The X-Rated Videotape Star Index II

A Guide to Your Favorite Adult Film Stars

Patrick Riley

The X-Rated Videotape Star Index II

Prometheus Books

59 John Glenn Drive
Amherst, NewYork 14228-2197

Published 1997 by Prometheus Books

The X-Rated Videotape Star Index II. Copyright © 1997 Patrick Riley.

Inquiries should be addressed to Prometheus Books, 59 John Glenn Drive, Amherst, New York 14228–2197, 716–691–0133. FAX: 716–691–0137. To place an order call: 800–421–0351

01 00 99 98   5 4 3 2

Riley, Patrick.
    The x-rated videotape star index II / Patrick Riley.
        p.   cm.
    ISBN 1–57392–168–8 (paper : alk. paper)
    1. Erotic films—Catalogs. 2. Motion picture actors and actresses—Credits. I. Title.
PN1995.9.S45R55   1997
016.79143′6538—dc21   97–27750
                                                            CIP

Printed in the United States of America on acid-free paper

Contents

Introduction

Welcome to *The X-Rated Videotape Star Index II*, a work which attempts to list all performers in nongay porno movies and the movies in which they appear. All these terms have specific meanings or considerations which will be discussed as we continue, but if you feel like plunging in straightaway without reading the manual, go right ahead. When you do so and then ask, "Why isn't my favorite star listed?" you might want to return here and do it the old-fashioned way.

Companion Books

The X-Rated Videotape Guide in six volumes contains reviews and synopses of many of the movies listed in this work, and all six are in print and available from the publisher, Prometheus Books (see the copyright page) or from wherever you bought this *Index*. Volumes I (1984) and II (1991) were written by Robert H. Rimmer, volumes III (1993) and IV (1994) were a joint work of Rimmer and Riley, and volumes V (1995) and VI (1996) were by Riley alone. The dates are the publication dates, meaning that you will not get a movie made (for example) in 1995 in a volume earlier than volume V; however, you may (and do) get reviews and re-reviews of movies from (say) 1981 in volumes later than volume I. The rule is for any movie: Look at the latest volume; if you don't find the movie, go to the next back in sequence, then the next, etc. Volume VI has an index to prior volumes, which makes life easier.

The listings for performers whose entry has remained unchanged from *The X-Rated Videotape Star Index I* (primarily "one-shot wonders") are not repeated in the *Star Index II* except for an indication at an appropriate point in the listings that they have an entry in the *Star Index I*. For those striving for completeness, the *Star Index I* is in print and available from the same sources as the *Guides*.

X-Rated Videotape

A slight misnomer that unfortunately we're all stuck with. Back in the early seventies the Motion Picture Association of America (the people who issue the ratings) actually issued some X ratings to movies of the era, the most famous being **Easy Rider**; however, the explicit-sex industry quickly jumped on the bandwagon and applied its own X, the result being that no self-respecting movie theater would book an X movie—the kiss of death for mainstream movies. Porno manufacturers even applied a minisystem of X for simulated sex and XXX for explicit sex, and you still hear people talk of and see titles with "Triple X" or "XXX". More information on the "X" question can be found in the introductions to volumes I and V of the *Guides*. For the purpose of this *Index* and the *Guides,* you should consider an X-rated videotape to be a porno videotape.

The word "videotape" however is important. The *Index* includes only movies released commercially in the United States on consumer-level videotape. It does not include TV appearances, alternate names of movies used in cable presentations, CD-ROMs, stage appearances of performers, movies only released theatrically, under-the-counter movies of celebrities screwing, or movies only obtainable from foreign sources. In other words it covers what you could possibly find in your local video store or adult bookstore.

Porno Movies

Porno is a very common contraction of pornographic especially when used in combination with the word "movies". *Webster's* defines pornography as "1. Writings, pictures, etc, intended primarily to arouse sexual desire" and that's the definition used for this *Index*: movies intended primarily to arouse sexual desire that are or were available to the consumer on videotape. Clear, no? Unfortunately not quite so clear especially when it comes to movies that contain only simulated sex and do have some story or characterization and especially when those movies are not issued by a traditional porno manufacturer.

Let's take a couple of examples. There's an underground twelve-minute movie from 1995 called **The Operation** which includes a complete explicit screw, perhaps even more explicit than normal because the movie is photographed in infrared and you can really see the details. Is that a porno movie? What was the intent of the movie-maker? I suspect that will depend on who is asking. For the art-house crowd, of course not; for the guy who wants to get turned on, probably. My solution is that any explicit-sex movie gets included as a porno movie no matter how "arty", underground, clinical, or high-brow. If you can see penetration, it's a porno

How about **Red Shoe Diaries**, a 1992 plotted movie with reasonable characterization from Republic with only simulated sex? Pretty girl and quite arousing but was it intended "primarily to arouse"? Hard to answer the question but since I'm the one deciding, the rule I use is: Can the director plausibly deny that the movie is "primarily to arouse"? If he can, it's not a porno and in this case **Red Shoe Diaries** has plausible deniability.

Some of the considerations as to plausibility are: Has the movie a plot? and Would anyone but guys wanting to get aroused rent or buy the movie?—which bring us to the third example, **Hot Sexy Strippers** from DGD Entertainment, a movie that consists of segments of strippers stripping. No sex, not even simulated, but it's a porno, guys. I'll point out right away that the *Guides* and *Index* are very poor in this area due probably to the low level of information available. Even manufacturers such as *Penthouse* and *Playboy* fail to provide information such as cast lists, and some of the smaller producers are very transient.

Gay Porno Movies

For the purpose of this *Index* and the *Guides* "gay" refers to homosexual activity between two males, not girl/girl sex. Why the average heterosexual would see boy/boy sex as more threatening and girl/girl sex as acceptable is a subject for the introduction to one of the *Guides*, not here. But taking it on a practical level, the presumption is that most heterosexuals are not interested in boy/boy sex and therefore those movies that only show boy/boy sex will be excluded even if the performer is a "porno star" (see below). Thus, under Peter North you will not find the gay movies he did as Matt Ramsey. There's a minor exception for a couple of the gay movies of John Holmes because of his death from AIDS (people trying to deny his gay performances) and for females (e.g., Sharon Kane) who have appeared in gay movies. This latter exception leads to the unfortunate result that some exclusively gay males will be listed for those explicit sex but gay movies in which a female appears. Ultimately I'll get this corrected, but for the moment just ignore them.

Bisexual movies, that is, movies where there is boy/girl sex as well as boy/boy sex, are in and so are the performers, meaning that you will get listings for otherwise exclusively gay males for their bisexual movies. Same problem as before and same solution.

She-male movies include transsexuals, transvestites, anyone who is actually male and pretends to be female. These performers are included as though they were actually female and the gay males (i.e., the ones not pretending to be female) will be included for their bisexual and she-male roles only.

Commercial Movies

A commercial movie is one that is sold through the normal commercial outlets (adult bookstore, mail order from someone like Excalibur, etc) and could usually be found in your local video store. If they don't have it or have never had it in the past, it's because the owner made a commercial decision not to buy it from his distributor. All that sounds simple, but there are things to watch for.

This *Index* and the *Guides* generally don't list "under the counter" movies, that is, movies usually containing illegal materials (e.g., kiddie porn), quasilegal items (e.g., defecation tapes), or celebrity porn, which are only available if you "know someone". OK, there are some places in NYC where not much "knowing" is necessary, but you're on your own there.

Apart from these there are perfectly legitimate amateur movies sold by individuals out of their homes or small businesses usually by mail order or directly to a small geographic subset of video stores. Unless there is a known porno star in a tape and there is adequate information available, these movies are not listed in the *Guides* and the participants are not listed in the *Index*. Where they are listed, most of these movies commence with the name of the issuer rather than a proper movie title.

Another type of movie is the "fan club movie", sold along with the used panties and pubic hair offcuts (pity the dog) at an extortionate price to members of the fan club. Unless these tapes are also sold to others or represent an attempt at a real movie (the Chessie Moore gang bang movies come to mind) they and the participants will not be listed.

Compilations

The category of "compilation" is attributed on the basis of the whole movie and not on the basis of an individual scene. From the perspective of the viewer who desires to see all footage of a particular actress, a problem arises when the manufacturer mixes new footage with previously released extracts. Similarly, in themed compilations (not many, I agree) you can get scenes from movies that your local video store doesn't carry or where the original company has gone out of business. To deal with this, compilations are divided into two types: the "bookstore compilation" you will usually find on sale by mail order or in the adult bookstore along with the dildoes and blow-up dolls; and the regular compilation. Bookstore compilations (e.g., the **Raunch-O-Rama** series) are almost certainly 100 percent old footage and although sometimes advertised as "themed", usually the theme seems to be more what the editor has on hand than any attempt to construct a quality product. Regular compilations cover the "quality" compilations plus those which are likely to have some new footage. Both types are listed in the *Guides,* but due to space limitations the bookstore compilations do not appear in the *Index.*

Porno Performers or Stars

Establishing whether a movie is a porno movie determines whether it goes into the *Guides* (the *Guides* also include movies with a high sexual content which would not be classed as porno movies under the tests above); so one would think that a performer in such movies is a porno performer or porno star, the word "star" having no greater meaning than to indicate appearance in the tape. Not quite. A porno star (one that will be listed in the *Index*) has to perform explicit sex or be part of a fellatio-type annual act to be classed as a porno star. The classification of a person as a porno star has the consequence that I will pick up and list any videotape appearance of that star, including nonsexual ones. For nonporno stars who appear in porno movies only their porno movie performances and appearances in other movies in which there is also a porno star will be listed.

Clear as mud? Let's try some examples.

Marilyn Chambers performed explicit sex on screen; of that there is no doubt. Therefore every movie on videotape in which she appears, regardless of what she actually does, will be listed including **The Owl And The Pussycat**, the Barbra Streisand movie in which Marilyn had a bit part. You won't find a listing for Barbra, however, because **Owl** is not a porno movie and to my knowledge Barbra never appeared in a porno movie (thank God!).

Aldo Ray had a nonsex role as a bad guy in a porno movie, **Sweet Savage**; so he and that movie will be listed. He also appeared in hundreds of other Hollywood movies, most of which don't interest this *Index,* but among them were four other movies that in addition to having Aldo also had a qualifying porno star: **Biohazard** (Angelique Pettijohn), **Evils Of The Night** (Amber Lynn), **Shock 'Em**

Dead (Traci Lords), and **The Sicilian** (Ron Jeremy). He's listed for all five (at least).

There are a small number of nonporno stars who, either because of demand or because I personally want to track them, will appear. Uschi Digart and Marsha Jordan are two of the "demand" performers who have never done explicit sex on screen but are listed, and Jane March and Alyssa Milano are a couple of my personal preferences.

For nude appearances of nonporno stars and occasional porno stars you should get *The Bare Facts Video Guide*, available from the same bookstores where *The X-Rated Videotape Star Index* is sold or directly from:

The Bare Facts
PO Box 3255
Santa Clara CA 95055-3255

They also sell some scream queen movies and ancillary listings.

Completeness and Accuracy

If the world were a perfect place, every movie would have a complete and correct cast list on the box and in the movie or it would be available from the manufacturer on demand. Every review and every advertisement would be correct to the smallest detail. Every porno star would acquire a unique stage name before entering the business and would never change that name and it would be that name that would appear in the complete and correct cast list. Every movie would be established as a complete and fixed unity, no scenes would ever be added or removed, the name would never change, and no scenes would ever be copied onto another tape without full disclosure.

But we don't live in a perfect world. And the porno movie industry and the associated review industry are some of the least perfect parts of that world. Some of the problems with movies and their manufacturers:

- Titles that are reused for a totally different movie, sometimes by a different company in the same year.
- Movies where the box title, the movie-credits title, and even the cassette title are different.
- Movies made in one year but not released until years later without any indication of the age of the product.
- Movies advertised as being manufacturer X but which finally appear under manufacturer Y.
- Movies that are advertised but never appear.
- Older movies with one or more scenes chopped out, sometimes replaced with other scenes, and these movies are then sold under the old name with no external indication of any changes having been made. Sometimes this chopping is done to remove an underage actress (e.g., the Traci Lords problem), but other times it's an indication of spinelessness (e.g., removal of a mild B&D scene from an explicit sex tape) or for commercial advantage. Note that in the *Guides* and this *Index* cast and scene detail are of the original tape unless otherwise

noted. Because of the replacement factor and other minor items such as credits, running times are rarely a good guide to whether you have a complete movie.

- Movies that are advertised as features but are recycled clips from other movies.
- No credits, particularly in foreign and pro-am movies.
- Credits on the box that don't match the credits in the movie and may not even correspond to the number and sex of the people appearing.
- Performers credited under other names, sometimes new pseudonyms, sometimes their real names, and sometimes the name of another performer. Worst here is the intent to deceive, where an actress thinks she'll get more work under a new name.

Reviews in the monthly magazines frequently add to the problem very often by assigning a reviewer who has no idea of the cast and can't be bothered to try to identify them. Particularly annoying are cases where the credits to the movies did list the complete cast, but for whatever reason the reviewer decided not to put the names in his review.

The author makes no claim to have seen all the movies listed in this *Index* and relies for unseen movies on other peoples' contemporaneous reviews, on advertisements, press releases, movies announced by the performer him/herself or listed by a fan club or shown in other listings of performers' movies, on interviews and articles in various magazines and books and increasingly in postings on such internet newsgroups as rec.arts.movies.erotica. All of these sources present the risk of introducing error and are not blindly accepted, especially when several sources conflict, but the vast majority of entries, even from the first edition, have held up to public scrutiny.

Movies the author has personally seen are of course 100 percent correct in every particular! NOT! Unlike certain over-ego'ed porn historians and sometime-workers for industry magazines, the author makes no claims to divinity, perfection, or even that he could identify Bill Clinton if he fell over him. All you get here are best efforts and while I'm always willing to correct errors, I'm not going to get too upset (neither should you) if I didn't know that Fred Stud, an occasional seventies performer, was in the orgy ooono In **Debbie Does Dallas #34** and was credited under the name Fred Dick. Frankly, being that pedantic about collecting performers' appearances indicates a possible personality defect. Perhaps you should get away from the VCR and out into the real world a little more.

The utility of these listings is far more along these lines: "I've seen Jennifer Smith, a gorgeous little creature, in **Debbie Does Dallas #34** and **Just-Starting Girls #21**. Does she appear in any other movies?" Well, yes, she's in these five other movies that you may have to search for because your video store didn't bother to buy them. If she's in 155 movies, you should have had your fill of her by now (see above about getting out a little more). If you're interested in all the performances of Fred Stud, maybe you should reconsider your purchase of this book, which is devoted to heterosexuals.

The cutoff date for this book is March 31, 1997. That means movies released after that date will not be included, nor will performers who first appeared in movies released after that date. There may be movies included that were advertised but not yet released as of March 31, 1997, but you shouldn't try to see these as complete (cast may be tentative, etc).

Where To Get Movies

The author does not run a duplication service. Neither he nor Prometheus is connected with the video companies listed below and neither he nor Prometheus warrants their performance in any way. The author will not act as an intermediary to purchase tapes for residents of Bible Belt states, nor provide lists of stores that stock the more, ahem, risky tapes, nor does he undertake searches for hard-to-find tapes. Three general suppliers are provided without comment:

Movies Unlimited
6736 Castor Ave
Philadelphia PA 19149-2184
Tel: 1-800-4MOVIES (24 hours)

Great Pictures Inc
150-50 Coolidge Ave
Jamaica NY 11432
Tel: 1-800-445-6662

Excalibur Films
3621 W Commonwealth
Fullerton CA 92633
Tel: 1-800-BUY-MOVIES

For very early tapes (seventies and sometimes early eighties) you should try:

SVE
PO Box 797
Macomb IL 61455

Something Weird Video
PO Box 33664
Seattle WA 98133

Alpha Blue Archives Inc
PO Box 16072
Oakland CA 94610

Magazines such as *Cult Movies* and *Psychotronic* cover the sexploitation field and contain advertisements from video companies that specialize in this area. These video duplicators frequently also sell explicit sex movies and foreign movies.

The Internet

The internet seems to be an ideal place to find information covering the porno movie field and even to locate sources of hard-to-find tapes. Most manufacturers maintain web sites and there are many official and unofficial fan sites. Probably the most comprehensive set of links including links to other pages of links is provided by Jeff Knapp (Director) at:

http://www.gti.net/director/links/

Also of note is The Adult Film Database at:

http://homepage.eznet.net/~rwilhelm/asm/dbsearch.html

The database provides similar information to this Index in an on-line form and is maintained by Peter van Aarle.

For discussion of matters related to porno movies and the latest in breaking news you should check the moderated (no advertising) newsgroup rec.arts.movies.erotica. You might even run into me there.

Acknowledgments

To all those who have assisted in providing corrections to the first edition and have taken the time and trouble to help your fellow man by writing to me with updates and new information I want to extend a heartfelt thanks. There are literally hundreds of you out there, but I particularly want to thank Scott Lawrence of Louisiana, Felix Miata of Florida, JU of NJ, RN of PA, RW of AZ, SN of FL, TA of NY, TT of GA, BS of DC, JC of FL, FG of NY, GH of IL, PK of NY, FM of TX, FS of PA, GF of GA, GM of CA, RS of CA and, internationally, FL and GS, both of Germany, and TE, BC, and EA, all of the UK. With a couple of exceptions, this list is the same as that in volume VI of the *Guide,* as the correction of errors or additions that led to a relisting in volume VI most often resulted in a change to the performer lists.

To Contact the Author

If you have information to add or you wish to complain about my nonappreciation of the love of your life, you can contact me at:

Challenge Press
PO Box 180263
Brooklyn NY 11218-0263
E-Mail: p_riley@pipeline.com

Some rules about writing, however. I answer mail such as this in one big batch once a month (E-Mail is quicker), so if you just miss a cycle, you might wait almost two months for a reply. I try to answer all mail even if it's just to say "I don't know" and I don't require a self-addressed, stamped envelope, but if you do send one, it makes life a little easier (#10 folded in three please). Do not send money and if you send documents (catalogs, photos, videotape, etc.), make sure you say if you want them back; if you say nothing, I'll just keep or trash them. Tell me which book you're commenting on and keep a copy of your letter because often I'll reply, "On your fourth item...." I will not, however, answer abusive letters and I am not offering to become a pen pal. In return for replying to questions I expect you to tell me what you know (i.e., this is a two-way street). For example, if you are a devotee of Edith Smith and want to know if she does an anal in **The Great Orgy**, I expect you to tell me the names of all the movies you know she's in, unless I already have them all listed.

If you're looking for a fan club, or want to contact an actress or a video company, you should get a current copy of *Video Xcitement* (most adult bookstores), *Hustler Erotic Video Guide*, or *Adam Film World* or one of its derivatives (the latter two on your local newsstand). All three expend lots of time and effort in keeping the listings current, something that would be pointless in a book such as this. If you want to meet with the love of your life, there's no point in asking me for an introduction. Plan on attending the CES in January each year or the East Coast Video Show in Atlantic City, where, if she's a current actress, you may find her signing slicks.

Patrick Riley
April 1997

How to Read the Index

This section deals with the minutiae of the listings; what's included and how they got there are in the introduction.

Performers (Stars) Names

The performers are sequenced by their entire name (considered as an undifferentiated string of characters) because of the porno industry's practice of frequently crediting performers by their first name only. Thus, Amber Lynn will be found under "A" and not "L". Over the period of time since the *Star Index I,* I have had the opportunity to listen to the pros and cons of this method of listing and some initially passionate wails from the more traditional reader. At first it seems to shock people, but after a while they become quite acclimatized to the idea, a couple of them actually adapting their database (albeit smaller) to the method. The initial wails have now died down to nothing and apart from one recent comment on my "peculiar form of alphabetization", I've heard nothing about it over the last two years. I still consider it to be the better form for this industry.

You will occasionally find widely spread dates in the listing of a particular star. The later dates may be compilations of earlier scenes or there are two different people using the same name. The latter is particularly true for the males where nobody really cares if there was a Johnny Smith around in 1976 and another in 1986. Single names (e.g., "Lynn") should be considered as catch-alls and movies listed under such may well feature completely different people with the same name.

Where a known performer or performers are noted in a movie but there is no clearly established correspondence with the names in the credits, then both "performers" will be listed for that one movie. Similarly, where the performers in the movie credits and those on the box differ and cannot be reconciled, then all will be listed. One movie in the early seventies has the distinction of eighteen separate names in the cast lists but only six actual people in the movie.

Performers acquire their names in the first movie in which I see them or in which they are identified by another reviewer, provided that the name is a sensible name with a sensible spelling and does not conflict with another performer. Where there is a conflict or it's a silly name, a future name change to a better name will cause that later name to be adopted for all movies of the performer. The silly or conflicting names will appear as alternates. For example, Sahara Sands started out as just "Sahara", but finally, after about twenty movies (fast, these porno people), someone pointed out the confusion with Sahara, a black girl from the mid eighties, and the 1993 version added the "Sands".

Who determines what is sensible? Well, I guess I do, but if performers want a hint, names should consist of a first name and a last name (both required at all relevant times), neither of which should mean anything, and both should be spelt the most common way. If you want the ideal, examine the cast lists of the regular movies of the fifties and earlier (don't duplicate them): Tom Wayne, Harry Wayne, Michael Wayne, Nigel Wayne, Martin Wayne, Marcus Wayne, Sean Wayne,...Is there really a reason to produce silliness such as Rasta or Big Herc? And for females: Jennifer Ryan, Martha Ryan, Marilyn Ryan, Mary Ryan, Anne Ryan,...Do we really need Vixxxen, Foxy, Sexy Black, Tia, and a whole lot of one-name wonders?

Alternate Star Names

These are generally derived from the performer being credited in a movie or in a publication under another name but usually not an easily recognizable spelling variation. In some cases one of the alternate names might be their real (birth) name, but in most cases I don't know if it is or not. Only if the real name has been publicly stated as such, will I disclose it. Real names supplied to me in private communications or as part of the 2257 disclosures (see volume VI) will not be listed.

Biographical Data

This information is not intended to be complete and was accumulated as an aide-memoire to assist me when I'm trying to identify an uncredited or differently credited performer, or it's simply a bit of gossip that may come in handy later on. If you think it's hard on the actresses, remember that without "ugly" there can be no "pretty"; so those magazines that tell you every actress is "lovely" or "beautiful" are really saying nothing and are not helping you, the viewer, to find the girl you want to fantasize about. They might as well save the print space.

Movie Titles

Every movie title including the year (note: new in the *Star Index II*) is unique, even if the manufacturer didn't see fit to note that there was an already existing title and do the right thing and change his. Where there were two movies of the same name in the same year the name of the manufacturer has been added. Movies with sequels will have the #1 added to the prequel title so as to affirm which one we are talking about. Got that! For example, you will not find a box for **Backdoor To Hollywood #1**; it will say, **Backdoor To Hollywood** (without the #1), but the "#1" is added in the listing.

Apart from these variations, you will also find that some movies have alternate names (see the alternate-name listing at the end of the book). Some of these are genuine alternates—the movie has been released under two totally different names at different times. Most of them, however, are because the manufacturer has difficulty making up his mind what he wants to call the movie. It isn't unusual for the box, the cassette label, and the movie credits to have three quite different titles. In other cases, the box (which is what usually takes precedence) can be read with two (or more) interpretations as to what the name of the movie is. I'll pick the most obvious or most logical (to me) and the other will be shown as an alternate.

Be especially careful of adult-bookstore alternates reissued in the last few years where the alternate may not be exactly the same as the original. Similarly, sexploitation tapes from the seventies may have been through multiple versions, some of which may include explicit inserts.

For movie boxes which emphasize the name of the manufacturer (primarily the amateurs) the title will be preceded by some abbreviation of the manufacturer's name and it will be sequenced appropriately.

At the end of the listing of many stars you will notice that the titles begin again in alphabetical sequence except that the names are all preceded by a square bracket ([) and many of these titles lack distributor, year, and sometimes even a type. These movies are ones in which someone at some point has alleged that the star in question appears, but there is little or no confirmation, nor have there been any reviews of the movie which would allow some level of confidence in even the existence of the movie.

For example, Candy Samples allegedly appeared in a takeoff of **Charlie's Angels** called **Candy's Angels,** but apart from a comment by a reader of the original *Star Index* and a passing reference in a magazine article (which may have been the source for the reader) no other confirmation has come to light. Perhaps it was a projected movie that was never made, perhaps it appeared under some other title, or perhaps it appeared and then disappeared without review or listing anywhere.

Year

For original material, the year is supposed to be the year in which the movie was substantially finished; for compilations, it's the year of release. Often, it's not possible to tell and these movies have a "19??" or a "cr75" (circa 1975) or some other guess at a year. Many reviewers list the year as the year of release, so don't be surprised if you find earlier dates in the *Guides* and *Index.*

Distributor/Manufacturer

The two- or three-character code for the distributor corresponds to the listing at the end of the book. Recent movies are probably correct and obtainable but some of the older ones have been through a number of different "owners" and may no longer be with the distributor/manufacturer listed. Note that I am not interested in adding distributor/manufacturer codes where that knowledge doesn't make it easier to obtain the movie today and is merely of historical interest. For example, the fact that a movie was obtainable from Blue Video at some stage in its life doesn't help today's consumer who will just spend fruitless hours trying to find the extinct Blue Video; the information that the movie is currently available from (say) Video Search Of Miami does help.

Type

This is the last piece of information for each movie which, in the *Star Index I*, was called "Confidence Level". Nobody liked the concept of confidence level, so I've changed it to reflect the type of movie listed. Emphasis on TYPE OF MOVIE—it does NOT refer to the performance of the star you're looking at in that movie. For example the scene with Tom Byron and Draghixa in **Sodomania: The Baddest Of The Best** is an original scene (good too), but the overall movie is a compilation. If you want more details on the types (or classifications) see *The X-Rated Videotape Guide,* volume V (available at your friendly bookstore).

Each of the types below works in cascade. If it falls into one category as it goes along it's not even considered for the others.

- C: Compilations
- G: Gay—includes bi-sexual, she-male, gay.
- B: B&D—includes B&D, Tickling, Catfighting, Enema.
- F: Female—includes all-girl and single girl.
- S: Simulated—includes both no-sex and simulated sex movies.
- M: All the others—includes cartoons, segments, loops, smokers, big tits, documentaries and, of course, features.

Movie Names' Cross-References

If you can't find a particular movie listed under your favorite performer, but you know she/he's in it or you want to know if the movie you are searching for has been issued under any other names, this list is the place to look. The list can be used for both the main name (nonslanted typeface) and the alternate name (italics) in the same manner by simply looking up the name. If it's an alternate, the following title will be the main name; if it's a main name, it will be followed by a list of known alternates. If no entry exists, to my knowledge there is only one name for the movie.

Distributor/Manufacturer Listing

This list supplies the expanded name corresponding to the three (or two) character code which can be found after each movie in the main section. Many of the distributors listed are no longer in business, but if you wish to contact those that are, you should get a current copy of *Hustler Erotic Video Guide* or *Adam Film World* from your local newsstand. Most manufacturers no longer produce catalogs and many of them no longer make direct sales, so your best bet for purchasing movies are the retailers listed in the introduction. Of special interest is the emergence of specialists in the early seventies movies who are also listed there.

Star Index

A. HAWG
Welcome To Bondage: Lorrin Mick / 1993 / BON / B • Welcome To Bondage: Starlets #2 / 1994 / BON / C

A. RYDELL see Star Index I

A.D.
Asses Galore #1: From L.A. To Brazil / 1996 / DFI / M • Best Gang Bangs / 1996 / DFI / C • Waiting For The Man / 1996 / VT / M • Waiting To XXX-Hale / 1996 / MET / M

A.J. COHEN
The Anals Of History #1 / 1991 / MID / M • The Last Act / 1995 / VI / M

A.J. FUGAZI see Star Index I

A.J. MARTIN JR
The Catwoman / 1988 / VC / M • Hot Scalding / 1989 / VC / M • Oh, What A Night! / 1990 / VC / M • The Pillowman / 1988 / VC / M • Strange Curves / 1989 / VC / M

A.P. ANTHONY see J.P. Anthony

AARON
Pearl Necklace: Amorous Amateurs #19 / 1992 / SEE / M • Pearl Necklace: Amorous Amateurs #35 / 1993 / SEE / M • Pearl Necklace: Premier Sessions #01 / 1993 / SEE / M

AARON AUSTIN
B-Witched / 1994 / PEP / G • Bi-Athelon / 1993 / BIL / G • Inside Karl Thomas / 1994 / STA / G • Switch Hitters #7 / 1994 / IN / G

AARON BARON
Eat At Dave's #7 / 1996 / SP / M

AARON BRANDT
Marine Code Of Silence: Don't Ask Don't Tell / 1996 / BHE / G

AARON COLT *(Aaron Gold)*
Boyfriend of Julia Ann.
Casanova #3 / 1993 / SC / M • Casanova #4 / 1993 / SC / M • Elements Of Desire / 1994 / ULI / M • Harlots / 1993 / MID / M • Les Femmes Erotiques / 1993 / BFP / M • Penthouse: Forum Letters #2 / 1994 / A*V / S • The Pink Lady Detective Agency: Case Of The Twisted Sister / 1994 / IN / M • Pussyman #03: The Search Continues / 1993 / SNA / M • Raunch #09 / 1993 / CC / M • The Seduction Of Julia Ann / 1993 / VT / M

AARON GAGE
Bi-Heat #08 To #10 / 1988 / ZA / G • Techsex / 1988 / VXP / M

AARON GOLD see Aaron Colt

AARON HAUCHART
[S.S. Bordello / 1978 / … / M

AARON PARKER

The Submission Of Johns / 1995 / RB / B

AARON SCOTT see Star Index I

AARON STORM see Star Index I

AARON STUART *(Eric Stuart, Ralph Quail)*
American Pie / 1980 / SE / M • Aunt Peg's Fulfillment / 1980 / CV / M • Behind The Brown Door / 1986 / VCR / C • Beyond Shame / 1980 / VEP / M • Beyond Your Wildest Dreams / 1980 / CAT / M • The Blonde / 1980 / VCX / M • Coed Fever / 1980 / CA / M • Coffee, Tea Or Me / 1984 / CV / M • Daisy May / 1979 / VC / M • The Dancers / 1981 / VCX / M • Deep Rub / 1979 / VC / M • Delicious / 1981 / VXP / M • Educating Nina / 1984 / AT / M • The Erotic World Of Vanessa #2 / 1984 / VCR / C • Extremes / 1981 / CA / M • Fantasy / 1978 / VCX / M • Forbidden Entry / 1984 / VCR / M • Foxholes / 1983 / SE / M • Inside Desiree Cousteau / 1979 / VCX / M • Limited Edition #15 / 1980 / AVC / M • The Mistress #1 / 1983 / CV / M • Nothing To Hide #1 / 1981 / CV / M • Oriental Lust / 1983 / GO / M • Peaches And Cream / 1982 / SE / M • Shaved / 1984 / VCR / M • Showgirl #05: Crystal Dawn's Fantasies / 1983 / VCR / M • Showgirl #08: Serena's Fantasies / 1983 / VCR / M • Showgirl #14: Kitty Shane's Fantasies / 1983 / VCR / M • Showgirl #15: Taylor Evans' Fantasies / 1983 / VCR / M • Skin On Skin / 1981 / CV / M • Skintight / 1981 / CA / M • Small Town Girls / 1979 / CXV / M • Summer School / 1979 / VCX / M • Swedish Erotica #24 / 1980 / CA / M • Sweet Dreams Suzan / 1980 / CA / M • Tales Of The Backside / 1985 / VCR / C • Talk Dirty To Me #01 / 1980 / CA / M • Three Faces Of Angel / 1987 / CV / M • Three Ripening Cherries / 1979 / HIF / M • Two Senoritas / 197? / VHL / M • Tycoon's Daughter / cr73 / SVE / M • Urban Cowgirls / 1980 / CA / M • Vista Valley PTA / 1980 / CV / M • Yummy Nymphs / 1983 / TGA / C • [Grant Takes Richmond / 1981 / … / M

AARON WADD
They Shall Overcome / 1974 / VST / M

ABALONIA
Lesbian Love Dolls / 1995 / LIP / F • Mother Nature's Bulging Bellies / 1995 / LIP / F

ABBEY JEWELS
The Go-Go Girls / 1994 / EVN / M

ABBEY LANE see Abby Rhodes

ABBIE TREVOR see Star Index I

ABBY

Ateball: Linda's West Coast Talent Search / 1996 / ATE / M • Blue Vanities #521 / 1993 / FFL / M • Next Door Neighbors #05 / 1989 / BON / M

ABBY ANDREWS
Eight Babes A Week / 1996 / DGD / F • Red Rumpers #01 / 1996 / LBO / B • Sex, Truth & Videotape #1 / 1995 / DOC / M

ABBY GAIL see Abby Rhodes

ABBY GALE see Abby Rhodes

ABBY LAYNE see Abby Rhodes

ABBY LOVE see Abby Rhodes

ABBY RHODES *(Abby Gail, Abby Gale, Abby Love, Abbey Lane, Abby Layne)*
Older (under 30 according to her) blonde with a taut body, marginal face, small tits and hair around her ears and back of neck shaved. 5'5" tall. De-virginized at 16.
Amateurs Exposed #07 / 1995 / CV / M • Anal 247 / 1995 / CC / M • Anal Camera #08 / 1995 / EVN / M • Anal Freaks / 1994 / KWP / M • Anal Hellraiser #1 / 1995 / ROB / M • Anal Insatiable / 1995 / ROB / M • Anal Nurses / 1996 / LBO / M • Anal Therapy #4 / 1996 / FD / M • Anna Malle Exposed / 1996 / WV / M • Attack Of The Killer Dildos / 1996 / RAS / M • Bang City #4: Gina's Anal Gang Bang / 1995 / SC / M • Big Murray's New-Cummers #29: Tools Of The Trade / 1995 / FD / M • Birthday Bash / 1995 / BOT / M • Bootylicious: Trailer Trash / 1996 / JMP / M • Bootylicious: White Trash / 1995 / JMP / M • Brothers Bangin' / 1995 / ANA / M • Butt Hunt #04 / 1995 / LEI / M • The Butt Sisters Do The Twin Cities / 1996 / MID / M • Buttslammers #10: Lust On The Internet / 1995 / BS / F • Casting Couch Tips / 1996 / MP0 / M • Compulsion (Fat Dog) / 1996 / FD / M • Deep Inside Anal Camera / 1996 / EVN / C • Dildo Debutantes / 1995 / CA / F • Dirty & Kinky Mature Women #07 / 1996 / C69 / M • Dirty Tails / 1996 / SC / M • Double Dicked #1 / 1996 / RAS / M • Dream Butt / 1995 / VMX / M • Fishin' For Lust / 1996 / WST / M • Forbidden Subjects #4 / 1995 / FC / M • Gang Bang Bitches #05 / 1995 / PP / M • Gold Coast / 1996 / FD / M • Golden Oldies #6 / 1996 / TTV / M • The Hardwood Chronicles / 1995 / XCI / M • Hidden Camera #22 / 1994 / JMP / M • Hollywood Amateurs #24 / 1995 / MID / M • Hometown Girl / 1994 / VEX / M • Horny Old Broads / 1995 / FPI / M • In My Ass, Please! / 1996 / SP / M • Indiscreet! Video Magazine #1 / 1995 / FH / M • Lesbian Lust Bust / 1995 / GLI / F •

Lessons In Love / 1995 / SPI / M • Lips / 1994 / FC / M • Mike Hott: #273 Cunt of the Month: Abby 10-94 / 1994 / MHV / M • Mike Hott: #282 Three-Sum Sluts #01 / 1995 / MHV / M • Mike Hott: #283 Sahara / 1994 / MHV / M • Mike Hott: #315 Cum In My Mouth #02 / 1995 / MHV / C • Mike Hott: #317 Girls Who Swallow Cum #01 / 1995 / MHV / C • Mike Hott: #320 Three-Sum Sluts #06 / 1995 / MHV / M • Mike Hott: #321 Lesbian Sluts #20 / 1995 / MHV / F • Mike Hott: #367 Girls Who Lap Cum From Cunts #02 / 1996 / MHV / M • More Dirty Debutantes #36 / 1994 / 4P / M • Nasty Newcummers #07 / 1995 / MET / M • Older And Anal #2 / 1995 / FC / M • Orgies Orgies Orgies / 1994 / WV / A • Prime Choice #8 / 1996 / RAS / M • Profiles #01 / 1995 / XPR / M • Pussyman Auditions #04 / 1995 / SNA / M • Reel People #10 / 1995 / PP / M • Reverse Gang Bang / 1995 / JMP / M • Ron Hightower's White Chicks #15 / 1994 / LBO / M • Rump Man: Forever / 1995 / HW / M • Sam Gets Shafted / 1996 / MP0 / M • Shaving Mr. One Eye / 1996 / FC / M • Slutsville U.S.A. / 1995 / VMX / M • Special Attention / 1996 / MP0 / M • Stuff Your Face #1 / 1994 / JMP / M • Temptation / 1994 / VC / M • Tight Fit #15 / 1996 / GO / M • Triple Penetration Debutante Sluts #2 / 1996 / BAC / M • Underground #1 / 1996 / SC / M • Video Virgins #17 / 1994 / NS / M • The Violation Of Paisley Hunter / 1996 / JMP / F • Willie Wanker At The Fudge Packing Factory / 1995 / FD / M • Young And Anal #6 / 1996 / JMP / M

ABE KALISH
Sodom & Gomorrah / 1974 / MIT / M
ABE RICH
All The Loving Couples / 1979 / KIT / M
ABE THEIMBE see Star Index I
ABEL CAINE see Star Index I
ABEL FERRARA
Nine Lives Of A Wet Pussycat / 1975 / VCX / M
ABIGAIL CLAYTON (Gail Lawrence, Gail Wezke)
First movie was **Dixie**. Too big framed girl with originally small tits which were later enhanced to cantaloupe size and rigidity. Flattish face. Not a tight body.
The Best Of Alex De Renzy #1 / 1983 / VC / C • Blue Ribbon Blue / 1984 / CA / C • Bye Bye Monkey / 1977 / LUM / S • Classic Swedish Erotica #11 / 1986 / CA / C • A Coming Of Angels / 1977 / CA / M • Desires Within Young Girls / 1977 / CA / M • Dixie / 1976 / VHL / M • Femmes De Sade / 1976 / ALP / M • The Girls In The Band / 1976 / SVE / M • Good To The Last Drop / 1986 / VCS / C • The Health Spa / 1978 / SE / M • Hot Cookies / 1977 / WWV / M • Legends Of Porn #1 / 1987 / CV / C • Love Lips / 1976 / VC / M • Maniac / 1980 / MED / S • Marilyn Chambers' Private Fantasies #1 / 1983 / CA / M • Mary! Mary! / 1977 / SE / M • Me, Myself & I / 1987 / SE / C • Midnight Hustle / 1978 / VC / M • Naked Afternoon / 1976 / CV / M • October Silk / 1980 / COM / M • Once Upon A Time/Cave Woman / 1978 / VI / M • Only The Best #1 / 1986 / CV / C • Only The Best #2 / 1989 / CV / C • Only The Best #3 / 1990 / CV / C • Seven Into Snowy / 1977 / VC / M • Sex World / 1978 / SE / M • So

Fine / 1981 / WAR / S • The Spirit Of Seventy Six / 1976 / NGV / M • That's Porno / 1979 / CV / C • True Legends Of Adult Cinema: The Cult Superstars / 1993 / VC / C • True Legends Of Adult Cinema: Unsung Superstars / 1993 / VC / C • The Untamed / 1978 / VCX / M • VCA Previews #1 / 1988 / VC / C • With Love, Annette / 1985 / CA / C
ABIGAIL HEATH see Star Index I
ABIGAIL REED see Star Index I
ABLE
Bad Bad Gang / 1972 / SOW / M • Bucky Beaver's XXX Dragon Art Theatre Double Feature #07 / 1996 / SOW / M
ABRAXA
Magma: Dirty Diana / 1994 / MET / M
ABUNDANCY JONES
Genital Hospital / 1987 / SE / M
ABUNDAVITA see Shawn Devereaux
ACE HOLDEN
Like Father Like Son / 1996 / AWV / G
ACHILLE LALONDE
Ancient Secrets Of Sexual Ecstasy / 1996 / HIG / M
ACHIM NEUMANN
[Junge Madchen Mogen's HeiB, Hausfrauen Noch HeiBer / 1973 / ... / M
ADAM
Anal Virgins Of America #08 / 1994 / FOR / M • Nasty Newcummers #05 / 1994 / MET / M • Pearl Necklace: Amorous Amateurs #08 / 1992 / SEE / M
ADAM CARR see Star Index I
ADAM DEHAVEN
Bad Penny / 1978 / QX / M • Blonde Ambition / 1981 / QX / M • Bon Appetit / 1980 / QX / M • Devil In Miss Jones #2 / 1983 / VC / M • Firestorm #1 / 1984 / COM / M • Games Women Play #1 / 1980 / CA / M • In Love / 1983 / VC / M • Jack 'n' Jill #1 / 1979 / VXP / M • Misbehavin' / 1979 / VXP / M • Roommates / 1982 / VXP / M
ADAM FRANK
Taboo American Style #4: The Exciting Conclusion / 1985 / VC / M
ADAM HIGGINS see Star Index I
ADAM JAMES
[Snow Balling / 197? / ... / M
ADAM K.
Screamers / 1994 / HW / M
ADAM OLA see Star Index I
ADAM OREN LADD see Will Jarvis
ADAM PHILLIPS see Star Index I
ADAM RICHARDS see Star Index I
ADAM SLATER
N.Y. Video Magazine #04 / 1995 / OUP / M
ADAM VOUGHAN see John Decker
ADAM VOUGHN see John Decker
ADAM WARD
Satan's Sex Slaves / 1971 / ALP / M • Tonga: God Of Love & Lust / 1971 / ALP / M
ADAM WILD
Badgirls #4: Jayebird / 1995 / VI / M • Best Gang Bangs / 1996 / DFI / C • Blonde Justice #3 / 1994 / VI / M • Every Woman Has A Fantasy #3 / 1995 / VC / M • Gang Bang Pussycat / 1992 / ROB / M • My Sister's Husband / 1996 / AWV / G • Once In A Lifetime / 1996 / VC / C • Supermodel #2 / 1994 / VI / M • The Voyeur #1 / 1994 / EA / M
ADDENDA
Hard Core Beginners #08 / 1995 / LEI / M
ADEL MOUSK see Star Index I

ADELE
Private Gold #07: Kruger Park / 1996 / OD / M • Private Gold #12: The Pyramid #2 / 1996 / OD / M • Triple X Video Magazine #14 / 1996 / OD / M • Triple X Video Magazine #15 / 1996 / OD / M
ADELE CHARTS see Lisa K. Loring
ADELE LAMBERT see Star Index I
ADELE SLOAN see Star Index I
ADIA see Star Index I
ADOLPH A. SCHWARTZ see Russ Meyer
ADOLPH ROBBINS see Star Index I
ADONIS
Passionate Partners: The Guide For Daring Lovers / 1993 / PHV / S • Perversity In Paris / 1994 / AVI / M
ADORITA
San Francisco Lesbians #4 / 1993 / PL / F
ADREEN
Kinky College Cunts #20 / 1993 / NS / F
ADRIAN (JILL KELLY) see Jill Kelly
ADRIAN ADONIS
Bright Tails #8 / 1996 / STP / B • Sweet Surrender / 1980 / VCX / M
ADRIAN ASANTE
Video Virgins #29 / 1996 / NS / M
ADRIAN DUBUOIS
Sex #1 (Vca) / 1994 / VC / M
ADRIAN MICHAELS
Hungry Eyed Woman / cr71 / VCX / M
ADRIANA
Caribbean Sunset / 1996 / PL / M • Keep On Fucking / 1995 / XHE / M • Sexhibition #3 / 1996 / SUF / M • Sunset In Paradise / 1996 / PL / M • Women Who Control The Family Jewels #4 / 1995 / STM / B
ADRIANI see Zumira
ADRIANNA
Sodomania #09: Doin' Time / 1994 / EL / M
ADRIANNE CHRISTIAN
Back East Babes #1 / 1996 / NIT / M • Back East Babes #2 / 1996 / NIT / M • Back East Babes #3 / 1996 / NIT / M
ADRIANO
Private Film #19 / 1994 / OD / M
ADRIANO VUCCINI
Impulse #05: When I Was 20... / 1995 / MBP / M
ADRIENNE
Private Gold #12: The Pyramid #2 / 1996 / OD / M
ADRIENNE ALTENHAUS
Hardcore: The Films Of Richard Kern #1 / 1991 / FTV / M
ADRIENNE BELLAIRE (Terri Benoum)
Terri Benoum is from **Golden Girls**. Doe eyed swarthy innocent looking girl who may be Middle Eastern.
Between Lovers / 1983 / CA / M • Blue Ice / 1985 / CA / M • Deviations / 1983 / SE / M • Golden Girls, The Movie / 1984 / SE / M • Good To The Last Drop / 1986 / VCS / C • Wild In The Wilderness / 1984 / GO / M
ADRIENNE CARRIER see Star Index I
ADRIENNE PLUSHETTE see Star Index I
AFRICA SIMMS see Star Index I
AFRIKA
Black Gangbangers #10 / 1996 / HW / M • Licorice Lollipops: Summer Break / 1996 / HW / M • Vivid Raw #1 / 1996 / VI / M
AFRODISIAC see Heidi Nelson
AFTON PARISH see Star Index I
AGNATIA

Lesbian Sleaze / 1994 / PL / F
AGNES
Blue Vanities #538 / 1993 / FFL / M •
Magma: Live And Learn / 1995 / MET / M
AGNES BREV *see Star Index I*
AGNES FALODI
Private Film #24 / 1995 / OD / M
AGNES MAGYAR TELEGDI
True Stories #1 / 1993 / SC / M • True Stories #2 / 1993 / SC / M
AGNES NYRI
Skin #5: The 5th Column / 1996 / ERQ / M
AGNES SIVEI *see Star Index I*
AGNES SZABO
True Stories #1 / 1993 / SC / M • True Stories #2 / 1993 / SC / M
AGNES TILLI
Private Film #25 / 1995 / OD / M • Private Film #26 / 1995 / OD / M • Private Video Magazine #25 / 1995 / OD / M • Triple X Video Magazine #01 / 1995 / OD / M • Triple X Video Magazine #02 / 1995 / OD / M • Triple X Video Magazine #03 / 1995 / OD / M • Triple X Video Magazine #06 / 1995 / OD / M
AGNESE JADESH
Prima #14: Hotel Europa / 1996 / MBP / M
AIDA VARGAS
[Je Brule De Partout / 1978 / ... / M
AIDEN SHAW
Bimbo Boys / 1995 / PL / C
AIESHA *see lesha*
AIKO
Big Black Bang / 1996 / HW / M
AILEEN FERRARI *see Alena Ferrari*
AIMEE
Toe Tales #27 / 1995 / GOT / B
AIMEE LEIGH *see Hillary Summers*
AIOKA SUGIMI *see Star Index I*
AISHA
Banned In Britain / 1995 / VC / M •
Magma: Anal Teenies / 1994 / MET / M
AISHA (IESHA) *see lesha*
AISHA HANN *see Star Index I*
AISSA BLUE *see Anesa Blue*
AIVARR VILKMAA
Sex-A-Holic Lady / 1995 / PL / M
AJA *(Lucia Luciano)*
First movie was **Wild in the Woods**. Has 2 kids; aged 25 in 1989; lives in Fort Lauderdale, Florida. Started with small tits (35-23-34) and later had them enhanced (badly). Little girl voice and quite vulnerable sounding. Did her first anal with (at the time alleged) husband in **With A Wiggle In Her Walk**.
4F Dating Service / 1989 / AR / M • 69 Pump Street / 1988 / ZA / M • Aja / 1988 / PL / M • The All American Girl / 1989 / FAN / M • All For One / 1988 / CIN / M • Anal Angels #2 / 1990 / VEX / C • Anal Intruder #03 / 1989 / CC / M • Angel Of The Island / 1988 / IN / M • Angel Rising / 1988 / IN / M • Army Brat #2 / 1989 / VI / M • At The Pornies / 1989 / VC / M • Aussie Bloopers / 1993 / OD / M • Aussie Maid In America / 1990 / PM / M • Backfield In Motion / 1990 / PV / M • Best Of Bruce Seven #3 / 1990 / BIZ / C • Best Of Bruce Seven #4 / 1990 / BIZ / C • Bi Mistake / 1989 / VI / G • The Big Pink / 1989 / VWA / M • Big Titted Tarts / 1994 / PL / C • Bizarre Mistress Series: Sharon Mitchell / 1992 / BIZ / C • Black Beauty (Ebony & Ivory) / 1989 / E&I / M • Black Rage / 1988 / ZA / M • Black Widow / 1988 / WV / M • Bloopers #2 / 1991 / GO

/ C • Blue Angel / 1992 / AFV / M • Blue Angel / 1992 / AFV / M • The Bondage Society / 1991 / LON / B • The Book / 1990 / IF / M • Brat Force / 1989 / VI / M • Breast Collection #03 / 1995 / LBO / C • Breast Worx #23 / 1992 / LBO / M • Breast Worx #27 / 1992 / LBO / M • Breast Worx #32 / 1992 / LBO / M • Breast Worx #33 / 1992 / LBO / M • Broadway Brat / 1988 / VI / M • Bubble Butts #10 / 1992 / LBO / M • Call Girl Academy / 1990 / V99 / M • The Case Of The Sensuous Sinners / 1988 / ME / M • Chills / 1989 / LV / M • Club Head (EVN) #2 / 1989 / EVN / C • Coming In America / 1988 / VEX / M • Company Ball / 1988 / V99 / C • The De Renzy Tapes / 1990 / CA / C • Deep Throat #3 / 1989 / AR / M • Depraved / 1990 / IN / M • The Desk Top Dolls / 1990 / BAD / C • Dial A Sailor / 1990 / PM / M • Dirty Books / 1990 / V99 / M • Dirty Diane / 1989 / V99 / M • Dreams Bi-Night / 1989 / PL / G • Dresden Diary #03 / 1989 / BIZ / B • Dresden Diary #04 / 1989 / BIZ / B • The Dungeon Master / 1992 / BS / B • The Ebony Garden / 1988 / ZA / M • Ebony Love / 1992 / VT / C • The Erotic Adventures Of Chi Chi Chan / 1988 / VWA / M • Family Thighs / 1989 / AR / M • Fast Girls #2 / 1988 / DIS / M • Feel The Heat / 1989 / VEX / M • Filet-O-Breast / 1988 / AVC / M • A Fistful Of Bimbos / 1988 / FAZ / M • Flame / 1989 / ARG / M • Foxes / 1992 / FL / M • From Japan With Love / 1990 / SLV / M • Gazongas #03 / 1991 / VEX / M • Get Bi Tonight / 1991 / PL / G • Getting Off On Broadway / 1989 / IN / M • Ghostest With The Mostest / 1988 / CA / M • Girls Of The Double D #04 / 1989 / CDI / M • Girls Of The Double D #09 / 1989 / CDI / M • The God Daughter #3 / 1992 / AFV / M • The God Daughter #4 / 1992 / AFV / M • Good Morning Saigon / 1988 / ZA / M • Head Again / 1992 / AFV / M • Heather / 1989 / VWA / M • Hollywood Hustle #2 / 1990 / V99 / M • Homegrown Video #345 / 1991 / HOV / M • Hometown Honeys #3 / 1989 / VEX / M • Hot Flesh, Cold Chains / 1992 / HOM / B • Hunchback Of Notre Dame / 1991 / PL / M • Illicit Affairs / 1989 / VD / M • Innocence Lost / 1988 / CA / M • Innocent Bi Standers / 1989 / LV / G • Inside Sharon Mitchell / 1989 / ZA / C • Invasion Of The Samurai Sluts From Hell / 1988 / FAZ / M • Jungle Beaver / 1991 / HIO / M • Just Between Friends / 1988 / VEX / M • Kascha & Friends / 1988 / CIN / M • Keyhole #168: Bustin' The Royal Hienies / 1990 / LA / M • Kiss And Tell / 1992 / AFV / M • Ladies Lovin' Ladies #2 / 1992 / AR / F • The Last Temptation / 1988 / VD / M • The Last Temptation Of Kristi / 1988 / ME / M • Laying Down The Law #1 / 1992 / AFV / M • Laying Down The Law #2 / 1992 / AFV / M • Lays Of Our Lives / 1988 / ZA / M • Legal Tender (1990-X) / 1990 / VC / M • Legends Of Porn #3 / 1991 / MET / C • Lick Bush / 1992 / VD / C • Life Is Butt A Dream / 1989 / V99 / M • Lingerie Busters / 1991 / FH / M • Lost In Paradise / 1990 / CA / M • Mad Love / 1988 / VC / M • Madame X / 1989 / EVN / M • The Maltese Phallus / 1990 / V99 / M • Matters In Hand / 1989 / STA / G • Midnight Baller / 1989 / PL / M • Midnight Fantasies / 1989 / VEX / M • Missy Impos-

sible / 1989 / CAR / M • Moonstroked / 1988 / 3HV / M • More Than A Handful / 1993 / CA / C • More Than Friends / 1989 / FAZ / M • Most Wanted / 1991 / GO / M • My Bare Lady / 1989 / ME / M • Mystery Of The Golden Lotus / 1989 / HU / M • The Naked Stranger / 1988 / VI / M • Natural Pleasure / 1994 / ... / M • Naughty Neighbors / 1989 / CA / M • No Man's Land #03 / 1989 / VT / F • Nookie Court / 1992 / AFV / M • Nothing But Girls, Girls, Girls / 1988 / CDI / M • Office Girls / 1989 / CA / M • The Only Game In Town / 1991 / VC / M • Only The Very Best On Video / 1992 / VC / C • Open House (CDI) / 1989 / CDI / M • Oriental Treatment #3: The Lost Empress / 1991 / AFV / M • Oriental Treatment #4: The Demon Lover / 1992 / AFV / M • The Oversexual Tourist / 1989 / VEX / M • Paris Blues / 1990 / WV / C • Paris Burning / 1989 / CC / M • Phantom X / 1989 / VC / M • The Pillowman / 1988 / VC / M • Playing With A Full Dick / 1988 / PL / M • Power Play (Venus 99) / 1990 / V99 / M • Prom Girls / 1988 / CA / M • Pumping Ethel / 1988 / PV / M • Puppy Love / 1992 / AFV / M • Quickies / 1992 / AFV / M • Rachel Ryan Exposed / 1990 / WV / C • Rainwoman #01 / 1989 / CC / M • Riding Miss Daisy / 1990 / VEX / M • Risque Business / 1989 / V99 / M • Roll-X Girls / 1989 / DYV / M • Romeo And Juliet #2 / 1988 / WV / M • Secret Dreams / 1991 / VEX / M • Seduction / 1990 / VEX / M • Sex Crazy / 1989 / FAN / C • Sextectives / 1989 / CIN / M • Sexual Fantasies / 1993 / ... / C • Seymore Butts In The Love Shack / 1992 / FH / M • She-Male Encounters #19: Toga Party / 1989 / MET / G • Silver Seduction / 1992 / VT / M • Simply Irresistible / 1988 / CC / M • Singles Holiday / 1990 / PM / M • Snatched / 1989 / VI / M • Special Request #2 / 1991 / HOM / B • Splash / 1990 / WV / C • Splash Shots / 1989 / CC / M • Stairway To Paradise / 1990 / VC / M • Stand-In Studs / 1989 / V99 / M • Still The Brat / 1988 / VI / M • Stolen Kisses / 1989 / VD / M • Sucker / 1988 / VWA / M • Surfside Sex / 1988 / CA / M • Suzie Superstar #3 / 1989 / CV / M • Swedish Erotica Featurettes #1 / 1989 / CA / M • Taste For Submission / 1991 / LON / C • A Taste Of Trinity Loren / 1990 / PIN / C • Taylor Made / 1989 / DR / M • Temptations / 1989 / DR / M • This Dick For Hire / 1989 / ZA / M • Tinseltown Wives / 1992 / AFV / M • Too Hot To Stop / 1989 / V99 / M • Uninhibited / 1989 / VC / G • Virgins / 1989 / CAR / M • Wanda Does Transylvania / 1990 / V99 / M • Westside Tori / 1989 / ERO / M • Wet Pink / 1989 / PL / F • Wetness For The Prosecution / 1989 / LV / M • Where The Girls Play / 1992 / CC / F • Who Reamed Rosie Rabbit? #2 / 1989 / FAN / M • Who Shaved Aja? / 1989 / EX / M • Wild Fire / 1990 / WV / C • Wild In The Woods / 1988 / VEX / M • With A Wiggle In Her Walk / 1989 / WV / M • A Woman's Touch / 1988 / ZA / F
AJA DEVORE
The Best Little He/She House In Texas / 1993 / HSV / G • Cocks In Frocks #2 / 1996 / TTV / G • Dragon Lady / 1995 / SPO / G • Dragula: Queen Of Darkness / 1996 / HSV / G • Gentlemen Prefer She-Males / 1995 / CDI / G • I'm A Curious She-Male /

1993 / HSV / G • Interview With A She-Male / 1995 / PL / G • Lady Dick / 1993 / HSV / G • Malibu She Males / 1994 / MET / G • Married With She-Males / 1993 / PL / G • Nydp Trannie / 1996 / WP / G • The Prize Package / 1993 / HSV / G • Samurai She-Males / 1994 / HSV / G • She Male Devil / 1996 / HSV / G • She Male Dicktation / 1994 / HEA / G • She-Mails / 1993 / PL / G • She-Male Call Girls / 1996 / BIZ / G • She-Male Encounters #21: Psychic She Males / 1994 / MET / G • She-Male Sex Stories / 1996 / STA / G • She-Male Shenanigans / 1994 / HSV / G • She-Male Trouble / 1994 / HEA / G • She-Male Vacation / 1993 / HSV / G • The She-Male Who Stole Christmas / 1993 / HSV / G • Showgirl She-Male / 1996 / HSV / G • Surprise Package / 1993 / HSV / G • Tranny Hill: Sweet Surrender / 1994 / HSV / G • Trans America / 1993 / TSS / G • Transitions (TV) / 1993 / HSV / G • Transsexual Try Outs / 1993 / HSV / G • Transvestite Tour Guide / 1993 / HSV / G • TV Dildo Fantasy #2 / 1996 / BIZ / G • TV Evangelist / 1993 / HSV / G

AJITO see Star Index I

AKAN BELKIRAN
Toredo / 1996 / ROX / M

AKASKA
GRG: Busty Beauties / 1994 / GRG / F

AKIM
Private Film #27 / 1995 / OD / M • Triple X Video Magazine #09 / 1995 / OD / M

AKIRA TANAKA see Star Index I

AL
Illusions Of A Lady / 1972 / VSH / M

AL BANESE see Star Index I

AL BOGAS see Alex San Paolo

AL BORDA
Chunky director/promoter who performs in his own movies.
Al Borda's Brazilian Adventures / 1996 / BEP / M • Because I Can / 1995 / BEP / M • Butt Love / 1995 / AB / M • Dirty Video / 1996 / AB / M • Girly Video Magazine #1 / 1995 / BEP / M • Girly Video Magazine #2 / 1995 / BEP / M • Girly Video Magazine #3 / 1995 / BEP / M • Girly Video Magazine #4 / 1996 / BEP / M • Girly Video Magazine #5 / 1996 / BEP / M • Only Video Magazine #6 / 1996 / AB / M • Indecent Interview / 1995 / PL / F • Major Fucking Slut / 1995 / BIP / M • Major Fucking Whore / 1995 / BEP / M • Paisley Hunter: The Girl Just Can't Help It / 1996 / BEP / M • Sinboy #1 / 1996 / SC / M • Sinboy #2: Yo' Ass Is Mine / 1996 / SC / M • Sinboy #3: The Island Of Dr. Moron / 1996 / SC / M • Sinboy #4: Bareass Barbecue / 1996 / SC / M • The Stranger / 1996 / BEP / M • Whore'n / 1996 / AB / M

AL BROWN see Peter North

AL CHAN
The Girls In The Band / 1976 / SVE / M

AL CHIURRIZZI see Star Index I

AL E. GATOR
Latex #1 / 1994 / VC / M

AL GOLDSTEIN
Publisher of *Screw* magazine. Born January 10, 1936.
All About Annette / 1982 / SE / C • All About Sex / 1970 / AR / M • American Garter / 1993 / VC / M • Buzzzz! / 1993 / OD / M • Dirty Looks / 1982 / VC / C • Honeypie / 1975 / VC / M • I Wanna Be A Porn Star #1 / 1996 / 4P / M • It Happened In

Hollywood / 1973 / WWV / M • Let My Puppets Come / 1975 / CA / M • The Love Witch / 1973 / AR / M • Midnight Blue #2 / 1980 / VXP / M • Midnight Blue: Rob Lowe, The Go-Go's, and Chuck Berry / 1990 / SVE / M • Only The Very Best On Film / 1992 / VC / C • Peepshow / 1994 / OD / M • S.O.S. / 1975 / QX / M • Screw / 1985 / CV / M • Tales From The Clit / 1993 / OD / M • Thrilled To Death / 1988 / REP / S • The Tongue / 1995 / OD / M • Vow Of Passion / 1991 / VI / M • [Screwed / 1996 / ... / S

AL GORK see Gerard Damiano

AL KRAMMER see Star Index I

AL LAVINSKY see Roger Caine

AL LAWRENCE
Dirty Hairy's Shove It Up My Ass / 1996 / GOT / M

AL LEVINSKY see Roger Caine

AL LEVITSKY see Roger Caine

AL LEWIS see Star Index I

AL MILLER
Over Eighteen #02 / 1997 / HW / M

AL MOORE
Baby Doll / 1975 / AR / M

AL NULLI see Star Index I

AL PACKER
Meatball / 1972 / VCX / M

AL PITTMAN
Matinee Idol / 1984 / VC / M

AL PITTSBURGH
Her Wicked Ways / 1983 / CA / M

AL POE (Al Pole, Dick Pole)
Clean shaven black male with an afro.
Coming Attractions / 1976 / VEP / M • Erotic Fantasies #3 / 1983 / CV / C • A Party In My Tight Pussy / 1994 / MET / M • Sally's Palace Of Delight / cr76 / CV / M • Tongue / 1974 / ALP / M

AL POLE see Al Poe

AL RAND
Resurrection Of Eve / 1973 / MIT / M

AL RUSSO see Star Index I

AL SELTZER see Star Index I

AL TEREGO (Ken DeLucia)
Introducer for the **Sodomania** and similar series.
Bottom Dweller: The Final Voyage / 1996 / EL / M • Double Anal Alternatives / 1996 / FI / M • Sodomania #16: Sexxy Pistols / 1996 / EL / M • Sodomania #17: Simply Makes U Tingle / 1996 / EL / M • Sodomania #18: Shame Based / 1996 / EL / M

AL THORNTON see King Tung

AL VON RONK see Star Index I

ALABAMA
Anal Camera #11 / 1995 / EVN / M • Borderline (Vivid) / 1995 / VI / M • California Sluts / 1995 / ZA / M • Deep Inside Anal Camera / 1996 / EVN / C • Hollywood Amateurs #21 / 1995 / MID / M • Hot Amateur Nights / 1996 / WV / M • Humpkin Pie / 1995 / HW / M • Joe Elliot's College Girls #40 / 1995 / JOE / F • Mike Hott: #308 Bonus Cunt: Alabama / 1995 / MHV / M • Mike Hott: #313 Three-Sum Sluts #05 / 1995 / MHV / M • Mike Hott: #314 Cum In My Cunt #05 / 1995 / MHV / M • My First Time #1 / 1995 / NS / M • Nasty Newcummers #11 / 1995 / MET / M • Sorority Sluts Passed Out / 1995 / ZA / M • Virgin Killers: The Killing Spree / 1995 / PEP / M

ALAIN
Magma: Anal Teenies / 1994 / MET / M • Magma: Perverse Games / 1995 / MET /

M • Magma: Swinger / 1995 / MET / M

ALAIN D'LYLE
The Voyeur #7: Live In Europe #1 / 1996 / JLP / M

ALAIN DELOIN
Private Film #15 / 1994 / OD / M • Private Film #17 / 1994 / OD / M • Private Film #27 / 1995 / OD / M • Private Film #28 / 1995 / OD / M • Private Gold #05: Cape Town #1 / 1996 / OD / M • Private Gold #06: Cape Town #2 / 1996 / OD / M • Private Gold #11: The Pyramid #1 / 1996 / OD / M • Private Gold #12: The Pyramid #2 / 1996 / OD / M • Private Gold #13: The Pyramid #3 / 1996 / OD / M • Private Gold #14: Sweet Lady #1 / 1997 / OD / M • Triple X Video Magazine #12 / 1996 / OD / M

ALAIN LYE
Magma: Hot Service / 1995 / MET / M • Triple X Video Magazine #09 / 1995 / OD / M

ALAIN PATANSAN
Impulse #06: / 1996 / MBP / M

ALAIN SAURY see Star Index I

ALAN
Alex Jordan's First Timers #05 / 1994 / OD / M • Soft Places / 1978 / CXV / M

ALAN ADRIAN (Spike Adrian, John A. Mozzer)
John A. Mozzer is the publisher of *Weird Smut Comics*.
ABA: Double Feature #4 / 1996 / ALP / M • Aphrodesia's Diary / 1984 / CA / M • Babylon Blue / 1983 / VXP / M • Beyond The Blue / cr78 / SVE / M • The Bizarre World Of F.J. Lincoln / 19?? / VHL / C • Black Sister, White Brother / 1987 / AT / M • Blue Ecstasy / 1980 / CA / M • Caught From Behind #01 / 1982 / HO / M • Centerfold Fever / 1981 / VXP / M • Confessions Of A Middle Aged Nympho / 1986 / WET / M • The Correct Ritual / 1995 / JAM / B • Debbie Does Dallas #2 / 1980 / VC / M • Devil In Miss Jones #2 / 1983 / VC / M • Dirty Blonde / 1984 / VXP / M • Dr Bizarro / 1978 / ALP / B • Dr Love And His House Of Perversions / 1978 / VC / M • Every Man's Fancy / 1983 / BIZ / B • Fashion Fantasies / 1986 / VC / M • First Time At Cherry High / 1984 / VC / M • Four X Feeling / 1986 / QX / M • Foxtrot / 1982 / COM / M • G-Strings / 1984 / COM / M • The Gimmo / 1983 / CA / M • Hot Stuff / 1984 / VXP / M • House Of Pleasure / 1984 / CA / M • Inside Little Oral Annie / 1984 / VXP / M • Jabberwalk #2 / 1982 / ... / S • Kneel Before Me! / 1983 / ALP / B • Little Oral Annie Takes Manhattan / 1985 / VXP / M • Lustfire / 1991 / LA / C • Maneaters / 1983 / VC / M • Mistresses At War #01 / 1993 / BIZ / B • Mistresses At War #02 / 1993 / BIZ / B • Nasty Girls (1983-VCX) / 1983 / VCX / M • Never Sleep Alone / 1984 / CA / M • Night Hunger / 1983 / AVC / M • Oriental Techniques Of Pain And Pleasure / 1983 / ALP / B • Painmania / 1983 / AVO / B • Parted Lips / 1986 / QX / M • Pink Clam / 1986 / RLV / M • The Pink Ladies / 1980 / VC / M • The Pleasures Of Innocence / 1985 / VC / M • Princess Seka / 1980 / VC / M • Pussy Power #02 / 1989 / BTO / M • Secluded Passion / 1983 / VHL / M • Seka Is Tara / 1981 / VC / M • Sexcapades / 1983 / VC / M • Spiked Heels / cr83 / BIZ / B • Stray Cats / 1985 / VXP / M • That's My Daughter / 1982 / NGV / M • Thirst For

Passion / 1988 / TRB / M • True Legends Of Adult Cinema: The Golden Age / 1992 / VC / C • Urges In Young Girls / 1984 / VC / M • Vanessa...Maid In Manhattan / 1984 / VC / M • White Women / 1986 / CC / M • Wild Innocents / 1982 / VCX / M • Women At Play / 1984 / SE / M • [The Gang's All Here / cr85 / STM / M

ALAN BASSINGER see Alan Bosshart

ALAN BOSSHART (Allen Bassenger, Alan Bassinger)
Beach Blanket Brat / 1989 / VI / M • The Bride / 1986 / WV / M • Bringing Up Brat / 1987 / VI / M • The Enchantress / 1990 / VI / M • The Pink Pussycat / 1992 / CA / M • Raquel Released / 1991 / VI / M • Realities #1 / 1991 / ZA / M • Risque Burlesque #1 / 1994 / IN / M • Sin Asylum / 1995 / CV / M • Taboo #10 / 1992 / IN / M • Torch #1 / 1990 / VI / M

ALAN CANDY
Twilight / 1996 / ESN / M

ALAN CLEMENT(S) see Jake Teague

ALAN DARK
Aroused / 1985 / VIV / M

ALAN FRENCH see Star Index I
ALAN GOLDBERG see Star Index I
ALAN GORDON see Star Index I
ALAN GROGAN see Star Index I

ALAN KATZ
Sex Boat / 1980 / VCX / M

ALAN LACOSTA see Star Index I
ALAN LEVITT see Roger Caine

ALAN LOGAN
Cherry Hustlers / 1977 / VEN / M • Night After Night / 1973 / BL / M • Reunion (Vanessa Del Rio's) / 1977 / LIM / M • Sensuous Flygirls / cr72 / VHL / M • Sweet Wet Lips / 1974 / PVX / M

ALAN MALAPROF
The Girls In The Band / 1976 / SVE / M

ALAN MARIO see Alan Marlow
ALAN MARLO see Alan Marlow

ALAN MARLOW (Alan Mario, Alan Marlo, Alex Mario)
ABA: Double Feature #2 / 1996 / ALP / M • Angela, The Fireworks Woman / 1975 / VC / M • Barbara Broadcast / 1977 / VC / M • The Bite / 1975 / SVE / M • Defiance / 1974 / ALP / B • Divine Obsession / 1976 / TVX / M • Fannie / 1975 / ALP / M • French Shampoo / 1978 / VXP / M • Funk / 1977 / ... / M • Maraschino Cherry / 1978 / QX / M • My Master, My Love / 1975 / BL / B • Naked Came The Stranger / 1975 / VC / M • Once...And For All / 1979 / HLV / M • Oriental Blue / 1975 / ALP / M • The Passions Of Carol / 1975 / VXP / M • The Private Afternoons Of Pamela Mann / 1974 / TVX / M • Slip Up / 1974 / ALP / M • Wet Rainbow / 1973 / AR / M • When A Woman Calls / 1975 / VXP / M

ALAN MARTIN
Dark Dreams / 1971 / ALP / M

ALAN NORTH see Star Index I

ALAN OLIVER
Girls With Curves #1 / 1985 / CV / M

ALAN RAINY
Intense Perversions #4 / 1996 / PL / M

ALAN ROYCE
Backstage Pass / 1983 / VC / M • Centerfold Celebrities #3 / 1983 / VC / M • GVC: Suburban Lust #128 / 1983 / GO / M • GVC: Women Who Seduce Men #123 / 1982 / GO / M • Layover / 1985 / HO / M • Love Bites / 1985 / CA / M • Malibu Summer / 1983 / VC / M • Mile High Club / 1983 / CV / M • Perfect Fit / 1985 / DR / M • Rich Bitch / 1985 / HO / M • Shades Of Ecstasy / 1983 / HO / M • Six Faces Of Samantha / 1984 / AA / M

ALAN SPITZ see Star Index I
ALAN STERLING see Star Index I

ALANA (Alana Patch, Alana Night, Alona (Alana))
Frizzy haired not too pretty blonde with something wrong with her eyes and on occasion her rear end (surpassing acne). Large but not humongous inflated tits. Appeared on the August 1982 (yes, 1982) issue of Chic.
Alana: A Gang Bang Fantasy / 1993 / FC / M • Anal Avenue / 1992 / LV / M • Anal Nature / 1993 / AFD / M • Behind The Blinds / 1992 / VIM / M • Black Orchid / 1993 / WV / M • Bobby Hollander's Sweet Cheeks #102 / 1992 / WV / M • Breast Worx #34 / 1992 / LBO / M • Bubble Butts #19 / 1992 / LBO / M • Butt Bongo Bonanza / 1993 / FC / M • Butts Afire / 1992 / PMV / M • Desperado / 1994 / SC / M • I Am Desire / 1992 / WV / M • Joe Elliot's Latin College Girls #01 / 1995 / JOE / M • Madame A / 1992 / LV / M • Pearl Necklace: Thee Bush League: The Best Of Oral #01 / 1993 / SEE / C • Pearl Necklace: Thee Bush League #04 / 1992 / SEE / M • Principles Of Lust / 1992 / WV / M • Sex Fantasy / 1993 / PPR / M • Seymore Butts Swings / 1992 / FH / M • Tight Pucker / 1992 / WV / M • Two Sisters / 1992 / WV / M • Welcome To Bondage: Alana Patch / 1993 / BON / B

ALANA BLUE (Victoria Pagan, Arlana Blue)
Emaciated brunette, long black hair, medium tits, not too pretty, overly long eyelashes.
Bloodsucking Freaks / 1975 / VES / B • Coming Through The Window / cr75 / VXP / F • Confessions Of A Young American Housewife / 1973 / ALP / S • Happy Days / 1974 / IHV / M • Honeypie / 1975 / VC / M • How To Score With Girls / 1980 / ... / S • Thunderbuns / 1976 / VCX / C

ALANA FERRARI see Alena Ferrari
ALANA NIGHT see Alana
ALANA PATCH see Alana

ALBA BONN
Dracula Exotica / 1980 / TVX / M

ALBAN CERAY (Allan Ceray)
Bedside Manor / 1986 / CA / M • Diamond Snatch / 1977 / COM / M • Evil Mistress / 1984 / VIP / M • Exces Pornographiques / 1977 / ... / M • Hot Close-Ups / 1985 / CA / M • House Of 1001 Pleasures / 1985 / VC / M • Pussy Talk #2 / 1977 / CV / M • The Seduction Of Tessa / cr86 / CA / M • Sextasy / 1978 / COM / M • Sexual Circles / 1977 / VD / M • Traci, I Love You / 1987 / CA / M • [Cathy, Fille Soumise / 1977 / ... / M • [Indecences 1930 / 1977 / ... / M • [Vibrations Sensuelles / 1976 / ... / M

ALBERT
Magma: Sperm-Crazy / 1994 / MET / M

ALBERT DAVIS
Bad Girls #4 / 1984 / GO / M

ALBERT GORK see Gerard Damiano

ALBERT JOHNSON
Purely Physical / 1982 / SE / M

ALBERT LONDON
Erotic Fantasies #2 / 1983 / CV / C • The Joy Of Fooling Around / 1978 / CV / M

ALBERT PATH

Old Guys & Dolls #1 / 1995 / PL / M

ALBERTO
Julie's Diary / 1995 / LBO / M • Swedish Sex / 1996 / PL / M

ALBERTO FERRO see Lasse Braun

ALBERTO LOUIS
Midnight Obsession / 1995 / XC / M

ALBERTO REY
Buttman's Bouncin' British Babes / 1994 / EA / M • Penetrator #2: Grudge Day / 1995 / PL / M • Private Film #13 / 1994 / OD / M • Private Film #15 / 1994 / OD / M • Private Film #25 / 1995 / OD / M • Private Gold #01: Study In Sex / 1995 / OD / M • Private Gold #02: Friends In Sex / 1995 / OD / M • Private Gold #03: The Chase / 1996 / OD / M • Private Stories #01 / 1995 / OD / M • Private Stories #02 / 1995 / OD / M • Private Stories #03 / 1995 / OD / M • Private Stories #08 / 1996 / OD / M • Private Video Magazine #26 / 1995 / OD / M • Sodomania #08: The London Sessions / 1994 / EL / M • Triple X Video Magazine #07 / 1995 / OD / M • Triple X Video Magazine #10 / 1995 / OD / M

ALBERTO SANCHEZ
Don Salvatore: The Last Sicilian / 1995 / XC / M • Paprika / 1995 / XC / M • Private Film #06 / 1994 / OD / M • Private Film #10 / 1994 / OD / M • Virility / 1996 / XC / M

ALDO RAY
Biohazard / 1984 / MNT / S • Evils Of The Night / 1985 / LIV / S • Human Experiments / 1980 / VAM / S • Shock 'em Dead / 1990 / AE / S • The Sicilian / 1987 / LIV / S • Sweet Savage / 1978 / ALP / M

ALDO SNEED see Star Index I

ALEC AZOUS
Bucky Beaver's XXX Dragon Art Theatre Double Feature #10 / 1996 / SOW / M • Sins Of Sandra / cr72 / SOW / M

ALEC DANES
Lost In Vegas / 1996 / AWV / G

ALEC FREDERICK
Taboo American Style #3: Nina Becomes An Actress / 1985 / VC / M • Taboo American Style #4: The Exciting Conclusion / 1985 / VC / M

ALEC GROSSI see Star Index I

ALEC METRO
Alumni Girls / 1996 / GO / M • Angels In Flight / 1995 / NIT / M • Babe Watch #3 / 1995 / SC / M • Babe Watch #4 / 1995 / SC / M • The Bottom Line / 1995 / NIT / M • Carnal Invasions / 1996 / NIT / M • The Doll House / 1995 / CV / M • Erotic Visions / 1995 / ULI / M • Every Woman Has A Fantasy #3 / 1995 / VC / M • Fellatio Fanatics / 1996 / NIT / M • For Your Mouth Only / 1995 / GO / M • Forbidden / 1996 / SC / M • Generation X / 1995 / WAV / M • Hawaii / 1995 / VI / M • Hotel California / 1995 / MID / M • Innocence Lost / 1995 / GO / M • Jizz Glazed Goo Guzzlers #2 / 1996 / NIT / C • Kia Unmasked / 1995 / LE / M • Killer Tits / 1995 / LE / M • Kissing Kaylan / 1995 / CC / M • Lady Luck / 1995 / PMV / M • Lisa / 1997 / SC / M • Maui Waui / 1996 / PE / M • Mickey Ray's Sex Search #01: Sliding In / 1994 / WIV / M • My First Time #2 / 1996 / NS / M • Mysteria / 1995 / NIT / M • The Other Woman / 1996 / VC / M • Penetrator #2: Grudge Day / 1995 / PL / M • Philmore Butts Adventures In Paradise / 1996 / SUF / M • Private Dancers / 1996 / RAS / M • Promises &

Lies / 1995 / SS / M • Pussyman Auditions #07 / 1995 / SNA / M • Rear Window / 1996 / NIT / M • Rebel Cheerleaders / 1995 / VI / M • Ripe & Ready (Infinity) / 1995 / IF / M • Russian Roulette / 1995 / NIT / M • Scorched / 1995 / ONA / M • Screamers (Gourmet) / 1995 / ONA / M • The Sex Therapist / 1995 / GO / M • Shane's World #7 / 1996 / OD / M • Snatch Motors / 1995 / VC / M • Takin' It To The Limit #6 / 1995 / BS / M • Texas Crude / 1995 / NIT / M • Three Hearts / 1995 / CC / M • Thunder Boobs / 1995 / BTO / M • The Tigress / 1995 / VIM / M • Twists Of The Heart / 1995 / NIT / M • Up Close & Personal #2 / 1996 / IPI / M • Venom #7 / 1996 / VD / M • Wedding Night Blues / 1995 / EMC / M

ALEC POWERS
All-Star Softball Game / 1995 / SAB / G • Driven Home / 1995 / CSP / G • Nydp Trannie / 1996 / WP / G • Please Don't Tell / 1995 / CEN / G • Revenge Of The Bi Dolls / 1994 / CAT / G

ALEECIA *see Star Index I*

ALEEN MAI *see Star Index I*

ALEENA FERRARI *see Alena Ferrari*

ALEINA FERRARI *see Alena Ferrari*

ALEISHA LASHLEY *see Sade*

ALEJANDRA EGEA
Club Privado / 1995 / KP / M

ALEKSANDRA NICE
6969 Mel'hose Place / 1995 / VG0 / M • Barby's On Butt Row / 1996 / ABS / M • Dirty Dave's #1 / 1996 / VG0 / M • Dirty Dave's #3 / 1996 / XPR / M • Eat At Dave's #7 / 1996 / SP / M • Hardcore Debutantes #01 / 1996 / TEP / M • Interview's Foreign Affair / 1996 / LV / M • Old Bitches / 1996 / GLI / M • Pick Up Lines #09 / 1996 / OD / M • Sin-A-Matic / 1996 / VI / M • Video Virgins #33 / 1996 / NS / M

ALENA FERRARI *(Allena Ferrari, Aleena Ferrari, Aileen Ferrari, Aleina Ferrari, Alana Ferrari)*
Looks a bit like April West but with a big ass. Blondes On Fire / 1987 / VCR / C • Cat 'nipped / 1995 / PLV / B • Dialing For Desires / 1988 / 4P / M • Enemarathon / 1987 / BIZ / B • Flying High With Rikki Lee / 1992 / VEX / C • Flying High With Tracey Adams / 1987 / VEX / M • Friday The 13th #1: A Nude Beginning / 1987 / VD / M • Let's Get Naked / 1987 / VEX / M • Loose Lifestyles / 1988 / CA / M • Lucy Makes It Big / 1987 / ME / M • Magic Fingers / 1987 / ME / M • Sex For Secrets / 1987 / VCR / M • Sexperiences / 1987 / VEX / M • Space Vixens / 1987 / V99 / M • Tailspin / 1987 / AVC / M • Wet Weekend / 1987 / MAC / M

ALESKI TOMORKA
Sex-A-Holic Lady / 1995 / PL / M

ALESSANDRA
Ejacula #1 / 1992 / VC / M • Ejacula #2 / 1992 / VC / M

ALESSANDRO SELVAGGIO
Private Film #19 / 1994 / OD / M

ALEX
Anabolic Import #01: Anal X / 1994 / ANA / M • Bobby Hollander's Rookie Nookie #03 / 1993 / SFP / M • British Babe Hunt / 1996 / VC / M • Cat Walk / 1994 / KBR / S • Diamond's Outdoor Adventures / 1995 / DIP / M • Hazards In Heels / 1991 / RSV / S • HomeGrown Video #448: Look Who's

Cumming For Dinner / 1995 / HOV / M • Joe Elliot's College Girls #42 / 1995 / JOE / M • Kinky College Cunts #04 / 1993 / NS / F • Lee Nover: The Search For The Perfect Butt / 1996 / IP / M • Pearl Necklace: Thee Bush League: The Best Of Oral #01 / 1993 / SEE / C • The Reel Sex World #02 / 1994 / WP / M • S&M On The Ranch: Training The New Pony Girl / 1994 / VER / B • Shane's World #6: Slumber Party / 1996 / OD / F • Shaved #02 / 1992 / RB / F • Shaved #03 / 1992 / RB / F • Stevi's: Solo Squirts / 1994 / SSV / F • Stevi's: The Gusher / 1992 / SSV / M • Thermonuclear Sex / 1996 / EL / M • Uncle Roy's Amateur Home Video #09 / 1992 / VIM / M • Wild Desires / 1994 / MAX / M

ALEX (FEMALE)
New Faces, Hot Bodies #19 / 1995 / STP / M

ALEX (JAY ASHLEY) *see Jay Ashley*

ALEX (MALE)
New Faces, Hot Bodies #19 / 1995 / STP / M

ALEECIA — *[see above]*

ALEX ALLEY *see Star Index I*

ALEX APOLLO *see Alex San Paolo*

ALEX BEHAN
Julie's Diary / 1995 / LBO / M

ALEX BERRY
Anal Alice / 1992 / AFV / M • Anal House Party / 1993 / IP / M • Big Murray's New-Cummers #15: Rump Humpers / 1993 / FD / M • Bobby Hollander's Sweet Cheeks #108 / 1993 / QUA / M • Bubble Butts #24 / 1993 / LBO / M • The Gang Bang Story / 1993 / IP / M • Hometown Honeys #4 / 1993 / VEX / M • The Last American Sex Goddess / 1993 / IF / M • Mickey Ray's Sex Search #02: Tight Spots / 1994 / WIV / M • Summertime Boobs / 1994 / LEI / M

ALEX BLOKE *see Star Index I*

ALEX BROWN
Anna Amore's Fantasy Gang Bang / 1996 / FC / M • Oldies But Goodies / 1995 / WIV / M • Tailz From Da Hood #2 / 1995 / AVI / M

ALEX CARRINGTON
The Bi Spy / 1991 / STA / G • Inside Of Me / 1993 / PL / G • Lost In Vegas / 1996 / AWV / G

ALEX CARSON *see Star Index I*

ALEX DANE *(Loni (Alex Dane), Lonnie (Alex Dane), Dela Cucchi, Alex Dayne, Alexandria Dane, Alexus Dane, Olivia (Alex Dane), Maganda, Luna, Apolonia, Appolonia (Alex D.), Alexia Dane)*
Petite, pretty tomboy with a great personality, big deep coals for eyes, long straight black hair, very endearing smile and laugh but unfortunately, not a tight waist. Was 25 years old in 1994 and was 16 when de-virginized. Trained as a ballet dancer and then became a choreographer with a rock band. Was married at one stage. Not to be confused with the pretty blonde, Annabelle Dayne. Abducted / 1996 / ZA / M • Adam & Eve's House Party #1 / 1995 / VC / M • The Adventures Of Studman #3 / 1994 / AFV / M • American Fan Club Prowl / 1996 / VT / M • Anal Cum Queens / 1995 / ZA / M • Anal Delinquent #3 / 1995 / ROB / M • Anal Fireball / 1996 / ROB / M • Anal Load Lickers / 1996 / ROB / M • Anal Sex / 1996 / ZA / M • Anal Talisman / 1996 / ZA / M • Anal Trashy Ass / 1995 / ROB / M • Analtown USA #05 / 1995 / NIT / M • Arizona Gold / 1996 / KLP / M • Assy Sassy #3 /

1995 / ROB / F • Bad Company / 1994 / VI / M • Bad Luck For Bad Girls / 1996 / EXQ / B • Badgirls #3: Cell Block 69 / 1994 / VI / M • Bangkok Dreams / 1996 / SUF / M • Bangkok Nights / 1994 / VI / M • Beyond Reality #3: Stand Erect! / 1996 / EXQ / M • Black Jack City #4 / 1994 / HW / M • Booty Ho #3 / 1995 / ROB / M • Bootylicious: White Trash / 1995 / JMP / M • Bordello / 1995 / VI / M • Bun Busters #18 / 1994 / LBO / M • Bun Busters #19 / 1994 / LBO / M • Burlesxxx / 1996 / VT / M • Butt Bandits #4 / 1996 / VD / C • Butt Hunt #05 / 1995 / LEI / M • Butt Jammers #01 / 1995 / SC / F • Butt Jammers #05 / 1996 / SC / F • The Butt Sisters Do Boston / 1995 / MID / M • Butt Sluts #5 / 1995 / ROB / F • Buttslammers #12: Anal Madness / 1996 / BS / F • Buttslammers #13: The Madness Continues / 1996 / BS / F • California Swingers / 1996 / LV / M • Carnal Garden / 1996 / KLP / M • Casting Call #14 / 1995 / SO / M • Casting Call #18 / 1996 / SO / M • The Cathouse / 1994 / VI / M • Caught From Behind #21 / 1995 / HO / M • Caught Looking / 1995 / CC / M • Checkmate / 1996 / SNA / M • Cherry Poppers #15: Mischievous Maidens / 1996 / ZA / M • Compulsion (Fat Dog) / 1996 / FD / M • Conjugal Visits / 1995 / EVN / M • Conquest / 1996 / WP / M • Creme De Femme / 1994 / 4P / F • Creme De La Face #02 / 1994 / OD / M • Creme De La Face #05 / 1994 / OD / M • Cumback Pussy #2: Crawling Back For More / 1996 / EL / M • Cumback Pussy #5: Groopin' / 1996 / EL / M • The Cumm Brothers #03: Go To Traffic School / 1994 / OD / M • Dangerous / 1996 / SNA / M • The Decadent Adventures Of Generation XXX / 1994 / MAX / M • Deep Focus / 1995 / VC / M • Deep Inside Nikki Sinn / 1996 / VC / C • Desert Moon / 1994 / SPI / M • Dirty Dating Service #06 / 1994 / WP / M • Dirty Diner #3 / 1996 / SC / M • Dirty Doc's Housecalls #20 / 1994 / LV / M • The Doctor Is In #3: Achy Breaky Tarts / 1995 / NIT / M • Dr Finger's House Of Lesbians / 1996 / SC / M • Dreams Of A Gigolo / 1996 / SNA / M • Entangled / 1996 / KLP / M • Erotic Desires / 1994 / MAX / M • Eternal Lust / 1996 / VC / M • Family Affair / 1996 / XC / M • Far East Fantasy / 1995 / SUF / M • Finger Sluts #1 / 1996 / LV / F • First Time Lesbians #20 / 1994 / JMP / F • First Whores Club / 1996 / ERA / M • Forbidden Cravings / 1996 / VC / M • Forever Young / 1994 / VI / M • Full Metal Babes / 1995 / LE / M • Gang Bang Butthole Surfin' / 1996 / ROB / M • Gangbang Girl #15 / 1995 / ANA / M • Hardcore Schoolgirls #1: Sweet Young Things / 1995 / XPR / M • Hidden Camera #19 / 1994 / JMP / M • The Hitch-Hiker #13: Highway To Hell / 1995 / VIM / M • Hollywood Amateurs #12 / 1994 / MID / M • Hollywood Sex Tour / 1995 / VC / M • The Horny Hiker / 1995 / LE / M • Hot Tight Asses #14 / 1995 / TCK / M • Hot Tight Asses #15 / 1996 / TCK / M • Hot Tight Asses #16 / 1996 / TCK / M • Hotel Fantasy / 1995 / IN / M • Indecent Obsessions / 1995 / BBE / M • Interview's Southern Cumfort / 1996 / LV / M • Interviews At The Hard Wok Cafe / 1996 / LOF / M • Jenna Ink / 1996 / WP / M • Kink Show / 1997 / BON / B • Lesbian Climax / 1995 / ROB / F • Lust & Money / 1995 / SUF / M • Lust In

Time / 1996 / ONA / M • Midget Goes Hawaiian / 1995 / FC / M • Midget On Milligan's Island / 1995 / FC / M • More Dirty Debutantes #36 / 1994 / 4P / M • More Dirty Debutantes #38 / 1995 / 4P / M • Mr. Peepers Amateur Home Videos #88: A For Effort / 1994 / LBO / M • Mr. Peepers Amateur Home Videos #92: M-Ass-terpieces / 1994 / LBO / M • Muff Divers #1 / 1996 / TV / F • Mystic Tales Of The Orient / 1994 / PRK / M • The Naked Truth / 1995 / VI / M • Nasty Nymphos #06 / 1994 / ANA / M • Nektar / 1996 / BAC / M • The New Butt Hunt #12 / 1995 / LEI / C • Night Tales / 1996 / VC / M • Nightmare Visions / 1994 / ERA / M • No Man's Land #15 / 1996 / VT / F • Nothing Like A Dame #1 / 1995 / IN / M • Orgies Orgies Orgies / 1994 / WV / M • Out Of Love / 1995 / VI / M • Pai Gow Video #07: East Meets West / 1995 / EVN / M • Paradise / 1995 / FD / M • Perverted Stories #03 / 1995 / JMP / M • Perverted Stories #06 / 1996 / JMP / M • Philmore Butts Las Vegas Vacation / 1995 / SUF / M • Pick Up Lines #01 / 1995 / 4P / M • Pick Up Lines #02 / 1995 / 4P / M • Pick Up Lines #04 / 1995 / 4P / M • Pick Up Lines #06 / 1996 / OD / M • Private Desires / 1995 / LE / M • Puritan Video Magazine #05 / 1996 / LE / M • Pussyman #14: Dreams Of A Gigolo / 1996 / SNA / M • Raw Footage / 1996 / VC / M • The Scam / 1996 / LV / M • Selena Under Siege / 1995 / XCI / M • Sex Suites / 1995 / TP / M • Sex, Truth & Videotape #2 / 1996 / DOC / M • Sexhibition #1 / 1996 / SUF / M • The Shocking Truth #2 / 1996 / DWO / M • Snatch Patch / 1995 / LE / M • The Social Club / 1995 / LE / M • Sodomania #15: Warning! / 1996 / EL / M • Sodomania: Slop Shots / 1996 / EL / C • Some Like It Wet / 1995 / LE / M • Sorority Sex Kittens #3 / 1996 / VC / M • Streetwalkers / 1995 / HO / M • Student Fetish Videos: Bondage #02 / 1996 / PRE / B • Student Fetish Videos: Catfighting #16 / 1996 / PRE / B • Student Fetish Videos: The Enema #20 / 1996 / PRE / B • Surf Babes / 1995 / LE / M • Sweet Revenge / 1997 / KBE / M • Tail Taggers #128: / 1994 / WV / M • Takin' It To The Limit #8: Hooked On Crack / 1996 / BS / M • Teacher's Pet #2 / 1994 / WMG / M • Temple Of Love / 1995 / SUF / M • Tootsies & Footsies / 1994 / LBO / M • Ultimate Sensations / 1996 / NIT / M • Venom #5 / 1996 / VD / M • Venom #7 / 1996 / VD / M • Vibrating Vixens #2 / 1996 / TV / F • Video Virgins #14 / 1994 / NS / M • The Violation Of Alexandria Dane / 1995 / JMP / F • Virgin Hotline / 1996 / LVP / F • What You Are In The Dark / 1995 / KLP / M • Where The Girls Sweat...Not The Sequel / 1996 / EL / F • Whispered Secrets Of The Call Girls / 1995 / TVE / F • Wicked Fantasies / 1996 / CO2 / M • Yin Yang Oriental Love Bang #3: Bangkok Dreams / 1996 / SUF / M • Young & Natural #01 / 1995 / PRE / F • Young & Natural #02 / 1995 / PRE / F • Young & Natural #03 / 1995 / PRE / F • Young & Natural #08 / 1995 / PRE / F • Young & Natural #09 / 1995 / PRE / C

ALEX DAYNE *see* **Alex Dane**
ALEX DERENZY *(Rex Borsky)*
Director. The name Rex Boorski is a character played by the actor George Flower in **Video**

Vixens.
ALEX DOESEMALL
6969 Mel'hose Place / 1995 / VG0 / M
ALEX EKDAB *see Star Index I*
ALEX FIGUEROA *see Star Index I*
ALEX FLOWER
The Tale Of Tiffany Lust / 1981 / CA / M
ALEX GABOR *see* **Sasha Gabor**
ALEX GRECO *(Alexis Greco, Alexandria Greco, Alexandra Grecco, Alex Rocco (Greco), Joanne Greco, Joanna (Greco))*
Joanna is from **Unnatural Phenonomen #1**.
1001 Erotic Nights #2 / 1987 / VC / M • Acts Of Love / 1989 / ... / M • Adultery / 1986 / DR / M • Amanda By Night #2 / 1987 / CA / M • Bionic Babes / 1986 / 4P / M • Blazing Matresses / 1986 / AVC / M • Brat On The Run / 1987 / VI / M • Cheri's On Fire / 1986 / V99 / M • Debbie Does Dishes #1 / 1985 / AVC / M • Debbie Does Dishes #3 / 1987 / AVC / M • Dr Lust / 1987 / VC / M • Dream Girls / 1986 / VC / M • Dynamic Vices / 1987 / VC / M • Glamour Girls / 1987 / SE / M • Hay Fever / 1988 / TIG / F • Hot And Nasty! / 1986 / V99 / C • Hot Rocks / 1986 / WET / M • Hottest Parties / 1988 / VC / C • Irresistible #2 / 1986 / SE / M • Love At First Sight / 1987 / SE / C • Lover's Lane / 1986 / SE / M • Mouthwatering / 1986 / BRA / M • Nasty Nights / 1988 / PL / C • Naughty Girls Like It Big / 1986 / ELH / M • The Pleasure Maze / 1986 / PL / M • Rated Sex / 1986 / SE / M • The Red Garter / 1986 / SE / M • Screwdriver / 1988 / CC / C • Sex And The Secretary / 1988 / PP / M • Sin City / 1986 / WET / M • Talk Dirty To Me #05 / 1987 / DR / M • The Ultimate Lover / 1986 / VD / M • Unnatural Phenomenon #1 / 1985 / WV / M • Unnatural Phenomenon #2 / 1986 / WV / M • Unveiled / 1987 / VC / M • Woman In The Window / 1986 / TEM / M
ALEX HORN *(Alexander Horn, Axel Horn, Alex Schwart, Alex Wolf)*
Bazooka County #2 / 1989 / CC / M • The Chameleon / 1989 / VC / M • De Blond / 1989 / EA / M • Falcon Head / 1990 / ARG / M • Hollywood Knights #3 / 1991 / PCP / M • My Friend, My Lover / 1990 / FIR / M • My Sensual Body / 1989 / WET / M • The Outlaw / 1989 / VD / M • Paris Burning / 1989 / CC / M • Purple Haze / 1991 / WV / M • Rock 'n' Roll Heaven / 1989 / EA / M • The Swap #1 / 1990 / VI / M • Taylor Made / 1989 / DR / M • Torrid Without A Cause #2 / 1990 / VI / M
ALEX JORDAN *(Karen Hughes)*
Blonde with small tits, passable but older face and nice tight body. She married Justin Case on May 2, 1992. She used to be a deep sea diver working out of Liverpool (U.K.). She went to Australia and married a Britisher. She returned to Florida to the salvage business. (All of this seems rather unbelievable, so take it for what it's worth.) Committed suicide on July 2, 1995 by hanging herself. Her real name is Karen Elizabeth Hughes and she was 31 (born September 20, 1967) when she died.
1-900-FUCK #1 / 1995 / SO / M • Adult Video Nudes / 1993 / VC / M • The Adventures Of Seymore Butts / 1992 / FH / M • Alex Jordan's First Timers #01 / 1993 / OD / M •

Alex Jordan's First Timers #02 / 1993 / OD / M • Alex Jordan's First Timers #03 / 1993 / OD / M • Alex Jordan's First Timers #04 / 1994 / OD / M • Alex Jordan's First Timers #05 / 1994 / OD / M • Alex Jordan's First Timers #06 / 1994 / OD / M • Alex On My Mind / 1992 / VAL / M • America's Raunchiest Home Videos #13: Beauty And The Beach / 1992 / ZA / M • America's Raunchiest Home Videos #47: / 1993 / ZA / M • Anal Ecstacy Girls #1 / 1993 / ROB / F • The Anal-Europe Series #01: The Fisherman's Wife / 1992 / LV / M • B.L.O.W. / 1992 / LV / M • Bare Market / 1993 / VC / M • Beach Bum Amateur's #04 / 1992 / MID / M • Bedtime Tales / 1995 / IF / M • Bend Over Babes #3 / 1992 / EA / M • Best Butt(e) In The West #1 / 1992 / CC / M • The Best Of Buttslammers / 1995 / BS / C • Beverly Hills 90269 / 1992 / LV / M • Beverly Hills Madam / 1993 / FH / F • Biff Malibu's Totally Nasty Home Videos #04 / 1992 / ANA / M • Biff Malibu's Totally Nasty Home Videos #07 / 1992 / ANA / M • Biff Malibu's Totally Nasty Home Videos #14 / 1992 / ANA / M • The Bitches / 1993 / LIP / F • Bitches In Heat / 1994 / PL / C • Blonde Justice #1 / 1993 / VI / M • Blonde Justice #2 / 1993 / VI / M • Blow For Blow / 1992 / ZA / M • Body And Soul / 1992 / OD / M • Body And Soul / 1995 / BON / B • Bondage Memories #04 / 1994 / BON / C • Bonnie & Clyde #1 / 1992 / VI / M • Bonnie & Clyde #2 / 1992 / VI / M • The Booty Guard / 1993 / IP / M • Box Of Slavegirls / 1995 / LON / B • Breast Worx #36 / 1992 / LBO / M • Buffy Malibu's Totally Nasty All-Girl Home Videos #01 / 1992 / ANA / F • Butt Freak #2 / 1996 / EA / M • Butt Sluts #1 / 1993 / ROB / F • Buttslammers #01 / 1993 / BS / F • Cheating / 1994 / VI / M • Cheerleader Nurses #1 / 1993 / VC / M • Cheerleader Nurses #2 / 1993 / VC / M • Club Anal #1 / 1993 / ROB / F • Club Midnight / 1992 / LV / M • Crazy Times / 1995 / BS / B • The D.J. / 1992 / VC / M • The Darker Side Of Shayla #1 / 1993 / PL / M • Day Dreams / 1993 / CV / M • Dear John / 1993 / VI / M • Deep Inside Crystal Wilder / 1995 / VC / C • Deep Inside Nicole London / 1995 / VC / C • Deep Inside Nikki Dial / 1994 / VC / C • Deep Inside Nina Hartley / 1993 / VC / M • Depraved / 1993 / BS / B • Dick At Nite / 1993 / MET / M • Dirty Bob's #03: Xplicit Interviews / 1992 / FLP / S • Domination / 1994 / WP / M • Dream Teams / 1992 / VAL / M • Electro Sex / 1994 / FPI / M • Eleventh Annual AVN Awards / 1994 / VC / M • Endlessly / 1993 / VI / M • Fantasy Escorts / 1993 / FOR / M • Feds In Bed / 1993 / HO / M • Felicia's Fantasies / 1995 / HOM / B • Femme Fatale / 1993 / SC / M • The Fluffer #2 / 1993 / FD / M • For The Money #1 / 1993 / FH / M • For The Money #2 / 1993 / FH / M • Forbidden Obsessions / 1993 / BS / B • Forbidden Pleasures / 1995 / ERA / M • Frat Girls / 1993 / VC / M • Fun & Games / 1994 / FD / C • Gangbang Girl #16 / 1995 / ANA / M • Good Vibrations / 1993 / ZA / M • The Good, The Bad & The Nasty / 1992 / VC / M • Gorgeous / 1995 / MET / M • Hard Talk / 1992 / VC / M • Hard To Stop #2 / 1992 / VC / M • Hard Whips For Soft Bodies / 1993 / NTP / B • Heaven Scent (Las Vegas) / 1993 / LV / M • Hidden

Agenda / 1992 / XCI / M • Hypnotic Passions / 1993 / FOR / M • Inferno #1 / 1993 / SC / M • Inferno #2 / 1993 / SC / M • Insatiable Nurses / 1992 / VIM / M • Interview With A Vamp / 1994 / ANA / M • Intimate Spys / 1992 / FOR / M • Jasmine's Girls / 1995 / LON / B • Jennifer 69 / 1992 / PL / M • Jennifer Ate / 1993 / XCI / F • The Joi Fuk Club / 1993 / WV / M • Junkyard Dykes #02 / 1994 / ZA / F • Knight Shadows / 1992 / BS / B • Kym Wilde Sessions #3 / 1993 / RB / B • Kym Wilde's Ocean View / 1993 / BON / B • Kym Wilde's On The Edge #01 / 1993 / RB / B • Kym Wilde's On The Edge #19 / 1995 / RB / B • Kym Wilde's On The Edge #21 / 1995 / RB / B • Laguna Nights / 1995 / FH / M • Layover / 1994 / VI / M • Lethal Lolita / 1993 / LE / M • Licking Legends #1 / 1992 / LE / F • Licking Legends #2 / 1992 / LE / F • Madame A / 1992 / LV / M • Maneater (1992-Las Vegas) / 1992 / LV / M • Mike Hott: #195 Cunt of the Month: Alex Jordan / 1992 / MHV / F • Mike Hott: #196 Lesbian Sluts #01 / 1992 / MHV / F • Mike Hott: #202 Horny Couples #02 / 1992 / MHV / M • Mind Shadows #1 / 1993 / FD / M • Mind Shadows #2 / 1993 / FD / M • Mistress Of Shadows / 1995 / HOM / B • Misty @ Midnight / 1995 / LE / M • Misty's First Whipping / 1994 / LON / B • Mortal Passions / 1995 / FD / M • Mr. Peepers Amateur Home Videos #55: Anal Antics / 1992 / LBO / M • Naked Truth #1 / 1993 / FH / M • Nasty Nymphos #08 / 1995 / ANA / M • Nasty Nymphos #12 / 1996 / ANA / M • Neighborhood Watch #24: Nice Sticky Stuff / 1992 / LBO / M • Neighbors / 1994 / LE / M • Night Train / 1993 / VI / M • Nightvision / 1995 / VI / M • Nikki At Night / 1993 / LE / M • Odyssey 30 Min: #159: Blonde Beauty And The Beast / 1991 / OD / M • Odyssey 30 Min: #232: / 1992 / OD / M • One Of Our Porn Stars Is Missing / 1993 / OD / M • Oral Majority #10 / 1993 / WV / C • Our Bang #01 / 1992 / GLI / M • Our Bang #09 / 1993 / GLI / M • Painful Lessons (Bruce Seven) / 1992 / BS / B • Parlor Games / 1993 / VI / M • The Party / 1992 / CDI / M • Party Pack #2 / 1994 / LE / F • Phantom Pain / 1993 / BON / D • Pink Champagne #1: Pink Sundae / 1992 / PCV / M • Playin' With Fire / 1993 / LV / M • Profiles #04: Lust Lessons / 1995 / XPR / M • Pubic Eye / 1992 / HW / M • Pure Filth / 1995 / RV / M • Radical Affairs Video Magazine #04 / 1992 / ME / M • Ready Freddy? / 1992 / FH / M • Rears In Windows / 1993 / FH / M • Red Hot Coeds / 1993 / VIM / M • Ride The Pink Lady / 1993 / WV / M • Roto-Rammer / 1993 / LV / M • Rump Humpers #01 / 1992 / GLI / M • A Scent Of A Girl / 1993 / LV / M • Sex Police 2000 / 1992 / AFV / M • Sex Stories / 1992 / VC / M • Seymore Butts & The Honeymooners / 1992 / FH / M • Seymore Butts In The Love Shack / 1992 / FH / M • Seymore Butts Rides Again / 1992 / FH / M • Seymore Butts: Bustin' Out My Best Anal / 1995 / FH / C • Shades Of Blue / 1992 / VC / M • Silent Stranger / 1992 / VI / M • Single White Woman / 1992 / FD / M • Sittin' Pretty #2 / 1992 / DR / M • Skin To Skin / 1993 / LE / M • Slave Of Fashion / 1993 / LON / B • A Slow Hand / 1992 / FD / M • Sneek Peeks #2 / 1993 / OCV / M •

The Spanking Pact / 1995 / CAA / B • Spermacus / 1993 / PI / M • Surrogate Lover / 1992 / TP / M • Tailiens #2 / 1992 / FD / M • Tailiens #3 / 1992 / FD / M • Talk Dirty To Me #09 / 1992 / DR / M • Tenth Annual Adult Video News Awards / 1993 / VC / M • Titty Slickers #2 / 1994 / LE / M • Too Hot To Touch #2 / 1993 / CV / M • Topless Lightweight Spectacular: Alex Jordan Vs. Tina... / 1994 / VSL / B • Torture Clinic / 1995 / LON / B • Two Sisters / 1992 / WV / M • Ultimate Orgy #2 / 1992 / GLI / M • Ultimate Orgy #3 / 1992 / GLI / M • The Unashamed / 1993 / FD / M • Uncle Roy's Amateur Home Video #01 / 1992 / VIM / M • Uncle Roy's Amateur Home Video #02 / 1992 / VIM / M • Uncle Roy's Amateur Home Video #07 / 1992 / VIM / M • Uncle Roy's Amateur Home Video #10 / 1992 / VIM / M • Uncle Roy's Best Of The Best: Red Hots / 1993 / VIM / C • Uninhibited Love / 1994 / VPN / M • Vampire's Kiss / 1993 / AVI / M • Victoria's Amateurs #03 / 1992 / VGA / M • The Way They Wuz / 1996 / SHS / C • A Way With Wood / 1995 / HOM / B • Welcome To Bondage: Alex Jordan With Justin Case / 1992 / BON / B • Welcome To Bondage: Starlets #1 / 1993 / BON / C • Whispered Lies / 1993 / LBO / M • White Chicks Can't Hump / 1992 / FD / M • Why Things Burn / 1994 / LBO / M • Wicked Thoughts / 1992 / PL / M • Wicked Ways #2: Education Of A D.P. Virgin / 1995 / WP / M • Wild Girls / 1993 / LV / F • Wilder At Heart / 1993 / ANA / M • The Wrath Of Kane / 1995 / BON / B • Zena, Mistress Of The Universe / 1995 / HOM / B • [Private Moments #16 / 199? / ... / C • [Private Moments #21 / 199? / ... / C • [Surfside Sex / 1992 / PER / M

ALEX KATZ *(Felix)*
Head of In X-Cess Productions; aged 24 in 1994; Russian immigrant.
Demolition Woman #1 / 1994 / IP / M • Kinky Debutante Interviews #01 / 1994 / IP / M • Kinky Debutante Interviews #02 / 1994 / IP / M • Kinky Debutante Interviews #03 / 1994 / IP / M • Kinky Debutante Interviews #04 / 1994 / IP / M • Kinky Debutante Interviews #05 / 1994 / IP / M • Kinky Debutante Interviews #06 / 1994 / IP / M • Kinky Debutante Interviews #07 / 1994 / IP / M • Kinky Debutante Interviews #08 / 1995 / IP / M • Kinky Debutante Interviews #09 / 1995 / IP / M • Kinky Debutante Interviews #10 / 1995 / IP / M • Midnight Obsession / 1995 / XC / M

ALEX KENWOOD
The Mating Game / 1992 / PL / G

ALEX LINDSTROM
Sexual Customs In Scandinavia / cr73 / QX / M

ALEX MANN
All About Sex / 1970 / AR / M • I Drink Your Blood / 1971 / SOW / S • Invasion Of The Love Drones / 1977 / ALP / M • Keyholes Are For Peeping / 1972 / SOW / S • Sometime Sweet Susan / 1974 / ALP / M • Swing Tail / 1969 / SOW / S

ALEX MANTEGNA
Buttman In Barcelona / 1996 / EA / M

ALEX MARIO *see* Alan Marlow

ALEX MARTIN *see* Star Index I

ALEX MATHEWS
Butt Freak #1 / 1992 / EA / M • Buttman Vs Buttwoman / 1992 / EL / M • Buttman's Re-

venge / 1992 / EA / M • Complain, Complain / 1993 / BON / B

ALEX NULL
Tobianna: A Gang Bang Fantasy / 1993 / FC / M

ALEX PABLO *see* Alex San Paolo

ALEX PROFFIT
Intervidnet #2: French Made / 1994 / IVN / M

ALEX ROCCO (GRECO) *see* Alex Greco

ALEX SAN PAOLO *(Johnny Janiero, Johnny Janairo, Alex Apollo, Alex Pablo, Al Bogas, John Janeiro, John Janiero)*
Heavy set Hispanic male.
100% Amateur #02: Back Door And More / 1995 / OD / M • Aged To Perfection #3 / 1995 / TTV / M • Amateur Nights #11 / 1996 / HO / M • Amateur Nights #15 / 1997 / HO / M • Anal Asian Fantasies / 1996 / HO / M • Asian Boom Boom Girls / 1997 / HO / M • Big Boob Bangeroo #1 / 1995 / TTV / M • Big Boob Bangeroo #2 / 1995 / TTV / M • Big Boob Bangeroo #3 / 1996 / TTV / M • Big Boob Bangeroo #4 / 1995 / TTV / M • Big Boob Bangeroo #5 / 1996 / TTV / M • Big Boob Bangeroo #6 / 1996 / TTV / M • Big Boob Bangeroo #7 / 1996 / TTV / M • Big Boob Bangeroo #8 / 1996 / TTV / M • Butt Bangers Ball #1 / 1996 / TTV / M • Butt Bangers Ball #2 / 1996 / TTV / M • Cute Cuddly Bubbly Butts / 1996 / TTV / M • Cutie Pies / 1995 / TTV / M • Dirty & Kinky Mature Women #07 / 1996 / C69 / M • Dirty & Kinky Mature Women #09 / 1996 / C69 / M • East Vs West: Battle Of The Gang Bangs / 1994 / TTV / M • Face Dance #1 / 1992 / EA / M • Golden Oldies #1 / 1995 / TTV / M • Golden Oldies #2 / 1995 / TTV / M • Golden Oldies #3 / 1995 / TTV / M • Golden Oldies #4 / 1996 / TTV / M • Golden Oldies #5 / 1996 / TTV / M • Golden Oldies #6 / 1996 / TTV / M • Hershe Highway #5: Backdoor Blues / 1996 / HO / M • Hidden Camera #20 / 1994 / JMP / M • Hooters In The 'hood / 1995 / TTV / M • Lactamania #2: The Squirt Fest / 1995 / TTV / M • Las Vegas Big Boob Hospitality Sweet / 1997 / HO / M • Latin Fever #1 / 1996 / C69 / M • Latin Fever #2 / 1996 / C69 / M • Latin Plump Humpers #1 / 1995 / TTV / M • Latin Plump Humpers #2 / 1995 / TTV / M • Latin Plump Humpers #3 / 1995 / TTV / M • Lil' Latin Cutie Pies / 1996 / CDI / M • Love Chunks / 1996 / TTV / M • More To Love #2 / 1995 / TTV / M • Muffmania / 1995 / TTV / M • The Night Of The Coyote / 1993 / MED / M • Ready To Drop #08 / 1995 / FC / M • Ready To Drop #09 / 1995 / FC / M • Ready To Drop #10 / 1996 / FC / M • Ready To Drop #12 / 1996 / FC / M • Rollie Pollie Chicks / 1996 / TTV / M • Salsa & Spice #1 / 1995 / TTV / M • Salsa & Spice #2: Latin Lust / 1996 / TTV / M • Salsa & Spice #3 / 1996 / TTV / M • Salsa & Spice #4 / 1996 / TTV / M • Salsa & Spice #5 / 1997 / TTV / M • Sexual Harassment / 1996 / TTV / M • Slut Safari #3 / 1994 / FC / M • SVE: Dyana Does The Tag Team / 1994 / SVE / M • Sweet Black Cherries #2 / 1996 / TTV / M • Sweet Black Cherries #3 / 1996 / TTV / M • Sweet Black Cherries #4 / 1996 / TTV / M • Sweet Black Cherries #5 / 1996 / TTV / M • Sweet Black Cherries #6 / 1996 / TTV / M • Taxi Girls #3: Killer On The Loose / 1993 / MED / M •

Taxi Girls #4: Daughter Of Lust / 1994 / CA / M

ALEX SANDERS *(Scott Boisvert, Scott C.)*

Well built male with long blonde curly hair.

1-900-FUCK #3 / 1995 / SO / M • 13th Annual Adult Video News Awards / 1996 / VC / S • The 4th Vixxen / 1995 / EMC / M • A List / 1996 / SO / M • Abducted / 1996 / ZA / M • Abused / 1996 / ZA / M • Adam & Eve's House Party #1 / 1995 / VC / M • Adam & Eve's House Party #2: Bachelor Party / 1996 / VC / M • Adult Affairs / 1994 / VC / M • After Midnight / 1994 / IN / M • Airotica / 1996 / SC / M • All "A" / 1994 / SFP / C • All Amateur Perfect 10's / 1995 / LEI / M • All That Jism / 1994 / VD / M • Allure / 1996 / WP / M • Amateurs Exposed #04 / 1994 / CV / M • American Blonde / 1993 / VI / M • American Tushy! / 1996 / ULI / M • The Anal Adventures Of Suzy Super Slut #3 / 1994 / IPI / M • Anal Angels #3 / 1995 / VEX / C • Anal Anonymous / 1994 / ZA / M • Anal Aristocrat / 1995 / KWP / M • Anal Arsenal / 1994 / OD / M • Anal Asian #2: The Won-Ton Woman / 1994 / IN / M • Anal Asspirations / 1993 / LV / M • Anal Bandits / 1996 / SO / M • The Anal Diary Of Misty Rain / 1993 / EL / M • Anal Freaks / 1994 / KWP / M • Anal Fugitive / 1995 / PEP / M • Anal Gang Bangers #02 / 1993 / GLI / M • Anal Glamour Girls / 1995 / ME / M • Anal Invader / 1995 / PEP / M • Anal League / 1996 / IN / M • Anal Maniacs #1 / 1994 / WP / M • Anal Maniacs #2 / 1994 / WP / M • Anal Maniacs #4 / 1995 / WP / M • Anal Maniacs #5 / 1996 / WP / M • Anal Misconduct / 1995 / VD / M • Anal Nitrate / 1995 / PE / M • The Anal Nurse Scam / 1995 / CA / M • Anal Persuasion / 1994 / EX / M • Anal Playground / 1995 / CA / M • Anal Portrait / 1996 / ZA / M • Anal Princess #2 / 1996 / VC / M • Anal Runaway / 1996 / ZA / M • Anal Secrets (After Dark) / 1994 / AFD / M • Anal Secrets (Metro) / 1994 / IN / M • Anal Sex / 1996 / ZA / M • Anal Vision #11 / 1993 / LBO / M • Anal Vision #13 / 1993 / LBO / M • Anal Vision #18 / 1993 / LBO / M • Anal Vision #22 / 1993 / LBO / M • Anal Vision #25 / 1994 / LBO / M • The Anal-Europe Series #05: Anal European Vacation / 1993 / LV / M • Angel Baby / 1995 / SC / M • Animal Instinct / 1993 / VI / M • Ariana's Dirty Dancers: The Professionals / 1996 / 4P / M • The Artist / 1994 / HO / M • Ass Kisser: A Love Story / 1995 / PEP / M • Ass Openers! #1 / 1995 / TCK / C • Ass Poppers / 1995 / VMX / M • Assmania!! #1 / 1994 / ME / M • Attic Toys / 1994 / ERA / M • Attitude / 1995 / VC / M • Back Door Babewatch / 1995 / IF / C • Back Door Mistress / 1994 / GO / M • Back In Style / 1993 / VI / M • Badgirls #1: Lockdown / 1994 / VI / M • Badlands #1 / 1994 / PEP / M • Badlands #2: Back Into Hell / 1994 / PEP / M • Bangkok Boobarella / 1996 / BTO / M • Bare Ass In The Park / 1995 / PEP / M • Bareback / 1996 / LE / M • The Bashful Blonde From Beautiful Bendover / 1993 / PEP / M • The Basket Trick / 1993 / PL / M • Batbabe / 1995 / PL / M • Bedlam / 1995 / WAV / M • Bedtime Stories / 1996 / VC / M • Beeping Miss Buffy / 1995 / CDI / M • Big Bust Babes #15 / 1993 / AFI / M • The Big One / 1995 / HO / M • Big Tit Racket /

1995 / PEP / M • Black Bamboo / 1995 / IN / M • Black Nurse Fantasies / 1994 / CA / M • Black Satin / 1994 / IN / M • Black Tie Affair / 1993 / VEX / M • Blackbroad Jungle / 1994 / IN / M • Blaze / 1996 / WAV / M • Blonde Forces #2 / 1994 / CC / M • Blonde In Blue Flannel / 1995 / CA / M • Blue Movie / 1995 / WP / M • Blue Saloon / 1996 / ME / M • Bobby Hollander's Maneaters #06 / 1993 / SFP / M • Bobby Sox / 1996 / VI / S • Body Of Love / 1994 / ERA / M • Boobs A Poppin' / 1994 / TTV / M • Boobwatch #2 / 1997 / SC / M • Boogie In The Butt / 1993 / WIV / M • The Bottom Dweller Part Deux / 1994 / EL / M • Bra Busters #03 / 1993 / LBO / M • Breast Collection #04 / 1995 / LBO / C • Breastman Does The Himalayas / 1993 / EVN / M • Breastman's Anal Adventure / 1993 / EVN / M • Breastman's Bikini Pool Party / 1995 / EVN / M • Breastman's Wet T-Shirt Contest / 1994 / EVN / M • Breastman's Wild West Adventure / 1995 / EVN / M • Breeders / 1996 / MET / M • Brenda: Back To Beverly Hills 9021A / 1994 / CA / M • Buck Naked In The 21st Century / 1993 / EVN / M • Buffy's Anal Adventure / 1996 / CDI / M • Buffy's Bare Ass Barbecue / 1996 / CDI / M • Buffy's First Encounter / 1995 / CIN / M • Buffy's Malibu Adventure / 1995 / CDI / M • Buffy's New Boobs / 1996 / CIN / M • Bun Busters #04 / 1993 / LBO / M • Bunmasters / 1995 / VC / M • Busty Backdoor Nurses / 1996 / PL / M • The Butt Connection / 1993 / TIW / M • The Butt Detective / 1994 / VC / M • Butt Freak #2 / 1996 / EA / M • The Butt Sisters Do Baltimore / 1995 / MID / M • The Butt Sisters Do Cleveland / 1994 / MID / M • The Butt Sisters Do Detroit / 1993 / MID / M • The Butt Sisters Do Los Angeles / 1993 / MID / M • The Butt Sisters Do Sturgis / 1994 / MID / M • Butt Watch #06 / 1994 / FH / M • Butt Whore / 1994 / WIV / M • Butt's Motel #6 / 1994 / EX / M • Butt's Up, Doc #4 / 1994 / GO / M • Butterfly / 1993 / OD / M • Butthead Dreams: Down In The Bush / 1995 / FH / M • Buttman's Wet Dream / 1994 / EA / M • Caged Beauty / 1994 / FD / M • Call Of The Wild / 1995 / AFI / M • Careless / 1993 / PP / M • Carlita's Backway / 1993 / OD / M • Carnival Of Flesh / 1996 / NIT / M • Centerfold Strippers / 1994 / ME / M • Chateau Du Cheeks / 1994 / VC / M • Cherry Poppers #01 / 1993 / ZA / M • Christmas Carol / 1993 / LV / M • Chug-A-Lug Girls #6 / 1995 / VT / M • Cinesex #1 / 1995 / CV / M • Cinesex #2 / 1994 / CV / M • A Clockwork Orgy / 1995 / PL / M • Club Kiss / 1995 / ONA / M • Cold As Ice / 1994 / IN / M • Color Me Anal / 1995 / ME / M • Colossal Orgy #1 / 1993 / HW / M • Colossal Orgy #3 / 1994 / HW / M • Coming Attractions / 1995 / WHP / M • Compulsive Behavior / 1995 / PI / M • Conquest / 1996 / WP / M • The Corner / 1994 / VT / M • The Coven #1 / 1993 / VI / M • The Coven #2 / 1993 / VI / M • Covergirl / 1994 / WP / M • Crew Sluts / 1994 / KWP / M • Cumback Pussy #6: All-Star Poop Chute Salute / 1997 / EL / M • Dance Naked / 1995 / PEP / M • Dangerous Games / 1995 / VI / M • Dare You / 1995 / CA / M • The Darker Side / 1994 / HO / M • Daydreams, Nightdreams / 1996 / VC / M • De Sade / 1994 / SC / M • Deadly Sin / 1996 / ONA / M •

Dear Diary / 1995 / WP / M • Deceit / 1996 / ZA / M • Deep Behind The Scenes With Seymore Butts #1 / 1995 / ULI / M • Deep Inside Kaitlyn Ashley / 1995 / VC / C • Deep Seven / 1996 / VC / M • Delaid Delivery / 1995 / EX / M • Demolition Woman #1 / 1994 / IP / M • Demolition Woman #2 / 1994 / IP / M • The Deviant Doctor / 1996 / NS / M • Devil In A Wet T-Shirt / 1995 / SPI / M • Dick & Jane Big Breast Adventure / 1993 / AVI / M • Dick & Jane In The Mountains / 1994 / AVI / M • Dick & Jane Sneak On The Set / 1993 / AVI / M • Dirty Dancers #8 / 1996 / 4P / M • Dirty Diner #03 / 1993 / GLI / M • Dirty Diner #3 / 1996 / SC / M • Dirty Laundry #2 / 1994 / CV / M • Dirty Little Ass Slut / 1995 / KWP / M • Dirty Little Secrets / 1995 / WAV / M • Dirty Looks / 1994 / VI / M • Dirty Work / 1995 / VC / M • Dog Walker / 1994 / EA / M • Doin' The Rounds / 1995 / VC / M • Domination / 1994 / WP / M • Domination Nation / 1996 / VI / M • Double D Amateurs #09 / 1993 / JMP / M • Double Load #2 / 1994 / HW / M • Dp #2: The Mighty Fhucks / 1994 / FC / M • Draghixa With An X / 1994 / EX / M • The Dragon Lady #7: Tales From The Bed #6 / 1994 / WV / M • Dreams / 1995 / VC / M • Dukes Of Anal / 1996 / VC / M • Eighteen #3 / 1996 / SC / M • Eleventh Annual AVN Awards / 1994 / VC / M • Employee's Entrance In The Rear / 1996 / CC / M • Erotic Appetites / 1995 / IN / M • Erotic Escape / 1995 / FH / M • Erotic Newcummers Vol 1 #3: Anal Adventures / 1996 / DR / M • Ethnic Cheerleader Search #1 / 1996 / WIC / M • Every Nerd Has A Fantasy / 1996 / FC / M • Evil Temptations #2 / 1995 / ULP / M • Exit In Rear / 1993 / XCI / M • Explicit Entry / 1995 / LE / M • Exposure / 1995 / WAV / M • Extreme Passion / 1993 / WP / M • Extreme Sex #2: The Dungeon / 1994 / VI / M • The F Zone / 1995 / WP / M • The Face / 1994 / PP / M • Face To Face / 1995 / ME / M • Fantasies Of Persia / 1995 / VT / M • Fantasy Chamber / 1994 / ULI / M • Fantasy Inc. / 1995 / CV / M • Fast Forward / 1995 / CA / M • Firecrackers / 1994 / HW / M • Firm Offer / 1995 / SC / M • Fixing A Hole / 1995 / XCI / M • Flesh / 1996 / EA / M • Flesh For Fantasy / 1994 / CV / M • Fleshmates / 1994 / ERA / M • Flexxx #1 / 1994 / VT / M • Flexxx #2 / 1995 / VT / M • Flexxx #3 / 1995 / VT / M • Flexxx #4 / 1995 / VT / M • The Flirt / 1995 / GO / M • Florence Hump / 1994 / AFI / M • Freak Dat Booty / 1994 / WP / M • Freaknic / 1996 / IN / M • Frendz? #1 / 1996 / RAS / M • Frendz? #2 / 1996 / RAS / M • Fresh Meat (John Leslie) #2 / 1995 / EA / M • Gang Bang Bitches #10 / 1995 / PP / M • Gazongo / 1995 / PEP / M • Generation X / 1995 / WAV / M • Geranalmo / 1994 / PL / M • Get Lucky / 1996 / NIT / M • Ghosts / 1994 / EMC / M • The Girl In Room 69 / 1994 / VC / M • A Girl Like You / 1995 / LE / M • The Girl Next Door #1 / 1994 / VT / M • The Girl Next Door #2 / 1994 / VT / M • The Girls From Butthole Ridge / 1994 / ZA / M • Girls Of Sorority Row / 1994 / VT / M • The Girls Of Spring Break / 1995 / VT / M • The Girls Of Summer / 1995 / VT / M • Girls Of The Athletic Department / 1995 / VT / M • Girls Of The Ivy Leagues / 1994 / VT / M • Girls Of The Packed Ten / 1994 / VT / M • Girls

Of The Panty Raid / 1995 / VT / M • Girls Of The Very Big Eight / 1994 / VT / M • Girls Off Duty / 1994 / LE / M • Golddiggers #2 / 1995 / VC / M • The Great Pretenders / 1994 / FD / M • Greek Week / 1994 / CV / M • Hard Squeeze / 1994 / EMC / M • Hardcore / 1994 / VI / M • Harder, She Craved / 1995 / VC / M • Heart Breaker / 1994 / CA / M • Heavenly / 1995 / IF / M • Heavenly Yours / 1995 / CV / M • Heidi's Girls / 1995 / GO / M • Helen & Louise / 1996 / HDE / M • Hillbilly Honeys / 1996 / WP / M • Hollywood Boulevard / 1995 / CV / M • Hollywood Ho' House / 1994 / VC / M • Hollywood Legs / 1996 / NIT / M • Hollywood Spa / 1996 / WP / M • Hookers Of Hollywood / 1994 / LE / M • Hot Blooded / 1994 / ERA / M • Hot Tight Asses #06 / 1994 / TCK / M • Hot Tight Asses #07 / 1994 / TCK / M • Hot Tight Asses #09 / 1994 / TCK / M • Hot Tight Asses #11 / 1995 / TCK / M • Hot Tight Asses #13 / 1995 / TCK / M • Hot Wishes / 1995 / LE / M • Hotel California / 1995 / MID / M • Hotel Sodom #01 / 1995 / SNA / M • Hotel Sodom #02 / 1995 / SNA / M • Hotel Sodom #04: Free Parking In Rear / 1995 / SNA / M • Hotel Sodom #05: Tammi Ann Bends Over / 1995 / SNA / M • Hotel Sodom #07 / 1995 / SNA / M • Hotel Sodom #08 / 1995 / SNA / M • Hotel Sodom #09 / 1996 / SNA / M • Hotel Sodom #10 / 1996 / SNA / M • House Of Hoochies / 1996 / DDP / M • How To Deep Throat Your Lover / 1994 / A&E / M • Howard Sperm's Private Parties / 1994 / LBO / M • The Hungry Heart / 1996 / AOP / M • Immortal Desire / 1993 / VI / M • In Search Of The Perfect Blow Job / 1995 / OD / M • Incantation / 1996 / FC / M • Incocknito / 1993 / VIM / M • Intense Perversions #1 / 1995 / PL / M • Intercourse With The Vampyre #1 / 1994 / SC / M • Intercourse With The Vampyre #2 / 1994 / SC / M • International Analists / 1994 / AFD / M • Invitation For Lust / 1995 / C69 / M • Jaded Love / 1994 / CA / M • Jenna Ink / 1996 / WP / M • Jenna Loves Rocco / 1996 / WAV / M • Jinx / 1996 / WP / M • Ji̶ll Ohio̶al Oo̶ Guzzlers #1 / 1996 / NIT / C • Jordan Lee: Anal Queen / 1997 / SC / C • Kept Women / 1995 / LE / M • Keyholes / 1995 / OD / M • Kinky Cameraman #2 / 1996 / LEI / C • Kissing Kaylan / 1995 / CC / M • Ladies In Leather / 1995 / GO / M • Lady's Choice / 1995 / VD / M • The Last Act / 1995 / VI / M • The Last Anal Hero / 1993 / OD / M • Last Tango In Paradise / 1995 / ERA / M • Latex And Lace / 1996 / BBE / M • Lay Of The Land / 1995 / LE / M • Leena Is Nasty / 1994 / OD / M • Leg Tease #1 / 1995 / VT / M • Legend #5: The Legend Continues / 1994 / LE / M • The Legend Of Barbi-Q And Little Fawn / 1994 / CA / M • Legs / 1996 / ZA / M • Let's Dream On / 1994 / FD / M • Lingerie / 1995 / SC / M • Live Sex / 1994 / LE / M • Lollipop Shoppe #2 / 1996 / SC / M • Lollipops #2 / 1996 / SC / M • Lonely Hearts / 1995 / VC / M • Loose Morals / 1995 / EX / M • Lost Angels / 1997 / WP / M • Love Dancers / 1995 / ME / M • Love Exchange / 1995 / DR / M • Love Spice / 1995 / ERA / M • Lover Under Cover / 1995 / ERA / M • Lust What The Doctor Ordered / 1994 / WIV / M • Made For A Gangbang / 1995 /

ZA / M • Man Killer / 1996 / SC / M • Masque / 1995 / VC / M • Masquerade / 1995 / HO / M • The Mating Pot / 1994 / LBO / M • Memories / 1996 / ZA / M • Mickey Ray's Sex Search #02: Tight Spots / 1994 / WIV / M • Mickey Ray's Sex Search #03: Deep Heat / 1994 / WIV / M • The Mile High Club / 1995 / PL / M • Mile High Thrills / 1995 / VIM / M • Mixed-Up Marriage / 1995 / CV / M • More Than A Handful #4 / 1994 / MET / M • Motel Matches / 1996 / LE / M • The Mountie / 1994 / PP / M • Mutual Consent / 1995 / VC / M • My Boyfriend's Black / 1994 / FD / M • My Surrender / 1996 / A&E / M • Naked Scandal #1 / 1995 / SPI / M • Naked Scandal #2 / 1996 / SPI / M • Never Say Never, Again / 1994 / SC / M • The New Ass Masters #10 / 1996 / LEI / C • The New Ass Masters #15 / 1996 / LEI / C • The New Butt Hunt #15 / 1995 / LEI / C • The New Butt Hunt #19 / 1996 / LEI / C • New Pussy Hunt #24 / 1996 / LEI / C • New Pussy Hunt #25 / 1996 / LEI / C • New Wave Hookers #4 / 1994 / VC / M • The Night Shift / 1995 / LE / M • Nikki's Bon Voyage / 1993 / VC / M • Nikki's Last Stand / 1993 / VC / M • Nookie Of The Year / 1993 / HW / M • Nothing To Hide #2 / 1993 / CV / M • On The Rise / 1994 / EX / M • On The Run / 1995 / SC / M • Ona Z's Star Search #03 / 1993 / GLI / M • Oral Addiction / 1995 / VI / M • Organic Facials / cr91 / GLI / M • The Orgy #3 / 1993 / EMC / M • The Original Wicked Woman / 1993 / WP / M • The Other Side / 1995 / ERA / M • Pajama Party X #3 / 1994 / VC / M • The Palace Of Pleasure / 1995 / ULI / M • Passenger 69 #1 / 1994 / IP / M • Passion / 1996 / SC / M • Patent Leather / 1995 / CA / M • Pearl Of The Orient / 1995 / IN / M • Peepshow / 1994 / OD / M • Performer Of The Year / 1994 / WP / M • Perplexed / 1994 / FD / M • Persuasion / 1995 / LE / M • The Phantom Of The Montague Stage / 1997 / HO / M • Photo Play / 1995 / VI / M • Pick Up Lines #01 / 1995 / 4P / M • Pick Up Lines #05 / 1996 / OD / M • Pick Up Lines #08 / 1996 / OD / M • Pick Up Lines #10 / 1997 / OD / M • Pick Up Lines #11 / 1997 / OLI / M • Pick Up Lines #12 / 1997 / OD / M • Plaything #2 / 1995 / VI / M • Pleasure Dome: The Genesis Chamber / 1994 / AFV / M • Plumb And Dumber / 1995 / PP / M • A Pool Party At Seymores #1 / 1995 / ULI / M • A Pool Party At Seymores #2 / 1995 / ULI / M • Pounding Ass / 1995 / VMX / M • Precious Cargo / 1993 / VIM / M • Primarily Yours / 1996 / CA / M • Private Eyes / 1995 / LE / M • Private Label / 1993 / GLI / M • Private Matters / 1995 / EMC / M • Private Stories #12 / 1996 / OD / M • Private Video Magazine #02 / 1993 / OD / M • Profiles #08: Triple Ecstacy / 1996 / XPR / M • Provocative / 1994 / LE / M • Pulp Friction / 1994 / PP / M • Pussy Whipped / 1994 / FOR / M • Pussyclips #01 / 1994 / SNA / M • Pussyclips #05 / 1994 / SNA / M • Pussyclips #06 / 1995 / SNA / M • Pussyclips #07 / 1995 / SNA / M • Pussyclips #10 / 1995 / SNA / M • Pussyman #04: The Celebration / 1993 / SNA / M • Pussyman #05: Captive Audience / 1994 / SNA / M • Pussyman #06: House Of Games / 1994 / SNA / M • Pussyman #07: On The Dark Side / 1994 /

SNA / M • Pussyman #09: Feeding Frenzy / 1995 / SNA / M • Pussyman #10: Butts, Butts & More Butts / 1995 / SNA / M • Pussyman #11: Prime Cuts / 1995 / SNA / C • Pussyman #12: Sticky Fingers / 1995 / SNA / M • Pussyman #13: Lips / 1996 / SNA / M • Pussyman Auditions #02 / 1995 / SNA / M • Pussyman Auditions #08 / 1995 / SNA / M • Pussyman Auditions #11 / 1995 / SNA / M • Radical Affairs Video Magazine #08 / 1994 / ME / M • Rainwoman #07: In The Rainforest / 1993 / CC / M • Rainwoman #08 / 1994 / CC / M • Rainwoman #09: Wetlands / 1995 / CC / M • Raunch #09 / 1993 / CC / M • Raw Footage / 1996 / VC / M • Raw Talent: Deep Inside Lydia's Ass / 1993 / FH / M • Razor's Edge / 1995 / ONA / M • The Real Story Of Tonya & Nancy / 1994 / EX / M • Reckless Passion / 1995 / WAV / M • Red Hots / 1996 / PL / M • Reel People #05 / 1994 / PP / M • Reel People #07 / 1995 / PP / M • Reel People #08 / 1995 / PP / M • Reel People #09 / 1995 / PP / M • The Reel Sex World #04: Laid In Hawaii / 1994 / WP / M • Reel Sex World #05 / 1994 / WP / M • The Reel World #1 / 1994 / FOR / M • The Reel World #2 / 1994 / FOR / M • Reflections / 1996 / ZA / M • Release Me / 1996 / VT / M • Renegades #1 / 1994 / SC / M • Ring Of Passion / 1994 / ERA / M • Rising Buns / 1993 / HW / M • Rockhard (Coast) / 1996 / CC / M • Rod Wood / 1995 / LE / M • A Round Behind / 1995 / PEP / M • Rump Humpers #16 / 1993 / GLI / M • The Savage / 1994 / SC / M • The Secret Life Of Nina Hartley / 1994 / VC / M • Secret Rendez-Vous / 1994 / XCI / M • Sensations #1 / 1996 / SC / M • Seriously Anal / 1996 / ONA / M • Sex #3: After Seven (Vivid) / 1994 / VI / M • Sex Academy #2: The Art Of Talking Dirty / 1994 / ONA / M • Sex Academy #3: The Art Of Real Sex / 1994 / ONA / M • Sex Academy #4: The Art Of Anal / 1994 / ONA / M • Sex Academy #5: The Art Of Pulp Fiction / 1994 / ONA / M • Sex Bandits / 1995 / VC / M • Sex Freaks / 1995 / EA / M • Sex Kitten / 1995 / SC / M • Sex Therapy Ward / 1995 / LBO / M • Sexual Impulse / 1995 / VD / M • Sexual Instinct #2 / 1994 / DR / M • Seymore & Shane Do Ireland / 1994 / PI / M • Seymore & Shane Playing With Fire / 1994 / ULI / M • Shades Of Lust / 1993 / TP / M • Shameless / 1995 / VC / M • Shane's World #1 / 1996 / OD / M • Shave Tails #1 / 1994 / SO / M • Shave Tails #2 / 1994 / SO / M • Shave Tails #3 / 1994 / SO / M • Shave Tails #4 / 1995 / SO / M • Shayla's Gang / 1994 / WP / M • A Shot In The Pants / 1995 / HO / M • The Show / 1995 / VI / M • Show & Tell / 1996 / VI / M • Silky Thighs / 1994 / ERA / M • Simply Blue / 1995 / WAV / M • Sin Asylum / 1995 / CV / M • The Sin-A-Bun Girls / 1995 / OD / M • Sinnocence / 1995 / CDI / M • Sister Snatch #1 / 1994 / SNA / M • Sister Snatch #2 / 1995 / SNA / M • Ski Bunnies #1 / 1994 / HW / M • Ski Bunnies #2 / 1994 / HW / M • Skin Hunger / 1995 / MET / M • Sleaze Please! —August Edition / 1994 / FH / M • Sleaze Please! —September Edition / 1994 / FH / M • Sleaze Please! —October Edition / 1994 / FH / M • Sleaze Please! —November Edition / 1994 / FH / M • Slippery Slopes / 1995 / ME / M •

Sloppy Seconds / 1994 / PE / M • Smoke Screen / 1995 / WAV / M • Smooth Ride / 1996 / WP / M • Snake Pit / 1996 / DWO / M • Snatch Masters #03 / 1994 / LEI / M • Snatch Masters #04 / 1995 / LEI / M • Snatch Masters #07 / 1995 / LEI / M • So You Want To Be In The Movies? / 1994 / VC / M • Sodomania #04: Further On Down The Road / 1993 / EL / M • Sodomania #05: Euro-American Style / 1993 / EL / M • Sodomania #07: Deep Down Inside / 1993 / EL / M • Sodomania #12: Raw Filth / 1995 / EL / M • Sodomania #13: Your Lucky Number / 1995 / EL / M • Sodomania: Slop Shots / 1996 / EL / C • Something Blue / 1995 / CC / M • Sorority Cheerleaders / 1996 / PL / M • Spinners #1 (Wicked) / 1995 / WP / M • Spinners #2 (Wicked) / 1996 / WP / M • Spirit Guide / 1995 / IN / M • Spread The Wealth / 1993 / DR / M • Stacked Deck / 1994 / IN / M • Stand By Your Man / 1994 / CV / M • The Stand-Up / 1994 / VC / M • The Star / 1995 / CC / M • Starbangers #02 / 1993 / BIG / M • Starbangers #05 / 1993 / FPI / M • Starbangers #07 / 1995 / FPI / M • Stardust #1 / 1996 / VI / M • Stardust #2 / 1996 / VI / M • Stardust #4 / 1996 / VI / M • Starting Over / 1995 / WAV / M • Steamy Windows / 1993 / VI / M • The Stiff / 1995 / WAV / M • Stories Of Seduction / 1996 / MID / M • Straight A Students / 1993 / MET / M • Street Workers / 1995 / ME / M • Stretchin' The Rear / 1995 / PE / M • Strip Poker / 1995 / PEP / M • Strip Show / 1996 / CA / M • Stripper Nurses / 1994 / PE / M • Strippers Inc. #2 / 1994 / ONA / M • Strippers Inc. #3 / 1994 / ONA / M • Strippers Inc. #5 / 1995 / ONA / M • Stud Finders / 1995 / ONA / M • Stupid And Stupider / 1995 / SO / M • Style #2 / 1994 / VT / M • Subway / 1994 / SC / M • Supermodel #1 / 1994 / VI / M • Supermodel #2 / 1994 / VI / M • Superstar Sex Challenge #1 / 1994 / VC / M • Surprise!!! / 1994 / VI / M • Swallow / 1994 / VI / M • The Swap #2 / 1994 / VI / M • Swedish Erotica #80 / 1994 / CA / M • Swedish Erotica #84 / 1995 / CA / M • Sweet A$ Money / 1994 / MID / M • Tactical Sex Force / 1994 / IN / M • Tail Taggers #112 / 1993 / WV / M • Tail Taggers #116 / 1993 / WV / M • Tails Of Tribeca / 1993 / HW / M • Take It Inside / 1995 / PEP / M • Take This Wad And Shove It! / 1994 / ZA / M • Takin' It To The Limit #1 / 1994 / BS / M • Thin Ice / 1996 / ONA / M • The Three Muskatits / 1994 / PL / M • Tight Lips / 1994 / CA / M • The Time Machine / 1996 / WP / M • Tit Tease #1 / 1995 / VT / M • Titanic Orgy / 1995 / PEP / M • Tits A Wonderful Life / 1994 / CV / M • Tonya's List / 1994 / FD / M • Too Hot To Touch #2 / 1993 / CV / M • Top Debs #4: Sex Boat / 1993 / GO / M • Topless Window Washers / 1996 / LE / M • Torrid Tales / 1995 / VI / M • Totally Naked / 1994 / VC / M • Totally Real / 1996 / CA / M • The Toy Box / 1996 / ONA / M • Trading Partners / 1995 / GO / M • Trapped / 1996 / VI / M • Tricky Business / 1995 / AFI / M • Twist Of Fate / 1996 / WP / M • Two Sides Of A Lady / 1994 / HDE / M • The Ultimate Fantasy / 1995 / CV / M • Ultimate Sensations / 1996 / NIT / M • Underground #1 / 1996 / SC / M • Underground #2: Subway To Sodom / 1996 / SC / M • Underground #3: Sit On This / 1996 /

SC / M • Undress To Thrill / 1994 / VI / M • Up And Cummers #03 / 1993 / 4P / M • Up And Cummers #05 / 1993 / 4P / M • Up And Cummers #09 / 1994 / 4P / M • Up And Cummers #14 / 1994 / 4P / M • Up And Cummers #16 / 1994 / 4P / M • Up And Cummers #17 / 1994 / 4P / M • Up And Cummers #27 / 1996 / ERW / M • Up And Cummers #31 / 1996 / 4P / M • Up And Cummers #37 / 1996 / 4P / M • Up The Ying Yang #2 / 1995 / CC / M • The Usual Anal Suspects / 1996 / CC / M • Valentina: Princess Of The Forest / 1996 / SC / M • Valley Cooze / 1996 / SC / M • Venom #1 / 1995 / VD / M • Venom #2 / 1996 / VD / M • Venom #3 / 1996 / VD / M • Venom #5 / 1996 / VD / M • Venom #6 / 1996 / CA / M • Victoria With An "A" / 1994 / PL / M • Virgin Killers: Second Rampage / 1995 / PEP / M • Virgin Killers: The Killing Spree / 1995 / PEP / M • Virtual Reality Sixty Nine / 1995 / WP / M • Vivid Raw #2 / 1996 / VI / M • Voices In My Bed / 1993 / VI / M • The Voyeur #1 / 1994 / EA / M • Wad Gobblers #06 / 1993 / GLI / M • Wad Gobblers #07 / 1993 / GLI / M • Wad Gobblers #09 / 1993 / GLI / M • Wendy Whoppers: Psychic Healer / 1994 / PEP / M • Western Nights / 1994 / WP / M • Wet Faces #1 / 1997 / SC / C • Wet In The Saddle / 1994 / ME / M • White Shadow / 1994 / VC / M • Whoomp! There She Is / 1993 / AVI / M • Wicked Ways #1: Interview With The Anal Queen / 1994 / WP / M • Wicked Ways #2: Education Of A D.P. Virgin / 1995 / WP / M • Wicked Ways #3: An All-Anal Slutfest / 1995 / WP / M • Wild & Wicked #4 / 1994 / VT / M • Wild & Wicked #7 / 1996 / VT / M • Wild Roomies / 1994 / VC / M • Wildcats / 1995 / WP / M • Willie Wanker At The Fudge Packing Factory / 1995 / FD / M • Willie Wanker At The Sushi Bar / 1995 / FD / M • Witness For The Penetration / 1994 / PEP / M • A Woman Scorned / 1995 / CA / M • Women Behaving Badly / 1996 / RAS / M • Woodworking 101: Nina Hartley's Guide To Better Fellatio / 1994 / A&E / M • X-Tales / 1995 / VIM / M • Xcitement: The Movie / 1993 / XCI / M • Young Girls Do #2: Sweet Meat / 1995 / CDI / M

ALEX SCARRY
Becky Bound / 1994 / GAL / B • Love Is A Stranger #2 / 1994 / SV / B • Medieval Whines / 1994 / SV / B • Paint Balled / 1993 / SV / B • Schoolgirls In Disgrace / 1993 / SV / B

ALEX SCHWART *see* **Alex Horn**
ALEX STORM *(Alexis Storm, Alice Storm)*
Assuming The Position / 1989 / V99 / M • Bat Bitch #1 / 1989 / FAZ / M • Beach Blanket Brat / 1989 / VI / M • Behind The Backdoor #3 / 1989 / EVN / M • Belle Of The Ball / 1989 / V99 / M • Betty & Juice Possessed / 1995 / CA / M • Buns And Roses (V9) / 1990 / V99 / M • Class Act / 1989 / WAV / M • Club Lez / 1990 / PL / F • Debbie Does 'em All #3 / 1989 / CV / M • Deep In Deanna Jones / 1989 / EVN / M • Delicate Matters / 1989 / VEX / M • Diamond For Sale / 1990 / EVN / M • Entangled / 1996 / KLP / M • Fantasy Drive / 1990 / VEX / M • Farmer's Daughter / 1989 / FAZ / M • Frat Brats / 1990 / VC / M • Heart Breaker / 1989 / LE / M • Hidden Pleasures / 1990 / VEX / M • Hollywood

Hustle #1 / 1990 / V99 / M • Immorals #1: Broken Hearts / 1989 / AR / M • Immorals #2: The Good, The Bad, And The Banged / 1990 / AR / M • In The Flesh / 1990 / IN / M • It Happened At Midnight / 1990 / IN / M • Jailhouse Blue / 1990 / SO / M • Keep It Cumming / 1990 / V99 / M • Lost Lovers / 1990 / VEX / M • More Unbelievable Orgies / 1989 / EVN / C • Mr. Fun's Mondo Adventure / 1993 / VC / M • Nymphobrat / 1989 / VI / M • One For The Road / 1989 / V99 / M • Oral Addiction / 1989 / LV / M • Oriental Treatment #2: The Pearl Divers / 1989 / AR / M • Play Me / 1989 / VI / M • Raquel Untamed / 1990 / CIN / M • Real Magnolias / 1990 / AWV / M • Sea Of Lust / 1990 / FAN / M • Sex She Wrote / 1991 / VEX / M • She's America's Most Wanted / 1990 / VEX / M • Snow White And The Seven Weenies / 1989 / FAN / M • Space Virgins / 1990 / VEX / M • Storm Warning / 1989 / LV / M • Sweet Tease / 1990 / VEX / M • Ticket To Ride / 1990 / LV / M • Treacherous / 1995 / VD / M • Undercover Carol / 1990 / FAN / M • White Lies / 1990 / VEX / M • Wives Of The Rich And Famous / 1989 / V99 / M • The X-Rated OJ Truth... / 1995 / MID / M

ALEX STROBYE
1001 Danish Delights / cr68 / AR / M
ALEX STUART
Tomboy / 1983 / VCX / M
ALEX SUMMERS
So You Wanna Be A Porn Star #1: The Russians Are Cumming / 1994 / WHP / M
ALEX WARREN
Secrets Of Bondage / 1995 / SBP / B
ALEX WEAVER
Beverly She-Males / 1994 / PL / G • Karen's Bi-Line / 1989 / MET / G • Shaved She-Males / 1994 / PL / G
ALEX WILLIAMS
Bi Claudius / 1994 / BIL / G • Bi Dream Of Genie / 1994 / BIL / G • Bi George / 1994 / BIL / G • He-She Hangout / 1995 / HSV / G • Hot Bi Summer / 1994 / BIL / G • Little Shop Of She-Males / 1994 / HSV / G • Melrose Trannie / 1995 / HEA / G • The Princess With A Penis / 1994 / HSV / G • She Male Devil / 1996 / HSV / G • She-Male Loves Me / 1995 / VC / G • She-Male Slut House / 1994 / HEA / G • Showgirl She-Male / 1996 / HSV / G • Super Bi Bowl / 1995 / BIL / G • Trannie Love / 1995 / HSV / G • Tranny Hill: Sweet Surrender / 1994 / HSV / G • Transister Act / 1994 / HSV / G • Virtual She-Male / 1995 / HSV / G
ALEX WOLF *see* **Alex Horn**
ALEX ZANDRIA *see* **Star Index I**
ALEXA
The Betrayal Of Innocence #1: The Awakening Of Marika / 1993 / CC / M • The Betrayal Of Innocence #2: The Decadence / 1993 / CC / M • The Betrayal Of Innocence #3: The Choice / 1993 / CC / M • Joe Elliot's Asian College Girls #02 / 1995 / JOE / M • Meltin' The Burgh / 1996 / DGD / F • Pearl Necklace: Amorous Amateurs #01 / 1992 / SEE / M • Pearl Necklace: Amorous Amateurs #02 / 1992 / SEE / M • Pearl Necklace: Amorous Amateurs #04 / 1992 / SEE / M • Singapore Sluts / 1994 / ORE / C • The Witch's Tail / 1994 / GOU / M
ALEXA DANIS
True Stories #1 / 1993 / SC / M • True Sto-

ries #2 / 1993 / SC / M

ALEXA JAQUES

Sex Off The Runway / 1991 / GMI / M

ALEXA PARK *(Alexa Parks, Alexa Praval)*

Alexa Praval: **Ladies Room**. First movie was **Caught By Surprise**.

The Adultress / 1987 / CA / M • Angel's Gotta Have It / 1988 / FAN / M • The Art Of Passion / 1987 / CA / M • Babylon Pink #2 / 1988 / COM / M • Babylon Pink #3 / 1988 / COM / M • Bi-Surprise / 1988 / MET / G • The Bitches Of Westwood / 1987 / CA / M • Blowing The Whistle / 1986 / VIP / M • Breakin' All The Rules / 1987 / SE / M • The Catwoman / 1988 / VC / M • Caught By Surprise / 1987 / CDI / M • Debbie Does Dallas #4 / 1988 / VEX / M • Deep Inside Keisha / 1994 / VC / C • Deep Throat Fantasies / 1989 / VD / M • Easy Access / 1988 / ZA / M • Erotic Television Video / 1988 / VD / M • Erotic Therapy / 1987 / CDI / M • Fatal Erection / 1988 / SEV / M • The Fun House / 1988 / SEV / C • Games Couples Play / 1987 / HO / M • Get Me While I'm Hot / 1988 / PV / M • Ginger Does Them All / 1988 / CV / M • The Godmother #1 / 1987 / VC / M • The Godmother #2 / 1988 / VC / M • The Great Sex Contest #1 / 1988 / LV / M • HHHHot! TV #1 / 1988 / CDI / M • Hyapatia Lee's Arcade Series #01 / 1988 / ZA / C • The Joy Of Sec's / 1989 / VEX / M • Kiss My Asp / 1989 / EXH / M • Krystal Balling / 1988 / PL / M • The Ladies Room / 1987 / CA / M • Le Hot Club / 1987 / WV / M • Love Hammer / 1988 / VXP / M • Love On The Borderline / 1987 / IN / M • Lucy Has A Ball / 1987 / ME / M • Only The Very Best On Video / 1992 / VC / C • Oral Majority Black #1 / 1987 / WV / C • Parliament: Blondes Have More Fun / 1989 / PM / C • Parliament: Licking Lesbians #1 / 1988 / PM / F • Party Animals / 1987 / VEX / M • Party Animals / 1994 / VEX / C • Phone Sex Girls #1 / 1987 / VT / M • Primary Pleasure / 1987 / VXP / M • Sex Contest / 1988 / LV / M • Soul Games / 1988 / PV / C • St. X-Where #2 / 1988 / VD / M • Starship Intercourse / 1987 / DR / M • Surf, Sand And Üüll / 1üü I / 4F / M   • Suzie Superstar...The Search Continues / 1988 / CV / M • Tales Of The Uncensored / 1987 / FAN / M • A Taste Of Alexa / 1989 / PIN / C • Tracy Takes Paris / 1987 / VIP / M • Video Tramp #2 / 1988 / TME / M

ALEXA PARKS *see* **Alexa Park**

ALEXA PRAVAL *see* **Alexa Park**

ALEXANDER

Magma: Horny Bulls / 1994 / MET / M

ALEXANDER FALKEN

[Madchen, Die Sich Selbst, Bedienen / 1974 / ... / M

ALEXANDER GABOR *see* **Sasha Gabor**

ALEXANDER HORN *see* **Alex Horn**

ALEXANDER JAMES

Black Jailbait / 1984 / PL / M • Black To Africa / 1987 / PL / C • Ebony Orgies / 1987 / SE / C • Hot Chocolate #1 / 1984 / TAG / M

ALEXANDER KINGSFORD

Hot Dallas Nights / 1981 / VCX / M

ALEXANDER STEVENS

Gangbang Girl #02 / 1992 / ANA / M

ALEXANDER TITUS

Backdoor Club / 1986 / CA / M

ALEXANDRA

Alexandra The Greatest / 1990 / NAP / F • Alexandra's Pampered Pet / 1993 / LEO / G • Buttman's Big Butt Backdoor Babes / 1995 / EA / M • Mike Hott: #156 Alexandra And Midnight #1 / 1991 / MHV / F • Mike Hott: #157 Alexandra And Midnight #2 / 1991 / MHV / F • Mike Hott: #158 Alexandra Solo / 1991 / MHV / F • Night Watch Woman / 199? / NAP / B • Quebec Perversity #5 / 1996 / INO / M • Sperm Injection / 1995 / PL / M • Straight A Students / 1993 / MET / M • Triumph Of The Flesh / 1990 / NAP / B • Underdog / 1990 / NAP / B

ALEXANDRA (1976) *see* **Alexandria (1976)**

ALEXANDRA D'ORR *see* **Star Index I**

ALEXANDRA DAY *see* **Sunny Daye**

ALEXANDRA DREA

Young Sluts In Heat #2 / 1996 / PL / M

ALEXANDRA GRECCO *see* **Alex Greco**

ALEXANDRA LYNN

Hand Jobs #1 / 1994 / MAV / M

ALEXANDRA LYON *see* **Star Index I**

ALEXANDRA SAND

Flesh Fever / 1978 / CV / M

ALEXANDRA SILK *(Alexandre Silk)*

Petite brunette with long hair, marginal face with lots of freckles, medium tits, not a tight body. In 1996 she said she was 24 years old (looks older), was de-virginized at 13 and came from Las Vegas.

A List / 1996 / SO / M • Addicted To Lust / 1996 / NIT / M • Allure / 1996 / WP / M • Anal Auditions #1 / 1996 / XPR / M • Anal Explosions #2 / 1996 / NIT / M • Anal Institution #3 / 1996 / ZA / M • Anal League / 1996 / IN / M • Anal Territory / 1996 / AVD / M • Around Frisco / 1996 / SUF / M • Buffy's Nude Camera-Party / 1996 / CIN / M • Butt Sluts #6 / 1996 / ROB / F • California Swingers / 1996 / LV / M • Carnal Country / 1996 / NIT / M • Caught From Behind #22 / 1995 / HO / M • Caught From Behind #24 / 1996 / HO / M • The Clock Strikes Bizarre On Butt Row / 1996 / ABS / M • Cumback Pussy #3: Coast To Coast Rump Romp / 1996 / EL / M • Cumback Pussy #5: Groopin' / 1996 / EL / M • Deep Throat Girls #15 / 1995 / GO / M • Dirty Tails / 1996 / SC / M • Double Penetration Virgins. DF Therapy / 100ú / JMIF / M • Di Peter Proctor's House Of Anal Delights / 1996 / HO / M • Eternal Lust / 1996 / VC / M • Frendz? #1 / 1996 / RAS / M • Hardcore Confidential #1 / 1996 / TEP / M • Hardcore Fantasies #2 / 1996 / LV / M • Hardcore Fantasies #4 / 1996 / LV / M • Head Nurse / 1996 / RAS / M • Heavy Breathing / 1996 / NIT / M • Hershe Highway #5: Backdoor Blues / 1996 / HO / M • The Hitch-Hiker #17: Dead End / 1996 / VIM / M • Hot Parts / 1996 / NIT / M • Hot Tight Asses #17 / 1996 / TCK / M • Indecent Exposures / 1996 / MID / M • Ir4: In-rearendence Day / 1996 / HW / M • Legs / 1996 / ZA / M • Lesbian Pooper Sluts / 1996 / ROB / F • Philmore Butts Lake Poontang / 1996 / SUF / M • Promises And Lies / 1996 / NIT / M • Pussyman #15: The Bone Voyage Bash / 1997 / SNA / M • Pussyman Auditions #22 / 1996 / SNA / M • Reflections / 1996 / ZA / M • Risque Burlesque #2 / 1996 / IN / M • Rumpman In And Out Of Africa / 1996 / HW / M • Sex Drivers / 1996 / VMX / M • Sinister Sister / 1997 / WP / M • Sodomania #20: For

Members Only / 1997 / EL / M • Tight Fit #15 / 1996 / GO / M • Up Close & Personal #3 / 1996 / IPI / M • Valley Cooze / 1996 / SC / M • Video Virgins #30 / 1996 / NS / M • Wild Widow / 1996 / NIT / M

ALEXANDRA SMITH *see* **Star Index I**

ALEXANDRA TESSIER

Private Film #04 / 1993 / OD / M

ALEXANDRE SILK *see* **Alexandra Silk**

ALEXANDREA *see* **Star Index I**

ALEXANDRI

Buttman's Big Tit Adventure #3 / 1995 / EA / M

ALEXANDRIA

Bizarre Encounters / 1986 / 4P / B • Classical Gams / 1994 / LAG / F • Hollywood Amateurs #01 / 1994 / MID / M • I Love High Heels / 1994 / LAG / F • Match #3: Battling Babes / 1995 / NPA / B • Mr. Peepers Amateur Home Videos #70: New Tits On The Block / 1993 / LBO / M • Mr. Peepers Amateur Home Videos #77: Facial Coverage / 1993 / LBO / M • On Golden Heels / 1993 / LAG / B

ALEXANDRIA (1976) *(Alexandra (1976), Nina (Alexandria), Sonia Flicker)*

Very petite emaciated girl with long dark brown hair, small (not tiny) tits, tight waist, can look pretty (**Temptations**) or only passable. On drugs but nevertheless seems to like the sex. In **Breaker Beauties** she is credited as Alexandra. In **Heat Wave** and **Intimate Desires** she is credited as Nina. Sonia Flicker is from **Secret Dreams Of Mona Q**.

Blonde Velvet / 1976 / COL / M • Blue Vanities #523 / 1993 / FFL / M • Breaker Beauties / 1977 / VHL / M • Heat Wave / 1977 / COM / M • Intimate Desires / 1978 / VEP / M • Low Jinks / 1976 / REG / M • Secret Dreams Of Mona Q / 1977 / AR / M • Temptations / 1976 / VXP / M

ALEXANDRIA (BLISS) *see* **Beverly Bliss**

ALEXANDRIA (M. PAGE) *see* **Mona Page**

ALEXANDRIA DANE *see* **Alex Dane**

ALEXANDRIA DUNN *see* **Alexandria Quinn**

ALEXANDRIA GRECO *see* **Alex Greco**

ALEXANDRIA QUINN *(Alexandria Stewart, Alexandra Dunn, Victoria Quinn, Dianne Stewart, Diane Stewart)*

Hefty blonde bimbo with teased hair. Looks a bit like an overweight Tasha Voux. Has had boobs enhanced with scars in **Two Times A Virgin**. Real name is Dianne Stewart. Born Mar 25, 1973; tapes prior to Mar 25, 1991 are underage. Returned in November 1996 with a slimmed down body.

Adult Video News 1991 Awards / 1991 / VC / M • The Adventures Of Billy Blues / 1990 / HO / M • Alexandria, I Love You / 1993 / AFV / M • Alley Cat / 1991 / CIN / M • Amateur Lesbians #13: Brandi / 1991 / GO / F • Amateur Lesbians #16: Lorraine / 1991 / GO / F • Anal Climax #1 / 1991 / ROB / M • Anal Revolution / 1991 / ROB / M • Any Port In The Storm / 1991 / LV / M • Autoerotica #1 / 1991 / EX / M • Bangin' With The Home Girls / 1991 / AFV / M • Bend Over Babes #2 / 1991 / EA / M • Bite / 1991 / LE / M • Black On White / 1991 / VT / F • Blazing Butts / 1991 / LV / M • Blonde Savage / 1991 / CDI / M • Breaking And Entering / 1991 / AFV / M • Bush Pilots #1 / 1990 / VC / M • The Butt Stops Here / 1991 / LV / M • Buttman's Ultimate Workout / 1990 / EA / M • Call Girl / 1991 / AFV / M • Chicks On Sex / 1991 / FH / M • Club Head / 1990 / CA / M • Crude / 1991 / IN / M • Curse Of The Catwoman / 1990 / VC / M • Cyrano / 1991 / PL / M • The Dane Harlow Story / 1990 / IF / M • Dane's Brothel / 1990 / IF / G • The Danger Zone / 1990 / SO / M • Deep Cheeks #1 / 1991 / ROB / M • Deep Dreams / 1990 / IN / M • Devil's Agenda & Miss Jones / 1991 / AR / M • Double Cum / 1992 / IF / C • Double Penetration #4 / 1991 / WV / C • Dream Cream'n / 1991 / AR / M • East L.A. Law / 1991 / WV / M • Easy Pussy / 1991 / ROB / M • The Easy Way / 1990 / VC / M • Eat 'em And Smile / 1990 / ME / M • Edward Penishands #1 / 1991 / VT / M • Everything Butt #2 / 1991 / EX / C • Famous Anus #1 / 1990 / EX / M • Forbidden Desires / 1991 / CIN / F • Fortysomething #2 / 1991 / LE / M • Gazongas #03 / 1991 / VEX / M • Groupies / 1993 / AFV / F • Hot Diggity Dog / 1990 / ME / M • Hot Tight Asses #18 / 1996 / TCK / M • I Want To Be Nasty / 1991 / XCV / M • An Innocent Woman / 1991 / FAZ / M • Just Friends / 1991 / AFV / M • Laid In Heaven / 1991 / VC / M • Lingerie Busters / 1991 / FH / M • Lust For Love / 1991 / VC / M • Manbait #1 / 1991 / VC / M • Manbait #2 / 1992 / VC / M • The Midas Touch / 1991 / VT / M • Mischief / 1991 / WV / M • Mystified / 1991 / V99 / M • A Night At The Waxworks / 1990 / IF / M • Oral Addiction / 1989 / LV / M • The Pawnbroker / 1990 / IF / M • The Perfect Pair / 1991 / LE / M • Personalities / 1991 / PL / M • Purple Haze / 1991 / WV / M • Randy And Dane / 1991 / IF / G • Rapture / 1990 / SC / M • Renegade / 1990 / CIN / M • Rock Me / 1990 / LE / F • The Rookies / 1991 / VC / M • Screwballs / 1991 / AFV / M • Send Me An Angel / 1990 / V99 / M • Shameless / 1991 / SC / M • Shot From Behind / 1992 / FAZ / M • Skin Deep / 1991 / CIN / M • Space Virgins / 1990 / VEX / M • Special Treatment / 1991 / AFV / M • Student Fetish Videos: Catfighting #02 / 1991 / PLV / B • Student Fetish Videos: The Enema #02 / 1990 / SFV / B • Summer Lovers / 1991 / VEX / M • Sweet Poison / 1991 / CDI / M • Taboo #08 / 1990 / IN / M • Taboo #09 / 1991 / IN / M • Tiger Eye: Alexandria's Back / 1996 / TEV / F • Troublemaker / 1991 / VEX / M • Twin Cheeks #3 / 1991 / CIN / M • Twin Cheeks #4 / 1991 / CIN / M • Two Times A Virgin / 1991 / AR / M • Venus: Wings Of Seduction / 1991 / CDI / M • Virgin Spring / 1991 / FAZ / M • Wenches / 1991 / VT / F • Wild Side / 1991 / GO / M • [Golden Ring / 1992 / ... / M

ALEXANDRIA RYDER
Cheerleader Bondage Hell / 1995 / OUP / B • N.Y. Video Magazine #06 / 1995 / OUP / M • New York City Lesbian Gang Bang / 1995 / OUP / F • Streets Of New York #06 / 1996 / PL / M

ALEXANDRIA STEWART *see* **Alexandria Quinn**

ALEXIA
Sodomania #15: Warning! / 1996 / EL / M • Up And Cummers #31 / 1996 / 4P / M

ALEXIA DANE *see* **Alex Dane**

ALEXIS

Bondage Classix #03: Alexis In Bondage / 198? / BON / B • Bondage Classix #08: Alexis Slave Lessons / 198? / BON / B • Bondage Memories #03 / 1994 / BON / C • Bottoms Up (1993-Bon Vue) / 1993 / BON / B • Dark Desire / 1995 / STM / F • Double D Dykes #02 / 1992 / GO / F • Eighteen #3 / 1996 / SC / M • Feet First / 1988 / BIZ / S • Gallery Of Pain / 1995 / BON / B • Hot Body Competition: Bikinis & Bikes Contest / 1996 / CG / F • Hot Body Video Magazine: Sweet Dreams / 1996 / CG / F • House Of Sex #07: Banging Alexis / 1994 / RTP / M • House Of Sex #08: Banging Wendy / 1994 / RTP / M • A Lacy Affair #4 / 1991 / HO / F • Neighborhood Watch #15: All Worked Up / 1992 / LBO / M • Pearl Necklace: Facial #01 / 1994 / SEE / C • Spy Trap / 1995 / BON / B • The Story Of Pain / 1992 / PL / B • Take All Cummers / 1996 / HO / M

ALEXIS (SAKI) *see* **Saki**
ALEXIS (X) *see* **Alexis X**
ALEXIS BELLASIRE
Country & Western Cuties #2: Naked Pie Eating Contest / 1996 / AVN / M • The Cumm Brothers #14: Buttdraft / 1995 / OD / M • Fresh Faces #12 / 1996 / EVN / M

ALEXIS CHRISTIAN
Head To Head / 1996 / VI / M • Introducing Alexis / 1996 / VI / M • Penthouse: 25th Anniversary Swimsuit Video / 1994 / A*V / F • Where The Boys Aren't #8 / 1996 / VI / F • Where The Boys Aren't #9 / 1996 / VI / F

ALEXIS DEL LARGO
Take Off / 1978 / VXP / M
ALEXIS DEVELL *(Alexis Leslie)*
Enhanced too-big tits and lots of moles with curly long brown/blonde hair . Not particularly tight body. 21 years old in 1992. Grew up in Loveland, Colorado. Small tits as Alexis Leslie in **I Creme With Genie**.
Adult Video Nudes / 1993 / VC / M • Anal Ecstacy Girls #2 / 1993 / ROB / F • Ass Freaks #1 / 1993 / ROB / F • Assent Of A Woman / 1993 / DR / M • Borderline (Vivid) / 1995 / VI / M • Breastman Goes To Breastland #1 / 1993 / EVN / M • Burn / 1991 / LE / M • Butt Sluts #2 / 1993 / ROB / F • Caged Heat #2: Stripped Of Freedom / 1994 / NEH / S • Candy Factory / 1994 / PE / M • Checkmate / 1992 / CDI / M • The Cockateer #1 / 1991 / LE / M • The Cockateer #2 / 1992 / LE / M • Collectible / 1991 / LE / M • Curious / 1992 / LE / M • Deep Inside Kelly O'Dell / 1994 / VC / C • Dirty Looks / 1994 / VI / M • Eleventh Annual AVN Awards / 1994 / VC / M • Fantasy Girls / 1994 / PME / F • For The Money #1 / 1993 / FH / M • Foreign Affairs / 1991 / LE / M • Hungry #1 / 1992 / SC / M • Hungry #2 / 1993 / SC / M • I Creme With Genie / 1991 / PL / M • Jack The Stripper / 1992 / ME / M • Jennifer Ate / 1993 / XCI / F • Jezebel #1 / 1993 / SC / M • Jezebel #2 / 1993 / SC / M • Kadillac & Devell / 1993 / ZA / M • Kittens #2 / 1991 / CC / F • The Lady In Red / 1993 / VC / M • Lather / 1991 / LE / M • No Motive / 1994 / MID / M • The Original Wicked Woman / 1993 / WP / M • The Perfect Pair / 1991 / LE / M • Poor Little Rich Girl #1 / 1992 / XCI / M • Poor Little Rich Girl #2 / 1992 / XCI / M • The Prince Of Lies / 1992 / LE / M • Radical Affairs Video Magazine #04 / 1992 /

ME / M • See-Thru / 1992 / LE / M • The Servants Of Midnight / 1992 / CDI / M • Sexed / 1993 / HO / M • A Slow Hand / 1992 / FD / M • Sorority Sex Kittens #1 / 1992 / VC / M • Sorority Sex Kittens #2 / 1993 / VC / M • Southern Exposure / 1991 / LE / M • The Strip / 1992 / SC / M • Stripper Nurses / 1994 / PE / M • Toppers #17 / 1993 / TV / M • Toppers #18 / 1993 / TV / M • Toppers #20 / 1993 / TV / M • Toppers #22 / 1993 / TV / C • Unforgettable / 1992 / HO / M • Wild In Motion / 1992 / PL / M • Wild Innocence / 1992 / PL / M • Within & Without You / 1993 / WP / M

ALEXIS FIRESTONE
Bad Attitude / 1987 / CC / M • Close Friends / 1987 / CC / G • Deep Throat #2 / 1986 / AR / M • Dreams Of Desire / 1988 / BIZ / F • Fresh! / 1987 / VXP / M • Horneymooners #1 / 1988 / VXP / M • My Party Doll / 1987 / VXP / M • The Pleasure Machine / 1987 / VXP / M • Poltergash / 1987 / AVC / M • Sex Tips For Modern Women / 1987 / VXP / M • Sweet Revenge / 1986 / ZA / M • A Taste Of Ambrosia / 1987 / FEM / M • A Tasty Kind Of Love / 1987 / LV / M

ALEXIS FONTAINE
Passable face with very wide mouth, long reddish brown straight hair, lithe but not ultratight body, cantaloupes, shaven pussy, tongue pin, belly button ring, large tattoo in the middle of her back and a small one on her left butt, thin legs. 19 years old in 1997.
Cumback Pussy #5: Groopin' / 1996 / EL / M • Nasty Nymphos #16 / 1996 / ANA / M • Real Sex Magazine #02 / 1997 / HO / M

ALEXIS GOLD *(Julie Juggs)*
Pudgy big-titted amateur brunette born March 20, 1955 (ancient and looks it).
40 The Hard Way / 1991 / OD / M • Big & Bound #2 / 1992 / SBP / B • Body Slammers #01 / 1993 / SBP / B • Breast Wishes #03 / 1991 / LBO / M • Breast Worx #03 / 1991 / LBO / M • Breast Worx #05 / 1991 / LBO / M • Breast Worx #09 / 1991 / LBO / M • Bums Away / 1995 / PRE / C • Cage Cats / 1993 / SBP / B • Clean Out / 1991 / PRE / B • Day Of Reckoning / 1994 / CS / B • Deep Cleavage #1 / 1994 / AFI / F • Fear In The Forest / 1993 / CS / B • Frankenfoot / 1993 / SBP / B • The French Tickler / 1994 / CS / B • The Happy Woodcutter / 1993 / CS / B • High Fives / 1991 / PRE / B • The Intruders: The Next Stop / 1994 / VTF / B • Katrina's Bondage Memories #1 / 1994 / BON / C • Latex Bound #01 / 1993 / BON / B • Latex S&M Games / 1994 / SBP / B • Leg...Ends #05 / 1991 / PRE / F • Lost On Maneuvers / 1994 / VTF / B • Medieval Dungeon Master / 1993 / BON / B • Mistress Of The Dungeon / 1994 / VTF / B • Mr. Wilkes' Caning Academy / 1994 / VTF / B • Positively Pagan #01 / 1991 / ATA / M • Professor Butts / 1994 / SBP / F • Rump Roasts / 1991 / PRE / B • Slave Training (Vid Tech) / 1994 / VTF / B • Spanked! / 1995 / VTF / B • Start At The Bottom / 1993 / CS / B • Student Enemas / 1996 / PRE / C • Student Fetish Videos: Best of Enema #02 / 1992 / PRE / C • Student Fetish Videos: Best Of Foot Worship #02 / 1994 / PRE / C • Student Fetish Videos: The Enema #08 / 1992 / PRE / B • Student Fetish Videos: Tickling #05 / 1992 / SFV / B • Super Enemates #1 / 1994 / PRE / C • Tabatha's Super Video / 1993 /

H&S / S • Three For The Whip / 1995 / VTF / B • Tickle Thy Slaves / 1995 / SBP / B • Tied & Teased / 1993 / BON / B • Toppers #01 / 1992 / TV / F • Toppers #04 / 1993 / TV / M • Toppers #10 / 1993 / TV / M • Toppers #11 / 1993 / TV / C • Toppers #12 / 1993 / TV / C • The Very Best Of Breasts #3 / 1996 / H&S / S • Whipped And Waxed / 1993 / SBP / B • Wild Cats / 1991 / PRE / B

ALEXIS GRECO *see Alex Greco*

ALEXIS HART

More Dirty Debutantes #35 / 1994 / 4P / M

ALEXIS KIRBY *see Star Index I*

ALEXIS LESLIE *see Alexis DeVell*

ALEXIS PAINE *see Alexis Payne*

ALEXIS PAYNE *(Alexis Paine)*

Adler Shoots: The Reality Behind The Legend / cr90 / BON / B • Alexis Goes To Hell / 1996 / EXQ / B • Bad Luck For Bad Girls / 1996 / EXQ / B • The Bedford Wives / 1994 / LON / B • Bedroom Bondage / 1994 / LON / B • Beg For Mercy / 1993 / LBO / B • Bondage Cheerleaders / 1993 / LON / B • Bound For Stardom / cr94 / LON / B • Bruce Seven: A Compendium Of His Most Graphic Scenes Vol 3 / 1992 / BS / C • Bruce Seven: A Compendium Of His Most Graphic Scenes Vol 4 / 1993 / BS / C • Bruce Seven: A Compendium Of His Most Graphic Scenes Vol 5 / 1994 / BS / C • Bruce Seven: A Compendium Of His Most Graphic Scenes Vol 6 / 1994 / BS / C • Captive Housewife / 1994 / CS / B • Chateau Payne / 1995 / HOM / B • Cries From The Dungeon / cr94 / HOM / B • Desire & Submission #2 / 1994 / HAC / B • Dracula's Dungeon / 1995 / HOM / B • Dungeon Delight / 1995 / LON / B • The Dungeon Master / 1992 / BS / B • Dungeon Of The Borgias / 1993 / HOM / B • The Ecstasy Of Payne / 1994 / BS / B • The Face Of Fear / 1990 / BS / B • Forever Payne / 1994 / BS / B • Girls Next Door / 1995 / SHL / B • Hard Discipline #1 / 1993 / SHL / B • Hard Discipline #2: The Lady's Maid / 1993 / SHL / B • Hard Whips For Soft Bodies / 1993 / NTP / B • Her Darkest Desire / 1993 / HOM / B • Hot Rod To Hell #1 / 1991 / BIZ / B • In This The Oncala Wa Get / 1993 / CAA / B • A Journey Into Darkness / 1991 / BS / B • Kym Wilde's On The Edge #16 / 1994 / RB / B • Kym Wilde's On The Edge #18 / 1995 / RB / B • Man Handling / 1995 / RB / B • Mind Shadows #1 / 1993 / FD / M • Mind Shadows #2 / 1993 / FD / M • The Mystery Of Payne / 1991 / BS / B • A Night Of Hell / 1993 / LBO / B • Nurses Know Best / 1994 / SHL / B • Our Sorority / 1993 / SHL / B • Party Of Payne / 1993 / BS / B • Payne In Amsterdam / 1993 / STM / B • Payne-Full Revenge / 1995 / BS / B • The Perils Of Prunella #2 / 1991 / BIZ / B • The Power Of Summer #1: Revenge / 1992 / BS / B • The Price Of Curiosity / 1993 / LON / B • Princess Of Pain / 1996 / LBO / B • Prisoners In The House From Hell / 1995 / LON / B • Prisoners Of Payne / 1995 / NIT / B • Punished Princess / 1992 / HOM / B • Queen Of The Lash / 1993 / LON / B • Sinderella's Revenge / 1992 / HOM / B • Slave Of Fashion / 1993 / LON / B • Slavegirl Of Zor / 1996 / LON / B • The Slaves Of Alexis Payne / 1995 / LON / B • Special Request #3 / 1993 / HOM / B • Stolen Fantasies / 1995 /

LON / B • Strictly For Pleasure / 1994 / ONA / B • Submission To Ecstasy / 1995 / NTP / B • Takin' It To The Limit #1 / 1994 / BS / M • Terrors Of The Inquisition / 1992 / HOM / B • Tied & Tickled #18 / 1992 / CS / B • Torture Clinic / 1995 / LON / B • Torturer's Apprentice / 1996 / LBO / B • Trained By Payne / 1994 / ONA / B • A Twist Of Payne / 1993 / BS / B • Velma And Clarice/What Are Friends For / 1994 / HAC / B • A Way With Wood / 1995 / HOM / B • Whacked! / 1993 / BS / B • Will Of Iron / 1991 / HOM / B • Women Who Spank Men / 1995 / SHL / B • Zena, Mistress Of The Universe / 1995 / HOM / B

ALEXIS REID

Desire & Submission #1 / 1994 / HAC / B

ALEXIS ROSS *see Star Index I*

ALEXIS SERVICE *see Alexis X*

ALEXIS STAR *see Star Index I*

ALEXIS STORM *see Alex Storm*

ALEXIS VOGEL

The Rebel / 1990 / CIN / M

ALEXIS WHITE (BLACK)

All Night Long / 1990 / NWV / C • Black Bimbos In Heat / 1989 / MIR / C • Friday The 13th #1: A Nude Beginning / 1987 / VD / M • Hot Number / 1987 / WET / M • I Cream Of Genie / 1988 / SE / M • The Kiss / 1986 / SC / M • Wild Stuff / 1987 / WET / M • You Bring Out The Animal In Me / 1987 / MIR / M

ALEXIS WOLF

Adorable tight bodied brunette with small firm beautifully-shaped tits, tight waist, tight boy-like butt, good skin and a wonderful smile.

69th Street / 1993 / VIM / M • Biff Malibu's Totally Nasty Home Videos #27 / 1992 / ANA / M • Bitch / 1993 / VIM / M • Buffy Malibu's Totally Nasty All-Girl Home Videos #04 / 1993 / ANA / F • Incocknito / 1993 / VIM / M • Inner Pink #3 / 1994 / LIP / F • Madame Hiney: The Beverly Hills Butt Broker / 1993 / STR / M • Undercover Lover / 1992 / CV / M

ALEXIS X *(Alexis Service, Alexis (X))*

Brunette with short straight hair, medium slightly droopy tits, marginal body.

Alley Cat / 1993 / VC / M • Babylon Blue / 1983 / VXP / M • Corruption / 1983 / VC / M • Flash Pants / 1983 / VC / M • Getting Ahead / 1983 / PL / M • Glitter / 1983 / CA / M • Lady Lust / 1984 / CA / M • Maneaters / 1983 / VC / M • Once Upon A Secretary / 1983 / GO / M • Show Your Love / 1984 / VC / M

ALEXISS

Big Girl Workout / 1991 / BTO / M • Huge Ladies #10 / 1991 / BTO / M

ALEXUS DANE *see Alex Dane*

ALEXXI

Santa Is Coming All Over Town / 1996 / EVN / M

ALEXXX KNIGHT

Amateur Nights #13 / 1996 / HO / M • Asses Galore #5: T.T. Vs The World / 1996 / DFI / M • Butthole Bunnies / 1996 / ROB / F • Deep Dippin' Anal Babes / 1996 / ROB / F • Filthy First Timers #2: Innocence Lost / 1996 / EL / M • Generation Sex #2: Nature's Revenge / 1996 / VT / M • Max #11: Tunnel Of Lust / 1996 / LE / M • Neighborhood Nookie #1 / 1996 / RAS / M • Nineteen #6 / 1996 / FOR / M • No Man's Land #15 / 1996 / VT / F • Puritan Video Maga-

zine #04 / 1996 / LE / M • Sex For Hire / 1996 / ONA / M • Sodomania: Slop Shots / 1996 / EL / C • Thermonuclear Sex / 1996 / EL / M • Undercover / 1996 / VC / M • Young Tails / 1996 / LV / M

ALFRED B.

Screamers / 1994 / HW / M

ALGERNON HATE

Bitch School / 1996 / BON / B • Your Cheatin' Butt / 1996 / BON / B

ALI

A&B AB#247: Bizy-Arre Those Girls / 1991 / A&B / F • A&B AB#248: Ali / 1991 / A&B / M • A&B AB#252: Grandma Is In The Ali Again! / 1991 / A&B / F • A&B AB#258: Spanked Intruder / 1991 / A&B / M • A&B AB#267: Lingerie Party / 1991 / A&B / S • A&B AB#269: Red Asses / 1991 / A&B / M • A&B AB#276: Smoking Rods #2 / 1994 / A&B / M • Bobby Hollander's Rookie Nookie #10 / 1993 / MET / M • Mike Hott: #113 Jan And Ali / 1990 / MHV / F • Mike Hott: #114 Jan, Ali And Paul / 1990 / MHV / M • Mike Hott: #116 Ali And Pam-Ann And Dusty And Paul / 1990 / MHV / M • Private Gold #10: Sins / 1996 / OD / M • Seymore & Shane Playing With Fire / 1994 / ULI / M • Video Virgins #14 / 1994 / NS / M

ALI MOORE *(Kristi Bryant, Christie Bryant, Cristy Brian)*

Brunette with a pretty face, large natural, very nicely shaped breasts, tight waist and tight body. Gerri Orlando or Joy Glenn in **If My Mother Only Knew**. Not the same as Gina Martell. Was married for a while to Gary Sheene.

Aerobisex Girls #1 / 1983 / LIP / F • Aroused / 1985 / VIV / M • B.Y.O.B. / 1984 / VD / M • Best Of Caught From Behind #1 / 1987 / HO / C • Caught From Behind #03 / 1985 / HO / M • The Debutante / 1986 / BEA / M • Deep & Wet / 1986 / VD / M • Dirty Letters / 1984 / VD / M • Evil Angel / 1986 / VCR / M • Firestorm #2: The Angel Blade / 1986 / COM / M • Firestorm #3 / 1986 / COM / M • Gettin' Ready / 1985 / CDI / M • The Girls Of Malibu / 1986 / ACV / S • Girls Of Paradise #1 / 1986 / PV / C • The Girls Of The A Team #1 / 1985 / WV / M • Hollywood Undercover / 1989 / BWV / C • Hot Tails / 1984 / VEN / M • I Know What Girls Like / 1986 / WET / G • If My Mother Only Knew / 1985 / CA / M • Layover / 1985 / HO / M • Lottery Fever / 1985 / BEA / M • Love Bites / 1985 / CA / M • Lust Bug / 1985 / HO / M • Lust In Space / 1985 / PV / M • Naughty Cheerleaders / 1985 / HO / M • Only The Best Of Breasts / 1987 / CV / C • Only The Best Of Women With Women / 1988 / CV / C • Rich Bitch / 1985 / HO / M • Sex Crimes 2084 / 1985 / SE / M • Skin Dive / 1988 / AVC / M • Starlet Screen Test / 1990 / NST / S • Sweet Cheeks / 1987 / VCR / C • Temptations Of The Flesh / 1986 / VD / M • The Whore Of The Worlds / 1985 / PV / M • Wild Things #1 / 1985 / CV / M • Working Girls / 1985 / CA / M • WPINK-TV #1 / 1985 / PV / M • Yank My Doodle, It's A Dandy / 1985 / GOM / M

ALIANA

Freshness Counts / 1996 / EL / M

ALICE

Amateur Nights #10 / 1990 / HO / M • Blue Vanities #505 / 1992 / FFL / M • Double D Dykes #02 / 1992 / GO / F • Hard Core Beginners #04 / 1995 / LEI / M • Joe Elliot's College Girls #42 / 1995 / JOE / M • Kinky College Cunts #04 / 1993 / NS / F • Lesbian Pros And Amateurs #06 / 1992 / GO / F • Swingers Confidential #1 / 1995 / FC / M

ALICE ARNO
[The Loves Of Irina / 1973 / PS / S
ALICE BREEZY see Alice Springs
ALICE CLARK
Resurrection Of Eve / 1973 / MIT / M
ALICE ENOCH see Star Index I
ALICE ENRIGHT
One Last Score / 1978 / CDI / M
ALICE FAIRCHILD see Star Index I
ALICE HAMMER
Wet Wilderness / 1975 / VCX / B
ALICE HARVEY (Carolyn Anderson)
Brunette with medium enhanced tits, pretty face, tight waist, nice skin, lithe body but a bit too tall.
Strap-On Sally #01: Strap-On Psycho / 1993 / PL / F • Strap-On Sally #02: Ariana Bottoms Out / 1993 / PL / F • Streets Of New York #01 / 1994 / PL / M
ALICE HOLTZER see Star Index I
ALICE KAUFMAN see Star Index I
ALICE MILLER see Arcie Miller
ALICE NOBLE see Star Index I
ALICE NOLAND (Lisa Sanders)
Late sixties / early seventies soft core actress.
After The Ball Was Over / 1967 / SOW / S • Three Sexateers / 1970 / SOW / S
ALICE NORWOOD
Doogan's Woman / 1978 / S&L / M
ALICE SPRINGS (Allison Springs, Alice Breezy, Judy Blue(A.Springs))
Rather pudgy brunette with large tits. Australian. Alice Breezy: **Red Hot And Ready**.
1-800-934-BOOB / 1992 / VD / C • Acts Of Confession / 1991 / PP / M • Aussie Bloopers / 1993 / OD / M • Aussie Exchange Girls / 1990 / PM / M • Aussie Maid In America / 1990 / PM / M • Aussie Vice / 1989 / PM / M • Australian Connection / 1989 / PM / M • Blonde Ice #1 / 1990 / EX / M • Boobs, Butts And Bloopers #2 / 1990 / HO / M • Bushwackers / 1990 / PM / M • Casey At The Bat / 1991 / LV / M • Catalina: Sabotage / 1991 / CDI / M • Catalina: Undercover / 1991 / CIN / M • Caught From Behind #14 / 1990 / HO / M • City Girls / 1991 / VC / M • Cum On Line / 1991 / XPI / M • The Danger Zone / 1990 / SO / M • Dial A Sailor / 1990 / PM / M • Dick Tracer / 1990 / PM / M • Dream Lover / 1991 / WV / M • Dyke Bar / 1991 / PL / F • The Easy Way / 1990 / VC / M • Edge Of Sensation / 1990 / LE / M • Fantasy In Blue / 1991 / VI / M • The Fire Down Below / 1990 / IN / M • Friends & Lovers #1 / 1991 / VT / M • In Excess / 1991 / CA / M • Indiscretions / 1991 / PP / M • Joint Effort / 1992 / SEX / C • L.A. Stories / 1990 / VI / M • Lost In Paradise / 1990 / CA / M • Lusty Dusty / 1990 / VI / M • Mirage #1 / 1991 / VC / M • Nothing Serious / 1990 / EX / M • One Night Stand / 1990 / LE / M • Oral Majority #08 / 1990 / WV / C • Orgy On The Ranch / 1991 / NLE / M • Outback Assignment / 1991 / VD / M • The Outlaw / 1991 / WV / M • A Paler Shade Of Blue / 1991 / CC / M • Phone Sex Girls: Australia / 1989 / PM / M • A Portrait Of Christy / 1990 / VI / M • Rapture / 1990 / SC / M • Raunch #02 / 1990 / CC / M • Ravaged Ri-

valry / 1990 / HO / M • Rear Burner / 1990 / IN / M • Red Hot And Ready / 1990 / V99 / M • Safecracker / 1991 / CC / M • Sexual Healer / 1991 / CA / M • Singles Holiday / 1990 / PM / M • Sleepwalker / 1990 / XCI / M • Sophisticated Lady / 1991 / CIN / M • The Specialist / 1990 / HO / M • Splash / 1990 / WV / C • Steal Breeze / 1990 / SO / M • Street Walkers / 1990 / PL / M • Take Me / 1991 / NLE / M • Tell Me What To Do / 1991 / CA / M • Three Men And A Geisha / 1990 / HO / M • True Blue / 1989 / PM / M • The Two Janes / 1990 / WV / M • The War Of The Hoses / 1991 / NLE / M • Young Buns #2 / 1990 / WV / M
ALICE STORM see Alex Storm
ALICE THATCH see Star Index I
ALICE WRAY
Loving Friends / 1975 / AXV / M • Made To Order / 1975 / AXV / M
ALICIA
A&B AB#245: Older Couples Love Young Girls / 1991 / A&B / M • AVP #9120: The Therapist / 1991 / AVP / M • Blue Vanities #548 / 1994 / FFL / M • Frat Girls / 1993 / VC / M • Mike Hott: #200 Lesbian Sluts #03 / 1992 / MHV / F • Mike Hott: Apple Asses #15 / 1992 / MHV / F • Northwest Pecker Trek #3: Ducks & Dicks / 1994 / LBO / M • Pearl Necklace: Premier Sessions #04 / 1994 / SEE / M • Sorority Slumber Sluts / 1995 / WIV / F
ALICIA ADAMS see Le Le Adams
ALICIA HUNT
Slip Of The Tongue (Vxp) / 19?? / VXP / M
ALICIA JOHNSON
Basic Desire / cr85 / STM / B
ALICIA LASHLEY see Sade
ALICIA LEE see Bobbi Lee
ALICIA LELE see Bobbi Lee
ALICIA MONET (Holly Wood (Alicia), Alisha Monet)
Against All Bods / 1988 / ZA / M • Angel Gets Even / 1987 / FAN / M • Backside To The Future #2 / 1988 / ZA / M • Beauty And The Beast #1 / 1988 / VC / M • Boom Boom Valdez / 1988 / CA / M • California Native / 1988 / CDI / M • The Case Of The Mad Tickler / 1988 / ME / M • Caught In The Act / 1987 / WV / M • Conflict / 1988 / VD / M • Debbie Class Of '88 / 1987 / CC / M • Debbie Class Of '89 / 1989 / CC / M • Debbie For President / 1988 / CC / M • Debbie Goes To Hawaii / 1988 / VD / C • Deep Inside Keisha / 1994 / VC / C • Divine Decadence / 1988 / CA / M • Double Penetration #2 / 1986 / WV / C • Easy Access / 1988 / ZA / M • The Eleventh Commandment / 1987 / WAV / M • The Erotic Adventures Of Bonnie & Clyde / 1988 / GO / M • Erotic Television Video / 1988 / VD / M • Fatal Erection / 1988 / SEV / M • Fatal Passion / 1988 / CC / M • The Final Taboo / 1988 / CA / M • First Time Lesbians (Gourmet) / 1987 / GO / F • For Your Love / 1988 / IN / M • Ginger Does Them All / 1988 / CV / M • Goin' Down Slow / 1988 / VC / M • Good Evening Vietnam / 1987 / WV / M • Hawaii Vice #6 / 1989 / CDI / M • Hitler Sucks / 1988 / GO / M • Hyapatia Lee's Arcade Series #02 / 1988 / ZA / C • Inn Of Sin / 1988 / VT / M • La Bimbo / 1987 / PEN / M • Little Red Riding Hood / 1988 / WV / M • Love Lies / 1988 / FH / M • Lust Connection / 1988 / VT / M • Made In Germany / 1988 / FAZ / M • The Main At-

traction / 1988 / 4P / M • Making Ends Meet / 1988 / VT / M • The Master Of Pleasure / 1988 / VD / M • Naked Stranger / 1987 / CDI / M • Nasty Girls #1 (1989-Plum) / 1989 / PP / C • Once Upon A Temptress / 1988 / CA / M • Only The Best Of Oral / 1989 / CV / C • Outlaw Ladies #2 / 1988 / VC / M • Outrageous Foreplay / 1987 / WV / M • Phone Mates / 1988 / CA / M • Piece Of Heaven / 1988 / CDI / M • The PTX Club / 1988 / GO / M • Ramb-Ohh #2 / 1988 / PV / M • A Rare Starlet / 1987 / ME / M • Ride 'em Cow Girl / 1995 / VI / C • Robofox #1 / 1987 / FAN / M • Romeo And Juliet #1 / 1987 / WV / M • Samantha And The Deep Throat Girls / 1988 / CV / M • Satisfaction Jackson / 1988 / CA / M • The Sex Life Of Mata Hari / 1989 / GO / M • Sextrology / 1987 / CA / M • Sexual Power / 1988 / CV / M • She's So Fine #2 / 1988 / VC / M • The Slut / 1988 / FAN / M • Snapshots: Confessions Of A Video Voyeur / 1988 / CC / M • So Deep, So Good / 1988 / NSV / M • Surf, Sand And Sex / 1987 / SE / M • Suzie Superstar...The Search Continues / 1988 / CV / M • Sweat #2 / 1988 / PP / M • Switch Hitters #2: Swinging Both Ways / 1987 / IN / G • Taboo #06 / 1988 / IN / M • Toys 4 Us #2 / 1987 / WV / C • Twentysomething #1 / 1988 / VI / M • Twentysomething #2 / 1988 / VI / M • Video Voyeur #1 / 1988 / VT / C • Wet Dream On Maple Street / 1988 / FAN / M • White Chocolate / 1987 / PEN / M • Wise Girls / 1989 / IN / C • Woman To Woman / 1989 / ZA / C
ALICIA NOVEL see Star Index I
ALICIA RIO (Kora, Alyssa Rio)
Marginal face, medium/large tits, thick body, and lots of black hair. Born in La Capita, Mexico. Used to be a city employee. 5'2" tall. Married to Rex (or Steve) Houston. Allegedly tried to commit suicide in mid 1996 by jumping from a hotel window but settled for cutting herself with the broken glass and ending up in the hospital.
Adult Video Nudes / 1993 / VC / M • Almost Home Alone / 1993 / SFP / M • America's Dirtiest Home Videos #07 / 1991 / VEX / M • America's Dirtiest Home Videos #08 / 1992 / VEX / M • The Anal Diary Of Misty Rain / 1993 / EL / M • Anal Romance / 1993 / LV / M • Anal Vision #11 / 1993 / LBO / M • The Anal-Europe Series #05: Anal European Vacation / 1993 / LV / M • The Anals Of History #2 / 1992 / MID / M • Ass Openers! #1 / 1995 / TCK / C • Ass-Capades / 1992 / HW / M • Assy Sassy #1 / 1994 / ROB / F • Attack Of The 50 Foot Hooker / 1994 / OD / M • The Babe / 1992 / EX / M • Barrio Bitches / 1994 / SC / F • Batwoman & Catgirl / 1992 / HW / M • Bazooka County #5: The Jugs / 1993 / CC / M • Bedrooms And Boardrooms / 1992 / DR / M • Behind The Scenes: The Making Of The Wil & Ed Movies / 1992 / MID / M • Best Gang Bangs / 1996 / DFI / C • Betrayal / 1992 / XCI / M • Bi Bitches In Heat / 1996 / BIZ / F • Big Titted Tarts / 1994 / PL / C • Bikini Beach #1 / 1993 / CC / M • Bikini Beach #2 / 1993 / CC / M • Bikini Beach #3 / 1993 / CC / F • Bimbonese 101 / 1993 / PL / M • The Bitches / 1993 / LIP / F • Black Men Can Hump / 1992 / FH / M • Blue Bayou / 1993 / VC / M • Bobby Hollander's Maneaters #05 / 1993 / SFP / M •

Borderline (Vivid) / 1995 / VI / M • Bruise Control / 1993 / PRE / B • Bubble Butts #02 / 1992 / LBO / M • Bubble Butts #08 / 1992 / LBO / M • Bun Busters #12 / 1993 / LBO / M • Burning Desire / 1992 / CDI / M • The Butt Connection / 1993 / TIW / M • Butt Naked #2 / 1994 / OD / M • The Butt Sisters Do Las Vegas / 1994 / MID / M • Buttsizer, King Of Rears #2 / 1992 / EVN / M • Buttslammers #03: The Ultimate Dream / 1993 / BS / F • Caught & Bound / 1993 / BON / B • The Cellar Dweller / 1996 / EL / M • Checkmate / 1992 / CDI / M • Chronicles Of Pain #2 / 1996 / BIZ / B • Chug-A-Lug Girls #1 / 1993 / VT / M • Close Quarters / 1992 / ME / M • Club Anal #2 / 1993 / ROB / F • Coming Clean / 1992 / ME / M • Cum & Get Me / 1995 / PL / F • The D.P. Man #2 / 1992 / FD / M • Dear Bridgette / 1992 / ZA / M • Deep Inside Kelly O'Dell / 1994 / VC / C • Dial N For Nikki / 1993 / PEP / M • Dick & Jane Go To Hollywood #1 / 1993 / AVI / M • Dickin' Around / 1994 / VEX / M • Dirty Looks / 1994 / VI / M • Dirty Thoughts / 1992 / LE / M • Do The White Thing / 1992 / ZA / M • Dorm Girls / 1992 / VC / M • Double D Dykes #05 / 1992 / GO / F • The Dragon Lady #4: Tales From The Bed #3 / 1992 / WV / M • The Dream Team / 1995 / VT / M • The Erotic Artist / 1995 / VC / M • Erotica / 1992 / CC / M • Erotica Optique / 1994 / SUF / M • Everybody's Playmates / 1992 / CA / C • Falling Stars / 1996 / PRE / C • Fantasies Of Alicia / 1995 / VT / M • Fast Track / 1992 / LIP / F • Frathouse Sexcapades / 1993 / SFP / M • The Freak Club / 1994 / VMX / M • Full Throttle Girls: Boredom Pulled The Trigger / 1993 / VIM / M • Future Doms #1 / 1996 / BIZ / B • Gang Bang Fury #1 / 1992 / ROB / M • Gerein' Up / 1992 / VC / M • The Girls' Club / 1993 / VD / C • Girlz N The Hood #2 / 1992 / HW / M • Guttman's Hollywood Adventure / 1993 / PL / M • Hangin' Out / 1992 / IF / M • Heel's Angels / 1995 / PRE / B • The Hills Have Thighs / 1992 / MID / C • Hits & Misses / 1992 / PRE / B • Hollywood Scandal: The Heidi Flesh Story / 1993 / IP / M • Hookers Of Hollywood / 1994 / IF / M • Hooter Ho-Down / 1994 / LV / M • Hot Tight Asses #01 / 1992 / TCK / M • Hungry #1 / 1992 / SC / M • Hungry #2 / 1993 / SC / M • In Loving Color #2 / 1992 / VT / M • In Loving Color #3 / 1992 / VT / M • In Your Face #1 / 1992 / PL / M • Inferno #2 / 1993 / SC / M • Inside Job / 1992 / ZA / M • Junkyard Dykes #02 / 1994 / ZA / F • Just A Gigolo / 1992 / SC / M • KBBS: Weekend With Alicia Rio & Sheila Stone / 1992 / KBB / M • Kittens #4: Bodybuilding Bitches / 1993 / CC / F • Kym Wilde's On The Edge #12 / 1994 / RB / B • La Princesa Anal / 1993 / ROB / M • Lacy's Hot Anal Summer / 1992 / LV / M • The Last Good Sex / 1992 / FD / M • Latin Lust / 1992 / HW / C • A League Of Their Moan / 1992 / EVN / M • Leg...Ends #08 / 1993 / PRE / F • Lesbian Bitches #1 / 1994 / ROB / F • Lesbian Castle: No Kings Allowed / 1994 / LIP / F • Let's Party / 1993 / VC / M • Lez Go Crazy / 1992 / HW / C • Live Sex / 1994 / LE / M • The Love Doctor / 1992 / HIP / M • Love Hurts / 1992 / VD / M • Love Me, Love My Butt #1 / 1994 / ROB / F • Love Potion / 1993 / WV / M • Lovebone Invasion / 1993 / PL / M • Lovin' Spoonfuls #8 / 1996 / 4P / C • M Series #08 / 1993 / LBO / M • M Series #13 / 1993 / LBO / M • Maliboobies / 1993 / CDI / F • Marked #2 / 1993 / FD / M • Memories / 1992 / LE / M • Midnight Confessions / 1992 / XCI / M • Mind Shadows #1 / 1993 / FD / M • Mind Shadows #2 / 1993 / FD / M • Mindsex / 1993 / MPA / M • More Dirty Debutantes #12 / 1991 / 4P / M • Mr. Peepers Amateur Home Videos #50: All That Glitters / 1992 / LBO / M • Murphie's Brown / 1992 / LV / M • My Anal Sister / 1994 / XCI / M • My Cousin Ginny / 1993 / MET / M • My Favorite Rear / 1993 / PEP / M • My Secret Lover / 1992 / XCI / M • Naked Edge / 1992 / LE / M • The Naked Pen / 1992 / VC / M • Naked Truth #2 / 1993 / FH / M • Nasty Cracks / 1992 / PRE / B • Neighborhood Watch #21 / 1992 / LBO / M • Never Never Land / 1992 / PL / M • Night And Day #1 / 1993 / VT / M • Night Creatures / 1992 / PL / M • The Night Of The Coyote / 1993 / MED / M • No Fly Zone / 1993 / LE / F • No Man's Land #11 / 1995 / VT / F • Nookie Cookies / 1993 / CDI / F • Nookie Of The Year / 1993 / HW / M • Nympho Zombie Coeds / 1993 / VIM / M • Oreo A Go-Go #1 / 1992 / FH / M • Oreo A Go-Go #2 / 1992 / FH / M • Pajama Party X #1 / 1994 / VC / M • Pajama Party X #2 / 1994 / VC / M • Party Girl / 1995 / LV / M • Patriot Dames / 1992 / ZA / M • Poor Little Rich Girl #1 / 1992 / XCI / M • Poor Little Rich Girl #2 / 1992 / XCI / M • Pornographic Priestess / 1992 / CA / M • The Power & The Passion / 1993 / CDI / M • Pristine #1 / 1996 / CA / M • Private Dancer (Caballero) / 1992 / CA / M • Private Video Magazine #09 / 1994 / OD / M • Public Places #1 / 1994 / SC / M • A Pussy Called Wanda #1 / 1992 / DR / M • Pussy Galore / 1993 / VD / C • A Pussy To Die For / 1992 / CA / M • Pussyman #03: The Search Continues / 1993 / SNA / M • Pussyman #04: The Celebration / 1993 / SNA / M • Pussyman #05: Captive Audience / 1994 / SNA / M • Pussyman #06: House Of Games / 1994 / SNA / M • Pussyman #11: Prime Cuts / 1995 / SNA / C • Pussywoman #1: Sisters In Sin / 1994 / CC / M • Rahnwoman #00: Wailango / 1995 / CC / M • Raw Talent: Bang 'er 24 Times / 1992 / RTP / M • Raw Talent: Bang 'er 25 Times / 1992 / RTP / M • Raw Talent: Bang 'er 26 Times / 1992 / RTP / M • Raw Talent: Bang 'er Megamix 1 / 1994 / RTP / C • Read My Lips: No More Bush / 1992 / HW / M • Rears In Windows / 1993 / FH / M • Reflections Of Rio / 1993 / WP / M • Risque Burlesque #1 / 1994 / IN / M • Satisfaction / 1992 / LE / M • Sean Michaels On The Road #01: The Barrio / 1993 / VT / M • Seduced / 1992 / VD / M • See-Thru / 1992 / LE / M • Sensations #1 / 1996 / SC / M • The Serpent's Dream / 1993 / VC / M • Sex Bandits / 1992 / ZA / M • Sex Helst / 1992 / WV / M • Sex Trek #3: The Wrath Of Bob / 1992 / ME / M • Sexual Olympics #1: The Trials / 1992 / VT / M • Seymore Butts In The Love Shack / 1992 / FH / M • Seymore Butts Is Blown Away / 1993 / FH / M • Seymore Butts: Bustin' Out My Best Anal / 1995 / FH / C • A Shaver Among Us / 1992 / ZA / M • Shipwrecked / 1992 / CDI / M • Show Business / 1995 / LV / M • Ski Bunnies #1 / 1994 / HW / M • Ski Bunnies #2 / 1994 / HW / M • Skid Row / 1994 / SC / M • Slippery When Wet / 1994 / LEI / C • Sneek Peeks #1 / 1993 / FL / M • So You Want To Be In The Movies? / 1994 / VC / M • Sodomania #03: Foreign Objects / 1993 / EL / M • Sodomania: Slop Shots / 1996 / EL / C • Sole Search / 1996 / PRE / B • Sorority Sex Kittens #2 / 1993 / VC / M • The Spa / 1993 / VC / M • Spanish Fly / 1992 / LE / M • Steam / 1993 / AMP / M • Strike Three / 1996 / PRE / B • Student Fetish Videos: Best of Enema #02 / 1992 / PRE / C • Student Fetish Videos: Best Of Spanking #02 / 1993 / PRE / C • Student Fetish Videos: The Enema #09 / 1992 / PRE / B • Student Fetish Videos: Spanking #08 / 1992 / PRE / B • Student Fetish Videos: Tickling #06 / 1992 / SFV / B • The Submission Of Alicia Rio / 1996 / BIZ / B • Summer Games / 1992 / HW / M • Supermarket Babes In Heat / 1992 / OD / M • Surfer Girl / 1992 / PP / M • Sweet Alicia Rio / 1992 / FH / M • Sweet Cheerleaders Spanked / 1996 / BIZ / B • Takin' It To The Limit #4 / 1995 / BS / M • Taxi Girls #3: Killer On The Loose / 1993 / MED / M • Taxi Girls #4: Daughter Of Lust / 1994 / CA / M • Thinking Of You / 1992 / LV / F • Tickled Pink / 1993 / LE / F • The Tiffany Minx Affair / 1992 / FOR / M • Toppers #02 / 1992 / TV / M • Tori Welles Goes Behind The Scenes / 1992 / FD / M • Trashy Ladies / 1993 / LIP / F • Twin Freaks / 1992 / ZA / M • Under The Pink / 1994 / ROB / F • Unfaithful Entry / 1992 / DR / M • Voyeur Video / 1992 / ZA / M • Wad Gobblers #04 / 1992 / GLI / M • Wad Gobblers #13 / 1994 / GLI / M • Wanderlust / 1992 / LE / M • Waterbabies #2 / 1992 / CC / M • Waterworld: The Enema Club / 1996 / BIZ / B • Wet In The Saddle / 1994 / ME / M • White Men Can Hump / 1992 / EVN / M • Whorelock / 1993 / LV / M • Wild & Wicked #6 / 1995 / VT / M • Willing Women / 1993 / VD / C • Within & Without You / 1993 / WP / M • Women Of Influence / 1993 / LV / F • X-TV / 1992 / CA / C • [European Invasion / cr93 / A&E / M

ALICIA ROBBINS *see* **Star Index I**

ALICIA SANBORN
Blue Vanities #105 (New) / 1996 / FFL / M • Blue Vanities #165 (Old) / 1991 / FFL / M • Blue Vanities #166 (Old) / 1991 / FFL / M

ALICIA TRENT
ABA: Double Feature #2 / 1996 / ALP / M • Fannie / 1975 / ALP / M

ALICYN *see* **Alicyn Sterling**

ALICYN STERLING *(Mandy White, Allison Sterling, Alyce Sterling, Alicyn, Cheri Bonet, Lynette Sterling, Alicyn Storm, Carrie Bittner, Carrie Breeze, Carrie Cruise, Carrie Mitchell)*
Blonde with tendency to red. Very white body. Uncredited in **Twisted**. Mandy White: **Torch #2, Positions Wanted**. Cheri Bonet: **Rockin' the Boat**. In **Lethal Woman** she has had her breasts enlarged to grotesque proportions. Lynette Sterling: **No Time for Love**. First movie was **Sudden Urge**.

Americans Most Wanted / 1991 / HO / M • Anal Adventures #2: Bodacious Buns / 1991 / VC / M • Anal Leap / 1991 / ZA / M • Angels / 1992 / VC / M • Assault With A Friendly Weapon / 1990 / DAY / M • The Back Doors (Western) / 1991 / WV / M • Backdoor Black #1 / 1992 / WV / C • Bad

Influence / 1991 / CDI / M • Bedrooms And Boardrooms / 1992 / DR / M • Bend Over Babes #2 / 1991 / EA / M • Bi Madness / 1991 / STA / G • Bikini Summer #2 / 1992 / PME / S • Bite / 1991 / LE / M • Blonde Ambition / 1991 / CIN / M • Blow Job Betty / 1991 / CC / M • Brandy & Alexander / 1991 / VC / M • Breast Worx #02 / 1991 / LBO / M • Breast Worx #04 / 1991 / LBO / M • Bruce Seven: A Compendium Of His Most Graphic Scenes Vol 4 / 1993 / BS / C • Business And Pleasure / 1992 / AFV / M • The Butler Did It / 1991 / FH / M • The Chains Of Torment / 1991 / BS / B • Cream Dream / 1991 / ZA / M • Deep Cheeks #2 / 1991 / ROB / M • Desert Fox / 1990 / VD / M • The Determinator #1 / 1991 / VIM / M • The Determinator #2 / 1991 / VIM / M • Don't Bother To Knock / 1991 / FAZ / M • Easy Pussy / 1991 / ROB / M • Eternity / 1991 / CDI / M • Evil Woman / 1990 / LE / M • The Exhibitionist / 1991 / VD / M • The Eye Of The Needle / 1991 / CIN / M • Forbidden Desires / 1991 / CIN / F • Fortysomething #2 / 1991 / LE / M • Girls Just Wanna Have Toys / 1993 / PL / F • Girls Will Be Boys #3 / 1991 / PL / F • The God Daughter #1 / 1991 / AFV / M • Good Vibrations #2: A Couples Guide To Vibrator Use / 1991 / VT / M • Heatseekers / 1991 / IN / M • Home But Not Alone / 1991 / WV / M • How To Love Your Lover / 1992 / XII / S • Inferno / 1991 / XCI / M • The Innocent And The Guilty / 1994 / PEP / C • An Innocent Woman / 1991 / FAZ / M • Jail Babes #2: Bustin' Out / 1992 / PL / F • Just For The Hell Of It / 1991 / CA / M • The Key to Love / 1992 / ZA / M • Killer Looks / 1991 / VI / M • Kiss And Tell / 1992 / AFV / M • Last Tango In Rio / 1991 / DR / M • Lather / 1991 / LE / M • Lethal Woman / 1991 / CIN / M • Lingerie Busters / 1991 / FH / M • A Little Christmas Tail / 1991 / ZA / M • Little Miss Curious / 1991 / CA / M • Lust For Love / 1991 / VC / M • The Midnight Hour / 1991 / VT / M • The New Kid On The Block / 1991 / VD / M • Night Rhythms / 1992 / IMP / S • No Time For Love / 1991 / VI / M • Nothing Serious / 1990 / EX / M • Nurse Nancy / 1991 / CA / M • One Million Years DD / 1992 / CC / M • Oriental Treatment #3: The Lost Empress / 1991 / AFV / M • Oriental Treatment #4: The Demon Lover / 1992 / AFV / M • Penthouse: Satin & Lace #1 / 1992 / PET / F • Positions Wanted / 1990 / VI / M • Prisoner Of Love / 1991 / ME / M • Private Dancer (Caballero) / 1992 / CA / M • Puppy Love / 1992 / AFV / M • Purple Haze / 1991 / WV / M • Queen Of Hearts #3: Heartless / 1992 / PL / M • Rebel / 1991 / ZA / M • Rockin' The Boat / 1990 / VI / M • Selena's Secrets / 1991 / MIN / M • Sex Liners / 1991 / CIN / M • Sex Sting / 1992 / FD / M • Shameless / 1991 / SC / M • Shattered / 1991 / LE / M • Silver Elegance / 1992 / VT / M • Sittin' Pretty #1 / 1990 / DR / M • Sizzle / 1990 / PP / M • Something New / 1991 / FH / M • Sophisticated Lady / 1991 / CIN / M • Sudden Urge / 1990 / IN / M • Sun Bunnies #1 / 1991 / SC / M • Sweet Licks / 1991 / MID / M • Switch Hitters #6: Back In The Bull Pen / 1991 / IN / G • Taboo #09 / 1991 / IN / M • Temptation Eyes / 1991 / VT / M • Torch #2 / 1990 / VI / M • Truth And Bare / 1991 / LV / M • Twin Cheeks #1 / 1990 / CIN / M •

Twin Cheeks #3 / 1991 / CIN / M • Twisted / 1990 / VI / M • Two Of A Kind / 1991 / ZA / M • A Vision In Heather / 1991 / VI / M • Wild & Wicked #1 / 1991 / VT / M • [Malibu Summer / 1991 / ... / S

ALICYN STORM *see* **Alicyn Sterling**
ALIDA LEIGH
[Kink, Hollywood Style / 197? / ... / M
ALIEA PEARS
Bend Over Babes #4 / 1996 / EA / M • Pick Up Lines #05 / 1996 / OD / M
ALIEN
The Desert Cafe / 1996 / NIT / M
ALINA *see* **Lana Sands**
ALINA KOVAIENCO *see* **Lana Sands**
ALINA KOVALENCO *see* **Lana Sands**
ALINA KOVELENCO *see* **Lana Sands**
ALIONA
Marquis De Sade / 1995 / IP / M
ALISA
Dorm Girls / 1992 / VC / M • Hot Close-Ups / 1984 / WV / M • Private Film #27 / 1995 / OD / M • Private Film #28 / 1995 / OD / M • Sleeping Booty / 1995 / EL / M • Sodomania #15: Warning! / 1996 / EL / M • Sodomania: Slop Shots / 1996 / EL / C
ALISA MONET *see* **Isabella Rovetti**
ALISA TROY *see* **Star Index I**
ALISE
Invitation Only / 1989 / AMB / M
ALISE MELL
Anal Magic / 1995 / XC / M • The Sex Clinic / 1995 / WIV / M
ALISHA (SADE) *see* **Sade**
ALISHA BRIGETTE
Hard Core Beginners #09 / 1995 / LEI / M • The New Butt Hunt #13 / 1995 / LEI / C
ALISHA JORDEAN *see* **Sharise**
ALISHA LASHLEY *see* **Sade**
ALISHA LITTLETON *see* **Star Index I**
ALISHA MONET *see* **Alicia Monet**
ALISON KAYE
Bondage Boot Camp / 1988 / TAN / B • The Bondage Club #5 / 1990 / LON / B
ALISON LEPRIOL *see* **Kascha**
ALISON PARISH
Belly Of The Beast / 1993 / ZFX / B • Dance Macabre / 1993 / ZFX / B • Dirty Deeds Done Cheap / 1993 / ZFX / B • Erotic Bondage Confessions / 1992 / ZFX / B • Futureshock / 1993 / ZFX / B • Guinea Pigs #2 / 1993 / ZFX / B • Highway To Hell / 1993 / ZFX / B • Meanstreak / 1993 / ZFX / B • Night Prowler #1 / 1993 / ZFX / B • Pretty Tied Up / 1993 / ZFX / B • Spread Eagle / 1992 / ZFX / B • Squealer / 1993 / ZFX / B • Tiffany Twisted / 1993 / ZFX / B • X-Tractor / 1993 / ZFX / B
ALISTAIR CHRISTINE *see* **Star Index I**
ALIZA
Private Film #20 / 1995 / OD / M • Private Film #21 / 1995 / OD / M • Private Film #23 / 1995 / OD / M • Triple X Video Magazine #03 / 1995 / OD / M
ALLA
Joe Elliot's College Girls #27 / 1994 / JOE / M
ALLAIN
Magma: Nymphettes / 1993 / MET / M • Magma: Trans-Games / 1995 / MET / G
ALLAN CERAY *see* **Alban Ceray**
ALLAN COMMIE *see* **Star Index I**
ALLAN EDWARDS *see* **Star Index I**
ALLAN FOX *see* **Star Index I**
ALLAN JACOBS
Prisoner Of Pleasure / 1981 / ALP / B

ALLAN NICKS
The Family Jewels / cr76 / GO / M
ALLAN NOVAK *see* **Star Index I**
ALLAN TODD *see* **Star Index I**
ALLANAH
Magma: Old And Young / 1995 / MET / M
ALLEN
Homegrown Video #314 / 1990 / HOV / M • HomeGrown Video #458: Cream Pie For Dessert / 1995 / HOV / C • HomeGrown Video #466: Loot The Booty / 1996 / HOV / M
ALLEN BASSENGER *see* **Alan Bosshart**
ALLEN GARFIELD *(Allen Goorwitz)*
Cry Uncle / 1971 / VCX / S • Night Visitor / 1989 / MGM / S • One From The Heart / 1982 / C3S / S • The Owl And The Pussycat / 1970 / GTE / S
ALLEN GOORWITZ *see* **Allen Garfield**
ALLEN GREGORY *see* **Star Index I**
ALLENA FERRARI *see* **Alena Ferrari**
ALLEY CAT *see* **Heidi Nelson**
ALLEY CAT ANDERSON
Anal Annie And The Backdoor Housewives / 1984 / LIP / F • The Best Of Anal Annie: The Girl-Girl Adventures / 1993 / LIP / C
ALLISON
Blue Vanities #572 / 1995 / FFL / M • Breast Of Britain #2 / 1987 / BTO / M • California Girl: Amateur Nude Auditions / 1995 / PME / S • Eric Kroll's Bondage #1 / 1994 / ERK / M • Eric Kroll's Fetish #1 / 1994 / ERK / M • Hot Body Video Magazine: Red Hot / 1995 / CG / S • Joe Elliot's College Girls #30 / 1994 / JOE / M • Pearl Necklace: Premier Sessions #04 / 1994 / SEE / M • Pussy Power #01 / 1991 / BTO / M
ALLISON BRACH *see* **Greta Carlson**
ALLISON CODY *see* **Star Index I**
ALLISON KAYE
The Bondage Club #4 / 1990 / LON / B
ALLISON LOUISE DOWNE *see* **Vicki Miles**
ALLISON PINK *see* **Star Index I**
ALLISON RAND
The Sexaholic / 1988 / VC / M
ALLISON ROYCE *see* **Star Index I**
ALLISON SPRINGS *see* **Alice Springs**
ALLISON STERLING *see* **Alicyn Sterling**
ALLISON WRIGHT *see* **Star Index I**
ALLISTER EVANS
Once...And For All / 1979 / HLV / M
ALLSTYNE VON BUSCH
Bad Penny / 1978 / QX / M • Pussycat Ranch / 1978 / CV / M
ALLYSON ANGEL *see* **Star Index I**
ALMA DOUCET
That Lady From Rio / 1976 / VXP / M
ALMA KATZ *see* **Star Index I**
ALMA MAIZE *see* **Star Index I**
ALMA POIA *see* **Star Index I**
ALONA
Fazano's Student Bodies / 1995 / EL / M
ALONA (ALANA) *see* **Alana**
ALONA KNIGHT *see* **Star Index I**
ALPHONSE *see* **Star Index I**
ALTA
Blue Vanities #508 / 1992 / FFL / M
ALVA HARRIS
Hard Action / 1975 / AXV / M
ALVIN
Home Movie Production #06 / 1990 / DR / M
ALYCE *see* **Star Index I**
ALYCE STERLING *see* **Alicyn Sterling**
ALYCIN SANBORN

Blue Vanities #514 / 1992 / FFL / M

ALYSSA
A&B GB#043: How To Pick Up Girls / 1992 / A&B / M • BCS: Tools Of The Trade / 1995 / BCS / F • Inner Pink #4 / 1995 / LIP / F • Pearl Necklace: Facial #01 / 1994 / SEE / C

ALYSSA ALLURE
Amazing Hardcore #1: Blow Jobs / 1997 / MET / M • Anal Booty Burner / 1996 / ROB / M • Anal Cornhole Cutie / 1996 / ROB / M • Anal Honeypie / 1996 / ROB / M • Anal Lickers And Cummers / 1996 / ROB / M • Ass, Gas & The Mystical GLOP / 1997 / EL / M • Barby's On Butt Row / 1996 / ABS / M • Brunette Roulette / 1996 / LE / M • The Crackster / 1996 / OUP / M • Deep Inside Dirty Debutantes #11 / 1996 / 4P / M • Eighteen #2 / 1996 / SC / M • Escape From Anal Lost Angels / 1996 / HO / M • Fuck Jasmin / 1997 / MET / M • Hardcore Debutantes #02 / 1996 / TEP / M • Puritan Video Magazine #05 / 1996 / LE / M • Pussyman Auditions #17 / 1995 / SNA / M • Real Sex Magazine #01 / 1996 / HO / M • Sodomania #18: Shame Based / 1996 / EL / M • Up And Cummers #29 / 1996 / ERW / M

ALYSSA HART
Pearl Necklace: Amorous Amateurs #40 / 1994 / SEE / M • Pearl Necklace: Premier Sessions #03 / 1994 / SEE / M • Pearl Necklace: Thee Bush League #30 / 1994 / SEE / M

ALYSSA JARREAU *(Alyssa Jeareau, Elyssa Jarrea, Susan Ferral)*
Brunette with small slightly droopy breasts, quite pretty face. Looks a bit like Mandi Wine without the rolls of flab; eyes are very small. Married to Tim Lake and was 5'4", 115 lbs, 27 yrs old in 1991 (**MDD #13**). Susan Ferral in **Raquel Released**.
America's Raunchiest Home Videos #06: Fuck Frenzy / 1992 / ZA / M • The Dirty Little Mind of Martin Fink / 1991 / ME / M • Elvis Slept Here / 1992 / LE / M • Frankie And Joanie / 1991 / HW / M • Hooray For Hineywood / 1991 / MID / M • Hot Summer Knights / 1991 / LV / M • Hunchback Of Notre Dame / 1991 / PL / M • More Dirty Debutantes #13 / 1992 / 4P / M • Naked Goddess #1 / 1991 / VC / M • Pearl Necklace: Amorous Amateurs #07 / 1992 / SEE / M • Pearl Necklace: Amorous Amateurs #08 / 1992 / SEE / M • The Pink Persuader / 1992 / LBO / M • Portrait Of Lust / 1992 / WV / M • Princess Orgasma #1 / 1991 / PP / M • Raquel Released / 1991 / VI / M • Sorority Sex Kittens #2 / 1993 / VC / M • Walking Small / 1992 / ZA / M • Welcome To Dallas / 1991 / VI / M

ALYSSA JEAREAU *see* Alyssa Jarreau

ALYSSA LOVE
Cumback Pussy #7: NUGIRLZ / 1997 / EL / M • More Dirty Debutantes #64 / 1997 / SBV / M

ALYSSA MALONE
Amateurs Exposed #06 / 1995 / CV / M • Bobby Hollander's Maneaters #08 / 1993 / SFP / M • Harry Horndog #11: Love Puppies #2 / 1992 / ZA / M • Lawnmower Woman / 1992 / MID / M • Mr. Peepers Amateur Home Videos #61: Four Play For Four / 1992 / LBO / M • Nasty Newcummers #06 / 1995 / MET / M • Odyssey Triple Play #53: Butt-Fuck Bash / 1993 /

OD / M

ALYSSA MILANO
Not a porno star.
Deadly Sins / 1994 / WAR / S • Embrace Of The Vampire / 1994 / NLH / S • Fear / 1996 / MCA / S • Poison Ivy #2 / 1995 / NLH / S

ALYSSA RIO *see* Alicia Rio

AMADEUS DEE *see* Star Index I

AMALIA COLIN
Private Gold #04: Amazonas / 1996 / OD / M • Private Stories #06 / 1995 / OD / M

AMALIN
Ancient Secrets Of Sexual Ecstasy / 1996 / HIG / M

AMANDA
Alley Cats / 1995 / VC / M • Amanda's Bondage Adventure / 1994 / GAL / B • Anal Camera #05 / 1995 / EVN / M • Back East Babes #2 / 1996 / NIT / M • Back East Babes #3 / 1996 / NIT / M • Blue Vanities #555 / 1994 / FFL / M • Collectors Series #01 / 1991 / TAO / B • Dirty Doc's Housecalls #03 / 1993 / LV / M • FTV #11: Tough Girl Boxing / 1996 / FT / B • Girls Games Of Summer #4 / 1994 / NIV / S • Hidden Camera #09 / 1993 / JMP / M • Intimate Interviews #3 / 1996 / NIT / M • Joe Elliot's College Girls #46 / 1996 / JOE / M • Keyholes / 1995 / OD / M • Kinky College Cunts #13 / 1993 / NS / F • Kinky College Cunts #14 / 1993 / NS / F • Kinky College Cunts #19 / 1993 / NS / F • Lewd In Liverpool / 1995 / VC / M • Luscious Lickin' Lesbians / 1995 / TIE / F • Mike Hott: #161 Amanda Solo / 1991 / MHV / F • Mike Hott: #162 Barbi And Amanda #1 / 1991 / MHV / F • Mike Hott: #163 Barbi And Amanda #2 / 1991 / MHV / F • Mike Hott: #275 Cunt of the Month: Amanda 1-95 / 1995 / MHV / M • Mondo Extreme / 1996 / SHS / M • Pearl Necklace: Amorous Amateurs #41 / 1994 / SEE / M • Pearl Necklace: Premier Sessions #03 / 1994 / SEE / M • Seymore & Shane Do Ireland / 1994 / ULI / M • Triple X Video Magazine #09 / 1995 / OD / M • Up And Cummers #06 / 1993 / 4P / M • Video Virgins #15 / 1994 / NS / M • The Watering Hole / 1994 / HO / M

AMANDA (S/M)
XXX Bondage Adventure / 1994 / TTV / M • Bad She-Males / 1994 / HSV / G • Corporate Bi Out / 1994 / BIL / G • Freaky Flix / 1995 / TTV / C • Sex Starved She-Males / 1995 / MET / G • She-Male Loves Me / 1995 / VC / G • She-Male Seduction / 1995 / MET / G • Sizzling She Males / 1995 / MET / G • Spring Trannie / 1995 / VC / G • Trannie Love / 1995 / HSV / G • Transexual Blvd / 1994 / PL / G • Transister Act / 1994 / HSV / G

AMANDA ADAMS *see* Amanda Stone

AMANDA ADDAMS *see* Amanda Stone

AMANDA BLAKE
Betrayal / 1974 / JFF / S • Blue's Velvet / 1979 / ECV / M • Getting Off / 1979 / VIP / M • Teenage Cowgirls / 1973 / ALP / M

AMANDA CHASE PARKER
Bound To Tease #4 / 1989 / BON / C

AMANDA GIER
Dildo Bitches / 1995 / LAF / F

AMANDA HUNTER
Seymore & Shane Meet Kathy Willets, The Naughty Nymph / 1994 / ULI / M

AMANDA HUNTER (HOL) *see* Jim Holliday

AMANDA HURT
Twilight / 1996 / ESN / M

AMANDA JAMES *see* Amanda Jane Adams

AMANDA JANE *see* Amanda Jane Adams

AMANDA JANE ADAMS *(Amanda Jane, Amanda James)*
Pretty blonde with small/medium tits.
Age Of Consent / 1985 / AVC / M • Genie's Dirty Girls / 1987 / VCX / M • Indecent Wives / 1985 / HO / M • Let's Get It On With Amber Lynn / 1986 / VC / M • Midnight Pink / 1987 / WV / M • The Pleasure Seekers / 1985 / AT / M • Video Paradise / 1988 / ZA / M

AMANDA LAVER *see* Star Index I

AMANDA LOVE
Perfect Endings / 1994 / PLV / B • Tip Tap Toe / 1995 / PRE / C • Toe Nuts / 1994 / PRE / B

AMANDA MARIE
Finger Pleasures #1 / 1995 / PL / F • Housemother's Discipline #6 / 1994 / RB / B • Shaved #07 / 1995 / RB / F

AMANDA MORRISON
The Adventures Of Bebe / 1995 / SHL / B • Amanda's Punishment / 1994 / BON / B • Bi Stander / 1995 / BIN / G • Bip Shoots #2 / 1994 / BON / B • Body And Soul / 1995 / BON / B • Bound By Design / 1995 / BON / B • The Continuing Adventures Of Bebe / 1995 / SHL / B • Cum On Inn / 1995 / TEG / M • Delivered For Discipline / 1995 / BON / B • Final Orgy / 1996 / BON / B • A Girl's Affair #06 / 1995 / FD / F • Hard Discipline #2: The Lady's Maid / 1993 / SHL / B • Heels & Toes #2 / 1994 / BON / F • The Initiate / 1995 / BON / B • Jasmine's Girls / 1995 / LON / B • Just Eat Me, Damn It! / 1995 / BVW / F • Kiss Of The Whip / 1996 / BON / B • Knot Of Eroticism / 1995 / VTF / B • Kym Wilde's On The Edge #17 / 1995 / RB / B • Kym Wilde's On The Edge #19 / 1995 / RB / B • Labyrinth Of The Lash / 1996 / BON / B • Little Girl Lost / 1995 / SC / M • Mike Hott: #337 Chanell Pregnant / 1996 / MHV / F • Mis-Fortune / 1995 / VTF / B • No Mercy / 1996 / VTF / B • Phantom Pain / 1995 / BON / B • Picture Me Bound / 1995 / LON / B • Ready To Drop #12 / 1996 / FC / M • S&M Lockout / 1996 / VTF / B • S&M Sessions / 1996 / VTF / B • Spank & Spank Again / 1995 / BON / B • Stand By Your Man / 1994 / CV / M • Torture Clinic / 1995 / LON / B • Tricked & Tied / 1996 / VTF / B • The Violation Of Kia / 1995 / JMP / F

AMANDA RAE
Blonde with crinkly hair, small tits, reasonably pretty face, belly button jewelery, tight body, nice smile.
Anal Justice / 1994 / ROB / M • Ass Openers! #2 / 1995 / TCK / C • Assy Sassy #2 / 1994 / ROB / F • Butt Sluts #3 / 1994 / ROB / F • The Darker Side / 1994 / HO / M • Dream Strokes / 1994 / WIV / M • Gang Bang Wild Style #2 / 1994 / ROB / M • Hot Tight Asses #07 / 1994 / TCK / M • Legend #5: The Legend Continues / 1994 / LE / M • Love Thrust / 1995 / ERA / M • Love Tryst / 1995 / VPN / M • Mr. Peepers Amateur Home Videos #87: Groupie Therapy / 1994 / LBO / M • Party Pack #2 / 1994 / LE / F • Performer Of The Year / 1994 / WP / M • Pussyclips #01 / 1994 / SNA / M • Rain-

woman #07: In The Rainforest / 1993 / CC / M • Rainwoman #08 / 1994 / CC / M • The Reel Sex World #04: Laid In Hawaii / 1994 / WP / M • Reel Sex World #05 / 1994 / WP / M • Silky Thighs / 1994 / ERA / M • Witness For The Penetration / 1994 / PEP / M

AMANDA RAE (MINDY) *see* Mindy Rae
AMANDA READY
Motel Sex #2 / 1995 / FAP / M
AMANDA SHEAR
Blue Cabaret / 1989 / VTO / M • Dancing Angels / 1989 / PL / M • [Berlin Caper / 1989 / ... / M
AMANDA SHELL *see* Star Index I
AMANDA STONE *(Camile, Camille (A. Stone), Amanda Adams, Amanda Addams, Emily Moore)*
Camile (**Torch #2**). Emily Moore in **Taste of Ecstasy**. After an absence of three to four years returned in late 1994 with a boob job (large, rock solid) and perhaps some work on her nose under the name Amanda Addams or some misspelling thereof.
After Midnight / 1994 / IN / M • Anal Addicts / 1994 / KWP / M • Anal Freaks / 1994 / KWP / M • Anal Maniacs #2 / 1994 / WP / M • Big Knockers #08 / 1994 / TV / M • Big Knockers #10 / 1995 / TV / M • Big Knockers #14 / 1995 / TV / M • Big Knockers #20 / 1995 / TV / C • Big Knockers #21: Best Of Lesbian #2 / 1995 / TV / C • Big Thingiees / 1996 / BEP / M • Butt Sluts #4 / 1995 / ROB / F • Butthead Dreams: Big Boating Bonanza / 1994 / FH / M • Chasin' The Fifties / 1994 / WP / M • The Devil In Miss Jones #5: The Inferno / 1994 / VC / M • Dirty Bob's #16: Hoosier Hooters! / 1994 / FLP / S • Double D Amateurs #21 / 1994 / JMP / M • Dreams / 1995 / VC / M • Erotic Appetites / 1995 / IN / M • Evil Temptations #2 / 1995 / ULP / M • First Time Lesbians #22 / 1994 / JMP / F • The Girl Next Door #1 / 1994 / VT / M • Girls Of The Ivy Leagues / 1994 / VT / M • Intersextion / 1994 / HO / M • King Tung Is The Egyptian Lover / 1990 / LA / M • Life's A Beach, Then You're Fucked / 1995 / FRM / M • Lingerie / 1995 / SC / M • Lonely Hearts / 1995 / VC / M • The Mile High Club / 1995 / PL / M • The Model / 1991 / HO / M • Naughty By Night / 1995 / DR / M • New Wave Hookers #2 / 1991 / VC / M • New Wave Hookers #4 / 1994 / VC / M • No Tell Motel / 1995 / CV / M • Ona Zee's Black Label #1: Sex Hunger / 1996 / ONA / C • Ona Zee's Doll House #3 / 1995 / ONA / F • The Other Side / 1995 / ERA / M • Patriot X / 1995 / LE / M • A Rising Star / 1991 / HO / M • Sapphire / 1995 / ERA / M • Scream In The Middle Of The Night / 1990 / CC / M • Sex Academy #3: The Art Of Real Sex / 1994 / ONA / M • Sex Liners / 1991 / CIN / M • Shock / 1995 / LE / M • Silent Women / 1995 / ERA / M • Sin Asylum / 1995 / CV / M • Sizzle / 1990 / PP / M • Solo Adventures / 1996 / AB / F • Stretchin' The Rear / 1995 / PE / M • Strip Search / 1995 / CV / M • Student Fetish Videos: Best of Catfighting #03 / 1995 / PRE / C • Student Fetish Videos: Catfighting #14 / 1994 / PRE / B • Student Fetish Videos: The Enema #19 / 1995 / PRE / B • Student Fetish Videos: Foot Worship #15 / 1995 / PRE / B • Supertung / 1990 / LA / M • Tactical Sex Force / 1994 / IN / M • A

Taste Of Ecstasy / 1991 / CIN / M • Taxi Girls #3: Killer On The Loose / 1993 / MED / M • Temptation Of Serenity / 1994 / WP / M • The Thief / 1994 / SC / M • Torch #2 / 1990 / VI / M • Visions #1 / 1995 / ERA / M • Wet In The Saddle / 1994 / ME / M
AMANDA TAYLOR *see* Amanda Tyler
AMANDA TYLER *(Valentina (A. Tyler), Havana, Amanda Taylor)*
976-STUD / 1989 / LV / M • Backdoor Black #1 / 1992 / WV / C • Backing In #3 / 1991 / WV / C • The Big Rock / 1988 / FOV / M • Blacks & Blondes #58 / 1989 / WV / M • Born To Burn / 1987 / HOT / M • Broadcast Nudes / 1988 / EVN / M • Caught From Behind #08 / 1988 / HO / M • Dana Lynn's Hot All Over / 1987 / V99 / M • The Days Of Our Wives / 1988 / GO / M • Deep Throat #3 / 1989 / AR / M • Every Man's Fancy / 1988 / SEX / M • Every Man's Fancy / 1991 / V99 / M • Fondle With Care / 1989 / VEX / M • Fun In The Sun / 1988 / EVN / C • The Girls Of Cooze / 1992 / V99 / C • The Godmother #2 / 1988 / VC / M • Hard Road To Victory / 1989 / WV / C • Her Every Wish / 1988 / GO / M • Hospitality Sweet / 1988 / WV / M • Hot To Swap / 1988 / VEX / M • Introducing Kascha / 1988 / CDI / M • Lesbian Lingerie Fantasy #1 / 1988 / ESP / F • Lesbian Lovers / 1988 / GO / F • Lesbian Nymphos / 1988 / GO / C • Love In Reverse / 1988 / FAZ / M • No Way In / 1988 / EVN / M • Passion Princess / 1991 / VEX / M • Sex Lies / 1988 / FAN / M • Sex Sluts In The Slammer / 1988 / FAN / M • She's No Angel #1 / 1990 / V99 / M • Sophisticated Lady / 1988 / SEX / M • The Squirt / 1988 / AR / M • Steam Heat / 1989 / VEX / M • Tails Of The Town / 1988 / WV / M • Three Men And A Lady / 1988 / EVN / M • Under The Law / 1989 / AFV / M • The Wacky World Of X-Rated Bloopers / 1989 / GO / M • The Way They Were / 1990 / CDI / M • Young And Innocent / 1987 / HO / M
AMANDA VICTORIA
Amanda Victoria's Sultry Sessions #1 / 1995 / GLI / F • Amanda Victoria's Sultry Sessions #2 / 1995 / GLI / F • Amanda Victoria's Sultry Sessions #3 / 1995 / GLI / M • Kym Wilde's On The Edge #36 / 1996 / RB / B • Porno Bizarro / 1995 / GLI / M • Swap Meat / 1995 / GLI / M • A Tall Tail / 1996 / FC / M • Wild Cherries / 1996 / SC / F
AMAYO SMITH
Ancient Amateurs #1 / 1996 / LOF / M
AMBAR
Private Gold #04: Amazonas / 1996 / OD / M • Private Stories #08 / 1996 / OD / M • Triple X Video Magazine #10 / 1995 / OD / M
AMBER
A&B GB#010: Double Creamer / 1992 / A&B / M • A&B GB#066: Debbie And Amber / 1992 / A&B / M • America's Raunchiest Home Videos #53: / 1993 / ZA / M • Black Cheerleader Search #04 / 1996 / ROB / M • Blue Vanities #571 / 1995 / FFL / M • Feels Like Silk / 1983 / SE / M • Hardcore Schoolgirls #5: Virgin Killers / 1996 / XPR / M • Ho Duzzit Model Agency #2 / 1993 / AFV / M • Hot Body Competition: Lusty Lingerie Contest / 1996 / CG / F • Meltin' The Burgh / 1996 / DGD / F • Nothing Butt Amateurs #01 / 1993 / AFI / M • Reel Life Video #32: / 1995 / RLF / M •

Reel Life Video: Britt & Iron John / 1995 / RLF / F • She Studs #05 / 1990 / BIZ / G • She-Male Friends #2 / cr94 / TTV / G • Star Struck / 1992 / VEX / M • Street Fantasies / 1993 / AFV / M • Student Fetish Videos: The Enema #13 / 1994 / PRE / B • Student Fetish Videos: Spanking #12 / 1994 / PRE / B • Student Fetish Videos: Tickling #08 / 1994 / SFV / B • Trisexual Encounters #11 / 1990 / PL / G • Under The Skirt #1 / 1995 / KAE / F • Virgins Of Video #06 / 1993 / YDI / M • Virgins Of Video #09 / 1993 / YDI / M
AMBER AUTO *see* Star Index I
AMBER CALLAHAN *see* Star Index I
AMBER DEE
[Mountain Orgy / 197? / ... / M
AMBER HUNT
Blonde with masses of curly long hair, prominent overbite, marginal face, lithe body, medium tits, large clit. Seems to have a pleasant personality.
Auto-Erotic Practices / 1980 / VCR / F • Baby Face #1 / 1977 / VC / M • Blue Vanities #030 / 1988 / FFL / M • Blue Vanities #059 / 1988 / FFL / M • Candy Stripers #1 / 1978 / ALP / M • A Coming Of Angels / 1977 / CA / M • Cry For Cindy / 1976 / AR / M • Fiona On Fire / 1978 / VC / M • Lipps & Mccain / 1978 / VC / M • Long Jeanne Silver / 1977 / VC / M • Once Upon A Time/Cave Woman / 1978 / VI / M • Sex World / 1978 / SE / M • Superstar John Holmes / 1979 / AVC / M • Triple Header / 1986 / SE / C • True Legends Of Adult Cinema: Unsung Superstars / 1993 / VC / C • Yuppies In Heat / 1988 / CHA / C • [Bare Knuckles / 1980 / ... / M
AMBER JADE *see* Star Index I
AMBER JOHNSON *see* Star Index I
AMBER KELLY
Anal Virgins Of America #04 / 1993 / FOR / M • Casting Call (Venus 99) / 1993 / V99 / M
AMBER LEE
Hard Sell / 1990 / VC / M • Mysterious Jane / 1981 / LUN / S
AMBER LOVELAND
Eight Babes A Week / 1996 / DGD / F • Red Rumpers #01 / 1996 / LBO / B
AMBER LYNN *(Amber Lynn Adams)*
Passable face, lithe body, blonde. Sister of Buck Adams but fortunately doesn't look like him. First movies had her with natural tits and then they were enhanced to a larger although still reasonable size. Was 21 in 1986 and comes from Southern California. By her return in 1995 the tits seem to have grown even more to large rock solid cantaloupes and her body has started to deteriorate. Note that according to her she has never done anal on screen—the apparent ones you see are not her.
The $50,000,000 Cherry / 1987 / VD / M • 52 Pick-Up / 1986 / MED / S • Adult 45 #01 / 1985 / DR / C • All For His Ladies / 1987 / PP / C • Amazing Sex Stories #2 / 1987 / SUV / C • Amber & Sharon Do Paris #1 / 1985 / PAA / M • Amber & Sharon Do Paris #2 / 1985 / PAA / M • Amber Aroused / 1985 / CA / M • Amber Lynn's Hotline 976 / 1987 / VCR / M • Amber Lynn's Personal Best / 1986 / VD / M • Amber Lynn's Peter Meter / 1988 / 3HV / C • Amber Lynn: She's Back / 1995 / TTV / C • Amber Lynn: The Ultimate Experience / 1990 / VIP / F •

Amber Pays The Rent / 1986 / VT / M • Amber Waves / 1992 / VT / C • Amber's Desires / 1985 / CA / M • Amberella / 1986 / GO / M • The Angel In Mr. Holmes / 1988 / WV / C • Babe Watch #3 / 1995 / SC / M • Babe Watch #4 / 1995 / SC / M • Ball Street / 1988 / CA / M • Battle Of The Titans / 1986 / AVC / M • The Best Little Whorehouse In San Francisco / 1984 / LA / M • Best Of Talk Dirty To Me #02 / 1991 / DR / C • Beverly Hills Wives / 1985 / CV / M • Bi-Sexual Fantasies / 1984 / LAV / G • The Black Anal-ist #1 / 1988 / VEX / M • Black Girls Do It Better / 1986 / CV / M • Blonde Desire / 1984 / AIR / M • Blondes! Blondes! Blondes! / 1986 / VCS / C • Blowing The Whistle / 1986 / VIP / M • Bodies By Jackie / 1985 / IVP / M • Body Shop / 1984 / VCX / M • Boobs, Butts And Bloopers #1 / 1990 / HO / M • Bootsie / 1984 / CC / M • Bordello...House Of The Rising Sun / 1985 / SE / M • Both Ends Burning / 1987 / VC / M • Can't Get Enough / 1985 / CA / M • Celebrity Presents Celebrity / 1986 / VEP / C • Centerfold Celebrities #4 / 1983 / VC / M • Centerfold Celebrities #5 / 1983 / VC / M • Charmed And Dangerous / 1987 / VI / M • Chastity And The Starlets / 1986 / RAV / M • Cheek To Cheek / 1986 / VEX / M • Circus Acts / 1987 / SE / C • Cock Robin / 1989 / SUE / M • Cocktales / 1985 / AT / M • Color Me Amber / 1985 / VC / M • Commando Lovers / 1986 / SUV / M • Corporate Assets / 1985 / SE / M • Cottontail Club / 1985 / HO / M • Crocodile Blondee #1 / 1987 / CA0 / M • Cum Shot Revue #3 / 1988 / HO / C • Dangerous When Wet (Amber Lynn Is) / 1987 / VCX / M • Dangerous Women / 1987 / WET / M • Dear Fanny / 1984 / CV / M • Desire / 1990 / VC / M • Devil In Miss Jones #3: A New Beginning / 1986 / VC / M • The Devil In Mr Holmes / 1988 / PV / M • Dickman & Throbbin / 1985 / WV / M • Dirty 30's Cinema: Amber Lynn / 1986 / PV / C • Dirty Dreams / 1987 / CA / M • The Doorman Always Comes Twice / cr84 / AIR / C • Double Penetration #2 / 1986 / WV / C • Double Penetration #3 / 1986 / WV / C • Dream Girls / 1986 / VC / M • Ebony & Ivory Fantasies / 1988 / VD / U • Ebony Orgies / 1987 / SE / C • End Of Innocence / 1986 / AR / M • The End Zone / 1987 / LA / C • Endless Passion / 1987 / LIM / C • Erotic City / 1985 / CV / M • Erotic Dreams / 1987 / HO / M • Erotic Gold / 82 / 1985 / VEN / M • Evils Of The Night / 1985 / LIV / S • Female Aggressors / 1986 / LAV / M • The Filthy Rich / 1989 / LA / M • First Annual XRCO Awards / 1984 / AVC / C • Four X Feeling / 1986 / QX / M • Friday The 13th #1: A Nude Beginning / 1987 / VD / M • From Paris With Lust / 1985 / PEN / M • Future Sex / 1984 / NSV / M • Getting LA'd / 1986 / PV / M • Ginger On The Rocks / 1985 / VI / M • Ginger's Greatest Girl/Girl Hits / 1986 / VI / C • Girl Toys / 1986 / DR / M • The Girl With The Hungry Eyes / 1984 / ECS / M • Girls Of The Night / 1985 / CA / M • The Girls On F Street / 1986 / AVC / M • Girls On Girls / 1987 / SE / C • Going Down With Amber / 1987 / 4P / M • The Good, The Bad, And The Horny / 1985 / VCX / M • The Grafenberg Spot / 1985 / MIT / M • Harlem Candy / 1987 / WET / M • Headgames / 1985 / WV / M • Holly Does Hollywood #1 / 1985 / VEX / M • Hollywood Harlots / 1986 / VEX / C • Hollywood Heartbreakers / 1985 / VEX / M • Honeybuns #2: Grecian Formula / 1987 / WV / C • Honeymoon Harlots / 1986 / AVC / M • Hot Amber Nights / 1987 / CC / M • Hot Holes / 1992 / IF / C • Hot Tails / 1984 / VEN / M • Hot Wire / 1985 / VXP / M • Hottest Ticket / 1987 / WV / C • Hyapatia Lee's Arcade Series #02 / 1988 / ZA / C • I Love A Girl In A Uniform / 1989 / VC / C • I Love LA #1 / 1986 / PEN / C • I Love LA #2 / 1989 / PEN / C • If My Mother Only Knew / 1985 / CA / M • In And Out (In Beverly Hills) / 1986 / WV / M • Inches For Keisha / 1988 / WV / C • The Initiation Of Cynthia / 1985 / VXP / M • Jane Bond Meets Octopussy / 1986 / VD / M • Jane Bond Meets The Man With The Golden Rod / 1987 / VD / M • Just The Two Of Us / 1985 / WV / M • Kinky Sluts / 1988 / MIR / C • Le Sex De Femme #4 / 1989 / AFI / C • Legends Of Porn #2 / 1989 / CV / C • Les Lesbos Of Paris #1 / 1985 / LIP / F • Les Lesbos Of Paris #2 / 1985 / LIP / F • Let's Get It On With Amber Lynn / 1986 / VC / M • Lifestyles Of The Blonde And Dirty / 1987 / WET / M • Lip Service / 1987 / BIK / C • Liquid Love / 1988 / CA / M • Living Doll / 1987 / WV / M • Lonely Lady / 1984 / VC / M • Looking For Mr Goodsex / 1984 / CC / M • The Lost Angel / 1989 / KIS / C • Love At First Sight / 1987 / SE / C • Love Bites / 1985 / CA / M • Love Button / 1985 / AVC / M • Love Probe / 1986 / VT / M • Love Scenes For Loving Couples / 1987 / CV / C • Loving Spoonfulls / 1987 / 4P / C • Luscious Lucy In Love / 1986 / AVC / M • Lusty Adventurer / 1985 / GO / M • Mammary Lane / 1988 / VT / C • The Many Shades Of Amber / 1986 / LIM / M • Marina Heat / 1985 / CV / M • Me, Myself & I / 1987 / SE / C • Miami Spice #1 / 1987 / CA / M • Miami Spice #2 / 1988 / CA / M • Mrs. Rodger's Neighborhood / 1988 / EVN / C • Nightclub / 1996 / SC / M • Nina's Knockouts / 1987 / AVC / C • No Man's Land #01 / 1988 / VT / C • Only The Best Of Anal / 1992 / MET / C • Only The Best Of Girls With Curves / 1992 / CV / C • Only The Best Of Men's And Women's Fantasies / 1988 / CV / C • Only The Best Of Oral / 1989 / CV / C • Only The Best Of The Erotic Eighties / 1992 / VC / C • Only The Best Of Women With Women / 1988 / CV / C • Oral Majority #02 / 1987 / WV / C • Oral Majority #03 / 1986 / WV / C • Oral Majority #04 / 1987 / WV / C • Oral Majority #06 / 1988 / WV / C • Orgies / 1987 / WV / C • Parliament: Bare Assets / 1988 / PM / F • Parliament: Eating Pussy #1 / 1989 / PM / C • Parliament: Finger Friggin' #1 / 1988 / PM / F • Parliament: Fuckin' Superstars #1 / 1990 / PM / C • Parliament: Lesbian Lovers #1 / 1986 / PM / F • Parliament: Woman's Touch / 1988 / PM / F • Passionate Heiress / 1987 / CA / M • Passionate Lee / 1984 / CRE / M • Perfect Partners / 1986 / CV / M • Personal Touch #3 / 1983 / AR / M • Phone Sex Girls #1 / 1987 / VT / M • Pink And Pretty / 1986 / CA / M • Please Don't Stop / 1986 / CV / M • The Pleasure Maze / 1986 / PL / M • The Poonies / 1985 / VI / M • Porn In The USA #1 / 1986 / WV / C • Porn In The USA #2 / 1987 / VEN / M • Provocative Pleasures / 1988 / VC / C • The Rise Of The Roman Empress #1 / 1986 / PV / M • Rocky-X #2 / 1988 / PEN / M • Rubdown / 1985 / VCX / M • Screen Play / 1984 / XTR / M • Screw / 1985 / CV / M • Sex Asylum #2 / 1986 / VI / M • Sex Life Of A Porn Star / 1986 / ELH / M • Sexual Odyssey / 1985 / VC / M • Shacking Up / 1985 / VXP / M • Shauna: Every Man's Fantasy / 1985 / CA / C • She Comes In Colors / 1987 / AMB / M • She's A Boy Toy / 1985 / DR / M • Sheer Bedlam / 1986 / VI / M • Slip Into Ginger & Amber / 1986 / MAP / C • Some Kind Of Woman / 1985 / CA / M • Space Virgins / 1984 / CRE / M • Splashing / 1986 / VCS / C • Starlets / 1985 / 4P / M • Street Heat / 1984 / VC / M • Sweat #1 / 1986 / PP / M • Sweat #2 / 1988 / PP / M • Swedish Erotica #57 / 1984 / CA / M • Swedish Erotica #66 / 1985 / CA / M • Swedish Erotica Hard #17: Amber & Christy's Sex Party / 1992 / OD / C • Sweet Cream / 1991 / VC / C • The Sweetest Taboo / 1986 / SE / M • Taboo #05 / 1986 / IN / M • Talk Dirty To Me #03 / 1986 / DR / M • A Taste Of Amber / 1988 / PIN / C • A Taste Of Black / 1987 / WET / M • A Taste Of Pink / 1985 / VXP / M • A Taste Of Tiffanie / 1990 / PIN / C • A Taste Of White / 1987 / WET / M • Teasers: Heavenly Bodies / 1988 / MET / M • Teasers: Hot Pursuit / 1988 / MET / M • Ten Little Maidens / 1985 / EXF / M • Things / 1990 / 3WO / S • Those Lynn Girls / 1989 / WV / C • To Lust In LA / 1986 / LA / M • Toys 4 Us #1 / 1987 / WV / C • Toys 4 Us #2 / 1987 / WV / C • Traci Who? / 1987 / AVC / C • Tracy Takes Paris / 1987 / VIP / M • Trashy Lady / 1985 / MAP / M • Tres Riche / 1986 / CLV / M • A Tribute To The King / 1985 / VCX / C • True Legends Of Adult Cinema: The Erotic Eighties / 1992 / VC / C • Tuff Stuff / 1987 / WET / M • The Ultimate Lover / 1986 / VD / M • Unleashed Lust / 1989 / VC / C • VCA Previews #4 / 1988 / VC / C • Video Voyeur #1 / 1988 / VT / C • Vixens In Heat / 1984 / ECS / M • The Wacky World Of X-Rated Bloopers / 1989 / GO / M • Wet Workout / 1987 / VEX / M • Where The Boys Aren't #6 / 1995 / VI / F • Wild Things #2 / 1986 / CV / M • The Wild Wild West / 1986 / SE / M • Women Without Men #1 / 1985 / VXM / F • The World According To Ginger / 1985 / VI / M • WPINK-TV #2 / 1986 / PV / M • X-Rated Bloopers #1 / 1984 / AR / M • Yellow Fever / 1984 / PL / M • [Centerfolds & Covergirls #1 / 19?? / ... / M • [Supermaschio Per Mogli Viziose / 19?? / ... / M

AMBER LYNN ADAMS *see* Amber Lynn

AMBER MIDNIGHT *see* Sukoya

AMBER NEKTOR
Naughty Schoolgirls Revenge / 1994 / BIZ / B

AMBER NIGHTENGALE *see Star Index I*

AMBER PHILLIPS *see Star Index I*

AMBER REY
Student Fetish Videos: Best of Enema #03 / 1994 / PRE / C • Student Fetish Videos: Catfighting #08 / 1993 / PRE / B • Student Fetish Videos: Spanking #11 / 1993 / PRE / B

AMBER ROE *see Star Index I*

AMBER ROSE
GVC: The Therapist #101 / 1986 / GO / M • Hot Cherries / 1990 / CC / F

AMBER ROSE KNIGHT

FTV #36: Power Boxing / 1996 / FT / B •
FTV #37: Power Wrestling / 1996 / FT / B •
FTV #38: Wrestling Tough / 1996 / FT / B

AMBER SAVAGE *see* **Sukoya**

AMBER SCOTT
Schoolgirl Fannies On Fire / 1994 / BIZ / B

AMBER SMITH
Bel Air Babes / 1996 / SUF / M • Black
Dirty Debutantes / 1993 / 4P / M • Joe El-
liot's College Girls #37 / 1994 / JOE / M •
Lovin' Spoonfuls #4 / 1995 / 4P / C • More
Dirty Debutantes #31 / 1994 / 4P / M

AMBER SMYTHE
Dreams Are Forever / cr72 / AVC / M • Oh
Doctor / cr72 / ADU / M

AMBER SUNN
Winner Takes All / 1995 / LON / B

AMBER WOODS *see* **Sharise**

AMBRE
Perversity In Paris / 1994 / AVI / M

AMBROSIA
The Best Of Fabulous Flashers / 1996 /
DGD / F • The Bride's Initiation / 1976 /
VIP / M • The Horny Housewife / 1996 /
HO / M

AMBROSIA FOX *(Laurie Ambrosia, Lori
Ambrosia)*
Blonde with shoulder length unwashed hair,
not too good skin, small tits, lithe (perhaps
skinny) body, marginal face.
Dr Bizarro / 1978 / ALP / B • Forgive Me, I
Have Sinned / 1982 / ALP / B • Island Love
/ 1983 / SHO / M • Kneel Before Me! /
1983 / ALP / B • Oriental Techniques Of
Pain And Pleasure / 1983 / ALP / B •
School Daze / 1983 / … / M • Sex Stalker /
1983 / MPP / M • The Story Of Prunella /
1982 / AVO / M • Tales Of The Bizarre /
1983 / ALP / B • The Taming Of Rebecca /
1982 / SVE / B • Twilight Pink #2 / 1982 /
VC / M

AMBROSIA LE STAT
Boot Camp / 1996 / PRE / B • Road Kill /
1995 / CA / M • Venom #1 / 1995 / VD / M

AMEIKO *see* **Star Index I**

AMELIA
Dick & Jane Go To Mexico / 1994 / AVI / M
• Hollywood Amateurs #06 / 1994 / MID /
M

AMELIA BIBB *see* **Star Index I**

AMELIA CANON
Bobby Hollander's Maneaters #02 / 1993 /
SFP / M • More Dirty Debutantes #20 /
1993 / 4P / M • Mr. Peepers Amateur
Home Videos #65: Suckaterial Skills /
1993 / LBO / M • Uncle Roy's Amateur
Home Video #09 / 1992 / VIM / M

AMELIA SPRINGFIELDS
Tycoon's Daughter / cr73 / SVE / M

AMELISE *see* **Star Index I**

AMER
College Video Virgins #04 / 1996 / AOC /
M

AMEY MOUR *see* **Star Index I**

AMI
Asian Connection Video #103 / 1996 / AC0
/ B

AMI RODGERS *see* **Amy Rogers**

AMI ROGERS *see* **Amy Rogers**

AMI WHITE
Parting Shots / 1990 / VD / M

AMICA
Sirens / 1995 / GOU / M

AML NITRATE
The Love Witch / 1973 / AR / M

AMNESIA

Black Cheerleader Jungle Jerk-Off / 1996 /
WIC / F • Black Cheerleader Search #01 /
1996 / ROB / M • Black Cheerleader
Search #03 / 1996 / ROB / M

AMORE PERTUTI
Personal Services / 1975 / CV / M

AMY
A&B AB#123: Sexy Blondes / 1990 / A&B /
F • Alex Jordan's First Timers #06 / 1994 /
OD / M • Blue Vanities #569 / 1996 / FFL /
M • British Cunts Are Cumming! / 1996 /
SPL / M • Eye On You: Amy / 1996 / EOY /
F • HomeGrown Video #465: Bong The
Schlong / 1996 / HOV / M • Joe Elliot's
College Girls #45 / 1996 / JOE / M • Micro
X Video #3 / 1992 / YDI / M • Mr. Peepers
Amateur Home Videos #31: Ginger
Thomas / 1991 / LBO / M • Neighbor Girls
T59 / 1992 / NEI / F • Reel Life Video #02:
Becky, Julie & Amy / 1994 / RLF / M •
Stevi's: Amy's Dreamy Threesome / 1996 /
SSV / M • Stevi's: Amy's First Time Bi /
1994 / SSV / F • Stevi's: Amy's Wet Solo /
1994 / SSV / F • Stevi's: Your Turn / 1994 /
SSV / B • Tight Security / 1995 / BON / B •
Wrestling Vixens / 1991 / CDP / B

AMY (KEANNA) *see* **Keanna**

AMY (POLISH) *see* **Tiffany (Polish)**

AMY (S/M)
TV's And The Houseboy / 1993 / GOT / G •
TV's Dilemma / 1993 / GOT / G

AMY ALLISON *(Amy Grant)*
Tall, long curly dark brown hair, small tits, lithe
body, passable face. Amy Grant is from
Lingerie.
Corrupt Desires / 1984 / MET / M • Lingerie / 1983 / CDI / M • Stud Hunters /
1984 / CA / M

AMY BERENS *see* **Tawny Downs**

AMY COPELAND *see* **Star Index I**

AMY FRIEDMAN
Pleasure Productions #01 / 1984 / VCR /
M

AMY GRANT *see* **Amy Allison**

AMY HUNTER *see* **Star Index I**

AMY KOOIMAN *see* **Zara Whites**

AMY LAWSON
Girls On Girls / 1983 / VC / F

AMY LYNN
Pussy Hunt #08 / 1995 / LEI / M

AMY MATHIEU *see* **Star Index I**

AMY MICHELLE *see* **Star Index I**

AMY RAPP *see* **Star Index I**

AMY RIVERS *see* **Amy Rogers**

AMY ROBERTS *see* **Star Index I**

AMY ROGERS *(Ami Rodgers, Ami
Rogers, Amy Rivers)*
Not too pretty, curly dark blonde hair, large
droopy tits, too tall and a bit womanly,
mole on right shoulder top.
Blonde Desire / 1984 / AIR / M • Breastog-
raphy, Lesson #1 / 1987 / VCR / M • Com-
ing Holmes / 1985 / VD / M • Desperately
Seeking Suzie / 1985 / VD / M • Dirty Pic-
tures / 1985 / SUP / M • Foot Show / 1989
/ BIZ / B • The Girls Of The A Team #1 /
1985 / WV / M • Head & Tails / 1988 / VD /
M • Hot Merchandise / 1985 / AVC / M •
Jubilee Of Eroticism / 1985 / GO / M • Kiss
Of The Gypsy / 1986 / WV / M • Lust In
Space / 1985 / PV / M • Marilyn Chambers'
Private Fantasies #5 / 1985 / CA / M •
Naked Night / 1985 / VCR / M • Naughty
Girls In Heat / 1986 / SE / M • The Poonies
/ 1985 / VI / M • Sailing Into Ecstasy / 1986
/ VCX / M • Strange Bedfellows / 1985 / PL

/ M • Swedish Erotica #62 / 1984 / CA / M •
Swedish Erotica #63 / 1985 / CA / M •
Taboo #04 / 1985 / IN / M • We Love To
Tease / 1985 / VD / M • Wet 'n' Bare With
Barbara Dare / 1988 / NEO / C

AMY SCOTT *see* **Star Index I**

AMY STONE
A Girl Like That / 1979 / CDC / M • The
Sexpert / 1975 / VEP / M

AMY TURNER
Hardcore: The Films Of Richard Kern #1 /
1991 / FTV / M

AMY WELLS *see* **Day Jason**

ANA
Hollywood Amateurs #05 / 1994 / MID / M
• Penetration (Anabolic) #2 / 1995 / ANA /
M

ANAIS
Freshness Counts / 1996 / EL / M • Jura
Sexe / 1995 / JP / G • Private Film #20 /
1995 / OD / M • Private Film #21 / 1995 /
OD / M

ANAL ANNIE *see* **Nina Hartley**

ANALISA
The Cumm Brothers #10: Night Of The
Giving Head / 1995 / OD / M • The Doctor
Is In #2: Pussy Pox / 1995 / NIT / M •
Pussy Fest Of The Northwest #5 / 1995 /
NIT / M • The Sodomizer #4 / 1996 / SC /
M • Teacher's Pet #4 / 1995 / APP / M

ANALMASTER
Anal Asian / 1994 / VEX / M

ANALU
Mike Hott: #240 Carmel And Analu / 1991 /
MHV / F

ANAOS
Private Video Magazine #22 / 1995 / OD /
M

ANASIS
Ass, Gas & The Mystical GLOP / 1997 / EL
/ M

ANASTANIA
Rosa / Francesca / 1995 / XC / M

ANASTASIA
The Anal Adventures Of Suzy Super Slut
#2 / 1994 / AFV / M • Anal Injury / 1994 /
ZA / M • Beach Bum Amateur's #37 / 1993
/ MID / M • Beach Bum Amateur's #43 /
1993 / MID / M • Cats In A Storm / 199? /
NAP / B • Clan Of The Cave Woman /
1992 / NAP / B • Cleopatra Meets The
Czarina / 199? / NAP / B • Czarina On Fire
/ 199? / NAP / B • Dr Caligari / 1991 / SGV
/ S • The Drowning / 199? / NAP / B •
Harry Horndog #17: Love Puppies #5 /
1993 / ZA / M • Jura Sexe / 1995 / JP / G •
The Penetrator #1 / 1991 / PL / M • Valleys
Of The Moon / 1991 / SC / M

ANASTASIA (HUNGARY)
Anita / 1996 / BLC / M

ANDRAS
Private Stories #11 / 1996 / OD / M • Thermonuclear Sex / 1996 / EL / M

ANDRAS KOLZAS
True Stories #1 / 1993 / SC / M • True Stories #2 / 1993 / SC / M

ANDRE
Russian Model Magazine #1 / 1996 / IP /
M

ANDRE ALLEN *see* **Sean Michaels**

ANDRE BOLE *see* **Andre Bolla**

ANDRE BOLLA *(Andre Bole)*
Slim short black guy.
Beaverly Hills Cop / 1985 / SE / M • Be-
yond The Senses / 1986 / AVC / M • Black
Bunbusters / 1985 / VC / M • Black Dy-

nasty / 1985 / VD / M • Chocolate Cherries #1 / 1984 / LA / M • Ebony Ecstacy / 1988 / HIO / C • Ebony Superstars / 1988 / VC / C • Hooters / 1986 / AVC / M • Love Bites / 1985 / CA / M • Marilyn Chambers' Private Fantasies #6 / 1985 / CA / M • Wetness For The Prosecution / 1989 / LV / M

ANDRE BOVA *see Star Index I*

ANDRE CARTER *see Star Index I*

ANDRE CHAZEL
Bel Ami / 1976 / VXP / M • Je Suis Une Nymphomane / 1970 / ... / S • [Molly / 1977 / ... / S

ANDRE GRAY *see Star Index I*

ANDRE KAY *see Star Index I*

ANDRE MISTRAL
Juicy Virgins / 1995 / WIV / M

ANDRE NELSON
Dr Bizarro / 1978 / ALP / B • The Story Of Prunella / 1982 / AVO / M • Tales Of The Bizarre / 1983 / ALP / B • The Taming Of Rebecca / 1982 / SVE / B

ANDRE POST *see Star Index I*

ANDRE THE ARRANGER *see Star Index I*

ANDREA
100% Amateur #24: Dildos And Toys / 1996 / OD / M • Blows Job / 1989 / BIZ / B • Blue Vanities #506 / 1992 / FFL / M • Blue Vanities #583 / 1996 / FFL / M • Creme De Femme #2 / 1981 / AVC / C • Ebony Dancer / 1994 / HBE / M • Fondle With Care / 1989 / VEX / M • Global Girls / 1996 / GO / F • International Love And The Dancer / 1995 / PME / S • Jura Sexe / 1995 / JP / G • Lesbian Pros And Amateurs #26 / 1993 / GO / F • Lovin' Spoonfuls #3 / 1995 / 4P / C • Missy Impossible / 1989 / CAR / M • More Dirty Debutantes #55 / 1996 / 4P / M • Mr. Peepers Nastiest #4 / 1995 / LBO / C • Mr. Peepers Nastiest #6 / 1995 / LBO / C • Mystery Of The Maletease Dildo / 1992 / STR / M • Nasty Travel Tails #01 / 1993 / CC / M • Prague By Night #2 / 1996 / EA / M • Private Film #20 / 1995 / OD / M • Private Film #21 / 1995 / OD / M • Private Gold #08: The Longest Night / 1996 / OD / M • Private Gold #10: Sins / 1996 / OD / M • Private Gold #12: The Pyramid #2 / 1996 / OD / M • Private Stories #10 / 1996 / OD / M • Private Stories #11 / 1996 / OD / M • Private Video Magazine #24 / 1995 / OD / M • The Reel Sex World #02 / 1994 / WP / M • The Reel Sex World #03 / 1994 / WP / M • Rocco Goes To Prague / 1995 / EA / M • Slap Happy / 1994 / PRE / B • Sluts 'n' Angels In Budapest / 1994 / EL / M • Sodomania #11: In Your Face / 1994 / EL / M • Sorority Lingerie Party / 1995 / NIV / F • Southern: Previews #1 / 1992 / SSH / C • Transvestite Tour Guide / 1993 / HSV / G • Triple X Video Magazine #01 / 1995 / OD / M

ANDREA (BRAZIL)
Amazon Heat #1 / 1996 / CC / M • The Bottom Dweller 33 1/3 / 1995 / EL / M

ANDREA (DINA) *see Dina Pearl*

ANDREA (ENGLISH)
English Muffins / 1995 / VC / M

ANDREA (TEXAS M) *see Texas Milly*

ANDREA ADAMS
Female Sensations / 1984 / VC / M • Loose Times At Ridley High / 1984 / VCX / M • Saturday Matinee Series #4 / 1996 / VCX / C

ANDREA AMORE
Adam & Eve's House Party #1 / 1995 / VC / M • Casting Call #16 / 1995 / SO / M • Cherry Poppers #10: Sweet And Sassy / 1995 / ZA / M • Dirty Bob's #23: Tampa Teasers / 1995 / FLP / S • Dirty Bob's #24: The Big O! / 1996 / FLP / M • Dirty Bob's #25: Porn Never Sleeps! / 1996 / FLP / S • Dirty Dancers #7 / 1996 / 4P / M • New Faces, Hot Bodies #20 / 1996 / STP / M

ANDREA BRITTIAN *see Jessica Longe*

ANDREA BRITTON *see Jessica Longe*

ANDREA CASTILLE
Her Personal Touch / 1996 / STM / F • Lesbian Sex, Power & Money / 1994 / STM / F • Pussy Hunt #04 / 1994 / LEI / M

ANDREA CSEPKE *see Dina Pearl*

ANDREA DRYER
More Dirty Debutantes #09 / 1991 / 4P / M

ANDREA FEIEK
Prima #09: ASSassins / 1995 / MBP / M

ANDREA FEJES
Lil' Women: Vacation / 1996 / EUR / M

ANDREA HART *see Star Index I*

ANDREA HUSZAR
True Stories #1 / 1993 / SC / M • True Stories #2 / 1993 / SC / M

ANDREA LANGE *see Star Index I*

ANDREA MAISON
Love Theatre / cr80 / VC / M

ANDREA MARTIN *see Star Index I*

ANDREA MITRIK
Sperm Injection / 1995 / PL / M

ANDREA MOFFIT
Italian Game / 1994 / CS / B

ANDREA MOLNOR
Juicy Virgins / 1995 / WIV / M • A Private Love Affair / 1996 / IP / M

ANDREA NASCHAK *see April Rayne*

ANDREA NOBILI
1001 Nights / 1996 / IP / M • Erotic Dreams / 1992 / VTV / M • Essence Of A Woman / 1995 / ONA / M • Hotel Fear / 1996 / ONA / M • Juliet & Romeo / 1996 / XC / M • The Last Vamp / 1996 / IP / M • Robin Thief Of Wives / 1996 / XC / M • Rosa / Francesca / 1995 / XC / M • Sex Penitentiary / 1996 / XC / M

ANDREA NORTH *(Andrea Shane)*
First seen in **Nasty Girls #3 (1990-CDI)**. In More Dirty Debutantes #4 she is credited as Andrea Shane. Very tight nice body with small tits—a typical mall girl.
More Dirty Debutantes #04 / 1990 / 4P / M • Nasty Girls #3 (1990-CDI) / 1990 / CDI / M

ANDREA OUQ
Private Gold #02: Friends In Sex / 1995 / OD / M

ANDREA PARDUCCI
Sex Boat / 1980 / VCX / M • Ultraflesh / 1980 / GO / M

ANDREA PATET *see Star Index I*

ANDREA ROLAND *see Jessica Longe*

ANDREA ROTHCHILD *see Star Index I*

ANDREA SHANE *see Andrea North*

ANDREA SUTTON *see Star Index I*

ANDREA SZABO
Private Film #27 / 1995 / OD / M • Private Film #28 / 1995 / OD / M • Private Stories #02 / 1995 / OD / M • Triple X Video Magazine #03 / 1995 / OD / M

ANDREA TRAVIS *see Andrea True*

ANDREA TRUE *(Inger Kissen, Singh Low, Andrea Travis)*
Not too pretty older female with reddish blonde hair, freckles, small to medium droopy tits and lithe body.
ABA: Double Feature #3 / 1996 / ALP / M • Babylon Gold / 1983 / COM / C • The Big Thing / 1973 / VHL / M • The Bite / 1975 / SVE / M • Blue Vanities #002 / 1987 / FFL / M • Blue Vanities #256 / 1996 / FFL / M • Blue Vanities #521 / 1993 / FFL / M • Both Ways / 1976 / VC / G • The Chamber Mades / 1975 / EVI / M • Christy / 1975 / CA / M • Classic Erotica #2 / 1980 / SVE / M • Dance Of Love / cr70 / BL / M • Debbie Does Las Vegas / 1982 / KOV / M • Devil's Due / 1974 / ALP / M • Double Header / cr73 / BL / M • Dr Teen Dilemma / 1973 / VHL / M • Employee Benefits / 1983 / AMB / M • Every Inch A Lady / 1975 / QX / M • Exotic French Fantasies / 1974 / PVX / M • Fast Ball / cr73 / VXP / M • French Wives / 1970 / VC / M • Go Fly A Kite / cr73 / VHL / M • The Hardy Girls / cr71 / ALP / M • Have Blower Will Travel / 1975 / SOW / M • Head Nurse / cr74 / VXP / M • Heavy Load / 1975 / COM / M • Hot Channels / 1973 / AR / M • Hypnorotica / 1972 / EVI / M • Illusions Of A Lady / 1972 / VSH / M • Inside Andrea True / cr75 / BL / M • International Intrigue / 1983 / AMB / M • Keep On Truckin' / cr73 / BL / M • Kinky Potpourri #32 / 199? / SVE / C • Lady On The Couch / 1978 / SVE / M • Limited Edition #23 / 1983 / AVC / M • Little Orphan Sammy / 1976 / VC / M • MASH'ed / cr75 / ALP / M • Maxine's Dating Service / 1974 / VHL / M • Meatball / 1972 / VCX / M • The Millionairess / cr74 / CDC / M • Once Over Nightly / 197? / VXP / M • Once...And For All / 1979 / HLV / M • Open For Business / 1983 / AMB / M • Overexposure / cr73 / GO / M • Pleasure Cruise / 1972 / WV / M • Prurient Interest / 1974 / BL / M • Psyched For Sex / cr73 / BL / M • Road Service / cr73 / VHL / M • The Russians Are Coming / cr69 / VST / M • Seduction / 1974 / VXP / M • The Seduction Of Lyn Carter / 1974 / ALP / M • Sexual Freedom In The Ozarks / 1971 / VHL / M • Sophie Says No / 1975 / VHL / M • The Sorceress / 1974 / BL / M • South Of The Border / 1977 / VC / M • Summer Session / cr75 / BL / M • Swedish Erotica #09 / 1980 / CA / M • Sweet Wet Lips / 1974 / PVX / M • Switchcraft / 1975 / VHL / M • Teenage Nurses / 1975 / QX / M • True Legends Of Adult Cinema: The Cult Superstars / 1993 / VC / C • The True Way / 1975 / SVE / M • Tycoon's Daughter / cr73 / SVE / M • Weekend Cowgirls / 1983 / CA / M • The Wetter The Better / 1975 / VST / M • Winter Of 1849 / cr73 / BL / M • [Grant Takes Richmond / 1981 / ... / M • [Love Express / 1974 / ... / M • [Spikey's Magic Wand / 1973 / ... / S

ANDREA WOLFE
Up And Cummers #38 / 1996 / RWP / M

ANDREAS K.
Private Gold #09: Private Dancer / 1996 / OD / M

ANDREAS MANNKOPF
The Young Seducers / 1971 / BL / M

ANDREAS WESTPHAL *see Star Index I*

ANDRES MONTANO
Queens From Outer Space / 1993 / HSV / G

ANDRES RUDIVOKA
Sex-A-Holic Lady / 1995 / PL / M

ANDREW

Mr. Peepers Amateur Home Videos #77: Facial Coverage / 1993 / LBO / M • Private Gold #10: Sins / 1996 / OD / M • Stevi's: The Gusher / 1992 / SSV / M

ANDREW BLAKE *(Paul Nevitt)*
Normally a director. The Paul Nevitt name was used to direct the **Penthouse** videos.

ANDREW LOAD
Ass, Gas & The Mystical GLOP / 1997 / EL / M • The Cellar Dweller / 1996 / EL / M • Nice Fuckin' Movie / 1997 / EL / M • Sodomania #20: For Members Only / 1997 / EL / M • Sodomania #21: Degenerate Lifestyles! / 1997 / EL / M

ANDREW MCVEEN *see* **Star Index I**
ANDREW MICHAELS *see* **Star Index I**
ANDREW MONTANA
Bi 'n' Large / 1994 / PL / G • My She-Male Valentine / 1994 / HSV / G • She-Male Surprise / 1995 / CDI / G • Toys Bi Us / 1993 / BIL / G

ANDREW NICHOLS *(Andy Nichols)*
Cafe Flesh / 1982 / VC / M • Devil In Miss Jones #3: A New Beginning / 1986 / VC / M • Night Of The Living Babes / 1987 / MAE / S • Nightdreams #1 / 1981 / CA / M • Wimps / 1987 / LIV / S

ANDREW STANWAY
The Lover's Guide: Advanced Sexual Techniques / 1994 / PME / M • The Lover's Guide: Better Orgasms / 1994 / PME / M

ANDREW THOMAS *see* **Star Index I**
ANDREW WADE *(Grey Waters)*
SO of Brooke Waters.
19 & Naughty #2 / 1995 / SKV / M • 50 And Still Gangbangin'! / 1995 / EMC / M • Addictive Desires / 1994 / OD / M • The Butt Sisters Do Boston / 1995 / MID / M • Dirty Doc's Housecalls #19 / 1994 / LV / M • A Dirty Western #2: Smoking Guns / 1994 / CV / M • Dreams Of Desires / 1995 / ONA / M • Erotic World Of Anne Spice / 1995 / WV / M • Fashion Plate / 1995 / WAV / M • The Flirt / 1995 / GO / M • High Heel Harlots #05 / 1994 / SFP / M • Hollywood Amateurs #05 / 1994 / MID / M • Kinky Debutante Interviews #04 / 1994 / IP / M • Man Handling / 1995 / RB / B • Mastering The Male / 1995 / RB / B • Mr. Peepers Amateur Home Videos #91: Hole Lot'a Humping Goin / 1994 / LBO / M • Nightmare On Lesbian Street / 1995 / LIP / F • Odyssey Triple Play #99: Hail, Hail, The GangBang's Here #2 / 1995 / OD / M • Orgies Orgies Orgies / 1994 / WV / M • Private Audition / 1995 / EVN / M • Screamers (Ona Zee) / 1995 / ONA / M • Sex Academy #2: The Art Of Talking Dirty / 1994 / ONA / M • Top Debs #6: Rear Entry Girls / 1995 / GO / M • Vagina Beach / 1995 / FH / M • While You Were Dreaming / 1995 / WV / M • Who's In Charge (Titan) / 1995 / TEG / M • Wild Orgies #15 / 1995 / AFI / M

ANDREW YOUNG *see* **Star Index I**
ANDREW YOUNGMAN
Drop Sex: Wipe The Floor / 1997 / JLP / M • Penetration (Anabolic) #2 / 1995 / ANA / M • The Thief, The Girl & The Detective / 1996 / HDE / M

ANDREY
Private Stories #05 / 1995 / OD / M
ANDRIA COLLINS *see* **Star Index I**
ANDY
Blue Vanities #538 / 1993 / FFL / M • Full Moon Video #35: Wild Side Couples: The School HeadMaste / 1995 / FAP / M • Private Stories #03 / 1995 / OD / M • Private Stories #06 / 1995 / OD / M

ANDY (DICK NASTY) *see* **Dick Nasty (Brit)**
ANDY (SHAWN RICKS) *see* **Shawn Ricks**
ANDY ABRAMS *see* **Randy West**
ANDY ADLER
Adler Shoots: The Reality Behind The Legend / cr90 / BON / B
ANDY BROWN *see* **Paul Scharf**
ANDY DEER *see* **Randy West**
ANDY ESPOSITO
Seduce Me Tonight / 1984 / AT / M
ANDY FIELDS
Boiling Point / 1978 / SE / M
ANDY GREY
Sweet Savage / 1978 / ALP / M
ANDY HARDY
Cheri's On Fire / 1986 / V99 / M • Glamour Girls / 1987 / SE / M • Love At First Sight / 1987 / SE / C
ANDY HAYES *see* **Star Index I**
ANDY KUFF
G...They're Big / 1981 / TGA / C • Girls & Guys & Girls Or Guys / 19?? / REG / M • Yamahama Mamas / 1983 / TGA / C
ANDY MILBERG
Ancient Secrets Of Sexual Ecstasy / 1996 / HIG / M
ANDY NICHOLS *see* **Andrew Nichols**
ANDY PRISCILLA
Private Gold #03: The Chase / 1996 / OD / M
ANDY TYLER *see* **Star Index I**
ANE TASK
And Then Came Eve / cr72 / VCX / M • Fantastic Voyeur / 1975 / AVC / M
ANEKO
Max #07: French Kiss / 1995 / XPR / M
ANESA BLUE *(Aissa Blue)*
Falling apart body, 25 years old in 1995, de-virginized at 18, not too pretty, Greek origin.
Birthday Bash / 1995 / BOT / M • Girlz Towne #07 / 1995 / FC / F • Stuff Your Face #1 / 1994 / JMP / M • Video Virgins #17 / 1994 / NS / M
ANETTE ALM
Swedish Vip Magazine #1 / 1995 / PL / M • Swedish Vip Magazine #2 / 1995 / PL / M
ANGEL
Angel Pays Her Bill / 1994 / VIG / B • Any Way They're Tied / 1993 / HAC / B • AVP #7018: Special Services / 1990 / AVP / M • AVP #9111: The Pass / 1991 / AVP / M • Backstreet: Spring Break '96 / 1996 / BST / F • Big Busted Lesbians At Play / 1991 / BIZ / F • Blue Vanities #512 / 1992 / FFL / M • Blue Vanities #529 / 1993 / FFL / M • Blue Vanities #534 / 1993 / FFL / M • Blue Vanities #554 / 1994 / FFL / M • Candyman #05: Virgin Dream / 1993 / GLI / M • Dirty Dancers #2 / 1994 / 4P / M • Disciplined By Catfighters / 1993 / STM / B • The Fantasy Realm #1 / 1990 / RUM / M • First Training / 1987 / BIZ / B • Flogged For His Sins / 1993 / STM / B • The French Canal / 1995 / DVP / G • Full Moon Video #30: Rainy Day Lays / 1994 / FAP / M • Hard Licks / 1993 / GOT / B • Hog Tied And Spanked / 1991 / BIZ / B • Hot Body Competition: Beverly Hill's Miniskirt Madness Cont. / 1996 / CG / F • Itsy Bitsy Gang Bang / 1996 / HW / M • Leather Lair #3 / 1993 / STM / B • Micro X Video #a / 1993 / YDI / M • Mommie Severest / 1992 /

STM / B • More Dirty Debutantes #17 / 1992 / 4P / M • More Dirty Debutantes #18 / 1992 / 4P / M • Mr. Peepers Amateur Home Videos #91: Hole Lot'a Humping Goin / 1994 / LBO / M • Northwest Pecker Trek #1 / 1994 / LBO / M • OUTS: Brandy & Angel / 1994 / OUT / F • Pearl Necklace: Premier Sessions #05 / 1994 / SEE / M • Penetration (Flash) #1 / 1995 / FLV / M • Severe Penalties / 1993 / GOT / B • The Slaves Of Alexis Payne / 1995 / LON / B • Somewhere Under The Rainbow #1 / 1995 / HW / M • Spanked Ecstasy / 1991 / BIZ / B • Sweet Sunshine / 1995 / IF / M • Tickling Scenes / 1991 / TAO / C • Toe Tales #11 / 1993 / GOT / B • Toe Tales #12 / 1994 / GOT / C • Tormented / 1993 / GOT / B • Up And Cummers: The Movie / 1994 / 4P / M

ANGEL (1984) *(Brandee, Jennifer James)*
Very pretty brunette with a lithe body and small to medium tits. Nice smile and nice personality in her 84/85 movies but had turned into a hard-as-nails blonde in her 87/88 attempt at a comeback. **Pretty Girl;** (an original loop) was her first movie. **Sherri's Gotta Have It, Shoppe Of Temptations,** and **Out Of Towner** are not this Angel. She was a model for *Seventeen.*
The 8th Annual Erotic Film Awards / 1984 / SE / C • Adult Video News Magazine / 1985 / ZEB / M • Angel Of The Island / 1988 / IN / M • Angel Of The Night / 1985 / IN / M • Angel Rising / 1988 / IN / M • Angel's Back / 1988 / IN / M • Angel's Revenge / 1985 / IN / M • Blonde Heat (VCA) / 1985 / VC / M • Dangerous Stuff / 1985 / COM / M • Debbie Does 'em All #1 / 1985 / CV / M • For Your Thighs Only / 1985 / WV / M • Ginger Rides Again / 1988 / KIS / C • Girls Like Us / cr88 / IN / C • Girls On Fire / 1985 / VCX / M • Holiday For Angels / 1987 / IN / M • Honkytonk Angels / 1988 / IN / C • Hot Blooded / 1983 / CA / M • L'Amour / 1984 / CA / M • The Last X-Rated Movie #1 / 1990 / COM / M • The Last X-Rated Movie #2 / 1990 / COM / M • The Last X-Rated Movie #4 / 1990 / COM / M • Legends Of Porn #2 / 1989 / CV / C • The Lost Angel / 1989 / KIS / C • Love Scenes For Loving Couples / 1987 / CV / C • Matinee Idol / 1984 / VC / M • Only The Best Of Debbie / 1992 / MET / C • Only The Best Of Women With Women / 1988 / CV / C • Oral Majority #01 / 1986 / WV / C • Oral Majority #02 / 1987 / WV / C • Passions / 1985 / MIT / M • Playmate #01 / 1984 / VC / M • The Pleasures Of Innocence / 1985 / VC / M • Pretty Girl / 1984 / VIS / M • Star Angel / 1986 / COM / M • Three Faces Of Angel / 1987 / CV / M • Too Hot To Touch #1 / 1985 / CV / M • Too Naughty To Say No / 1984 / CA / M • Tower Of Power / 1985 / CV / M • Undercover Angel / 1988 / IN / M • VCA Previews #3 / 1988 / VC / C • VCA Previews #4 / 1988 / VC / C • Wise Girls / 1989 / IN / C

ANGEL (HARLEY) *see* **Harley Haze**
ANGEL (HUNGARIAN)
The Betrayal Of Innocence #1: The Awakening Of Marika / 1993 / CC / M • The Betrayal Of Innocence #2: The Decadence / 1993 / CC / M • The Betrayal Of Innocence #3: The Choice / 1993 / CC / M • Depravity On The Danube / 1993 / EL / M • Somewhere Under The Rainbow #2 / 1995 / HW

/ M
ANGEL (S/M)
French-Pumped Femmes #1 / 1989 / RSV / G • High Heel Slave / 1989 / LEO / B • My Girl: Transaction #2 / 1993 / SC / G • Power Games / 1992 / STM / B • She-Male Whorehouse / 1988 / VD / G • She-Males Behind Closed Doors / 1991 / RSV / G • Taste For Submission / 1991 / LON / C
ANGEL (VIXXEN) *see* Vixxen
ANGEL ARMSTRONG
Sex Mountain / cr80 / VCX / M
ANGEL ASH
Anal Sluts & Sweethearts #2 / 1993 / ROB / M • Bad Habits / 1993 / VC / M • Best Gang Bangs / 1996 / DFI / C • Face Dance #1 / 1992 / EA / M • Face Dance #2 / 1992 / EA / M • Gang Bang Cummers / 1993 / ROB / M • Nurse Tails / 1994 / VC / M • Pussy Tails #01 / 1993 / CDY / M • Slave To Love / 1993 / ROB / M
ANGEL BABY
Mistress In Training / 1996 / STM / B • P.L.O.W.: Punk Ladies Of Wrestling / 1996 / GOT / B
ANGEL BARRERA *see Star Index I*
ANGEL BARRETT
Alice In Wonderland / 1976 / CA / M • Couples / 1976 / VHL / M • Highway Hookers / 1976 / SVE / M • The Naughty Victorians / 1975 / VC / M • The Night Of The Spanish Fly / 1978 / CV / M
ANGEL BLONDEE
Big-Busted Cat-Fight Fantasy / 1990 / NAP / B • Cat-Fight Angels / 1990 / NAP / B
ANGEL BO
Club Privado / 1995 / KP / M
ANGEL BUST
Huge inflated titted (55-23-38) not too pretty girl. 22 years old and tiny height-wise.
976-76DD / 1993 / VI / M • The Adventures Of Buck Naked / 1994 / OD / M • Beverly Hills Sex Party / 1993 / EX / M • Big Boob Bikini Bash / 1995 / BTO / M • Big Bust Babes #14 / 1993 / AFI / M • Big Bust Bangers #1 / 1994 / AMP / M • The Big Busteddd / 1993 / AFD / M • The Boob Tube / 1993 / MET / M • Booberella / 1992 / BTO / M • Bra Busters #01 / 1993 / LBO / M • Breast Wishes #14 / 1888 / LBO / M • Bust A Move / 1993 / SC / M • The Bust Things In Life Are Free / 1994 / NAP / S • The Butt Sisters Do Detroit / 1993 / MID / M • Carlita's Backway / 1993 / OD / M • Deep Inside Dirty Debutantes #08 / 1993 / 4P / M • Dick & Jane Big Breast Adventure / 1993 / AVI / M • Double D Dreams / 1996 / NAP / S • Double D Dykes #10 / 1993 / GO / F • Double Load #2 / 1994 / HW / M • Double-D Reunion / 1995 / BTO / M • Falling In Love Again / 1993 / PMV / M • The Girls From Hootersville #02 / 1993 / SFP / M • Heavenly Bodies / 1993 / NAP / B • In X-Cess / 1994 / LV / M • L.A. Topless / 1994 / LE / M • More Than A Mouthful / 1995 / LBO / C • Natural Wonders / 1993 / VI / M • Needful Sins / 1993 / WV / M • No Fly Zone / 1993 / LE / F • Precious Cargo / 1993 / VIM / M • Sarah Jane's Love Bunnies #02 / 1993 / FPI / F • She Quest / 1994 / OD / M • The Three Muskatits / 1994 / PL / M • Tit City #1 / 1993 / SC / M • Toppers #11 / 1993 / TV / C • Toppers #14 / 1993 / TV / M • Toppers #15 / 1993 / TV / M • Toppers #17 / 1993 / TV / M • Toppers

#22 / 1993 / TV / C • Toppers #30 / 1994 / TV / C • Twin Action / 1993 / LE / M • Wendy Whoppers: Prison Love Doll / 1994 / PEP / M • Wet Nurses #1 / 1994 / LE / M • What About Boob? / 1993 / CV / M
ANGEL CAKE
She-Male Slut House / 1994 / HEA / G
ANGEL CASH *(Nancy Racetor)*
Nancy Racetor is from **Ultraflesh**.
All About Angel Cash / 1982 / VXP / M • Best Of Caught From Behind #1 / 1987 / HO / C • Beyond The Valley Of The Ultra Milkmaids / 1984 / 4P / F • Big Bust Babes #02 / 1984 / AFI / M • Blue Vanities #029 / 1988 / FFL / M • Blue Vanities #030 / 1988 / FFL / M • Blue Vanities #070 / 1988 / FFL / M • Blue Vanities #253 / 1996 / FFL / M • Caught From Behind #01 / 1982 / HO / M • Caught From Behind #02: The Sequel / 1983 / HO / M • Dream Girls #2 / 1983 / CA / C • The Erotic Adventures Of Dr Storm / 1983 / XTR / M • Erotic Interlude / 1981 / CA / M • The Erotic World Of Angel Cash / 1983 / VXP / M • Fantasy Peeps: Sensuous Delights / 1984 / 4P / M • Getting Ahead / 1983 / PL / M • A Girl Named Angel / 19?? / ... / M • Hard Worker / cr80 / AVC / M • A Lacy Affair #1 / 1983 / HO / F • Ladies In Love / 19?? / PLY / C • Limited Edition #23 / 1983 / AVC / M • Limited Edition #25 / 1984 / AVC / M • Little Orphan Dusty #2 / 1981 / VIS / M • Loving Spoonfulls / 1987 / 4P / C • Milky Mama / cr72 / ... / S • The Right Stiff / 1983 / AMB / M • Romancing The Bone / 1984 / VC / M • Spanking Scenes #01 / 1983 / TAO / C • Ultraflesh / 1980 / GO / M • Wine Me, Dine Me, 69 Me / 1989 / COL / C
ANGEL COLLINS
Adorable, very pretty face, long fine dark blonde hair, small/medium very nicely shaped tits, tight waist, tight little butt, good skin, smiles nicely, good personality but a liar. Supposedly 22 years old in 1995 and from Nebraska. Not the same as Harley Haze (watch the moles) despite some resemblance.
Ass Masters (Leisure) #06 / 1995 / LEI / M • The Girls Of Spring Break / 1995 / VT / M • Island Of Lust / 1995 / XCI / M • Snatch Masters #06 / 1996 / LEI / M • Work Of Art / 1995 / LE / M
ANGEL CRUZ
Back To Black #1 / 1988 / VEX / M • Bright Lights, Big Titties / 1989 / CA / M • Double D Roommates / 1989 / BTO / M • Girls Of The Double D #05 / 1988 / CIN / M • Pussy Power #02 / 1989 / BTO / M • Stormi / 1988 / LV / M • Toys, Not Boys #3 / 1991 / FC / C
ANGEL DESMOND *see* Angel Ducharme
ANGEL DUCHARME *(Angel Desmond)*
Mrs. Rodger's Neighborhood / 1988 / EVN / C • Stormy / 1980 / CV / M • Swedish Erotica #10 / 1980 / CA / M • Swedish Erotica #12 / 1980 / CA / M • Tangerine / 1979 / CXV / M • Telefantasy / 1978 / AR / M
ANGEL EYES
FTV #70: Outcall Outcry / 1996 / FT / B • FTV #76: Bundy Bashout / 1996 / FT / B • FTV #77: TV Fight / 1996 / FT / B • FTV #78: Cat's Claws / 1996 / FT / B
ANGEL FACE *see Star Index I*
ANGEL GIONELLI *see Star Index I*
ANGEL HALL *see* Jeannie Pepper

ANGEL HARRIS
Angel's TV & TS Harlots / 1993 / RSV / G • The National Transsexual / 1990 / GO / G • She-Male Encounters #17: Sorority / 1987 / MET / G • She-Male Encounters #18: Murder She-Male Wrote / 1987 / MET / G • She-Male Solos: Angel / 1991 / LEO / G • Trisexual Encounters #05 / 1986 / PL / G
ANGEL HART
Kiss Ass / 1996 / AMP / M
ANGEL HAWKE
The Queen Of Mean / 1992 / FC / M • Totally Tasteless Video #01 / 1994 / TTV / M
ANGEL KELLY *(Sugar Brown)*
Black girl (5'7" 36-20-34).
Addicted To Love / 1988 / WAV / M • Alice In Blackland / 1988 / VC / M • Alice In Whiteland / 1988 / VC / M • Amazing Sex Stories #1 / 1986 / SUV / M • Angel Gets Even / 1987 / FAN / M • Angel Kelly Raw / 1987 / FAN / M • Angel's Gotta Have It / 1988 / FAN / M • Backing In #1 / 1990 / WV / C • Backing In #2 / 1990 / WV / C • The Barlow Affairs / 1991 / XCI / M • Behind The Scenes With Angela Baron / 1988 / FAZ / C • The Best Of Black White & Pink Inside / 1996 / CV / C • The Best Of Ron Jeremy / 1990 / WET / C • Big Gulp #2 / 1987 / VIP / C • Biloxi Babes / 1988 / WV / M • Black Angel / 1987 / CC / M • Black Cherries / 1993 / EVN / C • Black Girls Do It Better / 1986 / CV / M • Black Magic / 1986 / DR / M • Black Magic Sex Clinic / 1987 / DOX / M • The Black Mystique / 1986 / CV / M • Black On White / 1987 / PL / C • Black Satin Nights / 1988 / DR / C • Black Taboo #2 / 1986 / SE / M • Black To Africa / 1987 / PL / C • Black Valley Girls #1 / 1986 / 4R / M • Black Voodoo / 1987 / FOV / M • Blackman & Anal Woman #1 / 1990 / PL / M • Blowing The Whistle / 1986 / VIP / M • The Boss / 1987 / FAN / M • The Bottom Line / 1986 / WV / M • Built For Sex (Angela Baron's) / 1988 / FAZ / C • The Call Girl / 1986 / VD / M • Cheating / 1986 / SEV / M • Chocolate Delights #1 / 1985 / TAG / C • Chocolate Delights #2 / 1985 / TAG / C • Creatures Of The Night / 1987 / FAN / M • Debbie Class Of '88 / 1987 / CC / M • Debbie Does Dishes #3 / 1987 / AVC / M • Debbie Goes To Hawaii / 1988 / VD / C • Detroit Dames / 1988 / DR / C • Devil In Miss Dare / 1986 / AVC / C • Doin' The Harlem Shuffle / 1986 / CA / M • Double Black Fantasy / 1987 / CC / C • Dr Lust / 1987 / VC / M • Ebony & Ivory Fantasies / 1988 / VD / C • Ebony & Ivory Sisters / 1985 / PL / C • Ebony Dreams / 1988 / PIN / C • Ebony Love / 1992 / VT / C • Ebony Orgies / 1987 / SE / C • End Of Innocence / 1986 / AR / M • Even More Dangerous / 1990 / SO / M • Fantasy Couples / 1989 / FAZ / C • Fatal Passion / 1988 / CC / M • The Girls On F Street / 1986 / AVC / M • Guess Who Came At Dinner? / 1987 / FAN / M • Harlem Candy / 1987 / WET / M • HHH-Hot! TV #1 / 1988 / CDI / M • HHHHot! TV #2 / 1988 / CDI / M • Hill Street Blacks #2 / 1988 / DR / M • Honeymoon Harlots / 1986 / AVC / M • Hot And Nasty! / 1986 / V99 / C • Hot Chocolate #2 / 1986 / PLY / M • Hot Rocks / 1986 / WET / M • Hotter Chocolate / 1986 / AVC / M • House Of Sexual Fantasies / 1987 / GO / M • I Am Curious Black

/ 1986 / WET / M • I Cream Of Genie / 1988 / SE / M • In And Out Of Africa / 1986 / EVN / M • Jumpin' Black Flesh / 1987 / BTV / C • Jungle Juice / 1988 / EXP / C • Just The Two Of Us / 1985 / WV / M • A Lacy Affair #3 / 1989 / HO / F • Lady In Black / 1989 / FAZ / C • Let's Get Wet / 1987 / WV / M • Lethal Passion / 1991 / PL / M • Little Miss Dangerous / 1989 / SO / M • Living In A Wet Dream / 1986 / PEN / C • The Load Warriors #1 / 1987 / VD / M • The Load Warriors #2 / 1987 / VD / M • Love Probe / 1986 / VT / M • Lust Connection / 1988 / VT / M • Making Ends Meet / 1988 / VT / M • Mardi Gras Passions / 1987 / MET / M • Material Girl / 1986 / VD / M • More Chocolate Candy / 1986 / VD / M • The More the Merrier / 1989 / VC / C • Naughty Girls Like It Big / 1986 / ELH / M • Night Games / 1986 / WV / M • No Man's Land #01 / 1988 / VT / C • Only The Best Of Barbara Dare / 1990 / CV / C • Only The Best Of Girls With Curves / 1992 / CV / C • Oral Majority #07 / 1989 / WV / C • Out Of Control / 1987 / SE / M • The Out Of Towner / 1987 / CDI / M • Parliament: Dark & Sweet #1 / 1991 / PM / C • Parliament: Hot Foxes #1 / 1988 / PM / F • Parliament: Three Way Lust / 1988 / PM / M • Partners In Sex / 1988 / FAN / M • Phone Sex Girls #2 / 1987 / VT / M • Play It Again, Samantha / 1986 / EVN / M • Porn In The USA #2 / 1987 / VEN / C • Princess Charming / 1987 / AVC / C • Pumping Irene #1 / 1986 / FAN / M • Pumping Irene #2 / 1986 / FAN / M • The Red Hot Roadrunner / 1987 / VD / M • Restless Nights / 1987 / SEV / M • Saturday Night Beaver / 1986 / EVN / M • Secrets Behind The Green Door / 1987 / SE / M • Sexy Delights #2 / 1987 / CLV / M • The Sins Of Angel Kelly / 1987 / FAN / C • Sins Of The Wealthy #2 / 1986 / CLV / M • Sorority Pink #1 / 1989 / CV / M • Sorority Pink #2 / 1989 / CV / M • Soul Games / 1988 / PV / C • A Sticky Situation / 1987 / CA / M • Sweat #1 / 1986 / PP / M • Swedish Erotica #71 / 1986 / CA / M • Swedish Erotica #72 / 1986 / CA / M • Swedish Erotica Featurettes #1 / 1989 / CA / M • Swedish Erotica Featurettes #2 / 1989 / CA / M • Sweet Chocolate / 1987 / VD / M • Sweet Things / 1987 / VC / M • Taija Is Sizzling Hot / 1986 / VT / M • Tales Of The Uncensored / 1987 / FAN / M • A Taste Of Angel / 1989 / PIN / C • A Taste Of Sahara / 1990 / PIN / C • Three For All / 1988 / PL / M • The Thrill Of It / 1986 / CAT / M • To Lust In LA / 1986 / LA / M • Torrid Zone / 1987 / MIR / M • Tracy Takes Paris / 1987 / VIP / M • Trampire / 1987 / FAN / M • Weird Fantasy / 1986 / LA / M • Welcome To The Jungle / 1988 / FAZ / C • Wet Kink / 1989 / CDI / M • Where There's Smoke There's Fire / 1987 / FAN / M • [Cherry Pickers / 19?? / ... / M • [Dick Tales / 19?? / ... / M • [Encyclopedia Sexualis / 1986 / ... / M • [Foxy Ladies / 19?? / ... / M • [I Love You, Molly Flynn / 1988 / ... / M • [Lust Incorporated / 1988 / ... / M • [Wild Sex Stories / 1985 / ... / M

ANGEL LA MONICA *see* **Casey (Angel L.M.)**

ANGEL LOVE
The Awakening Of Sally / 1984 / VCR / M

ANGEL MARSHALL

Lady Zazu's Daughter / 1971 / ALP / M

ANGEL MARTINE
Sharon In The Rough-House / 1976 / LA / M

ANGEL NICOLET *see* **Star Index I**

ANGEL PARRISH
Match #1: The Main Event / 1995 / NPA / B • Match #2: Savage Heat / 1995 / NPA / B

ANGEL PAYSON *see* **Jeanna Fine**

ANGEL ROOLE
Love Airlines / 1978 / SE / M

ANGEL RUSH *see* **Jeanna Fine**

ANGEL SELBY
Cafe Flesh / 1982 / VC / M

ANGEL SMITH
N.Y. Video Magazine #10 / 1996 / OUP / M

ANGEL SNOW *(Snow, Lexi Leigh)*
Blonde with long hair, 18 years old in 1995, de-virginized at 14, comes from LA, passable face, medium tits, belly button jewel, not a tight waist, flower wreath tattoo on her ankle and another just above her ass crack (sunburst) surmounted by the word "Snow".

Anal League / 1996 / IN / M • Anal Runaway / 1996 / ZA / M • The Blowjob Adventures Of Doctor Fellatio / 1997 / EL / M • Bootylicious: Yo Bitch / 1996 / JMP / M • Buttman In The Crack / 1996 / EA / M • Cirque Du Sex #2 / 1996 / VT / M • Cumback Pussy #5: Groopin' / 1996 / EL / M • Dick & Jane Go To A Bachelor Party (#17) / 1996 / AVI / M • Dirty Tricks #1: Just A Bunch Of Whores / 1995 / EA / M • Dirty Tricks #2: This Ain't Love / 1996 / EA / M • Domination Nation / 1996 / VI / M • Erotic Newcummers Vol 1 #3: Anal Adventures / 1996 / DR / M • Fashion Sluts #3 / 1995 / ABS / M • Golden Rod / 1996 / SPI / M • Hard Core Beginners #09 / 1995 / LEI / M • Hardcore Fantasies #2 / 1996 / LV / M • Hardware / 1996 / ZA / M • Hypnotic Hookers #1 / 1996 / NIT / M • Innocence Lost / 1995 / GO / M • Intense Perversions #3 / 1996 / PL / M • Jizz Glazed Goo Guzzlers #1 / 1996 / NIT / C • Legs / 1996 / ZA / M • Loose Jeans / 1996 / GO / M • Monkey Gang Bang / 1996 / NOT / M • My First Time #1 / 1995 / NS / M • Mystique / 1996 / SC / M • Nineteen #3 / 1996 / FOR / M • Nothing Sacred / 1995 / LE / M • Passage To Pleasure / 1995 / LE / M • Perverted Stories #10 / 1996 / JMP / M • Puritan Video Magazine #04 / 1996 / LE / M • Raw Sex #02 / 1995 / ERW / M • Screamers (Gourmet) / 1995 / ONA / M • The Sex Therapist / 1995 / GO / M • Show & Tell / 1996 / VI / M • Sticky Fingers / 1996 / WV / M • Summer Dreams / 1996 / TEP / M • Titty Slickers #3 / 1996 / LE / M • Video Virgins #21 / 1995 / NS / M • White Trash Whore / 1996 / JMP / M

ANGEL STARR *see* **Star Index I**

ANGEL STEEL
Canadian Beaver Hunt #1 / 1996 / PL / M

ANGEL STREET
Fringe Benefits / 1975 / IHV / M

ANGEL VENISE *see* **Star Index I**

ANGEL WEST *(Equinette, Donna Joyce, Debbie Merritt)*
Debbie Merritt: **Secrets**. Pretty, tiny child-like body with a nice personality but the acting ability of a rock. Small tits. Sounds like she's on drugs most of the time.

Age Of Consent / 1985 / AVC / M • Bachelorette Party / 1984 / JVV / M • Confes-

sions Of A Candystriper / 1984 / VC / M • Dial F For Fantasy / 1984 / PL / M • Flesh For Fantasies / 1986 / TAM / M • Gettin' Ready / 1985 / CDI / M • Getting Lucky / 1983 / CA / M • Hot Tails / 1984 / VEN / M • I Love A Girl In A Uniform / 1989 / VC / C • Intimate Couples / 1984 / VCX / M • Jean Genie / 1985 / CA / M • Joys Of Erotica #113 / 1984 / VCR / C • A Little Dynasty / 1985 / CIV / M • Little Girls, Dirty Desires / 1984 / JVV / M • Lonely Lady / 1984 / VC / M • The Loves Of Lolita / 1984 / VC / M • Secrets / 1984 / HO / M • Sex Waves / 1984 / EXF / M • Shaved Sinners #1 / 1988 / VT / M • Shaved Sinners #2 / 1987 / VT / M • She's A Good Lust Charm / 1987 / LA / C • Taboo #03 / 1983 / IN / M • Treasure Chest / 1985 / GO / M

ANGEL WHITE *see* **Star Index I**

ANGELA
Angel's Revenge / 1987 / VER / B • Anita / 1996 / BLC / M • Beach Bum Amateur's #33 / 1993 / MID / M • Big Busty #22 / 198? / H&S / S • Bizarre World Of Scott Baker / 1992 / CAS / B • Blue Vanities #169 (New) / 1996 / FFL / M • Blue Vanities #169 (Old) / 1991 / FFL / M • Blue Vanities #503 / 1992 / FFL / M • Blue Vanities #554 / 1994 / FFL / M • Buttman Goes To Rio #2 / 1991 / EA / M • Depravity On The Danube / 1993 / EL / M • Fabulous Footwear / 1993 / LEO / B • Ginger Lynn Allen's Lingerie Gallery #1 / 1994 / UNI / F • Girls Just Wanna Have Cum / 1995 / HO / M • Hardcore Male/Female Oil Wrestling / 1996 / JSP / M • HomeGrown Video #463: Cum And Get It / 1995 / HOV / M • How To Make A Model #06: Many Happy Returns / 1995 / LBO / M • Lesbian Pros And Amateurs #08 / 1992 / GO / F • Odyssey 30 Min: Three Way Interracial Fucks / 1992 / OD / M • Private Film #19 / 1994 / OD / M • Private Video Magazine #22 / 1995 / OD / M • RSK: Angela #2: The Voyeur / 1993 / RSK / F • S&M On The Ranch: Training The New Pony Girl / 1994 / VER / B • Samuels: Angela's Xxxx Time / 1990 / SAM / M • Sodomania #05: Euro-American Style / 1993 / EL / M • Spanked Shopper & Other Tales / 1991 / BON / C • True Stories #1 / 1993 / SC / M • True Stories #2 / 1993 / SC / M

ANGELA AMBRUS
Sexhibition #3 / 1996 / SUF / M

ANGELA BARON
Teutonic blonde with originally medium but later enhanced (good job) large tits, a reasonable if a little hard face, and a nice trim body with a tight waist. Born Dec 31, 1962 in Dussledorf, Germany.

20th Century Fox / 1989 / FAZ / M • Angela Baron Series #1 / 1988 / VD / C • Angela Baron Series #2 / 1988 / VD / C • Angela Baron Series #3 / 1988 / VD / C • Angela Baron Series #4 / 1988 / VD / C • Angela Baron Series #5 / 1988 / VD / C • Angela Baron Series #6 / 1988 / VD / C • Angela Takes A Dare / 1988 / FAZ / M • Back In Style / 1993 / VI / M • Back On Top / 1988 / FAZ / M • Behind The Scenes With Angela Baron / 1988 / FAZ / C • Best Body In Town / 1989 / FAZ / F • The Bitch / 1988 / FAN / M • The Bitch Is Back / 1988 / FAN / M • Built For Sex (Angela Baron's) / 1988 / FAZ / C • Cat Scratch Fever / 1989 / FAZ / M • Fantasy Couples / 1989 / FAZ / C •

Fantasy Exchange / 1993 / VI / M • Fantasy World / 1991 / NWV / C • Final Farewell / 1990 / FAZ / C • For Her Pleasure Only / 1989 / FAZ / M • For Your Lips Only / 1989 / FAZ / M • The Girl With The Blue Jeans Off / 1989 / FAZ / M • Good Enough To Eat / 1988 / FAZ / M • Guess Who Came At Dinner? / 1987 / FAN / M • Hustler Honeys #3 / 1988 / VC / S • Immortal Desire / 1993 / VI / M • Love In Reverse / 1988 / FAZ / M • Made In Germany / 1988 / FAZ / M • More Than Friends / 1989 / FAZ / M • Partners In Sex / 1988 / FAN / M • Porn Star's Day Off / 1990 / FAZ / M • Postcards From Abroad / 1991 / CA / C • Pure Sex / 1988 / FAN / C • The Red Baron / 1989 / FAN / M • Robofox #1 / 1987 / FAN / M • Robofox #2 / 1988 / FAN / M • Sex Lies / 1988 / FAN / M • Tales Of The Uncensored / 1987 / FAN / M • Taste Of Angela Baron / 1989 / VD / C • Trampire / 1987 / FAN / M • Where There's Smoke There's Fire / 1987 / FAN / M • [Kingsized Knockers / 19?? / ... / M • [Secrets Of The International Sex Vixens / 19?? / ... / M

ANGELA BERGON *see Star Index I*

ANGELA BLUE

Worksex / 1980 / ... / M

ANGELA CASTLE *see Star Index I*

ANGELA DAVIS *see Melanie Moore*

ANGELA DAY *see Star Index I*

ANGELA DERMER *see Toni Scott*

ANGELA DICKEY

Most Valuable Slut / 1973 / HLV / M

ANGELA DORIAN *see Victoria Vetri*

ANGELA DUNLAP *(Angelique Dunlap, Angelica Dunlap, Angelica Dunlup)*

House Of Lust / 1984 / VD / M • Sex Play / 1984 / SE / M • Society Affairs / 1982 / CA / M • Undressed Rehearsal / 1984 / VD / M

ANGELA FAITH

Flabby, curly-haired not-too-pretty blonde with medium droopy tits and an out-of-condition body.

AHV #18: Wild Time / 1992 / EVN / M • Amateur A Cuppers / 1993 / VEX / C • Amateur Orgies #07 / 1992 / AFI / M • Amateur Orgies #15 / 1992 / AFI / M • Angela In Bondage / 1994 / BON / B • As Sweet As They Come / 1992 / V99 / M • Backstage Entrance #1 / 1992 / FH / M • The Backway Inn #1 / 1992 / FD / M • The Backway Inn #2 / 1992 / FD / M • Bad To The Bone / 1992 / LE / M • Bareback Riders / 1992 / VEX / M • Beach Bum Amateur's #05 / 1992 / MID / M • Bi 'n' Large / 1994 / PL / G • Bi Chill / 1994 / BIL / G • Biggies #04 / 1992 / XPI / M • Blue Moon / 1992 / AFV / M • The Bodacious Boat Orgy #1 / 1993 / GLI / M • The Bodacious Boat Orgy #2 / 1993 / GLI / M • Body Slammers #01 / 1993 / SBP / B • Bondage Fantasy #2 / 1995 / BON / B • Bondage Fantasy #3 / 1995 / BON / B • Bone Alone / 1993 / MID / M • Bound Destiny / 1994 / LON / B • Bums Away / 1995 / PRE / C • Butt Jammers #03 / 1995 / SC / F • Butts Up / 1994 / CA / M • Casting Call #01 / 1993 / SO / M • Catfighting Students / 1995 / PRE / C • Chug-A-Lug Girls #2 / 1993 / VT / M • Corporate Bi Out / 1994 / BIL / G • Cult Of The Whip / 1995 / LON / B • Dead Ends / 1992 / PRE / B • Deep Inside Brittany O'connell / 1996 / VC / C • Defiance: Spanking And Beyond / 1993 / PRE / B • Defiance: The Ultimate Spanking / 1993 / BIZ / B • Direc-

tor Dilemma #1 / 1995 / BON / B • Director Dilemma #2 / 1995 / BON / B • Dirty Bob's #03: Xplicit Interviews / 1992 / FLP / S • The Disciplinarians / 1996 / LON / B • Dominating Girlfriends #1 / 1992 / PL / B • Double D Dykes #05 / 1992 / GO / F • Double Detail / 1992 / SO / M • Erotika / 1994 / WV / M • Feathermates / 1992 / PRE / B • Finger Pleasures #4 / 1995 / FL / F • Flood Control / 1992 / PRE / B • The Foot Client / 1993 / SBP / B • Forbidden Forrest / 1994 / BON / B • Full Service Woman / 1992 / V99 / M • A Girl's Affair #01 / 1992 / FD / F • Girls Will Be Boys #6 / 1993 / PL / F • Gold: What? Another Week / 1993 / GCG / F • Good Bi Girl / 1994 / BIL / G • Hillary Vamp's Private Collection #31 / 1992 / HOV / M • Hits & Misses / 1992 / PRE / B • I Was An Undercover Slave / 1994 / HOM / B • Infamous Crimes Against Nature / 1993 / SUM / M • Inferno #2 / 1993 / SC / M • Joy-Fm #11 / 1994 / BHS / M • Joy-Fm #12 / 1994 / BHS / M • Just Bondage / 1993 / CS / B • Kane Video #4: Customer Satisfaction / 1995 / VTF / B • Kinky Lesbians #02 / 1993 / BIZ / B • L.A.D.P. / 1991 / PL / M • Late On Arrival / 1994 / CS / B • Laugh Factory / 1995 / PRE / C • Leather And Tether / 1993 / STM / C • Leather Obsession / 1996 / BON / B • Leg...Ends 09 / 1994 / PRE / F • Long Dan Silver / 1992 / IF / M • Lucky Ladies #109 / 1992 / STI / M • Lust / 1993 / FH / M • M Series 04 / 1993 / LBO / M • Maid Service / 1993 / FL / M • Mike Hott: #177 Margie Solo / 1991 / MHV / F • Mike Hott: #197 Lesbian Sluts #02 / 1992 / MHV / F • Mike Hott: #203 Horny Couples #03 / 1992 / MHV / M • Mike Hott: Apple Asses #06 / 1992 / MHV / F • Mocha Magic / 1992 / FH / M • Monkee Business / 1994 / CS / B • Mr. Peepers Amateur Home Videos #37: Stairway to Heaven / 1991 / LBO / M • Mr. Peepers Amateur Home Videos #56: Hindsight Is Brownish / 1992 / LBO / M • Neighborhood Watch #18: Smokin' In Bed / 1992 / LBO / M • Neighborhood Watch #25: / 1992 / LBO / M • Neighborhood Watch #26: / 1992 / LBO / M • Neighborhood Watch #28 / 1992 / LBO / M • Next Door Neighbors #36 / 1991 / BON / M • Nothing Personal / 1993 / CA / M • Obey Thy Feet / 1994 / SBP / B • Odyssey Amateur #30: Angela & Ted's Anal Adventure / 1991 / OD / M • On Your Bare Bottom / 1992 / BON / B • Oreo A Go-Go #1 / 1992 / FH / M • The Other End Of The Whip / 1994 / LON / B • Our Bang #01 / 1992 / GLI / M • Our Bang #02 / 1992 / GLI / M • Our Bang #03 / 1992 / GLI / M • Our Bang #05 / 1992 / GLI / M • Our Bang #07 / 1992 / GLI / M • Paper Tiger / 1992 / VI / M • The Perversionist / 1995 / HOM / B • Photo Bound / 1994 / VTF / B • The Poetry Of The Flesh / 1993 / PEP / M • Positively Pagan #05 / 1993 / ATA / M • The Power Dykes / 1993 / BIZ / B • Professor Butts / 1994 / SBP / F • Professor Sticky's Anatomy 3X #03 / 1992 / FC / M • Quality Control / 1996 / VTF / B • Raging Waters / 1992 / PRE / B • Rare Ends / 1996 / PRE / C • Raw Talent Compilations: Gang Bang #2 / 1995 / RTP / C • Raw Talent: Bang 'er 16 Times / 1992 / RTP / M • Raw Talent: Bang 'er 33 Times / 1992 / RTP / M • Raw Talent: Bang 'er 34 Times / 1992 / RTP / M

• Raw Talent: Bang 'er 100 Times / 1992 / RTP / M • Raw Talent: Lust / 1993 / FH / M • Raw Talent: Swing Rave / 1993 / FH / M • Raw Talent: Voyeurism / 1994 / FH / M • Rear Ended / 1992 / CS / B • The Rehearsal / 1993 / VC / M • Return To Leather Lair / 1993 / STM / B • S&M Latex: The Bitch / 1995 / SBP / B • Sam Shaft's Anal Thrusts #3 / 1993 / RTP / M • School For Wayward Wives / 1993 / BIZ / B • Semper Bi / 1994 / PEP / G • She's My Cherry Pie / 1992 / V99 / M • Shockers / 1996 / SBP / B • Slave Training (Vid Tech) / 1994 / VTF / B • Slipping It In / 1992 / FD / M • Sole Survivors / 1996 / PRE / C • Spank & Spank Again / 1995 / BON / B • Spanking Tails / 1993 / BON / B • Stolen Fantasies / 1995 / LON / B • Student Fetish Videos: Catfighting #03 / 1991 / PRE / B • Student Fetish Videos: Catfighting #04 / 1992 / PRE / B • Student Fetish Videos: The Enema #07 / 1992 / PRE / B • Student Fetish Videos: Tickling #04 / 1992 / SFV / B • Sweet Things / 1992 / VEX / M • Swing Rave / 1993 / EVN / M • The Tickle Shack / 1995 / SBP / B • Tied & Tickled Classics #12 / 1996 / CS / C • Toe Hold / 1992 / PRE / B • Too Fast For Love / 1992 / IF / M • Ultimate Orgy #3 / 1992 / GLI / M • Uncle Roy's Amateur Home Video #01 / 1992 / VIM / M • Uncle Roy's Amateur Home Video #03 / 1992 / VIM / M • Uncle Roy's Amateur Home Video #05 / 1992 / VIM / M • Uncle Roy's Amateur Home Video #07 / 1992 / VIM / M • Uncle Roy's Best Of The Best: Brazen Brunettes / 1993 / VIM / C • Uncle Roy's Best Of The Best: Cornhole Classics / 1992 / VIM / C • Under The Hood: Nina Hartley's Guide To Better Cunnilingus / 1994 / A&E / M • Underground #3: Sit On This / 1996 / SC / M • Voyeurism #1 / 1993 / FH / M • Winner Takes All / 1995 / LON / B • You Said A Mouthful / 1992 / IF / M • Your Cheatin' Butt / 1996 / BON / B

ANGELA FOUROSTIE *see Star Index I*

ANGELA HAZE *(Erica Strauss)*

Quite pretty slim girl with small tits and afro-type curly light brown hair.

Baby Face #1 / 1977 / VC / M • Baby Love & Beau / 1979 / TVX / M • The Best Of Alex De Renzy #1 / 1983 / VC / C • Do You Wanna Be Loved? / 1977 / AR / M • Little Orphan Dusty #2 / 1981 / VIS / M • Mary! Mary! / 1977 / SE / M • Please, Please Me / 1976 / AR / M • The Spirit Of Seventy Six / 1976 / NGV / M • Student Bodies / 1975 / VC / M

ANGELA JONES

As Nature Intended / 1958 / SOW / S • Blue Vanities #532 / 1993 / FFL / M

ANGELA LEAH

Girls Of The Double D #14 / 1990 / CIN / M • Giving It To Barbii / 1990 / TOR / M • International Phone Sex Girls #5 / 1991 / PM / M • Phone Sex Girls #5 / 1990 / TOR / M • Stunt Woman / 1990 / LIP / F • Titillation #2 / 1990 / SE / M

ANGELA MARTIN

Treasure Chest / 1985 / GO / M

ANGELA O'DAY *see Star Index I*

ANGELA PARKER

B*A*S*H / 1989 / BIZ / C • The Conquest / 1988 / NAP / B • Ebony Boxes / 1988 / NAP / B • Gent Video Covergirls #1: Angela Parker / 1996 / ... / F • Maid To Fight /

1988 / NAP / B • Pool Frolic / 1988 / NAP / B • Return Match / 1988 / NAP / B • Sole Kisses / 1987 / BIZ / S • Tooth And Nail / 1988 / NAP / B

ANGELA PRIMA *see Star Index I*

ANGELA SAVAGE
Many Faces Of Shannon / 1988 / VC / C

ANGELA SCHENK *see Star Index I*

ANGELA STEIGER *see Star Index I*

ANGELA SUMMERS *(Stella Blue)*
Blonde with large inflated tits and a big butt. Originally from CA; 36-24-36; 5'3" tall; first movie was **Wild Goose Chase**.
Adult Video News 1992 Awards / 1992 / VC / M • The Adventures Of Seymore Butts / 1992 / FH / M • Amateur American Style #23 / 1992 / AR / M • Amateur Lesbians #11: Rusty / 1991 / GO / F • America's Dirtiest Home Videos #01 / 1991 / VEX / M • America's Dirtiest Home Videos #08 / 1992 / VEX / M • Anal Illusions / 1991 / LV / M • Angels / 1992 / VC / M • As Bad As She Wants To Be / 1992 / IF / M • B&D Sorority / 1991 / BON / B • Back Seat Bush / 1992 / LV / M • Bazooka County #4 / 1992 / CC / M • Behind The Scenes: The Making Of The Wil & Ed Movies / 1992 / MID / M • Bend Over Babes #2 / 1991 / EA / M • Bend Over Babes #3 / 1992 / EA / M • Best Of Buttman #1 / 1991 / EA / C • Best Of Buttman #2 / 1993 / EA / C • Best Of Edward Penishands / 1993 / VT / C • Big Titted Tarts / 1994 / PL / C • Black On White / 1991 / VT / F • Blonde Riders / 1991 / CC / M • Blue Angel / 1991 / SE / M • Book Of Love / 1992 / VC / M • Breast Worx #18 / 1992 / LBO / M • Bruce Seven's Favorite Endings #1 / 1991 / EL / C • Butt Freak #1 / 1992 / EA / M • Buttman Goes To Rio #2 / 1991 / EA / M • Buttman's Inferno / 1993 / EA / M • Call Girl / 1991 / AFV / M • Candy Factory / 1994 / PE / M • Cat Lickers #1 / 1990 / ME / F • Clean And Dirty / 1990 / ME / M • Cyrano / 1991 / PL / M • Dances With Foxes / 1991 / CC / M • Deep Inside Centerfold Girls / 1991 / VC / M • Dirty Business / 1992 / CV / M • Dirty Looks / 1994 / VI / M • Dirty Tricks / 1993 / CC / M • Edward Penishands #2 / 1991 / VT / M • Eleventh Annual AVN Awards / 1994 / VC / M • Erotic Angel / 1994 / ERA / M • Female Persuasion / 1990 / SO / F • First Time Ever #1 / 1995 / PE / F • Forbidden Desires / 1991 / CIN / F • Girls Gone Bad #3: Back To The Slammer / 1991 / GO / F • Girls Gone Bad #5: Mexican Justice / 1991 / GO / F • Gorgeous / 1990 / CA / M • A Handful Of Summers / 1991 / ME / M • Heatwave #1 / 1992 / FH / F • Her Obsession / 1991 / MID / M • In The Can With Oj / 1994 / HCV / M • In The Jeans Again / 1990 / ME / M • Just For The Hell Of It / 1991 / CA / M • Laying The Ghost / 1991 / VC / M • Lesbians In Tight Shorts / 1992 / LV / F • A Little Christmas Tail / 1991 / ZA / M • Lust For Love / 1991 / VC / M • Made In Heaven / 1991 / PP / M • Malibu Spice / 1991 / VC / M • The Mark Of Zara / 1990 / XCI / M • Meat Market / 1992 / SEX / C • Miss 21st Century / 1991 / ZA / M • More Dirty Debutantes #05 / 1990 / 4P / M • Nasty Jack's Homemade Vid. #09 / 1991 / CDI / M • Next Door Neighbors #39 / 1992 / BON / M • Next Door Neighbors #40 / 1992 / BON / M • Night Cap / 1990 / EX / M • No Tell Motel / 1990 / ZA / M • Obses-sion / 1991 / CDI / M • The Only Game In Town / 1991 / VC / M • The Penetrator #1 / 1991 / PL / M • Personalities / 1991 / PL / M • Puttin' Her Ass On The Line / 1991 / DR / M • Queen Of Hearts #3: Heartless / 1992 / PL / M • Radical Affairs Video Magazine #05 / 1993 / ME / M • Radical Affairs Video Magazine #08 / 1994 / ME / M • Rocket Girls / 1993 / VC / M • Safecracker / 1991 / CC / M • Sex Scenes / 1992 / VD / C • The Sex Symbol / 1991 / GO / M • Sexual Olympics #1: The Trials / 1992 / VT / M • Shot From Behind / 1992 / FAZ / M • Sloppy Seconds / 1994 / PE / M • Snatched To The Future / 1991 / EL / F • Sorority Sex Kittens #1 / 1992 / VC / M • Sorority Sex Kittens #2 / 1993 / VC / M • Stripper Nurses / 1994 / PE / M • Summer's End / 1991 / ROB / M • Sun Bunnies #1 / 1991 / SC / M • Take My Wife, Please / 1993 / WP / M • Talk Dirty To Me #08 / 1990 / DR / M • A Taste Of K.C. Williams / 1992 / VD / C • Titty Slickers #1 / 1991 / LE / M • Tori Welles Goes Behind The Scenes / 1992 / FD / M • Twice As Hard / 1992 / IF / M • Wenches / 1991 / VT / F • Where The Girls Play / 1992 / CC / F • Wild Goose Chase / 1990 / EA / M • Will And Ed's Bogus Gang Bang / 1992 / MID / M • Wire Desire / 1991 / XCI / M • X-Rated Blondes / 1992 / VD / C

ANGELA TUFFS
The Analyst / 1975 / ALP / M

ANGELA VERDI
Impulse #06: / 1996 / MBP / M

ANGELA WELLS
Rise And Fall Of Sparkle / 19?? / BL / M

ANGELA WHORENEY
Adventures Of The DP Boys: Sicilian Sluts / 1995 / HW / M • Butt Hunt #11 / 1995 / LEI / M • Hard Core Beginners #01 / 1995 / LEI / M • Hard Core Beginners #06 / 1995 / LEI / M • Jug Humpers / 1995 / V99 / C • Nasty Nymphos #08 / 1995 / ANA / M • Pussy Hunt #15 / 1995 / LEI / M • The Ultimate Pleasure / 1995 / LEI / M

ANGELA WILDER *see Star Index I*

ANGELIA PRINCE *see Star Index I*

ANGELICA
Angel In Bondage / 1983 / CA / B • Aqua Brats / 1996 / NAP / B • Asian Connection Video #098 / 1996 / AC0 / B • Back Down / 1996 / RB / B • Bend Over Brazilian Babes #1 / 1993 / EA / M • Big Busted Goddesses Of Beverly Hills / 1996 / NAP / S • Broadway Fannie Rose / 1986 / CA / M • Dick & Jane Do The Strip / 1994 / AVI / M • Dirty Doc's Housecalls #05 / 1993 / LV / M • Little Orphan Dusty #2 / 1981 / VIS / M • Nutts About Butts / 1994 / LE / M • Private Film #16 / 1994 / OD / M • Seven Year Bitch / 1996 / ALI / M • Sodomania #17: Simply Makes U Tingle / 1996 / EL / M • Triple X Video Magazine #15 / 1996 / OD / M

ANGELICA (L. ARMANI) *see Louise Armani*

ANGELICA (T. MINX) *see Tiffany Minx*

ANGELICA (V. GOLD) *see Victoria Gold*

ANGELICA BELLA *(Gabriella Dari)*
Very pretty Italian girl with dark hair, large droopy tits, and a tight waist. Looks a little like Laura Antonelli in her prime.
The Anal-Europe Series #01: The Fisherman's Wife / 1992 / LV / M • The Anal-Europe Series #02: Fantasies / 1992 / LV / M

• Angel's Vengeance / 1995 / VMX / M • Kinky Villa / 1995 / PL / M • Screamers / 1994 / HW / M • [Eccitazione Fatale / cr93 / ... / M • [European Invasion / cr93 / A&E / M • [Oscenita Selvaggia / cr93 / ... / M

ANGELICA BENDER
Sexual Customs In Scandinavia / cr73 / QX / M

ANGELICA DUNLAP *see Angela Dunlap*

ANGELICA DUNLUP *see Angela Dunlap*

ANGELICA FOX *see Anjelica Fox*

ANGELICA MIRAI
Private Gold #11: The Pyramid #1 / 1996 / OD / M • Private Gold #12: The Pyramid #2 / 1996 / OD / M • Private Gold #13: The Pyramid #3 / 1996 / OD / M

ANGELICA RAIN *(Anjelica Rain, Teri Lynn (A. Rain))*
Brunette/dark blonde, tall (same height as Tom Byron), medium inflated tits, very tight waist, nice boy-like butt, dark tan with bikini bottom tan lines, light blue/blue grey eyes, mole on left buttock, reasonably pretty but not adorable. Was 21 years old in 1993.
Day Dreams / 1993 / CV / M • Pouring It On / 1993 / CV / M • Southern: Anjelica's Dance & Lingerie / 1994 / SSH / F • Southern: Anjelica's Photo Session / 1994 / SSH / F • Too Hot To Touch #2 / 1993 / CV / M

ANGELICA TOMLINSON *see Star Index I*

ANGELIKA
Buttwoman Back In Budapest / 1993 / EL / M • Drop Sex: Wipe The Floor / 1997 / JLP / M

ANGELINA
Up And Cummers #33 / 1996 / 4P / M • Up And Cummers #34 / 1996 / 4P / M

ANGELINA CLETA *see Star Index I*

ANGELINA FLORES
Angel Buns / 1981 / QX / M

ANGELINA REY
Ancient Amateurs #2 / 1996 / LOF / M

ANGELINA ROMERO
Angel Buns / 1981 / QX / M

ANGELINE
Blue Vanities #553 / 1994 / FFL / M • Little Big Girls / 1996 / VC / M

ANGELINE APRINE *see Star Index I*

ANGELIQUE
Amsterdam Nights #2 / 1996 / VC / M • Black Mystique #02 / 1993 / VT / F • Black Silk Stockings / 1978 / SE / C • Blue Vanities #526 / 1993 / FFL / M • Bondage Cheerleaders / 1993 / LON / B • Busty Brittany Takes London / 1996 / H&S / M • Casting Call #10 / 1994 / MET / M • Cherry Poppers #08: Tender And Tight / 1994 / ZA / M • Cherry Poppers #09: Misbehavin' / 1995 / ZA / M • French Open / 1993 / PV / M • French Open Part Deux / 1993 / MET / M • Girls Around The World #29 / 1995 / BTO / M • Gode-Party / 1994 / RUM / M • Jamie's French Debutantes / 1992 / PL / B • Magma: Sperma / 1994 / MET / M • N.Y. Video Magazine #07 / 1996 / OUP / M • On The Prowl In Paris / 1992 / SC / M • Pumping Up With Angelique / 1995 / H&S / S • The Royal Court Collection / 1993 / VER / S • Streets Of New York #07 / 1996 / PL / M • Tania's Lustexzesse / 1994 / MET / M • Thunder Boobs / 1995 / BTO / M • The Touch Of Her Flesh / 1967 / SOW / S • World Sex Tour #2 / 1995 / ANA / M • [Tape Busters #4 / 19?? / ... / M

ANGELIQUE (BLACK)
Black Cheerleader Search #05 / 1996 / IVC / M • Black Cream Queens / 1996 / APP / F

ANGELIQUE (T. WYNN) see Tracey Wynn

ANGELIQUE BROWN see Star Index I

ANGELIQUE DEMOLINE
The Stewardesses / 1969 / SOW / S • The Stewardesses / 1981 / CA / M

ANGELIQUE DUNLAP see Angela Dunlap

ANGELIQUE NOVOU
Samurai She-Males / 1994 / HSV / G • The She-Male Who Stole Christmas / 1993 / HSV / G • Trannie Love / 1995 / HSV / G • Transsexual Try Outs / 1993 / HSV / G

ANGELIQUE PETTIJOHN *(Heaven St John, Angelique Pettyjohn)*
Heaven St John: **Titillation**. Huge boobed not too pretty girl. Died Feb 28, 1992 from cancer in Las Vegas.
Biohazard / 1984 / MNT / S • Body Talk / 1982 / VCX / M • Childish Things / 1969 / ... / S • Clambake / 1967 / MGM / S • The Curious Female / 1969 / SOW / S • Famous Ta-Ta's #1 / 1986 / VCS / C • G.I. Executioner / 1971 / VES / S • Heaven With A Gun / 1969 / MGM / S • Hell's Belles / 1968 / ... / S • The Lost Empire / 1983 / LIV / S • The Mad Doctor Of Blood Island / 1968 / ... / S • Mother / 1970 / ... / S • Repo Man / 1983 / MCA / S • Stalag 69 / 1982 / VHL / S • Takin' It Off / 1984 / VES / S • Titillation #1 / 1982 / SE / M • The Wizard Of Speed And Time / 1988 / WTV / S • [Just Tell Me That You Love Me, Junie Moon / 1970 / ... / S

ANGELIQUE PETTYJOHN see Angelique Pettijohn

ANGELIQUE RICARD
Nasty Habits Are Hard To Break / 1986 / 4P / M • The National Transsexual / 1990 / GO / G • The Sex Change Girls / 1987 / 4P / G • She Studs #02 / 1991 / BIZ / G • Taking It To The Streets / 1987 / CDI / M • Trisexual Encounters #01 / 1985 / PL / G • Trisexual Encounters #02 / 1985 / PL / G • Viva Vanessa The Undresser / 1984 / VC / M

ANGELLA
Collected Spankings #1 / 1992 / BON / C • Collected Spankings #2 / 1992 / BON / C

ANGELO
Blow Bi Blow / 1988 / MET / G • Erotic Dimensions: Explicit / 1982 / NSV / M • Erotic Dimensions: The Wild Life / 1982 / NSV / M • Nightclub / 1996 / SC / M

ANGELO (STASHA) see Stasha

ANGELO MATHIO
Score Of Sex / 1995 / BAC / G

ANGELO RIVERA
Deep Passage / 1984 / VCR / C

ANGIE
Anal Dynomite / 1995 / ROB / M • Anal Senorita #2 / 1995 / ROB / M • Analtown USA #08 / 1995 / NIT / M • Angie, Trish, Linda, Samantha / 1990 / PLV / B • Blue Vanities #520 / 1993 / FFL / M • Blue Vanities #545 / 1994 / FFL / M • Blue Vanities #577 / 1995 / FFL / M • California Girl: Amateur Nude Auditions / 1995 / PME / S • Cum Buttered Corn Holes #1 / 1996 / NIT / C • Eurotica #10 / 1996 / XC / M • Girls Of The Ivy League / 1994 / NIV / F • Hot Legs #1 / 1990 / PLV / B • Wet Mask / 1995 / SC

/ M

ANGIE CARAT
Sperm Injection / 1995 / PL / M

ANGIE DEE see Star Index I

ANGIE DEMAZO see Star Index I

ANGIE DICKENS
The Girls In The Band / 1976 / SVE / M

ANGIE DICKS
The Devil's Playground / 1974 / VC / M

ANGIE FERREIRA see Star Index I

ANGIE LAI
She-Male Encounters #10: She-Male Vacation / 1986 / MET / G

ANGIE MARTSONI see Star Index I

ANGIE MEYERS see Star Index I

ANGIE SANTINI
Finger Pleasures #2 / 1995 / PL / F

ANGIE VAN
Tales Of A High Class Hooker / 19?? / VXP / M

ANGLE CINSALO see Star Index I

ANGUS MACDUIHNE
Conquest / 1996 / WP / M

ANGUS MIRAMBA see Star Index I

ANIA
Triple X Video Magazine #02 / 1995 / OD / M

ANICA
More Dirty Debutantes #63 / 1997 / SBV / M

ANIKA KARNAL
Diamonds / 1996 / HDE / M

ANIKO KAPOS
Lil' Women: Vacation / 1996 / EUR / M

ANIKO SPREAD
Private Gold #01: Study In Sex / 1995 / OD / M • Private Gold #02: Friends In Sex / 1995 / OD / M

ANIKU
Fazano's Student Bodies / 1995 / EL / M • Sluts 'n' Angels In Budapest / 1994 / EL / M • Sodomania #11: In Your Face / 1994 / EL / M • Sodomania: Slop Shots / 1996 / EL / C

ANIMAL see Star Index I

ANINE
Private Gold #14: Sweet Lady #1 / 1997 / OD / M

ANISA *(Naomi Wang, Kimi Lee)*
Oriental, from the Phillipines. Aged 19 in 1991. Appeared in **More Dirty Debutantes #12** under the name Naomi Wang. Boyfriend is in the army. Very pretty but had bands on her teeth in **MDD #12**.
The A Chronicles / 1992 / CC / M • America's Raunchiest Home Videos #24: Suck My Thumb / 1992 / ZA / M • Anal Adventures #2: Bodacious Buns / 1991 / VC / M • Anal Cuties #1 / 1992 / ROB / M • Anal Delights #2 / 1992 / ROB / M • Anal Fury / 1992 / ROB / M • Anal Leap / 1991 / ZA / M • Anal Lover #2 / 1993 / ROB / M • Anal Rampage #1 / 1992 / ROB / M • Anal Savage #1 / 1992 / ROB / M • Anal Siege / 1993 / ROB / M • Anal Sluts & Sweethearts #1 / 1992 / ROB / M • Anal Thrills / 1992 / ROB / M • Anal Thunder #1 / 1993 / ROB / M • Anal With An Oriental Slant / 1993 / ROB / M • Asian Heat #01: Cherry Blossom Tales / 1993 / SC / M • Asian Heat #03: Tales Of The Golden Lotus / 1993 / SC / M • Asian Silk / 1992 / VI / M • Best Gang Bangs / 1996 / DFI / C • The Best Of Oriental Anal #1 / 1994 / ROB / C • Bubble Butts #03 / 1992 / LBO / M • Bunz-Eye / 1992 / ROB / M • Deep Inside Dirty Debu-

tantes #10 / 1993 / 4P / M • Defenseless / 1992 / CDI / M • Dial A Nurse / 1992 / VD / M • Disoriented / 1992 / VI / M • Dr Butts #2 / 1992 / 4P / M • The Final Secret / 1992 / SO / M • Fortune Cookie / 1992 / VI / M • Gang Bang Fury #1 / 1992 / ROB / M • Gang Bang Pussycat / 1992 / ROB / M • La Princesa Anal / 1993 / ROB / M • Lovin' Spoonfuls #3 / 1995 / 4P / C • Lovin' Spoonfuls #4 / 1995 / 4P / C • Lovin' Spoonfuls #8 / 1996 / 4P / C • Madam X / 1992 / HO / M • Mind Games / 1992 / CDI / M • Moist To The Touch / 1991 / DR / M • More Dirty Debutantes #12 / 1991 / 4P / M • More Dirty Debutantes #27 / 1993 / 4P / M • More Dirty Debutantes #37 / 1995 / 4P / M • Mr. Peepers Amateur Home Videos #24: The Sleazy Riders / 1991 / LBO / M • Neighborhood Watch #12 / 1991 / LBO / M • New Ends #01 / 1993 / 4P / M • New Ends #02 / 1993 / 4P / M • New Ends #03 / 1993 / 4P / M • New Ends #04 / 1993 / 4P / M • New Ends #05 / 1993 / 4P / M • New Ends #06 / 1994 / 4P / M • New Ends #07 / 1994 / 4P / M • New Ends #08 / 1994 / 4P / M • New Ends #09 / 1994 / 4P / M • New Ends #10 / 1995 / 4P / M • Odyssey Amateur #60: Hawaiian Paradise / 1991 / OD / M • Odyssey Amateur #73: Lori's Oral Luau / 1991 / OD / M • Ready, Willing & Anal (Cv) / 1993 / CV / C • Reel Sex #05: Lesbian Toy Part / 1994 / SPP / F • The Secret Garden #1 / 1992 / XCI / M • Seoul Train / 1991 / IN / M • Sin City: The Movie / 1992 / SC / M • The Strip / 1992 / SC / M • Sweet Dreams / 1991 / VC / M • Tailspin #3 / 1992 / VT / M • Up And Cummers: The Movie / 1994 / 4P / M • Up For Grabs / 1991 / FH / M

ANISA BLUE
Knocked-Up Nymphos #1 / 1996 / GLI / M • Pussy Hunt #07 / 1994 / LEI / M

ANISSA
Forbidden Fantasies #3 / 1995 / ZA / M • Hollywood Amateurs #13 / 1994 / MID / M • Hollywood Amateurs #14 / 1995 / MID / M • Interstate 95 Amateurs #1 / 1995 / RHV / M • Nasty Newcummers #07 / 1995 / MET / M

ANITA
Blue Vanities #527 / 1993 / FFL / M • Blue Vanities #554 / 1994 / FFL / M • Dildo Bitches / 1995 / LAF / F • Drop Out / 1972 / ... / S • Girls Around The World #05 / 1992 / BTO / S • Homegrown Video #245 / 1990 / HOV / M • Homegrown Video #357 / 1991 / HOV / M • Magma: Anita #2 / 1996 / MET / M • Magma: Bizarre Games / 1996 / MET / M • Mammary Manor / 1992 / BTO / M • Plastic Workshop / 1995 / LAF / M • Private Stories #06 / 1995 / OD / M • Sey-Mar Butts: My Travels With The Tramp / 1994 / FH / M • Tit To Tit #1 / 1994 / BTO / M

ANITA ANDERSON see Anita Ericsson

ANITA BERENSON see Star Index I

ANITA BLONDE *(Anita Kelly)*
Medium slightly droopy tits, short blonde hair, OK body and a passable face.
Anal Palace / 1995 / VC / M • Anita / 1996 / BLC / M • Big Babies In Budapest / 1996 / EL / M • Dirty Stories #4 / 1995 / PE / M • Paris Chic / 1996 / SAE / M • Passion In Venice / 1995 / ULI / M • Private Film #24 / 1995 / OD / M • Private Film #25 / 1995 / OD / M • Private Film #26 / 1995 / OD / M •

Private Stories #02 / 1995 / OD / M • Private Video Magazine #18 / 1994 / OD / M • Profiles #10: / 1997 / XPR / M • Rock 'n' Roll Rocco / 1997 / EA / M • Sodomania #17: Simply Makes U Tingle / 1996 / EL / M • Sodomania #20: For Members Only / 1997 / EL / M • Triple X Video Magazine #01 / 1995 / OD / M • Triple X Video Magazine #02 / 1995 / OD / M • The Voyeur #8: Live In Europe #2 / 1996 / JLP / M • World Sex Tour #1 / 1995 / ANA / M

ANITA CHRIS *see* **Anita Ericsson**

ANITA COLLYER
Blue Vanities #581 / 1996 / FFL / M

ANITA COSTO *see Star Index I*

ANITA CREST *see* **Vicky Lindsay**

ANITA DARK
Hotel Fear / 1996 / ONA / M • Private Stories #09 / 1996 / OD / M • Profiles #10: / 1997 / XPR / M • Rock 'n' Roll Rocco / 1997 / EA / M • Sodomania #20: For Members Only / 1997 / EL / M • The Voyeur #8: Live In Europe #2 / 1996 / JLP / M • World Sex Tour #6 / 1996 / ANA / M

ANITA ERICSSON *(Anita Anderson, Anita Chris)*
Blue Vanities #514 / 1992 / FFL / M • Erotic Fantasies #1 / 1983 / CV / C • Practice Makes Perfect / 1975 / QX / M • [Hungry Young Women / 1977 / ALP / M • [Laura's Toys / 1975 / ... / S • [Molly / 1977 / ... / S

ANITA F.
Euro Extremities #17 / 199? / SVE / C • Euro Extremities #28 / 199? / SVE / C • Euro Extremities #29 / 199? / SVE / C • Euro Extremities #42 / 199? / SVE / C

ANITA KELLY *see* **Anita Blonde**

ANITA MAUN *see Star Index I*

ANITA RANIERI *see* **Anita Rinaldi**

ANITA RINALDI *(Anita Ranieri)*
Blonde with medium to large tits. Anabolic Import #03: Oral X / 1994 / ANA / M • Betty Bleu / 1996 / IP / M • Erotic Rondo / 1996 / IP / M • The Last Train #1 / 1995 / BHE / M • The Last Train #2 / 1995 / BHE / M • The Last Vamp / 1996 / IP / M • Midnight Obsession / 1995 / XC / M • Miss Liberty / 1996 / IP / M • Paradise Villa / 1995 / WIV / M • A Private Love Affair / 1996 / IP / M • True Stories #1 / 1993 / SC / M • True Stories #2 / 1993 / SC / M

ANITA ROSE
Sore Throat / 1985 / GO / M

ANITA SANDS *see Star Index I*

ANITA SIMONE
Bound And Gagged #02 / 1991 / RB / B • The Doctor's Remedy / 1992 / RB / B • Punished Cheeks / 1992 / RB / B • Shaved #04 / 1992 / RB / F

ANITA THRILL
Finger Pleasures #2 / 1995 / PL / F • San Francisco Lesbians #3 / 1993 / PL / F • San Francisco Lesbians #4 / 1993 / PL / F

ANITA TYMES *see Star Index I*

ANJA *see* **Axinia**

ANJA SCHREINER *see* **Tanya DeVries**

ANJELA JAMES *see Star Index I*

ANJELICA FOX *(Angelica Fox)*
Not too pretty humongous titted Irish girl. Tits were natural in **Buttman's Moderately Big Tit Adventure** and enhanced in later movies. 26 years old in 1994, 42DD-24-34, 108lbs.
All Amateur Perfect 10's / 1995 / LEI / M • Anal Innocence #3 / 1994 / ROB / M • Ass

Busters Incorporated / 1996 / BLC / M • Booty Queen / 1995 / ROB / M • Buttman's British Moderately Big Tit Adventure / 1994 / EA / M • Full Moon Fever / 1994 / LBO / M • Heavenly / 1995 / IF / M • Hot Tight Asses #09 / 1994 / TCK / M • Snatch Masters #03 / 1994 / LEI / M • Sodomania: Slop Shots / 1996 / EL / C • The Theory Of Relativity / 1994 / EL / M • Video Virgins #19 / 1994 / NS / M

ANJELICA RAIN *see* **Angelica Rain**

ANKA-BEATRICE PREDA
True Stories #1 / 1993 / SC / M • True Stories #2 / 1993 / SC / M

ANN
Anabolic Import #07: Anal X / 1995 / ANA / M • Ash Prod: We Aim To Tease / 1995 / ASH / M • Girls Around The World #11 / 199? / BTO / S • Hollywood Amateurs #13 / 1994 / MID / M • Lesbian Pros And Amateurs #09 / 1992 / GO / F • Lesbian Pros And Amateurs #10 / 1992 / GO / F

ANN BANKS *see* **Tempest Storm**

ANN BARDOT *see Star Index I*

ANN BRADY *see Star Index I*

ANN BROWN *see Star Index I*

ANN CARTER *see Star Index I*

ANN D. PIERCE
The Bizarre World Of F.J. Lincoln / 19?? / VHL / C • Carnal Olympics / 1983 / CA / M • I Liko To Watch / 1982 / CA / M • Kinky Couples / 1980 / BIZ / B • A Lady At Last / cr80 / BIZ / G • Man To Maiden / 1984 / BIZ / B • Talk Dirty To Me #02 / 1982 / CA / M

ANN DEVIN
Bucky Beaver's XXX Dragon Art Theatre Double Feature #15 / 1996 / SOW / M • Left At The Altar / 1974 / SOW / M

ANN DICKERSON *see* **Blake Mitchell**

ANN DROJENY
Bad She-Males / 1994 / HSV / G • Cocks In Frocks #1 / 1996 / TTV / G • Cocks In Frocks #2 / 1996 / TTV / G • Come Back Little She-Male / 1994 / HSV / G • Dungeons & Drag Queens / 1994 / HSV / G • Gentlemen Prefer She-Males / 1995 / CDI / G • He-She Haw / 1996 / HSV / G • Las Vegas She-Males / 1995 / BCP / G • Primal She-Male / 1996 / HSV / G • She Male Dicktation / 1994 / HEA / G • She Male Jail / 1994 / HSV / G • Trannie Angel / 1995 / HSV / G • Trannie Get Your Gun / 1994 / HSV / G • Tranny Hill: Sweet Surrender / 1994 / HSV / G • Transsexual Prostitutes #1 / 1996 / DFI / G

ANN HESS *see Star Index I*

ANN HOOVER *see Star Index I*

ANN K.
Blue Vanities #509 / 1992 / FFL / M

ANN KLEIN
The Untamed Vixens / 1976 / VHL / M

ANN LOGAN *see Star Index I*

ANN MARSHALL
The Love Witch / 1973 / AR / M

ANN MILLER
Blue Vanities #555 / 1994 / FFL / M

ANN PIERCE
Every Man's Fancy / 1983 / BIZ / B

ANN REESE
Blue Vanities #558 / 1994 / FFL / M

ANN RODGERS *see Star Index I*

ANN SAPP
Hot Property (AVC) / 1975 / AVC / M • Last Of The Wild / 1975 / CA / M • Tattooed Lady (AVC) / 19?? / BIZ / M

ANN ST JAMES
Bedtime Video #09 / 1984 / GO / M

ANN SYLMAR
Love Secrets / 1976 / VIP / M • Sweet Folds Of Flesh / 19?? / AST / M

ANN TAUSSIE *see Star Index I*

ANN WALKER
Blue Vanities #581 / 1996 / FFL / M • Hollywood Hot Tubs / 1984 / VES / S

ANN WHITING *see Star Index I*

ANN WOODS *see Star Index I*

ANN YOUNG
The Altar Of Lust / 1971 / SOW / S • Creme De La Face #18: Cum Mops / 1997 / OD / M

ANNA
Bend Over Brazilian Babes #1 / 1993 / EA / M • Black Street Hookers #2 / 1996 / DFI / M • Blue Vanities #578 / 1995 / FFL / M • Homegrown Video #418: Looks As Good As It Feels / 1994 / HOV / M • Lollipop Shoppe #2 / 1996 / SC / M • Magma: Puszta Teenies / 1995 / MET / M • More Dirty Debutantes #16 / 1992 / 4P / M • Painless Steel #3 / 1996 / FLV / M • Prima #13: Dr. Max Back To Budapest / 1995 / MBP / M • Private Gold #12: The Pyramid #2 / 1996 / OD / M • Private Gold #14: Sweet Lady #1 / 1997 / OD / M • Private Video Magazine #01 / 1993 / OD / M • Ready To Drop #07 / 1995 / FC / M • Southern Belles #5 / 1995 / XPR / M • Tit To Tit #3 / 1995 / BTO / M

ANNA AMORE *(Stormy Weathers (AA))*
Black with coffee colored skin (looks like a dark version of Lovette) 27 years old in 1995 and de-virginized at 17. 38DD-24-36 and comes from Michigan.
Anal Anarchy / 1995 / VC / M • Anna Amore At Mi-Sex / 1996 / ... / S • Anna Amore's Fantasy Gang Bang / 1996 / FC / M • Big Knockers #16 / 1995 / TV / M • Big Knockers #18 / 1995 / TV / M • Big Knockers #19 / 1995 / TV / M • Big Knockers #21: Best Of Lesbian #2 / 1995 / TV / C • Bite The Black Bullets / 1995 / ME / M • Black & Blue / 1995 / NAP / B • Black Centerfolds #1 / 1996 / DR / M • Black Centerfolds #2 / 1996 / DR / M • Black Knockers #01 / 1995 / TV / M • Black Knockers #10 / 1995 / TV / M • Black Leather / Black Skin / 1995 / VT / B • Black Mamas At War / 1996 / NAP / B • Black Mystique #14 / 1995 / VT / F • Black Power / 1996 / LEI / C • Black Pussyman Auditions #1 / 1996 / SNA / M • Black Snatch Fever / 1995 / ME / M • Blacks N' Blue / 1995 / VT / B • Camp Fire Tramps / 1995 / LOT / M • The Case Of The Black Booty / 1996 / LV / M • Cat Lickers #3 / 1995 / ME / F • Dark Desires (Factory-1995) / 1995 / FH / M • Different Strokes / 1996 / VC / M • Doin' The Nasty / 1996 / AVI / M • Every Nerd Has A Fantasy / 1996 / FC / M • Fashion sluts #5: Ethnic Ecstasy / 1995 / ABS / M • Foot Masters / 1995 / PRE / B • Ganggstas Paradise / 1995 / AVI / M • Home Runs / 1995 / PRE / C • Interracial Escorts / 1995 / GO / M • The Kiss / 1995 / WP / M • The Magnificence Of Minka / 1996 / NAP / S • Miss Judge / 1997 / VI / M • My Baby Got Back #05 / 1995 / VT / M • New Pussy Hunt #16 / 1995 / LEI / M • The New Snatch Masters #15 / 1995 / LEI / C • The Return Of Dr Blacklove / 1996 / CC / M • Rumpman In And Out Of Africa / 1996 / HW / M • Sista!

#5 / 1996 / VT / F • So Bad / 1995 / VT / M • Tailz From Da Hood #1 / 1995 / AVI / M • Toot Z Roll / 1995 / WP / M • Video Virgins #25 / 1995 / NS / M • Waiting To XXX-Hale / 1996 / MET / M • Wrestling Queens / 1996 / NAP / B

ANNA BELMAN
Tomboy / 1983 / VCX / M
ANNA CHOW LING *see Star Index I*
ANNA DAVIS *see* Crystal Sync
ANNA DJUKEVITCH *see* Star Index I
ANNA E. *see* Star Index I
ANNA GIANI *see Star Index I*
ANNA GODATPE
Immortal Desire / 1993 / VI / M
ANNA GUILLEMET *see Star Index I*
ANNA HARVEY
Ancient Secrets Of Sexual Ecstasy / 1996 / HIG / M
ANNA KAREYNA *see Star Index I*
ANNA LINGUS
Sleaze Please!—December Edition / 1994 / FH / M
ANNA LISA PEARSON
Talk Dirty To Me #02 / 1982 / CA / M
ANNA LIVIA PLURABELL *see Star Index I*
ANNA MALLE
Not too pretty Hispanic girl with rock hard large tits, de-virginized at 13. Curly black hair. A purple and green tattoo on her left tit and another on her belly at the pussy hair line. Married to (or SO of) Hank Armstrong.
A Is For Asia / 1996 / 4P / M • The Adventures Of Studman #2 / 1994 / AFV / M • Airotica / 1996 / SC / M • The Anal Adventures Of Max Hardcore: Full Throttle / 1994 / ZA / M • The Anal Adventures Of Suzy Super Slut #2 / 1994 / AFV / M • Anal Agony / 1994 / ZA / M • Anal Angels #6 / 1996 / VEX / C • Anal Dynomite / 1995 / ROB / M • Anal Freaks / 1994 / KWP / M • Anal Generation / 1995 / PE / M • Anal Maniacs #2 / 1994 / WP / M • Anal Plaything #2 / 1995 / ROB / M • Anal Senorita #2 / 1995 / ROB / M • Anal Torture / 1994 / ZA / M • Animal Instinct / 1996 / DTV / M • Anna Malle Exposed / 1996 / WV / M • Ashlyn Rising / 1995 / VI / M • Ann Mootoon (Leisure) #05 / 1995 / LEI / M • Assmania!! #1 / 1994 / ME / M • Babes Behind Bars / 1996 / CNP / F • Backing In #6 / 1994 / WV / C • Backing In #7 / 1995 / WV / C • The Backway Inn #5 / 1993 / FD / M • Bad Company / 1994 / VI / M • Battling Bitches #2 / 1995 / BIZ / B • Beauty's Punishment / 1996 / BIZ / B • Beauty's Revenge / 1996 / BIZ / B • The Big Stick-Up / 1994 / WV / M • Bizarre's Dracula #1 / 1995 / BIZ / B • Bizarre's Dracula #2 / 1995 / BIZ / B • Bloopers & Boners / 1996 / VI / M • Boob Acres / 1996 / HW / M • Breeders / 1996 / MET / M • Buffy's Anal Adventure / 1996 / CDI / M • Bunmasters / 1995 / VC / M • Butt Freak #2 / 1996 / EA / M • Butt Hunt #08 / 1995 / LEI / M • The Butt Sisters Do Denver / 1994 / MID / M • Butthead Dreams: Exposed / 1995 / FH / M • Buttman's Wet Dream / 1994 / EA / M • Casting Call #07 / 1994 / SO / M • The Cathouse / 1994 / VI / M • Caught In The Act (1995-Wave) / 1995 / WAV / M • Checkmate / 1995 / WAV / M • Chronicles Of Pain #1 / 1996 / BIZ / B • Club Erotica / 1996 / IN / M • Club Kiss / 1995 / ONA / M

• Compulsive Behavior / 1995 / PI / M • Corporate Affairs / 1996 / CC / M • Crazy Love / 1995 / VI / M • Cumback Pussy #3: Coast To Coast Rump Romp / 1996 / EL / M • Cunthunt / 1995 / AB / F • Cybersex / 1996 / WAV / M • Cynthia And The Pocket Rocket / 1995 / CV / M • Decadence / 1996 / VC / M • Deep Cheeks #5 / 1995 / ROB / M • Deep Throat Girls #11 / 1995 / GO / M • The Delegate / 1996 / RAS / M • Desert Moon / 1994 / SPI / M • Dirty Bob's #27: Laid Back In L.A.! / 1996 / FLP / S • Diva #1: Caught In The Act / 1996 / VC / F • Dominant Jean / 1996 / CC / M • Double D Amateurs #20 / 1994 / JMP / M • Dream House / 1995 / XPR / M • Dresden Diary #13: / 1995 / BIZ / B • Dresden Diary #14: Ecstasy In Hell / 1996 / BIZ / B • Dresden Diary #15: / 1996 / BIZ / B • Dresden Diary #16: / 1996 / BIZ / B • Encore / 1995 / VI / M • The Enema Bandit Strikes Again / 1995 / BIZ / B • Evil Temptations #2 / 1995 / ULP / M • Exposure / 1995 / WAV / M • Extreme Sex #4: The Experiment / 1995 / VI / M • Eye On You: Anna Meets The Rabbit / 1995 / EOY / F • Eye On You: Michelle Meets Anna Malle / 1995 / EOY / M • Fantasy Chamber / 1994 / ULI / M • Final Obsession / 1996 / LE / M • Finger Sluts #1 / 1996 / LV / F • First Time Lesbians #21 / 1994 / JMP / F • Frankenstein / 1994 / SC / M • Frontin' Da Booty / 1994 / WP / M • Gangbang Girl #14 / 1994 / ANA / M • Girls Of The Very Big Eight / 1994 / VT / M • Glory Days / 1996 / IN / M • The Gypsy Queen / 1996 / CC / M • Hard Feelings / 1995 / VI / M • Heavy Breathing / 1996 / NIT / M • Heidi's Girls / 1995 / GO / M • The Hitch-Hiker #05: Traffic Jam / 1994 / WMG / M • Hollywood Boulevard / 1995 / CV / M • Homegrown Video: Here Comes Anna Malle / 1994 / HOV / M • Hotel Sodom #01 / 1995 / SNA / M • Hotel Sodom #02 / 1995 / SNA / M • Hotel Sodom #07 / 1995 / SNA / M • Hotel Sodom #10 / 1996 / SNA / M • Independence Night / 1996 / SC / M • Jenna Loves Rocco / 1996 / WAV / M • Jizz Glazed Goo Guzzlers #1 / 1996 / NIT / C • Kissing Kaylani / 1997 / OD / M • Kym Wilde's On The Edge #39 / 1996 / RB / B • Latex And Lace / 1996 / BBE / M • Leather Bound Dykes From Hell #6 / 1995 / BIZ / B • Leather Bound Dykes From Hell #7 / 1996 / BIZ / B • Let's Play Doctor / 1994 / PV / M • Lost Angels / 1997 / WP / M • Lovin' Spoonfuls #3 / 1995 / 4P / C • Macin' #2: Macadocious / 1996 / SMP / M • The Many Faces Of P.J. Sparxx / 1996 / WP / M • Mask Of Innocence / 1996 / WP / B • Matawhore / 1996 / RAS / M • Max #01 / 1994 / FWE / M • Max Gold #1 / 1996 / XPR / C • More Dirty Debutantes #37 / 1995 / 4P / M • Naked Desert / 1995 / VI / M • Nasty Nymphos #05 / 1994 / ANA / M • Nasty Nymphos #09 / 1995 / ANA / M • Natural Born Thrillers / 1994 / LV / M • The New Butt Hunt #15 / 1995 / LEI / C • The New Butt Hunt #19 / 1996 / LEI / C • New Positions / 1994 / PV / M • Nina Hartley's Guide To Anal Sex / 1996 / A&E / M • Nina Hartley's Guide To Swinging / 1996 / A&E / M • Nina Hartley's Lifestyles Party / 1995 / FRM / M • No Man's Land #11 / 1995 / VT / F • On Her Back / 1994 / VI / M • Ona Zee's Doll House #3 / 1995 / ONA / F •

Open Lips / 1994 / WV / M • The Other Woman / 1996 / VC / M • Passion / 1996 / SC / M • Phantasm / 1995 / WP / M • Philmore Butts Las Vegas Vacation / 1995 / SUF / M • Photo Play / 1995 / VI / M • Private Stories #02 / 1995 / OD / M • Public Access / 1995 / VC / M • Pure Smut / 1996 / GO / M • Pussy Hunt #14 / 1995 / LEI / M • Pussyclips #07 / 1995 / SNA / M • Pussyman #09: Feeding Frenzy / 1995 / SNA / M • Razor's Edge / 1995 / ONA / M • The Secret Life Of Nina Hartley / 1994 / VC / M • Sex Academy #5: The Art Of Pulp Fiction / 1994 / ONA / M • Sex Trek #4: The Next Orgasm / 1994 / ME / M • Sexual Harassment / 1996 / TTV / M • Shane's World #5 / 1996 / OD / M • Shave Tails #1 / 1994 / SO / M • A Shot In The Pants / 1995 / HO / M • Simply Blue / 1995 / WAV / M • Six Degrees Of Penetration / 1996 / PP / M • Skin #6: The 6th Sense / 1996 / ERQ / M • Skin Dive / 1996 / SC / M • Southern Comfort #1 / 1995 / DWV / M • Southern Comfort #2 / 1995 / DWV / M • Spiked Heel Diaries #4 / 1995 / BIZ / B • Spiked Heel Diaries #5 / 1995 / BIZ / B • Starting Over / 1995 / WAV / M • Strap-On Sally #05: Chantilly's French Kiss / 1995 / PL / F • Strap-On Sally #06: Triple Penetration Trollop / 1995 / PL / F • Street Legal / 1995 / WAV / M • Streets Of New York #08 / 1996 / PL / M • Sweet As Honey / 1996 / NIT / M • Taboo #14: Kissing Cousins / 1995 / IN / M • Tail Taggers #125 / 1994 / WV / M • Takin' It To The Limit #4 / 1995 / BS / M • Thin Ice / 1996 / ONA / M • To Snatch A Thief / 1996 / BON / B • Twist Of Fate / 1996 / WP / M • Vice / 1994 / WAV / M • Video Virgins #14 / 1994 / NS / M • Waterworld: The Enema Movie / 1996 / BIZ / B • Wild Widow / 1996 / NIT / M • Wildcats / 1995 / WP / M • Witches Are Bitches / 1996 / NIT / M • XXX / 1996 / TEP / M

ANNA MARIA
Kisses From Romania / 1995 / NIT / M • Private Gold #12: The Pyramid #2 / 1996 / OD / M • Private Stories #07 / 1996 / OD / M • Private Stories #09 / 1996 / OD / M • World Sex Tour #3 / 1995 / ANA / M

ANNA MARCHE CAPICHIA *see* VANESSA del Rio

ANNA MARIE
So Deep, So Good / 1988 / NSV / M

ANNA MARIE TYLER
Black Bottom Girlz / 1994 / CA / M • Butthead Dreams / 1994 / FH / M • Butts Up / 1994 / CA / M • Mike Hott: #281 Cunt of the Month: Anna Marie / 1995 / MHV / M • Natural Born Dominants / 1995 / IBN / B • No Reservations / 1995 / MN0 / G • Perverted #1: The Babysitters / 1994 / ZA / M • Slave Quarters / 1995 / PRE / B • Student Fetish Videos: Best Of Foot Worship #03 / 1995 / PRE / C • Student Fetish Videos: The Enema #17 / 1995 / PRE / B • Student Fetish Videos: Foot Worship #14 / 1995 / PRE / B • Student Fetish Videos: Spanking #18 / 1995 / PRE / B • Tail Taggers #126 / 1994 / WV / M • Wasted / 1995 / PRE / B

ANNA MARJE
Joe Elliot's College Girls #29 / 1994 / JOE / M

ANNA MARLIE
Swinging Ski Girls / 1981 / VCX / M • Swinging Sorority / 1976 / VCX / S

ANNA MARTI
House Of Chicks: Masturbation Memoirs #2 / 1995 / HOC / F

ANNA MAY
Secret Desires / 1994 / ORE / C

ANNA MONROE
Sex On The Strip: The Lusty Ladies Of Las Vagas / 1993 / CPG / F

ANNA NICOLE
Very pretty black girl with lithe body, small tits, gap in front teeth, short straight black hair, narrow hips, nice butt, and tight waist. As of end-1996 she says she's 5'7" tall, 20 years old, was de-virginized at 19 and was currently going to college.
The Adventures Of Peeping Tom #4 / 1997 / OD / M • Black Cheerleader Search #07 / 1996 / IVC / M • Dreamgirls: Fort Lauderdale / 1996 / DR / M • Pick Up Lines #08 / 1996 / OD / M • Up And Cummers #39 / 1996 / RWP / M

ANNA NOELLE
Eric Kroll's Bondage #1 / 1994 / ERK / M • Eric Kroll's Fetish #2 / 1994 / ERK / M

ANNA OCH FREDRIK
Screamers / 1994 / HW / M

ANNA PIERCE see Linda Shaw

ANNA RIVA see Roberta Findlay

ANNA ROMERO
Zazel / 1996 / CV / M

ANNA ST JAMES
Bad Penny / 1978 / QX / M

ANNA TURNER see Star Index I

ANNA VALKO see Star Index I

ANNA VENTURA (Jasmine DuBay, Jasmine DuBois)
Brunette with passable face, medium to large tits, not a particularly tight body. 20 years old in 1981 and measured 38-23-36, 5'5" tall and 110lbs.
Bad Girls #1 / 1981 / GO / M • Best Of Richard Rank #2 / 1987 / GO / F • Big Bust Babes #02 / 1984 / AFI / M • Caballero Preview Tape #3 / 1984 / CA / C • Classic Erotica #9 / 1996 / SVE / M • Daddy's Little Girls / 1983 / CA / M • Devil In Miss Jones #2 / 1983 / VC / M • Hot Dreams / 1983 / CA / M • Ladies With Big Boobs / 1984 / AMB / M • Lusty Ladies #02 / 1983 / 4P / M • Lusty Ladies #03 / 1983 / SVE / M • Lusty Ladies #08 / 1984 / 4P / M • Lusty Ladies #11 / 1984 / 4P / M • Never Sleep Alone / 1984 / CA / M • The Oui Girls / 1981 / VHL / M • That's Outrageous / 1983 / CA / M • When She Was Bad / 1983 / CA / M • Wild Dallas Honey / 1985 / VCX / M • Wine Me, Dine Me, 69 Me / 1989 / COL / C

ANNA WATICAN
[The Loves Of Irina / 1973 / PS / S

ANNA WEBB
Old Wave Hookers #2 / 1995 / PL / M

ANNA-LISA
Canned Heat / 1996 / TCK / M • Older & Bolder In San Francisco / 1996 / TEP / M

ANNA-MARIA
Divine Decadence / 1988 / CA / M • Private Gold #10: Sins / 1996 / OD / M • Samantha And The Deep Throat Girls / 1988 / CV / M • Sexual Power / 1988 / CV / M

ANNABEL CHONG
Oriental, cute pretty, medium enhanced tits, lithe body. Born May 22, 1972 in London, England and lost her virginity at 13.
All I Want For Christmas Is A Gangbang / 1994 / AMP / M • Anal Queen / 1994 / FPI

/ M • The Best Of Annabel Chong / 1995 / FPI / C • Candy / 1995 / MET / M • Dementia / 1995 / IP / M • Depraved Fantasies #3 / 1994 / FPI / M • Dirt Bags / 1994 / FPI / M • Don't Try This At Home / 1994 / FPI / M • Dragxina, Queen Of The Underworld / 1995 / MET / G • Guess Again / 1994 / FPI / G • Guess What? / 1994 / FPI / G • I Can't Believe I Did The Whole Team! / 1994 / FPI / M • Intense / 1996 / MET / M • Love Bunnies #09 / 1994 / FPI / F • More Dirty Debutantes #37 / 1995 / 4P / M • Mr. Madonna / 1994 / FPI / G • Out Of My Mind / 1995 / PL / M • Possessed / 1996 / MET / M • Queen Of The Bizarre / 1994 / AMP / G • Sgt. Peckers Lonely Hearts Club Gang Bang / 1995 / AMP / M • Sordid Stories / 1994 / AMP / M • Straight A's / 1994 / AMP / M • Vortex / 1995 / MET / M • What's A Nice Girl Like You Doing In An Anal Movie? / 1995 / AMP / M • The World's Biggest Gang Bang #1 / 1995 / FPI / M

ANNABELLA
Penetration (Flash) #1 / 1995 / FLV / M

ANNABELLE
Hardcore: The Films Of Richard Kern #1 / 1991 / FTV / M • Magma: Claudine In Action / 1996 / MET / M • Sex Museum / 1976 / AXV / M • Wrasslin She-Babes #05 / 1996 / SOW / M

ANNABELLE DANE see Annabelle Dayne

ANNABELLE DAYNE (Annabelle Dane)
Very pretty blonde with long straight hair, small tits, large clit, tight waist and a very nice smile. On the defect side, she has some cellulite in the rear and the tops of her thighs. 23 years old in 1994.
Amateur Dreams #1 / 1994 / DR / M • Anal Addicts / 1994 / KWP / M • Anal Innocence #3 / 1994 / ROB / M • Anal Misconduct / 1995 / VD / M • Anal Pool Party / 1996 / PE / M • Anal Sweetheart / 1994 / ROB / M • Beaver Hunt #03 / 1994 / LEI / M • Black Nurse Fantasies / 1994 / CA / M • Booty Queen / 1995 / ROB / M • Buttslammers #09: Fade To Anal / 1995 / BS / F • Cold As Ice / 1994 / IN / M • The Cumm Brothers #12: Two GOOS For Every Girl / 1995 / OD / M • Deep Inside Nikki Sinn / 1996 / VC / C • Deep Seven / 1996 / VC / M • Dirty Doc's Housecalls #17 / 1994 / LV / M • Fantasy Du Jour / 1995 / FH / M • Fantasy Flings #03 / 1995 / WP / M • Fresh Meat (John Leslie) #1 / 1994 / EA / M • Girls Of The Very Big Eight / 1994 / VT / M • Green Piece Of Ass #2 / 1994 / RTP / M • Heartbeat / 1995 / PP / M • Hotel Sodom #07 / 1995 / SNA / M • House Of Sex #16: Dirty Oral Three Ways / 1994 / RTP / M • The Legend Of Barbi-Q And Little Fawn / 1994 / CA / M • Lucky Lady / 1995 / CV / M • M Series #23 / 1994 / LBO / M • Mr. Peepers Amateur Home Videos #93: Creative Fornication / 1994 / LBO / M • New Pussy Hunt #26 / 1996 / LEI / C • The New Snatch Masters #22 / 1996 / LEI / C • Northwest Pecker Trek #2: Evergreen, Ever Horny / 1994 / LBO / M • Odyssey Triple Play #90: Black & White In Loving Color / 1995 / OD / M • Paradise Found / 1995 / LE / M • Paradise Lost / 1995 / LE / M • Renegades #1 / 1994 / SC / M • Simply Kia / 1994 / LE / M • Swing Into...Spring / 1995 / KWP / M • Where The Girls

Sweat...Not The Sequel / 1996 / EL / F

ANNAH MARIE
Decadence / 1996 / VC / M • No Man's Land #14 / 1996 / VT / F • The Seduction Of Annah Marie / 1996 / VT / M • Style #3 / 1996 / VT / M • Wild & Wicked #7 / 1996 / VT / M

ANNASTASIA
Melrose Trannie / 1995 / HEA / G • Virtual She-Male / 1995 / HSV / G

ANNE
Blue Vanities #531 / 1993 / FFL / M • Blue Vanities #584 / 1996 / FFL / M • Lesbian Pros And Amateurs #01 / 1992 / GO / F • Lesbian Pros And Amateurs #03 / 1992 / GO / F • More Dirty Debutantes #16 / 1992 / 4P / M

ANNE BARR see Star Index I

ANNE BEATY see Star Index I

ANNE BEIKNAP
The Anger In Jennie / 1975 / VHL / M

ANNE BOIRONS
Les Chaleurs De La Gyneco / 1996 / FAP / F

ANNE BRADY
Satisfaction Guaranteed / 1972 / AXV / M

ANNE BRIME
Erotic Dimensions: Bold Fantasies / 1982 / NSV / M

ANNE CHOVIE
Class Reunion / cr77 / BL / F

ANNE CHRISTIAN
ABA: Double Feature #3 / 1996 / ALP / M • Christy / 1975 / CA / M

ANNE CUMMINGS
Inside Little Oral Annie / 1984 / VXP / M

ANNE DICKENS
Just Deserts / 1991 / BIZ / B

ANNE FAULKNER
Garters And Lace / 1975 / SE / M

ANNE FISHER see Star Index I

ANNE GALE
The Openings / 1975 / BL / M

ANNE GRAF
[Schulmadchen-Report 4: Was Eltern Oft Verzweifeln LaBt / 1972 / ... / M

ANNE LIBERT
[Le Journal Intime D'Une Nymphomane / 1972 / ... / M • [Vice And Virtue / 1963 / ... / S

ANNE LIEBERT
Five Kittens / 19?? / ... / M

ANNE MAGLE
Practice Makes Perfect / 1975 / QX / M • [Molly / 1977 / ... / S

ANNE MARIE
Beneath The Valley Of The Ultra-Vixens / 1979 / RMV / S • Supervixens / 1975 / RMV / S • Ultimate Fantasy / 1993 / BON / B • [Black & White & Brutal #1 / 1996 / ... / S • [Black & White & Brutal #2 / 1996 / ... / S

ANNE MARIE (TAE) see Brooke Ashley

ANNE MARIE JACKSON see Victoria Jackson

ANNE NEVENS
Love Lips / 1976 / VC / M

ANNE PERRY
Casanova #2 / 1976 / CA / M

ANNE PROTO see Star Index I

ANNE SANDS see Annie Sprinkle

ANNE SHMALL
Violated / 1973 / PVX / M

ANNE SILVERS
Bucky Beaver's XXX Dragon Art Theatre Double Feature #11 / 1996 / SOW / M •

Teenage Fantasies #1 / 1972 / SOW / M

ANNE THOMAS *see Star Index I*

ANNE YOUNG
More Dirty Debutantes #58 / 1996 / 4P / M

ANNE-MARIE
Frank Thring's Double Penetration #2 / 1996 / XPR / M

ANNETTE
Annette: Horny Secretary / 1990 / LOD / F • Blue Vanities #541 / 1994 / FFL / M • Lil' Women: Vacation / 1996 / EUR / M • Magma: Anal Wedding / 1995 / MET / M • Magma: Nymphettes / 1993 / MET / M • Private Video Magazine #01 / 1993 / OD / M • Samuels: Annette: 21 And Ready / 1990 / SAM / F • Sex Appeal / 1984 / ABV / M • Unnatural Phenomenon #1 / 1985 / WV / M • Unnatural Phenomenon #2 / 1986 / WV / M • Wrasslin She-Babes #14 / 1996 / SOW / M

ANNETTE CHANG
The Masseuse #2 / 1994 / VI / M

ANNETTE DUROUSTER *see Star Index I*

ANNETTE HAVEN *(Annette Robinson)*
Light brown or dark blonde hair, passable face, elegant, medium/large natural tits, tight waist, flat belly, spindly legs, a little too wide on the hips. The paradigm of white and one of the very few reasonable looking porno stars of the seventies but unfortunately she's an ice princess. Was a nurse's aide, then worked in a massage parlor and finally became a dancer before doing her first movie (**Lady Freaks**) in 1973 for Alex DeRenzy. As of 1991 was 37 and living in Marin County with her husband, Billy.
1001 Erotic Nights #1 / 1982 / VC / M • 8 To 4 / 1981 / CA / M • The 8th Annual Erotic Film Awards / 1984 / SE / C • Adult 45 #01 / 1985 / DR / C • All About Annette / 1982 / SE / C • Anna Obsessed / 1978 / ALP / M • Ape Over Love / 197? / BL / M • The Autobiography Of A Flea / 1976 / MIT / M • Barbara Broadcast / 1977 / VC / M • Best Of Talk Dirty To Me #01 / 1991 / DR / C • Between The Sheets / 1982 / CA / M • The Bigger The Better / 1986 / SE / C • Black Silk Stockings / 1978 / SE / C • The Blonde / 1980 / VCX / M • Blue Ribbon Blue / 1984 / CA / C • Blue Vanities #042 (New) / 1988 / FFL / M • Blue Vanities #042 (Old) / 1988 / FFL / M • Blue Vanities #046 (New) / 1988 / FFL / M • Blue Vanities #046 (Old) / 1988 / FFL / M • Blue Vanities #064 / 1988 / FFL / M • Blue Vanities #912 / 1993 / FFL / M • Blue Vanities #589 / 1996 / FFL / M • Bodies In Heat #1 / 1983 / CA / M • Bodies In Heat #2 / 1989 / DR / M • A Brief Affair / 1982 / CA / M • Caballero Preview Tape #1 / 1982 / CA / C • Caballero Preview Tape #2 / 1983 / CA / C • Caballero Preview Tape #3 / 1984 / CA / C • Caballero Preview Tape #4 / 1985 / CA / C • Carnal Haven / 1976 / SVE / M • Centerspread Girls / 1982 / CA / M • Charli / 1981 / VCX / M • Charm School / 1986 / VI / M • China Girl / 1974 / SE / M • Classic Swedish Erotica #06 / 1986 / CA / C • Coed Fever / 1980 / CA / M • A Coming Of Angels / 1977 / CA / M • A Coming Of Angels, The Sequel / 1985 / CA / M • Critics' Choice #1 / 19?? / SE / C • Deep Rub / 1979 / VC / M • Deep Tango / 1973 / VEP / M • Desires Within Young Girls / 1977 / CA / M • Dungeon Of Lust / 197? / AVC / M •

Easy Alice / 1976 / VC / M • Electric Blue: World Nudes Tonight / 1985 / CA / C • Erotic Fantasies #2 / 1983 / CV / C • Erotic Fantasies: Women With Women / 1984 / CV / C • Erotic Gold #2 / 1985 / VEN / M • Exhausted / 1981 / CA / C • F / 1980 / GO / M • Fantastic Orgy / 197? / ... / M • Female Athletes / 1977 / VXP / M • Femmes De Sade / 1976 / ALP / M • Fetish Fever / 1993 / CA / C • First Annual XRCO Awards / 1984 / AVC / C • For The Love Of Pleasure / 1979 / SE / M • The Girl From S.E.X. / 1982 / CA / M • Good To The Last Drop / 1986 / VCS / C • The Grafenberg Spot / 1985 / MIT / M • High School Memories / 1980 / VCX / M • Honkytonk Angels / 1988 / IN / C • Hot Girls In Love / 1984 / VIV / C • Hot Pursuit / 1983 / VC / M • The Huntress / 1987 / IN / M • Kym Wilde's On The Edge #13 / 1994 / RB / B • Kym Wilde's On The Edge #23 / 1995 / RB / B • Kym Wilde's On The Edge #30 / 1995 / RB / B • Ladies Nights / 1980 / VC / M • Lady Freaks / 1973 / ... / M • Legends Of Porn #1 / 1987 / CV / C • Legends Of Porn #2 / 1989 / CV / C • Limited Edition #01 / 1979 / AVC / M • Limited Edition #11 / 1980 / AVC / M • Love Scenes For Loving Couples / 1987 / CV / C • Love You / 1980 / CA / M • Lust At First Bite / 1978 / VC / M • Maraschino Cherry / 1978 / QX / M • Marilyn Chambers' Private Fantasies #1 / 1983 / CA / M • Memphis Cathouse Blues / 1982 / CA / M • Naked Afternoon / 1976 / CV / M • The Nicole Stanton Story #1 / 1989 / CA / M • Once Upon A Time/Cave Woman / 1978 / VI / M • One Of A Kind / 1976 / SVE / M • Only The Best #1 / 1986 / CV / C • Only The Very Best On Film / 1992 / VC / C • Overnight Sensation / 1976 / AR / M • Pajama Party / 1993 / CV / C • The Passion Within / 1986 / MAP / M • Peaches And Cream / 1982 / SE / M • Private Thighs / 1987 / AVC / C • Public Affairs / 1984 / CA / M • Reflections / 1977 / VCX / M • Seka In Heat / 1988 / BMV / C • The Seven Seductions Of Madame Lau / 1981 / EVI / M • The Sex Game / 1987 / SE / C • Sex Loose / 1982 / VC / M • Sex World / 1978 / SE / M • Sexsations / 1984 / NSV / M • Sheer Haven / 1989 / DR / C • Sheer Panties / 1979 / SE / C • Skintight / 1981 / CA / M • Soft Places / 1978 / CXV / M • Sound Of Love / 1981 / CA / M • The Spirit Of Seventy Six / 1976 / NGV / M • Splashing / 1986 / VCS / C • Summer Of '72 / 1982 / CA / M • Swedish Erotica #02 / 1980 / CA / M • Swedish Erotica #05 / 1980 / CA / M • Swedish Erotica #22 / 1980 / CA / M • Swedish Erotica #45 / 1983 / CA / M • Swedish Erotica #46 / 1983 / CA / M • Swedish Erotica Superstar #2: Brigette Monet / 1983 / CA / C • Take Off / 1978 / VXP / M • Talk Dirty To Me #06 / 1989 / DR / M • Tapestry Of Passion / 1976 / SE / M • Teenage Sex Therapist / 1977 / ... / M • Tell Them Johnny Wadd Is Here / 1975 / QX / M • That's Erotic / 1979 / CV / C • That's Porno / 1979 / CV / C • Thunderbuns / 1976 / VCX / C • Tower Of Power / 1985 / CV / M • True Legends Of Adult Cinema: The Golden Age / 1992 / VC / C • The Ultimate Pleasure / 1977 / HIF / M • V—The Hot One / 1978 / CV / M • VCA Previews #2 / 1988 / VC / C • Visions Of Clair / 1977 / WWV / M • Wicked Sensa-

tions #1 / 1981 / CA / M • Wine Me, Dine Me, 69 Me / 1989 / COL / C • With Love, Annette / 1985 / CA / C • With Love, Lisa / 1985 / CA / C • The World Of Henry Paris / 1981 / VC / C • [Best Of Annette Haven / 1986 / ... / C • [Crazy Town / 1976 / ... / M

ANNETTE HEINZ *(Annette Hines)*
Brooke Does College / 1984 / VC / M • Burlexxx / 1984 / VC / M • The Casting Couch / 1983 / GO / M • Consenting Adults / 1981 / VXP / M • Dangerous Stuff / 1985 / COM / M • Down & Out In New York City / 1986 / SE / M • Firebox / 1986 / VXP / M • G-Strings / 1984 / COM / M • Getting Ahead / 1983 / PL / M • Hot Lips / 1984 / VC / M • Hypersexuals / 1984 / VC / M • Lady Lust / 1984 / CA / M • Parted Lips / 1986 / QX / M • Piggies / 1984 / VC / M • Pink Clam / 1986 / RLV / M • Pleasure Channel / 1984 / VC / M • Public Affairs / 1984 / CA / M • Pussycat Galore / 1984 / VC / M • Rimshot / 1987 / CDI / M • Scenes They Wouldn't Let Me Shoot / 1984 / VC / M • Sex Spa USA / 1984 / VC / M • Sheer Rapture / 1984 / ... / M • Show Your Love / 1984 / VC / M • Succulent / 1983 / VXP / M • Teaser / 1986 / RLV / M • Three Daughters / 1986 / FEM / M • Whose Fantasy Is It, Anyway? / 1983 / AVC / M

ANNETTE HINES *see* **Annette Heinz**

ANNETTE LINDER *see Star Index I*

ANNETTE PETERS *see Star Index I*

ANNETTE ROBINSON *see* **Annette Haven**

ANNICA SALOMONSSON
The Second Coming Of Eva / 1974 / ALP / M

ANNIE
AVP #9140: The Fitting / 1991 / AVP / M • Blue Vanities #509 / 1992 / FFL / M • Blue Vanities #555 / 1994 / FFL / M • Double Adventure / 1993 / EA / M • Fantasy Photography: Making Babies / 1995 / FAP / M • Girls Around The World #04 / 1991 / BTO / M • Girls Around The World #11 / 199? / BTO / S • Harlem Honies #2: Nasty In New York / 1994 / CC / M • Kitty Foxx's Kinky Kapers #01 / 1995 / TTV / M • Wrasslin She-Babes #12 / 1996 / SOW / M

ANNIE AMPLE
The Best Of Big Busty / 1986 / L&W / C • Busty Nymphos / 1984 / BTO / S • Electric Blue #009 / 1983 / CA / S • The Last Horror Film / 1982 / VTR / S

ANNIE ANAL
Odyssey Triple Play #69: Prick & Pussy Pairs / 1994 / OD / M

ANNIE BLAKER
Vanessa's Hot Nights / 1984 / SVE / M

ANNIE CORDAY
A Merry Widow / 1996 / SPI / M

ANNIE CROSS *see* **Dina DeVille**

ANNIE DARLING *see Star Index I*

ANNIE GERARD *see Star Index I*

ANNIE HALL *see* **Rene Bond**

ANNIE LAWRENCE
The Family Jewels / cr76 / GO / M

ANNIE MARS
Bedtime Video #03 / 1984 / GO / M

ANNIE MAXUM *see Star Index I*

ANNIE MORROW
Toys, Not Boys #1 / 1991 / FC / C

ANNIE OWEN *see* **Little Oral Annie**

ANNIE OWENS *see* **Little Oral Annie**

ANNIE SANDS *see* **Annie Sprinkle**

ANNIE SPRINKLE *(Anne Sands, Annie Sands, Ellen Steinberg)*
Quite pretty but fat girl with black hair and huge tits. 40 years old in 1994. Small tattoo on her right hip.
ABA: Double Feature #2 / 1996 / ALP / M • ABA: Double Feature #4 / 1996 / ALP / M • ABA: Double Feature #5 / 1996 / ALP / M • The Affairs Of Janice / 1975 / ALP / M • Annie Gets Ready / 1992 / ANN / F • Annie Sprinkle's Fantasy Salon / 1990 / VER / B • Bang Bang You Got It / 1975 / VXP / M • Bazooka County Population 38D / 1987 / CC / F • The Best Of Big Busty / 1986 / L&W / C • Big Busty #03 / 1985 / CPL / S • Bizarre Styles / 1981 / ALP / B • Blow Some My Way / 1977 / VHL / M • Blue Vanities #200 / 1993 / FFL / M • Blue Vanities #220 / 1994 / FFL / M • Blue Vanities #244 / 1995 / FFL / M • Call Me Angel, Sir / 1976 / ALP / M • Centerfold Fever / 1981 / VXP / M • Cherry Hustlers / 1977 / VEN / M • Come With Me, My Love / 1976 / PVX / M • Consenting Adults / 1981 / VXP / M • Debbie Does 'em All #1 / 1985 / CV / M • Deep Inside Annie Sprinkle / 1981 / VXP / M • The Devil Inside Her / 1977 / ALP / M • Dirty Looks / 1982 / VC / C • The Double Exposure Of Holly / 1977 / TVX / M • Dreams Of Desire / 1988 / BIZ / F • Ecstasy In Blue / 1976 / ALP / M • Electric Blue #015 / 1984 / CA / S • Erotic Tattooing And Piercing #1 / 1986 / FLV / M • Expose Me, Lovely / 1976 / QX / M • Fannie / 1975 / ALP / M • Female Misbehavior / 1992 / FRV / S • For Richer, For Poorer / 1979 / CXV / M • Forbidden Photographs / cr91 / FLV / M • Frank Henenlotter's XXX Hardcore Horrors #05 / 1996 / SOW / M • French Shampoo / 1978 / VXP / M • Funk / 1977 / … / M • Historic Erotica #2: Hippies In Heat / 1992 / GMI / M • A History Of Corsets / 1987 / VER / S • Honeypie / 1975 / VC / M • Horneymooners #1 / 1988 / VXP / M • Hotter Than July / 1988 / CC / F • House Of Chicks: Masturbation Memoirs #2 / 1995 / HOC / F • Interlude / 1983 / CA / B • Intimate Action #1 / 1983 / INP / M • Intimate Action #2 / 1983 / INP / M • Jack 'n' Jill #1 / 1979 / VXP / M • Kathy's Graduation Present / 1975 / SVE / M • Kinky Potpourri #33 / 1997 / SVE / C • Kneel Before Me! / 1983 / ALP / B • Lifestyles Convention / 1992 / PKP / S • Linda, Les And Annie / 1990 / AJA / G • The Lingerie Shop / 1987 / VER / G • MASH'ed / cr75 / ALP / M • Mature Women #02 / 1991 / BTO / M • Midnight Blue #2 / 1980 / VXP / M • My Father Is Coming / 1991 / FRV / S • My Master, My Love / 1975 / BL / B • Mystical Fetish / 1989 / KEE / B • Night Of Submission / 1976 / BIZ / M • Night On The Town / 1982 / KEN / S • Once Over Nightly / 197? / VXP / M • Oriental Techniques Of Pain And Pleasure / 1983 / ALP / B • Painmania / 1983 / AVO / B • Pandora's Mirror / 1981 / CA / M • Pinned And Smothered / 1992 / BIZ / B • Pornocopia Sensual / 1976 / VHL / M • Rites Of Passion / 1988 / FEM / M • Satan Was A Lady / 1977 / ALP / M • The Satisfiers Of Alpha Blue / 1980 / AVC / M • Seduction / 1974 / VXP / M • She Comes In Colors / 1987 / AMB / M • She-Male Encounters #05: Orgy At The Poysinberry Bar #1 / 1987 / MET / G • Sherlick Holmes /

cr75 / SVE / M • Slippery When Wet / 1976 / VXP / M • Spitfire / 1984 / COM / M • Sue Prentiss, R.N. / cr76 / CDC / M • Sunset Strip Girls / 1975 / TGA / M • Sweet Revenge / 1986 / ZA / M • Teenage Cover Girl / 1975 / VCX / M • Teenage Deviates / 1975 / SVE / M • Teenage Masseuse / 197? / BL / M • Throat...12 Years After / 1984 / VC / M • Too Hot To Handle / 1975 / CDC / M • Triple Header / 1987 / AIR / C • Twilight Pink #1 / 1980 / AR / M • Unwilling Lovers / 197? / SVE / M • Wimps / 1987 / LIV / S • Women Without Men #2 / 1988 / VXP / F • Young Nurses In Love / 1986 / VES / S • [Cathy's Graduation / 197? / … / M • [Deep Deconstruction / 199? / … / S • [Doll / 197? / … / M • [Mondo New York / 1987 / … / S • [My Erotic Fantasies / 197? / … / M • [Portrait Of A Porno Star—Inmost, Inside Annie Sprinkle / 199? / … / S • [Sacred Sex / 199? / … / S • [Shadows In The City / 1991 / … / S • [Sluts And Goddesses / 199? / … / M • [Temple Of The Fetus / 199? / … / S • [Tiger's Leap / 197? / … / M • [War Is Menstrual Envy / 1991 / … / S • [Wet X-Mas / 197? / … / M

ANNIE YOUNG
What's A Nice Girl Like You... / 1981 / … / M

ANTHONY
Dirty Dancers #3 / 1995 / 4P / M • Eternal Lust / 1996 / VC / M • Inside Seka / 1980 / VXP / M • Nightshift Nurses #2 / 1996 / VC / M • Shayla's Gang / 1994 / WP / M • Shayla's Swim Party / 1997 / VC / M • Sorority Sex Kittens #3 / 1996 / VC / M • Streets Of New York #08 / 1996 / PL / M • Striptease #2 / 1995 / PL / M

ANTHONY CASINO *see* **Star Index I**

ANTHONY CRANE *(Martin London)*
SO of Nicole London.
Adventures Of The DP Boys: The Pool Service / 1993 / HW / M • Badgirls #3: Cell Block 69 / 1994 / VI / M • Badgirls #4: Jayebird / 1995 / VI / M • Bed & Breakfast / 1995 / WAV / M • Debi's Darkest Desires / 1996 / BIZ / B • Desert Moon / 1994 / SPI / M • Dirty Laundry #2 / 1994 / CV / M • The Domination Of Summer #1 / 1994 / BIZ / B • Double Cross (Wicked) / 1995 / WP / M • Dresden Diary #12: / 1995 / BIZ / B • The Enema Bandit / 1994 / BIZ / B • The Enema Bandit Returns / 1995 / BIZ / B • Enema Obedience #2 / 1994 / BIZ / B • Enema Obedience #3: The Ultimate Punishment / 1994 / BIZ / B • Hard Evidence / 1996 / WP / M • Hexxxed / 1994 / VT / M • Hostile Takeover: Bitch Bosses / 1995 / BIZ / B • Hot In The Saddle / 1994 / ERA / M • The Hypnotist / 1994 / SBP / B • Laguna Nights / 1995 / FH / M • Mind Set / 1996 / VI / M • Naughty Nicole / 1994 / SC / M • Porsche Lynn, Vault Mistress #2 / 1994 / BIZ / B • Prisoners Of Pain / 1994 / BIZ / B • Revelations / 1993 / FEM / M • The Room Mate / 1995 / EX / M • Shelby's Forbidden Fears / 1995 / BIZ / B • The Stiff / 1995 / WAV / M • Taboo #12 / 1994 / MET / M • Taboo #13 / 1994 / IN / M • The Tongue / 1995 / OD / M

ANTHONY DEBRAY *see* **Star Index I**

ANTHONY DILLEN
Courting Libido / 1995 / HIV / G

ANTHONY FORTUNADA
Mafia Girls / 1972 / SOW / M

ANTHONY FRAYNE

Introducing Alexis / 1996 / VI / M

ANTHONY GALLO
Inside Karl Thomas / 1994 / STA / G • Secret Sex #3: The Takeover / 1994 / CAT / G

ANTHONY GATELIFT *see* **Star Index I**

ANTHONY LAWTON *(Steven Chase)*
Older male from the bondage movies.
Battling Bitches / 1993 / SBP / B • Body Slammers #03 / 1993 / SBP / B • The Bondage Adventures Of Randy Ranger / 1994 / SBP / B • Day Of Reckoning / 1994 / CS / B • Double Cross (Vid Tech) / 1995 / VTF / B • Double Xx Cross / 1995 / VTF / B • Dungeon Of Despair / 199? / CS / B • Feet For The Master / 1994 / SBP / B • Frankentickle / 1993 / CS / B • The Intruders: The Next Stop / 1994 / VTF / B • Kane Video #1: The Riding Crop / 1993 / VTF / B • Kane Video #2 / 1994 / VTF / B • Latex Bound #01 / 1993 / BON / B • Latex Bound #02 / 1993 / BON / B • Latex S&M Games / 1994 / SBP / B • Lost On Maneuvers / 1994 / VTF / B • Master Of De'feet / 1993 / SBP / B • Medieval Dungeon Master / 1993 / BON / B • The Missing Report / 1992 / CS / B • Monkee Business / 1994 / CS / B • Photo Bound / 1994 / VTF / B • Professor Butts / 1994 / SBP / F • Rear Ended / 1992 / CS / B • Rubber Dungeon Of Pain / 1993 / SBP / B • Rubber Foot Slave / 1993 / SBP / B • Rubber Me Butt! / 1994 / SBP / B • S&M Latex: The Bitch / 1995 / SBP / B • Slave Training (Vid Tech) / 1994 / VTF / B • Spanked! / 1995 / VTF / B • Spanking Good Reason / 1994 / VTF / B • Spanking Good Salary / 1993 / VTF / B • Start At The Bottom / 1993 / CS / B • Three For The Whip / 1995 / VTF / B • Tickled And Teased / 1994 / SBP / B • Tied & Tickled #18 / 1992 / CS / B • Tied & Tickled #23: Tickling Dick / 1994 / CS / B • Tied & Tickled #28: Tickling Dr. Cripley / 1995 / CS / B • Time For Action / 1993 / CS / B

ANTHONY LINDERO *see* **J.P. Anthony**

ANTHONY LLAMA *see* **Star Index I**

ANTHONY MARKO *see* **Star Index I**

ANTHONY MATTEI
Chronicles Of Pain #3: Slave Traders / 1996 / BIZ / B

ANTHONY MCCLOUD
Foxx Tales / 1996 / TTV / M

ANTHONY MICHAELS
Club Kiss / 1995 / ONA / M • Razor's Edge / 1995 / ONA / M • Sex For Hire / 1996 / ONA / M

ANTHONY PERRAINO *see* **Lou Perry**

ANTHONY RAY *see* **Star Index I**

ANTHONY RICHARD *see* **Robert Bullock**

ANTHONY SHAWN
Sabrina Starlet / 1994 / SC / M

ANTHONY SPINELLI *(George Spelvin (AS), Sybil Kidd, Wendy Lions, Wes Brown, Sam Weston (Spin))*
George Spelvin: **Exposed**. His son, Mitchell Spinelli, is also in the business, under that name and also as Michael Ellis.
Cheating American Style / 1988 / WV / M • Easy / 1978 / CV / M • Exposed / 1980 / SE / M • Nothing To Hide #1 / 1981 / CV / M • Portrait Of An Affair / 1988 / VD / M • Sizzle / 1990 / PP / M • Skin On Skin / 1981 / CV / M • Talk Dirty To Me #01 / 1980 / CA / M • Vista Valley PTA / 1980 / CV / M • [One Potato, Two Potato / 1964 / … / S

ANTHONY STILLITI *see Star Index I*

ANTHONY VENUTI
Undercovers / 1982 / CA / M

ANTHONY WONG
The Vixens Of Kung Fu: A Tale Of Yin Yang / 1975 / VC / M

ANTHONY ZEUS *see Damian Zeus*

ANTIQUE
Blue Vanities #569 / 1996 / FFL / M

ANTOINE *(Frenchy (Antoine), Fx)*
Small male who sounds French and has a small but very hard dick. He seems to be the boyfriend of Kiki (blonde).
Anal 247 / 1995 / CC / M • Dirty Dating Service #06 / 1994 / WP / M • Mr. Peepers Amateur Home Videos #87: Groupie Therapy / 1994 / LBO / M • New Faces, Hot Bodies #13 / 1994 / STP / M • New Faces, Hot Bodies #15 / 1994 / STP / M

ANTOINE DRAKE
Love Theatre / cr80 / VC / M

ANTOINETTE
Blue Vanities #508 / 1992 / FFL / M • French Heat / 1975 / VC / M • Lunch / 1972 / VC / M • Mistress Cleopatra Rules / 1993 / NEP / B • Onanie #2 / 1995 / MET / F • Victim Of Her Thighs / 1993 / STM / B

ANTOINETTE (GABRIEL) *see Gabriella (Portugal)*

ANTOINETTE TURQUOIS *see Star Index I*

ANTON
Frank Thring's Double Penetration #3 / 1996 / XPR / M

ANTON RETOR *see Star Index I*

ANTON VAGAS *see Star Index I*

ANTONETTE
Blue Vanities #504 / 1992 / FFL / M

ANTONIA
Under The Skirt #2 / 1995 / KAE / F

ANTONIA AMORE
The Wild Women / 1996 / PL / M

ANTONIO
AVP #5002: Naive And Naughty / 1990 / AVP / M • Behind The Blinds / 1992 / VIM / M • The Convict / 1995 / TAO / B • Eat At Dave's / 5 / 1996 / SP / M • Fresh Faces #06 / 1995 / EVN / M • Girlz N The Hood #2 / 1992 / HW / M • Old Bitches / 1996 / OLI / M • R/H Production: Interview For A Roommate / 1995 / R/H / M

ANTONIO CRABBE
Dames / 1985 / SE / M • Showgirls / 1985 / SE / M • Suzie Superstar #2 / 1985 / CV / M

ANTONIO VALENTINO
Zazel / 1996 / CV / M

ANTONIO VEGA
Ready To Drop #04 / 1994 / FC / M

ANTONO VEGAS
Natural Response / 1996 / GPI / G

APHRODESIA
Midget Goes Hawaiian / 1995 / FC / M

APHRODISIAC *see Heidi Nelson*

APHRODITE *see Fallon*

APOLLO STAR *see Star Index I*

APOLONIA *see Alex Dane*

APPOLONIA
FTV #12: Two Against A Wimp / 1996 / FT / B • FTV #20: Pizza Brawl / 1996 / FT / B

APPOLONIA (ALEX D.) *see Alex Dane*

APRIL
Any Way They're Tied / 1993 / HAC / B • April In Bondage / 1993 / BON / B • Babe Watch #3 / 1995 / SC / M • Babe Watch #4 / 1995 / SC / M • Babe Watch #5 / 1996 /

VC / M • Babes Illustrated #4 / 1995 / IN / F • Backhand / 1995 / SC / M • Beaver & Buttface / 1995 / SC / M • Blade / 1996 / MID / M • Blonde / 1995 / LE / M • Blonde Justice #3 / 1994 / VI / M • Breast Wishes #01 / 1991 / LBO / M • Celebrity Sluts And Tabloid Tramps / 1996 / LV / M • Chained Heat / 1996 / APP / M • Crazy Love / 1995 / VI / M • Destiny & April In Bondage / 1993 / BON / B • Euro Studs / 1996 / SC / C • Evil Temptations #1 / 1995 / ULP / M • Evil Temptations #2 / 1995 / ULP / M • Forbidden / 1996 / SC / M • Girls Next Door / 1996 / ANE / M • The Golden Touch / 1995 / WP / M • Hot Body Competition: Bikinis & Bikes Contest / 1996 / CG / F • Little Girl Lost / 1995 / SC / M • Lollipops #1 / 1996 / SC / M • More Dirty Debutantes #36 / 1994 / 4P / M • Pick Up Lines #09 / 1996 / OD / M • Pristine #1 / 1996 / CA / M • Pristine #2 / 1996 / CA / M • Real People Real Bondage #1 / 1995 / BON / C • Renegades #2 / 1995 / SC / M • Silent Women / 1995 / ERA / M • Some Like It Hard / 1995 / VC / M • Tainted Love / 1996 / VC / M • This Year's Blonde / 1995 / LE / M • Thunder Road / 1995 / SC / M • Tranny Claus / 1994 / HEA / G • Up And Cummers #16 / 1994 / 4P / M • Vivid Raw #3: Double Header / 1996 / VI / M • Wet Workout: Shape Up, Then Strip Down / 1995 / PME / S

APRIL ADAMS
Filth / 1996 / SPI / M • The Romeo Syndrome / 1995 / SC / M

APRIL BLOOM
Sista! #4 / 1996 / VT / F

APRIL COLLINS *see Star Index I*

APRIL DANCER *(Ivy English)*
Reddish blonde (dark) girl with small (maybe tiny) tits, lithe tight body, pretty face when she smiles, sulky when she doesn't, nice butt, good skin, large tattoo on her left neck, other tattoos on right shoulder back (question mark?) and left belly, belly button ring, tongue pin.
Beauty's Punishment / 1996 / BIZ / B • Beauty's Revenge / 1996 / BIZ / B • Bizarre's Dracula #1 / 1995 / BIZ / B • Bizarre's Dracula #2 / 1996 / BIZ / B • Burning Desires / 1994 / BS / B • Buttslammers #07: Indecent Decadence / 1994 / BS / F • Buttslammers #08: The Ultimate Invasion / 1994 / BS / F • Chronicles Of Pain #1 / 1996 / BIZ / B • Chronicles Of Pain #2 / 1996 / BIZ / B • Chronicles Of Submission / 1995 / BON / B • Defiance: The Art Of Spanking / 1996 / BIZ / B • Dresden Diary #13: / 1995 / BIZ / B • Dresden Diary #14: Ecstasy In Hell / 1996 / BIZ / B • Dresden Diary #15: / 1996 / BIZ / B • The Enema Bandit Strikes Again / 1995 / BIZ / B • Forbidden Awakenings / 1996 / BON / B • Forever Payne / 1994 / BS / B • Future Doms #1 / 1996 / BIZ / B • Futuro Doms #2 / 1996 / BIZ / B • Goldilocks And The 3 Bares / 1996 / LBO / B • Leather Bound Dykes From Hell #6 / 1995 / BIZ / B • Leather Bound Dykes From Hell #7 / 1996 / BIZ / B • Leather Bound Dykes From Hell #8 / 1996 / BIZ / B • Mistress Kane: Lessons In Terror / 1996 / BIZ / B • Mistress Kane: Town In Torment / 1996 / BIZ / B • Obsession / 1994 / BS / B • Princess Of Pain / 1996 / LBO / B • Punishment Of The Liars / 1996 / LBO / B •

Revolt Of The Slaves / 1996 / LBO / B • Spiked Heel Diaries #4 / 1995 / BIZ / B • Spiked Heel Diaries #5 / 1995 / BIZ / B • Stalking Of Slave Laura / 1996 / BIZ / B • Starlet / 1994 / VI / M • The Submission Of Alicia Rio / 1996 / BIZ / B • Supermodel #2 / 1994 / VI / M • Sweet Cheerleaders Spanked / 1996 / BIZ / B • Taste For Submission / 1996 / VTF / B • A Touch Of Leather / 1994 / BS / B • Vagablonde / 1994 / VI / M • Video Dominatrix / 1996 / LON / B • Waterworld: The Enema Movie / 1996 / BIZ / B • Wheel Of Obsession / 1996 / TWP / B • The Whipping Post / 1995 / BS / B

APRIL DAVIS *see Star Index I*

APRIL DIAMONDS *(Brazil (April D), Brazil Newporte, April Lee)*
Long messy dark brown or black hair, lots of facial acne but otherwise a passable face, lithe body, small tits, nasty Caesarian scar.
Ateball: Linda's West Coast Talent Search / 1996 / ATE / M • Babes Behind Bars / 1996 / CNP / F • Behind The Scenes / 1996 / GO / M • Casting Call #15 / 1995 / SO / M • Caught In The Act (1995-Lv) / 1995 / LV / M • Creme De La Face #10: Cum Dome / 1995 / OD / M • The Cumm Brothers #14: Buttdraft / 1995 / OD / M • Delinquents On Butt Row / 1996 / EA / M • Dirty Bob's #19: Over The Boardwalk! / 1995 / FLP / S • Fantasy Fuchs / 1996 / PLP / C • Finger Pleasures #6 / 1996 / PL / F • A Girl's Affair #09 / 1996 / FD / F • Hardcore Fantasies #1 / 1996 / LV / M • Here Comes Magoof #1 / 1995 / VC / M • Hollywood Amateurs #32 / 1996 / MID / M • Hollywood Starlets Adventure #05 / 1995 / AVS / M • In My Ass, Please! / 1996 / SP / M • Interview: Caught In The Act / 1996 / LV / M • Interview: New And Natural / 1995 / LV / M • Kool Ass / 1996 / BOT / M • Kym Wilde's On The Edge #31 / 1996 / RB / B • Latin Fever #1 / 1996 / C69 / M • Leather Unleashed / 1995 / GO / M • Lil' Latin Cutie Pies / 1996 / CDI / M • Lingerie / 1996 / RAS / M • Mike Hott: #332 Girls Who Swallow Cum #02 / 1995 / MHV / C • Mike Hott: #339 Cum In My Mouth #04 / 1996 / MHV / C • Mike Hott #343 Lesbian Dildo #20 / 1996 / MHV / F • Mike Hott: #353 Bonus Cunt: April Lee / 1996 / MHV / M • Mike Hott: #356 Girls Who Lap Cum From Cunts #01 / 1996 / MHV / M • Mike Hott: #362 Fuck The Boss #7 / 1996 / MHV / M • Mike Hott: #366 Lactating Lesbians / 1996 / MHV / F • Mike Hott: #368 Three-Sum Sluts #13 / 1996 / MHV / M • Mrs. Buttfire / 1995 / SUF / M • Nasty Newcummers #14 / 1995 / MET / M • Nineteen #1 / 1996 / FOR / M • No Man's Land #13 / 1996 / VT / F • Paradise / 1995 / FD / M • Pussyman Auditions #14 / 1995 / SNA / M • Salsa & Spice #2: Latin Lust / 1996 / TTV / M • The Sodomizor #2 / 1995 / SC / M • The Spa / 1996 / RAS / M

APRIL DIVINE
Temptation: The Story Of A Lustful Bride / 1983 / NSV / M

APRIL FURNUGEN *see Star Index I*

APRIL GRANT *(Lois Grant)*
Bottoms Up #04 / 1983 / AVC / C • Camp Beaverlake #1 / 1984 / AR / M • A Dirty Western #1 / 1973 / AR / M • High School Fantasies / 1974 / EVI / M • John Holmes, The Lost Films / 1988 / PEN / C • Little Or-

phan Dusty #1 / 1978 / ALP / M • Lust Flight 2000 / 1378 / VHL / M • Saturday Matinee Series #3 / 1996 / VCX / C • That's Erotic / 1979 / CV / C • Wham Bam Thank You Spaceman / 1973 / BPI / S

APRIL HARPER
The Likes Of Louise / 197? / BL / M

APRIL LACE *see* **Star Index I**

APRIL LEE *see* **April Diamonds**

APRIL MAYE
The French Tickler / 1994 / CS / B • Latex Bound #02 / 1993 / BON / B • Monkee Business / 1994 / CS / B • Tied & Tickled #28: Tickling Dr. Cripley / 1995 / CS / B

APRIL MAYE (1985) *(Collette Marin)*
Dildo Lesbian Bondage / 1986 / BIZ / B • Kiss Of The Gypsy / 1986 / WV / M • Layover / 1985 / HO / M • Lust American Style / 1985 / WV / M • Only The Best Of Oral / 1989 / CV / C • Rich Bitch / 1985 / HO / M • Savage Fury #1 / 1985 / VEX / M • Suzie Superstar #2 / 1985 / CV / M

APRIL MAYE (70S)
Candy Lips / 1975 / CXV / M • Erecter Sex #4: Pole Position / cr70 / AR / M • Oh Those Nurses / 1982 / VC / M

APRIL O'TOOLE
America's Dirtiest Home Videos #05 / 1991 / VEX / M • America's Dirtiest Home Videos #06 / 1991 / AMA / M • In Pursuit Of Passion / 1990 / V99 / M • Lonely And Blue / 1990 / VEX / M • Send Me An Angel / 1990 / V99 / M

APRIL RAIN *see* **April Rayne**

APRIL RAYNE *(April Rain, Valerie Harte, Andrea Naschak)*
Was 19 in 1991. Had breast implant surgery in Utah which also fixed her nose. This cost $1900. Appears in an unrated movie, **Hold Me, Thrill Me, Kiss Me**, as Andrea Naschak.
The Adventures Of Buttgirl & Wonder Wench / 1991 / AFV / M • Amateur Lesbians #03: April / 1991 / GO / F • Amateur Lesbians #12: Kimberly / 1991 / GO / F • America's Dirtiest Home Videos #03 / 1991 / VEX / M • Anal Attraction #2 / 1993 / AFV / C • Anal Encounters #3: Back In The Dark One / 1991 / VC / M • Another Rear View / 1990 / LE / M • Autobiography Of A Whip / 1991 / BS / B • Back To Back #2 / 1992 / FC / C • Backdoor To Harley-Wood #2 / 1990 / AFV / M • The Backpackers #2 / 1990 / IN / M • Bitches In Heat / 1994 / PL / C • Black Mariah / 1991 / FC / M • Black On White / 1991 / VT / F • Blonde Riders / 1991 / CC / M • The Breast Things In Life Are Free / 1991 / LV / M • Bruce Seven's Favorite Endings #1 / 1991 / EL / C • Bung-Ho Babes / 1991 / FC / M • Butt Naked #1 / 1990 / OD / M • Can't Touch This / 1991 / PL / M • Clean And Dirty / 1990 / ME / M • Cyrano / 1991 / PL / M • Deep Inside Jeanna Fine / 1992 / VC / C • Deep Inside Savannah / 1993 / VC / C • Dr Butts #1 / 1991 / 4P / M • Dream Cream'n / 1991 / AR / M • Ebony Love / 1992 / VT / C • Ecstasy / 1991 / LE / M • Edward Penishands #2 / 1991 / VT / M • Eternal Bliss / 1990 / AFV / M • The Face Of Fear / 1990 / BS / B • Friends & Lovers #1 / 1991 / VT / M • Girl Friends / 1990 / PL / F • Girls Of Silicone Valley / 1991 / FC / M • A Handful Of Summers / 1991 / ME / M • The Harley Girls / 1991 / AR / F • Headbangers Balls / 1991 / PL / M • Hold Me, Thrill Me, Kiss Me

/ 1993 / LIV / S • Hot Shots / 1992 / VD / C • I Love X / 1992 / FC / C • I Said A Butt Light #2 / 1990 / LV / M • Inferno / 1991 / XCI / M • The Last Blonde / 1991 / IN / M • Lesbian Lingerie Fantasy #4 / 1990 / ESP / F • Little Miss Curious / 1991 / CA / M • Moon Godesses #1 / 1992 / VIM / M • My 500 Pound Vibrator / 1991 / LV / C • Nasty Jack's Homemade Vid. #26 / 1991 / CDI / M • The New Kid On The Block / 1991 / VD / M • New Wave Hookers #2 / 1991 / VC / M • No Tell Motel / 1990 / ZA / M • Personalities / 1991 / PL / M • Putting It All Behind #1 / 1991 / IN / M • Raunch #01 / 1990 / CC / M • Rayne Storm / 1991 / VI / M • Rear Admiral / 1990 / ZA / M • Ride 'em Cowgirl / 1991 / V99 / M • Single Girl Masturbation #4 / 1990 / ESP / F • Skippy, Jiff & Jam / 1990 / CIA / M • Snatched To The Future / 1991 / EL / F • Street Walkers / 1990 / PL / M • Sweet Poison / 1991 / CDI / M • Tori Welles Goes Behind The Scenes / 1992 / FD / M • Toys, Not Boys #1 / 1991 / FC / C • Toys, Not Boys #3 / 1991 / FC / C • Two Times A Virgin / 1991 / AR / M • The Ultimate Pleasure / 1991 / MET / G • Vegas #5: Blackjack / 1991 / CIN / M • Vegas Reunion / 1992 / TOP / M • Virgin Spring / 1991 / FAZ / M • Wenches / 1991 / VT / F • Wild & Wicked #1 / 1991 / VT / M

APRIL SOMMERS *see* **Desiree Fox**

APRIL SUMMER
Private Film #07 / 1994 / OD / M • Private Film #08 / 1994 / OD / M • Private Film #17 / 1994 / OD / M • Private Video Magazine #08 / 1994 / OD / M

APRIL SUMMER (1976)
Divine Obsession / 1976 / TVX / M

APRIL SUMMER (FOX) *see* **Desiree Fox**

APRIL SUMMERS *see* **Desiree Fox**

APRIL WEST *(Jennifer Miles)*
Pretty blone with medium tits and a slightly too big a butt.
976-STUD / 1989 / LV / M • The Chameleon / 1989 / VC / M • Cheating American Style / 1988 / WV / M • Erotic Tales / 1989 / V99 / M • The First of April / 1988 / VI / M • Horneymooners #2 / 1988 / VXP / M • Hot Scalding / 1989 / VC / M • The Pearl Divers / 1988 / VWA / M • The Perfect Brat / 1989 / VI / M • Raw Talent #3 / 1988 / VC / M • Second Skin / 1989 / VC / M • Sex In Dangerous Places / 1988 / VI / M • Sleeping Beauty Aroused / 1989 / VI / M • Strange Curves / 1989 / VC / M • The Sweet Spurt Of Youth / 1988 / WV / M • Torrid / 1989 / VI / M • Torrid Without A Cause #1 / 1989 / VI / M • True Confessions Of Hyapatia Lee / 1989 / VI / M • True Confessions Of Tori Welles / 1989 / VI / M • True Love / 1989 / VI / M • Twentysomething #3 / 1989 / VI / M • Where The Boys Aren't #1 / 1989 / VI / F

APRIL WINE *see* **Star Index I**

ARA
Pumps In Da Rump #2 / 1996 / HW / M

ARABIAN TREASURE CHT *see* **Nikki King**

ARCADIA
Eurotica #01 / 1995 / XC / M

ARCADIA (LAKE) *see* **Arcadia Lake**

ARCADIA BLUE *see* **Arcadia Lake**

ARCADIA LAKE *(Arcadia Blue, Arcadia Small, Arcadia (Lake))*
Pretty, black hair, small breasts, lithe tight body. SO of Eric Edwards at one time. Died

of a drug OD in the eighties.
Amanda By Night #1 / 1981 / CA / M • American Pie / 1980 / SE / M • Babylon Gold / 1983 / COM / C • Babylon Pink #1 / 1979 / COM / M • Backdoor Girls / 1983 / VCR / C • Bedtime Video #03 / 1984 / GO / M • Behind The Brown Door / 1986 / VCR / C • Bella / 1980 / AR / M • Between The Sheets / 1982 / CA / M • Blonde In Black Silk / 1979 / QX / M • Blue Vanities #087 / 1988 / FFL / M • Bottoms Up #01 / 1983 / AVC / C • Centerspread Girls / 1982 / CA / M • Charli / 1981 / VCX / M • Classic Erotica Special / 1985 / SVE / M • Debbie Does Dallas #1 / 1978 / VC / M • Diamond Collection #39 / 1983 / CDI / M • Erotic Fantasies: Women With Women / 1984 / CV / C • Fascination / 1980 / QX / M • Flight Sensations / 1983 / VC / C • French Kiss / 1979 / PVX / M • Girls In Passion / 1979 / VHL / M • Honey Throat / 1980 / CV / M • Indecent Exposure / 1981 / CA / M • Irresistible #1 / 1982 / SE / M • Limited Edition #01 / 1979 / AVC / M • Loose Threads / 1979 / S&L / M • Love-In Arrangement / 1981 / VXP / M • Misbehavin' / 1979 / VXP / M • Neon Nights / 1981 / COM / M • October Silk / 1980 / COM / M • Only The Best Of Women With Women / 1988 / CV / C • Passion Toys / 1985 / VCR / C • Pussycat Ranch / 1978 / CV / M • Randy, The Electric Lady / 1978 / VC / M • Robin's Nest / 1979 / BL / M • Satin Suite / 1979 / QX / M • Secrets Of A Willing Wife / 1979 / VXP / M • Showgirl #07: Arcadia Lake's Fantasies / 1983 / VCR / M • Steamy Sirens / 1984 / AIR / C • Summertime Blue / 1979 / VCX / M • Suze's Centerfolds #4 / 1981 / CA / M • That's My Daughter / 1982 / NGV / M • What Would Your Mother Say? / 1981 / HAV / M • Young, Wild And Wonderful / 1980 / VCX / M • [Flesh Fantasy / 1981 / … / M

ARCADIA SMALL *see* **Arcadia Lake**

ARCHIE
Homegrown Video #193 / 1990 / HOV / M

ARCHIE FLYNN
Too Hot To Handle / 1975 / CDC / M

ARCIE MILLER *(R.C. Miller, Alice Miller, Rachel Miller, Arcie Simpson)*
White girl with black hair—a little pudgy. Looks similar to Devon Shire with bushy eyebrows.
Belle Of The Ball / 1989 / V99 / M • Between A Rock And A Hot Place / 1989 / VEX / M • Bi Cycling / 1989 / FC / G • Bionca, Just For You / 1989 / BON / F • Blows Job / 1989 / BIZ / B • Blue Fire / 1991 / V99 / M • Body Triple / 1991 / VC / M • Bondage Memories #03 / 1994 / BON / C • Camera Shy / 1990 / IN / M • Depraved / 1990 / IN / M • Dirty Diane / 1989 / V99 / M • Drainman / 1989 / BIZ / B • Earthquake Girls / 1990 / CC / M • Easy Lover / 1989 / EX / M • Ever Binding Love / 199? / CS / B • The Girl With The Blue Jeans Off / 1989 / FAZ / M • Hawaii Vice #3 / 1988 / CIN / M • Hawaii Vice #7 / 1989 / CDI / M • Hawaii Vice #8 / 1990 / CIN / M • The Heat Of The Moment / 1990 / IN / M • Hot In The City / 1989 / VEX / M • Keep It Cumming / 1990 / V99 / M • Kisses Don't Lie / 1989 / PL / M • Lonely Is The Night / 1990 / V99 / M • Lost Lovers / 1990 / VEX / M • Love Button / 1989 / VD / M • Master Plan / 198? / BON / B • My Pleasure / 1992 / CS / B • The New

Barbarians #1 / 1990 / VC / M • The New Barbarians #2 / 1990 / VC / M • Passion Prescription / 1990 / V99 / M • Playing Dirty / 1989 / VEX / M • Raw Sewage / 1989 / FC / M • Say Something Nasty / 1989 / CC / M • Secret Cravings / 1989 / V99 / M • Secret Obsession / 1990 / V99 / M • Seduction / 1990 / VEX / M • Sex Charades / 1990 / VEX / M • Sex Crazed / 1989 / VEX / M • She's A Boy / 1989 / LV / G • She's America's Most Wanted / 1990 / VEX / M • She-Male Nurse / 1989 / LV / S • Shoe Horny / 1989 / BIZ / B • The Squirt Bunny / 1989 / ERU / M • Squirt On The Hunt / 1989 / ERU / M • Stephanie, Just For You / 1989 / BON / F • Suzie Superstar #3 / 1989 / CV / M • Ticket To Ride / 1990 / LV / M • Toys, Not Boys #3 / 1991 / FC / C • Unforgivable / 1989 / IN / M • Victoria's Secret / 1989 / SO / M • Wildfire / 1989 / EVN / M • [The Devil In Barbara Dare / 1990 / VEX / M

ARCIE SIMPSON *see Arcie Miller*
ARI ADLER
China De Sade / 1977 / ALP / M
ARI(ANA) *see Ariana*
ARIA ARSIKAINEN *see Star Index I*
ARIANA *(Ari(ana), Ariane(a))*
Born Nov 3, 1958 in Brooklyn NY. Brunette with bulbous eyes and a squarish body. Enhanced hard canteloupes. SO of Luc Wilder. Rumor has it they have broken up in mid 1996.
The Adventures Of Buttwoman #2: Behind Bars / 1992 / EL / F • All That Jism / 1994 / VD / M • Amateur Lesbians #29: Ari / 1992 / GO / F • American Garter / 1993 / VC / M • Anal Island #2 / 1996 / VC / M • Anal Therapy #2 / 1993 / FD / M • Ariana's Bondage / 1993 / BON / B • Ariana's Dirty Dancers: The Professionals / 1996 / 4P / M • Ariana's Domain / 1996 / GOT / B • Ariana's Torment / 1995 / BON / B • Backlash / 1992 / GOT / B • Battling Bitches #1 / 1995 / BIZ / B • Beauty's Punishment / 1996 / BIZ / B • Beauty's Revenge / 1996 / BIZ / B • The Best Of Buttslammers / 1995 / BS / C • Beverly Hills Madam / 1993 / FH / F • Bizarre's Dracula #1 / 1995 / BIZ / B • Bizarre's Dracula #2 / 1995 / BIT / B • Black Flava / 1994 / EX / M • Black Orchid / 1993 / WV / M • Bondage Fantasy #2 / 1995 / BON / B • Bondage Journey / 1995 / STM / B • Bondage Memories #05 / 1994 / BON / C • Bondage Of The Rising Sun / 1996 / BON / B • Booty In The House / 1993 / WP / M • Breast Collection #03 / 1995 / LBO / C • The Breast Of Breastmen / 1995 / EVN / C • Breast Wishes #10 / 1992 / LBO / M • Breast Wishes #11 / 1993 / LBO / M • Breast Worx #27 / 1992 / LBO / M • Bruce Seven: A Compendium Of His Most Graphic Scenes Vol 5 / 1994 / BS / C • Buffy The Vamp / 1992 / FD / M • Bull Dyke Humiliation / 1993 / PL / B • Butt Bandits #4 / 1996 / VD / C • The Butt Detective / 1994 / VC / M • Butts Up / 1994 / CA / M • Buttslammers #01 / 1993 / BS / F • Buttslammers #04: Down And Dirty / 1993 / BS / F • Buttslammers #06: Over The Edge / 1994 / BS / F • Buttslammers #08: The Ultimate Invasion / 1994 / BS / F • Buttslammers #09: Fade To Anal / 1995 / BS / F • Captive #1 / 1995 / BON / B • Captive Sessions / 1994 / GOT / B • Casting Call #01 / 1993 / SO / M • Chained / 1995 /

SC / M • Chasey Revealed / 1994 / WP / M • Chronicles Of Submission / 1995 / BON / B • Chug-A-Lug Girls #4 / 1994 / VT / M • Cinderella Society / 1993 / GO / M • Club Midnight / 1992 / LV / M • Colossal Orgy #1 / 1993 / HW / M • Coming Attractions / 1995 / WHP / M • Covergirl / 1996 / LE / M • The Crimson Kiss / 1993 / WV / M • Date With A Mistress / 1995 / BIZ / B • Daughters Of Discipline / 1993 / GOT / B • Debi Diamond: Mega Mistress / 1995 / BIZ / B • Deep Inside Ariana / 1995 / VC / C • Depraved / 1993 / BS / B • Desert Moon / 1994 / SPI / M • The Devil In Miss Jones #5: The Inferno / 1994 / VC / M • Diamond Likes It Rough / 1995 / BON / B • Dirty Bob's #19: Over The Boardwalk! / 1995 / FLP / S • Dirty Bob's #23: Tampa Teasers / 1995 / FLP / S • Dirty Dancers #1 / 1994 / 4P / M • Dirty Dancers #2 / 1994 / 4P / M • Dirty Dancers #3 / 1995 / 4P / M • Dirty Dancers #4 / 1995 / 4P / M • Dirty Dancers #5 / 1995 / 4P / M • Dirty Dancers #6 / 1995 / 4P / M • Dirty Dancers #7 / 1996 / 4P / M • Dirty Dancers #8 / 1996 / 4P / M • Dirty Laundry #1 / 1994 / CV / M • Dirty Laundry #2 / 1994 / CV / M • Doctors Of Pain / 1995 / BIZ / B • Double Load #2 / 1994 / HW / M • Dr Of Pain / 1995 / BIZ / B • Dreams Of Desires / 1995 / ONA / M • Dresden Diary #09 / 1993 / BIZ / B • Dresden Diary #10: Punishment For Their Sins / 1993 / BIZ / B • Dresden Diary #13: / 1995 / BIZ / B • Dresden Diary #14: Ecstasy In Hell / 1996 / BIZ / B • Dresden Diary #15: / 1996 / BIZ / B • Dungeon Brats / 1994 / STM / B • Dungeon Punishment / 1995 / STM / B • Elegant Bargain / 1994 / FD / C • The Enema Bandit Strikes Again / 1995 / BIZ / B • Erotica / 1992 / CC / M • Every Woman Has A Fantasy #3 / 1995 / VC / M • Everything Is Not Relative / 1994 / EL / M • Expose Me Again / 1996 / CV / M • Extreme Sex #4: The Experiment / 1995 / VI / M • A Fairy's Tail / 1996 / TTV / M • Firecrackers / 1994 / HW / M • Flesh For Fantasy / 1994 / CV / M • Fleshmates / 1994 / ERA / M • Flexxx #1 / 1994 / VT / M • The Fluffer #1 / 1993 / FD / M • The Fluffer #2 / 1993 / FD / M • Forbidden Awakenings / 1996 / BON / B • Forbidden Obsessions / 1993 / BS / B • Fundgeon Of The Mind #1 / 1994 / BON / B • A Girl's Affair #03 / 1993 / FD / F • Happy Endings / 1994 / WP / M • Hard Hand Luc / 1994 / STM / B • Hard Licks / 1993 / GOT / B • Heart Breaker / 1994 / CA / M • Herman's Other Head / 1992 / LV / M • Hollywood Swingers #02 / 1992 / LBO / M • Hot Tight Asses #10 / 1995 / TCK / M • Hypnotic Passions / 1993 / FOR / M • The Illustrated Woman / 1995 / CA / M • Infamous Crimes Against Nature / 1993 / SUM / M • The Initiation / 1995 / FD / M • Invitation For Lust / 1995 / C69 / M • Kinky Cameraman #1 / 1996 / LEI / C • Kittens #6 / 1994 / CC / F • Kittens #7 / 1995 / CC / F • Kym Wilde's On The Edge #07 / 1994 / RB / B • Kym Wilde's On The Edge #16 / 1994 / RB / B • Kym Wilde's On The Edge #20 / 1995 / RB / B • Leather Bound Dykes From Hell #5 / 1995 / BIZ / B • Leather Bound Dykes From Hell #6 / 1995 / BIZ / B • Leather Bound Dykes From Hell #7 / 1996 / BIZ / B • Leather For Lovers #2 / 1995 / VEG / M • Lolita / 1995 / SC / M • Love Doll Lucy #1 /

1994 / PL / F • Love Doll Lucy #2 / 1994 / PL / F • Lydia's Web / 1994 / TWP / B • M Series #08 / 1993 / LBO / M • The Maltese Bimbo / 1993 / FD / M • Marked #1 / 1993 / FD / M • Marked #2 / 1993 / FD / M • Masquerade (1992-Usa) / 1992 / SC / M • Masquerade / 1995 / HO / M • The Master And The Mistress / 1993 / GOT / B • Masters Of Dominance / 1996 / GOT / C • Mistress Of The Whip / 1996 / GOT / C • Misty Rain: Wrestling Terror / 1995 / BIZ / B • More Than A Handful #5: California Or Bust / 1994 / MET / M • Mr. Peepers Amateur Home Videos #51: Bun Burners / 1992 / LBO / M • Neighborhood Watch #27 / 1992 / LBO / M • Night Of Seduction / 1994 / VC / M • Night Seduction / 1995 / VC / M • Nina Hartley's Guide To Swinging / 1996 / A&E / M • No Man's Land #09 / 1994 / VT / F • Nobody's Looking / 1993 / VC / M • Obsession / 1994 / BS / B • Odyssey 30 Min: #187: She Loves the Two Cock System / 1991 / OD / M • Odyssey 30 Min: #201: / 1992 / OD / M • Oral Majority #12 / 1994 / WV / C • The Orgy #1 / 1993 / EMC / M • The Orgy #2 / 1993 / EMC / M • The Orgy #3 / 1993 / EMC / M • Painful Lessons (Bruce Seven) / 1992 / BS / B • Peepshow / 1994 / OD / M • The Princess Slave / 1994 / BIZ / B • Profiles #03: House Dick / 1995 / XPR / M • Public Enemy / 1995 / GO / M • Public Places #1 / 1994 / SC / M • Public Places #2 / 1995 / SC / M • Pussy Tamer #1 / 1993 / BIZ / B • Pussy Tamer #2 / 1993 / BIZ / B • Reckless Passion / 1995 / WAV / M • The Right Connection / 1995 / VC / M • Sex Between The Scenes / 1994 / LAP / M • Sex Ranch / 1993 / VC / M • Sex Scientist / 1992 / FD / M • Single White Woman / 1992 / FD / M • Slave Girls' Agony / 1993 / PL / B • Sleeping Booty / 1995 / EL / M • Sodomania: Slop Shots / 1996 / EL / C • Spiked Heel Diaries #3 / 1995 / BIZ / B • Spiked Heel Diaries #4 / 1995 / BIZ / B • Spiked Heel Diaries #5 / 1995 / BIZ / B • The Spirit Of My Master / 1994 / BIZ / B • Stardust #2 / 1996 / VI / M • Steady As She Blows / 1993 / LV / M • Strap-On Sally #01: Strap-On Psycho / 1993 / PL / F • Strap-On Sally #02: Ariana Bottoms Out / 1993 / PL / F • Strap-On Sally #03: Thigh Harness Terror / 1994 / PL / F • Strap-On Sally #04: Double Penetration Dykes / 1994 / PL / F • Strip Search / 1995 / CV / M • Striptease / 1995 / SPI / M • Submission Of Ariana / 1995 / BIZ / B • The Submission Of Felecia / 1993 / BS / B • Submissive Exposure Profile #5: Keli Thomas / 1996 / STM / C • Taboo #15 / 1995 / IN / M • Takin' It To The Limit #5 / 1995 / BS / M • Tangled / 1994 / PL / M • Telephone Expose / 1995 / VC / M • Third Degree / 1992 / GOT / B • Tight Asses / 1994 / RB / B • Tight Shots #1 / 1994 / VI / M • Titanic Orgy / 1995 / PEP / M • Toe Tales #01 / 1992 / GOT / B • Toe Tales #04 / 1992 / GOT / B • Toe Tales #12 / 1994 / GOT / C • Toe Tales #18 / 1994 / GOT / B • Toe Tales #24 / 1995 / GOT / C • Tricky Business / 1995 / AFI / M • A Trip Through Pain / 1995 / BS / B • Ultimate Orgy #1 / 1992 / GLI / M • The Unashamed / 1993 / FD / M • Uncle Roy's Amateur Home Video #11 / 1992 / VIM / M • Undeniable Urge / 1996 / HAC / B • Waterworld: The Enema Movie / 1996 / BIZ / B • Web Of Darkness /

1993 / BS / B • Weekend At Joey's / 1995 / ERA / M • Welcome To Bondage: Ari / 1993 / BON / B • Welcome To Bondage: Starlets #1 / 1993 / BON / C • Where The Girls Sweat...Not The Sequel / 1996 / EL / F • The Whipping Post / 1995 / BS / B • Whips And Chains / 1995 / BS / B • Willing & Wilder / 1995 / BON / B • Without Pity / 1995 / GOT / B • Working Stiffs / 1993 / FD / M • A World Of Hurt / 1994 / BS / B • Yvonne's Odyssey / 1995 / BS / B

ARIANA (HUNG)
Sodomania #10: Euro/American Again / 1994 / EL / M

ARIANE(A) see Ariana

ARIAOLA see Star Index I

ARICK
New Faces, Hot Bodies #14 / 1994 / STP / M • New Faces, Hot Bodies #22 / 1996 / STP / M

ARIEL
Real Women...Real Fantasies! / 1996 / WSD / F • Supermodel #1 / 1994 / VI / M • A Whole Lotta Crushin' Going On / 1995 / IBN / B

ARIEL ANDERSON *(Samantha (Ariel))*
Passable face, small/medium tits, long wavy brown hair, lithe body, tattoos around belly button (2), and another on right shoulder back, and belly button ring. Says she's 28 years old in 1996 and was de-virginized at 18. Despite the tattoos around the belly button she should not be confused with the Samantha from **Green Piece Of Ass #1**.
My First Time #7 / 1996 / NS / M

ARIEL COLE
Dr Dominatrix / 1996 / LBO / B • Little Shop Of Tortures / 1996 / LBO / B • The Spank Master / 1996 / PRE / B • The Story Of Ouch! / 1996 / LBO / B • Wet Screams / 1996 / BON / B

ARIEL DAYE
Redhead (natural judging by pubic hair) but blonde in 1995 appearances with dead white skin, small tits, flat butt, flower tattoo on the left buttock, groucho black eyebrows, not pretty but not ugly either. 25 in 1993 and was de-virginized at 17. As of mid 1996 was allegedly undergoing chemotherapy for toxoplasmosis and can no longer do sex scenes. According to the *Merck Manual* toxoplasmosis of adult onset rarely needs treatment and when it does "chemotherapy" is just medication like for any other non-cancerous disease. There is no impact that would mean no sex. On the other hand, toxoplasmosis is one of the classic opportunistic infections associated with AIDS, where because of the compromised immune system, the disease does require agressive treatment. Hmmm!
Anal Island #1 / 1996 / VC / M • Anal Princess #2 / 1996 / VC / M • Anal Virgins Of America #03 / 1993 / FOR / M • Arizona Gold / 1996 / KLP / M • Assy Sassy #3 / 1995 / ROB / F • Between The Cheeks #3 / 1993 / VC / M • Black And White Revisited / 1995 / VT / F • Bubble Butts #28 / 1993 / LBO / M • Buffy's Bare Ass Barbecue / 1996 / CDI / M • Butt Sluts #5 / 1995 / ROB / F • Camera Shy / 1993 / FOR / M • Carnal Garden / 1996 / KLP / M • Caught From Behind #21 / 1995 / HO / M • Christmas Carol / 1993 / LV / M • Covergirl / 1996 / LE / M • Cum Swappers / 1995 / ZA / M • Dirty Tricks #1: Just A Bunch Of

Whores / 1995 / EA / M • Dream House / 1995 / XPR / M • Erotic Bondage / 1996 / ONA / B • Forbidden Cravings / 1996 / VC / M • Foreign Tongues #1: Going Down / 1995 / VI / M • Golddiggers #2 / 1995 / VC / M • Hard Core Beginners #01 / 1995 / LEI / M • The Heist / 1996 / WAV / M • Hollywood In Your Face / 1993 / VC / M • Indiscreet! Video Magazine #3 / 1995 / FH / M • Induced Pleasure / 1995 / ERA / M • Intense Perversions #2 / 1996 / PL / M • Interview With A Vibrator / 1996 / WAV / M • Make My Wife Please... / 1993 / VC / M • The Man Who Loves Women / 1994 / VC / M • Mystique / 1996 / SC / M • New Pussy Hunt #25 / 1996 / LEI / C • Night Tales / 1996 / VC / M • No Man's Land #14 / 1996 / VT / F • Nothing Butt The Truth / 1993 / AFV / M • Nympho Zombie Coeds / 1993 / VIM / M • Oral Obsession #2 / 1995 / VI / M • Party House / 1995 / WAV / M • Plaything #2 / 1995 / VI / M • Profiles #04: Lust Lessons / 1995 / XPR / M • Profiles #05: Planet Lust / 1995 / XPR / M • Pussyman Auditions #10 / 1995 / SNA / M • Real Tickets #1 / 1994 / VC / M • Real Tickets #2 / 1994 / VC / M • The Right Connection / 1995 / VC / M • Road Kill / 1995 / CA / M • Saturday Night Porn #3 / 1993 / AFV / M • Savage Liasons / 1995 / BEP / F • The Seduction Of Annah Marie / 1996 / VT / M • Sex Gallery / 1995 / WAV / M • Sex Machine / 1994 / VT / M • Silver Screen Confidential / 1996 / WP / M • The Tantric Guide To Sexual Potency And Extended Orgasm / 1994 / A&E / M • The Toy Box / 1996 / ONA / M • Vibrating Vixens #2 / 1996 / TV / F • Video Virgins #04 / 1993 / NS / M • Virtual Sex / 1993 / VC / M • The Wanderer #2: Slippery When Wet / 1995 / CDI / M • What's Butt Got To Do With It? / 1993 / HW / M • Wild & Wicked #6 / 1995 / VT / M • Young & Natural #03 / 1995 / PRE / F • Young & Natural #04 / 1995 / PRE / F • Young & Natural #05 / 1995 / PRE / F • Young & Natural #08 / 1995 / PRE / F • Young & Natural #09 / 1995 / PRE / C

ARIEL KNIGHT *(Tami White, Donna Leigh, Donna Leight, Demi Evris, Demi White, Donna Leah, Tammy White, Tamara White, Demi Eras, Donna Lee, Ariel Storm)*
1001 Erotic Nights #2 / 1987 / VC / M • 20th Century Fox / 1989 / FAZ / M • Amazing Tails #2 / 1987 / CA / M • Amazing Tails #3 / 1987 / CA / M • Anal Angels / 1996 / PRE / B • Angel's Revenge / 1985 / IN / M • Back To Back #1 / 1987 / 4P / C • Backdoor To Hollywood #01 / 1986 / CDI / M • Backside To The Future #1 / 1986 / ZA / M • Beauty And The Beast #2 / 1990 / VC / M • Best Of Foot Worship #3 / 1992 / BIZ / C • The Big Tease #1 / 1990 / VC / M • The Big Tease #2 / 1990 / VC / M • Black Widow / 1988 / WV / M • Blacks & Blondes #20 / 1986 / WV / M • Body And Sole / 1990 / BIZ / B • Boobs, Butts And Bloopers #1 / 1990 / HO / M • The Booby Prize #2 / 1988 / PL / F • Breaking It #2 / 1989 / GO / M • Bum Rap / 1990 / PLV / B • Busty Wrestling Babes / 1986 / VD / M • Campfire Girls / 1988 / SE / M • Candy's Little Sister Sugar / 1988 / VD / M • Cat 'nipped / 1995 / PLV / B • Classic Pics / 1988 / PP / C • Coming On America / 1989 / VWA / M • Crocodile Blondee #2 / 1988 / VCX / M •

Crystal Balls / 1986 / DR / M • Daddy's Darling Daughters / 1986 / PL / M • The Days Of Our Wives / 1988 / GO / M • Dead Ends / 1992 / PRE / B • Debbie For President / 1988 / CC / M • Deep Inside Barbie / 1989 / CDI / C • Deep Inside Keisha / 1994 / VC / C • The Desk Top Dolls / 1990 / BAD / C • Dirty Harriet / 1986 / SAT / M • Dirty Laundry / 1988 / PP / M • Double Insertion / 1986 / 4P / M • Drainman / 1989 / BIZ / B • Dy-Nasty / 1988 / SE / M • End Results / 1991 / PRE / C • Enemaced / 1988 / PLV / B • Enematews #02 / 1989 / BIZ / B • Enemates #12 / 1996 / BIZ / B • Fatal Erection / 1988 / SEV / M • Flash Floods / 1991 / PRE / C • Foot Teasers / 1988 / BIZ / B • Frat Brats / 1990 / VC / M • French Cleaners / 1986 / VCR / M • From Sweden With Love / 1989 / ZA / M • Genital Hospital / 1987 / SE / M • Girls Of The Double D #04 / 1989 / CDI / M • Girls! Girls! Girls! #2 / 1986 / VCS / C • Good Morning Taija Rae / 1988 / VCX / M • Gourmet Premier: Side Pocket / Headline Sex #910 / cr85 / GO / M • Gourmet Premier: Swinging Singles / Sizzling Stripper #907 / cr85 / GO / M • Hawaii Vice #2 / 1989 / CDI / M • Hawaii Vice #3 / 1988 / CIN / M • Hawaii Vice #6 / 1989 / CDI / M • Helpless Coeds / 1987 / BIZ / B • Hyapatia Lee's Arcade Series #01 / 1988 / ZA / C • Immoral Majority / 1986 / HTV / M • In The Flesh / 1990 / IN / M • Innocent Seduction / 1988 / VC / M • Island Girls #3: Rip Tide / 1991 / CDI / C • Jane Bond Meets Thunderthighs / 1988 / VD / M • Kascha's Blues / 1988 / CDI / M • Kascha's Days & Nights / 1989 / CDI / M • KTSX-69 / 1988 / CA / M • La Boomba / 1987 / VCX / M • The Ladies Room / 1987 / CA / M • The Last Condom / 1988 / PP / M • The Last Temptation / 1988 / VD / M • Leather & Lace / 1987 / SE / C • Leg...Ends #01 / 1988 / BIZ / F • Lethal Woman #1 / 1988 / SEV / M • License To Thrill / 1985 / VD / M • A Live Nude Girl / 1989 / VWA / M • The Magic Shower / 1989 / CDI / M • Making Charli / 1989 / CDI / M • Mantrap / 1986 / BAN / M • Maxine / 1987 / EXF / M • Me, Myself & I / 1987 / SE / C • More Chocolate Candy / 1986 / VD / M • More Unbelievable Orgies / 1989 / EVN / C • My Wildest Dreams / 1988 / IN / C • The Naked Stranger / 1988 / VI / M • Nasty Girls #1 (1989-Plum) / 1989 / PP / C • Nasty Girls #3 (1990-Plum) / 1990 / PP / M • Night Games / 1986 / WV / M • No Man's Land #02 / 1988 / VT / F • Office Girls / 1989 / CA / M • Oh! You Beautiful Doll / 1990 / ZA / M • Oral Majority #07 / 1989 / WV / C • Parliament: Lesbian Lovers #2 / 1988 / PM / F • Parliament: Samantha Strong #1 / 1986 / PM / M • Parliament: Teasers #2 / 1988 / PM / F • Parliament: Woman's Touch / 1988 / PM / F • Political Party / 1985 / AVC / M • Portrait Of A Nymph / 1988 / PP / M • Pretty Peaches #2 / 1987 / VC / M • Red Bottoms / 1988 / BIZ / B • Romeo And Juliet #2 / 1988 / WV / M • Rough Draft / 1986 / VEN / M • Ruthless Women / 1988 / SE / M • Scent Of A Woman / 1985 / GO / M • Scorching Secrets / 1988 / IN / M • Shaved Pink / 1986 / WET / M • Shaved Sinners #1 / 1988 / VT / M • Shoe Horny / 1989 / BIZ / B • Sleazy Rider / 1990 / FOV / M • Sleeping Beauty Aroused / 1989 / VI / M •

The Slutty Professor / 1989 / VWA / M • Sole Goal / 1996 / PRE / B • Sole-Ohs / 1989 / BIZ / F • Still The Brat / 1988 / VI / M • Student Fetish Videos: Best Of Foot Worship #02 / 1994 / PRE / C • Student Fetish Videos: Foot Worship #05 / 1992 / PRE / B • Super Ball / 1989 / VWA / M • Super Leg-Ends / 1992 / PRE / C • Surf, Sand And Sex / 1987 / SE / M • Tail Of The Scorpion / 1990 / ELP / M • A Taste Of Ariel / 1989 / PIN / C • Three Men And A Lady / 1988 / EVN / M • Thy Neighbour's Wife / 1986 / DR / M • Tickle Power / 1987 / PLV / B • Tickle Time / 1987 / BIZ / B • Tickled! / 1989 / BIZ / C • Tip Of The Tongue / 1985 / V20 / M • Top Buns / 1986 / HO / M • Torrid Without A Cause #1 / 1989 / VI / M • Traci Who? / 1987 / AVC / C • User Friendly #1 / 1990 / LV / M • User Friendly #2 / 1990 / LV / M • Veil / 1990 / VI / M • Virgin Cheeks / 1986 / VD / M • The Wacky World Of X-Rated Bloopers / 1989 / GO / M • Watersgate / 1994 / PRE / C • What's Up Doc / 1988 / SEV / M • When Love Came To Town / 1989 / EVN / M • Wild Fire / 1990 / WV / C • Woman To Woman / 1989 / ZA / C • A Woman's Touch / 1988 / ZA / F • Young Cheeks / 1990 / BEB / B • [Devil Women / 1989 / … / M • [Edible Vegetables / 1988 / EVN / M

ARIEL LEE *see Star Index I*
ARIEL STORM *see Ariel Knight*
ARIELE COLE
The Best Of Fabulous Flashers / 1996 / DGD / F • Eight Babes A Week / 1996 / DGD / F • Fantasy Abduction / 1997 / BON / B • Interrogation South American Style / 1995 / LBO / B • Kidnapped By Pirates / 1995 / LON / B • Kym Wilde's On The Edge #25 / 1995 / RB / B • Kym Wilde's On The Edge #26 / 1995 / RB / B • Kym Wilde's On The Edge #31 / 1996 / RB / B • Never Trust A Slave / 1996 / BON / B • Pain In The Rent / 1996 / BON / B • The Perversionist / 1995 / HOM / B • Portraits Of Pain / 1995 / B&D / B • S&M Latex: The Bitch / 1995 / SBP / B • Student Fetish Videos: Bondage #02 / 1996 / PRE / B • Student Fetish Videos: Tickling #12 / 1995 / SFV / B • Unruly Gloves #1 / 1995 / BON / B • Unruly Slaves #2 / 1995 / BON / B
ARIELLE
Up And Cummers #22 / 1995 / RWP / M
ARIES
Butt Sluts #6 / 1996 / ROB / F • Cherry Poppers #14: Teeny Tongues / 1996 / ZA / M • Dirty Dirty Debutantes #5 / 1996 / 4P / M • Hot Amateur Nights / 1996 / WV / M • Lesbian Pooper Sluts / 1996 / ROB / F • Malibu Butt Sluts / 1996 / ROB / F • Trouble In Paradise / 1996 / ULP / M • Video Virgins #27 / 1996 / NS / M
ARIES (SEVENTIES)
Sexual Awareness / cr72 / CDC / M
ARISTIDE MASSACCESI *see Joe D'Amato*
ARIZONA *see Star Index I*
ARIZONA ALICE
Eric Kroll's Fetish #2 / 1994 / ERK / M • Eric Kroll's Fetish #3: Female Hygiene / 1994 / ERK / M
ARLANA BLUE *see Alana Blue*
ARLEEN DUPREE *see Star Index I*
ARLEEN GODDMAN *see Star Index I*
ARLENE
A&B AB#279: Ecstasy And Agony / 1991 /

A&B / M • A&B AB#285: Marge / 1991 / A&B / M • A&B AB#289: My Ass Is Red / 1991 / A&B / B
ARLENE AUBER
Sex U.S.A / 1970 / SEP / M
ARLENE HUNTER
The Marilyn Monroe double.
The Art Of Burlesque / 1968 / SOW / S • Baghdad After Midnight / cr65 / SOW / S • Big Bust Loops #02 / 1993 / SOW / M • Big Bust Loops #12 / 1993 / SOW / M • Bare Vanities #008 / 1988 / FFL / M • Electric Blue #003 / 1981 / CA / S • Glamour Girls U.S.A. #01 / 1995 / SOW / M • Grindhouse Follies: First Row #01 / 1993 / SOW / M • GVC: Shauna, Blonde Superstar #132 / 1984 / GO / C • Madness / cr80 / VTE / S • Nostalgic Sex Series #2 / 1980 / WWV / M • Nudie Classics #3 / 1993 / VDM / M • Olde Time Erotica #2 / 1990 / PL / M • Only The Best Of Oral / 1989 / CV / C • Only The Best Of Women With Women / 1988 / CV / C • Our Sexual History / 1992 / A&E / M • Striporama #2 / 1993 / VDM / S • A Virgin In Hollywood / cr68 / SOW / S
ARLENE JAMISON
One Last Score / 1978 / CDI / M
ARLENE MANHATTAN
The 8th Annual Erotic Film Awards / 1984 / SE / C • Aphrodesia's Diary / 1984 / CA / C • Girls With Curves #1 / 1985 / CV / M • The Tale Of Tiffany Lust / 1981 / CA / M • [Making Out / 1976 / … / M
ARLENE PHILLIPS
Blue Vanities #056 / 1988 / FFL / M • Blue Vanities #524 / 1993 / FFL / M • Blue Vanities #585 / 1996 / FFL / M
ARLENE ROSS
Woman Of The Night / 1971 / SVE / M
ARLENE STEWARD
Star Of The Orient / 1978 / VIP / M
ARMAND
Bored Games / 1988 / ALF / M • Tania's Lustexzesse / 1994 / MET / M
ARMAND ELLISON
The Joy Of Fooling Around / 1978 / CV / M
ARMAND PIERRE LASCAU *see Star Index I*
ARMAND YEROUN
Amour / 1978 / VC / M
ARMELLE BLUES
Anal Boat / 1996 / P69 / M
ARMIN
Der Mosen-Pflucker / 1995 / KRM / M
ARNE LARSON
Garters And Lace / 1975 / SE / M
ARNELLE
Absolute Anal / 1996 / XC / M
ARNIE POLLOCK *see Star Index I*
ARNO *see Star Index I*
ARNOLD SCHWARTZ
Viola Video #107: Private Party / 1995 / PEV / M
ARNOLD SCHWARTZPECKE *(Arnold Squirtz)*
The name should be "Arnold Schwartzpecker" or some variant thereof.
19 & Naughty #1 / 1994 / SKV / M • 9-Ball: Geisha Gang Bang / 1994 / PL / M • Adventures Of The DP Boys: South Of The Border / 1995 / HW / M • Anal 247 / 1995 / CC / M • Bang City #1: Kelly's Anal Gang Bang / 1995 / SC / M • Bang City #4: Gina's Anal Gang Bang / 1995 / SC / M • Bar-B-Que Gang Bang / 1994 / JMP / M •

Ben Dover & Barbie / 1995 / SUF / M • Big Murray's New-Cummers #17: Age Before Beauty / 1993 / FD / M • Bubble Butts Gold #2 / 1994 / LBO / M • Butt Hole In-One / 1994 / AFV / M • Come And Get It! / 1995 / LBO / M • D.P. Party Tonite / 1995 / JMP / M • Dirty And Kinky Mature Women #1 / 1995 / C69 / M • Dirty Doc's Housecalls #03 / 1993 / LV / M • Dirty Doc's Housecalls #06 / 1993 / LV / M • Dirty Doc's Housecalls #07 / 1994 / LV / M • Dirty Doc's Housecalls #09 / 1994 / LV / M • Dixie Downes Gang Bang / 1996 / FC / M • Double Crossed / 1994 / MID / M • East Vs West: Battle Of The Gang Bangs / 1994 / TTV / M • Electro Sex / 1994 / FPI / M • Emerald: Princess Of The Night / 1996 / FC / M • Gang Bang Bitches #01 / 1994 / PP / M • Gang Bang Bitches #02 / 1994 / PP / M • Gang Bang Bitches #03 / 1994 / PP / M • Gang Bang Bitches #04 / 1995 / PP / M • Gang Bang Bitches #05 / 1995 / PP / M • Gang Bang Bitches #06 / 1995 / PP / M • Gang Bang Bitches #07 / 1995 / PP / M • Gang Bang Bitches #08 / 1995 / PP / M • Gang Bang Bitches #09 / 1995 / PP / M • Gang Bang Bitches #10 / 1995 / PP / M • Gang Bang Diaries #3 / 1994 / SFP / M • Gang Bang Virgin #1 / 1994 / HO / M • Gang Bang Virgin #2 / 1995 / HO / M • Ganggstas Paradise / 1995 / AVI / M • Grateful Grandma's Gang Bang / 1994 / FC / M • Green Piece Of Ass #1 / 1994 / RTP / M • Green Piece Of Ass #2 / 1994 / RTP / M • Holly's Holiday Gang Bang / 1994 / LBO / M • Horny Henry's Oriental Adventure / 1994 / TTV / M • Horny Henry's Peeping Adventures / 1994 / TTV / M • Horny Henry's Snowballing Adventure / 1995 / TTV / M • Kinky Debutante Interviews #03 / 1994 / IP / M • Kinky Debutante Interviews #05 / 1994 / IP / M • Lady M's Anal Gang Bang / 1995 / FC / M • Lessons 'n' Love / 1994 / LBO / M • M Series #24 / 1994 / LBO / M • M Series #25 / 1994 / LBO / M • Monkey Gang Bang / 1996 / NOT / M • Neighborhood Watch #39: / 1993 / LBO / M • Nena Cherry's Dp Gang Bang / 1996 / NIT / M • Next...! / 1995 / ... / M • Nici Sterling's Dp Gang Bang / 1996 / FC / M • Nydp Pink / 1994 / HW / M • Over Forty Gang Bang / 1994 / RTP / M • Patty Plenty's Gang Bang / 1995 / NIT / M • Please Take A Number / 1996 / CDI / M • Raw Sex #02 / 1995 / ERW / M • Reel People #06 / 1995 / PP / M • Reel People #07 / 1995 / PP / M • Roxy: A Gang Bang Fantasy / 1994 / FC / M • Rump Man: Forever / 1995 / HW / M • Rumpman In And Out Of Africa / 1996 / HW / M • Sex Circus / 1994 / VIM / M • Sofia: A Gang Bang Fantasy / 1994 / FC / M • The Spa / 1996 / RAS / M • Studio Bust Out / 1994 / BTO / M • Stuff Your Ass #3 / 1996 / JMP / M • Stuff Your Face #1 / 1994 / JMP / M • Stuff Your Face #2 / 1995 / JMP / M • Tia's Holiday Gang Bang / 1995 / HO / M • Tight Fit #03 / 1994 / GO / M • Tight Fit #07 / 1994 / GO / M • Titanic Orgy / 1995 / PEP / M • Ultimate Anal Gang Bang #3 / 1995 / HW / M • Wicked Waxxx Worxxx / 1995 / HW / M • Wild Orgies #08 / 1994 / AFI / M
ARNOLD SQUIRTZ *see Arnold Schwartzpecke*
ARNOLD STRANGLER
The Tale Of Tiffany Lust / 1981 / CA / M

ARNOLD SWARTZ
Cheri's On Fire / 1986 / V99 / M • Glamour Girls / 1987 / SE / M • Love At First Sight / 1987 / SE / C

ARNY SCHWARTZ *see Star Index I*

ARRILA TIMEA
Somewhere Under The Rainbow #2 / 1995 / HW / M

ARROW GARRETT *see Nikki Wylde*

ART CLAYBOURNE
Pink Champagne / 1979 / CV / M

ART DECKO
Showgirl She-Male / 1996 / HSV / G

ART DOLORES
Bucky Beaver's XXX Dragon Art Theatre Double Feature #11 / 1996 / SOW / M • Teenage Fantasies #1 / 1972 / SOW / M

ART JORDAN
Pornocopia Sensual / 1976 / VHL / M

ART LONDON
Badgirls #2: Strip Search / 1994 / VI / M

ART NORTH
Sticky Situation / 1975 / VXP / M

ART ROBERTS
The Pleasure Palace / 1978 / CV / M

ART SAUNDERS *see Mark Saunders*

ART STEVENS *see Star Index I*

ART THANASH
Never So Deep / 1981 / VCX / M

ARTEMIS ANTOINE *see Artemis Antone*

ARTEMIS ANTONE *(Artemis Antoine)*
Quite pretty but a little on the heavy side. 5'2" tall and supposedly 22 years old in 1997 but she also says her birthday is 10/20/70 which would make her 26 (information from the same movie). Also works with her mother, Jennifer Antone.
Anal Gang Bangers #01 / 1992 / GLI / M • At The Mercy Of Mistress Jacqueline / 1993 / STM / B • Behind The Backdoor #5 / 1992 / EVN / M • Bondage Fantasy #1 / 1995 / BON / B • Bondage Fantasy #3 / 1995 / BON / B • Bondage Is Our Pleasure / 1996 / BON / B • The Computer Date / 1994 / ATO / B • Dazzling Dominants / 1991 / RSV / B • Depths Of Domination / 1993 / NAP / B • Facesitting Frenzy / 1995 / IBN / B • Foot Licking Fantasy / 1993 / SSP / B • In Your Face / 1995 / IBN / B • Lazy Boy / 1995 / ATO / B • Lessons From The Mistress / 1994 / BON / B • The Luxury Of Servitude / 1994 / BON / B • Magical Mistresses: Jennifer And Artemis / 1993 / RSV / B • More Dirty Debutantes #62 / 1997 / SBV / M • Mother & Daughter From Hell / 1996 / ATO / B • Personal Trainer (Ibn) / 1995 / IBN / B • Playtoys For Mistress Artemis / 1992 / RSV / B • Queen Dominatrix / 1993 / NAP / B • Real People Real Bondage #2 / 1996 / BON / C • Slaves Of Artemis / 1996 / BON / B • Spectator Sport / 1993 / VVO / B • Taped, Tied & Tormented / 1994 / ATO / B • Trainer's Turnabout / 1994 / BON / B • Trample Bimbo / 1995 / IBN / B • Vixen Takes Control / 1993 / VER / B

ARTHUR (C. JAMMER) *see Cal Jammer*

ARTHUR FENTON *see Jim Holliday*

ARTHUR GREENSPAN
All About Sex / 1970 / AR / M

ARTHUR IRVING
All About Sex / 1970 / AR / M

ARTHUR KNIGHT
Bad Girls #2 / 1983 / GO / M

ARTHUR POTTS *see Star Index I*

ARTHUR WEST *see Jerry Butler*

ARTIE
Dirty Dancers #1 / 1994 / 4P / M • Intimate Interviews #4 / 1996 / NIT / M

ARTIE MITCHELL
Shot to death by his brother, Jim in 1991. Jim was later convicted of voluntary manslaughter. Part owner of the O'Farrell Theatre in SFO.
Behind The Green Door #1 / 1972 / MIT / M • Reckless Claudia / 1971 / MIT / M

ARTII CHOKE
Comeback / 1995 / VI / M • The Devil In Miss Jones #5: The Inferno / 1994 / VC / M • Sexy Nurses #2 / 1994 / CV / M

ARTURO MILLHOUSE
Bionca, Just For You / 1989 / BON / F • Midnight Desires / 1976 / VXP / M • The Passions Of Carol / 1975 / VXP / M

ASAMI KOBAYASHI
Love Melody / 1983 / ORC / M

ASH
HomeGrown Video #466: Loot The Booty / 1996 / HOV / M

ASHA DAS *see Star Index I*

ASHELY WINTERS
Girls Around The World #27 / 1995 / BTO / M

ASHEYA *see Mauvais DeNoire*

ASHLEE *see Star Index I*

ASHLEE COLORS
California Blacks / 1994 / V99 / M • Chocolate Bunnies #04 / 1995 / LBO / C • Ebony Erotica #06: Black Essence / 1993 / GO / M • Ebony Erotica #09: Bronze Thrills / 1993 / GO / M • Ebony Erotica #12: Pussy Posse / 1993 / GO / M • M Series #03 / 1993 / LBO / M • Much More Than A Mouthful #3 / 1993 / VEX / M • Rump-Shaker #1 / 1993 / HW / M • Sex Machine / 1994 / VT / M • Tight Home Girls / 1993 / EVN / C

ASHLEE LYONS
One of three girls in **Nasty Girls #3 (1990-CDI)**. May be either a Nina De Ponca look-a-like or an ugly blonde.
Nasty Girls #3 (1990-CDI) / 1990 / CDI / M

ASHLEE SCENE
Positively Pagan #01 / 1991 / ATA / M • Positively Pagan #02 / 1991 / ATA / M • Positively Pagan #04 / 1991 / ATA / M • Positively Pagan #06 / 1993 / ATA / M

ASHLEIGH (BRITISH)
Filthy First Timers #6 / 1997 / EL / M

ASHLEIGH TAYLOR
Eight Babes A Week / 1996 / DGD / F • Hot Body Video Magazine: Sweet Dreams / 1996 / CG / F • The Spank Master / 1996 / PRE / B

ASHLEY
The Applicant / 1988 / BON / B • AVP #4004: A Girl's Best Friend / 1990 / AVP / F • Bubbles / 1993 / KBR / S • Cat Walk / 1994 / KBR / S • Dr Pussy's Tasty Tails #1 / 1993 / SHV / F • Facesitting Frenzy / 1995 / IBN / B • Flash Backs / 1990 / BON / B • Full Moon Video #19: Toys For Twats / 1994 / FAP / F • Girls Next Door / 1996 / ANE / M • Homegrown Video #342 / 1991 / HOV / M • HomeGrown Video #458: Cream Pie For Dessert / 1995 / HOV / C • Lucky Ladies #101 / 1992 / STI / M • Nasty Fuckin' Movies #24 / 1994 / RUM / M • Nasty Newcummers #10 / 1995 / MET / M • New Faces, Hot Bodies #09 / 1993 / STP

/ M • Odyssey Triple Play #98: Three Ways To Sunday / 1995 / OD / M • Pearl Necklace: Premier Sessions #01 / 1993 / SEE / M • Pussy Hunt #01 / 1994 / LEI / M • Southern: Previews #1 / 1992 / SSH / C • Student Fetish Videos: The Enema #10 / 1993 / PRE / B • Student Fetish Videos: Spanking #10 / 1993 / PRE / B • Student Fetish Videos: Tickling #07 / 1992 / SFV / B • Top It Off / 1990 / VC / M • Unlaced / 1992 / PL / M • Up And Cummers #17 / 1994 / 4P / M

ASHLEY ALLEN *see Crystal Deveraux*

ASHLEY BRITTON *see Stacey Donovan*

ASHLEY BROOKS
Gourmet Premier: Swinging Singles / Sizzling Stripper #907 / cr85 / GO / M • Tinsel Town / 1980 / VC / M • The Wacky World Of X-Rated Bloopers / 1989 / GO / M

ASHLEY BROWN *see Taylor Evans*

ASHLEY BUST
Big Boob Bikini Bash / 1995 / BTO / M • Girls Around The World #20: Deena Duos & Friends / 1994 / BTO / M

ASHLEY COLE *see Ashley Nicole*

ASHLEY DARK
AVP #9109: Have-A-Ball Bar / 1991 / AVP / M

ASHLEY DAVIDSON *see Star Index I*

ASHLEY DAWN *see Ashley Dunn*

ASHLEY DOWNING *see Ashley Dunn*

ASHLEY DUBOIS
Inside Seka / 1980 / VXP / M

ASHLEY DUNN *(Ashley Dawn, Ashley Downing)*
First seen in **True Sin** where she had small breasts. They were subsequently enlarged in a K-Mart job which left visible scars. Slightly Oriental looking but quite pretty.
The A Chronicles / 1992 / CC / M • Amateur Nights #03 / 1990 / HO / M • Another Secret / 1990 / SO / M • As Sweet As They Come / 1992 / V99 / M • Assault With A Friendly Weapon / 1990 / DAY / M • Avenging Angeli / 1990 / CC / M • Body & Soul / 1995 / IF / M • Cape Rear / 1992 / WV / M • Deep Dreams / 1990 / IN / M • Deep Inside Samantha Strong / 1992 / CDI / C • Dream Girls / 1990 / CIN / M • The Dream Merchants / 1990 / CDI / M • The Easy Way / 1990 / VC / M • Erectnophobia #1 / 1991 / MID / M • Forbidden Games / 1990 / CDI / M • Girls Will Be Boys #2 / 1990 / PL / F • Girly Video Magazine #6 / 1996 / AB / M • Hot Meat / 1990 / V99 / M • Inner Pink #4 / 1995 / LIP / F • Jugsy (Western) / 1992 / WV / M • Lady In Blue / 1990 / CIN / M • Lambody / 1990 / CDI / M • Lethal Love / 1990 / DAY / M • Love In An Elevator / 1990 / CC / M • Mr. Peepers Amateur Home Videos #03: Satin 'n' Face / 1991 / LBO / M • Nasty Ladies / 1990 / PP / C • Oral Clinic / 1990 / DAY / M • The Pawnbroker / 1990 / IF / M • Rapture / 1990 / SC / M • Red Hot / 1990 / EX / M • Sexual Intent / 1990 / PP / M • The Sexual Limits / 1992 / VC / M • Snatch Masters #01 / 1994 / LEI / M • True Sin / 1990 / PP / M • Vampirass / 1992 / VC / M

ASHLEY FAIR
Private Film #08 / 1994 / OD / M

ASHLEY FIELDS
Bound Before Xmas / 1995 / VTF / B • Knot Of Eroticism / 1995 / VTF / B • Little Shop Of Tickle / 1995 / SBP / B • Secrets Of Bondage / 1995 / SBP / B • Shockers /

1996 / SBP / B • Student Fetish Videos: Bondage #01 / 1995 / PRE / B • Student Fetish Videos: Tickling #12 / 1995 / SFV / B

ASHLEY GRANT *see* Taylor Evans
ASHLEY KING *see* Star Index I
ASHLEY KNIGHT
Dirty & Kinky Mature Women #08 / 1996 / C69 / M

ASHLEY LAUREN *(Kristen (A. Lauren))*
Pretty blonde with a petite body and small natural tits. Unfortunately, in none of her appearances does she do more than masturbate. Is either Kristen or Valerie Stone in **House of Dreams** and **Secrets** and I've presumed for the purposes of attribution that she is Kristen.
Andrew Blake's Girls / 1992 / CA / C • California Blondes #06 / 1992 / VD / C • Desire / 1990 / VC / M • Erotic Eye / 1995 / DGD / S • House Of Dreams / 1990 / CA / M • Little Miss Curious / 1991 / CA / M • Penthouse: Great Pet Hunt #2 / 1993 / NIV / F • Secrets / 1990 / CA / M
ASHLEY LIBERTY *see* Lady Ashley Liberty
ASHLEY MOORE *(C. Moore Ashley, Seymour Ashley, Steve Tucker)*
Tall male with a moustache.
Babylon Gold / 1983 / COM / C • The Bimbo #1 / 1985 / VXP / M • The Bimbo #2: The Homecoming / 1986 / RLV / M • Bizarre Styles / 1981 / ALP / B • Black Licorice / 1985 / CDI / M • Bon Appetit / 1980 / QX / M • Candy Stripers #2 / 1985 / AR / M • Candy Stripers #3 / 1986 / AR / M • China Doll / 1976 / VC / M • Chocolate Bon-Bons / 1985 / PL / M • The Collegiates / 1971 / BL / M • Cravings / 1987 / VC / M • Daddy's Little Girls / 1983 / CA / M • Deep Throat #2 / 1986 / AR / M • Devil In Miss Jones #2 / 1983 / VC / M • Dominatrix Without Mercy / 1976 / ALP / B • Down & Out In New York City / 1986 / SE / M • Erotic Moments / 1985 / CDI / C • The Erotic World Of Angel Cash / 1983 / VXP / M • Feel The Heat / 1985 / AAH / M • A Girl Like That / 1979 / CDC / M • Glitter / 1983 / CA / M • Hidden Fantasies / 1986 / VD / M • The Houseplayer / 1987 / OXH / M • Honeypie / 1975 / VC / M • Hot Dreams / 1983 / CA / M • House Of Sin / 1982 / AVO / M • Inside Seka / 1980 / VXP / M • Justine: A Matter Of Innocence / 1980 / SAT / M • Krazy 4 You / 1987 / 4P / M • Lady Madonna / 1985 / RLV / M • The Love Tapes / 1980 / BL / M • Miami Vice Girls / 1984 / RLV / M • Mouth To Mouth / 1986 / CC / M • Nasty Girls (1983-VCX) / 1983 / VCX / M • Neon Nights / 1981 / COM / M • Never Sleep Alone / 1984 / CA / M • Only The Very Best On Film / 1992 / VC / C • Pandora's Mirror / 1981 / CA / M • A Passage Thru Pamela / 1985 / VC / G • The Passions Of Carol / 1975 / VXP / M • Platinum Paradise / 1980 / COM / M • The Playgirl / 1982 / CA / M • Prisoner Of Pleasure / 1981 / ALP / B • Private School Girls / 1983 / CA / M • Quicksilver / 1987 / CDI / M • Raw Talent #2 / 1987 / VC / M • Rimshot / 1987 / CDI / M • Roommates / 1982 / VXP / M • Secret Mistress / 1986 / VD / M • Sex Crimes 2084 / 1985 / SE / M • Sharon / 1977 / AR / M • Silky / 1980 / VXP / M • Slave Of Pleasure / 1978 / BL / M • Sleazy Susan / 1986 / VXP / M • Sugar

Britches / 1980 / VCX / C • Suzie's Take Out Service / 1975 / CDC / M • Temptations Of The Flesh / 1986 / VD / M • Three Daughters / 1986 / FEM / M • Thunderstorm / 1987 / VC / M • Times Square Comes Alive / 1984 / VC / M • Tongue 'n Cheek (Red Light) / 1984 / RLV / M • Too Many Pieces / 1975 / LA / M • Ultrasex / 1987 / VC / M • Voluptuous Predators / cr76 / VHL / M • Wanda Whips Wall Street / 1982 / VXP / M • Whatever Happened To Miss September? / 1973 / ALP / M • White Women / 1986 / CC / M • The Widespread Scandals Of Lydia Lace / 1983 / CA / M • Wrecked 'em / 1985 / CC / M • Young Nympho's / 1986 / VD / M

ASHLEY MORRISON
Hidden Camera #15 / 1994 / JMP / M • Mr. Peepers Amateur Home Videos #83: Roni And The Private's / 1994 / LBO / M • New Ends #06 / 1994 / 4P / M • Pleasure Dome: The Genesis Chamber / 1994 / AFV / M • Swinging Couples #03 / 1994 / GO / M • Vivid At Home #02 / 1994 / VI / M
ASHLEY NICKOLE *see* Ashley Nicole
ASHLEY NICOLE *(Ashley Cole, Ashley Nickole)*
Acts Of Confession / 1991 / PP / M • Adult Video News 1992 Awards / 1992 / VC / M • Amateur American Style #19 / 1992 / AFV / M • America's Dirtiest Home Videos #03 / 1991 / VEX / M • America's Dirtiest Home Videos #08 / 1992 / VEX / M • Anal Blitz / 1991 / MID / M • Anal Dawn / 1991 / AMB / M • Anal Nation #2 / 1990 / CC / M • Another Rear View / 1990 / LE / M • The Back Doors (Executive) / 1991 / EX / M • The Backpackers #3 / 1991 / IN / M • Ball Busters / 1991 / FH / M • Bazooka County #3 / 1991 / CC / M • The Best Of The Gangbang Girl Series / 1995 / ANA / C • Black Balled / 1990 / ZA / M • Bonfire Of The Panties / 1990 / CC / M • Breasts And Beyond #2 / 1991 / ME / M • The Butt Stops Here / 1991 / LV / M • Cum Blasted Cuties / 1993 / GO / C • Cumming Clean / 1991 / FL / M • Curse Of The Catwoman / 1990 / VC / M • Dances With Foxes / 1991 / CC / M • Dirty Business / 1992 / CV / M • Drugie Hasan The World's Youngest Gynaecologist / 1990 / VT / M • Dr Butts #1 / 1991 / 4P / M • Edward Penishands #1 / 1991 / VT / M • The Enchantress / 1990 / VI / M • The Eternal Idol / 1992 / CDI / M • Eternity / 1991 / CDI / M • Foxx Hunt / 1991 / GO / M • Gangbang Girl #05 / 1992 / ANA / M • Gangbang Girl #06 / 1992 / ANA / M • Good Vibrations #1: Self Satisfaction With A Vibrator / 1991 / VT / M • Hot Shots / 1992 / VD / C • Imagine / 1991 / LV / M • In The Jeans Again / 1990 / ME / M • Inferno / 1991 / XCI / M • The Journey: Oral Majority / 1991 / WV / M • The Lascivious Ladies Of Dr Lipo / 1991 / OD / M • Leena Goes Pro / 1992 / VT / M • Legend #3 / 1991 / LE / M • A Little Nookie / 1991 / VD / M • Most Wanted / 1991 / GO / M • Nasty Jack's Homemade Vid. #15 / 1991 / CDI / M • Nasty Jack's Homemade Vid. #16 / 1991 / CDI / M • New Wave Hookers #2 / 1991 / VC / M • No Time For Love / 1991 / VI / M • Nothing But Trouble / 1991 / CIN / M • Odyssey Amateur #47: Gangbang-A-Gram / 1991 / OD / M • The Perfect Pair / 1991 / LE / M • Punished Princess / 1992 / HOM / B • Raunch #03 /

1991 / CC / M • Screwballs / 1991 / AFV / M • Selena's Secrets / 1991 / MIN / M • Sensuous / 1991 / LV / M • Sex Asylum #4 / 1991 / VI / M • Sex Express / 1991 / SE / M • Shake Well Before Using / 9990 / LV / M • Silver Sensations / 1992 / VT / M • Sittin' Pretty #1 / 1990 / DR / M • Special Treatment / 1991 / AFV / M • Step To The Rear / 1991 / VD / M • Sudden Urge / 1990 / IN / M • Sweat Shop / 1991 / EVN / M • Taste For Submission / 1991 / LON / C • Things That Go Hump in the Night / 1991 / LV / M • Three Men And A Hooker / 1991 / WV / M • Titillation #3 / 1991 / SE / M • Titty-Titty Bang-Bang / 1992 / FC / C • Top It Off / 1990 / VC / M • Toys, Not Boys #1 / 1991 / FC / C • A Trip Down Mammary Lane / 1991 / FC / M • Two Of A Kind / 1990 / LV / M • Two Of A Kind / 1991 / ZA / M • We're Having A Party / 1991 / EVN / M • Wicked / 1991 / XCI / M • Wicked Fascination / 1991 / CIN / M • Wild & Wicked #1 / 1991 / VT / M • Wild Side / 1991 / GO / M • The Wild Wild Chest #1 / 1990 / HO / M • The Wright Stuff / 1991 / AFV / M • [Quodoushka / 1991 / VI / M
ASHLEY NIGER *see* Ashley Winger
ASHLEY O'BRIEN *see* Star Index I
ASHLEY PHILLIPS (CL) *see* Christie Leeds
ASHLEY RENE *(Micki Marsaille, Miki Marsalli)*
Pretty brunette with large tits and a tight body. Was 28 in 1995, comes from Hollywood CA, and was de-virginized at 15. .
976 Video #2: The Brunettes / 1994 / TZV / F • Alexis Goes To Hell / 1996 / EXQ / B • The Ambassador File / 1995 / HOM / B • Arch Worship / 1995 / PRE / B • Ashley Rene & Veronica: Bondage Buddies / 1994 / BON / B • Ashley Renee In Jeopardy / 1991 / HOM / B • Audition For Pain / 1996 / VTF / B • Bad Girls Get Punished / 1994 / NTP / B • Bad Slaves / 1995 / HOM / B • Bare-Chested, Bare-Breasted, Big-Busted, Wet T-Shirt Video / 1990 / NAP / B • Bedside Cats / 1989 / NAP / B • Beg For Mercy / 1993 / LBO / B • Big Boob Conflict / 1994 / NAP / B • Big Bust Bikini Battle / 1991 / NAP / B • Bigger is Better / 1992 / NAP / B • The Blonde And The Brunette / 1989 / NAP / B • Body Vs. Body / 1989 / NAP / B • Bondage Cheerleaders / 1993 / LON / B • Bondage Memories #01 / 1993 / BON / C • Bondage Memories #04 / 1994 / BON / C • The Bondage Society / 1991 / LON / B • Bound Before Xmas / 1995 / VTF / B • Bound To Tease #4 / 1989 / BON / C • Breast Friends, Breast Enemies / 1994 / NAP / B • Bun Runners / 1994 / PRE / B • The Cat In Danielle / 1993 / NAP / B • Cat-Fight Audition / 1990 / NAP / B • The Cats of Club Napali / 1990 / NAP / B • Caught From Behind #21 / 1995 / HO / M • Clash / 1989 / NAP / B • Club Sadismo / 1993 / LON / B • Compelled By Restraints / 1996 / VTF / B • Contract / 1995 / LON / B • Corporate Affairs / 1996 / CC / M • Dance To The Whip / 1996 / LBO / B • Defiance: The Art Of Spanking / 1996 / BIZ / B • Detective Covergirls / 1996 / CUC / B • Dirty Dancers #6 / 1995 / 4P / M • Dirty Dancers #9 / 1996 / HO / M • Dirty Tails / 1996 / SC / M • Diva #2: Deep In Glamour / 1996 / VC / F • The Divine Marquis / 1995 / ONA / B • Double Trouble Spanking /

1993 / BON / B • Duel Of The Cats / 1990 / NAP / B • Dungeon Delight / 1995 / LON / B • Eighteen #2 / 1996 / SC / M • Eighteen #3 / 1996 / SC / M • Th Fanny / 1997 / WP / M • Felicia's Fantasies / 1995 / HOM / B • The Fine Art Of Hairpulling / 1993 / NAP / B • Finger Pleasures #6 / 1996 / PL / F • Fist Of Leather / 1989 / NAP / B • Gang-bang Bitches / 1996 / LON / B • A Girl's Affair #08 / 1995 / FD / F • A Girl's Affair #10 / 1996 / FD / F • Goldilocks And The 3 Bi Bears / 1997 / TTV / G • A Grand Obses-sion / 1992 / B&D / B • Grand Slam / 1990 / PRE / B • Hot Flesh, Cold Chains / 1992 / HOM / B • Hot Rod To Hell #2 / 1992 / BS / B • Interrogation South American Style / 1995 / LBO / B • Introducing Cindy Kramer / 1989 / NAP / F • Introducing Micki Mar-saille / 1990 / NAP / F • It Takes Hair To Be A Woman / 1995 / NAP / B • Jane Bondage Is Captured / 1993 / LON / B • Jasmine's Girls / 1995 / LON / B • The Joi Of Tit Fighting / 199? / NAP / B • Knot Of Eroticism / 1995 / VTF / B • Kym Wilde's On The Edge #31 / 1996 / RB / B • Leather Bound Dykes From Hell #8 / 1996 / BIZ / B • Leg...Ends #12 / 1994 / PRE / F • Lip Service / 1995 / WP / M • Magnificent Seven / 1991 / NAP / F • Maid For Bondage / 1993 / BON / B • Mean Streak / 1994 / NAP / B • Melissa's Wish / 1993 / LON / B • Mellon Man #04 / 1995 / AVI / M • Mellon Man #07 / 1996 / AVI / M • Micki Meets Her Match / 1992 / NAP / B • Micki's Big Bust / 199? / NAP / B • Mis-Fortune / 1995 / VTF / B • Miss Matches / 1996 / PRE / C • Mistress Kane: Lessons In Terror / 1996 / BIZ / B • Mistress Of Cruelty / cr94 / HOM / B • Mistress Of Hair Pulling / 1993 / NAP / B • Mistress Of Misery / 1996 / LBO / B • Modern Torture / 1992 / PL / B • No Man's Land #13 / 1996 / VT / F • No Man's Land #14 / 1996 / VT / F • No Man's Land #15 / 1996 / VT / F • Nude Secre-taries / 1994 / EDE / S • Pain Puppets / 1996 / LBO / B • Picture Me Bound / 1995 / LON / B • Prescription For Pain #1 / 1992 / BON / B • Punishment Of Ashley Renee / 1993 / BON / B • Pussyclips #09 / 1995 / SNA / M • Pussyman's House Party #1 / 1996 / SNA / M • Pussyman's House Party #2 / 1996 / SNA / M • Queen Of The Lash / 1993 / LON / B • Rendezvous With A BBS Mistress / 1995 / IBN / B • Roommates / 1989 / BON / B • S&M Locked / 1996 / VTF / B • S&M Sessions / 1996 / VTF / B • Scared Stiff / 1992 / PL / B • Sexual Ha-rassment / 1996 / TTV / M • Sexual HerASSment / 1995 / IBN / B • Shooting Gallery / 1996 / EL / M • Slap Happy / 1994 / PRE / B • Spankology 101a / 1994 / BON / B • Spankology 101b / 1994 / BON / B • Stories Of Seduction / 1996 / MID / M • Strictly For Pleasure / 1994 / ONA / B • Student Fetish Videos: Best of Catfighting #02 / 1994 / PRE / C • Student Fetish Videos: Best of Catfighting #03 / 1995 / PRE / C • Student Fetish Videos: Best Of Foot Worship #03 / 1995 / PRE / C • Stu-dent Fetish Videos: Bondage #03 / 1996 / PRE / B • Student Fetish Videos: Catfight-ing #09 / 1994 / PRE / B • Student Fetish Videos: Catfighting #11 / 1994 / PRE / B • Student Fetish Videos: Foot Worship #12 / 1994 / PRE / B • Student Fetish Videos: Spanking #14 / 1994 / PRE / B • Student

Fetish Videos: Spanking #22 / 1996 / PRE / B • Student Fetish Videos: Tickling #13 / 1996 / SFV / B • Tarts In Torment / 1993 / LBO / B • Tau Kappa Ticklers / 1995 / HAC / B • Threshold Of Fear / 1993 / BON / B • The Thrill Of Competition / 1989 / NAP / B • Tickling Vamps / 1995 / SBP / B • Topless Window Washers / 1996 / LE / M • Toppers #19 / 1993 / TV / M • Toppers #21 / 1993 / TV / C • Tortured Passions / 1994 / PL / B • The Torturous Infidel / 1994 / PL / B • The Tower Of Lyndon / 1994 / LON / B • Tri-umph Of The Flesh / 1990 / NAP / B • Up And Cummers #23 / 1995 / 4P / M • Victo-ria Victorious / 1990 / NAP / B • Video Vir-gins #28 / 1996 / NS / M • Violation / 1996 / LE / M • Wheel Of Obsession / 1996 / TWP / B • When Big Busted Cats Tangle / 1990 / NAP / B • When Mams Collide / 1992 / NAP / B • The Whips & Chains Af-fair / 1994 / HOM / B • White Slavers / 1996 / LBO / B • Wild Cherries / 1996 / SC / F • Winner Takes All / 1995 / LON / B • The Wrath Of Kane / 1995 / BON / B • Wylder Nights / 1996 / BON / B

ASHLEY SHYE
Brown hair, passable face, tiny tits with swollen areola, loss of belly muscle tone, nice butt. Seems to have a nice tomboyish personal-ity. 19 years old in 1996 and de-virginized at 17.

Anal Auditions #3 / 1996 / LE / M • Anal Reunion / 1996 / EVN / M • Analtown USA #09 / 1995 / NIT / M • Casting Call #16 / 1995 / SO / M • Casting Call #17 / 1996 / SO / M • Cherry Poppers #15: Mischievous Maidens / 1996 / ZA / M • Country & West-ern Cuties #1 / 1996 / EVN / M • Creme De La Face #12: Pretty Faces To Cum On / 1995 / OD / M • The Cumm Brothers #17: Goo Guy Gone Bad / 1996 / OD / M • Delinquents On Butt Row / 1996 / EA / M • Filthy First Timers #1 / 1996 / EL / M • Fresh Faces #10 / 1996 / EVN / M • Hard-core Schoolgirls #4: Little Kittens / 1996 / XPR / M • Hardcore Schoolgirls #5: Virgin Killers / 1996 / XPR / M • The Hitch-Hiker #16: Dirty Low Down / 1996 / VIM / M • Hollywood Amateurs #28 / 1996 / MID / M • Innocent Girls Of Legal Age #3 / 1996 / MP0 / M • Interview With A Mistress / 1996 / BON / B • Mike Hott: #360 Cum In My Cunt #08 / 1995 / MHV / C • Mike Hott: #365 Lesbian Sluts #26 / 1996 / MHV / F • Mike Hott: #369 Cum In My Mouth #05 / 1996 / MHV / C • Mike Hott: #373 Three-Sum Sluts #14 / 1996 / MHV / M • Mike Hott: #376 Cunt Of The Month: Ashley Shye / 1996 / MHV / M • Mike Hott: #380 Girls Who Lap Cum From Cunts #03 / 1996 / MHV / C • Nineteen #2 / 1996 / FOR / M • Nineteen #3 / 1996 / FOR / M • Nineteen #5 / 1996 / FOR / M • Nothing Like Nurse Nookie #4 / 1996 / NIT / M • Pretty Anal Ladies / 1996 / ANE / M • Sex Lessons / 1996 / NIT / M • The Sodomizer #2 / 1995 / SC / M • While The Cat's Away / 1996 / NIT / M • Witches Are Bitches / 1996 / NIT / M

ASHLEY ST JOHN *see* **Lisa Lake**
ASHLEY STEPHENS *see* **Star Index I**
ASHLEY SUMMER *see* **Rachel Ashley**
ASHLEY SYNCLAIRE *see* **Star Index I**
ASHLEY VAN SLOANE
Backdoor Brides #1 / 1985 / PV / M
ASHLEY WAGNER *see* **Ashley Winger**

ASHLEY WAYNE *see* **Star Index I**
ASHLEY WELLES *see* **Taylor Evans**
ASHLEY WEST *see* **Taylor Evans**
ASHLEY WINGER *(Ashley Niger, Ashley Wagner, Lola (Ashley Winger))*
Looks like Virginia Lane.
Blind Date / 1989 / E&I / M • Cum Rain, Cum Shine / 1989 / FAZ / M • Dirty Books / 1990 / V99 / M • Heart Of Stone / 1990 / FAN / M • I Want Your Sex / 1990 / FAZ / M • The Legend Of Sleepy Hollow / 1989 / LE / M • My Wildest Date / 1989 / FOV / M • Office Girls / 1989 / CA / M • Riding Miss Daisy / 1990 / VEX / M • Undercover Angel / 1988 / IN / M • Wanda Does Transylvania / 1990 / V99 / M • Wanda Whips The Dragon Lady / 1990 / V99 / M • Words Of Love / 1989 / LE / M
ASHLEY WINTERS
Babes Of The Bay #1 / 1994 / LIP / F • Butt Jammers #01 / 1995 / SC / F • Butt Jam-mers #02 / 1995 / SC / F • Sin City Cycle Sluts #1 / 1995 / SC / F • Sin City Cycle Sluts #2 / 1995 / SC / F
ASHLEY YOUNG *see* **Kitty Yung**
ASHLEY YUNG *see* **Kitty Yung**
ASHLEY/SIDNEY
My First Time #7 / 1996 / NS / M
ASHLY BRITTON *see* **Stacey Donovan**
ASHLY JALLAY
Babes Of The Bay #2 / 1995 / LIP / F
ASHLYN
Raw Talent: Fetish Of The Month #05 / 1994 / RTP / G
ASHLYN GERE *(Kim McKamy, Kimberly Patton, Kimberly Marshall)*
Not too pretty older (supposedly born 9/14/1967 but looks older than this would imply and some non-sex roles make this date impossible) brunette with enhanced tits. Very hard shell but not slutty. First anal seems to have been **Scream In The Night**. Supposedly has a BA in acting from the University of Las Vegas (mail order?).
Adult Video News 1991 Awards / 1991 / VC / M • Adult Video News 1992 Awards / 1992 / VC / M • The Adventures Of Billy Blues / 1990 / HO / M • The Adventures Of Mikki Finn / 1991 / CA / M • All That Sex / 1990 / LE / M • Andrew Blake's Girls / 1992 / CA / C • Angel #3: The Final Chap-ter / 1988 / NWW / S • Animal Instinct / 1993 / VI / M • Anonymous / 1993 / VI / M • Aroused #1 / 1994 / VI / M • Aroused #2 / 1995 / VI / M • Ashlyn Gere: The Savage Mistress / 1992 / BIZ / B • Ashlyn Rising / 1995 / VI / M • Auction #1 / 1992 / BIZ / B • Auction #2 / 1992 / BIZ / B • Bad / 1990 / VC / M • Bedrooms And Boardrooms / 1992 / DR / M • The Best Of Andrew Blake / 1993 / CA / C • The Best Of Ashlyn Gere / 1995 / BIZ / C • Betrayal / 1992 / XCI / M • The Bigger They Come / 1993 / VD / C • Bikini Brats / 199? / NAP / B • Black Stock-ings / 1990 / VD / M • Body And Soul / 1992 / OD / M • Bonnie & Clyde #1 / 1992 / VI / M • Bonnie & Clyde #2 / 1992 / VI / M • Boobs, Butts And Bloopers #1 / 1990 / HO / M • Boobs, Butts And Bloopers #2 / 1990 / HO / M • Bruce Seven: A Compendium Of His Most Graphic Scenes Vol 2 / 1991 / BS / C • Bruce Seven: A Compendium Of His Most Graphic Scenes Vol 3 / 1992 / BS / C • Bruce Seven: A Compendium Of His Most Graphic Scenes Vol 4 / 1993 / BS / C • Bun For The Money / 1990 / FH / M •

Bush Pilots #1 / 1990 / VC / M • Bush Pilots #2 / 1991 / VC / M • Captain Butt's Beach / 1992 / LV / M • Chameleons: Not The Sequel / 1991 / VC / M • Cheating / 1994 / VI / M • Cheeks #5: The Ultimate Butt / 1991 / CC / M • Club Head / 1990 / CA / M • Creation Of Karen: Tormented & Transformed / 1993 / BIZ / B • Creepozoids / 1987 / UCV / S • Decadence / 1996 / VC / M • Deep Inside Centerfold Girls / 1991 / VC / M • Deep Inside Deidre Holland / 1993 / VC / C • Deep Inside Kelly O'Dell / 1994 / VC / C • Deep Inside Tyffany Million / 1995 / VC / C • Dirty Books / 1992 / VC / M • Dirty Looks / 1994 / VI / M • Dr Jeckel & Ms Hide / 1990 / LV / M • Dreamaniac / 1986 / WIZ / S • Dresden Diary #06: The Hellfire Legend / 1992 / BIZ / B • Dresden Diary #07 / 1992 / BIZ / B • Dresden Diary #08 / 1992 / BIZ / B • Dripping Wet Video / 1993 / NAP / F • The Education Of Karen / 1993 / BIZ / B • Eleventh Annual AVN Awards / 1994 / VC / M • Eternity / 1990 / SC / M • Evil Laugh / 1986 / CEL / S • Extreme Sex #4: The Experiment / 1995 / VI / M • Fatal Instinct / 1992 / NLH / S • Gere Up / 1991 / LV / C • Gerein' Up / 1992 / VC / M • Hot Rod To Hell #1 / 1991 / BS / B • Hot Shots / 1992 / VD / C • House Of Dreams / 1990 / CA / M • Ice Woman #1 / 1993 / VI / M • Ice Woman #2 / 1993 / VI / M • Imagine / 1991 / LV / M • Internal Affairs / 1995 / VI / M • Just For Tonight / 1992 / VC / M • Laid In Heaven / 1991 / VC / M • Laid Off / 1990 / CA / M • The Last Resort / 1990 / VC / M • Legend #3 / 1991 / LE / M • Lick Bush / 1992 / VD / C • The Lonely Lady / 1983 / MCA / S • Magnificent Seven / 1991 / NAP / F • Malibu Spice / 1991 / VC / M • The Masseuse #2 / 1994 / VI / M • Mirage #1 / 1991 / VC / M • Mirage #2 / 1992 / VC / M • Miss 21st Century / 1991 / ZA / M • The Model / 1991 / HO / M • The Mystery Of Payne / 1991 / BS / B • N.Y. Video Magazine #09 / 1996 / OUP / M • New Lovers / 1993 / VI / M • Night Train / 1993 / VI / M • Nightvision / 1995 / VI / M • Paper Tiger / 1992 / VI / M • Photo Play / 1995 / VI / M • The Tenth Pussyout / 1992 / OA / M • Pink To Pink / 1993 / VI / C • The Pleasure Seekers / 1990 / VD / M • Private Video Magazine #18 / 1994 / OD / M • Pussy Galore / 1993 / VD / C • Put It In Gere / 1991 / CA / M • Realities #1 / 1991 / ZA / M • Realities #2 / 1992 / ZA / M • Ride 'em Cow Girl / 1995 / VI / C • A Rising Star / 1991 / HO / M • Scream In The Middle Of The Night / 1990 / CC / M • The Secret Garden #1 / 1992 / XCI / M • The Secret Garden #2 / 1992 / XCI / M • Secrets / 1990 / CA / M • Sex #3: After Seven (Vivid) / 1994 / VI / M • Sex Scenes / 1992 / VD / C • Sexual Instinct #1 / 1992 / DR / M • Shifting Gere / 1990 / VT / M • Simply Blue / 1005 / WAV / M • Sleeping Around / 1991 / CA / M • Slow Burn / 1991 / VC / M • Someone Else / 1992 / VC / M • Sorority Sex Kittens #1 / 1992 / VC / M • Sorority Sex Kittens #2 / 1993 / VC / M • Sorority Sex Kittens #3 / 1996 / VC / M • Sporting Illustrated / 1990 / HO / M • Steamy Windows / 1993 / VI / M • Street Angels / 1992 / LV / M • Sunrise Mystery / 1992 / FD / M • Swedish Erotica Featurettes #5 / 1990 / CA / M • Sweet Angel Ass / 1990 / FH / M • Tailiens #2 / 1992 / FD / M • Tailiens #3 / 1992 / FD / M • Talk Dirty To Me #08 / 1990 / DR / M • Talk Dirty To Me #09 / 1992 / DR / M • A Taste Of Ashlyn Gere / 1990 / PIN / C • The Tease / 1990 / VC / M • Tenth Annual Adult Video News Awards / 1993 / VC / M • Total Reball / 1990 / CC / M • True Legends Of Adult Cinema: The Golden Age / 1992 / VC / C • True Legends Of Adult Cinema: The Modern Era / 1992 / VC / C • True Legends Of Adult Cinema: Unsung Superstars / 1993 / VC / C • True Sin / 1990 / PP / M • Two Women / 1992 / ROB / M • Voices In My Bed / 1993 / VI / M • Waterbabies #1 / 1992 / CC / M • The Witching Hour / 1992 / FOR / M • With Love From Ashlyn / 1991 / HO / C • Wrapped Up / 1992 / VD / C • [High Society Centerspread #16 / 199? / ... / S • [Lunchmeat / 1987 / TVD / S

ASHTON POWERS see Star Index I

ASHTON TAYLOR

Gorgeous little black girl with a small slim body, tiny tits but a very nice smile and personality. First movie: **Twice As Nice**. Appears to have a tattoo on her right bicep in **The Crack Of Dawn** and another on her back just above her right buttock.

The Crack Of Dawn / 1989 / GLE / M • Down 4 Busine$$ / 1989 / GMI / M • Heather Hunter's Bedtime Stories / 1991 / GLE / C • Twice As Nice / 1989 / VWA / M

ASIA

The Dragon Lady #1 / 1988 / WV / C • Oriental Sexpress / 1984 / WV / M

ASIA CARRERA see Asia Carrera

ASIA CARRERA *(Asia Carerra, Jessica Bennett)*

Oriental-looking (half Japanese and half German), quite pretty, 20 years old in 1994 (born 8/6/73 in NYC), lithe body, small tits, reasonably tight waist, long straight black hair. Unfortunately, she is quite passionless, and seems incapable of letting go although she says she can't have an orgasm in nearly every scene (sure!). Originally a runaway she then became a dancer in New Jersey and then went to CA to get into porn. As of early 1995 she has had her tits enhanced to medium/large size; it was a reasonable job and they look quite flexible with only a small scar visible under the left areola. Supposedly a member of MENSA and a classical pianist.

A Is For Asia / 1996 / 4P / M • The Adventures Of Studman #1 / 1994 / AFV / M • Always Anal / 1995 / AVI / C • The Anal Adventures Of Suzy Super Slut #1 / 1994 / AFV / M • Aroused #1 / 1994 / VI / M • Aroused #2 / 1995 / VI / M • The Art Of Deception / 1996 / BON / B • Babe Magnet / 1994 / IN / M • Babe Watch #1 / 1994 / SC / M • Babe Watch #2 / 1994 / SC / M • Backstage Pass / 1994 / SC / M • Badgirls #1: Lockdown / 1994 / VI / M • Bangkok Boobarella / 1996 / BTO / M • Bangkok Nights / 1994 / VI / M • Barrio Bitches / 1994 / SC / F • Beauty's Punishment / 1996 / BIZ / B • Beauty's Revenge / 1996 / BIZ / B • Bed & Breakfast / 1995 / WAV / M • Biography: Asia Carrera / 1995 / SC / C • Bloopers & Boners / 1996 / VI / M • Blue Dreams / 1996 / SC / M • Bonnie & Clyde #3 / 1994 / VI / M • Bonnie & Clyde #4 / 1994 / VI / M • Breeders / 1996 / MET / M • Butt Watch #03 / 1994 / FH / M • The Cathouse / 1994 / VI / M • Chemical Reaction / 1995 / CC / M • Chinatown / 1994 / SC / M • Chow Down / 1994 / VI / M • Chronicles Of Pain #1 / 1996 / BIZ / B • Cinesex #1 / 1995 / CV / M • Cinesex #2 / 1994 / CV / M • Cloud 9 / 1995 / VI / M • Comeback / 1995 / VI / M • Coming Of Age / 1995 / VEX / C • Conquest / 1996 / WP / M • Corporate Affairs / 1996 / CC / M • Crazy Love / 1995 / VI / M • Crazy With The Heat #3 / 1994 / CV / M • Cross Cuntry Vacation / 1995 / CC / M • Cumback Pussy #6: All-Star Poop Chute Salute / 1997 / EL / M • Cumming Clean (1996—Caballero) / 1996 / CA / M • Daydreams, Nightdreams / 1996 / VC / M • Deep Inside Misty Rain / 1995 / VC / C • Defending Your Soul / 1995 / EX / M • The Dinner Party #1 / 1994 / ULI / M • Dominant Jean / 1996 / CC / M • Dresden Diary #14: Ecstasy In Hell / 1996 / BIZ / B • Dresden Diary #15: / 1996 / BIZ / B • Elements Of Desire / 1994 / ULI / M • Encore / 1995 / VI / M • Forever Young / 1994 / VI / M • Gemini / 1994 / SC / M • Growing Apart / 1996 / XCI / M • Hawaii / 1995 / VI / M • Her Name Is Asia / 1996 / SUF / M • Hollywood Hookers / 1996 / DWV / M • Hollywood Spa / 1996 / WP / M • The Illustrated Woman / 1995 / CA / M • Internal Affairs / 1995 / VI / M • International Affairs / 1994 / PL / M • Interview With A Vamp / 1994 / ANA / M • It's Blondage, The Video / 1994 / VI / M • Ladies Room / 1994 / SC / F • The Last Act / 1995 / VI / M • Latex And Lace / 1996 / BBE / M • Layover / 1994 / VI / M • Leather Bound Dykes From Hell #7 / 1996 / BIZ / B • Lipstick Lesbians #1: Massage Parlor Dykes / 1994 / ZA / F • Mask Of Innocence / 1996 / WP / B • Masque / 1995 / VC / M • The Masseuse #2 / 1994 / VI / M • Mighty Man #1: Virgins In The Forest / 1994 / LE / M • The Mountie / 1994 / PP / M • Mystique / 1996 / SC / M • New Positions / 1994 / PV / M • Night Nurses / 1995 / WAV / M • No Motive / 1994 / MID / M • Off Duty Porn Stars / 1994 / VC / M • Once In A Lifetime / 1996 / VC / C • Phantonm / 1006 / WP / M • The Player / 1995 / VI / M • Primarily Yours / 1996 / CA / M • Private Performance / 1994 / EX / M • Public Places #1 / 1994 / SC / M • Putting It All Behind #2: Star Treatment / 1994 / IN / M • R & R / 1994 / VC / M • Radical Affairs Video Magazine #07 / 1994 / ME / M • Red Hots / 1996 / PL / M • Red Light / 1994 / SC / S • Ride 'em Cow Girl / 1995 / VI / C • Satin & Lace / 1994 / WP / M • Satyr / 1996 / WP / M • Scandal / 1995 / VI / M • Scrue / 1995 / VI / M • Secret Rendez-Vous / 1994 / XCI / M • Secret Urges (Vidco) / 1994 / VD / C • Sensual Recluse / 1994 / EX / M • Sex #1 (Vca) / 1994 / VC / M • Sex #2: Fate (Vca) / 1995 / VC / M • Sex And Money / 1994 / DGD / S • Sex On The Saddle: Wicked Women Of The Wild West / 1994 / CPG / S • Sexual Healing / 1994 / VI / M • Sexual Misconduct / 1994 / VD / C • Shame / 1994 / VI / M • Sista Act / 1994 / AVI / M • Spiked Heel Diaries #5 / 1995 / BIZ / B • The Stand-Up / 1994 / VC / M • Suite 18 / 1994 / VI / M • Superboobs / 1994 / LE / M • Supermodel #1 / 1994 / VI / M • Supermodel #2 / 1994 / VI / M • The Swap #2 / 1994 / VI / M • Sweet Revenge / 1997 /

KBE / M • Taboo #13 / 1994 / IN / M • Tempted / 1994 / VI / M • This Year's Model / 1996 / WAV / M • Tight Lips / 1994 / CA / M • Titty Bar #2 / 1994 / LE / M • Tongue In Cheek / 1994 / LE / M • Trouble Maker / 1995 / VI / M • Unleashed / 1996 / SAE / M • Up And Cummers #09 / 1994 / 4P / M • Up And Cummers: The Movie / 1994 / 4P / M • Vagablonde / 1994 / VI / M • Waterworld: The Enema Movie / 1996 / BIZ / B • Western Nights / 1994 / WP / M • Where The Boys Aren't #7 / 1995 / VI / F • Wild & Wicked #4 / 1994 / VT / M

ASIA DIAMOND
Old Wave Hookers #1 / 1995 / PL / M

ASS MASTER
Forbidden Fantasies #2 / 1995 / ZA / M

ASS PUMPIN
Diary Of A Bed / 1979 / HOE / M

ASTRID see Star Index I

ASTRID BONER
Vanessa / 1977 / VAM / S • [Junge Madchen Mogen's HeiB, Hausfrauen Noch HeiBer / 1973 / … / M

ASTRID GORDON see Star Index I

ASTRID LARSON see Star Index I

ASTRID LILLIMOR see Uschi Digart

ATHENA
Anal Rescue 811 / 1992 / PL / M • Angels With Sticky Faces / 1991 / VD / M • Bloopers & Behind The Scenes / 1995 / LEI / M • Girls From Girdleville / 1992 / ERK / M • John Wayne Bobbitt Uncut / 1994 / LEI / M • Pearl Necklace: Amorous Amateurs #13 / 1992 / SEE / M • Pearl Necklace: Facial #01 / 1994 / SEE / C • Pussy Fest Of The Northwest #4 / 1995 / NIT / M • Pussy Hunt / #04 / 1994 / LEI / M

ATHENA LEE see Athena Star

ATHENA STAR *(Athena Lee)*
Bottle blonde (strawberry) with passable face, petite body, small tits. Athena Lee is from **Shape Up For Sensational Sex**.
Bi-Ceps / 1986 / LA / C • The Big Switch / 1985 / LAV / G • Blacks Have More Fun / 1985 / AVC / M • Bodies By Jackie / 1985 / IVP / M • Celebrity Presents Celebrity / 1986 / VEP / C • Centerfold Celebrities #2 / 1983 / VC / M • Centerfold Celebrities #4 / 1983 / VC / M • Centerfold Celebrities #6 / 1983 / VC / M • Charming Cheapies #6: Red Tide / 1985 / 4P / M • Deep Throat Girls / 1986 / ELH / M • Erotic Zones #3 / 1986 / CA / M • Flash Pants / 1983 / VC / M • Garter Charter Tours / 1986 / AVC / M • Girls Of The Third Reich / 1985 / FC / M • Glitter / 1983 / CA / M • Golden Globes / 1989 / VEX / M • Hot Cars, Nasty Women / 1985 / WV / M • Hot Lips / 1984 / VC / M • Hot Merchandise / 1985 / AVC / M • I Never Say No / 1983 / VC / M • Joys Of Erotica #108 / 1984 / VCR / C • License To Thrill / 1985 / VD / M • More Chocolate Candy / 1986 / VD / M • Night Games / 1986 / WV / M • Parliament: Bare Assets / 1988 / PM / F • Parliament: Teasers #1 / 1986 / PM / F • Photoflesh / 1984 / HO / M • Piggies / 1984 / VC / M • Pleasure Channel / 1984 / VC / M • Pleasure Productions #08 / 1984 / VCR / M • The Pregnant Babysitter / 1984 / WV / M • Private School Girls / 1983 / CA / M • Radio K-KUM / 1984 / HO / M • Rear Entry / 1985 / VCR / C • Red Tide / 19?? / … / M • Salt & Pepper / 1986 / VCS / C • The Sex Change Girls / 1987 / 4P / G • Sex Toys / 1985 / CA

/ M • Shape Up For Sensational Sex / 1985 / SE / M • Slumber Party / 1984 / HO / M • Street Heat / 1984 / VC / M • Suze's Centerfolds #8 / 1984 / CA / M • Taija Is Sizzling Hot / 1986 / VT / M • A Taste Of Genie / 1986 / 4P / M • Throat...12 Years After / 1984 / VC / M • Up & In / 1985 / AA / M • Voyeur's Delight / 1986 / VCS / C • Wings Of Passion / 1984 / HO / M • With Love From Ginger / 1986 / HO / C • With Love From Susan / 1988 / HO / C • The Wizard Of AHH's / 1985 / SE / M • [Trailer Park Twats / 1986 / … / M

ATILLA
Itsy Bitsy Gang Bang / 1996 / HW / M

ATLANTA RIZZEN *(Candi Lace, Candy Lace)*
Slutty looking blonde with a tattoo (rabbit and a flower) just above her right tit. Not too pretty, medium enhanced tits. 26 years old in 1994.
Anal Virgins Of America #08 / 1994 / FOR / M • Booby Prize / 1995 / PEP / M • Brassiere To Eternity / 1994 / PEP / F • Call Me / 1995 / CV / M • Deep Throat Girls #03 / 1994 / GO / M • Dirty Dominique / 1994 / V99 / M • Girls With Curves #2 / 1994 / CV / M • HomeGrown Video #445: Sex Kittens / 1995 / HOV / M • Housewife Lust #1 / 1995 / TV / F • Leg...Ends #15 / 1995 / PRE / F • Mellon Man #03 / 1994 / AVI / M • My Desire / 1996 / NIT / M • New Faces, Hot Bodies #16 / 1994 / STP / M • New Girls In Town #6 / 1994 / CC / M • Pussy Hunt #04 / 1994 / LEI / M • Southern Belles #3 / 1995 / HOV / M • Star Crossed / 1995 / VC / M • Temptation / 1994 / VC / M • Video Virgins #15 / 1994 / NS / M • Wildfire: #05 Candi / 1994 / WIF / F

ATLAS
Black Juice Bombs / 1996 / NIT / C • Jus' Knockin' Boots #1: Fade To Black / 1996 / NIT / M • Jus' Knockin' Boots #2: Black On Line / 1996 / NIT / M

ATLAS D.
Private Gold #09: Private Dancer / 1996 / OD / M

ATTILA
Magma: Puszta Teenies / 1995 / MET / M • Mission Hard / 1995 / XC / M • Passion In Venice / 1995 / ULI / M • Plastic Workshop / 1995 / LAF / M • Private Gold #10: Sins / 1996 / OD / M • Private Stories #07 / 1996 / OD / M • Private Stories #08 / 1996 / OD / M • Private Stories #09 / 1996 / OD / M • Sorority House Party / 1992 / APE / S • Triple X Video Magazine #09 / 1995 / OD / M

ATTILA DONI
Anita / 1996 / BLC / M • The Coming Of Nikita / 1995 / EL / M • Sodomania #14: C**t Lickin', C*m Drinkin' Bitches / 1995 / EL / M • True Stories #1 / 1993 / SC / M • True Stories #2 / 1993 / SC / M

ATTILA GLAS
Private Gold #02: Friends In Sex / 1995 / OD / M • Thermonuclear Sex / 1996 / EL / M

ATTILA GREY
Love Slave / 1995 / WIV / M

ATTILA SCHULTER
Jungle Heat / 1995 / LUM / M

ATTILA SCHUSZTER
Diamonds / 1996 / HDE / M • A Merry Widow / 1996 / SPI / M • Prima #09: As-

Sassins / 1995 / MBP / M • Sodomania #15: Warning! / 1996 / EL / M • Sodomania: Slop Shots / 1996 / EL / C • True Stories #1 / 1993 / SC / M • True Stories #2 / 1993 / SC / M

ATTILLA
Dick & Jane Return To Hungary / 1993 / OAP / M • Private Gold #04: Amazonas / 1996 / OD / M • Sluts 'n' Angels In Budapest / 1994 / EL / M • Sodomania #11: In Your Face / 1994 / EL / M

ATTY F.
Private Gold #09: Private Dancer / 1996 / OD / M

AUBREY
Up And Cummers #22 / 1995 / RWP / M

AUBREY NICHOLS *(Diane Darlington)*
Blonde, medium tits, womanly body, big butt and hefty thighs, passable face.
800 Fantasy Lane / 1979 / GO / M • The Beauty Pageant / 1981 / AVC / M • Blue Vanities #536 / 1993 / FFL / M • Creme De Femme #4 / 1981 / AVC / C • Heavenly Desire / 1979 / WV / M • Limited Edition #04 / 1979 / AVC / M • One Way At A Time / 1979 / CA / M • Sissy's Hot Summer / 1979 / CA / M • Steamy Sirens / 1984 / AIR / C • Taxi Girls #1 / 1980 / WV / M • Triple Header / 1987 / AIR / C

AUBREY TURNER see Star Index I

AUDE LECOEUR see Star Index I

AUDRA see Star Index I

AUDRA TESS see Star Index I

AUDREY LANE see Valhalla

AUDREY LANG see Susan Adle

AUDREY LORD see Star Index I

AUDREY QWEST
Cocks In Frocks #2 / 1996 / TTV / G

AUDREY ROSE
Fresh Faces #04 / 1995 / EVN / M • Hardcore: The Films Of Richard Kern #1 / 1991 / FTV / M

AUDREY YOUNG
GVC: Blonde Heat #136 / 1985 / GO / M

AUDRY KYLE
Lovin' Spoonfuls #4 / 1995 / 4P / C

AUDRY LONGO
Boiling Point / 1978 / SE / M

AUDRY SOLMES
More Dirty Debutantes #32 / 1994 / 4P / M

AUGUST WEST see Star Index I

AUNT GOLDIE see Star Index I

AUNT PEG see Juliet Anderson

AUNT PEG NORTON see Juliet Anderson

AURA
Black Casting Couch #1 / 1993 / WP / M

AURELIE
Eurotica #08 / 1996 / XC / M

AUROA LEE see Aurora

AURORA *(Aurora Lee, Treonna, Auroa Lee, Auroura, Treanna)*
Very short blonde hair, passable face, medium tits, small tattoo just above the left one, nice skin, not a tight waist.
Aurora's Secret Diary / 1985 / LA / M • Between The Cheeks #1 / 1985 / VC / M • Bi And Beyond #3 / 1989 / INH / G • The Big Tease / 1987 / 1990 / VC / M • Born To Suck Cock / 1994 / MET / C • Candy Stripers #2 / 1985 / AR / M • Dames / 1985 / SE / M • Desperate Women / 1986 / VD / M • Dirty Diane / 1989 / V99 / M • Erotic City / 1985 / CV / M • Erotic Zones #2 / 1985 / CA / M • Flash Trance / 1985 / IVP / M • Forbidden Entry / 1984 / VCR / M • Girls! Girls! Girls!

#1 / 1986 / VCS / C • Headgames / 1985 / WV / M • Heartthrobs / 1985 / CA / M • Hershe Highway #2 / 1989 / HO / M • How Do You Like It? / 1985 / CA / M • I Love A Girl In A Uniform / 1989 / VC / C • Icy Hot / 1990 / MID / M • Inside Candy Samples / 1984 / CV / M • No Man's Land #03 / 1989 / VT / F • Only The Best Of Women With Women / 1988 / CV / C • Oriental Jade / 1985 / VC / M • The Return Of Indiana Joan / 1989 / PL / M • Schoolgirl By Day / 1985 / LA / M • Sex Crazed / 1989 / VEX / M • Sexual Odyssey / 1985 / VC / M • Shave Tail / 1984 / AMB / M • Single Girl Masturbation #2 / 1989 / ESP / F • Swedish Erotica #60 / 1984 / CA / M • Tales Of The Backside / 1985 / VCR / C • Taste Of The Best #3 / 1988 / PIN / C • Thought You'd Never Ask / 1986 / CA / M • Toys 4 Us #2 / 1987 / WV / C • With A Wiggle In Her Walk / 1989 / WV / M • You're The Boss / 1985 / VD / M

AURORA (1996)
Country & Western Cuties #2: Naked Pie Eating Contest / 1996 / EVN / M • Filthy First Timers #3: Tearing Down The Walls Of Shame / 1996 / EL / M • Here Comes Elska / 1997 / XPR / M

AURORA (DEST. LANE) see Destini Lane

AURORA LEE see Aurora

AURORE
Hot Bodies (Caballero) / 1984 / CA / M

AUROURA see Aurora

AUSTIN
Big Boob Bikini Bash / 1995 / BTO / M

AUSTIN MCCLOUD
The Happy Office / 1996 / NIT / M • In Your Face #4 / 1996 / PL / M • Keyholes / 1995 / OD / M • Renegades #2 / 1995 / SC / M • Titties 'n Cream #3 / 1995 / FC / M • Video Virgins #22 / 1995 / NS / M

AUSTIN MOORE *(Roger Karns)*
One time husband of Erica Boyer.
Adventures Of The DP Boys: Down At The Sunset Grill / 1993 / HW / M • All That Glitters / 1992 / LV / M • Anal Island / 1992 / LV / M • The Anals Of History #1 / 1991 / MID / M • Any Port In The Storm / 1991 / LV / M • As Sweet As Can Be / 1993 / V99 / M • Back To Black #2 / 1992 / VEX / C • Back To The Orient / 1992 / HW / M • The Backdoor Club / 1992 / LV / M • Big Bust Babes #11 / 1992 / AFI / M • Big Murray's New-Cummers #11: Willing & Able / 1993 / FD / M • Big Murray's New-Cummers #12: In The Pink / 1993 / FD / M • Body Fire / 1991 / LV / M • Breast Worx #39 / 1992 / LBO / M • Bung-Ho Babes / 1991 / FC / M • Buns And Roses (LV) / 1990 / LV / M • Butt Light: Queen Of Rears / 1992 / STR / M • Crash In The Rear / 1992 / HW / C • Dark Corners / 1991 / LV / M • Encino Woman / 1992 / VIM / M • Final Anal Tease / 1992 / MID / M • Freaks Of Leather #1 / 1993 / IF / M • Frenzy / 1992 / SC / M • Girls Of Silicone Valley / 1991 / FC / M • Hometown Honeys #4 / 1993 / VEX / M • I Dream Of Tiffany / 1993 / IF / M • Just One Look / 1993 / V99 / M • The Last Temptation Of Teri / 1991 / IF / M • Miracle On 69th Street / 1992 / HW / M • Moon Godesses #1 / 1992 / VIM / M • Nina's Toys And Boys / 1991 / LV / C • Nothing Else Matters / 1992 / V99 / C • Passion From Behind / 1990 / LV / M • The Pick Up

/ 1993 / MID / M • Pump It Up / 1990 / LV / M • R & R / 1994 / VC / M • Renegades #1 / 1994 / SC / M • Rocco Unleashed / 1994 / SC / M • Star Struck / 1992 / VEX / M • Stocking Stuffers / 1992 / LV / M • Tempting Tianna / 1992 / V99 / M • Tight Pucker / 1992 / WV / M • Too Cute For Words / 1992 / V99 / M • Top Heavy / 1993 / IF / M • Transparent Desires / 1991 / LV / M • Ultimate Sensations / 1996 / NIT / M • Wendy Whoppers: Environmental Attorney / 1993 / PEP / M • Wild Dreams / 1995 / V99 / M • Will & Ed's Keister Easter / 1992 / MID / M • Willie Wanker And The Fun Factory / 1994 / FD / M • Women's Penitentiary / 1992 / VIM / M • The Wonder Rears / 1990 / SO / M • Working Girl / 1993 / VI / M

AUSTIN TANNER
Body & Soul / 1995 / IF / M • Gang Bang Bitches #05 / 1995 / PP / M • Hollywood Amateurs #11 / 1994 / MID / M • Indiscreet! Video Magazine #1 / 1995 / FH / M • Lady's Choice / 1995 / VD / M • Mickey Ray's Sex Search #04: Long And Hard / 1994 / WIV / M • Oriental Girls In Heat / 1995 / IF / M • Revenge Of The Pussy Suckers From Mars / 1994 / PP / M

AUTUMN
Forbidden Session / 1996 / VTF / B

AUTUMN (C. LEEDS) see Christie Leeds

AUTUMN DAYE *(Tanya Tashara)*
Blonde, older, reasonably pretty, small tits, belly button ring, tight waist, nice smile.
The Anal Adventures Of Max Hardcore: Cafe Life / 1994 / ZA / M • Anal Angels #4 / 1995 / VEX / C • Anal Destroyer / 1994 / ZA / M • Anal Maniacs #2 / 1994 / WP / M • Assmania!! #1 / 1994 / ME / M • Backdoor Boogie / 1994 / TEG / M • Butt Hunt #10 / 1995 / LEI / M • Casting Call #08 / 1994 / SO / M • Doin' The Rounds / 1995 / VC / M • Evil Temptations #1 / 1995 / ULP / M • The Hitch-Hiker #10: Rolling & Reaming / 1995 / WMG / M • Hotel Sodom #01 / 1995 / SNA / M • Hotel Sodom #03 / 1995 / SNA / M • In Search Of The Brown Eye: An Anal Adventure / 1995 / MAX / M • Itty Bitty Blonde Committee / 1995 / V99 / M • Masquerade / 1995 / HO / M • May #02 / 1994 / FWE / M • Max Gold #1 / 1996 / XPR / C • Orgies Orgies Orgies / 1994 / WV / M • Pussy Hunt #11 / 1995 / LEI / M • Rectal Rodeo / 1994 / ZA / M • Safari Jane / 1995 / ERA / M • Satyriasis / 1995 / PL / M • Slammed / 1995 / PV / M • Tail Taggers #130 / 1994 / WV / M • The Violation Of Alexandria Dane / 1995 / JMP / F

AUTUMN FAIRCHILD
Bi The Rear Window / 1994 / BIL / G

AUTUMN JONES
Sex And The Cheerleaders / 1983 / XTR / M

AUTUMN TRUE
Cafe Flesh / 1982 / VC / M

AVA
The Best Of Fabulous Flashers / 1996 / DGD / F • Blue Vanities #509 / 1992 / FFL / M

AVA (ORLOWSKI) see Eva Orlowski

AVA (S/M)
Dressing For Leisure / 1992 / STM / G • Seductive TV / 1995 / GOT / G • She-Male Solos #07: Ava / 1992 / LEO / G • Transvestite Ordeal / 1994 / GOT / G • TV Roommate / 1996 / GOT / G • TV's And The Houseboy / 1993 / GOT / G • TV's

Dilemma / 1993 / GOT / G

AVA DAY
Pussy Fest Of The Northwest #1 / 1995 / NIT / M

AVA GRACE see Star Index I

AVA GUERIN see Star Index I

AVA HOLLYWOOD
3 Mistresses Of The Mansion / 1994 / STM / B • A Peek Over The Wall / 1995 / STM / G • Power Games / 1992 / STM / B • Profiles In Discipline #02: Naughty Angel / 1994 / STM / C • She Studs #02 / 1991 / BIZ / G • She-Male By Choice / 1993 / STM / G • Spanking Tea Party / 1994 / STM / B • Trained Transvestites / 1995 / STM / B • Trisexual Encounters #01 / 1985 / PL / G

AVA LUSTRA
Girls Around The World #29 / 1995 / BTO / M • Thunder Boobs / 1995 / BTO / M

AVA MARIA see Melissa Melendez

AVA ORLOUSKYU see Eva Orlowski

AVA ORLOWSKY see Eva Orlowski

AVALON see Avalone

AVALON (1995)
Ass Masters (Leisure) #04 / 1995 / LEI / M • HomeGrown Video #473: Furpie Feast #3 / 1997 / HOV / C

AVALON (1996)
The Adventures Of Peeping Tom #3 / 1996 / OD / M • Pick Up Lines #09 / 1996 / OD / M • Pick Up Lines #10 / 1997 / OD / M • Pick Up Lines #11 / 1997 / OD / M

AVALON (AMAT) see Star Index I

AVALONE *(Avalon, Liz Golden)*
Small tattoo on the right shoulder. Looks like Keli Richards but teeth are better and she is slightly fatter.
The Adventures Of Buttgirl & Wonder Wench / 1991 / AFV / M • Amateur Lesbians #10: Stephanie / 1991 / GO / F • Amateur Lesbians #12: Kimberly / 1991 / GO / F • Amateur Lesbians #13: Brandi / 1991 / GO / F • Amateur Lesbians #14: Kristin / 1991 / GO / F • Amateur Lesbians #25: International Budapest / 1992 / GO / F • Amateur Lesbians #30: Randi / 1992 / GO / F • Amateur Lesbians #35: Meo / 1993 / GO / F • Anal Commander / 1990 / ZA / M • Black & Blue / 1990 / SO / M • Blonde Temptation / 1995 / IF / M • Breast Wishes #04 / 1991 / LBO / M • Casual Sex / 1991 / GO / M • Dreams Of Candace Hart / 1991 / VI / M • Foxx Hunt / 1991 / GO / M • Girls In Heat / 1991 / ZA / F • Hollywood Teasers #01 / 1992 / LBO / F • I Said A Butt Light #2 / 1990 / LV / M • In Too Deep / 1992 / AFD / M • Lust Never Sleeps / 1991 / FAZ / M • Most Wanted / 1991 / GO / M • Nightfire / 1991 / CIN / M • The Other Side Of Debbie / 1991 / CC / M • Prisoner Of Love / 1991 / ME / M • Putting It All Behind #1 / 1991 / IN / M • Raw Talent: Bang 'er 07 Times / 1992 / RTP / M • Scream In The Middle Of The Night / 1990 / CC / M • The Spectacle / 1991 / IN / M • The Stranger Beside Me / 1991 / WV / M • Transformed / 1991 / MET / M • Twin Cheeks #1 / 1990 / CIN / M • Two Of A Kind / 1990 / LV / M • Wicked Thoughts / 1991 / AFV / M • The Wonder Rears / 1990 / SO / M

AVIA ANITA
More Dirty Debutantes #32 / 1994 / 4P / M

AXEL
Neighborhood Watch #07: Made Up To Go Down / 1991 / LBO / M

AXEL GARRET *see Star Index I*

AXEL HORN *see Alex Horn*

AXEL WOLF *see Star Index I*

AXINIA *(Anja, Xenia (Axinia))*
German girl with quite a pretty face and large natural tits. Generally bad skin. Brunette or dark blonde. Nice smile. As of the end of 1994, her body has died.
Amateur Orgies #23 / 1993 / AFI / M • Amateur Orgies #28 / 1993 / AFI / M • America's Raunchiest Home Videos #60: / 1993 / ZA / M • Beyond Passion / 1993 / IF / M • Bi-Bi Love Amateurs #3 / 1993 / QUA / G • Bobby Hollander's Rookie Nookie #04 / 1993 / SFP / M • Bobby Hollander's Rookie Nookie #06 / 1993 / SFP / M • Bra Busters #01 / 1993 / LBO / M • Breast Collection #03 / 1995 / LBO / C • Breast Worx #42 / 1993 / LBO / M • Buffy Malibu's Totally Nasty All-Girl Home Videos #03 / 1992 / ANA / F • Butt Bongo Bonanza / 1993 / FC / M • Der Mosen-Pflucker / 1995 / KRM / M • Dirty Dating Service #01 / 1993 / WP / M • Double D Dykes #08 / 1993 / GO / F • The Ebony Connection #2 / 1994 / LBO / C • Gazonga Goddess #1 / 1993 / IF / M • Gazongas #05 / 1993 / VEX / C • Hard To Hold / 1993 / IF / M • Harry Horndog #21: Birthday Orgy / 1993 / ZA / M • Hidden Camera #05 / 1993 / JMP / M • More Dirty Debutantes #36 / 1994 / 4P / M • Nasty Newcummers #01 / 1993 / MET / M • Nasty Nymphos #02 / 1994 / ANA / M • Odyssey Triple Play #59: Two On Two Fuckfest / 1994 / OD / M • The Orgy #2 / 1993 / EMC / M • Pearl Necklace: Thee Bush League #17 / 1993 / SEE / M • Prime Offender / 1993 / PEP / M • Princess Of Persia / 1993 / IP / M • Sean Michaels On The Road #07: New York / 1993 / VT / M • Sodomania #03: Foreign Objects / 1993 / EL / M • Spanish Fly / 1993 / VEX / M • Tail Taggers #121: Behind The Lens / 1994 / WV / M • Tit Tales #4 / 1993 / FC / M • Uncle Roy's Amateur Home Video #22 / 1993 / VIM / M • Wad Gobblers #09 / 1993 / GLI / M

AXLE HOSE *see Star Index I*

AYA MISAWA *see Star Index I*

AYAKO MITSUI *see Star Index I*

AYLA
Creme De La Face #14: Kiss My Cum / 1996 / OD / M

AYSHA HART
Private Film #01 / 1993 / OD / M

AZURE TE *see Star Index I*

B. BEANE
Ms. Fix-It / 1994 / PRK / M

B. BERNARD BEHAN *see Bruce Seven*

B. DONNA
San Francisco Lesbians #2 / 1992 / PL / F

B. FORE
Private Film #12 / 1994 / OD / M

B. LOGAN
Blue Vanities #540 / 1994 / FFL / M

B. MARTIN
Blue Vanities #540 / 1994 / FFL / M

B. RON ELLIOT *see Byron Maybe*

B. SERVANT
Chocolate Bon-Bons / 1985 / PL / M

B.A. DREAMER *see Star Index I*

B.B. LONG *see Star Index I*

B.B. WOOD SR
Sex #1 (Vca) / 1994 / VC / M

B.B. ZARR *see Star Index I*

B.D. CADD

Internal Affairs / 1995 / VI / M • Nylon / 1995 / VI / M

B.J.
A&B AB#082: Cum On Me / 1990 / A&B / M • A&B AB#343: Foot Lovers And How To Stuff A Wild Pussy / 1991 / A&B / M • Wrasslin She-Babes #09 / 1996 / SOW / M • Wrasslin She-Babes #10 / 1996 / SOW / M

B.J. BAILY *see Jack Baker*

B.J. BOGGS
Gina, The Foxy Lady / cr79 / COV / M • Too Many Cocks In Me! / 1992 / MET / M

B.J. DYKE *see Star Index I*

B.J. SLATER
AC/DC #2 / 1994 / HP / G • Bi 'n' Large / 1994 / PL / G • Bi Chill / 1994 / BIL / G • The Bi Valley / 1994 / BIL / G • Gentlemen Prefer She-Males / 1995 / CDI / G • Good Bi Girl / 1994 / BIL / G • My She-Male Valentine / 1994 / HSV / G • Samurai She-Males / 1994 / HSV / G • Semper Bi / 1994 / PEP / G • She-Male Swish Bucklers / 1994 / HSV / G • She-Male Valentine / 1996 / HSV / G • The She-Male Who Stole Christmas / 1993 / HSV / G • Trannie Get Your Gun / 1994 / HSV / G • Transsexual Try Outs / 1993 / HSV / G

BABA
Blue Vanities #519 / 1993 / FFL / M

BABBIE BALL
Sharon In The Rough-House / 1976 / LA / M

BABE
Joe Elliot's College Girls #26 / 1994 / JOE / M • Joe Elliot's College Girls #27 / 1994 / JOE / M • Joe Elliot's College Girls #37 / 1994 / JOE / M • New Faces, Hot Bodies #01 / 1992 / STP / M • New Faces, Hot Bodies #02 / 1992 / STP / M • New Faces, Hot Bodies #03 / 1992 / STP / M

BABETTE
Alice In Pornoland / 1996 / IP / M • Ejacula #1 / 1992 / VC / M • Ejacula #2 / 1992 / VC / M • FTV #45: Mother Knows Best / 1996 / FT / B • FTV #49: Crooked Cats / 1996 / FT / B • FTV #50: Double-D Duo / 1996 / FT / B • Impulse #01: Memories Of An Italian Slut / 1995 / MBP / M • Impulse #06: / 1996 / MBP / M • Impulse #07: / 1996 / MBP / M • Impulse #08: The A Channel / 1996 / MBP / M • Lettre Da Rimini / 1995 / MID / M • Magma: Lust Excesses / 1995 / MET / M • Magma: Nymphettes / 1993 / MET / M • Magma: Pussy Jobs / 1994 / MET / M • Magma: Sperm Dreams / 1990 / MET / M • Magma: Young & Old / 1995 / MET / M • Old Bitches / 1996 / GLI / M

BABETTE BURE
Illusions Within Young Girls / 1981 / VEP / M

BABETTE DUBOIS
San Francisco Lesbians #2 / 1992 / PL / F

BABS
Biff Malibu's Totally Nasty Home Videos #37 / 1993 / ANA / M

BABS DU *see Star Index I*

BABS SILLS
All The Loving Couples / 1979 / KIT / M

BABSY DIONESIS
Julie's Diary / 1995 / LBO / M

BABSY MILES
Twilight / 1996 / ESN / M

BABY
Amazing Hardcore #1: Blow Jobs / 1997 / MET / M • Knock Outs / 1992 / HHV / S •

VGA: Bureau Of Discipline #1 / 1993 / VGA / B • VGA: Bureau Of Discipline #2 / 1993 / VGA / B • VGA: Bureau Of Discipline #3 / 1993 / VGA / B

BABY (VERCINIA) *see Vercinia*

BABY BROOKE
She-Male Cocksuckers / 1993 / LEO / G • She-Male Solos #10 / 1992 / LEO / G • TV Training Center / 1993 / LEO / G

BABY DOE
Hot Lips / 1984 / VC / M • Naked Scents / 1984 / VC / M • Throat...12 Years After / 1984 / VC / M • Twilight Pink #2 / 1982 / VC / M • White Hot / 1984 / VXP / M

BABY DOLL
Big Babies In Budapest / 1996 / EL / M

BABY DYNAMITE
East Coast Sluts #05: North Carolina / 1995 / PL / M

BABY SUE YOUNG
Fetish Fever / 1993 / CA / C • Jezebel / 1979 / CV / M • Naughty Network / 1981 / CA / M • Porn In The USA #1 / 1986 / WV / C

BABYGIRL *see Vercinia*

BACARDI BREEZE
Black Cheerleader Search #05 / 1996 / IVC / M • Black Fantasies #14 / 1996 / HW / M • Menaja's House Party / 1996 / HW / M

BACKEY JACKIE
Amadeus Mozart / 1996 / XC / M • Buttman's European Vacation #3 / 1995 / EA / M • Passion In Venice / 1995 / ULI / M • Sex Scandals / 1995 / XC / M • Twilight / 1996 / ESN / M

BAD
Sorority Stewardesses #1 / 1995 / PE / M

BAD BRIDGETT
Mistress Elsa's Latex Sex Camp / 1994 / PL / F

BAD ERNIE *see Star Index I*

BAD MAMA JAMA
Adventures Of Bad Mama Jama #1 / 1984 / CPL / M • Adventures Of Bad Mama Jama #2 / 1985 / CPL / M • Adventures Of Bad Mama Jama #3 / 1985 / CPL / M • Bad Mama Jama And The Fat Ladies Of The Evening / 1989 / VT / M • Loving Large / 1994 / VT / C

BAILEY
Alpine Affairs / 1995 / LE / M • Beach Bum Amateur's #42 / 1995 / MID / M • Butt Hunt #09 / 1995 / LEI / M • Cabin Fever / 1995 / ERA / M • Cum Tv / 1996 / NIT / M • The Cumm Brothers #07: Honeymoon On Uranus / 1995 / OD / M • The Cumm Brothers #12: Two GOOS For Every Girl / 1995 / OD / M • Cutie Pies / 1995 / TTV / M • Forbidden Fantasies #3 / 1995 / ZA / M • Fresh Faces #04 / 1995 / EVN / M • Full Metal Babes / 1995 / LE / M • Hollywood Amateurs #15 / 1995 / MID / M • Hot Body Competition: Lusty Lingerie Contest / 1996 / CG / F • Interview: New And Natural / 1995 / LV / M • Mickey Ray's Sex Search #05: Deep Inside / 1995 / WIV / M • Nasty Newcummers #09 / 1995 / MET / M • Perverted Stories #01 / 1995 / JMP / M • Pizzas, Hot Tubs & Bimbos / 1995 / SUF / M • Private Diaries #1: Christina / 1995 / AVI / M • Pussy Hunt #11 / 1995 / LEI / M • Pussy Hunt #12 / 1995 / LEI / M • Reminiscing / 1995 / LE / M • Romance & Fantasy / 1995 / VEX / M • Savage Liasons / 1995 / BEP / F • The Seductive Secretary /

1995 / GO / M • Stuff Your Face #3 / 1995 / JMP / M • Teacher's Pet #3 / 1995 / APP / M • Tinsel Town Tales / 1995 / NOT / M • Video Virgins #21 / 1995 / NS / M • The Violation Of Kia / 1995 / JMP / F • Young And Anal #3 / 1995 / JMP / M

BAILEY PARRISH
Real Tickets #1 / 1994 / VC / M

BAILEY THOMAS
A Is For Asia / 1996 / 4P / M • More Dirty Debutantes #42 / 1995 / 4P / M • More Dirty Debutantes #43 / 1995 / 4P / M

BAILLAT
Perversity In Paris / 1994 / AVI / M

BAJA see Star Index I

BAKER
Raw Talent: Bang 'er 26 Times / 1992 / RTP / M

BALJIT
British Babe Hunt / 1996 / VC / M

BAM BAM
Done In The Desert Sun / 1995 / OUP / M • House Of Anal / 1995 / NOT / M • Pick Up Lines #01 / 1995 / 4P / M • Top Debs #6: Rear Entry Girls / 1995 / GO / M

BAMBAMBA
Odyssey Triple Play #46: Ass-Splitting Sex / 1993 / OD / M

BAMBI
Anal Analysis (Heatwave) / 1992 / HW / M • AVP #8004: Missy's Surprise / 1990 / AVP / F • Blue Vanities #531 / 1993 / FFL / M • Blue Vanities #583 / 1996 / FFL / M • Bubble Butts #24 / 1993 / LBO / M • Bubbles / 1993 / KBR / S • Buffy Malibu's Nasty Girls #11 / 1996 / ANA / F • Candyman #01: 1-900-Fantasies / 1992 / GLI / M • Candyman #02 / 1992 / GLI / M • Candyman #03 / 1993 / GLI / M • Candyman Virgin Dream / 1993 / GLI / M • Candyman #07: Favorite Sweets / 1993 / GLI / M • The Convict / 1995 / TAO / B • Dirty & Kinky Mature Women #10 / 1996 / C69 / M • Gangbang Girl #16 / 1995 / ANA / M • Girls Around The World #27 / 1995 / BTO / M • Girls Around The World #28 / 1995 / BTO / S • Golden Oldies #6 / 1996 / TTV / M • H&S: Bambi / 199? / H&S / S • Harry Horndog #08: Anal Lovers #1 / 1992 / ZA / M • Harsha Highway #5: Backdoor Blues / 1996 / HO / M • High Heel Harlots #01 / 1993 / SFP / M • Nasty Nymphos #11 / 1995 / ANA / M • The Older Women's Sperm Bank #4 / 1996 / SUF / M • The Older Women's Sperm Bank #5 / 1996 / SUF / M • Parliament: Lesbian Seduction #1 / 1990 / PM / F • Pussy Tails #01 / 1993 / CDY / M • Shaved #02 / 1992 / RB / F • Sin City Cycle Sluts #2 / 1995 / SC / F • Street Fantasies / 1993 / AFV / M • SVE: Spank'er Butt #3 / 1994 / SVE / B • Swedish Erotica #37 / 1981 / CA / M • Swedish Erotica #40 / 1981 / CA / M • Taboo #02 / 1982 / IN / M • Why Do You Want To be In An Adult Vidoo / 1000 / PM / F

BAMBI ALLEN
Charm School / 1986 / VI / M • Come Ring My Chimes / 19?? / ... / M • Dream Jeans / 1987 / CA / M • The Hot Box Invasion / 1987 / AMB / M • Hot Seat / 1986 / AVC / M • Lash Of Lust / 1968 / ... / S • Nudes At Eleven #1 / 1986 / AVC / M • Revenge Of The Babes #2 / 1987 / PL / M • Rio Heat / 1986 / VD / M • Saturday Night Beaver / 1986 / EVN / M • Sex Machine / 1986 / LA

/ M • Sex-O-Gram / 1986 / LA / M • Star Gazers / 1986 / CA / M • Summer Lovers / 1987 / WET / M • Tickled! / 1989 / BIZ / C • Weird Fantasy / 1986 / LA / M

BAMBI BACH see Star Index I

BAMBI BAXTER
Naughty Schoolgirls Revenge / 1994 / BIZ / B

BAMBI CUMMINGS see Star Index I

BAMBI DEER
Call Me Angel, Sir / 1976 / ALP / M

BAMBI HAMILTON
Blue Vanities #514 / 1992 / FFL / M

BAMBI LEIGH
Blue Vanities #586 / 1996 / FFL / M • Lusty Ladies #03 / 1983 / SVE / M

BAMBI LOVE
Arsenal Of Fear / 1993 / BS / B • Blame It On Bambi / 1992 / BS / B • Cruel Passions / 1992 / BS / B • The Power Of Summer #2: Reward / 1992 / BS / B • Roommate's Revenge / 1992 / RB / B

BAMBI SNYDER see Star Index I

BAMBI WOODS
Caballero Preview Tape #2 / 1983 / CA / C • Debbie Does Dallas #1 / 1978 / VC / M • Debbie Does Dallas #2 / 1980 / VC / M • Debbie Does Dallas #3 / 1985 / VC / M • Swedish Erotica #12 / 1980 / CA / M

BAMBINO BROWN
Black Gangbangers #12 / 1996 / HW / M

BAMBY KAY
Anal Magic / 1995 / XC / M • Bedtime Story Italiano / 1995 / UGO / M

BAN
Global Girls / 1996 / GO / F

BARB
On Your Bare Bottom / 1992 / BON / B • Teaserama / 1954 / SOW / S

BARBARA
A&B AB#304: Stripping Lesbians / 1991 / A&B / F • AVP #9132: Barbara Likes It Hard / 1991 / AVP / M • Barby's On Butt Row / 1996 / ABS / M • Blue Vanities #508 / 1992 / FFL / M • Blue Vanities #527 / 1993 / FFL / M • Blue Vanities #541 / 1994 / FFL / M • Blue Vanities #578 / 1995 / FFL / M • Body Tease / 1992 / VER / F • Eurotica #03 / 1995 / XC / M • Eurotica #05 / 1996 / XC / M • French-Pumped Femmes #1 / 1989 / RSV / G • French-Pumped Femmes #3 / 1991 / RSV / G • Hardcore Schoolgirls #4: Little Kittens / 1996 / XPR / M • Joe Elliot's College Girls #32 / 1994 / JOE / M • Magma: Hot Shots / 1995 / MET / M • Older And Anal #1 / 1995 / FC / M • Penetration (Flash) #1 / 1995 / FLV / M • Penetration (Flash) #2 / 1995 / FLV / M • Private Film #20 / 1995 / OD / M • Private Film #23 / 1995 / OD / M • Sodomania #02: More Tails / 1992 / EL / M • Totally Disgusting / 1995 / GAL / B

BARBARA ALTON
10 Years Of Big Busts #2 / 1990 / BTO / C • The Best Of Big Busty / 1986 / L&W / C • Big Busty #05 / 198? / BTO / M • Changing Places / 1984 / AVC / M

BARBARA AMES see Star Index I

BARBARA BARTON
Beyond Fulfillment / 1975 / SE / M • Ecstasy / 1979 / SE / M • Fulfillment / 1973 / SE / M • Garters And Lace / 1975 / SE / M

BARBARA BELKIN
Waterpower / 1975 / VHL / M

BARBARA BILLS see Delania Ruffino

BARBARA BLAIR

Philmore Butts Meets The Palm Beach Nymphomaniac Kathy Wille / 1995 / SUF / M

BARBARA BOSQUET
Blonde In Black Lace / 1975 / VCX / M

BARBARA BOURBON
Candy Tangerine Man / 1975 / UNV / S • A Dirty Western #1 / 1973 / AR / M • The Erotic Adventures Of Peter Galore / 1973 / ALP / M • I Spit On Your Corpse / 1974 / REP / S • The Private Afternoons Of Pamela Mann / 1974 / TVX / M • Saturday Matinee Series #3 / 1996 / VCX / C • True Legends Of Adult Cinema: Unsung Superstars / 1993 / VC / C • The World Of Henry Paris / 1981 / VC / C

BARBARA BRAUN see Star Index I

BARBARA BRYAN see Star Index I

BARBARA BUSH
Sharon In The Rough-House / 1976 / LA / M

BARBARA CARON
Amber & Sharon Do Paris #1 / 1985 / PAA / M • Amber & Sharon Do Paris #2 / 1985 / PAA / M • Cock Robin / 1989 / SUE / M • Drop Out / 1972 / ... / S • From Paris With Lust / 1985 / PEN / M • Les Lesbos Of Paris #1 / 1985 / LIP / F • Wild, Free And Hungry / 1970 / SOW / S

BARBARA CARSON
Night After Night / 1973 / BL / M

BARBARA CLOUDS *(Barbara Harold, Barbara Klouds)*
Chopstix / 1979 / TVX / M • Las Vegas Lady / 1981 / VCX / M • Little Girls Blue #2 / 1983 / VCX / M

BARBARA COLE see Star Index I

BARBARA COLLINS see Star Index I

BARBARA D'ANTONI see Star Index I

BARBARA DAHL
Karin & Barbara Superstars / 1988 / PL / M

BARBARA DANIELS see Star Index I

BARBARA DARE *(Kim Wylde (B. Dare), Kim Wilde (B. Dare), Kimberly Dare, Kimberly Pare, Stacey Nix)*
Shaggy haired pretty very petite hard blonde who obviously prefers women. First movies were Lilith Unleashed and The Oddest Couple. Stacey Nix is from Evil Toons. Born Feb 27, 1963 according to one report.
10 1/2 Weeks / 1986 / SE / M • Adult Video News 1991 Awards / 1991 / VC / M • Aerobics Girls Club / 1986 / 4P / F • Aerobisex Girls #2 / 1989 / LIP / F • Angela Takes A Dare / 1988 / FAZ / M • The Autobiography Of Herman Flogger / 1986 / AVC / M • Back To Back #1 / 1987 / 4P / C • Barbara Dare's Bad / 1988 / SE / C • Barbara Dare's Prime Choice / 1987 / SE / C • Barbara Dare's Roman Holiday / 1987 / SE / M • Barbara The Barbarian / 1987 / SE / M • Behind Closed Doors / 1990 / VI / M • The Best Little Whorehouse In Beverly Hills / 1986 / CDI / M • The Best Little Whorehouse In Hong Kong / 1987 / SE / M • Blame It On Ginger / 1986 / VI / M • Blow By Blow / 1984 / QX / M • Bratgirl / 1989 / VI / M • Circus Acts / 1987 / SE / C • Corporate Affairs / 1986 / SE / M • Debbie Class Of '88 / 1987 / CC / M • Debbie Does 'em All #3 / 1989 / CV / M • Debbie Goes To College / 1986 / ELH / M • Deep Inside Keisha / 1994 / VC / C • Deep Throat Girls / 1986 / ELH / M • Devil In

Miss Dare / 1986 / AVC / C • Diaries Of Fire And Ice #1 / 1989 / VC / M • Diaries Of Fire And Ice #2 / 1989 / VC / M • Dig It / 1994 / FD / C • Dirty Diane / 1989 / V99 / M • Dirty Harriet / 1986 / SAT / M • Double Dare / 1986 / SE / M • Dr Lust / 1987 / VC / M • Dynamic Vices / 1987 / VC / M • E.X. / 1986 / SUP / M • Evil Toons / 1990 / PRS / S • Fantasy Couples / 1989 / FAZ / C • Fatal Erection / 1988 / SEV / M • Femmes On Fire / 1988 / VC / F • For Her Pleasure Only / 1989 / FAZ / M • For Your Lips Only / 1989 / FAZ / M • The Fun House / 1988 / SEV / C • Ginger And Spice / 1986 / VI / M • Ginger Then And Now / 1990 / VI / C • Girl Crazy / 1989 / CDI / F • Girls, Girls, Girls, Girls / 1993 / FD / C • Girlworld #4 / 1989 / LIP / F • The Greatest American Blonde / 1987 / WV / C • Hanna Does Her Sisters / 1986 / HUR / M • Harem Girls / 1986 / SE / M • The Honeydrippers / 1987 / VXP / M • Hot And Nasty! / 1986 / V99 / C • Hot Property / 1989 / EXH / C • Hyapatia Lee's Arcade Series #01 / 1988 / ZA / C • Inches For Keisha / 1988 / WV / C • The Insatiable Hyapatia Lee / 1987 / SE / C • L.A. Stories / 1990 / VI / M • Leather & Lace / 1987 / SE / C • Legends Of Porn #2 / 1989 / CV / C • Legends Of Porn #3 / 1991 / MET / C • Lick Bush / 1992 / VD / C • Lilith Unleashed / 1986 / VC / M • Lover's Lane / 1986 / SE / M • Lust Italian Style / 1987 / CA / M • Mantrap / 1986 / BAN / M • Mardi Gras / 1986 / SE / M • Miami Spice #1 / 1987 / CA / M • The Naked Stranger / 1988 / VI / M • Nasty Nights / 1988 / PL / C • The Oddest Couple / 1986 / VC / M • Only The Best Of Barbara Dare / 1990 / CV / C • Only The Best Of Debbie / 1992 / MET / C • Only The Best Of The Erotic Eighties / 1992 / VC / C • Oral Majority #01 / 1986 / WV / C • Phantom Of The Cabaret #1 / 1989 / VC / M • Phantom Of The Cabaret #2 / 1989 / VC / M • Playpen / 1987 / VC / M • Porsche / 1990 / NSV / M • Provocative Pleasures / 1988 / VC / C • Red Hot Fire Girls / 1989 / VD / M • Ride A Pink Lady / 1986 / SE / M • Sex Asylum #2 / 1986 / VI / M • Sex Beat / 1985 / WV / M • The Sex Game / 1987 / SE / C • Sex In Dangerous Places / 1988 / VI / M • Sheer Bedlam / 1986 / VI / M • Simply Outrageous / 1989 / VC / C • Sin City / 1986 / WET / M • Sinful Sisters / 1986 / VEX / M • Slippery When Wet / 1986 / PL / M • Sophisticated Women / 1986 / BAN / M • Sorority Pink #1 / 1989 / CV / M • Sorority Pink #2 / 1989 / CV / M • Star Tricks / 1988 / WV / M • Surf, Sand And Sex / 1987 / SE / M • Suzie Superstar #3 / 1989 / CV / M • Tail For Sale / 1988 / VD / M • Taste Of The Best #2 / 1988 / PIN / C • Tongue 'n Cheek (Red Light) / 1984 / RLV / M • Torrid / 1989 / VI / M • Triangle / 1989 / VI / M • True Legends Of Adult Cinema: The Cult Superstars / 1993 / VC / C • True Legends Of Adult Cinema: The Erotic Eighties / 1992 / VC / C • True Love / 1989 / VI / M • Two Into One #1 / 1988 / PIN / C • Ultrasex / 1987 / VC / M • Valet Girls / 1987 / ... / S • VCA Previews #4 / 1988 / VC / C • Video Voyeur #1 / 1988 / VT / C • Video Voyeur #2 / 1989 / VT / C • Wet 'n' Bare With Barbara Dare / 1988 / NEO / C • Wet Pink / 1989 / PL / C • Where The Boys Aren't #1 / 1989 / VI / F • Where The Boys Aren't #2 /

1989 / VI / F • Wild In The Wilderness / 1988 / SE / M • The Wild Wild West / 1986 / SE / M • Woman To Woman / 1989 / ZA / C • Women Who Love Men, Men Who Love Women / 1993 / FD / C • The Zebra Club / 1986 / VSE / M • [Barbara Dare's Greatest Hits / 1988 / ... / C • [The Devil In Barbara Dare / 1990 / VEX / M • [Good Neighbors Come in All Colors / 1989 / ... / M • [High Society Centerspread #10 / 1988 / ... / S

BARBARA DAVIES see Star Index I
BARBARA DOBSON
Jungle Heat / 1995 / LUM / M
BARBARA DOLL
French girl. Blonde with long straight hair, passable face, small tits, reasonable hard body, 21 years old in 1994. In April 1995 tested positive for HIV. Lots of speculation on how she got it ranging from intravenous drugs (she denies) to those dirty Europeans via forged HIV test certificates. The industry went bananas insisting on condoms for everyone but then breathed a collective sigh of relief when it was reported that later tests showed she was HIV negative. Back to business as usual but for Doll her career in the US was over so she moved back to France. Some scurrilous rumormongers hinted that there may have been a little payment involved to get her out of the country—out of sight and out of mind—but, not coming from an industry-approved source those rumors were officially frowned upon. Lo and behold, in 1997 during the Stagliano disclosure, it's finally admitted that Doll "might be" HIV+ after all.
113 Cherry Lane / 1994 / FOR / M • The Adventures Of Major Morehead / 1994 / SC / M • Adventures Of The DP Boys: At The French Riviera / 1994 / HW / M • The Anal Adventures Of Bruce Seven / 1996 / BS / C • The Anal Adventures Of Suzy Super Slut #2 / 1994 / AFV / M • Anal Exchange / 1995 / C69 / M • Anal Planet / 1994 / CC / M • Anal Pow Wow / 1995 / XC / M • The Anal-Europe Series #07: / 1994 / LV / M • Ass Dweller / 1994 / WIV / M • Back Door Mistress / 1994 / GO / M • Backdoor Club #1 / 1996 / VEX / C • Backstage Pass / 1994 / SC / M • Behind The Brown Door / 1994 / PE / M • Buffy Malibu's Nasty Girls #06 / 1994 / ANA / F • Butt Banged Bicycle Babes / 1994 / ANA / M • Butts Of Steel / 1994 / BLC / M • Buttslammers #05: Quake, Rattle & Roll! / 1994 / BS / F • Candy's Custom Car Wash / 1995 / FC / M • Canned Heat / 1995 / IN / M • Cat Lickers #2 / 1994 / ME / F • Cat Lickers #3 / 1995 / ME / F • Chemical Reaction / 1995 / CC / M • Cloud 9 / 1995 / VI / M • Deep Inside Ariana / 1995 / VC / C • The Devil In Miss Jones #5: The Inferno / 1994 / VC / M • Dick & Jane Go To Northridge / 1994 / AVI / M • Dick & Jane Penetrate Paris / 1994 / AVI / M • Dick & Jane Up, Down And All Around / 1994 / AVI / M • The Dickheads #2 / 1993 / MID / M • Domination / 1994 / WP / M • Erotic World Of Anne Spice / 1995 / WV / M • Explicit Entry / 1995 / LE / M • Fantasy Chamber / 1994 / ULI / M • Filthy Sleazy Scoundrels / 1994 / HW / M • French Doll / 1994 / ME / M • French Roommate / 1995 / C69 / M • French Twist / 1995 / IN / M • French Vanilla / 1994 / HW / M • The French Way /

1994 / HOV / M • Games Women Play / 1995 / XC / M • The Grind / 1995 / XC / M • Heartbeat / 1995 / PP / M • Homegrown Video #419: Reigning Pussycats And Horndogs / 1994 / HOV / M • Hot Tight Asses #09 / 1994 / TCK / M • Hotel Sodom #08 / 1995 / SNA / M • Hotel Sodom #10 / 1996 / SNA / M • The Inseminator #1 / 1994 / LBO / M • The Inseminator #2: Domination Day / 1994 / LBO / M • International Affairs / 1994 / PL / M • Koko Is Cumin' At Cha / 1994 / AVI / M • La Femme Vanessa / 1995 / SC / M • Latex #1 / 1994 / VC / M • Let's Play Doctor / 1994 / PV / M • Long Dark Shadow / 1994 / LE / M • Loving You Always / 1994 / IN / M • M Series #22 / 1994 / LBO / M • Masturbation Ages 20 To 45 / 1996 / C69 / F • Miss Anal #1 / 1995 / C69 / M • Miss Anal #2 / 1995 / C69 / M • Miss Anal #3 / 1995 / C69 / M • Natural Born Thriller / 1994 / CC / M • The New Ass Masters #08 / 1996 / LEI / C • The New Butt Hunt #15 / 1995 / LEI / C • New Positions / 1994 / PV / M • New Wave Hookers #4 / 1994 / VC / M • The Nurses Are Cumming #2 / 1996 / LBO / C • Nurses Do It With Care / 1995 / EVN / M • Orgies Orgies Orgies / 1994 / WV / M • Paris Taxis / 1995 / XYS / M • Passenger 69 #1 / 1994 / IP / M • The Passion / 1995 / IP / M • Perversity In Paris / 1994 / AVI / M • Picture Perfect (Cal Vista) / 1995 / CV / M • Private Film #15 / 1994 / OD / M • Public Places #1 / 1994 / SC / M • Public Places #2 / 1995 / SC / M • Pussyman #06: House Of Games / 1994 / SNA / M • Pussyman #11: Prime Cuts / 1995 / SNA / C • Radical Affairs Video Magazine #08 / 1994 / ME / M • Reality & Fantasy / 1994 / DR / M • A Rear And Pleasant Danger / 1995 / PP / M • Rocco Unleashed / 1994 / SC / M • Rock Me / 1994 / CC / M • The Scarlet Woman / 1994 / WP / M • Secret Of Her Suckcess / 1994 / VC / M • Sex Trek #5: Deep Space Sex / 1994 / ME / M • Silk Stockings: The Black Widow / 1994 / SPI / M • Skin #1 / 1994 / EUR / M • Skin #2 / 1995 / ERQ / M • Skin Hunger / 1995 / MET / M • Sleaze Please!—November Edition / 1994 / FH / M • Stretchin' The Rear / 1995 / PE / M • Sweat 'n' Bullets / 1995 / MID / M • Sweet A$ Money / 1994 / MID / M • Swinging Couples #04 / 1994 / GO / M • Taboo #13 / 1994 / IN / M • Takin' It To The Limit #2 / 1994 / BS / M • Tommyknockers / 1994 / CC / M • Up And Cummers #07 / 1994 / 4P / M • The Valley Girl Connection / 1994 / IN / M • The Violation Of Alexandria Dane / 1995 / JMP / F • While You Were Dreaming / 1995 / WV / M • Young Nurses In Lust / 1994 / LBO / M
BARBARA ERICSON see Star Index I
BARBARA FELL
The Beat Goes On / 1987 / VCR / C
BARBARA FORD see Star Index I
BARBARA GATES see Star Index I
BARBARA GORDON
Jail Bait / 1976 / VC / M
BARBARA HALSWORTH
Blue Vanities #517 / 1992 / FFL / M
BARBARA HAROLD see Barbara Clouds
BARBARA HAUSER see Star Index I
BARBARA HAWKS
Blue Vanities #517 / 1992 / FFL / M
BARBARA HESS

Older Women Younger Men #3 / 1993 / CC / M

BARBARA HUGHES *see Star Index I*

BARBARA JASON *see Star Index I*

BARBARA JONES
Best Butt(e) In The West #1 / 1992 / CC / M

BARBARA JOY *see Lorna Maitland*

BARBARA KLOUDS *see Barbara Clouds*

BARBARA LEIGH
Chained / cr76 / BIZ / B • Famous T & A / 1982 / WIZ / C • Seven / 1979 / LIV / S

BARBARA LESTER *see Star Index I*

BARBARA LOVELYNN *see Star Index I*

BARBARA MADISON *see Star Index I*

BARBARA MARTIN
Journal Of Love / 1970 / ALP / M

BARBARA MILLER *see Star Index I*

BARBARA MILLS
Chain Gang Women / 1971 / AE / S • Come Ring My Chimes / 19?? / ... / M • Love Garden / 1971 / SOW / S • Sweet Georgia / 1970 / SOW / S • [The Suckers / 1969 / ... / S

BARBARA MOLATH
Private Film #24 / 1995 / OD / M • Private Film #26 / 1995 / OD / M • Private Stories #03 / 1995 / OD / M • Private Video Magazine #26 / 1995 / OD / M • Triple X Video Magazine #01 / 1995 / OD / M • Triple X Video Magazine #02 / 1995 / OD / M

BARBARA MOOSE
Come Play With Me #2 / 1980 / PS / S • Girls U.S.A. / 1980 / AIR / M • [La Rabatteuse / 1977 / ... / M

BARBARA NICHOLS
Blue Vanities #580 / 1996 / FFL / M

BARBARA NIVEN
Under Lock And Key / 1994 / IMP / S

BARBARA NORDON
Blue Vanities #546 / 1994 / FFL / M

BARBARA O'FARRELL *see Star Index I*

BARBARA PECKINPAUGH *see Susanna Britton*

BARBARA PEYRET *see Star Index I*

BARBARA POMERANZ *see Star Index I*

BARBARA REDDING
The Bite / 1975 / SVE / M

BARBARA RIOKEI
Inside Marilyn / 1984 / CA / M

BARBARA ROBERTS *see Star Index I*

BARBARA SALK
The Girls In The Band / 1976 / SVE / M

BARBARA SAMPLES *see Star Index I*

BARBARA SEAVER
Her Total Response / 1975 / SVE / M

BARBARA SELLER *see Star Index I*

BARBARA SMITH
Violated / 1973 / PVX / M

BARBARA STANEK
[Krankenschwestern-Report / 1972 / ... / M

BARBARA STEPHENS *see Star Index I*

BARBARA STRASBERG
For Members Only / 1980 / LIM / M

BARBARA SUMMERS
The Erotic Adventures Of Alladin X / 1995 / IP / M • Naughty Sisters #1 / 1992 / RB / B • She Had It Coming / 1991 / RB / B

BARBARA TEIL
Lovin' Spoonfuls #7 / 1996 / 4P / C • More Dirty Debutantes #32 / 1994 / 4P / M

BARBARA WALLACE
I Am Always Ready / 1978 / HIF / M

BARBARA WELLS

Debutantes Discipline / Please Cane Me / 1993 / CS / B

BARBARA WOOD (TRIX) *see Trixie Tyler*

BARBARA WOODS
This is a catchall name for actresses who haven't decided on a name yet.

BARBARA WOODS (DSHIR *see Devon Shire*

BARBARA WOODS (MONA) *see Mona Lisa*

BARBARELLA
Alice In Pornoland / 1996 / IP / M • Cherry Busters / 1995 / WIV / M • Private Film #19 / 1994 / OD / M • Private Video Magazine #21 / 1995 / OD / M

BARBARITO
Reel Life Video #52: Crystal Fox & The Plumber / Barbarito / 1996 / RLF / M

BARBARZ WETT
Eat At Dave's #5 / 1996 / SP / M • Old Bitches / 1996 / GLI / M

BARBERELLA *see Star Index I*

BARBETTE
Impulse #02: The Film / 1995 / MBP / M

BARBI
6000 Lash Lane / 1994 / LON / B • Bubbles / 1993 / KBR / S • Exposed / 1993 / HOM / B • Latex Submission #2 / 1992 / BIZ / B • Punished Embezzler / 1993 / BON / B • The Tower Of Lyndon / 1994 / LON / B

BARBI BOND
Country & Western Cuties #2: Naked Pie Eating Contest / 1996 / EVN / M • Harry Horndog #30: Love Puppies #7 / 1995 / FPI / M • Here Comes Magoof #1 / 1995 / VC / M • Mike Hott: #339 Cum In My Mouth #04 / 1996 / MHV / C • Mike Hott: #345 Cum In My Cunt #07 / 1995 / MHV / C • Mike Hott: #349 Girls Who Swallow Cum #03 / 1996 / MHV / C • Mike Hott: #356 Girls Who Lap Cum From Cunts #01 / 1996 / MHV / M • Mike Hott: #357 Bonus Cunt: Barbie Bond / 1996 / MHV / M • Mike Hott: #362 Fuck The Boss #7 / 1996 / MHV / M • Mike Hott: #368 Three-Sum Sluts #13 / 1996 / MHV / M • The Nympho Files / 1995 / NIT / M • Pizza Sluts: They Deliver / 1995 / XCI / M • Sex Truth & Videotape #1 / 1996 / DOC / M • Snatch Masters #02 / 1994 / LEI / M • Texas Crude / 1995 / NIT / M • The Tickle Shack / 1995 / SBP / B • Twists Of The Heart / 1995 / NIT / M

BARBI DAHL (S/M)
The Best Of Hot Heels / 1992 / BIZ / B • Fantasies Of A Transsexual / 1991 / BIZ / G • She-Mails / 1993 / PL / G • She-Males In Torment #2 / 1992 / BIZ / G • TV Blondes Do It Best / 1992 / BIZ / G • TV Ladies Room / 1993 / BIZ / G • TV Reform School / 1992 / BIZ / G • TVs Teased And Tormented / 1995 / BIZ / G

BARBI JAMES *see Star Index I*

BARBI MILLER
Pussy Showdown / 1994 / WIV / M

BARBI SVENSON *see Merle Michaels*

BARBIE
A&B AB#182: Watch Me Spank Me / 1990 / A&B / M • A&B AB#199: My Girl Barbie / 1990 / A&B / M • A&B AB#200: Bachelor Party / 1990 / A&B / M • A&B AB#201: Pussy Galore / 1990 / A&B / F • A&B AB#205: Strippers Choice / 1990 / A&B / M • A&B AB#332: Barbie Again / 1991 / A&B / F • A&B AB#371: Wild Woman #1 /

1991 / A&B / M • Bitter She-Males / 1992 / BIZ / G • Bus Stop Tales #03 / 1989 / PRI / M • The Cellar Dweller / 1996 / EL / M • Eye On You: Anna Meets The Rabbit / 1995 / EOY / F • Hot Legs #2 / 1990 / PLV / B • Hot Shoes / 1992 / BIZ / B • Kinky College Cunts #06 / 1993 / NS / F • Latex Submission #1 / 1992 / BIZ / B • Stevi's: Baby Barbie / 1996 / SSV / F • Stevi's: Barbie Spreads / 1993 / SSV / M • Stevi's: Naughty Girls / 1993 / SSV / F • Stevi's: Toys R Barbie / 1995 / SSV / F • Tails From The Whip / 1991 / HOM / B

BARBIE ANGEL *(Barbie Brochant)*
Petite blonde, who can look very young some-times, with a shaven pussy, tight waist, small droopy tits, fleshy labia, passable face.
Al Borda's Brazilian Adventures / 1996 / BEP / M • Anal Auditions #3 / 1996 / LE / M • Analtown USA #11 / 1996 / NIT / M • Casting Call #18 / 1996 / SO / M • Hardcore Schoolgirls #4: Little Kittens / 1996 / XPR / M • Hardcore Schoolgirls #5: Virgin Killers / 1996 / XPR / M • Max #09: Where Danger Lurks / 1996 / XPR / M • Max #10: Dirty Deeds / 1996 / XPR / M • Max #11: Tunnel Of Lust / 1996 / LE / M • Max Gold #1 / 1996 / XPR / C • Max World #3: Formula 1 / 1996 / XPR / M • Max World #4: Let's Party / 1996 / XPR / M • Puritan Video Magazine #03 / 1996 / LE / M • Sinboy #4: Bareass Barbecue / 1996 / SC / M

BARBIE BENDUM
Doing It / 1982 / SE / M • Playboy Video Magazine #09 / 1985 / PLA / S

BARBIE BENTZ *see Star Index I*

BARBIE BLAKE *(Bunny Blake, Bunny Lake, Barbie Lake)*
Blonde with curly hair, small/medium tits and a marginal face.
Another Kind Of Love / 1985 / CV / M • The Autobiography Of Herman Flogger / 1986 / AVC / M • Back To Back #1 / 1987 / 4P / C • Backdoor Brides #1 / 1985 / PV / M • Cavalcade Of Stars / 1985 / VCR / C • Devil In Miss Dare / 1986 / AVC / C • Dirty Tricks / 1986 / 4P / M • Ecstasy / 1986 / PP / M • Girls, Girls, Girls, Girls / 1993 / FD / C • Hanna Does Her Sisters / 1986 / HUR / M • Heavy Breathing / 1986 / CV / M • Indecent Itch / 1985 / VCR / M • Jewels Of The Night / 1986 / SE / M • The Magic Touch / 1985 / CV / M • Pleasure Spot / 1986 / CA / M • Ramb-Ohh #1 / 1986 / PV / M • Rambone Does Hollywood / 1986 / WET / M • Rump Humpers / 1985 / WET / M • Shiela's Deep Desires / 1986 / HO / M • Star 85: Kari Fox / 1985 / VEX / M • This Butt's For You / 1986 / PME / M • Tip Of The Tongue / 1985 / V20 / M • To Live & Shave In LA / 1986 / WET / M

BARBIE BROCHANT *see Barbie Angel*

BARBIE BROOKES
Barbii's Painful Examination / 1995 / GAL / B • East Coast Sluts #04: New York City / 1995 / PL / M • East Coast Sluts #06: Philadelphia / 1995 / PL / M • N.Y. Video Magazine #10 / 1996 / OUP / M • Slapped Around Sluts / 1995 / PL / B • Streets Of New York #05 / 1995 / PL / M • Striptease #1 / 1995 / PL / M • Striptease #2 / 1995 / PL / M • Using Your Assets To Get A Head / 1996 / OUP / F

BARBIE CONRAD
Cover Girl Fantasies #2 / 1983 / VCR / C

BARBIE DAHL
Small-titted, very hard brunette.
The Bimbo #1 / 1985 / VXP / M • Blow By Blow / 1984 / QX / M • Broadway Fannie Rose / 1986 / CA / M • Candy Stripers #3 / 1986 / AR / M • Cravings / 1987 / VC / M • Decadence / 1986 / VD / M • Down & Dirty Scooter Trash / 1988 / CA / M • Eaten Alive / 1985 / VXP / M • Fashion Dolls / 1985 / LA / M • Girl Busters / 1985 / VC / M • The Honeydrippers / 1987 / VXP / M • Indiana Joan In The Black Hole Of Mammoo / 1984 / VC / M • Krazy 4 You / 1987 / 4P / M • Lustfire / 1991 / LA / C • Miami Vice Girls / 1984 / RLV / M • Moans & Groans / 1987 / 4P / M • Mouth To Mouth / 1986 / CC / M • A Passage Thru Pamela / 1985 / VC / G • Pleasure Party (Gourmet) / 1985 / GO / M • Romancing The Bone / 1984 / VC / M • A Taste Of Pink / 1985 / VXP / M • This Babe's Pen / 1984 / TAR / M • Tight Fit / 1987 / V99 / M • Tight Fit / 1991 / VEX / C • Times Square Comes Alive / 1984 / VC / M • Tongue 'n Cheek (Red Light) / 1984 / RLV / M • TV Dildo Fantasy #1 / 1992 / BIZ / G • The Vamp / 1986 / AVC / M • Vas-O-Line Alley / 1985 / VC / M • Wrecked 'em / 1985 / CC / M • The Year Of The Sex Dragon / 1986 / PV / M • You Make Me Wet / 1985 / SVE / M • [The Gang's All Here / cr85 / STM / M

BARBIE DALE *see Star Index I*

BARBIE DOLL *(Michelle Matell, Jerrii Sinclaire, Michele Martin)*
California blonde. Brainless but a nice body. Jerrii Sinclaire is from **The Wild Wild West**.
18 Candles / 1989 / LA / M • All The Way / 1989 / LIM / C • America's Raunchiest Home Videos #69: / 1993 / ZA / M • Backdoor To Hollywood #04 / 1988 / CDI / M • Bad Attitude / 1992 / CDI / M • Bad Side Of Town / 1993 / AFD / M • Batteries Included / 1988 / 3HV / M • Bedtime Stories / 1992 / CDI / M • Between Her Thighs / 1992 / CDI / M • Bi And Beyond #1 / 1988 / LAV / G • Black, White And Blue / 1989 / E&I / M • Blackballed / 1994 / VI / C • Blonde Fantasy / 1988 / CC / M • Body Slam / 1987 / 4P / B • Broadcast Nudes / 1988 / EVN / M • Bubbles / 1991 / IF / M • Bums Away / 1995 / PRE / C • California Blondes #01 / 1986 / VEX / M • California Blondes #02 / 1987 / VEX / M • California Cherries / 1987 / EVN / M • The Case Of The Mad Tickler / 1988 / ME / M • Caught From Behind #08 / 1988 / HO / M • Decadent / 1991 / WV / M • Doctor Feelgood / 1988 / CDI / M • The Elixir / 1992 / CDI / M • Expert Tease / 1988 / CC / M • Feel The Heat / 1989 / VEX / M • The Fire Down Below / 1992 / CDI / M • Full Metal Bikini / 1988 / PEN / M • Girls Will Be Boys #4 / 1991 / PL / F • Giving It To Barbii / 1990 / TOR / M • Golden Arches / 1992 / PRE / B • Golden Globes / 1989 / VEX / M • Heartbreaker / 1992 / CDI / M • Hot Blondes / 1988 / VEX / M • Hot Dreams / 1989 / VEX / M • Hot Dreams / 1991 / VEX / M • Hot Pink And Chocolate Brown / 1988 / PV / M • In Charm's Way / 1987 / IN / M • International Phone Sex Girls #5 / 1991 / PM / M • Laid In The USA / 1988 / CC / M • Leg...Ends #07 / 1993 / PRE / F • Love In Reverse / 1988 / FAZ / M • The Luv Game / 1988 / VCX / M • Magic Pool / 1988 / VD / M •

Mind Games / 1992 / CDI / M • The Moon Girls / 1990 / ME / C • Nasty Newshounds / 1988 / ME / M • No Way In / 1988 / EVN / M • Oral Majority Black #2 / 1988 / WV / C • Oriental Spice / 1990 / SE / M • The Out Of Towner / 1987 / CDI / M • Passionate Lips / 1990 / OD / M • Phone Sex Girls #5 / 1990 / TOR / M • Platinum Princess / 1988 / VEX / M • A Rare Starlet / 1987 / ME / M • Red Velvet / 1988 / PV / M • The Secret Diaries / 1990 / V99 / M • Sex Lies / 1988 / FAN / M • The Smart Aleck / 1990 / PM / M • Soul Games / 1988 / PV / C • Spanish Fly / 1987 / CA / M • Spellbound / 1991 / CDI / M • Street Heat / 1992 / CDI / M • Student Fetish Videos: The Enema #06 / 1992 / PRE / B • Student Fetish Videos: Spanking #05 / 1991 / SFV / B • Student Fetish Videos: Tickling #03 / 1992 / SFV / B • Super Blondes / 1989 / VEX / M • Suzy Cue / 1988 / VI / M • Sweet Cheeks (1991-Prestige) / 1991 / PRE / B • A Taste Of Pleasure / 1988 / AVC / M • Two Women & A Man / 1988 / VEX / M • Two Women & A Man / 1991 / VEX / C • Wet Tails / 1989 / PL / M • The Wild Wild West / 1986 / SE / M • Young And Innocent / 1987 / HO / M • [Blondes Have More Cum / 1989 / ... / M

BARBIE DOLL (OTHER)
Amateur Night / 1988 / CC / M • Do It American Amateur Style / 1992 / EAA / M • Horney Housewives / 1989 / EDV / M

BARBIE HALL
The Best Of Hot Heels / 1992 / BIZ / B • Enema Diary / 1989 / BIZ / B • Home Runs / 1995 / PRE / C

BARBIE LAKE *see Barbie Blake*

BARBIE LEE
Hot Savannah Nights / 1991 / VEX / M • Leading Lady / 1991 / V99 / M

BARBIE LEIGH
Let's Talk Sex / 1982 / CA / M

BARBIE MATHEWS *see Sharon Kane*

BARBIE TURNER
Goodbye My Love / 1980 / CA / M

BARBIE WINER *see Star Index I*

BARBII *(Michelle Verran)*
Very pretty blonde with an adorable body, medium tits and a very tight waist. **Barbii** aka **Introducing Barbii** was first movie. **Broadway Fannie Rose** is Barbie Dahl. Husband (Joe Pornales) committed suicide in 1989.
A.S.S.(Anal Security Squad) / 1988 / VD / M • B*A*S*H / 1989 / BIZ / C • Backdoor To Hollywood #04 / 1988 / CDI / M • Barbii Bound / 1988 / BON / B • Barbii Unleashed / 1988 / 4P / M • The Best Of Backdoor To Hollywood / 1990 / CIN / C • Best Of Foot Worship #2 / 1989 / BIZ / C • Bound To Tease #2 / 1989 / BON / C • Catfighting Cheerleaders / 1989 / BIZ / B • Crackdown / 1988 / BIZ / B • Deep Inside Barbie / 1989 / CDI / C • Dump Site / 1989 / BIZ / C • Eye Of The Tigress / 1988 / VD / M • Floor Play / 1989 / PLV / B • Friday The 13th #2 / 1989 / VD / M • From Rags To Riches / 1988 / CDI / M • Hot Buns / 1988 / BIZ / B • Hustler Honeys #1 / 1988 / VC / S • I Can't Get No...Satisfaction / 1988 / CDI / M • Introducing Barbii / 1987 / CDI / M • Legs And Lingerie #1 / 1990 / BIZ / F • Loose Ends #5: The New Generation / 1988 / 4P / M • Lusty Desires / 1988 / CDI / M • Miami Spice #1 / 1987 / CA / M • Rip Off #1 / 1988 / BIZ / B • Rip Off #2 / 1988 /

PLV / B • Rollover & Cell Blocks / 1988 / PLV / B • Sex And The Happy Landlord / 1988 / CDI / M • Sorority House Massacre #2: Nighty Nightmare / 1990 / WAR / S • Spend The Holidays With Barbii / 1987 / CDI / M • Tight Fit (Foot Fet) / 1988 / BIZ / B

BARBII (1992)
The Best Of Doctor Butts / 1994 / 4P / C • Two Women / 1992 / ROB / M

BARBRA BRAZILLE
Cleopatra Vs. The Indian Princess / 199? / NAP / B • Two Busty Barbies: Wet And Wild / 199? / NAP / F

BARBRA STREISAND (X)
Blue Vanities #007 / 1988 / FFL / M • Blue Vanities #124 / 1990 / FFL / M • Blue Vanities #181 / 1993 / FFL / M • Blue Vanities #210 / 1994 / FFL / M

BARBY DOLL
Most Valuable Slut / 1973 / HLV / M

BARBY MULLER
San Francisco Lesbians #5 / 1994 / PL / F

BARDOT
Backstage Pass / 1992 / VEX / M • Bardot / 1991 / VI / M • Breast Worx #10 / 1991 / LBO / M • Circus Of Lesbians / 1995 / VI / C • Neighborhood Watch #05 / 1991 / LBO / M • Pajama Party / 1993 / CV / C • Welcome To Dallas / 1991 / VI / M

BARK STAR *see T.T. Boy*

BARNABE *see Star Index I*

BARNEY *see Star Index I*

BARNEY WILSON
Body Slammers #03 / 1993 / SBP / B • Cabin Fever (B&D) / 1993 / BON / B • Medieval Dungeon Master / 1993 / BON / B • Tie Me, Tease Me / 1994 / CS / B

BARON VON TITAN *see Star Index I*

BARONESS SILVER *see Star Index I*

BARRY
Big Murray's New-Cummers #02: Las Vegas Swingers / 1992 / FD / M

BARRY (SHANE HUNTER) *see Shane Hunter*

BARRY BANG
Black On White / 1972 / CVX / M

BARRY BEAR
Full Moon Video #35: Wild Side Couples: The School HeadMaste / 1995 / FAP / M • Master's Touch #1: Dog House Slut / 1994 / FAP / B • Master's Touch #3: A Dream Or A Nightmare / 1995 / FAP / B • Master's Touch #5: Slave Revolt / 1995 / FAP / B

BARRY BOND
Deadly Sin / 1996 / ONA / M

BARRY CHRISTIAN
Farewell Scarlett / 1976 / COM / M • Honeypie / 1975 / VC / M • Loose Threads / 1979 / S&L / M • Ms. Woman Of The Year / 1980 / BL / M

BARRY FRYE *see Star Index I*

BARRY GARNETT
Inside Desiree Cousteau / 1979 / VCX / M

BARRY GILLIS *see Jamie Gillis*

BARRY HALL *see Jay Serling*

BARRY KUKLER
The Girls In The Band / 1976 / SVE / M

BARRY LINEHAN
Suburban Wives / 19?? / VST / M

BARRY LONG *see Star Index I*

BARRY LOOSE
She Male Sex Kittens / 1995 / MET / G

BARRY MCKAY *see Star Index I*

BARRY O'RILEY
Matinee Idol / 1984 / VC / M

BARRY PRIMUS
[Night Dreams / 1980 / ... / M
BARRY TONE
The End Zone / 1993 / PRE / B • Red Bottoms / 1988 / BIZ / B • Sole Kisses / 1987 / BIZ / S
BARRY W.C. *see Star Index I*
BARRY WOOD
Arches Of Triumph / 1995 / PRE / S • Best Of Foot Worship #2 / 1989 / BIZ / C • Feet First / 1988 / BIZ / S • Girls Of Treasure Island / 1988 / CV / M
BART
Intimate Interviews #1 / 1996 / NIT / M
BART CHRISTIAN *see Star Index I*
BART FRIEDMAN
Erotic Tattooing And Piercing #1 / 1986 / FLV / M
BARTOS
The Betrayal Of Innocence #1: The Awakening Of Marika / 1993 / CC / M • The Betrayal Of Innocence #2: The Decadence / 1993 / CC / M • The Betrayal Of Innocence #3: The Choice / 1993 / CC / M
BARUCH
Breaker Beauties / 1977 / VHL / M
BASH *see Star Index I*
BASIL
The French Canal / 1995 / DVP / G
BATSOA
Black Knockers #14 / 1995 / TV / M
BAUMER TREE *see* **Beerbohn Tree**
BAYBEE CAKES
Big Babies In Budapest / 1996 / EL / M • Sodomania #17: Simply Makes U Tingle / 1996 / EL / M
BAYIS MEIR *see Star Index I*
BEA
Bedtime Story Italiano / 1995 / UGO / M • The Erotic Misadventures Of Harry Johnson / 1992 / ZA / M • The Mastering Of Bea / 1995 / BON / B • Sex Scandals / 1995 / XC / M
BEA GENESTE *see Star Index I*
BEA MOORE
Tale Of Bearded Clam / cr71 / PYR / M
BEAN
New Faces, Hot Bodies #10 / 1993 / STP / M
BEATA
Private Gold #08: The Longest Night / 1996 / OD / M • Private Stories #06 / 1995 / OD / M • Private Stories #08 / 1996 / OD / M
BEATE *see* **Deborah Wells**
BEATE FRIEDMAN *see Star Index I*
BEATRICE
Magma: Horny Bulls / 1994 / MET / M
BEATRICE ANN
Erotic Dimensions: Explode / 1982 / NSV / M
BEATRICE HARNOIS
Felicia / 1975 / QX / M • Les Deux Gouines / 1975 / ... / M • Pussy Talk #1 / 1975 / TVX / M • [Making Out / 1976 / ... / M
BEATRICE LANCEL *see Star Index I*
BEATRICE M *see Star Index I*
BEATRICE POKITAN *see Star Index I*
BEATRICE SALL
Ejacula #1 / 1992 / VC / M • Ejacula #2 / 1992 / VC / M
BEATRICE TUCKER
The Erotic Adventures Of Alladin X / 1995 / IP / M
BEATRICE VALLE *(Patrice Valle)*
Passable face, black hair, medium/large tits,

voluptuous body. French.
10,000 Anal Maniacs #1 / 1993 / FOR / M • America's Raunchiest Home Videos #61: / 1993 / ZA / M • Anal Angels #3 / 1995 / VEX / C • Anal Angels #6 / 1996 / VEX / C • Anal Arsenal / 1994 / OD / M • Anal Ecstacy Girls #1 / 1993 / ROB / F • Anal Planet / 1994 / CC / M • Anal Pow Wow / 1995 / XC / M • Anal Sexual Silence / 1993 / IP / M • Anal Vision #15 / 1993 / LBO / M • The Anal-Europe Series #03: The Museum Of The Living Art / 1993 / LV / M • The Anal-Europe Series #04: Anal Recall / 1993 / LV / M • The Analizer / 1994 / VD / M • Ass Openers! #1 / 1995 / TCK / C • Ass Openers! #2 / 1995 / TCK / C • The Beverly Thrillbillies / 1993 / ZA / M • The Big Busteddd / 1993 / AFD / M • Bondage Proposal / 1993 / STM / B • The BoobyGuard / 1993 / FOR / M • Bun Busters #02 / 1993 / LBO / M • Butt's Motel #6 / 1994 / EX / M • Butts Afire / 1992 / PMV / M • The Can Can / 1993 / LV / M • Cannes 93: Broads Abroad / 1993 / ELP / M • Chain Gang / 1994 / OD / F • Deep Inside Debi Diamond / 1995 / VC / C • Dial A For Anal / 1994 / CA / M • Dirty Doc's Housecalls #11 / 1994 / LV / M • Doggie Style / 1994 / CA / M • Dungeon De Sade / 1993 / FC / B • Essence Of A Woman / 1993 / FOR / M • Euro Extremities #54 / 199? / SVE / C • Euro-Max #1: Frisky In France / 1995 / SC / M • Euroslut #2 / 1994 / CC / M • Father Of The Babe / 1993 / ZA / M • Gangbang Girl #13 / 1994 / ANA / M • Girls Just Wanna Have Girls #3 / 1994 / HIO / F • The Grind / 1995 / XC / M • Guttman's Paris Vacation / 1993 / PL / M • Hardcore Copy / 1993 / PL / M • Harry Horndog #19: Anal Lovers #3 / 1993 / ZA / M • Hot Tight Asses #04 / 1993 / TCK / M • Hot Tight Asses #06 / 1994 / TCK / M • Impulse #01: Memories Of An Italian Slut / 1995 / MBP / M • Impulse #05: When I Was 20... / 1995 / MBP / M • Impulse #08: The A Channel / 1996 / MBP / M • Impulse #09: / 1996 / MBP / M • Infamous Crimes Against Nature / 1993 / SUM / M • Interactive / 1993 / VD / M • International Analists / 1994 / AFD / M • Knockin' Da Booty / 1993 / WP / M • Leather And Tether / 1993 / STM / C • Lesbian Pros And Amateurs #24 / 1993 / GO / F • Magma: Bizarre Games / 1996 / MET / M • Magma: Spezial: Anal / 1994 / MET / M • Maidens Of Servitude #1 / 1993 / STM / B • Miss Nude International / 1993 / LE / M • Model's Memoirs / 1993 / IP / M • The New Butt Hunt #15 / 1995 / LEI / C • The Original Wicked Woman / 1993 / WP / M • Plan 69 From Outer Space / 1993 / CA / M • Pudsucker / 1994 / MID / M • Pussywoman #2 / 1994 / CC / M • Radical Affairs Video Magazine #06 / 1993 / ME / M • Sarah Jane's Love Bunnies #01 / 1993 / FPI / F • Secret Urges (Starmaker) / 1994 / STM / F • Sexophrenia / 1993 / VC / M • Sharon Mitchell's Sex Clinic #01 / 1993 / FC / M • Slave To Love / 1993 / ROB / M • Sniff Doggy Style / 1994 / PL / M • Sodomania #03: Foreign Objects / 1993 / EL / M • Sodomania: The Baddest Of The Best...And Then Some / 1994 / EL / C • Steele Butt / 1993 / AFV / M • Submissive Flashbacks / 1995 / STM / C • Susse Pussies / 199? / SVE / M • Sweet Tarts / 1993 / STM / B • Tommyknockers / 1994 /

CC / M • Trash In The Can / 1993 / LV / M • Victoria With An "A" / 1994 / PL / M • Video Virgins #02 / 1992 / NS / M • The Women / 1993 / CAT / F • [European Invasion / cr93 / A&E / M
BEAU DA'CIOUS
She Male Devil / 1996 / HSV / G • Showgirl She-Male / 1996 / HSV / G
BEAU GARRETTE *see* **Beau Michaels**
BEAU JAMES *see Star Index I*
BEAU LOVEJOY
L.A. Tool & Die / 1979 / TMX / G
BEAU MATHEWS *see Star Index I*
BEAU MICHAELS *(Steven Taylor (Beau), Sebastian (Beau Mic), Beau Garrette, George Wylde, Orgie Georgie, Orgy George, Hugh Hardon, Greg Holmer)*
SO of Nikki Wylde; later divorced. Greg Holmer is from **More Dirty Debutantes #8**.
Backfire / 1991 / GO / M • The Best Of Andrew Blake / 1993 / CA / C • Biff Malibu's Totally Nasty Home Videos #08 / 1992 / ANA / M • Blue Views / 1990 / CDI / M • Bonfire Of The Panties / 1990 / CC / M • Cheek Busters / 1990 / FH / M • Club Head / 1990 / CA / M • Confessions Of Christy / 1991 / CAY / M • Eve Of Seduction / 1991 / CDI / M • Headbangers Balls / 1991 / PL / M • Hollywood Studs / 1993 / FD / M • House Of Dreams / 1990 / CA / M • Intimate Obsession / 1992 / NIV / S • L.A.D.P. / 1991 / PL / M • The Lethal Squirt / 1990 / AR / M • Married With Hormones #1 / 1991 / PL / M • Married With Hormones #2 / 1992 / PL / M • More Dirty Debutantes #08 / 1991 / 4P / M • Naked Bun 2 1/2 / 1991 / WV / M • A Night At The Waxworks / 1990 / IF / M • Nightmare On Dyke Street / 1992 / PL / M • Oral Clinic / 1990 / DAY / M • The Passion Of Heather Lear / 1990 / AFV / M • The Pawnbroker / 1990 / IF / M • The Penetrator #1 / 1991 / PL / M • Private & Confidential / 1990 / AR / M • Sensuous / 1991 / LV / M • Shaved Sinners #3 / 1990 / VT / M • The Smart Ass Vacation / 1990 / VT / M • Snatches Of Pink / 1991 / NAN / M • Sweat Shop / 1991 / EVN / M • Swing & Swap #02 / 1990 / CDI / M • Total Reball / 1990 / CC / M • Twin Peeks / 1990 / DR / M • Video Virgins #06 / 1993 / NS / M • The Wild And The Innocent / 1990 / CC / M • Wilde At Heart / 1992 / VEX / M
BEAU SHERIDAN
Melrose Trannie / 1995 / HEA / G
BEAUTY *see Star Index I*
BEAVER
America's Raunchiest Home Videos #08: Who Was That Masked Mn / 1991 / ZA / M
BEBE
Big Butt Babes #1 / 1994 / BTO / M
BEBE BOPPER *see Star Index I*
BEBE LEBADD
The Ambassador File / 1995 / HOM / B • Autobiography Of A Slave / 1993 / PL / B • Badd Girl's Spanking / 1994 / SIM / B • Bondage Asylum / 1995 / LON / B • Bound Destiny / 1994 / LON / B • The Building Of Mistress Simone's Dungeon Of Pleasure / 1991 / BIZ / B • Chains Of Passion / 1993 / PL / B • Defiance, The Spanking Saga / 1992 / BIZ / B • Diary Of A Mistress / 1995 / HOM / B • Dynamic Duo / 1992 / BIZ / B • Fantasy Doctor / 1993 / PL / B • Hot Flesh, Cold Chains / 1992 / HOM / B • House Of

Correction / 1991 / HOM / B • Kidnapped By Pirates / 1995 / LON / B • Lesbians, Bondage & Blackjack / 1991 / BIZ / B • Lessons In Humiliation / 1991 / BIZ / B • Melissa's Wish / 1993 / LON / B • Mistress Rules / 1995 / STM / B • Mistress Sharon's Girl Toy / 1995 / STM / B • Nightmare Of Discipline / 1993 / NTP / B • The Other End Of The Whip / 1994 / LON / B • Paddled Payoff / 1993 / STM / B • Prescription For Lust / 1995 / NIT / M • Slave Exchange / 1995 / STM / B • Student Fetish Videos: Best of Enema #03 / 1994 / PRE / C • Student Fetish Videos: Catfighting #08 / 1993 / PRE / B • Student Fetish Videos: Spanking #11 / 1993 / PRE / B • Submissive Exposure Profile #5: Keli Thomas / 1996 / STM / C • Suck Channel / 1991 / VIM / M • Tails From The Whip / 1991 / HOM / B • Tarts In Torment / 1993 / LBO / B • A Taste Of Torment / 1995 / NIT / B • Their Absolute Property / 1994 / STM / B • The Tower Of Lyndon / 1994 / LON / B • Trapped By The Mistress / 1991 / BIZ / B • Trial By Bondage / 1991 / LON / B

BECCA
Becky S: Becky And Becca / 1993 / BEC / F

BECCA CHOW
Vivid Raw #2 / 1996 / VI / M

BECKIE
Butt Freak #2 / 1996 / FA / M

BECKY
Amateur Hours #04 / 1989 / AFI / M • Amateur Hours #07 / 1990 / AFI / M • Becky Bound / 1994 / GAL / B • Blue Vanities #520 / 1993 / FFL / M • Blue Vanities #530 / 1993 / FFL / M • Blue Vanities #554 / 1994 / FFL / M • Bondage Models #1 / 1996 / JAM / B • Creme De Femme #2 / 1981 / AVC / C • Lesbian Lust Bust / 1995 / GLI / F • Reel Life Video #02: Becky, Julie & Amy / 1994 / RLF / M

BECKY (P. CARLSON) *see* **Paige Carlson**

BECKY ANN THORNTON
Beyond The Blue / cr78 / SVE / M • Insane Desires / cr78 / … / M • The Last Sex Act / cr78 / S&L / M

BECKY AUSTIN
Blue Vanities #090 / 1988 / FFL / M

BECKY BARDOT *see* **Rebecca Bardoux**
BECKY BITTER *see* **Becky Savage**
BECKY BLU
Intervidnet #1: Special Delivery / 1994 / IVN / M • Intervidnet #2: French Made / 1994 / IVN / M

BECKY CLAY *see* **Becky Savage**
BECKY COWAN
Spanking Video #2: Naval Discipline / 1995 / MET / B

BECKY CUMMINGS
Many Faces Of Shannon / 1988 / VC / C

BECKY EASTON *see* **Star Index I**
BECKY HALL *see* **Becky Savage**
BECKY LAINE *see* **Star Index I**
BECKY LEBEAU *(Sharona Bonner)*
Beverly Hills Girls / 1985 / HID / S • Bikini Drive-In / 1995 / … / S • Body Chemistry #3: Point Of Seduction / 1994 / NEH / S • Dinosaur Island / 1993 / NEH / S • For Love And Money / 1987 / CV / S • Hollywood Hot Tubs / 1984 / VES / S • It's Your Move / 1990 / TAO / B • Not Of This Earth / 1994 / MGM / S • Nudity Required / 1989 / AE / S • Ring Wise / 1990 / TAO / B • Sins

Of Desire / 1993 / C3S / S • Soft Bodies / 1988 / SB / F • Soft Bodies: Beyond Blonde / 1995 / SB / F • Soft Bodies: Curves Ahead / 1991 / SB / F • Soft Bodies: Double Exposure / 1994 / SB / F • Soft Bodies: Invitational / 1990 / SB / F • Soft Bodies: Party Favors / 1992 / SB / F • Soft Bodies: Pillow Talk / 1992 / SB / F • Soft Bodies: Show 'n Tell / 1995 / SB / F • Soft Bodies: Squeeze Play / 1993 / SB / F • Soft Bodies: Takin' It All Off / 1987 / VES / S • [Jake Spanner, Private Eye / 1989 / … / S

BECKY MCLAIN
Blue Vanities #555 / 1994 / FFL / M

BECKY O'GRADY *see* **Star Index I**
BECKY SAUNDERS *see* **Star Index I**
BECKY SAVAGE *(Rebecca Savage, Becky Hall, Becky Clay, Laura Sands, Becky Bitter)*
Shoulder length curly brown hair, medium tits, passable face, lithe body. Becky Clay is from **Blue Vanities #221**. First mvoie was F. Becky Bitter is from **L.A. Tool & Die**.
10 Years Of Big Busts #1 / 1989 / BTO / C • Aerobisex Girls #1 / 1983 / LIP / F • All The Action / 1980 / TVX / M • The Best Little Cathouse In Las Vegas / 1982 / HO / M • The Blonde Next Door / 1982 / GO / M • Blue Interview / 1983 / VCR / M • Blue Vanities #221 / 1994 / FFL / M • Bob's Lesson / 1984 / BIZ / B • Burning Desire / 1983 / HO / M • Cafe Flesh / 1982 / VC / M • California Valley Girls / 1983 / HO / M • Cathouse Fever / 1984 / VC / M • Centerfold Celebrities #2 / 1983 / VC / M • Challenge Of Desire / 1983 / NSV / M • D-Cup Delights / 1987 / VCR / M • Erotic Dimensions #9: The Fantasy Trade / 1982 / NSV / M • Erotic Dimensions: I Want To Watch / 1982 / NSV / M • Erotic Interlude / 1981 / CA / M • Erotic Radio WSEX / 1983 / VC / M • The Erotic World Of Sylvia Benedict (#5) / 1983 / VCR / C • F / 1980 / GO / M • Fantasy Follies #1 / 1983 / VC / M • Fantasy Follies #2 / 1983 / VC / M • Forbidden Dreams / 1984 / BIZ / G • Foreplay / 1982 / VC / M • Free And Foxy / 1986 / VCX / C • French Erotica: Inside Hollywood / 1980 / AR / M • Gimme An X / 1993 / VD / C • The Girls Of Klit House / 1984 / LIP / F • Go For It / 1984 / VC / M • Golden Girls #22 / 1984 / CA / M • Golden Girls #35 / 1988 / CA / M • Greatest Cathouse In Las Vegas / 1983 / EVI / M • GVC: Danielle's Girlfriends #116 / cr83 / GO / F • GVC: Summer Beach House #106 / 1980 / GO / M • Intimate Lessons / 1982 / VC / M • Intimate Realities #2 / 1983 / VC / M • Kiss And Tell / 1980 / CA / M • L.A. Tool & Die / 1979 / TMX / G • A Lacy Affair #1 / 1983 / HO / F • Let's Talk Sex / 1982 / CA / M • Maximum #1 / 1982 / CA / M • Maximum #4 / 1983 / CA / M • Mrs. Smith's Erotic Holiday / 1982 / VCX / M • Nanci Blue / 1979 / SE / M • Nasty Nurses / 1983 / CA / M • Outlaw Women / 1983 / LIP / F • Philappetite / 19?? / … / M • The Piercing Of Jamie / 1983 / BIZ / B • Plato's, The Movie / 1980 / SE / M • Sex Games / 1983 / CA / M • Sex Loose / 1982 / VC / M • Snow Honeys / 1983 / VC / M • Sweet Alice / 1983 / VCX / M • Sweet Cheeks / 1980 / VCX / M • Tales From The Chateau / 1987 / BON / B • Too Much Too Soon / 1983 / VCX / M • Touch Me In The Morning / 1982 / CA / M • Twice A Virgin / 1984 / PL / G • Undercovers /

1982 / CA / M • Wet, Wild And Wicked / 1984 / SE / M

BECKY SUNSHINE
Becky S: Becky And Becca / 1993 / BEC / F • Becky S: Becky And Bonnie #1 / 1993 / BEC / F • Becky S: Becky And Bonnie #3 / 1995 / BEC / F • Becky S: Becky And Cherry / 1994 / BEC / F • Becky S: Becky And Edy / 1995 / BEC / F • Becky S: Becky Makes A Salad / 1994 / BEC / F • Becky S: Becky Meets A Fan / 1994 / BEC / M • Becky S: Becky Meets Super Klitty / 1994 / BEC / F • Becky S: Becky Sunshine & Dani Ashe / 1993 / BEC / F • Becky S: Becky's Bald Beaver / 1994 / BEC / F • Becky S: Becky's First Modeling Session / 1994 / BEC / F • Becky S: Becky's Tongue Bath / 1994 / BEC / M • Becky S: Inside And Out / 1994 / BEC / F • Becky S: Let The Sunshine In / 1993 / BEC / C • Becky S: Lingerie And Lace / 1994 / BEC / F • Becky S: Meet Cherry / 1995 / BEC / F • Becky S: Super Becky / 1994 / BEC / F • Becky S: Sweet, Sweet Becky / 1995 / BEC / F • Becky S: The Making Of Passenger 69 / 1995 / BEC / M • The Booty Guard / 1993 / IP / M • Dirty Bob's #06: NiCESt NoviCES / 1992 / FLP / S • Dirty Bob's #07: DanCES With OrifiCES / 1992 / FLP / S • Dirty Bob's #10: Sleeping Late In Seattle / 1993 / FLP / S • Good Day With Becky Sunshine / 199? / H&S / S • Lady Love / 1996 / ODI / F • Passenger 69 #1 / 1994 / IP / M • Passenger 69 #2 / 1994 / IP / M • Tit To Tit #3 / 1995 / BTO / M • Toppers #15 / 1993 / TV / M • Toppers #19 / 1993 / TV / M • Toppers #20 / 1993 / TV / M • Toppers #22 / 1993 / TV / C • Toppers & Whoppers #2 / 1994 / PRE / C

BECKY VOSS
Donna Young: Becky Voss #1 / 1995 / DY / F

BEERBOHN TREE *(Baumer Tree, Max Birnbaum)*
Anyone But My Husband / 1975 / VC / M • The Naughty Victorians / 1975 / VC / M • The Night Of The Spanish Fly / 1978 / CV / M • Skin Flicks / 1978 / AVC / M • The Untamed Vixens / 1976 / VHL / M

BEHOP
We Be Bangin' 24/7 / 1996 / FD / M

BELA
Prima #13: Dr. Max Back To Budapest / 1995 / MBP / M

BELINDA
Blue Vanities #004 / 1987 / FFL / M • Buttman In Barcelona / 1996 / EA / M • Candyman #01: 1-900-Fantasies / 1992 / GLI / M • Lesbian Lingerie Fantasy #1 / 1988 / ESP / F • Showgirls / 1985 / SE / M • Single Girl Masturbation #1 / 1988 / ESP / F • Titanic Tits #10 / 198? / L&W / S • Toe Tales #06 / 1993 / GOT / B

BELINDA BAYER
Bottom Dweller: The Final Voyage / 1996 / EL / M • Sodomania #17: Simply Makes U Tingle / 1996 / EL / M

BELINDA BUTTERFIELD
Shape Up For Sensational Sex / 1985 / SE / M

BELINDA ROSS
Rise And Fall Of Sparkle / 19?? / BL / M

BELLA BLANCHE *see* **Star Index I**
BELLA DONNA *(Lisa Canary, Lisa La More, Lisa Lamore, Diamond (Bella))*
Not too pretty, masses of tousled blonde hair,

medium tits, pudgy. Born in 1966 and is the daughter of David Canary of the soap opera **All My Children**. Started at a age 17 in **Stiff Competition** where she only does nudity and then returned four years later for the real thing. Then returned again in the mid-nineties under the name Diamond with huge enhanced tits. She also uses (1996) the name Lisa Lamore or Lisa La More.
18 Candles / 1989 / LA / M • A List / 1996 / SO / M • Anal Explosions #1 / 1996 / NIT / M • The Battle Of the Breast Queens / 1989 / INS / C • Beaver Hunt #01 / 1994 / LEI / M • Best Of Buttman #1 / 1991 / EA / C • Best Of Buttman #2 / 1993 / EA / C • Big Boob Bangeroo #7 / 1996 / TTV / M • Big Boob Bangeroo #8 / 1996 / TTV / M • Big Bust Babes #24 / 1994 / AFI / M • Big Knockers #05 / 1994 / TV / M • Big Knockers #08 / 1994 / TV / M • Big Knockers #10 / 1995 / TV / M • Big Knockers #20 / 1995 / TV / C • Big Knockers #21: Best Of Lesbian #2 / 1995 / TV / C • Black Hollywood Amateurs #09 / 1995 / MID / M • The Butt Sisters Do Las Vegas / 1994 / MID / M • The Butt, The Boobs, The Lips / 1996 / C69 / M • Butthole Bunnies / 1996 / ROB / F • Camp Fire Tramps / 1995 / LOT / M • Caught From Behind #20 / 1995 / HO / M • Centerfold Strippers / 1994 / ME / M • Cum Buttered Corn Holes #2 / 1996 / NIT / C • Dark Eyes / 1995 / FC / M • Deep Dippin' Anal Babes / 1996 / ROB / F • Diamond Goes Haywire / 1995 / DIP / M • Diamond Keeps Cumming / 1995 / DIP / F • Diamond Meets Valeria / 1995 / DIP / F • Diamond's Outdoor Adventures / 1995 / DIP / M • Diamond's Pleasure House / 1995 / DIP / F • The Dinner Party #2: The Buffet / 1996 / ULI / M • Double D Amateurs #21 / 1994 / JMP / M • Ebony Assets / 1994 / VBE / M • Fantasy Girls / 1988 / CA / M • First Time Lesbians #21 / 1994 / JMP / F • First Time Lesbians #22 / 1994 / JMP / F • French Doll / 1994 / ME / M • Fresh Faces #11 / 1996 / EVN / M • Girlz Towne #10 / 1995 / FC / F • Gypsy Queen / 1995 / CC / M • Hometown Honeys #2 / 1988 / VEX / M • I Can't Get No...Satisfaction / 1988 / CDI / M • Inspector Croissant: The Case Of The Missing Pinky / 1995 / FC / M • Interview's Hard Bodied Harlots / 1996 / LV / M • Life's A Beach, Then You're Fucked / 1995 / FRM / M • Little French Maids / 1988 / VEX / M • Look What I Found On The Street #01 / 1996 / CC / M • My First Time #2 / 1996 / NS / M • My First Time #3 / 1996 / NS / M • My Wildest Dreams / 1988 / IN / C • Nasty Dancing / 1989 / VEX / M • A New Experience / 1995 / DIP / M • Only The Strong Survive / 1988 / ZA / M • Party Wives / 1988 / CDI / M • Prime Choice #1 / 1995 / RAS / M • Private Dancers / 1996 / RAS / M • Profiles #01 / 1995 / XPR / M • Pure Anal / 1996 / MET / M • Pussy Galore / 1996 / DIP / F • Pussy Hunt #01 / 1994 / LEI / M • Pussyman Auditions #14 / 1995 / SNA / M • Pussyman's Nite Club Party #1 / 1996 / SNA / M • Pussyman's Nite Club Party #2 / 1997 / SNA / M • Quest For Pleasure / 1996 / DIP / F • Rippin' 'n' Strippin' #1 / 1987 / BON / B • Rippin' 'n' Strippin' #2 / 1988 / BON / B • Rockin' The Captain's Boat / 1996 / DIP / M • Sorority Bound / 1988 / BON / B • The Spa / 1996 / RAS / M • Stiff Competition #1

/ 1984 / CA / M • Streetwalkers / 1995 / HO / M • Totally Tasteless Video #01 / 1994 / TTV / M • Tricks Of The Trade / 1988 / CA / M • Valentino's Euro-Invasion / 1997 / SC / M • Wet Wonderland / 1988 / VEX / M • While The Cat's Away / 1996 / NIT / M

BELLA DONNA (1980)
Girls U.S.A. / 1980 / AIR / M

BELLA RIO see Chelsea Ann

BELLA STARR see Star Index I

BELLE CLAUDET
Sweet Paradise / 1980 / ELV / M

BELLE NORTH see Star Index I

BELLE STEVENS see Star Index I

BELYNDA
Agony & Extacy / 1993 / GOT / B • Inhuman Bondage / 1993 / GOT / B • The Maltese Bimbo / 1993 / FD / M • Third Degree / 1992 / GOT / B • Toe Tales #04 / 1992 / GOT / B

BEN
100% Amateur #09: Asians & Latinas / 1995 / OD / M

BEN (NICK RAGE) see Nick Rage

BEN B. BONG see Star Index I

BEN DARE
Hollywood Amateurs #24 / 1995 / MID / M • Nikki Arizona's Tomboys / 1995 / GAL / M

BEN DAVIDSON see Star Index I

BEN DOVER (70S)
Nostalgia Blue / 1976 / VC / M

BEN DOVER (R.WELLES) see Ray Welles

BEN DOVER (S. PERRY) see Steve Perry

BEN FISHER see Star Index I

BEN GLEANER see Star Index I

BEN HANDY see Steve Hatcher

BEN LOVING
Fan Fuxxx #1 / 1996 / DWV / M

BEN OVER
Bondage Love Slave / 1994 / SBP / B

BEN PIERCE
Bad Penny / 1978 / QX / M • Debbie Does Dallas #1 / 1978 / VC / M

BEN RIDGE
[Rear End Crashes / 197? / ... / M

BEN T.
Dirty & Kinky Mature Women #07 / 1996 / C69 / M

BEN WAH
Bubble Butts #12 / 1992 / LBO / M

BENDEGO see Star Index I

BENEDICT CANYON
The 900 Club / 1993 / BON / B • Gangbang Girl #10 / 1993 / ANA / M • Gangbang Girl #11 / 1993 / ANA / M • Gangbang Girl #16 / 1995 / ANA / M

BENICIO TEQUILLES
Private Film #12 / 1994 / OD / M

BENJI
Big Murray's New-Cummers #20: Hot Honies In Heat / 1993 / FD / M • Crazy On You / 1991 / IF / M • Dirty Deeds / 1992 / IF / M • Exooutive Positions / 1991 / V99 / M • School Dayze / 1987 / BON / B • Twice As Hard / 1992 / IF / M • Viviana's Dude Ranch / 1992 / IF / M

BENNETT
Raw Talent: Bang 'er 32 Times / 1992 / RTP / M • Raw Talent: Fetish of the Month Club #03 / 1992 / RTP / M

BENNETT HALL see Star Index I

BENNETT SURF
Great Grandma Gets Her Cookies / 1995 /

FC / M

BENNY
Odyssey Triple Play #63: Orient Express / 1994 / OD / M

BENNY HANSEN see Star Index I

BENNY MOORE (Jack Harris)
Guy looks a bit like Michael Gaunt and has a bald spot and a moustache. Jack Harris comes from **Coming Attractions**.
Coming Attractions / 1976 / VEP / M

BENNY OVER
Cyber-Sex Love Junkies / 1996 / BBE / M

BENOIT
Private Film #27 / 1995 / OD / M • Private Film #28 / 1995 / OD / M

BENT ROHWEDER
Sensations / 1975 / ALP / M

BENT WARBURG
Bel Ami / 1976 / VXP / M • Danish Pastries / 1972 / QX / M • Keyhole / 1977 / SE / M • [Justine Och Juliette / 1975 / ... / S

BENTLEY CHRISTMAS
Resurrection Of Eve / 1973 / MIT / M

BERGIE
Striptease #1 / 1995 / PL / M

BERIT AGEDAHL
The Second Coming Of Eva / 1974 / ALP / M

BERLIN (Ines (Berlin), Lady Berlin, Monika (Berlin), Lucy Love)
German brunette with big tits, 24 years old, not too pretty.
Amateur Orgies #23 / 1993 / AFI / M • Anal Camera #03 / 1994 / EVN / M • Anal Camera #04 / 1995 / EVN / M • Anal Hounds & Bitches / 1994 / ROB / M • Anal Vision #07 / 1993 / LBO / M • The Anal-Europe Series #03: The Museum Of The Living Art / 1993 / LV / M • The Anal-Europe Series #04: Anal Recall / 1993 / LV / M • The Ass Master #04 / 1993 / GLI / M • Backdoor Black #2 / 1993 / WV / C • Backdoor To The City Of Sin / 1993 / ANA / M • Backing In #5 / 1994 / WV / C • Beach Bum Amateur's #36 / 1993 / MID / M • Bi-Wicked / 1994 / BIN / G • Big Murray's New-Cummers #15: Rump Humpers / 1993 / FD / M • Big Murray's New-Cummers #16: Frat Boys #2 / 1993 / FD / M • Black Detail #2 / 1994 / VT / M • Bobby Hollander's Rookie Nookie #05 / 1993 / SFP / M • Bobby Hollander's Sweet Cheeks #108 / 1993 / QUA / M • Buffy Malibu's Totally Nasty All-Girl Home Videos #03 / 1992 / ANA / F • Bun Busters #02 / 1993 / LBO / M • Bun Busters #06 / 1993 / LBO / M • Bun Busters #22 / 1994 / LBO / M • Burn It Up / 1994 / VEX / M • Butt Hunt #01 / 1994 / LEI / M • Captain Bob's Lust Boat #2 / 1993 / FCP / M • Cluster Fuck #03 / 1994 / MAX / M • The Cumm Brothers #01 / 1993 / OD / M • Deep Inside Anal Camera / 1996 / EVN / C • Dirty Doc's Housecalls #07 / 1994 / LV / M • End Of Innocence / 1994 / WIV / M • Erotic Desires / 1994 / MAX / M • Extreme Sex #2: The Dungeon / 1994 / VI / M • Fantastic Facials / 1995 / PEV / C • First Time Lesbians #13 / 1994 / JMP / F • Forbidden Subjects #1 / 1994 / FC / M • Frankenstein / 1994 / SC / M • Gang Bang Bitches #01 / 1994 / PP / M • Gang Bang In Vedova / 1995 / WIV / M • Gangbang Girl #11 / 1993 / ANA / M • Gangbang Sluts / 1994 / VMX / M • Harry Horndog #19: Anal Lovers #3 / 1993 / ZA / M • Hidden Camera #04 / 1993 / JMP / M • High

Heel Harlots #03 / 1994 / SFP / M • House Of Sex #16: Dirty Oral Three Ways / 1994 / RTP / M • Lovin' Spoonfuls #5 / 1996 / 4P / C • M Series #05 / 1993 / LBO / M • M Series #06 / 1993 / LBO / M • The Mad D.P. Tea Party / 1994 / FC / M • Mistress Of The Mansion / 1994 / CV / M • New Ends #04 / 1993 / 4P / M • Odyssey 30 Min: #301: / 1993 / OD / M • Odyssey Triple Play #58: Anal Insanity / 1994 / OD / M • Odyssey Triple Play #60: Interracial Facial / 1994 / OD / M • Odyssey Triple Play #81: Copulation Intergration / 1994 / OD / M • The Orgy #2 / 1993 / EMC / M • Pearl Necklace: Thee Bush League #18 / 1993 / SEE / M • Ron Hightower's White Chicks #04 / 1993 / LBO / M • Ron Hightower's White Chicks #09 / 1994 / LBO / M • Ron Hightower's White Chicks #15 / 1994 / LBO / M • Rump Humpers #16 / 1993 / GLI / M • Sexual Trilogy #01 / 1993 / SFP / M • Ski Bunnies #1 / 1994 / HW / M • Sleaze Please!—August Edition / 1994 / FH / M • Sleaze Please!—September Edition / 1994 / FH / M • Sodomania #03: Foreign Objects / 1993 / EL / M • Stylin' / 1994 / FD / M • The Sweet Sweet Back #3: Sho' Nuff Got Dat Woodski / 1994 / FH / M • Tail Taggers #101 / 1993 / WV / M • Tail Taggers #102 / 1993 / WV / M • Tight Tushies #2 / 1994 / MET / M • U Witness: Video Three-Pak #3 / 1995 / MSP / M • Ultimate Anal Gang Bang #3 / 1995 / HW / M • Up The Ying Yang #1 / 1994 / CC / M • Walk On The Wild Side / 1994 / VIM / M • Wet Deal / 1994 / FD / M

BERLIN (BLACK)
Black Cheerleader Search #04 / 1996 / ROB / M • Black Cheerleader Search #08 / 1996 / IVC / M • Black Knockers #10 / 1995 / TV / M

BERLYNN
Kym Wilde's On The Edge #36 / 1996 / RB / B • Wild Cherries / 1996 / SC / F

BERN H.
Foreign Exchange Sluts / 1995 / TNT / M

BERNADETTE
Dirty Stories #4 / 1995 / PE / M • Magma: Anita #2 / 1996 / MET / M • Magma: Double #2 / 1995 / MET / M • Magma: Tits Practice / 1995 / MET / M • Passion In Venice / 1995 / ULI / M • Private Film #21 / 1995 / OD / M • Roman Orgy / 1991 / PL / M • Sodomania #14: C**t Lickin', C*m Drinkin' Bitches / 1995 / EL / M • Sodomania: Slop Shots / 1996 / EL / C • Southern: Previews #1 / 1992 / SSH / C • World Sex Tour #4 / 1996 / ANA / M

BERNADETTE COLE
Looking Good / 1984 / ABV / M

BERNADETTE MANFREDI
Anal Palace / 1995 / VC / M

BERNADETTE TYREE see Star Index I

BERNADINE
Magma: Fuck Me Diana / 1994 / MET / M

BERNADINE LEE see Star Index I

BERNADOTTE
The Sex Clinic / 1995 / WIV / M

BERNARD ADDISON see Star Index I

BERNARD CLIFF see Star Index I

BERNARD DANIELS see Star Index I

BERNARD TALBIN
Erotic Pleasures / 1976 / CA / M

BERND WILCZEWSKI
The Young Seducers / 1971 / BL / M

BERND ZAHN

The Young Seducers / 1971 / BL / M

BERNEDETTE PETERS
Open Lips / 1983 / AVO / M

BERNHARD
Magma: Old And Young / 1995 / MET / M

BERNICE see Star Index I

BERNIE
Older And Anal #1 / 1995 / FC / M • Slaves Of Artemis / 1996 / BON / B

BERNIE BOYLE
Thundercrack! / 1974 / LUM / M

BERNIE DIX
Blue Bayou / 1993 / VC / M • The Secret Life Of Nina Hartley / 1994 / VC / M

BERNIE GREENSTEIN
Campus Girl / 1972 / VXP / M

BERNIE HOWARD see Star Index I

BERNIE RICHARDS see Star Index I

BERNIE SCHITZ
Bucky Beavers #074 / 1995 / SOW / M • The Psychiatrist / 1971 / SOW / M

BERRY
Homegrown Video #414: Pussy Hairstylist / 1994 / HOV / M

BERRY SWEET
Anal Witness #1 / 1996 / LBO / M

BERT
Big Busty #19 / 198? / H&S / M

BERT BLAKE
American Sex Fantasy / 1975 / IHV / M

BERT HENRY see Star Index I

BERT HUPLEY see Star Index I

BERT LEWISON
Postgraduate Course In Sexual Love / 1975 / QX / M

BERT SCHMIDT see Star Index I

BERT STRINGWRONG see Star Index I

BERT WILLIS
Eruption / 1977 / VCX / M

BERTA RUSS see Star Index I

BERTH MILTON
The Porn Brokers / 1977 / VAE / M

BERTHA
Porno Screentests / 1982 / VC / M

BERTHA (LAYLA) see Layla LaShell

BERTHA JONES
The Collegiates / 1971 / BL / M

BERTRAND CORNE see Star Index I

BESS
Blue Vanities #512 / 1992 / FFL / M

BESSI
Puritan Video Magazine #05 / 1996 / LE / M

BETA G.
Private Gold #09: Private Dancer / 1996 / OD / M

BETAYROK
The Witch's Tail / 1994 / GOU / M

BETH ANN
Mike Hott: #292 Three-Sum Sluts #03 / 1995 / MHV / M

BETH ANNA *(Beth Anne, Joanna Miquel, Joan Miquel)*
Beach House / 1981 / CA / C • Chorus Call / 1978 / TVX / M • Classic Erotica #5 / 1985 / SVE / M • Dirty Lilly / 1975 / VXP / M • Dirty Looks / 1982 / VC / C • Disco Madness / cr80 / VST / S • From Holly With Love / 1977 / CA / M • High School Bunnies / 1978 / VC / M • Intimate Desires / 1978 / VEP / M • Kinky Tricks / 1978 / VEP / M • Limited Edition #02 / 1979 / AVC / M • The Love Couch / 1977 / VC / M • The Nite Bird / 1978 / BL / M • The Seduction Of Cindy / 1980 / VC / M • She's No Angel / cr75 / AXV / M • Skin Flicks / 1978

/ AVC / M • Summertime Blue / 1979 / VCX / M • Sweet Savage / 1978 / ALP / M • Sweet Throat / 1979 / CV / M • Take Off / 1978 / VXP / M • Wet Shots (Vcr) / 1983 / VCR / C • [Flesh Fantasy / 1981 / ... / M • [Fuck Me, Suck Me, Eat Me / 1990 / ... / M

BETH ANNE see Beth Anna

BETH B.
Ace In The Hole / 1995 / PL / M

BETH DAYLOR
Angel Hard / 1996 / STV / M

BETH FIX see Shauna Evans

BETH KIMMEL
Blue Vanities #580 / 1996 / FFL / M

BETH LAWS see Star Index I

BETH MCDYER
[El Paso Wrecking Corp / 1977 / TMX / G

BETH RATZER
Take Off / 1978 / VXP / M

BETH RODERICK see Star Index I

BETH ROSEN see Star Index I

BETH RUBERMAN see Star Index I

BETH SANDERS
K-Sex / 1976 / VCR / M

BETH SVENSON see Star Index I

BETH WILSON
The Girls Of Mr X / 1978 / CA / M

BETHANY BUSTIN
Big Boob Lottery / 1993 / BTO / M • Big Boob Pajama Party / 1993 / BTO / F • On Location In The Bahamas / 1996 / H&S / S

BETHANY LANDERS
Harlem Harlots #2 / 1995 / AVS / M

BETSY
Blue Vanities #540 / 1994 / FFL / M

BETSY ANN SUMMERS
Erotic Dimensions: A Woman's Lust / 1982 / NSV / M

BETSY BOUDOIR see Star Index I

BETSY MILBERG
Ancient Secrets Of Sexual Ecstasy / 1996 / HIG / M

BETSY WARD see T.J. Carson

BETTE PAIN
Orgy Of Pain / 1995 / BON / B

BETTIE PAGE see Betty Page

BETTY
AVP #9116: And Gina Makes Three / 1991 / AVP / M • Blue Vanities #527 / 1993 / FFL / M • Blue Vanities #554 / 1994 / FFL / M • Fetish High Heels And Corsets / 1987 / RSV / G • High Heels In Heat #3 / 1989 / RSV / F • HomeGrown Video #473: Furpie Feast #3 / 1997 / HOV / C • Il Medico Della Coppie / 1996 / TNT / M • Painless Steel #4 / 1996 / FLV / M • Pearl Necklace: Amorous Amateurs #11 / 1992 / SEE / M • Pearl Necklace: Amorous Amateurs #12 / 1992 / SEE / M • Pearl Necklace: Facial #01 / 1994 / SEE / C • Private Film #20 / 1995 / OD / M • Private Gold #12: The Pyramid #2 / 1996 / OD / M • Sexual Harassment / 1996 / TTV / M

BETTY ALEXANDER
Viola Video #109: Backdoor Bavarian Babes / 1995 / PEV / M

BETTY ANDERSON
Dirty Stories #5 / 1996 / PE / M • The Voyeur #7: Live In Europe #1 / 1996 / JLP / M

BETTY BEAVER see Star Index I

BETTY BIRD
The Older Women's Sperm Bank #6 / 1996 / SUF / M

BETTY BLUE (D.NORT.) see Debbie Northrup

BETTY BOOBS
The Battle Of the Breast Queens / 1989 / INS / C • Big Tit Hookers / 1989 / BTO / M • Big Tit Orgy #03 / 1991 / BTO / C • Big Top Cabaret #2 / 1989 / BTO / M • Diamond Head / 1987 / AVC / M • Double D Harem / 1988 / L&W / M • Hometown Honeys #2 / 1988 / VEX / M • Incorrigible / 1996 / MET / M • A Little Bit Of Honey / 1987 / WET / M • Little French Maids / 1988 / VEX / M • Viper's Place / 1988 / VD / M • Who's Dat Girl / 1987 / VEX / M

BETTY BOPP
Fantasy Photography: Mail Call / 1995 / FAP / F

BETTY BROOK
Visions / 1977 / QX / M

BETTY BUSH see Star Index I

BETTY CARSON
Love Airlines / 1978 / SE / M

BETTY CHAN
Headmaster's Study Part I & Ii / 1993 / CS / B

BETTY CHILDS
A Climax Of Blue Power / 1974 / EVI / M

BETTY DE MUIR
Blackmail For Daddy / 1976 / VCX / M

BETTY DODSON see Star Index I

BETTY FRENCH
The Loves Of Mary Jane / 1989 / BWV / C • A Touch Of Sex / 1972 / AR / M

BETTY GABOR
The Bodyguard / 1995 / SC / M • Private Video Magazine #02 / 1993 / OD / M • Top Model / 1995 / SC / M

BETTY HUNT see Star Index I

BETTY JEAN BRADLEY see Star Index I

BETTY LOU see Star Index I

BETTY MIDNIGHT see Star Index I

BETTY PAGE (Bettie Page)
Glamor pin-up girl.
Blue Vanities #132 / 1991 / FFL / M • Classic Films Of Irving Klaw / 1984 / LON / M • Striporama #1 / 1952 / SOW / S • Teaserama / 1954 / SOW / S • Varietease / 1955 / SOW / S

BETTY QUILL
All The Loving Couples / 1979 / KIT / M

BETTY RAGL see Star Index I

BETTY ROCKET
Black Jack City #4 / 1994 / HW / M

BETTY SCOTT
Tales Of A High Class Hooker / 19?? / VXP / M

BETTY SINCLAIR
Aphrodesia's Diary / 1984 / CA / M

BETTY STYLES see Star Index I

BETTY WARD
Erotic Interlude / 1981 / CA / M

BETTY WELLS
The Untamed Vixens / 1976 / VHL / M

BETTY WHITMAN
Karla / 19?? / ... / M

BEV
Blue Vanities #168 (New) / 1996 / FFL / M • Blue Vanities #168 (Old) / 1991 / FFL / M

BEV JACKSON
Teenage Party People / 19?? / ... / M

BEVERLEE HILLS see Gina Gianetti

BEVERLY
AVP #7010: Get It In The Rear / 1991 / AVP / M • Blue Vanities #507 / 1992 / FFL / M • Blue Vanities #532 / 1993 / FFL / M • Cheerleader Strippers / 1996 / PE / M • Eternal Bonds / 1995 / RHV / B • First

Time Lesbians #08 / 1993 / JMP / F • Mother Nature's Bulging Bellies / 1995 / LIP / F • Skintight / 1991 / VER / F

BEVERLY BLAIR see Beverly Bliss

BEVERLY BLISS (Beverly Blair, Alexandria (Bliss))
Brunette, medium tits, passable face, a little thick around the waist.
Amazing Tails #5 / 1990 / CA / M • Best Of Bruce Seven #1 / 1990 / BIZ / C • Best Of Bruce Seven #4 / 1990 / BIZ / C • Blue Dream Lover / 1985 / TAR / M • Bondage Interludes #2 / 1983 / BIZ / B • Camp Beaverlake #1 / 1984 / AR / M • Confessions Of A Candystriper / 1984 / VC / M • Confessions Of Candy / 1984 / VC / M • Dirty Shary / 1985 / VD / M • Double Penetration Fever / 1989 / MIR / C • Erotic Zones #1 / 1985 / CA / M • Every Man's Fantasy / 1985 / IN / M • Evil Angel / 1986 / VCR / M • Fox Fever's Catfight Action / 1984 / VCR / B • Ginger's Private Party / 1985 / VI / M • Ginger: The Movie / 1988 / PV / C • Girls Just Want To...Have Fun / 1984 / SE / M • Head Waitress / 1984 / VC / M • Headhunters / 1984 / VC / M • Hollywood Harlots / 1986 / VEX / C • Hollywood Heartbreakers / 1985 / VEX / M • Hot Flashes / 1984 / VC / M • Hot Sweet Honey / 1985 / VEP / M • Hot Tails / 1984 / VEN / M • The Idol / 1985 / WV / M • Intimate Couples / 1984 / VCX / M • Jean Genie / 1985 / CA / M • Let's Talk Sex / 1982 / CA / M • Little Often Annie / 1984 / VC / M • The Lover Girls / 1985 / VEX / M • Lust In The Fast Lane / 1984 / PV / M • Mistresses And Slaves: The Best Of Bruce Seven / 1991 / BEB / C • Mouthful Of Love / 1984 / VC / M • Naughty Angels / 1984 / VC / M • Naughty Nanette / 1984 / VC / M • Naughty Nurses / 1986 / VEX / M • Pleasure Party (Gourmet) / 1985 / GO / M • Raffles / 1988 / VC / M • The Ribald Tales Of Canterbury / 1986 / CA / M • Rich Quick, Private Dick / 1984 / CA / M • Savage Fury #1 / 1985 / VEX / M • Shaved / 1984 / VCR / M • Spreading Joy / 1988 / VC / M • Squalor Motel / 1985 / SE / M • Summer Break / 1985 / VEX / M • Suzie Superstar #2 / 1985 / CV / M • Swedish Erotica #59 / 1984 / CA / M • Taking Off / 1984 / VC / M • Tongue 'n Cheek (Vca) / 1984 / VC / M • Up In The Air / 1984 / CDI / M • Water Nymph / 1987 / LIM / M • Young Nurses In Love / 1987 / VC / M

BEVERLY BOVY
Dear Pam / 1976 / CA / M

BEVERLY DOOM see Star Index I

BEVERLY GLASS see Star Index I

BEVERLY GLEN (Whitney Prince, Whitney Price, Freda (B. Glen), Jamie Lee (B. Glen))
Rather hard looking blonde who normally has short hair, medium/large (natural, I think) breasts and a tight body, considering her age.
Amateur Orgies #30 / 1993 / AFI / M • Amateur Orgies #33 / 1993 / AFI / M • Amateur Orgies #35 / 1993 / AFI / M • America's Raunchiest Home Videos #64: / 1993 / ZA / M • Anal Crybabies / 1996 / BAC / M • Anal Delinquent #2 / 1994 / ROB / M • Anal Overtures / 1993 / AFD / M • Anal Virgins Of America #03 / 1993 / FOR / M • Anal Virgins Of America #05 / 1993 / FOR / M • Anal Vision #01 / 1992 / LBO / M • Arch

Villains / 1994 / PRE / B • Arch Worship / 1995 / PRE / B • Bad Girls #5 / 1994 / GO / M • The Beat Goes On / 1987 / VCR / C • The Beaverly Hillbillies / 1993 / IP / M • The Big Switch / 1985 / LAV / G • Breastography, Lesson #1 / 1987 / VCR / M • The Bridges Of Anal County / 1996 / PVO / C • Bubble Butts #19 / 1992 / LBO / M • Bun Runners / 1994 / PRE / B • Butt Darling / 1994 / WIV / M • The Butt Detective / 1994 / VC / M • Butt's Up, Doc #4 / 1994 / GO / M • Charmed And Dangerous / 1987 / VI / M • The Cumm Brothers #01 / 1993 / OD / M • Deep Inside Rachel Ashley / 1987 / VEX / M • Deep Inside Viviana / 1992 / VEX / C • Dirty Doc's Housecalls #01 / 1993 / LV / M • Doin' The Nasty / 1996 / AVI / M • Double Black Fantasy / 1987 / CC / C • Dr Fraud's Female Fantasies / 1993 / AM / M • Eclipse / 1993 / SC / M • The Fantasy Booth / 1993 / ONA / M • First Time Lesbians (Gourmet) / 1987 / GO / F • Flash Trance / 1985 / IVP / M • Flesh In Ecstasy #05: Rachel Ashley / 1987 / GO / C • Flesh In Ecstasy #08: Traci Adams / 1987 / GO / C • Fun "4" All / 1994 / PRE / B • Gang Bang Bitches #01 / 1994 / PP / M • Gang Bang Jizz Jammers / 1994 / ROB / M • Gold: I Need A Cum / 1993 / GCG / F • Hard Ride / 1986 / VT / M • Harry Horndog #11: Love Puppies #2 / 1992 / ZA / M • Hidden Camera #08 / 1993 / JMP / M • Hollywood '94: Butts Abound / 1993 / ELP / M • Hollywood Scandal: The Heidi Flesh Story / 1993 / IP / M • Hot Tight Asses #06 / 1994 / TCK / M • Hot Touch / 1984 / VCX / M • Imaginary Lovers / 1986 / ME / M • Incocknito / 1993 / VIM / M • Invasion Of The Lust Snatchers / 1988 / 4P / M • Jane Bond Meets Thunderballs / 1986 / VD / M • The Joi Fuk Club / 1993 / WV / M • Junkyard Dykes #01 / 1994 / ZA / F • The Last X-Rated Movie #1 / 1990 / COM / M • The Last X-Rated Movie #3 / 1990 / COM / M • Leg...Ends #11 / 1994 / PRE / F • Lessons With My Aunt / 1986 / SHO / M • Lip Service / 1987 / BIK / C • Love Probe / 1986 / VT / M • Lube Job / 1994 / PRE / B • Lucy Has A Ball / 1987 / ME / M • Lust In America / 1985 / VCX / M • Madame Hiney: The Beverly Hills Butt Broker / 1993 / STR / M • Mother's Pride / 1985 / DIM / M • My Pretty Go Between / 1985 / VC / M • Nature Girls #2: Get Wet / 1995 / WIV / F • Nikki And The Pom-Pom Girls / 1987 / VEX / M • No Man's Land #01 / 1988 / VT / C • Odyssey Triple Play #72: Backdoor Score / 1994 / OD / M • Ona Zee's Learning The Ropes #09: The Training Continues / 1992 / ONA / B • Parliament: Lesbian Lovers #2 / 1988 / PM / F • Parliament: Lesbian Seduction #1 / 1990 / PM / F • Part-Time Stewardesses / 1989 / VCR / M • Perplexed / 1994 / FD / M • Phone Sex Girls #1 / 1987 / VT / M • Professor Sticky's Anatomy 3X #03 / 1992 / FC / M • Red On The Noodle Like A Swance On A Poodle / 1990 / FC / C • Reel Sex #02: Splash Party / 1994 / SPP / M • Reel Sex #05: Lesbian Toy Part / 1994 / SPP / F • Ride The Pink Lady / 1993 / WV / M • Rocco Unleashed / 1994 / SC / M • Sean Michaels On The Road #10: Seattle / 1994 / VT / M • Sensuous Singles: Whitney Prince / 1987 / VCR / F • Sex Drive / 1993 / VEX / M • Sex Search / 1988 / IN / S • Sinners #3 / 1989 / COM /

M • Slap Happy / 1994 / PRE / B • Snake Eyes #2 / 1987 / COM / M • Sodomania #07: Deep Down Inside / 1993 / EL / M • Sugarpussy Jeans / 1986 / TEM / M • Superstar Sex Challenge #1 / 1994 / VC / M • Superstar Sex Challenge #2 / 1994 / VC / M • Superstar Sex Challenge #3 / 1994 / VC / M • Switch Hitters #1 / 1987 / IN / G • Tail Taggers #107 / 1993 / WV / M • Tail Taggers #109 / 1993 / WV / M • Tail Taggers #110 / 1993 / WV / M • Tail Taggers #112 / 1993 / WV / M • Tail Taggers #114: Booty Brunch / 1994 / WV / M • A Taste Of Cherry / 1985 / CV / M • Tight Fit #08 / 1994 / GO / M • Title Shots / 1995 / PRE / B • Toys, Not Boys #3 / 1991 / FC / C • Vegas Brats / 1990 / WV / M • Video Virgins #09 / 1993 / NS / M • Video Virgins #10 / 1993 / NS / M • Weak-Ends / 1995 / PRE / B • What's Butt Got To Do With It? / 1993 / HW / M • Whorelock / 1993 / LV / M • Wicked Wenches / 1988 / LA / M • Wild & Wicked #4 / 1994 / VT / M • Wild Orgies #01 / 1994 / AFI / M • Wild Orgies #10 / 1994 / AFI / M

BEVERLY HUTTON see Star Index I
BEVERLY MAYS
Prisoner Of Pleasure / 1981 / ALP / B
BEVERLY ROGERS
K-Sex / 1976 / VCR / M
BEVERLY SIRENS
Waterfront Honey / 19?? / XTR / M
BEVERLY STEIG
Waterpower / 1975 / VHL / M
BIANCA
Bow Down Backstreet / 1996 / HW / M • Ginger Lynn Allen's Lingerie Gallery #2: Private Screening / 1994 / UNI / F • Hot Body Hall Of Fame: Christy Carrera / 1996 / CG / F • Hot Body Video Magazine: Beverly Hills Wet T-Shirt Contest / 1994 / CG / F • Hot Body Video Magazine: Wild Thing / 1996 / CG / F • Pearl Necklace: Thee Bush League #20 / 1993 / SEE / M • Sodomania #12: Raw Filth / 1995 / EL / M • Sodomania #15: Warning! / 1996 / EL / M • Sodomania: Slop Shots / 1996 / EL / C • Student Fetish Videos: Best Of Foot Worship #03 / 1995 / PRE / C
BIANCA (BIONCA) see Bionca
BIANCA BRADLEY see Bionca
BIANCA CORJAY
The Experiment / 1983 / BIZ / B • Master Control / 1985 / CS / B
BIANCA GOLD see Bionca
BIANCA LANE
Cluster Fuck #01 / 1993 / MAX / M • Pearl Necklace: Amorous Amateurs #33 / 1992 / SEE / M
BIANCA LEE
American Pie / 1980 / SE / M
BIANCA LUZ
Bottoms Up #03 / 1983 / AVC / C • Limited Edition #03 / 1979 / AVC / M
BIANCA MOORE see Star Index I
BIANCA TRUMP (Bionca Trump, Wendy C. Iwanow)
Brunette with bimbo like qualities and enormous enhanced boobs of which she is very proud. Born Tacoma, Washington Nov 7, 1972. Arrested for armed robbery in 1995 in connection with the burglary of a john's apartment (aged 22 at the time). Wendy Christine Iwanow is her real name.
The Adventures Of Seymore Butts / 1992 / FH / M • America's Dirtiest Home Videos

#09 / 1992 / VEX / M • Anal Al's Adventures / 1995 / PL / M • Anal Asian / 1994 / VEX / M • Anal Blues / 1994 / PEP / M • Anal Encounters #4: Tales From The Crack / 1992 / VC / M • Babe Watch #1 / 1994 / SC / M • Babe Watch #2 / 1994 / SC / M • Backstage Pass / 1992 / VEX / M • Beauty And The Beach / 1991 / CC / M • Bianca Trump's Towers / 1992 / LV / M • Biff Malibu's Totally Nasty Home Videos #21 / 1992 / ANA / M • Big Knockers #02 / 1994 / TV / M • Big Knockers #03 / 1994 / TV / M • Big Knockers #04 / 1994 / TV / M • Big Knockers #12 / 1995 / TV / C • Bigger / 1991 / PL / M • Bodies In Motion / 1994 / IF / M • Brassiere To Eternity / 1994 / PEP / F • Breast Collection #04 / 1995 / LBO / C • The Breast Files #1 / 1994 / AVI / M • Breast Wishes #13 / 1993 / LBO / M • Breast Worx #22 / 1992 / LBO / M • Breast Worx #32 / 1992 / LBO / M • Breast Worx #33 / 1992 / LBO / M • Buffy Malibu's Totally Nasty All-Girl Home Videos #03 / 1992 / ANA / F • A Cameo Appearence / 1992 / VI / M • The Cockateer #1 / 1991 / LE / M • Collectible / 1991 / LE / M • Delicious (VCX-1993) / 1993 / VCX / M • The Determinator #2 / 1991 / VIM / M • Double D Dykes #06 / 1992 / GO / F • Down & Dirty / 1995 / NAP / B • Dr Rear / 1995 / CC / M • Dyno-Mite / 1992 / IF / M • Edward Penishands #3 / 1991 / VT / M • Endangered / 1992 / PP / M • Foreskin Gump / 1994 / LE / M • The Girl In Room 69 / 1994 / VC / M • Girl Gone Bad #6: On Parole / 1992 / GO / F • Girls Just Wanna Have Toys / 1993 / PL / F • Glitz Tits #06 / 1993 / GLI / M • Good Pussy / 1994 / VIM / M • Greek Week / 1994 / CV / M • Guttman's Hollywood Adventure / 1993 / PL / M • Harry Horndog #06: Girls On Girls #2 / 1992 / ZA / F • Ho' Style Takeover / 1993 / FH / M • Hot & Horny Amateurs #1 / 1994 / … / M • Hot Blooded / 1994 / ERA / M • Hot Tight Asses #08 / 1994 / TCK / M • Hot Wishes / 1995 / LE / M • Illusions #2 / 1992 / IF / M • In Loving Color #1 / 1992 / VT / M • Inner Pink #3 / 1994 / LIP / F • Innocence Found / 1991 / PAL / G • It's A Wonderful Sexlife / 1991 / LE / M • Jail Babes #2: Bustin' Out / 1992 / PL / F • The Last Action Whore / 1993 / LV / M • Lather / 1991 / LE / M • Leena Is Nasty / 1994 / OD / M • Lesbian Bitches #1 / 1994 / ROB / F • Lesbian Pros And Amateurs #05 / 1992 / GO / F • Lust What The Doctor Ordered / 1994 / WIV / M • Maid Service / 1993 / FL / M • Masked Ball / 1992 / IF / M • Mike Hott: #189 Bianca Trump Solo / 1991 / MHV / F • Mike Hott: Apple Asses #12 / 1992 / MHV / F • The Mountie / 1994 / PP / M • Mr. Peepers Amateur Home Videos #27: The Backdoor Babysitter / 1991 / LBO / M • Mr. Peepers Amateur Home Videos #32: Fingers in the Honey Po / 1991 / LBO / M • Mr. Peepers Nastiest #6 / 1995 / LBO / C • Neighborhood Watch #18: Smokin' In Bed / 1992 / LBO / M • Nightmare On Dyke Street / 1992 / PL / M • One In A Million / 1992 / HW / M • One Night Love Affair / 1991 / IF / M • Oral Madness #2 / 1992 / OD / M • Peekers / 1993 / MID / M • Penthouse: Satin & Lace #1 / 1992 / PET / F • Private Request / 1994 / GLI / M • Pulse / 1994 / EX / M • Put 'em On Da Glass / 1994 / VT / M • Rainbows / 1992 / VT / F • Raquel

Released / 1991 / VI / M • Raunch #04: Silver Melts / 1991 / CC / M • Ready, Willing & Anal / 1992 / OD / M • Rent-A-Butt / 1992 / VC / M • The Savannah Affair / 1993 / CDI / M • Seoul Train / 1991 / IN / M • Sex Symphony / 1992 / VC / M • Seymore Butts In The Love Shack / 1992 / FH / M • Seymore Butts Rides Again / 1992 / FH / M • Seymore Butts: Bustin' Out My Best Anal / 1995 / FH / C • Someone Else / 1992 / VC / M • Stick It In The Rear #2 / 1993 / PL / M • Tit For Tat / 1994 / PEP / M • Too Cute For Words / 1992 / V99 / M • Trump Your Ass / 1996 / NAP / B • Two Of A Kind / 1991 / ZA / M • Valleys Of The Moon / 1991 / SC / M • Wendy Whoppers: Brain Surgeon / 1993 / PEP / M • Women Of Color #2 / 1994 / ANA / M • Women Of Color / 1991 / PL / F • Yankee Rose / 1994 / LE / M
BIANCHI FASINI
The Desirous Wife / 1988 / PL / M
BIBI
Heat Wave / 1977 / COM / M
BIC JOHNSON
Sweet Brown Sugar / 1994 / AVI / M
BIE WARBURG
Bel Ami / 1976 / VXP / M
BIF MALONE see Biff Malibu
BIFF see Star Index I
BIFF BARKER see Biff Parker
BIFF MALIBU (Dick Nasty (Malibu), Bif Malone, Chris Alexander, Christopher Alexande, Chris K.)
Blonde surfer type male who is looking a bit dissolute in 1992. Married to Buffy Malibu (Marie Mason).
The Adventures Of Buttgirl & Wonder Wench / 1991 / AFV / M • AHV #01: Three Way Wonders / 1991 / EVN / M • Amateur American Style #17 / 1991 / AR / M • Amateur American Style #29 / 1992 / AR / M • Amateur Nights #02 / 1989 / HO / M • Amateur Nights #03 / 1990 / HO / M • Ambushed / 1990 / SE / M • America's Raunchiest Home Videos #01: Some Serious Sex / 1991 / ZA / M • America's Raunchiest Home Videos #02: Cooking with Hot Sauce / 1991 / ZA / M • America's Raunchiest Home Videos #04: Recipes for Hot Sex / 1991 / ZA / M • America's Raunchiest Home Videos #05: Sasha Gets Stuffed / 1992 / ZA / M • America's Raunchiest Home Videos #06: Fuck Frenzy / 1992 / ZA / M • America's Raunchiest Home Videos #12: Bimbo Ballers From Brt / 1992 / ZA / M • America's Raunchiest Home Videos #13: Beauty And The Beach / 1992 / ZA / M • America's Raunchiest Home Videos #15: Outrageous Reaming / 1992 / ZA / M • America's Raunchiest Home Videos #16: Sophia's Yankee Doodle / 1992 / ZA / M • America's Raunchiest Home Videos #32: Model of Lust / 1992 / ZA / M • America's Raunchiest Home Videos #34: The Big Splash / 1992 / ZA / M • Anal Attack / 1991 / ZA / M • Anal Attraction #2 / 1993 / AFV / C • Anal Gang Bangers #01 / 1992 / GLI / M • Anal Ski Vacation / 1993 / ANA / M • The Anals Of History #1 / 1991 / MID / M • Animal Instincts / 1991 / VEX / M • The Applicant / 1988 / BON / B • B.L.O.W. / 1992 / LV / M • Back In Action / 1992 / FD / M • Backdoor To Cannes / 1993 / VC / M • Backdoor To Harley-Wood #1 / 1990 / AFV

/ M • Backdoor To Harley-Wood #2 / 1990 / AFV / M • Backdoor To Russia #3 / 1993 / VC / M • Backdoor To The City Of Sin / 1993 / ANA / M • Backstage Entrance #1 / 1992 / FH / M • The Backway Inn #2 / 1992 / FD / M • Bangin' With The Home Girls / 1991 / AFV / M • Beach Bum Amateur's #03 / 1992 / MID / M • Beach Bum Amateur's #06 / 1992 / MID / M • Beach Bum Amateur's #08 / 1992 / MID / M • Beach Bum Amateur's #10 / 1992 / MID / M • Beach Bum Amateur's #11 / 1992 / MID / M • Beach Bum Amateur's #12 / 1992 / MID / M • Beach Bum Amateur's #14 / 1992 / MID / M • Beaverjuice / 1992 / LV / M • Behind The Scenes: The Making Of The Wil & Ed Movies / 1992 / MID / M • Best Butt(e) In The West #1 / 1992 / CC / M • Biff Malibu's Totally Nasty Home Videos #01 / 1992 / ANA / M • Biff Malibu's Totally Nasty Home Videos #02 / 1992 / ANA / M • Biff Malibu's Totally Nasty Home Videos #03 / 1992 / ANA / M • Biff Malibu's Totally Nasty Home Videos #04 / 1992 / ANA / M • Biff Malibu's Totally Nasty Home Videos #05 / 1992 / ANA / M • Biff Malibu's Totally Nasty Home Videos #06 / 1992 / ANA / M • Biff Malibu's Totally Nasty Home Videos #07 / 1992 / ANA / M • Biff Malibu's Totally Nasty Home Videos #08 / 1992 / ANA / M • Biff Malibu's Totally Nasty Home Videos #09 / 1992 / ANA / M • Biff Malibu's Totally Nasty Home Videos #10 / 1992 / ANA / M • Biff Malibu's Totally Nasty Home Videos #11 / 1992 / ANA / M • Biff Malibu's Totally Nasty Home Videos #12 / 1992 / ANA / M • Biff Malibu's Totally Nasty Home Videos #13 / 1992 / ANA / M • Biff Malibu's Totally Nasty Home Videos #14 / 1992 / ANA / M • Biff Malibu's Totally Nasty Home Videos #15 / 1992 / ANA / M • Biff Malibu's Totally Nasty Home Videos #16 / 1992 / ANA / M • Biff Malibu's Totally Nasty Home Videos #17 / 1992 / ANA / M • Biff Malibu's Totally Nasty Home Videos #19 / 1992 / ANA / M • Biff Malibu's Totally Nasty Home Videos #20 / 1992 / ANA / M • Biff Malibu's Totally Nasty Home Videos #21 / 1992 / ANA / M • Biff Malibu's Totally Nasty Home Videos #23 / 1992 / ANA / M • Biff Malibu's Totally Nasty Home Videos #24 / 1992 / ANA / M • Biff Malibu's Totally Nasty Home Videos #25 / 1992 / ANA / M • Biff Malibu's Totally Nasty Home Videos #26 / 1992 / ANA / M • Biff Malibu's Totally Nasty Home Videos #27 / 1992 / ANA / M • Biff Malibu's Totally Nasty Home Videos #28 / 1992 / ANA / M • Biff Malibu's Totally Nasty Home Videos #29 / 1993 / ANA / M • Biff Malibu's Totally Nasty Home Videos #30 / 1993 / ANA / M • Biff Malibu's Totally Nasty Home Videos #31 / 1993 / ANA / M • Biff Malibu's Totally Nasty Home Videos #32 / 1993 / ANA / M • Biff Malibu's Totally Nasty Home Videos #33 / 1993 / ANA / M • Biff Malibu's Totally Nasty Home Videos #34 / 1993 / ANA / M • Biff Malibu's Totally Nasty Home Videos #35 / 1993 / ANA / M • Biff Malibu's Totally Nasty Home Videos #36 / 1993 / ANA / M • Biff Malibu's Totally Nasty Home Videos #37 / 1993 / ANA / M • Biff Malibu's Totally Nasty Home Videos #38 / 1993 / ANA / M • Biff Malibu's Totally Nasty Home Videos #39 / 1993 / ANA / M • Biff Malibu's Totally Nasty Home

Videos #40 / 1993 / ANA / M • Blue Fox / 1991 / VI / M • Blue Jeans Brat / 1991 / VI / M • Boobs, Butts And Bloopers #2 / 1990 / HO / M • Boobytrap...The Next Generation / 1992 / HW / M • Breaking And Entering / 1991 / AFV / M • Breast Friends / 1991 / PL / M • Breast Worx #03 / 1991 / LBO / M • Breast Worx #12 / 1991 / LBO / M • Breast Worx #22 / 1992 / LBO / M • Buns And Roses (LV) / 1990 / LV / M • Business And Pleasure / 1992 / AFV / M • The Butler Did It / 1991 / FH / M • Butt Naked #1 / 1990 / OD / M • Butt Woman #2 / 1992 / FH / M • Butt's Up, Doc #1 / 1992 / GO / M • The Buttnicks #2 / 1991 / HIO / M • Call Girl / 1991 / AFV / M • Camp Beaverlake #2 / 1991 / AFV / M • Candy Stripers #4 / 1990 / AR / M • Cannes Heat / 1992 / FD / M • Catalina Sixty-Nine / 1991 / AR / M • Christy In The Wild / 1992 / VI / M • Club Midnight / 1992 / LV / M • The Coach's Daughter / 1991 / AR / M • Cocktails / 1990 / HO / M • Dallas Does Debbie / 1992 / PL / M • Dark Star / 1991 / VI / M • Deep Butt / 1994 / MID / C • Deep Dreams / 1990 / IN / M • Deep Throat #6 / 1992 / AFV / M • Desert Heat / 1992 / BON / B • Devil's Agenda & Miss Jones / 1991 / AR / M • Dial 666 For Lust / 1991 / AFV / M • Dirty Dave's American Amateurs #14 / 1992 / AR / M • Dream Lover / 1991 / WV / M • Dreams Cum True / 1990 / HO / M • Easy Pickin's / 1990 / LV / M • Erotic Heights / 1991 / AR / M • Eternal Bliss / 1990 / AFV / M • Flame / 1989 / ARG / M • Flash Backs / 1990 / BON / B • Flashpoint / 1991 / AFV / M • The Flintbones / 1992 / FR / M • Fox Fever / 1991 / LV / M • Foxes / 1992 / FL / M • Freak Show / 1991 / FC / M • Gangbang Girl #01 / 1992 / ANA / M • Gangbang Girl #02 / 1992 / ANA / M • Gangbang Girl #03 / 1992 / ANA / M • Gangbang Girl #13 / 1994 / ANA / M • Gangbang Girl #16 / 1995 / ANA / M • Gangbang Girl #17 / 1995 / ANA / M • Gettin' Wet / 1990 / VC / M • Girls Around The World #04 / 1991 / BTO / M • Guess Who Came To Dinner / 1992 / AFV / M • Hard Bodies / 1989 / CDI / M • The Harder Way / 1991 / AR / M • Hollywood's Hills / 1992 / LV / M • Hot Summer Knights / 1991 / LV / M • Hotel Sex / 1992 / AFV / M • Hump Up The Volume / 1991 / AR / M • I Said A Butt Light #2 / 1990 / LV / M • In Pursuit Of Passion / 1990 / V99 / M • Indian Summer #1 / 1991 / VI / M • Indian Summer #2: Sandstorm / 1991 / VI / M • It Happened At Midnight / 1990 / IN / M • Junk Yard Dogs / 1991 / FC / M • L.A. Rear / 1992 / FD / M • Laying Down The Law #1 / 1992 / AFV / M • Laying Down The Law #2 / 1992 / AFV / M • The Lethal Squirt / 1990 / AR / M • Looks Like A Million / 1992 / LV / M • Love Button / 1989 / VD / M • Love On The Line / 1990 / SO / M • Madame A / 1992 / LV / M • Tho Many Loves Of Jennifer / 1991 / VCO / S • Married With Hormones #1 / 1991 / PL / M • Midnight Caller / 1992 / MID / M • Miss 21st Century / 1991 / ZA / M • Mistress Sondra's Playthings / 1990 / BON / B • Moon Godesses #1 / 1992 / VIM / M • Mr. Peepers Amateur Home Videos #33: Great Balls A' Fire / 1991 / LBO / M • Mr. Peepers Nastiest #4 / 1995 / LBO / C • Muffy The Vampire Layer / 1992 / LV / M • Murphie's Brown / 1992 / LV / M • My 500

Pound Vibrator / 1991 / LV / C • My Mistress...Her Slave / 1990 / PL / B • Nasty Reputation / 1991 / VEX / M • Neighborhood Watch #03 / 1991 / LBO / M • Neighborhood Watch #14: The Beaver Cleaver / 1991 / LBO / M • Next Door Neighbors #17 / 1990 / BON / M • Next Door Neighbors #41 / 1993 / BON / M • Nookie Court / 1992 / AFV / M • Odyssey Amateur #75: Sindy! / 1991 / OD / M • Orgy On The Ranch / 1991 / NLE / M • The Pawnbroker / 1990 / IF / M • Peekers / 1993 / MID / M • Penetrating Thoughts / 1992 / LV / M • The Penetrator #1 / 1991 / PL / M • Pink Card / 1991 / FH / M • Purple Rubber / 1993 / STM / B • Racquel In Paradise / 1990 / VC / M • Racquel In The Wild / 1992 / VI / M • Raquel Released / 1991 / VI / M • Rear View / 1989 / LE / M • Riviera Heat / 1993 / FD / M • Rock & Roll Fantasies / 1992 / FL / M • Roman Goddess / 1992 / HW / M • Runnin' Hot / 1992 / LV / M • Screwballs / 1991 / AFV / M • Sex Acts & Video Tape / 1990 / AFV / M • Sex In A Singles Bar / 1992 / VC / M • Sex Police 2000 / 1992 / AFV / M • The Sex Symbol / 1991 / GO / M • Sexual Healing / 1992 / LV / M • Skippy, Jiff & Jam / 1990 / CIA / M • Slipping It In / 1992 / FD / M • The Smart Ass Enquirer / 1990 / VT / M • Smarty Pants / 1992 / VEX / M • Southern Side Up / 1992 / LV / M • Special Treatment / 1991 / AFV / M • The Spectacle / 1991 / IN / M • Stocking Stuffers / 1992 / LV / M • Stolen Hearts / 1991 / AFV / M • Surf City Sex / 1991 / CIA / M • A Tale Of Two Titties #1 / 1990 / AR / M • A Tale Of Two Titties #2 / 1992 / AFV / M • Tinseltown Wives / 1992 / AFV / M • Titty-Titty Bang-Bang / 1992 / FC / C • Tropic Of Kahlia / 1991 / VI / M • Truth And Bare / 1991 / LV / M • Twin Cheeks (Arrow) / 1991 / AR / M • Twin Peaks / 1993 / PL / M • Two Of A Kind / 1990 / LV / M • Two Times A Virgin / 1991 / AR / M • The Ultimate / 1991 / BON / B • Ultimate Orgy #2 / 1992 / GLI / M • Ultimate Orgy #3 / 1992 / GLI / M • Where There's Sparxx, There's Fire / 1991 / LV / M • Wicked Thoughts / 1991 / AFV / M • Wil And Ed's Excellent Boner Christmas / 1991 / MID / M • Wild Girl / 1991 / GO / M • Will & Ed Are Geeks In Heat / 1994 / MID / M • Will & Ed's Keister Easter / 1992 / MID / M • Will And Ed's Bogus Gang Bang / 1992 / MID / M • Will And Ed: The Curse Of Poona / 1994 / MID / C • The Wonder Rears / 1990 / SO / M • Zane's World / 1992 / ZA / M

BIFF PARKER *(Biff Barker, Mike Parker)*
Blue Vanities #003 / 1987 / FFL / M • Frat House / 1979 / NGV / M • Nanci Blue / 1979 / SE / M • October Silk / 1980 / COM / M • Pink Champagne / 1979 / CV / M • Pro Ball Cheerleaders / 1979 / AVC / M

BIFF WILSON *see* **Ted Wilson**

BIG AL
Brown Sugar / 1984 / VC / M • Something For Everybody / 1975 / ... / M

BIG BAKE
As Sweet As They Come / 1992 / V99 / M • Breakfast At Tiffany's / 1994 / IF / M

BIG BERTHA *see* **Star Index I**

BIG BOB
Jane Bond Meets Thunderthighs / 1988 / VD / M

BIG BOY *see* **Chi Chi La Rue**

BIG BUTT JILL

Fat Fannies #13 / 1995 / BTO / F
BIG DAVE *see* **David Angel**
BIG DICK POWERS *see* ***Star Index I***
BIG ED
Sparkling Champagne / 1994 / FH / M
BIG ED SIMMS *see* ***Star Index I***
BIG EDDIE *see* ***Star Index I***
BIG HERC (Hercules)
Big black male.
8-Ball: Westside Gang Bang / 1995 / PL / M • The Best Little Whorehouse In Tijuana / 1995 / HBE / M • Black Ass Masters #1 / 1995 / GLI / M • Black Ass Masters #2 / 1995 / GLI / M • Black Ass Masters #3 / 1995 / GLI / M • Black Gangbangers #04 / 1995 / HW / M • Black Gangbangers #05 / 1995 / HW / M • Black Gangbangers #06 / 1995 / HW / M • Black Gangbangers #09 / 1995 / HW / M • Black Gangbangers #10 / 1996 / HW / M • Black Hollywood Amateurs #03 / 1995 / MID / M • Black Hollywood Amateurs #13 / 1995 / MID / M • Black Hollywood Amateurs #15 / 1995 / MID / M • Black Hollywood Amateurs #17 / 1995 / MID / M • Black Orgies #34 / 1995 / GO / M • Blonde Temptation / 1995 / IF / M • Boob Tube Lube / 1996 / RAS / M • Casting Call #12 / 1995 / MET / M • Gangbang Girl #15 / 1995 / ANA / M • Hard Core Beginners #03 / 1995 / LEI / M • In The Can With Oj / 1994 / HCV / M • LA Nasty / 1995 / SP / M • Maverdick / 1995 / WV / M • Nasty Newcummers: Black Edition / 1995 / MET / M • Nasty Nymphos #12 / 1996 / ANA / M • Opie Goes To South Central / 1995 / PP / M • Rump-Shaker #4 / 1995 / HW / M • Shades Of Color #2 / 1995 / LBO / M • Takin' It To The Limit #4 / 1995 / BS / M • Wet & Slippery / 1995 / WV / M
BIG JACK
Sandy's: Bicycle Trail Humpers / 1994 / SM / F
BIG JIM SLADE
America's Raunchiest Home Videos #70: / 1993 / ZA / M • Winter Heat / 1994 / MID / M
BIG JIM THORNTON *see* ***Star Index I***
BIG JOHN
The Coming Of Angie / cr73 / TGA / M • Denni O' #3: Fanta-Sea Of Cum / 1996 / SP / M • The Spectacular Denni O'Brien / 1995 / SP / M • There's Magic In The Air / 1987 / AR / M
BIG JON FALLUS *see* **John C. Holmes**
BIG LYNN
Bust Lust / cr83 / BIZ / B • Smothering Boobs / cr83 / BIZ / B
BIG MAMA JACKSON *see* ***Star Index I***
BIG MAN
Black Bush Bashers / 1996 / LOK / M
BIG MIKE *see* ***Star Index I***
BIG RANDY ROD *see* ***Star Index I***
BIG RED
50 And Still Gangbangin'! / 1995 / EMC / M • Big Bust Strippers #01 / 1990 / BTO / F • Catfighting Cheerleaders / 1989 / BIZ / B • Tickled In Pink / 1988 / BIZ / B
BIG RODNEY *see* ***Star Index I***
BIG SUE
Blue Vanities #555 / 1994 / FFL / M
BIG T.
Jinx / 1996 / WP / M • The Time Machine / 1996 / WP / M
BIG TITS MALLOY *see* ***Star Index I***
BIG VIC
Cum To Drink Of It / 1996 / BCP / M • Hard

Cum Cafe / 1996 / BCP / M • Pussy Fest Of The Northwest #4 / 1995 / NIT / M
BIGG JOHN *see* ***Star Index I***
BIGGI FREYER
The Ideal Marriage / 1971 / SOW / M
BIGI DOREE
Dirty Business / 1995 / WIV / M
BIGUS DICKUS
The Fantasy Booth / 1993 / ONA / M
BIJOU DELUXE
Primal She-Male / 1996 / HSV / G • She Male Devil / 1996 / HSV / G • Showgirl She-Male / 1996 / HSV / G
BIJOU RAVAGE
Teach Me / 1984 / VD / M
BIKER BILL
Easy Binder / 1994 / VTF / B
BILL
Bi-Bi Love Amateurs #4 / 1994 / QUA / G • China Lee's Bachelorette Party / 1995 / RHV / M • Dirty Dancers #4 / 1995 / 4P / M • Doin' The Nasty / 1996 / AVI / M • FTV #59: Butt Bash Party / 1996 / FT / B • Mismatch / 1995 / TVI / M
BILL ADAMS *see* ***Star Index I***
BILL AMERSON (Bill Williams)
Normally a director.
The Divorcee / 1969 / PS / S • Girls On Fire / 1985 / VCX / M • Never Enough / 1971 / VCX / M • Night Of The Zombies / 1981 / PRS / S • Saturday Matinee Series #3 / 1996 / VCX / C • Secret Games #2: The Escort / 1993 / IMP / S • Taboo American Style #3: Nina Becomes An Actress / 1985 / VC / M • Taboo American Style #4: The Exciting Conclusion / 1985 / VC / M
BILL ANDERSON *see* ***Star Index I***
BILL BARRY *see* **Herschel Savage**
BILL BERRY *see* **Herschel Savage**
BILL BLACKMAN *see* **Ron Jeremy**
BILL BROWN *see* ***Star Index I***
BILL BUCK
Ring Of Desire / 1981 / SE / M
BILL CALDWELL
Sexy Ties & Videotape / 1992 / STM / B • Stern Auditor / 1992 / STM / B
BILL CHAMBERS
Hot Cookies / 1977 / WWV / M
BILL CODY
Rise And Fall Of Sparkle / 19?? / BL / M
BILL CONEY *see* ***Star Index I***
BILL CORLY
Love Mexican Style / cr75 / BLT / M
BILL CORT
Farmers Daughters / 1975 / VC / M • Legends Of Porn #2 / 1989 / CV / C
BILL CRAWFORD *see* **Richard Logan**
BILL DOLLAR *see* ***Star Index I***
BILL DURHAM *see* ***Star Index I***
BILL ELIOT *see* ***Star Index I***
BILL FALCONI
The Girls From Hootersville #06 / 1994 / SFP / M
BILL FENWAY
Black And White And Red All Over / 1994 / STM / B • The Boss's Boy Toy / 1992 / STM / B • Case Studies Of The Punishing Nurse / 1992 / STM / B • Chambers Of Discipline / 1992 / PL / B • Corrected Deception / 1994 / STM / B • Dangerous Lessons / 1994 / STM / C • Dark Reality #1 / 1995 / STM / B • Dark Reality #2 / 1995 / STM / B • Deck His Balls With Holly / 1992 / STM / B • Disciplinary Action / 1995 / STM / B • Disciplined Sissy / 1992 / PL / B • Dragon Lady's Domination Technique /

1995 / STM / B • Dungeon Builder's Punishment / 1994 / STM / B • Dungeon Training / 1995 / STM / B • Humiliating Bind / 1996 / STM / B • Kimbra's Wimps / 1995 / STM / B • Kimbra, Slave Trainer / 1993 / STM / B • Latex, Leather & Lace / 1993 / STM / B • Lauren's Adventures In Bondageland #1: Mistress Lauren / 1994 / STM / C • Leather Master / 1996 / STM / B • Masked Mistress / 1994 / STM / B • Matronly Stern Spankings / 1994 / STM / B • Mistress Lauren's Bizarre Picnic / 1992 / STM / B • Oriental Dominatrix / 1995 / STM / B • Power Games / 1992 / STM / B • Produce Or Suffer / 1994 / STM / B • Profiles In Discipline #02: Naughty Angel / 1994 / STM / C • Profiles In Discipline #03: Mistress Franchesca / 1994 / STM / C • Profiles In Discipline #04: Mistress Domino / 1994 / STM / C • Proper Penance / 1992 / STM / B • Punishment Playpen / 1995 / STM / B • Red Boot Diaries / 1992 / STM / B • Secret Retreat #1 / 1991 / STM / B • Secret Retreat #2 / 1991 / STM / B • Sentence Of Pain / 1994 / STM / B • She Who Must Be Obeyed / cr85 / STM / B • She-Male By Choice / 1993 / STM / G • Smothered, Bound & Tickled / 1993 / STM / B • Spanked By Santa / 1992 / STM / B • Toe-Tally Foot-Age / 1992 / STM / C • Trained Transvestites / 1995 / STM / B • Transvestite Academy / 1991 / PL / G • Transvestite Secrets Revealed / 1993 / STM / G • TS Trains TV Hubby / 1994 / STM / G • TV Sorority Sister / 1996 / STM / G • TV Trained To Perform / 1994 / STM / G • Two Trained For Obedience / 1993 / STM / B • Virgil To Virginia / 1993 / STM / G • Virginia's TV Initiation / 1992 / STM / G • Women Who Control The Family Jewels #2 / 1993 / STM / C • Women Who Control The Family Jewels #4 / 1995 / STM / B
BILL FLAGSTAFF
All About Teri Weigel / 1996 / XCI / M
BILL GROAN *see* ***Star Index I***
BILL HARRISON *see* ***Star Index I***
BILL HEADCLOVER *see* ***Star Index I***
BILL HORNER
ABA: Double Feature #5 / 1996 / ALP / M • Night Of Submission / 1976 / BIZ / M
BILL HOUSTON
Bondage Shoots / 1993 / BON / B • Criss-Cross / 1993 / BON / B • Deception (1995-B&D) / 1995 / BON / B • Hot Daze #04: Timid Feelings / 1993 / BON / B • Katrina's Bondage Memories #2 / 1994 / BON / C • Spanking Tails / 1993 / BON / B • Tanya Fox's Bondage Fantasies / 1993 / BON / B • Your Cheatin' Butt / 1996 / BON / B
BILL HUNTER
She-Male Encounters #17: Sorority / 1987 / MET / G • She-Male Encounters #18: Murder She-Male Wrote / 1987 / MET / G
BILL JOHN
Erotic Dimensions: Bold Fantasies / 1982 / NSV / M
BILL KISHNER
Casanova #2 / 1976 / CA / M
BILL LANDIS *see* **Bobby Spector**
BILL LARRIE *see* ***Star Index I***
BILL LEE *see* ***Star Index I***
BILL LEWIS *see* ***Star Index I***
BILL MAJORS
Bev's Bondage Torment / 1994 / BON / B • Birds Of Prey / cr79 / BON / B • Bondage Classix #06: Class Of 86 #1 / 1986 / BON /

B • Bondage Classix #09: Andrea's Fault / 1987 / BON / B • Bondage Classix #11: Karen's B&D Phone Sex / 1984 / BON / B • Bondage Classix #13: Class Of 86 #2 / 1991 / BON / B • Bondage Classix #16: Tough Task / 1987 / BON / B • Bondage Classix #18: Gwen And Debbie's Torments / 198? / BON / B • Bondage Memories #01 / 1993 / BON / C • Bondage Memories #02 / 1993 / BON / C • Bondage Memories #04 / 1994 / BON / C • The Bondage Producer / 1991 / BON / B • Bound To Be Punk / 1990 / BON / B • Captured Cop #1: Deadly Explosion / 1991 / BON / B • Double Whipping / 198? / BON / B • Fantasy Valley Ranch #1 / 1987 / BON / B • Forbidden Fantasies / 1991 / BON / B • Fundgeon Of The Mind #1 / 1994 / BON / B • Greta Carlson Sessions #1 / 1994 / BON / B • Greta Carlson Sessions #2 / 1994 / BON / B • Greta Carlson Sessions #3 / 1994 / BON / B • Greta Carlson Sessions #4 / 1995 / BON / B • Greta's Ultimate Penalty #1 / 1995 / BON / B • Greta's Ultimate Penalty #2: The Real Thing / 1995 / BON / B • Home Maid Memories #2 / 1994 / BON / C • Judi's B&D Slave School / 1980 / BON / B • Kym Wilde Bound On Stage #1 / 1993 / BON / B • Kym Wilde Bound On Stage #2 / 1993 / BON / B • Kym Wilde Bound On Stage #3 / 1993 / BON / B • Kym Wilde Sessions #1 / 1991 / B&D / B • The Luxury Of Servitude / 1994 / BON / B • Major Submission / 1996 / BON / B • The Mastering Of Bea / 1995 / BON / B • Pet Hotel #1 / 1988 / BON / B • Pet Hotel #2 / 1988 / BON / B • Prescription For Pain #1 / 1992 / BON / B • Real Breasts Real Torment / 1995 / BON / C • Real People Real Bondage #2 / 1996 / BON / C • School Dayze / 1987 / BON / B • Sessions With A Slave / cr90 / BON / B • Shades Of Bondage / 1991 / BON / B • Slave Bea, Basement Bound / 1993 / BON / B • Slave Slut #1 / 1993 / BON / B • Slave Slut #2 / 1993 / BON / B • Slaves On Loan / 1995 / BON / B • Surrogate Master / 1996 / BON / B • The Taming Of Kitty / 1996 / BON / B • Tanya Foxx: A Diary Of Torment / 1995 / BON / B • Tanya Foxx: Suspended In Time / 1996 / BON / C • Tortured Present / cr8? / BON / B • Trainer's Turnabout / 1994 / BON / B • Trouble For Two / 1994 / BON / B • Volunteer Victim #1 / 1993 / BON / B • Volunteer Victim #2 / 1994 / BON / B • Willing & Wilder / 1995 / BON / B

BILL MARGOLD *see* **William Margold**

BILL MARLOW
Cherry Busters / 1995 / WIV / M

BILL MARLOWE
Bi Intruder / 1991 / STA / G • Bi-Swingers / 1991 / PL / G • Black Knockers #05 / 1995 / TV / M • Dominique Goes Bi / 1994 / STA / G • Entertainment Bi-Night / 1989 / PL / G • Inside Karl Thomas / 1994 / STA / G • Live Bi-Me / 1990 / PL / G • Party Partners / 1994 / STA / G • Switch Hitters #7 / 1994 / IN / G • Switch Hitters #8 / 1995 / IN / G

BILL MCKEAN
Inside Seka / 1980 / VXP / M • The Satisfiers Of Alpha Blue / 1980 / AVC / M • Twilight Pink #1 / 1980 / AR / M

BILL MICHAELS
Silk, Satin & Sex / 1983 / SE / M

BILL MILL
Young Sluts In Heat #1 / 1996 / PL / M

BILL MILLER
Deep Inside Centerfold Girls / 1991 / VC / M

BILL MORGAN *see Star Index I*
BILL MULLANEY *see Star Index I*
BILL NUNNERY
C.O.D. / 1981 / VES / S • Take Off / 1978 / VXP / M

BILL ORR
Steamy Dreams / cr70 / CVX / M

BILL OWEN
Sex Boat / 1980 / VCX / M

BILL PUGGETT
One Last Score / 1978 / CDI / M

BILL RATHER
Lusty Ladies #04 / 1983 / 4P / M

BILL RICE
Hardcore: The Films Of Richard Kern #1 / 1991 / FTV / M

BILL RILEY
GVC: Valley Vixens #124 / 1983 / GO / M

BILL SMITH
The Nite Bird / 1978 / BL / M

BILL SPECTOR *see* **Bobby Spector**

BILL STANLEY
Erotic Fantasies #5 / 1983 / CV / C

BILL STEWART
From Russia With Lust / 1984 / VC / M

BILL THORPE *see Star Index I*
BILL VAN LOAN *see Star Index I*
BILL W. *see Star Index I*
BILL WESTON
Pleasures Of A Woman / 1983 / CA / M

BILL WILDE
Black Detail #1 / 1994 / VT / M • Black Detail #2 / 1994 / VT / M • New Girls In Town #5 / 1994 / CC / M • Vienna's Place / 1996 / VCX / M

BILL WILLIAMS *see* **Bill Amerson**
BILL WILSON *see Star Index I*
BILL WRIGHT *see* **Frank Thring**
BILLE
Reel Life Video #49: / 1996 / RLF / F

BILLI BEST
Bucky Beaver's XXX Dragon Art Theatre Double Feature #01 / 1996 / SOW / M • Hitler's Harlots / cr73 / SOW / M

BILLIE
Blue Vanities #044 (New) / 1988 / FFL / M • Blue Vanities #055 / 1988 / FFL / M • Mr. Peepers Amateur Home Videos #50: Insight Is Brownish / 1992 / LBO / M

BILLIE BLUE *see Star Index I*
BILLIE ROBINSON
Resurrection Of Eve / 1973 / MIT / M

BILLIE SLEE *see Star Index I*
BILLY
Charm School / 1986 / VI / M • Filthy First Timers #3: Tearing Down The Walls Of Shame / 1996 / EL / M • Intimate Interviews #2 / 1996 / NIT / M • Mr. Peepers Amateur Home Videos #42: Great American Tails / 1992 / LBO / M • Stevi's: Jennifer's Cream Pie / 1996 / SSV / M

BILLY (D. CANNON) *see* **David Cannon**
BILLY BELL *see* **Herschel Savage**
BILLY BEST *see Star Index I*
BILLY BLACK
Erotic Dimensions: Bold Fantasies / 1982 / NSV / M

BILLY BLUE *see Star Index I*
BILLY BONER *see Star Index I*
BILLY BRONCO *see Star Index I*
BILLY BUDDE *see Star Index I*
BILLY CLUB
Anal Camera #07 / 1995 / EVN / M •

Beach Bum Amateur's #38 / 1993 / MID / M

BILLY COMAS
Body Talk / 1982 / VCX / M

BILLY DANIELS *see* **Billy Dee**
BILLY DEAN *see Star Index I*
BILLY DEE *(Obi Wahn, Billy Daniels, Larry (Billy Dee))*
Billy Daniels is from **Open Lips**. Was married to Suzannah French at one stage.
The 8th Annual Erotic Film Awards / 1984 / SE / C • 976-STUD / 1989 / LV / M • The Adventures Of Dick Black, Black Dick / 1987 / DR / M • The Affairs Of Miss Roberts / 19?? / ... / M • After The Lights Go Out / 1989 / VEX / M • Alice In Blackland / 1988 / VC / M • Alice In Whiteland / 1988 / VC / M • All American Girls #1 / 1982 / CA / M • All Night Long / 1990 / NWV / C • Amanda By Night #2 / 1987 / CA / M • Amber Aroused / 1985 / CA / M • Amber Lynn's Personal Best / 1986 / VD / M • Amos & Candy / 1987 / VCR / C • Anal Intruder #02 / 1988 / CC / M • Anal Intruder #03 / 1989 / CC / M • The Anal-ist #2 / 1986 / VEX / M • Angel Kelly Raw / 1987 / FAN / M • Angel's Gotta Have It / 1988 / FAN / M • Another Kind Of Love / 1985 / CV / M • Any Time, Any Place / 1981 / CA0 / M • The Art Of Passion / 1987 / CA / M • Baby Cakes / 1982 / SE / M • Backdoor Romance / 1984 / VIV / M • Backing In #2 / 1990 / WV / C • Ball Street / 1988 / CA / M • Barbara Dare's Prime Choice / 1987 / SE / C • Barbara The Barbarian / 1987 / SE / M • Bare Elegance / 1984 / MAP / M • Bare Essence / 1989 / EA / M • Battle Of The Stars #1 / 1985 / NSV / M • Battle Of The Stars #3: Stud Wars / 1985 / NSV / M • Beverly Hills Cox / 1986 / CA / M • Beverly Hills Exposed / 1985 / SE / M • Beverly Hills Heat / 1985 / VEP / M • Beyond Desire / 1986 / VC / M • Beyond Shame / 1980 / VEP / M • The Bitch / 1988 / FAN / M • The Bitches Of Westwood / 1987 / CA / M • The Black Anal-ist #1 / 1988 / VEX / M • Black Baby Dolls / 1985 / TAG / M • Black Girls Do It Better / 1986 / CV / M • Black Magic / 1985 / WET / M • Black Magic / 1986 / DR / M • Black Magic Sex Clinic / 1987 / DOX / M • Black On White / 1987 / PL / C • Black Hage / 1988 / ZA / M • Black Taboo #1 / 1984 / JVV / M • Black Taboo #2 / 1986 / SE / M • Blackballed / 1994 / VI / C • Blonde Heat (VCA) / 1985 / VC / M • Blondes Have More Fun / 1980 / SE / M • Blow Job Babes / 1988 / BEV / C • Blue Movie / 1989 / VD / M • Bo-Dacious / 1989 / V99 / M • Bodies In Heat #1 / 1983 / CA / M • Bodies In Heat #2 / 1989 / DR / M • Body Games / 1987 / DR / M • Body Magic / 1982 / SE / M • Body Talk / 1982 / VCX / M • Boobs, Butts And Bloopers #1 / 1990 / HO / M • Bootsie / 1984 / CC / M • Born To Run / 1985 / WV / M • The Boss / 1987 / FAN / M • Breakin' All The Rules / 198? / SE / M • Bring On The Virgins / 1989 / CA / M • Broadcast Nudes / 1988 / EVN / M • Brown Sugar / 1984 / VC / M • Built For Sex (Angela Baron's) / 1988 / FAZ / C • But...Can She Type? / 1989 / CDI / M • The Buttnicks #1 / 1990 / VEX / M • California Blondes #01 / 1986 / VEX / M • California Blondes #03 / 1988 / VEX / M • California Native / 1988 / CDI / M • The Call Girl / 1986 / VD / M • Camp Beaver-

lake #1 / 1984 / AR / M • Captain Hooker & Peter Porn / 1987 / VD / M • Caught From Behind #05: Blondes & Blacks / 1986 / HO / M • Caught From Behind #07 / 1987 / HO / M • Caught In The Act / 1987 / WV / M • Charli / 1981 / VCX / M • Cheating / 1986 / SEV / M • Cheek To Cheek / 1986 / VEX / M • Cherry Busters / 1984 / VIV / M • China Bitch / 1989 / PV / C • China White / 1986 / WV / M • Chocolate Chips / 1987 / VD / M • Chocolate Cream / 1984 / SUP / M • Chocolate Delights #1 / 1985 / TAG / C • Chocolate Delights #2 / 1985 / TAG / C • The Chocolate Fudge Factory / 1987 / PIN / M • Circus Acts / 1987 / SE / C • Classic Swedish Erotica #05 / 1986 / CA / C • Classic Swedish Erotica #11 / 1986 / CA / C • Classic Swedish Erotica #21 / 1986 / CA / C • Classic Swedish Erotica #30 / 1987 / CA / C • Club Exotica #1 / 1985 / WV / M • Club Exotica #2 / 1985 / WV / M • Club Sex / 1989 / GO / M • Coffee, Tea Or Me / 1984 / CV / M • Coming Alive / 1988 / LV / M • Commando Lovers / 1986 / SUV / M • Corporate Affairs / 1986 / SE / M • Cummin' Alive / 1984 / VC / M • Daddy's Darling Daughters / 1986 / PL / M • Dana Lynn's Hot All Over / 1987 / V99 / M • Dancing Angels / 1989 / PL / M • Dark Desires / 1989 / BMV / C • Dear Fanny / 1984 / CV / M • Debbie 4 Hire / 1988 / AVC / M • Debbie Class Of '8R / 1987 / CC / M • Debbie Does Dishes #1 / 1985 / AVC / M • Debbie Goes To Hawaii / 1988 / VD / C • Deep Chill / cr85 / AT / M • Deep Obsession / 1987 / WV / M • Deep Throat #3 / 1989 / AR / M • Deep Throat Fantasies / 1989 / VD / M • Desert Foxes / 1989 / SE / M • Desperately Seeking Suzie / 1985 / VD / M • Deviations / 1983 / SE / M • Deviled X / 1987 / 4P / M • Diamond Collection #80 / 1986 / CDI / M • Diamond Head / 1987 / AVC / M • Dirty Dr. Feelgood / 1988 / VEX / M • Dirty Movies / 1989 / VD / M • Dirty Pictures / 1988 / CA / M • Dirty Shary / 1985 / VD / M • Doctor Desire / 1984 / VD / M • Doin' The Harlem Shuffle / 1986 / CA / M • Doing It / 1982 / SE / M • Double Dare / 1986 / SE / M • Double Desires / 1988 / PIN / C • Double Pleasure / 1985 / VCR / M • Double Your Pleasure / 1989 / VEX / M • Dr Blacklove #1 / 1987 / CC / M • Dr Juice's Lust Potion / 1986 / TEM / M • Dr Lust / 1987 / VC / M • Dr Strange Sex / 1985 / CA / M • The Dragon Lady #1 / 1988 / WV / C • Dynamic Vices / 1987 / VC / M • E.X. / 1986 / SUP / M • Ebony & Ivory Fantasies / 1988 / VD / C • Ebony Ecstacy / 1988 / HIO / C • Ebony Orgies / 1987 / SE / C • Ebony Superstars / 1988 / VC / C • Educating Nina / 1984 / AT / M • The Eleventh Commandment / 1987 / WAV / M • The End Zone / 1987 / LA / C • Endless Passion / 1987 / LIM / C • The Erotic Adventures Of Bonnie & Clyde / 1988 / GO / M • Erotic Dimensions #1: Ripe / 1982 / NSV / M • Erotic Dimensions: Aggressive Women / 1982 / NSV / M • Erotic Dimensions: I Want To Watch / 1982 / NSV / M • Erotic Dimensions: The Wild Life / 1982 / NSV / M • Erotic Rendezvous / 1988 / VEX / M • The Erotic World Of Linda Wong / 1985 / VIV / M • Erotic Zones #2 / 1985 / CA / M • Extra Sensual Pleasure / 1983 / PAC / M • Fantasy Land / 1984 / LA / M • Fashion Passion / 1985 / VD / M • Fatal

Passion / 1988 / CC / M • Find Your Love / 1988 / CV / M • The Fire Inside / 1988 / VC / C • Fireball / 1988 / IN / M • Flasher / 1986 / VD / M • Flesh For Frankenstein / 1987 / VEX / M • Fondle With Care / 1989 / VEX / M • For Your Love / 1988 / IN / M • French Letters / 1984 / CA / M • Friday The 13th #1: A Nude Beginning / 1987 / VD / M • Friday The 13th #2 / 1989 / VD / M • Frisky Fables / 1988 / LV / M • The Fun House / 1988 / SEV / C • Furburgers / 1987 / VD / M • Future Sex / 1984 / NSV / M • Gazongas #02 / 1988 / VEX / M • The Girl From S.E.X. / 1982 / CA / M • Girl Toys / 1986 / DR / M • Girls That Talk Dirty / 1986 / VCS / C • Go For It / 1984 / VC / M • Golden Girls, The Movie / 1984 / SE / M • Good 'n' Plenty / 1987 / AVC / M • The Good Time Girls / 1985 / VEX / M • Good Vibrations / 1991 / PM / M • The Good, The Bad, And The Horny / 1985 / VCX / M • Grind / 1988 / CV / M • Guess Who Came At Dinner? / 1987 / FAN / M • A Hard Act To Swallow / 1988 / VT / M • Hard At Work / 1989 / VEX / M • Head Trips / cr88 / EXH / C • Hitler Sucks / 1988 / GO / M • Hollywood Harlots / 1986 / VEX / C • Hometown Honeys #1 / 1986 / VEX / M • Hometown Honeys #2 / 1988 / VEX / M • Honkytonk Angels / 1988 / IN / C • Hot And Nasty! / 1986 / V99 / C • Hot Black Moon Rising Forever / 1988 / ZA / M • The Hot Box Invasion / 1987 / AMB / M • Hot Chocolate #2 / 1986 / PLY / M • Hot In The City / 1989 / VEX / M • Hot Number / 1987 / WET / M • Hot Ones / 1982 / SUP / C • Hot Rocks / 1986 / WET / M • House Of Lust / 1984 / VD / M • How To Get A "Head" / 1988 / CV / M • The Huntress / 1987 / IN / M • Hyapatia Lee's Sexy / 1986 / SE / M • I Cream Of Genie / 1988 / SE / M • I Found My Thrill On Cheri Hill / 1988 / PL / M • Illusions Of Ecstasy / 1985 / NSV / M • In All The Right Places / 1986 / VD / M • Indecent Proposals / 1988 / SEX / M • Indecent Proposals / 1991 / V99 / M • Inflamed / 1984 / NSV / M • Inn Of Sin / 1988 / VT / M • Inner Blues / 1987 / VD / M • Innocent Taboo / 1986 / VD / M • Inside Sharon Mitchell / 1989 / ZA / C • Irresistible #1 / 1982 / SE / M • Jack Hammer / 1987 / ZA / M • Jewels Of The Night / 1986 / SE / M • Joanna's Dreams / 1988 / SEV / M • John Holmes, The Man, The Legend / 1995 / EVN / C • K.U.N.T.-TV / 1988 / WV / M • The Ladies In Lace Party / 1985 / MAP / M • Ladies Nights / 1980 / VC / M • Las Vegas Lady / 1981 / VCX / M • Le Hot Club / 1987 / WV / M • The Legend Of Lady Blue / 1978 / VCX / M • Legends Of Porn #1 / 1987 / CV / C • Lessons In Lust / 1987 / LA / M • Let's Get Wet / 1987 / WV / M • Lifestyles Of The Black And Famous / 1986 / WET / M • Lips: The Passage To Pleasure / 1981 / CA / M • Liquid Love / 1988 / CA / M • A Little Bit Of Honey / 1987 / WET / M • Little French Maids / 1988 / VEX / M • Little Muffy Johnson / 1985 / VEP / M • Little Shop Of Whores / 1987 / VI / M • Living In A Wet Dream / 1986 / PEN / C • Looking For Mr Goodsex / 1984 / CC / M • Loose Ends #4 / 1988 / 4P / M • Loose Lifestyles / 1988 / CA / M • Lorelei / 1984 / CV / M • Lost Innocence / 1988 / PV / M • Lost Lovers / 1990 / VEX / M • Love Lies / 1988 / IN / M • Love On The Run / 1989 / CA / M

• Lover's Lane / 1986 / SE / M • Lucky In Love #2 / 1988 / SEV / M • Lust Connection / 1988 / VT / M • Lustfully Seeking Susan / 1985 / PLY / M • Mad About You / 1987 / VC / M • Mad Sex / 1986 / VD / M • Makeout / 1988 / VT / M • Mammary Lane / 1988 / VT / C • Mantrap / 1986 / BAN / M • The Many Shades Of Amber / 1986 / LIM / M • Mardi Gras / 1986 / SE / M • Mardi Gras Passions / 1987 / MET / M • Marilyn Chambers' Private Fantasies #4 / 1983 / CA / M • Marilyn Chambers' Private Fantasies #5 / 1985 / CA / M • Marina Heat / 1985 / CV / M • Marina Vice / 1985 / PEN / M • The Master Of Pleasure / 1988 / VD / M • Matched Pairs / 1988 / VEX / M • Max Bedroom / 1987 / ZA / M • Midnight Fantasies / 1989 / VEX / M • The Mischief Maker / 1987 / SE / M • Missing Pieces / 1985 / IN / M • Mistaken Identity / 1990 / CC / M • Moonlusting #2 / 1987 / WV / M • More Than A Handful #1 / 1985 / CV / C • Motel Sweets / 1987 / VD / M • Much More Than A Mouthful #1 / 1987 / VEX / M • Mystic Pieces / 1989 / EA / M • Naked Stranger / 1987 / CDI / M • Nasty / 1985 / NSV / M • Nasty Nights / 1988 / PL / C • A Natural Woman / 1989 / IN / M • Naughty Cheerleaders / 1985 / HO / M • Naughty Girls In Heat / 1986 / SE / M • Naughty Nymphs / 1986 / VEX / M • Naughty Nymphs / 1991 / VEX / C • New Sensations / 1990 / CC / M • The Night Before / 1987 / WV / M • Night Moves / 1983 / SUP / M • Nudes At Eleven #2 / 1987 / AVC / M • Object(s) Of My Desire / 1988 / V99 / M • On White Satin / 1980 / VCX / M • One For The Road / 1989 / V99 / M • One More Time / 1990 / VEX / M • One Wife To Give / 1989 / ZA / M • Only The Best Of Anal / 1992 / MET / C • Only The Best Of Barbara Dare / 1990 / CV / C • Open House (Vid Exc) / 1989 / VEX / M • Open Lips / 1983 / AVO / M • The Oui Girls / 1981 / VHL / M • Out Of Control / 1987 / SE / M • Parliament: Blondes Have More Fun / 1989 / PM / C • Parting Shots / 1990 / VD / M • Party Animals / 1987 / VEX / M • Party Animals / 1994 / VEX / C • Party Girls / 1988 / MAP / M • Passion Chain / 1987 / ZA / M • Passion Pit / 1985 / SE / M • The Passion Within / 1986 / MAP / M • Passionate Heiress / 1987 / CA / M • Peach Fuzz / 1976 / CDI / M • Peek-A-Boo / 1987 / VEX / M • Peepers / 1988 / CV / M • Peeping Passions / 1989 / CAE / M • Perils Of Paula / 1989 / CA / M • Phone Sex Girls #2 / 1987 / VT / M • Physical #1 / 1981 / SUP / M • Physical #2 / 1985 / SUP / M • Piece Of Heaven / 1988 / CDI / M • The Pink Panties / 1985 / NSV / M • Platinum Princess / 1988 / VEX / M • Play Me Again, Vanessa / 1986 / VC / M • Playing Dirty / 1989 / VEX / M • Playpen / 1987 / VC / M • Please Me! / cr86 / LIM / M • The Pleasure Game / 1988 / CA / M • The Pleasure Hunt #1 / 1984 / NSV / M • The Pleasure Hunt #2 / 1985 / NSV / M • The Pleasure Maze / 1986 / PL / M • Pleasure Principle / 1988 / VEX / M • Pleasure Spot / 1986 / CA / M • Pleasures Of A Woman / 1983 / CA / M • Plenty Of Pleasure / 1990 / WET / M • Porno Screentests / 1982 / VC / M • Porsche Lynn, Every Man's Dream / 1988 / CC / C • Pretty Peaches #2 / 1987 / VC / M • Private Moments / 1983 / CV / M • The

PTX Club / 1988 / GO / M • Queen Of Hearts #1 / 1987 / PL / M • Rachel Ryan / 1988 / WV / C • Raising Hell / 1987 / VD / M • Ramb-Ohh #2 / 1988 / PV / M • Rambone Does Hollywood / 1986 / WET / M • Reamin' Reunion / 1988 / CC / M • Rearbusters / 1988 / LVI / C • Red Hot Pepper / 1986 / V99 / M • Restless Nights / 1987 / SEV / M • The Return Of Dr Blacklove / 1996 / CC / M • The Return Of Johnny Wadd / 1986 / PEN / M • Robofox #1 / 1987 / FAN / M • Rock Hard / 1985 / CV / M • Salt & Pepper / 1986 / VCS / C • Satin Dolls / 1985 / CV / M • Screen Play / 1984 / XTR / M • Screw / 1985 / CV / M • Screwdriver / 1988 / CC / C • Secret Of My Sex-Cess / 1988 / CV / M • Secrets Behind The Green Door / 1987 / SE / M • The Seductress / 1982 / VC / M • Sex Asylum #3 / 1988 / VI / M • Sex Charades / 1990 / VEX / M • Sex Crimes 2084 / 1985 / SE / M • Sex F/X / 1986 / VPE / M • Sex Life Of A Porn Star / 1986 / ELH / M • The Sex Life Of Mata Hari / 1989 / GO / M • Sex Slaves / 1986 / VEX / M • Sex Wars / 1984 / EXF / M • Sextrology / 1987 / CA / M • Sexy Delights #2 / 1987 / CLV / M • Shameless / 1982 / SVE / M • Sheer Haven / 1989 / DR / C • Sheri's Gotta Have It / 1985 / LIM / C • Sheri's Wild Dream / 19?? / LIM / C • Showgirl #14: Kitty Shane's Fantasies / 1983 / VCR / M • Sin City / 1986 / WET / M • Sinful Pleasures / 1987 / HO / C • Sinful Sisters / 1986 / VEX / M • Sinset Boulevard / 1987 / WV / M • Skintight / 1981 / CA / M • Sky Foxes / 1987 / VC / M • Snapshots: Confessions Of A Video Voyeur / 1988 / CC / M • Soaking Wet / 1985 / CV / M • Sophisticated Women / 1986 / BAN / M • Soul Games / 1988 / PV / C • Soul Kiss This / 1988 / VCR / C • Sound F/X / 1989 / V99 / M • St. X-Where #2 / 1988 / VD / M • Star Tricks / 1988 / WV / M • The Stimulators / 1983 / VC / M • Stormi / 1988 / LV / M • Stormy / 1980 / CV / M • Strange Love / 1987 / WV / M • Strictly Business / 1987 / VD / M • Strip Search / 1987 / SEV / M • Suite Sensations / 1988 / SEX / M • Super Models Do LA / 1000 / ,KL / M • •••••••••• •••••• • 11 / 1980 / CA / M • Swedish Erotica #18 / 1980 / CA / M • Swedish Erotica #33 / 1980 / CA / M • Swedish Erotica #47 / 1983 / CA / M • Swedish Erotica #65 / 1985 / CA / M • Swedish Erotica #66 / 1985 / CA / M • Swedish Erotica #68 / 1985 / CA / M • Swedish Erotica #69 / 1985 / CA / M • Swedish Erotica #71 / 1986 / CA / M • Swedish Erotica #72 / 1986 / CA / M • Sweet Sensations / 1989 / SEX / M • Sweet Temptations / 1989 / V99 / M • Sweet Things / 1987 / VC / M • Sweet Tricks / 1987 / TEM / M • Taboo #05 / 1986 / IN / M • Tales Of The Uncensored / 1987 / FAN / M • Tamara's Dreams / 1989 / VEX / M • A Taste Of Black / 1987 / WET / M • A Taste Of Laurel / 1990 / PIN / C • A Taste Of Sahara / 1990 / PIN / C • A Taste Of Taija Rae / 1989 / PIN / C • Taste Of The Best #2 / 1988 / PIN / C • Taste Of The Best #3 / 1988 / PIN / C • A Taste Of Vanessa De Rio / 1990 / PIN / C • A Taste Of White / 1987 / WET / M • Tease Me / 1986 / VC / M • Telemates / 1988 / STA / M • Telemates / 1991 / V99 / M • Tell Me Something Dirty / 1991 / NWV / M • Temp-

tation: The Story Of A Lustful Bride / 1983 / NSV / M • Temptations Of An Angel / 1989 / PEN / M • Terms Of Employment / 1984 / LA / M • This Is Your Sex Life / 1987 / VD / M • Three For All / 1988 / PL / M • Tight Fit / 1987 / V99 / M • Tight Fit / 1991 / VEX / C • Tight Squeeze / 1986 / AVC / M • Torrid Zone / 1987 / MIR / M • The Touchables / 1988 / CC / M • Trading Partners / 1983 / AIR / M • True Legends Of Adult Cinema: The Golden Age / 1992 / VC / C • Two Into One #1 / 1988 / PIN / C • The Ultimate O / 1985 / NSV / M • Undressed For Success / 1990 / V99 / M • Undulations / 1980 / VC / M • Uniform Behavior / 1989 / ZA / M • Unveiled / 1987 / VC / M • VCA Previews #4 / 1988 / VC / C • Video Voyeur #1 / 1988 / VT / C • Viper's Place / 1988 / VD / M • Virginia / 1983 / CA / M • Voyeur's Delight / 1986 / VCS / C • Wet 'n' Bare With Barbara Dare / 1988 / NEO / C • Wet Kink / 1989 / CDI / M • Wet Kisses / 1988 / V99 / M • What A Country / 1989 / PL / M • Where There's Smoke There's Fire / 1987 / FAN / M • Who Came In The Backdoor? / 1987 / PV / M • Who's Dat Girl / 1987 / VEX / M • Wild Black Erotica #4 / cr89 / VD / C • Wild In The Wilderness / 1984 / GO / M • Wild Oral Erotica / 1988 / VD / C • Wild Stuff / 1987 / WET / M • Wild Things #1 / 1985 / CV / M • Wild Toga Party / 1985 / VD / M • Wildheart / 1989 / IN / M • With Love, Lisa / 1985 / CA / C • WPINK-TV #3 / 1988 / PV / M • XXX Workout / 1987 / VEX / M • Yank My Doodle, It's A Dandy / 1985 / GOM / M • Yiddish Erotica #1 / 1986 / SE / C • You Bring Out The Animal In Me / 1987 / MIR / M • The Young And The Wrestling #2 / 1989 / PL / M • Young Girls Do / 1984 / ELH / M • Young Girls In Tight Jeans / 1989 / VD / M • Young Nympho's / 1986 / VD / M • [Berlin Caper / 1989 / ... / M

BILLY DIGGET
Let's Talk Sex / 1982 / CA / M

BILLY FRANK
Freak Show / 1991 / FC / M • Lady Avenger / 1987 / ... / S • Nudity Required / 1989 / AE / S

BILLY GLYDE
Quietwark Pussy #7: NUGIRLZ / 1997 / FI / M • Fresh Faces #08 / 1995 / EVN / M • Living On The Edge / 1997 / DWO / M • Monkey Gang Bang / 1996 / NOT / M • Over Eighteen #02 / 1997 / HW / M • Perverted Stories #10 / 1996 / JMP / M • Pick Up Lines #11 / 1997 / OD / M • Planet X #1 / 1996 / HW / M • Puritan Video Magazine #04 / 1996 / LE / M • Puritan Video Magazine #05 / 1996 / LE / M • Puritan Video Magazine #10 / 1997 / LE / M • Real Sex Magazine #02 / 1997 / HO / M • Rockhard (Sin City) / 1996 / SC / M • Shane's World #7 / 1996 / OD / M • The Swing / 1996 / VI / M • Young And Anal #6 / 1996 / JMP / M

BILLY JAMES see Star Index I

BILLY JOE
Heavy Load / 1975 / COM / M • MASH'ed / cr75 / ALP / M

BILLY JOE BROWN
Ring Of Desire / 1981 / SE / M

BILLY JOE FIELDS
Cunning Coeds / 1985 / IVP / M • Deliveries In The Rear #1 / 1985 / AVC / M • Dirty 30's Cinema: Heather Wayne / 1985 / PV / C • Headgames / 1985 / WV / M • Hot Sweet Honey / 1985 / VEP / M • Little

American Maid / 1987 / VCX / M • Sexeo / 1985 / PV / M

BILLY JOE FOX see Star Index I

BILLY MAE MARSHALL
Jezebel / 1979 / CV / M

BILLY PARADISE
Thundercrack! / 1974 / LUM / M

BILLY ROCKET
Carnal Interludes / 1995 / NOT / M • Cyberanal / 1995 / VC / M • In Search Of The Perfect Blow Job / 1995 / OD / M • Peepshow / 1994 / OD / M • Western Nights / 1994 / WP / M

BILLY SAVAGE see Star Index I

BILLY SHADE
Big Boys Toy / 1994 / SV / B

BILLY SLATER
Driven Home / 1995 / CSP / G • Long Play / 1995 / 3XP / G • No Reservations / 1995 / MN0 / G

BILLY SLAUGHTER
When The Fat Lady Sings / 1996 / EX / M

BILLY STAVNEY see Star Index I

BILLY TAPP
M Series #29 / 1994 / LBO / M

BILLY TEVE
Candy's Custom Car Wash / 1995 / FC / M

BILLY THE KID
Bobby Hollander's Rookie Nookie #07 / 1993 / SFP / M • GVC: The Babysitter #107 / 1983 / GO / M • Neighborhood Watch #39: / 1993 / LBO / M • Stevi's: Kiss My Feet / 1993 / SSV / M • VGA: Bureau Of Discipline #1 / 1993 / VGA / B • VGA: Bureau Of Discipline #2 / 1993 / VGA / B • VGA: Bureau Of Discipline #3 / 1993 / VGA / B

BILLY THORNBERG
Dixie Ray Hollywood Star / 1983 / CA / M

BILLY TOP
Anal Camera #02 / 1994 / EVN / M • Sparkling Champagne / 1994 / FH / M

BILLY WEDGE
The Debutante / 1986 / BEA / M

BILLY WILSON see Star Index I

BILLY WYMP
Domination In Black & White / 19?? / BIZ / B

BILLY YOUNG
Orgy Camera #2 / 1996 / EVN / M

BINKY BISH
Resurrection Of Eve / 1973 / MIT / M

BIONCA *(Bionica Bradley, Bianca Bradley, Bionica, Bianca Gold, Bianca (Bionca))*
Not too pretty, hard brunette with small/medium tits who was once the SO of Bruce Seven. First movie was **Teacher's Pet (1985)** at age of 19.
A.S.S.(Anal Security Squad) / 1988 / VD / M • AC/DC #1 / 1991 / LA / G • The Adventures Of Buttman / 1989 / EA / M • Adventures Of Buttwoman #1 / 1991 / EL / F • Aerobics Girls Club / 1986 / 4P / F • Aerobisex Girls #2 / 1989 / LIP / F • Amazons From Burbank / 1990 / PL / F • The Anal Adventures Of Bruce Seven / 1996 / BS / C • Anal Attraction #1 / 1988 / 3HV / M • Anal Climax #2 / 1991 / ROB / M • The Anal Diary Of Misty Rain / 1993 / EL / M • Anal Encounters #3: Back In The Dark One / 1991 / VC / M • Anal Extasy / 1992 / ROB / M • Anal Fury / 1992 / ROB / M • Anal Heat / 1990 / ZA / M • Anal Intruder #05: The Final Outrage / 1990 / CC / M • Anal Madness / 1992 / ROB / M • Anal Nation #1 / 1990 / CC / M • Anal Nation #2 / 1990

/ CC / M • The Analizer / 1994 / VD / M • Angels Bi Day, Devils Bi Night / 1990 / FC / G • Anus & Andy / 1993 / ZA / M • The Anus Family / 1991 / CC / M • Around The World With Samantha Strong / 1989 / V99 / M • Ass Openers! #1 / 1995 / TCK / C • Attitude / 1995 / VC / M • Autobiography Of A Whip / 1991 / BS / B • Autoerotica #2 / 1991 / EX / M • Bachelor Party #1 / 1993 / FPI / M • Back To Back #1 / 1987 / 4P / C • Badgirls #2: Strip Search / 1994 / VI / M • Badgirls #4: Jayebird / 1995 / VI / M • Bar-bii Unleashed / 1988 / 4P / M • Batteries Included / 1988 / 3HV / M • Bend Over Babes #1 / 1990 / EA / M • Best Of Bruce Seven #3 / 1990 / BIZ / C • Best Of Bruce Seven #4 / 1990 / BIZ / C • The Best Of Buttslammers / 1995 / BS / C • The Best Of Doctor Butts / 1994 / 4P / C • Between The Cheeks #2 / 1990 / VC / M • Beyond It All / 1991 / PAL / G • Bi And Beyond #5 / 1990 / INH / G • Bi Medicine / 1991 / STA / G • Bi-Guy / 1990 / LA / G • Bi-Surprise / 1988 / MET / G • Bionca On Fire / 1988 / 4P / M • Bionca, Just For You / 1989 / BON / F • Black & Beyond: The Darker Sid / 1990 / INH / G • Blackman & Anal Woman #2 / 1990 / PL / M • Blame It On The Heat / 1989 / VC / M • Blazing Nova / 1989 / LV / M • Blowing In Style / 1989 / EA / M • Body Slam / 1987 / 4P / B • Bondage Memories #01 / 1993 / BON / C • The Boneheads / 1992 / PL / M • Boobs, Butts And Bloopers #1 / 1990 / HO / M • Bossy Babes / 1993 / TCK / M • Both Ends Burning / 1987 / VC / M • The Bottom Dweller Part Deux / 1994 / EL / M • Bound For Pleasure / 1991 / BS / B • Bruce Seven's Favorite Endings #1 / 1991 / EL / C • Bruce Seven: A Compendium Of His Most Graphic Scenes Vol 1 / 1991 / BS / C • Bruce Seven: A Compendium Of His Most Graphic Scenes Vol 3 / 1992 / BS / C • Bruce Seven: A Compendium Of His Most Graphic Scenes Vol 4 / 1993 / BS / C • Bustin' Thru / 1993 / LV / M • Buttman Vs Buttwoman / 1992 / EL / M • Buttman's Big Tit Adventure #3 / 1995 / EA / M • Buttslammers #01 / 1993 / BS / F • Buttslammers #03: The Ultimate Dream / ~~1993 / BS / F •~~ ~~Buttslammers #04: Down~~ And Dirty / 1993 / BS / F • Buttslammers #06: Over The Edge / 1994 / BS / F • Buttslammers #08: The Ultimate Invasion / 1994 / BS / F • California Gigolo / 1987 / VD / M • Car Wash Angels / 1995 / VC / M • Carnival Of Knowledge / 1992 / XCI / M • Cat Lickers #2 / 1994 / ME / F • Catfighting Lesbians / 1991 / BIZ / F • Centerfold Celebrities '94 #2 / 1994 / SFP / M • The Chains Of Torment / 1991 / BS / B • The Challenge / 1990 / EA / B • Chatsworth Hall / 1989 / BIZ / B • Cheap Shots / 1994 / PRE / B • Cheerleader Nurses #1 / 1993 / VC / M • Cheerleader Nurses #2 / 1993 / VC / M • Chocolate Cherries #1 / 1984 / LA / M • Circus Of Lesbians / 1995 / VI / C • Clinique / 1989 / VC / M • Club Bed / 1987 / CIX / M • Club Ginger / 1986 / VI / M • Collectible / 1991 / LE / M • The Contessa / 1989 / VC / M • Corruption / 1990 / CC / M • Courting Libido / 1995 / HIV / G • Creme De Femme / 1994 / 4P / F • Croco-dile Blondee #2 / 1988 / VCX / M • Cyrano / 1991 / PL / M • Dangerous When Wet (Amber Lynn Is) / 1987 / VCX / M • Dark

Destiny / 1992 / BS / B • Dark Interludes / 1991 / BS / B • Deep Cheeks #3 / 1992 / ROB / M • Deep Inside Jeanna Fine / 1992 / VC / C • Deep Inside Misty Rain / 1995 / VC / C • Deep Inside Nicole London / 1995 / VC / C • Deep Inside Nikki Dial / 1994 / VC / C • Deep Inside Tyffany Million / 1995 / VC / C • Depraved Fantasies #1 / 1993 / FPI / M • Depraved Fantasies #2 / 1994 / FPI / M • Designing Babes / 1990 / GOT / M • Dial A For Anal / 1994 / CA / M • Dia-mond In The Raw / 1996 / XCI / M • Di-aries Of Fire And Ice #1 / 1989 / VC / M • Diaries Of Fire And Ice #2 / 1989 / VC / M • Ding Dung School / 1994 / PLV / B • Dou-ble Down / 1993 / LBO / M • Double Pene-tration #4 / 1991 / WV / C • Down Bi Law / 1992 / CAT / G • Dr Butts #2 / 1992 / 4P / M • Dresden Diary #03 / 1989 / BIZ / B • Dresden Diary #04 / 1989 / BIZ / B • Dun-geon Dykes #1 / 1994 / FPI / F • Dungeon Dykes #2 / 1994 / FPI / F • Ebony Ecstacy / 1988 / HIO / C • The Ecstasy Girls #2 / 1986 / CA / M • Enemates #08 / 1993 / BIZ / B • Everybody Wants Some / 1996 / EXQ / F • Extreme Heat / 1987 / ME / M • Ex-treme Sex #1: The Club / 1994 / VI / M • Extreme Sex #2: The Dungeon / 1994 / VI / M • Extreme Sex #3: Wired / 1994 / VI / M • Extreme Sex #4: The Experiment / 1995 / VI / M • Fantasy Chamber / 1994 / ULI / M • Fat Ends / 1989 / 4P / M • Femmes On Fire / 1988 / VC / F • The Finer Things In Life / 1990 / PL / F • Firm / 1993 / MID / M • First Time Ever #1 / 1995 / PE / F • Foot Hold / 1994 / PRE / B • Foreign Bodies / 1991 / IN / M • The French Connexxxion / 1991 / VC / M • From Rags To Riches / 1988 / CDI / M • Fun "4" All / 1994 / PRE / B • G Squad / 1990 / SO / G • Gentlemen Prefer Ginger / 1985 / VI / M • Ghost Lus-ters / 1990 / EL / F • Ghostly Estate / 1989 / BON / B • Gillie's Isle / 1990 / GOT / M • Ginger's Greatest Boy/Girl Hits / 1987 / VI / C • Ginger's Greatest Girl/Girl Hits / 1986 / VI / C • Ginger's Private Party / 1985 / VI / M • Girl Crazy / 1989 / CDI / F • Girl Friends / 1990 / PL / F • Girls Just Wanna Have Girls #2 / 1990 / HIO / F • Girls Of Oil / 1991 / PL / A • ~~Girls Of Treasure~~ ~~Is-~~ land / 1988 / CV / M • Godmother / 1991 / AWV / F • Growing Up / 1990 / GO / M • Guilty By Seduction / 1993 / PI / M • Happy Endings / 1994 / WP / M • Hard On The Press / 1991 / AWV / M • Hard To Stop #1 / 1992 / VV / M • Hard To Stop #2 / 1992 / VC / M • Haunted Passions / 1990 / FC / M • Hawaii Vice #1 / 1988 / CIN / M • Hawaii Vice #3 / 1988 / CIN / M • Headbangers Balls / 1991 / PL / M • Heads Or Tails? / 1993 / PL / M • Heartbeats / 1992 / LE / M • Home But Not Alone / 1991 / WV / M • Honkytonk Angels / 1988 / IN / C • Hot Bodies In Bondage / 1993 / LBO / B • The Hot Lick Cafe / 1990 / AMB / M • Hot Scalding / 1989 / VC / M • Hot Tight Asses #01 / 1992 / TCK / M • Hot Tight Asses #03 / 1993 / TCK / M • Hot Tight Asses #04 / 1993 / TCK / M • Hot Tight Asses #05 / 1994 / TCK / M • Hot Tight Asses #07 / 1994 / TCK / M • House Of Dark Dreams #1 / 1990 / BS / B • House Of Dark Dreams #2 / 1990 / BS / B • How To Deep Throat Your Lover / 1994 / A&E / M • I Touch Myself / 1992 / IN / M • Indecent Offer / 1993 / AFV / M • Infidelity / 1988 /

4P / M • Invitation Only / 1989 / AMB / M • Island Girls #2: Fun In The Sun / 1990 / CDI / C • Island Girls #3: Rip Tide / 1991 / CDI / C • Jaded / 1989 / 4P / M • Jane Bond Meets The Man With The Golden Rod / 1987 / VD / M • Jealous Lovers / 1989 / CDI / M • Junk Yard Dogs / 1991 / FC / M • Kinky Roommates / 1992 / TP / M • Kinkyvision #2 / 1988 / VC / M • Kittens #1 / 1990 / CC / F • Kittens #4: Bodybuild-ing Bitches / 1993 / CC / F • The Kitty Kat Club / 1990 / PL / F • Knight Shadows / 1992 / BS / B • Lace / 1989 / VT / F • The Last Girl Scout / 1992 / PL / M • Last Rumba In Paris / 1989 / VC / M • Laugh Factory / 1995 / PRE / C • Le Sex De Femme #5 / 1990 / AFI / C • Leather / 1989 / VT / F • Leather And Lace / 1989 / VT / F • Leather For Lovers #1 / 1992 / LFL / M • Leena's Early Experiences / 1995 / OD / C • The Legend Of Reggie D. / 1989 / EA / M • Lesbian Catfights / 1990 / BIZ / B • Lesbian Dildo Bondage #2 / 1990 / BIZ / B • Lesbian Lingerie Fantasy #1 / 1988 / ESP / F • Lesbian Love Connection / 1992 / LIP / F • Letters From The Heart / 1991 / AWV / M • Licensed To Thrill / 1990 / VC / M • Lips On Lips / 1989 / LIP / F • Little Miss Dangerous / 1989 / SO / M • Loose Ends #2 / 1986 / 4P / M • Loose Ends #3 / 1987 / BS / M • Loose Ends #4 / 1988 / 4P / M • Loose Ends #5: The New Generation / 1988 / 4P / M • Loose Ends #6 / 1989 / 4P / M • The Lottery / 1989 / CIN / M • Love Bunnies #06 / 1994 / FPI / F • Love Bunnies #07 / 1994 / FPI / F • Lust Con-nection / 1988 / VT / M • Mad Jack Beyond Thunderdome / 1986 / WET / M • The Makeup Room #1 / 1992 / VC / M • The Makeup Room #2 / 1992 / VC / M • Male Domination #15: Women In Suspension / 1990 / BIZ / C • Married With Hormones #1 / 1991 / PL / M • Married With Hormones #2 / 1992 / PL / M • Masturbation Madness / 1991 / 5KS / F • The Mating Pot / 1994 / LBO / M • Memories / 1992 / LE / M • Mind Trips / 1992 / FH / M • Miss Anal America / 1993 / LV / M • Mistresses And Slaves: The Best Of Bruce Seven / 1991 / BEP / C • Monaco Falls / 1997 / VC / M • Night And Day / 1993 / VT / M • The Night Of The Headhunter / 1985 / WV / M • Night Of The Living Debbies / 1989 / EX / M • Nightshift Nurses #1 / 1988 / VC / M • Nightshift Nurses #2 / 1996 / VC / M • No Man's Land #08: Eight Women Who Ate Women / 1993 / VT / F • On Your Honor / 1989 / LE / M • The Only Game In Town / 1991 / VC / M • Only The Best #3 / 1990 / CV / C • Only The Best Of Barbara Dare / 1990 / CV / C • Only The Very Best On Video / 1992 / VC / C • The Orgy #1 / 1993 / EMC / M • The Orgy #2 / 1993 / EMC / M • The Orgy #3 / 1993 / EMC / M • Other People's Pussy / 1993 / LV / M • Painful Initiation / 1992 / PL / B • Paris Burning / 1989 / CC / M • Party Doll A Go-Go #1 / 1991 / VC / M • Party Doll A Go-Go #2 / 1991 / VC / M • Party Wives / 1988 / CDI / M • Performer Of The Year / 1994 / WP / M • Phantom Of The Cabaret #1 / 1989 / VC / M • Phantom Of The Cabaret #2 / 1989 / VC / M • The Poonies / 1985 / VI / M • Pornocchio / 1987 / ME / M • A Portrait Of Dorian / 1992 / OD / M • Precious Gems / 1988 / CV / M • The Price Was Right / 1994 / PAE / M •

Project Ginger / 1985 / VI / M • Pussyman #01: The Search / 1993 / CC / M • Pussyman #02: The Prize / 1993 / CC / M • Pussyman #08: The Squirt Queens / 1994 / SNA / M • Pussyman #11: Prime Cuts / 1995 / SNA / C • R.E.A.L. #1 / 1994 / LV / F • Rainwoman #01 / 1989 / CC / M • Rainwoman #07: In The Rainforest / 1993 / CC / M • Ravaged / 1990 / CIN / M • Ready, Willing & Anal (Cv) / 1993 / CV / C • Realities #2 / 1992 / ZA / M • The Rising / 1987 / SUV / M • The Rocky Porno Video Show / 1986 / 4P / M • Sacrificed To Love / 1986 / CDI / M • Salsa Break / 1989 / EA / M • Saturday Night Special / 1989 / DR / M • Secret Lessons #2 / 1989 / BIZ / B • Sex Appraisals / 1990 / HO / M • Sex Asylum #1 / 1985 / VI / M • Sex In Strange Places: The Sphincter Zone / 1994 / FPI / M • Shadows In The Dark / 1990 / 4P / M • Silk Elegance / 1991 / VIM / M • Single Girl Masturbation #1 / 1988 / ESP / F • Slippery When Wet / 1994 / LEI / C • Sloppy Seconds / 1994 / PE / M • Smeers / 1992 / PL / M • Sodomania #05: Euro-American Style / 1993 / EL / M • Sodomania: Slop Shots / 1996 / EL / C • Sodomania: The Baddest Of The Best...And Then Some / 1994 / EL / C • Some Like It Hotter / 1989 / CDI / M • Sorority Pink #2 / 1989 / CV / M • Sorority Sex Kittens #1 / 1992 / VC / M • Sorority Sex Kittens #2 / 1993 / VC / M • St. Tropez Lust / 1990 / VC / M • Steam / 1993 / AMP / M • Stephanie, Just For You / 1989 / BON / F • Sterling Silver / 1992 / CC / M • The Sting Of Ecstasy / 1991 / BS / B • Strange Sex In Strange Places / 1994 / ZA / M • Stripper Nurses / 1994 / PE / M • Stroke Play / 1994 / PLV / B • Student Fetish Videos: Best of Enema #03 / 1994 / PRE / C • Student Fetish Videos: The Enema #14 / 1994 / PRE / B • Student Fetish Videos: Foot Worship #09 / 1994 / PRE / B • Student Fetish Videos: Tickling #09 / 1994 / SFV / B • Studio Sex / 1990 / FH / M • Sunny After Dark / 1990 / WV / M • Super Enemates #2 / 1996 / PRE / C • Superstar Masturbation / 1990 / BIZ / F • Swallow / 1994 / VI / M • Sweet Nothings / 1987 / HO / M • Switch Hitters #1 / 1987 / IN / G • Switch Hitters #5: The Night Games / 1990 / IN / G • Taboo #11: Crazy On You / 1993 / IN / M • Takin' It To The Limit #1 / 1994 / BS / M • Takin' It To The Limit #2 / 1994 / BS / M • Takin' It To The Limit #3 / 1994 / BS / M • Takin' It To The Limit #4 / 1995 / BS / M • Takin' It To The Limit #5 / 1995 / BS / M • Takin' It To The Limit #7: Debauched / 1996 / BS / M • Tales By Taylor / 1989 / AMB / M • A Taste Of Genie / 1986 / 4P / M • The Teacher's Pet / 1985 / WV / M • Throbbin' Hood / 1987 / VD / M • Tip Tap Toe / 1995 / PRE / C • Too Hot To Handle / 1989 / WET / F • Tori Welles Goes Behind The Scenes / 1992 / FD / M • Toys, Not Boys #3 / 1991 / FC / C • True Legends Of Adult Cinema: The Modern Era / 1992 / VC / C • Tush / 1992 / ZA / M • Two Women / 1992 / ROB / M • Undercover Lover / 1993 / VC / M • Uninhibited Love / 1994 / VPN / M • Used And Abused #2 / 1994 / SFP / M • Val Girls / 1990 / PL / F • Visions Of Desire / 1993 / HO / M • Watersgate / 1994 / PRE / C • Weak-Ends / 1995 / PRE / B • Wenches / 1991 / VT / F • Where The Girls Play /

1992 / CC / F • Where The Girls Sweat #1 / 1990 / EA / F • Who Framed Ginger Grant? / 1989 / CC / M • Wicked Pleasures / 1995 / BS / B • Wicked Sensations #2 / 1989 / DR / M • Wild In Motion / 1992 / PL / M • The Wild Thing / 1992 / HO / M • With The Devil In Her Rear / 1992 / WV / M • The World According To Ginger / 1985 / VI / M • You Bet Your Ass / 1991 / EA / B

BIONCA PASTORA
Lovin' Spoonfuls #7 / 1996 / 4P / C • More Dirty Debutantes #32 / 1994 / 4P / M

BIONICA see Bionca

BIONICA (S/M) see Star Index I

BIONICA BRADLEY see Bionca

BIONICA TRUMP see Bianca Trump

BIP
Bip Shoots #1 / 1994 / BON / B • Bip Shoots #2 / 1994 / BON / B • Delivered For Discipline / 1995 / BON / B • Final Orgy / 1996 / BON / B • Katrina's Awakening #3 / 1994 / BON / B • Orgy Of Pain / 1995 / BON / B • Spank-O-Rama / 1994 / BON / B • Vagabondage / 1996 / B&D / B

BIRDIE JORDAN
Jezebel / 1979 / CV / M

BIRGIT BERGEN
[Junge Madchen Mogen's HeiB, Hausfrauen Noch HeiBer / 1973 / ... / M

BIRGIT TETZLAFF
[Schulmadchen-Report 4: Was Eltern Oft Verzweifeln LaBt / 1972 / ... / M

BISHOP THE HORSE
Rusty Boner's Late Night Videos #1 / 1995 / RHV / M

BJORN BECK
Casanova #2 / 1976 / CA / M

BJORN REY
Private Film #04 / 1993 / OD / M

BJORN TORVAIT
Little Darlings / 1981 / VEP / M

BLACK BOMBSHELL
The Best Little Whorehouse In Tijuana / 1995 / HBE / M • Made In The Hood / 1995 / HBE / M

BLACK CHERRY
Juicy's Houseparty / 1995 / HW / M • Ron Hightower's Casting Couch #2 / 1995 / FC / M

BLACK COBRA
Black Knockers #11 / 1995 / TV / M

BLACK COFFEE
Black Hollywood Amateurs #23 / 1996 / MID / M • Black Hollywood Amateurs #24 / 1996 / MID / M • Black Knockers #03 / 1995 / TV / M

BLACK HAWK BILL
Oriental Techniques Of Pain And Pleasure / 1983 / ALP / B

BLACK ICE
Beg For It / 1995 / GOT / B • Beyond Domination / 1996 / GOT / B

BLACK JACK
Amsterdam Nights #2 / 1996 / VC / M • Diamonds / 1996 / HDE / M • Magma: Spezial: Black & White #3 / 1995 / MET / M

BLACK LYNN
Karin & Barbara Superstars / 1988 / PL / M

BLACK MASTER MARC
Black Masters: Black Obsession / 1995 / GOT / B • Black Masters: Den Of Punishment / 1996 / GOT / B • Black Masters: Red Flesh / 1996 / GOT / B • Black Masters: Restrained / 1995 / GOT / B • Black Masters: Trapped / 1995 / GOT / B • Mas-

ters Of Dominance / 1996 / GOT / C

BLACK ORCHID
Dark Passions #01 / 1993 / AFV / M • Hot Summer In The City / 1976 / SVE / M

BLACK SAPPHIRE
Let Me Tell Ya 'Bout Black Chicks / 1985 / VC / M • Let Me Tell Ya 'Bout White Chicks / 1985 / VC / M

BLACK WIDOW see Star Index I

BLACKEY JAVIC
Dangerous Pleasure / 1995 / WIV / M

BLACKIE see Star Index I

BLACKIE FRANK
Magma: Huge Cum Shots / 1995 / MET / M

BLACKSTAR see Star Index I

BLADE BARON
Bar-B-Que Gang Bang / 1994 / JMP / M • Dance Naked / 1995 / PEP / M • Foreskin Gump / 1994 / LE / M • Girl's School / 1994 / ERA / M • Holly's Holiday Gang Bang / 1994 / LBO / M • Pulp Friction / 1994 / PP / M • Tits A Wonderful Life / 1994 / CV / M

BLADE THOMPSON
Driven Home / 1995 / CSP / G • Nydp Trannie / 1996 / WP / G

BLAINE BYGRAVE see Star Index I

BLAINE EDMONDS see Star Index I

BLAINE HARRIS see Blair Harris

BLAIR CASTLE see Brooke Fields

BLAIR DAVIS see Blair Harris

BLAIR HARRIS *(Blair Davis, Eric Blair, Blaine Harris, Blair Morris, David Blair, Blair Morgan, Thomas Francini)*
The Thomas Francini is from **Teeny Buns**. Very easy to confuse with David Morris but according to one contempory Blair is over six feet tall and much taller than David which doesn't help much because it's very hard to tell heights on video.

San Francisco Cosmopolitan Club Amateur Night / 1983 / WV / M • American Pie / 1980 / SE / M • Anal Annie And The Willing Husbands / 1984 / LIP / M • Baby Cakes / 1982 / SE / M • Baby Face #1 / 1977 / VC / M • Backdoor Bandits / 1989 / MIR / C • Backdoor Romance / 1984 / VIV / M • Beauty / 1981 / VC / M • Behind The Brown Door / 1986 / VCR / C • The Best Of Alex De Renzy #1 / 1983 / VC / C • Beyond Shame / 1980 / VEP / M • Beyond Taboo / 1984 / VIV / M • Black, White & Red All Over / 1984 / EXF / C • The Blonde / 1980 / VCX / M • Blue Confessions / 1983 / VCR / M • Blue Heat / 1975 / IVP / M • Body Candy / 1980 / VIS / M • Boiling Point / 1978 / SE / M • Bon Appetite / 1985 / TGA / C • Bound / 1979 / BIZ / B • Bubblegum / 1982 / VC / M • Bucky Beaver's XXX Dragon Art Theatre Double Feature #03 / 1996 / SOW / M • Butter Me Up / 1984 / CHX / M • Challenge Of Desire / 1983 / NSV / M • Champagne For Breakfast / 1980 / SE / M • Cheri's On Fire / 1986 / V99 / M • Cinderella / 1985 / VEL / M • Color Me Amber / 1985 / VC / M • Daisy May / 1979 / VC / M • Dark Angel / 1983 / VC / M • Deep Passage / 1984 / VCR / C • Dirty Girls / 1984 / MIT / M • Double Pleasure / 1985 / VCR / M • Erotic Dimensions: Aggressive Women / 1982 / NSV / M • Erotic Dimensions: Explicit / 1982 / NSV / M • Erotic Encounters / 1985 / LIM / C • Erotic Penetration / 1987 / HO / C • The Erotic World Of Linda Wong / 1985

/ VIV / M • Expectations / 1977 / SE / M • Exploring Young Girls / 1978 / ALP / M • Exposed / 1980 / SE / M • Extra Sensual Pleasure / 1983 / PAC / M • Female Athletes / 1977 / VXP / M • Femme Fatale / 1984 / VIV / M • For The Love Of Pleasure / 1979 / SE / M • Foreplay / 1982 / VC / M • A Formal Faucett / 1978 / VC / M • Getting Personal / 1986 / CA / M • Girl On The Run / 1985 / VC / M • Glamour Girls / 1987 / SE / M • The Greatest American Blonde / 1987 / WV / C • Hard Soap, Hard Soap / 1977 / EVI / M • Hard Times / 1985 / WV / M • Hot Close-Ups / 1984 / WV / M • Hot Legs / 1979 / VCX / M • Illusions Of Ecstasy / 1985 / NSV / M • Inflamed / 1984 / NSV / M • Inspiration / 1981 / CHX / M • Island Of Dr Love / 1977 / S&L / M • K-Sex / 1976 / VCR / M • The Last Taboo / 1984 / VIV / M • The Legend Of King Karl / 1986 / AR / M • The Legend Of Lady Blue / 1978 / VCX / M • Little Girls Blue #1 / 1977 / VCX / M • Love At First Sight / 1987 / SE / C • Love Secrets / 1976 / VIP / M • Love You / 1980 / CA / M • Moments Of Love / 1983 / MID / M • My First Time / 1976 / GO / M • Nasty / 1985 / NSV / M • Nasty Lady / 1984 / CV / M • A Night On The Wild Side / 1986 / VC / M • On White Satin / 1980 / VCX / M • Once Upon A Time/Cave Woman / 1978 / VI / M • Oriental Sexpress / 1984 / WV / M • Oriental Taboo / 1985 / CDI / M • The Other Side Of Julie / 1978 / CV / M • Pink Lips / 1977 / VCX / M • Playing With Fire / 1983 / IN / M • Please, Mr Postman / 1981 / VC / M • The Pleasure Hunt #1 / 1984 / NSV / M • Pretty Girl / 1984 / VIS / M • Pretty Peaches #1 / 1978 / MIT / M • Private Moments / 1983 / CV / M • Private Teacher / 1983 / CA / M • Saturday Matinee Series #1 / 1996 / VCX / C • School For Hookers / 1974 / SOW / M • Screwples / 1979 / CA / M • Seka's Fantasies / 1981 / CA / M • Sensuous Moments / 1983 / VIV / M • Serena, An Adult Fairy Tale / 1979 / VEN / M • Sex Loose / 1982 / VC / M • Sexsations / 1984 / NSV / M • Shameless / 1982 / SVE / M • Shoppe Of Temptation / 1979 / AR / M • Sleepless Nights / 1984 / VIV / M • Small Town Girls / 1979 / CXV / M • Snow Honeys / 1983 / *[illegible]* / M • *[illegible]* ...Sweet As Honey / 1984 / SE / M • Swedish Erotica #45 / 1983 / CA / M • Sweet Dreams Suzan / 1980 / CA / M • Sweet Young Foxes / 1984 / VCX / M • Talk Dirty To Me #02 / 1982 / CA / M • A Taste Of Money / 1983 / AT / M • Teeny Buns / 1977 / VC / M • Telefantasy / 1978 / AR / M • Temptation: The Story Of A Lustful Bride / 1983 / NSV / M • Too Hot To Touch #1 / 1985 / CV / M • Triangle Of Lust / 1983 / VCR / M • Tropic Of Desire / 1979 / WWV / M • Urban Cowgirls / 1980 / CA / M • Victoria's Secret Desires / 1983 / S&L / C • Water Nymph / 1987 / LIM / M • You Turn Me On / 1986 / LIM / M

BLAIR HIGGINS see Blake Palmer

BLAIR JEFFERSON
Two Way Mirror / 1985 / CV / M

BLAIR MORGAN see Blair Harris

BLAIR MORRIS see Blair Harris

BLAIR MORSE
Skintight / 1981 / CA / M

BLAIR ROGERS
Inside Desiree Cousteau / 1979 / VCX / M

BLAIR SAVALI

Old Guys & Dolls #1 / 1995 / PL / M

BLAIRE see Star Index I

BLAIRE POWERS see Star Index I

BLAIRE RICHMOND see Tamara Long-ley

BLAISE NAGEL see Star Index I

BLAISE PASCAL
Chickie / 1975 / CA / M

BLAKE
HomeGrown Video #462: Motion In The Backfield / 1995 / HOV / M

BLAKE EDWARDS see Blake Palmer

BLAKE HUNTER see Blake Palmer

BLAKE MCDONALD see Star Index I

BLAKE MITCHELL *(Ann Dickerson)*
Humongous enhanced tits, ugly face, large hefty body, 36DD-24-36, 5'5" tall, 125lbs, 35 years old in 1996.

American Fan Club Prowl / 1996 / VT / M • Ass Masters (Leisure) #05 / 1995 / LEI / M • The Babes Of Bonerville / 1995 / VEX / C • Bedroom Bruises / 1996 / NAP / B • Big & Busty Superstars / 1996 / DGD / F • Big Boob Bangeroo #4 / 1995 / TTV / M • Big Knockers #19 / 1995 / TV / M • Big Knockers #22 / 1995 / TV / M • Brian Sparks: Virtually Unreal #1 / 1996 / ALD / M • Crunch Bunch / 1995 / PRE / C • Cyber-Sex Love Junkies / 1996 / BBE / M • Debbie Class Of '95 / 1995 / CC / M • Dirty & Kinky Mature Women #08 / 1996 / C69 / M • Donna Young: Ann & Heather's Oil VIdeo / 1995 / DY / F • Donna Young: Ann & Heather's First Lesbian Video #1 / 1996 / DY / F • Donna Young: Ann & Kathy's First Lesbian Video #1 / 1995 / DY / F • Donna Young: Just Girls / 1995 / DY / F • Dream House / 1995 / XPR / M • Electropussy / 1995 / CC / M • Fortysomething And Still Hot / 1995 / SUF / M • Fresh Faces #11 / 1996 / EVN / M • Fresh Meat (John Leslie) #3 / 1996 / EA / M • FTV #56: Leg Lock Of Love / 1996 / FT / B • FTV #57: Birthday Boxing Bash / 1996 / FT / B • FTV #58: Jab-O-Rama / 1996 / FT / B • FTV #59: Butt Bash Party / 1996 / FT / B • FTV #60: Big Bust Punch Out / 1996 / FT / B • FTV #61: Boss Lady #1 / 1996 / FT / B • FTV #62: Boss Lady #2 / 1996 / FT / B • FTV #66: Squeeze Me Tighter / 1996 / FT / B • FTV #67: Carry I Hurt You / 1996 / FT / B • FTV #68: Topless Boob Torture / 1996 / FT / B • FTV #69: Boxing Boob Bash / 1996 / FT / B • FTV #71: Bully Girl / 1996 / FT / B • FTV #72: Massage Mayhem / 1996 / FT / B • FTV #74: Big Bust Challenge #1 / 1996 / FT / B • FTV #75: Big Bust Challenge #2 / 1996 / FT / B • The Generation Gap / 1996 / LV / M • Hawaiian Buttwatch / 1995 / SUF / M • Here Comes Magoof #2 / 1995 / VC / M • Hollywood Amateurs #19 / 1995 / MID / M • Hot Tight Asses #12 / 1995 / TCK / M • House Of Leather / 1995 / GO / M • House On Paradise Beach / 1996 / VC / M • Interview's Big Boob Bonanza / 1996 / LV / M • Jizz Glazed Goo Guzzlers #1 / 1996 / NIT / C • Kym Wilde's On The Edge #35 / 1996 / RB / B • LA, Citadel Of The Busty Angels / 1995 / NAP / S • Latent Image: Ann Dickerson / 1994 / LAT / F • Lesbian Lust Bust / 1995 / GLI / F • Make Me Over, Baby / 1996 / LOF / M • Marathon Woman / 1996 / CAW / B • The Meatman / 1995 / OUP / M • Mellon Man #04 / 1995 / AVI / M • Mike Hott: #297 Cunt of the Month: Blake / 1995 / MHV / M •

Mike Hott: #384 Three-Sum Sluts #16 / 1996 / MHV / M • Mike Hott: #390 / 1996 / MHV / M • Mike Hott: #392 / 1996 / MHV / M • Ona Zee's Doll House #2 / 1995 / ONA / F • Outlaw Sluts / 1996 / RAS / M • Paradise / 1995 / FD / M • Perverted Stories #03 / 1995 / JMP / M • Perverted Stories #04 / 1995 / JMP / M • Philmore Butts Hawaiian Anal Adventure / 1995 / SUF / M • Philmore Butts Strikes Gold / 1996 / SUF / M • Pizzas, Hot Tubs & Bimbos / 1995 / SUF / M • Playtex / 1996 / GLI / M • Prescription For Lust / 1995 / NIT / M • Profiles #04: Lust Lessons / 1995 / XPR / M • Pussyman Auditions #06 / 1995 / SNA / M • Rear Window / 1996 / NIT / M • Russian Roulette / 1995 / NIT / M • Sex On The Beach Hawaiian Style #1 / 1995 / ULP / M • Sex On The Beach Hawaiian Style #2 / 1995 / ULP / M • Sex On The Beach Hawaiian Style #3 / 1995 / ULP / M • Sex, Truth & Videotape #2 / 1996 / DOC / M • Shaving Mr. One Eye / 1996 / FC / M • Slutsville U.S.A. / 1995 / VMX / M • Snatch Masters #09 / 1995 / LEI / M • Sole Goal / 1996 / PRE / B • Stowaway / 1995 / LE / M • Swat Team / 1995 / PRE / B • Tied & Tickled Classics #12 / 1996 / CS / C • Too Hot / 1996 / LV / M • Trick Shots / 1995 / PV / M • Tripper Stripper / 1995 / VMX / M • Tropical Taboo / 1995 / HO / M • Using Your Assets To Get A Head / 1996 / OUP / F • Video Virgins #23 / 1995 / NS / M • The Voyeur #6 / 1996 / EA / M • Water Wars / 1996 / NAP / B • Whammin' & Jammin' At The Hard Cock Ole / 1996 / GLI / M • What's In It 4 Me / 1995 / TEG / M • Wild Cherries / 1996 / SC / F

BLAKE PALMER *(Blake Edwards, Brian Palmer, Donald Pagen, Skip Stroke, Blake Hunter, Skip Robbins, Skip Layton, Skip Stokey, Blair Higgins)*
Blonde male, going bald in the mid-nineties with a dick that tapers from a point at the end to quite thick where it joins the rest of his body. He has been called "the wedge" because of this phenonomen.

10 Years Of Big Busts #1 / 1989 / BTO / C • 18 Candles / 1989 / LA / M • 2 Baggers / 1994 / *[illegible]* / M • *[illegible]* / 1997 / M / M • 976-STUD / 1989 / LV / M • Addicted To Lust / 1996 / NIT / M • The Adventures Of Dick Black, Black Dick / 1987 / DR / M • After The Lights Go Out / 1989 / VEX / M • All American Girls #2: In Heat / 1983 / CA / M • All For One / 1988 / CIN / M • Amazing Tails #2 / 1987 / CA / M • Anal House Party / 1993 / IP / M • Anal Pandemonium / 1994 / TTV / M • Anal Playground / 1995 / CA / M • Anal Witness #2: No Prisoners / 1996 / LBO / M • Angel's Revenge / 1985 / IN / M • Anna Malle Exposed / 1996 / WV / M • The Arabian Treasure Chest / 1987 / L&W / C • Ateball: Linda & Friends #2 / 1995 / ATE / M • Ateball: Linda's West Coast Talent Search / 1996 / ATE / M • B.Y.O.B. / 1984 / VD / M • Babenet / 1995 / VC / M • Bachelor Party #1 / 1993 / FPI / M • Backdoor To Harley-Wood #1 / 1990 / AFV / M • Backdoor To Hollywood #05 / 1988 / CDI / M • Backing In #3 / 1991 / WV / C • Backing In #6 / 1994 / WV / C • Bang City #7: Carolina's Anal Gang Bang / 1995 / SC / M • The Battle Of The Breast Queens / 1989 / INS / C • Beauties And The Beast / 1990 / AFV / M • Behind Blue Eyes #2 / 1988 / ZA

/ M • Behind The Backdoor #2 / 1989 / EVN / M • The Best Of Blondes / 1986 / VCR / C • Best Of Buttman #2 / 1993 / EA / C • Betty & Juice Possessed / 1995 / CA / M • Between Her Thighs / 1992 / CDI / M • Between My Breasts #02 / 1986 / L&W / S • Between My Breasts #06 / 1989 / BTO / M • Between The Cheeks #2 / 1990 / VC / M • Beyond Reality #3: Stand Erect! / 1996 / EXQ / M • Beyond The Senses / 1986 / AVC / M • Big Bust Babes #04 / 1988 / AFI / M • Big Bust Bangers #1 / 1994 / AMP / M • Big Bust Bangers #2 / 1994 / AMP / M • Big Busty #21 / 1987 / H&S / M • The Big Pink / 1995 / MID / M • The Big Tease #2 / 1990 / VC / M • Big Tit Orgy #01 / 1987 / H&S / M • Big Top Cabaret #1 / 1986 / BTO / M • Black Cobra / 1989 / WV / M • Black Reamers / 1986 / 4P / M • Black Video Virgins #1 / 1996 / NS / M • Blacks Have More Fun / 1985 / AVC / M • Blonde Desire / 1984 / AIR / M • Blonde Fantasy / 1988 / CC / M • Blue Dream Lover / 1985 / TAR / M • Blue Vanities #057 / 1988 / FFL / M • Blue Vanities #058 / 1988 / FFL / M • Blue Vanities #098 / 1988 / FFL / M • Blue Vanities #176 / 1992 / FFL / M • Boobs, Butts And Bloopers #1 / 1990 / HO / M • The Bottom Line / 1995 / NIT / M • Bottoms Up #06 / 1986 / AVC / C • Breaking It #2 / 1989 / GO / M • Breast Of Britain #2 / 1987 / BTO / M • Broadcast Nudes / 1988 / EVN / M • Bunny Bleu: A Gang Bang Fantasy / 1994 / FC / M • Bursting Bras / 1990 / BTO / C • Butt Bandits #4 / 1996 / VD / C • Cajun Heat / 1993 / SC / M • California Cherries / 1987 / EVN / M • Campfire Girls / 1988 / SE / M • Candy Snacker / 1993 / WIV / M • Candy's Custom Car Wash / 1995 / FC / M • Cape Rear / 1992 / WV / M • Career Girls / 1996 / OUP / M • Carolina's D.P. Anal Gangbang / 1996 / FC / M • The Case Of The Mad Tickler / 1988 / ME / M • Casino Of Lust / 1984 / AT / M • The Catwoman / 1988 / VC / M • Caught From Behind #11 / 1989 / HO / M • Chestmates / 1988 / VEX / M • Chills / 1989 / LV / M • China Girl / 1989 / V99 / M • Club DV8 #2 / 1993 / SC / M • Club Head (EVN) #2 / 1989 / EVN / C • Coming Out / 1993 / VD / M • Compulsive Behavior / 1995 / PI / M • Convenience Store Girls / 1986 / VD / M • Cram Session / 1986 / V99 / M • Creamy Cheeks / 1986 / VEX / M • Crocodile Blondee #2 / 1988 / VCX / M • Daddy's Darling Daughters / 1986 / PL / M • Dare You / 1995 / CA / M • The De Renzy Tapes / 1990 / CA / C • Debbie Does Dallas Again / 1994 / AFV / M • Deep Inside Debi Diamond / 1995 / VC / C • Deep Inside Ginger Lynn / 1986 / SE / C • Deep Inside Tracey / 1987 / CDI / C • Deep Throat #5 / 1990 / AR / M • Delicate Matters / 1989 / VEX / M • Depraved Fantasies #4 / 1995 / FPI / M • Desert Fox / 1990 / VD / M • Desert Foxes / 1989 / SE / M • Dial F For Fantasy 1984 / PL / M • Diamond Collection #65 / 1984 / CDI / M • Diamond Collection #70 / 1985 / CDI / M • Diamond For Sale / 1990 / EVN / M • Diamond In The Rough / 1993 / BIA / C • Diary Of A Geisha / 1995 / WV / C • Dick & Jane Look For Pussy In The Park / 1995 / AVI / M • Dirty 30's Cinema: Heather Wayne / 1985 / PV / C • Dirty Looks / 1990 / IN / M • Dirty Tricks #1: Just A Bunch Of Whores / 1995 / EA / M • Dou-

ble Anal Alternatives / 1996 / EL / M • Double Trouble / 1988 / V99 / M • Double Whammy / 1986 / LA / M • Dr Truth's Great Sex / 1986 / VD / M • The Dragon Lady #2: Tales From the Bed / 1992 / WV / M • Dream Lust / 1995 / NIT / M • East Vs West: Battle Of The Gang Bangs / 1994 / TTV / M • Eat At The Blue Fox / 1983 / VC / M • Ebony Humpers #4 / 1988 / VEX / M • Electric Blue: World Nudes Tonight / 1985 / CA / C • The Enchantress / 1990 / VI / M • Enemaced / 1988 / PLV / B • Entangled / 1996 / KLP / M • Erotic Dreams / 1987 / HO / M • Erotic Tales / 1989 / V99 / M • Erotic Therapy / 1987 / CDI / M • The Erotic World Of Candy Shields / 1984 / VCR / C • The Erotic World Of Cody Nicole / 1984 / VCR / C • The Erotic World Of Rene Summers / 1984 / VCR / C • The Erotic World Of Sylvia Benedict (#5) / 1983 / VCR / C • Every Woman Has A Fantasy #1 / 1984 / VC / M • Fade To Black / 1988 / CDI / M • Falcon Head / 1990 / ARG / M • Fantasies Of Alicia / 1995 / VT / M • Fantasies Unltd. / 1985 / CDI / M • Fantasy Club #41: Luscious Lolita / 1984 / WV / M • Fast Girls #2 / 1988 / DIS / M • Fatal Seduction / 1988 / CDI / M • Femme Fatale / 1984 / VIV / M • Femme Fatale / 1993 / SC / M • Filet-O-Breast / 1988 / AVC / M • The Fire Down Below / 1990 / IN / M • Firefoxes / 1985 / PLY / M • Flesh And Boner / 1993 / WV / M • Flesh For Fantasies / 1986 / TAM / M • Flesh Palace / 1995 / LBO / M • Fondle With Care / 1989 / VEX / M • Foot Teasers / 1988 / BIZ / B • For Your Love / 1988 / IN / M • Friday Night Fever / 1989 / LV / M • Friendly Fire / 1996 / EDP / M • Full Metal Bikini / 1988 / PEN / M • Fun In A Bun / 1990 / LV / M • Fun In The Sun / 1988 / EVN / C • The Fury / 1993 / WIV / M • Future Sodom / 1988 / VD / M • The Gang Bang Story / 1993 / IP / M • Gang Bangs #2 / 1989 / EA / M • Gangbang At The O.K. Corral / 1994 / FPI / M • Gazongas #02 / 1988 / VEX / M • Gazongas Galore #1 / 1996 / NIT / C • Ghostest With The Mostest / 1988 / CA / M • The Girl From S.E.X. / 1982 / CA / M • Girls Of The Bamboo Palace / 1989 / VEX / M • Girls Of The Double D #03 / 1988 / CDI / M • Girls Of The Double D #04 / 1989 / CDI / M • Girls Of The Double D #09 / 1989 / CDI / M • Girls Of Treasure Island / 1988 / CV / M • The Godmother #2 / 1988 / VC / M • Golden Globes / 1989 / VEX / M • Gourmet Quickies: Stacey Donovan #706 / 1985 / GO / C • Granny Bangers / 1995 / MET / M • The Great Sex Contest #2 / 1989 / LV / M • GVC: Lost In Lust #134 / 1984 / GO / M • Hardbreak Ridge / 1990 / WV / M • Harlem Candy / 1987 / WET / M • Harry Horndog #28: Fabulous Squirt Queens / 1994 / FPI / M • Harry Horndog #29: Anal Lovers #5 / 1995 / FPI / M • Heartthrobs / 1985 / CA / M • Heidi A / 1985 / PL / M • Hellfire / 1995 / MET / M • Her Every Wish / 1988 / GO / M • Hershe Highway #2 / 1989 / HO / M • Hershe Highway #3 / 1990 / HO / M • Hidden Camera #01 / 1993 / JMP / M • Hidden Camera #20 / 1994 / JMP / M • Holly Does Hollywood #1 / 1985 / VEX / M • Hollywood Amateurs #19 / 1995 / MID / M • Hollywood Temps / 1993 / ZA / M • The Honeymoon: The Bride's Running Behind /

1990 / 4P / M • Hot Blondes / 1988 / VEX / M • Hot Dreams / 1989 / VEX / M • Hot Dreams / 1991 / VEX / M • Hot Licks At The Pussycat Club / 1990 / WV / C • Hot Scalding / 1989 / VC / M • Hot Shorts: Susan Hart / 1986 / VCR / C • Hot Shorts: Sylvia Benedict / 1986 / VCR / C • Hot To Swap / 1988 / VEX / M • Hot Yachts / 1987 / VEX / M • I Dream Of Ginger / 1985 / VI / M • I Want A Divorce / 1993 / ZA / M • I Want To Be Bad / 1984 / CV / M • Inches For Keisha / 1988 / WV / C • Innocent Obsession / 1989 / FC / M • Interracial Anal #03: Black And White All Over / 1995 / AFI / M • Intimate Realities #2 / 1983 / VC / M • Introducing Kascha / 1988 / CDI / M • Jack Hammer / 1987 / ZA / M • Jizz Glazed Goo Guzzlers #1 / 1996 / NIT / C • Jizz Glazed Goo Guzzlers #2 / 1996 / NIT / C • Juggs / 1984 / VCR / M • Just Between Friends / 1988 / VEX / M • Kascha & Friends / 1988 / CIN / M • Keyhole #168: Robo-Cocks / 1989 / KEH / M • L.A. Fantasies / 1990 / WV / C • The Last Temptation Of Kristi / 1988 / ME / M • Late Night For Lovers / 1989 / ME / M • Let's Talk Dirty / 1987 / SE / M • Lingerie / 1983 / CDI / M • Lip Service / 1988 / LV / C • Little Girls Of The Streets / 1984 / CV / M • Loco Motion / 1988 / VSX / C • Loose Lifestyles / 1988 / CA / M • Love Button / 1989 / VD / M • Love Letters / 1991 / VI / M • Love To Mother / 1984 / VIV / M • Lust At The Top / 1985 / CDI / M • Lust Letters / 1988 / CA / M • Lusty Couples (Come To) / cr85 / CHX / M • Lusty Ladies #11 / 1984 / 4P / M • The Luv Bang / 1994 / SC / M • Made In Japan / 1992 / VI / M • The Main Attraction / 1988 / 4P / M • Make My Night / 1985 / CIN / M • Making It Big / 1984 / CV / M • Mandii's Magic / 1988 / CDI / M • Marilyn Chambers' Private Fantasies #2 / 1983 / CA / M • Max Bedroom / 1987 / ZA / M • Maximum Head / 1987 / SE / M • Middle Aged Sex Maniacs / 1995 / SUF / M • Mike Hott: #369 Cum In My Mouth #05 / 1996 / MHV / C • Mike Hott: #375 Girls Who Swallow Cum #05 / 1996 / MHV / C • More Unbelievable Orgies / 1989 / EVN / C • Mrs. Rodger's Neighborhood / 1988 / EVN / C • My Friend, My Lover / 1990 / FIR / M • My Way / 1993 / CA / M • My Wildest Dreams / 1988 / IN / C • Naked Mockey-Rayna / 1996 / EVN / M • Nasty Habits Are Hard To Break / 1986 / 4P / M • Nasty Lovers / 1987 / SE / C • Nasty Newshounds / 1988 / ME / M • Naturally Sweet / 1989 / VEX / M • Naughty Neighbors / 1986 / VEX / M • The Naughty Ninja Girls / 1987 / LA / M • The New Babysitter / 1995 / GO / M • A New Girlfriend / 1991 / XPI / M • New Pussy Hunt #26 / 1996 / LEI / C • Night Moods / 1985 / AVC / M • Nighttime Stories / 1991 / LE / M • Nina's Toys And Boys / 1991 / LV / C • Nothing Personal / 1993 / CA / M • The Nympho Files / 1995 / NIT / M • Older & Bolder In San Francisco / 1996 / TEP / M • One For The Gusher / 1995 / AMP / M • Only The Best #3 / 1990 / CV / C • Oral Majority #01 / 1986 / WV / C • Oral Majority #08 / 1990 / WV / C • Oriental Gang Bang Fantasy / 1994 / FC / M • Oriental Girls In Heat / 1995 / IF / M • Oriental Jade / 1985 / VC / M • Oriental Temptations / 1992 / WV / M • Outlaws / 1993 / SC / M • The Oversexual Tourist / 1989 / VEX / M •

Paradise / 1995 / FD / M • Paris Blues / 1990 / WV / C • Paris Burning / 1989 / CC / M • Party In The Rear / 1989 / LV / M • Passages #1 / 1991 / VI / M • Passion From Behind / 1990 / LV / M • Peep Land / 1992 / FH / M • Penthouse: The Girls Of Penthouse #1 / 1984 / VES / S • The Perfect Brat / 1989 / VI / M • Personal Touch #1 / 1983 / AR / M • Perverted #1: The Babysitters / 1994 / ZA / M • Perverted #2: The Virgins / 1995 / ZA / M • Perverted Stories #04 / 1995 / JMP / M • Pipe Dreams / 1985 / 4P / M • Plan 69 From Outer Space / 1993 / CA / M • Playing The Field / 1990 / VEX / M • Pleasure #4 / 1990 / BTO / M • Pleasure Productions #03 / 1984 / VCR / M • Pleasure Productions #04 / 1984 / VCR / M • Pleasure Productions #06 / 1984 / VCR / M • Pleasure Productions #11 / 1985 / VCR / M • Porn On The 4th Of July / 1990 / IN / M • Power Play (Venus 99) / 1990 / V99 / M • Precious Gems / 1988 / CV / M • Prescription For Lust / 1995 / NIT / M • Pretty As You Feel / 1984 / PV / M • Private Video Magazine #08 / 1994 / OD / M • Profiles #06: Super Model Orgy / 1996 / XPR / M • Profiles #07: Sexworld / 1996 / XPR / M • Prom Girls / 1988 / CA / M • Pussyclips #07 / 1995 / SNA / M • A Rare Starlet / 1987 / ME / M • Raunch #07 / 1993 / CC / M • Raven / 1985 / VCR / M • The Red Hot Roadrunner / 1987 / VD / M • Red Velvet / 1988 / PV / M • Reel Sex #02: Splash Party / 1994 / SPP / M • Ride A Pink Lady / 1986 / SE / M • Rxx For A Gangbang / 1994 / ZA / M • Same Time Every Year / 1981 / VHL / M • The Satisfiers Of Alpha Blue / 1980 / AVC / M • Savage Fury #2 / 1989 / CAY / M • Scandalous / 1989 / CC / M • Scorching Secrets / 1988 / IN / M • Secret Cravings / 1989 / V99 / M • The Seduction Of Lana Shore / 1984 / PL / M • Sensuous Tales / 1984 / VCR / C • Sex Asylum #4 / 1991 / VI / M • Sex Busters / 1984 / PLY / M • The Sex Change Girls / 1987 / 4P / C • Sex In The Great Outdoors / 1987 / SE / C • Sex Lives Of The Rich And Beautiful / 1988 / CA / M • Sexeo / 1985 / PV / M • Sexscape / 1986 / CA / M • The Carnal Fiend / 1984 / LA / M • Sgt. Peckers Lonely Hearts Club Gang Bang / 1995 / AMP / M • Shameless Desire / 1989 / VEX / M • She's A Good Lust Charm / 1987 / LA / C • Shipwrecked / 1991 / VEX / C • The Shocking Truth #1 / 1996 / DWO / M • Showtime / 1996 / VT / M • Six-Nine Love / 1990 / LV / M • Skippy, Jiff & Jam / 1990 / CIA / M • Slumber Party / 1984 / HO / M • Sordid Stories / 1994 / AMP / M • Sore Throat / 1985 / GO / M • Spanish Fly / 1993 / VEX / M • Splash Dance / 1987 / AR / M • Springtime In The Rockies / 1984 / CIN / M • Squirt Squad / 1995 / AMP / M • Stairway To Heaven / 1989 / ME / M • Starbangers #02 / 1993 / BIG / M • Starbangers #03 / 1993 / ZA / M • Starbangers #04 / 1993 / FPI / M • Starbangers #05 / 1993 / FPI / M • Starbangers #10 / 1997 / ZA / M • Stephanie's Outrageous / 1988 / LV / C • Strong Language / 1989 / IN / M • Stud Hunters / 1984 / CA / M • Summer Dreams / 1996 / TEP / M • Sunstroke Beach / 1990 / WV / M • Super Blondes / 1989 / VEX / M • Suze's Centerfolds #4 / 1981 / CA / M • Suze's Centerfolds #7 /

1983 / CA / M • Swedish Erotica #75 / 1994 / CA / M • Sweet Little Things / 1985 / COL / M • Sweet Nothings / 1987 / HO / M • Swinging Shift / 1985 / CDI / M • Switch Hitters #1 / 1987 / IN / G • Taboo #03 / 1983 / IN / M • Tail Taggers #113: Behind The Scenes / 1994 / WV / M • Tail Taggers #123 / 1994 / WV / M • Tail Taggers #124 / 1994 / WV / M • Take The A Train / 1993 / MID / M • Takin' It To The Limit #2 / 1994 / BS / M • Tales Of The Backside / 1985 / VCR / C • A Taste Of Genie / 1986 / 4P / M • A Taste Of Pleasure / 1988 / AVC / M • A Taste Of Stephanie / 1990 / PIN / C • Taste Of The Best #2 / 1988 / PIN / C • Telemates / 1988 / STA / M • Telemates / 1991 / V99 / M • Temperatures Rising / 1986 / VT / M • These Buns For Hire / 1990 / LV / M • This Is Your Sex Life / 1987 / VD / M • Three Men And A Lady / 1988 / EVN / M • Tight Fit #07 / 1994 / GO / M • Tight Fit #12 / 1995 / GO / M • Too Hot To Stop / 1989 / V99 / M • Top Buns / 1986 / HO / M • Top Debs #6: Rear Entry Girls / 1995 / GO / M • Top Heavy / 1988 / VD / M • Tracie Lords / 1984 / CIT / M • Tracy In Heaven (Orig 1985) / 1985 / WV / M • Treacherous / 1995 / VD / M • Tricks Of The Trade / 1988 / CA / M • Tropical Taboo / 1995 / HO / M • Truth And Bare / 1991 / LV / M • Twentysomething #3 / 1989 / VI / M • Venus Of The Nile / 1991 / WV / M • Very Sexy Ballet / 1988 / CA / M • Video Virgins #02 / 1992 / NS / M • Virgin Heat / 1986 / TEM / M • Voluptuous / 1993 / CA / M • Vortex / 1995 / MET / M • The Wacky World Of X-Rated Bloopers / 1989 / GO / M • Welcome To Dallas / 1991 / VI / M • Whiplash / 1996 / DFI / M • Who Shaved Aja? / 1989 / EX / M • The Whole Diamond / 1990 / EVN / M • The Whore / 1989 / CA / M • Wild & Wicked #2 / 1992 / VT / M • Wild In The Wilderness / 1988 / SE / M • Wild Orgies #12 / 1994 / AFI / M • Wild Orgies #14 / 1994 / AFI / M • Wild Orgies #16 / 1995 / AFI / M • Willie Wanker And The Fun Factory / 1994 / FD / M • The Woman Who Loved Men / 1984 / SE / M • Working Girl Gang Bang / 1995 / GLI / M • The World's Biggest Gang Bang #1 / 1995 / FPI / M • WPINK-TV #3 / 1988 / PV / M • X-Rated Bloopers #1 / 1984 / AR / M • The X-Rated OJ Truth... / 1995 / MID / M • X-TV #1 / 1986 / PL / C • The Zebra Club / 1986 / VSE / M

BLAKE SMYTHE see Blake West

BLAKE STERLING
GRG: Busty Beauties / 1994 / GRG / F • GRG: Finger Fucking Females / 1994 / GRG / F • GRG: Kinky Kunts / 1994 / GRG / F • GRG: Office Gang Bang / 1993 / GRG / M

BLAKE STORM
Kitty's Kinky Capers / 1996 / TTV / M

BLAKE WEST (Blake Smythe, Chris Stock, Charles Stark, Charles Stork, Chris McDonald, Chris Blake)
Blake Smythe (**Mamm's The Word**). Chris Stock comes from **Edward Penishands #2**. Charles Stark comes from **Blue Jeans Brat**. Chris McDonald is from **Buttnicks #2**.
America's Raunchiest Home Videos #26: Tiptoe Thru The 2 Lips / 1992 / ZA / M • Between The Cheeks #2 / 1990 / VC / M •

Blue Jeans Brat / 1991 / VI / M • Butt's Motel #5 / 1990 / EX / M • The Buttnicks #2 / 1991 / HIO / M • Catalina: Undercover / 1991 / CIN / M • Cum On Line / 1991 / XPI / M • Deep Inside Centerfold Girls / 1991 / VC / M • Desire / 1990 / VC / M • East L.A. Law / 1991 / WV / M • Edward Penishands #2 / 1991 / VT / M • The Erotic Adventures Of Fanny Annie / 1991 / WV / M • Foxx Hunt / 1991 / GO / M • G Squad / 1990 / SO / G • Gangbang Girl #01 / 1992 / ANA / M • Gangbang Girl #02 / 1992 / ANA / M • Have I Got A Girl For You / 1989 / VEX / M • Headbangers Balls / 1991 / PL / M • Introducing Danielle / 1990 / CDI / M • Lambody / 1990 / CDI / M • Mamm's The Word / 1991 / ZA / M • Personalities / 1991 / PL / M • Possession / 1990 / CIN / M • Princess Of The Night / 1990 / VD / M • Sex Appraisals / 1990 / HO / M • Tailgate Party / 1990 / HO / M • Three's A Crowd / 1990 / HO / M • Twin Peeks / 1990 / DR / M • Untamed Passion / 1991 / VEX / M

BLAKE YOUNG (Kobe Tai)
Oriental, long black hair, medium enhanced tits, lithe body, passable face. Married in November 1996 to Mark Davis. As of 1996 her measurements were 32-22-32, 5'2" tall, 90lbs. Born 1/15/72 in Taipei Taiwan.
Adam & Eve's House Party #2: Bachelor Party / 1996 / VC / M • Asian Pussyman Auditions / 1996 / SNA / M • Dirty Dancers #8 / 1996 / 4P / M • Executions On Butt Row / 1996 / EA / M • Lethal Affairs / 1996 / VI / M • Lotus / 1996 / VI / M • Show & Tell / 1996 / VI / M • Stardust #4 / 1996 / VI / M • Stardust #5 / 1996 / VI / M • Trapped / 1996 / VI / M • Vivid Raw #2 / 1996 / VI / M

BLANCA
Frat House / 1979 / NGV / M • Prague By Night #2 / 1996 / EA / M

BLANCHE DU BROD
Melrose Trannie / 1995 / HEA / G

BLAZE
Cirque Du Sex #1 / 1996 / VT / M • Creme De La Face #11: Cum Plasterers / 1995 / OD / M • Creme De La Face #14: Kiss My Cum / 1996 / OD / M • Hollywood Amateurs #26 / 1995 / MID / M • Hollywood Amateurs #28 / 1996 / MID / M • Intimate Interviews #3 / 1996 / NIT / M • Nookie Professor #2 / 1996 / AVS / M • Nothing Like Nurse Nookie #1 / 1995 / NIT / M • Possessed / 1996 / MET / M • Sex Lessons / 1996 / NIT / M • The Violation Of Felecia / 1995 / JMP / F • Young And Anal #3 / 1995 / JMP / M

BLAZE (ROXANNE) see Roxanne Blaze

BLAZE KRAY
Live Sex Net / 1996 / SPR / M

BLAZE STARR (Fannie Belle Fleming)
Blue Vanities #552 / 1994 / FFL / M • Blue Vanities #556 / 1994 / FFL / M • Buxom Beautease / 19?? / SOW / S • Nature Girl / 1962 / SOW / S

BLONDE AMAZON
Lesbian Love Slave / 1989 / KEE / B

BLONDE DEE
A Is For Asia / 1996 / 4P / M • Lovin' Spoonfuls #5 / 1996 / 4P / C • More Dirty Debutantes #34 / 1994 / 4P / M • More Dirty Debutantes #35 / 1994 / 4P / M • World Famous Dirty Debutantes / 1995 / 4P / S

BLONDE ICE
Dirty Dixie / 1992 / IF / M • One Night Love

Affair / 1991 / IF / M • Party Dolls / 1992 / VEX / M • Rear Entry / 1995 / LEI / M • Southern Accents / 1992 / VEX / M

BLONDEE see Blondi

BLONDI (Blondee, Blondie (Blondi), Blondi Bee, Majorie Miller)

First movie was **Cheerleader Academy** in which her boobs were not enhanced. She later had them expanded to grotesque proportions in a K-Mart job that made them look like cantaloupes. Otherwise her body was very tight and her face was very pretty. She only worked with her then current boyfriend, Tony Montana (what taste!).

The Adultress / 1987 / CA / M • Amber Lynn's Hotline 976 / 1987 / VCR / M • The Beat Goes On / 1987 / VCR / C • Black Sensations / 1987 / VEX / M • Blondes On Fire / 1987 / VCR / C • Blue Lace / 1986 / SE / M • Body Slam / 1987 / 4P / B • The Bottom Line / 1986 / WV / M • The Brazilian Connection / 1988 / CA / M • Breastography, Lesson #1 / 1987 / VCR / M • California Blondes #01 / 1986 / VEX / M • California Blondes #03 / 1991 / VD / C • California Blondes #06 / 1992 / VD / C • Cheerleader Academy / 1986 / PL / M • Coed Oil Wrestling / 1987 / MAI / B • Cream Dreams / 1986 / VEX / M • Creamy Cheeks / 1986 / VEX / M • Cum Blasted Cuties / 1993 / GO / C • The Desk Top Dolls / 1990 / BAD / C • Dirty Blondes / 1986 / CDI / M • Erica Boyer: Non-Stop / 1988 / VD / C • Erotic Dreams / 1987 / HO / M • Flesh In Ecstasy #01: Blondie / 1987 / GO / C • Flesh In Ecstasy #12: Blondie / 1987 / GO / C • The Gentlemen's Club / 1986 / WV / M • The Girls Of Malibu / 1986 / ACV / S • Hard Choices / 1987 / CA / M • Hard Rockin' Babes / 1987 / VD / F • Honkytonk Angels / 1988 / IN / C • Hooters / 1986 / AVC / M • Hot 'n' Nasty / 1989 / XCE / M • Hyapatia Lee's Sexy / 1986 / SE / M • In Search Of The Perfect 10 / 1987 / MAE / S • Invasion Of The Lust Snatchers / 1988 / 4P / M • Jane Bond Meets Octopussy / 1986 / VD / M • Keyhole #167: Ass Eaters / 1989 / KEH / M • Kittens #2 / 1991 / CC / F • The Ladies Room / 1987 / CA / M • Little Shop Of Whores / 1987 / VI / M • Loose Lifestyles / 1988 / CA / M • Love On The Borderline / 1987 / IN / M • Loving Spoonfulls / 1987 / 4P / C • Lucy Has A Ball / 1987 / ME / M • Lucy Makes It Big / 1987 / ME / M • Lust Letters / 1988 / CA / M • Miami Spice #1 / 1987 / CA / M • The Moon Girls / 1990 / ME / C • Naughty Neighbors / 1986 / VEX / M • Night Of The Living Babes / 1987 / MAE / S • Parliament: Blondes Have More Fun / 1989 / PM / C • Parliament: California Blondes #1 / 1987 / PM / F • Parliament: Finger Friggin' #2 / 1988 / PM / F • Party Favors / 1989 / VES / S • Primal Urge / 1992 / VEX / M • Pumping Irene #1 / 1986 / FAN / M • Pumping Irene #2 / 1986 / FAN / M • Reckless Passion / 1986 / ME / M • Sensuous Singles: Keisha / 1987 / VCR / F • Sex Aliens / 1987 / CA / M • Sheets Of San Francisco / 1986 / AVC / M • Space Vixens / 1987 / V99 / M • Spend The Holidays With Barbii / 1987 / CDI / M • Supersluts Of Wrestling / 1986 / VD / M • Swedish Erotica #73 / 1986 / CA / M • Sweet Cheeks / 1987 / VCR / C • Taija's Satin Seduction / 1987 / CDI / M • A Taste Of

Amber / 1988 / PIN / C • Teasin' & Pleasin' / 1988 / LBO / F • Wet And Wild #1 / 1986 / VEX / M • Whatever Turns You On / 1987 / CA / M • X-TV #1 / 1986 / PL / C • XXX Workout / 1987 / VEX / M • [T&A #01 / 1989 / ... / C

BLONDI BEE see Blondi

BLONDIE

A&B AB#296: Blondie Takes It All / 1991 / A&B / M • A&B AB#303: Blondie Is A Whore / 1991 / A&B / M • Blue Vanities #194 / 1993 / FFL / M • Blue Vanities #195 / 1993 / FFL / M • Blue Vanities #504 / 1992 / FFL / M • Blue Vanities #516 / 1992 / FFL / M • Blue Vanities #584 / 1996 / FFL / M • Danielle's Dirty Deeds / 1991 / CC / M • G-Strings / 1984 / COM / M • Homegrown Video #350 / 1991 / HOV / M • Orgies Orgies Orgies / 1994 / WV / M • Private Gold #05: Cape Town #1 / 1996 / OD / M • Private Gold #06: Cape Town #2 / 1996 / OD / M • Video Kixs Magazine #6 / 1983 / GLD / M

BLONDIE (BLONDI) see Blondi

BLONDIE DOLL

Cheatin' Hearts / 1991 / VEX / M • Jewel Of The Orient / 1991 / VEX / M

BLONDINA

Itsy Bitsy Gang Bang / 1996 / HW / M • Somewhere Under The Rainbow #2 / 1995 / HW / M

BLONDINE

Magma: Chateau Extreme / 1995 / MET / M

BLONDY

Anal 247 / 1995 / CC / M

BLOSSOM LEI

Formula 69 / 1984 / JVV / M • Girls On Fire / 1985 / VCX / M • Lip Service / 1987 / BIK / C

BLU (CRAYOLA) see Crayola Blue

BLU-SILK (Katmandu)

Tall Oriental girl with very tiny tits but a nice smiling diposition.

The Best Of Fabulous Flashers / 1996 / DGD / F • Fantasy Flings #02 / 1994 / WP / M • First Time Lesbians #20 / 1994 / JMP / F • Mr. Peepers Amateur Home Videos #94: Calendar Cleavage / 1994 / LBO / M • Northwest Pecker Trek #1 / 1994 / LBO / M • Northwest Pecker Trek #4: Laid In Latte Land / 1994 / LBO / M • Odyssey Triple Play #79: Dildos Dykes & Dicks / 1994 / OD / M

BLUE

Video Virgins #03 / 1993 / NS / M

BLUE BLAKE

Night Walk / 1995 / HIV / G • Our Trespasses / 1996 / AWV / G

BLUE STEEL

Beettlejizum / 1991 / PL / M

BO

AVP #8011: Initiating Shannon / 1990 / AVP / M • Hard Core Beginners #10 / 1995 / LEI / M • Private Places / 1995 / IF / M

BO AUSTIN

Marine Code Of Silence: Don't Ask Don't Tell / 1996 / BHE / G

BO BRIDGET

Wet Dreams / 1980 / WWV / M

BO DEREK (Kathleen Collins, Mary Kathleen Collin, Cathleen Collins)

Cathleen Collins is from **Fantasies (1973)**. Her maiden name is Mary Kathleen Collins.

10 / 1979 / WAR / S • Bolero / 1984 / LIV / S • Fantasies / 1973 / CBS / S • Woman Of

Desire / 1993 / VMA / S

BO GARRET

Who Shaved Cassi Nova? / 1989 / EX / M

BO HALLDOFF

The Second Coming Of Eva / 1974 / ALP / M

BO HANON

Pleasures Of A Woman / 1983 / CA / M

BO REGAN

American Pie / 1980 / SE / M

BO ROBERTS

Forbidden Dreams / 1984 / BIZ / G • Twice A Virgin / 1984 / PL / G

BO STALLION

All-Star Softball Game / 1995 / SAB / G • Driven Home / 1995 / CSP / G • Man Made Pussy / 1994 / HEA / G • Mr. Blue / 1996 / JSP / G

BO SUMMERS

Bi-Ology: The Making Of Mr Right / 1992 / CAT / G • Remembering Times Gone Bi / 1995 / AWV / G

BO THORPE

Stick Pussy / 1992 / HSV / G

BOB

A&B AB#013: Interracial Trio / 1990 / A&B / M • Abused / 1996 / ZA / M • AVP #7014: Dealin' With Dicks / 1991 / AVP / M • AVP #9116: And Gina Makes Three / 1991 / AVP / M • Big Murray's New-Cummers #02: Las Vegas Swingers / 1992 / FD / M • Bound Fantasies / 1994 / VIG / B • Hardcore: The Films Of Richard Kern #1 / 1991 / FTV / M • Homegrown Video #418: Looks As Good As It Feels / 1994 / HOV / M • HomeGrown Video #435: Seasoned To Perfection / 1994 / HOV / M • Mistress Cleopatra Rules / 1993 / NEP / B

BOB BAKER

3 Mistresses Of The Mansion / 1994 / STM / B • Dragon Lady's Domination Technique / 1995 / STM / B • Lauren's Adventures In Bondageland #1: Mistress Lauren / 1994 / STM / C • Lauren's Adventures In Bondageland #2: Mistress Shane / 1994 / STM / C • Masked Mistress / 1994 / STM / B • Oriental Dominatrix / 1995 / STM / B • Produce Or Suffer / 1994 / STM / B • Sentence Of Pain / 1994 / STM / B • A Touch Of Danger / 1994 / STM / B • Women Who Control The Family Jewels #4 / 1995 / STM / B

BOB BALHATCHET

The Bite / 1975 / SVE / M

BOB BERNHARDING

Easy / 1978 / CV / M

BOB BLACK

The Girls In The Band / 1976 / SVE / M

BOB BLOUNT

L.A. Tool & Die / 1979 / TMX / G

BOB BLUECLOUD

Once Upon A Time/Cave Woman / 1978 / VI / M

BOB BONER

Great Grandma Gets Her Cookies / 1995 / FC / M

BOB CABEZA GRANDE

The Bite / 1975 / SVE / M

BOB CARR

China Girl / 1974 / SE / M

BOB CECCHINI

Resurrection Of Eve / 1973 / MIT / M

BOB CHINN

Exhausted / 1981 / CA / C • The History Of Pornography / 1970 / SOW / M • Pizza Girls (We Deliver) / 1978 / VCX / M • Pri-

vate Thighs / 1987 / AVC / C
BOB CRAWFORD
The Starmaker / 1982 / VC / M
BOB CRESSE *(Robert W. Cresse, R.W. Cresse)*
Late sixties / early seventies B movie actor and an associate of Ed Wood Jr.
Bummer! / 1972 / SOW / S • The Erotic Adventures Of Zorro / 1969 / SOW / S • The Forbidden / 1966 / SOW / S • House On Bare Mountain / 1962 / SOW / S • Love Camp 7 / 1968 / SOW / S • The Pick-Up / 1968 / BOC / S • Surftide 77 / 1962 / SOW / S
BOB CRYSTON
Down Bi Law / 1992 / CAT / G
BOB DAMON
L.A. Tool & Die / 1979 / TMX / G
BOB DAWG
Intervidnet #1: Special Delivery / 1994 / IVN / M • Intervidnet #2: French Made / 1994 / IVN / M
BOB DIXON
Dreams Are Forever / cr72 / AVC / M
BOB FORTE
Peepholes / 1982 / AVC / M
BOB FOSTER
The Divorce / 1986 / VC / G • Professor Probe And The Spirit Of Sex / 1986 / ADU / M
BOB FRENCH
Eat At Dave's #5 / 1996 / SP / M
BOB GLEN
Sissy's Hot Summer / 1979 / CA / M
BOB HARREL
Girls Next Door / 1995 / SHL / B
BOB J.
Man Training / 1993 / RB / B
BOB JACKSON
Conflict Of Interest / 1994 / FST / G
BOB KIRK
Jane Bond And The Girl From AUNTIE / 1979 / VCI / M
BOB KISH
Bucky Beaver's XXX Dragon Art Theatre Double Feature #11 / 1996 / SOW / M • San Francisco Ball / 1971 / SOW / S
BOB KNIGHT
Rearing Rachel / 1990 / 7A / M
BOB LANCE
██████████ ████ / ██ / M
BOB LASH
Lollipop Palace / 1973 / VCX / M
BOB LONG
Interview With A Tramp / 1996 / SP / M
BOB LOWE
Bi & Large / 1994 / STA / G • Bi-Inferno / 1992 / VEX / G • Easy Way Out / 1989 / OD / M • The Eyes Of A Stranger / 1992 / CDI / G • Fire & Ice / 1992 / CDI / G • House Of Spartacus #1 / 1993 / IF / M • Masked Ball / 1992 / IF / M • More Than A Woman / 1992 / CDI / G • Shaved She-Males / 1992 / STA / G • Switch Hitters #8 / 1995 / IN / G • Switch Hitters #9 / 1995 / IN / G • Tonight's The Night / 1992 / V99 / M
BOB MACINTOSH
Foxy Boxing / 1982 / AVC / M
BOB MAGNUM
Anal Princess #2 / 1996 / VC / M • Exotic Car Models #1 / 1996 / IN0 / F • Male Order Brides / 1996 / RAS / M • Microslut / 1996 / TTV / M • N.Y. Video Magazine #01 / 1994 / OUP / M • Nina Hartley's Guide To Swinging / 1996 / A&E / M
BOB MARSHALL

Quality Control / 1996 / VTF / B
BOB MARTIN
Throbbin' Hood / 1987 / VD / M
BOB MIGLIANO
Carnal Haven / 1976 / SVE / M • One Of A Kind / 1976 / SVE / M
BOB MORRIS
Resurrection Of Eve / 1973 / MIT / M
BOB NIMITZ
Jezebel / 1979 / CV / M
BOB ONIT
The Adventures of Marilyn Ohno / 1996 / GLI / M
BOB ORCHS
Sweet Humility / 1995 / STM / B • Toe Tales #29 / 1995 / GOT / B
BOB PHILLIPS
Deep Throat #1 / 1972 / AR / M
BOB PRIESTLY
Blonde In Black Silk / 1979 / QX / M • The Good Girls Of Godiva High / 1979 / VCX / M
BOB ROBBINS
Bucky Beaver's XXX Dragon Art Theatre Double Feature #09 / 1996 / SOW / M • Up In Flames / 1973 / SOW / M
BOB ROBERTS
Erotic Tattooing And Piercing #1 / 1986 / FLV / M
BOB ROGERS
Eat At Dave's #7 / 1996 / SP / M • Jingle Balls / 1996 / EVN / M
BOB ROSE
3 A.M. / 1975 / ALP / M • The Goodbye Girls / 1979 / CDI / M • Little Me & Marla Strangelove / 1979 / ALP / M • One Last Score / 1978 / CDI / M • Oriental Treatment #1 / 1978 / AR / M • Star Of The Orient / 1978 / VIP / M
BOB RUSSELL
The Erotic World Of Vanessa #1 / 1983 / VCR / C • The Erotic World Of Vanessa #2 / 1984 / VCR / C
BOB RUSSO
Bon Appetite / 1985 / TGA / C • The Erotic World Of Seka / 1983 / VCR / C • Showgirl #14: Kitty Shane's Fantasies / 1983 / VCR / M • Torch Of Desire / 1983 / REG / M
BOB SCOTT
The █████████ ████ █ █████ █ ██ / M
BOB SEXTON
Living On The Edge / 1997 / DWO / M
BOB SKID
Amateur Night / 1988 / CC / M
BOB SPIREY
Beyond The Valley Of The Ultra Milkmaids / 1984 / 4P / F
BOB ST CLAIR
Cry Rape / 1975 / ASR / M
BOB STEIN
Sex Resort / 1986 / 4P / M
BOB STONE
Harry Horndog #10: Love Puppies #1 / 1992 / ZA / M • Spermacus / 1993 / PI / M
BOB SUMNER
In Love / 1983 / VC / M
BOB TALMADGE
Old Guys & Dolls #1 / 1995 / PL / M
BOB TURNER
Flash / 1980 / CA / M
BOB TYLER *see* **Rob Tyler**
BOB VERNA
Midsummer Love Story / 1993 / WV / M • Sex Wish / 1992 / WV / M • Taxi Girls #3: Killer On The Loose / 1993 / MED / M
BOB WALTERS *see* **Harry Reems**

BOB WHITE
The Little French Maid / 1981 / VCX / M
BOB WILMA
Brown Sugar / 1984 / VC / M
BOB WOLF *see* **Lawrence T. Cole**
BOBBI
Blue Vanities #129 / 1990 / FFL / M
BOBBI BOOBES
The Beauty Pageant / 1981 / AVC / M
BOBBI BRANDT
Bondage Asylum / 1995 / LON / B • Domestic Discipline / 1995 / HAC / B • Fetish Finishing School / 1995 / HOM / B • Lessons In Bondage / 1995 / HOM / B • Runaway Slaves / 1995 / HOM / B • A Touch Of Leather / 1994 / BS / B • A World Of Hurt / 1994 / BS / B
BOBBI HALL
Blue Vanities #576 / 1995 / FFL / M
BOBBI JACKSON *see* **Tara Aire**
BOBBI LEE *(Bobbie Lee, Alicia Lele, Alicia Lee)*
Ugly fat blonde in the style of Samantha Strong.
Ambushed / 1990 / SE / M • Animal Instincts / 1991 / VEX / M • Breast Wishes #04 / 1991 / LBO / M • Dreams Cum True / 1990 / HO / M • Female Persuasion / 1990 / SO / F • Incorrigible / 1996 / MET / M • Precious Peaks / 1990 / ZA / M • Rainwoman #04 / 1990 / CC / M • Unzipped / 1991 / WV / M
BOBBI SOXX
Blonde, flat ass, enhanced medium tits, marginal face, womanly body.
Aja / 1988 / PL / M • America's Raunchiest Home Videos #15: Outrageous Reaming / 1992 / ZA / M • Big Bust Babes #04 / 1988 / AFI / M • Buffy Malibu's Totally Nasty All-Girl Home Videos #01 / 1992 / ANA / F • Cab-O-Lay / 1988 / PL / M • Fantasy Girls / 1988 / CA / M • Girls Of The Double D #03 / 1988 / CDI / M • Home Bodies / 1988 / VEX / M • Leather For Lovers #1 / 1992 / LFL / M • Midnight Fantasies / 1989 / VEX / M • Miss Adventures / 1989 / VEX / M • On The Make / 1988 / V99 / M • Only In Your Dreams / 1988 / VEX / M • Overexposed / 1988 / VEX / M • Playing WITH A Full Dick / 1988 / PL / M • Reflections Of Innocence / 1988 / SEX / M • Reflections Of Innocence / 1991 / VEX / C • Surfside Sex / 1988 / CA / M • Turn Up The Heat / 1988 / SEX / M • Turn Up The Heat / 1991 / VEX / C • Wild In The Woods / 1988 / VEX / M
BOBBI SOXX (1995)
Catching Snapper / 1995 / XCI / M • Fresh Faces #09 / 1996 / EVN / M • Mike Hott: #310 Cunt Of The Month: Bobbi Soxx / 1995 / MHV / M • Mike Hott: #314 Cum In My Cunt #05 / 1995 / MHV / M • My First Time #1 / 1995 / NS / M • Nasty Newcummers #11 / 1995 / MET / M
BOBBI SOXX (HOLLY W) *see* **Holly White**
BOBBIE
At Home With Stan And Bobbie / 1996 / SHL / B • Blue Vanities #521 / 1993 / FFL / M • Blue Vanities #539 / 1993 / FFL / M • Hot Body Competition: Lusty Lingerie Contest / 1996 / CG / F
BOBBIE BLAKE
Dirty Tricks / 1986 / 4P / M • Double Whammy / 1986 / LA / M • In Search Of The Wild Beaver / 1986 / DR / M

BOBBIE BURNS
Centerfold Fever / 1981 / VXP / M • Inside Seka / 1980 / VXP / M • Manhattan Mistress / 1980 / VBM / M • The Starmaker / 1982 / VC / M

BOBBIE BURTON
A Scent Of Heather / 1981 / VXP / M

BOBBIE HALL
Auditions / 1978 / MEA / S • Blue Vanities #250 / 1996 / FFL / M • John Holmes And The All-Star Sex Queens / 1984 / AMB / M • Venture Into The Bizarre / cr78 / VHL / M

BOBBIE JACKSON *see* **Tara Aire**

BOBBIE LEE *see* **Bobbi Lee**

BOBBIE LILLY
Nina Hartley's Professional Amateur Tournament #2 / 1990 / BKD / M

BOBBIE LONG
Best Of Bruce Seven #1 / 1990 / BIZ / C

BOBBY
Amateur Night #02 / 1990 / HME / M • Big Murray's New-Cummers #02: Las Vegas Swingers / 1992 / FD / M • Bizarre Mistress Series: Mistress Jacqueline / 1992 / BIZ / C • Blue Vanities #500 / 1992 / FFL / M • Blue Vanities #511 / 1992 / FFL / M • Double D Dykes #08 / 1993 / GO / F • Satisfaction Guaranteed / 1972 / AXV / M • Up And Cummers #06 / 1993 / 4P / M

BOBBY ASTOR
Hong Kong Hookers / 1984 / AMB / M

BOBBY ASTYR
The Affairs Of Janice / 1975 / ALP / M • Afternoon Delights / 1981 / CA / M • American Babylon / 1985 / PV / M • And Four To Go / cr70 / REG / M • Angie, Undercover Cop / 1980 / MSI / M • Babylon Gold / 1983 / COM / C • Babylon Pink #1 / 1979 / COM / M • Backdoor Girls / 1983 / VCR / C • Barbara Broadcast / 1977 / VC / M • Betty Blue (X) / 19?? / BL / M • Black, White & Red All Over / 1984 / EXF / C • Blonde In Black Silk / 1979 / QX / M • Blonde Velvet / 1976 / COL / M • Blue Ecstasy / 1980 / CA / M • Breaker Beauties / 1977 / VHL / M • Bunny's Office Fantasies / 1984 / VC / M • Burlexxx / 1984 / VC / M • Candi Girl / 1979 / PVX / M • Candy Stripers #2 / 1985 / AR / M • Captain Lust And The Amorous Contessa / 1977 / IHV / M • Centerfold Fever / 1981 / VXP / M • Cherry Hustlers / 1977 / VEN / M • Chorus Call / 1978 / TVX / M • Come To Me / cr80 / AIR / C • Confessions Of Seka / 1981 / SAT / M • Corruption / 1983 / VC / M • Dark Passions / 1984 / VCR / C • Decendance Of Grace / 1977 / CA / M • Devil In Miss Jones #2 / 1983 / VC / M • Dinner With Samantha / 1983 / PTV / M • Dirty Looks / 1982 / VC / C • The Double Exposure Of Holly / 1977 / TVX / M • Double Your Pleasure / 1978 / CV / M • Dr Love And His House Of Perversions / 1978 / VC / M • Dracula Exotica / 1980 / TVX / M • Ecstasy In Blue / 1976 / ALP / M • Electric Blue: World Nudes Tonight / 1985 / CA / C • Erotic Fantasies #2 / 1983 / CV / C • Executive Secretary / 1975 / CA / M • Expose Me, Lovely / 1976 / QX / M • Fantasy Club Of America / 1980 / BL / M • Feelings / 1977 / VC / M • For Richer, For Poorer / 1979 / CXV / M • Foxtrot / 1982 / COM / M • French Classmates / 1977 / PVI / M • French Shampoo / 1978 / VXP / M • French Teen / 1977 / CV / M • A Girl's Best Friend / 1981 / QX / M • Goodbye My Love

/ 1980 / CA / M • GVC: Strange Family / 1977 / GO / M • Her Name Was Lisa / 1979 / VC / M • Honeymoon Haven / 1977 / QX / M • Honeypie / 1975 / VC / M • Honeysuckle Rose / 1979 / CA / M • Hot Child In The City / 1979 / PVX / M • Hypersexuals / 1984 / VC / M • Inside Little Oral Annie / 1984 / VXP / M • Intensive Care / 1974 / BL / M • It Happened In Hollywood / 1973 / WWV / M • Joint Venture / 1977 / ELV / M • Limited Edition #01 / 1979 / AVC • Limited Edition #11 / 1980 / AVC / M • Liquid A$$ets / 1982 / CA / M • Little Oral Annie Takes Manhattan / 1985 / VXP / M • The Love Syndrome / 1978 / CV / M • Love-In Arrangement / 1981 / VXP / M • Love-In Maid / cr72 / CDC / M • Mascara / 1982 / CA / M • Midnight Blue #1 / 1980 / VXP / M • More / 1973 / BL / M • New York Babes / 1979 / AR / M • October Silk / 1980 / COM / M • Odyssey / 1977 / VC / M • Once Upon A Secretary / 1983 / GO / M • Only The Very Best On Film / 1992 / VC / C • Oriental Blue / 1975 / ALP / M • Outlaw Ladies #1 / 1981 / VC / M • Painful Desires / 19?? / BL / B • Peepholes / 1982 / AVC / M • People / 1978 / QX / M • The Pitfalls Of Bunny / cr76 / SVE / M • Platinum Paradise / 1980 / COM / M • The Playgirl / 1982 / CA / M • Please Me! / cr86 / LIM / M • The Pleasure Palace / 1978 / CV / M • Princess Seka / 1980 / VC / M • Pussycat Galore / 1984 / VC / M • Roommates / 1982 / VXP / M • Satan Was A Lady / 1977 / ALP / M • Schoolgirl's Reunion / 1975 / VHL / M • Secret Dreams Of Mona Q / 1977 / AR / M • The Seduction Of Cindy / 1980 / VC / M • Seka Is Tara / 1981 / VC / M • Sex Spa USA / 1984 / VC / M • Sharon / 1977 / AR / M • Sherlick Holmes / cr75 / SVE / M • Silky / 1980 / VXP / M • Sizzle / 1979 / QX / M • Small Change / 1978 / CDC / M • The Story Of Eloise / 1976 / SVE / M • Sue Prentiss, R.N. / cr76 / CDC / M • Swap / 19?? / ... / M • Teenage Cousins / cr76 / SOW / M • Teenage Housewife / 1976 / BL / M • Teenage Runaways / 1977 / WWV / M • That Lady From Rio / 1976 / VXP / M • That's Erotic / 1979 / CV / C • This Lady Is A Tramp / 1980 / CV / M • Thrilling Drilling / 1974 / SVE / M • Through The Looking Glass / 1976 / ALP / M • Thunderbuns / 1976 / VCX / C • Tigresses...And Other Man-Eaters / 1979 / VXP / M • Times Square Comes Alive / 1984 / VC / M • Too Hot To Handle / 1975 / CDC / M • Too Many Pieces / 1975 / LA / M • Too Young To Care / cr73 / BOC / M • Undercovers / 1982 / CA / M • Vanessa's Bed Of Pleasure / 1983 / SVE / M • VCA Previews #2 / 1988 / VC / C • The Vixens Of Kung Fu: A Tale Of Yin Yang / 1975 / VC / M • Way Down Deep / cr78 / PYR / M • When A Woman Calls / 1975 / VXP / M • Women In Love / 1980 / CA / M • The World Of Henry Paris / 1981 / VC / C • [Fuck Me, Suck Me, Eat Me / 1990 / ... / M

BOBBY BLAKE
Goldilocks And The 3 Bi Bears / 1997 / TTV / G

BOBBY BRIGANIE
Seka Is Tara / 1981 / VC / M

BOBBY BROWN
Frat Girls / 1993 / VC / M • Red Hot Coeds / 1993 / VIM / M • Uncle Roy's Amateur Home Video #07 / 1992 / VIM / M

BOBBY BULLOCK *see* **Robert Bullock**

BOBBY CARDY
Bodies By Jackie / 1985 / IVP / M

BOBBY CORDOVA
The Rod Garetto Story / 1995 / FC / C

BOBBY DARLIN
Sensuous Flygirls / cr72 / VHL / M

BOBBY DEE *see* **Robbie Dee**

BOBBY FRIEDMAN
Rampaging Nurses / 1971 / MIT / M

BOBBY GOLDEN
Debbie Does Dallas #2 / 1980 / VC / M

BOBBY HATTON
The Erotic World Of Angel Cash / 1983 / VXP / M

BOBBY HOLLANDER
Director who was hospitalized for lung cancer in 1994. Was married to (and may still be) Gloria Leonard.

All About Gloria Leonard / 1978 / VXP / M • Bloopers #2 / 1991 / GO / C • Bobby Hollander's Maneaters #05 / 1993 / SFP / M • Bobby Hollander's Maneaters #09 / 1993 / SFP / M • Bobby Hollander's Rookie Nookie #02 / 1993 / SFP / M • Bubble Butts #07 / 1992 / LBO / M • Centerfold Celebrities #1 / 1982 / VC / M • Centerfold Celebrities #2 / 1983 / VC / M • Centerfold Celebrities #3 / 1983 / VC / M • Centerfold Celebrities #4 / 1983 / VC / M • Centerfold Celebrities #5 / 1983 / VC / M • Centerfold Celebrities '94 #1 / 1994 / SFP / M • Centerfold Celebrities '94 #2 / 1994 / SFP / M • Chorus Call / 1978 / TVX / M • The Girls From Hootersville #04 / 1993 / SFP / M • Growing Up / 1990 / GO / M • GVC: Paper Dolls #117 / 1983 / GO / F • GVC: The Therapist #101 / 1986 / GO / M • High Heel Harlots #02 / 1993 / SFP / M • Hollywood Legs / 1996 / NIT / M • How To Make A Model #02: Got Her In Bed / 1993 / QUA / M • Hustler Honeys #1 / 1988 / VC / S • Hustler Honeys #2 / 1988 / VC / S • Hustler Honeys #3 / 1988 / VC / S • Hustler Honeys #4 / 1988 / VC / S • Intimate Desires / 1978 / VEP / M • Million Dollar Buns / 1996 / MYS / M • New York Babes / 1979 / AR / M • Ninja Cheerleaders / 1990 / GO / M • Personal Touch #1 / 1983 / AR / M • Personal Touch #2 / 1983 / AR / M • Personal Touch #3 / 1983 / AR / M • Personal Touch #4 / 1989 / AR / M • Shauna Grant: The Early Years / 1988 / PV / C • Used And Abused #2 / 1994 / SFP / M • Vow Of Passion / 1991 / VI / M • The Wacky World Of X-Rated Bloopers / 1989 / GO / M • X-Rated Bloopers #1 / 1984 / AR / M

BOBBY HUNTER
Anal Maniacs #5 / 1996 / WP / M • Busted-D-D In Las Vegas / 1996 / LV / M • Dilton: Dilton De002 / 1996 / DIL / F • Dirty Bob's #25: Porn Never Sleeps! / 1996 / FLP / S • Dirty Dave's #4 / 1996 / XPR / M • Southern Belles #7 / 1996 / XPR / M • Western Whores Hotel / 1996 / VG0 / M • Young And Anal #4 / 1996 / JMP / M

BOBBY JACKSON *see* **Tara Aire**

BOBBY JAMES
New Girls In Town #1 / 1990 / CC / M

BOBBY JO
Mike Hott: #122 Bobby Jo And Shelly / 1990 / MHV / F • Stevi's: Bobby Jo's Raised Skirt / 1996 / SSV / F

BOBBY JO TOWNSHEND
Creme De La Face #03 / 1994 / OD / M

BOBBY KASBY *see* **Bobby Kassner**

BOBBY KASSNER *(Robby Kasby)*
Mystique / 1979 / CA / M
BOBBY LAND
The Story of Bobby / cr80 / BIZ / B
BOBBY LASNER
Campus Girl / 1972 / VXP / M
BOBBY LEE
Up And Cummers #37 / 1996 / 4P / M
BOBBY LILLY
Positively Pagan #04 / 1991 / ATA / M
BOBBY LONDON
Assumed Innocence / 1990 / AR / M •
More Dirty Debutantes #03 / 1990 / 4P / M
• Nasty Jack's Homemade Vid. #14 / 1990
/ CDI / M • Strangers When We Meet /
1990 / VCR / M
BOBBY MARTIN
Extreme Heat / 1987 / ME / M
BOBBY MILNE
Secrets Of A Willing Wife / 1979 / VXP / M
BOBBY MOORE
Bedroom Bedlam / 1973 / VHL / M
BOBBY NEUWAVE *see* **Mark Kernes**
BOBBY NEWWAVE *see* **Mark Kernes**
BOBBY PARISI
Beyond The Blue / cr78 / SVE / M
BOBBY REED
Downstairs, Upstairs / 1980 / SE / M • Fox-
holes / 1983 / SE / M
BOBBY RODEO
A Dirty Western #2: Smoking Guns / 1994
/ CV / M
BOBBY SOCCIE
Deep Inside Annie Sprinkle / 1981 / VXP /
M • The Erotic World Of Angel Cash / 1983
/ VXP / M
BOBBY SOX (MALE)
Pai Gow Video #06: New Wave Orientals /
1994 / EVN / M
BOBBY SPECTOR *(Bill Spector, Bill Lan-
dis)*
69th Street Vice / 1984 / VC / M • Black
Flesh / 1986 / LA / M • Black Licorice /
1985 / CDI / M • Bordello...House Of The
Rising Sun / 1985 / SE / M • Chocolate
Bon-Bons / 1985 / PL / M • Cravings /
1987 / VC / M • Erotic Moments / 1985 /
CDI / C • Fannie's Fantail / 1985 / VC / M •
Flash Pants / 1983 / VC / M • Hot Lips /
1984 / VC / M • Krazy 4 You / 1987 / 4P /
M • Mouth & Groans / 1987 / 4P / M •
Mouth To Mouth / 1986 / CC / M • Over-
sexed / 1986 / VXP / M • Parted Lips /
1986 / QX / M • Pink Clam / 1986 / RLV /
M • Return To Alpha Blue / 1984 / AVC / M
• Seven Minutes In Heaven / 1986 / VXP /
M • Sex Crimes 2084 / 1985 / SE / M •
Times Square Comes Alive / 1984 / VC / M
• Ultrasex / 1987 / VC / M • Vas-O-Line
Alley / 1985 / VC / M • Wrecked 'em / 1985
/ CC / M
BOBBY SUE *see* **Shelby Stevens**
BOBBY SUNDERLAND
Freedom Of Choice / 1984 / VHL / M
BOBBY TAYLOR
House Of Green Desire / cr78 / CPL / M
BOBBY THICKE
Mocha Magic / 1992 / FH / M
BOBBY VITALE
1-900-FUCK #3 / 1995 / SO / M • Anal An-
archy / 1995 / VC / M • Anal Aristocrat /
1995 / KWP / M • Anal Chiropractor / 1995
/ PEP / M • Anal Dynomite / 1995 / ROB /
M • Anal Island #1 / 1996 / VC / M • Anal
Island #2 / 1996 / VC / M • Anal Plaything
#2 / 1995 / ROB / M • Anal Princess #1 /

1996 / VC / M • Anal Princess #2 / 1996 /
VC / M • Anal Talisman / 1996 / ZA / M •
Anal Webb / 1995 / ZA / M • Babe Watch
#3 / 1995 / SC / M • Babe Watch #4 / 1995
/ SC / M • Backhand / 1995 / SC / M • Bad-
girls #5: Maximum Babes / 1995 / VI / M •
Badgirls #6: Ridin' Into Town / 1995 / VI /
M • Bang City #5: Lennox's Anal Gang
Bang / 1995 / SC / M • Beeping Miss Buffy
/ 1995 / CDI / M • Betty & Juice Possessed
/ 1995 / CA / M • Blade / 1996 / MID / M •
Bloopers & Boners / 1996 / VI / M • Bobby
Sox / 1996 / VI / S • Body Language /
1995 / VI / M • Borderline (Vivid) / 1995 /
VI / M • Born Bad / 1996 / WAV / M •
Breastman's Bikini Pool Party / 1995 /
EVN / M • The Butt Sisters Do Chicago /
1995 / MID / M • The Butt Sisters Do
Philadelphia / 1995 / MID / M • Car Wash
Angels / 1995 / VC / M • Centerfold / 1995
/ SC / M • Chasey Loves Rocco / 1996 / VI
/ M • Cheap Shot / 1995 / WAV / M • Club
Kiss / 1995 / ONA / M • Cybersex / 1996 /
WAV / M • Deep Inside Debi Diamond /
1995 / VC / C • Deep Inside Kaitlyn Ashley
/ 1995 / VC / C • Diamond In The Raw /
1996 / XCI / M • Dirty Tricks #1: Just A
Bunch Of Whores / 1995 / EA / M • Dream
Butt / 1995 / VMX / M • Electropussy /
1995 / CC / M • The End / 1995 / VI / M •
Erotic Visions / 1995 / ULI / M • Expose
Me Again / 1996 / CV / M • Fashion Plate /
1995 / WAV / M • Fast Forward / 1995 / CA
/ M • Foreign Tongues #1: Going Down /
1995 / VI / M • French Vanilla / 1994 / HW /
M • Gang Bang Bitches #09 / 1995 / PP /
M • Gangbang Girl #16 / 1995 / ANA / M •
Gangbang Girl #17 / 1995 / ANA / M •
Ghost Town / 1995 / WAV / M • A Girl Like
You / 1995 / LE / M • The Girl With The
Heart-Shaped Tattoo / 1995 / WAV / M •
Hard Core Beginners #02 / 1995 / LEI / M •
Hard Core Beginners #10 / 1995 / LEI / M •
Hard Evidence / 1996 / WP / M • Hard
Feelings / 1995 / VI / M • Hawaii / 1995 /
VI / M • Head To Head / 1996 / VI / M •
Head Trip / 1995 / CV / M • Heatseekers /
1996 / PE / M • The Heist / 1996 / WAV / M
• Hornet's Nest / 1996 / ONA / M • House
Of Leather / 1995 / CC / M • House On
Paradise Beach / 1995 / VC / M • I Want It
All / 1995 / WAV / M • Illicit Entry / 1995 /
WAV / M • Interview With A Milkman / 1996
/ VI / M • Interview With A Vibrator / 1996 /
WAV / M • Interview: Doin' The Butt / 1995
/ LV / M • Introducing Alexis / 1996 / VI / M
• Jenna Loves Rocco / 1996 / WAV / M •
Jenteal Loves Rocco / 1996 / VI / M • Last
Tango In Paradise / 1995 / ERA / M • Lay-
over / 1994 / VI / M • Lethal Affairs / 1996 /
VI / M • Lust Runner / 1995 / VC / M •
Made For A Gangbang / 1995 / ZA / M •
Man Killer / 1996 / SC / M • Masque / 1995
/ VC / M • Mutual Consent / 1995 / VC / M
• My Wildest Date / 1995 / HO / M • Naked
Scandal #1 / 1995 / SPI / M • Naked Scan-
dal #2 / 1996 / SPI / M • The Naked Truth /
1995 / VI / M • Nasty Nymphos #12 / 1996
/ ANA / M • Nasty Nymphos #13 / 1996 /
ANA / M • Nasty Nymphos #14 / 1996 /
ANA / M • The New Butt Hunt #12 / 1995 /
LEI / C • New Pussy Hunt #25 / 1996 / LEI
/ C • Night Nurses / 1995 / WAV / M • Night
Play / 1995 / WAV / M • The Night Shift /
1995 / LE / M • Nightclub / 1996 / SC / M •
Nylon / 1995 / VI / M • The Panty Parlor /

1996 / VIM / M • Party House / 1995 / WAV
/ M • Passion / 1996 / SC / M • The Pawn
Shop / 1996 / MID / M • Philmore Butts
Meets The Freak / 1995 / SUF / M • Photo
Play / 1995 / VI / M • Pizzas, Hot Tubs &
Bimbos / 1995 / SUF / M • Pleasureland /
1996 / VI / M • Power Of The Pussy / 1995
/ LEI / M • Primal Instinct / 1996 / SNA / M
• Pristine #2 / 1996 / CA / M • Pussyclips
#09 / 1995 / SNA / M • Pussyman #13:
Lips / 1996 / SNA / M • Pussyman Audi-
tions #14 / 1995 / SNA / M • Pussyman Au-
ditions #15 / 1995 / SNA / M • Pussyman
Auditions #17 / 1995 / SNA / M • Pussy-
man Auditions #19 / 1996 / SNA / M •
Pussyman Auditions #21 / 1996 / SNA / M
• Pussyman Auditions #23 / 1996 / SNA /
M • Razor's Edge / 1995 / ONA / M • Rebel
Cheerleaders / 1995 / VI / M • Rolling
Thunder / 1995 / VI / M • A Round Behind /
1995 / PEP / M • Scrue / 1995 / VI / M •
Sex Academy #5: The Art Of Pulp Fiction /
1994 / ONA / M • Sex Gallery / 1995 /
WAV / M • The Sexual Solution #1 / 1995 /
LE / M • The Sexual Solution #2 / 1995 /
LE / M • Shave Tails #4 / 1995 / SO / M •
Silk Stockings: The Black Widow / 1994 /
SPI / M • Simply Blue / 1995 / WAV / M •
Skin Dive / 1996 / SC / M • Some Like It
Wet / 1995 / LE / M • Sperm Bitches / 1995
/ ZA / M • Star Crossed / 1995 / VC / M •
Stardust #1 / 1996 / VI / M • Stardust #3 /
1996 / VI / M • Stardust #4 / 1996 / VI / M •
Starting Over / 1995 / WAV / M • The Stiff /
1995 / WAV / M • Stiletto / 1994 / WAV / M
• Street Legal / 1995 / WAV / M • Strippers
Inc. #5 / 1995 / ONA / M • Striptease /
1995 / SPI / M • Stupid And Stupider /
1995 / SO / M • Style #3 / 1996 / VT / M •
Suggestive Behavior / 1996 / VI / M • Surf
Babes / 1995 / LE / M • Sweet Revenge /
1996 / WAV / M • Tainted Love / 1996 / VC
/ M • Temptation / 1994 / VC / M • Thin Ice
/ 1996 / ONA / M • This Year's Model /
1996 / WAV / M • The Tongue / 1995 / OD /
M • The Toy Box / 1996 / ONA / M • Vice /
1994 / WAV / M • View Point / 1995 / VI / M
• Vivid Raw #2 / 1996 / VI / M • The Voyeur
#5 / 1995 / EA / M • The Voyeur #6: Luv In
A Hot Tub #2 / 1996 / JLP / M • A Woman
Scorned / 1995 / CA / M • Work Of Art /
1995 / LE / M
BOBBY WEST
More Dirty Debutantes #31 / 1994 / 4P / M
BOBBY WHITE
Honey, I Blew Everybody #2 / 1992 / MID /
M
BOBBY-JO
Full Moon Video #22: Elite Fantasy Girls /
1992 / FAP / F
BOBI HALL
Urgent Desires / 1983 / AMB / M
BOBINA *see* **Zumira**
BOBY PAXTON
Cocks In Frocks #1 / 1996 / TTV / G
BOGIE
Tits A Wonderful Life / 1994 / CV / M
BON SHOT
Beyond Passion / 1993 / IF / M
BON-BON
Big Busty #19 / 198? / H&S / M
BONES
New Ends #03 / 1993 / 4P / M
BONITA
Small girl with black hair, looks Hispanic in
origin, small tits, tight body, slightly wide

waist, but very, very pretty and has a very pleasant personality. 22 years old in 1993 and was de-virginized at 16.

A Is For Asia / 1996 / 4P / M • The Best Of Doctor Butts / 1994 / 4P / C • Creme De Femme / 1994 / 4P / F • Deep Inside Dirty Debutantes #07 / 1993 / 4P / M • Deep Inside Dirty Debutantes #09 / 1993 / 4P / M • Lovin' Spoonfuls #3 / 1995 / 4P / C • Lovin' Spoonfuls #4 / 1995 / 4P / C • More Dirty Debutantes #21 / 1993 / 4P / M • More Dirty Debutantes #22 / 1993 / 4P / M • More Dirty Debutantes #23 / 1993 / 4P / M • More Dirty Debutantes #24 / 1993 / 4P / M • More Dirty Debutantes #29 / 1994 / 4P / M • More Dirty Debutantes #30 / 1994 / 4P / M • More Dirty Debutantes #33 / 1994 / 4P / M • More Dirty Debutantes #43 / 1995 / 4P / M • More Dirty Debutantes #46 / 1995 / 4P / M • More Dirty Debutantes #49 / 1995 / 4P / M • New Ends #03 / 1993 / 4P / M • New Ends #06 / 1994 / 4P / M • New Ends #07 / 1994 / 4P / M • Up And Cummers: The Movie / 1994 / 4P / M

BONITA (FIFTIES)
Blue Vanities #542 / 1994 / FFL / M

BONITA DYAN
Sweet Captive / 1979 / EVI / M • Sweet Dreams Suzan / 1980 / CA / M

BONNIE
Becky S: Becky And Bonnie #1 / 1993 / BEC / F • Becky S: Becky And Bonnie #3 / 1995 / BEC / F • Blue Vanities #522 / 1993 / FFL / M • Blue Vanities #557 / 1994 / FFL / M • Blue Vanities #559 / 1994 / FFL / M • Limited Edition #19 / 1980 / AVC / M • Limited Edition #20 / 1980 / AVC / M • Odyssey Triple Play #93: Satisfaction Via Gang Bang / 1995 / OD / M • Pussy Power #01 / 1991 / BTO / M • Superstar Masturbation / 1990 / BIZ / F • Women On Women #2 / 1994 / MAV / F

BONNIE BANKS
Voluptuous #5 / 1996 / H&S / M

BONNIE BELLE
The Red Garter / 1986 / SE / M

BONNIE BELLES
Blue Vanities #556 / 1994 / FFL / M

BONNIE BENSON
Ultraflesh / 1980 / GO / M

BONNIE BREA
Black Beauties #1 / 1992 / VIM / M

BONNIE BRIGHT
Wet Mask / 1995 / SC / M

BONNIE BROWN
[Kindergarten Teachers Who Take It Up the Ass / 1974 / ... / M

BONNIE FAYETTE
Lady Luck / 1975 / VCX / M

BONNIE HAMMER
Avalon Calling / cr72 / AXV / M

BONNIE HOLLIDAY *(Bonnie Hollyday, Bonnie Stewart)*
Petite brunette or dark blonde with long hair, pretty face, small tits, tight waist, and heavy-lidded eyes.

11 / 1980 / VCX / M • All About Annette / 1982 / SE / C • Beyond Shame / 1980 / VEP / M • The Blonde / 1980 / VCX / M • Carnal Haven / 1976 / SVE / M • Champagne For Breakfast / 1980 / SE / M • Champagne Orgy / cr78 / HIF / M • China Girl / 1974 / SE / M • Desires Within Young Girls / 1977 / CA / M • The Devil's Playground / 1974 / VC / M • Dream Girl / 1974 / AVC / M • The Erotic World Of Vanessa

#1 / 1983 / VCR / C • The Erotic World Of Vanessa #2 / 1984 / VCR / C • Exhausted / 1981 / CA / C • Fantasy Girls / 1974 / VC / M • Female Athletes / 1977 / VXP / M • A History Of The Blue Movie / 1970 / CAL / M • Hot Lunch / 1978 / SE / M • Hot Pink / 1983 / VC / C • The Jade Pussycat / 1977 / CA / M • K-Sex / 1976 / VCR / M • Lady Freaks / 1973 / ... / M • Legends Of Porn #2 / 1989 / CV / C • Love Dreams / 1981 / CA / M • One Of A Kind / 1976 / SVE / M • Only The Best #3 / 1990 / CV / C • The Perfect Gift / 1979 / LOV / M • Physical #1 / 1981 / SUP / M • Please, Please Me / 1976 / AR / M • Reflections / 1977 / VCX / M • Rolls Royce #04 / 1980 / ... / C • Seven Into Snowy / 1977 / VC / M • Showgirl #13: Chris Cassidy's Fantasies / 1983 / SVE / M • Small Town Girls / 1979 / CXV / M • Teenage Madam / 1979 / CXV / M • Teenage Playmates / 1979 / LOV / M • Triplets / 1985 / VCR / M • True Legends Of Adult Cinema: The Golden Age / 1992 / VC / C • True Legends Of Adult Cinema: Unsung Superstars / 1993 / VC / C • The Ultimate Kiss / 1984 / ZA / M • Visions Of Clair / 1977 / WWV / M • Working Girls / 1984 / BMQ / M

BONNIE HOLLYDAY see Bonnie Holliday

BONNIE JEAN
Nurses Of The 407th / 1982 / CA / M

BONNIE JEAN BRADLEY
Blow Job Bonnie / 1992 / CC / M

BONNIE KING
The Vixens Of Kung Fu: A Tale Of Yin Yang / 1975 / VC / M

BONNIE LAIN see Spring Finlay

BONNIE LAMBERT
Girls Just Wanna Have Girls #2 / 1990 / HIO / F

BONNIE LOCKE
Blue Vanities #585 / 1996 / FFL / M

BONNIE LOGAN
Blue Vanities #514 / 1992 / FFL / M

BONNIE MICHAELS
No Man's Land #14 / 1996 / VT / F

BONNIE MILLER
Lesbian Dildo Bondage #2 / 1990 / BIZ / B • Lesbian Obsession / 1990 / BIZ / B

BONNIE MULFORD
Teenage Pony Girls / 1977 / VCX / M

BONNIE PARKER
Black Beauties #2 / 1992 / VIM / M

BONNIE SALLOR
Hot Action! / 1982 / CA / M

BONNIE STEWART see Bonnie Holliday

BONNIE WALKER
Taboo #07 / 1980 / IN / M

BONNIE WATERS
Blue Vanities #516 / 1992 / FFL / M • Blue Vanities #552 / 1994 / FFL / M

BONNIE WEBB
Fade To Rio / 1984 / VHL / M

BONNY
Black Mystique #02 / 1993 / VT / F • Blue Vanities #533 / 1993 / FFL / M • Blue Vanities #564 / 1994 / FFL / M

BOOTS
Blue Vanities #559 / 1994 / FFL / M • My First Time #4 / 1996 / NS / M

BORIS
FTV #05: Spy Vs. Spy / 1996 / FT / B • Wrasslin She-Babes #06 / 1996 / SOW / M • Wrasslin She-Babes #09 / 1996 / SOW / M

BORIS SMITH
Odyssey / 1977 / VC / M

BOSS KINGPIN
Cham Pain / 1991 / DCV / B • Field Of Screams / 1991 / DOM / B • Slave Shock / 1991 / DCV / B • White Slavery / 1991 / DCV / B

BOSTON BERTHA
The Best Of Wild Bill's Big Ladies / 1996 / H&S / C • Between My Breasts #07 / 1989 / L&W / M

BOY TOY see Woody Long

BOYD LEE
Nikki Arizona's Tomboys / 1995 / GAL / M • Trading Partners / 1995 / GO / M

BOYEO
Blush: Bathroom Slut / 1993 / FAT / F

BRAD
Amateur Nights #08 / 1990 / HO / M • America's Raunchiest Home Videos #50: / 1993 / ZA / M • HomeGrown Video #465: Bong The Schlong / 1996 / HOV / M

BRAD (DERRICK LANE) see Derrick Lane

BRAD ALEXANDER see Brad Armstrong

BRAD ARMSTRONG *(Brad Alexander)*
SO of Dyanna Lauren. In the mid-nineties graduated to directing.

Amazing Tails #4 / 1990 / CA / M • Anal Planet / 1994 / CC / M • Anal Pussycat / 1995 / ROB / M • Arizona Gold / 1996 / KLP / M • Back To Anal Alley / 1994 / ME / M • Bad Company / 1994 / VI / M • The Beverly Thrillbillies / 1993 / ZA / M • Bimbo Bowlers From Boston / 1990 / ZA / M • Boiling Point / 1994 / WAV / M • Breeders / 1996 / MET / M • Checkmate / 1995 / WAV / M • Chug-A-Lug Girls #3 / 1993 / VT / M • The Complete Guide To Sexual Positions / 1996 / PME / S • Conquest / 1996 / WP / M • Cover To Cover / 1995 / WP / M • Dick & Jane Go To Hollywood #2 / 1993 / AVI / M • Dirty Little Secrets / 1995 / WAV / M • Double Cross (Wicked) / 1995 / WP / M • Dr Butts #3 / 1993 / 4P / M • Erotic Visions / 1995 / ULI / M • Exposure / 1995 / WAV / M • Extreme Sex #1: The Club / 1994 / VI / M • Fashion Plate / 1995 / WAV / M • The Finishing Touch / 1994 / DR / M • Gangbang Girl #16 / 1995 / ANA / M • Hard Evidence / 1996 / WP / M • Hardcore / 1994 / VI / M • Head Lock / 1989 / VD / M • Heat / 1995 / WAV / M • Illicit Entry / 1995 / WAV / M • Immortal Desire / 1993 / VI / M • Jenna Ink / 1996 / WP / M • Lip Service / 1995 / WP / M • Nasty Newcummers #10 / 1995 / MET / M • Nightbreed / 1995 / VI / M • No Motive / 1994 / MID / M • Nothing To Hide #2 / 1993 / CV / M • Once In A Lifetime / 1996 / VC / C • Oral Obsession #1 / 1994 / VI / M • Passionate Partners: The Guide For Daring Lovers / 1993 / PHV / S • Perplexed / 1994 / FD / M • Plan 69 From Outer Space / 1993 / CA / M • Poison / 1994 / VI / M • The Proposal / 1993 / HO / M • Raunch #08 / 1993 / CC / M • Ride 'em Cow Girl / 1995 / VI / C • Satyr / 1996 / WP / M • Sex Gallery / 1995 / WAV / M • Sex Magic / 1996 / CAW / B • Sex Raiders / 1996 / WAV / M • Shaved Sinners #4 / 1993 / VT / M • Sheepless In Montana / 1993 / FOR / M • Sins Of Tami Monroe / 1991 / CA / C • Ski Bunnies #2 / 1994 / HW / M • Spiked Heel Diaries #5 / 1995 / BIZ / B • The Star / 1995 / CC / M • Star

Struck / 1994 / ERA / M • Starlet / 1994 / VI / M • Steamy Windows / 1993 / VI / M • The Stiff / 1995 / WAV / M • A Stripper Named Desire / 1993 / CC / M • Striptease / 1995 / SPI / M • Swallow / 1994 / VI / M • The Swap #2 / 1994 / VI / M • This Year's Model / 1996 / WAV / M • Undress To Thrill / 1994 / VI / M • Up And Cummers #16 / 1994 / 4P / M • Weird Sex / 1995 / GO / M • White Shadow / 1994 / VC / M • Wildcats / 1995 / WP / M

BRAD ASHLEY
Las Vegas Girls / 1983 / HIF / M

BRAD BRANDEN
The Hottest Show In Town / 1974 / … / M

BRAD CARLTON
Every Which Way / 1990 / V10 / G

BRAD DANIELS
Natural Response / 1996 / GPI / G

BRAD EVANS
Calendar Girl '83 / 1983 / CXV / M

BRAD EVERWOOD
Cheeks #5: The Ultimate Butt / 1991 / CC / M

BRAD FULLER
Barbie's Fantasies / 1974 / VHL / M

BRAD GERIG
Desire / 1990 / VC / M

BRAD GUNCH
Heavenly / 1995 / IF / M

BRAD HARDING
All Over Me / 1991 / VC / M

BRAD HILL
The Fine Line / 1990 / SO / M

BRAD MICHAELS
Lost In Vegas / 1996 / AWV / G • Mr. Peepers Amateur Home Videos #06: The Patriots / 1991 / LBO / M

BRAD MORGAN
The Best Little He/She House In Texas / 1993 / HSV / G • Bi Anonymous / 1993 / BIL / G • Bi-Golly / 1993 / BIL / G • Gilligan's Bi-Land / 1994 / PL / G • Inside Of Me / 1993 / PL / G • Married With She-Males / 1993 / PL / G • She-Male Vacation / 1993 / HSV / G • TV Evangelist / 1993 / HSV / G

BRAD PEARSON
The Ultimate She-Male / 1995 / LEO / G

BRAD PHELPS
Black, White & Red All Over / 1984 / EXF / C • The Erotic World Of Seka / 1983 / VCR / C • Triangle Of Lust / 1983 / VCR / M

BRAD PHILLIPS
Bi Mistake / 1989 / VI / G • Bi-Swingers / 1991 / PL / G • Budding Blondes / 1979 / TGA / C • The Offering / 1988 / INH / G • Party Doll / 1990 / VC / M • Switch Hitters #4: The Grand Slam / 1989 / IN / G

BRAD SINGER see Brett Singer

BRAD STEELE
Up And Cummers #38 / 1996 / RWP / M

BRAD STEVENS
Play It Again, Samantha / 1986 / EVN / M

BRAD STONE
Bi And Beyond #2 / 1989 / CAT / G

BRAD VALE
In And Out Of Africa / 1986 / EVN / M

BRAD WILCOX
Ass Tales / 1991 / PL / M • Brittany's Getaway / 1992 / PL / M • Class Ass / 1992 / PL / M • Danielle's Dirty Deeds / 1991 / CC / M • The Fantasy Realm #1 / 1990 / RUM / M • Mr. Big / 1991 / PL / M • Unlaced / 1992 / PL / M

BRADFORD ARMDEXTER

Alice In Wonderland / 1976 / CA / M

BRADFORD NEELY
Teddy Bare / 1977 / CA / M

BRADI SUMMERS
She-Male Swish Bucklers / 1994 / HSV / G

BRADLEY PICKLESIMER
Lost In Vegas / 1996 / AWV / G

BRADY T. SCOTT
Love Office Style / 19?? / BOC / M

BRAM ARNOLD
Firestorm #1 / 1984 / COM / M

BRAM STROKER
Dragula: Queen Of Darkness / 1996 / HSV / G

BRANDEE see Angel (1984)

BRANDI
100% Amateur #24: Dildos And Toys / 1996 / OD / M • Amateur Lesbians #13: Brandi / 1991 / GO / F • AVP #9153: The Monday Night Game / 1991 / AVP / M • Bubble Butts #09 / 1992 / LBO / M • Doc Bondage / 1992 / ZFX / B • First Time Lesbians #09 / 1993 / JMP / F • Hustler Video Magazine #1 / 1983 / SE / M • Hustler Video Magazine #2 / 1984 / SE / M • Interview's Backdoor To The Orient / 1996 / LV / M • Meanstreak / 1993 / ZFX / B • Neighborhood Watch #27 / 1992 / LBO / M • New Faces, Hot Bodies #10 / 1993 / STP / M • New Faces, Hot Bodies #11 / 1993 / STP / M • Red Riding She Male / 1995 / PL / G • Sex Police 2000 / 1992 / AFV / M • Southern Discomfort / 1992 / ZFX / B • Story Of Sweet Nicole / 1992 / ZFX / B • The Tasting / 1991 / EX / M • Wicked Stepmother / 1993 / NAP / B • Wilde At Heart / 1992 / VEX / M

BRANDI (BLACK)
Black Video Virgins #1 / 1996 / NS / M • Dirty Dirty Debutantes #2 / 1996 / 4P / M • More Black Dirty Debutantes / 1994 / 4P / M • More Black Dirty Debutantes #3 / 1994 / 4P / M • More Black Dirty Debutantes #5 / 1995 / 4P / M • More Dirty Debutantes #34 / 1994 / 4P / M

BRANDI MOANS
Drainman / 1989 / BIZ / B • Flash Floods / 1991 / PRE / C • Grand Slam / 1990 / PRE / B

BRANDI OANS
Forbidden Fantasies #3 / 1995 / ZA / M • Huge Grant On The Sunset Strip / 1995 / EVN / M

BRANDI SOMMERS
Little Shop Of She-Males / 1994 / HSV / G • Melrose Trannie / 1995 / HEA / G • Primal She-Male / 1996 / HSV / G • She-Male Surprise / 1995 / CDI / G • She-Male Valentine / 1996 / HSV / G

BRANDI WILLIAMS
Virtual She-Male / 1995 / HSV / G

BRANDI WINE
Angel Puss / 1988 / VC / M • Barbii Unleashed / 1988 / 4P / M • Batteries Included / 1988 / 3HV / M • Behind Blue Eyes #2 / 1988 / ZA / M • Beverly Hills Seduction / 1988 / WV / M • Bi And Beyond #2 / 1989 / CAT / G • Black Dreams / 1988 / CDI / M • Broadcast Nudes / 1988 / EVN / M • The Case Of The Sensuous Sinners / 1988 / ME / M • The Casting Whip / 1990 / PL / B • Charlie's Girls #1 / 1988 / CC / M • Educating Kascha / 1989 / CIN / M • Find Your Love / 1988 / CV / M • From Kascha With Love / 1988 / CDI / M • Hawaii Vice #2 / 1989 / CDI / M • Hawaii Vice #3 / 1988

/ CIN / M • Hawaii Vice #8 / 1990 / CIN / M • Hot & Heavy / 1989 / PL / M • Hot To Swap / 1988 / VEX / M • I Can't Get No...Satisfaction / 1988 / CDI / M • Inner Pink #2 / 1989 / LIP / F • Innocence Lost / 1988 / CA / M • Introducing Kascha / 1988 / CDI / M • Island Girls #1 / 1990 / CDI / C • Island Girls #2: Fun In The Sun / 1990 / CDI / C • Kascha & Friends / 1988 / CIN / M • Laid In The USA / 1988 / CC / M • The Legend Of Reggie D. / 1989 / EA / M • Lesbian Co-Ed Watersports / 1992 / BIZ / B • Love Ghost / 1990 / WV / M • Love In Reverse / 1988 / FAZ / M • Mad Love / 1988 / VC / M • Mandii's Magic / 1988 / CDI / M • Nasty Dancing / 1989 / VEX / M • Nightmare On Porn Street / 1988 / ME / M • Parting Shots / 1990 / VD / M • The Pillowman / 1988 / VC / M • Precious Gems / 1988 / CV / M • Proposals / 1988 / CC / M • Red Velvet / 1988 / PV / M • Ruthless Women / 1988 / SE / M • Salsa Break / 1989 / EA / M • Secret Of My Sex-Cess / 1988 / CV / M • Sex Lies / 1988 / FAN / M • Sex Sounds / 1989 / PL / M • Shameless Desire / 1989 / VEX / M • Soft Caresses / 1988 / VEX / M • Spread Eagle / 1992 / ZFX / B • Surfside Sex / 1988 / CA / M • Suzy Cue / 1988 / VI / M • Sweet Addiction / 1988 / CIN / M • Twisted Sisters / 1988 / ZA / M • Wet Wonderland / 1988 / VEX / M • Wrong Arm Of The Law / 1987 / ZA / M

BRANDIE
Nookie Professor #2 / 1996 / AVS / M

BRANDIE RIO
Girly Video Magazine #4 / 1996 / BEP / M • In Your Face #3 / 1995 / PL / M • Kittens & Vamps #2 / 1995 / ROB / F • Mike Hott: #324 Bonus Cunt: Brandie Rio / 1996 / MHV / M • Mike Hott: #330 Three-Sum Sluts #08 / 1995 / MHV / M • Mike Hott: #331 Lesbian Sluts #21 / 1996 / MHV / F • Mike Hott: #339 Cum In My Mouth #04 / 1996 / MHV / C • Sexual Healing / 1996 / SC / M

BRANDON
Memoirs Of A Chambermaid / 1987 / FIR / M • Mr. Peepers Amateur Home Videos #61: Four Play For Four / 1992 / LBO / M • Primal / 1994 / PHV / S • Uncle Roy's Amateur Home Video #17 / 1993 / VIM / M • Wet / 1994 / PHV / F • Working Women / 1994 / PHV / S

BRANDON HALL see Dan T. Mann

BRANDON HARRIS
The Long Ranger / 1987 / VCX / M

BRANDON IRON
Bonfire Of The Panties / 1990 / CC / M • Canadian Beaver Hunt #2 / 1996 / PL / M • Cirque Du Sex #1 / 1996 / VT / M • Mellon Man #06 / 1995 / AVI / M • Nasty Newcummers #10 / 1995 / MET / M • Philmore Butts Meets The Palm Beach Nymphomaniac Kathy Wille / 1995 / SUF / M • Screamers (Gourmet) / 1995 / ONA / M • Stuff Your Face #3 / 1995 / JMP / M • Young And Anal #2 / 1995 / JMP / M

BRANDON T.
Anita / 1996 / BLC / M

BRANDON WILDE
Buck's Excellent Transsexual Adventure / 1989 / STA / G • The Last Good-Bi / 1990 / CDI / G

BRANDY
Amateur Black: Sexpots / 1996 / SUF / M • Black Women, White Men #5 / 1995 / FC /

M • Black Women, White Men #6 / 1995 / FC / M • Blue Vanities #511 / 1992 / FFL / M • Bubble Butts Gold #1 / 1994 / LBO / M • Dirty Doc's Housecalls #02 / 1993 / LV / M • Forbidden Fantasies #2 / 1995 / ZA / M • GM #151: Inside Brandy / 1994 / GMV / F • Hidden Camera #04 / 1993 / JMP / M • Hollywood Amateurs #20 / 1995 / MID / M • Homegrown Video #179 / 1990 / HOV / M • Homegrown Video #408: Hot Anal Action! / 1993 / HOV / C • Homegrown Video #425: The Best Of Brandy / 1994 / HOV / M • An Innocent Woman / 1991 / FAZ / M • The Lustful Turk / 1968 / SOW / S • Mike Hott: #201 Lesbian Sluts #04 / 1992 / MHV / F • The New Snatch Masters #22 / 1996 / LEI / C • On The Prowl #2 / 1991 / SC / M • OUTS: Brandy & Angel / 1994 / OUT / F • Penthouse: 25th Anniversary Pet Of The Year Spectacular / 1994 / A*V / F • Singapore Sluts / 1994 / ORE / C • Starlet Screen Test / 1990 / NST / S • Uncle Roy's Amateur Home Video #09 / 1992 / VIM / M • Up 'n' Coming / 1983 / CA / M

BRANDY (S/M)
Transsexual Prostitutes #1 / 1996 / DFI / G • Transsexual Prostitutes #2 / 1997 / DFI / G

BRANDY ALEXANDER *(Brandy Alexandre)*
Marginal face, blonde curly hair, small tits and an attitude. Born 7/17/1964. 5'2" tall.
Adult Video News 1992 Awards / 1992 / VC / M • Bare Essence / 1989 / EA / M • Behind You All The Way #2 / 1990 / SO / M • Bend Over Babes #1 / 1990 / EA / M • Bend Over Babes #2 / 1991 / EA / M • Best Butt(e) In The West #1 / 1992 / CC / M • Best Of Buttman #1 / 1991 / EA / C • Best Of Buttman #2 / 1993 / EA / C • Bikini City / 1991 / CC / M • Blowing In Style / 1989 / EA / M • Boobs, Butts And Bloopers #1 / 1990 / HO / M • Born To Be Wild / 1987 / SE / M • Boxed Lunches / 1989 / ... / M • Buttman Goes To Rio #1 / 1990 / EA / M • Call Girls In Action / 1989 / CV / M • Cat & Mouse #1 / 1992 / XCI / M • Caught From Behind #09 / 1988 / HO / M • Chameleons: Not The Sequel / 1991 / VC / M • Cheeks #4: A Backstreet Affair / 1991 / CC / M • Cheeks #5: The Ultimate Butt / 1991 / CC / M • Cum Shot Revue #5 / 1988 / HO / C • Dance Fire / 1989 / EA / M • De Blond / 1989 / EA / M • Debbie Class Of '89 / 1989 / CC / M • Debbie Does The Devil In Dallas / 1987 / SE / M • Diamond In The Rough / 1989 / EX / M • Dreams In The Forbidden Zone / 1989 / PCP / M • Earthquake Girls / 1990 / CC / M • Fantasy Girls / 1988 / CA / M • Foolish Pleasures / 1989 / ME / M • Girls And Guns / 1992 / KBR / M • Hawaii Vice #8 / 1990 / CIN / M • The Hindlick Maneuver / 1991 / CC / M • Honey, I Blew Everybody / 1992 / MID / M • Hyapatia Lee's Arcade Series #01 / 1988 / ZA / C • Hyapatia Lee's Arcade Series #02 / 1988 / ZA / C • In Your Face #2 / 1992 / PL / M • Island Girls #1 / 1990 / CDI / C • The Kink / 1988 / WV / M • Kinky Business #2 / 1989 / DR / M • Late Night For Lovers / 1989 / ME / M • Lawyers In Heat / 1989 / CDI / M • Love On The Run / 1989 / CA / M • Love Shack / 1990 / CC / M • Making Tracks / 1990 / DR / M • My Wildest Date / 1989 / FOV / M • Mystic Pieces / 1989 / EA / M • Nightdreams #2 / 1990 / VC / M • Only The

Strong Survive / 1988 / ZA / M • Private Places / 1992 / VC / M • Pussyman #02: The Prize / 1993 / CC / M • Puttin' Her Ass On The Line / 1991 / DR / M • Rock 'n' Roll Heaven / 1989 / EA / M • Satania / 1986 / DR / M • Saturday Night Special / 1989 / DR / M • Search For An Angel / 1988 / WV / M • Sexual Olympics #2: The Finals / 1992 / VT / M • The Sexual Zone / 1989 / EX / M • Seymore Butts In The Love Shack / 1992 / FH / M • Seymore Butts: Bustin' Out My Best Anal / 1995 / FH / C • Shadow Dancers #1 / 1989 / EA / M • Shadow Dancers #2 / 1989 / EA / M • Soft Tail / 1991 / IN / M • Sumo Sue And The Fat Ladies Of Wrestling / 1988 / FAN / M • Talk Dirty To Me #07 / 1990 / DR / M • Talk Dirty To Me #08 / 1990 / DR / M • Taylor Made / 1989 / DR / M • Tori Welles Goes Behind The Scenes / 1992 / FD / M • Toy Box Lingerie Show / 1991 / ESP / S • Tricks Of The Trade / 1988 / CA / M • Twin Peeks / 1990 / DR / M • Unchain My Heart / 1990 / CC / M • When Larry Ate Sally / 1989 / EX / M • Who Shaved Aja? / 1989 / EX / M • Whore Of The Roses / 1990 / AFV / M • [Best Friends #2 / 198? / ... / G

BRANDY ALEXANDER-83
Camp Beaverlake #1 / 1984 / AR / M • Centerfold Celebrities #4 / 1983 / VC / M • Centerfold Celebrities #5 / 1983 / VC / M • Charming Cheapies #2: No Holes Barred / 1985 / 4P / M • Fantasy Land / 1984 / LA / M • Showdown / 1985 / BON / B

BRANDY ALEXANDRE *see* **Brandy Alexander**

BRANDY BENT
America's Raunchiest Home Videos #31: Miss Dream Tits / 1992 / ZA / M

BRANDY BLAXX
Vampirass / 1992 / VC / M

BRANDY BOSWORTH *(Delta Force)*
This is a female.
900 Desert Strip / 1991 / XPI / M • Ambitious Blondes / 1992 / VIM / M • Ambushed / 1990 / SE / M • Bad Influence / 1991 / CDI / M • Bazooka County #3 / 1991 / CC / M • Beauty & The Body Builder / 199? / NAP / B • Black & Blue / 1990 / SO / M • Blonde Ambition / 1991 / CIN / M • Boobs, Butts And Bloopers #2 / 1990 / HO / M • Dr Hooters / 1991 / PL / M • Dripping Wet Video / 1993 / NAP / F • Dyke Bar / 1991 / PL / F • The Fire Down Below / 1992 / CDI / M • Images Of Desire / 1990 / PM / M • Lesbo A Go-Go / 1990 / PL / F • Magnificent Seven / 1991 / NAP / F • Malibu Spice / 1991 / VC / M • On Stage And In Color / 1991 / VIP / M • Queen Challenged / 199? / NAP / B • Radioactive / 1990 / VIP / M • Shake Well Before Using / 9990 / LV / M • Surf City Sex / 1991 / CIA / M • Three's A Crowd / 1990 / HO / M • Transsexual 6900 / 1990 / LV / G • Wild Goose Chase / 1990 / EA / M

BRANDY DANIELS
Kittens #3 / 1992 / CC / F

BRANDY DELIGHT
Babes Of The Bay #1 / 1994 / LIP / F

BRANDY GOLD
Living Doll / 1992 / CDI / M • Southern: Brandy Gold / 1992 / SSH / F • Southern: Previews #2 / 1992 / SSH / C • Wanderlust / 1992 / LE / M

BRANDY HALL
Dr Pussy's Tasty Tails #2 / 1993 / SHV / F

BRANDY HANES
America's Raunchiest Home Videos #32: Model of Lust / 1992 / ZA / M • Biff Malibu's Totally Nasty Home Videos #11 / 1992 / ANA / M

BRANDY KANE
Creme De La Face #03 / 1994 / OD / M

BRANDY LAWRENCE
The Starmaker / 1982 / VC / M

BRANDY LEE
Trisexual Encounters #06 / 1987 / PL / G

BRANDY LONG
Blue Vanities #514 / 1992 / FFL / M • Not Tonite Henry! / 1958 / SOW / S

BRANDY LUCK
Cocktails / 1990 / HO / M

BRANDY MARTIN
The Experiment / 1983 / BIZ / B • The Trainers / cr83 / BIZ / B

BRANDY MCDANIELS
Hard For The Money / 1984 / CV / M • Parliament: Hard TV #1 / 1988 / PM / G • Teeny Talk / 1995 / DBM / M

BRANDY MICHAELS
Trisexual Encounters #08 / 1988 / PL / G

BRANDY MOANS
Title Shots / 1995 / PRE / B

BRANDY O'SHEA
All American Girls #1 / 1982 / CA / M

BRANDY SMITH
Hot Lunch / 1978 / SE / M

BRANDY SUMMERVILLE *see* **Lexus**

BRANDY TYLER
Caribbean Sunset / 1996 / PL / M

BRANDY WEST
Hot Cherries / 1990 / CC / F • Putting On The Ritz / 1990 / VEX / M

BRANDY WILLOWS
Breakin' All The Rules / 1987 / SE / M • Wet Kink / 1989 / CDI / M

BRANEY TRAMBLE
Take Off / 1978 / VXP / M

BRAS LEWISON
Postgraduate Course In Sexual Love / 1975 / QX / M

BRAZIL *(Tanya Tucker, Sandra Clinton)*
Very hard looking and sounding blonde who first appeared in **Harry Horndog #14** under the name Tanya Tucker.
Butt Woman #5 / 1993 / FH / M • Casting Call #01 / 1993 / SO / M • From Brazil With Love / 1992 / ZA / M • The Goddess / 1993 / ZA / M • Harry Horndog #14: Love Puppies #3 / 1992 / ZA / M • Heatwave #2 / 1993 / FH / F • Sarah Jane's Love Bunnies #01 / 1993 / FPI / F • Seymore Butts Meets The Cumback Brat / 1993 / FH / M • Top Debs #1: Prom Night / 1992 / GO / M • Toppers #06 / 1993 / TV / M • Toppers #07 / 1993 / TV / M • Toppers #08 / 1993 / TV / M • Toppers #12 / 1993 / TV / C • Toppers & Whoppers #1 / 1994 / PRE / C • Untamed Cowgirls Of The Wild West #01: The Pillow Biters / 1992 / ZA / M • Who Killed Holly Hollywood? / 1993 / VC / M

BRAZIL (APRIL D) *see* **April Diamonds**

BRAZIL MERCEDES
Harry Horndog #10: Love Puppies #1 / 1992 / ZA / M • Spermacus / 1993 / PI / M

BRAZIL NEWPORTE *see* **April Diamonds**

BREA *see* **Zumira**

BREANNA
Anal Witness #2: No Prisoners / 1996 / LBO / M • Club Deb #4 / 1996 / MET / M • Numba 1 Ass Fucka / 1996 / ROB / M

BREANNA MALLOY *(Briana Malloy, Brionna Malloy, Brenda Malloy, Mary Arnold)*
Could be your mother—ugly, falling apart body, small/medium tits, bad skin, aged.
Adventures Of The DP Boys: D.P. Nurses / 1995 / HW / M • Adventures Of The DP Boys: Sicilian Sluts / 1995 / HW / M • Anal Camera #05 / 1995 / EVN / M • Anal Torture / 1994 / ZA / M • Backdoor Smugglers / 1994 / JAV / M • Big Murray's New-Cummers #17: Age Before Beauty / 1993 / FD / M • Big Murray's New-Cummers #28: Rump Humpers #2 / 1995 / FD / M • Birthday Bash / 1995 / BOT / M • Bootylicious: Trailer Trash / 1996 / JMP / M • Butt Hunt #01 / 1994 / LEI / M • Casting Call #07 / 1994 / SO / M • The Cumm Brothers #05: These Nuts For Hire / 1994 / OD / M • Different Strokes / 1994 / PRE / B • Dixie Downes Gang Bang / 1996 / FC / M • Exstasy / 1995 / WV / M • Gas Works / 1994 / PRE / B • The Go-Go Girls / 1994 / EVN / M • Here Comes Magoof #1 / 1995 / VC / M • Hidden Camera #20 / 1994 / JMP / M • Hollywood Amateurs #08 / 1994 / MID / M • Hollywood Amateurs #16 / 1995 / MID / M • Hollywood Amateurs #23 / 1995 / MID / M • Hollywood Starlets Adventure #01 / 1995 / AVS / M • In My Ass, Please! / 1996 / SP / M • Indiscreet! Video Magazine #3 / 1995 / FH / M • Kane Video #4: Customer Satisfaction / 1995 / VTF / B • Kink Inc. / 1996 / MP0 / M • Mike Hott: #360 Cum In My Cunt #08 / 1995 / MHV / C • Mike Hott: #362 Fuck The Boss #7 / 1996 / MHV / M • Mike Hott: #375 Girls Who Swallow Cum #05 / 1996 / MHV / C • Nasty Newcummers: Black Edition / 1995 / MET / M • Natural Born Dominants / 1995 / IBN / B • Orgies Orgies Orgies / 1994 / WV / M • Poop Shute Debutantes / 1995 / LBO / M • Reverse Gang Bang / 1995 / JMP / M • Ron Hightower's White Chicks #16 / 1994 / LBO / M • Swedish Erotica #74 / 1994 / CA / M • Swedish Erotica #80 / 1994 / CA / M • Tail Taggers #130 / 1994 / WV / M • Tight Fit #09 / 1994 / GO / M • Tight Fit #11 / 1995 / GO / M • Triple Flay / 1995 / PRE / B • Triple Play / 1994 / PRE / B • Wet & Misled / Iooo / I AR / I III • Wild Orgies #13 / 1994 / AFI / M • Wild Orgies #14 / 1994 / AFI / M • Wild Orgies #16 / 1995 / AFI / M • Wild Orgies #17 / 1995 / AFI / M • The World's Biggest Gang Bang #1 / 1995 / FPI / M

BREANNON
The Girls Of Summer / 1995 / VT / M

BREE ANTHONY *(Sue Richards, Sue Rowan)*
Brunette, medium tits, OK body but sometimes shows a tendency to fat, passable face.
Alice In Wonderland / 1976 / CA / M • Anyone But My Husband / 1975 / VC / M • Beach House / 1981 / CA / C • Cheryl Surrenders / cr77 / VHL / M • Classic Erotica #6 / 1985 / SVE / M • Divine Obsession / 1976 / TVX / M • The Double Exposure Of Holly / 1977 / TVX / M • Highway Hookers / 1976 / SVE / M • Honeypie / 1975 / VC / M • Invasion Of The Love Drones / 1977 / ALP / M • Kinky Potpourri #32 / 199? / SVE / C • Midnight Desires / 1976 / VXP / M • More / 1973 / BL / M • One Last Fling / cr76 / CPL / M • Oriental Blue / 1975 / ALP / M • Reunion (Vanessa Del Rio's) / 1977 /

LIM / M • Satan Was A Lady / 1977 / ALP / M • Sexteen / 1975 / VC / M • Street Girls Of Ny / 19?? / SIL / M • Sugar Britches / 1980 / VCX / C • The Taking Of Christina / 1975 / NGV / M • Thunderbuns / 1976 / VCX / C • The Vixens Of Kung Fu: A Tale Of Yin Yang / 1975 / VC / M • Wet Rocks / 1975 / BL / M • When A Woman Calls / 1975 / VXP / M • Winter Heat / 1975 / AVC / M

BREEZY see Crystal Breeze
BREEZY KANE see Breezy Lane
BREEZY LANE *(Breezy Kane)*
Petite blonde with slightly droppy medium tits, tight body, nice smile and pretty face.
Amberella / 1986 / GO / M • The Beat Goes On / 1987 / VCR / C • Breastography, Lesson #1 / 1987 / VCR / M • California Taboo / 1986 / VC / M • Divorce Court Expose #2 / 1987 / VD / M • Don't Get Them Wet / 1987 / VD / M • The First Taboo / 1989 / LA / M • Flesh For Fantasies / 1986 / TAM / M • Furburgers / 1987 / VD / M • The Gentlemen's Club / 1986 / WV / M • In All The Right Places / 1986 / VD / M • Innocence Lost / 1987 / CAT / G • Mitzi's Honor / 1987 / TAM / M • Nikki And The Pom-Pom Girls / 1987 / VEX / M • Nudes At Eleven #1 / 1986 / AVC / M • Nymphette #2 / 1986 / WV / M • Pacific Intrigue / 1987 / AMB / M • Satania / 1986 / DR / M • Sensuous Singles: Whitney Prince / 1987 / VCR / F • Sex Derby / 1986 / GO / M • Sex Machine / 1986 / LA / M • She-Male Encounters #13: She-Male Reformatory / 1987 / MET / G • She-Male Encounters #14: She-Male Wrestlers / 1987 / MET / G • Snapshots: Confessions Of A Video Voyeur / 1988 / CC / M • Sweet Cheeks / 1987 / VCR / C • The Switch Is On / 1985 / CAT / G • Teasin' & Pleasin' / 1988 / LBO / F • Two On The Tongue / 1988 / TAM / C • Venus Of The Nile / 1991 / WV / M • The Wacky World Of X-Rated Bloopers / 1989 / GO / M • Weird Fantasy / 1986 / LA / M

BREI
Joe Elliot's College Girls #40 / 1995 / JOE / F

BRENDA
AVP #81/1: A Gifl's Night In / 1990 / AVP / F • Big Bust Vixens / 1984 / BTO / S • Blue Vanities #579 / 1995 / FFL / M • Classic Swedish Erotica #11 / 1986 / CA / C • College Video Virgins #07 / 1996 / AOC / M • Granada Affair / 1984 / JAN / B • Homegrown Video #418: Looks As Good As It Feels / 1994 / HOV / M • Joe Elliot's College Girls #31 / 1994 / JOE / M • Joe Elliot's College Girls #33 / 1994 / JOE / M • Joe Elliot's College Girls: Brenda Uncut / 1994 / JOE / M • Skirts & Flirts #01 / 1997 / XPR / F • Wrasslin She-Babes #10 / 1996 / SOW / M

BRENDA ARTHUR
18 And Anxious / cr78 / CDI / M

BRENDA B. BADD
Licorice Twists / 1985 / WET / M

BRENDA BASSIE
Powerbone / 1976 / VC / M • Teenage Cousins / cr76 / SOW / M

BRENDA BITCHIN
Techsex / 1988 / VXP / M

BRENDA BROOKS
Angel Buns / 1981 / QX / M

BRENDA CARIN see Holli Woods (1989)

BRENDA CHENG
Red Glow Of Revenge / 1992 / RB / B

BRENDA DARLING
Ultraflesh / 1980 / GO / M

BRENDA HALE
Jezebel / 1979 / CV / M

BRENDA KAN see Crystal Sync

BRENDA LEE
Student Fetish Videos: Bondage #01 / 1995 / PRE / B • Student Fetish Videos: Catfighting #16 / 1996 / PRE / B • Student Fetish Videos: Foot Worship #17 / 1995 / PRE / B

BRENDA LOCKWOOD
Candi Girl / 1979 / PVX / M • Hot Child In The City / 1979 / PVX / M

BRENDA MALLOY see Breanna Malloy

BRENDA MOORE
Fantasy Peeps: Black On White / 1985 / 4P / M

BRENDA RAM
Hard Candy / 1977 / ... / M

BRENDA SCHALL
Girls In Passion / 1979 / VHL / M

BRENDA STARR
California Blondes #01 / 1986 / VEX / M • Cream Dreams / 1986 / VEX / M • Lust At Sea / 1986 / VD / M

BRENDA STEWART
Randy, The Electric Lady / 1978 / VC / M

BRENDA VARGO
Prisoner Of Paradise / 1980 / VCX / M

BRENDA VIXEN
Redliners / 1980 / VXP / M

BRENDAN
Club Kiss / 1995 / ONA / M

BRENDAN REED
Kinky Ladies Of Bourbon Street / 1976 / LUM / M

BRENDON RORIE
Mean Ass Bitch / 1996 / RB / B • Young Sluts In Heat #2 / 1996 / PL / M

BRENNAN
I Am Desire / 1992 / WV / M

BRENT
On The Prowl #2 / 1991 / SC / M

BRENT BECKETT
Return Engagement / 1995 / VI / M

BRET
UI Di Love Amateurs #1 / 1993 / SFP / G • Dick & Jane In San Francisco / 1996 / AVI / M • Uncle Roy's Amateur Home Video #13 / 1992 / VIM / M

BRET HANKS
Bedtime Video #06 / 1984 / GO / M

BRET ROTH
Lactamania #3 / 1995 / TTV / M

BRET STEVENS
Lessons In Lust / 1987 / LA / M

BRET STING see Jordan Smith

BRETT
Alex Jordan's First Timers #03 / 1993 / OD / M • Bubble Butts #19 / 1992 / LBO / M • Fresh Faces #10 / 1996 / EVN / M • Harry Horndog #14: Love Puppies #3 / 1992 / ZA / M • HomeGrown Video #464: Liza, We Love You / 1995 / HOV / M • Neighborhood Watch #38: Pearlie's Curlie's / 1993 / LBO / M

BRETT BRADSHAW
Bubble Butts #13 / 1992 / LBO / M

BRETT BRENNAN
Bone Therapy / 1992 / LV / M • Freaks Of Leather #1 / 1993 / IF / M • Freaks Of Leather #2 / 1994 / IF / C • Gazongas #04 / 1993 / LEI / C • Lust For Leather / 1993 /

IF / M • Much More Than A Mouthful #4 / 1994 / VEX / M • Nothing Else Matters / 1992 / V99 / C • Pleasure Chest / 1993 / IF / M • Tight Pucker / 1992 / WV / M

BRETT DAILEY
Final Blow / 19?? / BL / M

BRETT FORD
4 Bi 4 / 1994 / BIN / G • Long Play / 1995 / 3XP / G

BRETT LAND *see* **Brett Next**

BRETT NEILSON
More Than A Handful #1 / 1985 / CV / C

BRETT NEXT *(Dean James, Brett Land)*
America's Dirtiest Home Videos #04 / 1991 / VEX / M • America's Dirtiest Home Videos #05 / 1991 / VEX / M • America's Dirtiest Home Videos #14 / 1992 / VEX / M • Between A Rock And A Hot Place / 1989 / VEX / M • The Big Gun / 1989 / FAN / M • Debbie Does 'em All #3 / 1989 / CV / M • Delicate Matters / 1989 / VEX / M • Drink Of Love / 1990 / V99 / M • Head Nurse / 1990 / V99 / M • Heartless / 1989 / REB / M • Heather's Secrets / 1990 / VEX / M • The Honeymoon: The Bride's Running Behind / 1990 / 4P / M • A Little Bit Pregnant / 1995 / SO / M • Lonely And Blue / 1990 / VEX / M • Lonely Is The Night / 1990 / V99 / M • Playing Dirty / 1989 / VEX / M • Ready To Drop #10 / 1996 / FC / M • Rituals / 1989 / V99 / M • Seduction / 1990 / VEX / M • Space Cadet / 1989 / IN / M • Space Virgins / 1990 / VEX / M • Storm Warning / 1989 / LV / M • Tequila Sunset / 1989 / V99 / M • This Bun's For You / 1989 / FAN / M • Tied & Tickled #14: Count Tickula / 1986 / CS / B • Tropical Temptations / 1989 / VEX / M

BRETT RYAN
Bobby Hollander's Maneaters #02 / 1993 / SFP / M • Letters From The Heart / 1991 / AWV / M • Worthy Women / 1990 / AWV / M

BRETT SAY
All The Loving Couples / 1979 / KIT / M

BRETT SIMS
Bi-Heat #08 To #10 / 1988 / ZA / G • Deep Inside Trading / 1986 / AR / M • She Studs #03 / 1991 / BIZ / G • She-Male Encounters #05: Orgy At The Poysinberry Bar #1 / 1987 / MET / G • She-Male Encounters #12: Orgy At The Poysinberry #2 / 1987 / MET / G • Trisexual Encounters #07 / 1988 / PL / G • Trisexual Encounters #08 / 1988 / PL / G • Trisexual Encounters #12 / 1990 / PL / G

BRETT SINGER *(Brad Singer)*
9-Ball: Geisha Gang Bang / 1994 / PL / M • Anal Anarchy / 1995 / VC / M • Anal Witness #1 / 1996 / LBO / M • The Fucking Elvises / 1994 / GLI / M • Generation Sex #2: Nature's Revenge / 1996 / VT / M • The Hardwood Chronicles / 1995 / XCI / M • Here Comes Magoof #2 / 1995 / VC / M • Hot Wired / 1996 / VC / M • Hotwired / 1996 / VC / M • House Of Anal / 1995 / NOT / M • Lollipop Shoppe #1 / 1996 / SC / M • Nineteen #2 / 1996 / FOR / M • Oral Addiction / 1995 / VI / M • Phantom X / 1989 / VC / M • Pizza Sluts: They Deliver / 1995 / XCI / M • Shayla's Swim Party / 1997 / VC / M • Sorority Sluts Passed Out / 1995 / ZA / M • Summer Dreams / 1996 / TEP / M • Temple Of Love / 1995 / SUF / M • Underground #3: Sit On This / 1996 / SC / M • View Point / 1995 / VI / M •

Wicked Fantasies / 1996 / CO2 / M • Wicked Ways #2: Education Of A D.P. Virgin / 1995 / WP / M • Working Girl Gang-Bang / 1995 / GLI / M

BRETT STEVENS
The Other Woman / 1996 / VC / M • Outlaw Sluts / 1996 / RAS / M

BRETT STEWART
Toying Around / 1992 / FL / M

BRETT TRUE
Behind Closed Doors / 1990 / VI / M • L.A. Stories / 1990 / VI / M • True Love / 1989 / VI / M

BRETT WILLIAMS
Stasha's Adult School / 1993 / CDI / G

BREWSTER COCBURN *see* **Woody Long**

BREWSTER JAMES
Family Affair / 1979 / MIT / M

BRI
Breast Of Britain #2 / 1987 / BTO / M

BRIAN
Club Doma #2 / 1994 / VER / B • Homegrown Video #193 / 1990 / HOV / M • Homegrown Video #371 / 1991 / HOV / M • Homegrown Video #373 / 1991 / HOV / M • Naughty Butt Nice / 1993 / IF / M • Pearl Necklace: Premier Sessions #01 / 1993 / SEE / M

BRIAN ALLEN
Leather Persuasion / 1980 / BIZ / B

BRIAN BROOKS
Mother's Wishes / 1974 / GO / M

BRIAN CURTIN *see* **Woody Long**

BRIAN CURTIS *see* **Woody Long**

BRIAN DAVIDSON
Kinky Ladies Of Bourbon Street / 1976 / LUM / M • The Seduction Of Amy / 1975 / THT / S

BRIAN ESTERVEZ
Crossover / 1989 / STA / G • Hung Guns / 1988 / STA / G • Incessant / 1988 / CAD / G

BRIAN GELB
P.L.O.W.: Punk Ladies Of Wrestling / 1996 / GOT / B

BRIAN JENSEN
Las Vegas Girls / 1983 / HIF / M

BRIAN KIDD
Like Father Like Son / 1996 / AWV / G • My Sister's Husband / 1996 / AWV / G

BRIAN LEDER
Submission (Knight) / 1994 / KNF / B

BRIAN LONG *(Carl Mann)*
This male is a director and appears in **Field Of Wet Dreams**.
Field Of Wet Dreams / 1992 / EVN / M • Lady & The Champ / 1991 / AFV / M • Santa Comes Again / 1990 / GLE / M

BRIAN MAXON
The Big Switch / 1985 / LAV / G

BRIAN MAXX
Night Walk / 1995 / HIV / G

BRIAN MORAN
Hardcore: The Films Of Richard Kern #1 / 1991 / FTV / M

BRIAN PALMER *see* **Blake Palmer**

BRIAN ROOKER
Beaver & Buttcheeks / 1993 / DR / M

BRIAN SMITH
Her Total Response / 1975 / SVE / M

BRIAN SUREWOOD
Anal Runaway / 1996 / ZA / M • Director's Wet Dreams / 1996 / BBE / M • Friendly Fire / 1996 / EDP / M • From The Heart / 1996 / XCI / M • Hollywood Hookers / 1996

/ DWV / M • In The Line Of Desire / 1996 / MID / M • Nice Fuckin' Movie / 1997 / EL / M • The Night Of The Living Bed / 1996 / LE / M • Shadows Of Lust / 1996 / NIT / M • Starbangers #09 / 1996 / ZA / M • Titty Slickers #3 / 1996 / LE / M

BRIAN WILSON
Treasure Chest / 1985 / GO / M

BRIAN WOOD
The Psychiatrist / 1978 / VC / M

BRIAN YOUNG
Domina #4 / 1996 / LBO / G

BRIANA (LYNN) *see* **Brianna Lynn**

BRIANA MALLOY *see* **Breanna Malloy**

BRIANE
Joe Elliot's College Girls #28 / 1994 / JOE / M

BRIANNA
Biff Malibu's Totally Nasty Home Videos #31 / 1993 / ANA / M • Dirty Old Men #2 / 1995 / IP / M • Domina #6 / 1996 / LBO / B • Double D Dykes #21 / 1995 / GO / F • Hot Body Video Magazine: Wild Thing / 1996 / CG / F • LA Nasty / 1995 / SP / M • Sex 4 Life / 1995 / XPR / M

BRIANNA BLISS
Cherry Poppers #13: Anal Pajama Party / 1996 / ZA / M • Deep Dish Booty Pie / 1996 / ROB / M • Hardcore Fantasies #2 / 1996 / LV / M • Hot Amateur Nights / 1996 / WV / M • Innocence Lost / 1995 / GO / M • My First Time #2 / 1996 / NS / M • Mystique / 1996 / SC / M • New Hardcore Beginners #20 / 1996 / LEI / C • New Pussy Hunt #28 / 1997 / LEI / C • Nineteen #3 / 1996 / FOR / M • The Violation Of Paisley Hunter / 1996 / JMP / F

BRIANNA LEE
Assy #2 / 1996 / JMP / M • Catch Of The Day #3 / 1996 / VG0 / M • The Erotic Diaries Of Briana Lee / 1996 / XPR / M • The Letter X #2 / 1996 / MID / M • Lustful Letters #1 / 1996 / BLE / M • Sorority Sex Kittens #3 / 1996 / VC / M

BRIANNA LYNN *(Briana (Lynn))*
Beach Bum Amateur's #11 / 1992 / MID / M • Boobs, Butts And Bloopers #2 / 1990 / HO / M • Dane's Party / 1991 / IF / G • Dreams Cum True / 1990 / HO / M • Hard Feelings / 1991 / V99 / M • Lady Of The House / 1990 / VEX / M • Opportunity Knocks / 1990 / HO / M • Ravaged Rivalry / 1990 / HO / M • Red Hot And Ready / 1990 / V99 / M • Ride 'em Cowgirl / 1991 / V99 / M • The Rock Hard Files / 1991 / VEX / M • A Touch Of Mink / 1990 / V99 / M • The Wild Wild Chest #1 / 1990 / HO / M

BRIANNA MARIE
Intimate Affairs / 1990 / VEX / M

BRIANNA RAE *see* **Heather Lere**

BRIANNON
Beverly Hills Blondes #1 / 1995 / LV / M • Foreign Fucks / 1995 / FOR / M • Humpkin Pie / 1995 / HW / M • Indiscreet! Video Magazine #3 / 1995 / FH / M • Mike Hott: #304 Cunt of the Month: Briannon / 1995 / MHV / M • Mike Hott: #336 Three-Sum Sluts #09 / 1995 / MHV / M

BRICE *see* **Madelyn Knight**

BRICK MAJORS
Anonymous / 1993 / VI / M • Babewatch #2 / 1994 / CC / M • Bang City #7: Carolina's Anal Gang Bang / 1995 / SC / M • Big Tit Racket / 1995 / PEP / M • Blonde / 1995 / LE / M • Carolina's D.P. Anal Gang-

bang / 1996 / FC / M • The Deviant Doctor / 1996 / NS / M • Double Cross (Wicked) / 1995 / WP / M • Fast Forward / 1995 / CA / M • Flexxx #3 / 1995 / VT / M • Fresh Meat (John Leslie) #2 / 1995 / EA / M • Heartbeat / 1995 / PP / M • Jailhouse Nurses / 1995 / SC / M • Kia Unmasked / 1995 / LE / M • Lady's Choice / 1995 / VD / M • Latex #1 / 1994 / VC / M • Lay Of The Land / 1995 / LE / M • Legal Briefs / 1996 / EX / M • Mickey Ray's Sex Search #05: Deep Inside / 1995 / WIV / M • Nasty Dreams / 1994 / PRK / M • On The Rise / 1994 / EX / M • Perverted Women / 1995 / SC / M • Please Take A Number / 1996 / CDI / M • Private Eyes / 1995 / LE / M • Rod Wood / 1995 / LE / M • Sex Academy #2: The Art Of Talking Dirty / 1994 / ONA / M • Sex Academy #3: The Art Of Real Sex / 1994 / ONA / M • Sex Academy #4: The Art Of Anal / 1994 / ONA / M • Sexhibition #1 / 1996 / SUF / M • Sexhibition #2 / 1996 / SUF / M • The Star / 1995 / CC / M • Star Crossed / 1995 / VC / M • Starbangers #09 / 1996 / ZA / M • Strip Poker / 1995 / PEP / M • Strip Search / 1995 / CV / M • The Strippers / 1995 / GO / M • Temptation / 1994 / VC / M • The Thrill Of It / 1986 / CAT / M • Titanic Orgy / 1995 / PEP / M • Transformation / 1996 / XCI / M • The Usual Anal Suspects / 1996 / CC / M • A Woman Scorned / 1995 / CA / M • Work Of Art / 1995 / LE / M

BRIDGET
A&B AB#134: Panties Girl / 1990 / A&B / S • A&B AB#138: Shaved Teen / 1990 / A&B / M • A&B AB#177: Pizza Nerd / 1990 / A&B / M • A&B AB#225: Outdoor Sex Queen / 1990 / A&B / M • A&B AB#337: Home Movies / 1991 / A&B / M • A&B AB#354: All Day Cock / 1991 / A&B / M • A&B AB#361: The Birthday Gift / 1991 / A&B / M • A&B AB#447: Kinky Lady / 1996 / A&B / F • A&B AB#472: Bridget / 1994 / A&B / F • A&B AB#476: Bridget / 1994 / A&B / F • A&B AB#547: Sexy Bridget Masturbates / 1995 / A&B / F • A&B AB#548: Sexy Bridget Outdoors / 1995 / A&B / F • Babewatch Video Magazine #2 / 1994 / ERI / F • Limited Edition #25 / 1984 / AVC / M

BRIDGETT
Bondage Daydream / 1994 / BON / B • Peaches Poses / 1988 / BON / B

BRIDGETT MONROE see Brigitte Monroe

BRIDGETTE
Blue Vanities #512 / 1992 / FFL / M • Blue Vanities #513 / 1992 / FFL / M • Blue Vanities #576 / 1995 / FFL / M • Bubbles / 1993 / KBR / S • Butt Hunt #07 / 1995 / LEI / M • Catch Of The Day #6 / 1996 / VG0 / M • Deep Inside Anal Camera / 1996 / EVN / C • Filthy First Timers #1 / 1996 / EL / M • Girls Around The World #26 / 1995 / BTO / S • Pole Cats / 1993 / KBR / S • SVE: Greta Gets Off / 1994 / SVE / M • Too Fast For Love / 1992 / IF / M

BRIDGETTE (MAIER) see Brigitte Maier

BRIDGETTE (S/M)
The Clock Strikes Bizarre On Butt Row / 1996 / ABS / M • Deep Obsession / 1987 / WV / M • French-Pumped Femmes #1 / 1989 / RSV / G • French-Pumped Femmes #4 / 1991 / RSV / G

BRIDGETTE BELLE (Chrissy (Br. Belle))

Pretty, shoulder length reddish black straight hair, medium tits with very large areola, not particularly tight body, meaty labia. She says she's 20 years old in 1996 and is a mixture of Welsh and black. Appears with her SO Ray Swaze (or Swayze).

Dirty Dirty Debutantes #8 / 1996 / 4P / M • Ethnic Cheerleader Search #1 / 1996 / WIC / M • Fame Is A Whore On Butt Row / 1996 / ABS / M • Hollywood Amateurs #18 / 1995 / MID / M • I Wanna Be A Porn Star #1 / 1996 / 4P / M • I Wanna Be A Porn Star #2 / 1996 / 4P / M • More Dirty Debutantes #52 / 1996 / 4P / M • More Dirty Debutantes #54 / 1996 / 4P / M • More Dirty Debutantes #62 / 1997 / SBV / M • Up And Cummers #28 / 1996 / ERW / M • Up And Cummers #31 / 1996 / 4P / M • Up And Cummers #36 / 1996 / 4P / M

BRIDGETTE BLUE see Champagne

BRIDGETTE HANSONE
Disciplined Sissy / 1992 / PL / B • Women Who Control The Family Jewels #2 / 1993 / STM / C

BRIDGETTE MONEY see Brigitte Monet

BRIDGITT MENDOSA
The Missing Report / 1992 / CS / B

BRIDGITTE LEON
Caught In The Act / 1978 / MAP / M

BRIGADE VAN MEERHAEG see Brigitte LaHaye

BRIGETTE
Anal Cum Queens / 1995 / ZA / M • Buffy Malibu's Totally Nasty All-Girl Home Videos #04 / 1993 / ANA / F • The Exotic Dreams Of Casanova / 1970 / SOW / S

BRIGETTE BLUE see Champagne

BRIGETTE DEPALMA
Pleasure So Deep / 1983 / AT / M

BRIGETTE LAHAYE see Brigitte LaHaye

BRIGETTE LANNING see Karine Gambier

BRIGETTE LYNNE
Take Off / 1978 / VXP / M

BRIGIDA
Prague By Night #1 / 1996 / EA / M

BRIGIT
Penetration (Flash) #1 / 1995 / FLV / M

BRIGITTA
Love Slave / 1995 / WIV / M • Prague By Night #1 / 1996 / EA / M

BRIGITTE
Anal Camera #09 / 1995 / EVN / M • Beach Bum Amateur's #03 / 1992 / MID / M • Bedtime Story Italiano / 1995 / UGO / M • Games Women Play / 1995 / XC / M • Golden Arches / 1992 / PRE / B • Harry Horndog 23: The Final Flick / 1993 / ZA / M • Magma: Anita #2 / 1996 / MET / M • Magma: Spezial: Black & White #3 / 1995 / MET / M • Magma: Test Fuck / 1995 / MET / M • One Night Love Affair / 1991 / IF / M • Popped Tarts / 1992 / RB / B • Swimming Pool Orgy / 1995 / FRF / M • World Class Ass / 1995 / FC / M

BRIGITTE (ZUMIRA) see Zumira

BRIGITTE AIME (Vixene, Jacqueline Warner, Chantal LeMaire, Jennifer Gold, Sandi (Brig. Aime))

Not too pretty French-Canadian brunette with a thick body (not fat) and small tits. The tits were later enhanced to rock solid grapefruit. Jacqueline Warner in **Making It** (1990); Vixene in **Untamed Passion;** Chantal Lemaire in **Buns & Roses (LV)** and **Shake Well Before Using.**

AC/DC #2 / 1994 / HP / G • The Adventures Of Mr. Tootsie Pole #1 / 1995 / LBO / M • Adventures Of The DP Boys: Hooter County / 1995 / HW / M • Adventures Of The DP Boys: Janet And Da Boyz / 1994 / HW / M • All For You, Baby / 1990 / VEX / M • Amateur American Style #20 / 1992 / AFV / M • Amateur Lesbians #19: Sophia / 1992 / GO / F • Amateurama #05 / 1993 / RTP / F • Anal Assassins / 1991 / IN / M • Anal Blitz / 1991 / MID / M • Anal Climax #2 / 1991 / ROB / M • Anal Encounters #1 / 1991 / VC / M • Anal Encounters #2 / 1991 / VC / M • Anal Gang Bangers #01 / 1992 / GLI / M • Anal Heat / 1990 / ZA / M • Anal Illusions / 1991 / LV / M • Anal Legend / 1994 / ROB / M • Anal Lover #1 / 1992 / ROB / M • Anal Orgy / 1993 / DRP / M • Anal Revolution / 1991 / ROB / M • Anal Starlets / 1991 / ROB / M • Anal Summer / 1994 / ROB / M • Anal Therapy #1 / 1992 / FD / M • Anal Vision #04 / 1992 / LBO / M • Angels / 1992 / VC / M • Art Of Sex / 1992 / FD / M • As Time Goes Bi / 1993 / WMG / G • Ashlyn Gere: The Savage Mistress / 1992 / BIZ / B • Auction #1 / 1992 / BIZ / B • Auction #2 / 1992 / BIZ / B • Autobiography Of A Slave / 1993 / PL / B • Back In Action / 1992 / FD / M • Back In The Pen / 1992 / FH / M • Back Seat Bush / 1992 / LV / M • The Backdoor Club / 1992 / LV / M • Backdoor Suite / 1992 / EX / M • Backing In #3 / 1991 / WV / C • Backstage Entrance #2 / 1992 / FH / M • Badgirls #1: Lockdown / 1994 / VI / M • Battle Of The Superstars / 1993 / VI / M • Begging For Bondage / 1993 / PL / B • The Best Of Oriental Anal #1 / 1994 / ROB / C • Between The Bars / 1992 / FH / M • Bi And Busty / 1991 / STA / G • Bi Bi Birdie / 1993 / BIL / G • Bi Claudius / 1994 / BIL / G • Bi Intruder / 1991 / STA / G • Bi The Rear Window / 1994 / BIL / G • Bi Watch / 1994 / BIN / G • The Bi-Analyst / 1991 / STA / G • Bi-Inferno / 1992 / VEX / G • Biff Malibu's Totally Nasty Home Videos #31 / 1993 / ANA / M • Big Boob Ball / 1995 / IF / C • The Big One / 1992 / GO / M • Black Is Back / 1993 / HW / M • Black Jack City #01 / HW / M • Black Men Can Hump / 1992 / FH / M • Booty Mistress / 1994 / ROB / M • The Box / 1992 / EX / M • Breast Wishes #12 / 1993 / LBO / M • Bubble Butts #08 / 1992 / LBO / M • Bunmasters / 1995 / VC / M • Buns And Roses (LV) / 1990 / LV / M • Butt Camp / 1993 / HW / C • The Butt Sisters Do Cleveland / 1994 / MID / M • Butt's Up, Doc #1 / 1992 / GO / M • Butt's Up, Doc #2 / 1992 / GO / M • Butties / 1992 / VC / M • Buttsizer, King Of Rears #2 / 1992 / EVN / M • Buttwiser / 1992 / HW / M • Carnal Possessions / 1991 / VEX / M • Cliff Banger / 1993 / HW / M • Crash In The Rear / 1992 / HW / C • Creation Of Karen: Tormented & Transformed / 1993 / BIZ / B • Dallas Does Debbie / 1992 / PL / M • Dane Gets It Good / 1991 / IF / G • Days Gone Bi / 1994 / BIN / G • Deep C Diver / 1992 / LV / M • Deep Cheeks #1 / 1991 / ROB / M • Deep Cheeks #2 / 1991 / ROB / M • Deep Inside Savannah / 1993 / VC / C • Destination Moon / 1992 / GO / C • Dial N Again / 1993 / PEP / M • Dial N For Nikki / 1993 / PEP / M • Dirty Doc's Housecalls #12 / 1994 / LV / M • Doggie Style / 1994 /

CA / M • Don't Bother To Knock / 1991 / FAZ / M • Dorm Girls / 1992 / VC / M • Double Penetration #4 / 1991 / WV / C • Double Penetration #5 / 1992 / WV / C • Dougie Hoser: The World's Youngest Gynaecologist / 1990 / VT / M • Dreams Cum True / 1990 / HO / M • Dresden Diary #06: The Hellfire Legend / 1992 / BIZ / B • Dresden Diary #07 / 1992 / BIZ / B • Dresden Diary #08 / 1992 / BIZ / B • Drive Bi / 1994 / BIL / G • Dyke Bar / 1991 / PL / F • East L.A. Law / 1991 / WV / M • The End / 1992 / SC / M • Faithless Companions / 1992 / WV / M • Fast Cars And Fast Women / 1992 / LV / M • Fit To Be Tied / 1993 / PL / B • Florence Hump / 1994 / AFI / M • For Sale Bi Owner / 1994 / ... / G • Foreign Affairs / 1992 / VT / C • Foreign Bodies / 1991 / IN / M • Girls And Guns / 1992 / KBR / M • Girls Will Be Boys #4 / 1991 / PL / F • Girlz N The Hood #1 / 1991 / HW / M • Glen And Glenda / 1994 / CA / M • Good Bi Girl / 1994 / BIL / G • The Great Pretenders / 1994 / FD / M • Group Therapy / 1992 / TP / M • Guess Who? / 1991 / EX / M • Halloweenie / 1991 / PL / M • Hangin' Out / 1992 / IF / M • Hard Core Cafe / 1991 / PL / M • Harness Hannah At The Strap-On Ho Down / 1994 / WIV / F • Holly's Hollywood / 1992 / STM / F • Hollywood Connection / 1992 / ... / M • Home But Not Alone / 1991 / WV / M • Homegrown Video #314 / 1990 / HOV / M • Homegrown Video #385 / 1992 / HOV / M • Home-Grown Video #458: Cream Pie For Dessert / 1995 / HOV / C • Hot Flushes / 1992 / PRE / B • Hotel Sodom #05: Tammi Ann Bends Over / 1995 / SNA / M • House Of Torture / 1993 / PL / B • I Wanna Be A Lesbian / 1993 / HSV / F • In Too Deep / 1992 / AFD / M • In Your Wildest Dreams / 1993 / STY / M • Jeff Stryker's Favorite Sexual Positions / 1993 / STY / C • The Journey: Oral Majority / 1991 / WV / M • Just A Gigolo / 1992 / SC / M • L.A.D.P. / 1991 / PL / M • Laying The Ghost / 1991 / VC / M • Leg...Ends #06 / 1992 / PRE / F • Lipstick Lesbians / 1993 / STM / F • M Series #05 / 1993 / LBO / M • Madame A / 1992 / LV / M • Making It / 1990 / FH / M • The Mark Of Zara / 1990 / XCI / M • Midnight Angel / 1992 / CDI / M • Mistress Memoirs #2 / 1993 / PL / C • Mocha Magic / 1992 / FH / M • Moon Godesses #1 / 1992 / VIM / M • My Mistress...Her Slave / 1990 / PL / B • N.Y.D.P. / 1994 / PEP / M • Naked Buns 8 1/2 / 1992 / CC / M • Night Cap / 1990 / EX / M • Night Deposit / 1991 / VC / M • Nipples / 1994 / FOR / F • Nydp Pink / 1994 / HW / M • On The Job Training / 1991 / RB / B • Ona Zee's Learning The Ropes #10: Chains Of Love / 1994 / ONA / B • Oreo A Go-Go #1 / 1992 / FH / M • Oreo A Go-Go #2 / 1992 / FH / M • Orgy Attack / 1993 / DRP / M • The Outlaw / 1991 / WV / M • Paging Betty / 1994 / VC / M • Penetrating Thoughts / 1992 / LV / M • The Penetrator #1 / 1991 / PL / M • The Perfect Girl / 1992 / CDI / G • Power Play (Bruce Seven) / 1990 / BS / B • Private Film #18 / 1994 / OD / M • Put It In Gere / 1991 / CA / M • Red Hot And Ready / 1990 / V99 / M • Remembering Times Gone Bi / 1995 / AWV / G • Ride 'em Hard / 1992 / LV / M • Rim Job Rita / 1994 / SC / M • The Rock Hard Files / 1991 / VEX / M • Runnin' Hot / 1992

/ LV / M • Sabotage / 1994 / CA / M • Sex Drive / 1993 / VEX / M • Sexorcist / 1994 / HW / M • Sexual Healing / 1992 / LV / M • Shake Well Before Using / 9990 / LV / M • Shameless / 1991 / SC / M • Shave Me / 1994 / RTP / F • Shoot To Thrill / 1992 / WV / M • Simply Irresistible / 1991 / CIN / M • Slave Connection / 1993 / PL / B • Sleaze Please!—December Edition / 1994 / FH / M • Sodom & Gomorrah / 1992 / OD / M • Something New / 1991 / FH / M • Southern Side Up / 1992 / LV / M • Spank! / 1992 / STM / B • The Stand-Up / 1994 / VC / M • The Story Of Pain / 1992 / PL / B • Succulent Toes / 1995 / STM / B • Summer's End / 1991 / ROB / M • Sweet Cheeks (1991-Prestige) / 1991 / PRE / B • Tailiens #2 / 1992 / FD / M • Tailiens #3 / 1992 / FD / M • Tails From The Tower / 1993 / AFI / M • The Tasting / 1991 / EX / M • Thighs & Dolls / 1993 / PEP / M • Three Men And A Hooker / 1991 / WV / M • Three's A Crowd / 1990 / HO / M • Tiffany Lords Straps One On #1 / 1994 / WIV / F • Tiffany Lords Straps One On #2 / 1994 / WIV / F • Tight Squeeze / 1992 / SC / M • Tight Tushies #2 / 1994 / MET / M • Titty City #1 / 1995 / TIW / M • To The Rear / 1992 / VC / M • A Touch Of Mink / 1990 / V99 / M • Transparent Desires / 1991 / LV / M • Untamed Passion / 1991 / VEX / M • Up Against It / 1993 / ZA / M • Wendy's Bi Adventure / 1994 / STA / M • Women's Penitentiary / 1992 / VIM / M • Zane's World / 1992 / ZA / M

BRIGITTE ASHLEY-WARN
Private Film #03 / 1993 / OD / M

BRIGITTE BAKO
Red Shoe Diaries #1 / 1992 / REP / S • Strange Days / 1995 / FXV / S • [Replikator / 1994 / ... / S

BRIGITTE BORDEAUX
Casting Call #07 / 1994 / SO / M • Hot Action! / 1982 / CA / M

BRIGITTE GRAHAM
Love Airlines / 1978 / SE / M

BRIGITTE HAMPTON
Babes Of The Bay #1 / 1994 / LIP / F

BRIGITTE HILL
Open For Business / 1983 / AMB / M

BRIGITTE HUNTER
Anal Vision #11 / 1993 / LBO / M

BRIGITTE LAHAIE *see* **Brigitte LaHaye**

BRIGITTE LAHAYE *(Brigette LaHaye, Brigitte Lahaie, Brigade Van Meerhaeg, Brigitte Simonin)*
Born October 12, 1955, real name Brigade Van Meerhaegue (truncated in alternate names). The Big Orgy / cr81 / VD / M • Clarissa / 1978 / LUM / S • Come Play With Me #1 / 1979 / PS / S • Come Play With Me #2 / 1980 / PS / S • Dark Mission / 1987 / LUM / S • Diva / 1981 / AR0 / S • Education Of The Baroness / 1980 / CA / B • Emmanuelle #3 / 1977 / ... / S • Evenings Of A Voyeur Couple / 1979 / LUM / M • Exces Pornographiques / 1977 / ... / M • Faceless / 1988 / LUM / S • Fascination / 1979 / VS / S • French Erotic Fantasies / 1978 / ... / M • French Lessons / 1985 / VD / M • Friendly Favors / 1983 / PS / S • Henry & June / 1990 / MCA / S • Illusions Within Young Girls / 1981 / VEP / M • Island Women / 1976 / LUM / S • Joy #2 (French) / 1985 / VC0 / S • La Nuit Des Traquees / 1980 / ... / S • Secrets Of A French Maid /

cr75 / ... / S • Two At Once / 1978 / CV / M • Untamed Sex / 1979 / ... / S • [Cathy, Fille Soumise / 1977 / ... / M • [Education Anglaise / 1982 / ... / S • [I...Comme Icare / 1979 / ... / S • [Indecences 1930 / 1977 / ... / M • [Inonde Mon Ventre / 1977 / ... / M • [Je Brule De Partout / 1978 / ... / M • [Je Suis Une Belle Salope / 1977 / ... / M • [Jouir Jusqu'au Delire / 1977 / ... / M • [Jouissances / 1976 / ... / M • [L'Executrice / 1986 / ... / S • [La Rabatteuse / 1977 / ... / M • [Le Diable Rose / 1987 / ... / S • [Les Plaisirs Fous / 1976 / ... / M • [Les Raisins De La Mort / 1978 / VS / S • [Paul Raymond's Erotica / 1981 / ... / S • [Rentre C'est Bon / 1977 / ... / M • [S.S. Bordello / 1978 / ... / M • [Segrete Espereinze Di Luca E Fanny / 1980 / ... / S • [Suivez Mon Regard / 1986 / ... / S • [Swedish Erotic Sensations / 1980 / ... / S • [Vibrations Sensuelles / 1976 / ... / M • [Whirlpool / 1981 / ... / S

BRIGITTE LAVAL
The Rise Of The Roman Empress #1 / 1986 / PV / M

BRIGITTE MAIER *(Bridgette (Maier))*
Born August 7, 1952 in Austria (another source says Schleswig-Holstein, Germany) and came to the US when she was four. Quite pretty with reddish hair, medium tits, very white skin, tits look unnaturally firm. *Penthouse* pet in 1974 and *Playboy* spread in December 1975. As of 1995 she supposedly lives in NY.

Anal Assault / 197? / ALP / M • Blue Vanities #015 (New) / 1988 / FFL / M • Blue Vanities #089 / 1988 / FFL / M • Caballero Preview Tape #3 / 1984 / CA / C • Erotic Fantasies: Women With Women / 1984 / CV / C • French Blue / 1974 / ... / M • How Sweet It Is / 1974 / SE / M • Kinkorama / 1975 / CA / M • Love Lies Waiting / 1974 / AXV / M • Marriage And Other Four Letter Words / 1974 / VC / M • Penetration / 1975 / SAT / M • Puss-O-Rama / 1975 / BLT / C • The Second Coming Of Eva / 1974 / ALP / M • Sensations / 1975 / ALP / M • Tongue / 1974 / ALP / M • The True Way / 1975 / SVE / M • The Virgin Cowboy / 1975 / ALP / S • [Justine Och Juliette / 1975 / ... / S

BRIGITTE MONET *(Bridgette Money, Dana Cannon, Tina (B. Monet), Diana Diamond)*
Tall, large, not too pretty brunette in the Lauren Bacall style, with a big butt. Diana Diamond is from **Babylon Blue**.

Babylon Blue / 1983 / VXP / M • Beverly Hills Cox / 1986 / CA / M • Beverly Hills Wives / 1985 / CV / M • Big Tits And Fat Fannies #01 / 1989 / BTO / M • Blue Ribbon Blue / 1984 / CA / C • Blue Vanities #015 (Old) / 1988 / FFL / M • Blue Vanities #018 (Old) / 1988 / FFL / M • Blue Vanities #128 / 1990 / FFL / M • Bodacious Ta Ta's / 1984 / CA / M • A Brief Affair / 1982 / CA / M • Caballero Preview Tape #2 / 1983 / CA / C • Collection #03 / 1983 / SVE / M • Collection #04 / 1983 / CA / M • Collection #05 / 1984 / CA / M • Collection #06 / 1984 / CA / M • Erotic Interlude / 1981 / CA / M • Expressions Of Love / 1984 / CAV / M • For Services Rendered / 1984 / CA / M • The Girl From S.E.X. / 1982 / CA / M • Girls That Love Girls / 1984 / CA / F • Golden Girls #04 / 1981 / CA / M • Hustler Video Magazine #1 / 1983 / SE / M • I Like

To Watch / 1982 / CA / M • Indecent Pleasures / 1984 / CA / M • Legends Of Porn #1 / 1987 / CV / C • Lesbian Lust / 19?? / BIZ / C • Let's Talk Sex / 1982 / CA / M • Letters Of Love / 1985 / CA / M • Maximum #4 / 1983 / CA / M • Maximum #6 / 1983 / CA / M • Nightlife / 1983 / CA / M • Only The Best Of Girls With Curves / 1992 / CV / C • Porno Screentests / 1982 / VC / M • Pussy Galore / 1993 / VD / C • Screw / 1985 / CV / M • Shame On Shanna / 1989 / DR / C • Sorority Sweethearts / 1983 / CA / M • Stiff Competition #1 / 1984 / CA / M • Summer Of '72 / 1982 / CA / M • Suze's Centerfolds #4 / 1981 / CA / M • Swedish Erotica #15 / 1980 / CA / M • Swedish Erotica #34 / 1980 / CA / M • Swedish Erotica #41 / 1982 / CA / M • Swedish Erotica #42 / 1982 / CA / M • Swedish Erotica #44 / 1982 / CA / M • Swedish Erotica #46 / 1983 / CA / M • Swedish Erotica Superstar #2: Brigette Monet / 1983 / CA / C • Talk Dirty To Me #02 / 1982 / CA / M • Triangle Of Lust / 1983 / VCR / M • An Unnatural Act #1 / 1984 / DR / M • Up Up And Away / 1984 / CA / M • With Love, Lisa / 1985 / CA / C

BRIGITTE MONROE *(Paulina (B. Monroe), Paulina Down, Paulina Downs, Bridgett Monroe)*
Very pretty girl with a tattoo on the right shoulder and also the inside of the right ankle. De-virginized at 15. First was blonde, then black hair and has now gone red. Returned after an absence of a couple of years with **Casanova #1** but her body has really gone to seed and she has had her tits enhanced. Further, her face looks coarse. The moral: never come back!
19 And Nasty / 1990 / ME / M • A Is For Asia / 1996 / 4P / M • Amazing Tails #5 / 1990 / CA / M • Anal Alley Cat / 1996 / KWP / M • Anal Interrogation / 1995 / ZA / M • Anal Nation #1 / 1990 / CC / M • Beeping Miss Buffy / 1995 / CDI / M • Between A Rock And A Hot Place / 1989 / VEX / M • Big Knockers #15 / 1995 / TV / M • Big Knockers #21: Best Of Lesbian #2 / 1995 / TV / C • Big Knockers #22 / 1995 / TV / M • The Big One / 1995 / HO / M • The Bigger They Come / 1000 / VD / C • Bitches In Heat #2: On Vacation / 1995 / ZA / M • Black Stockings / 1990 / VD / M • Body Language / 1995 / VI / M • Boobs, Butts And Bloopers #1 / 1990 / HO / M • Borderline (Vivid) / 1995 / VI / M • Bruce Seven's Favorite Endings #1 / 1991 / EL / C • Candy Ass / 1990 / V99 / M • Casanova #1 / 1993 / SC / M • Circus Sluts / 1995 / LV / M • Club Head / 1990 / CA / M • The Comix / 1995 / VI / M • Confessions Of Christy / 1991 / CAY / M • Conjugal Visits / 1995 / EVN / M • Delicate Matters / 1989 / VEX / M • Desire / 1990 / VC / M • Dirty Looks / 1990 / IN / M • Double D Dykes #19 / 1995 / GO / F • Double D Dykes #20 / 1995 / GO / F • Dr Finger's House Of Lesbians / 1996 / SC / M • Dream Reamin' / 1995 / LV / M • Driving Miss Daisy Crazy #1 / 1990 / WV / M • The Exhibitionist / 1991 / VD / M • Fantasy Inc. / 1995 / CV / M • Fire & Ice / 1995 / LV / M • The Fire Down Below / 1990 / IN / M • Gangbusters / 1995 / VC / M • Getting Personal / 1995 / PE / M • Girls Of The Athletic Department / 1995 / VT / M • Hollywood Hustle #2 / 1990 / V99 / M • The

Horny Housewife / 1996 / HO / M • Hot Cargo / 1990 / MID / M • The House On Chasey Lane / 1995 / VI / M • Housewife Lust #2 / 1995 / TV / F • I'm No Brat / 1990 / FAZ / M • Indiscreet! Video Magazine #2 / 1995 / FH / M • Induced Pleasure / 1995 / ERA / M • Keep It Cumming / 1990 / V99 / M • Ladies Man / 1990 / REB / M • Lady's Choice / 1995 / VD / M • Legal Briefs / 1996 / EX / M • Legend #2 / 1990 / LE / M • Lick-A-Thon #2 / 1996 / HW / C • Little Girl Lost / 1995 / SC / M • Live Bait / 1990 / IN / M • Mellon Man #05 / 1995 / AVI / M • Meltdown / 1990 / LV / M • Midget Goes Hawaiian / 1995 / FC / M • Model Wife / 1991 / CA / M • Nasty Jack's Homemade Vid. #08 / 1990 / CDI / M • Naughty Nights / 1996 / PLP / C • Night Trips #2 / 1990 / CA / M • Nude Awakenings / 1996 / PP / M • Odyssey Amateur #37: Cumming To America / 1991 / OD / M • Oriental Spice / 1990 / SE / M • Passionate Lips / 1990 / OD / M • Phantasm / 1995 / WP / M • Philmore Butts Meets The Freak / 1995 / SUF / M • Playing The Field / 1990 / VEX / M • A Pool Party At Seymores #1 / 1995 / ULI / M • The Pump / 1991 / CC / M • Pussyman #09: Feeding Frenzy / 1995 / SNA / M • Raquel On Fire / 1990 / VC / M • Rear Burner / 1990 / IN / M • Road Kill / 1995 / CA / M • Rolling Thunder / 1995 / VI / M • Shave Tails #2 / 1994 / SO / M • She's America's Most Wanted / 1990 / VEX / M • Ski Sluts / 1995 / LV / M • The Smart Aleck / 1990 / PM / M • Snatch Masters #04 / 1995 / LEI / M • Spellbound / 1991 / CDI / M • Star 90 / 1990 / CAY / M • Star Spangled Banner / 1990 / FAZ / M • The Strippers / 1995 / GO / M • The Swap #1 / 1990 / VI / M • Swedish Erotica #80 / 1994 / CA / M • Sweet Miss Fortune / 1990 / LE / M • Sweet Tease / 1990 / VEX / M • The Taming Of Tami / 1990 / CA / M • The Temple Of Poon / 1996 / PE / M • Torrid Tales / 1995 / VI / M • Torrid Without A Cause #2 / 1990 / VI / M • Trading Partners / 1995 / GO / M • Trick Tracey #1 / 1990 / CC / M • Trick Tracy #2: Tracy Loves Dick / 1990 / CC / M • Triple Header #1990 / VXP / M • Hollisland / 1989 / FAN / C • Undercover Carol / 1990 / FAN / M • Venom #1 / 1995 / VD / M • Whackers / 1995 / PP / M • Where The Girls Sweat #1 / 1990 / EA / F • Where The Girls Sweat...Not The Sequel / 1996 / EL / F • Whispered Secrets Of The Call Girls / 1995 / TVE / F • Wire Desire / 1991 / XCI / M • WPINK-TV #5 / 1993 / PV / M • Zara's Revenge / 1991 / XCI / M

BRIGITTE MOREAU
The Devil In Mr Holmes / 1988 / PV / M

BRIGITTE OLSEN
Hot Lunch / 1978 / SE / M

BRIGITTE PARIS
More Dirty Debutantes #34 / 1994 / 4P / M

BRIGITTE ROYALE
Aerobisex Girls #1 / 1983 / LIP / F • Best Of Bruce Seven #3 / 1990 / BIZ / C • Bondage Interludes #1 / 1983 / BIZ / B • Bondage Interludes #2 / 1983 / BIZ / B • Bouncing Buns / 1983 / VC / M • Bound For Slavery / 1983 / BLB / B • Mistresses And Slaves: The Best Of Bruce Seven / 1991 / BEB / C • Outlaw Women / 1983 / LIP / F • Rear Action Girls #1 / 1984 / LIP / F • Women's Secret Desires / 1983 / LIP /

F

BRIGITTE SIMONIN *see* **Brigitte LaHaye**

BRIGITTE TETZLAFF
[Krankenschwestern-Report / 1972 / ... / M

BRIONNA MALLOY *see* **Breanna Malloy**

BRITNY
Real People Real Bondage #1 / 1995 / BON / C

BRITT
Reel Life Video #32: / 1995 / RLF / M • Reel Life Video: Britt & Iron John / 1995 / RLF / F

BRITT ENGLISH *see* **Brittania**

BRITT MORGAN *(Brittany Morgan, Jacy Bodean)*
Not too good looking blonde who seems to take it up the butt without any problems. Small tits. Older looking. Married to Jace Rocker. Split up in 1993.
A&B AB#027: Gang Bang Girl / 1990 / A&B / M • A&B AB#028: Britt Takes On 35 / 1990 / A&B / M • A&B AB#415: Sex Club #2 / 1993 / A&B / M • Adult Video News 1992 Awards / 1992 / VC / M • The Adventures Of Mikki Finn / 1991 / CA / M • Anything Goes / 1993 / VD / C • As The Spirit Moves You / 1990 / LV / M • AVP #9110: Eight Balls & Peeping Toms / 1991 / AVP / M • Bad Attitude / 1987 / CC / M • Beaver Ridge / 1991 / VC / M • Bend Over Babes #1 / 1990 / EA / M • Best Of Brittany Morgan / cr90 / STM / B • Beyond Innocence / 1990 / VCR / F • The Big Tease #1 / 1990 / VC / M • The Bigger They Come / 1993 / VD / C • Blow Job Betty / 1991 / CC / M • Blow Job Bonnie / 1992 / CC / M • The Bod Squad / 1989 / VT / M • Brandy & Alexander / 1991 / VC / M • Bush Wacked / 1991 / ZA / M • Carnal College / 1987 / VT / M • The Case Of The Sensuous Sinners / 1988 / ME / M • Case Studies Of The Punishing Nurse / 1992 / STM / B • The Cat Club / 1987 / SE / M • Catfights #3 / 1987 / OHV / B • Caught From Behind #14 / 1990 / HO / M • Cheeks #2: The Bitter End / 1989 / CC / M • Cheeks #4: A Backstreet Affair / 1991 / CC / M • Close Friends / 1991 / OD / M • Creepshow Hooters / 1987 / VXP / M • Dark Corners / 1991 / LV / M • Deep Inside Nina Hartley / 1993 / VC / M • Dirty Movies / 1989 / VD / M • Dirty Tricks / 1993 / CC / M • Domination & Fantasies / 1992 / BIZ / B • Eleventh Annual AVN Awards / 1994 / VC / M • The Erotic Adventures Of The Three Musketeers / 1992 / CEL / S • Even More Dangerous / 1990 / SO / M • Executive Suites / 1993 / PL / M • Extreme Heat / 1987 / ME / M • The Fine Line / 1990 / SO / M • Finely Back / 1990 / PL / F • The Flintbones / 1992 / FR / M • For His Eyes Only / 1989 / PL / M • Future Sodom / 1988 / VD / M • Genie In A Bikini / 1991 / ZA / M • Girl Lovers / 1990 / BIZ / F • Girls Don't Lie / 1990 / IN / F • Girls Just Wanna Have Girls #1 / 1988 / HIO / F • Girls Just Wanna Have Girls #2 / 1990 / HIO / F • Girls Just Wanna Have Toys / 1993 / PL / F • The Girls Of Porn / 1989 / FRV / F • Good Vibrations #1: Self Satisfaction With A Vibrator / 1991 / VT / M • Halloweenie / 1991 / PL / M • Haunted Nights / 1993 / WP / M • Heatwave #1 / 1992 / FH / F • Holly's Hollywood / 1992 / STM / F • Homegrown Video: At Home With Britt Morgan / 1990 /

HOV / M • How To Have Anal Sex / 1993 / A&E / M • How To Have Oral Sex / 1993 / A&E / M • How To Love Your Lover / 1992 / XII / S • I Found My Thrill On Cheri Hill / 1988 / PL / M • Imagine / 1991 / LV / M • In Excess / 1991 / CA / M • In Your Face #1 / 1992 / PL / M • Infidelity / 1988 / 4P / M • Interactive / 1994 / SC / M • Jail Babes #1 / 1990 / PL / F • Jail Babes #2: Bustin' Out / 1992 / PL / F • Joy-Fm #07 / 1994 / BHS / M • Joy-Fm #10 / 1994 / BHS / M • Joy-Fm #11 / 1994 / BHS / M • Joy-Fm #12 / 1994 / BHS / M • Kinky Lesbians #01 / 1992 / BIZ / B • Leena Goes Pro / 1992 / VT / M • Lesbian Dildo Bondage #2 / 1990 / BIZ / B • Lesbian Dildo Fever #2 / 1989 / BIZ / F • Lesbian Fantasies / 1990 / BIZ / F • Lesbian Kink Trilogy #1 / 1992 / STM / F • Lesbian Obsession / 1990 / BIZ / B • Lesbian Thrills / 1992 / BIZ / B • Let's Talk Dirty / 1987 / SE / M • Lick Bush / 1992 / VD / C • Lingerie Busters / 1991 / FH / M • Lips On Lips / 1989 / LIP / F • A Little Dove-Tale / 1987 / IN / M • Loose Ends #6 / 1989 / 4P / M • Love Lotion #9 / 1987 / VXP / M • Lucky Ladies #104 / 1992 / STI / M • Lurid Trios / 1994 / CA / C • Mad Love / 1988 / VC / M • Maximum Head / 1987 / SE / M • Mirage #2 / 1992 / VC / M • The Moon Girls / 1990 / ME / C • Mystic Pieces / 1989 / EA / M • Native Tongue / 1993 / VI / M • The New Kid On The Block / 1991 / VD / M • Night With A Vampire / 1992 / MID / M • Nightmare On Porn Street / 1988 / ME / M • No Man's Land #01 / 1988 / VT / C • No Man's Land #05 / 1992 / VT / F • On Trial #1: In Defense Of Savannah / 1991 / VI / M • On Trial #2: Oral Arguments / 1991 / VI / M • One Wife To Give / 1989 / ZA / M • The Only Game In Town / 1991 / VC / M • Only The Best Of Barbara Dare / 1990 / CV / C • P.S.: Back Alley Cats #01 / 1992 / PSP / F • Passion Chain / 1987 / ZA / M • Pearl Necklace: Amorous Amateurs #02 / 1992 / SEE / M • Pearl Necklace: Amorous Amateurs #14 / 1992 / SEE / M • Pearl Necklace: Thee Bush League: The Best Of Oral #01 / 1993 / SEE / C • Pearl Necklace: Thee Bush League #02 / 1992 / SEE / M • Perils Of Paula / 1989 / CA / M • The Pillowman / 1988 / VC / M • Playing For Passion / 1987 / IN / M • Porn Star Home Video Series 1 / 1990 / HOV / M • Pornocchio / 1987 / ME / M • Private Lessons / 1989 / STM / B • Private Pleasures / 1994 / STM / F • Queen Of Hearts #1 / 1987 / CL / M • Queen Of Hearts #2: Hearts On Fire / 1990 / PL / M • Queen Of Hearts #3: Heartless / 1992 / PL / M • Radical Affairs Video Magazine #02 / 1992 / ME / M • Radio-Active / 1992 / SC / M • Rainwoman #03 / 1990 / CC / M • Ruthless Women / 1988 / SE / M • Safecracker / 1991 / CC / M • Secret Fantasies Of Submissive Women / 1992 / BIZ / B • Secrets Behind The Green Door / 1987 / SE / M • Sexpionage / 1987 / VXP / M • Sexpot / 1987 / VXP / M • Sinderella #1 / 1992 / VI / M • Sinderella #2 / 1992 / VI / M • Slip Of The Tongue / 1990 / SE / M • Sorority Pink #1 / 1989 / CV / M • Sorority Pink #2 / 1989 / CV / M • Space Cadet / 1989 / IN / M • Spanked Students / 1989 / PLV / B • Spellbound / 1991 / CDI / M • St. X-Where #2 / 1988 / VD / M • Street Angels / 1992 / LV / M • Stud Puppy / 1992 / STM / B • Style #1 / 1992 / VT / M • Sugar

Tongues / 1992 / STM / C • Superstar Masturbation / 1990 / BIZ / F • Sweet Seduction / 1990 / LV / M • Taboo #06 / 1988 / IN / M • Tailspin #1 / 1991 / VT / M • Tailspin #2 / 1991 / VT / M • Take My Wife, Please / 1993 / WP / M • A Taste Of Viper / 1990 / PIN / C • The Three Musketeers #1 / 1992 / FD / M • The Three Musketeers #2 / 1992 / FD / M • Throbbin' Hood / 1987 / VD / M • Tongues Of Fire / 1987 / BIZ / F • Trampled / 1993 / STM / B • Transvestites Ruled By Desire / cr88 / STM / G • TVs Ruled By Women / 1992 / BIZ / G • Two In The Bush / 1991 / EX / M • Two On The Tongue / 1988 / TAM / C • Uniform Behavior / 1989 / ZA / M • What A Country / 1989 / PL / M • What's Up Doc / 1988 / SEV / M • Wicked / 1991 / XCI / M • Wise Girls / 1989 / IN / C • The Witching Hour / 1992 / FOR / M • Women Who Control The Family Jewels #2 / 1993 / STM / C • Women Who Control The Family Jewels #3 / 1995 / STM / C • WPINK-TV #5 / 1993 / PV / M • The Young And The Wrestling #1 / 1988 / PL / M • The Young And The Wrestling #2 / 1989 / PL / M • [Brittany's Bosom Buddies / 1990 / … / M • [High Society Centerspread #05 / 1987 / … / S • [High Society Centerspread #07 / 1988 / … / S

BRITT NEILSON
Cummin' Alive / 1984 / VC / M

BRITT REED
A Party In My Tight Pussy / 1994 / MET / M • Sally's Palace Of Delight / cr76 / CV / M

BRITT RONSTADT
Sounds Of Sex / 1985 / CA / M

BRITT SIMMS
She Studs #04 / 1991 / BIZ / G

BRITTA VOSS
Von Sex Gier Besessen / 1995 / PF / M

BRITTANI PARIS *see* **Tori Welles**

BRITTANIA *(Britt English, Gina Brittania)*
Tall English girl with small droopy tits and reddish-brown hair. Can't act.
The Backpackers #3 / 1991 / IN / M • Bedtime For Byron / 1991 / ME / M • Buttman's Bouncin' British Babes / 1994 / EA / M • Foreign Bodies / 1991 / IN / M • A Handful Of Summers / 1991 / ME / M • More Dirty Debutantes #09 / 1991 / 4P / M • Private Film #11 / 1994 / OD / M • Private Film #13 / 1994 / OD / M • Private Video Magazine #11 / 1994 / OD / M • Private Video Magazine #14 / 1994 / OD / M • Private Video Magazine #18 / 1994 / OD / M • Sodomania #08: The London Sessions / 1994 / EL / M • Sodomania: Slop Shots / 1996 / EL / C

BRITTANY *(Tiffany (Brittany))*
Tiffany in **Butts Motel #4**. This is supposedly Paula Price's sister which is probably true because she looks as ugly. She's married to director Jim Enright.
19 And Nasty / 1990 / ME / M • Amateur Lesbians #41: Kelli / 1993 / GO / F • Anal Alley / 1990 / ME / M • Back To Nature / 1990 / CA / M • Behind You All The Way #1 / 1990 / SO / M • Boa: Mainly Bound Outside / 1992 / BON / B • Breast Side Story / 1990 / LE / M • Breaststroke #3 / 1989 / EX / M • The Bust Blondes In The USA / 1995 / NAP / F • Butt's Motel #4 / 1989 / EX / M • Cheaters / 1990 / LE / M • The Devil Made Her Do It / 1992 / HO / M • Family Affairs / 1990 / VD / M • Famous Anus #1 / 1990 / EX / M • Female Persua-

sion / 1990 / SO / F • Friday Night Fever / 1989 / LV / M • Girls Of The Double D #12 / 1990 / CDI / M • Haunted Nights / 1993 / WP / M • Head Co-Ed Society / 1989 / VT / M • Homegrown Video #430 / 1994 / HOV / M • Hot Spot / 1990 / PL / F • Jail Babes #1 / 1990 / PL / F • Jailhouse Blue / 1990 / SO / M • Juggernaut / 1990 / EX / M • King Tung: The Tongue Squad / 1990 / LA / M • Kinky Couples / 1990 / VD / M • Legend #1 / 1990 / LE / M • Long Dan Silver / 1992 / IF / M • Lover's Trance / 1990 / LE / M • Money Honey / 1990 / TOR / M • Porn On The 4th Of July / 1990 / IN / M • Precious Peaks / 1990 / ZA / M • Pussywoman #1: Sisters In Sin / 1994 / CC / M • Pussywoman #2 / 1994 / CC / M • Racquel's Treasure Hunt / 1990 / VC / M • The Rebel / 1990 / CIN / M • The Secret (USA) / 1990 / SO / M • Sex & Other Games / 1990 / CIN / M • She's Got The Juice / 1990 / CDI / M • The Smart Ass #2: Rusty's Revenge / 1990 / VT / M • The Smart Ass Vacation / 1990 / VT / M • Some Like It Hot / 1989 / CDI / M • Steal Breeze / 1990 / SO / M • Student Fetish Videos: Best of Enema #03 / 1994 / PRE / C • Student Fetish Videos: The Enema #13 / 1994 / PRE / B • Student Fetish Videos: Tickling #08 / 1994 / SFV / B • Switch Hitters #5: The Night Games / 1990 / IN / G • Trouble / 1989 / VD / M • Vegas #3: Let It Ride / 1990 / CIN / M • Victoria's Secret / 1989 / SO / M • Where The Sun Never Shines / 1990 / IN / C • Wicked / 1991 / XCI / M • Wire Desire / 1991 / XCI / M • Wise Ass! / 1990 / FH / M • You Said A Mouthful / 1992 / IF / M

BRITTANY (GIDGETTE) *see* **Gidgette**

BRITTANY (O'CONNELL) *see* **Brittany O'Connell**

BRITTANY (OTHER)
Hot Body Competition: The Beverly Hill's Naughty Nightie C. / 1995 / CG / F • Silver Screen Confidential / 1996 / WP / M

BRITTANY ANDREWS *(Brittany Edwards)*
Blonde with huge tits, long hair, marginal face, looks like she has been around. Not to be confused with Busty Brittany who also has big tits (obviously) but is shorter.
The Art Of Deception / 1996 / BON / B • Badgirls #5: Maximum Babes / 1995 / VI / M • Bedroom Bruises / 1996 / NAP / B • The Best Of Fabulous Flashers / 1996 / DGD / F • Big Busty Major Babes / 1996 / NAP / F • Bob's Video #101: City Of Angels / 1996 / BOV / F • Bob's Video #103: Soft And Sexy / 1996 / BOV / F • Bondage Of The Rising Sun / 1996 / BON / B • Boobtown / 1995 / VC / M • City Girl / 1996 / LEI / C • Cloud 900 / 1996 / EYE / M • Deep Focus / 1995 / VC / M • Th Fanny / 1997 / WP / M • Finger Sluts #1 / 1996 / LV / F • Forbidden / 1996 / SC / M • Golden Rod / 1996 / SPI / M • Hard Core Beginners #11 / 1995 / LEI / M • Hawaii / 1995 / VI / M • Hot Body Competition: Beverly Hill's Miniskirt Madness Cont. / 1996 / CG / F • In Your Face / 1995 / IBN / B • Internal Affairs / 1995 / VI / M • Jenna's Built For Speed / 1997 / WP / F • Jiggly Queens #3 / 1996 / LE / M • Lingerie Lust: The Catfight / 1996 / NAP / B • Mellon Man #07 / 1996 / AVI / M • Motel Matches / 1996 / LE / M • The Naked Truth / 1995 / VI / M • New Pussy Hunt #20 / 1996 / LEI / C • New Pussy Hunt #24 / 1996 / LEI / C • Night

Nurses / 1995 / WAV / M • The Other Woman / 1996 / VC / M • Out Of Love / 1995 / VI / M • Philmore Butts Goes Hollyweird / 1996 / SUF / M • Playtime / 1996 / VI / M • Portraits Of Pain / 1995 / B&D / B • Power Of The Pussy / 1995 / LEI / M • Scandal / 1995 / VI / M • Sex Detectives / 1996 / SUF / M • Stone: Brittany: Worship My Butt / 1996 / SCS / F • Student Fetish Videos: Bondage #03 / 1996 / PRE / B • Student Fetish Videos: Catfighting #17 / 1996 / PRE / B • Student Fetish Videos: Foot Worship #18 / 1995 / PRE / B • Trample Bimbo / 1995 / IBN / B • Unruly Slaves #1 / 1995 / BON / B • Unruly Slaves #2 / 1995 / BON / B • Venom #2 / 1996 / VD / M • Water Wars / 1996 / NAP / B

BRITTANY BARDO *see* **Regina Bardot**
BRITTANY BARDOT *see* **Regina Bardot**
BRITTANY BARENT *see* **Regina Bardot**
BRITTANY DUNN *see* **Brooke Dunn**
BRITTANY EDWARDS *see* **Brittany Andrews**
BRITTANY FOX
Bare Essentials / 1995 / NIV / F • The Best Of Fabulous Flashers / 1996 / DGD / F • Breast Worx #08 / 1991 / LBO / M • Fabulous Flashers #2 / 1996 / DGD / F • Heidi's High Heeled Hookers / 1995 / BBE / M • More Dirty Debutantes #40 / 1995 / 4P / M • Naked Dolls / 1995 / NIV / F • Paradise Found / 1995 / LE / M • Private Eyes / 1995 / LE / M • Reality & Fantasy / 1994 / DR / M

BRITTANY GOLD
Lovin' Spoonfuls #7 / 1996 / 4P / C
BRITTANY LAINE *see* **Linda York**
BRITTANY LANE *see* **Linda York**
BRITTANY MORGAN *see* **Britt Morgan**
BRITTANY O'CONNELL *(Brittany (O'Connell), Brittany (O'Conner)*
Blonde/redhead with a nice body and a sweet smile. Was 19 and 5'2" in 1992 and is married and comes from Phoenix AZ. She was born Dec 6, 1972 in Panorama City, CA. Well, it's confusing but maybe it's possible. Had her tits enhanced around May 1995 to watermelon size (they were medium firm before).
Addictive Desires / 1994 / OD / M • Adult Video Nudes / 1993 / VC / M • The Adventures Of Major Morehead / 1994 / SC / M • The Adventures Of Mr. Tootsie Pole #1 / 1995 / LBO / M • Affairs Of The Heart / 1993 / VI / M • After Midnight / 1994 / IN / M • America's Raunchiest Home Videos #45: The Bigger They Cum / 1992 / ZA / M • America's Raunchiest Home Videos #46: / 1993 / ZA / M • American Connection Video Magazine #01 / 1992 / ZA / M • American Garter / 1993 / VC / M • Anal Attitude / 1993 / HO / M • Anal Centerfold / 1995 / ROB / M • Anal Ecstacy Girls #1 / 1993 / ROB / F • Anal Hellraiser #1 / 1995 / ROB / M • Anal Nitrate / 1995 / PE / M • Anal Shame / 1995 / VD / M • Anal Siege / 1993 / ROB / M • Anal Urge / 1993 / ROB / M • Anal Vision #10 / 1993 / LBO / M • Anal Vision #13 / 1993 / LBO / M • Assent Of A Woman / 1993 / DR / M • Attic Toys / 1994 / ERA / M • Babe Patrol / 1993 / FOR / M • Babe Watch #1 / 1994 / SC / M • Babe Watch #2 / 1994 / SC / M • Babes / 1993 / HO / M • Baby Doll / 1994 / SC / M • Backdoor Diaries / 1995 / BBE / M • Bad Girls #5 / 1994 / GO / M • Battlestar Orgasmica

/ 1992 / EVN / M • Between The Cheeks #3 / 1993 / VC / M • Big Murray's New-Cummers #19: The Ass Grabber / 1993 / FD / M • The Big One / 1995 / HO / M • Birthday Bash / 1995 / BOT / M • Blue Bayou / 1993 / VC / M • Body Language / 1995 / VI / M • Both Ends Burning / 1993 / HW / M • Bringing Up The Rear / 1993 / VD / C • Brittany O'Connell: Champagne Taste / 1996 / BRO / F • Brothers Bangin' / 1995 / ANA / M • Bubble Butts #22 / 1993 / LBO / M • Butt Bongo Babes / 1993 / VD / M • The Butt Sisters Do Cleveland / 1994 / MID / M • Butt Sluts #1 / 1993 / ROB / F • Butthead Dreams: Mission Impenetrable / 1994 / FH / M • Buzzzz! / 1993 / OD / M • Charm School / 1993 / PEP / M • Chateau Du Cheeks / 1994 / VC / M • Cheerleader Strippers / 1996 / PE / M • Chemical Reaction / 1995 / CC / M • Chicks, Licks And Dirty Tricks / 1993 / ME / F • Cinnamon Twist / 1993 / OD / M • Constant Craving / 1992 / VD / M • Corn Hole Kittens / 1996 / ROB / F • The Coven #1 / 1993 / VI / M • The Coven #2 / 1993 / VI / M • The Crack / 1994 / LV / M • De Sade / 1994 / SC / M • Deep Inside Brittany O'connell / 1996 / VC / C • Deep Inside Keisha / 1994 / VC / C • Deep Inside Misty Rain / 1995 / VC / C • A Dirty Western #2: Smoking Guns / 1994 / CV / M • Double Decadence / 1995 / NOT / M • Double Penetration Virgins #03 / 1994 / LE / M • The Dragon Lady #6: Tales From The Bed #5 / 1993 / WV / M • Dreams Of Desires / 1995 / ONA / M • The Drifter / 1995 / CV / M • The Ebony Connection #4 / 1994 / LBO / C • Eleventh Annual AVN Awards / 1994 / VC / M • Erotic Angel / 1994 / ERA / M • Essence Of A Woman / 1993 / FOR / M • Exit In Rear / 1993 / XCI / M • Extreme Sex #3: Wired / 1994 / VI / M • Face Dance #1 / 1992 / EA / M • Face Dance #2 / 1992 / EA / M • The Farmer's Daughters / 1994 / LV / M • Fireball #1 / 1994 / VI / C • Flashback / 1993 / SC / M • Flexxx #2 / 1995 / VT / M • The Fluffer #1 / 1993 / FD / M • The Fluffer #2 / 1993 / FD / M • Foolproof / 1994 / VC / M • Frankenstein / 1994 / SC / M • From Brazil With Love / 1992 / ZA / M • Full Moon Bay / 1993 / VI / M • Gang Bang Cummers / 1993 / ROB / M • Ghosts / 1995 / WV / M • Gimme An X / 1993 / VD / C • Girls Will Be Boys #5 / 1993 / PL / F • The Goddess / 1993 / ZA / M • The Governess / 1993 / WP / M • Happy Ass Lesbians / 1994 / ROB / F • The Hooker / 1995 / LOT / M • Hot For Teacher / 1993 / VD / M • The Hustlers / 1993 / MID / M • I Married An Anal Queen / 1993 / MID / M • Ice Woman #1 / 1993 / VI / M • Ice Woman #2 / 1993 / VI / M • If These Walls Could Talk (Director's Cut) / 1993 / MET / M • If These Walls Could Talk #1: Wicked Whispers / 1993 / MET / M • Indecent / 1993 / XCI / M • Indecent Obsessions / 1995 / BBE / M • Intersextion / 1994 / HO / M • Intimate Spys / 1992 / FOR / M • Into The Fire / 1994 / ZA / M • Jailhouse Cock / 1993 / IP / M • Jam / 1993 / PL / M • Kelly Eighteen #1 / 1993 / LE / M • Kelly Eighteen #2 / 1993 / LE / M • Kink #1 / 1995 / ROB / M • Last Tango In Paradise / 1995 / ERA / M • Leena Meets Frankenstein / 1993 / OD / M • Lesbian Bitches #1 / 1994 / ROB / F • Lesbian C*Nt Whores / 1996 / ROB / F • The Lovers /

1993 / HO / M • Make Me Watch / 1994 / PV / M • The Man Who Loved Women / 1993 / SC / M • Maneater / 1995 / ERA / M • Mask / 1993 / VI / M • Midnight Madness / 1993 / DR / M • Mighty Man #1: Virgins In The Forest / 1994 / LE / M • Mind Shadows #2 / 1993 / FD / M • Mr. Peepers Amateur Home Videos #63: Sexual Soiree / 1992 / LBO / M • Mr. Peepers Amateur Home Videos #68: A Tough Load To Swallow / 1993 / LBO / M • Ms. Behaved / 1994 / SC / M • Naked Reunion / 1993 / VI / M • Nasty Pants / 1995 / SUF / M • Neighborhood Watch #36 / 1992 / LBO / M • Neutron Man / 1993 / HO / M • Never Say Never, Again / 1994 / SC / M • The New Ass Masters #07 / 1996 / LEI / C • The New Ass Masters #10 / 1996 / LEI / C • New Lovers / 1993 / VI / M • The New Snatch Masters #13 / 1995 / LEI / C • New Wave Hookers #3 / 1993 / VC / M • Night Train / 1993 / VI / M • Nightmare Visions / 1994 / ERA / M • Nightshift Nurses #2 / 1996 / VC / M • Nightvision / 1993 / TP / M • Nikki's Bon Voyage / 1993 / VC / M • Nikki's Last Stand / 1993 / VC / M • No Motive / 1994 / MID / M • Nurse Tails / 1994 / VC / M • The One And Only / 1993 / FD / M • One Of Our Porn Stars Is Missing / 1993 / OD / M • The Orgy #1 / 1993 / EMC / M • The Orgy #2 / 1993 / EMC / M • The Orgy #3 / 1993 / EMC / M • The Other Side / 1995 / ERA / M • The Other Side Of Chelsea / 1993 / XCI / M • Pajama Party X #1 / 1994 / VC / M • Pajama Party X #2 / 1994 / VC / M • Parlor Games / 1993 / VI / M • The Pink Lady Detective Agency: Case Of The Twisted Sister / 1994 / IN / M • Private Film #12 / 1994 / OD / M • Private Film #14 / 1994 / OD / M • Private Film #18 / 1994 / OD / M • Private Video Magazine #04 / 1993 / OD / M • Private Video Magazine #11 / 1994 / OD / M • Private Video Magazine #15 / 1994 / OD / M • Promises & Lies / 1995 / SS / M • The Psychic / 1993 / CC / M • Public Places #1 / 1994 / SC / M • Public Places #2 / 1995 / SC / M • R.E.A.L. #2 / 1994 / LV / F • Radical Affairs Video Magazine #05 / 1993 / ME / M • Radical Affairs Video Magazine / 1994 / LV / M • Real Tickets #2 / 1994 / VC / M • Real Tickets #2 / 1994 / VC / M • Reel Life / 1993 / ZA / M • The Rehearsal / 1993 / VC / M • Release Me / 1996 / VT / M • Risque Burlesque #1 / 1994 / IN / M • Sapphire / 1995 / ERA / M • The Savage / 1994 / SC / M • Sean Michaels On The Road #03: Beverly Hills / 1993 / VT / M • The Secret Life Of Nina Hartley / 1994 / VC / M • Seven Good Women / 1993 / HO / F • Sex Bandits / 1995 / VC / M • Sexophrenia / 1993 / VC / M • Sharon Starlet / 1993 / WIV / M • Shooting Star / 1993 / XCI / M • Silent Stranger / 1992 / VI / M • The Sin-A-Bun Girls / 1995 / OD / M • Slave To Love / 1993 / ROB / M • So You Want To Be In The Movies? / 1994 / VC / M • The Social Club / 1995 / LE / M • Sodomania #01: Tales Of Perversity / 1992 / EL / M • Sodomania #04: Further On Down The Road / 1993 / EL / M • Sorority Sex Kittens #3 / 1996 / VC / M • Stardust #1 / 1996 / VI / M • Stardust #2 / 1996 / VI / M • Stardust #3 / 1996 / VI / M • Stardust #4 / 1996 / VI / M • Stardust #5 / 1996 / VI / M • Steal This Heart #1 / 1993 / CV / M • Steal This Heart

#2 / 1993 / CV / M • Steal This Heart (Director's) / 1993 / CV / M • Stiff Competition #2 / 1994 / CA / M • Stiletto / 1994 / WAV / M • Stuff Your Face #1 / 1994 / JMP / M • Taboo #12 / 1994 / MET / M • Tails Of Desire / 1995 / GO / M • Taxi Girls #3: Killer On The Loose / 1993 / MED / M • Teri Diver's Bedtime Tales / 1993 / FD / M • The Thief / 1994 / SC / M • Thighs & Dolls / 1993 / PEP / M • Tongue In Cheek / 1994 / LE / M • Top Debs #1: Prom Night / 1992 / GO / M • Top Debs #3: Riding Academy / 1993 / GO / M • True Sex / 1994 / EMC / M • Two Sides Of A Lady / 1994 / HDE / M • Untamed Cowgirls Of The Wild West #01: The Pillow Biters / 1992 / ZA / M • The Valley Girl Connection / 1994 / IN / M • Video Virgins #03 / 1993 / NS / M • The Violation Of Alexandria Dane / 1995 / JMP / F • Virgin / 1993 / HW / M • Virtual Reality / 1993 / EX / M • Visions #1 / 1995 / ERA / M • Visions #2 / 1995 / ERA / M • Voices In My Bed / 1993 / VI / M • Web Of Darkness / 1993 / BS / B • Welcome To Bondage: Brittany / 1993 / BON / B • What's Up, Tiger Pussy? / 1995 / VC / M • White Shadow / 1994 / VC / M • Who Killed Holly Hollywood? / 1993 / VC / M • Wild & Wicked #3 / 1993 / VT / M • Wild Breed / 1995 / SC / M • Wild Things #4 / 1994 / CV / M • Wilde Palms / 1994 / XCI / M • Working Stiffs / 1993 / FD / M

BRITTANY O'CONNER *see* **Brittany O'- Connell**

BRITTANY O'NEIL
Burbank Sperm Bank / 1996 / CIN / M • Femme Fatale / 1996 / CIN / M • Gun Runner / 1996 / CIN / M

BRITTANY SAKS
Anal Rescue 811 / 1992 / PL / M • Angels With Sticky Faces / 1991 / VD / M • Beettlejizum / 1991 / PL / M • Brittany's Getaway / 1992 / PL / M • Class Ass / 1992 / PL / M • Danielle's Dirty Deeds / 1991 / CC / M • I Creme With Genie / 1991 / PL / M • Journey Into Latex / 1992 / STM / B • Kittens #2 / 1991 / CC / F • Kittens #3 / 1992 / CC / F • Mr. Big / 1991 / PL / M • Rick's Bondage Playmate #1 / 1992 / BON / B • Sex Between The Scenes / 1994 / LAP / M • Unlaced / 1992 / PL / M

BRITTANY STONE
Erotic Newcummers Vol 1 #2: Texas Twisters / 1993 / DR / M • Hot Body Hall Of Fame: Christy Carrera / 1996 / CG / F • Love Scenes #3 / 1993 / B/F / S • Margarita On The Rocks / 1994 / SFP / M • The Other Side Of Melinda / 1995 / LON / B • Sean Michaels On The Road #08: Chicago / 1993 / VT / M • Swinging Couples #01 / 1993 / GO / M

BRITTANY STRYKER *(Judy Jones)*
All For His Ladies / 1987 / PP / C • Amber Lynn's Peter Meter / 1988 / 3HV / C • Angel Of The Night / 1985 / IN / M • Backdoor Brides #1 / 1985 / PV / M • Backdoor Summer #1 / 1988 / PV / C • Backdoor To Hollywood #02 / 1986 / CDI / M • Banana Splits / 1987 / 3HV / M • Beyond The Casting Couch / 1986 / VD / M • The Brat / 1986 / VI / M • California Gigolo / 1987 / VD / M • Cavalcade Of Stars / 1985 / VCR / C • Charmed And Dangerous / 1987 / VI / M • Circus Of Lesbians / 1995 / VI / C • Despicable Dames / 1986 / CC / M • Devil In Miss Dare / 1986 / AVC / C • Dirty 30's Cin-

ema: Brittany Stryker / 1986 / PV / C • Dirty Blondes / 1986 / CDI / M • Dr Penetration / 1986 / WET / M • Erotic Therapy / 1987 / CDI / M • Flasher / 1986 / VD / M • Flesh In Ecstasy #07: Brittany Stryker / 1987 / GO / C • Flying High With Rikki Lee / 1992 / VEX / C • Flying High With Tracey Adams / 1987 / VEX / M • For Your Thighs Only / 1985 / WV / M • Get Me While I'm Hot / 1988 / PV / M • Ginger's Greatest Girl/Girl Hits / 1986 / VI / C • Girls Like Us / cr88 / IN / C • Hard Ride / 1986 / VT / M • Having It All / 1985 / IN / M • Honeybuns #1 / 1987 / WV / C • Hot Nights At The Blue Note Cafe / 1985 / WV / M • Hottest Ticket / 1987 / WV / C • I Am Curious Black / 1986 / WET / M • Indecent Itch / 1985 / VCR / M • Kinkyvision #1 / 1986 / 3HV / M • Kiss Of The Dragon Lady / 1986 / SEV / M • Late After Dark / 1985 / BAN / M • Let's Get It On With Amber Lynn / 1986 / VC / M • Lucky In Love #1 / 1985 / BAN / M • Lust At Sea / 1986 / VD / M • Lusty Layout / 1986 / PV / M • Meat Market / 1992 / SEX / C • Nasty Girls #2 (1990-Plum) / 1990 / PP / M • Naughty Nymphs / 1986 / VEX / M • Naughty Nymphs / 1991 / VEX / C • No Man's Land #01 / 1988 / VT / C • Pumping Irene #1 / 1986 / FAN / M • Pumping Irene #2 / 1986 / FAN / M • Raunch #01 / 1990 / CC / M • Raunch #02 / 1990 / CC / M • Rears / 1987 / VI / M • Restless Passion / 1987 / HO / M • Sex Asylum #1 / 1985 / VI / M • The Sins Of Angel Kelly / 1987 / FAN / C • Sky Foxes / 1987 / VC / M • Sleeping With Everybody / 1992 / MID / C • Soul Games / 1988 / PV / C • Submissive Women / 1989 / ... / C • Supersluts Of Wrestling / 1986 / VD / M • Sweet Cheeks / 1987 / VCR / C • Switch Hitters #1 / 1987 / IN / G • Tailgunners / 1985 / WET / M • Tailspin / 1987 / AVC / M • Taking It To The Streets / 1987 / CDI / M • Talk Dirty To Me One More Time #1 / 1985 / PP / M • Virgin Heat / 1986 / TEM / M • White Trash / 1986 / PV / M • Wild Oral Erotica / 1988 / VD / C • Wise Girls / 1989 / IN / C

BRITTANY TYLER
Cat 'nipped / 1995 / PLV / B

BRITTICE
Dirty Blue Movies #03 / 1992 / JTV / M

BRITTON HILL
Daddy's Darling Daughters / 1986 / PL / M

BROCK STEWART
Where The Girls Are / 1984 / VEX / M

BROCKTON O'TOOLE *(Buckston O'- Toole, Buck O'Toole)*
Grey haired, not unpleasant old codger who generally introduces or does non-sex roles in Evil and Elegant Angel movies.
C-Hunt / 1985 / PL / M • De Blond / 1989 / EA / M • Depravity On The Danube / 1993 / EL / M • Evil Angel / 1986 / VCR / M • Face Dance #1 / 1992 / EA / M • A Fairy's Tail / 1996 / TTV / M • The Godmother #2 / 1988 / VC / M • Innocent Obsession / 1989 / FC / M • Nasty Habits Are Hard To Break / 1986 / 4P / M • Sex For Secrets / 1987 / VCR / M • Shadow Dancers #1 / 1989 / EA / M • Sodomania #02: More Tails / 1992 / EL / M • Sodomania #03: Foreign Objects / 1993 / EL / M • Sodomania #04: Further On Down The Road / 1993 / EL / M • Sodomania #05: Euro-American Style / 1993 / EL / M • Sodomania #06: Gangs And Bangs And Other Thangs / 1993 / EL /

M • Sodomania #07: Deep Down Inside / 1993 / EL / M • Sodomania #08: The London Sessions / 1994 / EL / M • Sodomania #09: Doin' Time / 1994 / EL / M • Sodomania #10: Euro/American Again / 1994 / EL / M • Sodomania #11: In Your Face / 1994 / EL / M • Sodomania #12: Raw Filth / 1995 / EL / M • Sodomania #15: Warning! / 1996 / EL / M • Sodomania #19: Sweet Cream / 1996 / EL / M • Sodomania #20: For Members Only / 1997 / EL / M • Sodomania #21: Degenerate Lifestyles! / 1997 / EL / M • Sodomania: The Baddest Of The Best...And Then Some / 1994 / EL / C • A Taste Of Genie / 1986 / 4P / M • The Teacher's Pet / 1985 / WV / M • Tit Tales #2 / 1990 / FC / M

BRODERICK STERLING
Mandy's Executive Sweet / 1982 / AVC / M

BRODIE BURKE
Going Down Under / 1993 / OD / M

BRON WHITE
Candy Stripers #1 / 1978 / ALP / M

BROOK
AVP #7002: Hard Dick, Wet Pussy And Wine / 1990 / AVP / M • Hot Body Competition: Bikinis & Bikes Contest / 1996 / CG / F

BROOK LONDON *(Tina Lynn (B.London))*
Assumed Innocence / 1990 / AR / M • More Dirty Debutantes #03 / 1990 / 4P / M • Nasty Jack's Homemade Vid. #14 / 1990 / CDI / M • Strangers When We Meet / 1990 / VCR / M

BROOK OWEN
The Horny Housewife / 1996 / HO / M

BROOK PETERS
Love Lips / 1976 / VC / M

BROOK TAYLOR
The Disciplinarians / 1996 / LON / B

BROOKE
Cherry Poppers #16: Cuddly Cunts / 1996 / ZA / M • Chronicles Of Lust #2 / 1996 / XPR / M • Girly Video Magazine #3 / 1995 / BEP / M • Rocco Unleashed / 1994 / SC / M • She-Male Bride Exposed / 1992 / LEO / G • Sluthunt #3 / 1996 / BIP / F • Stevi's: Brooke's Favorite Toy / 1996 / SSV / F • Student Fetish Videos: Foot Worship #09 / 1994 / PRE / B • Student Fetish Videos: Tickling #09 / 1994 / SFV / B • Titan's Gonzo Video Magazine #02 / 1996 / TEG / M • Weak-Ends / 1995 / PRE / B • Whore'n / 1996 / AB / M • Whoreos' / 1996 / BEP / M

BROOKE ASHLEY *(Fantasia (Tae), China Lakke, Anne Marie (Tae), Fantasia Lee, Tae)*
Kittenish girl with slightly Oriental look. Pretty face with a hard body and small breasts, good skin. After some time in the business in 1991/2 she blew up into a pudgy but still pretty girl and then disappeared. She returned in 1993 in a slimmed-down version as Brooke Ashley.
The Adventures Of Peeping Tom #3 / 1996 / OD / M • Amateur Lesbians #43: Poppy / 1993 / GO / F • America's Raunchiest Home Videos #17: This Butt's For You / 1992 / ZA / M • America's Raunchiest Home Videos #19: Bedroom Farce / 1992 / ZA / M • The Anal Adventures Of Max Hardcore: Adventures In Shopping / 1992 / ZA / M • Anal Analysis / 1992 / ZA / M • Anal Cuties #1 / 1992 / ROB / M • Anal Cuties #2 / 1992 / ROB / M • Anal Cuties

#3 / 1992 / ROB / M • Anal Lover #1 / 1992 / ROB / M • Anal Vision #18 / 1993 / LBO / M • Anal Vision #23 / 1994 / LBO / M • Asian Heat #02: Satin Angels / 1993 / SC / M • Asian Heat #04: House Of The Rising Sun / 1993 / SC / M • Asian Pussyman Auditions / 1996 / SNA / M • Assford Wives / 1992 / ATL / M • Bangkok Dreams / 1996 / SUF / M • The Best Of Oriental Anal #1 / 1994 / ROB / C • Big Murray's New-Cummers #22: Exotic Erotica / 1993 / FD / M • Bitches In Heat / 1994 / PL / C • Bobby Hollander's Sweet Cheeks #110 / 1994 / WV / M • Buffy Malibu's Totally Nasty All-Girl Home Videos #05 / 1993 / ANA / F • The Burma Road #1 / 1994 / LBO / C • The Burma Road #2 / 1994 / LBO / C • Cherry Poppers #02: Barely Legal / 1994 / ZA / M • Committed / 1992 / LE / M • Curious / 1992 / LE / M • Dial A Nurse / 1992 / VD / M • Dirty Video #1 / 1996 / AB / M • Disoriented / 1992 / VI / M • Double Crossing / 1991 / IN / M • Double Penetration Virgins #03 / 1994 / LE / M • Dr Peter Proctor's House Of Anal Delights / 1996 / HO / M • Dungeon Dykes #2 / 1994 / FPI / F • Feathermates / 1992 / PRE / B • First Time Lesbians #14 / 1994 / JMP / F • Flood Control / 1992 / PRE / B • Fortune Cookie / 1992 / VI / M • A Geisha's Secret / 1993 / VI / M • Gutter Mouths / 1996 / JMP / M • Hard As A Rock / 1992 / ZA / M • Her Name Is Asia / 1996 / SUF / M • Hillary Vamp's Private Collection #31 / 1992 / HOV / M • Hits & Misses / 1992 / PRE / B • Hooked / 1992 / SC / M • House Of The Rising Sun / 1993 / VT / M • Inside Job / 1992 / ZA / M • Intervidnet #1: Special Delivery / 1994 / IVN / M • Jack The Stripper / 1992 / ME / M • Midnight Fantasies / 1992 / VIM / M • More Dirty Debutantes #28 / 1994 / 4P / M • N.Y. Video Magazine #09 / 1996 / OUP / M • Nasty Cracks / 1992 / PRE / B • Naughty Nicole / 1994 / SC / M • Naughty Nurses / 1992 / VD / C • Never Never Land / 1992 / PL / M • Oriental Anal Sluts / 1993 / WV / C • Pai Gow Video #03: Egg Foo Kitty Yung / 1993 / EVN / M • Perks / 1992 / ZA / M • Perverted Stories #09 / 1996 / JMP / M • Pick Up Lines #07 / 1995 / OD / M • Pick Up Lines #08 / 1996 / OD / M • Pick Up Lines #12 / 1997 / OD / M • Portrait Of Lust / 1992 / WV / M • Puritan Video Magazine #02 / 1996 / LE / M • Puritan Video Magazine #05 / 1996 / LE / M • Rice Burners / 1996 / NOT / M • Romancing The Butt / 1992 / ATL / M • Sabrina Starlet / 1994 / SC / M • The Seduction Of Sabrina / 1996 / AVD / M • See-Thru / 1992 / LE / M • Sex Trek #3: The Wrath Of Bob / 1992 / ME / M • Sexual Trilogy #05 / 1994 / SFP / M • The Shocking Truth / 2 / 1996 / DWO / M • Showtime / 1996 / VT / M • Spanish Fly / 1992 / LE / M • Student Fetish Videos: The Enema #08 / 1992 / PRE / B • Student Fetish Videos: Tickling #05 / 1992 / SFV / B • Sweet Target / 1992 / CDI / M • Taboo #10 / 1992 / IN / M • Tori Welles Goes Behind The Scenes / 1992 / FD / M • Two Women / 1992 / ROB / M • Victoria's Secret Life / 1992 / WV / M • Voices In My Bed / 1993 / VI / M • Wet Faces #1 / 1997 / SC / C • With The Devil In Her Rear / 1992 / WV / M • Yin Yang Oriental Love Bang #3: Bangkok Dreams / 1996 / SUF / M • You

Assed For It / 1996 / NOT / M • Young And Anal #5 / 1996 / JMP / M • Young And Anal #6 / 1996 / JMP / M

BROOKE BENNETT *(Joan Victoria)*
The Blonde Next Door / 1982 / GO / M • Blue Jeans / 1982 / VXP / M • C.T. Coed Teasers / 1978 / VXP / M • Daddy's Little Girls / 1983 / CA / M • Expose Me Now / 1982 / CV / M • The Oui Girls / 1981 / VHL / M

BROOKE CAMPBELL
Dirty Dave's #1 / 1996 / VG0 / M • Dirty Debutantes #4 / 1996 / 4P / M • Fresh Meat (John Leslie) #3 / 1996 / EA / M • How To Make A College Co-Ed / 1995 / VG0 / M • Sinboy #2: Yo' Ass Is Mine / 1996 / SC / M

BROOKE DUNN *(Brittany Dunn, Brooke St. Lee, Nancy (Brooke Dunn))*
Blonde with large inflated tits, pretty face, lithe body except for the tits, flat rear end, facially similar to Victoria Paris. Seems to have a scar across the top of her pubic bone which may be an old Caesarian.
Adventures Of The DP Boys: Back In Town / 1994 / HW / M • The Anal Adventures Of Max Hardcore: Grand Prix / 1994 / ZA / M • Anal Camera #02 / 1994 / EVN / M • Anal Torture / 1994 / ZA / M • Anal Virgins Of America #09 / 1994 / FOR / M • Big Boob Bangeroo #2 / 1995 / TTV / M • Big Boob Bangeroo #3 / 1996 / TTV / M • Big Boob Bangeroo #7 / 1996 / TTV / M • Big Murray's New-Cummers #25: / 1994 / FD / M • Butt Bangers Ball #2 / 1996 / TTV / M • Butt Hunt #02 / 1994 / LEI / M • Casting Call #10 / 1994 / MET / M • Caught From Behind #20 / 1995 / HO / M • Cherry Poppers #07: Li'l Darlin's / 1994 / ZA / M • The Cumm Brothers #04: Laid Off & Laid / 1994 / OD / M • The Dickheads #2 / 1993 / MID / M • Double D Nurses / 1994 / PV / M • Freeway Love / 1994 / FD / M • Gang Bang In Vedova / 1995 / WIV / M • Harness Hannah At The Strap-On Palace / 1994 / WIV / F • Horny Henry's Strange Adventure / 1995 / TTV / M • Hotel Sodom #06 / 1995 / SNA / M • Kinky Debutante Interviews #02 / 1994 / IP / M • Kinky Orientals / 1994 / FH / M • Lesbian Workout #1 / 1994 / GO / F • Lesbian Workout #2 / 1994 / GO / F • Lovin' Every Minute Of It / 1994 / VEX / C • Mellon Man #02 / 1994 / AVI / M • Midnight Dreams / 1994 / WV / M • Mike Hott: #277 Cum In My Cunt #2 / 1994 / MHV / M • Mike Hott: #287 Bonus Cunt: Brooke Dunn / 1995 / MHV / M • Older And Anal #1 / 1995 / FC / M • Pussy Showdown / 1994 / WIV / M • Ron Hightower's White Chicks #14 / 1994 / LBO / M • Slut Safari #3 / 1994 / FC / M • Tight Fit #08 / 1994 / GO / M • Titties 'n Cream #2 / 1995 / FC / M • TV Nation #1 / 1995 / HW / G • Welcome To Bondage: Brooke / 1994 / BON / B • Wild Orgies #11 / 1994 / AFI / M

BROOKE FIELDS *(Blair Castle)*
The Awakening Of Sally / 1984 / VCR / M • Bad Girls #2 / 1983 / GO / M • Brooke Does College / 1984 / VC / M • Centerfold Celebrities #2 / 1983 / VC / M • Hostage Girls / 1984 / VC / M • Hypersexuals / 1984 / VC / M • Ice Cream #1: Tuesday's Lover / 1983 / VC / M • Ice Cream #2: French Postcard / 1983 / VC / M • Jack 'n' Jill #2 / 1984 / VC / M • Lady Lust / 1984 / CA / M • Love Champions / 1987 / VC / M •

Lust And The Law / 1991 / GO / C • New Wave Hookers #1 / 1984 / VC / M • Piggies / 1984 / VC / M • Pleasure Channel / 1984 / VC / M • Pussycat Galore / 1984 / VC / M • Sex Spa USA / 1984 / VC / M • Snake Eyes #1 / 1984 / COM / M • Stray Cats / 1985 / VXP / M • Summer Camp Girls / 1983 / CA / M • Turn On With Kelly Nichols / 1984 / CA / M • Vanessa...Maid In Manhattan / 1984 / VC / M

BROOKE HARLOW
Essence / 1996 / SO / M • Freaknic / 1996 / IN / M • Waiting To XXX-Hale / 1996 / MET / M

BROOKE LANE
Zazel / 1996 / CV / M

BROOKE LEE *(Silk)*
Vietnamese, small tits, child-like face (passable), not a tight waist, reddish brown hair, 5'2" tall, 25 years old in 1996, 34-24-34. Has a three word tattoo on her left shoulder back. Came to the USA in 1975.
Anal Witness #1 / 1996 / LBO / M • Asses Galore #4: Extreme Noise Terror / 1996 / DFI / M • Dirty Diner #3 / 1996 / SC / M • Dirty Dirty Debutantes #4 / 1996 / 4P / M • I Wanna Be A Porn Star #2 / 1996 / 4P / M • Lovin' Spoonfuls #6 / 1996 / 4P / C • More Dirty Debutantes #50 / 1996 / 4P / M • More Dirty Debutantes #51 / 1996 / 4P / M • Up And Cummers #37 / 1996 / 4P / M • Up And Cummers #38 / 1996 / RWP / M • Valentina: Princess Of The Forest / 1996 / SC / M

BROOKE LUV
Beaver Hunt #02 / 1994 / LEI / M • Butt Hunt #01 / 1994 / LEI / M • Pussy Hunt #02 / 1994 / LEI / M • Pussyclips #03 / 1994 / SNA / M • Reel People #07 / 1995 / PP / M • Welcome To Paradise / 1994 / IF / M

BROOKE MEADOWFIELD
Jail Bait / 1976 / VC / M

BROOKE ST. LEE *see* **Brooke Dunn**

BROOKE SUMMERS
The Beverly Thrillbillies / 1987 / EVN / M • City Of Rage / 1989 / EVN / M • Find Your Love / 1988 / CV / M • Frisky Fables / 1988 / LV / M • The Girls Of Ball Street / 1988 / VEX / M • The Heat Is On / 1989 / VEX / M

BROOKE WATERS
Long curly reddish brown hair, small tits, lithe body, freckles, reasonably pretty face, 22 years old in 1995, married to Andrew Wade, de-virginized at 13, mother of two girls.
19 & Naughty #2 / 1995 / SKV / M • Anal Witness #2: No Prisoners / 1996 / LBO / M • Ass Thrashing / 1995 / RB / B • Attitude / 1995 / VC / M • Babe Watch #1 / 1994 / SC / M • Babe Watch #2 / 1994 / SC / M • Babes Illustrated #2 / 1994 / IN / F • Beaver Hunt #03 / 1994 / LEI / M • Bizarre Desires / 1995 / ROB / F • Buffy Malibu's Nasty Girls #07 / 1994 / ANA / F • Buffy's New Boobs / 1996 / CIN / M • Bunmasters / 1995 / VC / M • Butt Jammers #03 / 1995 / SC / F • Butt Jammers #04 / 1995 / SC / F • The Butt Sisters Do Boston / 1995 / MID / M • Butt Watch #06 / 1994 / FH / M • Buttslammers #08: The Ultimate Invasion / 1994 / BS / F • Call Me Mistress / 1996 / ATO / B • Cheeks #8 / 1995 / CC / M • Cheeky Response / 1995 / RB / B • Cinderella In Chains #1 / 1996 / LBO / B • Coming Attractions / 1995 / WHP / M •

Cumming Unscrewed / 1995 / TEG / F • The Dean Of Discipline / 1996 / HAC / B • Debbie Class Of '95 / 1995 / CC / M • Delaid Delivery / 1995 / EX / M • Desire Kills / 1996 / SUM / M • Devil In A Wet T-Shirt / 1995 / SPI / M • Diamond In The Raw / 1996 / XCI / M • Dirty Bob's #23: Tampa Teasers / 1995 / FLP / S • Dirty Doc's Housecalls #19 / 1994 / LV / M • A Dirty Western #2: Smoking Guns / 1994 / CV / M • Dreams Of Desires / 1995 / ONA / M • Dungeon Play / 1995 / IBN / B • Dungeon Punishment / 1995 / STM / B • Erotic World Of Anne Spice / 1995 / WV / M • Facesitting Frenzy / 1995 / IBN / B • Fantasy Abduction / 1997 / BON / B • Fashion Plate / 1995 / WAV / M • Fatal Illusion / 1995 / WIV / M • The Fetish Files / 1995 / IBN / B • Finger Pleasures #4 / 1995 / PL / F • First Time Lesbians #21 / 1994 / JMP / F • The Flirt / 1995 / GO / M • Forever Young / 1994 / VI / M • Freak Of The Week / 1996 / LIP / F • The Go-Go Girls / 1994 / EVN / M • Her Personal Touch / 1996 / STM / F • High Heel Harlots #05 / 1994 / SFP / M • Hollywood Amateurs #05 / 1994 / MID / M • Hourman Is Here / 1994 / CC / M • If You Can't Lick 'em...Join 'em / 1996 / BAC / F • Jenna Loves Rocco / 1996 / WAV / M • Kittens #6 / 1994 / CC / F • Kym Wilde's On The Edge #15 / 1994 / RB / B • Kym Wilde's On The Edge #16 / 1994 / RB / B • Kym Wilde's On The Edge #18 / 1995 / RB / B • Kym Wilde's On The Edge #21 / 1995 / RB / B • Lesbian Bitches #2 / 1994 / ROB / F • Lesbian Mystery Theatre: The Case Of The Deadly Dyke / 1994 / LIP / F • Lesbian Social Club / 1995 / ROB / F • Lonely Hearts / 1995 / VC / M • Love Bunnies #09 / 1994 / FPI / F • Love Spice / 1995 / ERA / M • Maid To Beat / 1994 / PL / B • Major Exposure / 1995 / PL / F • Man Handling / 1995 / RB / B • Mastering The Male / 1995 / RB / B • Mistress Of Misery / 1996 / LBO / B • Mistress Rules / 1995 / STM / B • Mistress Sharon's Girl Toy / 1995 / STM / B • Mr. Peepers Amateur Home Videos #91: Hole Lot'a Humping Goin / 1994 / LBO / M • The New Ass Masters #08 / 1996 / LEI / C • Nightmare On Lesbian Street / 1995 / LIP / F • Nina Hartley's Lifestyles Party / 1995 / FRM / M • Odyssey Triple Play #99: Hail, Hail, The Gang-Bang's Here #2 / 1995 / OD / M • Ona Zee's Learning The Ropes #10: Chains Of Love / 1994 / ONA / B • Orgies Orgies Orgies / 1994 / WV / M • Pain Is The Price / 1996 / LBO / B • Pain Puppets / 1996 / LBO / B • Paradise Lost / 1995 / LE / M • Persuasion / 1995 / LE / M • Private Audition / 1995 / EVN / M • Screamers (Ona Zee) / 1995 / ONA / M • Secret Games / 1995 / BON / B • Sex Academy #2: The Art Of Talking Dirty / 1994 / ONA / M • Sex Academy #4: The Art Of Anal / 1994 / ONA / M • Sex Lives Of Clowns / 1994 / VC / M • Shaved #09 / 1995 / RB / F • Simply Kia / 1994 / LE / M • Sister Snatch #2 / 1995 / SNA / M • Slave Exchange / 1995 / STM / B • Smokin' Mistress / 1995 / IBN / B • Strip For The Whip / 1997 / BON / B • Student Fetish Videos: The Enema #16 / 1994 / PRE / B • Student Fetish Videos: Spanking #17 / 1994 / PRE / B • Student Fetish Videos: Tickling #10 / 1994 / SFV / B • Submissive Exposure

Profile #5: Keli Thomas / 1996 / STM / C • Succulent Toes / 1995 / STM / B • Sweet A$ Money / 1994 / MID / M • Take It Inside / 1995 / PEP / M • Titan's Amateur Video Magazine #03 / 1995 / TEG / M • To Bi For / 1996 / PL / G • Top Debs #6: Rear Entry Girls / 1995 / GO / M • Torturer's Apprentice / 1996 / LBO / B • Transformation / 1996 / XCI / M • Vagablonde / 1994 / VI / M • Vagina Beach / 1995 / FH / M • What's The Lesbian Doing In My Pirate Movie? / 1995 / LIP / F • While You Were Dreaming / 1995 / WV / M • The Whipping Post / 1995 / BS / B • Who's In Charge (Titan) / 1995 / TEG / M • Wild Orgies #15 / 1995 / AFI / M • Winter Heat / 1994 / MID / M

BROOKE WEST
Pudgy, not too pretty blonde with a birthmark halfway up her spine.
11 / 1980 / VCX / M • Amanda By Night #1 / 1981 / CA / M • Audra's Ordeal / 1983 / BIZ / B • The Blonde / 1980 / VCX / M • Blue Ribbon Blue / 1984 / CA / C • Caballero Preview Tape #1 / 1982 / CA / C • Caballero Preview Tape #2 / 1983 / CA / C • Centerfold Celebrities #5 / 1983 / VC / M • Coed Fever / 1980 / CA / M • The Doorman Always Comes Twice / cr84 / AIR / C • Double Pleasure / 1985 / VCR / M • Erotic Dimensions #4: The Exhibitionist / 1982 / NSV / M • Extremes / 1981 / CA / M • Fantasy / 1978 / VCX / M • French Finishing School / 1980 / CA / M • Garage Girls / 1981 / CV / M • The Girl From S.E.X. / 1982 / CA / M • I'm Yours / 1983 / AIR / C • Intimate Explosions / 1982 / ... / C • Le Sex De Femme #3 / 1989 / AFI / C • Lips: The Passage To Pleasure / 1981 / CA / M • The Mistress #1 / 1983 / CV / M • Nasty Nurses / 1983 / CA / M • Never So Deep / 1981 / VCX / M • Playing With Fire / 1983 / IN / M • Rockin' With Seka / 1980 / WV / M • Showgirl #08: Serena's Fantasies / 1983 / VCR / M • Showgirl #13: Chris Cassidy's Fantasies / 1983 / SVE / M • Swedish Erotica #23 / 1980 / CA / M • Taboo #01 / 1980 / VCX / M • Wild Dallas Honey / 1985 / VCX / M

BROOKE WEST(T.EVANS) *see* **Taylor Evans**

BROOKE YOUNG
One part of a pair of identical twins (the other is Taylor Young) who is one of the very few good looking females of the seventies. Brunette with tight body and small tits.
ABA: Double Feature #3 / 1996 / ALP / M • Cannonball Run / 1981 / 2CF / S • Cherry Hustlers / 1977 / VEN / M • Double Your Pleasure / 1978 / CV / M • Erotic Fantasies #1 / 1983 / CV / C • Saturday Matinee Series #2 / 1996 / VCX / C • Stardust #3 / 1996 / VI / M • Sweet Cakes / 1976 / VC / M • Teenage Twins / 1976 / VCX / M • Thunderbuns / 1976 / VCX / C

BROTHER LOVE
Orgies Orgies Orgies / 1994 / WV / M

BROTHER THEODORE
Gums / 1976 / AVC / M

BROWN BOMBER
Blue Vanities #519 / 1993 / FFL / M

BROWN SUGAR
Bubble Butts #12 / 1992 / LBO / M

BROWN T. GOOD
Kink: Police Chronicles / 1995 / ROB / M

BROWN THUNDER
Kitty Foxx's Kinky Kapers #02 / 1995 / TTV

/ M

BRUCE
Bi-Bi Love Amateurs #3 / 1993 / QUA / G • Cindy Puts Out / 1996 / OLL / M • Ona Zee's Date With Dallas / 1992 / ONA / M

BRUCE ANGEL
Heat Wave / 1977 / COM / M

BRUCE BROWN
Highway Hookers / 1976 / SVE / M

BRUCE COOPER
Is The Dr In? / 1979 / AXV / M

BRUCE DARWIN
Limited Edition #03 / 1979 / AVC / M

BRUCE GATES
Hidden Obsessions / 1992 / BFP / M

BRUCE GILCHRIST *see* **Harry Reems**

BRUCE HARDWELL
Lust Inferno / 1982 / CA / M

BRUCE KERNS *see* **Jack Mann**

BRUCE KIRK
Anatomy Of A Male Stripper / 1990 / 4P / S • Erotic Radio WSEX / 1983 / VC / M

BRUCE LEI *(Ho Chung)*
Oriental seedy-looking male.
The Anal Adventures Of Max Hardcore: The Resurrection / 1995 / ZA / M • Asian Angel / 1993 / VEX / C • Ben Dover & Barbie / 1995 / SUF / M • Body & Soul / 1995 / IF / M • Bootylicious: China Town / 1995 / JMP / M • Butt Hunt #04 / 1995 / LEI / M • Butt Hunt #05 / 1995 / LEI / M • Butt Hunt #06 / 1995 / LEI / M • Butt Hunt #07 / 1995 / LEI / M • Butt Hunt #08 / 1995 / LEI / M • Butt Hunt #09 / 1995 / LEI / M • Butt Hunt #10 / 1995 / LEI / M • Butt Hunt #11 / 1995 / LEI / M • Cherry Poppers #11: California Co-Eds / 1995 / ZA / M • Dirty Mind / 1995 / VEX / M • Exotic Tastes / 1995 / VEX / C • Forbidden Fantasies #1 / 1995 / ZA / M • Freaks Of Leather #1 / 1993 / IF / M • Gazongas #05 / 1993 / VEX / C • Hard Core Beginners #09 / 1995 / LEI / M • Hard Core Beginners #11 / 1995 / LEI / M • Heavenly / 1995 / IF / M • Hometown Girl / 1994 / VEX / M • Hometown Honeys #5 / 1993 / VEX / M • Hot Box / 1995 / V99 / C • House Of Anal / 1995 / NOT / M • House Of Spartacus #1 / 1993 / IF / M • House Of Spartacus #2 / 1993 / IF / M • Jug Humpers / 1995 / V99 / C • Much More Than A Mouthful #3 / 1993 / VEX / M • The New Snatch Masters #14 / 1995 / LEI / C • Party Favors / 1993 / VEX / M • Pleasure Chest / 1993 / IF / M • Pretty Young Things Escort Service / 1995 / ZA / M • Pussy Hunt #06 / 1994 / LEI / M • Pussy Hunt #08 / 1995 / LEI / M • Pussy Hunt #09 / 1995 / LEI / M • Pussy Hunt #10 / 1995 / LEI / M • Pussy Hunt #11 / 1995 / LEI / M • Pussy Hunt #12 / 1995 / LEI / M • Pussy Hunt #13 / 1995 / LEI / M • Pussy Hunt #14 / 1995 / LEI / M • Pussy Hunt #15 / 1995 / LEI / M • Pussyclips #04 / 1994 / SNA / M • She's No Angel #2 / 1995 / V99 / M • Spanish Fly / 1993 / VEX / M • Sweet Cheeks (1991-Vid Excl) / 1991 / VEX / C • Sweet Things / 1992 / VEX / M • Up The Middle / 1995 / V99 / M

BRUCE LONG
Take Off / 1978 / VXP / M

BRUCE MAGNUM
Bi 'n' Sell / 1990 / VC / G

BRUCE MURPHY
Carnal Olympics / 1983 / CA / M

BRUCE SEVEN *(B. Bernard Behan)*
Born in Torrington, Connecticut but moved to

CA in 1945 and was a special effects man in the regular movies. Had a stroke in October 1995 that has left him partially paralyzed.

Arsenal Of Fear / 1993 / BS / B • Bend Over Babes #2 / 1991 / EA / M • Beyond Reality #2: Anal Expedition / 1996 / EXQ / M • Blame It On Bambi / 1992 / BS / B • Blind Innocence / 1993 / BS / B • Bondage Interludes #1 / 1983 / BIZ / B • Bondage Interludes #2 / 1983 / BIZ / B • The Bottom Dweller / 1993 / EL / M • The Bottom Dweller Part Deux / 1994 / EL / M • The Bottom Dweller 33 1/3 / 1995 / EL / M • Bruce Seven: A Compendium Of His Most Graphic Scenes Vol 5 / 1994 / BS / C • Bruce Seven: A Compendium Of His Most Graphic Scenes Vol 6 / 1994 / BS / C • Burning Desires / 1994 / BS / B • Buttman Goes To Rio #2 / 1991 / EA / M • Buttman Vs Buttwoman / 1992 / EL / M • Buttman's Big Tit Adventure #1 / 1992 / EA / M • Buttman's Big Tit Adventure #3 / 1995 / EA / M • Caught In The Act / 1993 / BS / B • The Chains Of Torment / 1991 / BS / B • Conflict / 1988 / VD / M • Crazy Times / 1995 / BS / B • Dances With Pain / 1992 / BS / B • Dangerous Assignment / 1993 / BS / B • Dark Destiny / 1992 / BS / B • Depraved / 1993 / BS / B • The Distress Factor / 1992 / BS / B • Dr Butts #2 / 1992 / 4P / M • The Ecstasy Of Payne / 1994 / BS / B • Eleventh Annual AVN Awards / 1994 / VC / M • Eye Of The Tigress / 1988 / VD / M • Face Dance #1 / 1992 / EA / M • Fallen Angels / 1983 / VES / M • Felecia's Folly / 1993 / BS / B • Fit To Be Tied / 1991 / BS / B • Forbidden Obsessions / 1993 / BS / B • Gang Bangs #1 / 1985 / VCR / M • Hang 'em High / 1995 / BS / B • Hot Rod To Hell #1 / 1991 / BS / B • Knight Shadows / 1992 / BS / B • Leather Revenge / 1983 / BIZ / B • Obsession / 1994 / BS / B • Overkill / 1994 / BS / B • The Pain Connection / 1994 / BS / B • Painful Cheeks / 1994 / BS / B • Painful Lessons (Bruce Seven) / 1992 / BS / B • Painful Pleasures / 1993 / BS / B • Party Of Payne / 1993 / BS / B • The Power Of Summer #1: Revenge / 1992 / BS / B • The Power Of Summer #2: Reward / 1992 / BS / B • Punished / 1994 / BS / B • Rear Ended / 1985 / WV / M • Shane's Ultimate Fantasy / 1994 / BS / B • Starlets / 1985 / 4P / M • Strange Passions / 1993 / BS / B • The Submission Of Felecia / 1993 / BS / B • Takin' It To The Limit #1 / 1994 / BS / M • Takin' It To The Limit #2 / 1994 / BS / M • Takin' It To The Limit #3 / 1994 / BS / M • Takin' It To The Limit #4 / 1995 / BS / M • Takin' It To The Limit #5 / 1995 / BS / M • Takin' It To The Limit #7: Debauched / 1996 / BS / M • A Touch Of Leather / 1994 / BS / B • A Twist Of Payne / 1993 / BS / B • Web Of Darkness / 1993 / BS / B • Wicked Moments / 1996 / BS / B • Wicked Pleasures / 1995 / BS / B • A World Of Hurt / 1994 / BS / B • Yvonne's Odyssey / 1995 / BS / B

BRUCE STALLION
Angel Of The Island / 1988 / IN / M

BRUCE WALSH
Bucky Beaver's XXX Dragon Art Theatre Double Feature #11 / 1996 / SOW / M • San Francisco Ball / 1971 / SOW / S

BRUCE WEST

Bacchanale / 1972 / ALP / M

BRUCE WILLING
Cry Hard / 1990 / DOM / B

BRUNA
Buttman's Big Butt Backdoor Babes / 1995 / EA / M

BRUNO
Adultress / 1995 / WIV / M • The French Canal / 1995 / DVP / G • Triple X Video Magazine #09 / 1995 / OD / M

BRUNO AISSIX
Anal Virgins #01 / 1996 / NS / M • Buttman In The Crack / 1996 / EA / M • Executions On Butt Row / 1996 / EA / M • Family Affair / 1996 / XC / M • Illicit Affairs / 1996 / XC / M • Miss Anal #3 / 1995 / C69 / M • Paris Chic / 1996 / SAE / M • Unleashed / 1996 / SAE / M • Video Virgins #26 / 1996 / NS / M

BRUNO BIX
Thief Of Passion / 1996 / P69 / M

BRUNO HUBER
[Madchen, Die Sich Selbst, Bedienen / 1974 / ... / M

BRUNO KOHLS
The Beat Goes On / 1987 / VCR / C

BRUNO RENTAUSKAS
Teresa, The Woman Who Loves Men / 1985 / CV / M

BRUNO RUDITIS
Professional Janine / 1984 / CA / M

BRUSTER
Anal 247 / 1995 / CC / M

BRUTUS
Sandra's Submission / 1994 / GAL / B

BRYAN ALLAN
Ms. Fix-It / 1994 / PRK / M

BRYAN AUSTIN
Every Which Way / 1990 / V10 / G

BRYAN COBB *see* **Tony Tedeschi**

BRYAN DUNHILL
Subject Nine / 1995 / ZFX / B • The Worm / 1995 / ZFX / B

BRYAN KURTIS *see* **Woody Long**

BRYAN LONDON
Horny Henry's London Adventure / 1995 / TTV / M

BRYAN YOUNG
Behind The Backdoor #7 / 1995 / EVN / M • Tit In A Wringer / 1990 / FC / M

BRYCE
Painful Madness / 1995 / BS / B

BRYCE DENIM
Bi Watch / 1994 / BIN / G

BRYLE BRITTON
A Guide To Making Love / 1973 / VES / M

BRYSE
To Bi For / 1996 / PL / G

BUBBA
Cherry Poppers #15: Mischievous Maidens / 1996 / ZA / M

BUBBA BLUE
Vegas Brats / 1990 / WV / M

BUBBA BRANDO
Buttman's Ultimate Workout / 1990 / EA / M • Oreo A Go-Go #2 / 1992 / FH / M

BUBBA THE BLACK
Let Me Tell Ya 'Bout White Chicks / 1985 / VC / M

BUBBALICIOUS
Booty And The Ho' Bitch / 1995 / JMP / M • Bootylicious: Booty & The Ho Bitch / 1996 / JMP / M

BUBBLES
Bubbles / 1993 / KBR / S • HomeGrown Video #473: Furpie Feast #3 / 1997 / HOV

/ C • Resurrection Of Eve / 1973 / MIT / M

BUBBLES DARLING
Nooner / 1985 / AMB / M

BUBBLES LA TOUCHE
Mondo Extreme / 1996 / SHS / M

BUCK
Big Boob Celebration / 1994 / BTO / M

BUCK ADAMS *(Buick Adams, Charles Allen, D.A. Adams, Charles S. Allen)*
Charles Allen in **Uninhibited**. The guy looks like a prizefighter and is the brother of Amber Lynn. Married to Janette Littledove at one stage.

2002: A Sex Odyssey / 1985 / DR / M • Above And Beyond / 1990 / PNP / G • Adult Video News 1992 Awards / 1992 / VC / M • The Adultress / 1987 / CA / M • The Adventures Of Major Morehead / 1994 / SC / M • Alien Lust / 1985 / AVC / M • The All American Girl / 1991 / PP / M • All The President's Women / 1994 / LV / M • All The Way Down / 1991 / ZA / M • Alley Cat / 1991 / CIN / M • Amazing Sex Stories #1 / 1986 / SUV / M • Amber Aroused / 1985 / CA / M • Amber Lynn's Personal Best / 1986 / VD / M • Amberella / 1986 / GO / M • The Amorous Adventures Of Janette Littledove / 1988 / AR / M • The Anal Adventures Of Suzy Super Slut #1 / 1994 / AFV / M • Anal Angels #2 / 1990 / VEX / C • Anal Attack / 1991 / ZA / M • Anal Attraction #1 / 1988 / 3HV / M • Anal Blitz / 1991 / MID / M • Anal Climax #1 / 1991 / ROB / M • Anal Fury / 1992 / ROB / M • Anal Leap / 1991 / ZA / M • Anal Revolution / 1991 / ROB / M • The Anal-Europe Series #05: Anal European Vacation / 1993 / LV / M • The Anal-Europe Series #06: Anal Luck / 1993 / LV / M • Around The World With Samantha Strong / 1989 / V99 / M • Aroused #1 / 1994 / VI / M • Assy #2 / 1996 / JMP / M • Babe Watch #1 / 1994 / SC / M • Babe Watch #2 / 1994 / SC / M • Babe Watch #3 / 1995 / SC / M • Babe Watch #4 / 1995 / SC / M • Babe Watch #5 / 1996 / VC / M • Babe Watch Beach / 1996 / SC / M • Backdoor Brides #2: The Honeymoon / 1986 / PV / M • Backdoor Romance / 1984 / VIV / M • Backhand / 1995 / SC / M • Bare Ass Beach / 1994 / TP / M • The Barlow Affairs / 1991 / XCI / M • The Battle Of the Breast Queens / 1989 / INS / C • Bazooka County #2 / 1989 / CC / M • Beach Ball / 1994 / SC / M • Beaver & Buttface / 1995 / SC / M • Behind Closed Doors / 1990 / VI / M • The Best Little Whorehouse In San Francisco / 1984 / LA / M • Best Of Caught From Behind #5 / 1991 / HO / C • The Best Of Oriental Anal #1 / 1994 / ROB / C • Beverly Hills Heat / 1985 / VEP / M • Beverly Hills Seduction / 1988 / WV / M • The Big Bang #1 / 1993 / LV / M • The Big Bang #2 / 1994 / LV / M • The Big Rock / 1988 / FOV / M • Bigger / 1991 / PL / M • Bimbo Bowlers From Buffalo / 1989 / ZA / M • Biography: Kaitlyn Ashley / 1996 / SC / C • Bite / 1991 / LE / M • Black Girls Do It Better / 1986 / CV / M • Black In The Saddle Again / 1991 / ZA / M • Black Lava / 1986 / WET / M • Blacks & Blondes #57 / 1989 / WV / M • Blade / 1996 / MID / M • Blazing Bedrooms / 1987 / LA / M • Blazing Butts / 1991 / LV / M • Blonde Angel / 1994 / VI / M • Body Shop / 1984 / VCX / M • The Boneheads / 1992 / PL / M • Bonnie & Clyde #3 / 1994 / VI / M • Bonnie & Clyde

vate Dancer (CDI) / 1992 / CDI / M • Pro Ball / 1991 / VD / M • Proposals / 1988 / CC / M • Public Enemy / 1990 / VIP / M • Public Places #2 / 1995 / SC / M • Pump It Up / 1990 / LV / M • Purely Sexual / 1991 / HO / M • Purple Haze / 1991 / WV / M • Push It To The Limit / 1988 / EVN / M • R & R / 1994 / VC / M • Radioactive / 1990 / VIP / M • Raunch #03 / 1991 / CC / M • Ravaged Rivalry / 1990 / HO / M • Raw Talent #2 / 1987 / VC / M • The Real Story Of Tonya & Nancy / 1994 / EX / M • Realities #1 / 1991 / ZA / M • Red Hot Pepper / 1986 / V99 / M • Red Light / 1994 / SC / S • Renegades #1 / 1994 / SC / M • Renegades #2 / 1995 / SC / M • Restless Passion / 1987 / HO / M • The Return Of Johnny Wadd / 1986 / PEN / M • Rio Heat / 1986 / VD / M • Rituals / 1989 / V99 / M • Rituals / 1993 / SC / M • Rock Me / 1994 / CC / M • Rocky-X #1 / 1986 / PEN / M • Rocky-X #2 / 1988 / PEN / M • Roxy / 1991 / VC / M • Sailing Into Ecstasy / 1986 / VCX / M • Satania / 1986 / DR / M • The Savage / 1994 / SC / M • The Scarlet Bride / 1989 / VI / M • Schoolgirl By Day / 1985 / LA / M • Secret Cravings / 1989 / V99 / M • Sensuous / 1991 / LV / M • Sex And The Single Girl / 1990 / FAN / M • Sex Crazed / 1989 / VEX / M • The Sex Dancer / 1986 / NSV / M • Sex Derby / 1986 / GO / M • Sex Drive / 1984 / VXP / M • Sex In The Great Outdoors / 1987 / SE / C • Sex On The Town / 1989 / V99 / M • Sexaholics / 1987 / VCX / M • Sexual Healing / 1994 / VI / M • Sexual Healing / 1996 / SC / M • Shameless / 1991 / SC / M • Shameless Desire / 1989 / VEX / M • She's A Boy Toy / 1985 / DR / M • She's A Good Lust Charm / 1987 / LA / C • She's No Angel #1 / 1990 / V99 / M • Sheri's Gotta Have It / 1985 / LIM / C • Shooting Star / 1993 / XCI / M • A Shot In The Mouth #2 / 1991 / ME / M • Silver Elegance / 1992 / VT / M • Skid Row / 1994 / SC / M • Skin Dive / 1996 / SC / M • Sleazy Rider / 1990 / FOV / M • Sleeping Around / 1991 / CA / M • Smooth Operator / 1986 / AR / M • Snow Bunnies #1 / 1995 / SC / M • Snow Bunnies #2 / 1995 / SC / M • Soaking Wet / 1985 / CV / M • [illegible] Sweet Cream / 1996 / EL / M • Sodomania: Slop Shots / 1996 / EL / C • Sophisticated Lady / 1988 / SEX / M • Speedtrap / 1992 / VC / M • Spread Sheets / 1991 / DR / M • Spread The Wealth / 1993 / DR / M • Starved For Affection / 1985 / AVC / M • Step To The Rear / 1991 / VD / M • Sticky Lips / 1993 / EX / M • Stolen Kisses / 1989 / VD / M • Storm Warning / 1989 / LV / M • Strange Curves / 1989 / VC / M • Stranger At The Backdoor / 1994 / CC / M • Subway / 1994 / SC / M • Summer Heat / 1991 / CIN / M • Summer Lovers / 1987 / WET / M • Super Blondes / 1989 / VEX / M • Super Hornio Brothers #1 / 1993 / MID / M • Super Hornio Brothers #2 / 1993 / MID / M • Superboobs / 1994 / LE / M • Supermodel #1 / 1994 / VI / M • Supermodel #2 / 1994 / VI / M • Suzy's Birthday Bang / 1985 / CDI / M • Swedish Erotica #61 / 1984 / CA / M • Swedish Erotica #65 / 1985 / CA / M • Swedish Erotica #67 / 1985 / CA / M • Swedish Erotica #69 / 1985 / CA / M • Sweet Summer / 1986 / AMO / M • Sweet Temptations / 1989 / V99 / M • Switch Hitters #6: Back In The Bull Pen / 1991 / IN / G • Taboo #05 / 1986 / IN / M • Taboo #09 / 1991 / IN / M • Taboo #12 / 1994 / MET / M • Taboo #13 / 1994 / IN / M • Tail For Sale / 1988 / VD / M • Tails Of The Town / 1988 / WV / M • Tamara's Dreams / 1989 / VEX / M • A Taste Of Porsche / 1988 / PIN / C • A Taste Of Taija Rae / 1989 / PIN / C • Taste Of The Best #1 / 1988 / PIN / C • Taste Of The Best #2 / 1988 / PIN / C • Taste Of The Best #3 / 1988 / PIN / C • A Taste Of Victoria Paris / 1990 / PIN / C • Temptation Eyes / 1991 / VT / M • This Bun's For You / 1989 / FAN / M • This Stud's For You / 1986 / MAP / C • Three Men And A Barbi / 1989 / FAN / M • Thunder And Lightning / 1996 / MID / M • Thunder Road / 1995 / SC / M • Titty Bar #2 / 1994 / LE / M • Tongue In Cheek / 1994 / LE / M • Tori Welles Goes Behind The Scenes / 1992 / FD / M • Total Exposure / 1992 / CDI / M • Traci Who? / 1987 / AVC / C • Triple Xposure / 1986 / VD / M • True Legends Of Adult Cinema: The Modern Era / 1992 / VC / C • True Sex / 1994 / EMC / M • Twin Cheeks #3 / 1991 / CIN / M • Twin Cheeks #4 / 1991 / CIN / M • Two Of A Kind / 1991 / ZA / M • Two Women & A Man / 1988 / VEX / M • Two Women & A Man / 1991 / VEX / C • The Ultimate Climax / 1989 / V99 / M • Ultimate Gang Bang #1 / 1994 / HW / M • Under The Law / 1989 / AFV / M • Uninhibited / 1993 / ANT / S • Valleys Of The Moon / 1991 / SC / M • VCA Previews #4 / 1988 / VC / C • Visions #1 / 1995 / ERA / M • Visions #2 / 1995 / ERA / M • Vixens In Heat / 1984 / ECS / M • The Wacky World Of X-Rated Bloopers / 1989 / GO / M • Walk On The Wild Side / 1994 / VIM / M • Wet And Wild #2 / 1995 / VEX / M • Wet Dreams 2001 / 1987 / VD / M • Wet Kisses / 1986 / SE / M • What Are Friends For? / 1985 / MAP / M • The Whore Of The Worlds / 1985 / PV / M • Whorelock / 1993 / LV / M • Wicked Fascination / 1991 / CIN / M • Wild & Wicked #2 / 1992 / VT / M • Wild Desires / 1994 / MAX / M • Wild Things #1 / 1985 / CV / M • Wild Toga Party / 1985 / VD / M • Willie Wanker And The Fun Factory / 1994 / FD / [illegible] / 1988 / AR / M • WPINK-TV #2 / 1986 / PV / M • X Factor: The Next Generation / 1991 / HO / M • Zara's Revenge / 1991 / XCI / M • [Transsexual Obsession / 1989 / ... / G

BUCK EVERETT

Bi-Bi Love Amateurs #2 / 1993 / SFP / G

BUCK FLOWER *see* George Flower

BUCK FLOWERS *see* George Flower

BUCK LACEY

Resurrection Of Eve / 1973 / MIT / M

BUCK O'TOOLE *see* Brockton O'Toole

BUCK O. ROGERS

Bad Attitude / 1987 / CC / M • Black Flesh / 1986 / LA / M • Black Voodoo / 1987 / FOV / M • Carnal College / 1987 / VT / M • Close Friends / 1987 / CC / G • A Little Dove-Tale / 1987 / IN / M • Lucy Makes It Big / 1987 / ME / M • Pornocchio / 1987 / ME / M • Throbbin' Hood / 1987 / VD / M

BUCK SIMPSON

A Rising Star / 1991 / HO / M

BUCK STRADLIN

Marine Code Of Silence: Don't Ask Don't Tell / 1996 / BHE / G

BUCK TAYLOR

Harlem Honies #1 / 1993 / CC / M • Harlem Honies #2: Nasty In New York / 1994 / CC / M • Teenage Cheerleader / 1978 / VXP / M

BUCK WILLIAMS

Director's Punishment / 1996 / GOT / B

BUCKEROO

Heart Breaker / 1985 / TAR / C • Thunderstorm / 1987 / VC / M • Ultrasex / 1987 / VC / M

BUCKKO

Bust Lust / cr83 / BIZ / B

BUCKLEY

HomeGrown Video #462: Motion In The Backfield / 1995 / HOV / M

BUCKO RYAN

Robofox #2 / 1988 / FAN / M

BUCKSTON O'TOOLE *see* Brockton O'-Toole

BUD CARRERA *see* Bud Lee

BUD GREENE

In Love / 1983 / VC / M

BUD LEE *(Bud Carrera, Tony Lee)*

Married to Hyapatia but split up in 1993. Married Asia Carrera in 1995. 42 years old in 1996.

A Is For Asia / 1996 / 4P / M • Badgirls #6: Ridin' Into Town / 1995 / VI / M • Blue Dreams / 1996 / SC / M • Body Girls / 1983 / SE / M • The Enchantress / 1990 / VI / M • Forever Young / 1994 / VI / M • Frendz? #2 / 1996 / RAS / M • Heavenly Hyapatia / 1990 / VI / M • Hyapatia Lee's Secret Dreams / 1986 / SE / M • I Do #1 / 1989 / VI / M • Indian Summer #1 / 1991 / VI / M • Indian Summer #2: Sandstorm / 1991 / VI / M • Kelly Jaye Close-Up / 1994 / VI / M • The Last Act / 1995 / VI / M • Nylon / 1995 / VI / M • On Her Back / 1994 / VI / M • The Red Garter / 1986 / SE / M • The Ribald Tales Of Canterbury / 1986 / CA / M • Sleeping Beauty Aroused / 1989 / VI / M • Strip Show / 1996 / CA / M • Sweet Young Foxes / 1984 / VCX / M • Triangle / 1989 / VI / M • True Confessions Of Hyapatia Lee / 1989 / VI / M • Twist Of Fate / 1996 / WP / M • The Young Like It Hot / 1983 / CA / M

BUD WEISER

The Beauty Pageant / 1981 / AVC / M

BUD WIPP

Portraits Of Pleasure / 1974 / BL / M

BUD WISE *(Slim Grady)*

800 Fantasy Lane / 1979 / GO / M • Hot Dallas Nights / 1981 / VCX / M

BUDDY

Odyssey Amateur #15: Robyn and Buddy's Backdoor Bash / 1991 / OD / M • Venture Into The Bizarre / cr78 / VHL / M

BUDDY BOONE

Campus Girl / 1972 / VXP / M

BUDDY DAVID

Behind The Backdoor #7 / 1995 / EVN / M

BUDDY DAVIS

Blackmail For Daddy / 1976 / VCX / M • Penthouse: Forum Letters #2 / 1994 / A*V / S

BUDDY GRANT

Dollface / 1987 / CV / M

BUDDY HATTON

Alley Cat / 1983 / VC / M • Consenting Adults / 1981 / VXP / M • Deep Inside Annie Sprinkle / 1981 / VXP / M • Down & Dirty Scooter Trash / 1988 / CA / M • Intimate Realities #1 / 1983 / VC / M • Rites Of Passion / 1988 / FEM / M

BUDDY JACKSON

Nattie's Pleasure Palace / cr70 / AVC / M

BUDDY LOVE

All Night Long / 1990 / NWV / C • Amber Lynn's Hotline 976 / 1987 / VCR / M • Amber Lynn's Personal Best / 1986 / VD / M • Backside To The Future #2 / 1988 / ZA / M • Best Of Caught From Behind #5 / 1991 / HO / C • Big, Bad & Beautiful / 1988 / MIR / C • Black To The Future / 1986 / VD / M • Blondes! Blondes! Blondes! / 1986 / VCS / C • Born To Be Bad / 1987 / CV / M • Both Ends Burning / 1987 / VC / M • Caddy Shack-Up / 1986 / VD / M • California Gigolo / 1987 / VD / M • Captain Hooker & Peter Porn / 1987 / VD / M • Careena #1 / 1987 / WV / C • Casing The Crack / 1987 / V99 / M • The Catwoman / 1988 / VC / M • Caught From Behind #09 / 1988 / HO / M • Cheeks #1 / 1988 / CC / M • China White / 1986 / WV / M • Coming Alive / 1988 / LV / M • Cram Session / 1986 / V99 / M • Crocodile Blondee #2 / 1988 / VCX / M • Dangerous When Wet (Amber Lynn Is) / 1987 / VCX / M • Debbie Does 'em All #2 / 1988 / CV / M • Deeper! Harder! Faster! / 1986 / VCS / C • Divorce Court Expose #1 / 1986 / VD / M • Divorce Court Expose #2 / 1987 / VD / M • Doctor Blacklove / 1987 / CC / M • Dream Jeans / 1987 / CA / M • End Of Innocence / 1986 / AR / M • Every Man's Fancy / 1988 / SEX / M • Every Man's Fancy / 1991 / V99 / M • Fantasy Girls / 1988 / CA / M • Fatal Seduction / 1988 / CDI / M • Find Your Love / 1988 / CV / M • Furburgers / 1987 / VD / M • G Spot Girls / 1988 / V99 / M • The Girls On F Street / 1986 / AVC / M • Grafenberg Girls Go Fishing / 1987 / MIT / M • Here's Looking At You / 1988 / V99 / M • Honeymoon Harlots / 1986 / AVC / M • Hot & Heavy / 1989 / PL / M • Hot 'n' Nasty / 1989 / XCE / M • Hot Number / 1987 / WET / M • Hot Rocks / 1986 / WET / M • Hot Rods / 1988 / VEX / M • Hot Summer Nites / 1988 / VEX / M • I Cream Of Genie / 1988 / SE / M • In Charm's Way / 1987 / IN / M • Innocent Seduction / 1988 / VC / M • Interracial Sex / 1987 / M&M / M • The Joys Of Masturbation / 1988 / M&M / M • Karate Girls / 1987 / VCR / M • Kinky / 1987 / SE / M • The Kiss / 1986 / SC / M • Laid In The USA / 1988 / CC / M • The Load Warriors #2 / 1987 / VD / M • Lover's Lane / 1986 / SE / M • Lucky In Love #2 / 1988 / SEV / M • Lust And The Law / 1991 / GO / C • Lust Tango In Paris / 1987 / PEN / M • Mammary Lane / 1988 / VT / C • Maximum Head / 1987 / SE / M • Maxine / 1987 / EXF / M • The Mile High Girls / 1987 / CA / M • Nasty Nights / 1988 / PL / C • Naughty Girls Like It Big / 1986 / ELH / M • Only The Strong Survive / 1988 / ZA / M • Only The Very Best On Video / 1992 / VC / C • Oral Majority #03 / 1986 / WV / C • Pacific Intrigue / 1987 / AMB / M • The Penetration Of Elle Rio / 1987 / GO / M • Princess Charming / 1987 / AVC / C • Raising Hell / 1987 / VD / M • Ramb-Ohh #1 / 1986 / PV / M • Real Men Eat Keisha / 1986 / VC / M • Ride A Pink Lady / 1986 / SE / M • Rio Heat / 1986 / VD / M • The Scent Of Samantha / 1988 / VEX / C • The Sex Game / 1987 / SE / C • Sex Machine / 1986 / LA / M • Sex Sounds / 1989 / PL / M • Sex-O-Gram / 1986 / LA / M • Sexaholics / 1987 / VCX / M • Sinderotica /

1985 / HO / M • Sins Of Nina Hartley / 1989 / MIR / C • Snapshots: Confessions Of A Video Voyeur / 1988 / CC / M • Soft Caresses / 1988 / VEX / M • Soft Warm Rain / 1987 / VD / M • Spend The Holidays With Barbii / 1987 / CDI / M • Spooked / 1989 / VEX / M • Steam Heat / 1989 / VEX / M • Strip Search / 1987 / SEV / M • Summer Lovers / 1987 / WET / M • Suzy Cue / 1988 / VI / M • The Thrill Of It / 1986 / CAT / M • Tricks Of The Trade / 1988 / CA / M • Very Sexy Ballet / 1988 / CA / M • Video Store Vixens / 1986 / PL / M • The Wacky World Of X-Rated Bloopers / 1989 / GO / M • Weird Fantasy / 1986 / LA / M • Wet Kisses / 1988 / V99 / M • The Zebra Club / 1986 / VSE / M

BUDDY OWEN

Ultraflesh / 1980 / GO / M

BUDDY SIMS

Slit Skirts / 1983 / VXP / M

BUFF PUFF

Sex #1 (Vca) / 1994 / VC / M

BUFFY

Fantasy Photography: Buffy And The Boys / 1995 / VG0 / M • Love Bunnies #10 / 1994 / FPI / F • Pussy Fest Of The Northwest #2 / 1995 / NIT / M

BUFFY (S/M)

Bitter She-Males / 1992 / BIZ / G • Chicks With Dicks #1: A Slick And Slippery Oil Orgy / 1992 / BIZ / B • Fantasies Of A Transsexual / 1991 / BIZ / G • Sharon Kane's TV Tamer / 1993 / BIZ / G • She-Male Mistress / 1992 / BIZ / G • She-Males In Torment #2 / 1992 / BIZ / G • Shopping With A Transvestite: In A Boy, Out A Girl / 1992 / BIZ / G • Transvestite Tour Guide / 1993 / HSV / G • TV Blondes Do It Best / 1992 / BIZ / G • TV Dildo Fantasy #1 / 1992 / BIZ / G • TV Dungeon / 1992 / BIZ / G • TV Ladies Room / 1993 / BIZ / G • TV Phone Sex / 1992 / BIZ / G • TV Reform School / 1992 / BIZ / G • TV Room / 1993 / BIZ / G • TV Shoestore Fantasy #1 / 1991 / BIZ / G • TV Terrorists: Hostage Sluts / 1993 / BIZ / G • TVs In Control / 1991 / BIZ / G • TVs In Trouble #2 / 1991 / BIZ / G • TVs Plaything / 1992 / BIZ / G • TVs Teased And Tormented / 1995 / BIZ / G

BUFFY DAVIS *(Buffy Marie, Buffy Shinshay, Page Turner, Buffy Martin, Buffy M.)*

A blonde porker. First movie was **Love Bites**. May be the same as Brenda Starr.

1001 Erotic Nights #2 / 1987 / VC / M • Age Of Consent / 1985 / AVC / M • Amazing Tails #1 / 1987 / CA / M • Amazing Tails #2 / 1987 / CA / M • Amazing Tails #3 / 1987 / CA / M • Anal Angels #1 / 1986 / VEX / M • Angel Of The Night / 1985 / IN / M • Angels Of Mercy / 1985 / HO / M • Attack Of The Monster Mammaries / 1987 / LA / C • Back To Back #1 / 1987 / 4P / C • Backdoor Lust / 1987 / CV / C • Behind The Backdoor #1 / 1986 / EVN / M • Best Of Caught From Behind #1 / 1987 / HO / C • Best Of Caught From Behind #2 / 1988 / HO / C • Beyond The Casting Couch / 1986 / VD / M • Beyond The Denver Dynasty / 1988 / CA / M • Blue Lace / 1986 / SE / M • Bondage Playmates / Taut Adventure / 1987 / BIZ / B • Boobs, Butts And Bloopers #1 / 1990 / HO / M • The Brazilian Connection / 1988 / CA / M • Busty Wrestling Babes / 1986 / VD / M • Califor-

nia Blondes #06 / 1992 / VD / C • The Call Girl / 1986 / VD / M • Caught From Behind #03 / 1985 / HO / M • Caught From Behind #04: Nasty Young Girls / 1985 / HO / M • Caught From Behind #05: Blondes & Blacks / 1986 / HO / M • Collection #10 / 1987 / CA / M • Cram Session / 1986 / V99 / M • Cream Dreams / 1986 / VEX / M • Crystal Blue / 1987 / VD / M • Daddy's Darling Daughters / 1986 / PL / M • Dark Side Of The Moon / 1986 / VD / M • Deliveries In The Rear #1 / 1985 / AVC / M • Despicable Dames / 1986 / CC / M • Diamond Collection #80 / 1986 / CDI / M • Double Dare / 1986 / SE / M • Double Penetration #1 / 1985 / WV / M • Double Penetration #2 / 1986 / WV / C • Double Whammy / 1986 / LA / M • Ebony Humpers #1 / 1986 / VEX / M • Erotic Penetration / 1987 / HO / C • Family Heat / 1985 / AT / M • Farmers Daughters / 1985 / WV / M • Forbidden Bodies / 1986 / HU / M • The Fun House / 1988 / SEV / C • Future Voyeur / 1985 / SUV / M • Genie's Dirty Girls / 1987 / VCX / M • Genital Hospital / 1987 / SE / M • The Girls Of The A Team #1 / 1985 / WV / M • Girls Of The Double D #01 / 1986 / CDI / M • GVC: Companions #122 / 1983 / GO / F • GVC: Danielle's Girlfriends #116 / cr83 / GO / F • GVC: Women Who Love Women #115 / cr83 / GO / F • GVC: Women's Fantasies #108 / 1983 / GO / F • Hometown Honeys #1 / 1986 / VEX / M • Honeybuns #1 / 1987 / WV / C • Honeybuns #2: Grecian Formula / 1987 / WV / C • Hot Ones / 1988 / HO / C • The Hottest Show In Town / 1987 / VIP / M • House Of Blue Dreams / 1985 / WV / M • House Of The Rising Moon / 1986 / VD / M • Humongous Squirting Knockers / 1992 / CA / C • I Wanna Be A Bad Girl / 1986 / PP / M • Immoral Majority / 1986 / HTV / M • In Search Of The Wild Beaver / 1986 / DR / M • Indecent Wives / 1985 / HO / M • Innocent Taboo / 1986 / VD / M • Interracial Anal Bonanza / 1993 / CA / C • The Ladies Room / 1987 / CA / M • Lessons In Lust / 1987 / LA / M • Like A Virgin #2 / 1986 / AT / M • Love Bites / 1985 / CA / M • The Love Scene / 1985 / CDI / M • Lust American Style / 1985 / WV / M • The Lust Potion Of Doctor F / 1985 / WV / M • The Magic Touch / 1985 / CV / M • Mantrap / 1986 / BAN / M • Midnight Pink / 1987 / WV / M • Nasty Habits Are Hard To Break / 1986 / 4P / M • Oral Majority #01 / 1986 / WV / C • Oral Majority #02 / 1987 / WV / C • Oral Majority #04 / 1987 / WV / C • Orgies / 1987 / WV / C • Parliament: Anal Babes #1 / 1989 / PM / F • Parliament: Queens Of Double Penetration #1 / 1991 / PM / F • Parliament: Strip Tease #1 / 1986 / PM / F • A Passage To Ecstasy / 1985 / CDI / M • Playing For Passion / 1987 / IN / M • Rambone Does Hollywood / 1986 / WET / M • Rambone Meets The Double Penetrators / 1987 / WET / M • Rated Sex / 1986 / SE / M • Rear Ended / 1985 / WV / M • Return To Sex 5th Avenue / 1985 / WV / M • The Ribald Tales Of Canterbury / 1986 / CA / M • Screaming Rage / 1988 / LV / C • Sex In The Great Outdoors / 1987 / SE / C • Sex Lives Of The Rich And Beautiful / 1988 / CA / M • Sexscape / 1986 / CA / M • Shaved Pink / 1986 / WET / M • She

Comes Undone / 1987 / AIR / C • Sophisticated Women / 1986 / BAN / M • Soul Games / 1988 / PV / C • Sweat #1 / 1986 / PP / M • Swedish Erotica #73 / 1986 / CA / M • Taxi Girls #2: In Search Of Toni / 1986 / ELD / M • Thanks For The Mammaries / 1987 / CA / M • They Call My Sugar Candie / 1989 / SUE / M • Tickle Time / 1987 / BIZ / B • Top Buns / 1986 / HO / M • Toys 4 Us #1 / 1987 / WV / C • Toys 4 Us #2 / 1987 / WV / C • VCA Previews #4 / 1988 / VC / C • Video Paradise / 1988 / ZA / M • We Love To Tease / 1985 / VD / M • The Whore Of The Worlds / 1985 / PV / M • A Woman's Touch / 1988 / ZA / F • [Little Combinations Of Mirandez / 19?? / ... / M • [Take My Body / 1989 / ... / M • [Tastes Like Candy / 1987 / ... / M

BUFFY M. *see* **Buffy Davis**
BUFFY MALIBU *see* **Marie Mason**
BUFFY MARIE *see* **Buffy Davis**
BUFFY MARTIN *see* **Buffy Davis**
BUFFY MAST
Eyes Of A Dreamer / 1983 / S&L / M
BUFFY MOSELLE
Sinners #2 / 1988 / COM / M • Sinners #3 / 1989 / COM / M
BUFFY SHINSHAY *see* **Buffy Davis**
BUFFY ST JOHN *see* **Sylvia Benedict**
BUFFY ST JOHNS *see* **Sylvia Benedict**
BUI'T RAYMOND
Potpourri / 1981 / TGA / M • Service Entrance / 1979 / REG / C • Sex Ed With Lil' Red / 1983 / TGA / M
BUICK ADAMS *see* **Buck Adams**
BULL
Video Virgins #04 / 1993 / NS / M
BULLET
Bi Bi Banjee Boyz / 1994 / PL / G
BUNNY
Bunny's Bind / 1994 / GAL / B • Golden Moments / 1985 / BAK / F • On The Prowl #2 / 1991 / SC / M • Raw Talent: Bang 'er 31 Times / 1992 / RTP / M • Wall To Wall Bondage / 1993 / BON / B • Yellow Waters #1 / 1985 / BAK / F • Yellow Waters #2 / 1985 / BAK / F
BUNNY BLAKE *see* **Barbie Blake**
BUNNY BLEU *(Kimberly Warner, Kim Warner, Ruby Smart, Kristi Warner)*
Brunette   with grotesque proportions. In 1988's **The Brazilian Connection** she is analed by Marc Wallice. Originally I thought this was Jerrii Sinclaire in **The Wild Wild West** but now I think that was Barbie Doll. As of late 1994, her dimensions were 50F-22-33, 5'3" tall. Kristi Warner is from **Loose Times At Ridley High**.
1-900-FUCK #1 / 1995 / SO / M • 1-900-FUCK #3 / 1995 / SO / M • 1001 Erotic Nights #2 / 1987 / VC / M • 21 Hump Street / 1988 / VWA / M • Adult 45 #01 / 1985 / DR / C • Aerobisex Girls #1 / 1983 / LIP / F • Age Of Consent / 1985 / AVC / M • Aggressive Lesbians / 1995 / STM / C • America's Raunchiest Home Videos #71: / 1993 / ZA / M • Anal Addicts / 1994 / KWP / M • Anal Angels #5 / 1996 / VEX / C • Anal Centerfold / 1995 / ROB / M • Anal Dynomite / 1995 / ROB / M • Anal Hellraiser #1 / 1995 / ROB / M • Anal Insatiable / 1995 / ROB / M • Anal Maniacs #2 / 1994 / WP / M • Anal Rescue 811 / 1992 / PL / M • Anal Senorita #2 / 1995 / ROB / M • Ateball: More Than A Mouthful / 1995 / ATE /

F • Attic Toys / 1994 / ERA / M • B*A*S*H / 1989 / BIZ / C • Back To Class #1 / 1984 / DR / M • Backdoor To Brooklyn / 1992 / PL / M • Beach Bunny / 1994 / V99 / M • Best Of Bruce Seven #3 / 1990 / BIZ / C • Best Of Bruce Seven #4 / 1990 / BIZ / C • Best Of Foot Worship #2 / 1989 / BIZ / C • Beverly Hills Exposed / 1985 / SE / M • Big Boob Bangeroo #1 / 1995 / TTV / M • Big Boob Boat Ride #1 / 1992 / FC / M • Big Breast Beach / 1995 / LV / M • Big Bust Babes #27 / 1995 / AFI / M • Big Bust Babes #33 / 1995 / AFI / M • Big Knockers #01 / 1994 / TV / M • Big Knockers #19 / 1995 / TV / M • Big Knockers #22 / 1995 / TV / M • The Big Pink / 1989 / VWA / M • The Big Switch / 1985 / LAV / G • Big Titted Tarts / 1994 / PL / C • The Bigger The Better / 1986 / SE / C • Bizarre Mistress Series: Mistress Jacqueline / 1992 / BIZ / C • Blonde Desire / 1984 / AIR / M • Blondes! Blondes! / 1986 / VCS / C • Bodacious Ta Ta's / 1984 / CA / M • Boiling Desires / 1986 / VC / M • Bond-Aid / 1992 / STM / B • Bondage Fantasies #1 / 1989 / BIZ / B • Bondage Fantasies #2 / 1989 / BIZ / B • Boobs A Poppin' / 1994 / TTV / M • Boobwatch #2 / 1997 / SC / M • Bound And Punished / 1984 / BIZ / B • Bound And Spanked / cr94 / STM / B • Bound Biker Babes #1 / 1991 / STM / B • Bound For Slavery / 1983 / BLB / B • The Brazilian Connection / 1988 / CA / M • Breaking It #1 / 1984 / COL / M • Breast Wishes #10 / 1992 / LBO / M • Breastman's Triple X Cellent Adventure / 1995 / EVN / M • Breastman's Wet T-Shirt Contest / 1994 / EVN / M • Bringing Up The Rear / 1993 / VD / C • Bruise Control / 1993 / PRE / B • Bunnie's Bondage Land / 1994 / STM / C • Bunny Bleu: A Gang Bang Fantasy / 1994 / FC / M • Bunny's Lesson In Pain / 1992 / PL / B • C-Hunt / 1985 / PL / M • Cabaret Sin / 1987 / IN / M • California Blondes #06 / 1992 / VD / C • California Fever / 1987 / CV / M • Cat Alley / 1986 / AVC / M • Catfighting Cheerleaders / 1989 / BIZ / B • Chatsworth Hall / 1989 / BIZ / B • Cheerleader Academy / 1986 / PL / M • Chocolate Kisses / 1986 / CA / M • Chug-A-Lug Girls #5 / 1994 / VT / M • Circus Acts / 1987 / SE / C • Classical Romance / 1984 / MAP / M • Cocksuckers #2 / 1994 / FPI / M • Coming Attractions / 1995 / WHP / M • Competent People / 1994 / FD / C • Cover Girls / 1985 / VEX / C • Crackdown / 1988 / BIZ / B • Cram Session / 1986 / V99 / M • Cum Shot Revue #2 / 1985 / HO / C • The Cumshot Caper / 1986 / ... / M • Cunning Coeds / 1985 / IVP / M • Control / 1994 / MID / F • Daddy's Girls / 1985 / LA / M • Dangerous Pleasure / 1995 / WIV / M • The Debutante / 1986 / BEA / M • Deeper! Harder! Faster! / 1986 / VCS / C • Demolition Woman #1 / 1994 / IP / M • Demolition Woman #2 / 1994 / IP / M • Desire / 1983 / VCX / M • Dial A Dick / 1986 / AVC / M • Dial F For Fantasy / 1984 / PL / M • Diamond Collection #57 / 1984 / CIN / M • Dirty / 1993 / FD / C • Dirty 30's Cinema: Heather Wayne / 1985 / PV / C • Dirty Blondes / 1986 / CDI / M • Dirty Shary / 1985 / VD / M • Disciples Of Bondage / 1992 / STM / B • Don't Tell Daddy #1 / 1985 / PL / C • Double D Amateurs #19 / 1994 / JMP / M • Double D Dykes #17 /

1995 / GO / F • Double D Dykes #18 / 1995 / GO / F • Double D Dykes #19 / 1995 / GO / F • Double D Dykes #22 / 1995 / GO / F • Double Dare / 1986 / SE / M • Double Down / 1985 / AMB / M • Double Standards / 1986 / VC / M • Dr Truth's Great Sex / 1986 / VD / M • Dresden Mistress #1 / 1988 / BIZ / B • Dresden Mistress #2 / 1989 / BIZ / B • Dresden Mistress #3 / 1989 / BIZ / B • E Three / 1985 / GO / M • Empire Of The Sins / 1988 / IN / M • Erotic Aerobics / 1984 / VC / M • Erotic Express / 1983 / CV / M • Erotic Penetration / 1987 / HO / C • Erotic Radio WSEX / 1983 / VC / M • Erotic Therapy / 1987 / CDI / M • Experiment In Ecstasy / 1996 / LEI / M • Fantasies Unltd. / 1985 / CDI / M • First Annual XRCO Awards / 1984 / AVC / C • First Time Lesbians (Gourmet) / 1987 / GO / F • Flaming Tongues #1 / 1984 / MET / F • Flesh In Ecstasy #15: Bunny Bleu / 1988 / GO / C • Flexxx #1 / 1994 / VT / M • Floor Play / 1989 / PLV / B • Forbidden Dildo Taboos / 1992 / STM / F • Forbidden Fruit / 1985 / PV / M • Free And Foxy / 1986 / VCX / C • Freeway Honey / 1985 / VC / M • Fun In The Sun / 1988 / EVN / C • Gemini / 1994 / SC / M • Getting LA'd / 1986 / PV / M • Ghosts / 1995 / WV / M • Ginger In Ecstasy / 1987 / GO / C • Ginger's Private Party / 1985 / VI / M • Girl Games / 1987 / PL / C • Girl Toys / 1986 / DR / M • Girls Just Wanna Have Girls #2 / 1990 / HIO / F • Girls On Girls / 1987 / SE / C • Girls That Love Girls / 1984 / CA / F • Glamour Girl #2 / 1984 / CDI / M • Golddiggers #1 / 1985 / VC / M • Golden Girls #26 / 1985 / CA / M • Golden Girls #30 / 1985 / CA / M • The Good, The Bad, And The Horny / 1985 / VCX / M • Gourmet Premier: Heather & Bunny / Around the World #906 / cr85 / GO / M • Gourmet Premier: Lust X 4 / Raven's Rendezvous #901 / cr85 / GO / M • GVC: The Bad Bride #135 / 1985 / GO / M • GVC: Broadcast Babes #138 / 1985 / GO / M • Hard Squeeze / 1994 / EMC / M • Head & Tails / 1988 / VD / M • Heavy Breathing / 1986 / CV / M • Hollywood Pink / 1985 / HO / M • Hooked / 1992 / PHE / B • The Honeymooners / 1986 / CDI / M • Horny Henry's Peeping Adventures / 1994 / TTV / M • Horny Henry's Strange Adventure / 1995 / TTV / M • Horny Henry's Swinging Adventures / 1994 / TTV / M • Hot Buns / 1988 / BIZ / B • Hot Merchandise / 1985 / AVC / M • Hot Tails / 1984 / VEN / M • Hot Tight Asses #09 / 1994 / TCK / M • Hot To Trot / 1994 / IF / M • Hotel Sodom #05: Tammi Ann Bends Over / 1995 / SNA / M • Hottest Parties / 1988 / VC / C • Hustler Video Magazine #1 / 1983 / SE / M • I Dream Of Ginger / 1985 / VI / M • I Love LA #1 / 1986 / PEN / C • I Love LA #2 / 1989 / PEN / C • I Wanna Be Teased / 1984 / SE / M • I Want It All / 1984 / VD / M • Ice Cream #3: Naked Eyes / 1984 / VC / M • Impulse #01: Memories Of An Italian Slut / 1995 / MBP / M • In-N-Out With John Leslie / 1988 / WV / C • Infidelity / 1988 / 4P / M • Initiation Of Kylie / 1995 / VT / M • Interview: Doin' The Butt / 1995 / LV / M • It's Incredible / 1985 / SE / M • Journey Into Pain #2 / 1989 / BIZ / B • Journey Into Submission / 1990 / BIZ / B • Joys Of Erotica #111 / 1984 / VCR / C • Jug Humpers / 1995 / V99 / C • Kept

Women / 1995 / LE / M • L.A. Topless / 1994 / LE / M • The Ladies In Lace Party / 1985 / MAP / M • Ladies Room / 1994 / SC / F • Last Tango In Paradise / 1995 / ERA / M • Leather Lust Mistress / 1989 / BIZ / B • Leg...Ends #01 / 1988 / BIZ / F • Leg...Ends #09 / 1994 / PRE / F • Lesbian Dildo Bondage #2 / 1990 / BIZ / B • Lesbian Kink Trilogy #1 / 1992 / STM / F • Lesbian Nymphos / 1988 / GO / C • Lesbian Obsession / 1990 / BIZ / B • Lesbian Pussy Power / 1992 / BIZ / B • Let's Do It / 1994 / V99 / M • Let's Get It On With Amber Lynn / 1986 / VC / M • Like A Virgin #2 / 1986 / AT / M • Limited Edition #29 / 1984 / AVC / M • Lip Service / 1987 / BIK / C • Lip Service / 1988 / LV / C • Little American Maid / 1987 / VCX / M • A Little Bit Of Hanky Panky / 1984 / GO / M • Little Girls Talking Dirty / 1984 / VCX / M • Little Girls, Dirty Desires / 1984 / JVV / M • Loose Times At Ridley High / 1984 / VCX / M • Lottery Lust / 1986 / PEN / M • Love Button / 1985 / AVC / M • The Lover Girls / 1985 / V99 / M • Loving Lips / 1987 / AMB / C • Lucky At Lust / 1989 / SDP / M • Lucky Charm / 1986 / AVC / C • Lucy Has A Ball / 1987 / ME / M • The Lust Detector / 1986 / PIN / M • Lusty Adventurer / 1985 / GO / M • Lusty Layout / 1986 / PV / M • Making It In New York / 1989 / PLD / M • Male Domination #14 / 1990 / BIZ / C • Male Domination #15: Women In Suspension / 1990 / BIZ / C • Melts In Your Mouth / 1984 / ROY / M • Mind Mirror / 1994 / LAP / M • More Than A Mouthful #1 / 1995 / VEX / F • Mrs. Rodger's Neighborhood / 1988 / EVN / C • Muff Diving Usa / 1986 / EVN / C • Murder By Sex / 1993 / LAP / M • N.Y. Video Magazine #07 / 1996 / OUP / M • Naked Lust / 1985 / SE / M • Nasty Dancers #2 / 1996 / STM / B • Nasty Lovers / 1987 / SE / C • Nasty Nymphos #07 / 1994 / ANA / M • Naughty Nurses / 1986 / VEX / M • The New Ass Masters #07 / 1996 / LEI / C • Nice 'n' Tight / 1985 / AIR / M • Nina's Knockouts / 1987 / AVC / C • No Man's Land #09 / 1994 / VT / F • Obsessions In Lace / 1994 / PL / M • Older Men With Young Girls / 1985 / CC / M • On The Rise / 1994 / EX / M • Oral Majority #04 / 1987 / WV / C • Orgy Attack / 1993 / DRP / M • Oriental Lesbian Fantasies / 1984 / PL / F • Our Major Is Sex / 1984 / VD / M • Parliament: Bare Assets / 1988 / PM / F • Parliament: Dildo Babes #2 / 1988 / PM / F • Parliament: Eating Pussy #1 / 1989 / PM / C • Parliament: Finger Friggin' #1 / 1986 / PM / F • Parliament: Fuckin' Superstars #1 / 1990 / PM / C • Parliament: Strip Tease #1 / 1986 / PM / F • Party Girls / 1988 / MAP / M • Passion By Fire / 1986 / LAV / G • Passionate Lee / 1984 / CRE / M • Pearl Necklace: Amorous Amateurs #15 / 1992 / SEE / M • Pearl Necklace: Amorous Amateurs #16 / 1992 / SEE / M • Pearl Necklace: Amorous Amateurs #32 / 1993 / SEE / F • Pearl Necklace: Facial #01 / 1994 / SEE / C • Penetration #2 / 1984 / AVC / M • Penitentiary / 1995 / HW / M • Perfect Fit / 1985 / DR / M • Personal Touch #3 / 1983 / AR / M • Physical Attraction / 1984 / MAP / M • Pleasure Productions #04 / 1984 / VCR / C / M • Pleasure Spot / 1986 / CA / M • Pocahotass #2 / 1996 / FD / M • Political Party / 1985 / AVC / M • Positively Pagan #06 / 1993 / ATA / M • The Postman Always Comes Twice / 1986 / AMB / M • Pretty As You Feel / 1984 / PV / M • Private Showings / 1992 / STM / B • Professor Probe And The Spirit Of Sex / 1986 / ADU / M • The Proposal / 1993 / HO / M • Pulsating Flesh / 1986 / VC / M • Pussyman #13: Lips / 1996 / SNA / M • Raging Waters / 1992 / PRE / B • The Return Of Johnny Wadd / 1986 / PEN / M • Rich Quick, Private Dick / 1984 / CA / M • Rip Off #1 / 1988 / BIZ / B • Rock 'n' Roll Bondage Sluts / 1992 / STM / B • Rockin' Erotica / 1987 / SE / C • Rollover & Cell Blocks / 1988 / PLV / B • Rubdown / 1985 / VCX / M • Rump Man: Forever / 1995 / HW / M • Salt & Pepper / 1986 / VCS / C • Sappho Sextet / 1983 / LIP / F • Satin Dolls / 1985 / CV / M • Saturday Matinee Series #4 / 1996 / VCX / C • Savage Discipline / 1993 / STM / C • Savage Fury #1 / 1985 / VEX / M • Scandal In The Mansion / 1985 / CDI / M • Scandalous Simone / 1985 / SE / M • The Scarlet Woman / 1994 / WP / M • Secret Lessons #1 / 1986 / BIZ / B • Secret Lessons #2 / 1989 / BIZ / B • Secret Of Her Suckcess / 1994 / VC / M • Secret Retreat #1 / 1991 / STM / B • Secret Retreat #2 / 1991 / STM / B • Sex Between The Scenes / 1994 / LAP / M • The Sex Game / 1987 / SE • Sex Star Competition / 1985 / PL / M • Sex Starved / 1986 / VWA / M • Sex Toys / 1985 / CA / M • Sexeo / 1985 / PV / M • Sexplorations / 1991 / VC / C • Sexy Delights #1 / 1986 / CLV / M • She's A Good Lust Charm / 1987 / LA / C • Show Them No Mercy #1 / 1991 / STM / B • Show Them No Mercy #2 / 1991 / STM / B • Sins Of The Wealthy #1 / 1986 / CLV / M • Sissy Spanked In Red Panties / 1992 / STM / B • Slammed / 1995 / PV / M • Sleeping With Everybody / 1992 / MID / C • Slip Into Ginger & Amber / 1986 / MAP / C • Sordid Stories / 1994 / AMP / M • Splashing / 1986 / VCS / C • Star 85: Kari Fox / 1985 / VEX / M • A Star Is Porn / 1985 / PL / M • A Sticky Situation / 1987 / CA / M • Stiff Competition #1 / 1984 / CA / M • Student Fetish Videos: Best of Catfighting #02 / 1994 / PRE / C • Student Fetish Videos: Best of Enema #03 / 1994 / PRE / C • Student Fetish Videos: Best Of Foot Worship #03 / 1995 / PRE / C • Student Fetish Videos: Best Of Spanking #02 / 1993 / PRE / C • Student Fetish Videos: Catfighting #06 / 1992 / PRE / B • Student Fetish Videos: Catfighting #10 / 1994 / PRE / B • Student Fetish Videos: The Enema #14 / 1994 / PRE / B • Student Fetish Videos: Foot Worship #09 / 1994 / PRE / B • Student Fetish Videos: Spanking #09 / 1993 / PRE / B • Student Fetish Videos: Tickling #07 / 1992 / SFV / B • Student Fetish Videos: Tickling #09 / 1994 / SFV / B • Submissive Flashbacks / 1995 / STM / C • Sucker / 1988 / VWA / M • Summer Break / 1985 / VEX / M • Super Leg-Ends / 1992 / PRE / C • Super Models Do LA / 1986 / AT / M • Superstar Masturbation / 1990 / BIZ / F • Suzie Superstar #2 / 1985 / CV / M • Swedish Erotica #54 / 1984 / CA / M • Sweet Little Things / 1985 / COL / M • Sweet Surrender / 1985 / AVC / M • Taija's Satin Seduction / 1987 / CDI / M • Tails From The Crack / 1995 / HW / M • Take It Off / 1986 / TIF / M • Taking It To The Streets / 1987 / CDI / M • Tales Of Taija Rae / 1989 / DR / M • Talk Dirty To Me #03 / 1986 / DR / M • A Taste Of Bunny / 1988 / PIN / C • Taste Of The Best #1 / 1988 / PIN / C • Taste Of The Best #2 / 1988 / PIN / C • Teenage Games / 1985 / HO / M • Temperatures Rising / 1986 / VT / M • Terms Of Endowment / 1986 / PV / M • This Stud's For You / 1986 / MAP / C • Tight And Tender / 1985 / CA / M • Tight Fit (Foot Fet) / 1988 / BIZ / B • Titanic Orgy / 1995 / PEP / M • To Snatch A Thief / 1989 / PLD / M • Toe Hold / 1992 / PRE / B • Toe-Tally Foot-Age / 1992 / STM / C • Tongue In Cheek #02 / 1995 / HO / C • Tonya's List / 1994 / FD / M • Too Good To Be True / 1984 / MAP / M • Too Naughty To Say No / 1984 / CA / M • Too Young To Know / 1984 / CC / M • Toppers #01 / 1992 / TV / F • Toppers #02 / 1992 / TV / M • Toppers #04 / 1993 / TV / M • Toppers #09 / 1993 / TV / M • Toppers #12 / 1993 / TV / C • Toppers #28 / 1994 / TV / M • Toppers #29 / 1994 / TV / M • Toppers #32 / 1994 / TV / C • Traci Who? / 1987 / AVC / C • Trashy Lady / 1985 / MAP / M • Trick Or Treat / 1985 / ELH / M • Triple Play / 1983 / HO / M • Twins / 1986 / WV / M • The Ultimate Thrill / 1988 / PIN / C • An Unnatural Act #1 / 1984 / DR / M • Unnatural Act #2 / 1986 / DR / M • Unthinkable / 1984 / SE / M • Up Up And Away / 1984 / CA / M • Vegas Brats / 1990 / WV / M • Video Store Vixens / 1986 / PL / M • Visions Of Desire / 1993 / HO / M • Voyeur's Delight / 1986 / VCS / C • The Wacky World Of X-Rated Bloopers / 1989 / GO / M • Wall To Wall / 1985 / VD / M • Water Nymph / 1987 / LIM / M • Weak-Ends / 1995 / PRE / B • Wet Nurses #1 / 1994 / LE / M • Wet Science / 1986 / PLY / M • Wet Sex / 1984 / CA / M • What Gets Me Hot / 1984 / ISV / M • What's The Lesbian Doing In My Pirate Movie? / 1995 / LIP / F • Wicked Wenches / 1988 / LA / M • Wicked Woman / 1994 / HO / M • Wide World Of Sex / 1987 / CLV / C • Wild & Wicked #4 / 1994 / VT / M • Wild Nurses In Lust / 1986 / PLY / M • Wild Orgies #12 / 1994 / AFI / M • Wild Orgies / 1986 / SE / C • Women Who Love Girls / 1989 / CLV / C • WPINK-TV #1 / 1985 / PV / M • WPINK-TV #2 / 1986 / PV / M • X-Rated Bloopers #1 / 1984 / AR / M • X-Rated Bloopers #2 / 1986 / AR / M • X-TV #1 / 1986 / PL / C • You Make Me Wet / 1985 / SVE / M • [Abracadabra / 1989 / ... / M • [Ahpa: Vicky Vs Christy / 199? / AHP / B • [Candy Palace / 19?? / ... / M • [Dick Tales / 19?? / ... / M • [Dolls And Dragons / 19?? / ... / M • [Edible Vegetables / 1988 / EVN / M • [Emerald Dimples / 19?? / ... / M • [Good Love / 1988 / ... / M • [Mixed Company / 1986 / ... / M • [My Private Party / 1985 / VI / M • [My Sweetheart / 1986 / ... / M • [Night Of Legends / 1985 / AVC / M • [Sex Spirit / 1991 / NGV / M • [Uncensored Submission / 1990 / BIZ / B • [Woman's Desires / 1983 / ... / M

BUNNY BRODY
Resurrection Of Eve / 1973 / MIT / M

BUNNY DOWNE *see* Vicki Miles

BUNNY GLAMAZON
Big Bust Blondes / 1992 / BTO / F • Big Busty #36 / 198? / H&S / S • Exposure Images #12: Bunny Glamazon / 1992 / EXI /

F • Tit To Tit #2 / 1994 / BTO / M

BUNNY HATTON
Alley Cat / 1983 / VC / M • Consenting Adults / 1981 / VXP / M • Deep Inside Annie Sprinkle / 1981 / VXP / M • The Erotic World Of Angel Cash / 1983 / VXP / M • Intimate Realities #1 / 1983 / VC / M

BUNNY LAKE *see* **Barbie Blake**

BUNNY ROSE
Rears / 1987 / VI / M

BUNNY SAVAGE
Lollipop Palace / 1973 / VCX / M

BUNNY TAYLOR
Tight Fit / 1987 / V99 / M • Tight Fit / 1991 / VEX / C

BURGUNDY DAYE
[Bewitched Sex / 197? / ... / M

BURGUNDY GRANT
People / 1978 / QX / M

BURNT AMBER
The Affairs Of Miss Roberts / 19?? / ... / M

BURT ALLEN
Loveland / 1973 / VST / M

BURT ARMSTRONG
Clock House / 1990 / FC / M

BURT LONG
Nina's Knockouts / 1987 / AVC / C

BURT REICH
Heartless / 1989 / REB / M

BURT SHIELDS
The Model / 1991 / HO / M

BURTON GOLDWATER
Sex U.S.A / 1970 / SEP / M

BUSTER
Kym Wilde's Bondage House Party #2 / 1993 / BON / B • Ready To Drop #02 / 1992 / FC / M • Uncle Roy's Amateur Home Video #10 / 1992 / VIM / M

BUSTER CHERI *(Rod Ryker)*
Identified as both Rod Ryker and Buster Cheri in **Bush Pilots #2**. Rayne's boyfriend or husband.
Beauty And The Beach / 1991 / CC / M • Bush Pilots #1 / 1990 / VC / M • Bush Pilots #2 / 1991 / VC / M • The Girl Has Assets / 1990 / LV / M • Hard Deck / 1991 / XPI / M • Mickey Ray's Sex Search #03: Deep Heat / 1994 / WIV / M • Prisoner Of Love / 1991 / ME / M • The Pump / 1991 / CC / M • Racquel In Paradise / 1990 / VC / M • Read My Lips / 1990 / FH / M • Red Line / 1991 / PL / M • Slip Of The Tongue / 1990 / SE / M • Slow Burn / 1991 / VC / M • A Taste Of K.C. Williams / 1992 / VD / C

BUSTER COCKBURN *see* **Woody Long**

BUSTER HYMAN
Loose Ends #6 / 1989 / 4P / M

BUSTER HYMEN *see* **Jamie Gillis**

BUSTER LONDON
Young Sluts In Heat #1 / 1996 / PL / M

BUSTER RAMSES
Big Boys Toy / 1994 / SV / B • Paint Balled / 1993 / SV / B

BUSTER ROUSE
Ropemasters / cr90 / BON / B

BUSTY BELL *see* **Busty Belle**

BUSTY BELLE *(Busty Bell)*
10 Years Of Big Busts #1 / 1989 / BTO / C • B-Witched / 1994 / PEP / G • Backdoor To Harley-Wood #2 / 1990 / AFV / M • The Battle Of the Breast Queens / 1989 / INS / C • Belle Of The Ball / 1989 / V99 / M • Between My Breasts #09 / 1990 / BTO / M • Between My Breasts #10 / 1990 / BTO / M • Bi & Large / 1994 / STA / G • Bi 'n' Large / 1994 / PL / G • Bi And Busty / 1991 / STA

/ G • Bi Chill / 1994 / BIL / G • The Bi-Linguist / 1993 / BIL / G • Bi-Athelon / 1993 / BIL / G • Bi-Golly / 1993 / BIL / G • Bi-Inferno / 1992 / VEX / G • Big Bust Strippers #01 / 1990 / BTO / F • Big Busty #30 / 198? / H&S / S • Breast Wishes #03 / 1991 / LBO / M • Breathless / 1989 / CIN / M • Buffy Malibu's Totally Nasty All-Girl Home Videos #04 / 1993 / ANA / F • Bursting Bras / 1990 / BTO / C • Charlie's Girls #2 / 1989 / CC / M • Chills / 1989 / LV / M • Cumming Clean / 1991 / FL / M • Deep Inside Barbie / 1989 / CDI / C • Dominique Goes Bi / 1994 / STA / G • Double Jeopardy / 1990 / HO / M • Dream Dates / 1990 / V99 / M • Family Thighs / 1989 / AR / M • Gilligan's Bi-Land / 1994 / PL / G • Girls Of The Double D #06 / 1989 / CIN / M • Girls Of The Double D #08 / 1989 / CDI / M • Girls Of The Double D #10 / 1989 / CDI / M • Girls Of The Double D #11 / 1990 / CIN / M • Goodtime Charli / 1989 / CIN / M • The Harley Girls / 1991 / AR / F • Heather Hunter On Fire / 1988 / VWA / M • Hollywood Teasers #04 / 1992 / LBO / F • Inside Of Me / 1993 / PL / G • The Last Good-Bi / 1990 / CDI / G • Lick Bush / 1992 / VD / C • The Lottery / 1989 / CIN / M • Love Button / 1989 / VD / M • The Magic Shower / 1989 / CDI / M • Missy Impossible / 1989 / CDI / M • More Than A Woman / 1992 / CDI / G • My 500 Pound Vibrator / 1991 / LV / C • A Night At The Waxworks / 1990 / IF / M • The Oversexual Tourist / 1989 / VEX / M • The Pleasure Chest / 1988 / VWA / M • Racquel's Treasure Hunt / 1990 / VC / M • Retail Slut / 1989 / LV / M • Sex Flex / 1989 / CDI / M • Sex Sluts From Beyond The Galaxy / 1991 / LBO / C • Smothering Tits And Pussy #3 / 199? / H&S / M • Space Cadet / 1989 / IN / M • Succulent Toes / 1994 / PL / B • A Taste Of Victoria Paris / 1990 / PIN / C • Too Hot To Stop / 1989 / V99 / M • Virgins / 1989 / CAR / M • X Dreams / 1989 / CA / M

BUSTY BRITTANY
Blonde with humongous tits. Not to be confused with Brittany Andrews who is taller.
Anally Insatiable / 1995 / KWP / M • Ass Masters (Leisure) #04 / 1995 / LEI / M • Big Boob Bikini Bash / 1995 / BTO / M • Big Breast Beach / 1995 / LV / M • Big Knockers #15 / 1995 / TV / M • Big Knockers #16 / 1995 / TV / M • Big Knockers #19 / 1995 / TV / M • Big Knockers #20 / 1995 / TV / C • Big Knockers #21: Best Of Lesbian #2 / 1995 / TV / C • The Boob Tube / 1993 / MET / M • Breast Collection #01 / 1995 / LBO / C • Breast Worx #23 / 1992 / LBO / M • Breast Worx #25 / 1992 / LBO / M • Breast Worx #26 / 1992 / LBO / M • Busty Brittany Takes London / 1996 / H&S / M • Busty Porno Stars #1 / 1995 / H&S / M • Double D Dreams / 1996 / NAP / S • Duke Of Knockers #2 / 1995 / BTO / M • Harlots From Hootersville / 1994 / BLC / M • Hollywood Teasers #03 / 1992 / LBO / M • Hot Box / 1995 / V99 / C • Interview's Big Boob Bonanza / 1996 / LV / M • Lesbian Nights / 1996 / AVI / F • Mellon Man #04 / 1995 / AVI / M • Mellon Man #06 / 1995 / AVI / M • Mellon Man #07 / 1996 / AVI / M • Natural Wonders / 1993 / VI / M • Philmore Butts Goes Wild! / 1996 / SUF / M • Scandal / 1995 / VI / M • Snatch Masters #08 / 1995 / LEI / M • Spread It Wide / 1996 /

AVI / M • Tit To Tit #2 / 1994 / BTO / M • What About Boob? / 1993 / CV / M

BUSTY BROWN
Reel Classics #2 / 1996 / H&S / M • Reel Classics #3 / 1996 / H&S / M

BUSTY DUSTY
Big Busty #47 / 1994 / BTO / S • Big Tit Roundup #1 / 199? / H&S / S • Double D-Cup Dates / 1994 / BTO / M • Girls Around The World #28 / 1995 / BTO / S • H&S: Busty Dusty / 199? / H&S / S • Score Busty Covergirls #4 / 1995 / BTO / S

BUTCH
Beach Bum Amateur's #25 / 1993 / MID / M • Bi-Bi Love Amateurs #4 / 1994 / QUA / G • HomeGrown Video #470: Heroes, Torpedoes & Grinders / 1996 / HOV / M • Learn Your Lessons / 1992 / BIZ / M • Ona Zee's Date With Dallas / 1992 / ONA / M • A Pool Party At Seymores #1 / 1995 / ULI / M • Transsexual Try Outs / 1993 / HSV / G

BUTCH (T.T. BOY) *see* **T.T. Boy**

BUTCH BEELER
[No Mo' Hoes / cr70 / ... / M • [Ooze Dripping Wimmins / cr70 / ... / M

BUTCH BERGER
Submission Position #608 / 1988 / CTS / B

BUTCH BERKELY
Sin City: The Movie / 1992 / SC / M

BUTCH BERKLY
Inspector Croissant: The Case Of The Missing Pinky / 1995 / FC / M

BUTCH BRADY
Barbie's Fantasies / 1974 / VHL / M

BUTCH HARDON
Bi The Time You Get Back / 1995 / BIN / G • Tranny Claus / 1994 / HEA / G

BUTCH KATAZAKAIS
Resurrection Of Eve / 1973 / MIT / M

BUTCH TAYLOR
Bi Mistake / 1989 / VI / G • The Offering / 1988 / INH / G • Switch Hitters #4: The Grand Slam / 1989 / IN / G

BUTCH WILLIAMS
Anal Assassins / 1991 / IN / M • Anal Commander / 1990 / ZA / M

BUTLER JAMES
Full Service Butler / 1993 / KEE / B • Rich Bitches / 1993 / KEE / B

████████████
Black Street Hookers #2 / 1996 / DFI / M

BUTTMAN *see* **John Stagliano**

BUZZ
GRG: Buzz & Karen / 1993 / GRG / M

BYRON LONG
The Adventures Of Peeping Tom #2 / 1996 / OD / M • The Adventures Of Peeping Tom #3 / 1996 / OD / M • Amateur Black: Starlets / 1995 / SUF / M • Anal, Facial & Interracial / 1996 / FC / M • Asses Galore #1: From L.A. To Brazil / 1996 / DFI / M • Asses Galore #4: Extreme Noise Terror / 1996 / DFI / M • Back Rent / 1996 / MP0 / M • Big Black Bang / 1996 / HW / M • Big Murray's New-Cummers #29: Tools Of The Trade / 1995 / FD / M • The Black Butt Sisters Do Boston / 1995 / MID / M • The Black Butt Sisters Do Houston / 1996 / MID / M • The Black Butt Sisters Do Seattle / 1995 / MID / M • Black Cheerleader Search #04 / 1996 / ROB / M • Black Cheerleader Search #06 / 1996 / IVC / M • Black Cheerleader Search #08 / 1996 / IVC / M • Black Fantasies #09 / 1995 / HW / M • Black Fantasies #10 / 1995 / HW / M • Black Fantasies #13 / 1996 / HW / M •

Black Fantasies #14 / 1996 / HW / M •
Black Fantasies #16 / 1996 / HW / M •
Black Gangbangers #08 / 1995 / HW / M •
Black Gangbangers #10 / 1996 / HW / M •
Black Gangbangers #11 / 1996 / HW / M •
Black Gangbangers #12 / 1996 / HW / M •
Black Hollywood Amateurs #19 / 1995 /
MID / M • Black Hollywood Amateurs #22 /
1996 / MID / M • Black Hollywood Ama-
teurs #23 / 1996 / MID / M • Black Holly-
wood Amateurs #25 / 1996 / MID / M •
Black Hollywood Amateurs #26 / 1996 /
MID / M • Black Knockers #01 / 1995 / TV /
M • Black Knockers #02 / 1995 / TV / M •
Black Knockers #03 / 1995 / TV / M • Black
Knockers #04 / 1995 / TV / M • Black
Knockers #05 / 1995 / TV / M • Black
Knockers #06 / 1995 / TV / M • Black
Knockers #11 / 1995 / TV / M • Black
Knockers #12 / 1995 / TV / M • Black
Knockers #13 / 1995 / TV / M • Black
Knockers #14 / 1995 / TV / M • Black Lube
Job Girls / 1995 / SUF / M • Black Sensa-
tions: Models In Heat / 1995 / SUF / M •
Black Talez N Da Hood / 1996 / APP / M •
The Body System / 1996 / FD / M • Booty
Bang #1 / 1996 / HW / M • Bootylicious:
Baby Got Booty 1996 / JMP / M • Bootyli-
cious: Big Badd Booty / 1995 / JMP / M •
Bootylicious: Bitches & Ho's / 1996 / JMP /
M • Bootylicious: Booty & The Ho Bitch /
1996 / JMP / M • Bootylicious: China Town
/ 1995 / JMP / M • Bootylicious: It's A
Bootyful Thing / 1996 / JMP / M • Bootyli-
cious: Trailer Trash / 1996 / JMP / M •
Bootylicious: Yo Bitch / 1996 / JMP / M •
Bow Down Backstreet / 1996 / HW / M •
Butt-Nanza / 1995 / WV / M • Byron Long
At Large / 1995 / VC / M • Champagne's
House Party / 1996 / HW / M • China's
House Party / 1996 / HW / M • Cindy's
House Party / 1996 / HW / M • Climax At
The Melting Pot #2 / 1996 / AVS / M •
Fashion Passion / 1997 / TEP / M • Git Yo'
Ass On Da Bus! / 1996 / HW / M • Hard-
core Confidential #2 / 1996 / TEP / M •
Here Comes Magoof #1 / 1995 / VC / M •
Here Comes Magoof #2 / 1995 / VC / M •
Hooter Tutor / 1996 / APP / M • Juicy's
Houseparty / 1995 / HW / M • Kimberly
Kupps Gets Black Balled / 1996 / NIT / M •
Latin Fever #1 / 1996 / C69 / M • A Low-
down Dirty Game / 1996 / LBO / M •
Menaja's House Party / 1996 / HW / M •
Miss Judge / 1997 / VI / M • My Baby Got
Back #07 / 1995 / VT / M • My Baby Got
Back #08 / 1996 / VT / M • My Baby Got
Back #09 / 1996 / VT / M • My First Time
#5 / 1996 / NS / M • Old Wives' Tails / 1995
/ EMC / M • Perverted Stories #03 / 1995 /
JMP / M • Perverted Stories #07 / 1996 /
JMP / M • Primal Rear / 1996 / TIW / M •
Puritan Video Magazine #04 / 1996 / LE /
M • Ron Hightower's Casting Couch #2 /
1995 / FC / M • Show & Tell / 1996 / VI / M
• Snatch Shot / 1996 / LBO / M • Stuff Your
Ass #1 / 1995 / JMP / M • Stuff Your Ass #2
/ 1995 / JMP / M • Stuff Your Ass #3 / 1996
/ JMP / M • Stuff Your Face #3 / 1995 /
JMP / M • Stuff Your Face #4 / 1996 / JMP
/ M • Two Can Chew / 1995 / FD / M • Two-
Pac / 1996 / VT / M • Vivid Raw #1 / 1996 /
VI / M • Vivid Raw #4 / 1996 / VI / M • Wait-
ing 2 XX Hale / 1996 / APP / M • White
Trash Whore / 1996 / JMP / M • Young And
Anal #3 / 1995 / JMP / M

BYRON LORD
Coed Fever / 1980 / CA / M • Scarlet Neg-
ligee / 1968 / ALP / S
BYRON MAYBE *(B. Ron Elliot)*
The Defilers / 1964 / SOW / S
BYRON PRESTON
Bavarian Cream & Other Delights / 1985 /
PV / M
BYRON STRESS
MASH'ed / cr75 / ALP / M
C
The Crack Of Dawn / 1989 / GLE / M
C. BAUGHMAN
Blue Vanities #580 / 1996 / FFL / M
C. KNIGHT
Blue Vanities #555 / 1994 / FFL / M
C. MOORE ASHLEY *see* **Ashley Moore**
C.B. DEMILLE *see* **Star Index I**
C.C. CHERRY
Butt Hunt #04 / 1995 / LEI / M
C.C. EDWARDS *see* **Star Index I**
C.C. MALONE *see* **Jennifer West**
C.C. MOORE
Big Bust Strippers #03 / 1991 / BTO / F •
Big Busted Goddesses Of L.A. / 1991 /
NAP / S • Biggest Sexiest Boobs In The
USA Contest / 1989 / NAP / F • D-Cup Hol-
iday / 1991 / BTO / M • Girls Around The
World #03 / 1990 / BTO / M • Girls Around
The World #13: Lynn LeMay And Friends /
1994 / BTO / M • Girls Of Sundance Spa:
Hardcore Plumpers #1 / 1992 / BTO / M •
Tit To Tit #2 / 1994 / BTO / M
C.C. SADIST
Whipped And Shaved / 1995 / FLV / B
C.D. LAFLEUER *see* **George Flower**
C.J.
M.O. #1 / 1995 / STP / F • New Faces, Hot
Bodies #18 / 1995 / STP / M • Toy Time #5:
/ 1996 / STP / F
C.J. BENNETT *(Jessie Jean, Judy (C.J.
Bennett))*
Small brunette, who in her first few perfor-
mances, looked very attractive and seemed
to have a tight little body. After about five
movies she seemed to deteriorate into a
body that looks more like Madison (except
for the tits which are still small). Personality wise she seems to be quite pleasant and
seems to enjoy sex. Was 18 in 1993 and got
de-virginized at 17.
30 Days In The Hole / 1993 / ZA / M • 4 Bi 4
/ 1994 / BIN / G • Adventures Of The DP
Boys: Down At The Sunset Grill / 1993 / HW
/ M • Adventures Of The DP Boys: The Hollywood Bubble Butts / 1993 / HW / M • Amateur Dreams #2 / 1994 / DR / M • Amateur
Orgies #33 / 1993 / AFI / M • Amateur Orgies #34 / 1993 / AFI / M • Anal Breakdown
/ 1994 / ROB / M • Anal Crack Master / 1994
/ ROB / M • The Anal Diary Of Misty Rain /
1993 / EL / M • Anal Hounds & Bitches /
1994 / ROB / M • Anal Idol / 1994 / ROB / M
• Anal Plaything #1 / 1994 / ROB / M • Anal
Virgins Of America #05 / 1993 / FOR / M •
Backdoor Magic / 1994 / LV / M • Backdoor
To Harley-Wood #3 / 1993 / AFV / M • Back-
stage Pass / 1994 / SC / M • Beach Bum
Amateur's #35 / 1993 / MID / M • Bi
Claudius / 1994 / BIL / G • Bi George / 1994
/ BIL / G • Bi On The Fourth Of July / 1994 /
BIL / G • Bi-Sexual Anal #2 / 1994 / RTP / G
• Black Attack / 1994 / ZA / M • Bobby Hol-
lander's Sweet Cheeks #109 / 1994 / WV /
M • Bodywaves / 1994 / ELP / M • Bun
Busters #09 / 1993 / LBO / M • Bun Busters

#10 / 1993 / LBO / M • Bun Busters #13 /
1994 / LBO / M • Butt Bangers Ball / 1994 /
FPI / M • Butt Of Steel / 1994 / LV / M • Cast-
ing Call #05 / 1994 / SO / M • Climax At The
Melting Pot #1 / 1996 / AVS / M • The Cumm
Brothers #02: Goin' To A Ho' Down / 1994 /
OD / M • Cuntz #1 / 1994 / RTP / M • Cuntz
#2 / 1994 / RTP / M • Cuntz #3 / 1994 / RTP
/ M • Cuntz #4 / 1994 / RTP / M • Dirt Bags
/ 1994 / FPI / M • Dirty Doc's Housecalls #07
/ 1994 / LV / M • Double D Dykes #13 / 1994
/ GO / F • Double Penetration Virgins #05:
Go To Hell / 1994 / BB0 / M • Dungeon
Dykes #2 / 1994 / FPI / F • Electro Sex /
1994 / FPI / M • Fantasy Flings #02 / 1994 /
WP / M • First Time Lesbians #12 / 1993 /
JMP / F • Good Pussy / 1994 / VIM / M •
Guess Again / 1994 / FPI / G • Hidden Cam-
era #14 / 1994 / JMP / M • Hidden Camera:
Interracial Special / 1994 / JMP / M • Holly-
wood Starlets Adventure #03 / 1995 / AVS /
M • House Of Sex #15: Dirty Anal Three
Ways / 1994 / RTP / M • Kinky Orientals /
1994 / FH / M • Little Magicians / 1993 / ANA
/ M • Little Shop Of She-Males / 1994 / HSV
/ G • Lovin' Spoonfuls #6 / 1996 / 4P / C •
Mike Hott: #259 Cunt Of The Month: C.J.
Bennett 2-94 / 1994 / MHV / M • More Dirty
Debutantes #29 / 1994 / 4P / M • Mr.
Madonna / 1994 / FPI / G • My Boyfriend's
Black / 1994 / FD / M • My Cum Is Oozing
From C.J.'s Pussy / 1994 / RTP / M • Nasty
Nymphos #01 / 1993 / ANA / M • Odyssey
Triple Play #76: Double Penetration, Triple
Present. / 1994 / OD / M • Oriental Oddballs
#2 / 1994 / FH / M • Pearl Necklace: Thee
Bush League #28 / 1994 / SEE / M • Private
Request / 1994 / GLI / M • Private Video
Magazine #09 / 1994 / OD / M • Pussy Tales
/ 1993 / SC / F • Queen Of The Bizarre /
1994 / AMP / G • Ron Hightower's White
Chicks #03 / 1993 / LBO / M • Ron High-
tower's White Chicks #11 / 1994 / LBO / M •
Savage Fury #3 / 1994 / VEX / M • She Male
Sex Kittens / 1995 / MET / G • Show & Tell /
1994 / ELP / M • Slut Safari #2 / 1994 / FC /
M • Sodomania: Slop Shots / 1996 / EL / C
• A Step Beyond / 1994 / AMP / G • Stolen
Fantasies / 1995 / LON / B • Strap On Anal
Attitude / 1994 / SCL / M • Stylin' / 1994 / FD
/ M • Super Bi Bowl / 1995 / BIL / G • The
Sweet Sweet Back #3: Sho' Nuff Got Dat
Woodski / 1994 / FH / M • Swinging Couples
#01 / 1993 / GO / M • Take This Wad And
Shove It! / 1994 / ZA / M • Tight Fit #02 /
1994 / GO / M • Up And Cummers #12 /
1994 / 4P / M • Video Virgins #07 / 1993 /
NS / M • Willie Wanker And The Fun Factory
/ 1994 / FD / M
C.J. CARSON *see* **Star Index I**
C.J. HALL
Bondage Memories #04 / 1994 / BON / C •
Nancy Crew Meets Dr. Freidastein / cr90 /
BON / B • Wild Thing / 1989 / BON / B
C.J. LAING *(Gwen Star, C.J. Lainge,
Jessy Lang, C.J. Lange, Jessie Sav-
age, Lisa Collins (CJL))*
Dark short-haired blonde with lithe body, small
tits but too big a nose to be deemed pretty.
Although she doesn't smile very much, she
seems quite vulnerable and down-to-earth
and, depending on the movie, can generate
some erotic excitement. As of 1995 is sup-
posedly dead.
ABA: Double Feature #4 / 1996 / ALP / M •
ABA: Double Feature #5 / 1996 / ALP / M *

The Affairs Of Janice / 1975 / ALP / M • The Anger In Jennie / 1975 / VHL / M • Anyone But My Husband / 1975 / VC / M • Art School / cr70 / VHL / M • Baby Oil / 1974 / SOW / M • Bang Bang You Got It / 1975 / VXP / M • Barbara Broadcast / 1977 / VC / M • Barbie's Fantasies / 1974 / VHL / M • Beach House / 1981 / CA / C • Blue Vanities #079 / 1988 / FFL / M • Bucky Beaver's XXX Dragon Art Theatre Double Feature #15 / 1996 / SOW / M • Carnal Games / 1978 / BL / M • Cracked Ice / 1977 / PVX / M • Daughters Of Discipline #1 / 197? / AVO / B • Dear Pam / 1976 / CA / M • Dirty Lilly / 1975 / VXP / M • Dirty Looks / 1982 / VC / C • Dominatrix Without Mercy / 1976 / ALP / B • Ecstasy In Blue / 1976 / ALP / M • Erotic Dr Jekyll / 1975 / VXP / M • Erotic Fantasies #2 / 1983 / CV / C • Erotic Fantasies #4 / 1983 / CV / C • Erotic Gold #2 / 1985 / VEN / M • Executive Secretary / 1975 / CA / M • Farewell Scarlett / 1976 / COM / M • Go Fly A Kite / cr73 / VHL / M • The Honeymooners / 1978 / CV / M • Jawbreakers / 1985 / VEN / C • Legends Of Porn #1 / 1987 / CV / C • Little Orphan Sammy / 1976 / VC / M • Maraschino Cherry / 1978 / QX / M • Midnight Desires / 1976 / VXP / M • The New York City Woman / 1979 / VC / C • Night Of Submission / 1976 / BIZ / M • Odyssey / 1977 / VC / M • Only The Very Best On Film / 1992 / VC / C • Oriental Blue / 1975 / ALP / M • Satan Was A Lady / 1977 / ALP / M • Schoolgirl's Reunion / 1975 / VHL / M • Sex Wish / 1976 / CV / M • Sexteen / 1975 / VC / M • Slave Of Pleasure / 1978 / BL / M • Slippery When Wet / 1976 / VXP / M • Sweet Punkin...I Love You / 1975 / VC / M • The Taking Of Christina / 1975 / NGV / M • Teenage Pajama Party / 1977 / VC / M • Too Hot To Handle / 1975 / CDC / M • Two Senoritas / 197? / VHL / M • Unwilling Lovers / 197? / SVE / M • VCA Previews #12 / 1988 / VC / C • The Vixens Of Kung Fu: A Tale Of Yin Yang / 1975 / VC / M • Waterpower / 1975 / VHL / M • Women In Uniform / 1977 / VHL / M • The World Of Henry Paris / 1981 / VC / C • [Best Of Annette Haven / 1986 / ... / C • [Dark Side Of [Fantacy] / 19/0 / VBJ / M • [Gladys And Her All-Girl Band / cr75 / ... / M

C.J. LAINGE *see* **C.J. Laing**

C.J. LANGE *see* **C.J. Laing**

C.J. WILLIAMS
Bi Dream Of Genie / 1994 / BIL / G

C.J.X.
Dirty Dancers #1 / 1994 / 4P / M

C.R. KING
Suzie's Take Out Service / 1975 / CDC / M

CA SEE (WILLIAMS) *see* **Casey Williams**

CABO
Heavenly / 1995 / IF / M • Private Places / 1995 / IF / M

CAERAGE *see* **Star Index I**

CAESAR BALSTIC *see* **Star Index I**

CAESAR RINALDI
Every Nerd Has A Fantasy / 1996 / FC / M

CAESAR WAYLONS *see* **Star Index I**

CAGEY BEE
Show & Tell / 1994 / ELP / M • Sleeping Single / 1994 / CC / M • So You Wanna Be A Porn Star #1: The Russians Are Cumming / 1994 / WHP / M

CAILLE AIMES *see* **Shauna Grant**

CAITLYN LEWIS *see* **Pamela Rose**

CAJUN QUEEN
Ataack Of The Giant Mutant Tits / 1996 / H&S / S • Big Busty #20 / 198? / H&S / M • Big Tit Orgy #01 / 1987 / H&S / M • Big Top Cabaret #1 / 1986 / BTO / M • Breast Of Britain #2 / 1987 / BTO / M • Fat Fannies #08 / 1992 / BTO / M

CAL EAST *see* **Cal Jammer**

CAL FOURNY
Midnight Hustle / 1978 / VC / M

CAL JAMA *see* **Cal Jammer**

CAL JAMMER *(Cal Jana, Chris Douglas, Cal East, Cal Jama, Kal Jammer, Tim Johnson, Arthur (C. Jammer), Randy Potes)*
Chris Douglas in **Sweet Misfortune**, Cal Jana in **The Big Tease**. Tim Johnson in **Talk Dirty To Me #7**. Committed suicide on January 25, 1995 by blowing his brains out apparently because of relationship problems with his SO, Jill Kelly. 34 years old in 1995 from Bethesda MD.
9-Ball: Geisha Gang Bang / 1994 / PL / M • A Is For Anal / 1993 / LV / M • Above The Knee / 1994 / WAV / M • Adult Affairs / 1994 / VC / M • Adventures In Paradise / 1992 / VEX / M • The Adventures Of Buttgirl & Wonder Wench / 1991 / AFV / M • Adventures Of The DP Boys: Back In The Bush / 1993 / HW / M • Adventures Of The DP Boys: Down At The Sunset Grill / 1993 / HW / M • Against All Bods / 1991 / VEX / M • All In The Name Of Love / 1992 / IF / M • All That Glitters / 1992 / LV / M • Amazing Tails #4 / 1990 / CA / M • America's Dirtiest Home Videos #05 / 1991 / VEX / M • Anal Attraction #2 / 1993 / AFV / C • Anal Avenue / 1992 / LV / M • Anal Blitz / 1991 / MID / M • Anal Dawn / 1991 / AMB / M • Anal Destroyer / 1994 / ZA / M • Anal Distraction / 1993 / PEP / M • Anal Encounters #2 / 1991 / VC / M • Anal Encounters #6 / 1992 / VC / M • Anal Encounters #7: Enter Through The Rear / 1992 / VC / M • Anal Encounters #8 / 1992 / VC / M • Anal Future / 1992 / VC / M • Anal Heat / 1990 / ZA / M • Anal Intruder #04 / 1990 / CC / M • Anal Island / 1992 / LV / M • Anal Nation #1 / 1990 / CC / M • Anal Nation #2 / 1990 / CC / M • Anal Madness / 1990 / AFD / M • Anal Romance / 1993 / LV / M • Anal Therapy #1 / 1992 / FD / M • Anal Therapy #2 / 1993 / FD / M • Anal Woman #2 / 1993 / PL / M • The Anal-Europe Series #02: Fantasies / 1992 / LV / M • The Anal-Europe Series #03: The Museum Of The Living Art / 1993 / LV / M • The Anal-Europe Series #04: Anal Recall / 1993 / LV / M • Anything Goes / 1993 / VD / C • Art Of Sex / 1992 / FD / M • The Artist / 1994 / HO / M • As Sweet As They Come / 1992 / V99 / M • Asian Invasion / 1993 / IP / M • Asian Persuasion / 1993 / WV / M • Ass-Capades / 1992 / HW / M • Assumed Innocence / 1990 / AR / M • Assuming The Position / 1989 / V99 / M • Aussie Exchange Girls / 1990 / PM / M • Aussie Maid In America / 1990 / PM / M • B.L.O.W. / 1992 / LV / M • The Babe / 1992 / EX / M • Babe Watch #1 / 1994 / SC / M • Babe Watch #2 / 1994 / SC / M • The Back Doors (Executive) / 1991 / EX / M • The Back Doors (Western) / 1991 / WV / M • Back In Action / 1992 / FD / M • Back Seat Bush / 1992 / LV / M • Back To The Orient / 1992 / HW / M • Backdoor Brides #4 / 1993 / PV / M • The Backdoor

Club / 1992 / LV / M • Backdoor Suite / 1992 / EX / M • Backdoor To Russia #2 / 1993 / VC / M • Backdoor To Russia #3 / 1993 / VC / M • Backing In #6 / 1994 / WV / C • The Backpackers #1 / 1990 / IN / M • Backstage Entrance #1 / 1992 / FH / M • Backstage Entrance #2 / 1992 / FH / M • Backstage Pass / 1992 / VEX / M • The Backway Inn #2 / 1992 / FD / M • Bardot / 1991 / VI / M • Bare Ass Beach / 1994 / TP / M • The Bare Truth / 1994 / FD / C • Battlestar Orgasmica / 1992 / EVN / M • Beach Blanket Brat / 1989 / VI / M • Beaverjuice / 1992 / LV / M • Bed, Butts & Breakfast / 1990 / LV / M • Bedazzled / 1993 / OD / M • Bedtime Tales / 1995 / IF / M • Behind The Backdoor #5 / 1992 / EVN / M • Behind The Backdoor #6 / 1993 / EVN / M • Behind The Scenes: The Making Of The Wil & Ed Movies / 1992 / MID / M • Between The Bars / 1992 / FH / M • Beverly Hills 90269 / 1992 / LV / M • Beverly Hills Geisha / 1992 / V99 / M • Beverly Hills Sex Party / 1993 / EX / M • Big Murray's New-Cummers #21: Double Penetration One / 1993 / FD / M • Big Murray's New-Cummers #22: Exotic Erotica / 1993 / FD / M • The Big One / 1992 / GO / M • The Big Tease #1 / 1990 / VC / M • Black & White In Living Color / 1992 / WV / M • Black Analyst #2 / 1995 / VEX / M • Black Jack City #2: Black's Revenge / 1992 / HW / M • Black Orchid / 1993 / WV / M • Blackman & Anal Woman #2 / 1990 / PL / M • Blonde Beaver Bonanza / 1992 / TCP / M • Blonde Bombshell / 1991 / CC / M • Blonde Ice #2 / 1993 / EX / M • Blonde Temptation / 1995 / IF / M • Blow For Blow / 1992 / ZA / M • Blow Out / 1991 / IF / M • Blue Angel / 1991 / SE / M • Blue Angel / 1992 / AFV / M • Body And Soul / 1992 / OD / M • Body Fire / 1991 / LV / M • Boiling Point / 1994 / WAV / M • The Book / 1990 / IF / M • Boomeranal / 1992 / CC / M • Born For Porn / 1989 / FAZ / M • Both Ends Burning / 1993 / HW / M • The Bottom Dweller / 1993 / EL / M • The Box / 1992 / EX / M • Breast Wishes #09 / 1992 / LBO / M • Breast Wishes #10 / 1992 / LBO / M • Breast Wishes #13 / 1992 / LBO / M • Breast Wishes #13 / 1993 / LBO / M • Breast Worx #17 / 1991 / LBO / M • Breast Worx #20 / 1992 / LBO / M • Breastman Goes To Breastland #1 / 1993 / EVN / M • Bubble Butts #10 / 1992 / LBO / M • Bubble Butts #13 / 1992 / LBO / M • Bubble Butts #23 / 1992 / LBO / M • Buns And Roses (V9) / 1990 / V99 / M • Burn It Up / 1994 / VEX / M • Bustin' Thru / 1993 / LV / M • But...Can She Type? / 1989 / CDI / M • The Butt Connection / 1993 / TIW / M • The Butt Sisters Do Denver / 1994 / MID / M • Butt's Up, Doc #1 / 1992 / GO / M • Butt's Up, Doc #2 / 1992 / GO / M • Butties / 1992 / VC / M • Buttsizer, King Of Rears #2 / 1992 / EVN / M • Buttwiser / 1992 / HW / M • California Taxi Girls / 1991 / AFV / M • The Can Can / 1993 / LV / M • Candy Stripers #4 / 1990 / AR / M • Cape Rear / 1992 / WV / M • Casting Call #01 / 1993 / SO / M • Charm School / 1993 / PEP / M • Cheek Busters / 1990 / FH / M • Cheeks #2: The Bitter End / 1989 / CC / M • Cheeks #7: Mirror Image / 1994 / CC / M • Compulsive Behavior / 1995 / PI / M • Crash In The Rear / 1992 / HW / C • Crazy On You / 1991 / IF / M • The Crimson Kiss / 1993 /

WV / M • Cumming Clean / 1991 / FL / M • Dallas Does Debbie / 1992 / PL / M • Dark Dreams / 1992 / WV / M • Dark Obsessions / 1993 / WV / M • Dark Star / 1991 / VI / M • Date Night / 1992 / V99 / M • Decadent Delights / 1992 / IF / M • Deep Dreams / 1990 / IN / M • Deep In The Bush / 1990 / KIS / M • Deep Inside Ariana / 1995 / VC / C • Deep Inside Charli / 1990 / CDI / C • Deep Inside Ona Zee / 1992 / VC / C • Deep Throat #5 / 1990 / AR / M • Desert Fox / 1990 / VD / M • The Devil In Miss Jones #5: The Inferno / 1994 / VC / M • Devil's Agenda & Miss Jones / 1991 / AR / M • Dial 666 For Lust / 1991 / AFV / M • Diamond In The Rough / 1993 / BIA / C • Diary Of A Porn Star / 1993 / FOR / M • The Dickheads #1 / 1993 / MID / M • Digital Lust / 1990 / SE / M • Dirty Deeds / 1992 / IF / M • Dirty Dixie / 1992 / IF / M • Double Load #1 / 1993 / HW / M • Double Penetration #4 / 1991 / WV / C • Double Penetration #5 / 1992 / WV / C • Double Penetration #6 / 1993 / WV / C • Dr Hooters / 1991 / PL / M • The Dragon Lady #2: Tales From the Bed / 1992 / WV / M • The Dragon Lady #3: Tales From The Bed #2 / 1992 / WV / M • Dream Dates / 1990 / V99 / M • Dreams Of Candace Hart / 1991 / VI / M • Driving Miss Daisy Crazy #1 / 1990 / WV / M • Driving Miss Daisy Crazy #2 / 1992 / WV / M • Dutch Masters / 1990 / IN / M • Ebony Princess / 1994 / IN / M • Eleventh Annual AVN Awards / 1994 / VC / M • The End / 1992 / SC / M • Erectnophobia #2 / 1992 / MID / M • The Erotic Adventures Of Fanny Annie / 1991 / WV / M • Erotic Heights / 1991 / AR / M • Excitable / 1992 / IF / M • Falling In Love Again / 1993 / PMV / M • Fast Cars And Fast Women / 1992 / LV / M • Final Anal Tease / 1992 / MID / M • The Finishing Touch / 1994 / DR / M • Foreskin Gump / 1994 / LE / M • Forever / 1991 / LE / M • Foxes / 1992 / FL / M • Friday Night Fever / 1989 / LV / M • Fringe Benefits / 1992 / IF / M • From China With Love / 1993 / ZA / M • Full Service Woman / 1992 / V99 / M • Gangbang Girl #01 / 1992 / ANA / M • Gangbang Girl #02 / 1992 / ANA / M • Gangbang Girl #03 / 1992 / ANA / M • Gangbang Girl #04 / 1992 / ANA / M • Gangbang Girl #05 / 1992 / ANA / M • Gangbang Girl #07 / 1992 / ANA / M • Gangbang Girl #08 / 1992 / ANA / M • Gangbang Girl #10 / 1993 / ANA / M • Gangbang Girl #11 / 1993 / ANA / M • Ghost To Ghost / 1991 / CC / M • Girlz N The Hood #1 / 1991 / HW / M • The Good, The Bed, And The Snuggly / 1993 / ZA / M • Guess Who? / 1991 / EX / M • Hangin' Out / 1992 / IF / M • Hard At Work / 1989 / VEX / M • Hard Core Cafe / 1991 / PL / M • The Hard Line / 1993 / PEP / M • Hard Ride / 1992 / WV / M • Hard To Hold / 1993 / IF / M • Hard To Thrill / 1991 / CIN / M • Head Again / 1992 / AFV / M • Head Lines / 1992 / SC / M • Head Talk / 1991 / ZA / M • Heads Or Tails? / 1993 / PL / M • Heartbreaker / 1991 / IF / M • Holly's Holiday Gang Bang / 1994 / LBO / M • Hollywood Assets / 1990 / FH / M • Hollywood Bikini Party Girls / 1989 / VC / M • Hollywood Ho' House / 1994 / VC / M • Hollywood Hustle #2 / 1990 / V99 / M • Hollywood Temps / 1993 / ZA / M • Hollywood's Hills / 1992 / LV / M • Hometown Honeys #5 / 1993 /

VEX / M • Hot Box / 1995 / V99 / C • Hot Cargo / 1990 / MID / M • Hot Meat / 1990 / V99 / M • Hot Savannah Nights / 1991 / VEX / M • Hot Spot / 1991 / CDI / M • House Of Spartacus #2 / 1993 / IF / M • House Pet / 1992 / V99 / M • The Howard Sperm Show / 1993 / LV / M • Hump Up The Volume / 1991 / AR / M • Hungry #1 / 1992 / SC / M • Hurts So Good / 1991 / VEX / M • I Am Desire / 1992 / WV / M • I Dream Of Teri / 1993 / IF / M • I Want A Divorce / 1993 / ZA / M • I Want To Be Nasty / 1991 / XCV / M • If Looks Could Kill / 1992 / V99 / M • If These Walls Could Talk (Director's Cut) / 1993 / MET / M • If These Walls Could Talk #1: Wicked Whispers / 1993 / MET / M • If These Walls Could Talk #2: Burning Secrets / 1993 / CV / M • Illusions #1 / 1992 / IF / M • Images Of Desire / 1990 / PM / M • Inferno #2 / 1993 / SC / M • The Journey: Oral Majority / 1991 / WV / M • The Joy Dick Club / 1994 / MID / M • Jugsy (Western) / 1992 / WV / M • Junk Yard Dogs / 1991 / FC / M • Just A Guigol / 1992 / SC / M • Just For The Hell Of It / 1991 / CA / M • King Tung Is The Egyptian Lover / 1990 / LA / M • King Tung: The Tongue Squad / 1990 / LA / M • A Kiss Before Dying / 1993 / CDI / M • L.A. Rear / 1992 / FD / M • L.A. Stories / 1990 / VI / M • L.A.D.P. / 1991 / PL / M • Lacy's Hot Anal Summer / 1992 / LV / M • The Last American Sex Goddess / 1993 / IF / M • The Last Good Sex / 1992 / FD / M • The Last Of The Muff Divers / 1992 / MID / M • Latex #1 / 1994 / VC / M • A League Of Their Moan / 1992 / EVN / M • Lick My Lips / 1990 / LV / M • Lies Of Passion / 1992 / LV / M • A Little Nookie / 1991 / VD / M • Long Dan Silver / 1992 / IF / M • Looking For Love / 1991 / VEX / M • Looks Like A Million / 1992 / LV / M • Love On The Line / 1990 / SO / M • Love Potion / 1993 / WV / M • Lust Crimes / 1992 / WV / M • Lust Fever / 1991 / FH / M • Lust For Leather / 1993 / IF / M • The Luv Bang / 1994 / SC / M • Maid For Service / 1990 / LV / M • Maid Service / 1993 / FL / M • The Makeup Room / 1992 / VC / M • Making It / 1990 / FH / M • Manbait #2 / 1992 / VC / M • Maneater (1992-Las Vegas) / 1992 / LV / M • Marked #1 / 1993 / FD / M • Marked #2 / 1993 / FD / M • Mickey Ray's Sex Search #04: Long And Hard / 1994 / WIV / M • Miss 21st Century / 1991 / ZA / M • Miss Directed / 1990 / VI / M • Mix Up / 1992 / IF / M • Mona Lisa / 1992 / LV / M • Monday Nite Ball / 1990 / VT / M • More Dirty Debutantes #08 / 1991 / 4P / M • More Dirty Debutantes #13 / 1992 / 4P / M • More Dirty Debutantes #19 / 1993 / 4P / M • Motel Hell / 1992 / PL / M • Much More Than A Mouthful #3 / 1993 / VEX / M • Muffy The Vampire Layer / 1992 / LV / M • Mummy Dearest #1 / 1990 / LV / M • Mummy Dearest #3: The Parting / 1991 / LV / M • My 500 Pound Vibrator / 1991 / LV / C • My Anal Valentine / 1993 / FD / M • My Favorite Rear / 1993 / PEP / M • Mystery Of The Maletease Dildo / 1992 / STR / M • Mystified / 1991 / V99 / M • N.Y.D.P. / 1994 / PEP / M • Naked Goddess #1 / 1991 / VC / M • The Naked Truth / 1990 / SE / M • Nasty Nymphos #07 / 1994 / ANA / M • Naughty Butt Nice / 1993 / IF / M • Naughty By Nature / 1992 / IF / M • Neighborhood Watch #05 / 1991 / LBO / M

• Neighborhood Watch #14: The Beaver Cleaver / 1991 / LBO / M • New Wave Hookers #2 / 1991 / VC / M • New Wave Hookers #3 / 1993 / VC / M • Night And Day #1 / 1993 / VT / M • A Night At The Waxworks / 1990 / IF / M • Night Creatures / 1992 / PL / M • Night Of Passion / 1993 / BIA / C • Night Wish / 1992 / CDI / M • Nightmare Visions / 1994 / ERA / M • Nikki's Last Stand / 1993 / VC / M • Ninja Cheerleaders / 1990 / GO / M • Nothing Butt The Truth / 1993 / AFV / M • Nothing Else Matters / 1992 / V99 / C • Objective: D.P. / 1993 / PEP / M • Odyssey Amateur #75: Sindy! / 1991 / OD / M • On A Platter / 1994 / FD / M • On The Rise / 1994 / EX / M • One Lay At A Time / 1992 / V99 / M • One Night Love Affair / 1991 / IF / M • One Of A Kind / 1992 / VEX / M • Open Lips / 1994 / WV / M • Opposite Attraction / 1992 / VEX / M • Oral Majority #08 / 1990 / WV / C • Oriental Anal Sluts / 1993 / WV / C • Pajama Party X #3 / 1994 / VC / M • Parlor Games / 1992 / VT / M • Party Animals / 1994 / VEX / C • Passages #3 / 1991 / VI / M • Passion From Behind / 1990 / LV / M • Passion Prescription / 1990 / V99 / M • The Pawnbroker / 1990 / IF / M • Peekers / 1993 / MID / M • Penetrating Thoughts / 1992 / LV / M • Performance / 1990 / VI / M • Playin' With Fire / 1993 / LV / M • Pleasure Chest / 1993 / IF / M • Pointers / 1990 / LV / M • Pops / 1994 / PL / M • Portrait Of Lust / 1992 / WV / M • Positions Wanted / 1990 / VI / M • The Power & The Passion / 1993 / CDI / M • Principles Of Lust / 1992 / WV / M • Private & Confidential / 1990 / AR / M • The Pump / 1991 / CC / M • Pussy Galore / 1993 / VD / C • Queen Of Hearts #2: Hearts On Fire / 1990 / PL / M • Queen Of Hearts #3: Heartless / 1992 / PL / M • Queen Of Midnight / 1991 / V99 / M • Raising Kane / 1992 / FD / M • Rayne Storm / 1991 / VI / M • Read My Lips: No More Bush / 1992 / HW / M • Ready, Willing & Anal (Cv) / 1993 / CV / C • Red Beaver Bonanza / 1992 / TCP / M • Red Hot / 1990 / EX / M • Retail Slut / 1989 / LV / M • Revenge Of The Pussy Suckers From Mars / 1994 / PP / M • Ring Of Passion / 1993 / WV / M • Ringside Knockout / 1990 / DR / M • Rock & Roll Fantasies / 1992 / FL / M • Rocky Mountains / 1991 / IF / M • Roto-Rammer / 1993 / LV / M • Runnin' Hot / 1992 / LV / M • The Savannah Affair / 1993 / CDI / M • Savannah R.N. / 1992 / HW / M • Scarlet Fantasy / 1990 / VI / M • A Scent Of Leather / 1992 / IF / M • Scorcher / 1992 / GO / M • Screwed On The Job / 1991 / XPI / M • Secret Of Her Suckcess / 1994 / VC / M • Secret Services / 1993 / PEP / M • The Seductress / 1992 / ZA / M • Sex About Town / 1990 / LV / M • Sex Academy #4: The Art Of Anal / 1994 / ONA / M • Sex Express / 1991 / SE / M • Sex Heist / 1992 / WV / M • Sex Lives Of Clowns / 1994 / VC / M • Sex Lives On Porno Tape / 1992 / VC / C • Sex Scientist / 1992 / FD / M • Sex Sting / 1992 / FD / M • The Sex Symbol / 1991 / GO / M • Sex Symphony / 1992 / VC / M • Sex Toy / 1993 / CA / C • Sexlock / 1992 / XPI / M • Sexual Healing / 1992 / LV / M • She's My Cherry Pie / 1992 / V99 / M • Shoot To Thrill / 1992 / WV / M • Silence Of The Buns / 1992 / WV / M • Sin City: The Movie / 1992 / SC / M • Single Tight Female / 1992 / LV / M • Six Plus One #2 / 1993 / VEX / C • Sleeping Around / 1991 / CA / M • Sleeping With Emily / 1991 / LE / M • Sleepwalker / 1990 / XCI / M • Slipping It In / 1992 / FD / M • Smarty Pants / 1992 / VEX / M • Snatch Masters #05 / 1995 / LEI / M • Snow White And The Seven Weenies / 1989 / FAN / M • So I Married A Lesbian / 9993 / WV / M • Soda Jerk / 1992 / ZA / M • Sodomania: The Baddest Of The Best...And Then Some / 1994 / EL / C • Sofia: A Gang Bang Fantasy / 1994 / FC / M • Soft And Wild / 1991 / LV / M • Something New / 1991 / FH / M • Southern Accents / 1992 / VEX / M • Space Cadet / 1989 / IN / M • Spanish Fly / 1993 / VEX / M • Spanish Rose / 1991 / VEX / M • Splatman / 1992 / FR / M • Spring Break / 1992 / PL / M • Squirt 'em Cowgirl / 1990 / ERU / M • Star Struck / 1992 / VEX / M • Stick It In The Rear #2 / 1993 / PL / M • Stocking Stuffers / 1992 / LV / M • Strangers When We Meet / 1990 / VCR / M • Street Girl Named Desire / 1992 / FD / M • Summertime Boobs / 1994 / LEI / M • The Swap #1 / 1990 / VI / M • Sweet A$ Money / 1994 / MID / M • Sweet Alicia Rio / 1992 / FH / M • Sweet Cheeks (1991-Vid Excl) / 1991 / VEX / C • Sweet Miss Fortune / 1990 / LE / M • Sweet Poison / 1991 / CDI / M • Sweet Things / 1992 / VEX / M • Taboo #10 / 1992 / IN / M • Taboo #11: Crazy On You / 1993 / IN / M • Tail Taggers #103 / 1993 / WV / M • Tail Taggers #107 / 1993 / WV / M • Tails Of Tribeca / 1993 / HW / M • Tales From The Backside / 1993 / VC / M • Talk Dirty To Me #07 / 1990 / DR / M • A Tall Dark Stranger / 1990 / LV / M • The Taming Of Tami / 1990 / CA / M • Tempting Tianna / 1992 / V99 / M • Teri Diver's Bedtime Tales / 1993 / FD / M • Texas Towers / 1993 / IF / M • This Bun's For You / 1989 / FAN / M • This Butt Lite Is For You / 1992 / ATL / M • This Could Be The Night / 1993 / IF / M • Three Men And A Hooker / 1991 / WV / M • Tight Pucker / 1992 / WV / M • Tit For Tat / 1994 / PEP / M • Titanic Orgy / 1995 / PEP / M • To Shave And Shave Not / 1994 / PEP / M • To The Rear / 1992 / VC / M • Tomboy / 1991 / V99 / M • Tonight's The Night / 1994 / V99 / M • Too Cute For Words / 1992 / V99 / M • Too Fast For Love / 1992 / IF / M • Top Heavy / 1993 / IF / M • Torch #2 / 1990 / VI / M • Torrid Tonisha / 1992 / VEX / M • Total Exposure / 1992 / CDI / M • Totally Teri / 1992 / IF / M • Transparent Desires / 1991 / LV / M • Trash In The Can / 1993 / LV / M • Tropic Of Kahlia / 1991 / VI / M • Troublemaker / 1991 / VEX / M • True Sex / 1994 / EMC / M • Tunnel Of Lust / 1993 / LV / M • Two Sisters / 1992 / WV / M • The Unauthorized Biography Of Rob Blow / 1990 / LV / M • Undercover Lover / 1993 / VC / M • Unsolved Double Penetration / 1993 / PEP / M • Unveil My Love / 1991 / HO / M • Upbeat Love #1 / 1994 / CV / M • Veil / 1990 / VI / M • Victoria's Secret Life / 1992 / WV / M • Virgin / 1993 / HW / M • Virgin Spring / 1991 / FAZ / M • A Vision In Heather / 1991 / VI / M • Viviana's Dude Ranch / 1992 / IF / M • Voodoo Vixens / 1991 / IF / M • War Of The Tulips / 1990 / IN / M • Washington D.P. / 1993 / PEP / M • Waves Of Passion / 1993 / PL / M • We're Having A Party / 1991 / EVN / M • Wee Wee's Big Misadventure /

1991 / FH / M • Welcome To Paradise / 1994 / IF / M • Wet Memories / 1993 / WV / M • Where The Boys Aren't #2 / 1989 / VI / F • Where The Boys Aren't #3 / 1990 / VI / F • White Shadow / 1994 / VC / M • Wicked Ways #1: Interview With The Anal Queen / 1994 / WP / M • Wil And Ed's Excellent Boner Christmas / 1991 / MID / M • Wild & Wicked #1 / 1991 / VT / M • Wild In Motion / 1992 / PL / M • Wilde At Heart / 1992 / VEX / M • Wilde Palms / 1994 / XCI / M • Will & Ed Are Geeks In Heat / 1994 / MID / M • Will & Ed's Back To Class / 1992 / MID / M • Will & Ed's Keister Easter / 1992 / MID / M • Will And Ed's Bogus Gang Bang / 1992 / MID / M • Will And Ed: The Curse Of Poona / 1994 / MID / C • Words Of Love / 1989 / LE / M • You Bet Your Buns / 1992 / ZA / M

CAL JANA *see* **Cal Jammer**
CAL MARTIN *see* **Rusty Boner**
CALAWAY HOLMES
ABA: Double Feature #1 / 1996 / ALP / M • Fanny Hill / 1975 / TGA / M
CALDWELL ARTHUR
Rainwoman #03 / 1990 / CC / M
CALENE
Wedding Rituals / 1995 / DVP / M
CALI CATAINE
Girls Of The Very Big Eight / 1994 / VT / M
CALIE
Mike Hott: #328 Cunt Of The Month: Calie / 1995 / MHV / M • Nookie Professor #1 / 1996 / AVS / M
CALIF PALM *see* **Star Index I**
CALINE
Aerienne's Surprise / 1995 / WIV / M
CALIPH
Nba: Nuttin' Butt Ass / 1996 / SMP / M
CALISTA J. *see* **Jill Kelly**
CALLE
Voluptuous #2 / 199? / H&S / M • Voluptuous #3 / 199? / H&S / M • Voluptuous #5 / 1996 / H&S / M
CALLE NISKA
The Wild Women / 1996 / PL / M
CALLIE
Blue Vanities #539 / 1993 / FFL / M
CALLIE AIMS *see* **Shauna Grant**
CALVIN BULVER *see* **Jeff Hannover**
CALVIN VICTOR
Mona The Virgin Nymph / 1970 / ALP / M
CAMARO
Orgies Orgies Orgies / 1994 / WV / M
CAMELIA
Rebecca Lord's World Tour #1: French Edition / 1995 / WP / M
CAMEO *(Katrina (Cameo), Kelly Page, Kameo)*
Small breasted pretty blonde first seen in **Performance**. As of **Flashpoint** (about August 1991) she has had her breasts enhanced. Used to be the steady girlfriend of Cal Jammer but allegedly she was married early in 1992 to the former husband of Trixie Tyler. Born April 25, 1967 and supposedly has one or two kids (depending on the source) from before porn.
The Adventures Of Buttgirl & Wonder Wench / 1991 / AFV / M • Anal Encounters #2 / 1991 / VC / M • Anal Intruder #10 / 1995 / CC / M • Anal Nation #1 / 1990 / CC / M • Assumed Innocence / 1990 / AR / M • Behind Closed Doors / 1990 / VI / M • Behind You All The Way #1 / 1990 / SO / M • Beverly Hills Madam / 1993 / FH / F • The

Bimbo #1 / 1992 / AFV / M • The Bimbo #2 / 1992 / AFV / M • Boobs, Butts And Bloopers #1 / 1990 / HO / M • Business And Pleasure / 1992 / AFV / M • The Buttnicks #3 / 1992 / CC / M • California Taxi Girls / 1991 / AFV / M • Call Girl / 1991 / AFV / M • A Cameo Appearence / 1992 / VI / M • Camp Beaverlake #2 / 1991 / AFV / M • Candy Stripers #4 / 1990 / AR / M • Carnal College #1 / 1991 / AFV / F • Catalina Sixty-Nine / 1991 / AR / M • Club Josephine / 1991 / AR / F • The Coach's Daughter / 1991 / AR / M • Deep In The Bush / 1990 / KIS / M • Deep Inside Charli / 1990 / CDI / C • Deep Throat #5 / 1990 / AR / M • Desert Fox / 1990 / VD / M • Devil's Agenda & Miss Jones / 1991 / AR / M • Dial 666 For Lust / 1991 / AFV / M • Dick-Tation / 1991 / AFV / M • Digital Lust / 1990 / SE / M • Dream Cream'n / 1991 / AR / M • Erotic Heights / 1991 / AR / M • Every Man Should Have One / 1991 / VEX / M • Fantasy In Blue / 1991 / VI / M • Fireball #1 / 1994 / VI / C • Flashpoint / 1991 / AFV / M • Flesh Mountain / 1994 / VI / C • Foxes / 1992 / FL / M • Gere Up / 1991 / LV / C • Girl Friends / 1990 / PL / F • Girls Will Be Boys #1 / 1990 / PL / F • The Girls' Club / 1990 / VC / F • The God Daughter #1 / 1991 / AFV / M • The God Daughter #2 / 1991 / AFV / M • The God Daughter #3 / 1992 / AFV / M • The God Daughter #4 / 1992 / AFV / M • Graduation From F.U. / 1992 / FOR / M • Groupies / 1993 / AFV / F • The Harder Way / 1991 / AR / M • Head Again / 1992 / AFV / M • Hotel Sex / 1992 / AFV / M • Hump Up The Volume / 1991 / AR / M • I Do #2 / 1990 / VI / M • If Dreams Come True / 1991 / AFV / M • Immoral Support / 1992 / AFV / M • Juicy Lips / 1991 / PL / F • Just Friends / 1991 / AFV / M • King Tung Is The Egyptian Lover / 1990 / LA / M • King Tung: The Tongue Squad / 1990 / LA / M • Kiss And Tell / 1992 / AFV / M • Knight Shadows / 1992 / BS / B • Ladies Lovin' Ladies #2 / 1992 / AR / F • Ladies Lovin' Ladies #4 / 1992 / AFV / F • Laying Down The Law #1 / 1992 / AFV / M • Laying Down The Law #2 / 1992 / AFV / M • Lick My Lips / 1990 / LV / M • Loose Lips / 1990 / VC / M • Love On The Line / 1990 / SO / M • The Luscious Baker Girls / 1990 / VD / M • Making It / 1990 / FH / M • Masterpiece / 1990 / VI / M • Modern Love #1 / 1991 / HOP / S • More Dirty Debutantes #08 / 1991 / 4P / M • Mummy Dearest #1 / 1990 / LV / M • The Naked Truth / 1990 / SE / M • New Wave Hookers #2 / 1991 / VC / M • A Night At The Waxworks / 1990 / IF / M • Night Trips #2 / 1990 / CA / M • Nightdreams #2 / 1990 / VC / M • Nightdreams #3 / 1991 / VC / M • Nightvision / 1993 / TP / M • Ninja Cheerleaders / 1990 / GO / M • Nipples / 1994 / FOR / F • Nookie Court / 1992 / AFV / M • Odyssey Amateur #63: Pussy, Pussy Everywhere! / 1991 / OD / M • Opening Night / 1991 / AR / M • Pajama Party / 1993 / CV / C • Patriot Dames / 1992 / ZA / M • The Pawnbroker / 1990 / IF / M • Performance / 1990 / VI / M • Pointers / 1990 / LV / M • Positions Wanted / 1990 / VI / M • Private & Confidential / 1990 / AR / M • Pulse / 1994 / EX / M • The Pump / 1991 / CC / M • Puppy Love / 1992 / AFV / M • Pussywoman #3 / 1995 / CC / M • Putting It All

Behind #1 / 1991 / IN / M • Quickies / 1992 / AFV / M • Rainwoman #03 / 1990 / CC / M • Rayne Storm / 1991 / VI / M • Red Hot / 1990 / EX / M • Revealed / 1992 / VT / M • Ringside Knockout / 1990 / DR / M • Rock & Roll Fantasies / 1992 / FL / M • Rock Me / 1990 / LE / F • Rumors / 1992 / FL / M • Scarlet Fantasy / 1990 / VI / M • Sex She Wrote / 1991 / VEX / M • Sleepwalker / 1990 / XCI / M • Sorority Pink #3 / 1992 / SP / M • Squirt 'em Cowgirl / 1990 / ERU / M • Stolen Hearts / 1991 / AFV / M • Strangers When We Meet / 1990 / VCR / M • A Tall Dark Stranger / 1990 / LV / M • Taylor Wayne's World / 1992 / AFV / M • Tinseltown Wives / 1992 / AFV / M • Trick Tracey #1 / 1990 / CC / M • Two Times A Virgin / 1991 / AR / M • The Unauthorized Biography Of Rob Blow / 1990 / LV / M • Up The Gulf / 1991 / AR / M • V.I.C.E. #1 / 1991 / AFV / M • V.I.C.E. #2 / 1991 / AFV / M • Veil / 1990 / VI / M • A Vision In Heather / 1991 / VI / M • The Wild And The Innocent / 1990 / CC / M • Women In Need / 1990 / HO / M

CAMERON *see* **Krista Lane**

CAMERON KELLY
Bi Day...Bi Night / 1988 / PV / G • She-Male Encounters #19: Toga Party / 1989 / MET / G • Sulka's Nightclub / 1989 / VT / G • Transitory States / 1989 / STA / G

CAMERON MITCHELL
Dixie Ray Hollywood Star / 1983 / CA / M • Terror On Tape / cr85 / CO1 / S • Titillation #1 / 1982 / SE / M • The Tomb / 1986 / TRW / S • The Toolbox Murders / 1978 / VTR / S

CAMERON RILEY
Sex Off The Runway / 1991 / GMI / M

CAMERON SIMS *see* **Krista Lane**

CAMI
Kinky College Cunts #22 / 1993 / NS / F

CAMI GRAHAM
Take Off / 1978 / VXP / M

CAMILA GORDON *see* **Star Index I**

CAMILE *see* **Amanda Stone**

CAMILLA
Swedish Sex / 1996 / PL / M

CAMILLA (STACEY D) *see* **Stacey Donovan**

CAMILLA BRYANT
Ultraflesh / 1980 / GO / M

CAMILLA FRANKLIN
Sex Boat / 1980 / VCX / M

CAMILLE
Bootyville / 1994 / EVN / M • Joe Elliot's Black College Girls #01 / 1995 / JOE / M

CAMILLE (A. STONE) *see* **Amanda Stone**

CAMILLE (STEP. PAGE) *see* **Stephanie Page**

CAMILLE SANDS *see* **Star Index I**

CAN CAN MAGGIE
The Ass Master #01 / 1993 / GLI / M • Dirty Diner #01 / 1993 / GLI / M • Dirty Diner #02 / 1993 / GLI / M • Dirty Diner #03 / 1993 / GLI / M

CANDACE (1984)
Reel People #02 / 1984 / AR / M

CANDACE (1995) *see* **Candace Berg**

CANDACE (BERG) *see* **Candace Berg**

CANDACE BERG *(Candace Waters, Kandace Bunn, Candace (Berg), Kandace, Candace (1995))*
Brunette with shoulder length hair, passable tomboyish face, small/medium tits, nice

smile, tongue pin, belly button ring, narrow hips, bouffant hair style, tattoo on left tit which looks like a shamrock growing out of her nipple and another small one on her left belly at the bikini line, mole on belly just beneath her right tit. 20 years old in 1995, de-virginized at 13, comes from Arizona and wears rings on her toes.
Anal Camera #08 / 1995 / EVN / M • The Best Of Fabulous Flashers / 1996 / DGD / F • Butt Hunt #10 / 1995 / LEI / M • Butt Pumpers / 1995 / FH / M • Casting Call #11 / 1995 / MET / M • Cherry Poppers #09: Misbehavin' / 1995 / ZA / M • Executions On Butt Row / 1996 / EA / M • In Through The Out Door / 1995 / PE / M • Interview's Backdoor To The Orient / 1996 / LV / M • Max #04: The Harder They Come / 1995 / FWE / M • Miss Anal #1 / 1995 / C69 / M • Pussy Hunt #13 / 1995 / LEI / M • Pussy Lotto / 1995 / WIV / M • Teacher's Pet #3 / 1995 / APP / M • Video Virgins #20 / 1995 / NS / M • World Class Ass / 1995 / FC / M • Yellow Orchid / 1996 / SUF / M

CANDACE BOWEN
The Psychiatrist / 1978 / VC / M

CANDACE CHAMBERS *see* **Candida Royale**

CANDACE DALEY *see* **Mistress Candice**

CANDACE HART *see* **Candice Hart**

CANDACE LIPTON
Two Way Mirror / 1985 / CV / M

CANDACE WATERS *see* **Candace Berg**

CANDI
Amateur Lesbians #36: Candi / 1993 / GO / F • Amateur Lesbians #37: Gretta / 1993 / GO / F • Amateur Lesbians #38: Jessica / 1993 / GO / F • HomeGrown Video #466: Loot The Booty / 1996 / HOV / M • Hot Shorts: Ginger Lynn / 1986 / VCR / C • Luscious Lips / 1994 / ORE / C • Max Gold #1 / 1996 / XPR / C • New Faces, Hot Bodies #17 / 1995 / STP / M • The Pleasure Hunt #1 / 1984 / NSV / M • Young Cheeks / 1990 / BEB / B

CANDI (EVANS) *see* **Candie Evans**

CANDI BARBO
Bon Appetite / 1985 / TGA / C • Service Entrance / 1979 / REG / C

CANDI BARR
Dungeons & Drag Queens / 1994 / HSV / G • She Male Dicktation / 1994 / HEA / G • She-Mails / 1993 / PL / G

CANDI BELL *see* **Star Index I**

CANDI CASH *see* **Kandi Connor**

CANDI COAT
[The Raw Report / 1978 / ... / M

CANDI LACE *see* **Atlanta Rizzen**

CANDI LICKS
Buttslammers #11: / 1996 / BS / F • Buttslammers #12: Anal Madness / 1996 / BS / F • Lesbian Connection / 1996 / SUF / F • Motel Sex #3 / 1995 / RAP / M • Night Prowler #3: Master Of Reality / 1995 / ZFX / B • Night Prowler #5 / 1995 / ZFX / B • Phantacide Peepshow / 1996 / ZFX / B • Philmore Butts Goes Wild! / 1996 / SUF / M • Sensuous Torture / 1996 / BS / B • Stuff Your Face #4 / 1996 / JMP / M • Takin' It To The Limit #7: Debauched / 1996 / BS / M • Video Pirates #5: A Bullet To Bite / 1995 / ZFX / B

CANDICE
Blue Vanities #530 / 1993 / FFL / M • Bust Lust / cr83 / BIZ / B • Honeypie / 1975 / VC

/ M • Hot Body Competition: Bikinis & Bikes Contest / 1996 / CG / F • Yin Yang Oriental Love Bang #2 / 1996 / SUF / M • Yin Yang Oriental Love Bang #4: Yellow Orchid / 1996 / SUF / M

CANDICE (HART) *see* **Candice Hart**

CANDICE (MISTRESS) *see* **Mistress Candice**

CANDICE BALL *see* **Candida Royale**

CANDICE BOTTOMS *see* **Star Index I**

CANDICE CHAMBERS *see* **Candida Royale**

CANDICE EVANS *see* **Candie Evans**

CANDICE HART *(Candice Smith, Candice (Hart), Candice Heart, Candace Hart, Loretta Sterling, Candice Walker, Laura Dean, Carolyn Monroe)*
Small-titted blonde who bears some resemblance to Madonna. Born September 17, 1968 in Bloomington, Indiana. SO of Jordan Smith, at least in her earlier movies. Had her breasts enhanced to rock solid cantaloupes and changed her name to Carolyn Monroe. As of the mid-nineties lives in Italy and has her own production company. Candice Smith in the **Newcummers**. Loretta Sterling in **Passages #1** & **#2**.
Adventures In Paradise / 1992 / VEX / M • The Adventures Of Seymore Butts / 1992 / FH / M • Alley Cat / 1991 / CIN / M • America's Dirtiest Home Videos #05 / 1991 / VEX / M • America's Dirtiest Home Videos #06 / 1991 / AMA / M • Anal Addiction #3 / 1991 / SO / M • Anal Adventures (Dragon) / 1992 / DRP / M • Anal Climax #1 / 1991 / ROB / M • Anal Leap / 1991 / ZA / M • Anal Nation #2 / 1990 / CC / M • Anal Revolution / 1991 / ROB / M • Angel's Vengeance / 1995 / VMX / M • The Back Doors (Executive) / 1991 / EX / M • Backfire / 1991 / GO / M • Backing In #4 / 1993 / WV / C • Bedtime Tales / 1995 / IF / M • Bend Over Babes #2 / 1991 / EA / M • The Best Of Oriental Anal #1 / 1994 / ROB / C • Beyond It All / 1991 / PAL / G • Beyond Passion / 1993 / IF / M • Biff Malibu's Totally Nasty Home Videos #07 / 1992 / ANA / M • Black & White In Living Color / 1992 / WV / M • Blonde City / 1992 / IN / M • Blonde Forces #1 / 1991 / CC / M • Blonde Riders / 1991 / CC / M • Blonde Savage / 1991 / CDI / M • Can't Touch This / 1991 / PL / M • The Chains Of Torment / 1991 / BS / B • Chameleons: Not The Sequel / 1991 / VC / M • Collectible / 1991 / LE / M • Coming Clean / 1992 / ME / M • Crude / 1991 / IN / M • Dark Star / 1991 / VI / M • Debbie Does Wall Street / 1991 / VC / M • Destination Moon / 1992 / GO / C • Dr Butts #1 / 1991 / 4P / M • Dr Butts #2 / 1992 / 4P / M • Dream Date / 1992 / HO / M • The Dream Machine / 1992 / CDI / M • Dreams Of Candace Hart / 1991 / VI / M • Ecstasy / 1991 / LE / M • Ejacula #1 / 1992 / VC / M • Ejacula #2 / 1992 / VC / M • Every Woman Has A Secret / 1991 / ROB / M • Everybody's Playmates / 1992 / CA / C • The Eye Of The Needle / 1991 / CIN / M • Family Affair / 1996 / XC / M • Fatal Illusion / 1995 / WIV / M • Fever / 1992 / CA / M • Forbidden Desires / 1991 / CIN / F • French Open / 1990 / OD / M • Friends & Lovers #2 / 1991 / VT / M • Full Moon Fever / 1992 / PEP / M • Girls Will Be Boys #3 / 1991 / PL / F • Girls Will Be Boys #4 / 1991 / PL / F • The Girls' Club / 1993 / VD / C • Great Expectations /

1992 / VEX / C • A Handful Of Summers / 1991 / ME / M • Hard Core Cafe Revisited / 1991 / PL / M • Heads Or Tails? / 1993 / PL / M • Hot Diamond / 1995 / LE / M • Hot Spot / 1991 / CDI / M • Hothouse Rose #2 / 1992 / VC / M • How To Love Your Lover / 1992 / XII / S • If Looks Could Kill / 1992 / V99 / M • Illicit Affairs / 1996 / XC / M • Images Of Desire / 1990 / PM / M • Impulse #01: Memories Of An Italian Slut / 1995 / MBP / M • Impulse #05: When I Was 20... / 1995 / MBP / M • Impulse #09: / 1996 / MBP / M • Internal Affairs / 1992 / CDI / M • It's Only Love / 1992 / VEX / M • Jungle Beaver / 1991 / HIO / M • The Last Blonde / 1991 / IN / M • Lick-A-Thon #2 / 1996 / HW / C • Long Dan Silver / 1992 / IF / M • Made In Heaven / 1991 / PP / M • Magma: Tits Practice / 1995 / MET / M • Main Street, U.S.A. / 1992 / PP / M • Midnight Angel / 1992 / CDI / M • Mind Trips / 1992 / FH / M • Mischief / 1991 / WV / M • The Newcummers / 1990 / 4P / M • Nighttime Stories / 1991 / LE / M • Nothing Else Matters / 1992 / V99 / C • Once In A Blue Moon / 1991 / CC / M • One Million Years DD / 1992 / CC / M • The Only Game In Town / 1991 / VC / M • Painful Initiation / 1992 / PL / B • The Party / 1992 / CDI / M • Passages #1 / 1991 / VI / M • Passages #2 / 1991 / VI / M • The Pink Pussycat / 1992 / CA / M • Pink To Pink / 1993 / VI / C • Pornographic Priestess / 1992 / CA / M • Private Dancer (Caballero) / 1992 / CA / M • Purely Sexual / 1991 / HO / M • Puttin' Her Ass On The Line / 1991 / DR / M • Raunch #03 / 1991 / CC / M • Regarding Hiney / 1991 / CC / M • Sarah's Inheritance / 1995 / WIV / M • Shameless / 1991 / SC / M • Shipwrecked / 1992 / CDI / M • Shoot To Thrill / 1992 / WV / M • Shot From Behind / 1992 / FAZ / M • Skin Deep / 1991 / CIN / M • Sleeping With Emily / 1991 / LE / M • Stepsister's Discipline / 1992 / RB / B • Sun Bunnies #1 / 1991 / SC / M • Switch Hitters #6: Back In The Bull Pen / 1991 / IN / G • Talk Dirty To Me #08 / 1990 / DR / M • The Tasting / 1991 / EX / M • To The Rear / 1992 / VC / M • Unlike A Virgin / 1991 / HO / M • Venus: Wings Of Seduction / 1991 / CDI / M • Virgin Spring / 1991 / FH / M • The Vision / 1991 / LE / M • Voodoo Vixens / 1991 / IF / M • Voyeur Video / 1992 / ZA / M • Wacs / 1992 / PP / M • Wet Faces #1 / 1997 / SC / C • White Men Can Hump / 1992 / EVN / M • Wild Goose Chase / 1990 / EA / M • Wrapped Up / 1992 / VD / C • You Bet Your Butt / 1992 / VC / M

CANDICE HEART *see* **Candice Hart**
CANDICE LEE *see* **Star Index I**
CANDICE RAE *see* **Star Index I**
CANDICE SMITH *see* **Candice Hart**
CANDICE STEWART
GVC: Anything Goes #119 / 1983 / GO / M
CANDICE WALKER *see* **Candice Hart**
CANDIDA ROBBINS
The Bride's Initiation / 1976 / VIP / M
CANDIDA ROYALE *(Candice Chambers, Candice Ball, Candace Chambers)*
In the seventies, brunette with long slightly curly hair, large droopy tits, flabby belly, womanly body, passable face. In the nineties...well, you don't want to know.
The Analyst / 1975 / ALP / M • Baby Rosemary / 1975 / SE / M • Ball Game / 1980 / CA / M • Blue Ecstasy / 1980 / CA / M •

Blue Magic / 1981 / QX / M • Blue Vanities #536 / 1993 / FFL / M • Bustin' In The Back Door / 1987 / VEP / C • Carnal Haven / 1976 / SVE / M • Champagne For Breakfast / 1980 / SE / M • Classic Swedish Erotica #02 / 1986 / CA / C • Creme De Femme #1 / 1981 / AVC / C • Creme De Femme #4 / 1981 / AVC / C • Delicious / 1981 / VXP / M • Easy Alice / 1976 / VC / M • Erotic Fantasies: Women With Women / 1984 / CV / C • Exhausted / 1981 / CA / C • Fascination / 1980 / QX / M • Femmes De Sade / 1976 / ALP / M • Forbidden Worlds / 1988 / GO / C • Hard Soap, Hard Soap / 1977 / EVI / M • Hot Rackets / 1979 / CV / M • International Intrigue / 1983 / AMB / M • Kinky Tricks / 1978 / VEP / M • Legends Of Porn #1 / 1987 / CV / C • The Liberation Of Honeydoll Jones / 1978 / VCX / M • Limited Edition #03 / 1979 / AVC / M • Limited Edition #04 / 1979 / AVC / M • Love Secrets / 1976 / VIP / M • Lovers, An Intimate Portrait #1: Sydney & Ray / 1993 / FEM / M • Lovers, An Intimate Portrait #2: Jennifer & Steve / 1994 / FEM / M • Masterpiece / cr78 / VEP / M • Midnight Blue #2 / 1980 / VXP / M • My Surrender / 1996 / A&E / M • New York Babes / 1979 / AR / M • Night Hunger / 1983 / AVC / M • October Silk / 1980 / COM / M • Olympic Fever / 1979 / AR / M • Only The Best Of Women With Women / 1988 / CV / C • Our Naked Eyes / 1988 / TME / M • Outlaw Ladies #1 / 1981 / VC / M • Pizza Girls (We Deliver) / 1978 / VCX / M • The Playgirl / 1982 / CA / M • Pleasure #3 / 1988 / BTO / M • Pleasure #4 / 1990 / BTO / M • Pro Ball Cheerleaders / 1979 / AVC / M • Sex Appeal / 1986 / VES / S • Sexcapades / 1983 / VC / M • Showgirl #10: Candida Royale's Fantasies / 1983 / VCR / M • Sissy's Hot Summer / 1979 / CA / M • Sizzle / 1979 / QX / M • The Starlets / 1976 / RAV / M • Studio Of Lust / 1984 / HO / C • Sunny / 1979 / VC / M • The Tale Of Tiffany Lust / 1981 / CA / M • Taxi Girls #1 / 1980 / WV / M • Teenage Pony Girls / 1977 / VCX / M • That Lucky Stiff / 1979 / QX / M • Thoroughly Amorous Amy / 1978 / VCX / M • Three Daughters / 1986 / FEM / M • The Tiffany Minx / 1991 / CAT / M • Ultraflesh / 1980 / GO / M • Urban Heat / 1985 / FEM / M • VCA Previews #2 / 1988 / VC / C • Wine Me, Dine Me, 69 Me / 1989 / COL / C • [Successful Seducer / 1995 / ... / M
CANDIE
Frat House / 1979 / NGV / M
CANDIE DEANGELO *see* **Star Index I**
CANDIE EVANS *(Candice Evans, Candie Evens, Candi (Evans), Jean Poremba)*
Very sweet blonde with a pretty face and a nice body except for the tits which look like another K-Mart job. **Crystal Balls** was first movie. Rumor has it that as of 1996 she is married to the character "Laser" (aka Ken Starr) from the TV show **American Gladiators**, has two kids and lives in Orlando FL.
All For His Ladies / 1987 / PP / C • Amazing Tails #1 / 1987 / CA / M • Amazing Tails #2 / 1987 / CA / M • And I Do Windows Too / 1986 / PP / M • Baby Face #2 / 1987 / VC / M • Backside To The Future #1 / 1986 / ZA / M • Behind The Backdoor #1 / 1986 / EVN / M • Beyond The Senses / 1986 / AVC / M • Blue Lace / 1986 / SE / M • Boiling Desires / 1986 / VC / M • Born To Run

/ 1985 / WV / M • The Bottom Line / 1986 / WV / M • Butt's Motel #1 / 1989 / EX / M • Cabaret Sin / 1987 / IN / M • California Fever / 1987 / CV / M • Careena #1 / 1987 / WV / C • Careena #2: A Star On The Rise / 1988 / WV / C • Cat Alley / 1986 / AVC / M • Cheerleader Academy / 1986 / PL / M • Classic Swedish Erotica #01 / 1986 / CA / C • Classic Swedish Erotica #02 / 1986 / CA / C • Classic Swedish Erotica #03 / 1986 / CA / C • Classic Swedish Erotica #04 / 1986 / CA / C • Classic Swedish Erotica #05 / 1986 / CA / C • Classic Swedish Erotica #06 / 1986 / CA / C • Classic Swedish Erotica #07 / 1986 / CA / C • Classic Swedish Erotica #08 / 1986 / CA / C • Classic Swedish Erotica #09 / 1986 / CA / C • Classic Swedish Erotica #10 / 1986 / CA / C • Classic Swedish Erotica #11 / 1986 / CA / C • Classic Swedish Erotica #12 / 1986 / CA / C • Classic Swedish Erotica #13 / 1986 / CA / C • Classic Swedish Erotica #14 / 1986 / CA / C • Classic Swedish Erotica #15 / 1986 / CA / C • Classic Swedish Erotica #16 / 1986 / CA / C • Classic Swedish Erotica #17 / 1986 / CA / C • Classic Swedish Erotica #18 / 1986 / CA / C • Classic Swedish Erotica #19 / 1986 / CA / C • Classic Swedish Erotica #20 / 1986 / CA / C • Classic Swedish Erotica #21 / 1986 / CA / C • Classic Swedish Erotica #22 / 1986 / CA / C • Classic Swedish Erotica #23 / 1986 / CA / C • Classic Swedish Erotica #24 / 1986 / CA / C • Club Head (EVN) #1 / 1987 / EVN / C • Coming In America / 1988 / VEX / M • Crystal Balls / 1986 / DR / M • Cum Shot Revue #2 / 1985 / HO / C • Cum Shot Revue #3 / 1988 / HO / C • Cum Shot Revue #4 / 1988 / HO / C • Cum Shot Revue #5 / 1988 / HO / C • The Desk Top Dolls / 1990 / BAD / C • Devil In Miss Dare / 1986 / AVC / C • Dirty Harriet / 1986 / SAT / M • Divorce Court Expose #1 / 1986 / VD / M • Dr Juice's Lust Potion / 1986 / TEM / M • Dream Girls / 1986 / VC / M • Ebony & Ivory Fantasies / 1988 / VD / C • Empire Of The Sins / 1988 / IN / M • Farmers Daughters / 1985 / WV / M • Flesh In Ecstasy #14: Candy Evans / 1988 / GO / C • Forbidden Bodies / 1986 / HU / M • Genital Hospital / 1987 / SE / M • The Greatest American Blonde / 1987 / WV / C • Having It All / 1985 / IN / M • Hooters / 1986 / AVC / M • Hot Gun / 1986 / CA / M • Hottest Ticket / 1987 / WV / C • Immoral Majority / 1986 / HTV / M • In And Out (In Beverly Hills) / 1986 / WV / M • In Search Of The Golden Bone / 1986 / CA / M • In Search Of The Wild Beaver / 1986 / DR / M • Inside Sharon Mitchell / 1989 / ZA / C • Irresistible #2 / 1986 / SE / M • Les Be Friends / 1988 / WV / C • Lingerie Party / 1987 / SE / C • Lucky Charm / 1986 / AVC / C • Lust And The Law / 1991 / GO / C • Lust At Sea / 1986 / VD / M • The Lust Potion Of Doctor F / 1985 / WV / M • Mad Jack Beyond Thunderdome / 1986 / WET / M • Miami Spice #1 / 1987 / CA / M • Miami Spice #2 / 1988 / CA / M • The Moon Girls / 1990 / ME / C • Nasty Romances / 1985 / HO / C • Night Of The Living Babes / 1987 / MAE / S • Open Up Tracy / 1984 / VD / M • Oral Majority #02 / 1987 / WV / C • Parliament: Fanny / 1987 / PM / F • Parliament: Finger Friggin' #1 / 1986 / PM / F • Parliament: Lesbian Lovers #1 / 1986 / PM

/ F • Parliament: Lonesome Ladies #1 / 1987 / PM / F • Party Favors / 1989 / VES / S • Playing For Passion / 1987 / IN / M • Princess Charming / 1987 / AVC / C • Ramb-Ohh #1 / 1986 / PV / M • Reckless Passion / 1986 / ME / M • Sex Aliens / 1987 / CA / M • Sex Asylum #2 / 1986 / VI / M • Sex Beat / 1985 / WV / M • The Sex Game / 1987 / SE / C • The Sex Goddess / 1984 / GO / M • Sexscape / 1986 / CA / M • Sexy Delights #1 / 1986 / CLV / M • Sheer Bedlam / 1986 / VI / M • Sheets Of San Francisco / 1986 / AVC / M • Slippery When Wet / 1986 / PL / M • Spies / 1986 / PL / M • Splash Dance / 1987 / AR / M • Stag Party / 1986 / ACV / S • Starlet Screen Test / 1990 / NST / S • Swedish Erotica #73 / 1986 / CA / M • Tailgunners / 1985 / WET / M • Take It Off / 1986 / TIF / M • Takin' It All Off / 1987 / VES / S • A Taste Of Candie Evans / 1989 / PIN / C • They Call My Sugar Candie / 1989 / SUE / M • Traci Who? / 1987 / AVC / C • Tunnel Of Love / 1986 / CLV / M • Up All Night / 1986 / CC / M • VCA Previews #4 / 1988 / VC / C • Wet Science / 1986 / PLY / M • Wild Oral Erotica / 1988 / VD / C • Woman In The Window / 1986 / TEM / M • Women In Uniform / 1986 / TEM / M • X-TV #1 / 1986 / PL / C • You Can't Hurry Love / 1988 / VES / S • [Foxy Ladies / 19?? / ... / M • [Tastes Like Candy / 1987 / ... / M

CANDIE EVENS *see* **Candie Evans**

CANDRA

C-Hunt #03: Sunny Delights / 1995 / PEV / M

CANDY

A&B AB#160: Candy's Delight / 1990 / A&B / F • A&B AB#563: Candy's Treats / 1995 / A&B / M • Anal Exchange / 1995 / C69 / M • Angie, Trish, Linda, Samantha / 1990 / PLV / B • Asian Connection Video #098 / 1996 / AC0 / B • AVP #1001: Candy's Fantasy—The Robbery / 1987 / AVP / M • AVP #1006: Candy's Debut / 1987 / AVP / M • AVP #1009: A Living Doll / 1990 / AVP / M • AVP #9147: Candy Can / 1990 / AVP / M • AVP #9148: Candy's Gang Bang / 1990 / AVP / M • Before She Says I Do / 1984 / MAP / M • Best Of Buttman #1 / 1991 / EA / C • Big Bust Babes #15 / 1993 / AFI / M • Black Casting Couch #2 / 1994 / WP / M • Blue Vanities #525 / 1993 / FFL / M • Blue Vanities #576 / 1995 / FFL / M • Bobby Hollander's Rookie Nookie #08 / 1993 / SFP / M • Body And Sole / 1990 / BIZ / B • Dance Fever / 1985 / VCR / M • Doctor Desire / 1984 / VD / M • Homegrown Video #260 / 1990 / HOV / M • Hot Girls In Love / 1985 / VXP / M • Hot Legs #1 / 1990 / PLV / B • Hotel Lesbos / 1986 / LIP / F • The Hunt Is On / 1994 / HU / F • Maidens Of Servitude #1 / 1993 / STM / B • Midnight Angels #03 / 1993 / MID / F • A Midsummer Night's Bondage / 1993 / ARL / B • Pearl Necklace: Amorous Amateurs #02 / 1992 / SEE / M • Pearl Necklace: Amorous Amateurs #03 / 1992 / SEE / M • Pearl Necklace: Facial #01 / 1994 / SEE / C • RSK: Candy #1 / 1992 / RSK / F • RSK: Candy #2 / 1993 / RSK / F • RSK: Candy #3 / 1993 / RSK / F • Sex Busters / 1984 / PLY / M • Shaved #03 / 1992 / RB / F • Slut Safari #2 / 1994 / FC / M • Snatch Masters #03 / 1994 / LEI / M • Splato: Sexual Fantasies #06 / 1996 / SPL / M • SVE: Spank'er Butt #2 / 1994 /

SVE / B • Tongue Twisters / 1986 / VXP / M • Tootsies & Footsies / 1994 / LBO / M • Video Virgins #13 / 1994 / NS / M • Women Without Men #1 / 1985 / VXP / F

CANDY (CAREENA C.) *see* **Careena Collins**

CANDY (CARNAL DEL) *see* **Carnal Delight**

CANDY (KELLI DYLAN) *see* **Kelli Dylan**

CANDY APPLES

The Anal Adventures Of Max Hardcore: The Resurrection / 1995 / ZA / M • Anal Institution #2 / 1996 / ZA / M • Anal Toy Story / 1996 / MP0 / M • Ben Dover & Barbie / 1995 / SUF / M • Best Exotic Dancers In The Usa / 1995 / PME / S • Blondes / 1995 / MET / M • The Blowjob Adventures Of Doctor Fellatio / 1997 / EL / M • Booty Bitch / 1995 / ROB / M • Candy / 1995 / MET / M • Cherry Poppers #11: California Co-Eds / 1995 / ZA / M • Cumback Pussy #1 / 1996 / EL / M • Delirium / 1996 / MET / M • Dirty Dave's #2 / 1996 / XPR / M • Dirty Dave's #4 / 1996 / XPR / M • Dirty Tricks #1: Just A Bunch Of Whores / 1995 / EA / M • Emerald: Princess Of The Night / 1996 / FC / M • Explicit / 1995 / MET / M • Forbidden Fantasies #1 / 1995 / ZA / M • Fuck Jasmin / 1997 / MET / M • GM #186: Spring Break Copper Canyon '96 / 1996 / GMV / M • Hellfire / 1995 / MET / M • Huge Grant On The Sunset Strip / 1995 / EVN / M • Incorrigible / 1996 / MET / M • Mall Slut / 1997 / SC / M • More Dirty Debutantes #62 / 1997 / SBV / M • Nasty Pants / 1995 / SUF / M • Notorious / 1995 / MET / M • Nymphos / 1995 / MET / M • Perverted Stories #02 / 1995 / JMP / M • Perverted Stories #06 / 1996 / JMP / M • Perverted Stories #09 / 1996 / JMP / M • Perverted Stories #10 / 1996 / JMP / M • Planet X #1 / 1996 / HW / M • Primal / 1995 / MET / M • Raunch Ranch / 1995 / LE / M • Sexual Atrocities / 1996 / EL / M • Stuff Your Ass #2 / 1995 / JMP / M • Stuff Your Face #4 / 1996 / JMP / M • Triple Penetration Debutante Sluts #1 / 1996 / BAC / M • White Trash Whore / 1996 / JMP / M • The World's Biggest Gang Bang #2 / 1996 / FPI / M • Young And Anal #6 / 1996 / JMP / M

CANDY AUSTIN

Bondage Pleasures #1 / 1981 / 4P / B • How To Make Love To A Woman / 19?? / VV0 / M

CANDY BARBOUR *see* **Kandy Barbour**

CANDY BARBOUR (ASS) *see* **Star Index I**

CANDY BARK

Good Morning, Little Schoolgirl / cr75 / BL / M

CANDY BARR *(Juanita Slusher, Carol Barr)*

Very early (fifties) performer in loops. Famous for the loop **Smart Alec**.

All About Sex / 1970 / AR / M • Big Bust Loops #02 / 1993 / SOW / M • Big Bust Loops #06 / 1993 / SOW / M • Big Bust Loops #07 / 1993 / SOW / M • Big Bust Loops #12 / 1993 / SOW / M • Blue Vanities #006 / 1987 / FFL / M • Blue Vanities #096 / 1988 / FFL / M • Blue Vanities #115 / 1988 / FFL / M • Classics Erotica From The Past #3 / 1990 / PL / M • Grindhouse Follies #08 / 1993 / SOW / M • Grindhouse Follies #10 / 1993 / SOW / M • Grindhouse Follies #11 / 1993 / SOW / M • Grindhouse

Follies: First Row #01 / 1993 / SOW / M • A History Of The Blue Movie / 1970 / CAL / M • Naughty Nostalgia #10 / 1981 / CLX / M • Naughty Peeps And Stags #4 / 1993 / SOW / M • Nostalgia Blue / 1976 / VC / M • Nudie Cuties #023 / 1993 / SOW / S • Nudie Cuties #026 / 1993 / SOW / S • Nudie Cuties #027 / 1993 / SOW / S • Nudie Cuties #035 / 1993 / SOW / S • Only The Best #3 / 1990 / CV / C • Our Sexual History / 1992 / A&E / M • Panties Inferno / 1964 / SOW / S • Striporama 2 / 1993 / VDM / S • When Sex Was Dirty #2 / 1991 / FC / M

CANDY BARR (S/M)

Cocks In Frocks #1 / 1996 / TTV / G • Las Vegas She-Males / 1995 / BCP / G • Pom Pom She-Males / 1994 / HEA / G • TV Nation #2 / 1995 / HW / G

CANDY BURROUGHS *see* **Star Index I**

CANDY CAIN *see* **Star Index I**

CANDY CANTELOUPES

Booberella / 1992 / BTO / M • Girls Around The World #21: Tawny Peaks & Friends / 1995 / BTO / M • Score Busty Covergirls #8 / 1995 / BTO / S

CANDY CARR

Pleasure Productions #12 / 1985 / VCR / M

CANDY CASH *see* **Kandi Connor**

CANDY CONNOR *see* **Kandi Connor**

CANDY CONNORS *see* **Kandi Connor**

CANDY COXX

The Big One / 1995 / HO / M

CANDY CRUIZE *see* **Laurel Canyon**

CANDY CUMMINGS *see* **Star Index I**

CANDY DAKOTA

Butt Busting / 1996 / RB / B • Fashion Sluts #8 / 1996 / ABS / M • Young Sluts In Heat #1 / 1996 / PL / M

CANDY DALLAS *see* **Star Index I**

CANDY DELANY

Top Debs #4: Sex Boat / 1993 / GO / M

CANDY ESSEX

A Little Bit Pregnant / 1995 / SO / M

CANDY HART

GRG: Candy Gets Gang Banged / 1993 / GRG / M • GRG: Candy Hart / 1995 / GRG / M • Harness Hannah At The Strap-On Palace / 1994 / WIV / F

CANDY HEART *see* **Star Index I**

CANDY HILLER

Pink Champagne / 1979 / CV / M

CANDY JOHNSON *see* **Star Index I**

CANDY K.

Dirty Dancers #3 / 1995 / 4P / M

CANDY KANE *(Candye Kane, Kandy Kane)*

10 Years Of Big Busts #1 / 1989 / BTO / C • The Best Of Big Busty / 1986 / L&W / C • Between My Breasts #03 / 1986 / L&W / S • Big Busty #03 / 1985 / CPL / S • Big Busty #05 / 1987 / BTO / M • Big Busty #14 / 198? / H&S / S • Big Busty #17 / 198? / H&S / M • Big Tit Orgy #04 / 1991 / BTO / C • Blue Vanities #221 / 1994 / FFL / M • Blue Vanities #579 / 1995 / FFL / M • Bouncin' In The U.S.A. / 1986 / H&S / S • Bursting Bras / 1990 / BTO / C • Busen #02 / 1988 / L&W / M • Candy's Back / 199? / H&S / M • I Want It All / 1984 / VD / M • Let Me Tell Ya 'Bout Fat Chicks #1 / 1986 / 4P / C • Two Tons Of Fun #1 / 1985 / 4P / C • The Velvet Edge / cr76 / SE / M • The Very Best Of Breasts #3 / 1996 / H&S / S

CANDY KORN

The Loves Of Mary Jane / 1989 / BWV / C

• A Touch Of Sex / 1972 / AR / M

CANDY LACE *see* **Atlanta Rizzen**

CANDY LANE

Dirty Dancers #4 / 1995 / 4P / M • Homecoming / 1981 / CA / M

CANDY LOVE

Sex Wish / 1976 / CV / M • Sexteen / 1975 / VC / M • Teenage Pajama Party / 1977 / VC / M • Too Many Pieces / 1975 / LA / M • Worksex / 1980 / ... / M

CANDY LUV *see* **Star Index I**

CANDY MAJORS

Her Total Response / 1975 / SVE / M

CANDY MARIE *see* **Destini Lane**

CANDY MARIE SAINT

The Masseuse #2 / 1994 / VI / M

CANDY MASON *see* **Justina Lynn**

CANDY MATHEWS

Cherry Poppers #04: Ripe 'n' Ready / 1994 / ZA / M • Tied, Trained And Transformed / 19?? / BIZ / B

CANDY MORE *see* **Star Index I**

CANDY MORRISON

Reel Classics #1 / 1996 / H&S / M

CANDY NICHOLS

Starlet Nights / 1982 / XTR / M

CANDY NIXON *see* **Candy Vegas**

CANDY ROBBINS

Bunbusters / 1984 / VCR / M

CANDY SAMPLES *(Mary Gavin)*

Blonde and huge breasted. 5'4" tall, 48-24-36 in 1984.

10 Years Of Big Busts #1 / 1989 / BTO / C • 40 Plus / 1987 / MFM / M • The 8th Annual Erotic Film Awards / 1984 / SE / C • Adult Movie Bloopers / 1983 / VIN / C • All The Way In / 1984 / VC / M • Attack Of The Monster Mammaries / 1987 / LA / C • Beneath The Valley Of The Ultra-Vixens / 1979 / RMV / S • Best Chest In The West / 1984 / ACV / S • The Best Little Whorehouse In San Francisco / 1984 / LA / M • Big Bust Babes #01 / 1984 / AFI / M • Big Bust Babes #06 / 1991 / AFI / F • Big Bust Loops #08 / 1993 / SOW / M • Big Bust Loops #14 / 1994 / SOW / M • Big Bust Loops #15 / 1994 / SOW / M • Big Busty #05 / 198? / BTO / M • Big Busty #13 / 198? / H&S / S • Blue Vanities #004 / 1987 / FFL / M • Blue Vanities #005 / 1987 / FFL / M • Blue Vanities #020 (New) / 1300 / FFL / M • Blue Vanities #039 (Old) / 1988 / FFL / M • Blue Vanities #042 (Old) / 1988 / FFL / M • Blue Vanities #046 (Old) / 1988 / FFL / M • Blue Vanities #051 / 1988 / FFL / M • Blue Vanities #058 / 1988 / FFL / M • Blue Vanities #125 / 1990 / FFL / M • Blue Vanities #129 / 1990 / FFL / M • Blue Vanities #130 / 1990 / FFL / M • Blue Vanities #132 / 1991 / FFL / M • Blue Vanities #240 / 1995 / FFL / M • Blue Vanities #241 / 1995 / FFL / M • Blue Vanities #250 / 1996 / FFL / M • Blue Vanities #559 / 1994 / FFL / M • Blue Vanities #584 / 1996 / FFL / M • Bouncin' In The U.S.A. / 1986 / H&S / S • Brabusters #1 / 1981 / CA / S • Bucky Beaver's Double Softies #02 / 1996 / SOW / S • Bucky Beaver's XXX Dragon Art Theatre Double Feature #21 / 1996 / SOW / M • Busen #03 / 1989 / BTO / M • Busty Beauties / 199? / SVE / M • Candy Get Your Gun / cr75 / SOW / S • Candy Samples' Video Review / 1984 / 4P / M • The Candy Store / cr71 / GO / M • Candy's Bedtime Story / 1983 / CA / M • Candy's Candy / 1976 / BL / M • Candy's Cat House / cr75 / SOW / M •

Candy's Sweet Interview / 1982 / DIM / C • Cock Robin / 1989 / SUE / M • The Cocktail Hostesses / 1972 / ... / S • Collection #01 / 1982 / CA / M • Down And Dirty / 1985 / LBO / M • Electric Blue #015 / 1984 / CA / S • The Elevator / 1972 / ALP / M • Fantasm / 1976 / VS / S • Fantasm Cums Again / 1977 / VS / S • Flesh Gordon #1 / 1974 / FAC / S • Girls In Passion / 1979 / VHL / M • Gourmet Quickies: Candy Samples #713 / 1985 / GO / C • Inside Candy Samples / 1984 / CV / M • Is There Sex After Marriage? / 1972 / SOW / S • John Holmes And The All-Star Sex Queens / 1984 / AMB / M • Last Days Of Pompeii / 1975 / ... / S • Le Sex De Femme #4 / 1989 / AFI / C • Legends Of Porn #1 / 1987 / CV / C • Liberty / 197? / CID / M • Love Boccaccio Style / 1970 / SOW / S • Maximum #1 / 1982 / CA / M • Maximum #3 / 1983 / CA / M • Maximum #4 / 1983 / CA / M • Mondo Topless #2 / 1966 / RMV / S • More Than A Handful #1 / 1985 / CV / C • Nipples / 1973 / ALP / M • Only The Best Of Breasts / 1987 / CV / C • Only The Best Of Women With Women / 1988 / CV / C • Oriental Ecstasy Girls / 1974 / ... / M • Pleasure Unlimited / 1972 / PS / S • Robot Love Slaves / cr71 / SOW / S • Sex As You Like It / 1972 / SVE / M • Superchick / 1971 / PRS / S • Superknockers / 1979 / ALP / M • A Taste Of Candy / 1985 / LA / M • Tough Guns / 1972 / ALP / S • True Legends Of Adult Cinema: The Cult Superstars / 1993 / VC / C • Two Tons Of Fun #1 / 1985 / 4P / C • Unleashed Lust / 1989 / VC / C • Up! / 1976 / RMV / S • VCA Previews #3 / 1988 / VC / C • [Candy's Angels / cr75 / ... / M • [Hey, There's Naked Bodies On My TV / 1978 / ... / S • [Madam's House / 1972 / ... / M

CANDY SHIELDS

The Erotic World Of Candy Shields / 1984 / VCR / C • Forbidden Fruit / 1985 / PV / M • Joys Of Erotica / 1984 / VCR / M • Joys Of Erotica #107 / 1984 / VCR / C • Joys Of Erotica #109 / 1984 / VCR / C • Pleasure Productions #04 / 1984 / VCR / M • Pleasure Productions #06 / 1984 / VCR / M

CANDY SHORT

Odyssey / 1977 / VC / M

CANDY OMITII *see* **Star Index I**

CANDY SNOW

Creme De La Face #04 / 1994 / OD / M • Dangerous / 1989 / PV / M • Swedish Erotica #74 / 1994 / CA / M

CANDY SPLIT *see* **Star Index I**

CANDY SPOTS

Swedish Erotica #63 / 1985 / CA / M

CANDY STATON

Bitch Queendom / 1987 / BIZ / B • Black Angels / 1985 / VC / M • Black Clits And White Dicks / cr86 / JAN / M • Carnal College / 1987 / VT / M • Mistress Candy / cr80 / BIZ / G • Secret Loves / 1986 / CDI / M • Slit Skirts / 1983 / VXP / M • Sulka And Candy / 1992 / BIZ / C

CANDY STORM *see* **Star Index I**

CANDY STRAPP

Agony Of Love, Lace And Lash / cr73 / SOW / M • Bucky Beaver's XXX Dragon Art Theatre Double Feature #14 / 1996 / SOW / M

CANDY STRONG

Smooth Operator / 1986 / AR / M • Tight Fit / 1987 / V99 / M • Tight Fit / 1991 / VEX / C

CANDY SUE

Bedtime Video #06 / 1984 / GO / M

CANDY SUMMER

800 Fantasy Lane / 1979 / GO / M

CANDY VAGAS *see* **Candy Vegas**

CANDY VEGAS *(Candy Nixon, Candy Vagas, Cindy (Candy Vegas), Jesse Lang, Jesse Lange, Jessica Lange (X), Jessie Lange, Jessie Land)*

Older, blonde, marginal face, loss of belly muscle tone, small droopy tits, small tattoo in the middle of her back at waist level.

100% Amateur #19: / 1996 / OD / M • Anal Fantasy / 1996 / SUF / M • Anal Sex Freaks / 1996 / ZA / M • Anal Witness #2: No Prisoners / 1996 / LBO / M • Analtown USA #10 / 1996 / NIT / M • Ass Busters / 1995 / VMX / C • Bareback / 1996 / LE / M • Bi And Beyond #6: Authentic / 1996 / FD / G • Bi The Book / 1996 / MID / G • The Blowjob Adventures Of Doctor Fellatio / 1997 / EL / M • Booty Sister #2 / 1996 / ROB / M • Buffy's Bare Ass Barbecue / 1996 / CDI / M • Butt Hunt #06 / 1995 / LEI / M • Creme De La Face #13: Nine Nasty Nymphs / 1995 / OD / M • Cum On Inn / 1995 / TEG / M • Cummin' 'round The Mountain / 1996 / BCP / M • Devil In A Wet T-Shirt / 1995 / SPI / M • Domina #5: Whipper Snapper / 1996 / LBO / B • Domina #7 / 1996 / LBO / B • Double Anal Alternatives / 1996 / EL / M • Emerald: Princess Of The Night / 1996 / FC / M • Fresh Faces #06 / 1995 / EVN / M • The Girl With The Heart-Shaped Tattoo / 1995 / WAV / M • A Girl's Affair #06 / 1995 / FD / F • Hard Core Beginners #04 / 1995 / LEI / M • House Of Leather / 1995 / GO / M • In Through The Out Door / 1995 / PE / M • Interview's Anal Queens / 1996 / LV / M • Lady M's Anything Nasty #01: Pink Pussy Party / 1996 / AVI / F • Masturbation Ages 20 To 45 / 1996 / C69 / F • Mile High Thrills / 1995 / VIM / M • Miss Anal #1 / 1995 / C69 / M • Mrs. Buttfire / 1995 / SUF / M • Nasty Newcummers #14 / 1995 / MET / M • The New Ass Masters #09 / 1996 / LEI / C • The New Ass Masters #10 / 1996 / LEI / C • The New Butt Hunt #13 / 1995 / LEI / C • Nude Awakenings / 1996 / PP / M • Perverted Stories #11 / 1996 / JMP / M • Pussyman Auditions #12 / 1996 / SNA / M • Pussyman Auditions #14 / 1995 / SNA / M • Pussyman's Nite Club Party #1 / 1996 / SNA / M • Pussyman's Nite Club Party #2 / 1997 / SNA / M • Rare Ends / 1996 / PRE / C • Sexhibition #1 / 1996 / SUF / M • Sittin' On Da Krome / 1995 / HW / M • Slutsville U.S.A. / 1995 / VMX / M • Sodom Chronicles / 1995 / FH / M • Sodomania: Slop Shots / 1996 / EL / C • The Sodomizer #3 / 1996 / SC / M • Sole Survivors / 1996 / PRE / C • Spazm #1: Point Blank / 1996 / LBO / M • The Stiff / 1995 / WAV / M • Throbbing Threesomes / 1996 / NIT / M • The Tigress / 1995 / VIM / M • Triple Penetration Debutante Sluts #2 / 1996 / BAC / M • Under The Cum Cum Tree / 1996 / BCP / M • Underground #2: Subway To Sodom / 1996 / SC / M • Vienna's Place / 1996 / VCX / M • Where The Girls Sweat...Not The Sequel / 1996 / EL / F

CANDY WONG *see* **Star Index I**

CANDY YORK

Campus Girl / 1972 / VXP / M

CANDYE KANE *see* **Candy Kane**

CANE

Bad Bad Gang / 1972 / SOW / M • Bucky

Beaver's XXX Dragon Art Theatre Double Feature #07 / 1996 / SOW / M

CANMORE MCBAINE
Conquest / 1996 / WP / M

CAP LINCOLN
Sweet Young Foxes / 1984 / VCX / M

CAP WELLS *see Star Index I*

CAPPY *see Star Index I*

CAPRI
The Executive's Wives / 1970 / ALP / S • Her Odd Tastes / 1969 / SOW / S • Parliament: Hard TV #2 / 1990 / PM / G

CAPRI DANELL
Desire / 1990 / VC / M

CAPTAIN BOB
AHV #22: Hello, I Love You / 1992 / EVN / M • Amateur Orgies #19 / 1992 / AFI / M • Amateur Orgies #20 / 1992 / AFI / M • America's Raunchiest Home Videos #09: Orgasmic Oriental / 1992 / ZA / M • The Bodacious Boat Orgy #2 / 1993 / GLI / M • Buttsizer #3: Return Of The King Of Rears / 1995 / EVN / M • Captain Bob's Lust Boat #1 / 1993 / FCP / M • Captain Bob's Lust Boat #2 / 1993 / FCP / M • Captain Bob's Pussy Patrol / 1993 / FCP / M • Cluster Fuck #05 / 1994 / MAX / M • Crazy On You / 1991 / IF / M • Dirty & Kinky Mature Women #06 / 1995 / C69 / M • Dirty Old Men #1 / 1995 / FPI / M • Dixie Downes Gang Bang / 1996 / FC / M • Dr Fraud's Female Fantasies / 1993 / AM / M • Fresh Faces #11 / 1996 / EVN / M • Geriatric Valley Girls / 1995 / FC / M • Hillary Vamp's Private Collection #04 / 1992 / HVD / M • Hillary Vamp's Private Collection #11 / 1992 / HVD / M • Looking For Love / 1991 / VEX / M • Masquerade (1992-Usa) / 1992 / SC / M • Our Bang #01 / 1992 / GLI / M • Our Bang #07 / 1992 / GLI / M • Our Bang #08 / 1992 / GLI / M • Positively Pagan #01 / 1991 / ATA / M • Rump Humpers #06 / 1992 / GLI / M • Rump Humpers #07 / 1992 / GLI / M • Rump Humpers #18 / 1994 / GLI / M • She's No Angel / 1996 / ERA / S • Six Plus One #2 / 1993 / VEX / C • Southern Accents / 1992 / VEX / M • Sugar Daddies / 1995 / FPI / M • Ultimate Orgy #2 / 1992 / GLI / M • Viviana's Dude Ranch / 1992 / IF / M • Way Inside Lee Caroll / 1992 / VIM / M

CAPTAIN LATEX *see Star Index I*

CAPTAIN VIDEO *see Star Index I*

CAPTAIN X *see Star Index I*

CARA
Amateur Hours #24 / 1990 / AFI / M

CARA DAVIS *see Cara Lott*

CARA GAGE
[Tender Loving Care / 197? / … / M

CARA LOTT *(Daisy Downes, Pam Weston, Carie Evans, Kara Lott, Cara Davis, Charlene Stone, Dawn Robbins, Pamela Weston)*
Short-haired blonde with thin body, passable face, medium tits and large areola. Cara Davis in **Shades of Ecstasy**. Charlene Stone in **Talk Dirty To Me #2**. Was involved in a sting operation in Orange County CA where she was charged with prostitution. The judge in the case mysteriously dismissed the charges, however, leading to speculation that she had supplied him with sexual favors.
1-800-TIME / 1990 / IF / M • Aerobics Girls Club / 1986 / 4P / F • Against All Bods / 1988 / ZA / M • Ass Lover's Special / 1996

/ PE / M • Backstage Pass / 1983 / VC / M • Bad Girls #4 / 1984 / GO / M • The Best Of Blondes / 1986 / VCR / C • Best Of Bruce Seven #3 / 1990 / BIZ / C • Best Of Bruce Seven #4 / 1990 / BIZ / C • Bi-Coastal / 1985 / LAV / G • Bi-Heat #01 / 1987 / ZA / G • Bi-Heat #02 / 1987 / ZA / G • Bi-Heat #03 / 1987 / ZA / G • Bi-Heat #04 / 1987 / ZA / G • Bi-Sexual Fantasies / 1984 / LAV / G • Big Top Cabaret #1 / 1986 / BTO / M • Bitches In Heat / 1994 / PL / C • Blondes On Fire / 1987 / VCR / C • Blondie / 1985 / TAR / M • Blow Job Babes / 1988 / BEV / C • Blue Interview / 1983 / VCR / M • Blue Vanities #067 / 1988 / FFL / M • Body Double / 1984 / C3S / S • Caught By Surprise / 1987 / CDI / M • China & Silk / 1984 / MAP / M • Club Head (EVN) #1 / 1987 / EVN / C • Club Taboo / 1987 / MET / G • Collection #10 / 1987 / CA / M • The Color of Honey / 1987 / SUV / M • Cum Shot Revue #1 / 1985 / HO / C • Cum Shot Revue #2 / 1985 / HO / C • Daddy Doesn't Know / 1984 / HO / M • Daddy's Girls / 1985 / LA / M • Days Gone Bi / 1988 / ZA / G • The Days Of Our Wives / 1988 / GO / M • Deep Inside Trading / 1986 / AR / M • The Deep Insiders / 1987 / VXP / M • Desperately Seeking Suzie / 1985 / VD / M • Devil In Miss Dare / 1986 / AVC / C • Diamond Collection #60 / 1984 / CDI / M • Dirty Harriet / 1986 / SAT / M • Dirty Pictures / 1985 / SUP / M • Do It In The Road / 1990 / LV / M • Double Agents / 1988 / VXP / M • Double Down / 1985 / AMB / M • The Erotic Adventures Of Dr Storm / 1983 / XTR / M • Fantasy Drive / 1990 / VEX / M • Fireball / 1988 / IN / M • Flesh In Ecstasy #16: Cara Lott / 1988 / GO / C • Fleshdance Fever / 1984 / SAT / M • Foreplay / 1982 / VC / M • Frat Brats / 1990 / VC / M • Free And Foxy / 1986 / VCX / C • Frisky Business / 1984 / VC / M • From Russia With Lust / 1984 / VC / M • Fuck This / 1988 / BEV / C • The Fun House / 1988 / SEV / C • Getting Lucky / 1983 / CA / M • The Ginger Effect / 1985 / VI / M • Ginger's Greatest Girl/Girl Hits / 1986 / VI / C • Girls Of Sin / 1994 / PL / C • Glamour Girl #5 / 1985 / CDI / M • Golden Girls #11 / 1983 / CA / M • Golden Girls #24 / 1984 / CA / M • Golden Girls #26 / 1985 / CA / M • The Good Time Girls / 1985 / VEX / M • Gourmet Quickies: Cara Lott #715 / 1985 / GO / C • GVC: Bizarre Women #129 / 1982 / GO / M • GVC: Companions #122 / 1983 / GO / F • GVC: Paper Dolls #117 / 1983 / GO / F • GVC: Real Estate #109 / 198? / GO / M • GVC: Women Who Seduce Men #123 / 1982 / GO / M • Hard To Handle / 19?? / GO / C • The Heat Is On / 1985 / WV / M • Hot Blooded / 1983 / CA / M • Hot Rods / 1988 / VEX / M • Hot Shorts: Cara Lott / 1986 / VCR / C • Hot Spa / 1984 / CA / M • I Like To Be Watched / 1984 / VD / M • Incessant / 1988 / CAD / G • Inside Little Oral Annie / 1984 / VXP / M • Internal Affair / 1990 / V99 / M • Intimate Realities #1 / 1983 / VC / M • It's My Body / 1985 / CDI / M • Joined: The Siamese Twins / 1989 / PL / M • Joys Of Erotica #112 / 1984 / VCR / C • Joys Of Erotica #113 / 1984 / VCR / C • Lace / 1989 / VT / F • Ladies In Heat / 1986 / PV / F • Le Sex De Femme #5 / 1990 / AFI / C • Leather / 1989 / VT / F • Leather And Lace / 1989 / VT / F • Let's Talk Sex / 1982

/ CA / M • Loving Spoonfulls / 1987 / 4P / C • The Maltese Phallus / 1990 / V99 / M • Mandy's Executive Sweet / 1982 / AVC / M • Mantrap / 1986 / BAN / M • Matched Pairs / 1988 / VEX / M • Maximum #2 / 1982 / CA / M • A Mid-Slumber's Night Dream / 1985 / 4P / M • Mistresses And Slaves: The Best Of Bruce Seven / 1991 / BEB / C • Monkey Business / 1987 / SEV / M • My Party Doll / 1987 / VXP / M • Nasty Habits Are Hard To Break / 1986 / 4P / M • The Newcomers / 1983 / VCX / M • Night Prowlers / 1985 / MAP / M • No More Mr Nice Guy / 1989 / GO / M • Only The Best Of Barbara Dare / 1990 / CV / C • Our Naked Eyes / 1988 / TME / M • Panting At The Opera / 1988 / VXP / M • Parliament: Blondes Have More Fun / 1989 / PM / C • Passion For Bondage / 1983 / BIZ / B • Pay The Lady / 1987 / VXP / M • Peeping Passions / 1989 / CAE / M • Physical #2 / 1985 / SUP / M • Playing With Fire / 1983 / IN / M • The Pleasure Machine / 1987 / VXP / M • Pleasure Principle / 1988 / VEX / M • Pleasure Productions #02 / 1984 / VCR / M • Pleasure Productions #03 / 1984 / VCR / M • Pleasure Productions #04 / 1984 / VCR / M • Ravaged / 1990 / CIN / M • Rear Action Girls #1 / 1984 / LIP / F • Satisfactions / 1983 / CA / M • Scent Of A Wild Woman / 1993 / EVN / C • Secretaries / 1990 / PL / F • Separated / 1989 / INH / M • Sex And The Single Girl / 1990 / FAN / M • The Sex Change Girls / 1987 / 4P / G • Sex Shoot / 1985 / AT / M • Shades Of Ecstasy / 1983 / HO / M • Shave Tail / 1984 / AMB / M • She's A Good Lust Charm / 1987 / LA / C • Sizzling Suburbia / 1985 / CDI / M • Sno Bunnies / 1990 / PL / F • Snow Honeys / 1983 / VC / M • Sophisticated Women / 1986 / BAN / M • Sounds Of Sex / 1985 / CA / M • Spermbusters / 1984 / AT / M • Star 84: Tina Marie / 1984 / VEX / M • Stolen Lust / 1985 / AAH / M • Striptease / 1983 / VC / M • Suze's Centerfolds #5 / 1981 / CA / M • Suze's Centerfolds #6 / 1981 / CA / M • Swedish Erotica #37 / 1981 / CA / M • Swedish Erotica #38 / 1981 / CA / M • Sweet Young Foxes / 1984 / VCX / M • Taboo #02 / 1982 / IN / M • Tailhouse Rock / 1985 / WV / M • Tales Of The Golden Pussy / 1989 / RUM / M • Talk Dirty To Me #02 / 1982 / CA / M • A Taste Of Pleasure / 1988 / AVC / M • A Tasty Kind Of Love / 1987 / LV / M • Toppers #22 / 1993 / TV / C • Toys / 1982 / INF / M • Tracie Lords / 1984 / CIT / M • Trashy Lady / 1985 / MAP / M • Unbelievable Orgies #1 / 1987 / EVN / C • Up To No Good / 1986 / CDI / M • The Wacky World Of X-Rated Bloopers / 1989 / GO / M • Watch My Lips / 1985 / AAH / M • Wet 'n' Bare With Barbara Dare / 1988 / NEO / C • Where The Girls Are / 1984 / VEX / M • Wicked Wenches / 1988 / LA / M • Women At Play / 1984 / SE / M • Women Without Men #2 / 1988 / VXP / F • [Danny Does 'Em All / 1989 / … / G • [Party Doll / 1987 / VXP / M

CARAMELLE
Private Film #19 / 1994 / OD / M • Private Video Magazine #20 / 1995 / OD / M • Private Video Magazine #21 / 1995 / OD / M

CAREENA COLLINS *(Coreena Collins, Casee, Candy (Careena C.))*
Petite brunette with a rather hard face and small tits. Depending on the movie she some-

times looks a little barrel-shaped around the belly. First movie was **Snatchbuckler**. The gap in her appearences (1987 to 1994) was due to her attendence at college to get a law degree.

13th Annual Adult Video News Awards / 1996 / VC / S • The Anal Adventures Of Bruce Seven / 1996 / BS / C • Anal Breakdown / 1994 / ROB / M • Anal Deep Rider / 1994 / ROB / M • Anal Heartbreaker / 1995 / ROB / M • Anal Innocence #3 / 1994 / ROB / M • Anal Lover #3 / 1994 / ROB / M • Anal Plaything #1 / 1994 / ROB / M • Anal Spitfire / 1994 / ROB / M • Anal Sweetheart / 1994 / ROB / M • Baby Face #2 / 1987 / VC / M • Best Gang Bangs / 1996 / DFI / C • Beyond Reality #1 / 1995 / EXQ / M • Booty Ho #2 / 1995 / ROB / M • Born To Run / 1985 / WV / M • The Bottom Dweller 33 1/3 / 1995 / EL / M • Brooklyn Nights / 1994 / OD / M • Bruce Seven: A Compendium Of His Most Graphic Scenes Vol 1 / 1991 / BS / C • Bruce Seven: A Compendium Of His Most Graphic Scenes Vol 2 / 1991 / BS / C • Buttslammers #09: Fade To Anal / 1995 / BS / F • Car Wash Angels / 1995 / VC / M • Careena #1 / 1987 / WV / C • Careena #2: A Star On The Rise / 1988 / WV / C • Club Exotica #1 / 1985 / WV / M • Club Exotica #2 / 1985 / WV / M • Dark Interludes / 1991 / BS / B • Deep Cheeks #5 / 1995 / ROB / M • Devil In Miss Jones #3: A New Beginning / 1986 / VC / M • Dressed To Thrill / 1986 / CDI / M • The Ecstasy Of Payne / 1994 / BS / B • The Face Of Fear / 1990 / BS / B • Farmers Daughters / 1985 / WV / M • Fast Girls #1 / 1987 / GBX / M • Gang Bang Nymphette / 1994 / ROB / M • Gangbang Girl #19 / 1996 / ANA / M • Gimme An X / 1993 / VD / C • Hang 'em High / 1995 / BS / B • Honeybuns #1 / 1987 / WV / C • Hot Licks At The Pussycat Club / 1990 / WV / C • Hottest Ticket / 1987 / WV / C • House Of Blue Dreams / 1985 / WV / M • Hyapatia Lee's Secret Dreams / 1986 / SE / M • In Search Of The Golden Bone / 1986 / CA / M • In-N-Out With John Leslie / 1988 / WV / C • Kink #1 / 1995 / ROB / M • Les Be Friends / 1988 / WV / C • Little Miss Anal / [illegible] • The Lust Potion Of Doctor F / 1985 / WV / M • Mad Jack Beyond Thunderdome / 1986 / WET / M • Masochistic Tendencies: The First Night / 1995 / BS / B • The Mystery Of Payne / 1991 / BS / B • Nymphette #1 / 1986 / WV / M • Nymphette #2 / 1986 / WV / M • Oral Majority #01 / 1986 / WV / C • Oral Majority #02 / 1987 / WV / C • Oral Majority #03 / 1986 / WV / C • Oral Majority #04 / 1987 / WV / C • Oral Majority #05 / 1987 / WV / C • Oral Majority #06 / 1988 / WV / C • Orgies / 1987 / WV / C • Painful Cheeks / 1994 / BS / B • Payne-Full Revenge / 1995 / BS / B • Power Play (Bruce Seven) / 1990 / BS / B • Ramb-Ohh #1 / 1986 / PV / M • Rated Sex / 1986 / SE / M • Return To Sex 5th Avenue / 1985 / WV / M • Science Friction / 1986 / AXT / M • Sherlock Homie / 1995 / IN / M • Snatchbuckler / 1985 / DR / M • Sodomania: Slop Shots / 1996 / EL / C • Sodomania: Smokin' Sextions / 1996 / EL / C • Takin' It To The Limit #2 / 1994 / BS / M • Takin' It To The Limit #3 / 1994 / BS / M • Takin' It To The Limit #5 / 1995 / BS / M • Takin' It To The Limit #6 / 1995 / BS / M • Thrill Seekers / 1990 / BS / B • Toys 4 Us #2 / 1987 / WV / C • Toys 4 Us #3: Follow The Leader / 1990 / WV / C • Twins / 1986 / WV / M • Unnatural Phenomenon #1 / 1985 / WV / M • Unnatural Phenomenon #2 / 1986 / WV / M • Whips And Chains / 1995 / BS / B • Wild Fire / 1990 / WV / C • A World Of Hurt / 1994 / BS / B • Yvonne's Odyssey / 1995 / BS / B

CARESS

A&B AB#013: Interracial Trio / 1990 / A&B / M • A&B AB#140: Black Is Better / 1990 / A&B / F • A&B AB#141: Black Seduction / 1990 / A&B / F • A&B AB#192: Home Shopping Club / 1990 / A&B / M • A&B AB#341: Inter-Racial Lesbians / 1991 / A&B / F • New Ends #10 / 1995 / 4P / M

CARESSA CHANG ***see*** **Connie Yung**

CARESSA NATURE

You're The Boss / 1985 / VD / M

CARESSA NATURE (SR) ***see*** **Summer Rose**

CARESSA SAVAGE *(Coressa Savage, Caressa Stone)*

Not too pretty blonde with a chunky body. Originally had small tits (see **Doin' The Rounds**) but later had them enhanced.

A Is For Asia / 1996 / 4P / M • Anal Glamour Girls / 1995 / ME / M • Anal Princess #1 / 1996 / VC / M • Assmania!! #2 / 1995 / ME / M • Babes Behind Bars / 1996 / CNP / F • Babes Illustrated #5 / 1996 / IN / F • Bad Attitude #1 / 1995 / LV / M • Beach Mistress / 1994 / XCI / M • Best Butt(e) In The West #2 / 1995 / CC / M • Beyond Reality #2: Anal Expedition / 1996 / EXQ / M • Beyond Reality #3: Stand Erect! / 1996 / EXQ / M • Blaze / 1996 / WAV / M • The Butt Sisters Do Philadelphia / 1995 / MID / M • The Butt Sisters Do The Twin Cities / 1996 / MID / M • Buttslammers #11: / 1996 / BS / F • Buttslammers #12: Anal Madness / 1996 / BS / F • Buttslammers #13: The Madness Continues / 1996 / BS / F • Captive Coeds / 1996 / LON / B • Car Wash Angels / 1995 / VC / M • Cat Lickers #3 / 1995 / ME / F • Cheerleader Strippers / 1996 / PE / M • Cyberanal / 1995 / VC / M • Deep Behind The Scenes With Seymore Butts #1 / 1995 / [illegible] / VC / C • Doin' The Rounds / 1995 / VC / M • DPTV: Double Penetration Television / 1996 / SUF / M • Eternal Lust / 1996 / VC / M • Everybody Wants Some / 1996 / EXQ / F • First Time Ever #1 / 1995 / PE / F • Flesh / 1996 / EA / M • Forever / 1995 / SC / M • Generation Sex #1 / 1996 / VT / M • Generation Sex #2: Nature's Revenge / 1996 / VT / M • A Girl's Affair #09 / 1996 / FD / F • Hellriders / 1995 / SC / M • Hot Tight Asses #13 / 1995 / TCK / M • If You Can't Lick 'em...Join 'em / 1996 / BAC / F • In Search Of The Perfect Blow Job / 1995 / OD / M • Jinx / 1996 / WP / M • Journal Of O #1: Servant Slave / 1994 / ONA / B • Juicy Cheerleaders / 1995 / LE / M • Last Tango In Paradise / 1995 / ERA / M • Latex #2 / 1995 / VC / M • Lesbian Connection / 1996 / SUF / F • Lesbian Debutante #02 / 1996 / IP / F • Maneater / 1995 / ERA / M • Mystique / 1996 / SC / M • N.Y. Video Magazine #07 / 1996 / OUP / M • Naughty Nights / 1996 / PLP / C • New Pussy Hunt #19 / 1996 / LEI / C • Nightshift Nurses #2 / 1996 / VC / M • No Man's Land #14 / 1996 / VT / F • Ona Zee's Doll House #1 / 1995 / ONA / F • The Palace Of Pleasure / 1995 / ULI / M • Passion / 1996 / SC / M • Poop Shute Debutantes / 1995 / LBO / M • Puritan Video Magazine #01 / 1996 / LE / M • Pussyclips #08 / 1995 / SNA / M • Pussyman #09: Feeding Frenzy / 1995 / SNA / M • Pussyman #10: Butts, Butts & More Butts / 1995 / SNA / M • Pussyman #12: Sticky Fingers / 1995 / SNA / M • Pussyman #13: Lips / 1996 / SNA / M • Pussyman's Nite Club Party #1 / 1996 / SNA / M • Pussyman's Nite Club Party #2 / 1997 / SNA / M • Radical Affairs Video Magazine #09 / 1995 / ME / M • Rainwoman #10: The Tenth Anniversary Edition / 1996 / CC / M • Raw Footage / 1996 / VC / M • Raw Sex #02 / 1995 / ERW / M • Rockhard (Coast) / 1996 / CC / M • Savage Liasons / 1995 / BEP / F • Selena Under Siege / 1995 / XCI / M • Sensuous Torture / 1996 / BS / B • Sex Freaks / 1995 / EA / M • Sex Raiders / 1996 / WAV / M • The Sexual Solution #2 / 1995 / LE / M • Shane's World #1 / 1996 / OD / M • Shane's World #3 / 1996 / OD / M • Skye's The Limit / 1995 / BON / B • Sluthunt #2 / 1995 / BIP / F • Solo Adventures / 1996 / AB / F • Sorority Sex Kittens #3 / 1996 / VC / M • Sorority Stewardesses #1 / 1995 / PE / M • Sorority Stewardesses #2 / 1995 / PE / M • Spinners #2 (Wicked) / 1996 / WP / M • Student Fetish Videos: The Enema #19 / 1995 / PRE / B • Student Fetish Videos: Tickling #11 / 1995 / SFV / B • The Toy Box / 1996 / ONA / M • Ultimate Sensations / 1996 / NIT / M • Undercover / 1996 / VC / M • Up And Cummers #24 / 1995 / 4P / M • The Violation Of Felecia / 1995 / JMP / F • The Violation Of Missy / 1996 / JMP / F • The Violation Of Paisley Hunter / 1996 / JMP / F • The Voyeur #5 / 1995 / EA / M • Wet 'n' Wicked / 1995 / BEP / F • Where The Girls Sweat...Not The Sequel / 1996 / EL / F • Whore D'erves / 1996 / OUP / F

CARESSA STONE ***see*** **Caressa Savage**

CARESSE NEVA

[The Horny Artist / 197? / ... / M

CAREY CARNSWORGH

American Pie / 1980 / SF / M

[illegible] ***see Star Index I***

CARI FOX ***see*** **Kari Fox**

CARIE EVANS ***see*** **Cara Lott**

CARINA ***see Star Index I***

CARINE STEPHEN ***see Star Index I***

CARL DAVENPORT

Conflict Of Interest / 1994 / FST / G

CARL ESSER

Primarily screenwriter. Died in 1995 of a heart attack.

City Of Sin / 1991 / LV / M • Crazed #1 / 1992 / VI / M • Crazed #2 / 1992 / VI / M • The Fluffer #2 / 1993 / FD / M • On Trial #1: In Defense Of Savannah / 1991 / VI / M • On Trial #2: Oral Arguments / 1991 / VI / M • Stiff Competition #2 / 1994 / CA / M • Street Angels / 1992 / LV / M • Telesex #1 / 1992 / VI / M • Veil / 1990 / VI / M

CARL IRWIN ***see*** **Carl Regal**

CARL LANGER ***see Star Index I***

CARL LINCOLN ***see Star Index I***

CARL MANN ***see*** **Brian Long**

CARL MONSON ***see*** **Carlos Monsoya**

CARL PARKER ***see Star Index I***

CARL REGAL *(Carl Irwin)*

Desires Within Young Girls / 1977 / CA / M • Do You Wanna Be Loved? / 1977 / AR /

M • Girls In Blue / 1987 / VCX / C • Little Girls Blue #1 / 1977 / VCX / M • Once Upon A Time/Cave Woman / 1978 / VI / M • Pizza Girls (We Deliver) / 1978 / VCX / M • Seven Into Snowy / 1977 / VC / M • Talk Dirty To Me #01 / 1980 / CA / M

CARL ROSS
Fantastic Voyeur / 1975 / AVC / M

CARL STEELE
AC/DC #2 / 1994 / HP / G

CARL STONE
My Baby Got Back #02 / 1993 / VT / M

CARL YOUNG see Star Index I

CARLA
Biff Malibu's Totally Nasty Home Videos #13 / 1992 / ANA / M • Blue Vanities #539 / 1993 / FFL / M • The Bondage File / 19?? / BIZ / C • Dirty Dave's American Amateurs #05 / 1992 / AR / M • Inside Seka / 1980 / VXP / M • My Name Is Carla / 1986 / BIZ / B • Naughty New Orleans / 1962 / SOW / S • Odyssey Amateur #77: Carla's Close Shave / 1991 / OD / M • The Royal Court Collection / 1993 / VER / S

CARLA BANKS see Star Index I

CARLA BLAS
Suzie's Take Out Service / 1975 / CDC / M

CARLA BLY
Bavarian Cream & Other Delights / 1985 / PV / M

CARLA CAPRI
Casting Call #16 / 1995 / SO / M • Max #08: The Fugitive / 1995 / XPR / M

CARLA CHASEN see Star Index I

CARLA CRABBE see Star Index I

CARLA DAWN see Star Index I

CARLA FERRARI
Breast Of Britain #9 / 1990 / BTO / M • Bright Lights, Big Titties / 1989 / CA / M • Bustin' Out / 1988 / VEX / M • Coming In America / 1988 / VEX / M • Double D Roommates / 1989 / BTO / M • Girls Don't Lie / 1990 / IN / F • Kinkyvision #2 / 1988 / VC / M • Reflections Of Innocence / 1988 / SEX / M • Reflections Of Innocence / 1991 / VEX / C • Splendor In The Ass #1 / 1989 / CA / M • Sumo Sue And The Fat Ladies Of Wrestling / 1988 / FAN / M • Turn Up The Heat / 1988 / SEX / M • Turn Up The Heat / 1991 / VEX / C

CARLA MCKIZZICK
Ring Of Desire / 1981 / SE / M

CARLA MESSINA see Star Index I

CARLA MONTGOMERY
Loveland / 1973 / VST / M

CARLA RUSSELL see Star Index I

CARLA THOMAS
Rise And Fall Of Sparkle / 19?? / BL / M

CARLA TURNER
Erotic Fantasies #4 / 1983 / CV / C • The Other Side Of Julie / 1978 / CV / M

CARLA WAYNE see Star Index I

CARLA YOUNG
Sweet Sixteen / 1974 / SVE / M • Women In Uniform / 1977 / VHL / M

CARLEINE
Lesbian Workout #1 / 1994 / GO / F

CARLIE
The girl is the same but the camerawork and lighting seems to have a major effect on her looks. Either long straight dark brown or black hair, small/medium firm natural or enhanced tits with a nipple ring in the left one, white skin, poor dentition or just an overbite, jutting jaw *a la* Janine or a not-too-pretty face, flat belly, shaven pussy. As

of 1996 she doesn't seem to have done men.
Chronicles Of Pain #3: Slave Traders / 1996 / BIZ / B • Dirty Tricks #2: This Ain't Love / 1996 / EA / M • Fresh Meat (John Leslie) #3 / 1996 / EA / M • Joe Elliot's College Girls #31 / 1994 / JOE / M • Leather Bound Dykes From Hell #8 / 1996 / BIZ / B • Mistress Kane: Lessons In Terror / 1996 / BIZ / B • Mistress Kane: Town In Torment / 1996 / BIZ / B • Stalking Of Slave Laura / 1996 / BIZ / B • Ultimate Sensations / 1996 / NIT / M • Wicked Fantasies / 1996 / CO2 / M

CARLIE ZACHS see Star Index I

CARLITO AYALA see Star Index I

CARLO
Hillary Vamp's Private Collection #06 / 1992 / HVD / M

CARLO MANUGUERRA
Body Love / 1976 / CA / M

CARLO PONCE
Amateur Nights #15 / 1997 / HO / M • Amateur Nights #16 / 1997 / HO / M • Asian Boom Boom Girls / 1997 / HO / M

CARLOS see Star Index I

CARLOS BALAJO
L.A. Tool & Die / 1979 / TMX / G

CARLOS CHET see Jon Dough

CARLOS MONSOYA *(Carl Monson, Charles Monsoya)*
Booby Trap / 1970 / SOW / S

CARLOS RADILLO
Bi Bi Banjee Boyz / 1994 / PL / G

CARLOS SANDER see Star Index I

CARLOS TOBALINA *(Troy Benny, Efrain Tobalina)*
Normally a director. Owned HIFCOA (Hollywood International Film Corporation of America).
Casanova #2 / 1976 / CA / M • Champagne Orgy / cr78 / HIF / M • Dr Teen Dilemma / 1973 / VHL / M • Flesh & Laces #1 / 1983 / CA / M • Flesh & Laces #2 / 1983 / CA / M • Flesh Pond / 1983 / VC / M • Lady Dynamite / 1983 / VC / M • Love Champions / 1987 / VC / M • Mai Lin Vs Serena / 1982 / HIF / M • Marathon / 1982 / CA / M • Sensual Fire / 1979 / HIF / M • Sexual Odyssey / 1985 / VC / M • Wild Nurses In Lust / 1986 / PLY / M

CARLOS VALENTINO see Star Index I

CARLOTTA
Blue Vanities #547 / 1994 / FFL / M

CARLOTTA (LORRIN M) see Lorrin Mick

CARLY
Creme De La Face #04 / 1994 / OD / M • Hidden Camera #19 / 1994 / JMP / M • HomeGrown Video #470: Heroes, Torpedoes & Grinders / 1996 / HOV / M • M Series #30 / 1994 / LBO / M • Mr. Peepers Amateur Home Videos #24: The Sleazy Riders / 1991 / LBO / M • Southern Belles #2 / 1995 / HOV / M • Teacher's Pet #1 / 1994 / WMG / M

CARLY SEMEN
Odyssey Triple Play #93: Satisfaction Via Gang Bang / 1995 / OD / M

CARLYN SAND
The Satisfiers Of Alpha Blue / 1980 / AVC / M

CARMAN
Blue Vanities #510 / 1992 / FFL / M

CARMEL CARSON see Star Index I

CARMEL CENTRE
San Francisco Lesbians #6 / 1994 / PL / F

CARMEL MONTEREY
ABA: Double Feature #1 / 1996 / ALP / M • Fanny Hill / 1975 / TGA / M

CARMEL NOUGAT see Crystal Starr

CARMEL O'SHEA see Carmel St Clair

CARMEL SNOW see Pia Snow

CARMEL ST CLAIR *(Carmel O'Shea)*
Hispanic girl with black hair and droopy medium tits but she exudes sex. 5'3" tall and comes from Honduras. In the beginning of 1994 she had large silicone implants added. Rumored to be married to Rick O'Shea.
American Connection Video Magazine #02 / 1992 / ZA / M • Anal Climax #3 / 1993 / ROB / M • Anal Co-Ed / 1993 / ROB / M • Anal Sensation / 1993 / ROB / M • Anal Vision #11 / 1993 / LBO / M • Babewatch #1 / 1993 / CC / M • Beach Bum Amateur's #39 / 1993 / MID / M • Biff Malibu's Totally Nasty Home Videos #30 / 1993 / ANA / M • Black Orgies #11 / 1993 / AFI / M • Bobby Hollander's Maneaters #08 / 1993 / SFP / M • The Bodacious Boat Orgy #1 / 1993 / GLI / M • The Bodacious Boat Orgy #2 / 1993 / GLI / M • Bubble Butts #20 / 1992 / LBO / M • Buttslammers #03: The Ultimate Dream / 1993 / BS / F • Chocolate Bunnies #02 / 1995 / LBO / C • Colossal Orgy #1 / 1993 / HW / M • Colossal Orgy #3 / 1994 / HW / M • Dark Alleys #20 / 1993 / FC / M • Deep Inside Dirty Debutantes #05 / 1993 / 4P / M • The Devil In Grandma Jones / 1994 / FC / M • Dirty Bob's #13: Getting Lucky In Vegas / 1994 / FLP / S • Dollars And Yen / 1994 / FH / M • Double D Amateurs #15 / 1994 / JMP / M • Ebony Erotica #05: Black Obsessions / 1993 / GO / M • Ebony Erotica #10: Dark Eyes / 1993 / GO / M • First Time Lesbians #14 / 1994 / JMP / F • Frathouse Sexcapades / 1993 / SFP / M • Gazongas #05 / 1993 / VEX / C • Hedonism #01 / 1993 / FH / M • Hidden Camera #01 / 1993 / JMP / M • How To Make A Model #01 / 1992 / MET / M • Kiss Is A Rebel With A Cause / 1993 / WV / M • Kitty Kat Club / 1994 / SC / F • Lesbian Pros And Amateurs #25 / 1993 / GO / F • Lust / 1993 / FH / M • M Series #02 / 1993 / LBO / M • Mike Hott: #240 Carmel And Analu / 1991 / MHV / F • Mike Hott: #252 Horny Couples #15 / 1994 / MHV / M • Mike Hott: #263 Lesbian Sluts #16 / 1994 / MHV / F • Mike Hott: #292 Three-Sum Sluts #03 / 1995 / MHV / M • Mike Hott: #331 Lesbian Sluts #21 / 1996 / MHV / F • Mike Hott: #366 Lactating Lesbians / 1996 / MHV / F • Money, Money, Money / 1993 / FD / M • More Dirty Debutantes #20 / 1993 / 4P / M • Mr. Peepers Amateur Home Videos #59: The Ball Of The Wild / 1992 / LBO / M • Mr. Peepers Amateur Home Videos #69: Love Tunnel / 1993 / LBO / M • The Night Of The Coyote / 1993 / MED / M • Objective: D.P. / 1993 / PEP / M • Odyssey 30 Min: #263: Carmel's 4-Way Dating Game / 1992 / OD / M • Odyssey 30 Min: #264: / 1992 / OD / M • Odyssey 30 Min: #279: Carmel's Anal Party / 1992 / OD / M • Odyssey Triple Play #51: Anal Party / 1993 / OD / M • Odyssey Triple Play #59: Two On Two Fuckfest / 1994 / OD / M • Odyssey Triple Play #70: Three By Threeway / 1994 / OD / M • Party Of Payne / 1993 / BS / B • Pearl Necklace: Thee Bush League #07 / 1992 / SEE / M • Pussy Posse / 1993 / CC / M • Raw Talent:

Hedonism #1 / 1993 / FH / M • Shear Ecstasy / 1993 / PEP / M • Sheer Ecstasy / 1993 / IF / M • Sodomania #04: Further On Down The Road / 1993 / EL / M • Stylin' / 1994 / FD / M • Swinging Couples #02 / 1993 / GO / M • This Could Be The Night / 1993 / IF / M • Ultimate Gang Bang #1 / 1994 / HW / M • Virgins Of Video #02 / 1993 / YDI / M • Washington D.P. / 1993 / PEP / M • Xcitement: The Movie / 1993 / XCI / M

CARMELLA
Odyssey Triple Play #09: Interracial Lovefest / 1992 / OD / M

CARMELLA (MELBA C.) see Melba Cruz

CARMELO PETIX
Body Love / 1976 / CA / M • Kinky Ladies Of Bourbon Street / 1976 / LUM / M

CARMEN
Afternoon Delights / 1995 / FC / M • Blue Vanities #543 / 1994 / FFL / M • Blue Vanities #554 / 1994 / FFL / M • Blue Vanities #572 / 1995 / FFL / M • Dirty Dirty Debutantes #6 / 1996 / 4P / M • HomeGrown Video #455 / 1995 / HOV / M • Little Big Hole #1 / 199? / SVE / M • Little Big Hole #2 / 199? / SVE / M • Little Big Hole #3 / 199? / SVE / M • Slave Traders / 1995 / GOT / B

CARMEN ALMADA see Star Index I

CARMEN BASE
The Awakening Of Sally / 1984 / VCR / M

CARMEN DE LA TORRE
GVC: The Babysitter #107 / 1983 / GO / M

CARMEN FANCHON see Star Index I

CARMEN JACKEL
[Schulmadchen-Report 4: Was Eltern Oft Verzweifeln LaBt / 1972 / … / M

CARMEN MONREPOS
Ass Attack / 1995 / PL / M

CARMEN REATTA see Star Index I

CARMEN ROYALE see Star Index I

CARMEN SANDS
Lovin' Spoonfuls #7 / 1996 / 4P / C • More Dirty Debutantes #31 / 1994 / 4P / M

CARMEN SOUZA
Ready To Drop #01 / 1990 / FC / M

CARMINE see Devin DeRay

CARMINE DELVECHIO see Star Index I

CARMINE VALENTINO see Star Index I

CARNAL
100% Amateur #19: / 1996 / OD / M

CARNAL CANDY
Dude Looks Like A Lady / 1993 / SC / G • She-Male Encounters #01: Tanatalizing Toni / 1981 / MET / G • She-Male Encounters #02: Carnal Candy / 1981 / MET / G • True Crimes Of Passion / 1983 / CA / G

CARNAL DELIGHT (Candy (Carnal Del))
Short haired blonde.
Harry Horndog #30: Love Puppies #7 / 1995 / FPI / M • Rump Man: Sex On The Beach / 1995 / HW / M

CARO KEFF
Girl Service / 1972 / CV / M • Strange Experiences Cockfucking / 1994 / MET / M

CAROL
Amateur Hours #01 / 1989 / AFI / M • Blue Vanities #195 / 1993 / FFL / M • Blue Vanities #520 / 1993 / FFL / M • Blue Vanities #554 / 1994 / FFL / M • Blue Vanities #557 / 1994 / FFL / M • Creme De Femme #2 / 1981 / AVC / C • Eurotica #06 / 1996 / XC / M • Homegrown Video #317 / 1990 / HOV / M • HomeGrown Video #458: Cream Pie For Dessert / 1995 / HOV / C • Match #4:

Hellcats / 1995 / NPA / B • Swingers Confidential #1 / 1995 / FC / M

CAROL ANN
Bottom Busters / 1973 / BLT / M

CAROL ANN JACKSON
Fast Cars, Fast Women / 1979 / SE / M • Golden Girls #01 / 1981 / CA / M • Golden Girls #02 / 1981 / SVE / M

CAROL ANNE see Stephanie Hart-Roger

CAROL BARR see Candy Barr

CAROL BART
Girls U.S.A. / 1980 / AIR / M

CAROL BIGBY
Fantasy Girls / 1974 / VC / M

CAROL BOSHOLM
Inside Seka / 1980 / VXP / M

CAROL BRUCE
A Party In My Tight Pussy / 1994 / MET / M • Revenge Of A Motorcycle Mama / 1972 / ALP / M

CAROL BURNS
Family Affair / 1979 / MIT / M

CAROL CARRS see Star Index I

CAROL CHRISTY see Star Index I

CAROL CONNERS (Carol Kaiser)
Angular, not too pretty blonde.
The Best Of Gail Palmer / 1981 / WWV / C • The Bride's Initiation / 1976 / VIP / M • Candy Goes To Hollywood / 1979 / VCX / M • The Confessions Of Linda Lovelace / 1974 / AR / C • Consenting Adults / 1981 / VXP / M • Cousin Betty / cr70 / AXV / M • Daddy's Rich / 1972 / ALP / M • Deep Throat #1 / 1972 / AR / M • Desire For Men / 1981 / MIT / M • The Erotic Adventures Of Candy / 1978 / VCX / M • For Services Rendered / 1986 / VD / M • Midnight Blue #2 / 1980 / VXP / M • My Bed Is Crowded / cr75 / VCI / M • Road Of Death / cr72 / … / S • School Teacher's Weekend Vacation / cr72 / SVE / M • Sweet Savage / 1978 / ALP / M • Water People / cr72 / AXV / M • Weekend Tail / 1987 / VD / M • [Catalina Caper / 1968 / … / S • [The Super Salesman / 1975 / … / M

CAROL CONNERS (KAND) see Kandi Connor

CAROL CROSS (Gwendolen Roth)
[text unclear] College / 1984 / VC / M • Burlexxx / 1984 / VC / M • Christine's Secret / 1986 / FEM / M • Climax / 1985 / CA / M • Decadence / 1986 / VD / M • Deep & Wet / 1986 / VD / M • Dirty Blonde / 1984 / VXP / M • Double Trouble / 1986 / DRV / M • Femme / 1984 / VC / M • First Time At Cherry High / 1984 / VC / M • Flasher / 1986 / VD / M • Give It To Me / 1984 / SE / M • Good Girl, Bad Girl / 1984 / SE / M • Great Sexpectations / 1984 / VC / M • Hot Licks / 1984 / SE / M • Hot Stuff / 1984 / VXP / M • Hypersexuals / 1984 / VC / M • Inside Little Oral Annie / 1984 / VXP / M • Jack 'n' Jill #2 / 1984 / VC / M • Make Me Feel It / 1984 / SE / M • The Pleasures Of Innocence / 1985 / VC / M • Poltergash / 1987 / AVC / M • Pussycat Galore / 1984 / VC / M • Rambone: The First Time / 1985 / JOH / M • Sex Crimes 2084 / 1985 / SE / M • Slammer Girls / 1987 / LIV / S • Supergirls Do General Hospital / 1984 / VC / M • Supergirls Do The Navy / 1984 / VC / M • Sweet Spread / 1986 / VXP / M • The T & A Team / 1984 / VC / M • Taboo American Style #3: Nina Becomes An Actress / 1985 / VC / M • Taboo American

Style #4: The Exciting Conclusion / 1985 / VC / M • Three Daughters / 1986 / FEM / M • Urban Heat / 1985 / FEM / M • Wet Dreams / 1984 / CA / M

CAROL CUMMINGS (Carol Cummins)
Hard as nails older female with enhanced medium tits.
20th Century Fox / 1989 / FAZ / M • The All American Girl / 1989 / FAN / M • All The Right Motions / 1990 / DR / M • America's Most Wanted Girl / 1989 / IN / M • As Nasty As She Wants To Be / 1990 / IN / M • Bad Medicine / 1990 / VEX / M • Beeches / 1990 / KIS / M • Behind The Backdoor #3 / 1989 / EVN / M • Bet Black / 1989 / CDI / M • Between A Rock And A Hot Place / 1989 / VEX / M • The Big Gun / 1989 / FAN / M • The Bikini Carwash Company #1 / 1990 / IMP / S • Blacks & Blondes: The Movie / 1989 / WV / M • Blame It On The Heat / 1989 / VC / M • Blind Date / 1989 / E&I / M • Bloopers #2 / 1991 / GO / C • Bo-Dacious / 1989 / V99 / M • Bodies In Heat #2 / 1989 / DR / M • Boobs, Butts And Bloopers #1 / 1990 / HO / M • Born For Porn / 1989 / FAZ / M • Boxed Lunches / 1989 / … / M • Busting Loose / 1989 / AMB / F • Butt's Motel #1 / 1989 / EX / M • Call Girls In Action / 1989 / CV / M • Candy Ass / 1990 / V99 / M • Cat Scratch Fever / 1989 / FAZ / M • Club Head (EVN) #3 / 1992 / EVN / C • Con Jobs / 1990 / V99 / M • Cum For Me, Carol / 1990 / FAZ / C • Cum Rain, Cum Shine / 1989 / FAZ / M • Dangerous / 1989 / PV / M • Debbie Does 'em All #3 / 1989 / CV / M • Dirty Lingerie / 1990 / VD / M • Executive Suites / 1990 / VEX / M • Fantasy Couples / 1989 / FAZ / C • The First Taboo / 1989 / LA / M • Foolish Pleasures / 1989 / ME / M • For Her Pleasure Only / 1989 / FAZ / M • The Girl With The Blue Jeans Off / 1989 / FAZ / M • The Girls Are Bustin' Loose / 1988 / AMB / F • Girls Like Us / cr88 / IN / C • Girls Of The Double D #06 / 1989 / CIN / M • Handle With Care / 1989 / FAZ / M • Hard At Work / 1989 / VEX / M • Head Nurse / 1990 / V99 / M • Hershe Highway #2 / 1989 / HO / M • Hidden Desire / 1989 / HO / M • Holly Does Hollywood #4 / 1990 / CAY / M • Hollywood Bikini Party Girls / 1989 / VC / M • Hollywood Knights #3 / 1991 / PCP / M • Hollywood X-Posed #1 / 1992 / VIM / C • Hot Cargo / 1990 / MID / M • Hot Palms / 1989 / GO / M • I Dream Of Christy / 1989 / CAY / M • Imagination X-Posed / 1989 / 4P / M • Jealous Lovers / 1989 / CDI / M • Keep It Cumming / 1990 / V99 / M • Kinky Nurses / 1995 / VEX / C • Kisses Don't Lie / 1989 / PL / M • Ladies Man / 1990 / REB / M • Le Sex De Femme #1 / 1989 / AFI / C • Live In, Love In / 1989 / ME / M • Love Button / 1989 / VD / M • More Than Friends / 1989 / FAZ / M • Night Lessons / 1990 / V99 / M • No Strings Attached / 1990 / ERO / M • On Stage And In Color / 1991 / VIP / M • One Flew Over The Cuckoo's Breast / 1989 / FAZ / M • Only The Best Of Debbie / 1992 / MET / C • Pajama Party / 1993 / CV / C • Passion Prescription / 1990 / V99 / M • Playing Dirty / 1989 / VEX / M • Plenty Of Pleasure / 1990 / WET / M • Public Enemy / 1990 / VIP / M • Radioactive / 1990 / VIP / M • Raunchy Ranch / 1991 / AFV / M • The Red Baron / 1989 / FAN / M • Rituals / 1989 / V99 / M • The Scarlet

Bride / 1989 / VI / M • Seduction / 1990 / VEX / M • Sex And The Single Girl / 1990 / FAN / M • Sex Crazy / 1989 / FAN / C • Sex Lives On Porno Tape / 1992 / VC / C • Sexy Nurses #1 On And Off Duty / 1990 / CV / M • She's America's Most Wanted / 1990 / VEX / M • She's No Angel #1 / 1990 / V99 / M • Six-Nine Love / 1990 / LV / M • The Smart Aleck / 1990 / PM / M • Soft And Wild / 1991 / LV / M • Spellbound / 1989 / LV / M • Studio Sex / 1990 / FH / M • Sweet Darlin' / 1990 / VEX / M • Sweet Tease / 1990 / VEX / M • Temptations / 1989 / DR / M • Tequila Sunset / 1989 / V99 / M • Torrid House / 1989 / VI / M • Toys 4 Us #3: Follow The Leader / 1990 / WV / C • The Unauthorized Biography Of Rob Blow / 1990 / LV / M • Unclassified Carol / 1989 / FAN / C • Undercover Carol / 1990 / FAN / M • War Of The Tulips / 1990 / IN / M • Weekend Blues / 1990 / IN / M • White Lies / 1990 / VEX / M • Who Shaved Trinity Loren? / 1988 / EX / M • Wildheart / 1989 / IN / M • Women In Charge / 1990 / VEX / M • X-Rated Bloopers #2 / 1986 / AR / M • [City Lickers / 1990 / … / M • [Girls In The Mist / 1989 / … / M • [Hot Squack #2 / 1990 / … / M • [Kingsized Knockers / 19?? / … / M

CAROL CUMMINS *see* **Carol Cummings**

CAROL DAVIS
C.O.D. / 1981 / VES / S • Love Airlines / 1978 / SE / M

CAROL DEE BOIS *see* **Carole DuBois**

CAROL DEMPSEY *see Star Index I*

CAROL DODA
Head / 1968 / … / S • Honkytonk Nights / 1978 / TWV / S • Never So Deep / 1981 / VCX / M • Playboy Video Magazine #03 / 1983 / PLA / S • The Seven Seductions Of Madame Lau / 1981 / EVI / M • Trashi / 1980 / CA / M

CAROL DOWNS *see* **Carol Titian**

CAROL FERRARI *see Star Index I*

CAROL FIELD
Teenage Pajama Party / 1977 / VC / M

CAROL FRAZIER *see* **Nikki Randall**

CAROL HILLER
Sunny / 1979 / VC / M

CAROL HINES
[Home From The Sea / 19?? / … / M

CAROL HUNT
Dirty & Kinky Mature Women #06 / 1995 / C69 / M

CAROL JENKA *see Star Index I*

CAROL JONES
The Kiss-O-Gram Girls / 1986 / L&W / S • Older Women Younger Men #3 / 1993 / CC / M

CAROL KAISER *see* **Carol Conners**

CAROL KAY *see Star Index I*

CAROL LARSON *see Star Index I*

CAROL LYNN
The Cross Of Lust / 1995 / CL0 / M • Euromania #2 / 1996 / AOC / M • Eurotique Sexualis / 1995 / AOC / M • Letters From A Slave / 1995 / AOC / M • Skin #1 / 1994 / EUR / M • Skin #2 / 1995 / ERQ / M

CAROL MARKS
I Love Pain / 1995 / GOT / B • Rough Games / 1994 / GOT / B

CAROL MILLER
Big Bust Babes #02 / 1984 / AFI / M • Caged Heat #1 / 1974 / ST0 / S

CAROL NASH
Alice In Pornoland / 1996 / IP / M • The

Best Of The Gangbang Girl Series / 1995 / ANA / C • Extraterrestrial Virgins / 1995 / VIT / M • Gangbang Girl #09 / 1993 / ANA / M • Hamlet: For The Love Of Ophelia #1 / 1996 / IP / M • Hamlet: For The Love Of Ophelia #2 / 1996 / IP / M • On The Prowl In Paris / 1992 / SC / M • A Private Love Affair / 1996 / IP / M

CAROL PARSONS
The French Maid's Flogging / 1995 / BIZ / B

CAROL QUEEN
Blush: How To Female Ejaculate / 1992 / BLV / F • Erotica S.F. / 1994 / ORP / M

CAROL RICHARD
Dresden Diary #01 / 1986 / BIZ / B

CAROL ROBBINS
Sex For Sale / 1972 / BWV / M

CAROL RUSSA *see* **Susan Sloan**

CAROL RUSSO *see* **Susan Sloan**

CAROL SANDS *see Star Index I*

CAROL SMITH *see Star Index I*

CAROL STAHL
Erotic Dimensions: Aggressive Women / 1982 / NSV / M

CAROL TALBOT
Backside To The Future #2 / 1988 / ZA / M

CAROL TATUM *see Star Index I*

CAROL TAYLOR
Blue Vanities #030 / 1988 / FFL / M • Blue Vanities #534 / 1993 / FFL / M

CAROL TITIAN *(Titian, Zylecko Princess, Carol Downs, Fantasia (Carol Tit))*
Ugly face, deteriorated body, large tits (may be enhanced), blonde curly hair.
Amber Lynn's Personal Best / 1986 / VD / M • Anal Annie And The Magic Dildo / 1984 / LIP / F • Big, Bad & Beautiful / 1988 / MIR / C • Black Bimbos In Heat / 1989 / MIR / C • Body Games / 1987 / DR / M • Boobs, Butts And Bloopers #1 / 1990 / HO / M • Built For Sex (Angela Baron's) / 1988 / FAZ / C • Caught From Behind #07 / 1987 / HO / M • Cream Puff / 1986 / VSE / M • Depraved Innocent / 1986 / VD / M • Girlworld #2 / 1988 / LIP / F • The Hot Lunch Club / 1985 / WV / M • Hot Nights And Hard Bodies / 1986 / VD / M • I Cream Of Genie / 1988 / SE / M • Joanna's Dreams / 1988 / SEV / M • The Kiss / 1986 / SC / M • Legacy Of Lust / 1985 / CA / M • The Legend Of King Karl / 1986 / AR / M • Liquid Love / 1988 / CA / M • Nina Does 'em All / 1988 / 3HV / C • The Pleasure Game / 1988 / CA / M • Red Hot Pepper / 1986 / V99 / M • Rockin' Erotica / 1987 / SE / C • Sex Academy / 1985 / PLY / M • Sins Of Nina Hartley / 1989 / MIR / C • Sweet Surrender / 1985 / AVC / M • Sweet Things / 1987 / VC / M • Tales Of The Uncensored / 1987 / FAN / M • Teacher's Pets / 1985 / AVC / M • Tell Me Something Dirty / 1991 / NWV / M • Torrid Zone / 1987 / MIR / M • Trampire / 1987 / FAN / M • Wet Panties / 1989 / MIR / C • Wild Stuff / 1987 / WET / M • You Bring Out The Animal In Me / 1987 / MIR / M

CAROL TONG *see Star Index I*

CAROL TROY
The Older Women's Sperm Bank #2 / 1996 / SUF / M

CAROL VAUGHAN
Blue Vanities #580 / 1996 / FFL / M

CAROL WELK
The Virgin Forest / 1975 / AXV / M • Weekend Lovers / 1975 / AVC / M

CAROL WESTWOOD *see Star Index I*

CAROL WITT
Blue Vanities #577 / 1995 / FFL / M

CAROLA
S&M On The Ranch: Training The New Pony Girl / 1994 / VER / B

CAROLE
Eurotica #11 / 1996 / XC / M • Eurotica #12 / 1996 / XC / M • Triple X Video Magazine #11 / 1995 / OD / M • Wrasslin She-Babes #12 / 1996 / SOW / M

CAROLE COMES
Older & Bolder In San Francisco / 1996 / TEP / M • Senior Sexcapades #1 / 1995 / PL / M

CAROLE D.
Kidnapped And Trained / 1997 / BON / B • Service After Sale / 1996 / BON / B

CAROLE DUBOIS *(Carol Dee Bois)*
French. Short black hair, marginal face, medium tits, lithe but not thin body, small (appendectomy?) scar on her right belly, and tattoos everywhere as follows: large sparse tattoo covering the left side of her back, wings on the right shoulder top, waist just above right butt, and a squiggle on her left breast.
Chasey Loves Rocco / 1996 / VI / M • Get Lucky / 1996 / NIT / M • Private Gold #05: Cape Town #1 / 1996 / OD / M • Private Gold #07: Kruger Park / 1996 / OD / M • Triple X Video Magazine #12 / 1996 / OD / M • The Voyeur #6 / 1996 / EA / M

CAROLE HAYNES
Blue Vanities #582 / 1996 / FFL / M

CAROLE HOLLAND *see Star Index I*

CAROLE MILLER
Old Wave Hookers #2 / 1995 / PL / M

CAROLE PARKER *see Star Index I*

CAROLE TROY
Alumni Girls / 1996 / GO / M

CAROLE ZABOR *see Star Index I*

CAROLINA
Ancient Amateurs #2 / 1996 / LOF / M • Bang City #7: Carolina's Anal Gang Bang / 1995 / SC / M • Carolina's D.P. Anal Gangbang / 1996 / FC / M • Dirty & Kinky Mature Women #10 / 1996 / C69 / M • Dirty Stories #1 / 1995 / PE / M • Filthy First Timers #5 / 1997 / EL / M • War Whores / 1996 / EL / M

CAROLINA (BRAZ) *see Star Index I*

CAROLINA KNOWLES
The Trainers / cr83 / BIZ / B

CAROLINE
Blue Vanities #544 / 1994 / FFL / M • The Girls Of Daytona / 1993 / BTO / S • International Love And The Dancer / 1995 / PME / S • Little Big Girls / 1996 / VC / M • Magma: Dirty Twins / 1994 / MET / M • Onanie #2 / 1995 / MET / F • Sappho Connection / 19?? / LIP / F • Tania's Lustexzesse / 1994 / MET / M • The Thief, The Girl & The Detective / 1996 / HDE / M • Tied & Tickled / 1996 / GAL / B • The Voyeur #8: Live In Europe #2 / 1996 / JLP / M

CAROLINE BELL
Snatch Masters #10 / 1995 / LEI / M

CAROLINE CHAMBERS *see* **Megan Leigh**

CAROLINE CONNELLY *see* **Carolyn Connelly**

CAROLINE DU BARRE *see Star Index I*

CAROLINE LAURIE
Diaries Of Fire And Ice #1 / 1989 / VC / M • Diaries Of Fire And Ice #2 / 1989 / VC / M

• Phantom Of The Cabaret #1 / 1989 / VC / M • Phantom Of The Cabaret #2 / 1989 / VC / M

CAROLINE MAY
[Cousin Betty / 197? / ... / M

CAROLINE MUIR
Ancient Secrets Of Sexual Ecstasy / 1996 / HIG / M

CAROLINE PARKS see Star Index I

CAROLINE RAAB
Letters From A Slave / 1995 / AOC / M

CAROLINE SHIELDS
Penitent Wife / Miss Armstrong / 1993 / CS / B

CAROLINE SIDNEY
Dirty Lilly / 1975 / VXP / M

CAROLYN
976 Video #2: The Brunettes / 1994 / TZV / F • Blue Vanities #129 / 1990 / FFL / M • Wrasslin She-Babes #08 / 1996 / SOW / M

CAROLYN ANDERSON see Alice Harvey

CAROLYN BRANDT *(Jane Bond)*
Brunette, passable face.
The Erotic Adventures Of Pinocchio / 1971 / JLT / S • Frank Henenlotter's XXX Hardcore Horrors: Mad Love... / 1996 / SOW / M • The Mad Love Of The Red Hot Vampire / 1971 / SOW / M • Perverted Passions / 1974 / ALP / M • The Thrill Killers / 1965 / CAM / S • [Body Fever / 1969 / ... / S

CAROLYN CHAMBERS *see* **Megan Leigh**

CAROLYN CONNELLY *(Caroline Connelly)*
Bouncin' In The U.S.A. / 1986 / H&S / S • Honeybuns #1 / 1987 / WV / C • In All The Right Places / 1986 / VD / M • Karate Girls / 1987 / VCR / M • Mitzi's Honor / 1987 / TAM / M • Nymphette #2 / 1986 / WV / M • Oral Majority #02 / 1987 / WV / C • Sexaholics / 1987 / VCX / M • St. X-Where #1 / 1986 / VD / M • Summer Lovers / 1987 / WET / M • Weird Fantasy / 1986 / LA / M

CAROLYN DREW
Prime Choice #1 / 1995 / RAS / M

CAROLYN GRACE see Star Index I

CAROLYN KELLY
Bullwhip: Art Of The Single-Tail Whip / 1996 / BN / B

CAROLYN LATTER see Star Index I

CAROLYN MONROE see Candice Hart

CAROLYN SAND see Star Index I

CARON GARDENER
Blue Vanities #517 / 1992 / FFL / M

CARON SHIELDS
Schoolgirl Fannies On Fire / 1994 / BIZ / B

CARRAH MAJOR-MINOR *see* **Star Index I**

CARRESSA see Summer Rose

CARRESSA NATURE (SR) see Summer Rose

CARRI STEPHENS see Star Index I

CARRIE
Blue Vanities #544 / 1994 / FFL / M • Blue Vanities #569 / 1996 / FFL / M • Erotic Eye / 1995 / DGD / S • HomeGrown Video #470: Heroes, Torpedoes & Grinders / 1996 / HOV / M • Horny Henry's London Adventure / 1995 / TTV / M • Love Letters / 1992 / ELP / F • Mr. Peepers Amateur Home Videos #42: Great American Tails / 1992 / LBO / M • Mr. Peepers Nastiest #4 / 1995 / LBO / C

CARRIE (DOWNS) see Kerri Downs

CARRIE (NIKKI WYLDE) *see* **Nikki Wylde**

CARRIE BITTNER see Alicyn Sterling

CARRIE BREEZE see Alicyn Sterling

CARRIE CONAFFE
Loving Friends / 1975 / AXV / M • Made To Order / 1975 / AXV / M

CARRIE CRUISE see Alicyn Sterling

CARRIE DOWNS
19 & Naughty #1 / 1994 / SKV / M

CARRIE EVANS
GVC: Real Estate #109 / 198? / GO / M

CARRIE FISHER
Amazon Women On The Moon / 1987 / MCA / S • As Cute As They Cum / 1990 / VEX / M • Hollywood Hustle #1 / 1990 / V99 / M • Shampoo / 1975 / CRC / S

CARRIE FOX see Kari Fox

CARRIE JONES
Adult Video News 1992 Awards / 1992 / VC / M • Alley Cats / 1995 / VC / M • American Buttman In London / 1991 / EA / M

CARRIE LEWIN see Star Index I

CARRIE LYONS see Crystal Sync

CARRIE MALONE see Star Index I

CARRIE MITCHELL see Alicyn Sterling

CARRIE STEVENS see Star Index I

CARRIE VASALLE
Creme De Femme / 1994 / 4P / F • More Dirty Debutantes #29 / 1994 / 4P / M • More Dirty Debutantes #33 / 1994 / 4P / M • World Famous Dirty Debutantes / 1995 / 4P / S

CARRY WELTON see Star Index I

CARTER COURTNEY
The Bite / 1975 / SVE / M

CARTER STEVENS *(Steven Mitchell, Steve Mitchell, Mal Worob, Malcolm S. Worob, Gordon O. Duvall, Gordon Duvall, Peter Sutinov)*
Normally an East Coast director with a penchant for B&D but has occasionally performed, including sex, in his own and others' productions.
ABA: Double Feature #5 / 1996 / ALP / M • Ball & Chain / 1994 / GOT / B • Beach House / 1981 / CA / C • Blow Some My Way / 1977 / VHL / M • Candi Girl / 1979 / PVX / M • Cheerleaders In Bondage #2 / 1995 / GOT / B • The Crack Of Dawn / 1989 / CLE / M • Dallas Odyssey: Child / 1995 / VCX / M • Dangerous Desires (Gotham) / 1994 / GOT / B • Dracula Exotica / 1980 / TVX / M • Final Test / 1993 / GOT / B • Forbidden Ways / 1994 / GOT / B • From Holly With Love / 1977 / CA / M • The Fury Inside / 1994 / GOT / B • High School Honeys / 1974 / SOW / M • Home For Unwed Mothers / 1984 / AMB / F • Honeysuckle Rose / 1979 / CA / M • Hot Child In The City / 1979 / PVX / M • Hot Dreams / 1983 / CA / M • Inside Jennifer Welles / 1977 / VXP / M • Losing Control / 1995 / GOT / B • The Love Couch / 1977 / VC / M • Master Of Masters #1 / 1995 / BBB / B • Master's Frenzy / 1994 / GOT / B • Masters Of Dominance / 1996 / GOT / C • Mistress Electra / 1983 / AVO / B • Night Of Submission / 1976 / BIZ / M • Pandora's Mirror / 1981 / CA / M • The Passions Of Carol / 1975 / VXP / M • Platinum Paradise / 1980 / COM / M • Prisoner Of Pleasure / 1981 / ALP / B • Ravaged / 1994 / GOT / B • Raw Deal / 1994 / GOT / B • Salon For Seduction / 1986 / LA / M • Severe Penalties / 1993 / GOT / B • Show No Mercy / 1993 / GOT / B • Slave Traders / 1995 / GOT / B • Spanking It Red / 1993 / GOT / B • Street Girls Of Ny / 19?? / SIL

/ M • Take Off / 1978 / VXP / M • The Tiffany Minx / 1981 / SAT / M • Tormented / 1993 / GOT / B • Twilight Pink #1 / 1980 / AR / M • Twilight Pink #2 / 1982 / VC / M • Twisted Rage / 1995 / GOT / B • Wild Girls / 1994 / GOT / B • [Intimidation / 197? / ... / M

CARTER TWEASEDALE
Daddy's Little Girls / 1983 / CA / M

CARTER WARD
Breastman's Wild West Adventure / 1995 / EVN / M • Hot In The Saddle / 1994 / ERA / M • Safari Jane / 1995 / ERA / M

CARY BLASTUM see Star Index I

CARY CORMAN see Enjil Von Bergdorf

CARY EVANS
My Sister's Husband / 1996 / AWV / G

CARY GAINEY
American Pie / 1980 / SE / M

CARY LACY see Catherine Burgess

CARY MONROE
She-Male Encounters #13: She-Male Reformatory / 1987 / MET / G

CARYN
HomeGrown Video #472: Everyday People / 1996 / HOV / M

CASANDRA
Blue Vanities #569 / 1996 / FFL / M

CASANOVA
Anal Magic / 1995 / XC / M • Mission Hard / 1995 / XC / M • Sex Scandals / 1995 / XC / M

CASEE see Careena Collins

CASEY
A&B AB#506: You Squirt I Squirt #1 / 1995 / A&B / M • A&B AB#514: Elizabeth & Casey & Their Male Sex Slave / 1995 / A&B / M • Breast Worx #10 / 1991 / LBO / M • Intimate Interviews #2 / 1996 / NIT / M • Odyssey 30 Min: Casey And Friend / 1992 / OD / M • Ona Zee's Date With Dallas / 1992 / ONA / M • Rear Entry / 1995 / LEI / M

CASEY (ANGEL L.M.) *(Angel La Monica)*
Pretty brunetten or dark blonde, small tits, tight body and waist, tattoo on left shoulder back and another on left shoulder outside. 20 years old in 1995 but looks younger. Probably around 5'7" based on her height relative to other people. Hard to tell and measures 34-24-34.
Butt Hunt #10 / 1995 / LEI / M • Cherry Poppers #13: Anal Pajama Party / 1996 / ZA / M • Dirty Dirty Debutantes #2 / 1996 / 4P / M • Fashion Sluts #6 / 1995 / ABS / M • Girls Of The Panty Raid / 1995 / VT / M • Interview's Southern Cumfort / 1996 / LV / M • Pick Up Lines #03 / 1995 / 4P / M • Pussy Hunt #11 / 1995 / LEI / M • Up And Cummers #24 / 1995 / 4P / M • Up And Cummers #25 / 1995 / 4P / M • Young Girls Do #2: Sweet Meat / 1995 / CDI / M

CASEY (KRISTA) see Krista

CASEY (WILLIAMS) see Casey Williams

CASEY COOL see K.C. Cool

CASEY DONOVAN *(Calvin Culver)*
Major gay actor of the seventies who appeared in such movies as **Boys In The Sand** and **The Back Row**. Now (1995) dead of AIDS.
L.A. Tool & Die / 1979 / TMX / G • The Opening Of Misty Beethoven / 1976 / VC / M • Score / 1975 / AUD / S

CASEY EDWARDS
Switch Hitters #2: Swinging Both Ways / 1987 / IN / G

CASEY EWING
Weird Fantasy / 1986 / LA / M

CASEY FOX *see* **Casey Williams**

CASEY JONES
New Girls In Town #7 / 1994 / CC / M • Reel Sex #02: Splash Party / 1994 / SPP / M

CASEY JORDON
Driven Home / 1995 / CSP / G • Score Of Sex / 1995 / BAC / G

CASEY KING *see* **Star Index I**

CASEY O'BRIEN
Bi-Athelon / 1993 / BIL / G • Bi-Sex Pleasures / 1993 / PL / G • I'm A Curious She-Male / 1993 / HSV / G • Lady Dick / 1993 / HSV / G • Semper Bi / 1994 / PEP / G • Transsexual Try Outs / 1993 / HSV / G • TV Evangelist / 1993 / HSV / G

CASEY O'TOOLE *see* **Star Index I**

CASEY SHADOWS *see* **Star Index I**

CASEY ST JAMES
Fresh Meat (John Leslie) #2 / 1995 / EA / M • Head Trip / 1995 / VC / M • Virgin Killers: Second Rampage / 1995 / PEP / M

CASEY WILLIAMS *(Casey (Williams), K.C. Williams, Ca See (Williams), Pace Barlow, Tracy (Casey Will.), Casey Fox, Tracey Wolfe, Tracy Wolfe)*
Pace Barlow in **Black On White**. 5'7", 34C-24-34, 21 in 1991. Had breasts enhanced to look like grapefruit in early 1992 (went to 36C).
Acts Of Confession / 1991 / PP / M • Adventures Of Buttwoman #1 / 1991 / EL / F • The Adventures Of Mikki Finn / 1991 / CA / M • The All American Girl / 1991 / PP / M • All That Sex / 1990 / LE / M • Alley Cat / 1991 / CIN / M • Amateur Lesbians #13: Brandi / 1991 / GO / F • Amateur Lesbians #15: Courtney / 1991 / GO / F • Amateur Lesbians #30: Randi / 1992 / GO / F • Americans Most Wanted / 1991 / HO / M • Anal Addiction #3 / 1991 / SO / M • Anal Adventures #1: Anal Executive / 1991 / VC / M • Anal Encounters #8 / 1992 / VC / M • Anything Goes / 1993 / VD / C • As The Spirit Moves You / 1990 / LV / M • Ass Backwards / 1991 / ME / M • Baccarat #2 / 1991 / FH • Beaver Ridge / 1991 / VC / M • Bedtime For Byron / 1991 / ME / M • The Best Of Doctor Butts / 1994 / 4P / C • Big Titted Tarts / 1994 / PL / C • The Big Winner #1 / 1991 / CDP / B • Bigger / 1991 / PL / M • Black On White / 1991 / VT / F • Blonde Ice #1 / 1990 / EX / M • The Boneheads / 1992 / PL / M • Brainteasers / 1991 / ZA / M • Brandy & Alexander / 1991 / VC / M • Breast Wishes #09 / 1992 / LBO / M • Bruce Seven: A Compendium Of His Most Graphic Scenes Vol 1 / 1991 / BS / C • Bubbles / 1991 / IF / M • Bum Rap / 1990 / PLV / B • Bush Pilots #2 / 1991 / VC / M • Bush Wacked / 1991 / ZA / M • Casey At The Bat / 1991 / LV / M • Cat Lickers #1 / 1990 / ME / F • Charlie's Girls #3 / 1991 / CC / M • The Cockateer #2 / 1992 / LE / M • Cream Dream / 1991 / ZA / M • Cyrano / 1991 / PL / M • Debbie Does Wall Street / 1991 / VC / M • Deception / 1991 / XCI / M • Deep Inside Nina Hartley / 1993 / VC / M • Desire / 1990 / VC / M • Digital Lust / 1990 / SE / M • Door To Door / 1990 / EX / M • Double Take / 1991 / BIZ / B • Dr Butts #1 / 1991 / 4P / M • Ebony Love / 1992 / VT / C • Edge Of Sensation / 1990 / LE / M • Edward Penishands #2 / 1991 / VT / M • Edward Penishands #3 / 1991 / VT / M • Eternity / 1991 / CDI / M • Everything Goes /

1990 / SE / M • The Final Secret / 1992 / SO / M • Four Alarm / 1991 / SE / M • Friends & Lovers #2 / 1991 / VT / M • Girls Gone Bad #3: Back To The Slammer / 1991 / GO / F • Girls Just Wanna Have Toys / 1993 / PL / F • Girls Of Sin / 1994 / PL / C • Gorgeous / 1990 / CA / M • Head Talk / 1991 / ZA / M • Heatseekers / 1991 / IN / M • Hot Shots / 1992 / VD / C • Hothouse Rose #1 / 1991 / VC / M • How To Love Your Lover / 1992 / XII / S • Hunchback Of Notre Dame / 1991 / PL / M • Imagine / 1991 / LV / M • In The Jeans Again / 1990 / ME / M • Innocence Found / 1991 / PAL / G • Jail Babes #2: Bustin' Out / 1992 / PL / F • Killer Looks / 1991 / VI / M • Lethal Passion / 1991 / PL / M • Lick My Lips / 1990 / LV / M • Lifeguard / 1991 / VI / M • Little Big Dong / 1992 / ZA / M • A Little Christmas Tail / 1991 / ZA / M • Live Bait / 1990 / IN / M • Loose Lips / 1990 / VC / M • Madame X / 1990 / EX / M • Made In Heaven / 1991 / PP / M • Malibu Spice / 1991 / VC / M • Manbait #2 / 1992 / VC / M • The Mark Of Zara / 1990 / XCI / M • Married With Hormones #1 / 1991 / PL / M • Meat Market / 1992 / SEX / C • The Midas Touch / 1991 / VT / M • Mirage #2 / 1992 / VC / M • Miss 21st Century / 1991 / ZA / M • More Dirty Debutantes #05 / 1990 / 4P / M • More Dirty Debutantes #12 / 1991 / 4P / M • Naked Goddess #2 / 1991 / VC / M • Never Never Land / 1992 / PL / M • Night With A Vampire / 1992 / MID / M • No Man's Land #05 / 1992 / VT / F • No Time For Love / 1991 / VI / M • Nothing But Trouble / 1991 / CIN / M • Nothing Personal / 1990 / IN / M • Object Of Desire / 1991 / FAZ / M • Only The Very Best On Video / 1992 / VC / C • Oral Clinic / 1990 / DAY / M • The Pamela Principle #1 / 1992 / IMP / S • Party Pack #1 / 1990 / LE / F • Penthouse: 1993 Pet Of The Year Playoff / 1993 / PET / F • Penthouse: 1993 Pet Of The Year Winners / 1993 / PET / F • Penthouse: The Girls Of Penthouse #3 / 1995 / PET / S • Prisoner Of Lust / 1991 / VC / F • Puttin' Her Ass On The Line / 1991 / DR / M • Puttin' Out / 1992 / VD / M • Rainbows / 1992 / VT / F • Satin Shadows / 1991 / CIN / M • Scenes From A Crystal Ball / 1992 / ZA / M • The Screamer / 1991 / CA / M • Sex Scenes / 1992 / VD / C • Sexual Intent / 1990 / PP / M • Shanna's Final Fling / 1991 / ME / M • Shattered / 1991 / LE / M • She Likes To Watch / 1992 / EVN / M • A Shot In The Mouth #2 / 1991 / ME / M • Silk Elegance / 1991 / VIM / M • Simply Irresistible / 1991 / CIN / M • Slow Burn / 1991 / VC / M • The Smart Ass Vacation / 1990 / VT / M • Soft Tail / 1991 / IN / M • Southern Comfort / 1991 / CIN / M • Speedtrap / 1992 / VC / M • Spread Sheets / 1991 / DR / M • Stake Out / 1991 / CIN / M • Starr / 1991 / CA / M • Steal Breeze / 1990 / SO / M • Summer Break / 1991 / PP / C • Talk Dirty To Me #08 / 1990 / DR / M • A Taste Of K.C. Williams / 1992 / VD / C • The Tasting / 1991 / EX / M • Temptation Eyes / 1991 / VT / M • Tori Welles Goes Behind The Scenes / 1992 / FD / M • Total Exposure / 1992 / CDI / M • True Legends Of Adult Cinema: The Modern Era / 1992 / VC / C • Uninhibited / 1993 / ANT / S • Used Cars / 1990 / CDI / M • Vegas #4: Joker's Wild / 1990 / CDI / M • The Vision / 1991 / LE / M • Walking Small

/ 1992 / ZA / M • Warm To The Touch / 1990 / CDI / M • Wenches / 1991 / VT / F • Where The Girls Sweat #2 / 1991 / EL / F • Wild & Wicked #2 / 1992 / VT / M • Wild Goose Chase / 1990 / EA / M • Women Of Color / 1991 / PL / F • Wrapped Up / 1992 / VD / C

CASEY WINTERS *see* **Star Index I**

CASH (BLACK)
Black Cheerleader Search #07 / 1996 / IVC / M • Black Street Hookers #1 / 1996 / DFI / M • I Wanna Be A Porn Star #1 / 1996 / 4P / M

CASH (SUE) *see* **Sue Cash**

CASH HAMILTON
Devil's Ecstasy / 1974 / VCX / M

CASH MARKMAN
Goldenbush / 1996 / AVI / M

CASHA (SUE) *see* **Sue Cash**

CASHA RAE *see* **Star Index I**

CASHMERE
Girlz Towne #09 / 1995 / FC / F • Pussy Power #04 / 1992 / BTO / M

CASMIR ROSE *see* **Star Index I**

CASPER
AVP #2003: Menage A Trois #2 / 1990 / AVP / M • AVP #3002: The Good Bi Girls / 1990 / AVP / M • AVP #7029: Not Just Another Saturday Night / 1991 / AVP / M • AVP #9109: Have-A-Ball Bar / 1991 / AVP / M • Back East Babes #2 / 1996 / NIT / M

CASSANDRA
Bum Rap / 1990 / PLV / B • Cassandra's Punishment #1 / 1994 / GAL / B • Crazy Lust / 1994 / ORE / C • Double Take / 1991 / BIZ / B • Eurotica #08 / 1996 / XC / M • For The Hell Of It / 1992 / BS / B • Girls Around The World #11 / 199? / BTO / S • Golden Arches / 1992 / PRE / B • H&S: Cassandra / 199? / H&S / M • Hot Foot / 1991 / PLV / B • Mickey Ray's Sex Search #01: Sliding In / 1994 / WIV / M • More Than Friends / 1989 / FAZ / M • Popped Tarts / 1992 / RB / B • Private Film #18 / 1994 / OD / M • Pussyman Auditions #17 / 1995 / SNA / M • Rusty Boner's Late Night Videos #1 / 1995 / RHV / M • Severity / 1996 / BON / B • Studio Of Lust / 1984 / HO / C • Tailz From Da Hood #4 / 1996 / AVI / M • Tailz From Da Hood #5 / 1996 / AVI / M • Titty-Titty Bang-Bang / 1992 / FC / C • Topless Lightweight Spectacular: Alex Jordan Vs. Tina... / 1994 / VSL / B • Tropic Of Passion / 1971 / NGV / M • Virgins Of Video #06 / 1993 / YDI / M • Whoeros' / 1996 / BEP / M

CASSANDRA (DARK) *see* **Cassandra Dark**

CASSANDRA CAPPUCI *(Cassandra Capucci)*
Boobs, Butts And Bloopers #2 / 1990 / HO / M • Down And Out / 1995 / PRE / B • The Eliminators / 1991 / BIZ / B • Happy Endings / 1990 / BIZ / B • Hot Flushes / 1992 / PRE / B • Leg...Ends #06 / 1992 / PRE / F • The Specialist / 1990 / HO / M • Sweet Cheeks (1991-Prestige) / 1991 / PRE / B • Three Men And A Geisha / 1990 / HO / M

CASSANDRA CAPUCCI *see* **Cassandra Cappuci**

CASSANDRA CURTIS
Dream Lust / 1995 / NIT / M

CASSANDRA CURVES
Black & Blue / 1995 / NAP / B • Black Bamboo / 1995 / IN / M • Black Hollywood Amateurs #24 / 1996 / MID / M • Black Jack

City #5 / 1995 / HW / M • Black Juice Bombs / 1996 / NIT / C • Black Knockers #03 / 1995 / TV / M • Black Knockers #09 / 1995 / TV / M • Black Knockers #14 / 1995 / TV / M • Black Mamas At War / 1996 / NAP / B • Busty Porno Stars #2 / 1996 / H&S / M • Dangerous Behinds #1 / 1995 / HW / M • Dark Eyes / 1995 / FC / M • Girlz N The Hood #5 / 1995 / HW / M • Hooter Tutor / 1996 / APP / M • Interview: Chocolate Treats / 1995 / LV / M • Mistress 'n Da Hood / 1995 / VT / B • Nasty Newcummers #11 / 1995 / MET / M • The Panty Parlor / 1996 / VIM / M • Pussyman Auditions #10 / 1995 / SNA / M • Sista! #3 / 1995 / VT / F • Sistaz In Chains / 1995 / VT / B • Sittin' On Da Krome / 1995 / HW / M • Wacky Weekend / 1995 / SUF / M

CASSANDRA DARK *(Cassandra (Dark), Raven Bates, Lucinda (C. Dark), Cassandra Lin, China (C. Dark))*
Brunette with slightly Oriental overtones.
Amateur Lesbians #01: Leanna / 1991 / GO / F • Amateur Lesbians #03: April / 1991 / GO / F • Amateur Lesbians #12: Kimberly / 1991 / GO / F • Amateur Lesbians #29: Ari / 1992 / GO / F • Amateur Nights #02 / 1989 / HO / M • Amazons From Burbank / 1990 / PL / F • Anal Cuties #1 / 1992 / ROB / M • Anal Cuties #2 / 1992 / ROB / M • Anal Cuties #3 / 1992 / ROB / M • The Audition / 1992 / BON / B • Babes With Attitudes / 1990 / EVN / M • Behind You All The Way #2 / 1990 / SO / M • Between My Breasts #11 / 1990 / BTO / M • Bionca, Just For You / 1989 / BON / F • Bloopers #2 / 1991 / GO / C • Bondage Cheerleaders / 1993 / LON / B • Bondage Memories #03 / 1994 / BON / C • Boobs, Butts And Bloopers #2 / 1990 / HO / M • Bottoms Up (1993-Bon Vue) / 1993 / BON / B • Bus Stop Tales #05 / 1989 / PRI / M • Bus Stop Tales #07 / 1989 / PRI / M • Bus Stop Tales #11 / 1990 / 4P / M • Busted / 1989 / CA / M • Crunch Bunch / 1995 / PRE / C • Deep Inside Dirty Debutantes #06 / 1993 / 4P / M • Deep Inside Victoria / 1992 / CDI / C • Disoriented / 1992 / VI / M • Dr Finger's House Of Forbidden Dreams / 1992 / VI / M • Girls Of The Double D #07 / 1989 / CIN / M • Girls, Girls And More Girls / 1990 / LV / F • Grand Slam / 1990 / PRE / B • Hawaii Vice #7 / 1989 / CDI / M • Hawaii Vice #8 / 1990 / CIN / M • The Heat Of The Moment / 1990 / IN / M • The Honeymoon: The Bride's Running Behind / 1990 / 4P / M • Hot Cherries / 1990 / CC / F • I'll Take The Whip / 1993 / BON / B • In The Can / 1990 / EX / M • Innocent Obsession / 1989 / FC / M • The Magic Box / 1990 / SO / M • Master Plan / 198? / BON / B • Mike Hott: #153 Cassandra Solo / 1991 / MHV / F • Mike Hott: #154 Cassandra And Dusty #1 / 1991 / MHV / F • Mike Hott: #155 Cassandra And Dusty #2 / 1991 / MHV / F • Moondance / 1991 / WV / M • More Dirty Debutantes #08 / 1991 / 4P / M • More Dirty Debutantes #12 / 1991 / 4P / M • More Dirty Debutantes #14 / 1992 / 4P / M • Next Door Neighbors #08 / 1990 / BON / M • Odyssey 30 Min: #112: / 1991 / OD / M • Odyssey Amateur #63: Pussy, Pussy Everywhere! / 1991 / OD / M • Odyssey Amateur #66: Eat The One You're With / 1991 / OD / M • Old Fashioned

Spankings / 1991 / BON / B • Party Pack #1 / 1990 / LE / F • Passionate Lips / 1990 / OD / M • Pleasure Is My Business / 1989 / EX / M • Rock Me / 1990 / LE / F • Sex Crazy / 1989 / FAN / C • Stephanie, Just For You / 1989 / BON / F • Sudden Urge / 1990 / IN / M • Taboo #08 / 1990 / IN / M • Tit Tales #1 / 1989 / 4P / M • Val Girls / 1990 / PL / F • Vegas #1: Royal Flush / 1990 / CIN / M • Wicked Wenches / 1991 / LV / M • Wild Fire / 1990 / WV / C • Will And Ed's Bogus Gang Bang / 1992 / MID / M

CASSANDRA DEAN *see Star Index I*

CASSANDRA DEL RIO *(Kassandra del Rio, Cassandra Del Rio)*
This is a she-male.
Kiss It Goodbye / 1991 / SE / M • The National Transsexual / 1990 / GO / G • Parliament: Hard TV #1 / 1988 / PM / G • She-Male Encounters #13: She-Male Reformatory / 1987 / MET / G • She-Male Sex Clinic / 1991 / VC / G • She-Male Showgirls / 1992 / STA / G • She-Male Solos #06 / 1990 / LEO / G • She Male Spirits Of The Night / 1991 / VC / G • Trisexual Encounters #05 / 1986 / PL / G • Trisexual Encounters #06 / 1987 / PL / G • The Ultimate Sex / 1992 / MET / G

CASSANDRA DEL RIO *see* **Cassandra del Rio**

CASSANDRA LEE (VICT) *see* **Victoria Lee**

CASSANDRA LEIGH
Not to be confused with Lisa Boyle(s) who used the name Cassandra Leigh in **Midnight Tease**.
Bunny's Office Fantasies / 1984 / VC / M • Caged Heat 3000 / 1995 / NEH / S • Candy Stripers 3 / 1986 / AR / M • Decadence / 1986 / VD / M • Driller / 1984 / VC / M • The Hot Tip / 1986 / VXP / M • Playpen / 1987 / VC / M • Public Affairs / 1984 / CA / M • Pussycat Galore / 1984 / VC / M • Raw Talent #1 / 1984 / VC / M • Raw Talent #2 / 1987 / VC / M • Sex Spa USA / 1984 / VC / M • Snake Eyes #1 / 1984 / COM / M • Urban Heat / 1985 / FEM / M • VCA Previews #4 / 1988 / VC / C

CASSANDRA LIN *see* **Cassandra Dark**

CASSANDRA O.
Cum To Drink Of It / 1996 / BCP / M • The Cumm Brothers #10: Night Of The Giving Head / 1995 / OD / M • The Doctor Is In #3: Achy Breaky Tarts / 1995 / NIT / M • Hard Cum Cafe / 1996 / BCP / M • Pussy Fest Of The Northwest #4 / 1995 / NIT / M • Pussy Fest Of The Northwest #5 / 1995 / NIT / M • Sex Lessons / 1996 / NIT / M • The Sodomizer #2 / 1995 / SC / M

CASSANDRA PETERS *see Star Index I*

CASSANDRA STARK *see Star Index I*

CASSANDRA VIPER
The Ultimate She-Male / 1995 / LEO / G

CASSE
Crazy Times / 1995 / BS / B

CASSIDY *(Rebecca (Cassidy))*
Brunette with good skin, pretty face, small but adequate breasts—a little hefty on the thighs. Under the Rebecca name she's a blonde (also in **Anal Storm**). As of mid 1993, she swas supposedly working for Sean Michaels in some administrative capacity.
The A Chronicles / 1992 / CC / M • Alice In Hollywierd / 1992 / ZA / M • Amateur Lesbians #22: Cassidy / 1992 / GO / F • Amer-

ica's Raunchiest Home Videos #18: Anal Crunch / 1992 / ZA / M • Anal Intruder #06: The Anal Twins / 1992 / CC / M • Anal Storm / 1991 / ZA / M • The Anals Of History #1 / 1991 / MID / M • Anything That Moves / 1992 / VC / M • Ass-Capades / 1992 / HW / M • Back In The Pen / 1992 / FH / M • The Backway Inn #1 / 1992 / FD / M • The Bare-Assed Naked Gun / 1992 / MID / M • Betrayal / 1992 / XCI / M • Biff Malibu's Totally Nasty Home Videos #02 / 1992 / ANA / M • Biggies #04 / 1992 / XPI / M • Book Of Love / 1992 / VC / M • Butt Woman #3 / 1992 / FH / M • Butt's Up, Doc #3 / 1992 / GO / M • Buttman Vs Buttwoman / 1992 / EL / M • Cat & Mouse #1 / 1992 / XCI / M • Committed / 1992 / LE / M • Cumming Clean / 1991 / FL / M • Diver Down / 1992 / CC / M • Erotica / 1992 / CC / M • The Exhibitionist / 1991 / VD / M • Fast Girls #3 / 1992 / XPI / M • Full Blown / 1992 / GO / M • Gerein' Up / 1992 / VC / M • Girlz N The Hood #2 / 1992 / HW / M • Head Talk / 1991 / ZA / M • Hot Pie Delivery / 1993 / AFV / M • In Your Face #2 / 1992 / PL / M • Jungle Jive / 1992 / VD / M • Just For Tonight / 1992 / VC / M • Laying Down The Law #2 / 1992 / AFV / M • Lesbians In Tight Shorts / 1992 / LV / F • Miss 21st Century / 1991 / ZA / M • Mr. Peepers Amateur Home Videos #02: Bachelorette Party / 1991 / LBO / M • Mr. Peepers Amateur Home Videos #43: Gym-Nastiness / 1992 / LBO / M • Mr. Peepers Amateur Home Videos #49: Up And Cumming #2 / 1992 / LBO / M • Night Creatures / 1992 / PL / M • Nurse Nancy / 1991 / CA / M • A Pussy Called Wanda #1 / 1992 / DR / M • Ready Freddy? / 1992 / FH / M • Romancing The Butt / 1992 / ATL / M • The Seduction Of Mary / 1992 / VC / M • Sex Under Glass / 1992 / VC / M • Sexual Instinct #1 / 1992 / DR / M • Silver Sensations / 1992 / VT / M • Spanish Fly / 1992 / LE / M • Tickets To Paradise / 1992 / XPI / M • Uncle Roy's Amateur Home Video #03 / 1992 / VIM / M • Uncle Roy's Amateur Home Video #04 / 1992 / VIM / M • Uncle Roy's Best Of The Best: Brown Eyes Only / 1992 / VIM / C • Up For Grabs / 1991 / FH / M • Waterbabies #2 / 1992 / CC / M • White Men Can't Hump / 1992 / CC / M

CASSIDY (1996)
Decadent Dreams / 1996 / ME / M • Lisa / 1997 / SC / M • New Pussy Hunt #18 / 1995 / LEI / C • Pick Up Lines #11 / 1997 / OD / M • Sweet Things / 1996 / FF / C

CASSIE
A&B AB#355: Pantyhose Lovers / 1991 / A&B / M • Butt Bangers Ball #2 / 1996 / TTV / M • Mistress Memoirs #2 / 1993 / PL / C

CASSIE BLAKE *see* **Gina Gianetti**
CASSIE NOVA *see* **Kassi Nova**
CASSIE WILLIAMS
Velvet / 1995 / SPI / M

CASSIEY
Women Behaving Badly / 1996 / RAS / M
CASSINOVA *see* **Kassi Nova**
CASSIS POIVRE
The French Touch / 1984 / NSV / M

CAT
Bondage Models #2 / 1996 / JAM / B • Dirty & Kinky Mature Women #09 / 1996 / C69 / M • Homegrown Video #395 / 1993 / HOV / M • HomeGrown Video #458: Cream Pie

For Dessert / 1995 / HOV / C
CAT DALTON *see Star Index I*
CAT GERLIN
Sweet Paradise / 1980 / ELV / M
CAT TAILER
Score Busty Centerfolds #2 / 1995 / BTO / M
CAT THOMAS *see Star Index I*
CATALINA (BLACK)
African Angels #1 / 1996 / NIT / M
CATALINA (CRYSTAL G) *see* **Crystal Gold**
CATALINA D'AMOUR
American Sushi / 1996 / CHP / F • Best Exotic Dancers In The Usa / 1995 / PME / S • Blonde Busty & Bound / 1996 / VTF / B • Bondage Check-Up / 1996 / VTF / B • Catalina D'Amour: Beach Bunny Masturbator / 1996 / CHP / F • Catalina D'Amour: Bound & Tickled In San Francisco / 1996 / CLA / B • Catalina D'Amour: Hawaii Sex-O / 1996 / CLA / M • Catalina D'Amour: Screwing Uncle Mike / 1996 / CLA / M • Catalina D'Amour: Sexercise / 1996 / CHP / F • Catalina Bound / 1996 / VTF / B • Charm: Dominant Bitch #1 / 1996 / CHP / M • Charm: Hot Nympho Slut / 1996 / CHP / M • Hostage Bound / 1996 / VTF / B • Porsche's Ordeal / 1996 / LBO / B • Shockers / 1996 / SBP / B
CATALINE BULLOCKS
Private Gold #01: Study In Sex / 1995 / OD / M • Private Gold #02: Friends In Sex / 1995 / OD / M • Private Stories #03 / 1995 / OD / M • Private Stories #07 / 1996 / OD / M
CATERINA ALTIERI
Juliet & Romeo / 1996 / XC / M • Robin Thief Of Wives / 1996 / XC / M
CATERINA RINALDI
All Grown Up / 1996 / XC / M • Pussyman #14: Dreams Of A Gigolo / 1996 / SNA / M • Virility / 1996 / XC / M
CATHERINE
Erotic Westernscapes / 1994 / PHV / S • Euromania #2 / 1996 / AOC / M • Northwest Pecker Trek #6: Two Girls For Every Boy / 1995 / LBO / M
CATHERINE BURGESS *(Cary Lacy, Catherine Earnshaw, Catherine Erhardt)*
Passable face, wiry blonde hair, medium droopy tits, womanly body, good tan lines. Catherine Erhardt is from **Cinderella 2000** and Cary Lacy from **Expose Me Lovely**.
Cinderella 2000 / 1977 / SVI / S • The Double Exposure Of Holly / 1977 / TVX / M • Expose Me, Lovely / 1976 / QX / M • Through The Looking Glass / 1976 / ALP / M
CATHERINE CASTEL
[Vibrations Sensuelles / 1976 / ... / M
CATHERINE COMBAS *see Star Index I*
CATHERINE CRYSTAL *see* **Shannon (s/m)**
CATHERINE DREW
Sinderotica / 1985 / HO / M • The Wizard Of AHH's / 1985 / SE / M
CATHERINE DRICHESSE *see Star Index I*
CATHERINE EARNSHAW *see* **Catherine Burgess**
CATHERINE ERHARDT *see* **Catherine Burgess**
CATHERINE FARRONI *see Star Index I*
CATHERINE KELLY

Creme De La Face #07 / 1995 / OD / M • Creme De La Face #11: Cum Plasterers / 1995 / OD / M • Cum To Drink Of It / 1996 / BCP / M • The Cumm Brothers #13: Rump Rangers / 1996 / OD / M • The Cumm Brothers #16: Deja Goo / 1996 / OD / M • High Heeled & Horny #2 / 1995 / LBO / M • Nothing Like Nurse Nookie #3 / 1996 / NIT / M • Nothing Like Nurse Nookie #5 / 1996 / NIT / M • Sex Lessons / 1996 / NIT / M • Sorority Slumber Sluts / 1995 / WIV / F • Teacher's Pet #2 / 1994 / WMG / M
CATHERINE MARIE *see Star Index I*
CATHERINE MARSILE *see Star Index I*
CATHERINE OSBORNE
Love Lips / 1976 / VC / M
CATHERINE REYNOLDS
Feels Like Silk / 1983 / SE / M
CATHERINE RIVET *see Star Index I*
CATHERINE WARREN *see Star Index I*
CATHLEEN COLLINS *see* **Bo Derek**
CATHLEEN RAYMOND *see* **Gabrielle Scream**
CATHLYN MOORE *see* **Cher Delight**
CATHY
Amateur Nights #10 / 1990 / HO / M • Blue Vanities #112 / 1988 / FFL / M • Blue Vanities #505 / 1992 / FFL / M • Blue Vanities #507 / 1992 / FFL / M • Blue Vanities #525 / 1993 / FFL / M • Blue Vanities #527 / 1993 / FFL / M • Blue Vanities #541 / 1994 / FFL / M • Blue Vanities #566 / 1995 / FFL / M • Blue Vanities #579 / 1995 / FFL / M • Bottoms Up #04 / 1983 / AVC / C • Girls Of France / 1991 / BTO / M • Tit To Tit #2 / 1994 / BTO / M
CATHY CARTWRIGHT *see Star Index I*
CATHY CHO
Snared For Submission / 1995 / BON / B
CATHY COFER
Flesh & Laces #1 / 1983 / CA / M
CATHY COLLINS
Against All Bods / 1991 / VEX / M • Much More Than A Mouthful #4 / 1994 / VEX / M • Pony Girl #1: In Harness / 1985 / CS / B • Positively Pagan #01 / 1991 / ATA / M • Positively Pagan #05 / 1993 / ATA / M • Positively Pagan #11 / 1993 / ATA / M • Positively Pagan #12 / 1993 / ATA / M • Robin Head / 1991 / CC / M • Sweet Stuff / 1991 / V99 / M
CATHY CUNNSUGLER
Love In Strange Places / 1977 / CA / M
CATHY EBELT
Ultraflesh / 1980 / GO / M
CATHY GOLDBERG
Girl Crazy / 1989 / CDI / F
CATHY GRENIER *see Star Index I*
CATHY MENARD
Diamond Snatch / 1977 / COM / M • French Taboo / 1985 / ABV / M • Hot Bodies (Caballero) / 1984 / CA / M • Laura's Desires / 1978 / CA / M • Naughty Fantasy / 1986 / CA / M • Sexual Initiation Of A Married Woman / 1984 / VD / M • Take My Body / 1984 / SE / M
CATHY NELLMAN *see Star Index I*
CATHY PARKER
The Love Witch / 1973 / AR / M
CATHY PATRICK
Big Bust Scream Queens / 1994 / BTO / M • Girls Around The World #14 / 199? / BTO / M • Plumper Therapy / 1995 / BTO / M • Studio Bust Out / 1994 / BTO / M • Zena Hardcore Special / 1994 / BTO / M
CATHY REMUND

Ultraflesh / 1980 / GO / M
CATHY SPILLANE
[Sex Secretaries / 197? / ... / M
CATHY STEVENS *see Star Index I*
CATHY STEWART
Come Play With Me #1 / 1979 / PS / S • French Taboo / 1985 / ABV / M • Looking Good / 1984 / ABV / M • Sextasy / 1978 / COM / M • Two At Once / 1978 / CV / M
CATHY TAVEL *see Star Index I*
CATHY WALKER
The Case Of The Full Moon Murders / 1971 / SOW / M
CATHY ZURITS
Ready To Drop #01 / 1990 / FC / M
CATLYN ASHLEY *see* **Kaitlyn Ashley**
CATMAN
More Dirty Debutantes #60 / 1997 / SBV / M
CATRINA
Frat House / 1979 / NGV / M • Sodomania #13: Your Lucky Number / 1995 / EL / M
CATRINA JAMES *see Star Index I*
CATUCHITA *see Star Index I*
CAZANDER ZIM *see Star Index I*
CECE MALONE *see* **Jennifer West**
CECELIA WILSON
On White Satin / 1980 / VCX / M
CECIL B. WATKINS
Kym Wilde's On The Edge #33 / 1996 / RB / B
CECIL HOWARD *(H. Oscar Ward, Ward Summers)*
Normally a director.
Fantasex / 1976 / COM / M • Firestorm #1 / 1984 / COM / M • Foxtrot / 1982 / COM / M • Georgia Peach / 1977 / COM / M • Heat Wave / 1977 / COM / M • Justine: A Matter Of Innocence / 1980 / SAT / M • Neon Nights / 1981 / COM / M • Platinum Paradise / 1980 / COM / M • Scoundrels / 1982 / COM / M
CECIL JOHNSON *see* **Scott Johnson**
CECILA
Anal Tramps / 1996 / LIP / F • Blush: Dykestyles #2: Dress Up For Daddy / 1993 / FAT / F
CECILE
Black small girl, nice body, light skin, braces on teeth and a scar on her right abdomen.
Black Valley Girls #2 / 1989 / DR / M
CECILE (EUROPE)
Jamie's French Debutantes / 1992 / PL / B • On The Prowl In Paris / 1992 / SC / M • Penetration (Anabolic) #1 / 1995 / ANA / M • Triple X Video Magazine #14 / 1996 / OD / M
CECILE DEVILLE
Layover / 1985 / HO / M • Naughty Cheerleaders / 1985 / HO / M • Society Affairs / 1982 / CA / M • Working Girls / 1985 / CA / M
CECILIA GARDNER *see Star Index I*
CECILIA GROUT
Private Gold #06: Cape Town #2 / 1996 / OD / M • Private Gold #07: Kruger Park / 1996 / OD / M • Triple X Video Magazine #13 / 1996 / OD / M • Triple X Video Magazine #15 / 1996 / OD / M
CECILLE MORLES *see Star Index I*
CECILY *see Star Index I*
CEDAR HOUSTON
Lickity Split / 1974 / COM / M
CELENE
Anal Alley / 1996 / FD / M
CELESTE

Not too pretty big brunette with small tits and a hefty body. Some say she resembles Cindy Crawford but I can't see it myself. Had her tits enhanced to rock-solid cantaloupe size and her nose fixed. Comes from Stillwater MN and in 1995 her measurements were 34DD-23-34. Worked as a dancer in Deja Vu in Minneapolis. SO of Woody Long then mid-1995 divorced from Woody and married Paul Norman. Has at least one child by Paul Norman but now separated or divorced from him.

10,000 Anal Maniacs #1 / 1993 / FOR / M • Alexandria, I Love You / 1993 / AFV / M • America's Raunchiest Home Videos #37: Learning Her Lesson / 1992 / ZA / M • Anal Ski Vacation / 1993 / ANA / M • Anniversary / 1992 / FOR / M • Back To Anal Alley / 1994 / ME / M • Backdoor Brides #4 / 1993 / PV / M • Backdoor To Harley-Wood #3 / 1993 / AFV / M • Badgirls #6: Ridin' Into Town / 1995 / VI / M • Bedlam / 1995 / WAV / M • The Best Of Buttslammers / 1995 / BS / C • The Bet / 1993 / VT / M • Biff Malibu's Totally Nasty Home Videos #18 / 1992 / ANA / M • Big Town / 1993 / PP / M • Black Tie Affair / 1993 / VEX / M • Borderline (Vivid) / 1995 / VI / M • Bosoms Are For Loving / 1994 / NAP / C • Breast Worx #37 / 1992 / LBO / M • Buffy Malibu's Totally Nasty All-Girl Home Videos #01 / 1992 / ANA / F • Buffy Malibu's Totally Nasty All-Girl Home Videos #02 / 1992 / ANA / F • The Bust Things In Life Are Free / 1994 / NAP / S • Bustin' Thru / 1993 / LV / M • Butt Freak #1 / 1992 / EA / M • Buttslammers #02: The Awakening Of Felicia / 1993 / BS / F • Captured Beauty / 1995 / SAE / B • Casanova #3 / 1993 / SC / M • Caught In The Act (1995-Wave) / 1995 / WAV / M • Chain Gang / 1994 / OD / F • Chateau Du Cheeks / 1994 / VC / M • Crazy With The Heat #3 / 1994 / CV / M • Dangerous Curves / 1995 / VC / M • Deep Cover / 1993 / WP / M • Deep Inside Nicole London / 1995 / VC / C • Defending Your Sex Life / 1992 / LE / M • Dial N Again / 1993 / PEP / M • Dial N For Nikki / 1993 / PEP / M • The Dinner Party #1 / 1994 / ULI / M • Dripping With Desire / 1992 / DR / M • Elements Of Desire / 1994 / VI / M • 1994 Annual AVN Awards / 1994 / VC / M • Erotic Eye / 1995 / DGD / S • Euroslut #1: French Tart / 1993 / CC / M • Exposure / 1995 / WAV / M • Haunted Nights / 1993 / WP / M • Heavenscent / 1993 / ZA / M • Heidi Does Hollywood / 1993 / AFV / M • Hidden Obsessions / 1992 / BFP / M • Hollywood Ho' House / 1994 / VC / M • Hollywood Scandal: The Heidi Flesh Story / 1993 / IP / M • Hot & Horny Amateurs #4 / 1994 / … / M • I Made Marian / 1993 / PEP / M • Immortal Desire / 1993 / VI / M • Just A Gigolo / 1992 / SC / M • Kinky Cameraman #4 / 1996 / LEI / C • Lacy's Hot Anal Summer / 1992 / LV / M • Leena Goes Pro / 1992 / VT / M • The Look / 1993 / WP / M • The Makeup Room #2 / 1992 / VC / M • My Secret Lover / 1992 / XCI / M • The Natural / 1993 / VT / M • Never On A Sunday / 1995 / CVI / C • No Man's Land #06 / 1992 / VT / F • Nobody's Looking / 1993 / VC / M • Notorious / 1992 / SC / M • Nylon / 1995 / VI / M • The Orgy #1 / 1993 / EMC / M • The Orgy #2 / 1993 / EMC / M • The Orgy #3 / 1993 / EMC / M • The Original Wicked Woman /

1993 / WP / M • Pajama Party X #2 / 1994 / VC / M • Penthouse: Forum Letters #2 / 1994 / A*V / S • Plan 69 From Outer Space / 1993 / CA / M • The Poetry Of The Flesh / 1993 / PEP / M • Poison / 1994 / VI / M • Poor Little Rich Girl #1 / 1992 / XCI / M • Poor Little Rich Girl #2 / 1992 / XCI / M • Porn In The Pen / 1993 / LE / F • Pussyman #03: The Search Continues / 1993 / SNA / M • Pussyman #04: The Celebration / 1993 / SNA / M • Radio-Active / 1992 / SC / M • Raunch #08 / 1993 / CC / M • Reckless Passion / 1995 / WAV / M • Reds / 1993 / LE / F • Saturday Night Porn #3 / 1993 / AFV / M • The Seduction Of Julia Ann / 1993 / VT / M • Sex On The Strip: The Lusty Ladies Of Las Vagas / 1993 / CPG / F • Sex Under Glass / 1992 / VC / M • Sexdrive #1: Topdown Girl / 1993 / OD / M • Sexual Athlete / 1993 / CAW / B • Sexy Nurses #2 / 1994 / CV / M • Seymore Butts In The Love Shack / 1992 / FH / M • Seymore Butts: Bustin' Out My Best Anal / 1995 / FH / C • Shiver / 1993 / FOR / M • Sindy Does Anal / 1993 / AFV / M • Sindy Does Anal Again / 1994 / AFV / M • Sindy's Sexercise Workout / 1994 / AFV / M • Single Tight Female / 1992 / LV / M • Soap Me Up! / 1993 / FD / M • Southern Cumfort / 1993 / HO / M • Stasha's Adult School / 1993 / CDI / G • Stocking Stuffers / 1992 / LV / M • Student Fetish Videos: Best of Catfighting #02 / 1994 / PRE / C • Student Fetish Videos: Best Of Foot Worship #02 / 1994 / PRE / C • Student Fetish Videos: Best Of Spanking #02 / 1993 / PRE / C • Student Fetish Videos: Catfighting #06 / 1992 / PRE / B • The Submission Of Felecia / 1993 / BS / B • Thinking Of You / 1992 / LV / F • Tongue In Cheek #02 / 1995 / HO / C • Toppers #18 / 1993 / TV / M • Toppers #19 / 1993 / TV / M • Toppers #21 / 1993 / TV / C • Toppers #24 / 1994 / TV / M • Toppers #32 / 1994 / TV / C • Toppers & Whoppers #2 / 1994 / PRE / C • Tortured Passions / 1994 / PL / B • The Torturous Infidel / 1994 / PL / B • Trouble Maker / 1995 / VI / M • Ultimate Orgy #1 / 1992 / GLI / M • Ultra Head / 1992 / CA / M • Unfaithful Entry / 1992 / DR / M • Unnatural / 1992 / CC / M • Up And Cummers #04 / 1993 / 4P / M • War Of The Big Busted Bondo Babes / 1994 / NAP / B • Warm Pink / 1992 / LE / M • Welcome To Bondage: Celeste / 1993 / BON / B • Wicked Women / 1993 / ME / M • Wild Innocence / 1992 / PL / M • [Digtown / 1993 / PP / M

CELESTE (BLACK)
African Angels #2 / 1996 / NIT / M • Amateur Black: Whores / 1996 / SUF / M • Black Cheerleader Search #03 / 1996 / ROB / M • Black Juice Bombs / 1996 / NIT / C • Creme De La Face #13: Nine Nasty Nymphs / 1995 / OD / M

CELESTE (EARLY)
Blue Vanities #116 / 1988 / FFL / M • John Holmes, The Lost Films / 1988 / PEN / C • A Party In My Tight Pussy / 1994 / MET / M • Sally's Palace Of Delight / cr76 / CV / M

CELESTE CREW *see Star Index I*
CELESTE WILLINGS
Under The Cum Cum Tree / 1996 / BCP / M

CELIA
Breast Worx #28 / 1992 / LBO / M • Magma: Anal Teenies / 1994 / MET / M

CELIA DARGENT *see Star Index I*
CELIA VETTI *see Star Index I*
CELIA YOUNG
Committed suicide in early 1992.
All That Sex / 1990 / LE / M • Cat Lickers #1 / 1990 / ME / F • Dr Jeckel & Ms Hide / 1990 / LV / M • Party Pack #1 / 1990 / LE / F • Wet 'n' Working / 1990 / EA / F

CELINA
Deep Behind The Scenes With Seymore Butts #2 / 1995 / ULI / M

CELINA (SELINA ST) *see Selina St Clair*
CELINE
Magma: Nymphettes / 1993 / MET / M • Magma: Olympus Of Lust / 1994 / MET / M • Magma: Young & Old / 1995 / MET / M

CELINE DE VOUX *(Celine Devaux, Seline De Voux, Celine Deavoux)*
Blonde with long hair, medium firm tits (might be enhanced but if they are it was an excellent job), tight curvaceous body, belly button ring, shaven pussy, passable face, quiet personality, 20 years old in 1995, 38-26-36, de-virginized at 15, a little too tall. Comes from Virginia Beach VA but doesn't have an accent.

Anal Disciples #2: The Anal Conflict / 1996 / ZA / M • Anal Tight Ass / 1995 / ROB / M • Anal Trashy Ass / 1995 / ROB / M • Anal Virgins #01 / 1996 / NS / M • Another Fuckin' Anal Movie / 1996 / ROB / M • As Easy As A Bunch Of Cunts / 1996 / ROB / F • Babes Illustrated #5 / 1996 / IN / F • Cirque Du Sex #1 / 1996 / VT / M • Corn Hole Kittens / 1996 / ROB / F • Cum Buttered Corn Holes #2 / 1996 / NIT / C • Delirium / 1996 / MET / M • Dirty Tricks #2: This Ain't Love / 1996 / EA / M • Fashion Sluts #6 / 1995 / ABS / M • Freaky Tailz / 1996 / AVI / M • Fuck U: Girls Of The Packed-10 / 1995 / ZA / M • Hard Feelings / 1995 / VI / M • Hardcore Schoolgirls #5: Virgin Killers / 1996 / XPR / M • Hit Parade / 1996 / PRE / B • Hot Tight Asses #16 / 1996 / TCK / M • Hot Wired / 1996 / VC / M • Hotwired / 1996 / VC / M • Hypnotic Hookers #1 / 1996 / NIT / M • In Your Face #4 / 1996 / PL / M • Interview: Barely Legal / 1995 / LV / M • Leo Endo #17 / 1996 / FD / M • Dian C Nt Whores / 1996 / ROB / F • Macin' #2: Macadocious / 1996 / SMP / M • Mind Set / 1996 / VI / M • More Dirty Debutantes #48 / 1995 / 4P / M • My First Time #7 / 1996 / NS / M • N.Y. Video Magazine #09 / 1996 / OUP / M • Naked & Nasty / 1995 / WP / M • Ona Zee's Doll House #2 / 1995 / ONA / C • Philmore Butts On The Prowl / 1995 / SUF / M • Pleasureland / 1996 / VI / M • Pocahotass #1 / 1996 / FD / M • Puritan Video Magazine #01 / 1996 / LE / M • Pussyclips #10 / 1995 / SNA / M • Sluts, Butts And Pussy / 1996 / DFI / M • Sodomania #16: Sexxy Pistols / 1996 / EL / M • Stardust #3 / 1996 / VI / M • Toes 'n' Cons / 1996 / PRE / S • Using Your Assets To Get A Head / 1996 / OUP / F • Video Virgins #26 / 1996 / NS / M • Video Virgins #33 / 1996 / NS / M • Virgin Bar Maids / 1996 / VMX / M • The Voyeur #6 / 1996 / EA / M • Voyeur Strippers / 1996 / PL / F • Whitey's On The Moon / 1996 / ROB / M • Young & Natural #10 / 1995 / PRE / F • Young & Natural #12 / 1996 / TV / F • Young & Natural #13 / 1996 / TV / F

CELINE DEAVOUX *see Celine De Voux*
CELINE DEVAUX *see Celine De Voux*

CELINE LEMONT *see Star Index I*

CELLY *see Star Index I*

CENDRINE
Magma: Chateau Extreme / 1995 / MET / M • Magma: Spezial: Anal Ii / 1994 / MET / M

CERAN MORRIS
Bend Over Babes #4 / 1996 / EA / M • Pick Up Lines #02 / 1995 / 4P / M • Pick Up Lines #05 / 1996 / OD / M • Venom #2 / 1996 / VD / M

CERES LU
Old Wave Hookers #1 / 1995 / PL / M

CESAR
Sodomania #09: Doin' Time / 1994 / EL / M

CHAD
The Absolute Worst Of Amateur #1 / 1993 / VEX / M • AVP #2002: Meange A Trois #1 / 1990 / AVP / M • Bi-Bi Love Amateurs #1 / 1993 / SFP / G • Bobby Hollander's Rookie Nookie #03 / 1993 / SFP / M • Eighteen #3 / 1996 / SC / M • My First Time #7 / 1996 / NS / M • Streets Of New York #05 / 1995 / PL / M • Uncle Roy's Amateur Home Video #20 / 1993 / VIM / M

CHAD CHATSWORTH *see Star Index I*

CHAD CONNERS
Night Walk / 1995 / HIV / G

CHAD DAVIS
American Sex Fantasy / 1975 / IHV / M

CHAD DONOVAN
Secret Sex #2: The Sex Radicals / 1994 / CAT / G

CHAD KNIGHT
Big Switch #3: Bachelor Party / 1991 / CAT / G • The Eyes Of A Stranger / 1992 / CDI / G • A Family Affair / 1991 / AWV / G • Lust Horizons / 1992 / PL / G • The Mating Game / 1992 / PL / G • Remembering Times Gone Bi / 1995 / AWV / G • Steel Garters / 1992 / CAT / G

CHAD LAMBERT
The Devil Inside Her / 1977 / ALP / M • Frank Henenlotter's XXX Hardcore Horrors #05 / 1996 / SOW / M

CHAD LOWE
Trans America / 1993 / TSS / G

CHAD MOORE
Tranny Claus / 1994 / HEA / G

CHAD RAD *see Chad Thomas*

CHAD SANDERS *see Jon Dough*

CHAD STEEL
Bi Bi Birdie / 1993 / BIL / G • The Crying Flame / 1993 / HSV / G • The Prize Package / 1993 / HSV / G • She Male Service / 1994 / HEA / G • She-Male Encounters #21: Psychic She Males / 1994 / MET / G • She-Male Surprise / 1995 / CDI / G • Surprise Package / 1993 / HSV / G • Transitions (TV) / 1993 / HSV / G • TV Evangelist / 1993 / HSV / G

CHAD TAYLOR
Be Careful What You Wish For / 1993 / VC / G

CHAD THOMAS *(Chad Rad)*
Boyfriend or husband of Misty Rain. Horrible facial skin.
Addictive Desires / 1994 / OD / M • America's Raunchiest Home Videos #59: / 1993 / ZA / M • Anal Arsenal / 1994 / OD / M • The Anal Diary Of Misty Rain / 1993 / EL / M • Anal Therapy #3 / 1994 / FD / M • Anal Vision #06 / 1992 / LBO / M • Backdoor Magic / 1994 / LV / M • Beach Bum Amateur's #26 / 1993 / MID / M • Bi-Athelon / 1993 / BIL / G • Bi-Golly / 1993 / BIL / G •

Big Murray's New-Cummers #07: Swinging in the "A" / 1993 / FD / M • Butt Banged Bicycle Babes / 1994 / ANA / M • Butt Banged Cycle Sluts / 1995 / ANA / M • Deep Inside Misty Rain / 1995 / VC / C • Deep Space 69 / 1994 / HW / M • Director's Wet Dreams / 1996 / BBE / M • Dream House / 1995 / XPR / M • The French Way / 1994 / HOV / M • Gangbang Girl #15 / 1995 / ANA / M • Gangbang Girl #16 / 1995 / ANA / M • Geranalmo / 1994 / PL / M • GM #173: Memorial Weekend T&A 1995 / 1995 / GMV / S • Hard Core Beginners #10 / 1995 / LEI / M • Here Comes Elska / 1997 / XPR / M • Misty Rain's Anal Orgy / 1994 / FRM / M • Money, Money, Money / 1993 / FD / M • Nasty Nymphos #05 / 1994 / ANA / M • Nightshift Nurses #2 / 1996 / VC / M • Odyssey Triple Play #61: Rump Humpers / 1994 / OD / M • Profiles #02 / 1995 / XPR / M • Profiles #03: House Dick / 1995 / XPR / M • Pure Filth / 1995 / RV / M • Satyriasis / 1995 / PL / M • Sex 4 Life / 1995 / XPR / M • Sodom Chronicles / 1995 / FH / M • Sodomania #04: Further On Down The Road / 1993 / EL / M • Sorority Sex Kittens #3 / 1996 / VC / M • Stand By Your Man / 1994 / CV / M • The Swap #2 / 1994 / VI / M • Telephone Expose / 1995 / VC / M • Truck Stop Angel / 1994 / CC / M • Up And Cummers #04 / 1993 / 4P / M • Video Virgins #03 / 1993 / NS / M • The Voyeur #2 / 1994 / EA / M

CHAD TYLER *see Star Index I*

CHAKA *see Star Index I*

CHAMICE
Mike Hott: #141 Chamice Solo / 1991 / MHV / F • Mike Hott: #142 Sissy And Chamice #1 / 1991 / MHV / F • Mike Hott: #143 Sissy And Chamice #2 / 1991 / MHV / F

CHAMONIE *see Channone*

CHAMONIQUE
San Francisco Lesbians #3 / 1993 / PL / F

CHAMPAGNE *(Bridgette Blue, Brigette Blue, Lynn Connelly)*
White girl with large tits, blonde hair and reasonably pretty face, tattoo of a cat on her belly.
The Adventures Of Buttman / 1989 / EA / M • The Affairs Of Miss Roberts / 19?? / ... / M • Anal Addiction #1 / 1990 / SO / M • Anal Attraction #1 / 1988 / 3HV / M • Army Brat #2 / 1989 / VI / M • Backdoor Summer #1 / 1988 / PV / C • Backdoor To Harley-Wood #1 / 1990 / AFV / M • Backdoor To Hollywood #05 / 1988 / CDI / M • Backdoor To Hollywood #06 / 1989 / CIN / M • Backdoor To Hollywood #07 / 1989 / CIN / M • Backdoor To Hollywood #08 / 1989 / CIN / M • Bare Essence / 1989 / EA / M • Beach Blanket Brat / 1989 / VI / M • Bend Over Babes #1 / 1990 / EA / M • Best Of Buttman #1 / 1991 / EA / C • Best Of Foot Worship #3 / 1992 / BIZ / C • Big Boob Made / 199? / NAP / B • The Big E #09 / 1990 / BIZ / B • The Big Winner #1 / 1991 / CDP / B • Bionca, Just For You / 1989 / BON / F • Body And Sole / 1990 / BIZ / B • Bored Housewife / 1989 / CIN / M • The Bottom Line / 1990 / AMB / M • Breaststroke #1 / 1988 / EX / M • Bruce Seven's Favorite Endings #1 / 1991 / EL / C • Bum Rap / 1990 / PLV / B • Bush League #1 / 1990 / CC / M • Caught From Behind #10 / 1989 / HO / M • Champagne Bound At Home /

cr90 / BON / B • Circus Of Lesbians / 1995 / VI / C • Class Act / 1989 / WAV / M • Club Lez / 1990 / PL / F • Competition / 1989 / BON / B • Dance Fire / 1989 / EA / M • Do It In The Road / 1990 / LV / M • Don't Worry Be Sexy / 1989 / EVN / C • Double Take / 1991 / BIZ / B • Double Trouble / 1988 / V99 / M • Dr Jeckel & Ms Hide / 1990 / LV / M • Drainman / 1989 / BIZ / B • Dreams In The Forbidden Zone / 1989 / PCP / M • The Drowning / 199? / NAP / B • Dutch Masters / 1990 / IN / M • The Ebony Connection #4 / 1994 / LBO / C • End Results / 1991 / PRE / C • Flash Floods / 1991 / PRE / C • Flesh Mountain / 1994 / VI / C • Funny Ladies / 1996 / PRE / B • Gazongas #02 / 1988 / VEX / M • Gazongas #03 / 1991 / VEX / M • Girls Of The Double D #05 / 1988 / CIN / M • The Girls' Club / 1990 / VC / F • Hard Sell / 1990 / VC / M • Hot Foot / 1991 / PLV / B • Hot Spot / 1990 / PL / F • House Of Dark Dreams #2 / 1990 / BS / B • I Said A Butt Light #1 / 1990 / LV / M • Itty Bitty Titty Committee #1 / 1990 / PL / F • Juicy Lips / 1991 / PL / F • Kinkyvision #2 / 1988 / VC / M • Lawyers In Heat / 1989 / CDI / M • Leave It To Cleavage #2 / 1989 / EVN / M • Legs And Lingerie #1 / 1990 / BIZ / F • The Love Mistress / 1989 / WV / M • Maiden Heaven #1 / 1992 / MID / F • Miss Adventures / 1989 / VEX / M • Nymphobrat / 1989 / VI / M • Party Pack #1 / 1990 / LE / F • Play Me / 1989 / VI / M • Positive Positions / 1989 / VEX / M • Rachel Ryan Exposed / 1990 / WV / C • Real Breasts Real Torment / 1995 / BON / C • Single Girl Masturbation #2 / 1989 / ESP / F • Six-Nine Love / 1990 / LV / M • Slap Shots / 1991 / PRE / B • The Smart Ass #2: Rusty's Revenge / 1990 / VT / M • Steal Breeze / 1990 / SO / M • Stephanie, Just For You / 1989 / BON / F • Swingers Ink / 1990 / VC / M • Talk Dirty To Me #07 / 1990 / DR / M • Taylor Made / 1989 / DR / M • Val Girls / 1990 / PL / F • Wet 'n' Working / 1990 / EA / F • The Whole Diamond / 1990 / EVN / M • Wild Goose Chase / 1990 / EA / M • Women's Penitentiary / 1992 / VIM / M • [Girls Doin' Girls #01 / cr90 / A&E / M

CHAMPAGNE (PENDARV.) *see Champagne Pendarvis*

CHAMPAGNE PENDARVIS *(Champagne (Pendarv.), Champagne Pendavis, Sasha Pendavis, Shaka)*
Tall (5'8") black girl with slightly pudgy body, large natural tits, reasonably pretty face, strong thighs. Used to work as a secretary to a private investigator before becoming a stripper and then moving into porn. Not the same as Yasmine Pendarvis. Born March 23, 1970.
Always Anal / 1995 / AVI / C • Big Bust Babes #20 / 1994 / AFI / M • Black Beauty (Coast To Coast) / 1994 / CC / M • Black Beauty (Las Vegas) / 1995 / LV / M • Black Cheerleader Search #02 / 1996 / ROB / M • Black Knockers #01 / 1995 / TV / M • Blackdoor Babes / 1994 / TIW / M • Blacks N' Blue / 1995 / VT / B • The Blues #2 / 1994 / VT / M • Booty In The House / 1993 / WP / M • The Bottom Dweller Part Deux / 1994 / EL / M • Brothers Bangin' / 1995 / ANA / M • Bump 'n' Grind / 1994 / HW / M • Champagne's House Party / 1996 / HW / M • Chocolate Bunnies #01 / 1995 / LBO /

C • Dark Alleys #24 / 1994 / FC / M • Dark Alleys #28 / 1994 / FC / M • Dark Discipline / 1994 / STM / B • Dick & Jane Sneak On The Set / 1993 / AVI / M • Dirty Bob's #09: Orlando Orgasms / 1993 / FLP / S • Dirty Bob's #11: Vegas Blues #1 / 1994 / FLP / S • Dirty Dating Service #03 / 1994 / WP / M • Dollars And Yen / 1994 / FH / M • Eleventh Annual AVN Awards / 1994 / VC / M • Girlz In The Hood #3: Erotic Justice / 1993 / HW / M • In Loving Color #1 / 1992 / VT / M • M Series #18 / 1994 / LBO / M • Maverdick / 1995 / WV / M • Mistress 'n Da Hood / 1995 / VT / B • Paint It Black / 1995 / EVN / M • The Players Club / 1994 / HW / M • Primal Rear / 1996 / TIW / M • Private Video Magazine #09 / 1994 / OD / M • Pussy Posse / 1993 / CC / M • Put 'em On Da Glass / 1994 / VT / M • Racially Motivated / 1994 / LV / M • Radical Affairs Video Magazine #07 / 1994 / ME / M • Rump-Shaker #2 / 1993 / HW / M • Rump-Shaker #3 / 1994 / HW / M • Shades Of Erotica #03 / 1994 / GLI / M • Sista Act / 1994 / AVI / M • Sista! #1 / 1993 / VT / F • Sistaz In Chains / 1995 / VT / B • Sparkling Champagne / 1994 / FH / M • Truck Stop Angel / 1994 / CC / M • Up And Cummers #05 / 1993 / 4P / M • Video Virgins #08 / 1993 / NS / M • Whoomp! There She Is / 1993 / AVI / M • Women Who Control The Family Jewels #4 / 1995 / STM / B • The World's Biggest Gang Bang #1 / 1995 / FPI / M • Yo Yo Yo: A Very Black Christmas Tale! / 1994 / HW / M • You Said A Mouthful / 1992 / IF / M • [Amazing Grace / 1994 / ... / M • [Black In The Sack / 1995 / EVN / M

CHAMPAGNE PENDAVIS *see* **Champagne Pendarvis**

CHANCE

Big Boob Bikini Bash / 1995 / BTO / M • Pearl Necklace: Thee Bush League #03 / 1992 / SEE / M

CHANCE (CHANEL) *see* **Chanel (1992)**

CHANCE CALDWELL

Anything You Ever Wanted To Know About Sex / 1993 / VEX / M • Bi & Large / 1994 / STA / G • The Bi-Linguist / 1993 / BIL / G • Bi Madness / 1991 / STA / G • Bi-Inferno / 1992 / VEX / G • Big Switch #3: Bachelor Party / 1991 / CAT / G • The Dildo Tube / 1993 / MET / M • In Your Wildest Dreams / 1993 / STY / M • Letters From The Heart / 1991 / AWV / M • More Than A Woman / 1992 / CDI / G • Mr. Blue / 1996 / JSP / G • Night Walk / 1995 / HIV / G • Passion For Fashion / 1992 / PEP / G • Sex Bi-Lex / 1993 / CAT / G • She-Male Instinct / 1995 / BCP / G • Sinderella She-Males / 1994 / HEA / G • Stasha's Last Kiss / 1992 / VEX / G • Stasha: Portrait Of A Swinger / 1992 / CDI / G • Transsexual Prostitutes #2 / 1997 / DFI / G • Wendy's Bi Adventure / 1994 / STA / M

CHANCE KUFFS

Blonde Busty & Bound / 1996 / VTF / B

CHANCE ROTHCHILD *see* ***Star Index I***

CHANCE RYDER

Bi And Beyond #6: Authentic / 1996 / FD / G • EXXXtra Parts: Interview With a Hermaphrodite / 1995 / PL / M • Sex Freaks / 1995 / EA / M

CHANCE WILDER *see* ***Star Index I***

CHANDLER STEELE

Marginal face, long red or dark brown hair depending on the movie, lithe body,

small/medium tits with erectible nipples, diamond-shaped tattoo around belly button, not a tight waist, and a shaven pussy. Personality leaves something to be desired.

Asses Galore #7: Lunatic Fringe / 1996 / DFI / M • Cherry Poppers: The College Years #01 / 1997 / ZA / M • Cumback Pussy #4: Get Some!!! / 1996 / EL / M • Fame Is A Whore On Butt Row / 1996 / ABS / M • Filthy First Timers #3: Tearing Down The Walls Of Shame / 1996 / EL / M • More Dirty Debutantes #60 / 1997 / SBV / M • More Dirty Debutantes #62 / 1997 / SBV / M • Puritan Video Magazine #10 / 1997 / LE / M • Sodomania #19: Sweet Cream / 1996 / EL / M • Up And Cummers #37 / 1996 / 4P / M • Up And Cummers #38 / 1996 / RWP / M • Up And Cummers #39 / 1996 / RWP / M • War Whores / 1996 / EL / M

CHANDRA FAYME

Best Chest 14 / 1994 / CAW / B • Busted By The Boss / 1995 / CAW / B

CHANDRA SAX *see* ***Star Index I***

CHANDRA SWEET *(Shaundra Sweet)*

Blonde with an adorable little body and a very pretty face, medium natural tits, tight waist, was 18 in 1993. Subsequent to her **Pearl Necklace** stint she put on weight and now falls into the marginal class (pity).

Anal Assault / 1995 / PEV / C • Anal Vision #16 / 1993 / LBO / M • Backstreet: Mardi Gras '96 / 1996 / BST / S • Beyond Driven #3 / 1996 / ZFX / B • Blunt Trauma #2 / 1996 / ZFX / B • Bound And Abused / 1993 / SV / B • Bunny Tails / 1994 / SV / B • Dirty Bob's #09: Orlando Orgasms / 1993 / FLP / S • Dirty Bob's #10: Sleeping Late In Seattle / 1993 / FLP / S • Disciplz Of Pain / 1995 / ZFX / B • The Ebony Connection #3 / 1994 / LBO / C • Fair Warning / 1995 / ZFX / B • Gangland #5 / 1995 / ZFX / B • Innocent Exile / 1995 / ZFX / B • Intervidnet #2: French Made / 1994 / IVN / M • M Series #14 / 1993 / LBO / M • Mincemeat Pie / 1996 / ZFX / B • Mr. Peepers Amateur Home Videos #73: Carnal Capture / 1993 / LBO / M • Mr. Peepers Nastiest #1 / 1995 / LBO / C • The Necklace #1 / 1994 / ZFX / B • The Necklace #2 / 1994 / ... / U / I • Pearl Necklace: Amorous Amateurs #30 / 1993 / SEE / M • Pearl Necklace: Amorous Amateurs #31 / 1993 / SEE / M • Pearl Necklace: Amorous Amateurs #32 / 1993 / SEE / F • Pearl Necklace: Amorous Amateurs #34 / 1992 / SEE / M • Pearl Necklace: Amorous Amateurs #35 / 1993 / SEE / M • Pearl Necklace: Premier Sessions #01 / 1993 / SEE / M • Pearl Necklace: Thee Bush League #18 / 1993 / SEE / M • Pearl Necklace: Thee Bush League #19 / 1993 / SEE / M • Pearl Necklace: Thee Bush League #23 / 1993 / SEE / M • Subject Nine / 1995 / ZFX / B • Tech: Chandra Sweet #1 / 1993 / TWA / M • Tech: Chandra Sweet #2 / 1993 / TWA / M • Tech: Chandra Sweet #3 / 1993 / TWA / M • Video Pirates #1 / 1995 / ZFX / B • Video Pirates #2 / 1995 / ZFX / B • Video Pirates #5: A Bullet To Bite / 1995 / ZFX / B • War Pigs #1 / 1996 / ZFX / B • War Pigs #2 / 1996 / ZFX / B • The Worm / 1995 / ZFX / B

CHANEL **(1992)** *(Shanel, Chance (Chanel), Chenel, Chantel (Chanel), Sasha (Chanel), Jane Reddix, Valerie*

Van Owen)

Tight bodied brunette who seems to go from small tits to larger ones and then back again. Maybe she had them marginally enhanced and the movies are seen out of sequence. Quite pretty and very athletic but has an elephant ears pussy and talks dirty. Got married to Jake Williams at the Las Vegas Convention in 1992. Born April 13, 1966 in Louisville Kentucky (25 in 1992). Got de-virginized at age 17. Says she's double jointed. Split up with Jake in 1993. Jane Reddix is from **The Erotic Adventures Of The Three Musketeers**. Valerie Van Owen is a name used in the Harmony Concepts B&D movies. Got pregnant in 1995 and blew up like a balloon. Gave birth to a baby in early 1996, father unknown.

1-900-SPANKME Ext.1 / 1994 / BON / B • 1-900-SPANKME Ext.2 / 1994 / BON / B • Amateur Orgies #33 / 1993 / AFI / M • Anal Virgins Of America #03 / 1993 / FOR / M • The Art Of Spanking / 1995 / VTF / B • Attack Of The 50 Foot Hooker / 1994 / OD / M • Balling Instinct / 1992 / FH / M • Beverly Hills Madam / 1993 / FH / F • Biff Malibu's Totally Nasty Home Videos #30 / 1993 / ANA / M • Bip Shoots #2 / 1994 / BON / B • Black To Basics / 1992 / ZA / M • Body And Soul / 1995 / BON / B • Bodywaves / 1994 / ELP / M • Bondage Fantasy #3 / 1995 / BON / B • Broad Of Directors / 1992 / PEP / M • Buffy Malibu's Totally Nasty All-Girl Home Videos #01 / 1992 / ANA / F • Buffy Malibu's Totally Nasty All-Girl Home Videos #05 / 1993 / ANA / F • Butt Jammers / 1994 / WIV / M • Buttmasters / 1994 / AMP / M • Casanova #4 / 1993 / SC / M • Colossal Orgy #1 / 1993 / HW / M • Curious / 1992 / LE / M • The D.J. / 1992 / VC / M • Deep Inside Deidre Holland / 1993 / VC / C • Deep Inside Tiffany Mynx / 1994 / VC / C • Double A Dykes / 1992 / GO / F • Double D Dykes #04 / 1992 / GO / F • Elegant Bargain / 1994 / FD / C • The Erotic Adventures Of The Three Musketeers / 1992 / CEL / S • Flying High #1 / 1992 / HO / M • For The Money #2 / 1993 / FH / M • Forbidden Dreams / 1993 / UDP / D • A Girl's Affair #04 / 1994 / FD / F • The Girls' Club / 1993 / VD / C • The Good, The Bad & The Nasty / 1992 / VC / M • Graduation From F.U. / 1992 / FOR / M • Harlots / 1993 / MID / M • Heels & Toes #1 / 1994 / BON / F • Heels & Toes #2 / 1994 / BON / F • I'm Too Sexy / 1992 / CA / M • Jack The Stripper / 1992 / ME / M • Joe Elliot's College Girls #26 / 1994 / JOE / M • Just Deserts / 1994 / BON / B • Katrina's Awakening #1 / 1994 / BON / B • Katrina's Awakening #2 / 1994 / BON / B • Katrina's Awakening #3 / 1994 / BON / B • Kitty Kat Club / 1994 / SC / F • Kym Wilde's On The Edge #13 / 1994 / RB / B • Kym Wilde's On The Edge #16 / 1994 / RB / B • Leave It To Bondage / 1994 / BON / B • Legend #4: Critic's Choice / 1992 / LE / M • Lesbian Love Connection / 1992 / LIP / F • Lipstick Lesbians #1: Massage Parlor Dykes / 1994 / ZA / F • The Man Who Loved Women / 1993 / SC / M • Mike Hott: #337 Chanell Pregnant / 1996 / MHV / F • Mocha Magic / 1992 / FH / M • More Dirty Debutantes #33 / 1994 / 4P / M • Nasty Nymphos #02 / 1994 / ANA / M • Native Tongue / 1993 / VI / M • No Bust Babes /

1992 / AFI / M • Oreo A Go-Go #2 / 1992 / FH / M • Private Dancer (CDI) / 1992 / CDI / M • Professor Sticky's Anatomy 3X #01 / 1992 / FC / M • Radical Affairs Video Magazine #01 / 1992 / ME / M • Radio-Active / 1992 / SC / M • Ready To Drop #11 / 1996 / FC / M • Ready To Drop #12 / 1996 / FC / M • Reel Sex #05: Lesbian Toy Part / 1994 / SPP / F • Revealed / 1992 / VT / M • Rituals / 1993 / SC / M • Rump Reamers / 1994 / TTV / M • Saints & Sinners / 1992 / PEP / M • Saturday Night Porn #3 / 1993 / AFV / M • Savannah's Last Stand / 1993 / VI / M • The Secret Life Of Herbert Dingle / 1994 / TTV / M • See-Thru / 1992 / LE / M • Sexorcist / 1994 / HW / M • Sexvision / 1992 / HO / M • Seymore Butts & The Honeymooners / 1992 / FH / M • A Shaver Among Us / 1992 / ZA / M • Shayla's Home Repair / 1993 / EVN / M • Sin City: The Movie / 1992 / SC / M • Sound Of Tickling / 1995 / SBP / B • Spank-O-Rama / 1994 / BON / B • Spankology 101a / 1994 / BON / B • Spankology 101b / 1994 / BON / B • Student Fetish Videos: Best of Catfighting #02 / 1994 / PRE / C • Student Fetish Videos: Best of Enema #03 / 1994 / PRE / C • Student Fetish Videos: The Enema #15 / 1994 / PRE / B • Student Fetish Videos: Spanking #16 / 1994 / PRE / B • Student Fetish Videos: Tickling #10 / 1994 / SFV / B • Superstar Sex Challenge #2 / 1994 / VC / M • Suspended / 1995 / VTF / B • Swinging Couples #02 / 1993 / GO / M • Tailiens #1 / 1992 / FD / M • Tailiens #2 / 1992 / FD / M • Tailiens #3 / 1992 / FD / M • The Three Musketeers #1 / 1992 / FD / M • The Three Musketeers #2 / 1992 / FD / M • Too Sexy / 1992 / MID / M • Tori Welles Goes Behind The Scenes / 1992 / FD / M • Witness For The Penetration / 1994 / PEP / M • Women On Fire / 1995 / LBO / M

CHANEL (EUROPEAN)
Magma: Spezial: Anal / 1994 / MET / M • The Voyeur #8: Live In Europe #2 / 1996 / JLP / M

CHANEL (OTHER)
Bondage Fantasy #1 / 1995 / BON / B • Hot Body Competition: Beverly Hill's Miniskirt Madness Cont. / 1996 / CG / F

CHANEL (PRICE) see Chanel Price
CHANEL (T.TAYLOR) see Tianna Taylor
CHANEL LINDSAY
Chuck & Di In Heat / 1986 / DR / M • Night Of Loving Dangerously / 1984 / PV / M • On Golden Blonde / 1984 / PV / M

CHANEL PRICE *(Chanel (Price))*
An Amazon. In 1988 was going to a bachelor party by helicopter. When she got out she put her hands up in the air and had a finger chopped off.
Adler Shoots: The Reality Behind The Legend / cr90 / BON / B • Angel's Revenge / 1985 / IN / M • Battle Of The Beast Women / 1995 / ... / M • Best Of Caught From Behind #2 / 1988 / HO / C • Black Bunbusters / 1985 / VC / M • Black Magic / 1986 / DR / M • Black Magic Sex Clinic / 1987 / DOX / M • Black Satin Nights / 1988 / DR / C • Blonde On The Run / 1985 / PV / M • Caught From Behind #05: Blondes & Blacks / 1986 / HO / M • Caught From Behind #07 / 1987 / HO / M • Caught From Behind #10 / 1989 / HO / M • Classic Pics / 1988 / PP / C • Daddy's Darling Daughters / 1986 / PL / M • Deep And Dark / 1986

/ PLV / B • Devil In Miss Jones #3: A New Beginning / 1986 / VC / M • Ecstasy / 1986 / PP / M • Escort To Ecstasy / 1987 / 3HV / M • Hill Street Blacks #1 / 1985 / 4R / M • Honeybuns #2: Grecian Formula / 1987 / WV / C • Krazy 4 You / 1987 / 4P / M • License To Thrill / 1985 / VD / M • Lifestyles Of The Black And Famous / 1986 / WET / M • Moans & Groans / 1987 / 4P / M • Mouth To Mouth / 1986 / CC / M • Night Moods / 1985 / AVC / M • Only The Best Of Women With Women / 1988 / CV / C • The Pillowman / 1988 / VC / M • Queen Of Spades / 1986 / VD / M • Rear Ended / 1985 / WV / M • Rears / 1987 / VI / M • Sex Star Competition / 1985 / PL / M • Sexplorations / 1991 / VC / C • Slummin' Hood Girlz / 1993 / CA / M • Taija's Satin Seduction / 1987 / CDI / M • The Wedding / 1986 / VC / M • Wild Things #2 / 1986 / CV / M • The X-Terminator / 1986 / PV / M

CHANG
Cindy Prince #7 / 1995 / BON / B

CHANNEL
Dungeon Queens / 1995 / BIZ / G • Suspend Thy Slaves / 1996 / VTF / B

CHANNENE see Channone

CHANNONE *(Chamonie, Chaonnone, Channene)*
French, not too pretty, very short hair, medium (may be enhanced) tits, nice butt. Later movies she has let her hair grow long (or uses a wig) and has a large tattoo on her right butt.
The Anal Adventures Of Max Hardcore: Cafe Life / 1994 / ZA / M • Anal Angels #3 / 1995 / VEX / C • Anal Angels #5 / 1996 / VEX / C • Ass Freaks #2 / 1995 / ROB / F • Ass Masters (Leisure) #06 / 1995 / LEI / M • Backdoor Diaries / 1995 / BBE / M • Backdoor Imports / 1995 / LV / M • Batbabe / 1995 / PL / M • Big & Busty Centerfolds / 1996 / DGD / F • Buffy Malibu's Nasty Girls #09 / 1995 / ANA / F • Butt Hunt #07 / 1995 / LEI / M • The Butt Sisters Do Houston / 1996 / MID / M • Buttslammers #10: Lust On The Internet / 1995 / BS / F • Club Anal #3 / 1995 / ROB / F • Club Privado / 1995 / KP / M • Cyberanal / 1995 / VC / M • The Deviant Doctor / 1996 / NS / M • Dirty Tricks #1: Just A Bunch Of Whores / 1995 / EA / M • Double Anal Alternatives / 1996 / EL / M • Euro Studs / 1996 / SC / C • Face To Face / 1995 / ME / M • Fire & Ice: Caught In The Act / 1995 / WP / M • Flesh / 1996 / EA / M • Foreign Asses / 1996 / MP0 / M • French Roommate / 1995 / C69 / M • Gang Bang Fury #2 / 1996 / ROB / M • A Girl's Affair #09 / 1996 / FD / F • Goldenbush / 1996 / AVI / M • Hard Core Beginners #02 / 1995 / LEI / M • Hard Core Beginners #09 / 1995 / LEI / M • Hard Evidence / 1996 / WP / M • Hawaiian Buttwatch / 1995 / SUF / M • Heavenly Yours / 1995 / CV / M • Heidi's High Heeled Hookers / 1995 / BBE / M • The Hitch-Hiker #11: / 1995 / WMG / M • Hot Tight Asses #10 / 1995 / TCK / M • Indecent Obsessions / 1995 / BBE / M • Interview: Silicone Sisters / 1996 / LV / M • Julia Ann: Superstar / 1995 / WAV / M • Kink: Police Chronicles / 1995 / ROB / M • Kittens & Vamps #2 / 1995 / ROB / F • Lollipops #1 / 1996 / SC / M • Lunachick / 1995 / VI / M • Max #05: The Harder They Fall / 1995 / FRM / M • Mixed-Up Marriage / 1995 / CV / M •

Night Stalker / 1995 / BBE / M • Nightbreed / 1995 / VI / M • Paradise / 1995 / FD / M • Perverted Stories #04 / 1995 / JMP / M • Philmore Butts Hawaiian Anal Adventure / 1995 / SUF / M • Playmates Of The Rich And Famous / 1995 / BBE / M • Private Video Magazine #20 / 1995 / OD / M • Private Video Magazine #23 / 1995 / OD / M • Profiles #06: Super Model Orgy / 1996 / XPR / M • Pussy Hunt #15 / 1995 / LEI / M • Pussyman Auditions #11 / 1995 / SNA / M • Rebecca Lord's World Tour #1: French Edition / 1995 / WP / M • Sensations #2 / 1996 / SC / M • Sex On The Beach Hawaiian Style #1 / 1995 / ULP / M • Sex On The Beach Hawaiian Style #2 / 1995 / ULP / M • Sex On The Beach Hawaiian Style #3 / 1995 / ULP / M • Sex Secrets Of A Mistress / 1995 / VI / M • A Shot In The Pink / 1995 / BBE / M • Snatch Masters #10 / 1995 / LEI / M • Sodomania #13: Your Lucky Number / 1995 / EL / M • Sodomania #14: C**t Lickin', C*m Drinkin' Bitches / 1995 / EL / M • Sodomania: Slop Shots / 1996 / EL / C • Southern Comfort #1 / 1995 / DWV / M • Southern Comfort #2 / 1995 / DWV / M • Suzi Bungholeo / 1995 / ROB / M • Sweet As Honey / 1996 / NIT / M • Takin' It To The Limit #5 / 1995 / BS / M • Takin' It To The Limit #6 / 1995 / BS / M • Topless Window Washers / 1996 / LE / M • Turnabout / 1996 / CTP / M • Unbridled / 1995 / PPI / M • Up And Cummers #28 / 1996 / ERW / M • Venom #3 / 1996 / VD / M • Western Whores Hotel / 1996 / VG0 / M • Where The Girls Sweat...Not The Sequel / 1996 / EL / F • The Wicked One / 1995 / WP / M • Wild & Wicked #6 / 1995 / VT / M

CHANTAINE see Leanna Foxxx
CHANTAL
Black Mystique #13 / 1995 / VT / F • Tailz From Da Hood #3 / 1996 / AVI / M

CHANTAL (SHALIMAR) see Shalimar
CHANTAL LEMAIRE see Brigitte Aime
CHANTAL VIRAPIN
Body Love / 1976 / CA / M • Perverse / 1984 / CA / M

CHANTE *(Chantel (Chante), Vanessa (Chante))*
Tall Hispanic girl with dark hair (sometimes reddish) a very tight waist, tight butt, large enhanced tits and a reasonably pretty face. 34DD-22-34 and 21 years old in 1994.
Ace In The Hole / 1995 / PL / M • Adventures Of The DP Boys: At The French Riviera / 1994 / HW / M • America's Raunchiest Home Videos #59: / 1993 / ZA / M • Anal Angel / 1994 / EX / M • Big Murray's New-Cummers #26: Real Tits / 1994 / FD / M • Bobby Hollander's Sweet Cheeks #111 / 1994 / WV / M • Bun Busters #16 / 1994 / LBO / M • Bun Busters #21 / 1994 / LBO / M • Butt Hole In-One / 1994 / AFV / M • Butt Hunt #02 / 1994 / LEI / M • Canadian Beaver Hunt #2 / 1996 / PL / M • Creme De La Face #02 / 1994 / OD / M • Deep Throat Girls #04 / 1994 / GO / M • Dirty Dating Service #05 / 1994 / WP / M • Dirty Doc's Housecalls #11 / 1994 / LV / M • Dirty Dominique / 1994 / V99 / M • Double D Amateurs #15 / 1994 / JMP / M • Double D Amateurs #16 / 1994 / JMP / M • Freeway Love / 1994 / FD / M • The Girls From Hootersville #06 / 1994 / SFP / M • Hard-On Copy / 1994 / WV / M • Harness Hannah At The Strap-On Ho Down / 1994 / WIV / F •

The Hollywood Starlet Search / 1995 / SC / M • Horny Henry's French Adventure / 1994 / TTV / M • Horny Henry's Oriental Adventure / 1994 / TTV / M • Max World #6: Rolling + Reaming! / 1996 / LE / M • Mr. Peepers Amateur Home Videos #89: Stiffy Stuffer / 1994 / LBO / M • Mr. Peepers Amateur Home Videos #92: M-Ass-terpieces / 1994 / LBO / M • Nasty Fuckin' Movies #22 / 1994 / RUM / M • Nasty Newcummers #04 / 1994 / MET / M • New Ends #07 / 1994 / 4P / M • No Motive / 1994 / MID / M • Nydp Pink / 1994 / HW / M • Odyssey 30 Min: #431: / 1994 / OD / M • Paging Betty / 1994 / VC / M • Pops / 1994 / PL / M • Pussyclips #02 / 1994 / SNA / M • The Quest / 1994 / SC / M • Reel Sex #02: Splash Party / 1994 / SPP / M • Reel Sex World #05 / 1994 / WP / M • Rump Humpers #05 / 1992 / GLI / M • Sindy Does Anal Again / 1994 / AFV / M • Sister Snatch #1 / 1994 / SNA / M • Sleaze Please!—November Edition / 1994 / FH / M • So You Wanna Be A Porn Star #1: The Russians Are Cumming / 1994 / WHP / M • Stewardesses Behind Bars / 1994 / HW / M • Streets Of New York #04 / 1995 / PL / M • Summer Vacation #1 / 1996 / RAS / M • Summer Vacation #2 / 1996 / RAS / M • Supermodel #1 / 1994 / VI / M • Supermodel #2 / 1994 / VI / M • Swinging Couples #03 / 1994 / GO / M • Tail Taggers #117 / 1993 / WV / M • Tail Taggers #122: Anal Delight / 1994 / WV / M • Taxi Girls #4: Daughter Of Lust / 1994 / CA / M • Top Debs #5: Deb Of The Month / 1994 / GO / M

CHANTEL
As Nasty As She Wants To Be / 1990 / IN / M • Bend Over Babes #1 / 1990 / EA / M • Dirty Dixie / 1992 / IF / M • Executive Suites / 1990 / VEX / M • Girls, Girls And More Girls / 1990 / LV / F • Girlz N The Hood #1 / 1991 / HW / M • Playing The Field / 1990 / VEX / M • Star 90 / 1990 / CAY / M
CHANTEL (CHANEL) see **Chanel (1992)**
CHANTEL (CHANTE) see **Chante**
CHANTEL DUCLOS see **Star Index I**
CHANTEL LANE see **Star Index I**
CHANTEL LEE
Doin' The Nasty / 1996 / AVI / M
CHANTEL NAUHA see **Star Index I**
CHANTEL TROBERT see **Star Index I**
CHANTELL
America's Raunchiest Home Videos #43: Cum Blow My Horn / 1992 / ZA / M • The Satisfiers Of Alpha Blue / 1980 / AVC / M
CHANTELLE
Anal Virgins Of America #07 / 1994 / FOR / M • Creme De La Face #16: Ladies Licking / 1996 / OD / M • Hollywood Amateurs #24 / 1995 / MID / M • Kinky Ladies Of London / 1995 / VC / M • New Girls In Town #8 / 1994 / CC / M • Public Enemy / 1990 / VIP / M • Swedish Erotica #76 / 1994 / CA / M
CHANTELLE (CHARLI) see **Charli**
CHANTILLY LACE
All-Star Anal Interviews #1 / 1995 / LEI / M • Anal Woman #2 / 1993 / PL / M • Anal Woman #3 / 1995 / PL / M • Ass Tales / 1991 / PL / M • The Big Shave / 1993 / PEP / M • Class Ass / 1992 / PL / M • Dirty Bob's #18: Under The Boardwalk! / 1995 / FLP / S • Dirty Bob's #19: Over The Boardwalk! / 1995 / FLP / S • Double D Dykes #08 / 1993 / GO / F • Full Service Woman / 1992

/ V99 / M • Herman's Other Head / 1992 / LV / M • Hometown Girl / 1994 / VEX / M • Just My Imagination / 1993 / WP / M • Lonely Is The Night / 1990 / V99 / M • Love Doll Lucy #1 / 1994 / PL / F • Love Doll Lucy #2 / 1994 / PL / F • Mr. Big / 1991 / PL / M • Obsessions In Lace / 1994 / PL / M • Oral Support / 1989 / V99 / M • Secret Admirer / 1992 / VEX / M • She's My Cherry Pie / 1992 / V99 / M • Stick It In The Rear #1 / 1991 / PL / M • Stick It In The Rear #2 / 1993 / PL / M • Strap-On Sally #01: Strap-On Psycho / 1993 / PL / F • Strap-On Sally #02: Ariana Bottoms Out / 1993 / PL / F • Strap-On Sally #03: Thigh Harness Terror / 1994 / PL / F • Strap-On Sally #04: Double Penetration Dykes / 1994 / PL / F • Strap-On Sally #05: Chantilly's French Kiss / 1995 / PL / F • Strap-On Sally #06: Triple Penetration Trollop / 1995 / PL / F • Strap-On Sally #07: Face Dildo Frenzy / 1995 / PL / F • Strap-On Sally #08: Strap-On Cock Fight / 1995 / PL / F • Strap-On Sally #09 / 1996 / PL / F • Transitions: An Anal Adventure / 1993 / PL / M • Unlaced / 1992 / PL / M
CHANZE
Latex #1 / 1994 / VC / M
CHAONNONE see **Channone**
CHARA STASHIA
The Crying Flame / 1993 / HSV / G • Married With She-Males / 1993 / PL / G • She-Male Slut House / 1994 / HEA / G
CHARDONNAY
Black Centerfolds #1 / 1996 / DR / M • Black Centerfolds #2 / 1996 / DR / M • Black Knockers #09 / 1995 / TV / M • Booty Bang #1 / 1996 / HW / M • The Cumm Brothers #12: Two GOOS For Every Girl / 1995 / OD / M • Fashion Sluts #7 / 1996 / ABS / M • Girly Video Magazine #4 / 1996 / BEP / M • Interview's Foreign Affair / 1996 / LV / M • Mike Hott: #354 Three-Sum Sluts #12 / 1996 / MHV / M • Mike Hott: #358 Cunt Of The Month: Chardonnay / 1996 / MHV / M • Nasty Newcummers #13 / 1995 / MET / M • Stripping / 1995 / NIT / M • Western Whores Hotel / 1996 / VG0 / M • Whiplash / 1996 / DFI / M
CHARGER see **Star Index I**
CHARISE see **Charise**
CHARISMA (Kitty Luv, Love (Charisma), Karisma, Kitty Love)
Ugly girl with some traces of black. Mother's name is Lolita Arquette. Has what looks to be a 5 year old boy (**Current Affair** 060591). Has had her boobs enhanced to grotesque proportions in mid-1991.
Amateur Lesbians #09: Meschel / 1991 / GO / F • Amateur Lesbians #11: Rusty / 1991 / GO / F • Amateur Lesbians #21: Daphne / 1992 / GO / F • Amazons From Burbank / 1990 / PL / F • Assinine / 1990 / CC / M • Assuming The Position / 1989 / V99 / M • Bareback Riders / 1992 / VEX / M • Bazooka County #3 / 1991 / CC / M • Beaverjuice / 1992 / LV / M • Big Boob Made / 199? / NAP / B • Big Bust Babes #07 / 1991 / AFI / M • Big Bust Babes #08 / 1991 / AFI / M • Bigger Is Better / 1992 / NAP / B • Biggies #04 / 1992 / XPI / M • Bikini City / 1991 / CC / M • Black By Popular Demand / 1992 / ZA / M • Black Jack City #1 / 1991 / VT / M • Black Mariah / 1991 / FC / M • Blow Out / 1991 / IF / M • Booby Prize / 1995 / PEP / M • Breast

Worx #03 / 1991 / LBO / M • Breast Worx #04 / 1991 / LBO / M • Breast Worx #05 / 1991 / LBO / M • Breast Worx #06 / 1991 / LBO / M • Breast Worx #12 / 1991 / LBO / M • Breast Worx #28 / 1992 / LBO / M • Breaststroke #3 / 1989 / EX / M • Buck's Excellent Transsexual Adventure / 1989 / STA / G • Corruption / 1990 / CC / M • Cycle Sluts / 1992 / CC / M • Dances With Foxes / 1991 / CC / M • Dark Double D-Lites / 1993 / HW / C • Deep In Deanna Jones / 1989 / EVN / M • Devil In The Blue Dress / 1989 / ME / M • Double D Dykes #02 / 1992 / GO / F • Dutch Masters / 1990 / IN / M • Earthquake Girls / 1990 / CC / M • For Your Lips Only / 1989 / FAZ / M • Girl Country / 1990 / CC / F • Girlz N The Hood #1 / 1991 / HW / M • Great Balls Of Fire / 1989 / FAZ / M • Heart Breaker / 1989 / LE / M • Hollywood Teasers #02 / 1992 / LBO / F • In Your Face #2 / 1992 / PL / M • Into The Gap / 1991 / LE / M • It Happened At Midnight / 1990 / IN / M • Lesbian Lingerie Fantasy #2 / 1989 / ESP / F • Lesbian Lingerie Fantasy #3 / 1989 / ESP / F • Lethal Passion / 1991 / PL / M • Little Big Dong / 1992 / ZA / M • Lonely Is The Night / 1990 / V99 / M • Long Dan Silver / 1992 / IF / M • Love Shack / 1990 / CC / M • Low Blows: The Private Collection / 1989 / ME / M • The Maddams Family / 1991 / XCI / M • Made In Hollywood / 1990 / VEX / M • Mike Hott: #182 Charisma / 1990 / MHV / M • Mike Hott: Apple Asses #03 / 1992 / MHV / F • Mistaken Identity / 1990 / CC / M • Mo' Booty #1 / 1992 / HW / C • New Sensations / 1990 / CC / M • Oral Addiction / 1989 / LV / M • The Other Side Of Debbie / 1991 / CC / M • Play Christy For Me / 1990 / CAY / M • Pussy Power #05 / 1992 / BTO / M • Rainwoman #02 / 1990 / CC / M • Robin Head / 1991 / CC / M • Rocky Mountains / 1991 / IF / M • Seduction / 1990 / VEX / M • Sex On Location / 1989 / KIS / M • Sex Wish / 1992 / WV / M • Sexlock / 1992 / XPI / M • Sexual Healing / 1992 / LV / M • Silk Elegance / 1991 / VIM / M • Single Girl Masturbation #3 / 1989 / ESP / F • Snow White And The Seven Weenies / 1989 / FAN / M • Sterling Silver / 1992 / CC / M • Sweet Temptations / 1989 / V99 / M • Tit Tales #3 / 1991 / FC / M • Tits And Tongues / 1993 / NAP / B • Titty-Titty Bang-Bang / 1992 / FC / C • Tropical Temptations / 1989 / VEX / M • Tug O' Love / 1990 / CC / M • Wanda Does Transylvania / 1990 / V99 / M • Wanda Whips The Dragon Lady / 1990 / V99 / M • Who Reamed Rosie Rabbit? #2 / 1989 / FAN / M • Wild Side / 1991 / GO / M • Wives Of The Rich And Famous / 1989 / V99 / M
CHARITY
Best Butt(e) In The West #1 / 1992 / CC / M • Black Knockers #01 / 1995 / TV / M • Blue Vanities #576 / 1995 / FFL / M • Butt-Nanza / 1995 / WV / M • Harlem Harlots #3 / 1996 / AVS / M • My First Time #5 / 1996 / NS / M
CHARIZ
Sodomania #10: Euro/American Again / 1994 / EL / M
CHARLA MISS 42
Count The Ways / 1976 / CA / M
CHARLEEN
Blue Vanities #115 / 1988 / FFL / M
CHARLENE

Blue Vanities #510 / 1992 / FFL / M • Busty Nymphos / 1984 / BTO / S • Keep On Fucking / 1995 / XHE / M • Mike Hott: #110 Lin Shia And Charlene / 1990 / MHV / F • Mike Hott: #111 Lin Shia, Charlene And Paul / 1990 / MHV / M • Sacred Doll / 1995 / FRF / M • Wrasslin She-Babes #08 / 1996 / SOW / M • Wrasslin She-Babes #14 / 1996 / SOW / M

CHARLENE (SHELENE) *see* Shelene

CHARLENE CODY *see Star Index I*

CHARLENE MILLS
College Girls / cr73 / VXP / M

CHARLENE ROBEN
Magma: Happy Anal / 1995 / MET / M

CHARLENE STONE *see* Cara Lott

CHARLES
Buttwoman In Budapest / 1992 / EA / M • FTV #54: Punch Me Harder / 1996 / FT / B • Magma: Anita #2 / 1996 / MET / M • Sharon's House Party / 1995 / HW / M • Thermonuclear Sex / 1996 / EL / M

CHARLES ALLEN *see* Buck Adams

CHARLES ANTHONY *see Star Index I*

CHARLES BELL *see Star Index I*

CHARLES BOND *see Star Index I*

CHARLES BREEN *see Star Index I*

CHARLES BROWN *see Star Index I*

CHARLES CALDWELL
Violated / 1973 / PVX / M

CHARLES CANYON *see* Chris Chittell

CHARLES COLTEN *see Star Index I*

CHARLES DARNEL *see Star Index I*

CHARLES DE SANTOS *see Star Index I*

CHARLES DIAMOND
Three Men And A Geisha / 1990 / HO / M

CHARLES EGGLESTON
After Hours Bondage / 1993 / BON / B • Home Maid Memories #2 / 1994 / BON / C

CHARLES ENGEL
Resurrection Of Eve / 1973 / MIT / M

CHARLES F. KANE
Overnight Sensation / 1976 / AR / M

CHARLES GATEWOOD
Erotic Tattooing And Piercing #1 / 1986 / FLV / M • Erotic Tattooing And Piercing #5 / 1991 / FLV / M

CHARLES HOOPER *see Star Index I*

CHARLES KOUTZ
Sweet Savage / 1978 / ALP / M

CHARLES LEE
Black & White Bondage / 1991 / BON / B • Home Maid Memories #2 / 1994 / BON / C

CHARLES LONG *see Star Index I*

CHARLES MONSOYA *see* Carlos Monsoya

CHARLES MUIR
Ancient Secrets Of Sexual Ecstasy / 1996 / HIG / M

CHARLES NEAL *see Star Index I*

CHARLES POPOL *see Star Index I*

CHARLES S. ALLEN *see* Buck Adams

CHARLES SCHREINER
Everything Goes / 1975 / CA / M • I Want What I See / 1985 / VC / M • Love Play / 1977 / CA / M • Young Widows / 1981 / CA / M

CHARLES SMALL *see Star Index I*

CHARLES SMITH
Sacrilege / 1971 / AXV / M

CHARLES STARK *see* Blake West

CHARLES STERN
All The Loving Couples / 1979 / KIT / M

CHARLES STORK *see* Blake West

CHARLES SULLIVAN *see Star Index I*

CHARLES SYKES

Sodom & Gomorrah / 1974 / MIT / M

CHARLES V. DINGLEY *see* Chuck Vincent

CHARLES WARDEN *see Star Index I*

CHARLEY *see Star Index I*

CHARLEY LOWS
Taboo American Style #4: The Exciting Conclusion / 1985 / VC / M

CHARLEY ST. ELMO
Nice 'n' Tight / 1985 / AIR / M

CHARLEY X *see Star Index I*

CHARLI *(Chantelle (Charli), Farrah (Charli))*
Adorable little girl with small to medium breasts, a pretty face and a very pleasant personality. Farrah in **X Dreams**.
Backdoor To Hollywood #08 / 1989 / CIN / M • Backdoor To Hollywood #09 / 1989 / CIN / M • Bimbo Bowlers From Buffalo / 1989 / ZA / M • Breathless / 1989 / CIN / M • Deep Inside Charli / 1990 / CDI / C • Delicious (VCX-1993) / 1993 / VCX / M • From Sweden With Love / 1989 / ZA / M • Goodtime Charli / 1989 / CIN / M • Inner Pink #3 / 1994 / LIP / F • Introducing Charli / 1989 / CIN / M • Making Charli / 1989 / CDI / M • Porn On The 4th Of July / 1990 / IN / M • She's Ready / 1990 / CDI / M • Slick Honey / 1989 / VC / M • Strange Curves / 1989 / VC / M • X Dreams / 1989 / CA / M

CHARLI WATERS
Died 1989 of homicide (carved up by a john). Backdoor To Hollywood #05 / 1988 / CDI / M • Carnal Possessions / 1988 / VEX / M • Carnal Possessions / 1991 / VEX / M • Every Man's Fancy / 1988 / SEX / M • Every Man's Fancy / 1991 / V99 / M • Fantasy Girls / 1988 / CA / M • First Time Lesbians (Gourmet) / 1987 / GO / F • The Godmother #1 / 1987 / VC / M • The Godmother #2 / 1988 / VC / M • Her Every Wish / 1988 / GO / M • Kascha & Friends / 1988 / CIN / M • Keyhole #168: Robo-Cocks / 1989 / KEH / M • Lesbian Nymphos / 1988 / GO / C • Megasex / 1988 / EVN / M • Parliament: Bottoms #2 / 1988 / PM / C • Parliament: Licking Lesbians #1 / 1988 / PM / F • Raging Weekend / 1988 / GO / M • Reflections Of Innocence / 1988 / SEX / M • Reflections Of Innocence / 1991 / VEX / C • The Scent Of Samantha / 1988 / VEX / C • Sex Sluts In The Slammer / 1988 / FAN / M • Sweet Addiction / 1988 / CIN / M • Three Men And A Lady / 1988 / EVN / M • Turn Up The Heat / 1988 / SEX / M • Turn Up The Heat / 1991 / VEX / C • The Wacky World Of X-Rated Bloopers / 1989 / GO / M

CHARLIE
Come With Me / 1995 / GOT / M • Magma: Anal Wedding / 1995 / MET / M • Magma: Insatiable Lust / 1995 / MET / M

CHARLIE (1996)
The Attendant / 1996 / SC / M • Cumback Pussy #4: Get Some!!! / 1996 / EL / M • More Dirty Debutantes #60 / 1997 / SBV / M

CHARLIE ANN
Bus Stop Tales #11 / 1990 / 4P / M

CHARLIE BOY
Secret Sex #3: The Takeover / 1994 / CAT / G

CHARLIE BRIGGS
Bad Penny / 1978 / QX / M

CHARLIE BUCK *see* Jonathan Younger

CHARLIE CALICO
Stevi's: Anal Photographer / 1994 / SSV /

M • Stevi's: Charlie's Sexy Tease / 1996 / SSV / M • Stevi's: Cum Together / 1994 / SSV / F • Stevi's: How Short Do You Want It? / 1994 / SSV / F • Stevi's: Pantyhose Superheroes / 1995 / SSV / F

CHARLIE ELVEGARD
Bel Ami / 1976 / VXP / M

CHARLIE HIGH
Birthday Bash / 1995 / BOT / M

CHARLIE JAMES
Against All Bods / 1991 / VEX / M • Animal Instincts / 1991 / VEX / M • Every Man Should Have One / 1991 / VEX / M • Hot Savannah Nights / 1991 / VEX / M • Queen Of Midnight / 1991 / V99 / M

CHARLIE LATOUR
This is an not-too-pretty old pudgy blonde female.
Anal Rescue 811 / 1992 / PL / M • Confessions Of A Middle Aged Nympho / 1986 / WET / M • Deep & Wet / 1986 / VD / M • Director's Punishment / 1996 / GOT / B • Every Body / 1992 / LAP / M • Fashion Fantasies / 1986 / VC / M • Hidden Fantasies / 1986 / VD / M • Hot Licks / 1984 / SE / M • Lilith Unleashed / 1986 / VC / M • Long Hard Nights / 1984 / ELH / M • Mind Mirror / 1994 / LAP / M • Murder By Sex / 1993 / LAP / M • Ripe And Ready #02 / 1994 / BTO / M • Santa Comes Again / 1990 / GLE / M • Sex Between The Scenes / 1994 / LAP / M • Silence Of The G.A.M.S. / 1992 / CA / M • Temptations Of The Flesh / 1986 / VD / M • Thunderstorm / 1987 / VC / M • Toe Tales #01 / 1992 / GOT / B • VCA Previews #4 / 1988 / VC / C • White Hot / 1984 / VXP / M • Wild In The Sheets / 1984 / WET / M

CHARLIE MACK
Up And Cummers #33 / 1996 / 4P / M • Up And Cummers #34 / 1996 / 4P / M

CHARLIE MARIE
Limited Edition #21 / 1981 / AVC / M

CHARLIE SHOES
The Oval Office / 1991 / LV / M

CHARLIE ST CYR
America's Most Wanted Girl / 1989 / IN / M • Bodies In Heat #2 / 1989 / DR / M • Bring On The Virgins / 1989 / CA / M • Call Girl Academy / 1990 / V99 / M • The Case Of The Crooked Cathouse / 1989 / ME / M • The Last Temptation Of Kristi / 1988 / ME / M • My Bare Lady / 1989 / ME / M • Push It To The Limit / 1988 / EVN / M • Rocky-X #2 / 1988 / PEN / M • Second Skin / 1989 / VC / M • Temptations Of An Angel / 1989 / PEN / M

CHARLIE STONE *see* Eric Price

CHARLIE W. *see Star Index I*

CHARLIE WARNER *see Star Index I*

CHARLOTTA
Magma: Spezial: Black & White #3 / 1995 / MET / M

CHARLOTTE
Beauties In Bondage / 199? / CS / B • M Series #29 / 1994 / LBO / M • Magma: Dreams Of Lust / 1994 / MET / M

CHARLOTTE ANN *see Star Index I*

CHARLOTTE HOLSTEIN
ABA: Double Feature #1 / 1996 / ALP / M • Fanny Hill / 1975 / TGA / M

CHARLOTTE LEE *see* Charlotte O'Hara

CHARLOTTE LEIGH *see* Charlotte O'Hara

CHARLOTTE O'HARA *(Charlotte Leigh, Charlotte Lee)*

Ugly and fat.
As Nasty As She Wants To Be / 1990 / IN / M • Assuming The Position / 1989 / V99 / M • Blonde Temptation / 1995 / IF / M • Dream Dates / 1990 / V99 / M • Gold Diggers / 1993 / IN / M • Hard At Work / 1989 / VEX / M • Hardbreak Ridge / 1990 / WV / M • Heather's Secrets / 1990 / VEX / M • Ladies Lovin' Ladies #3 / 1993 / AFV / F • Oral Hijinx / 1990 / ERU / M • Playing Dirty / 1989 / VEX / M • Raunchy Ranch / 1991 / AFV / M • Riding Miss Daisy / 1990 / VEX / M • Sorority Pink #3 / 1992 / SP / M • Space Cadet / 1989 / IN / M • Sunstroke Beach / 1990 / WV / M • Tropical Temptations / 1989 / VEX / M • The Ultimate Climax / 1989 / V99 / M

CHARLY
Magma: Horny For Cock / 1990 / MET / M

CHARLY RULE
Inside Desiree Cousteau / 1979 / VCX / M

CHARLY SPARK
Hot Diamond / 1995 / LE / M • Up Your Ass #1 / 1996 / ANA / M

CHARLYNE
Older & Bolder In San Francisco / 1996 / TEP / M

CHARLZ see Star Index I

CHARMAINE
Bionic Babes / 1986 / 4P / M • Blue Vanities #555 / 1994 / FFL / M

CHARMEN see Star Index I

CHARMILA see Star Index I

CHARRON PEIPER
Sex Spa USA / 1984 / VC / M

CHASE
More Dirty Debutantes #64 / 1997 / SBV / M

CHASE (, CHRISTIAN) see Christian Chase

CHASE (FEMALE) see Vanessa Chase

CHASE (MALE)
Alexandria, I Love You / 1993 / AFV / M • Cheeks #7: Mirror Image / 1994 / CC / M • Special Reserve / 1994 / VC / M

CHASE ALLEN
Our Trespasses / 1996 / AWV / G

CHASE MANHATTAN (Chayse Manhattan)
[Originally a film involving blonde with real solid cantaloupes but sometimes has dark red hair (still the same cantaloupes) and looks reasonably pretty. Either way the rest of her body is nice and lithe. Spidery looking tattoo on her right belly which consists of a hand and another design plus the words "Rochelle" and "Garret". 20 years old in 1993. In 1996 she has had further tit expansion.
Ace Mulholland / 1995 / ERA / M • Anal Al's Adventures / 1995 / PL / M • Anal Breakdown / 1994 / ROB / M • Anal Delights #3 / 1993 / ROB / M • Anal Plaything #1 / 1994 / ROB / M • Anal Thunder #2 / 1993 / ROB / M • Attitude Adjustment / 1993 / BS / B • The Basket Trick / 1993 / PL / M • Behind The Brown Door / 1994 / PE / M • Booty Sister #1 / 1993 / ROB / M • Both Ends Burning / 1993 / HW / M • Brassiere To Eternity / 1994 / PEP / F • Bruce Seven: A Compendium Of His Most Graphic Scenes Vol 5 / 1994 / BS / C • Bun Busters #08 / 1993 / LBO / M • Butt Watch #04 / 1994 / FH / M • Butthunt / 1994 / AFV / F • Carnal Garden / 1996 / KLP / M • Circus Of Lesbians / 1995 / VI / C • Colossal Orgy #2 /

1994 / HW / M • Eleventh Annual AVN Awards / 1994 / VC / M • Extreme Sex #1: The Club / 1994 / VI / M • Fantasy Fuchs / 1996 / PLP / C • The Girls From Hootersville #05 / 1994 / SFP / M • Girls With Curves #2 / 1994 / CV / M • Gypsy Queen / 1995 / CC / M • Hay Fever / 1988 / TIG / F • Heidigate / 1993 / HO / M • Hello Norma Jeane / 1994 / VT / M • Hot Blooded / 1994 / ERA / M • Indecent Interview / 1995 / PL / F • Kym Wilde's On The Edge #33 / 1996 / RB / B • Leena Is Nasty / 1994 / OD / M • Maui Waui / 1996 / PE / M • Misfits / 1994 / CV / M • New Ends #05 / 1993 / 4P / M • Nipples / 1994 / FOR / F • No Motive / 1994 / MID / M • Private Film #20 / 1995 / OD / M • Private Film #21 / 1995 / OD / M • Private Performance / 1994 / EX / M • Pussyman #03: The Search Continues / 1993 / SNA / M • Pussyman #04: The Celebration / 1993 / SNA / M • The Quest / 1994 / SC / M • Rocco Unleashed / 1994 / SC / M • Sex-A-Fari / 1994 / LV / M • Shaved Sinners #4 / 1993 / VT / M • Sheepless In Montana / 1993 / FOR / M • Steady As She Blows / 1993 / LV / M • Stevi's: Stevi's Second Shaved Shoot / 1995 / SSV / S • Stretchin' The Rear / 1995 / PE / M • Super Ball Sunday / 1994 / LBO / M • A Taste Of Fanny / 1994 / FH / M • The Teacher's Pet / 1993 / LV / M • A Touch Of Leather / 1994 / BS / B • Ultimate Gang Bang #1 / 1994 / HW / M • Venom #4 / 1996 / VD / M • Virgin / 1993 / HW / M • Wild Cherries / 1996 / SC / F • Wild Roomies / 1994 / VC / M

CHASEY (VANESSA) see Vanessa Chase

CHASEY LAINE (Tiffany Anne (CLA))
Discovered by Alexis DeVell and managed by Lucky Smith. She was a dancer and from Florida. Pretty face, nice smile, long light brown/blonde hair, medium droopy tits which she gets inflated during **The Original Wicked Woman** going from a perfectly adequate size to large cantaloupes. From **Chasey Revealed:** 22 years old, 34D-23-34, hazel eyes. First movie was **County Line,** then **Real Tickets** and tit enhancement during **The Original Wicked Woman.** First g/g was with P.J. Sparkxx. Credited as Tiffany Anne in **Tales From The Crypt: Demon Knight.** Married to Justin Sterling.
13th Annual Adult Video News Awards / 1996 / VC / S • Big Busted Dream Girls / 1995 / PME / S • Bloopers & Boners / 1996 / VI / M • Captured On Camera / 1997 / BON / B • Chasey Loves Rocco / 1996 / VI / M • Chasey Revealed / 1994 / WP / M • Chasey Saves The World / 1996 / VI / M • Chasin' The Fifties / 1994 / WP / M • County Line / 1993 / PEP / M • Covergirl / 1994 / WP / M • Domination / 1994 / WP / M • Eleventh Annual AVN Awards / 1994 / VC / M • Erotic Eye / 1995 / DGD / S • Film Buff / 1994 / WP / M • Hawaii / 1995 / VI / M • Hot Bodies In Bondage / 1993 / LBO / B • The House On Chasey Lane / 1995 / VI / M • Internal Affairs / 1995 / VI / M • Interview With A Vibrator / 1996 / WAV / M • Lethal Affairs / 1996 / VI / M • New Wave Hookers #4 / 1994 / VC / M • Once In A Lifetime / 1996 / VC / C • The Original Wicked Woman / 1993 / WP / M • Real Tickets #1 / 1994 / VC / M • Real Tickets #2 / 1994 / VC / M • Restrained By Desire /

1994 / NTP / B • Scrue / 1995 / VI / M • Sex #1 (Vca) / 1994 / VC / M • Sex #2: Fate (Vca) / 1995 / VC / M • Strictly For Pleasure / 1994 / ONA / B • Submission / 1994 / WP / M • Tales From The Crypt Presents Demon Knight / 1994 / NEH / S • View Point / 1995 / VI / M • Viewpoint / 1996 / VI / M • Where The Boys Aren't #9 / 1996 / VI / F • White Wedding / 1995 / VI / M • Wicked As She Seems / 1993 / WP / M • Wicked At Heart / 1995 / WP / M

CHASI
Cum Buttered Corn Holes #3 / 1996 / NIT / C

CHASTITY
Rather a misnomer for a girl in this business, eh? Chastity is black with a passable (pretty in some movies) face, tight body, small tits, narrow hips, small scar in upper left quadrant, nice butt, tattoo on right calf and another on left forearm (both names of ex boyfriends) and a belly button ring. 18 years old in 1995 and de-virginized at 16.
Afro American Dream Girls #1 / 1996 / DR / M • Afro American Dream Girls #2 / 1996 / DR / M • Analtown USA #04 / 1995 / NIT / M • Arcade Slut / 1994 / PSE / B • The Black Butt Sisters Do Boston / 1995 / MID / M • Black Centerfolds #3 / 1996 / MID / M • Black Cheerleader Search #01 / 1996 / ROB / M • Black Jack City #5 / 1995 / HW / M • Bondage "Sybian" Rides / 1994 / PSE / B • Bootylicious: Baby Got Booty / 1996 / JMP / M • Dangerous Behinds #2 / 1996 / HW / M • Eighteen #3 / 1996 / SC / M • Girls II Women / 1996 / AVI / M • Girlz N The Hood #5 / 1995 / HW / M • Hot Flesh, Cold Chains / 1992 / HOM / B • Interview: Barely Legal / 1995 / LV / M • Licorice Lollipops: Back To School / 1996 / HW / M • More Dirty Debutantes #45 / 1995 / 4P / M • My First Time #3 / 1996 / NS / M • N.Y. Video Magazine #09 / 1996 / OUP / M • Penthouse: Satin & Lace #1 / 1992 / PET / F • Sista! #5 / 1996 / VT / F • Sweet Black Cherries #1 / 1996 / TTV / M • Up And Cummers #30 / 1996 / 4P / M • Video Virgins #25 / 1995 / NS / M

CHASTITY QUAOE see Joni Ashley

CHASTITY X
San Francisco Lesbians #2 / 1992 / PL / F

CHASYDEE
Sweet Black Cherries #1 / 1996 / TTV / M

CHATAQUE
Harlem Harlots #2 / 1995 / AVS / M

CHAYSE MANHATTAN see Chase Manhattan

CHAZ CARLTON
Driven Home / 1995 / CSP / G

CHAZ CHASE
Anal Party Girls / 1996 / GV / M • Badgirls #5: Maximum Babes / 1995 / VI / M • Big Boob Ball / 1995 / IF / C • Camp Fire Tramps / 1995 / LOT / M • Catch Of The Day #4 / 1996 / VG0 / M • Caught From Behind #20 / 1995 / HO / M • Dirty Dancers #6 / 1995 / 4P / M • The Erotic Artist / 1995 / VC / M • Girly Video Magazine #4 / 1996 / BEP / M • Hard Core Beginners #02 / 1995 / LEI / M • Hard Core Beginners #04 / 1995 / LEI / M • Hollywood Sex Tour / 1995 / VC / M • Hose Jobs / 1995 / VEX / M • Innocence Lost / 1995 / GO / M • Jug Humpers / 1995 / V99 / C • Killer Tits / 1995 / LE / M • The Last Act / 1995 / VI / M • Lust & Desire / 1996 / WV / M • Mike Hott: #340 Cunt

Of The Month: Westin Chase / 1996 / MHV / M • Mike Hott: #349 Girls Who Swallow Cum #03 / 1996 / MHV / C • Rebel Cheerleaders / 1995 / VI / M • Sex Bandits / 1995 / VC / M • Starbangers #07 / 1995 / FPI / M • Stuff Your Face #3 / 1995 / JMP / M • Three Hearts / 1995 / CC / M • Video Virgins #19 / 1994 / NS / M • Video Virgins #20 / 1995 / NS / M • The Voyeur #4 / 1995 / EA / M

CHAZ DONATELLO

Pearl Necklace: Amorous Amateurs #19 / 1992 / SEE / M • Pearl Necklace: Thee Bush League #11 / 1993 / SEE / M

CHAZ ST PETERS

King Dong / 1985 / SAT / M

CHAZ VIDAL

Biff Malibu's Totally Nasty Home Videos #37 / 1993 / ANA / M • Ona Z's Star Search #01 / 1993 / GLI / M • Ona Z's Star Search #03 / 1993 / GLI / M • Uncle Roy's Amateur Home Video #20 / 1993 / VIM / M

CHAZ VINCENT

Passable face, dark reddish/brownish hair, medium tits, lithe body. Nice personality. SO of Dizzy Blonde.

1-800-934-BOOB / 1992 / VD / C • All-Star Anal Interviews #1 / 1995 / LEI / M • Amateur Nights #03 / 1990 / HO / M • Anal Dawn / 1991 / AMB / M • Anal Ecstacy Girls #2 / 1993 / ROB / F • Anal Intruder #04 / 1990 / CC / M • The Analizer / 1990 / LV / M • Ass Freaks #1 / 1993 / ROB / F • Babes / 1993 / HO / M • Beauty And The Beast #2 / 1990 / VC / M • Black Detail #1 / 1994 / VT / M • Bloopers #2 / 1991 / GO / C • Bossy Babes / 1993 / TCK / M • Bottoms Up (1993-Hollywood) / 1993 / HO / M • Buzzzz! / 1993 / OD / M • Charmed Again / 1989 / VI / M • Chaz & Dizzy Bound At Home / 1990 / BON / B • Cheek Busters / 1990 / FH / M • Coming Of Age / 1989 / CA / M • Crossing Over / 1990 / IN / M • Day Dreams / 1993 / CV / M • Double Impact / 1992 / CDI / G • Fantasy Escorts / 1993 / FOR / M • Flesh / 1996 / EA / M • Fun In A Bun / 1990 / LV / M • The Hardriders / 1990 / 4P / M • Have I Got A Girl For You / 1989 / VEX / M • Heidigate / 1993 / HO / M • Hollywood Assets / 1990 / FH / M • Honey, I Blew Everybody #1 / 1992 / HIO / M • I Do #2 / 1990 / VI / M • I'll Do Anything But... / 1992 / CA / M • In Your Face #2 / 1992 / PL / M • In Your Face #3 / 1995 / PL / M • International Phone Sex Girls #5 / 1991 / PM / M • Kinky Couples / 1990 / VD / M • Ladies Man / 1990 / REB / M • Lips / 1994 / FC / M • Making Tracks / 1990 / DR / M • Mr. Peepers Amateur Home Videos #01: Hot And Nasty / 1991 / LBO / M • Muff Divers #3 / 1996 / TV / F • Nasty Girls #1 (1990-CDI) / 1990 / CIN / M • Nasty Girls #3 (1990-CDI) / 1990 / CDI / M • Ninja Cheerleaders / 1990 / GO / M • No Man's Land #08: Eight Women Who Ate Women / 1993 / VT / F • Nookie Cookies / 1993 / CDI / F • Not So Innocent / 1989 / VEX / M • Not So Innocent / 1990 / HO / M • The Nymphette / 1993 / CA / M • Obsession / 1991 / CDI / M • Odyssey 30 Min: #095: Cream Rises To The Top / 1991 / OD / M • Odyssey Triple Play #13: Girls On Girls / 1992 / OD / F • The Outlaw / 1989 / VD / M • Phone Sex Girls #5 / 1990 / TOR / M • Possession / 1990 / CIN / M • Real People Real Bondage #2 / 1996 / BON / C • Rear-

ing Rachel / 1990 / ZA / M • The Rebel / 1990 / CIN / M • Reel Life / 1993 / ZA / M • Sea Of Lust / 1990 / FAN / M • Sex Punk 2000 / 1993 / FOR / M • She's Got The Juice / 1990 / CDI / M • She's Ready / 1990 / CDI / M • Space Virgins / 1990 / VEX / M • Squirt 'em Cowgirl / 1990 / ERU / M • A Stripper Named Desire / 1993 / CC / M • Surfer Girl / 1992 / PP / M • Swing & Swap #02 / 1990 / CDI / M • Taboo #12 / 1994 / MET / M • Taboo #13 / 1994 / IN / M • Take It To The Limit / 1990 / V99 / M • These Buns For Hire / 1990 / LV / M • Tight Spot / 1992 / VD / M • Tit In A Wringer / 1993 / FC / M • Touched / 1990 / VI / M • True Legends Of Adult Cinema: The Modern Era / 1992 / VC / C • Tug O' Love / 1990 / CC / M • Two Women / 1992 / ROB / M • Vampire's Kiss / 1993 / AVI / M • Veil / 1990 / VI / M • Voices In My Bed / 1993 / VI / M • Wicked Woman / 1994 / HO / M • Young & Natural #06 / 1995 / PRE / F • Young & Natural #08 / 1995 / PRE / F • Young & Natural #09 / 1995 / PRE / C • Young & Natural #11 / 1995 / PRE / F • Young & Natural #12 / 1996 / TV / F

CHE-NE-NE

Fucking Pregnant Babes #1: Che-Ne-Ne's Pelvic Exam / 1995 / AVS / M

CHEEZBOY

KBBS: Weekend With Laurel Canyon / 1992 / KBB / M • Painful Mistake (Dungeon) / 1993 / PL / B

CHELLE

Adorable. Very pretty face, slim body, medium nicely shaped tits, tight waist, nice smile, total body tan.

Anal Playground / 1995 / CA / M • Arches Of Triumph / 1995 / PRE / S • Chained / 1995 / SC / M • Club Kiss / 1995 / ONA / M • Deep Inside Kaitlyn Ashley / 1995 / VC / C • Doin' The Rounds / 1995 / VC / M • Girls Of The Athletic Department / 1995 / VT / M • Hit Ladies / 1995 / PRE / B • Hollywood Sex Tour / 1995 / VC / M • Keyholes / 1995 / OD / M • Lolita / 1995 / SC / M • Masquerade / 1995 / HO / M • Seymore & Shane Live On Tour / 1995 / ULI / M • Swat Team / 1995 / PRE / B • The Voyeur #5 / 1995 / EA / M

CHELLE (SUPREME) *see* **Chelly Supreme**

CHELLY CASEY *see* **Chelly Supreme**

CHELLY KCEE *see* **Chelly Supreme**

CHELLY SUPREME *(Chelly Kcee, Chelly Casey, Shelly Supreme, Chelle (Supreme))*

Older, dark red hair with very white body, humongous enhanced tits, not too pretty.

Adventures Of The DP Boys: Triple Penetration Girls / 1993 / HW / M • America's Raunchiest Home Videos #02: Cooking with Hot Sauce / 1991 / ZA / M • America's Raunchiest Home Videos #31: Miss Dream Tits / 1992 / ZA / M • Anal Takeover / 1993 / PEP / M • Assinine / 1990 / CC / M • Backdoor To Paradise / 1990 / ELV / M • Beach Bum Amateur's #10 / 1992 / MID / M • Big Boob Bangeroo #3 / 1996 / TTV / M • Big Bust Babes #08 / 1991 / AFI / M • Big Bust Babes #13 / 1993 / AFI / M • Big Bust Babes #17 / 1993 / AFI / M • Bobby Hollander's Sweet Cheeks #101 / 1992 / WV / M • Bobby Hollander's Sweet Cheeks #108 / 1993 / QUA / M • Boobytrap...The Next Generation / 1992 / HW / M • Breast Col-

lection #02 / 1995 / LBO / C • Breast Wishes #14 / 1993 / LBO / M • Breast Worx #35 / 1992 / LBO / M • Breast Worx #38 / 1992 / LBO / M • Breastman's Anal Adventure / 1993 / EVN / M • The Butt Connection / 1993 / TIW / M • Candy Ass / 1990 / V99 / M • Confessions #2 / 1992 / OD / M • The Devil In Grandma Jones / 1994 / FC / M • Dirty & Kinky Mature Women #09 / 1996 / C69 / M • Double D Amateurs #01 / 1993 / JMP / M • The Ebony Connection #1 / 1994 / LBO / C • A Few Good Rears / 1993 / IN / M • Foxxxy Lady / 1992 / HW / M • Fresh Tits Of Bel Air / 1992 / OD / M • Golden Oldies #3 / 1995 / TTV / M • Harry Horndog #08: Anal Lovers #1 / 1992 / ZA / M • Harry Horndog #09: Anal Orgy #2 / 1992 / ZA / M • Hollywood Swingers #05 / 1992 / LBO / M • Hot Amateur Nights / 1996 / WV / M • In Pursuit Of Passion / 1990 / V99 / M • It's Only Love / 1992 / VEX / M • Lesbian Lingerie Fantasy #7 / 1991 / ESP / F • Lonely And Blue / 1990 / VEX / M • Mike Hott: #122 Bobby Jo And Shelly / 1990 / MHV / F • Mike Hott: #124 Three Girl Oil Party / 1990 / MHV / F • Mike Hott: #125 Three Girl Lingerie Party / 1990 / MHV / F • Mike Hott: #126 Three Girl Spanking Party #1 / 1990 / MHV / F • Mike Hott: #127 Three Girl Spanking Party #2 / 1990 / MHV / F • Mike Hott: #128 Sex Potpourri / 1990 / MHV / M • Mike Hott: #129 Shelly Gets Sucked / 1990 / MHV / M • Mike Hott: #130 Shelly's Black Gang Bang #1 / 1990 / MHV / M • Mike Hott: #131 Shelly's Black Gang Bang #2 / 1990 / MHV / M • Mike Hott: #164 Jamie Lee And Shelly #1 / 1991 / MHV / F • Mike Hott: #165 Jamie Lee And Shelly #2 / 1991 / MHV / F • Mike Hott: #210 Horny Couples #05 / 1992 / MHV / M • Mike Hott: Apple Asses #04 / 1992 / MHV / F • Mike Hott: Cum Cocktails #2 / 1995 / MHV / C • More Than A Handful #3 / 1993 / MET / M • Mr. Peepers Amateur Home Videos #04: Hot English Muff / 1991 / LBO / M • Mr. Peepers Amateur Home Videos #59: The Ball Of The Wild / 1992 / LBO / M • Nikki's Nightlife / 1992 / IN / M • Objective: D.P. / 1993 / PEP / M • Odyssey 30 Min: #243: / 1992 / OD / M • Odyssey Triple Play #46: Ass-Splitting Sex / 1993 / OD / M • Odyssey Triple Play #47: Backdoor Bingers / 1993 / OD / M • Odyssey Triple Play #53: Butt-Fuck Bash / 1993 / OD / M • Old Throat And D.P. / 1993 / FC / M • Pearl Necklace: Thee Bush League #06 / 1992 / SEE / M • A Reason To Die / 1994 / PEP / M • Ron Hightower's White Chicks #07 / 1993 / LBO / M • Sex Circus / 1994 / VIM / M • Seymore Butts & His Mystery Girl / 1993 / FH / M • Seymore Butts Swings / 1992 / FH / M • Six Plus One #2 / 1993 / VEX / C • Slummin' Hood Girlz / 1993 / CA / M • Star Struck / 1992 / VEX / M • Straight A Students / 1993 / MET / M • Straight A's / 1993 / VC / M • Tails Of Tribeca / 1993 / HW / M • Too Cute For Words / 1992 / V99 / M • Toppers #03 / 1993 / TV / M • Toppers #04 / 1993 / TV / M • Toppers #08 / 1993 / TV / M • Toppers #12 / 1993 / TV / C • Toppers & Whoppers #1 / 1994 / PRE / C • Uncle Roy's Amateur Home Video #15 / 1992 / VIM / M • Uncle Roy's Amateur Home Video #17 / 1993 / VIM / M • Welcome To Bondage: Chelly / 1993 / BON / B • White

Wedding / 1994 / V99 / M

CHELSEA
AHV #22: Hello, I Love You / 1992 / EVN / M • Black Knockers #05 / 1995 / TV / M • Butt Hunt #08 / 1995 / LEI / M • Cat Walk / 1994 / KBR / S • Facial Attraction / 1988 / BEE / C • Fresh Faces #05 / 1995 / EVN / M • Girls Next Door / 1996 / ANE / M • The Godmother #2 / 1988 / VC / M • High Heel Harlots #01 / 1993 / SFP / M • Hollywood Amateurs #18 / 1995 / MID / M • How To Make Love To A Black Woman #1: You Gotta Have Rhythm / 1996 / VCX / M • Meltin' The Burgh / 1996 / DGD / F • The New Ass Masters #10 / 1996 / LEI / C • Pearl Necklace: Thee Bush League #02 / 1992 / SEE / M • Pussy Hunt #13 / 1995 / LEI / M • Sex Lives On Porno Tape / 1992 / VC / C • Skirts & Flirts #01 / 1997 / XPR / F • Swedish Erotica #70 / 1985 / CA / M • Wacked Waitresses / 1986 / CS / B

CHELSEA (ANGEL) see Star Index I
CHELSEA (ENGLISH) see Star Index I
CHELSEA (LYNX) see Chelsea Lynx
CHELSEA ANN (Bella Rio, Simone Taylor)
Quite pretty Hispanic brunette with rock hard enhanced tits. Not adverse to anals and always seems to appear with a wimpy moustachioed male (Jack Mann). Aged 25 in 1993.
Anal Vision #10 / 1993 / LBO / M • Beach Bum Amateur's #25 / 1993 / MID / M • Bobby Hollander's Sweet Cheeks #106 / 1993 / QUA / M • Butt Woman #4 / 1993 / FH / M • Casting Call #03 / 1993 / SO / M • The Girls From Hootersville #01 / 1993 / SFP / M • Heatwave #2 / 1993 / FH / F • Margarita On The Rocks / 1994 / SFP / M • Midnight Angels #01 / 1993 / MID / F • Midnight Angels #02 / 1993 / MID / F • Nympho Zombie Coeds / 1993 / VIM / M • Pearl Necklace: Thee Bush League: The Best Of Oral #01 / 1993 / SEE / C • Pearl Necklace: Thee Bush League #09 / 1993 / SEE / M • Private Video Magazine #03 / 1993 / OD / M • Sodomania #04: Further On Down The Road / 1993 / EL / M

CHELSEA BLAKE
American Babylon / 1985 / PV / M • Burlexxx / 1984 / VC / M • Can't Get Enough / 1000 / CA / M • Christine's Secret / 1986 / FEM / M • Climax / 1985 / CA / M • Cravings / 1987 / VC / M • Dick Of Death / 1985 / VCR / M • First Time At Cherry High / 1984 / VC / M • Great Sexpectations / 1984 / VC / M • Inside Everybody / 1984 / AVC / M • Jailhouse Girls / 1984 / VC / M • Pleasure Island / 1984 / AR / M • Public Affairs / 1984 / CA / M • Pussycat Galore / 1984 / VC / M • Raw Talent #1 / 1984 / VC / M • Return To Alpha Blue / 1984 / AVC / M • Shauna: Every Man's Fantasy / 1985 / CA / C • Succulent / 1983 / VXP / M • Supergirls Do General Hospital / 1984 / VC / M • Tight Delight / 1985 / VXP / M • Turn On With Kelly Nichols / 1984 / CA / M • Urban Heat / 1985 / FEM / M • Vanessa...Maid In Manhattan / 1984 / VC / M • VCA Previews #4 / 1988 / VC / C

CHELSEA BLUE
Anal Inquisition / 1996 / ZA / M • Anal Party Girls / 1996 / GV / M • Analtown USA #09 / 1995 / NIT / M • Another Fuckin' Anal Movie / 1996 / ROB / M • Anything Goes / 1996 / OUP / M • As Easy As A Bunch Of Cunts / 1996 / ROB / F • Ass Lover's Special /

1996 / PE / M • Bobby Sox / 1996 / VI / S • Carnal Invasions / 1996 / NIT / M • The Contessa De Sade / 1996 / LBO / B • Corn Hole Kittens / 1996 / ROB / F • Cumback Pussy #5: Groopin' / 1996 / EL / M • Dirty Dirty Debutantes #6 / 1996 / 4P / M • Extreme Close-Up / 1996 / VI / M • Fashion Sluts #8 / 1996 / ABS / M • Head To Head VI / 1996 / VI / M • Introducing Alexis / 1996 / VI / M • Jizz Glazed Goo Guzzlers #2 / 1996 / NIT / C • Kym Wilde's On The Edge #34 / 1996 / RB / B • Leg Show #2 / 1996 / NIT / M • Lesbian C*Nt Whores / 1996 / ROB / F • Lovin' Spoonfuls #8 / 1996 / 4P / C • NYDP Blue / 1996 / WP / M • Pick Up Lines #04 / 1995 / 4P / M • Prime Choice #5 / 1996 / RAS / M • Pussyman Auditions #19 / 1996 / SNA / M • Raw Silk / 1996 / RAS / M • Return Of The Knickers Inspector / 1994 / CS / B • Silver Screen Confidential / 1996 / WP / M • The Sodomizer #2 / 1995 / SC / M • Whitey's On The Moon / 1996 / ROB / M • Wild Cherries / 1996 / SC / F

CHELSEA DALLAS see Star Index I
CHELSEA GRANT
Anal Receivers / 3996 / MP0 / M

CHELSEA LANE
Anal Vision #01 / 1992 / LBO / M

CHELSEA LANE (LYNX) see Chelsea Lynx

CHELSEA LYNX (Chelsea (Lynx), Lynx (Chelsea), Minx, Siska, Chelsea Lane (Lynx))
Adorable tight bodied girl from the Philippines (but says she is from Malaysia in Up And Cummers #05) with small tits, tight waist and nice boy-like butt. 18 years old in 1992 and has been in the US for about 6 years.
AHV #40: Whole Lotta Love / 1993 / EVN / M • America's Raunchiest Home Videos #41: Welcum Neighbor / 1992 / ZA / M • Asian Heat #01: Cherry Blossom Tales / 1993 / SC / M • Asian Heat #02: Satin Angels / 1993 / SC / M • Asian Invasion / 1993 / IP / M • Biff Malibu's Totally Nasty Home Videos #22 / 1992 / ANA / M • Blow For Blow / 1992 / ZA / M • Blow Job Baby / 1993 / CC / M • Casanova #4 / 1993 / SC / M • Geisha Gall Rill #11 / 1991 / CL / M • Deep Inside Dirty Debutantes #05 / 1993 / 4P / M • Euro Studs / 1996 / SC / C • Fantasy Exchange / 1993 / VI / M • Foxxxy Lady / 1992 / HW / M • Harry Horndog #11: Love Puppies #2 / 1992 / ZA / M • Intervidnet #1: Special Delivery / 1994 / IVN / M • Love Letters #1 / 1993 / SC / M • Lovin' Spoonfuls #4 / 1995 / 4P / C • Lovin' Spoonfuls #6 / 1996 / 4P / C • The Man Who Loved Women / 1993 / SC / M • More Dirty Debutantes #19 / 1993 / 4P / M • More Dirty Debutantes #20 / 1993 / 4P / M • More Dirty Debutantes #22 / 1993 / 4P / M • More Dirty Debutantes #24 / 1993 / 4P / M • More Dirty Debutantes #30 / 1994 / 4P / M • The Natural / 1993 / VT / M • Neighborhood Watch #38: Pearlie's Curlie's / 1993 / LBO / M • Oriental Sorority Secrets / 1992 / VIM / M • The Other Side Of Chelsea / 1993 / XCI / M • Pearl Necklace: Amorous Amateurs #33 / 1992 / SEE / M • Pudsucker / 1994 / MID / M • The Seduction Of Julia Ann / 1993 / VT / M • Sneek Peeks #2 / 1993 / OCV / M • Super Hornio Brothers / 1993 / MID / M • Super Hornio Brothers #2 / 1993 / MID / M •

Swinging Couples #02 / 1993 / GO / M • Up And Cummers #05 / 1993 / 4P / M

CHELSEA MANCHESTER (Tigr, Chelsea McClane, Tigr Minette, Tieger, Tigr Mennett, Tina Mennett)
Tigr Minette in **Lips**. Passable face, dark blonde with small to medium tits, erect nipples.
1001 Erotic Nights #1 / 1982 / VC / M • 8 To 4 / 1981 / CA / M • All About Annette / 1982 / SE / C • All Day Suckers / cr77 / BOC / M • All The King's Ladies / 1981 / SUP / M • Babes In Toyland / 1988 / COM / C • Bedtime Tales / 1985 / SE / M • Between The Sheets / 1982 / CA / M • Blue Vanities #031 / 1988 / FFL / M • Body Girls / 1983 / SE / M • C.T. Coed Teasers / 1978 / VXP / M • Caballero Preview Tape #2 / 1983 / CA / C • Caballero Preview Tape #3 / 1984 / CA / C • Campus Capers / 1982 / VC / M • Chastity Kidd / 1983 / COM / M • Daddy's Little Girls / 1983 / CA / M • Dangerous Women / 1987 / WET / M • Dark Angel / 1983 / VC / M • Diamond Collection #19 / 1982 / CDI / M • Down Under / 1986 / VIP / M • The Erotic Aventures Of Lolita / 1982 / VXP / M • Erotic Dimensions #3: My Way! / 1982 / NSV / M • Erotic Dimensions: Bold Fantasies / 1982 / NSV / M • Erotic Dimensions: Explicit / 1982 / NSV / M • Erotic Dimensions: The Wild Life / 1982 / NSV / M • F...It / 1987 / SE / C • Foreplay / 1982 / VC / M • Go For It / 1984 / VC / M • Her Wicked Ways / 1983 / CA / M • Hot School Reunion / 1984 / CHX / F • Hottest Parties / 1988 / VC / C • House Of Sin / 1982 / AVO / M • I Want To Be Bad / 1984 / CV / M • Indecent Exposure / 1981 / CA / M • Kamikaze Hearts / 1986 / FAC / S • Ladies Nights / 1980 / VC / M • Lips: The Passage To Pleasure / 1981 / CA / M • Little Girls Lost / 1982 / VC / M • Love Scenes For Loving Couples / 1987 / CV / C • Matinee Idol / 1984 / VC / M • Never Sleep Alone / 1984 / CA / M • Never So Deep / 1981 / VCX / M • Nightlife / 1983 / CA / M • Nothing To Hide #1 / 1981 / CV / M • Nurses Of The 407th / 1982 / CA / M • Open Lips / 1983 / AVO / M • Peaches And Cream / 1982 / SE / M • Please, Mr Postman / 1981 / VC / M • Purely Physical / 1982 / SE / M • Salt & Pepper / 1986 / VCS / C • San Fernando Valley Girls / 1983 / CA / M • Scoundrels / 1982 / COM / M • Spitfire / 1984 / COM / M • Star Angel / 1986 / COM / M • Stephanie's Lust Story / 1983 / VC / M • Sulka's Wedding / 1983 / MET / G • Suzie Superstar #1 / 1983 / CV / M • Taboo #07 / 1980 / IN / M • This Babe's For You / 1984 / TAR / M • Trashi / 1980 / CA / M • Undercovers / 1982 / CA / M • UPS / 1981 / ... / M • VCA Previews #1 / 1988 / VC / C • Water Nymph / 1987 / LIM / M • When She Was Bad / 1983 / CA / M • Wild Dallas Honey / 1985 / VCX / M • With Love, Loni / 1985 / CA / C • Women At Play / 1984 / SE / M • [Erotic Dimensions Vols 1 To 8 / 1983 / NSV / C

CHELSEA MCCLANE see Chelsea Manchester
CHELSEA PFEIFFER
Lessons Learned / 1994 / HAC / B • My Maid Maria / 1996 / SHL / B • Nurses Know Best / 1994 / SHL / B • Spanking Double Feature / 1994 / SHL / B

CHELSEA RAY
Behind Blue Eyes #1 / 1986 / ME / M • Dr

Juice's Lust Potion / 1986 / TEM / M •
Women In Uniform / 1986 / TEM / M
CHELSEA ROSE see Star Index I
CHELSEA RYAN
The Dinner Party / 1995 / ERA / M
CHELSEA WOLF see Star Index I
CHELSEY NOON
Desires Within Young Girls / 1977 / CA / M
CHENEL see Chanel (1992)
CHENELLE REEMO see Star Index I
CHENIN BLANC
Pick Up Lines #08 / 1996 / OD / M • Up And
Cummers #27 / 1996 / ERW / M
CHENISE
Tight Home Girls / 1993 / EVN / C
CHENISE SMITH
Black Lust / 1995 / UBP / M
CHENNEL
Joe Elliot's College Girls #29 / 1994 / JOE
/ M • Joe Elliot's College Girls #32 / 1994 /
JOE / M • Kinky College Cunts #24 / 1993
/ NS / M
CHER
A&B AB#444: Sexy Cher / 1994 / A&B / M
• A&B AB#445: Please Let Me Lick It Up /
1995 / A&B / M • Good Times / 1967 / ... /
S • Rump Humpers #03 / 1992 / GLI / M
CHER DELIGHT *(Kathryn Moore, Sher
Delight, Cathlyn Moore, Sheer Delight,
Kathlyn Moore, Denise Kelly)*
Big body, big tits, passable face, blonde. Had
her first child in June 1986. Denise Kelly is
from **Amber Aroused**.
Amber Aroused / 1985 / CA / M • Bedtime
Tales / 1985 / SE / M • Blonde On Black /
1986 / CC / F • Camp Beaverlake #1 / 1984
/ AR / M • Candy Stripers #2 / 1985 / AR /
M • Cavalcade Of Stars / 1985 / VCR / C •
Chocolate Delights #1 / 1985 / TAG / C •
The Eyes Of Eddie Mars / 1984 / CV / M •
For Your Thighs Only / 1985 / WV / M •
Four X Feeling / 1986 / QX / M • Gettin'
Ready / 1985 / CDI / M • Girl Busters /
1985 / VC / M • Heart Breaker / 1985 / TAR
/ C • Honeybuns #1 / 1987 / WV / C • Hot
Nights At The Blue Note Cafe / 1985 / WV
/ M • Hot Touch / 1984 / VCX / M • Inches
For Keisha / 1988 / WV / C • Indecent Itch
/ 1985 / VCR / M • The Initiation Of Cynthia
/ 1985 / VXP / M • The Melting Spot / 1985
/ VSE / M • Oral Majority #02 / 1987 / WV /
C • A Passage Thru Pamela / 1985 / VC /
G • Pulsating Flesh / 1986 / VC / M • Sex
Drive / 1984 / VXP / M • Showdown / 1985
/ BON / B • Snatchbuckler / 1985 / DR / M
• A Taste Of Genie / 1986 / 4P / M • Tip Of
The Tongue / 1985 / V20 / M
CHERANNE CASE see Kandi Jones
CHERELLE *(Scherell)*
Hard looking girl with piggy eyes who in **Hard
Core Beginners #01** says she's German
from Hamburg and in **Casting Call #12**
says she's French. Medium droopy tits,
womanly body.
Black Ass Masters #1 / 1995 / GLI / M • The
Breast Files #3 / 1994 / AVI / M • Busty
Backdoor Nurses / 1996 / PL / M • Casting
Call #12 / 1995 / MET / M • Cherry Poppers
#10: Sweet And Sassy / 1995 / ZA / M •
Hard Core Beginners #01 / 1995 / LEI / M
• Hard Core Beginners #07 / 1995 / LEI / M
• Heavenly / 1995 / IF / M • LA Nasty / 1995
/ SP / M • Nasty Nymphos #08 / 1995 / ANA
/ M • The New Ass Masters #08 / 1996 / LEI
/ C • Private Gold #04: Amazonas / 1996 /
OD / M • Show Business / 1995 / LV / M •

The Stranger / 1996 / BEP / M • Swedish
Erotica #85 / 1995 / CA / M • Triple X Video
Magazine #10 / 1995 / OD / M • Tropical
Taboo / 1995 / HO / M • Wet Mask / 1995 /
SC / M
CHERELLE MARIE
Blackman / 1989 / PL / M • Here...Eat This!
/ 1990 / FAZ / M
CHERI
Black Mystique #14 / 1995 / VT / F • Blue
Vanities #571 / 1995 / FFL / M • Bull Dyke
Humiliation / 1993 / PL / B • Dirty Doc's
Housecalls #06 / 1993 / LV / M • Fantasy
Photography: Cheri's Passion / 1995 / FAP
/ F • Pantyhose Teasers #2 / 1992 / JBV /
S • Pretty Soles And Toes / 1993 / JBV / B
• Pussy Tales / 1993 / SC / F • Slave Girls'
Agony / 1993 / PL / B
**CHERI (MARILYN ROSE) see Marilyn
Rose**
CHERI AMOUR see Star Index I
CHERI ANDERSON see Elaine Southern
CHERI BAINES see Star Index I
CHERI BONBON
Old Wave Hookers #2 / 1995 / PL / M
CHERI BONET see Alicyn Sterling
CHERI CARSON
Triple Play / 1983 / HO / M
CHERI CAVUER see Cheri Janvier
CHERI CHAMPAGNE *(Destiny Duval)*
Brunette, medium tits, passable face, lithe
body.
Dr Bizarro / 1978 / ALP / B • Forgive Me, I
Have Sinned / 1982 / ALP / B • Heaven's
Touch / 1983 / CA / M • Island Love / 1983
/ SHO / M • Luscious / 1980 / VXP / M •
Midnight Heat / 1982 / VC / M • Night
Hunger / 1983 / AVC / M • Open Lips / 1983
/ AVO / M • Peepholes / 1982 / AVC / M •
Puss 'n' Boots / 1982 / VXP / M • The
Pussy Burglar / 1983 / SHO / M • Sex
Stalker / 1983 / MPP / M • The Stimulators
/ 1983 / VC / M • The Story Of Prunella /
1982 / AVO / M • Sweet Little Sister/The
Dreamer / 1983 / SHO / M • Tales Of The
Bizarre / 1983 / ALP / B • The Taming Of
Rebecca / 1982 / SVE / B
CHERI CHARLENE see Cheri Janvier
CHERI GARNER see Cheri Janvier
CHERI GARNIER see Cheri Janvier
CHERI GENEVIEVE see Cheri Janvier
CHERI HILL *(Fawn Roberts)*
Fawn Roberts in **G Spot Girls**.
After The Lights Go Out / 1989 / VEX / M •
Bimbo Cheerleaders From Outer Space /
1988 / FAN / M • Blonde Temptation / 1995
/ IF / M • Can't Beat The Feeling / 1988 /
VEX / M • Eye Of The Tigress / 1988 / VD
/ M • Fantasy Girls / 1988 / CA / M • G Spot
Girls / 1988 / V99 / M • Hot Summer Nites
/ 1988 / VEX / M • I Found My Thrill On
Cheri Hill / 1988 / PL / M • The Legend Of
Reggie D. / 1989 / EA / M • Littledove's Cup
/ 1988 / FOV / M • My Wife Is A Call Girl /
1989 / FAZ / M • Porn Star's Day Off / 1990
/ FAZ / M • Port Holes / 1988 / AVC / M •
Proposals / 1988 / CC / M • Salsa Break /
1989 / EA / M • Sex On The Town / 1989 /
V99 / M • Shameless Desire / 1989 / VEX /
M • Steam Heat / 1989 / VEX / M • Suite
Sensations / 1988 / SEX / M • Sweet Addiction / 1988 / CIN / M • Sweet Sensations
/ 1989 / SEX / M • Three Men And A Barbi
/ 1989 / FAN / M • Two Women & A Man /
1988 / VEX / M
CHERI JANVIEL see Cheri Janvier

CHERI JANVIER *(Mon Cheri Janvier,
Cheri Garnier, Sheri Gavner, Cherri
Janvier, Cheri Cavuer, Cheri Janviel,
Cheri Genevieve, Cheri Garner, Cherri
Gardner, Cherie Cavuer, Cheri Char-
lene)*
Anal Reamers / 1986 / 4P / M • Back To
Back #1 / 1987 / 4P / C • Beaverly Hills Cop
/ 1985 / SE / M • Boobs, Butts And Bloop-
ers #2 / 1990 / HO / M • Carrie...Sex On
Wheels / 1985 / AA / M • Caught From Be-
hind #03 / 1985 / HO / M • Coming Holmes
/ 1985 / VD / M • Double Penetration #2 /
1986 / WV / C • Erotica Jones / 1985 / AVC
/ M • Firefoxes / 1985 / PLY / M • Girls Of
Cell Block F / 1985 / WV / M • The Girls Of
The A Team #1 / 1985 / WV / M • Hollywood
Pink / 1985 / HO / M • Just Another Pretty
Face / 1985 / AVC / M • A Little Dynasty /
1985 / CIV / M • Loose Morals / 1987 / HO
/ M • The Lover Girls / 1985 / VEX / M •
Lust American Style / 1985 / WV / M • Lust
Bug / 1985 / HO / M • Naked Lust / 1985 /
SE / M • Open Up Tracy / 1984 / VD / M •
Oral Majority #01 / 1986 / WV / C • Pipe
Dreams / 1985 / 4P / M • The Pornbirds /
1985 / VC / M • The Pussywillows / 1985 /
SUV / M • The Ribald Tales Of Canterbury
/ 1986 / CA / M • Surfside Sex / 1985 / PV
/ M • Toys 4 Us #1 / 1987 / WV / C • Toys 4
Us #2 / 1987 / WV / C • Trashy Lady / 1985
/ MAP / M • Woman Times Four / 1983 /
LIP / F
CHERI LAI-ME
Black Dynasty / 1985 / VD / M • Black Val-
ley Girls #1 / 1986 / 4R / M • Detroit Dames
/ 1988 / DR / C • Funky Brewster / 1986 /
DR / M • Let Me Tell Ya 'Bout Black Chicks
/ 1985 / VC / M • Licorice Twists / 1985 /
WET / M • Professor Probe And The Spirit
Of Sex / 1986 / ADU / M
CHERI LAINE
The Big E #08 / 1988 / BIZ / B
CHERI LARKIN see Star Index I
CHERI LEBLANC see Star Index I
CHERI LYNN see Cody O'Connor
CHERI MONTEREY *(Jette Montery)*
Adorable little brunette.
The Girls' Club / 1990 / VC / F • More Dirty
Debutantes #03 / 1990 / 4P / M • P.S.: Back
Alley Cats #04 / 1992 / PSP / F • P.S.: Back
Alley Cats #05 / 1992 / PSP / F
CHERI MOON see Star Index I
CHERI NICOLE see Star Index I
CHERI ROBERTS see Lisa Lake
CHERI ST CLAIR see Sheri St Clair
CHERI SWELLS
Dungeon De Sade / 1993 / FC / B • Life In
The Fat Lane #3 / 1990 / FC / M • Makin'
Bacon / 1994 / WIV / M
CHERI TAYLOR *(Cheryl Taylor)*
Not too pretty hard blonde with inflated large
tits. Born November 15, 1952 according to
Bloopers #2.
Adultery / 1989 / PP / M • As The Spirit
Moves You / 1990 / LV / M • Bend Over
Babes #1 / 1990 / EA / M • The Best Of An-
drew Blake / 1993 / CA / C • Best Of
Buttman #1 / 1991 / EA / C • Bimbo
Bowlers From Boston / 1990 / ZA / M •
Bloopers #2 / 1991 / GO / C • Boobs, Butts
And Bloopers #1 / 1990 / HO / M • Bruce
Seven's Favorite Endings #1 / 1991 / EL /
C • Busting Loose / 1989 / AMB / F • Cali-
fornia Blondes #03 / 1991 / VD / C • Cheri
Taylor Is Tasty And Tight / 1991 / ZA / M •

Club Lez / 1990 / PL / F • Coming Of Age / 1989 / CA / M • Cool Sheets / 1989 / PP / M • The Crack Of Dawn / 1989 / GLE / M • De Blond / 1989 / EA / M • Devil In The Blue Dress / 1989 / ME / M • The Dong Show #01 / 1990 / AMB / M • Down 4 Busine$$ / 1989 / GMI / M • Dreams Of The Everyday Housewife / 1990 / FAZ / M • The Easy Way / 1990 / VC / M • Flesh Mountain / 1994 / VI / C • Ghost Lusters / 1990 / EL / F • Girl Crazy / 1989 / CDI / F • The Girls Are Bustin' Loose / 1988 / AMB / F • Girls Of The Double D #14 / 1990 / CIN / M • Hard On The Press / 1991 / AWV / M • Head Lock / 1989 / VD / M • Heather Hunter's Bedtime Stories / 1991 / GLE / C • Heather's Home Movies / 1989 / VWA / M • Hot Palms / 1989 / GO / M • Hot Scalding / 1989 / VC / M • Hot Talk Radio / 1989 / VWA / M • I Do #1 / 1989 / VI / M • If You're Nasty / 1991 / PL / F • Inner Pink #2 / 1989 / LIP / F • Insatiable Immigrants / 1989 / VT / M • Invitation Only / 1989 / AMB / M • Itty Bitty Titty Committee #1 / 1990 / PL / F • Joint Effort / 1992 / SEX / C • Kinky Business #2 / 1989 / DR / M • Kiss My Grits / 1989 / CA / M • The Last Temptation / 1988 / VD / M • Le Sex De Femme #1 / 1989 / AFI / C • The Legend Of Sleepy Hollow / 1989 / LE / M • The Luscious Baker Girls / 1990 / VD / M • Manbait #2 / 1992 / VC / M • Meat Market / 1992 / SEX / C • Meltdown / 1990 / LV / M • Monday Nite Ball / 1990 / VT / M • Mystic Pieces / 1989 / EA / M • Nasty Girls #2 (1990-Plum) / 1990 / PP / M • Nasty Girls #3 (1990-Plum) / 1990 / PP / M • Naughty Neighbors / 1989 / CA / M • Never Enough / 1990 / PP / M • Night Trips #2 / 1990 / CA / M • Oh, What A Night! / 1990 / VC / M • On The Prowl #1 / 1989 / SC / M • One Night Stand / 1990 / LE / M • Out For Blood / 1990 / VI / M • The Perfect Brat / 1989 / VI / M • Personal Touch #4 / 1989 / AR / M • Rainwoman #02 / 1990 / CC / M • Raw Sewage / 1989 / FC / M • Real Magnolias / 1990 / AWV / M • Rock 'n' Roll Heaven / 1989 / EA / M • Saturday Night Special / 1989 / DR / M • Scandalous / 1989 / CC / M • The Scarlet Bride / 1989 / VI / M • Secrets / 1990 / VI / M • Selena's Secrets / 1991 / MIN / M • Sex And The Secretary / 1988 / PP / M • Sex Sluts From Beyond The Galaxy / 1991 / LBO / C • Sex Toy / 1993 / CA / C • Sexual Fantasies / 1993 / ... / C • Sexual Relations / 1990 / PP / M • Studio Sex / 1990 / FH / M • Swedish Erotica Featurettes #2 / 1989 / CA / M • Tales By Taylor / 1989 / AMB / M • A Taste Of Cheri / 1990 / PIN / C • Taylor Made / 1989 / DR / M • Temptations Of An Angel / 1989 / PEN / M • This Dick For Hire / 1989 / ZA / M • This One's For You / 1989 / AR / M • Triangle / 1989 / VI / M • True Confessions Of Hyapatia Lee / 1989 / VI / M • Unchain My Heart / 1990 / CC / M • Welcome To The House Of Fur Pi / 1989 / GO / M • Where The Boys Aren't #2 / 1989 / VI / F • Where The Boys Aren't #3 / 1990 / VI / F • Words Of Love / 1989 / LE / M • Worthy Women / 1990 / AWV / M • X-Rated Bloopers #2 / 1986 / AR / M

CHERIE CAVUER *see* **Cheri Janvier**
CHERIE KENT
School For Sex / cr72 / SOW / M
CHERIE SYLVAN *see* **Star Index I**
CHERISE

Dream House / 1995 / XPR / M
CHERISH
Bitch School / 1996 / BON / B • Final Orgy / 1996 / BON / B • Wet Screams / 1996 / BON / B
CHEROKEE *(Cleopatra (Cherokee))*
Black girl a masculine body, tiny tits, hairy pussy, a face that looks like it's a mask with lots of make-up, narrow hips, not a tight waist, 26 years old in 1996. In **More Black Dirty Debutantes #6** she's credited as and says her name is Cleopatra but she's not the same as any of the girls in **Innocent Little Girls** so one presumes there are several.
The Adventures Of Peeping Tom #2 / 1996 / OD / M • All That: Black Women's Fantasies / 1996 / VT / M • Anal Climax #4 / 1996 / ROB / M • Back Rent / 1996 / MP0 / M • Black Cheerleader Search #03 / 1996 / ROB / M • Black Hose Bag / 1996 / ROB / M • Black Pussyman Auditions #1 / 1996 / SNA / M • Black Video Virgins #1 / 1996 / NS / M • Booty Sister #2 / 1996 / ROB / M • Creme De La Face #13: Nine Nasty Nymphs / 1995 / OD / M • Creme De La Face #14: Kiss My Cum / 1996 / OD / M • Domination Nation / 1996 / VI / M • Essence / 1996 / SO / M • Harness Hannah At The Strap-On Palace / 1994 / WIV / F • More Black Dirty Debutantes #6 / 1996 / 4P / M • My Baby Got Back #08 / 1996 / VT / M • My Baby Got Back #09 / 1996 / VT / M • New Pussy Hunt #28 / 1997 / LEI / C • Primal Instinct / 1996 / SNA / M • Sumo Sue And The Fat Ladies Of Wrestling / 1988 / FAN / M • Tailz From Da Hood #4 / 1996 / AVI / M • Tailz From Da Hood #5 / 1996 / AVI / M • Up And Cummers #28 / 1996 / ERW / M • Vivid Raw #1 / 1996 / VI / M • Waiting For The Man / 1996 / VT / M • Whitey's On The Moon / 1996 / ROB / M
CHERRI BUSH *see* **Elaine Southern**
CHERRI GARDNER *see* **Cheri Janvier**
CHERRI HILL (LS) *see* **Laurie Smith**
CHERRI JANOVIER *see* **Cheri Janvier**
CHERRI ORCHARD
Cheerleaders In Bondage #1 / 1994 / GOT / B • Final Test / 1993 / GOT / B • Mistress Of The Whip / 1996 / GOT / C • Stroke Of Nine / 1994 / GOT / B • Toe Tales #08 / 1993 / GOT / B • Toe Tales #12 / 1994 / GOT / C • Trial And Error / 1994 / GOT / B
CHERRI SUMMERS *see* **Rene Summers**
CHERRI SWELLS
Rollie Pollie Chicks / 1996 / TTV / M
CHERRIE *see* **Star Index I**
CHERRIE KNIGHT
Blue Vanities #112 / 1988 / FFL / M
CHERRY
A&B AB#502: Cherry / 1995 / A&B / M • A&B Dr. Lisa #1: Oh Doctor Put It In / 1990 / A&B / M • A&B GB#002: Sperm Bank #1 / 1992 / A&B / M • A&B GB#053: Sperm Bank #2 / 1992 / A&B / M • After Hours Bondage / 1993 / BON / B • Becky S: Becky And Cherry / 1994 / BEC / F • Bound For Therapy / 1991 / BIZ / B • Ebony Assets / 1994 / VBE / M • Hard Ride / 1992 / WV / M • Home Maid Memories #2 / 1994 / BON / C • Strap-On Sally #03: Thigh Harness Terror / 1994 / PL / F • Strap-On Sally #04: Double Penetration Dykes / 1994 / PL / F • Thinking Of You / 1992 / LV / F
CHERRY (NIKKI PINK) *see* **Nikki Pink**
CHERRY ADAMS
Burning Desire / 1983 / HO / M • A Lacy Af-

fair #1 / 1983 / HO / F • Toys, Not Boys #3 / 1991 / FC / C • Why Gentlemen Prefer Blondes / 1983 / HO / C
CHERRY BEAUCHAMP *see* **Chrissy Beauchamp**
CHERRY BLOSSOM *see* **Suzie Suzuki**
CHERRY BOMB *see* **Star Index I**
CHERRY CHEN *see* **Lulu Chang**
CHERRY DEVINE *see* **Star Index I**
CHERRY DIVINE
GVC: Forbidden Ways #114 / 1978 / GO / M
CHERRY ELLAY *see* **Star Index I**
CHERRY GRAMME *see* **Star Index I**
CHERRY JAMES *see* **Star Index I**
CHERRY KNIGHT
Blue Vanities #506 / 1992 / FFL / M • Blue Vanities #515 / 1992 / FFL / M • Erotica / 1961 / RMV / S • Teaserama / 1954 / SOW / S • Varietease / 1955 / SOW / S
CHERRY LANSON *see* **Cherry Lawson**
CHERRY LAWSON *(Cherry Lanson)*
Not too good looking blonde with a falling apart body, very white skin and droopy medium tits.
Amateur Lesbians #28: Sharon / 1992 / GO / F • Amateur Orgies #08 / 1992 / AFI / M • Amateur Orgies #13 / 1992 / AFI / M • Amateurs Exposed #01 / 1993 / CV / M • America's Raunchiest Home Videos #29: Love Box / 1992 / ZA / M • Anal Therapy #1 / 1992 / FD / M • Art Of Sex / 1992 / FD / M • Backdoor To Russia #3 / 1993 / VC / M • Beach Bum Amateur's #08 / 1992 / MID / M • Biff Malibu's Totally Nasty Home Videos #11 / 1992 / ANA / M • Big Murray's New-Cummers #03: Orgy 'Til Dawn / 1992 / FD / M • Big Murray's New-Cummers #04: Booty Love / 1992 / FD / M • The Bodacious Boat Orgy #1 / 1993 / GLI / M • Breast Worx #30 / 1992 / LBO / M • Breast Worx #32 / 1992 / LBO / M • Bruise Control / 1993 / PRE / B • Daughters Of Discipline / 1993 / GOT / B • Double D Dykes #03 / 1992 / GO / F • Enemates #07 / 1992 / PRE / B • Flood Control / 1992 / PRE / B • Gang Bang Pussycat / 1992 / ROB / M • Gang Bang Thrills / 1992 / ROB / M • Glitz Tits #01 / 1992 / GLI / M • Horny Housedog #09. Anal Orgy #2 / 1992 / ZA / M • Honeymooned / 1992 / PRE / B • Leg...Ends #08 / 1993 / PRE / F • Lesbian Pros And Amateurs #15 / 1992 / GO / F • The Long & Short Of It / 1992 / RUM / F • The Maltese Bimbo / 1993 / FD / M • Manwiched / 1992 / FPI / M • Midnight Fantasies / 1992 / VIM / M • Motel Hell / 1992 / PL / M • Neighborhood Watch #34 / 1992 / LBO / M • Odyssey 30 Min: #202: / 1992 / OD / M • Odyssey 30 Min: #212: / 1992 / OD / M • Odyssey 30 Min: #229: / 1992 / OD / M • Odyssey 30 Min: #230: / 1992 / OD / M • Odyssey 30 Min: #242: / 1992 / OD / M • Odyssey Triple Play #33: 3 Back-Door Boinkers / 1993 / OD / M • Our Bang #06 / 1992 / GLI / M • Our Bang #07 / 1992 / GLI / M • Positively Pagan #01 / 1991 / ATA / M • Positively Pagan #04 / 1991 / ATA / M • Pudsucker / 1994 / MID / M • Raw Talent: Bang 'er 23 Times / 1992 / RTP / M • Raw Talent: Bang Kitty Foxx / 1994 / RTP / M • Raw Talent: Fetish Of The Month #04 / 1994 / RTP / G • Raw Talent: Top Bang / 1994 / RTP / M • Sailor Beware / 1993 / GOT / B • Spring Break / 1992 / PL / M • Suspension In Latex / 1992 / GOT / B • Toe

Tales #04 / 1992 / GOT / B • Twin Peaks / 1993 / PL / M • Ultimate Orgy #3 / 1992 / GLI / M • Vice Versa / 1992 / FD / M • Will & Ed's Keister Easter / 1992 / MID / M • Will And Ed: The Curse Of Poona / 1994 / MID / C • Women Who Love Men, Men Who Love Women / 1993 / FD / C • Yank Fest / 1994 / FD / C • Zane's World / 1992 / ZA / M

CHERRY PITT
Student Fetish Videos: Bondage #03 / 1996 / PRE / B • Student Fetish Videos: Catfighting #17 / 1996 / PRE / B • Student Fetish Videos: The Enema #16 / 1994 / PRE / B • Student Fetish Videos: Foot Worship #18 / 1995 / PRE / B • Student Fetish Videos: Spanking #17 / 1994 / PRE / B • Student Fetish Videos: Tickling #10 / 1994 / SFV / B

CHERRY SHANE
[The Surprised Coed / 197? / … / M

CHERRY SMITH see Star Index I
CHERRY STONE see Kaitlyn Ashley
CHERRY SUNDAE
Deeper Spikes / 1984 / BIZ / B • First Training / 1987 / BIZ / B

CHERRY SWELLS
Heavyweight Contenders / 1996 / HW / M

CHERRY WOOD
Pearl Necklace: Premier Sessions #05 / 1994 / SEE / M

CHERY MiYATA
Northwest Pecker Trek #4: Laid In Latte Land / 1994 / LBO / M

CHERYL
Blue Vanities #569 / 1996 / FFL / M • Eurotica #06 / 1996 / XC / M • Eurotica #11 / 1996 / XC / M • Magma: Bizarre Lust / 1995 / MET / M • Miss Nude America Contest And The Mr. Nude America Contest / 1975 / WIZ / S • Odyssey Triple Play #96: Anal Option #2 / 1995 / OD / M • Triple X Video Magazine #13 / 1996 / OD / M

CHERYL BERLINSKY
Seduce Me Tonight / 1984 / AT / M

CHERYL BLANK
Dungeon Of Lust / 197? / AVC / M

CHERYL BRITT see Star Index I
CHERYL COLLETTE see Star Index I
CHERYL HANSON see Star Index I
CHERYL HASS
Erotic Dimensions #8: Just For Me / 1982 / NSV / M

CHERYL LANDON see Star Index I
CHERYL PLAY see Star Index I
CHERYL ROSTAND
The Sex Machine / 1971 / SOW / M

CHERYL SMITH (Rainbeaux Smith)
The Best Of Sex And Violence / 1981 / WIZ / C • Caged Heat #1 / 1974 / ST0 / S • Cinderella / 1977 / VAM / S • Fantasm Cums Again / 1977 / VS / S • The Pom Pom Girls / 1976 / STM / S • Revenge Of The Cheerleaders / 1976 / LIV / S • Swinging Cheerleaders / 1974 / MV1 / S • Video Vixens / 1972 / VES / S

CHERYL SUNSET see Melba Cruz
CHERYL TAYLOR see Cheri Taylor
CHERYL W. SMYTHE
Agony Of Love, Lace And Lash / cr73 / SOW / M • Bucky Beaver's XXX Dragon Art Theatre Double Feature #14 / 1996 / SOW / M

CHERYL WHITE
ABA: Double Feature #5 / 1996 / ALP / M • Night Of Submission / 1976 / BIZ / M •

Teenage Pony Girls / 1977 / VCX / M

CHERYSSE (S/M) see Star Index I
CHESSE MOORE see Chessie Moore
CHESSIE ANN see Chrissy Ann
CHESSIE MOORE (Robin (Ches. Moore), Chesse Moore)
Ugly looking blonde with huge tits she throws over her shoulders. Alegedly in 1995 she was 66DDD. Robin in **Between My Breasts #14**.
A&B AB#073: Cum Eating Anal Fucking Gang Bang / 1990 / A&B / M • A&B GB#072: Chessie Does It / 1990 / A&B / M • A&B GB#074: Anal Gang Bang From Asia #1 / 1993 / A&B / M • Adventures Of The DP Boys: Hooter County / 1995 / HW / M • Alice In Pornoland / 1996 / IP / M • Amateur Hours #06 / 1990 / AFI / M • Anal Angels / 1996 / PRE / B • Anal Dawn / 1991 / AMB / M • Anal Intruder #05: The Final Outrage / 1990 / CC / M • Backdoor Lambada / 1990 / GO / M • Backdoor To Hollywood #13 / 1990 / CDI / M • The Backpackers #1 / 1990 / IN / M • Battle Of The Ultra Milkmaids / 1992 / LET / M • Bed, Butts & Breakfast / 1990 / LV / M • Best Of Foot Worship #3 / 1992 / BIZ / C • Between Breasts #14 / 1991 / BTO / S • Between My Breasts #15 / 1991 / BTO / M • Bi-Bi-Baby / 1990 / CDI / G • Big Boob Bangeroo #3 / 1996 / TTV / M • Big Boob Bangeroo #5 / 1996 / TTV / M • Big Bust Babes #05 / 1990 / AFI / F • Big Bust Babes #06 / 1991 / AFI / F • Big Bust Babes #07 / 1991 / AFI / M • Big Bust Babes #12 / 1993 / AFI / M • Big Busty #37 / 198? / H&S / S • Big Tit Torment / 1994 / SSP / B • Black & Gold / 1990 / CIN / M • Bobby Hollander's Sweet Cheeks #104 / 1993 / QUA / M • Breast Wishes #01 / 1991 / LBO / M • Breast Wishes #10 / 1992 / LBO / M • Breast Worx #24 / 1992 / LBO / M • Breastman Does The Himalayas / 1993 / EVN / M • Bum Rap / 1990 / PLV / B • Bums Away / 1995 / PRE / C • Butt's Motel #5 / 1990 / EX / M • Catfighting Students / 1995 / PRE / C • Cheeks #3 / 1990 / CC / M • Chessie's Home Videos #01: Oral #1 / 1994 / CHM / M • Chessie's Home Videos #02: Oral #2 / 1994 / CHM / M • Chessie's Home Videos #03: Cum Bandit / 1995 / CHM / M • Chessie's Home Videos #04: Titty Fucks / 1995 / CHM / M • Chessie's Home Videos #05: Anal / 1995 / CHM / M • Chessie's Home Videos #06: Double Insertion / 1995 / CHM / M • Chessie's Home Videos #07: Cumbath / 1995 / CHM / M • Chessie's Home Videos #08: Monster Cocks / 1995 / CHM / M • Chessie's Home Videos #09: Fuck-N-With The Fans / 1995 / CHM / M • Chessie's Home Videos #10: Members Only / 1995 / CHM / M • Chessie's Home Videos #11: Hot Shots #1 / 1995 / CHM / C • Chessie's Home Videos #12: Bust Out Party / 1994 / CHM / M • Chessie's Home Videos #13: Nasty As She Wants To Be / 1994 / CHM / M • Chessie's Home Videos #14: Hot Shots #1 / 1995 / CHM / C • Chessie's Home Videos #15: Pussy Pounder / 1995 / CHM / M • Chessie's Home Videos #16: Internal Cum Shots / 1995 / CHM / M • Chessie's Home Videos #17: C.E.S. Show / 1995 / CHM / M • Chessie's Home Videos #18: Then And Now / 1995 / CHM / M • Chessie's Home Videos #19: Girl On Girl / 1995 / CHM / F •

Chessie's Home Videos #20: Black Balled / 1995 / CHM / M • Chessie's Home Videos #21: Black Humpers / 1995 / CHM / M • Chessie's Home Videos #22: Black Gang Bang #1 / 1995 / CHM / M • Chessie's Home Videos #23: Black Gang Bang #2 / 1995 / CHM / M • Chessie's Home Videos #24: Black Gang Bang #3 / 1995 / CHM / M • Chessie's Home Videos #25: Chessie's Black Lovers / 1995 / CHM / F • Chessie's Home Videos #26: Little Big Man / 1994 / CHM / M • Chessie's Home Videos #27: Dark Meat / 1994 / CHM / M • Chessie's Home Videos #28: Black Internal Cum / 1994 / CHM / M • Chessie's Home Videos #29: Black Ass Masters / 1994 / CHM / M • Chessie's Home Videos #30: Kings Trade / 1994 / CHM / M • Chessie's Home Videos #31: Ebony And Ecstasy / 1995 / CHM / M • Chessie's Home Videos #32: Black On White / 1994 / CHM / M • Chessie's Home Videos #33: Toys #1 / 1994 / CHM / F • Chessie's Home Videos #34: Toys #2 / 1994 / CHM / F • Chessie's Home Videos #35: Toys #3 / 1995 / CHM / F • Chessie's Home Videos #36: Nature Girl / 1995 / CHM / F • Chessie's Home Videos #37: Big Boob Action / 1995 / CHM / F • Chessie's Home Videos #38: Masturbation / 1995 / CHM / F • Chessie's Home Videos #39: Bubble Bath / 1995 / CHM / F • Chessie's Home Videos #40: Strip Show / 1995 / CHM / F • Chessie's Home Videos #41: Lingerie Show / 1995 / CHM / F • Chessie's Home Videos #42: Workout / 1995 / CHM / F • Chessie's Home Videos #43: Hootermania / 1995 / CHM / F • Chessie's Home Videos #44: Boob Tube / 1995 / CHM / F • Chessie's Home Videos #45: Ultimate Whack-Off Tape / 1995 / CHM / F • Chessie's Home Videos #46: Chessie Live! / 1995 / CHM / F • Chessie's Home Videos #47A: Chessie In Charge / 1995 / CHM / B • Chessie's Home Videos #47B: The Taming Of Chessie / 1995 / CHM / B • Chessie's Home Videos #48: Big Boob Bondage / 1995 / CHM / B • Chessie's Home Videos #49: Close Shave / 1995 / CHM / M • Chessie's Home Videos #50: Goddess In Training / 1995 / CHM / F • Chessie's Home Videos #51: Mardi Gras '95 / 1995 / CHM / M • Chessie's Home Videos #52: Great Outdoors / 1994 / CHM / M • Chessie's Home Videos #53: Peek-A-Boo Chessie / 1994 / CHM / M • Chessie's Home Videos #54: Sheet Fighter / 1994 / CHM / B • Chessie's Home Videos: Foot Fantasies / 1995 / CHM / S • Chessie's Home Videos: Lip Service / 1995 / CHM / M • Crazy On You / 1991 / IF / M • Deep Inside Raquel / 1992 / CDI / C • Deep Throat #4 / 1990 / AR / M • Deep Throat #5 / 1990 / AR / M • Dirty Bob's #05: Vegas MasterpieCES / 1992 / FLP / S • Double D Dykes #01 / 1992 / GO / F • Double Detail / 1992 / SO / M • End Results / 1991 / PRE / C • Enemates #12 / 1996 / BIZ / B • Extraterrestrial Virgins / 1995 / VIT / M • Flash Floods / 1991 / PRE / C • Flush Dance / 1996 / PRE / C • Fortysomething #1 / 1990 / LE / M • Full Bodied: Trinity Loren / 1990 / H&S / S • Girls Around The World #21: Tawny Peaks & Friends / 1995 / BTO / M • The Girls From Hootersville #01 / 1993 / SFP / M • The Girls From Hootersville #07 / 1994 / SFP / M • Girls Of The Double D

#13 / 1990 / CDI / M • Girls Will Be Boys #1 / 1990 / PL / F • Girls Will Be Boys #2 / 1990 / PL / F • Girls Will Be Boys #3 / 1991 / PL / F • Girls Will Be Boys #4 / 1991 / PL / F • Glitz Tits #01 / 1992 / GLI / M • Gold Diggers / 1993 / IN / M • Hillary Vamp's Private Collection #03 / 1992 / HVD / M • Hillary Vamp's Private Collection #06 / 1992 / HOV / M • The Hind-Lick Maneuver / 1991 / GO / C • How To Make A Model #03: Sunshine & Melons / 1994 / QUA / M • Hump Chessie & Kimberly / 199? / H&S / M • Images Of Desire / 1990 / PM / M • Introducing Mishka / 1995 / H&S / S • Jailhouse Blue / 1990 / SO / M • Juggernaut / 1990 / EX / M • Kinky Nurses / 1995 / VEX / C • Lesbian Nights / 1996 / AVI / F • Lettre Da Rimini / 1995 / MID / M • Lonely Is The Night / 1990 / V99 / M • Looking For Love / 1991 / VEX / M • Lusty Lap Dancers #1 / 1994 / HO / M • Making It Big / 1990 / TOR / M • Mega-Tits / 1990 / NAP / F • Mike Hott: #132 Chessie And Satina #1 / 1991 / MHV / F • Mike Hott: #133 Chessie And Satina #2 / 1991 / MHV / F • Mike Hott: #135 Chessie Solo / 1991 / MHV / F • Mike Hott: #140 Sissy Solo / 1991 / MHV / F • Mike Hott: #151 Four Girl Spanking Session / 1991 / MHV / F • Mike Hott: Cum Cocktails #1 / 1995 / MHV / C • Mission Hard / 1995 / XC / M • Money Honey / 1990 / TOR / M • More Dirty Debutantes #07 / 1991 / 4P / M • The Naked Truth / 1990 / SE / M • Nasty Girls #2 (1990-CDI) / 1990 / CDI / M • The New Butt Hunt #19 / 1996 / LEI / C • New Girls In Town #1 / 1990 / CC / M • Night Vibes / 1990 / KNI / M • The Nurses Are Cumming #1 / 1996 / LBO / C • Ona Zee's Black Label #1: Sex Hunger / 1996 / ONA / C • Passion From Behind / 1990 / LV / M • The Pawnbroker / 1990 / IF / M • Pearl Necklace: Amorous Amateurs #25 / 1993 / SEE / M • Pearl Necklace: Amorous Amateurs #26 / 1993 / SEE / M • Positively Pagan #06 / 1993 / ATA / M • Prima #01: Anal Poker / 1995 / MBP / M • Private Video Magazine #03 / 1993 / OD / M • Pussy Power #02 / 1989 / BTO / M • Raquel Untamed / 1990 / CIN / M • Roamin' Hands / 1996 / RAS / M • Sex Acts & Video Tape / 1990 / AFV / M • Shaved Sinners #3 / 1990 / VT / M • Slip Of The Tongue / 1990 / SE / M • Smothering Tits And Pussy #3 / 199? / H&S / M • Sole Food / 1992 / PRE / B • Student Fetish Videos: Catfighting #01 / 1991 / PLV / B • Student Fetish Videos: Foot Worship #02 / 1990 / PRE / B • Student Fetish Videos: Spanking #02 / 1990 / SFV / B • Tail Taggers #121: Behind The Lens / 1994 / WV / M • A Tale Of Two Titties #1 / 1990 / AR / M • Tit In A Wringer / 1993 / FC / M • Tit Tales #2 / 1990 / FC / M • Tit Tales #4 / 1993 / FC / M • Tit To Tit #1 / 1994 / BTO / M • Tit To Tit #3 / 1995 / BTO / M • Titillation #2 / 1990 / SE / M • Titty City #1 / 1995 / TIW / M • Titty Town #1 / 1994 / HW / M • Titty-Titty Bang-Bang / 1992 / FC / C • Toppers #10 / 1993 / TV / M • Toppers #11 / 1993 / TV / C • Toys, Not Boys #1 / 1991 / FC / C • Toys, Not Boys #3 / 1991 / FC / C • Triple Header / 1990 / KNI / M • The Very Best Of Breasts #1 / 1996 / H&S / S • Wise Ass! / 1990 / FH / M

CHESTER SNAVLEY
Fatliners #2 / 1991 / EX / M

CHESTNUT
Bound Fantasies / 1994 / VIG / B • Bound Seductress / 1994 / VIG / B • Caught In The Act (1995-Galax) / 1995 / GAL / B

CHESTY LOVE
10 Years Of Big Busts #1 / 1989 / BTO / C • Between My Breasts #09 / 1990 / BTO / M • Big Bust Strippers #01 / 1990 / BTO / F

CHESTY MORGAN (Lillian Wilczkowsky)
Big Bust Loops #10 / 1993 / SOW / M • Big Bust Loops #15 / 1994 / SOW / M • Blue Vanities #526 / 1993 / FFL / M • Deadly Weapons / 1973 / SOW / S • Double Agent 73 / 1974 / SOW / S • The Immoral Three / 1973 / SOW / S • Sex Freaks / 1991 / TAB / M

CHESTY WEST
Pink Lips / 1977 / VCX / M

CHET ANUSZEZ see **Jon Dough**

CHET AZNIVOUR see **Jon Dough**

CHET SANDERS see **Jon Dough**

CHEUNCEY JAMES
Dr Juice's Lust Potion / 1986 / TEM / M • Nudes At Eleven #2 / 1987 / AVC / M • Women In Uniform / 1986 / TEM / M

CHEYANNE
Big & Busty Country Line Dancing / 1995 / SEM / S • More Black Dirty Debutantes #3 / 1994 / 4P / M

CHEYENNE (Gina (Cheyenne))
Tight bodied dark skinned girl with a slightly hooked nose and a resemblence to Crystal Breeze. Gina is the verbal credit in **Beach Bum Amateurs #18**. Was 29 in 1993 and is supposedly of Mexican/French/Indian ancestry.
69th Street / 1993 / VIM / M • America's Raunchiest Home Videos #50: / 1993 / ZA / M • Anal Nature / 1993 / AFD / M • The Anal-Europe Series #02: Fantasies / 1992 / LV / M • The Anal-Europe Series #04: Anal Recall / 1993 / LV / M • Beach Bum Amateur's #15 / 1992 / MID / M • Beach Bum Amateur's #18 / 1992 / MID / M • Bend Over Backwards / 1993 / VIM / M • Bitch / 1993 / VIM / M • Black Centerfold Celebrities / 1993 / MID / M • Black On Black (1994-Midnight) / 1994 / MID / C • Bobby Hollander's Maneaters #03 / 1993 / SFP / M • Dumb Therapy / 1992 / LV / M • Boomerwang / 1992 / MID / M • Brown Sugar From The Hood / 1996 / MID / M • The Butt Sisters Do New Orleans / 1995 / MID / M • The Buttnicks #4: The Black Buttnicks / 1993 / CC / M • Cheeks #6 / 1992 / CC / M • Danger-Ass / 1992 / MID / M • Dark Alleys #13 / 1993 / FC / M • Dark Alleys #16 / 1993 / FC / M • Ebony Erotica #03: Black Adonis / 1993 / GO / M • Ebony Erotica #10: Dark Eyes / 1993 / GO / M • Frathouse Sexcapades / 1993 / SFP / M • From A Whisper To A Scream / 1993 / GO / M • Gangbang Girl #12 / 1993 / ANA / M • Glitz Tits #02 / 1992 / GLI / M • Gone Wild / 1993 / LV / M • GRG: Pussy Licking Ladies / 1994 / GRG / F • Head Lines / 1992 / SC / M • Heavenly Hooters / 1994 / IF / M • Herman's Other Head / 1992 / LV / M • HomeGrown Video #442: / 1995 / HOV / M • Honey, I Blew Everybody #2 / 1992 / MID / M • The Howard Sperm Show / 1993 / LV / M • The Last Of The Muff Divers / 1992 / MID / M • Lesbian Pros And Amateurs #17 / 1992 / GO / F • Lesbian Pros And Amateurs #18 / 1993 / GO / F • Love Letters #1 / 1993 / SC / M • Major Slut /

1993 / LV / M • Miracle On 69th Street / 1992 / HW / M • Moon Godesses #2 / 1993 / VIM / M • More Dirty Debutantes #19 / 1993 / 4P / M • Mr. Peepers Amateur Home Videos #65: Suckaterial Skills / 1993 / LBO / M • Mr. Peepers Amateur Home Videos #81: It Beats A Rosy Palm / 1993 / LBO / M • My Anal Valentine / 1993 / FD / M • Neighborhood Watch #31: Sticking It To The Neighbors / 1992 / LBO / M • Neighborhood Watch #32 / 1992 / LBO / M • One Of Our Porn Stars Is Missing / 1993 / OD / M • Pearl Necklace: Amorous Amateurs #23 / 1993 / SEE / M • Picture Me Naked / 1993 / LE / M • Raw Talent: Top Bang / 1994 / RTP / M • Roto-Rammer / 1993 / LV / M • A Scent Of A Girl / 1993 / LV / M • Shaved #02 / 1992 / RB / F • She-Male Shenanigans / 1994 / HSV / G • Single Tight Female / 1992 / LV / M • The Sweet Sweet Back's Big Bone (#1) / 1994 / FH / M • Toyz / 1993 / MID / M • Tunnel Of Lust / 1993 / LV / M • Udderly Fantastic / 1993 / IF / M • Uncle Roy's Amateur Home Video #13 / 1992 / VIM / M • Wad Gobblers #01 / 1992 / GLI / M • Wad Gobblers #02 / 1992 / GLI / M • Wild Girls / 1993 / LV / F • Will & Ed's Back To Class / 1992 / MID / M • Will And Ed: The Curse Of Poona / 1994 / MID / C • Women Of Influence / 1993 / LV / F • The Wong Side Of Town / 1992 / LV / M

CHEYENNE (BLACK)
Black Mistress, White Slaves / 1992 / RB / B • Black Mystique #10 / 1994 / VT / F • Bound And Gagged #02 / 1991 / RB / B

CHEYENNE (EUROP)
Amadeus Mozart / 1996 / XC / M • Anal Palace / 1995 / VC / M • Juliet & Romeo / 1996 / XC / M • Never Say Never To Rocco Siffredi / 1995 / EA / M

CHEYENNE (MONIQUE) see **Monique DeMone**

CHEYNE BLANC
Pick Up Lines #08 / 1996 / OD / M • Up And Cummers #27 / 1996 / ERW / M

CHI CHI LA RUE (Big Boy, Larry Paciotti, Taylor Hudson)
Gross (6'1" 280lbs in 1995) she-male who has a good sense of humor. Born 1949 in Hibbing MN. Taylor Hudson was a name used as director.
Adult Video News 1992 Awards / 1992 / VC / M • Batwoman & Catgirl / 1992 / HW / M • Bitter She-Males / 1992 / BIZ / G • Book Of Love / 1992 / VC / M • The Cathouse / 1994 / VI / M • Crossing Over / 1990 / IN / M • Eleventh Annual AVN Awards / 1994 / VC / M • The Erotic Adventures Of The Three Musketeers / 1992 / CEL / S • Even More Dangerous / 1990 / SO / M • Extreme Sex #3: Wired / 1994 / VI / M • Female Mimics International: Behind The Scenes / 1988 / LEO / G • The French Canal / 1995 / DVP / G • Godmother / 1991 / AWV / F • Head Lock / 1989 / VD / M • Introducing Tracey Wynn / 1991 / PL / M • Lady & The Champ / 1991 / AFV / M • Laze / 1990 / ZA / M • Revenge Of The Bi Dolls / 1994 / CAT / G • She-Males In Torment #2 / 1992 / BIZ / G • Sinderella She-Males / 1994 / HEA / G • Stairway To Paradise / 1990 / VC / M • Steel Garters / 1992 / CAT / G • Tenth Annual Adult Video News Awards / 1993 / VC / M • The Three Musketeers #1 / 1992 / FD / M • The Three Musketeers #2 / 1992 / FD / M • Tori Welles Goes Behind The Scenes

/ 1992 / FD / M • TV Reform School / 1992 / BIZ / G

CHI CHI LING *see* **Jasmine**

CHI LOO
Yellow Fever / 1994 / ORE / C

CHICAGO
Black Snatch #2 / 1996 / DFI / F

CHICK WRIGHT
The Erotic Adventures Of Peter Galore / 1973 / ALP / M

CHICO
Bedtime Video #06 / 1984 / GO / M • Come With Me / 1995 / GOT / M

CHIKAKO KAWATABA *see* **Star Index I**

CHINA
Black Mystique #03 / 1994 / VT / F • Creme De France #2 / 1981 / AVC / C • For Your Lips Only / 1989 / FAZ / M • Hot Services / 1989 / WET / M • How To Have Oral Sex / 1993 / A&E / M • Limited Edition #24 / 1984 / AVC / M • Midnight Angels #03 / 1993 / MID / F • Sea Of Lust / 1990 / FAN / M • Who Reamed Rosie Rabbit? #2 / 1989 / FAN / M

CHINA (1994)
Butt Hunt #09 / 1995 / LEI / M • Love Doll Lucy #1 / 1994 / PL / F • Love Doll Lucy #2 / 1994 / PL / F

CHINA (C. DARK) *see* **Cassandra Dark**

CHINA CAT *see* **Stephanie Swift**

CHINA DOLL
Blue Vanities #512 / 1992 / FFL / M

CHINA DOLL (BLACK) *see* **Chyna Dahl**

CHINA JADE
A Taste Of Sugar / 1978 / AR / M

CHINA KITTY
She-Male Encounters #10: She-Male Vacation / 1986 / MET / G • She-Male Encounters #11: She-Male Roommates / 1986 / MET / G

CHINA LAKKE *see* **Brooke Ashley**

CHINA LEE *see* **Kristara Barrington**

CHINA LEE (1995)
2 Wongs Make A White / 1996 / FC / M • Anal Cannibals / 1996 / ZA / M • Anal Institution #2 / 1996 / ZA / M • Anal Princess #1 / 1996 / VC / M • Anal Professor / 1996 / ZA / M • Anal Shame / 1995 / VD / M • Analtown USA #10 / 1996 / NIT / M • Back Door Asians / 1995 / EVN / M • Bang City #2: China's Anal Gang Bang / 1995 / SC / M • Bang City #5: Lennox's Anal Gang Bang / 1995 / SC / M • Beyond Reality #2: Anal Expedition / 1996 / EXQ / M • Big Boob Boat Butt Ride / 1996 / FC / M • Blue Saloon / 1996 / ME / M • Busted-D-D In Las Vegas / 1996 / LV / M • The Butt Sisters Do Houston / 1996 / MID / M • Cherry Poppers #10: Sweet And Sassy / 1995 / ZA / M • China Lee's Bachelorette Party / 1995 / RHV / M • The Complete & Total Anal Workout #2 / 1996 / ZA / M • Cum Buttered Corn Holes #2 / 1996 / NIT / C • Deep Waterworld / 1995 / HW / M • The Dinner Party / 1995 / ERA / M • Dirty Old Men #2 / 1995 / IP / M • Do Me Nurses / 1995 / LE / M • Double Anal Alternatives / 1996 / EL / M • Double D Dykes #24 / 1995 / GO / F • Double Dicked #2 / 1996 / RAS / M • East Coast Sluts #01: New Jersey / 1995 / PL / M • Employee's Entrance In The Rear / 1996 / CC / M • Every Nerd's Big Boob Boat Butt Ride / 1996 / FC / M • Fresh Meat #2 / 1996 / PL / M • Gang Bang Virgin #2 / 1995 / HO / M • Hardcore Schoolgirls #1: Sweet Young Things / 1995 / XPR / M •

Hooters And The Blowjobs / 1996 / HW / M • Hot Tight Asses #11 / 1995 / TCK / M • Inspector Croissant: The Case Of The Missing Pinky / 1995 / FC / M • Interstate 95 Amateurs #1 / 1995 / RHV / M • Kink Inc. / 1996 / MP0 / M • Lollipops #2 / 1996 / SC / M • Lovin' Spoonfuls #8 / 1996 / 4P / C • Max #05: The Harder They Fall / 1995 / FRM / M • More Dirty Debutantes #39 / 1995 / 4P / M • Mr. Pink And The Hotel Harlots / 1996 / ORG / F • Muff Divers #2 / 1996 / TV / F • N.Y. Video Magazine #01 / 1994 / OUP / M • N.Y. Video Magazine #05 / 1995 / OUP / M • Nasty Newcummers #10 / 1995 / MET / M • Nasty Newcummers #12 / 1995 / MET / M • OUTS: China Lee / 1995 / OUT / F • Perverted #2: The Virgins / 1995 / ZA / M • Private Diaries #1: Christina / 1995 / AVI / M • Pro-Am Jam / 1996 / GLI / M • Profiles #03: House Dick / 1995 / XPR / M • Pussyman Auditions #07 / 1995 / SNA / M • A Round Behind / 1995 / PEP / M • Rusty Boner's Late Night Videos #1 / 1995 / RHV / M • Savage Lessons #2 / 1995 / BON / B • Senior Stimulation / 1996 / CC / M • Sodomania: Slop Shots / 1996 / EL / C • Surfin' The Net / 1996 / RAS / M • Temple Of Love / 1995 / SUF / M • Treacherous / 1995 / VD / M • Valentino's Asian Invasion / 1997 / SC / M • Video Virgins #21 / 1995 / NS / M • Virtual Reality Sixty Nine / 1995 / WP / M • Vivid Raw #2 / 1996 / VI / M • Waterworld Deep / 1995 / HW / M • Yin Yang Oriental Love Bang #2 / 1996 / SUF / M • Young & Natural #04 / 1995 / PRE / F • Young & Natural #05 / 1995 / PRE / F • Young & Natural #07 / 1995 / PRE / F • Young & Natural #08 / 1995 / PRE / F • Young & Natural #09 / 1995 / PRE / C

CHINA LEIGH *(Tina Wong, Tina Orchid (C.Leigh, Tina Austin)*
Adorable Oriental girl. Not in **Three Shades of Flesh**.
Beyond Shame / 1980 / VEP / M • China Sisters / 1978 / SE / M • A Formal Faucett / 1978 / VC / M • Hot Bodies (Ventura) / 1984 / VEN / C • House Of Kristina / cr78 / VCX / B • Jawbreakers / 1985 / VEN / C • Once Upon A Time/Cave Woman / 1978 / VI / M • Same Time Every Year / 1981 / VHL / M • Saturday Matinee Series #1 / 1996 / VCX / C • Serena, An Adult Fairy Tale / 1979 / VEN / M • Soft Places / 1978 / CXV / M • Teeny Buns / 1977 / VC / M • VCA Previews #1 / 1988 / VC / C

CHINA MAI
Anal Cuties #2 / 1992 / ROB / M • Anal Cuties #3 / 1992 / ROB / M • Asian Persuasion / 1993 / WV / M • The Best Of Oriental Anal #1 / 1994 / ROB / C • Biff Malibu's Totally Nasty Home Videos #20 / 1992 / ANA / M • Blow For Blow / 1992 / ZA / M • Bobby Hollander's Maneaters #07 / 1993 / SFP / M • Brother Act / 1992 / PL / M • The Burma Road #3 / 1996 / LBO / C • Dark Obsessions / 1993 / WV / M • Dirty Dating Service #01 / 1993 / WP / M • The Dragon Lady #4: Tales From The Bed #3 / 1992 / WV / M • Erotic Dripping Orientals / 1993 / WV / M • A Few Good Rears / 1993 / IN / M • From China With Love / 1993 / ZA / M • Kiss Is A Rebel With A Cause / 1993 / WV / M • The Magnificent 7 / 1994 / VTF / B • Mr. Peepers Amateur Home Videos #57: Super-Suckers Of Flight / 1992 / LBO / M • Neighborhood Watch #33 / 1992 /

LBO / M • The Night Of The Coyote / 1993 / MED / M • No Bust Babes / 1992 / AFI / M • Odyssey 30 Min: #239: / 1992 / OD / M • One Of Our Porn Stars Is Missing / 1993 / OD / M • Raw Talent: Hedonism #1 / 1993 / FH / M • Straight A Students / 1993 / MET / M • Taxi Girls #3: Killer On The Loose / 1993 / MED / M • Up The Ying Yang #1 / 1994 / CC / M • The Wong Side Of Town / 1992 / LV / M

CHINA MOON *see* **June Lee**

CHINA ROSE *see* **Star Index I**

CHINA THYMICKS
Alexis Goes To Hell / 1996 / EXQ / B • Dr Whacks Treatment / 1996 / VTF / B • Fit To Be Tied / 1996 / PL / B • Gangbang Bitches / 1996 / LON / B • Kym Wilde's On The Edge #38 / 1996 / RB / B • No Mercy For The Bitches / 1996 / LBO / B • Punishment Of The Liars / 1996 / LBO / B • Revolt Of The Slaves / 1996 / LBO / B • Roped & Ravished / 1996 / CS / B

CHINA WONG
The Bizarre World Of F.J. Lincoln / 19?? / VHL / C • Every Man's Fancy / 1983 / BIZ / B • Mama's Boy / 1984 / VD / M • Oriental Temptations / 1984 / CV / C • The Oui Girls / 1981 / VHL / M • Sex On The Orient Express / 1991 / VC / C • Too Much Too Soon / 1983 / VCX / M • Yes, My Lady / 1984 / VHL / B

CHINA WU CU UU
G...They're Big / 1981 / TGA / C • Girls & Guys & Girls Or Guys / 19?? / REG / M • Valley Girls Ferr Shurr / cr85 / EXF / M • Yamahama Mamas / 1983 / TGA / C

CHIP
AVP #2003: Menage A Trois #2 / 1990 / AVP / M

CHIP BUCKLEY *see* **Star Index I**

CHIP DALE
Breaking It #2 / 1989 / GO / M • Competition / 1989 / BON / B • Drainman / 1989 / BIZ / B • Enemates #02 / 1989 / BIZ / B • Flash Floods / 1991 / PRE / C • Mike Hott: #365 Lesbian Sluts #26 / 1996 / MHV / F • My Wildest Date / 1989 / FOV / M • Naughty Neighbors / 1989 / CA / M • Paula's Perils / 1989 / BON / B • Roll-X Girls / 1989 / DYV / M • Shoe Horny / 1989 / BIZ / B • Sole Goal / 1996 / PRE / B • Sole-Ohs / 1989 / BIZ / F • Taylor Made / 1989 / DR / M • Twentysomething #3 / 1989 / VI / M

CHIP DANIELS
All-Star Softball Game / 1995 / SAB / G • Please Don't Tell / 1995 / CEN / G

CHIP KNIGHTS *see* **Nick Rage**

CHIP STOKELY *see* **Star Index I**

CHIQUITA *see* **Star Index I**

CHIQUITA JOHNSON *see* **Star Index I**

CHIRSTY (CHRISSY A) *see* **Chrissy Ann**

CHIRSTY WILD *see* **Chrissy Ann**

CHISLIENNE AUPLAT *see* **Star Index I**

CHLOE
Babes Of The Bay #1 / 1994 / LIP / F • Booty Babes / 1993 / ROB / F • Bun Busters #14 / 1994 / LBO / M • Eurotica #12 / 1996 / XC / M • Grindhouse Follies #16 / 1993 / SOW / M • Odyssey 30 Min: #382: Dildo Dykes / 1993 / OD / M • Pony Girls / 1993 / ROB / F • RSK: Chloe #1: Screen Test / 1993 / RSK / F • Sweet Lips & Buns / 1993 / ROB / F • Thrill Seekers / 1993 / ROB / F

CHLOE (S/M)

Beverly She-Males / 1994 / PL / G • Bone Appetit: A She-Male Seduction / 1994 / BIZ / G • Chicks With Dicks #1: A Slick And Slippery Oil Orgy / 1992 / BIZ / B • Defiant TV's / 1994 / BIZ / G • Dungeons & Drag Queens / 1994 / HSV / G • Gentlemen Prefer She-Males / 1995 / CDI / G • Hollywood She Males / 1995 / MET / G • Malibu She Males / 1994 / MET / G • Red Riding She Male / 1995 / PL / G • Shaved She-Males / 1994 / PL / G • She's The Boss / 1993 / BIL / G • She-Male Mistress / 1992 / BIZ / G • She-Male Surprise / 1995 / CDI / G • She-Male Vacation / 1993 / HSV / G • She-Males In Torment #1 / 1992 / BIZ / G • Shopping With A Transvestite: In A Boy, Out A Girl / 1992 / BIZ / G • Stick Pussy / 1992 / HSV / G • Trannie Get Your Gun / 1994 / HSV / G • Tranny Jerk-Fest / 1995 / VC / G • Transexual Blvd / 1994 / PL / G • Transexual Passions #2 / 1994 / BIZ / G • TV Blondes Do It Best / 1992 / BIZ / G • TV Dungeon / 1992 / BIZ / G • TV Ladies Room / 1993 / BIZ / G • TV Nation #2 / 1995 / HW / G • TV Panty Party / 1994 / BIZ / G • TV Shaved Pink / 1992 / BIZ / G • TVs Teased And Tormented / 1995 / BIZ / G

CHLOE COLLINS
Sweet Black Cherries #4 / 1996 / TTV / M
CHLOE GREGORY
Sweet Paradise / 1980 / ELV / M
CHLOE JAMES
A-Z Of Lesbian Love / 1996 / PAL / F • Playboy: Intimate Workout for Lovers / 1992 / PLA / S • The Statesman's Wife / 1996 / PAL / M
CHLOE NICHOLE
Marginal brunette with shoulder length unkempt hair, tiny tits, and a petite body. Very serious about her sex. De-virginized at 11 by a 19 year old guy, according to her.
Anal Addict / 1995 / ROB / M • Anal Anarchy / 1995 / VC / M • Asses Galore #4: Extreme Noise Terror / 1996 / DFI / M • Barby's On Butt Row / 1996 / ABS / M • Bimbette: Adventures In Anal Land / 1996 / TEP / M • Bobby Sox / 1996 / VI / S • Boss Bitch From Bondage Hell / 1996 / LBO / B • Confessions Of Chloe / 1996 / BON / B • Cumback Pussy #1 / 1996 / EL / M • Dirty Dancers #9 / 1996 / HO / M • Eighteen #1 / 1996 / SC / M • Eighteen & Easy / 1996 / SC / M • Forbidden Awakenings / 1996 / BON / B • Gangbang Girl #17 / 1995 / ANA / M • The Generation Gap / 1996 / LV / M • Hardcore Schoolgirls #3: Legal And Eager / 1995 / XPR / M • I'm So Horny, Baby / 1997 / ROB / M • In Your Face #3 / 1995 / PL / M • Incarceration Of Chloe / 1996 / BON / B • Innocent's Initiation / 1996 / BON / B • Interview: Barely Legal / 1995 / LV / M • Lotus / 1996 / VI / M • Mike Hott: #356 Girls Who Lap Cum From Cunts #01 / 1996 / MHV / M • Mike Hott: #360 Cum In My Cunt #08 / 1995 / MHV / C • Mike Hott: #361 Girls Who Swallow Cum #04 / 1996 / MHV / C • Mike Hott: #362 Fuck The Boss #7 / 1996 / MHV / M • Mike Hott: #365 Lesbian Sluts #26 / 1996 / MHV / F • Mike Hott: #369 Cum In My Mouth #05 / 1996 / MHV / C • Mike Hott: #370 Cunt Of The Month: Chloe Nicole / 1996 / MHV / M • Mike Hott: #379 Three-Sum Sluts #15 / 1996 / MHV / M • Nasty Newcummers #13 / 1995 / MET / M • No Mercy For The Bitches / 1996 /

LBO / B • Porsche's Ordeal / 1996 / LBO / B • Pussyman Auditions #19 / 1996 / SNA / M • Rectal Raiders / 1997 / ROB / M • Rump-Shaker #5 / 1996 / HW / M • Sabrina The Booty Queen / 1997 / ROB / M • Satyr / 1996 / WP / M • Sexual Atrocities / 1996 / EL / M • The Shocking Truth #1 / 1996 / DWO / M • Sisters In Submission / 1996 / BON / B • Slavegirl Of Zor / 1996 / LON / B • Sodomania #21: Degenerate Lifestyles! / 1997 / EL / M • Tied Temptations / 1996 / BON / B • Young And Anal #1 / 1995 / JMP / M
CHLOE VEE see Chloe Vevrier
CHLOE VEVRIER (Chloe Vee, Chloe Zee) Humongous tits, short dark red hair, hefty body.
Bangkok Bangers / 1995 / BTO / M • Big Busty #49 / 1995 / BTO / S • Busty Bangkok Bangers / 1996 / H&S / M • Chloe In Japan / 199? / H&S / S • The Chloe Story / 1995 / H&S / S • Hirsute Lovers #2 / 1995 / BTO / M • Introducing Chloe / 199? / H&S / S • On Location In The Bahamas / 1996 / H&S / S • On Location: Boob Cruise / 1996 / H&S / S • Score Busty Centerfolds #2 / 1995 / BTO / M • Score Busty Covergirls #7 / 1995 / BTO / S • Sin City Cycle Sluts #1 / 1995 / SC / F • Sin City Cycle Sluts #2 / 1995 / SC / F • Tit To Tit #4 / 1996 / BTO / S
CHLOE ZEE see Chloe Vevrier
CHOCKLATE
Big Bad Biker Bitches / 1994 / TTV / M • More To Love #1 / 1994 / TTV / M
CHOCOLA
Dangerous Behinds #1 / 1995 / HW / M
CHOCOLATE
Black Babes In Heat / 1993 / VIM / M • Black Beauties #2 / 1992 / VIM / M • Black Magic #1 / 1993 / VIM / M • Dark Alleys #01 / 1992 / FC / M • Dark Passions #01 / 1993 / AFV / M • Dark Passions #02 / 1993 / AFV / M • The Lustful Turk / 1968 / SOW / S • More To Love #2 / 1995 / TTV / M • Pumps In Da Rump #2 / 1996 / HW / M • Tit In A Wringer / 1993 / FC / M
CHOCOLATE (HOOKER)
Black Street Hookers #1 / 1996 / DFI / M
CHOCOLATE TIE
Black Bush Bashers / 1996 / LOK / M • Black Fantasies #09 / 1995 / HW / M • Black Fantasies #10 / 1995 / HW / M • Black Knockers #10 / 1995 / TV / M
CHOP SHOP see Melinda Masglow
CHOPPER JOHN see Star Index I
CHOW CHEE
My Brother's Girl / 1996 / AVV / M
CHOY
Lovin' Spoonfuls #7 / 1996 / 4P / C • More Dirty Debutantes #16 / 1992 / 4P / M
CHRIMSON see Jacqueline
CHRIS
All Pain, No Gain / 1991 / NEP / B • AVP #2003: Menage A Trois #2 / 1990 / AVP / M • Beneath The Cane / 1992 / BON / B • Blue Vanities #167 (New) / 1996 / FFL / M • Blue Vanities #167 (Old) / 1991 / FFL / M • Blue Vanities #168 (New) / 1996 / FFL / M • Blue Vanities #168 (Old) / 1991 / FFL / M • Blue Vanities #549 / 1994 / FFL / M • Blush: Suburban Dykes / 1991 / BLV / F • Bubble Butts #09 / 1992 / LBO / M • Club Doma #2 / 1994 / VER / B • Eurotica #13 / 1996 / XC / M • Foxx Tales / 1996 / TTV / M • The Girls Of Fantasex #2 / 1996 / NIT

/ M • Hardcore Male/Female Oil Wrestling / 1996 / JSP / M • Hardcore: The Films Of Richard Kern #1 / 1991 / FTV / M • Hot Body Competition: Hot Pants Contest / 1996 / CG / F • N.Y. Video Magazine #08 / 1996 / OUP / M • Party Club / 1996 / C69 / M • Pearl Necklace: Amorous Amateurs #41 / 1994 / SEE / M • Pearl Necklace: Premier Sessions #03 / 1994 / SEE / M • Slave Julia / 1995 / VP0 / B • Totally Ona: The Best Of Ona Zee / 1996 / ONA / C
CHRIS (MARK SAUNDER) see Mark Saunders
CHRIS ALEXANDER see Biff Malibu
CHRIS ALLEN
Bi-Coastal / 1985 / LAV / G
CHRIS ANDERSON
800 Fantasy Lane / 1979 / GO / M • F / 1980 / GO / M
CHRIS B. SEPHARTIC (Chris Sifartic) Chris Sifartic is from **The Big Bang (1988)**. The Big Bang / 1988 / WET / M • The Sexaholic / 1988 / VC / M • The Sleazy Detective / 1988 / VD / M
CHRIS BERG see Star Index I
CHRIS BLAKE see Kyle West
CHRIS BLOOM see Star Index I
CHRIS BURNS see Star Index I
CHRIS CASSIDY see Cris Cassidy
CHRIS CHASE see Christian Chase
CHRIS CHITTEL
[Hungry Young Women / 1977 / ALP / M
CHRIS CHITTELL (Charles Canyon)
Practice Makes Perfect / 1975 / QX / M • [Molly / 1977 / … / S
CHRIS CLAYTON
She-Male Encounters #19: Toga Party / 1989 / MET / G
CHRIS COLLINS see Meo
CHRIS COLLINS (MALE)
Natural Response / 1996 / GPI / G
CHRIS CRAVEN see Star Index I
CHRIS DANO
Big Switch #3: Bachelor Party / 1991 / CAT / G • Sex Bi-Lex / 1993 / CAT / G
CHRIS DOUGH see Star Index I
CHRIS DOUGLAS see Cal Jammer
CHRIS EDWARDS see Star Index I
CHRIS ESTED see Star Index I
CHRIS GALLAGHER see Star Index I
CHRIS GARLAND
Ultraflesh / 1980 / GO / M
CHRIS GREEN
Courting Libido / 1995 / HIV / G • Long Play / 1995 / 3XP / G • Secret Sex #3: The Takeover / 1994 / CAT / G
CHRIS GREULICH
Sodom & Gomorrah / 1974 / MIT / M
CHRIS GUZZARDO
She-Male Encounters #17: Sorority / 1987 / MET / G
CHRIS HOPKINS see Dianne Holt
CHRIS IZZDAS
Fair Warning / 1995 / ZFX / B • The Necklace #3 / 1994 / ZFX / B • The Plant / 1995 / ZFX / B
CHRIS JACKSON
Satan Was A Lady / 1977 / ALP / M
CHRIS JONES
Bedtime Video #03 / 1984 / GO / M
CHRIS JORDAN
The Clamdigger's Daughter / 1972 / SOW / S • Confessions Of A Young American Housewife / 1973 / ALP / S • The Taking Of Christina / 1975 / NGV / M • [The Switch / 1974 / … / S

CHRIS K. *see* Biff Malibu

CHRIS KENNEDY *see Star Index I*

CHRIS KISSEN
Certified Mail / 1975 / CDC / M • Dance Of Love / cr70 / BL / M • Love-In Maid / cr72 / CDC / M • Referral Service / cr71 / BL / M • The Sorceress / 1974 / BL / M

CHRIS KNEWS *see* Kris Newz

CHRIS KNIHT
Private Film #22 / 1995 / OD / M

CHRIS KRIMSON
Bondage Memories #01 / 1993 / BON / C • Bound & Shaved / 1994 / BON / B • Canyon Capers / 1991 / BON / B • Katrina's Bondage Memories #2 / 1994 / BON / C • Switch / 1992 / BON / B

CHRIS LA FORTE *see Star Index I*

CHRIS LADD
Bi And Beyond #3 / 1989 / INH / G • Video Virgins #14 / 1994 / NS / M

CHRIS LARSEN *see Star Index I*

CHRIS LAVAE
Backdoor To Brooklyn / 1992 / PL / M • Every Body / 1992 / LAP / M • Transsexual Trouble / 1991 / CIN / G

CHRIS LEE
Beyond Passion / 1993 / IF / M • Hole In One / 1993 / IF / M • Humongous Hooters / 1993 / IF / M • Knockout / 1994 / VEX / M • Living For Love / 1993 / V99 / M • Summertime Boobs / 1994 / LEI / M

CHRIS LESLIE
Bip Tease / 1996 / BON / B

CHRIS LYNN *see Star Index I*

CHRIS MARLOW
Double Crossed / 1994 / MID / M

CHRIS MCDONALD *see* Blake West

CHRIS MILES
Twilight / 1996 / ESN / M

CHRIS NEWS *see* Kris Newz

CHRIS OFFERSEN
Euro-Snatch / 1996 / SNA / M

CHRIS OSCAR *see* Wild Oscar

CHRIS PARKER
Bi Stander / 1995 / BIN / G

CHRIS PARKER (KJ) *see* Kevin James

CHRIS PERRY
Le Parfum De Mathilde / 1994 / VI / M

CHRIS R. *see Star Index I*

CHRIS REED *(John Simmons, Jon Simmons)*
Amazing Tails #1 / 1987 / CA / M • Amazing Tails #3 / 1987 / CA / M • Beyond The Senses / 1986 / AVC / M • Black Magic / 1986 / DR / M • Black Magic Sex Clinic / 1987 / DOX / M • Busty Wrestling Babes / 1986 / VD / M • Caught From Behind #07 / 1987 / HO / M • Cram Session / 1986 / V99 / M • Deep Inside Tracey / 1987 / CDI / C • Goddess Of Love / 1986 / CDI / M • Heavy Breathing / 1986 / CV / M • The Honeymooners / 1986 / CDI / M • Hooters / 1986 / AVC / M • Kinkyvision #1 / 1986 / 3HV / M • A Little Romance / 1986 / HO / M

CHRIS RELLY
Superstar John Holmes / 1979 / AVC / M

CHRIS RIVERS
Bootylicious: Trailer Trash / 1996 / JMP / M • Hollywood Sex Tour / 1995 / VC / M • Young And Anal #6 / 1996 / JMP / M

CHRIS ROCKS
Starlet Nights / 1982 / XTR / M

CHRIS ROOS
Butt Naked #1 / 1990 / OD / M

CHRIS SIFARTIC *see* Chris B. Sephartic

CHRIS STERLING *see* Wild Oscar

CHRIS STOCK *see* Blake West

CHRIS STONE
Bi Anonymous / 1993 / BIL / G • Bi-Sex Pleasures / 1993 / PL / G • Lust Horizons / 1992 / PL / G • The Mating Game / 1992 / PL / G • Stasha's Last Kiss / 1993 / VEX / G

CHRIS THOMAS *see* Mark Saunders

CHRIS THOMPSON *see Star Index I*

CHRIS THUNDER
Like Father Like Son / 1996 / AWV / G

CHRIS THUNDERBOLT
East Coast Sluts #05: North Carolina / 1995 / PL / M

CHRIS TODD *see Star Index I*

CHRIS TYLER
Natural Response / 1996 / GPI / G

CHRIS VALENTINE *see Star Index I*

CHRIS WALTON
American Sex Fantasy / 1975 / IHV / M

CHRIS WARFIELD
Dixie Ray Hollywood Star / 1983 / CA / M

CHRIS WELLINGTON
Canadian Beaver Hunt #2 / 1996 / PL / M • Canadian Beaver Hunt #3 / 1996 / PL / M • Canadian Beaver Hunt #4 / 1996 / PL / M

CHRIS WEST *see Star Index I*

CHRIS WILSON
[Bewitched Sex / 197? / … / M

CHRIS YEAGER
To Bi For / 1996 / PL / G

CHRISSE ORCHIDE *see Star Index I*

CHRISSIE
Blue Vanities #116 / 1988 / FFL / M • Sex On The Saddle: Wicked Women Of The Wild West / 1994 / CPG / S

CHRISSIE SNOW *see Star Index I*

CHRISSY
100% Amateur #05: Threesomes & Group Scenes / 1995 / OD / M • P.L.O.W.: Punk Ladies Of Wrestling / 1996 / GOT / B • Wet 'n' Wild / 1995 / TVI / F

CHRISSY (ANN) *see* Chrissy Ann

CHRISSY (BR. BELLE) *see* Bridgette Belle

CHRISSY ANN *(Chrissy (Ann), Crissy (Ann), Chrissy Anne, Chirsty (Chrissy A), Christy Wild, Chirsty Wild, Chessie Ann)*
Very pretty blonde with great skin, blue eyes and tight body. Small breasts. 5'0" tall. Has a tattoo on her left belly just above the bikini line of what looks like rabbit ears with the words "eat me" underneath. Not to be confused with her sister, Christy Ann, who is very similar but has a bigger nose with a bulb on the end and freckles.

All That Glitters / 1992 / LV / M • America's Raunchiest Home Videos #21: Pumping Pussy / 1992 / ZA / M • Anal Intruder #06: The Anal Twins / 1992 / CC / M • Anal Kitten / 1992 / ROB / M • Anal Lover #2 / 1993 / ROB / M • Anal Romance / 1993 / LV / M • The Anal-Europe Series #02: Fantasies / 1992 / LV / M • Backdoor To Russia #1 / 1992 / VC / M • Backdoor To Russia #2 / 1993 / VC / M • Beach Bum Amateur's #03 / 1992 / MID / M • Beverly Hills 90269 / 1992 / LV / M • Biff Malibu's Totally Nasty Home Videos #08 / 1992 / ANA / M • The Big One / 1992 / GO / M • Black & White In Living Color / 1992 / WV / M • Bubble Butts #05 / 1992 / LBO / M • Bubble Butts #23 / 1992 / LBO / M • Cat & Mouse #1 / 1992 / XCI / M • Cat & Mouse #2 / 1993 / XCI / M • Dallas Does Debbie / 1992 / PL / M • Dou-

ble A Dykes / 1992 / GO / F • Dripping With Desire / 1992 / DR / M • Face Dance #1 / 1992 / EA / M • Face Dance #2 / 1992 / EA / M • Fast Girls #3 / 1992 / XPI / M • Gang Bang Fury #1 / 1992 / ROB / M • Gang Bang Pussycat / 1992 / ROB / M • Gang Bang Thrills / 1992 / ROB / M • Harry Horndog #10: Love Puppies #1 / 1992 / ZA / M • Heads Or Tails? / 1993 / PL / M • How To Make A Model #04: Facial Cream Girls / 1994 / LBO / M • Lacy's Hot Anal Summer / 1992 / LV / M • Lovin' Spoonfuls #7 / 1996 / 4P / C • Modern Torture / 1992 / PL / B • More Dirty Debutantes #14 / 1992 / 4P / M • Naughty By Nature / 1992 / IF / M • No Bust Babes / 1992 / AFI / M • Parlor Games / 1992 / VT / M • Penetrating Thoughts / 1992 / LV / M • A Pussy Called Wanda #2 / 1992 / DR / M • Scared Stiff / 1992 / PL / B • The Seduction Of Mary / 1992 / VC / M • The Seductress / 1992 / ZA / M • Shoot To Thrill / 1992 / WV / M • Silence Of The Buns / 1992 / WV / M • Soda Jerk / 1992 / ZA / M • Splatman / 1992 / FR / M • Street Girl Named Desire / 1992 / FD / M • Talk Dirty To Me #09 / 1992 / DR / M • Uncle Roy's Amateur Home Video #01 / 1992 / VIM / M • Uncle Roy's Best Of The Best: Cornhole Classics / 1992 / VIM / C • Victoria's Secret Life / 1992 / WV / M • The Visualizer / 1992 / VC / M • Women Of Influence / 1993 / LV / F

CHRISSY ANNE *see* Chrissy Ann

CHRISSY BEAUCHAMP *(Cherry Beauchamp, Jennifer Russell, Gabrielle Behar)*
Adorable brunette (sometimes blonde) with tight body, medium tits and a nice smile.

Blue Interview / 1983 / VCR / M • GVC: Companions #122 / 1983 / GO / F • GVC: Paper Dolls #117 / 1983 / GO / F • Heartthrobs / 1985 / CA / M • Oriental Jade / 1985 / VC / M • Satisfactions / 1983 / CA / M • Up Up And Away / 1984 / CA / M

CHRISSY CARNAL
Inner Pink #4 / 1995 / LIP / F

CHRISSY ELLIS
Pearl Necklace: Amorous Amateurs #27 / 1993 / SEE / M • Pearl Necklace: Amorous Amateurs #28 / 1993 / SEE / M • Pearl Necklace: Amorous Amateurs #30 / 1993 / SEE / M • Pearl Necklace: Amorous Amateurs #31 / 1993 / SEE / M

CHRISSY JISUM
2 Baggers / 1994 / ZA / M

CHRISSY LEE *(Chrissy Ly)*
Korean girl with little English. Pretty face, long straight dark blonde hair, lithe petite body, medium natural tits, tight waist, nice butt. In 1997 she says she is 21 years old and was de-virginized at 18.

Creme De La Face #18: Cum Mops / 1997 / OD / M • Ethnic Cheerleader Search #1 / 1996 / WIC / M • More Dirty Debutantes #63 / 1997 / SBV / M • White Men Can't Iron On Butt Row / 1997 / ABS / M

CHRISSY LY *see* Chrissy Lee

CHRISSY MAX
Las Vegas Big Boob Hospitality Sweet / 1997 / HO / M

CHRISSY PETERSON *(Elaine Welles)*
Shoulder length curly dark hair, passable face, medium tits, not a tight waist, bit flat on the butt.

Chopstix / 1979 / TVX / M • Expensive Taste / 1978 / VCX / M • Girls In Blue /

CHRISSY SAVAGE *see Star Index I*

CHRISSY WILLIAMS
Flash Pants / 1983 / VC / M

CHRISSY WILLIAMS-CRS *see* **Crystal Sync**

CHRISTA
Bikini Watch / 1996 / PHV / F • Bobby Hollander's Rookie Nookie #12 / 1993 / SFP / M • Joe Elliot's College Girls #29 / 1994 / JOE / M • Kinky College Cunts #14 / 1993 / NS / F • Kinky College Cunts #25 / 1993 / NS / M • Made In The Hood / 1995 / HBE / M

CHRISTA ANDERSON *see* **Crystal Sync**

CHRISTA BELL
Love Roots / 1987 / LIM / M • Love Under 16 / cr75 / VST / M

CHRISTA COLLINS
Ready To Drop #04 / 1994 / FC / M

CHRISTA DUNCAN
Intimate Desires / 1978 / VEP / M • The Nite Bird / 1978 / BL / M

CHRISTA FEE
[Madchen, Die Sich Selbst, Bedienen / 1974 / ... / M

CHRISTA LINDER
Bel Ami / 1976 / VXP / M

CHRISTA R. *see* **Christa Rain**

CHRISTA RAIN *(Krista Rain, Christa R.)*
Shoulder length blonde hair in ringlets, small to medium tits, small tattoo on right belly, slightly chubby, marginal face, flabby belly, shaven pussy.
Butt Hunt #09 / 1995 / LEI / M • Comeback / 1995 / VI / M • Hard Core Beginners #02 / 1995 / LEI / M • New Faces, Hot Bodies #18 / 1995 / STP / M • Senior Stimulation / 1996 / CC / M

CHRISTA UNTERKIRCHNE *see Star Index I*

CHRISTANA BELL *see Star Index I*

CHRISTARRAH KNIGHT *see* **Kristarrah Knight**

CHRISTEL
Magma: Body Cocktails / 1995 / MET / M

CHRISTEL LOVING *see* **Crystal Lovin**

CHRISTEL S.
Foreign Exchange Sluts / 1995 / INT / M

CHRISTELLE
Anabolic Import #01: Anal X / 1994 / ANA / M • Eurotica #09 / 1996 / XC / M • Magma: Old And Young / 1995 / MET / M • Private Video Magazine #04 / 1993 / OD / M

CHRISTEN
Fun Zone / 1994 / PRE / B

CHRISTEN CARSON
California Taboo / 1986 / VC / M

CHRISTI
Joe Elliot's College Girls #26 / 1994 / JOE / M • Sex On The Strip: The Lusty Ladies Of Las Vagas / 1993 / CPG / F

CHRISTI KAYE *see Star Index I*

CHRISTI LAKE *(Crista Lake)*
Blonde with an slim body, passable face, overbite, small to medium tits, shaven pussy, fleshy labia. Much too pushy, personalitywise. 5'9" tall, 105/110 lbs, 34C-24-34, 33 years old in 1996.
Abused / 1996 / ZA / M • Adam & Eve's House Party #3: Swing Party / 1996 / VC / M • Angels In Flight / 1995 / NIT / M • Asses Galore #1: From L.A. To Brazil / 1996 / DFI / M • The Backline Reporter / 1996 / ZA / M

• Bend Over Babes #4 / 1996 / EA / M • Call Of The Wild / 1995 / AFI / M • Chug-A-Lug Girls #6 / 1995 / VT / M • Cyber-Sex Love Junkies / 1996 / BBE / M • Deep Behind The Scenes With Seymore Butts #1 / 1995 / ULI / M • Deep Seven / 1996 / VC / M • Director's Wet Dreams / 1996 / BBE / M • Dirty Bob's #24: The Big O! / 1996 / FLP / M • Dirty Bob's #27: Laid Back In L.A.! / 1996 / FLP / S • Dirty Dancers #5 / 1995 / 4P / M • Dirty Stories #3 / 1995 / PE / M • Dominant Jean / 1996 / CC / M • Dominique's Inheritance / 1996 / CVC / M • Everybody Wants Some / 1996 / EXQ / F • Fan Fuxxx #1 / 1996 / DWV / M • Fashion Plate / 1995 / WAV / M • Forbidden Cravings / 1996 / VC / M • Fresh Meat (John Leslie) #2 / 1995 / EA / M • Gang Bang Bitches #11 / 1995 / PP / M • Ghost Town / 1995 / WAV / M • The Girls Of Summer / 1995 / VT / M • Hard Core Beginners #09 / 1995 / LEI / M • Hard Core Beginners #12 / 1995 / LEI / M • Hollywood Hookers / 1996 / DWV / M • Jenteal Loves Rocco / 1996 / VI / M • Julia Ann: Superstar / 1995 / WAV / M • Lollipops #1 / 1996 / SC / M • Lust In Time / 1996 / ONA / M • My First Time #2 / 1996 / NS / M • Naked Scandal #1 / 1995 / SPI / M • Naked Scandal #2 / 1996 / SPI / M • New Pussy Hunt #18 / 1995 / LEI / C • Night Stalker / 1995 / BBE / M • Night Tales / 1996 / VC / M • Nina Hartley's Guide To Swinging / 1996 / A&E / M • The Palace Of Pleasure / 1995 / ULI / M • Please Take A Number / 1996 / CDI / M • Pocahotass #1 / 1996 / FD / M • Prime Choice #4 / 1995 / RAS / M • Pristine #2 / 1996 / CA / M • Profiles #08: Triple Ecstacy / 1996 / XPR / M • Rainwoman #09: Wetlands / 1995 / CC / M • The Right Connection / 1995 / VC / M • Rock 'n' Roll Rocco / 1997 / EA / M • Shane's World #2 / 1996 / OD / M • A Shot In The Pink / 1995 / BBE / M • Sleeping Booty / 1995 / EL / M • Smooth Ride / 1996 / WP / M • Sorority Sex Kittens #3 / 1996 / VC / M • Southern Comfort #1 / 1995 / DWV / M • Southern Comfort #2 / 1995 / DWV / M • Strap-On Sally #07: Face Dildo Frenzy / 1995 / PL / F • Streetwalkers / 1995 / PL / M • Streets Of New York #07 / 1996 / PL / M • Strippers Inc. #5 / 1995 / ONA / M • A Tall Tail / 1996 / FC / M • Telephone Expose / 1995 / VC / M • Triple X Video Magazine #17 / 1996 / OD / M • Up And Cummers #28 / 1996 / ERW / M • Up Close & Personal #1 / 1996 / IPI / M • The Usual Anal Suspects / 1996 / CC / M • Virgins / 1995 / ERA / M • Whore'n / 1996 / AB / M • Young & Natural #13 / 1996 / TV / F • Young & Natural #15 / 1996 / TV / F • Young & Natural #16 / 1996 / TV / F • Young & Natural #18 / 1996 / TV / C

CHRISTI LANE *see* **Kristie Leigh**

CHRISTIAN
Different Strokes / 1996 / VC / M • Dirty Girls / 1984 / MIT / M • Gigi Gives It Away / 1995 / FRF / M • Intimate Interviews #2 / 1996 / NIT / M • Lewd In Liverpool / 1995 / VC / M • Pearl Necklace: Thee Bush League #19 / 1993 / SEE / M • Prime Cuts #1 / 1994 / FOR / M • Prime Cuts #2 / 1994 / FOR / M

CHRISTIAN BOENER *see Star Index I*

CHRISTIAN CHASE *(Chase (, Christian), Chris Chase)*

1001 Erotic Nights #2 / 1987 / VC / M • 69 Park Avenue / 1985 / ELH / M • Big, Bad & Beautiful / 1988 / MIR / C • Chocolate Cream / 1984 / SUP / M • Color Me Amber / 1985 / VC / M • Erotic Encounters / 1985 / LIM / C • Love At First Sight / 1987 / SE / C • The Lust Potion Of Doctor F / 1985 / WV / M • On The Wet Side / 1987 / V99 / M • Rebecca's / 1983 / AVC / M • Showgirls / 1985 / SE / M • Sinderotica / 1985 / HO / M • Sleepless Nights / 1984 / VIV / M • Wild Things #2 / 1986 / CV / M

CHRISTIAN DOWD *see Star Index I*

CHRISTIAN FOX
Courting Libido / 1995 / HIV / G • Driven Home / 1995 / CSP / G • Long Play / 1995 / 3XP / G

CHRISTIAN GROVARD *see Star Index I*

CHRISTIAN HART
The Stewardesses / 1969 / SOW / S • The Stewardesses / 1981 / CA / M

CHRISTIAN MURPHY
Bi-Conflict / 1994 / FST / G • Conflict Of Interest / 1994 / FST / G • No Reservations / 1995 / MN0 / G

CHRISTIAN PARKER *(Ernst Hemmingway, Thomas Parker)*
Black & White In Living Color / 1992 / WV / M • Blue Fox / 1991 / VI / M • Double Penetration #6 / 1993 / WV / C • Down And Out / 1995 / PRE / B • The Eliminators / 1991 / BIZ / B • Happy Endings / 1990 / BIZ / B • Heads Or Tails? / 1993 / PL / M • In Pursuit Of Passion / 1990 / V99 / M • The Legend Of The Kama Sutra / 1990 / A&E / M • Love Letters / 1991 / VI / M • No Time For Love / 1991 / VI / M • Sex Asylum #4 / 1991 / VI / M • The Stroke / 1990 / SO / M

CHRISTIAN SARNER *see* **Paula Wain**

CHRISTIAN SARVER *see* **Paula Wain**

CHRISTIAN SCOTT
A Decent Proposal / 1993 / BIL / G

CHRISTIAN STEELE
Asses Galore #7: Lunatic Fringe / 1996 / DFI / M • Cherry Poppers: The College Years #01 / 1997 / ZA / M • Fame Is A Whore On Butt Row / 1996 / ABS / M • Filthy First Timers #3: Tearing Down The Walls Of Shame / 1996 / EL / M • Filthy First Timers #5 / 1997 / EL / M • More Dirty Debutantes #60 / 1997 / SBV / M • More Dirty Debutantes #62 / 1997 / SBV / M • Puritan Video Magazine #10 / 1997 / LE / M • Sodomania #19: Sweet Cream / 1996 / EL / M • Up And Cummers #37 / 1996 / 4P / M • Up And Cummers #39 / 1996 / RWP / M • War Whores / 1996 / EL / M

CHRISTIAN SUMMERS
Lovin' Spoonfuls #7 / 1996 / 4P / C

CHRISTIAN VAN BERGEN
[Schulmadchen-Report 4: Was Eltern Oft Verzweifeln LaBt / 1972 / ... / M

CHRISTIAN VERNON *see Star Index I*

CHRISTIE
First Time Lesbians #20 / 1994 / JMP / F

CHRISTIE (CREAM) *see* **Christy (Cream)**

CHRISTIE BARRINGTON *see* **Kristara Barrington**

CHRISTIE BRYANT *see* **Ali Moore**

CHRISTIE FORD *(Misty Winter, Christin Ford)*
Pretty blonde with small tits and lithe body except for too wide hips.
Afternoon Delights / 1981 / CA / M • Babes In Toyland / 1988 / COM / C • Debbie Does Dallas #1 / 1978 / VC / M • Dirty Looks /

1982 / VC / C • Fascination / 1980 / QX / M • A Girl's Best Friend / 1981 / QX / M • Inside Seka / 1980 / VXP / M • Justine: A Matter Of Innocence / 1980 / SAT / M • Love-In Arrangement / 1981 / VXP / M • Manhattan Mistress / 1980 / VBM / M • New York Babes / 1979 / AR / M • The Nite Bird / 1978 / BL / M • October Silk / 1980 / COM / M • Platinum Paradise / 1980 / COM / M • Satin Suite / 1979 / QX / M • A Scent Of Heather / 1981 / VXP / M • Seka Is Tara / 1981 / VC / M • Steamy Sirens / 1984 / AIR / C • Twilight Pink #1 / 1980 / AR / M • Velvet High / 1980 / VC / M • Women In Love / 1980 / CA / M

CHRISTIE KEITH *see* **Christy Keith**
CHRISTIE LANE *see* **Kristie Leigh**
CHRISTIE LEEDS *(Christine (C.Leeds), Autumn (C. Leeds), Ashley Phillips (CL), Christine St Clair)*
Tiny breasted girl with the figure of a 14 year old, long brown straight hair, 22 years old in 1993, dancer, comes from Pennsylvania originally. Not too good in the skin department. Generally appears with husband Doug Warr who has a Svengali like beard.
America's Raunchiest Home Videos #35: Nothing Butt / 1992 / ZA / M • Biff Malibu's Totally Nasty Home Videos #10 / 1992 / ANA / M • Bobby Hollander's Sweet Cheeks #102 / 1992 / WV / M • Bubble Butts #17 / 1992 / LBO / M • Bubble Butts #18 / 1992 / LBO / M • Deep Inside Dirty Debutantes #05 / 1993 / 4P / M • Double D Dykes #03 / 1992 / GO / F • Hollywood Swingers #02 / 1992 / LBO / M • Hollywood's Hills / 1992 / LV / M • Mr. Peepers Amateur Home Videos #49: Up And Cumming #2 / 1992 / LBO / M • Odyssey Triple Play #51: Anal Party / 1993 / OD / M • Pearl Necklace: Thee Bush League: The Best Of Oral #01 / 1993 / SEE / C • Real People Real Bondage #2 / 1996 / BON / C • Rump Humpers #08 / 1992 / GLI / M • Sex Police 2000 / 1992 / AFV / M • Uncle Roy's Amateur Home Video #13 / 1992 / VIM / M • Uncle Roy's Amateur Home Video #14 / 1992 / VIM / M • Welcome To Bondage: Christie / 1993 / BON / B • Welcome To Bondage: Starlets #2 / 1994 / BON / C • White Men Can't Hump / 1992 / CC / M
CHRISTIE LEIGH *see* **Kristie Leigh**
CHRISTIE MICHAELS
She-Male Encounters #14: She-Male Wrestlers / 1987 / MET / G • Trisexual Encounters #05 / 1986 / PL / G • Trisexual Encounters #06 / 1987 / PL / G
CHRISTIE ROBBINS
21 Hump Street / 1988 / VWA / M • Back To Rears / 1988 / VI / M • Ball In The Family / 1988 / VWA / M • Breaststroke #2 / 1989 / EX / M • But...Can She Type? / 1989 / CDI / M • Butt's Motel #2 / 1989 / EX / M • Debbie's Love Spell / 1988 / STM / M • The Flirt / 1987 / VWA / M • The Girls Of The B.L.O. / 1988 / VWA / M • Lays Of Our Lives / 1988 / ZA / M • Roll-X Girls / 1989 / DYV / M • Shoot To Thrill / 1988 / VWA / M • Sugar Tongues / 1992 / STM / C • Suzie Creamcheese / 1988 / VWA / M
CHRISTIN FORD *see* **Christie Ford**
CHRISTINA
Backdoor Club #1 / 1996 / VEX / C • Ben Dover & Barbie / 1999 / SUF / M • Buttman's European Vacation #3 / 1995 / EA / M • Cheap Tricks #1 / 1996 / PAV / M

• European Sex TV / 1996 / EL / M • Hot Body Video Magazine: Brunette Power / 1994 / CG / F • A Merry Widow / 1996 / SPI / M • Pussyman Auditions #06 / 1995 / SNA / M • Rear Entry / 1995 / LEI / M • Sunset Rides Again / 1995 / VC / M • Take All Cummers / 1996 / HO / M • World Sex Tour #4 / 1996 / ANA / M
CHRISTINA (1992)
A&B GB#031: Spoon Lover #1 / 1992 / A&B / M • A&B GB#038: Spoon It Up Honey #1 / 1992 / A&B / M • A&B GB#039: Spoon It Up Honey #2 / 1992 / A&B / M • A&B GB#041: The Surpise Party #1 / 1992 / A&B / M • America's Raunchiest Home Videos #25: Victoria's Secretions / 1992 / ZA / M • Biff Malibu's Totally Nasty Home Videos #18 / 1992 / ANA / M • Lesbian Pros And Amateurs #12 / 1992 / GO / F
CHRISTINA (FRENCH) *see* **Star Index I**
CHRISTINA (KING) *see* **Krystina King**
CHRISTINA (S/M) *see* **Star Index I**
CHRISTINA ANGEL *(Christy (C. Angel))*
Reasonably pretty strawberry blonde *Playboy* bunny type with medium enhanced tits, bad facial skin, tattoo on left belly, slightly too big across the hips. Was originally a librarian and then became a dancer at Goldfingers in NYC prior to getting into the business. Later added a vertical tattoo between her shoulder blades.
American Beauty #1 / 1993 / FOR / M • American Beauty #2 / 1994 / FOR / M • Angel Baby / 1995 / SC / M • Angel Eyes / 1995 / IN / M • Animal Instinct / 1993 / VI / M • Back To Anal Alley / 1994 / ME / M • The Bottom Dweller Part Deux / 1994 / EL / M • Butt Hunt #09 / 1995 / LEI / M • Butt Jammers #03 / 1995 / SC / F • Butt Jammers #04 / 1995 / SC / F • Casting Call #13 / 1995 / SO / M • Cat Lickers #2 / 1994 / ME / F • Catwalk #1 / 1995 / SC / M • Catwalk #2 / 1995 / SC / M • Cheating / 1994 / VI / M • Dial A For Anal / 1994 / CA / M • The Doctor Is In #2: Pussy Pox / 1995 / NIT / M • Dog Walker / 1994 / EA / M • Done In The Desert Sun / 1995 / OUP / M • Double Penetration Virgins #06: DP Diner / 1995 / JMP / M • Dungeon Dykes #2 / 1994 / FPI / F • Eleventh Annual AVN Awards / 1994 / VC / M • Exstasy / 1995 / WV / M • Finger Pleasures #4 / 1995 / PL / F • Happy Ass Lesbians / 1994 / ROB / F • Hard Cum Cafe / 1996 / BCP / M • Hookers Of Hollywood / 1994 / LE / M • Horny Henry's Snowballing Adventure / 1995 / TTV / M • I Love Lesbians / 1995 / ERW / F • Intercourse With The Vampyre #1 / 1994 / SC / M • Intercourse With The Vampyre #2 / 1994 / SC / M • Jizz Glazed Goo Guzzlers #1 / 1996 / NIT / C • Kym Wilde's On The Edge #25 / 1995 / RB / B • Kym Wilde's On The Edge #26 / 1995 / RB / B • Kym Wilde's On The Edge #39 / 1996 / RB / B • Lesbian Bitches #1 / 1994 / ROB / F • Live Sex / 1994 / LE / M • Long Dark Shadow / 1994 / LE / M • Night Train / 1993 / VI / M • Pretending / 1993 / CV / M • Pussy Hunt #15 / 1995 / LEI / M • Pussywoman #2 / 1994 / CC / M • Radical Affairs Video Magazine #07 / 1994 / ME / M • Raunch #10: Uncut Jewel / 1994 / CC / M • Raw Sex #01 / 1994 / ERW / M • The Reel World #1 / 1994 / FOR / M • The Reel World #2 / 1994 / FOR / M • Rumpman: Caught In An Anal Avalanche / 1995 / HW / M • Sex Kitten / 1995 / SC /

M • Sex On The Saddle: Wicked Women Of The Wild West / 1994 / CPG / S • Sex On The Strip: The Lusty Ladies Of Las Vagas / 1993 / CPG / F • Sex Secrets Of High Priced Call Girls / 1995 / MID / M • Sleeping Single / 1994 / CC / M • Sodom Chronicles / 1995 / FH / M • Spin For Sex / 1994 / IN / M • The Swap #2 / 1994 / VI / M • Under The Pink / 1994 / ROB / F • Undress To Thrill / 1994 / VI / M • Up And Cummers #09 / 1994 / 4P / M • The Violation Of Kia / 1995 / JMP / F • Wet Faces #1 / 1997 / SC / C
CHRISTINA APPLELEIGH *see* **Christine Applelay**
CHRISTINA APPLELEIR *see* **Christine Applelay**
CHRISTINA BOUVER
Sexhibition #3 / 1996 / SUF / M
CHRISTINA CLARK *see* **Trinity Lane**
CHRISTINA CRUISE *see* **Rebecca Wild**
CHRISTINA DE'OAR *see* **Christina Dior**
CHRISTINA DEVEAUX *see* **Star Index I**
CHRISTINA DIOR *(Dior, Christina De'Oar)*
Tall (5'8") blonde with small tits and cellulite in her rear. Sounds like she needs a bit of psychiatric help.
Arabian Nights / 1993 / WP / M • Backdoor To The City Of Sin / 1993 / ANA / M • Harry Horndog #16: Love Puppies #4 / 1992 / ZA / M • The Pain Connection / 1994 / BS / B • Songbird / 1993 / AMP / M • Up And Cummers #06 / 1993 / 4P / M • Who Killed Holly Hollywood? / 1993 / VC / M
CHRISTINA DUPONTE *see* **Tiffany DuPont**
CHRISTINA EVOL *(Kristina Evol)*
Pudgy blonde who looks like she's dirty (i.e. hasn't washed recently).
Changing Partners / 1989 / FAZ / M • Delicate Matters / 1989 / VEX / M • Dream Dates / 1990 / V99 / M • Head Nurse / 1990 / V99 / M • Heartless / 1989 / REB / M • Heather's Secrets / 1990 / VEX / M • The Honeymoon: The Bride's Running Behind / 1990 / 4P / M • Internal Affair / 1990 / V99 / M • Ladies Man / 1990 / REB / M • Lonely Is The Night / 1990 / V99 / M • Night Lessons / 1990 / V99 / M • Night Watch / 1990 / VEX / M • Oral Addiction / 1989 / LV / M • Playing Dirty / 1989 / VEX / M • Rituals / 1989 / V99 / M • Space Cadet / 1989 / IN / M • Sweet Tease / 1990 / VEX / M • Tequilla Sunset / 1989 / V99 / M • This Bun's For You / 1989 / FAN / M • Tropical Temptations / 1989 / VEX / M • Undercover Carol / 1990 / FAN / M
CHRISTINA FERRARA
Wild Innocents / 1982 / VCX / M
CHRISTINA GRANTHAM
Schoolgirl Fannies On Fire / 1994 / BIZ / B
CHRISTINA HELLMAN
Bel Ami / 1976 / VXP / M
CHRISTINA HILL
Bondage-Gram / 1983 / BIZ / B • The Girls Of Klit House / 1984 / LIP / F • Happy Birthday Bondage Gram / 1983 / BIZ / B • Jane Bonda's Bizarre Workout / 1984 / BIZ / B • Lusty Couples (Come To) / cr85 / CHX / M • Mama's Boy / 1984 / VD / M
CHRISTINA HOWARD *see* **Roxanne Rolland**
CHRISTINA HULTBERG
The Psychiatrist / 1978 / VC / M
CHRISTINA LAKE
Body Shop / 1984 / VCX / M

CHRISTINA LAREINA see Star Index I
CHRISTINA LINDBERG
[Schulmadchen-Report 4: Was Eltern Oft Verzweifeln LaBt / 1972 / ... / M
CHRISTINA MARTON see Star Index I
CHRISTINA MESEOROS
Juicy Virgins / 1995 / WIV / M
CHRISTINA ROSE
Anal Camera #11 / 1995 / EVN / M • Cum Swappers / 1995 / ZA / M
CHRISTINA RUSSELL see Tina Russell
CHRISTINA SEA see Kristine Sea
CHRISTINA TYLER see Tina Tyler
CHRISTINA VALENTI
The Joy Club / 1996 / XC / M
CHRISTINA WEST see Kristina West
CHRISTINA WOODS
Horny Henry's Strange Adventure / 1995 / TTV / M • Nasty Backdoor Nurses / 1994 / LBO / M
CHRISTINA Z.
Up And Cummers #38 / 1996 / RWP / M
CHRISTINE
100% Amateur #18: / 1995 / OD / M • Adultress / 1995 / WIV / M • Big Murray's New-Cummers #23: Naughty Nymphettes / 1993 / FD / M • Blue Vanities #524 / 1993 / FFL / M • Bosom Buddies / 1990 / BTO / F • Christine's Bondage Fantasies / 1996 / JAM / B • Christine: All Day All Night / 1996 / GLI / M • Dirty Blue Movies #04 / 1993 / JTV / F • Hot Chicks Do L.A. / 1994 / EVN / F • Magma: Deep Inside Janine / 1994 / MET / M • Neighborhood Watch #23: Sinsational Sex / 1992 / LBO / M • The Nibblers / 1979 / TVX / M • Odyssey 30 Min: Christine's Anal Deflowering / 1992 / OD / M • Penthouse: Great Pet Hunt #1 / 1992 / PET / F • Reel People #04 / 1994 / PP / M • Spank Me, Spank Me, Spank Me / 199? / BON / B
CHRISTINE (C.LEEDS) see Christie Leeds
CHRISTINE (S/M) see Star Index I
CHRISTINE ALBEROLA
Felicia / 1975 / QX / M
CHRISTINE AMEN see Star Index I
CHRISTINE APPLELAY (Christina Appleleir, Christina Appleleigh, Kristine Apple)
Blonde with nice long hair, a thickening body and small natural breasts. Also has a double chin.
AHV #16: Let It Loose / 1992 / EVN / M • American Built / 1992 / LE / M • Anal House Party / 1993 / IP / M • The Anals Of History #2 / 1992 / MID / M • The Awakening / 1992 / SC / M • Biff Malibu's Totally Nasty Home Videos #26 / 1992 / ANA / M • The Big E #10 / 1992 / PRE / B • Big Murray's New-Cummers #06: Men & Women / 1993 / FD / M • Blonde Beaver Bonanza / 1992 / TCP / M • Bobby Hollander's Rookie Nookie #02 / 1993 / SFP / M • Buffy Malibu's Totally Nasty All-Girl Home Videos #02 / 1992 / ANA / F • Butt Woman #2 / 1992 / FH / M • Butt Woman #3 / 1992 / FH / M • Butt Woman #4 / 1993 / FH / M • Casting Call #01 / 1993 / SO / M • Cat Fight / 1992 / ONH / M • The Creasemaster / 1993 / VC / M • Dark Justice / 1992 / ZA / M • Defending Your Sex Life / 1992 / LE / M • Dream Date / 1992 / HO / M • Elvis Slept Here / 1992 / LE / M • Feathermates / 1992 / PRE / B • Final Anal Tease / 1992 / MID / M • Fire & Ice / 1992 / CDI / G • Forget Me Not

/ 1994 / FH / M • Funny Ladies / 1996 / PRE / B • The Gang Bang Story / 1993 / IP / M • Harry Horndog #05: Sex Hungry Couples #1 / 1992 / ZA / M • Heatwave #1 / 1992 / FH / F • How To Make A Model #02: Got Her In Bed / 1993 / QUA / M • Lust Horizons / 1992 / PL / G • Malibu Blue / 1992 / LE / M • The Merry Widows / 1993 / VC / M • Mr. Peepers Amateur Home Videos #32: Fingers in the Honey Po / 1991 / LBO / M • New Girls In Town #2 / 1992 / CC / M • Positively Pagan #07 / 1993 / ATA / M • Raging Hormones / 1992 / LE / M • Ride 'em Hard / 1992 / LV / M • Savannah R.N. / 1992 / HW / M • The Seducers / 1992 / ZA / M • See-Thru / 1992 / LE / M • Talk Dirty To Me #09 / 1992 / DR / M • Uncle Roy's Amateur Home Video #10 / 1992 / VIM / M • Waterbabies #2 / 1992 / CC / M
CHRISTINE BAER
Sex Roulette / 1979 / CA / M
CHRISTINE BEAUGRAND see Star Index I
CHRISTINE BERG see Star Index I
CHRISTINE CARR
Little Me & Marla Strangelove / 1979 / ALP / M
CHRISTINE CLARK see Trinity Lane
CHRISTINE CLARK (FR)
Girl With The Million $ Legs / 1987 / PL / M
CHRISTINE CLENNE see Star Index I
CHRISTINE CRAIG see Star Index I
CHRISTINE DE B.
Anal In The Alps / 1996 / P69 / M • Cunt Of Monte Cristo / 1996 / SPL / M
CHRISTINE DE BEAUSSA see Star Index I
CHRISTINE DE SHAEFFR (Jessica Teal)
Blonde, not too pretty face, shoulder length curly hair, womanly body, tiny tattoo on right belly just near pubic hair, small tits.
Blue Ecstasy / 1980 / CA / M • Blue Vanities #055 / 1988 / FFL / M • The Budding Of Brie / 1980 / TVX / M • Classic Swedish Erotica #30 / 1987 / CA / C • Classic Swedish Erotica #32 / 1987 / CA / C • Dracula Exotica / 1980 / TVX / M • Dungeons Of Pain / or80 / BIZ / B • An Erotic Trilogy / cr81 / GO / M • Helpless Coeds / 1987 / BIZ / B • Hot Lunch / 1978 / SE / M • Justine: A Matter Of Innocence / 1980 / SAT / M • Last Of The Wild / 1975 / CA / M • The Live Show / 1979 / SVE / M • Loving Friends / 1975 / AXV / M • Mortgage Of Sin / 1975 / CA / M • October Silk / 1980 / COM / M • Oh Doctor / cr72 / ADU / M • The Pink Ladies / 1980 / VC / M • Pizza Girls (We Deliver) / 1978 / VCX / M • A Scent Of Heather / 1981 / VXP / M • Sex Museum / 1976 / AXV / M • Silky / 1980 / VXP / M • Sunny / 1979 / VC / M • Swedish Erotica #12 / 1980 / CA / M • Tattooed Lady (Twilight) / 1980 / TWI / M • Teenage Cruisers / 1977 / VCX / M • Telefantasy / 1978 / AR / M • Weekend Fantasy / 1980 / VCX / M
CHRISTINE DELINAR see Star Index I
CHRISTINE FELDE see Star Index I
CHRISTINE GLENNE see Star Index I
CHRISTINE GYHAGEN
Bel Ami / 1976 / VXP / M • [Molly / 1977 / ... / S
CHRISTINE HELLER (Cindy Johnson, Karen Kushman, Karen Cusick, Dolores Coubron, Paula Thomas (Ch He), Kathy Thomas, Kathy Kane, Kathy Kirk,

Kathy Kline, Kathy Collins (CH), Kathy Carlton, Kathy Christian, Kathy Kusick, Karen Kusick (Hellr), Kristine Heller, Dolores Colburn, Karen Custer, Kathy Marsh)
Distinctive face, passable, small tits, a little womanly, allegedly Australian. A real nut crusher.
Baby Face #1 / 1977 / VC / M • The Best Of Alex De Renzy #1 / 1983 / VC / C • Ceremony, The Ritual Of Love / 1976 / AVC / M • Classic Swedish Erotica #12 / 1986 / CA / C • Classic Swedish Erotica #25 / 1987 / CA / C • Confessions Of A Woman / 1976 / SE / M • Do You Wanna Be Loved? / 1977 / AR / M • The Erotic Adventures Of Candy / 1978 / VCX / M • Foxy Lady / 1978 / CV / M • Good To The Last Drop / 1986 / VCS / C • Inside Babysitter / 1977 / MID / M • Joint Venture / 1977 / ELV / M • Legends Of Porn #1 / 1987 / CV / C • Legends Of Porn #2 / 1989 / CV / C • Lipps & Mccain / 1978 / VC / M • Little Girls Blue #1 / 1977 / VCX / M • Long Jeanne Silver / 1977 / VC / M • Mary! Mary! / 1977 / SE / M • Masterpiece / cr78 / VEP / M • Only The Best #1 / 1986 / CV / C • The Other Side Of Julie / 1978 / CV / M • Pink Lips / 1977 / VCX / M • Pretty Peaches #1 / 1978 / MIT / M • Reflections / 1977 / VCX / M • Seven Into Snowy / 1977 / VC / M • Sexsations / 1984 / NSV / M • Shiela's Deep Desires / 1986 / HO / M • The Spirit Of Seventy Six / 1976 / NGV / M • Swedish Erotica #05 / 1980 / CA / M • Taboo #02 / 1982 / IN / M • Teenage Desires / 1975 / IVP / M • Teenage Madam / 1979 / CXV / M • Teeny Buns / 1977 / VC / M • Thoroughly Amorous Amy / 1978 / VCX / M • True Legends Of Adult Cinema: Unsung Superstars / 1993 / VC / C • The Ultimate Pleasure / 1977 / HIF / M • The Untamed / 1978 / VCX / M • V—The Hot One / 1978 / CV / M
CHRISTINE HOWARD
Aroused / 1985 / VIV / M • High Price Spread / 1986 / PV / C
CHRISTINE HUTTON see Star Index I
CHRISTINE JUSTICE see Star Index I
CHRISTINE KEELER
Blue Vanities #006 / 1987 / FFL / M • Blue Vanities #096 / 1988 / FFL / M
CHRISTINE KELLY
Beyond The Blue / cr78 / SVE / M • Blue Heat / 1975 / IVP / M • The Fur Trap / 1973 / AVC / M • Insane Desires / cr78 / ... / M • Oriental Babysitter / 1976 / SE / M • Reflections / 1977 / VCX / M • Sexsations / 1984 / NSV / M • The Untamed / 1978 / VCX / M
CHRISTINE LOUIS
Body Love / 1976 / CA / M
CHRISTINE MARLBERG
Sex Mountain / cr80 / VCX / M
CHRISTINE MORLUR
Bondage Wildcats / 1993 / NAP / B
CHRISTINE MULLER see Star Index I
CHRISTINE ROBERTS
Born Erect / cr80 / CA / M
CHRISTINE SARVER see Paula Wain
CHRISTINE ST CLAIR see Christie Leeds
CHRISTINE SUSHI see Star Index I
CHRISTINE TYLER see Nikki Tyler
CHRISTINE VON STRATO
Confessions Of A Blue Movie Star / 1974 / CTH / S • [Junge Madchen Mogen's HeiB,

Hausfrauen Noch HeiBer / 1973 / ... / M
CHRISTINE WILLIAMS *see* **Crystal Sync**
CHRISTINE WOODS *(Sierra Blaze)*
Dark blonde who seems to often wear glasses. Small slightly droopy breasts with small nipples, very petite, tight body, lots of facial acne, a bit flat on rear.
Anal Anonymous / 1994 / ZA / M • Anal Vision #26 / 1994 / LBO / M • Bobby Hollander's Sweet Cheeks #112 / 1994 / QUA / M • Cherry Poppers #03: School's Out / 1994 / ZA / M • The Hitch-Hiker #03: No Exit / 1994 / WMG / M • Muffmania / 1995 / TTV / M • The Nurses Are Cumming #1 / 1996 / LBO / C • The Real Deal #1 / 1994 / FC / M • So You Wanna Be A Porn Star #1: The Russians Are Cumming / 1994 / WHP / M
CHRISTINNA SNOW
Enforcing The Code / 1994 / TVI / B
CHRISTIVA *see Star Index I*
CHRISTOFF DUBET
The Rise Of The Roman Empress #1 / 1986 / PV / M
CHRISTOPH *see* **Christophe Clark**
CHRISTOPHE CLARK *(Christopher Clark, Christoph, Kris Klark, Kriss Klark)*
Blonde, older looking French male.
1001 Nights / 1996 / IP / M • All Inside Eva / 1991 / PL / M • Anabolic Import #02: Anal X / 1991 / ANA / M • Angel Wolf / 1995 / WIV / M • Barbara Dare's Roman Holiday / 1987 / SE / M • Buttman's European Vacation #1 / 1991 / EA / M • Club Ecstasy / 1987 / CA / M • The Coming Of Nikita / 1995 / EL / M • Deep Blue / 1989 / PV / M • Della Borsa / 1995 / WIV / M • The Desirous Wife / 1988 / PL / M • The Devil In Mr Holmes / 1988 / PV / M • Diamonds / 1996 / HDE / M • Dirty Stories #4 / 1995 / PE / M • Doctor, Doctor: Show Me Everything / 1995 / VMX / M • Double Desires / 1988 / PIN / C • Dr Max And The Anal Girls / 1994 / WIV / M • The Erotic Adventures Of Alladin X / 1995 / IP / M • Euro Bondage #1 / 1995 / ONA / B • Euro Studs / 1996 / SC / C • Euroflesh: Dentro II Vulcano / 1996 / SC / M • Gode-Party / 1994 / RUM / M • Grand Prixxx / 1987 / CA / M • Hamlet: For The Love Of Ophelia #1 / 1996 / IP / M • Hamlet: For The Love Of Ophelia #2 / 1996 / IP / M • Hot Hideaway / 1986 / CA / M • The Husband / 1995 / WIV / M • Infidel / 1996 / WV / M • Karin & Barbara Superstars / 1988 / PL / M • Ladies In Leather / 1995 / GO / M • Lady By Night / 1987 / CA / M • The Last Train #1 / 1995 / BHE / M • The Last Train #2 / 1995 / BHE / M • Le Parfum De Mathilde / 1994 / VI / M • Lollipops #1 / 1996 / SC / M • Lollipops #2 / 1996 / SC / M • Lust Italian Style / 1987 / CA / M • Lusting, London Style / 1992 / VC / M • Magma: Anal Teenies / 1994 / MET / M • Magma: Bizarre Lust / 1995 / MET / M • Magma: Sperm Dreams / 1990 / MET / M • Magma: Trans-Games / 1995 / MET / G • Marquis De Sade / 1995 / IP / M • A Merry Widow / 1996 / SPI / M • Nasty Nymphos #10 / 1995 / ANA / M • Nasty Nymphos #11 / 1995 / ANA / M • Nasty Nymphos #12 / 1996 / ANA / M • On My Lips / 1989 / PV / M • Penetration (Anabolic) #1 / 1995 / ANA / M • Penetration (Anabolic) #2 / 1995 / ANA / M • Penetration (Anabolic) #3 / 1995 / ANA / M • Penetration (Anabolic) #4 / 1996 / ANA / M • Porsche / 1990 / NSV / M • Prima #09: ASSassins / 1995 / MBP / M •

Prima #14: Hotel Europa / 1996 / MBP / M • Sensations #1 / 1996 / SC / M • Sensations #2 / 1996 / SC / M • Sluts 'n' Angels In Budapest / 1994 / EL / M • Sodomania #10: Euro/American Again / 1994 / EL / M • Sodomania #11: In Your Face / 1994 / EL / M • Sodomania: Slop Shots / 1996 / EL / C • Sperm Injection / 1995 / PL / M • A Very Debauched Girl / 1988 / PL / M • World Sex Tour #3 / 1995 / ANA / M • World Sex Tour #4 / 1996 / ANA / M • Young And Anal #1 / 1995 / JMP / M
CHRISTOPHE GIL *see Star Index I*
CHRISTOPHER
Bi-Bi Love Amateurs #1 / 1993 / SFP / G • Blonde Butt Babes / 1994 / LV / M • Butt Freak #2 / 1996 / EA / M • Seymore & Shane Live On Tour / 1995 / ULI / M • Up And Cummers #27 / 1996 / ERW / M
CHRISTOPHER ADAMS *see Star Index I*
CHRISTOPHER ALEXANDE *see* **Biff Malibu**
CHRISTOPHER CHARM *see Star Index I*
CHRISTOPHER CLARK *see* **Christophe Clark**
CHRISTOPHER CRUISE
Delinquents On Butt Row / 1996 / EA / M • Desert Island Buttwatch / 1996 / SUF / M • East Coast Sluts #07: Tampa Bay / 1995 / PL / M • Fresh Meat #1 / 1996 / PL / M • Philmore Butts Spring Break / 1996 / SUF / M • Tampa Spice / 1996 / SUF / M • Up And Cummers #18 / 1995 / 4P / M
CHRISTOPHER GILBERT *see Star Index I*
CHRISTOPHER GREGORY *see Star Index I*
CHRISTOPHER GROSSO *see Star Index I*
CHRISTOPHER JAMES
Private Film #05 / 1993 / OD / M • Private Film #09 / 1994 / OD / M
CHRISTOPHER KERSEN *see Star Index I*
CHRISTOPHER L'AIDE
The French Touch / 1984 / NSV / M
CHRISTOPHER LADD
Summer Of '69 / 1994 / MID / M • Visual Fantasies / 1995 / LE / M • Wet & Wicked / 1995 / PRK / M
CHRISTOPHER MAN *see Star Index I*
CHRISTOPHER NORRIS
Agony Of Love, Lace And Lash / cr73 / SOW / M • Bucky Beaver's XXX Dragon Art Theatre Double Feature #14 / 1996 / SOW / M
CHRISTOPHER PARKER *see Star Index I*
CHRISTOPHER SHARP
Cyber-Sex Love Junkies / 1996 / BBE / M • Dreams Of Desires / 1995 / ONA / M • Mile High Thrills / 1995 / VIM / M • Penetrator #2: Grudge Day / 1995 / PL / M • Plaything #1 / 1995 / VI / M • Prime Choice #7 / 1996 / RAS / M • Wet Daydreams / 1996 / XCI / M
CHRISTOPHER SUSS
Erotic Rondo / 1996 / IP / M • The Last Vamp / 1996 / IP / M
CHRISTY
Amateur Hours #02 / 1989 / AFI / M • Amatour Hours #05 / 1990 / AFI / M • Amateur Night #03 / 1990 / HME / F • Amateur Night #04 / 1990 / HME / M • Blue Vanities #555 / 1994 / FFL / M • Christy: Pantyhose Delight / 1990 / LOD / S • Everything Goes /

1975 / CA / M • The Girls Of Daytona / 1993 / BTO / S • J.E.G.: Christy, Tim And Scott / 1995 / JEG / M • More Dirty Debutantes #45 / 1995 / 4P / M • More Dirty Debutants #46 / 1995 / 4P / M • Mr. Peepers Amateur Home Videos #24: The Sleazy Riders / 1991 / LBO / M • Mr. Peepers Nastiest #5 / 1995 / LBO / C • New Faces, Hot Bodies #12 / 1993 / STP / M • New Faces, Hot Bodies #16 / 1994 / STP / M • Next Door Neighbors #01 / 1989 / BON / M • Paris Models / 1987 / CDI / M • Spreading Joy / 1984 / IN / M • Under The Skirt #2 / 1995 / KAE / F
CHRISTY (C. ANGEL) *see* **Christina Angel**
CHRISTY (CREAM) *(Christie (Cream), Cream (Christie))*
OK looking blonde with small tits who seems to be associated with the Stevi's Secrets and the VGA group. Was 24 in 1992 and had her first sexual experience at 13.
A&B AB#116: Blowjobs For All / 1990 / A&B / M • All "A" / 1994 / SFP / C • AVP #9131: Kelly Doubles Up / 1991 / AVP / M • Big Murray's New-Cummers #01: Blondes Have More... / 1992 / FD / M • Bobby Hollander's Rookie Nookie #07 / 1993 / SFP / M • Bobby Hollander's Sweet Cheeks #107 / 1993 / QUA / M • Butter Up My Butt-Hole / 1992 / RUM / M • Christy In Bondage / 1993 / BON / B • Full Moon Video #22: Elite Fantasy Girls / 1992 / FAP / F • Full Moon Video #28: Christy Cremes—Bottoms Up! / 1994 / FAP / M • Gemini: Sex Packs #01 / 1993 / FAP / M • Gemini: Sex Packs #03 / 1993 / FAP / M • Gemini: Sex Packs #04 / 1993 / FAP / M • House Play (Bon Vue) / 1994 / BON / B • Mistress Gretchen And Christy / 1993 / BON / B • Mr. Peepers Amateur Home Videos #68: A Tough Load To Swallow / 1993 / LBO / M • Nasty Fuckin' Movies #08: Blow Jobs For Everybody / 1992 / RUM / M • Nasty Fuckin' Movies #10: Bend For A Friend / 1992 / RUM / M • Neighborhood Watch #39: / 1993 / LBO / M • Pearl Necklace: Thee Bush League: The Best Of Oral #01 / 1993 / SEE / C • Pearl Necklace: Thee Bush League #04 / 1992 / SEE / M • Seymore Butts & His Mystery Girl / 1993 / FH / M • Spooky Night / 1993 / BON / B • Stevi's: All Butts About It / 1993 / SSV / M • Stevi's: Candi's First Time Bi / 1996 / SSV / F • Stevi's: Carl's Christy Cream's Customs / 1995 / SSV / M • Stevi's: Carl's Christy Customs / 1992 / SSV / M • Stevi's: Christy's Anal Lover / 1992 / SSV / M • Stevi's: Christy's Garterbelt Dance / 1992 / SSV / F • Stevi's: Dildo Duet / 1994 / SSV / F • Stevi's: Good Vibrations / 1994 / SSV / M • Stevi's: Hot Night / 1993 / SSV / F • Stevi's: How Short Do You Want It? / 1994 / SSV / F • Stevi's: Oral Lover's Delight / 1992 / SSV / M • Stevi's: Pantyhose Superheroes / 1995 / SSV / F • Stevi's: Rear Assets / 1992 / SSV / M • Stevi's: Slip Sliding Away / 1993 / SSV / F • Stevi's: Smoke Screen / 1996 / SSV / F • Stevi's: Spanked Debutantes / 1992 / SSV / B • Stevi's: Stevi's XXX Sex Previews / 1995 / SSV / C • SVE: Lusty Lady In Waiting / 1993 / SVE / M • Upper Class Bondage / 1993 / BON / B • VGA: Bureau Of Discipline #1 / 1993 / VGA / B • VGA: Bureau Of Discipline #2 / 1993 / VGA / B •

VGA: Bureau Of Discipline #3 / 1993 / VGA / B

CHRISTY (KRYSTI)LYNN *see* **Krysti Lynn**

CHRISTY (S/M)
Transsexual Prostitutes #1 / 1996 / DFI / G

CHRISTY ANN
Twin sister to Chrissy Ann—looks much more rangy. Expecting a child as of mid-1992.
America's Raunchiest Home Videos #26: Tiptoe Thru The 2 Lips / 1992 / ZA / M • The Anal Adventures Of Max Hardcore: Sunset Boulevard / 1992 / ZA / M • Anal Intruder #06: The Anal Twins / 1992 / CC / M • Biff Malibu's Totally Nasty Home Videos #08 / 1992 / ANA / M • Blonde Butt Babes / 1994 / LV / M • Lovin' Spoonfuls #7 / 1996 / 4P / C • More Dirty Debutantes #14 / 1992 / 4P / M • Penetrating Thoughts / 1992 / LV / M

CHRISTY BATES
Rough Games / 1994 / GOT / B • Ruling Methods / 1994 / GOT / B • Toe Tales #15 / 1994 / GOT / B • Toe Tales #16 / 1994 / GOT / B • Toe Tales #24 / 1995 / GOT / C

CHRISTY BAYE
Disciples Of Bondage / 1992 / STM / B • East Coast Sluts #01: New Jersey / 1995 / PL / M • Journey Into Latex / 1992 / STM / B • Nasty Dancers #1 / 1996 / STM / B • Red Boot Diaries / 1992 / STM / B • Rick's Bondage Playmate #2 / 1993 / HMV / B • Strap-On Sally #01: Strap-On Psycho / 1993 / PL / F • Strap-On Sally #02: Ariana Bottoms Out / 1993 / PL / F • Streets Of New York #01 / 1994 / PL / M • Toe Tales #18 / 1994 / GOT / B • Trained Transvestites / 1995 / STM / B • Transvestite Academy / 1991 / PL / G

CHRISTY BRIAN *see* **Gail Force**

CHRISTY CANYON *(Sara Wine, Tara Wine)*
Not too pleasant brunette with huge natural droopy tits and an attitude. As of June 1993, she has supposedly quit to marry Tom Sinopoli of Visual Images. Later divorced. Was 18 in 1984. 5'7" and 36DD-24-36 in 1995. Married Jeremy Stone of *AFW* in mid 1996.
10 Years Of Big Busts #2 / 1990 / BTO / C • 11th Annual Adult Video News Awards / 1996 / VC / S • Adult Video News 1991 Awards / 1991 / VC / M • Adult Video News 1992 Awards / 1992 / VC / M • Attack Of The Monster Mammaries / 1987 / LA / C • Back To Class #1 / 1984 / DR / M • Bardot / 1991 / VI / M • Battle Of The Stars #1 / 1985 / NSV / M • The Beat Goes On / 1987 / VCR / C • The Best Of Big Busty / 1986 / L&W / C • Best Of Hot Shorts #01 / 1987 / VCR / C • Between My Breasts #01 / 1986 / BTO / S • Big Bust Babes #06 / 1991 / AFI / F • Big Bust Black Legends / 1991 / BTO / C • Big Busty #10 / 198? / H&S / M • Billionaire Girls Club / 1988 / LVI / C • Black Throat / 1985 / VC / M • Bloopers & Boners / 1996 / VI / M • Breastography, Lesson #1 / 1987 / VCR / M • Bursting Bras / 1990 / BTO / C • Cavalcade Of Stars / 1985 / VCR / C • Christy Canyon: She's Back / 1995 / TTV / C • Christy In The Wild / 1992 / VI / M • Comeback / 1995 / VI / M • The Coming Of Christy / 1990 / CAY / M • Confessions Of Christy / 1991 / CAY / M • Crazed #1 / 1992 / VI / M • Crazed #2 / 1992 / VI / M • Cum Shot Revue #2 / 1985 / HO / C • Deep Inside Christy / 1992 / CDI / C • Deep

Inside Traci / 1986 / CDI / C • Diamond Collection #65 / 1984 / CDI / M • Diamond Collection #67 / 1985 / CDI / M • Diamond Collection #76 / 1985 / CDI / M • Dirty 30's Cinema: Christy Canyon / 1986 / PV / C • Dirty Letters / 1984 / VD / M • Dirty Shary / 1985 / VD / M • Dixie Dynamite / 1992 / IF / C • Doctor Desire / 1984 / VD / M • Domination Nation / 1996 / VI / M • Dreams Of Candace Hart / 1991 / VI / M • Educating Mandy / 1985 / CDI / M • The Enchantress / 1985 / 4P / M • Erotica Jones / 1985 / AVC / M • Evil Angel / 1986 / VCR / M • Exposure Images #16: Christy Canyon / 1992 / EXI / F • Famous Ta-Ta's #1 / 1986 / VCS / C • Fantasies Unltd. / 1985 / CDI / M • Fantasy In Blue / 1991 / VI / M • Fantasy World / 1991 / NWV / C • Flesh And Ecstasy / 1985 / VD / M • Flesh Mountain / 1994 / VI / C • Gang Bangs #1 / 1985 / VCR / M • Ginger On The Rocks / 1985 / VI / M • Ginger: The Movie / 1988 / PV / C • Girls Of Paradise #1 / 1986 / PV / C • Girls Together / 1985 / GO / C • The Good, The Bad, And The D-Cup / 1991 / GO / C • Gourmet Quickies: Christy Canyon #719 / 1985 / GO / C • Gourmet Quickies: Christy Canyon / Ellie Rio #730 / 1985 / GO / C • Gourmet Quickies: Marie Sharp / Christy Canyon #729 / 1985 / GO / C • Harlequin Affair / 1985 / CIX / M • Holly Does Hollywood #1 / 1985 / VEX / M • Holly Does Hollywood #4 / 1990 / CAY / M • Hot In The City / 1989 / VEX / M • Hot Shorts: Christy Canyon / 1987 / VCR / C • Hot Women / 1989 / E&I / C • How To Love Your Lover / 1992 / XII / S • Hypnotic Sensations / 1985 / GO / M • I Dream Of Christy / 1989 / CAY / M • I Dream Of Ginger / 1985 / VI / M • I Like To Be Watched / 1984 / VD / M • It's My Body / 1985 / CDI / M • Jubilee Of Eroticism / 1985 / GO / M • Kiss My Asp / 1989 / EXH / M • Kiss Of The Gypsy / 1986 / WV / M • Kissin' Cousins / 1984 / PL / M • The Ladies In Lace Party / 1985 / MAP / M • Le Sex De Femme #1 / 1989 / AFI / C • Le Sex De Femme #3 / 1989 / AFI / C • The Legend Of The Kama Sutra / 1990 / A&E / M • Lick Bush / 1992 / VD / C • Little Girls Of The Streets / 1984 / CV / M • Lovin' USA / 1989 / EXH / C • Loving Spoonfuls / 1987 / 4P / C • Marilyn Chambers' Private Fantasies #6 / 1985 / CA / M • A Mid-Slumber's Night Dream / 1985 / 4P / M • More Than A Handful / 1993 / CA / C • Night Of Loving Dangerously / 1984 / PV / M • Nightbreed / 1995 / VI / M • On Golden Blonde / 1984 / PV / M • On Trial #1: In Defense Of Savannah / 1991 / VI / M • On Trial #2: Oral Arguments / 1991 / VI / M • One Hot Night Of Passion / 1985 / COL / C • Only The Best Of Breasts / 1987 / CV / C • Only The Best Of Women With Women / 1988 / CV / C • Oral Addiction / 1995 / VI / M • Orifice Party / 1985 / GOM / M • Parliament: Super Head #1 / 1989 / PM / C • Party Girls / 1988 / MAP / M • Passages #1 / 1991 / VI / M • Passages #2 / 1991 / VI / M • Passages #3 / 1991 / VI / M • Passages #4 / 1991 / VI / M • Perfect Fit / 1985 / DR / M • Play Christy For Me / 1990 / CAY / M • A Portrait Of Christy / 1990 / VI / M • Pretty In Peach / 1992 / VI / M • Princess Charming / 1987 / AVC / C • Racquel In The Wild / 1992 / VI / M • Ready, Willing & Anal (Cv) / 1993 / CV

/ C • Savage Fury #1 / 1985 / VEX / M • Savage Fury #2 / 1989 / CAY / M • Seduction Of Christy / 19?? / GO / C • Sex #2 (Vivid) / 1993 / VI / M • Sex 5th Avenue / 1985 / WV / M • Sex Asylum #4 / 1991 / VI / M • The Sex Goddess / 1984 / GO / M • Sex Secrets Of A Mistress / 1995 / VI / M • The Show / 1995 / VI / M • Sinful Pleasures / 1987 / HO / C • Sinfully Yours / 1984 / HO / M • Sore Throat / 1985 / GO / M • Star 90 / 1990 / CAY / M • Starlets / 1985 / 4P / M • Swedish Erotica #57 / 1984 / CA / M • Swedish Erotica #58 / 1984 / CA / M • Swedish Erotica Hard #17: Amber & Christy's Sex Party / 1992 / OD / C • Sweet Cheeks / 1987 / VCR / C • A Taste Of Tawnee / 1988 / LV / C • Taste Of The Best #2 / 1988 / PIN / C • Three By Three / 1989 / LV / C • Traci Who? / 1987 / AVC / C • Tracy In Heaven (Orig 1985) / 1985 / WV / M • Treasure Chest / 1985 / GO / M • The Trouble With Traci / 1984 / CHA / C • Twisted / 1990 / VI / M • Two Tons Of Fun #1 / 1985 / 4P / C • VCA Previews #4 / 1988 / VC / C • Victim Of Love #1 / 1992 / VI / M • Victim Of Love #2 / 1992 / VI / M • Video Tramp #1 / 1985 / AA / M • The Wacky World Of X-Rated Bloopers / 1989 / GO / M • Where The Boys Aren't #5 / 1992 / VI / F • Where The Boys Aren't #6 / 1995 / VI / F • Where The Boys Aren't #7 / 1995 / VI / F • Where The Boys Aren't #9 / 1996 / VI / F • Wild Things #1 / 1985 / CV / M • The Woman In Pink / 1984 / SE / M • WPINK-TV #1 / 1985 / PV / M • X-TV #1 / 1986 / PL / C • You Make Me Wet / 1985 / SVE / M

CHRISTY DAWN *see* **Star Index I**
CHRISTY KAYE *see* **Star Index I**
CHRISTY KEITH *(Christie Keith)*
Ambushed / 1990 / SE / M • Dane's Party / 1991 / IF / G • Dane's Surprise / 1991 / IF / G • Hard Feelings / 1991 / V99 / M • Lady Badass / 1990 / V99 / M • Wild Goose Chase / 1990 / EA / M

CHRISTY KLUVER *see* **Star Index I**
CHRISTY KNIGHTS *see* **Kristarrah Knight**

CHRISTY LANE (BLACK)
Casting Couch Tips / 1996 / MP0 / M • Innocent Little Girls #1 / 1996 / MP0 / M • Vivid Raw #1 / 1996 / VI / M

CHRISTY LEE *see* **Kristie Leigh**
CHRISTY LEIGH *see* **Kristie Leigh**
CHRISTY LOVE
The Beat Goes On / 1987 / VCR / C • Caballero Preview Tape #2 / 1983 / CA / C • Erotic Dimensions #2: Black Desire / 1982 / NSV / M • Heavenly Nurse / 1984 / CA / M • [Bizarre Sex Bazaar / 197? / ... / M

CHRISTY LYNN *see* **Star Index I**
CHRISTY STORM
Bad She-Males / 1994 / HSV / G • Dungeons & Drag Queens / 1994 / HSV / G • He-She Hangout / 1995 / HSV / G • My She-Male Valentine / 1994 / HSV / G • Samurai She-Males / 1994 / HSV / G • She-Male Swish Bucklers / 1994 / HSV / G • She-Male Valentine / 1996 / HSV / G • Trannie Get Your Gun / 1994 / HSV / G • Tranny Hill: Sweet Surrender / 1994 / HSV / G • Transister Act / 1994 / HSV / G

CHRISTY STRAY
The Best Of Fabulous Flashers / 1996 / DGD / F • Eight Babes A Week / 1996 /

DGD / F • The Spank Master / 1996 / PRE / B

CHRISTY WAAY *see* **Kursti Way**

CHRISTY WAY *see* **Kursti Way**

CHRISTY WILD *see* **Chrissy Ann**

CHRISY BELLO
The Stand-Up / 1994 / VC / M

CHROME HELMUT *see* **Star Index I**

CHRYSO DAVID
Latex #1 / 1994 / VC / M

CHRYSTAL
Ron Hightower's White Chicks #12 / 1994 / LBO / M • Seymore & Shane On The Loose / 1994 / ULI / M

CHRYSTAL LOVEN *see* **Crystal Lovin**

CHRYSTY
Private Gold #12: The Pyramid #2 / 1996 / OD / M

CHU-CHU
Blue Vanities #516 / 1992 / FFL / M

CHUCK
AVP #9152: Three Man Slut / 1991 / AVP / M • Blue Vanities #538 / 1993 / FFL / M • Slammin' Granny In The Fanny / 1995 / GLI / M

CHUCK BARRON *see* **Star Index I**

CHUCK BAYLES
Resurrection Of Eve / 1973 / MIT / M

CHUCK BERRY
Midnight Blue: Rob Lowe, The Go-Go's, and Chuck Berry / 1990 / SVE / M

CHUCK CEE *see* **Robert Bullock**

CHUCK CORD
L.A. Tool & Die / 1979 / TMX / G

CHUCK DAWSON
Dixie Ray Hollywood Star / 1983 / CA / M

CHUCK FABRAE *see* **Star Index I**

CHUCK GLORE *see* **Chuck Scott**

CHUCK HOWARD
Sophisticated Pleasure / 1984 / WV / M

CHUCK LAKIRK
Once...And For All / 1979 / HLV / M

CHUCK MARTIN *see* **Tony Martino**

CHUCK MARTINO *see* **Tony Martino**

CHUCK MORRISON *see* **Michael Morrison**

CHUCK SCOTT *(Chuck Glore)*
Moonshine Mountain / 1965 / SOW / S

CHUCK SPEAR
Lady Luck / 1975 / VCX / M

CHUCK STARR
Football Widow / 1979 / SCO / M • French Erotica: Love Story / 1980 / AR / M • French Erotica: Report Card / 1980 / AR / M • Love Story / 1979 / SCO / M

CHUCK STONE
Big Boob Bangeroo #1 / 1995 / TTV / M • Black Bush Bashers / 1996 / LOK / M • The Black Butt Sisters Do Detroit / 1995 / MID / M • The Black Butt Sisters Do Seattle / 1995 / MID / M • Black Fantasies #12 / 1996 / HW / M • Black Hollywood Amateurs #11 / 1995 / MID / M • Black Jack City #5 / 1995 / HW / M • Black Knockers #01 / 1995 / TV / M • Black Orgies #02 / 1993 / AFI / M • Black Orgies #10 / 1993 / AFI / M • Ebony Erotica #03: Black Adonis / 1993 / GO / M • Ebony Erotica #04: Ebony Gods / 1993 / GO / M • Ebony Erotica #05: Black Obsessions / 1993 / GO / M • Mo' Honey / 1993 / FH / M • Ona Z's Star Search #01 / 1993 / GLI / M • Ready To Drop #03 / 1994 / FC / M • Rump-Shaker #2 / 1993 / HW / M • Sex Machine / 1994 / VT / M • Totally Tasteless Video #01 / 1994 / TTV / M

CHUCK VINCENT *(Marc Ubell, Martha Ubell, Felix Miguel Arroyo, Larry Revene, Charles V. Dingley)*
Normally a director. Died of Aids in 1991 after taking an odd health cure in Ecuador.
The 8th Annual Erotic Film Awards / 1984 / SE / C • C.O.D. / 1981 / VES / S • Devil In Miss Jones #2 / 1983 / VC / M • Fantasex / 1976 / COM / M • Georgia Peach / 1977 / COM / M • Porn Star Of The Year Contest / 1984 / VWA / M • The Voyeur / 1985 / VC / M • Wimps / 1987 / LIV / S

CHUISHA *see* **Cumisha Amado**

CHULA HENRY
Sunny / 1979 / VC / M

CHYNA BLUE
Macin' #1 / 1996 / SMP / M

CHYNA DAHL *(China Doll (black))*
Black girl.
Big Black & Beautiful Gang Bang / 1995 / HO / M • Black Anal Dreams / 1995 / WV / M • Black Fantasies #12 / 1996 / HW / M • Black Hollywood Amateurs #03 / 1995 / MID / M • Black Hollywood Amateurs #08 / 1995 / MID / M • Black Hollywood Amateurs #11 / 1995 / MID / M • Black Knockers #04 / 1995 / TV / M • Black Knockers #11 / 1995 / TV / M • Bootylicious: Ghetto Booty / 1996 / JMP / M • Bootylicious: Yo Bitch / 1996 / JMP / M • Butt Hunt #09 / 1995 / LEI / M • Champagne's House Party / 1996 / HW / M • China's House Party / 1996 / HW / M • Ebony Dancer / 1994 / HBE / M • Girlz Towne #07 / 1995 / FC / F • Girlz Towne #08 / 1995 / FC / F • Hooter Tutor / 1996 / APP / M • Hooters In The 'hood / 1995 / TTV / M • Interview: Dark And Delicious / 1996 / LV / M • A Lowdown Dirty Game / 1996 / LBO / M • Maverdick / 1995 / WV / M • Miss Nude International / 1993 / LE / M • Primal Rear / 1996 / TIW / M • Pussy Hunt #08 / 1995 / LEI / M • Reverse Gang Bang / 1995 / JMP / M • Rump-Shaker #5 / 1996 / HW / M

CHYNA WHITE
Lotus Blossoms / 1996 / SUF / M • Yin Yang Oriental Love Bang #5: Lotus Blossoms / 1996 / SUF / M

CICCI *see* **Star Index I**

CICCIOLINA *(Ilona Staller)*
Although thought of as Italian, she was actually born (12/26/51) in Budapest and moved to Italy in 1976 as a teenager. Did a lot of porno movies and then in 1987 was elected to the Italian parliament but only served one term. She married an artist, Jeff Koons, in 1991 and was divorced in 1994 with lots of wrangling over their child.
Backdoor Summer #1 / 1988 / PV / C • Backdoor Summer #2 / 1989 / PV / C • Backfield In Motion / 1990 / PV / M • Cicciolina Gang Bang / 19?? / TLV / M • Cicciolina In Heat / 19?? / TLV / M • Euro Extremities #17 / 199? / SVE / C • Euro Extremities #19 / 199? / SVE / C • Inhibition / 1976 / MED / S • Maiden Italy #1 / 1992 / ... / C • Maiden Italy #2 / 1992 / ... / C • Passionate Lovers / 1991 / PL / M • The Rise Of The Roman Empress #1 / 1986 / PV / M • The Rise Of The Roman Empress #2 / 1990 / PV / M • Skin Deep / 1979 / ... / S • World Cup / 1990 / PL / M • Yellow Emmanuelle / 1971 / UNV / S • [Bedtime Stories / 19?? / MAJ / S • [Due Porno Diue Per Uomini / 19?? / HOB / M • [H'perversioni Deglie Angeli / 19?? / HOB / M • [La Conchiglia Dei Desideri / 19?? / PUB / M • [Palm Springs Weekend / 19?? / ... / M • [Replikator / 1994 / ... / S • [Una Partita Senza Carte / 19?? / PUB / M • [Vizi E Stravizi Di Moana E Cicciolina / 19?? / BMA / M

CICI *see* **Star Index I**

CICI (VERONICA LAKE) *see* **Veronica Lake**

CIE CIE
Alley Cat Showdown / 1990 / NAP / B • Broadcast Nudes / 1988 / EVN / M • Claws And Fangs / 1990 / NAP / B • House Of Correction / 1991 / HOM / B • Roommates / 1989 / BON / B • Tails From The Whip / 1991 / HOM / B • Tied & Tickled #28: Tickling Dr. Cripley / 1995 / CS / B

CIERA *(Sierra Stuart)*
Pudgy, almost fat, brunette with large tits, small in height, pleasant but not pretty face.
Binding Contract / 1992 / ZFX / B • Doc Bondage / 1992 / ZFX / B • The Misadventures Of Lois Payne / 1995 / ZFX / B • Sorority Bondage Hazing / 1990 / BON / B • Southern Discomfort / 1992 / ZFX / B • Story Of Sweet Nicole / 1992 / ZFX / B • Z F/X #4 / 1993 / BON / B • ZFX: Nastiest Bound Babes / 1996 / BON / C

CIERA BROOKS
Cute, pretty face, small/tiny tits, narrow hips, tight butt, shaven pussy, small tattoo on her right belly. Seems to hate facials (wise girl).
The Adventures Of Peeping Tom #1 / 1996 / OD / M • Cheek To Cheek / 1997 / EL / M • Cherry Poppers #14: Teeny Tongues / 1996 / ZA / M • Compulsion (Amazing) / 1996 / MET / M • Corn Hole Kittens / 1996 / ROB / F • Hit Parade / 1996 / PRE / B • Leg...Ends #17 / 1996 / PRE / F • Lesbian C*Nt Whores / 1996 / ROB / F • Ona Zee's Doll House #3 / 1995 / ONA / F • Pick Up Lines #08 / 1996 / OD / M • Sodomania #16: Sexxy Pistols / 1996 / EL / M • Toes 'n' Cons / 1996 / PRE / S • Venom #3 / 1996 / VD / M • Venom #4 / 1996 / VD / M • Whore D'erves / 1996 / OUP / F • Young & Natural #14 / 1996 / TV / F • Young & Natural #16 / 1996 / TV / F • Young & Natural #18 / 1996 / TV / C • Young & Natural #19 / 1996 / TV / F

CIERA NIGHT
Big, Bad Bulging Bazooms / 1993 / NAP / F • Boobs On Fire / 1993 / NAP / F • Humiliating Defeat / 1996 / NAP / B • Kelly Eighteen #1 / 1993 / LE / M • One Million Heels B.C. / 1993 / SVE / S • The Taming Of Ciera / 1993 / NAP / B

CIERA ROSE
Cheap Tricks #1 / 1996 / PAV / M • Fresh Meat #1 / 1996 / PL / M

CILLA PINK
Swap Meet / 1984 / VD / M

CILYA MEDVEDEVOVA
Russian Girls / 1996 / WV / M

CINAMON
The Best Of Wild Bill's Big Ladies / 1996 / H&S / C • Hard Ride / 1992 / WV / M

CINAMON (CINNAMON) *see* **Cinnamon**

CINDAY *see* **Star Index I**

CINDEE COX *see* **Sindee Coxx**

CINDEE SUMMERS *(Cyndee Summers, Cindy Summers, Deborah Whitney, Elizabeth Winters)*
Reddish blonde with medium tits and a thick body. Elizabeth Winters is from **An Act Of Confession**.
An Act Of Confession / 1972 / ALP / M • Ad-

ventures Of Flash Beaver / 1972 / CLX / S • Around The World With Johnny Wadd / 1975 / ALP / C • Attack Of The Monster Mammaries / 1987 / LA / C • Blue Vanities #045 (New) / 1988 / FFL / M • Blue Vanities #045 (Old) / 1988 / FFL / M • Blue Vanities #089 / 1988 / FFL / M • Bucky Beaver's Double Softies #04 / 1996 / SOW / S • Classic Swedish Erotica #04 / 1986 / CA / C • Classified Sex / 1975 / CPL / M • Collection #06 / 1984 / CA / M • Collection #08 / 1984 / CA / M • Desperate Women / 1986 / VD / M • Devil's Ecstasy / 1974 / VCX / M • Divorce Court Expose #2 / 1987 / VD / M • Don't Tell Mama / 1974 / VIP / M • Dresden Diary #01 / 1986 / BIZ / B • Dresden Diary #02 / 1986 / BIZ / B • Ecstasy / 1979 / SE / M • The Erotic Adventures Of Peter Galore / 1973 / ALP / M • Erotic Zones #1 / 1985 / CA / M • For Services Rendered / 1984 / CA / M • Fun In The Sun / cr70 / ... / M • Garter Charter Tours / 1986 / AVC / M • House Of Pleasure / 1984 / CA / M • Legends Of Porn #1 / 1987 / CV / C • Letters Of Love / 1985 / CA / M • The Liars / cr71 / AXV / M • The Long Ranger / 1987 / VCX / M • Love Lies Waiting / 1974 / AXV / M • Love Picnic / cr70 / ... / M • The Loves Of Mary Jane / 1989 / BWV / C • More Than A Handful #1 / 1985 / CV / C • More Than Friends / 1973 / AXV / M • Mother's Wishes / 1974 / GO / M • Older Women With Young Boys / 1984 / CC / M • The Other Side Of Lianna / 1984 / LA / M • Panorama Blue / 1974 / ALP / S • Panty Girls / 1972 / BMV / M • Penthouse Passions / 1975 / BLT / M • Personal Services / 1975 / CV / M • Poor Cecily / 1973 / ALF / S • Satin Dolls / 1985 / CV / M • Sex In The Comics / 1973 / VC / M • Sex Prophet / 1973 / ALP / M • Sexual Therapist / cr71 / CLX / M • Stiff Competition #1 / 1984 / CA / M • Studs 'n' Stars / 1989 / VC / C • Super Models Do LA / 1986 / AT / M • Swedish Erotica #56 / 1984 / CA / M • Swedish Erotica Featurettes #5 / 1990 / CA / M • Taboo #04 / 1985 / IN / M • Taste Of The Best #3 / 1988 / PIN / C • Teenage Bride / 1970 / SOW / S • A Touch Of Sex / 1972 / AR / M • The Training #1 / 1984 / BIZ / B • True Legends Of Adult Cinema: The Golden Age / 1992 / VC / C • Wine Me, Dine Me, 69 Me / 1989 / COL / C • The Winning Stroke / 1975 / VIS / M • [The Professionals / cr72 / ... / M

CINDERELLA
Explore With Coralie / 1996 / C69 / M

CINDI
Big Murray's New-Cummers #17: Age Before Beauty / 1993 / FD / M • Big Murray's New-Cummers #20: Hot Honies In Heat / 1993 / FD / M • Naughty Nights / 1996 / PLP / C • Reel Life Video #33: New Mom In Town / 1995 / RLF / M

CINDI (MINT) see Cindy Mint
CINDI BARBOUR see Kandy Barbour
CINDI CONNOR see Kandi Connor
CINDI SNOW see Tanya Storm
CINDI VALENTINE see Kandi Valentine
CINDY
A&B AB#499: Slutty Cindy / 1995 / A&B / M • A&B AB#564: Cindy Oh Cindy / 1995 / A&B / M • Alex Jordan's First Timers #06 / 1994 / OD / M • America's Raunchiest Home Videos #01: Some Serious Sex / 1991 / ZA / M • Anal In The Alps / 1996 / P69 / M • Biff Malibu's Totally Nasty Home Videos #09 / 1992 / ANA / M • Biff Malibu's Totally Nasty Home Videos #34 / 1993 / ANA / M • Big Murray's New-Cummers #21: Double Penetration One / 1993 / FD / M • The Black Butt Sisters Do Detroit / 1995 / MID / M • Blue Vanities #542 / 1994 / FFL / M • Blue Vanities #560 / 1994 / FFL / M • Bound & Mastered #1 Thru #4 / 1986 / VER / B • Bright Tails #3 / 1994 / STP / B • Bright Tails #4 / 1994 / STP / B • Bright Tails #7 / 1995 / STP / B • Cherry Poppers #08: Tender And Tight / 1994 / ZA / M • Cindy Puts Out / 1996 / OLL / M • Cindy's House Party / 1996 / HW / M • Complain, Complain / 1993 / BON / B • The Cross Of Lust / 1995 / CLO / M • Diva #2: Deep In Glamour / 1996 / VC / F • European Sex TV / 1996 / EL / M • Fbi In Search Of Bondage #1 / 1991 / BON / B • Final Orgy / 1996 / BON / B • Freaky Flix / 1995 / TTV / C • Girls From Girdleville / 1992 / ERK / M • The Girls Of Malibu / 1986 / ACV / S • Horny Henry's Swinging Adventures / 1994 / TTV / M • Hot Body Competition: Lusty Lingerie Contest / 1996 / CG / F • Interview: Chocolate Treats / 1995 / LV / M • Introducing Micki Marsaille / 1990 / NAP / F • Lesbian Pros And Amateurs #26 / 1993 / GO / F • More To Love #2 / 1995 / TTV / M • New Faces, Hot Bodies #14 / 1994 / STP / M • New Faces, Hot Bodies #15 / 1994 / STP / M • New Faces, Hot Bodies #16 / 1994 / STP / M • New Faces, Hot Bodies #17 / 1995 / STP / M • Rollie Pollie Chicks / 1996 / TTV / M • Skin #2 / 1995 / ERQ / M • Stevi's: Spanked Debutantes / 1992 / SSV / B • Swimming Pool Orgy / 1995 / FRF / M • Toy Time #2: Nasty Solos / 1994 / STP / F • Up And Cummers #21 / 1995 / RWP / M • Wildfire: Shaving Beauties / 1996 / WIF / F • Wrestling Vixens / 1991 / CDP / B

CINDY #5 see Star Index I
CINDY (CANDY VEGAS) see Candy Vegas
CINDY (JAPANESE) see Star Index I
CINDY (SUZIE MATHEW) see Suzie Mathews
CINDY ADAMS
Big Boob Bangeroo #3 / 1996 / TTV / M • Life In The Fat Lane #1 / 1990 / FC / M • Life In The Fat Lane #2 / 1990 / FC / M • Tit Tales #2 / 1990 / FC / M • Titty-Titty Bang-Bang / 1992 / FC / C

CINDY ADAMS (STOKES) see Cindy Stokes
CINDY ARHH see Jennifer Noxt
CINDY ARRGH see Jennifer Noxt
CINDY BALL
Never Enough / 1971 / VCX / M • Saturday Matinee Series #3 / 1996 / VCX / C
CINDY BARR see Star Index I
CINDY BARRON see Star Index I
CINDY BELL
All The Way / 1980 / CDC / M • Fastlane Fuck-Holes! / 1994 / MET / M
CINDY BERLIN
Badgirls #2: Strip Search / 1994 / VI / M
CINDY BLACK see Star Index I
CINDY BROOKS see Cynthia Brooks
CINDY CAIN see Cindy Carver
CINDY CARRERA
The Thief, The Girl & The Detective / 1996 / HDE / M
CINDY CARVER (Cindy Cain)
Blonde Heat (VCA) / 1985 / VC / M •

Chocolate Cream / 1984 / SUP / M • Diary Of A Bad Girl / 1986 / SUP / M • E.X. / 1986 / SUP / M • The Erotic World Of Linda Wong / 1985 / VIV / M • The House Of Strange Desires / 1985 / NSV / M • The Last Taboo / 1984 / VIV / M • Little Showoffs / 1984 / VC / M • Missing Pieces / 1985 / IN / M • Radio K-KUM / 1984 / HO / M • Sex Wars / 1984 / EXF / M • Star Tricks / 1988 / WV / M • Sweet Young Foxes / 1984 / VCX / M • Two On The Tongue / 1988 / TAM / C • Wet 'n' Bare With Barbara Dare / 1988 / NEO / C • Wild In The Wilderness / 1984 / GO / M
CINDY CINDY
Never Trust A Slave / 1996 / BON / B
CINDY ESSEX
Ready To Drop #08 / 1995 / FC / M • Ready To Drop #09 / 1995 / FC / M • Ready To Drop #10 / 1996 / FC / M
CINDY FIELDS
California Heat / cr75 / BL / M
CINDY GRANT see Star Index I
CINDY HOPKINS see Cindy Stokes
CINDY JAMES
Fade To Rio / 1984 / VHL / M
CINDY JENSEN see Star Index I
CINDY JILL
Tale Of Bearded Clam / cr71 / PYR / M
CINDY JOHNSON see Christine Heller
CINDY JONES
Buttman's Inferno / 1993 / EA / M
CINDY KITTY
China's House Party / 1996 / HW / M
CINDY KRAMER
Bed-Side Cats / 1989 / NAP / B • Clash / 1989 / NAP / B • Introducing Cindy Kramer / 1989 / NAP / F • Lingerie Kittens / 1989 / NAP / B • The Thrill Of Competition / 1989 / NAP / B
CINDY LABARE (Lindy LaBare, Cindy Labarre)
Dirty blonde with a cute face and fantastic tight body. Inverted nipples. Seems to always appear with Suzanne St. Lorraine.
Knights In Black Satin / 1990 / VEX / M • Living In Sin / 1990 / VEX / M • Perfect Girl / 1991 / VEX / M • Suzanne's Grand Affair / 1990 / CV / M
CINDY LABARRE see Cindy LaBare
CINDY LAKE see Star Index I
CINDY LANE see Jenny Lane
CINDY LAUDER
Filthy First Timers #4 / 1996 / EL / M
CINDY LEE see Sonja
CINDY LEWIS
Seka's Fantasies / 1981 / CA / M
CINDY LOU HAMMER
Insane Desires / cr78 / ... / M
CINDY LOVE
Amateur Black: Sexpots / 1996 / SUF / M • Big Man's Ebony Dreams / 1996 / LOK / M • The Black Butt Sisters Do Houston / 1996 / MID / M • The Black Butt Sisters Do New Orleans / 1996 / MID / M • The Black Butt Sisters Do Seattle / 1995 / MID / M • Black Cheerleader Search #03 / 1996 / ROB / M • Black Fantasies #14 / 1996 / HW / M • Black Hollywood Amateurs #11 / 1995 / MID / M • Black Hollywood Amateurs #12 / 1995 / MID / M • Black Snatch #1 / 1996 / DFI / F • Booty Bang #1 / 1996 / HW / M • Bootylicious: Ghetto Booty / 1996 / JMP / M • The Case Of The Black Booty / 1996 / LV / M • Champagne's House Party / 1996 / HW / M • Chocolate Bunnies #06 / 1996 /

LBO / C • In Da Booty / 1996 / LV / M • Licorice Lollipops: Back To School / 1996 / HW / M • Menaja's House Party / 1996 / HW / M • Orgy Camera #2 / 1996 / EVN / M • Primal Rear / 1996 / TIW / M • Pumps In Da Rump #2 / 1996 / HW / M • Snatch Shot / 1996 / LBO / M • Waiting 2 XX Hale / 1996 / APP / M • Young And Anal #3 / 1995 / JMP / M

CINDY LYNN *see Star Index I*

CINDY MACREEDY
The Art Of Darkness / 1996 / ZFX / B

CINDY MARGOLIS
Shape Up For Sensational Sex / 1985 / SE / M

CINDY MARSHALL
Cover Girl Fantasies #2 / 1983 / VCR / C

CINDY MARX *see Star Index I*

CINDY MINT *(Cindi (Mint))*
Brunette with very white skin and firm small breasts—not very pretty.
Breast Collection #03 / 1995 / LBO / C • The Cumm Brothers #01 / 1993 / OD / M • A Girl's Affair #02 / 1993 / FD / F • Harry Horndog #11: Love Puppies #2 / 1992 / ZA / M • Harry Horndog #12: Harry's Xmas Party / 1992 / ZA / M • Intimate Spys / 1992 / FOR / M • Mike Hott: #245 Cunt of the Month: Cyndi 7-93 / 1993 / MHV / M • Mr. Peepers Amateur Home Videos #75: Trio In Rio / 1993 / LBO / M • Mr. Peepers Nastiest #3 / 1995 / LBO / C • Split Decision / 1993 / FD / M • Straight A Students / 1993 / MET / M • Top Debs #2: The Reunion / 1993 / GO / M • Voluptuous / 1993 / CA / M

CINDY MONTGOMERY *see Star Index I*

CINDY MORGAN *see Star Index I*

CINDY NEAL
Blue Vanities #567 / 1995 / FFL / M • Blue Vanities #581 / 1996 / FFL / M

CINDY NELSON
10 Years Of Big Busts #1 / 1989 / BTO / C • The Best Of Big Busty / 1986 / L&W / C • Busty Nymphos / 1984 / BTO / S • Down Mammary Lane #4 / 1989 / BTO / F

CINDY PICKETT
[Night Dreams / 1980 / ... / M

CINDY PRICE *see Star Index I*

CINDY PRINCE
Bondage Classix #14: Four Lives Of Cindy / 1989 / BON / B • Bondage Memories #03 / 1994 / BON / C • Cindy Prince #1 / 1993 / BON / B • Cindy Prince #2 / 1993 / BON / B • Cindy Prince #3 / 1993 / BON / B • Cindy Prince #4 / 1993 / BON / B • Cindy Prince #5 / 1994 / BON / B • Cindy Prince #6 / 1994 / BON / B • Cindy Prince #7 / 1995 / BON / B • Cindy Prince #8 / 1995 / BON / B • The Good Stuff / 1989 / BON / C

CINDY REEMS *see Cindy West*

CINDY RIGDON *see Star Index I*

CINDY ROME
Shape Up For Sensational Sex / 1985 / SE / M

CINDY SCORSESE
Don Salvatore: The Last Sicilian / 1995 / XC / M • Virility / 1996 / XC / M

CINDY SEAY *see Star Index I*

CINDY SHEPARD *see Star Index I*

CINDY SHINN *see Lulu Chang*

CINDY SNOW *see Tanya Storm*

CINDY SPITTLER
Rabin's Revenge / 1971 / MIT / M

CINDY STERLING *see Jamie Summers*

CINDY STEVENS *see Roxanne Hall*

CINDY STOKES *(Cindy Adams (Stokes),*
Suzanne Fields, Cindy Hopkins)*
Bucky Beaver's XXX Dragon Art Theatre Double Feature #11 / 1996 / SOW / M • Double Exposure / 1972 / VCX / M • Flesh Gordon #1 / 1974 / FAC / S • Hollywood Babylon / 1972 / AIR / S • Nicole: The Story Of O / 1972 / CLX / M • Teenage Fantasies #1 / 1972 / SOW / M • [I Am Curious But Not Yellow / 197? / ... / M

CINDY SUMMERS *see Cindee Summers*

CINDY SWIFT *see Star Index I*

CINDY TAYLOR
Beach Blanket Bango / 1975 / EVI / M • High School Fantasies / 1974 / EVI / M • Teenage Throat / 1974 / ... / M

CINDY THOMPSON *see Star Index I*

CINDY TRAVERS *see Star Index I*

CINDY TYLER
Blue Vanities #551 / 1994 / FFL / M

CINDY WEBER *see Star Index I*

CINDY WEST *(Cindy Reems)*
Long dark blonde hair, womanly body, medium droopy tits, marginal face.
ABA: Double Feature #3 / 1996 / ALP / M • Airport Girls / 1975 / VXP / M • Betty Blue (X) / 19?? / BL / M • Christy / 1975 / CA / M • Devil's Due / 1974 / ALP / M • Executive Secretary / 1975 / CA / M • Happy Days / 1974 / IHV / M • Head Nurse / cr74 / VXP / M • Keep On Truckin' / cr73 / BL / M • Love-In Maid / cr72 / CDC / M • Sticky Situation / 1975 / VXP / M • The Young Nymphs / 1973 / ... / M

CINDY ZONE *see Star Index I*

CINNAMON *(Cinnamon Dream, Cinamon (Cinnamon), Sinamon (Cinnamon))*
Small black girl.
Avenged / 1986 / CS / B • Chocolate Delights #1 / 1985 / TAG / C • Dance Fever / 1985 / VCR / M • Ebony Superstars / 1988 / VC / C • Hot Chocolate #1 / 1984 / TAG / M • Samurai Dick / 1984 / VC / M • Take It Off / 1986 / TIF / M

CINNAMON (OTHER)
A&B AB#484: Kitty's Desire #1 / 1995 / A&B / M • A&B AB#487: Kitty Gets A Reaming #2 / 1995 / A&B / M • A&B AB#493: Marilyn's Kinky Dreams #2 / 1995 / A&B / M • A&B AB#494: Marilyn's Kinky Dreams #3 / 1995 / A&B / M • Black Mystique #02 / 1993 / VT / F

CINNAMON (SINNAMON) *see Sinnamon*

CINNAMON DREAM *see Cinnamon*

CINTHIA
Midnight Obsession / 1995 / XC / M

CINTYA RAFFAELL
Jungle Heat / 1995 / LUM / M

CIQUITA
Brunette with small breasts.
Lost In Paradise / 1990 / CA / M

CIRIG
Latex #1 / 1994 / VC / M

CIRO PALLANDINO
Ejacula #1 / 1992 / VC / M • Ejacula #2 / 1992 / VC / M

CISCO
Bi Bi Banjee Boyz / 1994 / PL / G

CISSY ST JAMES *see Star Index I*

CLAIR DIA *(Vanessa Jorson, Emily Smith)*
Reddish blonde hair, small tits, lithe body, passable face.
3 A.M. / 1975 / ALP / M • Classic Erotica #5 / 1985 / SVE / M • Desires Within Young Girls / 1977 / CA / M • The Journey Of O / 1975 / TVX / M • Naked Afternoon / 1976 / CV / M • What About Jane? / 1971 / ALP /
M

CLAIR JAMES *(Diamond Lil, Crystal Lil, Patty Redding)*
Fantasy Girls / 1974 / VC / M • The Pleasure Masters / 1975 / AST / M • South Of The Border / 1977 / VC / M

CLAIR LOOSE
The Divorce / 1986 / VC / G • The House / cr86 / TEM / G • The Scam / 1986 / TEM / G

CLAIR LUCERNE *see Star Index I*

CLAIR LUMIERE *see Judith Hamilton*

CLAIR TYLER *see Jacqueline*

CLAIR VOYANT
Bondage Memories #03 / 1994 / BON / C • Final Exam #1 / 1987 / BON / B • Final Exam #2 / 1988 / BON / B

CLAIR WRIGHT *see Star Index I*

CLAIRE
Alley Cats / 1995 / VC / M • Jamie Gillis: The Private Collection Vol #1 / 1991 / SC / F • Magma: Lust Excesses / 1995 / MET / M • Magma: Sperm Dreams / 1990 / MET / M • Magma: Trans-Games / 1995 / MET / G • Triple X Video Magazine #11 / 1995 / OD / M

CLAIRE DE LOOM *see Cleopatra*

CLAIRE FORESTIER
The Seduction Of Tessa / cr86 / CA / M

CLAIRE FRANKLIN *see Star Index I*

CLAIRE KRUMPERT
Personal Services / 1975 / CV / M

CLAIRE LAWRENCE *see Star Index I*

CLAIRE ORCHIDEA
Private Film #19 / 1994 / OD / M

CLAIROL SCHNAPPS
Sin City Cycle Sluts #1 / 1995 / SC / F • Sin City Cycle Sluts #2 / 1995 / SC / F

CLANCE THOMAS
Kitty's Kinky Capers / 1996 / TTV / M

CLARENCE PERCY
Another Roll In The Hay / 1985 / COL / M

CLARICE STARLING
Papa's Got A Brand New Jag / 1995 / GOT / M

CLARISSA
Biff Malibu's Totally Nasty Home Videos #14 / 1992 / ANA / M • Fallen Angels / 1983 / VES / M • Kittens #7 / 1995 / CC / F • Odyssey 30 Min: #190: The Other Fucking Roommate / 1991 / OD / M • Odyssey 30 Min: Clarissa's 4-Way Return / 1992 / OD / M • Snatch Masters #07 / 1995 / LEI / M

CLARISSA (M. MONET) *see Melissa Monet*

CLARISSA BRUNI
Never Say Never To Rocco Siffredi / 1995 / EA / M

CLARISSA CATZ
Amateur Gay Girls / 1995 / LEI / C • The Best Of Buttslammers / 1995 / BS / C • Hard Core Beginners #11 / 1995 / LEI / M • Lolita / 1995 / SC / M • Nasty Nymphos #09 / 1995 / ANA / M • Private Audition / 1995 / EVN / M • Reel People #09 / 1995 / PP / M

CLARISSA HAMILTON *see Star Index I*

CLARISSA MARIE
Young And Anal #1 / 1995 / JMP / M

CLARISSA RUE
Freaky Flix / 1995 / TTV / C • Horny Henry's Swinging Adventures / 1994 / TTV / M

CLARISSA STARLOVE *see Star Index I*

CLARK IRVING
Betrayed / 1996 / WP / M

CLARK SHARP *see Star Index I*

CLARKE DAVY
Five Kittens / 19?? / ... / M
CLARKE WATERS see Star Index I
CLAUDE
Cindy Puts Out / 1996 / OLL / M • Gigi
Gives It Away / 1995 / FRF / M • Julie's
Diary / 1995 / LBO / M • Letters From A
Slave / 1995 / AOC / M
CLAUDE BACH see Star Index I
CLAUDE BASSEUR
[Let's Make A Dirty Movie / 1980 / ... / M
CLAUDE IRRISON see Star Index I
CLAUDE LOIR see Star Index I
CLAUDE MARTIN see Star Index I
CLAUDE MILLER see Star Index I
CLAUDE OLIVIER
Jura Sexe / 1995 / JP / G
CLAUDE SUCE see Star Index I
CLAUDE VALMONT see Star Index I
CLAUDE WINCHEL see Star Index I
CLAUDETTE
Magma: Horny For Cock / 1990 / MET / M
• Magma: Huge Cum Shots / 1995 / MET /
M • Magma: Pussy Jobs / 1994 / MET / M
CLAUDETTE ARLY see Star Index I
CLAUDETTE DENISE see Star Index I
CLAUDIA
The Betrayal Of Innocence #1: The Awakening Of Marika / 1993 / CC / M • The Betrayal Of Innocence #2: The Decadence /
1993 / CC / M • The Betrayal Of Innocence
#3: The Choice / 1993 / CC / M • Blue Vanities #504 / 1992 / FFL / M • Blue Vanities
#529 / 1993 / FFL / M • Czech, Please #1 /
1996 / BAC / F • Discipline / 1994 / TVI / B
• Nasty Travel Tails #01 / 1993 / CC / M •
Penetration (Anabolic) #1 / 1995 / ANA / M
CLAUDIA (HISPANIC)
Long reddish brown hair, initially thought to be
not too pretty but in later movies upgraded
to passable, plucked eyebrows, poor facial
skin, small tits, very long nipples, hairy
pussy, lithe body, tattoo on left ankle outside. Some loss of belly muscle tone indicating probable infant production. 25 years
old in 1996 and says she comes from Central America and was de-virginized at 21.
The Blowjob Adventures Of Doctor Fellatio
/ 1997 / EL / M • Fashion Passion / 1997 /
TEP / M • I'm So Horny, Baby / 1997 / ROB
/ M • Interracial Video Virgins #01 / 1996 /
NS / M • Lady Sterling Takes It Up The
Arse / 1997 / ROB / M • More Dirty Debutantes #60 / 1997 / SBV / M • Pick Up Lines
#13 / 1997 / OD / M
CLAUDIA BROOKS see Star Index I
CLAUDIA BUDWELL
Fireworks / 1981 / CA / M
CLAUDIA CLEMENTE
Top Secret / 1995 / XHE / M
CLAUDIA COLOGNE see Star Index I
CLAUDIA COSTE see Star Index I
CLAUDIA CRAWFORD see Star Index I
CLAUDIA FIELERS
Confessions Of A Blue Movie Star / 1974 /
CTH / S • [Die Madchenhandler / 1972 / ...
/ M • [Junge Madchen Mogen's HeiB,
Hausfrauen Noch HeiBer / 1973 / ... / M •
[Krankenschwestern-Report / 1972 / ... / M
• [Madchen, Die Sich Selbst, Bedienen /
1974 / ... / M • [Schulmadchen-Report 4:
Was Eltern Oft Verzweifeln LaBt / 1972 / ...
/ M
CLAUDIA GRAYSON see Linda McDowell
CLAUDIA GROSSO

Sirens / 1995 / GOU / M
CLAUDIA JAIMES
The Voyeur #7: Live In Europe #1 / 1996 /
JLP / M
CLAUDIA NOBEL see Star Index I
CLAUDIA PETERSEN
Dirty Stories #5 / 1996 / PE / M
CLAUDIA PETERSON
Up And Cummers #32 / 1996 / 4P / M
CLAUDIA WARTON see Star Index I
CLAUDIA ZANTE
Dangerous Passion / 1978 / VC / M • Made
In France / 1974 / VC / M
CLAUDINE
Adultress / 1995 / WIV / M • Magma: Claudine In Action / 1996 / MET / M • Magma:
Double #2 / 1995 / MET / M
CLAUDINE BECCAIRE
Emilienne / 1975 / LUM / S • Exhibition /
1975 / ... / M • French Blue / 1974 / ... / M
• Inhibition / 1976 / MED / S • Les Deux
Gouines / 1975 / ... / M • Mafia Girls / 1975
/ ... / M • Penetration / 1975 / SAT / M
CLAUDINE GRAYSON see Linda Mc-Dowell
CLAUDIO CAZZO (Sergio (Claudio C),
Claudio Bergamin)
Italian SO of Gina Rome. Yul Brynner/Kojak
type.
100% Amateur #27: / 1996 / OD / M • Adam
& Eve's House Party #3: Swing Party /
1996 / VC / M • Anal, Facial & Interracial /
1996 / FC / M • Analtown USA #10 / 1996 /
NIT / M • Anna Malle Exposed / 1996 / WV
/ M • Ass, Gas & The Mystical GLOP / 1997
/ EL / M • Black Women, White Men #5 /
1995 / FC / M • Bushwoman: She Takes
Two / 1996 / RAS / M • Conquest / 1996 /
WP / M • Dirty Old Men #2 / 1995 / IP / M •
Dixie Downes Gang Bang / 1996 / FC / M
• Dream House / 1995 / XPR / M • Fantasy
Fuchs / 1996 / PLP / C • Fresh Faces #04
/ 1995 / EVN / M • Gangland Bangers /
1995 / VC / M • Hard Core Beginners #11 /
1995 / LEI / M • Hard Evidence / 1996 / WP
/ M • Here Comes Jenny St. James / 1996
/ HOV / M • Here Comes Magoof #1 / 1995
VC / M • Hollywood Amateurs #17 / 1996 /
MID / M • Hot Diamond / 1995 / LE / M • Illicit Affairs / 1996 / XC / M • Kinky Debutante Interviews #10 / 1995 / IP / M • Living
On The Edge / 1997 / DWO / M • Make Me
Over, Baby / 1996 / LOF / M • Male Order
Brides / 1996 / RAS / M • Mickey Ray's Sex
Search #06 / 1996 / WIV / M • Mike Hott:
#322 Cunt of the Month: Gina / 1995 / MHV
/ M • Mike Hott: #367 Girls Who Lap Cum
From Cunts #02 / 1996 / MHV / M • My
Surrender / 1996 / A&E / M • Nasty Newcummers #08 / 1995 / MET / M • New
Pussy Hunt #17 / 1995 / LEI / M • Nice
Fuckin' Movie / 1997 / EL / M • Nineteen #3
/ 1996 / FOR / M • Pay 4 Play / 1996 / RAS
/ M • Perverted Stories #08 / 1996 / JMP /
M • Pizza Sluts: They Deliver / 1995 / XCI
/ M • Planet X #1 / 1996 / HW / M • A Pool
Party At Seymores #1 / 1995 / ULI / M • Private Dancers / 1996 / RAS / M • Private Diaries #1: Christina / 1995 / AVI / M • Puritan Video Magazine #03 / 1996 / LE / M •
Raw Silk / 1996 / RAS / M • Reel People
#04 / 1994 / PP / M • Saki's Bedtime Stories / 1995 / TTV / M • Senior Stimulation /
1996 / CC / M • The Sex Therapist / 1995 /
GO / M • Shades Of Color #2 / 1995 / LBO

/ M • Shaving Grace / 1996 / GO / M •
Shayla's Swim Party / 1997 / VC / M • The
Shocking Truth #1 / 1996 / DWO / M • The
Shocking Truth #2 / 1996 / DWO / M •
Show & Tell / 1996 / VI / M • Sodomania
#12: Raw Filth / 1995 / EL / M • Sodomania: Slop Shots / 1996 / EL / C • Stripping /
1995 / NIT / M • Stuff Your Ass #2 / 1995 /
JMP / M • Stuff Your Face #4 / 1996 / JMP
/ M • Trapped / 1996 / VI / M • Triple Penetration Debutante Sluts #1 / 1996 / BAC / M
• While The Cat's Away / 1996 / NIT / M
CLAUDIO MELONIE
Anal Maidens Three / 1996 / BOT / M •
Anal Pool Party / 1996 / PE / M • Assy #2 /
1996 / JMP / M • Behind The Scenes /
1996 / GO / M • Buttsizer #3: Return Of
The King Of Rears / 1995 / EVN / M • Dirty
Business / 1995 / WIV / M • Miss Anal #2 /
1995 / C69 / M • Nasty Nymphos #10 /
1995 / ANA / M • Party Club / 1996 / C69 /
M • Skin #5: The 5th Column / 1996 / ERQ
/ M • Sleeping Booty / 1995 / EL / M • Stowaway / 1995 / LE / M • Young And Anal #1
/ 1995 / JMP / M
CLAUDIO ROSSO
French Blue / 1974 / ... / M • Penetration /
1975 / SAT / M • Sensations / 1975 / ALP /
M
CLAUS BOSSY
Letters From A Slave / 1995 / AOC / M
CLAUS MINDER
Flesh...And The Fantasies / 1991 / BIZ / B
CLAUS TINNEY
[Krankenschwestern-Report / 1972 / ... / M
CLAY see Star Index I
CLAY HYDE
Resurrection Of Eve / 1973 / MIT / M •
Seven Into Snowy / 1977 / VC / M • The
Spirit Of Seventy Six / 1976 / NGV / M
CLAY HYDE (HOLLIDAY) see Jim Holliday
CLAY TANNING see Star Index I
CLEA CARSON
Pretty brunette with medium to large tits and a
tight little body.
ABA: Double Feature #2 / 1996 / ALP / M •
Bad Penny / 1978 / QX / M • Carnal Games
/ 1977 / DL / M • Doughhakes Of Grace /
1977 / CA / M • Dirty Susan / 1979 / CPL /
M • French Teen / 1977 / CV / M • Here
Comes The Bride / 1977 / CV / M • High
School Bunnies / 1978 / VC / M • Limited
Edition #01 / 1979 / AVC / M • Maraschino
Cherry / 1978 / QX / M • Revenge & Punishment / 1996 / ALP / M • Rip-Off Of Millie
/ cr78 / VHL / M • Seduction Of Joyce /
1977 / BL / M • Sharon In The Roughhouse / 1976 / LA / M • Small Change /
1978 / CDC / M • Stand By Your Woman /
cr80 / HOR / M • Swedish Sorority Girls /
1978 / CV / M • Sweet Throat / 1979 / CV /
M • Take Off / 1978 / VXP / M • Teenage
Runaways / 1977 / WWV / M • Triple
Header / 1987 / AIR / C • Vanessa's Hot
Nights / 1984 / SVE / M • [Untamed Desires / 1985 / ... / M
CLEDE see Star Index I
CLEMENS
Magma: Horny For Cock / 1990 / MET / M
CLEMENTINE MAYOL see Star Index I
CLEO
Black Snatch #2 / 1996 / DFI / F • Blue
Vanities #517 / 1992 / FFL / M • Buttman
Goes To Rio #2 / 1991 / EA / M • Gold
Coast / 1996 / FD / M • Up And Cummers

CLEO CATALINA
Cheeky Response / 1995 / RB / B • Finger Pleasures #1 / 1995 / PL / F

CLEO NICHOLE
Sisters In Submission / 1996 / BON / B

CLEO PATRA see **Cleopatra**

CLEO SIMMONDS
Blue Vanities #517 / 1992 / FFL / M

CLEOPATRA *(Cleo Patra, Claire De Loom)*
There seem to be several Cleopatra's around one of which is Cherokee but in at least one other case the Cleopatra is probably a pudgy white girl.
Amateur Nights #15 / 1997 / HO / M • Big Murray's New-Cummers #31: / 1996 / FD / M • Checkmate / 1996 / SNA / M • Country & Western Cuties #2: Naked Pie Eating Contest / 1996 / EVN / M • Dangerous / 1996 / SNA / M • Fresh Faces #10 / 1996 / EVN / M • Hardcore Debutantes #01 / 1996 / TEP / M • Hollywood Amateurs #27 / 1996 / MID / M • Innocent Little Girls #1 / 1996 / MP0 / M • Orgy Camera #2 / 1996 / EVN / M • Rimmers #1 / 1996 / MP0 / M • Rimmers #2 / 1996 / MP0 / M • Super Sampler #5 / 1994 / LOD / C • Young And Anal #4 / 1996 / JMP / M

CLEOPATRA (CHEROKEE) see **Cherokee**

CLIFF
Anal Ski Vacation / 1993 / ANA / M • AVP #9118: Just Another F—Film The Couple / 1991 / AVP / M • Bi-Bi Love Amateurs #3 / 1993 / QUA / G • Full Moon Video #30: Rainy Day Lays / 1994 / FAP / M

CLIFF PARKER
Night Walk / 1995 / HIV / G

CLIFF RAVEN
Erotic Tattooing And Piercing #1 / 1986 / FLV / M

CLIMAX
Amateur Black: Whores / 1996 / SUF / M • Black Fantasies #13 / 1996 / HW / M • Git Yo' Ass On Da Bus! / 1996 / HW / M • Interracial Affairs / 1996 / FC / M • So Bad / 1995 / VT / M • Whammin' & Jammin' At The Hard Cock Ole / 1996 / GLI / M

CLINT
Alex Jordan's First Timers #02 / 1993 / OD / M • Ona Zee's Date With Dallas / 1992 / ONA / M

CLINT HUGHES see **Star Index I**

CLINT LONGLEY
Manhattan Mistress / 1980 / VBM / M • Never Sleep Alone / 1984 / CA / M

CLINT PARKER see **Star Index I**

CLINT RAIN
Hardcore: The Films Of Richard Kern #1 / 1991 / FTV / M

CLINT SUREFIRE
Made In The Hood / 1995 / HBE / M

CLINT WESTWOOD
The Good, The Bad & The Dirty / cr75 / 4P / M • Three Men And A Lady / 1988 / EVN / M

CLINTON DARKE see **Star Index I**

CLIO
GRG: Clio's Climax / 1996 / GRG / F

CLOE
Fantasy Flings #02 / 1994 / WP / M • Mr. Peepers Amateur Home Videos #94: Calendar Cleavage / 1994 / LBO / M • Odyssey Triple Play #79: Dildos Dykes & Dicks / 1994 / OD / M • Sexual Trilogy #04

/ 1994 / SFP / M

CLOE COLLINS
Sweet Black Cherries #2 / 1996 / TTV / M

CLOE DUPONT
Top Model / 1995 / SC / M

CLORISSA
Extreme Guilt / 1996 / GOT / B

CLOTHILDE
Magma: Insatiable Lust / 1995 / MET / M

CLOVER
Foxy Boxing / 1982 / AVC / M

CLYDE CLONE
Wet Dreams / 1980 / WWV / M

CLYDE CLUTH
Nipples / 1973 / ALP / M • [Madam Satan / 19?? / ... / M

CLYDE FRAZEE see **Star Index I**

CLYDE GERARD see **Star Index I**

CLYDE LORAN
Caught! / 1985 / BIZ / B

CLYDE WILCOX
Ultraflesh / 1980 / GO / M

COBRA
Bondage Memories #04 / 1994 / BON / C • The Bondage Producer / 1991 / BON / B • Shades Of Bondage / 1991 / BON / B

COCA see **Star Index I**

COCCO BUTTA
Catch Of The Day #5 / 1996 / VG0 / M

COCHISE see **Star Index I**

COCK VAN DER MEER see **Star Index I**

COCO
Adventures Of The DP Boys: Backyard Boogie / 1994 / HW / M • Bay City Hot Licks / 1993 / ROB / F • Black Anal Dreams / 1995 / WV / M • Bootylicious: EZ Street / 1995 / JMP / M • Bootylicious: It's A Butt Thang / 1994 / JMP / M • Coco's House Party / 1995 / HW / M • The Girls From Hootersville #08 / 1994 / SFP / M • Nasty Nymphos #13 / 1996 / ANA / M • Pony Girls / 1993 / ROB / F • Sexual Trilogy #04 / 1994 / SFP / M • Wet & Slippery / 1995 / WV / M

COCO (DOMINIQUE) see **Dominique Simone**

COCO CHANEL
Be Careful What You Wish For / 1993 / VC / G • Coco In Private / 1991 / RSV / G • French-Pumped Femmes #1 / 1989 / RSV / G • French-Pumped Femmes #3 / 1991 / RSV / G • French-Pumped Femmes #4 / 1991 / RSV / G • The Mysteries Of Transsexualism Explored #2 / 1990 / LEO / G • She-Male Cocksuckers / 1993 / LEO / G • She-Male Encounters #19: Toga Party / 1989 / MET / G • She-Male Showgirls / 1992 / STA / G • She-Male Solos #04: Coco / 1990 / LEO / G • She-Male Tales / 1990 / MET / G • SM TV #2 / 1995 / FC / G • Sulka's Nightclub / 1989 / VT / G • TV Training Center / 1993 / LEO / G

COCOA
Adventures Of The DP Boys: Big Black Booty / 1994 / HW / M • Behind The Black Door #2 / 1993 / MID / M • Black 'n' White In Color / 1987 / VCR / C • Black Lube Job Girls / 1995 / SUF / M • The Good The Fat & The Ugly / 1995 / OD / M • Helpless Coeds / 1987 / BIZ / B • Plato's, The Movie / 1980 / SE / M

COCOA (EBONY AYES) see **Ebony Ayes**

COCOJA see **Star Index I**

CODY
Full Moon Video #4F: The Submission Of Cody / 1994 / FAP / B • More Dirty Debu-

tantes #64 / 1997 / SBV / M

CODY (T. RIVERS) see **Tanya Rivers**

CODY ADAMS *(Craig Adams, Jon Tiffany)*
Wimpy blonde male with a pony tail who is the boyfriend or husband of Tiffany Minx.
Butt Jammers / 1994 / WIV / M • Butt Of Steel / 1994 / LV / M • The Butt Sisters Do Sturgis / 1994 / MID / M • Cheek To Cheek / 1997 / EL / M • Cumback Pussy #4: Get Some!!! / 1996 / EL / M • Deep Inside Debi Diamond / 1995 / VC / C • Deep Inside Tiffany Mynx / 1994 / VC / C • The Fantasy Booth / 1993 / ONA / M • The Quest / 1994 / SC / M • Real Tickets #1 / 1994 / VC / M • Real Tickets #2 / 1994 / VC / M • Sodomania #09: Doin' Time / 1994 / EL / M • Superstar Sex Challenge #2 / 1994 / VC / M • Wicked As She Seems / 1993 / WP / M • Wilder At Heart / 1993 / ANA / M

CODY FOSTER *(Ginger Bush)*
Blonde with short hair and a peaches and cream facial complexion (body wise she isn't so good). Looks a bit prim. Small tits and tight body. 19 years old in 1993 from Oceanside CA.
Bi-Ology: The Making Of Mr Right / 1992 / CAT / G • Depraved Fantasies #2 / 1994 / FPI / M • Dirty Old Men #1 / 1995 / FPI / M • Love Bunnies #07 / 1994 / FPI / F • More Dirty Debutantes #28 / 1994 / 4P / M

CODY JAMES see **Star Index I**

CODY LOREN see **Corey Cox**

CODY LYON see **Star Index I**

CODY NICOLE *(Roxanne Potts, Roxanne Cody Nichole, Roxanne (Cody N))*
Tall blonde, pretty face, medium tits.
The Beat Goes On / 1987 / VCR / C • Bloopers #1 / cr90 / GO / C • Bondage Pleasures #1 / 1981 / 4P / B • Bondage Pleasures #2 / 1981 / 4P / B • Brooke Does College / 1984 / VC / M • Caballero Preview Tape #4 / 1985 / CA / C • Celebrity Presents Celebrity / 1986 / VEP / C • Centerfold Celebrities #1 / 1982 / VC / M • Centerfold Celebrities #2 / 1983 / VC / M • Climax / 1985 / CA / M • Deep Passion / 19?? / REG / C • Dirty Blonde / 1984 / VXP / M • Dirty Girls / 1984 / MIT / M • Dominated By Desire #1 / 1984 / 4P / B • Dream Girls #4 / 1984 / CA / C • Endless Passion / 1987 / LIM / C • The Erotic World Of Cody Nicole / 1984 / VCR / C • A Family Affair / 1984 / AVC / M • Femme Fatale / 1984 / VIV / M • From Russia With Lust / 1984 / VC / M • Girls On Fire / 1985 / VCX / M • Girls That Love Girls / 1984 / CA / F • Girls Together / 1985 / GO / C • Golden Girls #02 / 1981 / SVE / M • Golden Girls #23 / 1984 / CA / M • Golden Girls #27 / 1985 / CA / M • Golden Girls #34 / 1988 / CA / M • Gourmet Premier: Sex School / Centerfold Layout #909 / cr84 / GO / M • Gourmet Quickies: Cody Nicole #702 / 1984 / GO / C • GVC: Blonde Heat #136 / 1985 / GO / M • GVC: Suburban Lust #128 / 1983 / GO / M • GVC: Valley Vixens #124 / 1983 / GO / M • Holly Does Hollywood #1 / 1985 / VEX / M • Holly Rolling / 1984 / AVC / M • Hot Line / 1980 / CA / M • Hot Shorts: Cody Nicole / 1987 / VCR / C • Hot Stuff / 1984 / VXP / M • House Of Pleasure / 1984 / CA / M • How To Make Love To A Woman / 19?? / VV0 / M • Hypersexuals / 1984 / VC / M • Love Champions / 1987 / VC / M • A Loving Bind / 1986 / 4P / B • The Many Shades Of Amber / 1986 / LIM / M • Parliament: Super

Head #1 / 1989 / PM / C • Personal Touch #2 / 1983 / AR / M • Pleasure Productions #03 / 1984 / VCR / M • Pleasure Productions #04 / 1984 / VCR / M • Rope Burn / 1984 / 4P / B • Sensuous Tales / 1984 / VCR / C • Sex Boat / 1980 / VCX / M • Sex Games / 1983 / CA / M • Squalor Motel / 1985 / SE / M • Star 84: Tina Marie / 1984 / VEX / M • Stray Cats / 1985 / VXP / M • Suze's Centerfolds #9 / 1985 / CA / M • Too Naughty To Say No / 1984 / CA / M • Triangle Of Lust / 1983 / VCR / M • Up 'n' Coming / 1983 / CA / M • Up Up And Away / 1984 / CA / M • Wet Dreams / 1984 / CA / M • Wet Panties / 1989 / MIR / C • Where The Girls Are / 1984 / VEX / M • X-Rated Bloopers #1 / 1984 / AR / M

CODY O'CONNOR *(Cheri Lynn)*
Redhead with medium to large tits and a little bit of pudge around the middle (depends on the movie). As of late 1994 she has become a blonde and looks much better.
Battlestar Orgasmica / 1992 / EVN / M • Black Velvet #2 / 1993 / CC / M • The BoobyGuard / 1993 / FOR / M • Breastman Goes To Breastland #1 / 1993 / EVN / M • Buffy Malibu's Totally Nasty All-Girl Home Videos #01 / 1992 / ANA / F • Chug-A-Lug Girls #1 / 1993 / VT / M • Face Dance #1 / 1992 / EA / M • Face Dance #2 / 1992 / EA / M • French Twist / 1995 / IN / M • From A Whisper To A Scream / 1993 / GO / M • The Good, The Bed, And The Snuggly / 1993 / ZA / M • Heartbeat / 1995 / PP / M • In The Can With Oj / 1994 / HCV / M • A Kiss Before Dying / 1993 / CDI / M • Money, Money, Money / 1993 / FD / M • New Wave Hookers #3 / 1993 / VC / M • Playin' With Fire / 1993 / LV / M • A Pussy Called Wanda #2 / 1992 / DR / M • The Rehearsal / 1993 / VC / M • Revenge Of The Pussy Suckers From Mars / 1994 / PP / M • Rugburn / 1993 / LE / M • The Sex Connection / 1993 / VC / M • Sexophrenia / 1993 / VC / M • Sodomania #01: Tales Of Perversity / 1992 / EL / M • Sodomania #02: More Tails / 1992 / EL / M • Sodomania #10: Euro/American Again / 1994 / EL / M • Sodomania: Slop Shots / 1996 / EL / C • Sodomania: The Baddest Of The Best...And Then Some / 1994 / EL / C • Temptation / 1994 / VC / M • Tunnel Of Lust / 1993 / LV / M • Video Virgins #02 / 1992 / NS / M • Virgin Tales #01 / 1993 / 4P / M • Wendy Whoppers: Brain Surgeon / 1993 / PEP / M • Wendy Whoppers: Razorwoman / 1993 / PEP / M

CODY SUE
The Coming Of Angie / cr73 / TGA / M
COL. ALBERT LEA
Private Film #12 / 1994 / OD / M
COLE CARPENTER *see Star Index I*
COLE FURY *see Ray Victory*
COLE PHILLIPS
B-Witched / 1994 / PEP / G • Bi Chill / 1994 / BIL / G • Days Gone Bi / 1994 / BIN / G
COLE REECE
Bi The Book / 1996 / MID / G • Mixed Apples / 1996 / APP / G
COLE REESE
Cocks In Frocks #1 / 1996 / TTV / G
COLE STEVENS *see Jordan Smith*
COLE TAYLOR *see Star Index I*
COLETTE
High Heels In Heat #1 / 1988 / RSV / F • High Heels In Heat #4 / 1989 / RSV / F •

Magma: Sperm-Crazy / 1994 / MET / M
COLIN BEARDSLEY
American Sexual Revolution / 1970 / SOW / M
COLIN LANEFORD
Taboo American Style #3: Nina Becomes An Actress / 1985 / VC / M • Taboo American Style #4: The Exciting Conclusion / 1985 / VC / M
COLIN LEWIS
Sex Over 40 #1 / 1994 / PL / M
COLIN MATHEWS *see Star Index I*
COLIN TAYLOR *see Star Index I*
COLLEEN ANDERSON *see Heather Young*
COLLEEN APPLEGATE *see Shauna Grant*
COLLEEN BAILY
Blue Vanities #192 / 1993 / FFL / M
COLLEEN BRENNAN *(Sharon Kelly, Oyga Vault)*
Not too pretty reddish blonde with a womanly body and medium to large tits. Sharon Kelly was the name used in early soft core such as **Sassy Sue**. Oyga is from **Raw Talent #2**.
69 Park Avenue / 1985 / ELH / M • The 8th Annual Erotic Film Awards / 1984 / SE / C • Alice Goodbody / 1975 / MED / S • All For His Ladies / 1987 / PP / C • The Animal In Me / 1985 / IN / M • The Beauties And The Beast / 1973 / AP0 / S • Bedtime Tales / 1985 / SE / M • Beverly Hills Exposed / 1985 / SE / M • The Bigger The Better / 1986 / SE / C • Blondie / 1985 / TAR / M • The Boob Tube / 1975 / VIG / S • Candy Stripers #2 / 1985 / AR / M • Carnal Olympics / 1983 / CA / M • Caught From Behind #04: Nasty Young Girls / 1985 / HO / M • China & Silk / 1984 / MAP / M • Circus Acts / 1987 / SE / C • Club Ecstasy / 1987 / CA / M • A Coming Of Angels, The Sequel / 1985 / CA / M • Coming Together / 1984 / CA / M • Computer Girls / 1983 / LIP / F • Corrupt Desires / 1984 / MET / M • Country Girl / 1985 / AVC / M • Cummin' Alive / 1984 / VC / M • Daisy Chain / 1984 / IN / M • Delinquent School Girls / 1974 / NWW / S • Dirty Girls / 1984 / MIT / M • The Dirty Mind Of Young Sally / 1973 / SOW / S • Dirty Shary / 1985 / VD / M • Down And Dirty In Beverly Hills / 1986 / CV / M • Family Secrets / 1985 / AMB / M • Famous Ta-Ta's #1 / 1986 / VCS / C • Famous Ta-Ta's #2 / 1986 / SE / C • Fantasy Land / 1984 / LA / M • First Annual XRCO Awards / 1984 / AVC / C • Flesh And Ecstasy / 1985 / VD / M • Four X Feeling / 1986 / QX / M • The Fur Trap / 1973 / AVC / M • Getting Personal / 1986 / CA / M • Girls Of The Night / 1985 / CA / M • Good Girl, Bad Girl / 1984 / SE / M • Home Movies Ltd #2 / 1985 / SE / M • Hot Blooded / 1983 / CA / M • Hustle / 1975 / PAR / S • Hustler Video Magazine #1 / 1983 / SE / M • Hustler Video Magazine #2 / 1984 / SE / M • I Wanna Be A Bad Girl / 1986 / PP / M • Ilsa, Keeper Of The Oil Sheik's Harem / 1975 / AME / S • Ilsa, She Wolf Of The SS / 1974 / VID / S • The Initiation Of Cynthia / 1985 / VXP / M • Innocent Taboo / 1986 / VD / M • Joint Effort / 1992 / SEX / C • Lady By Night / 1987 / CA / M • Lady Dynamite / 1983 / VC / M • Le Sex De Femme #4 / 1989 / AFI / C • Leather & Lace / 1987 / SE / C • Legends Of Porn #1 / 1987 / CV / C • Little Kimmi

Johnson / 1983 / VEP / M • Love Champions / 1987 / VC / M • Love Roots / 1987 / LIM / M • Loving Lips / 1987 / AMB / C • Mafia Girls / 1972 / SOW / M • Matinee Idol / 1984 / VC / M • Maximum #5 / 1983 / CA / M • Meat Market / 1992 / SEX / C • The Mob Job / cr72 / SOW / S • More Than A Handful #1 / 1985 / CV / C • Mother's Pride / 1985 / DIM / M • Nice 'n' Tight / 1985 / AIR / M • One Night At A Time / 1984 / PV / M • Only The Best Of Men's And Women's Fantasies / 1988 / CV / C • Only The Best Of Oral / 1989 / CV / C • Perfect Fit / 1985 / DR / M • Raw Talent #2 / 1987 / VC / M • Rearbusters / 1988 / LVI / C • The Red Garter / 1986 / SE / M • Red On The Noodle Like A Swance On A Poodle / 1990 / FC / C • The Red Room And Other Places / 1992 / COM / C • The Ribald Tales Of Canterbury / 1986 / CA / M • Sassy Sue / 1972 / SOW / S • Scared Stiff / 1984 / PV / M • Screaming Rage / 1988 / LV / C • Secret Mistress / 1986 / VD / M • Sex Crimes 2084 / 1985 / SE / M • The Sex Game / 1987 / SE / C • Sex-A-Vision / 1985 / DR / M • Shampoo / 1975 / CRC / S • Six Faces Of Samantha / 1984 / AA / M • Slammer Girls / 1987 / LIV / S • Some Kind Of Woman / 1985 / CA / M • Squalor Motel / 1985 / SE / M • Star Angel / 1986 / COM / M • Street Heat / 1984 / VC / M • Striptease / 1983 / VC / M • Sulka's Daughter / 1984 / MET / G • Supervixens / 1975 / RMV / S • Suzy's Birthday Bang / 1985 / CDI / M • Swedish Erotica #59 / 1984 / CA / M • Taboo #03 / 1983 / IN / M • Taboo #05 / 1986 / IN / M • Talk Dirty To Me #03 / 1986 / DR / M • Talk Dirty To Me One More Time #1 / 1985 / PP / M • Taste Of The Best #1 / 1988 / PIN / C • Teenage Bride / 1970 / SOW / S • Tower Of Power / 1985 / CV / M • Trinity Brown / 1984 / CV / M • Unnatural Act #2 / 1986 / DR / M • Up Up And Away / 1984 / CA / M • Vanessa...Maid In Manhattan / 1984 / VC / M • Voyeur's Delight / 1986 / VCS / C • Wet, Wild And Wicked / 1984 / SE / M • [Carnal Madness / 1975 / ... / S
COLLEEN COX
Blue Vanities #222 / 1994 / FFL / M
COLLEEN DAVIS *see Heather Young*
COLLEEN JEWELL
Bedtime Video #04 / 1984 / GO / M
COLLEEN MERCURY
Golden Girls, The Movie / 1984 / SE / M
COLLETTE COBAR
Blue Vanities #552 / 1994 / FFL / M
COLLETTE CONNER
Centerfold Fever / 1981 / VXP / M • In Love / 1983 / VC / M
COLLETTE DUBARGE *see Star Index I*
COLLETTE MAREVIL
House Of Love / cr77 / VC / M • Salon D'amour / 19?? / IHV / M
COLLETTE MARIN *see April Maye (1985)*
COLLETTE ROBERTS *see Star Index I*
COLLIN JAMES
I'm A Curious She-Male / 1993 / HSV / G • She Male Jail / 1994 / HSV / G
COLLIN WEST
Pick Up Lines #10 / 1997 / OD / M
COLT 45
Girls Around The World #22: Letha Weapons & Friends / 1995 / BTO / M • Girls Around The World #25 / 1995 / BTO /

S

COLT JACKSON *see Star Index I*

COLT STEELE
Airotica / 1996 / SC / M • American Blonde / 1993 / VI / M • Anal Virgins Of America #03 / 1993 / FOR / M • Anal Virgins Of America #04 / 1993 / FOR / M • Ashlyn Rising / 1995 / VI / M • Backdoor Play / 1996 / AVI / M • Bad Company / 1994 / VI / M • Boiling Point / 1994 / WAV / M • Boobwatch #1 / 1996 / SC / M • Boobwatch #2 / 1997 / SC / M • Bordello / 1995 / VI / M • The Cathouse / 1994 / VI / M • Caught From Behind #21 / 1995 / HO / M • Chasin' The Fifties / 1994 / WP / M • Cheating / 1994 / VI / M • Chow Down / 1994 / VI / M • Cumback Pussy #2: Crawling Back For More / 1996 / EL / M • The Desert Cafe / 1996 / NIT / M • The Devil In Miss Jones #5: The Inferno / 1994 / VC / M • Dick & Jane Go To A Bachelor Party (#17) / 1996 / AVI / M • Double Crossed / 1994 / MID / M • Eighteen #3 / 1996 / SC / M • Eighteen & Easy / 1996 / SC / M • Explicit Entry / 1995 / LE / M • Gazongas Galore #1 / 1996 / NIT / C • The Go-Go Girls / 1994 / EVN / M • Hawaii / 1995 / VI / M • Hollywood Spa / 1996 / WP / M • How To Deep Throat Your Lover / 1994 / A&E / M • I Cream On Jeannie / 1995 / AVI / M • Immortal Desire / 1993 / VI / M • Jinx / 1996 / WP / M • Latex #1 / 1994 / VC / M • Lollipop Shoppe #1 / 1996 / SC / M • Lollipop Shoppe #2 / 1996 / SC / M • Lotus / 1996 / VI / M • Manhandled! / 1997 / BON / B • The Many Faces Of P.J. Sparxx / 1996 / WP / M • Naked Ambition / 1995 / VC / M • New Girls In Town #4 / 1993 / CC / M • New Girls In Town #5 / 1994 / CC / M • The Night Of The Living Bed / 1996 / LE / M • Night Train / 1993 / VI / M • Nightvision / 1995 / VI / M • On Her Back / 1994 / VI / M • The Player / 1995 / VI / M • Playtime / 1996 / VI / M • Pretending / 1993 / CV / M • Promises And Lies / 1996 / NIT / M • Reckless Passion / 1995 / WAV / M • Rockhard (Sin City) / 1996 / SC / M • Spin For Sex / 1994 / IN / M • Steamy Sins / 1996 / IN / M • Stiletto / 1994 / WAV / M • Strip Search / 1995 / CV / M • Surprise!!! / 1994 / VI / M • Swallow / 1994 / VI / M • Tailz From Da Hood #5 / 1996 / AVI / M • The Time Machine / 1996 / WP / M • Undress To Thrill / 1994 / VI / M • Unleashed / 1996 / SAE / M • Unmistakably You / 1995 / CV / M • Upbeat Love #1 / 1994 / CV / M • Valentina: Princess Of The Forest / 1996 / SC / M • Video Virgins #17 / 1994 / NS / M • Whispered Lies / 1993 / LBO / M • Wild Orgies #02 / 1994 / AFI / M • XXX Channel / 1996 / VT / M

COMBAT MIKE
Bondage Classix #08: Alexis Slave Lessons / 198? / BON / B

COMFORT
Best Butt(e) In The West #1 / 1992 / CC / M

COMINIC LECROIX *see Star Index I*

COMISHA *see Cumisha Amado*

COMMANDER
The Necklace #1 / 1994 / ZFX / B

CON COVERT
The Ecstasy Girls #1 / 1979 / CA / M • A Scream In The Streets / 1971 / SOW / S

CONCHITA ALONSO
Up And Cummers #10 / 1994 / 4P / M

CONCHITA COSTELLO *see Star Index I*

CONNER HENRY *see Ted Wilson*

CONNIE
A&B GB#022 / 1992 / A&B / M • Amateur Nights #10 / 1990 / HO / M • Blue Vanities #546 / 1994 / FFL / M • Blue Vanities #555 / 1994 / FFL / M • Blue Vanities #573 / 1996 / FFL / M • Creme De La Face #17: Semen For Seven / 1996 / OD / M • Dirty & Kinky Mature Women #05 / 1995 / C69 / M • House Of Sex #06: Banging Wendy, Kitty, Corby and Connie / 1994 / RTP / M • Magma: Perverse Games / 1995 / MET / M • Mr. Peepers Nastiest #6 / 1995 / LBO / C • Raw Talent: Bang 'er 32 Times / 1992 / RTP / M • Sex Scientist / 1992 / FD / M

CONNIE ALLEN
Finger Pleasures #1 / 1995 / PL / F

CONNIE BENET
GVC: Pool Service #105 / cr84 / GO / M • GVC: The Therapist #101 / 1986 / GO / M • The Wacky World Of X-Rated Bloopers / 1989 / GO / M

CONNIE BURNETT *see Star Index I*

CONNIE CAMPBELL
Bedtime Video #04 / 1984 / GO / M

CONNIE CHAN
Yellow Orchid / 1996 / SUF / M

CONNIE CHILDS
Dirty & Kinky Mature Women #07 / 1996 / C69 / M • Geriatric Valley Girls / 1995 / FC / M • Golden Oldies #4 / 1996 / TTV / M • Golden Oldies #5 / 1996 / TTV / M • Lactamania #2: The Squirt Fest / 1995 / TTV / M • The Real Deal #2 / 1995 / FC / M • The Real Deal #3 / 1996 / FC / M

CONNIE COOMBS *see Star Index I*

CONNIE COX *see Star Index I*

CONNIE DOUGLAS *see Connie Peterson*

CONNIE FREEMAN
Toys, Not Boys #1 / 1991 / FC / C

CONNIE HOWEL
[Snow Balling / 197? / ... / M

CONNIE KRUMPERT
Personal Services / 1975 / CV / M

CONNIE LAUREN
Transsexual Dynasty / 1996 / BIZ / G

CONNIE LINDSTROM *see Star Index I*

CONNIE LINGUS *see Star Index I*

CONNIE NEILSEN *see Star Index I*

CONNIE PETERS *see Connie Peterson*

CONNIE PETERSON *(Connie Douglas, Connie Peters, Connie Sievers, Connie Severs, Gloria Roberts, Jill Johns, Susan Blue)*
Blonde, poor skin with lots of freckles, medium to large tits, smile but a wouldn't say it's a nice smile, lithe body, not a tight waist, small tattoo on her right forearm.
Backdoor Romance / 1984 / VIV / M • Ball Game / 1980 / CA / M • Blue Vanities #016 (Old) / 1988 / FFL / M • Blue Vanities #048 / 1988 / FFL / M • Blue Vanities #062 / 1988 / FFL / M • Blue's Velvet / 1979 / ECV / M • Body Candy / 1980 / VIS / M • Bottoms Up #02 / 1983 / AVC / C • Bottoms Up #04 / 1983 / AVC / C • Bottoms Up #05 / 1986 / AVC / C • Caballero Preview Tape #1 / 1982 / CA / C • Classic Swedish Erotica #21 / 1986 / CA / C • Classic Swedish Erotica #35 / 1987 / CA / C • Come Under My Spell / cr78 / HIF / M • Cover Girl Fantasies #1 / 1983 / VCR / C • Daisy May / 1979 / VC / M • Diamond Collection #01 / 1979 / SVE / M • Flash / 1980 / CA / M • Flight Sensations / 1983 / VC / C • Frat House /

1979 / NGV / M • Getting Off / 1979 / VIP / M • Goodbye My Love / 1980 / CA / M • Homecoming / 1981 / CA / M • Hot Rackets / 1979 / CV / M • I Am Always Ready / 1978 / HIF / M • John Holmes, The Lost Films / 1988 / PEN / C • Kiss And Tell / 1980 / CA / M • Legends Of Porn #1 / 1987 / CV / C • Limited Edition #05 / 1979 / AVC / M • Limited Edition #06 / 1979 / AVC / M • Limited Edition #09 / 1980 / AVC / M • The Little French Maid / 1981 / VCX / M • Mrs. Rodger's Neighborhood / 1988 / EVN / C • Nanci Blue / 1979 / SE / M • Olympic Fever / 1979 / AR / M • Only The Best #1 / 1986 / CV / C • Oriental Babysitter / 1976 / SE / M • The Other Side Of Julie / 1978 / CV / M • Pink Champagne / 1979 / CV / M • Seka's Fantasies / 1981 / CA / M • Skintight / 1981 / CA / M • Stormy / 1980 / CV / M • Swedish Erotica #05 / 1980 / CA / M • Swedish Erotica #10 / 1980 / CA / M • Swedish Erotica #24 / 1980 / CA / M • Swedish Erotica #26 / 1980 / CA / M • Swedish Erotica #30 / 1980 / CA / M • Swedish Erotica Superstar #3: Janey Robbins / 1984 / CA / C • Taboo #01 / 1980 / VCX / M • That's Erotic / 1979 / CV / C • Trouble Down Below / 1981 / CA / M • [Burning Wild / 1979 / SIL / M • [Chain Letter / 1978 / ... / M • [Three For Love / 1983 / ... / M

CONNIE SEVERS *see Connie Peterson*

CONNIE SIEVERS *see Connie Peterson*

CONNIE YUNG *(Karessa Chang, Caressa Chang)*
Oriental with the standard black hair, small/medium tits, not too pretty face and loss of belly muscle tone.
2 Wongs Make A White / 1996 / FC / M • Around Frisco / 1996 / SUF / M • Catch Of The Day #5 / 1996 / VG0 / M • Dirty Dave's #2 / 1996 / XPR / M • Finger Pleasures #2 / 1995 / PL / F • Her Name Is Asia / 1996 / SUF / M • Old Guys & Dolls #2 / 1995 / PL / M • Older & Bolder In San Francisco / 1996 / TEP / M • The Real Deal #4 / 1996 / FC / M • Shaved #09 / 1995 / RB / F • Vienna's Place / 1996 / VCX / M • Yellow Orchid / 1996 / SUF / M • Yin Yang Oriental Love Bang #4: Yellow Orchid / 1996 / SUF / M

CONNOR *see Star Index I*

CONNY HUNDT *see Star Index I*

CONRAD EAST
Swedish Erotica #80 / 1994 / CA / M

CONRAD I. PICKLEBUTT
Adult Affairs / 1994 / VC / M

CONRAD WEST
Sex Over 40 #1 / 1994 / PL / M • Young Sluts In Heat #2 / 1996 / PL / M

CONSTANCE DREW
1001 Erotic Nights #2 / 1987 / VC / M

CONSTANCE MERCY
Constance & Eric At It Again / cr90 / BON / B • Constance & Eric Bound At Home / 1990 / BON / B • Home Maid Memories #1 / 1994 / BON / C • Real People Real Bondage #1 / 1995 / BON / C • Suspension Of Disbelief #1 / 1989 / BON / B • Suspension Of Disbelief #2 / 1989 / BON / B

CONSTANCE MONEY *(Susan Jensen)*
Pretty long haired dark blonde with medium tits.
Anna Obsessed / 1978 / ALP / M • Barbara Broadcast / 1977 / VC / M • Confessions Of A Teenage Peanut Butter Freak / 1974 /

LIM / M • Hustler Video Magazine #2 / 1984 / SE / M • The Joy Of Letting Go / 1976 / SE / M • Legends Of Porn #1 / 1987 / CV / C • Maraschino Cherry / 1978 / QX / M • Mary! Mary! / 1977 / SE / M • Only The Very Best On Film / 1992 / VC / C • The Opening Of Misty Beethoven / 1976 / VC / M • San Francisco Original 200s #9 / 1980 / SVE / M • Sex Maniacs / 1987 / JOY / C • A Taste Of Money / 1983 / AT / M • That's Porno / 1979 / CV / C • True Legends Of Adult Cinema: The Cult Superstars / 1993 / VC / C • Wild Orgies / 1986 / SE / C

CONSTANCE MURRAY
The Bride's Initiation / 1976 / VIP / M

CONSTANCE PENNY *see* **Copper Penny**

CONSTANCE PENNY (EW) *see* **Eileen Welles**

CONSTANCE WHITEBREAD
The Starmaker / 1982 / VC / M

CONSUELLA
Blue Vanities #501 / 1992 / FFL / M

COOKIE (M. MASGLOW) *see* **Melinda Masglow**

COOKIE FRENCH
The Satisfiers Of Alpha Blue / 1980 / AVC / M

COOKIE HOOKER *see* **Star Index I**

COOKIE MUFFIN
Black Fantasies #13 / 1996 / HW / M

COOL G.
Span's Garden Party / 1996 / HW / M

COON DOG
Bondage Memories #03 / 1994 / BON / C • Bondage Shoots / 1993 / BON / B • Flash Backs / 1990 / BON / B • Master Plan / 198? / BON / B

COPPER PENNY *(Constance Penny)*
Tall girl with copper colored hair including pubic. Small tits. Face a little like Serena. White body.
All American Girls #1 / 1982 / CA / M • C.T. Coed Teasers / 1978 / VXP / M • Classic Erotica #6 / 1985 / SVE / M • The Erotic Aventures Of Lolita / 1982 / VXP / M • House Of Sin / 1982 / AVO / M • Maximum #5 / 1983 / CA / M • Scoundrels / 1982 / COM / M • The Starmaker / 1982 / VC / M • Taking It To The Streets / 1987 / CDI / M

CORA
Black Casting Couch #2 / 1994 / WP / M • Chocolate Bunnies #02 / 1995 / LBO / C • M Series #26 / 1994 / LBO / M

CORA LEE *see* **Coralie**

CORAL CIE
On White Satin / 1980 / VCX / M • Same Time Every Year / 1981 / VHL / M • The Satisfiers Of Alpha Blue / 1980 / AVC / M

CORAL SANDS
Filthy First Timers #5 / 1997 / EL / M • Filthy First Timers #7 / 1997 / EL / M • A Week And A Half In The Life Of A Prostitute / 1997 / EL / M

CORALIE *(Cora Lee)*
French, pretty, long straight black hair, medium firm but not enhanced tits, lithe body but not a particularly tight waist, good skin, totally shaven pussy.
Cindy Puts Out / 1996 / OLL / M • Dirty Stories #1 / 1995 / PE / M • Eurotica #02 / 1995 / XC / M • Eurotica #13 / 1996 / XC / M • Explore With Coralie / 1996 / C69 / M • Fashion Sluts #1 / 1995 / ABS / M • Gigi Gives It Away / 1995 / FRF / M • Hienie's Heroes / 1995 / VC / M • Mickey Ray's Sex

Search #05: Deep Inside / 1995 / WIV / M • The New Butt Hunt #14 / 1995 / LEI / C • Paris Chic / 1996 / SAE / M • Private Film #23 / 1995 / OD / M • Pussyman Auditions #02 / 1995 / SNA / M • The Streets Of Paris / 1996 / SC / M • Triple X Video Magazine #02 / 1995 / OD / M • World Sex Tour #1 / 1995 / ANA / M • World Sex Tour #2 / 1995 / ANA / M

CORBY WELLS *see* **Natalie Harris**

CORD COLBY
Bi Intruder / 1991 / STA / G

COREEN
Blue Vanities #558 / 1994 / FFL / M

COREENA COLLINS *see* **Careena Collins**

COREENA TAYLOR *see* **Josalynn Taylor**

CORESSA SAVAGE *see* **Caressa Savage**

COREY *see* **Star Index I**

COREY CAINE
Amateur Gay Girls / 1995 / LEI / C • Black Masters: Black Obsession / 1995 / GOT / B • Black Masters: Restrained / 1995 / GOT / B • The Dean's Spanking / 1995 / STM / B • Dragon Lady's Domination Technique / 1995 / STM / B • East Coast Sluts #04: New York City / 1995 / PL / M • Last Resort / 1994 / GOT / B • Lesbian Kink Trilogy #2 / 1995 / STM / F • Masters Of Dominance / 1996 / STM / C • Moist Thighs / 1995 / STM / F • On Your Knees / 1995 / GOT / B • Oriental Dominatrix / 1995 / STM / B • Slapped Around Sluts / 1995 / PL / B • Slave Traders / 1995 / GOT / B • Strap-On Sally #03: Thigh Harness Terror / 1994 / PL / F • Strap-On Sally #04: Double Penetration Dykes / 1994 / PL / F • Toe Tales #20 / 1995 / GOT / B • Toe Tales #21 / 1995 / GOT / B • Toe Tales #23 / 1995 / GOT / B • Toe Tales #29 / 1995 / GOT / B • Very Bad Girls / 1995 / GOT / B • Video Virgins #19 / 1994 / NS / M • Without Pity / 1995 / GOT / B

COREY COX *(Cody Loren)*
Mousy looking blonde with a passable face, medium droppy tits, lithe body, very flat large areola. Cody Loren is from **Day Dreams**.
Biff Malibu's Totally Nasty Home Videos #34 / 1993 / ANA / M • Black Is Back / 1993 / HW / M • Breastman Does The Himalayas / 1993 / EVN / M • Casting Call (Venus 99) / 1993 / V99 / M • Day Dreams / 1993 / CV / M • Freaks Of Leather #2 / 1994 / IF / C • Heavenly Hooters / 1994 / IF / M • Hometown Honeys #4 / 1993 / VEX / M • Hot Pie Delivery / 1993 / AFV / M • I Want A Divorce / 1993 / ZA / M • Juranal Park / 1993 / OD / M • Just My Imagination / 1993 / WP / M • The Last Anal Hero / 1993 / OD / M • Pearl Necklace: Amorous Amateurs #28 / 1993 / SEE / M • Seymore Butts Swings / 1992 / FH / M • To Shave And Shave Not / 1994 / PEP / M • Udderly Fantastic / 1993 / IF / M • The Worst Porno Ever Made With The Best Sex / 1993 / PL / M

COREY FRICTION
She-Males In Torment #2 / 1992 / BIZ / G • TV Blondes Do It Best / 1992 / BIZ / G • TV Ladies Room / 1993 / BIZ / G • TV Reform School / 1992 / BIZ / G • TVs Teased And Tormented / 1995 / BIZ / G

COREY GATES *(Nicki (Corey Gates), Cori Gates, Nicki Gates)*
Brrr! Weightlifter female with muscles and

hefty thighs, large tits, not too pretty face, short curly blonde hair, large protruding clit probably due to steroid use.
Ass Angels / 1996 / PAL / F • Boudoir Babe / 1996 / VMX / M • Butt Jammers #05 / 1996 / SC / F • Buttslammers #10: Lust On The Internet / 1995 / BS / F • The Cumm Brothers #14: Buttdraft / 1995 / OD / M • Dirty Dave's #3 / 1996 / XPR / M • Hollywood Amateurs #24 / 1995 / MID / M • Hollywood Amateurs #31 / 1996 / MID / M • Hungry Humpers / 1996 / SP / M • Interview's Hard Bodied Harlots / 1996 / LV / M • Lesbian Debutante #01 / 1996 / IP / F • Lesbian Nights / 1996 / AVI / F • Mike Hott: #338 Lesbian Sluts #22 / 1996 / MHV / F • Mike Hott: #345 Cum In My Cunt #07 / 1995 / MHV / C • Mike Hott: #354 Three-Sum Sluts #12 / 1996 / MHV / M • Mike Hott: #356 Girls Who Lap Cum From Cunts #01 / 1996 / MHV / M • Mike Hott: #366 Lactating Lesbians / 1996 / MHV / F • New York Bound #1 / 1996 / GAL / B • New York Bound #2: The Next Day / 1996 / GAL / B • Nikki Arizona's Tomboys / 1995 / GAL / M • Nineteen #1 / 1996 / FOR / M • Old Guys & Dolls #1 / 1995 / PL / M • Pierced Punctured And Perverted / 1995 / FC / M • Pussyman Auditions #13 / 1995 / SNA / M • Rimmers #1 / 1996 / MP0 / M • Sex, Truth & Videotape #2 / 1996 / DOC / M • Slutsville U.S.A. / 1995 / VMX / M • The Sodomizer #3 / 1996 / SC / M • The Tigress / 1995 / VIM / M • Tripper Stripper / 1995 / VMX / M • Turnabout / 1996 / CTP / M

COREY KIDD
Inside Seka / 1980 / VXP / M

COREY NIXON
Charade / 1993 / HSV / G • Single White She-Male / 1993 / PL / G • Transfigured / 1993 / HSV / G

COREY PAINE
Toe Tales #27 / 1995 / GOT / B

COREY SCOTT
A Decent Proposal / 1993 / BIL / G • Queens From Outer Space / 1993 / HSV / G • She's The Boss / 1993 / BIL / G

CORI GATES *see* **Corey Gates**

Blue Vanities #547 / 1994 / FFL / M

CORINA
Hot Body Competition: Bikinis & Bikes Contest / 1996 / CG / F • Shannon Shows Off / 1993 / HAC / G

CORINA CHAN
Yin Yang Oriental Love Bang #4: Yellow Orchid / 1996 / SUF / M

CORINNA *see* **Valeria**

CORINNA TAYLOR *see* **Valeria**

CORINNE *see* **Star Index I**

CORINNE CLERY *see* **Corrine Clery**

CORKY JAMES
Alumni Girls / 1996 / GO / M • The Fabulous 50's Girls Ride Again / 1994 / EMC / M • The Generation Gap / 1996 / LV / M • Hard Core Beginners #01 / 1995 / LEI / M • Lactamania #2: The Squirt Fest / 1995 / TTV / M • Lactamania #3 / 1995 / TTV / M • Middle Aged Maidens / 1995 / GLI / M • Older Women With Younger Ideas / 1995 / GLI / M • The Older Women's Sperm Bank #2 / 1996 / SUF / M • The Ultimate Fantasy / 1995 / CV / M

CORNELL HAYES *see* **Herschel Savage**

CORRINA
Dick & Jane Go To Hong Kong / 1995 / AVI

/ M
CORRINA (J. WELLS) *see* **Jenna Wells**
CORRINA (V. GOLD) *see* **Victoria Gold**
CORRINA LINDERO *see* **Valeria**
CORRINE
Blue Vanities #574 / 1996 / FFL / M • Impulse #08: The A Channel / 1996 / MBP / M
CORRINE CLERY *(Corinne Clery)*
Very pretty with shoulder length wavy dark brown hair, medium tits, tight waist, a little big on the butt. There seems to be no standard way of spelling her name with different guides and publicity spelling it with one or two "r"'s. Maybe someone should ask her.
The Con Artists / 1978 / HHV / S • Covert Action / 1978 / ... / S • Dangerous Obsession / 1986 / AIP / S • Fatal Fix / 1983 / ... / S • The Humanoid / 1978 / RCA / S • I Hate Blondes / 1981 / ... / S • Insanity / 1982 / ... / S • Kleinhoff Hotel / 1977 / ... / S • Love By Appointment / 1976 / NLH / S • Moonraker / 1979 / MGM / S • The Story Of O #1 / 1975 / LOR / S • Yor, The Hunter From The Future / 1983 / C3S / S • [Autostop Rosso Sangue / 1978 / ... / S • [Fade Out / 1979 / ... / S
CORRY MCCABE
Bi-Conflict / 1994 / FST / G • Conflict Of Interest / 1994 / FST / G
CORT STEVENS
Revenge Of The Bi Dolls / 1994 / CAT / G
CORTKNEE
Pretty blonde with white skin and nice tight waist, endhanced (very bad job—nipples are misplaced) medium tits and a humongous clit. Speaks with a husky voice but there's nothing else about her to indicate she might be a post-op transsexual. She says in 1996 she's 23 years old, was de-viginized at 16, did her first anal at 20 and comes from Valencia, CA.
Anal Auditions #1 / 1996 / XPR / M • Anal Crash Test Dummies / 1997 / ROB / M • Anal Fantasy / 1996 / SUF / M • Anal Fever / 1996 / ROB / M • Anal Fireball / 1996 / ROB / M • Anal Institution #3 / 1996 / ZA / M • Anal Load Lickers / 1996 / ROB / M • Anal Lovebud / 1996 / ROB / M • Anal Sex Freaks / 1996 / ZA / M • Anal Virgins #03 / 1996 / NS / M • Canned Heat / 1996 / TCK / M • Career Girls / 1996 / OUP / M • The Cumm Brothers #15: Hot Primal Sex / 1996 / OD / M • The Dinner Party #2: The Buffet / 1996 / ULI / M • Diva #2: Deep In Glamour / 1996 / VC / F • Every Woman Wants A Penis #2 / 1996 / MID / M • The Hitch-Hiker #17: Dead End / 1996 / VIM / M • Hot Tight Asses #18 / 1996 / TCK / M • Innocent Girls Of Legal Age #3 / 1996 / MP0 / M • Intense Perversions #4 / 1996 / PL / M • Just Do It! / 1996 / RAS / M • Living On The Edge / 1997 / DWO / M • Lockdown / 1996 / NIT / M • Max #10: Dirty Deeds / 1996 / XPR / M • Max #12: Spread Eagle / 1996 / LE / M • Naked Mockey-Rayna / 1996 / EVN / M • Nineteen #2 / 1996 / FOR / M • Nineteen #3 / 1996 / FOR / M • The Phantom Of The Montague Stage / 1997 / HO / M • Puritan Video Magazine #03 / 1996 / LE / M • Puritan Video Magazine #04 / 1996 / LE / M • Pussyman's Nite Club Party #1 / 1996 / SNA / M • Pussyman's Nite Club Party #2 / 1997 / SNA / M • Raw Footage / 1996 / VC / M • Reflections / 1996 / ZA / M • Roller Babes / 1996 / ERA

/ M • Sex Hungry Butthole Sluts / 1996 / ROB / M • Seymore Butts: Big Boobs In Buttsville / 1996 / FH / M • Shooting Gallery / 1996 / EL / M • Sinboy #4: Bareass Barbecue / 1996 / SC / M • Sodom Bottoms / 1996 / SP / M • Squirters / 1996 / ULI / M • Triple Penetration Debutante Sluts #1 / 1996 / BAC / M • Venom #6 / 1996 / CA / M • Video Virgins #32 / 1996 / NS / M
CORTNEY *see* **Courtney**
CORTNEY CHAMBERS
Latent Image: Cortney Chambers / 1994 / LAT / F
CORVINA *see* **Jenna Wells**
CORY *see* **Star Index I**
CORY BRANDON
Auditions / 1978 / MEA / S • Dialing For Desires / 1988 / 4P / M • Dreams Of Desires / 1995 / ONA / M
CORY CUMMINGS *see* **Star Index I**
CORY MARJON
Debbie Does 'em All #1 / 1985 / CV / M • The Seductress / 1982 / VC / M
CORY MILES
No Reservations / 1995 / MN0 / G
CORY MONROE
Bi Day...Bi Night / 1988 / PV / G • Bi Night / 1989 / PL / G • Bi-Dacious / 1989 / PL / G • Bi-Swingers / 1991 / PL / G • Bi-Ways / 1991 / PL / G • By Day Bi Night / 1989 / LV / G • Dominated Dudes / 1992 / PL / B • Dreams Bi-Night / 1989 / PL / G • Entertainment Bi-Night / 1989 / PL / G • Get Bi Tonight / 1991 / PL / G • Hotel Transylvania #1 / 1990 / LIP / G • The National Transsexual / 1990 / GO / G • Parliament: Hard TV #1 / 1988 / PM / G • Split Decision / 1989 / MET / G • Trans Europe Express / 1989 / VC / G • Trisexual Encounters #03 / 1986 / PL / G • Trisexual Encounters #05 / 1986 / PL / G • Trisexual Encounters #06 / 1987 / PL / G • Uninhibited / 1989 / VC / G
CORY WOLF *(Kamry Wood)*
Large nosed brunette with medium tits; a little pudgy around the waist.
Asspiring Actresses / 1989 / CA / M • Chills / 1989 / LV / M • Love Button / 1989 / VD / M • Party In The Rear / 1989 / LV / M • Power Play (Venus 99) / 1990 / V99 / M • Sweet Temptations / 1989 / V99 / M • Switch Hitters #4: The Grand Slam / 1989 / IN / G • Tamara's Dreams / 1989 / VEX / M • Who Reamed Rosie Rabbit? #1 / 1989 / FAN / M • Young Girls In Tight Jeans / 1989 / VD / M
COSMO TOPPER
Adventures Of The DP Boys: Berlin Butt Babes / 1993 / HW / M • All "A" / 1994 / SFP / C • Beach Bum Amateur's #37 / 1993 / MID / M • Bobby Hollander's Maneaters #04 / 1993 / SFP / M • Bobby Hollander's Maneaters #06 / 1993 / SFP / M • Bubble Butts #18 / 1992 / LBO / M • Butt Bongo Bonanza / 1993 / FC / M • The Cumm Brothers #02: Goin' To A Ho' Down / 1994 / OD / M • Double Penetration Virgins #03 / 1994 / LE / M • Erotic Newcummers Vol 1 #1: Capitol Desires / 1993 / DR / M • Fresh Meat (John Leslie) #1 / 1994 / EA / M • GRG: Forced Anal / 1994 / GRG / M • Hollywood Swingers #08 / 1993 / LBO / M • Pearl Necklace: Amorous Amateurs #35 / 1993 / SEE / M • Pearl Necklace: Thee Bush League #15 / 1993 / SEE / M • Sharon Mitchell's Sex Clinic #01 / 1993 / FC / M • Stiff Competition #2 / 1994 / CA /

M • Straight A Students / 1993 / MET / M • Taboo #12 / 1994 / MET / M • Taboo #13 / 1994 / IN / M • Totally Tasteless Video #02 / 1994 / TTV / M • Video Virgins #02 / 1992 / NS / M
COTTON MATHER
Chickie / 1975 / CA / M
COUGAR *see* **Marie Mason**
COUNTESS ANGELIQUE
Slave Mansion / 1980 / BIZ / B • The Story of Bobby / cr80 / BIZ / B • Transvestite Castle / 1980 / BIZ / G
COURNETY *see* **Courtney**
COURTENEY *see* **Courtney**
COURTNEY *(Courtney, Cortney, Natasha (Courtney), Truly Scrumptious, Cournety, Natasia (Courtney), Nasty Natasia, Natasha Zimmerman, Eden (Courtney))*
Not too pretty tiny blonde with small tits. In about 1992 she had her tits enhanced to rock-solid cantaloupe size. Born Feb 5, 1958 in Los Angeles CA.
4 Bi 4 / 1994 / BIN / G • 69th Street / 1993 / VIM / M • The A Chronicles / 1992 / CC / M • A Is For Anal / 1993 / LV / M • Adults Only / 1995 / BOT / M • Adventures Of The DP Boys: Back In The Bush / 1993 / HW / M • AHV #16: Let It Loose / 1992 / EVN / M • AHV #18: Wild Time / 1992 / EVN / M • Amateur Hours #65 / 1994 / AFI / M • Amateur Lesbians #15: Courtney / 1991 / GO / F • Amateur Lesbians #16: Lorraine / 1991 / GO / F • Amateur Lesbians #18: Jamie / 1992 / GO / F • Amateur Lesbians #20: Flame / 1992 / GO / F • Amateur Lesbians #22: Cassidy / 1992 / GO / F • Amateur Lesbians #23: Sherri / 1992 / GO / F • Amateur Lesbians #37: Gretta / 1993 / GO / F • Amateurs Exposed #01 / 1993 / CV / M • Ambitious Blondes / 1992 / VIM / M • America's Raunchiest Home Videos #04: Recipes for Hot Sex / 1991 / ZA / M • America's Raunchiest Home Videos #62: / 1993 / ZA / M • American Connection Video Magazine #01 / 1992 / ZA / M • American Connection Video Magazine #02 / 1992 / ZA / M • American Swinger Video Magazine #04 / 1993 / ZA / M • Anal Adventures #1: Anal Executive / 1991 / VC / M • Anal Adventures #2: Bodacious Buns / 1991 / VC / M • Anal Analysis (Heatwave) / 1992 / HW / M • Anal Angel / 1991 / ZA / M • Anal Distraction / 1993 / PEP / M • Anal Encounters #6 / 1992 / VC / M • Anal Intruder #08: Rich Girls Gone Bad / 1993 / CC / M • Anal Leap / 1991 / ZA / M • Anal Ski Vacation / 1993 / ANA / M • Anal Takeover / 1993 / PEP / M • Anal Thunder #1 / 1993 / ROB / M • Anal Vision #06 / 1992 / LBO / M • Anal With An Oriental Slant / 1993 / ROB / M • Anals, Inc / 1995 / ZA / M • The Anus Family / 1991 / CC / M • Baccarat #1 / 1991 / FH / M • Baccarat #2 / 1991 / FH / M • Backdoor Brides #4 / 1993 / PV / M • Backstage Pass / 1992 / VEX / M • The Backway Inn #4 / 1993 / FD / M • The Bashful Blonde From Beautiful Bendover / 1993 / PEP / M • Behind The Backdoor #4 / 1990 / EVN / M • Behind The Backdoor #6 / 1993 / EVN / M • Behind The Scenes: The Making Of The Wil & Ed Movies / 1992 / MID / M • Beyond Passion / 1993 / IF / M • The Bi-Linguist / 1993 / BIL / G • Bi The Rear Window / 1994 / BIL / G • Bi This! / 1995 / BIL / G • Bi-Sex Pleasures / 1993 /

PL / G • Biff Malibu's Totally Nasty Home Videos #01 / 1992 / ANA / M • Biff Malibu's Totally Nasty Home Videos #33 / 1993 / ANA / M • Biff Malibu's Totally Nasty Home Videos #37 / 1993 / ANA / M • Bitter She-Males / 1992 / BIZ / G • Bizarre Mistress Series: Mistress Jacqueline / 1992 / BIZ / C • Blazing Butts / 1991 / LV / M • Bobby Hollander's Sweet Cheeks #114 / 1994 / QUA / M • Bone Alone / 1993 / MID / M • Bone Therapy / 1992 / LV / M • Both Ends Burning / 1993 / HW / M • Breast Worx #32 / 1992 / LBO / M • Breastman Does The Himalayas / 1993 / EVN / M • Breastman Does The Twin Towers / 1993 / EVN / M • Breathless / 1991 / WV / M • Bubble Butts #15 / 1992 / LBO / M • Bubble Butts #24 / 1993 / LBO / M • Bushwoman: She Takes Two / 1996 / RAS / M • Bustline / 1993 / LE / M • The Butt Boss / 1993 / VD / M • Butt Love / 1995 / AB / M • Butthead Dreams / 1994 / FH / M • The Buttnicks #2 / 1991 / HIO / M • Cannes Heat / 1992 / FD / M • Captain Bob's Pussy Patrol / 1993 / FCP / M • Caught From Behind #15 / 1991 / HO / M • Cheeks #7: Mirror Image / 1994 / CC / M • Cluster Fuck #06 / 1994 / MAX / M • Covergirl / 1996 / LE / M • Cream Pies #01 / 1993 / ZA / M • The Crimson Kiss / 1993 / WV / M • Cyber-Sex Love Junkies / 1996 / BBF / M • Cyberanal / 1995 / VC / M • Decadent / 1991 / WV / M • Deep Butt / 1994 / MID / C • Delivered For Discipline / 1995 / BON / B • Derrier / 1991 / CC / M • Dirty Blue Movies #02 / 1992 / JTV / M • Dirty Dating Service #01 / 1993 / WP / M • Dirty Laundry / 1994 / HOH / M • Diver Down / 1992 / CC / M • Double D Amateurs #06 / 1993 / JMP / M • End Of Innocence / 1994 / WIV / M • Enema Bondage / 1992 / BIZ / B • Enema Obedience #1 / 1992 / BIZ / B • Erectnophobia #1 / 1991 / MID / M • European Debutantes #01 / 1995 / IP / M • The Fluffer #2 / 1993 / FD / M • For The Hell Of It / 1992 / BS / B • For Your Mouth Only / 1995 / GO / M • Forever Payne / 1994 / BS / B • Fox Fever / 1991 / LV / M • French Open / 1993 / PV / M • French Open Part Deux / 1993 / MFT / M • Gang-bang Girl #00 / 1953 / ANA / M • The Girls From Hootersville #08 / 1994 / SFP / M • Girls Will Be Boys #4 / 1991 / PL / F • The Go-Go Girls / 1994 / EVN / M • Gold LeMay / 1991 / VIM / M • Gone Wild / 1993 / LV / M • The Hard Line / 1993 / PEP / M • Harness Hannah At The Strap-On Ho Down / 1994 / WIV / F • Heaven Scent (Las Vegas) / 1993 / LV / M • Hershe Highway #4 / 1991 / HO / M • Hillary Vamp's Private Collection #01 / 1991 / HVD / M • Hooray For Hineywood / 1991 / MID / M • Hootermania / 1994 / VC / M • Hot Spot / 1991 / CDI / M • Hot Tight Asses #13 / 1995 / TCK / M • Hot To Trot / 1994 / IF / M • The Howard Sperm Show / 1993 / LV / M • Hush...My Mother Might Hear Us / 1993 / FL / M • If You Can't Lick 'em...Join 'em / 1996 / BAC / F • Incocknito / 1993 / VIM / M • Indecent / 1993 / XCI / M • Indecent Proposition / 1993 / LV / M • It's Only Love / 1992 / VEX / M • Just Bondage / 1993 / CS / B • Kinky Debutante Interviews #04 / 1994 / IP / M • Kittens #4: Bodybuilding Bitches / 1993 / CC / F • Lady M's Anything Nasty #01: Pink Pussy Party / 1996 / AVI / F • Late On Arrival / 1994 / CS / B • Lesbian Appliance Guide: Tools, Toys

& Tits #2 / 1994 / GO / F • Lesbian Lingerie Fantasy #7 / 1991 / ESP / F • Lesbian Workout #1 / 1994 / GO / F • Lessons 'n' Love / 1994 / LBO / M • Letters From The Heart / 1991 / AWV / M • Long Dan Silver / 1992 / IF / M • Lusty Lawyers / 1995 / PRK / M • Major Slut / 1993 / LV / M • Masked Ball / 1992 / IF / M • Midnight Caller / 1992 / MID / M • Mike Hott: #208 Cunt of the Month: Courtney / 1995 / MHV / M • Mike Hott: #272 Jack Off On My Cunt #01 / 1994 / MHV / M • Mike Hott: #279 Fuck The Boss #4 / 1995 / MHV / M • Mistress Jacqueline's Slave School / 1992 / BIZ / B • Mona Lisa / 1992 / LV / M • Moore, Moore, Moore: An Anal Explosion / 1992 / IN / M • MR. Peepers Amateur Home Videos #30: Bearded Clam On the Hal / 1991 / LBO / M • Mr. Peepers Amateur Home Videos #33: Great Balls A' Fire / 1991 / LBO / M • Mr. Peepers Amateur Home Videos #38: Bringing Up the Rear / 1991 / LBO / M • Mr. Peepers Amateur Home Videos #56: Hindsight Is Brownish / 1992 / LBO / M • Mr. Peepers Amateur Home Videos #62: Private Pussy Party / 1992 / LBO / M • Mr. Peepers Amateur Home Videos #64: Proposition 69 / 1992 / LBO / M • Mr. Peepers Amateur Home Videos #94: Calendar Cleavage / 1994 / LBO / M • Mr. Peepers Nastlest #4 / 1995 / LBO / C • N.Y.D.P. / 1994 / PEP / M • Neighborhood Watch #09: Dial-A-Slut / 1991 / LBO / M • Neighborhood Watch #11 / 1991 / LBO / M • New Hardcore Beginners #20 / 1996 / LEI / C • New Pussy Hunt #25 / 1996 / LEI / C • Nothing Personal / 1993 / CA / M • Objective: D.P. / 1993 / PEP / M • Odyssey Triple Play #67: Girls Who Love It Up The Ass / 1994 / OD / M • Ona Z's Star Search #01 / 1993 / GLI / M • Ona Z's Star Search #03 / 1993 / GLI / M • One Night Love Affair / 1991 / IF / M • Open Lips / 1994 / WV / M • Oral Madness #1 / 1991 / OD / M • Pearl Necklace: Amorous Amateurs #04 / 1992 / SEE / M • Pearl Necklace: Amorous Amateurs #05 / 1992 / SEE / M • Pearl Necklace: Thee Bush League: The Best Of Oral #01 / 1992 / SEE / C • Pearl Necklace: Thee Bush League: The Best Of Oral #01 / 1994 / SEE / C • Pearl Necklace: Thee Bush League #03 / 1992 / SEE / M • Peekers / 1993 / MID / M • Penthouse: Great Pet Hunt #1 / 1992 / PET / F • Perverted #3: The Parents / 1995 / ZA / M • Precious Cargo / 1993 / VIM / M • Prime Choice #7 / 1996 / RAS / M • Purely Sexual / 1991 / HO / M • Pussyman #07 / 1992 / CC / M • A Reason To Die / 1994 / PEP / M • Reel Sex #05: Lesbian Toy Part / 1994 / SPP / F • Reflections Of Rio / 1993 / WP / M • Regarding Hiney / 1991 / CC / M • Remembering Times Gone Bi / 1995 / AWV / G • Rites Of Passage: Transformation Of A Student To A Slave / 1992 / BIZ / B • Riviera Heat / 1993 / FD / M • Roman Goddess / 1992 / HW / M • Rump Humpers #07 / 1992 / GLI / M • Rump Humpers #14 / 1993 / GLI / M • Sex Drive / 1993 / VEX / M • Sex In A Singles Bar / 1992 / VC / M • Sex Scientist / 1992 / FD / M • Sexlock / 1992 / XPI / M • Sharon Mitchell's Sex Clinic #01 / 1993 / FC / M • She's The Boss / 1992 / VIM / M • She-Male Voyager / 1994 / HEA / G • Shooting Star / 1993 / XCI / M • Silk 'n' Spanking / 1994 / VER / M • Single Girl Masturbation

#7 / 1991 / ESP / F • Snatch Masters #04 / 1995 / LEI / M • Soap Me Up! / 1993 / FD / M • Special Reserve / 1994 / VC / M • Spinners #2 (Wicked) / 1996 / WP / M • Star Struck / 1991 / AFV / M • A Strict Affair...Lessons in Discipline and Obedience / 1992 / BIZ / B • Student Fetish Videos: Tickling #09 / 1994 / SFV / B • Suburban Nymphos / 1994 / ATL / M • Super Hornio Brothers #1 / 1993 / MID / M • Super Hornio Brothers #2 / 1993 / MID / M • SVE: Cheap Thrills #4: Woman To Woman / 1992 / SVE / F • SVE: Three On A Couch / 1992 / SVE / M • Sweet Dreams / 1991 / VC / M • Tail Taggers #101 / 1993 / WV / M • Tail Taggers #102 / 1993 / WV / M • Tail Taggers #108: Vibro Love / 1993 / WV / M • Titty Bar #1 / 1993 / LE / M • To Bi For / 1996 / PL / G • Too Fast For Love / 1992 / IF / M • Totally Ona: The Best Of Ona Zee / 1996 / ONA / C • Transparent Desires / 1991 / LV / M • Trash In The Can / 1993 / LV / M • Tunnel Of Lust / 1993 / LV / M • Twice As Hard / 1992 / IF / M • Twin Cheeks #3 / 1991 / CIN / M • Twin Cheeks #4 / 1991 / CIN / M • Venus: Wings Of Seduction / 1991 / CDI / M • Voyeur's Fantasies / 1996 / C69 / M • Wendy Whoppers: Razorwoman / 1993 / PEP / M • Wet Daydreams / 1996 / XCI / M • Whore There's Sparxx, There's Fire / 1991 / LV / M • Wil And Ed's Excellent Boner Christmas / 1991 / MID / M • Wild Fire / 1990 / WV / C • Will And Ed's Bogus Gang Bang / 1992 / MID / M • Will And Ed: The Curse Of Poona / 1994 / MID / C • Women Who Love Men, Men Who Love Women / 1993 / FD / C • You Said A Mouthful / 1992 / IF / M • [Three On A Couch / 1992 / ... / M

COURTNEY (1992) *see Star Index I*

COURTNEY (1995)
Raw Sex #02 / 1995 / ERW / M

COURTNEY (OTHER)
GRG: Born To Do Porn / 1996 / GRG / M • GRG: Courtney's Cunt Is Hot / 1996 / GRG / M

COURTNEY BISHOP
Belly Of The Beast / 1993 / ZFX / B • Dirty Hoode Dana Uhcap / 1555 / ZFX / B • Futureshock / 1993 / ZFX / B • Highway To Hell / 1993 / ZFX / B • Night Prowler #1 / 1993 / ZFX / B

COURTNEY CAMERON
Executions On Butt Row / 1996 / EA / M • Philmore Butts Spring Break / 1996 / SUF / M

COURTNEY COUNTEE III
Resurrection Of Eve / 1973 / MIT / M

COURTNEY FOXX
Strap-On Sally #09: / 1996 / PL / F

COURTNEY HILL *see* **Tammy Monroe**

COURTNEY LOVE
[The People vs. Larry Flynt / 1996 / C3S / S

COUSIN PHIL *see* **Tony Martino**

COUSIN THELMA
Fat Fannies #13 / 1995 / BTO / F

COWBOY
Diamonds / 1996 / HDE / M • Penetration (Anabolic) #2 / 1995 / ANA / M

COWBOY BOB
Giggles / 1992 / PRE / B • Laugh Factory / 1995 / PRE / C

COWBOY JOE *see* **Joe Verducci**

COY DECKER
Please Don't Tell / 1995 / CEN / G

COZY EDMUNDSON
Resurrection Of Eve / 1973 / MIT / M

CRAIG ADAMS *see* **Cody Adams**

CRAIG BAUMGARTEN
Sometime Sweet Susan / 1974 / ALP / M

CRAIG CENTURIAN
Shape Up For Sensational Sex / 1985 / SE / M

CRAIG EDWARDS *see* **Craig Roberts**

CRAIG ESPOSITO
Midnight Desires / 1976 / VXP / M • Waterpower / 1975 / VHL / M

CRAIG ROBERTS *(Craig Edwards, Gerry Randolph, Greg Ruffner, Steve Dante, Gary Sikes)*
Gerry Randolph is ex **Blowoff**. Steve Dante comes from **Pretty As You Feel** but this could be wrong as the camerawork isn't good enough to see clearly. This is also Neal Devero or Bill Rather but not possible to tell which—see **Lusty Ladies #04**.
Amber Aroused / 1985 / CA / M • The Animal In Me / 1985 / IN / M • The Best Of Blondes / 1986 / VCR / C • Black Throat / 1985 / VC / M • Blowoff / 1985 / CA / M • Blue Dream Lover / 1985 / TAR / M • Bodacious Ta Ta's / 1984 / CA / M • Carrie...Sex On Wheels / 1985 / AA / M • Centerfold Celebrities #4 / 1983 / VC / M • Charming Cheapies #6: Red Tide / 1985 / 4P / M • Coffee & Cream / 1984 / AVC / M • Come As You Are / 1985 / SUV / M • Coming Together / 1984 / CA / M • Diamond Collection #68 / 1985 / CDI / M • Diamond Collection #79 / 1986 / CDI / M • Dirty Letters / 1984 / VD / M • Double Messages / 1987 / MOV / M • Dream Lovers / 1980 / MET / G • Educating Mandy / 1985 / CDI / M • The Erotic World Of Cody Nicole / 1984 / VCR / C • Flesh In Ecstasy #04: Jeanna Fine / 1987 / GO / C • Future Voyeur / 1985 / SUV / M • Gang Bangs #1 / 1985 / VCR / M • Getting Lucky / 1983 / CA / M • GVC: Anything Goes #119 / 1983 / GO / M • GVC: Broadcast Babes #138 / 1985 / GO / M • GVC: Dreams Of Pleasure #120 / 1983 / GO / M • GVC: Suburban Lust #128 / 1983 / GO / M • GVC: Valley Vixens #124 / 1983 / GO / M • Head & Tails / 1988 / VD / M • Hindsight / 1985 / IN / M • Holly Does Hollywood #1 / 1985 / VEX / M • Hollywood Harlots / 1986 / VEX / C • Hollywood Heartbreakers / 1985 / VEX / M • Insatiable #2 / 1984 / CA / M • Just Another Pretty Face / 1985 / AVC / M • Letters Of Love / 1985 / CA / M • The Lover Girls / 1985 / VEX / M • Lust At The Top / 1985 / CDI / M • Lusty Ladies #03 / 1983 / SVE / M • Lusty Ladies #04 / 1983 / 4P / M • Lusty Ladies #11 / 1984 / 4P / M • Making It Big / 1984 / CV / M • Miss Passion / 1984 / VD / M • Naughty Nurses / 1986 / VEX / M • Only The Best Of Anal / 1992 / MET / C • Parliament: Shauna Grant #1 / 1988 / PM / C • Personal Touch #3 / 1983 / AR / M • Photoflesh / 1984 / HO / M • Pleasure Productions #01 / 1984 / VCR / M • Pleasure Productions #04 / 1984 / VCR / M • Pleasure Productions #06 / 1984 / VCR / M • Pretty As You Feel / 1984 / PV / M • Savage Fury #1 / 1985 / VEX / M • Scandal In The Mansion / 1985 / CDI / M • Sensuous Tales / 1984 / VCR / C • Sex Star / 1983 / CA / M • Sex Toys / 1985 / CA / M • She-Male Encounters #03: Juicy Jennifer / 1981 / MET / G • She-Male Encounters #10: She-Male Vacation / 1986 / MET

/ G • The Shoe Store / 1985 / BIZ / B • Silk Elegance / 1991 / VIM / M • Six Faces Of Samantha / 1984 / AA / M • Slave Exchange / 1985 / BIZ / B • Slumber Party / 1984 / HO / M • Snack Time / 1983 / HO / M • Springtime In The Rockies / 1984 / CIN / M • Squalor Motel / 1985 / SE / M • Stiff Competition #1 / 1984 / CA / M • Stud Hunters / 1984 / CA / M • Sulka's Daughter / 1984 / MET / G • Sulka's Wedding / 1983 / MET / G • Suze's Centerfolds #8 / 1984 / CA / M • Suze's Centerfolds #9 / 1985 / CA / M • Taboo #02 / 1982 / IN / M • Taboo #03 / 1983 / IN / M • Taboo #04 / 1985 / IN / M • Tarot Temptress / 1985 / AA / M • Teasers / 1984 / HO / M • Too Good To Be True / 1984 / MAP / M • Too Naughty To Say No / 1984 / CA / M • Up Up And Away / 1984 / CA / M • The Wacky World Of X-Rated Bloopers / 1989 / GO / M • Wet Sex / 1984 / CA / M • Where The Girls Are / 1984 / VEX / M • Where The Sun Never Shines / 1990 / IN / C • Wicked Whispers / 1985 / VD / M • With Love From Susan / 1988 / HO / C • X-Rated Bloopers #1 / 1984 / AR / M • You're The Boss / 1985 / VD / M

CRAIG TECHNIQUES
New Girls In Town #7 / 1994 / CC / M

CRAIG WILLIAMS *see* **Star Index I**

CRAYOLA BLUE *(Blu (Crayola), Krayola Blue)*
Blonde with a Barbra Streisand face, large tattoo on left bicep, pussy rings, belly button post, medium/large tits, thick body. 21 years old in 1996 and de-virginized at 14.
Anal Academy / 1996 / ZA / M • Anal Sex Freaks / 1996 / ZA / M • Butthole Bunnies / 1996 / ROB / F • By Myself / 1996 / PL / F • The Complete & Total Anal Workout #2 / 1996 / ZA / M • Deep Dippin' Anal Babes / 1996 / ROB / F • In The Line Of Desire / 1996 / MID / M • Lesbian Debutante #03 / 1996 / IP / F • Macin' #1 / 1996 / SMP / M • Muff Divers #1 / 1996 / TV / F • Night Vision / 1996 / WP / M • No Fear / 1996 / IN / F • Over Exposed / 1996 / ULP / M • Perverted Stories #09 / 1996 / JMP / M • Playtime / 1996 / VI / M • Puritan Video Magazine #03 / 1996 / LE / M • Samantha & Company / 1996 / PL / M • The Scam / 1996 / LV / M • Sexperiment / 1996 / ULP / M • Sinboy #2: Yo' Ass Is Mine / 1996 / SC / M • Sinboy #4: Bareass Barbecue / 1996 / SC / M • Six Degrees Of Penetration / 1996 / PP / M • Skeezers / 1996 / LV / M • Solo Adventures / 1996 / AB / F • Strong Sensations / 1996 / PL / M • Totally Depraved / 1996 / SC / M • Venom #5 / 1996 / VD / M • Video Virgins #27 / 1996 / NS / M • Young & Natural #19 / 1996 / TV / F • Young & Natural #21 / 1996 / TV / F

CRAZY ACE *see* **Star Index I**

CRAZY KARLOTTA
The Trainers / cr83 / BIZ / B

CREAM
The Black Butt Sisters Do Houston / 1996 / MID / M

CREAM (CHRISTIE) *see* **Christy (Cream)**

CREAM COCOA
Buttman's Big Tit Adventure #3 / 1995 / EA / M

CREIG RUSSELL
Her Total Response / 1975 / SVE / M

CRICKET
Spotlight: Poke Her / 1994 / SPV / M • Valentine's Challenge / 1992 / LIP / F •

Valentine's Wonderland / 1992 / LIP / F

CRIKILA
Star Crossed / 1995 / VC / M

CRIMSON *see* **Jacqueline**

CRIS BREWER
Lickity Split / 1974 / COM / M

CRIS CASSIDY *(Suzette Holland, Montana (C. Cassidy), Montana Brent, Monti Stevens, Chris Cassidy, Martina Holland, Suzanne Myers, Suzanne Wright, Montana Station)*
Ugly too-tall hard blonde with pudgy waist, enhanced large tits, lousy skin and usually, hairy armpits. First film was **Sex World**.
All Day Suckers / cr77 / BOC / M • Baby Love & Beau / 1979 / TVX / M • Backdoor Girls / 1983 / VCR / C • Behind The Scenes Of An Adult Movie / 1983 / CV / M • Blonde At Both Ends / 1993 / TGA / M • Blondes Have More Fun / 1980 / SE / M • Blue Heat / 1975 / IVP / M • Blue Vanities #017 (New) / 1988 / FFL / M • Blue Vanities #018 (New) / 1988 / FFL / M • Blue Vanities #048 / 1988 / FFL / M • Blue Vanities #065 / 1988 / FFL / M • Blue Vanities #071 / 1988 / FFL / M • Blue Vanities #091 / 1988 / FFL / M • Blue Vanities #120 / 1990 / FFL / M • Blue Vanities #585 / 1996 / FFL / M • Caballero Preview Tape #2 / 1983 / CA / C • Candy Stripers #1 / 1978 / ALP / M • The China Cat / 1978 / CA / M • Classic Swedish Erotica #01 / 1986 / CA / C • Classic Swedish Erotica #12 / 1986 / CA / C • Classic Swedish Erotica #28 / 1987 / CA / C • Cum Shot Revue #1 / 1985 / HO / C • Cum Shot Revue #2 / 1985 / HO / C • Diamond Collection #02 / 1979 / CDI / M • Diamond Collection #06 / 1979 / CDI / M • Double Pleasure / 1985 / VCR / M • The Erotic Adventures Of Candy / 1978 / VCX / M • Erotic Fantasies #1 / 1983 / CV / C • Erotic Fantasies #5 / 1983 / CV / C • Erotic In Nature / 1985 / TIG / F • Exhausted / 1981 / CA / C • Expectations / 1977 / SE / M • Fantasm / 1976 / VS / S • Female Athletes / 1977 / VXP / M • For Services Rendered / 1984 / CA / M • Games Women Play #1 / 1980 / CA / M • Garage Girls / 1981 / CV / M • Hay Fever / 1988 / TIG / F • Honkytonk Nights / 1978 / TWV / S • Hot Pink / 1983 / VC / C • Hot Rackets / 1979 / CV / M • Hot Teenage Assets / 1978 / WWV / M • In Love / 1983 / VC / M • Le Sex De Femme #3 / 1989 / AFI / C • Legends Of Porn #1 / 1987 / CV / C • Lipps & Mccain / 1978 / VC / M • The Live Show / 1979 / SVE / M • Loving Friends / 1975 / AXV / M • The Milky Way / 1981 / ... / M • National Pornographic #1: Lesbians / 1987 / 4P / C • National Pornographic #5: / 1987 / 4P / C • Once Upon A Time/Cave Woman / 1978 / VI / M • The Perfect Weekend / 1984 / AVC / M • Pink Punk / 19?? / ECO / C • Rolls Royce #04 / 1980 / ... / C • Rolls Royce #05 / 1980 / ... / C • Rolls Royce #06 / 1980 / ... / C • Sadie / 1980 / EVI / M • Screwples / 1979 / CA / M • Seka's Fantasies / 1981 / CA / M • Sensual Encounters Of Every Kind / 1978 / SE / M • Sex Prophet / 1973 / ALP / M • Sex World / 1978 / SE / M • Showgirl #01: Leslie Bovee's Fantasies / 1981 / VCR / M • Showgirl #13: Chris Cassidy's Fantasies / 1983 / SVE / M • Skintight / 1981 / CA / M • Soft Places / 1978 / CXV / M • Splashing / 1986 / VCS / C • Star Of The Orient / 1978 / VIP / M •

Stormy / 1980 / CV / M • Swedish Erotica #11 / 1980 / CA / M • Swedish Erotica #12 / 1980 / CA / M • Swedish Erotica #26 / 1980 / CA / M • Swedish Erotica #28 / 1980 / CA / M • Sweet Sister / 1974 / SIL / M • Talk Dirty To Me #01 / 1980 / CA / M • Talk Dirty To Me #05 / 1987 / DR / M • Treasure Box / 1981 / VC / M • True Legends Of Adult Cinema: The Cult Superstars / 1993 / VC / C • Valerie / 1975 / VCX / M • Wet Shots (Vcr) / 1983 / VCR / C • Where There's Smoke / 1986 / TIG / F • Wicked Sensations #1 / 1981 / CA / M • Young Doctors In Lust / 1979 / NSV / M • Yuppies In Heat / 1988 / CHA / C • [Pleasure Isle / cr75 / DIV / S

CRIS COLLINS *see* **Meo**

CRIS RIVERS

D.P. Party Tonite / 1995 / JMP / M • Zena's Gang Bang / 1995 / HO / M

CRISSI

Creme De Femme #4 / 1981 / AVC / C

CRISSI STEVENS

Blue Vanities #537 / 1993 / FFL / M • Blue Vanities #560 / 1994 / FFL / M • Bottoms Up #05 / 1986 / AVC / C • Creme De Femme #2 / 1981 / AVC / C • Free And Foxy / 1986 / VCX / C • Limited Edition #21 / 1981 / AVC / M • Limited Edition #22 / 1981 / AVC / M • Love Goddesses / 1981 / VC / M

CRISSY

Blue Vanities #539 / 1993 / FFL / M • Blue Vanities #573 / 1996 / FFL / M

CRISSY (ANN) *see* **Chrissy Ann**

CRISSY CANFIELD

Boobwatch #1 / 1996 / SC / M

CRISSY DALTON

Little Darlings / 1981 / VEP / M

CRISSY LEE *see* **Star Index I**

CRISTA

Black Playhouse / 1995 / HBE / M • Dirty Blue Movies #02 / 1992 / JTV / M • Joe Elliot's College Girls #35 / 1994 / JOE / M

CRISTA LAKE *see* **Christi Lake**

CRISTANN KING

The Blowjob Adventures Of Doctor Fellatio / 1997 / EL / M

CRISTARA BARRINGTON *see* **Kristara Barrington**

CRISTEL *see Star Index I*

CRISTIANN

Filthy First Timers #6 / 1997 / EL / M

CRISTINA (KING) *see* **Krystina King**

CRISTINA COLECCHIA *see* **Manya**

CRISTINA GANZ

Paprika / 1995 / XC / M

CRISTINA ROSS

Midnight Obsession / 1995 / XC / M

CRISTINA VALENTI

Sex Penitentiary / 1996 / XC / M

CROW

Domina #4 / 1996 / LBO / G

CROWN PRINCESS

Amateur Black: Honeys / 1995 / SUF / M • Amateur Black: Starlets / 1995 / SUF / M • Anal Virgins #01 / 1996 / NS / M • Bad Attitude #2 / 1995 / LV / M • Black Bush Bashers / 1996 / LOK / M • The Black Butt Sisters Do Boston / 1995 / MID / M • The Black Butt Sisters Do Chicago / 1995 / MID / M • The Black Butt Sisters Do New York / 1995 / MID / M • The Black Butt Sisters Do Seattle / 1995 / MID / M • Black Fantasies #07 / 1995 / HW / M • Black Fantasies #12 / 1996 / HW / M • Black Hollywood Amateurs

#07 / 1995 / MID / M • Black Hollywood Amateurs #08 / 1995 / MID / M • Black Hollywood Amateurs #15 / 1995 / MID / M • Black Hollywood Amateurs #18 / 1995 / MID / M • Black Hollywood Amateurs #19 / 1995 / MID / M • Black Hollywood Amateurs #22 / 1996 / MID / M • Black Talez N Da Hood / 1996 / APP / M • Buffy's Malibu Adventure / 1995 / CDI / M • Butt-Nanza / 1995 / WV / M • Dirty Dirty Debutantes #3 / 1996 / 4P / M • Ebony Erotica #34: Mellow Moprene / 1995 / GO / M • Girlz Towne #05 / 1995 / FC / F • Liar's Poke Her / 1995 / NIW / M • Orgy Camera #1 / 1995 / EVN / M • Rump Man: Forever / 1995 / HW / M • Shake Your Booty / 1996 / EVN / M • Sittin' On Da Krome / 1995 / HW / M • Tails From The Hood / 1995 / FH / M • Video Virgins #24 / 1996 / NS / M • You Go Girl! (Video Team) / 1995 / VT / M

CROZE CURTIS

Limited Edition #12 / 1980 / AVC / M

CRUELLA DEVILLE

Hardcore: The Films Of Richard Kern #1 / 1991 / FTV / M

CRYSTAL

A&B AB#096: The Seduction / 1990 / A&B / M • Amateur Hours #01 / 1989 / AFI / M • Amateur Hours #05 / 1990 / AFI / M • Amateur Hours #09 / 1990 / AFI / M • Amateur Hours #21 / 1990 / AFI / M • American Connection Video Magazine #03 / 1993 / ZA / M • AVP #2002: Meange A Trois #1 / 1990 / AVP / M • AVP #7022: 1 + 2 = 3 Times The Fun / 1991 / AVP / M • AVP #7025: Cum Specialist / 1991 / AVP / M • Black Casting Couch #1 / 1993 / WP / M • Blue Vanities #168 (New) / 1996 / FFL / M • Blue Vanities #168 (Old) / 1991 / FFL / M • Blue Vanities #546 / 1994 / FFL / M • The Good The Fat & The Ugly / 1995 / OD / M • M Series #19 / 1994 / LBO / M • Mother Nature's Bulging Bellies / 1995 / LIP / F • Mr. Peepers Amateur Home Videos #55: Anal Antics / 1992 / LBO / M • Mr. Peepers Amateur Home Videos #84: She Put the Bra in Braz / 1994 / LBO / M • Mr. Peepers Nastiest #1 / 1995 / LBO / C • New Faces, Hot Bodies #04 / 1992 / STP / M • New Faces, Hot Bodies #07 / 1992 / STP / M • New Faces, Hot Bodies #09 / 1993 / STP / M • New Faces, Hot Bodies #17 / 1995 / STP / M • New Faces, Hot Bodies #21 / 1996 / STP / C • Reel Life Video #37: Heavy Honies / 1995 / RLF / M • She-Male Friends #1 / cr94 / TTV / G • Slut Safari #1 / 1994 / FC / M • Southern Belles #1 / 1994 / HOV / M

CRYSTAL (SAM. HALL) *see* **Samantha Hall**

CRYSTAL BLUE *see* **Crystal Breeze**

CRYSTAL BREEZE *(Breezy, Crystal Blue, Lisa Marie (Crys B), Debbie Cole (Crys B), Lisa Breeze, Lisa Marie Stagno)*

Brunette, curvaceous body, medium tits, passable face. SO of Jay Serling who was very jealous. Broke up in late eighties and returned in 1996 doing g/g scenes only. Rumor has it that she was only 16 when she started in porn and that she went to the same LA high school as Christy Canyon.

Adam & Eve's House Party #1 / 1995 / VC / M • Adult 45 #01 / 1985 / DR / C • Amber Aroused / 1985 / CA / M • Anal Anarchy / 1995 / VC / M • Anal Princess #2 / 1996 / VC / M • Ashley Renee In Jeopardy / 1991 / HOM / B • Avenged / 1986 / CS / B •

Babes Behind Bars / 1996 / CNP / F • Bad Girls #3 / 1984 / COL / M • Bare Elegance / 1984 / MAP / M • Best Of Hot Shorts #01 / 1987 / VCR / C • Best Of Talk Dirty To Me #02 / 1991 / DR / C • Biography: Kaitlyn Ashley / 1996 / SC / C • Bloopers #2 / 1991 / GO / C • Body Shop / 1984 / VCX / M • Born Bad / 1996 / WAV / M • Breezy / 1985 / VCR / M • Camp Beaverlake #1 / 1984 / AR / M • Car Wash Angels / 1995 / VC / M • Casino Of Lust / 1984 / AT / M • Crystal Blue / 1987 / VD / M • Cum Shot Revue #2 / 1985 / HO / C • Cummin' Alive / 1984 / VC / M • Daisy Chain / 1984 / IN / M • Dick & Jane Go To A Bachelor Party (#17) / 1996 / AVI / M • Dirty 30's Cinema: Crystal Breeze / 1986 / PV / C • Dirty Bob's #27: Laid Back In L.A.! / 1996 / FLP / S • Endless Passion / 1987 / LIM / C • Every Man's Fantasy / 1985 / IN / M • Ex-Connection / 1986 / SEV / M • Extra Sensual Pleasure / 1983 / PAC / M • Flaming Tongues #1 / 1984 / MET / F • Flesh In Ecstasy #05: Rachel Ashley / 1987 / GO / C • Flesh In Ecstasy #07: Brittany Stryker / 1987 / GO / C • Fresh Meat (John Leslie) #2 / 1995 / EA / M • Ginger's Hawaiian Scrapbook / 1988 / GO / C • Ginger: The Movie / 1988 / PV / C • Girls Just Want To...Have Fun / 1984 / SE / M • Girls! Girls! Girls! #1 / 1986 / VCS / C • Golden Girls, The Movie / 1984 / SE / M • Head Shots / 1995 / VI / M • Head Waitress / 1984 / VC / M • Headhunters / 1984 / VC / M • The Heist / 1996 / WAV / M • High Price Spread / 1986 / PV / C • Hot Flashes / 1984 / VC / M • Hot Flesh, Cold Chains / 1992 / HOM / B • Hot Girls In Love / 1985 / VXP / M • Hot Pink / 1985 / VCR / F • The Idol / 1985 / WV / M • Inside China Lee / 1984 / VC / M • Joys Of Erotica #109 / 1984 / VCR / C • Joys Of Erotica #114 / 1984 / VCR / C • Kinky Business #1 / 1984 / DR / M • Lair Of The Bondage Bandits / 1991 / HOM / B • Legend #6: / 1996 / LE / M • Liquid Dreams / 1992 / AE / S • Love Champions / 1987 / VC / M • The Loves Of Lolita / 1984 / VC / M • Lust For Freedom / 1987 / AIP / S • Lust In The Fast Lane / [...] / M • The Many Shades Of Amber / 1986 / LIM / M • Miss Passion / 1984 / VD / M • Monkey Business / 1987 / SEV / M • Mouthful Of Love / 1984 / VC / M • Naughty Angels / 1984 / VC / M • Naughty Nanette / 1984 / VC / M • No Man's Land #13 / 1996 / VT / F • Open Up Tracy / 1984 / VD / M • Oral Majority #03 / 1986 / WV / C • Panty Raid / 1984 / GO / M • Parliament: Anal Babes #1 / 1989 / PM / F • Parliament: Bottoms #1 / 1987 / PM / F • Parliament: Dildo Babes #1 / 1986 / PM / F • Parliament: Finger Friggin' #1 / 1986 / PM / F • Parliament: Finger Friggin' #2 / 1988 / PM / F • Parliament: Lonesome Ladies #1 / 1987 / PM / F • Parliament: Super Head #1 / 1989 / PM / C • Parliament: Sweet Starlets #1 / 1986 / PM / F • Party House / 1995 / WAV / M • Perfect Fit / 1985 / DR / M • The Pink Lagoon: A Sex Romp In Paradise / 1984 / GO / M • Playing For Passion / 1987 / IN / M • Pleasure Productions #07 / 1984 / VCR / M • Pleasure Productions #09 / 1985 / VCR / M • Pleasure Productions #12 / 1985 / VCR / M • Pony Girl #2: At The Ranch / 1986 / CS / B • Private Love Affairs / 1985 / VCR / C • Raffles / 1988 / VC / M • Raven / 1985 / VCR / M • Sex For

Hire / 1989 / HOE / C • The Sex Game / 1987 / SE / C • Sex In The Great Outdoors / 1987 / SE / C • Sex-A-Vision / 1985 / DR / M • Sexual Healing / 1996 / SC / M • Shape Up For Sensational Sex / 1985 / SE / M • Sister Dearest / 1984 / DR / M • The Sperminator / 1985 / VXP / M • Spreading Joy / 1988 / VC / M • Stephanie's Outrageous / 1988 / LV / C • The Strippers / 1995 / GO / M • Taking Off / 1984 / VC / M • Talk Dirty To Me #03 / 1986 / DR / M • Taste Of The Best #3 / 1988 / PIN / C • Teasers: Heavenly Bodies / 1988 / MET / M • Teasers: Hot Pursuit / 1988 / MET / M • Terms Of Endowment / 1986 / PV / M • Tongue 'n Cheek (Vca) / 1984 / VC / M • Tongue Twisters / 1986 / VXP / M • Trial By Bondage / 1991 / LON / B • Triplets / 1985 / VCR / M • Tropical Nights / 1988 / GO / C • Up In The Air / 1984 / CDI / M • Vixens In Heat / 1984 / ECS / M • The Wild Ones / 1996 / CC / M • Wild Weekend / 1984 / HO / M • Will Of Iron / 1991 / HOM / B • Winner Take All / 1986 / SEV / M • With Love From Ginger / 1986 / HO / C • Women Without Men #1 / 1985 / VXP / F • Young Nurses In Love / 1987 / VC / M • [Army Of One / 1993 / ... / S • [T&A #01 / 1989 / ... / C

CRYSTAL CINC see Crystal Sync

CRYSTAL CLEAR

Creme De La Face #02 / 1994 / OD / M • Tootsies & Footsies / 1994 / LBO / M

CRYSTAL CLUSTER see Star Index I

CRYSTAL COX see Star Index I

CRYSTAL CRAWFORD

Bi Watch / 1994 / BIN / G • Bi-Conflict / 1994 / FST / G • Conflict Of Interest / 1994 / FST / G • Courting Libido / 1995 / HIV / G • Hollywood She Males / 1995 / MET / G • Lady Dick / 1993 / HSV / G • Las Vegas She-Males / 1995 / BCP / G • Man Made Pussy / 1994 / HEA / G • Nydp Trannie / 1996 / WP / G • Pom Pom She-Males / 1994 / HEA / G • Score Of Sex / 1995 / BAC / G • She Male Service / 1994 / HEA / G • She-Male Instinct / 1995 / BCP / G • She-Male Sex Stories / 1996 / STA / G • She-Male Trouble / 1994 / HEA / G • She-Male Vacation / 1993 / HSV / G • Sinderella She-Males / 1994 / HEA / G • To Bi For / 1996 / PL / G • Wings Of Change / 1993 / HSV / G

CRYSTAL DAWN

Back To Back #1 / 1987 / 4P / C • Backdoor Girls / 1983 / VCR / C • Behind The Brown Door / 1986 / VCR / C • Black 'n' White In Color / 1987 / VCR / C • Black Beauty (Playtime) / 19?? / PLY / C • Blue Vanities #087 / 1988 / FFL / M • Blue Vanities #534 / 1993 / FFL / M • Bottoms Up #01 / 1983 / AVC / C • Bottoms Up #03 / 1983 / AVC / C • Bottoms Up #05 / 1986 / AVC / C • Budding Blondes / 1979 / TGA / C • Bunbusters / 1984 / VCR / M • Candy Girls #1 / 19?? / AVC / M • Cover Girl Fantasies #1 / 1983 / VCR / C • Cover Girl Fantasies #2 / 1983 / VCR / C • Double Pleasure / 1985 / VCR / M • Ebony Erotica / 1985 / SVE / C • The Erotic World Of Crystal Dawn (#3) / 1983 / VCR / C • Erotic Zones #3 / 1986 / CA / M • Female Athletes / 1977 / VXP / M • Hot School Reunion / 1984 / CHX / F • Inside Desiree Cousteau / 1979 / VCX / M • Limited Edition #07 / 1979 / AVC / M • Loving Lesbos / 1983 / VCR / C • Lusty Ladies #11 / 1984 / 4P / M • Seka's Fantasies / 1981 /

CA / M • Shaved / 1984 / VCR / M • Showgirl #03: Vanessa Del Rio's Fantasies / 1981 / VCR / M • Showgirl #05: Crystal Dawn's Fantasies / 1983 / VCR / M • Showgirl #13: Chris Cassidy's Fantasies / 1983 / SVE / M • Snack Time / 1983 / HO / M • Swedish Erotica #49 / 1983 / CA / M • Triangle Of Lust / 1983 / VCR / M • Wet Shots (Vcr) / 1983 / VCR / C

CRYSTAL DAY see Star Index I

CRYSTAL DEVERAUX *(Ashley Allen)*

Tall dark redhead with huge tits and a not-too-pretty face.

Bodies In Motion / 1994 / IF / M • Centerfold Strippers / 1994 / ME / M

CRYSTAL EVANS

Amateur Coed Frolics / 1985 / SUN / M • Bi Bi Love / 1986 / LAV / G • Divine Decadence / 1988 / CA / M • Legs / 1986 / AMB / M • Lifestyles Of The Black And Famous / 1986 / WET / M • Samantha And The Deep Throat Girls / 1988 / CV / M • The Sex Change Girls / 1987 / 4P / G • So Deep, So Good / 1988 / NSV / M

CRYSTAL FIRE see Star Index I

CRYSTAL FOX

Reel Life Video #52: Crystal Fox & The Plumber / Barbarito / 1996 / RLF / M

CRYSTAL GOLD *(Catalina (Crystal G))*

Blonde with marginal face, tall lithe body, huge enhanced tits and the personality of a rock. Definitely not the same as Jordan St. James, although they both have the rock-hard tits.

All-Star Anal Interviews #1 / 1995 / LEI / M • Anal Hellraiser #2 / 1995 / ROB / M • Babe Watch #5 / 1996 / VC / M • Backdoor Diaries / 1995 / BBE / M • Bareback / 1996 / LE / M • Beverly Hills Blondes #2 / 1995 / LV / M • Big Bust Babes #26 / 1995 / AFI / M • Big Bust Babes #36 / 1996 / AFI / M • Big Bust Babes #38 / 1996 / AFI / M • Big Knockers #13 / 1995 / TV / M • Big Knockers #14 / 1995 / TV / M • Big Knockers #16 / 1995 / TV / M • Big Knockers #18 / 1995 / TV / M • Big Knockers #19 / 1995 / TV / M • Big Knockers #20 / 1995 / TV / C • Big Knockers #21: Best Of Lesbian #2 / 1995 / TV / C • Blade / 1996 / MID / M • Bloopers & Behind The Scenes / 1995 / LEI / M • Boobtown / 1995 / VC / M • The Breast Files #2 / 1994 / AVI / M • Breastman's Wild West Adventure / 1995 / EVN / M • Butt Hunt #03 / 1994 / LEI / M • Butthead Dreams / 1994 / FH / M • Casting Couch Tips / 1996 / MP0 / M • College Cuties / 1995 / LE / M • The Crackster / 1996 / OUP / M • Crystal Images / 1995 / INB / M • Cybersex / 1996 / WAV / M • Deep Behind The Scenes With Seymore Butts #1 / 1995 / ULI / M • Deep Waterworld / 1995 / HW / M • The Dinner Party #1 / 1994 / ULI / M • Double D Dykes #14 / 1994 / GO / F • Double D Dykes #16 / 1995 / GO / F • Double D Dykes #25 / 1995 / GO / F • Drilling For Gold / 1995 / ME / M • Final Obsession / 1996 / LE / M • Freak Of The Week / 1996 / LIP / F • Gang Bang Jizz Queen / 1995 / ROB / M • A Girl Like You / 1995 / LE / M • Gold Coast / 1996 / FD / M • Golddiggers #3 / 1995 / VC / M • The Golden Touch / 1995 / WP / M • Hollywood Hillbillies / 1996 / LE / M • Hollywood Hookers / 1996 / DWV / M • House Of Leather / 1995 / GO / M • In Bloom / 1995 / INB / M • Inner Pink #4 / 1995 / LIP / F • Interview's Blonde Bombshells / 1995 / LV / M • John Wayne Bobbitt

Uncut / 1994 / LEI / M • Lady Luck / 1995 / PMV / M • Lesbian Love Dolls / 1995 / LIP / F • Lust Behind Bars / 1996 / GO / M • Lustful Obsessions / 1996 / NOT / M • Malibu Madam / 1995 / CC / M • Mission Phenomenal / 1996 / HIP / M • My Wildest Date / 1995 / HO / M • New Girls In Town #6 / 1994 / CC / M • Nightmare On Lesbian Street / 1995 / LIP / F • Nude Awakenings / 1996 / PP / M • Nudist Colony Vacation / 1996 / NIT / M • Pajama Party X #1 / 1994 / VC / M • The Palace Of Pleasure / 1995 / ULI / M • Penitentiary / 1995 / HW / M • Persuasion / 1995 / LE / M • Philmore Butts Strikes Gold / 1996 / SUF / M • Private Dancers / 1996 / RAS / M • Profiles #05: Planet Lust / 1995 / XPR / M • Pumphouse Slut / 1996 / CC / M • Pumphouse Sluts / 1996 / CC / M • Pussy Hunt #04 / 1994 / LEI / M • Pussy Hunt #05 / 1994 / LEI / M • Pussyman Auditions #09 / 1995 / SNA / M • Reckless Passion / 1995 / WAV / M • Red Hot Honeys / 1994 / IF / M • Reservoir Bitches / 1994 / BIP / M • Revenge Of The Bi Dolls / 1994 / CAT / G • Road Kill / 1995 / CA / M • Roommates To Lovers / 1995 / LIP / F • Samantha & Company / 1996 / PL / M • Scorched / 1995 / ONA / M • Secret Seductions #1 / 1995 / LV / M • Secret Seductions #2 / 1995 / ULP / M • Seriously Anal / 1996 / ONA / M • Seymore & Shane Playing With Fire / 1994 / ULI / M • Shaving Grace / 1996 / GO / M • A Shot In The Pink / 1995 / BBE / M • The Strippers / 1995 / GO / M • A Taste Of Fanny / 1994 / FH / M • Topless Window Washers / 1996 / LE / M • Tricky Business / 1995 / AFI / M • Trouble Maker / 1995 / VI / M • Two Sides Of A Lady / 1994 / HDE / M • Up Close & Personal #1 / 1996 / IPI / M • The Usual Anal Suspects / 1996 / CC / M • Venom #6 / 1996 / CA / M • Waterworld Deep / 1995 / HW / M • What's The Lesbian Doing In My Pirate Movie? / 1995 / LIP / F • Whore House / 1995 / IPI / M • Whore'n / 1996 / AB / M

CRYSTAL HARRIS see Crystal Sync

CRYSTAL HART see Star Index I

CRYSTAL HOLLAND see Star Index I

CRYSTAL JADE

HHHHot! TV #1 / 1988 / CDI / M

CRYSTAL JORDAN

Old Wave Hookers #1 / 1995 / PL / M • Old Wave Hookers #2 / 1995 / PL / M

CRYSTAL JOY

Erotic Tattooing And Piercing #1 / 1986 / FLV / M

CRYSTAL KAYE

The Erotic Adventures Of Dr Storm / 1983 / XTR / M

CRYSTAL KNIGHT *(Jennifer (Crystal K))*

Pretty black (perhaps) girl who appeared in 1994 with her SO Sam Strong. In this appearance she had fairly large floppy tits on a very petite high quality body (tight waist, nice butt, tattoo of an eagle on her right butt). Then she got pregnant and of course the tits expanded along with the belly. After birth she obviously had difficulty removing the weight but by 1997 she had it down to a level where she could be said to have a lithe body but never as tight as before. Post birth she also had her tits enhanced and is probably one of the very few for whom it was a wise move. In 1997 she has firm medium sized ones which look reasonably natural.

Very nice friendly personality. Cuban/Dominican origin, 21 years old in 1994, devirginized at 15.
The Adventures Of Peeping Tom #3 / 1996 / OD / M • Black Mystique #12 / 1995 / VT / F • Bootylicious: It's A Butt Thang / 1994 / JMP / M • Eighteen & Easy / 1996 / SC / M • I Love Lesbians / 1995 / ERW / F • Knight In Shining Panties / 1996 / ME / M • Lactamania #2: The Squirt Fest / 1995 / TTV / M • Lactamania #3 / 1995 / TTV / M • More Black Dirty Debutantes / 1994 / 4P / M • More Black Dirty Debutantes #3 / 1994 / 4P / M • More Black Dirty Debutantes #4 / 1995 / 4P / M • More Black Dirty Debutantes #5 / 1995 / 4P / M • Pick Up Lines #08 / 1996 / OD / M • Ready To Drop #05 / 1995 / FC / M • Ready To Drop #06 / 1995 / FC / M • Ready To Drop #07 / 1995 / FC / M • Ready To Drop #08 / 1995 / FC / M • Up And Cummers #13 / 1994 / 4P / M
CRYSTAL LAKE *(Crystal Lee, Crystal Lane (Lake), Crystal Lee Curtis)*
Short haired blonde with thin body, small tits, bit flat on butt, quite pretty. Crystal Lee in **Backdoor To Hollywood #01**. Is this also Christina Lake in **Body Shop**?
The Awakening Of Sally / 1984 / VCR / M • Backdoor Bandits / 1989 / MIR / C • Backdoor To Hollywood #01 / 1986 / CDI / M • Black Heat / 1986 / VCR / C • Caught In The Middle / 1985 / CDI / M • Crunch Bunch / 1995 / PRE / C • Dangerous Curves / 1985 / CV / M • Ebony Erotica / 1985 / SVE / C • Erotic Aerobics / 1984 / VC / M • The Erotic World Of Crystal Lake (#4) / 1984 / VCR / C • Fantasy Follies #1 / 1983 / VC / M • Flesh & Laces #1 / 1983 / CA / M • Grand Slam / 1990 / PRE / B • Groupies Galore / 1983 / VC / M • Intimate Realities #2 / 1983 / VC / M • Joys Of Erotica / 1984 / VCR / M • Joys Of Erotica #107 / 1984 / VCR / C • Joys Of Erotica #112 / 1984 / VCR / C • Joys Of Erotica #113 / 1984 / VCR / C • Malibu Summer / 1983 / VC / M • Maximum #5 / 1983 / CA / M
CRYSTAL LANE (KL) *see* **Krista Lane**
CRYSTAL LANE (LAKE) *see* **Crystal Lake**
CRYSTAL LEA *see* **Roxanne Blaze**
CRYSTAL LEE *see* **Crystal Lake**
CRYSTAL LEE CURTIS *see* **Crystal Lake**
CRYSTAL LIL *see* **Clair James**
CRYSTAL LONDON
Holly Does Hollywood #3 / 1989 / VEX / M • The Whole Diamond / 1990 / EVN / M
CRYSTAL LOVIN *(Chrystal Loven, Christel Loving, Crystal Loving, Krystal Love)*
Reddish blonde with a marginal face, medium droopy tits, womanly body. Probably French.
Backdoor Romance / 1984 / VIV / M • The Beat Goes On / 1987 / VCR / C • Celebrity Presents Celebrity / 1986 / VEP / C • Centerfold Celebrities #2 / 1983 / VC / M • Centerfold Celebrities #3 / 1983 / VC / M • Golden Girls #09 / 1983 / CA / M • Ice Cream #2: French Postcard / 1983 / VC / M • Mile High Club / 1983 / CV / M • Only The Best Of Anal / 1992 / MET / C • Personal Touch #2 / 1983 / AR / M • X-Rated Bloopers #1 / 1984 / AR / M • Young And Restless / 1983 / VIV / M • [Erotic Dimensions Vols 1 To 8 / 1983 / NSV / C
CRYSTAL LOVING *see* **Crystal Lovin**

CRYSTAL MANNERS *see* **Star Index I**
CRYSTAL MANNING
Pink Champagne / 1979 / CV / M
CRYSTAL ONYX
Swedish Erotica #71 / 1986 / CA / M • Swedish Erotica #72 / 1986 / CA / M
CRYSTAL PEACH *see* **Star Index I**
CRYSTAL PEARL *see* **Pearl**
CRYSTAL ROYCE
Blue's Velvet / 1979 / ECV / M • Getting Off / 1979 / VIP / M
CRYSTAL SHELDON
An Unnatural Act #1 / 1984 / DR / M
CRYSTAL SLADE
White Hot / 1984 / VXP / M
CRYSTAL SLIM *see* **Star Index I**
CRYSTAL STARR *(Carmel Nougat)*
Blonde with huge droopy tits (44-30-43) and a marginal face. 24 years old in 1983. She says her real name is Carmel Nougat (sure!) and she comes from South Carolina.
Between My Breasts #05 / 1988 / BTO / S • Big Busty #24 / 198? / H&S / S • Big Tit Orgy #04 / 1991 / BTO / C • The Boarding House / 1983 / WV / M • Busen Extra #1 / 1991 / BTO / M • Fantasy Follies #1 / 1983 / VC / M
CRYSTAL SYNC *(Christa Anderson, Christine Williams, Ellen Williams, Sandy Long, Brenda Kan, Erica Baron, Crystal Cinc, Chrissy Williams-CRS, Carrie Lyons, Mary Beth Johnson, Anna Davis, Erica Johnson, Crystal Harris)*
Slim brunette with small tits and a marginal face. Sounds English and is a little on the expressionless side. Slim body but a bit flat on the butt and in some positions she looks like she has lost muscle tone in her belly. In **Breaker Beauties** she is credited as Mary Beth Johnson and has a horrible afro but other movies have a prettier hair style.
The Affairs Of Janice / 1975 / ALP / M • Blow Dry / 1977 / SVE / M • Breaker Beauties / 1977 / VHL / M • Classic Erotica Special / 1985 / SVE / M • Dear Pam / 1976 / CA / M • Doctor Yes / 1978 / VIS / M • Ecstasy In Blue / 1976 / ALP / M • French Kittens / 1977 / CA / M • Girl Scout Cookies / 197? / SVE / M • Hot Nurses / 1977 / CA / M • Hot Wives / 19?? / VXP / M • In Too Deep / 1979 / CDC / M • Love In Strange Places / 1977 / CA / M • Magic Girls / 1983 / SVE / M • Maraschino Cherry / 1978 / QX / M • The New York City Woman / 1979 / VC / C • Odyssey / 1977 / VC / M • A Scent Of Heather / 1981 / VXP / M • Sharon In The Rough-House / 1976 / LA / M • Slippery When Wet / 1976 / VXP / M • Sweet Punkin...I Love You / 1975 / VC / M • That Lady From Rio / 1976 / VXP / M • The Tiffany Minx / 1981 / SAT / M • The Trouble With Young Stuff / 1976 / VC / M • Vanessa's Bed Of Pleasure / 1983 / SVE / M • VCA Previews #2 / 1988 / VC / C • The Violation Of Claudia / 1977 / QX / M • A Woman's Torment / 1977 / VC / M
CRYSTAL VALENTINE *see* **Star Index I**
CRYSTAL WATERS *see* **Tami Lee Curtis**
CRYSTAL WILDER *(Krystal Wilder)*
Girl who looks a bit like Marilyn Rose but with a feminist attitude (well, maybe—in her first movies she sounded like this but later seemed to be more of a practical tomboy) and huge tits which she says are real but I

don't believe her. Her boyfriend/husband is Terry Thomas. Born September 13, 1967 in Brooking, South Dakota. First movie was **Masquerade**. First on screen anal was with Ron Jeremy in **Sun Bunnies #2**.
10,000 Anal Maniacs #1 / 1993 / FOR / M • Adult Video Nudes / 1993 / VC / M • Anal Babes / 1995 / PPR / M • Anal Ecstasy Girls #2 / 1993 / ROB / F • Anal Intruder #07 / 1993 / CC / M • Anal Sexual Silence / 1993 / IP / M • Anal Taboo / 1993 / ROB / M • The Anal Team / 1993 / LV / M • Ass Freaks #1 / 1993 / ROB / F • Ass Openers! #2 / 1995 / TCK / C • Babes Illustrated #2 / 1994 / IN / F • Babes Illustrated #3 / 1995 / IN / F • Bazooka County #5: The Jugs / 1993 / CC / M • The Bet / 1993 / VT / M • Big Bust Casting Call / 1993 / PME / S • The Big Stick-Up / 1994 / WV / M • Bikini Beach #1 / 1993 / CC / M • Bikini Beach #2 / 1993 / CC / M • Bikini Beach #3 / 1993 / CC / F • Black Booty / 1993 / ZA / M • A Blaze Of Glory / 1993 / ME / M • Blinded By Love / 1993 / OD / M • Blow For Blow / 1992 / ZA / M • Bobby Hollander's Sweet Cheeks #101 / 1992 / WV / M • Body Work / 1993 / MET / M • Boogie In The Butt / 1993 / WIV / M • The Boss / 1993 / VT / M • Bossy Babes / 1993 / TCK / M • Breast Worx #37 / 1992 / LBO / M • Breastman's Anal Adventure / 1993 / EVN / M • Bringing Up The Rear / 1993 / VD / C • Bronco Millie / 1992 / ZA / M • The Brothel / 1993 / OD / M • Bruise Control / 1993 / PRE / B • Bubble Butts #14 / 1992 / LBO / M • Burgundy Blues / 1993 / MET / M • Bush League #2 / 1992 / CC / M • Butt Darling / 1994 / WIV / M • Butt Hole Boulevard / 1993 / CA / M • The Butt Sisters / 1993 / MID / M • The Butt Sisters Do Las Vegas / 1994 / MID / M • Butt Sluts #2 / 1993 / ROB / F • Butts Afire / 1992 / PMV / M • Caged Fury / 1993 / DR / M • Catfighting Students / 1995 / PRE / C • Cheeks #6 / 1992 / CC / M • Cheerleader Nurses #1 / 1993 / VC / M • Cheerleader Nurses #2 / 1993 / VC / M • Cinnamon Twist / 1993 / OD / M • Cooler Girls / 1994 / MID / C • Cum Backed And Loaded / 1994 / BCP / M • Deep Butt / 1994 / MID / C • Deep Inside Crystal Wilder / 1995 / VC / C • Deep Inside Nikki Dial / 1994 / VC / C • Dial N Again / 1993 / PEP / M • Diary Of A Porn Star / 1993 / FOR / M • Dick & Jane Do The Strip / 1994 / AVI / M • Dirty Bob's #17: Tampa Teasers! / 1994 / FLP / S • Dirty Laundry #1 / 1994 / CV / M • Dirty Little Lies / 1993 / VT / M • The Dragon Lady #4: Tales From The Bed #3 / 1992 / WV / M • Dream House / 1995 / XPR / M • Dream Strokes / 1994 / WIV / M • Eleventh Annual AVN Awards / 1994 / VC / M • En Garde / 1993 / DR / M • Endlessly / 1993 / VI / M • Erotica / 1992 / CC / M • Essence Of A Woman / 1993 / FOR / M • Fantasy Girls / 1994 / PME / F • First Time Ever #1 / 1995 / PE / F • Fleshmates / 1994 / ERA / M • The Fluffer #1 / 1993 / FD / M • Frenzy / 1992 / SC / M • From Brazil With Love / 1992 / ZA / M • Gang Bang Wild Style #1 / 1993 / ROB / M • Gangbang Girl #12 / 1993 / ANA / M • Gimme An X / 1993 / VD / C • The Go-Go Girls / 1994 / EVN / M • The Governess / 1993 / WP / M • Hard To Stop #1 / 1992 / VC / M • Hard To Stop #2 / 1992 / VC / M • Harry Horndog #10: Love Pup-

pies #1 / 1992 / ZA / M • Hollywood Temps / 1993 / ZA / M • Hootermania / 1994 / VC / M • Hot For Teacher / 1993 / VD / M • Hot Tight Asses #02 / 1993 / TCK / M • Hyapatia Obsessed / 1993 / EX / M • Interactive / 1993 / VD / M • Juranal Park / 1993 / OD / M • Kadillac & Devell / 1993 / ZA / M • Knockin' Da Booty / 1993 / WP / M • The Last Anal Hero / 1993 / OD / M • Lawnmower Woman / 1992 / MID / M • Leg...Ends #08 / 1993 / PRE / F • Lesbian Dating Game / 1993 / LIP / F • Licking Legends #2 / 1992 / LE / F • Loopholes / 1993 / TP / M • Malcolm XXX / 1992 / OD / M • Masquerade (1992-Usa) / 1992 / SC / M • The Mistress (1993-Caballero) / 1993 / CA / M • Mistress To Sin / 1994 / LV / M • Model's Memoirs / 1993 / IP / M • Molly B-Goode / 1994 / FH / M • More Than A Handful / 1993 / CA / C • Nasty Cracks / 1992 / PRE / B • Neighborhood Watch #36 / 1992 / LBO / M • Never Say Never, Again / 1994 / SC / M • New Wave Hookers #3 / 1993 / VC / M • Night Creatures / 1992 / PL / M • No Man's Land #06 / 1992 / VT / F • No Man's Land #07 / 1993 / VT / F • Objective: D.P. / 1993 / PEP / M • Odyssey 30 Min: #205: / 1992 / OD / M • Odyssey Triple Play #33: 3 Back-Door Boinkers / 1993 / OD / M • Odyssey Triple Play #48: Rear End Reaming / 1993 / OD / M • One Of Our Porn Stars Is Missing / 1993 / OD / M • Oral Majority #13 / 1995 / WV / C • P.J. Sparxx On Fire / 1992 / MID / C • Pajama Party X #1 / 1994 / VC / M • Pajama Party X #2 / 1994 / VC / M • Panties / 1993 / VD / M • Passenger 69 #2 / 1994 / IP / M • Passion's Prisoners / 1994 / LV / M • Poison Ivory / 1993 / MID / F • Poor Little Rich Girl #1 / 1992 / XCI / M • Poor Little Rich Girl #2 / 1992 / XCI / M • Professor Sticky's Anatomy 3X #02 / 1992 / FC / M • Public Places #1 / 1994 / SC / M • Public Places #2 / 1995 / SC / M • Pulp Friction / 1994 / PP / M • Pussy Galore / 1993 / VD / C • A Pussy To Die For / 1992 / CA / M • Radical Affairs Video Magazine #05 / 1993 / ME / M • Raging Waters / 1992 / PRE / B • Rainwoman #06 / 1993 / CC / M • Rear Entry / 1995 / LEI / M • Ring Of Passion / 1993 / WV / M • Secret Services / 1993 / PEP / M • Seduced / 1992 / VD / M • Seven Good Women / 1993 / HO / F • Sex #1 (Vivid) / 1993 / VI / M • Sex #2 (Vivid) / 1993 / VI / M • Sex Lives Of Clowns / 1994 / VC / M • Sexdrive #1: Topdown Girl / 1993 / OD / M • Sharon Starlet / 1993 / WIV / M • Shear Ecstasy / 1993 / PEP / M • Shooting Star / 1993 / XCI / M • Single White Nympho / 1992 / MID / M • A Slow Hand / 1992 / FD / M • The Smart Ass Returns / 1993 / VT / M • Sole Survivors / 1996 / PRE / C • Sparxx / 1993 / MID / F • Stacked Deck / 1994 / IN / M • Star Crossed / 1995 / VC / M • A Stripper Named Desire / 1993 / CC / M • Stripper Nurses / 1994 / PE / M • Student Fetish Videos: Best of Enema #02 / 1992 / PRE / C • Student Fetish Videos: Best Of Foot Worship #02 / 1994 / PRE / C • Student Fetish Videos: Catfighting #05 / 1992 / PRE / B • Student Fetish Videos: The Enema #10 / 1993 / PRE / B • Student Fetish Videos: Foot Worship #08 / 1992 / PRE / B • Sun Bunnies #2: The Pink Cheek Tales / 1992 / SC / M • The Taming Of Savannah / 1993 / VI / M • Teri's Fantasies /

1993 / VEX / M • Titties 'n Cream #3 / 1995 / FC / M • Toe Hold / 1992 / PRE / B • Topless Stewardesses / 1995 / PV / M • Toppers #02 / 1992 / TV / M • Toppers #19 / 1993 / TV / M • Toppers #20 / 1993 / TV / M • Toppers #22 / 1993 / TV / C • Toppers #26 / 1994 / TV / M • Toppers #30 / 1994 / TV / C • Toppers #31 / 1994 / TV / C • Toppers & Whoppers #2 / 1994 / PRE / C • Treasure Chest / 1994 / LV / M • Truth Or Dare / 1993 / VI / M • The Unashamed / 1993 / FD / M • Unchained Melanie / 1992 / VC / M • Unsolved Double Penetration / 1993 / PEP / M • Untamed Cowgirls Of The Wild West #01: The Pillow Biters / 1992 / ZA / M • Untamed Cowgirls Of The Wild West #02: Jammy Glands... / 1993 / ZA / M • Up And Coming Executive / 1993 / TP / M • The Uptown Girl / 1992 / ZA / M • Virtual Reality / 1993 / EX / M • Washington D.P. / 1993 / PEP / M • Web Of Desire / 1993 / OD / M • Welcome To Bondage: Crystal Wilder / 1993 / BON / B • Welcome To Bondage: Starlets #1 / 1993 / BON / C • Wet Faces #1 / 1997 / SC / C • White Shadow / 1994 / VC / M • Who Killed Holly Hollywood? / 1993 / VC / M • Wicked Waxxx Worxxx / 1995 / HW / M • Wilder At Heart / 1993 / ANA / M • Working Girl / 1993 / VI / M • You Bet Your Buns / 1992 / ZA / M

CUBBIE
Sorority Stewardesses #1 / 1995 / PE / M

CUDDLES
Black Fantasies #11 / 1996 / HW / M • Bootylicious: Big Badd Booty / 1995 / JMP / M

CUDDLIE
Girlz Towne #08 / 1995 / FC / F • Girlz Towne #11 / 1995 / FC / F

CUM JUDD *see Star Index I*

CUMISHA AMADO *(Cunisha Amado, Mara Amado, Myra Amado, Nancy (Cum. Amado), Leila LaVeau, Comisha, Kumisha, Kisha, Chuisha)*
An ugly Oriental-looking woman.
A&B AB#480: Kisha / 1994 / A&B / M • A&B GB#072: Chessie Does It / 1990 / A&B / M • A&B GB#074: Anal Gang Bang From Asia #1 / 1993 / A&B / M • A&B GB#075: Anal Gang Bang From Asia #2 / 1993 / A&B / M • AC/DC #2 / 1994 / HP / G • Adventures Of The DP Boys: South Of The Border / 1995 / HW / M • Adventures Of The DP Boys: Tokyo Tramps / 1994 / HW / M • Adventures Of The DP Boys: Triple Penetration Girls / 1993 / HW / M • Amateur Lesbians #39: Tiffany / 1993 / GO / F • Amateur Lesbians #40: Sunset / 1993 / GO / F • Amateur Lesbians #44: Cumisha / 1993 / GO / F • Amateur Orgies #22 / 1993 / AFI / M • Amateur Orgies #31 / 1993 / AFI / M • American Connection Video Magazine #01 / 1992 / ZA / M • American Connection Video Magazine #02 / 1992 / ZA / M • American Connection Video Magazine #03 / 1993 / ZA / M • The Anal Adventures Of Max Hardcore: Suzy Superslut / 1992 / ZA / M • Anal Annie's All-Girl Escort Service / 1990 / LIP / F • Anal Asian Fantasies / 1996 / HO / M • Anal Distraction / 1993 / PEP / M • Anal Gang Bangers #02 / 1993 / GLI / M • Anal Nature / 1993 / AFD / M • Anal Nymphettes / 1995 / LIP / F • Anal Pandemonium / 1994 / TTV / M • Anal Reunion / 1996 / EVN / M • The Anal Team / 1993 /

LV / M • Anal Therapy #3 / 1994 / FD / M • Anal Variations #02 / 1993 / FH / M • Anal Vision #04 / 1992 / LBO / M • Anal Witness #2: No Prisoners / 1996 / LBO / M • Anal, Facial & Interracial / 1996 / FC / M • Animal Attraction / 1994 / IF / M • Anything You Ever Wanted To Know About Sex / 1993 / VEX / M • Asian Angel / 1993 / VEX / C • Asian Heat #02: Satin Angels / 1993 / SC / M • Asian Heat #03: Tales Of The Golden Lotus / 1993 / SC / M • Asian Heat #05: The Joy Suck Club / 1994 / SC / M • Bachelor Party #1 / 1993 / FPI / M • Backing In #7 / 1995 / WV / C • Bad She-Males / 1994 / HSV / G • Bangkok Nights / 1994 / VI / M • Beach Bum Amateur's #24 / 1993 / MID / M • Beach Bum Amateur's #29 / 1993 / MID / M • Beverly Hills Sex Party / 1993 / EX / M • Beyond Reality #2: Anal Expedition / 1996 / EXQ / M • Bi This! / 1995 / BIL / G • Bi-Bi Love Amateurs #3 / 1993 / QUA / G • Bi-Conflict / 1994 / FST / G • Bi-Nanza / 1994 / BIL / G • Biff Malibu's Totally Nasty Home Videos #32 / 1993 / ANA / M • Big Murray's New-Cummers #18: Crazy Cuties / 1993 / FD / M • Big Murray's New-Cummers #21: Double Penetration One / 1993 / FD / M • Black Ass Masters #1 / 1995 / GLI / M • Black Bamboo / 1995 / IN / M • Black Booty / 1993 / ZA / M • Blonde Angel / 1994 / VI / M • Blow Job Blvd #1 / 1993 / SC / M • Boob Tube Lube / 1996 / RAS / M • The Booty Bandit / 1994 / FC / M • Bootylicious: China Town / 1995 / JMP / M • Bordello / 1995 / VI / M • Both Ends Burning / 1993 / HW / M • Bubble Butts #23 / 1992 / LBO / M • Bun Busters #03 / 1993 / LBO / M • Bun Busters #22 / 1994 / LBO / M • The Burma Road #1 / 1994 / LBO / C • The Burma Road #2 / 1994 / LBO / C • Butt Hole Boulevard / 1993 / CA / M • Butt Jammers #01 / 1995 / SC / F • Butt Jammers #05 / 1996 / SC / F • Buttslammers #13: The Madness Continues / 1996 / BS / F • Candyman #03 / 1993 / GLI / M • Candyman #07: Favorite Sweets / 1993 / GLI / M • Captain Bob's Lust Boat #1 / 1993 / FCP / M • Casting Call #03 / 1993 / SO / M • Caught From Behind #17 / 1992 / HO / M • Cluster Fuck #01 / 1993 / MAX / M • Colossal Orgy #1 / 1993 / HW / M • Colossal Orgy #2 / 1994 / HW / M • Colossal Orgy #3 / 1994 / HW / M • Confessions Of A Slutty Nurse / 1994 / VIM / M • Conflict Of Interest / 1994 / FST / C • Cream Pies #01 / 1993 / ZA / M • Cream Pies #02 / 1993 / ZA / M • Creme De Femme / 1994 / 4P / F • Creme De La Face #01 / 1994 / OD / M • Deep Inside Debi Diamond / 1995 / VC / C • Deep Inside The Orient / 1993 / LV / M • Deep Space 69 / 1994 / HW / M • Deliciously Teri / 1993 / IF / M • Desert Moon / 1994 / SPI / M • Diary Of A Geisha / 1995 / WV / C • Dirt Bags / 1994 / FPI / M • Dirty Danyel / 1994 / V99 / M • Dirty Dating Service #01 / 1993 / WP / M • Dirty Panties / 1994 / SCL / M • Double Butts / 1994 / RTP / M • Double D Dykes #07 / 1992 / GO / F • Double D Dykes #08 / 1993 / GO / F • Double Wong Dong / 1995 / LV / M • Dp #2: The Mighty Fhucks / 1994 / FC / M • Drive Bi / 1994 / BIL / G • The End Zone / 1993 / PRE / B • Enemates #07 / 1992 / PRE / B • Erotic Dripping Orientals / 1993 / WV / M • Erotica Optique / 1994 / SUF / M • Everybody Wants Some / 1996 / EXQ / F • Fan-

CYRINA STETSON
Adventures Of The DP Boys: Berlin Butt Babes / 1993 / HW / M • Anal Virgins Of America #01 / 1993 / FOR / M • Biff Malibu's Totally Nasty Home Videos #32 / 1993 / ANA / M • Bobby Hollander's Rookie Nookie #06 / 1993 / SFP / M • Harry Horndog #19: Anal Lovers #3 / 1993 / ZA / M • Hollywood Swingers #10 / 1993 / LBO / M • Pearl Necklace: Thee Bush League #21 / 1993 / SEE / M • Russian Seduction / 1993 / IP / M • Sean Michaels On The Road #07: New York / 1993 / VT / M • Take It Like A Man / 1994 / IF / M

CYRUS JAMES see Star Index I

D'ANNE
Erotic Dimensions: A Woman's Lust / 1982 / NSV / M

D'ELLIOT MARCUSSI
Cafe Flesh / 1982 / VC / M

D. BABY
TV Birdcage Rage #2 / 1996 / GLI / G

D. BOBER
Channel Blonde / 1994 / VI / M

D. DICKMAN see Star Index I

D. ENGLISH see Derrick Taylor

D. FRANCESCO
Take Off / 1978 / VXP / M

D. HARTMAN
Double Your Pleasure / 1978 / CV / M

D. HUNTER
Blue Vanities #555 / 1994 / FFL / M

D. NIG
AVP #1001: Candy's Fantasy—The Robbery / 1987 / AVP / M • AVP #1006: Candy's Debut / 1987 / AVP / M • AVP #8007: First Moves / 1991 / AVP / M

D.A. ADAMS see Buck Adams

D.D. BURK see Star Index I

D.D. SIMMONS
Dracula Exotica / 1980 / TVX / M

D.D. WINTERS *(Denise Mathews, Vanity (D.D. Wint))*
Canadian model, real name Denise Mathews, who appeared in some Canadian B movies as D.D. Winters and then became involved with the singer Prince. He changed her name to Vanity (not to be confused with the porn star also called Tisa) and she did some records. Went on to a series of almost-A movies and an appearance in *Playboy*. Finally married a football player from the L.A. Rams and became a born-again Christian, ashamed of her past.
52 Pick-Up / 1986 / MED / S • The Best Of Sex And Violence / 1981 / WIZ / C • Famous T & A / 1982 / WIZ / C • Tanya's Island / 1980 / ... / S

D.E. BOYD
Two Can Chew / 1995 / FD / M

D.J HOUSTON
Dream Slave / 199? / CS / B • Pony Girl #1: In Harness / 1985 / CS / B

D.J. see Dee Jay

D.J. ALDEN
Tall quite pretty dark blonde with long straight hair, lithe body, medium enhanced tits with almost no areola, small tattoo on her left shoulder back, large tattoo on her right buttock next to a large birthmark.
The Darker Side / 1994 / HO / M • Jaded Love / 1994 / CA / M • Love Thrust / 1995 / ERA / M • Mickey Ray's Sex Search #02: Tight Spots / 1994 / WIV / M • My Generation / 1994 / HO / M • Reel People #07 / 1995 / PP / M • The Reel Sex World #04:

Laid In Hawaii / 1994 / WP / M • Reel Sex World #05 / 1994 / WP / M • Tight Lips / 1994 / CA / M

D.J. CONE *(D.J. Morgan)*
Amber's Desires / 1985 / CA / M • Beyond Desire / 1986 / VC / M • Blacks & Blondes #02 / 1986 / WV / M • Candy's Little Sister Sugar / 1988 / VD / M • For Your Love / 1988 / IN / M • Legacy Of Lust / 1985 / CA / M • Nightshift Nurses #1 / 1988 / VC / M • Play Me Again, Vanessa / 1986 / VC / M

D.J. HOUSTON
Fear In The Forest / 1993 / CS / B • Monkee Business / 1994 / CS / B

D.J. LAINE
Sensuous Moments / 1983 / VIV / M

D.J. MICHAELS
Latin Fever #2 / 1996 / C69 / M

D.J. MORGAN see D.J. Cone

D.J. STAR see Star Index I

D.J. YUKON
G...They're Big / 1981 / TGA / C • Girls & Guys Or Guys / 19?? / REG / M • Yamahama Mamas / 1983 / TGA / C

D.J.X.
Raw Sex #02 / 1995 / ERW / M • Up And Cummers #25 / 1995 / 4P / M • Up And Cummers #31 / 1996 / 4P / M • Up And Cummers #34 / 1996 / 4P / M • Up And Cummers #39 / 1996 / RWP / M

DADDY GREG
She-Male Slut House / 1994 / HEA / G

DAGI KING
Dangerous Pleasure / 1995 / WIV / M • Double Pleasure / 1995 / XYS / M

DAGMAR
Der Spritz-Treff / 1995 / KRM / M • Private Video Magazine #18 / 1994 / OD / M

DAGOBERT WALTER
The Erotic Adventures of Hansel And Gretel / 1971 / SOW / S • [Krankenschwestern-Report / 1972 / ... / M

DAHLIA GREY see Jamie Dion

DAHVIANNA
Asses Galore #6: Fallen Angels / 1996 / DFI / M • Black Cheerleader Search #09 / 1996 / IVC / M • Ethnic Cheerleader Search #1 / 1996 / WIC / M

DAISY
American Dream Girls #2 / 1994 / LEI / M • Club Doma #2 / 1994 / VER / B • Pantyhose Teasers #1 / 1991 / JBV / S • Private Gold #14: Sweet Lady #1 / 1997 / OD / M • Red Hot Honeys / 1994 / IF / M • Salsa & Spice #1 / 1995 / TTV / M • Up And Cummers #20 / 1995 / 4P / M • Up And Cummers #22 / 1995 / RWP / M

DAISY (J.R. CARR.) see J.R. Carrington

DAISY (JENNA J.) see Jenna Jameson

DAISY DOWNES see Cara Lott

DAISY JEFFERSON see Star Index I

DAISY JONES see Star Index I

DAISY LAY
Bucky Beavers #074 / 1995 / SOW / M • The Psychiatrist / 1971 / SOW / M

DAISY MAE
Full Moon Video #27: Welcum Wagon / 1994 / FAP / M • Pussycat Ranch / 1978 / CV / M

DAISY MAYO see Star Index I

DAISY MILES
Big Titted Tarts / 1994 / PL / C

DAISY SINCLAIR
The Initiate / 1995 / BON / B • Interviews At The Hard Wok Cafe / 1996 / LOF / M • Just Eat Me, Damn It! / 1995 / BVW / F • Sugar

Mommies / 1995 / FPI / M

DAJILLA see Zumira

DAKOTA
Back Rent / 1996 / MP0 / M • Hot Body Competition: Beverly Hill's Miniskirt Madness Cont. / 1996 / CG / F • Innocent Little Girls #1 / 1996 / MP0 / M • Pearl Necklace: Amorous Amateurs #08 / 1992 / SEE / M • Rodney's Rookies #1 / 1996 / NIT / M

DAKOTA (JANINE) see Janine Lindemulder

DAKOTA TRISHE
Debi Diamond's Dirty Dykes #1 / 1995 / FD / F • Foreign Asses / 1996 / MP0 / M • Fresh Faces #07 / 1995 / EVN / M • In Your Face #4 / 1996 / PL / M • Mrs. Buttfire / 1995 / SUF / M

DAKTARI LORENZ see Star Index I

DALANA BISSONNETTE see Star Index I

DALE
AVP #7020: Bubbles In The Smokies / 1991 / AVP / M • Dirty Tricks #2: This Ain't Love / 1996 / EA / M • Harry Horndog #29: Anal Lovers #5 / 1995 / FPI / M • Home-Grown Video #455 / 1995 / HOV / M • Rump Humpers #02 / 1992 / GLI / M

DALE DANIELS see Star Index I

DALE DAVIS
Sodomania #08: The London Sessions / 1994 / EL / M

DALE MEADOR
18 And Anxious / cr78 / CDI / M • The Autobiography Of A Flea / 1976 / MIT / M • Baby Rosemary / 1975 / SE / M • Bad Company / 1978 / CV / M • The China Cat / 1978 / CA / M • China De Sade / 1977 / ALP / M • Lipps & Mccain / 1978 / VC / M • Peaches And Cream / 1982 / SE / M • Resurrection Of Eve / 1973 / MIT / M • Sodom & Gomorrah / 1974 / MIT / M

DALE PRESLEY see Star Index I

DALE WEINBERG
House Of Anal / 1995 / NOT / M • Planet X #1 / 1996 / HW / M

DALIA see Star Index I

DALILA
The Way Of Sex / 1995 / DBV / M • Boys R' Us / 1995 / WIV / M • Dildo Bitches / 1995 / LAF / F • Sex For Hire / 1996 / ONA / M • The Shocking Truth #2 / 1996 / DWO / M

DALLAS
Booty Babes / 1993 / ROB / F • Meltin' The Burgh / 1996 / DGD / F • Red Hot Honeys / 1994 / IF / M • Sweet Lips & Buns / 1993 / ROB / F • Titties 'n Cream #3 / 1995 / FC / M

DALLAS (1991) *(Dallas DeNiro)*
Big blonde in the style of Debi Diamond—poorly dyed hair.
The Anus Family / 1991 / CC / M • Bardot / 1991 / VI / M • Cries From The Dungeon / cr94 / HOM / B • Double D Dykes #02 / 1992 / GO / F • Fast Track / 1992 / LIP / F • Gazongas Galore #1 / 1996 / NIT / C • Girls Of Sin / 1994 / PL / C • Hot Flesh, Cold Chains / 1992 / HOM / B • In Your Face #1 / 1992 / PL / M • Jungle Beaver / 1991 / HIO / M • Never Never Land / 1992 / PL / M • Regarding Hiney / 1991 / CC / M • Sexual Olympics #2: The Finals / 1992 / VT / M • Tori Welles Goes Behind The Scenes / 1992 / FD / M • Welcome To Dallas / 1991 / VI / M

DALLAS (1994) *(Dallas Whitaker)*

Blonde with a pretty face but huge enhanced tits, 26 years old in 1995 and 19 when de-virginized. Married to Austin McCloud.
Altered Paradise / 1995 / LE / M • Amateur Gay Girls / 1995 / LEI / C • Anal Anarchy / 1995 / VC / M • Anal Aristocrat / 1995 / KWP / M • Anal Intruder #10 / 1995 / CC / M • Anal Tight Ass / 1995 / ROB / M • Anal Trashy Ass / 1995 / ROB / M • Aroused #2 / 1995 / VI / M • Ass Angels / 1996 / PAL / F • Ass Freaks #2 / 1995 / ROB / F • Back Door Mistress / 1994 / GO / M • The Back-door Bradys / 1995 / PL / M • Bare Ass In The Park / 1995 / PEP / M • The Best Of Strippers Inc / 1996 / ONA / C • Big & Busty Superstars / 1996 / DGD / F • Big Bust Babes #26 / 1995 / AFI / M • Big Knockers #13 / 1995 / TV / M • Big Knockers #14 / 1995 / TV / M • Big Knockers #20 / 1995 / TV / C • Big Knockers #21: Best Of Lesbian #2 / 1995 / TV / C • Bigger Than Life / 1995 / IF / M • Blue Movie / 1995 / WP / M • Booby Prize / 1995 / PEP / M • Bunmasters / 1995 / VC / M • The Butt Sisters Do Philadelphia / 1995 / MID / M • Butthead Dreams: Down In The Bush / 1995 / FH / M • Cat Lickers #3 / 1995 / ME / F • Cheek To Cheek / 1997 / EL / M • Circus Of Lesbians / 1995 / VI / C • Circus Sluts / 1995 / LV / M • Club Anal #3 / 1995 / ROB / F • Cold As Ice / 1994 / IN / M • Color Me Anal / 1995 / ME / M • Comeback / 1995 / VI / M • Dance Naked / 1995 / PEP / M • The Devil In Miss Jones #5: The Inferno / 1994 / VC / M • Double D Dykes #18 / 1995 / GO / F • Dream Lust / 1995 / NIT / M • Fixing A Hole / 1995 / XCI / M • Flexxx #4 / 1995 / VT / M • For Love Or Money / 1994 / AFI / M • Four Weddings And A Honeymoon / 1995 / PL / M • Gang Bang Bitches #05 / 1995 / PP / M • Gangbusters / 1995 / VC / M • Gangland Bangers / 1995 / VC / M • The Girl Next Door #2 / 1994 / VT / M • Girl's School / 1994 / ERA / M • Girls Of The Ivy Leagues / 1994 / VT / M • The Golden Touch / 1995 / WP / M • The Happy Office / 1996 / NIT / M • Harry Horndog #29: Anal Lovers #5 / 1995 / FPI / M • Hollywood Amateurs #11 / 1994 / MID / M • Hollywood Boulevard / 1995 / CV / M • Hot Tight Asses #14 / 1994 / TCK / M • Hotel Sodom #07 / 1995 / SNA / M • In Your Face #4 / 1996 / PL / M • In-ternal Affairs / 1995 / VI / M • Keyholes / 1995 / OD / M • Kia Unmasked / 1995 / LE / M • Killer Tits / 1995 / LE / M • Kinky Cam-eraman #4 / 1996 / LEI / C • Kittens & Vamps #2 / 1995 / ROB / F • Lady's Choice / 1995 / VD / M • Lonely Hearts / 1995 / VC / M • Many Happy Returns / 1995 / NIT / M • Mickey Ray's Sex Search #04: Long And Hard / 1994 / WIV / M • More Than A Hand-ful #6: Life Under The Big Top / 1994 / MET / M • Nasty Nymphos #10 / 1995 / ANA / M • Nina Hartley's Guide To Swinging / 1996 / A&E / M • Nothing Like A Dame #2 / 1995 / IN / M • Nurses Do It With Care / 1995 / EVN / M • On The Rise / 1994 / EX / M • The Passion Potion / 1995 / WP / M • Pey-ton's Place / 1996 / ULP / M • Photo Play / 1995 / VI / M • Plumb And Dumber / 1995 / PP / M • Prescription For Lust / 1995 / NIT / M • Pro-Am Jam / 1996 / GLI / M • Puri-tan Video Magazine #07 / 1996 / LE / M • Pussy Hunt #05 / 1994 / LEI / M • Red Hots / 1996 / PL / M • Renegades #2 / 1995 / SC / M • Revenge Of The Pussy Suckers From

Mars / 1994 / PP / M • Satyriasis / 1995 / PL / M • Scandal / 1995 / VI / M • Secret Services / 1995 / CV / M • Sensual Spirits / 1995 / LE / M • Sex Academy #2: The Art Of Talking Dirty / 1994 / ONA / M • Sex Academy #3: The Art Of Real Sex / 1994 / ONA / M • Sex Academy #4: The Art Of Anal / 1994 / ONA / M • Simply Blue / 1995 / WAV / M • The Sin-A-Bun Girls / 1995 / OD / M • Sluthunt #1 / 1995 / BIP / F • Snatch Masters #03 / 1994 / LEI / M • Spirit Guide / 1995 / IN / M • Stacked Deck / 1994 / IN / M • Star Crossed / 1995 / VC / M • Starting Over / 1995 / WAV / M • Strip-pers Inc. #4 / 1995 / ONA / M • Student Fetish Videos: Catfighting #14 / 1994 / PRE / B • Student Fetish Videos: The Enema #19 / 1995 / PRE / B • Student Fetish Videos: Foot Worship #15 / 1995 / PRE / B • Sure Bet / 1995 / CV / M • Taboo #15 / 1995 / IN / M • Take It Inside / 1995 / PEP / M • Temptation / 1994 / VC / M • Texas Crude / 1995 / NIT / M • Thunder Road / 1995 / SC / M • Tight Fit #10 / 1994 / GO / M • Timepiece / 1994 / CV / M • Top-less Brain Surgeons / 1995 / LE / M • Un-bridled / 1995 / PPI / M • Unplugged / 1995 / CC / M • Upbeat Love #2 / 1995 / CV / M • Video Virgins #22 / 1995 / NS / M • Vi-sions #1 / 1995 / ERA / M • Waterbabies #3 / 1996 / CC / M • Wot Faces #1 / 1997 / SC / C • Wet Nurses #2 / 1995 / LE / M • Where The Girls Sweat...Not The Sequel / 1996 / EL / F • Wild & Wicked #6 / 1995 / VT / M • Wild Orgies #15 / 1995 / AFI / M • Willie Wanker At The Fudge Packing Factory / 1995 / FD / M • Willie Wanker At The Sushi Bar / 1995 / FD / M • A Woman Scorned / 1995 / CA / M • The X-Rated OJ Truth... / 1995 / MID / M

DALLAS (MIKO) *see* Dallas Miko
DALLAS COURT
[Sexy Twins / 19?? / ... / M
DALLAS D'AMOUR *(Lili Xiang)*
Ugly pudgy Oriental (worse than Cumisha) with medium to large droopy tits, cunt ring, large tattoos on her right upper outside thigh and her upper right butt. 5'9" tall, 23 years old and 38-24-38 all as of early 1996. De-flighized at 12.
100% Amateur #02: Back Door And More / 1995 / OD / M • 9-Ball: Geisha Gang Bang / 1994 / PL / M • The Anal Adventures Of Max Hardcore: Grand Prix / 1994 / ZA / M • Anal All Stars / 1994 / CA / M • Anal Hunger / 1994 / ROB / M • Anal Savage #2 / 1994 / ROB / M • The Anal-Europe Series #07: / 1994 / LV / M • Analtown USA #09 / 1995 / NIT / M • Analtown USA #11 / 1996 / NIT / M • Ass Masters (Leisure) #02 / 1995 / LEI / M • Babes Of The Bay #1 / 1994 / LIP / F • Back Door Asians / 1995 / EVN / M • The Backway Inn #5 / 1993 / FD / M • Birthday Bash / 1995 / BOT / M • Black Studs & Little White Trash / 1995 / ROB / M • The Bottom Line / 1995 / NIT / M • Brooklyn Nights / 1994 / OD / M • Butt Jammers #01 / 1995 / SC / F • Butt Jam-mers #02 / 1995 / SC / F • Butt Jammers #05 / 1996 / SC / F • Casting Call #10 / 1994 / MET / M • The Cheater / 1994 / XCI / M • Color Me Anal / 1995 / ME / M • The Cumm Brothers #14: Buttdraft / 1995 / OD / M • Dance Naked / 1995 / PEP / M • De-fying The Odds / 1995 / OD / M • Dick & Jane In San Francisco / 1996 / AVI / M •

Dirty Bob's #23: Tampa Teasers / 1995 / FLP / S • Do Me Nurses / 1995 / LE / M • Dr Freckle & Mr Jive / 1995 / IN / M • Face To Face / 1995 / ME / M • Flesh Palace / 1995 / LBO / M • French Twist / 1996 / HO / M • Gang Bang Bitches #06 / 1995 / PP / M • Gazongas Galore #1 / 1996 / NIT / C • Girl's School / 1994 / ERA / M • Gorgeous / 1995 / MET / M • Hard Squeeze / 1994 / EMC / M • Horny Henry's Euro Adventure / 1995 / TTV / M • Hotel Sodom #03 / 1995 / SNA / M • If You Can't Lick 'em...Join 'em / 1996 / BAC / F • Inspector Croissant: The Case Of The Missing Pinky / 1995 / FC / M • Jizz Glazed Goo Guzzlers #1 / 1996 / NIT / C • Kinky Cameraman #2 / 1996 / LEI / C • Kinky Debutante Interviews #05 / 1994 / IP / M • Lovin' Spoonfuls #7 / 1996 / 4P / C • Mike Hott: #289 Three-Sum Sluts #02 / 1995 / MHV / M • Mysteria / 1995 / NIT / M • Nasty Dreams / 1994 / PRK / M • National Boom Boom's European Vacation / 1994 / HW / M • New Ends #10 / 1995 / 4P / M • The Nympho Files / 1995 / NIT / M • Opie Goes To South Central / 1995 / PP / M • Or-gies Orgies Orgies / 1994 / WV / M • Ori-ental Gang Bang / 1995 / HO / M • Outcall Outlaws / 1995 / CC / M • Pai Gow Video #07: East Meets West / 1995 / EVN / M • Pearl Of The Orient / 1995 / IN / M • Pre-scription For Lust / 1995 / NIT / M • Pulp Friction / 1994 / PP / M • Pussy Lotto / 1995 / WIV / M • Rebel Cheerleaders / 1995 / VI / M • Safari Jane / 1995 / ERA / M • Secret Diary #2 / 1995 / MID / M • Sex House / 1995 / AFV / M • Sexual Misconduct / 1994 / VD / C • Sweet Brown Sugar / 1994 / AVI / M • Tail Taggers #127: / 1994 / WV / M • Temple Of Love / 1995 / SUF / M • Tight Fit #12 / 1995 / GO / M • Titanic Orgy / 1995 / PEP / M • Tits A Wonderful Life / 1994 / CV / M • Tricky Business / 1995 / AFI / M • Un-plugged / 1995 / CC / M • Whore House / 1995 / IPI / M • Willie Wanker At The Sushi Bar / 1995 / FD / M

DALLAS DENIRO *see* Dallas (1991)
DALLAS MIKO *(Yoko Seki, Dallas (Miko))*
California Reaming / 1985 / WV / M • Hot Cars, Nasty Women / 1985 / 4WD / M • Lage / 1986 / AMB / M • Satin Finish / 1985 / SUV / M • Sexual Pursuit / 1985 / AT / M • Sins Of The Wealthy #1 / 1986 / CLV / M • We Love To Tease / 1985 / VD / M • WPINK-TV #1 / 1985 / PV / M
DALLAS SAWYER
The Misadventures Of Lois Payne / 1995 / ZFX / B • Southern Discomfort / 1992 / ZFX / B
DALLAS SHERRY
Miss Bondwell's Reformatory / 1994 / LON / B
DALLAS ST CLAIRE *(Jennifer Stone)*
Fat and not too pretty with masses of curly blonde hair and a tattoo on her left tit.
America's Raunchiest Home Videos #20: Penthouse Pussy Power / 1992 / ZA / M • Anal Asian #1 / 1992 / IN / M • Anal Climax #2 / 1991 / ROB / M • Anal Delights #2 / 1992 / ROB / M • Anal Thrills / 1992 / ROB / M • Biff Malibu's Totally Nasty Home Videos #07 / 1992 / ANA / M • Blonde Ice #1 / 1990 / EX / M • Breast Worx #15 / 1992 / LBO / M • Breast Worx #20 / 1992 / LBO / M • Bunz-Eye / 1992 / ROB / M • Dark Dreams / 1992 / WV / M • Eat My Cherry / 1994 / BHS / M • Jugsy (Western)

/ 1992 / WV / M • The Key to Love / 1992 / ZA / M • Long Hot Summer / 1992 / CDI / M • Mr. Peepers Amateur Home Videos #10: Red Rider & Little Shav / 1991 / LBO / M • Mr. Peepers Amateur Home Videos #38: Bringing Up the Rear / 1991 / LBO / M • Nasty Jack's Homemade Vid. #31 / 1991 / CDI / M • Night Of Passion / 1993 / BIA / C • Oral Majority #09 / 1992 / WV / C • Tush / 1992 / ZA / M

DALLAS STARR *see Star Index I*

DALLAS TAYLOR
Courting Libido / 1995 / HIV / G • Long Play / 1995 / 3XP / G • Married Men With Men On The Side / 1996 / BHE / G • Mr. Blue / 1996 / JSP / G • Revenge Of The Bi Dolls / 1994 / CAT / G

DALLAS WHITAKER *see* **Dallas (1994)**

DALNY MARGA
Anal Institution #2 / 1996 / ZA / M • Anal Sex / 1996 / ZA / M • Anal Talisman / 1996 / ZA / M • Analtown USA #12 / 1996 / NIT / M • Ass Masters (Leisure) #03 / 1995 / LEI / M • Bootylicious: Trailer Trash / 1996 / JMP / M • The Bottom Line / 1995 / NIT / M • Butt Wackers / 1995 / FH / M • Butt X Files #2: Anal Abduction / 1995 / WIV / M • Butthead Dreams: Down In The Bush / 1995 / FH / M • Buttslammers #10: Lust On The Internet / 1995 / BS / F • Casting Call #16 / 1995 / SO / M • Contrast / 1995 / CA / M • The Crackster / 1996 / OUP / M • Cum Buttered Corn Holes #1 / 1996 / NIT / C • Dr Freckle & Mr Jive / 1995 / IN / M • Eternal Bonds / 1995 / RHV / B • Femme Fatale / 1996 / CIN / M • Forbidden Fantasies #1 / 1995 / ZA / M • Freak Of The Week / 1996 / LIP / F • Hot Wired / 1996 / VC / M • Hotwired / 1996 / VC / M • Legs / 1996 / ZA / M • Lovin' Spoonfuls #8 / 1996 / 4P / C • Max World #4: Let's Party / 1996 / XPR / M • More Dirty Debutantes #39 / 1995 / 4P / M • Mother Nature's Bulging Bellies / 1995 / LIP / F • Muff Divers #1 / 1996 / TV / F • Muff Divers #3 / 1996 / TV / F • My Ass #1 / 1996 / NOT / M • Perverted Stories #07 / 1996 / JMP / M • Pretty Young Things Escort Service / 1995 / ZA / M • Pure Anal / 1996 / MET / M • Pussyman Auditions #01 / 1995 / SNA / M • Reverse Gang Bang / 1995 / JMP / M • Rice Burners / 1996 / NOT / M • Ring Of Desire / 1995 / LBO / M • Rumpman: Caught In An Anal Avalanche / 1995 / HW / M • Sex Academy #5: The Art Of Pulp Fiction / 1994 / ONA / M • Shave Tails #3 / 1994 / SO / M • Snatch Masters #08 / 1995 / LEI / M • Sorority Sex Kittens #3 / 1996 / VC / M • Spazm #1: Point Blank / 1996 / LBO / M • Sperm Bitches / 1995 / ZA / M • Tender Loins / 1996 / PE / M • Top Debs #6: Rear Entry Girls / 1995 / GO / M • Vibrating Vixens #2 / 1996 / TV / F • What's The Lesbian Doing In My Pirate Movie? / 1995 / LIP / F • White Wedding / 1995 / VI / M • Young & Natural #01 / 1995 / PRE / F • Young & Natural #02 / 1995 / PRE / F • Young & Natural #07 / 1995 / PRE / F • Young & Natural #08 / 1995 / PRE / F • Young & Natural #09 / 1995 / PRE / C

DAMEAN (WOLF) *see* **Damian Wolf**

DAMIAN
Anal 247 / 1995 / CC / M • Big Bust Babes #13 / 1993 / AFI / M • Big Bust Babes #14 / 1993 / AFI / M • The Black Butt Sisters Do Los Angeles / 1995 / MID / M • D.P. Party

Tonite / 1995 / JMP / M • Girls II Women / 1996 / AVI / M • Hidden Camera #15 / 1994 / JMP / M • Laguna Nights / 1995 / FH / M • More Dirty Debutantes #46 / 1995 / 4P / M • New Faces, Hot Bodies #06 / 1993 / STP / M • New Faces, Hot Bodies #07 / 1993 / STP / M • New Faces, Hot Bodies #08 / 1993 / STP / M • New Faces, Hot Bodies #09 / 1993 / STP / M • New Faces, Hot Bodies #10 / 1993 / STP / M • New Faces, Hot Bodies #11 / 1993 / STP / M • New Faces, Hot Bodies #12 / 1993 / STP / M • New Faces, Hot Bodies #13 / 1994 / STP / M • New Faces, Hot Bodies #14 / 1994 / STP / M • New Faces, Hot Bodies #16 / 1994 / STP / M • New Faces, Hot Bodies #17 / 1995 / STP / M • New Faces, Hot Bodies #18 / 1995 / STP / M • New Faces, Hot Bodies #19 / 1995 / STP / M • New Faces, Hot Bodies #20 / 1996 / STP / M • New Faces, Hot Bodies #21 / 1996 / STP / C • New Girls In Town #6 / 1994 / CC / M • Odyssey Triple Play #31: Double Penetration Babes / 1993 / OD / M • Odyssey Triple Play #46: Ass-Splitting Sex / 1993 / OD / M • Video Virgins #10 / 1993 / NS / M • The Voyeur #2 / 1994 / EA / M • Wad Gobblers #11 / 1994 / GLI / M

DAMIAN CASTELLANDS *see* **Damien Cashmere**

DAMIAN WOLF *(Damien (Wolf), Damien Wolf, Damean (Wolf))*
Dangerous looking male who looks like he's a cross between a black and a Hispanic.
A&B GB#072: Chessie Does It / 1990 / A&B / M • Action In Black / 1993 / FD / M • Adventures Of The DP Boys: Back In Town / 1994 / HW / M • Amateurs Exposed #05 / 1995 / CV / M • America's Raunchiest Home Videos #57 / 1993 / ZA / M • America's Raunchiest Home Videos #66: / 1993 / ZA / M • Anal Gang Bangers #02 / 1993 / GLI / M • Bachelor Party #2 / 1993 / FPI / M • Beach Bum Amateur's #16 / 1992 / MID / M • Beach Bum Amateur's #19 / 1992 / MID / M • Beach Bum Amateur's #22 / 1993 / MID / M • Beach Bum Amateur's #26 / 1993 / MID / M • Beach Bum Amateur's #27 / 1993 / MID / M • Beach Bum Amateur's #28 / 1993 / MID / M • Beach Bum Amateur's #29 / 1993 / MID / M • Big Bust Babes #23 / 1994 / AFI / M • Big Bust Bangers #1 / 1994 / AMP / M • Big Bust Bangers #2 / 1994 / AMP / M • Black Orgies #01 / 1993 / AFI / M • Black Orgies #21 / 1994 / GO / M • Black Orgies #22 / 1994 / GO / M • Black Orgies #33 / 1995 / GO / M • Black Orgies #36 / 1995 / GO / M • Bobby Hollander's Maneaters #02 / 1993 / SFP / M • Bobby Hollander's Rookie Nookie #06 / 1993 / SFP / M • Bobby Hollander's Rookie Nookie #08 / 1993 / SFP / M • Bobby Hollander's Sweet Cheeks #102 / 1992 / WV / M • Bone Alone / 1993 / MID / M • Bra Busters #02 / 1993 / LBO / M • Breast Worx #35 / 1992 / LBO / M • Bun Busters #02 / 1993 / LBO / M • California Blacks / 1994 / V99 / M • Candy / 1995 / MET / M • Candyman #06 / 1993 / GLI / M • Club DV8 #1 / 1993 / SC / M • Deep Throat Girls #03 / 1994 / GO / M • Deliciously Teri / 1993 / IF / M • Depraved Fantasies #1 / 1993 / FPI / M • Depraved Fantasies #2 / 1994 / FPI / M • Depraved Fantasies #3 / 1994 / FPI / M • Dick & Jane Do The Slopes In Ass Spin / 1994 / AVI / M •

Dirt Bags / 1994 / FPI / M • Dirty Dating Service #05 / 1994 / WP / M • Double Penetration Virgins #03 / 1994 / LE / M • Ebony Erotica #05: Black Obsessions / 1993 / GO / M • Ebony Erotica #06: Black Essence / 1993 / GO / M • Ebony Erotica #07: Sepia Salute / 1993 / GO / M • Ebony Erotica #08: Indigo Moods / 1993 / GO / M • Ebony Erotica #25: Java Jive / 1994 / GO / M • Ebony Erotica #26: Night Shift / 1994 / GO / M • Ebony Erotica #34: Mellow Moprene / 1995 / GO / M • Freaks Of Leather #2 / 1994 / IF / C • The Fucking Elvises / 1994 / GLI / M • Gangbang Girl #16 / 1995 / ANA / M • Grateful Grandma's Gang Bang / 1994 / FC / M • Green Piece Of Ass #3 / 1994 / RTP / M • Harry Horndog #19: Anal Lovers #3 / 1993 / ZA / M • Hispanic Orgies #01 / 1993 / GO / M • Hispanic Orgies #02 / 1993 / GO / M • Hometown Honeys #5 / 1993 / VEX / M • Hot Amateur Nights / 1996 / WV / M • House Of Sex #14: All Black Gang Bang / 1994 / RTP / M • House Of Sex #16: Dirty Oral Three Ways / 1994 / RTP / M • House Of Spartacus #1 / 1993 / IF / M • Lactamania #1 / 1994 / TTV / M • Living For Love / 1993 / V99 / M • Love Letters #1 / 1993 / SC / M • Love Letters #2 / 1993 / SC / M • M Series #04 / 1993 / LBO / M • M Series #06 / 1993 / LBO / M • M Series #07 / 1993 / LBO / M • M Series #21 / 1994 / LBO / M • M Series #30 / 1994 / LBO / M • Mellon Man #04 / 1995 / AVI / M • Mike Hott: #213 Horny Couples #07 / 1992 / MHV / M • Mr. Peepers Amateur Home Videos #58: Penthouse Pussy Power / 1992 / LBO / M • Mr. Peepers Amateur Home Videos #59: The Ball Of The Wild / 1992 / LBO / M • Nasty Newcummers #05 / 1994 / MET / M • Nasty Newcummers #08 / 1995 / MET / M • Nasty Nymphos #01 / 1993 / ANA / M • Naughty Nicole / 1994 / SC / M • Neighborhood Watch #33 / 1992 / LBO / M • Nici Sterling's DP Gang Bang / 1996 / FC / M • Odyssey 30 Min: #242: / 1992 / OD / M • Odyssey 30 Min: #263: Carmel's 4-Way Dating Game / 1992 / OD / M • Odyssey 30 Min: #264: / 1992 / OD / M • Odyssey 30 Min: #282: / 1992 / OD / M • Odyssey 30 Min: #325: / 1993 / OD / M • Odyssey 30 Min: #328: / 1993 / OD / M • Odyssey Triple Play #53: Butt-Fuck Bash / 1993 / OD / M • Odyssey Triple Play #70: Three By Threeway / 1994 / OD / M • Odyssey Triple Play #74: Conjugal Couples / 1994 / OD / M • Odyssey Triple Play #81: Copulation Intergration / 1994 / OD / M • Ona Z's Star Search #01 / 1993 / GLI / M • Ona Zee's Black Label #1: Sex Hunger / 1996 / ONA / C • One For The Gusher / 1995 / AMP / M • Oriental Gang Bang / 1995 / HO / M • Patty Plenty's Gang Bang / 1995 / NIT / M • Pearl Necklace: Amorous Amateurs #25 / 1993 / SEE / M • Pearl Necklace: Amorous Amateurs #26 / 1993 / SEE / M • Pearl Necklace: Thee Bush League: The Best Of Oral #01 / 1993 / SEE / C • Positively Pagan #01 / 1991 / ATA / M • Positively Pagan #06 / 1993 / ATA / M • Raw Talent: Bang 'er 15 Times / 1992 / RTP / M • Ready And Willing / 1993 / VEX / M • Ron Hightower's White Chicks #09 / 1994 / LBO / M • Ron Hightower's White Chicks #12 / 1994 / LBO / M • Ron Hightower's White Chicks #14 / 1994 / LBO / M • Rosie: The Neighborhood Slut / 1994 /

VIM / M • Rump Humpers #16 / 1993 / GLI / M • Savage Fury #3 / 1994 / VEX / M • Sex Fantasy / 1993 / PPR / M • Sgt. Peckers Lonely Hearts Club Gang Bang / 1995 / AMP / M • Slummin' Hood Girlz / 1993 / CA / M • Spanish Fly / 1993 / VEX / M • Starbangers #02 / 1993 / BIG / M • Starbangers #06 / 1994 / FPI / M • Stiff Competition #2 / 1994 / CA / M • Tails From The Tower / 1993 / AFI / M • Tight Fit #02 / 1994 / GO / M • Udderly Fantastic / 1993 / IF / M • The Ultimate Squirting Machine / 1994 / FPI / M • Uncle Roy's Amateur Home Video #17 / 1993 / VIM / M • Vortex / 1995 / MET / M • Witchcraft 2000 / 1994 / GLI / M • The World's Biggest Gang Bang #1 / 1995 / FPI / M

DAMIAN WOLF (1985)
Girls Of The Third Reich / 1985 / FC / M

DAMIAN ZEUS *(Anthony Zeus, Zeus, Damien Zeus)*
Young blonde male.
Bachelor Party #1 / 1993 / FPI / M • Bachelor Party #2 / 1993 / FPI / M • Black Detail #1 / 1994 / VT / M • Black Detail #2 / 1994 / VT / M • Bunny Bleu: A Gang Bang Fantasy / 1994 / FC / M • Butt Bangers Ball / 1994 / FPI / M • Cherry Poppers #03: School's Out / 1994 / ZA / M • For The Money #1 / 1993 / FH / M • Gangbang At The O.K. Corral / 1994 / FPI / M • Gangbang Sluts / 1994 / VMX / M • I Can't Believe I Did The Whole Team! / 1994 / FPI / M • Naked Truth #1 / 1993 / FH / M • Silent Stranger / 1992 / VI / M • Starbangers #02 / 1993 / BIG / M • Starbangers #04 / 1993 / FPI / M • Starbangers #05 / 1993 / FPI / M • Super Ball Sunday / 1994 / LBO / M • The Swap #2 / 1994 / VI / M • Titan's Amateur Video Magazine #03 / 1995 / TEG / M • Top Debs #2: The Reunion / 1993 / GO / M • Virgin / 1993 / HW / M

DAMIEN
Bimbo Boys / 1995 / PL / C • Bizarre Mistress Series: Sharon Mitchell / 1992 / BIZ / C • Black Power / 1996 / LEI / C • Dirty & Kinky Mature Women #09 / 1996 / C69 / M • The Fabulous 50's Girls Ride Again / 1994 / EMC / M • The Fine Line / 1990 / SO / M • Geriatric Volley Girls / 1995 / FH • Hardcore Confidential #1 / 1996 / TEP / M • Incantation / 1996 / FC / M • Latin Fever #1 / 1996 / C69 / M • The Mating Game / 1992 / PL / G • Naughty Senorita / 1994 / WIV / M • The Pleasure Girl / 1994 / GO / M • Steel Garters / 1992 / CAT / G • Sugar Mommies / 1995 / FPI / M • Triple Penetration Debutante Sluts #1 / 1996 / BAC / M • When The Fat Lady Sings / 1996 / EX / M

DAMIEN (WOLF) *see* **Damian Wolf**

DAMIEN CASHMERE *(Damian Castellands, Damon Cashmere, Damien Kashmir, Damion Cashmere)*
Against All Bods / 1988 / ZA / M • Angel's Back / 1988 / IN / M • Angela Takes A Dare / 1988 / FAZ / M • Back To Rears / 1988 / VI / M • Bad Attitude / 1987 / CC / M • Beyond The Denver Dynasty / 1988 / CA / M • Big Top Cabaret #2 / 1989 / BTO / M • The Bitch Is Back / 1988 / FAN / M • Bondage Games #1 / 1991 / BIZ / B • Bondage Games #2 / 1991 / BIZ / B • Bustin' Out / 1988 / VEX / M • Casabanga / 1991 / NAN / M • Charmed Forces / 1987 / VI / M • Cheating American Style / 1988 / WV / M • Coming In America / 1988 / VEX / M •

Creatures Of The Night / 1987 / FAN / M • Critical Positions / 1987 / VXP / M • Deep Inside Ona Zee / 1992 / VC / C • Deep Inside Trading / 1986 / AR / M • Double Agents / 1988 / VXP / M • Double Black Fantasy / 1987 / CC / C • Every Body / 1992 / LAP / M • Extreme Heat / 1987 / ME / M • Fannie's Fantail / 1985 / VC / M • Firebox / 1986 / VXP / M • Flesh In Ecstasy #04: Jeanna Fine / 1987 / GO / C • Flesh In Ecstasy #05: Rachel Ashley / 1987 / GO / C • Flesh In Ecstasy #07: Brittany Stryker / 1987 / GO / C • The Flirt / 1987 / VWA / M • Flying High With Rikki Lee / 1992 / VEX / C • Flying High With Tracey Adams / 1987 / VEX / M • Fondle With Care / 1989 / VEX / M • Fresh! / 1987 / VXP / M • The Golden Gals / 1989 / BTO / M • Good Evening Vietnam / 1987 / WV / M • Hard Ball / 1991 / NAN / M • Hard Times / 1990 / GLE / M • The Heiress / 1988 / VI / M • Hot & Heavy / 1989 / PL / M • Hot Scalding / 1989 / VC / M • The Hot Tip / 1986 / VXP / M • Hot To Swap / 1988 / VEX / M • Inside Sharon Mitchell / 1989 / ZA / C • Kiss Thy Mistress' Feet #1 / 1990 / BIZ / B • Krystal Balling / 1988 / PL / M • Let's Get Naked / 1987 / VEX / M • Little Red Riding Hood / 1988 / WV / M • Love Hammer / 1988 / VXP / M • Love Lotion #9 / 1987 / VXP / M • Mad Love / 1988 / VC / M • Mind Mirror / 1994 / LAP / M • My Party Doll / 1987 / VXP / M • Nikki And The Pom-Pom Girls / 1987 / VEX / M • Object(s) Of My Desire / 1988 / V99 / M • Only The Very Best On Video / 1992 / VC / C • Panting At The Opera / 1988 / VXP / M • Passion Chain / 1987 / ZA / M • The Pleasure Machine / 1987 / VXP / M • Porked / 1986 / VXP / M • Pornocchio / 1987 / ME / M • Princess Of Penetration / 1988 / VXP / M • The Screwables / 1992 / RUM / M • Second Skin / 1989 / VC / M • Sex In Dangerous Places / 1988 / VI / M • Sex Sounds / 1989 / PL / M • Sex Tips For Modern Women / 1987 / VXP / M • Sex World Girls / 1987 / AR / M • Sexpot / 1987 / VXP / M • Sexual Odyssey / 1985 / VC / M • Shoot To Thrill / 1988 / VWA / M • Silence Of The G.A.M.S. / 1992 / CA / M • Strange Revenge / 1988 / ZA / M • The Sweet Spurt Of Youth / 1988 / WV / M • Tailspin / 1987 / AVC / M • Teaser / 1986 / RLV / M • Throbbin' Hood / 1987 / VD / M • Thunderstorm / 1987 / VC / M • Tight End / 1988 / VXP / M • Trapped By The Mistress / 1991 / BIZ / B • Walk On The Wild Side / 1987 / CDI / M • Wet Tails / 1989 / PL / M • What Kind Of Girls Do You Think We Are? / 1986 / VEX / M • What Kind Of Girls Do You Think We Are? / 1991 / VEX / C • Wishbone / 1988 / VXP / M • Wrong Arm Of The Law / 1987 / ZA / M

DAMIEN HARRIS *see* **Star Index I**

DAMIEN KASHMIR *see* **Damien Cashmere**

DAMIEN MICHAELS
Adults Only / 1995 / BOT / M • Amateur Dreams #4 / 1994 / DR / M • Anal Camera #06 / 1995 / EVN / M • Anal Camera #14 / 1996 / EVN / M • Anal Reunion / 1996 / EVN / M • Ancient Amateurs #1 / 1996 / LOF / M • Ancient Amateurs #2 / 1996 / LOF / M • Attack Of The Killer Dildos / 1996 / RAS / M • Bang City #6: Bugger's Banquet / 1995 / SC / M • Bang City #7: Carolina's Anal Gang Bang / 1995 / SC / M •

Bedtime Stories / 1996 / VC / M • Birthday Bash / 1995 / BOT / M • Blue Saloon / 1996 / ME / M • Booty And The Ho' Fish / 1996 / RAS / M • Breastman's Triple X Cellent Adventure / 1995 / EVN / M • Career Girls / 1996 / OUP / M • Carolina's D.P. Anal Gangbang / 1996 / FC / M • Cyber-Sex Love Junkies / 1996 / BBE / M • Dark Eyes / 1995 / FC / M • Decadent Dreams / 1996 / ME / M • Dirty & Kinky Mature Women #07 / 1996 / C69 / M • Double Dicked #1 / 1996 / RAS / M • Double Dicked #2 / 1996 / RAS / M • Fresh Faces #10 / 1996 / EVN / M • Fresh Meat (John Leslie) #1 / 1994 / EA / M • Gang Bang Diaries #5 / 1994 / SFP / M • Grateful Grandma's Gang Bang / 1994 / FC / M • Head Nurse / 1996 / RAS / M • Hollywood Hookers / 1996 / DWV / M • Home Nurses Anal Adventure / 1994 / LBO / M • Interviews At The Hard Wok Cafe / 1996 / LOF / M • Kimberly Kupps Gets 5 A's / 1996 / NIT / M • Lingerie / 1996 / RAS / M • Lockdown / 1996 / NIT / M • Mickey Ray's Sex Search #03: Deep Heat / 1994 / WIV / M • Mike Hott: #327 Older Gals #12 / 1995 / MHV / F • Mike Hott: #339 Cum In My Mouth #04 / 1996 / MHV / C • Mike Hott: #342 Three-Sum Sluts #10 / 1995 / MHV / M • Monkey Gang Bang / 1996 / NOT / M • Mutiny On The Booty / 1996 / FC / M • Nena Cherry's Dp Gang Bang / 1996 / NIT / M • Nineteen #4 / 1996 / FOR / M • Old Wave Hookers #1 / 1995 / PL / M • Old Wave Hookers #2 / 1995 / PL / M • Orgy Camera #2 / 1996 / EVN / M • Patty Plenty's Gang Bang / 1995 / NIT / M • Pay 4 Play / 1996 / RAS / M • Planet X #1 / 1996 / HW / M • Prime Choice #4 / 1995 / RAS / M • Prime Choice #6 / 1996 / RAS / M • Prime Choice #7 / 1996 / RAS / M • Private Film #24 / 1995 / OD / M • Private Film #26 / 1995 / OD / M • Private Stories #01 / 1995 / OD / M • Private Stories #02 / 1995 / OD / M • Private Stories #03 / 1995 / OD / M • Private Video Magazine #25 / 1995 / OD / M • Pussy Showdown / 1994 / WIV / M • The Real Deal #3 / 1996 / FC / M • The Real Deal #4 / 1996 / FC / M • Sex Over 40 #1 / 1994 / PL / M • The Annointment #1 / 1994 / PL / M • Starbangers #09 / 1996 / ZA / M • Summer Dreams / 1996 / TEP / M • Summer Vacation #1 / 1996 / RAS / M • Summer Vacation #2 / 1996 / RAS / M • Surfin' The Net / 1996 / RAS / M • Tia's Holiday Gang Bang / 1995 / HO / M • Triple X Video Magazine #06 / 1995 / OD / M • Voyeur's Fantasies / 1996 / C69 / M • Wet & Wicked / 1995 / PRK / M • Wild Orgies #09 / 1994 / AFI / M

DAMIEN MISCHIEF
The Savage / 1994 / SC / M • Wet Faces #1 / 1997 / SC / C

DAMIEN WOLF *see* **Damian Wolf**

DAMIEN ZEUS *see* **Damian Zeus**

DAMION CASHMERE *see* **Damien Cashmere**

DAMION WHITE
Kitty Foxx's Kinky Kapers #01 / 1995 / TTV / M

DAMON
Bizarre Mistress Series: Mistress Destiny / 1992 / BIZ / C • Caught, Punished And Caged / 1991 / BIZ / B • A Date With Destiny / 1992 / BIZ / B • Sweet Surrender / 1991 / BIZ / B • Sweet Surrender / 1991 / BIZ / B

DAMON CASHMERE *see* **Damien Cashmere**

DAMON CHRISTIAN *(Fred Stifflerin, Richard Aldrich)*
Normally a director but occasionally appears in his own movies.
American Pie / 1980 / SE / M • Debbie Does Dishes #1 / 1985 / AVC / M • Disco Lady / 1978 / EVI / M • Goin' Down / 1985 / VC / M • Nudes At Eleven #2 / 1987 / AVC / M • Private Thighs / 1987 / AVC / C • The Seductress / 1982 / VC / M • Sheets Of San Francisco / 1986 / AVC / M • Tell Them Johnny Wadd Is Here / 1975 / QX / M • Tracey's Love Chamber / 1987 / AR / M • Yank My Doodle, It's A Dandy / 1985 / GOM / M • Yuppies In Heat / 1988 / CHA / C

DAMON GERARD
Wet Wilderness / 1975 / VCX / B

DAMON JONES
White Hot / 1984 / VXP / M

DAMONA MARIN
Resurrection Of Eve / 1973 / MIT / M

DAN
Dark Alleys #01 / 1992 / FC / M • The French Canal / 1995 / DVP / G • Homegrown Video #402 / 1993 / HOV / M

DAN CARTER
Anal Angels #2 / 1990 / VEX / C • Falcon Head / 1990 / ARG / M • Open House (CDI) / 1989 / CDI / M • Sodom & Gomorrah / 1974 / MIT / M

DAN COOPER
College Girl / 1990 / VEX / M • The Lethal Squirt / 1990 / AR / M • Littledove's Cup / 1995 / DBM / M • Rainwoman #03 / 1990 / CC / M • Salsa Break / 1989 / EA / M • Satisfaction / 1974 / CDC / M • The Squirt / 1988 / AR / M • Squirt 'em Cowgirl / 1990 / ERU / M • The Squirt Bunny / 1989 / ERU / M • Squirt On The Hunt / 1989 / ERU / M

DAN D. LYON
Depraved Fantasies #3 / 1994 / FPI / M • Kitty Foxx's Kinky Kapers #01 / 1995 / TTV / M • Kitty Foxx's Kinky Kapers #02 / 1995 / TTV / M • Positively Pagan #05 / 1993 / ATA / M

DAN DANCING
Hot Country / cr83 / WV / M

DAN DELGADO
Sorority Stewardesses #1 / 1995 / PE / M

DAN EGAN
Expensive Taste / 1978 / VCX / M

DAN FISHER
Flesh & Laces #1 / 1983 / CA / M • Flesh & Laces #2 / 1983 / CA / M • Layover / 1985 / HO / M • Marathon / 1982 / CA / M • Miss American Dream / 1985 / CIV / M • Rich Bitch / 1985 / HO / M

DAN HARDMAN *see* **David Hardman**
DAN HOOPER *see* **Star Index I**
DAN HOWARD *see* **Star Index I**
DAN ISUZU *see* **Star Index I**
DAN IZUSU
Tied & Tickled #14: Count Tickula / 1986 / CS / B

DAN JOHNSON *see* **Star Index I**
DAN MILO *see* **Star Index I**
DAN O'NEILL
Resurrection Of Eve / 1973 / MIT / M

DAN PACE
L.A. Tool & Die / 1979 / TMX / G

DAN POLE
The Kowloon Connection / 1973 / VCX / M

• Oriental Kitten / 1973 / VCX / M
DAN QUICK *see* **Star Index I**
DAN ROBERTS
Baby Face #1 / 1977 / VC / M • The Best Of Alex De Renzy #1 / 1983 / VC / C

DAN ROCKHARD
Screamers (Ona Zee) / 1995 / ONA / M

DAN SILVER *see* **Dan Steele**
DAN SIR *see* **Star Index I**
DAN SLAVIN *see* **Star Index I**
DAN SOLON *see* **Star Index I**
DAN STEAL *see* **Dan Steele**
DAN STEEK *see* **Dan Steele**
DAN STEELE *(Dan Stone, Dan Steek, Dan Silver, Dan Steal, Dr. Dan)*
Construction worker type who was the boyfriend of Suzanne St Lorraine and as of 1994 is the boyfriend of Jasmine Aloha—blonde hair, big muscles. Dan Stone in **In Pursuit Of Passion**. Dr. Dan in **Fire & Ice: Caught In The Act**.
Anal Asian / 1994 / VEX / M • Anything You Ever Wanted To Know About Sex / 1993 / VEX / M • Bangkok Nights / 1994 / VI / M • Beaver Hunt #02 / 1994 / LEI / M • Begging For Bondage / 1993 / PL / B • Big Boob Ball / 1995 / IF / C • Blue Fire / 1991 / V99 / M • Bodies In Motion / 1994 / IF / M • Breakfast At Tiffany's / 1994 / IF / M • The Breast Of Breastmen / 1995 / EVN / C • Breastman Goes To Breastland #2 / 1993 / EVN / M • Burn It Up / 1994 / VEX / M • Cluster Fuck #01 / 1993 / MAX / M • College Girl / 1990 / VEX / M • Defending Your Soul / 1995 / EX / M • Delicate Matters / 1989 / VEX / M • Deliciously Teri / 1993 / IF / M • Dick & Jane Do The Slopes In Ass Spin / 1994 / AVI / M • Double Load #2 / 1994 / HW / M • An Evening At Mistress Dominos / 1990 / PL / B • Fire & Ice: Caught In The Act / 1995 / WP / M • Flexxx #1 / 1994 / VT / M • Fortune Nookie / 1994 / PPP / M • Gazonga Goddess #2 / 1994 / IF / M • Hometown Honeys #5 / 1993 / VEX / M • The Hustlers / 1993 / MID / M • I Married An Anal Queen / 1993 / MID / M • In Pursuit Of Passion / 1990 / V99 / M • Knights In Black Satin / 1990 / VEX / M • Living In Sin / 1990 / VEX / M • Long Dan Silver / 1992 / IF / M • Man Of Steel / 1992 / IF / M • Nasty Nymphos #04 / 1994 / ANA / M • Night Watch / 1990 / VEX / M • No Motive / 1994 / MID / M • Perfect Girl / 1991 / VEX / M • Physically Fit / 1991 / V99 / C • Playing The Field / 1990 / VEX / M • Romance & Fantasy / 1995 / VEX / M • Secret Dreams / 1991 / VEX / M • Six Plus One #2 / 1993 / VEX / C • Spanish Fly / 1993 / VEX / M • Stewardesses Behind Bars / 1994 / HW / M • Summer Dreams / 1990 / VEX / M • Sweet Sunshine / 1995 / IF / M • Sweet Tease / 1990 / VEX / M • Teach Me Tonight / 1990 / VEX / M • Thunder And Lightning / 1996 / MID / M • Voodoo Vixens / 1991 / IF / M • Welcome To Paradise / 1994 / IF / M • Wet, Wild And Willing / 1993 / V99 / M • Wild Thing / 1994 / IF / M • You Can Touch This / 1991 / EVN / M

DAN STEPHENS
Daddy's Little Girls / 1983 / CA / M • Flash Pants / 1983 / VC / M • Hypersexuals / 1984 / VC / M • In Love / 1983 / VC / M • Night Hunger / 1983 / AVC / M • Piggies / 1984 / VC / M • Pleasure Channel / 1984 / VC / M • Private School Girls / 1983 / CA / M • Throat...12 Years After / 1984 / VC / M

DAN STONE *see* **Dan Steele**
DAN STYLE
Gangbang Girl #04 / 1992 / ANA / M
DAN T. MANN *(Lee Cooper, Brandon Hall, Danny Mann)*
Lee Cooper (**La Bimbo**—as director). Rough looking male with tattos on his left arm at shoulder level. Sandy/dark hair. Brandon Hall is the box credits for **Too Hot To Touch**.
69 Park Avenue / 1985 / ELH / M • Amber Lynn: She's Back / 1995 / TTV / C • Anal Annie And The Willing Husbands / 1984 / LIP / M • Anal Reamers / 1986 / 4P / M • Angel Of The Night / 1985 / IN / M • Backdoor Babes / 1985 / WET / M • Backstage / 1988 / CDI / M • Ball Busters / 1984 / CV / M • Beyond Taboo / 1984 / VIV / M • The Big Bang / 1988 / WET / M • Blonde Heat (VCA) / 1985 / VC / M • Blue Dream Lover / 1985 / TAR / M • Butter Me Up / 1984 / CHX / M • The Case Of The Sensuous Sinners / 1988 / ME / M • Chocolate Cream / 1984 / SUP / M • The Color of Honey / 1987 / SUV / M • Crystal Blue / 1987 / VD / M • Debbie Does 'em All #1 / 1985 / CV / M • Deep Chill / cr85 / AT / M • Deep Inside Keisha / 1994 / VC / C • Deep Inside Rachel Ashley / 1987 / VEX / M • Deep Inside Samantha Strong / 1992 / CDI / C • Deep Inside Viviana / 1992 / VEX / C • Deliveries In The Rear #1 / 1985 / AVC / M • Desperately Seeking Suzie / 1985 / VD / M • Dialing For Desires / 1988 / 4P / M • Dirty Shary / 1985 / VD / M • Don't Tell Daddy #1 / 1985 / PL / C • Dreams / 1987 / AR / M • E Three / 1985 / GO / M • Educating Nina / 1984 / AT / M • The Enchantress / 1985 / 4P / M • The Fire Inside / 1988 / VC / C • Firefoxes / 1985 / PLY / M • Flesh And Ecstasy / 1985 / VD / M • Flesh In Ecstasy #04: Jeanna Fine / 1987 / GO / C • Flesh In Ecstasy #05: Rachel Ashley / 1987 / GO / C • Flesh In Ecstasy #08: Traci Adams / 1987 / GO / C • Flying High With Rikki Lee / 1992 / VEX / C • Flying High With Tracey Adams / 1987 / VEX / M • French Cleaners / 1986 / VCR / M • Future Sex / 1984 / NSV / M • Future Sodom / 1988 / VD / M • Gang Bangs #1 / 1985 / VCR / M • Girl On The Run / 1985 / VC / M • Going Down With Amber / 1987 / 4P / M • Gourmet Quickies: Rikki Blake #721 / 1985 / GO / C • Harlequin Affair / 1985 / CIX / M • Headgames / 1985 / WV / M • Heidi A / 1985 / PL / M • Holly Does Hollywood #1 / 1985 / VEX / M • Holly Does Hollywood #2 / 1987 / VEX / M • Hot Amber Nights / 1987 / CC / M • Hot Close-Ups / 1984 / WV / M • Hot Flashes / 1984 / VC / M • Hot School Reunion / 1984 / CHX / F • Hot Yachts / 1987 / VEX / M • House Of Lust / 1984 / VD / M • Hustler #17 / 1984 / CA0 / M • Hyapatia Lee's Arcade Series #01 / 1988 / ZA / C • Hyapatia Lee's Arcade Series #02 / 1988 / ZA / C • Imaginary Lovers / 1986 / ME / M • Indecent Pleasures / 1984 / CA / M • Inflamed / 1984 / NSV / M • La Bimbo / 1987 / PEN / M • The Ladies In Lace Party / 1985 / MAP / M • Ladies Of The 80's / 1985 / PV / M • Legends Of Porn #2 / 1989 / CV / C • Let Me Tell Ya 'Bout Black Chicks / 1985 / VC / M • Let's Get Naked / 1987 / VEX / M • License To Thrill / 1985 / VD / M • Like A Virgin #1 / 1985 / AT / M • A Little Dynasty / 1985 / CIV / M • Looking For Lust / 1984 /

THE X-RATED VIDEOTAPE STAR INDEX   **169**

VEL / M • Loose Caboose / 1987 / 4P / M • Lorelei / 1984 / CV / M • Love Bites / 1985 / CA / M • The Love Scene / 1985 / CDI / M • Lovin' USA / 1989 / EXH / C • Lucy Has A Ball / 1987 / ME / M • Lustfully Seeking Susan / 1985 / PLY / M • Lusty / 1986 / CDI / M • A Mid-Slumber's Night Dream / 1985 / 4P / M • Misadventures Of The Bang Gang / 1987 / AR / M • Naughty Nymphs / 1986 / VEX / M • Naughty Nymphs / 1991 / VEX / C • Nice 'n' Tight / 1985 / AIR / M • Nicki / 1987 / VI / M • On The Wet Side / 1987 / V99 / M • Parliament: Blondes Have More Fun / 1989 / PM / C • Parliament: Samantha Strong #1 / 1986 / PM / M • Party Girls / 1988 / MAP / M • Passion Pit / 1985 / SE / M • Passions / 1985 / MIT / M • Pipe Dreams / 1985 / 4P / M • Play Me Again, Vanessa / 1986 / VC / M • Playing For Passion / 1987 / IN / M • Playmate #01 / 1984 / VC / M • The Pleasure Hunt #1 / 1984 / NSV / M • The Pleasure Seekers / 1985 / AT / M • The Plumber Cometh / 1985 / 4P / M • Precious Assets / cr87 / VEX / M • Princess Of Darkness / 1987 / VEX / M • Rambone Does Hollywood / 1986 / WET / M • Rearbusters / 1988 / LVI / C • The Red Hot Roadrunner / 1987 / VD / M • Rump Humpers / 1985 / WET / M • Screwdriver / 1988 / CC / C • Sex Asylum #1 / 1985 / VI / M • The Sex Goddess / 1984 / GO / M • Sex Search / 1988 / IN / S • Sexperiences / 1987 / VEX / M • Shave Tail / 1984 / AMB / M • Shipwrecked / 1991 / VEX / C • Sizzling Summer / 1984 / VC / M • Sore Throat / 1985 / GO / M • Splash Dance / 1987 / AR / M • A Star Is Porn / 1985 / PL / M • Starlets / 1985 / 4P / M • Stephanie's Outrageous / 1988 / LV / C • Summer Break / 1985 / VEX / M • Supersluts Of Wrestling / 1986 / VD / M • Surf, Sand And Sex / 1987 / SE / M • Tailgunners / 1985 / WET / M • Tailspin / 1987 / AVC / M • Taking Off / 1984 / VC / M • A Taste Of Cherry / 1985 / CV / M • Tease Me / 1986 / VC / M • This Butt's For You / 1986 / PME / M • Three Faces Of Angel / 1987 / CV / M • Tight Fit / 1987 / V99 / M • Tight Fit / 1991 / VEX / C • Tongue 'n Cheek (Vca) / 1991 / VC / M • Too Hot To Touch #1 / 1985 / CV / M • Traci Who? / 1987 / AVC / C • Tracy In Heaven (Orig 1985) / 1985 / WV / M • Two Tons Of Fun #1 / 1985 / 4P / C • Up To No Good / 1986 / CDI / M • Virgin Heat / 1986 / TEM / M • Wet Weekend / 1987 / MAC / M • Wet Workout / 1987 / VEX / M • White Chocolate / 1987 / PEN / M • You're The Boss / 1985 / VD / M • [Centerfolds & Covergirls #1 / 19?? / ... / M

DAN THE FAN
More Dirty Debutantes #31 / 1994 / 4P / M
DAN TOWERS
Missing Pieces / 1985 / IN / M
DAN VOGEL
Intimate Desires / 1978 / VEP / M
DAN WEST
No Reservations / 1995 / MN0 / G
DAN WHITE *see Star Index I*
DAN WILCOX *see Star Index I*
DANA
AVP #9500: The Long Hard Ride / 1991 / AVP / M • Black Bound Beauty / 1995 / GAL / B • Shaved #01 / 1991 / RB / F • The Wacky World Of X-Rated Bloopers / 1989 / GO / M
DANA ANDES *see Star Index I*

DANA CANNON *see* **Brigitte Monet**
DANA DENNIS *(Dana Doe)*
Dana Doe is from **Kiss And Tell**.
Kiss And Tell / 1980 / CA / M • Sex Boat / 1980 / VCX / M
DANA DEVILLE *see* **Dina DeVille**
DANA DILLON *see* **Dana Dylan**
DANA DOE *see* **Dana Dennis**
DANA DOUGLAS
Club Ecstasy / 1987 / CA / M • Despicable Dames / 1986 / CC / M • I Was A She-Male For The FBI / 1987 / SEA / G • Mardi Gras Passions / 1987 / MET / M • Parliament: Hard TV #1 / 1988 / PM / G • Queens Are Wild #1 / 1992 / VIM / G • The Riding Mistress / 1983 / BIZ / B • Screw / 1985 / CV / M • She Studs #01 / 1990 / BIZ / G • She Studs #02 / 1991 / BIZ / G • She-Male Encounters #05: Orgy At The Poysinberry Bar #1 / 1987 / MET / G • She-Male Encounters #12: Orgy At The Poysinberry #2 / 1987 / MET / G • She-Male Encounters #18: Murder She-Male Wrote / 1987 / MET / G • Simply Outrageous / 1989 / VC / C • Trisexual Encounters #02 / 1985 / PL / G • Trisexual Encounters #03 / 1986 / PL / G • Tropical Lust / 1987 / MET / M
DANA DYLAN *(Shari Sloane, Dana Dillon, Diana Dylan, Shari Sloan, Sheri Sloan, Dana Williams)*
The $50,000,000 Cherry / 1987 / VD / M • 10 1/2 Weeks / 1986 / SE / M • Addicted To Love / 1988 / WAV / M • Anal Intruder #02 / 1988 / CC / M • Bi-Heat #02 / 1987 / ZA / G • Bi-Heat #03 / 1987 / ZA / G • Bi-Heat #04 / 1987 / ZA / G • Black Heat / 1986 / VC / M • Blacks & Blondes #49 / 1987 / WV / M • The Boss / 1987 / FAN / M • Catfights #3 / 1987 / OHV / B • The Color of Honey / 1987 / SUV / M • The De Renzy Tapes / 1990 / CA / C • Debbie Does Dallas #4 / 1988 / VEX / M • Double Black Fantasy / 1987 / CC / C • Dump Site / 1989 / BIZ / C • Enemarathon / 1987 / BIZ / B • Fantasy Chamber / 1987 / VT / M • Furburgers / 1987 / VD / M • Goin' Down Slow / 1988 / VC / M • Going Down With Amber / 1987 / 4P / M • Grafenberg Girls Go Fishing / 1987 / MIT / M • Little Red Riding Hood / 1988 / WV / M • Loose Caboose / 1987 / 4P / M • Love Lotion #9 / 1987 / VXP / M • The Million Dollar Screw / 1987 / VT / M • Nightshift Nurses #1 / 1988 / VC / M • Nikki And The Pom-Pom Girls / 1987 / VEX / M • No Man's Land #01 / 1988 / VT / C • Raising Hell / 1987 / VD / M • Restless Passion / 1987 / HO / M • Sexpionage / 1987 / VXP / M • Sexy Delights #2 / 1987 / CLV / M • The Sins Of Angel Kelly / 1987 / FAN / C • Smooth As Silk / 1987 / VIP / M • Star 88: Dana Lynn / 1988 / VEX / C • Techsex / 1988 / VXP / M • Tongues Of Fire / 1987 / BIZ / F • Toothless People / 1988 / SUV / M • Tres Riche / 1986 / CLV / M • Twin Cheeks (Arrow) / 1991 / AR / M • Two On The Tongue / 1988 / TAM / C • Warm Bodies, Hot Nights / 1988 / PV / M
DANA FOX *see Star Index I*
DANA FULLER
Resurrection Of Eve / 1973 / MIT / M
DANA LYNN
Pretty short haired blonde with medium tits and a small tattoo on her right shoulder back. She's a tiny bit chubby.
Aja / 1988 / PL / M • Amos & Candy / 1987 / VCR / C • Anal Intruder #02 / 1988 / CC /

M • Anal Pleasures / 1988 / AVC / M • Backdoor Brides #3 / 1988 / PV / M • Backdoor Summer #1 / 1988 / PV / C • Batteries Included / 1988 / 3HV / M • Blonde Fantasy / 1988 / CC / M • Blow Job Babes / 1988 / BEV / C • California Blondes #01 / 1986 / VEX / M • California Blondes #02 / 1987 / VEX / M • The Catwoman / 1988 / VC / M • Cherry Cheerleaders / 1987 / VEX / M • Coming Alive / 1988 / LV / M • Dana Lynn's Hot All Over / 1987 / V99 / M • Debbie Does Dallas #4 / 1988 / VEX / M • Dump Site / 1989 / BIZ / C • Educating Kascha / 1989 / CIN / M • Enema Diary / 1989 / BIZ / B • Fireball / 1988 / IN / M • Flesh For Frankenstein / 1987 / VEX / M • Flesh In Ecstasy #10: Dana Lynn / 1987 / GO / C • Flesh In Ecstasy #11: Frankie Leigh / 1987 / GO / C • From Kascha With Love / 1988 / CDI / M • Fuck This / 1988 / BEV / C • Gazongas #01 / 1987 / VEX / M • Ghostest With The Mostest / 1988 / CA / M • The Girls Of Cooze / 1992 / V99 / C • Goin' Down Slow / 1988 / VC / M • The Great Sex Contest #1 / 1988 / LV / M • High Rollers / 1987 / VEX / M • Hollywood Harlots / 1986 / VEX / C • Home Runs / 1995 / PRE / C • Hot & Heavy / 1989 / PL / M • Hot 'n' Nasty / 1989 / XCE / M • How To Get A "Head" / 1988 / CV / M • Innoconce Lost / 1988 / CA / M • Introducing Barbii / 1987 / CDI / M • The Joy Of Sec's / 1989 / VEX / M • Just Between Friends / 1988 / VEX / M • Kascha & Friends / 1988 / CIN / M • Kascha's Blues / 1988 / CDI / M • Laid In The USA / 1988 / CC / M • Lesbian Nymphos / 1988 / GO / C • Lip Service / 1988 / LV / C • Lust In Bloom / 1988 / LV / M • Lusty Detective / 1988 / VEX / M • Magic Pool / 1988 / VD / M • Matched Pairs / 1988 / VEX / M • Moonstroked / 1988 / 3HV / M • Nasty Dancing / 1989 / VEX / M • Nothing But Girls, Girls, Girls / 1988 / CDI / M • Parliament: Ass Parade #1 / 1988 / PM / F • Parliament: Blondes Have More Fun / 1989 / PM / C • Party Animals / 1987 / VEX / M • Party Animals / 1994 / VEX / C • Platinum Princess / 1988 / VEX / M • Playing With A Full Dick / 1988 / PL / M • Pleasure Principle / 1988 / VEX / M • Prom Girls / 1988 / CA / M • Screwing Around / 1988 / LV / M • The Secret Diaries / 1990 / V99 / M • Secret Of My Sex-Cess / 1988 / CV / M • Sex Sounds / 1989 / PL / M • Shaved Sinners #1 / 1988 / VT / M • Shaved Sinners #2 / 1987 / VT / M • Sound F/X / 1989 / V99 / M • Spooked / 1989 / VEX / M • Star 88: Dana Lynn / 1988 / VEX / C • Suzy Cue / 1988 / VI / M • A Taste Of Pleasure / 1988 / AVC / M • Tight Fit (Foot Fet) / 1988 / BIZ / B • Tracey's Love Chamber / 1987 / AR / M • Tricks Of The Trade / 1988 / CA / M • Wet Wonderland / 1988 / VEX / M • Who's Dat Girl / 1987 / VEX / M
DANA MANN *see Star Index I*
DANA MOORE *see Star Index I*
DANA STAR *see* **Kahlia**
DANA STONE
Bella / 1980 / AR / M
DANA VAN NESS
Seduce Me Tonight / 1984 / AT / M
DANA WILLIAMS *see* **Dana Dylan**
DANA WOODS *see* **Rebecca Sloan**
DANDY THOMAS *see Star Index I*
DANE DEVOID *see Star Index I*
DANE GROSS *see Star Index I*

DANE HARLOW
The Dane Harlow Story / 1990 / IF / M • Dane's Brothel / 1990 / IF / G • Dane's Party / 1991 / IF / G • Hermaphrodites / 1996 / REB / C • Randy And Dane / 1991 / IF / G

DANE TARSON
Night Walk / 1995 / HIV / G

DANELLA DI ORICI see Day Jason

DANGER see Sydney Dance

DANGER (BLACK)
Women Who Control The Family Jewels #4 / 1995 / STM / B

DANI
Depravity On The Danube / 1993 / EL / M • Pussy Fest Of The Northwest #3 / 1995 / NIT / M

DANI ASHE *(Danielle Ashe)*
Bangkok Bangers / 1995 / BTO / M • Becky S: Becky Sunshine & Dani Ashe / 1993 / BEC / F • Boobs On Fire / 1993 / NAP / F • Bulging Babes At War / 1994 / NAP / B • Bustline Collision / 1994 / NAP / B • Busty Bangkok Bangers / 1996 / H&S / M • The Cat In Danielle / 1993 / NAP / B • Dirty Bob's #04: SliCES Of ViCES / 1992 / FLP / S • Dirty Bob's #06: NiCESt NoviCES / 1992 / FLP / S • Dripping Wet Video / 1993 / NAP / F • Exploding Fists / 1994 / NAP / B • H&S: Danni Ashe / 199? / H&S / S • H&S: Danni Ashe (#35) / 199? / H&S / S • H&S: Trisha / 199? / H&S / S • Humongous Hooters / 1995 / PME / F • The Mountainous Mams Of Alyssa Alps / 1993 / NAP / S • On Location: Boob Cruise / 1996 / H&S / S • Score Busty Centerfolds #2 / 1995 / BTO / M • Soft Bodies: Double Exposure / 1994 / SB / F • Soft Bodies: Pillow Talk / 1992 / SB / F • Tiger Eye: An Evening With Danielle / 1994 / TEV / F • Tiger Eye: Danni Ashe Catfight / 1995 / TEV / B • Tiger Eye: Wind In Her Sails / 1994 / TEV / F • Tit To Tit #3 / 1995 / BTO / M • Tit To Tit #4 / 1996 / H&S / S • The Very Best Of Breasts #1 / 1996 / H&S / S • Voluptuous #4 / 199? / H&S / M

DANI HERBELIN
Barbara Dare's Roman Holiday / 1987 / SE / M • Grand Prixxx / 1987 / CA / M

DANI SEXTON
Amazing Hardcore #1: Blow Jobs / 1997 / MET / M • Pure Anal / 1996 / MET / M

DANI WILLIAMS see Star Index I

DANICA RAY see Danica Rhae

DANICA RHAE *(Danica Ray)*
3 Beauties And A Maid / cr82 / LIP / F • Best Of Bruce Seven #1 / 1990 / BIZ / C • Bizarre Fantasies / 1983 / BIZ / B • Blowoff / 1985 / CA / M • Bound By Desire / 1983 / BIZ / B • Caballero Preview Tape #4 / 1985 / CA / C • Erotic Penetration / 1987 / HO / C • Golden Girls #18 / 1984 / CA / M • Hot Girls In Love / 1984 / VIV / C • Loose Morals / 1987 / HO / M • Photoflesh / 1984 / HO / M • Radio K-KUM / 1984 / HO / M • Sensuous Moments / 1983 / VIV / M • Sex Maniacs / 1987 / JOY / C • Sex Play / 1984 / SE / M • Sex Star / 1983 / CA / M • Slumber Party / 1984 / HO / M • Sulka's Daughter / 1984 / MET / G • Surfside Sex / 1985 / PV / M • Wet Panties / 1989 / MIR / C • With Love From Ginger / 1986 / HO / C • X Factor / 1984 / HO / M • You Turn Me On / 1986 / LIM / M • Young And Restless / 1983 / VIV / M

DANICA WOOD see Star Index I

DANIEL
Amazon Heat #1 / 1996 / CC / M • Big Bust Babes #29 / 1995 / AFI / M • Duke Of Knockers #2 / 1995 / BTO / M • Private Film #16 / 1994 / OD / M • Tight Fit #13 / 1995 / GO / M • Veronica The Screenwriting Hooker / 1996 / LE / M

DANIEL CLAIR see Star Index I

DANIEL ELMSLIE
The Doll House / 1995 / CV / M

DANIEL FITZGERALD
The Taking Of Christina / 1975 / NGV / M

DANIEL HUSONG
The Jade Pussycat / 1977 / CA / M

DANIEL KANE
Dixie Debutantes #1 / 1996 / MYS / M

DANIEL LOIRE see Star Index I

DANIEL PAGANO see Star Index I

DANIEL RYAN
Private Film #01 / 1993 / OD / M

DANIEL TRABERT
Extreme Close-Up / 1981 / VC / M

DANIELA (BRAZ) see Star Index I

DANIELA DI ORIGI see Day Jason

DANIELE BOLLA
Impulse #02: The Film / 1995 / MBP / M

DANIELE DELAUDE
[La Rabatteuse / 1977 / … / M

DANIELLA
Anal Maidens Three / 1996 / BOT / M • Anal Pool Party / 1996 / PE / M • Assy #2 / 1996 / JMP / M • The Kiss / 1995 / WP / M • Masturbation Ages 20 To 45 / 1996 / C69 / F • Miss Anal #2 / 1995 / C69 / M • Nasty Nymphos #10 / 1995 / ANA / M • Party Club / 1996 / C69 / M • Penetration (Anabolic) / #2 / 1995 / ANA / M • Sleeping Booty / 1995 / EL / M • Stowaway / 1995 / LE / M • Triple X Video Magazine #05 / 1995 / OD / M • Up And Cummers #15 / 1994 / 4P / M • Up And Cummers #21 / 1995 / RWP / M

DANIELLA (1980)
Debbie Does Dallas #2 / 1980 / VC / M

DANIELLA D'ORICI see Day Jason

DANIELLA DARIUS see Star Index I

DANIELLE *(Danielle Martin)*
Blonde with a hard face and medium tits. Born Sacramento. 32 years old in 1994—18 when she started with **Nightdreams** and **The Blonde Next Door**.
Amber Lynn's Personal Best / 1986 / VD / M • Backdoor Club / 1986 / CA / M • Bedroom Thighs / 1986 / VXP / M • Behind The Scenes Of An Adult Movie / 1983 / CV / M • Black 'n' White In Color / 1987 / VCR / C • The Blonde Next Door / 1982 / GO / M • Blue Ice / 1985 / CA / M • Blue Vanities #061 / 1988 / FFL / M • Blue Vanities #121 / 1990 / FFL / M • Bondage Boot Camp / 1988 / TAN / B • The Bottom Line / 1986 / WV / M • Caballero Preview Tape #2 / 1983 / CA / C • California Blondes #03 / 1991 / VD / C • Can Heat / 1988 / PLV / B • Carnal Olympics / 1983 / CA / M • Casing The Crack / 1987 / V99 / M • Chicks In Black Leather / 1989 / VC / C • Collection #05 / 1984 / CA / M • Dear Fanny / 1984 / CV / M • Dirty Blonde / 1984 / VXP / M • Dirty Dr. Feelgood / 1988 / VEX / M • Down & Out In New York City / 1986 / SE / M • End Of Innocence / 1986 / AR / M • The End Zone / 1987 / LA / C • Erotic Dimensions #3: My Way! / 1982 / NSV / M • Erotic Dimensions: Aggressive Women / 1982 / NSV / M • Erotic Dimensions: I Want To Watch / 1982 / NSV / M • Erotic Dimensions: Macho

Women / 1982 / NSV / M • Erotic Gold #1 / 1985 / VEN / M • The Erotic World Of Angel Cash / 1983 / VXP / M • Expose Me Now / 1982 / CV / M • Fashion Fantasies / 1986 / VC / M • Feet First / 1988 / BIZ / S • Flasher / 1986 / VD / M • Flesh In Ecstasy #13: Danielle / 1988 / GO / C • Forbidden Worlds / 1988 / GO / C • The Girls Of Malibu / 1986 / ACV / S • Gourmet Quickies: Danielle #709 / 1985 / GO / C • Gourmet Quickies: Trinity Loren / Jacquelyn Brooks #726 / 1985 / GO / C • GVC: The Babysitter #107 / 1983 / GO / M • GVC: Danielle's Girlfriends #116 / cr83 / GO / F • GVC: Danielle, Blonde Superstar #131 / 1983 / GO / C • GVC: Lust Weekend #103 / 1980 / GO / M • GVC: Party Girl #102 / 1981 / GO / M • GVC: Summer Beach House #106 / 1980 / GO / M • GVC: Sweet Dominance #127 / 1983 / GO / B • GVC: The Therapist #101 / 1986 / GO / M • GVC: Women's Fantasies #108 / 1983 / GO / F • Horny Toed / 1989 / BIZ / S • Hostage Girls / 1984 / VC / M • Hot Shorts: Danielle / 1987 / VCR / C • Hot Stuff / 1984 / VXP / M • Hottest Ticket / 1987 / WV / C • Indecent Pleasures / 1984 / CA / M • Inside Danielle / 1985 / VC / C • Inside Little Oral Annie / 1984 / VXP / M • Inspiration / 1981 / CHX / M • Intimate Lessons / 1982 / VC / M • Just The Two Of Us / 1985 / WV / M • Karate Girls / 1987 / VCR / M • Leather & Lace / 1987 / SE / C • Leg...Ends #02 / 1988 / BIZ / F • Legends Of Porn #2 / 1989 / CV / C • Lessons In Lust / 1987 / LA / M • The Life & Loves Of Nikki Charm / 1986 / MAL / M • Limo Connection / 1983 / VC / M • The Lingerie Shop / 1987 / VER / G • Little Oral Annie Takes Manhattan / 1985 / VXP / M • Love Champions / 1987 / VC / M • Lucky In Love #2 / 1988 / SEV / M • Lust Squad / 1988 / … / M • Lusty Ladies #14 / 1984 / 4P / F • Memphis Cathouse Blues / 1982 / CA / M • Miami Spice #1 / 1987 / CA / M • Miami Spice #2 / 1988 / CA / M • Mks: Date With Danielle / 1994 / MKS / M • Moments Of Love / 1983 / MID / M • Much More Than A Mouthful #2 / 1988 / VEX / M • My Sinful Life / 1983 / HIF / M • My Therapist / 1983 / MED / S • New York Vice / 1984 / CC / M • Nicki / 1987 / VI / M • Nightdreams #1 / 1981 / CA / M • The Oddest Couple / 1986 / VC / M • Only The Best #2 / 1989 / CV / C • Oral Majority #02 / 1987 / WV / C • Oral Majority #05 / 1987 / WV / C • Oral Majority #06 / 1988 / WV / C • Oriental Hawaii / 1982 / CA / M • Penthouse: The Girls Of Penthouse #1 / 1984 / VES / S • Pink And Pretty / 1986 / CA / M • Porn In The USA #1 / 1986 / WV / C • Porn In The USA #2 / 1987 / VEN / C • Pumping Flesh / 1985 / CA / M • Pussycat Galore / 1984 / VC / M • Rambone: The First Time / 1985 / JOH / M • Raw Talent #1 / 1984 / VC / M • Real Breasts Real Torment / 1995 / BON / C • Roxbury #1 / 1982 / VHL / B • Scented Secrets / 1990 / CIN / M • The Sex Detective / 1987 / GO / M • Sex F/X / 1986 / VPE / M • Sex Pistol / 1990 / CDI / M • Sex Spa USA / 1984 / VC / M • Sexually Altered States / 1986 / VC / M • St. X-Where #1 / 1986 / VD / M • Stiff Competition #1 / 1984 / CA / M • Stray Cats / 1985 / VXP / M • Strip Search / 1987 / SEV / M • Summer Camp Girls / 1983 / CA / M • Suze's Centerfolds #4 / 1981 / CA / M • Swedish Erotica #41 / 1982

/ CA / M • Sweet Spread / 1986 / VXP / M • The Switch Is On / 1985 / CAT / G • The Thrill Of It / 1986 / CAT / M • True Legends Of Adult Cinema: Unsung Superstars / 1993 / VC / C • Turn On Blondie / 19?? / COL / M • Unnatural Phenomenon #1 / 1985 / WV / M • Unnatural Phenomenon #2 / 1986 / WV / M • Untamed Passions / 1987 / CV / C • Vanessa...Maid In Manhattan / 1984 / VC / M • VCA Previews #4 / 1988 / VC / C • The Wacky World Of X-Rated Bloopers / 1989 / GO / M • Wet Dreams 2001 / 1987 / VD / M • Wet Kisses / 1988 / V99 / M • White Women / 1986 / CC / M • With Love, Annette / 1985 / CA / C • Women At Play / 1984 / SE / M • Working It Out / 1983 / CA / M • X-Rated Bloopers #2 / 1986 / AR / M • Young Nympho's / 1986 / VD / M

DANIELLE (OTHER)
AVP #9118: Just Another F—Film The Couple / 1991 / AVP / M • Behind The Scenes / 1996 / GO / M • Blood Bath / 1995 / FLV / B • Buttsizer #3: Return Of The King Of Rears / 1995 / EVN / M • Casanova #2 / 1976 / CA / M • Cross Cuntry Vacation / 1995 / CC / M • The Cumm Brothers #3: Deja Goo / 1996 / OD / M • Dr Pussy's Tasty Tails #1 / 1993 / SHV / F • Hot Body Competition: Bikinis & Bikes Contest / 1996 / CG / F • Nothing Like Nurse Nookie #5 / 1996 / NIT / M • Odyssey Triple Play #94: Triple Decker Sex Sandwich / 1995 / OD / M • Royal Ass Force / 1996 / VC / M • The Sodomizer #5: Destination Moon / 1996 / SC / M • The Sodomizer #6 / 1996 / SC / M • Superfox: Danielle / 1992 / SFO / F • Young And Anal #1 / 1995 / JMP / M

DANIELLE (S/M)
French-Pumped Femmes #1 / 1989 / RSV / G • French-Pumped Femmes #3 / 1991 / RSV / G • Night For Dressing / 1987 / VER / G

DANIELLE (SLOAN) see Denise Sloan
DANIELLE (SPEC)
Bondage Classix #01: Making Danielle Talk / 1987 / BON / B • Bondage Classix #02: Krysta's Nightmare #1 / 1987 / BON / B • Bondage Classix #16: Tough Tank / 1987 / BON / B • The Bondage Club #4 / 1990 / LON / B • The Bondage Club #5 / 1990 / LON / B • Bondage Memories #01 / 1993 / BON / C • Bondage Memories #02 / 1993 / BON / C • Shaved #01 / 1991 / RB / F

DANIELLE ASHE see Dani Ashe
DANIELLE ASHLEY
Sex Over 40 #2 / 1994 / PL / M
DANIELLE BASTION
Private Film #03 / 1993 / OD / M
DANIELLE BOLLA
Impulse #06: / 1996 / MBP / M • Prima #01: Anal Poker / 1996 / MBP / M
DANIELLE DARLING see Star Index I
DANIELLE DUPREE
Muffmania / 1995 / TTV / M • Swap / 19?? / ... / M
DANIELLE GUEGUARD
The Card Game / 1985 / CA / M • The Making Of A Porno Movie / 1984 / CA / M • Naughty Fantasy / 1986 / CA / M • Never Enough / 1983 / SE / M
DANIELLE HELL see Star Index I
DANIELLE HERBST
Euro-Snatch / 1996 / SNA / M
DANIELLE HUNNEE

Boiling Point / 1978 / SE / M
DANIELLE L. KELSON
Bend Over Babes #4 / 1996 / EA / M
DANIELLE LEMAN
Karla / 19?? / ... / M
DANIELLE MARTIN see Danielle
DANIELLE MCNEIL
My Pleasure / 1992 / CS / B • Sinderella's Revenge / 1992 / HOM / B • The Slaves Of Alexis Payne / 1995 / LON / B
DANIELLE RAYE
Tinsel Town / 1980 / VC / M
DANIELLE ROGERS (Rene Le Vellers, Vicki (D. Rogers))
Tall very pretty brunette (except for the huge siliconized boobs). Vicki in **Lifeguard**. Renne Le Vellers in **Ringside Knockout**. Married Randy Spears in 1991 and retired from the business. Had a baby in May 1992, a daughter named Amanda Jane.
All That Sex / 1990 / LE / M • Beat The Heat / 1990 / VI / M • Breaking And Entering / 1991 / AFV / M • Burn / 1991 / LE / M • Bust A Move / 1993 / SC / M • Camp Beaverlake #2 / 1991 / AFV / M • Carnal College #1 / 1991 / AFV / F • Catalina Sixty-Nine / 1991 / AR / M • Collectible / 1991 / LE / M • The Come On: Skip's Video Guide To Scoring Chicks / 1991 / LE / M • The Creasemaster's Wife / 1993 / VC / M • Danielle's Dirty Deeds / 1991 / CC / M • Deception / 1991 / XCI / M • Deep Inside Danielle / 1990 / CDI / C • Denim / 1991 / LE / M • Dick-Tation / 1991 / AFV / M • Dream Girls / 1990 / CIN / M • Edge Of Sensation / 1990 / LE / M • Erectnophobia #1 / 1991 / MID / M • Flashpoint / 1991 / AFV / M • Forbidden Games / 1990 / CDI / M • Ghost Writer / 1992 / LE / M • Heart To Heart / 1990 / LE / M • Hooray For Hineywood / 1991 / MID / M • House Of Dreams / 1990 / CA / M • I Creme With Genie / 1991 / PL / M • If Dreams Come True / 1991 / AFV / M • Introducing Danielle / 1990 / CDI / M • Juggernaut / 1990 / EX / M • Just For The Hell Of It / 1991 / CA / M • Kittens #2 / 1991 / CC / F • Lifeguard / 1990 / VI / M • The Masseuse #1 / 1990 / VI / M • More Dirty Debutantes #01 / 1990 / 4P / M • Naked Buns 8 1/2 / 1992 / CC / M • Naked Edge / 1992 / LE / M • New Wave Hookers #2 / 1991 / VC / M • Nighttime Stories / 1991 / LE / M • On The Loose / 1991 / LV / M • On Trial #3: Takin' It To The Jury / 1992 / VI / M • One Night Stand / 1990 / LE / M • Opening Night / 1991 / AR / M • The Orgy #1 / 1993 / EMC / M • The Orgy #2 / 1993 / EMC / M • The Orgy #3 / 1993 / EMC / M • Party Pack #1 / 1990 / LE / F • The Passion Of Heather Lear / 1990 / AFV / M • A Portrait Of Christy / 1990 / VI / M • Prisoner Of Love / 1991 / ME / M • Private Places / 1992 / VC / M • Ringside Knockout / 1990 / DR / M • Roadgirls / 1990 / DR / M • Satisfaction / 1992 / LE / M • Secrets / 1990 / CA / M • Sex In A Singles Bar / 1992 / VC / M • Sex Trek #2: The Search For Sperm / 1991 / ME / M • A Shot In The Mouth #2 / 1991 / ME / M • The Smart Ass Enquirer / 1990 / VT / M • Sodom & Gomorrah / 1992 / OD / M • Someone Else / 1992 / VC / M • Southern Exposure / 1991 / LE / M • Steamy Windows / 1990 / VC / M • Stolen Hearts / 1991 / AFV / M • Sweet Dreams / 1991 / VC / M • Sweet Miss Fortune / 1990 / LE / M • Tailspin #2 / 1991 / VT / M • This

Year's Blonde / 1990 / LE / M • Tit City #1 / 1993 / SC / M • Tit City #2 / 1993 / SC / M • V.I.C.E. #1 / 1991 / AFV / M • V.I.C.E. #2 / 1991 / AFV / M • Victim Of Love #1 / 1992 / VI / M • Victim Of Love #2 / 1992 / VI / M • The Wild One / 1990 / LE / M • Women In Need / 1990 / HO / M
DANIELLE STEEL see Star Index I
DANIELLE WILDE see Star Index I
DANILEE D'ORICI see Day Jason
DANISE see Star Index I
DANNY
Bobby Hollander's Rookie Nookie #10 / 1993 / MET / M • The Girls Of Fantasex #2 / 1996 / NIT / M • Kinky Ladies Of London / 1995 / VC / M • M Series #04 / 1993 / LBO / M • Reed: Danny #1 / 1991 / RED / F • Reed: Danny #2 / 1991 / RED / M • Rump Humpers #16 / 1993 / GLI / M • Sexual Trilogy #01 / 1993 / SFP / M
DANNY BOY
Breast Worx #08 / 1991 / LBO / M • Payne In The Behind / 1993 / AMF / C • The World Of Payne / 1991 / STM / B
DANNY BROWN
Bi-Dacious / 1989 / PL / G • Blow Bi Blow / 1988 / MET / G • Innocent Bi Standers / 1989 / LV / G • Matters In Hand / 1989 / STA / G • Swing Shift / 1989 / PL / G
DANNY D. see Star Index I
DANNY DALLAS
Blonde Heaven / 1994 / TLE / S • Double Cross (Wicked) / 1995 / WP / M • Up And Cummers #04 / 1993 / 4P / M
DANNY DANIELS see Star Index I
DANNY DEMEATO
Backdoor Play / 1996 / AVI / M • Captain Bob's Pussy Patrol / 1993 / FCP / M • I Cream On Jeannie / 1995 / AVI / M • Into The Fire / 1994 / ZA / M • Suburban Nymphos / 1994 / ATL / M • Voyeur's Fantasies / 1996 / C69 / M • Wedding Vows / 1994 / ZA / M
DANNY FLYNN see Star Index I
DANNY GIBSON
The Rod Garetto Story / 1995 / FC / C
DANNY HAZELWOOD see Star Index I
DANNY HUSSONG see David Hunter
DANNY RAMON
A Decent Proposal / 1993 / BIL / G • Queens From Outer Space / 1993 / HSV / G • She's The Boss / 1993 / BIL / G • Toys Bi Us / 1993 / BIL / G
DANNY LAZARRE see Star Index I
DANNY MANN see Dan T. Mann
DANNY RAY see Star Index I
DANNY ROMANO
Bi Madness / 1991 / STA / G
DANNY SILMAN
Postgraduate Course In Sexual Love / 1975 / QX / M
DANNY SOMMERS
Sex Bi-Lex / 1993 / CAT / G
DANNY SPATS
Inside Desiree Cousteau / 1979 / VCX / M
DANNY STEVENS see Star Index I
DANNY THE WONDER PON
Case Studies Of The Punishing Nurse / 1992 / STM / B • Chambers Of Discipline / 1992 / PL / B • Disciplinary Action / 1995 / STM / B • The Mistress And The Prince / 1995 / STM / B • Oriental Dominatrix / 1995 / STM / B • Pony Boy / 1993 / STM / C • Trampled / 1993 / STM / B • Victim Of Her Thighs / 1993 / STM / B
DANNY WEIDLMAN see Star Index I

DANTE
Ganggstas Paradise / 1995 / AVI / M • Heat
Wave / 1977 / COM / M • The Stand-Up /
1994 / VC / M • Toot Z Roll / 1995 / WP / M
DANY BERGER *see Star Index I*
DANY BROWN
The Rod Garetto Story / 1995 / FC / C
DANY VERNEUILLE *see Star Index I*
DANYEL CHEEKS
Ugly looking blonde with a gone-to-seed body
and huge inflated tits. Measures 38DD-24-
36. Born in Paoli, Indiana. As of late 1994
she has a large tattoo on her right tit. As of
1996 married to Jim Sparks (aka Sam John-
son).
A Is For Anal / 1993 / LV / M • The Adven-
tures Of Buttwoman #2: Behind Bars /
1992 / EL / F • All-Star Anal Interviews #1 /
1995 / LEI / M • The Anal Adventures Of
Bruce Seven / 1996 / BS / C • Anal Delights
#3 / 1993 / ROB / M • Anal Thunder #2 /
1993 / ROB / M • Anal-Holics / 1993 / AFV
/ M • Backing In #6 / 1994 / WV / C • Bend
Over Babes #3 / 1992 / EA / M • The Best
Of Buttslammers / 1995 / BS / C • Big &
Busty Superstars / 1996 / DGD / F • The
Big Pink / 1995 / MID / M • Big Thingiees /
1996 / BEP / M • Breast Collection #01 /
1995 / LBO / C • Breast Wishes #13 / 1993
/ LBO / M • Bring On The Night / 1994 /
VEX / M • Bruce Seven: A Compendium Of
His Most Graphic Scenes Vol 6 / 1994 / BS
/ C • Bunmasters / 1995 / VC / M • Butt
Freak #1 / 1992 / EA / M • Butt Freak #2 /
1996 / EA / M • Butt Watch #03 / 1994 / FH
/ M • Butt Watch #04 / 1994 / FH / M •
Buttslammers #04: Down And Dirty / 1993
/ BS / F • Buttslammers #05: Quake, Rattle
& Roll! / 1994 / BS / F • Buttslammers #07:
Indecent Decadence / 1994 / BS / F •
Buttslammers #09: Fade To Anal / 1995 /
BS / F • The Can Can / 1993 / LV / M • Car-
nal College #2 / 1993 / AFV / M • Cheek To
Cheek / 1993 / LV / B • Desire Kills / 1996
/ SUM / M • Dirty Danyel / 1994 / V99 / M •
Everything Is Not Relative / 1994 / EL / M •
A Few Good Women / 1993 / CC / M •
Flesh Shopping Network #1 / 1995 / MID /
M • For Love Or Money / 1994 / AFI / M •
The Girls Of Bel Air / 1995 / NIT / M • Hang
'em High / 1995 / BS / B • Hootermania /
1994 / VC / M • House Of Spartacus #1 /
1993 / IF / M • Infamous Crimes Against
Nature / 1993 / SUM / M • Jiggly Queens
#2 / 1994 / LE / M • Just Lesbians / 1995 /
NOT / F • Just One Look / 1993 / V99 / M •
Kinky Cameraman #4 / 1996 / LEI / C • The
Legend Of Barbi-Q And Little Fawn / 1994
/ CA / M • Lust For Leather / 1993 / IF / M
• Needful Sins / 1993 / WV / M • New Wave
Hookers #3 / 1993 / VC / M • Oral Majority
#12 / 1994 / WV / C • Painful Cheeks /
1994 / BS / B • Private Film #01 / 1993 /
OD / M • Private Video Magazine #03 /
1993 / OD / M • Public Access / 1995 / VC
/ M • Pussywoman #1: Sisters In Sin / 1994
/ CC / M • Rainwoman #07: In The Rain-
forest / 1993 / CC / M • Rainwoman #08 /
1994 / CC / M • Ready And Willing / 1993 /
VEX / M • Sex Detective / 1994 / LV / M •
Sex Punk 2000 / 1993 / FOR / M • Sey-
more Butts & His Mystery Girl / 1993 / FH /
M • Seymore Butts Is Blown Away / 1993 /
FH / M • Seymore Butts Swings / 1992 / FH
/ M • Seymore Butts: Bustin' Out My Best
Anal / 1995 / FH / C • Shane's Ultimate

Fantasy / 1994 / BS / B • Sister Snatch #2
/ 1995 / SNA / M • So I Married A Lesbian /
9993 / WV / M • Sodomania #08: The London Sessions / 1994 / EL / M • Sodomania:
Slop Shots / 1996 / EL / C • Sodomania:
Smokin' Sextions / 1996 / EL / C • Solo Ad-
ventures / 1996 / AB / F • Split Decision /
1993 / FD / M • Superboobs / 1994 / LE / M
• Takin' It To The Limit #1 / 1994 / BS / M •
Takin' It To The Limit #3 / 1994 / BS / M •
The Theory Of Relativity / 1994 / EL / M •
Titty Bar #2 / 1994 / LE / M • Toppers #21 /
1993 / TV / C • Toppers #23 / 1994 / TV / M
• Toppers #25 / 1994 / TV / M • Toppers #26
/ 1994 / TV / M • Toppers #30 / 1994 / TV /
C • Toppers #31 / 1994 / TV / C • Toppers
#32 / 1994 / TV / C • Wet Event / 1992 / IF
/ M • Winter Heat / 1994 / MID / M • Wit-
ness For The Penetration / 1994 / PEP / M
DANYELLE STEELE
Bad She-Males / 1994 / HSV / G
DAPHNE
Hard Deck / 1991 / XPI / M
DAPHNE (FRANKS) *see Daphne Franks*
DAPHNE (SLOAN) *see Diane Sloan*
DAPHNE BLISS *see Star Index I*
DAPHNE FRANKS *(Daphne (Franks))*
Not too pretty with scarred hanging tits, wom-
anly body, reddish black hair, large tattoo
on left hip and another behind her left ear.
Adventures Of The DP Boys: The Holly-
wood Bubble Butts / 1993 / HW / M • Ama-
teur Lesbians #21: Daphne / 1992 / GO / F
• Amateur Lesbians #29: Ari / 1992 / GO /
F • Amateur Lesbians #30: Randi / 1992 /
GO / F • Amateur Lesbians #43: Poppy /
1993 / GO / F • America's Raunchiest
Home Videos #05: Sasha Gets Stuffed /
1992 / ZA / M • America's Raunchiest
Home Videos #34: The Big Splash / 1992 /
ZA / M • Anal Attraction #2 / 1993 / AFV / C
• Anal Gang Bangers #01 / 1992 / GLI / M
• Another Dirty Western / 1992 / AFV / M •
Backstage Pass / 1992 / VEX / M • Biff Mal-
ibu's Totally Nasty Home Videos #16 /
1992 / ANA / M • Big Boob Bangeroo #1 /
1995 / TTV / M • Big Boob Bangeroo #7 /
1996 / TTV / M • Big Bust Babes #09 / 1992
/ AFI / M • Big Bust Babes #19 / 1994 / AFI
/ M • Big Bust Babes #30 / 1995 / AFI / M •
Black & White In Living Color / 1992 / WV
/ M • Blow Out / 1991 / IF / M • Blue Moon
/ 1992 / AFV / M • Bodies In Motion / 1994
/ IF / M • Boobs On Fire / 1993 / NAP / F •
Breakfast At Tiffany's / 1994 / IF / M •
Breastman's Wild West Adventure / 1995 /
EVN / M • Bun Busters #11 / 1993 / LBO /
M • Business And Pleasure / 1992 / AFV /
M • The Bust Things In Life Are Free / 1994
/ NAP / S • Busty Babes In Heat #3 / 1995
/ BTO / M • Butt Seriously Folks / 1994 /
AFV / M • California Covet / 1995 / CA / M
• Chug-A-Lug Girls #4 / 1994 / VT / M •
Creme De La Face #04 / 1994 / OD / M •
The Cumm Brothers #02: Goin' To A Ho'
Down / 1994 / OD / M • Dementia / 1995 /
IP / M • Devil's Agenda & Miss Jones /
1991 / AR / M • Dirty Dating Service #03 /
1994 / WP / M • Dirty Doc's Housecalls #09
/ 1994 / LV / M • Double D Dykes #03 /
1992 / GO / F • Double D Dykes #16 / 1995
/ GO / F • Double Penetration #6 / 1993 /
WV / C • First Time Lesbians #10 / 1993 /
JMP / F • Fun & Games / 1994 / FD / C •
The Girls From Hootersville #04 / 1993 /
SFP / M • Girls, Girls, Girls, Girls / 1993 /

FD / C • The God Daughter #3 / 1992 / AFV
/ M • The God Daughter #4 / 1992 / AFV /
M • Head Again / 1992 / AFV / M • Head
First / 1995 / OD / M • Hillary Vamp's Pri-
vate Collection #11 / 1992 / HVD / M • Hot
Pie Delivery / 1993 / AFV / M • House Of
Spartacus #2 / 1993 / IF / M • Hush...My
Mother Might Hear Us / 1993 / FL / M •
Kinky Debutante Interviews #07 / 1994 / IP
/ M • Kiss And Tell / 1992 / ATV / M • Ladies
Lovin' Ladies #2 / 1992 / AR / F • Ladies
Lovin' Ladies #4 / 1992 / AFV / F • Laying
Down The Law #1 / 1992 / AFV / M • Lay-
ing Down The Law #2 / 1992 / AFV / M •
Leg...Ends #16 / 1996 / PRE / F • Maid For
Bondage / 1993 / LBO / B • Masked Ball /
1992 / IF / M • Mike Hott: #261 Horny Cou-
ples #17 / 1994 / MHV / M • Mix Up / 1992
/ IF / M • The Mountainous Mams Of Alyssa
Alps / 1993 / NAP / S • Ms. Fix-It / 1994 /
PRK / M • Musical Bedrooms / 1993 / AFV
/ M • The New Snatch Masters #21 / 1996
/ LEI / C • Nookie Court / 1992 / AFV / M •
Nurses Do It With Care / 1995 / EVN / M •
Phone Fantasy #2 / 1992 / ATL / M • Pun-
ishment Of Ashley Renee / 1993 / BON / B
• Quickies / 1992 / AFV / M • Rock & Roll
Fantasies / 1992 / FL / M • Rump Humpers
#02 / 1992 / GLI / M • Score 4 Me / 1991 /
XPI / M • Sex In Dangerous Places / 1994
/ OD / M • Sex In Strange Places: The
Sphincter Zone / 1994 / FPI / M • Shaved
Sinners #4 / 1993 / VT / M • Southern Ac-
cents / 1992 / VEX / M • Student Fetish
Videos: Best of Catfighting #03 / 1995 /
PRE / C • Student Fetish Videos: Foot
Worship #16 / 1995 / PRE / B • Student
Fetish Videos: Spanking #20 / 1995 / PRE
/ B • Sunrise Mystery / 1992 / FD / M • A
Tale Of Two Titties #2 / 1992 / AFV / M •
Tinseltown Wives / 1992 / AFV / M • Top
Debs #6: Rear Entry Girls / 1995 / GO / M
• Toying Around / 1992 / FL / M • Wet Day-
dreams / 1996 / XCI / M • What's Up, Tiger
Pussy? / 1995 / VC / M • Wicked Wenches
/ 1991 / LV / M
DAPHNE JONES *see Star Index I*
DARA 1
Catch Of The Day #1 / 1995 / VG0 / M
DARA 2
Catch Of The Day #1 / 1995 / VG0 / M
DARBY DOUBLE *see Jeff Scott*
DARBY FOX
Alien Probe #2 / 1994 / ZFX / B • Gangland
#5 / 1995 / ZFX / B • Specter / 1994 / ZFX
/ B
DARBY LLOYD RAINS *(Darby Rains)*
Older, ugly, flabby, small breasted female.
The $50,000 Climax Show / 1975 / ... / M •
All About Sex / 1970 / AR / M • Amos &
Candy / 1987 / VCR / C • Angel On Fire /
1974 / ALP / M • Beneath The Mermaids /
1975 / ... / M • Bordello / 1973 / AR / M •
Both Ways / 1976 / VC / G • Chorus Call /
1978 / TVX / M • College Girls / cr73 / VXP
/ M • Dark Dreams / 1971 / ALP / M • Devil's
Due / 1974 / ALP / M • Erotic Fantasies #5
/ 1983 / CV / C • The Erotic Memoirs Of A
Male Chauvinist Pig / 1973 / QX / M • Every
Inch A Lady / 1975 / QX / M • Farewell
Scarlett / 1976 / COM / M • Fast Ball / cr73
/ VXP / M • Flight Sensations / 1983 / VC /
C • The French Connection / 1971 / 2CF /
S • French Kiss / 1979 / PVX / M • French
Shampoo / 1978 / VXP / M • Fringe Bene-
fits / 1975 / IHV / M • Heavy Load / 1975 /

COM / M • Hot Channels / 1973 / AR / M •
Inside Georgina Spelvin / 1974 / VC / M •
Intimate Teenagers / 1974 / BL / M • Lady
On The Couch / 1978 / SVE / M • Legends
Of Porn #1 / 1987 / CV / C • The Felines /
1975 / VCX / M • Lovelace Meets Miss
Jones / 1975 / AVC / M • Lust Flight 2000 /
1978 / VHL / M • Memories Within Miss
Aggie / 1974 / VHL / M • My Master, My
Love / 1975 / BL / B • Naked Came The
Stranger / 1975 / VC / M • Night After Night
/ 1973 / BL / M • Personals / 1972 / COM /
M • Practice Makes Perfect / 1975 / QX / M
• The Private Afternoons Of Pamela Mann
/ 1974 / TVX / M • Prurient Interest / 1974 /
BL / M • Referral Service / cr71 / BL / M •
Saturday Matinee Series #2 / 1996 / VCX /
C • Sex U.S.A / 1970 / SEP / M • Sleepy-
head / 1973 / VXP / M • Slip Up / 1974 /
ALP / M • Steamy Sirens / 1984 / AIR / C •
Sticky Situation / 1975 / VXP / M • Teenage
Cheerleader / 1978 / VXP / M • Teenage
Stepmother / cr74 / SVE / M • Triple
Header / 1987 / AIR / C • True Legends Of
Adult Cinema: The Golden Age / 1992 / VC
/ C • True Legends Of Adult Cinema: Un-
sung Superstars / 1993 / VC / C • Virgin
And The Lover / 1973 / ALP / M • The
World Of Henry Paris / 1981 / VC / C •
[Love Express / 1974 / … / M • [Molly /
1977 / … / S • [Voices Of Desire / 1973 / …
/ M

DARBY MICHAELS see Star Index I
DARBY RAINS see Darby Lloyd Rains
DARCEY
Alley Cats / 1995 / VC / M
DARCIE see Star Index I
DARCIE PETERS
Inside Desiree Cousteau / 1979 / VCX / M
DARCY DERRINGER see Tammy Mon-
roe
DARCY MCDANIELS
Huge (5'9" tall, 260 lbs). Has been in the busi-
ness since 1986 and is David Hardman's
sister.
Carnival / 1995 / PV / M • Dementia / 1995
/ IP / M • The Devil In Miss Jones #5: The
Inferno / 1994 / VC / M • The Good The Fat
& The Ugly / 1995 / OD / M • More To Love
#1 / 1995 / TTV / M
DARCY NICHOLS see Tantala Ray
DARCY NYCHOLS see Tantala Ray
DARCY QUIMBY
Exotic Tastes / 1995 / VEX / C • Pussy
Hunt #04 / 1994 / LEI / M
DARIAN HAZE
Fbi In Search Of Bondage #1 / 1991 / BON
/ B • Masters Of Dominance / 1996 / GOT
/ C • No Mercy For The Witches / 1992 /
HOM / B • Phantom Image / 1991 / BON /
B • Punishment Of Ashley Renee / 1993 /
BON / B • The Punishment Of Red Riding
Hood / 1996 / LBO / B • The Queens Of
Mean / 1994 / NTP / B • Slave's Revenge /
cr94 / LON / B • Special Request #3 / 1993
/ HOM / B • The Tower Of Lyndon / 1994 /
LON / B
DARIAN LAQUOIX
Creme De La Face #15: Showroom Sex /
1996 / OD / M • Fame Is A Whore On Butt
Row / 1996 / ABS / M • Nothing Like Nurse
Nookie #5 / 1996 / NIT / M • Sodomania
#18: Shame Based / 1996 / EL / M
DARIEN
Dirty Stories #2 / 1995 / PE / M • Toe Tales
#28 / 1995 / GOT / B • Toe Tales #29 / 1995

/ GOT / B
DARIO see Rocco Siffredi
DARIONE BETANCOURT
Fair Warning / 1995 / ZFX / B • The Plant /
1995 / ZFX / B
DARK DICK see Star Index I
DARK KNIGHT
Big Man's Ebony Dreams / 1996 / LOK / M
• The Black Butt Sisters Do Baltimore /
1995 / MID / M • The Black Butt Sisters Do
Boston / 1995 / MID / M • The Black Butt
Sisters Do Detroit / 1995 / MID / M • Black
Gangbangers #10 / 1996 / HW / M • Black
Hollywood Amateurs #01 / 1995 / MID / M
• Black Hollywood Amateurs #14 / 1995 /
MID / M • Coco's House Party / 1995 / HW
/ M • Shades Of Color #1 / 1995 / LBO / M
• Shades Of Color #2 / 1995 / LBO / M
DARK VICTORY
Legal Tender (1990-X) / 1990 / VC / M
DARLA
AVP #9119: Darla's Dream / 1991 / AVP / M
• Real Men Eat Keisha / 1986 / VC / M
DARLA BARTUN see Star Index I
DARLA BOND
Dressed For Bondage / 1993 / BON / B •
Real People Real Bondage #2 / 1996 /
BON / C
DARLA CRANE
Anything Goes / 1995 / NAP / B • Bad Girls
Get Punished / 1994 / NTP / B • Because
She Loves It! / 1993 / HAV / B • Bondage
Wildcats / 1993 / NAP / B • Bosoms Are For
Loving / 1994 / NAP / C • Defeat And Hu-
miliate / 1995 / NAP / B • Delightfully Darla!
/ 1993 / PAN / B • Lessons Learned / 1994
/ HAC / B • Oriental Conquest / 1995 / NAP
/ B • The Other End Of The Whip / 1994 /
LON / B • A Play On History / 1993 / HAC /
B • Tau Kappa Ticklers / 1995 / HAC / B •
War Of The Big Busted Bondo Babes /
1994 / NAP / B
DARLA DERRIERE
The Adventures Of Seymore Butts / 1992 /
FH / M • Bruce Seven's Favorite Endings
#1 / 1991 / EL / C • Buttman's Ultimate
Workout / 1990 / EA / M • Where The Girls
Sweat #1 / 1990 / EA / F
DARLA KENT
Vanessa's Hot Nights / 1984 / SVE / M
DARLA LANE
Bound And Gagged #05 / 1992 / RB / B
DARLA O'BRIAN see Shelene
DARLA O'BRIEN see Shelene
DARLA PHILLIPS
Most Valuable Slut / 1973 / HLV / M
DARLA RASCAL see Star Index I
DARLEEN see Star Index I
DARLENE
Between My Breasts #14 / 1991 / BTO / S
• Big Busty #37 / 198? / H&S / S • Bras And
Panties #1 / 199? / H&S / S • Dark Alleys
#02 / 1992 / FC / M • The Doorman Always
Comes Twice / cr84 / AIR / C • French-
Pumped Femmes #1 / 1989 / RSV / G •
Girls Around The World #11 / 199? / BTO /
S • Water Nymph / 1987 / LIM / M
DARLENE DAHL
The Beat Goes On / 1987 / VCR / C •
Breastography, Lesson #1 / 1987 / VCR /
M • Classic Swedish Erotica #29 / 1987 /
CA / C • Sensuous Singles: Whitney Prince
/ 1987 / VCR / F • Sweet Cheeks / 1987 /
VCR / C • Teasin' & Pleasin' / 1988 / LBO /
F
DARLENE DAY

Switch Hitters #2: Swinging Both Ways /
1987 / IN / G
DARLENE DESIRE
Snatch Masters #03 / 1994 / LEI / M
DARLENE DESTINY
Sista! #2 / 1994 / VT / F
DARLENE DEVON
Bucky Beaver's XXX Dragon Art Theatre
Double Feature #10 / 1996 / SOW / M •
Sins Of Sandra / cr72 / SOW / M
DARLENE ENGLISH see Star Index I
DARLENE LEWIS
Bottom Busters / 1973 / BLT / M
DARLENE MEAD see Star Index I
DARLENE SAUNDERS
The Loves Of Mary Jane / 1989 / BWV / C
• A Touch Of Sex / 1972 / AR / M
DARLING
Blue Vanities #554 / 1994 / FFL / M
DARLING DARLA see Star Index I
DARLING DESIRES
Girls With Big Jugs / 1995 / V99 / M •
Pussy Hunt #09 / 1995 / LEI / M
DARMEN see Star Index I
DARNELL
100% Amateur #03: On The Dark Side /
1995 / OD / M
DARNELL MASON see Star Index I
DARRELL
Odyssey Triple Play #09: Interracial Love-
fest / 1992 / OD / M
DARRELL JOHNSON
Sweet Young Sins / 1973 / SIL / M
DARREN see Star Index I
DARREN DARE
Seymore Butts: My Travels With The
Tramp / 1994 / FH / M
DARREN ROCK
The Hippy Hooker / 19?? / … / M
DARRICK see Derrick Taylor
DARRIEN DUCATI
N.Y. Video Magazine #01 / 1994 / OUP / M
• Streets Of New York #04 / 1995 / PL / M
DARRIEN HART see Eric Starr
DARRIN A. GOOD
Kink: Police Chronicles / 1995 / ROB / M
DARRIN BLUE see Star Index I
DARRIN LEE see Star Index I
DARRYL BROOK
Secret Sex #3: The Takeover / 1994 / CAT
/ G
DARRYL EDWARDS (Daryle Edwards,
Kong)
Kong is from **Sex & Other Games**.
Charlie's Girls #1 / 1988 / CC / M • Fade To
Black / 1988 / CDI / M • Sex & Other
Games / 1990 / CIN / M • That Ole Black
Magic / 1988 / CDI / M • Tower Of Power /
1989 / E&I / C • Weekend Delights / 1992 /
V99 / M
DARRYL FELD see Star Index I
DARRYL SPANNER
Sodomania #08: The London Sessions /
1994 / EL / M
DARTANIAN
Rainwoman #10: The Tenth Anniversary
Edition / 1996 / CC / M
DARWIN BURKE
Postgraduate Course In Sexual Love /
1975 / QX / M
DARYL BROCK
My Sister's Husband / 1996 / AWV / G •
Secret Sex #2: The Sex Radicals / 1994 /
CAT / G
DARYLE EDWARDS see Darryl Edwards
DARYLL GRIFFIN see Star Index I

DAS SILBEY
Intimate Secrets Of Sex & Spirit / 1995 / TMM / M
DASHEL
Homegrown Video #112 / 1990 / HOV / M
DASHILL MIGUELE
Sweet Savage / 1978 / ALP / M
DATSE WIROUT
Private Film #27 / 1995 / OD / M • Private Film #28 / 1995 / OD / M
DAVE
Breast Worx #23 / 1992 / LBO / M • Czech Mate / 1996 / BAC / M • FTV #21: New Boss In Town / 1996 / FT / B • FTV #22: Muscle Thrill / 1996 / FT / B • Hollywood Amateurs #12 / 1994 / MID / M • Homegrown Video #294 / 1990 / HOV / M • HomeGrown Video #458: Cream Pie For Dessert / 1995 / HOV / C • Mammary Manor / 1992 / BTO / M • Mr. Peepers Amateur Home Videos #31: Ginger Thomas / 1991 / LBO / M • Mr. Peepers Amateur Home Videos #90: Back Door Bonanza / 1994 / LBO / M • Pearl Necklace: Amorous Amateurs #05 / 1992 / SEE / M • Pearl Necklace: Amorous Amateurs #34 / 1992 / SEE / M • Radical Affairs Video Magazine #06 / 1993 / ME / M • Radical Affairs Video Magazine #09 / 1995 / ME / M • SVE: Foxy's Audition / 1994 / SVE / M • SVE: Swing Time / 1993 / SVE / M • Worshipping Goddess Sondra / 1993 / VER / B
DAVE ANDERSON
Dun-Hur #1 / 1994 / SC / M
DAVE ARTHUR *see* **Kirdy Stevens**
DAVE BERRY *see* **Star Index I**
DAVE BLACK *see* **David Angel**
DAVE CANNON *see* **David Cannon**
DAVE CARSON *see* **Star Index I**
DAVE CONNER *see* **Dave Cummings**
DAVE COOPER *see* **Dave Copeland**
DAVE COPELAND *(Seymour Love, Dave Cooper)*
Coming On America / 1989 / VWA / M • The Crack Of Dawn / 1989 / GLE / M • The Erotic Adventures Of Bedman And Throbbin / 1989 / VWA / M • The Erotic Adventures Of Chi Chi Chan / 1988 / VWA / M • Heather Hunter On Fire / 1988 / VWA / M • My Party Doll / 1987 / VXP / M • The Naked Bun / 1989 / VWA / M • The Pleasure Chest / 1988 / VWA / M • The Slutty Professor / 1989 / VWA / M
DAVE CROSS *see* **Star Index I**
DAVE CUMMINGS *(Dave Conner, Malcolm Sands)*
Retired 57-year-old (as of 1997) army officer. Works as a loan officer for a mortgage company and a part-time porn star/director.
Anal & 3-Way Play / 1995 / GLI / M • Anal Anarchy / 1995 / VC / M • Anal Party Girls / 1996 / GV / M • Bang City #5: Lennox's Anal Gang Bang / 1995 / SC / M • Black Fantasies #04 / 1995 / HW / M • Black Street Hookers #3 / 1996 / DFI / M • The Body System / 1996 / FD / M • Delight Gang Bang / 1995 / GLI / M • Denni O' #3: Fanta-Sea Of Cum / 1996 / SP / M • The Devil In Miss Jones #5: The Inferno / 1994 / VC / M • Dirty Dave's #1 / 1996 / VG0 / M • Dirty Dave's #2 / 1996 / XPR / M • Dirty Dave's #3 / 1996 / XPR / M • Dirty Dave's #4 / 1996 / XPR / M • Dirty Old Men #2 / 1995 / IP / M • Dirty Tricks #1: Just A Bunch Of Whores / 1995 / EA / M • Dr Finger's House Of Lesbians / 1996 / SC / M • Eat At

Dave's #1 / 1995 / SP / M • Eat At Dave's #2 / 1995 / SP / M • Eat At Dave's #3 / 1995 / SP / M • Eat At Daves #4: Condo Cummers / 1995 / SP / M • Eat At Dave's #5 / 1996 / SP / M • Eat At Dave's #6 / 1996 / SP / M • Eat At Dave's #7 / 1996 / SP / M • Every Granny Has A Fantasy / 1996 / GLI / M • Every Woman Has A Fantasy #3 / 1995 / VC / M • Filthy First Timers #5 / 1997 / EL / M • Forbidden / 1996 / SC / M • The Generation Gap / 1996 / LV / M • Gimme Head Till I'm Dead / 1995 / GLI / M • Go Denni O: The Best Of Denni O'Brien / 1996 / GLI / C • Grinding Grannies / 1996 / GLI / M • Hardcore Debutantes #04 / 1997 / TEP / M • The Hardwood Chronicles / 1995 / XCI / M • Here Comes Elska / 1997 / XPR / M • Hollywood Confidential / 1996 / SC / M • Home Maid Muffins / 1996 / GLI / M • HVC: The Adventures Of The Old Man And The Stud / 1996 / HVP / M • HVC: An Interracial Portrait Of Black & White Sensuality / 1996 / HVP / M • HVC: Just What The Doctor Ordered / 1996 / HVP / M • HVC: The Lost Keys / 1996 / HVP / M • Kym Wilde's On The Edge #24 / 1995 / RB / B • Lollipops #2 / 1996 / SC / M • Middle Aged Maidens / 1995 / GLI / M • Mike Hott: #280 Horny Couples #18 / 1995 / MHV / M • Nightclub / 1996 / SC / M • Old Bitches / 1996 / GLI / M • Old Guys & Dolls #1 / 1995 / PL / M • Old Guys & Dolls #2 / 1995 / PL / M • The Older Women's Sperm Bank #2 / 1996 / SUF / M • Profiles #09: / 1996 / XPR / M • R/H Productions #5001: A Friendly Encounter Of A Sexual Kind / 1995 / R/H / M • R/H Productions #5002: An Interview For A Roommate / 1995 / R/H / M • Senior Stimulation / 1996 / CC / M • Sex Freaks / 1995 / EA / M • Slammin' Granny In The Fanny / 1995 / GLI / M • Sugar Daddies / 1995 / FPI / M • Swap Meat / 1995 / GLI / M • Temptation Eyes / 1996 / XCI / M • The World's Biggest Gang Bang #1 / 1995 / FPI / M • The World's Biggest Gang Bang #2 / 1996 / FPI / M • [Monstrous Boobs / 1996 / ... / M • [Second Wives Club / 1996 / ... / M • [Sin Tax / 1996 / ZA / M • [Tight Ends Anal Contest / 1996 / ... / M • [Wet Masks / 1996 / SC / M
DAVE D'ANGELO
Night Crawlers / 1994 / SC / M
DAVE DE LONG
Kitty Foxx's Kinky Kapers #01 / 1995 / TTV / M
DAVE DEBIN
Teenage Pajama Party / 1977 / VC / M
DAVE DESILVA
Taxi Girls #3: Killer On The Loose / 1993 / MED / M • Tight Fit #01 / 1994 / GO / M
DAVE DODGE
Bang City #7: Carolina's Anal Gang Bang / 1995 / SC / M • Carolina's D.P. Anal Gangbang / 1996 / FC / M • Country & Western Cuties #2: Naked Pie Eating Contest / 1996 / EVN / M • Da Booty Call / 1994 / HW / M • Dirty Minds / 1996 / NIT / M • Gang Bang Bitches #04 / 1995 / PP / M • Gang Bang Diaries #5 / 1994 / SFP / M • Kinky Debutante Interviews #02 / 1994 / IP / M • Kinky Debutante Interviews #03 / 1994 / IP / M • My Ass #1 / 1996 / NOT / M • Nydp Pink / 1994 / HW / M • Oriental Oddballs #1 / 1994 / FH / M • Perverted Stories #09 / 1996 / JMP / M • The Room Mate / 1995 / EX / M • Santa Is Coming All Over Town /

1996 / EVN / M • Stuff Your Face #2 / 1995 / JMP / M • Titanic Orgy / 1995 / PEP / M • Triple Penetration Debutante Sluts #2 / 1996 / BAC / M
DAVE ERDMAN
Resurrection Of Eve / 1973 / MIT / M
DAVE GOLDENROD
All American Super Bitches / 1984 / BIZ / B • Ebony Goddesses / 1985 / LON / B
DAVE HAMMER
High Heel Harlots #05 / 1994 / SFP / M
DAVE HARDMAN *see* **David Hardman**
DAVE HARTMAN *see* **David Morris**
DAVE HEAD *see* **Star Index I**
DAVE HILL *see* **Dave Rock**
DAVE JONATHAN
The Hustler / 1989 / CDI / M
DAVE LONGSHLONG *see* **Marc Stevens**
DAVE MILLER *see* **Star Index I**
DAVE MONTANA *see* **Star Index I**
DAVE NELSON
All About Teri Weigel / 1996 / XCI / M • Anal Angels #5 / 1996 / VEX / C • Backfield In Motion / 1995 / VT / M • New Pussy Hunt #24 / 1996 / LEI / C
DAVE NESOR *see* **Star Index I**
DAVE PHILLIPS *see* **Star Index I**
DAVE REUBEN *see* **Dave Ruby**
DAVE ROCK *(Dave Hill, David Hill)*
Long blonde hair.
Digital Lust / 1990 / SE / M • Lady Of The House / 1990 / VEX / M • Making It / 1990 / FH / M • Read My Lips / 1990 / FH / M • Shifting Gere / 1990 / VT / M • Sunny After Dark / 1990 / WV / M
DAVE RUBY *(David Rubenstein, Dave Rudy, David Rudy, Richard Hiller, Dave Reuben, Jonny Canuuk)*
Balding male with a muscular body.
18 And Anxious / cr78 / CDI / M • ABA: Double Feature #2 / 1996 / ALP / M • ABA: Double Feature #4 / 1996 / ALP / M • Afrodisiac #1 / 1987 / CC / M • Afternoon Delights / 1981 / CA / M • American Desire / 1981 / CA / M • Anal Intruder #01 / 1986 / CC / M • Angel In Distress / 1982 / AVO / B • Angela In Wonderland / 1986 / VD / M • Babylon Pink #1 / 1979 / COM / M • Bad Attitude / 1987 / CC / M • Bad Penny / 1978 / QX / M • Black Angels / 1985 / VC / M • Black Girls In Heat / 1985 / PL / M • Breaker Beauties / 1977 / VHL / M • Bunbusters / 1984 / VCR / M • Daughters Of Discipline #2 / 1983 / AVO / B • Decadence / 1986 / VD / M • Dirty Lilly / 1975 / VXP / M • Double Pleasure / 1985 / VCR / M • Double Your Pleasure / 1978 / CV / M • Dracula Exotica / 1980 / TVX / M • Erotic Moments / 1985 / CDI / C • Feels Like Silk / 1983 / SE / M • The Fur Trap / 1973 / AVC / M • Getting Ahead / 1983 / PL / M • A Girl's Best Friend / 1981 / QX / M • Girls U.S.A. / 1980 / AIR / M • Heaven's Touch / 1983 / CA / M • Her Total Response / 1975 / SVE / M • Hot Dreams / 1983 / CA / M • Hot Fudge / 1984 / VC / M • Insane Lovers / 1978 / VIS / M • Inside Jennifer Welles / 1977 / VXP / M • Inside Seka / 1980 / VXP / M • Jailhouse Girls / 1984 / VC / M • Justine: A Matter Of Innocence / 1980 / SAT / M • The Love Couch / 1977 / VC / M • Love-In Arrangement / 1981 / VXP / M • Lust Inferno / 1982 / COM / M • Manhattan Mistress / 1980 / VBM / M • Mistress Electra / 1983 / AVO / B • Mystique / 1979 / CA / M • N.Y. Video Magazine #02 / 1995 /

OUP / M • Nasty Girls (1983-VCX) / 1983 / VCX / M • Naughty Nurses / 1982 / VCR / M • The Nite Bird / 1978 / BL / M • October Silk / 1980 / COM / M • Open Lips / 1983 / AVO / M • Oriental Techniques Of Pain And Pleasure / 1983 / ALP / B • Painmania / 1983 / AVO / B • Pandora's Mirror / 1981 / CA / M • The Pink Ladies / 1980 / VC / M • Platinum Paradise / 1980 / COM / M • Please Me! / cr86 / LIM / M • The Pleasures Of Innocence / 1985 / VC / M • Princess Seka / 1980 / VC / M • Prisoner Of Pleasure / 1981 / ALP / B • Rambone: The First Time / 1985 / JOH / M • Rip-Off Of Millie / cr78 / VHL / M • Secrets Of A Willing Wife / 1979 / VXP / M • Show Your Love / 1984 / VC / M • Silence Of The G.A.M.S. / 1992 / CA / M • Silky / 1980 / VXP / M • Sizzle / 1979 / QX / M • Slave Of Pleasure / 1978 / BL / M • Small Change / 1978 / CDC / M • The Starmaker / 1982 / VC / M • The Stimulators / 1983 / VC / M • Sunny / 1979 / VC / M • Sweet Surrender / 1980 / VCX / M • The Tale Of Tiffany Lust / 1981 / CA / M • Urges In Young Girls / 1984 / VC / M • Vas-O-Line Alley / 1985 / VC / M • White Hot / 1984 / VXP / M • Wicked Schoolgirls / 1981 / SVE / M

DAVE RUDY *see* **Dave Ruby**
DAVE RUSSELL
Lost In Vegas / 1996 / AWV / G
DAVE SANDER *see* **David Sanders**
DAVE SANDERS *see* **David Sanders**
DAVE SCARBOROUGH *see* **Geoff Coldwater**
DAVE SMITH *see* **Star Index I**
DAVE W.
Rocco Unleashed / 1994 / SC / M
DAVE WATSON
Anal Reamers / 1986 / 4P / M • Black Reamers / 1986 / 4P / M • Down The Drain / 1986 / 4P / M • More To Love #2 / 1995 / TTV / M • Pipe Dreams / 1985 / 4P / M • The Plumber Cometh / 1985 / 4P / M
DAVE WILLETS
Seymore & Shane Meet Kathy Willets, The Naughty Nymph / 1994 / ULI / M
DAVEY JONES
The Collegiates / 1971 / BL / M • Illusions Of A Lady / 1972 / VSH / M
DAVI
Blue Vanities #547 / 1994 / FFL / M
DAVIA *see* **Star Index I**
DAVIA ARDELL *(Davia Arnell, Diavia, Stormy Weather (DA), Davida Ardell)*
Petite blonde, long straight hair, small conical tits, large areola, tight waist, nice butt, belly button ring, small tattoos on left shoulder back and right hip, and light down on her arms. Facially she looks a bit like C.J. Bennett with moles on both cheeks. She sounds very sweet. After a couple of appearances she had a boob job and increased her size to rock solid large canteloupes.
1-900-FUCK #3 / 1995 / SO / M • A List / 1996 / SO / M • The Anal Adventures Of Bruce Seven / 1996 / BS / C • Anal Booty Burner / 1996 / ROB / M • Anal Cum Queens / 1995 / ZA / M • Anal Fever / 1996 / ROB / M • Anal League / 1996 / IN / M • Anal Lickers And Cummers / 1996 / ROB / M • Anal Lovebud / 1996 / ROB / M • Anal Princess #2 / 1996 / VC / M • Anal Rippers #1: The Beginning / 1995 / ZA / M • Analtown USA #05 / 1995 / NIT / M • Babe Watch Beach / 1996 / SC / M • Beverly Hills

Bikini Company / 1996 / NIT / M • Bikini Beach #4 / 1996 / CC / M • Boobwatch #2 / 1997 / SC / M • Breastman's Bikini Pool Party / 1995 / EVN / M • Buffy Malibu's Nasty Girls #11 / 1996 / ANA / F • Butt Love / 1995 / AB / M • Buttman's Bubble Butt Babes / 1996 / EA / M • Buttslammers #12: Anal Madness / 1996 / BS / F • Casting Call #15 / 1995 / SO / M • Caught From Behind #23 / 1995 / HO / M • The Complete & Total Anal Workout #1 / 1995 / ZA / M • Cum Buttered Corn Holes #2 / 1996 / NIT / C • Cumback Pussy #1 / 1996 / EL / M • Cumback Pussy #6: All-Star Poop Chute Salute / 1997 / EL / M • Dirty Diner #3 / 1996 / SC / M • Dreams / 1995 / VC / M • Frendz? #2 / 1996 / RAS / M • Girls Of Sorority Row / 1994 / VT / M • Glory Days / 1996 / IN / M • Golddiggers #2 / 1995 / VC / M • Golddiggers #3 / 1995 / VC / M • Hang 'em High / 1995 / BS / B • Hard Core Beginners #06 / 1995 / LEI / M • Hot Tight Asses #12 / 1995 / TCK / M • Hot Tight Asses #13 / 1995 / TCK / M • Hot Tight Asses #14 / 1995 / TCK / M • Intense Perversions #2 / 1996 / PL / M • Interview: Barely Legal / 1995 / LV / M • Itty Bitty Blonde Committee / 1995 / V99 / M • Jenteal Loves Rocco / 1996 / VI / M • Joanie Pneumatic / 1996 / PL / M • Little Girl Blue / 1995 / RHS / M • Max #07: French Kiss / 1995 / XPR / M • Max #09: Where Danger Lurks / 1996 / XPR / M • Max #12: Spread Eagle / 1996 / LE / M • Max World #1 / 1995 / FRM / M • Max World #3: Formula 1 / 1996 / XPR / M • The New Ass Masters #14 / 1996 / LEI / C • Night Stalker / 1995 / BBE / M • Nikki Loves Rocco / 1996 / VI / M • Nineteen #6 / 1996 / FOR / M • Nineteen #7 / 1996 / FOR / M • Nymphos / 1995 / MET / M • Odyssey 30 Min: #551: / 1995 / OD / M • Prime Choice #7 / 1996 / RAS / M • Private Dancers / 1996 / RAS / M • Private Stories #12 / 1996 / OD / M • Profiles #08: Triple Ecstacy / 1996 / XPR / M • Pure Anal / 1996 / MET / M • Pussy Hunt #09 / 1995 / LEI / M • Pussyman #12: Sticky Fingers / 1995 / SNA / M • Pussyman Auditions #11 / 1995 / SNA / M • Reel People #09 / 1995 / PP / M • Rockhard (Coast) / 1996 / CC / M • The Scam / 1996 / LV / M • Sensations #1 / 1996 / SC / M • Seriously Anal / 1996 / ONA / M • Sex Drives Of The Rich And Famous / 1996 / ERA / M • Sex Hungry Butthole Sluts / 1996 / ROB / M • Silver Screen Confidential / 1996 / WP / M • Spinners #1 (Wicked) / 1995 / WP / M • Suburban Buttnicks Forever / 1995 / CC / M • Suggestive Behavior / 1996 / VI / M • Takin' It To The Limit #3 / 1994 / BS / M • Thunder And Lightning / 1996 / MID / M • The Time Machine / 1996 / WP / M • Unchained Marylin / 1996 / VT / M • Venom #2 / 1996 / VD / M • Venom #3 / 1996 / VD / M • Video Virgins #31 / 1996 / NS / M • Virgin Killers: The Killing Spree / 1995 / PEP / M • Vortex / 1995 / MET / M • The Wanderer #2: Slippery When Wet / 1995 / CDI / M • Waterbabies #3 / 1996 / CC / M • A Week And A Half In The Life Of A Prostitute / 1997 / EL / M • Wicked Ways #2: Education Of A D.P. Virgin / 1995 / WP / M • Wild Assed Pooper Slut / 1996 / ROB / M • XXX / 1996 / TEP / M • Young Girls Do #1: Troublemakers / 1995 / CDI / M • Young Girls Do #2: Sweet Meat / 1995 / CDI / M

DAVIA ARNELL *see* **Davia Ardell**
DAVID
Amateur Nights #15 / 1997 / HO / M • FTV #04: Tough Turf / 1996 / FT / B • Girls II Women / 1996 / AVI / M • N.Y. Video Magazine #08 / 1996 / OUP / M • Nest Of Joy / 19?? / GO / M • Private Request / 1994 / GLI / M • Shane's World #5 / 1996 / OD / M • Toe Tales #06 / 1993 / GOT / B
DAVID AARON CLARK
Back Down / 1996 / RB / B
DAVID ACKERMAN
Golden Girls, The Movie / 1984 / SE / M
DAVID ADAMS *see* **Star Index I**
DAVID ALLEN *see* **Star Index I**
DAVID AMBROSE *see* **Star Index I**
DAVID ANGEL *(David Black (Angel), Dave Black, Big Dave)*
SO of Tracey Wynn.
2 Hung 2 Tung / 1992 / MID / M • America's Raunchiest Home Videos #01: Some Serious Sex / 1991 / ZA / M • America's Raunchiest Home Videos #07: A Fucking Beauty / 1991 / ZA / M • The Anals Of History #1 / 1991 / MID / M • The Back Doors (Executive) / 1991 / EX / M • Between The Bars / 1992 / FH / M • Biff Malibu's Totally Nasty Home Videos #01 / 1992 / ANA / M • Biff Malibu's Totally Nasty Home Videos #06 / 1992 / ANA / M • The Erotic Adventures Of The Three Musketeers / 1992 / CEL / S • The Fine Line / 1990 / SO / M • French Open / 1990 / OD / M • Gangbang Girl #04 / 1992 / ANA / M • Gangbang Girl #07 / 1992 / ANA / M • Gangbang Girl #08 / 1992 / ANA / M • In Your Face #1 / 1992 / PL / M • In Your Face #2 / 1992 / PL / M • Oral Madness #1 / 1991 / OD / M • She-Male Sex Clinic / 1991 / VC / G • She Male Spirits Of The Night / 1991 / VC / G • Soft And Wild / 1991 / LV / M • Starr / 1991 / CA / M • Steel Garters / 1992 / CAT / G • The Three Musketeers #1 / 1992 / FD / M • The Three Musketeers #2 / 1992 / FD / M • The Ultimate Pleasure / 1991 / MET / G
DAVID ASHFIELD
Bi-Coastal / 1985 / LAV / G • Gidget Goes Bi / 1990 / STA / G • Mix-N-Match / 1990 / LV / G • She-Male Encounters #05: Orgy At The Poysinberry Bar #1 / 1987 / MET / G • She-Male Encounters #12: Orgy At The Poysinberry #2 / 1987 / MET / G • She-Male Salsa / 1987 / VC / G
DAVID BALFOUR
Volunteer Victim #1 / 1993 / BON / B • Volunteer Victim #2 / 1994 / BON / B
DAVID BATES *see* **Star Index I**
DAVID BLACK
Erotic Dimensions #7: Fulfilled / 1982 / NSV / M • Pearl Necklace: Amorous Amateurs #40 / 1994 / SEE / M • Pearl Necklace: Premier Sessions #03 / 1994 / SEE / M • Pearl Necklace: Thee Bush League #30 / 1994 / SEE / M
DAVID BLACK (ANGEL) *see* **David Angel**
DAVID BLAIR *see* **Blair Harris**
DAVID BOOK *(David Brook, Les Sek, David Jordan)*
Ugly looking guy with a foreign accent.
Agony Of Love, Lace And Lash / cr73 / SOW / M • Baby Doll / 1975 / AR / M • The Best Of Alex De Renzy #1 / 1983 / VC / C • Bucky Beaver's XXX Dragon Art Theatre Double Feature #14 / 1996 / SOW / M • Dental Nurse / 1973 / VXP / M • Dixie /

1976 / VHL / M • Fantasy Girls / 1974 / VC / M • Fortune Cookie Nookie / 1986 / VCS / C • Hardgore / 1973 / ALP / M • The Joy Of Letting Go / 1976 / SE / M • The Legend Of Lady Blue / 1978 / VCX / M • Midnight Hustle / 1978 / VC / M • Night Caller / 1975 / ALP / M • Night Pleasures / 1975 / WWV / M • Oriental Babysitter / 1976 / SE / M • Parochial Passion Princess / 1975 / ,,. / M • The Pleasure Masters / 1975 / AST / M

DAVID BROOK see David Book

DAVID CALVIN see Star Index I

DAVID CANNON (Dave Cannon, Billy (D. Cannon), David Smith)
Bridgette Monet's SO.
Babylon Blue / 1983 / VXP / M • Beverly Hills Wives / 1985 / CV / M • Blowoff / 1985 / CA / M • Bodacious Ta Ta's / 1984 / CA / M • A Brief Affair / 1982 / CA / M • Classical Romance / 1984 / MAP / M • Collection #05 / 1984 / CA / M • Expressions Of Love / 1984 / CAV / M • For Services Rendered / 1984 / CA / M • The Girl From S.E.X. / 1982 / CA / M • Her Wicked Ways / 1983 / CA / M • I Like To Watch / 1982 / CA / M • Indecent Pleasures / 1984 / CA / M • Legends Of Porn #2 / 1989 / CV / C • Let's Talk Sex / 1982 / CA / M • Letters Of Love / 1985 / CA / M • Lingerie / 1983 / CDI / M • Nightlife / 1983 / CA / M • Physical Attraction / 1984 / MAP / M • Porno Screentests / 1982 / VC / M • Screw / 1985 / CV / M • Sorority Sweethearts / 1983 / CA / M • Stiff Competition #1 / 1984 / CA / M • Stud Hunters / 1984 / CA / M • Summer Of '72 / 1982 / CA / M • Suze's Centerfolds #4 / 1981 / CA / M • Swedish Erotica #45 / 1983 / CA / M • Swedish Erotica Superstar #2: Brigette Monet / 1983 / CA / C • Swedish Erotica Superstar #4: Shauna Grant / 1984 / CA / C • Talk Dirty To Me #02 / 1982 / CA / M • Taste Of The Best #2 / 1988 / PIN / C • Working It Out / 1983 / CA / M

DAVID CASSIDY
Instant Karma / 1990 / MGM / S • Private Film #10 / 1994 / OD / M

DAVID CHANNING
Her Total Response / 1975 / SVE / M

DAVID CHASE see Star Index I

DAVID CHRISTOFF see David Christopher

DAVID CHRISTOPHER (Pussyman, The Great Waldo, David Christoff)
69th Street Vice / 1984 / VC / M • ABA: Double Feature #4 / 1996 / ALP / M • ABA: Double Feature #5 / 1996 / ALP / M • Afrodisiac #1 / 1987 / CC / M • All American Super Bitches / 1984 / BIZ / B • Alley Cat / 1983 / VC / M • Angel In Distress / 1982 / AVO / B • Angela, The Fireworks Woman / 1975 / VC / M • Asian Pussyman Auditions / 1996 / SNA / M • Backdoor Club #1 / 1996 / VEX / C • Bizarre Sorceress / 1979 / STM / B • Black Angels / 1985 / VC / M • Black Clits And White Dicks / cr86 / JAN / M • Black Girls In Heat / 1985 / PL / M • Black Pussyman Auditions #1 / 1996 / SNA / M • Black Sister, White Brother / 1987 / AT / M • Blonde Ambition / 1981 / QX / M • Blow Dry / 1977 / SVE / M • Bordello...House Of The Rising Sun / 1985 / SE / M • Brooke Does College / 1984 / VC / M • Busty Porno Stars #1 / 1995 / H&S / M • Busty Porno Stars #2 / 1996 / H&S / M • Chocolate Bon-Bons / 1985 / PL / M • Cocktales / 1985 / AT / M • Cravings / 1987 / VC / M • Dallas

School Girls / 1981 / VCX / M • Daughters Of Discipline #2 / 1983 / AVO / B • Dick Of Death / 1985 / VCR / M • Discipline Collectors #1: Deep Spikes / 1985 / BIZ / B • Down & Dirty Scooter Trash / 1988 / CA / M • Ebony Goddesses / 1985 / LON / B • Erotic Fantasies #3 / 1983 / CV / C • Fashion Dolls / 1985 / LA / M • The Final Test / 197? / RLV / B • The First Taboo / 1989 / LA / M • French Teen / 1977 / CV / M • Girl Busters / 1985 / VC / M • Hard Core Beginners #12 / 1995 / LEI / M • Head / 1985 / LA / M • Heat Wave / 1977 / COM / M • Here Comes The Bride / 1977 / CV / M • High School Bunnies / 1978 / VC / M • Hot Stuff / 1984 / VXP / M • Hot Tight Asses #10 / 1995 / TCK / M • Hotel Sodom #03 / 1995 / SNA / M • House Of Sin / 1982 / AVO / M • Hypersexuals / 1984 / VC / M • I Know What Girls Like / 1986 / WET / G • Isle Of The Amazon Women / 1992 / STM / B • Joint Venture / 1977 / ELV / M • Kneel Before Me! / 1983 / ALP / B • Krazy 4 You / 1987 / 4P / M • Mouth To Mouth / 1986 / CC / M • New Pussy Hunt #24 / 1996 / LEI / C • Night Of Submission / 1976 / BIZ / M • The Oddest Couple / 1986 / VC / M • Only The Very Best On Film / 1992 / VC / C • Oriental Techniques Of Pain And Pleasure / 1983 / ALP / B • Painmania / 1983 / AVO / B • A Passage Thru Pamela / 1985 / VC / G • Portrait / 1974 / SE / M • Punished Crossdressers / cr85 / STM / B • Pussy Power #01 / 1991 / BTO / M • Pussyclips #01 / 1994 / SNA / M • Pussyclips #02 / 1994 / SNA / M • Pussyclips #03 / 1994 / SNA / M • Pussyclips #04 / 1994 / SNA / M • Pussyclips #05 / 1994 / SNA / M • Pussyclips #06 / 1995 / SNA / M • Pussyclips #07 / 1995 / SNA / M • Pussyclips #08 / 1995 / SNA / M • Pussyclips #09 / 1995 / SNA / M • Pussyclips #10 / 1995 / SNA / M • Pussyman #01: The Search / 1993 / CC / M • Pussyman #02: The Prize / 1993 / CC / M • Pussyman #03: The Search Continues / 1993 / SNA / M • Pussyman #04: The Celebration / 1993 / SNA / M • Pussyman #05: Captive Audience / 1994 / SNA / M • Pussyman #06: House Of Games / 1994 / SNA / M • Pussyman #07: On The Dark Side / 1994 / SNA / M • Pussyman #08: The Squirt Queens / 1994 / SNA / M • Pussyman #09: Feeding Frenzy / 1995 / SNA / M • Pussyman #10: Butts, Butts & More Butts / 1995 / SNA / M • Pussyman #11: Prime Cuts / 1995 / SNA / C • Pussyman #12: Sticky Fingers / 1995 / SNA / M • Pussyman #13: Lips / 1996 / SNA / M • Pussyman #15: The Bone Voyage Bash / 1997 / SNA / M • Pussyman Auditions #01 / 1995 / SNA / M • Pussyman Auditions #02 / 1995 / SNA / M • Pussyman Auditions #03 / 1995 / SNA / M • Pussyman Auditions #04 / 1995 / SNA / M • Pussyman Auditions #05 / 1995 / SNA / M • Pussyman Auditions #06 / 1995 / SNA / M • Pussyman Auditions #07 / 1995 / SNA / M • Pussyman Auditions #08 / 1995 / SNA / M • Pussyman Auditions #09 / 1995 / SNA / M • Pussyman Auditions #10 / 1995 / SNA / M • Pussyman Auditions #11 / 1995 / SNA / M • Pussyman Auditions #12 / 1995 / SNA / M • Pussyman Auditions #13 / 1995 / SNA / M • Pussyman Auditions #14 / 1995 / SNA / M • Pussyman Auditions #15 / 1995 / SNA / M • Pussyman Auditions #16 / 1995 / SNA / M • Pussyman Auditions #17

/ 1995 / SNA / M • Pussyman Auditions #18 / 1996 / SNA / M • Pussyman Auditions #19 / 1996 / SNA / M • Pussyman Auditions #20 / 1996 / SNA / M • Pussyman Auditions #21 / 1996 / SNA / M • Pussyman Auditions #22 / 1996 / SNA / M • Pussyman Auditions #23 / 1996 / SNA / M • Pussyman's House Party #1 / 1996 / SNA / M • Pussyman's House Party #2 / 1996 / SNA / M • Pussyman's Nite Club Party #1 / 1996 / SNA / M • Romancing The Bone / 1984 / VC / M • Scenes They Wouldn't Let Me Shoot / 1984 / VC / M • Secluded Passion / 1983 / VHL / M • Sex Stalker / 1983 / MPP / M • Shameful Desires In Black & White Girls / 1984 / PL / M • Sharon / 1977 / AR / M • Sister Snatch #2 / 1995 / SNA / M • Smoker / 1983 / VC / M • Smothering Boobs / cr83 / BIZ / B • The Story Of Prunella / 1982 / AVO / M • Swedish Sorority Girls / 1978 / CV / M • Take Off / 1978 / VXP / M • The Tale Of Tiffany Lust / 1981 / CA / M • The Taming Of Rebecca / 1982 / SVE / B • Thirst For Passion / 1988 / TRB / M • This Lady Is A Tramp / 1980 / CV / M • Throbbin' Hood / 1987 / VD / M • Tongue 'n Cheek (Red Light) / 1984 / RLV / M • Twilight Pink #1 / 1980 / AR / M • The Untamed Vixens / 1976 / VHL / M • Vamp's Blackmail / cr83 / STM / B • Vas-O-Line Alley / 1985 / VC / M • Visions / 1977 / QX / M

DAVID CLARK see Star Index I

DAVID CORRELL see Star Index I

DAVID DAVIDSON
Angela, The Fireworks Woman / 1975 / VC / M • Foxtrot / 1982 / COM / M • Kink: Police Chronicles / 1995 / ROB / M

DAVID DEAN see Star Index I

DAVID DIAMANI
Club Taboo / 1987 / MET / G • Haulin' 'n' Ballin' / 1988 / MET / G • Switch Hitters #2: Swinging Both Ways / 1987 / IN / G

DAVID DIXON
Sweet Punkin...I Love You / 1975 / VC / M

DAVID DUKEHAM
Another Roll In The Hay / 1985 / COL / M • Bad Girls #2 / 1983 / GO / M • Bad Girls #3 / 1984 / COL / M • Jubilee Of Eroticism / 1985 / GO / M

DAVID DYKE see Star Index I

DAVID ELLIOT see Ron Jeremy

DAVID EPSTEIN
The Masseuse #2 / 1994 / VI / M

DAVID FERENC
Diamonds / 1996 / HDE / M

DAVID FINE see Star Index I

DAVID FLEX see Star Index I

DAVID FOX see Star Index I

DAVID FRIEDMAN (Davis Freeman)
T&A film director from the sixties.
Adult Video News Magazine / 1985 / ZEB / M • Bell, Bare And Beautiful / 1963 / SOW / S • Blonde Heat (VCA) / 1985 / VC / M • Bummer! / 1972 / SOW / S • The Erotic Adventures Of Zorro / 1969 / SOW / S • The Fabulous Bastard From Chicago / 1969 / SOW / S • For Adults Only / 1992 / KIP / S • Leather Persuasion / 1980 / BIZ / B • Love Camp 7 / 1968 / SOW / S • Matinee Idol / 1984 / VC / M • The Pick-Up / 1968 / BOC / S • Starlet / 1969 / SOW / S • Thar She Blows! / 1969 / SOW / S

DAVID GARNET see Star Index I

DAVID GLASER
Love Airlines / 1978 / SE / M

DAVID GREER see Star Index I

DAVID HABIB *see Star Index I*

DAVID HAND
Erotic Dimensions: A Woman's Lust / 1982 / NSV / M

DAVID HARDMAN *(Dan Hardman, Dave Hardman, Lance Hardman)*
Is the brother of Darcy McDaniels.
$ex 4 Fun & Profit / 1996 / SPR / M • 100% Amateur #25: / 1996 / OD / M • 50 And Still Gangbangin'! / 1995 / EMC / M • 50 And Still Pumping! / 1994 / EMC / M • 55 And Still Bangin' / 1995 / HW / M • Abducted / 1996 / ZA / M • Ace In The Hole / 1995 / PL / M • Addictive Desires / 1994 / OD / M • The Adventures Of Peeping Tom #4 / 1997 / OD / M • Adventures Of The DP Boys: Back In Town / 1994 / HW / M • Adventures Of The DP Boys: Berlin Butt Babes / 1993 / HW / M • Adventures Of The DP Boys: Big Black Booty / 1994 / HW / M • Adventures Of The DP Boys: Chocolate City / 1994 / HW / M • Adventures Of The DP Boys: D.P. Nurses / 1995 / HW / M • Adventures Of The DP Boys: Hooter County / 1995 / HW / M • Adventures Of The DP Boys: Sicilian Sluts / 1995 / HW / M • Adventures Of The DP Boys: South Of The Border / 1995 / HW / M • Adventures Of The DP Boys: The Golden Girls / 1995 / HW / M • Adventures Of The DP Boys: The Hollywood Bubble Butts / 1993 / HW / M • Adventures Of The DP Boys: Tokyo Tramps / 1994 / HW / M • Adventures Of The DP Boys: Triple Penetration Girls / 1993 / HW / M • Aged To Perfection #2 / 1995 / TTV / M • All I Want For Christmas Is A Gangbang / 1994 / AMP / M • Alumni Girls / 1996 / GO / M • Amateur Orgies #27 / 1993 / AFI / M • Amateur Orgies #29 / 1993 / AFI / M • Amateur Orgies #30 / 1993 / AFI / M • Amateur Orgies #33 / 1993 / AFI / M • Amateur Orgies #34 / 1993 / AFI / M • Amateurs Exposed #06 / 1995 / CV / M • Amazing Hardcore #1: Blow Jobs / 1997 / MET / M • Anal Academy / 1996 / ZA / M • Anal Agony / 1994 / ZA / M • Anal Alley / 1996 / FD / M • Anal Auditions / 1995 / VMX / M • Anal Camera #12 / 1995 / EVN / M • Anal Connection / 1996 / ZA / M • Anal Fantasy / 1996 / SUF / M • Anal Freaks / 1994 / KWP / M • Anal Inquisition / 1996 / ZA / M • Anal Institution #1 / 1996 / ZA / M • Anal Institution #2 / 1996 / ZA / M • Anal Institution #3 / 1996 / ZA / M • Anal Knights In Hollywood #1 / 1993 / MET / M • Anal Knights In Hollywood #2 / 1993 / MET / M • Anal Maidens Three / 1996 / BOT / M • Anal Misconduct / 1995 / VD / M • Anal Party Girls / 1996 / GV / M • Anal Portrait / 1996 / ZA / M • Anal Professor / 1996 / ZA / M • Anal Sex / 1996 / ZA / M • Anal Sex Freaks / 1996 / ZA / M • Anal Therapy #3 / 1994 / FD / M • Anal Virgins #01 / 1996 / NS / M • Anal Virgins #02 / 1996 / NS / M • Anal Virgins #03 / 1996 / NS / M • Anal Virgins Of America #09 / 1994 / FOR / M • Anal Virgins Of America #10 / 1994 / FOR / M • Anal Vision #25 / 1994 / LBO / M • Anal Webb / 1995 / ZA / M • Anal Witness #1 / 1996 / LBO / M • The Anal-Europe Series #07: / 1994 / LV / M • Anals, Inc / 1995 / ZA / M • Analtown USA #07 / 1995 / NIT / M • Analtown USA #11 / 1996 / NIT / M • Angel Eyes / 1995 / IN / M • Animal Instinct / 1996 / DTV / M • Asian Exotica / 1995 / EVN / M • Asian Pussyman Auditions / 1996 / SNA / M •

Back Door Asians / 1995 / EVN / M • Back Door Mistress / 1994 / GO / M • Backdoor Boogie / 1994 / TEG / M • Backdoor Diaries / 1995 / BBE / M • Backdoor Imports / 1995 / LV / M • Backdoor Play / 1996 / AVI / M • Backing In #4 / 1993 / WV / C • Backing In #5 / 1994 / WV / C • Backing In #6 / 1994 / WV / C • Backing In #7 / 1995 / WV / C • Bad Girls #5 / 1994 / GO / M • Bad To The Bone / 1996 / ULP / M • Badgirls #6: Ridin' Into Town / 1995 / VI / M • Bang City #2: China's Anal Gang Bang / 1995 / SC / M • Bang City #3: Fallon's Anal Gang Bang / 1995 / SC / M • Bang City #6: Bugger's Banquet / 1995 / SC / M • Bangkok Dreams / 1996 / SUF / M • Beach Bum Amateur's #38 / 1993 / MID / M • Beach Bum Amateur's #40 / 1993 / MID / M • Beach Bum Amateur's #42 / 1995 / MID / M • Bedtime Stories / 1996 / VC / M • Behind The Scenes / 1996 / GO / M • Bi And Beyond #6: Authentic / 1996 / FD / G • Bi Stander / 1995 / BIN / G • The Big Bang #2 / 1994 / LV / M • Big Black & Beautiful Gang Bang / 1995 / HO / M • Big Boob Boat Ride #2 / 1995 / FC / M • Big Bust Babes #19 / 1994 / AFI / M • Big Bust Babes #25 / 1995 / AFI / M • Big Bust Babes #33 / 1995 / AFI / M • Big Bust Babes #35 / 1996 / AFI / M • Big Bust Babes #36 / 1996 / AFI / M • Big Murray's New-Cummers #17: Age Before Beauty / 1993 / FD / M • Big Murray's New-Cummers #20: Hot Honies In Heat / 1993 / FD / M • The Big One / 1995 / HO / M • Bigger Than Life / 1995 / IF / M • Bimbette: Adventures In Anal Land / 1996 / TEP / M • Birthday Bash / 1995 / BOT / M • Bitches In Heat #1: Locked In The Basement / 1995 / ZA / M • Bitches In Heat #2: On Vacation / 1995 / ZA / M • Black Cheerleader Search #05 / 1996 / IVC / M • Black Cheerleader Search #09 / 1996 / IVC / M • Black Gangbangers #02 / 1995 / HW / M • Black Gangbangers #04 / 1995 / HW / M • Black Gangbangers #05 / 1995 / HW / M • Black Gangbangers #06 / 1995 / HW / M • Black Gangbangers #07 / 1995 / HW / M • Black Gangbangers #08 / 1995 / HW / M • Black Gangbangers #09 / 1995 / HW / M • Black Jack City #3 / 1994 / HW / M • Black Jack City #5 / 1995 / HW / M • Black Knockers #09 / 1995 / TV / M • Black Knockers #10 / 1995 / TV / M • Black Video Virgins #1 / 1996 / NS / M • Black Women, White Men #5 / 1995 / FC / M • Black Women, White Men #6 / 1995 / FC / M • Blondes / 1995 / MET / M • Blue Saloon / 1996 / ME / M • Bobby Hollander's Sweet Cheeks #110 / 1994 / WV / M • Bobby Hollander's Sweet Cheeks #111 / 1994 / WV / M • Bobby Hollander's Sweet Cheeks #112 / 1994 / QUA / M • Boob Acres / 1996 / HW / M • Boob Tube Lube / 1996 / RAS / M • Breast Collection #04 / 1995 / LBO / C • Breastman's Wild West Adventure / 1995 / EVN / M • The Bridges Of Anal County / 1996 / PVO / C • Bubble Butts Gold #1 / 1994 / LBO / M • Busted-D-D In Las Vegas / 1996 / LV / M • The Butt Detective / 1994 / VC / M • Butt Hole In-One / 1994 / AFV / M • The Butt Sisters Do Boston / 1995 / MID / M • The Butt Sisters Do Cleveland / 1994 / MID / M • The Butt Sisters Do Houston / 1996 / MID / M • The Butt Sisters Do New Orleans / 1995 / MID / M • Butt X Files #2: Anal Abduction / 1995 / WIV / M • Butthead

Dreams: Mission Impenetrable / 1994 / FH / M • The Cable Girl / 1996 / NIT / M • California Swingers / 1996 / LV / M • Call Of The Wild / 1995 / AFI / M • Camp Fire Tramps / 1995 / LOT / M • Candy's Custom Car Wash / 1995 / FC / M • Carnal Country / 1996 / NIT / M • Carnal Interludes / 1995 / NOT / M • Casting Call #11 / 1995 / MET / M • Casting Call #12 / 1995 / MET / M • Caught In The Act (1995-Lv) / 1995 / LV / M • Channel 69 / 1996 / CC / M • Cherry Poppers #02: Barely Legal / 1994 / ZA / M • Cherry Poppers #05: Playtime / 1994 / ZA / M • Cherry Poppers: The College Years #01 / 1997 / ZA / M • Cirque Du Sex #1 / 1996 / VT / M • Cirque Du Sex #2 / 1996 / VT / M • The Clock Strikes Bizarre On Butt Row / 1996 / ABS / M • Club Deb #1 / 1996 / MET / C • Club Deb #3 / 1996 / MET / M • Club Deb #4 / 1996 / MET / M • Club Erotica / 1996 / IN / M • Cluster Fuck #05 / 1994 / MAX / M • College Cruelty / 1995 / FFE / B • Come And Get It! / 1995 / LBO / M • The Come On / 1995 / EX / M • Command Performance / 1996 / ZA / M • The Complete & Total Anal Workout #1 / 1995 / ZA / M • The Complete & Total Anal Workout #2 / 1996 / ZA / M • Compulsion (Amazing) / 1996 / MET / M • Compulsion (Fat Dog) / 1996 / FD / M • Compulsive Behavior / 1995 / PI / M • Crimson Thighs / 1995 / HW / M • Cry Babies #1: Anal Scream / 1995 / ZA / M • Cum Buttered Corn Holes #1 / 1996 / NIT / C • Cum On Inn / 1995 / TEG / M • Cum Soaked And Loaded / 1994 / BCP / M • D.P. Party Tonite / 1995 / JMP / M • Debauchery / 1995 / MET / M • Decadence / 1995 / AMP / M • Deep Inside Ariana / 1995 / VC / C • Deep Waterworld / 1995 / HW / M • The Delegate / 1996 / RAS / M • Delirium / 1996 / MET / M • Dementia / 1995 / IP / M • The Devil In Miss Jones #5: The Inferno / 1994 / VC / M • Dim Sum (Eating Chinese) / 1996 / SUF / M • The Dinner Party / 1995 / ERA / M • Dirt Bags / 1994 / FPI / M • Dirty & Kinky Mature Women #08 / 1996 / C69 / M • Dirty And Kinky Mature Women #1 / 1995 / C69 / M • Dirty Dancers #9 / 1996 / HO / M • Dirty Doc's Housecalls #01 / 1993 / LV / M • Dirty Doc's Housecalls #07 / 1994 / LV / M • Dirty Doc's Housecalls #11 / 1994 / LV / M • Dirty Doc's Housecalls #17 / 1994 / LV / M • Dirty Tails / 1996 / SC / M • Dominant Jean / 1996 / CC / M • Don't Try This At Home / 1994 / FPI / M • Double D Amateurs #17 / 1994 / JMP / M • Double D Amateurs #21 / 1994 / JMP / M • Double D Amateurs #22 / 1994 / JMP / M • Double Decadence / 1995 / NOT / M • Double Dicked #1 / 1996 / RAS / M • Double Penetration Virgins #01 / 1993 / LE / M • Double Penetration Virgins #02: The Second Cumming / 1994 / LE / M • Double Penetration Virgins #03 / 1994 / LE / M • Double Penetration Virgins #05: Go To Hell / 1994 / BB0 / M • Double Penetration Virgins #06: DP Diner / 1995 / JMP / M • Double Penetration Virgins: DP Therapy / 1996 / JMP / M • Double Wong Dong / 1995 / LV / M • DPTV: Double Penetration Television / 1996 / SUF / M • The Dragon Lady #5: Tales From The Bed #4 / 1993 / WV / M • The Dragon Lady #6: Tales From The Bed #5 / 1993 / WV / M • Dream Butt / 1995 / VMX / M • Dream House / 1995 / XPR / M • Dreams Of A Gigolo / 1996 / SNA / M •

East Vs West: Battle Of The Gang Bangs / 1994 / TTV / M • Ebony Anal Gang Bang #2 / 1994 / RTP / M • Electro Sex / 1994 / FPI / M • Elodie Does The U.S.A. / 1995 / PPR / M • Enigma / 1995 / MET / M • Erotic Angel / 1994 / ERA / M • Erotic Desires / 1994 / MAX / M • Erotic Newcummers Vol 1 #3: Anal Adventures / 1996 / DR / M • Frotic Newcummers Vol 1 #5 / 1996 / DR / M • Every Nerd Has A Fantasy / 1996 / FC / M • Exstasy / 1995 / WV / M • The Fabulous 50's Girls #1 / 1994 / EMC / M • The Fabulous 50's Girls Ride Again / 1994 / EMC / M • A Fairy's Tail / 1996 / TTV / M • Far East Fantasy / 1995 / SUF / M • The Fat, The Bald & The Ugly / 1995 / JMP / M • Feature Speciale: The Ultimate Squirt / 1996 / ANE / M • Fire Down Below / 1994 / GO / M • Firecrackers / 1994 / HW / M • Flappers / 1995 / EMC / M • Flesh And Boner / 1993 / WV / M • The Flirt / 1995 / GO / M • Florence Hump / 1994 / AFI / M • For Love Or Money / 1994 / AFI / M • For Your Mouth Only / 1995 / GO / M • Forbidden Pleasures / 1995 / ERA / M • Forbidden Subjects #1 / 1994 / FC / M • Forbidden Subjects #2 / 1994 / FC / M • Forbidden Subjects #3 / 1995 / FC / M • Forbidden Subjects #4 / 1995 / FC / M • Fortysomething And Still Hot / 1995 / SUF / M • Fuck Jasmin / 1997 / MET / M • Fuck U: Girls Of The Packed-10 / 1995 / ZA / M • Full Metal Babes / 1995 / LE / M • Full Throttle Girls: Boredom Pulled The Trigger / 1993 / VIM / M • Gang Bang Bitches #02 / 1994 / PP / M • Gang Bang Diaries #1 / 1993 / SFP / M • Gang Bang Diaries #2 / 1993 / SFP / M • Gang Bang Diaries #3 / 1994 / SFP / M • Gang Bang Diaries #4 / 1994 / SFP / M • Gang Bang Party / 1994 / HW / M • Gang Bang Virgin #2 / 1995 / HO / M • Gangbang At The O.K. Corral / 1994 / FPI / M • Gangbang Girl #16 / 1995 / ANA / M • Generation Sex #2: Nature's Revenge / 1996 / VT / M • Geriatric Valley Girls / 1995 / FC / M • The Girls From Butthole Ridge / 1994 / ZA / M • Glory Days / 1996 / IN / M • Go Ahead...Eat Me! / 1995 / KWP / M • The Go-Go Girls / 1994 / EVN / M • Gonzo Groups & Gang Bangs / 1994 / GLI / M • Good Pussy / 1994 / VIM / M • Granny Bangers / 1995 / MET / M • Grateful Grandma's Gang Bang / 1994 / FC / M • Gutter Mouths / 1996 / JMP / M • Hardcore Confidential #1 / 1996 / TEP / M • Hardcore Fantasies #1 / 1996 / LV / M • Hardcore Fantasies #2 / 1996 / LV / M • Hardcore Fantasies #5 / 1996 / LV / M • Harry Horndog #29: Anal Lovers #5 / 1995 / FPI / M • Harry Horndog #30: Love Puppies #7 / 1995 / FPI / M • Head Nurse / 1996 / RAS / M • Heavyweight Contenders / 1996 / HW / M • Hedonism #01 / 1993 / FH / M • Heidi's Girls / 1995 / GO / M • Heidi's High Heeled Hookers / 1995 / BBE / M • Hell Hole / 1996 / ZA / M • Hellfire / 1995 / MET / M • Henry's Big Boob Adventure / 1996 / HO / M • Hidden Camera #05 / 1993 / JMP / M • Hidden Camera #10 / 1993 / JMP / M • High Heel Harlots #03 / 1994 / SFP / M • High Heel Harlots #04 / 1994 / SFP / M • The Hitch-Hiker #02: Dangerous Curves / 1994 / WMG / M • The Hitch-Hiker #06: Salty Dog / 1994 / WMG / M • The Hitch-Hiker #09: Back Road Detour / 1994 / WMG / M • Hollywood Amateurs #01 / 1994 / MID / M • Hollywood Amateurs #02 / 1994 / MID / M • Hollywood Amateurs #03 / 1994 / MID / M • Hollywood Amateurs #04 / 1994 / MID / M • Hollywood Amateurs #06 / 1994 / MID / M • Hollywood Amateurs #07 / 1994 / MID / M • Hollywood Amateurs #08 / 1994 / MID / M • Hollywood Amateurs #09 / 1994 / MID / M • Hollywood Amateurs #10 / 1994 / MID / M • Hollywood Amateurs #16 / 1994 / MID / M • Hollywood Amateurs #19 / 1995 / MID / M • Hollywood Amateurs #27 / 1995 / MID / M • Hollywood Amateurs #28 / 1996 / MID / M • Hollywood Amateurs #31 / 1996 / MID / M • Hollywood Amateurs #32 / 1996 / MID / M • Hollywood Amateurs #33 / 1996 / MID / M • Hollywood Legs / 1996 / NIT / M • The Hollywood Starlet Search / 1995 / SC / M • Home Nurses Anal Adventure / 1994 / LBO / M • HomeGrown Video #456 / 1995 / HOV / M • The Hooker / 1995 / LOT / M • Hooters And The Blowjobs / 1996 / HW / M • Hooters In The 'hood / 1995 / TTV / M • Horny Henry's Oriental Adventure / 1994 / TTV / M • Horny Henry's Peeping Adventures / 1994 / TTV / M • Horny Henry's Strange Adventure / 1995 / TTV / M • The Horny Hiker / 1995 / LE / M • The Horny Housewife / 1996 / HO / M • Hot In The Saddle / 1994 / ERA / M • Hot Parts / 1996 / NIT / M • Hot Tight Asses #09 / 1994 / TCK / M • Hot Tight Asses #17 / 1996 / TCK / M • Hotel Sodom #05: Tammi Ann Bends Over / 1995 / SNA / M • Hourman Is Here / 1994 / CC / M • House Of Anal / 1995 / NOT / M • House Of Leather / 1995 / GO / M • House Of Sex #16: Dirty Oral Three Ways / 1994 / RTP / M • House On Paradise Beach / 1996 / VC / M • The Hungry Heart / 1996 / AOP / M • The Hunt / 1996 / ULP / M • Hypnotic Hookers #2 / 1996 / NIT / M • I Can't Believe I Did The Whole Team! / 1994 / FPI / M • I Cream On Jeannie / 1995 / AVI / M • Illicit Affairs / 1996 / XC / M • The Illustrated Woman / 1995 / CA / M • In Your Face #3 / 1995 / PL / M • Incorrigible / 1996 / MET / M • Indecent Obsessions / 1995 / BBE / M • Indiscreet! Video Magazine #2 / 1995 / FH / M • Intense / 1996 / MET / M • Intense Perversions #4 / 1996 / PL / M • Interracial 247 / 1995 / CC / M • Interracial Escorts / 1995 / GO / M • Interracial Video Virgins #01 / 1996 / NS / M • Intersextion / 1994 / HO / M • Interview With A Vamp / 1994 / ANA / M • Interview's Anal Queens / 1996 / LV / M • Into The Fire / 1994 / ZA / M • Jizz Glazed Goo Guzzlers #2 / 1996 / NIT / C • Joanie Pneumatic / 1996 / PL / M • The Joi Fuk Club / 1993 / WV / M • Juliette's Desires / 1996 / LE / M • Kinky Debutante Interviews #01 / 1994 / IP / M • Kinky Debutante Interviews #03 / 1994 / IP / M • Kinky Debutante Interviews #05 / 1994 / IP / M • The Knocker Room / 1993 / GO / M • Kool Ass / 1996 / BOT / M • L.A. Topless / 1994 / LE / M • Lactamania #3 / 1995 / TTV / M • Ladies In Leather / 1995 / GO / M • A Lady / 1995 / FD / M • Lady M's Anal Gang Bang / 1995 / FC / M • Lady's Choice / 1995 / VD / M • Latin Fever #3 / 1996 / C69 / M • Leather Unleashed / 1995 / GO / M • Leg Show #1 / 1995 / NIT / M • Leg Show #2 / 1996 / NIT / M • Lessons 'n' Love / 1994 / LBO / M • The Line Up / 1996 / CDI / M • Lips / 1994 / FC / M • Little Girl Lost / 1995 / SC / M • Lonely Hearts / 1995 / VC / M • Lust / 1993 / FH / M • Lust Behind Bars / 1996 / GO / M • M Series #11 / 1993 / LBO / M • The Mad D.P. Tea Party / 1994 / FC / M • Major Fucking Whore / 1995 / BEP / M • Male Order Brides / 1996 / RAS / M • Maliboob Beach / 1995 / FH / M • Masquerade / 1995 / HO / M • The Meatman / 1995 / OUP / M • Mellon Man #05 / 1995 / AVI / M • Menaja's House Party / 1996 / HW / M • Mickey Ray's Sex Search #05: Deep Inside / 1995 / WIV / M • Microslut / 1996 / TTV / M • Mike Hott: #289 Three-Cum Sluts #02 / 1995 / MHV / M • Mike Hott: #347 Bonus Cunt: Jessica / 1995 / MHV / M • Million Dollar Buns / 1996 / MYS / M • Mind Games / 1995 / IMV / M • Miss Anal #1 / 1995 / C69 / M • Miss D.P. Butterfly / 1995 / TIW / M • Missed You / 1995 / RTP / M • Models Etc. / 1995 / LV / M • Monkey Gang Bang / 1996 / NOT / M • Motel Sex #2 / 1995 / FAP / M • Muffmania / 1995 / TTV / M • Mutual Consent / 1995 / VC / M • Mystic Tales Of The Orient / 1994 / PRK / M • Naked Ambition / 1995 / VC / M • Naked Scandal #1 / 1995 / SPI / M • Naked Scandal #2 / 1996 / SPI / M • Nasty Newcummers #02 / 1993 / MET / M • Nasty Newcummers #04 / 1994 / MET / M • Nasty Newcummers #06 / 1995 / MET / M • Nasty Newcummers #12 / 1995 / MET / M • Nasty Pants / 1995 / SUF / M • Naughty Nicole / 1994 / SC / M • Nektar / 1996 / BAC / M • New Girls In Town #4 / 1993 / CC / M • New Pussy Hunt #25 / 1996 / LEI / C • Nudist Colony Vacation / 1996 / NIT / M • Nurses Do It With Care / 1995 / EVN / M • Nymphos / 1995 / MET / M • Odyssey Triple Play #84: Anal Option / 1994 / OD / M • Odyssey Triple Play #88: Candid Couples / 1995 / OD / M • Odyssey Triple Play #99: Hail, Hail, The Gang-Bang's Here #2 / 1995 / OD / M • Old Wives' Tails / 1995 / EMC / M • Older And Anal #1 / 1995 / FC / M • Older And Anal #2 / 1995 / FC / M • One For The Gusher / 1995 / AMP / M • Open Lips / 1994 / WV / M • Oral Majority #13 / 1995 / WV / C • Orgies Orgies Orgies / 1994 / WV / M • Oriental Oddballs #1 / 1994 / FH / M • Oriental Oddballs #2 / 1994 / FH / M • Out Of My Mind / 1995 / PL / M • P.K. & Company / 1995 / CV / M • Pai Gow Video #07: East Meets West / 1995 / EVN / M • Paradise / 1995 / FD / M • Party Club / 1996 / C69 / M • Party Girl / 1995 / LV / M • Pearl Necklace: Thee Bush League #29 / 1994 / SEE / M • Perverted #1: The Babysitters / 1994 / ZA / M • Perverted Stories #01 / 1995 / JMP / M • Perverted Stories #02 / 1995 / JMP / M • Perverted Stories #03 / 1995 / JMP / M • Perverted Stories #04 / 1995 / JMP / M • Perverted Stories #05 / 1995 / JMP / M • Perverted Stories #06 / 1996 / JMP / M • Perverted Stories #08 / 1996 / JMP / M • Perverted Stories #09 / 1996 / JMP / M • Perverted Stories #10 / 1996 / JMP / M • Perverted Stories #11 / 1996 / JMP / M • Philmore Butts Meets The Palm Beach Nymphomaniac Kathy Wille / 1995 / SUF / M • Pizzas, Hot Tubs & Bimbos / 1995 / SUF / M • Playmates Of The Rich And Famous / 1995 / BBE / M • Please Take A Number / 1996 / CDI / M • Pocahotass #2 / 1996 / FD / M • Point Of Entry / 1996 / WP / M • Poop Shute Debutantes / 1995 / LBO / M • Positions Wanted: Experienced Only / 1993 / PV / M • Possessed / 1996 / MET

/ M • Pretty Anal Ladies / 1996 / ANE / M • Primal Rear / 1996 / TIW / M • Prime Choice #5 / 1996 / RAS / M • Prime Choice #8 / 1996 / RAS / M • Private Desires / 1995 / LE / M • Private Request / 1994 / GLI / M • Private Video Magazine #09 / 1994 / OD / M • Private Video Magazine #13 / 1994 / OD / M • Profiles #04: Lust Lessons / 1995 / XPR / M • Promises And Lies / 1996 / NIT / M • Public Enemy / 1995 / GO / M • Pure Anal / 1996 / MET / M • Pure Smut / 1996 / GO / M • Puritan Video Magazine #01 / 1996 / LE / M • Puritan Video Magazine #03 / 1996 / LE / M • Puritan Video Magazine #04 / 1996 / LE / M • Puritan Video Magazine #05 / 1996 / LE / M • Puritan Video Magazine #07 / 1996 / LE / M • Pussy Lotto / 1995 / WIV / M • Pussyclips #02 / 1994 / SNA / M • Pussyman #14: Dreams Of A Gigolo / 1996 / SNA / M • Pussyman Auditions #04 / 1995 / SNA / M • Pussyman Auditions #07 / 1995 / SNA / M • Pussyman Auditions #08 / 1995 / SNA / M • Pussyman Auditions #10 / 1995 / SNA / M • Pussyman Auditions #19 / 1996 / SNA / M • Pussyman Auditions #23 / 1996 / SNA / M • Pussyman's House Party #1 / 1996 / SNA / M • Pussyman's House Party #2 / 1996 / SNA / M • Pussyman's Nite Club Party #1 / 1996 / SNA / M • Pussyman's Nite Club Party #2 / 1997 / SNA / M • Q Balls #2 / 1996 / TTV / M • Rainwoman #09: Wetlands / 1995 / CC / M • Rainwoman #10: The Tenth Anniversary Edition / 1996 / CC / M • Raunch Ranch / 1995 / LE / M • Raw Footage / 1996 / VC / M • Ready To Drop #07 / 1995 / FC / M • Ready To Drop #10 / 1996 / FC / M • Ready To Drop #11 / 1996 / FC / M • Real Sex Magazine #01 / 1996 / HO / M • Real Sex Magazine #02 / 1997 / HO / M • Rectal Rodeo / 1994 / ZA / M • Red Door Diaries #1 / 1995 / ZA / M • Red Door Diaries #2 / 1996 / ZA / M • Reel People #06 / 1995 / PP / M • Reel Sex #02: Splash Party / 1994 / SPP / M • Reflections / 1996 / ZA / M • Reminiscing / 1995 / LE / M • Rice Burners / 1996 / NOT / M • Ride The Pink Lady / 1993 / WV / M • Rock Groupies In Heat / ⸮⸮⸮⸮ / ⸮⸮ / M • Rockhard (Coast) / 1996 / CC / M • Rollover / 1996 / NIT / M • Roly Poly Gang Bang / 1995 / HW / M • The Room Mate / 1995 / EX / M • Rosie: The Neighborhood Slut / 1994 / VIM / M • Roxy Rider Is In Control / 1996 / NIT / M • Rump Man: Forever / 1995 / HW / M • Rump Man: Sex On The Beach / 1995 / HW / M • Rump-Shaker #5 / 1996 / HW / M • Rumpman's Backdoor Sailing / 1996 / HW / M • Rumpman: Caught In An Anal Avalanche / 1995 / HW / M • Russian Girls / 1996 / WV / M • Sabrina Starlet / 1994 / SC / M • Saki's Bedtime Stories / 1995 / TTV / M • Samantha & Company / 1996 / PL / M • Sapphire / 1995 / ERA / M • Sarah's Inheritance / 1995 / WIV / M • The Scam / 1996 / LV / M • Sex Bandits / 1995 / VC / M • Sex Freaks / 1995 / EA / M • Sex Lives Of Clowns / 1994 / VC / M • Sex Suites / 1995 / TP / M • Sexperiment / 1996 / ULP / M • Sexual Atrocities / 1996 / EL / M • Sgt. Peckers Lonely Hearts Club Gang Bang / 1995 / AMP / M • Shameless / 1995 / VC / M • Shaving Mr. One Eye / 1996 / FC / M • The Shocking Truth #1 / 1996 / DWO / M • The Shocking Truth #2 / 1996 / DWO / M •

Shooting Gallery / 1996 / EL / M • A Shot In The Pink / 1995 / BBE / M • Show Business / 1995 / LV / M • Sideshow Freaks / 1996 / ZA / M • Sin-A-Matic / 1996 / VI / M • Sinister Sister / 1997 / WP / M • Sittin' On Da Krome / 1995 / HW / M • Slammed / 1995 / PV / M • Slammin' Granny In The Fanny / 1995 / GLI / M • Sluts In Suburbia / 1994 / GLI / M • Smooth As Silk / 1994 / EMC / M • So I Married A Lesbian / 9993 / WV / M • Sodom Chronicles / 1995 / FH / M • Sodomize Me!!! / 1996 / SPR / M • Sofia: A Gang Bang Fantasy / 1994 / FC / M • Sordid Stories / 1994 / AMP / M • Spazm #1: Point Blank / 1996 / LBO / M • Star Girl / 1996 / ERA / M • Starbangers #08 / 1996 / FPI / M • Starbangers #09 / 1996 / ZA / M • Starbangers #10 / 1997 / ZA / M • Steam / 1996 / ULP / M • Steamy Sins / 1996 / IN / M • Sticky Fingers / 1996 / WV / M • Straight A's / 1994 / AMP / M • Stripping / 1995 / NIT / M • Strong Sensations / 1996 / PL / M • Stuff Your Ass #2 / 1995 / JMP / M • Stuff Your Ass #3 / 1996 / JMP / M • Stuff Your Face #1 / 1994 / JMP / M • Stuff Your Face #2 / 1995 / JMP / M • Stuff Your Face #3 / 1995 / JMP / M • Stuff Your Face #4 / 1996 / JMP / M • Sugar Mommies / 1995 / FPI / M • Super Ball Sunday / 1994 / LBO / M • Swedish Erotica #84 / 1995 / CA / M • Sweet As Honey / 1996 / NIT / M • Sweet Black Cherries #1 / 1996 / TTV / M • Swinging Couples #01 / 1993 / GO / M • Tail Taggers #105 / 1993 / WV / M • Tail Taggers #110 / 1993 / WV / M • Tail Taggers #111 / 1993 / WV / M • Tail Taggers #114: Booty Brunch / 1994 / WV / M • Tails From The Crack / 1995 / HW / M • Tails Of Desire / 1995 / GO / M • Tailz From Da Hood #1 / 1995 / AVI / M • Take All Cummers / 1996 / HO / M • Take This Wad And Shove It! / 1994 / ZA / M • Talking Trash #1 / 1995 / HW / M • Talking Trash #2 / 1995 / HW / M • A Tall Tail / 1996 / FC / M • Temple Of Love / 1995 / SUF / M • Tight Fit #10 / 1994 / GO / M • Tight Tushies #2 / 1994 / MET / M • Titty Town #2 / 1995 / HW / M • The Tonya Hard-On Story / 1994 / GO / M • Top Debs #5: Deb Of The Month / 1994 / GO / M • Top Debs #6: Rear Entry Girls / 1995 / GO / M • Topless Window Washers / 1996 / LE / M • Triple Penetration Debutante Sluts #1 / 1996 / BAC / M • Triple Penetration Debutante Sluts #2 / 1996 / BAC / M • True Sex / 1994 / EMC / M • The Twin Peaks Of Mount Fuji / 1996 / SUF / M • Two Too Much / 1996 / MET / M • Ultimate Anal Gang Bang #3 / 1995 / HW / M • Under The Covers / 1996 / GO / M • Underground #1 / 1996 / SC / M • Vagabonds / 1996 / ERA / M • Vagina Beach / 1995 / FH / M • Video Virgins #04 / 1993 / NS / M • Video Virgins #06 / 1993 / NS / M • Video Virgins #07 / 1993 / NS / M • Video Virgins #08 / 1993 / NS / M • Video Virgins #10 / 1993 / NS / M • Video Virgins #11 / 1994 / NS / M • Video Virgins #12 / 1994 / NS / M • Video Virgins #13 / 1994 / NS / M • Video Virgins #14 / 1994 / NS / M • Video Virgins #15 / 1994 / NS / M • Video Virgins #16 / 1994 / NS / M • Video Virgins #17 / 1994 / NS / M • Video Virgins #21 / 1995 / NS / M • Video Virgins #22 / 1995 / NS / M • Video Virgins #23 / 1995 / NS / M • Video Virgins #24 / 1996 / NS / M • Video Virgins #25 / 1995 / NS / M • Video Virgins #26 / 1996 /

NS / M • Video Virgins #27 / 1996 / NS / M • Video Virgins #28 / 1996 / NS / M • Video Virgins #29 / 1996 / NS / M • Video Virgins #30 / 1996 / NS / M • Video Virgins #31 / 1996 / NS / M • Video Virgins #32 / 1996 / NS / M • Video Virgins #33 / 1996 / NS / M • Violation / 1996 / LE / M • Vivid At Home #01 / 1994 / VI / M • Vortex / 1995 / MET / M • War Whores / 1996 / EL / M • Waterbabies #3 / 1996 / CC / M • Waterworld Deep / 1995 / HW / M • Waves Of Passion / 1996 / ERA / M • Wedding Night Blues / 1995 / EMC / M • Wedding Vows / 1994 / ZA / M • Wet Mask / 1995 / SC / M • What Women Want / 1996 / SUF / M • What You Are In The Dark / 1995 / KLP / M • What's Butt Got To Do With It? / 1993 / HW / M • When The Fat Lady Sings / 1996 / EX / M • White Trash Whore / 1996 / JMP / M • Wicked Ways #3: An All-Anal Slutfest / 1995 / WP / M • Wild Desires / 1994 / MAX / M • Wild Orgies #01 / 1994 / AFI / M • Wild Orgies #04 / 1994 / AFI / M • Wild Orgies #05 / 1994 / AFI / M • Wild Orgies #10 / 1994 / AFI / M • Wild Orgies #11 / 1994 / AFI / M • Wild Orgies #14 / 1994 / AFI / M • Wild Orgies #16 / 1995 / AFI / M • Wild Orgies #17 / 1995 / AFI / M • Wild Orgies #21 / 1996 / AFI / M • Xxxanadu / 1994 / HW / M • Yin Yang Oriental Love Bang #1 / 1996 / SUF / M • Yin Yang Oriental Love Bang #2 / 1996 / SUF / M • Yin Yang Oriental Love Bang #3: Bangkok Dreams / 1996 / SUF / M • Yin Yang Oriental Love Bang #4: Yellow Orchid / 1996 / SUF / M • You Assed For It / 1996 / NOT / M • Young And Anal #3 / 1995 / JMP / M • Young And Anal #5 / 1996 / JMP / M • Young And Anal #6 / 1996 / JMP / M • Young Girls Do #1: Troublemakers / 1995 / CDI / M • Young Tails / 1996 / LV / M

DAVID HARTLEY
Nina Hartley's Lifestyles Party / 1995 / FRM / M • Positively Pagan #04 / 1991 / ATA / M • Under The Hood: Nina Hartley's Guide To Better Cunnilingus / 1994 / A&E / M

DAVID HATCHER
⸮⸮⸮⸮ ⸮⸮⸮⸮⸮⸮ ⸮⸮⸮⸮ / ⸮⸮⸮⸮ / ULP / M

DAVID HILL *see* **Dave Rock**

DAVID HOLMAN
Flash Backs / 1990 / BON / B • Overtime / 1993 / BON / B

DAVID HUGHES
The Rod Garretto Story / 1995 / FC / C • Trisexual Encounters #02 / 1985 / PL / G

DAVID HULL *see* **Star Index I**

DAVID HUNTER (Danny Hussong)
Handsome blonde male.
Summer Of Laura / 1975 / CXV / M

DAVID INNIS
Temptations / 1976 / VXP / M

DAVID ISRAEL-SANDLER *see* **David Sanders**

DAVID JAMES
Kinky Peep Shows: Anals & Orals / 1995 / SUF / M

DAVID JARMAN
Waterpower / 1975 / VHL / M

DAVID JORDAN *see* **David Book**

DAVID JOSEPH *see* **Star Index I**

DAVID KANE
The Likes Of Louise / 197? / BL / M

DAVID KERR *see* **Star Index I**

DAVID KLINE
Transsexual Prostitutes #1 / 1996 / DFI / G

DAVID KRAMER *see Star Index I*
DAVID LAMONT *see Star Index I*
DAVID LANE *see Star Index I*
DAVID LANG
Secrets Of A Willing Wife / 1979 / VXP / M
DAVID LARK
The Voyeur #7: Live In Europe #1 / 1996 / JLP / M
DAVID LECOGNEUR
Private Film #05 / 1993 / OD / M • Private Film #09 / 1994 / OD / M • Private Film #15 / 1994 / OD / M
DAVID LEE BYNUM
Lust At First Bite / 1978 / VC / M
DAVID LEONE
Bucky Beaver's XXX Dragon Art Theatre Double Feature #10 / 1996 / SOW / M • Sins Of Sandra / cr72 / SOW / M
DAVID LINDSEY
White Hot / 1984 / VXP / M
DAVID LIPMAN *see Star Index I*
DAVID MAC
Ole / 1971 / KIT / M
DAVID MACK
Sex Over 40 #1 / 1994 / PL / M
DAVID MANN
Foreplay / 1982 / VC / M
DAVID MARCUS *see Star Index I*
DAVID MAURICE
Inside Desiree Cousteau / 1979 / VCX / M
DAVID MESSA *see Star Index I*
DAVID MICHAELS
Beach Bum Amateur's #18 / 1992 / MID / M • Bobby Hollander's Sweet Cheeks #109 / 1994 / WV / M • California Taxi Girls / 1991 / AFV / M • Double Penetration Virgins #05: Go To Hell / 1994 / BB0 / M • Kiss It Goodbye / 1991 / SE / M • A Lover's Guide To Sexual Ecstasy / 1992 / PME / S • Modern Love #2 / 1992 / CPV / S • Old Guys & Dolls #2 / 1995 / PL / M • Pleasure Dome: The Genesis Chamber / 1994 / AFV / M • Sindy Does Anal Again / 1994 / AFV / M
DAVID MIDEAST *see Star Index I*
DAVID MIRANDA
Battle Of The Titans / 1986 / AVC / M
DAVID MORRIS *(David Morrison, Dave Hartman)*
1001 Erotic Nights #1 / 1982 / VC / M • All About Gloria Leonard / 1978 / VXP / M • All The Way In / 1984 / VC / M • Babylon Pink #1 / 1979 / COM / M • Backlash / 1992 / GOT / B • Bad Penny / 1978 / QX / M • Between My Breasts #10 / 1990 / BTO / M • Bi Bi American Style / cr85 / MET / G • The Big Pink / 1989 / VWA / M • Big Tit Hookers / 1989 / BTO / M • Big Top Cabaret #2 / 1989 / BTO / M • Black Flesh / 1986 / LA / M • Black Voodoo / 1987 / FOV / M • Blind Date / 1989 / E&I / M • The Blonde / 1980 / VCX / M • Blonde Ambition / 1981 / QX / M • Blue Ribbon Blue / 1984 / CA / C • Bondage Photo Session / 1990 / BIZ / B • CB Mamas / 1976 / MIT / M • Centerfold Fever / 1981 / VXP / M • Chain Of Command / 1991 / GOT / B • Champagne For Breakfast / 1980 / SE / M • Cheating American Style / 1988 / WV / M • Coming On America / 1989 / VWA / M • Daisy May / 1979 / VC / M • Daughters Of Discipline / 1993 / GOT / B • Days Gone Bi / 1988 / ZA / G • Debbie Does Dallas #1 / 1978 / VC / M • Deep Inside Trading / 1986 / AR / M • The Deep Insiders / 1987 / VXP / M • Deep Throat #2 / 1986 / AR / M • Double Your

Pleasure / 1978 / CV / M • Easy Access / 1988 / ZA / M • Emmanuelle Around The World / 1977 / WIZ / S • The Erotic Adventures Of Bedman And Throbbin / 1989 / VWA / M • Erotic Moments / 1985 / CDI / C • Every Woman Has A Fantasy #1 / 1984 / VC / M • Exposed / 1980 / SE / M • Family Thighs / 1989 / AR / M • Fannie's Fantail / 1985 / VC / M • Fantasy / 1978 / VCX / M • Fashion Fantasies / 1986 / VC / M • Feel The Heat / 1985 / AAH / M • Female Athletes / 1977 / VXP / M • Five Card Stud / 1990 / BIZ / B • Foxtrot / 1982 / COM / M • Garage Girls / 1981 / CV / M • The Golden Gals / 1989 / BTO / M • Heat Wave / 1977 / COM / M • Here Comes The Bride / 1977 / CV / M • High School Memories / 1980 / VCX / M • Hot & Heavy / 1989 / PL / M • Hot Ones / 1982 / SUP / C • Insatiable #1 / 1980 / CA / M • Kiss Thy Mistress' Feet #2 / 1990 / BIZ / B • Krystal Balling / 1988 / PL / M • Latex Slaves / cr87 / GOT / B • A Little Dove-Tale / 1987 / IN / M • A Live Nude Girl / 1989 / VWA / M • Magic Fingers / 1987 / ME / M • Mammary Lane / 1988 / VT / C • Misbehavin' / 1979 / VXP / M • Missy Impossible / 1989 / CAR / M • More Than Sisters / 1978 / VC / M • Ms. Magnificent / 1979 / SE / M • My Sister Seka / 1981 / CA / M • Nasty Lady / 1984 / CV / M • New York Babes / 1979 / AR / M • Night Shift Latex Slaves / 1991 / GOT / B • The Nite Bird / 1978 / BL / M • The Oddest Couple / 1986 / VC / M • Odyssey / 1977 / VC / M • Princess Of Penetration / 1988 / VXP / M • Quicksilver / 1987 / CDI / M • The Return Of Indiana Joan / 1989 / PL / M • Rimshot / 1987 / CDI / M • Rolls Royce #02 / 1980 / ... / C • San Fernando Valley Girls / 1983 / CA / M • Secret Lovers / 1986 / CDI / M • Sex Sounds / 1989 / PL / M • Sex World Girls / 1987 / AR / M • Small Town Girls / 1979 / CXV / M • Super Ball / 1989 / VWA / M • Sweet Surrender / 1980 / VCX / M • Temptation: The Story Of A Lustful Bride / 1983 / NSV / M • Three Ripening Cherries / 1979 / HIF / M • Thunderstorm / 1987 / VC / M • The Tiffany Minx / 1981 / SAT / M • Toe Tales #01 / 1992 / GOT / B • Toe Tales #03 / 1992 / GOT / B • Toe Tales #04 / 1992 / GOT / B • Toe Tales #09 / 1993 / GOT / B • Toothless People / 1988 / SUV / M • Tracey's Love Chamber / 1987 / AR / M • Ultrasex / 1987 / VC / M • Video Tramp #2 / 1988 / TME / M • Virgins / 1989 / CAR / M • Weekend Fantasy / 1980 / VCX / M • Wishbone / 1988 / VXP / M • With Love, Lisa / 1985 / CA / C • Young Doctors In Lust / 1979 / NSV / M • Yuppies In Heat / 1988 / CHA / C
DAVID MORRISON *see David Morris*
DAVID PARKER
Jacky's Revenge #1 / 1993 / BON / B • Jacky's Revenge #2 / 1994 / BON / B • Master's Touch #5: Slave Revolt / 1995 / FAP / B
DAVID PERRY
Chateau Duval / 1996 / HDE / M • Le Parfum De Mathilde / 1994 / VI / M • Paris Chic / 1996 / SAE / M • Private Film #16 / 1994 / OD / M • Private Film #19 / 1994 / OD / M • Private Film #20 / 1995 / OD / M • Private Film #21 / 1995 / OD / M • Private Film #23 / 1995 / OD / M • Private Gold #11: The Pyramid #1 / 1996 / OD / M • Private Gold #12: The Pyramid #2 / 1996 / OD / M • Pri-

vate Gold #13: The Pyramid #3 / 1996 / OD / M • Private Video Magazine #20 / 1995 / OD / M • Private Video Magazine #21 / 1995 / OD / M • Private Video Magazine #24 / 1995 / OD / M • Private Video Magazine #25 / 1995 / OD / M • Skin #4: The 4th Rite / 1995 / ERQ / M • Triple X Video Magazine #02 / 1995 / OD / M • Triple X Video Magazine #03 / 1995 / OD / M • Triple X Video Magazine #08 / 1995 / OD / M • Triple X Video Magazine #09 / 1995 / OD / M • Triple X Video Magazine #11 / 1995 / OD / M • The Voyeur #3 / 1995 / EA / M
DAVID PIERCE
Her Name Was Lisa / 1979 / VC / M • Pop-Porn: Safari Club / 1992 / 4P / M • Safari Club / 1977 / 4P / M • This Lady Is A Tramp / 1980 / CV / M
DAVID PINNEY
Boiling Point / 1978 / SE / M • Reflections / 1977 / VCX / M • V—The Hot One / 1978 / CV / M
DAVID PIRELL *see Star Index I*
DAVID POLLACK *see Star Index I*
DAVID POLLMEN
Dog Walker / 1994 / EA / M
DAVID PRIDAY
Sugar Mommies / 1995 / FPI / M
DAVID PUTNAM
Kitty's Kinky Capers / 1996 / TTV / M
DAVID RAMSDALE
Ancient Secrets Of Sexual Ecstasy / 1996 / HIG / M
DAVID REISEN *see Star Index I*
DAVID ROGERS
Pleasure Productions #06 / 1984 / VCR / M
DAVID ROSEN
Limited Edition #04 / 1979 / AVC / M • Tinsel Town / 1980 / VC / M • Ultraflesh / 1980 / GO / M
DAVID ROUZE
Private Film #13 / 1994 / OD / M
DAVID RUBENSTEIN *see Dave Ruby*
DAVID RUDY *see Dave Ruby*
DAVID SACHER
The World Of Payne / 1991 / STM / B
DAVID SAND *see Star Index I*
DAVID SANDERS *(Dave Sanders, Dave Sander, Steve Saunders, David Sandler, David Israel-Sandler, Steve Sanders)*
Generally unshaven male. Could be either Jim Hopson or Sal Langford in **Lusty Ladies #4** but not possible to tell which.
Animal Impulse / 1985 / AA / M • The Battle Of The Breast Queens / 1989 / INS / C • Blow Job Babes / 1988 / BEV / C • Carrie...Sex On Wheels / 1985 / AA / M • Casino Of Lust / 1984 / AT / M • Centerfold Celebrities #3 / 1983 / VC / M • Chance Meetings / 1988 / VEX / M • Changing Places / 1984 / AVC / M • Cherry Cheerleaders / 1987 / VEX / M • Coming Alive / 1988 / LV / M • Daddy Doesn't Know / 1984 / HO / M • Dana Lynn's Hot All Over / 1987 / V99 / M • Debbie Does 'em All #1 / 1985 / CV / M • Debbie Does 'em All #2 / 1988 / CV / M • Debbie Does Dallas #5 / 1988 / VEX / M • The Erotic World Of Sylvia Benedict (#5) / 1983 / VCR / C • Fast Girls #2 / 1988 / DIS / M • Femme / 1984 / VC / M • Flash Pants / 1983 / VC / M • Flesh For Frankenstein / 1987 / VEX / M • From Rags To Riches / 1988 / CDI / M • Ginger (1984-Vivid) / 1984 / VI / M • The Girls Of Cooze / 1992 / V99 / C • Girls Of The Bamboo

Palace / 1989 / VEX / M • Girls Of The Double D #03 / 1988 / CDI / M • Good Girls Do / 1984 / HO / M • GVC: The Bad Bride #135 / 1985 / GO / M • Hard For The Money / 1984 / CV / M • Holly Does Hollywood #3 / 1989 / VEX / M • Hollywood Harlots / 1985 / VEX / C • Hollywood Heartbreakers / 1985 / VEX / M • Home Bodies / 1988 / VEX / M • Hot Spa / 1984 / CA / M • Innocent Bi Standers / 1989 / LV / G • Intimate Realities #1 / 1983 / VC / M • Just Between Friends / 1988 / VEX / M • Lingerie / 1983 / CDI / M • Little Girls Of The Streets / 1984 / CV / M • The Lover Girls / 1985 / VEX / M • Lusty Ladies #04 / 1983 / 4P / M • Nasty Dancing / 1989 / VEX / M • Naughty Nurses / 1986 / VEX / M • Only In Your Dreams / 1988 / VEX / M • Overexposed / 1988 / VEX / M • Party Wives / 1988 / CDI / M • Pleasure Principle / 1988 / VEX / M • Positive Positions / 1989 / VEX / M • Pumping Ethel / 1988 / PV / M • Pure Energy / 1990 / VEX / M • Red Velvet / 1988 / PV / M • Reflections Of Innocence / 1988 / SEX / M • Reflections Of Innocence / 1991 / VEX / C • Rites Of Passion / 1988 / FEM / M • Savage Fury #1 / 1985 / VEX / M • Screwed On The Job / 1991 / XPI / M • Screwing Around / 1988 / LV / M • Shades Of Ecstasy / 1983 / HO / M • Silk, Satin & Sex / 1983 / SE / M • Suite Sensations / 1988 / SEX / M • Summer Break / 1985 / VEX / M • Suzie Superstar #3 / 1989 / CV / M • Sweet Sensations / 1989 / SEX / M • Turn Up The Heat / 1988 / SEX / M • Turn Up The Heat / 1991 / VEX / C • Urban Heat / 1985 / FEM / M • The Whole Diamond / 1990 / EVN / M • Wild Oats / 1988 / CV / M

DAVID SANDLER *see* David Sanders

DAVID SASHER *see Star Index I*

DAVID SAVAGE

Bang Bang You Got It / 1975 / VXP / M • Every Inch A Lady / 1975 / QX / M • Naked Came The Stranger / 1975 / VC / M • The Private Afternoons Of Pamela Mann / 1974 / TVX / M • Slip Up / 1974 / ALP / M

DAVID SCHAFER

Doctor Yes / 1978 / VIS / M

DAVID SCHROEDER

The Masseuse #1 / 1991 / VI / M

DAVID SCHWARTZ

Hustler Video Magazine #1 / 1983 / SE / M

DAVID SCOTT

Climax / 1985 / CA / M • Dangerous Stuff / 1985 / COM / M • Dirty Blonde / 1984 / VXP / M • Down & Out In New York City / 1986 / SE / M • Flesh And Fantasy / 1985 / VC / M • Freedom Of Choice / 1984 / VHL / M • Hot Stuff / 1984 / VXP / M • Pussycat Galore / 1984 / VC / M • Sex On The Set / 1984 / RLV / M • Sex Spa USA / 1984 / VC / M • Sexy Secrets Of The Sex Therapists / 1988 / L&W / M • Stray Cats / 1985 / VXP / M • Supergirls Do General Hospital / 1984 / VC / M • Supergirls Do The Navy / 1984 / VC / M • The T & A Team / 1984 / VC / M • Urban Heat / 1985 / FEM / M • Vanessa...Maid In Manhattan / 1984 / VC / M • Viva Vanessa The Undresser / 1984 / VC / M • Wet Dreams / 1984 / CA / M

DAVID SMITH *see* David Cannon

DAVID STEEL

Eat At Dave's #7 / 1996 / SP / M

DAVID STONE

The Dinner Party #2: The Buffet / 1996 / ULI / M • Dirty Tails / 1996 / SC / M • Lollipop Shoppe #1 / 1996 / SC / M

DAVID SUTTON *see Star Index I*

DAVID TANNER

The Love Couch / 1977 / VC / M

DAVID THOMPSON

Night Walk / 1995 / HIV / G

DAVID VALDEZ *see Star Index I*

DAVID VALENTINO *see Star Index I*

DAVID VALFER

Angel Buns / 1981 / QX / M

DAVID WASHINGTON *see Star Index I*

DAVID WATSON

Horny Henry's Swinging Adventures / 1994 / TTV / M • Positively Pagan #05 / 1993 / ATA / M

DAVID WAYNE *see Star Index I*

DAVID WELLS

A Foot Story / 1996 / OUP / B • Wild Cactus / 1993 / IMP / M

DAVID WILLIAMS

Fetishes Of Monique / cr76 / VHL / B • Kidnapped Girls Agency / cr86 / HOM / B • The Pitfalls Of Bunny / cr76 / SVE / M • Pornocopia Sensual / 1976 / VHL / M • Rollerbabies / 1976 / VC / M

DAVID WINGATE

Vivid At Home #02 / 1994 / VI / M

DAVID WOJNAROWITZ

Hardcore: The Films Of Richard Kern #1 / 1991 / FTV / M

DAVIDA ARDELL *see* Davia Ardell

DAVIS FREEMAN *see* David Friedman

DAVONA DAVISON *see Star Index I*

DAVY JONES *see Star Index I*

DAVY SCARBORGH *see* Geoff Coldwater

DAVY SCARBORO *see* Geoff Coldwater

DAVY SCARBOROUGH *see* Geoff Coldwater

DAVY SCARBOUGH *see* Geoff Coldwater

DAVY SCARBROUGH *see* Geoff Coldwater

DAWN

A&B AB#464: Dr. Dick's Skin Treatment #1 / 1994 / A&B / M • A&B AB#465: Four Anal Sluts / 1994 / A&B / M • A&B AB#466: Gang Bang Girls & Sexy Sluts / 1994 / A&B / M • Blue Vanities #546 / 1994 / FFL / M • British Babe Hunt / 1996 / VC / M • Bus Stop Tales #14 / 1990 / PRI / M • Caught From Behind #10 / 1989 / HO / M • Deep Inside Dirty Debutantes #05 / 1993 / 4P / M • Domina #3 / 1996 / LBO / G • Golden Moments / 1985 / BAK / F • HomeGrown Video #453: / 1995 / HOV / M • Hot Body Competition: Bikinis & Bikes Contest / 1996 / CG / F • Just The Way You Like It #1: Sandy's Milk / 1994 / JEG / M • Odyssey Amateur #52: Dawn's Anal Awakening / 1991 / OD / M • Raunch #10: Uncut Jewel / 1994 / CC / M • Sandy's: Young & Willing / 1995 / SM / F • Yellow Waters #1 / 1985 / BAK / F • Yellow Waters #2 / 1985 / BAK / F

DAWN ADAMS *see Star Index I*

DAWN AVALON *see Star Index I*

DAWN BURNING

Bad To The Bone / 1996 / ULP / M • Bikini Beach #4 / 1996 / CC / M • Breeders / 1996 / MET / M • The Clock Strikes Bizarre On Butt Row / 1996 / ABS / M • Double D Dykes #27 / 1995 / GO / F • Macin' #2: Macadocious / 1996 / SMP / M • Maui Waui / 1996 / PE / M • Ona Zee's Doll House #4 / 1996 / ONA / F • Pick Up Lines #05 / 1996

/ OD / M • Profiles #07: Sexworld / 1996 / XPR / M • Snake Pit / 1996 / DWO / M • Twist Of Fate / 1996 / WP / M • Underground #2: Subway To Sodom / 1996 / SC / M • Up And Cummers #30 / 1996 / 4P / M • XXX / 1996 / TEP / M

DAWN CHANDRA *see Star Index I*

DAWN CUMMINGS

Kinky Ladies Of Bourbon Street / 1976 / LUM / M • Only The Best From Europe / 1989 / CV / C • Peek Freak / 1987 / CV / M • Sensations / 1975 / ALP / M • Sexy / 1976 / SE / M

DAWN DEVINE *(Destiny (1996))*

Marginal face, brunette with long brown hair, braces on teeth, petite lithe body, tight waist, a little flab on the belly, and small/medium tits. She says (1996) she's 24 years old, was de-virginized at 19, and comes from North Carolina via Dallas TX. Seems to have a nice personality.

Affair With Destiny / 1996 / STM / F • Anal Virgins #03 / 1996 / NS / M • Cherry Poppers: The College Years #01 / 1997 / ZA / M • Creme De La Face #18: Cum Mops / 1997 / OD / M • Fellatio Fanatics / 1996 / NIT / M • More Dirty Debutantes #57 / 1996 / 4P / M • Nineteen #6 / 1996 / FOR / M • Nineteen #7 / 1996 / FOR / M • Puritan Video Magazine #07 / 1996 / LE / M • Pussyman's Nite Club Party #1 / 1996 / SNA / M • Pussyman's Nite Club Party #2 / 1997 / SNA / M • Rectal Raiders / 1997 / ROB / M • Sabrina The Booty Queen / 1997 / ROB / M

DAWN DEVINE (1994)

Coming Of Fortune / 1994 / EX / M

DAWN DIVINE

The Real Deal #1 / 1994 / FC / M • A Taste Of Genie / 1986 / 4P / M

DAWN FAIRCHILD *see Star Index I*

DAWN PERRY

The Master And Mrs. Johnson / 1980 / SAT / M

DAWN REBEL *see* Rebel Dean

DAWN ROBBINS *see* Cara Lott

DAWN SAVAGE

Double Trouble: Spanking English Style / 1996 / BIZ / B

DAWN STARR *see Star Index I*

DAWN SWENSON

Sex Boat / 1980 / VCX / M

DAWN WILLIAMS

Blue Vanities #582 / 1996 / FFL / M

DAY JASON *(Daniella D'Orici, Amy Wells, Danella Di Orici, Daniela Di Origi, Danilee D'Orici)*

Come Fly With Us / 1974 / QX / M • Defiance / 1974 / ALP / B • Joy Riders / 1975 / SAT / M • The Felines / 1975 / VCX / M • The Love Bus / 1974 / OSC / M • The Passions Of Carol / 1975 / VXP / M • The Private Afternoons Of Pamela Mann / 1974 / TVX / M • Teenage Stepmother / cr74 / SVE / M

DAYMON

Northwest Pecker Trek #3: Ducks & Dicks / 1994 / LBO / M

DAYN MORGAN *see Star Index I*

DAYNE CHRISTIAN *(Jake Dane)*

Presentable male who seems to be the boyfriend of Stacy Spelling.

Anal Heartbreaker / 1995 / ROB / M • Fashion Sluts #2 / 1995 / ABS / M • Fashion Sluts #8 / 1996 / ABS / M • The Voyeur

#4 / 1995 / EA / M

DAZI
Solo Adventures / 1996 / AB / F

DE DE MUNSON
American Pie / 1980 / SE / M

DE JE VOU *see* **Sharon Kane**

DE JU *see* **Lulu Brace**

DE NAVARRE
Sinister Servants / 1996 / CUC / B

DE-AHANA *see* **De-Ahna**

DE-AHNA *(De-Anna, De-Ahana)*
Bordello...House Of The Rising Sun / 1985 / SE / M • Feel The Heat / 1985 / AAH / M • Jack 'n' Jill #2 / 1984 / VC / M • Ultrasex / 1987 / VC / M

DE-ANNA *see* **De-Ahna**

DEACON BLUE
Audition For Pain / 1996 / VTF / B • Awol / 1994 / SBP / B • Battling Bitches / 1993 / SBP / B • Battling Bruisers / 1993 / SBP / B • Body Slammers #03 / 1993 / SBP / B • Bound For Cash / 1994 / SBP / B • Cage Cats / 1993 / SBP / B • Club DOM / 1994 / SBP / B • The Foot Client / 1993 / SBP / B • Foot Hookers / 1994 / SBP / B • Frankentickle / 1993 / CS / B • Little Shop Of Tickle / 1995 / SBP / B • Lost On Maneuvers / 1994 / VTF / B • The Magnificent 7 / 1994 / VTF / B • Medically Bound Tickle Team / 1996 / VTF / B • Monkee Business / 1994 / CS / B • Quality Control / 1996 / VTF / B • The Rack / 1994 / SBP / B • The Rock / 1994 / SBP / B • Roped & Ravished / 1996 / CS / B • Rubber Me Butt! / 1994 / SBP / B • Secrets Of Bondage / 1995 / SBP / B • Shockers / 1996 / SBP / B • Sound Of Tickling / 1995 / SBP / B • Taunted, Tied & Tickled / 1995 / SBP / B • The Tickle Shack / 1995 / SBP / B • Tickled And Teased / 1994 / SBP / B • Tickling Vamps / 1995 / SBP / B • Two Tied For Tickling / 1995 / SBP / B

DEADRA MARROW *see* **Dominique Simone**

DEADRE MARROW *see* **Dominique Simone**

DEAN
Amateur Nights #05 / 1990 / HO / M • Toe Tales #26 / 1995 / GOT / B • TV Shoestore Fantasy #1 / 1991 / BIZ / G • TVs In Trouble #2 / 1991 / BIZ / G

DEAN ALBA *see* **Wayne Summers**

DEAN CLASS
Bi-Ology: The Making Of Mr Right / 1992 / CAT / G

DEAN EDWARDS
American Sex Fantasy / 1975 / IHV / M

DEAN GARY *see* **Star Index I**

DEAN GLASS *see* **Star Index I**

DEAN HAYES
More Than A Voyeur / cr73 / SEP / M

DEAN JAMES *see* **Brett Next**

DEAN RICHMOND
Philappetite / 19?? / ... / M • The Piercing Of Jamie / 1983 / BIZ / B

DEAN ROBERSON
Latex #1 / 1994 / VC / M

DEAN RUSTIN *see* **Star Index I**

DEAN SPEEDE
Filthy First Timers #2: Innocence Lost / 1996 / EL / M • Filthy First Timers #3: Tearing Down The Walls Of Shame / 1996 / EL / M • Filthy First Timers #4 / 1996 / EL / M

DEAN TAIT
Both Ways / 1976 / VC / G • The Devil Inside Her / 1977 / ALP / M • Frank Henen-

lotter's XXX Hardcore Horrors #05 / 1996 / SOW / M

DEAN THOMAS
Ready To Drop #09 / 1995 / FC / M

DEANN GANDEZA *see* **Lei Lani**

DEANNA
Mike Hott: #292 Three-Sum Sluts #03 / 1995 / MHV / M

DEANNA BLONDE
FTV #39: Balls In A Bunch / 1996 / FT / B • FTV #41: Fight To The Finish / 1996 / FT / B • FTV #42: Three Is Not Company / 1996 / FT / B • FTV #43: The Enforcer / 1996 / FT / B • FTV #45: Mother Knows Best / 1996 / FT / B • FTV #47: Hold Me Hurt Me / 1996 / FT / B • FTV #48: Bare Breasted Boxing / 1996 / FT / B • FTV #49: Crooked Cats / 1996 / FT / B • FTV #50: Double-D Duo / 1996 / FT / B • FTV #51: Amazon Queen / 1996 / FT / B • FTV #52: Busty Blood Bath / 1996 / FT / B • FTV #55: Fight Time Fiesta / 1996 / FT / B • FTV #64: Blonde Bust Battle / 1996 / FT / B • FTV #67: Sorry I Hurt You / 1996 / FT / B

DEANNA DARBY *see* **Star Index I**

DEANNA DEVLIN
Mellon Man #01 / 1994 / AVI / M • Nasty Newcummers #08 / 1995 / MET / M • Nostalgic Stockinged Maidens / 1994 / VER / F • Wicked Waxxx Worxxx / 1995 / HW / M

DEANNA NIICHEL
The Cumm Brothers #04: Laid Off & Laid / 1994 / OD / M

DEANNE *see* **Star Index I**

DEANNE FORREST
Devil's Ecstasy / 1974 / VCX / M

DEANNE RHODES
Secret Retreat #1 / 1991 / STM / B • Show Them No Mercy #1 / 1991 / STM / B • Show Them No Mercy #2 / 1991 / STM / B

DEB
Full Moon Video #10: Squat City / 1994 / FAP / F

DEBBETT
Adventures Of The DP Boys: Back In Town / 1994 / HW / M • Anal Camera #03 / 1994 / EVN / M • Anal Pandemonium / 1994 / TTV / M • Ateball: More Than A Mouthful / 1995 / ATE / F • Bi Love Lucy / 1994 / PL / G • Bi On The Fourth Of July / 1994 / BIL / G • Butt Bangers Ball #1 / 1996 / TTV / M • Butt Hunt #01 / 1994 / LEI / M • Different Strokes / 1994 / PRE / B • Dirty Doc's Housecalls #18 / 1994 / LV / M • Enemates #09 / 1994 / BIZ / B • The Fabulous 50's Girls #1 / 1994 / EMC / M • First Time Lesbians #19 / 1994 / JMP / F • Fun Zone / 1994 / PRE / B • Gang Bang Diaries #5 / 1994 / SFP / M • Golden Oldies #2 / 1995 / TTV / M • Golden Oldies #4 / 1996 / TTV / M • Hot Bi Summer / 1994 / BIL / G • House Of Sex #02: Banging Debbett / 1994 / RTP / M • Just The Way You Like It #2: Watch Debette Do It / 1994 / JEG / M • Kinky Orientals / 1994 / FH / M • More Than A Mouthful #1 / 1995 / VEX / F • Mr. Peepers Amateur Home Videos #87: Groupie Therapy / 1994 / LBO / M • Oriental Oddballs #1 / 1994 / FH / M • Oriental Oddballs #2 / 1994 / FH / M • Over Forty Gang Bang / 1994 / RTP / M • Pussy Showdown / 1994 / WIV / M • The Real Deal #1 / 1994 / FC / M • Ron Hightower's White Chicks #11 / 1994 / LBO / M • Tail Taggers #125 / 1994 / WV / M • Triple Flay / 1995 / PRE / B • Triple Play / 1994 / PRE

/ B

DEBBI GENTRY *see* **Star Index I**

DEBBI VALE *see* **Star Index I**

DEBBIE
976-76DD / 1993 / VI / M • A&B AB#318: Let's Have An Orgy / 1991 / A&B / M • A&B GB#066: Debbie And Amber / 1992 / A&B / M • AHV #20: Give It To Me, Baby / 1992 / EVN / M • Amateur Night #04 / 1990 / HME / M • Blue Vanities #116 / 1988 / FFL / M • Blue Vanities #508 / 1992 / FFL / M • Body & Soul / 1995 / IF / M • Breast Of Britain #4 / 1990 / BTO / S • Buttman's European Vacation #1 / 1991 / EA / M • Canadian Beaver Hunt #4 / 1996 / PL / M • Gourmet Premier: Sex School / Centerfold Layout #909 / cr84 / GO / M • Innocence Bound / 1995 / GAL / B • Joe Elliot's College Girls #30 / 1994 / JOE / M • Lesbian Love Dolls / 1995 / LIP / F • Mike Hott: #120 Dildo Debbie, Dusty, Mike And Steve / 1990 / MHV / M • Neighborhood Watch #17: Burning The Sausage / 1992 / LBO / M • Odyssey Amateur #88: Debbie Does Greek / 1992 / OD / M • Odyssey Triple Play #08: Hot Wet & Wild / 1992 / OD / M • Pearl Necklace: Amorous Amateurs #33 / 1992 / SEE / M • Pussy Hunt #06 / 1994 / LEI / M • Stevi's: Debbie's Pantyhose Tease / 1994 / SSV / F

DEBBIE ANSON
Juggs / 1984 / VCR / M

DEBBIE BERLE *see* **Sheena Horne**

DEBBIE BLAISDELL *see* **Tracey Adams**

DEBBIE BLAZE
Stevi's: Debbie's Sex Combo / 1996 / SSV / M

DEBBIE BROOKS
Waterfront Honey / 19?? / XTR / M

DEBBIE COLE
Kneel Before Me! / 1983 / ALP / B • Oriental Techniques Of Pain And Pleasure / 1983 / ALP / B

DEBBIE COLE (CRYS B) *see* **Crystal Breeze**

DEBBIE CROFT *see* **Star Index I**

DEBBIE DARLING
Girls Just Want To...Have Fun / 1984 / SE / M • She-Male Encounters #05: Orgy At The Poysinberry Bar #1 / 1987 / MET / G • She-Male Encounters #12: Orgy At The Poysinberry #2 / 1987 / MET / G

DEBBIE DAVISON *see* **Star Index I**

DEBBIE DEE
Buttman's Big Tit Adventure #3 / 1995 / EA / M

DEBBIE DOES *see* **Debbie Hopkins**

DEBBIE DOWNS *see* **Star Index I**

DEBBIE DUZZIT
Ed Woody / 1995 / HBE / M • Ho Duzzit Model Agency #1 / 1993 / AFV / M

DEBBIE EVANS *see* **Star Index I**

DEBBIE FOLEY *see* **Kimberly Kane**

DEBBIE GARLAND *see* **Star Index I**

DEBBIE GREEN *see* **Debbie Northrup**

DEBBIE GUKEISEN
Inside Seka / 1980 / VXP / M

DEBBIE HAMILTON *see* **Monique Cardin**

DEBBIE HOPKINS *(Debbie Does)*
Very limber blonde with small droopy tits, small but not very hard body, and a tattoo on the back of her right hand.
The Anal Adventures Of Max Hardcore: Full Throttle / 1994 / ZA / M • Casting Call #06 / 1994 / SO / M • Cherry Poppers #04: Ripe 'n' Ready / 1994 / ZA / M

DEBBIE HOUSTON *see* **Sheena Horne**
DEBBIE HUPP *see* **Heather Thomas**
DEBBIE JACOBS *see* **Star Index I**
DEBBIE JAMES
Close Up / 19?? / BOC / M
DEBBIE JOHNSSON
Scandanavian Double Features #2 / 1996 / PL / M • Scandanavian Double Features #3 / 1996 / PL / M
DEBBIE JOINTED *see* **Debi Jointed**
DEBBIE JORDAN
10 Years Of Big Busts #1 / 1989 / BTO / C • Big Busty #49 / 1995 / BTO / S
DEBBIE LADD
Hot Child In The City / 1979 / PVX / M
DEBBIE LEE
Fetishes Of Monique / cr76 / VHL / B
DEBBIE LEE JONES
French Kiss / 1979 / PVX / M • Wild Innocents / 1982 / VCX / M
DEBBIE LESTER *see* **Debi Diamond**
DEBBIE LEWIS *see* **Star Index I**
DEBBIE LOVE
Squalor Motel / 1985 / SE / M
DEBBIE LYNN *see* **Debra Lynn**
DEBBIE MAJORS
Bondage Classix #13: Class Of 86 #2 / 1991 / BON / B • Bondage Classix #18: Gwen And Debbie's Torments / 198? / BON / B • Bondage Memories #02 / 1993 / BON / C • Double Whipping / 198? / BON / B • Real Breasts Real Torment / 1995 / BON / C • School Dayze / 1987 / BON / B • Tortured Present / cr87 / BON / B
DEBBIE MERRITT *see* **Angel West**
DEBBIE MICHAELS
Amateur Dreams #4 / 1994 / DR / M
DEBBIE MOORE *see* **Sheri St Clair**
DEBBIE NELSON
Blue Vanities #514 / 1992 / FFL / M
DEBBIE NORTHRUP *(Debbie Green, Lautrec, Betty Blue (D.Nort.), Debbie Thornton, Jessie Blu)*
Dark blonde or light brown shoulder length hair, droopy medium tits, passable face, overbite.
Back Road To Paradise / 1984 / CDI / M • Caught From Behind #01 / 1982 / HO / M • China & Silk / 1984 / MAB / M • Old Olympix Affair #137 / 1985 / GO / M • Inflamed / 1984 / NSV / M • Letters Of Love / 1985 / CA / M • Loco Motion / 1988 / VSX / C • Pretty As You Feel / 1984 / PV / M • Rear Action Girls #1 / 1984 / LIP / F • Sappho Sextet / 1983 / LIP / F • Shape Up For Sensational Sex / 1985 / SE / M • Springtime In The Rockies / 1984 / CIN / M • This Side Up / 1987 / VSX / C • The Wacky World Of X-Rated Bloopers / 1989 / GO / M • Wings Of Passion / 1984 / HO / M
DEBBIE PRESSMAN
Orgy At Rachel's Pad / 1975 / … / M
DEBBIE RAINIER *see* **Star Index I**
DEBBIE REVENGE
Babylon Pink #1 / 1979 / COM / M • Fetishes Of Monique / cr76 / VHL / B • For Richer, For Poorer / 1979 / CXV / M • Satin Suite / 1979 / QX / M
DEBBIE ROSE
Inside Desiree Cousteau / 1979 / VCX / M
DEBBIE ROSS *see* **Star Index I**
DEBBIE SANDS
The Velvet Edge / cr76 / SE / M
DEBBIE SHAW *see* **Star Index I**
DEBBIE THORNTON *see* **Debbie Northrup**

DEBBIE TRUELOVE
Debbie Does Las Vegas / 1982 / KOV / M • Indian Lady / 1983 / VC / M • Las Vegas Erotica / 1983 / MVI / M • Skin Deep / 1982 / CA / M • South Of The Border / 1977 / VC / M • Weekend Cowgirls / 1983 / CA / M
DEBBIE VAN GILS
Magma: Olympus Of Lust / 1994 / MET / M • Private Film #02 / 1993 / OD / M
DEBBIE WAHEWEE
Catch Of The Day #1 / 1995 / VG0 / M
DEBBIE WINTERS
Eat At Dave's #1 / 1995 / SP / M • The Superhawk Girls...And Their Fabulous Toys / 1996 / GLI / F
DEBBY
Amateur Hours #02 / 1989 / AFI / M • Busty Superstars #1 / 199? / H&S / S
DEBERA WELLS *see* **Deborah Wells**
DEBI
Blue Vanities #116 / 1988 / FFL / M • Blue Vanities #511 / 1992 / FFL / M • Young Cheeks / 1990 / BEB / B
DEBI DIAMOND *(Debi Hanson, Shelly Rey, Shelly Rae, Kaviar, Debbie Lester, Debra Diamond, Miss D.D., Debi Dymond, Josi Emerson)*
Started back in the early eighties as Shelly Rey and retired for a while, returning as Debi Diamond. Very enthusiastic about sex but of the grungy kind. Too tall and too big a frame, small tits, lean manish body, not ugly but not pretty facially. Debbie Lester in **Make Me Sweat**. Allegedly had breasts enhanced in 1990 but no difference noted. Born Jan 5, 1965. Josi Emerson in Lust Weekend (1987).
$exce$$ / 1993 / CA / M • 10,000 Anal Maniacs #2 / 1994 / FOR / M • 3 Wives / 1993 / VT / M • Above The Knee / 1994 / WAV / M • Addictive Desires / 1994 / OD / M • Adult Video News 1992 Awards / 1992 / VC / M • Adults Only / 1995 / BOT / M • The Adventures Of Studman #2 / 1994 / AFV / M • After Midnight / 1994 / IN / M • The All American Girl / 1991 / PP / M • All American Girls #2: In Heat / 1983 / CA / M • All The President's Women / 1994 / LV / M • Anal Al's Adventures / 1995 / PL / M • Anal Asspirations / 1993 / LV / M • Anal Attitude / 1993 / HO / M • Anal Babes / 1995 / PPR / M • Anal Mystique / 1994 / EMC / M • Anal Persuasion / 1994 / EX / M • Anal Secrets (Metro) / 1994 / IN / M • Anal Woman #3 / 1995 / PL / M • The Anal-Europe Series #08: / 1995 / LV / M • The Analizer / 1994 / VD / M • Angelica / 1989 / ARG / M • Anus & Andy / 1993 / ZA / M • Anything Goes / 1993 / VD / C • The Artist / 1994 / HO / M • Ass Dweller / 1994 / WIV / M • Ass Openers! #1 / 1995 / TCK / C • Ass Openers! #2 / 1995 / TCK / C • Attic Toys / 1994 / ERA / M • Baccarat #2 / 1991 / FH / M • Bachelor Party #1 / 1993 / FPI / M • Backdoor To Hollywood #09 / 1989 / CIN / M • Backing In #3 / 1991 / WV / C • Backing In #6 / 1994 / WV / C • Backing In #7 / 1995 / WV / C • Bad Girls #2 / 1983 / GO / M • Badgirls #1: Lockdown / 1994 / VI / M • Badgirls #2: Strip Search / 1994 / VI / M • Beauties And The Beast / 1990 / AFV / M • Bedtime Stories / 1992 / CDI / M • Bend Over Backwards / 1993 / VIM / M • The Best Of Backdoor To Hollywood / 1990 / CIN / C • Best Of Buttman #1 / 1991 / EA / C • The Best Of Buttslammers / 1995 / BS / C • Best Of

Caught From Behind #5 / 1991 / HO / C • Best Of Talk Dirty To Me #02 / 1991 / DR / C • The Best Of The Gangbang Girl Series / 1995 / ANA / C • The Bet / 1993 / VT / M • Between Her Thighs / 1992 / CDI / M • Between The Cheeks #2 / 1990 / VC / M • The Big Bang #2 / 1994 / LV / M • Big Boob Ball / 1995 / IF / C • The Big Tease #1 / 1990 / VC / M • The Big Tease #2 / 1990 / VC / M • The Bitches / 1993 / LIP / F • Black Butt Jungle / 1993 / ME / M • Black Cobra / 1989 / WV / M • Black For More / 1993 / ZA / M • Blacks & Blondes: The Movie / 1989 / WV / M • Blinded By Love / 1993 / OD / M • Blonde Butt Babes / 1994 / LV / M • Bloopers (Video Team) / 1994 / VT / M • Boiling Point / 1994 / WAV / M • Boobs, Butts And Bloopers #1 / 1990 / HO / M • The Book / 1990 / IF / M • Bottoms Up (1993-Hollywood) / 1993 / HO / M • Bratgirl / 1989 / VI / M • Breastman Does The Himalayas / 1993 / EVN / M • Breathless / 1989 / CIN / M • Buffy Malibu's Nasty Girls #07 / 1994 / ANA / F • Bunmasters / 1995 / VC / M • Burgundy Blues / 1993 / MET / M • Bustin' Thru / 1993 / LV / M • Butt Bandits #4 / 1996 / VD / C • The Butt Boss / 1993 / VD / M • Butt Jammers #04 / 1995 / SC / F • The Butt Sisters Do Los Angeles / 1993 / MID / M • Butt X Files #1 / 1995 / WIV / M • Butt's Motel #3 / 1989 / EX / M • Butthead Dreams: Mission Impenetrable / 1994 / FH / M • Butthunt / 1994 / AFV / F • The Buttnicks #1 / 1990 / VEX / M • Buttslammers #03: The Ultimate Dream / 1993 / BS / F • Buttslammers #04: Down And Dirty / 1993 / BS / F • Buttslammers #05: Quake, Rattle & Roll! / 1994 / BS / F • Buttslammers #06: Over The Edge / 1994 / BS / F • Buttslammers #07: Indecent Decadence / 1994 / BS / F • Caballero Preview Tape #4 / 1985 / CA / C • Cajun Heat / 1993 / SC / M • Candy Factory / 1994 / PE / M • Candy Snacker / 1993 / WIV / M • Cape Rear / 1992 / WV / M • The Case Of The Cockney Cupcake / 1989 / ME / M • Caught From Behind #13 / 1990 / HO / M • Caught From Behind #18 / 1993 / HO / M • Caught From Behind #19 / 1994 / HO / M • Centerfold Celebrities '94 #2 / 1994 / SFP / M • The Chameleon / 1989 / VC / M • Checkmate / 1995 / WAV / M • Cheeks #3 / 1990 / CC / M • Cheerleader Nurses #1 / 1993 / VC / M • Cheerleader Nurses #2 / 1993 / VC / M • Chocolate & Vanilla Twist / 1992 / PL / F • Christmas Carol / 1993 / LV / M • City Of Sin / 1991 / LV / M • Close To The Edge / 1994 / VI / M • Club DV8 #1 / 1993 / SC / M • Club DV8 #2 / 1993 / SC / M • Collection #06 / 1984 / CA / M • Coming Attractions / 1995 / WHP / M • Compulsive Behavior / 1995 / PI / M • The Corruption Of Christina / 1993 / WP / M • County Line / 1993 / PEP / M • Covergirl / 1994 / WP / M • Creme De Femme / 1994 / 4P / F • Cumming Of Ass / 1995 / TP / M • The Cumming Of Sarah Jane #2 / 1993 / AFV / M • Cunthunt / 1995 / AB / F • Dangerous Debi / 1993 / HO / C • Debbie Does Dallas Again / 1994 / AFV / M • Debi Diamond's Dirty Dykes #1 / 1995 / FD / F • Debi Diamond's Dirty Dykes #2 / 1995 / FD / F • Debi Diamond: Mega Mistress / 1995 / BIZ / B • Debi Does Girls / 1992 / PL / F • Debi's Darkest Desires / 1996 / BIZ / B • Decadence / 1994 / WHP / M • Deep Cheeks #1 / 1991 / ROB / M •

Deep Cheeks #2 / 1991 / ROB / M • Deep Cover / 1993 / WP / M • Deep Inside Debi Diamond / 1995 / VC / C • Deep Inside Misty Rain / 1995 / VC / C • Deep Inside P.J. Sparxx / 1995 / VC / C • Deep Inside Victoria / 1992 / CDI / C • Deep Throat #4 / 1990 / AR / M • Deep Throat #5 / 1990 / AR / M • Denim Dolls #1 / 1989 / CDI / M • Denim Dolls #2 / 1990 / CDI / M • Depraved Fantasies #1 / 1993 / FPI / M • Depraved Fantasies #2 / 1994 / FPI / M • Desert Foxes / 1989 / SE / M • Desert Moon / 1994 / SPI / M • Dial A For Anal / 1994 / CA / M • Diamond For Sale / 1990 / EVN / M • Diamond In The Raw / 1996 / XCI / M • Diamond In The Rough / 1989 / EX / M • Diamond In The Rough / 1993 / BIA / C • Diamond In The Rough / 1995 / FD / M • Diamond Likes It Rough / 1995 / BON / B • The Dickheads #1 / 1993 / MID / M • The Dinner Party #1 / 1994 / ULI / M • Dirty Longstocking / 1994 / GOU / M • Dirt Bags / 1994 / FPI / M • Dirty Laundry #2 / 1994 / CV / M • Dirty Little Lies / 1993 / VT / M • Dirty Little Movies / 1990 / … / M • Dirty Panties / 1994 / SCL / M • Doggie Style / 1994 / CA / M • Dollars And Yen / 1994 / FH / M • Double D Dykes #09 / 1993 / GO / F • Double Down / 1993 / LBO / M • Dp #2: The Mighty Fhucks / 1994 / FC / M • Dr Feelgood Sex Psychiatrist / 1994 / LV / M • The Dragon Lady #2: Tales From the Bed / 1992 / WV / M • Dresden Diary #11: Endangered Secrets / 1994 / BIZ / B • Dresden Diary #12: / 1995 / BIZ / B • Dungeon Dykes #1 / 1994 / FPI / F • Dungeon Dykes #2 / 1994 / FPI / F • Earth Girls Are Sleazy / 1990 / SO / M • Easy Pussy / 1991 / ROB / M • The Easy Way / 1990 / VC / M • Easy Way Out / 1989 / OD / M • Eleventh Annual AVN Awards / 1994 / VC / M • The End Of The Innocence / 1989 / IN / M • Essence Of A Woman / 1993 / FOR / M • The Eternal Idol / 1992 / CDI / M • Extreme Sex #2: The Dungeon / 1994 / VI / M • Extreme Sex #3: Wired / 1994 / VI / M • Extreme Sex #4: The Experiment / 1995 / VI / M • The Farmer's Daughters / 1994 / LV / M • Fatal Illusion / 1995 / WIV / M • Femme Fatale / 1993 / SC / M • Firecrackers / 1994 / HW / M • First Time Ever #1 / 1995 / PE / F • Forbidden Pleasures / 1995 / ERA / M • Frat Girls Of Double D / 1993 / PP / M • Friday Night Fever / 1989 / LV / M • Full Moon Fever / 1994 / LBO / M • Full Throttle Girls: Boredom Pulled The Trigger / 1993 / VIM / M • Fun In A Bun / 1990 / LV / M • The Fury / 1993 / WIV / M • Future Lust / 1989 / ME / M • Gang Bang Face Bath #1 / 1993 / ROB / M • Gang Bangs #2 / 1989 / EA / M • Gangbang Girl #03 / 1992 / ANA / M • Gangbang Girl #04 / 1992 / ANA / M • Girl Country / 1990 / CC / F • The Girl With The Heart-Shaped Tattoo / 1995 / WAV / M • A Girl's Affair #04 / 1994 / FD / F • Girls Of The Double D #11 / 1990 / CIN / M • Girls Will Be Boys #5 / 1993 / PL / F • Good Vibrations / 1993 / ZA / M • The Good, The Bed, And The Snuggly / 1993 / ZA / M • Goodtime Charli / 1989 / CIN / M • The Governess / 1993 / WP / M • Happy Endings / 1994 / WP / M • Hardbreak Ridge / 1990 / WV / M • Her Wicked Ways / 1983 / CA / M • Hershe Highway #2 / 1989 / HO / M • Hershe Highway #3 / 1990 / HO / M • High Heel Harlots #04 / 1994 / SFP / M •

Hole In One / 1994 / HO / M • Hollywood Temps / 1993 / ZA / M • The Honeymoon: The Bride's Running Behind / 1990 / 4P / M • Horny Henry's Snowballing Adventure / 1995 / TTV / M • Hose Jobs / 1995 / VEX / M • Hot Licks At The Pussycat Club / 1990 / WV / C • Hot Tight Asses #03 / 1993 / TCK / M • Hot Tight Asses #07 / 1994 / TCK / M • Hotel Paradise / 1989 / CA / M • Hotel Sodom #01 / 1995 / SNA / M • Hotel Sodom #08 / 1995 / SNA / M • Hourman Is Here / 1994 / CC / M • How To Deep Throat Your Lover / 1994 / A&E / M • Hump Up The Volume / 1991 / AR / M • Hypnotic Passions / 1993 / FOR / M • I Want A Divorce / 1993 / ZA / M • Icy Hot / 1990 / MID / M • If These Walls Could Talk (Director's Cut) / 1993 / MET / M • If These Walls Could Talk #2: Burning Secrets / 1993 / CV / M • Immortal Desire / 1993 / VI / M • In X-Cess / 1994 / LV / M • Introducing Charli / 1989 / CIN / M • Introducing Tabitha / 1990 / CIN / M • Jailhouse Cock / 1993 / IP / M • Just Lesbians / 1995 / NOT / F • Kadillac & Devell / 1993 / ZA / M • Kascha's Days & Nights / 1989 / CDI / M • Kinky Cameraman #1 / 1996 / LEI / C • Kinky Cameraman #2 / 1996 / LEI / C • Kym Wilde's On The Edge #13 / 1994 / RB / B • Kym Wilde's On The Edge #14 / 1994 / RB / B • Kym Wilde's On The Edge #15 / 1994 / RB / B • Kym Wilde's On The Edge #19 / 1995 / RB / B • Kym Wilde's On The Edge #21 / 1995 / RB / B • L.A. Fantasies / 1990 / WV / C • The Last Action Whore / 1993 / LV / M • The Last Good-Bi / 1990 / CDI / G • Latex #1 / 1994 / VC / M • Leather Bound Dykes From Hell #5 / 1995 / BIZ / B • The Legend Of Sleepy Hollow / 1989 / LE / M • Legs And Lingerie #2 / 1990 / BEB / F • Lesbian Castle: No Kings Allowed / 1994 / LIP / F • Lesbian Lingerie Fantasy #2 / 1989 / ESP / F • Lessons 'n' Love / 1994 / LBO / M • Lick Bush / 1992 / VD / C • A Little Christmas Tail / 1991 / ZA / M • A Little Irresistible / 1991 / ZA / M • The Look / 1993 / WP / M • Loopholes / 1993 / TP / M • Love Bunnies #06 / 1994 / FPI / F • Love Bunnies #07 / 1994 / FPI / F • The Love Doctor / 1992 / HIP / M • Low Blows: The Private Collection / 1989 / ME / M • Lust And The Law / 1991 / GO / C • Lust Weekend / 1987 / CA / M • Made In Japan / 1992 / VI / M • The Magic Shower / 1989 / CDI / M • Make Me Sweat / 1989 / CIN / M • Makin' It / 1994 / A&E / M • Malibook Beach / 1995 / FH / M • Maneaters (1992-Vidco) / 1992 / VD / C • The Mating Pot / 1994 / LBO / M • Mind Shadows #1 / 1993 / FD / M • Mindsex / 1993 / MPA / M • Miss Anal America / 1993 / LV / M • Mistaken Identity / 1990 / CC / M • Misty Rain's Anal Orgy / 1994 / FRM / M • Models Etc. / 1995 / LV / M • Moonglow / 1989 / IN / M • My Friend, My Lover / 1990 / FIR / M • Nasty Girls #1 (1990-CDI) / 1990 / CIN / M • Naughty 90's / 1990 / HO / M • Naughty In Nature / 1994 / PL / M • Neighbors / 1994 / LE / M • A New Girlfriend / 1991 / XPI / M • Night And Day #2 / 1993 / VT / M • A Night At The Waxworks / 1990 / IF / M • Night Nurses / 1995 / WAV / M • Nighttime Stories / 1991 / LE / M • Nightvision / 1993 / TP / M • No Man's Land #08: Eight Women Who Ate Women / 1993 / VT / F • No Man's Land #11 / 1995 / VT / F • Not So Innocent / 1990 / HO / M • Nothing

But Trouble / 1991 / CIN / M • Nothing Personal / 1993 / CA / M • Nurses Bound By Duty / 1996 / BIZ / B • On The Come Line / 1993 / MID / M • The Orgy #1 / 1993 / EMC / M • The Orgy #2 / 1993 / EMC / M • The Orgy #3 / 1993 / EMC / M • Oriental Temptations / 1992 / WV / M • Outlaws / 1993 / SC / M • Overnight Sensation / 1991 / XCI / M • A Paler Shade Of Blue / 1991 / CC / M • Paris Blues / 1990 / WV / C • Party In The Rear / 1989 / LV / M • Party Of Payne / 1993 / BS / B • The Passion / 1995 / IP / M • Passion From Behind / 1990 / LV / M • Peep Land / 1992 / FH / M • Peepshow / 1994 / OD / M • Performer Of The Year / 1994 / WP / M • Pin-Up / 1991 / BAD / C • Pouring It On / 1993 / CV / M • Precious Cargo / 1993 / VIM / M • Prescription For Pleasure / 1993 / HW / M • Princess Orgasma #1 / 1991 / PP / M • Prisoners Of Pain / 1994 / BIZ / B • Private & Perverse / 1994 / CA / C • Pussy Galore / 1993 / VD / C • Pussyman #03: The Search Continues / 1993 / SNA / M • Pussyman #04: The Celebration / 1993 / SNA / M • Pussyman #11: Prime Cuts / 1995 / SNA / M • R.E.A.L. #1 / 1994 / LV / F • Radical Affairs Video Magazine #07 / 1994 / ME / M • Rapture / 1990 / SC / M • Raquel On Fire / 1990 / VC / M • Raunch #08 / 1993 / CC / M • Raunchy Ranch / 1991 / AFV / M • Raw #2 / 1994 / AFV / M • Real Tickets #1 / 1994 / VC / M • Real Tickets #2 / 1994 / VC / M • Rear Entry / 1995 / LEI / M • Rears In Windows / 1993 / FH / M • Reds / 1993 / LE / F • The Reel World #2 / 1994 / FOR / M • Reflections / 1995 / FD / M • The Rehearsal / 1993 / VC / M • Reservoir Bitches / 1994 / BIP / M • Route 69 / 1989 / OD / M • Rumpman: Caught In An Anal Avalanche / 1995 / HW / M • San Fernando Valley Girls / 1983 / CA / M • Sapphire / 1995 / ERA / M • Saturday Night Porn #1 / 1993 / AFV / M • Saturday Night Porn #2 / 1993 / AFV / M • Say Something Nasty / 1989 / CC / M • Scandalous / 1989 / CC / M • The Screamer / 1991 / CA / M • Selina / 1993 / XCI / M • Send Me An Angel / 1990 / V99 / M • Sensual Exposure / 1993 / ULI / M • Sex #1 (Vca) / 1994 / VC / M • Sex #2: Fate (Vca) / 1995 / VC / M • Sex In Abissi / 1993 / WIV / M • Sex In Strange Places: The Sphincter Zone / 1994 / FPI / M • Sex Lives Of Clowns / 1994 / VC / M • Sex Nurses / 1991 / VIR / M • Sex Scandals / 1995 / XC / M • Sexmares / 1993 / FH / M • Sexophrenia / 1993 / VC / M • The Sexual Zone / 1989 / EX / M • Shame / 1994 / VI / M • Shameless / 1991 / SC / M • She's Ready / 1990 / CDI / M • Shear Ecstasy / 1993 / PEP / M • Shelby's Forbidden Fears / 1995 / BIZ / B • Shiver / 1993 / FOR / M • Shock / 1995 / LE / M • Single Girl Masturbation #2 / 1989 / ESP / F • Single Girl Masturbation #3 / 1989 / ESP / F • Six-Nine Love / 1990 / LV / M • Skin Dive / 1988 / AVC / M • Skippy, Jiff & Jam / 1990 / CIA / M • Slippery When Wet / 1994 / LEI / C • Sloppy Seconds / 1994 / PE / M • Slurp 'n' Gag / 1994 / CA / C • Sluthunt #1 / 1995 / BIP / F • Smart Ass Delinquent / 1993 / VT / M • So I Married A Lesbian / 9993 / WV / M • So You Want To Be In The Movies? / 1994 / VC / M • Soaked To The Bone / 1989 / IN / M • The Social Club / 1995 / LE

/ M • Sodomania #05: Euro-American Style / 1993 / EL / M • Sodomania #06: Gangs And Bangs And Other Thangs / 1993 / EL / M • Sodomania: Slop Shots / 1996 / EL / C • Sodomania: The Baddest Of The Best...And Then Some / 1994 / EL / C • Soft Tail / 1991 / IN / M • Some Like It Hot / 1989 / CDI / M • Songbird / 1993 / AMP / M • Spiked Heel Diaries #3 / 1995 / BIZ / B • Sporting Illustrated / 1990 / HO / M • Squirt 'em Cowgirl / 1990 / ERU / M • Stairway To Heaven / 1989 / ME / M • The Stand-Up / 1994 / VC / M • The Starlet / 1991 / PP / M • Steam / 1993 / AMP / M • Steamy Windows / 1990 / VC / M • Stiff Magnolias / 1990 / HO / M • Strange Sex In Strange Places / 1994 / ZA / M • Stranger At The Backdoor / 1994 / CC / M • Stripper Nurses / 1994 / PE / M • Stud Hunters / 1984 / CA / M • Student Nurses / 1991 / CA / M • Stuff Your Face #2 / 1995 / JMP / M • Submission Of Ariana / 1995 / BIZ / B • Suburban Nymphos / 1994 / ATL / M • Sunstroke Beach / 1990 / WV / M • Super Tramp / 1989 / VD / M • Surprise!!! / 1994 / VI / M • Suze's Centerfolds #1 / 1980 / CA / M • Suze's Centerfolds #7 / 1983 / CA / M • Suze's Centerfolds #9 / 1985 / CA / M • Swallow / 1994 / VI / M • Switch Hitters #8 / 1995 / IN / G • Tailgunners / 1990 / CDI / M • Tails Of Tribeca / 1993 / HW / M • Take The A Train / 1993 / MID / M • Takin' It To The Limit #1 / 1994 / BS / M • Talking Trash #1 / 1995 / HW / M • Talking Trash #2 / 1995 / HW / M • A Taste Of Debi / 1990 / PIN / C • Tender Loving Care / 1994 / BRI / S • These Buns For Hire / 1990 / LV / M • Three's A Crowd / 1990 / HO / M • Toys 4 Us #3: Follow The Leader / 1990 / WV / C • The Training #2 / 1994 / BIZ / B • Trashy Ladies / 1993 / LIP / F • Treasure Chest / 1994 / LV / M • True Love / 1989 / VI / M • Truth And Bare / 1991 / LV / M • Two Of A Kind / 1991 / ZA / M • The Tyffany Million Diaries / 1995 / IMV / C • Uncut Diamond / 1989 / IN / M • Unforgivable / 1989 / IN / M • Uninhibited Love / 1994 / VPN / M • Up And Away / 1984 / CA / M • Upbeat Love #1 / 1994 / CV / M • Used And Abused #1 / 1994 / SFP / M • Vagina Beach / 1995 / FH / M • Valleys Of The Moon / 1991 / SC / M • Vegas #2: Snake Eyes / 1990 / CIN / M • Venus Of The Nile / 1991 / WV / M • The Violation Of Alexandria Dane / 1995 / JMP / F • The Violation Of Kia / 1995 / JMP / F • The Violation Of Rachel Love / 1995 / JMP / F • Virtual Reality / 1993 / EX / M • Vixens / 1989 / LV / F • Wanted / 1995 / DR / M • Welcome To Dallas / 1991 / VI / M • Who Shaved Aja? / 1989 / EX / M • The Whole Diamond / 1990 / EVN / M • The Whore / 1989 / CA / M • Why Things Burn / 1994 / LBO / M • Wicked Waxxx Worxxx / 1995 / HW / M • Wild & Wicked #2 / 1992 / VT / M • Wild Breed / 1995 / SC / M • Wild Dreams / 1995 / V99 / M • Wild Fire / 1990 / WV / C • Willing & Wilder / 1995 / BON / B • The Women / 1993 / CAT / F • Words Of Love / 1989 / LE / M • WPINK-TV #5 / 1993 / PV / M • You're A Fucking Slut #1 / 1995 / TP / M • You're A Fucking Slut #2 / 1995 / TP / M • Young Girls In Tight Jeans / 1989 / VD / M • [Denim Dolls #3 / 1990 / ... / M • [Full Throttle Girls #2 / 1993 / VIM / M • [Video Roulette / 1994 / MID / M • [View To Thrill /

1993 / SFP / M

DEBI DYMOND *see* **Debi Diamond**

DEBI GUNTER *see* *Star Index I*

DEBI HANSON *see* **Debi Diamond**

DEBI JOINTED *(Tabitha Jordan, Debbie Jointed)*

What a stupid name! Lithe body with some cellulite in the rear. Brunette or reddish blonde depending on the movie, small to medium droopy tits. Two moles on her belly/chest and another to the left of her ass on her back. As of first quarter 1995 she has had her tits enhanced.

The Basket Trick / 1993 / PL / M • The Catburglar / 1994 / PL / M • Fair Warning / 1995 / ZFX / B • The Necklace #3 / 1994 / ZFX / B • Pearl Necklace: Amorous Amateurs #28 / 1993 / SEE / M • Pearl Necklace: Amorous Amateurs #29 / 1993 / SEE / M • Pearl Necklace: Amorous Amateurs #30 / 1993 / SEE / M • Pearl Necklace: Amorous Amateurs #36 / 1993 / SEE / M • Pearl Necklace: Thee Bush League #17 / 1993 / SEE / M • The Plant / 1995 / ZFX / B • Real Tickets #1 / 1994 / VC / M • Real Tickets #2 / 1994 / VC / M • Subterfuge / 1994 / ZFX / B • Super Groupie / 1993 / PL / M • Tech: Tabitha Jordan #1 / 1993 / TWA / F • The Van / 1995 / ZFX / B • Video Pirates #1 / 1995 / ZFX / B • Video Pirates #2 / 1995 / ZFX / B

DEBI LANE *see* *Star Index I*

DEBORAH

Buffy Malibu's Totally Nasty All-Girl Home Videos #03 / 1992 / ANA / F • Eurotica #10 / 1996 / XC / M • Il Medico Della Coppie / 1996 / TNT / M • Kinky College Cunts #17 / 1993 / NS / F

DEBORAH ASHIRA *see* *Star Index I*

DEBORAH BRAST

Sodom & Gomorrah / 1974 / MIT / M

DEBORAH CHRISTAL

Skin #4: The 4th Rite / 1995 / ERQ / M

DEBORAH CLEARBRANCH *see* **Desiree Cousteau**

DEBORAH CRYSTEL

The Way Of Sex / 1995 / DBV / M

DEBORAH D. ANNETTE *see* *Star Index I*

DEBORAH KARE *see* **Kitty Suckerman**

DEBORAH LACEY

Blue Vanities #582 / 1996 / FFL / M

DEBORAH LUNA *see* *Star Index I*

DEBORAH MORGAN

Cry Uncle / 1971 / VCX / S • Dirty Mary / cr77 / BL / M

DEBORAH PENSON

The Coming Of Joyce / 1977 / VIS / M • Decendance Of Grace / 1977 / CA / M • Pop-Porn: Safari Club / 1992 / 4P / M • Safari Club / 1977 / 4P / M

DEBORAH PHILLIPS *see* *Star Index I*

DEBORAH SCIRE

Not In My Neighborhood / 1993 / IPR / B

DEBORAH STEELE *see* **Rebecca Steele**

DEBORAH SULLIVAN

Sadie / 1980 / EVI / M

DEBORAH WELLS *(Beate, Debera Wells, Nicole Budvar)*

Hungarian with small tits and a lithe tanned body. 5'9" tall, flattish ass. Post-1994 she has returned to Europe and her body has spread a bit.

Alone / 1993 / OD / F • Amadeus Mozart / 1996 / XC / M • American Beauty #1 / 1993 / FOR / M • Anal Alice / 1992 / AFV / M •

Anal Palace / 1995 / VC / M • Angel's Vengeance / 1995 / VMX / M • Babe Patrol / 1993 / FOR / M • Bad Habits / 1993 / VC / M • Bend Over Backwards / 1993 / VIM / M • Bitch / 1993 / VIM / M • Buffy Malibu's Totally Nasty All-Girl Home Videos #05 / 1993 / ANA / F • The Butt Sisters / 1993 / MID / M • Club DV8 #1 / 1993 / SC / M • Club DV8 #2 / 1993 / SC / M • Colossal Orgy #1 / 1993 / HW / M • Eight Is Never Enough / 1993 / ZA / M • Erotic Dreams / 1992 / VTV / M • The Erotic Misadventures Of Harry Johnson / 1992 / ZA / M • Erotic Rondo / 1996 / IP / M • Facesitter #3 / 1994 / CC / M • Father Of The Babe / 1993 / ZA / M • Foolproof / 1994 / VC / M • Full Moon Bay / 1993 / VI / M • Gangbang Girl #11 / 1993 / ANA / M • Gangbang Girl #16 / 1995 / ANA / M • Head First / 1993 / LE / M • Heidi Does Hollywood / 1993 / AFV / M • Horny Orgy / 1993 / GOU / M • Hotel Fear / 1996 / ONA / M • Howard Sperm's Private Parties / 1994 / LBO / M • Hyapatia Obsessed / 1993 / EX / M • Ice Woman #1 / 1993 / VI / M • Ice Woman #2 / 1993 / VI / M • Indecent Offer / 1993 / AFV / M • Kittens #5 / 1994 / CC / F • Ladies Lovin' Ladies #3 / 1993 / AFV / F • The Last Vamp / 1996 / IP / M • Les Femmes Erotiques / 1993 / BFP / M • Matrimony Intrigue / 1995 / WIV / M • Miss Nude International / 1993 / LE / M • Moment To Moment / 1996 / ONA / M • Moon Goddesses #2 / 1993 / VIM / M • More Dirty Debutantes #22 / 1993 / 4P / M • Nurse Tails / 1994 / VC / M • Nylon / 1995 / VI / M • Passion In Venice / 1995 / ULI / M • Picture Me Naked / 1993 / LE / M • Poison Ivory / 1993 / MID / F • Prima #09: ASSassins / 1995 / MBP / M • Pussyman #04: The Celebration / 1993 / SNA / M • Radical Affairs Video Magazine #06 / 1993 / ME / M • Raincoat Fantasies / 1993 / ELP / M • Raunchy Remedy / 1993 / ELP / M • Sarah Jane's Love Bunnies #01 / 1993 / FPI / F • Sindy Does Anal / 1993 / AFV / M • Sparxx / 1993 / MID / F • Spin For Sex / 1994 / IN / M • Steal This Heart #1 / 1993 / CV / M • Steal This Heart #2 / 1993 / CV / M • Steal This Heart (Director's) / 1993 / CV / M • Surprise!!! / 1994 / VI / M • Tales From The Zipper #1 / 1993 / ME / M • Tickled Pink / 1993 / LE / F • Undress To Thrill / 1994 / VI / M • Up And Cummers: The Movie / 1994 / 4P / M • Video Virgins #05 / 1993 / NS / M • Virtual Sex / 1993 / VC / M • Woman 2 Woman #1 / 1993 / SOF / F • Working Girl / 1993 / VI / M • The Worst Porno Ever Made With The Best Sex / 1993 / PL / M • WPINK-TV #4 / 1993 / PV / M • WPINK-TV #5 / 1993 / PV / M

DEBORAH WHITNEY *see* **Cindee Summers**

DEBRA

Lick My Ink #7 / 1994 / TWP / M • Mr. Peepers Amateur Home Videos #47: Sigma Cum Louder / 1992 / LBO / M • She-Male Encounters #04: Jaded Jennifer / 1981 / MET / G • Stilettos And Spikes / 1991 / JBV / S • Working Women / 1994 / PHV / S

DEBRA ALLEN *see* *Star Index I*

DEBRA AREOLA

Bare Waves / 1986 / VD / M • Bionic Babes / 1986 / 4P / M • Born To Be Bad / 1987 / CV / M • The Lost Angel / 1989 / KIS / C • Nightfire / 1987 / LA / M • Smooth Operator / 1986 / AR / M • Tight Fit / 1987 / V99 / M

• Tight Fit / 1991 / VEX / C • Videobone / 1988 / WET / M

DEBRA DAE
Opening Night (Amateur) / 1991 / PRI / M

DEBRA DIAMOND *see Debi Diamond*

DEBRA FLEX
Psychoanal Therapy / 1994 / CA / M

DEBRA HALBERT *see Star Index I*

DEBRA HARDIN *see Star Index I*

DEBRA HOPKINS *see Dorothy Oh*

DEBRA JONES *see Star Index I*

DEBRA LYNN *(Vicki Larsen, Debbie Lynn, Vicky Larsen, Vicky (Debra Lynn))*
Long straight brown hair, elegant looking, passable face. Early performances had her with small tits (e.g., **Like A Virgin #1**) but later they seemed to be expanded to medium size.
Deeper! Harder! Faster! / 1986 / VCS / C • Dial F For Fantasy / 1984 / PL / M • Head Trips / cr88 / EXH / C • Hollywood Pink / 1985 / HO / M • Hot Tails / 1984 / VEN / M • Like A Virgin #1 / 1985 / AT / M • Lorelei / 1984 / CV / M • Naked Night / 1985 / VCR / M • Only The Best Of Women With Women / 1988 / CV / C • Parliament: Anal Babes #1 / 1989 / PM / F • Parliament: Bottoms #1 / 1987 / PM / F • Parliament: Dildo Babes #1 / 1986 / PM / F • The Ribald Tales Of Canterbury / 1986 / CA / M • Satin Dolls / 1985 / CV / M • Sex 5th Avenue / 1985 / WV / M • Super Models Do LA / 1986 / AT / M • Undressed Rehearsal / 1984 / VD / M

DEBRA LYON *see Star Index I*

DEBRA RAYE *see Star Index I*

DEBRA RUSH
Forbidden Entry / 1984 / VCR / M • Pleasure Productions #11 / 1985 / VCR / M • Pleasure Productions #12 / 1985 / VCR / M • Tales Of The Backside / 1985 / VCR / C

DEBRA STANDLE *see Star Index I*

DEBRA WONG
Loose Times At Ridley High / 1984 / VCX / M • Saturday Matinee Series #4 / 1996 / VCX / C

DEBRAH JACKSON
Golden Girls, The Movie / 1984 / SE / M

DEDE COLLINS *see Star Index I*

DEDE ST JEAN *see Star Index I*

DEDINA *see Zumira*

DEE
Limited Edition #21 / 1981 / AVC / M • Limited Edition #24 / 1984 / AVC / M • Voluptuous #1 / 199? / H&S / S

DEE DEE
Big Boob Tease / 1993 / NAP / F • Exposure Images #25: Dee Dee / 1995 / EXI / F • Student Fetish Videos: Best Of Foot Worship #02 / 1994 / PRE / C • Student Fetish Videos: Best Of Spanking #02 / 1993 / PRE / C • Student Fetish Videos: Tickling #03 / 1992 / SFV / B

DEE DEE DIAMOND *see Star Index I*

DEE DEE REEVES *(Shelly (Dee Dee))*
Humongous hooters.
Breast Worx #03 / 1991 / LBO / M • Breast Worx #11 / 1991 / LBO / M • Breast Worx #14 / 1992 / LBO / M • Butt Freak #1 / 1992 / EA / M • Buttman's Big Tit Adventure #1 / 1992 / EA / M • H&S: Dee Dee Reeves / 199? / H&S / S • Mike Hott: #187 Dee Dee Solo / 1991 / MHV / F • Mike Hott: Apple Asses #11 / 1992 / MHV / F • Student Fetish Videos: Spanking #06 / 1991 / PRE / B • Uncle Roy's Amateur Home Video #02

/ 1992 / VIM / M • Uncle Roy's Amateur Home Video #03 / 1992 / VIM / M • The Very Best Of Breasts #2 / 1996 / H&S / S

DEE DEE WATTS *see Star Index I*

DEE FINLEY
Hardcore: The Films Of Richard Kern #1 / 1991 / FTV / M

DEE GORDON
The Cathouse / 1994 / VI / M

DEE JAY *(D.J., Deejay)*
Small breasted blonde with a trim figure. Her breasts look empty even though she's about an A cup.
Amateur Nights #16 / 1997 / HO / M • The Dane Harlow Story / 1990 / IF / M • Dangerous / 1989 / PV / M • Dirty & Kinky Mature Women #09 / 1996 / C69 / M • Heartless / 1989 / REB / M • Love Champions / 1987 / VC / M • Masked Ball / 1992 / IF / M • Night Watch / 1990 / VEX / M • One For The Road / 1989 / V99 / M • One More Time / 1990 / VEX / M • Passion Prescription / 1990 / V99 / M • Randy And Dane / 1991 / IF / G • Secret Obsession / 1990 / V99 / M • Sexy Nurses #1 On And Off Duty / 1990 / CV / M • Sweet Tease / 1990 / VEX / M • Tamara's Dreams / 1989 / VEX / M • Tequilla Sunset / 1989 / V99 / M • Tomboy / 1991 / V99 / M • Undercover Carol / 1990 / FAN / M • Women In Charge / 1990 / VEX / M

DEE LOCKHART
Spank Me, Spank Me, Spank Me / 199? / BON / B

DEE LYTE *see Pamela Dee*

DEE SMOOTH
The Adventures Of Buck Naked / 1994 / OD / M • Aged To Perfection #1 / 1994 / TTV / M • Black Attack / 1994 / ZA / M • The Black Butt Sisters Do Los Angeles / 1995 / MID / M • Black Gangbangers #01 / 1994 / HW / M • Black Hollywood Amateurs #02 / 1995 / MID / M • Black Hollywood Amateurs #05 / 1995 / MID / M • Black Hollywood Amateurs #23 / 1996 / MID / M • Dirty Dating Service #05 / 1994 / WP / M • Gang Bang Diaries #4 / 1994 / SFP / M • Hooter Tutor / 1996 / APP / M • Kink: Police Chronicles / 1995 / ROB / M • Ron Hightower's White Chicks #05 / 1993 / LBO / M • Ron Hightower's White Chicks #06 / 1993 / LBO / M

DEE STROYER
The Anal Adventures Of Max Hardcore: The Resurrection / 1995 / ZA / M • Forbidden Fantasies #2 / 1995 / ZA / M • Forbidden Fantasies #3 / 1995 / ZA / M

DEE VINE *see Mindy Rae*

DEE-ANNE
Bedtime Video #04 / 1984 / GO / M • Junkyard Dykes #02 / 1994 / ZA / F

DEEDEE
Bondage Classix #02: Krysta's Nightmare #1 / 1987 / BON / B

DEEDRA HOLLAND *see Diedre Holland*

DEEJAY *see Dee Jay*

DEENA
Joe Elliot's College Girls #41 / 1996 / JOE / M

DEENA DUOS
Big Busty #50 / 1994 / BTO / S • Double-D Reunion / 1995 / BTO / M • Girls Around The World #20: Deena Duos & Friends / 1994 / BTO / M • On Location In Palm Springs / 1996 / H&S / S

DEIDRA MORROW *see Dominique Simone*

DEIDRE
I Love The Feeling / 1994 / CS / B • Ultimate Anal Gang Bang #3 / 1995 / HW / M

DEIDRE HOLLAND *see Diedre Holland*

DEIDRE HOPKINS *see Diedre Hopkins*

DEJA *see Misty Lynn*

DEJA (1996)
Black Juice Bombs / 1996 / NIT / C • C-Hunt #05: Wett Worx / 1996 / PEV / M • Fresh Meat #1 / 1996 / PL / M • Fresh Meat #2 / 1996 / PL / M • Jus' Knockin' Boots #1: Fade To Black / 1996 / NIT / M • Jus' Knockin' Boots #2: Black On Line / 1996 / NIT / M

DEJAVU
Red Riding She Male / 1995 / PL / G

DEJINA SPYCER
Makin' Bacon / 1994 / WIV / M

DEJU *see Lulu Brace*

DEL OCM *see Star Index I*

DELA
Black Beauty (Coast To Coast) / 1994 / CC / M

DELA CUCCHI *see Alex Dane*

DELAINE YOUNG *see Star Index I*

DELANIA RUFFINO *(Barbara Bills)*
Pretty brunette with small tits and a white body. Facially looks a little like Annette Haven.
California Gigolo / 1979 / WWV / M • Candy Goes To Hollywood / 1979 / VCX / M • Expectations / 1977 / SE / M • Extreme Close-Up / 1981 / VC / M • Hot Legs / 1979 / VCX / M • Summer In Heat / 1979 / VEP / M • Telefantasy / 1978 / AR / M • True Legends Of Adult Cinema: Unsung Superstars / 1993 / VC / C

DELFIN
Pick Up Lines #13 / 1997 / OD / M • White Men Can't Iron On Butt Row / 1997 / ABS / M

DELIA COSNER *see Star Index I*

DELIA MOORE *(Delilah (D. Moore))*
Was 23 in 1988.
Afrodisiac #1 / 1987 / CC / M • Bi And Beyond #1 / 1988 / LAV / G • Bitches In Heat / 1994 / PL / C • Deep Throat Fantasies / 1989 / VD / M • Erotic Television Video / 1988 / VD / M • A Girl Named Sam / 1988 / CC / M • Les Be Friends / 1988 / WV / C • The Master Of Pleasure / 1988 / VD / M • Peepers / 1988 / CV / M • Rippin' 'n' Strippin' #1 / 1987 / BON / B • Rippin' 'n' Strippin' #2 / 1988 / BON / B • Sorority Bound / 1988 / BON / B • Tough Girls Don't Dance / 1987 / SEV / M • Tricks Of The Trade / 1988 / CA / M • Very Sexy Ballet / 1988 / CA / M

DELICIOUS MILANO
Cumback Pussy #5: Groopin' / 1996 / EL / M

DELIGHT
Delight Gang Bang / 1995 / GLI / M

DELILAH
Florida Girls On Film / 1994 / DGD / F • Women In Charge / 1990 / VEX / M

DELILAH (D. MOORE) *see Delia Moore*

DELILAH DAWN
An old biddy who is allegedly Sabrina Dawn's mother.
Falcon Head / 1990 / ARG / M • Grandma Does Dallas / 1990 / FC / M • Hot Cherries / 1990 / CC / F • Rainwoman #03 / 1990 / CC / M • Things Mommy Taught Me / 1990 / KNI / M

DELILAH DAWN (1993)

Not to be confused with the old biddy of 1990 who was supposed to be Sabrina Dawn's mother, this one is a pretty dark blonde with green eyes, medium slightly droopy tits, tight waist, very white skin and a Holland Tunnel for a pussy.

Anal Vision #17 / 1993 / LBO / M • Madame Hollywood / 1993 / LE / M • Mr. Peepers Amateur Home Videos #77: Facial Coverage / 1993 / LBO / M • Sex Fugitives / 1993 / LE / M

DELILAH DEVIE see Star Index I
DELILAH KITT see Star Index I
DELILAH SAVAGE see Tina Tyler
DELLA
Blue Vanities #570 / 1995 / FFL / M
DELLA CAROL
Fashion Fantasy / 1972 / GO / M
DELLA DAMAGE see Lynx Cannon
DELLIAH see Star Index I
DELORES
Blue Vanities #511 / 1992 / FFL / M • Blue Vanities #554 / 1994 / FFL / M
DELORES (BLACK)
Black Cheerleader Search #09 / 1996 / IVC / M
DELORES DELUXE see Star Index I
DELORIS COMFORTH see James Lewis
DELPHIN
Creme De La Face #18: Cum Mops / 1997 / OD / M
DELPHY MEADE
Ultraflesh / 1980 / GO / M
DELTA BLUE
More Dirty Debutantes #43 / 1995 / 4P / M
DELTA DAVIES
Bump 'n' Grind / 1994 / HW / M • Rump-Shaker #3 / 1994 / HW / M
DELTA FORCE see Brandy Bosworth
DEMARCUS
Climax At The Melting Pot #1 / 1996 / AVS / M
DEMI
Feature Speciale: The Ultimate Squirt / 1996 / ANE / M • Mondo Extreme / 1996 / SHS / M
DEMI DEMAURIER see Demi Fairbanks
DEMI ERAS see Ariel Knight
DEMI EVRIS see Ariel Knight
DEMI FAIRBANKS *(Deeme Moorier, Demi DeMaurier)*
Passable face, shoulder length brown hair, 22 years old in 1995, comes from Scottsdale AZ, de-virginized at 16, large cantaloupes, faint tattoo on her left butt.

Erotic Newcummers Vol 1 #4 / 1996 / DR / M • The Horny Hiker / 1995 / LE / M • Pick Up Lines #02 / 1995 / 4P / M • Pick Up Lines #03 / 1995 / 4P / M • Pussyman Auditions #15 / 1995 / SNA / M • The Strippers / 1995 / GO / M • Up And Cummers #22 / 1995 / RWP / M • Video Virgins #24 / 1996 / NS / M • Virgins / 1995 / ERA / M • Wedding Night Blues / 1995 / EMC / M
DEMI RHODES
Breastman's Triple X Cellent Adventure / 1995 / EVN / M • Lesbian Debutante #02 / 1996 / IP / F
DEMI WHITE see Ariel Knight
DEMI WILLIS
Anal Anarchy / 1995 / VC / M • Anal Hellraiser #2 / 1995 / ROB / M • Anal Webb / 1995 / ZA / M • Buffy Malibu's Nasty Girls #09 / 1995 / ANA / F • Channel 69 / 1996 / CC / M • Fashion Sluts #4 / 1995 / ABS / M

• Gang Bang Jizz Queen / 1995 / ROB / M • Jingle Balls / 1996 / EVN / M • Muff Divers #2 / 1996 / TV / F • My First Time #3 / 1996 / NS / M • Nasty Nymphos #11 / 1995 / ANA / M • Nasty Nymphos #15 / 1996 / ANA / M • Red Hots / 1996 / PL / M • Young & Natural #06 / 1995 / PRE / F • Young & Natural #09 / 1995 / PRE / C • Young & Natural #11 / 1995 / PRE / F • Young & Natural #12 / 1996 / TV / F • Young & Natural #18 / 1996 / TV / C • Young And Anal #2 / 1995 / JMP / M
DEMIA MOORE
Private Gold #05: Cape Town #1 / 1996 / OD / M • Private Gold #06: Cape Town #2 / 1996 / OD / M • Private Gold #12: The Pyramid #2 / 1996 / OD / M • Triple X Video Magazine #08 / 1995 / OD / M • Triple X Video Magazine #13 / 1996 / OD / M
DEMIAN THORE see Star Index I
DEMITRI ZUKOV
Russian Girls / 1996 / WV / M
DEMONIC see Lauren Brice
DEN see Star Index I
DENA CRANE
Erotic Tattooing And Piercing #1 / 1986 / FLV / M
DENA FERARA see Star Index I
DENE see Star Index I
DENEA see Star Index I
DENESE
Liquid Lips #2 / 1994 / MAV / M
DENIS
HomeGrown Video #434: Forrest Hump / 1994 / HOV / M
DENISE
AVP #7005: Denise Does It Again / 1991 / AVP / M • Blue Vanities #168 (New) / 1996 / FFL / M • Blue Vanities #168 (Old) / 1991 / FFL / M • Blue Vanities #170 (New) / 1996 / FFL / M • Blue Vanities #170 (Old) / 1991 / FFL / M • Brabusters #1 / 1981 / CA / S • Creme De Femme #3 / 1981 / AVC / C • Hirsute Lovers #1 / 1995 / BTO / M • Hirsute Lovers / 1999? / H&S / F • Homegrown Video #431 / 1994 / HOV / M • Limited Edition #26 / 1984 / AVC / M • Master Of Masters #1 / 1995 / BBB / B • Neighborhood Watch #06: Extended Foreplay / 1991 / LBO / M • RSK: Denise #1 / 1993 / RSK / F • RSK: Denise #2 / 1993 / RSK / F • RSK: Julia's Teenage Spanking / 1995 / RSK / B • Sex Appeal / 1984 / ABV / M • Sex Clinic Girls / cr71 / SAT / M • Sizzling Latex / 1992 / VER / B • Teasedance Masturbation #3 / 1994 / MAV / F
DENISE (BRAZ) see Star Index I
DENISE BERRISON
Hard Worker / cr80 / AVC / M
DENISE CONNORS *(Denise Stevens)*
Alice In Whiteland / 1988 / VC / M • Debbie Class Of '89 / 1989 / CC / M • Debbie For President / 1988 / CC / M • Dirty Laundry / 1988 / PP / M • The Final Taboo / 1988 / CA / M • Here's Looking At You / 1988 / V99 / M • Hot Rods / 1988 / VEX / M • Phone Mates / 1988 / CA / M • Portrait Of A Nymph / 1988 / PP / M • Satisfaction Jackson / 1988 / CA / M • Split Decision / 1989 / MET / G • Strong Rays / 1988 / IN / M • Switch Hitters #3: Squeeze Play / 1988 / IN / G
DENISE DAMIANO
Carnal Olympics / 1983 / CA / M
DENISE DANIELS
Blue Vanities #059 / 1988 / FFL / M • Blue

Vanities #504 / 1992 / FFL / M • Blue Vanities #516 / 1992 / FFL / M • Blue Vanities #545 / 1994 / FFL / M • Blue Vanities #575 / 1995 / FFL / M • Erotica / 1961 / RMV / S • Mr. Peter's Pets / 1962 / SOW / S
DENISE DENEUVE see Denise Sloan
DENISE DUVELL see Star Index I
DENISE FEVIER
House Of Love / cr77 / VC / M • Made In France / 1974 / VC / M • Salon D'amour / 19?? / IHV / M
DENISE FLEYTOW see Star Index I
DENISE FORD
The Return Of Johnny Wadd / 1986 / PEN / M • Sailing Into Ecstasy / 1986 / VCX / M
DENISE HICKS
Blue Vanities #129 / 1990 / FFL / M
DENISE LAFRANCE see Star Index I
DENISE LYNN ROBERTS see Star Index I
DENISE MARTIN see Star Index I
DENISE MATHEWS see D.D. Winters
DENISE MCDOWE
Top Secret / 1995 / XHE / M
DENISE MUNSON
Girls On Fire / 1985 / VCX / M
DENISE O'BRIEN see Star Index I
DENISE PETERS
Not too pretty brunette with small tits and a lithe body. Chin pin, nipple rings, piercings everywhere. Tattoos everywhere too. The female version of Jack Hammer. Badly acne scarred face. Needs a face peel. 25 years old in 1996 and de-virginized at 18.

Ass, Gas & The Mystical GLOP / 1997 / EL / M • Filthy First Timers #5 / 1997 / EL / M • Interracial Video Virgins #01 / 1996 / NS / M
DENISE POWELL see Star Index I
DENISE ROBBINS
In-Flight Service / 19?? / BL / M
DENISE SCHWARTZ
Heat Wave / 1977 / COM / M
DENISE SEXTON
Trouble Down Below / 1981 / CA / M
DENISE SLOAN *(Denise Deneuve, Danielle (Sloan))*
One of indentical twins (Diane is the other). Denise Deneuve is from **Extreme Close-up**.

Dracula Exotica / 1980 / TVX / M • Extreme Close-Up / 1981 / VC / M • The Good Girls Of Godiva High / 1979 / VCX / M • The Love Tapes / 1980 / BL / M • Sunny / 1979 / VC / M • Tigresses...And Other Man-Eaters / 1979 / VXP / M
DENISE SNOW
Flight Sensations / 1983 / VC / C
DENISE STEVENS see Denise Connors
DENISE THOMAS see Star Index I
DENISE TRUDEAU see Star Index I
DENISE WILLIAMS
Hawaiian Sex-O / cr71 / AVC / M
DENLAILA WED
Helen Does Holland / 1996 / VC / M
DENNEA BENFONATE see Star Index I
DENNI O'BRIEN
The Adventures of Marilyn Ohno / 1996 / GLI / M • Christine: All Day All Night / 1996 / GLI / M • Denni O' #3: Fanta-Sea Of Cum / 1996 / SP / M • Denni O' #4: Beach Ballin' / 1996 / SP / M • Denni O' #5: / 1996 / SP / M • Denni's Special Pussy Hole Workout / 1996 / SP / F • Eat At Dave's #2 / 1995 / SP / M • Go Denni O: The Best Of Denni O'Brien / 1996 / GLI / C • Insatiable Denni

O' #2 / 1995 / SP / M • Mondo Extreme / 1996 / SHS / M • The Spectacular Denni O'Brien / 1995 / SP / M • Swap Meat / 1995 / GLI / M

DENNIS B. MANAS
Pristine #2 / 1996 / CA / M

DENNIS CONAN *see Star Index I*

DENNIS EAST *see Star Index I*

DENNIS HARTER
Worksex / 1980 / ... / M

DENNIS JOHNSON
Let Me Tell Ya 'Bout Fat Chicks #2 / 1988 / 4P / M • Life In The Fat Lane #1 / 1990 / FC / M

DENNIS JONES *see Star Index I*

DENNIS KANE
Mother's Wishes / 1974 / GO / M

DENNIS KEATS
Inside China Lee / 1984 / VC / M

DENNIS LONG
Sex On The Run #2 / 1994 / TTV / M

DENNIS MORGAN *see Star Index I*

DENNIS PARKER *see Wade Nichols*

DENNIS SOBIN *see Star Index I*

DENT WESTWOOD *see Star Index I*

DENTON *see Star Index I*

DEREK *see Star Index I*

DEREK AMANZA *see Star Index I*

DEREK BROWN
Mind Mirror / 1994 / LAP / M • Sex Between The Scenes / 1994 / LAP / M

DEREK CRUISE
Secret Sex #2: The Sex Radicals / 1994 / CAT / G

DEREK HARPER *see Derrick Lane*

DEREK HONDO *see Star Index I*

DEREK LANE *(Randy Fruth)*
Balding but quite handsome young male with large tits and an emaciated bottom half of his body. This is not Derrick Lane, Racquel's boyfriend and it's not Kato Kaelin, despite some dishonest advertising.
Barbara Dare's Prime Choice / 1987 / SE / C • Blonde Fantasy / 1988 / CC / M • Sex Search / 1988 / IN / S • Surf, Sand And Sex / 1987 / SE / M

DEREK MARTIN *see Star Index I*

DEREK RICE *see Star Index I*

DEREK SCOTT
Kiss My Asp / 1989 / EXH / M

DEREK TAYLOR *see Derrick Taylor*

DERI IZABELLE
Sirens / 1995 / GOU / M

DERICH TAYLOR *see Derrick Taylor*

DERICK COLBY
Sex Off The Runway / 1991 / GMI / M

DERICK WINTERS *see Star Index I*

DERIN *see Laurel Canyon*

DERIN DELIGHT *see Laurel Canyon*

DERK JOHNSON
Jenteal Loves Rocco / 1996 / VI / M

DERRICK
Bi The Time You Get Back / 1995 / BIN / G • Mondo Extreme / 1996 / SHS / M

DERRICK LANE *(Derek Harper, Brad (Derrick Lane))*
Boyfriend or husband of Racquel Darrian.
Above And Beyond / 1990 / PNP / G • Beauty And The Beach / 1991 / CC / M • Bitches In Heat / 1994 / PL / C • Blow Job Betty / 1991 / CC / M • Bonnie & Clyde #1 / 1992 / VI / M • Bonnie & Clyde #2 / 1992 / VI / M • Bonnie & Clyde #3 / 1994 / VI / M • Bonnie & Clyde #4 / 1994 / VI / M • The Catwoman / 1988 / VC / M • Charlie's Girls #3 / 1990 / CC / M • Cheeks #3 / 1990 / CC

/ M • Christy In The Wild / 1992 / VI / M • Class Act / 1989 / WAV / M • Cloud 9 / 1995 / VI / M • Curse Of The Catwoman / 1990 / VC / M • Dangerous Curves / 1995 / VC / M • Deep Inside Ariana / 1995 / VC / C • Deep Inside Racquel Darrian / 1994 / VC / C • Deep Inside Raquel / 1992 / CDI / C • Desire / 1990 / VC / M • Dream Girls / 1990 / CIN / M • The Dream Merchants / 1990 / CDI / M • Eleventh Annual AVN Awards / 1994 / VC / M • Exiles / 1991 / VT / M • The God Daughter #2 / 1991 / AFV / M • House Of Sexual Fantasies / 1987 / GO / M • Hyapatia Lee's Arcade Series #01 / 1988 / ZA / C • Hyapatia Lee's Arcade Series #02 / 1988 / ZA / C • In The Heat Of The Night / 1990 / CDI / M • Intimate Journey / 1993 / VI / M • Joined: The Siamese Twins / 1989 / PL / M • King Tongue Meets Anal Woman / 1990 / PL / M • Lambody / 1990 / CDI / M • Lunachick / 1995 / VI / M • Modern Love #1 / 1991 / HOP / S • More Dirty Debutantes #05 / 1990 / 4P / M • Night Games / 1986 / WV / M • Night Trips #2 / 1990 / CA / M • Not So Innocent / 1990 / HO / M • Nymphobrat / 1989 / VI / M • On Trial #3: Takin' It To The Jury / 1992 / VI / M • On Trial #4: The Verdict / 1992 / VI / M • Oral Madness #2 / 1992 / OD / M • The Orgy #2 / 1993 / EMC / M • Out For Blood / 1990 / VI / M • Racquel In Paradise / 1990 / VC / M • Racquel In The Wild / 1992 / VI / M • Racquel's Addiction / 1991 / VC / M • Racquel's Treasure Hunt / 1990 / VC / M • Raquel On Fire / 1990 / VC / M • Raquel Released / 1991 / VI / M • Raquel Untamed / 1990 / CIN / M • Raunch #02 / 1990 / CC / M • Ravaged / 1990 / CIN / M • Red Line / 1991 / PL / M • Renegade / 1990 / CIN / M • Ride 'em Cow Girl / 1995 / VI / C • Rolling Thunder / 1995 / VI / M • Sea Of Love / 1990 / CIN / M • Seoul Train / 1991 / IN / M • Separated / 1989 / INH / M • Servin' It Up / 1993 / VC / M • Sex Ranch / 1993 / VC / M • Sexmares / 1993 / FH / M • Silent Stranger / 1992 / VI / M • Silver Sensations / 1992 / VT / M • Sinderella #1 / 1992 / VI / M • Sinderella #2 / 1992 / VI / M • Spend The Holidays With Barbii / 1987 / CDI / M • Stake Out / 1991 / CIN / M • A Tall Dark Stranger / 1990 / LV / M • The Tiffany Minx Affair / 1992 / FOR / M • Top It Off / 1990 / VC / M • Torrid Tales / 1995 / VI / M • Tropic Of Kahlia / 1991 / VI / M • Two Hearts / 1991 / VI / M • Used Cars / 1990 / CDI / M • Vegas #3: Let It Ride / 1990 / CIN / M • Warm To The Touch / 1990 / CDI / M • Welcum To My Place / 1990 / ZA / M • Words Of Love / 1989 / LE / M

DERRICK STANTON
L.A. Tool & Die / 1979 / TMX / G

DERRICK TAYLOR *(Darrick, Derek Taylor, Derich Taylor, D. English)*
English male with 50 pence on the pound who has a huge dick.
2 Baggers / 1994 / ZA / M • Action In Black / 1993 / FD / M • Amateurs Exposed #01 / 1993 / CV / M • America's Raunchiest Home Videos #45: The Bigger They Cum / 1992 / ZA / M • American Swinger Video Magazine #04 / 1993 / ZA / M • American Swinger Video Magazine #06 / 1993 / ZA / M • American Swinger Video Magazine #07 / 1993 / ZA / M • Anal Gang Bangers #02 / 1993 / GLI / M • Anal Queen / 1994 / FPI / M • Bachelor Party #1 / 1993 / FPI /

M • Backdoor Play / 1996 / AVI / M • Biff Malibu's Totally Nasty Home Videos #24 / 1992 / ANA / M • Big Bust Babes #11 / 1992 / AFI / M • Big Bust Babes #13 / 1993 / AFI / M • Big Bust Babes #14 / 1993 / AFI / M • Big Bust Babes #15 / 1993 / AFI / M • Big Bust Bangers #1 / 1994 / AMP / M • Big Bust Bangers #2 / 1994 / AMP / M • Bun Busters #22 / 1994 / LBO / M • Butt Bangers Ball / 1994 / FPI / M • Depraved Fantasies #1 / 1993 / FPI / M • Depraved Fantasies #3 / 1994 / FPI / M • Dirty Dating Service #04 / 1994 / WP / M • Dirty Doc's Housecalls #12 / 1994 / LV / M • Don't Try This At Home / 1994 / FPI / M • Gang Bang Bitches #01 / 1994 / PP / M • Gang Bang Bitches #02 / 1994 / PP / M • Gang Bang Bitches #03 / 1994 / PP / M • Gang Bang Bitches #04 / 1995 / PP / M • Gang Bang Bitches #10 / 1995 / PP / M • Gang Bang Diaries #2 / 1993 / SFP / M • Gang Bang Diaries #3 / 1994 / SFP / M • Gangbang Girl #11 / 1993 / ANA / M • Gangbang Girl #12 / 1993 / ANA / M • Gangbang Girl #16 / 1995 / ANA / M • Harry Horndog #11: Love Puppies #2 / 1992 / ZA / M • Harry Horndog #13: Anal Lovers #2 / 1992 / ZA / M • Harry Horndog #14: Love Puppies #3 / 1992 / ZA / M • Harry Horndog #16: Love Puppies #4 / 1992 / ZA / M • Harry Horndog #17: Love Puppies #5 / 1993 / ZA / M • Harry Horndog #19: Anal Lovers #3 / 1993 / ZA / M • Harry Horndog #20: Love Puppies #6 / 1993 / ZA / M • Harry Horndog #21: Birthday Orgy / 1993 / ZA / M • Harry Horndog #23: The Final Flick / 1993 / ZA / M • Hollywood Swingers #03 / 1992 / LBO / M • Honey, I Blew Everybody #2 / 1992 / MID / M • I Can't Believe I Did The Whole Team! / 1994 / FPI / M • I Cream On Jeannie / 1995 / AVI / M • The Last Of The Muff Divers / 1992 / MID / M • Lawnmower Woman / 1992 / MID / M • Leena Is Nasty / 1994 / OD / M • Little Magicians / 1993 / ANA / M • More Dirty Debutantes #43 / 1995 / 4P / M • Mr. Peepers Amateur Home Videos #89: Stiffy Stuffer / 1994 / LBO / M • Nasty Nymphos #01 / 1993 / ANA / M • Neighborhood Watch #35 / 1992 / LBO / M • Neighborhood Watch #36 / 1992 / LBO / M • Odyssey 30 Min: #202: / 1992 / OD / M • Odyssey 30 Min: #231: / 1992 / OD / M • Odyssey 30 Min: #264: / 1992 / OD / M • Odyssey Triple Play #31: Double Penetration Babes / 1993 / OD / M • Odyssey Triple Play #33: 3 Back-Door Boinkers / 1993 / OD / M • Over 50 / 1994 / GLI / M • Starbangers #03 / 1993 / ZA / M • Starbangers #06 / 1994 / FPI / M • Ultimate Anal Gang Bang #3 / 1995 / HW / M

DES MENDEZ
Shape Up For Sensational Sex / 1985 / SE / M

DESI BOLLO
Catch Of The Day #1 / 1995 / VG0 / M

DESI DEANGELO *(Jasae, Elise DiMedici)*
Jasae is apparently her legal name.
1-900-SPANKME Ext.1 / 1994 / BON / B • 1-900-SPANKME Ext.2 / 1994 / BON / B • Bad Girls From Mars / 1990 / VMA / S • Big Busted Dream Girls / 1995 / PME / S • Bip Shoots #1 / 1994 / BON / B • Body Slammers #03 / 1993 / SBP / B • Bonda-Cize / 1988 / BON / B • Bound Destiny / 1994 / LON / B • Bound For Cash / 1994 / SBP / B • Bound To Be Tickled / 1994 / VTF / B •

Bruce Seven: A Compendium Of His Most Graphic Scenes Vol 3 / 1992 / BS / C • Bruce Seven: A Compendium Of His Most Graphic Scenes Vol 4 / 1993 / BS / C • Bruise Control / 1993 / PRE / B • Carnal Crimes / 1991 / MAE / S • Cave Girl / 1985 / C3S / S • Cinderella In Chains #1 / 1996 / LBO / B • Clean Out / 1991 / PRE / B • Clear And Present Anger / 1995 / IBN / B • Desi Bound / 1988 / BON / B • Director Dilemma #1 / 1995 / BON / B • Director Dilemma #2 / 1995 / BON / B • Doctor DeAngelo / 1994 / CS / B • Down And Out / 1995 / PRE / B • Drainman / 1989 / BIZ / B • Dungeon Of Despair / 1997 / CS / B • Fetish Finishing School / 1995 / HOM / B • Fit To Be Tied / 1991 / BS / B • Flash Floods / 1991 / PRE / C • Frankentickle / 1993 / CS / B • The Golden Dagger / 1993 / LON / B • Heel's Angels / 1995 / PRE / B • High Fives / 1991 / PRE / B • Hits & Misses / 1992 / PRE / B • House Of Correction / 1991 / HOM / B • Latex Bound #02 / 1993 / BON / B • Leg...Ends #05 / 1991 / PRE / F • Leg...Ends #08 / 1993 / PRE / F • Love Scenes #2 / 1992 / B/F / S • The Magnificent 7 / 1994 / VTF / B • The Missing Report / 1992 / CS / B • Mob Boss / 1990 / ... / S • My Maid Maria / 1996 / SHL / B • Nasty Cracks / 1992 / PRE / B • Nightmare Of Discipline / 1993 / NTP / B • No Mercy For The Witches / 1992 / HOM / B • Pain In The Rent / 1996 / BON / B • Prescription For Pain #3: Bad Medicine / 1993 / BON / B • The Price Of Curiosity / 1993 / LON / B • Punished Princess / 1992 / HOM / B • Rendezvous With A BBS Mistress / 1995 / IBN / B • Ring Revenge / 1990 / NAP / B • Ring Wise / 1990 / TAO / B • Rump Roasts / 1991 / PRE / B • Runaway Slaves / 1995 / HOM / B • The Secret Dungeon / 1993 / HOM / B • Sexual HerASSment / 1995 / IBN / B • Shape Up For Sensational Sex / 1985 / SE / M • Shoe Horny / 1989 / BIZ / B • Sluts In Slavery / 1995 / LBO / B • Sole Search / 1996 / PRE / B • Spanking Good Salary / 1993 / VTF / B • Spankology 101a / 1994 / BON / B • Spankology 101b / 1994 / BON / B • Spectator Sport / 1993 / VVO / B • Swindle / 1991 / CEL / S • Terrors Of The Inquisition / 1992 / HOM / B • Three Wishes #1 / 1991 / CDP / B • Three Wishes #2 / 1991 / CDP / B • Tied & Tickled #23: Tickling Dick / 1994 / CS / B • Toe Teasers #3 / 1994 / SBP / B • Tortured Passions / 1994 / PL / B • The Torturous Infidel / 1994 / PL / B • Turn Of Events / 1990 / NAP / B • Under Construction / 1988 / BON / B • Watersports Spree #2 / 1994 / BIZ / C • When East Meets West / 1990 / NAP / B • Who's Teaching Who? / 1990 / NAP / B • Wild Cats / 1991 / PRE / B • [Nude Aerobics #2 / 199? / ... / S

DESIRE
The Bondage File / 19?? / BIZ / C • Girl's Towne #1 / 1994 / FC / F • The Way Of Sex / 1995 / DBV / M

DESIRE BASTEREAUD
Sex Roulette / 1979 / CA / M

DESIRE DUPREE
Babewatch #2 / 1994 / CC / M • Black Booty / 1995 / UBP / M • Black Hollywood Amateurs #01 / 1995 / MID / M • Black Hollywood Amateurs #05 / 1995 / MID / M • Love Bunnies #10 / 1994 / FPI / F • More

Black Dirty Debutantes / 1994 / 4P / M • Naughty Senorita / 1994 / WIV / M • Yo Yo: A Very Black Christmas Tale! / 1994 / HW / M

DESIRE LOWE
The Real Deal #4 / 1996 / FC / M

DESIRE MOORE
The Girls Of Fantasex #2 / 1996 / NIT / M

DESIRE X. *see Star Index I*

DESIREE
America's Raunchiest Home Videos #58: / 1993 / ZA / M • Black Sensations: Models In Heat / 1995 / SUF / M • Girlz Towne #10 / 1995 / FC / F • Hot Body Competition: Lusty Lingerie Contest / 1996 / CG / F • Master's Touch #2: Punished Slave Girls / 1994 / FAP / B • Tropical Temptations / 1989 / VEX / M

DESIREE CARSON *see Desiree Lane*

DESIREE CLEARBRANCH *see Desiree Cousteau*

DESIREE COUSTEAU *(Desiree Clearbranch, Deborah Clearbranch)*
Short haired brunette with un-manageable hair, large tits, womanly body, little girl voice, marginal facially.
800 Fantasy Lane / 1979 / GO / M • Aphrodisia's Diary / 1984 / CA / M • Behind The Scenes Of An Adult Movie / 1983 / CV / M • The Best Of Alex De Renzy #1 / 1983 / VC / C • Blue Vanities #018 (New) / 1988 / FFL / M • Blue Vanities #034 / 1988 / FFL / M • Blue Vanities #046 (New) / 1988 / FFL / M • Blue Vanities #046 (Old) / 1988 / FFL / M • Blue Vanities #067 / 1988 / FFL / M • Blue Vanities #240 / 1995 / FFL / M • Blue Vanities #241 / 1995 / FFL / M • Blue's Velvet / 1979 / ECV / M • Boiling Point / 1978 / SE / M • Caballero Preview Tape #1 / 1982 / CA / C • Caballero Preview Tape #2 / 1983 / CA / C • Caged Heat #1 / 1974 / ST0 / S • Candy Goes To Hollywood / 1979 / VCX / M • Centerspread Girls / 1982 / CA / M • The China Cat / 1978 / CA / M • Classic Erotica #2 / 1980 / SVE / M • Classic Swedish Erotica #08 / 1986 / CA / C • Critics' Choice #2 / 1984 / SE / C • Daddy's Little Girl / 1977 / VCI / M • Deep Rub / 1979 / VC / M • Delicious / 1981 / VXP / M • Diamond Collection #05 / 1979 / CDI / M • Easy / 1978 / CV / M • The Ecstasy Girls #1 / 1979 / CA / M • Electric Blue #002 / 1986 / CA / S • Electric Blue #005 / 1982 / CA / S • Electric Blue: Desiree Cousteau / 1983 / CA / C • Erotic Fantasies #2 / 1983 / CV / C • Erotic Fantasies #4 / 1983 / CV / C • Erotic Gold #2 / 1985 / VEN / M • Female Athletes / 1977 / VXP / M • Flight Sensations / 1983 / VC / C • Forbidden Worlds / 1988 / GO / C • A Formal Faucett / 1978 / VC / M • Free And Foxy / 1986 / VCX / C • French Finishing School / 1980 / CA / M • Getting Off / 1979 / VIP / M • Gina, The Foxy Lady / cr79 / COV / M • Hot Lunch / 1978 / SE / M • Hot Pink / 1983 / VC / C • Hot Rackets / 1979 / CV / M • Inside Desiree Cousteau / 1979 / VCX / M • International Intrigue / 1983 / AMB / M • Legends Of Porn #1 / 1987 / CV / C • Legends Of Porn #2 / 1989 / CV / C • Ms. Magnificent / 1979 / SE / M • Nudes At Eleven #2 / 1987 / AVC / M • Only The Best Of Breasts / 1987 / CV / C • Pizza Girls (We Deliver) / 1978 / VCX / M • Pretty Peaches #1 / 1978 / MIT / M • Randy, The Electric Lady / 1978 / VC / M • Saturday Matinee Series #1 /

1996 / VCX / C • Sex In The Great Outdoors / 1987 / SE / C • Snow Honeys / 1983 / VC / M • Summer In Heat / 1979 / VEP / M • Swedish Erotica #06 / 1980 / CA / M • Swedish Erotica #15 / 1980 / CA / M • Swedish Erotica #23 / 1980 / CA / M • Swedish Erotica #26 / 1980 / CA / M • Swedish Erotica #27 / 1980 / CA / M • Swedish Erotica Hard #22: Seka & Desiree: Sex 101 / 1992 / OD / C • Swedish Erotica Superstar #2: Brigette Monet / 1983 / CA / C • Sweet Alice / 1983 / VCX / M • The Tale Of Tiffany Lust / 1981 / CA / M • Telefantasy / 1978 / AR / M • That's Erotic / 1979 / CV / C • That's Porno / 1979 / CV / C • Too Many Cocks In Me! / 1992 / MET / M • A Tribute To The King / 1985 / VCX / C • True Legends Of Adult Cinema: The Cult Superstars / 1993 / VC / C • VCA Previews #1 / 1988 / VC / C • Wild Orgies / 1986 / SE / C • Yuppies In Heat / 1988 / CHA / C • [Best Of Xxx / cr90 / ... / C

DESIREE DEMONA
Maximum Desade / 1995 / ZFX / B

DESIREE DOUGLAS *see Star Index I*

DESIREE DUVALLE *see Star Index I*

DESIREE ELMS *see Star Index I*

DESIREE FERRARI *see Star Index I*

DESIREE FONTAINE
Love Is A Stranger #1 / 1994 / SV / B • Love Is A Stranger #2 / 1994 / SV / B

DESIREE FOX *(Sasha (Desiree Fox), April Sommers, April Summers, April Summer (Fox))*
Sasha in **Breakstroke**.
All Hands On Dick / 1988 / STA / G • The Big Rock / 1988 / FOV / M • Bionca On Fire / 1988 / 4P / M • Caught From Behind #10 / 1989 / HO / M • The Dane Harlow Story / 1990 / IF / M • Desert Foxes / 1989 / SE / M • Double Penetration Fever / 1989 / MIR / C • Double Trouble / 1988 / V99 / M • Fire & Ice / 1988 / BON / B • Life Is Butt A Dream / 1989 / V99 / M • Personal Touch #4 / 1989 / AR / M • Pony Girl #2: At The Ranch / 1986 / CS / B • Positive Positions / 1989 / VEX / M • The Squirt / 1988 / AR / M • This One's For You / 1989 / AR / M • Twin Cheeks (Arrow) / 1991 / AR / M • Under The Law / 1989 / AFV / M • Wake-Up Call #1 / 1987 / BON / B • Wake-Up Call #2 / 1987 / BON / B • With A Wiggle In Her Walk / 1989 / WV / M

DESIREE HOPKINS *see Diedre Hopkins*

DESIREE LANE *(Desiree Carson, Desiree Ray)*
Pretty strawberry blonde, very nicely shaped medium tits, tight waist, nice personality. Rumor has it that she left the porno industry and became a Mormon.
Backdoor Bandits / 1989 / MIR / C • Backing In #2 / 1990 / WV / C • Best Of Atom / 1984 / AT / C • Beyond Taboo / 1984 / VIV / M • Black & White Affair / 1984 / VD / M • Blonde At Both Ends / 1993 / TGA / M • Bodies In Heat #1 / 1983 / CA / M • Body Girls / 1983 / SE / M • California Valley Girls / 1983 / HO / M • Celebrity Presents Celebrity / 1986 / VEP / C • Centerfold Celebrities #3 / 1983 / VC / M • Classical Romance / 1984 / MAP / M • Confessions Of A Candystriper / 1984 / VC / M • Confessions Of Candy / 1984 / VC / M • Critics' Choice #2 / 1984 / SE / C • Dark Angel / 1983 / VC / M • Deep Inside Ginger Lynn / 1986 / SE / C • Diamond Collection #55 /

1984 / CIN / M • Diamond Collection #79 / 1986 / CDI / M • Eat At The Blue Fox / 1983 / VC / M • Educating Eva / 1984 / VC / M • Endless Passion / 1987 / LIM / C • Erotic Aerobics / 1984 / VC / M • Erotic Encounters / 1985 / LIM / C • Erotic Radio WSEX / 1983 / VC / M • Every Man's Fantasy / 1985 / IN / M • F...It / 1987 / SE / C • Female Sensations / 1984 / VC / M • Flesh-dance / 1983 / SE / M • Fleshdance Fever / 1984 / SAT / M • Formula 69 / 1984 / JVV / M • Girls Just Want To...Have Fun / 1984 / SE / M • Girls On Girls / 1983 / VC / F • Girls On Girls / 1987 / SE / C • Girls! Girls! Girls! #1 / 1986 / VCS / C • Golden Girls #17 / 1984 / CA / M • Golden Girls #18 / 1984 / CA / M • Golden Girls #25 / 1984 / CA / M • Golden Girls #28 / 1985 / CA / M • Head Waitress / 1984 / VC / M • Home Movies Ltd #1 / 1983 / SE / M • Hot Flashes / 1984 / VC / M • Hot School Reunion / 1984 / CHX / F • Hyapatia Lee's Arcade Series #01 / 1988 / ZA / C • I Never Say No / 1983 / VC / M • Inside China Lee / 1984 / VC / M • The Last Taboo / 1984 / VIV / M • Lip Service / 1987 / BIK / C • Little Often Annie / 1984 / VC / M • Looking For Lust / 1984 / VEL / M • Making It Big / 1984 / CV / M • The Many Shades Of Amber / 1986 / LIM / M • Maximum #5 / 1983 / CA / M • Mouthful Of Love / 1984 / VC / M • Naughty Angels / 1984 / VC / M • Naughty Nanette / 1984 / VC / M • New Wave Hookers #1 / 1984 / VC / M • One Night At A Time / 1984 / PV / M • Raffles / 1988 / VC / M • Scandal In The Mansion / 1985 / CDI / M • Sex And The Cheerleaders / 1983 / XTR / M • The Sex Game / 1987 / SE / C • Sex In The Great Outdoors / 1987 / SE / C • Sex Play / 1984 / SE / M • Shades Of Ecstasy / 1983 / HO / M • Shaved / 1984 / VCR / M • Sheer Haven / 1989 / DR / C • Sizzling Summer / 1984 / VC / M • Squalor Motel / 1985 / SE / M • Street Heat / 1984 / VC / M • Stud Hunters / 1984 / CA / M • Sulka's Daughter / 1984 / MET / G • The Sweetest Taboo / 1986 / SE / M • Taking Off / 1984 / VC / M • Temptation: The Story Of A Lustful Bride / 1983 / NSV / M • Tongue 'n Cheek (Vca) / 1984 / VC / M • Two On The Tongue / 1988 / TAM / C • An Unnatural Act #1 / 1984 / DR / M • Up Desiree Lane / 1984 / VC / M • Vixens In Heat / 1984 / ECS / M • Why Gentlemen Prefer Blondes / 1983 / HO / C • [Reunion / 1984 / ... / M

DESIREE RAY *see* **Desiree Lane**
DESIREE ROCK *see* **Star Index I**
DESIREE ROXXE *see* **Star Index I**
DESIREE WEST *(Pat Lee, Patricia Lee)*
Black girl with a distinctive passable face and lithe body. Medium to large droopy tits.
All Night Long / 1975 / SE / M • Amos & Candy / 1987 / VCR / C • Angel On Fire / 1974 / ALP / M • Baby Face #1 / 1977 / VC / M • Back To Back #1 / 1987 / 4P / C • Black Beauties / 1987 / SE / C • Black Silk Stockings / 1978 / SE / C • Blue Vanities #056 / 1988 / FFL / M • Carnal Haven / 1976 / SVE / M • CB Mamas / 1976 / MIT / M • Ceremony, The Ritual Of Love / 1976 / AVC / M • Cherry Truckers / 1979 / ALP / M • China Lust / 1976 / VC / M • Classic Erotica #1 / 1980 / SVE / M • Classic Swedish Erotica #07 / 1986 / CA / C • Classic Swedish Erotica #11 / 1986 / CA / C • Com-

ing Attractions / 1976 / VEP / M • Count The Ways / 1976 / CA / M • Critics' Choice #2 / 1984 / SE / C • Daddy's Little Girl / 1977 / VCI / M • Dental Nurse / 1973 / VXP / M • The Devil's Playground / 1974 / VC / M • Do You Wanna Be Loved? / 1977 / AR / M • Ebony Erotica / 1985 / VCR / C • Ebony Lust / 19?? / HOR / C • Expectations / 1977 / SE / M • Fantastic Orgy / 197? / ... / M • Fantasy In Blue / 1975 / IHV / M • Female Athletes / 1977 / VXP / M • Femmes De Sade / 1976 / ALP / M • Fight Sensations / 1983 / VC / C • Garters And Lace / 1975 / SE / M • Girls! Girls! Girls! #1 / 1986 / VCS / C • The Gypsy Ball / 1979 / ENC / M • Her Last Fling / 1977 / HIF / M • Hot Bodies (Ventura) / 1984 / VEN / C • The Joy Of Letting Go / 1976 / SE / M • Legends Of Porn #1 / 1987 / CV / C • Lingerie Party / 1987 / SE / C • Love Lips / 1976 / VC / M • Love Slaves / 1976 / VCR / M • Meter Maids / 1974 / SIL / M • Most Valuable Slut / 1973 / HLV / M • National Pornographic #4: / 1987 / 4P / C • Night Pleasures / 1975 / WWV / M • Once Upon A Time/Cave Woman / 1978 / VI / M • One Of A Kind / 1976 / SVE / M • Only The Best Of Breasts / 1987 / CV / C • Physical #1 / 1981 / SUP / M • The Pleasure Masters / 1975 / AST / M • Randy, The Electric Lady / 1978 / VC / M • Rockin' With Seka / 1980 / WV / M • Salt & Pepper / 1986 / VCS / C • San Francisco Original 200s Special / 1980 / SVE / C • The Sex Game / 1987 / SE / C • Sex World / 1978 / SE / M • Sexsations / 1984 / NSV / M • The Sinful Pleasures Of Reverend Star / 1976 / ... / M • The Spirit Of Seventy Six / 1976 / NGV / M • The Starlets / 1976 / RAV / M • Swedish Erotica #43 / 1982 / CA / M • Sweet Cakes / 1976 / VC / M • Sweet Savage / 1978 / ALP / M • Tapestry Of Passion / 1976 / SE / M • Teen Angel / cr74 / CV / M • Teenage Madam / 1979 / CXV / M • Teenage Runaway / 1973 / AXV / M • That's Erotic / 1979 / CV / C • That's Porno / 1979 / CV / C • Torch Of Desire / 1983 / REG / M • Triangle Of Lust / 1983 / VCR / M • True Legends Of Adult Cinema: Unsung Superstars / 1993 / VC / C • The Hot One / 1978 / CV / M • Valley Girls Ferr Shurr / cr85 / EXF / M • Vanessa's Bed Of Pleasure / 1983 / SVE / M • Vista Valley PTA / 1980 / CV / M • [Best Of Xxx / cr90 / ... / C • [Cat Tails / 1976 / CVX / M • [Chain Letter / 1978 / ... / M • [Fire Under The Skin / 197? / ... / M

DESMON FLAME
Reel Life Video #08: Bachelor Party / 1994 / RLF / M • Reel Life Video #09 / 1994 / RLF / M

DESSIE STROND
Ready To Drop #04 / 1994 / FC / M

DESTIN
FTV #71: Bully Girl / 1996 / FT / B

DESTINI LANCE *see* **Destini Lane**
DESTINI LANE *(Destini Lance, Destiny (Lane), Destiny Lane, Nancy (Destiny Lane), Aurora (Dest. Lane), Shanna (Dest. Lane), Whitney Banks, Whitney (Dest. Lane), Whitley Banks, Candy Marie)*
Blue eyed blonde with the black roots showing, not great skin, small tits, freckles on chest, 20 years old in 1993, wears lots of silver rings. In **Nasty Nymphos #02** she says she's 19 years old and divorced from her

husband who she married at age 16.
30 Days In The Hole / 1993 / ZA / M • Amateurs Exposed #05 / 1995 / CV / M • Anal Justice / 1994 / ROB / M • Anal Vision #19 / 1993 / LBO / M • Beach Bum Amateur's #36 / 1993 / MID / M • Big Bust Babes #25 / 1995 / AFI / M • Bigger Than Life / 1995 / IF / M • The Blues #2 / 1994 / VT / M • Bobby Hollander's Sweet Cheeks #110 / 1994 / WV / M • Bodywaves / 1994 / ELP / M • Breastman's Wet T-Shirt Contest / 1994 / EVN / M • Butt Bandits #4 / 1996 / VD / C • Casting Call #04 / 1993 / SO / M • Caught From Behind #19 / 1994 / HO / M • Cheatin' / 1994 / FD / M • Cherry Poppers #01 / 1993 / ZA / M • Controlled / 1994 / FD / M • The Couch Trap / 1993 / ELP / M • Cousin Bubba Country Corn Porn #01 / 1994 / VIM / M • Dirty Doc's Housecalls #05 / 1993 / LV / M • Eclipse / 1993 / SC / M • First Time Lesbians #15 / 1994 / JMP / F • Four Screws And An Anal / 1994 / NEY / M • The Fucking Elvises / 1994 / GLI / M • Gang Bang Bitches #04 / 1995 / PP / M • Gang Bang Wild Style #2 / 1994 / ROB / M • A Girl's Affair #04 / 1994 / FD / F • Hidden Camera #12 / 1993 / JMP / M • The Hitch-Hiker #01: Wide Open Spaces / 1993 / WMG / M • Invitation To The Blues / 1994 / LE / M • Love Potion 69 / 1994 / VC / M • M Series #16 / 1993 / LBO / M • M Series #20 / 1994 / LBO / M • Mike Hott: #258 Horny Couples #16 / 1994 / MHV / M • Nasty Nymphos #02 / 1994 / ANA / M • The New Butt Hunt #19 / 1996 / LEI / C • Older Men With Younger Women #2 / 1994 / CC / M • Pearl Necklace: Premier Sessions #01 / 1993 / SEE / M • Private Film #12 / 1994 / OD / M • Private Film #14 / 1994 / OD / M • Private Video Magazine #08 / 1994 / OD / M • Private Video Magazine #10 / 1994 / OD / M • Private Video Magazine #19 / 1994 / OD / M • Pussy Tales / 1993 / SC / F • Pussyclips #02 / 1994 / SNA / M • Ron Hightower's White Chicks #05 / 1993 / LBO / M • Superstar Sex Challenge #1 / 1994 / VC / M • Superstar Sex Challenge #2 / 1994 / VC / M • Superstar Sex Challenge #3 / 1994 / VC / M • Swinging Couples #01 / 1993 / GO / M • Wet Deal / 1994 / FD / M • Wild Thing / 1994 / IF / M • Willie Wanker And The Fun Factory / 1994 / FD / M • Women Of Color #1 / 1994 / ANA / M

DESTINY
A&B AB#803: Flash And Fuck—Destiny / 1995 / A&B / M • Abduction Of A Salesman / 1990 / BIZ / B • Black Mystique #12 / 1995 / VT / F • The Bondage File / 19?? / BIZ / C • Box Of Slavegirls / 1995 / LON / B • Destiny & April In Bondage / 1993 / BON / B • An Editor's Nightmare / 1995 / LON / B • Facesitting Frenzy / 1995 / IBN / B • GRG: Dueling Dykes / 1994 / GRG / F • Interracial Affairs / 1996 / FC / M • Northwest Pecker Trek #2: Evergreen, Ever Horny / 1994 / LBO / M • Pussy Hunt #11 / 1995 / LEI / M • She Studs #04 / 1991 / BIZ / G • Show Them No Mercy #1 / 1991 / STM / B

DESTINY (1996) *see* **Dawn Devine**
DESTINY (H. DIVINE) *see* **Honeysuckle Divine**
DESTINY (LANE) *see* **Destini Lane**
DESTINY ANN
Dixie Debutantes #1 / 1996 / MYS / M
DESTINY COLLINS

The Bitch Biker #1: The Long Road Home / 1994 / RBP / F

DESTINY DEMOORE
Destiny / 1996 / BON / B • The Go-Go Girls / 1994 / EVN / M • Hollywood Starlets Adventure #04 / 1995 / AVS / M • Open Lips / 1994 / WV / M • Pussy Hunt #07 / 1994 / LEI / M • Samantha's Private Fantasies / 1994 / WV / M

DESTINY DEMOORE (HW) *see* **Honey Wells**

DESTINY DUVAL *see* **Cheri Champagne**

DESTINY LANE *see* **Destini Lane**

DESTINY MOORE (HW) *see* **Honey Wells**

DESTINY REIGNS
Raw Sex #02 / 1995 / ERW / M

DETLAS VAN BURG
Blue Ice / 1985 / CA / M • Lust At First Bite / 1978 / VC / M

DETROIT
Honey Drippers / 1992 / ROB / F • Kittens & Vamps #1 / 1993 / ROB / F • Lesbian Lockup / 1993 / ROB / F • Sweet Lips & Buns / 1993 / ROB / F • Two Women / 1992 / ROB / M

DEVA
Trading Partners / 1983 / AIR / M

DEVA STATION
Crew Sluts / 1996 / NOT / M • Sorority Sex Kittens #3 / 1996 / VC / M

DEVAN *see* **Josalynn Taylor**

DEVEL DREGGS
Black Playhouse / 1995 / HBE / M

DEVEN
Joe Elliot's College Girls: Deven Uncut / 1994 / JOE / M

DEVI
Video Virgins #12 / 1994 / NS / M

DEVIENCE
Climax At The Melting Pot #1 / 1996 / AVS / M

DEVIN
Bob's Video #101: City Of Angels / 1996 / BOV / F • Bob's Video #102: Hot Scenes From L.A. / 1996 / BOV / F • Bubble Butts #10 / 1992 / LBO / M • The Flintbones / 1992 / FR / M • Hard Core Beginners #03 / 1995 / LEI / M • Hollywood Swingers #04 / 1992 / LBO / M • Hose Jobs / 1995 / VEY / ?? • ??? City Cycle Sluts #?? / 1996 / OO / F • Zazel / 1996 / CV / M

DEVIN CALOWAY
Charming Cheapies #1: Joy's Many Loves / 1985 / 4P / M

DEVIN DEMOORE
Pick Up Lines #11 / 1997 / OD / M

DEVIN DERAY *(Carmine)*
Black or some variant therof which she refuses to discuss, ugly, huge watermelons, large womanly body, hard personality. She says she's 22 but looks 42.
Big Knockers #13 / 1995 / TV / M • Big Knockers #20 / 1995 / TV / C • Black Knockers #13 / 1995 / TV / M • Bow Down Backstreet / 1996 / HW / M • Busty Babes / 1995 / NAP / F • Double D Dreams / 1996 / NAP / S • My Black Ass / 1996 / NOT / M • Nasty Nymphos #16 / 1996 / ANA / M • Score Busty Centerfolds #1 / 1995 / BTO / S • Seymore Butts: Big Boobs In Buttsville / 1996 / FH / M • Up Your Ass #3 / 1996 / ANA / M

DEVIN DESOTO
San Francisco Lesbians #1 / 1992 / PL / F

DEVIN DEVANE

The Farmer's Daughter / 1995 / TEG / M

DEVIN DOUGHERTY
Reckless Claudia / 1971 / MIT / M

DEVIN KANE
Boot Camp / 1996 / PRE / B • Profiles #06: Super Model Orgy / 1996 / XPR / M

DEVIN LOVELACE
Three For The Whip / 1995 / VTF / B

DEVLIN WEED
The Adventures Of Peeping Tom #3 / 1996 / OD / M • Bedtime Stories / 1996 / VC / M • Big Man's Dream / 1996 / LOK / M • Black Bush Bashers / 1996 / LOK / M • The Black Butt Sisters Do Baltimore / 1995 / MID / M • The Black Butt Sisters Do Boston / 1995 / MID / M • The Black Butt Sisters Do Detroit / 1995 / MID / M • The Black Butt Sisters Do New Orleans / 1996 / MID / M • The Black Butt Sisters Do New York / 1995 / MID / M • The Black Butt Sisters Do Philadelphia / 1995 / MID / M • The Black Butt Sisters Do Seattle / 1995 / MID / M • Black Fantasies #07 / 1995 / HW / M • Black Fantasies #09 / 1995 / HW / M • Black Fantasies #10 / 1995 / HW / M • Black Fantasies #11 / 1996 / HW / M • Black Fantasies #12 / 1996 / HW / M • Black Fantasies #15 / 1996 / HW / M • Black Fantasies #16 / 1996 / HW / M • Black Gangbangers #10 / 1996 / HW / M • Black Hollywood Amateurs #02 / 1995 / MID / M • Black Hollywood Amateurs #04 / 1995 / MID / M • Black Hollywood Amateurs #06 / 1995 / MID / M • Black Hollywood Amateurs #07 / 1995 / MID / M • Black Hollywood Amateurs #08 / 1995 / MID / M • Black Hollywood Amateurs #10 / 1995 / MID / M • Black Hollywood Amateurs #11 / 1995 / MID / M • Black Hollywood Amateurs #12 / 1995 / MID / M • Black Hollywood Amateurs #14 / 1995 / MID / M • Black Hollywood Amateurs #15 / 1995 / MID / M • Black Hollywood Amateurs #16 / 1995 / MID / M • Black Hollywood Amateurs #17 / 1995 / MID / M • Black Hollywood Amateurs #19 / 1995 / MID / M • Black Hollywood Amateurs #20 / 1995 / MID / M • Black Hollywood Amateurs #21 / 1996 / MID / M • Black Hollywood Amateurs #22 / 1996 / MID / M • Black Hollywood Amateurs #24 / 1996 / MID / M • Black Hollywood Amateurs #25 / 1996 / MID / M • Black Hollywood Amateurs #26 / 1996 / MID / M • Black Knockers #09 / 1995 / TV / M • Black Knockers #10 / 1995 / TV / M • Black Knockers #11 / 1995 / TV / M • Black Knockers #13 / 1995 / TV / M • Black Orgies #23 / 1994 / GO / M • Black Orgies #27 / 1994 / GO / M • Black Orgies #28 / 1994 / GO / M • Black Orgies #36 / 1995 / GO / M • Black Talez N Da Hood / 1996 / APP / M • Bootylicious: Baby Got Booty / 1996 / JMP / M • Bootylicious: Bitches & Ho's / 1996 / JMP / M • Bootylicious: Trailer Trash / 1996 / JMP / M • Bootylicious: White Trash / 1995 / JMP / M • Bootylicious: Yo Bitch / 1996 / JMP / M • Bow Down Backstreet / 1996 / HW / M • Bun Busters #20 / 1994 / LBO / M • Conjugal Visits / 1995 / EVN / M • Dark Alleys #28 / 1994 / FC / M • Ebony Erotica #23: Black Betty / 1994 / GO / M • Ebony Erotica #24: Hot Chocolate / 1994 / GO / M • Ebony Erotica #25: Java Jive / 1994 / GO / M • Ebony Erotica #27: Caramel Lust / 1994 / GO / M • Ebony Erotica #34: Mellow

Moprene / 1995 / GO / M • Git Yo' Ass On Da Bus! / 1996 / HW / M • Gutter Mouths / 1996 / JMP / M • Hardcore Fantasies #5 / 1996 / LV / M • In Da Booty / 1996 / LV / M • Liar's Poke Her / 1995 / NIW / M • A Lowdown Dirty Game / 1996 / LBO / M • The Mad D.P. Tea Party / 1994 / FC / M • Miss Judge / 1997 / VI / M • My Ass #1 / 1996 / NOT / M • My Baby Got Back #09 / 1996 / VT / M • Perverted Stories #09 / 1996 / JMP / M • Primal Rear / 1996 / TIW / M • Puritan Video Magazine #04 / 1996 / LE / M • Ron Hightower's Casting Couch #1 / 1995 / FC / M • Ron Hightower's Casting Couch #2 / 1995 / FC / M • Ron Hightower's White Chicks #11 / 1994 / LBO / M • Ron Hightower's White Chicks #12 / 1994 / LBO / M • Ron Hightower's White Chicks #13 / 1994 / LBO / M • Ron Hightower's White Chicks #15 / 1994 / LBO / M • Ron Hightower's White Chicks #16 / 1994 / LBO / M • Shades Of Color #1 / 1995 / LBO / M • Sharon's House Party / 1995 / HW / M • Skeezers / 1996 / LV / M • Snatch Shot / 1996 / LBO / M • Stardust #5 / 1996 / VI / M • Triple Penetration Debutante Sluts #2 / 1996 / BAC / M • Waiting 2 XX Hale / 1996 / APP / M • Young And Anal #6 / 1996 / JMP / M

DEVO
Beverly She-Males / 1994 / PL / G

DEVON
Begging For Bondage / 1992 / BON / B • Booty Babes / 1993 / ROB / F • China Lee's Bachelorette Party / 1995 / RHV / M • Kinky College Cunts #02 / 1993 / NS / M • Mr. Peepers Nastiest #2 / 1995 / LBO / C • Pony Girls / 1993 / ROB / F • Shaved She-Males / 1994 / PL / G • Sweet Lips & Buns / 1993 / ROB / F • Thrill Seekers / 1993 / ROB / F

DEVON (HAWAII) *see* **Star Index I**

DEVON BLAKE
Sodomania: Slop Shots / 1996 / EL / C

DEVON DANIELS
10 Years Of Big Busts #3 / 199? / BTO / C • Big Busty #29 / 198? / H&S / S • Big Busty #31 / 1989 / BTO / S • H&S: Devon Daniels / 1988? / H&S / S

DEVON DELIGHT *see* **Laurel Canyon**

DEVON FERRARI
Breast Of Britain #9 / 1990 / BTO / M • Turn Up The Heat / 1988 / SEX / M • Turn Up The Heat / 1991 / VEX / C

DEVON HARRISON
Coed Fever / 1980 / CA / M

DEVON NICHOLS
Fair Warning / 1995 / ZFX / B

DEVON REXX
N.Y. Video Magazine #03 / 1995 / OUP / M • Primal Submission / A Glutton For Punishment / 1995 / OUP / B • Rusty Boner's Late Night Videos #1 / 1995 / RHV / M

DEVON SHIRE *(Jennifer Peace, Barbara Woods (DShir)*
Quite pretty brunette with medium well proportioned natural tits. First seen in **Lifeguard** where she says she's not turned on by men. Born in Pineville KY. Aged 21 in 1992. Appeared on **A Current Affair** on February 12, 1992 where she claims she is stopping her porno career and moving into regular movies (don't worry, she didn't—usual hype). Her real name is Jennifer Peace. Was mixed up with the O.J. Simpson affair via being the one-time girlfriend of

Al Cowlings. Took some time off because of the money she made on giving interviews about OJ and had a baby (father not disclosed and she says she has no intention of getting married). As of mid 1996 her tits are now slobby and she has lost belly muscle tone.
Ace In The Hole / 1995 / PL / M • All About Teri Weigel / 1996 / XCI / M • All In The Name Of Love / 1992 / IF / M • Amateur American Style #17 / 1991 / AR / M • Amateur Lesbians #13: Brandi / 1991 / GO / F • Amateur Lesbians #14: Avalon / 1991 / GO / F • Amateur Lesbians #25: International Budapest / 1992 / GO / F • Amateur Lesbians #35: Meo / 1993 / GO / F • Amateurama #01 / 1992 / RTP / M • American Dream Girls #2 / 1994 / LEI / M • Anal Aspirations / 1993 / LV / M • Angel Wolf / 1995 / WIV / M • Another Rear View / 1990 / LE / M • As Dirty As She Wants To Be / 1990 / ME / M • As Sweet As Can Be / 1993 / V99 / M • Backdoor Black #2 / 1993 / WV / C • Backfield In Motion / 1995 / VT / M • Bad Boy's Punishment / 1993 / BIZ / B • Between Her Thighs / 1992 / CDI / M • Beverly Hills Geisha / 1992 / V99 / M • Bi & Large / 1994 / STA / G • The Bimbo #1 / 1992 / AFV / M • The Bimbo #2 / 1992 / AFV / M • Bimbonese 101 / 1993 / PL / M • Bitches In Heat / 1994 / PL / C • Black On White / 1991 / VT / F • Blue Jeans Brat / 1991 / VI / M • Bobby Hollander's Rookie Nookie #14 / 1993 / SFP / M • Burn It Up / 1994 / VEX / M • Buttsizer, King Of Rears #1 / 1992 / EVN / M • Casey At The Bat / 1991 / LV / M • Cat Lickers #1 / 1990 / ME / F • Caught In The Act (1995-Lv) / 1995 / LV / M • Celebrity Sluts And Tabloid Tramps / 1996 / LV / M • Christmas Carol / 1993 / LV / M • The Come On: Skip's Video Guide To Scoring Chicks / 1991 / LE / M • The Couch Trap / 1993 / ELP / M • The Creasemaster / 1993 / VC / M • The Creasemaster's Wife / 1993 / VC / M • Cum On Line / 1991 / XPI / M • Dangerous Curves / 1995 / VC / M • Date Night / 1992 / V99 / M • Death Dancers / 1993 / 3SR / S • Debbie Does Wall Street / 1991 / VC / M • Decadent Delights / 1992 / IF / M • The Determinator #1 / 1991 / VIM / M • The Determinator #2 / 1991 / VIM / M • Dirty Dave's American Amateurs #08 / 1992 / AR / M • Dirty Dirty Debutantes #7 / 1996 / 4P / M • Dominique Goes Bi / 1994 / STA / G • Eat My Cherry / 1994 / BHS / M • The Eye Of The Needle / 1991 / CIN / M • Faithless Companions / 1992 / WV / M • Femme Fatale / 1993 / SC / M • Forbidden Desires / 1991 / CIN / F • Fortysomething #2 / 1991 / LE / M • Frenzy / 1992 / SC / M • Girls Just Wanna Have Toys / 1993 / PL / F • Girls Will Be Boys #6 / 1993 / PL / F • Guttman's Hollywood Adventure / 1993 / PL / M • Hard Deck / 1991 / XPI / M • Hardcore Copy / 1993 / PL / M • Heart To Heart / 1990 / LE / M • Heartbreaker / 1992 / CDI / M • Heatwave #1 / 1992 / FH / F • Hidden Camera #09 / 1993 / JMP / M • Homegrown Video #370 / 1991 / HOV / M • Hometown Girl / 1994 / VEX / M • Housewife From Hell / 1994 / TRI / S • How To Love Your Lover / 1992 / XII / S • It's A Wonderful Sexlife / 1991 / LE / M • Jail Babes #2: Bustin' Out / 1992 / PL / F • John Wayne Bobbitt Uncut / 1994 / LEI / M • Kinky Lesbians #02 /

1993 / BIZ / B • The Last Temptation Of Teri / 1991 / IF / M • Lesbian Pros And Amateurs #24 / 1993 / GO / F • Lifeguard / 1990 / VI / M • Lingerie Busters / 1991 / FH / M • Love Potion 69 / 1994 / VC / M • Lust For Love / 1991 / VC / M • Madame X / 1990 / EX / M • Make Me Sweat / 1994 / V99 / M • The Man Who Loved Women / 1993 / SC / M • Midnight Angel / 1992 / CDI / M • Mistre3aoc At War #01 / 1993 / BIZ / B • Mistresses At War #02 / 1993 / BIZ / B • Mr. Peepers Amateur Home Videos #78: She Dreams Of Weenie / 1993 / LBO / M • Mr. Peepers Nastiest #1 / 1995 / LBO / C • Nasty Jack's Homemade Vid. #31 / 1991 / CDI / M • Naughty By Nature / 1992 / IF / M • New Pussy Hunt #24 / 1996 / LEI / C • New Wave Hookers #3 / 1993 / VC / M • On Your Bare Bottom / 1992 / BON / B • Pajama Party / 1993 / CV / C • Party Pack #1 / 1990 / LE / F • Personalities / 1991 / PL / M • Perverted Stories #03 / 1995 / JMP / M • Phone Fantasy #1 / 1992 / ATL / M • The Power Dykes / 1993 / BIZ / B • Prisoner Of Lust / 1991 / VC / F • Queen Of Hearts #3: Heartless / 1992 / PL / M • Raincoat Fantasies / 1993 / ELP / M • Raunchy Remedy / 1993 / ELP / M • Raw Talent: Bang 'er 07 Times / 1992 / RTP / M • Ring Of Passion / 1993 / WV / M • Satin Shadows / 1991 / CIN / M • School For Wayward Wives / 1993 / BIZ / B • Secret Games #2: The Escort / 1993 / IMP / S • Sensual Exposure / 1993 / ULI / M • The Sex Connection / 1993 / VC / M • Sex Trek #1: The Next Peneration / 1990 / ME / M • Sexual Outlaws / 1994 / MON / S • Seymore Butts In Paradise / 1993 / FH / M • Seymore Butts: Bustin' Out My Best Anal / 1995 / FH / C • Shifting Gere / 1990 / VT / M • Simply Irresistible / 1991 / CIN / M • Smeers / 1992 / PL / M • Snakedance / 1992 / VI / M • Southern Comfort / 1991 / CIN / M • The Spa / 1993 / VC / M • Stasha's Diary / 1991 / CIN / G • Switch Hitters #6: Back In The Bull Pen / 1991 / IN / G • Switch Hitters #7 / 1994 / IN / G • Tail Taggers #104 / 1993 / WV / M • Tangled / 1994 / PL / M • The Teacher's Pet / 1993 / LV / M • Tight Pucker / 1992 / WV / M • Too Cute For Words / 1992 / V99 / M • Total Exposure / 1992 / CDI / M • Toys Bi Us / 1993 / BIL / G • Twin Cheeks #4 / 1991 / CIN / M • Twister / 1992 / CC / M • Viviana's Dude Ranch / 1992 / IF / M • Wicked / 1991 / XCI / M

DEVON SHORE
Brunette, not too pretty, small tits, very big butt, small tattoo on her right belly, bad dentition, womanly body. Supposedly a dancer from Texas.
Anal Fantasy / 1996 / SUF / M • Bottom Dweller: The Final Voyage / 1996 / EL / M • Butt Sluts #6 / 1996 / ROB / F • Casting Call #17 / 1996 / SO / M • Compulsion (Amazing) / 1996 / MET / M • Corporate Justice / 1996 / TEP / M • Delinquents On Butt Row / 1996 / EA / M • Dirty Dave's #2 / 1996 / XPR / M • Dirty Dave's #4 / 1996 / XPR / M • Eighteen #1 / 1996 / SC / M • Hardcore Confidential #1 / 1996 / TEP / M • Malibu Butt Sluts / 1996 / ROB / F • Million Dollar Buns / 1996 / MYS / M • More Dirty Debutantes #56 / 1996 / 4P / M • Nineteen #1 / 1996 / FOR / M • Nothing Like Nurse Nookie #4 / 1996 / NIT / M • Passion / 1996 / SC / M • Perverted Stories

#08 / 1996 / JMP / M • The Shocking Truth #1 / 1996 / DWO / M • Shooting Gallery / 1996 / EL / M • Summer Dreams / 1996 / TEP / M • Up And Cummers #29 / 1996 / ERW / M • Venom #6 / 1996 / CA / M • Virgin Bar Maids / 1996 / VMX / M • The Voyeur #8: Live In Europe #2 / 1996 / JLP / M • Whiplash / 1996 / DFI / M • Young Tails / 1996 / LV / M

DEVON/DEVIN
The Adventures Of Peeping Tom #2 / 1996 / OD / M • Club Deb #4 / 1996 / MEI / M • More Dirty Debutantes #55 / 1996 / 4P / M • Pick Up Lines #06 / 1996 / OD / M • Shane's World #3 / 1996 / OD / M • Valley Cooze / 1996 / SC / M • Video Virgins #32 / 1996 / NS / M • Whiplash / 1996 / DFI / M

DEWEY ALEXANDER *see* **Richard Pacheco**

DEXTER *see Star Index I*

DEY LATURE
Charming Cheapies #3: Day And Night / 1985 / 4P / M

DHAMRA
Babes Of The Bay #1 / 1994 / LIP / F

DHARMA
Blood Bath / 1995 / FLV / B

DIAMOND
Filthy First Timers #6 / 1997 / EL / M

DIAMOND (BELLA) *see* Bella Donna

DIAMOND (EUROPE)
Eurotica #01 / 1995 / XC / M

DIAMOND (JACKY PAGE) *see* **Jacky Page**

DIAMOND (OTHER)
A&B AB#367: Gang Bang Girls / 1991 / A&B / C • A&B AB#371: Wild Woman #1 / 1991 / A&B / M • A&B AB#372: Wild Woman #2 / 1991 / A&B / M • A&B AB#378: Fuck Me / 1991 / A&B / M • A&B AB#566: Diamond's Cum Pie / 1995 / A&B / M • A&B AB#567: Diamond Gets Slutty / 1995 / A&B / M • East Coast Sluts #10: Ohio / 1996 / PL / M

DIAMOND BELLE *see Star Index I*

DIAMOND BLACK
Freaky Flix / 1995 / TTV / C • Horny Henry's Swinging Adventures / 1994 / TTV / M • Kitty Foxx's Kinky Kapers #02 / 1995 / TTV / M

DIAMOND CARTIER *(Dymond Cartier)*
This is a male (may be black).
Detroit Dames / 1988 / DR / C • Magic Pool / 1988 / VD / M • The Secret Diaries / 1990 / V99 / M • Sex World Girls / 1987 / AR / M • Tight End / 1988 / VXP / M

DIAMOND DAVE
Dirty Dancers #3 / 1995 / 4P / M

DIAMOND GIRL
Rock And Roll Auditions / 1995 / CZV / M

DIAMOND LADY
Harlem Harlots #1 / 1995 / AVS / M

DIAMOND LANE
Taste For Submission / 1991 / LON / C

DIAMOND LIL *see* Clair James

DIANA
100% Amateur #03: On The Dark Side / 1995 / OD / M • A&B AB#395: Cum Dripping Ladies / 1990 / A&B / M • A&B AB#396: Cum All Over Me / 1990 / A&B / M • A&B AB#397: Cum Sisters / 1990 / A&B / M • A&B AB#399: Swingers Journey #1 / 1993 / A&B / M • A&B AB#400: Swingers Journey #2 / 1993 / A&B / M • A&B AB#406: I Want To Be Gang Banged / 1993 / A&B / M • A&B AB#409: Sex, Loves

And Videotape / 1993 / A&B / M • A&B AB#420: Diana's Sex Friends / 1993 / A&B / M • A&B AB#422: Cum Follow Me Or In Me! / 1993 / A&B / M • A&B AB#526 / 1995 / A&B / M • A&B FL#06 / 1995 / A&B / S • A&B FL#07: Preview Video / 1995 / A&B / C • Amateur Nights #16 / 1997 / HO / M • Blue Vanities #502 / 1992 / FFL / M • English Class / 1995 / VC / M • Fantasy In Oil #1 / 1996 / CAW / B • FTV #71: Bully Girl / 1996 / FT / B • FTV #73: Killer Kupps / 1996 / FT / B • Girl's Towne #1 / 1994 / FC / F • Limited Edition #26 / 1984 / AVC / M • Liquid Lips #2 / 1994 / MAV / M • Magma: Dirty Diana / 1994 / MET / M • Magma: Dirty Twins / 1994 / MET / M • Magma: Fuck Me Diana / 1994 / MET / M • Max Gold #1 / 1996 / XPR / C • Raw Talent: Bang 'er 45 Times / 1993 / RTP / M • Raw Talent: Murphy Bang / 1994 / RTP / M • Raw Talent: Voyeurism / 1994 / FH / M • Triple X Video Magazine #08 / 1995 / OD / M • Triple X Video Magazine #11 / 1995 / OD / M

DIANA (RICHARDS) see Diana Richards

DIANA BONET
R/H Productions #5001: A Friendly Encounter Of A Sexual Kind / 1995 / R/H / M • R/H Productions #5002: An Interview For A Roommate / 1995 / R/H / M • Raunchy Reggae / 1995 / SP / M

DIANA CHAMBERLAIN see Star Index I

DIANA CORCORAN see Star Index I

DIANA DEMARCO
Max #03 / 1995 / FWE / M

DIANA DENEUVE see Diane Sloan

DIANA DEVILLE see Star Index I

DIANA DIAMOND see Brigitte Monet

DIANA DYLAN see Dana Dylan

DIANA HARFIELD see Star Index I

DIANA HOLT see Dianne Holt

DIANA HUNTER see Star Index I

DIANA JOHNSON see Star Index I

DIANA JONATHAN
Daddy's Little Girls / 1983 / CA / M

DIANA KLINE
Sex Star / 1983 / CA / M

DIANA KNIGHT (Diane King)
Black girl, medium tits (may be enhanced as they look smaller in some movies), not too pretty, shaven pussy, nice personality.
Anal House Party / 1993 / IP / M • Black Babes In Heat / 1993 / VIM / M • Black Bitches In Heat #1 / 1995 / GDV / M • Black Cherries / 1993 / EVN / C • Black Dirty Debutantes / 1993 / 4P / M • Black Gangbangers #07 / 1995 / HW / M • Black Mystique #10 / 1994 / VT / F • The Bold, The Bald & The Beautiful / 1993 / VIM / M • Dark Passions #02 / 1993 / AFV / M • Dark Passions #03 / 1995 / AFV / M • The Gang Bang Story / 1993 / IP / M • Girlz Towne #01 / 1995 / FC / F • Girlz Towne #07 / 1995 / FC / F • Lovin' Spoonfuls #6 / 1996 / 4P / C • M Series #06 / 1993 / LBO / M • Odyssey Triple Play #81: Copulation Intergration / 1994 / OD / M • Oral Gang Bang Girls #1 / 1993 / FH / M • Oral Gang Bang Girls #2 / 1993 / FH / M • Prime Time Slime #03 / 1994 / GLI / M • The Reel Sex World #02 / 1994 / WP / M • Shades Of Erotica #01 / 1994 / GLI / M • Up And Cummers #24 / 1995 / 4P / M • Video Virgins #04 / 1993 / NS / M • What's Butt Got To Do With It? / 1993 / HW / M • [Anal Stud's Story / 1993 / IP / M

DIANA LARKIN
Steamy Dreams / cr70 / CVX / M

DIANA LEE
Diamonds / 1996 / HDE / M • The Statesman's Wife / 1996 / PAL / M

DIANA MAY
Angel Buns / 1981 / QX / M

DIANA PEARL
Diamonds / 1996 / HDE / M

DIANA REED
Private Gold #01: Study In Sex / 1995 / OD / M • Private Gold #02: Friends In Sex / 1995 / OD / M

DIANA RICHARDS (Diane Richards, Dianna Richards, Diana (Richards))
Old female.
50 And Still Pumping! / 1994 / EMC / M • Aged To Perfection #1 / 1994 / TTV / M • Ateball: More Than A Mouthful / 1995 / ATE / F • Dirty & Kinky Mature Women #07 / 1996 / C69 / M • The Fabulous 50's Girls Ride Again / 1994 / EMC / M • Freaky Flix / 1995 / TTV / C • Granny Bangers / 1995 / MET / M • Kitty Foxx's Kinky Kapers #03 / 1995 / TTV / M • Kitty's Kinky Capers / 1996 / TTV / M • More Than A Mouthful #1 / 1995 / VEX / F • Old Wives' Tails / 1995 / EMC / M • Older Women With Younger Ideas / 1995 / GLI / M • The Older Women's Sperm Bank #4 / 1996 / SUF / M • Slammln' Granny In The Fanny / 1995 / GLI / M • Sugar Mommies / 1995 / FPI / M • The Ultimate Climax / 1996 / EMC / M

DIANA ROGERS see Star Index I

DIANA SLOAN see Diane Sloan

DIANA SPICE
Latin Plump Humpers #1 / 1995 / TTV / M

DIANA STRAWBERRY see Star Index I

DIANA VAN LAAR
Sex Off The Runway / 1991 / GMI / M

DIANA VINCENT
Private Gold #06: Cape Town #2 / 1996 / OD / M • Triple X Video Magazine #15 / 1996 / OD / M

DIANE
A&B AB#468: Cum Girls / 1994 / A&B / M • Blue Vanities #509 / 1992 / FFL / M • Blue Vanities #512 / 1992 / FFL / M • Eurotica #00 / 1000 / VFG / M • Lazybody's Girl / 19?? / SOW / S • FTV #26: Smother Queen / 1996 / FT / B • The Hunt Is On / 1994 / HU / F • J.E.G.: Pair Of Precious Pregnants / 1995 / JEG / F • Pearl Necklace: Thee Bush League: The Best Of Oral #01 / 1993 / SEE / C • Sappho Connection / 19?? / LIP / F • Spank You Very Much / 1995 / IBN / B • SVE: Diane Solos Into Ecstasy / 1994 / SVE / F

DIANE (SUNSET T) see Sunset Thomas

DIANE BALSAM
Flipside: A Backdoor Adventure / 1985 / CV / M

DIANE BAXTER see Star Index I

DIANE BEATTY
[Tender Loving Care / 197? / ... / M

DIANE BERRY
[No More Dirty Deals / 1994 / V-I / S

DIANE CANNON
Busty Debutantes / 1996 / H&S / M • A Foot Story / 1996 / OUP / B • Over The Knee / 1996 / OUP / B

DIANE DALE
Little Me & Marla Strangelove / 1979 / ALP / M

DIANE DALTON see Jean Dalton

DIANE DARLINGTON see Aubrey Nichols

DIANE DRAKE
Dianna's Destiny / 19?? / BIZ / B

DIANE DUBOIS see Star Index I

DIANE DUGLAS see Star Index I

DIANE HURLEY see Dyanna Lauren

DIANE KING see Diana Knight

DIANE KORBEL see Star Index I

DIANE LEE see Rene Bond

DIANE MARTIN
Ring Of Desire / 1981 / SE / M

DIANE MASON
Blue Vanities #565 / 1995 / FFL / M

DIANE MILLER
One Page Of Love / 1980 / VCX / M • Paul, Lisa And Caroline / 1976 / SE / M • The Psychiatrist / 1978 / VC / M • Resurrection Of Eve / 1973 / MIT / M

DIANE O'DAINE (Victoria (D.O'Daine))
Dark blonde with too large a nose to be called pretty, big hips, reasonably slim waist, small tits, good tan lines, tattoo on left outside ankle. Not the same as Victoria Gunn.
Anal Brat / 1993 / FL / M • Anal Virgins Of America #02 / 1993 / FOR / M • Bobby Hollander's Rookie Nookie #10 / 1993 / MET / M • Captain Bob's Lust Boat #2 / 1993 / FCP / M • First Time Lesbians #05 / 1993 / JMP / F • Frathouse Sexcapades / 1993 / SFP / M • French Open / 1993 / PV / M • French Open Part Deux / 1993 / MET / M • Harry Horndog #21: Birthday Orgy / 1993 / ZA / M • Hidden Camera #04 / 1993 / JMP / M • Hot Pie Delivery / 1993 / AFV / M • Primal Desires / 1993 / EX / M • Real Tickets #1 / 1994 / VC / M • Real Tickets #2 / 1994 / VC / M • Sleeping With Seattle / 1993 / LV / M • Student Fetish Videos: Spanking #12 / 1994 / PRE / B • Suburban Nymphos / 1994 / ATL / M • Super Hornio Brothers #2 / 1993 / MID / M • Video Virgins #04 / 1993 / NS / M

DIANE PARKER
N.Y. Video Magazine #05 / 1995 / OUP / M • New York City Lesbian Gang Bang / 1995 / OUP / F • Pain Slut / 1995 / OUP / B • Savage Delights / 1995 / OUP / B • Strap-On Sally #01: Strap-On Psycho / 1993 / PL / F • Strap On Sally #02: Ariana Bottoms Out / 1993 / PL / F • Streets Of New York #04 / 1995 / PL / M

DIANE PRINCE see Star Index I

DIANE RACHEL see Rayne

DIANE RICHARDS see Diana Richards

DIANE ROCHELLE see Star Index I

DIANE SIMEONE
Family Affair / 1979 / MIT / M

DIANE SLOAN (Diana Sloan, Diana Deneuve, Daphne (Sloan))
One of identical twins (Denise is the other). Diana Deneuve is from Extreme Close-Up.
Dracula Exotica / 1980 / TVX / M • Extreme Close-Up / 1981 / VC / M • Fantasy Club #28: Cuntortionist / 1984 / WV / M • The Good Girls Of Godiva High / 1979 / VCX / M • Passions / 1985 / MIT / M • Smoker / 1983 / VC / M • Sophisticated Pleasure / 1984 / WV / M • Sunny / 1979 / VC / M • Tigresses...And Other Man-Eaters / 1979 / VXP / M

DIANE SMILEY
Sex Over 40 #1 / 1994 / PL / M

DIANE ST CLAIR
High School Honeys / 1974 / SOW / M • Marilyn And The Senator / 1974 / HIF / M

DIANE STEELE *see Star Index I*

DIANE STEWART *see Alexandria Quinn*

DIANE SUMMER
Bedtime Video #02 / 1984 / GO / M

DIANE WILDE *see Star Index I*

DIANE WILLIS
Dungeon Of Lust / 197? / AVC / M

DIANE WINTERS
Bedtime Video #07 / 1984 / GO / M

DIANNA
Bus Stop Tales #14 / 1990 / PRI / M • Lesbian Pros And Amateurs #01 / 1992 / GO / F

DIANNA BAKER *see Tina Russell*

DIANNA DIAMOND
Anal Sweetheart / 1994 / ROB / M • Booty Queen / 1995 / ROB / M

DIANNA LAUREN *see Dyanna Lauren*

DIANNA LOVE
Love Roots / 1987 / LIM / M • Love Under 16 / cr75 / VST / M

DIANNA RICHARDS *see Diana Richards*

DIANNA ROSE *see Erotica*

DIANNA SPICE
Latin Plump Humpers #3 / 1995 / TTV / M

DIANNE
Canadian Beaver Hunt #1 / 1996 / PL / M • Strange Diary / 1976 / AXV / M

DIANNE AMORED
The Final Test / 197? / RLV / B

DIANNE HOLT *(Chris Hopkins, Diana Holt)*
Passable face, dark blonde, small tits, good tan lines, tight waist. Smiles but it's more like a grin.
Adult 45 #01 / 1985 / DR / C • Beyond Shame / 1980 / VEP / M • Blondes Have More Fun / 1980 / SE / M • Caballero Preview Tape #1 / 1982 / CA / C • The Executive Lady / 1980 / TOT / M • French Letters / 1984 / CA / M • High School Memories / 1980 / VCX / M • Sadie / 1980 / EVI / M • Wicked Sensations #1 / 1981 / CA / M

DIANNE RICHARDS
House On Paradise Beach / 1996 / VC / M

DIANNE SELLARS
The Liars / cr71 / AXV / M

DIANNE SLEEK
Sexhibition #3 / 1996 / SUF / M

DIANNE STEWART *see Alexandria Quinn*

DIAVIA *see Davia Ardell*

DIC TRACY
Anything Goes / 1996 / OUP / M • Betrayed / 1996 / WP / M • Chasey Loves Rocco / 1996 / VI / M • Conquest / 1996 / WP / M • Jenteal Loves Rocco / 1996 / VI / M • Lactamania #4 / 1996 / TTV / M • Nina Hartley's Guide To Swinging / 1996 / A&E / M

DICK
Dick & Jane Penetrate Paris / 1994 / AVI / M • Dick & Jane Up, Down And All Around / 1994 / AVI / M • New Faces, Hot Bodies #22 / 1996 / STP / M • Nothing Like Nurse Nookie #5 / 1996 / NIT / M • Odyssey Triple Play #46: Ass-Splitting Sex / 1993 / OD / M

DICK BOGART
Pleasures Of A Woman / 1983 / CA / M

DICK BOLLA
Bon Appetite / 1985 / TGA / C

DICK BUNCH
Insatiable Denni O' #2 / 1995 / SP / M

DICK CANDOO *see Star Index I*

DICK CASSIDY *see Rick Cassidy*

DICK DALLAS *see Star Index I*

DICK DELONG *see Star Index I*

DICK DEXTER
It Could Happen To You / 1996 / HW / M

DICK DRIPPEN
Denni O' #4: Beach Ballin' / 1996 / SP / M • Denni O' #5: / 1996 / SP / M • Seven Year Bitch / 1996 / GLI / M

DICK DUNDEE
What Women Want / 1996 / SUF / M

DICK EVERHARD
Ace In The Hole / 1995 / PL / M

DICK FITZINIT
My First Time #4 / 1996 / NS / M • Young And Anal #1 / 1995 / JMP / M

DICK FULTON *see Star Index I*

DICK GALAN *see Star Index I*

DICK GORBY *see Jordan Smith*

DICK HARDCOCK
Cyber-Sex Love Junkies / 1996 / BBE / M

DICK HOWARD *(Jeremy Stone, Mack Howard, Tim Connelly)*
Under the name Dick Howard and Mack Howard was a porn stud and graduated to being the editor of *Adam Film Word* and its derivatives under the name Jeremy Stone. Married Christy Canyon in mid 1996.
Bedtime Tales / 1985 / SE / M • Black Girls In Heat / 1985 / PL / M • Black Sister, White Brother / 1987 / AT / M • Black To Africa / 1987 / PL / C • Blowing Your Mind / 1984 / RSV / M • Brooke Does College / 1984 / VC / M • Burlexxx / 1984 / VC / M • Coming In Style / 1986 / CA / M • The Doctor's In / 1986 / CDI / M • Double Trouble / 1986 / DRV / M • Driller / 1984 / VC / M • The Ecstasy Girls #2 / 1986 / CA / M • First Annual XRCO Awards / 1984 / AVC / C • Freedom Of Choice / 1984 / VHL / M • Getting Ahead / 1983 / PL / M • Give It To Me / 1984 / SE / M • Great Sexpectations / 1984 / VC / M • Hostage Girls / 1984 / VC / M • Hypersexuals / 1984 / VC / M • Jailhouse Girls / 1984 / VC / M • Pleasure Channel / 1984 / VC / M • Pleasure Island / 1984 / AR / M • Private School Girls / 1983 / CA / M • The Return Of Johnny Wadd / 1986 / PEN / M • Rising Star / 1985 / CA / M • Satin Finish / 1985 / SUV / M • Sinners #1 / 1988 / COM / M • Sinners #2 / 1988 / COM / M • Sinners #3 / 1989 / COM / M • Sodomania: Slop Shots / 1996 / EL / C • Supergirls Do General Hospital / 1984 / VC / M • Supergirls Do The Navy / 1984 / VC / M • Turn On With Kelly Nichols / 1984 / CA / M

DICK JAMES *see Star Index I*

DICK JASON
The Erotic World Of Vanessa #1 / 1983 / VCR / C • The Erotic World Of Vanessa #2 / 1984 / VCR / C

DICK KEESTER *see Star Index I*

DICK MASTERS *see Rick Masters*

DICK NASTY (BRIT) *(Kevin (Dick Nasty), Peter London, Andy (Dick Nasty))*
Blonde British male who is a surprisingly bad actor. SO of Stephanie DuValle.
19 & Naughty #1 / 1994 / SKV / M • 19 & Naughty #2 / 1995 / SKV / M • 30 Days In The Hole / 1993 / ZA / M • 55 And Still Bangin' / 1995 / HW / M • Addicted To Lust / 1996 / NIT / M • Adults Only / 1995 / BOT / M • Adventures Of The DP Boys: At The French Riviera / 1994 / HW / M • Adventures Of The DP Boys: Back In The Bush / 1993 / HW / M • Adventures Of The DP Boys: Back In Town / 1994 / HW / M • Adventures Of The DP Boys: Backyard Boogie / 1994 / HW / M • Adventures Of The

DP Boys: D.P. Nurses / 1995 / HW / M • Adventures Of The DP Boys: Sicilian Sluts / 1995 / HW / M • Adventures Of The DP Boys: The Golden Girls / 1995 / HW / M • Adventures Of The DP Boys: The Pool Service / 1993 / HW / M • Alpine Affairs / 1995 / LE / M • Amateur Orgies #19 / 1992 / AFI / M • Amateur Orgies #30 / 1993 / AFI / M • America's Raunchiest Home Videos #14: Janet's Big Lunch / 1992 / 7A / M • America's Raunchiest Home Videos #23: Video Virgin / 1992 / ZA / M • Anal Academy / 1996 / ZA / M • Anal Alice / 1992 / AFV / M • Anal Angels #3 / 1995 / VEX / C • Anal Angels #6 / 1996 / VEX / C • Anal Asspirations / 1993 / LV / M • Anal Camera #09 / 1995 / EVN / M • Anal Explosions #2 / 1996 / NIT / M • Anal Fantasy / 1996 / SUF / M • Anal Inquisition / 1996 / ZA / M • Anal Institution #1 / 1996 / ZA / M • Anal Institution #2 / 1996 / ZA / M • Anal Institution #3 / 1996 / ZA / M • Anal Nature / 1993 / AFD / M • Anal Nitrate / 1995 / PE / M • Anal Pandemonium / 1994 / TTV / M • Anal Rippers #2: The Unveiling / 1996 / ZA / M • Anal Sex Freaks / 1996 / ZA / M • The Anal Team / 1993 / LV / M • Anal Torture / 1994 / ZA / M • Anal Variations #01 / 1993 / FH / M • Anal Variations #02 / 1993 / FH / M • Anal Virgins #01 / 1996 / NS / M • Anal Virgins Of America #01 / 1993 / FOR / M • Anal Virgins Of America #02 / 1993 / FOR / M • Anal Virgins Of America #09 / 1994 / FOR / M • Anal Virgins Of America #10 / 1994 / FOR / M • Anal Vision #20 / 1993 / LBO / M • Anal Vision #21 / 1993 / LBO / M • The Anal-Europe Series #06: Anal Luck / 1993 / LV / M • Analtown USA #03 / 1995 / NIT / M • Analtown USA #06 / 1995 / NIT / M • Analtown USA #12 / 1996 / NIT / M • Anna Malle Exposed / 1996 / WV / M • Ass, Gas & The Mystical GLOP / 1997 / EL / M • Assy #2 / 1996 / JMP / M • Attack Of The Killer Dildos / 1996 / RAS / M • Babe Wire / 1996 / HW / M • Backdoor Imports / 1995 / LV / M • Backdoor Magic / 1994 / LV / M • Backdoor To Cannes / 1993 / VC / M • Bad To The Bone / 1996 / ULP / M • Bang City #2: China's Anal Gang Bang / 1995 / SC / M • Bang City #3: Fallon's Anal Gang Bang / 1995 / SC / M • Bang City #5: Lennox's Anal Gang Bang / 1995 / SC / M • Bang City #6: Bugger's Banquet / 1995 / SC / M • Beach Bum Amateur's #06 / 1992 / MID / M • Beach Bum Amateur's #17 / 1992 / MID / M • Beach Bum Amateur's #37 / 1993 / MID / M • Beverly Hills Bikini Company / 1996 / NIT / M • Biff Malibu's Totally Nasty Home Videos #16 / 1992 / ANA / M • Biff Malibu's Totally Nasty Home Videos #24 / 1992 / ANA / M • Biff Malibu's Totally Nasty Home Videos #26 / 1992 / ANA / M • Biff Malibu's Totally Nasty Home Videos #34 / 1993 / ANA / M • The Big Bang #1 / 1993 / LV / M • The Big Bang #2 / 1994 / LV / M • The Big Bang #3 / 1994 / LV / M • Big Bust Babes #13 / 1993 / AFI / M • Big Bust Babes #24 / 1994 / AFI / M • Big Bust Babes #26 / 1995 / AFI / M • Big Murray's New-Cummers #03: Orgy 'Til Dawn / 1992 / FD / M • Big Murray's New-Cummers #04: Booty Love / 1992 / FD / M • Big Murray's New-Cummers #05: Luscious Lesbos / 1993 / FD / M • Big Murray's New-Cummers #06: Men & Women / 1993 / FD / M • Bimbette: Adventures In Anal Land / 1996 /

TEP / M • Bitches In Heat #2: On Vacation / 1995 / ZA / M • Black Babes / 1995 / LV / M • Black Babes In Heat / 1993 / VIM / M • Black Gangbangers #02 / 1995 / HW / M • Black Gangbangers #07 / 1995 / HW / M • Black Gangbangers #09 / 1995 / HW / M • Black Juice Bombs / 1996 / NIT / C • The Blonde & The Beautiful #1 / 1993 / LV / M • The Blonde & The Beautiful #2 / 1993 / LV / M • Blonde Butt Babes / 1994 / LV / M • The Blowjob Adventures Of Doctor Fellatio / 1997 / EL / M • Blue Bayou / 1993 / VC / M • Blue Moon / 1992 / AFV / M • Bobby Hollander's Rookie Nookie #04 / 1993 / SFP / M • Bobby Hollander's Rookie Nookie #05 / 1993 / SFP / M • Bobby Hollander's Rookie Nookie #08 / 1993 / SFP / M • Bobby Hollander's Sweet Cheeks #110 / 1994 / WV / M • Bodywaves / 1994 / ELP / M • The Bold, The Bald & The Beautiful / 1993 / VIM / M • Boob Acres / 1996 / HW / M • Boob Tube Lube / 1996 / RAS / M • The Bottom Line / 1995 / NIT / M • Breast Collection #04 / 1995 / LBO / C • Breast Wishes #13 / 1993 / LBO / M • Breast Wishes #14 / 1993 / LBO / M • Breast Worx #30 / 1992 / LBO / M • Brian Sparks: Virtually Unreal #2 / 1996 / ALD / M • Broken Vows / 1996 / ULP / M • Bump 'n' Grind / 1994 / HW / M • Bun Busters #01 / 1993 / LBO / M • Bun Busters #02 / 1993 / LBO / M • Bun Busters #03 / 1993 / LBO / M • Bun Busters #09 / 1993 / LBO / M • Bun Busters #11 / 1993 / LBO / M • Bun Busters #12 / 1993 / LBO / M • Bun Busters #19 / 1994 / LBO / M • Bunny Bleu: A Gang Bang Fantasy / 1994 / FC / M • Busted-D-D In Las Vegas / 1996 / LV / M • Butt Hole In-One / 1994 / AFV / M • Butt Love / 1995 / AB / M • Butt Watch #01 / 1993 / FH / M • Butt Watch #02 / 1993 / FH / M • Cabin Fever / 1995 / ERA / M • The Cable Girl / 1996 / NIT / M • Camp Beaverlake #2 / 1991 / AFV / M • Cannes 93: Broads Abroad / 1993 / ELP / M • Cannes Heat / 1992 / FD / M • The Cannes Sex Fest / 1992 / SFP / M • Career Girls / 1996 / OUP / M • Casting Call #02 / 1993 / SO / M • Casting Call #05 / 1994 / SO / M • Casting Call #08 / 1994 / SO / M • Casting Call #09 / 1996 / GO / M • Casting Call #11 / 1995 / MET / M • Casting Call #15 / 1995 / SO / M • Casting Call #16 / 1995 / SO / M • Catalina Sixty-Nine / 1991 / AR / M • The Catburglar / 1994 / PL / M • Caught From Behind #23 / 1995 / HO / M • Caught In The Act (1995-Lv) / 1995 / LV / M • Cheating Hearts / 1994 / AFI / M • Chocolate Bunnies #02 / 1995 / LBO / C • A Clockwork Orgy / 1995 / PL / M • Club DV8 #2 / 1993 / SC / M • Colossal Orgy #1 / 1993 / HW / M • Colossal Orgy #2 / 1994 / HW / M • Colossal Orgy #3 / 1994 / HW / M • The Complete & Total Anal Workout #2 / 1996 / ZA / M • Corporate Justice / 1996 / TEP / M • The Couch Trap / 1993 / ELP / M • Country Girl / 1996 / VC / M • Cousin Bubba Country Corn Porn #01 / 1994 / VIM / M • Cracklyn / 1994 / HW / M • Crimson Thighs / 1995 / HW / M • Cum Buttered Corn Holes #3 / 1996 / NIT / C • Cuntz #1 / 1994 / RTP / M • D.P. Party Tonite / 1995 / JMP / M • Da Booty Call / 1994 / HW / M • Dangerous Behinds #1 / 1995 / HW / M • Dark Passions #01 / 1993 / AFV / M • Dark Tunnels / 1994 / LV / M • Deep Dreams / 1990 / IN / M • Deep Inside The Orient /

1993 / LV / M • Deep Space 69 / 1994 / HW / M • Deep Throat #6 / 1992 / AFV / M • Deep Throat Girls #15 / 1995 / GO / M • Deep Waterworld / 1995 / HW / M • The Delegate / 1996 / RAS / M • Designer Bodies / 1993 / VI / M • Dirty & Kinky Mature Women #08 / 1996 / C69 / M • Dirty And Kinky Mature Women #3 / 1995 / C69 / M • Dirty Diner #02 / 1993 / GLI / M • Dirty Diner #03 / 1993 / GLI / M • Dirty Doc's Housecalls #01 / 1993 / LV / M • Dirty Doc's Housecalls #02 / 1993 / LV / M • Dirty Doc's Housecalls #08 / 1994 / LV / M • Dirty Doc's Housecalls #09 / 1994 / LV / M • Dirty Doc's Housecalls #10 / 1994 / LV / M • Dirty Doc's Housecalls #11 / 1994 / LV / M • Dirty Doc's Housecalls #13 / 1994 / LV / M • Dirty Doc's Housecalls #14 / 1994 / LV / M • Dirty Minds / 1996 / NIT / M • Double Crossed / 1994 / MID / M • Double Dicked #2 / 1996 / RAS / M • Double Wong Dong / 1995 / LV / M • Dp #2: The Mighty Fhucks / 1994 / FC / M • Dr Peter Proctor's House Of Anal Delights / 1996 / HO / M • The Dragon Lady #5: Tales From The Bed #4 / 1993 / WV / M • Dream House / 1995 / XPR / M • Escape From Anal Lost Angels / 1996 / HO / M • Eskimo Gang Bang / 1994 / HW / M • Eternal Bliss / 1990 / AFV / M • Euro-Max #1: Frisky In France / 1995 / SC / M • Euro-Max #2. Cream n' Euro Sluts / 1995 / SC / M • Euro-Max #3: / 1995 / SC / M • Euro-Max #4: / 1995 / SC / M • Every Granny Has A Fantasy / 1996 / GLI / M • Exstasy / 1995 / WV / M • The Fanny Farm / 1996 / NIT / M • The Farmer's Daughters / 1994 / LV / M • Fashion Sluts #4 / 1995 / ABS / M • Filthy Sleazy Scoundrels / 1994 / HW / M • Fire & Ice: Caught In The Act / 1995 / WP / M • For Your Mouth Only / 1995 / GO / M • Forbidden / 1996 / SC / M • Foxxxy Lady / 1992 / HW / M • French Open / 1995 / PV / M • French Twist / 1996 / HO / M • The French Way / 1994 / HOV / M • Fresh Faces #05 / 1995 / EVN / M • Fresh Faces #09 / 1996 / EVN / M • Fuck U: Girls Of The Packed-10 / 1995 / ZA / M • Gang Bang Bitches #01 / 1994 / PP / M • Gang Bang Bitches #02 / 1994 / PP / M • Gang Bang Bitches #03 / 1994 / PP / M • Gang Bang Bitches #04 / 1995 / PP / M • Gang Bang Bitches #10 / 1995 / PP / M • Gang Bang Diaries #3 / 1994 / SFP / M • Gang Bang In Vedova / 1995 / WIV / M • Gangbang Girl #09 / 1993 / ANA / M • Gangbang Girl #10 / 1993 / ANA / M • Gangbang Girl #11 / 1993 / ANA / M • Gangbang Girl #14 / 1994 / ANA / M • Gangbang Girl #16 / 1995 / ANA / M • Gangbang Girl #17 / 1995 / ANA / M • Gazongas Galore #1 / 1996 / NIT / C • The Girls From Hootersville #07 / 1994 / SFP / M • Girlz N The Hood #5 / 1995 / HW / M • Glitz Tits #04 / 1992 / GLI / M • Glitz Tits #06 / 1993 / GLI / M • Golden Rod / 1996 / SPI / M • Guttman's Hollywood Adventure / 1993 / PL / M • Guttman's Paris Vacation / 1993 / PL / M • Hardcore Confidential #1 / 1996 / TEP / M • Hardcore Fantasies #1 / 1996 / LV / M • Hardcore Fantasies #3 / 1996 / LV / M • Hardcore Fantasies #5 / 1996 / LV / M • Haunting Dreams #2 / 1993 / LV / M • Heavy Breathing / 1996 / NIT / M • Henry's Big Boob Adventure / 1996 / HO / M • Hidden Camera #13 / 1994 / JMP / M • The Hitch-Hiker #01: Wide Open Spaces / 1993 / WMG / M •

The Hitch-Hiker #08: On The Trail / 1994 / WMG / M • The Hitch-Hiker #16: Dirty Low Down / 1996 / VIM / M • Ho' Style Takeover / 1993 / FH / M • Hollywood '94: Butts Abound / 1993 / ELP / M • Hollywood Amateurs #07 / 1994 / MID / M • Hollywood Amateurs #09 / 1994 / MID / M • Hollywood Amateurs #17 / 1995 / MID / M • Hollywood Swingers #08 / 1993 / LBO / M • Hooters And The Blowjobs / 1996 / HW / M • Horny Henry's Euro Adventure / 1995 / TTV / M • Horny Henry's French Adventure / 1994 / TTV / M • Horny Henry's London Adventure / 1995 / TTV / M • Horny Henry's Oriental Adventure / 1994 / TTV / M • Horny Henry's Peeping Adventures / 1994 / TTV / M • Horny Henry's Snowballing Adventure / 1995 / TTV / M • Horny Henry's Strange Adventure / 1995 / TTV / M • Horny Henry's Swinging Adventures / 1994 / TTV / M • Hot Diamond / 1995 / LE / M • Hot Leather #1 / 1995 / GO / M • Hotel Guard / 1995 / WIV / M • Hotel Sodom #06 / 1995 / SNA / M • House Of Anal / 1995 / NOT / M • House Of Sex #04: Banging Menette / 1994 / RTP / M • House Of Sex #16: Dirty Oral Three Ways / 1994 / RTP / M • Howard Sperm's Private Parties / 1994 / LBO / M • Humpkin Pie / 1995 / HW / M • The Hunt / 1996 / ULP / M • In X-Cess / 1994 / LV / M • In Your Face #3 / 1995 / PL / M • In Your Face #4 / 1996 / PL / M • Indecent Proposition / 1993 / LV / M • Inspector Croissant: The Case Of The Missing Pinky / 1995 / FC / M • Interracial Affairs / 1996 / FC / M • Interview's Anal Queens / 1996 / LV / M • Interview's Big Boob Bonanza / 1996 / LV / M • Interview's Hard Bodied Harlots / 1996 / LV / M • Interview: Bun Busters / 1995 / LV / M • Interview: Chocolate Treats / 1995 / LV / M • Interview: Dark And Delicious / 1996 / LV / M • Interview: Doin' The Butt / 1995 / LV / M • Interview: Naturals / 1995 / LV / M • Interview: New And Natural / 1995 / LV / M • Ir4: Inrearendence Day / 1996 / HW / M • It Happened At Midnight / 1990 / IN / M • The Joy Dick Club / 1994 / MID / M • Kimberly Kupps Gets 5 A's / 1996 / NIT / M • Interviews #05 / 1994 / IP / M • Kinky Debutante Interviews #06 / 1994 / IP / M • Kool Ass / 1996 / BOT / M • Lady Luck / 1995 / PMV / M • The Last Action Whore / 1993 / LV / M • Latin Fever #3 / 1996 / C69 / M • Lessons 'n' Love / 1994 / LBO / M • Lessons In Love / 1995 / SPI / M • A Little Bit Pregnant / 1995 / SO / M • Lockdown / 1996 / NIT / M • Lollipops #1 / 1996 / SC / M • Lollipops #2 / 1996 / SC / M • Lonely And Blue / 1990 / VEX / M • The Look / 1993 / WP / M • Loose Jeans / 1996 / GO / M • Love Potion 69 / 1994 / VC / M • Lovebone Invasion / 1993 / PL / M • Maid Service / 1993 / FL / M • Main Course / 1992 / FL / M • Major Fucking Whore / 1995 / BEP / M • Mall Slut / 1997 / SC / M • Mammary Manor / 1992 / BTO / M • The Man Who Loved Women / 1993 / SC / M • Mechanics Bi Day, Lube Job Bi Night / 1995 / SP0 / G • Middle Aged Maidens / 1995 / GLI / M • Midnight Caller / 1992 / MID / M • Mike Hott: #221 Horny Couples #09 / 1992 / MHV / M • Mike Hott: #244 Horny Couples #14 / 1993 / MHV / M • Mike Hott: #257 Cunt of the Month: Selina / 1993 / MHV / M • Mike Hott: #258 Horny Couples #16 /

1994 / MHV / M • Mike Hott: #267 Cunt of the Month: Nikki Tee / 1994 / MHV / M • Mike Hott: #268 Cum In My Mouth #01 / 1994 / MHV / C • Mike Hott: #271 Cunt of the Month: Rebecca / 1994 / MHV / M • Mike Hott: #272 Jack Off On My Cunt #01 / 1994 / MHV / M • Mike Hott: #277 Cum In My Cunt #2 / 1994 / MHV / M • Mike Hott: #280 Horny Couples #18 / 1995 / MHV / M • Mike Hott: #282 Three-Sum Sluts #01 / 1995 / MHV / M • Mike Hott: #287 Bonus Cunt: Brooke Dunn / 1995 / MHV / M • Mike Hott: #288 Cunt of the Month: Stephanie / 1995 / MHV / M • Mike Hott: #289 Three-Sum Sluts #02 / 1995 / MHV / M • Mike Hott: #298 Bonus Cunt: Candy Connor / 1995 / MHV / M • Mike Hott: #301 Three-Sum Sluts #04 / 1995 / MHV / M • Mike Hott: #304 Cunt of the Month: Briannon / 1995 / MHV / M • Mike Hott: #314 Cum In My Cunt #05 / 1995 / MHV / M • Mike Hott: #315 Cum In My Mouth #02 / 1995 / MHV / C • Mike Hott: #316 Cunt Of The Month: Liza Harper / 1995 / MHV / M • Mike Hott: #323 Three-Sum Sluts #07 / 1995 / MHV / M • Mike Hott: #324 Cum In My Cunt #06 / 1995 / MHV / C • Mike Hott: #325 Bonus Cunt: Shonna Lynn / 1995 / MHV / M • Mike Hott: #336 Three-Sum Sluts #09 / 1995 / MHV / M • Mike Hott: #339 Cum In My Mouth #04 / 1996 / MHV / C • Mike Hott: #341 Bonus Cunt: Julia / 1995 / MHV / M • Mike Hott: #345 Cum In My Cunt #07 / 1995 / MHV / C • Mike Hott: #349 Girls Who Swallow Cum #03 / 1996 / MHV / C • Mike Hott: #351 Three-Sum Sluts #11 / 1996 / MHV / M • Mike Hott: #354 Three-Sum Sluts #12 / 1996 / MHV / M • Mike Hott: #356 Girls Who Lap Cum From Cunts #01 / 1996 / MHV / M • Mike Hott: #358 Cunt Of The Month: Chardonnay / 1996 / MHV / M • Mike Hott: #359 Bonus Cunt: Sophia Rio / 1996 / MHV / M • Mike Hott: #360 Cum In My Cunt #08 / 1995 / MHV / C • Mike Hott: #361 Girls Who Swallow Cum #04 / 1996 / MHV / C • Mike Hott: #367 Girls Who Lap Cum From Cunts #02 / 1996 / MHV / M • Mike Hott: #368 Three-Sum Sluts #13 / 1996 / MHV / M • Mike Hott: #369 Cum In My Mouth #05 / 1996 / MHV / C • Mike Hott: #370 Cunt Of The Month: Chloe Nicole / 1996 / MHV / M • Mike Hott: #371 Horny Couples #19 / 1996 / MHV / M • Mike Hott: #373 Three-Sum Sluts #14 / 1996 / MHV / M • Mike Hott: #379 Three-Sum Sluts #15 / 1996 / MHV / M • Mike Hott: #380 Girls Who Lap Cum From Cunts #03 / 1996 / MHV / C • Mike Hott: #384 Three-Sum Sluts #16 / 1996 / MHV / M • Mike Hott: #386 / 1996 / MHV / M • Mike Hott: #387 Girls Who Lap Cum From Cunts #04 / 1996 / MHV / M • Mike Hott: #393 / 1996 / MHV / M • Mister Stickypants / 1996 / LV / M • The Most Dangerous Game / 1996 / HO / M • Mr. Peepers Amateur Home Videos #39: Cumming In Colors / 1992 / LBO / M • Mr. Peepers Amateur Home Videos #46: A Schnitzel In The Bush / 1992 / LBO / M • Mr. Peepers Amateur Home Videos #48: Dialing For Services / 1992 / LBO / M • Mr. Peepers Amateur Home Videos #55: Anal Antics / 1992 / LBO / M • Mr. Peepers Amateur Home Videos #56: Hindsight Is Brownish / 1992 / LBO / M • Mr. Peepers Amateur Home Videos #60: The Backdoor Is Open / 1992

/ LBO / M • Mr. Peepers Amateur Home Videos #62: Private Pussy Party / 1992 / LBO / M • Mr. Peepers Amateur Home Videos #66: Ready In Red / z993 / LBO / M • Mr. Peepers Amateur Home Videos #78: She Dreams Of Weenie / 1993 / LBO / M • Mr. Peepers Amateur Home Videos #81: It Beats A Rosy Palm / 1993 / LBO / M • Mr. Peepers Amateur Home Videos #82: Born To Swing! / 1993 / LBO / M • Musical Bedrooms / 1993 / AFV / M • Mysteria / 1995 / NIT / M • Naked Scandal #1 / 1995 / SPI / M • Naked Scandal #2 / 1996 / SPI / M • Nasty Newcummers #12 / 1995 / MET / M • Nasty Nymphos #02 / 1994 / ANA / M • Nasty Nymphos #07 / 1994 / ANA / M • Nasty Nymphos #09 / 1995 / ANA / M • Naughty / 1996 / LV / M • Naughty Senorita / 1994 / WIV / M • Neighborhood Slut / 1996 / LV / M • Neighborhood Watch #19 / 1992 / LBO / M • Neighborhood Watch #25: / 1992 / LBO / M • Neighborhood Watch #27 / 1992 / LBO / M • Neighborhood Watch #30 / 1992 / LBO / M • Neighborhood Watch #39: / 1993 / LBO / M • The New Ass Masters #11 / 1996 / LEI / C • The New Ass Masters #15 / 1996 / LEI / C • The New Butt Hunt #19 / 1996 / LEI / C • New Girls In Town #7 / 1994 / CC / M • New Pussy Hunt #24 / 1996 / LEI / C • The New Snatch Masters #14 / 1995 / LEI / C • The New Snatch Masters #20 / 1996 / LEI / C • The New Snatch Masters #22 / 1996 / LEI / C • Nice Fuckin' Movie / 1997 / EL / M • Nookie Ranch / 1996 / NIT / M • Nudist Colony Vacation / 1996 / NIT / M • Nydp Pink / 1994 / HW / M • The Nympho Files / 1995 / NIT / M • Nympho Zombie Coeds / 1993 / VIM / M • Old Bitches / 1996 / GLI / M • Ona Zee's Black Label #1: Sex Hunger / 1996 / ONA / C • Once Upon An Anus / 1993 / LV / M • One Night In The Valley / 1996 / CA / M • Oriental Gang Bang / 1995 / HO / M • Oriental Sorority Secrets / 1992 / VIM / M • Other People's Pussy / 1993 / LV / M • Our Bang #10 / 1993 / GLI / M • Over Exposed / 1996 / ULP / M • Over Forty Gang Bang / 1994 / RTP / M • Peekers / 1993 / MID / M • Penetrator #2: Grudge Day / 1995 / PL / M • Perverted #3: The Parents / 1995 / ZA / M • Perverted Stories #04 / 1995 / JMP / M • Perverted Stories #09 / 1996 / JMP / M • Peyton's Place / 1996 / ULP / M • Pick Up Lines #10 / 1997 / OD / M • Pierced Punctured And Perverted / 1995 / FC / M • Pleasure Dome: The Genesis Chamber / 1994 / AFV / M • Point Of Entry / 1996 / WP / M • Positively Pagan #02 / 1991 / ATA / M • Positively Pagan #04 / 1991 / ATA / M • Positively Pagan #07 / 1993 / ATA / M • Positively Pagan #11 / 1993 / ATA / M • Positively Pagan #12 / 1993 / ATA / M • Prime Choice #6 / 1996 / RAS / M • Private Label / 1993 / GLI / M • Private Video Magazine #03 / 1993 / OD / M • Private Video Magazine #16 / 1994 / OD / M • Profiles #01 / 1995 / XPR / M • Profiles #03: House Dick / 1995 / XPR / M • Profiles #08: Triple Ecstacy / 1996 / XPR / M • Pudsucker / 1994 / MID / M • Pumps In Da Rump #2 / 1996 / HW / M • Puritan Video Magazine #01 / 1996 / LE / M • Q Balls #1 / 1996 / TTV / M • Racially Motivated / 1994 / LV / M • Raincoat Fantasies / 1993 / ELP / M • Raunchy Porno Picture Show / 1992 / FC /

M • Raunchy Remedy / 1993 / ELP / M • Raw Talent: Bang 'er 05 Times / 1991 / RTP / M • Ready To Drop #06 / 1995 / FC / M • Ready To Drop #09 / 1995 / FC / M • Ready To Drop #11 / 1996 / FC / M • Ready To Drop #12 / 1996 / FC / M • The Real Deal #1 / 1994 / FC / M • Rear Window / 1996 / NIT / M • Rears In Windows / 1993 / FH / M • The Rehearsal / 1993 / VC / M • Rituals / 1003 / SC / M • Riviera Heat / 1993 / FD / M • Roller Babes / 1996 / ERA / M • Roly Poly Gang Bang / 1995 / HW / M • Roxy Rider Is In Control / 1996 / NIT / M • Rump Man: Forever / 1995 / HW / M • Rump Man: Goes To Cannes / 1995 / HW / M • Rump Man: Sex On The Beach / 1995 / HW / M • Rump-Shaker #3 / 1994 / HW / M • Rump-Shaker #4 / 1995 / HW / M • Rump-Shaker #5 / 1996 / HW / M • Rumpman In And Out Of Africa / 1996 / HW / M • Rumpman's Backdoor Sailing / 1996 / HW / M • Rumpman: Caught In An Anal Avalanche / 1995 / HW / M • Russian Roulette / 1995 / NIT / M • Samantha & Company / 1996 / PL / M • Sarah's Inheritance / 1995 / WIV / M • Satyriasis / 1995 / PL / M • Savannah R.N. / 1992 / HW / M • The Scam / 1996 / LV / M • Secret Diary #1 / 1994 / TAW / M • The Secret Life Of Herbert Dingle / 1994 / TTV / M • Sensations #1 / 1996 / SC / M • Sensations #2 / 1996 / SC / M • Sex Circus / 1994 / VIM / M • Sex Drives Of The Rich And Famous / 1996 / ERA / M • Sex Fugitives / 1993 / LE / M • Sex On The Beach Hawaiian Style #1 / 1995 / ULP / M • Sex Police 2000 / 1992 / AFV / M • Sexophrenia / 1993 / VC / M • Sexorcist / 1994 / HW / M • Sexperiment / 1996 / ULP / M • Shaving Grace / 1996 / GO / M • Shaving Mr. One Eye / 1996 / FC / M • Show & Tell / 1994 / ELP / M • Sinboy #3: The Island Of Dr. Moron / 1996 / SC / M • Sittin' On Da Krome / 1995 / HW / M • Skeezers / 1996 / LV / M • Sleeping With Seattle / 1993 / LV / M • Sneek Peeks #1 / 1993 / FL / M • Sneek Peeks #2 / 1993 / OCV / M • Soap Me Up! / 1993 / FD / M • Soap Opera Sluts / 1996 / AFI / M • The Social Club / 1995 / LE / M • Sodom Chronicles / 1995 / FH / M • Some Like It Wet / 1995 / LE / M • Sorority Sluts Passed Out / 1995 / ZA / M • The Spa / 1996 / RAS / M • Star Struck / 1991 / AFV / M • Starbangers #08 / 1996 / FPI / M • Steam / 1996 / ULP / M • Steele Butt / 1993 / AFV / M • Street Fantasies / 1993 / AFV / M • Studio Bust Out / 1994 / BTO / M • Stuff Your Ass #2 / 1995 / JMP / M • Stuff Your Ass #3 / 1996 / JMP / M • Stuff Your Face #2 / 1995 / JMP / M • Subway / 1994 / SC / M • Superstar Sex Challenge #1 / 1994 / VC / M • Superstar Sex Challenge #3 / 1994 / VC / M • Surf Babes / 1995 / LE / M • Surfin' The Net / 1996 / RAS / M • Sweat 'n' Bullets / 1995 / MID / M • Sweet Black Cherries #1 / 1996 / TTV / M • Tail Taggers #109 / 1993 / WV / M • Tail Taggers #128: / 1994 / WV / M • Tails Of Desire / 1995 / GO / M • Talking Trash #1 / 1995 / HW / M • The Teacher's Pet / 1993 / LV / M • This Could Be The Night / 1993 / IF / M • This Girl Is Freaky / 1996 / NIT / M • Tight Fit #08 / 1994 / GO / M • Tight Fit #11 / 1995 / GO / M • Tight Fit #13 / 1995 / GO / M • Tight Fit #15 / 1996 / GO / M • Tinsel Town Tales / 1995 / NOT / M • Titan's Amateur Video

Magazine #03 / 1995 / TEG / M • Titty City #1 / 1995 / TIW / M • Titty City #2 / 1995 / TIW / C • Titty Town #1 / 1994 / HW / M • Titty Town #2 / 1995 / HW / M • Too Hot / 1996 / LV / M • Triple Penetration Debutante Sluts #1 / 1996 / BAC / M • Trouble In Paradise / 1996 / ULP / M • Twists Of The Heart / 1995 / NIT / M • Ultimate Anal Gang Bang #3 / 1995 / HW / M • Ultimate Gang Bang #1 / 1994 / HW / M • Ultimate Orgy #3 / 1992 / GLI / M • Unbalanced Chemicals / 1996 / SUF / M • Velvet / 1995 / SPI / M • Video Virgins #06 / 1993 / NS / M • Video Virgins #15 / 1994 / NS / M • Video Virgins #23 / 1995 / NS / M • Waterworld Deep / 1995 / HW / M • Wet Daydreams / 1996 / XCI / M • What Women Want / 1996 / SUF / M • What's Butt Got To Do With It? / 1993 / HW / M • White Stockings / 1994 / BHS / M • Wicked Thoughts / 1992 / PL / M • Wild Orgies #11 / 1994 / AFI / M • Wild Orgies #17 / 1995 / AFI / M • Witchcraft 2000 / 1994 / GLI / M • The Worst Porno Ever Made With The Best Sex / 1993 / PL / M • The Wright Stuff / 1991 / AFV / M • Xxxanadu / 1994 / HW / M • Yin Yang Oriental Love Bang #1 / 1996 / SUF / M • Young And Anal #2 / 1995 / JMP / M • Young And Anal #3 / 1995 / JMP / M • Young Tails / 1996 / LV / M • Zena's Gang Bang / 1995 / HO / M

DICK NASTY (MALIBU) see Biff Malibu

DICK NASTY (S/M)
Dragon Lady / 1995 / SP0 / G

DICK NASTY (W. LONG) see Woody Long

DICK PAYNE
A Dirty Western #1 / 1973 / AR / M • Saturday Matinee Series #3 / 1996 / VCX / C • That's Erotic / 1979 / CV / C

DICK POLE see Al Poe

DICK POWERS
Bi Dream Of Genie / 1994 / BIL / G • Girls Come Too / 1963 / SOW / S • Little Shop Of She-Males / 1994 / HSV / G

DICK RAMBONE
Angels Of Mercy / 1985 / HO / M • Baby Face #2 / 1987 / VC / M • Backdoor Brides #1 / 1985 / PV / M • Best Of Caught From Behind #1 / 1987 / HO / C • Bloopers, Butts And Bloopers #1 / 1990 / HO / M • Caught From Behind #04: Nasty Young Girls / 1985 / HO / M • Caught From Behind #12 / 1989 / HO / M • Cavalcade Of Stars / 1985 / VCR / C • Double Penetration #1 / 1985 / WV / M • Double Penetration #2 / 1986 / WV / C • Dr Penetration / 1986 / WET / M • Erotic Penetration / 1987 / HO / C • Honeybuns #2: Grecian Formula / 1987 / WV / C • Let's Get It On With Amber Lynn / 1986 / VC / M • Love Scenes For Loving Couples / 1987 / CV / C • Only The Best Of Oral / 1989 / CV / C • Play Me Again, Vanessa / 1986 / VC / M • Rambone Does Hollywood / 1986 / WET / M • Rambone The Destroyer / 1985 / WET / M • Rambone Meets The Double Penetrators / 1987 / WET / M • Sex Star Competition / 1985 / PL / M • Shane's World #3 / 1996 / OD / M • Sins Of The Wealthy #1 / 1986 / CLV / M • Taxi Girls #2: In Search Of Toni / 1986 / ELD / M • White Bun Busters / 1985 / VC / M • Wild Things #2 / 1986 / CV / M

DICK RANGER see Star Index I

DICK SHARP see Star Index I

DICK SHERMAN see Star Index I

DICK TRICK
She-Male Encounters #21: Psychic She Males / 1994 / MET / G

DICK TURPIN see Star Index I

DICK WACKER
Kinky Debutante Interviews #02 / 1994 / IP / M • Kinky Debutante Interviews #03 / 1994 / IP / M

DICKY
Bi-Bi Love Amateurs #2 / 1993 / SFP / G

DICKY WHIPT
She Male Sluts / 1995 / KDP / G

DIDI
AVP #6969: Lights, Camera, Sexation / 1990 / AVP / M

DIDI WELLER
Bedside Brat / 1988 / VI / M

DIDIER
Adultress / 1995 / WIV / M

DIDIER AUBRICOT
[Je Brule De Partout / 1978 / ... / M

DIEDRA CARRERA
Disciplz Of Pain / 1995 / ZFX / B

DIEDRA CHLOE
More Dirty Debutantes #08 / 1991 / 4P / M

DIEDRA JAMES
Cream Pies #02 / 1993 / ZA / M

DIEDRE BLACK
Cheeks #2: The Bitter End / 1989 / CC / M

DIEDRE CARRERA
Innocent Exile / 1995 / ZFX / B

DIEDRE HOLLAND *(Deedra Holland, Martine Anuszek, Deidre Holland, Martine Helene, Valerie Stone)*

Passable face, lithe body, small/medium tits. Dutch, but imported from Australia after appearing in several of John Bone's productions. Married to Jon Dough in 1992 but divorced in 1994. In her last few movies she has had her tits enhanced to rock solid cantaloupes.

Aussie Bloopers / 1993 / OD / M • Aussie Vice / 1989 / PM / M • Australian Connection / 1989 / PM / M • Bad Habits / 1993 / VC / M • Beat The Heat / 1990 / VI / M • Behind Closed Doors / 1990 / VI / M • Best Of Diedre Holland / 1990 / PM / C • The Better Sex Video Series #1: The Better Sex Basics / 1991 / LEA / M • The Better Sex Video Series #2: Advanced Sex Techniques / 1991 / LEA / M • Beverly Hills 90269 / 1992 / LV / M • The Bigger They Come / 1993 / VD / C • The Blonde & The Beautiful #1 / 1993 / LV / M • The Blonde & The Beautiful #2 / 1993 / LV / M • Blonde Ice #2 / 1993 / EX / M • Bloopers (Video Team) / 1994 / VT / M • Blue Bayou / 1993 / VC / M • Bushwackers / 1990 / PM / M • Busted / 1992 / HO / M • Chameleons: Not The Sequel / 1991 / VC / M • City Of Sin / 1991 / LV / M • Deception / 1991 / XCI / M • Deep Inside Deidre Holland / 1993 / VC / C • Deep Throat #6 / 1992 / AFV / M • Dick Tracer / 1990 / PM / M • Diedre In Danger / 1990 / VI / M • Double Crossed / 1994 / MID / M • Elements Of Desire / 1994 / ULI / M • Eleventh Annual AVN Awards / 1994 / VC / M • Endangered / 1992 / PP / M • The Erotic Adventures Of The Three Musketeers / 1992 / CEL / S • Everybody's Playmates / 1992 / CA / C • Foreign Affairs / 1992 / VT / C • Forever Yours / 1992 / CDI / M • Frankie And Joanie / 1991 / HW / M • Full Throttle Girls: Boredom Pulled The Trigger / 1993 / VIM / M • The Girls' Club / 1993 / VD / C • The Good, The Bed, And

The Snuggly / 1993 / ZA / M • Hidden Obsessions / 1992 / BFP / M • Hot Sweet 'n' Sticky / 1992 / CA / C • House Of Dreams / 1990 / CA / M • I'm Too Sexy / 1992 / CA / M • Images Of Desire / 1990 / PM / M • Killer Looks / 1991 / VI / M • Let's Party / 1993 / VC / M • Lusty Dusty / 1990 / VI / M • The Maddams Family / 1991 / XCI / M • Malcolm Meadows P.I. / 1994 / VIM / M • Masterpiece / 1990 / VI / M • Midsummer Love Story / 1993 / WV / M • Mind Trips / 1992 / FH / M • Night And Day #1 / 1993 / VT / M • Only The Best Of The Erotic Eighties / 1992 / VC / C • Only The Very Best On Film / 1992 / VC / C • The Other Woman / 1992 / IMP / S • Pajama Party / 1993 / CV / C • Penthouse: Fast Cars, Fantasy Women / 1992 / PET / F • Penthouse: Satin & Lace #1 / 1992 / PET / F • Phone Sex Girls: Australia / 1989 / PM / M • Play Me / 1989 / VI / M • Princess Orgasma #1 / 1991 / PP / M • A Private Love Affair / 1996 / IP / M • A Pussy Called Wanda #1 / 1992 / DR / M • A Pussy Called Wanda #2 / 1992 / DR / M • Raunch #04: Silver Melts / 1991 / CC / M • Rebel / 1991 / ZA / M • Rhapsody / 1993 / VT / M • Rockin' The Boat / 1990 / VI / M • Secrets / 1990 / CA / M • Sensual Exposure / 1993 / ULI / M • The Serpent's Dream / 1993 / VC / M • Sex #1 (Vca) / 1994 / VC / M • Sex #2: Fate (Vca) / 1995 / VC / M • Sin City: The Movie / 1992 / SC / M • The Starlet / 1991 / PP / M • Student Nurses / 1991 / CA / M • Surrogate Lover / 1992 / TP / M • The Tantric Guide To Sexual Potency And Extended Orgasm / 1994 / A&E / M • Tenth Annual Adult Video News Awards / 1993 / VC / M • Things Change / 1992 / MET / M • Things Change #1: My First Time / 1992 / CV / M • Things Change #2: Letting Go / 1992 / CV / M • The Three Musketeers #1 / 1992 / FD / M • The Three Musketeers #2 / 1992 / FD / M • Tongue In Cheek #01 / 1995 / HO / C • Totally Naked / 1994 / VC / M • True Blue / 1989 / PM / M • True Legends Of Adult Cinema: The Cult Superstars / 1993 / VC / C • True Legends Of Adult Cinema: The Erotic Eighties / 1992 / VC / C • Unfinished 1994 / PV / M • The Uptown Girl / 1992 / ZA / M • Veil / 1990 / VI / M • Voices In My Bed / 1993 / VI / M • Where The Boys Aren't #2 / 1989 / VI / F • Wishful Thinking / 1992 / VC / M • The Women / 1993 / CAT / F • WPINK-TV #4 / 1993 / PV / M • WPINK-TV #5 / 1993 / PV / M • Wrapped Up / 1992 / VD / C • X-Rated Blondes / 1992 / VD / C • [Down Under / 1989 / ... / M • [Full Throttle Girls #2 / 1993 / VIM / M • [Wet And Wild Ones / 1993 / VIM / C

DIEDRE HOPKINS *(Deidre Hopkins, Desiree Hopkins)*
Bi-Coastal / 1985 / LAV / G • Dear Fanny / 1984 / CV / M • Double Standards / 1986 / VC / M • Free And Foxy / 1986 / VCX / C • Let Me Tell Ya 'Bout White Chicks / 1985 / VC / M • Little American Maid / 1987 / VCX / M • Palomino Heat / 1985 / COM / F • Samurai Dick / 1984 / VC / M • Street Heat / 1984 / VC / M • Video Store Vixens / 1986 / PL / M

DIEDRE O'RDURE
African Angels #1 / 1996 / NIT / M • Hard Cum Cafe / 1996 / BCP / M

DIENA
Homegrown Video #075 / 1990 / HOV / M

• Homegrown Video #079 / 1990 / HOV / M
• Homegrown Video #094 / 1990 / HOV / M
• Homegrown Video #112 / 1990 / HOV / M
• Homegrown Video #168 / 1990 / HOV / M
• HomeGrown Video #458: Cream Pie For Dessert / 1995 / HOV / C • HomeGrown Video #468: Lust American Style / 1996 / HOV / C

DIETER GROEST
[Krankenschwestern-Report / 1972 / … / M

DIGNA A. RAY
Flipside: A Backdoor Adventure / 1985 / CV / M • Ultrasex / 1987 / VC / M

DIJANA *(Jenna (Dijana), Jeanna (Dijana))*
A Rene Summers look-alike. Big girl, chubby body, large natural tits, marginal face, very curly long brown/sandy hair, young looking.
Cheek To Cheek / 1997 / EL / M • Intense Perversions #4 / 1996 / PL / M

DILLON
Cat Walk / 1994 / KBR / S • Hypno Sex / 1996 / ZA / M • Hypnosex / 1996 / ZA / M • New Girls In Town #4 / 1993 / CC / M • Nurse's Schoolgirl Enema / 1990 / BIZ / B

DIMILLA
Anabolic Import #07: Anal X / 1995 / ANA / M

DIMITRI
Russian Model Magazine #2 / 1996 / IP / M

DINA
Blue Vanities #527 / 1993 / FFL / M • Breast Of Britain #3 / 1987 / BTO / M • Breast Of Britain #4 / 1990 / BTO / S • Fresh Meat (John Leslie) #3 / 1996 / EA / M • Midnight Angels #03 / 1993 / MID / F • Oral Majority #03 / 1986 / WV / C

DINA DELICIOUS see Star Index I

DINA DEVILLE *(Dana DeVille, Annie Cross)*
Nice looking blonde with small too-firm tits, tight waist and a narrow hips who was married to Steve Drake at one stage.
Barbara The Barbarian / 1987 / SE / M • California Gigolo / 1987 / VD / M • The Dinner Party / 1986 / WV / M • Fantasy Chamber / 1987 / VT / M • Good Vibrations / 1991 / PM / M • HHHHot! TV #2 / 1988 / CDI / M • Liquid Love / 1988 / CA / M • Lust Weekend / 1987 / CA / M • Peggy Sue / 1987 / VT / M • Phone Sex Girls #2 / 1987 / VT / M • Private Encounters / 1987 / SE / M • Sweet Things / 1987 / VC / M • Wet Weekend / 1987 / MAC / M

DINA FLEM see Star Index I

DINA PEARL *(Andrea (Dina), Andrea Csepke)*
Hungarian, 20 years old in 1996, de-virginized at 14, short blonde hair, passable face, black eyebrows, medium enhanced cantaloupes, lithe body, nice little butt and a nice smile.
The Coming Of Nikita / 1995 / EL / M • The Fatal Bet / 1996 / VTV / M • Gangbang Girl #18 / 1996 / ANA / M • Hamlet: For The Love Of Ophelia #1 / 1996 / IP / M • Lil' Women: Grand Prix Holiday / 1996 / EUR / M • Lil' Women: Vacation / 1996 / EUR / M • Nasty Nymphos #15 / 1996 / ANA / M • Operation Sex / 1996 / XC / M • Paradise Villa / 1995 / WIV / M • Private Video Magazine #16 / 1994 / OD / M • Puritan Video Magazine #07 / 1996 / LE / M • Seduction Italiano / 1995 / WIV / M • Skin #5: The 5th Column / 1996 / ERQ / M • Sodomania: Slop Shots / 1996 / EL / C • The Thief, The

Girl & The Detective / 1996 / HDE / M • Triple X Video Magazine #03 / 1995 / OD / M • Up Your Ass #2 / 1996 / ANA / M • World Sex Tour #3 / 1995 / ANA / M • [Assassins Of The Danube / 1996 / … / M • [Der Kronzeuge / 1996 / … / M • [The Girl, The Thief & The Detective / 1996 / … / M • [Triangolo Mortale / 1996 / … / M

DINA RICE see Lacey Logan

DINAMIT
The Betrayal Of Innocence #1: The Awakening Of Marika / 1993 / CC / M • The Betrayal Of Innocence #2: The Decadence / 1993 / CC / M • The Betrayal Of Innocence #3: The Choice / 1993 / CC / M • Nasty Travel Tails #01 / 1993 / CC / M

DINKY DORA see Dora Dice

DINO see Wayne Summers

DINO ALBA see Wayne Summers

DINO ALEXANDER
Cupid's Arrow / 1984 / VCR / M • Dear Fanny / 1984 / CV / M • Dirty Shary / 1985 / VD / M • Double Standards / 1986 / VC / M • Erotica Jones / 1985 / AVC / M • Free And Foxy / 1986 / VCX / C • Garter Charter Tours / 1986 / AVC / M • The Girl With The Hungry Eyes / 1984 / ECS / M • Hot Buns / 1983 / VCX / M • The Hottest Show In Town / 1987 / VIP / M • The Idol / 1985 / WV / M • Intimate Couples / 1984 / VCX / M • Layover / 1985 / HO / M • Little American Maid / 1987 / VCX / M • Little Girls Of The Streets / 1984 / CV / M • Little Girls, Dirty Desires / 1984 / JVV / M • On Golden Blonde / 1984 / PV / M • Oral Majority #01 / 1986 / WV / C • The Other Side Of Lianna / 1984 / LA / M • Passionate Lee / 1984 / CRE / M • Princess Charming / 1987 / AVC / C • Rich Bitch / 1985 / HO / M • Sexual Pursuit / 1985 / AT / M • Teenage Games / 1985 / HO / M • Video Guide To Sexual Positions / 1984 / JVV / M • Vote Pink / 1984 / VD / M • You Make Me Wet / 1985 / SVE / M

DINO BAKER
The Rod Garetto Story / 1995 / FC / C

DINO DIMARCO
Lost In Vegas / 1996 / AWV / G • My Sister's Husband / 1996 / AWV / G • Night Walk / 1995 / HIV / G

DINO PHILLIPS
Please Don't Tell / 1995 / CEN / G • Score Of Sex / 1995 / BAC / G

DION WATSON
More To Love #1 / 1994 / TTV / M

DIONNA CASTRO see Star Index I

DIONNE WORSHIP
She-Male Encounters #21: Psychic She Males / 1994 / MET / G

DIOR see Christina Dior

DIOR (BLACK)
Anal Booty Burner / 1996 / ROB / M • Black Cheerleader Search #08 / 1996 / IVC / M • Black Street Hookers #3 / 1996 / DFI / M • The Blowjob Adventures Of Doctor Fellatio / 1997 / EL / M • Git Yo' Ass On Da Bus! / 1996 / HW / M • Wild Assed Pooper Slut / 1996 / ROB / M

DIRCH PASSER
1001 Danish Delights / cr68 / AR / M

DIRK FLETCHER
Courting Libido / 1995 / HIV / G

DIRK LAYE see Star Index I

DIRTY FRANK see Star Index I

DIRTY GARY see Gary Vann

DIRTY NADINE

Detention Cell #101 / 1995 / VTF / B

DISNEY
Real Women...Real Fantasies! / 1996 / WSD / F • San Francisco Lesbians #1 / 1992 / PL / F

DITA
Captured On Camera / 1997 / BON / B • Mike Hott: #391 / 1996 / MHV / M • Mike Hott: #393 / 1996 / MHV / M • Naked Mockey-Rayna / 1996 / EVN / M

DITSY
Corsets & Cords / 1994 / BON / B • Real People Real Bondage #1 / 1995 / BON / C

DITTA
Fashion Sluts #3 / 1995 / ABS / M

DIVA
Pretty black haired girl with medium, probably enhanced tits and a large mole or birthmark on her left chest between the top of her breast and her armpit. In later movies her breasts have been enhanced to large size and the mole has disappeared. Supposedly 26 years old in 1993.
The Basket Trick / 1993 / PL / M • Beaver Hunt #03 / 1994 / LEI / M • The Big Bang #1 / 1993 / LV / M • Black Mystique #11 / 1995 / VT / F • Bobby Hollander's Maneaters #08 / 1993 / SFP / M • Casanova #3 / 1993 / SC / M • The Catburglar / 1994 / CA / M • Christmas Carol / 1993 / LV / M • Contract For Service / 1994 / NTP / B • Cousin Bubba Country Corn Porn #01 / 1994 / VIM / M • Deep Inside Dirty Debutantes #10 / 1993 / 4P / M • Deep Inside Misty Rain / 1995 / VC / C • The Dinner Party #1 / 1994 / ULI / M • Dirty Doc's Housecalls #01 / 1993 / LV / M • Diva / 1993 / XCI / M • Dracula's Dungeon / 1995 / HOM / B • F-Channel / 1994 / AFV / F • Hard Core Beginners #06 / 1995 / LEI / M • Harlots / 1993 / MID / M • Hooter Hown / 1994 / LV / M • The Hustlers / 1993 / MID / M • I Married An Anal Queen / 1993 / MID / M • Immortal Desire / 1993 / VI / M • Latin Plump Humpers #3 / 1995 / TTV / M • Lovin' Spoonfuls #3 / 1995 / 4P / C • M Series #15 / 1993 / LBO / M • The Magnificence Of Minka / 1996 / NAP / S • Maid For Bondage / 1993 / LBO / B • The Man Who Loved Women / 1993 / SC / M • New Ends #05 / 1993 / 4P / M • Odyssey Triple Play #89: Group Sex Grab Bag / 1995 / OD / M • Positions Wanted: Experienced Only / 1993 / PV / M • Prison World / 1994 / NTP / B • Pussy Hunt #03 / 1994 / LEI / M • Raunch #09 / 1993 / CC / M • Sex #1 (Vca) / 1994 / VC / M • Sex #2: Fate (Vca) / 1995 / VC / M • Seymore Butts Goes Nuts / 1994 / FH / M • Slaves Of Passion / 1995 / HOM / B • Stacked With Honors / 1993 / DR / M • Super Groupie / 1993 / PL / M • Taxi Girls #3: Killer On The Loose / 1993 / MED / M • Up And Cummers #23 / 1995 / 4P / M • Video Virgins #07 / 1993 / NS / M • Video Virgins #08 / 1993 / NS / M • Wendy Whoppers: Ufo Tracker / 1994 / PEP / M

DIVA (1984)
A Little Bit Of Hanky Panky / 1984 / GO / M • Surrender In Paradise / 1984 / GO / M • Tropical Nights / 1988 / GO / C

DIVA WOLF
Amber's Desires / 1985 / CA / M • Dr Strange Sex / 1985 / CA / M • Fleshdance Fever / 1984 / SAT / M • Gourmet Premier: Beyond Arousal / Diva Does The Director 905 / cr85 / GO / M • Showdown / 1985 /

Screwples / 1979 / CA / M

DOLPH *see Star Index I*

DOLPH STOUBER
Marilyn Chambers' Private Fantasies #3 / 1983 / CA / M

DOM JUAN
Bi Claudius / 1994 / BIL / G • Drive Bi / 1994 / BIL / G • He-She Hangout / 1995 / HSV / G • The Princess With A Penis / 1994 / HSV / G

DOM SINCLAIR
The Best Of Both Worlds #2 / 1986 / MID / G • Primal She-Male / 1996 / HSV / G

DOMINA BLUE *see Star Index I*

DOMINA LADY IRIS
Skin #5: The 5th Column / 1996 / ERQ / M

DOMINATIA *see Star Index I*

DOMINATRIX BLUES *see Star Index I*

DOMINIC DOMINGUEZ
Visions / 1977 / QX / M

DOMINIC LE CROIX *see Star Index I*

DOMINIC SINCLAIR
Mixed Apples / 1996 / APP / G

DOMINIECE
Black Cheerleader Search #06 / 1996 / IVC / M • Black Cheerleader Search #11 / 1997 / IVC / M

DOMINIQUE
The Baroness / 1987 / VD / M • Big Bust Fantasies / 1995 / PME / F • Big Bust Vixens / 1984 / BTO / S • Blue Vanities #538 / 1993 / FFL / M • Caged Virgins / 1970 / VS / S • California Valley Girls / 1983 / HO / M • Centerfold Celebrities #3 / 1983 / VC / M • Duel Of The Show-Mates / 199? / NAP / B • Eat At The Blue Fox / 1983 / VC / M • Fire Down Below / 1994 / GO / M • Gland Slam / 1995 / PRE / B • GVC: Bizarre Women #129 / 1982 / GO / M • GVC: Sweet Dominance #127 / 1983 / GO / B • GVC: Women Who Seduce Men #123 / 1982 / GO / M • Hillary Vamp's Private Collection #06 / 1992 / HVD / M • Hot Body Competition: Bikinis & Bikes Contest / 1996 / CG / F • Hot Body Competition: Lusty Lingerie Contest / 1996 / CG / F • Hot Stuff / 1984 / VXP / M • Intimate Realities #1 / 1983 / VC / M • Juicy Virgins / 1995 / WIV / M • Malibu Summer / 1983 / VC / M • Marilyn, My Love / 1985 / ELH / M • Master's Touch #1: Dog House Slut / 1994 / FAP / B • Master's Touch #2: Punished Slave Girls / 1994 / FAP / B • Master's Touch #5: Slave Revolt / 1995 / FAP / B • Parliament: Ass Masters #1 / 1987 / PM / M • Pearl Necklace: Thee Bush League #9 / 1993 / SEE / M • Penthouse: Great Pet Hunt #1 / 1992 / PET / F • Personal Touch #1 / 1983 / AR / M • Raw Talent: Bang 'er Out Of Hell / 1994 / RTP / M • Regency #41: Jambo / cr81 / RHV / M • S&M On The Ranch: Training The New Pony Girl / 1994 / VER / B • Sabre's Last Stand / 1993 / NAP / B • Sex And The Cheerleaders / 1983 / XTR / M • Shave Me / 1994 / RTP / F • She-Male Slut House / 1994 / HEA / G • Swimming Pool Orgy / 1995 / FRF / M • Uninhibited / 1993 / ANT / S • The Wacky World Of X-Rated Bloopers / 1989 / GO / M • [Le Frisson Des Vampires / 1970 / VS / S

DOMINIQUE (LONI S) *see* Loni Sanders

DOMINIQUE (SIMONE) *see* Dominique Simone

DOMINIQUE ASHLEY
Black Trisexual Encounters #4 / 1986 / LA / G • Parliament: Hard TV #1 / 1988 / PM /

G • Queens Are Wild #1 / 1992 / VIM / G • Trisexual Encounters #04 / 1986 / PL / G

DOMINIQUE AVELINE
Erotic Pleasures / 1976 / CA / M • Flesh Fever / 1978 / CV / M • French Erotic Fantasies / 1978 / … / M • Sextasy / 1978 / COM / M

DOMINIQUE BOUCHE *see* Sydney Dance

DOMINIQUE BUZOT *see Star Index I*

DOMINIQUE CHARRON *see Star Index I*

DOMINIQUE DANCER
Loose Times At Ridley High / 1984 / VCX / M • Saturday Matinee Series #4 / 1996 / VCX / C

DOMINIQUE DESSEAUX
Cherry Busters / 1995 / WIV / M

DOMINIQUE DUGET *see Star Index I*

DOMINIQUE FRAZER *see Star Index I*

DOMINIQUE HUMBERT *see* Marilyn Jess

DOMINIQUE LEE *see Star Index I*

DOMINIQUE MONET
Coming Through The Window / cr75 / VXP / F

DOMINIQUE PERIGNON
Private Film #03 / 1993 / OD / M

DOMINIQUE SANDS *see Star Index I*

DOMINIQUE SANTOS
Nine Lives Of A Wet Pussycat / 1975 / VCX / M

DOMINIQUE SIMON *see* Dominique Simone

DOMINIQUE SIMONE *(Simone (Dominique), Dominique (Simone), Deadre Marrow, Monique Simone, Monique Simon, Domonique Symour, Domonique Simone, Coco (Dominique), Dominique Simon, Deadra Marrow, Deidra Morrow, Jennifer Rose)*
Black girl with a tight body except for the tits. Deadre Marrow is from **Wild At Heart.** Monique Simone in **Three Men And A Hooker.** Domonique Symour in **Nina Hartley: Wild Thing.** Coco in **Lesbian Lingerie Fantasy #4.** Born in Atltanta, GA on June 18, 1971. After breast enhancement is 34D-22-36 in a 5'5" body, 107lbs. Has had breasts enhanced twice.
900 Desert Strip / 1991 / XPI / M • Abused Husband / 1990 / PL / B • Acts Of Confession / 1991 / PP / M • Adult Video News 1992 Awards / 1992 / VC / M • The Adventures Of Breastman / 1992 / EVN / M • Amateur Lesbians #02: Dominique / 1991 / GO / F • Amateur Lesbians #04: Tera / 1991 / GO / F • Anal Angels #5 / 1996 / VEX / C • Anal Magic / 1995 / XC / M • Anal Orgy / 1993 / DRP / M • Anal Rampage #1 / 1992 / ROB / M • Anal Rookies #1 / 1992 / ROB / M • Anal Sluts & Sweethearts #1 / 1992 / ROB / M • The Anal Team / 1993 / LV / M • Animal Attraction / 1994 / IF / M • Assford Wives / 1992 / ATL / M • B.L.O.W. / 1992 / LV / M • Babes / 1991 / CIN / M • Back To Back #2 / 1992 / FC / C • Back To Black #2 / 1992 / VEX / C • Backdoor Play / 1996 / AVI / M • Bad Habits / 1990 / WV / M • Bangin' With The Home Girls / 1991 / AFV / M • Bazooka County #5: The Jugs / 1993 / CC / M • Behind The Backdoor #4 / 1990 / EVN / M • Behind The Scenes: The Making Of The Wil & Ed Movies / 1992 / MID / M • The Best Of Sean Michaels / 1994 / VT / C • Big & Busty Superstars / 1996 / DGD / F • The Big Bang / 1994 / FF

/ M • Big Knockers #01 / 1994 / TV / M • The Bimbo #1 / 1992 / AFV / M • The Bimbo #2 / 1992 / AFV / M • Black & Blue / 1990 / SO / M • Black & White In Living Color / 1992 / WV / M • Black Analyst #2 / 1995 / VEX / M • Black Balled / 1990 / ZA / M • Black Beach / 1995 / LV / M • Black Beauties #1 / 1992 / VIM / M • Black Butt Jungle / 1993 / ME / M • Black Buttman #01 / 1003 / CC / M • Black Centerfold Celebrities / 1993 / MID / M • Black Cream Queens / 1996 / APP / F • Black Flava / 1994 / EX / M • Black Is Back / 1993 / HW / M • Black Jack City #1 / 1991 / VT / M • Black Jack City #2: Black's Revenge / 1992 / HW / M • Black Mariah / 1991 / FC / M • Black Men Can Hump / 1992 / FH / M • Black Obsession / 1991 / ZA / M • Black On White / 1991 / VT / F • Black Power / 1996 / LEI / C • Black Streets / 1994 / LE / M • Black Velvet #1 / 1992 / CC / M • Black Velvet #2 / 1993 / CC / M • Black Velvet #3 / 1994 / CC / M • Blackbroad Jungle / 1994 / IN / M • Blacks & Whites #2 / 1995 / GO / M • Blow Job Bonnie / 1992 / CC / M • The Blues #1 / 1992 / VT / M • Body & Soul / 1995 / IF / M • Body Heat / 1990 / CDI / M • Boobs, Butts And Bloopers #2 / 1990 / HO / M • The BoobyGuard / 1993 / FOR / M • Boomeranal / 1992 / CC / M • Bootin' Up / 1995 / VT / B • Booty By Nature / 1994 / WP / M • Breaking And Entering / 1991 / AFV / M • Breast Worx #01 / 1991 / LBO / M • Bung-Ho Babes / 1991 / FC / M • Butt Woman #4 / 1993 / FH / M • Butt's Up, Doc #3 / 1992 / GO / M • The Buttnicks #4: The Black Buttnicks / 1993 / CC / M • Buttslammers #05: Quake, Rattle & Roll! / 1994 / BS / F • California Blacks / 1994 / V99 / M • California Taxi Girls / 1991 / AFV / M • Carnal Crimes / 1991 / MAE / S • Casanova #2 / 1993 / SC / M • Club Josephine / 1991 / AR / F • The Coach's Daughter / 1991 / AR / M • Coming Out Bi / 1995 / IN / G • Cycle Sluts / 1992 / CC / M • Dark Desires #2 (Infin—1996) / 1996 / IF / M • Dark Tunnels / 1994 / LV / M • Deep Cheeks #3 / 1992 / ROB / M • Dick & Jane Sneak On The Set / 1993 / AVI / M • Dirty Dominique / 1994 / V99 / M • Dominique Goes Bi / 1994 / STA / G • Dominique's Bi Adventure / 1995 / STA / G • Don Juan De-Marco / 1994 / NLH / S • Dream Lover / 1991 / WV / M • East L.A. Law / 1991 / WV / M • Ebony Princess / 1994 / IN / M • Edward Penishands #1 / 1991 / VT / M • The Erotic Adventures Of Fanny Annie / 1991 / WV / M • Eternal Bliss / 1990 / AFV / M • Even More Dangerous / 1990 / SO / M • Fantasy Duel / 1996 / NAP / B • Feathermates / 1992 / PRE / B • Fishbone / 1994 / WIV / F • Flood Control / 1992 / PRE / B • Foolish Pleasure / 1992 / VD / M • Forget Me Not / 1994 / FH / M • Foxes / 1992 / FL / M • Freak Dat Booty / 1994 / WP / M • Get You Wet / 1992 / NAP / S • Girl Friends / 1990 / PL / F • Girls Gone Bad #7: Misfits Of Society / 1992 / GO / F • Girlz N The Hood #2 / 1992 / HW / M • The God Daughter #2 / 1991 / AFV / M • Grand Slam / 1993 / … / B • Group Therapy / 1992 / TP / M • Groupies / 1993 / AFV / F • Guess Who Came To Dinner / 1992 / AFV / M • Harlots From Hootersville / 1994 / BLC / M • Head Again / 1992 / AFV / M • Heatwave #2 / 1993 / FH / F • Hidden Obsessions / 1992

/ BFP / M • Hits & Misses / 1992 / PRE / B • Hooter Heaven / 1992 / CA / M • Hot Licks / 1990 / CDI / M • Hotel Sex / 1992 / AFV / M • Howard Sperm's Private Parties / 1994 / LBO / M • I Cream On Jeannie / 1995 / AVI / M • I Dream Of Teri / 1993 / IF / M • If You're Nasty / 1991 / PL / F • Illusions #2 / 1992 / IF / M • Immoral Support / 1992 / AFV / M • Immorals #3: Stroked / 1991 / SC / M • In Loving Color #3 / 1992 / VT / M • In Too Deep / 1992 / AFD / M • Indecent / 1993 / XCI / M • Inside Job / 1992 / ZA / M • Into The Fire / 1994 / ZA / M • Jack The Stripper / 1992 / ME / M • The Journey: Oral Majority / 1991 / WV / M • Just Friends / 1991 / AFV / M • Kinky Cameraman #4 / 1996 / LEI / C • La Princesa Anal / 1993 / ROB / M • Ladies Lovin' Ladies #1 / 1990 / AR / F • Ladies Lovin' Ladies #4 / 1992 / AFV / F • Lady & The Champ / 1991 / AFV / M • Lady Badass / 1990 / V99 / M • Laying Down The Law #1 / 1992 / AFV / M • Leena Goes Pro / 1992 / VT / M • Leg...Ends #10 / 1994 / PRE / F • Lesbian Lingerie Fantasy #4 / 1990 / ESP / F • Lez Go Crazy / 1992 / HW / C • Love Is ... / 1990 / EVN / M • Maliboobies / 1993 / CDI / F • The Midas Touch / 1991 / VT / M • Mike Hott: #174 Dominique's Shoe Fetish / 1990 / MHV / F • Mirror Images #1 / 1991 / AE / S • Mission Hard / 1995 / XC / M • Mistress 'n Da Hood / 1995 / VT / B • Mistress To Sin / 1994 / LV / M • Mo' White Trash / 1993 / MET / M • Mocha Magic / 1992 / FH / M • The Model / 1991 / HO / M • Money, Money, Money / 1993 / FD / M • Mr. Peepers Amateur Home Videos #12: Like It! Lick It! / 1991 / LBO / M • Mr. Peepers Amateur Home Videos #15: When Company Comes / 1991 / LBO / M • Murphie's Brown / 1992 / LV / M • Musical Bedrooms / 1993 / AFV / M • My Baby Got Back #01 / 1992 / VT / M • My Baby Got Back #03 / 1993 / VT / M • My Baby Got Back #06 / 1995 / VT / M • Nasty Cracks / 1992 / PRE / B • Nina Hartley: Wild Thing / 1991 / QIN / M • Nookie Court / 1992 / AFV / M • Nothing But The Truth / 1993 / AFV / M • Nothing Serious / 1990 / EX / M • Notorious / 1992 / SC / M • NYDP Blue / 1996 / WP / M • One Million Years DD / 1992 / CC / M • Opie Goes To South Central / 1995 / PP / M • Oreo A Go-Go #1 / 1992 / FH / M • Oreo A Go-Go #2 / 1992 / FH / M • Party Favors / 1993 / VEX / M • The Passion / 1995 / IP / M • Positively Pagan #06 / 1993 / ATA / M • The Price Was Right / 1994 / PAE / M • Prima #01: Anal Poker / 1995 / MBP / M • The Psychic / 1993 / CC / M • Radical Affairs Video Magazine #02 / 1992 / ME / M • Radical Affairs Video Magazine #05 / 1993 / ME / M • Raging Waters / 1992 / PRE / B • Raunchy Porno Picture Show / 1992 / FC / M • Raw #1 / 1994 / AFV / M • Rock & Roll Fantasies / 1992 / FL / M • Screwballs / 1991 / AFV / M • Sean Michaels On The Road #07: New York / 1993 / VT / M • Sex Scandals / 1995 / XC / M • Sex Trek #3: The Wrath Of Bob / 1992 / ME / M • Shooting Star / 1993 / XCI / M • Silence Of The Buns / 1992 / WV / M • Single Girl Masturbation #4 / 1990 / ESP / F • Sista! #1 / 1993 / VT / F • Sista! #3 / 1995 / VT / F • Sista! #5 / 1996 / VT / F • Sistaz In Chains / 1995 / VT / B • Slummin' Hood Girlz / 1993 / CA / M •

Soft Tail / 1991 / IN / M • Special Treatment / 1991 / AFV / M • Starbangers #02 / 1993 / BIG / M • Step To The Rear / 1991 / VD / M • Stolen Hearts / 1991 / AFV / M • Student Fetish Videos: The Enema #01 / 1990 / PRE / B • Student Fetish Videos: The Enema #02 / 1990 / SFV / B • Student Fetish Videos: Foot Worship #01 / 1990 / PRE / B • Student Fetish Videos: Foot Worship #02 / 1990 / PRE / B • Student Fetish Videos: Spanking #01 / 1990 / PLV / B • Student Fetish Videos: Spanking #02 / 1990 / SFV / B • Superboobs / 1994 / LE / M • Switch Hitters #7 / 1994 / IN / G • Tailiens #1 / 1992 / FD / M • Tailiens #2 / 1992 / FD / M • Tailiens #3 / 1992 / FD / M • A Tale Of Two Titties #1 / 1990 / AR / M • Three Men And A Hooker / 1991 / WV / M • Toe Biz / 1993 / PRE / S • Too Fast For Love / 1992 / IF / M • Toppers #05 / 1993 / TV / M • Toppers #07 / 1993 / TV / M • Toppers #09 / 1993 / TV / M • Toppers #11 / 1993 / TV / C • Toppers #12 / 1993 / TV / C • Toppers #28 / 1994 / TV / M • Toppers #29 / 1994 / TV / M • Toppers #30 / 1994 / TV / C • Toppers #31 / 1994 / TV / C • Toppers #32 / 1994 / TV / C • Toppers & Whoppers #1 / 1994 / PRE / C • Toys, Not Boys #3 / 1991 / FC / C • Two Women / 1992 / ROB / M • Up And Coming Executive / 1993 / TP / M • V.I.C.E. #2 / 1991 / AFV / M • The Vision / 1991 / LE / M • We're No Angels / 1990 / CIN / M • Welcome To Bondage: Dominique / 1993 / BON / B • Welcome To Bondage: Starlets #1 / 1993 / BON / C • Wet Faces #1 / 1997 / SC / C • White Chicks Can't Hump / 1992 / FD / M • Whoopin' Her Behind / 1995 / VT / B • Wicked Thoughts / 1991 / AFV / M • Wild At Heart / 1990 / CDI / M • Wild Buck / 1993 / STY / M • Women Of Color #1 / 1994 / ANA / M • The X-Producers / 1991 / XPI / M • You Can Touch This / 1991 / EVN / M • [Black Bite #2 / 1993 / MID / M • [Black Booty Busters / 1995 / FC / C

DOMINIQUE ST CLAIR
Blondes Like It Hot / 1989 / ELL / M • Diaries Of Fire And Ice #1 / 1989 / VC / M • Diaries Of Fire And Ice #2 / 1989 / VC / M • Evil Mistress / 1984 / VIP / M • Girl With The Million $ Legs / 1987 / PL / M • Girls With Curves #1 / 1985 / CV / M • Hotel Lesbos / 1986 / LIP / F • House Of 1001 Pleasures / 1985 / VC / M • Sex Sleuth / cr80 / ... / M • Shared With Strangers / 1985 / CV / M • Skin #3 / 1995 / ERQ / M • Sweet Dreams / 1978 / CON / M • [Segrete Espereinze Di Luca E Fanny / 1980 / ... / S

DOMINIQUE ST PIERRE see Star Index I

DOMINIQUE STEELER
Serviced With A Smile / 1985 / VD / M

DOMINIQUE TORRES see Sydney Dance

DOMINIQUE TROY
Boarding School Lesbos / 1977 / LIP / F • Diamond Snatch / 1977 / COM / M

DOMINIQUE TROYES see Marilyn Jess

DOMINIQUE WEBB
Love Is A Stranger #1 / 1994 / SV / B • Love Is A Stranger #2 / 1994 / SV / B

DOMINIQUE WINTERS
Buffy Malibu's Nasty Girls #08 / 1995 / ANA / F • Dream House / 1995 / XPR / M • Misty Rain's Anal Orgy / 1994 / FRM / M • Nasty

Nymphos #05 / 1994 / ANA / M • Profiles #02 / 1995 / XPR / M • Profiles #03: House Dick / 1995 / XPR / M • R.E.A.L. #2 / 1994 / LV / F • Snatch Patch / 1995 / LE / M • Video Virgins #16 / 1994 / NS / M

DOMINO
Blue Vanities #530 / 1993 / FFL / M • Don't Get Them Wet / 1987 / VD / M • Made In Heaven / 1991 / PP / M • Meat Market / 1992 / SEX / C • Sodomania #08: The London Sessions / 1994 / EL / M • The Universal Ball / 1989 / LEO / G

DOMINO LEE
Older & Bolder In San Francisco / 1996 / TEP / M

DOMONIC RETTA
Blow By Blow / 1984 / QX / M • Sweet Spread / 1986 / VXP / M • Switch Hitters #2: Swinging Both Ways / 1987 / IN / G

DOMONICK
Back East Babes #2 / 1996 / NIT / M • Jus' Knockin' Boots #2: Black On Line / 1996 / NIT / M

DOMONIQUE SIMONE see Dominique Simone

DOMONIQUE SYMOUR see Dominique Simone

DON
Homegrown Video #112 / 1990 / HOV / M • Homegrown Video #191 / 1990 / HOV / M • Homegrown Video #373 / 1991 / HOV / M • Pearl Necklace: Amorous Amateurs #37 / 1993 / SEE / M • SVE: Tales From The Lewd Library #3 / 1994 / SVE / M

DON ALLEN
Dance Of Love / cr70 / BL / M • Intensive Care / 1974 / BL / M • Lady On The Couch / 1978 / SVE / M • Lickity Split / 1974 / COM / M • My Master, My Love / 1975 / BL / B • Not Just Another Woman / 1974 / ... / M • Referral Service / cr71 / BL / M

DON ANDREWS
Curiosity Excited The Kat / 1984 / BIZ / B

DON ARDEN see Star Index I

DON BRUCE
Flash / 1980 / CA / M

DON CARTER see Star Index I

DON DARINGER see Peter Elite

DON DERINGER see Peter Elite

DON FERNANDO (Leon Romero, Ron Gomez, Don Frederico)
1-800-TIME / 1990 / IF / M • 2 Wongs Make A White / 1996 / FC / M • 50 And Still Pumping! / 1994 / EMC / M • 55 And Still Bangin' / 1995 / HW / M • 976-76DD / 1993 / VI / M • 976-STUD / 1989 / LV / M • Aged To Perfection #1 / 1994 / TTV / M • Aged To Perfection #2 / 1995 / TTV / M • Aged To Perfection #3 / 1995 / TTV / M • Alice In Blackland / 1988 / VC / M • All For One / 1988 / CIN / M • All For You, Baby / 1990 / VEX / M • All The King's Ladies / 1981 / SUP / M • Amateur Lusty Latins #2 / 1997 / SUF / M • Amateur Orgies #22 / 1993 / AFI / M • Amateurs Exposed #05 / 1995 / CV / M • Ambitious Blondes / 1992 / VIM / M • America's Raunchiest Home Videos #63: / 1993 / ZA / M • America's Raunchiest Home Videos #68: / 1993 / ZA / M • America's Raunchiest Home Videos #69: / 1993 / ZA / M • Anal Addiction #2 / 1990 / SO / M • Anal Angels #3 / 1995 / VEX / C • Anal Angels #6 / 1996 / VEX / C • Anal Attraction #2 / 1993 / AFV / C • Anal Brat / 1993 / FL / M • Anal Camera #05 / 1995 / EVN / M • Anal Camera #08 / 1995 / EVN /

M • Anal Camera #09 / 1995 / EVN / M • Anal Carnival / 1992 / ROB / M • Anal Climax #2 / 1991 / ROB / M • Anal Destroyer / 1994 / ZA / M • Anal Exchange / 1995 / C69 / M • Anal Fury / 1992 / ROB / M • Anal Future / 1992 / VC / M • Anal Gang Bangers #01 / 1992 / GLI / M • Anal House Party / 1993 / IP / M • Anal Innocence #1 / 1991 / ROB / M • Anal Intruder #03 / 1980 / CC / M • Anal Intruder #05: The Final Outrage / 1990 / CC / M • Anal Intruder #06: The Anal Twins / 1992 / CC / M • Anal Magic / 1995 / XC / M • Anal Oriental Sorority / 1994 / LBO / M • Anal Pow Wow / 1995 / XC / M • The Anal Team / 1993 / LV / M • Anal Therapy #2 / 1993 / FD / M • Anal Torture / 1994 / ZA / M • Anal Virgins #01 / 1996 / NS / M • Anal Vision #05 / 1993 / LBO / M • Anal Vision #12 / 1993 / LBO / M • Anal Vision #20 / 1993 / LBO / M • Anal Vision #27 / 1994 / LBO / M • Anal Vision #28 / 1994 / LBO / M • The Analizer / 1990 / LV / M • Ancient Amateurs #2 / 1996 / LOF / M • Angel Wolf / 1995 / WIV / M • Animal Attraction / 1994 / IF / M • Around The World With Samantha Strong / 1989 / V99 / M • As Nasty As She Wants To Be / 1990 / IN / M • Asian Appetite / 1993 / HO / M • Asian Boom Boom Girls / 1997 / HO / M • Asian Exotica / 1995 / EVN / M • Asian Heat #02: Satin Angels / 1993 / SC / M • Asian Heat #03: Tales Of The Golden Lotus / 1993 / SC / M • Asian Heat #05: The Joy Suck Club / 1994 / SC / M • Asian Invasion / 1993 / IP / M • Assford Wives / 1992 / ATL / M • Assinine / 1990 / CC / M • Asspiring Actresses / 1989 / CA / M • Aussie Maid In America / 1990 / PM / M • The Babes Of Bonerville / 1995 / VEX / C • Babes With Attitudes / 1990 / EVN / M • Baccarat #1 / 1991 / FH / M • Baccarat #2 / 1991 / FH / M • Back To Nature / 1990 / CA / M • Backdoor Smugglers / 1994 / JAV / M • Backdoor To Hollywood #02 / 1986 / CDI / M • Backdoor To Hollywood #03 / 1987 / CDI / M • Backdoor To Hollywood #09 / 1989 / CIN / M • The Backpackers #1 / 1990 / IN / M • Backside To The Future #2 / 1988 / ZA / M • Backstage Entrance #1 / 1992 / FH / M • Backstage Entrance #2 / 1992 / FH / M • The Backway Inn #1 / 1992 / FD / M • Bad Medicine / 1990 / VEX / M • Ball Busters / 1991 / FH / M • Bang City #3: Fallon's Anal Gang Bang / 1995 / SC / M • Barbara Dare's Bad / 1988 / SE / C • Bare Waves / 1986 / VD / M • The Bare-Assed Naked Gun / 1992 / MID / M • The Battle Of the Breast Queens / 1989 / INS / C • Battle Of The Stars #2: East Versus West / 1985 / NSV / M • Beach Bum Amateur's #23 / 1993 / MID / M • Beach Bum Amateur's #24 / 1993 / MID / M • Beach Bum Amateur's #26 / 1993 / MID / M • Beach Bum Amateur's #28 / 1993 / MID / M • Beach Bunny / 1994 / V99 / M • The Beat Goes On / 1987 / VCR / C • Beaver Hunt #03 / 1994 / LEI / M • Beeches / 1990 / KIS / M • Behind The Backdoor #3 / 1989 / EVN / M • Behind The Backdoor #4 / 1990 / EVN / M • Behind The Backdoor #5 / 1992 / EVN / M • Behind The Black Door / 1987 / VEX / M • Belle Of The Ball / 1989 / V99 / M • Bend Over Backwards / 1993 / VIM / M • The Best Of Black Anal #1 / 1995 / ROB / C • Best Of Caught From Behind #5 / 1991 / HO / C • The Best Of Oriental Anal #1 /

1994 / ROB / C • Between My Breasts #07 / 1989 / L&W / M • Between My Breasts #10 / 1990 / BTO / M • Between The Bars / 1992 / FH / M • Beverly Hills Geisha / 1992 / V99 / M • Beyond Shame / 1980 / VEP / M • Biff Malibu's Totally Nasty Home Videos #17 / 1992 / ANA / M • Biff Malibu's Totally Nasty Home Videos #20 / 1992 / ANA / M • Biff Malibu's Totally Nasty Home Videos #39 / 1993 / ANA / M • Big Bad Biker Bitches / 1994 / TTV / M • The Big Bang / 1988 / WET / M • The Big Bang / 1994 / FF / M • Big Boob Boat Ride #1 / 1992 / FC / M • Big Butts Of The Wild West / 1993 / BTO / M • Big Murray's New-Cummers #09: Oriental Lovers / 1993 / FD / M • Big Murray's New-Cummers #21: Double Penetration One / 1993 / FD / M • Big Murray's New-Cummers #28: Rump Humpers #2 / 1995 / FD / M • Big Tit Country / 1988 / BTO / M • Big Tit Orgy #01 / 1987 / H&S / M • Big Top Cabaret #1 / 1986 / BTO / M • Bionic Babes / 1986 / 4P / M • The Bitch / 1988 / FAN / M • The Black Anal-ist #1 / 1988 / VEX / M • Black Angel / 1987 / CC / M • Black Cheerleader Search #02 / 1996 / ROB / M • Black Cheerleader Search #04 / 1996 / ROB / M • Black Cobra / 1989 / WV / M • Black Gangbangers #03 / 1995 / HW / M • Black Heat / 1986 / VC / M • Black Women, White Men #1 / 1995 / FC / M • Black Women, White Men #7 / 1995 / FC / M • Black Women, White Men #8 / 1995 / FC / M • Bloopers #2 / 1991 / GO / C • Blue Fire / 1991 / V99 / M • Blue Vanities #402 (New) / 1988 / FFL / M • Blue's Velvet / 1979 / ECV / M • Bo-Dacious / 1989 / V99 / M • The Boarding House / 1983 / WV / M • Bobby Hollander's Rookie Nookie #04 / 1993 / SFP / M • Bobby Hollander's Rookie Nookie #06 / 1993 / SFP / M • Bobby Hollander's Sweet Cheeks #104 / 1993 / QUA / M • Bobby Hollander's Sweet Cheeks #107 / 1993 / QUA / M • Body & Soul / 1995 / IF / M • Boiling Point / 1978 / SE / M • Bone Alone / 1993 / MID / M • Boobs, Butts And Bloopers #1 / 1990 / HO / M • Boobs, Butts And Bloopers #2 / 1990 / HO / M • Boomeranal / 1992 / CC / M • Bootylicious: China Town / 1995 / JMP / M • The Bottom Line / 1990 / AMB / M • Bottoms Up #05 / 1986 / AVC / C • Breakin' All The Rules / 1987 / SE / M • Breaking It #1 / 1984 / COL / M • Breast Wishes #13 / 1993 / LBO / M • Breast Worx #19 / 1992 / LBO / M • Breast Worx #28 / 1992 / LBO / M • Breast Worx #32 / 1992 / LBO / M • Breast Worx #34 / 1992 / LBO / M • Breast Worx #40 / 1992 / LBO / M • Breast Worx #42 / 1993 / LBO / M • Bring On The Night / 1994 / VEX / M • Bubble Butts #17 / 1992 / LBO / M • Bubble Butts #23 / 1992 / LBO / M • Bubble Butts #25 / 1993 / LBO / M • Bubble Butts #26 / 1993 / LBO / M • Bucky Beaver's XXX Dragon Art Theatre Double Feature #02 / 1996 / SOW / M • Bun Busters #20 / 1994 / LBO / M • Bunny Bleu: A Gang Bang Fantasy / 1994 / FC / M • The Burma Road #1 / 1994 / LBO / C • The Burma Road #2 / 1994 / LBO / C • Busen Extra #1 / 1991 / BTO / M • Bustin' Out / 1988 / VEX / M • Busty Babes In Heat #1 / 1993 / BTO / M • Busty Babes In Heat #2 / 1993 / BTO / M • The Butler Did It / 1991 / FH / M • Butt Bandits #4 / 1996 / VD / C • Butt Bongo Bo-

nanza / 1993 / FC / M • Butt Hunt #04 / 1995 / LEI / M • Butt Hunt #05 / 1995 / LEI / M • Butt Hunt #06 / 1995 / LEI / M • Butt Hunt #07 / 1995 / LEI / M • Butt Hunt #08 / 1995 / LEI / M • Butt Hunt #09 / 1995 / LEI / M • Butt Hunt #10 / 1995 / LEI / M • Butt Hunt #11 / 1995 / LEI / M • Butt Light: Queen Of Rears / 1992 / STR / M • Butt Pumpers / 1995 / FH / M • Butt Wackers / 1995 / FH / M • Butt X Files #2: Anal Abduction / 1995 / WIV / M • Butt's Motel #5 / 1990 / EX / M • The Buttnicks #1 / 1990 / VEX / M • California Cherries / 1987 / EVN / M • California Fever / 1987 / CV / M • California Gigolo / 1979 / WWV / M • California Taboo / 1986 / VC / M • Call Girl Academy / 1990 / V99 / M • Can't Beat The Feeling / 1988 / VEX / M • Candy Stripers #1 / 1978 / ALP / M • Captives / 1983 / BIZ / B • Carnal Carnival / 1992 / FC / M • Carnal Olympics / 1983 / CA / M • Carnal Possessions / 1988 / VEX / M • Carnal Possessions / 1991 / VEX / M • Casey At The Bat / 1991 / LV / M • Casting Call #09 / 1995 / SO / M • Casting Call #10 / 1994 / MET / M • Casting Call #11 / 1995 / MET / M • Casting Call #12 / 1995 / MET / M • Cat On A Hot Sin Roof / 1989 / LV / M • Caught From Behind #11 / 1989 / HO / M • Caught In The Act / 1978 / MAP / M • Cheek Busters / 1990 / FH / M • Cheek-A-Boo / 1988 / LV / M • Cheeks #1 / 1988 / CC / M • Cherry Poppers #10: Sweet And Sassy / 1995 / ZA / M • Chestmates / 1988 / VEX / M • Chills / 1989 / LV / M • China Bitch / 1989 / PV / C • China Girl / 1989 / V99 / M • China Sisters / 1978 / SE / M • Chocolate Chips / 1987 / VD / M • Cirque Du Sex #2 / 1996 / VT / M • Club Bed / 1987 / CIX / M • Coed Fever / 1980 / CA / M • Colossal Orgy #1 / 1993 / HW / M • Colossal Orgy #3 / 1994 / HW / M • Come And Get It! / 1995 / LBO / M • Coming Alive / 1988 / LV / M • Confessions / 1992 / PL / M • Confessions Of Candy / 1984 / VC / M • Corporate Affairs / 1986 / SE / M • Cottontail Club / 1985 / HO / M • Cream / 1993 / SC / M • Creatures Of The Night / 1987 / FAN / M • Cumming Clean / 1991 / FL / M • D.P. Grannies / 1995 / JMP / M • Dana Lynn's Hot All Over / 1987 / V99 / M • Dances With Foxes / 1991 / CC / M • The Dane Harlow Story / 1990 / IF / M • Dane's Party / 1991 / IF / G • Dark Angel / 1983 / VC / M • Dark Desires / 1989 / BMV / C • Debbie Does 'em All #3 / 1989 / CV / M • Debbie Does Dallas #5 / 1988 / VEX / M • Decadent Delights / 1992 / IF / M • Deep Butt / 1994 / MID / C • Deep In Deanna Jones / 1989 / EVN / M • Deep Inside Anal Camera / 1996 / EVN / C • Deep Inside Keisha / 1994 / VC / C • Deep Inside The Orient / 1993 / LV / M • Deep Throat #4 / 1990 / AR / M • Deep Undercover / 1989 / PV / M • Delicate Matters / 1989 / VEX / M • Derrier / 1991 / CC / M • Desire For Men / 1981 / MIT / M • Devil In Miss Jones #3: A New Beginning / 1986 / VC / M • Devil In Vanity / 1990 / CC / M • Diamond For Sale / 1990 / EVN / M • Dick & Jane Go To Mexico / 1994 / AVI / M • Dick & Jane Up, Down And All Around / 1994 / AVI / M • Dick-Tation / 1991 / AFV / M • Dirty Blondes / 1986 / CDI / M • Dirty Books / 1990 / V99 / M • Dirty Danyel / 1994 / V99 / M • Dirty Diane / 1989 / V99 / M • Dirty Dr. Feelgood / 1988 / VEX / M • Dirty Mind /

Snatch Masters #16 / 1995 / LEI / C • The New Snatch Masters #18 / 1996 / LEI / C • Nici Sterling's DP Gang Bang / 1996 / FC / M • Night Cap / 1990 / EX / M • Nightfire / 1987 / LA / M • Nina Does 'em All / 1988 / 3HV / C • Nineteen #4 / 1996 / FOR / M • Nineteen #8 / 1997 / FOR / M • Odyssey Triple Play #67: Girls Who Love It Up The Ass / 1994 / OD / M • Oh My Gush / 1995 / OD / M • Older And Anal #1 / 1995 / FC / M • Older And Anal #2 / 1995 / FC / M • On The Make / 1988 / V99 / M • One For The Road / 1989 / V99 / M • One More Time / 1990 / VEX / M • One Of These Nights / 1991 / V99 / M • One Way At A Time / 1979 / CA / M • Only The Best Of Anal / 1992 / MET / C • Open Lips / 1983 / AVO / M • Opening Night / 1991 / AR / M • Oral Addiction / 1989 / LV / M • Oral Majority #08 / 1990 / WV / C • Orgies Orgies Orgies / 1994 / WV / M • Oriental Oddballs #1 / 1994 / FH / M • Oriental Sexpress / 1984 / WV / M • Oriental Spice / 1990 / SE / M • Oriental Taboo / 1985 / CDI / M • The Other Side / 1995 / ERA / M • Out Of Control / 1987 / SE / M • Overexposed / 1988 / VEX / M • The Oversexual Tourist / 1989 / VEX / M • Pai Gow Video #09: Naked Asians / 1995 / EVN / M • Paradise Road / 1990 / WV / M • Paris Blues / 1990 / WV / C • Party Club / 1996 / C69 / M • Party Doll / 1990 / VC / M • Party In The Rear / 1989 / LV / M • Passion For Fashion / 1992 / PEP / G • Passion Pit / 1985 / SE / M • Passion Prescription / 1990 / V99 / M • Pearl Necklace: Amorous Amateurs #22 / 1993 / SEE / M • Pearl Necklace: Amorous Amateurs #28 / 1993 / SEE / M • Pearl Necklace: Thee Bush League #24 / 1993 / SEE / M • Pearl Necklace: Thee Bush League #25 / 1993 / SEE / M • Peeping Passions / 1989 / CAE / M • The Performers / 1986 / NSV / M • Personal Touch #4 / 1989 / AR / M • Physical #1 / 1981 / SUP / M • Pink Card / 1991 / FH / M • Pink Lips / 1977 / VCX / M • The Pink Panties / 1985 / NSV / M • The Players Club / 1994 / HW / M • Playing Dirty / 1989 / VEX / M • The Pleasure Hunt #1 / 1984 / NSV / M • The Pleasure Hunt #2 / 1985 / NSV / M • Pleasure Is My Business / 1989 / EX / M • The Pleasure Maze / 1986 / PL / M • Plenty Of Pleasure / 1990 / WET / M • Plumpers Of Sundance Spa / 1993 / BTO / M • Pointers / 1990 / LV / M • Pretty Peaches #3 / 1989 / VC / M • Prime Offender / 1993 / PEP / M • Private Video Magazine #02 / 1993 / OD / M • Private Video Magazine #13 / 1994 / OD / M • Profiles #06: Super Model Orgy / 1996 / XPR / M • Proposals / 1988 / CC / M • The PTX Club / 1988 / GO / M • Pumpkin Farm / 1983 / WV / M • Pure Energy / 1990 / VEX / M • Puritan Video Magazine #05 / 1996 / LE / M • Puritan Video Magazine #09 / 1997 / LE / M • Purple Haze / 1991 / WV / M • Pussy Hunt #05 / 1994 / LEI / M • Pussy Hunt #06 / 1994 / LEI / M • Pussy Hunt #07 / 1994 / LEI / M • Pussy Hunt #08 / 1995 / LEI / M • Pussy Hunt #09 / 1995 / LEI / M • Pussy Hunt #10 / 1995 / LEI / M • Pussy Hunt #11 / 1995 / LEI / M • Pussy Hunt #12 / 1995 / LEI / M • Pussy Hunt #13 / 1995 / LEI / M • Pussy Hunt #14 / 1995 / LEI / M • Pussy Hunt #15 / 1995 / LEI / M • Pussy Lotto / 1995 / WIV / M • Pussyclips #01 / 1994 / SNA / M • Pussyclips #02 /

1994 / SNA / M • Pussyman Auditions #22 / 1996 / SNA / M • Raising Kane / 1992 / FD / M • Randy And Dane / 1991 / IF / G • Rated Sex / 1986 / SE / M • Raunch #03 / 1991 / CC / M • The Real Deal #4 / 1996 / FC / M • Reamin' Reunion / 1988 / CC / M • Rear Entry / 1995 / LEI / M • Rectal Rodeo / 1994 / ZA / M • The Red Hot Roadrunner / 1987 / VD / M • Reflections Of Innocence / 1988 / SEX / M • Reflections Of Innocence / 1991 / VEX / C • Restless Passion / 1987 / HO / M • Revealed / 1992 / VT / M • Ripe & Ready (Infinity) / 1995 / IF / M • The Rise Of The Roman Empress #2 / 1990 / PV / M • The Rites Of Uranus / 1975 / SOW / M • Rituals / 1989 / V99 / M • Rock Me / 1994 / CC / M • Romancing The Butt / 1992 / ATL / M • Roto-Rammer / 1993 / LV / M • Salsa Break / 1989 / EA / M • Sea Of Lust / 1990 / FAN / M • Secret Cravings / 1989 / V99 / M • Secrets Behind The Green Door / 1987 / SE / M • The Seductress / 1992 / ZA / M • Sensual Seduction / 1986 / LBO / M • Sex About Town / 1990 / LV / M • Sex Aliens / 1987 / CA / M • Sex Dreams On Maple Street / 1985 / WV / M • Sex Express / 1991 / SE / M • Sex In Abissi / 1993 / WIV / M • Sex On Location / 1989 / KIS / M • Sex Scandals / 1995 / XC / M • Sex Scientist / 1992 / FD / M • Sexy Nurses #1 On And Off Duty / 1990 / CV / M • Shake Well Before Using / 9990 / LV / M • She's America's Most Wanted / 1990 / VEX / M • She's No Angel #2 / 1995 / V99 / M • She Male Spirits Of The Night / 1991 / VC / G • Simply Irresistible / 1988 / CC / M • Sins Of Nina Hartley / 1989 / MIR / C • Sins Of The Wealthy #2 / 1986 / CLV / M • Six-Nine Love / 1990 / LV / M • Sizzling Summer / 1984 / VC / M • The Sleazy Detective / 1988 / VD / M • Sleeping Beauty Aroused / 1989 / VI / M • Slip Of The Tongue / 1990 / SE / M • Slummin' Hood Girlz / 1993 / CA / M • Smooth Operator / 1986 / AR / M • Snakedance / 1992 / VI / M • Soft And Wild / 1991 / LV / M • Soft Caresses / 1988 / VEX / M • Something New / 1991 / FH / M • Space Virgins / 1990 / VEX / M • Splatman / 1992 / FR / M • Star 90 / 1990 / CAY / M • Star Spangled Blacks / 1994 / VEX / M • Starbangers #08 / 1996 / FPI / M • Stormy / 1980 / CV / M • Stowaway / 1995 / LE / M • Strong Rays / 1988 / IN / M • Stuff Your Face #2 / 1995 / JMP / M • Stylin' / 1994 / FD / M • Suburban Nymphos / 1994 / ATL / M • Summer Dreams / 1996 / TEP / M • Summer School / 1979 / VCX / M • Sumo Sue And The Fat Ladies Of Wrestling / 1988 / FAN / M • Sunrise Mystery / 1992 / FD / M • Super Blondes / 1989 / VEX / M • Super Hornio Brothers #1 / 1993 / MID / M • Super Hornio Brothers #2 / 1993 / MID / M • Superstar Sex Challenge #1 / 1994 / VC / M • Superstar Sex Challenge #2 / 1994 / VC / M • Superstar Sex Challenge #3 / 1994 / VC / M • Suzie Superstar #3 / 1989 / CV / M • Sweat Shop / 1991 / EVN / M • Swedish Erotica #35 / 1980 / CA / M • Swedish Erotica #82 / 1995 / CA / M • Sweet Addiction / 1988 / CIN / M • Sweet Chastity / 1990 / EVN / M • Sweet Summer / 1986 / AMO / M • Sweet Sunshine / 1995 / IF / M • Sweet Temptations / 1989 / V99 / M • Swing Rave / 1993 / EVN / M • Switch Hitters #2: Swinging Both Ways / 1987 / IN / G • Switch Hitters #3:

Squeeze Play / 1988 / IN / G • Switch Hitters #4: The Grand Slam / 1989 / IN / G • Taboo #01 / 1980 / VCX / M • Tail For Sale / 1988 / VD / M • Taking It To The Streets / 1987 / CDI / M • Tamara's Dreams / 1989 / VEX / M • A Taste Of Black / 1987 / WET / M • A Taste Of White / 1987 / WET / M • Taxi Girls #2: In Search Of Toni / 1986 / ELD / M • Teach Me Tonight / 1990 / VEX / M • Telefantasy / 1978 / AR / M • Temptation: The Story Of A Lustful Bride / 1983 / NSV / M • This One's For You / 1989 / AR / M • Tit Tales #4 / 1993 / FC / M • Titties 'n Cream #3 / 1995 / FC / M • Too Hot To Stop / 1989 / V99 / M • Too Hot To Touch #1 / 1985 / CV / M • Torrid Tonisha / 1992 / VEX / M • Totally Tasteless Video #02 / 1994 / TTV / M • A Touch Of Mink / 1990 / V99 / M • The Touchables / 1988 / CC / M • Trading Partners / 1983 / AIR / M • Trans Europe Express / 1989 / VC / G • Triple Header / 1990 / KNI / M • Triple Penetration Debutante Sluts #1 / 1996 / BAC / M • Triple Penetration Debutante Sluts #2 / 1996 / BAC / M • Tropic Of Desire / 1979 / WWV / M • Tuff Stuff / 1987 / WET / M • Turn Up The Heat / 1988 / SEX / M • Turn Up The Heat / 1991 / VEX / C • Two Women / 1992 / ROB / M • Type Cast / 1986 / AR / M • The Ultimate Climax / 1989 / V99 / M • The Ultimate O / 1985 / NSV / M • Uncle Roy's Amateur Home Video #21 / 1993 / VIM / M • Undercover Carol / 1990 / FAN / M • Undressed For Success / 1990 / V99 / M • Up The Gulf / 1991 / AR / M • Up The Middle / 1995 / V99 / M • V.I.C.E. #1 / 1991 / AFV / M • Vampirass / 1992 / VC / M • Video Virgins #18 / 1994 / NS / M • Video Virgins #19 / 1994 / NS / M • Video Virgins #20 / 1995 / NS / M • Video Virgins #21 / 1995 / NS / M • Video Virgins #25 / 1995 / NS / M • Video Virgins #26 / 1996 / NS / M • Videobone / 1988 / WET / M • Virgin Busters / 1989 / LV / M • Viviana's Dude Ranch / 1992 / IF / M • Vivid Raw #2 / 1996 / VI / M • Voodoo Vixens / 1991 / IF / M • Voyeurism #1 / 1993 / FH / M • Water Nymph / 1987 / LIM / M • Wedding Vows / 1994 / ZA / M • Weekend Blues / 1990 / IN / M • Welcome To Dallas / 1991 / VI / M • Welcome To Paradise / 1994 / IF / M • Westside Tori / 1989 / ERO / M • Wet & Wicked / 1992 / VEX / M • Wet And Wild #1 / 1986 / VEX / M • Wet And Wild #2 / 1995 / VEX / M • Wet Event / 1992 / IF / M • Wet Kink / 1989 / CDI / M • Wet Kisses / 1988 / V99 / M • Wetness For The Prosecution / 1989 / LV / M • Whammin' & Jammin' At The Hard Cock Ole / 1996 / GLI / M • White Men Can't Iron On Butt Row / 1997 / ABS / M • Who's Dat Girl / 1987 / VEX / M • Wild Oral Erotica / 1988 / VD / C • Wild Stuff / 1987 / WET / M • Wild Thing / 1994 / IF / M • Wild Widow / 1996 / NIT / M • Will And Ed's Bogus Gang Bang / 1992 / MID / M • Women In Uniform / 1986 / TEM / M • Women Who Love Men, Men Who Love Women / 1993 / FD / C • The Wong Side Of Town / 1992 / LV / M • World Class Ass / 1995 / FC / M • The X-Producers / 1991 / XPI / M • X-Rated Bloopers #2 / 1986 / AR / M • The X-Rated OJ Truth... / 1995 / MID / M • The Year Of The Sex Dragon / 1986 / PV / M • Yin Yang Oriental Love Bang #2 / 1996 / SUF / M • Yin Yang Oriental Love Bang #4: Yellow Orchid / 1996 / SUF / M •

Yin Yang Oriental Love Bang #5: Lotus Blossoms / 1996 / SUF / M • You Bet Your Buns / 1992 / ZA / M • You Bring Out The Animal In Me / 1987 / MIR / M • You Can Touch This / 1991 / EVN / M • Young And Anal #6 / 1996 / JMP / M • Young, Dumb & Full Of Cum / 1995 / GLI / M • Zena Hardcore Special / 1994 / BTO / M

DON FREDERICO *see* Don Fernando
DON GOMEZ *see* Don Fernando
DON HARDIN *see Star Index I*
DON HART *see* Mike Horner
DON HODGES
Classical Romance / 1984 / MAP / M • Hot Touch / 1984 / VCX / M • Looking For Love / 1985 / VCX / M • Pink Champagne / 1979 / CV / M • What Gets Me Hot / 1984 / ISV / M
DON HOLIDAY *see Star Index I*
DON HORNER *see* Mike Horner
DON HOUSTON
Hardcore: The Films Of Richard Kern #1 / 1991 / FTV / M
DON LAWRENCE
Erotic Mystique / 19?? / BL / M
DON LIASON *see Star Index I*
DON MANCHESTER
Golden Girls, The Movie / 1984 / SE / M
DON N. *see Star Index I*
DON NORMAN
Angel Buns / 1981 / QX / M
DON PATRICK
Kitty's Kinky Capers / 1996 / TTV / M
DON PETERSON
Bad Penny / 1978 / QX / M • Breaker Beauties / 1977 / VHL / M • The Double Exposure Of Holly / 1977 / TVX / M • Hot Nurses / 1977 / CA / M • Love In Strange Places / 1977 / CA / M • Odyssey / 1977 / VC / M • Pussycat Ranch / 1978 / CV / M • The Violation Of Claudia / 1977 / QX / M
DON QUAN
Sugar Daddies / 1995 / FPI / M
DON RITCHIE *see Star Index I*
DON ROBERTSON
Blue Confessions / 1983 / VCR / M
DON SHINA
Island Of Love / 1983 / CV / M
DON SILVA *see Star Index I*
~~RANI NNVMG see Star Index I~~
DON THE WIMP
Wrestling Sluts #3 / 1990 / NPA / B
DON TORETTA *see Star Index I*
DON WAND
Gangbang Girl #04 / 1992 / ANA / M
DON WATSON
The Virgin Forest / 1975 / AXV / M • Weekend Lovers / 1975 / AVC / M
DON WEBBER *see* Marc Wallice
DONA AMBROSE *see Star Index I*
DONA DENNIS
Hot Tight Asses #14 / 1995 / TCK / M
DONALD BLANK
Dracula Exotica / 1980 / TVX / M
DONALD CASALINA
Menage De Sade / 1987 / BIZ / B
DONALD DANZIG (SIC) *see* Zumira
DONALD LONG
Erotic Dimensions #2: Black Desire / 1982 / NSV / M
DONALD PAGEN *see* Blake Palmer
DONALD WRIGHT *see Star Index I*
DONDI BASTONE *see Star Index I*
DONELLA DANZIG *see* Zumira
DONELLA DANZING *see* Zumira
DONNA

A&B AB#401: Cum Orgy / 1993 / A&B / M • A&B AB#431: Cum Dripping Orgy / 1994 / A&B / M • Big Bust Black Legends / 1991 / BTO / C • Black & White Bondage / 1991 / BON / B • Blue Vanities #510 / 1992 / FFL / M • Blue Vanities #527 / 1993 / FFL / M • Blue Vanities #540 / 1994 / FFL / M • Bondage Classix #02: Krysta's Nightmare #1 / 1987 / BON / B • Bondage Classix #11: Karen's B&D Phone Sex / 1984 / BON / B • Bondage Classix #17: The Millionaire / 198? / BON / B • Bus Stop Tales #02 / 1989 / PRI / M • Dangerous Desires (Gotham) / 1994 / GOT / B • Frat House / 1979 / NGV / M • Fucking Pregnant Babes #2: I Re-Enter Mamma / 1995 / AVS / M • Gang Bang Bitches #04 / 1995 / PP / M • Girls Around The World #21: Tawny Peaks & Friends / 1995 / BTO / M • Home Maid Memories #2 / 1994 / BON / C • Homegrown Video #247 / 1990 / HOV / V • Limited Edition #06 / 1979 / AVC / M • Ravaged / 1994 / GOT / B • Rawhide / 1994 / BIZ / B • Reel Life Video #05 / 1994 / RLF / M • Skirts & Flirts #01 / 1997 / XPR / F • Swedish Erotica #17 / 1980 / CA / M
DONNA (BRITISH)
Filthy First Timers #6 / 1997 / EL / M
DONNA AMBROSE
Tit To Tit #1 / 1994 / BTO / M
DONNA ANNE *(Donna N., Scarlet La Rue)*
Very white girl with small tits and a flabby but not fat body. Curly black hair and a not pretty face.
976-STUD / 1989 / LV / M • Assuming The Position / 1989 / V99 / M • Behind The Backdoor #2 / 1989 / EVN / M • Behind The Black Door / 1987 / VEX / M • Body Triple / 1991 / VC / M • Bring On The Virgins / 1989 / CA / M • The Buttnicks #1 / 1990 / VEX / M • Caught From Behind #10 / 1989 / HO / M • Club Head (EVN) #2 / 1989 / EVN / C • Double Trouble / 1988 / V99 / M • Fat Ends / 1989 / 4P / M • Flesh In Ecstasy #01: Blondie / 1987 / GO / C • Flesh In Ecstasy #03: Purple Passion / 1987 / GO / C • Flesh In Ecstasy #12: Blondie / 1987 / GO / C • Girls Like Us / cr88 / IN / C • Hard At Work / 1989 / VEX / M • Have I Got A Girl For You / 1989 / VEX / M • Her Highway #1 / 1989 / HO / M • Hot Amber Nights / 1987 / CC / M • L.A. Fantasies / 1990 / WV / C • Life Is Butt A Dream / 1989 / V99 / M • Loose Caboose / 1987 / 4P / M • The Love Mistress / 1989 / WV / M • Lust Of Blacula / 1987 / VEX / M • Naturally Sweet / 1989 / VEX / M • Paradise Road / 1990 / WV / M • Pleasure Is My Business / 1989 / EX / M • Strong Language / 1989 / IN / M • Sweet Angel Ass / 1990 / FH / M • Tamara's Dreams / 1989 / VEX / M • Ticket To Ride / 1990 / LV / M • The Wacky World Of X-Rated Bloopers / 1989 / GO / M • Wet Workout / 1987 / VEX / M
DONNA BLUE *see Star Index I*
DONNA BREAUX *see Star Index I*
DONNA BROWN
Blue Vanities #553 / 1994 / FFL / M
DONNA BUCOLA *see Star Index I*
DONNA BUSTY BROWN
Blue Vanities #110 / 1988 / FFL / M
DONNA CAPRIS
Up 'n' Coming / 1983 / CA / M
DONNA CHRISTOPHER *see Star Index I*
DONNA DAWN

Young Love / 1973 / VCX / M
DONNA DERRIERE *see Star Index I*
DONNA DUKE
Juice / 19?? / COM / M
DONNA FERGUSON *see Star Index I*
DONNA GEIGER
One Last Fling / cr76 / CPL / M
DONNA HART
Lesbian Lingerie Fantasy #1 / 1988 / ESP / F • Single Girl Masturbation #1 / 1988 / ESP / F • Swinging Sorority / 1976 / VCX / S
DONNA JAMES
Big British Plumpers / 1989 / BTO / M • N.Y. Video Magazine #08 / 1996 / OUP / M
DONNA JORDAN *see Star Index I*
DONNA JOY *see Star Index I*
DONNA JOYCE *see* Angel West
DONNA LAWSON
Carnal Highways / 1980 / HIF / M
DONNA LEAH *see* Ariel Knight
DONNA LEE *see* Ariel Knight
DONNA LEIGH *see* Ariel Knight
DONNA LEIGHT *see* Ariel Knight
DONNA MALAT
American Pie / 1980 / SE / M
DONNA MALVIDO *see Star Index I*
DONNA N. *see* Donna Anne
DONNA PUSSIE
Bucky Beaver's XXX Dragon Art Theatre Double Feature #13 / 1996 / SOW / M • Tomatoes / cr70 / SOW / M
DONNA SAMPSON
Pleasure Productions #01 / 1984 / VCR / M
DONNA SCHELL
She-Male Encounters #13: She-Male Reformatory / 1987 / MET / G
DONNA SOYER *see Star Index I*
DONNA STANLEY
The Stewardesses / 1969 / SOW / S • The Stewardesses / 1981 / CA / M • Swamp Girl / cr70 / SOW / S
DONNA STARR
Private Film #01 / 1993 / OD / M
DONNA W.
Foreign Exchange Sluts / 1995 / TNT / M
DONNA WARNER
Family Affair / 1996 / XC / M • Horny Brits Take It In The Bum / 1997 / ROB / M • Nino Fuckin' Movie / 1997 / EL / M • Oodomania #21: Degenerate Lifestyles! / 1997 / EL / M
DONNA YOUNG
Afternoon Tease / cr72 / VCX / S • Blacksnake! / 1973 / ST0 / S • Donna Young: Behind The Scenes / 1995 / DY / F • Donna Young: Donna's Mistress/Slave #1 / 1995 / DY / B • Donna Young: Donna's Nurse Video #1 / 1995 / DY / F • Donna Young: Donna's Outdoor Video / 1995 / DY / F • Donna Young: Donna's Pussy Stuffing Video / 1995 / DY / F • Donna Young: Nurse Donna / 1996 / DY / F • Wild Honey / 1969 / SOW / S
DONNIE *see Star Index I*
DONNIE COCKTAILS *see Star Index I*
DONNIE LEE *see Star Index I*
DONNIE RUSSO
Long Play / 1995 / 3XP / G
DONZELLA DANZIG *see* Zumira
DOOBIE BROWN *see Star Index I*
DORA
A&B AB#350: The Dildo Salesman / 1991 / A&B / M
DORA DICE *(Dinky Dora)*
Fat ugly blonde with droopy medium sized tits. Looks like a younger version of Rene Sum-

mers.
Blue Moon / 1992 / AFV / M • Eternal Bliss / 1990 / AFV / M • The Exhibitionist / 1991 / VD / M • Kiss It Goodbye / 1991 / SE / M • Mike Hott: #173 Dora Dice / 1990 / MHV / M • Strange Behavior / 1991 / VD / M

DORA SEBRIN
Undulations / 1980 / VC / M

DORAN O'DARE see Regina Bardot

DORE
New Faces, Hot Bodies #10 / 1993 / STP / M

DOREEN
Blue Vanities #517 / 1992 / FFL / M • Blue Vanities #522 / 1993 / FFL / M • Blue Vanities #559 / 1994 / FFL / M • California Girl: Amateur Nude Auditions / 1995 / PME / S • FTV #20: Pizza Brawl / 1996 / FT / B • Kinky College Cunts #01 / 1993 / NS / F • Street Fantasies / 1993 / AFV / M

DOREEN BELMONT see Star Index I
DOREEN CORMIER see Star Index I
DOREEN DOUBLE DECKER
FTV #07: DD Destroyer / 1996 / FT / B • FTV #08: Topless Fighting Lesson / 1996 / FT / B • FTV #23: Catfighting Crooks / 1996 / FT / B • FTV #24: Secret Submission / 1996 / FT / B

DOREEN GRAY
The Sexaholic / 1988 / VC / M

DOREEN LAZLO
Binding Experience / 1994 / CS / B

DORENE
Blue Vanities #556 / 1994 / FFL / M

DORIA MANSON see Star Index I

DORIAN
Bi And Beyond #3 / 1989 / INH / G • Rivals In Submission / 1996 / BON / B • Up And Cummers #22 / 1995 / RWP / M

DORIAN COFFEY see Star Index I

DORIAN DENNIS
Blue Vanities #556 / 1994 / FFL / M • Buxom Beautease / 19?? / SOW / S

DORIAN GRANT *(Joy (Dorian Grant))*
Long black hair, medium to large tits, curvaceous body, small tattoo on right shoulder back and another around belly button, clit rings, passable face.
Asses Galore #2: No Remorse...No Repent / 1996 / DFI / M • Butt Sluts #6 / 1996 / ROB / F • Celebrity Sluts And Tabloid Tramps / 1996 / LV / M • Girls Around The World #04 / 1991 / BTO / M • Ona Zee's Doll House #4 / 1996 / ONA / F • Sleaze Please!—October Edition / 1994 / FH / M • Student Fetish Videos: Catfighting #13 / 1994 / PRE / B • Virgin Hotline / 1996 / LVP / F • Young & Natural #14 / 1996 / TV / F • Young & Natural #16 / 1996 / TV / F • Young & Natural #18 / 1996 / TV / C • Young & Natural #20 / 1996 / TV / F

DORIAN KUPL
Casanova #2 / 1976 / CA / M

DORIAN L'AMOUR
Hostage Bound / 1996 / VTF / B

DORIAN PATCH see Star Index I

DORICE see Misty Lynn

DORIK PERMAN
Opening Night (Amateur) / 1991 / PRI / M

DORINDA
Reel Life Video #47: Hairy Pussy Chronicles / 1996 / RLF / F

DORIS
Blue Vanities #538 / 1993 / FFL / M • Blue Vanities #577 / 1995 / FFL / M • Homegrown Video #373 / 1991 / HOV / M • Pri-

vate Gold #10: Sins / 1996 / OD / M

DORIS ARDEN
Carmen Baby / 1967 / AUD / S • [Krankenschwestern-Report / 1972 / ... / M

DORIS CLACTON
Horny Henry's London Adventure / 1995 / TTV / M

DORIS DEL RIO see Star Index I
DORIS FOLK see Star Index I
DORIS GRAY
The Ultimate Pleasure / 1977 / HIF / M

DORIS KEENE see Star Index I
DORIS LIGHT
Erotic Dimensions: Macho Women / 1982 / NSV / M

DORIS LONG
Bucky Beaver's XXX Dragon Art Theatre Double Feature #10 / 1996 / SOW / M • Sins Of Sandra / cr72 / SOW / M

DORIS NITTE
Lady Luck / 1975 / VCX / M

DORIS S.
Private Gold #09: Private Dancer / 1996 / OD / M

DORIS THOMAS
[Le Journal Intime D'Une Nymphomane / 1972 / ... / M

DORIS TYLER see Star Index I
DORIS WILEY
Hard Action / 1975 / AXV / M

DORIT HENKE
[Krankenschwestern-Report / 1972 / ... / M

DOROTHEA RAU
[Junge Madchen Mogen's Heiß, Hausfrauen Noch HeiBer / 1973 / ... / M • [Krankenschwestern-Report / 1972 / ... / M

DOROTHEA REDD see Star Index I
DOROTHY
Blue Vanities #505 / 1992 / FFL / M • Blue Vanities #520 / 1993 / FFL / M • Blue Vanities #548 / 1994 / FFL / M • Blue Vanities #554 / 1994 / FFL / M • Blue Vanities #573 / 1996 / FFL / M • Diane's Night Out / 1988 / VER / B • Neighborhood Watch #21 / 1992 / LBO / M

DOROTHY (HUNGARY)
The Adventures Of Peeping Tom #4 / 1997 / OD / M • Asses Galore #5: T.T. Vs The World / 1996 / DFI / M • Butt Row Unplugged / 1996 / ABS / M • Cumback Pussy #3: Coast To Coast Rump Romp / 1996 / EL / M • Cumback Pussy #4: Get Some!!! / 1996 / EL / M • Hot Tight Asses #18 / 1996 / TCK / M • Pick Up Lines #11 / 1997 / OD / M • War Whores / 1996 / EL / M

DOROTHY BREKEN
Violated / 1973 / PVX / M

DOROTHY COX
The Cumm Brothers #09: Chewin' The Bush / 1995 / OD / M

DOROTHY DE MOLY see Star Index I
DOROTHY H. PATTON see Seka
DOROTHY LAINE
Sinister Servants / 1996 / CUC / B

DOROTHY LE MAY *(Norma Gene, Dorothy Young, Norma Jean (D.LeMay))*
Not too pretty blonde with medium tits and a lithe body. Sounds retarded.
Bad Company / 1978 / CV / M • Bedtime Video #09 / 1984 / GO / M • Behind The Scenes Of An Adult Movie / 1983 / CV / M • Blonde Fire / 1979 / EVI / M • Blondes Have More Fun / 1980 / SE / M • Blondes On Fire / 1987 / VCR / C • Blue Heat / 1975 / IVP / M • Blue Vanities #054 / 1988 / FFL

/ M • Blue Vanities #080 / 1988 / FFL / M • Blue Vanities #086 / 1988 / FFL / M • Body Candy / 1980 / VIS / M • Caballero Preview Tape #2 / 1983 / CA / C • Caballero Preview Tape #3 / 1984 / CA / C • Champagne For Breakfast / 1980 / SE / M • Champagne Orgy / cr78 / HIF / M • Chopstix / 1979 / TVX / M • Classic Swedish Erotica #29 / 1987 / CA / C • Cum Shot Revue #2 / 1985 / HO / C • Deep Passage / 1984 / VCR / C • Erotic Fantasies #5 / 1983 / CV / C • Every Which Way She Can / 1981 / CA / M • Fantasy / 1978 / VCX / M • Female Athletes / 1977 / VXP / M • For The Love Of Pleasure / 1979 / SE / M • A Formal Faucett / 1978 / VC / M • Garage Girls / 1981 / CV / M • Gina, The Foxy Lady / cr79 / COV / M • High School Memories / 1980 / VCX / M • Hot Bodies (Ventura) / 1984 / VEN / C • Hot Ones / 1982 / SUP / C • House Of Desires / cr78 / BL / M • House Of Green Desire / cr78 / CPL / M • I Am Always Ready / 1978 / HIF / M • Inside Desiree Cousteau / 1979 / VCX / M • Irresistible #1 / 1982 / SE / M • Jawbreakers / 1985 / VEN / C • Legends Of Porn #1 / 1987 / CV / C • Memphis Cathouse Blues / 1982 / CA / M • Nightdreams #1 / 1981 / CA / M • Nightlife / 1983 / CA / M • Only The Best #2 / 1989 / CV / C • Only The Very Best On Film / 1992 / VC / C • Physical #1 / 1981 / SUP / M • Physical #2 / 1985 / SUP / M • Saturday Matinee Series #1 / 1996 / VCX / C • Sensual Encounters Of Every Kind / 1978 / SE / M • Sensual Fire / 1979 / HIF / M • Serena, An Adult Fairy Tale / 1979 / VEN / M • Small Town Girls / 1979 / CXV / M • Stalag 69 / 1982 / VHL / S • Sweet Captive / 1979 / EVI / M • Sweet Dreams Suzan / 1980 / CA / M • Taboo #01 / 1980 / VCX / M • Taboo #02 / 1982 / IN / M • Tales Of The Backside / 1985 / VCR / C • Talk Dirty To Me #01 / 1980 / CA / M • Three Ripening Cherries / 1979 / HIF / M • Too Many Cocks In Me! / 1992 / MET / M • Trashi / 1980 / CA / M • Triple Play / 1983 / HO / M • Tropic Of Desire / 1979 / WWV / M • True Legends Of Adult Cinema: Unsung Superstars / 1993 / VC / C • Vista Valley PTA / 1980 / CV / M • Wild Orgies / 1986 / SE / C • [Can't Stop Coming / 1984 / ... / M

DOROTHY MAY
Bucky Beaver's XXX Dragon Art Theatre Double Feature #03 / 1996 / SOW / M • School For Hookers / 1974 / SOW / M

DOROTHY MCNALLY see Star Index I
DOROTHY NEWKIRK see Laurien Dominique
DOROTHY O see Dorothy Oh
DOROTHY OH *(Joy Marchant, Joy Merchant, Dorothy O, Dorothy Onan, Debra Hopkins, Joy Kelly)*
Marginal looking brunette with small tits but a nice personality and good acting skills.
Back Road To Paradise / 1984 / CDI / M • Bare Elegance / 1984 / MAP / M • Bottoms Up #05 / 1986 / AVC / C • Bottoms Up #06 / 1986 / AVC / C • Casino Of Lust / 1984 / AT / M • Confessions Of A Candystriper / 1984 / VC / M • Cum Shot Revue #2 / 1985 / HO / C • Daddy Doesn't Know / 1984 / HO / M • Deep Inside Ginger Lynn / 1986 / SE / C • Diamond Collection #71 / 1985 / CDI / M • Diamond Collection #78 / 1985 / CDI / M • Educating Eva / 1984 / VC / M • Every Man's Fantasy / 1985 / IN / M • Girls Just

Want To...Have Fun / 1984 / SE / M • Head Waitress / 1984 / VC / M • Headhunters / 1984 / VC / M • Holiday For Angels / 1987 / IN / M • Hot Buns / 1983 / VCX / M • Hot Flashes / 1984 / VC / M • Inside China Lee / 1984 / VC / M • Little Often Annie / 1984 / VC / M • Make Me Want It / 1986 / CA / M • Mouthful Of Love / 1984 / VC / M • Naughty Angels / 1984 / VC / M • Naughty Nanette / 1984 / VC / M • Our Major Is Sex / 1984 / VD / M • The Perfect Weekend / 1984 / AVC / M • Pleasure Productions #04 / 1984 / VCR / M • Raffles / 1988 / VC / M • Simply Outrageous / 1989 / VC / C • Spreading Joy / 1988 / VC / M • Sunny Side Up / 1984 / VC / M • Swedish Erotica #54 / 1984 / CA / M • Up In The Air / 1984 / CDI / M • What Gets Me Hot / 1984 / ISV / M • Where The Sun Never Shines / 1990 / IN / C • The Woman Who Loved Men / 1984 / SE / M • Young Nurses In Love / 1987 / VC / M

DOROTHY ONAN see Dorothy Oh
DOROTHY ROBERTS
Strange Diary / 1976 / AXV / M
DOROTHY ROSE
Doctor Yes / 1978 / VIS / M
DOROTHY YOUNG see Dorothy Le May
DORRIE LANE
San Francisco Lesbians #6 / 1994 / PL / F
DORSEE LANE see Star Index I
DORY
Radical Affairs Video Magazine #06 / 1993 / ME / M
DORY DEVON see Star Index I
DORY LANE
House Of Chicks: Masturbation Memoirs #1 / 1995 / HOC / F • House Of Chicks: The Magic Of Female Ejaculation / 1992 / HOC / F
DOT
Blue Vanities #554 / 1994 / FFL / M
DOUG
Cum Soaked And Loaded / 1994 / BCP / M • Full Moon Video #35: Wild Side Couples: The School HeadMaste / 1995 / FAP / M • Hardcore Male/Female Oil Wrestling / 1996 / JSP / M • Homegrown Video #221 / 1000 / HOV / M • Homegrown Video #300 / 1995 / HOV / M • HomeGrown Video #458: Cream Pie For Dessert / 1995 / HOV / C • HomeGrown Video #468: Lust American Style / 1996 / HOV / C • House Play (California Star) / 1994 / CS / B • Ona Zee's Date With Dallas / 1992 / ONA / M • Radical Affairs Video Magazine #09 / 1995 / ME / M
DOUG BARRIS
Bad Girls #2 / 1983 / GO / M
DOUG BECT
Anal Virgins Of America #04 / 1993 / FOR / M
DOUG BENNETT
Confessions Of Candy / 1984 / VC / M • Educating Eva / 1984 / VC / M • Headhunters / 1984 / VC / M • Hot Flashes / 1984 / VC / M • Naughty Nanette / 1984 / VC / M • Raffles / 1988 / VC / M • Sizzling Summer / 1984 / VC / M • Spreading Joy / 1988 / VC / M • Taking Off / 1984 / VC / M • Tongue 'n Cheek (Vca) / 1984 / VC / M • Up Desiree Lane / 1984 / VC / M • Young Nurses In Love / 1987 / VC / M
DOUG BLACK
Switch Hitters #2: Swinging Both Ways / 1987 / IN / G

DOUG CHAPIN
Resurrection Of Eve / 1973 / MIT / M
DOUG DOUGLAS
Hooters In The 'hood / 1995 / TTV / M
DOUG FRANCOIS see Star Index I
DOUG HAMILTON
C.T. Coed Teasers / 1978 / VXP / M • The Erotic Aventures Of Lolita / 1982 / VXP / M
DOUG JACKSON see Sonny Landham
DOUG LEAR
Ultraflesh / 1980 / GO / M
DOUG MASTERS see Star Index I
DOUG NILES
Bi And Beyond #3 / 1989 / INH / G • Innocence Found / 1991 / PAL / G
DOUG PERRY
Courting Libido / 1995 / HIV / G
DOUG ROSS see Steve Douglas
DOUG ROSSI see Steve Douglas
DOUG WARR
America's Raunchiest Home Videos #35: Nothing Butt / 1992 / ZA / M • Deep Inside Dirty Debutantes #05 / 1993 / 4P / M • Mr. Peepers Amateur Home Videos #49: Up And Cumming #2 / 1992 / LBO / M • White Men Can't Hump / 1992 / CC / M
DOUGLAS DAWSON see Star Index I
DOUGLAS FAIRBANK
Sex Boat / 1980 / VCX / M
DOUGLAS STONE
Bottoms Up / 1974 / SOW / M • Bucky Beaver's XXX Dragon Art Theatre Double Feature #05 / 1996 / SOW / M • Too Many Cocks In Me! / 1992 / MET / M
DOUGLAS WOOD
Farewell Scarlett / 1976 / COM / M • Through The Looking Glass / 1976 / ALP / M
DOW
Global Girls / 1996 / GO / F
DR. BERNIE ZILBERGEL see Star Index I
DR. BIGGS
Doctor Feelgood / 1988 / CDI / M
DR. D see Star Index I
DR. DAN see Dan Steele
DR. DEACON see Rodney Moore
DR. DELLA FITZGERALD see Star Index I
DR. DICK see Rodney Moore
DR. INFINITY see Star Index I
DR. JESSIE POTTER see Star Index I
DR. JUDY SEIFER see Star Index I
DR. MARTY KLEIN see Star Index I
DR. MAX FITZGERALD see Star Index I
DR. ROGER LIBBY see Star Index I
DR. SADISTA see Star Index I
DR. SIEGFRIED
Deep Inside Centerfold Girls / 1991 / VC / M
DR. TECH see Star Index I
DR. YESSIR see Star Index I
DRAGHIXA *(Droghixa, Drajika Laurent, Dragica)*
French girl with minimal command of English. Blonde with gray undertones, medium to large breasts, tight waist (earlier European movies were not so tight), creamy skin, pretty face (although her eyes are a little small), nice personality. Small appendectomy scar. 20 years old in 1994, 1m73cm (5'7") tall. Used to be a hairdresser. Parents were Yugoslavian hence the name.
Anal Virgins Of America #06 / 1994 / FOR / M • Blonde Forces #2 / 1994 / CC / M • Body English / 1993 / PL / M • Buffy Mal-

ibu's Nasty Girls #06 / 1994 / ANA / F • Bun Busters #18 / 1994 / LBO / M • Butt Banged Bicycle Babes / 1994 / ANA / M • Circus Of Lesbians / 1995 / VI / C • Dick & Jane Up, Down And All Around / 1994 / AVI / M • Draghixa With An X / 1994 / EX / M • Elements Of Desire / 1994 / ULI / M • Euro-Max #2: Cream n' Euro Sluts / 1995 / SC / M • Euroslut #2 / 1994 / CC / M • Games Women Play / 1995 / XC / M • Gang Bang Face Bath #3 / 1994 / ROB / M • Gang Bang Wild Style #2 / 1994 / ROB / M • The Grind / 1995 / XC / M • International Analists / 1994 / AFD / M • Intervidnet #2: French Made / 1994 / IVN / M • Le Parfum De Mathilde / 1994 / VI / M • Magma: Nymphettes / 1993 / MET / M • Ms. Behaved / 1994 / SC / M • Off Duty Porn Stars / 1994 / VC / M • Older Men With Younger Women #2 / 1994 / CC / M • Omi Ist Die Scharfste / 199? / SVE / M • Private Film #06 / 1994 / OD / M • Private Film #07 / 1994 / OD / M • Private Video Magazine #06 / 1993 / OD / M • Private Video Magazine #07 / 1994 / OD / M • Private Video Magazine #08 / 1994 / OD / M • Radical Affairs Video Magazine #07 / 1994 / ME / M • Secrets Of Madame X #2 / 1995 / WIV / M • Seduction Italiano / 1995 / WIV / M • Sex And Money / 1994 / DGD / S • Shane's Ultimate Fantasy / 1994 / BS / B • Sodomania: The Baddest Of The Best...And Then Some / 1994 / EL / C • Stiff Competition #2 / 1994 / CA / M • Taboo #12 / 1994 / MET / M • Up And Cummers #07 / 1994 / 4P / M • The Voyeur #1 / 1994 / EA / M
DRAGICA see Draghixa
DRAGO
Anal Angel / 1994 / EX / M • Beach Bum Amateur's #29 / 1993 / MID / M • Careless / 1993 / PP / M • Rising Buns / 1993 / HW / M
DRAGON
TV Nation #1 / 1995 / HW / G
DRAJIKA LAURENT see Draghixa
DRAKE
Masochistic Tendencies: The First Night / 1995 / BS / B • A World Of Hurt / 1994 / BS / B
DREA
Very thin especially legs, passable face, black hair with a fringe, small tits.
Country Comfort / 1981 / SE / M • Doing It / 1982 / SE / M • Endless Lust / 1983 / VC / M • Erotic Aerobics / 1984 / VC / M • Erotic Radio WSEX / 1983 / VC / M • Fantasy Follies #1 / 1983 / VC / M • Flesh & Laces #2 / 1983 / CA / M • Flesh Pond / 1983 / VC / M • Fox Fever's Catfight Action / 1984 / VCR / B • Foxholes / 1983 / SE / M • The Girl From S.E.X. / 1982 / CA / M • The Good Time Girls / 1985 / VEX / M • Good To The Last Drop / 1986 / VCS / C • Las Vegas Girls / 1983 / HIF / M • Las Vegas Lady / 1981 / VCX / M • Leather & Lace / 1987 / SE / C • Marathon / 1982 / CA / M • The Midnight Zone / 1986 / IN / M • Modesty Gold / 19?? / MID / M • Pleasure Dome / 1982 / SE / M • Ring Of Desire / 1981 / SE / M • Sexcalibur / 1982 / SE / M • Shades Of Blue #1 / 1982 / ASV / M • Sheer Delight / 1984 / VC / M • Stephanie's Lust Story / 1983 / VC / M • Sweet Alice / 1983 / VCX / M • Too Much Too Soon / 1983 / VCX / M • Undercovers / 1982 / CA / M • Wet Dreams / 1980 / WWV / M • What

Would Your Mother Say? / 1981 / HAV / M
DREAM
Dream's House Party / 1995 / HW / M • Ebony Dancer / 1994 / HBE / M • Ebony Erotica #29: Dark Dreams / 1994 / GO / M • Ebony Erotica #30: Night Train / 1994 / GO / M • More Dirty Debutantes #31 / 1994 / 4P / M
DREW
Catch Of The Day #3 / 1996 / VG0 / M • Filthy First Timers #2: Innocence Lost / 1996 / EL / M • Male Domination #16 / 1990 / BIZ / C
DREW ANDREWS
Like Father Like Son / 1996 / AWV / G • Married Men With Men On The Side / 1996 / BHE / G • Our Trespasses / 1996 / AWV / G
DREW NOLAN
No Reservations / 1995 / MN0 / G
DREW PHOENIX
Aggressive Lesbians / 1995 / STM / C • Binding Contract / 1992 / ZFX / B • Bondage Imagination Unlimited / 1994 / BON / B • Bound For Therapy / 1991 / BIZ / B • Doc Bondage / 1992 / ZFX / B • Full Moon Video #24: Wild Side Couples / 1992 / FAP / M • Gangland #5 / 1995 / ZFX / B • Lesbian Co-Ed Watersports / 1992 / BIZ / B • The Necklace #3 / 1994 / ZFX / B • Slaves Of Passion / 1995 / HOM / B • Sorority Bondage Hazing / 1990 / BON / B • Spellbound (Bizarre) / 1991 / BIZ / B • Z F/X #1 / cr92 / BON / B • ZFX: Nastiest Bound Babes / 1996 / BON / C
DREW REESE
Zazel / 1996 / CV / M
DRINDA LA LUMIA
Take Off / 1978 / VXP / M
DROGHIXA see Draghixa
DRU BERRYMOOR
Short blonde hair, marginal face, small tits, not a tight body, looks young.
The Blowjob Adventures Of Doctor Fellatio / 1997 / EL / M • Bondage Brothel / 1996 / LBO / B • Cumback Pussy #5: Groopin' / 1996 / EL / M • Dungeon Brats / 1994 / STM / B • Dungeon Punishment / 1995 / STM / B • Dynasty's Anal Brat Pack / 1996 / OUP / F • Hard Hand Luc / 1994 / STM / B • Hot Crimson Buns / 1996 / STM / B • Kittens #6 / 1994 / CC / F • Lesbian Sex, Power & Money / 1994 / STM / F • Living On The Edge / 1997 / DWO / M • Lollipops #1 / 1996 / SC / M • Major Exposure / 1995 / PL / F • Mistress Sharon's Girl Toy / 1995 / STM / B • N.Y. Video Magazine #07 / 1996 / OUP / M • Nasty Dancers #1 / 1996 / STM / B • Painful Employment / 1996 / OUP / B • Painful Madness / 1995 / BS / B • Reality & Fantasy / 1994 / DR / M • Sharon's Painful Persuasions / 1996 / SIL / B • Slave Exchange / 1995 / STM / B • Student Fetish Videos: Catfighting #17 / 1996 / PRE / B • Student Fetish Videos: The Enema #20 / 1996 / PRE / B • Student Fetish Videos: Foot Worship #18 / 1995 / PRE / B • Submissive Exposure Profile #5: Keli Thomas / 1996 / STM / C • Takin' It To The Limit #5 / 1995 / BS / M • Titan's Amateur Video Magazine #01 / 1995 / TEG / M • TV Sorority Sister / 1996 / STM / G • Using Your Assets To Get A Head / 1996 / OUP / F • Whips And Chains / 1995 / BS / B • Wicked Moments / 1996 / BS / B • Wrath Of The Dungeon Brats / 1996 / OUP

/ B • Young Lips / 1996 / STM / F
DRUANNE
Eurotica #05 / 1996 / XC / M
DRUE
Catch Of The Day #6 / 1996 / VG0 / M
DRUNA
Triple X Video Magazine #10 / 1995 / OD / M
DUANE
Nina Hartley's Guide To Swinging / 1996 / A&E / M • Wet & Slippery / 1995 / WV / M
DUANE MARKS see Star Index I
DUCHESS
Best Butt(e) In The West #1 / 1992 / CC / M
DUCHESS VON STERN
Afrodisiac #1 / 1987 / CC / M • All American Super Bitches / 1984 / BIZ / B • The Best Of Trained Transvestites / 1990 / BIZ / G • Bizarre Mistress Series: Duchess Von Stern / 1992 / BIZ / C • Bizarre Sorceress / 1979 / STM / B • The Collector / cr83 / BIZ / B • Deeper Spikes / 1984 / BIZ / B • Discipline Collectors #1: Deep Spikes / 1985 / BIZ / B • Ebony Goddesses / 1985 / LON / B • The Full Treatment / cr85 / STM / B • Humiliated Husband / cr83 / BIZ / B • Isle Of The Amazon Women / 1992 / STM / B • Lesbian Dildo Fever #1 / 1989 / BIZ / F • Secluded Passion / 1983 / VHL / M • Top Control / cr85 / JAN / B • Trained Animal / 19?? / ... / B • Training Academy / 1984 / LA / B • TVs By Choice / 19?? / BIZ / G • Vamp's Blackmail / cr83 / STM / B
DUDA
Everything Is Not Relative / 1994 / EL / M
DUDLEY DARE see Star Index I
DUDLEY DINGLE
Northwest Pecker Trek #2: Evergreen, Ever Horny / 1994 / LBO / M
DUKE
Behind The Blinds / 1992 / VIM / M • Bubble Butts #11 / 1992 / LBO / M • A Few Good Rears / 1993 / IN / M • The Knocker Room / 1993 / GO / M • Odyssey Triple Play #47: Backdoor Bingers / 1993 / OD / M
DUKE DEVLIN see Star Index I
DUKE JOHNSON
Goldilocks And The 3 Bi Bears / 1997 / TTV / G • Hot Summer In The City / 1976 / SVE / M • She Male Service / 1994 / HEA / G
DUKE PELIGROSO
Her Wicked Ways / 1983 / CA / M
DUKE STRONG
Sex, Truth & Videotape #2 / 1996 / DOC / M
DULCE MANN
Defiance / 1974 / ALP / B • Farewell Scarlett / 1976 / COM / M • Heavy Load / 1975 / COM / M • Wimps / 1987 / LIV / S
DUNGEON DON
Julie: A First Time Submissive In A Dungeon / 1996 / DHP / B
DURWOOD SMALL see Star Index I
DUSCHA *(Dushka)*
Old biddy, probably in her fifties, Marine style hair cut with white color, medium tits, not too pretty, agressive.
Clock House / 1990 / FC / M • Duscha's Cult Classics #1 / 1995 / FC / C • Duscha's Cult Classics #2 / 1995 / FC / C • Getting Lucky / 1983 / CA / M • Girls Of The Third Reich / 1985 / FC / M • House Of Pleasure / 1984 / CA / M • Lady Domina / 1989 / FC / B • Sulka's Daughter / 1984 / MET / G •

Toys, Not Boys #3 / 1991 / FC / C • [Duscha's Bordello / 199? / FC / M • [Duscha's Fuckfest / 199? / FC / M • [A Voluptuous Lady / 199? / FC / M
DUSHKA see Duscha
DUSTIN see Star Index I
DUSTIN PARKER see Star Index I
DUSTY
A&B AB#224: Wild Women / 1990 / A&B / F • A&B AB#235: Yes, Yes, Nanette / 1994 / A&B / M • A&B AB#258: Spanked Intruder / 1991 / A&B / M • A&B AB#264: Smoking Suckers / 1991 / A&B / M • A&B AB#266: Baby Oil Party / 1991 / A&B / M • A&B AB#267: Lingerie Party / 1991 / A&B / S • A&B AB#269: Red Asses / 1991 / A&B / M • A&B AB#276: Smoking Rods #2 / 1994 / A&B / M • A&B AB#279: Ecstasy And Agony / 1991 / A&B / M • A&B AB#285: Marge / 1991 / A&B / M • A&B AB#289: My Ass Is Red / 1991 / A&B / B • A&B AB#533: Mom Knows Best / 1995 / A&B / M • A&B AB#536: Hairy Wet Pussies / 1995 / A&B / M • A&B AB#537: Drunken Lady / 1995 / A&B / M • Amateurama #02 / 1992 / RTP / F • Amateurama #03 / 1992 / RTP / F • Anal Sluts & Sweethearts #3 / 1995 / ROB / M • Big Girl Workout / 1991 / BTO / M • Black Ass Masters #2 / 1995 / GLI / M • Blue Vanities #574 / 1996 / FFL / M • Booty Ho #2 / 1995 / ROB / M • Creme De La Face #07 / 1995 / OD / M • The Cumm Brothers #08: Escape From Uranus / 1995 / OD / M • Cumm For Dinner / 1995 / BCP / M • The Doctor Is In #2: Pussy Pox / 1995 / NIT / M • Easy Binder / 1994 / VTF / B • Fashion Sluts #2 / 1995 / ABS / M • Hard Core Beginners #03 / 1995 / LEI / M • Hard Core Beginners #04 / 1995 / LEI / M • How To Make A Model #06: Many Happy Returns / 1995 / LBO / M • Huge Ladies #10 / 1991 / BTO / M • Kane Video #2 / 1994 / VTF / B • Lesbian Lust Bust / 1995 / GLI / F • Little House Of Pleasure / 1987 / WDD / S • Mike Hott: #105 Dusty And Paul / 1990 / MHV / M • Mike Hott: #106 Dusty And Lacy / 1990 / MHV / F • Mike Hott: #116 Ali And Pam-Ann And Dusty And Paul / 1990 / MHV / M • Mike Hott: #120 Dildo Debbie, Dusty, Mike And Steve / 1990 / MHV / M • Mike Hott: #123 Foot Fetish #1 / 1990 / MHV / M • Mike Hott: #124 Three Girl Oil Party / 1990 / MHV / F • Mike Hott: #125 Three Girl Lingerie Party / 1990 / MHV / F • Mike Hott: #126 Three Girl Spanking Party #1 / 1990 / MHV / F • Mike Hott: #127 Three Girl Spanking Party #2 / 1990 / MHV / F • Mike Hott: #128 Sex Potpourri / 1990 / MHV / M • Mike Hott: #152 Dusty Solo / 1991 / MHV / F • Mike Hott: #154 Cassandra And Dusty #1 / 1991 / MHV / F • Mike Hott: #155 Cassandra And Dusty #2 / 1991 / MHV / F • Mike Hott: #175 Dusty And Satina / 1991 / MHV / F • Mike Hott: #242 Fuck The Boss #02 / 1993 / MHV / M • Mike Hott: #358 Cunt Of The Month: Chardonnay / 1996 / MHV / M • Mike Hott: Cum Cocktails #3 / 1995 / MHV / C • Real People Real Bondage #2 / 1996 / BON / C • Stevi's: Your Turn / 1994 / SSV / B • Sushi Butts / 1994 / SCL / M • Titan's Gonzo Video Magazine #02 / 1996 / TEG / M
DUSTY (ROSE) see Dusty Rose
DUSTY DREAMS see Star Index I
DUSTY MCNAMARA
Pink Champagne / 1979 / CV / M

DUSTY MEADOWS *see Star Index I*

DUSTY RAVEN
Blue Vanities #003 / 1987 / FFL / M • Limited Edition #12 / 1980 / AVC / M

DUSTY REEVES
Limited Edition #05 / 1979 / AVC / M • Ring Of Desire / 1981 / SE / M

DUSTY RHODES *see Dusty Rose*

DUSTY ROSE *(Dusty (Rose), Dusty Rhodes)*
In mid 1991 KCBS-TV in LA said that this girl was HIV positive and had known about it for at least six years (i.e. turned positive in 1985). She says it's not true and the rumors are just sour grapes from her husband because she left him to live with Rick Savage. According to the trade press they have a medical report of October 1991 saying she's HIV negative.

900 Desert Strip / 1991 / XPI / M • All For You, Baby / 1990 / VEX / M • Amateur Lesbians #05: Missy / 1991 / GO / F • Amateur Lesbians #06: Taylor / 1991 / GO / F • America's Dirtiest Home Videos #06 / 1991 / AMA / M • America's Dirtiest Home Videos #14 / 1992 / VEX / M • As Nasty As She Wants To Be / 1990 / IN / M • B&D Sorority / 1991 / BON / B • Babes / 1991 / CIN / M • Backdoor Lambada / 1990 / GO / M • Backdoor To Hollywood #11 / 1990 / CIN / M • Backdoor To Paradise / 1990 / ELV / M • Bad Medicine / 1990 / VEX / M • Bi-Guy / 1990 / LA / G • Bizarre Master Series: Rick Savage / 1992 / BIZ / C • Bizarre Master Series: Sir Michael / 1992 / BIZ / C • Bizarre Mistress Series: Mistress Destiny / 1992 / BIZ / C • Bizarre Mistress Series: Sharon Mitchell / 1992 / BIZ / C • Black In The Saddle / 1990 / ZA / M • Blonde Temptation / 1995 / IF / M • Bondage Academy #1 / 1991 / BON / B • Bondage Academy #2 / 1991 / BON / B • Bondage Games #1 / 1991 / BIZ / B • Bondage Games #2 / 1991 / BIZ / B • Bondage Memories #01 / 1993 / BON / C • Bound Tickled Tied / cr90 / BON / B • Bun For The Money / 1990 / FH / M • The Butt Stops Here / 1991 / LV / M • Butt Woman #1 / 1990 / FH / M • Captured

Cop #1: Deadly Explosion / 1991 / BON / B • Captured Cop #2: The Stakeout / 1991 / BON / B • Captured Cop #3: Double Cross / 1991 / BON / B • Caught, Punished And Caged / 1991 / BIZ / B • College Girl / 1990 / VEX / M • Dane's Surprise / 1991 / IF / G • Defiance, The Spanking Saga / 1992 / BIZ / B • Do It American Amateur Style / 1992 / EAA / M • Double Penetration #4 / 1991 / WV / C • Dresden Diary #05: Invasion of Privacy / 1992 / BIZ / B • Dusty Bound At Home / 1994 / BON / B • East L.A. Law / 1991 / WV / M • The Erotic Adventures Of Fanny Annie / 1991 / WV / M • The Girl Has Assets / 1990 / LV / M • Hollywood Assets / 1990 / FH / M • Hot Sweet 'n' Sticky / 1992 / CA / C • Imagine / 1991 / LV / M • In Pursuit Of Passion / 1990 / V99 / M • It Happened At Midnight / 1990 / IN / M • King Tung Is The Egyptian Lover / 1990 / LA / M • Lady Badass / 1990 / V99 / M • Lady Of The House / 1990 / VEX / M • Laid Off / 1990 / CA / M • Lesbians, Bondage & Blackjack / 1991 / BIZ / B • A Little Nookie / 1991 / VD / M • Lonely And Blue / 1990 / VEX / M • Lonely Is The Night / 1990 / V99 / M • Love Ghost / 1990 / WV / M • Lust Fever / 1991 / FH / M • Maid For

Service / 1990 / LV / M • My Mistress...Her Slave / 1990 / PL / B • Nasty Calendar / 1991 / XPI / M • Next Door Neighbors #12 / 1990 / BON / M • Next Door Neighbors #39 / 1992 / BON / M • Oral Majority #08 / 1990 / WV / C • Orgy On The Ranch / 1991 / NLE / M • The Outlaw / 1991 / WV / M • P.S.: Back Alley Cats #02 / 1992 / PSP / F • P.S.: Back Alley Cats #06 / 1992 / PSP / F • Paris By Night / 1990 / IN / M • Putting On The Ritz / 1990 / VEX / M • Rainy Days #1 / 1991 / BON / B • Rainy Days #2 / 1991 / BON / B • Rear Admiral / 1990 / ZA / M • Ride 'em Cowgirl / 1991 / V99 / M • Saki's House Party / 1990 / KNI / M • Sex Kittens / 1990 / VEX / F • Sex Pistol / 1990 / CDI / M • She-Male Sex Clinic / 1991 / VC / G • A Slave For The Bride / 1991 / BIZ / B • Space Virgins / 1990 / VEX / M • Spank Me Darling / 1993 / VTF / B • The Stranger Beside Me / 1991 / WV / M • Summer Heat / 1991 / CIN / M • Supertung / 1990 / LA / M • Suzanne's Grand Affair / 1990 / CV / M • Sweet Darlin' / 1990 / VEX / M • Sweet Poison / 1991 / CDI / M • Sweet Surrender / 1991 / BIZ / B • Teach Me Tonight / 1990 / VEX / M • Torrid Tonisha / 1992 / VEX / M • Triple Header / 1990 / KNI / M • TVs In Trouble #2 / 1991 / BIZ / G • Twin Cheeks #2 / 1991 / CIN / M • The War Of The Hoses / 1991 / NLE / M • We're No Angels / 1990 / CIN / M • Young Buns #2 / 1990 / WV / M

DUSTY ROSE (1996)
Filthy First Timers #1 / 1996 / EL / M • Filthy First Timers #3: Tearing Down The Walls Of Shame / 1996 / EL / M

DWARF *see Star Index I*

DWAYNE
AVP #6003: Lynn's Desire / 1991 / AVP / M

DWIGHT
Foxx Tales / 1996 / TTV / M

DWIGHT FRYE *see Star Index I*

DWIGHT LIGHTNING *see Steve Drake*

DYANA
SVE: Dyana Does The Tag Team / 1994 / SVE / M

DYANNA LAUREN *(Dianna Lauren, Dyanna Laurence, Diane Hadley)*
Blonde with enhanced tits (not too bad) and a rose tattoo on her midline just above her pussy. Quite pretty but has teased hair and sounds slutty. Supposedly has a degree in music and was 21 before she first got laid. Only screws her boyfriend, Brad Armstrong, but has made exceptions for the likes of Marc Wallice with a condom.

13th Annual Adult Video News Awards / 1996 / VC / S • Anal Planet / 1994 / CC / M • Assy Sassy #1 / 1994 / ROB / F • Babes Illustrated #1 / 1994 / IN / F • Back To Anal Alley / 1994 / ME / M • Bad Girls Get Punished / 1994 / NTP / B • Bad Habits / 1993 / VC / M • Badgirls #5: Maximum Babes / 1995 / VI / M • The Best Of Doctor Butts / 1994 / 4P / C • The Bet / 1993 / VT / M • Beverly Hills Sex Party / 1993 / EX / M • The Beverly Thrillbillies / 1993 / ZA / M • Big Busted Dream Girls / 1995 / PME / S • Big Knockers #02 / 1994 / TV / M • Big Knockers #03 / 1994 / TV / M • Big Knockers #04 / 1994 / TV / M • Big Knockers #12 / 1995 / TV / C • Blind Spot / 1993 / VI / M • Boiling Point / 1994 / WAV / M • Bonnie & Clyde #3 / 1994 / VI / M • Bonnie & Clyde #4 / 1994 / VI / M • Cat Lickers #2 / 1994 /

ME / F • The Cathouse / 1994 / VI / M • Checkmate / 1995 / WAV / M • Chug-A-Lug Girls #3 / 1993 / VT / M • Circus Of Lesbians / 1995 / VI / C • Club Anal #2 / 1993 / ROB / F • Club DV8 #1 / 1993 / SC / M • Delicious Passions / 1993 / ROB / F • Designs On Women / 1994 / IN / F • Dick & Jane Go To Hollywood #2 / 1993 / AVI / M • Double Decadence / 1995 / NOT / M • Double Penetration Virgins #05: Go To Hell / 1994 / BB0 / M • Dr Butts #3 / 1993 / 4P / M • Elements Of Desire / 1994 / ULI / M • Eleventh Annual AVN Awards / 1994 / VC / M • The End Zone / 1993 / PRE / B • Extreme Sex #1: The Club / 1994 / VI / M • Father Of The Babe / 1993 / ZA / M • The Finishing Touch / 1994 / DR / M • Grand Slam / 1993 / ... / B • The Great American Boobs To Kill For Dance Contest / 1995 / PEP / C • Hard Feelings / 1995 / VI / M • Hardcore / 1994 / VI / M • Hawaii / 1995 / VI / M • I Love Juicy / 1993 / ZA / M • Immortal Desire / 1993 / VI / M • In Cold Sweat / 1996 / VI / M • Island Fantasies / 1993 / NIV / S • It's Blondage, The Video / 1994 / VI / M • Killer Looks / 1994 / IMP / S • Kym Wilde's On The Edge #06 / 1993 / RB / B • The Last Act / 1995 / VI / M • Leg...Ends #11 / 1994 / PRE / F • Love Me, Love My Butt #1 / 1994 / ROB / F • Miss Nude International / 1993 / LE / M • The Mistress (1993-Caballero) / 1993 / CA / M • Night Play / 1995 / WAV / M • No Motive / 1994 / MID / M • Nothing To Hide #2 / 1993 / CV / M • On Her Back / 1994 / VI / M • Oral Obsession #1 / 1994 / VI / M • Pajama Party X #2 / 1994 / VC / M • Passionate Partners: The Guide For Daring Lovers / 1993 / PHV / S • Perplexed / 1994 / FD / M • Plan 69 From Outer Space / 1993 / CA / M • Poison / 1994 / VI / M • The Proposal / 1993 / HO / M • Pussyman #04: The Celebration / 1993 / SNA / M • Raunch #08 / 1993 / CC / M • Red Light / 1994 / SC / S • The Reel World #1 / 1994 / FOR / M • The Reel World #2 / 1994 / FOR / M • The Rehearsal / 1993 / VC / M • Sarah Jane's Love Bunnies #04 / 1993 / FPI / F • Sex Magic / 1994 / BWV / B • Sex In The Studio / 1994 / CPG / S • Sexual Athlete / 1993 / CAW / B • Shame / 1994 / VI / M • Shaved Sinners #4 / 1993 / VT / M • Sheepless In Montana / 1993 / FOR / M • Ski Bunnies #1 / 1994 / HW / M • Ski Bunnies #2 / 1994 / HW / M • Split Tail Lovers / 1994 / ROB / F • The Star / 1995 / CC / M • Star Struck / 1994 / ERA / M • Stardust #3 / 1996 / VI / M • Steamy Windows / 1993 / VI / M • A Stripper Named Desire / 1993 / CC / M • Swallow / 1994 / VI / M • The Swap #2 / 1994 / VI / M • The Swing / 1996 / VI / M • Taste Of Shame / 1994 / ROB / F • The Tattle Tail / 1993 / ME / M • Tip Tap Toe / 1995 / PRE / C • Toe Biz / 1993 / PRE / S • Toppers #07 / 1993 / TV / M • Toppers #16 / 1993 / TV / M • Toppers #18 / 1993 / TV / M • Toppers #19 / 1993 / TV / M • Toppers #22 / 1993 / TV / C • Toppers & Whoppers #2 / 1994 / PRE / C • The Truth Laid Bare / 1993 / ZA / M • Twelfth Annual Avn Awards / 1995 / VC / M • Undress To Thrill / 1994 / VI / M • Up And Cummers #04 / 1993 / 4P / M • Up And Cummers #16 / 1994 / 4P / M • Venus' Playhouse / 1994 / VDL / S • Web Of Desire / 1993 / OD / M • Weird Sex /

1995 / GO / M • Where The Boys Aren't #7 / 1995 / VI / F • Where The Boys Aren't #8 / 1996 / VI / F • Where The Boys Aren't #9 / 1996 / VI / F • White Shadow / 1994 / VC / M • WPINK-TV #4 / 1993 / PV / M
DYANNA LAWSON see Dyanna Lauren
DYLAN
The Girls Of Fantasex #2 / 1996 / NIT / M • Julie's Diary / 1995 / LBO / M
DYLAN FOX see Star Index I
DYLAN MONTANA see Star Index I
DYLAN RAGE
Bi The Time You Get Back / 1995 / BIN / G • Tranny Claus / 1994 / HEA / G
DYMOND CARTIER see Diamond Cartier
DYNAMITE
Black & Wet Private Parts / 1994 / STM / F • Dark Angels / 1996 / STM / F • Dark Desire / 1995 / STM / F • Disciplinary Action / 1995 / STM / B • Ebony Erotica #19: Ebony Angels / 1994 / GO / M • Girlz Towne #12 / 1995 / FC / F • Harlem Honies #1 / 1993 / CC / M • Harlem Honies #2: Nasty In New York / 1994 / CC / M • Hoetown / 1994 / STM / F • Lesbian Kink Trilogy #2 / 1995 / STM / F • Vivid Raw #4 / 1996 / VI / M • Women Who Control The Family Jewels #4 / 1995 / STM / B • [Chocolate Waitress / 199? / ... / M
DYNAMO HUM see Heidi Nelson
DYNASTI see Tessa Kahn
DYNASTY
Act Of Submission / 1995 / OUP / B • Dirty Bob's #18: Under The Boardwalk! / 1995 / FLP / S • Dirty Bob's #19: Over The Boardwalk! / 1995 / FLP / S • Dynasty's Anal Brat Pack / 1996 / OUP / F • Dynasty's S&M Initiation / 1994 / OUP / B • East Coast Sluts #10: Ohio / 1996 / PL / M • Magic Moments: Dynasty's Magic Moments / 1996 / MM1 / F • N.Y. Video Magazine #01 / 1994 / OUP / M • N.Y. Video Magazine #02 / 1995 / OUP / M • N.Y. Video Magazine #06 / 1995 / OUP / M • New York City Lesbian Gang Bang / 1995 / OUP / F • Painful Employment / 1996 / OUP / B • Pearl Necklace: Premier Sessions #04 / 1994 / SEE / M • The Punishment Of Dynasty / 1995 / OUP / B • Southern Belles #6 / 1996 / XPR / M • Southern Belles: Sugar Magnolias / 1996 / XPR / M
E. COLI
White Hot / 1984 / VXP / M
E. THUMPER see Stephanie DuValle
E.J. VEX
Beaver & Buttcheeks / 1993 / DR / M
E.R. HUXLEY see Star Index I
E.T. SQUARED
Tight Spot / 1996 / WV / M
E.Z. RYDER (Easy Ryder, Nigel Wild)
Was at one time engaged to Holly Ryder. 51 years old in 1993.
Adult Video News 1991 Awards / 1991 / VC / M • The Adventures Of Studman #1 / 1994 / AFV / M • Anal Addiction #2 / 1990 / SO / M • Backdoor To Harley-Wood #2 / 1990 / AFV / M • Beyond It All / 1991 / PAL / G • Blue Bayou / 1993 / VC / M • Blue Dreams / 1996 / SC / M • Bondage Proposal / 1993 / STM / B • Bottoms Up (1993-Bon Vue) / 1993 / BON / B • Cheap Shots / 1994 / PRE / B • Conquest / 1996 / WP / M • Corporate Affairs / 1996 / CC / M • Criss-Cross / 1993 / BON / B • Cyrano / 1991 / PL / M • Deep Inside P.J. Sparxx /

1995 / VC / C • Diamond In The Rough / 1993 / BIA / C • Ding Dung School / 1994 / PLV / B • Double Trouble Spanking / 1993 / BON / B • Erotika / 1994 / WV / M • Foolproof / 1994 / VC / M • Foot Hold / 1994 / PRE / B • Forever Young / 1994 / VI / M • French Open / 1993 / PV / M • French Open Part Deux / 1993 / MET / M • The Girl With The Heart-Shaped Tattoo / 1995 / WAV / M • Hard Ride / 1992 / WV / M • Harlots / 1993 / MID / M • Holly Ryder Tied At Home / 1992 / BON / B • Hothouse Rose #1 / 1991 / VC / M • I'll Take The Whip / 1993 / BON / B • Internal Affairs / 1995 / VI / M • Jugsy (X-Citement) / 1992 / XCI / M • Junk Yard Dogs / 1991 / FC / M • Kym Wilde's On The Edge #02 / 1993 / RB / B • Lap Of Luxury / 1994 / WIV / M • Leather And Tether / 1993 / STM / C • Leather Lair #1 / 1992 / STM / B • Leather Lair #3 / 1993 / STM / B • Lethal Passion / 1991 / PL / M • Lucky Lady / 1995 / CV / M • Make My Wife Please... / 1993 / VC / M • The Many Loves Of Jennifer / 1991 / VC0 / S • Mike Hott: Cum Cocktails #1 / 1995 / MHV / C • Mind Set / 1996 / VI / M • More Dirty Debutantes #08 / 1991 / 4P / M • Naked Goddess #1 / 1991 / VC / M • The Newcummers / 1990 / 4P / M • Nikki's Bon Voyage / 1993 / VC / M • Nikki's Last Stand / 1993 / VC / M • Odds 'n' Ends / 1992 / PRE / B • Paddle Tales / 1992 / BON / B • Paging Betty / 1994 / VC / M • The Party / 1992 / CDI / M • Peepshow / 1994 / OD / M • The Phoenix #1 / 1992 / VI / M • Prescription For Pleasure / 1993 / HW / M • Profiles In Discipline #02: Naughty Angel / 1994 / STM / C • Rare Ends / 1996 / PRE / C • Razor's Edge / 1995 / ONA / M • Real People Real Bondage #2 / 1996 / BON / C • Road Kill / 1995 / CA / M • Scandal / 1995 / VI / M • Scorched / 1995 / ONA / M • The Seduction Of Marylin Star / 1995 / VT / M • Servin' It Up / 1993 / VC / M • Sexophrenia / 1993 / VC / M • Silk Stockings: The Black Widow / 1994 / SPI / M • Sisters / 1993 / ZA / M • Sole Survivors / 1996 / PRE / C • Sorority Sex Kittens #1 / 1992 / VC / M • Sorority Sex Kittens #2 / 1993 / VC / M • Street Fantasies / 1993 / AFV / M • Strippers Inc. #1 / 1994 / ONA / M • Strippers Inc. #4 / 1995 / ONA / M • Stroke Play / 1994 / PLV / B • Student Fetish Videos: Best of Enema #03 / 1994 / PRE / C • Sweat Shop / 1991 / EVN / M • Tales From Leather Lair: The Leather Master / 1992 / STM / B • Tami Monroe Tied At Home / 1993 / BON / B • Tempted / 1994 / VI / M • Thin Ice / 1996 / ONA / M • A Touch Of Mink / 1990 / V99 / M • Unplugged / 1995 / CC / M • Venus Of The Nile / 1991 / WV / M • Vivid At Home #01 / 1994 / VI / M • Vivid At Home #02 / 1994 / VI / M • Vow Of Passion / 1991 / VI / M • Watersgate / 1994 / PRE / C • Web Of Desire / 1993 / OD / M • Welcome To Bondage: Alana Patch / 1993 / BON / B • Welcome To Bondage: Alex Jordan With Justin Case / 1992 / BON / B • Welcome To Bondage: Ari / 1993 / BON / B • Welcome To Bondage: Brittany / 1993 / BON / B • Welcome To Bondage: Brooke / 1994 / BON / B • Welcome To Bondage: Celeste / 1993 / BON / B • Welcome To Bondage: Chelly / 1993 / BON / B • Welcome To Bondage:

Christie / 1993 / BON / B • Welcome To Bondage: Crystal Wilder / 1993 / BON / B • Welcome To Bondage: Dominique / 1993 / BON / B • Welcome To Bondage: Eva / 1993 / BON / B • Welcome To Bondage: Francesca Le / 1992 / BON / B • Welcome To Bondage: Gabrill / 1993 / BON / B • Welcome To Bondage: Jasper / 1994 / BON / B • Welcome To Bondage: Kelli & Sharp / 1993 / BON / B • Welcome To Bondage: Miyoshi / 1992 / BON / B • Welcome To Bondage: Nikki / 1993 / BON / B • Welcome To Bondage: Pantera / 1994 / BON / B • Welcome To Bondage: Paramour & Quinn / 1993 / BON / B • Welcome To Bondage: Rebecca And Julian / 1993 / BON / B • Welcome To Bondage: Sahara / 1994 / BON / B • Welcome To Bondage: Sami / 1993 / BON / B • Welcome To Bondage: Starlets #1 / 1993 / BON / C • Welcome To Bondage: Starlets #2 / 1994 / BON / C • Welcome To Bondage: Sunset Thomas / 1993 / BON / B • Welcome To Bondage: Tara Gold / 1992 / BON / B • Welcome To Bondage: Tiffany Taylor / 1992 / BON / B • Whispered Lies / 1993 / LBO / M • Wild Innocence / 1992 / PL / M • Women On Top / 1995 / BON / B
EARL RAWLINGS see Star Index I
EARL ROBBINS see Star Index I
EARL WHITE
Erotic Fantasies #5 / 1983 / CV / C
EARTHA QUAKE
Heavyweight Contenders / 1996 / HW / M • Horny Henry's Strange Adventure / 1995 / TTV / M • More To Love #1 / 1994 / TTV / M • More To Love #2 / 1995 / TTV / M • Q Balls #1 / 1996 / TTV / M • Q Balls #2 / 1996 / TTV / M • When The Fat Lady Sings / 1996 / EX / M
EASTMAN PRICE
Love Boccaccio Style / 1970 / SOW / S • Swingers Massacre / 1975 / SVE / S • An Unnatural Act #1 / 1984 / DR / M
EASY ED
FTV #24: Secret Submission / 1996 / FT / B • FTV #25: Big Bust Domination / 1996 / FT / B • FTV #26: Smother Queen / 1996 / FT / B • FTV #27: Secretaries' Revenge & Twist & Shout / 1996 / FT / B • FTV #29: Boss Lady And Black & Blue / 1996 / FT / B • FTV #32: Fist Filet / 1996 / FT / B • FTV #35: Kimberly Kupps Konquest #2 / 1996 / FT / B • FTV #44: Tight Tamali And Bam Jam / 1996 / FT / B • FTV #50: Double-D Duo / 1996 / FT / B • FTV #61: Boss Lady #1 / 1996 / FT / B • FTV #62: Boss Lady #2 / 1996 / FT / B • FTV #63: DD Domination #1 / 1996 / FT / B • FTV #65: DD Domination #2 / 1996 / FT / B • FTV #70: Outcall Outcry / 1996 / FT / B • FTV #72: Massage Mayhem / 1996 / FT / B • FTV #76: Bundy Bashout / 1996 / FT / B
EASY RYDER see E.Z. Ryder
EBENEZER BARTHOLOMU
The Spirit Of Seventy Six / 1976 / NGV / M
EBER HARD
Club Kiss / 1995 / ONA / M
EBONI WILSON
Chocolate Candy #1 / 1984 / VD / M
EBONY
Booty In Da House / 1995 / EVN / M • Hardcore Male/Female Oil Wrestling / 1996 / JSP / M
EBONY ASS

Dangerous Behinds #1 / 1995 / HW / M
EBONY AYERS *see* **Ebony Ayes**
EBONY AYES *(Ebony Ayers, Ebony Eyes, Phylis Roberts, Cocoa (Ebony Ayes))*
Ugly black girl with diseased-looking skin. Phylis Roberts is from **Innocent Seduction.**
10 Years Of Big Busts #1 / 1989 / BTO / C • Afrodisiac #2 / 1989 / CC / M • Amos & Candy / 1987 / VCR / C • Angelica / 1989 / ARG / M • Babes At War / 1990 / NAP / B • Backfield In Motion / 1990 / PV / M • Bedroom Showdown / 1988 / NAP / B • Behind The Black Door / 1987 / VEX / M • Best In Bed / 1988 / NAP / B • Between My Breasts #04 / 1986 / L&W / S • Beyond The Senses / 1986 / AVC / M • Big Bust Babes #04 / 1988 / AFI / M • Big Bust Babes #06 / 1991 / AFI / F • The Big E #07 / 1988 / BIZ / B • Big Tit Hookers / 1989 / BTO / M • Big Tit Orgy #03 / 1991 / BTO / C • Big Top Cabaret #2 / 1989 / BTO / M • Big-Busted Cell-Mates / 1990 / NAP / B • The Bigger The Better / 1986 / SE / C • The Bigger They Come, The Harder They fall / 1990 / NAP / B • Biggest And The Best / 1988 / NAP / B • Black & Gold / 1990 / CIN / M • Black 'n' Blew / 1988 / VC / M • Black Angel / 1987 / CC / M • Black Cat Rumble / 1988 / NAP / B • Black Chicks In Heat / 1988 / VC / M • Black Fox / 1988 / CC / M • Black Goddesses / cr85 / STM / B • Black Madam Sadista / 1992 / BIZ / B • Black On White / 1988 / NAP / B • Black Valley Girls #2 / 1989 / DR / M • Blackman / 1989 / PL / M • Blonde Bitch, Black Bitch / 1988 / NAP / B • Blonde Jail-Bait / 1989 / NAP / B • Body Vs. Body / 1989 / NAP / B • Bondage Thrills / cr85 / STM / B • The Booby Prize #1 / 1988 / PL / F • The Booby Prize #2 / 1988 / PL / F • Busen Extra #1 / 1991 / BTO / M • Busen Extra #2 / 1990 / BTO / M • Bustline Collision / 1994 / NAP / B • Busty Bitches / 1990 / BIZ / S • Campfire Girls / 1988 / SE / M • Cat-Fight Queen / 1988 / NAP / B • Charlie's Girls #1 / 1988 / CC / M • Chocolate Dreams (Venus 99) / 1987 / V99 / M • Cleopatra Meets The Czarina / 199? / NAP / ㅐ ⬝ Cleopatra Vs. The Indian Princess / 199? / NAP / B • Closet Nazi / 1988 / NAP / B • The Conquest / 1988 / NAP / B • Czarina On Fire / 199? / NAP / B • Dance Challenge / 1988 / NAP / B • Die Supergeilen Raubritter / 1995 / CL0 / M • Dildoe Action / cr85 / STM / B • Dominated / 1988 / NAP / B • Double D Delights / 1989 / VCR / C • Double D Roommates / 1989 / BTO / M • Dr Juice's Lust Potion / 1986 / TEM / M • Dream Match / 1989 / NAP / B • Duel Of The Bustlines / 1988 / NAP / B • Duel Of The Love Goddesses / 1990 / NAP / B • Ebony And The Blonde / 1988 / NAP / B • Ebony Boxes / 1988 / NAP / B • Ebony Humpers #1 / 1986 / VEX / M • Ebony Humpers #3 / 1987 / VEX / M • Ebony Humpers #4 / 1988 / VEX / M • Educating Kascha / 1989 / CIN / M • EE 7 / 1991 / NAP / S • Exploding Fists / 1994 / NAP / B • Fight For Supremacy / 1989 / NAP / B • Filet-O-Breast / 1988 / AVC / M • The Final Match / 1988 / NAP / B • Fireball / 1988 / IN / M • Fist Of Leather / 1989 / NAP / B • Flesh For Frankenstein / 1987 / VEX / M • Forbidden Dildo Taboos / 1992 / STM / F • French Cleaners / 1986 / VCR /

M • Friendly Persuasion / 1988 / NAP / B • Get Bi Tonight / 1991 / PL / G • Girls Of The Double D #01 / 1986 / CDI / M • Girls Of The Double D #02 / 1987 / CDI / M • Girls Of The Double D #03 / 1988 / CDI / M • Girls Of The Double D #04 / 1989 / CDI / M • Girls Of The Double D #08 / 1989 / CDI / M • Girls Of The Double D #12 / 1990 / CDI / M • The Godmother #1 / 1987 / VC / M • The Godmother #2 / 1988 / VC / M • Good 'n' Plenty / 1987 / AVC / M • Good Golly, Miss Molly / 1987 / CDI / M • Hooters / 1986 / AVC / M • How To Get A "Head" / 1988 / CV / M • Hyapatia Lee's Sexy / 1986 / SE / M • Hypnotized / 1988 / NAP / B • I Can't Get No...Satisfaction / 1988 / CDI / M • Innocent Seduction / 1988 / VC / M • Introducing Melissa Mounds / 1989 / NAP / F • Introducing Micki Marsaille / 1990 / NAP / F • Just Between Friends / 1988 / VEX / M • Just Ebony / 1988 / NAP / F • Kascha & Friends / 1988 / CIN / M • Kascha's Blues / 1988 / CDI / M • Kicking Ass / 1988 / NAP / B • Kiss Thy Mistress' Feet #1 / 1990 / BIZ / B • Knight Of Conquest / 1994 / NAP / B • La Boomba / 1987 / VCX / M • Lesbian Dildo Fever #2 / 1989 / BIZ / F • Lesbian Fantasies / 1990 / BIZ / F • Lesbian She Fights #1 / 1992 / BIZ / B • Lesbian She Fights #2 / 1992 / BIZ / B • Lucky Charm / 1986 / AVC / C • Lust Letters / 1988 / CA / M • Lust Of Blacula / 1987 / VEX / M • Magma: Splash Of Sperm / 1990 / MET / M • Mandii's Magic / 1988 / CDI / M • Matched Pairs / 1988 / VEX / M • Mega-Tits / 1990 / NAP / F • More Than A Mouthful #1 / 1991 / VEX / M • Much More Than A Mouthful #1 / 1987 / VEX / M • My Sensual Body / 1989 / WET / M • Nasty Blacks / 1988 / VEX / M • National Pornographic #4: / 1987 / 4P / C • Nooner / 1986 / AVC / M • Nothing But Girls, Girls, Girls / 1988 / CDI / M • Office Dispute / 1988 / NAP / B • Oral Majority #06 / 1988 / WV / C • Over-Matched / 199? / NAP / B • Parliament: Dildo Babes #2 / 1988 / PM / F • Parliament: Three Way Lust / 1988 / PM / M • Parliament: Tops & Bottoms #1 / 1988 / PM / F • Party Wagon / 1988 / CDI / M • Peal Frolic / 1988 / NAP / B • Post Party Mayhem / 1988 / NAP / B • Queen Challenged / 199? / NAP / B • Red Hot Fire Girls / 1989 / VD / M • Return Match / 1988 / NAP / B • The Rise Of The Roman Empress #2 / 1990 / PV / M • Roman-Afro Wrestling / 1989 / NAP / B • Ruling The Roost / 1990 / NAP / B • Rumble-Cats / 1989 / NAP / B • Scorching Secrets / 1988 / IN / M • Sex With A Stranger / 1986 / AVC / M • The Sexaholic / 1988 / VC / M • Some Like It Hotter / 1989 / CDI / M • Special Massage / 1989 / NAP / B • Strong-Willed / 1995 / NAP / B • Swing Shift / 1989 / PL / G • Taking It To The Streets / 1987 / CDI / M • The Taking Of Reno / 1988 / NAP / B • A Taste Of Ebony / 1990 / PIN / C • That Ole Black Magic / 1988 / CDI / M • This Dick For Hire / 1989 / ZA / M • Tickle Power / 1987 / PLV / B • Top Heavy / 1988 / VD / M • Tower Of Power / 1989 / E&I / C • The Trainee / 1989 / NAP / B • Travelling Companion / 1989 / NAP / B • Warrior Queen Of The Zulus / 1993 / NAP / B • White Chocolate / 1987 / PEN / M • Working Girls / 1988 / NAP / B • Wrestling Challenge / 1990 /

NAP / B • Wrestling Queen Of The Nile / 1993 / NAP / B • Wrestling Queens / 1989 / NAP / B • [Berlin Caper / 1989 / ... / M • [The Best Of Double D's / 1989 / VD / C • [Black Beauties / 1986 / ... / M • [The Blacks Next Door / 1988 / VD / M • [Casino Fortune / 1988 / ... / M • [Feuchte Lust / 1989 / ... / M • [Horny Heatwaves / 1989 / VTO / M • [Washington Affairs / 1988 / ... / M • [Weekend In Fist Fuck Land / 1988 / ... / M
EBONY CLARK *see* **Star Index I**
EBONY EYES *see* **Ebony Ayes**
EBONY PARKS *see* **Sade**
EBONY REESE
Black Lust / 1995 / UBP / M
EBONY ROCK
AVP #9129: The Rumor Police / 1991 / AVP / M
EBONY ROD
The Adventures of Marilyn Ohno / 1996 / GLI / M • Denni O' #4: Beach Ballin' / 1996 / SP / M • Seven Year Bitch / 1996 / GLI / M
EBONY SMILES
Sweet Black Cherries #4 / 1996 / TTV / M
ED
Big Murray's New-Cummers #07: Swinging in the "A" / 1993 / FD / M • Porno Screentests / 1992 / VC / M • Savage Fury #3 / 1994 / VEX / M
ED BOA *see* **Star Index I**
ED BUCKS
Justine: A Matter Of Innocence / 1980 / SAT / M
ED DE ROO *see* **Loretta Sterling (M)**
ED DELONG
Mr. Blue / 1996 / JSP / G
ED DOUSSET
Positively Pagan #01 / 1991 / ATA / M • Positively Pagan #02 / 1991 / ATA / M • Positively Pagan #04 / 1991 / ATA / M • Positively Pagan #06 / 1993 / ATA / M
ED HAMILTON
ABA: Double Feature #5 / 1996 / ALP / M • Night Of Submission / 1976 / BIZ / M
ED HARDY
Erotic Tattooing And Piercing #1 / 1986 / FLV / M
ED LAROUX
Funk / 1977 / ... / M
ED LINCOLN
All The King's Ladies / 1981 / SUP / M
ED MARSHALL
Come With Me, My Love / 1976 / PVX / M • MASH'ed / cr75 / ALP / M
ED MASTERS *see* **Star Index I**
ED MICHAELS *see* **Star Index I**
ED NAVARRO
Bucky Beaver's XXX Dragon Art Theatre Double Feature #02 / 1996 / SOW / M • The Rites Of Uranus / 1975 / SOW / M
ED OAKS *see* **Mickey (Missy)**
ED PARKS
Bedtime Video #05 / 1984 / GO / M
ED PASTRAM *see* **Star Index I**
ED POWERS *(Mark Arnold)*
If you don't know who Ed is and what he looks like...well, just rent a **More Dirty Debutantes** tape. He frequently uses the name Mark Arnold as a director, comes from Brooklyn and was born 10/25/54.
A Is For Asia / 1996 / 4P / M • The Audition / 1992 / BON / B • Autobiography Of A Whip / 1991 / BS / B • Barbi Bound 1988 / BON / B • Barbii Unleashed / 1988 / 4P /

M • Behind The Backdoor #5 / 1992 / EVN / M • The Best Of Doctor Butts / 1994 / 4P / C • Big Boob Boat Ride #1 / 1992 / FC / M • Black Dirty Debutantes / 1993 / 4P / M • Black To Basics / 1992 / ZA / M • Body Slam / 1987 / 4P / B • Bonda-Cize / 1988 / BON / B • The Bottom Dweller Part Deux / 1994 / EL / M • Bus Stop Tales #01 / 1989 / PRI / M • Bus Stop Tales #02 / 1989 / PRI / M • Bus Stop Tales #03 / 1989 / PRI / M • Bus Stop Tales #04 / 1989 / PRI / M • Bus Stop Tales #05 / 1989 / PRI / M • Bus Stop Tales #06 / 1989 / PRI / M • Bus Stop Tales #07 / 1989 / PRI / M • Bus Stop Tales #08 / 1990 / PRI / M • Bus Stop Tales #09 / 1990 / PRI / M • Bus Stop Tales #10 / 1990 / PRI / M • Bus Stop Tales #11 / 1990 / 4P / M • Bus Stop Tales #12 / 1990 / 4P / M • Bus Stop Tales #13 / 1990 / 4P / M • Bus Stop Tales #14 / 1990 / PRI / M • The Challenge / 1990 / EA / B • Controlled / 1990 / BS / B • Cruel Passions / 1992 / BS / B • Debutante Dreams / 1995 / 4P / M • Deep Inside Dirty Debutantes #01 / 1992 / 4P / M • Deep Inside Dirty Debutantes #02 / 1992 / 4P / M • Deep Inside Dirty Debutantes #03 / 1992 / 4P / M • Deep Inside Dirty Debutantes #04 / 1992 / 4P / M • Deep Inside Dirty Debutantes #05 / 1993 / 4P / M • Deep Inside Dirty Debutantes #06 / 1993 / 4P / M • Deep Inside Dirty Debutantes #07 / 1993 / 4P / M • Deep Inside Dirty Debutantes #08 / 1993 / 4P / M • Deep Inside Dirty Debutantes #09 / 1993 / 4P / M • Deep Inside Dirty Debutantes #10 / 1993 / 4P / M • Deep Inside Dirty Debutantes #11 / 1996 / 4P / M • Dirty Bob's #23: Tampa Teasers / 1995 / FLP / S • Dirty Bob's #27: Laid Back In L.A.! / 1996 / FLP / S • Dirty Dancers #1 / 1994 / 4P / M • Dirty Dancers #2 / 1994 / 4P / M • Dirty Debutantes / 1990 / 4P / M • Dirty Dirty Debutantes #1 / 1995 / 4P / M • Dirty Dirty Debutantes #2 / 1996 / 4P / M • Dirty Dirty Debutantes #3 / 1996 / 4P / M • Dirty Dirty Debutantes #4 / 1996 / 4P / M • Dirty Dirty Debutantes #5 / 1996 / 4P / M • Dirty Dirty Debutantes #6 / 1996 / 4P / M • Dirty Dirty Debutantes #7 / 1996 / 4P / M • Dirty Dirty Debutantes #8 / 1996 / 4P / M • Dr Butts #1 / 1991 / 4P / M • Dr Butts #2 / 1992 / 4P / M • Dr Butts #3 / 1993 / 4P / M • Dr Hooters / 1991 / PL / M • The Face Of Fear / 1990 / BS / B • The Fear Zone / 1991 / BS / B • For The Hell Of It / 1992 / BS / B • Gangbang Girl #05 / 1992 / ANA / M • Gangbang Girl #06 / 1992 / ANA / M • The Hardriders / 1990 / 4P / M • House Of Dark Dreams #1 / 1990 / BS / B • House Of Dark Dreams #2 / 1990 / BS / B • I Wanna Be A Porn Star #1 / 1996 / 4P / M • I Wanna Be A Porn Star #2 / 1996 / 4P / M • Imagination X-Posed / 1989 / 4P / M • Jaded / 1989 / 4P / M • Junk Yard Dogs / 1991 / FC / M • Just For The Hell Of It / 1991 / CA / M • Lollipop Shoppe #1 / 1996 / SC / M • Lollipop Shoppe #2 / 1996 / SC / M • Loose Ends #5: The New Generation / 1988 / 4P / M • Loose Ends #6 / 1989 / 4P / M • Love Chunks / 1996 / TTV / M • Lovin' Spoonfuls #3 / 1995 / 4P / C • Lovin' Spoonfuls #4 / 1995 / 4P / C • Lovin' Spoonfuls #5 / 1996 / 4P / C • Lovin' Spoonfuls #6 / 1996 / 4P / C • Lovin' Spoonfuls #7 / 1996 / 4P / C • Lovin' Spoonfuls #8 / 1996 / 4P / C • Makin' It / 1994 / A&E / M • Manbait #1 /

1991 / VC / M • Manbait #2 / 1992 / VC / M • Married With Hormones #2 / 1992 / PL / M • Meltdown / 1990 / LV / M • More Black Dirty Debutantes / 1994 / 4P / M • More Black Dirty Debutantes #3 / 1994 / 4P / M • More Black Dirty Debutantes #4 / 1995 / 4P / M • More Black Dirty Debutantes #5 / 1995 / 4P / M • More Black Dirty Debutantes #6 / 1996 / 4P / M • More Dirty Debutantes / 1990 / PRI / M • More Dirty Debutantes #03 / 1990 / 4P / M • More Dirty Debutantes #04 / 1990 / 4P / M • More Dirty Debutantes #05 / 1990 / 4P / M • More Dirty Debutantes #06 / 1990 / 4P / M • More Dirty Debutantes #07 / 1991 / 4P / M • More Dirty Debutantes #08 / 1991 / 4P / M • More Dirty Debutantes #09 / 1991 / 4P / M • More Dirty Debutantes #10 / 1991 / 4P / M • More Dirty Debutantes #11 / 1991 / 4P / M • More Dirty Debutantes #12 / 1991 / 4P / M • More Dirty Debutantes #13 / 1992 / 4P / M • More Dirty Debutantes #14 / 1992 / 4P / M • More Dirty Debutantes #15 / 1992 / 4P / M • More Dirty Debutantes #16 / 1992 / 4P / M • More Dirty Debutantes #17 / 1992 / 4P / M • More Dirty Debutantes #18 / 1992 / 4P / M • More Dirty Debutantes #19 / 1993 / 4P / M • More Dirty Debutantes #20 / 1993 / 4P / M • More Dirty Debutantes #21 / 1993 / 4P / M • More Dirty Debutantes #22 / 1993 / 4P / M • More Dirty Debutantes #23 / 1993 / 4P / M • More Dirty Debutantes #24 / 1993 / 4P / M • More Dirty Debutantes #25 / 1993 / 4P / M • More Dirty Debutantes #26 / 1993 / 4P / M • More Dirty Debutantes #27 / 1993 / 4P / M • More Dirty Debutantes #28 / 1994 / 4P / M • More Dirty Debutantes #29 / 1994 / 4P / M • More Dirty Debutantes #30 / 1994 / 4P / M • More Dirty Debutantes #31 / 1994 / 4P / M • More Dirty Debutantes #32 / 1994 / 4P / M • More Dirty Debutantes #33 / 1994 / 4P / M • More Dirty Debutantes #34 / 1994 / 4P / M • More Dirty Debutantes #35 / 1994 / 4P / M • More Dirty Debutantes #36 / 1994 / 4P / M • More Dirty Debutantes #37 / 1995 / 4P / M • More Dirty Debutantes #38 / 1995 / 4P / M • More Dirty Debutantes #39 / 1995 / 4P / M • More Dirty Debutantes #40 / 1995 / 4P / M • More Dirty Debutantes #41 / 1995 / 4P / M • More Dirty Debutantes #42 / 1995 / 4P / M • More Dirty Debutantes #43 / 1995 / 4P / M • More Dirty Debutantes #44 / 1995 / 4P / M • More Dirty Debutantes #45 / 1995 / 4P / M • More Dirty Debutantes #46 / 1995 / 4P / M • More Dirty Debutantes #47 / 1995 / 4P / M • More Dirty Debutantes #48 / 1995 / 4P / M • More Dirty Debutantes #49 / 1995 / 4P / M • More Dirty Debutantes #50 / 1996 / 4P / M • More Dirty Debutantes #51 / 1996 / 4P / M • More Dirty Debutantes #52 / 1996 / 4P / M • More Dirty Debutantes #53 / 1996 / 4P / M • More Dirty Debutantes #54 / 1996 / 4P / M • More Dirty Debutantes #55 / 1996 / 4P / M • More Dirty Debutantes #56 / 1996 / 4P / M • More Dirty Debutantes #57 / 1996 / 4P / M • More Dirty Debutantes #58 / 1996 / 4P / M • More Dirty Debutantes #59 / 1996 / SBV / M • More Dirty Debutantes #60 / 1997 / SBV / M • More Dirty Debutantes #61 / 1997 / SBV / M • More Dirty Debutantes #62 / 1997 / SBV / M • More Dirty Debutantes

#63 / 1997 / SBV / M • More Dirty Debutantes #64 / 1997 / SBV / M • More Dirty Debutantes #65 / 1997 / SBV / M • Naked Goddess #1 / 1991 / VC / M • The Naked Truth / 1990 / SE / M • Nasty Habits Are Hard To Break / 1986 / 4P / M • National Pornographic #2: Orientals / 1987 / 4P / C • New Ends #01 / 1993 / 4P / M • New Ends #02 / 1993 / 4P / M • New Ends #03 / 1993 / 4P / M • New Ends #04 / 1993 / 4P / M • New Ends #05 / 1993 / 4P / M • New Ends #06 / 1994 / 4P / M • New Ends #07 / 1994 / 4P / M • New Ends #08 / 1994 / 4P / M • New Ends #09 / 1994 / 4P / M • New Ends #10 / 1995 / 4P / M • The Newcummers / 1990 / 4P / M • Oriental Gang Bang Fantasy / 1994 / FC / M • Pick Up Lines #01 / 1995 / 4P / M • Pick Up Lines #02 / 1995 / 4P / M • Pick Up Lines #03 / 1995 / 4P / M • Pick Up Lines #04 / 1995 / 4P / M • Pop-Porn: Safari Club / 1992 / 4P / M • Pussy Whipped / 1991 / PL / B • Ready To Drop #07 / 1995 / FC / M • Romancing The Butt / 1992 / ATL / M • Shadows In The Dark / 1990 / 4P / M • She Asked For It! / 1992 / RB / B • Steal Breeze / 1990 / SO / M • Sun Bunnies #1 / 1991 / SC / M • The Tasting / 1991 / EX / M • Tenth Annual Adult Video News Awards / 1993 / VC / M • Tight Shots #1 / 1994 / VI / M • Tight Shots #2 / 1994 / VI / M • Top Heavy / 1988 / VD / M • Totally Tasteless Video #02 / 1994 / TTV / M • Under Construction / 1988 / BON / B • Up And Cummers #03 / 1993 / 4P / M • Up And Cummers #10 / 1994 / 4P / M • Up And Cummers: The Movie / 1994 / 4P / M • Valentina: Princess Of The Forest / 1996 / SC / M • Virgin Tales #01 / 1993 / 4P / M • The Wacky World Of Ed Powers / 1996 / 4P / C • Where The Boys Aren't #6 / 1995 / VI / F • Wicked / 1991 / XCI / M • World Famous Dirty Debutantes / 1995 / 4P / S • You Bet Your Ass / 1991 / EA / B

ED SHANNON *see Star Index I*

ED SONNER
Let's Talk Sex / 1982 / CA / M

ED STARK
Fantasy Fever / 1975 / AVC / M • Mortgage Of Sin / 1975 / CA / M • Pleasure Island / 1975 / TGA / M • Sex Museum / 1976 / AXV / M

ED STIFFLER
[So Many Men, So Little Time / 19?? / BL / G

ED THOMPSON *see Star Index I*

ED, THE HEAD
Breast Wishes #06 / 1991 / LBO / M • Bubble Butts #03 / 1992 / LBO / M • Bubble Butts #07 / 1992 / LBO / M • E Three / 1985 / GO / M

EDA HALLECK
Boiling Point / 1978 / SE / M

EDD SLED
Night Crawlers / 1994 / SC / M

EDDIE
Cindy Puts Out / 1996 / OLL / M • Older & Bolder In San Francisco / 1996 / TEP / M • Rocky Mountains / 1991 / IF / M • Tight Ties / 1994 / BON / B • Transsexual Escorts / 1990 / BIZ / G

EDDIE CANNON *see Star Index I*

EDDIE CRANE
AC/DC #1 / 1991 / LA / G

EDDIE D
Tail Taggers #121: Behind The Lens / 1994

/ WV / M
EDDIE EVANS *see Star Index I*
EDDIE FIERCE
More Black Dirty Debutantes #6 / 1996 /
4P / M • Raw Silk / 1996 / RAS / M • Tailz
From Da Hood #4 / 1996 / AVI / M
EDDIE FORTUNATO
Innocent Seduction / 1988 / VC / M
EDDIE MARCUS
The Little French Maid / 1981 / VCX / M
EDDIE MARINARA
Angel Of The Night / 1985 / IN / M
EDDIE VALENS *see Star Index I*
EDDY *see Star Index I*
EDDY CANNON
Sweet Savage / 1978 / ALP / M
EDDY CRANE *see Star Index I*
EDDY LAAN *see Star Index I*
EDDY PIERCE *see Star Index I*
EDDY SHAW
Erotic Dimensions: Aggressive Women /
1982 / NSV / M
EDEE
Nasty Girls (1983-VCX) / 1983 / VCX / M
EDEN
Anal Auditions #3 / 1996 / LE / M • Assy
Sassy #3 / 1995 / ROB / F • Cheeks #8 /
1995 / CC / M • Dirty Video #1 / 1996 / AB
/ M • Girly Video Magazine #1 / 1995 / BEP
/ M • Las Vegas She-Males / 1995 / BCP /
G • Lesbian Climax / 1995 / ROB / F •
Major Fucking Whore / 1995 / BEP / M
EDEN (COURTNEY) *see Courtney*
EDGAR EAGER *see Star Index I*
EDGAR READY
Motel Sex #1 / 1995 / FAP / M
EDGAR WIDOES
White Hot / 1984 / VXP / M
EDGEY JONES *see Star Index I*
EDIE SWENSON *see Uschi Digart*
EDIE ZAMORA
Interview's Backdoor To The Orient / 1996
/ LV / M
EDINA
Fazano's Student Bodies / 1995 / EL / M •
Frank Thring's Double Penetration #1 /
1995 / XPR / M • Frank Thring's Double
Penetration #3 / 1996 / XPR / M • Love
Slave / 1995 / WIV / M • Private Video
Magazine #21 / 1995 / OD / M
EDIT BOTOS
True Stories #1 / 1993 / SC / M • True Sto-
ries #2 / 1993 / SC / M
EDITH
Frank Thring's Double Penetration #2 /
1996 / XPR / M • Miss Nude America Con-
test And The Mr. Nude America Contest /
1975 / WIZ / S • Mr. Peepers Amateur
Home Videos #46: A Schnitzel In The Bush
/ 1992 / LBO / M
EDITH ARGENTINA
Love Theatre / cr80 / VC / M
EDITH BUCKHOLTZ
Private Film #08 / 1994 / OD / M
EDITH GOLDFARB
Romeo And Juliet #2 / 1988 / WV / M
EDMOND SEARLE *see Star Index I*
EDMOUND HORNSBY
Midnight Hustle / 1978 / VC / M
EDNA
Blue Vanities #130 / 1990 / FFL / M
EDNA BARDO
Doogan's Woman / 1978 / S&L / M
EDSEL *see Star Index I*
EDUARDA
Buttman's Big Butt Backdoor Babes / 1995

/ EA / M
EDUARDO
Long Play / 1995 / 3XP / G
EDUARDO CONTE
Prima #01: Anal Poker / 1995 / MBP / M
EDUARDO MARTINEZ *see Star Index I*
EDWARD B. DAVIS
Feelings / 1977 / VC / M
EDWARD ELECTRIC
Car Wash Angels / 1995 / VC / M
EDWARD ELITE
Pleasures Of A Woman / 1983 / CA / M
EDWARD FRENCH
Angel Buns / 1981 / QX / M
EDWARD HAZZARD
F / 1980 / GO / M
EDWARD HILLEGAR *see Star Index I*
EDWARD NORTON
[The People vs. Larry Flynt / 1996 / C3S /
S
EDWARD PENISHANDS *see Sikki Nixx*
EDWARD ROEHM
Candy Tangerine Man / 1975 / UNV / S •
Fulfillment / 1973 / SE / M • Ilsa, Keeper Of
The Oil Sheik's Harem / 1975 / AME / S •
Ilsa, She Wolf Of The SS / 1974 / VID / S
EDWIGE DAVIS
Perverse / 1984 / CA / M
EDWIN BUSH
The Theory Of Relativity / 1994 / EL / M
EDWINA BETH WILLIAMS *see Edy
Williams*
EDWINA THORNE
Black Angels / 1985 / VC / M • Sex Appeal
/ 1986 / VES / S
EDY WILLIAMS *(Edwina Beth Williams)*
In 1995 was a wizened old crone which is un-
derstandable considering that she was born
in 1942 in Salt Lake City and married to
Russ Meyer for a while.
An Almost Perfect Affair / 1979 / PAR / S •
Amateur Gay Girls / 1995 / LEI / C • Bad
Girls From Mars / 1990 / VMA / S • Bad
Manners / 1984 / STM / S • Becky S:
Becky And Edy / 1995 / BEC / F • The Best
Of Sex And Violence / 1981 / WIZ / C • Be-
yond The Valley Of The Dolls / 1970 / CBS
/ S • Caballero Preview Tape #4 / 1985 /
CA / C • Chained Heat #1 / 1983 / VES / S
• Dirty Laundry / 1987 / ... / S • Dr Alien /
1989 / PAR / S • Dr Minx / 1975 / CO1 / S •
Famous T & A / 1982 / WIZ / C • Good
Times / 1967 / ... / S • Hellhole / 1985 /
C3S / S • Hollywood Hot Tubs / 1984 /
VES / S • A House Is Not A Home / 1964 /
EHE / S • Lady Lust / 1984 / CA / M •
Mankillers / 1987 / C3S / S • The Naked
Kiss / 1964 / HVC / S • Nudity Required /
1989 / AE / S • The Pad And How To Use It
/ 1966 / MCA / S • Rented Lips / 1988 /
AVD / S • The Secret Life Of An American
Wife / 1968 / FOX / S • The Seven Minutes
/ 1971 / STO / S • Snatch Masters #06 /
1995 / LEI / M • [I Sailed To Tahiti With An
All Girl Crew / 1968 / ... / S • [Jake Span-
ner, Private Eye / 1989 / ... / S • [Where
It's At / 1969 / ... / S
EFRAIN TOBALINA *see Carlos Tobalina*
EGGPLANT *see Star Index I*
EILEEN
Blue Vanities #501 / 1992 / FFL / M •
Bondage Classix #02: Krysta's Nightmare
#1 / 1987 / BON / B • Steel Cage Bondage
/ 1995 / GAL / B
EILEEN ALLEN
Blue Vanities #552 / 1994 / FFL / M

EILEEN WALES *see Eileen Welles*
EILEEN WELLES *(Mary Ann Evans, Con-
stance Penny (EW), Ilene Wells, Eileen
Wales)*
Small to medium floppy tits to the point that
they look like empty sacks on occasion,
dark blonde/brunette, lean body that looks
well used, hard personality, marginal face.
Credited as Constance Penny in **Boiling
Point** and Mary Ann Evans in **Expensive
Taste.**
Baby Love & Beau / 1979 / TVX / M • Boil-
ing Point / 1978 / SE / M • Candy Stripers
#1 / 1978 / ALP / M • The China Cat / 1978
/ CA / M • The Erotic Adventures Of Candy
/ 1978 / VCX / M • Expensive Taste / 1978
/ VCX / M • The Girl From S.E.X. / 1982 /
CA / M • Heavenly Desire / 1979 / WV / M
• Hot Teenage Assets / 1978 / WWV / M •
The Legend Of Lady Blue / 1978 / VCX / M
• Pretty Peaches #1 / 1978 / MIT / M •
Rolls Royce #02 / 1980 / ... / C • Stormy /
1980 / CV / M • Sweet Savage / 1978 /
ALP / M • A Taste Of Sugar / 1978 / AR / M
• The Tender Trap / 1978 / IHV / M
EKKEHARDT BELLE
[Junge Madchen Mogen's Heiß, Haus-
frauen Noch HeiBer / 1973 / ... / M
EL
First Time Lesbians #16 / 1994 / JMP / F
ELAINA LANE
Kym Wilde's On The Edge #14 / 1994 / RB
/ B
ELAINE
Blue Vanities #130 / 1990 / FFL / M • Blue
Vanities #197 / 1993 / FFL / M • Blue Vani-
ties #501 / 1992 / FFL / M • Brabusters #2
/ 1982 / CA / S • HomeGrown Video #465:
Bong The Schlong / 1996 / HOV / M • Joe
Elliot's College Girls #32 / 1994 / JOE / M •
Joe Elliot's College Girls #41 / 1996 / JOE
/ M • Titanic Tits #01 / 1984 / L&W / S •
Under The Skirt #2 / 1995 / KAE / F
ELAINE DARBY
Love Roots / 1987 / LIM / M • Love Under
16 / cr75 / VST / M
ELAINE FREEMAN *see Star Index I*
ELAINE JONES
Blue Vanities #514 / 1992 / FFL / M • Blue
Vanities #551 / 1994 / FFL / M • Erotica /
1961 / RMV / S • The Touchables / 1961 /
SOW / S
ELAINE SMITH *see Star Index I*
ELAINE SOUTHERN *(Elaine Suterland,
Sherry Anderson, Cheri Anderson,
Elaine Sutherland, Cherri Bush)*
Bare Elegance / 1984 / MAP / M • Dirty
Dreams / 1987 / CA / M • Good Girls Do /
1984 / HO / M • Love Lessons / 1986 / HO
/ M • Return To Sex 5th Avenue / 1985 /
WV / M • Shadows In The Dark / 1990 / 4P
/ M • Shave Tail / 1984 / AMB / M • The
Twilight Moan / 1985 / WV / M • Wild
Weekend / 1984 / HO / M • With Love
From Ginger / 1986 / HO / C • Young And
Naughty / 1984 / HO / M
ELAINE SUTERLAND *see Elaine South-
ern*
ELAINE SUTHERLAND *see Elaine
Southern*
ELAINE WELLES *see Chrissy Peterson*
ELAINE WOOD
Black Magic / 1985 / WET / M • Blue Vani-
ties #517 / 1992 / FFL / M
ELANNA *see Lana Sands*
ELANORA TAYLOR *see Star Index I*

ELEANNA
Buttman's Big Tit Adventure #3 / 1995 / EA / M

ELEANOR
Prague By Night #1 / 1996 / EA / M • Prague By Night #2 / 1996 / EA / M

ELEANOR BARNES
Waterpower / 1975 / VHL / M

ELEANOR M.
Lesbian Sleaze / 1994 / PL / F

ELEANORA
Cool It Baby / 1967 / SOW / S • More Dirty Debutantes #16 / 1992 / 4P / M

ELEC VAUGHAN
Semper Bi / 1994 / PEP / G

ELECTRA
Blue Vanities #115 / 1988 / FFL / M • Dirty Bob's #01: Xcellent Adventure / 1991 / FLP / S • Positively Pagan #01 / 1991 / ATA / M • Positively Pagan #02 / 1991 / ATA / M

ELECTRA BLUE
Le Striptease / 1983 / GLD / S • Secrets Of A Willing Wife / 1979 / VXP / M

ELECTRA GLIDE
Night Crawlers / 1994 / SC / M

ELEKTRE
San Francisco Lesbians #3 / 1993 / PL / M

ELENA
Blue Vanities #112 / 1988 / FFL / M • Buttman's Orgies / 1996 / EA / M • Rocco Goes To Prague / 1995 / EA / M • Sandy Insatiable / 1995 / EA / M • Thermonuclear Sex / 1996 / EL / M • Triple X Video Magazine #13 / 1996 / OD / M

ELEONER LIQUORE see Star Index I
ELEXIS see Star Index I
ELEYNA see Star Index I
ELFRIEDE PAYER
[Schulmadchen-Report 4: Was Eltern Oft Verzweifeln LaBt / 1972 / ... / M

ELI
Hard Core Beginners #07 / 1995 / LEI / M

ELIE SHEER
Teenage Party People / 19?? / ... / M

ELIN SVENSSON
Swedish Vip Magazine #1 / 1995 / PL / M

ELINORE
Blue Vanities #583 / 1996 / FFL / M

ELINORE DEVERAUX
Women In Uniform / 1977 / VHL / M

ELISA
San Francisco Lesbians #4 / 1993 / PL / F

ELISA (M. MELENDEZ) see Melissa Melendez

ELISA FLOREZ see Missy Manners
ELISABETH
Depravity On The Danube / 1993 / EL / M • Ejacula #1 / 1992 / VC / M • Ejacula #2 / 1992 / VC / M • Eurotica #09 / 1996 / XC / M • Lee Nover: The Search For The Perfect Butt / 1996 / IP / M • World Sex Tour #3 / 1995 / ANA / M

ELISABETH KING
Angel's Vengeance / 1995 / VMX / M • Anita / 1996 / BLC / M • Behind The Mask / 1995 / XC / M • Flamenco Ecstasy / 1996 / UEF / M • Sodomania #14: C**t Lickin', C*m Drinkin' Bitches / 1995 / EL / M • Sodomania: Slop Shots / 1996 / EL / C • The Thief, The Girl & The Detective / 1996 / HDE / M • The Voyeur #7: Live In Europe #1 / 1996 / JLP / M

ELISABETH SANCHEZ
Who's In Charge / 1995 / JAM / B

ELISABETH VOLKMANN

[Junge Madchen Mogen's HeiB, Hausfrauen Noch HeiBer / 1973 / ... / M • [Krankenschwestern-Report / 1972 / ... / M

ELISABETH WELT
French Blue / 1974 / ... / M • Penetration / 1975 / SAT / M

ELISABETH WELZ
[Krankenschwestern-Report / 1972 / ... / M

ELISE see Nikki Valentine
ELISE ALINE see Nikki Valentine
ELISE DIMEDICI see Desi DeAngelo
ELISE VANDERBILT see Sade
ELISHA see Star Index I
ELISSA VANDERBILT see Sade
ELIZABETH
A&B AB#501: Squirter / 1995 / A&B / M • A&B AB#502: Cherry / 1995 / A&B / M • A&B AB#503: Squirting Sluts / 1995 / A&B / M • A&B AB#506: You Squirt I Squirt #1 / 1995 / A&B / M • A&B AB#509: How To Squirt / 1995 / A&B / C • A&B AB#510: Can I Cum For You / 1995 / A&B / M • A&B AB#512: I Am Wet & Sexy / 1995 / A&B / F • A&B AB#513: Pick Up Girl / 1995 / A&B / M • A&B AB#514: Elizabeth & Casey & Their Male Sex Slave / 1995 / A&B / M • A&B AB#515: Put Out The Fire / 1995 / A&B / F • A&B FL#20: 4 Girl Flashing / 1995 / A&B / M • American Connection Video Magazine #03 / 1993 / ZA / M • AVP #9130: Tailor Made / 1991 / AVP / M • Blonde Busty & Bound / 1996 / VTF / B • Blue Vanities #194 / 1993 / FFL / M • Blue Vanities #507 / 1992 / FFL / M • Homegrown Video #414: Pussy Hairstylist / 1994 / HOV / M • Prima #13: Dr. Max Back To Budapest / 1995 / MBP / M • Shockers / 1996 / SBP / B

ELIZABETH (JAMA) see Elizabeth Jama
ELIZABETH ANASTASIA
Cafe Flesh / 1982 / VC / M

ELIZABETH AUBREY see Star Index I
ELIZABETH BURE
Educating Tricia / 1984 / VD / M • Sexual Initiation Of A Married Woman / 1984 / VD / M

ELIZABETH BURET
Everything Goes / 1975 / CA / M

ELIZABETH COX
Anal Vision #13 / 1993 / LBO / M • Bra Busters #02 / 1993 / LBO / M • Breastman Does The Himalayas / 1993 / EVN / M • More Than A Mouthful / 1995 / LBO / C

ELIZABETH DRANCOURT
Five Kittens / 19?? / ... / M

ELIZABETH ELDRIDGE see Star Index I
ELIZABETH ENGLISH see Star Index I
ELIZABETH GRAY
Prisoner Of Pleasure / 1981 / ALP / B

ELIZABETH HEMMINGWAY
[Je Brule De Partout / 1978 / ... / M

ELIZABETH JAMA *(Elizabeth (Jama), Tatianna (E. Jama))*
Black girl with pretty smiling face and firm but not enhanced small tits. Laughs all the time.
Action In Black / 1993 / FD / M • Babewatch #1 / 1993 / CC / M • Black Velvet #2 / 1993 / CC / M • Ebony Erotica #02: Midnight Madness / 1993 / GO / M • Ebony Erotica #04: Ebony Gods / 1993 / GO / M • Ebony Erotica #06: Black Essence / 1993 / GO / M • Harry Horndog #22: Huge Hooters / 1993 / ZA / M • My Baby Got Back #02 / 1993 / VT / M • Red Hot Honeys /

1994 / IF / M • Six Plus One #1 / 1993 / VEX / M • Six Plus One #2 / 1993 / VEX / C

ELIZABETH MARR see Monique Hall
ELIZABETH RANDOLPH see Star Index I
ELIZABETH SEXTON see Star Index I
ELIZABETH SHAY
Buttman In Barcelona / 1996 / EA / M • Buttman's British Extremely Big Tit Adventure / 1996 / EA / M

ELIZABETH SUROQUER see Star Index I
ELIZABETH WINTERS see Cindee Summers
ELIZABETHA
Deep Behind The Scenes With Seymore Butts #2 / 1995 / ULI / M

ELKAL SWARTZA see Star Index I
ELKE STEIN
Fantasy Club: Luau Orgy / 1980 / WV / M • Pumpkin Farm / 1983 / WV / M

ELKE VON see Uschi Digart
ELLA
Blue Vanities #526 / 1993 / FFL / M • Blue Vanities #530 / 1993 / FFL / M • Kisses From Romania / 1995 / NIT / M

ELLA BUTLER
Too Hot To Handle / 1975 / CDC / M

ELLA RYME see Star Index I
ELLE LEGEN
Going Down Under / 1993 / OD / M

ELLE RIO *(Elle Rios)*
All For His Ladies / 1987 / PP / C • Amberella / 1986 / GO / M • And I Do Windows Too / 1986 / PP / M • Ball Street / 1988 / CA / M • Beyond The Denver Dynasty / 1988 / CA / M • Big Bust Babes #06 / 1991 / AFI / F • The Black Chill / 1986 / WET / M • Born For Love / 1987 / ... / M • Cabaret Sin / 1987 / IN / M • Careena #2: A Star On The Rise / 1988 / WV / C • Cheating / 1986 / SEV / M • Cheeks #1 / 1988 / CC / M • China White / 1986 / WV / M • Diamond Head / 1987 / AVC / M • Divorce Court Expose #2 / 1987 / VD / M • Double Black Fantasy / 1987 / CC / C • Double Play / 1993 / CA / C • Dr Blacklove #1 / 1987 / CC / M • Empire Of The Sins / 1988 / IN / M • Flesh In Ecstasy #06: Elle Rio / 1987 / GO / C • Forbidden Bodies / 1986 / HU / M • Foreign Affairs / 1992 / VT / C • The Fun House / 1988 / SEV / C • Gourmet Quickies: Christy Canyon / Ellie Rio #730 / 1985 / GO / C • Grafenberg Girls Go Fishing / 1987 / MIT / M • Kiss Of The Dragon Lady / 1986 / SEV / M • Le Sex De Femme #4 / 1989 / AFI / C • Les Be Friends / 1988 / WV / C • Love Probe / 1986 / VT / M • Lust Letters / 1988 / CA / M • Mammary Lane / 1988 / VT / C • Monkey Business / 1987 / SEV / M • Nina Does 'em All / 1988 / 3HV / C • Nymphette #1 / 1986 / WV / M • Nymphette #2 / 1986 / WV / M • Only The Best #3 / 1990 / CV / C • Only The Best Of Oral / 1989 / CV / C • Oral Majority #03 / 1986 / WV / C • The Other Side Of Pleasure / 1987 / SEV / M • Pacific Intrigue / 1987 / AMB / M • Passion Chain / 1987 / ZA / M • Passionate Heiress / 1987 / CA / M • The Penetration Of Elle Rio / 1987 / GO / M • Postcards From Abroad / 1991 / CA / C • Pumping Irene #1 / 1986 / FAN / M • Pumping Irene #2 / 1986 / FAN / M • The Red Hot Roadrunner / 1987 / VD / M • Restless Nights / 1987 /

SEV / M • The Return Of Dr Blacklove / 1996 / CC / M • Rio Heat / 1986 / VD / M • Screwdriver / 1988 / CC / C • The Sex Game / 1987 / SE / C • Sex Lives Of The Rich And Beautiful / 1988 / CA / M • She Comes In Colors / 1987 / AMB / M • The Sins Of Angel Kelly / 1987 / FAN / C • Sins Of The Wealthy #2 / 1986 / CLV / M • Sweet Chocolate / 1987 / VD / M • The Switch Is On / 1985 / CAT / G • Toys 4 Us #1 / 1987 / WV / C • Toys 4 Us #2 / 1987 / WV / C • Two To Tango / 1987 / TEM / M • The Wacky World Of X-Rated Bloopers / 1989 / GO / M • What Kind Of Girls Do You Think We Are? / 1986 / VEX / M • What Kind of Girls Do You Think We Are? / 1991 / VEX / C • Who Came In The Backdoor? / 1987 / PV / M • Wild Fire / 1990 / WV / C • Wild Things #1 / 1985 / CV / M

ELLE RIOS *see* **Elle Rio**

ELLEN
Blue Vanities #512 / 1992 / FFL / M • HomeGrown Video #465: Bong The Schlong / 1996 / HOV / M

ELLEN BERLIN
Cowgirls / 1996 / GLI / M

ELLEN BURDEN
Midnight Desires / 1976 / VXP / M

ELLEN EARL *see* **Star Index I**

ELLEN EDDINGTON *see* **Star Index I**

ELLEN NOEL *see* **Star Index I**

ELLEN PLENTY
Jail Bait / 1976 / VC / M

ELLEN RAIN *see* **Star Index I**

ELLEN RAMSDALE
Ancient Secrets Of Sexual Ecstasy / 1996 / HIG / M

ELLEN STEINBERG *see* **Annie Sprinkle**

ELLEN WELLES
Snack Time / 1983 / HO / M

ELLEN WILLIAMS *see* **Crystal Sync**

ELLES
S&M On The Ranch: Training The New Pony Girl / 1994 / VER / B • VGA: Spanks-A-Lot / 1993 / VGA / B

ELLIE MAY JACKSON *see* **Taylor Evans**

ELLIE SWENSON
Blue Vanities #585 / 1996 / FFL / M

ELLINOR LEIPERT
[Schulmadchen-Report 4: Was Eltern Oft Verzweifeln LaBt / 1972 / ... / M

ELLIOT
Bi-Bi Love Amateurs #4 / 1994 / QUA / G

ELLIOT ANTHONY *see* **Star Index I**

ELLIOT LEWIS *see* **Star Index I**

ELLIOT SEAGAL
The Girls From Hootersville #06 / 1994 / SFP / M

ELLIOTT ALLAN *see* **Star Index I**

ELLYN GRANT *see* **Star Index I**

ELMER FOX *(Elmo Lavino, Elmo Tiger, Elmo Friar, St Elmo, Elmo Loving, Heinz Mueller)*
Heinz Mueller is ex **Prisoner Of Paradise**. Beneath The Valley Of The Ultra-Vixens / 1979 / RMV / S • Debbie Does 'em All #1 / 1985 / CV / M • Matinee Idol / 1984 / VC / M • Prisoner Of Paradise / 1980 / VCX / M • The Ribald Tales Of Canterbury / 1986 / CA / M • Sex Life Of A Porn Star / 1986 / ELH / M • Yank My Doodle, It's A Dandy / 1985 / GOM / M

ELMER PASTA *see* **Star Index I**

ELMO FRIAR *see* **Elmer Fox**

ELMO LAVINO *see* **Elmer Fox**

ELMO LOVING *see* **Elmer Fox**

ELMO TIGER *see* **Elmer Fox**

ELODIE
Anal Exchange / 1995 / C69 / M • Dick & Jane Look For Pussy In The Park / 1995 / AVI / M • Elodie Does The U.S.A. / 1995 / PPR / M • French Ed. #1 / 1994 / PAE / M • French Ed. #2 / 1995 / C69 / M • French Vanilla / 1994 / HW / M • Games Women Play / 1995 / XC / M • Horny Henry's French Adventure / 1994 / TTV / M • Hot Tight Asses #09 / 1994 / TCK / M • Le Parfum De Mathilde / 1994 / VI / M • Magma: Horny & Greedy / 1993 / MET / M • Mellon Man #04 / 1995 / AVI / M • Mission Hard / 1995 / XC / M • Orgies Orgies Orgies / 1994 / WV / M • Secrets Of Madame X #2 / 1995 / WIV / M • The Streets Of Paris / 1996 / SC / M

ELODIE GAUCHER
Angel's Vengeance / 1995 / VMX / M • Seduction Italiano / 1995 / WIV / M • Skin #1 / 1994 / EUR / M

ELON DISERE
Amsterdam Nights #1 / 1996 / BLC / M • Amsterdam Nights #2 / 1996 / VC / M • Cyberanal / 1995 / VC / M • Diamonds / 1996 / HDE / M • Dirty Tricks #2: This Ain't Love / 1996 / EA / M • Fresh Meat (John Leslie) #3 / 1996 / EA / M • Heavenly Yours / 1995 / CV / M • Hose Jobs / 1995 / VEX / M • Private Gold #04: Amazonas / 1996 / OD / M • Private Gold #08: The Longest Night / 1996 / OD / M • Private Gold #10: Sins / 1996 / OD / M • Rear Entry / 1995 / LEI / M • The Voyeur #3 / 1995 / EA / M • The Voyeur #6 / 1996 / EA / M

ELONE R.
Private Gold #09: Private Dancer / 1996 / OD / M

ELROY JONES *see* **Star Index I**

ELS *see* **Star Index I**

ELSA
Limited Edition #18 / 1980 / AVC / M

ELSA MCDONALD
Pleasure So Deep / 1983 / AT / M

ELSKA
Here Comes Elska / 1997 / XPR / M • Profiles #10: / 1997 / XPR / M

ELVIRA
The Best Of Sex And Violence / 1981 / WIZ / C • Famous T & A / 1982 / WIZ / C • How To Make A Model #05: Back To Innocence / 1994 / LBO / M • Magma: Perverse Games / 1995 / MET / M

ELVIRA CLARK *see* **Star Index I**

ELVIS *see* **Star Index I**

ELYSE ALEXANDER *see* **Star Index I**

ELYSSA JARREA *see* **Alyssa Jarreau**

ELYSSE
Kiss My Grits / 1989 / CA / M

EMANUELA CRISTALDI
Euroflesh: Dentro Il Vulcano / 1996 / SC / M • Girls In Heat / 1995 / WIV / M

EMBER HAZE
Petite redhead with a very child-like emaciated body, 20 years old, 87lbs, (in 1995), passable (in some movies, pretty) face, narrow hips, tight waist. Comes from Kalamazoo, MI and was de-virginized at 14.
Executions On Butt Row / 1996 / EA / M • Flesh / 1996 / EA / M • Glory Days / 1996 / IN / M • Hollywood Hillbillies / 1996 / LE / M • Lovin' Spoonfuls #8 / 1996 / 4P / C • More Dirty Debutantes #49 / 1995 / 4P / M • My First Time #4 / 1996 / NS / M • Private Desires / 1995 / LE / M • Star Girl / 1996 /

ERA / M • Taboo #16 / 1996 / CV / M • Video Virgins #24 / 1996 / NS / M • Wedding Night Blues / 1995 / EMC / M

EMERALD ESTRADA *(Esmerelda Estrada)*
Reddish blonde or light brown hair, enhanced rock-solid large tits, elegant face, nice little butt.
The Anal-Europe Series #07: / 1994 / LV / M • Attitude / 1995 / VC / M • Babewatch #2 / 1994 / CC / M • Brenda: Back To Beverly Hills 9021A / 1994 / CA / M • The Butt Sisters Do Cleveland / 1994 / MID / M • Casting Couch #1 / 1994 / KV / M • Latex #1 / 1994 / VC / M • Nasty Dreams / 1994 / PRK / M • Swedish Erotica #80 / 1994 / CA / M • Temptation Of Serenity / 1994 / WP / M

EMESE EROS
Diamonds / 1996 / HDE / M

EMIKO
Adventures Of The DP Boys: Tokyo Tramps / 1994 / HW / M • Miss D.P. Butterfly / 1995 / TIW / M

EMILE
Eurotica #07 / 1996 / XC / M

EMILE A. DEVOIS *see* **Star Index I**

EMILE BREN *see* **Star Index I**

EMILIA
Kisses From Romania / 1995 / NIT / M

EMILIE ROSE
The Girls Of Spring Break / 1995 / VT / M

EMILIO ROCKO *see* **Star Index I**

EMILIO SANCEZ
Sex Penitentiary / 1996 / XC / M

EMILY
Adorable lithe tight bodied girl with long silky light brown hair, small tits, and a pretty face.
Sensuous / 1991 / LV / M • Snatches Of Pink / 1991 / NAN / M

EMILY (BIG TITS)
Girls Of France / 1991 / BTO / M

EMILY (OTHER)
My First Time #4 / 1996 / NS / M • New Faces, Hot Bodies #05 / 1992 / STP / M

EMILY (SEVENTIES)
Blue Vanities #545 / 1994 / FFL / M

EMILY DIXON *see* **Star Index I**

EMILY HILL *(M, Evona, Lady M.)*
Tall white skinned blonde with lots of curly hair. Under the M name she has small to medium natural tits and under the Emily or Emily Hill names she has had them enhanced but not so that they're rock solid. She's identifiable by a mole on her inside right breast, another on the top and others below the breast. Marginal face.
Anal Interrogation / 1995 / ZA / M • Anal Misconduct / 1995 / VD / M • Anal Squeeze / 1993 / FOR / M • Anal Webb / 1995 / ZA / M • Ass Poppers / 1995 / VMX / M • Backdoor Play / 1996 / AVI / M • Bun Busters #03 / 1993 / LBO / M • Bushwoman: She Takes Two / 1996 / RAS / M • Butt Hunt #10 / 1995 / LEI / M • The Butt Sisters Do Washington D.C. / 1995 / MID / M • Car Wash Angels / 1995 / VC / M • Club Kiss / 1995 / ONA / M • Come And Get It! / 1995 / LBO / M • Creme De La Face #05 / 1994 / OD / M • Creme De La Face #09: Princess Of Cream / 1995 / OD / M • Creme De La Face #14: Kiss My Cum / 1996 / OD / M • The Delegate / 1996 / RAS / M • Eighteen #1 / 1996 / SC / M • Girls Of The Athletic Department / 1995 /

VT / M • High Heeled & Horny #2 / 1995 / LBO / M • I Cream On Jeannie / 1995 / AVI / M • Incantation / 1996 / FC / M • Independence Night / 1996 / SC / M • Into The Fire / 1994 / ZA / M • Jizz Glazed Goo Guzzlers #2 / 1996 / NIT / C • Lady M's Anal Gang Bang / 1995 / FC / M • Lady M's Anything Nasty #01: Pink Pussy Party / 1996 / AVI / F • Lady M's Anything Nasty #02: Meat Substitute / 1996 / AVI / F • Mile High Thrills / 1995 / VIM / M • The New Ass Masters #09 / 1996 / LEI / C • The New Ass Masters #11 / 1996 / LEI / C • Nightmare On Lesbian Street / 1995 / LIP / F • Nothing Like Nurse Nookie #4 / 1996 / NIT / M • Outlaw Sluts / 1996 / RAS / M • Passion / 1996 / SC / M • Pay 4 Play / 1996 / RAS / M • Perverted #1: The Babysitters / 1994 / ZA / M • The Princess Of Cream / 1995 / OD / M • Pussyman Auditions #05 / 1995 / SNA / M • Pussyman Auditions #23 / 1996 / SNA / M • Raw Silk / 1996 / RAS / M • Razor's Edge / 1995 / ONA / M • Red Door Diaries #1 / 1995 / ZA / M • Reel People #09 / 1995 / PP / M • Samuels: Lesbian Lust / 1990 / SAM / F • Sex Academy #2: The Art Of Talking Dirty / 1994 / ONA / M • Sex Academy #4: The Art Of Anal / 1994 / ONA / M • Sex Academy #5: The Art Of Pulp Fiction / 1994 / ONA / M • Sex Drives Of The Rich And Famous / 1996 / ERA / M • The Sodomizer #4 / 1996 / SC / M • Sordid Stories / 1994 / AMP / M • Sue / 1995 / VC / M • Summer Vacation #2 / 1996 / RAS / M • Swedish Erotica #84 / 1995 / CA / M • Underground #2: Subway To Sodom / 1996 / SC / M • Wedding Vows / 1994 / ZA / M • Wet Faces #1 / 1997 / SC / C • Whore D'erves / 1996 / OUP / F • Wicked Ways #3: An All-Anal Slutfest / 1995 / WP / M • Witches Are Bitches / 1996 / NIT / M

EMILY MOORE *see Amanda Stone*

EMILY REUER
[Krankenschwestern-Report / 1972 / ... / M

EMILY SMITH *see Clair Dia*

EMILY STAR
Anal Shame / 1995 / VD / M

EMMA
Blue Vanities #542 / 1994 / FFL / M • Lesbian Lust Bust / 1995 / GLI / F

EMMA BOVARY *see Pia Snow*

EMMA NIXON
The Quest #1 / 1996 / CAW / B • The Quest #2 / 1996 / CAW / B

EMMANUEL *see Mr. Emmanuel*

EMMANUELLE
Diva #2: Deep In Glamour / 1996 / VC / F • Hollywood Spa / 1996 / WP / M • Veronica The Screenwriting Hooker / 1996 / LE / M

EMMANUELLE PAREZE
Introductions / 1977 / VCR / M • Shocking / 1984 / SE / M

EMMANUELLE PAREZEE
Love Play / 1977 / CA / M

EMMELINE PARKHURST
Chickie / 1975 / CA / M

EMMY
Private Video Magazine #07 / 1994 / OD / M • Private Video Magazine #08 / 1994 / OD / M

EMMY VAN DER MEER *see Star Index I*

EMPRESS LAREY
The Mysteries Of Transsexualism Explored #2 / 1990 / LEO / G

EMPRESS XANTHIA
Jacklyn's Attitude Adjustment / 1995 / JAM / B

EMY
Asses Galore #6: Fallen Angels / 1996 / DFI / M • Der Mosen-Pflucker / 1995 / KRM / M

ENI *(Enny)*
Dutch girl, 20 years old, big natural tits, pudgy, not too pretty, mousey hair, big butt. Supposedly owns a model agency in Holland with her 42 year old boyfriend or husband (she wears a wedding ring).
New Ends #05 / 1993 / 4P / M • Up And Cummers #05 / 1993 / 4P / M

ENIKO
Triple X Video Magazine #01 / 1995 / OD / M • Triple X Video Magazine #05 / 1995 / OD / M • Triple X Video Magazine #07 / 1995 / OD / M

ENIKO SZANGI
True Stories #1 / 1993 / SC / M • True Stories #2 / 1993 / SC / M

ENJIL VON BERGDORF *(Cary Corman)*
Blonde male who looks and sounds like he might swing both ways.
Femmes De Sade / 1976 / ALP / M • Liquid Lips / 1976 / EVI / M • Love Slaves / 1976 / VCR / M • Night Caller / 1975 / ALP / M • The Pleasure Masters / 1975 / AST / M

ENNY *see Eni*

ENORA
Absolute Anal / 1996 / XC / M

ENRICO SIQUERRES
Private Film #12 / 1994 / OD / M

ENZI FUCHS
[Junge Madchen Mogen's HeiB, Hausfrauen Noch HeiBer / 1973 / ... / M

ENZO S. *see Star Index I*

EPIPHANY
Cinderella In Chains #3 / 1996 / LBO / B • Punishment Of The Liars / 1996 / LBO / B • White Slavers / 1996 / LBO / B

EQUINETTE *see Angel West*

ERIC
Butt Banged Bicycle Babes / 1994 / ANA / M • Forbidden Ways / 1994 / GOT / B • Magma: Bizarre Lust / 1995 / MET / M • Magma: Nymphettes / 1993 / MET / M • Magma: Shopping Anal / 1994 / MET / M • Magma: Sperm-Crazy / 1994 / MET / M • New Faces, Hot Bodies #05 / 1992 / STP / M • Pearl Necklace: Premier Sessions #01 / 1993 / SEE / M

ERIC ADAMS
East Coast Sluts #09: / 1995 / PL / M

ERIC APACHE
Dixie Debutantes #1 / 1996 / MYS / M • Gutter Mouths / 1996 / JMP / M • My Ass #1 / 1996 / NOT / M • Perverted Stories #11 / 1996 / JMP / M

ERIC BLAIR *see Blair Harris*

ERIC BOTELLI *see Star Index I*

ERIC BRAUN
Born Erect / cr80 / CA / M

ERIC CLARK
Constance & Eric At It Again / cr90 / BON / B • Constance & Eric Bound At Home / 1990 / BON / B • Home Maid Memories #1 / 1994 / BON / C • I Know What Girls Like / 1986 / WET / G • Real People Real Bondage #1 / 1995 / BON / C • Suspension Of Disbelief #1 / 1989 / BON / B • Suspension Of Disbelief #2 / 1989 / BON / B

ERIC COWARDS *see Eric Edwards*

ERIC DAHL *see Star Index I*

ERIC DAVID *see Star Index I*

ERIC DEGEORGIO *see Star Index I*

ERIC DRAY *see Star Index I*

ERIC DURO *see Eric Stein*

ERIC DURON *see Eric Stein*

ERIC DYLAN *see Star Index I*

ERIC EAST *see Star Index I*

ERIC EDWARDS *(Eric Roberts (Edward, Rob Everett, Rob Evert, Eric Cowards, Rob Emmett)*
As of 1997, the longest performing male actor—started in 1969 with Linda Lovelace. Eric Roberts in **Maraschino Cherry**.
2 Wongs Make A White / 1996 / FC / M • 20th Century Fox / 1989 / FAZ / M • 4F Dating Service / 1989 / AR / M • The 8th Annual Erotic Film Awards / 1984 / SE / C • ABA: Double Feature #3 / 1996 / ALP / M • Abigail Leslie Is Back In Town / 1974 / HOE / S • Afternoon Delights / 1981 / CA / M • Airotica / 1996 / SC / M • Alexandra / 1984 / VC / M • All The Way In / 1984 / VC / M • Amanda By Night #1 / 1981 / CA / M • Amanda By Night #2 / 1987 / CA / M • America's Most Wanted Girl / 1989 / IN / M • American Pie / 1980 / SE / M • Angel On Fire / 1974 / ALP / M • Angela, The Fireworks Woman / 1975 / VC / M • Angie, Undercover Cop / 1980 / MSI / M • Another Kind Of Love / 1985 / CV / M • Another Roll In The Hay / 1985 / COL / M • Anyone But My Husband / 1975 / VC / M • Babylon Gold / 1983 / COM / C • Babylon Pink #1 / 1979 / COM / M • Backdoor Bandits / 1989 / MIR / C • Backdoor Girls / 1983 / VCR / C • Backdoor To Hollywood #01 / 1986 / CDI / M • The Backpackers #1 / 1990 / IN / M • Badge 69 / cr74 / SVE / M • Bedrooms And Boardrooms / 1992 / DR / M • Bedtime Video #03 / 1984 / GO / M • Behind Blue Eyes #1 / 1986 / ME / M • Behind The Brown Door / 1986 / VC / C • Bella / 1980 / AR / M • Best Of Caught From Behind #1 / 1987 / HO / C • Between The Sheets / 1982 / CA / M • The Bite / 1975 / SVE / M • Bizarre Encounters / 1986 / 4P / B • Black On White / 1987 / PL / C • Black To Africa / 1987 / PL / C • Blonde Ambition / 1981 / QX / M • Blonde In Black Silk / 1979 / QX / M • Bloopers #2 / 1991 / GO / C • Blowoff / 1985 / CA / M • Blue Ecstasy / 1980 / CA / M • Blue Ribbon Blue / 1984 / CA / C • Blue Summer / 1973 / ALP / S • Blue Vanities #062 / 1988 / FFL / M • Bodies In Heat #1 / 1983 / CA / M • Bodies In Heat #2 / 1989 / DR / M • Body Games / 1987 / DR / M • Body Girls / 1983 / SE / M • Body Music #2 / 1990 / DR / M • Boobs, Butts And Bloopers #1 / 1990 / HO / M • Bottoms Up #01 / 1983 / AVC / C • Bottoms Up #03 / 1983 / AVC / C • Bottoms Up / 1974 / SOW / M • The Breast Files #3 / 1994 / AVI / M • A Brief Affair / 1982 / CA / M • Bubblegum / 1982 / VC / M • Bucky Beaver's XXX Dragon Art Theatre Double Feature #05 / 1996 / SOW / M • The Budding Of Brie / 1980 / TVX / M • Bunny's Office Fantasies / 1984 / VC / M • Butterflies / 1974 / CA / M • C-Hunt / 1985 / PL / M • California Valley Girls / 1983 / HO / M • Candy's Bedtime Story / 1983 / CA / M • Casino Of Lust / 1984 / AT / M • Caught By Surprise / 1987 / CDI / M • Caught From

PP / M • Shadows Of Lust / 1996 / NIT / M • Shape Up For Sensational Sex / 1985 / SE / M • Shauna Grant: The Early Years / 1988 / PV / C • Sheer Haven / 1989 / DR / C • Showgirl #02: Seka's Fantasies / 1981 / VCR / M • Showgirl #04: Tina Russell Classics / 1981 / VCR / M • Showgirl #07: Arcadia Lake's Fantasies / 1983 / VCR / M • Showgirls / 1985 / SE / M • Sinfully Yours / 1984 / HO / M • Slightly Used / 1987 / VD / M • Slip Into Silk / 1985 / CA / M • Slip Up / 1974 / ALP / M • Slumber Party / 1984 / HO / M • Smoker / 1983 / VC / M • Sophie Says No / 1975 / VHL / M • The Sorceress / 1974 / BL / M • Spanish Fly / 1987 / CA / M • Special Order / cr75 / BL / M • Spitfire / 1984 / COM / M • Splashing / 1986 / VCS / C • Stacey's Hot Rod / 1983 / CV / M • Stand By Your Woman / cr80 / HOR / M • Star Girl / 1996 / ERA / M • A Star Is Porn / 1985 / PL / M • Steamy Sirens / 1984 / AIR / C • Stephanie's Outrageous / 1988 / LV / C • Strange Bedfellows / 1985 / PL / M • Sugar Britches / 1980 / VCX / C • Sulka's Daughter / 1984 / MET / G • Summer Camp Girls / 1983 / CA / M • Summer Of Laura / 1975 / CXV / M • Summertime Blue / 1979 / VCX / M • Sunny Side Up / 1984 / VC / M • Suze's Centerfolds #5 / 1981 / CA / M • Suze's Centerfolds #7 / 1983 / CA / M • Swedish Erotica #52 / 1984 / CA / M • Sweet Angel Ass / 1990 / FH / M • Sweet Punkin...I Love You / 1975 / VC / M • Sweet Sixteen / 1974 / SVE / M • Sweet Throat / 1979 / CV / M • Sweet Wet Lips / 1974 / PVX / M • Sweet Young Foxes / 1984 / VCX / M • Taboo #02 / 1982 / IN / M • Tailhouse Rock / 1985 / WV / M • Take Off / 1978 / VXP / M • The Taking Of Christina / 1975 / NGV / M • Tales From The Chateau / 1987 / BON / B • Talk Dirty To Me #07 / 1990 / DR / M • Talk Dirty To Me #10 / 1996 / DR / M • A Taste Of Bette / 1978 / VHL / M • A Taste Of Janey / 1990 / PIN / C • A Taste Of Taija Rae / 1989 / PIN / C • Teenage Runaways / 1977 / WWV / M • Teenage Stepmother / cr74 / SVE / M • Teenage Twins / 1976 / VCX / M • Ten Little Maidens / 1985 / EXF / M • Thanks For The Mammaries / 1987 / CA / M • That's Erotic / 1979 / CV / C • That's My Daughter / 1982 / NGV / M • That's Porno / 1979 / CV / C • Thrilling Drilling / 1974 / SVE / M • Throat...12 Years After / 1984 / VC / M • Thy Neighbour's Wife / 1986 / DR / M • Tickled Pink / 1985 / VC / M • Tigresses...And Other Man-Eaters / 1979 / VXP / M • Tinsel Town / 1980 / VC / M • Tit Tales #1 / 1989 / 4P / M • Titillation #1 / 1982 / SE / M • To Lust In LA / 1986 / LA / M • Too Many Cocks In Me! / 1992 / MET / M • Too Naughty To Say No / 1984 / CA / M • Tracy Takes Paris / 1987 / VIP / M • Treasure Box / 1981 / VC / M • Trick Or Treat / 1985 / ELH / M • True Legends Of Adult Cinema: The Erotic Eighties / 1992 / VC / C • True Legends Of Adult Cinema: Unsung Superstars / 1993 / VC / C • Twin Peeks / 1990 / DR / M • Two Timer / 19?? / BL / M • Udderly Fantastic / 1983 / TGA / C • The Ultimate Lover / 1986 / VD / M • An Unnatural Act #1 / 1984 / DR / M • Unthinkable / 1984 / SE / M • Urban Cowgirls / 1980 / CA / M • Urges In Young Girls / 1984 / VC / M • Vanessa's Hot Nights / 1984 / SVE / M • Vanessa...Maid In Man-

hattan / 1984 / VC / M • VCA Previews #2 / 1988 / VC / C • VCA Previews #4 / 1988 / VC / C • Virgin And The Lover / 1973 / ALP / M • Virgin Snow / 1976 / VXP / M • Virgins / 1995 / ERA / M • The Visualizer / 1992 / VC / M • Viva Vanessa The Undresser / 1984 / VC / M • Voyeur's Delight / 1986 / VCS / C • The Wacky World Of X-Rated Bloopers / 1989 / GO / M • Waterpower / 1975 / VHL / M • Wedding Night Blues / 1995 / EMC / M • Wet Dreams / 1984 / CA / M • Wet Paint / 1990 / CA / M • Wet Shots (Vcr) / 1983 / VCR / C • Whatever Happened To Miss September? / 1973 / ALP / M • Whose Fantasy Is It, Anyway? / 1983 / AVC / M • Wild Dallas Honey / 1985 / VCX / M • Wild Orgies / 1986 / SE / C • The Wild Wild West / 1986 / SE / M • With Love From Ginger / 1986 / HO / C • The Woman Who Loved Men / 1984 / SE / M • Working It Out / 1983 / CA / M • The World Of Henry Paris / 1981 / VC / C • X Factor / 1984 / HO / M • X Factor: The Next Generation / 1991 / HO / M • X-TV #1 / 1986 / PL / C • Yiddish Erotica #1 / 1986 / SE / C • The Young Like It Hot / 1983 / CA / M • Young, Wild And Wonderful / 1980 / VCX / M • Yummy Nymphs / 1983 / TGA / C • [Go On Your Own Way / 19?? / ASR / M • [Laura's Toys / 1975 / ... / S • [Molly / 1977 / ... / S • [The Switch / 1974 / ... / S

ERIC ESTRELLA *see Star Index I*

ERIC EVANS
Bi-Conflict / 1994 / FST / G • Conflict Of Interest / 1994 / FST / G • Sex Bi-Lex / 1993 / CAT / G

ERIC EVOL *see Star Index I*

ERIC GRANGER *see Star Index I*

ERIC HOLMES
Deadly Sin / 1996 / ONA / M

ERIC HUMPHREY *see Star Index I*

ERIC JETER
N.Y. Video Magazine #10 / 1996 / OUP / M • Streets Of New York #08 / 1996 / PL / M

ERIC LAMACHO
N.Y. Video Magazine #08 / 1996 / OUP / M

ERIC LEE
Respect And Obey / 1993 / GOT / B • Tender And Wild / 1989 / MTP / M

ERIC LONGMUIR *see Star Index I*

ERIC MARIN *see Jon Martin*

ERIC MARTIN *see Jon Martin*

ERIC MONROE
Pom Pom She-Males / 1994 / HEA / G

ERIC MONTE *(Eric Monti)*
First video was **Once Upon A Secretary** in 1983.
America's Dirtiest Home Videos #05 / 1991 / VEX / M • Assinine / 1990 / CC / M • Blowing Your Mind / 1984 / RSV / M • Candy Stripers #3 / 1986 / AR / M • Candy Stripers #4 / 1990 / AR / M • Colossal Orgy #1 / 1993 / HW / M • Colossal Orgy #2 / 1994 / HW / M • Colossal Orgy #3 / 1994 / HW / M • Double Trouble / 1986 / DRV / M • Fashion Fantasies / 1986 / VC / M • Good Girl, Bad Girl / 1984 / SE / M • Hot & Heavy / 1989 / PL / M • Lonely And Blue / 1990 / VEX / M • Mind Trips / 1992 / FH / M • Murder By Sex / 1993 / LAP / M • Naughty In Nature / 1994 / PL / M • Once Upon A Secretary / 1983 / GO / M • Over 50 / 1994 / GLI / M • Oversexed / 1986 / VXP / M • Perfect Girl / 1991 / VEX / M • Poltergash / 1987 / AVC / M • Positively Pagan #06 / 1993 / ATA / M • Seven Min-

utes In Heaven / 1986 / VXP / M • Sex Sounds / 1989 / PL / M • Sinners #1 / 1988 / COM / M • Sinners #2 / 1988 / COM / M • Thunderstorm / 1987 / VC / M • Ultimate Gang Bang #1 / 1994 / HW / M • Undercover Carol / 1990 / FAN / M • XXX Workout / 1987 / VEX / M

ERIC MONTI *see* **Eric Monte**

ERIC NORD
Resurrection Of Eve / 1973 / MIT / M

ERIC PAUL
Draghixa With An X / 1994 / EX / M • Euroslut #2 / 1994 / CC / M

ERIC PRICE *(Charlie Stone)*
Bisexual actor who was married to or the boyfriend of Paula Price.
1-800-934-BOOB / 1992 / VD / C • 19 And Nasty / 1990 / ME / M • 50 Ways To Lick Your Lover / 1989 / ZA / M • Adam & Eve's House Party #2: Bachelor Party / 1996 / VC / M • All The Right Motions / 1990 / DR / M • All The Way Down / 1991 / ZA / M • Ambushed / 1990 / SE / M • Anal Addiction #1 / 1990 / SO / M • Anal Intruder #05: The Final Outrage / 1990 / CC / M • Anal Leap / 1991 / ZA / M • Anal Storm / 1991 / ZA / M • The Analizer / 1990 / LV / M • Ass Ventura: Crack Detective / 1996 / PL / M • The Backpackers #2 / 1990 / IN / M • Bad Habits / 1990 / WV / M • Bat Bitch #1 / 1989 / FAZ / M • Behind Blue Eyes #3 / 1989 / ME / M • Behind The Backdoor #4 / 1990 / EVN / M • Bend Over Babes #1 / 1990 / EA / M • The Better Sex Video Series #7: Advanced Sexual Fantasies / 1992 / LEA / M • Bi Night / 1989 / PL / G • Bi-Ways / 1991 / PL / C • Bimbo Bowlers From Boston / 1990 / ZA / M • Blackman & Anal Woman #1 / 1990 / PL / M • Blazing Nova / 1989 / LV / M • Blue Views / 1990 / CDI / M • Body Music #1 / 1989 / DR / M • Body Triple / 1991 / VC / M • Boobs, Butts And Bloopers #1 / 1990 / HO / M • Bored Housewife / 1989 / CIN / M • Bratgirl / 1989 / VI / M • Breast Side Story / 1990 / LE / M • Breasts And Beyond #1 / 1991 / ME / M • Breasts And Beyond #2 / 1991 / ME / M • Breaststroke #3 / 1989 / EX / M • Bush Wacked / 1991 / ZA / M • Butt Naked #1 / 1990 / OD / M • Butt Woman #1 / 1990 / FH / M • Butt's Motel #3 / 1989 / EX / M • Butt's Motel #4 / 1989 / EX / M • Candy Stripers #4 / 1990 / AR / M • Cheek Busters / 1990 / FH / M • City Girls / 1991 / VC / M • Class Act / 1989 / WAV / M • D-Cup Dating Service / 1991 / ME / M • Deep Inside Danielle / 1990 / CDI / C • Deep Inside Nina Hartley / 1993 / VC / M • Deep Inside Selena Steele / 1993 / VC / C • Deep Inside Victoria Paris / 1993 / VC / C • Denim Dolls #1 / 1989 / CDI / M • Denim Dolls #2 / 1990 / CDI / M • Derrier / 1991 / CC / M • Desert Foxes / 1989 / SE / M • Do It In The Road / 1990 / LV / M • Door To Door / 1990 / EX / M • Double Detail / 1992 / SO / M • Double Penetration Virgins: DP Therapy / 1996 / JMP / M • Double The Pleasure / 1990 / SE / M • The Dream Team / 1995 / VT / M • Earth Girls Are Sleazy / 1990 / SO / M • Exiles / 1991 / VT / M • Falcon Head / 1990 / ARG / M • Famous Anus #1 / 1990 / EX / M • Fantasy In Blue / 1991 / VI / M • Farmer's Daughter / 1989 / FAZ / M • Fortysomething #1 / 1990 / LE / M • Friday Night Fever / 1989 / LV / M • Get Bi Tonight / 1991 / PL / G •

Getting Off On Broadway / 1989 / IN / M • Girls In The Night / 1990 / LE / M • Giving It To Barbii / 1990 / TOR / M • Graduation Ball / 1989 / CAE / M • Hard Core Cafe Revisited / 1991 / PL / M • The Hardriders / 1990 / 4P / M • Hate To See You Go / 1990 / VC / M • Haunted Passions / 1990 / FC / M • Head Co-Ed Society / 1989 / VT / M • Head Lock / 1989 / VD / M • Heart Of Stone / 1990 / FAN / M • Heatseekers / 1996 / PE / M • Hienie's Heroes / 1995 / VC / M • Hollywood Confidential / 1996 / SC / M • Hot Meat / 1990 / V99 / M • Hot Palms / 1989 / GO / M • How To Love Your Lover / 1992 / XII / S • In The Can / 1990 / EX / M • Introducing Danielle / 1990 / CDI / M • The Last Good-Bi / 1990 / CDI / G • The Last Temptation / 1988 / VD / M • Layover / 1994 / VI / M • Legend #1 / 1990 / LE / M • The Legend Of The Kama Sutra / 1990 / A&E / M • Living On The Edge / 1997 / DWO / M • Lover's Trance / 1990 / LE / M • Lunar Lust / 2990 / HO / M • Lust Fever / 1991 / FH / M • Madame X / 1990 / EX / M • The Magic Box / 1990 / SO / M • Making It Big / 1990 / TOR / M • Making The Grade / 1989 / IN / M • Miss Directed / 1990 / VI / M • Mix-N-Match / 1989 / LV / G • Monday Nite Ball / 1990 / VT / M • Moondance / 1991 / WV / M • Naked Juice / 1995 / OD / G • National Poontang's Summer Vacation / 1990 / FC / M • The New Barbarians #2 / 1990 / VC / M • Night Trips #2 / 1990 / CA / M • No Man's Land #14 / 1996 / VT / F • Not So Innocent / 1989 / VEX / M • Nymphobrat / 1989 / VI / M • The Offering / 1988 / INH / G • Office Girls / 1989 / CA / M • Oh, What A Night! / 1990 / VC / M • On Trial #3: Takin' It To The Jury / 1992 / VI / M • On Trial #4: The Verdict / 1992 / VI / M • One Million Years DD / 1992 / CC / M • Only With A Married Woman / 1990 / LE / M • Oral Addiction / 1989 / LV / M • Out For Blood / 1990 / VI / M • The Outlaw / 1989 / VD / M • Passionate Angels / 1990 / HO / M • Passionate Lovers / 1991 / PL / M • Personal Touch #4 / 1989 / AR / M • Pick Up Lines #04 / 1995 / ... / M • Pleasure Island / 1990 / VI / M • The Pleasure Seekers / 1990 / VD / M • Porn On The 4th Of July / 1990 / IN / M • Pretty Peaches #3 / 1989 / VC / M • The Price Is Right / 1992 / VT / C • Private & Confidential / 1990 / AR / M • Pumping It Up / 1993 / ... / M • Pussywoman #1: Sisters In Sin / 1994 / CC / M • Ready, Willing & Anal (Cv) / 1993 / CV / C • Roadgirls / 1990 / DR / M • Robin Head / 1991 / CC / M • Route 69 / 1989 / OD / M • Scarlet Fantasy / 1990 / VI / M • The Scarlet Mistress / 1990 / VI / M • The Search For Pink October / 1990 / EX / M • Seoul Train / 1991 / IN / M • Sex Symphony / 1990 / VI / M • Sex Toy / 1993 / CA / C • A Shot In The Mouth #1 / 1990 / ME / M • Sirens / 1991 / VC / M • The Smart Aleck / 1990 / PM / M • Snatch Masters #04 / 1995 / LEI / M • Sorceress / 1990 / GO / M • Stacked With Honors / 1993 / DR / M • Strangers When We Meet / 1990 / VCR / M • Strykin' It Deep / 1989 / V10 / M • Style #1 / 1992 / VT / M • The Swap #1 / 1990 / VI / M • Swedish Erotica Featurettes #1 / 1989 / CA / M • Swing Shift / 1989 / PL / G • Switch Hitters #5: The Night Games / 1990 / IN / G • Tailspin #2 / 1991 / VT / M • A

Taste Of Tami Monroe / 1990 / PIN / C • A Taste Of Tori Welles / 1990 / PIN / C • Tattle Tales / 1989 / SE / M • Temptations / 1989 / DR / M • This One's For You / 1989 / AR / M • Titillation #2 / 1990 / SE / M • Titillation #3 / 1991 / SE / M • Tori Welles Exposed / 1990 / VD / C • Trouble Maker / 1995 / VI / M • True Love / 1989 / VI / M • User Friendly / 1992 / VT / M • Vanity / 1992 / HO / M • Vegas #1: Royal Flush / 1990 / CIN / M • Vogue / 1994 / VD / C • Waterbabies #2 / 1992 / CC / M • Waves Of Passion / 1996 / ERA / M • Welcome To The House Of Fur Pi / 1989 / GO / M • Wet Paint / 1990 / DR / M • Where The Sun Never Shines / 1990 / IN / C • The Wild One / 1990 / LE / M • Wildfire / 1989 / EVN / M • Women In Need / 1990 / HO / M • World Cup / 1990 / PL / M • The Wrong Woman / 1990 / LE / M

ERIC ROBERTS
The Best Of The Best #2 / 1983 / FOX / S • Mondo Bitches / 1991 / LBO / B • Sensation / 1994 / C3S / S

ERIC ROBERTS (EDWARD *see* **Eric Edwards**

ERIC ROHM *see* **Eric Rome**

ERIC ROME *(Eric Rohm)*
The Bitch / 1988 / FAN / M • Robofox #1 / 1987 / FAN / M • Sex Asylum #3 / 1988 / VI / M

ERIC RYAN
Bi-Heat #08 To #10 / 1988 / ZA / G • The Bikini Carwash Company #1 / 1990 / IMP / S • Dallas School Girls / 1981 / VCX / M • Days Gone Bi / 1988 / ZA / G • Games Women Play #1 / 1980 / CA / M • Techsex / 1988 / VXP / M • Velvet High / 1980 / VC / M

ERIC SCHUNN
Up And Cummers #14 / 1994 / 4P / M

ERIC STANNOUS *see* **Star Index I**

ERIC STARR *(Darrien Hart)*
The Boneheads / 1992 / PL / M • Cycle Sluts / 1992 / CC / M • Insatiable Nurses / 1992 / VIM / M • Midsummer Love Story / 1993 / WV / M • Queen Of Hearts #3: Heartless / 1992 / PL / M • Ready Freddy? / 1992 / WV / M • Temple Of Lust / 1992 / VC / M • Teri Diver's Bedtime Tales / 1993 / FD / M • Virtual Sex / 1993 / VC / M

ERIC STEIN *(Eric Duro, Eric Duron, Eric Stien)*
Bad Company / 1978 / CV / M • Coed Fever / 1980 / CA / M • Every Which Way She Can / 1981 / CA / M • Garage Girls / 1981 / CV / M • Hot Line / 1980 / CA / M • Memphis Cathouse Blues / 1982 / CA / M • Nothing To Hide #1 / 1981 / CV / M • On White Satin / 1980 / VCX / M • Purely Physical / 1982 / SE / M • Summer School / 1979 / VCX / M • With Love, Lisa / 1985 / CA / C

ERIC STEVENS *see* **Star Index I**

ERIC STIEN *see* **Eric Stein**

ERIC STONE
Anna Amore's Fantasy Gang Bang / 1996 / FC / M • Black For More / 1993 / ZA / M • Hollywood Swingers #08 / 1993 / LBO / M • In Loving Color #4 / 1993 / VT / M • Loose Ends #4 / 1988 / 4P / M • M Series #11 / 1993 / LBO / M • Rocks / 1993 / VT / M

ERIC STUART *see* **Aaron Stuart**

ERIC SWENSON *see* **Steve Powers**

ERIC TAYLOR *see* **Star Index I**

ERIC VON BULOW *see* **Star Index I**

ERIC WEDEKIND
[Junge Madchen Mogen's HeiB, Hausfrauen Noch HeiBer / 1973 / ... / M

ERIC WEISS
International Analists / 1994 / AFD / M • Le Parfum De Mathilde / 1994 / VI / M • Magma: Old And Young / 1995 / MET / M • Private Film #06 / 1994 / OD / M • Private Film #07 / 1994 / OD / M

ERIC WILLENBRINK
Hardcore: The Films Of Richard Kern #1 / 1991 / FTV / M

ERIC YORK
Conflict Of Interest / 1994 / FST / G • Courting Libido / 1995 / HIV / G • Driven Home / 1995 / CSP / G

ERICA
Blue Vanities #518 / 1993 / FFL / M • C-Hunt #03: Sunny Delights / 1995 / PEV / M • First Time Lesbians #16 / 1994 / JMP / F • Global Girls / 1996 / GO / F • How To Have Anal Sex / 1993 / A&E / M • New Faces, Hot Bodies #08 / 1993 / STP / M • New Faces, Hot Bodies #21 / 1996 / STP / C

ERICA (JALYNN) *see* **Jalynn**

ERICA ADAMS
The Boarding House / 1983 / WV / M

ERICA BARON *see* **Crystal Sync**

ERICA BEE *see* **Erica Boyer**

ERICA BOWDEN
Big Mamas / 1981 / ... / C • Blue Vanities #536 / 1993 / FFL / M

ERICA BOYER *(Erica Bee)*
Hard ball-busting not too pretty older female. Born in 1956 according to **Bloopers #2**. Was married to Austin Moore at one stage but is now believed to be divorced.
69 Park Avenue / 1985 / ELH / M • Adult Video Therapist / 1987 / CLV / C • Aerobics Girls Club / 1986 / 4P / F • All That Glitters / 1992 / LV / M • Amazing Tails #4 / 1990 / CA / M • Anal Island / 1992 / LV / M • Angel Kelly Raw / 1987 / FAN / M • Angel's Gotta Have It / 1988 / FAN / M • Another Kind Of Love / 1985 / CV / M • Any Port In The Storm / 1991 / LV / M • The Arabian Treasure Chest / 1987 / L&W / C • Aunt Peg's Fulfillment / 1980 / CV / M • The Autobiography Of Herman Flogger / 1986 / AVC / M • Back To Back #1 / 1987 / 4P / C • Backdoor Babes / 1985 / WET / M • The Backdoor Club / 1992 / LV / M • Backdoor Summer #1 / 1988 / PV / C • Backside To The Future #1 / 1986 / ZA / M • Barbara Dare's Bad / 1988 / SE / C • Barbara Dare's Prime Choice / 1987 / SE / C • Barbara The Barbarian / 1987 / SE / M • The Beat Goes On / 1987 / VCR / C • Before She Says I Do / 1984 / MAP / M • The Best Little Whorehouse In Beverly Hills / 1986 / CDI / M • The Best Little Whorehouse In Hong Kong / 1987 / SE / M • Best Of Bruce Seven #3 / 1990 / BIZ / C • Best Of Bruce Seven #4 / 1990 / BIZ / C • Best Of Hot Shorts #01 / 1987 / VCR / C • Beyond De Sade / 1979 / MIT / M • Big House Babes / 19?? / VC / M • Billionaire Girls Club / 1988 / LVI / C • Bimbo Bowlers From Boston / 1990 / ZA / M • Bionca On Fire / 1988 / 4P / M • The Bitch / 1988 / FAN / M • Black Throat / 1985 / VC / M • Black To The Future / 1986 / VD / M • Blazing Bedrooms / 1987 / LA / M • Bloopers

#2 / 1991 / GO / C • Blue Vanities #056 / 1988 / FFL / M • Body Fire / 1991 / LV / M • Body Girls / 1983 / SE / M • Body Music #1 / 1989 / DR / M • Born To Be Bad / 1987 / CV / M • Breast Worx #18 / 1992 / LBO / M • Breast Worx #20 / 1992 / LBO / M • Breastography, Lesson #1 / 1987 / VCR / M • Bruce Seven's Favorite Endings #1 / 1991 / EL / C • Buns And Roses (LV) / 1990 / LV / M • Cagney & Stacey / 1984 / AT / M • Calendar Girl '83 / 1983 / CXV / M • Campus Capers / 1982 / VC / M • Cavalcade Of Stars / 1985 / VCR / C • Cells Of Passion / 1981 / VD / M • Cheerleader Academy / 1986 / PL / M • Chicks In Black Leather / 1989 / VC / C • China White / 1986 / WV / M • Christy Canyon: She's Back / 1995 / TTV / C • Coffee, Tea Or Me / 1984 / CV / M • Dance Fever / 1985 / VCR / M • The Danger Zone / 1990 / SO / M • Dark Corners / 1991 / LV / M • Dark Interludes / 1991 / BS / B • Debbie Goes To Hawaii / 1988 / VD / C • The Debutante / 1986 / BEA / M • Deep Inside Vanessa Del Rio / 1986 / VC / M • Desire For Men / 1981 / MIT / M • Devil In Miss Dare / 1986 / AVC / C • Devil In Miss Jones #4: The Final Outrage / 1987 / VC / M • Diamond Head / 1987 / AVC / M • Dirty 30's Cinema: Patti Petite / 1986 / PV / C • Down The Drain / 1986 / 4P / M • Dr Blacklove #1 / 1987 / CC / M • Dreams In The Forbidden Zone / 1989 / PCP / M • Easy Pickin's / 1990 / LV / M • The Eleventh Commandment / 1987 / WAV / M • The Enchantress / 1985 / 4P / M • The End Zone / 1987 / LA / C • Erica Boyer: Non-Stop / 1988 / VD / C • Erotic Fantasies: Women With Women / 1984 / CV / C • Every Man's Dream, Every Woman's Nightmare / 1988 / CC / C • Every Woman Has A Fantasy #1 / 1984 / VC / M • Evil Angel / 1986 / VCR / M • Fantasy Club: The Boarding House / 1984 / WV / M • Fantasy World / 1991 / NWV / C • The Fine Art Of Anal Intercourse / 1985 / VCR / M • Flesh Fire / 1985 / AVC / M • For Your Thighs Only / 1985 / WV / M • From Sweden With Love / 1989 / ZA / M • Funky Brewster / 1986 / DR / M • Furburgers / 1987 / VD / M • Gang Bangs #1 / 1985 / VCR / M • Gentlemen Prefer Ginger / 1985 / VI / M • Ginger On The Rocks / 1985 / VI / M • Ginger Then And Now / 1990 / VI / C • Girl Games / 1987 / PL / C • Girl Toys / 1986 / DR / M • Girls Don't Lie / 1990 / IN / F • Girls Gone Bad #1 / 1990 / GO / F • Girls Gone Bad #2: The Breakout / 1990 / GO / F • The Girls Of Porn / 1989 / FRV / F • Girls U.S.A. / 1980 / AIR / M • Girls! Girls! Girls! #1 / 1986 / VCS / C • Girls, Girls, Girls, Girls / 1993 / FD / C • The Good Time Girls / 1985 / VEX / M • Gourmet Premier: Ginger's Hot Massage / Photo Orgy #912 / cr85 / GO / M • Gourmet Premier: Throbbing Threesome / Hot Wife's Hunger 902 / cr86 / GO / M • Gourmet Quickies: Erica Boyer / Rikki Blake #727 / 1985 / GO / C • Grand Opening / 1985 / AT / M • Gym Coach In Bondage / 1980 / VDS / B • Hanna Does Her Sisters / 1986 / HUR / M • Hard Rockin' Babes / 1987 / VD / F • Hard To Swallow / 1985 / PV / M • Head Lock / 1989 / VD / M • Holly Does Hollywood #1 / 1985 / VEX / M • Honeybuns #2: Grecian Formula / 1987 / WV / C • The Honeymooners / 1986 / CDI / M • Hooters

/ 1986 / AVC / M • Hot Licks At The Pussycat Club / 1990 / WV / C • Hot Nights At The Blue Note Cafe / 1985 / WV / M • Hot Property / 1989 / EXH / C • Hot Shorts: Christy Canyon / 1987 / VCR / C • How To Enlarge Your Penis / 1985 / VCR / M • Hustler Honeys #2 / 1988 / VC / S • I Said A Butt Light #1 / 1990 / LV / M • Imagine / 1991 / LV / M • The Immoral Miss Teeze / 1987 / CV / M • Inches For Keisha / 1988 / WV / C • Indecent Pleasures / 1984 / CA / M • Inside Sharon Mitchell / 1989 / ZA / C • Jamie Loves Jeff #1 / 1987 / VI / M • Just The Two Of Us / 1985 / WV / M • Le Sex De Femme #5 / 1990 / AFI / C • Legends Of Porn #2 / 1989 / CV / C • Les Be Friends / 1988 / WV / C • Lesbo Power Tools / 1994 / CA / C • Let's Get Physical (Hyapatia Lee's) / 1984 / CA / M • Loose Ends #1 / 1984 / 4P / M • Loose Ends #2 / 1986 / 4P / M • Loose Ends #3 / 1987 / BS / M • Loose Ends #4 / 1988 / 4P / M • Loose Ends #5: The New Generation / 1988 / 4P / M • Losing Control / 1985 / CDI / M • The Magic Touch / 1985 / CV / M • Maiden Heaven #2 / 1992 / MID / F • Manhattan Mistress / 1980 / VBM / M • Masturbation Madness / 1991 / 5KS / F • A Mid-Slumber's Night Dream / 1985 / 4P / M • The Mile High Girls / 1987 / CA / M • Mistresses And Slaves: The Best Of Bruce Seven / 1991 / BEB / C • The Modelling Studio / 1984 / GO / M • The Moon Girls / 1990 / ME / C • Naked Night / 1985 / VCR / M • Nasty Lady / 1984 / CV / M • The Night Of The Headhunter / 1985 / WV / M • Night Trips #2 / 1990 / CA / M • Nina's Toys And Boys / 1991 / LV / C • Nothing To Hide #1 / 1981 / CV / M • Once Upon A Madonna / 1985 / PV / M • Only The Best #3 / 1990 / CV / C • Only The Best Of Barbara Dare / 1990 / CV / C • Only The Best Of The Erotic Eighties / 1992 / VC / C • Only The Very Best On Video / 1992 / VC / C • Open Up Tracy / 1984 / VD / M • Oral Majority #01 / 1986 / WV / C • Oral Majority #03 / 1986 / WV / C • Oral Majority #04 / 1987 / WV / C • Oral Majority #05 / 1987 / WV / C • Palomino Heat / 1985 / COM / F • Passion For Bondage / 1983 / BIZ / B • Passion From Behind / 1990 / LV / M • The Performers / 1986 / NSV / M • Pipe Dreams / 1985 / 4P / M • Please, Mr Postman / 1981 / VC / M • Pleasure Party (Gourmet) / 1985 / GO / M • Porsche Lynn, Every Man's Dream / 1988 / CC / C • Pump It Up / 1990 / LV / M • Pumping Flesh / 1985 / CA / M • Pussyman #06: House Of Games / 1994 / SNA / M • Read My Lips: No More Bush / 1992 / HW / M • Rear Action Girls #1 / 1984 / LIP / F • Reckless Passion / 1986 / ME / M • Rio Heat / 1986 / VD / M • Robofox #1 / 1987 / FAN / M • Rolls Royce #05 / 1980 / ... / C • Rolls Royce #06 / 1980 / ... / C • Samantha, I Love You / 1988 / WV / C • Screwdriver / 1988 / CC / C • Seduction Of Jennifer / 1986 / HO / M • Sex Asylum #2 / 1986 / VI / M • Sex Asylum #3 / 1988 / VI / M • The Sex Dancer / 1986 / NSV / M • Sex For Hire / 1989 / HOE / C • Sex Games / 1983 / CA / M • Sex Loose / 1982 / VC / M • Sexy Delights #1 / 1986 / CLV / M • Shave Tail / 1984 / AMB / M • Sheer Bedlam / 1986 / VI / M • Sheets Of San Francisco / 1986 / AVC / M • Simply Outra-

geous / 1989 / VC / C • Sins Of Tami Monroe / 1991 / CA / C • Skin Games / 1986 / VEX / M • Skin Games / 1991 / VEX / C • Skin On Skin / 1981 / CV / M • Slippery When Wet / 1986 / PL / M • Snatched To The Future / 1991 / EL / F • Soul Kiss This / 1988 / VCR / C • Star 84: Tina Marie / 1984 / VEX / M • Swedish Erotica #51 / 1983 / CA / M • Sweet Cheeks / 1987 / VCR / C • Tailenders / 1985 / WET / M • Talk Dirty To Me #04 / 1986 / DR / M • Taste Of The Best #1 / 1988 / PIN / C • Tawnee...Be Good! / 1988 / LV / M • The Teacher's Pet / 1985 / WV / M • These Buns For Hire / 1990 / LV / M • This Butt's For You / 1986 / PME / M • Thrill Seekers / 1990 / BS / B • Tori Welles Exposed / 1990 / VD / C • Toys 4 Us #1 / 1987 / WV / C • Toys 4 Us #3: Follow The Leader / 1990 / WV / C • Trading Partners / 1983 / AIR / M • Transparent Desires / 1991 / LV / M • Trashy Ladies / 1993 / LIP / F • True Legends Of Adult Cinema: The Erotic Eighties / 1992 / VC / C • Unnatural Act #2 / 1986 / DR / M • Unveiled / 1987 / VC / M • VCA Previews #4 / 1988 / VC / C • Viper's Place / 1988 / VD / M • Virgin Cheeks / 1986 / VD / M • Wet Science / 1986 / PLY / M • Where The Girls Are / 1984 / VEX / M • Where The Sun Never Shines / 1990 / IN / C • White Bun Busters / 1985 / VC / M • The Whore Of The Worlds / 1985 / PV / M • The Wild Brat / 1988 / VI / M • Wild Toga Party / 1985 / VD / M • Woman To Woman / 1989 / ZA / C • A Woman's Touch / 1988 / ZA / F • The Wonder Rears / 1990 / SO / M • Working Girl / 1993 / VI / M • Working It Out / 1983 / CA / M • X Factor / 1984 / HO / M • X-Rated Bloopers #2 / 1986 / AR / M • X-TV #1 / 1986 / PL / C • Young Girls Do / 1984 / ELH / M • [Best Of Nina Hartley / 19?? / ... / C • [Ginger's Hot Massage / 1985 / ... / C • [I Love You, Molly Flynn / 1988 / ... / M • [Perfect Stranger / 1988 / ... / M

ERICA COLLINS
Dear Fanny / 1984 / CV / M • Only The Best Of Men's And Women's Fantasies / 1988 / CV / C

ERICA COOL
Everything Goes / 1975 / CA / M • [Cathy, Fille Soumise / 1977 / ... / M • [S.S. Bordello / 1978 / ... / M

ERICA DEMURE
Doctors Of Pain / 1995 / BIZ / B • Leather Bound Dykes From Hell #5 / 1995 / BIZ / B • Nurses Bound By Duty / 1996 / BIZ / B • Spiked Heel Diaries #3 / 1995 / BIZ / B • Submission Of Ariana / 1995 / BIZ / B

ERICA EATON
Angela, The Fireworks Woman / 1975 / VC / M • Bon Appetit / 1980 / QX / M • Every Inch A Lady / 1975 / QX / M • Love-In Maid / cr72 / CDC / M • Outlaw Ladies #1 / 1981 / VC / M • The Satisfiers Of Alpha Blue / 1980 / AVC / M

ERICA ERICKSON *see* **Veronica Erickson**
ERICA ESTRADA *see* **Francesca Le**
ERICA FOX *see* **Star Index I**
ERICA FUNN
6969 Mel'hose Place / 1995 / VG0 / M
ERICA HASS
Old Wave Hookers #1 / 1995 / PL / M
ERICA HAVENS *(Karen Havens, Karen St Joy)*

Brunette, shoulder length hair, hairy pussy, small tits, Passable face.
The Coming Of Joyce / 1977 / VIS / M • Decendance Of Grace / 1977 / CA / M • Devil In Miss Jones #1 / 1972 / VC / M • Doogan's Woman / 1978 / S&L / M • Erotic Fantasies #3 / 1983 / CV / C • Erotic Fantasies: Women With Women / 1984 / CV / C • Exploring Young Girls / 1978 / ALP / M • Here Comes The Bride / 1977 / CV / M • Honeymoon Haven / 1977 / QX / M • Saturday Matinee Series #1 / 1996 / VCX / C • Swedish Sorority Girls / 1978 / CV / M

ERICA IDOL
Ball Busters / 1984 / CV / M • The Big Bang / 1988 / WET / M • Blonde Heat (VCA) / 1985 / VC / M • Future Sex / 1984 / NSV / M • Illusions Of Ecstasy / 1985 / NSV / M • The Last Taboo / 1984 / VIV / M • Soft As Silk...Sweet As Honey / 1984 / SE / M

ERICA JOHNSON *see* **Crystal Sync**
ERICA JULLIETT
Prima #08: Sex Camping / 1995 / MBP / M
ERICA LOCKETT
Anal Hanky-Panky / 1997 / ROB / M • Ass, Gas & The Mystical GLOP / 1997 / EL / M • Raw Naked In Your Face / 1997 / ROB / M • Suzi's Wild Anal Ride / 1997 / ROB / M
ERICA MADOU *see* **Star Index I**
ERICA MEAD
Dinner With Samantha / 1983 / PTV / M
ERICA NILE *see* **Star Index I**
ERICA PIRI
Private Film #07 / 1994 / OD / M
ERICA RAKOSOY
Private Film #11 / 1994 / OD / M
ERICA RED
Private Film #13 / 1994 / OD / M
ERICA RICHARDSON
Blonde In Black Silk / 1979 / QX / M • Mystique / 1979 / CA / M • That Lucky Stiff / 1979 / QX / M
ERICA ROBERTS
Anal Virgins #02 / 1996 / NS / M • Undercover / 1996 / VC / M
ERICA ROBERTS (1993)
Sneek Peeks #1 / 1993 / FL / M
ERICA ROSS
Blue Lace / 1986 / OE / M • Corporate Affairs / 1986 / SE / M • Girls Of The Chorus Line / 1986 / CLV / M • Irresistible #2 / 1986 / SE / M • Science Friction / 1986 / AXT / M • To Live & Shave In LA / 1986 / WET / M
ERICA STONE
Angel Hard / 1996 / STV / M
ERICA STRAUSS *see* **Angela Haze**
ERICA SWANSON
Erotic Fantasies: Women With Women / 1984 / CV / C • The Joy Of Fooling Around / 1978 / CV / M
ERICK CASHMAN
Hollywood Amateurs #23 / 1995 / MID / M • Hollywood Amateurs #24 / 1995 / MID / M
ERICK LUEDERS
Take Off / 1978 / VXP / M
ERICK STAUFF
The Black Mystique / 1986 / CV / M • She-Male Encounters #11: She-Male Roommates / 1986 / MET / G
ERIK
Magma: Bizarre Games / 1996 / MET / M
ERIK ANDERSON *(Odus Hamlin)*
ERIK SILVA

Jezebel / 1979 / CV / M
ERIK SOMMET
Sharon In The Rough-House / 1976 / LA / M
ERIK VON SEROKHARDT *see* **Rocky Millhouse**
ERIKA
Blue Vanities #507 / 1992 / FFL / M • Blue Vanities #532 / 1993 / FFL / M • Cheap Tricks #1 / 1996 / PAV / M • Dirty Dancers #6 / 1995 / 4P / M • Feuchte Muschies / 1995 / KRM / M • Flesh Fever / 1978 / CV / M • International Love And The Dancer / 1995 / PME / S • Neighbor Girls T46 / 1991 / NEI / F • Sodomania: Slop Shots / 1996 / EL / C • World Sex Tour #4 / 1996 / ANA / M
ERIKA BELLA
Butt Banged Cycle Sluts / 1995 / ANA / M • Erika Bella: Euroslut / 1995 / EL / M • Hot Diamond / 1995 / LE / M • The Joy Club / 1996 / XC / M • Midnight Obsession / 1995 / XC / M • Paprika / 1995 / XC / M • Private Video Magazine #12 / 1994 / OD / M • Private Video Magazine #15 / 1994 / OD / M • The Sex Clinic / 1995 / WIV / M • The Thief, The Girl & The Detective / 1996 / HDE / M • World Sex Tour #1 / 1995 / ANA / M
ERIKA FOXX *see* **Jerrika Foxxx**
ERIKA GRANT
Sex Drivers / 1996 / VMX / M
ERIKA KOOL *see* **Star Index I**
ERIKA STONE
Le Parfum De Mathilde / 1994 / VI / M
ERIKA TOTH
Diamonds / 1996 / HDE / M
ERIKA VON JOCKISCH
[Schulmadchen-Report 4: Was Eltern Oft Verzweifeln LaBt / 1972 / ... / M
ERIKO *see* **Star Index I**
ERIN
Blue Vanities #505 / 1992 / FFL / M • The Bondage Club #1 / 1987 / LON / B • The Bondage Club #2 / 1987 / LON / B • Eric Kroll's Fetish #2 / 1994 / ERK / M • Erotic Eye / 1995 / DGD / S • Hot Body Competition: Hot Pants Contest / 1996 / CG / F
ERIN CANE
Beyond Driven #3 / 1996 / ZFX / B • War Pigs #1 / 1996 / ZFX / B • War Pigs #2 / 1996 / ZFX / B
ERIN KING
Up And Cummers #25 / 1995 / 4P / M • Up And Cummers #26 / 1996 / 4P / M
ERLING HITT
L.A. Tool & Die / 1979 / TMX / G
ERMINIO FASANI *see* **Star Index I**
ERNEST GREEN *(Ira Levine)*
One of the co-authors of Stoller's book, *Coming Attractions*.
Bondage Boot Camp / 1988 / TAN / B • Bondage Cheerleaders / 1993 / LON / B • The Bondage Club #4 / 1990 / LON / B • The Bondage Club #5 / 1990 / LON / B • Bound To Tease #4 / 1989 / BON / C • Captured On Camera / 1997 / BON / B • Chronicles Of Submission / 1995 / BON / B • Confessions of Chloe / 1996 / BON / B • Controlled / 1990 / BS / B • Couples Club #1 / 1988 / BON / B • Couples Club #2 / 1989 / BON / B • The Exchange / 1995 / BON / B • Final Exam #1 / 1987 / BON / B • Final Exam #2 / 1988 / BON / B • Fundgeon Of The Mind #1 / 1994 / BON / B • Incarceration Of Chloe / 1996 / BON / B • In-

ferno #2 / 1993 / SC / M • Phantom And The Whip / 1993 / VTF / B • The Story Of Pain / 1992 / PL / B • Theatre Of Seduction #1 / 1990 / BON / B • Theatre Of Seduction #2 / 1990 / BON / B • Tortured Passions / 1994 / PL / B • The Torturous Infidel / 1994 / PL / B • Trained By Payne / 1994 / ONA / B
ERNEST KRAUS *see* **Star Index I**
ERNIE STEAM *see* **Star Index I**
ERNIE TARZAN *see* **Star Index I**
ERNST HEMMINGWAY *see* **Christian Parker**
ERON *see* **Wild Oscar**
EROS BARSOTTI
Selen / 1996 / HW / M
EROS BELOTTI
Betty Bleu / 1996 / IP / M
EROS RYAN *see* **Star Index I**
EROTICA *(Dianna Rose)*
Black girl, 26 years old in 1996, 5'3" tall, passable sometimes pretty face, rose tattoo above left breast and another small tattoo on left shoulder front, narrow hips, meaty labia, long straight black hair, ugly scar (probably a Caesarian) running through her belly button which she tries to keep covered at all times.
Amazing Hardcore #1: Blow Jobs / 1997 / MET / M • Black Cheerleader Search #04 / 1996 / ROB / M • Bootylicious: Bitches & Ho's / 1996 / JMP / M • Creme De La Face #13: Nine Nasty Nymphs / 1995 / OD / M • Fresh Faces #11 / 1996 / EVN / M • Hershe Highway #5: Backdoor Blues / 1996 / HO / M • More Black Dirty Debutantes #6 / 1996 / 4P / M • The Sodomizer #3 / 1996 / SC / M • Sweet Black Cherries #5 / 1996 / TTV / M
ERVIN ELEKES
True Stories #1 / 1993 / SC / M • True Stories #2 / 1993 / SC / M
ERWIN RADBOY *see* **Star Index I**
ESA MARIE
Anal Camera #07 / 1995 / EVN / M • Bar-B-Que Gang Bang / 1994 / JMP / M • Black Hollywood Amateurs #04 / 1995 / MID / M • Butt Hunt #05 / 1995 / LEI / M • Comp. Fire. Tramps / 1995 / LOT / M • Dusting Ball #08 / 1994 / OD / M • Ebony Poppers #11: California Co-Eds / 1995 / ZA / M • Coco's House Party / 1995 / HW / M • The Cumm Brothers #06: Hook, Line And Sphincter / 1995 / OD / M • Cute Cuddly Bubbly Butts / 1996 / TTV / M • Cutie Pies / 1995 / TTV / M • Dirty Mind / 1995 / VEX / M • Forbidden Fantasies #1 / 1995 / ZA / M • Hard Core Beginners #04 / 1995 / LEI / M • The Hitch-Hiker #08: On The Trail / 1994 / WMG / M • Hollywood Amateurs #11 / 1994 / MID / M • Horny Henry's Strange Adventure / 1995 / TTV / M • I Cream On Jeannie / 1995 / AVI / M • Nasty Newcummers #07 / 1995 / MET / M • Orgies Orgies Orgies / 1994 / WV / M • Perverted Stories #01 / 1995 / JMP / M • Pussy Hunt #10 / 1995 / LEI / M • Rear Entry / 1995 / LEI / M • Roommates To Lovers / 1995 / LIP / F • Shades Of Color #1 / 1995 / LBO / M • Swedish Erotica #82 / 1995 / CA / M • Tail Taggers #128: / 1994 / WV / M • Video Virgins #20 / 1995 / NS / M
ESELLE FERRAND *see* **Lynn Ray**
ESMAY MONROE
Fantasy Follies #1 / 1983 / VC / M • Horror

In The Wax Museum / 1983 / TAO / B • Intimate Realities #2 / 1983 / VC / M
ESMERELDA
Attention: Ropes & Gags / 1994 / BON / B • Coed Fever / 1980 / CA / M • Driller / 1984 / VC / M • Patio Bondage / 1994 / BON / B
ESMERELDA ESTRADA see Emerald Estrada
ESMERELDA STANTON
Smoke & Mirrors / 1996 / PL / M
ESSENCE
African Angels #3 / 1996 / NIT / M • Shaved #02 / 1992 / RB / F
ESTELLA MCNALLY see Star Index I
ESTELLE
Jura Sexe / 1995 / JP / G • Magma: Hot Service / 1995 / MET / M • Triple X Video Magazine #08 / 1995 / OD / M
ESTELLE MARTIN
Black Cheerleader Search #07 / 1996 / IVC / M
ESTER SILS
Steamy Dreams / cr70 / CVX / M
ESTHER
Bizarre Dildo Obsession / 1989 / BIZ / B • Lesbian Pros And Amateurs #02 / 1992 / GO / F • Painless Steel #3 / 1996 / FLV / M
ESTHER ROBERTS see Star Index I
ESTHER STUDER
[Madchen, Die Sich Selbst, Bedienen / 1974 / ... / M
ESTHER WALKER
All Night Long / 1975 / SE / M
ESTRELLA see Star Index I
ESTRELLA DEL SOL
Toredo / 1996 / ROX / M
ETERNITY see Kim Eternity
ETHAN MICHAEL AYERS
Our Trespasses / 1996 / AWV / G
ETHYL SUPREME see Star Index I
ETIENNE
Magma: Old And Young / 1995 / MET / M
EUGENE SCOTT see Star Index I
EUNICE see Star Index I
EUREKA GOLD
Black Knockers #03 / 1995 / TV / M • Black Knockers #11 / 1995 / TV / M
EUROPA see Star Index I
EUROPE DICHAN
10 Years Of Big Busts #2 / 1990 / BTO / C • Big Bust Strippers #01 / 1990 / BTO / F • Busty Nymphos / 1996 / H&S / M • H&S Devon Dichan / 199? / H&S / S • On Location: Boob Cruise / 1996 / H&S / S
EVA
Bright Tails #4 / 1994 / STP / B • Czech, Please #1 / 1996 / BAC / F • Depravity On The Danube / 1993 / EL / M • Dick & Jane Return To Hungary / 1993 / OAP / M • Eurotica #11 / 1996 / XC / M • Hollywood Swingers #07 / 1993 / LBO / M • Home-Grown Video #473: Furpie Feast #3 / 1997 / HOV / C • Hose Jobs / 1995 / VEX / M • New Faces, Hot Bodies #19 / 1995 / STP / M • Private Gold #10: Sins / 1996 / OD / M • Private Gold #12: The Pyramid #2 / 1996 / OD / M • San Francisco Lesbians #4 / 1993 / PL / F • Sodomania #05: Euro-American Style / 1993 / EL / M • Sodomania #14: C**t Lickin', C*m Drinkin' Bitches / 1995 / EL / M • Student Fetish Videos: Bondage #03 / 1996 / PRE / B • Student Fetish Videos: Catfighting #17 / 1996 / PRE / B • Student Fetish Videos: Foot Worship #18 / 1995 / PRE / B

EVA ADAMS see Star Index I
EVA ALLEN *(Marlena Bond, Farron Heights, Farryn Heights, Natasha Nash, Monique DuBois)*
Monique DuBois is from **Sex On The Town**.
A.S.S.(Anal Security Squad) / 1988 / VD / M • Bimbo Cheerleaders From Outer Space / 1988 / FAN / M • Boobs, Butts And Bloopers #1 / 1990 / HO / M • The De Renzy Tapes / 1990 / CA / C • A Fistful Of Bimbos / 1988 / FAZ / M • Ghostest With The Mostest / 1988 / CA / M • Invasion Of The Samurai Sluts From Hell / 1988 / FAZ / M • Jane Bond Meets Thunderthighs / 1988 / VD / M • Loose Ends #5: The New Generation / 1988 / 4P / M • My Wife Is A Call Girl / 1989 / FAZ / M • The Nicole Stanton Story #1 / 1989 / CA / M • The Nicole Stanton Story #2 / 1989 / CA / M • Prom Girls / 1988 / CA / M • Saddletramp / 1988 / VD / M • The Scent Of Samantha / 1988 / VEX / C • Sex Lives Of The Rich And Famous #1 / 1988 / VC / M • Sex Lives Of The Rich And Famous #2 / 1989 / VC / M • Sex On The Town / 1989 / V99 / M • Shaved Sinners #1 / 1988 / VT / M • Shaved Sinners #2 / 1987 / VT / M • A Taste Of Eva Allen / 1989 / PIN / C • Three Men And A Barbi / 1989 / FAN / M • Two Women & A Man / 1988 / VEX / M • Two Women & A Man / 1991 / VEX / C • Wild Oats / 1988 / CV / M
EVA AXEN
Bel Ami / 1976 / VXP / M • [Justine Och Juliette / 1975 / ... / S • [Molly / 1977 / ... / S
EVA BEREIN see Star Index I
EVA BOND
Essence Of A Woman / 1995 / ONA / M
EVA BRAWN
Bi-Nanza / 1994 / BIL / G
EVA CHRISTIAN
The Ideal Marriage / 1971 / SOW / M
EVA DESTRUCTION
Diary Of A Tormented TV / 1995 / BIZ / G • Domina #2: Every Inch A Lady / 1996 / LBO / G • Domina #3 / 1996 / LBO / G • Dungeon Queens / 1995 / BIZ / G • Painful Secrets Of A TV / 1996 / BIZ / G • She Males Enslaved / 1996 / BIZ / G • She-Male She Devils / 1996 / BIZ / G • She-Males In Torment #3 / 1995 / BIZ / G • TVs In Leather And Pain / 1996 / BIZ / G
EVA DIONISIO
Juliet & Romeo / 1996 / XC / M • Robin Thief Of Wives / 1996 / XC / M
EVA FALK
Paris Chic / 1996 / SAE / M
EVA FEVER
Private Film #25 / 1995 / OD / M
EVA FLOWERS see Eva Tiffany
EVA GAINS
Steamy Dreams / cr70 / CVX / M
EVA GAULANT
Sexorcist Devil / 1974 / CXV / M
EVA HENDERSON
Blonde Velvet / 1976 / COL / M • Feelings / 1977 / VC / M • Jail Bait / 1976 / VC / M • Odyssey / 1977 / VC / M
EVA HENGER
True Stories #1 / 1993 / SC / M • True Stories #2 / 1993 / SC / M
EVA HOLLYWOOD
The National Transsexual / 1990 / GO / G • She-Male Desires / 1989 / VC / C • TS Trains TV Hubby / 1994 / STM / G

EVA HOUSEMAN
Erotic Fantasies: John Leslie / 1985 / CV / C • Skin On Skin / 1981 / CV / M • Three Faces Of Angel / 1987 / CV / M
EVA KLEBER
Diamond Snatch / 1977 / COM / M • Evil Mistress / 1984 / VIP / M • The French Touch / 1984 / NSV / M • Sappho Connection / 19?? / LIP / F
EVA KLEPKOVA
Dirty Stories #4 / 1995 / PE / M
EVA KOHLER
Anabolic Import #03: Oral X / 1994 / ANA / M
EVA KRISS see Star Index I
EVA LATIO
Invasion Of The Love Drones / 1977 / ALP / M
EVA MORGAN see Star Index I
EVA ORLOWSKI *(Ava (Orlowski), Ava Orlowsky, Ava Orlouskyu)*
Italian.
All Inside Eva / 1991 / PL / M • Crossing Over / 1990 / IN / M • Erotic Games / 1992 / PL / M • The Housewife In Heat / 1991 / PL / M • Live Bait / 1990 / IN / M • Sexy Country Girl / 1991 / PL / M
EVA PAUREY see Star Index I
EVA QUANG
Douce Penetrations / 1975 / LUM / M • Sensations / 1975 / ALP / M
EVA ST CLAIR
Afrodisiac #2 / 1989 / CC / M • Creme De La Face #08: Wanna Blow Job / 1995 / OD / M • Cum To Drink Of It / 1996 / BCP / M • Pussy Fest Of The Northwest #2 / 1995 / NIT / M
EVA TIFFANY *(Eva Flowers, Tiffany (Eva Fl))*
Brunette with small (some people would say tiny) conical tits with large areola and a small tattoo on the left one. Thin body, slightly flat on the butt, long face, long nose, good skin. Seems to have a nice personality.
Anal Bad Girls / 1994 / ROB / F • Anal Breakdown / 1994 / ROB / M • Anal Candy Ass / 1994 / ROB / M • Anal Injury / 1994 / ZA / M • Anal Plaything #1 / 1994 / ROB / M • Beaver Hunt #01 / 1994 / LEI / M • Bi-Wicked / 1994 / BIN / G • Big Murray's New-Cummers #26: Real Tits / 1994 / FD / M • Butt Sluts #4 / 1995 / ROB / F • Cherry Pie / 1994 / SC / M • Chug-A-Lug Girls #5 / 1994 / VT / M • Cluster Fuck #05 / 1994 / MAX / M • Decadence / 1994 / WHP / M • Dirty Doc's Housecalls #20 / 1994 / LV / M • Dr Rear / 1995 / CC / M • Fantasy Du Jour / 1995 / FH / M • Freeway Love / 1994 / FD / M • Fresh Meat (John Leslie) #1 / 1994 / EA / M • Gang Bang Nymphette / 1994 / ROB / M • Girl's School / 1994 / ERA / M • Happy Ass Lesbians / 1994 / ROB / F • Hard Squeeze / 1994 / EMC / M • Hollywood Amateurs #01 / 1994 / MID / M • Hollywood Lesbians / 1995 / ROB / F • Homegrown Video #420: Straight Into The Corner Pocket / 1994 / HOV / M • Hotel Sodom #01 / 1995 / SNA / M • Kept Women / 1995 / LE / M • Kym Wilde's On The Edge #15 / 1994 / RB / B • Lesbian Workout #1 / 1994 / GO / F • Lesbian Workout #2 / 1994 / GO / F • Mike Hott: #265 Cunt Of The Month: Eva / 1994 / MHV / M • Ms. Fix-It / 1994 / PRK / M • My Evil Twin / 1994 / LE / M • Obsessions

In Lace / 1994 / PL / M • On The Rise / 1994 / EX / M • Paradise Lost / 1995 / LE / M • Perverted #1: The Babysitters / 1994 / ZA / M • Psychoanal Therapy / 1994 / CA / M • Reckless / 1995 / NOT / M • Reel Sex #02: Splash Party / 1994 / SPP / M • Seekers / 1994 / CA / M • Simply Kia / 1994 / LE / M • Under The Pink / 1994 / ROB / F • The Voyeur #2 / 1994 / EA / M • Women Of Color #2 / 1994 / ANA / M

EVA TOMINELLI
Prima #14: Hotel Europa / 1996 / MBP / M

EVA WHISHAW
Suburban Wives / 19?? / VST / M

EVA Z.
Screamers / 1994 / HW / M

EVAN
Intimate Interviews #2 / 1996 / NIT / M

EVAN DANIELS
Aroused #2 / 1995 / VI / M

EVAN HUES see Star Index I

EVAN TAYLOR see Star Index I

EVE
Adorable creamy skinned girl with black hair, tight firm body, tight waist and medium firm (but not enhanced) tits. Very nice smile and a slight overbite. Small tattoo on her left shoulder back which looks like an eye, a fish or a gull in flight. 20 years old in 1993. Comes from Daytona Beach Florida where she was a college student.
Beach Bum Amateur's #30 / 1993 / MID / M • Frathouse Sexcapades / 1993 / SFP / M • Green Piece Of Ass #3 / 1994 / RTP / M • Hole In One / 1993 / IF / M • Jezebel #1 / 1993 / SC / M • Jezebel #2 / 1993 / SC / M • Love Letters #1 / 1993 / SC / M • Love Letters #2 / 1993 / SC / M • The Man Who Loved Women / 1993 / SC / M • Mike Hott: #230 Cunt Of The Month: Eve 1-93 / 1993 / MHV / M • Ona Zee's Black Label #1: Sex Hunger / 1996 / ONA / C • Pearl Necklace: Amorous Amateurs #03 / 1992 / SEE / M • Pearl Necklace: Facial #01 / 1994 / SEE / C • Princess Of Persia / 1993 / IP / M • Raw Talent: Bang 'er 32 Times / 1992 / RTP / M • Raw Talent: Murphy Bang / 1994 / RTP / M • Russian Seduction / 1993 / IP / M • Up And Cummers #02 / 1993 / 4P / M • Up And Cummers #03 / 1993 / 4P / M • Up And Cummers #04 / 1993 / 4P / M • Video Virgins #05 / 1993 / NS / M

EVE (1972)
Bad Bad Gang / 1972 / SOW / M • Bucky Beaver's XXX Dragon Art Theatre Double Feature #07 / 1996 / SOW / M

EVE (1976)
Blue Vanities #565 / 1995 / FFL / M • Pornocopia Sensual / 1976 / VHL / M

EVE (1987)
Out Of The Closet / 1989 / NUV / B • The Party / 1987 / VER / B

EVE (EUROPE)
Global Girls / 1996 / GO / F

EVE (HUNGARIAN)
Buttwoman Back In Budapest / 1993 / EL / M • Sodomania: Slop Shots / 1996 / EL / C

EVE BYRNA
Ultraflesh / 1980 / GO / M

EVE EVANS
Sex Boat / 1980 / VCX / M

EVE JARRE
Girls With Curves #1 / 1985 / CV / M

EVE MEYER
Blue Vanities #552 / 1994 / FFL / M • Eve

And The Handyman / 1960 / RMV / S

EVE PIRELLI
Gode-Party / 1994 / RUM / M

EVE ST. JOHN
What's A Nice Girl Like You... / 1981 / ... / M

EVE STERNBERG see Star Index I

EVE SUMMERS
Candi Girl / 1979 / PVX / M

EVELYN
100% Amateur #19: / 1996 / OD / M • Anal Heartbreaker / 1995 / ROB / M • Anal Pussycat / 1995 / ROB / M • Anal Senorita #1 / 1994 / ROB / M • Blue Vanities #554 / 1994 / FFL / M • Hard To Hold / 1993 / IF / M • Hot Hideaway / 1986 / CA / M • Kink #1 / 1995 / ROB / M

EVELYN ASHLEY
She-Male Encounters #17: Sorority / 1987 / MET / G • She-Male Sanitarium / 1988 / VD / G

EVELYN VALADE
The Card Game / 1985 / CA / M

EVELYN WEST
Blue Vanities #115 / 1988 / FFL / M • Grindhouse Follies #16 / 1993 / SOW / M

EVELYNE GRAUX see Star Index I

EVELYNE TRAEGER
The Swingin' Stewardesses / 1971 / VCX / S • The Young Seducers / 1971 / BL / M

EVENYT
Blue Vanities #129 / 1990 / FFL / M

EVERETT DRURY see Star Index I

EVETTE
Ebony Anal Gang Bang #2 / 1994 / RTP / M

EVIANNA
Lana Exposed / 1995 / VT / M

EVIL EVE
Euro-Max #3: / 1995 / SC / M • Euro-Max #4: / 1995 / SC / M

EVON
Overkill / 1994 / BS / B • Wad Gobblers #11 / 1994 / GLI / M

EVON CRAWFORD (Minerva, Rosie (Evon Crawfor), Venessa Steele, Vanessa Steele (EC))
Pudgy girl who looks somewhat like Sydney Dance, but not as pretty and poorly placed by pencil lines. Sullen look on her face. Black hair, slobby belly, medium tits.
Babewatch #2 / 1994 / CC / M • Black Hollywood Amateurs #01 / 1995 / MID / M • Black Orgies #28 / 1994 / GO / M • Buffy Malibu's Totally Nasty All-Girl Home Videos #04 / 1993 / ANA / F • Buttslammers #06: Over The Edge / 1994 / BS / F • Ebony Erotica #26: Night Shift / 1994 / GO / M • Ebony Erotica #27: Caramel Lust / 1994 / GO / M • Hollywood Amateurs #07 / 1994 / MID / M • Home Nurses Anal Adventure / 1994 / LBO / M • The Hooker / 1995 / LOT / M • Junkyard Anal / 1994 / JAV / M • Latin Plump Humpers #1 / 1995 / TTV / M • Lips / 1994 / FC / M • Naughty Senorita / 1994 / WIV / M • The Nurses Are Cumming #1 / 1996 / LBO / C • Swedish Erotica #79 / 1994 / CA / M

EVONA see Emily Hill

EVONE TAYLOR see Star Index I

EWA WITT
Private Film #25 / 1995 / OD / M

EWERT GRANHOLM
Bel Ami / 1976 / VXP / M

EXENE
Dyke's Discipline / 1994 / PL / F

EXOTICA see Star Index I

EXOTICA BLACK
Hollywood Amateurs #19 / 1995 / MID / M

EXTACY
Babes Of The Bay #2 / 1995 / LIP / F • Black Women, White Men #1 / 1995 / FC / M • We Be Bangin' 24/7 / 1996 / FD / M

EYESHA SOLARIO see Iesha

EZTER
Private Gold #08: The Longest Night / 1996 / OD / M • Private Gold #10: Sins / 1996 / OD / M • Private Stories #08 / 1996 / OD / M

F. MAURO
The Desirous Wife / 1988 / PL / M

F. MEAT
3 Mistresses Of The Chateau / 1995 / STM / B • Chateau Of Torment / 1995 / STM / B • Dungeon Discipline / 1996 / STM / B • Dungeon Training / 1995 / STM / B • Mistress Rules / 1995 / STM / B

F. POWERS GIREAU see Star Index I

F. SHAY
Blue Vanities #165 (New) / 1996 / FFL / M

F.E. CAMPBELL
Bondage Classix #10: Painful Mistake / 1993 / BON / B

F.M. BRADLEY see Field Marsh Bradley

F.M. ROB
Tale Of Bearded Clam / cr71 / PYR / M

F.T.
Profiles #03: House Dick / 1995 / XPR / M

FABIAN FUEGO see Star Index I

FABIEN STUART
Every Inch A Lady / 1975 / QX / M

FABIENNE
Just One Day / 1995 / DBM / M • Magma: Horny Bulls / 1994 / MET / M

FABIENNE PARC see Star Index I

FABIO
Toe Tales #18 / 1994 / GOT / B

FABIO DIMARTINO see Star Index I

FABRICCO TOWERS
She-Male Surprise / 1995 / CDI / G • She-Male Swish Bucklers / 1994 / HSV / G

FABULOUS PHYLLIS
She-Mails / 1993 / PL / G

FAITH
Green Piece Of Ass #4 / 1994 / RTP / M

FAITH FONTAYNE
Sweet Black Cherries #2 / 1996 / TTV / M • Sweet Black Cherries #3 / 1996 / TTV / M

FAITH LAVETTE
Anal Romp / 1995 / LIP / F • Ass Angels / 1996 / PAL / F • Bay City Hot Licks / 1993 / ROB / F • Butt Jammers #05 / 1996 / SC / F • Butt Sluts #1 / 1993 / ROB / F • Butt Sluts #5 / 1995 / ROB / F • Dick & Jane In San Francisco / 1996 / AVI / M • Honey Drippers / 1992 / ROB / F • Kittens & Vamps #1 / 1993 / ROB / F • Lesbian Climax / 1995 / ROB / F • Lesbian Lockup / 1993 / ROB / F • Pony Girls / 1993 / ROB / F • San Francisco Lesbians #5 / 1994 / PL / F • San Francisco Lesbians #6 / 1994 / PL / F • Thrill Seekers / 1993 / ROB / F

FAITH MARIE
Up And Cummers #35 / 1996 / 4P / M • Up And Cummers #36 / 1996 / 4P / M

FAITH TURNER
Bi-Dacious / 1989 / PL / G • Bimbo Bowlers From Buffalo / 1989 / ZA / M • Girlworld #3 / 1989 / LIP / F • Girlworld #4 / 1989 / LIP / F • Leading Lady / 1991 / V99

/ M • Moonglow / 1989 / IN / M • Oh! You Beautiful Doll / 1990 / ZA / M • Tail For Sale / 1988 / VD / M • Wet Pink / 1989 / PL / F

FAKIDA KNIGHT LEE see Star Index I

FAKIR MUSAFUR

Corsetry 101 / 1996 / ESF / B • Erotica S.F. / 1994 / ORP / M • Forbidden Photographs / cr91 / FLV / M

FAKIRRO

Thermonuclear Sex / 1996 / EL / M

FALCON

Casting Couch Cuties #1 / 1994 / WP / M • Vivid At Home #02 / 1994 / VI / M

FALLON *(Robin Lee, Lauren Hall (Fallon), Aphrodite, Joanna Stewart, Laurie Peacock, Lori Peacock, Squirt, Laurie P., Robin Lee Fallon, Lisa (Fallon))*

Pretty face, very droopy small tits, brunette. Lauren Hall is from **Backdoor to Hollywood #03**.

1-800-TIME / 1990 / IF / M • A.S.S.(Anal Security Squad) / 1988 / VD / M • Acts Of Love / 1989 / ... / M • After The Lights Go Out / 1989 / VEX / M • Alpine Affairs / 1995 / LE / M • Babes With Attitudes / 1990 / EVN / M • Back On Top / 1988 / FAZ / M • Backdoor To Harley-Wood #2 / 1990 / AFV / M • Backdoor To Hollywood #03 / 1987 / CDI / M • Bang City #3: Fallon's Anal Gang Bang / 1995 / SC / M • Bare Essence / 1989 / EA / M • Behind The Green Door #2: The Sequel / 1985 / MIT / M • Bi Day...Bi Night / 1988 / PV / G • Biloxi Babes / 1988 / WV / M • The Black Anal-ist #1 / 1988 / VEX / M • Black Studies / 1992 / GO / M • Black With Sugar / 1989 / CIN / M • Blowing In Style / 1989 / EA / M • Bone Alone / 1993 / MID / M • Boobs, Butts And Bloopers #1 / 1990 / HO / M • Boom Boom Valdez / 1988 / CA / M • Bootylicious: Trailer Trash / 1996 / JMP / M • Bound For Pleasure / 1991 / BS / B • By Day Bi Night / 1989 / LV / G • Cabin Fever / 1995 / ERA / M • The Cat Club / 1987 / SE / M • Catfights #3 / 1987 / OHV / B • Caught From Behind #08 / 1988 / HO / M • Club Bed / 1987 / CIX / M • College Girl / 1990 / VEX / M • Coming Alive / 1988 / LV / M • Con Jobs / 1990 / V99 / M • Crossover / 1989 / STA / G • Cum On Inn / 1995 / TEG / M • D.P. Party Tonite / 1995 / JMP / M • Debbie Does 'em All #2 / 1988 / CV / M • Debbie Does Dallas #5 / 1988 / VEX / M • Deep In The Bush / 1990 / KIS / M • The Deep Insiders / 1987 / VXP / M • Deep Throat #4 / 1990 / AR / M • A Dirty Western #2: Smoking Guns / 1994 / CV / M • Dr F #2: Bad Medicine / 1990 / WV / M • Dream Lover / 1991 / WV / M • Dreams / 1987 / AR / M • Easy Lovers / 1987 / SE / M • Feature Speciale: The Ultimate Squirt / 1996 / ANE / M • Flesh In Ecstasy #01: Blondie / 1987 / GO / C • Flesh In Ecstasy #02: Samantha Strong / 1987 / GO / C • For Your Lips Only / 1989 / FAZ / M • Full Blown / 1992 / GO / M • G Spot Girls / 1988 / V99 / M • Girl Country / 1990 / CC / F • The Girls Of Porn / 1989 / FRV / F • Girls Of The Double D #02 / 1987 / CDI / M • Girls Will Be Girls / 1988 / LV / F • The Godmother #1 / 1987 / VC / M • The Godmother #2 / 1988 / VC / M • Good Golly, Miss Molly / 1987 / CDI / M • Good Morning Taija Rae / 1988 / VCX / M • Growing Up / 1990 / GO / M • Hard Core Beginners #11 / 1995 / LEI / M • HH-

HHot! TV #1 / 1988 / CDI / M • HHHHot! TV #2 / 1988 / CDI / M • Hidden Pleasures / 1990 / VEX / M • Hollywood Hustle #1 / 1990 / V99 / M • Hot & Heavy / 1989 / PL / M • Hot 'n' Nasty / 1989 / XCE / M • Hot Ones / 1988 / HO / C • Hot Summer Nites / 1988 / VEX / M • Hot To Swap / 1988 / VEX / M • Hump Up The Volume / 1991 / AR / M • I Married A Bimbo / 1990 / BAD / C • Imagination X-Posed / 1989 / 4P / M • J.E.G.: Just The Way You Like It #28 / 1995 / JEG / M • J.E.G.: Kum Shot Kumpendium #17 / 1995 / JEG / C • J.E.G.: Pregnant Expose #2 (#32) / 1996 / JEG / F • Kinky / 1987 / SE / M • Kinky Lesbians #02 / 1993 / BIZ / B • Knocked-Up Nymphos #2 / 1996 / GLI / M • Latex Foot Torture / 1993 / SBP / B • Layover / 1985 / HO / M • The Legend Of Reggie D. / 1989 / EA / M • Lesbian Lingerie Fantasy #1 / 1988 / ESP / F • Let Me Tell Ya 'Bout Black Chicks / 1985 / VC / M • Let's Talk Dirty / 1987 / SE / M • The Lethal Squirt / 1990 / AR / M • Lip Service / 1988 / LV / C • Littledove's Cup / 1988 / FOV / M • Living In Sin / 1990 / VEX / M • Loose Ends #4 / 1988 / 4P / M • The Lover Girls / 1985 / VEX / M • Lust, Ties & Videotape / 1993 / BON / B • Maximum Head / 1987 / SE / M • Mechanics Bi Day, Lube Job Bi Night / 1995 / SP0 / G • Midnight Angels #03 / 1993 / MID / F • The Million Dollar Screw / 1987 / VT / M • Misadventures Of The Bang Gang / 1987 / AR / M • Moonstroked / 1988 / 3HV / M • My Wife Is A Call Girl / 1989 / FAZ / M • Naked Lust / 1985 / SE / M • Nasty Jack's Homemade Vid. #25 / 1991 / CDI / F • Naughty Ninja Girls / 1987 / LA / M • Nina's Toys And Boys / 1991 / LV / C • Ninja Cheerleaders / 1990 / GO / M • No Man's Land #01 / 1988 / VT / C • One Of These Nights / 1991 / V99 / M • Only In Your Dreams / 1988 / VEX / M • Oral Majority #06 / 1988 / WV / C • Oral Majority #08 / 1990 / WV / C • Parliament: Hot Foxes #1 / 1988 / PM / F • Pay The Lady / 1987 / VXP / M • Perfect Girl / 1991 / VEX / M • Perverted Stories #01 / 1995 / JMP / M • Perverted Stories #05 / 1995 / JMP / M • Perverted Stories #08 / 1996 / JMP / M • Pleasure Is My Business / 1989 / EX / M • Porn Star's Day Off / 1990 / FAZ / M • Port Holes / 1988 / AVC / M • The Power Dykes / 1993 / BIZ / B • Prime Time Slime #02 / 1994 / GLI / M • Prince Of Beverly Hills #1 / 1987 / VEX / M • Pure Energy / 1990 / VEX / M • Pussy Hunt #12 / 1995 / LEI / M • Pussyman #08: The Squirt Queens / 1994 / SNA / M • Rainwoman #01 / 1989 / CC / M • Rainwoman #03 / 1990 / CC / M • Rainwoman #04 / 1990 / CC / M • Rainwoman #05 / 1992 / CC / M • Rainwoman #07: In The Rainforest / 1993 / CC / M • Rainwoman #09: Wetlands / 1995 / CC / M • Raw #2 / 1994 / AFV / M • Ready To Drop #02 / 1992 / FC / M • Restless Passion / 1987 / HO / M • The Return Of The A Team / 1988 / WV / M • Salsa Break / 1989 / EA / M • Satisfaction Jackson / 1988 / CA / M • School For Wayward Wives / 1993 / BIZ / B • Score 4 Me / 1991 / XPI / M • Secrets / 1990 / CA / M • Sensual Spirits / 1995 / LE / M • Sex Asylum #3 / 1988 / VI / M • Sex Slaves / 1986 / VEX / M • Sex Sounds / 1989 / PL / M • Sexy And 18 / 1987 / SE / M • She's No Angel #1 / 1990 / V99 / M •

Simply Irresistible / 1988 / CC / M • Single Girl Masturbation #1 / 1988 / ESP / F • Sleazy Rider / 1990 / FOV / M • Slumber Party Reunion / 1987 / AR / M • Spanish Fly / 1987 / CA / M • Splatman / 1992 / FR / M • The Squirt / 1988 / AR / M • Squirt 'em Cowgirl / 1990 / ERU / M • The Squirt Bunny / 1989 / ERU / M • Squirt On The Hunt / 1989 / ERU / M • Squirt Squad / 1995 / AMP / M • The Squirt's Last Drop / 1989 / ERU / C • Student Fetish Videos: Best of Enema #02 / 1992 / PRE / C • Student Fetish Videos: Best Of Spanking #02 / 1993 / PRE / C • Student Fetish Videos: The Enema #09 / 1992 / PRE / B • Student Fetish Videos: Spanking #08 / 1992 / PRE / B • Student Fetish Videos: Tickling #06 / 1992 / SFV / B • Stuff Your Face #2 / 1995 / JMP / M • Suite Sensations / 1988 / SEX / M • Sweet Chastity / 1990 / EVN / M • Sweet Sensations / 1989 / SEX / M • Telemates / 1988 / STA / M • Telemates / 1991 / V99 / M • Three Men And A Barbi / 1989 / FAN / M • Tickets To Paradise / 1992 / XPI / M • Tight Spot / 1996 / WV / M • Tools Of The Trade / 1990 / WV / M • Transverse Tail / 1987 / CDI / M • Trinity, Just For You / 1989 / BON / F • The Two Janes / 1990 / WV / M • Two Women & A Man / 1988 / VEX / M • Two Women & A Man / 1991 / VEX / C • Under The Law / 1989 / AFV / M • Unzipped / 1991 / WV / M • The Violation Of Alexandria Dane / 1995 / JMP / F • The Violation Of Kia / 1995 / JMP / F • The Violation Of Missy / 1996 / JMP / F • Weekend Blues / 1990 / IN / M • Where The Boys Aren't #1 / 1989 / VI / F • White Satin Nights / 1991 / V99 / M • White Trash, Black Splash / 1988 / WET / M • Wild Orgies #19 / 1995 / AFI / M • Young And Innocent / 1987 / HO / M • [Mrs. Robbins / 1988 / ... / M • [Queen Of Double Penetration / 1990 / ... / M • [Rhine Waltz / 1988 / ... / M • [Who Dun Who / 1988 / ... / M

FAMKA

LA Nasty / 1995 / SP / M

FANESSA

The Older Women's Sperm Bank #5 / 1996 / SUF / M

FANNIE BELLE FLEMING see Blaze Starr

FANNY

Through The Looking Glass / 1976 / ALP / M • The Voyeur #7: Live In Europe #1 / 1996 / JLP / M

FANNY FATALE see Star Index I

FANNY WOLFE see Veri Knotty

FANTASIA

Big Knockers #18 / 1995 / TV / M • The Bust Blondes In The USA / 1995 / NAP / F • Leg...Ends #15 / 1995 / PRE / F • The Magnificence Of Minka / 1996 / NAP / S

FANTASIA (CAROL TIT) see Carol Titian

FANTASIA (TAE) see Brooke Ashley

FANTASIA JONES

Girls Of The Third Reich / 1985 / FC / M

FANTASIA LEE see Brooke Ashley

FANTASY

A&B AB#008: Sexaholics #1 / 1990 / A&B / M • A&B AB#015: / 1990 / A&B / M • A&B AB#016: Bachelor Party / 1990 / A&B / M • A&B AB#019: / 1990 / A&B / M • A&B AB#025: Day Dreamer / 1990 / A&B / M • AHV #20: Give It To Me, Baby / 1992 / EVN / M • Amateur Hours #49 / 1992 / AFI / M • Amateur Hours #50 / 1992 / AFI / M •

Exotic Tastes / 1995 / VEX / C • Flogged For His Sins / 1993 / STM / B • Hispanic Orgies #07 / 1994 / GO / M • Hollywood Swingers #10 / 1993 / LBO / M • Mr. Peepers Amateur Home Videos #67: Backdoor Fantasy / 1993 / LBO / M • Mr. Peepers Nastiest #2 / 1995 / LBO / C • Odyssey Triple Play #58: Anal Insanity / 1994 / OD / M • Ron Hightower's White Chicks #07 / 1993 / LBO / M • Snatch Masters #05 / 1995 / LEI / M • Student Fetish Videos: Tickling #05 / 1992 / SFV / B

FARAH
Philmore Butts Spring Break / 1996 / SUF / M

FARAH FELLATIO
Blue Vanities #561 / 1994 / FFL / M

FARAH LEE *see Star Index I*

FARAH WALTON *see Star Index I*

FARRAH
Babe Watch #5 / 1996 / VC / M • Babe Watch Beach / 1996 / SC / M • Desert Island Buttwatch / 1996 / SUF / M • First Whores Club / 1996 / ERA / M • The Heart Breaker / 1996 / MID / M • Maui Waui / 1996 / PE / M • Mickey Ray's Sex Search #06 / 1996 / WIV / M • Philmore Butts Adventures In Paradise / 1996 / SUF / M • Philmore Butts All American Butt Search / 1996 / SUF / M • Philmore Butts Goes Hollyweird / 1996 / SUF / M • Philmore Butts Lake Poontang / 1996 / SUF / M • Pussyman Auditions #23 / 1996 / SNA / M • Roller Babes / 1996 / ERA / M • She's No Angel / 1996 / ERA / S • Skin Dive / 1996 / SC / M • Tampa Spice / 1996 / SUF / M • Thunder And Lightning / 1996 / MID / M • Tight Spot / 1996 / WV / M • Wet Faces #1 / 1997 / SC / C

FARRAH (CHARLI) *see Charli*

FARRAH TAP *see Star Index I*

FARRAN HYTES *see Taylor Wayne*

FARRELL TIMLAKE *see Tim Lake*

FARRON
Ona Zee's Date With Dallas / 1992 / ONA / M

FARRON HEIGHTS *see Eva Allen*

FARRON HYTES *see Taylor Wayne*

FARRYN TIMLAITE *see Eva Allen*

FASCHA
Corsetry 101 / 1996 / ESF / B

FAST EDDIE
Kinky Business #1 / 1984 / DR / M • Perfect Fit / 1985 / DR / M

FAST EDDIE JACKSON *see Star Index I*

FAST STEPPIN FREDDIE *see Star Index I*

FATINA
Swedish Erotica #09 / 1980 / CA / M

FAUNA
Dance To The Whip / 1996 / LBO / B • Master's Touch #6: Dom's In Distress / 1995 / FAP / B • White Slavers / 1996 / LBO / B

FAUSTIE
Working It Out / 1983 / CA / M

FAWN DELL
Centerfold Celebrities #5 / 1983 / VC / M • The Girls Of Klit House / 1984 / LIP / F • Gum Me Bare #1 / 1994 / GLI / M • More Dirty Debutantes #03 / 1990 / 4P / M • Oriental Oddballs #1 / 1994 / FH / M

FAWN DESMOND
Kym Wilde's On The Edge #30 / 1995 / RB / B

FAWN FARR

[Kink, Hollywood Style / 197? / ... / M

FAWN LITTLE DEAR
More Dirty Debutantes #43 / 1995 / 4P / M

FAWN MILLER
Breast Worx #09 / 1991 / LBO / M • Breast Worx #10 / 1991 / LBO / M • Breast Worx #18 / 1992 / LBO / M • Buttman's Big Tit Adventure #1 / 1992 / EA / M • Chameleons: Not The Sequel / 1991 / VC / M • Dirty Bob's #02: Xciting XperienCES / 1992 / FLP / S • Hardcore Plumpers / 1991 / BTO / M • Hollywood Teasers #01 / 1992 / LBO / F • Homegrown Video #426: Best Big Breasted Women / 1994 / HOV / C • More Dirty Debutantes #11 / 1991 / 4P / M • Southern: Previews #2 / 1992 / SSH / C

FAWN PARIS
Back Road To Paradise / 1984 / CDI / M • Backdoor Romance / 1984 / VIV / M • Bare Elegance / 1984 / MAP / M • Camp Beaverlake #1 / 1984 / AR / M • Casino Of Lust / 1984 / AT / M • Cherry Busters / 1984 / VIV / M • Diamond Collection #79 / 1986 / CDI / M • Hot Touch / 1984 / VCX / M • Wet Sex / 1984 / CA / M • The Woman Who Loved Men / 1984 / SE / M

FAWN ROBERTS *see Cheri Hill*

FAWNA
The Ambassador File / 1995 / HOM / B • Bondage In The Bastille / 1994 / HOM / B • Bound Destiny / 1994 / LON / B • Contract / 1995 / LON / B • Dungeon Of The Borgias / 1993 / HOM / B • Female Fury / 199? / NAP / B • Frankentickle / 1993 / CS / B • The Golden Dagger / 1993 / LON / B • Hellfire Society / 19?? / HOM / B • Hot Bodies In Bondage / 1993 / LBO / B • Jane Bondage Is Captured / 1993 / LON / B • Lingerie Lust: The Catfight / 1996 / NAP / B • Magnificent Seven / 1991 / NAP / F • Punishment Of Ashley Renee / 1993 / BON / B • Slave Of Fashion / 1993 / LON / B • The Tale Of The Rope / 1993 / CS / B • Tied And Feathered / 1993 / VTF / B • Till She Screams / 1992 / HOM / B

FAWNTANA
The Black Butt Sisters Do Houston / 1996 / MID / M • Black Hollywood Amateurs #25 / 1996 / MID / M • Hollywood Starlets Adventure #04 / 1995 / AVS / M • Love Chunks / 1996 / TTV / M • Ron Hightower's White Chicks #13 / 1994 / LBO / M • Ron Hightower's White Chicks #16 / 1994 / LBO / M • Titties 'n Cream #1 / 1994 / FC / M

FAY
Blue Vanities #546 / 1994 / FFL / M

FAY BURD *(Phaery Burd, Tres Dover, Isolde, Isolde Jensen, Phae Bird, Jacklin Morina)*
Shoulder length blonde hair, lithe body, small to medium tits, flat belly, passable face. Jacklin Morina is from *Stormy*.
1001 Erotic Nights #1 / 1982 / VC / M • All About Annette / 1982 / SE / C • Blonde Fire / 1979 / EVI / M • Blondes Have More Fun / 1980 / SE / M • Candy Goes To Hollywood / 1979 / VCX / M • Dixie Ray Hollywood Star / 1983 / CA / M • Erotic Fantasies #1 / 1983 / CV / C • Exhausted / 1981 / CA / C • Expensive Taste / 1978 / VCX / M • Go For It / 1984 / VC / M • The Health Spa / 1978 / SE / M • Hot Cookies / 1977 / WWV / M • Kamikaze Hearts / 1986 / FAC / S • Ladies Nights / 1980 / VC / M •

Nasty Lady / 1984 / CV / M • Only The Best #1 / 1986 / CV / C • Please, Mr Postman / 1981 / VC / M • Purely Physical / 1982 / SE / M • Same Time Every Year / 1981 / VHL / M • The Seven Seductions Of Madame Lau / 1981 / EVI / M • Stormy / 1980 / CV / M • Swedish Erotica #09 / 1980 / CA / M

FAYE LITTLE
Wet Wilderness / 1975 / VCX / B

FAYE YOUNG *see Star Index I*

FAYRIN HEITZ *see Taylor Wayne*

FEFE *see Fi Fi Bardot*

FEFE BARDOT *see Fi Fi Bardot*

FELASHIA
Scratch: Return To Witch Fountain / 1993 / SCR / M • Scratch: Synergy #1: The Catch / 1992 / SCR / M • Scratch: Synergy #2: The Match / 1992 / SCR / M • Scratch: Synergy #3: The Make / 1992 / SCR / M

FELECIA *(Felicia, Felecia Danay)*
Small breasted, very pretty, tight body with a tight waist, perky nipples, long light brown wavy hair, 21 years old in 1993, former high school cheerleader. Supposedly discovered by Bruce Seven. Will only do g/g's but does give her boyfriend a BJ in **Tight Shots #1**. Felecia Danay is from the no-sex video **Nude Nurses**. Comes from Tacoma, WA.
13th Annual Adult Video News Awards / 1996 / VC / S • A Is For Asia / 1996 / 4P / M • Adam & Eve's House Party #1 / 1995 / VC / M • The Adventures Of Studman #3 / 1994 / AFV / M • The Anal Adventures Of Bruce Seven / 1996 / BS / C • The Anal Adventures Of Suzy Super Slut #3 / 1994 / IPI / M • Attitude Adjustment / 1993 / BS / B • Babe Watch #5 / 1996 / VC / M • Babenet / 1995 / VC / M • Babes Illustrated #1 / 1994 / IN / F • Babes Illustrated #2 / 1994 / IN / F • Babes Illustrated #3 / 1995 / IN / F • Babes Illustrated #4 / 1995 / IN / F • Babes Illustrated #5 / 1996 / IN / F • Bad Company / 1994 / VI / M • Bangkok Nights / 1994 / VI / M • Bare Ass Beach / 1994 / TP / M • Bare Essentials / 1995 / NIV / F • Bedlam / 1995 / WAV / M • The Best Of Buttslammers / 1995 / BS / C • Beyond Reality #1 / 1995 / EXQ / M • Black And White Revisited / 1995 / VT / F • Blaze / 1996 / WAV / M • Bordello / 1995 / VI / M • Borderline (Vivid) / 1995 / VI / M • Bruce Seven: A Compendium Of His Most Graphic Scenes Vol 5 / 1994 / BS / C • Bruce Seven: A Compendium Of His Most Graphic Scenes Vol 6 / 1994 / BS / C • Buffy Malibu's Nasty Girls #10 / 1996 / ANA / F • Buttslammers #02: The Awakening Of Felicia / 1993 / BS / F • Buttslammers #03: The Ultimate Dream / 1993 / BS / F • Buttslammers #04: Down And Dirty / 1993 / BS / F • Buttslammers #12: Anal Madness / 1996 / BS / F • Buttslammers #13: The Madness Continues / 1996 / BS / F • Carnal Garden / 1996 / KLP / M • Cat Lickers #2 / 1994 / ME / F • Cat Lickers #4 / 1995 / ME / F • Caught Looking / 1995 / CC / M • Checkmate / 1995 / WAV / M • Cheerleader Strippers / 1996 / PE / M • Cloud 9 / 1995 / VI / M • Club Decca / 1996 / BAC / F • Creme De Femme / 1994 / 4P / F • Crime Doesn't Pay / 1993 / BS / B • Cumback Pussy #1 / 1996 / EL / M • Cumback Pussy #2: Crawling Back For More / 1996 / EL / M • Cumback Pussy #4: Get Some!!! / 1996 / EL / M • Dangerous

Assignment / 1993 / BS / B • Dear Diary / 1995 / WP / M • Deep Behind The Scenes With Seymore Butts #1 / 1995 / ULI / M • Deep Inside Felecia / 1996 / VC / C • Deep Inside Misty Rain / 1995 / VC / C • The Devil In Miss Jones #5: The Inferno / 1994 / VC / M • Dirty Dirty Debutantes #8 / 1996 / 4P / M • Dirty Laundry #1 / 1994 / CV / M • Diva #2: Deep In Glamour / 1996 / VC / F • Do Me Nurses / 1995 / LE / M • DPTV: Double Penetration Television / 1996 / SUF / M • Eleventh Annual AVN Awards / 1994 / VC / M • Erotic Obsession / 1994 / IN / M • Erotic Visions / 1995 / ULI / M • Eternal Lust / 1996 / VC / M • Every Woman Has A Fantasy #3 / 1995 / VC / M • Extreme Sex #3: Wired / 1994 / VI / M • Fantasies Of Alicia / 1995 / VT / M • Fantasies Of Marylin / 1995 / VT / M • Fantasies Of Persia / 1995 / VT / M • Fantasy Chamber / 1994 / ULI / M • Fantasy Inc. / 1995 / CV / M • Far East Fantasy / 1995 / SUF / M • Fashion Plate / 1995 / WAV / M • Felecia's Folly / 1993 / BS / B • First Time Ever #1 / 1995 / PE / F • Frankenstein / 1994 / SC / M • Fresh Meat (John Leslie) #1 / 1994 / EA / M • Ghost Town / 1995 / WAV / M • The Girl With The Heart-Shaped Tattoo / 1995 / WAV / M • A Girl's Affair #07 / 1995 / FD / F • Glory Days / 1996 / IN / M • Golden Rod / 1996 / SPI / M • Hard Feelings / 1995 / VI / M • Hawaii / 1995 / VI / M • Hawaiian Heat #1 / 1995 / CC / M • Hawaiian Heat #2 / 1995 / CC / M • Heavenscent / 1993 / ZA / M • Here Comes Elska / 1997 / XPR / M • Hollywood Spa / 1996 / WP / M • Hot Body Competition: Bikinis & Bikes Contest / 1996 / CG / F • Hotel California / 1995 / MID / M • Hotel Sodom #07 / 1995 / SNA / M • Hotel Sodom #09 / 1996 / SNA / M • Housewife Lust #1 / 1995 / TV / F • Housewife Lust #2 / 1995 / TV / F • I Love Lesbians / 1995 / ERW / F • Illicit Affairs / 1996 / XC / M • In Cold Sweat / 1996 / VI / M • Indecent / 1993 / XCI / M • The Initiation / 1995 / FD / M • Jenna Ink / 1996 / WP / M • Jenna's Built For Speed / 1997 / WP / F • Killer Tits / 1995 / LE / M • Latex #2 / 1995 / VC / M • Leg Sex In The Sun / 1996 / H&S / S • Lethal Affairs / 1996 / VI / M • Lovin' Spoonfuls #4 / 1995 / 4P / C • Lustful Obsessions / 1996 / NOT / M • The Meatman / 1995 / OUP / M • Micky Ray's Hot Shots #01 / 1996 / DIG / M • Mind Set / 1996 / VI / M • Misty Rain's Anal Orgy / 1994 / FRM / M • More Black Dirty Debutantes #3 / 1994 / 4P / M • More Dirty Debutantes #62 / 1997 / SBV / M • More Dirty Debutantes #65 / 1997 / SBV / M • Naked & Nasty / 1995 / WP / M • Naked Dolls / 1995 / NIV / F • New Ends #08 / 1994 / 4P / M • Night Play / 1995 / WAV / M • Night Tales / 1996 / VC / M • Night Vision / 1996 / WP / M • Nightclub / 1996 / SC / M • Nightshift Nurses #2 / 1996 / VC / M • No Fear / 1996 / IN / F • No Man's Land #10 / 1994 / VT / F • Nude Nurses / 1993 / EDE / S • Ona Zee's Doll House #1 / 1995 / ONA / F • Ona Zee's Doll House #3 / 1995 / ONA / F • Once In A Lifetime / 1996 / VC / C • The Orgy #1 / 1993 / EMC / M • The Orgy #2 / 1993 / EMC / M • The Other Side / 1995 / ERA / M • The Pain Connection / 1994 / BS / B • The Palace Of Pleasure / 1995 / ULI / M • The Passion / 1995 / IP / M •

Payne-Full Revenge / 1995 / BS / B • Peepshow / 1994 / OD / M • Photo Play / 1995 / VI / M • Pick Up Lines #02 / 1995 / 4P / M • Playboy: The Girls Of Radio / 1995 / UNI / F • Porn In The Pen / 1993 / LE / F • Private Stories #01 / 1995 / OD / M • Puritan Video Magazine #06 / 1996 / LE / M • Pussyman #12: Sticky Fingers / 1995 / SNA / M • Radical Affairs Video Magazine #08 / 1994 / ME / M • Renegades #1 / 1994 / SC / M • The Right Connection / 1995 / VC / M • Rolling Thunder / 1995 / VI / M • Rumpman Goes To Cannes / 1996 / HW / M • The Savage / 1994 / SC / M • Secret Lives / 1994 / SC / F • Sensations #2 / 1996 / SC / M • Sex #3: After Seven (Vivid) / 1994 / VI / M • Simply Blue / 1995 / WAV / M • Sinister Sister / 1997 / WP / M • Sistal #5 / 1996 / VT / F • Sleaze Please!—December Edition / 1994 / FH / M • Sluthunt #3 / 1996 / BIP / F • Smells Like...Sex / 1995 / VC / M • Sorority Stewardesses #1 / 1995 / PE / M • Sorority Stewardesses #2 / 1995 / PE / M • Splattered / 1996 / MET / M • Star Attraction / 1995 / VT / M • Starting Over / 1995 / WAV / M • Street Workers / 1995 / ME / M • Strip Search / 1995 / CV / M • Strong Sensations / 1996 / PL / M • Style #3 / 1996 / VT / M • The Submission Of Felecia / 1993 / BS / B • Sunset's Anal & D.P. Gangbang / 1996 / PL / M • Takin' It To The Limit #6 / 1995 / BS / M • Takin' It To The Limit #8: Hooked On Crack / 1996 / BS / M • Telephone Expose / 1995 / VC / M • This Year's Model / 1996 / WAV / M • Three Hearts / 1995 / CC / M • Tight Shots #1 / 1994 / VI / M • A Touch Of Leather / 1994 / BS / B • A Twist Of Payne / 1993 / BS / B • Up And Cummers #01 / 1993 / 4P / M • Up And Cummers #02 / 1993 / 4P / M • Up And Cummers #16 / 1994 / 4P / M • Up And Cummers #17 / 1994 / 4P / M • Up And Cummers #26 / 1996 / 4P / M • Up And Cummers #34 / 1996 / 4P / M • Up And Cummers #39 / 1996 / RWP / M • Up And Cummers: The Movie / 1994 / 4P / M • Valentina: Princess Of The Forest / 1996 / SC / M • Vibrating Vixens #1 / 1996 / TV / F • The Violation Of Felecia / 1995 / JMP / F • The Violation Of Missy / 1996 / JMP / F • Virgin Hotline / 1996 / LVP / F • Visions #2 / 1995 / ERA / M • Visions Of Seduction / 1994 / SC / M • The Wacky World Of Ed Powers / 1996 / 4P / C • What You Are In The Dark / 1995 / KLP / M • Wicked Women / 1993 / ME / M • Wide Open Spaces / 1995 / VC / F • Wildcats / 1995 / WP / M • Wilde Palms / 1994 / XCI / M • World Famous Dirty Debutantes / 1995 / 4P / S • The XXX Files: Lust In Space / 1995 / IMV / M • Young & Natural #05 / 1995 / PRE / F • Young & Natural #08 / 1995 / PRE / F

FELECIA (OTHER)
California Sluts / 1995 / ZA / M
FELECIA DANAY see Felecia
FELECIEN ROLAND
Aerienne's Surprise / 1995 / WIV / M
FELENE see Nina DePonca
FELICIA see Felecia
FELICIA (EIGHTIES)
Lucky In Love #2 / 1988 / SEV / M • Strip Search / 1987 / SEV / M • Swedish Erotica #49 / 1983 / CA / M
FELICIA (K. KING) see Krystina King

FELICIA BERET see Star Index I
FELICIA BLACK see Star Index I
FELICIA CARTER see Star Index I
FELICIA GREEN
The Joy Of Fooling Around / 1978 / CV / M
FELICIA LOVING
The Pleasure Shoppe / 1980 / CA / M
FELICIA SANDA
Exhausted / 1981 / CA / C • Tell Them Johnny Wadd Is Here / 1975 / QX / M
FELICIEN ROLAND
Wedding Rituals / 1995 / DVP / M
FELICITY BROWNING
The Bite / 1975 / SVE / M
FELINA
Bootylicious: White Trash / 1995 / JMP / M • Transformation / 1996 / XCI / M
FELINA FABRE see Selina Fabre
FELINE see Nina DePonca
FELIPE *(Vinnie Demarco, Vinny La Marca)* Brazilian male brought to the US by John Stagliano.
America's Raunchiest Home Videos #02: Cooking with Hot Sauce / 1991 / ZA / M • America's Raunchiest Home Videos #21: Pumping Pussy / 1992 / ZA / M • The Barlow Affairs / 1991 / XCI / M • Bend Over Babes #2 / 1991 / EA / M • Bend Over Brazilian Babes #1 / 1993 / EA / M • Bend Over Brazilian Babes #2 / 1993 / EA / M • Best Of Buttman #2 / 1993 / EA / C • Butt Freak #1 / 1992 / EA / M • Buttman Goes To Rio #2 / 1991 / EA / M • Buttman Goes To Rio #3 / 1992 / EA / M • Buttman Goes To Rio #4 / 1993 / EA / M • Buttman's Big Tit Adventure #1 / 1992 / EA / M • Buttman's Double Adventure / 1993 / EA / M • Buttman's Revenge / 1992 / EA / M • Dirty Tricks / 1993 / CC / M • Gangbang Girl #01 / 1992 / ANA / M • Gangbang Girl #02 / 1992 / ANA / M • Gangbang Girl #03 / 1992 / ANA / M • Gangbang Girl #04 / 1992 / ANA / M • Impulse #01: Memories Of An Italian Slut / 1995 / MBP / M • Magma: Insatiable Lust / 1995 / MET / M • The Maltese Bimbo / 1993 / FD / M • Safecracker / 1991 / CC / M • Silver Sensations / 1992 / VT / M • With Love / 1995 / FD / M
FELIX see Alex Katz
FELIX FRANCHY
Massage Parlor / 1972 / SOW / S • [Justine Och Juliette / 1975 / ... / S • [Krankenschwestern-Report / 1972 / ... / M
FELIX HELIX see Star Index I
FELIX KRULL
The Erotic World Of Angel Cash / 1983 / VXP / M • A Scent Of Heather / 1981 / VXP / M
FELIX MIGUEL ARROYO see Chuck Vincent
FELIX SIMMONS see Star Index I
FELIX SLEED
On White Satin / 1980 / VCX / M
FELIX WURTMAN see Star Index I
FELIZIA
Eurotica #02 / 1995 / XC / M
FELLONIA
Anal Camera #06 / 1995 / EVN / M
FELONIOUS MONK
Latex Goddess / 1995 / IBN / B
FERENC
Love Slave / 1995 / WIV / M
FERENC CSEKLYE
Private Film #22 / 1995 / OD / M • True Stories #2 / 1993 / SC / M
FERENC DOMOTOR

True Stories #1 / 1993 / SC / M • True Stories #2 / 1993 / SC / M

FERENC ILSIJK
Private Film #10 / 1994 / OD / M

FERENC JUHASZ
Private Film #22 / 1995 / OD / M • Private Film #24 / 1995 / OD / M • Private Film #25 / 1995 / OD / M • Private Stories #01 / 1995 / OD / M • Private Stories #02 / 1995 / OD / M • Private Video Magazine #25 / 1995 / OD / M • Private Video Magazine #26 / 1995 / OD / M • True Stories #1 / 1993 / SC / M • True Stories #2 / 1993 / SC / M

FERNANDA
Asses Galore #4: Extreme Noise Terror / 1996 / DFI / M • Buttman Goes To Rio #3 / 1992 / EA / M

FERNANDA BRAZIL
Asses Galore #5: T.T. Vs The World / 1996 / DFI / M

FERNANDO
Cindy Puts Out / 1996 / OLL / M

FERNANDO FORTES
Carnal Highways / 1980 / HIF / M • Come Under My Spell / cr78 / HIF / M • I Am Always Ready / 1978 / HIF / M • Lusty Princess / 1978 / HIF / M

FERNECIA C.
Private Gold #09: Private Dancer / 1996 / OD / M

FERRELL TIMLAKE *see* **Tim Lake**

FERRIS WEAL
Up 'n' Coming / 1983 / CA / M

FETISH *see* **Heather Lere**

FI FI BARDOT *(Fefe, Fifi Le Feux, Fifi (Bardot), Fifi LaRue, Suzette LeFevre, Fefe Bardot)*
Suzette LeFevre is from **I Ream A Genie**. Started with small breasts but had them enhanced to grotesque proportions.
Best Of Buttman / 1991 / EA / C • Bi And Beyond #3 / 1989 / INH / G • Bimbo Bowlers From Buffalo / 1989 / ZA / M • Blame It On The Heat / 1989 / VC / M • Deep In Deanna Jones / 1989 / EVN / M • Deep Inside Keisha / 1994 / VC / C • Girlworld #3 / 1989 / LIP / F • Girlworld #4 / 1989 / LIP / F • Have I Got A Girl For You / 1989 / VEX / M • Hot Meat / 1990 / V99 / M • I Ream A Jeannie / 1990 / GLE / M • I Want Your Sex / 1990 / FAZ / M • Kinky Business #2 / 1989 / DR / M • Midnight Baller / 1989 / PL / M • Oh! You Beautiful Doll / 1990 / ZA / M • Paris Burning / 1989 / CC / M • The Penthouse / 1989 / PP / M • Pretty Peaches #3 / 1989 / VC / M • Rainwoman #01 / 1989 / CC / M • Red Hot Fire Girls / 1989 / VD / M • Rock 'n' Roll Heaven / 1989 / EA / M • Slumber Party / 1990 / LV / M • Space Virgins / 1990 / VEX / M • Tail For Sale / 1988 / VD / M • Take It To The Limit / 1990 / V99 / M • Ticket To Ride / 1990 / LV / M • Trans Europe Express / 1989 / VC / G • Wet Pink / 1989 / PL / F

FIAMMETTA
Girlfriends / 1983 / MIT / M • Hustler Video Magazine #1 / 1983 / SE / M

FIANA
Sex Between The Scenes / 1994 / LAP / M

FIDEL FOOTMAN *see* **Star Index I**

FIELD MARSH BRADLEY *(F.M. Bradley)*
Tall (6'3") male who looks like he just got out of jail.
The Adventures Of Dick Black, Black Dick / 1987 / DR / M • Behind The Black Door / 1987 / VEX / M • The Best Little Whorehouse In Beverly Hills / 1986 / CDI / M • The Best Of Black White & Pink Inside / 1996 / CV / C • The Black Anal-ist #1 / 1988 / VEX / M • Black Baby Dolls / 1985 / TAG / M • Black Beauties / 1987 / SE / C • Black Beauty (Coast To Coast) / 1994 / CC / M • Black Bimbos In Heat / 1989 / MIR / C • Black Booty / 1993 / ZA / M • Black Bunbusters / 1985 / VC / M • Black Chicks In Heat / 1988 / VC / M • The Black Chill / 1986 / WET / M • Black Dynasty / 1985 / VD / M • Black Gangbangers #02 / 1995 / HW / M • Black Heat / 1986 / VC / M • Black Jailbait / 1984 / PL / M • Black Lava / 1986 / WET / M • Black On White / 1987 / PL / C • Black Orgies #05 / 1993 / AFI / M • Black Orgies #07 / 1993 / AFI / M • Black Orgies #10 / 1993 / AFI / M • Black Orgies #22 / 1994 / GO / M • Black Rage / 1988 / ZA / M • Black Sensations / 1987 / VEX / M • Black Taboo #2 / 1986 / SE / M • Black To Africa / 1987 / PL / C • Black To Basics / 1992 / ZA / M • Black Velvet #2 / 1993 / CC / M • Blacks & Blondes #12 / 1986 / WV / M • Blacks & Blondes #13 / 1986 / WV / M • Blacks & Blondes #32 / 1986 / WV / M • Boobs, Butts And Bloopers #1 / 1990 / HO / M • Breakin' All The Rules / 1987 / SE / M • Broadcast Nudes / 1988 / EVN / M • The Butt Boss / 1993 / VD / M • The Buttnicks #4: The Black Buttnicks / 1993 / CC / M • Caddy Shack-Up / 1986 / VD / M • Caught From Behind #05: Blondes & Blacks / 1986 / HO / M • Cheeks #1 / 1988 / CC / M • Chocolate Cherries #1 / 1984 / LA / M • Chocolate Chips / 1987 / VD / M • Chocolate Delights #1 / 1985 / TAG / C • Chocolate Dreams (Venus 99) / 1987 / V99 / M • Club Exotica #1 / 1985 / WV / M • Club Exotica #2 / 1985 / WV / M • The Color Black / 1986 / WET / M • Dark Alleys #07 / 1992 / FC / M • Dark Alleys #08 / 1992 / FC / M • Dark Alleys #25 / 1994 / FC / M • Dark Brothers, Dark Sisters / 1986 / VCS / C • Dark Desires / 1989 / BMV / C • Dark Side Of The Moon / 1986 / VD / M • Deep Inside Traci / 1986 / CDI / C • Depraved Fantasies #1 / 1993 / FPI / M • Detroit Dames / 1988 / DR / C • Devil In Miss Jones #3: A New Beginning / 1986 / VC / M • Devil In Miss Jones #4: The Final Outrage / 1987 / VC / M • Diamond Collection #80 / 1986 / CDI / M • Dick & Jane Go To Hollywood #1 / 1993 / AVI / M • Dirty Pictures / 1985 / SUP / M • The Doctor's In / 1986 / CDI / M • Double Black Fantasy / 1987 / CC / C • Double Penetration #2 / 1986 / WV / C • Double Penetration #3 / 1986 / WV / C • Dr Blacklove #1 / 1987 / CC / M • Dr Penetration / 1986 / WET / M • Ebony Ecstasy / 1988 / HIO / C • Ebony Erotica #01: Black Narcissys / 1993 / GO / M • Ebony Erotica #02: Midnight Madness / 1993 / GO / M • Ebony Erotica #03: Black Adonis / 1993 / GO / M • Ebony Erotica #04: Ebony Gods / 1993 / GO / M • Ebony Erotica #07: Sepia Salute / 1993 / GO / M • Ebony Erotica #08: Indigo Moods / 1993 / GO / M • Ebony Erotica #09: Bronze Thrills / 1993 / GO / M • Ebony Erotica #14: Black & Tan / 1994 / GO / M • Ebony Erotica #15: Chocolate Kisses / 1994 / GO / M • Ebony Erotica #18: Soul Kiss / 1994 / GO / M • Ebony Erotica #21: Cordon Negro / 1994 / GO / M • Ebony Erotica #22: Fade To Black / 1994 / GO / M • Ebony Humpers #3 / 1987 / VEX / M • Ebony Orgies / 1987 / SE / C • Erotic Television Video / 1988 / VD / M • Even More Dangerous / 1990 / SO / M • Falcon Breast / 1987 / CDI / M • Fatal Passion / 1988 / CC / M • The Final Taboo / 1988 / CA / M • Flesh In Ecstasy #03: Purple Passion / 1987 / GO / C • Foxy Brown / 1984 / VC / M • From A Whisper To A Scream / 1993 / GO / M • Get Me While I'm Hot / 1988 / PV / M • The Girls Of The A Team #1 / 1985 / WV / M • Good Golly, Miss Molly / 1987 / CDI / M • Harlem Candy / 1987 / WET / M • Hedonism #01 / 1993 / FH / M • Hill Street Blacks #1 / 1985 / 4R / M • Hot Black Moon Rising Forever / 1988 / ZA / M • Humongous Squirting Knockers / 1992 / CA / C • The Hunger / 1993 / FOR / M • Hyapatia Lee's Arcade Series #02 / 1988 / ZA / C • Hyapatia Lee's Secret Dreams / 1986 / SE / M • I Am Curious Black / 1986 / WET / M • In A Crystal Fantasy / 1988 / VD / M • Interracial Sex / 1987 / M&M / M • Jam / 1993 / PL / M • Kink World: The Seduction Of Nena / 1993 / PL / M • The Kiss / 1986 / SC / M • Kiss My Asp / 1989 / EXH / M • Knights In White Satin / 1987 / SUV / C • Legends Of Porn #2 / 1989 / CV / C • Lessons In Lust / 1987 / LA / M • Lust / 1993 / FH / M • Lust Connection / 1988 / VT / M • Lust Of Blacula / 1987 / VEX / M • The Lust Potion Of Doctor F / 1985 / WV / M • M Series #25 / 1994 / LBO / M • Mad Love / 1988 / VC / M • Mo' White Trash / 1993 / MET / M • More Chocolate Candy / 1986 / VD / M • Moving In / 1986 / CV / M • My Boyfriend's Black / 1994 / FD / M • Naked Stranger / 1987 / CDI / M • Nasty Dreams / 1994 / PRK / M • The Night Before / 1987 / WV / M • Night Games / 1986 / WV / M • Nikki And The Pom-Pom Girls / 1987 / VEX / M • Old Throat And D.P. / 1993 / FC / M • Only The Best Of Anal / 1992 / MET / C • Oral Majority Black #1 / 1987 / WV / C • Oral Majority Black #2 / 1988 / WV / C • Orgies / 1987 / WV / C • Out Of Control / 1987 / SE / M • Outcall Outlaws / 1995 / CC / M • Parliament: Dark & Sweet #1 / 1991 / PM / C • The Pillowman / 1988 / VC / M • Pretty Peaches #2 / 1987 / VC / M • Psychoanal Therapy / 1994 / CA / M • Queen Of Spades / 1986 / VD / M • Reamin' Reunion / 1988 / CC / M • The Return Of Dr Blacklove / 1996 / CC / M • The Ribald Tales Of Canterbury / 1986 / CA / M • Ron Hightower's White Chicks #06 / 1993 / LBO / M • Ron Hightower's White Chicks #09 / 1994 / LBO / M • Salt & Pepper #1 / 1989 / AMB / C • Satisfaction Jackson / 1988 / CA / M • Sean Michaels On The Road #02: Da Hood / 1993 / VT / M • Seekers / 1994 / CA / M • Slummin' Hood Girlz / 1993 / CA / M • The Slut / 1988 / FAN / M • Smooth As Silk / 1987 / VIP / M • Snapshots: Confessions Of A Video Voyeur / 1988 / CC / M • Soul Games / 1988 / PV / C • Spanish Fly / 1987 / CA / M • Starbangers #02 / 1993 / BIG / M • Strange Love / 1987 / WV / M • Sweet Chocolate / 1987 / VD / M • Swing Rave / 1993 / EVN / M • Taija / 1986 / WV / C • Tailhouse Rock / 1985 / WV / M • A Taste Of Angel / 1989 / PIN / C • A Taste Of Black

/ 1987 / WET / M • A Taste Of White / 1987 / WET / M • Tell Me Something Dirty / 1991 / NWV / M • The Touchables / 1988 / CC / M • Ubangis On Uranus / 1987 / WV / M • Up & In / 1985 / AA / M • VCA Previews #4 / 1988 / VC / C • Voyeurism #1 / 1993 / FH / M • White Trash / 1986 / PV / M • White Trash, Black Splash / 1988 / WET / M • Wild Black Erotica #4 / cr89 / VD / C • Wild Oral Erotica / 1988 / VD / C • Wild Stuff / 1987 / WET / M • Yankee Seduction / 1984 / WV / M

FIFI
Black Cheerleader Search #04 / 1996 / ROB / M • Plan 69 From Outer Space / 1993 / CA / M

FIFI (BARDOT) see Fi Fi Bardot
FIFI ALDERCY
Eruption / 1977 / VCX / M

FIFI DUBOIS see Star Index I
FIFI L'AMOUR
Muff Diving French Riviera / 1986 / EVN / C

FIFI LARUE see Fi Fi Bardot
FIFI LASTRANGE
School For Sex / cr72 / SOW / M

FIFI LE FEUX see Fi Fi Bardot
FIFI SAUCISSON
A Clockwork Orgy / 1995 / PL / M

FIFI WATSON
Mona The Virgin Nymph / 1970 / ALP / M

FIM MILES
Euro-Snatch / 1996 / SNA / M

FIOLA
Bondage Bigtop / 1996 / CS / B

FIONA (KAHLIA) see Kahlia
FIONA VAN CLEEF
Kinky Villa / 1995 / PL / M

FIORELLA
A Merry Widow / 1996 / SPI / M

FIRE
Amateur Black: Hot Flesh / 1996 / SUF / M • Black Hollywood Amateurs #04 / 1995 / MID / M • Black Hollywood Amateurs #09 / 1995 / MID / M • Bootylicious: Bitches & Ho's / 1996 / JMP / M

FIREHAWK see Star Index I
FISH see Star Index I
FISHIE
Sweet Dreams / 1994 / ORE / C

FLAME
Redhead with small tits and a flood of freckles all over her upper back and on her face. Born 3/20/72.

1-800-934-BOOB / 1992 / VD / C • 40 The Hard Way / 1991 / OD / M • The Adventures Of Buttwoman #2: Behind Bars / 1992 / EL / F • Amateur Lesbians #05: Missy / 1991 / GO / F • Amateur Lesbians #20: Flame / 1992 / GO / F • Amateur Orgies #06 / 1992 / AFI / M • Anal Attack / 1991 / ZA / M • Anal Commander / 1990 / ZA / M • Anal Delights #2 / 1992 / ROB / M • Anal Extasy / 1992 / ROB / M • Anal Fever / 1991 / AMB / M • Anal Inferno / 1992 / ROB / M • Anal Madness / 1992 / ROB / M • Anal Romance / 1993 / LV / M • Anal Rookies #1 / 1992 / ROB / M • Anal Sluts & Sweethearts #1 / 1992 / ROB / M • Anal Thrills / 1992 / ROB / M • The Anal-Europe Series #03: The Museum Of The Living Art / 1993 / LV / M • Anything That Moves / 1992 / VC / M • Ashlyn Gere: The Savage Mistress / 1992 / BIZ / B • Auction #1 / 1992 / BIZ / B • Auction #2 / 1992 / BIZ / B • Ball Busters / 1991 / FH / M • Bat-

tle Of The Superstars / 1993 / VI / M • Bedtime Tales / 1995 / IF / M • Behind The Scenes: The Making Of The Wil & Ed Movies / 1992 / MID / M • Best Butt(e) In The West #1 / 1992 / CC / M • The Best Of Ashlyn Gere / 1995 / BIZ / C • The Best Of Flame / 1994 / BIZ / C • The Best Of Hot Heels / 1992 / BIZ / B • The Best Of Oriental Anal #1 / 1994 / ROB / C • Bi Bi Birdie / 1993 / BIL / G • The Bi-Linguist / 1993 / BIL / G • The Bi-Ologist / 1993 / ... / G • Bianca Trump's Towers / 1992 / LV / M • Bizarre Master Series: Rick Savage / 1992 / BIZ / C • Bizarre Mistress Series: Mistress Jacqueline / 1992 / BIZ / C • Bizarre Mistress Series: Sharon Mitchell / 1992 / BIZ / C • Black Jack City #1 / 1991 / VT / M • Black Obsession / 1991 / ZA / M • Blazing Butts / 1991 / LV / M • Blonde Ice #2 / 1993 / EX / M • Bloopers (Video Team) / 1994 / VT / M • Bubbles / 1991 / IF / M • Buffy Malibu's Totally Nasty All-Girl Home Videos #01 / 1992 / ANA / F • A Cameo Appearence / 1992 / VI / M • Casanova #1 / 1993 / SC / M • Caught From Behind #15 / 1991 / HO / M • City Of Sin / 1991 / LV / M • Colossal Orgy #1 / 1993 / HW / M • Colossal Orgy #2 / 1994 / HW / M • Confessions / 1992 / PL / M • Crazed #1 / 1992 / VI / M • Crazed #2 / 1992 / VI / M • Creation Of Karen: Tormented & Transformed / 1993 / BIZ / B • Cummin' Together / 1991 / JEF / M • Deep Butt / 1994 / MID / C • Deep Inside Savannah / 1993 / VC / C • Defiance, The Spanking Saga / 1992 / BIZ / B • Defiance: Spanking And Beyond / 1993 / PRE / B • Defiance: The Ultimate Spanking / 1993 / BIZ / B • Destination Moon / 1992 / GO / C • Dominique Goes Bi / 1994 / STA / G • Double D Dykes #01 / 1992 / GO / F • Dream Lover / 1991 / WV / M • Dresden Diary #05: Invasion of Privacy / 1992 / BIZ / B • Dresden Diary #06: The Hellfire Legend / 1992 / BIZ / B • Dresden Diary #07 / 1992 / BIZ / B • Dresden Diary #08 / 1992 / BIZ / B • Dresden Diary #09 / 1993 / BIZ / B • Dresden Diary #10: Punishment For Their Sins / 1993 / BIZ / B • The Education Of Karen / 1993 / BIZ / B • Enema Bondage / 1992 / BIZ / B • Enema Obedience #1 / 1992 / BIZ / B • Erectnophobia #1 / 1991 / MID / M • Erotic Encounters (Interludes) / 1993 / NIV / S • A Family Affair / 1991 / AWV / G • Flame's Bondage Bash / 1994 / BIZ / B • Girl Gone Bad #6: On Parole / 1992 / GO / F • Girls In Heat / 1991 / ZA / F • Girls Will Be Boys #3 / 1991 / PL / F • Graduation From F.U. / 1992 / FOR / M • Halloweenie / 1991 / PL / M • Hellraiser #3: Hell On Earth / 1992 / PAR / S • Hindfeld / 1993 / PI / M • Hollywood Teasers #03 / 1992 / LBO / M • Hooray For Hineywood / 1991 / MID / M • Hot Shoes / 1992 / BIZ / B • House Of Sleeping Beauties #1 / 1992 / VI / M • Impulse #07: / 1996 / MBP / M • In Your Wildest Dreams / 1993 / STY / M • Inside Karl Thomas / 1994 / STA / G • Jeff Stryker's Favorite Sexual Positions / 1993 / STY / C • Just For The Hell Of It / 1991 / CA / M • Kinky Lesbians #02 / 1993 / BIZ / B • Kym Wilde's On The Edge #07 / 1994 / RB / B • Kym Wilde's On The Edge #09 / 1994 / RB / B • The Lascivious Ladies Of Dr Lipo / 1991 / OD / M • Latex Submission #1 / 1992 / BIZ / B • Leather Bound

Dykes From Hell #2 / 1994 / BIZ / F • Leather Bound Dykes From Hell #3 / 1994 / BIZ / F • Leather Bound Dykes From Hell #4 / 1995 / BIZ / F • Lesbian Pros And Amateurs #01 / 1992 / GO / F • Lesbian Pros And Amateurs #04 / 1992 / GO / F • Lesbian Pros And Amateurs #05 / 1992 / GO / F • Lesbian Pros And Amateurs #06 / 1992 / GO / F • Maiden Heaven #2 / 1992 / MID / F • Master's Touch #4: Pain's World / 1995 / FAP / B • Miss Bondwell's Reformatory / 1994 / LON / B • Mistress Jacqueline's Slave School / 1992 / BIZ / B • Mistresses At War #01 / 1993 / BIZ / B • Mistresses At War #02 / 1993 / BIZ / B • Mr. Fun's Mondo Adventure / 1993 / VC / M • Mr. Peepers Amateur Home Videos #05: Hot To Trot / 1991 / LBO / M • Mr. Peepers Nastiest #5 / 1995 / LBO / C • Naked Goddess #1 / 1991 / VC / M • Naked Goddess #2 / 1991 / VC / M • Nasty Jack's Kloset Klassics #04 / 1991 / CDI / M • Night And Day #1 / 1993 / VT / M • Obey Me Bitch #3 / 1992 / BIZ / B • Obey Me Bitch #4 / 1993 / BIZ / B • Office Heels / 1992 / BIZ / B • The One And Only / 1993 / FD / M • Oral Madness #1 / 1991 / OD / M • Paper Tiger / 1992 / VI / M • Party Partners / 1994 / STA / G • Peep Land / 1992 / FH / M • The Penetrator #1 / 1991 / PL / M • The Pink Pussycat / 1992 / CA / M • Playin' With Fire / 1993 / LV / M • Possessions / 1992 / HW / M • Pouring It On / 1993 / CV / M • The Power Dykes / 1993 / BIZ / B • The Princess Slave / 1994 / BIZ / B • Pro Ball / 1991 / VD / M • Pussy Galore / 1993 / VD / C • Red Beaver Bonanza / 1992 / TCP / M • Rites Of Passage: Transformation Of A Student To A Slave / 1992 / BIZ / B • Roman Goddess / 1992 / HW / M • Rump Humpers #04 / 1992 / GLI / M • Satin Shadows / 1991 / CIN / M • Savannah R.N. / 1992 / HW / M • School For Wayward Wives / 1993 / BIZ / B • Scorcher / 1992 / GO / M • Sean Michaels On The Road #08: Chicago / 1993 / VT / M • The Secret Garden #1 / 1992 / XCI / M • The Secret Garden #2 / 1992 / XCI / M • Sex Scenes / 1992 / VD / C • Seymore Butts In The Love Shack / 1992 / FH / M • Shaved #06 / 1993 / RB / F • Sleeping Around / 1991 / CA / M • Sorority Sex Kittens #2 / 1993 / VC / M • Spiked Heel Diaries #1 / 1994 / BIZ / B • Spiked Heel Diaries #2 / 1994 / BIZ / B • The Spirit Of My Master / 1994 / BIZ / B • Street Angels / 1992 / LV / M • A Strict Affair...Lessons in Discipline and Obedience / 1992 / BIZ / B • Student Fetish Videos: Best of Catfighting #02 / 1994 / PRE / C • Student Fetish Videos: Best of Catfighting #03 / 1995 / PRE / C • Student Fetish Videos: Best of Enema #03 / 1994 / PRE / C • Student Fetish Videos: Best Of Spanking #03 / 1995 / PRE / C • Student Fetish Videos: Catfighting #09 / 1994 / PRE / B • Student Fetish Videos: Catfighting #12 / 1994 / PRE / B • Student Fetish Videos: The Enema #12 / 1994 / PRE / B • Student Fetish Videos: The Enema #15 / 1994 / PRE / B • Student Fetish Videos: Spanking #15 / 1994 / PRE / B • Switch Hitters #7 / 1994 / IN / G • Taboo #09 / 1991 / IN / M • Taboo #10 / 1992 / IN / M • Taboo #11: Crazy On You / 1993 / IN / M • Take Me...Use Me...Make Me Your Slave / 1994 / BIZ / B • The Taming Of Flame / 1992 / BIZ / B • Teri Diver's Bedtime Tales / 1993 / FD / M • Things Change / 1992 / MET / M • Things Change #1: My First Time / 1992 / CV / M • Tight Asses / 1994 / RB / B • Tight Spot / 1992 / VD / M • Transformed / 1991 / MET / M • Twin Cheeks #2 / 1991 / CIN / M • Ultimate Orgy #1 / 1992 / GLI / M • Valley Of The Sluts / 1991 / OD / M • VGA: Blazing Pussies / 1992 / VGA / B • VGA: Cutting Room Floor #1 / 1993 / VGA / M • VGA: Spanking Sampler #2 / 1992 / VGA / B • Watersports Spree #1 / 1992 / BIZ / C • A Weekend In Bondage / 1994 / BIZ / B • Where The Girls Sweat #2 / 1991 / EL / F • Wicked Thoughts / 1992 / PL / M • Wil And Ed's Excellent Boner Christmas / 1991 / MID / M • Wild Girls / 1993 / LV / F • Will And Ed: The Curse Of Poona / 1994 / MID / C • WPINK-TV #4 / 1993 / PV / M

FLAME (1995)
Butt Hunt #07 / 1995 / LEI / M • The New Ass Masters #10 / 1996 / LEI / C • Nookie Professor #2 / 1996 / AVS / M • Pussy Hunt #14 / 1995 / LEI / M

FLASH
Homegrown Video #291 / 1990 / HOV / M • HomeGrown Video #458: Cream Pie For Dessert / 1995 / HOV / C

FLAVIA VOLTAGE see Star Index I

FLEX GAMBLE
Marine Code Of Silence: Don't Ask Don't Tell / 1996 / BHE / G • Trans America / 1993 / TSS / G

FLICCA see Star Index I

FLINT CAGNEY see Star Index I

FLIP FOE
The Swing Thing / 1973 / TGA / M

FLIP LAURENT see Star Index I

FLO
Max World #3: Formula 1 / 1996 / XPR / M

FLO RIVERS see Star Index I

FLO ZEASILY see Star Index I

FLORA
Eurotica #01 / 1995 / XC / M • Eurotica #13 / 1996 / XC / M • Triple X Video Magazine #08 / 1995 / OD / M

FLORA MCINTOSH see Star Index I

#! ! #@@
Hot Babes / cr78 / CIG / M

FLORENCE
Eurotica #02 / 1995 / XC / M • Eurotica #03 / 1995 / XC / M • Impulse #08: The A Channel / 1996 / MBP / M • Magma: Horny & Greedy / 1993 / MET / M • Magma: Sperm-Crazy / 1994 / MET / M • Magma: Tits Practice / 1995 / MET / M

FLORENCE COUVRAT see Star Index I

FLOSSIE O'GRADY
Match #1: The Main Event / 1995 / NPA / B • Match #2: Savage Heat / 1995 / NPA / B

FLOUNDER
Wild Desires / 1994 / MAX / M

FLOYD THOMAS
Matinee Idol / 1984 / VC / M

FLUFFY LABUSCHE
The Love Couch / 1977 / VC / M

FOLSOM JACKSON
Tight Spot / 1996 / WV / M

FONDA FRENCH
Anal Cannibals / 1996 / ZA / M • Anal Delinquent #3 / 1995 / ROB / M • Anal Trashy Ass / 1995 / ROB / M • Black Video Virgins #1 / 1996 / NS / M • Bootylicious: Big Badd Booty / 1995 / JMP / M • By Myself / 1996 / PL / F • Dirty Dirty Debutantes

#3 / 1996 / 4P / M • Interracial Anal #06 / 1995 / AFI / M • Interview: Chocolate Treats / 1995 / LV / M • Lesbian Pooper Sluts / 1996 / ROB / F • Malibu Butt Sluts / 1996 / ROB / F • Mister Stickypants / 1996 / LV / M • My Baby Got Back #08 / 1996 / VT / M • My Baby Got Back #09 / 1996 / VT / M • Rumpman In And Out Of Africa / 1996 / HW / M • Samantha & Company / 1996 / PL / M • Sinboy #3: The Island Of Dr. Moron / 1996 / SC / M • Steam / 1996 / ULP / M • Takin' It To The Limit #7: Debauched / 1996 / BS / M • Toot Z Roll / 1995 / WP / M • Up And Cummers #25 / 1995 / 4P / M

FONDA PETERS
Bucky Beavers #074 / 1995 / SOW / M • The Psychiatrist / 1971 / SOW / M

FONDLE
House Of Sex #13: Interracial Gang Bang / 1994 / RTP / M

FONTANA
Hooters In The 'hood / 1995 / TTV / M • The Mad D.P. Tea Party / 1994 / FC / M

FORREST
Hollywood Amateurs #22 / 1995 / MID / M

FOSTER THOMAS see Star Index I

FOSTER WAINE
A Scent Of Heather / 1981 / VXP / M

FOUR HUCK see Star Index I

FOX see Star Index I

FOXINA see Star Index I

FOXY
Black Streets / 1994 / LE / M • Fishbone / 1994 / WIV / F • Hidden Camera #20 / 1994 / JMP / M • Horror In The Wax Museum / 1983 / TAO / B • Jane Bond Meets Thunderthighs / 1988 / VD / M • SVE: Foxy's Audition / 1994 / SVE / M

FOXY LADY
Climax At The Melting Pot #1 / 1996 / AVS / M

FOZ see George Kaplan

FOZZI see George Kaplan

FOZZIE see George Kaplan

FRACK see Star Index I

FRAINE TESSIER
Horny Henry's Euro Adventure / 1995 / IIV / M

FRAN
Blue Vanities #554 / 1994 / FFL / M • Blue Vanities #564 / 1994 / FFL / M • Blue Vanities #568 / 1995 / FFL / M • HomeGrown Video #435: Seasoned To Perfection / 1994 / HOV / M • HomeGrown Video #465: Bong The Schlong / 1996 / HOV / M • HomeGrown Video #470: Heroes, Torpedoes & Grinders / 1996 / HOV / M • The Mistake / 1989 / CDP / B • Swedish Sex / 1996 / PL / M

FRAN BAKER
Defiance / 1974 / ALP / B

FRAN BATES see Star Index I

FRAN CARLSTADT
ABA: Double Feature #1 / 1996 / ALP / M • Fanny Hill / 1975 / TGA / M

FRAN CARSTON
Postgraduate Course In Sexual Love / 1975 / QX / M

FRAN CASTANIO see Star Index I

FRAN COOPER see Star Index I

FRAN ESSEX
Expensive Taste / 1978 / VCX / M

FRAN FOX
Starlet Nights / 1982 / XTR / M

FRAN FRANCIS see Star Index I

FRAN HANCOCK
Prisoner Of Pleasure / 1981 / ALP / B

FRAN LANE see Star Index I

FRAN ROGERS
Bedtime Video #05 / 1984 / GO / M

FRAN SPECTOR
San Francisco Original 200s #7 / 1980 / SVE / M • [Harlot / cr70 / ... / M

FRANCE
Bedside Brat / 1988 / VI / M • Magma: Body Cocktails / 1995 / MET / M

FRANCE DANTIX
Gode-Party / 1994 / RUM / M

FRANCE LAROUSSE
Bucky Beaver's XXX Dragon Art Theatre Double Feature #02 / 1996 / SOW / M • The Rites Of Uranus / 1975 / SOW / M

FRANCE LOWREY see Star Index I

FRANCEISE FARLET see Star Index I

FRANCES LOPEZ
Dream Lovers / 1980 / MET / G

FRANCES NATIVIDAD see Kitten Natividad

FRANCES PARKS see Star Index I

FRANCES ROCK see Star Index I

FRANCESCA
Cheerleaders In Bondage #1 / 1994 / GOT / B • The Fury Inside / 1994 / GOT / B • Pussy Fest Of The Northwest #3 / 1995 / NIT / M • Raw Deal / 1994 / GOT / B • Toe Tales #14 / 1994 / GOT / B • Toe Tales #15 / 1994 / GOT / B • Toe Tales #24 / 1995 / GOT / C

FRANCESCA (GINA R) see Gina Rome

FRANCESCA (ROXY) see Roxy (Francesca)

FRANCESCA HAMILTON
The Psychiatrist / 1978 / VC / M

FRANCESCA LE *(Erica Estrada, Francesca Lee)*
Adorable with an exceedingly tight waist, pretty face, small tits, and great boy-like butt. Only defect is that she has the tendency to talk dirty and to pout. Born Dec 28, 1970 in LA. Dropped out of high school. Erica Estrada is from **Telesex**. In **MDD #18** (1992) she says she's 21, Hispanic and lost her virginity at 13.
1-800-934-DOOD / 1992 / VD / O • The 900 Club / 1993 / BON / B • Alice In Hollywierd / 1992 / ZA / M • America's Raunchiest Home Videos #28: Anal Aerobics / 1992 / ZA / M • The Anal Adventures Of Max Hardcore: Between The Lines / 1993 / ZA / M • Anal Angels #6 / 1996 / VEX / C • The Anal Diary Of Misty Rain / 1993 / EL / M • Anal Kitten / 1992 / ROB / M • Anal Lover #2 / 1993 / ROB / M • Anal Rampage #1 / 1992 / ROB / M • Anal Rookies #1 / 1992 / ROB / M • Anal Savage #1 / 1992 / ROB / M • Anal Vision #05 / 1993 / LBO / M • Anal Woman #2 / 1993 / PL / M • Ass Freaks #1 / 1993 / ROB / F • Ass Openers! #1 / 1995 / TCK / C • Ass Openers! #2 / 1995 / TCK / C • Back In The Pen / 1992 / FH / M • Backing In #3 / 1991 / WV / C • Ball & Chain / 1994 / GOT / B • Bare Market / 1993 / VC / M • Best Gang Bangs / 1996 / DFI / C • The Best Of The Gangbang Girl Series #2 / 1995 / ANA / C • Bip Shoots #2 / 1994 / BON / B • Bonnie & Clyde #1 / 1992 / VI / M • Bonnie & Clyde #2 / 1992 / VI / M • Buffy Malibu's Totally Nasty All-Girl Home Videos #01 / 1992 / ANA / F • Buffy Malibu's Totally Nasty All-Girl Home Videos #05 / 1993 /

ANA / F • Buffy Malibu's Nasty Girls #08 / 1995 / ANA / F • Bush League #2 / 1992 / CC / M • Butt Banged Bicycle Babes / 1994 / ANA / M • Butt Sluts #2 / 1993 / ROB / F • Buttslammers #04: Down And Dirty / 1993 / BS / F • Carnival Of Knowledge / 1992 / XCI / M • Centerfold / 1992 / VC / M • Cherry Redder / 1993 / RB / B • Cinnamon Twist / 1993 / OD / M • The Cockateer #2 / 1992 / LE / M • Crime Doesn't Pay / 1993 / BS / B • A Cum Sucking Whore Named Francesca / 1995 / ANA / C • The D.P. Man #1 / 1992 / FD / M • The D.P. Man #2 / 1992 / FD / M • The Darker Side Of Shayla #1 / 1993 / PL / M • Deep Inside Dirty Debutantes #05 / 1993 / 4P / M • Double Crossing / 1991 / IN / M • Dream Bound / 1995 / BON / B • Dungeon Brats / 1994 / STM / B • Dungeon Punishment / 1995 / STM / B • The Erotic Adventures Of The Three Musketeers / 1992 / CEL / S • Erotica / 1992 / CC / M • Face Dance #1 / 1992 / EA / M • Face Dance #2 / 1992 / EA / M • Fast Track / 1992 / LIP / F • Femme Fatale / 1993 / SC / M • Forbidden / 1992 / FOR / M • Gang Bang Thrills / 1992 / ROB / M • Gangbang Girl #12 / 1993 / ANA / M • Gangbang Girl #13 / 1994 / ANA / M • The Girls Of Summer / 1992 / FOR / M • Hard As A Rock / 1992 / ZA / M • Hard Hand Luc / 1994 / STM / B • Hard Rider / 1992 / IN / M • Heels & Toes #1 / 1994 / BON / F • Heels & Toes #2 / 1994 / BON / F • Her Personal Touch / 1996 / STM / F • Hidden Obsessions / 1992 / BFP / M • Hot Bodies In Bondage / 1993 / LBO / B • Hot Tight Asses #02 / 1993 / TCK / M • Hot Tight Asses #05 / 1994 / TCK / M • House Of Sleeping Beauties #1 / 1992 / VI / M • I Made Marian / 1993 / PEP / M • Immaculate Erection / 1992 / VD / M • Inferno #1 / 1993 / SC / M • Inferno #2 / 1993 / SC / M • Just Deserts / 1994 / BON / B • Kittens #4: Bodybuilding Bitches / 1993 / CC / F • Kym Wilde's On The Edge #16 / 1994 / RB / B • Leave It To Bondage / 1994 / BON / B • Leena / 1992 / VT / M • Leg...Ends #11 / 1994 / PRE / F • Lesbian Dating Game / 1993 / LIP / F • Lesbian Love Connection / 1992 / LIP / F • Little Magicians / 1993 / ANA / M • Lovin' Spoonfuls #3 / 1995 / 4P / C • More Dirty Debutantes #18 / 1992 / 4P / M • The Naked Pen / 1992 / VC / M • Nasty Nymphos #03 / 1994 / ANA / M • Nasty Nymphos #11 / 1995 / ANA / M • The New Ass Masters #11 / 1996 / LEI / C • New Wave Hookers #3 / 1993 / VC / M • Nikki Never Says No / 1992 / LE / M • The Nymphette / 1993 / CA / M • The Orgy #1 / 1993 / EMC / M • Overkill / 1994 / BS / B • The Pain Connection / 1994 / BS / B • Patriot Dames / 1992 / ZA / M • Perfect Endings / 1994 / PLV / B • Pornographic Priestess / 1992 / CA / M • Professor Sticky's Anatomy 3X #01 / 1992 / FC / M • Pure Filth / 1995 / RV / M • Raunch #05 / 1992 / CC / M • Ride 'em Cow Girl / 1995 / VI / C • Roommate Humiliation / 1993 / PL / B • See-Thru / 1992 / LE / M • Sexual Olympics #1: The Trials / 1992 / VT / M • Sexual Olympics #2: The Finals / 1992 / VT / M • Shades Of Blue / 1992 / VC / M • Shaved Sinners #4 / 1993 / VT / M • Slave Wages / 1995 / PRE / B • Sodomania #01: Tales Of Perversity / 1992 / EL / M • Sodomania #02: More Tails / 1992 / EL / M • Sodomania: Slop Shots / 1996 / EL / C • Sodomania: The Baddest Of The Best...And Then Some / 1994 / EL / C • Stick It In The Rear #2 / 1993 / PL / M • Student Fetish Videos: Best of Catfighting #02 / 1994 / PRE / C • Student Fetish Videos: Best Of Foot Worship #03 / 1995 / PRE / C • Student Fetish Videos: Foot Worship #09 / 1994 / PRE / B • The Taming Of Savannah / 1993 / VI / M • Telesex #1 / 1992 / VI / M • Teri Diver's Bedtime Tales / 1993 / FD / M • Things Change / 1992 / MET / M • Things Change #2: Letting Go / 1992 / CV / M • The Three Musketeers #1 / 1992 / FD / M • The Three Musketeers #2 / 1992 / FD / M • Tight Spot / 1992 / VD / M • Tip Tap Toe / 1995 / PRE / C • Toe Nuts / 1994 / PRE / B • Toe Tales #18 / 1994 / GOT / B • Toe Tales #22 / 1995 / GOT / B • Too Sexy / 1992 / MID / M • Transitions: An Anal Adventure / 1993 / PL / M • Two Women / 1992 / ROB / M • Wanderlust / 1992 / LE / M • Waves Of Passion / 1993 / PL / M • Welcome To Bondage: Francesca Le / 1992 / BON / B • Welcome To Bondage: Starlets #1 / 1993 / BON / C • Where The Boys Aren't #4 / 1992 / VI / F • Where The Boys Aren't #5 / 1992 / VI / F • The Wild Thing / 1992 / HO / M • Wilder At Heart / 1993 / ANA / M • The Witching Hour / 1992 / FOR / M

FRANCESCA LEE *see* **Francesca Le**

FRANCESCA MALCOLM
Secrets Of Madame X #2 / 1995 / WIV / M • The Sex Clinic / 1995 / WIV / M

FRANCESCA NATIVIDAD *see* **Kitten Natividad**

FRANCESCIA *see* **Meekah**

FRANCESCO
Lipstick / 1976 / PAR / S • Private Film #19 / 1994 / OD / M • Private Film #27 / 1995 / OD / M • Private Film #28 / 1995 / OD / M • World Sex Tour #2 / 1995 / ANA / M

FRANCESCO AVON
Essence Of A Woman / 1995 / ONA / M

FRANCESCO MALCOLM
All Grown Up / 1996 / XC / M • Angel Hard / 1996 / STV / M • Betty Bleu / 1996 / IP / M • Don Salvatore: The Last Sicilian / 1995 / XC / M • Erotic Dreams / 1992 / VTV / M • Essence Of A Woman / 1995 / ONA / M • Hot Diamond / 1995 / LE / M • Il Medico Della Coppie / 1996 / TNT / M • Prima #09: ASSassins / 1995 / MBP / M • Prima #14: Hotel Europa / 1996 / MBP / M • Toredo / 1996 / ROX / M • Virility / 1996 / XC / M

FRANCESCO TRULLI
The Coming Of Nikita / 1995 / EL / M • Sleeping Booty / 1995 / EL / M • Sodomania #14: C**t Lickin', C*m Drinkin' Bitches / 1995 / EL / M • Sodomania: Slop Shots / 1996 / EL / C

FRANCHI MARINO
Thunder Boobs / 1995 / BTO / M

FRANCIE FRENCH *see* **Star Index I**

FRANCINE
Between My Breasts #07 / 1989 / L&W / M • Blue Vanities #521 / 1993 / FFL / M • Blue Vanities #578 / 1995 / FFL / M • David Friedman's Road Show Shorts #07 / 1994 / SOW / S • Dr Butts #3 / 1993 / 4P / M • The Gypsy / 1996 / NIT / M • Home-Grown Video #455 / 1995 / HOV / M • Intimate Interviews #4 / 1996 / NIT / M • Junk Yard Dogs / 1991 / FC / M • Magma: Anal Wedding / 1995 / MET / M • Magma: Bizarre Lust / 1995 / MET / M • Magma: Horny For Cock / 1990 / MET / M • Magma: Huge Cum Shots / 1995 / MET / M • Magma: Lust Excesses / 1995 / MET / M • Max World #2: Europa Issue / 1995 / XPR / M

FRANCINE ALBOTT
Juicy Virgins / 1995 / WIV / M

FRANCINE LOWERY *see* **Star Index I**

FRANCINE PIESTE *see* **Star Index I**

FRANCINE STAR
Hot Fudge / 1984 / VC / M

FRANCIS *see* **Star Index I**

FRANCIS HAID
Von Sex Gier Besessen / 1995 / PF / M

FRANCIS LEA
The Aroused / 1989 / IN / M • Doctor Yes / 1978 / VIS / M • Pure Sex / 1988 / FAN / C

FRANCIS X. BUSH
Lickity Split / 1974 / COM / M

FRANCK
Cindy Puts Out / 1996 / OLL / M • Gigi Gives It Away / 1995 / FRF / M

FRANCK BALARD
Born For Love / 1987 / ... / M

FRANCO ARMANI
Alana: A Gang Bang Fantasy / 1993 / FC / M • Amateur A Cuppers / 1993 / VEX / C • Angel Eyes / 1995 / IN / M • Bachelor Party #2 / 1993 / FPI / M • Bareback Riders / 1992 / VEX / M • Beach Bum Amateur's #09 / 1992 / MID / M • Black Magic #1 / 1993 / VIM / M • The Bold, The Bald & The Beautiful / 1993 / VIM / M • Bun Busters #06 / 1993 / LBO / M • Club DV8 #2 / 1993 / SC / M • D.P. Party Tonite / 1995 / JMP / M • Dirty Doc's Housecalls #14 / 1994 / LV / M • The Doll House / 1995 / CV / M • Frenzy / 1992 / SC / M • Gang Bang Bitches #04 / 1995 / PP / M • Gang Bang Diaries #3 / 1994 / SFP / M • Harry Horndog #11: Love Puppies #2 / 1992 / ZA / M • Harry Horndog #13: Anal Lovers #2 / 1992 / ZA / M • Harry Horndog #14: Love Puppies #3 / 1992 / ZA / M • Hidden Camera #20 / 1994 / JMP / M • Hollywood Amateurs #13 / 1994 / MID / M • Illusions #2 / 1992 / IF / M • Jezebel #1 / 1993 / SC / M • The Mad D.P. Tea Party / 1994 / FC / M • Mr. Peepers Amateur Home Videos #67: Backdoor Fantasy / 1993 / LBO / M • Mr. Peepers Amateur Home Videos #75: Trio In Rio / 1993 / LBO / M • Much More Than A Mouthful #4 / 1994 / VEX / M • Neighborhood Watch #22: In The Pink And Wet / 1992 / LBO / M • Nothing Else Matters / 1992 / V99 / C • Odyssey Triple Play #62: Gang Bangs All Around / 1994 / OD / M • Odyssey Triple Play #75: Interracial Anal Threesome / 1994 / OD / M • Saturday Night Porn #2 / 1993 / AFV / M • Split Decision / 1993 / FD / M • Stuff Your Face #1 / 1994 / JMP / M • WPINK-TV #5 / 1993 / PV / M

FRANCO CINI
Impulse #05: When I Was 20... / 1995 / MBP / M

FRANCO LOMAY *see* **Star Index I**

FRANCO MONTINI
Selen / 1996 / HW / M

FRANCO ROCCAFORTE
Helen Does Holland / 1996 / VC / M • The Thief, The Girl & The Detective / 1996 / HDE / M

FRANCOIS

Homegrown Video #431 / 1994 / HOV / M • Magma: Pussy Jobs / 1994 / MET / M • Mrs. Rodger's Neighborhood / 1988 / EVN / C • Superstar Sex Challenge #3 / 1994 / VC / M

FRANCOIS (PAPPILION) see Francois Pappilion

FRANCOIS CANNON see Star Index I

FRANCOIS CLOUSOT

Max #08: The Fugitive / 1995 / XPR / M

FRANCOIS DUMAS see Francois Pappilion

FRANCOIS LOVELL see Star Index I

FRANCOIS PAPPILION (Francois (Pappilion), Jean-Jacques LeBon, Francois Dumas, Pappilion, Frank Pappilion)

Blonde body builder type male who was or is the SO of Kascha.

1001 Erotic Nights #2 / 1987 / VC / M • Adult Video Therapist / 1987 / CLV / C • All The Way In / 1984 / VC / M • Attack Of The Monster Mammaries / 1987 / LA / C • Baby Face #2 / 1987 / VC / M • Bachelorette Party / 1986 / ACV / S • Backdoor Lust / 1987 / CV / C • Backdoor To Hollywood #05 / 1988 / CDI / M • Backdoor To Hollywood #06 / 1989 / CIN / M • Backdoor To Hollywood #07 / 1989 / CIN / M • Backside To The Future #1 / 1986 / ZA / M • Bare Elegance / 1984 / MAP / M • Bedtime Stories / 1989 / WV / M • Before She Says I Do / 1984 / MAP / M • Bet Black / 1989 / CDI / M • Beverly Hills Cox / 1986 / CA / M • Beyond Desire / 1986 / VC / M • Big Gulp #2 / 1987 / VIP / C • Blonde Desire / 1984 / AIR / M • Blowing The Whistle / 1986 / VIP / M • Blue Ice / 1985 / CA / M • Bodies By Jackie / 1985 / IVP / M • Body Girls / 1983 / SE / M • California Reaming / 1985 / WV / M • Caught By Surprise / 1987 / CDI / M • Charlie's Girls #1 / 1988 / CC / M • Charm School / 1986 / VI / M • Club Exotica #1 / 1985 / WV / M • Club Exotica #2 / 1985 / WV / M • Club Ginger / 1986 / VI / M • Corporate Assets / 1985 / SE / M • Daisy Chain / 1984 / IN / M • Dance Fever / 1985 / VCR / M • Dark Angel / 1983 / VC / M • Deep Inside Vanessa Del Rio / 1986 / VC / M • Dirty Girls / 1984 / MIT / M • Double Messages / 1987 / MOV / M • Double Penetration #1 / 1985 / WV / M • Double Penetration #2 / 1986 / WV / C • Dr Lust / 1987 / VC / M • Dream Girls / 1986 / VC / M • Dream Lover / 1985 / CDI / M • Dressed To Thrill / 1986 / CDI / M • Dynamic Vices / 1987 / VC / M • E Three / 1985 / GO / M • Ebony & Ivory Fantasies / 1988 / VD / C • The Ecstasy Girls #2 / 1986 / CA / M • Educating Eva / 1984 / VC / M • Educating Kascha / 1989 / CIN / M • Educating Mandy / 1985 / CDI / M • Erica Boyer: Non-Stop / 1988 / VD / C • Erotic Dreams / 1987 / HO / M • Escort To Ecstasy / 1987 / 3HV / M • Europe On Two Guys A Day / 1987 / PV / M • Every Man's Fantasy / 1985 / IN / M • Every Woman Has A Fantasy #1 / 1984 / VC / M • Fade To Black / 1988 / CDI / M • Fantasy Chamber / 1987 / VT / M • Fashion Passion / 1985 / VD / M • Fatal Seduction / 1988 / CDI / M • French Letters / 1984 / CA / M • From Kascha With Love / 1988 / CDI / M • Future Voyeur / 1985 / SUV / M • Gimme An X / 1993 / VD / C • The Ginger Effect / 1985 / VI / C • The Girls Of Rodeo Drive / 1987 /

BAD / M • Girls Of The Chorus Line / 1986 / CLV / M • Girls Of The Double D #05 / 1988 / CIN / M • Girls Of The Double D #07 / 1989 / CIN / M • Girls Of The Double D #08 / 1989 / CDI / M • Girls Of The Third Reich / 1985 / FC / M • Girls Of Treasure Island / 1988 / CV / M • Good Morning Saigon / 1988 / ZA / M • The Good, The Bad, And The Horny / 1985 / VCX / M • Hard To Swallow / 1985 / PV / M • Hawaii Vice #1 / 1988 / CIN / M • Hawaii Vice #2 / 1989 / CDI / M • Hawaii Vice #3 / 1988 / CIN / M • Hawaii Vice #4 / 1989 / CIN / M • Hawaii Vice #5 / 1989 / CDI / M • Hawaii Vice #6 / 1989 / CDI / M • Hawaii Vice #7 / 1989 / CDI / M • Hawaii Vice #8 / 1990 / CIN / M • Hawaii Vice: Reflections / 1990 / CIN / C • Head Waitress / 1984 / VC / M • Headgames / 1985 / WV / M • Headhunters / 1984 / VC / M • Honkytonk Angels / 1988 / IN / C • Hot And Nasty! / 1986 / V99 / C • Hot Flashes / 1984 / VC / M • Hot Wire / 1985 / VXP / M • Hottest Parties / 1988 / VC / C • Hustler #17 / 1984 / CA0 / M • In All The Right Places / 1986 / VD / M • In And Out Of Africa / 1986 / EVN / M • In Search Of The Golden Bone / 1986 / CA / M • Inside China Lee / 1984 / VC / M • Introducing Kascha / 1988 / CDI / M • Irresistible #2 / 1986 / SE / M • Island Girls #1 / 1990 / CDI / C • Island Girls #2: Fun In The Sun / 1990 / CDI / C • Island Girls #3: Rip Tide / 1991 / CDI / C • Jealous Lovers / 1989 / CDI / M • The Joy-Stick Girls / 1986 / CLV / M • Karate Girls / 1987 / VCR / M • Kascha & Friends / 1988 / CIN / M • Kascha's Blues / 1988 / CDI / M • Kascha's Days & Nights / 1989 / CDI / M • Kiss My Asp / 1989 / EXH / M • Lessons In Lust / 1987 / LA / M • Let's Get Physical (Hyapatia Lee's) / 1984 / CA / M • A Little Dove-Tale / 1987 / IN / M • A Little Dynasty / 1985 / CIV / M • Looking For Lust / 1984 / VEL / M • Looking For Mr Goodsex / 1984 / CC / M • Loose Ends #1 / 1984 / 4P / M • Loose Ends #2 / 1986 / 4P / M • Loose Ends #3 / 1987 / BS / M • Love Champions / 1987 / VC / M • Lust In Space / 1985 / PV / M • Lust On The Orient X Press / 1986 / CA / M • Mad Jack Beyond Thunderdome / 1986 / WET / M • Mammary Lane / 1988 / VT / C • Mandii's Magic / 1988 / CDI / M • Material Girl / 1986 / VD / M • The Melting Spot / 1985 / VSE / M • Merry X Miss / 1986 / VIP / M • Miami Spice #2 / 1988 / CA / M • Nasty Habits Are Hard To Break / 1986 / 4P / M • Nasty Nights / 1988 / PL / C • Naughty Angels / 1984 / VC / M • Naughty Nanette / 1984 / VC / M • Nicki / 1987 / VI / M • Nudes At Eleven #1 / 1986 / AVC / M • Once Upon A Madonna / 1985 / PV / M • The Other Side Of Pleasure / 1987 / SEV / M • Perfect Fit / 1985 / DR / M • The Performers / 1986 / NSV / M • Phone Sex Fantasies / 1984 / QX / M • Pink And Pretty / 1986 / CA / M • Play Me Again, Vanessa / 1986 / VC / M • Playing For Passion / 1987 / IN / M • Pumping Flesh / 1985 / CA / M • Raffles / 1988 / VC / M • Ramb-Ohh #1 / 1986 / PV / M • Rated Sex / 1986 / SE / M • Rear Ended / 1985 / WV / M • Rearbusters / 1988 / LVI / C • Rock Hard / 1985 / CV / M • The Rocky Porno Video Show / 1986 / 4P / M • Rough Draft / 1986 / VEN / M • Sacrificed To Love / 1986 / CDI / M • Samantha, I Love You /

1988 / WV / C • Satin Dolls / 1985 / CV / M • Schoolgirl By Day / 1985 / LA / M • Science Friction / 1986 / AXT / M • Sex 5th Avenue / 1985 / WV / M • Sex Appeal / 1984 / ABV / M • Sex Asylum #1 / 1985 / VI / M • The Sex Change Girls / 1987 / 4P / G • Sex Machine / 1986 / LA / M • Sex-O-Gram / 1986 / LA / M • Sexaholics / 1987 / VCX / M • Shauna: Every Man's Fantasy / 1985 / CA / C • Shaved Pink / 1986 / WET / M • She Comes In Colors / 1987 / AMB / M • She Comes Undone / 1987 / AIR / C • Sins Of Wealthy Wives / 1989 / CDI / C • Sizzling Suburbia / 1985 / CDI / M • Sizzling Summer / 1984 / VC / M • Sounds Of Sex / 1985 / CA / M • Spreading Joy / 1988 / VC / M • Star 85: Kari Fox / 1985 / VEX / M • Starlets / 1985 / 4P / M • Super Models Do LA / 1986 / AT / M • Super Sex / 1986 / MAP / M • Taboo #04 / 1985 / IN / M • Taking Off / 1984 / VC / M • A Taste Of Paradise / 1984 / HO / M • A Taste Of Taija Rae / 1989 / PIN / C • Taste Of The Best #2 / 1988 / PIN / C • Taste Of The Best #3 / 1988 / PIN / C • Teenage Games / 1985 / HO / M • That Ole Black Magic / 1988 / CDI / M • This Stud's For You / 1986 / MAP / C • Too Naughty To Say No / 1984 / CA / M • Top Buns / 1986 / HO / M • Tracy Takes Paris / 1987 / VIP / M • Trading Partners / 1983 / AIR / M • Trashy Lady / 1985 / MAP / M • Tunnel Of Love / 1986 / CLV / M • Two To Tango / 1987 / TEM / M • Unveiled / 1987 / VC / M • Up All Night / 1986 / CC / M • Up Desiree Lane / 1984 / VC / M • Up In The Air / 1984 / CDI / M • VCA Previews #4 / 1988 / VC / C • Virgin Cheeks / 1986 / VD / M • Voyeur's Delight / 1986 / VCS / C • Weird Fantasy / 1986 / LA / M • Wet 'n' Bare With Barbara Dare / 1988 / NEO / C • Woman In The Window / 1986 / TEM / M • Working It Out / 1983 / CA / M • The World According To Ginger / 1985 / VI / M • Young Nurses In Love / 1987 / VC / M

FRANCOISE

Magma: Anita #2 / 1996 / MET / M • Magma: Deep Inside Janine / 1994 / MET / M • Magma: Sperma / 1994 / MET / M • Mobile Home Girls / 1985 / VC / M

FRANCOISE AVRIL see Star Index I

FRANCOISE DUCHARME

Telefantasy / 1978 / AR / M

FRANCOISE GERMAINE see Star Index I

FRANK

AVP #7012: Sex Collections / 1991 / AVP / M • Bi-Bi Love Amateurs #1 / 1993 / SFP / G • Big Bust Babes #17 / 1993 / AFI / M • Buttwoman In Budapest / 1992 / EA / M • Catch Of The Day #3 / 1996 / VG0 / M • Fresh Faces #07 / 1995 / EVN / M • Fresh Meat #1 / 1996 / PL / M • Magma: Deep Inside Janine / 1994 / MET / M • Magma: Sperma / 1994 / MET / M • Magma: Trans-Games / 1995 / MET / G • Private Film #16 / 1994 / OD / M • S&M On The Ranch: Training The New Pony Girl / 1994 / VER / B • Seymore Butts: My Travels With The Tramp / 1994 / FH / M • Shades Of Erotica #03 / 1994 / GLI / M • Swedish Erotica #37 / 1981 / CA / M

FRANK ACADE see Frank James

FRANK ADAMS

Dirty Looks / 1982 / VC / C • Games Women Play #1 / 1980 / CA / M • This Lady Is A Tramp / 1980 / CV / M

FRANK ALLAN *see* **Frank James**

FRANK BALLPARK
Jingle Balls / 1996 / EVN / M • Orgy Camera #1 / 1995 / EVN / M

FRANK BALZAC
Super Bi Bowl / 1995 / BIL / G

FRANK BREED
Good Morning, Little Schoolgirl / cr75 / BL / M

FRANK BUCKQUID
The Butt Sisters Do Washington D.C. / 1995 / MID / M • The Night Of The Living Bed / 1996 / LE / M • Passions Of Sin / 1996 / NIT / M • Rebel Without A Condom / 1996 / ERA / M • Shadows Of Lust / 1996 / NIT / M • She's No Angel / 1996 / ERA / S

FRANK BUFFDERM
Little Girls Blue #2 / 1983 / VCX / M

FRANK C.
Foreign Exchange Sluts / 1995 / TNT / M

FRANK CANNES
The Hitch-Hiker #05: Traffic Jam / 1994 / WMG / M

FRANK CHAPUIS
Wedding Rituals / 1995 / DVP / M

FRANK D'MICO
New Girls In Town #6 / 1994 / CC / M • Video Virgins #19 / 1994 / NS / M

FRANK DAWRY
Mile High Club / 1983 / CV / M

FRANK DELLA *see* **Star Index I**

FRANK DYUTAY *see* **Star Index I**

FRANK E. MOVATO
Debutante Dreams / 1995 / 4P / M

FRANK FURTER
Anal, Facial & Interracial / 1996 / FC / M

FRANK GIZHEH *see* **Star Index I**

FRANK GOTTI
Nightclub / 1996 / SC / M

FRANK GUNN
Despite the name this is a young Hungarian male. May be the same as the Hungarian, Frank Mallone.
Big Babies In Budapest / 1996 / EL / M • Bottom Dweller: The Final Voyage / 1996 / EL / M • Russian Model Magazine #2 / 1996 / IP / M • Sexhibition #3 / 1996 / SUF / M • Sodomania #21: Degenerate Lifestyles! / 1997 / EL / M • The Voyeur #7: Live In Europe #1 / 1996 / JLP / M • The Voyeur #8: Live In Europe #2 / 1996 / JLP / M

FRANK HALLOWELL
Amanda By Night #1 / 1981 / CA / M • Centerspread Girls / 1982 / CA / M • Coed Fever / 1980 / CA / M • Crazy With The Heat #1 / 1986 / CV / M • Desires Within Young Girls / 1977 / CA / M • The Ecstasy Girls #1 / 1979 / CA / M • The Ecstasy Girls #2 / 1986 / CA / M • Girls On Fire / 1985 / VCX / M • Joanna Storm On Fire / 1985 / VIV / M • Rated Sex / 1986 / SE / M • Society Affairs / 1982 / CA / M • Summer Camp Girls / 1983 / CA / M

FRANK HARRIS
Reel People #03 / 1989 / PP / M

FRANK HOLBY
Bottom Busters / 1973 / BLT / M

FRANK HUNGARIS
Private Film #13 / 1994 / OD / M

FRANK JAMES *(Frank Allan, Frank Acade)*
Frank Allan is from **Eat At The Blue Fox** and Frank Acade from **Dinner With Samantha**.
Adult Video Therapist / 1987 / CLV / C •

American Dream Girls #1 / 1986 / VEX / M • Anal Angels #1 / 1986 / VEX / M • Anal Intruder #02 / 1988 / CC / M • The Anal-ist #2 / 1986 / VEX / M • The Babes Of Bonerville / 1995 / VEX / C • Backdoor Brides #3 / 1988 / PV / M • Backdoor To Hollywood #02 / 1986 / CDI / M • Ball Street / 1988 / CA / M • Bare Essentials / 1987 / VEX / M • The Battle Of the Breast Queens / 1989 / INS / C • Beeches / 1990 / KIS / M • The Best Little Whorehouse In Beverly Hills / 1986 / CDI / M • The Best Of Blondes / 1986 / VCR / C • Between A Rock And A Hot Place / 1989 / VEX / M • Beyond The Denver Dynasty / 1988 / CA / M • The Big Gun / 1989 / FAN / M • Big Tit Orgy #01 / 1987 / H&S / M • Big Top Cabaret #1 / 1986 / BTO / M • Black Angel / 1987 / CC / M • Black Heat / 1986 / VC / M • Black Magic / 1986 / DR / M • Black To The Future / 1986 / VD / M • Blonde Fantasy / 1988 / CC / M • Born To Be Wild / 1987 / SE / M • Buns And Roses (V9) / 1990 / V99 / M • Caddy Shack-Up / 1986 / VD / M • California Blondes #01 / 1986 / VEX / M • California Blondes #02 / 1987 / VEX / M • California Cherries / 1987 / EVN / M • California Fever / 1987 / CV / M • Caught From Behind #07 / 1987 / HO / M • Celebrity Presents Celebrity / 1986 / VEP / C • Charmed Forces / 1987 / VI / M • Cheek To Cheek / 1986 / VEX / M • Cheeks #1 / 1988 / CC / M • Cream Dreams / 1986 / VEX / M • Creamy Cheeks / 1986 / VEX / M • Creatures Of The Night / 1987 / FAN / M • Dancing Angels / 1989 / PL / M • Debbie Does Dallas #4 / 1988 / VEX / M • Debbie Does The Devil In Dallas / 1987 / SE / M • Deep Inside Ona Zee / 1992 / VC / C • Depraved / 1990 / IN / M • Diamond Collection #80 / 1986 / CDI / M • Dinner With Samantha / 1983 / PTV / M • Dirty Blondes / 1986 / CDI / M • Dirty Prancing / 1987 / EVN / M • Dirty Tricks / 1986 / 4P / M • Doctor Feelgood / 1988 / CDI / M • The Doctor's In / 1986 / CDI / M • Double Black Fantasy / 1987 / CC / C • Dr Truth's Great Sex / 1986 / VD / M • Eat At The Blue Fox / 1983 / VC / M • Ebony Humpers #1 / 1986 / VEX / M • Ebony Humpers #3 / 1987 / VEX / M • Erotic Therapy / 1987 / CDI / M • The Erotic World Of Cody Nicole / 1984 / VCR / C • The Erotic World Of Crystal Lake (#4) / 1984 / VCR / C • The Erotic World Of Rene Summers / 1984 / VCR / C • The Erotic World Of Sylvia Benedict (#5) / 1983 / VCR / C • Every Man Should Have One / 1991 / VEX / M • Every Man's Fancy / 1988 / SEX / M • Every Man's Fancy / 1991 / V99 / M • Ex-Connection / 1986 / SEV / M • Fireball / 1988 / IN / M • Flesh For Frankenstein / 1987 / VEX / M • Fuck This / 1988 / BEV / C • Fun In The Sun / 1988 / EVN / C • Furburgers / 1987 / VD / M • Future Sodom / 1988 / VD / M • Gazongas #01 / 1987 / VEX / M • The Gentlemen's Club / 1986 / WV / M • Get Me While I'm Hot / 1988 / PV / M • Girls Just Wanna Have Boys / 1986 / AMB / M • Girls Of The Chorus Line / 1986 / CLV / M • Girls Of The Double D #01 / 1986 / CDI / M • Golden Girls #12 / 1984 / CA / M • Good 'n' Plenty / 1987 / AVC / M • Great Expectations / 1992 / VEX / C • The Great Sex Contest #1 / 1988 / LV / M • Groupies Ga-

lore / 1983 / VC / M • Hard Ride / 1986 / VT / M • Having It All / 1985 / IN / M • Having It All / 1991 / VEX / M • High Rollers / 1987 / VEX / M • Hollywood Hustle #2 / 1990 / V99 / M • Home Bodies / 1988 / VEX / M • Home Movies Ltd #1 / 1983 / SE / M • Hometown Honeys #1 / 1986 / VEX / M • Hometown Honeys #2 / 1988 / VEX / M • The Honeymooners / 1986 / CDI / M • Hot Pink And Chocolate Brown / 1988 / PV / M • Hot Spa / 1984 / CA / M • Hot Summer Nites / 1988 / VEX / M • House Of The Rising Moon / 1986 / VD / M • How To Get A "Head" / 1988 / CV / M • Hyapatia Lee's Arcade Series #01 / 1988 / ZA / C • Hyapatia Lee's Arcade Series #02 / 1988 / ZA / C • I Am Curious Black / 1986 / WET / M • The Immoral Miss Teeze / 1987 / CV / M • In Search Of The Wild Beaver / 1986 / DR / M • Introducing Barbii / 1987 / CDI / M • Joys Of Erotica / 1984 / VCR / M • The Joy Of Sec's / 1989 / VEX / M • Keep It Cumming / 1990 / V99 / M • Keyhole #168: Robo-Cocks / 1989 / KEH / M • Kiss Of The Dragon Lady / 1986 / SEV / M • Knights In Black Satin / 1990 / VEX / M • La Bimbo / 1987 / PEN / M • Little French Maids / 1988 / VEX / M • Lost Lovers / 1990 / VEX / M • Loving Lips / 1987 / AMB / C • Lust Letters / 1988 / CA / M • Lusty Layout / 1986 / PV / M • Matched Pairs / 1988 / VEX / M • Maximum #5 / 1983 / CA / M • Maximum Head / 1987 / SE / M • Megasex / 1988 / EVN / M • Misadventures Of The Bang Gang / 1987 / AR / M • Monkey Business / 1987 / SEV / M • Much More Than A Mouthful #1 / 1987 / VEX / M • Nasty Habits Are Hard To Break / 1986 / 4P / M • Naughty Neighbors / 1986 / VEX / M • Naughty Nymphs / 1986 / VEX / M • Naughty Nymphs / 1991 / VEX / C • Not So Innocent / 1989 / VEX / M • The Out Of Towner / 1987 / CDI / M • Passion Princess / 1991 / VEX / M • Passionate Heiress / 1987 / CA / M • Playing Dirty / 1989 / VEX / M • Playing For Passion / 1987 / IN / M • Playing The Field / 1990 / VEX / M • Pleasure Principle / 1988 / VEX / M • Pleasure Productions #01 / 1984 / VCR / M • Prince Of Beverly Hills #1 / 1987 / VEX / M • Queen Of Spades / 1986 / VD / M • Raising Hell / 1987 / VD / M • Rambone Meets The Double Penetrators / 1987 / WET / M • Reckless Passion / 1986 / ME / M • The Red Hot Roadrunner / 1987 / VD / M • Reel People #02 / 1984 / AR / M • Retail Slut / 1989 / LV / M • Riding Miss Daisy / 1990 / VEX / M • The Rising / 1987 / SUV / M • Rituals / 1989 / V99 / M • The Scent Of Samantha / 1988 / VEX / C • Secrets Behind The Green Door / 1987 / SE / M • Send Me An Angel / 1990 / V99 / M • Sensuous Moments / 1983 / VIV / M • Sensuous Tales / 1984 / VCR / C • Sex Aliens / 1987 / CA / M • Sex Lives Of The Rich And Beautiful / 1988 / CA / M • Sex She Wrote / 1991 / VEX / M • Sex Slaves / 1986 / VEX / M • Shaved Sinners #2 / 1987 / VT / M • She's No Angel #1 / 1990 / V99 / M • Sinful Sisters / 1986 / VEX / M • Sleeping With Everybody / 1992 / MID / C • Soul Games / 1988 / PV / C • Splash Dance / 1987 / AR / M • Spooked / 1989 / VEX / M • Stand-In Studs / 1989 / V99 / M • Star 84: Tina Marie / 1984 / VEX / M • Star 88: Dana Lynn / 1988 / VEX / C • Star

90 / 1990 / CAY / M • Steam Heat / 1989 / VEX / M • Sugarpussy Jeans / 1986 / TEM / M • Suite Sensations / 1988 / SEX / M • Summer Dreams / 1990 / VEX / M • Supersluts Of Wrestling / 1986 / VD / M • Suze's Centerfolds #7 / 1983 / CA / M • Swedish Erotica Featurettes #5 / 1990 / CA / M • Sweet Darlin' / 1990 / VEX / M • Sweet Nothings / 1987 / HO / M • Sweet Sensations / 1989 / SEX / M • Sweet Temptations / 1989 / V99 / M • Taboo #06 / 1988 / IN / M • Taija's Satin Seduction / 1987 / CDI / M • Tailgunners / 1985 / WET / M • Teach Me Tonight / 1990 / VEX / M • Tequilla Sunset / 1989 / V99 / M • Tough Girls Don't Dance / 1987 / SEV / M • Toys 4 Us #1 / 1987 / WV / C • Tracey's Love Chamber / 1987 / AR / M • The Ultimate Climax / 1989 / V99 / M • Up All Night / 1986 / CC / M • The Vanessa Obsession / 1987 / VCX / C • Weekend Blues / 1990 / IN / M • What Kind Of Girls Do You Think We Are? / 1986 / VEX / M • What Kind of Girls Do You Think We Are? / 1991 / VEX / C • Whatever Turns You On / 1987 / CA / M • White Chocolate / 1987 / PEN / M • Winner Take All / 1986 / SEV / M • [Berlin Caper / 1989 / ... / M

FRANK JAMES (OTHER)
Desert Island Buttwatch / 1996 / SUF / M • Philmore Butts Spring Break / 1996 / SUF / M • Streets Of New York #07 / 1996 / PL / M • Sunset In Paradise / 1996 / PL / M • Tampa Spice / 1996 / SUF / M

FRANK JONATHON *see Star Index I*
FRANK JONES
Seka's Fantasies / 1981 / CA / M • Sex And The Happy Landlord / 1988 / CDI / M

FRANK KNOWLL
Lusty Ladies #04 / 1983 / 4P / M

FRANK LARSON
The Voyeur #8: Live In Europe #2 / 1996 / JLP / M

FRANK LEE
Bucky Beaver's XXX Dragon Art Theatre Double Feature #09 / 1996 / SOW / M • Up In Flames / 1973 / SOW / M

FRANK LEE SAWRY
Oral Addiction / 1995 / VI / M

FRANK MALLONE
Anal Palace / 1995 / VC / M • Dirty Stories #4 / 1995 / PE / M • Dirty Stories #5 / 1996 / PE / M • Erika Bella: Euroslut / 1995 / EL / M • Mission Hard / 1995 / XC / M • Passion In Venice / 1995 / ULI / M • Russian Model Magazine #1 / 1996 / IP / M • The Sex Clinic / 1995 / WIV / M • The Thief, The Girl & The Detective / 1996 / HDE / M

FRANK MARINO
Ace Mulholland / 1995 / ERA / M • Dial A For Anal / 1994 / CA / M • Goldenbush / 1996 / AVI / M • A Peek Over The Wall / 1995 / STM / G • The Reel World #2 / 1994 / FOR / M • Western Nights / 1994 / WP / M

FRANK MARKS
Bucky Beaver's XXX Dragon Art Theatre Double Feature #09 / 1996 / SOW / M • Up In Flames / 1973 / SOW / M

FRANK MARRIN *see Star Index I*
FRANK MARTINEZ *see Star Index I*
FRANK MATEO
Deep Rub / 1979 / VC / M

FRANK MAURO *see Star Index I*
FRANK MAZARS
Cunt Of Monte Cristo / 1996 / SPL / M •

Foxy Lady #3 / 1986 / PL / M

FRANK METAIRIE
The Voyeur #3 / 1995 / EA / M

FRANK MICELLI
The Italian Stallion / 1970 / ELH / S • Love Secrets / 1976 / VIP / M

FRANK N. STEIN
Sex Dreams / 1995 / C69 / M

FRANK NOSSACK
[Krankenschwestern-Report / 1972 / ... / M

FRANK PAPILLON *see Francois Pappilion*
FRANK PENN
The Return Of Johnny Wadd / 1986 / PEN / M • Street Heat Orgy / 1986 / ERR / S

FRANK RHODES
All American Hustler / cr73 / SOW / M • Bucky Beaver's XXX Dragon Art Theatre Double Feature #28 / 1996 / SOW / M

FRANK RIMMER
Sweat 'n' Bullets / 1995 / MID / M

FRANK RIVERA
The Love Couch / 1977 / VC / M

FRANK ROSE *see Star Index I*
FRANK ROWNEY
Bucky Beaver's XXX Dragon Art Theatre Double Feature #02 / 1996 / SOW / M • The Rites Of Uranus / 1975 / SOW / M

FRANK RYAN *see Star Index I*
FRANK SERRONE
Barely Legal / 1985 / CDI / M • Christine's Secret / 1986 / FEM / M • Coming In Style / 1986 / CA / M • Deep Throat #2 / 1986 / AR / M • Driller / 1984 / VC / M • Girl Busters / 1985 / VC / M • Give It To Me / 1984 / SE / M • Harem Girls / 1986 / SE / M • Hot Licks / 1984 / SE / M • The Hot Tip / 1986 / VXP / M • Jailhouse Girls / 1984 / VC / M • A Passage Thru Pamela / 1985 / VC / G • Playpen / 1987 / VC / M • Porked / 1986 / VXP / M • Sex Tips For Modern Women / 1987 / VXP / M • Star Angel / 1986 / COM / M • Supergirls Do General Hospital / 1984 / VC / M • Supergirls Do The Navy / 1984 / VC / M • Taboo American Style #1: The Ruthless Beginning / 1985 / VC / M • Taboo American Style #4: The Exciting Conclusion / 1985 / VC / M • Ultrasex / 1987 / VC / M

FRANK SHAFT
Filthy First Timers #4 / 1996 / EL / M

FRANK SIMMONS
The Taking Of Christina / 1975 / NGV / M

FRANK STARR
Private Film #08 / 1994 / OD / M

FRANK STRONG *see Star Index I*
FRANK T. LANE
Anal Intruder #01 / 1986 / CC / M • Romancing The Bone / 1984 / VC / M

FRANK TESSIER
French Twist / 1996 / HO / M

FRANK THOMAS
Behind The Scenes / 1996 / GO / M

FRANK THRING *(Bill Wright)*
Sleazy English male with glasses and a head of white hair.
Alvin Rides Again / 1974 / NWW / S • French Twist / 1996 / HO / M • Horny Henry's Euro Adventure / 1995 / TTV / M • Lee Nover: The Search For The Perfect Butt / 1996 / IP / M • Private Film #01 / 1993 / OD / M • Private Film #19 / 1994 / OD / M • Private Video Magazine #12 /

1994 / OD / M • Private Video Magazine #14 / 1994 / OD / M • Russian Model Magazine #1 / 1996 / IP / M • Russian Model Magazine #2 / 1996 / IP / M • Sodomania #16: Sexxy Pistols / 1996 / EL / M • Sodomania: Slop Shots / 1996 / EL / C • Up The Gulf / 1991 / AR / M

FRANK TOWERS
Very large and well-built blonde guy.
9-Ball: Geisha Gang Bang / 1994 / PL / M • Addictive Desires / 1994 / OD / M • The Adventures Of Peeping Tom #1 / 1996 / OD / M • The Adventures Of Peeping Tom #2 / 1996 / OD / M • Amateur Orgies #29 / 1993 / AFI / M • Amateur Orgies #34 / 1993 / AFI / M • Amateur Orgies #36 / 1993 / AFI / M • American Pie / 1995 / WAV / M • Ass Busters / 1995 / VMX / C • Babe Wire / 1996 / HW / M • The Backdoor Bradys / 1995 / PL / M • Bare Ass In The Park / 1995 / PEP / M • Beeping Miss Buffy / 1995 / CDI / M • The Big One / 1995 / HO / M • Booby Prize / 1995 / PEP / M • Brunette Roulette / 1996 / LE / M • Burbank Sperm Bank / 1996 / CIN / M • Catching Snapper / 1995 / XCI / M • Channel 69 / 1996 / CC / M • Cold As Ice / 1994 / IN / M • Compulsive Behavior / 1995 / PI / M • Dance Naked / 1995 / PEP / M • Decadent Obsession / 1995 / OD / M • Deep Focus / 1995 / VC / M • The Devil In Miss Jones #5: The Inferno / 1994 / VC / M • Diamond In The Raw / 1996 / XCI / M • The Dinner Party #1 / 1994 / ULI / M • Dirty Doc's Housecalls #08 / 1994 / LV / M • The Doll House / 1995 / CV / M • Exstasy / 1995 / WV / M • Fixing A Hole / 1995 / XCI / M • Flexxx #1 / 1994 / VT / M • Flexxx #3 / 1995 / VT / M • Flexxx #4 / 1995 / VT / M • Foreskin Gump / 1994 / LE / M • Gang Bang Bitches #01 / 1994 / PP / M • Gang Bang Bitches #05 / 1995 / PP / M • Gang Bang Bitches #06 / 1995 / PP / M • Gang Bang Bitches #08 / 1995 / PP / M • Gang Bang Bitches #09 / 1995 / PP / M • Gang Bang Diaries #3 / 1994 / SFP / M • Generation Sex #2: Nature's Revenge / 1996 / VT / M • The Great American Boobs To Kill For / 1996 / ... / M • Hollywood Hillbillies / 1996 / LE / M • Hot Amateur Nights / 1996 / WV / M • Humpkin Pie / 1995 / HW / M • Indiscreet! Video Magazine #2 / 1995 / FH / M • Indiscreet! Video Magazine #3 / 1995 / FH / M • Kissing Kaylan / 1995 / CC / M • Lady M's Anal Gang Bang / 1995 / FC / M • Legal Briefs / 1996 / EX / M • Lust & Desire / 1996 / WV / M • Made For A Gangbang / 1995 / ZA / M • More Than A Handful #6: Life Under The Big Top / 1994 / MET / M • My First Time #2 / 1996 / NS / M • Nasty Newcummers #13 / 1995 / MET / M • Nothing Sacred / 1995 / LE / M • Nude Awakenings / 1996 / PP / M • Nudist Colony Vacation / 1996 / NIT / M • Oh My Gush / 1995 / OD / M • Opie Goes To South Central / 1995 / PP / M • Orgies Orgies Orgies / 1994 / WV / M • Passage To Pleasure / 1995 / LE / M • Pearl Of The Orient / 1995 / IN / M • Performer Of The Year / 1994 / WP / M • Persuasion / 1995 / LE / M • Pick Up Lines #01 / 1995 / 4P / M • Pick Up Lines #04 / 1995 / 4P / M • Pick Up Lines #06 / 1996 / OD / M • Pick Up Lines #09 / 1996 / OD / M • Pick Up Lines #10 / 1997 / OD / M • Pick Up Lines #11 / 1997 / OD / M • Pick

Up Lines #13 / 1997 / OD / M • Private Film #24 / 1995 / OD / M • Private Film #25 / 1995 / OD / M • Private Film #26 / 1995 / OD / M • Private Stories #01 / 1995 / OD / M • Private Video Magazine #26 / 1995 / OD / M • Pulp Friction / 1994 / PP / M • Real Sex Magazine #01 / 1996 / HO / M • Real Sex Magazine #02 / 1997 / HO / M • Reel People #10 / 1995 / PP / M • Reel People #11 / 1995 / PP / M • Rockhard (Sin City) / 1996 / SC / M • Rxx For A Gangbang / 1994 / ZA / M • Sex Bandits / 1995 / VC / M • Sex Freaks / 1995 / EA / M • Shades Of Erotica #02 / 1994 / GLI / M • A Shot In The Pants / 1995 / HO / M • The Sin-A-Bun Girls / 1995 / OD / M • Smoke & Mirrors / 1996 / PL / M • Star Crossed / 1995 / VC / M • Tail Taggers #129: / 1994 / WV / M • Talking Trash #2 / 1995 / HW / M • Telephone Expose / 1995 / VC / M • Three Hearts / 1995 / CC / M • Titanic Orgy / 1995 / PEP / M • Topless Window Washers / 1996 / LE / M • Triple X Video Magazine #01 / 1995 / OD / M • Triple X Video Magazine #06 / 1995 / OD / M • Undercover / 1996 / VC / M • Up And Cummers #38 / 1996 / RWP / M • Upbeat Love #2 / 1995 / CV / M • Violation / 1996 / LE / M • The Wanderer #2: Slippery When Wet / 1995 / CDI / M • Waterbabies #3 / 1996 / CC / M • Wendy Whoppers: Ufo Tracker / 1994 / PEP / M • Whackers / 1995 / PP / M • Wicked Waxxx Worxxx / 1995 / HW / M • Willie Wanker At The Sushi Bar / 1995 / FD / M

FRANK VERDUCCI *see* **Joe Verducci**

FRANK VERSACE
Private Film #21 / 1995 / OD / M • Private Film #23 / 1995 / OD / M • Private Film #27 / 1995 / OD / M • Private Film #28 / 1995 / OD / M • Private Gold #12: The Pyramid #2 / 1996 / OD / M • Private Gold #14: Sweet Lady #1 / 1997 / OD / M • Private Gold #15: Sweet Lady #2 / 1997 / OD / M • Triple X Video Magazine #02 / 1995 / OD / M • Triple X Video Magazine #03 / 1995 / OD / M

FRANK WARD *see* **Star Index I**

FRANK WASHINGTON
Ebony Erotica / 1985 / SVE / C

FRANK WELLES
Dreams Bi-Night / 1989 / PL / G • Trans Europe Express / 1989 / VC / G

FRANK ZEE *(Frankie Flowers)*
Husband of Ona Zee.
A&B BD#01: Submissive Slaves / 1991 / A&B / B • A&B BD#02: Submissive Wife #1 / 1991 / A&B / B • A&B BD#03: Male Slave / 1991 / A&B / B • A&B BD#06: Submissive Wife #2 / 1991 / A&B / B • A&B BD#07: Submissive Husband / 1991 / A&B / B • Afternoon With Goddess Sondra / 1992 / SSP / B • Birthday Surprise / 1988 / BON / B • Bondage Boot Camp / 1988 / TAN / B • The Bondage Club #2 / 1987 / LON / B • The Bondage Club #4 / 1990 / LON / B • The Bondage Club #5 / 1990 / LON / B • Covergirl / 1994 / WP / M • Dazzling Dominants / 1991 / RSV / B • Deadly Sin / 1996 / ONA / B • The Divine Marquis / 1995 / ONA / B • The Good Stuff / 1989 / BON / C • High Heels In Heat #1 / 1988 / RSV / F • Journal Of O #1: Servant Slave / 1994 / ONA / B • Journal Of O #2 / 1994 / ONA / B • Nikki's Last Stand / 1993 / VC / M • Ona Zee's Date With Dallas / 1992 / ONA /

M • Ona Zee's Learning The Ropes #01: Male Submissive / 1992 / ONA / B • Ona Zee's Learning The Ropes #02: Male Submissive / 1992 / ONA / B • Ona Zee's Learning The Ropes #03: Male Submissive / 1992 / ONA / B • Ona Zee's Learning The Ropes #04: Female Submissive / 1992 / ONA / B • Ona Zee's Learning The Ropes #05: Female Submissive / 1992 / ONA / B • Ona Zee's Learning The Ropes #07: At Lady Laura's / 1992 / ONA / B • Ona Zee's Learning The Ropes #08: Slaves In Training / 1992 / ONA / B • Ona Zee's Learning The Ropes #09: The Training Continues / 1992 / ONA / B • Ona Zee's Learning The Ropes #10: Chains Of Love / 1994 / ONA / B • Ona Zee's Learning The Ropes #11: Chains Required / 1994 / ONA / B • Ona Zee's Learning The Ropes #12: Couples / 1995 / ONA / B • Ona Zee's Learning The Ropes #13: Best Of Male Submission / 1996 / ONA / C • Razor's Edge / 1995 / ONA / M • Sex Academy #1 / 1993 / ONA / M • Sex Academy #2: The Art Of Talking Dirty / 1994 / ONA / M • Sex Academy #3: The Art Of Real Sex / 1994 / ONA / M • Sex Academy #4: The Art Of Anal / 1994 / ONA / M • Tangled / 1994 / PL / M • Totally Ona: The Best Of Ona Zee / 1996 / ONA / C • Welcome To Bondage: Mona Lisa / 1992 / BON / B

FRANK(IE) LEE *see* **Frankie Leigh**

FRANKIE
Blue Vanities #583 / 1996 / FFL / M • Neighborhood Watch #21 / 1992 / LBO / M • Positively Pagan #02 / 1991 / ATA / M • Sean Michaels On The Road #09: St. Louis / 1994 / VT / M • Stretchin' The Rear / 1995 / PE / M • Wrestling Classics #4 / 1993 / CDP / B

FRANKIE ANN
Strap-On Sally #09: / 1996 / PL / F

FRANKIE D'ANGELO *see* **Star Index I**

FRANKIE D. *see* **Star Index I**

FRANKIE DONUT *see* **Johnny Warner**

FRANKIE FAIN
Great Grandma Gets Her Cookies / 1995 / FC / M

FRANKIE FEVER
Pearl Necklace: Amorous Amateurs #27 / 1993 / SEE / M • Pearl Necklace: Amorous Amateurs #28 / 1993 / SEE / M • Pearl Necklace: Amorous Amateurs #31 / 1993 / SEE / M

FRANKIE FLOWERS *see* **Frank Zee**

FRANKIE LAYNE
Cheerleader type reminiscent of Nikki Charm with long blonde hair, small tits, aged skin weathered by the sun, petite body, tight waist, good tan lines, nice butt. A little too pushy.
Backdoor Diaries / 1995 / BBE / M • Beverly Hills Blondes #1 / 1995 / LV / M • Big Breast Beach / 1995 / LV / M • Caught In The Act (1995-Lv) / 1995 / LV / M • Dirty Dancers #5 / 1995 / 4P / M • Fashion Sluts #1 / 1995 / ABS / M • Hawaiian Buttwatch / 1995 / SUF / M • Indecent Obsessions / 1995 / BBE / M • Interview: Naturals / 1995 / LV / M • Malibu Heat / 1995 / HO / M • Muff Divers #3 / 1996 / TV / F • Paradise / 1995 / FD / M • Party Girl / 1995 / LV / M • Perverted Stories #03 / 1995 / JMP / M • Philmore Butts Hawaiian Anal Adventure / 1995 / SUF / M • Philmore Butts Las Vegas

Vacation / 1995 / SUF / M • Philmore Butts Meets The Freak / 1995 / SUF / M • Pick Up Lines #03 / 1995 / 4P / M • Pussy Hunt #12 / 1995 / LEI / M • Sex On The Beach Hawaiian Style #2 / 1995 / ULP / M • Sex On The Beach Hawaiian Style #3 / 1995 / ULP / M • Sex, Truth & Videotape #1 / 1995 / DOC / M • Student Fetish Videos: Bondage #01 / 1995 / PRE / B • Student Fetish Videos: Catfighting #16 / 1996 / PRE / B • Student Fetish Videos: Foot Worship #17 / 1995 / PRE / B • Tropical Taboo / 1995 / HO / M • Trouble In Paradise / 1996 / ULP / M • Vibrating Vixens #1 / 1996 / TV / F • Video Virgins #21 / 1995 / NS / M • Young & Natural #03 / 1995 / PRE / F • Young & Natural #04 / 1995 / PRE / F • Young & Natural #07 / 1995 / PRE / F • Young & Natural #08 / 1995 / PRE / F • Young & Natural #09 / 1995 / PRE / C

FRANKIE LEE *see* **Frankie Leigh**

FRANKIE LEIGH *(Hope (Frankie Leigh), Frankie Lee, Frank(ie) Lee, Hope Lynn, Sparkle Densmore, Hope Richards, Hope Summers (Lee), Cynthia Hope, Hope Geller)*
Pretty face, medium tits (may be enhanced), good tan lines, flat butt, dark brown curly hair, large areola. Hope is from **Vegas Brats** and Hope Lynn from **Teasers: Champagne Reunion**.
Aerobisex Girls #2 / 1989 / LIP / F • All Hands On Dick / 1988 / STA / G • The Aroused / 1989 / IN / M • Bare Essentials / 1987 / VEX / M • The Beverly Thrillbillies / 1987 / EVN / M • Bi And Beyond #1 / 1988 / LAV / G • Bi And Beyond #2 / 1989 / CAT / G • Biloxi Babes / 1988 / WV / M • Blow Job Babes / 1988 / BEV / C • Broadcast Nudes / 1988 / EVN / M • Butt's Motel #1 / 1989 / EX / M • Cat 'nipped / 1995 / PLV / B • Cherry Cheerleaders / 1987 / VEX / M • City Of Rage / 1989 / EVN / M • Cum Rain, Cum Shine / 1989 / FAZ / M • Dana Lynn's Hot All Over / 1987 / V99 / M • The Days Of Our Wives / 1988 / GO / M • The Divorce / 1986 / VC / G • Double Your Pleasure / 1989 / VEX / M • Facial Attraction / 1988 / BEE / C • First Time Lesbians (Gourmet) / 1987 / GO / F • Flesh In Ecstasy #11: Frankie Leigh / 1987 / GO / C • Fuck This / 1988 / BEV / C • Future Sodom / 1988 / VD / M • Gazongas #01 / 1987 / VEX / M • Girls Like Us / cr88 / IN / C • Girls Of Sin / 1994 / PL / C • Good Enough To Eat / 1988 / FAZ / M • High Rollers / 1987 / VEX / M • Holly Does Hollywood #2 / 1987 / VEX / M • Hollywood Harlots / 1986 / VEX / C • Hometown Honeys #2 / 1988 / VEX / M • The Honeymooners / 1986 / CDI / M • Hot Dreams / 1989 / VEX / M • Hot Dreams / 1991 / VEX / M • Hung Guns / 1988 / STA / G • In A Crystal Fantasy / 1988 / VD / M • In Charm's Way / 1987 / IN / M • In-N-Out With John Leslie / 1988 / WV / C • Inner Blues / 1987 / VD / M • Inner Pink #1 / 1988 / LIP / F • Jewel Of The Nite / 1986 / WV / M • Just Like Sisters / 1988 / VEX / M • K.U.N.T.-TV / 1988 / WV / M • KTSX-69 / 1988 / CA / M • The Legend Of Reggie D. / 1989 / EA / M • Little French Maids / 1988 / VEX / M • Littledove's Cup / 1988 / FOV / M • Love On The Run / 1989 / CA / M • Lucky At Lust / 1989 / SDP / M • Lust And The Law / 1991

/ GO / C • Lust Weekend / 1987 / CA / M •
Max Bedroom / 1987 / ZA / M • Miss Ad-
ventures / 1989 / VEX / M • More Than
Friends / 1989 / FAZ / M • Never Say Good
Bi / 1989 / STA / G • No More Mr Nice Guy
/ 1989 / GO / M • The Offering / 1988 / INH
/ G • Parliament: Dildo Babes #2 / 1988 /
PM / F • Parliament: Hot Legs #1 / 1988 /
PM / F • Parliament: Licking Lesbians #1 /
1988 / PM / F • Parliament: Licking Les-
bians #2 / 1989 / PM / F • Parting Shots /
1990 / VD / M • Partners In Sex / 1988 /
FAN / M • Party Animals / 1987 / VEX / M •
Party Animals / 1994 / VEX / C • Porn
Star's Day Off / 1990 / FAZ / M • Precious
Assets / cr87 / VEX / M • Princess Of
Darkness / 1987 / VEX / M • Raging Week-
end / 1988 / GO / M • Reamin' Reunion /
1988 / CC / M • The Return Of The A Team
/ 1988 / WV / M • Samantha, I Love You /
1988 / WV / C • Satin Angels / 1986 / WV /
M • The Scam / 1986 / TEM / G • Screwing
Around / 1988 / LV / M • Soft Caresses /
1988 / VEX / M • Sophisticated Lady /
1988 / SEX / M • Spellbound / 1989 / LV /
M • Splash Dance / 1987 / AR / M • Strong
Language / 1989 / IN / M • A Taste Of Pleasure / 1988 / AVC / M • Teasers: Champagne Reunion / 1988 / MET / M • Three
By Three / 1989 / LV / C • The Touchables
/ 1988 / CC / M • Tracey's Love Chamber /
1987 / AR / M • Two Women & A Man /
1988 / VEX / M • Two Women & A Man /
1991 / VEX / C • Under The Law / 1989 /
AFV / M • Vegas Brats / 1990 / WV / M •
The Wacky World Of X-Rated Bloopers /
1989 / GO / M • The Wedding / 1986 / VC /
M • Wet Weekend / 1987 / MAC / M • Who
Shaved Trinity Loren? / 1988 / EX / M •
[T&A #01 / 1989 / ... / C

FRANKIE RAY
Shame / 1994 / VI / M

FRANKLIN ANTHONY (Franklin Jones,
Noel Hemphill)
Just another stud. Shorter than John Leslie in
Coming Attractions from whence the
Jones name is derived. Appears in **An Act
Of Confession** as Noel Hemphill.
An Act Of Confession / 1979 / CLD / M •
Coming Attractions / 1976 / VEP / M • The
Life And Times Of Xavier Hollander / 1973
/ VXP / M • Marriage And Other Four Letter
Words / 1974 / VC / M

FRANKLIN CLEMENTE *see Star Index I*
FRANKLIN DOBBS *see Star Index I*
FRANKLIN JONES *see Franklin An-
thony*
FRANKO
American Swinger Video Magazine #04 /
1993 / ZA / M

FRANKY LAIME
Corporate Bi Out / 1994 / BIL / G

FRANKY VERACE
Private Film #15 / 1994 / OD / M

FRANNIE LEMAY *see Star Index I*
FRAPPE *see Star Index I*
FRAULEIN GOODENTIGHT *see Star
Index I*
FRAULINE
Master's Touch #5: Slave Revolt / 1995 /
FAP / B

FRED
Anabolic Import #01: Anal X / 1994 / ANA /
M • Rocks / 1993 / VT / M

FRED ADAMS
The Anger In Jennie / 1975 / VHL / M

FRED ANTON *see Jon Martin*
FRED BALLARD
An Unnatural Act #1 / 1984 / DR / M
FRED BAXTER
Submission (Knight) / 1994 / KNF / B
FRED BERGER *see Star Index I*
FRED C. DOBBS *see Star Index I*
FRED CLAY
All The Loving Couples / 1979 / KIT / M
FRED GREENBERG
Blackmail For Daddy / 1976 / VCX / M
FRED HALSTED
[El Paso Wrecking Corp / 1977 / TMX / G
FRED HAWKINS *see Star Index I*
FRED HEART *see Star Index I*
FRED HUBER
For Love Of Money / 1975 / CDC / M • The
Pleasure Bed / 1975 / IVP / M
FRED HURTS
Rice Burners / 1996 / NOT / M
FRED J. LINCOLN
Mainstream movie actor in the early seventies.
Became porno director in eighties and
nineties often with Patti Rhodes as screen-
writer or producer. He married her in the
early nineties but by mid-nineties they has
separated.
Barbara Dare's Roman Holiday / 1987 /
SE / M • Beauty's Punishment / 1996 / BIZ
/ B • Beauty's Revenge / 1996 / BIZ / B •
The Case Of The Full Moon Murders /
1971 / SOW / M • Coming Of Age / 1989 /
CA / M • Defiance / 1974 / ALP / B • Defi-
ance: Spanking And Beyond / 1993 / PRE
/ B • Devil In Miss Jones #2 / 1983 / VC / M
• Dominatrix Without Mercy / 1996 / ALP /
B • Edward Penishands #3 / 1991 / VT / M
• The Erotic Adventures Of The Three Mus-
keteers / 1992 / CEL / S • Fleshpots Of
42nd Street / 1971 / SOW / S • Freedom
Of Choice / 1984 / VHL / M • The French
Connection / 1993 / 2CF / S • Friday The
13th #1: A Nude Beginning / 1987 / VD / M
• Friday The 13th #2 / 1989 / VD / M • The
God Daughter #1 / 1991 / AFV / M • The
God Daughter #2 / 1991 / AFV / M • Hot-
house Rose #1 / 1991 / VC / M • Kinky
Couples / 1990 / VD / M • The Last House
On The Left / 1972 / VES / S • The Last
Temptation / 1988 / VD / M • Liquid A$$ets
/ 1982 / CA • Love Games / 1975 / SAT
/ M • Maneaters / 1983 / VC / M • Nasty
Girls   (1983-VCX) / 1983 / VCX / M •
Powerbone / 1976 / VC / M • Raunch #02 /
1990 / CC / M • Strange Behavior / 1991 /
VD / M • Swedish Erotica Featurettes #2 /
1989 / CA / M • Trick Tracy #2: Tracy
Loves Dick / 1990 / CC / M • The Ultimate
Fantasy / 1995 / CV / M • Viva Vanessa
The Undresser / 1984 / VC / M • Willie
Wanker And The Fun Factory / 1994 / FD /
M
FRED JAMES *see Star Index I*
FRED JONES
Love Bites / 1985 / CA / M
FRED KEITEL
Waterpower / 1975 / VHL / M
FRED L. MORRIS
ABA: Double Feature #1 / 1996 / ALP / M •
Fanny Hill / 1975 / TGA / M
FRED LORENZO
Beach Blanket Bango / 1975 / EVI / M •
High School Fantasies / 1974 / EVI / M •
Teenage Throat / 1974 / ... / M
FRED MARKS
Bucky Beaver's XXX Dragon Art Theatre

Double Feature #01 / 1996 / SOW / M •
Hitler's Harlots / cr73 / SOW / M
FRED MERTZ
Overnight Sensation / 1976 / AR / M
FRED PERNA *see Star Index I*
FRED PERSON
Private Film #05 / 1993 / OD / M • Private
Film #09 / 1994 / OD / M
FRED PICKSON *see Star Index I*
FRED POLE *see Star Index I*
FRED RAIN *see Star Index I*
FRED SAVAGE *see Rick Savage*
FRED SIMMONS *see Star Index I*
FRED STIFFLERIN *see Damon Christian*
FRED SUMMER
Little Girl Lost / 1995 / SC / M
FRED ZOTS
Lady Zazu's Daughter / 1971 / ALP / M •
The Weirdos And The Oddballs / 1968 /
CLX / M
FREDA
Blue Vanities #510 / 1992 / FFL / M • Blue
Vanities #539 / 1993 / FFL / M
FREDA (B. GLEN) *see Beverly Glen*
FREDDIE DIAMOND
Anal Anarchy / 1995 / VC / M • Bobby Hol-
lander's Rookie Nookie #01 / 1993 / SFP /
M • Bobby Hollander's Sweet Cheeks #103
/ 1992 / QUA / M • Bobby Hollander's
Sweet Cheeks #105 / 1993 / SFP / M •
Eighteen #2 / 1996 / SC / M • Hard-On
Copy / 1994 / WV / M • Road Kill / 1995 /
CA / M • Samantha's Private Fantasies /
1994 / WV / M • Taxi Girls #4: Daughter Of
Lust / 1994 / CA / M
FREDDIE SUMMERS
The Big Stick-Up / 1994 / WV / M
FREDDY KOHN *see Star Index I*
FREDDY STONE *see Star Index I*
FREDERIC
HomeGrown Video #466: Loot The Booty /
1996 / HOV / M
FREDERIC FOSTER
Beauty / 1981 / VC / M • Heaven's Touch /
1983 / CA / M • Pandora's Mirror / 1981 /
CA / M • Roommates / 1982 / VXP / M
FREDERIKA
Queens From Outer Space / 1993 / HSV /
G • She's The Boss / 1993 / RII / G
FREDERIQUE
Magma: Dirty Twins / 1994 / MET / M •
Magma: Live And Learn / 1995 / MET / M •
Magma: Nymphettes / 1993 / MET / M
FREDERIQUE BARRAI *see Star Index I*
FREDERIQUE SOUCHIER
Body Love / 1976 / CA / M
FREDRIC CARTON *see Star Index I*
FREE SAMPLES
Blue Vanities #514 / 1992 / FFL / M
FREEDOM
Canadian Beaver Hunt #3 / 1996 / PL / M •
Venus' Playhouse / 1994 / VDL / S •
World's Best Exotic Dancers #2 / 1995 /
PME / S
FRENCH MAID
Spanking Scenes #04 / cr80 / TAO / C
FRENCHI *see Star Index I*
FRENCHIE *see Star Index I*
FRENCHIE DEMAIN
Blue Vanities #552 / 1994 / FFL / M
FRENCHIE DIOR *see Star Index I*
FRENCHY
Intense Perversions #2 / 1996 / PL / M
FRENCHY (ANTOINE) *see Antoine*
FRICK *see Star Index I*
FRIDAY JONES *see Star Index I*

FRIDOLIN RING
Ass Attack / 1995 / PL / M
FRITZ KING
Frank Henenlotter's XXX Hardcore Horrors: Mad Love... / 1996 / SOW / M • The Mad Love Of The Red Hot Vampire / 1971 / SOW / M
FRITZ SOUTAG
Sex Dreams / 1995 / C69 / M
FRITZI ROSS see Star Index I
FUDGEE
Dirty & Kinky Mature Women #06 / 1995 / C69 / M
FUKUJI HASHIMOTO
Jacuzzi Lust / 1996 / AVE / M
FULIN
[No More Dirty Deals / 1994 / V-I / S
FUMIHIKO FUJIMOTO
Sexually Yours / 1996 / AVE / M
FUSAKO see Satomi Suzuki
FUSOKO see Satomi Suzuki
FX see Antoine
G SALE
Latin Plump Humpers #3 / 1995 / TTV / M • Salsa & Spice #1 / 1995 / TTV / M
G-DOG
Gangbang Girl #14 / 1994 / ANA / M
G-FANG
Women Of Color #2 / 1994 / ANA / M
G. COLE
Blue Vanities #516 / 1992 / FFL / M
G. HARRISON MARKS
Blue Vanities #581 / 1996 / FFL / M • Come Play With Me / 1977 / ... / S • Stinging Stewardesses / 1996 / BIZ / B
G. MONEY
Young Sluts In Heat #1 / 1996 / PL / M
G.G. PALMA
Visions / 1977 / QX / M
G.I. CANN
Meatball / 1972 / VCX / M
G.O. WEFUNK
The Hustler / 1989 / CDI / M
GABBY
Amateur Nights #15 / 1997 / HO / M • Amateur Nights #16 / 1997 / HO / M
GABCIA
Blue Vanities #500 / 1992 / FFL / M
GABI
Voluptuous #5 / 1996 / H&S / M
GABOR see Star Index I
GABRELLA
European Sex TV / 1996 / EL / M
GABRIEL see Star Index I
GABRIEL (PORTUGAL) see Gabriella (Portugal)
GABRIEL DONALD see Star Index I
GABRIEL LEE
Mr. Blue / 1996 / JSP / G
GABRIEL PONTELLO (Gabrielle Pontello, Gabriel Ponti)
Backdoor Club / 1986 / CA / M • Backdoor Lust / 1987 / CV / C • Bedside Manor / 1986 / CA / M • The Big Orgy / cr81 / VD / M • Blondes Like It Hot / 1984 / ELH / M • Breaking And Entering / 1984 / CA / M • Burning Snow / 1984 / CA / M • Call Girl / 1984 / CV / M • The Comeback Of Marilyn / 1986 / VC / M • Diamond Snatch / 1977 / COM / M • Double Desires / 1988 / PIN / C • Ebony Ecstacy / 1988 / HIO / C • Educating Tricia / 1984 / VD / M • Emmanuelle Goes To Cannes / 1984 / ECV / S • Erotic Intruders / 1985 / CA / M • For Love And Money / 1987 / CV / S • Foxy Lady #2 / 1986 / PL / M • Foxy Lady #3 / 1986 / PL /

M • French Postcard Girls / 1977 / VC / M • Girl With The Million $ Legs / 1987 / PL / M • Hot Bodies (Caballero) / 1984 / CA / M • Hot Close-Ups / 1985 / CA / M • Hot Desires / 1986 / VC / M • House Of 1001 Pleasures / 1985 / VC / M • Ladies Deluxe / 1978 / CON / M • Lusty Widow / 1987 / CA / M • Mimi / 1987 / CA / M • Mobile Home Girls / 1985 / VC / M • Mrs. Winter's Lover / 1984 / CA / M • Olinka, Goddess Of Love / 1987 / CA / C • Olinka, Grand Priestess Of Love / 1985 / CA / M • Only The Best From Europe / 1989 / CV / C • Passionate Pupil / 1986 / CA / M • Revolution / 1984 / CA / M • Shades Of Passion / 1985 / CA / M • Sharp Shooters / 1984 / CA / M • Spanish Fly / 1987 / CA / M • Sweet Dreams / 1978 / CON / M • Take My Body / 1984 / SE / M • A Taste Of Taija Rae / 1989 / PIN / C • Traci, I Love You / 1987 / CA / M • White Heat / 1981 / CA / M • Yacht Orgy / 1984 / CA / M • [Cathy, Fille Soumise / 1977 / ... / M
GABRIEL PONTI see Gabriel Pontello
GABRIELA
Skin #4: The 4th Rite / 1995 / ERQ / M
GABRIELA (PORTUGAL) see Gabriella (Portugal)
GABRIELLA (Jacqueline Roget, Gabrill)
Blonde, short hair, bit tits and a womanly body.
Beverly Hills Exposed / 1985 / SE / M • The Big Bang / 1988 / WET / M • Big, Bad & Beautiful / 1988 / MIR / C • Bootsie / 1984 / CC / M • The Butt Sisters Do The Twin Cities / 1996 / MID / M • Cowgirls / 1996 / GLI / M • Dangerous Women / 1987 / WET / M • Foot Mistress / 1986 / BIZ / B • Go For It / 1984 / VC / M • Gorgasm / 1992 / FTV / S • Hot Shorts: Gabriella / 1986 / VCR / C • Lifestyles Of The Blonde And Dirty / 1987 / WET / M • Lustfully Seeking Susan / 1985 / PLY / M • More Than A Handful #1 / 1985 / CV / C • Nudes At Eleven #2 / 1987 / AVC / M • Revenge By Lust / 1986 / VCR / M • Royally Flushed / 1987 / BIZ / B • Screen Play / 1984 / XTR / M • Secret Lessons #1 / 1986 / BIZ / B • Sensual Seduction / 1986 / LBO / M • Showdown / 1985 / BON / B • Soaking Wet / 1985 / CV / M • Sounds Of Sex / 1985 / CA / M • Student Fetish Videos: The Enema #16 / 1994 / PRE / B • Taste Of The Best #3 / 1988 / PIN / C • Tuff Stuff / 1987 / WET / M • Wild Toga Party / 1985 / VD / M • Yank My Doodle, It's A Dandy / 1985 / GOM / M
GABRIELLA (EARLY)
Blue Vanities #508 / 1992 / FFL / M
GABRIELLA (HUNG)
Buttwoman In Budapest / 1992 / EA / M • Never Say Never To Rocco Siffredi / 1995 / EA / M • Porno X-Treme #2: Club Bizarre / 1995 / SC / M • Porno X-Treme #4: Wet Dream / 1995 / SC / M • Private Gold #08: The Longest Night / 1996 / OD / M • Sirens / 1995 / GOU / M
GABRIELLA (OTHER)
Der Spritz-Treff / 1995 / KRM / M • Desert Island Buttwatch / 1996 / SUF / M • Global Girls / 1996 / GO / F • Philmore Butts Spring Break / 1996 / SUF / M
GABRIELLA (PORTUGAL) (Gabriel (Portugal), Gabriela (Portugal), Gabrielle (Portugal), Antoinette (Gabriel), Gabriella Solar)
Not too pretty girl with a swarthy skin and

black hair. Medium sized natural tits. 27 years old in 1993. She says she comes from Portugal hence the name to distinguish her from the mid-eighties girl.
Adventures Of The DP Boys: Berlin Butt Babes / 1993 / HW / M • Amateur Orgies #15 / 1992 / AFI / M • Amateur Orgies #19 / 1992 / AFI / M • Amateur Orgies #20 / 1992 / AFI / M • Amateur Orgies #24 / 1993 / AFI / M • Amateur Orgies #34 / 1993 / AFI / M • Amateur Orgies #36 / 1993 / AFI / M • America's Raunchiest Home Videos #22: City Lites / 1992 / ZA / M • America's Raunchiest Home Videos #49: Down In The Mouth / 1993 / ZA / M • American Garter / 1993 / VC / M • Anal Angel / 1994 / EX / M • Asian Angel / 1993 / VEX / C • Backing In #4 / 1993 / WV / C • Beach Bum Amateur's #16 / 1992 / MID / M • Beach Bunny / 1994 / V99 / M • Bend Over Backwards / 1993 / VIM / M • Big Murray's New-Cummers #03: Orgy 'Til Dawn / 1992 / FD / M • Big Murray's New-Cummers #04: Booty Love / 1992 / FD / M • Big Murray's New-Cummers #12: In The Pink / 1993 / FD / M • Big Murray's New-Cummers #19: The Ass Grabber / 1993 / FD / M • Bobby Hollander's Sweet Cheeks #104 / 1993 / QUA / M • The Breast Of Breastmen / 1995 / EVN / C • Breast Wishes #11 / 1993 / LBO / M • Breast Worx #40 / 1992 / LBO / M • Bring On The Night / 1994 / VEX / M • Burn It Up / 1994 / VEX / M • Butt Whore / 1994 / WIV / M • Cheap Shots / 1994 / PRE / B • Cream Pies #02 / 1993 / ZA / M • Creme De La Face #01 / 1994 / OD / M • Dickin' Around / 1994 / VEX / M • Dirty Blue Movies #04 / 1993 / JTV / F • Dirty Dating Service #05 / 1994 / WP / M • Dirty Deeds / 1992 / IF / M • Double D Dykes #14 / 1994 / GO / F • First Time Lesbians #03 / 1993 / JMP / F • Foot Hold / 1994 / PRE / B • Frathouse Sexcapades / 1993 / SFP / M • Gang Bang In Vedova / 1995 / WIV / M • Gazongas #04 / 1993 / LEI / C • Glitz Tits #04 / 1992 / GLI / M • Glitz Tits #05 / 1993 / GLI / M • Happy Ass Lesbians / 1994 / ROB / F • Harry Horndog #12: Harry's Xmas Party / 1992 / ZA / M • Harry Horndog #13: Anal Lovers #2 / 1992 / ZA / M • Hispanic Orgies #01 / 1993 / GO / M • Hispanic Orgies #07 / 1994 / GO / M • Hollywood Swingers #03 / 1992 / LBO / M • Home Nurses Anal Adventure / 1994 / LBO / M • Hometown Honeys #4 / 1993 / VEX / M • Hometown Honeys #5 / 1993 / VEX / M • Horny Henry's Oriental Adventure / 1994 / TTV / M • Hose Jobs / 1995 / VEX / M • Hot Blooded / 1994 / ERA / M • Hot Chicks Do L.A. / 1994 / EVN / F • House Of Spartacus #1 / 1993 / IF / M • House Of Spartacus #2 / 1993 / IF / M • How To Make A Model #03: Sunshine & Melons / 1994 / QUA / M • I Dream Of Tiffany / 1993 / IF / M • Incocknito / 1993 / VIM / M • Knockout / 1994 / VEX / M • Lesbian Bitches #1 / 1994 / ROB / F • Lovin' Every Minute Of It / 1994 / VEX / C • Mainstream / 1993 / PRE / B • Midnight Angels #01 / 1993 / MID / F • Midnight Angels #02 / 1993 / MID / F • Moon Godesses #2 / 1993 / VIM / M • Much More Than A Mouthful #4 / 1994 / VEX / M • Naughty Gabrielle / 1993 / VER / B • Nothing Else Matters / 1992 / V99 / C • The Nurses Are Cumming #1 / 1996 /

LBO / C • Nympho Zombie Coeds / 1993 / VIM / M • Odyssey 30 Min: #235: / 1992 / OD / M • Odyssey Triple Play #48: Rear End Reaming / 1993 / OD / M • One Lay At A Time / 1992 / V99 / M • One Of A Kind / 1992 / VEX / M • One Of Our Porn Stars Is Missing / 1993 / OD / M • Organic Facials / cr91 / GLI / M • Oriental Girls In Heat / 1995 / IF / M • Pearl Necklace: Thee Bush League: The Best Of Oral #01 / 1993 / SEE / C • Pleasure Chest / 1993 / IF / M • Pop-Porn: Safari Club / 1992 / 4P / M • Private Request / 1994 / GLI / M • Raw Talent: Deep Inside Gabriella's Ass (#4) / 1993 / FH / M • Ready And Willing / 1993 / VEX / M • Rears In Windows / 1993 / FH / M • Reel People #04 / 1994 / PP / M • A Scent Of Leather / 1992 / IF / M • Secret Admirer / 1992 / VEX / M • Seeing Red / 1993 / VI / M • Sex Drive / 1993 / VEX / M • Six Plus One #1 / 1993 / VEX / M • Smokin' Buns / 1993 / PRE / B • Strange Passions / 1993 / BS / B • Student Fetish Videos: Best of Enema #03 / 1994 / PRE / C • Student Fetish Videos: Catfighting #12 / 1994 / PRE / B • Student Fetish Videos: The Enema #13 / 1994 / PRE / B • Student Fetish Videos: Tickling #08 / 1994 / SFV / B • Sunset Rides Again / 1995 / VC / M • SVE: Going Solo / 1992 / SVE / F • Tail Taggers #116 / 1993 / WV / M • This Could Be The Night / 1993 / IF / M • Tip Tap Toe / 1995 / FC / M • Titties 'n Cream #2 / 1995 / FC / M • Toe Biz / 1993 / PRE / S • Twice As Hard / 1992 / IF / M • Ultimate Orgy #1 / 1992 / GLI / M • Uncle Roy's Amateur Home Video #16 / 1992 / VIM / M • Under The Pink / 1994 / ROB / F • Undercover Lover / 1992 / CV / M • Video Virgins #01 / 1992 / NS / M • Welcome To Bondage: Gabrill / 1993 / BON / B • Wendy Whoppers: Prison Love Doll / 1994 / PEP / M • Wet Memories / 1993 / WV / M • Wet, Wild And Willing / 1993 / V99 / M • Wicked Thoughts / 1992 / PL / M • Wild Dreams / 1995 / V99 / M • Wild Thing / 1994 / IF / M

GABRIELLA BLIQ
Private Gold #05: Cape Town #1 / 1996 / OD / M • Private Gold #09: Cape Town #2 / 1996 / OD / M • Triple X Video Magazine #12 / 1996 / OD / M • Triple X Video Magazine #15 / 1996 / OD / M

GABRIELLA DARI *see* **Angelica Bella**

GABRIELLA GOTTI
Anal Academy / 1996 / ZA / M • Anal Virgins #02 / 1996 / NS / M • Broken Vows / 1996 / ULP / M • Buffy Malibu's Nasty Girls #11 / 1996 / ANA / F • Butt Row Unplugged / 1996 / ABS / M • Buttman In The Crack / 1996 / EA / M • Cheap Tricks #1 / 1996 / PAV / M • Latin Fever #3 / 1996 / C69 / M • Nasty Nymphos #14 / 1996 / ANA / M • Philmore Butts All American Butt Search / 1996 / SUF / M • Profiles #08: Triple Ecstacy / 1996 / XPR / M • Tampa Spice / 1996 / SUF / M • Tight Spot / 1996 / WV / M • Video Virgins #29 / 1996 / NS / M • Wicked Fantasies / 1996 / CO2 / M

GABRIELLA SOLAR *see* **Gabriella (Portugal)**

GABRIELLE
Bone Alone / 1993 / MID / M • Bright Tails #2 / 1994 / STP / B • Kinky Cameraman #1 / 1996 / LEI / C • Neighbor Girls T77 / 1994 / NEI / F • Never Say No / 1983 / … / M • Pearl Necklace: Thee Bush League #03 /

1992 / SEE / M • Student Fetish Videos: Best of Catfighting #03 / 1995 / PRE / C • Student Fetish Videos: Spanking #16 / 1994 / PRE / B • Uncle Roy's Amateur Home Video #17 / 1993 / VIM / M • Up And Cummers #24 / 1995 / 4P / M

GABRIELLE (BLACK)
African Angels #3 / 1996 / NIT / M • Creme De La Face #16: Ladies Licking / 1996 / OD / M • The Sodomizer #5: Destination Moon / 1996 / SC / M

GABRIELLE (PORTUGAL) *see* **Gabriella (Portugal)**

GABRIELLE (ZUMIRA) *see* **Zumira**

GABRIELLE BEHAR *see* **Chrissy Beauchamp**

GABRIELLE MOLORE
European Sex Vacation / 1986 / VC / M

GABRIELLE MONIQUE
Teenage Playmates / 1979 / LOV / M

GABRIELLE PONTELLO *see* **Gabriel Pontello**

GABRIELLE SCREAM *(Cathleen Raymond)*
Lady Love / 1996 / ODI / F • The Pamela Principle #2: Seduce Me / 1994 / IMP / S • Penthouse: 25th Anniversary Swimsuit Video / 1994 / A*V / F • Penthouse: Pet Rocks / 1995 / PET / S • Perfect Gift / 1994 / BRI / S • Private Film #27 / 1995 / OD / M • Private Film #28 / 1995 / OD / M • Triple X Video Magazine #02 / 1995 / OD / M • Triple X Video Magazine #03 / 1995 / OD / M • Triple X Video Magazine #04 / 1995 / OD / M • Triple X Video Magazine #07 / 1995 / OD / M

GABRIELLE ST JAMES *see* **Star Index I**

GABRILL *see* **Gabriella**

GABY
Miss Anal #3 / 1995 / C69 / M • Triple X Video Magazine #11 / 1995 / OD / M

GABY B.
Private Gold #09: Private Dancer / 1996 / OD / M

GABY HILLER *see* **Star Index I**

GAEL
Anabolic Import #07: Anal X / 1995 / ANA / M

GAEL DIIULA
Thundercrack! / 1974 / LUM / M

GAELLE PERRERA *see* **Star Index I**

GAETAN
The French Canal / 1995 / DVP / G

GAGIT
Blue Vanities #555 / 1994 / FFL / M

GAIL
Blue Vanities #532 / 1993 / FFL / M • The Girls Of Malibu / 1986 / ACV / S • Homegrown Video #402 / 1993 / HOV / M • Mondo Extreme / 1996 / SHS / M • Wrasslin She-Babes #09 / 1996 / SOW / M

GAIL (ZUMIRA) *see* **Zumira**

GAIL ALLISON *see* **Star Index I**

GAIL ANDRE
Two At Once / 1978 / CV / M

GAIL BARIHART *see* **Star Index I**

GAIL FORCE *(Gail Storm, Gale Force, Heidi (Gail Force))*
Pretty with a very nice smile but droopy small to medium tits. Seemed to have a very nice personality. Later got a bit harder, had her tits done and married director Jim Powers. Gail Storm is from **Black To The Future**.
Amateur Lesbians #09: Meschel / 1991 / GO / F • Amateur Lesbians #10: Stephanie / 1991 / GO / F • Amateur Lesbians #15:

Courtney / 1991 / GO / F • Amateur Lesbians #16: Lorraine / 1991 / GO / F • Amateur Lesbians #18: Jamie / 1992 / GO / F • Amateur Lesbians #20: Flame / 1992 / GO / F • Amateur Lesbians #39: Tiffany / 1993 / GO / F • The Amateurs / 1984 / VCX / M • Amateurs Exposed #02 / 1993 / CV / M • Amber Lynn: She's Back / 1995 / TTV / C • Army Brat #1 / 1987 / VI / M • B.Y.O.B. / 1984 / VD / M • Backdoor Black #1 / 1992 / WV / C • The Bare-Assed Naked Gun / 1992 / MID / M • Bazooka County #4 / 1992 / CC / M • Beach Bum Amateur's #01 / 1992 / MID / M • Beach Bum Amateur's #02 / 1992 / MID / M • Black Angel / 1987 / CC / M • Black Encounters / 1992 / ZA / M • Black Rage / 1988 / ZA / M • Black To The Future / 1986 / VD / M • Blow Job Babes / 1988 / BEV / C • Blue Angel / 1991 / SE / M • Blue Angel / 1992 / AFV / M • Born To Be Wild / 1987 / SE / M • Bringing Up Brat / 1987 / VI / M • Broadcast Nudes / 1988 / EVN / M • Bubble Butts #12 / 1992 / LBO / M • Butt's Up, Doc #2 / 1992 / GO / M • Cabaret Sin / 1987 / IN / M • California Cherries / 1987 / EVN / M • Campfire Girls / 1988 / SE / M • Caught In The Middle / 1985 / CDI / M • Charmed Forces / 1987 / VI / M • Come As You Are / 1985 / SUV / M • Debbie Does Dallas #4 / 1988 / VEX / M • Debbie Does The Devil In Dallas / 1987 / SE / M • Decadent / 1991 / WV / M • Deep Inside Dirty Debutantes #05 / 1993 / 4P / M • Dirty Prancing / 1987 / EVN / M • Don't Tell Daddy #1 / 1985 / PL / C • Double Black Fantasy / 1987 / CC / C • The Ebony Garden / 1988 / ZA / M • Erectnophobia #2 / 1992 / MID / M • The Erotic Adventures Of Fanny Annie / 1991 / WV / M • Erotic Dreams / 1987 / HO / M • Erotic Therapy / 1987 / CDI / M • Fast Girls #1 / 1987 / GBX / M • Firm / 1993 / MID / M • Fun In The Sun / 1988 / EVN / C • Future Voyeur / 1985 / SUV / M • The Gentlemen's Club / 1986 / WV / M • Ginger Snaps / 1987 / VI / M • Girls Gone Bad #3: Back To The Slammer / 1991 / GO / F • Girls Gone Bad #5: Jailhouse Justice / 1991 / GO / F • Girls Like Us / cr88 / IN / C • Gold Diggers / 1993 / IN / M • The Great Sex Contest #1 / 1988 / LV / M • Hard As A Rock / 1992 / ZA / M • Having It All / 1985 / IN / M • The Hills Have Thighs / 1992 / MID / C • Hollywood Harlots / 1986 / VEX / C • Hot Black Moon Rising Forever / 1988 / ZA / M • The Huntress / 1987 / IN / M • Hyapatia Lee's Arcade Series #01 / 1988 / ZA / C • Hyapatia Lee's Arcade Series #02 / 1988 / ZA / C • I'm Too Sexy / 1992 / CA / M • Imaginary Lovers / 1986 / ME / M • In Your Face #2 / 1992 / PL / M • Inner Pink #1 / 1988 / LIP / F • Joanna's Dreams / 1988 / SEV / M • The Joy Of Sec's / 1989 / VEX / M • Kiss My Asp / 1989 / EXH / M • Kitty Kat Club / 1994 / SC / F • Knights In White Satin / 1987 / SUV / C • Ladies Lovin' Ladies #2 / 1992 / AR / F • Laguna Nights / 1995 / FH / M • Lesbian Love Connection / 1992 / LIP / F • Lesbian Pros And Amateurs #11 / 1992 / GO / F • Let's Get It On With Amber Lynn / 1986 / VC / M • Let's Get Wet / 1987 / WV / M • Let's Talk Dirty / 1987 / SE / M • Like A Virgin #1 / 1985 / AT / M • Lip Service / 1988 / LV / C • The Load Warriors #1 / 1987 / VD / M • Lost Innocence / 1988 / PV / M • Love Bites / 1985 / CA / M • Love Hurts / 1992 / VD / M • The Love Scene / 1985 / CDI / M • Lovin' USA / 1989 / EXH / C • Loving Spoonfulls / 1987 / 4P / C • Lust American Style / 1985 / WV / M • Lust In Bloom / 1988 / LV / M • Make My Night / 1985 / CIN / M • Manwiched / 1992 / FPI / M • Masquerade (1992-Usa) / 1992 / SC / M • The Million Dollar Screw / 1987 / VT / M • Mocha Magic / 1992 / FH / M • Muff 'n' Jeff / 1992 / ZA / M • Naughty Nymphs / 1986 / VEX / M • Naughty Nymphs / 1991 / VEX / C • Night Moods / 1985 / AVC / M • No One To Love / 1987 / PP / M • Oral Majority #04 / 1987 / WV / C • Oreo A Go-Go #2 / 1992 / FH / M • Orgies / 1987 / WV / C • Parliament: Three Way Lust / 1988 / PM / M • Perfection / 1985 / VD / M • Phone Sex Girls #1 / 1987 / VT / M • Pleasure Principle / 1988 / VEX / M • Pornographic Priestess / 1992 / CA / M • Professor Sticky's Anatomy 3X #02 / 1992 / FC / M • Put It In Gere / 1991 / CA / M • Puttin' Out / 1992 / VD / M • Rocco Unleashed / 1994 / SC / M • Schoolgirl By Day / 1985 / LA / M • Sex 5th Avenue / 1985 / WV / M • Sex Contest / 1988 / LV / M • The Sex Game / 1987 / SE / C • Sex Sting / 1992 / FD / M • Sleeping With Everybody / 1992 / MID / C • Sorority Pink #3 / 1992 / SP / M • Sound F/X / 1989 / V99 / M • Splash Dance / 1987 / AR / M • Starlets / 1988 / 4P / M • Starr / 1991 / CA / M • Starship Intercourse / 1987 / DR / M • Sugarpussy Jeans / 1986 / TEM / M • Sun Bunnies #2: The Pink Cheek Tales / 1992 / SC / M • Sweet Poison / 1991 / CDI / M • Sweet Tricks / 1987 / TEM / M • Switch Hitters #2: Swinging Both Ways / 1987 / IN / G • A Taste Of Tawnee / 1988 / LV / C • Tasty / 1985 / CA / M • Three By Three / 1989 / LV / C • Torrid Zone / 1987 / MIR / M • The Touchables / 1988 / CC / M • Two Into One #1 / 1988 / PIN / C • Vampirass / 1992 / VC / M • Vanity / 1992 / HO / M • Virgin Heat / 1986 / TEM / M • Virgin Spring / 1991 / FAZ / M • West Coast Girls / 19?? / ... / C • What Kind Of Girls Do You Think We Are? / 1986 / VEX / M • What Kind of Girls Do You Think We Are? / 1991 / VEX / C • White Trash, Black Splash / 1988 / WET / M • Wicked Thoughts / 1991 / AFV / M • Wild Hearts / 1992 / SC / M • Wild In The Wilderness / 1988 / SE / M • Willing Women / 1993 / VD / C • Woman To Woman / 1989 / ZA / C • X Factor: The Next Generation / 1991 / HO / M • X-Rated Blondes / 1992 / VD / C • X-Rated Bloopers #1 / 1984 / AR / M • X-Rated Bloopers #2 / 1986 / AR / M • XXX Workout / 1987 / VEX / M • [Total Eclipse Of The Moon / 1987 / ... / M

GAIL GARDEN *see Star Index I*

GAIL HARRIS *(Robyn Harris, Gail Thackray, Robin Harris)*
Angel #3: The Final Chapter / 1988 / NWW / S • Bottom Busters / 1973 / BLT / M • In Search Of The Perfect 10 / 1987 / MAE / S • Masseuse / 1996 / TRI / S • Nudity Required / 1989 / AE / S • Party Favors / 1989 / VES / S • Sins Of Desire / 1993 / C3S / S • Sorority House Massacre #2: Nighty Nightmare / 1990 / WAR / S • Takin' It All Off / 1987 / VES / S

GAIL LAWRENCE *see Abigail Clayton*

GAIL MEYER

Penetration #1 / 1984 / AVC / M

GAIL PALMER
The Erotic Adventures Of Candy / 1978 / VCX / M • The Italian Stallion / 1970 / ELH / S • Prisoner Of Paradise / 1980 / VCX / M • Shape Up For Sensational Sex / 1985 / SE / M

GAIL PARKER
The Stimulators / 1983 / VC / M

GAIL SCOTT *see Star Index I*

GAIL STARBRIGHT
Magma: Showtime Cunts / 1994 / MET / M

GAIL STERLING *(Gayle Sterling)*
Adultery / 1986 / DR / M • Anal Annie And The Magic Dildo / 1984 / LIP / F • And I Do Windows Too / 1986 / PP / M • The Art Of Passion / 1987 / CA / M • Bare Waves / 1986 / VD / M • Battle Of The Stars #2: East Versus West / 1985 / NSV / M • Battle Of The Stars #3: Stud Wars / 1985 / NSV / M • Blacks & Blondes #09 / 1986 / WV / M • Blacks & Blondes #14 / 1986 / WV / M • Carnal Olympics / 1983 / CA / M • Chocolate Chips / 1987 / VD / M • Chocolate Cream / 1984 / SUP / M • The Chocolate Fudge Factory / 1987 / PIN / M • Club Sex / 1989 / GO / M • Cream Puff / 1986 / VSE / M • Dangerous Desire / 1986 / NSV / M • Dark Angel / 1983 / VC / M • Deviled X / 1987 / 4P / M • The Erotic Adventures Of Bonnie & Clyde / 1988 / GO / M • First Time Lesbians (Gourmet) / 1987 / GO / F • For The Fun Of It / 1986 / SEV / M • The Fun House / 1988 / SEV / C • Future Sex / 1984 / NSV / M • The Greatest American Blonde / 1987 / WV / C • Grind / 1988 / CV / M • Heaven's Touch / 1983 / CA / M • Hitler Sucks / 1988 / GO / M • Hot Close-Ups / 1984 / WV / M • Hot Rocks / 1986 / WET / M • The House Of Strange Desires / 1985 / NSV / M • Irresistible #1 / 1982 / SE / M • Joanna's Dreams / 1988 / SEV / M • L.A. Raw / 1986 / SE / M • The Legend Of King Karl / 1986 / AR / M • Lesbian Lovers / 1988 / GO / F • A Lover For Susan / 1987 / CLV / M • Lust Inferno / 1982 / CA / M • Mouthwatering / 1986 / BRA / M • Nasty / 1985 / NSV / M • Nightlife / 1983 / CA / M • Oral Majority Black #1 / 1987 / WV / C • Passions / 1985 / MIT / M • Playmate #01 / 1984 / VC / M • Pretty Girl / 1984 / VIS / M • Private Encounters / 1987 / SE / M • The PTX Club / 1988 / GO / M • Rebecca's / 1983 / AVC / M • Red Hot Pepper / 1986 / V99 / M • Reel People #01 / 1983 / AR / M • Seduction By Fire / 1987 / VD / M • Sensual Seduction / 1986 / LBO / M • The Sex Dancer / 1986 / NSV / M • Sex Wars / 1984 / EXF / M • The Sleazy Detective / 1988 / VD / M • Spectators / 1984 / AVC / M • Spitfire / 1984 / COM / M • Starship Intercourse / 1987 / DR / M • Suzie Superstar #1 / 1983 / CV / M • Unnatural Phenomenon #1 / 1985 / WV / M • Unnatural Phenomenon #2 / 1986 / WV / M • Videobone / 1988 / WET / M • Wet 'n' Bare With Barbara Dare / 1988 / NEO / C

GAIL STEWART
Open Lips / 1983 / AVO / M

GAIL STORM *see Gail Force*

GAIL SUTRO *see Gina Gianetti*

GAIL THACKRAY *see Gail Harris*

GAIL TOWER
Tongue Of Velvet / 1985 / VCR / M

GAIL WEZKE *see Abigail Clayton*

GAILENE

Blue Vanities #528 / 1993 / FFL / M • Blue Vanities #557 / 1994 / FFL / M

GALATEA
Bound To Pay / 1995 / CS / B • Creme De La Face #04 / 1994 / OD / M • Lusty Lawyers / 1995 / PRK / M • Nasty Newcummers #06 / 1995 / MET / M • Pussy Hunt #09 / 1995 / LEI / M • Wet & Wicked / 1995 / PRK / M

GALAXY
Blue Balls / 1995 / VEX / C • Butt Hunt #09 / 1995 / LEI / M • Butt Pumpers / 1995 / FH / M • Pussy Hunt #11 / 1995 / LEI / M

GALE ANN *see Star Index I*

GALE FORCE *see Gail Force*

GALE WYNAN *see Star Index I*

GAN *see Star Index I*

GARDINA
Aged To Perfection #2 / 1995 / TTV / M • Butt Bangers Ball #1 / 1996 / TTV / M • Golden Oldies #1 / 1995 / TTV / M

GAREE TIGRAM
Tongue Of Velvet / 1985 / VCR / M

GARET ADKINS *see Sasha Gabor*

GARNET
Blue Vanities #547 / 1994 / FFL / M

GARRY VEE *see Star Index I*

GARTH PALMER
Angel Buns / 1981 / QX / M

GARY
Ancient Secrets Of Sexual Ecstasy / 1996 / HIG / M • Dangerous / 1996 / SNA / M • Horny For Anal / 1995 / TIE / M • Pearl Necklace: Thee Bush League #17 / 1993 / SEE / M • Primal Instinct / 1996 / SNA / M • Sharon Mitchell's Sex Clinic #02 / 1993 / FC / M • Tail Of The Scorpion / 1990 / ELP / M

GARY ALVARADO *see Star Index I*

GARY ANDERSON
Heat Of The Moment / 1983 / S&L / M

GARY AUSTIN *see Gerry Austin*

GARY BARKER *see Star Index I*

GARY BARON
Screwples / 1979 / CA / M • Serena, An Adult Fairy Tale / 1979 / VEN / M

GARY BLUSTONE *see Star Index I*

GARY BURBANK
The Sexaholic / 1988 / VC / M

GARY CONWAY *see Star Index I*

GARY COOK
Teenage Pajama Party / 1977 / VC / M

GARY DANA
On White Satin / 1980 / VCX / M • Sadie / 1980 / EVI / M • Yank My Doodle, It's A Dandy / 1985 / GOM / M

GARY DANE
Carnal Garden / 1996 / KLP / M

GARY DAVIS *see Star Index I*

GARY DEAN *see Star Index I*

GARY EVERHART
Las Vegas Lady / 1981 / VCX / M • Taboo #01 / 1980 / VCX / M

GARY GOODMAN *see Star Index I*

GARY GRAVER *see Robert McCallum*

GARY GRIMES
Candy Goes To Hollywood / 1979 / VCX / M

GARY JAMES *see Star Index I*

GARY LINDEN *see Star Index I*

GARY MARION *see Star Index I*

GARY RAY
Hardcore: The Films Of Richard Kern #1 / 1991 / FTV / M

GARY ROBERTS *see Star Index I*

GARY SHEENE

B.Y.O.B. / 1984 / VD / M • Charming Cheapies #2: No Holes Barred / 1985 / 4P / M

GARY SIKES *see* **Craig Roberts**

GARY VANN *(Dirty Gary)*
Is this the same as Gary Barker in **Dangerous Women**? The Big Bang / 1988 / WET / M • Born For Porn / 1989 / FAZ / M • Dangerous Women / 1987 / WET / M • The Divorce / 1986 / VC / G • Fantasy Girls / 1988 / CA / M • Head Nurse / 1990 / V99 / M • The House / cr86 / TEM / G • Lifestyles Of The Blonde And Dirty / 1987 / WET / M • The Scam / 1986 / TEM / G • Sensual Seduction / 1986 / LBO / M • Sex And The Single Girl / 1990 / FAN / M • Summer Dreams / 1990 / VEX / M • Tuff Stuff / 1987 / WET / M • The Wedding / 1986 / VC / M

GARY WATERS
Vagablonde / 1994 / VI / M

GARY WRIGHT
Bedtime Tales / 1985 / SE / M • Victims Of Love / 1975 / ALP / M

GATTA
Climax At The Melting Pot #1 / 1996 / AVS / M • Fresh Faces #01 / 1994 / EVN / M

GAVIN *see* **Star Index I**

GAVINO LEPRI
Love Slave / 1995 / WIV / M • Matrimony Intrigue / 1995 / WIV / M

GAYA
Sodomania #14: C**t Lickin', C*m Drinkin' Bitches / 1995 / EL / M • Sodomania: Slop Shots / 1996 / EL / C • World Sex Tour #2 / 1995 / ANA / M

GAYE GIBSON *see* **Star Index I**

GAYLE LEONARD *see* **Gloria Leonard**

GAYLE MICHELLE
27 in 1992 and looks it. Maried to Paul Cox who is the head of Total Video. Blonde with droopy tits and a small tattoo on her left chest.
Anal Squeeze / 1993 / FOR / M • Anniversary / 1992 / FOR / M • Babe Patrol / 1993 / FOR / M • Cumming Of Ass / 1995 / TP / M • Group Therapy / 1992 / TP / M • Hypnotic Passions / 1993 / FOR / M • Kinky R̲u̲m̲m̲a̲t̲e̲s̲ ̲/ 1992 / TP / M • L̲o̲o̲p̲h̲o̲l̲e̲s̲ ̲/ 1993 / TP / M • Odyssey Amateur #61: Gayle Loves Double Penetration / 1991 / OD / M • Odyssey Amateur #72: Three Cocks For Gayle / 1991 / OD / M • Prime Cuts #1 / 1994 / FOR / M • Prime Cuts #2 / 1994 / FOR / M • Surrogate Lover / 1992 / TP / M • SVE: Cheap Thrills #3: Self-Satisfaction / 1992 / SVE / F • Tight Ends In Motion / 1993 / TP / M • Total: Double Penetration / 1992 / TP / M • Total: Getting Stuck / 1992 / TP / M

GAYLE SCHAFFER
ABA: Double Feature #5 / 1996 / ALP / M • Night Of Submission / 1976 / BIZ / M

GAYLE STERLING *see* **Gail Sterling**

GAYLENE MARIE
Fever / 1982 / EVI / C • Greatest Cathouse In Las Vegas / 1983 / EVI / M • Interlude Of Lust / cr79 / HO / M • Marilyn Chambers' Private Fantasies #3 / 1983 / CA / M • The Younger The Better / 1982 / CA / M

GAZELLA SHELDON
Pink Champagne / 1979 / CV / M

GAZU
Triple X Video Magazine #09 / 1995 / OD / M

GEAN DAMAGE *see* **Lynx Cannon**

GEANNA FINE *see* **Jeanna Fine**

GEE WHIZ
Reel Classics #2 / 1996 / H&S / M

GELTER
Student Fetish Videos: Catfighting #13 / 1994 / PRE / B • Student Fetish Videos: The Enema #17 / 1995 / PRE / B • Student Fetish Videos: Foot Worship #13 / 1994 / PRE / B

GEMA (VALHALLA) *see* **Valhalla**

GEMA TALONS *see* **Valhalla**

GEMMA GIMENEZ
Body Love / 1976 / CA / M

GEN
Bun Busters #15 / 1994 / LBO / M • Hidden Camera #17 / 1994 / JMP / M

GEN X
Ona Zee's Learning The Ropes #09: The Training Continues / 1992 / ONA / B

GENA
Drastic Measures / 1996 / GOT / B

GENA LEE
Endless Lust / 1983 / VC / M • Little Girls Lost / 1982 / VC / M • A Little More Than Love / 1977 / SE / M • One Page Of Love / 1980 / VCX / M • Paul, Lisa And Caroline / 1976 / SE / M • The Psychiatrist / 1978 / VC / M • Ring Of Desire / 1981 / SE / M • Stephanie's Lust Story / 1983 / VC / M • A Very Small Case Of Rape / 1977 / TRP / M

GENAVIEVE LEFLEUR *see* **Genevieve LaFleur**

GENDER
Return Engagement / 1995 / VI / M • Striptease / 1995 / SPI / M

GENE
Fuckin' Reamin' Screamin' / 1995 / TIE / M

GENE BENSON *see* **Star Index I**

GENE CAGE
Diary Of A Bed / 1979 / HOE / M

GENE CARRERA (MALE) *see* **Star Index I**

GENE CARRIER
All The Action / 1980 / TVX / M • California Cowgirls / 1982 / CA / M • Heavenly Desire / 1979 / WV / M • Steamy Sirens / 1984 / AIR / C

GENE CLAYTON *see* **Star Index I**

GENE DAMAGE *see* **Lynx Cannon**

GENE DUQUENE
Bad Girls #1 / 1981 / GO / M

GENE GIANO *see* **Star Index I**

GENE LAMAR
Bi & Large / 1994 / STA / G • Goldilocks And The 3 Bi Bears / 1997 / TTV / G • Sinderella She-Males / 1994 / HEA / G

GENE MEDLIN
Hungry Eyed Woman / cr71 / VCX / M

GENE MILLER *see* **Star Index I**

GENE O'BRIAN *see* **Star Index I**

GENE POOL
The Big One / 1995 / HO / M

GENE POOLE
The Night Shift / 1995 / LE / M

GENE PRESTON *see* **Star Index I**

GENE ROSS
Editor at the industry advertising magazine.
Ace Mulholland / 1995 / ERA / M • Adult Video Nudes / 1993 / VC / M • Guilty By Seduction / 1993 / PI / M • One Of Our Porn Stars Is Missing / 1993 / OD / M • Pussyman #01: The Search / 1993 / CC / M • Pussyman #03: The Search Continues / 1993 / SNA / M • Sex Academy #1 / 1993 / ONA / M • Sodom & Gomorrah / 1992 / OD / M

GENEE
More Dirty Debutantes #64 / 1997 / SBV / M

GENERAL LEE
Devil In A Wet T-Shirt / 1995 / SPI / M • Foreskin Gump / 1994 / LE / M • Sex Circus / 1994 / VIM / M

GENEVA
Dungeon Of The Borgias / 1993 / HOM / B • Enemates #03 / 1991 / BIZ / B • Fbi In Search Of Bondage #1 / 1991 / BON / B • Gland Slam / 1995 / PRE / B • The Slaves Of Alexis Payne / 1995 / LON / B • Student Fetish Videos: Best Of Foot Worship #02 / 1994 / PRE / C • Student Fetish Videos: Catfighting #06 / 1992 / PRE / B • Toe Biz / 1993 / PRE / S • Transsexual Prostitutes #2 / 1997 / DFI / G • Women On Top / 1995 / BON / B

GENEVIEVE AUBORD *see* **Star Index I**

GENEVIEVE BOUVIER
Cheap Sluts And The Guys Who Fuck Them / 1994 / MET / M • Connie & Floyd / 1973 / SVE / M

GENEVIEVE LAFLEUR *(Genavieve Lefleur, Genivive Le Flur, Genevieve LaFlex)*
Slim girl who looks a bit like Valeria but is not the same. She has small tits, blue eyes, gray-blonde hair, and tight body. 19 years old in 1993 and was de-virginized at the age of 14.
America's Raunchiest Home Videos #78: Stairway To Anal / 1993 / ZA / M • Anal Vision #20 / 1993 / LBO / M • As Sweet As Can Be / 1993 / V99 / M • Beach Bum Amateur's #33 / 1993 / MID / M • Black Buttman #01 / 1993 / CC / M • Bobby Hollander's Maneaters #11 / 1994 / SFP / M • Bobby Hollander's Rookie Nookie #14 / 1993 / SFP / M • Bring On The Night / 1994 / VEX / M • Cream / 1993 / SC / M • Dr Fraud's Female Fantasies / 1993 / AM / M • High Heel Harlots #03 / 1994 / SFP / M • Much More Than A Mouthful #4 / 1994 / VEX / M • Nasty Nymphos #02 / 1994 / ANA / M • Pussy Posse / 1993 / CC / M • Pussy Tales / 1993 / SC / F • Raincoat Fantasies / 1993 / ELP / M • Raunchy Remedy / 1993 / ELP / M • Ron Hightower's White Chicks #04 / 1993 / LBO / M • Sex Drive / 1993 / VEX / M • Tales From The Clit / 1993 / OD / M • Video Virgins #06 / 1993 / NS / M

GENEVIEVE LAFLEX *see* **Genevieve LaFleur**

GENIE *see* **Star Index I**

GENIVIVE LE FLUR *see* **Genevieve LaFleur**

GENO *see* **Star Index I**

GENOA *see* **Star Index I**

GENOA STRANGELAND
Girlfriends / 1983 / MIT / M

GENTILE GYPSY *see* **Star Index I**

GENTLE GYPSY
The Payne Principle / 1995 / COC / B

GEOFF COLDWATER *(Jeff Coldwater, Davy Scarborough, Davy Scarbrough, Davy Scarboro, Davy Scarbough, Davy Scarborgh, Dave Scarborough)*
Curly haired male with a nipple ring in which he sometimes wears a whistle.
19 & Naughty #1 / 1994 / SKV / M • 19 & Naughty #2 / 1995 / SKV / M • Adventures Of The DP Boys: At The French Riviera / 1994 / HW / M • Adventures Of The DP

Boys: Janet And Da Boyz / 1994 / HW / M • Backdoor To Paradise / 1990 / ELV / M • The Big Bang #2 / 1994 / LV / M • Big Murray's New-Cummers #06: Men & Women / 1993 / FD / M • The Big Winner #1 / 1991 / CDP / B • Black Babes In Heat / 1993 / VIM / M • Black Beauties #1 / 1992 / VIM / M • Black Beauties #2 / 1992 / VIM / M • Black Fantasies #14 / 1996 / HW / M • Black Fire / 1993 / VIM / M • Black Gangbangers #02 / 1995 / HW / M • Black Jack City #2: Black's Revenge / 1992 / HW / M • Black Magic #1 / 1993 / VIM / M • Blue Moon / 1992 / AFV / M • The Bold, The Bald & The Beautiful / 1993 / VIM / M • Boobytrap...The Next Generation / 1992 / HW / M • Buttwiser / 1992 / HW / M • Byron Long At Large / 1995 / VC / M • Cannes Heat / 1992 / FD / M • The Cannes Sex Fest / 1992 / SFP / M • Chocolate Bunnies #02 / 1995 / LBO / C • Colossal Orgy #1 / 1993 / HW / M • Colossal Orgy #3 / 1994 / HW / M • Cousin Bubba Country Corn Porn #02 / 1994 / VIM / M • Dangerous Behinds #1 / 1995 / HW / M • Dark Passions #01 / 1993 / AFV / M • Dark Passions #02 / 1993 / AFV / M • Dirty Doc's Housecalls #06 / 1993 / LV / M • Dirty Doc's Housecalls #07 / 1994 / LV / M • Dirty Doc's Housecalls #10 / 1994 / LV / M • Dirty Doc's Housecalls #12 / 1994 / LV / M • Dreams Of Desires / 1995 / ONA / M • Dun-Hur #1 / 1994 / SC / M • Eternal Bliss / 1990 / AFV / M • Field Of Wet Dreams / 1992 / EVN / M • Filthy Sleazy Scoundrels / 1994 / HW / M • The Flirt / 1992 / EVN / M • Foxxxy Lady / 1992 / HW / M • From Japan With Love / 1990 / SLV / M • Gang Bang Bitches #02 / 1994 / PP / M • Gang Bang Bitches #03 / 1994 / PP / M • Gang Bang Diaries #3 / 1994 / SFP / M • The Go-Go Girls / 1994 / EVN / M • Hardcore Debutantes #01 / 1996 / TEP / M • Horny Henry's Swinging Adventures / 1994 / TTV / M • House Of Sex #04: Banging Menette / 1994 / RTP / M • Hush...My Mother Might Hear Us / 1993 / FL / M • Immorals #3: Stroked / 1991 / SC / M • Inner Blues / 1987 / VD / M • The Joy Dick Club / 1994 / MID / M • Kink #1 / 1995 / ROB / M • Kinky Debutante Interviews #05 / 1994 / IP / M • M Series #14 / 1993 / LBO / M • Maid Service / 1993 / FL / M • Main Course / 1992 / FL / M • Megasex / 1988 / EVN / M • Mr. Peepers Amateur Home Videos #13: Backdoor Doctor / 1991 / LBO / M • Mr. Peepers Amateur Home Videos #37: Stairway to Heaven / 1991 / LBO / M • Mr. Peepers Amateur Home Videos #39: Cumming In Colors / 1992 / LBO / M • Mr. Peepers Amateur Home Videos #43: Gym-Nastiness / 1992 / LBO / M • Mr. Peepers Amateur Home Videos #47: Sigma Cum Louder / 1992 / LBO / M • Mr. Peepers Amateur Home Videos #49: Up And Cumming #2 / 1992 / LBO / M • Neighborhood Watch #05 / 1991 / LBO / M • Neighborhood Watch #23: Sinsational Sex / 1992 / LBO / M • Neighborhood Watch #24: Nice Sticky Stuff / 1992 / LBO / M • Neighborhood Watch #26: / 1992 / LBO / M • Next Door Neighbors #10 / 1990 / BON / M • Nympho Zombie Coeds / 1993 / VIM / M • Oriental Gang Bang Fantasy / 1994 / FC / M • Oriental Sorority Secrets / 1992 / VIM / M • Our Bang #05 / 1992 / GLI / M • Over Forty

Gang Bang / 1994 / RTP / M • Pubic Eye / 1992 / HW / M • Pudsucker / 1994 / MID / M • Raunchy Porno Picture Show / 1992 / FC / M • Riviera Heat / 1993 / FD / M • Rump-Shaker #3 / 1994 / HW / M • Shaving Mr. One Eye / 1996 / FC / M • Sneek Peeks #1 / 1993 / FL / M • Sneek Peeks #2 / 1993 / OCV / M • So Bad / 1995 / VT / M • Steele Butt / 1993 / AFV / M • Stuff Your Face #2 / 1995 / JMP / M • Sweet Black Cherries #1 / 1996 / TTV / M • Toying Around / 1992 / FL / M • Ultimate Anal Gang Bang #3 / 1995 / HW / M • Wendy Is Watching / 1993 / ELP / M • Winter Heat / 1994 / MID / M • Women Who Love Men, Men Who Love Women / 1993 / FD / C • The Wright Stuff / 1991 / AFV / M

GEOFF CONRAD
Bottoms Up #04 / 1983 / AVC / C • Intimate Lessons / 1982 / VC / M

GEOFF GANN *see Karen Dior*

GEOFF REARDON
Telefantasy / 1978 / AR / M

GEOFF WAFT
Sex The Hard Way / 1985 / CV / M

GEOFFREY BIANCHI
Dirty Hairy's Back To Black / 1996 / GOT / M

GEOFFREY G. WRATH
Interracial Affairs / 1996 / FC / M

GEOFFREY PARKER
A Dirty Western #1 / 1973 / AR / M • Saturday Matinee Series #3 / 1996 / VCX / C

GEORG SCHIMANKI
Viola Video #101: Anal #7 / 1995 / PEV / M

GEORGE
Buttwoman In Budapest / 1992 / EA / M • The Girls Of Fantasex #1 / 1996 / NIT / M • Homegrown Video #418: Looks As Good As It Feels / 1994 / HOV / M • Lee Nover: The Search For The Perfect Butt / 1996 / IP / M • Lunch / 1972 / VC / M • Nasty Travel Tails #01 / 1993 / CC / M • Neighborhood Watch #40: / 1993 / LBO / M

GEORGE ALLEN *see Star Index I*

GEORGE APPLEGATE
Debutantes Discipline / Please Cane Me / 1993 / CS / B

GEORGE ARTHUR
MASH'ed / cr75 / ALP / M

GEORGE BARTIENEFF
Big Thumbs / 1978 / ... / M

GEORGE BEAUMONT *see Star Index I*

GEORGE BUNDY *see Star Index I*

GEORGE CHUMWAY
Overnight Sensation / 1976 / AR / M

GEORGE COX
Charming Cheapies #3: Day And Night / 1985 / 4P / M

GEORGE FLOWER *(Buck Flower, Buck Flowers, C.D. LaFleuer)*
Plays a character called Rex Boorski in **Video Vixens**.
Alice Goodbody / 1975 / MED / S • Below The Belt / 1971 / SOW / S • Candy Tangerine Man / 1975 / UNV / S • Cheerleader Camp / 1987 / PAR / S • Deep Jaws / 1976 / SOW / S • Delinquent School Girls / 1974 / NWW / S • The Dirty Mind Of Young Sally / 1973 / SOW / S • Do You Wanna Be Loved? / 1977 / AR / M • Drive-In Massacre / 1976 / WIZ / S • Ilsa, Keeper Of The Oil Sheik's Harem / 1975 / AME / S • Ilsa, She Wolf Of The SS / 1974 / VID / S • My Therapist / 1983 / MED / S • Norma Isn't Quite Normal / 1969 / SOW / S • Party

Favors / 1989 / VES / S • Playboy: Inside Out #2 / 1992 / PLA / S • Plughead Rewired: Circuitry Man #2 / 1993 / C3S / S • Sorority Babes In The Slimeball Bowl-O-Rama / 1988 / UCV / S • Summer Camp / 1980 / MED / S • Takin' It All Off / 1987 / VES / S • Touch Me / 1971 / SE / M • The Turn On / 1989 / NEH / S • Video Vixens / 1972 / VES / S • The Witch Who Came From The Sea / 1976 / UNV / S

GEORGE FRIDAY
Flesh Fever / 1978 / CV / M

GEORGE GUNN *see Star Index I*

GEORGE HAUCKS *see Star Index I*

GEORGE IRON
All American Super Bitches / 1984 / BIZ / B • Ebony Goddesses / 1985 / LON / B • Humiliating Bind / 1996 / STM / B • Kimbra's Wimps / 1995 / STM / B • Training Academy / 1984 / LA / B

GEORGE KAN *see Star Index I*

GEORGE KAPLAN *(Fozzi, Fozzie, Foz)*
Non-performing chubby male who, rumor has it, is or was a real actor in B movies before taking up doing bit parts and writing pornos.
Arizona Gold / 1996 / KLP / M • Body Language / 1995 / VI / M • Borderline (Vivid) / 1995 / VI / M • Cheap Shot / 1995 / WAV / M • Conquest / 1996 / WP / M • Cynthia And The Pocket Rocket / 1995 / CV / M • Entangled / 1996 / KLP / M • Forbidden Cravings / 1996 / VC / M • Gangbusters / 1995 / VC / M • Ghost Town / 1995 / WAV / M • Hillbilly Honeys / 1996 / WP / M • Jenteal Loves Rocco / 1996 / VI / M • Julia Ann: Superstar / 1995 / WAV / M • Lonely Hearts / 1995 / VC / M • Night Tales / 1996 / VC / M • Nightclub / 1996 / SC / M • Nothing Like A Dame #2 / 1995 / IN / M • Party House / 1995 / WAV / M • The Passion Potion / 1995 / WP / M • Return Engagement / 1995 / VI / M • Suggestive Behavior / 1996 / VI / M • Virtual Reality Sixty Nine / 1995 / WP / M

GEORGE KUCHAR
Thundercrack! / 1974 / LUM / M • [Sparkles Tavern / 1976 / ... / S

GEORGE LEE
Hellraiser #3: Hell On Earth / 1992 / PAR / S • Lust At First Bite / 1978 / VC / M

GEORGE LING
Chinese Blue / 1976 / ... / M

GEORGE MACELLARO
The Statesman's Wife / 1996 / PAL / M

GEORGE MARTIN
C.H.U.D. Cannibalistic Humanoid Underground Dwellers / 1983 / MED / S • Sexual Communication / 19?? / HIF / M

GEORGE MAXWELL
Nylon / 1995 / VI / M

GEORGE MITCHELL
Ultraflesh / 1980 / GO / M

GEORGE NEWHOUSE *see Star Index I*

GEORGE NIEVES *see Star Index I*

GEORGE O'HARA *see Star Index I*

GEORGE PAIN *see George Payne*

GEORGE PAYNE *(Mike Payne, George Pain, Sir George Payne, Master G.P.)*
Was 38 in 1989 and according to him first had sex at age 7 (!).
Afrodisiac #1 / 1987 / CC / M • Afternoon Delights / 1981 / CA / M • All About Gloria Leonard / 1978 / VXP / M • American Desire / 1981 / CA / M • Angel Buns / 1981 / QX / M • Angel In Distress / 1982 / AVO / B

• Aphrodesia's Diary / 1984 / CA / M • Auction #1 / 1992 / BIZ / B • Auction #2 / 1992 / BIZ / B • Babe / 1982 / AR / M • Backdoor Girls / 1983 / VCR / C • Beauty / 1981 / VC / M • Beauty And The Biker / 1993 / GOT / B • Black Angels / 1985 / VC / M • Black Girls In Heat / 1985 / PL / M • Black Sister, White Brother / 1987 / AT / M • Blonde Ambition / 1981 / QX / M • Blue Ecstasy / 1980 / CA / M • Blue Magic / 1981 / QX / M • Bon Appetit / 1980 / QX / M • Bunny's Office Fantasies / 1984 / VC / M • Burlexxx / 1984 / VC / M • Can't Get Enough / 1985 / CA / M • The Chamber Maids / 1993 / GOT / B • Cheap Thrills / 1984 / RLV / M • Cherry Cheesecake / 1984 / AR / M • Christine's Secret / 1986 / FEM / M • Classic Erotica Special / 1985 / SVE / M • Climax / 1985 / CA / M • Coming In Style / 1986 / CA / M • Corruption / 1983 / VC / M • Cover Girl Fantasies #1 / 1983 / VCR / C • Crack Up / 1994 / GOT / B • Creation Of Karen: Tormented & Transformed / 1993 / BIZ / B • Dallas School Girls / 1981 / VCX / M • Death Wish #1 / 1974 / MGM / S • Decadence / 1986 / VD / M • Delicious / 1981 / VXP / M • Devil In Miss Jones #2 / 1983 / VC / M • Diabolic Demands / 1992 / GOT / B • Dick Of Death / 1985 / VCR / M • Dirty Blonde / 1984 / VXP / M • Double Pleasure / 1985 / VCR / M • Dr Bizarro / 1978 / ALP / B • Driller / 1984 / VC / M • Eaten Alive / 1985 / VXP / M • The Erotic World Of Vanessa #1 / 1983 / VCR / C • The Erotic World Of Vanessa #2 / 1984 / VCR / C • Fashion Fantasies / 1986 / VC / M • Femme / 1984 / VC / M • The Filthy Rich / 1981 / CA / M • Firestorm #1 / 1984 / COM / M • First Time At Cherry High / 1984 / VC / M • Flash Pants / 1983 / VC / M • Forgive Me, I Have Sinned / 1982 / ALP / B • G-Strings / 1984 / COM / M • Girls That Talk Dirty / 1986 / VCS / C • Girls U.S.A. / 1980 / AIR / M • Goin' Down / 1985 / VC / M • Good Girl, Bad Girl / 1984 / SE / M • Great Sexpectations / 1984 / VC / M • Harem Girls / 1986 / SE / M • Head / 1985 / LA / M • Hostage Girls / 1984 / VC / [illegible] / 1984 / SE / M • Hot Rockers / 1985 / IVP / M • Hot Stuff / 1984 / VXP / M • Hot Wire / 1985 / VXP / M • Hypersexuals / 1984 / VC / M • Indiana Joan In The Black Hole Of Mammoo / 1984 / VC / M • The Initiation Of Cynthia / 1985 / VXP / M • Inside Everybody / 1984 / AVC / M • Inside Little Oral Annie / 1984 / VXP / M • Inside Seka / 1980 / VXP / M • Jack 'n' Jill #1 / 1979 / VXP / M • Jailhouse Girls / 1984 / VC / M • Kneel Before Me! / 1983 / ALP / B • Ladies Of The Knight / 1984 / GO / M • Lady Lust / 1984 / CA / M • The Latex Dungeon / 1992 / GOT / B • Lay Down And Deliver / 1989 / VWA / M • Long Hard Nights / 1984 / ELH / M • Maneaters / 1983 / VC / M • Manhattan Mistress / 1980 / VBM / M • Mascara / 1982 / CA / M • Masters Of Dominance / 1996 / GOT / C • Mistress Electra / 1983 / AVO / B • Murder By Sex / 1993 / LAP / M • Naughty Nurses / 1982 / VCR / M • Never Sleep Alone / 1984 / CA / M • New York Vice / 1984 / CC / M • Night Hunger / 1983 / AVC / M • The Nite Bird / 1978 / BL / M • The Nurses Are Coming / 1985 / VCR / C • October Silk / 1980 / COM / M • Only The Best #2 / 1989 / CV / C • Oriental Techniques Of Pain And Pleasure / 1983 / ALP / B • Pandora's Mirror / 1981 / CA / M • The Payoff / 1994 / GOT / B • Peepholes / 1982 / AVC / M • Phone Sex Fantasies / 1984 / QX / M • The Playgirl / 1982 / CA / M • Pleasure Channel / 1984 / VC / M • The Pleasures Of Innocence / 1985 / VC / M • Potpourri / 1981 / TGA / M • Prisoner Of Pleasure / 1981 / ALP / B • Public Affairs / 1984 / CA / M • Puss 'n' Boots / 1982 / VXP / M • Pussycat Galore / 1984 / VC / M • Rambone: The First Time / 1985 / JOH / M • Rearbusters / 1988 / LVI / C • Return To Alpha Blue / 1984 / AVC / M • Romancing The Bone / 1984 / VC / M • The Satisfiers Of Alpha Blue / 1980 / AVC / M • Scenes They Wouldn't Let Me Shoot / 1984 / VC / M • Scoundrels / 1982 / COM / M • Secluded Passion / 1983 / VHL / M • Sex Spa USA / 1984 / VC / M • Sex Stalker / 1983 / MPP / M • Sex Styles Of The Rich & Famous / 1986 / VXP / M • Sexcapades / 1983 / VC / M • Shacking Up / 1985 / VXP / M • Shauna: Every Man's Fantasy / 1985 / CA / C • Silky / 1980 / VXP / M • Sizzle / 1979 / QX / M • Snake Eyes #1 / 1984 / COM / M • The South Bronx Story / 1986 / CC / M • The Sperminator / 1985 / VXP / M • The Story Of Prunella / 1982 / AVO / M • Stray Cats / 1985 / VXP / M • Succulent / 1983 / VXP / M • Supergirls Do General Hospital / 1984 / VC / M • Supergirls Do The Navy / 1984 / VC / M • The T & A Team / 1984 / VC / M • The Tale Of Tiffany Lust / 1981 / CA / M • Tales Of The Bizarre / 1983 / ALP / B • The Taming Of Rebecca / 1982 / SVE / B • Thirst For Passion / 1988 / TRB / M • This Lady Is A Tramp / 1980 / CV / M • Throat...12 Years After / 1984 / VC / M • Tigresses...And Other Man-Eaters / 1979 / VXP / M • Tongue Twisters / 1986 / VXP / M • Transvestite Humiliation / 1992 / GOT / G • Triangle Of Lust / 1983 / VCR / M • TV Nurse / 1993 / GOT / G • Vanessa...Maid In Manhattan / 1984 / VC / M • Vas-O-Line Alley / 1985 / VC / M • Viva Vanessa The Undresser / 1984 / VC / M • The Voyeur / [illegible] / 1982 / VXP / M • Wet Dreams / 1980 / WWV / M • When She Was Bad / 1983 / CA / M • White Hot / 1984 / VXP / M • Women At Play / 1984 / SE / M • Young Nympho's / 1986 / VD / M • Young, Wild And Wonderful / 1980 / VCX / M • [The Gang's All Here / cr85 / STM / M

GEORGE RODRIGUEZ *see Star Index I*

GEORGE S. MCDONALD

Behind The Green Door #1 / 1972 / MIT / M • Blue Vanities #031 / 1988 / FFL / M • Easy Woman / 1980 / MIT / M • Flesh Factory / 1970 / AVC / M • Inside Marilyn Chambers / 1975 / MIT / M • Rabin's Revenge / 1971 / MIT / M • Rampaging Nurses / 1971 / MIT / M • Reckless Claudia / 1971 / MIT / M • School Girl / 1970 / ALP / M • Sodom & Gomorrah / 1974 / MIT / M • Wild Campus / 1970 / ... / M

GEORGE SAIBER

Anal Pow Wow / 1995 / XC / M • Angel's Vengeance / 1995 / VMX / M • Buttwoman Back In Budapest / 1993 / EL / M • Depravity On The Danube / 1993 / EL / M • Games Women Play / 1995 / XC / M • The Grind / 1995 / XC / M • Sluts 'n' Angels In Budapest / 1994 / EL / M

GEORGE SMITH

Ejacula #1 / 1992 / VC / M • Ejacula #2 / 1992 / VC / M

GEORGE SPELVIN

Oral Addiction / 1995 / VI / M

GEORGE SPELVIN (AS) *see* Anthony Spinelli

GEORGE SPENCER

If You Don't Stop It You'll Go Blind / 1977 / MED / S • Take Off / 1978 / VXP / M

GEORGE TORO *see Star Index I*

GEORGE WYLDE *see* Beau Michaels

GEORGE Z.

Private Gold #09: Private Dancer / 1996 / OD / M

GEORGES BLUE *see Star Index I*

GEORGES GUERRET *see Star Index I*

GEORGES MALU

Love Slaves / 1976 / VCR / M

GEORGETA

Kisses From Romania / 1995 / NIT / M

GEORGETTE

Alley Cats / 1995 / VC / M • A Shaver Among Us / 1992 / ZA / M • World Sex Tour #6 / 1996 / ANA / M • World Sex Tour #7 / 1996 / ANA / M

GEORGETTE JENNINGS

Bone Up My Hole / 1994 / MET / M • Saturday Night Special / 1980 / CV / M

GEORGETTE POPE

Have Blower Will Travel / 1975 / SOW / M

GEORGETTE SANDERS *(Michelle DuBois, Georgette Saunders)*

Michelle DuBois is from **Sweet Surrender**. Very pretty black haired girl with small tits, tight waist and nice smile. She has a hairy ass crack.

Babylon Pink #1 / 1979 / COM / M • Bad Penny / 1978 / QX / M • Debbie Does Dallas #1 / 1978 / VC / M • Dirty Susan / 1979 / CPL / M • Limited Edition #02 / 1979 / AVC / M • Lusty Ladies #03 / 1983 / SVE / M • Misbehavin' / 1979 / VXP / M • Sweet Surrender / 1980 / VCX / M • White Fire / 1980 / VC / M

GEORGETTE SAUNDERS *see* Georgette Sanders

GEORGETTE TEAPS

Most Valuable Slut / [illegible] / M

GEORGI

Der Mosen-Pflucker / 1995 / KRM / M

GEORGIA

Blue Vanities #512 / 1992 / FFL / M • Enemates #09 / 1994 / BIZ / B • Everything Is Not Relative / 1994 / EL / M • Magma: Hot Shots / 1995 / MET / M • Mike Hott: #256 Linda And Georgia / 1994 / MHV / F • Mr. Peepers Amateur Home Videos #71: I Dream Of Creamy / 1993 / LBO / M • Odyssey Triple Play #42: Pussy-Pumping Gang Bang / 1993 / OD / M

GEORGIA ANGELS

Infidel / 1996 / WV / M

GEORGIA ANGHELA

Marco Polo / 1995 / SC / M

GEORGIA DRUGG *see Star Index I*

GEORGIA GOLD

End Around / 1994 / PRE / B • Fun Zone / 1994 / PRE / B • Gas Works / 1994 / PRE / B • Leg...Ends #13 / 1995 / PRE / F • Nurses Know Best / 1994 / SHL / B • Spanking Double Feature / 1994 / SHL / B • Student Fetish Videos: Best of Catfighting #03 / 1995 / PRE / C • Student Fetish Videos: Best Of Foot Worship #03 / 1995 / PRE / C • Student Fetish Videos: Best Of

Spanking #03 / 1995 / PRE / C • Student Fetish Videos: Catfighting #09 / 1994 / PRE / B • Student Fetish Videos: Catfighting #11 / 1994 / PRE / B • Student Fetish Videos: Foot Worship #12 / 1994 / PRE / B • Student Fetish Videos: Spanking #12 / 1994 / PRE / B • Student Fetish Videos: Spanking #15 / 1994 / PRE / B

GEORGIA HOLDEN
Blue Vanities #115 / 1988 / FFL / M • Blue Vanities #552 / 1994 / FFL / M

GEORGIA ILENE DUG see Star Index I

GEORGIA PEACH see Star Index I

GEORGIA SPAIN
Switch Hitters #2: Swinging Both Ways / 1987 / IN / G

GEORGIA SPELVIN *see* Georgina Spelvin

GEORGIA TECK
Body Candy / 1980 / VIS / M

GEORGIA VAN HELSING
Betrayed / 1985 / CAL / B • Caught! / 1985 / BIZ / B • Master Control / 1985 / CS / B • Tourist Trap / 1984 / CS / B

GEORGIANA
Somewhere Under The Rainbow #1 / 1995 / HW / M

GEORGIE
Blue Vanities #544 / 1994 / FFL / M • Georgie's Ordeal / 1993 / LED / B

GEORGIE LITTLE
F / 1980 / GO / M

GEORGIE VEGAS
Ultraflesh / 1980 / GO / M

GEORGINA
Busen Wunder / 199? / L&W / M • Plumper Therapy / 1995 / BTO / M

GEORGINA (HUNGARY)
Sodomania #11: In Your Face / 1994 / EL / M

GEORGINA DAY
American Nympho In London / 1987 / VD / M • The Baroness / 1987 / VD / M • Hard Core Cafe / 1988 / VD / M • Hot Nights And Dirty Days / 1988 / VD / M • International Phone Sex Girls #1 / 1988 / VD / M

GEORGINA SPELVIN *(Ruth Raymond, Georgia Spelvin, Shelley Abels)*
Georgia Spelvin is from **The Jade Pussycat** (box). Brunette, marginal face, thick body, flat ass, older. Born in Texas and had polio as a child. Was a dancer in **Hello Dolly** on Broadway and the dance double for Shirley MacLaine in **Sweet Charity**. Was 36 years old when she starred in **The Devil In Miss Jones**. First movie was **High Priestess** which may also be called **Devil's Due**. As of 1996 she has been divorced twice and now lives with a boyfriend, John Welch a TV and commercial actor, and works in the graphics arts business. Was also called Ona Tural and Claudi Clitoris.
3 A.M. / 1975 / ALP / M • 6 To 9 Black Style / 1987 / LIM / C • The 8th Annual Erotic Film Awards / 1984 / SE / C • All The Way / 1980 / CDC / M • Babylon Pink #1 / 1979 / COM / M • Bad Blood / 1989 / AE / S • Bedroom Bedlam / 1973 / VHL / M • Bedtime Video #102: Free & Easy / 1984 / GO / M • Behind The Scenes Of An Adult Movie / 1983 / CV / M • The Best Of Gail Palmer / 1981 / WWV / C • Between Lovers / 1983 / CA / M • Birds And Beads / 1974 / VC / M • Blue Vanities #239 / 1995 / FFL / M • Blue Vanities #244 / 1995 / FFL / M • Blue Vanities #248 / 1995 / FFL / M •

Caballero Preview Tape #3 / 1984 / CA / C • Caballero Preview Tape #4 / 1985 / CA / C • Career Bed / 1969 / SOW / S • Centerspread Girls / 1982 / CA / M • The Confessions Of Linda Lovelace / 1974 / AR / C • Country Comfort / 1981 / SE / M • Cum Shot Revue #2 / 1985 / HO / C • The Dancers / 1981 / VCX / M • Desires Within Young Girls / 1977 / CA / M • Devil In Miss Jones #1 / 1972 / VC / M • Devil In Miss Jones #2 / 1983 / VC / M • Devil's Due / 1974 / ALP / M • Dirty Looks / 1982 / VC / C • Easy / 1978 / CV / M • The Ecstasy Girls #1 / 1979 / CA / M • Electric Blue: Caribbean Cruise / 1984 / CA / S • Endless Lust / 1983 / VC / M • The Erotic Adventures Of Candy / 1978 / VCX / M • Erotic Fantasies: Women With Women / 1984 / CV / C • The Erotic Memoirs Of A Male Chauvinist Pig / 1973 / QX / M • Exhausted / 1981 / CA / C • Fantasy / 1978 / VCX / M • Fantasy In Blue / 1975 / IHV / M • Fastlane Fuck-Holes! / 1994 / MET / M • First Annual XRCO Awards / 1984 / AVC / C • Flight Sensations / 1983 / VC / C • For Richer, For Poorer / 1979 / CXV / M • Free And Foxy / 1986 / VCX / C • French Kiss / 1979 / PVX / M • Fringe Benefits / 1975 / IHV / M • Garage Girls / 1981 / CV / M • Guess Who's Coming / 19?? / VSH / M • GVC: Teacher's Pet #112 / 1983 / GO / M • Happy Days / 1974 / IHV / M • High Priestess / cr71 / ... / M • Honeymoon Suite / 1974 / VHL / M • Honkytonk Nights / 1978 / TWV / S • I Spit On Your Corpse / 1974 / REP / S • Indecent Exposure / 1981 / CA / M • Inside Georgina Spelvin / 1974 / VC / M • The Jade Pussycat / 1977 / CA / M • The Journey Of O / 1975 / TVX / M • Lecher / 1980 / COM / M • Legends Of Porn #1 / 1987 / CV / C • Limited Edition #01 / 1979 / AVC / M • Limited Edition #02 / 1979 / AVC / M • Limited Edition #11 / 1980 / AVC / M • Lip Service / 1974 / VHL / M • Love Airlines / 1978 / SE / M • Lovelace Meets Miss Jones / 1975 / AVC / M • Midnight Blue #2 / 1980 / VXP / M • Mount Of Venus / 1975 / ... / M • Mystique / 1979 / CA / M • The New York City Woman / 1979 / VC / C • The Newcomers / 1973 / VSH / M • Only The Best #1 / 1986 / CV / C • Only The Best #3 / 1990 / CV / C • Overexposure / cr73 / GO / M • Police Academy / 1984 / WAR / S • Police Academy #2 / 1985 / WAR / S • The Private Afternoons Of Pamela Mann / 1974 / TVX / M • Private Thighs / 1987 / AVC / C • Ring Of Desire / 1981 / SE / M • The Russians Are Coming / cr69 / VST / M • S.O.S. / 1975 / QX / M • Saturday Matinee Series #1 / 1996 / VCX / C • Saturday Matinee Series #2 / 1996 / VCX / C • Sensual Encounters Of Every Kind / 1978 / SE / M • The Seven Seductions Of Madame Lau / 1981 / EVI / M • Sexual Witchcraft / 1973 / IHV / M • Skin On Skin / 1981 / CV / M • Sleepyhead / 1973 / VXP / M • Snow Honeys / 1983 / VC / M • Take Off / 1978 / VXP / M • Teachers And Cream / cr70 / BOC / M • That's Erotic / 1979 / CV / C • That's Porno / 1979 / CV / C • Tropic Of Desire / 1979 / WWV / M • True Legends Of Adult Cinema: The Golden Age / 1992 / VC / C • The Twilight Girls / 1958 / SVE / S • Urban Cowgirls / 1980 / CA / M • VCA Previews #2 / 1988 / VC / C • Wet Rainbow / 1973 /

AR / M • When She Was Bad / 1983 / CA / M • The World Of Henry Paris / 1981 / VC / C • [Parental Guidance / 1972 / ... / M • [S-X By Appointment / 196? / ... / S • [Spikey's Magic Wand / 1973 / ... / S • [Well Of Frenzy / 1973 / ... / M

GEORIA GOLD
Poor Little Rich Girls / 1994 / SHL / B

GEOS SAAVADNI see Star Index I

GERALD ELLIOT
Evil Angel / 1986 / VCR / M • Shape Up For Sensational Sex / 1985 / SE / M

GERALD GRANT see Star Index I

GERALD GREGORY
Marilyn, My Love / 1985 / ELH / M

GERALD GREYSTONE
Eat At The Blue Fox / 1983 / VC / M • Resurrection Of Eve / 1973 / MIT / M • She's A Boy Toy / 1985 / DR / M

GERALD KOHEN see Star Index I

GERALD LUIG see Star Index I

GERALD PEIK see Gerry Pike

GERALDINA
Penetration (Anabolic) #1 / 1995 / ANA / M

GERALDINE
Blue Vanities #531 / 1993 / FFL / M • Magma: Bizarre Lust / 1995 / MET / M • Magma: Claudine In Action / 1996 / MET / M

GERALDINE BEDECKER see Star Index I

GERALDINE BOETICHER see Star Index I

GERARD
M Series #26 / 1994 / LBO / M

GERARD BROULARD
Evil Come Evil Go / 1972 / ST0 / S • Sacrilege / 1971 / AXV / M

GERARD COURE see Star Index I

GERARD DAMIANO *(Albert Gork, Al Gork, Jerry Gerard)*
The legendary director who started it all with **Deep Throat**. Albert Gork is from **The Devil In Miss Jones #1**. Al Gork is from **Meatball**.
All About Sex / 1970 / AR / M • Bed, Butts & Breakfast / 1990 / LV / M • Bottoms Up / 1974 / SOW / M • Bucky Beaver's XXX Dragon Art Theatre Double Feature #05 / 1996 / SOW / M • Cheeks #2: The Bitter End / 1989 / CC / M • Come On Baby, Light My Fire / 1969 / SOW / S • Deep Throat #1 / 1972 / AR / M • Devil In Miss Jones #1 / 1972 / VC / M • Inside Everybody / 1984 / AVC / M • Joint Venture / 1977 / ELV / M • Just For The Hell Of It / 1991 / CA / M • Let My Puppets Come / 1975 / CA / M • Lethal Passion / 1991 / PL / M • Meatball / 1972 / VCX / M • Midnight Blue #2 / 1980 / VXP / M • Never So Deep / 1981 / VCX / M • People / 1978 / QX / M • Saturday Matinee Series #1 / 1996 / VCX / C • Sex U.S.A / 1970 / SEP / M • Skin Flicks / 1978 / AVC / M • The Story Of Joanna / 1975 / VHL / M • Too Many Cocks In Me! / 1992 / MET / M • We All Go Down / 1969 / SOW / S • Whose Fantasy Is It, Anyway? / 1983 / AVC / M

GERARD DAMIANO, JR
All About Sex / 1970 / AR / M

GERARD GREGORY see Star Index I

GERARD MENOUD
Cindy Puts Out / 1996 / OLL / M

GERARD T. HURLEY
Tender And Wild / 1989 / MTP / M

GERBIL BOY

4 Of A Kind / 1995 / BON / B • Call Me Mistress / 1996 / ATO / B • The Fetish Files / 1995 / IBN / B • Full House / 1995 / BON / B • Mistress Jennifer / 1995 / IBN / B • Mistress Katrina / 1995 / IBN / B • Overruled / 1995 / IBN / B • Reel Domination Series #1: Mistress Katrina / 1995 / IBN / B • Reel Domination Series #2: Mistress Jennifer / 1995 / IBN / B • Right On Track / 1995 / IBN / B • Smokin' Mistress / 1995 / IBN / B

GERD BRABSCH
Viola Video #107: Private Party / 1995 / PEV / M

GERD DAUER
Viola Video #105: / 1995 / PEV / M

GERD GOSEBREXHT
Viola Video #102: Anal #8 / 1995 / PEV / M

GERD HOLLRICH
Viola Video #101: Anal #7 / 1995 / PEV / M

GERD VAN HART
Twilight / 1996 / ESN / M

GERDA
Blue Vanities #580 / 1996 / FFL / M

GERI
Blue Vanities #512 / 1992 / FFL / M • Blue Vanities #526 / 1993 / FFL / M

GERI ALCOTT *see Star Index I*

GERI DAFFRON *see Star Index I*

GERI MILLER
High Rise / 1973 / QX / M • [Andy Warhol's Flesh / 1968 / ... / S

GERI PETTY
Fashion Fantasy / 1972 / GO / M

GERI REEVES
10 Years Of Big Busts #2 / 1990 / BTO / C • The Best Of Big Busty / 1986 / L&W / C • Big Bust Vixens / 1984 / BTO / S

GERNOT MOHNER
[Krankenschwestern-Report / 1972 / ... / M

GERONTE SEBEZIO
The Husband / 1995 / WIV / M

GERRI A. TRICK
Dirty Hairy's Over 50 Meets Mr. Black 18 Inches / 1996 / GOT / M

GERRY
Blue Vanities #516 / 1992 / FFL / M

GERRY AUSTIN *(Gary Austin)*
Blonde Velvet / 1976 / COL / M • Fotishes Of Monique / 8776 / VHL / B • Slave Of Pleasure / 1978 / BL / M • Two Lives Of Jennifer / 1979 / VHL / M

GERRY JOHN *see Star Index I*

GERRY PACKARD
Telefantasy / 1978 / AR / M

GERRY PIKE *(Jerry Pike, Gerry Pyke, Gerald Peik, Jerry Pine)*
Young blonde male with long hair and tattoo on his right forearm. Supposedly Australian.
The Adventures Of Studman #2 / 1994 / AFV / M • All "A" / 1994 / SFP / C • Alpine Affairs / 1995 / LE / M • The Anal Adventures Of Suzy Super Slut #1 / 1994 / AFV / M • The Anal Adventures Of Suzy Super Slut #2 / 1994 / AFV / M • Anal Agony / 1994 / ZA / M • Anal Anonymous / 1994 / ZA / M • The Anal Diary Of Misty Rain / 1993 / EL / M • Anal Injury / 1994 / ZA / M • Anal Vision #21 / 1993 / LBO / M • Anal Vision #26 / 1994 / LBO / M • The Anal-Europe Series #05: Anal European Vacation / 1993 / LV / M • The Anal-Europe Series #08: / 1995 / LV / M • Baby Doll / 1994 / SC / M • The Backway Inn #4 / 1993 / FD / M • Bad Attitude #1 / 1995 / LV / M • Bad Attitude #2 / 1995 / LV / M • Badgirls #6:

Ridin' Into Town / 1995 / VI / M • Beach Ball / 1994 / SC / M • Beverly Hills Blondes #1 / 1995 / LV / M • Beverly Hills Blondes #2 / 1995 / LV / M • Big Breast Beach / 1995 / LV / M • Big Bust Babes #20 / 1994 / AFI / M • Black Beach / 1995 / LV / M • Black Velvet #3 / 1994 / CC / M • Blonde Forces #2 / 1994 / CC / M • Bobby Hollander's Maneaters #09 / 1993 / SFP / M • Body English / 1993 / PL / M • Both Ends Burning / 1993 / HW / M • Buffy's Bare Ass Barbecue / 1996 / CDI / M • Bun Busters #13 / 1994 / LBO / M • Butt Banged Bicycle Babes / 1994 / ANA / M • Butt Bangers Ball / 1994 / FPI / M • The Butt Sisters Do Baltimore / 1995 / MID / M • The Butt Sisters Do Chicago / 1995 / MID / M • The Butt Sisters Do Daytona / 1995 / MID / M • The Butt Sisters Do Hawaii / 1995 / MID / M • The Butt Sisters Do New Orleans / 1995 / MID / M • The Butt Sisters Do Philadelphia / 1995 / MID / M • The Butt Sisters Do Seattle / 1995 / MID / M • Butt Watch #04 / 1994 / FH / M • Butt Watch #06 / 1994 / FH / M • Butt's Motel #6 / 1994 / EX / M • Butthead Dreams: Exposed / 1995 / FH / M • Buttman's Inferno / 1993 / EA / M • Cabin Fever / 1995 / ERA / M • Casting Call #07 / 1994 / SO / M • Cheating / 1994 / VI / M • Chemical Reaction / 1995 / CC / M • Cherry Pie / 1994 / SC / M • Cherry Poppers #02: Barely Legal / 1994 / ZA / M • Colossal Orgy #1 / 1993 / HW / M • Confessions Of A Slutty Nurse / 1994 / VIM / M • Cover To Cover / 1995 / WP / M • Deep Inside Debi Diamond / 1995 / VC / C • Deep Inside Misty Rain / 1995 / VC / C • Deep Inside Tyffany Million / 1995 / VC / C • Depraved Fantasies #3 / 1994 / FPI / M • Designer Bodies / 1993 / VI / M • The Dinner Party #1 / 1994 / ULI / M • Dirty Dancers #4 / 1995 / 4P / M • Dirty Stories #1 / 1995 / PE / M • Dog Walker / 1994 / EA / M • Double Load #2 / 1994 / HW / M • Dr Butts #3 / 1993 / 4P / M • Dream Reamin' / 1995 / LV / M • Dynamite Brat / 1995 / LV / M • Erotic Visions / 1995 / ULI / M • Erotica Optique / 1994 / SUF / M • Every Woman Has A Fantasy #3 / 1995 / VC / M • Exstasy / 1995 / WV / M • Fantasy Du Jour / 1995 / FH / M • Forever / 1995 / SC / M • Gangbang Girl #15 / 1995 / ANA / M • Gemini / 1994 / SC / M • Geranalmo / 1994 / PL / M • Glen And Glenda / 1994 / CA / M • Gypsy Queen / 1995 / CC / M • The Gypsy Queen / 1996 / CC / M • Hard Core Beginners #04 / 1995 / LEI / M • Helen & Louise / 1996 / HDE / M • Hello Norma Jeane / 1994 / VT / M • Hellriders / 1995 / SC / M • The Hitch-Hiker #01: Wide Open Spaces / 1993 / WMG / M • The Hitch-Hiker #04: Max Overdrive / 1994 / WMG / M • Hollywood Amateurs #14 / 1995 / MID / M • Hollywood Amateurs #15 / 1995 / MID / M • Hollywood Ho' House / 1994 / VC / M • Hollywood In Your Face / 1993 / VC / M • Hollywood Sex Tour / 1995 / VC / M • Immortal Desire / 1993 / VI / M • Infidel / 1996 / WV / M • Intercourse With The Vampyre #1 / 1994 / SC / M • Intercourse With The Vampyre #2 / 1994 / SC / M • International Analists / 1994 / AFD / M • Killer Looks / 1994 / IMP / S • M Series #27 / 1994 / LBO / M • Malibu Heat / 1995 / HO / M • Max #02 / 1994 / FWE / M • Max #09: Where Danger Lurks

/ 1996 / XPR / M • Max Gold #1 / 1996 / XPR / C • Mickey Ray's Sex Search #02: Tight Spots / 1994 / WIV / M • Midnight Dreams / 1994 / WV / M • Mistress To Sin / 1994 / LV / M • My First Time #1 / 1995 / NS / M • My First Time #2 / 1996 / NS / M • Nasty Nymphos #03 / 1994 / ANA / M • Nasty Nymphos #09 / 1995 / ANA / M • Nasty Nymphos #10 / 1995 / ANA / M • New Girls In Town #4 / 1993 / CC / M • Night Crawlers / 1994 / SC / M • Pajama Party X #1 / 1994 / VC / M • Pajama Party X #2 / 1994 / VC / M • Passion's Prisoners / 1994 / LV / M • Photo Opportunity / 1994 / VC / M • Pick Up Lines #01 / 1995 / 4P / M • The Pink Lady Detective Agency: Case Of The Twisted Sister / 1994 / IN / M • Pleasure Dome: The Genesis Chamber / 1994 / AFV / M • Poop Dreams / 1995 / ULP / M • Private Performance / 1994 / EX / M • Pure Anal / 1996 / MET / M • Pussyman #05: Captive Audience / 1994 / SNA / M • Pussyman #06: House Of Games / 1994 / SNA / M • Pussyman #07: On The Dark Side / 1994 / SNA / M • Pussyman #10: Butts, Butts & More Butts / 1995 / SNA / M • Pussyman Auditions #01 / 1995 / SNA / M • Pussyman Auditions #05 / 1995 / SNA / M • Pussyman Auditions #07 / 1995 / SNA / M • Reckless / 1995 / NOT / M • Red Light / 1994 / SC / S • The Reel World #1 / 1994 / FOR / M • The Reel World #2 / 1994 / FOR / M • Reflections / 1995 / FD / M • Reverse Gang Bang / 1995 / JMP / M • Rolling Thunder / 1995 / VI / M • Samantha's Private Fantasies / 1994 / WV / M • Saturday Night Porn #3 / 1993 / AFV / M • Secret Services / 1995 / CV / M • Sensual Recluse / 1994 / EX / M • Sex #1 (Vca) / 1994 / VC / M • Sex #2: Fate (Vca) / 1995 / VC / M • Sex And Money / 1994 / DGD / S • Sex Circus / 1994 / VIM / M • Sex In Strange Places: The Sphincter Zone / 1994 / FPI / M • Sex Scandals / 1995 / XC / M • Sex Secrets Of High Priced Call Girls / 1995 / MID / M • Seymore & Shane On The Loose / 1994 / ULI / M • Ski Bunnies #1 / 1994 / HW / M • Ski Bunnies #2 / 1994 / HW / M • Sleaze Please!—August Edition / 1994 / FH / M • Sleaze Please!—September Edition / 1994 / FH / M • Sleaze Please!—November Edition / 1994 / FH / M • Sodomania #06: Gangs And Bangs And Other Thangs / 1993 / EL / M • Sodomania #07: Deep Down Inside / 1993 / EL / M • Some Like It Hard / 1995 / VC / M • Star Struck / 1994 / ERA / M • Stiff Competition #2 / 1994 / CA / M • Strange Sex In Strange Places / 1994 / ZA / M • Tail Taggers #117 / 1993 / WV / M • Tail Taggers #125 / 1994 / WV / M • Takin' It To The Limit #5 / 1995 / BS / M • The Thief, The Girl & The Detective / 1996 / HDE / M • Tommyknockers / 1994 / CC / M • Torrid Tales / 1995 / VI / M • Up And Cummers #11 / 1994 / 4P / M • Up And Cummers #18 / 1995 / 4P / M • Victoria With An "A" / 1994 / PL / M • Video Virgins #07 / 1993 / NS / M • Video Virgins #20 / 1995 / NS / M • Virgin / 1993 / HW / M • Visions Of Seduction / 1994 / SC / M • Visual Fantasies / 1995 / LE / M • Vortex / 1995 / MET / M • The Voyeur #1 / 1994 / EA / M • The Voyeur #5 / 1995 / EA / M • Wanted / 1995 / DR / M • Wendy Whoppers: Prison Love Doll / 1994 / PEP / M • Wild Things

#4 / 1994 / CV / M
GERRY PYKE *see* **Gerry Pike**
GERRY RANDOLPH *see* **Craig Roberts**
GHISLAIN VAN HOVE
Exces Pornographiques / 1977 / ... / M •
[La Rabatteuse / 1977 / ... / M
GIA
Bull Dyke Humiliation / 1993 / PL / B • Forbidden Dildo Taboos / 1992 / STM / F • Hot Body Hall Of Fame: Christy Carrera / 1996 / CG / F • Moon Beads / 1995 / STM / F • Slave Girls' Agony / 1993 / PL / B
GIA GRACE *see* **Star Index I**
GIA LUCCI
Disciples Of Bondage / 1992 / STM / B • Journey Into Latex / 1992 / STM / B • Nasty Dancers #1 / 1996 / STM / B • Red Tails #1 / 1993 / STM / B • Secret Urges (Starmaker) / 1994 / STM / F
GIANCARLO BINI
Ejacula #1 / 1992 / VC / M • Ejacula #2 / 1992 / VC / M • Family Affair / 1996 / XC / M • Impulse #02: The Film / 1995 / MBP / M • Impulse #05: When I Was 20... / 1995 / MBP / M • Impulse #06: / 1996 / MBP / M • Impulse #07: / 1996 / MBP / M
GIANFRANCO ROMAGNOLI
The Coming Of Nikita / 1995 / EL / M • True Stories #1 / 1993 / SC / M • True Stories #2 / 1993 / SC / M
GIANNA
Beauty And The Biker / 1993 / GOT / B • The Chamber Maids / 1993 / GOT / B • Diabolic Demands / 1992 / GOT / B • The Dominator / 1992 / GOT / B • Every Body / 1992 / LAP / M • Inhuman Bondage / 1993 / GOT / B • The Latex Dungeon / 1992 / GOT / B • The Maltese Bimbo / 1993 / FD / M • Masters Of Dominance / 1996 / GOT / C • Mind Mirror / 1994 / LAP / M • No Pain, No Gain / 1992 / GOT / B • Show No Mercy / 1993 / GOT / B • Stroke Of Nine / 1994 / GOT / B • Suspension In Latex / 1992 / GOT / B • Third Degree / 1992 / GOT / B • Toe Tales #02 / 1992 / GOT / B • Toe Tales #03 / 1992 / GOT / B • Toe Tales #04 / 1992 / GOT / B • Toe Tales #05 / 1993 / GOT / B • Toe Tales #06 / 1993 / GOT / B • Toe Tales #08 / 1993 / GOT / B • Toe Tales #09 / 1993 / GOT / B • Toe Tales #12 / 1994 / GOT / C • Wild Girls / 1994 / GOT / B • With Love / 1995 / FD / M
GIDGET THE MIDGET
A Fairy's Tail / 1996 / TTV / M • Microslut / 1996 / TTV / M • Midget Goes Hawaiian / 1995 / FC / M • Midget On Milligan's Island / 1995 / FC / M
GIDGETTE *(Mitica, Brittany (Gidgette))*
Like Angel West but not as pretty. Also called "Mitica" (**Cheek Busters**) and "Brittany" in **Backpackers #1** but not the same as Paula Price's sister. Has improved in the 1991 round to be absolutely adorable. Small tattoo on inside right ankle.
Amateur Nights #10 / 1990 / HO / M • Anal Nation #1 / 1990 / CC / M • The Backpackers #1 / 1990 / IN / M • Cheek Busters / 1990 / FH / M • Girls Will Be Boys #1 / 1990 / PL / F • Girls Will Be Boys #2 / 1990 / PL / F • Hot Diggity Dog / 1990 / ME / M • Hot Dreams / 1991 / VEX / M • The Lethal Squirt / 1990 / AR / M • Possession / 1990 / CIN / M • The Pump / 1991 / CC / M • Queen Of Midnight / 1991 / V99 / M • Sensuous / 1991 / LV / M • Wise Ass! / 1990 / FH / M

GIGI
Asian Connection Video #103 / 1996 / AC0 / B • The Best Of Fabulous Flashers / 1996 / DGD / F • Blue Vanities #506 / 1992 / FFL / M • Boss Bitch From Bondage Hell / 1996 / LBO / B • Catalina Bound / 1996 / VTF / B • The Contessa De Sade / 1996 / LBO / B • Gigi Gives It Away / 1995 / FRF / M • GRG: Pretty, Playful And Provocative / 1996 / GRG / F • Harlem Harlots #1 / 1995 / AVS / M • Hot Body Video Magazine: Red Hot / 1995 / CG / S • I Know What Girls Like / 1986 / WET / G • Pain Puppets / 1996 / LBO / B • The Punishment Of Red Riding Hood / 1996 / LBO / B • The Reunion / 1996 / CS / B • Tightly Secured / 1996 / CS / B
GIGI (JULIET ANDER.) *see* **Juliet Anderson**
GIGI FERAUD
Magma: Olympus Of Lust / 1994 / MET / M
GIGI KELLY
Detective Covergirls / 1996 / CUC / B
GIGI RIGOLETTO
Pleasures Of A Woman / 1983 / CA / M
GIL PERKINS *see* **Star Index I**
GIL PIERCE
Let's Talk Sex / 1982 / CA / M
GIL WARD *see* **Star Index I**
GILBERT GROSSO
Visions Of Lust / 1983 / GO / M
GILBERT MEZA *see* **Star Index I**
GILBERT PALMITIER
Teenage Pajama Party / 1977 / VC / M
GILBERT SERVIEN
Shocking / 1984 / SE / M
GILBERT STEEL
An Unnatural Act #1 / 1984 / DR / M
GILBERTO
Sunny / 1979 / VC / M
GILDA ARANCIO
Body Love / 1976 / CA / M • [The Loves Of Irina / 1973 / PS / S
GILDA GRANT
The Loves Of Mary Jane / 1989 / BWV / C • Teenage Sex Kitten / 1972 / CA / M • A Touch Of Sex / 1972 / AR / M
GILDA JACOBS *see* **Star Index I**
GILLES KARL
[Jouissances / 1976 / ... / M
GILLES KERVIZIC
Erotic Pleasures / 1976 / CA / M
GILLY SYKES
Diversions / 1976 / ALP / M
GINA
AVP #9116: And Gina Makes Three / 1991 / AVP / M • The Awakening Of Marika / 1993 / CC / M • The Betrayal Of Innocence #1: The Awakening Of Marika / 1993 / CC / M • The Betrayal Of Innocence #2: The Decadence / 1993 / CC / M • The Betrayal Of Innocence #3: The Choice / 1993 / CC / M • Blue Vanities #538 / 1993 / FFL / M • Blue Vanities #554 / 1994 / FFL / M • Breast Wishes #01 / 1991 / LBO / M • Breast Worx #08 / 1991 / LBO / M • California Girl: Amateur Nude Auditions / 1995 / PME / S • The Crack Of Dawn / 1989 / GLE / M • FTV #08: Topless Fighting Lesson / 1996 / FT / B • FTV #12: Two Against A Wimp / 1996 / FT / B • Gina Learns The Ropes / 1994 / VIG / B • Kinky College Cunts #02 / 1993 / NS / M • Kinky College Cunts #05 / 1993 / NS / F • Kisses From Romania / 1995 / NIT / M • Love Slave / 1995 / WIV / M • Magma: Live And Learn / 1995 / MET / M • Nasty Travel Tails #02 / 1993 / CC / M

• New Faces, Hot Bodies #20 / 1996 / STP / M • Private Gold #13: The Pyramid #3 / 1996 / OD / M • Southern: Previews #2 / 1992 / SSH / C • Stilettos And Spikes / 1991 / JBV / S
GINA (CHEYENNE) *see* **Cheyenne**
GINA B. *see* **Star Index I**
GINA BEDELL *see* **Star Index I**
GINA BLACK
[Soul Sex / 197? / ... / M
GINA BLAIR *see* **Star Index I**
GINA BRITTANIA *see* **Brittania**
GINA CARNALI *see* **Marie Sharp**
GINA CARRERA *(Julie Colt, Julia Colt, Julie Winchester, Victoria Wilde, Jenna Carrera)*
Blonde, curly hair, small tits, a little mannish.
Amazing Sex Stories #1 / 1986 / SUV / M • Ball Busters / 1984 / CV / M • Bedtime Tales / 1985 / SE / M • The Best Of Black White & Pink Inside / 1996 / CV / C • Beyond Desire / 1986 / VC / M • The Big E #08 / 1988 / BIZ / B • Black Girls Do It Better / 1986 / CV / M • Blonde Heat (VCA) / 1985 / VC / M • Blondie / 1985 / TAR / M • Body Slammers #03 / 1993 / SBP / B • Can Heat / 1988 / PLV / B • Can't Get Enough / 1985 / CA / M • Candy Girls #5 / 19?? / AVC / M • Catfights #3 / 1987 / OHV / B • Caught In The Act / 1993 / BS / B • Cavalcade Of Stars / 1985 / VCR / C • China & Silk / 1984 / MAP / M • Cleopatra's Bondage Revenge / cr85 / BIZ / B • Club Head (EVN) #1 / 1987 / EVN / C • Commando Lovers / 1986 / SUV / M • Confessions Of A Middle Aged Nympho / 1986 / WET / M • Dames / 1985 / SE / M • Dear Fanny / 1984 / CV / M • Desert Lesbian / 1985 / LIB / F • Dr Strange Sex / 1985 / CA / M • Drainman / 1989 / BIZ / B • The Enchantress / 1985 / 4P / M • The End Zone / 1993 / PRE / B • Erotic Zones #3 / 1986 / CA / M • Fantasy Mansion / 1983 / BIZ / B • Felecia's Folly / 1993 / BS / B • The Filthy Rich / 1989 / LA / M • First Annual XRCO Awards / 1984 / AVC / C • Foot Teasers / 1988 / BIZ / B • Footgames In Bondage / 1992 / BIZ / C • Future Voyeur / 1985 / SUV / M • Girl Toys / 1986 / DR / M • Glamour Girl #8 / 1985 / CDI / M • Gourmet Premier: Broker's Esctacy / Student Pleasure #908 / cr83 / GO / M • Gourmet Quickies: Cody Nicole #702 / 1984 / GO / C • Hard Bodies / 1989 / CDI / M • Hard For The Money / 1984 / CV / M • Heidi A / 1985 / PL / M • High Price Spread / 1986 / PV / C • Hot Buns / 1988 / BIZ / B • Hot Cars, Nasty Women / 1985 / WV / M • Hot Girls In Love / 1985 / VXP / M • Hot Nights And Hard Bodies / 1986 / VD / M • Hot Shorts: Gina Carrera / 1986 / VCR / C • Hot Wire / 1985 / VXP / M • Ice Cream #4: Touch Of Mischief / 1984 / VC / M • Jean Genie / 1985 / CA / M • Jewels Of The Night / 1986 / SE / M • Joy Toys / 1985 / WET / M • The Joy-Stick Girls / 1986 / CLV / M • Joys Of Erotica #110 / 1984 / VCR / C • Joys Of Erotica #114 / 1984 / VCR / C • Kinky Business #1 / 1984 / DR / M • Lay Down And Deliver / 1989 / VWA / M • Leg...Ends #01 / 1988 / BIZ / F • Leg...Ends #09 / 1994 / PRE / F • Lottery Lust / 1986 / PEN / M • Love Roots / 1987 / LIM / M • Loving Spoonfulls / 1987 / 4P / C • Lust In Space / 1985 / PV / M • Lust On The Orient X-Press / 1986 / CA / M • The

Magic Touch / 1985 / CV / M • Marina Heat / 1985 / CV / M • Marine Code Of Silence: Don't Ask Don't Tell / 1996 / BHE / G • The Mating Season / 1984 / VC / M • The Melting Spot / 1985 / VSE / M • The Midnight Zone / 1986 / IN / M • Mr. Blue / 1996 / JSP / G • New Wave Hookers #1 / 1984 / VC / M • New York Vice / 1984 / CC / M • On Golden Blonde / 1984 / PV / M • Only The Best Of Women With Women / 1988 / CV / C • Palm Spring Girls / 1986 / LIB / M • The Peek A Boo Gang / 1985 / COL / M • Penetration #4 / 1984 / AVC / M • Perversion / 1984 / AVC / M • Phone Sex Fantasies / 1984 / QX / M • Pleasure Productions #12 / 1985 / VCR / M • Pleasure Spot / 1986 / CA / M • Raven / 1985 / VCR / M • Rip Off #1 / 1988 / BIZ / B • Satin Dolls / 1985 / CV / M • Sex In The Great Outdoors / 1987 / SE / C • Sex Waves / 1984 / EXF / M • Sex-A-Vision / 1985 / DR / M • Shacking Up / 1985 / VXP / M • Shauna: Every Man's Fantasy / 1985 / CA / C • She's A Boy Toy / 1985 / DR / M • Showdown / 1986 / CA / M • Sky Pies / 1985 / GO / M • Smart Asses / 1992 / BIZ / B • Soul Kiss This / 1988 / VCR / C • Space Virgins / 1984 / CRE / M • Stiff Competition #1 / 1984 / CA / M • Student Fetish Videos: Catfighting #07 / 1993 / PRE / B • Student Fetish Videos: Spanking #10 / 1993 / PRE / B • Student Fetish Videos: Spanking #12 / 1994 / PRE / B • Student Fetish Videos: Tickling #08 / 1994 / SFV / B • Sunny Side Up / 1984 / VC / M • Super Models Do LA / 1986 / AT / M • Suzie Superstar #2 / 1985 / CV / M • Swedish Erotica #53 / 1984 / CA / M • Swedish Erotica #60 / 1984 / CA / M • Sweet Cheeks / 1987 / VCR / C • A Taste Of Pink / 1985 / VXP / M • Taste Of The Best #1 / 1988 / PIN / C • Teasers / 1984 / HO / M • Three Wishes #1 / 1991 / CDP / B • Three Wishes #2 / 1991 / CDP / B • Tickled In Pink / 1988 / BIZ / B • Tight And Tender / 1985 / CA / M • Tongue Twisters / 1986 / VXP / M • Tracie Lords / 1984 / CIT / M • Trading Places / 1985 / DR / M • Treasure Box / 1986 / PEN / M • Triplets / 1000 / WOP / M • The Ultimate Thrill / 1988 / PIN / C • Unbelievable Orgies #1 / 1987 / EVN / C • Undressed Rehearsal / 1984 / VD / M • VCA Previews #4 / 1988 / VC / C • Video Guide To Sexual Positions / 1984 / JVV / M • Watersports Spree #2 / 1994 / BIZ / C • Wet Kisses / 1986 / SE / M • White Women / 1986 / CC / M • The Whore Of The Worlds / 1985 / PV / M • Wild In The Sheets / 1984 / WET / M • Wish You Were Here / 1984 / VXP / M • Women Without Men #1 / 1985 / VXP / F • X-Rated Bloopers #1 / 1984 / AR / M • Yiddish Erotica #1 / 1986 / SE / C • [Bondage Broadcast / 1989 / ... / B • [Palm Springs Drifter / 1986 / ... / M • [Prisoners Of The Inquisition / 1989 / ... / M • [Screaming Desire / 1986 / ... / M

GINA DAWN see Star Index I

GINA DELANY

Brunette, long black curly hair, facially like Selina St. Clair, large enhanced tits, a bit womanly. 30 years old in 1995, de-virginized at 14 and comes from Spain.

Anal Camera #10 / 1995 / EVN / M • Anal Fugitive / 1995 / PEP / M • Anal Playground / 1995 / CA / M • Anal Plaything #2 / 1995 / ROB / M • Anal Senorita #2 / 1995

/ ROB / M • The Anal-Europe Series #08: / 1995 / LV / M • Ass Masters (Leisure) #04 / 1995 / LEI / M • Ass Poppers / 1995 / VMX / M • Bad Attitude #2 / 1995 / LV / M • Bang City #4: Gina's Anal Gang Bang / 1995 / SC / M • Boudoir Babe / 1996 / VMX / M • Butt Pumpers / 1995 / FH / M • The Butt Sisters Do Baltimore / 1995 / MID / M • Caught From Behind #20 / 1995 / HO / M • Double Penetration Virgins #06: DP Diner / 1995 / JMP / M • Gazongo / 1995 / PEP / M • The Girls Of Spring Break / 1995 / VT / M • In The Crack / 1995 / VMX / M • Indiscreet! Video Magazine #2 / 1995 / FH / M • Kinky Debutante Interviews #09 / 1995 / IP / M • Mutual Consent / 1995 / VC / M • Nasty Nymphos #13 / 1996 / ANA / M • Pussyman Auditions #05 / 1995 / SNA / M • Raunch Ranch / 1995 / LE / M • Rumpman: Caught In An Anal Avalanche / 1995 / HW / M • Shave Tails #4 / 1995 / SO / M • Snatch Masters #10 / 1995 / LEI / M • Sodom Chronicles / 1995 / FH / M • Stuff Your Ass #1 / 1995 / JMP / M • Taboo #14: Kissing Cousins / 1995 / IN / M • Video Virgins #20 / 1995 / NS / M • The Voyeur #5 / 1995 / EA / M • What's In It 4 Me / 1995 / TEG / M • World Class Ass / 1995 / FC / M

GINA DIVELLI see Star Index I

GINA FINE see Jeanna Fine

GINA FORNELLI see Star Index I

GINA FOX see Star Index I

GINA GALINA

Dripping Wet Video / 1993 / NAP / F • Get You Wet / 1992 / NAP / S • When Blondes Compete / 1993 / NAP / B

GINA GENO (Gina Genoa)

The Erotic World Of Seka / 1983 / VCR / C • The Erotic World Of Vanessa #1 / 1983 / VCR / C • The Erotic World Of Vanessa #2 / 1984 / VCR / C

GINA GENOA see Gina Geno

GINA GIANELLI see Gina Gianetti

GINA GIANETTI (Cassie Blake, Gina Gianelli, Gail Sutro, Beverlee Hills)

Older blonde with enormous inflated tits. 44 years old in 1994.

10 Years Of Big Busts #3 / 199? / BTO / C • All American Girls #1 / 1982? / CA / M • Babes At War / 1990 / NAP / B • Bare-Chested, Bare-Breasted, Big-Busted, Wet T-Shirt Video / 1990 / NAP / B • Between My Breasts #15 / 1991 / BTO / M • Big Busted Goddesses Of L.A. / 1991 / NAP / S • Biggest Sexiest Boobs In The USA Contest / 1989 / NAP / F • Breast Worx #02 / 1991 / LBO / M • Busen Extra #3 / 1987 / BTO / M • Caballero Preview Tape #2 / 1983 / CA / C • Cats Will Be Cats / 1988 / NAP / B • Critics' Choice 2 / 1984 / SE / C • D-Cup Holiday / 1991 / BTO / M • Duel Of The Love Goddesses / 1990 / NAP / B • EE 7 / 1991 / NAP / S • Firefoxes / 1985 / PLY / M • Girls Around The World #03 / 1990 / BTO / M • Girls Of Sundance Spa: Hardcore Plumpers #1 / 1992 / BTO / M • Golden Girls, The Movie / 1984 / SE / M • Hollywood Teasers #02 / 1992 / LBO / F • Introducing Gina Gianetti / 1989 / NAP / F • Introducing Melissa Mounds / 1989 / NAP / F • Irresistible #1 / 1982 / SE / M • Purr Of The Cats / 1988 / NAP / B • Roman-Afro Wrestling / 1989 / NAP / B • Ruling The Roost / 1990 / NAP / B • Saddletramp / 1988 / VD / M • Secrets Behind The Green Door / 1987 / SE / M • Slightly

Used / 1987 / VD / M • Stunt Woman / 1990 / LIP / F • Taboo #06 / 1988 / IN / M • A Taste Of Money / 1983 / AT / M • Temptation: The Story Of A Lustful Bride / 1983 / NSV / M • Titillation #1 / 1982 / SE / M • Too Much Too Soon / 1983 / VCX / M • TVs In Trouble #2 / 1991 / BIZ / G

GINA HARLOW

Baby Blue / 1978 / CIG / M • Skin Flicks / 1978 / AVC / M

GINA LA ROSTA see Star Index I

GINA LAMARCA

Breeders / 1996 / MET / M • Penthouse: 1995 Pet Of The Year Playoff / 1994 / PET / F • Penthouse: 1995 Pet Of The Year Winners / 1995 / A*V / F • Penthouse: 25th Anniversary Swimsuit Video / 1994 / A*V / F • Penthouse: Behind The Scenes / 1995 / PET / F • Penthouse: Miami Hot Talk / 1996 / PET / S • Penthouse: Women In & Out Of Uniform / 1994 / A*V / S • Zazel / 1996 / CV / M

GINA LO see Star Index I

GINA LOREN

Switch Hitters #2: Swinging Both Ways / 1987 / IN / G

GINA LORIN

Sex Off The Runway / 1991 / GMI / M

GINA LYNN see Star Index I

GINA MAGNANI see Star Index I

GINA MARTELL (Gina Martelli, Jeanna Martez, Gina Paulson)

Facially very similar to Ali Moore with either (depending on the movie) dark brown, light brown or blonde hair, small tits, very pretty face, nice smile, petite body, and tight waist. Jeanna Martez is from **Delusions** and Gina Paulson is from **Dinner With Samantha**.

All American Girls #2: In Heat / 1983 / CA / M • The Best Of Blondes / 1986 / VCR / C • Delusions / 1983 / PRC / M • Dinner With Samantha / 1983 / PTV / M • The Erotic World Of Cody Nicole / 1984 / VCR / C • The Erotic World Of Sylvia Benedict (#5) / 1983 / VCR / C • GVC: Sweet Dominance #127 / 1983 / GO / B • Home Movies Ltd #1 / 1983 / SE / M • Hot Girls In Love / 1984 / VIV / C • Hot Pink / 1983 / VCR / F • Hyapatia Lee's Arcade Series #02 / 1988 / ZA / C • Mile High Club / 1983 / CV / M • Pleasure Productions #01 / 1984 / VCR / M • Pleasure Productions #03 / 1984 / VCR / M • San Fernando Valley Girls / 1983 / CA / M • Sensuous Moments / 1983 / VIV / M • Sensuous Tales / 1984 / VCR / C • Shaved / 1984 / VCR / M • Terri Gets Her Wish / 1983 / BIZ / B

GINA MARTELLI see Gina Martell

GINA MONROE

Battling Bitches / 1993 / SBP / B • The Bedford Wives / 1994 / LON / B • The Keys Please / 1993 / TAO / B

GINA NARDEAU see Star Index I

GINA PAULSON see Gina Martell

GINA PETERS

Debutantes Discipline / Please Cane Me / 1993 / CS / B

GINA RAE

Great looking sweet dark haired chickie.

Tease Me / 1986 / VC / M

GINA RICCI see Star Index I

GINA RINI

The Openings / 1975 / BL / M

GINA ROME (Francesca (Gina R), Sona Rome, Tiziana Mervar)

Italian. Tall with long dark brown hair, lithe body, medium firm tits, passable face, a bit flat on the butt. SO is Claudio Cazzo. 30 years old in 1996 and de-virginized at 17.

100% Amateur #27: / 1996 / OD / M • Around Frisco / 1996 / SUF / M • Backdoor Imports / 1995 / LV / M • Bad Attitude #1 / 1995 / LV / M • Best Of Video Virgins / 1995 / NS / C • Beverly Hills Bikini Company / 1996 / NIT / M • Brunette Roulette / 1996 / LE / M • Byron Long At Large / 1995 / VC / M • Catching Snapper / 1995 / XCI / M • The Cumm Brothers #13: Rump Rangers / 1996 / OD / M • Cummin' 'round The Mountain / 1996 / BCP / M • Dirty Old Men #2 / 1995 / IP / M • Dream House / 1995 / XPR / M • Fresh Faces #04 / 1995 / EVN / M • Gangland Bangers / 1995 / VC / M • Hard Core Beginners #11 / 1995 / LEI / M • Hardcore Fantasies #3 / 1996 / LV / M • Here Comes Jenny St. James / 1996 / HOV / M • Here Comes Magoof #1 / 1995 / VC / M • Here Comes Magoof #2 / 1995 / VC / M • Hollywood Amateurs #17 / 1995 / MID / M • Hot Diamond / 1995 / LE / M • Kinky Debutante Interviews #09 / 1995 / IP / M • Kinky Debutante Interviews #10 / 1995 / IP / M • Latin Fever #3 / 1996 / C69 / M • Lesbian Debutante #02 / 1996 / IP / F • The Letter X #2 / 1996 / MID / M • Male Order Brides / 1996 / RAS / M • Mike Hott: #322 Cunt of the Month: Gina / 1995 / MHV / M • Mike Hott: #324 Cum In My Cunt #06 / 1995 / MHV / C • Mike Hott: #326 Cum In My Mouth #03 / 1995 / MHV / C • Mike Hott: #330 Three-Sum Sluts #08 / 1995 / MHV / M • Mike Hott: #349 Girls Who Swallow Cum #03 / 1996 / MHV / C • Mike Hott: #363 Lesbian Sluts #25 / 1996 / MHV / F • Mike Hott: #367 Girls Who Lap Cum From Cunts #02 / 1996 / MHV / M • My Surrender / 1996 / A&E / M • Nasty Newcummers #08 / 1995 / MET / M • New Pussy Hunt #17 / 1995 / LEI / M • The Night Of The Living Bed / 1996 / LE / M • Nineteen #1 / 1996 / FOR / M • Odyssey 30 Min: #513: / 1995 / OD / M • A Pool Party At Seymores #1 / 1995 / ULI / M • A Pool Party At Seymores #2 / 1995 / ULI / M • Prescription Bound / 1996 / VTF / B • Private Diaries #1: Christina / 1995 / AVI / M • Pussy Hunt #14 / 1995 / LEI / M • Reel People #04 / 1994 / PP / M • Reel People #11 / 1995 / PP / M • Ron Hightower's Casting Couch #2 / 1995 / FC / M • Sex Lessons / 1996 / NIT / M • The Sex Therapist / 1995 / GO / M • Sexual Atrocities / 1996 / EL / M • Sexual Impulse / 1995 / VD / M • Shades Of Color #2 / 1995 / LBO / M • Shaving Grace / 1996 / GO / M • Shayla's Swim Party / 1997 / VC / M • The Shocking Truth #1 / 1996 / DWO / M • Show & Tell / 1996 / VI / M • Sodomania #12: Raw Filth / 1995 / EL / M • Sodomania: Slop Shots / 1996 / EL / C • The Sodomizer #4 / 1996 / SC / M • Stripping / 1995 / NIT / M • Student Fetish Videos: Spanking #22 / 1996 / PRE / B • Student Fetish Videos: Tickling #13 / 1996 / SFV / B • Sweet Smell Of Excess / 1996 / CIN / M • The Tigress / 1995 / VIM / M • Too Hot / 1996 / LV / M • Totally Real / 1996 / CA / M • Trapped / 1996 / VI / M • Turnabout / 1996 / CTP / M • Undercover / 1996 / VC / M • Video Virgins #24 / 1996 / NS / M • While The Cat's Away / 1996 / NIT / M • Witches Are Bitches /

1996 / NIT / M • Your Cheatin' Butt / 1996 / BON / B

GINA SHARE
Jenteal Loves Rocco / 1996 / VI / M • Kym Wilde's On The Edge #25 / 1995 / RB / B • Student Fetish Videos: Foot Worship #17 / 1995 / PRE / B • Student Fetish Videos: Spanking #20 / 1995 / PRE / B • Whammin' & Jammin' At The Hard Cock Ole / 1996 / GLI / M

GINA SHORE
The Violation Of Juliette / 1996 / JMP / F

GINA STARR
Nina, Just For You / 1989 / BON / F • Trinity, Just For You / 1989 / BON / F

GINA STONE see Star Index I

GINA SWEETS
Beneath My Heels / 1990 / BEB / B • Bizarre World Of Scott Baker / 1992 / CAS / B • Cruel Turnabout / 1990 / PL / B • Domination Vacation / 1995 / COC / B • Payne In The Behind / 1993 / AMF / C • The Payne Principle / 1995 / COC / B • Slaves Night Out / 1995 / COC / B • Slaves' Night Out / 1990 / COC / B • VGA: Don't Defy Domino / 1991 / VGA / B • VGA: Spanks-A-Lot / 1993 / VGA / B

GINA VALENTINA see Gina Valentino

GINA VALENTINO *(Gina Valentina, LaGina Valentina)*
Extra-pretty Italian-looking brunette with lithe tight body, medium droopy tits and an exceptionally good personality.

All The Way / 1989 / LIM / C • The Animal In Me / 1985 / IN / M • Bachelorette Party / 1984 / JVV / M • Back To Back #1 / 1987 / 4P / C • Back To Class #1 / 1984 / DR / M • Before She Says I Do / 1984 / MAP / M • Bent Over The Rent / 1984 / SKJ / B • Between The Cheeks #1 / 1985 / VC / M • Billionaire Girls Club / 1988 / LVI / C • Blue Dream Lover / 1985 / TAR / M • Candy Girls #5 / 19?? / AVC / M • Changing Places / 1984 / AVC / M • Correction Of Julie / 1985 / CS / B • Cum Shot Revue #2 / 1985 / HO / C • Dance Fever / 1985 / VCR / M • Deep Inside Tracey / 1987 / CDI / C • Deep Inside Traci / 1986 / CDI / C • Diamond Collection #76 / 1985 / CDI / M • Don't Tell Daddy #1 / 1985 / PL / C • Educating Mandy / 1985 / CDI / M • The Enchantress / 1985 / 4P / M • Ginger's Private Party / 1985 / VI / M • Girls Together / 1985 / GO / C • Golddiggers #1 / 1985 / VC / M • The Heartbreak Girl / 1985 / GO / M • Heartthrobs / 1985 / CA / M • Hindsight / 1985 / IN / M • Holiday For Angels / 1987 / IN / M • Hollywood Harlots / 1986 / VEX / C • Hollywood Heartbreakers / 1985 / VEX / M • Hot Sweet Honey / 1985 / VEP / M • I Love A Girl In A Uniform / 1989 / VC / C • I Want It All / 1984 / VD / M • Lingerie Party / 1987 / SE / C • Little Girls Of The Streets / 1984 / CV / M • Little Girls, Dirty Desires / 1984 / JVV / M • The Lost Angel / 1989 / KIS / C • The Love Scene / 1985 / CDI / M • Loving Spoonfulls / 1987 / 4P / C • The Midnight Zone / 1986 / IN / M • Oral Majority #04 / 1987 / WV / C • Oriental Jade / 1985 / VC / M • The Peek A Boo Gang / 1985 / COL / M • Penetration #5 / 1984 / AVC / M • Perfect Fit / 1985 / DR / M • Perversion / 1984 / AVC / M • Portrait Of Lust / 1984 / CC / M • Prescription For Passion / 1984 / VD / M • Rear Entry / 1985 / VCR / C • Spreading Joy / 1984 / IN / M • Studs

'n' Stars / 1989 / VC / C • Summer Girls / 1986 / HO / C • This Side Up / 1987 / VSX / C • This Stud's For You / 1986 / MAP / C • Too Good To Be True / 1984 / MAP / M • Too Young To Know / 1984 / CC / M • Tracy In Heaven (Orig 1985) / 1985 / WV / M • Tracy In Heaven (Rewrite) / 1986 / WV / M • The Twilight Moan / 1985 / WV / M • The Ultimate Thrill / 1988 / PIN / C • The Wacky World Of X-Rated Bloopers / 1989 / GO / M • Wild Weekend / 1984 / HO / M • With Love From Ginger / 1986 / HO / C

GINA VELOUR
The Operation / 1995 / 210 / M

GINA VERNAY see Star Index I

GINA VERONACA see Star Index I

GINA WILDE
The Wild Women / 1996 / PL / M

GINA WINTERS
Seymore Butts: Slippin' In Through The Out Door / 1996 / FH / M • Squirters / 1996 / ULI / M

GINGER
100% Amateur #18: / 1995 / OD / M • America's Raunchiest Home Videos #70: / 1993 / ZA / M • Blue Vanities #129 / 1990 / FFL / M • Blue Vanities #531 / 1993 / FFL / M • Blue Vanities #548 / 1994 / FFL / M • Creme De Femme #2 / 1981 / AVC / C • Creme De Femme #3 / 1981 / AVC / C • HomeGrown Video #452: Make Me Cum! / 1995 / HOV / M • Hot Body Video Magazine: Red Hot / 1995 / CG / S • Lesbian Lust Bust / 1995 / GLI / F • Limited Edition #06 / 1979 / AVC / M • Older & Bolder In San Francisco / 1996 / TEP / M • Pearl Necklace: Thee Bush League #26 / 1993 / SEE / M • Real (Estate) Bondage #3: Ginger Returns / 1995 / GAL / B • Rump Humpers #03 / 1992 / GLI / M • Snatch Masters #10 / 1995 / LEI / M • What's The Lesbian Doing In My Pirate Movie? / 1995 / LIP / F

GINGER (1981)
Country Comfort / 1981 / SE / M • Nightlife / 1983 / CA / M • Summer Of '72 / 1982 / CA / M

GINGER BREAD
Blue Vanities #198 / 1993 / FFL / M • Limited Edition #12 / 1980 / AVC / M

GINGER BUSH see Cody Foster

GINGER DARLING
Senior Sexcapades #1 / 1995 / PL / M

GINGER DODGERS
Fresh Faces #10 / 1996 / EVN / M

GINGER FRANKLIN
The Burning Sensation / cr78 / ASR / B

GINGER GRAHAM
Fortysomething And Still Hot / 1995 / SUF / M • Middle Aged Maidens / 1995 / GLI / M • Mike Hott: #312 Lesbian Sluts #19 / 1995 / MHV / F • Secret Seductions #1 / 1995 / LV / M • Secret Seductions #2 / 1995 / ULP / M

GINGER GRANT
Intimate Interviews #1 / 1996 / NIT / M

GINGER HILL
Bizarre Desires / 1995 / ROB / F • Erotic Visions / 1995 / ULI / M • Lesbian Bitches #2 / 1994 / ROB / F • Lesbian Social Club / 1995 / ROB / F

GINGER HULSEY
Hungry Eyed Woman / cr71 / VCX / M

GINGER JAYE *(Jinger Jaye)*
Old biddy with saggy medium tits and a falling apart body. Marginal face.

Horny Old Broads / 1995 / FPI / M • Hot Dreams / 1983 / CA / M • House Of Sin / 1982 / AVO / M • Luscious / 1980 / VXP / M • Peepholes / 1982 / AVC / M • Wild Innocents / 1982 / VCX / M

GINGER JONES

Hot Oven / 1975 / VC / M • Midnite Follies / cr65 / SOW / S

GINGER LEE HAWKINS

The Hippy Hooker / 19?? / ... / M

GINGER LYNN *(Ginger Lynn Allen)*

5'3" tall, very pretty with small tits and a tight body. Not in **Country Comfort**. According to **Hard Copy** September 10, 1992, she was dating Charlie Sheen at one time. In 1992 was caught for tax evasion and while on probation, a urine sample showed the presence of drugs. This resulted in two weeks in jail. Was 22 years old in 1985 (Born: 12/14/62) and originally came from Rockford, IL. De-virginized at 13. First on-screen anal was in **Pretty As You Feel** with Jerry Butler. Has had tits enhanced since leaving the business. March 31, 1996 had a baby boy, father undisclosed but rumored to be the head of a major porno manufacturer.

Adult 45 #01 / 1985 / DR / C • Adult Video News Magazine / 1985 / ZEB / M • All The Way / 1989 / LIM / C • Back To Class #1 / 1984 / DR / M • Backdoor Summer #1 / 1988 / PV / C • Backdoor Summer #2 / 1989 / PV / C • Ball Busters / 1984 / CV / M • The Beat Goes On / 1987 / VCR / C • Bedtime Tales / 1985 / SE / M • Best Of Atom / 1984 / AT / C • The Best Of Blondes / 1986 / VCR / C • The Best Of Ron Jeremy / 1990 / WET / C • The Best Of Taboo / cr90 / IN / C • Best Of Talk Dirty To Me #01 / 1991 / DR / C • The Better Sex Video Series #6: Acting Out Your Fantasies / 1992 / LEA / M • Between The Cheeks #1 / 1985 / VC / M • Beverly Hills Cox / 1986 / CA / M • Billionaire Girls Club / 1988 / LVI / C • Blame It On Ginger / 1986 / VI / M • Bloopers & Boners / 1996 / VI / M • Blowoff / 1985 / CA / M • Bound And Gagged: A Love Story / 1993 / TRI / S • Bunbusters / 1984 / VCR / M • Buried Alive / 1989 / C3S / S • Caballero Double Tape #1 / 1990 / CA / C • Caged Fury / 1990 / C3S / S • Cavalcade Of Stars / 1985 / VCR / C • China & Silk / 1984 / MAP / M • Cleo/Leo / 1989 / NWW / S • Club Ginger / 1986 / VI / M • Collection #05 / 1984 / CA / M • Collection #07 / 1984 / CA / M • A Coming Of Angels, The Sequel / 1985 / CA / M • Command Performance / 1988 / DR / C • Connection Live #1 / 1986 / VD / C • Cum Shot Revue #2 / 1985 / HO / C • Cum Shot Revue #3 / 1988 / HO / C • Cum Shot Revue #5 / 1988 / HO / C • Dance Fever / 1985 / VCR / M • Deep Inside Ginger Lynn / 1986 / SE / C • Dirty 30's Cinema: Ginger Lynn / 1986 / PV / C • Double Penetration Fever / 1989 / MIR / C • Dr Alien / 1989 / PAR / S • Electric Blue #013: Campus Fever / 1984 / CA / C • Electric Blue #017 / 1984 / CA / S • Electric Blue: Caribbean Cruise / 1984 / CA / S • Erotic Penetration / 1987 / HO / C • Escort Girls #1 / 198? / LVI / C • Facial Attraction / 1988 / BEE / C • Fantasy World / 1991 / NWV / C • Far Out Man / 1989 / C3S / S • First Annual XRCO Awards / 1984 / AVC / C • Forbidden Entry / 1984 / VCR / M • Gentlemen Prefer Ginger / 1985 / VI / M • Ginger

(1984-Vivid) / 1984 / VI / M • Ginger And Spice / 1986 / VI / M • The Ginger Effect / 1985 / VI / M • Ginger In Ecstasy / 1987 / GO / C • Ginger Lynn Allen's Lingerie Gallery #1 / 1994 / UNI / F • Ginger Lynn Allen's Lingerie Gallery #2: Private Screening / 1994 / UNI / F • Ginger Lynn Allen's Superbody Workout / 1993 / JDS / S • Ginger Lynn And Company / 1989 / ... / C • Ginger Lynn—Non-Stop / 1988 / VD / C • Ginger On The Rocks / 1985 / VI / M • Ginger Rides Again / 1988 / KIS / C • Ginger Snaps / 1987 / VI / M • Ginger Then And Now / 1990 / VI / C • Ginger's Greatest Boy/Girl Hits / 1987 / VI / C • Ginger's Greatest Girl/Girl Hits / 1986 / VI / C • Ginger's Hawaiian Scrapbook / 1988 / GO / C • Ginger's Private Party / 1985 / VI / M • Ginger: The Movie / 1988 / PV / C • Girls Of Paradise #1 / 1986 / PV / C • Girls On Fire / 1985 / VCX / M • Girls Together / 1985 / GO / C • Gourmet Premier: Ginger's Hot Massage / Photo Orgy #912 / cr85 / GO / M • Gourmet Premier: Throbbing Threesome / Hot Wife's Hunger 902 / cr86 / GO / M • Gourmet Quickies: Ginger Lynn #720 / 1985 / GO / C • The Grafenberg Spot / 1985 / MIT / M • Hollywood Boulevard #2 / 1989 / MGM / S • Hollywood X-Posed #1 / 1992 / VIM / C • Hot Ones / 1988 / HO / C • Hot Shorts: Ginger Lynn / 1986 / VCR / C • Hustler Honeys #2 / 1988 / VC / S • Hustler Honeys #4 / 1988 / VC / S • Hypnotic Sensations / 1985 / GO / M • I Want It All / 1984 / VD / M • Illusions Of Ecstasy / 1985 / NSV / M • Inside Ginger Lynn / 1985 / VD / C • Instant Karma / 1990 / MGM / S • Jailhouse Girls / 1984 / VC / M • Joys Of Erotica / 1984 / VCR / M • Joys Of Erotica #107 / 1984 / VCR / C • Joys Of Erotica #109 / 1984 / VCR / C • Kinky Business #1 / 1984 / DR / M • L'Amour / 1984 / CA / M • Leather Jackets / 1990 / C3S / S • Legends Of Porn #1 / 1987 / CV / C • Legends Of Porn #2 / 1989 / CV / C • Letters Of Love / 1985 / CA / M • Lip Service / 1988 / LV / C • A Little Bit Of Hanky Panky / 1984 / MAP / M • A Lust In The Fast Lane / 1984 / PV / M • Midnight Heat / 1988 / PLP / C • Mind, Body & Soul / 1992 / AIP / S • Miss Passion / 1984 / VD / M • The Modelling Studio / 1984 / GO / M • New Wave Hookers #1 / 1984 / VC / M • Night Of Loving Dangerously / 1984 / PV / M • On Golden Blonde / 1984 / PV / M • Only The Best Of Anal / 1992 / MET / C • Only The Best Of The Erotic Eighties / 1992 / VC / C • Panty Raid / 1984 / GO / M • Parliament: Super Head #1 / 1989 / PM / C • Photoflesh / 1984 / HO / M • The Pink Lagoon: A Sex Romp In Paradise / 1984 / GO / M • Playmate #01 / 1984 / VC / M • The Pleasure Hunt #1 / 1984 / NSV / M • The Pleasure Hunt #2 / 1985 / NSV / M • Pleasure Productions #06 / 1984 / VCR / M • Pleasure Productions #09 / 1985 / VCR / M • Pleasure Productions #11 / 1985 / VCR / M • The Poonies / 1985 / VI / M • Pretty As You Feel / 1984 / PV / M • Pretty Girl / 1984 / VIS / M • Private Love Affairs / 1985 / VCR / C • Project Ginger / 1985 / VI / M • Raven / 1985 / VCR / M • Ready, Willing & Anal (Cv) / 1993 / CV / C • Rearbusters / 1988 / LVI / C • Satan's Storybook / 1989 / EST / S • Secret Se-

duction / 1991 / FLA / C • Sex Asylum #1 / 1985 / VI / M • The Sex Game / 1987 / SE / C • Shape Up For Sensational Sex / 1985 / SE / M • Sheer Heaven / 1990 / CEL / S • Sinful Pleasures / 1987 / HO / C • Sister Dearest / 1984 / DR / M • Skin Deep / 1989 / MED / S • Slip Into Ginger & Amber / 1986 / MAP / C • Slumber Party / 1984 / HO / M • Some Kind Of Woman / 1985 / CA / M • Spermbusters / 1984 / AT / M • Splashing / 1986 / VCS / C • Stephanie's Outrageous / 1988 / LV / C • The Stranger / 1994 / C3S / S • Supergirls Do General Hospital / 1984 / VC / M • Surrender In Paradise / 1984 / GO / M • Suze's Centerfolds #8 / 1984 / CA / M • Suzie Superstar #2 / 1985 / CV / M • Suzie Superstar...The Search Continues / 1988 / CV / M • Swedish Erotica Featurettes #4 / 1990 / CA / M • Sweet Cheeks / 1987 / VCR / C • The Sweetest Taboo / 1986 / SE / M • Taboo #04 / 1985 / IN / M • Talk Dirty To Me #03 / 1986 / DR / M • A Taste Of Ginger / 1990 / PIN / C • Teasers / 1984 / HO / M • Ten Little Maidens / 1985 / EXF / M • Those Lynn Girls / 1989 / WV / C • Those Young Girls / 1984 / PV / M • Too Good To Be True / 1984 / MAP / M • Too Naughty To Say No / 1984 / CA / M • Trashy Lady / 1985 / MAP / M • A Tribute To The King / 1985 / VCX / C • Triple Header / 1986 / SE / C • Tropical Nights / 1988 / GO / C • Trouble Bound / 1992 / FOX / S • True Legends Of Adult Cinema: The Erotic Eighties / 1992 / VC / C • Ultimate Taboo / 1994 / ROP / S • Undressed Rehearsal / 1984 / VD / M • An Unnatural Act #1 / 1984 / DR / M • Up Up And Away / 1984 / CA / M • VCA Previews #4 / 1988 / VC / C • Vice Academy #1 / 1988 / PRS / S • Vice Academy #2 / 1990 / PRS / S • Vice Academy #3 / 1991 / PRS / S • Vice Academy #4 / 1994 / PRS / S • Voyeur's Delight / 1986 / VCS / C • The Wacky World Of X-Rated Bloopers / 1989 / GO / M • Whore / 1991 / VMA / S • Wild Black Erotica #4 / cr89 / VD / C • Wild Man / 1988 / CEL / S • Wild Weekend / 1984 / HO / M • With Love From Ginger / 1986 / HO / C • The Woman Who Loved Men / 1984 / SE / M • The World According To Ginger / 1985 / VI / M • Young Guns #2 / 1990 / FOX / S • [Ahpa: Vicky Vs Christy / 199? / AHP / B • [Die Laughing / 199? / ... / M • [Get Off With Ginger Lynn / 198? / ... / C • [Get Off With Hyapatia Lee / 198? / ... / C • [Ginger Lynn Meets John Holmes / 1991 / ... / C • [Ginger's Hot Massage / 1985 / ... / C • [God's Lonely Man / 199? / ... / M • [Intimate Bedroom Secrets / 198? / ... / M • [Kiss & Tell / 199? / ... / M • [Let The Music Be / 199? / ... / S • [Mystique Of The Orient #2 / 198? / ... / C • [Party At Rick's / 198? / ... / S

GINGER LYNN ALLEN see Ginger Lynn

GINGER PEACHY see Star Index I

GINGER RHODES see Star Index I

GINGER ROGERS

Kink Inc. / 1996 / MP0 / M

GINGER SNAP *(Ginger Snaps (cr75), Ginger Stark, Sharon Boxworth)*

Ugly with a pudgy body, black hair, and medium tits.

The Bite / 1975 / SVE / M • Dear Pam / 1976 / CA / M • The Love Bus / 1974 / OSC / M • Penthouse Passions / 1975 / BLT / M • Slip Up / 1974 / ALP / M

GINGER SNAPS (CR75) *see* **Ginger Snap**

GINGER SNAPS(THOMAS) *see* **Ginger Thomas**

GINGER SNATCH
Bun Busters #08 / 1993 / LBO / M • Bun Busters #09 / 1993 / LBO / M • Dirty Dating Service #04 / 1994 / WP / M

GINGER STARK *see* **Ginger Snap**

GINGER SUMMERS
Sex Over 40 #2 / 1994 / PL / M

GINGER THOMAS *(Ginger Snaps(Thomas))*
Amateur. Ugly and wears glasses.
A&B AB#059: Ginger's Gang Bang / 1990 / A&B / M • A&B AB#351: Ginger And Friends / 1991 / A&B / M • A&B AB#438: Fuck Our Pussies / 1994 / A&B / M • A&B GB#002: Fuck My Girlfriend / 1992 / A&B / M • A&B GB#003: Cum Together—Velvet And Ginger / 1992 / A&B / M • A&B GB#004: Ginger Takes It All / 1992 / A&B / M • Amateur Lesbians #27: Megan / 1992 / GO / F • Amateur Lesbians #28: Sharon / 1992 / GO / F • Amateur Lesbians #31: Lacy / 1992 / GO / F • Amateur Orgies #07 / 1992 / AFI / M • America's Raunchiest Home Videos #27: Here Cums Ginger! / 1992 / ZA / M • America's Raunchiest Home Videos #42: Swimsuit Sherrie / 1992 / ZA / M • Angels With Sticky Faces / 1991 / VD / M • AVP #9103: The Ball Street Journal, PM Edition / 1991 / AVP / M • AVP #9104: Mirror, Mirror / 1990 / AVP / F • AVP #9105: Rude Awakening / 1991 / AVP / M • AVP #9106: The Dare / 1991 / AVP / M • AVP #9108: Alone In The Woods / 1991 / AVP / M • AVP #9139: At Home / 1991 / AVP / M • Awakening In Blue / 1991 / PL / M • The Ball Street Journal / 1990 / VAL / M • Biff Malibu's Totally Nasty Home Videos #15 / 1992 / ANA / M • The Chamber Maids / 1993 / GOT / B • Chocolate Creme / 1992 / RUM / M • Dirty Bob's #01: Xcellent Adventure / 1991 / FLP / S • Hillary Vamp's Private Collection #07 / 1992 / HVD / M • Lesbian Pros And Amateurs #15 / 1992 / GO / F • Mr. Peepers Amateur Home Videos #29: Going Down Payment / 1991 / LBO / M • Mr. Peepers Amateur Home Videos #31: Ginger Thomas / 1991 / LBO / M • Mr. Peepers Amateur Home Videos #45: Coming From Behind / 1992 / LBO / M • Nina Hartley's Professional Amateur Tournament #1 / 1990 / RUM / M • Nina Hartley's Professional Amateur Tournament #2 / 1990 / BKD / M • Our Bang #02 / 1992 / GLI / M • Our Bang #04 / 1992 / GLI / M • Positively Pagan #03 / 1991 / ATA / M • Scratch: Return To Witch Fountain / 1993 / SCR / M • Scratch: Synergy #1: The Catch / 1992 / SCR / M • Scratch: Synergy #2: The Match / 1992 / SCR / M • Scratch: Synergy #3: The Make / 1992 / SCR / M • Tickets To Paradise / 1992 / XPI / M

GINGI
The Betrayal Of Innocence #1: The Awakening Of Marika / 1993 / CC / M • The Betrayal Of Innocence #2: The Decadence / 1993 / CC / M • The Betrayal Of Innocence #3: The Choice / 1993 / CC / M

GINI DAVIS
Lenny's Comeback / cr78 / CIN / M • Small Change / 1978 / CDC / M

GINI RATH

Sound Of Love / 1981 / CA / M

GINJER MARTIN
Odyssey / 1977 / VC / M

GINNETTE FREELAND *see* **Star Index I**

GINNI LEWIS
50 And Still Pumping! / 1994 / EMC / M • 55 And Still Bangin' / 1995 / HW / M • Big Murray's New-Cummers #17: Age Before Beauty / 1993 / FD / M • The Devil In Grandma Jones / 1994 / FC / M • Golden Oldies #3 / 1995 / TTV / M • Lactamania #2: The Squirt Fest / 1995 / TTV / M • Old Throat And D.P. / 1993 / FC / M • Positively Pagan #05 / 1993 / ATA / M

GINNY
Blue Vanities #583 / 1996 / FFL / M

GINNY TABOR
Ole / 1971 / KIT / M

GINO
Anal & 3-Way Play / 1995 / GLI / M • Odyssey Triple Play #62: Gang Bangs All Around / 1994 / OD / M

GINO COLBERT *(Sam Schad, Sam Shad)*
Sometime actor and director of gay and bisex movies. Same Shad is from **Inside Seka**.
Bi Day...Bi Night / 1988 / PV / G • Bi Dream Of Genie / 1990 / BIN / G • By Day Bi Night / 1989 / LV / G • Club Taboo / 1987 / MET / G • Dane's Brothel / 1990 / IF / G • Inch Bi Inch / 1989 / STA / G • Innocent Bi Standers / 1989 / LV / G • Inside Seka / 1980 / VXP / M • The Last Good-Bi / 1990 / CDI / G • Promises In The Dark / 1991 / CIN / G • Queens Behind Bars / 1990 / STA / G • She's A Boy / 1989 / LV / G • She-Male Nurse / 1989 / LV / G • She-Male Undercover / 1990 / STA / G • Switch Hitters #8 / 1995 / IN / G • Taboo #09 / 1991 / IN / M • Transsexual 6900 / 1990 / LV / G • The Ultimate Sex / 1992 / MET / G

GINO GAMBIO
Tail Taggers #130 / 1994 / WV / M

GINO GRAND
Borderline (Vivid) / 1995 / VI / M • Catch Of The Day #5 / 1996 / VG0 / M • Hard-On Copy / 1994 / WV / M • Pizza Sluts: They Deliver / 1995 / XCI / M • Stiff Competition #2 / 1994 / CA / M

GINO GULTIER
Transsexual Prostitutes #2 / 1997 / DFI / G

GIO ROMANO
Night Walk / 1995 / HIV / G

GIORDANO
Catching Snapper / 1995 / XCI / M

GIORGIO FALCONI *see* **Star Index I**

GIOVANINA *see* **Joan Devlon**

GIOVANNI GRIZELLE *see* **Star Index I**

GIOVANNI MENENDEZ *see* **Star Index I**

GISALE
Butt Bangers Ball #2 / 1996 / TTV / M

GISELA
Magma: Perverse Games / 1995 / MET / M

GISELLE
Hollywood Amateurs #21 / 1995 / MID / M • Hollywood Starlets Adventure #05 / 1995 / AVS / M • Magma: Double #2 / 1995 / MET / M • Magma: Double Anal / 1994 / MET / M • Magma: Fucking Holidays / 1995 / MET / M • Magma: Nymphettes / 1993 / MET / M • Magma: Sperm Dreams / 1990 / MET / M • Magma: Trans-Games / 1995 / MET / G • Porno X-Treme #2: Club Bizarre / 1995 / SC / M • Porno X-Treme #4: Wet Dream / 1995 / SC / M

GISELLE CLIMAX *see* **Star Index I**

GISELLE CONNORS
The Gypsy / 1996 / NIT / M

GISSEL MASON
Fresh Faces #08 / 1995 / EVN / M

GITA KOBAR *see* **Star Index I**

GIULIA
Prague By Night #2 / 1996 / EA / M

GIUSY CARRARA
Midnight Obsession / 1995 / XC / M

GIZZELLA *see* **Star Index I**

GLADYS
Bend Over Brazilian Babes #2 / 1993 / EA / M • Blue Vanities #554 / 1994 / FFL / M

GLAUCIA GONZALEZ
Max #06: Going South / 1995 / FRM / M

GLAUCIA NUNES
The Anal Adventures Of Max Hardcore: Hombre / 1995 / ZA / M • Max World #1 / 1995 / FRM / M

GLEN
English Muffins / 1995 / VC / M • Flexxx #4 / 1995 / VT / M

GLEN GATTON
Vivid At Home #02 / 1994 / VI / M

GLEN JOSEPH
The Burning Sensation / cr78 / ASR / B • Doctor Yes / 1978 / VIS / M • In Too Deep / 1979 / CDC / M

GLENDA FARREL *see* **Star Index I**

GLENDA GRAHAM
Blue Vanities #514 / 1992 / FFL / M

GLENDA SIMON *see* **Star Index I**

GLENDA TURNER *see* **Star Index I**

GLENN *see* **Star Index I**

GLENN HOEFFNER
Shame / 1994 / VI / M

GLENN SWALLOW
All The Senator's Girls / 1977 / CA / M

GLINT
Liquid Lips #2 / 1994 / MAV / M

GLITTER
The Stand-Up / 1994 / VC / M

GLORIA
A&B AB#544: My Wife Wants Black Cocks To Suck / 1995 / A&B / M • A&B GB#102: Gloria Does The Masses / 1993 / A&B / M • A&B GB#103: 2+3+4=9 Cocks For Gloria / 1993 / A&B / M • A&B GB#104: Back To Back Gang Bangs / 1993 / A&B / M • A&B GB#105: Surprise Cock Party / 1993 / A&B / M • A&B GB#106: Thanksgiving Gang Bang / 1993 / A&B / M • A&B GB#107: Get Away Gang Bang / 1993 / A&B / M • A&B GB#108: Back To Back Gang Bang #2 / 1993 / A&B / M • A&B GB#109: Moving Out Gang Bang / 1993 / A&B / M • A&B GB#110: 8 Man Fuck Fest / 1993 / A&B / M • Big Busty #47 / 1994 / BTO / S • Blue Vanities #554 / 1994 / FFL / M • D-Cup Holiday / 1991 / BTO / M • Double D-Cup Dates / 1994 / BTO / M • Girls Around The World #03 / 1990 / BTO / M • Nasty New-cummers #01 / 1993 / MET / M • The Other Side Of Debbie / 1991 / CC / M • Robin Head / 1991 / CC / M

GLORIA ALAY *see* **Star Index I**

GLORIA DEL MONTE
Paradise Villa / 1995 / WIV / M

GLORIA HADDIT *see* **Star Index I**

GLORIA HARDY *see* **Star Index I**

GLORIA HARRISON *see* **Terri Dolan**

GLORIA HOPE
A Dirty Western #1 / 1973 / AR / M • Saturday Matinee Series #3 / 1996 / VCX / C • That's Erotic / 1979 / CV / C

GLORIA LEONARD *(Gayle Leonard)*

Jewish from the Bronx. Was 38 in 1978 and sometime publisher of *High Society*. She studied ballet for 11 years and got into porn in 1975. Even at that age was ugly with a womanly body, big tits and reddish brown curly hair. Was married to (and may still be) Bobby Hollander.
All About Gloria Leonard / 1978 / VXP / M • Bad Girls #4 / 1984 / GO / M • Bon Appetit / 1980 / QX / M • Burlexxx / 1984 / VC / M • Candy Lips / 1975 / CXV / M • Celebration / 1984 / GO / C • Dirty Looks / 1982 / VC / C • Executive Secretary / 1975 / CA / M • Extreme Close-Up / 1981 / VC / M • Farmers Daughters / 1975 / VC / M • Fiona On Fire / 1978 / VC / M • First Annual XRCO Awards / 1984 / AVC / C • Flesh In Ecstasy #15: Bunny Bleu / 1988 / GO / C • GVC: Bizarre Moods #111 / cr83 / GO / M • GVC: Real Estate #109 / 198? / GO / M • GVC: Summer Beach House #106 / 1980 / GO / M • Heat Wave / 1977 / COM / M • Hollywood Goes Hard / 19?? / AVO / B • Hot Wire / 1985 / VXP / M • Intimate Desires / 1978 / VEP / M • Joy / 1977 / QX / M • Kinky Potpourri #32 / 199? / SVE / C • Ladies Of The Knight / 1984 / GO / M • The Legend Of Lady Blue / 1978 / VCX / M • Legends Of Porn #1 / 1987 / CV / C • Legends Of Porn #3 / 1991 / MET / C • Lifestyles Convention / 1992 / PKP / S • The Little Blue Box / 1978 / BL / M • Made In Heaven / 1991 / PP / M • Magic Girls / 1983 / SVE / M • Maraschino Cherry / 1978 / QX / M • Misbehavin' / 1979 / VXP / M • Naked Goddess #1 / 1991 / VC / M • Naked Goddess #2 / 1991 / VC / M • New York Babes / 1979 / AR / M • New York Vice / 1984 / CC / M • October Silk / 1980 / COM / M • Odyssey / 1977 / VC / M • On Trial #3: Takin' It To The Jury / 1992 / VI / M • On Trial #4: The Verdict / 1992 / VI / M • Only The Very Best On Film / 1992 / VC / C • The Opening Of Misty Beethoven / 1976 / VC / M • Phone Sex Fantasies / 1984 / QX / M • Powerbone / 1976 / VC / M • Revenge Of The Bi Dolls / 1994 / CAT / G • Roommates / 1982 / VXP / M • Sex Anneal / 1986 / VES / S • Sho'e So Finn #1 / 1985 / VC / M • Silky / 1980 / VXP / M • Taboo American Style #1: The Ruthless Beginning / 1985 / VC / M • Taboo American Style #2: The Story Continues / 1985 / VC / M • Taboo American Style #3: Nina Becomes An Actress / 1985 / VC / M • Taboo American Style #4: The Exciting Conclusion / 1985 / VC / M • Temptations / 1976 / VXP / M • This Lady Is A Tramp / 1980 / CV / M • Three Daughters / 1986 / FEM / M • Thrilled To Death / 1988 / REP / S • The Trouble With Young Stuff / 1976 / VC / M • Twilight Pink #1 / 1980 / AR / M • Vanessa's Bed Of Pleasure / 1983 / SVE / M • Virgin Dreams / 1976 / BMV / M • Vow Of Passion / 1991 / VI / M • Waterpower! / 1975 / VHL / M • Wishman / 1993 / MON / S • The World Of Henry Paris / 1981 / VC / C

GLORIA POOLE
Tender And Wild / 1989 / MTP / M

GLORIA RICKOFF
That Lady From Rio / 1976 / VXP / M

GLORIA ROBERTS *see Connie Peterson*

GLORIA ROSE
Seduce Me Tonight / 1984 / AT / M

GLORIA SHOWER
Deep Throat Girls / cr75 / ... / M

GLORIA TANS *see Star Index I*

GLORIA THROATE *see Star Index I*

GLORIA TODD
All About Gloria Leonard / 1978 / VXP / M • Beyond The Blue / cr78 / SVE / M • Honeymoon Haven / 1977 / QX / M • Slave Of Pleasure / 1978 / BL / M • Suzie's Take Out Service / 1975 / CDC / M • Take Off / 1978 / VXP / M

GLORIA VERVER
Ultraflesh / 1980 / GO / M

GLORIA VON STUBEN
The Collegiates / 1971 / BL / M

GO *see Star Index I*

GODDESS
Dangerous Behinds #2 / 1996 / HW / M

GODDESS ATHENA *see Star Index I*

GODDESS CANDICE *see Star Index I*

GODDESS ROXANNE *see Star Index I*

GODDESS SONDRA *see Sondra Rey*

GODESS ROSEMARY
Dinner With Andres / 1991 / Z/N / B

GOERGIE BLAKE
A-Z Of Lesbian Love / 1996 / PAL / F

GOFF VAN LOON
Bi Bi European Style / 1990 / PL / G • Get Bi Tonight / 1991 / PL / G

GOLDEN JADE
Adventures Of The DP Boys: Big Black Booty / 1994 / HW / M • Adventures Of The DP Boys: The Blacks Are Back / 1994 / HW / M • Adventures Of The DP Boys: The Blacks Are Cumming / 1994 / HW / M • Amateur Black: Honeys / 1995 / SUF / M • Amateur Black: Whores / 1996 / SUF / M • Amateur Nights #13 / 1996 / HO / M • The Anal Adventures Of Max Hardcore: High Voltage / 1994 / ZA / M • Anal Virgins Of America #10 / 1994 / FOR / M • Analtown USA #03 / 1995 / NIT / M • Beach Bum Amateur's #42 / 1995 / MID / M • Big Man's Ebony Dreams / 1996 / LOK / M • Black Bush Bashers / 1996 / LOK / M • The Black Butt Sisters Do Baltimore / 1995 / MID / M • The Black Butt Sisters Do Houston / 1996 / MID / M • The Black Butt Black Fantasies #09 / 1995 / HW / M • Black Fantasies #10 / 1995 / HW / M • Black Fantasies #15 / 1996 / HW / M • Black Gangbangers #01 / 1994 / HW / M • Black Hollywood Amateurs #13 / 1995 / MID / M • Black Hollywood Amateurs #20 / 1995 / MID / M • Black Hollywood Amateurs #26 / 1996 / MID / M • Bobby Hollander's Maneaters #01 / 1993 / SFP / M • Bobby Hollander's Maneaters #03 / 1993 / SFP / M • Boob Tube Lube / 1996 / RAS / M • Booty Bang #2 / 1996 / HW / M • Bow Down Backstreet / 1996 / HW / M • Butt-Nanza / 1995 / WV / M • Cindy's House Party / 1996 / HW / M • Coochie's Under Fire / 1996 / HW / F • Cum Buttered Corn Holes #3 / 1996 / NIT / C • Da Booty Bang #2 / 1996 / HW / M • Ebony Erotica #31: Creme De Cocoa / 1995 / GO / M • Ed Woody / 1995 / HBE / M • Far East Fantasy / 1995 / SUF / M • A Few Good Rears / 1993 / IN / M • Forbidden Subjects #3 / 1995 / FC / M • Git Yo' Ass On Da Bus! / 1996 / HW / M • The Go-Go Girls / 1994 / EVN / M • Golden Rod / 1996 / SPI / M • The Grunge Girl Chronicles / 1995 / MAX / M • Hardcore Confidential #2 / 1996 / TEP

/ M • In Da Booty / 1996 / LV / M • Interview's Anal Queens / 1996 / LV / M • Kinky Debutante Interviews #05 / 1994 / IP / M • Mall Slut / 1997 / SC / M • Miss Sharon Mitchell's Diaries #1 / 1995 / STM / B • Nasty Newcummers #06 / 1995 / MET / M • Orgies Orgies Orgies / 1994 / WV / M • Pay 4 Play / 1996 / RAS / M • Perverted Stories #07 / 1996 / JMP / M • Perverted Stories #08 / 1996 / JMP / M • Perverted Stories #09 / 1996 / JMP / M • Rimmers #1 / 1996 / MP0 / M • Shades Of Color #1 / 1995 / LBO / M • She-Male Encounters #22: She-Male Mystique / 1995 / MET / G • Skeezers / 1996 / LV / M • Squirt Flirts / 1996 / RAS / M • SVE: Anally Made Jade / 1993 / SVE / M • Video Virgins #15 / 1994 / NS / M • The Violation Of Alexandria Dane / 1995 / JMP / F • Wild Orgies #13 / 1994 / AFI / M • Yo' Where's Homey? / 1996 / SUF / M

GOLDIE
AVP #9133: Plunger Power / 1991 / AVP / M • Back To The Orient / 1992 / HW / M • Blue Vanities #583 / 1996 / FFL / M • Cracklyn / 1994 / HW / M • Da Booty Call / 1994 / HW / M • Dirty Bob's #15: The Contest! / 1994 / FLP / S • HomeGrown Video #453: / 1995 / HOV / M • Ms. Fix-It / 1994 / PRK / M • Oriental Gang Bang Fantasy / 1994 / FC / M • Sex On The Beach!: Spring Break Texas Style / 1994 / CPG / F • Sweat 'n' Bullets / 1995 / MID / M

GOLDIE (HEATHER B.) *see Heather Bowe*

GOLDIE (S.ROSE) *see Summer Rose*

GOLDIE ARCH *see Star Index I*

GOLDIE GIBSON
Blue Vanities #580 / 1996 / FFL / M • Glamour Girls U.S.A. #02 / 1996 / SOW / M

GOLDIE HAWK *see Star Index I*

GOLDIE LAKE *see Heather Lere*

GOLDIE LOX *see Star Index I*

GOLDIE STAR
Bend Over Babes #4 / 1996 / EA / M • Deep Inside Dirty Debutantes #11 / 1996 / 4P / M • Everybody Wants Some / 1996 / EIA / F • The Hardy Tail Of Arnie Italy Dali / 1995 / CG / F • Hot Body Video Magazine: Beverly Hills Wet T-Shirt Contest / 1994 / CG / F • Ona Zee's Doll House #4 / 1996 / ONA / F • Phantasm / 1995 / WP / M • Pick Up Lines #02 / 1995 / 4P / M • Pick Up Lines #05 / 1996 / OD / M • Sex On The Strip: The Lusty Ladies Of Las Vagas / 1993 / CPG / F • Thin Ice / 1996 / ONA / M • Venom #2 / 1996 / VD / M • Video Virgins #29 / 1996 / NS / M • The Wicked Web / 1996 / WP / M

GONZO *see Star Index I*

GOR *see Star Index I*

GORDON
AVP #9152: Three Man Slut / 1991 / AVP / M • Homegrown Video #403 / 1993 / HOV / M

GORDON BARCLAY
Suck Channel / 1991 / VIM / M

GORDON DUVALL *see Carter Stevens*

GORDON LEE
Lust Weekend / 1967 / SOW / S • She-Male Call Girls / 1996 / BIZ / G

GORDON O. DUVALL *see Carter Stevens*

GORDON PARKER
Born For Love / 1987 / ... / M

GORDON WELLS
Penitent Wife / Miss Armstrong / 1993 / CS / B

GORDON WILSON see Star Index I

GOTCHA see Star Index I

GOTHA ANDERSON
Bordello / 1973 / AR / M

GOTHE GREFBO
Bel Ami / 1976 / VXP / M

GRACE
ABA: Double Feature #2 / 1996 / ALP / M • Joe Elliot's College Girls #34 / 1994 / JOE / M • Rip-Off Of Millie / cr78 / VHL / M

GRACE BILLIGS see Star Index I

GRACE CARTER see Star Index I

GRACE HARLOW
Zazel / 1996 / CV / M

GRACE HEART see Star Index I

GRACE SANTOS see Star Index I

GRACE SCOTT see Star Index I

GRACE TARPEY
All About Sex / 1970 / AR / M

GRACE TURLEY see Star Index I

GRACE WEST
Nasty / 1985 / NSV / M • Rear Action Girls #1 / 1984 / LIP / F • Rear Action Girls #2 / 1985 / LIP / F

GRACE WILD see Star Index I

GRACIE HOLLAND see Star Index I

GRACIELLA
Joe Elliot's College Girls #34 / 1994 / JOE / M

GRADY SUTTON see Paul Thomas

GRANDWOOD
Mistress Justine #2 / 1995 / VP0 / B • Slave Julia / 1995 / VP0 / B

GRANT
HomeGrown Video #465: Bong The Schlong / 1996 / HOV / M

GRANT DICKERSON
The Coach's Daughter / 1991 / AR / M

GRANT JONES
Mother's Pride / 1985 / DIM / M

GRANT KING see Star Index I

GRANT LARSEN
Secret Sex #3: The Takeover / 1994 / CAT / G

GRANT LARSON
Long Play / 1995 / 3XP / G • More Than Friends / 1995 / KDP / G

GRANT LOMBARD see Ken Scudder

GRANT STOCKTON see Ken Scudder

GREER SHAPIRO
Hot Dallas Nights / 1981 / VCX / M

GREG
Big Bust Babes #12 / 1993 / AFI / M • Big Murray's New-Cummers #30: Couples At Play / 1995 / FD / M • Blue Vanities #197 / 1993 / FFL / M • Bobby Hollander's Rookie Nookie #08 / 1993 / SFP / M • Crew Sluts / 1996 / NOT / M • Homegrown Video #342 / 1991 / HOV / M • HomeGrown Video #458: Cream Pie For Dessert / 1995 / HOV / C • HomeGrown Video #465: Bong The Schlong / 1996 / HOV / M

GREG AFARIS
Snack Time / 1983 / HO / M

GREG ALAN
Tongue Of Velvet / 1985 / VCR / M

GREG ALVERADO see Star Index I

GREG DEREK
Backdoor To Hollywood #01 / 1986 / CDI / M • Bare Elegance / 1984 / MAP / M • Behind Blue Eyes #1 / 1986 / ME / M • The Best Little Whorehouse In Beverly Hills / 1986 / CDI / M • Blondie / 1985 / TAR / M •

Blow For Blow / 1992 / ZA / M • Bodacious Ta Ta's / 1984 / CA / M • Cabaret Sin / 1987 / IN / M • Country Girl / 1985 / AVC / M • Dirty Letters / 1984 / VD / M • Empire Of The Sins / 1988 / IN / M • Erotic Express / 1983 / CV / M • Fantasies Unltd. / 1985 / CDI / M • Fast Girls #1 / 1987 / GBX / M • Female Sensations / 1984 / VC / M • Ginger (1984-Vivid) / 1984 / VI / M • Hard Ride / 1986 / VT / M • The Heat Is On / 1985 / WV / M • Heavy Breathing / 1986 / CV / M • Hollywood Pink / 1985 / HO / M • Hollywood Undercover / 1989 / BWV / C • Hot Spa / 1984 / CA / M • I Never Say No / 1983 / VC / M • I Want It All / 1984 / VD / M • Intimate Realities #1 / 1983 / VC / M • Intimate Realities #2 / 1983 / VC / M • Kiss Of The Dragon Lady / 1986 / SEV / M • Legs / 1986 / AMB / M • Letters Of Love / 1985 / CA / M • Limited Edition #26 / 1984 / AVC / M • Lingerie / 1983 / CDI / M • Loose Morals / 1987 / HO / M • Lust American Style / 1985 / WV / M • Maximum #5 / 1983 / CA / M • Nice 'n' Tight / 1985 / AIR / M • Nina's Knockouts / 1987 / AVC / C • Nooner / 1986 / AVC / M • Open Up Tracy / 1984 / VD / M • A Passage To Ecstasy / 1985 / CDI / M • Pleasure Spot / 1986 / CA / M • Pretty As You Feel / 1984 / PV / M • Radio K-KUM / 1984 / HO / M • Raw Talent #2 / 1987 / VC / M • Sex Maniacs / 1987 / JOY / C • Sex With A Stranger / 1986 / AVC / M • Sister Dearest / 1984 / DR / M • Stud Hunters / 1984 / CA / M • Sugarpussy Jeans / 1986 / TEM / M • Surfside Sex / 1985 / PV / M • Teasers / 1984 / HO / M • Traci's Big Trick / 1987 / VAS / M • Transaction #1 / 1986 / WET / M • Tres Riche / 1986 / CLV / M • The Twilight Moan / 1985 / WV / M • Virgin Heat / 1986 / TEM / M • Vote Pink / 1984 / VD / M • Where The Sun Never Shines / 1990 / IN / C

GREG FULLTEN
Anal Party Girls / 1996 / GV / M

GREG GOODIE
Anal Camera #05 / 1995 / EVN / M

GREG HART
Take Off / 1978 / VXP / M • Visions / 1977 / QX / M

GREG HOLMER see Beau Michaels

GREG HOLMES see Star Index I

GREG LIONS see Star Index I

GREG MICHAELS see Star Index I

GREG NETT see Star Index I

GREG ORY see Randy Spears

GREG PATRICK see Randy Spears

GREG RAMBO see Star Index I

GREG ROBINSON see Star Index I

GREG ROME *(Rocky Rome, Rock Rome)*
Adult 45 #01 / 1985 / DR / C • Amber Lynn: She's Back / 1995 / TTV / C • Angels Of Passion / 1986 / CDI / M • Back Road To Paradise / 1984 / CDI / M • The Beat Goes On / 1987 / VCR / C • Breezy / 1985 / VCR / M • Casino Of Lust / 1984 / AT / M • Catalina Five-O: White Coral, Blue Death / 1990 / CIN / M • Cavalcade Of Stars / 1985 / VCR / C • Deep Inside Traci / 1986 / CDI / C • Doctor Desire / 1984 / VD / M • Escort Girls #1 / 1987 / LVI / C • Flesh Fire / 1985 / AVC / M • Forbidden Fruit / 1985 / PV / M • Freak Show / 1991 / FC / M • Golddiggers #1 / 1985 / VC / M • Good Girls Do / 1984 / HO / M • GVC: Hot Numbers #133 / 1984 / GO / M • Head & Tails / 1988 / VD / M • Heartthrobs / 1985 / CA /

M • The Heat Is On / 1985 / WV / M • Hindsight / 1985 / IN / M • Holly Does Hollywood #1 / 1985 / VEX / M • Hollywood Harlots / 1986 / VEX / C • Hollywood Heartbreakers / 1985 / VEX / M • Hot Merchandise / 1985 / AVC / M • I Dream Of Ginger / 1985 / VI / M • I Like To Be Watched / 1984 / VD / M • I Want It All / 1984 / VD / M • The Idol / 1985 / WV / M • The Joy-Stick Girls / 1986 / CLV / M • Joys Of Erotica #110 / 1984 / VCR / C • Lady Cassanova / 1985 / AVC / M • Letters Of Love / 1985 / CA / M • Little Girls, Dirty Desires / 1984 / JVV / M • Loose Ends #1 / 1984 / 4P / M • Love At First Sight / 1987 / SE / C • The Lover Girls / 1985 / VEX / M • Lust American Style / 1985 / WV / M • Lusty / 1986 / CDI / M • Mad Sex / 1986 / VD / M • Make Me Want It / 1986 / CA / M • Mirage #1 / 1991 / VC / M • Miss Passion / 1984 / VD / M • The Modelling Studio / 1984 / GO / M • More Than A Handful / 1993 / CA / C • New Wave Hookers #1 / 1984 / VC / M • Older Women With Young Boys / 1984 / CC / M • Open Up Tracy / 1984 / VD / M • Oral Majority #03 / 1986 / WV / C • Oriental Jade / 1985 / VC / M • Our Major Is Sex / 1984 / VD / M • Penetration #1 / 1984 / AVC / M • Pleasure Productions #12 / 1985 / VCR / M • Prescription For Passion / 1984 / VD / M • Pretty As You Feel / 1984 / PV / M • Raven / 1985 / VCR / M • Satin Finish / 1985 / SUV / M • Sex Liners / 1991 / CIN / M • Sex Waves / 1984 / EXF / M • Sexaholic / 1985 / AVC / M • Sexpertease / 1985 / VD / M • Sister Dearest / 1984 / DR / M • Skin Games / 1986 / VEX / M • Skin Games / 1991 / VEX / C • Squalor Motel / 1985 / SE / M • Starlets / 1985 / 4P / M • Stiff Competition #1 / 1984 / CA / M • Summer Break / 1985 / VEX / M • Sweet Cheeks / 1987 / VCR / C • Tarot Temptress / 1985 / AA / M • Teasers / 1984 / HO / M • Tip Of The Tongue / 1985 / V20 / M • Titty-Titty Bang-Bang / 1992 / FC / C • Treasure Chest / 1985 / GO / M • Two Timing Tracie / 1985 / V20 / M • Up Up And Away / 1984 / CA / M • Vote Pink / 1984 / VD / M • Water Nymph / 1987 / LIM / M • We Love To Tease / 1985 / VD / M • Wet Sex / 1984 / CA / M • Where The Girls Are / 1984 / VEX / M • Where The Sun Never Shines / 1990 / IN / C • White Bun Busters / 1985 / VC / M • Wicked Whispers / 1985 / VD / M • You Make Me Wet / 1985 / SVE / M • You're The Boss / 1985 / VD / M • Young And Naughty / 1984 / HO / M

GREG RUFFNER see Craig Roberts

GREG SLAVIN see Randy Spears

GREG STUDMAN
The Best Little Whorehouse In Tijuana / 1995 / HBE / M • Ebony Dancer / 1994 / HBE / M • Ed Woody / 1995 / HBE / M • Made In The Hood / 1995 / HBE / M

GREG TAYLOR
Eat At Dave's #1 / 1995 / SP / M

GREG WALTERS
Party #1 / 1979 / NAT / M • Tattooed Lady (AVC) / 19?? / BIZ / M

GREG WILCOCKS *(Master Greg)*
SO of Vixxen Vaughan and usually performs with her.
Dirty Dancers #2 / 1994 / 4P / M • Drastic Measures / 1996 / GOT / B • Extreme Guilt / 1996 / GOT / B • On Your Knees / 1995 / GOT / B • Road Trippin' #03: New York City

/ 1994 / OUP / M • Very Bad Girls / 1995 / GOT / B

GREGG BROWN *see* **Gregory Dark**

GREGG DALE
L.A. Tool & Die / 1979 / TMX / G

GREGG MILES *see* *Star Index I*

GREGOR SAMSA *(Scott Wainwright, Scott Long (Gregor))*
Assuming The Position / 1989 / V99 / M • Back To Nature / 1990 / CA / M • Backdoor To Hollywood #10 / 1989 / CIN / M • Belle Of The Ball / 1989 / V99 / M • Blackman & Anal Woman #2 / 1990 / PL / M • Boobs, Butts And Bloopers #1 / 1990 / HO / M • Breast Side Story / 1990 / LE / M • Deep Throat #4 / 1990 / AR / M • Devil In The Blue Dress / 1989 / ME / M • Driving Miss Daisy Crazy #1 / 1990 / WV / M • The End Of The Innocence / 1989 / IN / M • Girls Of The Double D #12 / 1990 / CDI / M • Good Things Come In Small Packages / 1989 / CA / M • Graduation Ball / 1989 / CAE / M • Have I Got A Girl For You / 1989 / VEX / M • Heavenly Hyapatia / 1990 / VI / M • Hershe Highway #3 / 1990 / HO / M • Jug Humpers / 1995 / V99 / C • Laid Off / 1990 / CA / M • Life, Love And Divorce / 1990 / LV / M • Lunar Lust / 2990 / HO / M • Lust In The Woods / 1990 / VI / M • Miss Directed / 1990 / VI / M • Moondance / 1991 / WV / M • Next Door Neighbors #07 / 1989 / BON / M • Oral Addiction / 1989 / LV / M • Oriental Spice / 1990 / SE / M • Paradise Road / 1990 / WV / M • Racquel's Treasure Hunt / 1990 / VC / M • The Rise Of The Roman Empress #2 / 1990 / PV / M • The Scarlet Mistress / 1990 / VI / M • Seduction / 1990 / VEX / M • Sex & Other Games / 1990 / CIN / M • Sex Lives On Porno Tape / 1992 / VC / C • Sex On Location / 1989 / KIS / M • Stiff Magnolias / 1990 / HO / M • Tailgunners / 1990 / CDI / M • Tattle Tales / 1989 / SE / M • Trick Tracy #2: Tracy Loves Dick / 1990 / CC / M • Tug O' Love / 1990 / CC / M • Undercover Angel / 1988 / IN / M • Where The Sun Never Shines / 1990 / IN / C • X-Rated Blondes / 1992 / VD / C

GREGORY *see Star Index I*

GREGORY DARK *(Gregg Brown)*
Normally a director. Not actually related to the other Dark "brother"..
Fallen Angels / 1983 / VES / M

GREGORY LIONS *see* *Star Index I*

GREGORY MANN *see* *Star Index I*

GREGORY PATRICK *see* **Randy Spears**

GREGORY PHILLIPS *see* **Jon Dough**

GRETA
Blush: Clips / 1990 / BLV / F • Mike Hott: #358 Cunt Of The Month: Chardonnay / 1996 / MHV / M • The Secret Life Of Herbert Dingle / 1994 / TTV / M

GRETA CARLSON *(Sherri Graham, Sherri (G.Carlson), Greta Karlson, Leita, Allison Brach, Treasure Chest, Shary Graham)*
Hefty blonde with large enhanced tits.
Adventures In Paradise / 1992 / VEX / M • Amateur Lesbians #23: Sherri / 1992 / GO / F • Amateur Lesbians #37: Gretta / 1993 / GO / F • Amateur Lesbians #38: Jessica / 1993 / GO / F • America's Raunchiest Home Videos #03: Shake 'n' Bake / 1991 / ZA / M • AVP #9111: The Pass / 1991 / AVP / M • AVP #9150: Babes In Joyland / 1990 / AVP / F • Bad Girls From Mars /

1990 / VMA / S • Battling Bitches / 1993 / SBP / B • Beach Bum Amateur's #12 / 1992 / MID / M • The Bedford Wives / 1994 / LON / B • Bev's Bondage Torment / 1994 / BON / B • Biff Malibu's Totally Nasty Home Videos #17 / 1992 / ANA / M • Big Boob Bangeroo #1 / 1995 / TTV / M • Big Boob Bangeroo #2 / 1995 / TTV / M • Big Boob Bangeroo #4 / 1995 / TTV / M • Big Boob Bangeroo #7 / 1996 / TTV / M • Big Murray's New-Cummers #01: Blondes Have More... / 1992 / FD / M • Big Murray's New-Cummers #08: Blondes Have More #2 / 1993 / FD / M • Binders Keepers / 1993 / BON / B • Bip Tease / 1996 / BON / B • Bonda-Cize / 1988 / BON / B • Bondage Across The Border / 1993 / B&D / B • Bondage Memories #02 / 1993 / BON / C • Bound To Tease #5 / 1990 / BON / C • The Boy Toy / 1995 / BON / B • Breast Wishes #09 / 1992 / LBO / M • Breast Wishes #14 / 1993 / LBO / M • Breast Worx #03 / 1991 / LBO / M • Breast Worx #05 / 1991 / LBO / M • Breast Worx #06 / 1991 / LBO / M • Breast Worx #24 / 1992 / LBO / M • Breast Worx #31 / 1992 / LBO / M • Breast Worx #32 / 1992 / LBO / M • Cage Cats / 1993 / SBP / B • Carnal Crimes / 1991 / MAE / S • Casbah Fantasy / 1989 / BON / B • Caught In The Act / 1992 / BON / B • Cheap Shots / 1994 / PRE / B • Cherry Red / 1993 / RB / B • Contract For Torment / 1995 / BON / B • Corsets & Cords / 1994 / BON / B • Creme De La Face #01 / 1994 / OD / M • Creme De La Face #02 / 1994 / OD / M • Criss-Cross / 1993 / BON / B • Cult Of The Whip / 1995 / LON / B • Deception (1995-B&D) / 1995 / BON / B • Desert Heat / 1992 / BON / B • Deutsch Marks / 1992 / BON / B • Dominating Girlfriends #2 / 1992 / PL / B • Double D Nurses / 1994 / PV / M • Droid Gunner / 1995 / NEH / S • An Editor's Nightmare / 1995 / LON / B • Feet For The Master / 1994 / SBP / B • Girls And Guns / 1992 / KBR / M • The Girls From Hootersville #06 / 1994 / SFP / M • Greta Carlson Memories #1 / 1994 / BON / C • Greta Carlson Memories #2 / 1996 / BON / C • Greta Carlson Sessions #1 / 1994 / BON / B • Greta Carlson Sessions #2 / 1994 / BON / B • Greta Carlson Sessions #3 / 1994 / BON / B • Greta Carlson Sessions #4 / 1995 / BON / B • Greta's Ultimate Penalty #1 / 1995 / BON / B • Greta's Ultimate Penalty #2: The Real Thing / 1995 / BON / B • GRG: Dueling Dykes / 1994 / GRG / F • GRG: Greta's Sinful & Sexual Masturbation / 1994 / GRG / F • GRG: Nasty Naughty Nymphos / 1994 / GRG / F • GRG: Pain & Pleasure / 1994 / GRG / B • GRG: Two Mistresses And A Slave / 1994 / GRG / B • Harem Nights / 1996 / SHL / B • Haunting Fear / 1990 / ... / S • Heatwave #1 / 1992 / FH / F • High Heeled & Horny #1 / 1994 / LBO / M • Hollywood Teasers #04 / 1992 / LBO / F • Home Bound Slave / 1993 / VTF / B • Hot Box / 1995 / V99 / C • House Of Slaves / 1995 / HOM / B • How To Make A Model #02: Got Her In Bed / 1993 / QUA / M • I Obey You / 1993 / VTF / B • If Looks Could Kill / 1992 / V99 / M • Illusions #1 / 1992 / IF / M • Journal Of O #1: Servant Slave / 1994 / ONA / M • Kittens #6 / 1994 / CC / F • Lair Of The Bondage Bandits / 1991 / HOM / B • Leave

It To Bondage / 1994 / BON / B • Leita Bound / 1988 / BON / B • Lesbian Sex, Power & Money / 1994 / STM / F • Luscious Lickin' Lesbians / 1995 / TIE / F • Major Submission / 1996 / BON / B • Masseuse / 1996 / TRI / S • Master Of Ecstasy / 1997 / BON / B • Mike Hott: #160 Barbi Solo / 1991 / MHV / F • Mike Hott: #162 Barbi And Amanda #1 / 1991 / MHV / F • Mike Hott: #163 Barbi And Amanda #2 / 1991 / MHV / F • Mike Hott: #196 Lesbian Sluts #01 / 1992 / MHV / F • Mike Hott: #202 Horny Couples #02 / 1992 / MHV / M • Mike Hott: #242 Fuck The Boss #02 / 1993 / MHV / M • Mike Hott: #279 Fuck The Boss #4 / 1995 / MHV / M • Mike Hott: #282 Three-Sum Sluts #01 / 1995 / MHV / M • Mike Hott: #296 Jordan Hart & Friends #1 / 1995 / MHV / M • Mike Hott: #299 Jordan Hart & Friends #2 / 1995 / MHV / M • Mike Hott: #317 Girls Who Swallow Cum #01 / 1995 / MHV / C • Mike Hott: Apple Asses #07 / 1992 / MHV / F • Mike Hott: Cum Cocktails #1 / 1995 / MHV / C • Mike Hott: Cum Cocktails #3 / 1995 / MHV / C • Mob Boss / 1990 / ... / S • More On The Job Training / 1994 / RB / B • Mr. Peepers Amateur Home Videos #09: Western Panty Party / 1991 / LBO / M • Mr. Peepers Amateur Home Videos #93: Creative Fornication / 1994 / LBO / M • Naked Obsession / 1992 / VES / S • Nancy Crew Meets Dr. Freidastein / cr90 / BON / B • Next Door Neighbors #15 / 1990 / BON / M • Odyssey 30 Min: #294: / 1992 / OD / M • Odyssey 30 Min: #308: Greta And The Virgins Pt 2 / 1993 / OD / M • Odyssey Triple Play #60: Interracial Facial / 1994 / OD / M • Odyssey Triple Play #68: Threesomes And Moresomes / 1994 / OD / M • Office Ties / 1992 / BON / B • Older Women Younger Men #3 / 1993 / CC / M • Party Of The Dammed / 1996 / BON / B • Paula's Perils / 1989 / BON / B • Pearl Necklace: Thee Bush League: The Best Of Oral #01 / 1993 / SEE / C • Pearl Necklace: Thee Bush League #01 / 1992 / SEE / M • Prescription For Pain #1 / 1992 / BON / B • Prescription For Pain #2: The Ultimate Pain / 1993 / BON / B • Prescription For Pain #3: Bad Medicine / 1993 / BON / B • Prime Choice #2 / 1995 / RAS / M • Professor Butts / 1994 / SBP / F • Road Trippin' #03: New York City / 1994 / OUP / M • Rubber Foot Slave / 1993 / SBP / B • Rubber Slave Clinic / 1994 / SBP / B • Slaves On Loan / 1995 / BON / B • Spanking Good Reason / 1994 / VTF / B • Spell Of The Whip / 1994 / HOM / B • Surrogate Master / 1996 / BON / B • Suspension Of Disbelief #2 / 1989 / BON / B • SVE: Afternoon Surprise / 1992 / SVE / M • SVE: Cheap Thrills #3: Self-Satisfaction / 1992 / SVE / F • SVE: Greta Gets Off / 1994 / SVE / F • SVE: Screentest Sex #2 / 1992 / SVE / M • SVE: Spanks For The Memories / 1994 / SVE / B • Thinking Of You / 1992 / LV / F • Tickled And Teased / 1994 / SBP / B • Tied & Tickled #28: Tickling Dr. Cripley / 1995 / CS / B • Tit City #1 / 1993 / SC / M • Titties 'n Cream #2 / 1995 / FC / M • Toe Teasers #1 / 1993 / SBP / B • Too Fast For Love / 1992 / IF / M • Uncle Roy's Amateur Home Video #19 / 1993 / VIM / M • Under Construction / 1988 / BON / B • Velma And Clarice/What Are Friends For / 1994 / HAC

/ B • Where There's Sparxx, There's Fire /
1991 / LV / M • Wilde At Heart / 1992 /
VEX / M

GRETA DANE
Night Blooms / 1997 / BON / B

GRETA GEIST *see Star Index I*

GRETA GORBY *see Star Index I*

GRETA HERTZ
Razor's Edge / 1995 / ONA / M

GRETA KARLSON *see Greta Carlson*

GRETA LINDSTROM *see Star Index I*

GRETA MAYBERRY
Chinese Blue / 1976 / ... / M

GRETA PATRICK *see Star Index I*

GRETA SMITH
Frank Henenlotter's XXX Hardcore Hor-
rors: Mad Love... / 1996 / SOW / M • The
Mad Love Of The Red Hot Vampire / 1971
/ SOW / M

GRETCHEN
GRG: Bang My Bush / 1995 / GRG / M •
House Play (California Star) / 1994 / CS /
B • Mike Hott: #235 Gretchen / 1994 / MHV
/ M • Mike Hott: #261 Horny Couples #17 /
1994 / MHV / M • Titanic Tits #01 / 1984 /
L&W / S • Wrestling Classics #4 / 1993 /
CDP / B

GRETCHEN (SUZIE MAT) *see Suzie*
Mathews

GRETCHEN KOLBER *see Star Index I*

GRETCHEN MYER
Caballero Preview Tape #3 / 1984 / CA / C
• Secret Passions / 1982 / CA / M

GRETCHEN RAY
18 And Anxious / cr78 / CDI / M

GRETCHEN SWEET *see Star Index I*

GRETTA *see Star Index I*

GRETTA LYNN *see Star Index I*

GRETTE SZALONTAI
True Stories #1 / 1993 / SC / M • True Stories #2 / 1993 / SC / M

GREY ALVARADO
Badd Girl's Spanking / 1994 / STM / B

GREY MICHELS
Sex Boat / 1980 / VCX / M

GREY POUPON *see Star Index I*

GREY WATERS *see Andrew Wade*

GRIFFIN *see Star Index I*

GROCIER *see Zumira*

GROSEILLE *see Star Index I*

GROVER GRIFFITH
American Sex Fantasy / 1975 / IHV / M •
Dominatrix Without Mercy / 1976 / ALP / B
• Loose Threads / 1979 / S&L / M • Ms.
Woman Of The Year / 1980 / BL / M • Sex-
teen / 1975 / VC / M • Through The Look-
ing Glass / 1976 / ALP / M

GUADALUPE
New Ends #09 / 1994 / 4P / M • Video Virgins #04 / 1993 / NS / M

GUADALUPE SAN FRAN.
House Of Chicks: Masturbation Memoirs
#1 / 1995 / HOC / F

GUARDIAN ANGEL
Living Legend / 1995 / V99 / M • Snatch
Masters #01 / 1994 / LEI / M

GUILIA SANTOS
The Way Of Sex / 1995 / DBV / M

GUILIA SCHIAVO
Dr Max And The Oral Girls / 1995 / VIT / M

GUILLAUME
The French Canal / 1995 / DVP / G

GUNTHER MOHNER
[Junge Madchen Mogen's HeiB, Haus-
frauen Noch HeiBer / 1973 / ... / M •
[Schulmadchen-Report 4: Was Eltern Oft

Verzweifeln LaBt / 1972 / ... / M

GUNTHER STOLL
The Ideal Marriage / 1971 / SOW / M

GUS HOWE
Lady Luck / 1975 / VCX / M

GUS ROTTROCKS
Roxy: A Gang Bang Fantasy / 1994 / FC /
M

GUS SHORTS *see Star Index I*

GUS THOMAS
Devil's Due / 1974 / ALP / M • It Happened
In Hollywood / 1973 / WWV / M

GUSHA SEEMAN *see Star Index I*

GUSTAVO MONTOVA
Conflict Of Interest / 1994 / FST / G

GUY
Behind The Mask / 1995 / XC / M • Perversity In Paris / 1994 / AVI / M • Tampa Spice
/ 1996 / SUF / M • TV Dungeon / 1992 /
BIZ / G

GUY (RICK O'S) *see Rick O'Shea*

GUY BOYER *see Star Index I*

GUY CASPER *see Star Index I*

GUY CONNERS
[Chained, Whipped, Flogged, Beaten And
Peed On / 1976 / ... / M

GUY DESILVA
Light skinned small black guy. Has a brother,
Will Ravage, who is very similar looking
meaning that the two may be miscredited.
$ex 4 Fun & Profit / 1996 / SPR / M • 100%
Amateur #02: Back Door And More / 1995
/ OD / M • 100% Amateur #11: / 1995 / OD
/ M • 100% Amateur #18: / 1995 / OD / M •
Addicted To Lust / 1996 / NIT / M • Adven-
tures Of The DP Boys: Backyard Boogie /
1994 / HW / M • Adventures Of The DP
Boys: Big Black Booty / 1994 / HW / M •
Adventures Of The DP Boys: Chocolate
City / 1994 / HW / M • Adventures Of The
DP Boys: D.P. Nurses / 1995 / HW / M •
Adventures Of The DP Boys: Hooter
County / 1995 / HW / M • Adventures Of
The DP Boys: Sicilian Sluts / 1995 / HW /
M • Adventures Of The DP Boys: The
Blacks Are Back / 1994 / HW / M • Adven-
tures Of The DP Boys: Tokyo Tramps /
1994 / HW / M • Afro American Dream
Girls #1 / 1996 / DR / M • Afro American
Dream Girls #2 / 1996 / DR / M • All That:
Black Women's Fantasies / 1996 / VT / M •
Amateur Dreams #1 / 1994 / DR / M • Am-
ateur Nights #12 / 1996 / HO / M • Amateur
Nights #13 / 1996 / HO / M • Amateur Or-
gies #26 / 1993 / AFI / M • Amateur Orgies
#28 / 1993 / AFI / M • Amateurs Exposed
#07 / 1995 / CV / M • Anal Camera #03 /
1994 / EVN / M • Anal Camera #04 / 1995 /
EVN / M • Anal Explosions #1 / 1996 / NIT
/ M • Anal Party Girls / 1996 / GV / M • Anal
Pool Party / 1996 / PE / M • Anal Toy Story
/ 1996 / MPO / M • The Anal-Europe Series
#08: / 1995 / LV / M • Analtown USA #02 /
1995 / NIT / M • Analtown USA #08 / 1995
/ NIT / M • Ancient Amateurs #1 / 1996 /
LOF / M • Ancient Amateurs #2 / 1996 /
LOF / M • Aroused #2 / 1995 / VI / M • Ass
Dweller / 1994 / WIV / M • Ass Masters
(Leisure) #02 / 1995 / LEI / M • Attack Of
The Killer Dildos / 1996 / RAS / M • Babe
Wire / 1996 / HW / M • Backdoor Smug-
glers / 1994 / JAV / M • Badgirls #3: Cell
Block 69 / 1994 / VI / M • Bang City #1:
Kelly's Anal Gang Bang / 1995 / SC / M •
Bang City #2: China's Anal Gang Bang /
1995 / SC / M • Bang City #4: Gina's Anal

Gang Bang / 1995 / SC / M • Bang City #5:
Lennox's Anal Gang Bang / 1995 / SC / M
• Beach Bum Amateur's #35 / 1993 / MID /
M • Beyond Reality #3: Stand Erect! / 1996
/ EXQ / M • Bi Stander / 1995 / BIN / G •
Big Boob Bangeroo #5 / 1996 / TTV / M •
Big Boob Boat Butt Ride / 1996 / FC / M •
Big Boob Boat Ride #2 / 1995 / FC / M •
Big Bust Babes #21 / 1994 / AFI / M • Big
Murray's New-Cummers #16: Frat Boys #2
/ 1993 / FD / M • Black Attack / 1994 / ZA /
M • Black Beauty (Coast To Coast) / 1994 /
CC / M • Black Beauty (Las Vegas) / 1995
/ LV / M • Black Centerfolds #3 / 1996 /
MID / M • Black Flava / 1994 / EX / M •
Black Gangbangers #01 / 1994 / HW / M •
Black Gangbangers #07 / 1995 / HW / M •
Black Gangbangers #08 / 1995 / HW / M •
Black Jack City #3 / 1993 / HW / M • Black
Jack City #5 / 1995 / HW / M • Black
Knockers #05 / 1995 / TV / M • Black
Knockers #06 / 1995 / TV / M • Black Or-
gies #12 / 1993 / AFI / M • Black Orgies
#15 / 1993 / AFI / M • Black Orgies #16 /
1993 / AFI / M • Black Orgies #17 / 1993 /
AFI / M • Black Orgies #18 / 1993 / AFI / M
• Black Orgies #21 / 1994 / GO / M • Black
Orgies #22 / 1994 / GO / M • Black Orgies
#25 / 1994 / GO / M • Boob Tube Lube /
1996 / RAS / M • Borderline (Vivid) / 1995 /
VI / M • Brian Sparks: Virtually Unreal #1 /
1996 / ALD / M • Brooklyn Nights / 1994 /
OD / M • Bun Busters #11 / 1993 / LBO / M
• Butt Alley / 1995 / VMX / M • Butt Banged
Bicycle Babes / 1994 / ANA / M • Butt
Freak #2 / 1996 / EA / M • Butt X Files #2:
Anal Abduction / 1995 / WIV / M •
Buttman's Big Butt Backdoor Babes / 1995
/ EA / M • Buttman's Inferno / 1993 / EA /
M • The Cable Girl / 1996 / NIT / M • Cali-
fornia Blacks / 1994 / V99 / M • Call Me /
1995 / CV / M • Camp Fire Tramps / 1995 /
LOT / M • Candy / 1995 / MET / M • Carni-
val Of Flesh / 1996 / NIT / M • The Case Of
The Black Booty / 1996 / LV / M • Casting
Couch Tips / 1996 / MP0 / M • Caught
From Behind #24 / 1996 / HO / M • Choco-
late Bunnies #02 / 1995 / LBO / C • Cine-
sex #1 / 1995 / CV / M • Cinesex #2 / 1994
/ CV / M • Club Deb #1 / 1996 / MET / C •
Come And Get It! / 1995 / LBO / M • Cor-
porate Justice / 1996 / TEP / M • The
Crackster / 1996 / OUP / M • Creme De La
Face #03 / 1994 / OD / M • Cum Buttered
Corn Holes #1 / 1996 / NIT / C • Cum But-
tered Corn Holes #2 / 1996 / NIT / C • The
Cumm Brothers #01 / 1993 / OD / M • The
Cumm Brothers #04: Laid Off & Laid /
1994 / OD / M • Cyberanal / 1995 / VC / M
• D.P. Grannies / 1995 / JMP / M • Dark
Eyes / 1995 / FC / M • Debauchery / 1995
/ MET / M • Decadence / 1995 / AMP / M •
Deep Inside Anal Camera / 1996 / EVN / C
• Deep Throat Girls #15 / 1995 / GO / M •
Dick & Jane Go To Mexico / 1994 / AVI / M
• Dirty And Kinky Mature Women #4 / 1995
/ C69 / M • Dirty Dating Service #06 / 1994
/ WP / M • Dirty Doc's Housecalls #16 /
1994 / LV / M • Dirty Doc's Housecalls #17
/ 1994 / LV / M • Dirty Laundry / 1994 /
HOH / M • Dirty Minds / 1996 / NIT / M •
Dirty Panties / 1994 / SCL / M • Dirty Tricks
#1: Just A Bunch Of Whores / 1995 / EA /
M • Double D Amateurs #17 / 1994 / JMP /
M • Dream Butt / 1995 / VMX / M • Dukes
Of Anal / 1996 / VC / M • Ebony Erotica

#17: Black Power / 1994 / GO / M • Ebony Erotica #21: Cordon Negro / 1994 / GO / M • Ebony Erotica / 1995 / VT / M • Every Nerd's Big Boob Boat Butt Ride / 1996 / FC / M • The Fanny Farm / 1996 / NIT / M • Fantasy Flings #01 / 1993 / WP / M • Fantasy Flings #02 / 1994 / WP / M • Fishin' For Lust / 1996 / WST / M • Florence Hump / 1994 / AFI / M • Foreign Asses / 1996 / MP0 / M • Fortune Nookie / 1994 / PPP / M • Gang Bang Diaries #4 / 1994 / SFP / M • Gang Bang Virgin #1 / 1994 / HO / M • Gang Bang Virgin #2 / 1995 / HO / M • Gangbang At The O.K. Corral / 1994 / FPI / M • Gazongas Galore #1 / 1996 / NIT / C • The Generation Gap / 1996 / LV / M • Gimme Some Head / 1994 / VT / M • Granny Bangers / 1995 / MET / M • Green Piece Of Ass #1 / 1994 / RTP / M • Green Piece Of Ass #2 / 1994 / RTP / M • The Happy Office / 1996 / NIT / M • Hard Core Beginners #04 / 1995 / LEI / M • Hardcore Confidential #1 / 1996 / TEP / M • Hardcore Fantasies #1 / 1996 / LV / M • Hardcore Fantasies #3 / 1996 / LV / M • Hardcore Fantasies #4 / 1996 / LV / M • Head Nurse / 1996 / RAS / M • Hellfire / 1995 / MET / M • Hidden Camera #05 / 1993 / JMP / M • Hidden Camera #15 / 1994 / JMP / M • Hidden Camera #18 / 1994 / JMP / M • High Heeled & Horny #1 / 1994 / LBO / M • Hispanic Orgies #03 / 1993 / GO / M • Hispanic Orgies #06 / 1993 / GO / M • Hispanic Orgies #07 / 1994 / GO / M • The Hitch-Hiker #09: Back Road Detour / 1994 / WMG / M • Holly's Holiday Gang Bang / 1994 / LBO / M • The Hooker / 1995 / LOT / M • The Horny Hiker / 1995 / LE / M • Hot Parts / 1996 / NIT / M • Hot Tight Asses #07 / 1994 / TCK / M • Hotel California / 1995 / MID / M • House Of Sex #16: Dirty Oral Three Ways / 1994 / RTP / M • I Can't Believe I Did The Whole Team! / 1994 / FPI / M • In Da Booty / 1996 / LV / M • In Search Of The Brown Eye: An Anal Adventure / 1995 / MAX / M • In The Crack! / 1995 / VMX / M • In Through The Out Door / 1995 / PE / M • Indiscreet! Video Maga-zline #1 / 1008 / FH / M • Indiscreet! Video Magazine #2 / 1995 / FH / M • Indiscreet! Video Magazine #3 / 1995 / FH / M • Inspector Croissant: The Case Of The Missing Pinky / 1995 / FC / M • Ir4: Inrearendence Day / 1996 / HW / M • Jizz Glazed Goo Guzzlers #1 / 1996 / NIT / C • Jizz Glazed Goo Guzzlers #2 / 1996 / NIT / C • Kimberly Kupps Gets Balled / 1996 / NIT / M • Kool Ass / 1996 / BOT / M • Lady M's Anal Gang Bang / 1995 / FC / M • Las Vegas Big Boob Hospitality Sweet / 1997 / HO / M • Layover / 1994 / VI / M • Leather Unleashed / 1995 / GO / M • Lingerie / 1996 / RAS / M • Living On The Edge / 1997 / DWO / M • Lust Behind Bars / 1996 / GO / M • M Series #16 / 1993 / LBO / M • M Series #17 / 1993 / LBO / M • M Series #18 / 1994 / LBO / M • M Series #19 / 1994 / LBO / M • M Series #22 / 1994 / LBO / M • M Series #23 / 1994 / LBO / M • M Series #24 / 1994 / LBO / M • M Series #26 / 1994 / LBO / M • Makin' Bacon / 1994 / WIV / M • Maliboob Beach / 1995 / FH / M • Mike Hott: #356 Girls Who Lap Cum From Cunts #01 / 1996 / MHV / M • Mike Hott: #361 Girls Who Swallow Cum #04 / 1996 / MHV / C • Mike Hott: #369

Cum In My Mouth #05 / 1996 / MHV / C • Mike Hott: #382 Cunt Of The Month: Shawn E. / 1996 / MHV / M • Mike Hott: #387 Girls Who Lap Cum From Cunts #04 / 1996 / MHV / M • Mike Hott: #388 Cunt Of The Month: Lil Lee / 1996 / MHV / M • Miss Anal #1 / 1995 / C69 / M • Miss Anal #2 / 1995 / C69 / M • Miss D.P. Butterfly / 1995 / TIW / M • Miss Judge / 1997 / VI / M • Mo' Booty #4 / 1995 / TIW / M • The Most Dangerous Game / 1996 / HO / M • My Baby Got Back #04 / 1994 / VT / M • My Baby Got Back #09 / 1996 / VT / M • Nasty Newcummers #03 / 1994 / MET / M • Nasty Newcummers #05 / 1994 / MET / M • Nasty Newcummers #09 / 1995 / MET / M • Nasty Newcummers #13 / 1995 / MET / M • The New Butt Hunt #13 / 1995 / LEI / C • New Pussy Hunt #26 / 1996 / LEI / C • Odyssey 30 Min: #431: / 1994 / OD / M • Odyssey Triple Play #81: Copulation Intergration / 1994 / OD / M • Odyssey Triple Play #90: Black & White In Loving Color / 1995 / OD / M • Older And Anal #1 / 1995 / FC / M • Older And Anal #2 / 1995 / FC / M • Older Women Younger Men #3 / 1993 / CC / M • The Older Women's Sperm Bank #3: Red Hot Grandmas / 1996 / SUF / M • One Night In The Valley / 1996 / CA / M • Operation Snatch / 1996 / RAS / M • Out Of My Mind / 1995 / PL / M • Over Exposed / 1996 / ULP / M • P.K. & Company / 1995 / CV / M • Party Club / 1996 / C69 / M • Pay 4 Play / 1996 / RAS / M • Pounding Ass / 1995 / VMX / M • Prime Choice #1 / 1995 / RAS / M • Prime Choice #2 / 1995 / RAS / M • Prime Choice #4 / 1995 / RAS / M • Prime Choice #8 / 1996 / RAS / M • Private Dancers / 1996 / RAS / M • Private Video Magazine #09 / 1994 / OD / M • Pure Anal / 1996 / MET / M • Pussy Lotto / 1995 / WIV / M • Put 'em On Da Glass / 1994 / VT / M • The Real Deal #3 / 1996 / FC / M • The Return Of Dr Blacklove / 1996 / CC / M • Rollover / 1996 / NIT / M • Roxy Rider Is In Control / 1996 / NIT / M • Roxy: A Gang Bang Fantasy / 1994 / FC / M • Saki's Bedtime Stories / 1995 / TTV / M • Screamers (Gourmet) / 1995 / ONA / M • The Seductive Secretary / 1995 / GO / M • Sex Drives Of The Rich And Famous / 1996 / ERA / M • Sexual Trilogy #05 / 1994 / SFP / M • Sgt. Peckers Lonely Hearts Club Gang Bang / 1995 / AMP / M • Show Business / 1995 / LV / M • Skeezers / 1996 / LV / M • Skid Row / 1994 / SC / M • Slutsville U.S.A. / 1995 / VMX / M • So Bad / 1995 / VT / M • Sodomania #09: Doin' Time / 1994 / EL / M • Sodomize Me!!! / 1996 / SPR / M • Sofia: A Gang Bang Fantasy / 1994 / FC / M • The Spa / 1996 / RAS / M • Starbangers #10 / 1997 / ZA / M • Streetwalkers / 1995 / HO / M • Stripping / 1995 / NIT / M • Summer Of '69 / 1994 / MID / M • Summer Vacation #1 / 1996 / RAS / M • Summer Vacation #2 / 1996 / RAS / M • Swedish Erotica #85 / 1995 / CA / M • Tail Taggers #119 / 1994 / WV / M • Tails From The Hood / 1995 / FH / M • Taxi Girls #3: Killer On The Loose / 1993 / MED / M • Teacher's Pet #2 / 1994 / WMG / M • Tender Box / 1996 / MP0 / M • This Girl Is Freaky / 1996 / NIT / M • Tight Fit #07 / 1994 / GO / M • Tight Fit #13 / 1995 / GO / M • Tight Fit #15 / 1996 / GO / M • Titties 'n Cream #1 / 1994 / FC / M • Titties 'n

Cream #3 / 1995 / FC / M • Titty City #1 / 1995 / TIW / M • Toot Z Roll / 1995 / WP / M • Tootsies & Footsies / 1994 / LBO / M • Two-Pac / 1996 / VT / M • Video Virgins #08 / 1993 / NS / M • Video Virgins #12 / 1994 / NS / M • Video Virgins #14 / 1994 / NS / M • Video Virgins #24 / 1996 / NS / M • Vivid At Home #01 / 1994 / VI / M • Wild Orgies #05 / 1994 / AFI / M • Wild Orgies #13 / 1994 / AFI / M • Wild Widow / 1996 / NIT / M • World Class Ass / 1995 / FC / M • Yo' Where's Homey? / 1996 / SUF / M

GUY FABRAY *see Star Index I*

GUY FOSTER
Going Down Under / 1993 / OD / M

GUY LAURENT *see Star Index I*

GUY MAUMONT *see Star Index I*

GUY MISE
Bedtime Video #03 / 1984 / GO / M

GUY RANGER *see Star Index I*

GUY ROGER
Erotic Pleasures / 1976 / CA / M • Sexy / 1976 / SE / M

GUY ROYER
[Les Plaisirs Fous / 1976 / ... / M • [S.S. Bordello / 1978 / ... / M

GWEN
Blue Vanities #506 / 1992 / FFL / M • Bondage Classix #18: Gwen And Debbie's Torments / 198? / BON / B • Bondage Memories #02 / 1993 / BON / C • Double Whipping / 198? / BON / B • Gwen's Tit Torment / cr87 / BON / B • Tortured Present / cr87 / BON / B

GWEN FISHER *see Star Index I*

GWEN STAR *see C.J. Laing*

GWEN STEWARD *see Star Index I*

GWENDA
Eurotica #06 / 1996 / XC / M • Eurotica #11 / 1996 / XC / M

GWENDOLEN ROTH *see Carol Cross*

GWENDOLYN
Lesbian Pros And Amateurs #04 / 1992 / GO / F

GWENN
Blue Vanities #502 / 1992 / FFL / M

GWYN
Gwyn's Lakeside Ordeal / 1994 / BON / B • Real People Real Bondage #1 / 1995 / BON / C

GYANTY
Private Film #15 / 1994 / OD / M

GYLENE
Rump Man: Goes To Cannes / 1995 / HW / M

GYN SENG *(Solange)*
Pretty, French of Vietnamese extraction, very tight body, small tits, very nice little butt.
Skin #3 / 1995 / ERQ / M • [The Chastity Belt / 199? / ... / M • [The Education Of Anna / 199? / ... / M

GYONGI *see Star Index I*

GYORGY KARDOS
True Stories #1 / 1993 / SC / M • True Stories #2 / 1993 / SC / M

GYPSY
Beach Bum Amateur's #22 / 1993 / MID / M • Gazonga Goddess #1 / 1993 / IF / M • Gazongas #04 / 1993 / LEI / C • Hardcore Copy / 1993 / PL / M • Hometown Honeys #4 / 1993 / VEX / M • Just One Look / 1993 / V99 / M • Mr. Peepers Amateur Home Videos #63: Sexual Soiree / 1992 / LBO / M • Neighborhood Watch #35 / 1992 / LBO / M • Nothing Else Matters / 1992 / V99 / C • Payne In The Behind / 1993 /

AMF / C • Ready And Willing / 1993 / VEX / M

GYPSY (MISTY DAWN) *see* **Misty Dawn**
GYPSY LEE *see* **Star Index I**
GYPSY LYN *see* **Star Index I**
GYPSY MARR *see* **Star Index I**
GYPSY ROSE
The Outrageous Nurse / 1981 / VD / G • She-Male Encounters #05: Orgy At The Poysinberry Bar #1 / 1987 / MET / G • Unveil My Love / 1991 / HO / M

GYSELENE KER-DAVID *see* **Star Index I**
GYSELLE
J.E.G.: Maidens Of Masturbation #8 / 1995 / JEG / F

GYUIRI
The Witch's Tail / 1994 / GOU / M

H. OSCAR WARD *see* **Cecil Howard**
H.B.
Kitty's Kinky Capers / 1996 / TTV / M

H.C. *see* **Krista**
HABANA CARMEN *see* **Star Index I**
HADDA CLIMAX
Meatball / 1972 / VCX / M

HAGBARD
New Faces, Hot Bodies #04 / 1992 / STP / M • New Faces, Hot Bodies #05 / 1992 / STP / M • New Faces, Hot Bodies #09 / 1993 / STP / M • New Faces, Hot Bodies #21 / 1996 / STP / C

HAI SOO
Shang-Hai Slits / 1994 / ORE / C

HAIKU *see* **Loni Sanders**
HAILEY
Ron Hightower's White Chicks #05 / 1993 / LBO / M • Student Fetish Videos: The Enema #07 / 1992 / PRE / B • Student Fetish Videos: Tickling #04 / 1992 / SFV / B

HAILY DAVIDSON *see* **Harley Haze**
HAKAN
American Tushy! / 1996 / ULI / M • Deep Behind The Scenes With Seymore Butts #2 / 1995 / ULI / M • The Dinner Party #2: The Buffet / 1996 / ULI / M • Prague By Night #1 / 1996 / EA / M • Prague By Night #2 / 1996 / EA / M • Private Stories #06 / 1995 / OD / M • Rock 'n' Roll Rocco / 1997 / EA / M • Seymore Butts: Slippin' In Through The Out Door / 1996 / FH / M

HAKAN JOEL
All Grown Up / 1996 / XC / M • Don Salvatore: The Last Sicilian / 1995 / XC / M • Flamenco Ecstasy / 1996 / UEF / M • Virility / 1996 / XC / M

HAKIM
Triple X Video Magazine #11 / 1995 / OD / M

HAKIM SMITH *see* **Star Index I**
HAL BRUCK *see* **Star Index I**
HAL FREEMAN *see* **Star Index I**
HAL HALE
Steamy Dreams / cr70 / CVX / M

HAL ROTH
The Rod Garetto Story / 1995 / FC / C

HAL STEVENS
Deep Rub / 1979 / VC / M

HAL WALKER
Hard Candy / 1977 / ... / M

HAL WILLIAMS
Anal Anarchy / 1995 / VC / M

HALE
Tit To Tit #2 / 1994 / BTO / M

HALEY
Amateur Nights #05 / 1990 / HO / M • Dirty & Kinky Mature Women #05 / 1995 / C69 /

M • English Muffins / 1995 / VC / M • Odyssey Amateur #46: Haley's Backdoor Comet / 1991 / OD / M • Tight Ties / 1994 / BON / B • ZFX: Nastiest Bound Babes / 1996 / BON / C

HALEY KNIGHT
Finger Pleasures #3 / 1995 / PL / F • Old Guys & Dolls #2 / 1995 / PL / M • Shaved #09 / 1995 / RB / F • Sin City Cycle Sluts #2 / 1995 / SC / F

HALEY LYNN
Reel Life Video #49: / 1996 / RLF / F

HALEY STARR
Look What I Found On The Street #01 / 1996 / CC / M • Video Virgins #30 / 1996 / NS / M

HALIE *see* **Star Index I**
HAMP SHEPHERD
Angel Rising / 1988 / IN / M

HANA
Prague By Night #1 / 1996 / EA / M • Prague By Night #2 / 1996 / EA / M

HANAKO AOMORI
Tonight / 1985 / ORC / M

HANAKU *(Nini)*
Oriental girl with saggy small tits but a lithe body. Not ugly but not pretty either.
Asian Persuasion / 1993 / WV / M • Back To The Orient / 1992 / HW / M • Big Murray's New-Cummers #09: Oriental Lovers / 1993 / FD / M • Black Jack City #2: Black's Revenge / 1992 / HW / M • Buttwiser / 1992 / HW / M • Crash In The Rear / 1992 / HW / C • Diary Of A Geisha / 1995 / WV / C • Dungeon Of The Borgias / 1993 / HOM / B • L.A. Rear / 1992 / FD / M • Lust For Leather / 1993 / IF / M • Mr. Fun's Mondo Adventure / 1993 / VC / M • Oriental Sorority Secrets / 1992 / VIM / M • Pubic Eye / 1992 / HW / M • Street Girl Named Desire / 1992 / FD / M • Tails From The Tower / 1993 / AFI / M • Tonight's The Night / 1992 / V99 / M

HANK
Bangkok Boobarella / 1996 / BTO / M • Bobby Hollander's Rookie Nookie #09 / 1993 / SFP / M • Duke Of Knockers #2 / 1995 / BTO / M • HomeGrown Video #434: Forrest Hump / 1994 / HOV / M • How To Make Love To A Black Woman #1: You Gotta Have Rhythm / 1996 / VCX / M • Profiles #03: House Dick / 1995 / XPR / M

HANK ARMSTRONG
SO of Anna Malle.
Anna Malle Exposed / 1996 / WV / M • Ashlyn Rising / 1995 / VI / M • The Backway Inn #5 / 1993 / FD / M • Battling Bitches #2 / 1995 / BIZ / B • Beauty's Punishment / 1996 / BIZ / B • Beauty's Revenge / 1996 / BIZ / B • The Big Stick-Up / 1994 / WV / M • Bizarre's Dracula #1 / 1995 / BIZ / B • Bizarre's Dracula #2 / 1995 / BIZ / B • Boob Acres / 1996 / HW / M • Butthead Dreams: Exposed / 1995 / FH / M • Chronicles Of Pain #4: Tools Of The Trade / 1996 / BIZ / B • Compulsive Behavior / 1995 / PI / M • Conjugal Visits / 1995 / EVN / M • Cybersex / 1996 / WAV / M • Date With A Mistress / 1995 / BIZ / B • Decadence / 1996 / VC / M • The Delegate / 1996 / RAS / M • Dominant Jean / 1996 / CC / M • Dresden Diary #14: Ecstasy In Hell / 1996 / BIZ / B • Dresden Diary #15: / 1996 / BIZ / B • Dresden Diary #16: / 1996 / BIZ / B • East Coast Sluts #08: Atlantic City / 1995 / PL / M • The Enema Bandit

Strikes Again / 1995 / BIZ / B • Exposure / 1995 / WAV / M • Final Obsession / 1996 / LE / M • Gangbang Girl #14 / 1994 / ANA / M • Glory Days / 1996 / IN / M • Heavy Breathing / 1996 / NIT / M • Independence Night / 1996 / SC / M • Lactamania #4 / 1996 / TTV / M • Lost Angels / 1997 / WP / M • The Many Faces Of P.J. Sparxx / 1996 / WP / M • Naked Desert / 1995 / VI / M • Nina Hartley's Guide To Anal Sex / 1996 / A&E / M • Nina Hartley's Guide To Swinging / 1996 / A&E / M • Oral Majority #13 / 1995 / WV / C • The Other Woman / 1996 / VC / M • Passion / 1996 / SC / M • Philmore Butts Las Vegas Vacation / 1995 / SUF / M • Photo Play / 1995 / VI / M • Pure Smut / 1996 / GO / M • Pussyman #09: Feeding Frenzy / 1995 / SNA / M • Sex Academy #5: The Art Of Pulp Fiction / 1994 / ONA / M • Shane's World #5 / 1996 / OD / M • Simply Blue / 1995 / WAV / M • Southern Comfort #1 / 1995 / DWV / M • Southern Comfort #2 / 1995 / DWV / M • Spiked Heel Diaries #4 / 1995 / BIZ / B • Starting Over / 1995 / WAV / M • Street Legal / 1995 / WAV / M • Streets Of New York #08 / 1996 / PL / M • Sweet As Honey / 1996 / NIT / M • Tail Taggers #126 / 1994 / WV / M • Thin Ice / 1996 / ONA / M • Waterworld: The Enema Movie / 1996 / BIZ / B • Wild Widow / 1996 / NIT / M

HANK FONDER *see* **Star Index I**
HANK GOLDEN *see* **Star Index I**
HANK GREENE *see* **Star Index I**
HANK HEATHCLIFF *see* **Star Index I**
HANK HIGHTOWER
Conflict Of Interest / 1994 / FST / G • Courting Libido / 1995 / HIV / G • Dominique's Bi Adventure / 1995 / STA / G • Like Father Like Son / 1996 / AWV / G • Long Play / 1995 / 3XP / G • Lost In Vegas / 1996 / AWV / G • Night Walk / 1995 / HIV / G

HANK MCALLISTER
More Than Friends / 1995 / KDP / G

HANK ROSE *(Mr. Doo Doo, Mark (Hank Rose))*
Ugly looking pudgy white male. The Mr. Doo Doo is from **AHV #40**.
19 & Naughty #1 / 1994 / SKV / M • A&B GB#072: Chessie Does It / 1990 / A&B / M • Aged To Perfection #2 / 1995 / TTV / M • AHV #40: Whole Lotta Love / 1993 / EVN / M • Alana: A Gang Bang Fantasy / 1993 / FC / M • All That: Black Women's Fantasies / 1996 / VT / M • Amateur Dreams #1 / 1994 / DR / M • Amateur Dreams #4 / 1994 / DR / M • America's Raunchiest Home Videos #53: / 1993 / ZA / M • Anal Camera #06 / 1995 / EVN / M • Anal Camera #09 / 1995 / EVN / M • Anal Camera #10 / 1995 / EVN / M • Anal Camera #11 / 1995 / EVN / M • Anal Camera #14 / 1996 / EVN / M • Anal Gang Bangers #01 / 1992 / GLI / M • Angel Eyes / 1995 / IN / M • Backdoor To Paradise / 1990 / ELV / M • Behind The Backdoor #7 / 1995 / EVN / M • Big Bad Biker Bitches / 1994 / TTV / M • The Big Bang #1 / 1993 / LV / M • The Big Bang #2 / 1994 / LV / M • Big Black Bang / 1996 / HW / M • Big Murray's New-Cummers #18: Crazy Cuties / 1993 / FD / M • Black Fire / 1993 / VIM / M • Black Gangbangers #11 / 1996 / HW / M • Black Gangbangers #12 / 1996 / HW / M • The Bold, The Bald & The Beautiful / 1993 /

VIM / M • Booty Bang #2 / 1996 / HW / M • Breastman's Triple X Cellent Adventure / 1995 / EVN / M • Bubble Butts #21 / 1993 / LBO / M • Bunny Bleu: A Gang Bang Fantasy / 1994 / FC / M • Cindy's House Party / 1996 / HW / M • Club DV8 #1 / 1993 / SC / M • Colossal Orgy #1 / 1993 / HW / M • Colossal Orgy #2 / 1994 / HW / M • Colossal Orgy #3 / 1994 / HW / M • Da Booty Bang #2 / 1996 / HW / M • Dangerous Behinds #1 / 1995 / HW / M • Dangerous Behinds #2 / 1996 / HW / M • Dark Passions #01 / 1993 / AFV / M • Dark Passions #02 / 1993 / AFV / M • Deep Inside Anal Camera / 1996 / EVN / C • The Devil In Miss Jones #5: The Inferno / 1994 / VC / M • Dirty And Kinky Mature Women #3 / 1995 / C69 / M • Dirty Dating Service #01 / 1993 / WP / M • Dirty Doc's Housecalls #05 / 1993 / LV / M • Dirty Doc's Housecalls #12 / 1994 / LV / M • Dirty Doc's Housecalls #14 / 1994 / LV / M • The Doll House / 1995 / CV / M • Eclipse / 1993 / SC / M • The Erotic Adventures Of Johnny Soiree / 1995 / LBO / M • Frat Brats / 1990 / VC / M • Frenzy / 1992 / SC / M • Fresh Faces #04 / 1995 / EVN / M • Fresh Faces #05 / 1995 / EVN / M • Fresh Faces #06 / 1995 / EVN / M • Fresh Faces #07 / 1995 / EVN / M • Fresh Faces #08 / 1995 / EVN / M • Fresh Faces #10 / 1996 / EVN / M • Gang Bang Bitches #02 / 1994 / PP / M • Gang Bang Bitches #03 / 1994 / PP / M • Gang Bang Diaries #3 / 1994 / SFP / M • Gang Bang Diaries #4 / 1994 / SFP / M • Gangbang Girl #04 / 1992 / ANA / M • The Girls From Hootersville #01 / 1993 / SFP / M • Hidden Camera #01 / 1993 / JMP / M • Hidden Camera #20 / 1994 / JMP / M • Hollywood Swingers #10 / 1993 / LBO / M • House Of Sex #04: Banging Menette / 1994 / RTP / M • Huge Grant On The Sunset Strip / 1995 / EVN / M • Immorals #2: The Good, The Bad, And The Banged / 1990 / AR / M • Inner Blues / 1987 / VD / M • Innocent Little Girls #1 / 1996 / MP0 / M • Interracial Affairs / 1996 / FC / M • Jingle Balls / 1996 / EVN / M • Kink #2 / 1995 / ROB / M • Love From The Backside / 1989 / FAZ / M • Mr. Peepers Amateur Home Videos #75: Trio In Rio / 1993 / LBO / M • Mr. Peepers Amateur Home Videos #91: Hole Lot'a Humping Goin / 1994 / LBO / M • Next Door Neighbors #02 / 1989 / BON / M • Next Door Neighbors #10 / 1990 / BON / M • No Way In / 1988 / EVN / M • Nympho Zombie Coeds / 1993 / VIM / M • Odyssey 30 Min: #294: / 1992 / OD / M • Odyssey Triple Play #74: Conjugal Couples / 1994 / OD / M • Odyssey Triple Play #75: Interracial Anal Threesome / 1994 / OD / M • Orgy Camera #1 / 1995 / EVN / M • Orgy Camera #2 / 1996 / EVN / M • Oriental Gang Bang Fantasy / 1994 / FC / M • Our Bang #03 / 1992 / GLI / M • Our Bang #05 / 1992 / GLI / M • Pai Gow Video #01: Asian Beauties / 1993 / EVN / M • Pai Gow Video #02: Wok & Roll / 1993 / EVN / M • Pai Gow Video #04: Tails Of The Town / 1994 / EVN / M • Pleasure Dome: The Genesis Chamber / 1994 / AFV / M • Positively Pagan #05 / 1993 / ATA / M • Pumps In Da Rump #2 / 1996 / HW / M • Queen Of Hearts #3: Heartless / 1992 / PL / M • Raw Talent: Bang 'er 14 Times / 1992 / RTP / M • Raw Talent: Bang 'er 15 Times /

1992 / RTP / M • Raw Talent: Bang 'er 16 Times / 1992 / RTP / M • Raw Talent: Bang 'er 17 Times / 1992 / RTP / M • Raw Talent: Bang 'er 23 Times / 1992 / RTP / M • Raw Talent: Bang 'er 26 Times / 1992 / RTP / M • Raw Talent: Bang 'er 34 Times / 1992 / RTP / M • Raw Talent: Bang 'er 45 Times / 1993 / RTP / M • Saturday Night Porn #2 / 1993 / AFV / M • Sexophrenia / 1993 / VC / M • Span's Garden Party / 1996 / HW / M • Star Struck / 1991 / AFV / M • Stiff Competition #2 / 1994 / CA / M • Sweet Black Cherries #1 / 1996 / TTV / M • Three Men And A Lady / 1988 / EVN / M • Ultimate Anal Gang Bang #3 / 1995 / HW / M • Ultimate Gang Bang #1 / 1994 / HW / M • Uncle Roy's Amateur Home Video #07 / 1992 / VIM / M • Velvet / 1995 / SPI / M • While The Cat's Away / 1996 / NIT / M • Wild Orgies #19 / 1995 / AFI / M

HANNA ALLEN see Star Index I
HANNAH
Blue Vanities #570 / 1995 / FFL / M • Private Film #16 / 1994 / OD / M • Private Stories #10 / 1996 / OD / M • Private Video Magazine #14 / 1994 / OD / M • Private Video Magazine #21 / 1995 / OD / M • Private Video Magazine #25 / 1995 / OD / M • Veronica's Kiss / 1979 / VCI / M

HANS
Aerienne's Surprise / 1995 / WIV / M • Breast Worx #24 / 1992 / LBO / M • Gazonga Goddess #1 / 1993 / IF / M • Homegrown Video #317 / 1990 / HOV / M • HomeGrown Video #458: Cream Pie For Dessert / 1995 / HOV / C • Porno X-Treme #2: Club Bizarre / 1995 / SC / M • Porno X-Treme #4: Wet Dream / 1995 / SC / M • VGA: Spanks-A-Lot / 1993 / VGA / B • Wedding Rituals / 1995 / DVP / M

HANS BRINKER
Kitty's Pleasure Palace / 1971 / ALP / M
HANS ENGELS
The Girls Of Mr X / 1978 / CA / M
HANS LASCH
Bucky Beaver's XXX Dragon Art Theatre Double Feature #01 / 1996 / SOW / M • Hitler's Harlots / cr73 / SOW / M
HANS LAUTHEC
The Swing Thing / 1973 / TGA / M
HANS LOCKE see Star Index I
HANS MILLER see Hans Mueller
HANS MOSER JR see Star Index I
HANS MUELLER *(Hans Miller)*
1-800-TIME / 1990 / IF / M • AC/DC #1 / 1991 / LA / G • All For You, Baby / 1990 / VEX / M • As Cute As They Cum / 1990 / VEX / M • Backdoor To Hollywood #13 / 1990 / CDI / M • Bi & Large / 1994 / STA / G • Bi And Busty / 1991 / STA / G • Bi-Bi-Baby / 1990 / CDI / G • Bi-Inferno / 1992 / VEX / G • Buns And Roses (V9) / 1990 / V99 / M • Crossing The Line / 1993 / STA / G • Deep Dreams / 1990 / IN / M • Dominique Goes Bi / 1994 / STA / G • Europe On Two Guys A Day / 1987 / PV / M • Fag Hags / 1991 / FC / G • Freak Show / 1991 / FC / M • Holly Does Hollywood #4 / 1990 / CAY / M • Life In The Fat Lane #3 / 1990 / FC / M • Lonely Is The Night / 1990 / V99 / M • Lost Lovers / 1990 / VEX / M • More Dirty Debutantes / 1990 / PRI / M • More Than A Woman / 1992 / CDI / G • Mystery Date / 1992 / CDI / G • New Girls In Town #1 / 1990 / CC / M • Night Watch / 1990 / VEX / M • One More Time / 1990 / VEX / M

• Passion For Fashion / 1992 / PEP / G • Playing Dirty / 1989 / VEX / M • Retail Slut / 1989 / LV / M • Sexy Nurses #1 On And Off Duty / 1990 / CV / M • Shaved She-Males / 1992 / STA / G • Single She-Male Singles Bar / 1990 / STA / G • Sisters Of Sin / 1991 / VIM / G • Stasha's Diary / 1991 / CIN / G • Sweet Darlin' / 1990 / VEX / M • Tit Tales #4 / 1993 / FC / M • The Ultimate Pleasure / 1991 / MET / G • The Ultimate Sex / 1992 / MET / G • White Lies / 1990 / VEX / M • White Satin Nights / 1991 / V99 / M • Women In Charge / 1990 / VEX / M

HANS MUSSER
Ejacula #1 / 1992 / VC / M • Ejacula #2 / 1992 / VC / M
HANS SCHILLER
Private Film #08 / 1994 / OD / M
HANS SONTAG
Body Love / 1976 / CA / M
HANS STALLION see Star Index I
HANS VAN DYK see Star Index I
HAPI see Star Index I
HARD HAT see Star Index I
HARDEN LONGG
East Coast Sluts #03: South Florida / 1995 / PL / M
HARDY BULL see Star Index I
HARDY HARRISON see Star Index I
HARLEQUIN see Star Index I
HARLETTA
The Cumm Brothers #02: Goin' To A Ho' Down / 1994 / OD / M • The Cumm Brothers #05: These Nuts For Hire / 1994 / OD / M
HARLEY
Fabulous Flashers #2 / 1996 / DGD / F • Tightly Secured / 1996 / CS / B
HARLEY (KRYSTI LYNN) see Krysti Lynn
HARLEY (MALE) *(Lucky (Harley))*
Not to be confused with Kristie Lynn who also used the name Harley, this one is a male with a Svengali-like beard who appears with rocker-girl, Scarlett.
Anal Vision #22 / 1993 / LBO / M • Beach Bum Amateur's #31 / 1993 / MID / M • Biff Malibu's Totally Nasty Home Videos #40 / 1993 / ANA / M • Bun Busters #04 / 1993 / LBO / M • Casting Call #05 / 1994 / SO / M • Dirty Doc's Housecalls #03 / 1993 / LV / M • The Knocker Room / 1993 / GO / M • Lovin' Spoonfuls #3 / 1995 / 4P / C • Video Virgins #05 / 1993 / NS / M
HARLEY (SHEILA) *(Sheila Sanders)*
Dancer on vacation from Detroit MI according to her in **My First Time #6**. Pretty, long blonde hair, rock solid cantaloupes, slightly womanly body. De-virginized at 16.
My First Time #6 / 1996 / NS / M
HARLEY D.
Helen Does Holland / 1996 / VC / M
HARLEY DAVIDSON see Star Index I
HARLEY DAVIS
The Beverly Thrillbillies / 1987 / EVN / M • Carnal Possessions / 1988 / VEX / M • Cheek-A-Boo / 1988 / LV / M • City Of Rage / 1989 / EVN / M • Club Head (EVN) #1 / 1987 / EVN / C • Feel The Heat / 1989 / VEX / M • Fun In A Bun / 1990 / LV / M • The Girls Of Cooze / 1992 / V99 / C • Leave It To Cleavage #1 / 1988 / GO / M • The Legend Of Reggie D. / 1989 / EA / M • Megasex / 1988 / EVN / M • Surfside Sex / 1988 / CA / M • Unbelievable Orgies #1 /

1987 / EVN / C
HARLEY HAZE *(Angel (Harley), Haily Davidson)*
Petite pretty brunette with small tits, large areola, tight waist, and a nice butt. Her pubic hair is just a vertical slash. Allegedly under indictment in Denver CO for some fairly serious offense. Could be another waste (like Amy Fisher) if she goes to jail. Not the same as Angel Collins (watch the moles) despite some resemblance.
Hard Core Beginners #03 / 1995 / LEI / M •
Sorority Stewardesses #1 / 1995 / PE / M •
Sorority Stewardesses #2 / 1995 / PE / M
HARLOT RAE *see Star Index I*
HARMON FLETCHER *see Star Index I*
HARMONY
The Blonde / 1980 / VCX / M • The Love Couch / 1977 / VC / M • New Girls In Town #7 / 1994 / CC / M
HARMONY (SYDNEY D) *see* Sydney Dance
HAROAH AMOS
Melanie's Hot Line / 1975 / CDC / M • Strange Experiences Cockfucking / 1994 / MET / M
HAROLD
HomeGrown Video #452: Make Me Cum! / 1995 / HOV / M
HAROLD ADLER
Classical Romance / 1984 / MAP / M
HAROLD ALFONSE *see Star Index I*
HAROLD BLACK
Bucky Beaver's XXX Dragon Art Theatre Double Feature #04 / 1996 / SOW / M • Revelations / 1974 / SOW / M
HAROLD GREEN
Eat At The Blue Fox / 1983 / VC / M
HAROLD LIME *(Ted Paramore, Ramsey Karson, Richard Kanter)*
Director.
HAROLD MASON
[Home From The Sea / 19?? / ... / M
HARRE OWEN
Pink Lips / 1977 / VCX / M
HARRIET HART *see Star Index I*
HARRIET MURPHY
Golden Girls, The Movie / 1984 / SE / M
HARRIET SUMMERS
Fantasy Peeps: Black On White / 1985 / 4P / M
HARRIETT
Blue Vanities #543 / 1994 / FFL / M
HARRY
Odyssey Amateur #71: When Harry Wet Sally / 1991 / OD / M
HARRY ADAMS
Sheila's Payoff / 1977 / VCX / M
HARRY BAYMAN *see Star Index I*
HARRY BELLI *see Star Index I*
HARRY BIGGERSTAFF
Bushwoman: She Takes Two / 1996 / RAS / M • Kimberly Kupps Gets 5 A's / 1996 / NIT / M
HARRY CASH
Sharon In The Rough-House / 1976 / LA / M
HARRY COWAN *see* Herschel Savage
HARRY DANIEL *see Star Index I*
HARRY DICKINSIDER *see* Tom Elliot
HARRY DREAMZ
Naughty Network / 1981 / CA / M
HARRY DUTCHMAN *see Star Index I*
HARRY DUTCHMAN (TTB) *see* T.T. Boy
HARRY HARDER
Heavenly / 1995 / IF / M

HARRY HARWOOD *see Star Index I*
HARRY HODAS
Love Mexican Style / cr75 / BLT / M
HARRY HORNDOG *see* John T. Bone
HARRY JABARR *see Star Index I*
HARRY KINDNESS
As Cute As They Cum / 1990 / VEX / M • Night Lessons / 1990 / V99 / M • Sexy Nurses #1 On And Off Duty / 1990 / CV / M • Tequilla Sunset / 1989 / V99 / M
HARRY LINCOLN
Golden Girls, The Movie / 1984 / SE / M
HARRY LITMUS
Hungry Eyed Woman / cr71 / VCX / M
HARRY MAGNUM
The Untamed / 1978 / VCX / M
HARRY MORAN *see Star Index I*
HARRY MORGAN *see Star Index I*
HARRY PALM
Teenage Pajama Party / 1977 / VC / M
HARRY REEMS *(Tim Long, Herb Stryker, Bruce Gilchrist, Herb Striecher, Bob Walters)*
Herb Stryker is from **A Time To Love**. Bruce Gilchrist is from **Demented**. Bob Walters is from **Fleshpots Of 42nd Street**. Born 1947 in the Bronx, NY. As of 1995 was allegedly selling real estate in Utah. Real name is Herbert Streicher.
The 8th Annual Erotic Film Awards / 1984 / SE / C • ABA: Double Feature #3 / 1996 / ALP / M • All About Sex / 1970 / AR / M • All For His Ladies / 1987 / PP / C • The Altar Of Lust / 1971 / SOW / S • The Amateurs / 1984 / VCX / M • Angel's Revenge / 1985 / IN / M • Ape Over Love / 197? / BL / M • Back To Class #1 / 1984 / DR / M • Backdoor Brides #1 / 1985 / PV / M • The Beat Goes On / 1987 / VCR / C • Bel Ami / 1976 / VXP / M • Beverly Hills Exposed / 1985 / SE / M • Blue Vanities #093 / 1988 / FFL / M • Blue Vanities #120 / 1990 / FFL / M • Blue Vanities #248 / 1995 / FFL / M • Butterflies / 1974 / CA / M • Caballero Preview Tape #4 / 1985 / CA / C • Cartier Affair / 1984 / WAR / S • The Case Of The Full Moon Murders / 1971 / SOW / M • Cavalcade Of Stars / 1985 / VCR / C • China & Silk / 1984 / MAP / M • Christy / 1975 / CA / M • Club Ginger / 1986 / VI / M • College Girls / cr73 / VXP / M • The Collegiates / 1971 / BL / M • The Confessions Of Linda Lovelace / 1974 / AR / C • Corporate Assets / 1985 / SE / M • Cum Shot Revue #2 / 1985 / HO / C • Cum Shot Revue #4 / 1988 / HO / C • Dark Dreams / 1971 / ALP / M • Deadly Weapons / 1973 / SOW / S • Deep Chill / cr85 / AT / M • Deep Inside Traci / 1986 / CDI / C • Deep Throat #1 / 1972 / AR / M • Demented / 1980 / MED / S • Devil In Miss Jones #1 / 1972 / VC / M • Dirty 30's Cinema: Ginger Lynn / 1986 / PV / C • Dream Lover / 1985 / CDI / M • Educating Mandy / 1985 / CDI / M • The End Zone / 1987 / LA / C • Erecter Sex #3: Sex Ed 101 / cr70 / AR / M • Erecter Sex #4: Pole Position / cr70 / AR / M • Erotic City / 1985 / CV / M • Erotic Dr Jekyll / 1975 / VXP / M • Erotic Fantasies #2 / 1983 / CV / C • Erotica Jones / 1985 / AVC / M • Every Inch A Lady / 1975 / QX / M • Evil Angel / 1986 / VCR / M • Experiments In Ecstacy / 1975 / COS / M • Fantasies Unltd. / 1985 / CDI / M • Fantasy Land / 1984 / LA / M • Fast Ball / cr73 / VXP / M • The Filthiest Show In Town / 1975 / ... / M

• First Annual XRCO Awards / 1984 / AVC / C • Flasher / 1986 / VD / M • Fleshpots Of 42nd Street / 1971 / SOW / S • For Your Thighs Only / 1985 / WV / M • Forced Entry / 1972 / ALP / M • French Lessons / 1985 / VD / M • French Schoolgirls / 1973 / AVC / M • Ginger Lynn—Non-Stop / 1988 / VD / C • Ginger's Greatest Boy/Girl Hits / 1987 / VI / C • Ginger: The Movie / 1988 / PV / C • Girl In A Penthouse / cr75 / CLX / M • The Girls Of The A Team #1 / 1985 / WV / M • Girls Of The Night / 1985 / CA / M • Girls On Fire / 1985 / VCX / M • The Grafenberg Spot / 1985 / MIT / M • GVC: Hotel Hooker #113 / 1975 / GO / M • Having It All / 1985 / IN / M • Heartthrobs / 1985 / CA / M • High Rise / 1973 / QX / M • Holiday For Angels / 1987 / IN / M • Honeybuns #1 / 1987 / WV / M • Honkytonk Angels / 1988 / IN / C • Hot Blooded / 1983 / CA / M • Hot Nights At The Blue Note Cafe / 1985 / WV / M • I Love LA #1 / 1986 / PEN / C • I Love LA #2 / 1989 / PEN / C • Indecent Itch / 1985 / VCR / M • Intensive Care / 1974 / BL / M • It Happened In Hollywood / 1973 / WWV / M • L'Amour / 1984 / CA / M • Late After Dark / 1985 / BAN / M • Legends Of Porn #1 / 1987 / CV / C • Legends Of Porn #2 / 1989 / CV / C • Loose Ends #1 / 1984 / 4P / M • Losing Control / 1985 / CDI / M • Love Bites / 1985 / CA / M • The Love Syndrome / 1978 / CV / M • The Love Witch / 1973 / AR / M • Lovelace Meets Miss Jones / 1975 / AVC / M • Loving Daughter / 1976 / VHL / M • Lucky In Love #1 / 1985 / BAN / M • Lust In Space / 1985 / PV / M • Marilyn Chambers' Private Fantasies #4 / 1983 / CA / M • Marilyn Chambers' Private Fantasies #6 / 1985 / CA / M • Meatball / 1972 / VCX / M • Memories Within Miss Aggie / 1974 / VHL / M • Midnight Blue #2 / 1980 / VXP / M • Miss Nude America Contest And The Mr. Nude America Contest / 1975 / WIZ / S • Mondo Porno / cr70 / SOW / M • More / 1973 / BL / M • National Lampoon Goes To The Movies / 1981 / MUN / S • Naughty Nurses / 1986 / VEX / M • The Newcomers / 1973 / VSH / M • A Night On The Wild Side / 1986 / VC / M • Night Prowlers / 1985 / MAP / M • Obsession / 1985 / HO / M • Older Men With Young Girls / 1985 / CC / M • One Night At A Time / 1984 / PV / M • Only The Best #3 / 1990 / CV / C • Only The Best Of Men's And Women's Fantasies / 1988 / CV / C • Oral Majority #02 / 1987 / WV / C • Oriental Jade / 1985 / VC / M • Over Sexposure / 1974 / VHL / M • Overexposure / cr73 / GO / M • A Passage To Ecstasy / 1985 / CDI / M • Penetration / 1976 / MV1 / S • Pleasure Cruise / 1972 / WV / M • Pleasure Motel / 197? / CV / M • Porn In The USA #1 / 1986 / WV / C • Prurient Interest / 1974 / BL / M • Pulsating Flesh / 1986 / VC / M • R.S.V.P. / 1983 / VES / S • Revolving Teens / 1974 / SEP / M • Rubdown / 1985 / VCX / M • S.O.S. / 1975 / QX / M • Saturday Matinee Series #1 / 1996 / VCX / C • Selling It / 1971 / BL / M • Sex Asylum #1 / 1985 / VI / M • Sex U.S.A / 1970 / SEP / M • Sex Wish / 1976 / CV / M • Sherlick Holmes / cr75 / SVE / M • Showgirl #04: Tina Russell Classics / 1981 / VCR / M • Sister Dearest / 1984 / DR / M • Slip Into Ginger & Amber / 1986 / MAP / C • Society

Affairs / 1982 / CA / M • Some Kind Of Woman / 1985 / CA / M • Sometime Sweet Susan / 1974 / ALP / M • Sweet Cheeks / 1987 / VCR / C • Talk Dirty To Me One More Time #1 / 1985 / PP / M • Teenage Cheerleader / 1978 / VXP / M • Ten Little Maidens / 1985 / EXF / M • This Side Up / 1987 / VSX / C • This Stud's For You / 1986 / MAP / C • Those Young Girls / 1984 / PV / M • A Time To Love / 1971 / ALP / M • Too Good To Be True / 1984 / MAP / M • Too Naughty To Say No / 1984 / CA / M • A Touch Of Genie / 1974 / ... / M • Tower Of Power / 1985 / CV / M • Traci Who? / 1987 / AVC / C • Trashy Lady / 1985 / MAP / M • Violated / 1973 / PVX / M • Voyeur's Delight / 1986 / VCS / C • Wait Till He Comes In Me! / 1994 / MET / M • The Weirdos And The Oddballs / 1968 / CLX / M • Wet Rainbow / 1973 / AR / M • Wet Shots (Vcr) / 1983 / VCR / C • Wet, Wild And Wicked / 1984 / SE / M • The Whore Of The Worlds / 1985 / PV / M • With Love From Susan / 1988 / HO / C • WPINK-TV #1 / 1985 / PV / M • [Hot Dog Cops /]980 / ... / S • [Justine Och Juliette / 1975 / ... / S • [Love Shrink / 1971 / ... / M • [Spikey's Magic Wand / 1973 / ... / S • [Undercover Cops / 19?? / ... / M

HARRY SEIGEL
Overnight Sensation / 1976 / AR / M

HARRY TAYLOR
The Untamed Vixens / 1976 / VHL / M

HARRY VALENTINE *see Star Index I*

HARRY WATSON
American Sex Fantasy / 1975 / IHV / M

HARRY WILCOX
The Loves Of Mary Jane / 1989 / BWV / C • A Touch Of Sex / 1972 / AR / M

HARRY WILLIAMS
Private Film #12 / 1994 / OD / M

HARU YAMAUA
A Soldier's Desire / 1985 / ORC / M

HARUKO MATSUSHITA
Private Escort / 1996 / AVE / M

HARVEY (RICK BLAINE) *see* Rick Blaine

HARVEY COWAN *see Herschel Savage*

HARVEY DENT *see Star Index I*

HARVEY LOWELL *see Star Index I*

HARVEY WALLBANGER
Stuff Your Face #4 / 1996 / JMP / M

HASHOIL DAMMIT *see Star Index I*

HATCHER *see* Steve Hatcher

HATMAN
Buttman In Barcelona / 1996 / EA / M • Buttman In The Crack / 1996 / EA / M • Snake Pit / 1996 / DWO / M • Valentino's Euro-Invasion / 1997 / SC / M

HAULIHAN *see Star Index I*

HAVANA *see* Amanda Tyler

HAYLEY
World Sex Tour #6 / 1996 / ANA / M • World Sex Tour #7 / 1996 / ANA / M

HAYLEY SHORE
New Pussy Hunt #20 / 1996 / LEI / C

HAZEL
HomeGrown Video #462: Motion In The Backfield / 1995 / HOV / M

HAZEL PARKER
Blue Vanities #549 / 1994 / FFL / M

HAZEL SCOTT
Indiana Joan In The Black Hole Of Mammoo / 1984 / VC / M • Romancing The Bone / 1984 / VC / M

HAZEL TAYLOR

Blue Vanities #581 / 1996 / FFL / M

HEADY LA MARS
Dirty 30's Cinema: Heather Wayne / 1985 / PV / C • Sexeo / 1985 / PV / M

HEALE AIERRE-GUSTAVW
Miss Anal #3 / 1995 / C69 / M

HEALY
Video Virgins #13 / 1994 / NS / M

HEATHER
Back East Babes #1 / 1996 / NIT / M • Beneath The Cane / 1992 / BON / B • Biff Malibu's Totally Nasty Home Videos #26 / 1992 / ANA / M • Blue Vanities #583 / 1996 / FFL / M • Bottoms Up (1993-Bon Vue) / 1993 / BON / B • Butt Hunt #10 / 1995 / LEI / M • Donna Young: Ann & Heather's First Lesbian Video #1 / 1996 / DY / F • Donna Young: Just Girls / 1995 / DY / F • Eat At Dave's #3 / 1995 / SP / M • First Time Lesbians #07 / 1993 / JMP / F • Girlz Towne #09 / 1995 / FC / F • I'll Take The Whip / 1993 / BON / B • Kinky Ladies Of London / 1995 / VC / M • The Last Temptation / 1988 / VD / M • Lesbian Fantasies / 1990 / BIZ / F • Lesbian Pros And Amateurs #05 / 1992 / GO / F • Lickin' Good / 1995 / TVI / F • Neighbor Girls T18 / 1990 / NEI / F • Neighborhood Watch #16: Dirty Laundry / 1992 / LBO / M • New Faces, Hot Bodies #09 / 1993 / STP / M • New Faces, Hot Bodies #21 / 1996 / STP / C • Pussy Tails #01 / 1993 / CDY / M • Rapture Girls #2: Ona & Stephanie / 1991 / OD / M • She's No Angel #2 / 1995 / V99 / M • She-Male Sex Clinic / 1991 / VC / G • She-Male Solos #09 / 1991 / LEO / G • She Male Spirits Of The Night / 1991 / VC / G • Sisters Of Sin / 1991 / VIM / G • The Sodomizer #5: Destination Moon / 1996 / SC / M • The Ultimate Sex / 1992 / MET / G • VGA: Blazing Pussies / 1992 / VGA / B • VGA: Cutting Room Floor #1 / 1993 / VGA / M • VGA: Spanking Sampler #2 / 1992 / VGA / B • Video Virgins #04 / 1993 / NS / M • Wet 'n' Wild / 1995 / TVI / F

HEATHER (K. KNIGHT) *see* Kristarrah Knight

HEATHER (THIN)
Emaciated very pretty blonde with small tits and a large tattoo (looks like a flower) on her right hip. See also Roxxi Raye who has a very similar body style.
Dirty Dancers #2 / 1994 / 4P / M • Strap-On Sally #03: Thigh Harness Terror / 1994 / PL / F • Strap-On Sally #04: Double Penetration Dykes / 1994 / PL / F • Up And Cummers #17 / 1994 / 4P / M • Up And Cummers #19 / 1995 / 4P / M

HEATHER ADAMS *see Star Index I*

HEATHER AIREY
Bondage Memories #04 / 1994 / BON / C • The Bondage Producer / 1991 / BON / B • Shades Of Bondage / 1991 / BON / B

HEATHER AUSTIN *see Star Index I*

HEATHER BATES
Donna Young: Ann & Heather's Oil Video / 1995 / DY / F • Donna Young: Heather Bates #1 / 1995 / DY / F

HEATHER BOWE *(Goldie (Heather B.))*
Slim blonde who has an overbite and looks like a younger smaller version of Victoria Paris. She has lots of freckles and was 27 years old in 1993. Seems to work with her husband, Rick. Has quite a tight waist and small firm tits.
Deep Inside Dirty Debutantes #02 / 1992 /

4P / M • Pearl Necklace: Thee Bush League #24 / 1993 / SEE / M

HEATHER BROWN *see* Heather Hart

HEATHER CAULEY *see Star Index I*

HEATHER CHASEN
Suburban Wives / 19?? / VST / M

HEATHER DE STAHL *see Star Index I*

HEATHER DEELEY *see Star Index I*

HEATHER DOUGHERTY *see Star Index I*

HEATHER ELLAS
Defiance / 1974 / ALP / B • Loose Threads / 1979 / S&L / M • Ms. Woman Of The Year / 1980 / BL / M • Teenage Cousins / cr76 / SOW / M

HEATHER FIELDS
All About Annette / 1982 / SE / C • All The King's Ladies / 1981 / SUP / M • East Coast Sluts #10: Ohio / 1996 / PL / M • N.Y. Video Magazine #09 / 1996 / OUP / M • Southern Belles #6 / 1996 / XPR / M • Southern Belles: Sugar Magnolias / 1996 / XPR / M • Streets Of New York #07 / 1996 / PL / M • Using Your Assets To Get A Head / 1996 / OUP / F

HEATHER FONTAINE
The Mysteries Of Transsexualism Explored #1 / 1987 / OZE / G • The Mysteries Of Transsexualism Explored #2 / 1990 / LEO / G • She-Male Tales / 1990 / MET / G • Sulka's Daughter / 1984 / MET / G

HEATHER FOX
Best Exotic Dancers In The Usa / 1995 / PME / S • She-Male Call Girls / 1996 / BIZ / G • She-Male Showgirls / 1992 / STA / G • TV Dildo Fantasy #2 / 1996 / BIZ / G

HEATHER GORDON *see* Hillary Summers

HEATHER HARD *see* Heather Hart

HEATHER HART *(Heather Heart, Heather Brown, Heather Hunt, Heather Hard, Shannon White (Hart), Heather Mills)*
Marginal brunette with medium droopy tits. Says she was de-virginized at 12. Heather Brown is from Kiss It Goodbye. Heather Hunt is from **Titillation #3**. Shannon White is from **More Dirty Debutantes #07**. Heather Mills is from **Sittin' Pretty #1**.
The Absolute Worst Of Amateur #1 / 1993 / VEX / M • The Adventures Of Buttgirl & Wonder Wench / 1991 / AFV / M • Adventures Of Buttwoman #1 / 1991 / EL / F • All About Teri Weigel / 1996 / XCI / M • All In The Name Of Love / 1992 / IF / M • Amateur American Style #26 / 1992 / AR / M • Amateur Lesbians #06: Taylor / 1991 / GO / F • Amateur Lesbians #07: Holly / 1991 / GO / F • Amateur Lesbians #14: Avalon / 1991 / GO / F • Amateur Lesbians #17: Sharise / 1992 / GO / F • America's Dirtiest Home Videos #01 / 1991 / VEX / M • American Garter / 1993 / VC / M • Anal Attraction #2 / 1993 / AFV / C • Anal Kitten / 1992 / ROB / M • Anal Lover #2 / 1993 / ROB / M • Anal Orgy / 1993 / DRP / M • Anal Savage #1 / 1992 / ROB / M • Animal Instincts #2 / 1994 / AE / S • Animal Instincts / 1991 / VEX / M • Bad Girl Handling / 1993 / RB / B • The Bad News Brat / 1991 / VI / M • The Bare-Assed Naked Gun / 1992 / MID / M • Bazooka County #5: The Jugs / 1993 / CC / M • Bed & Breakfast / 1992 / VC / M • Behind The Backdoor #4 / 1990 / EVN / M • The Best Of The Gangbang Girl Series / 1995 / ANA / C • Bi & Large / 1994 / STA / G • The Bi-

Linguist / 1993 / BIL / G • The Bi Spy / 1991 / STA / G • Bi-Inferno / 1992 / VEX / G • Bi-Sex Pleasures / 1993 / PL / G • Biff Malibu's Totally Nasty Home Videos #01 / 1992 / ANA / M • Biff Malibu's Totally Nasty Home Videos #05 / 1992 / ANA / M • Blazing Boners / 1992 / MID / M • Blonde Bombshell / 1991 / CC / M • Brandy & Alexander / 1991 / VC / M • Breast Wishes #06 / 1991 / LBO / M • Breast Worx #21 / 1992 / LBO / M • Breasts And Beyond #1 / 1991 / ME / M • Bruce Seven's Favorite Endings #1 / 1991 / EL / C • Bruce Seven: A Compendium Of His Most Graphic Scenes Vol 2 / 1991 / BS / C • Bums Away / 1995 / PRE / C • Buttman's Big Tit Adventure #1 / 1992 / EA / M • Buttman's Revenge / 1992 / EA / M • The Buttnicks #2 / 1991 / HIO / M • Chicks, Licks And Dirty Tricks / 1993 / ME / F • Christy In The Wild / 1992 / VI / M • Clean Out / 1991 / PRE / B • Confessions #1 / 1992 / OD / M • Confessions #2 / 1992 / OD / M • The Creasemaster / 1993 / VC / M • Dark Destiny / 1992 / BS / B • Debbie Does Wall Street / 1991 / VC / M • Deep Inside Jeanna Fine / 1992 / VC / C • Deep Throat #6 / 1992 / AFV / M • Defiance: Spanking And Beyond / 1993 / PRE / B • Defiance: The Ultimate Spanking / 1993 / BIZ / B • Derrier / 1991 / CC / M • Dial N Again / 1993 / PEP / M • Dial N For Nikki / 1993 / PEP / M • Dirty Dave's American Amateurs #11 / 1992 / AR / M • Diver Down / 1992 / CC / M • Double Load #1 / 1993 / HW / M • Dr Hooters / 1991 / PL / M • Dreams Of Candace Hart / 1991 / VI / M • Dripping With Desire / 1992 / DR / M • Every Woman Has A Secret / 1991 / ROB / M • Evil Woman / 1990 / LE / M • Executive Suites / 1993 / PL / M • Faithless Companions / 1992 / WV / M • Forever / 1991 / LE / M • Foxes / 1992 / FL / M • Gangbang Girl #05 / 1992 / ANA / M • Gangbang Girl #06 / 1992 / ANA / M • Gerein' Up / 1992 / VC / M • Girls Will Be Boys #6 / 1993 / PL / F • The God Daughter #2 / 1991 / AFV / M • The God Daughter #3 / 1992 / AFV / M • The God Daughter #4 / 1992 / AFV / M • Hard Deck / 1991 / XPI / M • Hard To Thrill / 1991 / CIN / M • The Harder Way / 1991 / AR / M • Head Lines / 1992 / SC / M • Heartbreaker / 1992 / CDI / M • Heatseekers / 1991 / IN / M • Heavy Petting / 1991 / SE / M • Hidden Obsessions / 1992 / BFP / M • High Fives / 1991 / PRE / B • Hit Parade / 1996 / PRE / B • Homegrown Video #316 / 1990 / HOV / M • Homegrown Video #327 / 1991 / HOV / M • Homegrown Video #426: Best Big Breasted Women / 1994 / HOV / C • Hometown Girl / 1994 / VEX / M • Hot Blondes / 1991 / VEX / C • Hot Rod To Hell #2 / 1992 / BS / B • Hot Spot / 1991 / CDI / M • Immoral Support / 1992 / AFV / M • An Innocent Woman / 1991 / FAZ / M • It's Only Love / 1992 / VEX / M • Italian Game / 1994 / CS / B • Jug Humpers / 1995 / V99 / C • Just A Gigolo / 1992 / SC / M • Just For Tonight / 1992 / VC / M • Killer Looks / 1991 / VI / M • Kiss It Goodbye / 1991 / SE / M • Ladies Lovin' Ladies #1 / 1990 / AR / F • Ladies Lovin' Ladies #3 / 1993 / AFV / F • Ladies Lovin' Ladies #4 / 1992 / AFV / F • The Lady In Red / 1993 / VC / M • The Last Good Sex / 1992 / FD / M • Leena / 1992 / VT / M • Leg...Ends #06

/ 1992 / PRE / F • Lesbian Pros And Amateurs #06 / 1992 / GO / F • Love Letters / 1991 / VI / M • Love Letters / 1992 / ELP / F • Lust & Money / 1995 / SUF / M • Lust Never Sleeps / 1991 / FAZ / M • Manbait #2 / 1992 / VC / M • Married With Hormones #1 / 1991 / PL / M • Masquerade (1992-Usa) / 1992 / SC / M • The Midnight Hour / 1991 / VT / M • Mix Up / 1992 / IF / M • More Dirty Debutantes #07 / 1991 / 4P / M • Mr. Peepers Amateur Home Videos #11: Fur Pie Smorgasbord / 1991 / LBO / M • Much More Than A Mouthful #3 / 1993 / VEX / M • New Wave Hookers #3 / 1993 / VC / M • Night And Day #1 / 1993 / VT / M • No Fear / 1996 / IN / F • Notorious / 1992 / SC / M • Oral Majority #12 / 1994 / WV / C • Oriental Temptations / 1992 / WV / M • Oriental Treatment #3: The Lost Empress / 1991 / AFV / M • Oriental Treatment #4: The Demon Lover / 1992 / AFV / M • P.J. Sparxx On Fire / 1992 / MID / C • Passages #1 / 1991 / VI / M • Passages #2 / 1991 / VI / M • The Perfect Stranger / 1991 / IN / M • Petite & Sweet / 1994 / V99 / M • Phone Fantasy #1 / 1992 / ATL / M • Phone Fantasy #2 / 1992 / ATL / M • Physically Fit / 1991 / V99 / C • Pole Cats / 1993 / KBR / S • Positively Pagan #06 / 1993 / ATA / M • The Power Dykes / 1993 / BIZ / B • Prescription For Pain #2: The Ultimate Pain / 1993 / BON / B • The Psychic / 1993 / CC / M • Pumping It Up / 1993 / ... / M • Queen Of Hearts #3: Heartless / 1992 / PL / M • Radical Affairs Video Magazine #06 / 1993 / ME / M • Rayne Storm / 1991 / VI / M • Real Swinger Videos #05 / 1993 / ... / M • Rebel / 1991 / ZA / M • Rump Roasts / 1991 / PRE / B • School For Wayward Wives / 1993 / BIZ / B • Seduced / 1992 / VD / M • Sensual Exposure / 1993 / ULI / M • Sex Express / 1991 / SE / M • Sex In A Singles Bar / 1992 / VC / M • Sex Sting / 1992 / FD / M • Sexlock / 1992 / XPI / M • Shipwrecked / 1991 / VEX / C • Sirens / 1991 / VC / M • Sittin' Pretty #1 / 1990 / DR / M • Six Plus One #1 / 1993 / VEX / M • Smart Ass / 1992 / RB / B • The Social Club / 1995 / LE / M • Sodomania #02: More Tails / 1992 / EL / M • Sole Goal / 1996 / PRE / B • Southern Comfort / 1991 / CIN / M • Speedster / 1992 / VI / M • Stasha: Portrait Of A Swinger / 1992 / CDI / G • Step To The Rear / 1991 / VD / M • Strange Lesbian Tales / 1996 / BAC / F • Student Fetish Videos: The Enema #04 / 1991 / PRE / B • Student Fetish Videos: Foot Worship #03 / 1991 / PRE / B • Student Fetish Videos: Spanking #04 / 1991 / PRE / B • Summer Heat / 1991 / CIN / M • Sun Bunnies #2: The Pink Cheek Tales / 1992 / SC / M • Sweet Cheeks (1991-Vid Excl) / 1991 / VEX / C • Sweet Dreams / 1991 / VC / M • Switch Hitters #6: Back In The Bull Pen / 1991 / IN / G • Tailspin #3 / 1992 / VT / M • Temptation Eyes / 1991 / VT / M • Things Change / 1992 / MET / M • Things Change #2: Letting Go / 1992 / CV / M • Tight Pucker / 1992 / WV / M • Tinseltown Wives / 1992 / AFV / M • Titillation #3 / 1991 / SE / M • Toppers #03 / 1993 / TV / M • Toppers #05 / 1993 / TV / M • Toppers #07 / 1993 / TV / M • Toppers #12 / 1993 / TV / C • Toppers & Whoppers #1 / 1994 / PRE / C • Torrid Tonisha / 1992 / VEX / M • Total Exposure / 1992 / CDI / M • Trouble-

maker / 1991 / VEX / M • Twister / 1992 / CC / M • Unveil My Love / 1991 / HO / M • Up And Coming Executive / 1993 / TP / M • The Visualizer / 1992 / VC / M • We're Having A Party / 1991 / EVN / M • Wendy Is Watching / 1993 / ELP / M • Wet Faces #1 / 1997 / SC / C • Whoppers #3 / 1993 / VEX / F • Wild Cats / 1991 / PRE / B • Wild Flower #1 / 1992 / VI / M • Will & Ed Are Geeks In Heat / 1994 / MID / M • Will & Ed's Back To Class / 1992 / MID / M • Wishful Thinking / 1992 / VC / M • X Factor: The Next Generation / 1991 / HO / M • The X-Producers / 1991 / XPI / M • X-Rated Bloopers #2 / 1986 / AR / M • You Bet Your Ass / 1991 / EA / B • [Quodoushka] / 1991 / VI / M

HEATHER HARTMANN
Overnight Sensation / 1976 / AR / M
HEATHER HEART *see* **Heather Hart**
HEATHER HEATH
[Point Of View / cr75 / ... / M
HEATHER HOLMES
I Was A She-Male For The FBI / 1987 / SEA / G • She-Male Encounters #05: Orgy At The Poysinberry Bar #1 / 1987 / MET / G • She-Male Encounters #12: Orgy At The Poysinberry #2 / 1987 / MET / G
HEATHER HUNT *see* **Heather Hart**
HEATHER HUNTER
Adorable little body with a butt that is the standard by which all others should be measured. Pretty with long krinkly black hair. Only defect is that her boobs are a little too big for her frame and are a bit droopy. Smiles or laughs all the time. De-virginized at 16 and 26 in 1995. Performed as a dancer on **Soul Train** on regular TV. Rumor has it that in 1991 she was dating (and presumably screwing) Magic Johnson (HIV positive) although she denies it. Was also involved with Artie Mitchell before his death (see the book *X-Rated*). First movie was **Heather Hunter On Fire** which she shot on her 18th birthday. Married once but now (1995) divorced.

Blackballed / 1994 / VI / C • Bloopers & Boners / 1996 / VI / M • Blue Jeans Brat / 1991 / VI / M • The Brat Pack / 1989 / VWA / M • A Cameo Appearence / 1992 / VI / M • Coming On America / 1989 / VWA / M • Dear John / 1993 / VI / M • Designer Genes / 1990 / VI / M • The End / 1995 / VI / M • Fashion Plate / 1995 / WAV / M • Frankenhooker / 1990 / FAC / S • Frankenhunter, Queen Of The Porno Zombies / 1989 / GMI / M • Heat / 1995 / WAV / M • Heather / 1989 / VWA / M • Heather Hunted / 1990 / VI / M • Heather Hunter On Fire / 1988 / VWA / M • Heather Hunter's Bedtime Stories / 1991 / GLE / S • Heather's Home Movies / 1989 / VWA / M • Hot Talk Radio / 1989 / VWA / M • Hung Jury / 1989 / VWA / M • I Want It All / 1995 / WAV / M • Lusty Dusty / 1990 / VI / M • Miss Judge / 1997 / VI / M • Performance / 1990 / VI / M • Pink To Pink / 1993 / VI / C • Playboy: Inside Out #1 / 1992 / PLA / S • Positions Wanted / 1990 / VI / M • The Red Head / 1989 / VWA / M • Savannah's Last Stand / 1993 / VI / M • Screw The Right Thing / 1990 / VWA / M • The Stiff / 1995 / WAV / M • Telesex #2 / 1992 / VI / M • Torch #1 / 1990 / VI / M • Torch #2 / 1990 / VI / M • Twice As Nice / 1989 / VWA / M • A Vision In Heather / 1991 / VI /

M • Where The Boys Aren't #3 / 1990 / VI / F • [Heather Hunter's Hottest Hits / 1990 / ... / C

HEATHER JASMINE *see Star Index I*
HEATHER KEITH *see Star Index I*
HEATHER KENNEDY
Almost Sisters / 1991 / NWV / G • Hollywood Models / 1995 / PHV / S • Hot Body Video Magazine: Southern Belle / 1994 / CG / F • Raw Adventures At Bikini Point / 1995 / PHV / F • Soft Bodies: Beyond Blonde / 1995 / SB / F

HEATHER LANE
Seduce Me Tonight / 1984 / AT / M

HEATHER LEAR *see* Heather Lere

HEATHER LEATHER
Anal Health Club Babes / 1995 / EVN / M

HEATHER LEE *(Maria (H. Lee), Sabrina (H. Lee))*
Beefy girl with masses of blonde curly hair, not too pretty, 23 years old in 1993 (born October 31, 1969), 12 when de-virginized (no footage available), large enhanced tits, flat rear end. 34D-22-33, 4'11" tall, 100lbs. Popped out a kid when she was in ninth grade at high school.
'Ho! 'Ho! 'Ho! / 1993 / WP / M • 113 Cherry Lane / 1994 / FOR / M • The Adventures Of Mr. Tootsie Pole #2 / 1995 / LBO / M • Alpine Affairs / 1995 / LE / M • Anal Anonymous / 1995 / SO / M • Anal Aristocrat / 1995 / KWP / M • Anal Chiropractor / 1995 / PEP / M • Anal Delinquent #2 / 1994 / ROB / M • Anal Disciples #1 / 1996 / ZA / M • Anal Innocence #2 / 1993 / ROB / M • Anal Maniacs #3 / 1995 / WP / M • Anal Playground / 1995 / CA / M • Anal Rippers #1: The Beginning / 1995 / ZA / M • Anal Therapy #3 / 1994 / FD / M • Anally Insatiable / 1995 / KWP / M • Anything You Ever Wanted To Know About Sex / 1993 / VEX / M • Ass Busters Incorporated / 1996 / BLC / M • Assy Sassy #2 / 1994 / ROB / F • Babe Magnet / 1994 / IN / M • Backdoor To Harley-Wood #3 / 1993 / AFV / M • Best Butt(e) In The West #2 / 1995 / CC / M • Beyond Reality #2: Anal Expedition / 1996 / EXQ / M • Big Duct Buboo #L5 / 1995 / AFI / M • Big Bust Babes #39 / 1996 / AFI / M • Big Knockers #01 / 1994 / TV / M • Big Town / 1993 / PP / M • Black Buttman #01 / 1993 / CC / M • Black Buttwatch / 1995 / FH / M • Black Cream Queens / 1996 / APP / F • Black Tie Affair / 1993 / VEX / M • Blacks & Whites #2 / 1995 / GO / M • Blonde Angel / 1994 / VI / M • Bobby Hollander's Maneaters #11 / 1994 / SFP / M • Boob Acres / 1996 / HW / M • Bra Busters #06 / 1993 / LBO / M • Breast Collection #02 / 1995 / LBO / C • The Breast Files #2 / 1994 / AVI / M • The Breast Of Breastmen / 1995 / EVN / C • Breastman Does The Twin Towers / 1993 / EVN / M • Breastman's Bikini Pool Party / 1995 / EVN / M • Busty Babes / 1995 / NAP / F • Butt Busters / 1995 / EX / M • Butt Jammers #01 / 1995 / SC / F • Butt Jammers #02 / 1995 / SC / F • Butt Of Steel / 1994 / LV / M • Butt Sluts #3 / 1994 / ROB / F • Butt Watch #04 / 1994 / FH / M • Butt's Motel #6 / 1994 / EX / M • Butt's Up, Doc #4 / 1994 / GO / M • Butts Of Steel / 1994 / BLC / M • Cabin Fever / 1995 / ERA / M • Call Of The Wild / 1995 / AFI / M • Candy / 1995 / MET / M • Carnival / 1995 / PV / M •

Casting Call #16 / 1995 / SO / M • The Catburglar / 1994 / PL / M • The Cellar Dweller / 1996 / EL / M • Centerfold Celebrities '94 #1 / 1994 / SFP / M • Certifiably Anal / 1993 / ROB / M • Channel Blonde / 1994 / VI / M • Christmas Carol / 1993 / LV / M • Country Girl / 1996 / VC / M • Covergirl / 1994 / WP / M • The Cumming Of Sarah Jane #2 / 1993 / AFV / M • Dark Tunnels / 1994 / LV / M • Debauchery / 1995 / MET / M • Decadence / 1995 / AMP / M • Der Champion / 1995 / BTO / M • Designer Bodies / 1993 / VI / M • Designs On Women / 1994 / IN / F • Dick & Jane Do The Strip / 1994 / AVI / M • The Dickheads #1 / 1993 / MID / M • Do Me Nurses / 1995 / LE / M • Double D Dykes #12 / 1993 / GO / F • Double D Dykes #18 / 1995 / GO / F • Double Decadence / 1995 / NOT / M • Double Penetration Virgins #02: The Second Cumming / 1994 / LE / M • Dr Finger's House Of Lesbians / 1996 / SC / M • The Ebony Connection #4 / 1994 / LBO / C • Fantasy Inc. / 1995 / CV / M • Fast Forward / 1995 / CA / M • For Your Mouth Only / 1995 / GO / M • Frontin' Da Booty / 1994 / WP / M • Fuck U: Girls Of The Packed-10 / 1995 / ZA / M • Gang Bang Face Bath #2 / 1994 / ROB / M • Getting Personal / 1995 / PE / M • A Girl Like You / 1995 / LE / M • The Girls From Hootersville #08 / 1994 / SFP / M • Harlots / 1993 / MID / M • Haunting Dreams #1 / 1993 / LV / M • The Heart Breaker / 1996 / MID / M • Hellfire / 1995 / MET / M • Hollywood Halloween Sex Ball / 1996 / EUR / M • The Hooker / 1995 / LOT / M • Hooter Ho-Down / 1994 / LV / M • Hooters / 1996 / MID / C • Hootersville (Legend) / 1995 / LE / M • Hot Tight Asses #05 / 1994 / TCK / M • Hot Tight Asses #06 / 1994 / TCK / M • Hot Tight Asses #08 / 1994 / TCK / M • Hot Tight Asses #11 / 1995 / TCK / M • Hot Tight Asses #14 / 1995 / TCK / M • Hotel Sodom #05: Tammi Ann Bends Over / 1995 / SNA / M • Hotel Sodom #09 / 1996 / SNA / M • Hypnotic Hookers #2 / 1996 / NIT / M • I Married An Anal Queen / 1993 / MID / M • Intense Perversions #1 / 1995 / PL / M • Interview: Silicone Sisters / 1996 / LV / M • Island Of Lust / 1995 / XCI / M • Jailhouse Nurses / 1995 / SC / M • Kinky Cameraman #2 / 1996 / LEI / C • Kittens #5 / 1994 / CC / F • Last Tango In Paradise / 1995 / ERA / M • Let's Dream On / 1994 / FD / M • Lips / 1994 / FC / M • Love Me, Love My Butt #2 / 1994 / ROB / F • M Series #13 / 1993 / LBO / M • Macin' #2: Macadocious / 1996 / SMP / M • Maneater / 1995 / ERA / M • Mellon Man #05 / 1995 / AVI / M • More Than A Handful #4 / 1994 / MET / M • Mr. Peepers Amateur Home Videos #76: Sixty Nine Plus Seven / 1993 / LBO / M • Nasty Nymphos #07 / 1994 / ANA / M • The New Butt Hunt #19 / 1996 / LEI / C • New Ends #05 / 1993 / 4P / M • New Girls In Town #4 / 1993 / CC / M • Nude Secretaries / 1994 / EDE / S • Once Upon An Anus / 1993 / LV / M • Other People's Pussy / 1993 / LV / M • Out Of My Mind / 1995 / PL / M • Pajama Party X #3 / 1994 / VC / M • Persuasion / 1995 / LE / M • Perverted Women / 1995 / SC / M • Pleasure Dome: The Genesis Chamber / 1994 / AFV / M • Public Enemy / 1995 / GO / M • Pump Fiction / 1995 / VT / M • Pussyman

#07: On The Dark Side / 1994 / SNA / M • Pussyman #13: Lips / 1996 / SNA / M • Rim Job Rita / 1994 / SC / M • Rocco Unleashed / 1994 / SC / M • Ron Hightower's White Chicks #06 / 1993 / LBO / M • Rump Man: Forever / 1995 / HW / M • Rump-Shaker #4 / 1995 / HW / M • Rumpman Forever / 1996 / HW / M • Rumpman's Backdoor Sailing / 1996 / HW / M • Sean Michaels On The Road #10: Seattle / 1994 / VT / M • Sex Academy #1 / 1993 / ONA / M • Sex In Abissi / 1993 / WIV / M • Sexual Trilogy #01 / 1993 / SFP / M • Seymore Butts Goes Deep Inside Shane / 1994 / FH / M • Seymore Butts: My Travels With The Tramp / 1994 / FH / M • Shaving Grace / 1996 / GO / M • Sin City Cycle Sluts #1 / 1995 / SC / F • Sin City Cycle Sluts #2 / 1995 / SC / F • Sindy's Sexercise Workout / 1994 / AFV / M • Slammed / 1995 / PV / M • Sleaze Please!—August Edition / 1994 / FH / M • Sleaze Please!—September Edition / 1994 / FH / M • Sluthunt #3 / 1996 / BIP / F • Sodomania #09: Doin' Time / 1994 / EL / M • Suburban Buttnicks Forever / 1995 / CC / M • Super Groupie / 1993 / PL / M • Tailz From Da Hood #4 / 1996 / AVI / M • Tailz From Da Hood #5 / 1996 / AVI / M • The Temple Of Poon / 1996 / PE / M • Titty Town #1 / 1994 / HW / M • Titty Town #2 / 1995 / HW / M • Toppers #28 / 1994 / TV / M • Toppers #29 / 1994 / TV / M • Toppers #31 / 1994 / TV / C • Trick Shots / 1995 / PV / M • Video Virgins #05 / 1993 / NS / M • Video Virgins #06 / 1993 / NS / M • Weekend At Joey's / 1995 / ERA / M • Wendy Whoppers: Bomb Squad / 1993 / PEP / M • Wendy Whoppers: Psychic Healer / 1994 / PEP / M • White Stockings / 1994 / BHS / M • White Wedding / 1995 / VI / M • Xxxanadu / 1994 / HW / M • [Quodoushka / 1991 / VI / M

HEATHER LEE (CR75) *see Star Index I*
HEATHER LEE (LERE) *see* Heather Lere
HEATHER LEE (THIN)
Binding Contract / 1992 / ZFX / B • Doc Bondage / 1992 / ZFX / B • Sorority Bondage Hazing / 1990 / BON / B • Southern Discomfort / 1992 / ZFX / B

HEATHER LERE *(Brianna Rae, Heather Lear, Marie Monet, Fetish, Wendi (H.Lere), Goldie Lake, Heather Lee (Lere), Wendy (H.Lere))*
Pretty, small breasted blonde with a nice tight body. Had a reputation for being very difficult and un-hygienic to work with. Performed very often with her boyfriend, Rob Tyler, and supposedly had a drug problem. Marie Monet also Fetish in **Sexy Nurses On And Off Duty**. Wendi is a double billing in **Trick Tracy #2**. Goldie Lake in **Girls Gone Bad #2**.
1-800-TIME / 1990 / IF / M • Adventures Of Buttwoman #1 / 1991 / EL / F • All For You, Baby / 1990 / VEX / M • Amazing Tails #5 / 1990 / CA / M • Auction #1 / 1992 / BIZ / B • Auction #2 / 1992 / BIZ / B • Backstage Pass / 1992 / VEX / M • Between The Cheeks #2 / 1990 / VC / M • Boobs, Butts And Bloopers #1 / 1990 / HO / M • Bruce Seven's Favorite Endings #1 / 1991 / EL / C • Bus Stop Tales #11 / 1990 / 4P / M • Cape Lere / 1992 / CC / M • Club Head / 1990 / CA / M • Dear Bridgette / 1992 / ZA / M • Deep Inside Dirty Debutantes #06 / 1993 / 4P / M • Deep Throat #5 / 1990 /

AR / M • Dresden Diary #06: The Hellfire Legend / 1992 / BIZ / B • Dresden Diary #08 / 1992 / BIZ / B • Enemates #06 / 1992 / BIZ / B • For The Hell Of It / 1992 / BS / B • Girls Gone Bad #2: The Breakout / 1990 / GO / F • Having It All / 1991 / VEX / M • Hollywood Studs / 1993 / FD / M • Honey, I Blew Everybody #1 / 1992 / MID / M • Hot Rod To Hell #1 / 1991 / BS / B • How To Love Your Lover / 1992 / XII / S • I Touch Myself / 1992 / IN / M • Introducing Danielle / 1990 / CDI / M • Jugsy (X-Citement) / 1992 / XCI / M • Jungle Beaver #1 / 1991 / HIO / M • Kittens #1 / 1990 / CC / F • The Last Girl Scout / 1992 / PL / M • Leading Lady / 1991 / V99 / M • Leg...Ends #06 / 1992 / PRE / F • Lesbian Pros And Amateurs #18 / 1993 / GO / F • Main Street, U.S.A. / 1992 / PP / M • More Dirty Debutantes / 1990 / PRI / M • More Dirty Debutantes #03 / 1990 / 4P / M • More Dirty Debutantes #11 / 1991 / 4P / M • Night Trips #2 / 1990 / CA / M • Odds 'n' Ends / 1992 / PRE / B • Odyssey Amateur #63: Pussy, Pussy Everywhere! / 1991 / OD / M • One Of These Nights / 1991 / V99 / M • The Party / 1992 / CDI / M • Party Dolls / 1992 / VEX / M • The Passion Of Heather Lear / 1990 / AFV / M • Pleasure Principle / 1990 / FAZ / M • The Pleasure Seekers / 1990 / VD / M • Princess Of The Night / 1990 / VD / M • A Pussy Called Wanda #1 / 1992 / DR / M • Ready Freddy? / 1992 / FH / M • Sex Appraisals / 1990 / HO / M • Sexy Nurses #1 On And Off Duty / 1990 / CV / M • Shipwrecked / 1992 / CDI / M • Space Virgins / 1990 / VEX / M • Stairway To Paradise / 1990 / VC / M • Suite Sensations / 1988 / SEX / M • Summer Lovers / 1991 / VEX / M • Sweet Darlin' / 1990 / VEX / M • Taboo #10 / 1992 / IN / M • A Taste Of Julia Parton / 1992 / VD / C • Trick Tracy #2: Tracy Loves Dick / 1990 / CC / M • Tush / 1992 / ZA / M • Vegas #2: Snake Eyes / 1990 / CIN / M • Vegas #3: Let It Ride / 1990 / CIN / M • Wanda Whips The Dragon Lady / 1990 / V99 / M • Where The Girls Play / 1992 / CC / F • Where The Girls Sweat #1 / 1990 / EA / F • Where The Girls Sweat #2 / 1991 / EL / F • White Satin Nights / 1991 / V99 / M • The Wild One / 1990 / LE / M • Women In Charge / 1990 / VEX / M • The Wrong Woman / 1992 / IN / M
HEATHER LOCKSTAR *see Star Index I*
HEATHER LYNN
Because I Can / 1995 / BEP / M • Behind The Mask / 1995 / XC / M • Bitches In Heat #2: On Vacation / 1995 / ZA / M • Hard Core Beginners #10 / 1995 / LEI / M • Interview: Naturals / 1995 / LV / M • Nasty Pants / 1995 / SUF / M • Perverted Stories #02 / 1995 / JMP / M
HEATHER MANNFIELD *see Heather Mansfield*
HEATHER MANSFIELD *(Jill Hunter, Heather Mannfield)*
Black Bunbusters / 1985 / VC / M • Burning Desire / 1983 / HO / M • Good Girls Do / 1984 / HO / M • Mama's Boy / 1984 / VD / M • The Night Of The Headhunter / 1985 / WV / M • Salt & Pepper / 1986 / VCS / C • Tailenders / 1985 / WET / M • Thrill Street Blues / 1985 / WV / M • Two Timing Tracie / 1985 / V20 / M • Up & In / 1985 / AA / M
HEATHER MARTIN (IR) *see Isabella Rovetti*
HEATHER MARTIN (SR) *see Summer Rose*
HEATHER MILLS *see Heather Hart*
HEATHER MIST
Enemates #02 / 1989 / BIZ / B • Feet First / 1988 / BIZ / S • Flash Floods / 1991 / PRE / C • Rip Off #1 / 1988 / BIZ / B • Rip Off #2 / 1988 / PLV / B • Sole-Ohs / 1989 / BIZ / F
HEATHER NEWMAN *see Megan Leigh*
HEATHER O'CONNELL *see Star Index I*
HEATHER O'DELL *see Star Index I*
HEATHER SINCLAIR *see Heather St Clair*
HEATHER ST CLAIR *(Heather Sinclair, Heather Strong)*
A former Miss Nude something-or-other she has a fantastic body with a tight waist, nice butt and great tan lines. In 1994 she had her tits enhanced but it was a good job and they are still proportionate to her body. Facially she's only so so with a too-big nose and black eyebrows that don't go with her blonde (may be real) hair. She's also too tall being the same height as Tom Byron.
The Anal Adventures Of Bruce Seven / 1996 / BS / C • Anal Candy Ass / 1994 / ROB / M • The Analizer / 1994 / VD / M • Beat The Heat / 1990 / VI / M • Best Of Foot Worship #3 / 1992 / BIZ / C • Black Velvet #3 / 1994 / CC / M • Butt Freak #2 / 1996 / EA / M • Buttman's Wet Dream / 1994 / EA / M • The Corner / 1994 / VT / M • Hawaii Vice: Reflections / 1990 / CIN / C • Heartless / 1989 / REB / M • Heather Hunted / 1990 / VI / M • The Landlady / 1990 / VI / M • Lesbian Lingerie Fantasy #5 / 1991 / ESP / F • Lifeguard / 1990 / VI / M • Main Course / 1992 / FL / M • Midnight Dreams / 1994 / WV / M • More Dirty Debutantes #04 / 1990 / 4P / M • Mummy Dearest #2: The Unwrapping / 1990 / LV / M • Nasty Jack's Homemade Vid. #04 / 1990 / CDI / M • Nasty Jack's Homemade Vid. #29 / 1991 / CDI / M • Nasty Jack's Homemade Vid. #31 / 1991 / CDI / M • Red Light / 1994 / SC / S • Single Girl Masturbation #5 / 1991 / ESP / F • Skippy, Jiff & Jam / 1990 / CIA / M • Slip Of The Tongue / 1990 / SE / M • The Swap #1 / 1990 / VI / M • Tail Taggers #117 / 1993 / WV / M • Takin' It To The Limit #1 / 1994 / BS / M • Takin' It To The Limit #2 / 1994 / BS / M • Toying Around / 1992 / FL / M • Up And Cummers #12 / 1994 / 4P / M • Up And Cummers #14 / 1994 / 4P / M • Wicked Pleasures / 1995 / BS / B • Wild Buck / 1993 / STY / M
HEATHER STAR *see Star Index I*
HEATHER STRONG *see Heather St Clair*
HEATHER TABBETHA
Leg...Ends #03 / 1991 / BIZ / F
HEATHER THOMAS *(Debbie Hupp)*
Not too pretty dark blonde with a barrel-like body. The relation between Debbie Hupp and Heather Thomas is based on **Breaking It #1** but is by no means certain.
Breaking It #1 / 1984 / COL / M • Camp Beaverlake #1 / 1984 / AR / M • Cheap Thrills / 1984 / RLV / M • Cyclone / 1986 / C3S / S • Ladies Of The Knight / 1984 / GO / M • Lesbian Nymphos / 1988 / GO / C • Oriental Lesbian Fantasies / 1984 / PL / F • Prescription For Passion / 1984 / VD / M • Wicked Wenches / 1988 / LA / M
HEATHER TORRANCE *(Heather Torso)*
The Adventures Of Buttman / 1989 / EA / M • Beeches / 1990 / KIS / M • Best Of Buttman #1 / 1991 / EA / C • Bo-Dacious / 1989 / V99 / M • Gang Bangs #2 / 1989 / EA / M • Hard Bodies / 1989 / CDI / M • Haunted Passions / 1990 / FC / M • Heather's Secrets / 1990 / VEX / M • Hidden Desire / 1989 / HO / M • Kascha's Days & Nights / 1989 / CDI / M • Mistaken Identity / 1990 / CC / M • More Than A Handful / 1993 / CA / C • National Poontang's Summer Vacation / 1990 / FC / M • New Sensations / 1990 / CC / M • Office Girls / 1989 / CA / M • Playin' Dirty / 1990 / VC / M • Playing Dirty / 1989 / VEX / M • She-Male Nurse / 1989 / LV / G • Slick Honey / 1989 / VC / M • Sweet Temptations / 1989 / V99 / M • Tamara's Dreams / 1989 / VEX / M • The Ultimate Climax / 1989 / V99 / M • Undressed For Success / 1990 / V99 / M
HEATHER TORSO *see Heather Torrance*
HEATHER VESPER *see Patti Petite*
HEATHER WADE *see Star Index I*
HEATHER WAYNE *(Laura Lee (H. Wayne), Teal Dare)*
Laura Lee is from **Ginger**. Reddish brown curly hair, medium tits, nice smile, passable face, 21 years old in 1985, de-virginized at 14.
Amber Lynn: She's Back / 1995 / TTV / C • The Animal In Me / 1985 / IN / M • Battle Of The Stars #2: East Versus West / 1985 / NSV / M • Beaverly Hills Cop / 1985 / SE / M • Best Of Hot Shorts #01 / 1987 / VCR / C • Carrie...Sex On Wheels / 1985 / AA / M • Cavalcade Of Stars / 1985 / VCR / C • Chocolate Kisses / 1986 / CA / M • Christy Canyon: She's Back / 1995 / TTV / C • Deep Inside Tracey / 1987 / CDI / C • Deep Inside Traci / 1986 / CDI / C • Deeper! Harder! Faster! / 1986 / VCS / C • Desperately Seeking Suzie / 1985 / VD / M • Diamond Collection #63 / 1984 / CDI / M • Dirty 30's Cinema: Heather Wayne / 1985 / PV / C • Dirty Shary / 1985 / VD / M • Doctor Desire / 1984 / VD / M • The Ecstasy Girls #2 / 1986 / CA / M • Educating Mandy / 1985 / CDI / M • The Enchantress / 1985 / 4P / M • Erotic Dimensions: Bold Fantasies / 1982 / NSV / M • Erotic Dimensions: Macho Women / 1982 / NSV / M • Flaming Tongues #3 / 1988 / MET / F • Flesh And Ecstasy / 1985 / VD / M • Flesh Fire / 1985 / AVC / M • Flesh For Fantasies / 1986 / TAM / M • Gang Bangs #1 / 1985 / VCR / M • Ginger (1984-Vivid) / 1984 / VI / M • Ginger On The Rocks / 1985 / VI / M • Ginger's Greatest Girl/Girl Hits / 1986 / VI / C • Girls Together / 1985 / GO / C • Gourmet Premier: Heather & Bunny / Around the World #cr85 / GO / M • Gourmet Premier: Heather & The Hitchhiker / Jessica's Joy903 / cr85 / GO / M • Gourmet Quickies: Heather Wayne #722 / 1985 / GO / C • Gourmet Quickies: Stacey Donovan / Heather Wayne #728 / 1985 / GO / C • Hard For The Money / 1984 / CV / M • Harlequin Affair / 1985 / CIX / M • Headgames / 1985 / WV / M • The Heartbreak Girl / 1985 / GO / M • Hindsight / 1985 / IN / M • Holiday For Angels / 1987 / IN / M • Hot Rockers / 1986 / IVP / M • Hot Shorts: Heather Wayne / 1986 / VCR / C • Hot Shorts: Robin Cannes / 1986 / VCR /

C • House Of Lust / 1984 / VD / M • I Love A Girl In A Uniform / 1989 / VC / C • Inches For Keisha / 1988 / WV / C • Inside Candy Samples / 1984 / CV / M • It's Incredible / 1985 / SE / M • Joy Toys / 1985 / WET / M • Jubilee Of Eroticism / 1985 / GO / M • Kissin' Cousins / 1984 / PL / M • The Ladies In Lace Party / 1985 / MAP / M • Le Sex De Femme #2 / 1989 / AFI / C • Legends Of Porn #1 / 1987 / CV / C • License To Thrill / 1985 / VD / M • Like A Virgin #1 / 1985 / AT / M • Little Girls Of The Streets / 1984 / CV / M • Little Muffy Johnson / 1985 / VEP / M • Love Bites / 1985 / CA / M • Loving Spoonfulls / 1987 / 4P / C • Lust At The Top / 1985 / CDI / M • Lusty Adventurer / 1985 / GO / M • A Mid-Slumber's Night Dream / 1985 / 4P / M • The Modelling Studio / 1984 / GO / M • More Than A Handful #1 / 1985 / CV / C • The More the Merrier / 1989 / VC / C • Naked Night / 1985 / VCR / M • Night Prowlers / 1985 / MAP / M • Only The Best Of Men's And Women's Fantasies / 1988 / CV / C • Only The Best Of Women With Women / 1988 / CV / C • Oral Majority #01 / 1986 / WV / C • Oral Majority #03 / 1986 / WV / C • Party Girls / 1988 / MAP / M • The Peek A Boo Gang / 1985 / COL / M • Perfection / 1985 / VD / M • The Pleasure Seekers / 1985 / AT / M • The Poonies / 1985 / VI / M • Project Ginger / 1985 / VI / M • Rambone The Destroyer / 1985 / WET / M • Scent Of A Woman / 1985 / GO / M • Sex 5th Avenue / 1985 / WV / M • Sex Busters / 1984 / PLY / M • Sex Shoot / 1985 / AT / M • Sexeo / 1985 / PV / M • Sinderotica / 1985 / HO / M • Sinful Pleasures / 1987 / HO / C • Some Kind Of Woman / 1985 / CA / M • Sore Throat / 1985 / GO / M • Spermbusters / 1984 / AT / M • Splashing / 1986 / VCS / C • A Star Is Porn / 1985 / PL / M • Starlets / 1985 / 4P / M • Stephanie's Outrageous / 1988 / LV / C • Suzie Superstar #2 / 1985 / CV / M • Swedish Erotica #56 / 1984 / CA / M • Sweet Cheeks / 1987 / VCR / C • Tailhouse Rock / 1985 / WV / M • A Taste Of Genie / 1986 / SE / C • A Taste Of Tawnee / 1988 / LV / C • The Teaserama Pet / 1985 / WV / M • Thrill Street Blues / 1985 / WV / M • Toys 4 Us #2 / 1987 / WV / C • Tracy Dick / 1985 / WV / M • Tracy In Heaven (Orig 1985) / 1985 / WV / M • Treasure Chest / 1985 / GO / M • Trick Or Treat / 1985 / ELH / M • The Wacky World Of X-Rated Bloopers / 1989 / GO / M • Wild Orgies / 1986 / SE / C • Wise Girls / 1989 / IN / C • The Woman In Pink / 1984 / SE / M • X-TV #1 / 1986 / PL / C • [Angels With Gooey Faces / 1985 / … / M • [Bare Mountain / 1985 / GO / M • [Toga Party / 1985 / … / M

HEATHER WHITE *see* **Krystina King**
HEATHER WILDE *see* **Star Index I**
HEATHER YOUNG (Colleen Anderson, Colleen Davis, Kelly Mint, June Meadows, Lemon Young, Lemmon Yellow) Pretty blonde with shoulder length slightly curly hair, small (some would say tiny) tits, good tan lines, tight waist and a nice butt.
The Blonde Goddess / 1982 / VXP / M • Bucky Beaver's XXX Dragon Art Theatre Double Feature #09 / 1996 / SOW / M • Deep Inside Annie Sprinkle / 1981 / VXP / M • Erotic Fantasies #3 / 1983 / CV / C • Erotic Fantasies #7 / 1984 / CV / C • Erotic

Fantasies: Women With Women / 1984 / CV / C • The Fur Trap / 1973 / AVC / M • Here Comes The Bride / 1977 / CV / M • Hot Honey / 1977 / VXP / M • Legends Of Porn #1 / 1987 / CV / C • Loose Threads / 1979 / S&L / M • More Than Sisters / 1978 / VC / M • People / 1978 / QX / M • Pussycat Ranch / 1978 / CV / M • Satin Suite / 1979 / QX / M • Skin Flicks / 1978 / AVC / M • Swedish Sorority Girls / 1978 / CV / M • Sweet Surrender / 1980 / VCX / M • Tigresses...And Other Man-Eaters / 1979 / VXP / M • Up In Flames / 1973 / SOW / M • White Fire / 1980 / VC / M
HEAVEN
High Heeled & Horny #4 / 1995 / LBO / M • Hot Body Competition: Beverly Hill's Miniskirt Madness Cont. / 1996 / CG / F • Medically Bound Tickle Team / 1996 / VTF / B • More Dirty Debutantes #55 / 1996 / 4P / M • Nothing Like Nurse Nookie #2 / 1996 / NIT / M
HEAVEN LEA *see* **Star Index I**
HEAVEN LEE
Pick Up Lines #13 / 1997 / OD / M
HEAVEN ST JOHN *see* **Angelique Pettijohn**
HECTOR
Bobby Hollander's Rookie Nookie #03 / 1993 / SFP / M • HomeGrown Video #453: / 1995 / HOV / M
HECTOR GOMEZ
Borderline (Vivid) / 1995 / VI / M
HECTOR MORALES
Bad Penny / 1978 / QX / M
HECTOR NINNY
Transformation Of Alicia / 19?? / BIZ / G
HECTOR Z. *see* **Star Index I**
HEDGE *see* **Ron Jeremy**
HEDVIG KASER
Sexhibition #3 / 1996 / SUF / M
HEDY LASMOOCH
Blue Vanities #182 / 1993 / FFL / M
HEIDE *see* **Star Index I**
HEIDE VON HUNTER
The Best Of East Coast Sluts / 1995 / PL / C • East Coast Sluts #02: Syracuse, NY / 1995 / PL / M • Firm Hands / 1996 / GOT / U • Muffs In Cuffs / 1995 / FTL / U • N.Y. Video Magazine #10 / 1996 / OUP / M • Slapped Around Sluts / 1995 / PL / B • Streets Of New York #05 / 1995 / PL / M • Striptease #1 / 1995 / PL / M • Striptease #2 / 1995 / PL / M
HEIDI
Bottoms Up #03 / 1983 / AVC / C • Funny Ladies / 1996 / PRE / B • Hillary Vamp's Private Collection #08 / 1992 / HVD / M • Homegrown Video #414: Pussy Hairstylist / 1994 / HOV / M • Lips: The Passage To Pleasure / 1981 / CA / M • Magma: Dreams Of Lust / 1994 / MET / M • Naughty Nymphs / 1986 / VEX / M • Southern: Heidi Deluxe / 1995 / SSH / F • Superfox: Heidi #19 / 1992 / SFO / F
HEIDI (GAIL FORCE) *see* **Gail Force**
HEIDI (NELSON) *see* **Heidi Nelson**
HEIDI CAT *see* **Heidi Nelson**
HEIDI ELKA WICKS
Employee Benefits / 1983 / AMB / M
HEIDI HOOTERS
Tit To Tit #1 / 1994 / BTO / M
HEIDI KANCE
Blue Vanities #561 / 1994 / FFL / M
HEIDI KAT *see* **Heidi Nelson**
HEIDI L.

Cluster Fuck #01 / 1993 / MAX / M
HEIDI LAMM
Heidi & Elke / 1995 / SHL / B
HEIDI MAHLER
Caballero Preview Tape #3 / 1984 / CA / C • Secret Passions / 1982 / CA / M
HEIDI NEISS
Anal Disciples #1 / 1996 / ZA / M • Anal Disciples #2: The Anal Conflict / 1996 / ZA / M • Anals, Inc / 1995 / ZA / M • Analtown USA #11 / 1996 / NIT / M • Creme De La Face #13: Nine Nasty Nymphs / 1995 / OD / M • Dirty Dancers #5 / 1995 / 4P / M • Perverted Stories #05 / 1995 / JMP / M • Red Door Diaries #1 / 1995 / ZA / M
HEIDI NELSON (Treble Hart, Monique (H. Nelson), Heidi (Nelson), Heidi Cat, Heidi Kat, Aphrodisiac, Dynamo Hum, Afrodisiac, Alley Cat)
Not too pretty brunette with a thick body. Born March 11, 1971 in Burbank CA.
The Adventures Of Breastman / 1992 / EVN / M • Amateur Lesbians #33: Mackala / 1992 / GO / F • Amateur Lesbians #34: Honey / 1991 / GO / F • The Anal-Europe Series #01: The Fisherman's Wife / 1992 / LV / M • Anything That Moves / 1992 / VC / M • Arsenal Of Fear / 1993 / BS / B • Assford Wives / 1992 / ATL / M • Backdoor Suite / 1992 / EX / M • Bed & Breakfast / 1992 / VC / M • Bianca Trump's Towers / 1992 / LV / M • The Big E #10 / 1992 / PRE / B • Big Tits And Fat Fannies #10 / 1994 / BTO / M • Black Encounters / 1992 / ZA / M • Blonde City / 1992 / IN / M • Boobytrap...The Next Generation / 1992 / HW / M • Bubble Butts #01 / 1992 / LBO / M • Bubble Butts #02 / 1992 / LBO / M • Bubble Butts #13 / 1992 / LBO / M • Buffy The Vamp / 1992 / FD / M • Butt Woman #2 / 1992 / FH / M • Butt Woman #3 / 1992 / FH / M • Buttman Vs Buttwoman / 1992 / EL / M • Cape Lere / 1992 / CC / M • Casting Call #01 / 1993 / SO / M • Cat Fight / 1992 / ONH / M • Dear Bridgette / 1992 / ZA / M • Double Penetration #6 / 1993 / WV / C • Dream Date / 1992 / HO / M • The Eyes Of A Stranger / 1992 / CDI / G • Fat Fannies #10 / 1994 / BTO / M • Fuck mates / 1992 / PRE / B • The Final Secret / 1992 / SO / M • Fringe Benefits / 1992 / IF / M • The Girls Of Summer / 1992 / FOR / M • Glitz Tits #02 / 1992 / GLI / M • Journey Into Servitude: The Pleasures Of Ultimate Humil... / 1992 / BIZ / B • Jugsy (X-Citement) / 1992 / XCI / M • Just One Look / 1993 / V99 / M • The Key to Love / 1992 / ZA / M • L.A. Rear / 1992 / FD / M • The Last Girl Scout / 1992 / PL / M • Last Tango In Rio / 1991 / DR / M • Leg...Ends #07 / 1993 / PRE / F • Maneater (1992-Las Vegas) / 1992 / LV / M • Manwiched / 1992 / FPI / M • The Mating Game / 1992 / PL / G • Mike Hott: #205 Lesbian Sluts #06 / 1992 / MHV / F • Mike Hott: #213 Horny Couples #07 / 1992 / MHV / M • Mistress Jacqueline's Slave School / 1992 / BIZ / B • Mr. Peepers Amateur Home Videos #38: Bringing Up the Rear / 1991 / LBO / M • Mr. Peepers Amateur Home Videos #40: Creme D' Wiener / 1992 / LBO / M • Nothing Else Matters / 1992 / V99 / C • Our Bang #05 / 1992 / GLI / M • Our Bang #08 / 1992 / GLI / M • Our Bang #13 / 1993 / GLI / M • Our Bang #14 / 1993 / GLI / M • Parlor Games / 1992 / VT / M • Peep Land

/ 1992 / FH / M • Physically Fit / 1991 / V99 / C • A Pussy Called Wanda #1 / 1992 / DR / M • Romancing The Butt / 1992 / ATL / M • Savage Fury #3 / 1994 / VEX / M • The Seducers / 1992 / ZA / M • Seymore Butts Rides Again / 1992 / FH / M • Single Tight Female / 1992 / LV / M • Six Plus One #2 / 1993 / VEX / C • Sweet Things / 1992 / VEX / M • Tailiens #2 / 1992 / FD / M • Tailiens #3 / 1992 / FD / M • Totally Teri / 1992 / IF / M • Two Sisters / 1992 / WV / M • Uncle Roy's Amateur Home Video #12 / 1992 / VIM / M • Uncle Roy's Best Of The Best: Brazen Brunettes / 1993 / VIM / C • The Visualizer / 1992 / VC / M • Wet & Wicked / 1992 / VEX / M

HEIDI SOHLER *see* **Uschi Digart**

HEIDI VOODENSHU
More Dirty Debutantes #51 / 1996 / 4P / M

HEIDI-HO *see Star Index I*

HEIDIE
The Voyeur #3 / 1995 / EA / M

HEINZ MUELLER *see* **Elmer Fox**

HELDA HOLDERIN *see Star Index I*

HELEANA
Big Busty #47 / 1994 / BTO / S • Double D-Cup Dates / 1994 / BTO / M

HELEN
America's Raunchiest Home Videos #06: Fuck Frenzy / 1992 / ZA / M • Blue Vanities #529 / 1993 / FFL / M • Blue Vanities #542 / 1994 / FFL / M • Blue Vanities #554 / 1994 / FFL / M • Blue Vanities #564 / 1994 / FFL / M • Blue Vanities #572 / 1995 / FFL / M • Blue Vanities #578 / 1995 / FFL / M • Blue Vanities #584 / 1996 / FFL / M • Breast Of Britain #2 / 1987 / BTO / M • Prague By Night #1 / 1996 / EA / M

HELEN BEDD
Amateur Lesbians #22: Cassidy / 1992 / GO / F • Anal Encounters #7: Enter Through The Rear / 1992 / VC / M • Body Fire / 1991 / LV / M • Bound For Pleasure / 1991 / BS / B • Breast Worx #07 / 1991 / LBO / M • Casabanga / 1991 / NAN / M • Girls Will Be Boys #3 / 1991 / PL / F • Scorcher / 1992 / GO / M • Shanna's Final Fling / 1991 / ME / M • Sweet Licks / 1991 / MID / M

HELEN BLAZEZ *see Star Index I*

HELEN CARROL *see Star Index I*

HELEN DO
Chinese Blue / 1976 / ... / M

HELEN DUVAL
Amsterdam Nights #1 / 1996 / BLC / M • Amsterdam Nights #2 / 1996 / VC / M • Bedtime Stories / 1996 / VC / M • Helen Does Holland / 1996 / VC / M • Hot New Imports / 1996 / XC / M • House On Paradise Beach / 1996 / VC / M • Private Video Magazine #07 / 1994 / OD / M • Private Video Magazine #08 / 1994 / OD / M • Private Video Magazine #09 / 1994 / OD / M • Two Sides Of A Lady / 1994 / HDE / M

HELEN FUTON
Slip Of The Tongue (Vxp) / 19?? / VXP / M

HELEN HARDIE *see Star Index I*

HELEN HAYNES *see Star Index I*

HELEN HAZE
The Pillowman / 1988 / VC / M

HELEN JONES
Blue Vanities #132 / 1991 / FFL / M • Blue Vanities #567 / 1995 / FFL / M

HELEN MADIGAN (Jennifer Mason, Mary Madigan, Helen Madison)
Pretty (or passable depending on her age)

brunette with either long straight hair (hippie style) or shoulder length (later movies). Small to medium tits, overbite, lithe body. ABA: Double Feature #5 / 1996 / ALP / M • Afrodisiac #1 / 1987 / CC / M • Angela, The Fireworks Woman / 1975 / VC / M • The Bite / 1975 / SVE / M • Blow Dry / 1977 / SVE / M • Blue Vanities #048 / 1988 / FFL / M • Blue Vanities #079 / 1988 / FFL / M • Blue Vanities #103 / 1988 / FFL / M • Blue Vanities #207 / 1993 / FFL / M • Blue Vanities #229 / 1994 / FFL / M • Blue Vanities #244 / 1995 / FFL / M • Blue Vanities #248 / 1995 / FFL / M • Blue Vanities #521 / 1993 / FFL / M • Bridal Intrigue / 1975 / VHL / M • Classic Erotica #5 / 1985 / SVE / M • Classic Erotica #6 / 1985 / SVE / M • Come Softly / 1977 / TVX / M • Confessions Of A Teenage Peanut Butter Freak / 1974 / LIM / M • Contact / 1975 / VC / M • Cum Shot Revue #1 / 1985 / HO / C • Daughters Of Darkness / 1975 / ASR / M • Debbie Does Las Vegas / 1982 / KOV / M • Ebony & Ivory Sisters / 1985 / PL / C • Ecstasy In Blue / 1976 / ALP / M • The Erotic Memoirs Of A Male Chauvinist Pig / 1973 / QX / M • Family Fun / cr75 / ... / M • Feelings / 1977 / VC / M • French Shampoo / 1978 / VXP / M • Girl Scout Cookies / 197? / SVE / M • GVC: Teacher's Pet #112 / 1983 / GO / M • Heavy Load / 1975 / COM / M • Illusions Of A Lady / 1972 / VSH / M • Kinky Potpourri #32 / 199? / SVE / C • Kinky Tricks / 1978 / VEP / M • Lecher / 1980 / COM / M • Legends Of Porn #1 / 1987 / CV / C • Limited Edition #02 / 1979 / AVC / M • Little Orphan Sammy / 1976 / VC / M • Ms. Woman Of The Year / 1980 / BL / M • Mystique / 1979 / CA / M • Naked Came The Stranger / 1975 / VC / M • New York Babes / 1979 / AR / M • Night After Night / 1973 / BL / M • Night Of Submission / 1976 / BIZ / M • The Nurses Are Coming / 1985 / VCR / C • The Openings / 1975 / BL / M • Over Sexposure / 1974 / VHL / M • The Porn Brokers / 1977 / VAE / M • Possessed / 1976 / VCX / M • Revolving Teens / 1974 / SEP / M • Road Service / cr73 / VHL / M • S.O.S. / 1975 / QX / M • Secluded Passion / 1983 / VHL / M • Sizzle / 1979 / QX / M • South Of The Border / 1977 / VC / M • Summer Of Laura / 1975 / CXV / M • Sweet Wet Lips / 1974 / PVX / M • Sylvia / 1976 / VCX / M • Teachers And Cream / cr70 / BOC / M • That's Erotic / 1979 / CV / C • True Legends Of Adult Cinema: The Golden Age / 1992 / VC / C • Virgin And The Lover / 1973 / ALP / M • Wet Rocks / 1975 / BL / M • The Wetter The Better / 1975 / VST / M • Whatever Happened To Miss September? / 1973 / ALP / M • When A Woman Calls / 1975 / VXP / M • Winter Heat / 1975 / AVC / M • [Love Express / 1974 / ... / M • [Spikey's Magic Wand / 1973 / ... / S • [Wild Girls / cr73 / ... / M

HELEN MADISON *see* **Helen Madigan**

HELEN MILLS
Totally Tasteless Video #02 / 1994 / TTV / M

HELEN MUNOZ *see Star Index I*

HELEN NILSSON
Swedish Vip Magazine #1 / 1995 / PL / M

HELEN OLSEN
The Awakening Of Sally / 1984 / VCR / M

HELEN SHELLEY *see Star Index I*

HELEN W.
Private Gold #09: Private Dancer / 1996 / OD / M

HELENA
Helen & Louise / 1996 / HDE / M • Prague By Night #2 / 1996 / EA / M • Private Gold #10: Sins / 1996 / OD / M • Rocco Goes To Prague / 1995 / EA / M • Yacht Orgy / 1984 / CA / M • Zazel / 1996 / CV / M

HELENA HUNTER
Ass Masters (Leisure) #01 / 1995 / LEI / M • The Hitch-Hiker #10: Rolling & Reaming / 1995 / WMG / M • The New Snatch Masters #15 / 1995 / LEI / C

HELENA ROLL
Loose Times At Ridley High / 1984 / VCX / M • Saturday Matinee Series #4 / 1996 / VCX / C

HELENE
Vampire Cats / 1994 / NAP / B

HELENE DETROIT *see Star Index I*

HELENE SHIRLEY
The Seduction Of Tessa / cr86 / CA / M

HELENE SIMONE *see Star Index I*

HELGA
Helga Hir. #22 / 1996 / NMP / M • Odyssey Triple Play #77: Hail Hail The Gang Bangs Here / 1994 / OD / M • Porno X-Treme #2: Club Bizarre / 1995 / SC / M • Porno X-Treme #4: Wet Dream / 1995 / SC / M • Wrestling Vixens / 1991 / CDP / B

HELGA SCHMIDT *see Star Index I*

HELGA SVEN
Between My Breasts #01 / 1986 / BTO / S • Beyond Taboo / 1984 / VIV / M • Big, Bad & Beautiful / 1988 / MIR / C • Blue Ice / 1985 / CA / M • Busen #03 / 1989 / BTO / M • Centerfold Celebrities #4 / 1983 / VC / M • Cinderella / 1985 / VEL / M • Diamond Collection #58 / 1984 / CDI / M • Dirty Girls / 1984 / MIT / M • Double Standards / 1986 / VC / M • Family Heat / 1985 / AT / M • Free And Foxy / 1986 / VCX / C • Gourmet Premier: Lust X 4 / Raven's Rendezvous #901 / cr85 / GO / M • Hot Close-Ups / 1984 / WV / M • How Do You Like It? / 1985 / CA / M • Hustler #17 / 1984 / CA0 / M • The Idol / 1985 / WV / M • Little American Maid / 1987 / VCX / M • Make Me Want It / 1986 / CA / M • Pipe Dreams / 1985 / 4P / M • The Plumber Cometh / 1985 / 4P / M • Rearbusters / 1988 / LVI / C • Rich Quick, Private Dick / 1984 / CA / M • Scandal In The Mansion / 1985 / CDI / M • Spectators / 1984 / AVC / M • Thought You'd Never Ask / 1986 / CA / M • Thrill Street Blues / 1985 / WV / M • The Titty Committee / 1986 / SE / C • What Gets Me Hot / 1984 / ISV / M • Wild Nurses In Lust / 1986 / PLY / M • [Tape Busters #4 / 19?? / ... / M

HELGA TRIXI *see Star Index I*

HELLEN POLLARD *see Star Index I*

HELLMUTH HAUPT
[Schulmadchen-Report 4: Was Eltern Oft Verzweifeln LaBt / 1972 / ... / M

HELMAN TOBALINA *see Star Index I*

HELMUT RICHLER *see Star Index I*

HENRI CALVE *see Star Index I*

HENRI PACHARD (Ron Sullivan, Jackson St Louis, John Maddox)
The 8th Annual Erotic Film Awards / 1984 / SE / C • The Anal Nurse Scam / 1995 / CA / M • The Art Of Passion / 1987 / CA / M • Babylon Blue / 1983 / VXP / M • Babylon Pink #1 / 1979 / COM / M • Barflies / 1990

/ ZA / M • Beauty And The Beast #2 / 1990 / VC / M • The Big One / 1995 / HO / M • The Bitches Of Westwood / 1987 / CA / M • Boom Boom Valdez / 1988 / CA / M • The Butt Boss / 1993 / VD / M • City Of Sin / 1991 / LV / M • Conflict / 1988 / VD / M • Devil In Miss Jones #2 / 1983 / VC / M • Eclipse / 1993 / SC / M • Fantasy Exchange / 1993 / VI / M • The Fluffer #1 / 1993 / FD / M • The Fluffer #2 / 1993 / FD / M • Getting Personal / 1986 / CA / M • Ginger And Spice / 1986 / VI / M • Ginger Does Them All / 1988 / CV / M • Heart Breaker / 1994 / CA / M • Heatseekers / 1991 / IN / M • Hothouse Rose #1 / 1991 / VC / M • In Love / 1983 / VC / M • Interview With A Milkman / 1996 / VI / M • Jaded Love / 1994 / CA / M • Jane Bond Meets Thunderthighs / 1988 / VD / M • The Legend Of Barbi-Q And Little Fawn / 1994 / CA / M • Long Hard Nights / 1984 / ELH / M • Matinee Idol / 1984 / VC / M • Nasty Girls (1983-VCX) / 1983 / VCX / M • The New Barbarians #1 / 1990 / VC / M • The New Barbarians #2 / 1990 / VC / M • The New Kid On The Block / 1991 / VD / M • New York Vice / 1984 / CC / M • The Nicole Stanton Story #1 / 1989 / CA / M • The Nicole Stanton Story #2 / 1989 / CA / M • On Trial #1: In Defense Of Savannah / 1991 / VI / M • On Trial #2: Oral Arguments / 1991 / VI / M • Once Upon A Temptress / 1988 / CA / M • Oral Addiction / 1995 / VI / M • The Orgy #3 / 1993 / EMC / M • The Other Side Of Chelsea / 1993 / XCI / M • Outlaw Ladies #1 / 1981 / VC / M • Patent Leather / 1995 / CA / M • The Pink Pussycat / 1992 / CA / M • Porn Star Of The Year Contest / 1984 / VWA / M • Psychoanal Therapy / 1994 / CA / M • Punishing The Sluts / 1996 / RB / B • Raquel Untamed / 1990 / CIN / M • Roommates / 1982 / VXP / M • Sex Academy #1 / 1993 / ONA / M • Sex On The Run #1 / 1994 / TTV / M • Sextrology / 1987 / CA / M • Showdown / 1986 / CA / M • Slammer Girls / 1987 / LIV / S • Steal Breeze / 1990 / SO / M • Stiff Competition #2 / 1994 / CA / M • Supergilu By Oannal Haarilut / 1004 / 'VO / M • Surfside Sex #2 / 1992 / LV / M • Taboo #08 / 1990 / IN / M • Taboo American Style #1: The Ruthless Beginning / 1985 / VC / M • Taboo American Style #2: The Story Continues / 1985 / VC / M • Taboo American Style #4: The Exciting Conclusion / 1985 / VC / M • Tailiens #2 / 1992 / FD / M • Tailiens #3 / 1992 / FD / M • Temptation Eyes / 1991 / VT / M • Unnatural Phenomenon #2 / 1986 / WV / M • Vanessa...Maid In Manhattan / 1984 / VC / M • Venom #1 / 1995 / VD / M • Venom #2 / 1996 / VD / M • Venom #3 / 1996 / VD / M • Venom #4 / 1996 / VD / M • Viva Vanessa The Undresser / 1984 / VC / M • Voluptuous / 1993 / CA / M • Vow Of Passion / 1991 / VI / M • The Whore / 1989 / CA / M • Wicked Sensations #2 / 1989 / DR / M • Xcitement: The Movie / 1993 / XCI / M

HENRI PIERRE-GUSTAVE
Paris Chic / 1996 / SAE / M
HENRICH F.
Foreign Exchange Sluts / 1995 / TNT / M
HENRIETTA
Asses Galore #6: Fallen Angels / 1996 / DFI / M
HENRIETTE

Magma: Bizarre Lust / 1995 / MET / M
HENRY CONRAD
Blackmail For Daddy / 1976 / VCX / M
HENRY FLETCHER see Star Index I
HENRY GITE see Star Index I
HENRY HURT
Cham Pain / 1991 / DCV / B
HENRY LAMBERT
Hot Cookies / 1977 / WWV / M
HENRY MARGOLIS
The Erotic Aventures Of Lolita / 1982 / VXP / M
HENRY MORE
Easy Way Out / 1989 / OD / M
HENRY PARIS *(Radley Metzger)*
Director.
HENRY ROLLINS
The Chase / 1993 / FOX / S • Hardcore: The Films Of Richard Kern #1 / 1991 / FTV / M
HENRY ROSS
Karla / 19?? / … / M
HENRY VAN DAMP
Lil' Women: Vacation / 1996 / EUR / M
HENRY WILLS
Bucky Beaver's XXX Dragon Art Theatre Double Feature #06 / 1996 / SOW / M • Finishing School / 1975 / SOW / M
HENRY WOODS see Star Index I
HERB BENKMAN
Bad Girls #4 / 1984 / GO / M
HERB IVAN see Star Index I
HERB NITKE *(St Peter)*
Herb Nitke is the real name of the producer of Nibo Films—now dead.
Taboo American Style #4: The Exciting Conclusion / 1985 / VC / M
HERB SEAL
Total Sexual Power: Mastering Ejaculatory Control / 1994 / EPR / M • Total Sexual Power: The Ecstasy Of Female Orgasm / 1994 / EPR / M
HERB SILAS see Star Index I
HERB STRIECHER see Harry Reems
HERB STRYKER see Harry Reems
HERBERT KLUEVER
The Young Seducers / 1971 / BL / M
HERBIE CHAISELOUNGE
Cululuu Muuulun / 1000 / DIF / D
HERCULES see Big Herc
HERMANN ROEBELING
[Schulmadchen-Report 4: Was Eltern Oft Verzweifeln LaBt / 1972 / … / M
HEROS
Flamenco Ecstasy / 1996 / UEF / M
HERSCHEL RICHARD
MASH'ed / cr75 / ALP / M
HERSCHEL SAVAGE *(Joel Caine, Jack Black, Jack Blake, Joel Black, Hubert Savage, Vic Falcone, Paul Hues, Bill Berry, Billy Bell, Joel Laiter, Jack Baron, Bill Barry, Vic Falcon, Vic Falcoln, Joel Kane, Nick Barris, Cornell Hayes, Paul Hughs, Harvey Cowan, Harry Cowan, Joe Caine)*
1001 Erotic Nights #1 / 1982 / VC / M • 11 / 1980 / VCX / M • 2002: A Sex Odyssey / 1985 / DR / M • 52 Pick-Up / 1986 / MED / S • 6 To 9 Black Style / 1987 / LIM / C • 8 To 4 / 1981 / CA / M • Adult 45 #01 / 1985 / DR / C • The Adultress / 1987 / CA / M • The Adventures Of Dick Black, Black Dick / 1987 / DR / M • Amanda By Night #1 / 1981 / CA / M • Amanda By Night #2 / 1987 / CA / M • Amber Aroused / 1985 / CA / M • Amber Lynn's Hotline 976 / 1987 /

VCR / M • Amber Pays The Rent / 1986 / VT / M • Amber's Desires / 1985 / CA / M • Angel's Revenge / 1985 / IN / M • Animal Impulse / 1985 / AA / M • Attack Of The Monster Mammaries / 1987 / LA / C • The Awakening Of Emily / 1976 / CDI / M • Bachelor's Paradise / 1986 / VEX / M • Bachelorette Party / 1984 / JVV / M • Backdoor Club / 1986 / CA / M • Backdoor Girls / 1983 / VCR / C • Backdoor Lust / 1987 / CV / C • Bad Girls #2 / 1983 / GO / M • Ball Game / 1980 / CA / M • Barbara The Barbarian / 1987 / SE / M • Beauty / 1981 / VC / M • Bedtime Video #03 / 1984 / GO / M • Behind The Brown Door / 1986 / VCR / C • Behind The Scenes Of An Adult Movie / 1983 / CV / M • The Best Little Whorehouse In San Francisco / 1984 / LA / M • Betty Baby / cr70 / BL / M • Beverly Hills Wives / 1985 / CV / M • Beyond Your Wildest Dreams / 1980 / CAT / M • Big Gulp #2 / 1987 / VIP / C • Billionaire Girls Club / 1988 / LVI / C • Bizarre Encounters / 1986 / 4P / B • The Black Chill / 1986 / WET / M • Black To The Future / 1986 / VD / M • The Blonde / 1980 / VCX / M • Blonde At Both Ends / 1993 / TGA / M • Blonde In Black Silk / 1979 / QX / M • The Blonde Next Door / 1982 / GO / M • Blondes Have More Fun / 1980 / SE / M • Blowing The Whistle / 1986 / VIP / M • Blowing Your Mind / 1984 / RSV / M • Blowoff / 1985 / CA / M • Blue Dream Lover / 1985 / TAR / M • Blue Ice / 1985 / CA / M • Blue Ribbon Blue / 1984 / CA / C • Blue Vanities #106 / 1988 / FFL / M • Bodies In Heat #1 / 1983 / CA / M • Bodies In Heat #2 / 1989 / DR / M • Bold Obsession / 1983 / NSV / M • Bootsie / 1984 / CC / M • The Boss / 1987 / FAN / M • Bottoms Up #01 / 1983 / AVC / C • Bottoms Up #03 / 1983 / AVC / C • The Brazilian Connection / 1988 / CA / M • Breakin' In / 1986 / WV / M • The Bride / 1986 / WV / M • Brooke Does College / 1984 / VC / M • Bunbusters / 1984 / VCR / M • Busty Wrestling Babes / 1986 / VD / M • Caballero Preview Tape #2 / 1983 / CA / C • Caballero Preview Tape #4 / 1985 / CA / C • Oaluarel Olu / LAUT / Iid / M • Galifornia Valley Girls / 1983 / HO / M • Campus Capers / 1982 / VC / M • Candi Girl / 1979 / PVX / M • Candy Lips / 1975 / CXV / M • Carnal Olympics / 1983 / CA / M • The Cat Club / 1987 / SE / M • Cathouse Fever / 1984 / VC / M • Cells Of Passion / 1981 / VD / M • Challenge Of Desire / 1983 / NSV / M • Channel 69 / 1986 / LA / M • Charmed And Dangerous / 1987 / VI / M • Cheryl Hanson: Cover Girl / 1981 / SE / M • China & Silk / 1984 / MAP / M • Chocolate Kisses / 1986 / CA / M • Classical Romance / 1984 / MAP / M • Club Exotica #1 / 1985 / WV / M • Club Exotica #2 / 1985 / WV / M • Club Head (EVN) #1 / 1987 / EVN / C • Coffee, Tea Or Me / 1984 / CV / M • Collection #08 / 1984 / CA / M • A Coming Of Angels, The Sequel / 1985 / CA / M • Coming On Strong / 1989 / CA / C • Coming Together / 1984 / CA / M • Confessions Of A Nymph / 1985 / VCR / M • Corporate Assets / 1985 / SE / M • Country Girl / 1985 / AVC / M • Cream Of The Crop / 19?? / HOR / C • D-Cup Delights / 1987 / VCR / M • Dames / 1985 / SE / M • Dangerous Curves / 1985 / CV / M • Debbie Does Dallas #1 / 1978 / VC / M • Debbie

C • Stiff Competition #1 / 1984 / CA / M • Street Heat / 1984 / VC / M • Strip Search / 1987 / SEV / M • Stripteaser / 1986 / LA / M • Sulka's Daughter / 1984 / MET / G • Summer Camp Girls / 1983 / CA / M • Suze's Centerfolds #8 / 1984 / CA / M • Swedish Erotica #23 / 1980 / CA / M • Swedish Erotica #24 / 1980 / CA / M • Swedish Erotica #25 / 1980 / CA / M • Swedish Erotica #29 / 1980 / CA / M • Swedish Erotica #33 / 1980 / CA / M • Swedish Erotica #34 / 1980 / CA / M • Swedish Erotica #43 / 1982 / CA / M • Swedish Erotica #44 / 1982 / CA / M • Swedish Erotica #49 / 1983 / CA / M • Swedish Erotica #50 / 1983 / CA / M • Swedish Erotica #54 / 1984 / CA / M • Swedish Erotica #55 / 1984 / CA / M • Swedish Erotica #57 / 1984 / CA / M • Swedish Erotica #59 / 1984 / CA / M • Swedish Erotica #63 / 1985 / CA / M • Swedish Erotica #64 / 1985 / CA / M • Swedish Erotica #65 / 1985 / CA / M • Swedish Erotica #68 / 1985 / CA / M • Swedish Erotica #73 / 1986 / CA / M • Swedish Erotica Featurettes #4 / 1990 / CA / M • Swedish Erotica Featurettes #5 / 1990 / CA / M • Swedish Erotica Superstar #4: Shauna Grant / 1984 / CA / C • Taboo #07 / 1980 / IN / M • Taija / 1986 / WV / C • Take It Off / 1986 / TIF / M • Tales From The Chateau / 1987 / BON / B • A Taste Of Candy / 1985 / LA / M • A Taste Of Money / 1983 / AT / M • A Taste Of Tawnee / 1988 / LV / C • Taste Of The Best #1 / 1988 / PIN / C • A Taste Of Vanessa De Rio / 1990 / PIN / C • Tawnee...Be Good! / 1988 / LV / M • Teasers: Heavenly Bodies / 1988 / MET / M • Teasers: Hot Pursuit / 1988 / MET / M • Teasers: The Inheritance / 1988 / MET / M • Teenage Cover Girl / 1975 / VCX / M • Teenage Housewife / 1976 / BL / M • Temptation: The Story Of A Lustful Bride / 1983 / NSV / M • That's My Daughter / 1982 / NGV / M • That's Porno / 1979 / CV / C • This Butt's For You / 1986 / PME / M • This Is Your Sex Life / 1987 / VD / M • This Stud's For You / 1986 / MAP / C • Tight And Tender / 1985 / CA / M • Tigresses...And Other Man-Eaters / 1979 / VXP / M • The Titty Committee / 1986 / SE / C • Too Much Too Soon / 1983 / VCX / M • Tower Of Power / 1985 / CV / M • Tracie Lords / 1984 / CIT / M • Trading Places / 1985 / DR / M • Trashy Lady / 1985 / MAP / M • Triplets / 1985 / VCR / M • True Legends Of Adult Cinema: The Golden Age / 1992 / VC / C • Twins / 1986 / WV / M • Two Into One #1 / 1988 / PIN / C • The Ultimate Lover / 1986 / VD / M • The Ultimate O / 1985 / NSV / M • The Ultimate Thrill / 1988 / PIN / C • Unbelievable Orgies #1 / 1987 / EVN / C • United We Fall / 19?? / REG / C • Up 'n' Coming / 1983 / CA / M • VCA Previews #4 / 1988 / VC / C • Virginia / 1983 / CA / M • The Wacky World Of X-Rated Bloopers / 1989 / GO / M • Water Nymph / 1987 / LIM / M • Watermelon Babes / 1984 / VCR / M • Wet Shots (Vcr) / 1983 / VCR / C • What Gets Me Hot / 1984 / ISV / M • Whatever Turns You On / 1987 / CA / M • White Fire / 1980 / VC / M • White Trash / 1986 / PV / M • Wild Black Erotica #4 / cr89 / VD / C • Wild Nurses In Lust / 1986 / PLY / M • Wild Things #1 / 1985 / CV / M • Wine Me, Dine Me, 69 Me / 1989

/ COL / C • Winner Take All / 1986 / SEV / M • With Love, Lisa / 1985 / CA / C • Working Girls / 1984 / BMQ / M • Working It Out / 1983 / CA / M • WPINK-TV #3 / 1988 / PV / M • The X-Team / 1984 / CV / M • XXX Workout / 1987 / VEX / M • Yamahama Mamas / 1983 / TGA / C • Yank My Doodle, It's A Dandy / 1985 / GOM / M • Yiddish Erotica #1 / 1986 / SE / C • Young Girls Do / 1984 / ELH / M • The Young Like It Hot / 1983 / CA / M

HERVE
Adultress / 1995 / WIV / M • The Big Tease #1 / 1990 / VC / M • The Big Tease #2 / 1990 / VC / M • Dick & Jane Penetrate Paris / 1994 / AVI / M • Rebecca Lord's World Tour #1: French Edition / 1995 / WP / M • Rump Man: Goes To Cannes / 1995 / HW / M • Skin #2 / 1995 / ERQ / M

HERVE AMALOU
Bored Games / 1988 / ALF / M • Erotic Pleasures / 1976 / CA / M

HERVE PIERRE GUSTAVE
Betty Bleu / 1996 / IP / M • Sacred Doll / 1995 / FRF / M

HEYWOOD HYMEN see Star Index I
HI BALL see Star Index I
HIAWATHA MENDELSON
Tricked & Tied / 1996 / VTF / B

HIEDI HANDCOCK
Blue Vanities #198 / 1993 / FFL / M

HIFA see Star Index I
HIGH ROLLER
Anal House Party / 1993 / IP / M • The Gang Bang Story / 1993 / IP / M

HILARY
HomeGrown Video #462: Motion In The Backfield / 1995 / HOV / M • HomeGrown Video #463: Cum And Get It / 1995 / HOV / M

HILDA KAUFFMAN
Blue Confessions / 1983 / VCR / M

HILDA ROSS
Tale Of Bearded Clam / cr71 / PYR / M

HILDE see Star Index I
HILDY
HomeGrown Video #470: Heroes, Torpedoes & Grinders / 1996 / HOV / M

HILLAIRE
Ancient Secrets Of Sexual Ecstasy / 1996 / HIG / M

HILLARY
Blue Vanities #501 / 1992 / FFL / M • Limited Edition #13 / 1980 / AVC / M • Limited Edition #25 / 1984 / AVC / M

HILLARY DAWN see Star Index I
HILLARY GORDON see Hillary Summers
HILLARY SCOTT
Little Girls Lost / 1982 / VC / M • Prison Babies / 1976 / ... / M • Ring Of Desire / 1981 / SE / M

HILLARY SUMMERS (Aimee Leigh, Heather Gordon, Hillary Gordon)
Dark blonde with passable face, lithe body, and small tits. Boobs enhanced in 1981. Aimee Leigh is from **Pink Champagne**.
800 Fantasy Lane / 1979 / GO / M • Babes In Toyland / 1988 / COM / C • The Beauty Pageant / 1981 / AVC / M • Blue Vanities #016 (New) / 1988 / FFL / M • Blue Vanities #042 (New) / 1988 / FFL / M • Blue Vanities #048 / 1988 / FFL / M • Blue Vanities #088 / 1988 / FFL / M • Blue Vanities #197 / 1993 / FFL / M • Blue Vanities #537 / 1993 / FFL / M • Blue Vanities #576 /

1995 / FFL / M • Blue Vanities #586 / 1996 / FFL / M • The Budding Of Brie / 1980 / TVX / M • Classic Erotica #9 / 1996 / SVE / M • Creme De Femme #3 / 1981 / AVC / C • Daisy May / 1979 / VC / M • Dixie Ray Hollywood Star / 1983 / CA / M • Dream Girls #2 / 1983 / CA / C • Endless Lust / 1983 / VC / M • Flash / 1980 / CA / M • Foxholes / 1983 / SE / M • Frat House / 1979 / NGV / M • Golden Girls #22 / 1984 / CA / M • The Goodbye Girls / 1979 / CDI / M • Heavenly Desire / 1979 / WV / M • Hellraiser #3: Hell On Earth / 1992 / PAR / S • Hot Dallas Nights / 1981 / VCX / M • Intimate Explosions / 1982 / ... / C • John Holmes, The Lost Films / 1988 / PEN / C • Justine: A Matter Of Innocence / 1980 / SAT / M • A Little More Than Love / 1977 / SE / M • Mrs. Rodger's Neighborhood / 1988 / EVN / C • National Pornographic #1: Lesbians / 1987 / 4P / C • Olympic Fever / 1979 / AR / M • Pandora's Mirror / 1981 / CA / M • Pink Champagne / 1979 / CV / M • Platinum Paradise / 1980 / COM / M • Porn In The USA #1 / 1986 / WV / C • Remember Connie / 1984 / MAP / M • Ring Of Desire / 1981 / SE / M • The Satisfiers Of Alpha Blue / 1980 / AVC / M • Sex Boat / 1980 / VCX / M • Silky / 1980 / VXP / M • Star Virgin / 1979 / CXV / M • Taxi Girls #1 / 1980 / WV / M • Triple Header / 1987 / AIR / C • Urban Cowgirls / 1980 / CA / M • A Very Small Case Of Rape / 1977 / TRP / M • Young, Wild And Wonderful / 1980 / VCX / M

HILLARY TAME see Star Index I
HILLARY VAMP see Star Index I
HILLARY VAN WETTERIN
Creme De La Face #08: Wanna Blow Job / 1995 / OD / M • The Cumm Brothers #11: Oh Cum On Ye Faces / 1995 / OD / M • Cummin' 'round The Mountain / 1996 / BCP / M • The Doctor Is In #2: Pussy Pox / 1995 / NIT / M • Hard Cum Cafe / 1996 / BCP / M • Pussy Fest Of The Northwest #2 / 1995 / NIT / M • Pussy Fest Of The Northwest #4 / 1995 / NIT / M • The Sodomizer #1 / 1995 / SC / M

HILLARY WINTERS see Tanya Rivers
HILLY WATERS
Cafe Flesh / 1982 / VC / M

HINDO SAIJO
Club Fantasy / 1996 / AVE / M • Jacuzzi Lust / 1996 / AVE / M

HIROMI TANAKA
Ken Chan, The Laundry Man / 1984 / ORC / M

HITOMI KAIMAN see Star Index I
HITOMI TASHIRO
Hot Spa Sex / 1996 / AVE / M

HO CHUNG see Bruce Lei
HOLIDAY
Bootin' Up / 1995 / VT / B • Whoopin' Her Behind / 1995 / VT / B

HOLL E. WUD
Foxx Tales / 1996 / TTV / M

HOLLI WOODS (1989) (Brenda Carin)
Brenda Carin is from **Body Music #1**.
Blacks & Blondes: The Movie / 1989 / WV / M • Body Music #1 / 1989 / DR / M • Godmother / 1991 / AWV / F • The Honeymoon: The Bride's Running Behind / 1990 / 4P / M • Uncle Roy's Amateur Home Video #07 / 1992 / VIM / M

HOLLI WOODS (1997)
More Dirty Debutantes #64 / 1997 / SBV /

M

HOLLY

Amateurama #05 / 1993 / RTP / F • Blue Vanities #520 / 1993 / FFL / M • Blue Vanities #545 / 1994 / FFL / M • Blue Vanities #574 / 1996 / FFL / M • The Epic Adventures Of White Panties #2: Fast Girls, Cool Ca / 1996 / FSP / S • First Time Lesbians #15 / 1994 / JMP / F • Frank Thring's Double Penetration #1 / 1995 / XPR / M • Homegrown Video #403 / 1993 / HOV / M • Lesbian Pros And Amateurs #06 / 1992 / GO / F • Limited Edition #16 / 1980 / AVC / M • SVE: Going Solo / 1992 / SVE / F • Swinging Couples #04 / 1994 / GO / M • Toe Tales #28 / 1995 / GOT / B • Triple X Video Magazine #02 / 1995 / OD / M • Triple X Video Magazine #03 / 1995 / OD / M • Triple X Video Magazine #05 / 1995 / OD / M • Video Virgins #10 / 1993 / NS / M

HOLLY BLACK

Private Gold #03: The Chase / 1996 / OD / M • Private Stories #04 / 1995 / OD / M • Private Stories #14 / 1996 / OD / M • Thermonuclear Sex / 1996 / EL / M

HOLLY BODY *(Holly Morgan)*

Big titted (38DD-25-36) blonde with masses of hair. As of 1994 she became a brunette. Holly Morgan was the name she used as an amateur.

$ex 4 Fun & Profit / 1996 / SPR / M • All-Star Anal Interviews #1 / 1995 / LEI / M • Anal Booty Burner / 1996 / ROB / M • Anal Lickers And Cummers / 1996 / ROB / M • Anal Misconduct / 1995 / VD / M • The Anal Nurse Scam / 1995 / CA / M • Babe Watch #1 / 1994 / SC / M • Babe Watch #3 / 1995 / SC / M • Babe Watch #4 / 1995 / SC / M • Babe Watch #5 / 1996 / VC / M • Babe Watch Beach / 1996 / SC / M • The Babes Of Bonerville / 1995 / VEX / C • Backhand / 1995 / SC / M • Bad Girls #5 / 1994 / GO / M • Bare Ass Beach / 1994 / TP / M • Beach Mistress / 1994 / XCI / M • Beaver & Buttface / 1995 / SC / M • Big Bust Babes #21 / 1994 / AFI / M • Big Knockers #08 / 1994 / TV / M • Big Knockers #20 / 1995 / TV / C • Blade / 1996 / MID / M • Boobs A Poppin' / 1994 / TTV / M • Boobtown / 1995 / VC / M • Centerfold / 1995 / SC / M • De Sade / 1994 / SC / M • Doin' The Rounds / 1995 / VC / M • Double D Dykes #24 / 1995 / GO / F • Freaks Of Leather #2 / 1994 / IF / C • Fresh Meat (John Leslie) #2 / 1995 / EA / M • Gazongas #13 / 1993 / LEI / M • Girlfriends / 1995 / SC / M • Golddiggers #2 / 1995 / VC / M • Hellriders / 1995 / SC / M • Holly's Holiday Gang Bang / 1994 / LBO / M • Horny Brits Take It In The Bum / 1997 / ROB / M • Humongous Hooters / 1995 / PME / F • Intense Perversions #1 / 1995 / PL / M • Julie's Diary / 1995 / LBO / M • Killer Tits / 1995 / LE / M • Lust & Desire / 1996 / WV / M • Many Happy Returns / 1995 / NIT / M • Mellon Man #06 / 1995 / AVI / M • Micky Ray's Hot Shots #01 / 1996 / DIG / M • My Wildest Date / 1995 / HO / M • Naked Lunch / 1995 / LEI / M • The New Ass Masters #14 / 1996 / LEI / C • One Of A Kind / 1992 / VEX / M • Philmore Butts Meets The Freak / 1995 / SUF / M • Pretty Young Things Escort Service / 1995 / ZA / M • Priceless / 1995 / WP / M • Prime Choice #2 / 1995 / RAS / M • Private Eyes / 1995 / LE / M • Pussyclips #04 /

1994 / SNA / M • Pussyman #12: Sticky Fingers / 1995 / SNA / M • Renegades #2 / 1995 / SC / M • Rod Wood / 1995 / LE / M • Seymore & Shane Mount Tiffany / 1994 / FH / M • Snow Bunnies #1 / 1995 / SC / M • Snow Bunnies #2 / 1995 / SC / M • Some Like It Wet / 1995 / LE / M • Splattered / 1996 / MET / M • Strippers Inc. #4 / 1995 / ONA / M • Surf Babes / 1995 / LE / M • The Thief / 1994 / SC / M • Thunder Road / 1995 / SC / M • Too Cute For Words / 1992 / V99 / M • Top Debs #5: Deb Of The Month / 1994 / GO / M • True Sex / 1994 / EMC / M • Up The Middle / 1995 / V99 / M • Visions #2 / 1995 / ERA / M • Wilde Palms / 1994 / XCI / M

HOLLY BRICKELL

Bound To Tease #5 / 1990 / BON / C

HOLLY BUSH

Lickity Split / 1974 / COM / M

HOLLY CARSON *see* **Kimberly Carson**

HOLLY CAT

Student Fetish Videos: Catfighting #17 / 1996 / PRE / B • Student Fetish Videos: The Enema #20 / 1996 / PRE / B • Student Fetish Videos: Foot Worship #18 / 1995 / PRE / B

HOLLY CHRISTIAN *see* **Star Index I**

HOLLY DAVIDSON *see* **Sukoya**

HOLLY DAZE

Anal Addiction #3 / 1991 / SO / M • Belle Of The Ball / 1989 / V99 / M • The Big Gun / 1989 / FAN / M • The Bod Squad / 1989 / VT / M • Body Triple / 1991 / VC / M • Born For Porn / 1989 / FAZ / M • Camera Shy / 1990 / IN / M • Crossover / 1989 / STA / G • Dirty Movies / 1989 / VD / M • Double Your Pleasure / 1989 / VEX / M • Girls Don't Lie / 1990 / IN / F • Heart Of Stone / 1990 / FAN / M • Hot Meat / 1990 / V99 / M • Hung Guns / 1988 / STA / G • Ladies Man / 1990 / REB / M • Made In Hollywood / 1990 / VEX / M • Object(s) Of My Desire / 1988 / V99 / M • Perils Of Paula / 1989 / CA / M • Retail Slut / 1989 / LV / M • Sex Sluts From Beyond The Galaxy / 1991 / LBO / C • Shameless Desire / 1989 / VEX / M • Sophisticated Lady / 1988 / SEX / M • Space Virgins / 1990 / VEX / M • This Bun's For You / 1989 / FAN / M

HOLLY HEAT

Butt Bangers Ball / 1994 / FPI / M • California Blacks / 1994 / V99 / M • Cheatin' / 1994 / FD / M • Rump Humpers #17 / 1994 / GLI / M • Savage Fury #3 / 1994 / VEX / M

HOLLY HENDRIX *see* **Star Index I**

HOLLY HUMMER

Long dark brown/black hair, medium tits, small tattoo on her left belly and another on her right shoulder back, shaven pussy, passable face, lithe body. Seems to have a nice personality.

Anal Lickers And Cummers / 1996 / ROB / M • Borsky's Back Door Bitches / 1996 / ROB / M • Career Girls / 1996 / OUP / M • Eternal Lust / 1996 / VC / M • Nineteen #4 / 1996 / FOR / M • Nineteen #8 / 1997 / FOR / M • Risque Burlesque #2 / 1996 / IN / M • Sodomania #18: Shame Based / 1996 / EL / M • Wild Assed Pooper Slut / 1996 / ROB / M

HOLLY JOY *see* **Star Index I**

HOLLY LANDIS

Defiance / 1974 / ALP / B

HOLLY MASON

Delinquents On Butt Row / 1996 / EA / M • Extreme Close-Up / 1996 / VI / M

HOLLY MCCALL *(Holly Near, Mary Cruiser)*

Fat and ugly.

All The King's Ladies / 1981 / SUP / M • The Awakening Of Emily / 1976 / CDI / M • Beyond Your Wildest Dreams / 1980 / CAT / M • Blondes Have More Fun / 1980 / SE / M • Blue Vanities #046 (New) / 1988 / FFL / M • Blue Vanities #192 / 1993 / FFL / M • Classic Erotica #8 / 1985 / SVE / M • Fantasex Island / 1983 / NSV / M • Hot Ones / 1982 / SUP / C • Ms. Magnificent / 1979 / SE / M • Nothing To Hide #1 / 1981 / CV / M • Peaches And Cream / 1982 / SE / M • Please, Mr Postman / 1981 / VC / M • Pretty Peaches #1 / 1978 / MIT / M • Room Service / cr80 / IHV / M • Same Time Every Year / 1981 / VHL / M • Sex Loose / 1982 / VC / M • Showgirl #18: Holly McCall's Fantasies / 1983 / VCR / M • Swedish Erotica #03 / 1980 / CA / M • Taboo #01 / 1980 / VCX / M • Talk Dirty To Me #01 / 1980 / CA / M • Tangerine / 1979 / CXV / M • Wicked Sensations #1 / 1981 / CA / M • Working Girls / 1984 / BMQ / M • Young Doctors In Lust / 1979 / NSV / M • Yuppies In Heat / 1988 / CHA / C

HOLLY MORGAN *see* **Holly Body**

HOLLY NEAR *see* **Holly McCall**

HOLLY NORTH

$ex 4 Fun & Profit / 1996 / SPR / M

HOLLY PAGE

Beyond Your Wildest Dreams / 1980 / CAT / M • The Blonde / 1980 / VCX / M • Garage Girls / 1981 / CV / M • The Girl From S.E.X. / 1982 / CA / M • On White Satin / 1980 / VCX / M • The Satisfiers Of Alpha Blue / 1980 / AVC / M • Wicked Sensations #1 / 1981 / CA / M

HOLLY RIDER *see* **Holly Ryder**

HOLLY RYDER *(Holly Rider, Lisa Marie Abato, Pearl Houston)*

Was engaged (not married) to E.Z. Ryder at one stage. In mid 1993 she left the porno business and, with her boyfriend John Fitzgerald, tried to get an amendment to the California constitution to ban porno movies because of some "protect the runaway" idea. She came from Long Island, originally.

The 900 Club / 1993 / BON / B • Adult Video News 1991 Awards / 1991 / VC / M • The Adventures Of Buttgirl & Wonder Wench / 1991 / AFV / M • Amateur Lesbians #01: Leanna / 1991 / GO / F • Amateur Lesbians #02: Dominique / 1991 / GO / F • Amateur Lesbians #03: April / 1991 / GO / F • Amateur Lesbians #07: Holly / 1991 / GO / F • Amateur Lesbians #08: Trixie / 1991 / GO / F • Amateur Lesbians #09: Meschel / 1991 / GO / F • Amateur Lesbians #10: Stephanie / 1991 / GO / F • Anal Addiction #2 / 1990 / SO / M • Anal Fever / 1991 / AMB / M • Anal Illusions / 1991 / LV / M • Any Port In The Storm / 1991 / LV / M • Ass Backwards / 1991 / ME / M • B.K. #4: Lesbian Clean Up / 1991 / BKD / F • Backdoor To Harley-Wood #2 / 1990 / AFV / M • Banana Slits / 1993 / STM / F • Best Of Bi And Beyond / 1992 / PNP / C • The Best Of Flame / 1994 / BIZ / C • Beyond It All / 1991 / PAL / G • The Big E #10 / 1992 / PRE / B • Big Game / 1990 / LV / M • Bizarre Master Series: Rick Savage / 1992 / BIZ / C • Bizarre Master Series: Sir Michael / 1992 / BIZ / C • Bizarre Mistress Series: Sharon Mitchell / 1992 / BIZ / C • Blind Innocence / 1993 / BS / B • Blonde Forces #1 / 1991 / CC / M • Bondage Games #1 / 1991 / BIZ / B • Bondage Games #2 / 1991 / BIZ / B • Boss Bitch In Bondage / 199? / LON / B • Bottoms Up (1993-Bon Vue) / 1993 / BON / B • Bound Biker Babes #2 / 1993 / STM / B • The Building Of Mistress Simone's Dungeon Of Pleasure / 1991 / BIZ / B • California Taxi Girls / 1991 / AFV / M • Call Girl / 1991 / AFV / M • Cape Rear / 1992 / WV / M • The Chains Of Torment / 1991 / BS / B • Cheeks #5: The Ultimate Butt / 1991 / CC / M • Crazy On You / 1991 / IF / M • Cumming Clean / 1991 / FL / M • Deck His Balls With Holly / 1992 / STM / B • Defiance, The Spanking Saga / 1992 / BIZ / B • Diabolic Demands / 1992 / GOT / B • Diary Of A Submissive Slut / 1993 / STM / C • Dick-Tation / 1991 / AFV / M • Disciplined By Catfighters / 1993 / STM / B • Dresden Diary #05: Invasion of Privacy / 1992 / BIZ / B • Dynamic Duo / 1992 / BIZ / B • The Fear Zone / 1991 / BS / B • Forbidden Desires / 1991 / CIN / F • Forgive Them Not #01 / 1993 / STM / B • Forgive Them Not #02 / 1993 / STM / B • Four Alarm / 1991 / SE / M • A Girl's Affair #01 / 1992 / FD / F • Girls Gone Bad #4: Cell Block Riot / 1991 / GO / F • Girls Will Be Boys #4 / 1991 / PL / F • Girls, Girls And More Girls / 1990 / LV / F • Golden Arches / 1992 / PRE / B • Halloweenie / 1991 / PL / M • The Harder Way / 1991 / AR / M • The Harley Girls / 1991 / AR / F • Holly Ryder Tied At Home / 1992 / BON / B • Holly's Hollywood / 1992 / STM / F • Hot Flushes / 1992 / PRE / B • Hot Spot / 1991 / CDI / M • Hothouse Rose #1 / 1991 / VC / M • Hothouse Rose #2 / 1992 / VC / M • I'll Take The Whip / 1993 / BON / B • In Deep With The Devil / 1991 / ME / M • An Innocent Woman / 1991 / FAZ / M • Jail Babes #2: Bustin' Out / 1992 / PL / F • Junk Yard Dogs / 1991 / FC / M • The Latex Dungeon / 1992 / GOT / B • Latex, Leather & Lace / 1993 / STM / B • Lay Lady Lay / 1991 / VEX / M • Leather And Tether / 1993 / STM / C • Leather Lair #1 / 1992 / STM / B • Leg...Ends #07 / 1993 / PRE / F • Lesbian Lingerie Fantasy #5 / 1991 / ESP / F • Lesbian Pros And Amateurs #05 / 1992 / GO / F • Lesbian Pros And Amateurs #21 / 1993 / GO / F • Lesbians, Bondage & Blackjack / 1991 / BIZ / B • Lessons In Humiliation / 1991 / BIZ / B • Letters From The Heart / 1991 / AWV / M • Lick My Lips / 1990 / LV / M • Lipstick Lesbians / 1993 / STM / F • A Little Irresistible / 1991 / ZA / M • Love On The Line / 1990 / SO / M • Mike Hott: #166 Holly Ryder Solo / 1991 / MHV / F • Mike Hott: #167 Holly Ryder And Lisa Wilson #1 / 1991 / MHV / F • Mike Hott: #168 Holly Ryder And Lisa Wilson #2 / 1991 / MHV / F • Mike Hott: Cum Cocktails #1 / 1995 / MHV / C • More Dirty Debutantes #08 / 1991 / 4P / M • My 500 Pound Vibrator / 1991 / LV / C • Naked Goddess #1 / 1991 / VC / M • Nasty Reputation / 1991 / VEX / M • The Newcummers / 1990 / 4P / M • Odds 'n' Ends / 1992 / PRE / B • On The Loose / 1991 / LV / M • Opening Night / 1991 / AR / M • Oral Madness #1 / 1991 / OD / M • Popped Tarts / 1992 / RB / B •

Princess Orgasma #1 / 1991 / PP / M • Profiles In Discipline #02: Naughty Angel / 1994 / STM / C • Profiles In Discipline #04: Mistress Domino / 1994 / STM / C • Purple Rubber / 1993 / STM / B • Pussy Whipped / 1991 / PL / B • Queens In Danger / 1990 / STA / G • Raw Talent: Bang 'er 09 Times / 1992 / RTP / M • Red Hot Coeds / 1993 / VIM / M • Red Tails #1 / 1993 / STM / B • Return To Leather Lair / 1993 / STM / B • The Rock Hard Files / 1991 / VEX / M • Sex Express / 1991 / SE / M • Sex Nurses / 1991 / VIR / M • The Sexual Limits / 1992 / VC / M • Single Girl Masturbation #5 / 1991 / ESP / F • Soft Tail / 1991 / IN / M • Sole Food / 1992 / PRE / B • Spank! / 1992 / STM / B • Spanked By Santa / 1992 / STM / B • Split Personality / 1991 / CIN / G • Stepsister's Discipline / 1992 / RB / B • Stolen Hearts / 1991 / AFV / M • Strange Passions / 1993 / BS / B • Street Fantasies / 1993 / AFV / M • Stud Puppy / 1992 / STM / B • Suburban Seduction / 1991 / HO / M • Succulent Toes / 1995 / STM / B • Super Enemates / 1994 / PRE / C • Tales From Leather Lair: The Leather Master / 1992 / STM / B • Tight Squeeze / 1992 / SC / M • Toe Tales #03 / 1992 / GOT / B • Toe Tales #12 / 1994 / GOT / C • A Touch Of Mink / 1990 / V99 / M • Toy Box Lingerie Show / 1991 / ESP / S • Trapped By The Mistress / 1991 / BIZ / B • Troublemaker / 1991 / VEX / M • Twilight / 1991 / ZA / M • Virginia's TV Initiation / 1992 / STM / G • Vow Of Passion / 1991 / VI / M • The War Of The Hoses / 1991 / NLE / M • Welcome To Bondage: Starlets #2 / 1994 / BON / C • Welcome To Dallas / 1991 / VI / M • Where The Girls Sweat #2 / 1991 / EL / F • Wild Side / 1991 / GO / M • Wishful Thinking / 1992 / VC / M • [Anal Fantasies #1 / 1991 / ... / M

HOLLY SWEET
East Coast Sluts #04: New York City / 1995 / PL / M • Moon Beads / 1995 / STM / F • N.Y. Video Magazine #04 / 1995 / OUP / M • Primal Submission / A Glutton For Punishment / 1995 / OUP / B • Sweet Humility / 1995 / STM / B • Toe Tales #26 / 1995 / GOT / B

HOLLY TAUBER
Lil' Women: Vacation / 1996 / EUR / M

HOLLY TEEZE
Alumni Girls / 1996 / GO / M • Dirty & Kinky Mature Women #10 / 1996 / C69 / M • The Older Women's Sperm Bank #5 / 1996 / SUF / M • The Ultimate Climax / 1996 / EMC / M

HOLLY WAINWRIGHT
Sensuous Flygirls / cr72 / VHL / M

HOLLY WAY *see Star Index I*

HOLLY WESTON
Alien Probe #1 / 1993 / ZFX / B • Dance Macabre / 1993 / ZFX / B • Guinea Pigs #3 / 1993 / ZFX / B

HOLLY WHITE *(Rachel Mann, Rachael Mann, Robin Goebel, Bobbi Soxx (Holly W))*
Blonde in the style of Stephanie Rage with enhanced boobs but not so bad as to be obnoxious. The rest of her body is very tight. Arrested in 1995 for extortion in attempting to defraud a 72-year old patron of a nudie bar—received five years in prison.
Beauty And The Beach / 1991 / CC / M • House Of Correction / 1991 / HOM / B • In

Deep With The Devil / 1991 / ME / M • Mona Lisa / 1992 / LV / M • No Mercy For The Witches / 1992 / HOM / B • The Pink Pussycat / 1992 / CA / M • Sleeping With Emily / 1991 / LE / M

HOLLY WOOD
Girls Around The World #25 / 1995 / BTO / S • H&S: Hollywood / 199? / H&S / S • Raw Talent: Bang 'er 17 Times / 1992 / RTP / M • Sam Shaft's Public Flashing #1 / 1994 / RTP / M

HOLLY WOOD (ALICIA) *see* **Alicia Monet**

HOLLY WOODLAWN
Is There Sex After Death? / 1970 / ... / S • Take Off / 1978 / VXP / M

HOLLY WOULD
OUTS: Holly Would / 1995 / OUT / F

HOMIE
Mo' Booty #4 / 1995 / TIW / M

HONEY
Breast Of Britain #2 / 1987 / BTO / M • Breast Of Britain #4 / 1990 / BTO / S • Buttman Goes To Rio #4 / 1993 / EA / M • Cruel Heels / 1991 / SSP / B • Eye On You: Honey And A Friend / 1996 / EOY / M • Limited Edition #17 / 1980 / AVC / M • More Dirty Debutantes #57 / 1996 / 4P / M • Pearl Necklace: Facial #01 / 1994 / SEE / C • Shane's World #5 / 1996 / OD / M • Shane's World #6: Slumber Party / 1996 / OD / F

HONEY AMOUR
Bedtime Video #05 / 1984 / GO / M

HONEY BARE *see* **Nancy Dare**

HONEY BEE
Blue Vanities #514 / 1992 / FFL / M • Blue Vanities #556 / 1994 / FFL / M • Reel Classics #2 / 1996 / H&S / M

HONEY BEE (SASHA) *see* **Sasha Sweet**

HONEY BUNS
Freaky Tailz / 1996 / AVI / M

HONEY CHEEKS
The Birthday Ball / 1975 / VHL / M

HONEY DASH *see* **Honey Stevens**

HONEY DUE
The Bite / 1975 / SVE / M

HONEY JARRE
Action In Black / 1993 / FD / M • Amateur Lesbians #34: Honey / 1991 / GO / F • Back In Action / 1992 / FD / M • Bobby Hollander's Rookie Nookie #02 / 1993 / SFP / M • Casting Call #01 / 1993 / SO / M • A Girl's Affair #01 / 1992 / FD / F • Positively Pagan #07 / 1993 / ATA / M • Raising Kane / 1992 / FD / M • Yank Fest / 1994 / FD / C

HONEY LOVE
Bucky Beaver's XXX Dragon Art Theatre Double Feature #03 / 1996 / SOW / M • School For Hookers / 1974 / SOW / M

HONEY MALONE *see* **Paula Winters**

HONEY MELLONS
Lesbian Sleaze / 1994 / PL / F

HONEY MELONS
The Best Of Wild Bill's Big Ladies / 1996 / H&S / C

HONEY MOONS
Busty Debutantes / 1996 / H&S / M • Busty Porno Queens / 1996 / H&S / M • Duke Of Knockers #2 / 1995 / BTO / M • Girls Around The World #19 / 1994 / BTO / S • Girls Around The World #20: Deena Duos & Friends / 1994 / BTO / M • H&S: Honey Moons / 199? / H&S / S • Score Busty Covergirls #7 / 1995 / BTO / S • Tit To Tit #4 / 1996 / BTO / S

HONEY MORE
Coming Of Age / 1989 / CA / M • The Outlaw / 1989 / VD / M • Parliament: Lesbian Seduction #2 / 1990 / PM / C • Swedish Erotica Featurettes #2 / 1989 / CA / M • Why Do You Want To be In An Adult Video / 1990 / PM / F

HONEY POTT
Blue Vanities #586 / 1996 / FFL / M • Flash / 1980 / CA / M

HONEY ROSE *see* **Nikki Wylde**

HONEY STEVENS *(Honey Dash)*
Blonde with very short hair, medium tits, lithe body, passable face. Honey Dash is from **Bizarre Styles**.
Bizarre Styles / 1981 / ALP / B • House Of Sin / 1982 / AVO / M • Mistress Electra / 1983 / AVO / B

HONEY WELLS *(Destiny DeMoore (HW), Destiny Moore (HW), Rebecca (Honey W))*
Blonde with shoulder length straight hair, tall, medium tits, big butt, a bit pudgy, nose like Barbara Streisand, not too pretty facially. 24 years old in 1994. De-virginized at 18. 5'9" tall and 36-26-36 body measurements. In 1994 says she has a two year old child. Destiny DeMoore were the credits in **Hard-On Copy** but there's another girl (slightly later) who goes by that name. The other Destiny is taller, has white hair (Honey is a golden color), very white skin (Honey is tanned all over), small tits (Honey's are bigger), and lots of cellulite in her butt and upper thighs (if she has any Honey's is not noticable).
Anal Angel / 1994 / EX / M • Bubble Butts Gold #1 / 1994 / LBO / M • Dick & Jane Do The Slopes In Ass Spin / 1994 / AVI / M • Hard-On Copy / 1994 / WV / M • The Hitch-Hiker #08: On The Trail / 1994 / WMG / M • Hot Chicks Do L.A. / 1994 / EVN / F • Milli Vanilla / 1994 / TP / M • Nasty Newcummers #05 / 1994 / MET / M • New Ends #08 / 1994 / 4P / M • Rump Humpers #18 / 1994 / GLI / M • Video Virgins #12 / 1994 / NS / M

HONEY WILDER *(Shirley Thompson)*
Not too pretty, older with a womanly body and dark hair, medium tits. First movie was **Wild Dallas Honey**.
52 Pick-Up / 1986 / MED / S • American Dream Girls #1 / 1986 / VEX / M • Bad Girls #2 / 1983 / GO / M • Bedtime Tales / 1985 / SE / M • Beverly Hills Wives / 1985 / CV / M • Breakin' In / 1986 / WV / M • Bubblegum / 1982 / VC / M • Bunny's Office Fantasies / 1984 / VC / M • Burlexxx / 1984 / VC / M • Caballero Preview Tape #3 / 1984 / CA / C • Caballero Preview Tape #4 / 1985 / CA / C • Cheek To Cheek / 1986 / VEX / M • Deep Inside Ginger Lynn / 1986 / SE / C • Despicable Dames / 1986 / CC / M • Dirty Blonde / 1984 / VXP / M • Divorce Court Expose #1 / 1986 / VD / M • Don't Tell Daddy #1 / 1985 / PL / C • Double Standards / 1986 / VC / M • Erotic Zones #3 / 1986 / CA / M • Famous Ta-Ta's #1 / 1986 / VCS / C • Famous Ta-Ta's #2 / 1986 / SE / C • For Love And Money / 1987 / CV / S • Forbidden Fruit / 1985 / PV / M • Free And Foxy / 1986 / VCX / C • Freeway Honey / 1985 / VC / M • Frisky Business / 1984 / VC / M • Genital Hospital / 1987 / SE / M • The Golden Gals / 1989 / BTO / M • Great Sexpectations / 1984 / VC

/ M • Hot Girls In Love / 1985 / VXP / M • Hot Sweet Honey / 1985 / VEP / M • Hustler Video Magazine #1 / 1983 / SE / M • Hyapatia Lee's Arcade Series #01 / 1988 / ZA / C • If My Mother Only Knew / 1985 / CA / M • It's My Body / 1985 / CDI / M • Jewel Of The Nite / 1986 / WV / M • Jewels Of The Night / 1986 / SE / M • Kiss Of The Gypsy / 1986 / WV / M • Loving Spoonfulls / 1987 / 4P / C • Lust Tango In Paris / 1987 / PEN / M • Marilyn Chambers' Private Fantasies #4 / 1983 / CA / M • More Than A Handful #1 / 1985 / CV / C • Naughty Girls Need Love Too / 1983 / SE / M • Never Sleep Alone / 1984 / CA / M • Night Hunger / 1983 / AVC / M • Night Magic / 1984 / SE / M • Nightlife / 1983 / CA / M • Older Women With Young Boys / 1984 / CC / M • Only The Best Of Breasts / 1987 / CV / C • Only The Best Of Men's And Women's Fantasies / 1988 / CV / C • Only The Best Of Women With Women / 1988 / CV / C • Parliament: Lesbian Lovers #1 / 1986 / PM / F • A Passage To Ecstasy / 1985 / CDI / M • Peeping Tom / 1986 / CV / M • Personal Touch #2 / 1983 / AR / M • Play It Again, Samantha / 1986 / EVN / M • The Pleasures Of Innocence / 1985 / VC / M • Porn Star Of The Year Contest / 1984 / VWA / M • Private Moments / 1983 / CV / M • Private Teacher / 1983 / CA / M • Pussycat Galore / 1984 / VC / M • Rated Sex / 1986 / SE / M • Satin Angels / 1986 / WV / M • Satisfactions / 1983 / CA / M • Scenes They Wouldn't Let Me Shoot / 1984 / VC / M • Schoolgirl By Day / 1985 / LA / M • Sex Spa USA / 1984 / VC / M • Society Affairs / 1982 / CA / M • The Sperminator / 1985 / VXP / M • Splashing / 1986 / VCS / C • Summer Camp Girls / 1983 / CA / M • Swedish Erotica #39 / 1981 / CA / M • Sweet Alice / 1983 / VCX / M • Taboo #02 / 1982 / IN / M • Taboo #03 / 1983 / IN / M • Taboo #04 / 1985 / IN / M • A Taste Of Amber / 1988 / PIN / C • Teasers: Champagne Reunion / 1988 / MET / M • Thought You'd Never Ask / 1986 / CA / M • The Titty Committee / 1986 / SE / C • Tongue Twisters / 1986 / VXP / M • Triple Xposure / 1986 / VD / M • Unthinkable / 1984 / SE / M • Wet Kisses / 1986 / SE / M • Whose Fantasy Is It, Anyway? / 1983 / AVC / M • Wild Dallas Honey / 1985 / VCX / M • Wilder At Heart / 1991 / VC / C • [A Dream Cum True / 1990 / FOV / M • [Forbidden Fantasies / 1984 / ... / M • [Golden Gate Girls / 1985 / ... / M • [Wife In The Fast Lane / 1993 / SHO / M

HONEYBEAR
Ona Zee's Date With Dallas / 1992 / ONA / M

HONEYDEW *see* **Star Index I**

HONEYSUCKLE DEVINE *see* **Honeysuckle Divine**

HONEYSUCKLE DIVINE *(Honeysuckle Devine, Destiny (H. Divine))*
Fat blonde, not too pretty, big tits. Amazing control over her vagina, being able to eject ping pong balls and hand lotion.
Honeysuckle Devine, Live / 1979 / MIT / M • Mitchell Brothers Ultra Core Collection / 1996 / SVE / C • S.O.S. / 1975 / QX / M

HONEYSUCKLE ROSE
Burlexxx / 1984 / VC / M • Secret Life Of Transvestites / cr89 / STM / G • Trisexual Encounters #07 / 1988 / PL / G

HONNE
Freaky Flix / 1995 / TTV / C • Totally Tasteless Video #01 / 1994 / TTV / M

HOPE
Babes Of The Bay #1 / 1994 / LIP / F • Chessie's Home Videos #30: Kings Trade / 1994 / CHM / M • Wet Workout: Shape Up, Then Strip Down / 1995 / PME / S

HOPE (1986)
Professor Probe And The Spirit Of Sex / 1986 / ADU / M

HOPE (FRANKIE LEIGH) *see* **Frankie Leigh**

HOPE GELLER *see* **Frankie Leigh**

HOPE HATHAWAY
Blue Vanities #514 / 1992 / FFL / M

HOPE LYNN *see* **Frankie Leigh**

HOPE REIGNS
Cuntz #3 / 1994 / RTP / M • Cuntz #4 / 1994 / RTP / M

HOPE RICHARDS *see* **Frankie Leigh**

HOPE RISING *(Monica (Hope Ris))*
Tall brunette with tiny tits and small areola, long face, long nose, deep voice.
The Dickheads #2 / 1993 / MID / M • Swinging Couples #04 / 1994 / GO / M

HOPE SEXTON
That Lady From Rio / 1976 / VXP / M

HOPE STOCKTON
Not too pretty gray/blonde with shoulder length hair flabby body and floppy medium tits. Her skin is transluscent such that lots of veins (even on her face) show through.
Dominatrix Without Mercy / 1976 / ALP / B • Georgia Peach / 1977 / COM / M • Midnight Desires / 1976 / VXP / M • Slippery When Wet / 1976 / VXP / M • Temptations / 1976 / VXP / M • Virgin Snow / 1976 / VXP / M

HOPE SUMMERS (LEE) *see* **Frankie Leigh**

HORNY HENRY
Henry's Big Boob Adventure / 1996 / HO / M • Hooters In The 'hood / 1995 / TTV / M • Horny Henry's Euro Adventure / 1995 / TTV / M • Horny Henry's French Adventure / 1994 / TTV / M • Horny Henry's London Adventure / 1995 / TTV / M • Horny Henry's Oriental Adventure / 1994 / TTV / M • Horny Henry's Peeping Adventures / 1994 / TTV / M • Horny Henry's Snowballing Adventure / 1995 / TTV / M • Horny Henry's Strange Adventure / 1995 / TTV / M • Horny Henry's Swinging Adventures / 1994 / TTV / M • Sweat 'n' Bullets / 1995 / MID / M

HORSE MACHO
Deeper Spikes / 1984 / BIZ / B

HOSS CUMRIGHT
Sluts, Butts And Pussy / 1996 / DFI / M

HOSTESS KARIN
Club Doma Global #4 / 1994 / VER / B

HOT CHOCOLATE
Black Gangbangers #12 / 1996 / HW / M • Black Hollywood Amateurs #25 / 1996 / MID / M • Black Hollywood Amateurs #26 / 1996 / MID / M • Black Knockers #11 / 1995 / TV / M • Booty Bang #2 / 1996 / HW / M • Bootylicious: It's A Bootyful Thing / 1996 / JMP / M • Coochie's Under Fire / 1996 / HW / F • Da Booty Bang #2 / 1996 / HW / M • Sweet Black Cherries #5 / 1996 / TTV / M • Sweet Black Cherries #6 / 1996 / TTV / M

HOT CINNAMON *see* **Star Index I**

HOUSTON

Womanly muscular body with enhanced rock-solid cantaloupes, marginal face. 115lbs, 34D-25-35 and 26 years old in 1995. Devirginized at 16. Had corn rolls in earlier movies and later short blonde hair. As of 1995, had a two year old daughter.
Angels In Flight / 1995 / NIT / M • The Bottom Line / 1995 / NIT / M • Carnal Invasions / 1996 / NIT / M • Carnival Of Flesh / 1996 / NIT / M • The Desert Cafe / 1996 / NIT / M • Dream Lust / 1995 / NIT / M • Gazongas Galore #1 / 1996 / NIT / C • Get Lucky / 1996 / NIT / M • Hollywood Legs / 1996 / NIT / M • Jizz Glazed Goo Guzzlers #1 / 1996 / NIT / C • Lisa / 1997 / SC / M • Many Happy Returns / 1995 / NIT / M • Mysteria / 1995 / NIT / M • The Nympho Files / 1995 / NIT / M • Promises And Lies / 1996 / NIT / M • Russian Roulette / 1995 / NIT / M • Sorority Sex Kittens #3 / 1996 / VC / M • Sweet As Honey / 1996 / NIT / M • A Taste Of Torment / 1995 / NIT / B • Texas Crude / 1995 / NIT / M • Twists Of The Heart / 1995 / NIT / M • Ultimate Sensations / 1996 / NIT / M

HOWARD BEACH
Hard Core Cafe / 1991 / PL / M

HOWARD BLAKEY
A Time To Love / 1971 / ALP / M

HOWARD DARKLEY
Babylon Pink #2 / 1988 / COM / M • Expose Me Now / 1982 / CV / M • The Final Taboo / 1988 / CA / M • Goin' Down Slow / 1988 / VC / M • Inspiration / 1981 / CHX / M • The Pillowman / 1988 / VC / M • Screwdriver / 1988 / CC / C • Sex Wars / 1984 / EXF / M • Talk Dirty To Me #05 / 1987 / DR / M

HOWARD DECKER see **Star Index I**
HOWARD FILENE see **Star Index I**
HOWARD HUMPER see **Jeffrey Hurst**
HOWARD J. BRUBAKER
The Art Of Marriage / 1970 / SOW / M

HOWARD KAY see **Star Index I**
HOWARD NELSON see **Star Index I**
HOWARD NORTH see **Star Index I**
HOWARD PIERPONT see **Star Index I**
HOWARD STEIN
Waterpower / 1975 / VHL / M

HOWARD VERNON
Castle Of The Creeping Flesh / 1967 / LUM / S • Faceless / 1988 / LUM / S • Succubus / 1967 / ... / S • [Le Journal Intime D'Une Nymphomane / 1972 / ... / M

HOWARD WHITE
Almost Sisters / 1991 / NWV / G • Forced To Crossdress / 1993 / CAS / B • The Payne Principle / 1995 / COC / B • VGA: Spanks-A-Lot / 1993 / VGA / B

HOWARD WORTH
Fastlane Fuck-Holes! / 1994 / MET / M • Supercharger / cr75 / CV / M

HOWIE GORDON
Candy Goes To Hollywood / 1979 / VCX / M

HOWIE GREEN see **Star Index I**
HOWIE STRANGE
Hot Flashes / 1984 / VC / M • Spreading Joy / 1988 / VC / M • Young Nurses In Love / 1987 / VC / M

HOWIE WARNER
Blue Vanities #198 / 1993 / FFL / M

HUBERT GERALD
[S.S. Bordello / 1978 / ... / M

HUBERT SAVAGE see **Herschel Savage**
HUDACSEK

The Betrayal Of Innocence #1: The Awakening Of Marika / 1993 / CC / M • The Betrayal Of Innocence #2: The Decadence / 1993 / CC / M • The Betrayal Of Innocence #3: The Choice / 1993 / CC / M

HUGGY BEAR
Erotic Tattooing And Piercing #1 / 1986 / FLV / M

HUGH E. RECTION
Bi Mistake / 1989 / VI / G • The Necklace #1 / 1994 / ZFX / B • Rump Reamers / 1994 / TTV / M

HUGH GRIFFITH
Butt's Motel #5 / 1990 / EX / M • Gangbang Girl #01 / 1992 / ANA / M • Gangbang Girl #02 / 1992 / ANA / M • Gangbang Girl #03 / 1992 / ANA / M • Gangbang Girl #04 / 1992 / ANA / M • In Pursuit Of Passion / 1990 / V99 / M

HUGH HARDON see **Beau Michaels**
HUGH JARGON
The World's Biggest Gang Bang #1 / 1995 / FPI / M

HUGH JORDAN see **Star Index I**
HUGH WESTY see **Star Index I**
HUGO FELLER
Ejacula #1 / 1992 / VC / M • Ejacula #2 / 1992 / VC / M

HULK
The Erotic Adventures Of Peter Galore / 1973 / ALP / M

HUNK see **Star Index I**
HUNNY
Raw Talent: Bang 'er 31 Times / 1992 / RTP / M

HUNTER
Seymore & Shane Live On Tour / 1995 / ULI / M

HUNTER SCOTT
Bi-Conflict / 1994 / FST / G • Conflict Of Interest / 1994 / FST / G

HURRICANE MARTHA
Erotic Tattooing And Piercing #5 / 1991 / FLV / M

HYAPATIA LEE
Allegedly American Indian who developed rock hard large inflated tits and an attitude to match. Was married to Bud Lee but split up in 1993. The anal in **Swedish Erotica #52** is faked and looks like it was taken from **The Young Like It Hot**; it's really with Lili Marlene. Aged 22 in 1983.
The 8th Annual Erotic Film Awards / 1984 / SE / C • Adam & Eve's Guide To A G-Spot Orgasm / 1994 / VI / M • Adult Video News 1991 Awards / 1991 / VC / M • Adult Video News 1992 Awards / 1992 / VC / M • Adult Video News Magazine / 1985 / ZEB / M • Barbara Dare's Prime Choice / 1987 / SE / C • The Better Sex Video Series #7: Advanced Sexual Fantasies / 1992 / LEA / M • Body Girls / 1983 / SE / M • Bratgirl / 1989 / VI / M • Burgundy Blues / 1993 / MET / M • Buttman At Nudes A Poppin' #1 / 1992 / EA / S • Centerfold / 1992 / VC / M • Crazed #1 / 1992 / VI / M • Crazed #2 / 1992 / VI / M • Critics' Choice #2 / 1984 / SE / C • Dark Star / 1991 / VI / M • Deep Cover / 1993 / WP / M • The Enchantress / 1990 / VI / M • Fetish Fever / 1993 / CA / C • Forever Young / 1994 / VI / M • Full Moon Bay / 1993 / VI / M • Heavenly Hyapatia / 1990 / VI / M • The Hollywood Starlet Search / 1995 / SC / M • Humongous Squirting Knockers / 1992 / CA / C • Hustler Video Magazine #1 / 1983 / SE / M •

Hyapatia Lee's Arcade Series #01 / 1988 / ZA / C • Hyapatia Lee's Arcade Series #02 / 1988 / ZA / C • Hyapatia Lee's Secret Dreams / 1986 / SE / M • Hyapatia Lee's Sexy / 1986 / SE / M • Hyapatia Obsessed / 1993 / EX / M • I Do #1 / 1989 / VI / M • I Do #2 / 1990 / VI / M • I Do #3 / 1992 / VI / M • Indian Summer #1 / 1991 / VI / M • Indian Summer #2: Sandstorm / 1991 / VI / M • The Insatiable Hyapatia Lee / 1987 / SE / C • Killing Obsession / 1994 / TRI / S • The Landlady / 1990 / VI / M • Legends Of Porn #2 / 1989 / CV / C • Let's Get Physical (Hyapatia Lee's) / 1984 / CA / M • Love Letters / 1991 / VI / M • Lust In The Woods / 1990 / VI / M • Made In Japan / 1992 / VI / M • The Masseuse #1 / 1990 / VI / M • Meat Market / 1992 / SEX / C • Native Tongue / 1993 / VI / M • Naughty Girls Need Love Too / 1983 / SE / M • One Wife To Give / 1989 / ZA / M • Pajama Party / 1993 / CV / C • Postcards From Abroad / 1991 / CA / C • The Red Garter / 1986 / SE / M • The Ribald Tales Of Canterbury / 1986 / CA / M • Rockin' Erotica / 1987 / SE / C • Saddletramp / 1988 / VD / M • Savannah Superstar / 1992 / VI / M • The Sex Game / 1987 / SE / C • Sleeping Beauty Aroused / 1989 / VI / M • Slow Dancing / 1990 / VI / M • Snakedance / 1992 / VI / M • Swedish Erotica #52 / 1984 / CA / M • Sweet Young Foxes / 1984 / VCX / M • Sweethearts / 1986 / SE / C • Swingers: A Sexy Comedy / 1994 / KBR / S • Takin' It Off / 1994 / DGD / S • A Taste Of Hyapatia Lee / 1990 / PIN / C • Tasty / 1985 / CA / M • Telesex #1 / 1992 / VI / M • The Titty Committee / 1986 / SE / C • Triangle / 1989 / VI / M • Triple Header / 1986 / SE / C • True Confessions Of Hyapatia Lee / 1989 / VI / M • Truth Or Dare / 1993 / VI / M • Uniform Behavior / 1989 / ZA / M • The Wild Wild West / 1986 / SE / M • Women Who Love Girls / 1989 / CLV / C • The Young Like It Hot / 1983 / CA / M • [Hellroller / 1992 / ... / S

I.M. ZOROASTER
Chickie / 1975 / CA / M

I.N.L. FLYNN
The Unsuspecting Repairman #1 / 1995 / TVI / B • The Unsuspecting Repairman #2 / 1995 / TVI / B

I.O. SILVER see **Star Index I**
IAN
HomeGrown Video #463: Cum And Get It / 1995 / HOV / M • Royal Ass Force / 1996 / VC / M

IAN BLACK see **Ian Daniels**
IAN DANIELS (Ian Black, Tom Black, Ian MacDaniel)
Was the SO of Shelby Stevens.
1-900-FUCK #1 / 1995 / SO / M • 1-900-FUCK #2 / 1995 / SO / M • 100% Amateur #02: Back Door And More / 1995 / OD / M • 100% Amateur #10: / 1995 / OD / M • 100% Amateur #13: / 1995 / OD / M • 9-Ball: Geisha Gang Bang / 1994 / PL / M • Addictive Desires / 1994 / OD / M • Alex Jordan's First Timers #04 / 1994 / OD / M • Alex Jordan's First Timers #05 / 1994 / OD / M • All I Want For Christmas Is A Gangbang / 1994 / AMP / M • All That Jism / 1995 / TEG / M • America's Raunchiest Home Videos #71: / 1993 / ZA / M • Anal Agony / 1994 / ZA / M • Anal Health Club

Babes / 1995 / EVN / M • Anal Interrogation / 1995 / ZA / M • The Anal Nurse Scam / 1995 / CA / M • Anal Princess #2 / 1996 / VC / M • Anal Virgins Of America #08 / 1994 / FOR / M • Anal Webb / 1995 / ZA / M • Analtown USA #05 / 1995 / NIT / M • Asian Heat #04: House Of The Rising Sun / 1993 / SC / M • Asian Heat #05: The Joy Suck Club / 1994 / SC / M • Assy #2 / 1996 / JMP / M • Babe Watch Beach / 1996 / SC / M • Babe Wire / 1996 / HW / M • Backdoor Diaries / 1995 / BBE / M • Bedlam / 1995 / WAV / M • Beverly Hills Bikini Company / 1996 / NIT / M • Big Bust Babes #20 / 1994 / AFI / M • Big Bust Babes #21 / 1994 / AFI / M • Big Bust Babes #27 / 1995 / AFI / M • Big Bust Babes #39 / 1996 / AFI / M • Blonde Justice #3 / 1994 / VI / M • Blonde Temptation / 1995 / IF / M • Bobby Hollander's Maneaters #09 / 1993 / SFP / M • Bobby Hollander's Rookie Nookie #11 / 1993 / SFP / M • Body Language / 1995 / VI / M • Bodywaves / 1994 / ELP / M • Boob Tube Lube / 1996 / RAS / M • Boobs A Poppin' / 1994 / TTV / M • Bra Busters #04 / 1993 / LBO / M • The Breast Files #3 / 1994 / AVI / M • Breastman Does The Twin Towers / 1993 / EVN / M • Broken Vows / 1996 / ULP / M • Buffy's Nude Camera-Party / 1996 / CIN / M • Bun Busters #16 / 1994 / LBO / M • Butthead Dreams: Big Boating Bonanza / 1994 / FH / M • Butthead Dreams: Down In The Bush / 1995 / FH / M • Butthead Dreams: Exposed / 1995 / FH / M • Butthead Dreams: Mission Impenetrable / 1994 / FH / M • California Covet / 1995 / CA / M • California Swingers / 1996 / LV / M • Caught From Behind #23 / 1995 / HO / M • Centerfold Celebrities '94 #1 / 1994 / SFP / M • Channel 69 / 1996 / CC / M • Channel Blonde / 1994 / VI / M • The Cheater / 1994 / XCI / M • Cheatin' / 1994 / FD / M • Cinesex #1 / 1995 / CV / M • Cinesex #2 / 1994 / CV / M • Colossal Orgy #1 / 1993 / HW / M • Colossal Orgy #2 / 1994 / HW / M • Colossal Orgy #3 / 1994 / HW / M • Comeback / 1995 / VI / M • The Comix / 1995 / VI / M • The Complete & Total Anal Workout #1 / 1995 / ZA / M • Corporate Justice / 1996 / TEP / M • The Couch Trap / 1993 / ELP / M • Cream / 1993 / SC / M • Crew Sluts / 1994 / KWP / M • Deep Throat Girls #15 / 1995 / GO / M • Dick & Jane Go To Mexico / 1994 / AVI / M • Dirty Doc's Housecalls #02 / 1993 / LV / M • Dirty Doc's Housecalls #17 / 1994 / LV / M • A Dirty Western #2: Smoking Guns / 1994 / CV / M • Dollars And Yen / 1994 / FH / M • DPTV: Double Penetration Television / 1996 / SUF / M • Dream House / 1995 / XPR / M • Dukes Of Anal / 1996 / VC / M • Eighteen #1 / 1996 / SC / M • Electropussy / 1995 / CC / M • Erotic Fiction / 1995 / LE / M • Escape From Anal Lost Angels / 1996 / HO / M • Escape To The Party / 1994 / ELP / M • Euro Studs / 1996 / SC / C • Extreme Sex #3: Wired / 1994 / VI / M • Far East Fantasy / 1995 / SUF / M • Fashion Passion / 1997 / TEP / M • Fire & Ice / 1995 / LV / M • Flipside / 1996 / VI / M • Forbidden / 1996 / SC / M • The French Way / 1994 / HOV / M • Frendz? #2 / 1996 / RAS / M • Gang Bang Bitches #01 / 1994 / PP / M • Gang Bang Bitches #02 / 1994 / PP / M • Gangbang At The O.K. Corral /

1994 / FPI / M • Gangbang Girl #13 / 1994 / ANA / M • Gangbang Girl #14 / 1994 / ANA / M • Gangbang Girl #17 / 1995 / ANA / M • Generation Sex #1 / 1996 / VT / M • The Girls From Hootersville #04 / 1993 / SFP / M • The Girls From Hootersville #05 / 1994 / SFP / M • The Girls From Hootersville #06 / 1994 / SFP / M • The Girls From Hootersville #08 / 1994 / SFP / M • Girly Video Magazine #2 / 1995 / BEP / M • Go Ahead...Eat Me! / 1995 / KWP / M • Hardcore Fantasies #3 / 1996 / LV / M • Hardcore Fantasies #5 / 1996 / LV / M • Head To Head / 1996 / VI / M • Heart Breaker / 1994 / CA / M • Heidi's High Heeled Hookers / 1995 / BBE / M • Here Comes Jenny St. James / 1996 / HOV / M • Hidden Camera #12 / 1993 / JMP / M • Hidden Camera #15 / 1994 / JMP / M • Hidden Camera #16 / 1994 / JMP / M • High Heel Harlots #05 / 1994 / SFP / M • Hollywood '94: Butts Abound / 1993 / ELP / M • The Hooker / 1995 / LOT / M • I Can't Believe I Did The Whole Team! / 1994 / FPI / M • Interview With A Vamp / 1994 / ANA / M • Interview's Anal Queens / 1996 / LV / M • The Joy Dick Club / 1994 / MID / M • Juliette's Desires / 1996 / LE / M • Kelly Jaye Close-Up / 1994 / VI / M • Kinky Fantasies / 1994 / KWP / M • Lady's Choice / 1995 / VD / M • Latex And Lace / 1996 / BBE / M • Leather / 1995 / LE / M • Lollipops #1 / 1996 / SC / M • Lollipops #2 / 1996 / SC / M • Love Potion 69 / 1994 / VC / M • Lust Behind Bars / 1996 / GO / M • Maneater / 1995 / ERA / M • Mastering The Male / 1995 / RB / B • Mellon Man #03 / 1994 / AVI / M • Mike Hott: #247 Cunt of the Month: Shelby / 1993 / MHV / M • More Than A Handful #5: California Or Bust / 1994 / MET / M • Mr. Peepers Amateur Home Videos #74: C Foam Surfer / 1993 / LBO / M • Mr. Peepers Amateur Home Videos #83: Roni And The Private's / 1994 / LBO / M • Mr. Peepers Amateur Home Videos #85: Hand Puppet Job / 1994 / LBO / M • Mr. Peepers Amateur Home Videos #86: Tit A Ton / 1994 / LBO / M • Nasty Fuckin' Movies #24 / 1994 / RUM / M • Nasty Newcummers #09 / 1995 / MET / M • Neighborhood Slut / 1996 / LV / M • Neighbors / 1994 / LE / M • The New Ass Masters #07 / 1996 / LEI / C • New Pussy Hunt #26 / 1996 / LEI / C • Night Stalker / 1995 / BBE / M • Nightlife / 1997 / CA / M • Nikki Loves Rocco / 1996 / VI / M • Nookie Ranch / 1996 / NIT / M • Odyssey 30 Min: #551: / 1995 / OD / M • Odyssey Triple Play #91: Bone Appetite / 1995 / OD / M • Odyssey Triple Play #97: The Anal Game / 1995 / OD / M • Odyssey Triple Play #98: Three Ways To Sunday / 1995 / OD / M • Off Duty Porn Stars / 1994 / VC / M • Oh My Gush / 1995 / OD / M • The Older Women's Sperm Bank #6 / 1996 / SUF / M • Oral Addiction / 1995 / VI / M • Over Exposed / 1996 / ULP / M • Performer Of The Year / 1994 / WP / M • Peyton's Place / 1996 / ULP / M • Philmore Butts Strikes Gold / 1996 / SUF / M • Pleasure Dome: The Genesis Chamber / 1994 / AFV / M • Prime Choice #7 / 1996 / RAS / M • Private Film #24 / 1995 / OD / M • Private Film #26 / 1995 / OD / M • Private Stories #01 / 1995 / OD / M • Private Stories #09 / 1996 / OD / M • Private Video Magazine #16 /

1994 / OD / M • Profiles #01 / 1995 / XPR / M • Profiles #04: Lust Lessons / 1995 / XPR / M • Profiles #05: Planet Lust / 1995 / XPR / M • Profiles #06: Super Model Orgy / 1996 / XPR / M • Profiles #07: Sexworld / 1996 / XPR / M • Profiles #08: Triple Ecstacy / 1996 / XPR / M • Psychoanal Therapy / 1994 / CA / M • Pussyman Auditions #01 / 1995 / SNA / M • Raincoat Fantasies / 1993 / ELP / M • Raunch #09 / 1993 / CC / M • Raunchy Remedy / 1993 / ELP / M • Real Sex Magazine #01 / 1996 / HO / M • Red Door Diaries #1 / 1995 / ZA / M • Ridin' The Big One / 1994 / TEG / M • Rockhard (Coast) / 1996 / CC / M • Rockhard (Sin City) / 1996 / SC / M • Roxy: A Gang Bang Fantasy / 1994 / FC / M • Samantha & Company / 1996 / PL / M • The Scam / 1996 / LV / M • Scrue / 1995 / VI / M • Secret Diary #2 / 1995 / MID / M • Seekers / 1994 / CA / M • Sensations #1 / 1996 / SC / M • Sex Bandits / 1995 / VC / M • Sex Drives Of The Rich And Famous / 1996 / ERA / M • Sex Fugitives / 1993 / LE / M • Sex Party / 1995 / KWP / M • Sexperiment / 1996 / ULP / M • Sexual Atrocities / 1996 / EL / M • The Sexual Solution #1 / 1995 / LE / M • Sexual Trilogy #03 / 1994 / SFP / M • Shaving Grace / 1996 / GO / M • A Shot In The Pink / 1995 / BBE / M • Show & Tell / 1994 / ELP / M • Skin Hunger / 1995 / MET / M • Sleaze Please!—August Edition / 1994 / FH / M • Sleaze Please!—December Edition / 1994 / FH / M • Snatch Masters #05 / 1995 / LEI / M • Snatch Masters #11 / 1995 / LEI / M • Snatch Patch / 1995 / LE / M • Squirt Squad / 1995 / AMP / M • Stand By Your Man / 1994 / CV / M • Starbangers #06 / 1994 / FPI / M • Starbangers #07 / 1995 / FPI / M • Stiff Competition #2 / 1994 / CA / M • Stranger At The Backdoor / 1994 / CC / M • Streetwalkers / 1995 / HO / M • Super Ball Sunday / 1994 / LBO / M • Supermodel #1 / 1994 / VI / M • Sweet Brown Sugar / 1994 / AVI / M • Sweet Smell Of Excess / 1996 / CIN / M • Swing Into...Spring / 1995 / KWP / M • Swinging Couples #01 / 1993 / GO / M • Swinging Couples #02 / 1993 / GO / M • Taboo #13 / 1994 / IN / M • Tailz From Da Hood #1 / 1995 / AVI / M • Tailz From Da Hood #5 / 1996 / AVI / M • Temple Of Love / 1995 / SUF / M • Titanic Orgy / 1995 / PEP / M • Titty Slickers #2 / 1994 / LE / M • Titty Troop / 1995 / CC / M • Trouble Maker / 1995 / VI / M • Ultimate Anal Gang Bang #3 / 1995 / HW / M • Unchained Marylin / 1996 / VT / M • Under The Covers / 1996 / GO / M • Venom #2 / 1996 / VD / M • Venom #3 / 1996 / VD / M • Venom #7 / 1996 / VD / M • Video Virgins #09 / 1993 / NS / M • Video Virgins #11 / 1994 / NS / M • Video Virgins #13 / 1994 / NS / M • Waterbabies #3 / 1996 / CC / M • The Watering Hole / 1994 / HO / M • A Week And A Half In The Life Of A Prostitute / 1997 / EL / M • Wet & Wicked / 1995 / PRK / M • Wild Roomies / 1994 / VC / M • XXX / 1996 / TEP / M • Young And Anal #2 / 1995 / JMP / M • Young Tails / 1996 / LV / M

IAN MACDANIEL *see* Ian Daniels
IAN MACGREGOR *see Star Index I*
IAN MCALLISTER *see Star Index I*
IAN MCLAINE
Private Film #01 / 1993 / OD / M

IAN MOORS
Amanda's Punishment / 1994 / BON / B •
Bondage Memories #03 / 1994 / BON / C •
Capturing Katrina / 1994 / BON / B • Con-
tract For Torment / 1995 / BON / B • De-
ception (1995-B&D) / 1995 / BON / B • Ex-
treme Sex #2: The Dungeon / 1994 / VI / M
• Katrina's Awakening #1 / 1994 / BON / B
• Katrina's Awakening #2 / 1994 / BON / B
• Katrina's Awakening #3 / 1994 / BON / B
• Kym Wilde Sessions #2 / 1993 / BON / B
• The Penitent / 1992 / BON / B • Prescrip-
tion For Pain #1 / 1992 / BON / B • Pre-
scription For Pain #2: The Ultimate Pain /
1993 / BON / B • The Punisher / 1994 /
BON / B • Slaves On Loan / 1995 / BON /
B • Surrogate Master / 1996 / BON / B •
Tanya Fox's Bondage Fantasies / 1993 /
BON / B • Tanya Foxx After Hours / 1993 /
BON / B • Tanya Foxx: Suspended In Time
/ 1996 / BON / C

IAN MORLEY *see Star Index I*
IAN NIXON
Kitty's Kinky Capers / 1996 / TTV / M
IAN ROBERTS
Jiggly Queens #1 / 1993 / LE / M
IAN STUART
More Dirty Debutantes #63 / 1997 / SBV /
M • Pick Up Lines #13 / 1997 / OD / M
IAN SUMMERS *see Star Index I*
IANA
Rocco Goes To Prague / 1995 / EA / M
IBRAHIM ASLANKAN
[Krankenschwestern-Report / 1972 / ... /
M
ICE
Black girl with a pretty face, small to medium
tits, 34B-24-34, slim body, narrow hips,
nice butt, good skin, bubbly personality,
5'8" tall. De-virginized at 15.
The Adventures Of Peeping Tom #1 / 1996
/ OD / M • Backdoor Play / 1996 / AVI / M •
Black Cheerleader Jungle Jerk-Off / 1996 /
WIC / F • Black Cheerleader Search #02 /
1996 / ROB / M • Black Mystique #13 /
1995 / VT / F • Dark Desires (Factory-
1995) / 1995 / FH / M • Ebony Erotica /
1995 / VT / M • Fashion sluts #5: Ethnic
Ecstasy / 1995 / ABS / M • Gimme Some
Head / 1994 / VT / M • Hard Core Begin-
ners #10 / 1995 / LEI / M • Hollywood On
Ice / 1995 / VT / M • I Cream On Jeannie /
1995 / AVI / M • Interracial 247 / 1995 / CC
/ M • More Black Dirty Debutantes #6 /
1996 / 4P / M • My Baby Got Back #08 /
1996 / VT / M • Pussy Hunt #08 / 1995 /
LEI / M • Raunch #10: Uncut Jewel / 1994
/ CC / M • Rump-Shaker #5 / 1996 / HW /
M • Samuels: Lesbian Lust / 1990 / SAM /
F • Sex In Black & White / 1995 / OD / M •
Sista! #3 / 1995 / VT / F • Small Top
Bitches / 1996 / AVI / M • Tailz From Da
Hood #2 / 1995 / AVI / M • Vagabonds /
1996 / ERA / M • Video Virgins #17 / 1994
/ NS / M • You Go Girl! (Video Team) /
1995 / VT / M
ICE-T
Frankenpenis / 1995 / LEI / M
IDA *see Selina Fabre*
IDA KING
The Bite / 1975 / SVE / M
IDEKI MAYANATA *see Star Index I*
IDILKO
Hamlet: For The Love Of Ophelia #1 /
1996 / IP / M
IDLE WYLDE

Ron Hightower's White Chicks #14 / 1994 /
LBO / M
IDO
World Cup / 1990 / PL / M
IESHA *(Aiesha, Aisha (Iesha), Lesha, Eye-
sha Solario)*
A little pudgy brunette with a tattoo on the left
breast.
Bad / 1990 / VC / M • Bi-Swingers / 1991 /
PL / G • Candy Ass / 1990 / V99 / M • Col-
lege Girl / 1990 / VEX / M • Head Nurse /
1990 / V99 / M • The Maltese Phallus /
1990 / V99 / M • More Dirty Debutantes /
1990 / PRI / M • Paris By Night / 1990 / IN
/ M • Perfect Girl / 1991 / VEX / M • San
Francisco Lesbians #3 / 1993 / PL / F • Se-
cret Dreams / 1991 / VEX / M • Summer
Dreams / 1990 / VEX / M • Tail Of The
Scorpion / 1990 / ELP / M • Teach Me
Tonight / 1990 / VEX / M • A Touch Of Gold
/ 1990 / IN / M
IGOR *see Star Index I*
IGOR ELDER
Inside Seka / 1980 / VXP / M
IGOR PREGUN *see Star Index I*
IHATALIN BADAR
True Stories #2 / 1993 / SC / M
ILDIKO
Analtown USA #06 / 1995 / NIT / M • Cum
Buttered Corn Holes #2 / 1996 / NIT / C •
Love Slave / 1995 / WIV / M • Magma:
Puszta Teenies / 1995 / MET / M • Max
World #3: Formula 1 / 1996 / XPR / M •
Midnight Obsession / 1995 / XC / M •
Plumper Therapy / 1995 / BTO / M • Pri-
vate Gold #12: The Pyramid #2 / 1996 /
OD / M • The Witch's Tail / 1994 / GOU / M
• World Sex Tour #3 / 1995 / ANA / M
ILDIKO SCHILLER
Screamers / 1994 / HW / M
ILDIKU
Sluts 'n' Angels In Budapest / 1994 / EL /
M • Sodomania #11: In Your Face / 1994 /
EL / M
ILEANA CARENATI *see Lili Carati*
ILEGEDUS
True Stories #1 / 1993 / SC / M • True Sto-
ries #2 / 1993 / SC / M
ILENE WELLS *see Eileen Welles*
ILLANA MOOR
Hungarian, black hair, medium slightly droopy
tits, pretty, lithe body, large areola. 21 years
old in 1996.
Casting Call #17 / 1996 / SO / M • Dirty
Tricks #2: This Ain't Love / 1996 / EA / M •
Hardcore Schoolgirls #4: Little Kittens /
1996 / XPR / M • Penetration (Anabolic) #3
/ 1995 / ANA / M • Profiles #06: Super
Model Orgy / 1996 / XPR / M • Sodomania
#16: Sexxy Pistols / 1996 / EL / M • Sodo-
mania: Slop Shots / 1996 / EL / C
ILLONA
Ding Dong: A Night At The Moulin Rouge /
1995 / SOW / S • Lesbian Pros And Ama-
teurs #05 / 1992 / GO / F • The Peek
Snatchers / 1965 / SOW / S
ILONA BACH
For Members Only / 1980 / LIM / M
ILONA K.
Screamers / 1994 / HW / M
ILONA STALLER *see Cicciolina*
ILONKA LIST
[Die Madchenhandler / 1972 / ... / M
ILSA EPPLE *see Star Index I*
ILSA HOFHERR *see Star Index I*
ILSA STUPP *see Star Index I*

ILSE PETERSEN
Bordello / 1973 / AR / M
ILSE-MARIE
Swedish Vip Magazine #2 / 1995 / PL / M
IMA KOOZE
They Shall Overcome / 1974 / VST / M
IMA PUTZ
Comeback / 1995 / VI / M
IMA WHORE *see Star Index I*
IMELDA
Asian Connection Video #103 / 1996 / AC0
/ B
IMPERIAL SUGAR *see Ray Victory*
INA
Blue Vanities #544 / 1994 / FFL / M • Pri-
vate Stories #09 / 1995 / OD / M
INCA *see Marie Mason*
INDEXA
San Francisco Lesbians #5 / 1994 / PL / F
INDRA
Dark Passions #03 / 1995 / AFV / M • First
Time Lesbians #01 / 1993 / JMP / F • Mid-
night Angels #03 / 1993 / MID / F • Rocco
Goes To Prague / 1995 / EA / M • Sandy
Insatiable / 1995 / EA / M
INDRED *see Star Index I*
INDRID *see Star Index I*
INES (BERLIN) *see Berlin*
INEZ
Blue Vanities #549 / 1994 / FFL / M
INEZ ACKER
Gourmet Quickies: Inez #712 / 1985 / GO /
C • GVC: Suburban Lust #128 / 1983 / GO
/ M • GVC: Valley Vixens #124 / 1983 / GO
/ M • Parliament: Shauna Grant #1 / 1988 /
PM / C • The Wacky World Of X-Rated
Bloopers / 1989 / GO / M
INGA
Bubble Butts #08 / 1992 / LBO / M •
Gazonga Goddess #1 / 1993 / IF / M • The
Madame's Boudoir / 1993 / STM / B • Mr.
Peepers Nastiest #4 / 1995 / LBO / C •
Profiles In Discipline #01: The Mistress Is A
Lady / 1994 / STM / C • Succulent Toes /
1995 / STM / B • Wrasslin She-Babes #05
/ 1996 / SOW / M
INGA PANTERA *see Wild Pantera*
INGDRA
Black Magic #1 / 1993 / VIM / M • The
Bold, The Bald & The Beautiful / 1993 /
VIM / M
INGE PINSON *see Uschi Digart*
INGE SWENSON
Blow Some My Way / 1977 / VHL / M
INGER HANNS
The Beat Goes On / 1987 / VCR / C
INGER KISSEN *see Andrea True*
INGER OLSEN *see Star Index I*
INGER SCOTT
Worksex / 1980 / ... / M
INGERLISE GAARDE *see Star Index I*
INGO *see Ritchie Razor*
INGRID
Busty Debutantes / 1996 / H&S / M • Girls
Around The World #21: Tawny Peaks &
Friends / 1995 / BTO / M • Mr. Peepers
Amateur Home Videos #46: A Schnitzel In
The Bush / 1992 / LBO / M • Porno X-
Treme #2: Club Bizarre / 1995 / SC / M •
Porno X-Treme #4: Wet Dream / 1995 /
SC / M • Private Video Magazine #18 /
1994 / OD / M • Sappho Connection / 19??
/ LIP / F • U Witness: Video Three-Pak #3 /
1995 / MSP / M
INGRID (BRAZIL)
Asses Galore #4: Extreme Noise Terror /

1996 / DFI / M
INGRID ALLEN *see Star Index I*
INGRID BACK
The Ideal Marriage / 1971 / SOW / M
INGRID ELLIOTT *see Rachel Ryan*
INGRID FINE *see Star Index I*
INGRID JENNINGS
F / 1980 / GO / M
INGRID KAWA *see Star Index I*
INGRID LAROCHE
Magma: Hot Service / 1995 / MET / M
INGRID PETERSON
Sexual Customs In Scandinavia / cr73 / QX / M
INGRID PIERCE *see Star Index I*
INGRID ROB
Bucky Beaver's XXX Dragon Art Theatre Double Feature #01 / 1996 / SOW / M • Hitler's Harlots / cr73 / SOW / M
INGRID STEEGER
The Sex Adventures Of The Three Musketeers / 1971 / MED / S • The Swingin' Stewardesses / 1971 / VCX / S • The Young Seducers / 1971 / BL / M • [Junge Madchen Mogen's HeiB, Hausfrauen Noch HeiBer / 1973 / ... / M • [Krankenschwestern-Report / 1972 / ... / M • [Schulmadchen-Report 4: Was Eltern Oft Verzweifeln LaBt / 1972 / ... / M
INGRID STENDAHL *see Star Index I*
INGRID TARPE
The Erotic Adventures Of Alladin X / 1995 / IP / M
INNA
Private Video Magazine #22 / 1995 / OD / M
INNOCENT
Anal Virgins Of America #07 / 1994 / FOR / M • Girls With Big Jugs / 1995 / V99 / M • Hard Core Beginners #05 / 1995 / LEI / M • Video Virgins #17 / 1994 / NS / M
INYA *see Star Index I*
IRA
A&B AB#344: Senior Citizen Tramp / 1991 / A&B / M • A&B AB#345: Ira Takes It Backdoor / 1991 / A&B / M • Tropic Of Passion / 1971 / NGV / M
IRA LEVINE *see Ernest Green*
IRENE
A&B AB#294: Training Irene / 1991 / A&B / M • A&B AB#299: Irene's Anal Circuit Training / 1991 / A&B / M • A&B AB#300: The Body Builders / 1991 / A&B / M • A&B AB#383: Fill My Ass / 1991 / A&B / M • A&B AB#385: Let's Fuck / 1991 / A&B / M • Blue Vanities #540 / 1994 / FFL / M • Magma: Dirty Diana / 1994 / MET / M • Mike Hott: #101 Masturbating Housewife #1 / 1990 / MHV / F • Mike Hott: #102 Masturbating Housewife #2 / 1990 / MHV / F
IRENE BEST *see Maria Tortuga*
IRENE GIORGIO *see Star Index I*
IRENE SILVER *see Star Index I*
IRENE WENDLIN *see Star Index I*
IRINA
Private Video Magazine #08 / 1994 / OD / M
IRINA BALARINA
French Twist / 1996 / HO / M • Horny Henry's Euro Adventure / 1995 / TTV / M
IRINA KANT
[Junge Madchen Mogen's HeiB, Hausfrauen Noch HeiBer / 1973 / ... / M
IRINA KIROV
A Merry Widow / 1996 / SPI / M
IRIS *see Star Index I*

IRIS FLOURET *see Susan Sloan*
IRIS LATTIMER
Body Candy / 1980 / VIS / M
IRIS MEDINA
Fantastic Orgy / 197? / ... / M • Jungle Blue / 1978 / HIF / M • The Ultimate Pleasure / 1977 / HIF / M
IRIS NILE *see Isis Nile*
IRIS STAR *see Star Index I*
IRIS STERN
Laura's Desires / 1978 / CA / M
IRIS WOBKER
[Krankenschwestern-Report / 1972 / ... / M
IRISH
Dirty Hairy's Over 50 Meets Mr. Black 18 Inches / 1996 / GOT / M
IRON JOHN
Reel Life Video #32: / 1995 / RLF / M • Reel Life Video: Britt & Iron John / 1995 / RLF / F
IRV O'NEAL *see Star Index I*
IRVING KLAW
Irving Klaw's Bondage Classix / 1986 / BIZ / B
IRVING SCHWARTZ
The French Tickler / 1994 / CS / B • Tied & Tickled #28: Tickling Dr. Cripley / 1995 / CS / B
ISA
Eurotica #07 / 1996 / XC / M
ISA DERRY
The Comeback Of Marilyn / 1986 / VC / M • Hot Desires / 1986 / VC / M
ISA ROBETTI *see Isabella Rovetti*
ISABEL
Love Play / 1977 / CA / M • Penetration (Flash) #2 / 1995 / FLV / M • Woman 2 Woman #1 / 1993 / SOF / F
ISABEL (M.MASGLOW) *see Melinda Masglow*
ISABEL WEISS *see Star Index I*
ISABELA (BRAZ) *see Star Index I*
ISABELLA
Bedside Manor / 1986 / CA / M • Dirty Dirty Debutantes #3 / 1996 / 4P / M • Dirty Doc's Housecalls #01 / 1993 / LV / M • Forbidden Fantasies #2 / 1995 / ZA / M • Just For The Thrill Of It / 1989 / V99 / M • Knocked-Up Nymphos #1 / 1996 / GLI / M • Lovin' Spoonfuls #5 / 1996 / 4P / C • Never So Deep / 1981 / VCX / M • Up And Cummers #32 / 1996 / 4P / M
ISABELLA PERINI
More Dirty Debutantes #33 / 1994 / 4P / M
ISABELLA ROVELLI *see Isabella Rovetti*
ISABELLA ROVETTI *(Lisa Bright, Isabella Rovelli, Kendall Marx, Lisa Carrington, Issabella Raffelli, Isa Robetti, Karal Broderick, Alisa Monet, Heather Martin (IR), Tabitha Lombardo)*
Sweet brunette with small tits, tight waist and good skin. Nice smile. Not Lisa More. First movie was **Robofox**. Karal Broderick in **The Sleazy Detective**.
Angel Gets Even / 1987 / FAN / M • Angel Puss / 1988 / VC / M • Angel Rising / 1988 / IN / M • Angel's Back / 1988 / IN / M • Angel's Gotta Have It / 1988 / FAN / M • Beauty And The Beast #1 / 1988 / VC / M • Behind Blue Eyes #2 / 1988 / ZA / M • Biloxi Babes / 1988 / WV / M • Blue Movie / 1989 / VD / M • Caught In The Act / 1987 / WV / M • Cherry Cheerleaders / 1987 / VEX / M • The De Renzy Tapes / 1990 /

CA / C • Dirty Pictures / 1988 / CA / M • For Your Love / 1988 / IN / M • Ghostest With The Mostest / 1988 / CA / M • Hello Molly / 1989 / CA / M • Inn Of Sin / 1988 / VT / M • Love Lies / 1988 / IN / M • Mad Love / 1988 / VC / M • The Main Attraction / 1988 / 4P / M • The Nicole Stanton Story #1 / 1989 / CA / M • The Nicole Stanton Story #2 / 1989 / CA / M • Prom Girls / 1988 / CA / M • Robofox #1 / 1987 / FAN / M • Screwing Around / 1988 / LV / M • The Sleazy Detective / 1988 / VD / M • Switch Hitters #2: Swinging Both Ways / 1987 / IN / G • Talk Dirty to Me One More Time #2 / 1988 / PP / C • Tender And Wild / 1989 / MTP / M • Three By Three / 1989 / LV / C • Undercover Angel / 1988 / IN / M • Wet Tails / 1989 / PL / M • The Wild Brat / 1988 / VI / M • The Young And The Wrestling #1 / 1988 / PL / M
ISABELLE
J.E.G.: Pair Of Precious Pregnants / 1995 / JEG / F • Magma: Bizarre Games / 1996 / MET / M • Magma: Chateau Extreme / 1995 / MET / M • Magma: Dirty Twins / 1994 / MET / M • Magma: Horny For Cock / 1990 / MET / M • Magma: Sperm-Crazy / 1994 / MET / M • Magma: Tits Practice / 1995 / MET / M • Private Stories #05 / 1995 / OD / M
ISABELLE ADORATA
Kinky Villa / 1995 / PL / M
ISABELLE BRELL *see Star Index I*
ISABELLE CHRISTIE *see Star Index I*
ISABELLE FAUCHON *see Star Index I*
ISABELLE KRISTAL *see Star Index I*
ISABELLE LA GRANGE *see Star Index I*
ISABELLE LECROIX
Skin #1 / 1994 / EUR / M
ISABELLE SEALING *see Star Index I*
ISABELLE TORILLA *see Star Index I*
ISADORA ROSE
Badd Girl's Spanking / 1994 / STM / B • Big Reward / 1995 / CS / B • Captive Coeds / 1996 / LON / B • The Disciplinarians / 1996 / LON / B • Dracula's Dungeon / 1995 / HOM / B • Lessons In Bondage / 1995 / HOM / B • Man In Chains / 1995 / HOM / B • Mistress Of Shadows / 1995 / HOM / B • Mistress Rules / 1995 / STM / B • Sharon's Painful Persuasions / 1996 / SIL / B • Slavegirl Of Zor / 1996 / LON / B • Their Absolute Property / 1994 / STM / B • Torture Clinic / 1995 / LON / B • Video Dominatrix / 1996 / LON / B • When The Mistress Is Away... / 1995 / HAC / B
ISIS (NOT NILE)
Freshness Counts / 1996 / EL / M
ISIS NICE *see Isis Nile*
ISIS NILE *(Iris Nile, Isis Nice)*
Originally small to medium breasted and later large artifically titted, quite pretty girl. Started with what looks like a small afro and then got a more reasonable hair style. Supposedly she's German/Egyptian and was born Oct 5, 1969 in Van Nuys CA. Despite some resemblance this is not the same as Diva. 5'7" tall, 120lbs, 32C-22-35 before tit job in 1993.
'Ho! 'Ho! 'Ho! / 1993 / WP / M • 1-900-FUCK #2 / 1995 / SO / M • American Swinger Video Magazine #06 / 1993 / ZA / M • American Swinger Video Magazine #07 / 1993 / ZA / M • Anal Mystique / 1994 / EMC / M • Anal Vision #14 / 1993 / LBO / M • The Anal-Europe Series #06: Anal Luck

/ 1993 / LV / M • Ass Openers! #2 / 1995 / TCK / C • Babe Magnet / 1994 / IN / M • Badgirls #1: Lockdown / 1994 / VI / M • Badgirls #2: Strip Search / 1994 / VI / M • Bedroom Bondage / 1994 / LON / B • Beverly Hills Sex Party / 1993 / EX / M • Big Bust Babes #21 / 1994 / AFI / M • Big Murray's New-Cummers #22: Exotic Erotica / 1993 / FD / M • Black Satin / 1994 / IN / M • Black Streets / 1994 / LE / M • Blonde Angel / 1994 / VI / M • Bonnie & Clyde #3 / 1994 / VI / M • Bonnie & Clyde #4 / 1994 / VI / M • Booby Prize / 1995 / PEP / M • Both Ends Burning / 1993 / HW / M • The Bottom Dweller Part Deux / 1994 / EL / M • Brassiere To Eternity / 1994 / PEP / F • Breastman Goes To Breastland #2 / 1993 / EVN / M • Butt Watch #01 / 1993 / FH / M • Butt Watch #02 / 1993 / FH / M • Butterfly / 1993 / OD / M • Caged Fury / 1993 / DR / M • Carlita's Backway / 1993 / OD / M • Channel Blonde / 1994 / VI / M • Chateau Du Cheeks / 1994 / VC / M • A Clockwork Orgy / 1995 / PL / M • Club Anal #2 / 1993 / ROB / F • Cluster Fuck #06 / 1994 / MAX / M • Confessions Of A Slutty Nurse / 1994 / VIM / M • County Line / 1993 / PEP / M • Dark Room / 1994 / VT / M • Delicious Passions / 1993 / ROB / F • Demolition Woman #1 / 1994 / IP / M • Designs On Women / 1994 / IN / F • The Dickheads #1 / 1993 / MID / M • Dog Walker / 1994 / EA / M • Double D Dykes #14 / 1994 / GO / F • Double D Dykes #15 / 1995 / GO / F • Double Down / 1993 / LBO / M • Ebony Princess / 1994 / IN / M • Erotic Desires / 1994 / MAX / M • Erotica Optique / 1994 / SUF / M • Facesitter #3 / 1994 / CC / M • Gemini / 1994 / SC / M • A Girl's Affair #02 / 1993 / FD / F • Girls Off Duty / 1994 / LE / M • Girls On Duty / 1994 / LE / M • Gonzo Groups & Gang Bangs / 1994 / GLI / M • The Great American Boobs To Kill For Dance Contest / 1995 / PEP / C • Hard Squeeze / 1994 / EMC / M • Harry Horndog #23: The Final Flick / 1993 / ZA / M • Haunting Dreams #2 / 1993 / LV / M • Heartbeat / 1995 / PP / M • Hollywood Ho' House / 1994 / VC / M • The Hollywood Starlet Search / 1995 / SC / M • Hookers Of Hollywood / 1994 / LE / M • Hooter Ho-Down / 1994 / LV / M • Horny Henry's Strange Adventure / 1995 / TTV / M • Hot Tight Asses #05 / 1994 / TCK / M • Hot Wishes / 1995 / LE / M • House Of The Rising Sun / 1993 / VT / M • I Touch Myself / 1994 / IP / F • In The Bush / 1994 / PP / M • Interactive / 1993 / VD / M • International Affairs / 1994 / PL / M • Into The Fire / 1994 / ZA / M • Invitation For Lust / 1995 / C69 / M • Kittens #5 / 1994 / CC / F • Ladies Room / 1994 / SC / F • Let's Dream On / 1994 / FD / M • Let's Play Doctor / 1994 / PV / M • Live Sex / 1994 / LE / M • Lovin' Spoonfuls #3 / 1995 / 4P / C • M Series #08 / 1993 / LBO / M • Makin' It / 1994 / A&E / M • Mighty Man #1: Virgins In The Forest / 1994 / LE / M • Milli Vanilla / 1994 / TP / M • More Dirty Debutantes #28 / 1994 / 4P / M • More Than A Handful #4 / 1994 / MET / M • More Than A Handful #5: California Or Bust / 1994 / MET / M • The Mountie / 1994 / PP / M • Mr. Peepers Amateur Home Videos #72: Dirty Diary / 1993 / LBO / M • Mr. Peepers Nastiest #2 / 1995 / LBO / C • Mr. Peepers Nastiest #3 / 1995

/ LBO / C • Night Crawlers / 1994 / SC / M • No Man's Land #09 / 1994 / VT / F • Odyssey Triple Play #80: Couple Play / 1994 / OD / M • The Original Wicked Woman / 1993 / WP / M • Other People's Pussy / 1993 / LV / M • Pleasure Dome: The Genesis Chamber / 1994 / AFV / M • Pussyman #05: Captive Audience / 1994 / SNA / M • Pussyman #06: House Of Games / 1994 / SNA / M • Pussyman #11: Prime Cuts / 1995 / SNA / C • Pussywoman #1: Sisters In Sin / 1994 / CC / M • Raunch #08 / 1993 / CC / M • Reckless / 1995 / NOT / M • Red Light / 1994 / SC / S • Reds / 1993 / LE / F • The Reel Sex World #01 / 1993 / WP / M • Ride 'em Cow Girl / 1995 / VI / C • Rock Me / 1994 / CC / M • Sarah Jane's Love Bunnies #03 / 1993 / FPI / F • Sean Michaels On The Road #04: Chinatown / 1993 / VT / M • The Secret Life Of Nina Hartley / 1994 / VC / M • Sensual Recluse / 1994 / EX / M • Sex Circus / 1994 / VIM / M • Sex Punk 2000 / 1993 / FOR / M • Sexual Instinct #2 / 1994 / DR / M • Shame / 1994 / VI / M • Shave Tails #1 / 1994 / SO / M • Shiver / 1993 / FOR / M • Show & Tell / 1994 / ELP / M • Silky Thighs / 1994 / ERA / M • Skid Row / 1994 / SC / M • Sleepless / 1993 / VD / M • Southern Cumfort / 1993 / HO / M • Spread The Wealth / 1993 / DR / M • The Star / 1995 / CC / M • Subway / 1994 / SC / M • Supermodel #1 / 1994 / VI / M • The Swap #2 / 1994 / VI / M • Sweat 'n' Bullets / 1995 / MID / M • Take It Like A Man / 1994 / IF / M • Taste Of Shame / 1994 / ROB / F • The Teacher's Pet / 1993 / LV / M • Temptation / 1994 / VC / M • The Three Muskatits / 1994 / PL / M • Titanic Orgy / 1995 / PEP / M • Titty Bar #2 / 1994 / LE / M • Tongue In Cheek / 1994 / LE / M • Top Debs #4: Sex Boat / 1993 / GO / M • Toppers #25 / 1994 / TV / M • Toppers #26 / 1994 / TV / M • Toppers #27 / 1994 / TV / M • Toppers #30 / 1994 / TV / C • Toppers #31 / 1994 / TV / C • Toppers #32 / 1994 / TV / C • Truck Stop Angel / 1994 / CC / M • Up And Cummers #02 / 1993 / 4P / M • Up And Cummers: The Movie / 1994 / 4P / M • Vagina Town / 1993 / CA / M • Virgin / 1993 / HW / M • Wendy Whoppers: Psychic Healer / 1994 / PEP / M • Wendy Whoppers: Ufo Tracker / 1994 / PEP / M • Wet Deal / 1994 / FD / M • Whispered Lies / 1993 / LBO / M • Wild Roomies / 1994 / VC / M • [Double Duty / 1993 / LBO / M •

[Video Roulette / 1994 / MID / M

ISLAND BOY
Maui Waui / 1996 / PE / M • Too Hot / 1996 / LV / M

ISLOS
Severity / 1996 / BON / B

ISOBEL BEAUMONT
Diary Of My Secret Life / 19?? / HOE / M

ISOLDE *see* **Fay Burd**

ISOLDE JENSEN *see* **Fay Burd**

ISRAEL
Dark Passions #03 / 1995 / AFV / M • GRG: Jaguar And Israel / 1994 / GRG / M • Private Collection: #130: Key To Pleasure / 1992 / TOP / M

ISRAEL GONZALEZ *see* **Max DeNiro**

ISSABELLA RAFFELLI *see* **Isabella Rovetti**

ITDIAN STALLIAN
Bitches In Heat #1: Locked In the Base-

ment / 1995 / ZA / M

IVA
Erotica Optique / 1994 / SUF / M

IVAN
The Bottom Dweller Part Deux / 1994 / EL / M

IVAN TOOS
Sunny / 1979 / VC / M

IVANA
Southern Belles #1 / 1994 / HOV / M

IVANA LITEREKA
Lil' Women: Vacation / 1996 / EUR / M

IVANA LUSHBOTTOM
French-Pumped Femmes #1 / 1989 / RSV / G • Glittering Gartered Girls / 1993 / RSV / B • Hazards In Heels / 1991 / RSV / S • Ivana Lushbottom's Skyscrapers / 1990 / RSV / B • Long Legged Ladies / 1993 / VER / M • Stockings & Stilettos #1 / 1989 / RSV / G

IVON
Video Virgins #13 / 1994 / NS / M

IVORY
Dark Angels / 1996 / STM / F • Dark Desire / 1995 / STM / F • Disciplinary Action / 1995 / STM / B • Girlz Towne #12 / 1995 / FC / F • Lesbian Kink Trilogy #2 / 1995 / STM / F • Punishment Playpen / 1995 / STM / B • Women Who Control The Family Jewels #4 / 1995 / STM / B

IVORY (COAST) *see* **Ivory Coast**

IVORY (ESSEX) *see* **Ivory Essex**

IVORY COAST *(Ivory (Coast))*
Ugly fat black girl with big droopy tits, long curly black hair—masses of it—23 years old in 1994, de-virginized at 16, body looks like that of a 40-year old.
Big Boob Pajama Party / 1993 / BTO / F • Big Busty #44 / 1994 / BTO / S • Black & Wet Private Parts / 1994 / STM / F • Black And White And Red All Over / 1994 / STM / B • Corrected Deception / 1994 / STM / B • Dark Discipline / 1994 / STM / B • Dynamite Dominator / 1993 / STM / B • Girls Around The World #22: Letha Weapons & Friends / 1995 / BTO / M • Harlem Honies #1 / 1993 / CC / M • Hoetown / 1994 / STM / F • Video Virgins #13 / 1994 / NS / M

IVORY ESSEX *(Ivory (Essex))*
Corrupt Desires / 1984 / MET / M • L'Amour / 1984 / CA / M

IVORY SNOW
Ass Masters (Leisure) #05 / 1995 / LEI / M • Naked Lunch / 1995 / LEI / M • Snatch Masters #09 / 1995 / LEI / M

IVY
Blue Vanities #572 / 1995 / FFL / M • World Sex Tour #3 / 1995 / ANA / M

IVY CRYSTAL
Dirty Stories #5 / 1996 / PE / M • Private Gold #09: Private Dancer / 1996 / OD / M • Private Stories #04 / 1995 / OD / M • Private Stories #05 / 1995 / OD / M • Private Stories #07 / 1996 / OD / M • Private Stories #08 / 1996 / OD / M

IVY ENGLISH *see* **April Dancer**

IVY LANE
Anal Angels #4 / 1995 / VEX / C • Butt Hunt #05 / 1995 / LEI / M

IVY POYSON *see* **Star Index I**

IZUMA SHIMA
[Love Thy Neighbor's Wife / 19?? / ... / M

J-DOGS
Bootylicious: Baby Got Booty / 1996 / JMP / M

J. AHART

San Francisco Lesbians #6 / 1994 / PL / F
J. BANDIT *see* **Sasha Gabor**
J. BENT
Dixie Debutantes #1 / 1996 / MYS / M
J. BOOMER TIBBS
Private School Girls / 1983 / CA / M
J. BOWEN *see* **Star Index I**
J. HARTMAN
Double Your Pleasure / 1978 / CV / M
J. JOHNSON
Girls Just Want To...Have Fun / 1984 / SE / M
J. JONES
San Francisco Lesbians #5 / 1994 / PL / F • San Francisco Lesbians #6 / 1994 / PL / F
J. LEWIS MONFRIED
Heat Wave / 1977 / COM / M
J. PARMEND
Magma: Fuck Me Diana / 1994 / MET / M
J. PEACHBOTTOM
You're The Boss / 1985 / VD / M
J. REYNOLDS
Blue Vanities #519 / 1993 / FFL / M
J. SCOTT
Fresh Meat (John Leslie) #1 / 1994 / EA / M
J.B.
19 And Nasty / 1990 / ME / M • Anal Anarchy / 1995 / VC / M • Anal Planet / 1994 / CC / M • As Dirty As She Wants To Be / 1990 / ME / M • Ass Backwards / 1991 / ME / M • Bare Elegance / 1984 / MAP / M • Bedtime For Byron / 1991 / ME / M • Biker Chicks In Love / 1991 / LE / M • Breasts And Beyond #2 / 1991 / ME / M • Cat Lickers #1 / 1990 / ME / F • Chasey Loves Rocco / 1996 / VI / M • Chinatown / 1994 / SC / M • The Cockateer #1 / 1991 / LE / M • The Cockateer #2 / 1992 / LE / M • Coming Clean / 1992 / ME / M • Dear Diary / 1995 / WP / M • Denim / 1991 / LE / M • Dial A For Anal / 1994 / CA / M • The Dirty Little Mind of Martin Fink / 1991 / ME / M • Dirty Stories #1 / 1995 / PE / M • Flesh For Fantasy / 1994 / CV / M • Gangbusters / 1995 / VC / M • Ghosts / 1994 / EMC / M • Harder, She Craved / 1995 / VC / M • Hot Spa / 1984 / CA / M • Illicit Entry / 1995 / WAV / M • In Deep With The Devil / 1991 / ME / M • Introducing Alexis / 1996 / VI / M • It's A Wonderful Sexlife / 1991 / LE / M • Jiggly Queens #1 / 1993 / LE / M • Kelly Eighteen #1 / 1993 / LE / M • Kelly Eighteen #2 / 1993 / LE / M • Legend #4: Critic's Choice / 1992 / LE / M • Legend #5: The Legend Continues / 1994 / LE / M • The Legend Of Reggie D. / 1989 / EA / M • Lethal Lolita / 1993 / LE / M • Lingerie / 1995 / SC / M • Memories / 1992 / LE / M • Nikki At Night / 1993 / LE / M • One Of Our Porn Stars Is Missing / 1993 / OD / M • The Only Game In Town / 1991 / VC / M • Paradise Lost / 1995 / LE / M • Party House / 1995 / WAV / M • Penetrator #2: Grudge Day / 1995 / PL / M • The Prince Of Lies / 1992 / LE / M • Radical Affairs Video Magazine #01 / 1992 / ME / M • Radical Affairs Video Magazine #02 / 1992 / ME / M • Radical Affairs Video Magazine #03 / 1992 / ME / M • Radical Affairs Video Magazine #04 / 1992 / ME / M • Radical Affairs Video Magazine #05 / 1993 / ME / M • Radical Affairs Video Magazine #06 / 1993 / ME / M • Risque Burlesque #1 / 1994 / IN / M • Rod Wood / 1995 / LE / M • The Romeo Syn-

drome / 1995 / SC / M • See-Thru / 1992 / LE / M • Sex Gallery / 1995 / WAV / M • Sex Trek #2: The Search For Sperm / 1991 / ME / M • Sex Trek #3: The Wrath Of Bob / 1992 / ME / M • Shanna's Final Fling / 1991 / ME / M • A Shot In The Mouth #2 / 1991 / ME / M • Sodom & Gomorrah / 1992 / OD / M • The Starlet / 1995 / SC / M • Tales From The Zipper #1 / 1993 / ME / M • Temptation Of Serenity / 1994 / WP / M • Titty Slickers #2 / 1994 / LE / M • Vampire's Kiss / 1993 / AVI / M • Western Nights / 1994 / WP / M • Whoomp! There She Is / 1993 / AVI / M • Wild Breed / 1995 / SC / M • Wrasslin She-Babes #11 / 1996 / SOW / M
J.B. FINE
High School Bunnies / 1978 / VC / M
J.B. HUNTER
N.Y. Video Magazine #09 / 1996 / OUP / M
J.C.
The French Canal / 1995 / DVP / G
J.C. BENNETT
Oriental Gang Bang / 1995 / HO / M
J.C. HAMILTON *see* **Star Index I**
J.C. PHILLIPS *see* **Star Index I**
J.D. FERGUSON
Battling Bruisers / 1993 / SBP / B • Bondage Constrictor / 1994 / VTF / B • Desert Of Fear / 1993 / BON / B • Foot Hookers / 1994 / SBP / B • A Gift Of Sam / 1992 / YOE / M • Samantha's Two-Way Dream / 1992 / BRE / M • Spanked And Whipped / 1994 / VTF / B • Taboo #12 / 1994 / MET / M • Taboo #13 / 1994 / IN / M • Tight Rope / 1993 / VTF / B
J.D. RAM
Bondage Watch #2 / 1996 / STM / B • Nasty Newcummers #11 / 1995 / MET / M
J.J.
HomeGrown Video #473: Furpie Feast #3 / 1997 / HOV / C
J.J. FLASH *see* **Star Index I**
J.J. FLUFF
Snatch Patch / 1995 / LE / M
J.J. GOODBAR *see* **Star Index I**
J.J. JONES
MASH'ed / cr75 / ALP / M
J.J. L-COOL
Small Top Bitches / 1996 / AVI / M
J.P.
America's Raunchiest Home Videos #08: Who Was That Masked Mn / 1991 / ZA / M • Spotlight: Poke Her / 1994 / SPV / M
J.P. ANTHONY *(Jonathan Lindero, Anthony Lindero, J.R. Anthony, A.P. Anthony, John Paul Anthony, Trick Tony, Jonathan Linders)*
Male who seems to be the companion of Valeria and obviously has an inflated idea of his own importance as he keeps changing his name.
Act Of Submission / 1995 / OUP / B • Anal Vision #16 / 1993 / LBO / M • The Anal-Europe Series #06: Anal Luck / 1993 / LV / M • The Backdoor Bandit / 1994 / LV / M • Backdoor Boogie / 1994 / TEG / M • Boogie In The Butt / 1993 / WIV / M • The Bridges Of Anal County / 1996 / PVO / C • Butt Darling / 1994 / WIV / M • Butt Watch #02 / 1993 / FH / M • Captain Bob's Lust Boat #2 / 1993 / FCP / M • Cousin Bubba Country Corn Porn #01 / 1994 / VIM / M • The Crack / 1994 / LV / M • Deep Cover / 1993 / WP / M • Dick & Jane Do The Strip / 1994 / AVI / M • A Dirty Western #2: Smoking Guns / 1994 / CV / M • Eclipse /

1993 / SC / M • Eight Is Never Enough / 1993 / ZA / M • Erotic Newcummers Vol 1 #2: Texas Twisters / 1993 / DR / M • Eroslut #1: French Tart / 1993 / CC / M • Explicit Entry / 1995 / LE / M • Extreme Passion / 1993 / WP / M • Florence Hump / 1994 / AFI / M • Forever Young / 1994 / VI / M • Hot Tight Asses #04 / 1993 / TCK / M • In X-Cess / 1994 / LV / M • Old Throat And D.P. / 1993 / FC / M • Perverted #1: The Babysitters / 1994 / ZA / M • Pussy Posse / 1993 / CC / M • Release Me Please / 1995 / VTF / B • Sex Academy #1 / 1993 / ONA / M • Starbangers #04 / 1993 / FPI / M • Tail Taggers #111 / 1993 / WV / M • Two Of A Kind / 1993 / PL / M • Ultimate Gang Bang #1 / 1994 / HW / M • Valeria Gets Fucked / 1995 / DIP / M • Voices In My Bed / 1993 / VI / M • Wilder At Heart / 1993 / ANA / M • Working Girl Gang-Bang / 1995 / GLI / M • Working Girls / 1995 / FH / M
J.P. ARMAND *see* **Jean Pierre Armand**
J.P. PARRADINE
Farewell Scarlett / 1976 / COM / M
J.P. RONNOCO
Golden Rod / 1996 / SPI / M • Lessons In Love / 1995 / SPI / M
J.R.
Sexy And 18 / 1987 / SE / M
J.R. ANTHONY *see* **J.P. Anthony**
J.R. CARRINGTON *(J.R. Cartwright, Daisy (J.R. Carr.))*
Not too pretty blonde with large enhanced tits, marginal skin and an attitude. Divorced and has two children as of mid 1995. Was originally a Pan-Am stewardess.
Adam & Eve's House Party #4 / 1996 / VC / M • All Amateur Perfect 10's / 1995 / LEI / M • The Anal Adventures Of Max Hardcore: High Voltage / 1994 / ZA / M • Anal Bad Girls / 1994 / ROB / F • Anal Camera #07 / 1995 / EVN / M • Anal Centerfold / 1995 / ROB / M • Anal Generation / 1995 / PE / M • Anal Innocence #3 / 1994 / ROB / M • Anal Insatiable / 1995 / ROB / M • Anal Maniacs #2 / 1994 / WP / M • Anal Misconduct / 1995 / VD / M • The Anal Nurse Scam / 1995 / CA / M • Anal Sweetheart / 1994 / ROB / M • Babe Watch #3 / 1995 / SC / M • Babe Watch #4 / 1995 / SC / M • Best Butt(e) In The West #2 / 1995 / CC / M • Beverly Hills Blondes #1 / 1995 / LV / M • Big & Busty Centerfolds / 1996 / DGD / F • Big Bust Babes #25 / 1995 / AFI / M • Blade / 1996 / MID / M • Blonde In Blue Flannel / 1995 / CA / M • Booty Queen / 1995 / ROB / M • The Bottom Line / 1995 / NIT / M • Breastman's Wild West Adventure / 1995 / EVN / M • Busty Babes In Heat #4 / 1995 / BTO / M • Butt Motors / 1995 / VC / M • Butt Sluts #4 / 1995 / ROB / F • Casting Call #09 / 1995 / SO / M • The Cumm Brothers #05: These Nuts For Hire / 1994 / OD / M • Cumming Of Ass / 1995 / TP / M • The Erotic Artist / 1995 / VC / M • Erotic World Of Anne Spice / 1995 / WV / M • Fire Down Below / 1994 / GO / M • Flesh Palace / 1995 / LBO / M • Freak Of The Week / 1996 / LIP / F • French Twist / 1995 / IN / M • Full Moon Madness / 1995 / CA / M • Gangbusters / 1995 / VC / M • Gangland Bangers / 1995 / VC / M • Girls Of The Ivy Leagues / 1994 / VT / M • Girly Video Magazine #1 / 1995 / BEP / M • Go Ahead...Eat Me! / 1995 / KWP / M • Hard Core Beginners #09 / 1995

/ LEI / M • Harry Horndog #29: Anal Lovers #5 / 1995 / FPI / M • Hawaii / 1995 / VI / M • Heatseekers / 1996 / PE / M • Hollywood Confidential / 1996 / SC / M • Hollywood Lesbians / 1995 / ROB / F • Indiscreet! Video Magazine #1 / 1995 / FH / M • Jizz Glazed Goo Guzzlers #2 / 1996 / NIT / C • Lessons In Love / 1995 / SPI / M • Max #02 / 1994 / FWE / M • Max Gold #1 / 1996 / XPR / C • Mission Phenomenal / 1996 / HIP / M • Mystique / 1996 / SC / M • Naked Ambition / 1995 / VC / M • Nasty Nymphos #07 / 1994 / ANA / M • The New Ass Masters #09 / 1996 / LEI / C • Night Stalker / 1995 / BBE / M • The Pleasure Girl / 1994 / GO / M • Plumb And Dumber / 1995 / PP / M • A Pool Party At Seymores #2 / 1995 / ULI / M • Private Video Magazine #21 / 1995 / OD / M • Pulp Friction / 1994 / PP / M • Pussy Hunt #04 / 1994 / LEI / M • Pussyman Auditions #07 / 1995 / SNA / M • Rebel Cheerleaders / 1995 / VI / M • Rectal Rodeo / 1994 / ZA / M • The Reel World #3: Trouble In Paradise / 1995 / FOR / M • Sex Therapy Ward / 1995 / LBO / M • Slippery Slopes / 1995 / ME / M • Sorority Stewardesses #1 / 1995 / PE / M • Sorority Stewardesses #2 / 1995 / PE / M • Surf Babes / 1995 / LE / M • Swedish Erotica #83 / 1995 / CA / M • Swing Into...Spring / 1995 / KWP / M • Tender Loving Care / 1995 / WP / M • Titty Town #2 / 1995 / HW / M • Topless Brain Surgeons / 1995 / LE / M • Two Sides Of A Lady / 1994 / HDE / M • Wet Faces #1 / 1997 / SC / C • While You Were Dreaming / 1995 / WV / M • Whore House / 1995 / IPI / M • Wicked Ways #1: Interview With The Anal Queen / 1994 / WP / M • Wild Breed / 1995 / SC / M

J.R. CARTWRIGHT *see J.R. Carrington*
J.R. KUFAHL *see Star Index I*
J.T.
Pearl Necklace: Amorous Amateurs #41 / 1994 / SEE / M • Pearl Necklace: Premier Sessions #03 / 1994 / SEE / M • Pearl Necklace: Thee Bush League #30 / 1994 / SEE / M
J.T. AMBROSE *see Tish Ambrose*
J.T. DENVER *(John Todd)*
Passion By Fire / 1986 / LAV / G
J.T. JAMES *see Star Index I*
J.T. SLOAN
Night Walk / 1995 / HIV / G
J.T. TAYLOR *(Jay Taylor)*
Boyfriend or husband of Dallas (1991). Long haired blonde who could be considered prettier than her.
The Anus Family / 1991 / CC / M • In Your Face #1 / 1992 / PL / M • Jungle Beaver / 1991 / HIO / M • Never Never Land / 1992 / PL / M • Regarding Hiney / 1991 / CC / M • Sexual Olympics #2: The Finals / 1992 / VT / M
J.W. GACY
Renegades #2) 1995 / SC / M
JACE ROCKER
Best Butt(e) In The West #1 / 1992 / CC / M • Cheeks #2: The Bitter End / 1989 / CC / M • Chinatown / 1994 / SC / M • Flesh For Fantasy / 1994 / CV / M • Future Sodom / 1988 / VD / M • A Little Dove-Tale / 1987 / IN / M • Loose Ends #6 / 1989 / 4P / M • Nightmare On Porn Street / 1988 / ME / M • Perils Of Paula / 1989 / CA / M • Queen Of Hearts #1 / 1987 / PL / M • Queen Of Hearts #2: Hearts On Fire / 1990 / PL / M •

Risque Burlesque #1 / 1994 / IN / M • St. X-Where #2 / 1988 / VD / M • The Starlet / 1995 / SC / M • Tailspin #3 / 1992 / VT / M • Throbbin' Hood / 1987 / VD / M • The Time Machine / 1996 / WP / M • Western Nights / 1994 / WP / M • The Young And The Wrestling #2 / 1989 / PL / M
JACK
Amateur Nights #10 / 1990 / HO / M • Asian Pussyman Auditions / 1996 / SNA / M • AVP #4005: The Ball Street Journal / 1991 / AVP / M • AVP #7022: 1 + 2 = 3 Times The Fun / 1991 / AVP / M • AVP #9153: The Monday Night Game / 1991 / AVP / M • Bondage Classix #17: The Millionaire / 198? / BON / B • FTV #42: Three Is Not Company / 1996 / FT / B • HomeGrown Video #465: Bong The Schlong / 1996 / HOV / M • Mr. Peepers Amateur Home Videos #71: I Dream Of Creamy / 1993 / LBO / M • New Faces, Hot Bodies #16 / 1994 / STP / M • Profiles #02 / 1995 / XPR / M • Pussyman Auditions #12 / 1995 / SNA / M • Pussyman Auditions #15 / 1995 / SNA / M • Pussyman Auditions #16 / 1995 / SNA / M • Pussyman Auditions #22 / 1996 / SNA / M • Pussyman Auditions #23 / 1996 / SNA / M • Pussyman's House Party #2 / 1996 / SNA / M • Submission Of Susie / 1993 / BIZ / B • Swedish Sex / 1996 / PL / M • Uncle Roy's Amateur Home Video #14 / 1992 / VIM / M • Uncle Roy's Amateur Home Video #15 / 1992 / VIM / M
JACK ACORN *see Star Index I*
JACK ALDIS
Erotic Fantasies #5 / 1983 / CV / C • Eruption / 1977 / VCX / M
JACK ALMS *see Star Index I*
JACK AMBERG *see Star Index I*
JACK ARMSTRONG *see Star Index I*
JACK BAILY *see Jack Baker*
JACK BAKER *(B.J. Baily, Jack Baily, John Anthony Bailey)*
Black. Died Nov 13, 1994 from liver cancer, aged 47.
The Adventures Of Dick Black, Black Dick / 1987 / DR / M • Aussie Exchange Girls / 1990 / PM / M • Bare Essence / 1989 / EA / M • Between The Cheeks #1 / 1985 / VC / M • Big Bust Babes #20 / 1994 / AFI / M • Black & White Affair / 1984 / VD / M • Black Babes In Heat / 1993 / VIM / M • Black Bad Girls / 1985 / PLY / M • Black Beauties #1 / 1992 / VIM / M • Black Beauties #2 / 1992 / VIM / M • Black Beauty (Coast To Coast) / 1994 / CC / M • Black Bunbusters / 1985 / VC / M • Black Gangbangers #01 / 1994 / HW / M • Black Gangbangers #02 / 1995 / HW / M • Black Jack City #3 / 1993 / HW / M • Black Magic #1 / 1993 / VIM / M • Black Throat / 1985 / VC / M • Black Velvet #2 / 1993 / CC / M • Blacks & Blondes #05 / 1986 / WV / M • Blacks & Blondes: The Movie / 1989 / WV / M • Blacks Have More Fun / 1985 / AVC / M • Boomerwang / 1992 / MID / M • Born To Run / 1985 / WV / M • Breakin' In / 1986 / WV / M • Cheeks #2: The Bitter End / 1989 / CC / M • Chocolate Candy #1 / 1984 / VD / M • Chocolate Dreams (Venus 99) / 1987 / V99 / M • Cinderella / 1977 / VAM / S • Club Exotica #1 / 1985 / WV / M • Club Exotica #2 / 1985 / WV / M • Coffee & Cream / 1984 / AVC / M • The Color Black / 1986 / WET / M • Dance Fire / 1989 / EA / M • Danger-Ass / 1992 / MID / M • Dark Alleys #01 / 1992 / FC / M•

Debbie Class Of '88 / 1987 / CC / M • Debbie Does Dishes #3 / 1987 / AVC / M • Debbie For President / 1988 / CC / M • Debbie Goes To Hawaii / 1988 / VD / C • Deep Inside Keisha / 1994 / VC / C • Deep Throat Fantasies / 1989 / VD / M • Detroit Dames / 1988 / DR / C • Devil In Miss Jones #3: A New Beginning / 1986 / VC / M • Devil In Miss Jones #4: The Final Outrage / 1987 / VC / M • Double Penetration #2 / 1986 / WV / C • Double Penetration #3 / 1986 / WV / C • Double Penetration Virgins #03 / 1994 / LE / M • Dr Blacklove #1 / 1987 / CC / M • Dr F #2: Bad Medicine / 1990 / WV / M • Ebony Erotica #01: Black Narcissys / 1993 / GO / M • Ebony Orgies / 1987 / SE / C • Farmers Daughters / 1985 / WV / M • The Final Taboo / 1988 / CA / M • For Love And Money / 1987 / CV / S • Forbidden Bodies / 1986 / HU / M • Girlz In The Hood #3: Erotic Justice / 1993 / HW / M • The Godmother #1 / 1987 / VC / M • The Godmother #2 / 1988 / VC / M • Hill Street Blacks #1 / 1985 / 4R / M • Horror In The Wax Museum / 1983 / TAO / B • Hot Chocolate #1 / 1984 / TAG / M • Hot Nights At The Blue Note Cafe / 1985 / WV / M • Hotel California / 1986 / WV / M • Hotter Chocolate / 1986 / AVC / M • House Of Blue Dreams / 1985 / WV / M • In Search Of The Perfect 10 / 1987 / MAE / S • Inches For Keisha / 1988 / WV / C • Innocence Lost / 1988 / CA / M • Knights In White Satin / 1987 / SUV / C • The Legend Of Reggie D. / 1989 / EA / M • Let Me Tell Ya 'Bout White Chicks / 1985 / VC / M • A Little Bit Of Honey / 1987 / WET / M • Living Doll / 1987 / WV / M • The Lust Potion Of Doctor F / 1985 / WV / M • Malibu Spice / 1991 / VC / M • Marilyn Chambers' Private Fantasies #2 / 1983 / CA / M • The Master Of Pleasure / 1988 / VD / M • Money, Money, Money / 1993 / FD / M • New Wave Hookers #1 / 1984 / VC / M • New Wave Hookers #2 / 1991 / VC / M • The Nicole Stanton Story #1 / 1989 / CA / M • The Nicole Stanton Story #2 / 1989 / CA / M • The Night Of The Headhunter / 1985 / WV / M • Nymphette #1 / 1986 / WV / M • Obsession / 1985 / HO / M • Only The Very Best On Video / 1992 / VC / C • Oral Majority Black #1 / 1987 / WV / C • Pretty Peaches #3 / 1989 / VC / M • The Return Of Dr Blacklove / 1996 / CC / M • Return To Sex 5th Avenue / 1985 / WV / M • Rump-Shaker #2 / 1993 / HW / M • Salsa Break / 1989 / EA / M • Satisfaction Jackson / 1988 / CA / M • Screwdriver / 1988 / CC / C • Sex 5th Avenue / 1985 / WV / M • Sex Beat / 1985 / WV / M • Showgirls / 1985 / SE / M • Slut Safari #1 / 1994 / FC / M • Slut Safari #2 / 1994 / FC / M • Slut Safari #3 / 1994 / FC / M • Space Cadet / 1989 / IN / M • Star Struck / 1991 / AFV / M • Suck Channel / 1991 / VIM / M • Sweet Chocolate / 1987 / VD / M • Thrill Street Blues / 1985 / WV / M • Toys 4 Us #2 / 1987 / WV / C • Tracy In Heaven (Orig 1985) / 1985 / WV / M • Tracy In Heaven (Rewrite) / 1986 / WV / M • Truck Stop Angel / 1994 / CC / M • Ubangis On Uranus / 1987 / WV / M • VCA Previews #4 / 1988 / VC / C • Venus Of The Nile / 1991 / WV / M • White Bun Busters / 1985 / VC / M • White Trash, Black Splash / 1988 / WET / M • Yankee Seduction / 1984 / WV / M

JACK BARON see Herschel Savage
JACK BEAR see Star Index I
JACK BENSON see Star Index I
JACK BIRCH
Candy Goes To Hollywood / 1979 / VCX / M • Sweet Savage / 1978 / ALP / M
JACK BLACK see Herschel Savage
JACK BLAKE see Herschel Savage
JACK BRIER
Swap Meet / 1984 / VD / M
JACK BROWN see Star Index I
JACK CHRISTIANO
ABA: Double Feature #5 / 1996 / ALP / M • Night Of Submission / 1976 / BIZ / M
JACK CLARK
[Sex Secretaries / 197? / ... / M
JACK CUMMINGS
Dirty & Kinky Mature Women #06 / 1995 / C69 / M
JACK D'ARCY see Star Index I
JACK DEHAVEN see Star Index I
JACK DORAL
Huge Grant On The Sunset Strip / 1995 / EVN / M
JACK DROGON
Fan Fuxxx #1 / 1996 / DWV / M
JACK DUSQUESNE see Star Index I
JACK E. LAYTON
Domina #8 / 1996 / LBO / B
JACK ENTMAN see Star Index I
JACK FRANK
The Second Coming Of Eva / 1974 / ALP / M • [Molly / 1977 / ... / S
JACK GATT (Jack Gatteau, Jacques Gato, Jacques Gatos)
Body Love / 1976 / CA / M • A Change Of Partners / 1982 / CA / M • Erotic Pleasures / 1976 / CA / M • Extreme Close-Up / 1981 / VC / M • Hot Action! / 1982 / CA / M • [Education Anglaise / 1982 / ... / S • [Indecences 1930 / 1977 / ... / M
JACK GATTEAU see Jack Gatt
JACK GOFF see Jake Barnes
JACK GOODING see Star Index I
JACK HAMMER
Alumni Girls / 1996 / GO / M • Anal Party Girls / 1996 / GV / M • Anal Pool Party / 1996 / PE / M • Anal Talisman / 1996 / ZA / M • Anal, Facial & Interracial / 1996 / FC / M • Analtown USA #03 / 1995 / NIT / M • Analtown USA #05 / 1995 / NIT / M • Analtown USA #09 / 1995 / NIT / M • Analtown USA #12 / 1996 / NIT / M • Bel Air Babes / 1996 / SUF / M • Beyond Reality #2: Anal Expedition / 1996 / EXQ / M • Bi Bi American Style / cr85 / MET / G • Big Bust Babes #33 / 1995 / AFI / M • Big Bust Babes #35 / 1996 / AFI / M • Big Bust Babes #36 / 1996 / AFI / M • Brian Sparks: Virtually Unreal #2 / 1996 / ALD / M • Buffy's New Boobs / 1996 / CIN / M • Cherry Poppers #14: Teeny Tongues / 1996 / ZA / M • Cirque Du Sex #1 / 1996 / VT / M • Cockpit / 1996 / SC / M • Cum Buttered Corn Holes #1 / 1996 / NIT / C • Decadence / 1986 / VD / M • DPTV: Double Penetration Television / 1996 / SUF / M • EXXXtra Parts: Interview With A Hermaphrodite / 1995 / PL / M • Fashion sluts #5: Ethnic Ecstasy / 1995 / ABS / M • Fashion Sluts #6 / 1995 / ABS / M • Fashion Sluts #8 / 1996 / ABS / M • Final Obsession / 1996 / LE / M • Flesh / 1996 / EA / M • Fresh Meat (John Leslie) #2 / 1995 / EA / M • Gangbang Girl #16 / 1995 / ANA / M • Get Lucky / 1996 / NIT / M • Going Down Under / 1993

/ OD / M • Harem Girls / 1986 / SE / M • Hawaiian Buttwatch / 1995 / SUF / M • Hollywood Amateurs #22 / 1995 / MID / M • Hollywood Amateurs #25 / 1995 / MID / M • Hollywood Amateurs #26 / 1995 / MID / M • Hollywood Amateurs #29 / 1996 / MID / M • Hollywood Amateurs #30 / 1996 / MID / M • Hollywood Amateurs #31 / 1996 / MID / M • Hot Honey / 1977 / VXP / M • House Of Anal / 1995 / NOT / M • Illicit Affairs / 1996 / XC / M • In Your Face #3 / 1995 / PL / M • Interracial Anal #06 / 1995 / AFI / M • Interview's Hard Bodied Harlots / 1996 / LV / M • Interview: Chocolate Treats / 1995 / LV / M • Interview: Dark And Delicious / 1996 / LV / M • Kinky Debutante Interviews #08 / 1995 / IP / M • Kool Ass / 1996 / BOT / M • Lady Luck / 1995 / PMV / M • The Line Up / 1996 / CDI / M • Mike Hott: #342 Three-Sum Sluts #10 / 1995 / MHV / M • Mike Hott: #361 Girls Who Swallow Cum #04 / 1996 / MHV / C • Mike Hott: #376 Cunt Of The Month: Ashley Shye / 1996 / MHV / M • Naughty / 1996 / LV / M • The New Babysitter / 1995 / GO / M • Next...! / 1996 / CDI / M • Night Stalker / 1995 / BBE / M • Perverted Stories #03 / 1995 / JMP / M • Perverted Stories #04 / 1995 / JMP / M • Perverted Stories #07 / 1996 / JMP / M • Philmore Butts Goes Wild! / 1996 / SUF / M • Philmore Butts Hawaiian Anal Adventure / 1995 / SUF / M • Philmore Butts Las Vegas Vacation / 1995 / SUF / M • Pierced Punctured And Perverted / 1995 / FC / M • Poop Shute Debutantes / 1995 / LBO / M • Pretty Anal Ladies / 1996 / ANE / M • Pumphouse Sluts / 1996 / CC / M • Rambone: The First Time / 1985 / JOH / M • Roly Poly Gang Bang / 1995 / HW / M • Rumpman's Backdoor Sailing / 1996 / HW / M • Saki's Bedtime Stories / 1995 / TTV / M • Samantha & Company / 1996 / PL / M • Sex Freaks / 1995 / EA / M • Sex On The Beach Hawaiian Style #1 / 1995 / ULP / M • Sex On The Beach Hawaiian Style #2 / 1995 / ULP / M • Sexual Overdrive / 1996 / LE / M • The Spectacular Denni O'Brien / 1995 / SP / M • Steam / 1996 / ULP / M • The Strippers / 1995 / GO / M • Stripping / 1995 / NIT / M • Stuff Your Ass #2 / 1995 / JMP / M • Stuff Your Face #4 / 1996 / JMP / M • Trouble In Paradise / 1996 / ULP / M • The Twin Peaks Of Mount Fuji / 1996 / SUF / M • Unbalanced Chemicals / 1996 / SUF / M • Yin Yang Oriental Love Bang #2 / 1996 / SUF / M • Young And Anal #2 / 1995 / JMP / M • Young And Anal #3 / 1995 / JMP / M • Young And Anal #4 / 1996 / JMP / M
JACK HANDY see Star Index I
JACK HARRIS see Benny Moore
JACK HAYS see Star Index I
JACK HOFFMAN
A Is For Asia / 1996 / 4P/ M • Anal Anarchy / 1995 / VC / M • Cyberanal / 1995 / VC / M • Internal Affairs / 1995 / VI / M • Twist Of Fate / 1996 / WP / M
JACK LAROO
Teenage Pajama Party / 1977 / VC / M
JACK LENNAN
Prey Of A Call Girl / 1975 / ALP / M
JACK LEROY see Star Index I
JACK LIVERMORE see Ric Lutz
JACK LYNN
Bucky Beaver's XXX Dragon Art Theatre Double Feature #06 / 1996 / SOW / M •

Finishing School / 1975 / SOW / M
JACK MANN (Bruce Kerns)
Wimpy looking Hispanic male with a crew cut and a moustache who always seems to appear with Chelsea Ann.
Amazing Nympho Stories / 1995 / TEG / M • Anal Vision #10 / 1993 / LBO / M • Beach Bum Amateur's #25 / 1993 / MID / M • Bobby Hollander's Sweet Cheeks #106 / 1993 / QUA / M • Butt Woman #4 / 1993 / FH / M • Casting Call #03 / 1993 / SO / M • The Girls From Hootersville #01 / 1993 / SFP / M • Margarita On The Rocks / 1994 / SFP / M • Nympho Zombie Coeds / 1993 / VIM / M • Pearl Necklace: Thee Bush League #09 / 1993 / SEE / M • Sodomania #04: Further On Down The Road / 1993 / EL / M • What's In It 4 Me / 1995 / TEG / M
JACK MARLOWE see Star Index I
JACK MASON
Fantasy Follies #1 / 1983 / VC / M • Flesh Pond / 1983 / VC / M • Foxholes / 1983 / SE / M • Sensuous Moments / 1983 / VIV/ M • You Turn Me On / 1986 / LIM / M • Young And Restless / 1983 / VIV / M
JACK MEHOFF
R & R / 1994 / VC / M
JACK MICHAELS
Shape Up For Sensational Sex / 1985 / SE / M
JACK MONROE
Tigresses...And Other Man-Eaters / 1979 / VXP / M
JACK MORIN
Let's Talk Anal / 1996 / ESF / M
JACK NASH see Jim Holliday
JACK NEWTON see Star Index I
JACK NICHOLS
All About Sex / 1970 / AR / M • Satisfaction / 1974 / CDC / M • Sex U.S.A / 1970 / SEP / M
JACK NITE see Star Index I
JACK O'BRIEN
The Bride's Initiation / 1976 / VIP / M
JACK OFF see Star Index I
JACK RABBIT
Let's Talk Anal / 1996 / ESF / M
JACK RENAUD see Star Index I
JACK ROGERS
Backdoor Club / 1986 / CA / M
JACK ROVEN
Gina, The Foxy Lady / cr79 / COV / M • Too Many Cocks In Me! / 1992 / MET / M
JACK S. MARGOLIS
Classical Romance / 1984 / MAP / M • Death Dancers / 1993 / 3SR / S
JACK SHEEPE see Jake Steed
JACK SHUGG see Star Index I
JACK SHUTE
Kate And The Indians / 1980 / SE / M
JACK SLADE
Ole / 1971 / KIT / M
JACK SLATER
Fresh Meat (John Leslie) #3 / 1996 / EA / M • International Affairs / 1994 / PL / M
JACK SPRAT see Star Index I
JACK STEPHEN see Star Index I
JACK STRICKER
Private Film #05 / 1993 / OD / M • Private Film #09 / 1994 / OD / M • Private Film #17 / 1994 / OD / M • Private Film #23 / 1995 / OD / M
JACK STUART
Princess Seka / 1980 / VC / M
JACK TAYLOR
Eugenie...The Story Of Her Journey Into

Perversion / 1969 / ... / S • Succubus / 1967 / ... / S • Swedish Nympho Slaves / 1977 / LUM / S • Wild Child / 1991 / BRU / S • [The Loves Of Irina / 1973 / PS / S

JACK THOMAS *see* **Zake Thomas**

JACK THOMPSON
Flesh + Blood / 1985 / VES / S • The Taking Of Christina / 1975 / NGV / M

JACK TONAS *see Star Index I*

JACK TRIESTE *see Star Index I*

JACK U. LATE
Mondo Bitches / 1991 / LBO / B

JACK VITEK *see Star Index I*

JACK WEAVER *see Star Index I*

JACK WEBB *see Star Index I*

JACK WEBER
Old Fashioned Spankings / 1991 / BON / B

JACK WILD
Erotic Dimensions: Explicit / 1982 / NSV / M • [The Pied Piper / 1971 / ... / S

JACK WRANGLER *(Jamie St. John)*
Married to Margaret Whiting, supposedly a star from the forties.
The 8th Annual Erotic Film Awards / 1984 / SE / C • Blue Magic / 1981 / QX / M • Bon Appetit / 1980 / QX / M • C.O.D. / 1981 / VES / S • China Sisters / 1978 / SE / M • Debbie Does Dallas #2 / 1980 / VC / M • Devil In Miss Jones #2 / 1983 / VC / M • Dirty Looks / 1982 / VC / C • Electric Blue: Cosmic Coeds / 1985 / CA / M • Electric Blue: World Nudes Tonight / 1985 / CA / C • The Filthy Rich / 1981 / CA / M • Games Women Play #1 / 1980 / CA / M • In Love / 1983 / VC / M • Jack 'n' Jill #1 / 1979 / VXP / M • Jack 'n' Jill #2 / 1984 / VC / M • Misbehavin' / 1979 / VXP / M • Rising Star / 1985 / CA / M • Roommates / 1982 / VXP / M • Summer In Heat / 1979 / VEP / M • Twilight Pink #2 / 1982 / VC / M • The Voyeur / 1985 / VC / M

JACK WRIGHT *(Mark McGuire, Mark McIntyre)*
Mark McGuire is from **Cry For Cindy**.
Blondes Have More Fun / 1980 / SE / M • China Sisters / 1978 / SE / M • Cry For Cindy / 1976 / AR / M • Easy / 1978 / CV / M • Erotic Fantasies #4 / 1983 / CV / C • Expectations / 1977 / SE / M • My First Time / 1976 / GO / M • Naked Afternoon / 1976 / CV / M • One Way At A Time / 1979 / CA / M • Sex World / 1978 / SE / M

JACKE STAR
Why Gentlemen Prefer Blondes / 1983 / HO / C

JACKI ANNE *see Star Index I*

JACKI GEEWHIZ *see Star Index I*

JACKI OH *see Star Index I*

JACKIE
A&B GB#024: Black Lover / 1992 / A&B / M • Amateurama #01 / 1992 / RTP / M • Amateurama #04 / 1992 / RTP / M • Blue Vanities #511 / 1992 / FFL / M • Blue Vanities #526 / 1993 / FFL / M • Blue Vanities #538 / 1993 / FFL / M • Blue Vanities #542 / 1994 / FFL / M • Blue Vanities #564 / 1994 / FFL / M • Blue Vanities #574 / 1996 / FFL / M • Breast Of Britain #6 / 1990 / BTO / S • Breast Of Britain #9 / 1990 / BTO / M • British Butt Search / 1995 / VC / M • Erotic Eye / 1995 / DGD / S • The Good Stuff / 1989 / BON / C • Hollywood Amateurs #15 / 1995 / MID / M • Home Maid Memories #2 / 1994 / BON / C • Love Letters / 1992 / ELP / F • Odyssey Triple Play #03: Anal Olympics / 1992 / OD / M • Pearl Necklace:

Thee Bush League: The Best Of Oral #01 / 1993 / SEE / C • Raw Talent: Sam Shaft's Best Anal Thrusts / 1992 / RTP / C • Sam Shaft's Best Anal Thrusts / 1994 / RTP / C • Service Call Bondage / 199? / BON / B • Sex Slave / 1995 / FGV / B • Super Sampler #5 / 1994 / LOD / C • SVE: Jackie's Gang Bang / 1993 / SVE / M • SVE: Jackie's Job Interview / 1993 / SVE / M • Wake-Up Call #2 / 1987 / BON / B

JACKIE BEARDSLEY
American Sex Fantasy / 1975 / IHV / M

JACKIE BEAT
The Best Little He/She House In Texas / 1993 / HSV / G • Blue Movie / 1995 / WP / M • Stardust #1 / 1996 / VI / M

JACKIE BUSHKIN *see Star Index I*

JACKIE CHRISTINA *see Star Index I*

JACKIE DESMOND *see Star Index I*

JACKIE JONES *see Star Index I*

JACKIE LENZ *see Star Index I*

JACKIE LOREN
The Jackie Loren Makeup Video / 1991 / WOW / G

JACKIE LYNN
More Dirty Debutantes #40 / 1995 / 4P / M

JACKIE MORALS *see Star Index I*

JACKIE NURA *see Star Index I*

JACKIE O'MED *see Star Index I*

JACKIE O'NEILL *see Star Index I*

JACKIE RICHARDS
The Girl Grabbers / 1968 / SOW / S • Hungry Mouth / 19?? / VXP / M • Love Is Where It's At / 1967 / SOW / S • She Came On The Bus / 1969 / SOW / S

JACKIE SAIRS JAMES
Honeypie / 1975 / VC / M

JACKIE TRISTAN *see Star Index I*

JACKIE WEAVER *see Star Index I*

JACKLIN MORINA *see* **Fay Burd**

JACKLYN JOHNSON
Little Darlings / 1981 / VEP / M

JACKLYN LICK *see* **Jacqueline Lick**

JACKLYN PALMER
Bondage Magic / 1996 / JAM / B • Bondage Models #1 / 1996 / JAM / B • Bondage Models #2 / 1996 / JAM / B • Jacklyn's Attitude Adjustment / 1995 / JAM / B • Mistress Jacklyn's Bondage / 1995 / JAM / B • Who's In Charge / 1995 / JAM / B

JACKSON *see Star Index I*

JACKSON ST LOUIS *see* **Henri Pachard**

JACKY ARNAL *see Star Index I*

JACKY PAGE *(Jacky Rose, Diamond (Jacky Page))*
Not too pretty redhead with lots of tattoos and particularly serpents on her outside hips/thighs.
Jacky's Revenge #1 / 1993 / BON / B • Jacky's Revenge #2 / 1994 / BON / B • Twisted Jacky / 1993 / BON / B

JACKY RIGBY *see Star Index I*

JACKY ROSE *see* **Jacky Page**

JACLINE MOREAU *see Star Index I*

JACQUE
Club Deb #3 / 1996 / MET / M

JACQUELINE *(Clair Tyler, Jane Tyler (Jacquel), Janette Tyler, Crimson, Jacqueline St Clair, Chrimson, Jacqueline Gorman)*
Born June 13, 1965. In 1990 was 36-25-35 and 5'6 1/2".
American Garter / 1993 / VC / M • Another Dirty Western / 1992 / AFV / M • At The Mercy Of Mistress Jacqueline / 1993 / STM / B • Babes With Attitudes / 1990 / EVN / M

• Bat Bitch #1 / 1989 / FAZ / M • Bat Bitch #2 / 1990 / FAZ / M • The Big Tease #2 / 1990 / VC / M • The Bimbo #1 / 1992 / AFV / M • Bimbo Bowlers From Boston / 1990 / ZA / M • Black In The Saddle / 1990 / ZA / M • Blazing Nova / 1989 / LV / M • Blue Angel / 1992 / AFV / M • Blue Angel / 1992 / AFV / M • Blue Moon / 1992 / AFV / M • Born For Porn / 1989 / FAZ / M • Bound To Pay / 1995 / CS / B • Bratgirl / 1989 / VI / M • Business And Pleasure / 1992 / AFV / M • Butt Seriously Folks / 1994 / AFV / M • Class Act / 1989 / WAV / M • Club Head (EVN) #3 / 1992 / EVN / C • Date With The Devil / 1989 / FAZ / M • Devil In The Blue Dress / 1989 / ME / M • The French Connexxxion / 1991 / VC / M • Friday Night Fever / 1989 / LV / M • Gere Up / 1991 / LV / C • The God Daughter #2 / 1991 / AFV / M • Guess Who Came To Dinner / 1992 / AFV / M • Hate To See You Go / 1990 / VC / M • Head Again / 1992 / AFV / M • Heart Breaker / 1989 / LE / M • Heavenly Hyapatia / 1990 / VI / M • Hollywood Dreams / 1993 / ... / S • Housewife From Hell / 1994 / TRI / S • I Do #1 / 1989 / VI / M • Jailhouse Blue / 1990 / SO / M • Journey Into Submission / 1990 / BIZ / B • Kym Wilde's On The Edge #07 / 1994 / RB / B • Ladies Lovin' Ladies #2 / 1992 / AR / F • Ladies Lovin' Ladies #4 / 1992 / AFV / F • Laying Down The Law #1 / 1992 / AFV / M • Laying Down The Law #2 / 1992 / AFV / M • Leather Lust Mistress / 1989 / BIZ / B • Legend #1 / 1990 / LE / M • Lesson In Spanking / 1996 / VTF / B • Love Scenes #3 / 1993 / B/F / S • Low Blows: The Private Collection / 1989 / ME / M • Mad Maxine / 1992 / AFV / M • Masterpiece / 1990 / VI / M • Mummy Dearest #1 / 1990 / LV / M • Night At The Waxworks / 1990 / IF / M • No Boys Allowed / 1991 / VC / F • Nymphobrat / 1989 / VI / M • Oh, What A Night! / 1990 / VC / M • Oral Addiction / 1989 / LV / M • Oral Support / 1989 / V99 / M • Performance / 1990 / VI / M • Professor Butts / 1994 / SBP / F • Quickies / 1992 / AFV / M • Racquel's Addiction / 1991 / VC / M • Radioactive / 1990 / VIP / M • Retail Slut / 1989 / LV / M • Rites Of Passage: Trans formation Of A Slave / 1992 / BIZ / B • Rock & Roll Fantasies / 1992 / FL / M • Scandalous / 1989 / CC / M • Sex Charades / 1990 / VEX / M • Slumber Party / 1990 / LV / M • Sodomania: Slop Shots / 1996 / EL / C • Sorceress / 1990 / GO / M • Student Fetish Videos: Best of Enema #03 / 1994 / PRE / C • Student Fetish Videos: The Enema #13 / 1994 / PRE / B • Student Fetish Videos: Spanking #12 / 1994 / PRE / B • Student Fetish Videos: Tickling #08 / 1994 / SFV / B • Swedish Erotica Featurettes #3 / 1989 / CA / M • Swingers Ink / 1990 / VC / M • A Tall Dark Stranger / 1990 / LV / M • Tattle Tales / 1989 / SE / M • Taylor Wayne's World / 1992 / AFV / M • This Bun's For You / 1989 / FAN / M • Tight Asses / 1994 / RB / B • Tinseltown Wives / 1992 / AFV / M • Triangle / 1989 / VI / M • Trouble / 1989 / VD / M • True Love / 1989 / VI / M • Veil / 1990 / VI / M • Virgin Busters / 1989 / LV / M • Wildfire / 1989 / EVN / M

JACQUELINE (HUNG)
Buttwoman In Budapest / 1992 / EA / M • The Coming Of Nikita / 1995 / EL / M •

Hamlet: For The Love Of Ophelia #1 / 1996 / IP / M • The Hungarian Connection / 1992 / EA / M • Sluts 'n' Angels In Budapest / 1994 / EL / M • Sodomania #11: In Your Face / 1994 / EL / M

JACQUELINE (OTHER)
The Best Of East Coast Sluts / 1995 / PL / C • Magma: Anal Teenies / 1994 / MET / M • Victim / 1996 / JAM / B

JACQUELINE BARDOT *see Star Index I*

JACQUELINE BEUDANT *see Star Index I*

JACQUELINE BRODIE
Sodom & Gomorrah / 1974 / MIT / M

JACQUELINE BROOKS *(Lenora Bruce)*
Brunette with shoulder length curly hair, pretty face, medium/large tits, womanly body.
Backdoor Babes / 1985 / WET / M • Bad Girls #1 / 1981 / GO / M • Girls Of Cell Block F / 1985 / WV / M • Gourmet Quickies: Trinity Loren / Jacquelyn Brooks #726 / 1985 / GO / C • GVC: Party Girl #102 / 1981 / GO / M • This Butt's For You / 1986 / PME / M • Toys 4 Us #2 / 1987 / WV / C • Tracy Dick / 1985 / WV / M • Transaction #1 / 1986 / WET / M • Wine Me, Dine Me, 69 Me / 1989 / COL / C

JACQUELINE DUBONNET
The Starmaker / 1982 / VC / M

JACQUELINE DUPREE *see Star Index I*

JACQUELINE FOSKETT
Resurrection Of Eve / 1973 / MIT / M

JACQUELINE FOURNIER *see Star Index I*

JACQUELINE GORMAN *see Jacqueline*

JACQUELINE JANIN *see Jacqueline Laurent*

JACQUELINE LAURENT *(Jacqueline Janin, Madelaine Laforet)*
French, born 1920 in Brienne-le-Chateau.
Bel Ami / 1976 / VXP / M • Practice Makes Perfect / 1975 / QX / M • [Hungry Young Women / 1977 / ALP / M • [Le Journal Intime D'Une Nymphomane / 1972 / ... / M

JACQUELINE LICK *(Jacklyn Lick, Paisley Lick)*
Long straight brown hair, medium enhanced tits (scars visible), large multi-colored tattoo on outside left thigh and another on her right belly/pussy, flabby belly probably due to tint production, not a tight body, marginal face that looks like a coarser version of Rebecca Lord. 5'0" tall, 100lbs and 27 years old in 1996. Has been a dancer since the age of 18.
Airotica / 1996 / SC / M • Anal Maniacs #5 / 1996 / WP / M • Badgirls #7: Lust Confined / 1995 / VI / M • Crew Sluts / 1996 / NOT / M • Cumback Pussy #2: Crawling Back For More / 1996 / EL / M • Frendz? #2 / 1996 / RAS / M • Hollywood Spa / 1996 / WP / M • Jinx / 1996 / WP / M • Pick Up Lines #08 / 1996 / WP / M • Sinister Sister / 1997 / WP / M • Sunset's Anal & D.P. Gangbang / 1996 / PL / M • Waterbabies #3 / 1996 / CC / M

JACQUELINE LOREN *see Jacqueline Lorians*

JACQUELINE LORIANS *(Monique Perry, Jacqueline Loren)*
Not the same as the Monique Perry (or Perri) of the 92/93 era. Quite pretty but later a bit flabby brunette with large tits.
All American Girls #1 / 1982 / CA / M • Amos & Candy / 1987 / VCR / C • Anatomy Of A Male Stripper / 1990 / 4P / S • Angel

Gets Even / 1987 / FAN / M • Babylon Blue / 1983 / VXP / M • Bad Girls #2 / 1983 / GO / M • Ball Busters / 1984 / CV / M • Ball In The Family / 1988 / VWA / M • Ball Street / 1988 / CA / M • Beauty And The Beast #1 / 1988 / VC / M • Black Widow / 1988 / WV / M • The Blonde Goddess / 1982 / VXP / M • Blue Ice / 1985 / CA / M • Blue Vanities #029 / 1988 / FFL / M • Blue Vanities #055 / 1988 / FFL / M • Bouncin' In The U.S.A. / 1986 / H&S / S • Broadcast Nudes / 1988 / EVN / M • Caballero Preview Tape #2 / 1983 / CA / C • Caught In The Act / 1987 / WV / M • Charm School / 1986 / VI / M • Classical Romance / 1984 / MAP / M • Club Sex / 1989 / GO / M • Daddy's Darling Daughters / 1986 / PL / M • The Desk Top Dolls / 1990 / BAD / C • Devil In Miss Jones #2 / 1983 / VC / M • Dirty Girls / 1984 / MIT / M • Double Messages / 1987 / MOV / M • Erotic City / 1985 / CV / M • Erotic Encounters / 1985 / LIM / C • Fantasies Of Jennifer Faye / 1983 / GO / M • Gettin' Ready / 1985 / CDI / M • Girls Of The Hollywood Hills / 1983 / VD / M • Goin' Down / 1985 / VC / M • Golden Girls #04 / 1981 / CA / M • Golden Girls #12 / 1984 / CA / M • Golden Girls #21 / 1984 / CA / M • Golden Girls #22 / 1984 / CA / M • Good Evening Vietnam / 1987 / WV / M • The Good, The Bad, And The D-Cup / 1991 / GO / C • Gourmet Quickies: Monique Perry #716 / 1985 / GO / C • GVC: Pool Service #105 / cr84 / GO / M • GVC: Women Who Love Women #115 / cr83 / GO / F • Hot Girls In Love / 1984 / VIV / C • Hot Stuff / 1984 / VXP / M • I Want To Be Bad / 1984 / CV / M • The Idol / 1985 / WV / M • In The Pink / 1983 / CA / M • Intimate Couples / 1984 / VCX / M • Just Another Pretty Face / 1985 / AVC / M • K.U.N.T.-TV / 1988 / WV / M • Ladies Of The 80's / 1985 / PV / M • Lesbian Lovers / 1988 / GO / F • Lesbian Nymphos / 1988 / GO / C • The Life & Loves Of Nikki Charm / 1986 / MAL / M • Limited Edition #23 / 1983 / AVC / M • Little Red Riding Hood / 1988 / WV / M • Loose Lifestyles / 1988 / CA / M • Losing Control / 1985 / CDI / M • Love Roots / 1987 / LIM / M • The Love Scene / 1985 / CDI / M • Lust And The Law / 1991 / GO / C • Lusty Detective / 1988 / VEX / M • Lusty Ladies #02 / 1983 / 4P / M • Lusty Ladies #12 / 1984 / 4P / M • Lusty Ladies #14 / 1984 / 4P / F • Making It Big / 1984 / CV / M • Maximum #2 / 1982 / CA / M • Nicki / 1987 / VI / M • Night Moods / 1985 / AVC / M • Nightdreams #1 / 1981 / CA / M • One Hot Night Of Passion / 1985 / COL / C • Only The Best #2 / 1989 / CV / C • Only The Best Of Peepers / 1992 / CV / C • Only The Best Of Women With Women / 1988 / CV / C • Parliament: Dildo Babes #2 / 1988 / PM / F • Parliament: Tops & Bottoms #1 / 1988 / PM / F • Passionate Heiress / 1987 / CA / M • Peek-A-Boo / 1987 / VEX / M • The PTX Club / 1988 / GO / M • Reamin' Reunion / 1988 / CC / M • Romeo And Juliet #2 / 1988 / WV / M • Sex For Secrets / 1987 / VCR / M • Sexaholic / 1985 / AVC / M • Sleepless Nights / 1984 / VIV / M • Soul Kiss This / 1988 / VCR / C • Suze's Centerfolds #8 / 1984 / CA / M • Suzie Creamcheese / 1988 / VWA / M • Swedish Erotica #54 / 1984 / CA / M • A Taste Of Stephanie / 1990 / PIN / C • This Stud's For

You / 1986 / MAP / C • Thrilled To Death / 1988 / REP / S • The Touchables / 1988 / CC / M • Traci's Big Trick / 1987 / VAS / M • Tracy In Heaven (Orig 1985) / 1985 / WV / M • Tracy In Heaven (Rewrite) / 1986 / WV / M • True Legends Of Adult Cinema: Unsung Superstars / 1993 / VC / C • The Vanessa Obsession / 1987 / VCX / C • Who Came In The Backdoor? / 1987 / PV / M • Wild Fire / 1990 / WV / C • X-TV #1 / 1986 / PL / C • Young Girls Do / 1984 / ELH / M

JACQUELINE MARROWS *see Star Index I*

JACQUELINE ROGET *see Gabriella*

JACQUELINE SHEEN
The Best Rears Of Our Lives / 1992 / OD / M • China Black / 1992 / IN / M • Playboy: Playmates In Paradise / 1993 / UNI / S • Playboy: Wet & Wild #3 / 1991 / HBO / S

JACQUELINE ST CLAIR *see Jacqueline*

JACQUELINE WARNER *see Brigitte Aime*

JACQUELINE WILD
Diamonds / 1996 / HDE / M • Private Film #22 / 1995 / OD / M • Private Stories #02 / 1995 / OD / M • Private Stories #08 / 1996 / OD / M • The Sex Clinic / 1995 / WIV / M • Triple X Video Magazine #03 / 1995 / OD / M • Up Your Ass #1 / 1996 / ANA / M • World Sex Tour #1 / 1995 / ANA / M

JACQUES
The Hardwood Chronicles / 1995 / XCI / M • Magma: Fuck Me Diana / 1994 / MET / M • Perversity In Paris / 1994 / AVI / M • Pizza Sluts: They Deliver / 1995 / XCI / M • Snow Honeys / 1993 / VC / M

JACQUES CONTI *see Star Index I*

JACQUES COUDERC *see Star Index I*

JACQUES DEVOLE *see Star Index I*

JACQUES DUBAY
The Rise Of The Roman Empress #1 / 1986 / PV / M

JACQUES GATO *see Jack Gatt*

JACQUES GATOS *see Jack Gatt*

JACQUES INSERMANI
Introductions / 1977 / VCR / M • Kinky Ladies Of Bourbon Street / 1976 / LUM / M • The Felines / 1975 / VCX / M • Sexy / 1976 / SE / M • Shocking / 1984 / SE / M

JACQUES LARBI *see Star Index I*

JACQUES MARBEUF
Dangerous Passion / 1978 / VC / M • Diamond Snatch / 1977 / COM / M • Evil Mistress / 1984 / VIP / M • Fascination / 1979 / VS / S • For Love And Money / 1987 / CV / S • Girl With The Million $ Legs / 1987 / PL / M • House Of Love / cr77 / VC / M • Made In France / 1974 / VC / M • Salon D'amour / 19?? / IHV / M • The Seduction Of Tessa / cr86 / CA / M

JACQUES SANDERS *see Star Index I*

JACQUES TRONC *see Star Index I*

JACQUES VALE
Love Theatre / cr80 / VC / M

JACQUES WAYNE *see Star Index I*

JACQUETTE *see Star Index I*

JACQUIE BRODIE *see Star Index I*

JACQUIE CHENILLE *see Star Index I*

JACY ALLEN *(Justine Love)*
Blonde, medium droopy tits, good tan lines, pretty face. Rumor that in 1996 she was seen panhandling in LA, presumably menatally ill.
All American Girls #2: In Heat / 1983 / CA / M • Bodacious Ta Ta's / 1984 / CA / M •

Golden Girls #13 / 1984 / CA / M • Golden Girls #14 /1984 / CA / M •Golden Girls #21 / 1984 / CA / M • Hot Box / 1995 / V99 / C • A Little Bit Of Hanky Panky / 1984 / GO / M • Lusty Ladies #05 / 1983 / 4P / M • Making It Big / 1984 / CV / M • Six Plus One #2 / 1993 / VEX / C • Swedish Erotica #48 / 1983 / CA / M

JACY BODEAN *see* **Britt Morgan**

JADE

Big & Busty Country Line Dancing / 1995 / SEM / S • Black Lube Job Girls / 1995 / SUF / M • Boobs, Butts And Bloopers #1 / 1990 / HO / M • Catfighting Students / 1995 / PRE / C • Hard Core Beginners #07 / 1995 / LEI / M • Hollywood Biker Chicks / 1993 / PHV / F • Neighborhood Watch #38: Pearlie's Curlie's / 1993 / LBO / M • Odyssey Triple Play #55: Black & White & Up The Ass / 1994 / OD / M • Pole Cats / 1993 / KBR / S • San Francisco Lesbians #3 / 1993 / PL / F • San Francisco Lesbians #4 / 1993 / PL / F • Shane's World #6: Slumber Party / 1996 / OD / F • Student Fetish Videos: Catfighting #05 / 1992 / PRE / B

JADE CHEN *see Star Index I*

JADE DUNN

Pleasure Productions #06 / 1984 / VCR / M

JADE EAST *(Lin Shin)*

Not too pretty Oriental with medium tits and a flattish face. From **Deep Inside Dirty Debutantes #10**, she was 29 in 1994.

18 Candles / 1989 / LA / M • A&B AB#224: Wild Women / 1990 / A&B / F • After The Lights Go Out / 1989 / VEX / M • All For One / 1988 / CIN / M • Amateur Orgies #18 / 1992 / AFI / M • Anal Attraction #1 / 1988 / 3HV / M • Anal Intruder #03 / 1989 / CC / M • Angela Takes A Dare / 1988 / FAZ / M • As Sweet As They Come / 1992 / V99 / M • Back In Action / 1992 / FD / M • Backing In #3 / 1991 / WV / C • Beach Bum Amateur's #23 / 1993 / MID / M • Beefeaters / 1989 / PV / M • Behind The Backdoor #2 / 1989 / EVN / M • Best Body In Town / 1989 / FAZ / F • Best Of Caught From Behind #5 / 1991 / HO / C • Best Of Foot Worship #3 / 1992 / BIZ / C • Bi-Sex Pleasures / 1993 / PL / G • Blacks & Blondes #36 / 1986 / WV / M • Blow Bi Blow / 1988 / MET / G • Blows Job / 1989 / BIZ / B • Bondage Gymnasium / 198? / … / B • The Bondage Zone / 1994 / CS / B • Bored Housewife / 1989 / CIN / M • The Bottom Line / 1990 / AMB / M • Bound To Tease #3 / 1989 / BON / C • Breast Worx #40 / 1992 / LBO / M • Broadcast Nudes / 1988 / EVN / M • Bruise Control / 1993 / PRE / B • Bubble Butts #20 / 1992 / LBO / M • Buck's Excellent Transsexual Adventure / 1989 / STA / G • The Burma Road #4 / 1996 / LBO / C • But...Can She Type? / 1989 / CDI / M • Casbah Fantasy / 1989 / BON / B • Caught From Behind #10 / 1989 / HO / M • China Girl / 1989 / V99 / M • Competition / 1989 / BON / B • Control / 1993 / BON / B • Crunch Bunch / 1995 / PRE / C • Deep Inside Dirty Debutantes #10 / 1993 / 4P / M • Devil In Vanity / 1990 / CC / M • Dirty Deeds / 1992 / IF / M • The Dragon Lady #1 / 1988 / WV / C • Drainman / 1989 / BIZ / B • Dreams In The Forbidden Zone / 1989 / PCP / M • Dump Site / 1989 / BIZ / C • Enemates #02 / 1989 / BIZ / B • Enemates #07 / 1992 / PRE / B • Every Which Way /

1990 / V10 / G • Flash Floods / 1991 / PRE / C • Fun In A Bun / 1990 / LV / M • Getting Off On Broadway / 1989 / IN / M • Girl Crazy / 1989 / CDI / F • Girls Don't Lie / 1990 / IN / F • Girls Gone Bad #1 / 1990 / GO / F • Girls Of The Bamboo Palace / 1989 / VEX / M • Good Morning Saigon / 1988 / ZA / M • Grand Slam / 1990 / PRE / B • Hangin' Out / 1992 / IF / M • Hard Sell / 1990 / VC / M • Hawaii Vice #1 / 1988 / CIN / M • Hawaii Vice #2 / 1989 / CDI / M • Hawaii Vice #3 / 1988 / CIN / M • Hawaii Vice #5 / 1989 / CDI / M • Hawaii Vice #6 / 1989 / CDI / M • Hawaii Vice: Reflections / 1990 / CIN / C • Hometown Honeys #3 / 1989 / VEX / M • Honeymooned / 1992 / PRE / B • Horny Toed / 1989 / BIZ / S • Hospitality Sweet / 1988 / WV / M • House Of Spartacus #2 / 1993 / IF / M • Illusions #2 / 1992 / IF / M • In A Crystal Fantasy / 1988 / VD / M • Invitation Only / 1989 / AMB / M • Just Like Sisters / 1988 / VEX / M • Kinkyvision #2 / 1988 / VC / M • Leg...Ends 09 / 1994 / PRE / F • Legs And Lingerie #1 / 1990 / BIZ / F • Man Of Steel / 1992 / IF / M • Mischief In The Mansion / 1989 / LE / M • Miss Matches / 1996 / PRE / C • Moon Rivers / 1994 / PRE / B • More Unbelievable Orgies / 1989 / EVN / C • My Anal Valentine / 1993 / FD / M • My Sensual Body / 1989 / WET / M • The Nicole Stanton Story #1 / 1989 / CA / M • The Nicole Stanton Story #2 / 1989 / CA / M • Object(s) Of My Desire / 1988 / V99 / M • One Lay At A Time / 1992 / V99 / M • Open House (CDI) / 1989 / CDI / M • Orient Sexpress / 1996 / AVI / M • Oriental Anal Sluts / 1993 / WV / C • Oriental Treatment #2: The Pearl Divers / 1989 / AR / M • Party In The Rear / 1989 / LV / M • Personal Touch #4 / 1989 / AR / M • Plenty Of Pleasure / 1990 / WET / M • The Price Was Right / 1994 / PAE / M • Proposals / 1988 / CC / M • Queens In Danger / 1990 / STA / G • Risque Business / 1989 / V99 / M • Running Mates / 1993 / PRE / B • Sensual Solos #03 / 1994 / AVI / F • Sex Flex / 1989 / CDI / M • Sex Lives Of The Rich And Famous #1 / 1988 / VC / M • Sex Lives Of The Rich And Famous #2 / 1989 / VC / M • She Comes Undone / 1987 / AIR / C • Simply Irresistible / 1988 / CC / M • Six Plus One #1 / 1993 / VEX / M • Slap Happy / 1994 / PRE / B • Smoke Screen / 1990 / CA / M • Soaked To The Bone / 1989 / IN / M • Soft Caresses / 1988 / VEX / M • Stolen Kisses / 1989 / VD / M • Strong Language / 1989 / IN / M • Strykin' It Deep / 1989 / V10 / M • Switch Hitters #4: The Grand Slam / 1989 / IN / G • Tails Of The Town / 1988 / WV / M • Temptations / 1989 / DR / M • This Could Be The Night / 1993 / IF / M • This One's For You / 1989 / AR / M • Three Men And A Geisha / 1990 / HO / M • Toe Hold / 1992 / PRE / B • Turn Of Events / 1990 / NAP / B • Up The Ying Yang / 1991 / EVN / C • Virgin Busters / 1989 / LV / M • Vixens / 1989 / LV / F • Watersports Spree #2 / 1994 / BIZ / C • Wet Event / 1992 / IF / M • Wet Memories / 1993 / WV / M • When East Meets West / 1990 / NAP / B • With A Wiggle In Her Walk / 1989 / WV / M • Wives Of The Rich And Famous / 1989 / V99 / M

JADE EAST (1982)

Forgive Me, I Have Sinned / 1982 / ALP / B • Heaven's Touch / 1983 / CA / M • Puss 'n'

Boots / 1982 / VXP / M

JADE LANEER *see Star Index I*

JADE LEWIS *see Star Index I*

JADE MACISIO

Finger Pleasures #1 / 1995 / PL / F

JADE MOON

Joe Elliot's College Girls #36 / 1994 / JOE / M

JADE NICHOLS

Bodies By Jackie / 1985 / IVP / M • Casino Of Lust / 1984 / AT / M • Charming Cheapies #1: Joy's Many Loves / 1985 / 4P / M • Charming Cheapies #2: No Holes Barred / 1985 / 4P / M • Fantasies Unltd. / 1985 / CDI / M • Flash Trance / 1985 / IVP / M • Ginger's Private Party / 1985 / VI / M • Girls Of The Third Reich / 1985 / FC / M • Heartthrobs / 1985 / CA / M • Joys Of Erotica #108 / 1984 / VCR / C • Little Girls Of The Streets / 1984 / CV / M • Oriental Jade / 1985 / VC / M • Sex For Hire / 1989 / HOE / C • Too Good To Be True / 1984 / MAP / M • Tracy In Heaven (Orig 1985) / 1985 / WV / M

JADE O'CONNER *see Star Index I*

JADE O'RILEY *see Star Index I*

JADE STERLING

The Gypsy / 1996 / NIT / M • Intimate Interviews #1 / 1996 / NIT / M

JADE WONG

All About Annette / 1982 / SE / C • Cells Of Passion / 1981 / VD / M • Erotic Dimensions #1: Ripe / 1982 / NSV / M • Erotic Dimensions #3: My Way! / 1982 / NSV / M • Erotic Dimensions #4: The Exhibitionist / 1982 / NSV / M • Erotic Dimensions: I Want To Watch / 1982 / NSV / M • The Final Sin / 1977 / COM / M • Intimate Explosions / 1982 / … / C • Mai Lin Vs Serena / 1982 / HIF / M • Nasty Lady / 1984 / CV / M • Oriental Hawaii / 1982 / CA / M • Prisoner Of Paradise / 1980 / VCX / M • Purely Physical / 1982 / SE / M

JAELINA

Chronicles Of Lust #2 / 1996 / XPR / M

JAGGER HAIG

Positively Pagan #03 / 1991 / ATA / M

JAGUAR

A&B AB#027: Gang Bang Girl / 1990 / A&B / M • A&B FL#02: Flashing Journey / 1995 / A&B / S • A&B GB#071: Jaguar / 1993 / A&B / M • A&B GBG#03: Black And White—Jaguar / 1995 / A&B / M • Amateur Lesbians #27: Megan / 1992 / GO / F • Amateur Lesbians #28: Sharon / 1992 / GO / F • Amateur Orgies #02 / 1992 / AFI / M • America's Dirtiest Home Videos #07 / 1991 / VEX / M • Anal International / 1992 / HW / M • Ass-Capades / 1992 / HW / M • Beach Bum Amateur's #08 / 1992 / MID / M • Beach Bum Amateur's #12 / 1992 / MID / M • The Big E #10 / 1992 / PRE / B • Black & White In Living Color / 1992 / WV / M • Black Beauties #1 / 1992 / VIM / M • Black Jack City #2: Black's Revenge / 1992 / HW / M • Black Men Can Hump / 1992 / FH / M • Black Women, White Men #2 / 1995 / FC / M • Buttman's Double Adventure / 1993 / EA / M • Buttwiser / 1992 / HW / M • Cycle Sluts / 1992 / CC / M • Dark Double D-Lites / 1993 / HW / C • Dead Ends / 1992 / PRE / B • Double D Amateurs #08 / 1993 / JMP / M • Double D Dykes #06 / 1992 / GO / F • Double Penetration #6 / 1993 / WV / C • Enemates #06 / 1992 / BIZ / B • Feathermates / 1992 / PRE / B • GRG: Jaguar And

Israel / 1994 / GRG / M • Hard To Hold / 1993 / IF / M • Hillary Vamp's Private Collection #19 / 1992 / HOV / M • Hits & Misses / 1992 / PRE / B • Hollywood Connection / 1992 / … / M • Honey Drippers / 1992 / ROB / F • In Loving Color #1 / 1992 / VT / M • In Loving Color #2 / 1992 / VT / M • In Loving Color #3 / 1992 / VT / M • In Loving Color #4 / 1993 / VT / M • In Your Face #1 / 1992 / PL / M • Leg...Ends #07 / 1993 / PRE / F • Lesbian Pros And Amateurs #13 / 1992 / GO / F • Lesbian Pros And Amateurs #14 / 1992 / GO / F • Lez Go Crazy / 1992 / HW / C • Mike Hott: #211 Horny Couples #06 / 1992 / MHV / M • Mocha Magic / 1992 / FH / M • Odyssey 30 Min: #188: The Double Penetration Of A Black Babe / 1991 / OD / M • Our Bang #01 / 1992 / GLI / M • Our Bang #02 / 1992 / GLI / M • Our Bang #03 / 1992 / GLI / M • Our Bang #04 / 1992 / GLI / M • Our Bang #05 / 1992 / GLI / M • Our Bang #07 / 1992 / GLI / M • Our Bang #08 / 1992 / GLI / M • Raw Talent: Bang 'er 14 Times / 1992 / RTP / M • Rocks / 1993 / VT / M • Sam Shaft's Public Flashing #2 / 1994 / RTP / M • Sex Police 2000 / 1992 / AFV / M • Shoot To Thrill / 1992 / WV / M • Student Fetish Videos: Catfighting #04 / 1992 / PRE / B • Student Fetish Videos: The Enema #08 / 1992 / PRE / B • Student Fetish Videos: Tickling #05 / 1992 / SFV / B • Ultimate Orgy #2 / 1992 / GLI / M • Uncle Roy's Amateur Home Video #05 / 1992 / VIM / M • Uncle Roy's Amateur Home Video #08 / 1992 / VIM / M • Victoria's Amateurs #04 / 1992 / VGA / M

JAIME LEE *see* **Jamie Leigh**

JAIMI GILLIS *see* **Jamie Gillis**

JAKE

AVP #9127: The Doctor Is In / 1991 / AVP / M • The Black Butt Sisters Do Los Angeles / 1995 / MID / M • Female Domination #2 / 1991 / BIZ / B • Homegrown Video #035 / 1990 / HOV / M • Neighborhood Watch #37: Pelvic Thrusters / 1993 / LBO / M

JAKE ALLBEEF

Burn It Up / 1994 / VEX / M • Illusions #2 / 1992 / IF / M

JAKE ANDREWS

Secret Sex #3: The Takeover / 1994 / CAT / G

JAKE BARNES *(Jack Goff)*

Drive-In Massacre / 1976 / WIZ / S • Summer Camp / 1980 / MED / S • Takin' It All Off / 1987 / VES / S

JAKE DANE *see* **Dayne Christian**

JAKE EAST *see* **Steve Hatcher**

JAKE ERICKSON *see* **Star Index I**

JAKE HUDSON

American Sex Fantasy / 1975 / IHV / M

JAKE HUNTER

Anal Sluts & Sweethearts #3 / 1995 / ROB / M • Butt Busting / 1996 / RB / B • Dick & Jane In San Francisco / 1996 / AVI / M • Gang Bang Face Bath #4 / 1995 / ROB / M • Gang Bang Jizz Queen / 1995 / ROB / M • Young Sluts In Heat #1 / 1996 / PL / M

JAKE LARKIN *see* **Star Index I**

JAKE REMME

Slut Safari #3 / 1994 / FC / M

JAKE RIDER *see* **Steven St. Croix**

JAKE RODGERS

She-Male Encounters #10: She-Male Vacation / 1986 / MET / G

JAKE RYDER

The Adventures Of Buttgirl & Wonder Wench / 1991 / AFV / M • All "A" / 1994 / SFP / C • Bobby Hollander's Maneaters #03 / 1993 / SFP / M • Bobby Hollander's Sweet Cheeks #103 / 1992 / QUA / M • Bobby Hollander's Sweet Cheeks #105 / 1993 / SFP / M • The Buttnicks #4: The Black Buttnicks / 1993 / CC / M • For The Money #2 / 1993 / FH / M • Inferno #1 / 1993 / SC / M • Pearl Necklace: Thee Bush League #07 / 1992 / SEE / M • The Sex Connection / 1993 / VC / M • Slip Of The Tongue / 1993 / DR / M • The Spa / 1993 / VC / M • Straight A Students / 1993 / MET / M • Video Virgins #02 / 1992 / NS / M

JAKE SCOTT

Bi Bi Love / 1986 / LAV / G • She-Male Encounters #13: She-Male Reformatory / 1987 / MET / G • Unveiled / 1987 / VC / M

JAKE SETO *see* **Star Index I**

JAKE SNEAD *see* **Jake Steed**

JAKE STEED *(Tim Woodfield, Max Stead, Tim Whitfield, Tim Winfield, Jake Steele, Max Steed, Jake Snead, Tim Wakefield, Jack Sheepe, Mack Stead)*

Black male with a definite bend in his dick. As of mid-1994 rumor has it that he is in jail for armed robbery (I wondered about those haircuts).

Action In Black / 1993 / FD / M • The Adventures Of Peeping Tom #3 / 1996 / OD / M • Against All Bods / 1991 / VEX / M • All About Teri Weigel / 1996 / XCI / M • All For You, Baby / 1990 / VEX / M • All That: Black Women's Fantasies / 1996 / VT / M • Almost Home Alone / 1993 / SFP / M • Amateur Hours #06 / 1990 / AFI / M • Amushed / 1990 / SE / M • America's Dirtiest Home Videos #08 / 1992 / VEX / M • Anal Addict / 1995 / ROB / M • The Anal Adventures Of Max Hardcore: The Resurrection / 1995 / ZA / M • Anal Angels #4 / 1995 / VEX / C • Anal Anonymous / 1995 / SO / M • Anal Assassins / 1991 / IN / M • Anal Booty Burner / 1996 / ROB / M • Anal Climax #2 / 1991 / ROB / M • Anal Cornhole Cutie / 1996 / ROB / M • Anal Dynomite / 1995 / ROB / M • Anal Hanky-Panky / 1997 / ROB / M • Anal Honeypie / 1996 / ROB / M • Anal Lickers And Cummers / 1996 / ROB / M • Anal Load Lickers / 1996 / ROB / M • Anal Maniacs #3 / 1995 / WP / M • Anal Misconduct / 1995 / VD / M • The Anal Nurse Scam / 1995 / CA / M • Anal Playground / 1995 / CA / M • Anal Plaything #2 / 1995 / ROB / M • Anal Rippers #1: The Beginning / 1995 / ZA / M • Anal Senorita #2 / 1995 / ROB / M • Anal Sluts & Sweethearts #3 / 1995 / ROB / M • Anal Therapy #1 / 1992 / FD / M • Anal Vision #07 / 1993 / LBO / M • Anally Insatiable / 1995 / KWP / M • Analtown USA #01 / 1995 / NIT / M • Analtown USA #02 / 1995 / NIT / M • Angels / 1992 / VC / M • Another Fuckin' Anal Movie / 1996 / ROB / M • Anus & Andy / 1993 / ZA / M • Anything Butt Love / 1990 / PL / M • Art Of Sex / 1992 / FD / M • Asian Appetite / 1993 / HO / M • Ass Lover's Special / 1996 / PE / M • Ass Openers! #2 / 1995 / TCK / C • Asses Galore #4: Extreme Noise Terror / 1996 / DFI / M • Asses Galore #7: Lunatic Fringe / 1996 / DFI / M • Babes / 1991 / CIN / M • The Back Doors (Western) / 1991 / WV / M • Back In Action / 1992 / FD / M • Back To Black #2 / 1992 / VEX / C • Back-

door Ebony / 1995 / WV / M • Backdoor Suite / 1992 / EX / M • Backdoor To Russia #1 / 1992 / VC / M • Backdoor To Russia #3 / 1993 / VC / M • Backdoor To The City Of Sin / 1993 / ANA / M • The Backpackers #2 / 1990 / IN / M • The Backpackers #3 / 1991 / IN / M • Bad Attitude #1 / 1995 / LV / M • Bad Attitude #2 / 1995 / LV / M • Barby's On Butt Row / 1996 / ABS / M • Bardot / 1991 / VI / M • Bare Market / 1993 / VC / M • Bareback Riders / 1992 / VEX / M • Behind The Backdoor #4 / 1990 / EVN / M • Beverly Hills Blondes #1 / 1995 / LV / M • Beverly Hills Blondes #2 / 1995 / LV / M • Beverly Hills Geisha / 1992 / V99 / M • Big Bust Babes #19 / 1994 / AFI / M • Black & Blue / 1990 / SO / M • Black & White In Living Color / 1992 / WV / M • Black Anal Dreams / 1995 / WV / M • Black Balled / 1990 / ZA / M • Black Beach / 1995 / LV / M • Black Booty / 1993 / ZA / M • Black Centerfolds #1 / 1996 / DR / M • Black Centerfolds #2 / 1996 / DR / M • Black Cheerleader Search #10 / 1997 / IVC / M • Black Dirty Debutantes / 1993 / 4P / M • Black Encounters / 1992 / ZA / M • Black Hose Bag / 1996 / ROB / M • Black Juice Bombs / 1996 / NIT / C • Black Mariah / 1991 / FC / M • Black Men Can Hump / 1992 / FH / M • Black Obsession / 1991 / ZA / M • Black Power / 1996 / LEI / C • Black Pussyman Auditions #1 / 1996 / SNA / M • Black Street Hookers #1 / 1996 / DFI / M • Black Street Hookers #2 / 1996 / DFI / M • Black Street Hookers #3 / 1996 / DFI / M • Black Street Hookers #4: The Streets Of San Francisco / 1996 / DFI / M • Black Street Hookers #5: The Mean Streets Of Washington D.C. / 1997 / DFI / M • Black Studs & Little White Trash / 1995 / ROB / M • Black To Basics / 1992 / ZA / M • Booty Bitch / 1995 / ROB / M • Booty Ho #2 / 1995 / ROB / M • Booty Ho #3 / 1995 / ROB / M • Borsky's Back Door Bitches / 1996 / ROB / M • Bossy Babes / 1993 / TCK / M • The Bottom Dweller 33 1/3 / 1995 / EL / M • The Box / 1992 / EX / M • The Butler Did It / 1991 / FH / M • Butt Busters / 1995 / EX / M • Butt Motors / 1995 / VC / M • Butt Row Unplugged / 1996 / ABS / M • Butthole Sweetheart / 1996 / ROB / M • Butties / 1992 / VC / M • The Buttnicks #2 / 1991 / HIO / M • California Sluts / 1995 / ZA / M • Can't Touch This / 1991 / PL / M • Cape Rear / 1992 / WV / M • Car Wash Angels / 1995 / VC / M • Casey At The Bat / 1991 / LV / M • Casting Call #16 / 1995 / SO / M • Cheatin' Hearts / 1991 / VEX / M • China Black / 1992 / IN / M • Chocolate Cherries #2 / 1990 / CC / M • Chug-A-Lug Girls #1 / 1993 / VT / M • The Cockateer #1 / 1991 / LE / M • College Girl / 1990 / VEX / M • Coming Out Bi / 1995 / IN / G • Contrast / 1995 / CA / M • Crazy On You / 1991 / IF / M • Cum Buttered Corn Holes #1 / 1996 / NIT / C • Cumback Pussy #2: Crawling Back For More / 1996 / EL / M • Cumback Pussy #3: Coast To Coast Rump Romp / 1996 / EL / M • Cumback Pussy #5: Groopin' / 1996 / EL / M • Curse Of The Catwoman / 1990 / VC / M • Dallas Does Debbie / 1992 / PL / M • Debutante Dreams / 1995 / 4P / M • Decadent Dreams / 1996 / ME / M • Derrier / 1991 / CC / M • Designer Genes / 1990 / VI / M • Dial A Nurse / 1992 / VD / M • Dirty Deeds / 1992 / IF / M • Dirty Diner #3 / 1996 / SC / M •

1990 / LV / M • Untamed Passion / 1991 / VEX / M • Up And Cummers #17 / 1994 / 4P / M • Up And Cummers #23 / 1995 / 4P / M • Up And Cummers #24 / 1995 / 4P / M • Up Your Ass #3 / 1996 / ANA / M • The Uptown Girl / 1992 / ZA / M • Valentina: Princess Of The Forest / 1996 / SC / M • Vice Versa / 1992 / FD / M • Video Virgins #31 / 1996 / NS / M • Virgin Tales #01 / 1993 / 4P / M • Voodoo Vixens / 1991 / IF / M • The Voyeur #4 / 1995 / EA / M • Waiting For The Man / 1996 / VT / M • The War Of The Hoses / 1991 / NLE / M • Wet & Slippery / 1995 / WV / M • Wet & Wicked / 1992 / VEX / M • White Men Can't Iron On Butt Row / 1997 / ABS / M • Whitey's On The Moon / 1996 / ROB / M • Whoreo / 1995 / BIP / M • Wicked Wenches / 1991 / LV / M • Wild Assed Pooper Slut / 1996 / ROB / M • Wild At Heart / 1990 / CDI / M • Wild Things #3 / 1992 / MET / M • Wilde At Heart / 1992 / VEX / M • You Bet Your Butt / 1992 / VC / M • You Said A Mouthful / 1992 / IF / M

JAKE STEELE *see* **Jake Steed**

JAKE STRONG
Foxx Tales / 1996 / TTV / M

JAKE STUART *see* **Star Index I**

JAKE TEAGUE *(Tim Wakefield, Alan Clement(s))*
Alan Clement is from **American Desire**.
American Desire / 1981 / CA / M • Babylon Gold / 1983 / COM / C • Bella / 1980 / AR / M • Blonde In Black Silk / 1979 / QX / M • Blonde Velvet / 1976 / COL / M • Bon Appetit / 1980 / QX / M • The Budding Of Brie / 1980 / TVX / M • C.O.D. / 1981 / VES / S • Candy Lips / 1975 / CXV / M • Captain Lust And The Amorous Contessa / 1977 / IHV / M • Carnal Games / 1978 / BL / M • Debbie Does Dallas #1 / 1978 / VC / M • Deep Inside Annie Sprinkle / 1981 / VXP / .M • Double Your Pleasure / 1978 / CV / M • Foxtrot / 1982 / COM / M • Girls U.S.A. / 1980 / AIR / M • Joy / 1977 / QX / M • Kid Stuff / 1981 / … / M • The Little Blue Box / 1978 / BL / M • Little Darlings / 1981 / VEP / M • Loose Threads / 1979 / S&L / M • Mystique / 1979 / CA / M • Neon Nights / 1981 / COM / M • New York Babes / 1979 / AR / M • New York's Finest / 1988 / AE / S • October Silk / 1980 / COM / M • Oh Those Nurses / 1982 / VC / M • Pornocopia Sensual / 1976 / VHL / M • Powerbone / 1976 / VC / M • Satin Suite / 1979 / QX / M • Sunny / 1979 / VC / M • Temptations / 1976 / VXP / M • Twilight Pink #1 / 1980 / AR / M • VCA Previews #2 / 1988 / VC / C • A Woman's Torment / 1977 / VC / M • Women In Love / 1980 / CA / M • Young, Wild And Wonderful / 1980 / VCX / M

JAKE WEST
$ex 4 Fun & Profit / 1996 / SPR / M • Christine's Secret / 1986 / FEM / M • Confessions Of A Middle Aged Nympho / 1986 / WET / M • Hotel Transylvania #2 / 1990 / LIP / G • Make Me Feel It / 1984 / SE / M • Taboo American Style #3: Nina Becomes An Actress / 1985 / VC / M

JAKE WILLIAMS *see* **Steve Hatcher**

JAKI
Blue Vanities #130 / 1990 / FFL / M

JALYNN *(Jaylin, Roxanne (Jalynn), Taylnn, Erica (Jalynn))*
Good looking petite blonde with a tattoo on her chest just above her right breast. Small tits,

pretty face. 19 years old in 1993 (born in 1974), 32B-24-34 4'11" tall, 90lbs in 1993. Comes from Warren, Ohio.
Alexandria, I Love You / 1993 / AFV / M • Amateur Orgies #24 / 1993 / AFI / M • Amateur Orgies #25 / 1993 / AFI / M • Anal Brat / 1993 / FL / M • Anal Virgins Of America #01 / 1993 / FOR / M • Beach Bum Amateur's #33 / 1993 / MID / M • Beyond Passion / 1993 / IF / M • Carnal College #2 / 1993 / AFV / M • Falling In Love Again / 1993 / PMV / M • First Time Lesbians #02 / 1993 / JMP / F • First Time Lesbians #04 / 1993 / JMP / F • Full Throttle Girls: Boredom Pulled The Trigger / 1993 / VIM / M • Humongous Hooters / 1993 / IF / M • The Knocker Room / 1993 / GO / M • Nasty Newcummers #02 / 1993 / MET / M • Nasty Newcummers #12 / 1995 / MET / M • New Ends #02 / 1993 / 4P / M • Nothing Butt The Truth / 1993 / AFV / M • Odyssey Triple Play #72: Backdoor Score / 1994 / OD / M • Primal Desires / 1993 / EX / M • Real Tickets #1 / 1994 / VC / M • Real Tickets #2 / 1994 / VC / M • Slave To Love / 1993 / ROB / M • Video Virgins #03 / 1993 / NS / M • Virtual Sex / 1993 / VC / M

JAMAICA
Amateur Black: Hot Flesh / 1996 / SUF / M • Black Beauties #1 / 1992 / VIM / M • Black Cheerleader Jungle Jerk-Off / 1996 / WIC / F • Black Cheerleader Search #04 / 1996 / ROB / M • How To Make Love To A Black Woman #1: You Gotta Have Rhythm / 1996 / VCX / M • Sweet Black Cherries #5 / 1996 / TTV / M • Sweet Black Cherries #6 / 1996 / TTV / M • Vivid Raw #4 / 1996 / VI / M

JAMAL DAVIS
Bucky Beaver's XXX Dragon Art Theatre Double Feature #06 / 1996 / SOW / M • Finishing School / 1975 / SOW / M

JAMBALAYA
Sperm Injection / 1995 / PL / M

JAMELA *(Jamila, Jamilla)*
Black girl with droopy breasts and a small tattoo on the left breast.
All For You, Baby / 1990 / VEX / M • Back To Black #1 / 1988 / VEX / M • Blacks Have More Fun / 1985 / AVC / M • Chocolate Cherries #2 / 1990 / CC / M • Drink Of Love / 1990 / V99 / M • Having It All / 1991 / VEX / M • Hidden Pleasures / 1990 / VEX / M • Hollywood Hustle #2 / 1990 / V99 / M • Living In Sin / 1990 / VEX / M • One Of These Nights / 1991 / V99 / M • Passion Princess / 1991 / VEX / M • Sex She Wrote / 1991 / VEX / M • Sexual Persuasion / 1991 / V99 / M • Sexy Nurses #1 On And Off Duty / 1990 / CV / M • Sweet Darlin' / 1990 / VEX / M • Women In Charge / 1990 / VEX / M

JAMENA JEWELS *see* **Tameya Jewels**

JAMES
Amateurs Exposed #01 / 1993 / CV / M • Anatomy Of A Male Stripper / 1990 / 4P / S • Fantasy Photography: Buffy And The Boys / 1995 / VG0 / M • HomeGrown Video #453: / 1995 / HOV / M • Latex #1 / 1994 / VC / M • Pussy Hunt #15 / 1995 / LEI / M • Smarty Pants / 1992 / VEX / M

JAMES BANDIT *see* **Sasha Gabor**

JAMES BROWNE
Cracked Ice / 1977 / PVX / M

JAMES BUTLER
Black Gangbangers #03 / 1995 / HW / M

JAMES CROCKETT *see* **Star Index I**

JAMES CROWNE *see* **Star Index I**

JAMES DALTON *see* **Star Index I**

JAMES DEAN *see* **Jason Dean**

JAMES FERANTI
Sharon Mitchell's Sex Clinic #02 / 1993 / FC / M • Stuff Your Face #4 / 1996 / JMP / M

JAMES FONG *see* **Star Index I**

JAMES FOXE
Beyond Domination / 1996 / GOT / B • Corrected Deception / 1994 / STM / B • Dangerous Lessons / 1994 / STM / C • Lauren's Adventures In Bondageland #1: Mistress Lauren / 1994 / STM / C • Masked Mistress / 1994 / STM / B • Sweat 'n' Bullets / 1995 / MID / M

JAMES FULTON
Seka's Fantasies / 1981 / CA / M

JAMES GILLES *see* **Jamie Gillis**

JAMES GILLETTE
Naughty Nurses / 1982 / VCR / M

JAMES GILLIS *see* **Jamie Gillis**

JAMES HAMLING
Foxholes / 1983 / SE / M

JAMES HONG
Caged Fury / 1990 / C3S / S • China Girl / 1974 / SE / M

JAMES HUNTER
Women's Penitentiary / 1992 / VIM / M

JAMES JAMMER *see* **Star Index I**

JAMES KLEEMAN *see* **Jamie Gillis**

JAMES KRAL *see* **Star Index I**

JAMES LA FOOT
Anal Pandemonium / 1994 / TTV / M

JAMES LEWIS *(DeLoris Comforth)*
40 The Hard Way / 1991 / OD / M • Anal Encounters #2 / 1991 / VC / M • Anal Encounters #3: Back In The Dark One / 1991 / VC / M • Angels / 1992 / VC / M • Avenging Angeli / 1990 / CC / M • Bavarian Cream & Other Delights / 1985 / PV / M • Between The Cheeks #2 / 1990 / VC / M • Black Stockings / 1990 / VD / M • Catalina: Tiger Shark / 1991 / CDI / M • Club Head / 1990 / CA / M • Deep Inside Debi Diamond / 1995 / VC / C • Giving It To Barbii / 1990 / TOR / M • Heavy Petting / 1991 / SE / M • In Too Deep / 1992 / AFD / M • International Phone Sex Girls #5 / 1991 / PM / M • The Journey: Oral Majority / 1991 / WV / M • Kiss It Goodbye / 1991 / SE / M • The Lethal Squirt / 1990 / AR / M • Love In An Elevator / 1990 / CC / M • Making It Big / 1990 / TOR / M • Money Honey / 1990 / TOR / M • Odyssey Amateur #47: Gangbang-A-Gram / 1991 / OD / M • The Passion Of Heather Lear / 1990 / AFV / M • Phone Sex Girls #5 / 1990 / TOR / M • Princess Of The Night / 1990 / VD / M • Put It In Gere / 1991 / CA / M • Red Hot / 1990 / EX / M • Sex Acts & Video Tape / 1990 / AFV / M • Stairway To Paradise / 1990 / VC / M • The Stranger Beside Me / 1991 / WV / M • Titillation #3 / 1991 / SE / M • The Wild And The Innocent / 1990 / CC / M • Women In Charge / 1990 / VEX / M • Zara's Revenge / 1991 / XCI / M

JAMES LISTER *see* **Star Index I**

JAMES MARCH
The Pink Ladies / 1980 / VC / M

JAMES MARTIN *see* **Star Index I**

JAMES MICHAEL
Temptations / 1989 / DR / M

JAMES MILES *see* **Star Index I**

JAMES MORRISON *see* **Star Index I**

JAMES PATRICK
Wild Dallas Honey / 1985 / VCX / M

JAMES PAUL *see Star Index I*

JAMES PERRY *see Star Index I*

JAMES PETERS *see Star Index I*

JAMES PRICE *see Star Index I*

JAMES RUGMAN *see Jamie Gillis*

JAMES RUSH
Wicked Fantasies / 1996 / CO2 / M

JAMES SMITH
Buttman's Bouncin' British Babes / 1994 / EA / M

JAMES SOO
Alice In Analand / 1994 / SC / M • Bobby Hollander's Maneaters #01 / 1993 / SFP / M • The Night Shift / 1995 / LE / M

JAMES STAR *see Star Index I*

JAMES SULLIVAN *see Star Index I*

JAMES TOWERS
Oldies But Goodies / 1995 / WIV / M

JAMES TYLER *see Star Index I*

JAMES WAND *see Star Index I*

JAMES WEBB *see Star Index I*

JAMES WEST
America's Raunchiest Home Videos #33: Anal Engagement / 1992 / ZA / M • Bangkok Dreams / 1996 / SUF / M • Betrayed / 1996 / WP / M • Juliette's Desires / 1996 / LE / M • Moonglow / 1989 / IN / M • Night Vision / 1996 / WP / M • The Ultimate Climax / 1989 / V99 / M • Yin Yang Oriental Love Bang #3: Bangkok Dreams / 1996 / SUF / M

JAMEYA JEWELS *see Tameya Jewels*

JAMI HUNTER *see Star Index I*

JAMIE
Cherry Poppers #07: Li'l Darlin's / 1994 / ZA / M • Cherry Poppin #01 / 1994 / CDY / M • College Video Virgins #04 / 1996 / AOC / M • Jamie And Lana / 1992 / JBV / B • Joe Elliot's Asian College Girls #02 / 1995 / JOE / M • Joe Elliot's College Girls #26 / 1994 / JOE / M • Joe Elliot's College Girls #37 / 1994 / JOE / M • Joe Elliot's College Girls: Jamie Uncut / 1994 / JOE / M • Pantyhose Teasers #2 / 1992 / JBV / S • The Piercing Of Jamie / 1983 / BIZ / B • Real Sex Magazine #01 / 1996 / HO / M • Rump Humpers #06 / 1992 / GLI / M • Rump Humpers #17 / 1994 / GLI / M • Satisfaction Guaranteed / 1972 / AXV / M • Sorority Lingerie Party / 1995 / NIV / F • Uncle Roy's Amateur Home Video #05 / 1992 / VIM / M

JAMIE BLUE *see Star Index I*

JAMIE BLUME *see Star Index I*

JAMIE CARSON
Hotel Sodom #01 / 1995 / SNA / M • Hotel Sodom #02 / 1995 / SNA / M • Hotel Sodom #03 / 1995 / SNA / M • Hotel Sodom #04: Free Parking In Rear / 1995 / SNA / M • Hotel Sodom #05: Tammi Ann Bends Over / 1995 / SNA / M • Hotel Sodom #06 / 1995 / SNA / M • Hotel Sodom #07 / 1995 / SNA / M • Hotel Sodom #08 / 1995 / SNA / M • Hotel Sodom #09 / 1996 / SNA / M • Hotel Sodom #10 / 1996 / SNA / M

JAMIE CROSSE *see Star Index I*

JAMIE DARLING *see Star Index I*

JAMIE DEAN *see Jason Dean*

JAMIE DION *(Dahlia Grey)*
Not too pretty plasticized *Penthouse* pet.
Captured Beauty / 1995 / SAE / B • Hidden Obsessions / 1992 / BFP / M • Les Femmes Erotiques / 1993 / BFP / M • Penthouse: 1993 Pet Of The Year Playoff / 1993 / PET / F • Penthouse: 1993 Pet Of

The Year Winners / 1993 / PET / F • Penthouse: All-Pet Workout / 1993 / NIV / F • Penthouse: The Girls Of Penthouse #3 / 1995 / PET / S • Penthouse: Satin & Lace #2 / 1992 / PET / F • Sex And Money / 1994 / DGD / S • Unleashed / 1996 / SAE / M

JAMIE FISHER
Dirty Dancers #1 / 1994 / 4P / M

JAMIE GILLIS *(James Kleeman, Jamie Grill, James Rugman, Buster Hymen, Jaimi Gillis, Ronny Morgan, James Gillis, Jamie Kantor, Barry Gillis, James Gilles)*
1001 Erotic Nights #2 / 1987 / VC / M • 800 Fantasy Lane / 1979 / GO / M • The 8th Annual Erotic Film Awards / 1984 / SE / C • ABA: Double Feature #4 / 1996 / ALP / M • Abused Husband / 1990 / PL / B • Adult 45 #01 / 1985 / DR / C • The Adventures Of Buttman / 1989 / EA / M • Alien Space Avenger / 1991 / AIP / S • All About Annette / 1982 / SE / C • All About Gloria Leonard / 1978 / VXP / M • Amanda By Night #1 / 1981 / CA / M • American Sex Fantasy / 1975 / IHV / M • Anal Annie Just Can't Say No / 1984 / LIP / M • Anal Extasy / 1992 / ROB / M • Anal Inferno / 1992 / ROB / M • Anal Madness / 1992 / ROB / M • Anal Starlets / 1991 / ROB / M • Angel On Fire / 1974 / ALP / M • Angela, The Fireworks Woman / 1975 / VC / M • Angels / 1992 / VC / M • Anna Obsessed / 1978 / ALP / M • At The Pornies / 1989 / VC / M • Aunt Peg / 1980 / CV / M • Babes In Toyland / 1988 / COM / C • Baby Face #2 / 1987 / VC / M • Baby Oil / 1974 / SOW / M • Babylon Gold / 1983 / COM / C • Back Down / 1996 / RB / B • Bad / 1990 / VC / M • Bad Attitude / 1987 / CC / M • Bad Girl Handling / 1993 / RB / B • Bad Girls #4 / 1984 / GO / M • Ball Busters / 1984 / CV / M • Bang Bash / 1979 / … / M • Barbara Broadcast / 1977 / VC / M • Barbie's Fantasies / 1974 / VHL / M • Beauty / 1981 / VC / M • Bedtime Video #05 / 1984 / GO / M • Behind Blue Eyes #1 / 1986 / ME / M • Best Of Atom / 1984 / AT / C • The Best Of Blondes / 1986 / VCR / C • Best Of Talk Dirty To Me #01 / 1991 / DR / C • Beverly Hills Cox / 1986 / CA / M • Big Gulp #1 / 1986 / VIP / C • Big Thumbs / 1978 / … / M • The Bigger The Better / 1986 / SE / C • The Birthday Ball / 1975 / VHL / M • The Bite / 1975 / SVE / M • Black Cheerleader Search #06 / 1996 / IVC / M • Black Widow / 1988 / WV / M • Black, White & Red All Over / 1984 / EXF / C • Blackman / 1989 / PL / M • Blacks & Blondes #09 / 1986 / WV / M • Blame It On Ginger / 1986 / VI / M • Blonde Ambition / 1981 / QX / M • Blonde On The Run / 1985 / PV / M • Blow Dry / 1977 / SVE / M • Blue Angel / 1992 / AFV / M • Blue Angel / 1992 / AFV / M • Blue Ecstasy / 1980 / CA / M • Blue Ice / 1985 / CA / M • Blue Ribbon Blue / 1984 / CA / C • Blue Vanities #018 (Old) / 1988 / FFL / M • Blue Vanities #034 / 1988 / FFL / M • Blue Vanities #037 / 1988 / FFL / M • Blue Vanities #038 / 1988 / FFL / M • Blue Vanities #046 (Old) / 1988 / FFL / M • Blue Vanities #048 / 1988 / FFL / M • Blue Vanities #056 / 1988 / FFL / M • Blue Vanities #058 / 1988 / FFL / M • Blue Vanities #063 / 1988 / FFL / M • Blue Vanities #069 / 1988 / FFL / M • Blue Vanities #098 / 1988 / FFL / M • Blue Vanities #199 / 1993 / FFL / M • Blue Vanities #244 / 1995 / FFL / M •

Blue Vanities #246 / 1995 / FFL / M • Blue Vanities #254 / 1996 / FFL / M • Blue Voodoo / 1983 / VD / M • Bobby Sox / 1996 / VI / S • Bone Up My Hole / 1994 / MET / M • Bound / 1979 / BIZ / B • Bound And Punished / 1984 / BIZ / B • Breaking It #1 / 1984 / COL / M • Bruised Buns / 1992 / RB / B • Bucky Beaver's XXX Dragon Art Theatre Double Feature #15 / 1996 / SOW / M • Bucky Beaver's XXX Dragon Art Theatre Double Feature #28 / 1996 / SOW / M • Cab-O-Lay / 1988 / PL / M • Captain Butt's Beach / 1992 / LV / M • Captain Lust And The Amorous Contessa / 1977 / IHV / M • Carnal Encounters Of The Barest Kind / 1978 / VOY / C • The Casting Whip / 1990 / PL / B • Celebrity Presents Celebrity / 1986 / VEP / C • Centerfold Celebrities #2 / 1983 / VC / M • Centerfold Celebrities #3 / 1983 / VC / M • Centerfold Celebrities #4 / 1983 / VC / M • Centerfold Celebrities #5 / 1983 / VC / M • Chained / cr76 / BIZ / B • Cheeks #2: The Bitter End / 1989 / CC / M • Cherry-Ettes For Hire / 1984 / 4P / M • Chickie / 1975 / CA / M • Chocolate Cream / 1984 / SUP / M • Classic Erotica Special / 1985 / SVE / M • Classic Swedish Erotica #03 / 1986 / CA / C • Classic Swedish Erotica #05 / 1986 / CA / C • Classic Swedish Erotica #08 / 1986 / CA / C • Classic Swedish Erotica #16 / 1986 / CA / C • Classic Swedish Erotica #24 / 1986 / CA / C • Classic Swedish Erotica #27 / 1987 / CA / C • Classic Swedish Erotica #28 / 1987 / CA / C • Clinique / 1989 / VC / M • Cocktales / 1985 / AT / M • Coed Fever / 1980 / CA / M • Coffee, Tea Or Me / 1984 / CV / M • College Video Virgins #07 / 1996 / AOC / M • Come And Be Purified / cr77 / LA / M • Come Fly With Us / 1974 / QX / M • A Coming Of Angels / 1977 / CA / M • A Coming Of Angels, The Sequel / 1985 / CA / M • The Contessa / 1989 / VC / M • Corporate Assets / 1985 / SE / M • Corruption / 1983 / VC / M • Couples / 1976 / VHL / M • Curse Of The Catwoman / 1990 / VC / M • Daddy Gets Punished / 1990 / PL / B • Dances With Foxes / 1991 / CC / M • Dangerous Women / 1987 / WET / M • Dark Angel / 1983 / VC / M • Daughters Of Discipline #1 / 197? / AVO / B • Debbie Does 'em All #1 / 1985 / CV / M • Deep Inside Brittany O'-connell / 1996 / VC / C • Deep Throat #2 / 1986 / AR / M • Deranged / 1987 / REP / S • Devil's Due / 1974 / ALP / M • Diaries Of Fire And Ice #1 / 1989 / VC / M • Diaries Of Fire And Ice #2 / 1989 / VC / M • Diary Of A Bad Girl / 1986 / SUP / M • Dirty Bob's #27: Laid Back In L.A.! / 1996 / FLP / S • Dirty Debutantes / 1990 / 4P / M • Dirty Diner #3 / 1996 / SC / M • Dirty Dirty Debutantes #2 / 1996 / 4P / M • Dirty Dirty Debutantes #4 / 1996 / 4P / M • Dirty Dirty Debutantes #5 / 1996 / 4P / M • Dirty Dirty Debutantes #7 / 1996 / 4P / M • Dirty Girls / 1984 / MIT / M • Dirty Lingerie / 1990 / VD / M • Dog Walker / 1994 / EA / M • Dolls To Dragons / 19?? / … / M • Domestic Training / 1992 / RB / B • Dominatrix Without Mercy / 1976 / ALP / B • The Double Exposure Of Holly / 1977 / TVX / M • Double Trouble Spanking / 1993 / BON / B • Dr Butts #1 / 1991 / 4P / M • Dracula Exotica / 1980 / TVX / M • Dream Girls / 1986 / VC / M • Dy-Nasty / 1988 / SE / M • The Ecstasy Girls #1 / 1979 / CA / M • The Ecstasy Girls #2 /

VEP / M • Sunset Strip Girls / 1975 / TGA / M • Sweat #1 / 1986 / PP / M • Swedish Erotica #07 / 1980 / CA / M • Swedish Erotica #08 / 1980 / CA / M • Swedish Erotica #11 / 1980 / CA / M • Swedish Erotica #12 / 1980 / CA / M • Swedish Erotica #14 / 1980 / CA / M • Swedish Erotica #43 / 1982 / CA / M • Swedish Erotica Letters #2 / 1989 / CA / C • Swedish Erotica Superstar #1: Seka / 1983 / CA / C • Sweet Alice / 1983 / VCX / M • Sweet Revenge / 1986 / ZA / M • Sweet Wet Lips / 1974 / PVX / M • Taboo #04 / 1985 / IN / M • Taboo #05 / 1986 / IN / M • Taboo #07 / 1980 / IN / M • Taboo #09 / 1991 / IN / M • Taboo #11: Crazy On You / 1993 / IN / M • Tales Of Taija Rae / 1989 / DR / M • Talk Dirty To Me #03 / 1986 / DR / M • Talk Dirty To Me #06 / 1989 / DR / M • A Taste Of Misty / 1990 / CA / C • A Taste Of Money / 1983 / AT / M • The Tasting / 1991 / EX / M • Taxi Girls #1 / 1980 / WV / M • Taxi Girls #2: In Search Of Toni / 1986 / ELD / M • Teaching Her A Lesson / 1992 / RB / B • Teenage Cheerleader / 1978 / VXP / M • Teenage Playmates / 1979 / LOV / M • Teenage Stepmother / cr74 / SVE / M • Ten Little Maidens / 1985 / EXF / M • Terms Of Endowment / 1986 / PV / M • That Lady From Rio / 1976 / VXP / M • That's Erotic / 1979 / CV / C • That's Outrageous / 1983 / CA / M • That's Porno / 1979 / CV / C • Things / 1990 / 3WO / S • This Stud's For You / 1986 / MAP / C • Thought You'd Never Ask / 1986 / CA / M • Three Faces Of Angel / 1987 / CV / M • Thrill Street Blues / 1985 / WV / M • Through The Looking Glass / 1976 / ALP / M • Too Hot To Touch #1 / 1985 / CV / M • Too Many Pieces / 1975 / LA / M • Too Naughty To Say No / 1984 / CA / M • Tori Welles Exposed / 1990 / VD / C • Toys 4 Us #1 / 1987 / WV / C • Trans Europe Express / 1989 / VC / G • Trinity Brown / 1984 / CV / M • Triple Header / 1987 / AIR / C • Trouble / 1989 / VD / M • True Legends Of Adult Cinema: The Cult Superstars / 1993 / VC / C • True Legends Of Adult Cinema: The Erotic Eighties / 1992 / VC / C • True Legends Of Adult Cinema: The Golden Age / 1992 / VC / C • Two Senoritas / 197? / VHL / M • Ultraflesh / 1980 / GO / M • Uncle Jamie's Double Trouble / 1992 / RB / B • Undulations / 1980 / VC / M • Up Up And Away / 1984 / CA / M • VCA Previews #2 / 1988 / VC / C • VCA Previews #4 / 1988 / VC / C • The Violation Of Claudia / 1977 / QX / M • The Violation Of Tori Welles / 1990 / VD / C • Virgin Dreams / 1996 / EA / M • Virginia / 1983 / CA / M • Vista Valley PTA / 1980 / CV / M • The Vixens Of Kung Fu: A Tale Of Yin Yang / 1975 / VC / M • The Wacky World Of Ed Powers / 1996 / 4P / C • Wanda Whips Wall Street / 1982 / VXP / M • Waterpower / 1975 / VHL / M • A Week And A Half In The Life Of A Prostitute / 1997 / EL / M • Wet Rocks / 1975 / BL / M • Wet Shots (Vcr) / 1983 / VCR / C • When A Woman Calls / 1975 / VXP / M • The Whore / 1989 / CA / M • Wild In The Wilderness / 1984 / GO / M • Wild Things #1 / 1985 / CV / M • Wine Me, Dine Me, 69 Me / 1989 / COL / C • Winter Heat / 1975 / AVC / M • With Love, Annette / 1985 / CA / C • With Love, Lisa / 1985 / CA / C • With Love, Loni / 1985 / CA / C • Woman In The Win-

dow / 1986 / TEM / M • Women In Uniform / 1986 / TEM / M • Working Girls / 1985 / CA / M • The World Of Henry Paris / 1981 / VC / C • WPINK-TV #2 / 1986 / PV / M • Young Nurses In Love / 1986 / VES / S • [Cathy's Graduation / 197? / ... / M • [Hotel Flesh / 1983 / CV / M

JAMIE GRILL *see* **Jamie Gillis**
JAMIE HILTON *see* *Star Index I*
JAMIE KANTOR *see* **Jamie Gillis**
JAMIE LEE *see* **Jamie Leigh**
JAMIE LEE (B. GLEN) *see* **Beverly Glen**
JAMIE LEIGH *(Jamie Lee, Jaime Lee)*
Not-too-pretty short haired blonde who started with small tits and had them enhanced in 1991 to rock solid, medium to large size. Not to be confused with Beverly Glen who sometimes uses the same name.

Adam & Eve's House Party #3: Swing Party / 1996 / VC / M • Amateur Lesbians #04: Tera / 1991 / GO / F • Amateur Lesbians #18: Jamie / 1992 / GO / F • Americans Most Wanted / 1991 / HO / M • Anal Addiction #2 / 1990 / SO / M • Anal Alley / 1996 / FD / M • Anal Assassins / 1991 / IN / M • Anal Starlets / 1991 / ROB / M • Another Rear View / 1990 / LE / M • Anything Goes / 1996 / OUP / M • Ariana's Dirty Dancers: The Professionals / 1996 / 4P / M • Ass Freaks #2 / 1995 / ROB / F • The Attendant / 1996 / SC / M • Back To Back #2 / 1992 / FC / C • Bad Side Of Town / 1993 / AFD / M • Best Of Bi And Beyond / 1992 / PNP / C • Beyond It All / 1991 / PAL / G • Black On White / 1991 / VT / F • Blonde Riders / 1991 / CC / M • Blue Angel / 1991 / SE / M • Body Fire / 1991 / LV / M • Bondage Memories #04 / 1994 / BON / C • The Bondage Producer / 1991 / BON / B • Boobs, Butts And Bloopers #2 / 1990 / HO / M • The Breast Files #3 / 1994 / AVI / M • Bruce Seven's Favorite Endings #1 / 1991 / EL / C • Bung-Ho Babes / 1991 / FC / M • Buttman In The Crack / 1996 / EA / M • Carnal College #1 / 1991 / AFV / F • Cheeks #4: A Backstreet Affair / 1991 / CC / M • Clean And Dirty / 1990 / ME / M • Club Anal #3 / 1995 / ROB / F • Cockpit / 1996 / SC / M • Cream Dream / 1991 / ZA / M • Cyrano / 1991 / PL / M • Dark Interludes / 1991 / BS / B • Deep Inside Centerfold Girls / 1991 / VC / M • Double Penetration #4 / 1991 / WV / C • Double Penetration #5 / 1992 / WV / C • Edward Penishands #1 / 1991 / VT / M • Edward Penishands #2 / 1991 / VT / M • Edward Penishands #3 / 1991 / VT / M • Even More Dangerous / 1990 / SO / M • Exotic Car Models #2 / 1996 / IN0 / F • EXXXtra Parts: Interview With a Hermaphrodite / 1995 / PL / M • The Face Of Fear / 1990 / BS / B • Flexxx #4 / 1995 / VT / M • Girl Friends / 1990 / PL / F • Girls Of Silicone Valley / 1991 / FC / M • Girls, Girls And More Girls / 1990 / LV / F • Hard Core Cafe / 1991 / PL / M • Hard Feelings / 1991 / V99 / M • The Hindlick Maneuver / 1991 / CC / M • Hot Tight Asses #13 / 1995 / TCK / M • If You're Nasty / 1991 / PL / F • Images Of Desire / 1990 / PM / M • In Excess / 1991 / CA / M • In Your Face #3 / 1995 / PL / M • Innocence Found / 1991 / PAL / G • Interview's Big Boob Bonanza / 1996 / LV / M • Jamie Lee's Procedure / 1991 / FC / S • The Journey: Oral Majority / 1991 / WV / M • Juicy Sex Scandals / 1991 / VD / M • Kym Wilde's On The

Edge #33 / 1996 / RB / B • Lady Of The House / 1990 / VEX / M • A Little Nookie / 1991 / VD / M • Love On The Line / 1990 / SO / M • Lust Fever / 1991 / FH / M • Making It / 1990 / FH / M • Microslut / 1996 / TTV / M • The Midas Touch / 1991 / VT / M • The Midnight Hour / 1991 / VT / M • Mike Hott: #164 Jamie Lee And Shelly #1 / 1991 / MHV / F • Mike Hott: #165 Jamie Lee And Shelly #2 / 1991 / MHV / F • Mike Hott: #389 Jamie Lee Pregnant / 1996 / MHV / F • My Mistress...Her Slave / 1990 / PL / B • Mystery Date / 1992 / CDI / G • Nasty Jack's Homemade Vid. #10 / 1991 / CDI / M • New Wave Hookers #2 / 1991 / VC / M • Night Deposit / 1991 / VC / M • No Man's Land #05 / 1992 / VT / F • On The Loose / 1991 / LV / M • Oral Addiction / 1995 / VI / M • The Outlaw / 1991 / WV / M • The Pawn Shop / 1996 / MID / M • Pierced Punctured And Perverted / 1995 / FC / M • Purely Sexual / 1991 / HO / M • Read My Lips / 1990 / FH / M • Ride 'em Cowgirl / 1991 / V99 / M • A Rising Star / 1991 / HO / M • Sensations #1 / 1996 / SC / M • Seoul Train / 1991 / IN / M • Sex She Wrote / 1991 / VEX / M • Sexual Healing / 1996 / SC / M • Shades Of Bondage / 1991 / BON / B • Shifting Gere / 1990 / VT / M • Skin Games / 1991 / VEX / C • Snatched To The Future / 1991 / EL / F • Split Personality / 1991 / CIN / G • Steam / 1996 / ULP / M • Stuff Your Ass #3 / 1996 / JMP / M • Sun Bunnies #1 / 1991 / SC / M • Tailspin #1 / 1991 / VT / M • A Taste Of Ecstasy / 1991 / CIN / M • Three Men And A Hooker / 1991 / WV / M • Tit Tales #3 / 1991 / FC / M • Titty Slickers #1 / 1991 / LE / M • Toying Around / 1992 / FL / M • Toys, Not Boys #3 / 1991 / FC / C • Twin Cheeks #1 / 1990 / CIN / M • Twin Cheeks #2 / 1991 / CIN / M • Two In The Bush / 1991 / EX / M • Unlike A Virgin / 1991 / HO / M • Virgins / 1995 / ERA / M • Voyeur Strippers / 1996 / PL / F • Wedding Night Blues / 1995 / EMC / M • Wenches / 1991 / VT / F • X Factor: The Next Generation / 1991 / HO / M • You Can Touch This / 1991 / EVN / M

JAMIE LEIGH (1982) *see* *Star Index I*
JAMIE LING
Sulka's Wedding / 1983 / MET / G
JAMIE LYNN *(Jamie Lynn Sterling)*
Not too pretty blonde with small tits, shoulder length hair, tattoo on her right belly at the bikini line, another large tattoo across the small of her back and bad facial acne.

Girly Video Magazine #2 / 1995 / BEP / M • Girly Video Magazine #3 / 1995 / BEP / M • Profiles #05: Planet Lust / 1995 / XPR / M
JAMIE LYNN STERLING *see* **Jamie Lynn**
JAMIE MCCLANE *see* *Star Index I*
JAMIE MONROE
50 And Still Pumping! / 1994 / EMC / M • Aged To Perfection #2 / 1995 / TTV / M • Aged To Perfection #3 / 1995 / TTV / M • Forbidden Subjects #3 / 1995 / FC / M • Golden Oldies #1 / 1995 / TTV / M • Hillary Vamp's Private Collection #07 / 1992 / HVD / M • Makin' Bacon / 1994 / WIV / M • Oldies But Goodies / 1995 / WIV / M • The Real Deal #1 / 1994 / FC / M
JAMIE PALMS
First Time Lesbians (Gourmet) / 1987 / GO / F
JAMIE SOMMERS *see* **Jamie Summers**
JAMIE ST JAMES *see* *Star Index I*

JAMIE ST. JOHN see Jack Wrangler
JAMIE STAFFORD see Jamie Summers
JAMIE STEELE see Star Index I
JAMIE SUMMERS (Jamie Sommers, Cindy Sterling, Jamie Stafford)
Pretty blonde who played the **Brat** series to perfection (maybe her real personality?). In those movies her tits look natural but they were either a very good job or she has later had them enhanced.
The Adultress / 1987 / CA / M • Andrew Blake's Girls / 1992 / CA / C • Army Brat #1 / 1987 / VI / M • The Bad News Brat / 1991 / VI / M • Ball Street / 1988 / CA / M • Blackballed / 1991 / VI / C • Blue Jeans Brat / 1991 / VI / M • Born For Love / 1987 / ... / M • The Brat / 1986 / VI / M • Brat On The Run / 1987 / VI / M • Bringing Up Brat / 1987 / VI / M • California Blondes #06 / 1992 / VD / C • Careena #1 / 1987 / WV / C • Careena #2: A Star On The Rise / 1988 / WV / C • Caught In The Act / 1987 / WV / M • Cummin' Together / 1991 / JEF / M • Double Exposure / 1990 / BAD / C • The Eleventh Commandment / 1987 / WAV / M • Hot Licks At The Pussycat Club / 1990 / WV / C • Hotel California / 1986 / WV / M • House Of Sleeping Beauties #1 / 1992 / VI / M • House Of Sleeping Beauties #2 / 1992 / VI / M • Jamie Loves Jeff #1 / 1987 / VI / M • Jamie Loves Jeff #2 / 1991 / VI / M • L.A. Raw / 1986 / SE / M • The Ladies Room / 1987 / CA / M • Les Be Friends / 1988 / WV / C • Little Shop Of Whores / 1987 / VI / M • Love Letters / 1991 / VI / M • Milk 'n' Honey / 1991 / STY / M • Night Rhythms / 1992 / IMP / S • Night Trips #1 / 1989 / CA / M • Oral Majority #06 / 1988 / WV / C • Passionate Heiress / 1987 / CA / M • The Phoenix #1 / 1992 / VI / M • The Phoenix #2 / 1992 / VI / M • Pink To Pink / 1993 / VI / C • Princess Charming / 1987 / AVC / C • Raw Talent #2 / 1987 / VC / M • Ride 'em Cow Girl / 1995 / VI / C • Toys 4 Us #3: Follow The Leader / 1990 / WV / C • Twins / 1986 / WV / M • Victim Of Love #1 / 1992 / VI / M • Victim Of Love #2 / 1992 / VI / M • Where The Boys Aren't #2 / 1989 / VI / F • Where The Boys Aren't #3 / 1990 / VI / F • Where The Boys Aren't #4 / 1992 / VI / F • The Wild Brat / 1988 / VI / M • Wild Fire / 1990 / WV / C
JAMIE TAKALL
Prescription For Passion / 1984 / VD / M
JAMIE TREVOR see Star Index I
JAMILA see Jamela
JAMILLA see Jamela
JAMINE MALIBU
Summer Of '72 / 1982 / CA / M
JAMMIN' JIM
A Touch Of Mink / 1990 / V99 / M
JAMOO
Coming Out Bi / 1995 / IN / G • Dominique's Bi Adventure / 1995 / STA / G • Gilligan's Bi-Land / 1994 / PL / G • Please Don't Tell / 1995 / CEN / G
JAMY see Star Index I
JAN
Blue Vanities #528 / 1993 / FFL / M • Blue Vanities #570 / 1995 / FFL / M • Mike Hott: #113 Jan And Ali / 1991 / MHV / F • Mike Hott: #114 Jan, Ali And Paul / 1990 / MHV / M • S&M On The Ranch: Training The New Pony Girl / 1994 / VER / B
JAN (SELENA) see Selena
JAN ADAMS see Star Index I

JAN B.
Jan B: Girl Play / 1996 / JB0 / F • Jan B: Jan & Nina Hartley / 1995 / JB0 / F • Jan B: Jan & Sierra / 1995 / JB0 / F • Jan B: Jan In The Garden / 1996 / JB0 / F • Jan B: Midnight Swim / 1996 / JB0 / F
JAN CLAUDE
Erotic Fantasies #5 / 1983 / CV / C
JAN DAVIS see Star Index I
JAN DEAN see Jason Dean
JAN HEDIN
Private Gold #04: Amazonas / 1996 / OD / M
JAN JORDAN
Love Is Not Enough / cr75 / SIL / M
JAN MICHAELS see Sean Michaels
JAN PETERSON
Loose Times At Ridley High / 1984 / VCX / M • Saturday Matinee Series #4 / 1996 / VCX / C
JAN PIERCE see Star Index I
JAN RINKBERG
Sexual Customs In Scandinavia / cr73 / QX / M
JAN SANDERS see Jon Dough
JAN SNOW
Bedtime Video #03 / 1984 / GO / M
JAN WELLS
Eager Beaver / 1975 / AVC / M • Fantasy Fever / 1975 / AVC / M • Mortgage Of Sin / 1975 / CA / M • Y-All Come / 1975 / CDC / M
JANA
Buttman's Orgies / 1996 / EA / M • The Cumm Brothers #10: Night Of The Giving Head / 1995 / OD / M • Pussy Fest Of The Northwest #1 / 1995 / NIT / M
JANA (WELLS) see Jenna Wells
JANA KNOX
The Psychiatrist / 1978 / VC / M
JANA SAUNDERS see Star Index I
JANAI
Not too pretty, big frame, brown or dark blonde hair, clit ring, small/medium tits, 19 years old, 5'10" tall, and a C cup in 1996.
Asses Galore #3: Pure Evil / 1996 / DFI / M • Buffy Malibu's Nasty Girls #11 / 1996 / ANA / F • The Clock Strikes Bizarre On Butt Row / 1996 / ABS / M • Dirty Dirty Debutantes #5 / 1996 / 4P / M • Dr Peter Proctor's House Of Anal Delights / 1996 / HO / M • Nasty Nymphos #14 / 1996 / ANA / M • Puritan Video Magazine #10 / 1997 / LE / M • Shooting Gallery / 1996 / EL / M • Sodomania #18: Shame Based / 1996 / EL / M
JANAY
Liquid Lips #2 / 1994 / MAV / M
JANE
Blue Vanities #541 / 1994 / FFL / M • Creme De Femme #3 / 1981 / AVC / C • Dick & Jane Do The Slopes In Ass Spin / 1994 / AVI / M • Dick & Jane Do The Strip / 1994 / AVI / M • Dick & Jane Penetrate Paris / 1994 / AVI / M • Dick & Jane Up, Down And All Around / 1994 / AVI / M • Different Strokes / 1996 / VC / M • Girls In Heat / 1995 / WIV / M • Hometown Girls / 1984 / CDP / F • Kinky Ladies Of London / 1995 / VC / M • Limited Edition #19 / 1980 / AVC / M • Rare Ends / 1996 / PRE / C • Sole Survivors / 1996 / PRE / C
JANE (RENE BOND) see Rene Bond
JANE ABRAMS
Penthouse Pleasures / 19?? / VST / M
JANE ALLISON

Hollywood Babylon / 1972 / AIR / S • Triple Play / 1983 / HO / M
JANE BAKER
The Arrangement / 1984 / CV / M • Come Play With Me #2 / 1980 / PS / S • [Segrete Espereinze Di Luca E Fanny / 1980 / ... / S • [Swedish Erotic Sensations / 1980 / ... / S
JANE BARTON
An Unnatural Act #1 / 1984 / DR / M
JANE BAUER
Pain Is The Price / 1996 / LBO / B
JANE BEST see Star Index I
JANE BLACK
On White Satin / 1980 / VCX / M
JANE BOND see Carolyn Brandt
JANE BRANDON see Pia Snow
JANE BRYANT
The Last Vamp / 1996 / IP / M
JANE CASTAY
Seduce Me Tonight / 1984 / AT / M
JANE CLAYTON see Star Index I
JANE DANIEL see Nina DePonca
JANE DANIELS see Nina DePonca
JANE DAVIL see Nina DePonca
JANE DEVILLE see Nina DePonca
JANE GRAHAM see Star Index I
JANE HAMILTON see Veronica Hart
JANE HARWOOD see Jane March
JANE KELTON
All American Girls #1 / 1982 / CA / M • The Blonde Goddess / 1982 / VXP / M • Delicious / 1981 / VXP / M
JANE LEBEAU
Attractive small breasted blonde with a good sense of humor.
Ass Tales / 1991 / PL / M • Class Ass /1992 / PL / M • Mr. Big / 1991 / PL / M • Stick It In The Rear #1 / 1991 / PL / M • Unlaced / 1992 / PL / M
JANE LINDSAY
Fantasy / 1978 / VCX / M • Flash / 1980 / CA / M • Small Town Girls / 1979 / CXV / M
JANE MARCH (Jane Harwood)
Gorgeous, very pretty face, tight waist, narrow hips, boy-like butt. Slightly Oriental looking due to her mother being Vietnamese/Chinese. Born Mar 20, 1973 in Edgeware, England. 5'2" tall, 98lbs. Married to Carmine Zozzora (producer of The Color Of Night).
Color Of Night / 1994 / HPH / S • The Lover / 1991 / MGM / S • Never Ever / 1996 / ... / S • Tarzan And Jane / 1997 / ... / S
JANE MARSH
Cheri's On Fire / 1986 / V99 / M • Glamour Girls / 1987 / SE / M
JANE MILTON see Star Index I
JANE PAGAN
Blue Vanities #533 / 1993 / FFL / M • Seka's Fantasies / 1981 / CA / M
JANE QUATROU
Personal Trainer (Cs) / 1995 / CS / B
JANE REDDIX see Chanel (1992)
JANE RODEO
The Bondage Zone / 1994 / CS / B • Tied & Tickled #28: Tickling Dr. Cripley / 1995 / CS / B
JANE SAYMORE
The All Girl Anal Orgy / 1996 / BAC / F • Anal Crybabies / 1996 / BAC / M
JANE SEEMOUR see Star Index I
JANE SENTAS see Jane Tsentas
JANE SENTIS see Jane Tsentas
JANE TAYLOR
San Francisco Lesbians #3 / 1993 / PL / F
JANE TRACEY

Blue Vanities #514 / 1992 / FFL / M

JANE TSENTAS *(Jane Sentis, Jane Sentas)*
The Adult Version Of Dr Jekyll And Mr Hyde / 1971 / SOW / S • Blood Sabbath / 1972 / JLT / S • Blue Vanities #193 / 1993 / FFL / M • The Jekyll And Hyde Portfolio / 1972 / ... / S • The Loves Of Mary Jane / 1989 / BWV / C • Sacrilege / 1971 / AXV / M • A Touch Of Sex / 1972 / AR / M • Wild, Free And Hungry / 1970 / SOW / S

JANE TYLER *(Janet Silver)*
Great Balls Of Fire / 1989 / FAZ / M

JANE TYLER (JACQUEL) *see* **Jacqueline**

JANE WALTER *see* **Star Index I**

JANE WATERS *see* **Star Index I**

JANE WENSTEIN
Teenage Cowgirls / 1973 / ALP / M

JANE WEST
Something For Everybody / 1975 / ... / M

JANE WILLIAMS
Spanking Video #1: Sports College / 1995 / MET / B • Spanking Video #4: Sports Comeback / 1995 / MET / B

JANEE *see* **Missy Warner**

JANELLE *see* **Star Index I**

JANELLE LEIGH *see* **Star Index I**

JANET
A&B GB#060: Mary, Janet & Stacey / 1992 / A&B / M • Bi-Bi Love Amateurs #1 / 1993 / SFP / G • Big Girl Workout / 1991 / BTO / M • Big Tit Roundup #1 / 199? / H&S / S • Blue Vanities #501 / 1992 / FFL / M • Blue Vanities #533 / 1993 / FFL / M • Blue Vanities #557 / 1994 / FFL / M • Blue Vanities #566 / 1995 / FFL / M • Blue Vanities #571 / 1995 / FFL / M • Bobby Hollander's Rookie Nookie #03 / 1993 / SFP / M • HomeGrown Video #455 / 1995 / HOV / M • HomeGrown Video #456 / 1995 / HOV / M • Huge Ladies #10 / 1991 / BTO / M • Kinky College Cunts #06 / 1993 / NS / F • Neighborhood Watch #22: In The Pink And Wet / 1992 / LBO / M

JANET ACT
Family Affair / 1979 / MIT / M

JANET BALDWIN *see* **Jenny Baxter**

JANET BEAVER
That's Erotic / 1979 / CV / C

JANET CHAMPER *see* **Star Index I**

JANET GAUT
Bucky Beaver's XXX Dragon Art Theatre Double Feature #02 / 1996 / SOW / M • The Rites Of Uranus / 1975 / SOW / M

JANET GEEWHIZ *see* **Janet Jackme**

JANET HOLMAN
San Francisco Lesbians #6 / 1994 / PL / F

JANET JACKME *(Janet Jackmee, Janet Geewhiz, Nikki (J.Jackme))*
Tiffany Taylor (**Principles of Lust**) is not Janet Jackme. Janet is black with small to medium sized droopy tits, a not-pretty face and a flattish ass. About 20 years old in 1993.
'Ho! 'Ho! 'Ho! / 1993 / WP / M • Adventures Of The DP Boys: Janet And Da Boyz / 1994 / HW / M • Adventures Of The DP Boys: The Blacks Are Cumming / 1994 / HW / M • All The President's Women / 1994 / LV / M • Amateur Orgies #11 / 1992 / AFI / M • Amateur Orgies #18 / 1992 / AFI / M • Amateurs Exposed #02 / 1993 / CV / M • America's Raunchiest Home Videos #30: Hot Afternoon / 1992 / ZA / M • Anal Delights #3 / 1993 / ROB / M • Anal Delin-

quent #1 / 1993 / ROB / M • Anal International / 1992 / HW / M • Anal Legend / 1994 / ROB / M • Anal Thunder #2 / 1993 / ROB / M • Back Rent / 1996 / MP0 / M • Backdoor Black #2 / 1993 / WV / C • Behind The Blackout / 1993 / HW / M • The Best Of Black Anal #1 / 1995 / ROB / C • The Best Of Oriental Anal #1 / 1994 / ROB / C • Biff Malibu's Totally Nasty Home Videos #23 / 1992 / ANA / M • Black Anal Dreams / 1995 / WV / M • Black Beach / 1995 / LV / M • Black Beauties #2 / 1992 / VIM / M • Black Beauty (Coast To Coast) / 1994 / CC / M • Black Bottom Girlz / 1994 / CA / M • The Black Butt Sisters Do Baltimore / 1995 / MID / M • The Black Butt Sisters Do Detroit / 1995 / MID / M • Black Buttman #02 / 1994 / CC / M • Black Buttwatch / 1995 / FH / M • Black Cherries / 1993 / EVN / C • Black Dirty Debutantes / 1993 / 4P / M • Black Fire / 1993 / VIM / M • Black Flava / 1994 / EX / M • Black Hollywood Amateurs #16 / 1995 / MID / M • Black Is Back / 1993 / HW / M • Black Jack City #3 / 1993 / HW / M • Black Leather / Black Skin / 1995 / VT / B • Black Magic #1 / 1993 / VIM / M • Black Magic #2 / 1994 / VIM / M • Black Mystique #07 / 1994 / VT / F • Black Mystique #08 / 1994 / VT / F • Black Nurse Fantasies / 1994 / CA / M • Black On Black (1994-Midnight) / 1994 / MID / C • Black Orgies #35 / 1995 / GO / M • Black Playhouse / 1995 / HBE / M • Black Satin / 1994 / IN / M • Black Sensations: Models In Heat / 1995 / SUF / M • Black Velvet #1 / 1992 / CC / M • Black Velvet #2 / 1993 / CC / M • Black Velvet #3 / 1994 / CC / M • Black Women, White Men #5 / 1995 / FC / M • Blackbroad Jungle / 1994 / IN / M • Blackdoor Babes / 1994 / TIW / M • Blacks N' Blue / 1995 / VT / B • The Blues #2 / 1994 / VT / M • Bobby Hollander's Maneaters #03 / 1993 / SFP / M • The Bodacious Boat Orgy #1 / 1993 / GLI / M • The Bodacious Boat Orgy #2 / 1993 / GLI / M • Body Of Innocence / 1993 / WP / M • Boomerwang / 1992 / MID / M • Bootin' Up / 1995 / VT / B • Booty By Nature / 1994 / WP / M • Booty Ho #1 / 1993 / ROB / M • Booty In The House / 1993 / WP / M • Booty Mistress / 1994 / ROB / M • Booty Sister #1 / 1993 / ROB / M • Bootylicious: EZ Street / 1995 / JMP / M • Brooklyn Nights / 1994 / OD / M • Bubble Butts #19 / 1992 / LBO / M • Bump 'n' Grind / 1994 / HW / M • The Butt Boss / 1993 / VD / M • Butt Camp / 1993 / HW / C • Butt Jammers / 1994 / WIV / M • The Buttnicks #4: The Black Buttnicks / 1993 / CC / M • Buttwiser / 1992 / HW / M • Chocolate Bunnies #01 / 1995 / LBO / C • Chocolate Bunnies #02 / 1995 / LBO / C • Chocolate Bunnies #06 / 1996 / LBO / C • Cracklyn / 1994 / HW / M • Crew Sluts / 1994 / KWP / M • Crimson Thighs / 1995 / HW / M • Da Booty Call / 1994 / HW / M • Danger-Ass / 1992 / MID / M • Dark Alleys #01 / 1992 / FC / M • Dark Alleys #08 / 1992 / FC / M • Dark Alleys #12 / 1993 / FC / M • Dark Double D-Lites / 1993 / HW / C • Dark Room / 1994 / VT / M • Dark Tunnels / 1994 / LV / M • Deep Cheeks #4 / 1993 / ROB / M • Defying The Odds / 1995 / OD / M • Deja Vu / 1993 / XCI / M • Double Penetration Virgins #02: The Second Cumming / 1994 / LE / M • The Ebony Connection #2 / 1994 / LBO /

C • Ebony Erotica #04: Ebony Gods / 1993 / GO / M • Ebony Erotica / 1995 / VT / M • Erotic Desires / 1994 / MAX / M • Erotica / 1992 / CC / M • European Debutantes #03 / 1995 / IP / M • Exit In Rear / 1993 / XCI / M • Fantasy Inc. / 1995 / CV / M • A Few Good Rears / 1993 / IN / M • Freak Dat Booty / 1994 / WP / M • From A Whisper To A Scream / 1993 / GO / M • Gimme Some Head / 1994 / VT / M • Girlz In The Hood #3: Erotic Justice / 1993 / HW / M • Ho The Man Down / 1994 / WIV / M • Hollywood Swingers #06 / 1992 / LBO / M • Hollywood Swingers #07 / 1993 / LBO / C • Honey, I Blew Everybody #1 / 1992 / MID / M • Jam / 1993 / PL / M • Janet's House Party / 1995 / HW / M • Kiss Is A Rebel With A Cause / 1993 / WV / M • Knockin' Da Booty / 1993 / WP / M • Koko Is Cumin' At Cha / 1994 / AVI / M • Lips / 1994 / FC / M • M Series #14 / 1993 / LBO / M • The Man Who Loves Women / 1994 / VC / M • Maverdick / 1995 / WV / M • Miss Judge / 1997 / VI / M • Miss Nude International / 1993 / LE / M • Mo' Booty #1 / 1992 / HW / C • Mo' White Trash / 1993 / MET / M • Money, Money, Money / 1993 / FD / M • Mr. Peepers Amateur Home Videos #61: Four Play For Four / 1992 / LBO / M • My Baby Got Back #01 / 1992 / VT / M • My Baby Got Back #02 / 1993 / VT / M • My Baby Got Back #03 / 1993 / VT / M • My Baby Got Back #04 / 1994 / VT / M • My Baby Got Back #05 / 1995 / VT / M • My Baby Got Back #06 / 1995 / VT / M • Nasty Nymphos #08 / 1995 / ANA / M • The New Ass Masters #11 / 1996 / LEI / C • The New Butt Hunt #19 / 1996 / LEI / C • Outcall Outlaws / 1995 / CC / M • Pussyman #07: On The Dark Side / 1994 / SNA / M • Pussywoman #2 / 1994 / CC / M • Quantum Deep / 1993 / HW / M • Racially Motivated / 1994 / LV / M • Return To Melrose Place / 1993 / HW / M • Rump-Shaker #1 / 1993 / HW / M • Rump-Shaker #2 / 1993 / HW / M • Rump-Shaker #3 / 1994 / HW / M • Sean Michaels On The Road #02: Da Hood / 1993 / VT / M • Sex Secrets Of High Priced Call Girls / 1995 / MID / M • Sexual Misconduct / 1994 / VD / C • Shades Of Color #2 / 1995 / LBO / M • Sharon's House Party / 1995 / HW / M • Sherlock Homie / 1995 / IN / M • Sweet Brown Sugar / 1994 / AVI / M • The Sweet Sweet Back's Big Bone (#1) / 1994 / FH / M • Tight Pucker / 1992 / WV / M • The Tonya Hard-On Story / 1994 / GO / M • Two-Pac / 1996 / VT / M • Up And Cummers #02 / 1993 / 4P / M • Wet & Slippery / 1995 / WV / M • What's Butt Got To Do With It? / 1993 / HW / M • White Boys & Black Bitches / 1995 / ROB / M • Whoopin' Her Behind / 1995 / VT / B • Wilder At Heart / 1993 / ANA / M • Women Of Color #1 / 1994 / ANA / M • You Go Girl! (Video Team) / 1995 / VT / M

JANET JACKMEE *see* **Janet Jackme**

JANET JONES
Sexual Freedom In The Ozarks / 1971 / VHL / M • Tycoon's Daughter / cr73 / SVE / M

JANET JOY
Candy Girls #2 / 19?? / AVC / M

JANET LITTLEDAY *see* **Janette Littledove**

JANET LONG
Teddy Bare / 1977 / CA / M

JANET ROSS *see Star Index I*

JANET SANDS
The Angel In Mr. Holmes / 1988 / WV / C • Carnal's Cuties / cr79 / XTR / M

JANET SILVER *see Jane Tyler*

JANET SLADE *see Star Index I*

JANET STANSBURY *see Star Index I*

JANET SUCCATIT *see Star Index I*

JANET TAYLOR
Black Mistress, White Slaves / 1992 / RB / B • The Doctor's Orders / 1992 / RB / B • Domestic Training / 1992 / RB / B • Housemother's Discipline #1 / 1991 / RB / B • Housemother's Discipline #2 / 1992 / RB / B • Housemother's Discipline #3 / 1992 / RB / B • Housemother's Discipline #4 / 1992 / RB / B • Housemother's Discipline #5 / 1994 / RB / B • Housemother's Discipline #6 / 1994 / RB / B • Nasty Jack's Homemade Vid. #18 / 1991 / CDI / M • Old Wave Hookers #1 / 1995 / PL / M • Punished Housemother / 1991 / RB / B • Punishment And Revenge / 1992 / RB / B • Sex Over 40 #1 / 1994 / PL / M • Sex Over 40 #2 / 1994 / PL / M • Shaved #04 / 1992 / RB / F • Spanking Fantasy / 1992 / RB / B

JANET TRENT *see Jennifer Noxt*

JANET WASS
The Stewardesses / 1969 / SOW / S • The Stewardesses / 1981 / CA / M

JANETH
Asian Connection Video #103 / 1996 / AC0 / B

JANETTE
Magma: Dirty Twins / 1994 / MET / M

JANETTE LITTLEDOVE *(Jeanette Littledove, Little Dove, Janet Littleday)*
Not too pretty, pudgy, with large inflated tits. Supposedly part American Indian. Born in 1967. Married to Buck Adams at one stage.
Amazing Sex Stories #2 / 1987 / SUV / C • The Amorous Adventures Of Janette Littledove / 1988 / AR / M • Anal Angels #2 / 1990 / VEX / C • Angel Of The Night / 1985 / IN / M • Around The World With Samantha Strong / 1989 / V99 / M • Big Busted Goddesses Of L.A. / 1991 / NAP / S • Careena #1 / 1987 / WV / C • Careena #2: A Star On The Rise / 1988 / WV / C • Cat-Fight Dream / 1988 / NAP / B • Crazy With The Heat #1 / 1986 / CV / M • Dangerous When Wet (Amber Lynn Is) / 1987 / VCX / M • Dirty Tricks / 1990 / VEX / M • End Of Innocence / 1986 / AR / M • Erotic Dreams / 1987 / HO / M • Forbidden Bodies / 1986 / HU / M • Hometown Honeys #1 / 1986 / VEX / M • Honkytonk Angels / 1988 / IN / C • Hotel California / 1986 / WV / M • Hottest Ticket / 1987 / WV / C • Irresistible #2 / 1986 / SE / M • Keyhole #167: Ass Eaters / 1989 / KEH / M • Les Be Friends / 1988 / WV / C • A Little Dove-Tale / 1987 / IN / M • Littledove's Cup / 1988 / FOV / M • Living In A Wet Dream / 1986 / PEN / C • Love Notes / 1986 / HO / C • Mammary Lane / 1988 / VT / C • Miami Spice #1 / 1987 / CA / M • The Million Dollar Screw / 1987 / VT / M • Nymphette #2 / 1986 / WV / M • Only The Best Of Breasts / 1987 / CV / C • Oral Majority #05 / 1987 / WV / C • Pretty Peaches #2 / 1987 / VC / M • Rachel Ryan Exposed / 1990 / WV / C • Rear Enders / 1987 / SE / C • Restless Passion / 1987 / HO / M • Rocky-X #2 / 1988 / PEN / M • Satania / 1986 / DR / M • Sexaholics / 1987 / VCX / M • Summer Lovers / 1987 / WET /

M • A Taste Of Pleasure / 1988 / AVC / M • Topless Trio / 1988 / NAP / B • Toys 4 Us #2 / 1987 / WV / C • Triple Xposure / 1986 / VD / M • With Love, Littledove / 1988 / AR / M

JANETTE SINCLAIR *see Star Index I*

JANETTE STARION *see Jean Afrique*

JANETTE TYLER *see Jacqueline*

JANEY
Blue Vanities #504 / 1992 / FFL / M • Lunch / 1972 / VC / M

JANEY CARL *see Star Index I*

JANEY LAMB
Buttman's British Moderately Big Tit Adventure / 1994 / EA / M • Buttman's Wet Dream / 1994 / EA / M • Private Film #06 / 1994 / OD / M • Private Video Magazine #16 / 1994 / OD / M • Sodomania #08: The London Sessions / 1994 / EL / M

JANEY ROBBINS
Tall, agressive, marginal face, medium to large tits, large tattoo on her left shoulder back, black slightly curly hair.
Back To Back #1 / 1987 / 4P / C • Backdoor Bandits / 1989 / MIR / C • Black Silk Secrets / 1989 / VC / C • Blacks & Blondes #16 / 1986 / WV / M • Bodies In Heat #1 / 1983 / CA / M • Chicks In Black Leather / 1989 / VC / C • Classic Erotica #6 / 1985 / SVE / M • Cock Robin / 1989 / SUE / M • Coffee, Tea Or Me / 1984 / CV / M • Collection #06 / 1984 / CA / M • Dear Fanny / 1984 / CV / M • Dial F For Fantasy / 1984 / PL / M • Dirty 30's Cinema: Janey Robbins & Shantell / 1986 / PV / C • Down And Dirty / 1985 / LBO / M • Dreams Of Natasha / 1985 / AAH / M • Endless Passion / 1987 / LIM / C • Femme Fatale / 1984 / VIV / M • Fleshdance / 1983 / SE / M • Getting Lucky / 1983 / CA / M • Ginger Lynn—Non-Stop / 1988 / VD / C • Girlfriends / 1983 / MIT / M • Girls Of Paradise #1 / 1986 / PV / C • Golden Girls #08 / 1983 / CA / M • Golden Girls #09 / 1983 / CA / M • Her Wicked Ways / 1983 / CA / M • High Price Spread / 1986 / PV / C • I Love A Girl In A Uniform / 1989 / VC / C • I Want It All / 1984 / VD / M • Indecent Pleasures / 1984 / CA / M • Insatiable #2 / 1984 / CA / M • Inside Everybody / 1984 / AVC / M • Kinky Sluts / 1988 / MIR / C • The Legend Of King Karl / 1986 / AR / M • Loose Ends #1 / 1984 / 4P / M • Lust At The Top / 1985 / CDI / M • The Many Shades Of Amber / 1986 / LIM / M • Nasty Nurses / 1983 / CA / M • Nice 'n' Tight / 1985 / AIR / M • A Night On The Wild Side / 1986 / VC / M • On Golden Blonde / 1984 / PV / M • Only The Best Of Oral / 1989 / CV / C • Orgies / 1987 / WV / C • Pleasure Zone / 1984 / SE / M • Private Moments / 1983 / CV / M • Private Teacher / 1983 / CA / M • San Fernando Valley Girls / 1983 / CA / M • Sex Dreams On Maple Street / 1985 / WV / M • Sex On The Set / 1984 / RLV / M • Sexpertease / 1985 / VD / M • Shades Of Ecstasy / 1983 / HO / M • She-Male Encounters #07: Divine Atrocities #1 / 1981 / MET / G • She-Male Encounters #08: Divine Atrocities #2 / 1981 / MET / G • Sheer Haven / 1989 / DR / C • Slip Into Silk / 1985 / CA / M • Summer Camp Girls / 1983 / CA / M • Swedish Erotica #49 / 1983 / CA / M • Swedish Erotica #50 / 1983 / CA / M • Swedish Erotica Superstar #3: Janey Robbins / 1984 / CA / C • A Taste Of Janey / 1990 / PIN / C • Ten Lit-

tle Maidens / 1985 / EXF / M • Terms Of Endowment / 1986 / PV / M • Tower Of Power / 1985 / CV / M • True Crimes Of Passion / 1983 / CA / G • Two On The Tongue / 1988 / TAM / C • Virginia / 1983 / CA / M • Where The Girls Are / 1984 / VEX / M • Whose Fantasy Is It, Anyway? / 1983 / AVC / M • Working It Out / 1983 / CA / M • Yankee Seduction / 1984 / WV / M • You Make Me Wet / 1985 / SVE / M

JANEY RUNNY
Rear Ended / 1985 / WV / M

JANI *see Star Index I*

JANI GEORGE
Taboo American Style #4: The Exciting Conclusion / 1985 / VC / M

JANI LOGAN *see Star Index I*

JANICE
The Best Of Fabulous Flashers / 1996 / DGD / F • Blue Vanities #515 / 1992 / FFL / M • Blue Vanities #532 / 1993 / FFL / M • Blue Vanities #583 / 1996 / FFL / M • Joe Elliot's College Girls #45 / 1996 / JOE / M • Mike Hott: #146 Janice And Sukoya #1 / 1991 / MHV / F • Mike Hott: #147 Janice And Sukoya #2 / 1991 / MHV / F • Pussy Fest Of The Northwest #5 / 1995 / NIT / M • Ready To Drop #06 / 1995 / FC / M

JANICE DUPRE
Angel In Distress / 1982 / AVO / B

JANICE DUVAL
The Pleasure Palace / 1978 / CV / M

JANICE FLANDERS
Streets Of New York #03 / 1994 / PL / M

JANICE JAMES
Football Widow / 1979 / SCO / M • French Erotica: Love Story / 1980 / AR / M • French Erotica: Report Card / 1980 / AR / M • Love Story / 1979 / SCO / M

JANICE LESSEN
Sex Over 40 #1 / 1994 / PL / M

JANICE SUMMERS
Anal Vision #18 / 1993 / LBO / M • The Ass Master #05 / 1994 / GLI / M

JANICE WETPIECE
The Best Little Whorehouse In Tijuana / 1995 / HBE / M

JANIE LEE *see Star Index I*

JANIE LOVE
[Sex With Stars / 19?? / ... / M

JANINA
Magma: Horny Bulls / 1994 / MET / M

JANINE
Girls Of Sundance Spa: Hardcore Plumpers #1 / 1992 / BTO / M • Magma: Deep Inside Janine / 1994 / MET / M • Magma: Fuck Me Diana / 1994 / MET / M • Magma: Sperm-Crazy / 1994 / MET / M • New Busom Brits / 199? / H&S / S

JANINE (LINDEMULDER) *see Janine Lindemulder*

JANINE BITSCH *see Star Index I*

JANINE DALTON *see Jean Dalton*

JANINE LINDE *see Janine Lindemulder*

JANINE LINDEMULDER *(Dakota (Janine), Janine (Lindemulder), Jeanine, Janine Linde)*
Plasticized showgirl type blonde (big) ex *Penthouse* who was originally supposed to be called Dakota. She is 36-24-36, 5'8" tall, and was born in La Mirada, CA on November 14, 1968. She is supposedly married to a construction worker but as of early 1996 was getting a divorce. Arrested May 19, 1995 in Las Vegas with Julia Ann for obscenity (or some variant thereof). It seems

that her tits are enhanced although it was a good job. American Blonde / 1993 / VI / M • Badgirls #1: Lockdown / 1994 / VI / M • Bikini Watch / 1996 / PHV / F • Blonde Justice #1 / 1993 / VI / M • Blonde Justice #2 / 1993 / VI / M • Blonde Justice #3 / 1994 / VI / M • Bloopers & Boners / 1996 / VI / M • Body Language / 1991 / VI / M • Caged Fury / 1990 / C3S / S • Channel Blonde / 1994 / VI / M • The Comix / 1995 / VI / M • The Coven #1 / 1993 / VI / M • The Coven #2 / 1993 / VI / M • Eleventh Annual AVN Awards / 1994 / VC / M • Extreme Close-Up / 1996 / VI / M • Extreme Sex #3: Wired / 1994 / VI / M • Fantasy Girls / 1990 / ERI / S • Head Shots / 1995 / VI / M • Head To Head / 1996 / VI / M • Hidden Obsessions / 1992 / BFP / M • It's Blondage, The Video / 1994 / VI / M • Killer Looks / 1994 / IMP / S • Lady In Waiting / 1994 / AGF / S • Layover / 1994 / VI / M • Lethal Affairs / 1996 / VI / M • Moving Target / 1992 / HHV / S • The Naked Truth / 1995 / VI / M • Once In A Lifetime / 1994 / VC / C • Oral Obsession #1 / 1994 / VI / M • Parlor Games / 1993 / VI / M • Penthouse: DreamGirls / 1994 / A*V / F • Penthouse: The Girls Of Penthouse #2 / 1993 / PET / S • Penthouse: Passport To Paradise / 1991 / PET / F • Penthouse: Ready To Ride / 1992 / PET / F • Penthouse: Satin & Lace #1 / 1992 / PET / F • Penthouse: Satin & Lace #2 / 1992 / PET / F • Penthouse: Women In & Out Of Uniform / 1994 / A*V / S • Playboy: Stripsearch: San Francisco / 1996 / UNI / S • The Player / 1995 / VI / M • Positively Pagan #06 / 1993 / ATA / M • Spring Fever USA / 1988 / PRS / S • Stripping For Your Lover / 1995 / NIV / F • Suite 18 / 1994 / VI / M • Tight Shots #2 / 1994 / VI / M • Vagablonde / 1994 / VI / M • Where The Boys Aren't #6 / 1995 / VI / F • Where The Boys Aren't #7 / 1995 / VI / F • Where The Boys Aren't #8 / 1996 / VI / F • Where The Boys Aren't #9 / 1996 / VI / F

JANINE REYNAUD
Castle Of The Creeping Flesh / 1967 / LUM / S • Chambermaid's Dream / 1986 / PS / S • Frustration / 1970 / ... / S • Je Suis Une Nymphomane / 1970 / ... / S • Kiss Me, Monster / 1967 / LUM / S • La Coda Dello Scorpione / 1971 / LUM / S • The Felines / 1975 / VCX / M • Marianne Bouquet / 1979 / VCX / M • Sadisterotica / 1967 / ... / S • Six Days A Week / 1966 / ... / S • Succubus / 1967 / ... / S • [Assassinio Senza Volto / 1967 / ... / S • [L'Uomo Piu Velenoso Del Cobra / 1971 / ... / S • [La Main Noire / 1968 / ... / S

JANIS KING
Open For Business / 1983 / AMB / M • A Touch Of Desire / 1983 / VCR / C • Whatever Happened To Miss September? / 1973 / ALP / M

JANIS LAKE
Love Slaves / 1976 / VCR / M

JANN
The Satisfiers Of Alpha Blue / 1980 / AVC / M

JANNE
Swedish Vip Magazine #2 / 1995 / PL / M

JANNE HEDIN
The Wild Women / 1996 / PL / M

JANNETTE
Magma: Claudine In Action / 1996 / MET / M

JANNETTE CUMMINGS
Debbie Does Dallas #3 / 1985 / VC / M

JANNI H.
Foreign Exchange Sluts / 1995 / TNT / M

JANNIKA
Swedish Vip Magazine #2 / 1995 / PL / M

JAQUELINE
Magma: Double #2 / 1995 / MET / M

JAQUI ANNE
Carnal Possessions / 1988 / VEX / M • Carnal Possessions / 1991 / VEX / M • Flame / 1989 / ARG / M

JAQULIN
The Betrayal Of Innocence #1: The Awakening Of Marika / 1993 / CC / M • The Betrayal Of Innocence #2: The Decadence / 1993 / CC / M • The Betrayal Of Innocence #3: The Choice / 1993 / CC / M

JARA (TEXAS M) *see* **Texas Milly**
JARAD (R. MASTERS) *see* **Rick Masters**
JARED CLARK *see* **Star Index I**
JARIS LAVENTURE
Pussyman #03: The Search Continues / 1993 / SNA / M

JASAE *see* **Desi DeAngelo**
JASMIN
The Bitch Biker #1: The Long Road Home / 1994 / RBP / F • Magma: Shopping Anal / 1994 / MET / M

JASMIN (KASSI NOVA) *see* **Kassi Nova**
JASMINE *(Mai Ling, Chi Chi Ling, Mei Ling, Linda Lee (Jasmine))*
. There are so many girls (particulary Asian) that call themselves Jasmine or some misspelling therof that ID and alternate names are almost worthless here.

Booty Babes / 1993 / ROB / F • Bum Rap / 1990 / PLV / B • Creamy Cheeks / 1986 / VEX / M • Creme De La Face #03 / 1994 / OD / M • Dark Passions #02 / 1993 / AFV / M • Ebony Goddesses / 1985 / LON / B • Erotic Dimensions: Aggressive Women / 1982 / NSV / M • Golden Girls #08 / 1983 / CA / M • Golden Girls #11 / 1983 / CA / M • Groupies Galore / 1983 / VC / M • GVC: Sweet Dominance #127 / 1983 / GO / B • The Heat Is On / 1985 / WV / M • High Heel Harlots #04 / 1994 / SFP / M • High Heels In Heat #1 / 1988 / RSV / F • High Rollers / 1987 / VEX / M • Hot Foot / 1991 / PLV / B • Liquid Lips #2 / 1994 / MAV / M • Lust Letters / 1988 / CA / M • Mr. Peepers Amateur Home Videos #74: C Foam Surfer / 1993 / LBO / M • Odyssey Triple Play #62: Gang Bangs All Around / 1994 / OD / M • Ona Z's Star Search #03 / 1993 / GLI / M • Oriental Temptations / 1984 / CV / C • Payne In The Behind / 1993 / AMF / C • Penthouse: The Girls Of Penthouse #2 / 1993 / PET / S • Sweet Lips & Buns / 1993 / ROB / F • Thrill Seekers / 1993 / ROB / F • The Trouble With Traci / 1984 / CHA / C • We Love To Tease / 1985 / VD / M • Women On Women #2 / 1994 / MAV / F • You Turn Me On / 1986 / LIM / M

JASMINE (KASSI NOVA) *see* **Kassi Nova**
JASMINE (ORIENTAL)
100% Amateur #04: Oriental Orientation / 1995 / OD / M

JASMINE (OTHER)
Bay City Hot Licks / 1993 / ROB / F • The End / 1995 / VI / M • Funny Ladies / 1996 / PRE / B • Hot Body Competition: Hot Pants Contest / 1996 / CG / F • Reel Life Video #49: / 1996 / RLF / F • Skirts & Flirts #02 /

1997 / XPR / F

JASMINE (WHITE)
All Pain, No Gain / 1991 / NEP / B • Creme De La Face #04 / 1994 / OD / M • High Heels In Heat #3 / 1989 / RSV / F • Home-Grown Video #446: Slam Bam Thank You Ma'am! / 1995 / HOV / M • Sex Professionals / 1994 / LIP / F

JASMINE ALOHA
Bangkok Nights / 1994 / VI / M • Beaver Hunt #02 / 1994 / LEI / M • Blonde Conquest / 1995 / NAP / B • Bloopers & Behind The Scenes / 1995 / LEI / M • Body Of Love / 1994 / ERA / M • Buffy Malibu's Nasty Girls #07 / 1994 / ANA / F • The Busty Kittens / 1995 / NAP / F • Defending Your Soul / 1995 / EX / M • Dick & Jane Do The Slopes In Ass Spin / 1994 / AVI / M • Eruption Of Jealousy / 1996 / NAP / B • Flexxx #1 / 1994 / VT / M • Fortune Nookie / 1994 / PPP / M • John Wayne Bobbitt Uncut / 1994 / LEI / M • Latina Rumble / 1996 / NAP / B • Legend #5: The Legend Continues / 1994 / LE / M • Lovin' Spoonfuls #6 / 1996 / 4P / C • The Mauling / 1995 / NAP / B • Nasty Nymphos #04 / 1994 / ANA / M • New Ends #07 / 1994 / 4P / M • Pussy Hunt #02 / 1994 / LEI / M • Rainwoman #08 / 1994 / CC / M • Spies Get Trashed / 1995 / NAP / B • Stewardesses Behind Bars / 1994 / HW / M • Tiffany Lords Straps One On #1 / 1994 / WIV / F • Tiffany Lords Straps One On #2 / 1994 / WIV / F • Up And Cummers #10 / 1994 / 4P / M • Welcome To Paradise / 1994 / IF / M

JASMINE DUBAY *see* **Anna Ventura**
JASMINE DUBOIS *see* **Anna Ventura**
JASMINE FOXX
Biff Malibu's Totally Nasty Home Videos #26 / 1992 / ANA / M

JASMINE JADE
Creme De La Face #13: Nine Nasty Nymphs / 1995 / OD / M • Creme De La Face #16: Ladies Licking / 1996 / OD / M

JASMINE JENKINS
Black Lust / 1995 / UBP / M

JASMINE JOHNSON
Creme De La Face #10: Cum Dome / 1995 / OD / M • Creme De La Face #11: Cum Plasterers / 1995 / OD / M • Creme De La Face #15: Showroom Sex / 1996 / OD / M • Cum Tv / 1996 / NIT / M • The Cumm Brothers #13: Rump Rangers / 1996 / OD / M • The Cumm Brothers #16: Deja Goo / 1996 / OD / M • Hard Cum Cafe / 1996 / BCP / M • High Heeled & Horny #4 / 1995 / LBO / M • Pussy Fest Of The Northwest #3 / 1995 / NIT / M • Pussy Fest Of The Northwest #4 / 1995 / NIT / M • Pussy Fest Of The Northwest #5 / 1995 / NIT / M • The Sodomizer #4 / 1996 / SC / M • The Sodomizer #6 / 1996 / SC / M • Teacher's Pet #4 / 1995 / APP / M

JASMINE JONES *see* **Star Index I**
JASMINE LEE
Fear In The Forest / 1993 / CS / B • The Happy Woodcutter / 1993 / CS / B

JASMINE OBERA
House On Paradise Beach / 1996 / VC / M

JASMINE RHODES
Edge Of Sensation / 1990 / LE / M • Lost In Paradise / 1990 / CA / M • Outback Assignment / 1991 / VD / M • Singles Holiday / 1990 / PM / M

JASMINE ST. CLAIR *(Jasmine St. James)*
Not too pretty with long black hair, rock solid

cantaloupes, marginal body, mole on her right cheek. 23 years old in 1995 and (according to her) has a degree in International business from Columbia University. She worked for J.P. Morgan and then started her own antiques business finally becoming a nude model before going into the porno business. Now let's see: graduates high school at 18; four years at Columbia; that makes her 22 at least; and one year to do Morgan, antique business and nude modelling? Sure!
Compulsion (Amazing) / 1996 / MET / M • Degenerate / 1996 / AMP / M • Delirium / 1996 / MET / M • Fuck Jasmin / 1997 / MET / M • Hellfire / 1995 / MET / M • Just Jasmin / 1996 / AMP / M • Marilyn Chambers' Bedtime Stories / 1993 / PS / S • Naked Horror / 1995 / ... / S • New York Nights / 1994 / ... / S • Playboy: The Girls Of South Beach / 1996 / UNI / S • Playboy: The Girls Of Summer / 1996 / UNI / S • Playboy: Women Of Color / 1996 / UNI / S • Possessed / 1996 / MET / M • Punk Ass / 1996 / MET / M • Two Too Much / 1996 / MET / M • Vortex / 1995 / MET / M • The World's Biggest Gang Bang #2 / 1996 / FPI / M
JASMINE ST. JAMES *see* Jasmine St. Clair
JASMINE WATERS
Positively Pagan #08 / 1993 / ATA / M
JASON
America's Raunchiest Home Videos #21: Pumping Pussy / 1992 / ZA / M • Fantasy Photography: Buffy And The Boys / 1995 / VG0 / M • Homegrown Video #359 / 1991 / HOV / M • Housebroken / 1983 / BIZ / B • A Midsummer Night's Bondage / 1993 / ARL / B • My First Time #6 / 1996 / NS / M • New Faces, Hot Bodies #03 / 1992 / STP / M • Tight Security / 1995 / BON / B
JASON ASHLEY *see* Jay Ashley
JASON BRODERICK
Bi Love Lucy / 1994 / PL / G • Bi-Wicked / 1994 / BIN / G • Gilligan's Bi-Land / 1994 / PL / G • Semper Bi / 1994 / PEP / G
JASON BROOKS *see Star Index I*
JASON BUCKLEE *see Star Index I*
JASON CARLSON
Backside To The Future #2 / 1988 / ZA / M
JASON CARNS
A Climax Of Blue Power / 1974 / EVI / M
JASON CHARLES *see Star Index I*
JASON DEAN *(James Dean, Jan Dean, Jamie Dean)*
Butt's Motel #3 / 1989 / EX / M • Cat On A Hot Sin Roof / 1989 / LV / M • The Girls Of Ball Street / 1988 / VEX / M • Her Every Wish / 1988 / GO / M • Hershe Highway #1 / 1989 / HO / M • Open House (Vid Exc) / 1989 / VEX / M • Oral Support / 1989 / V99 / M • Pure Energy / 1990 / VEX / M • Slumber Party / 1990 / LV / M • Soda Jerk / 1992 / ZA / M • The Ultimate Climax / 1989 / V99 / M • The Wacky World Of X-Rated Bloopers / 1989 / GO / M
JASON FOX *see Star Index I*
JASON JEFFREY
Boiling Point / 1978 / SE / M
JASON JULES *(Jason Powell)*
The Big Bang / 1988 / WET / M • Cheri's On Fire / 1986 / V99 / M • Corporate Affairs / 1986 / SE / M • Devil In Miss Jones #3: A New Beginning / 1986 / VC / M • Dollface / 1987 / CV / M • Love At First Sight / 1987 / SE / C • The Mile High Girls / 1987 / CA /

M • Tight Fit / 1987 / V99 / M
JASON KANE *see Star Index I*
JASON LOWE *see Star Index I*
JASON LYNN *see Star Index I*
JASON MARKS *see Star Index I*
JASON MARTIN *see Star Index I*
JASON MCKAY
Stuff Your Face #4 / 1996 / JMP / M
JASON NIKAS
Mr. Blue / 1996 / JSP / G
JASON POWELL *see* Jason Jules
JASON PRIDE
Sex Starved She-Males / 1995 / MET / G • She-Male Seduction / 1995 / MET / G
JASON RILEY
Anal Virgins #02 / 1996 / NS / M • Hollywood Amateurs #23 / 1995 / MID / M • Sky Foxes / 1987 / VC / M • Unveiled / 1987 / VC / M
JASON ROBERTS
Caballero Preview Tape #4 / 1985 / CA / C • The Young And The Wrestling #2 / 1989 / PL / M
JASON ROWE
The Fantasy Booth / 1993 / ONA / M
JASON RUSSELL *(John Russell)*
Husband of Tina Russell.
The Debauchers / 1972 / QX / M • Defiance / 1974 / ALP / B • Dr Teen Dilemma / 1973 / VHL / M • Fantasy Peeps: Sensuous Delights / 1984 / 4P / M • Fantasy Peeps: Untamed Desires / 1985 / 4P / M • Personals / 1972 / COM / M • Sex U.S.A / 1970 / SEP / M • Showgirl #04: Tina Russell Classics / 1981 / VCR / M • Sleepyhead / 1973 / VXP / M • A Touch Of Desire / 1983 / VCR / C • Whatever Happened To Miss September? / 1973 / ALP / M • The Whistle Blowers / cr72 / ... / M
JASON SHAW
Bi Watch / 1994 / BIN / G • Days Gone Bi / 1994 / BIN / G
JASON STEELE *see Star Index I*
JASON STYLES
Live Sex Net / 1996 / SPR / M • Mile High Thrills / 1995 / VIM / M • My First Time #3 / 1996 / NS / M • Tailz From Da Hood #2 / 1995 / AVI / M
JASON THORPE
Coed Fever / 1980 / CA / M • Tight Assets / cr80 / VC / M
JASON TYSON
She-Male Loves Me / 1995 / VC / G
JASON VOYEUR *see Star Index I*
JASON WELLES *see* Tyler Horne
JASON WELLS *see* Tyler Horne
JASON WHITMAN
Bitter Sweet Revenge / 1985 / CAL / B
JASON WILLIAMS
Alice In Wonderland / 1976 / CA / M • Cheerleaders' Wild Weekend / cr77 / VES / S • Flesh Gordon #1 / 1974 / FAC / S
JASPER
Blonde with large inflated tits and curly hair, big butt, small tattoo of a heart and arrow on her belly and not so pretty face reminiscent of Britt Morgan. Born Sep 7, 1971 at Travis Air Force Base (wherever that is). Lost her virginity at 14. Was a nude dancer in Las Vegas prior to getting into the business.
The Adventures Of Mr. Tootsie Pole #1 / 1995 / LBO / M • Anal Blues / 1994 / PEP / M • Attic Toys / 1994 / ERA / M • Baby Doll / 1994 / SC / M • Black Detail #2 / 1994 / VT / M • Blackbroad Jungle / 1994 / IN / M

• Brassiere To Eternity / 1994 / PEP / F • The Breast Files #1 / 1994 / AVI / M • Buck Naked In The 21st Century / 1993 / EVN / M • Bun Runners / 1994 / PRE / B • Butt Freak #2 / 1996 / EA / M • Buttman's Inferno / 1993 / EA / M • Buttmasters / 1994 / AMP / M • Caged Beauty / 1994 / FD / M • Centerfold Celebrities '94 #2 / 1994 / SFP / M • Cuntrol / 1994 / MID / F • Deep Inside Kaitlyn Ashley / 1995 / VC / C • Defending Your Soul / 1995 / EX / M • Dirty Doc's Housecalls #10 / 1994 / LV / M • Dirty Laundry / 1994 / HOH / M • Doggie Style / 1994 / CA / M • End Around / 1994 / PRE / B • End Of Innocence / 1994 / WIV / M • The Face / 1994 / PP / M • Gang Bang Bitches #01 / 1994 / PP / M • The Girl In Room 69 / 1994 / VC / M • A Girl's Affair #05 / 1994 / FD / F • Harness Hannah At The Strap-On Palace / 1994 / WIV / F • Horny Henry's Peeping Adventures / 1994 / TTV / M • Invitation To The Blues / 1994 / LE / M • Jiggly Queens #2 / 1994 / LE / M • Laguna Nights / 1995 / FH / M • Leena Is Nasty / 1994 / OD / M • Leg...Ends #12 / 1994 / PRE / F • M Series #20 / 1994 / LBO / M • Mindsex / 1993 / MPA / M • New Pussy Hunt #24 / 1996 / LEI / C • Nipples / 1994 / FOR / F • Paging Betty / 1994 / VC / M • Pops / 1994 / PL / M • The Real Story Of Tonya & Nancy / 1994 / EX / M • The Reel Sex World #04: Laid In Hawaii / 1994 / WP / M • Reel Sex World #05 / 1994 / WP / M • Rocco Unleashed / 1994 / SC / M • Ron Hightower's White Chicks #08 / 1994 / LBO / M • The Search For Canadian Beaver / 1995 / LIP / F • Sex Professionals / 1994 / LIP / F • Silky Thighs / 1994 / ERA / M • Subway / 1994 / SC / M • Taboo #12 / 1994 / MET / M • The Theory Of Relativity / 1994 / EL / M • Tiger Eye: Jasper / 1995 / TEV / F • Totally Naked / 1994 / VC / M • Used And Abused #2 / 1994 / SFP / M • Vivid At Home #02 / 1994 / VI / M • Welcome To Bondage: Jasper / 1994 / BON / B • [More Than A Handful / 1991 / ... / M
JAVOS STUDI
Amadeus Mozart / 1996 / XC / M
JAY
Blush: Dykestyles #2: Dress Up For Daddy / 1993 / FAT / F • Canadian Beaver Hunt #1 / 1996 / PL / M • Debi Diamond's Dirty Dykes #1 / 1995 / FD / F • Der Mosenpflucker / 1995 / KRM / M • Private Film #16 / 1994 / OD / M • Private Video Magazine #14 / 1994 / OD / M
JAY ASHLEY *(Jay Down, Jay Jason, Shady O'Toole (Jay), Alex (Jay Ashley), Jason Ashley)*
Young male married to Kaitlyn Ashley.
1-900-FUCK #1 / 1995 / SO / M • 1-900-FUCK #3 / 1995 / SO / M • 9-Ball: Geisha Gang Bang / 1994 / PL / M • A List / 1996 / SO / M • Abducted / 1996 / ZA / M • Abused / 1996 / ZA / M • Adult Affairs / 1994 / VC / M • Amateur Orgies #23 / 1993 / AFI / M • Amateur Orgies #31 / 1993 / AFI / M • Amazon Heat #1 / 1996 / CC / M • Anal Academy / 1996 / ZA / M • Anal Disciples #1 / 1996 / ZA / M • Anal Disciples #2: The Anal Conflict / 1996 / ZA / M • Anal Fugitive / 1995 / PEP / M • Anal Inquisition / 1996 / ZA / M • Anal Institution #1 / 1996 / ZA / M • Anal Institution #2 / 1996 / ZA / M • Anal League / 1996 / IN / M • Anal Maniacs #4 / 1995 / WP / M • Anal Maniacs #5 / 1996 /

WP / M • Anal Overtures / 1993 / AFD / M • Anal Portrait / 1996 / ZA / M • Anal Rippers #2: The Unveiling / 1996 / ZA / M • Anal Sex / 1996 / ZA / M • Anal Talisman / 1996 / ZA / M • Anal Vision #16 / 1993 / LBO / M • The Analizer / 1994 / VD / M • Anals, Inc / 1995 / ZA / M • Ass Ventura: Crack Detective / 1996 / PL / M • Ass, Gas & The Mystical GLOP / 1997 / EL / M • Back In Style / 1993 / VI / M • Back To Anal Alley / 1994 / ME / M • The Backdoor Bradys / 1995 / PL / M • Bareback / 1996 / LE / M • Beach Bum Amateur's #30 / 1993 / MID / M • The Best Of Strippers Inc / 1996 / ONA / C • Bi-Bi Love Amateurs #3 / 1993 / QUA / G • Big Bust Babes #36 / 1996 / AFI / M • Big Bust Babes #38 / 1996 / AFI / M • The Big One / 1995 / HO / M • Blonde Forces #2 / 1994 / CC / M • Bobby Sox / 1996 / VI / S • Boogie In The Butt / 1993 / WIV / M • The Breast Of Breastmen / 1995 / EVN / C • Breastman's Wet T-Shirt Contest / 1994 / EVN / M • Bubble Butts #27 / 1993 / LBO / M • Buffy's Anal Adventure / 1996 / CDI / M • Buffy's First Encounter / 1995 / CIN / M • Burbank Sperm Bank / 1996 / CIN / M • Butt Freak #2 / 1996 / EA / M • Buttman's Wet Dream / 1994 / EA / M • Carnal Country / 1996 / NIT / M • Caught From Behind #19 / 1994 / HO / M • Caught From Behind #22 / 1995 / HO / M • Cherry Poppers #12: Playing Nookie / 1995 / ZA / M • Cherry Poppers #13: Anal Pajama Party / 1996 / ZA / M • Cherry Poppers #14: Teeny Tongues / 1996 / ZA / M • Cherry Poppers #15: Mischievous Maidens / 1996 / ZA / M • Cherry Poppers: The College Years #01 / 1997 / ZA / M • Cinesex #1 / 1995 / CV / M • Cinesex #2 / 1994 / CV / M • A Clockwork Orgy / 1995 / PL / M • The Come On / 1995 / EX / M • The Complete & Total Anal Workout #2 / 1996 / ZA / M • The Corner / 1994 / VT / M • The Darker Side / 1994 / HO / M • Decadent Obsession / 1995 / OD / M • Deceit / 1996 / ZA / M • Deep Behind The Scenes With Seymore Butts #1 / 1995 / ULI / M • Deep Inside Kaitlyn Ashley / 1995 / VC / C • Desire Kills / 1996 / SUM / M • Dick & Jane Do The Slopes In Ass Spin / 1994 / AVI / M • Dick & Jane In The Mountains / 1994 / AVI / M • Director's Wet Dreams / 1996 / BBE / M • Dirty Doc's Housecalls #05 / 1993 / LV / M • Dirty Laundry #1 / 1994 / CV / M • Dirty Laundry #2 / 1994 / CV / M • Dog Walker / 1994 / EA / M • Done In The Desert Sun / 1995 / OUP / M • Double Decadence / 1995 / NOT / M • Employee's Entrance In The Rear / 1996 / CC / M • Erotic Newcummers Vol 1 #1: Capitol Desires / 1993 / DR / M • Erotic Newcummers Vol 1 #2: Texas Twisters / 1993 / DR / M • Exit In Rear / 1993 / XCI / M • Femme Fatale / 1996 / CIN / M • Flesh / 1996 / EA / M • The Freak Club / 1994 / VMX / M • Frendz? #1 / 1996 / RAS / M • Frendz? #2 / 1996 / RAS / M • Fuck U: Girls Of The Packed-10 / 1995 / ZA / M • Gang Bang Bitches #01 / 1994 / PP / M • Gang Bang Bitches #02 / 1994 / PP / M • Gang Bang Bitches #03 / 1994 / PP / M • Gang Bang Bitches #04 / 1995 / PP / M • Gang Bang Bitches #08 / 1995 / PP / M • Gang Bang Bitches #10 / 1995 / PP / M • Gang Bang Bitches #11 / 1995 / PP / M • The Girls Of Summer / 1995 / VT / M • Girls Of The Panty Raid /

1995 / VT / M • Gun Runner / 1996 / CIN / M • Hardcore / 1994 / VI / M • Helen & Louise / 1996 / HDE / M • Hell Hole / 1996 / ZA / M • Hexxxed / 1994 / VT / M • Hollywood Hookers / 1996 / DWV / M • Hollywood In Your Face / 1993 / VC / M • Hollywood Scandal: The Heidi Flesh Story / 1993 / IP / M • Hollywood Sex Tour / 1995 / VC / M • Hot Tight Asses #07 / 1994 / TCK / M • Hotel Fantasy / 1995 / IN / M • Invitation For Lust / 1995 / C69 / M • Jenteal Loves Rocco / 1996 / VI / M • Leena Is Nasty / 1994 / OD / M • Legs / 1996 / ZA / M • Lollipops #2 / 1996 / SC / M • Loose Morals / 1995 / EX / M • Lust Runner / 1995 / VC / M • Masquerade / 1995 / HO / M • Memories / 1996 / ZA / M • More Dirty Debutantes #24 / 1993 / 4P / M • Motel Matches / 1996 / LE / M • The Naked Truth / 1995 / VI / M • Nice Fuckin' Movie / 1997 / EL / M • Nudist Colony Vacation / 1996 / NIT / M • Odyssey Triple Play #62: Gang Bangs All Around / 1994 / OD / M • Once In A Lifetime / 1996 / VC / C • Oral Obsession #1 / 1994 / VI / M • The Palace Of Pleasure / 1995 / ULI / M • Peepshow / 1994 / OD / M • Penetrator #2: Grudge Day / 1995 / PL / M • Performer Of The Year / 1994 / WP / M • Perverted Women / 1995 / SC / M • The Phantom Of The Montague Stage / 1997 / HO / M • Please Take A Number / 1996 / CDI / M • Pristine #1 / 1996 / CA / M • Private Stories #12 / 1996 / OD / M • Private Video Magazine #16 / 1994 / OD / M • Pumphouse Sluts / 1996 / CC / M • Pure Smut / 1996 / GO / M • Puritan Video Magazine #02 / 1996 / LE / M • Puritan Video Magazine #10 / 1997 / LE / M • Razor's Edge / 1995 / ONA / M • The Real Story Of Tonya & Nancy / 1994 / EX / M • Rebel Cheerleaders / 1995 / VI / M • Red Door Diaries #2 / 1996 / ZA / M • Reflections / 1996 / ZA / M • Release Me / 1996 / VT / M • Rice Burners / 1996 / NOT / M • Rump Man: Forever / 1995 / HW / M • Rxx For A Gangbang / 1994 / ZA / M • The Seductive Secretary / 1995 / GO / M • Seriously Anal / 1996 / ONA / M • Sex Bandits / 1995 / VC / M • The Shocking Truth #1 / 1996 / DWO / M • A Shot In The Pants / 1995 / HO / M • Sideshow Freaks / 1996 / ZA / M • The Sin-A-Bun Girls / 1995 / OD / M • Sinnocence / 1995 / CDI / M • Ski Bunnies #1 / 1994 / HW / M • Snatch Masters #05 / 1995 / LEI / M • Snatch Masters #10 / 1995 / LEI / M • Soap Opera Sluts / 1996 / AFI / M • Sodomania #06: Gangs And Bangs And Other Thangs / 1993 / EL / M • Spinners #1 (Wicked) / 1995 / WP / M • Spinners #2 (Wicked) / 1996 / WP / M • Starbangers #07 / 1995 / FPI / M • Starbangers #08 / 1996 / FPI / M • Starbangers #09 / 1996 / ZA / M • Starlet / 1994 / VI / M • Strippers Inc. #2 / 1994 / ONA / M • Stud Finders / 1995 / ONA / M • Sunset's Anal & D.P. Gangbang / 1996 / PL / M • Super Groupie / 1993 / PL / M • Supermodel #2 / 1994 / VI / M • Superstar Sex Challenge #2 / 1994 / VC / M • Sweet Smell Of Excess / 1996 / CIN / M • Tail Taggers #113: Behind The Scenes / 1994 / WV / M • Take It Inside / 1995 / PEP / M • Tales From The Clit / 1993 / OD / M • Top Debs #4: Sex Boat / 1993 / GO / M • Totally Naked / 1994 / VC / M • Totally Real / 1996 / CA / M • Ultimate Anal Gang Bang #3 / 1995 / HW / M • Ultimate

Sensations / 1996 / NIT / M • Uninhibited Love / 1994 / VPN / M • Up And Cummers #28 / 1996 / ERW / M • The Usual Anal Suspects / 1996 / CC / M • Venom #5 / 1996 / VD / M • Video Virgins #05 / 1993 / NS / M • Virgin Dreams / 1996 / EA / M • Virgin Killers: The Killing Spree / 1995 / PEP / M • The Voyeur #1 / 1994 / EA / M • What's Up, Tiger Pussy? / 1995 / VC / M • Wicked As She Seems / 1993 / WP / M • Wicked At Heart / 1995 / WP / M • Wicked Ways #1: Interview With The Anal Queen / 1994 / WP / M • Wicked Ways #2: Education Of A D.P. Virgin / 1995 / WP / M • Wicked Ways #3: An All-Anal Slutfest / 1995 / WP / M • A Woman Scorned / 1995 / CA / M • Women Behaving Badly / 1996 / RAS / M • Young Girls Do #1: Troublemakers / 1995 / CDI / M • Young Girls Do #2: Sweet Meat / 1995 / CDI / M

JAY ASTON
Coming Of Age / 1995 / VEX / C

JAY B. DAVID
Up 'n' Coming / 1983 / CA / M

JAY BAY
Dirty Looks / 1994 / VI / M

JAY BOND
Positively Pagan #05 / 1993 / ATA / M

JAY BONDY
Positively Pagan #12 / 1993 / ATA / M

JAY BREAMAN
Hawaiian Sex-O / cr71 / AVC / M

JAY BROWN
Senior Sexcapades #1 / 1995 / PL / M

JAY DANIELS
The Erotic Adventures Of Dr Storm / 1983 / XTR / M • Sex And The Cheerleaders / 1983 / XTR / M

JAY DEE
Binders Keepers / 1993 / BON / B • Bondage Across The Border / 1993 / B&D / B • Bondage Is My Pleasure #1 / 1994 / CS / B • Bondage Is My Pleasure #2 / 1994 / CS / B • Bondage Is My Pleasure #3 / 1994 / CS / B • Bondage Is My Pleasure #4 / 1994 / CS / B • Bondage Memories #04 / 1994 / BON / C • Bondage Photo Session / 1990 / BIZ / B • The Bondage Producer / 1991 / BON / B • Bondage Shoots / 1993 / BON / B • The Bride Stripped Bare / 1994 / BON / B • Captured Cop #1: Deadly Explosion / 1991 / BON / B • Captured Cop #2: The Stakeout / 1991 / BON / B • Captured Cop #3: Double Cross / 1991 / BON / B • Caught In The Act / 1992 / BON / B • Criss-Cross / 1993 / BON / B • Desert Heat / 1992 / BON / B • Deutsch Marks / 1992 / BON / B • Five Card Stud / 1990 / BIZ / B • Her First Time / cr90 / BON / B • Home Maid Memories #2 / 1994 / BON / C • The Janitor / 1995 / CS / B • Jay Dee's Bondage Notebook #1 / cr90 / BON / B • Jay Dee's Bondage Notebook #2 / cr90 / BON / B • Katrina And The Pros / 1992 / BON / B • Katrina's Bondage Memories #1 / 1994 / BON / C • Kiri Bound / 1988 / BON / B • Krystle's Surrender / 1988 / BON / B • Nancy Crew Meets Dr. Freidastein / cr90 / BON / B • Phantom Image / 1991 / BON / B • Rainy Days #2 / 1991 / BON / B • The Riding Master / 1989 / BON / B • Shanna's Bondage Fantasy #1 / 1993 / BON / B • Shanna's Bondage Fantasy #2 / 1993 / BON / B • Shared Moments With You / 1992 / CS / B • The Snoopy Niece / 1991 / BON / B • Spanking, Spanking And More /

1990 / BON / B • Threshold Of Fear / 1993 / BON / B • Tied & Tickled #18 / 1992 / CS / B • Wild Thing / 1989 / BON / B
JAY DOWN *see* **Jay Ashley**
JAY GAMBLE *see* **Star Index I**
JAY GIOVANNI *see* **Star Index I**
JAY GRANT
In-Flight Service / 19?? / BL / M
JAY GREEN
Heat Wave / 1977 / COM / M
JAY HALLADAY *see* **Star Index I**
JAY JASON *see* **Jay Ashley**
JAY JAY *see* **Star Index I**
JAY JONES *see* **Star Index I**
JAY KIRK
All The Loving Couples / 1979 / KIT / M
JAY LA BELLE
Boys R' Us / 1995 / WIV / M
JAY MICHAELS
C-Hunt #01: Pandemonium / 1995 / PEV / M • C-Hunt #02: Hot Pockets / 1995 / PEV / M • Caribbean Sunset / 1996 / PL / M • East Coast Sluts #09: / 1995 / PL / M • Fresh Meat #1 / 1996 / PL / M • Fresh Meat #2 / 1996 / PL / M • Jus' Knockin' Boots #1: Fade To Black / 1996 / NIT / M • Pearl Necklace: Amorous Amateurs #40 / 1994 / SEE / M • Pearl Necklace: Premier Sessions #02 / 1993 / SEE / M • Pearl Necklace: Premier Sessions #03 / 1994 / SEE / M • Pearl Necklace: Premier Sessions #04 / 1994 / SEE / M • Pearl Necklace: Premier Sessions #05 / 1994 / SEE / M • Pearl Necklace: Thee Bush League #29 / 1994 / SEE / M
JAY MILLOW *see* **Jaye Milo**
JAY NORTH
Please Don't Tell / 1995 / CEN / G
JAY PARKER
She-Male Slut House / 1994 / HEA / G
JAY RAINIER
Black Girls In Heat / 1985 / PL / M
JAY RANSOM
Filthy First Timers #5 / 1997 / EL / M
JAY RICHARDS
Natural Response / 1996 / GPI / G
JAY RODRIGUEZ *see* **Star Index I**
JAY SANDERS *see* **Jon Dough**
JAY SEEMON *see* **John Seeman**
JAY SERLING *(Barry Hall)*
SO of Crystal Breeze in the mid-eighties. The Barry Hall attribution comes from **The Erotic World Of Cody Nicole**.
Amber Aroused / 1985 / CA / M • Amberella / 1986 / GO / M • Bad Girls #3 / 1984 / COL / M • Bordello...House Of The Rising Sun / 1985 / SE / M • Camp Beaverlake #1 / 1984 / AR / M • Confessions Of A Candystriper / 1984 / VC / M • Confessions Of Candy / 1984 / VC / M • Cummin' Alive / 1984 / VC / M • The Days Of Our Wives / 1988 / GO / M • Dear Fanny / 1984 / CV / M • Debbie Does Dallas #3 / 1985 / VC / M • Desperate Women / 1986 / VD / M • Endless Passion / 1987 / LIM / C • Erotic City / 1985 / CV / M • The Erotic World Of Cody Nicole / 1984 / VCR / C • The Eyes Of Eddie Mars / 1984 / CV / M • Fantasy Land / 1984 / LA / M • Formula 69 / 1984 / JVV / M • Ginger's Hawaiian Scrapbook / 1988 / GO / C • The Girl With The Hungry Eyes / 1984 / ECS / M • Girls Of The Night / 1985 / CA / M • Headhunters / 1984 / VC / M • Hot Gypsy Love / 1985 / CDI / M • In All The Right Places / 1986 / VD / M • Joanna Storm On Fire / 1985 / VIV / M • Looking

For Mr Goodsex / 1984 / CC / M • The Loves Of Lolita / 1984 / VC / M • The Many Shades Of Amber / 1986 / LIM / M • Mouthful Of Love / 1984 / VC / M • My Pretty Go Between / 1985 / VC / M • Naughty Nanette / 1984 / VC / M • Panty Raid / 1984 / GO / M • The Pink Lagoon: A Sex Romp In Paradise / 1984 / GO / M • Pleasure Productions #01 / 1984 / VCR / M • Pleasure Productions #04 / 1984 / VCR / M • Pulsating Flesh / 1986 / VC / M • Raffles / 1988 / VC / M • Sensuous Tales / 1984 / VCR / C • Sex Derby / 1986 / GO / M • The Sex Detective / 1987 / GO / M • Sex-O-Gram / 1986 / LA / M • Shauna: Every Man's Fantasy / 1985 / CA / C • Sizzling Summer / 1984 / VC / M • Soaking Wet / 1985 / CV / M • Starved For Affection / 1985 / AVC / M • Suze's Centerfolds #8 / 1984 / CA / M • Suzy's Birthday Bang / 1985 / CDI / M • Taste Of The Best #3 / 1988 / PIN / C • Up Desiree Lane / 1984 / VC / M • Up In The Air / 1984 / CDI / M • Visions Of Jeannie / 1986 / VD / M • Vixens In Heat / 1984 / ECS / M • The Wacky World Of X-Rated Bloopers / 1989 / GO / M • Xstasy / 1986 / NSV / M • Yellow Fever / 1984 / PL / M • [Centerfolds & Covergirls #1 / 19?? / ... / M
JAY SHANAHAN *see* **Jim Enright**
JAY SHEEN
Casting Call #03 / 1993 / SO / M • Deep Inside Dirty Debutantes #07 / 1993 / 4P / M • Hollywood Swingers #09 / 1993 / LBO / M • Rugburn / 1993 / LE / M
JAY SHIELDS *see* **Star Index I**
JAY SILVER *see* **Star Index I**
JAY STANLEY *see* **Star Index I**
JAY STANTON *see* **Star Index I**
JAY STREET *see* **Star Index I**
JAY SWEET
Busty Nymphos / 1996 / H&S / M • Girls Around The World #13: Lynn LeMay And Friends / 1994 / BTO / M
JAY TAYLOR *see* **J.T. Taylor**
JAY TRIPPER
Scoundrels / 1982 / COM / M
JAY W.
Dirty Dancers #2 / 1994 / 4P / M
JAY WISEMAN
Welcome To SM / 1996 / ESF / B
JAY ZINK
18 And Anxious / cr78 / CDI / M
JAYDE
Filthy First Timers #6 / 1997 / EL / M
JAYE DOGG
Gangbang In The Fat Lane / 1996 / FC / M
JAYE MILO *(Jay Millow)*
Slutty looking blonde with large enhanced tits.
Big Boob Bikini Bash / 1995 / BTO / M • The Boob Tube / 1993 / MET / M • Busty Nymphos / 1996 / H&S / M • Double-D Reunion / 1995 / BTO / M • Dutchess: Fetish #1 Golden Goddess / 1995 / DSP / B • Forbidden / 1992 / FOR / M • Girls Around The World #29 / 1995 / BTO / M • Hotter Than July / 1988 / CC / F • More Than A Woman / 1994 / H&S / M • Natural Wonders / 1993 / VI / M • Raunch #07 / 1993 / CC / M • Strap-On Sally #01: Strap-On Psycho / 1993 / PL / F • Strap-On Sally #02: Ariana Bottoms Out / 1993 / PL / F • Undercover Lover / 1992 / CV / M • Voluptuous / 1993 / CA / M • What About Boob? / 1993 / CV / M
JAYLIN *see* **Jalynn**
JAYME LEE *see* **Star Index I**

JAYNE
Jayne: Blonde Goddess / 1990 / LOD / F • Joe Elliot's College Girls #38 / 1994 / JOE / M
JAYNE CASE
Pink Champagne / 1979 / CV / M
JAYNE MANSFIELD
Baring It All / 1995 / PEK / S • Blue Vanities #006 / 1987 / FFL / M • Blue Vanities #007 / 1988 / FFL / M • Blue Vanities #515 / 1992 / FFL / M • Blue Vanities #518 / 1993 / FFL / M • Electric Blue #004 / 1981 / CA / S • The Wild, Wild World Of Jayne Mansfield / cr74 / SOW / S
JAZMIN
My Baby Got Back #02 / 1993 / VT / M • Voluptuous #4 / 199? / H&S / M
JAZZ
Battle Of The Ultra Milkmaids / 1992 / LET / M • Black Hollywood Amateurs #23 / 1996 / MID / M • Black Hollywood Amateurs #24 / 1996 / MID / M • Black Knockers #14 / 1995 / TV / M • Bow Down Backstreet / 1996 / HW / M • Git Yo' Ass On Da Bus! / 1996 / HW / M • Hillary Vamp's Private Collection #06 / 1992 / HOV / M • Hooter Tutor / 1996 / APP / M • Kym Wilde's Bondage House Party #2 / 1993 / BON / B • Lovin' Spoonfuls #3 / 1995 / 4P / C • Mistress Memoirs #1 / 1993 / PL / C • Mr. Peepers Amateur Home Videos #48: Dialing For Services / 1992 / LBO / M • My Mistress...Her Slave / 1990 / PL / B • Raw Talent: Bang 'er 15 Times / 1992 / RTP / M • Ready To Drop #02 / 1992 / FC / M • Ropemasters / cr90 / BON / B • Sam Shaft's Anal Thrusts #2 / 1992 / RTP / M • Sex Over 40 #2 / 1994 / PL / M • Slave Connection / 1993 / PL / B • Span's Garden Party / 1996 / HW / M • Totally Tasteless Video #01 / 1994 / TTV / M • Uncle Roy's Amateur Home Video #10 / 1992 / VIM / M • Waiting 2 XX Hale / 1996 / APP / M
JAZZMINE
All In The Name Of Love / 1992 / IF / M • Bun Busters #22 / 1994 / LBO / M • Chicks With Dicks #1: A Slick And Slippery Oil Orgy / 1992 / BIZ / B • Dirty Deeds / 1992 / IF / M • Excitable / 1992 / IF / M • If Looks Could Kill / 1992 / V99 / M • The Last American Sex Goddess / 1993 / IF / M • The Last Temptation Of Teri / 1991 / IF / M • Man Of Steel / 1992 / IF / M • Mix Up / 1992 / IF / M • One Lay At A Time / 1992 / V99 / M • One Of A Kind / 1992 / VEX / M • Runnin' Hot / 1992 / LV / M • A Scent Of Leather / 1992 / IF / M • Seymore Butts & The Honeymooners / 1992 / FH / M • Seymore Butts: Bustin' Out My Best Anal / 1995 / FH / C • She's My Cherry Pie / 1992 / V99 / M • She-Male Mistress / 1992 / BIZ / G • Smarty Pants / 1992 / VEX / M • Solo Adventures / 1996 / AB / F • Sweet Things / 1992 / VEX / M • TV Shaved Pink / 1992 / BIZ / G • Uncle Roy's Amateur Home Video #12 / 1992 / VIM / M • Video Virgins #03 / 1993 / NS / M • Wet & Wicked / 1992 / VEX / M • Wilde At Heart / 1992 / VEX / M
JAZZMINE ROSE
Freaks Of Leather #1 / 1993 / IF / M • It's Only Love / 1992 / VEX / M • Nothing Else Matters / 1992 / V99 / C • Party Favors / 1993 / VEX / M • Spanish Fly / 1993 / VEX / M • Tender Loving Care / 1994 / BRI / S
JE T'AIME *see* **Je Taime Towser**
JE TAIM TOURSEAKE *see* **Je Taime**

Towser

JE TAIME *see* **Je Taime Towser**

JE TAIME TOWSER *(Je T'Aime, Je Taime, Je Taim Tourseake)*
Black On Black / 1987 / CDI / M • Cat Alley / 1986 / AVC / M • Deep Inside Traci / 1986 / CDI / C • Diamond Collection #80 / 1986 / CDI / M • Ebony Erotica / 1985 / SVE / C • Farmers Daughters / 1985 / WV / M • Goddess Of Love / 1986 / CDI / M • The Honeymooners / 1986 / CDI / M • House Of The Rising Moon / 1986 / VD / M • Spies / 1986 / PL / M • The Zebra Club / 1986 / VSE / M

JE'ANNA PICHE *see* **Star Index I**

JEAN
Blue Vanities #509 / 1992 / FFL / M • Blue Vanities #553 / 1994 / FFL / M • Blue Vanities #555 / 1994 / FFL / M • Blue Vanities #564 / 1994 / FFL / M • Homegrown Video #374 / 1992 / HOV / M • Magma: Anal Wedding / 1995 / MET / M • Magma: Dirty Diana / 1994 / MET / M • Magma: Dirty Twins / 1994 / MET / M • Magma: Fuck Me Diana / 1994 / MET / M • Magma: Horny & Greedy / 1993 / MET / M • Magma: Live And Learn / 1995 / MET / M • Magma: Nymphettes / 1993 / MET / M • Magma: Swinger / 1995 / MET / M • Magma: Tanja's Horny Nights / 1994 / MET / M

JEAN   AFRIQUE *(Janette   Starion, Jeanette Starion)*
Former "Miss Nude Holland" with huge tits and fuzzy blonde hair who was brought into the business by Ray Victory. He apparently married her and they now (1992) do live sex shows in Europe.
Back To Afrique / 1991 / VEX / M • Cats Are Also Pets / 1990 / NAP / B • Cuffed And Beaten / 1990 / NAP / B • The Girls Of Cooze / 1992 / V99 / C • Jeanette Starion #1 / 1993 / RUM / M • Jeanette Starion #2 / 1993 / RUM / M • Lay Lady Lay / 1991 / VEX / M • Morning To Jean / 1991 / VEX / M • Opposite Attraction / 1992 / VEX / M • The Rock Hard Files / 1991 / VEX / M • Scandanavian Double Features #1 / 1996 / PL / M • Scandanavian Double Features #2 / 1996 / PL / M • Tomboy / 1991 / V99 / M • [Happy Acres / 1991 / VEX / M

JEAN CARR *see* **Star Index I**

JEAN CHARLIE
Sweet Paradise / 1980 / ELV / M

JEAN CHARVIN
Hot Babes / cr78 / CIG / M

JEAN CINE *see* **Lisa Lake**

JEAN CLARKE *see* **Star Index I**

JEAN DALTON *(Jeannie Dalton, Janine Dalton, Diane Dalton)*
Small breasted girl who looks very young but has a face reminiscent of Karen Summer. Not particularly tight body. In **The Untamed Vixens** she has a tattoo in the middle of her chest and in **Breaker Beauties** she has a tattoo on her left butt.
ABA: Double Feature #2 / 1996 / ALP / M • Barbie's Fantasies / 1974 / VHL / M • Blue Vanities / #030 / 1988 / FFL / M • Blue Voodoo / 1983 / VD / M • Breaker Beauties / 1977 / VHL / M • Call Me Angel, Sir / 1976 / ALP / M • Classic Erotica #3 / 1980 / SVE / M • Fannie / 1975 / ALP / M • Fire In Francesca / cr77 / ASR / M • Georgia Peach / 1977 / COM / M • Girls In Passion / 1979 / VHL / M • Joe Rock Superstar / cr76 / ALP / M • Kinky Potpourri #32 / 199?

/ SVE / C • Rip-Off Of Millie / cr78 / VHL / M • The Story Of Eloise / 1976 / SVE / M • Sugar Britches / 1980 / VCX / C • Sweet Cakes / 1976 / VC / M • That Lady From Rio / 1976 / VXP / M • Too Many Pieces / 1975 / LA / M • A Touch Of Desire / 1983 / VCR / C • The Untamed Vixens / 1976 / VHL / M

JEAN DAMAGE *see* **Lynx Cannon**

JEAN DANOU *see* **Star Index I**

JEAN DE VILLROY *see* **Jean Villroy**

JEAN DEFORETS *see* **Star Index I**

JEAN FAUBERT *see* **Star Index I**

JEAN FERRERE
[Je Brule De Partout / 1978 / ... / M

JEAN FOURNE
Bend Over Babes #4 / 1996 / EA / M

JEAN FRENCH *see* **Star Index I**

JEAN GATTO *see* **Star Index I**

JEAN GENTRY
Resurrection Of Eve / 1973 / MIT / M

JEAN GERARD
Exces Pornographiques / 1977 / ... / M

JEAN GERARD SORLIN
Body Love / 1976 / CA / M

JEAN GUERIN *see* **Star Index I**

JEAN HARLOW *see* **Jeanette Harlow**

JEAN HENRI
Anal Intruder #01 / 1986 / CC / M • The South Bronx Story / 1986 / CC / M

JEAN JEFFRIES *see* **Star Index I**

JEAN JENNINGS *(Lynda Mantz)*
Not so pretty long straight haired natural blonde with medium tits, lithe body, too tall, marginal personality, horrible actress.
Auto-Erotic Practices / 1980 / VCR / F • The Autobiography Of A Flea / 1976 / MIT/ M • Blue Vanities #523 / 1993 / FFL / M • Blue Vanities #533 / 1993 / FFL / M • The Case Of The Full Moon Murders / 1971 / SOW / M • Defiance / 1974 / ALP / B • Fantasy Peeps: Solo Girls / 1985 / 4P / M • French Kittens / 1985 / VC / C • Sharon / 1977 / AR / M • Summertime Blue / 1979 / VCX / M • Sweetheart / 1976 / SVE / M • That's Erotic / 1979 / CV / C • That's Porno / 1979 / CV / C • Virgin Dreams / 1976 / BMV / M • Virgin Snow / 1976 / VXP / M

JEAN JILL
More Than A Voyeur / cr73 / SEP / M

JEAN JOSEPH
18 And Anxious / cr78 / CDI / M

JEAN KING
Sex Boat / 1980 / VCX / M

JEAN LANGSTON
Transsexual Secretary / 19?? / BIZ / G

JEAN LECASTEL
Amsterdam Nights #1 / 1996 / BLC / M • Amsterdam Nights #2 / 1996 / VC / M • Chateau Duval / 1996 / HDE / M • Cool Water / 1995 / DBM / M • Deep Inside Dirty Debutantes #07 / 1993 / 4P / M • Dirty Stories #4 / 1995 / PE / M • Dirty Tricks #2: This Ain't Love / 1996 / EA / M • Harry Horndog #17: Love Puppies #5 / 1993 / ZA / M • Magma: Hot Service / 1995 / MET / M • Private Film #19 / 1994 / OD / M • Private Film #20 / 1995 / OD / M • Private Film #21 / 1995 / OD / M • Private Film #27 / 1995 / OD / M • Private Film #28 / 1995 / OD / M • Private Gold #05: Cape Town #1 / 1996 / OD / M • Private Gold #06: Cape Town #2 / 1996 / OD / M • Private Gold #10: Sins / 1996 / OD / M • Private Gold #13: The Pyramid #3 / 1996 / OD / M • Private Gold #14: Sweet Lady #1 / 1997 / OD / M • Pri-

vate Video Magazine #20 / 1995 / OD / M • Private Video Magazine #24 / 1995 / OD / M • The Voyeur #6 / 1996 / EA / M

JEAN LOUIS
Dick & Jane Penetrate Paris / 1994 / AVI / M • Peek Freak / 1987 / CV / M

JEAN LOUIS AKIM
Private Film #27 / 1995 / OD / M • Private Film #28 / 1995 / OD / M

JEAN LUC PITARD *see* **Star Index I**

JEAN MARIE
Five Kittens / 19?? / ... / M

JEAN MARSH
Love At First Sight / 1987 / SE / C

JEAN MCCARTNEY *see* **Star Index I**

JEAN MICHEL
Family Affair / 1996 / XC / M

JEAN NETO
Blue Vanities #169 (New) / 1996 / FFL / M • Blue Vanities #169 (Old) / 1991 / FFL / M • Blue Vanities #503 / 1992 / FFL / M

JEAN PARKER *see* **Star Index I**

JEAN PAUL *see* **Star Index I**

JEAN PAUL BRIDE
Magma: Hot Service / 1995 / MET / M

JEAN PAUL GASTEAU
The Rise Of The Roman Empress #1 / 1986 / PV / M

JEAN PETTIT
French Schoolgirls / 1973 / AVC / M

JEAN PHILLIPS
Aunt Peg Goes To Hollywood / 1982 / CA / M

JEAN PIERRE ARMAND *(J.P. Armand, Jean-Paul Armand)*
Amber & Sharon Do Paris #1 / 1985 / PAA / M • Amber & Sharon Do Paris #2 / 1985 / PAA / M • The Arrangement / 1984 / CV / M • Ejacula #1 / 1992 / VC / M • Ejacula #2 / 1992 / VC / M • Forbidden Pleasures / 1987 / VC / M • From Paris With Lust / 1985 / PEN / M • Girls With Curves #1 / 1985 / CV / M • Impulse #01: Memories Of An Italian Slut / 1995 / MBP / M • Juicy Virgins / 1995 / WIV / M • Jura Sexe / 1995 / JP / G • Magma: Anita #2 / 1996 / MET / M • Magma: Bizarre Games / 1996 / MET / M • Magma: Body Cocktails / 1995 / MET / M • Magma: Horny Bulls / 1994 / MET / M • Magma: Hot Shots / 1995 / MET / M • Magma: Huge Cum Shots / 1995 / MET / M • Magma: Olympus Of Lust / 1994 / MET / M • Magma: Sperma / 1994 / MET / M • Magma: Tanja's Horny Nights / 1994 / MET / M • Magma: Trans-Games / 1995 / MET / G • Menage A Trois / 1981 / HLV / M • Private Film #27 / 1995 / OD / M • Private Film #28 / 1995 / OD / M • Rosa / Francesca / 1995 / XC / M • Secrets Of Madame X #2 / 1995 / WIV / M • Tania's Lustexzesse / 1994 / MET / M • Taxi Girls #2: In Search Of Toni / 1986 / ELD / M

JEAN PIERRE TOMEL *see* **Star Index I**

JEAN POREMBA *see* **Candie Evans**

JEAN QUHO
Hong Kong Hookers / 1984 / AMB / M

JEAN RAMARTVELLE *see* **Star Index I**

JEAN REXLER
Beach House / 1981 / CA / C • More Than Sisters / 1978 / VC / M • A Woman's Torment / 1977 / VC / M

JEAN ROCHE *see* **Star Index I**

JEAN SANDER
Teenage Runaways / 1977 / WWV / M

JEAN SERVAIN *see* **Star Index I**

JEAN SILVER *see* **Long Jean Silver**

JEAN SMITH
Housemother's Discipline #5 / 1994 / RB / B

JEAN TODD
The Psychiatrist / 1978 / VC / M

JEAN VALJEAN
Afrodisiac #2 / 1989 / CC / M • Anal Intruder #01 / 1986 / CC / M • Angela In Wonderland / 1986 / VD / M • Black Angels / 1985 / VC / M • Black Girls In Heat / 1985 / PL / M • Black Licorice / 1985 / CDI / M • Black To Africa / 1987 / PL / C • Black Velvet #3 / 1994 / CC / M • Black Voodoo / 1987 / FOV / M • Confessions Of A Middle Aged Nympho / 1986 / WET / M • Dirty Hairy's Amateurs #04: Black Dicks White Lips / 1995 / GOT / M • Harlem Honies #1 / 1993 / CC / M • Harlem Honies #2: Nasty In New York / 1994 / CC / M • Mind Mirror / 1994 / LAP / M • Murder By Sex / 1993 / LAP / M • Pretty In Black / 1986 / WET / M • Silence Of The G.A.M.S. / 1992 / CA / M • There's Magic In The Air / 1987 / AR / M

JEAN VILLROY *(Robert LeRay, Jean de Villroy, Robert Le Ray, Robert Leray)*
Caballero Preview Tape #1 / 1982 / CA / C • Dangerous Passion / 1978 / VC / M • French Blue / 1974 / ... / M • House Of Love / cr77 / VC / M • Love Airlines / 1978 / SE / M • Made In France / 1974 / VC / M • Penetration / 1975 / SAT / M • The Pleasure Shoppe / 1980 / CA / M • Sensations / 1975 / ALP / M • Sex Roulette / 1979 / CA / M

JEAN WOLF *see Star Index I*

JEAN YVES
Butt Banged Cycle Sluts / 1995 / ANA / M • Private Gold #09: Private Dancer / 1996 / OD / M • World Sex Tour #3 / 1995 / ANA / M

JEAN-BAPTISTE ORY
Erotic Pleasures / 1976 / CA / M

JEAN-CLAUDE
Magma: Old And Young / 1995 / MET / M

JEAN-CLAUDE LADIEN *see Star Index I*

JEAN-CLAUDE MARTIN *see Star Index I*

JEAN-FRANCOIS
Anabolic Import #01: Anal X / 1994 / ANA / M

JEAN-JACQUES LEBON *see Francois Pappilion*

JEAN-LOUIS VATTIER
French Erotic Fantasies / 1978 / ... / M • Illusions Within Young Girls / 1981 / VEP / M • Shocking / 1984 / SE / M • [Je Suis Une Belle Salope / 1977 / ... / M

JEAN-LUC MONTANT
Private Gold #16: Summer Wind / 1997 / OD / M

JEAN-MARIE PALLARDY
Emmanuelle #3 / 1977 / ... / S • Emmanuelle Goes To Cannes / 1984 / ECV / S • Kiss Me With Lust / cr75 / ... / M

JEAN-PAUL ARMAND *see Jean Pierre Armand*

JEAN-PIERRE
Magma: Claudine In Action / 1996 / MET / M • Magma: Dirty Twins / 1994 / MET / M • Magma: Horny & Greedy / 1993 / MET / M

JEAN-PIERRE ARMAND
Gode-Party / 1994 / RUM / M

JEAN-PIERRE BOURBON
[Le Journal Intime D'Une Nymphomane / 1972 / ... / M

JEAN-PIERRE BOUYXOU

[The Loves Of Irina / 1973 / PS / S

JEANA
Blue Vanities #559 / 1994 / FFL / M

JEANE BRAYANT
Il Medico Della Coppie / 1996 / TNT / M • Rosa / Francesca / 1995 / XC / M

JEANELLE *see Star Index I*

JEANETTE
Magma: Fuck Me Diana / 1994 / MET / M • Magma: Perverse Games / 1995 / MET / M • Mike Hott: #172 Hidden Job Interview / 1990 / MHV / M • Ripe And Ready #01 / 1993 / BTO / M

JEANETTE (S/M) *see Star Index I*

JEANETTE HARLOW *(Jean Harlow, Karen Harlow)*
Personal Touch #1 / 1983 / AR / M • Star Virgin / 1979 / CXV / M • The Starmaker / 1982 / VC / M • X-Rated Bloopers #1 / 1984 / AR / M

JEANETTE HEDDIG
Scandanavian Double Features #1 / 1996 / PL / M

JEANETTE JAMES *see Nicole Black*

JEANETTE LANGE
Private Film #02 / 1993 / OD / M

JEANETTE LITTLEDOVE *see Janette Littledove*

JEANETTE NICHOLS
Bucky Beaver's XXX Dragon Art Theatre Double Feature #11 / 1996 / SOW / M • Teenage Fantasies #1 / 1972 / SOW / M

JEANETTE SINCLAIR *see Star Index I*

JEANETTE ST MICHAEL *see Star Index I*

JEANETTE STARION *see Jean Afrique*

JEANIE *see Star Index I*

JEANINE *see Janine Lindemulder*

JEANINE OLDFIELD
10 Years Of Big Busts #3 / 199? / BTO / C • D-Cup Holiday / 1991 / BTO / M • Girls Around The World #03 / 1990 / BTO / M • Girls Around The World #04 / 1991 / BTO / M • Girls Around The World #06 / 1992 / BTO / M • Girls Around The World #15 / 1994 / BTO / S • Tit To Tit #1 / 1994 / BTO / M • Tit To Tit #2 / 1994 / BTO / M • Tit To Tit #3 / 1995 / BTO / M • The Very Best Of Breasts #1 / 1996 / H&S / S • The World Of Double-D #2 / 199? / H&S / S

JEANNA (DIJANA) *see Dijana*

JEANNA FINE *(Gina Fine, Geanna Fine, Virginia Paymore, Vanna Paymore, Angel Payson, Angel Rush)*
Blonde with a punk hairstyle, passable face and small tits. She was 33-24-33 and 5'7" tall in 1991. Born 9/29/65. Had tits enhanced to rock solid cantaloupes and changed to a brunette. In 1992 she retired from the business with SO Sikki Nixx. As of 1994, no longer with Sikki who seems to be on the run from the mob, she returned to the porn business.
13th Annual Adult Video News Awards / 1996 / VC / S • Adult Video News 1992 Awards / 1992 / VC / M • The Adventures Of Dick Black, Black Dick / 1987 / DR / M • Amber Lynn's Hotline 976 / 1987 / VCR / M • Amberella / 1986 / GO / M • American Pie / 1995 / WAV / M • Anal Intruder #05: The Final Outrage / 1990 / CC / M • Anal Starlets / 1991 / ROB / M • Andrew Blake's Girls / 1992 / CA / C • Angel Baby / 1995 / SC / M • Ashley Renee In Jeopardy / 1991 / HOM / B • Autobiography Of A Whip / 1991 / BS / B • The Backpackers #2 / 1990

/ IN / M • Badgirls #5: Maximum Babes / 1995 / VI / M • Badgirls #6: Ridin' Into Town / 1995 / VI / M • Barbara The Barbarian / 1987 / SE / M • Bed & Breakfast / 1992 / VC / M • Best Of Bi And Beyond / 1992 / PNP / C • Best Of Edward Penishands / 1993 / VT / C • Bi And Beyond #1 / 1988 / LAV / G • Bi And Beyond #6: Authentic / 1996 / FD / G • Big Switch #3: Bachelor Party / 1991 / CAT / G • Bitches In Heat / 1994 / PL / C • Blonde Fantasy / 1988 / CC / M • Bloopers #2 / 1991 / GO / C • Blue Dreams / 1996 / SC / M • Blue Jeans Brat / 1991 / VI / M • Blue Movie / 1995 / WP / M • Brandy & Alexander / 1991 / VC / M • Breakin' In / 1986 / WV / M • The Bride / 1986 / WV / M • Bruce Seven's Favorite Endings #1 / 1991 / EL / C • Bruce Seven: A Compendium Of His Most Graphic Scenes Vol 1 / 1991 / BS / C • Bunmasters / 1995 / VC / M • Butt Motors / 1995 / VC / M • Buttslammers #09: Fade To Anal / 1995 / BS / F • Buttslammers #11: / 1996 / BS / F • California Gigolo / 1987 / VD / M • California Taboo / 1986 / VC / M • Cat & Mouse #1 / 1992 / XCI / M • Cat & Mouse #2 / 1993 / XCI / M • Catfights #3 / 1987 / OHV / B • Catwalk #1 / 1995 / SC / M • Catwalk #2 / 1995 / SC / M • Caught From Behind #15 / 1991 / HO / M • The Challenge / 1990 / EA / B • Chasey Loves Rocco / 1996 / VI / M • Cheating / 1986 / SEV / M • Checkmate / 1996 / SNA / M • Chronicles Of Pain #4: Tools Of The Trade / 1996 / BIZ / B • City Of Sin / 1991 / LV / M • Club Decca / 1996 / BAC / F • Cold As Ice / 1994 / IN / M • Controlled / 1990 / BS / B • Courting Libido / 1995 / HIV / G • Crossing Over / 1990 / IN / M • Cumming Clean (1996—Caballero) / 1996 / CA / M • Cycle Sluts / 1992 / CC / M • The Damp Spot / 1993 / AFD / C • Dark Desires / 1989 / BMV / C • Dark Star / 1991 / VI / M • Dear Diary / 1995 / WP / M • Decadence / 1996 / VC / M • Decadent Delights / 1992 / IF / M • Decadent Obsession / 1995 / OD / M • Deep Inside Jeanna Fine / 1992 / VC / C • Deep Inside Juli Ashton / 1996 / VC / C • Deep Inside Kaitlyn Ashley / 1995 / VC / C • Deep Inside P.J. Sparxx / 1995 / VC / C • Desire / 1990 / VC / M • Desperate / 1995 / WP / M • Detroit Dames / 1988 / DR / C • The Devil In Miss Jones #5: The Inferno / 1994 / VC / M • Diva #1: Caught In The Act / 1996 / VC / F • Divorce Court Expose #1 / 1986 / VD / M • Divorce Court Expose #2 / 1987 / VD / M • Double Cross (Wicked) / 1995 / WP / M • Down & Out In New York City / 1986 / SE / M • Dream House / 1995 / XPR / M • Dream Jeans / 1987 / CA / M • Dreams / 1995 / VC / M • Dreams Of A Gigolo / 1996 / SNA / M • Dresden Diary #16: / 1996 / BIZ / B • Edward Penishands #1 / 1991 / VT / M • The Erotic Artist / 1995 / VC / M • Erotic Obsession / 1994 / IN / M • Erotic Visions / 1995 / ULI / M • Evil Woman / 1990 / LE / M • Expose Me Again / 1996 / CV / M • The Fanny Farm / 1996 / NIT / M • Fantasy Theatre #1 / 1989 / VWA / C • Fatal Erection / 1988 / SEV / M • The Fine Line / 1990 / SO / M • Finely Back / 1990 / PL / F • The Finer Things In Life / 1990 / PL / F • Finger Sluts #1 / 1996 / LV / F • Firebox / 1986 / VXP / M • The First Taboo / 1989 / LA / M • Flappers / 1995 / EMC / M • Flesh In Ecstasy #02: Samantha

Strong / 1987 / GO / C • Flesh In Ecstasy #04: Jeanna Fine / 1987 / GO / C • Forbidden / 1996 / SC / M • Fresh! / 1987 / VXP / M • Full Nest / 1992 / WV / C • The Fun House / 1988 / SEV / C • Generally Horny Hospital / 1995 / IMV / M • A Girl's Best Friend (Madison Is) / 1990 / PL / F • The Girls Are Bustin' Loose / 1988 / AMB / F • Girls On Girls / 1987 / SE / C • Girls Together / 1985 / GO / C • Girlworld #1 / 1987 / LIP / F • Golden Rod / 1996 / SPI / M • Good Vibrations / 1991 / PM / M • Grand Prixxx / 1987 / CA / M • Guttman's Paris Vacation / 1993 / PL / M • Hangin' Out / 1992 / IF / M • Hard Evidence / 1996 / WP / M • Hardcore Copy / 1993 / PL / M • Harem Girls / 1986 / SE / M • Heatwaves / 1987 / LAV / G • Hollywood Confidential / 1995 / TWP / B • The Hot Tip / 1986 / VXP / M • Hothouse Rose #1 / 1991 / VC / M • Hothouse Rose #2 / 1992 / VC / M • Hottest Ticket / 1987 / WV / C • House Of Dreams / 1990 / CA / M • The House On Chasey Lane / 1995 / VI / M • How To Deep Throat Your Lover / 1994 / A&E / M • Hustler Honeys #5 / 1988 / VC / M • Images Of Desire / 1990 / PM / M • Impact / 1995 / SC / M • In The Fast Lane / 1995 / LE / M • Innocent Seduction / 1988 / VC / M • Intense Perversions #2 / 1996 / PL / M • Ir4: Inrearendence Day / 1996 / HW / M • Jail Babes #1 / 1990 / PL / F • Jennifer Ate / 1993 / XCI / F • Jenteal Loves Rocco / 1996 / VI / M • The Kiss / 1986 / SC / M • Kittens #4: Bodybuilding Bitches / 1993 / CC / F • The Kitty Kat Club / 1990 / PL / F • Lair Of The Bondage Bandits / 1991 / HOM / B • Latex #1 / 1994 / VC / M • Latex #2 / 1995 / VC / M • Le Sex De Femme #4 / 1989 / AFI / C • Les Be Friends / 1988 / WV / C • Lesbian Bitches #2 / 1994 / ROB / F • Lesbian Liasons / 1990 / SO / F • Lesbian Social Club / 1995 / ROB / F • Lessons In Love / 1995 / SPI / M • Lessons In Lust / 1987 / LA / M • Let's Party / 1993 / VC / M • Like Father Like Son / 1996 / AWV / G • Lonely Hearts / 1995 / VC / M • Love Ghost / 1990 / WV / M • Love Triangle / 1986 / PLY / C • Lust Runner / 1995 / VC / M • Lust Tango In Paris / 1987 / PEN / M • Malibu Madam / 1995 / CC / M • Malibu Spice / 1991 / VC / M • Many Happy Returns / 1995 / NIT / M • The Mark Of Zara / 1990 / XCI / M • Money, Money, Money / 1993 / FD / M • Moonlusting #2 / 1987 / WV / M • My Surrender / 1996 / A&E / M • Naked Scandal #1 / 1995 / SPI / M • Naked Scandal #2 / 1996 / SPI / M • Naughty Ninja Girls / 1987 / LA / M • Neighborhood Slut / 1996 / LV / M • Night Games / 1986 / WV / M • Night Walk / 1995 / HIV / G • No Man's Land #04 / 1990 / VT / F • No Man's Land #11 / 1995 / VT / F • The Nympho Files / 1995 / NIT / M • On Trial #2: Oral Arguments / 1991 / VI / M • Ona Zee's Doll House #3 / 1995 / ONA / F • The Only Game In Town / 1991 / VC / M • Only The Very Best On Film / 1992 / VC / C • Oral Madness #1 / 1991 / OD / M • Oral Madness #2 / 1992 / OD / M • Oral Majority #03 / 1986 / WV / C • Oral Majority #05 / 1987 / WV / C • Oral Majority #06 / 1988 / WV / C • Oral Majority #09 / 1992 / WV / C • The Other Woman / 1996 / VC / M • Our Trespasses / 1996 / AWV / G • Oversexed / 1986 / VXP / M • Pajama Party / 1993 / CV / C • Parted Lips / 1986 / QX / M • Party

Doll A Go-Go #1 / 1991 / VC / M • Party Doll A Go-Go #2 / 1991 / VC / M • Pay 4 Play / 1996 / RAS / M • Phone Sex Girls #2 / 1987 / VT / M • Pink Clam / 1986 / RLV / M • Play It Again, Samantha / 1986 / EVN/ M • Play School / 1990 / SO / M • Porked / 1986 / VXP / M • Primarily Yours / 1996 / CA / M • Private Encounters / 1987 / SE / M • Public Access / 1995 / VC / M • Pure / 1996 / WP / M • Pussyman #13: Lips / 1996 / SNA / M • Pussyman #14: Dreams Of A Gigolo / 1996 / SNA / M • Queen Of Hearts #2: Hearts On Fire / 1990 / PL / M • Rachel Ryan / 1988 / WV / C • Rainbows / 1992 / VT / F • Razor's Edge / 1995 / ONA / M • Restless Nights / 1987 / SEV / M • Revenge Of The Babes #2 / 1987 / PL / M • Rites Of Passion / 1988 / FEM / M • Romance & Fantasy / 1995 / VEX / M • Roxy / 1991 / VC / M • Ruthless Affairs / 1995 / LE / M • Safecracker / 1991 / CC / M • Secret Admirer / 1992 / VEX / M • Secret Diary #2 / 1995 / MID / M • Secret Recipe / 1990 / PL / F • Secrets / 1990 / CA / M • Seduction Of Jenna / 19?? / GO / C • The Sensual Massage Video / 1993 / ... / M • Seven Minutes In Heaven / 1986 / VXP / M • Sex 4 Life / 1995 / XPR / M • Sex Bi-Lex / 1993 / CAT / G • Sex Derby / 1986 / GO / M • Sex Kitten / 1995 / SC / M • Sex Lives Of Clowns / 1994 / VC / M • Sex Pistol / 1990 / CDI / M • Sex Tips For Modern Women / 1987 / VXP / M • Sex Trek #1: The Next Peneration / 1990 / ME / M • Sexaholic / 1985 / AVC / M • Sexual Impulse / 1995 / VD / M • She Comes In Colors / 1987 / AMB / M • Sins Of Nina Hartley / 1989 / MIR / C • Skin Hunger / 1995 / MET / M • Sleepwalker / 1990 / XCI / M • Slip Of The Tongue / 1993 / DR / M • The Smart Ass Enquirer / 1990 / VT / M • Snatch Motors / 1995 / VC / M • So Fine / 1992 / VT / C • Starbangers #09 / 1996 / ZA / M • Stardust #1 / 1996 / VI / M • Stardust #2 / 1996 / VI / M • Stardust #3 / 1996 / VI / M • Steal Breeze / 1990 / SO / M • Street Angels / 1992 / LV / M • Summer's End / 1991 / ROB / M • Taboo #08 / 1990 / IN / M • A Taste Of Ambrosia / 1987 / FEM / M • Teaser / 1986 / RLV / M • Teasers: Blackmail Party / 1988 / MET / M • Teasers: Frustrated Housewife / 1988 / MET / M • Thrill Seekers / 1990 / BS / B • Thunderstorm / 1987 / VC / M • Tracey And The Bandit / 1987 / LA / M • True Legends Of Adult Cinema: The Golden Age / 1992 / VC / C • True Legends Of Adult Cinema: The Modern Era / 1992 / VC / C • True Legends Of Adult Cinema: Unsung Superstars / 1993 / VC / C • Two In The Bush / 1991 / EX / M • Ubangis On Uranus / 1987 / WV / M • Untamed Cowgirls Of The Wild West #01: The Pillow Biters / 1992 / ZA / M • Untamed Cowgirls Of The Wild West #02: Jammy Glands... / 1993 / ZA / M • Valleys Of The Moon / 1991 / SC / M • VCA Previews #4 / 1988 / VC / C • Velvet / 1995 / SPI / M • Venom #2 / 1996 / VD / M • Venom #3 / 1996 / VD / M • The Wacky World Of X-Rated Bloopers / 1989 / GO / M • Weekend At Joey's / 1995 / ERA / M • Wet 'n' Working / 1990 / EA / F • Wet Dreams 2001 / 1987 / VD / M • Wet Panties / 1989 / MIR / C • Wide Open Spaces / 1995 / VC / F • Wild Fire / 1990 / WV / C • Wild Goose Chase / 1990 / EA / M • Wild Stuff / 1987 /

WET / M • Wild Widow / 1996 / NIT / M • Willie Wanker At The Fudge Packing Factory / 1995 / FD / M • The Worst Porno Ever Made With The Best Sex / 1993 / PL / M • The XXX Files: Lust In Space / 1995 / IMV / M • You Bring Out The Animal In Me / 1987 / MIR / M

JEANNA LYNN
The Oversexual Tourist / 1989 / VEX / M • Switch Hitters #4: The Grand Slam / 1989 / IN / G • Vixens / 1989 / LV / F

JEANNA MARTEZ see Gina Martell
JEANNE COOPER
The Girls In The Band / 1976 / SVE / M • There Was A Crooked Man / 1970 / WAR / S

JEANNE FORD see Star Index I
JEANNE JOSEPH see Star Index I
JEANNE MARCHAND see Star Index I
JEANNE MONTANAN
The Satisfiers Of Alpha Blue / 1980 / AVC/ M

JEANNE SALIERI
White Hot / 1984 / VXP / M

JEANNE SILVER see Long Jean Silver
JEANNE TOLLER
The Tale Of Tiffany Lust / 1981 / CA / M

JEANNIE
Neighborhood Watch #08: Extended Foreplay / 1991 / LBO / M • Stevi's: Jeannie's Spreads / 1995 / SSV / F • Toppers #12 / 1993 / TV / C

JEANNIE ADAM see Star Index I
JEANNIE BROWN
San Francisco Lesbians #1 / 1992 / PL / F • San Francisco Lesbians #2 / 1992 / PL / F

JEANNIE DALTON see Jean Dalton
JEANNIE PEPPER *(Angel Hall)*
Married to a German photographer by the name of Mr Dragon.
Alice In Blackland / 1988 / VC / M • Anal Carnival / 1992 / ROB / M • Anal Innocence #1 / 1991 / ROB / M • Anal Lover #1 / 1992 / ROB / M • Anything Butt Love / 1990 / PL / M • Assuming The Position / 1989 / V99 / M • Bachelor Party / 1987 / VCX / M • Back To Back #1 / 1987 / 4P / C • Back To Back #2 / 1992 / FC / C • Back To Nature / 1990 / CA / M • Backdoor Ebony / 1995 / WV / M • Backing In #2 / 1990 / WV / C • Bare Waves / 1986 / VD / M • Behind The Scenes With Angela Baron / 1988 / FAZ / C • The Best Of Black Anal #1 / 1995 / ROB / C • The Best Of Black White & Pink Inside / 1996 / CV / C • Bi And Beyond #5 / 1990 / INH / G • Bi-Sexual Fantasies / 1984 / LAV / G • Bizarre Interview: Jeannie Pepper / 198? / SVE / M • Black & Beyond: The Darker Sid / 1990 / INH / G • Black 'n' White In Color / 1987 / VCR / C • Black Baby Dolls / 1985 / TAG / M • Black Bad Girls / 1985 / PLY / M • Black Cat Rumble / 1988 / NAP / B • Black Chicks In Heat / 1988 / VC / M • Black Flava / 1994 / EX / M • Black Girls Do It Better / 1986 / CV / M • Black Holes In Space / 1987 / 4P / M • Black Jack City #3 / 1993 / HW / M • Black Lava / 1986 / WET / M • Black Mariah / 1991 / FC / M • Black Mystique #14 / 1995 / VT / F • Black On Black / 1987 / CDI / M • Black Orgies #26 / 1994 / GO / M • Black Orgies #35 / 1995 / GO / M • Black Satin Nights / 1988 / DR / C • Black Taboo #1 / 1984 / JVV / M • Black Velvet #3 / 1994 / CC / M • Blackdoor Babes / 1994 / TIW / M

• Blackman / 1989 / PL / M • Blackman & Anal Woman #1 / 1990 / PL / M • Blackman & Anal Woman #2 / 1990 / PL / M • Blonde On Black / 1986 / CC / F • Blowing Your Mind / 1984 / RSV / M • Blush: Hungry Hearts / 1990 / BLV / F • Blush: Suburban Dykes / 1991 / BLV / M • Bodies By Jackie / 1985 / IVP / M • Booty In Da House / 1995 / EVN / M • Bung-Ho Babes / 1991 / FC / M • Busted By The Boss / 1995 / CAW / B • Cats Have Claws / 1988 / NAP / B • Chocolate Delights #1 / 1985 / TAG / C • The Chocolate Fudge Factory / 1987 / PIN / M • Chocolate Kisses / 1986 / CA / M • Cowgals And Injuns / 1988 / NAP / B • Cream Puff / 1986 / VSE / M • Dark Alleys #28 / 1994 / FC / M • Dark Brothers, Dark Sisters / 1986 / VCS / C • Date With The Devil / 1989 / FAZ / M • Defying The Odds / 1995 / OD / M • Depraved / 1990 / IN / M • Diamond Collection #80 / 1986 / CDI / M • Ebony & Ivory Fantasies / 1988 / VD / C • Ebony Dreams / 1988 / PIN / C • Ebony Ecstacy / 1988 / HIO / C • Ebony Erotica #16: Dark & Sweet / 1994 / GO / M • Ebony Humpers #3 / 1987 / VEX / M • Ebony Orgies / 1987 / SE / C • Ebony Superstars / 1988 / VC / C • Eromania #1 / 1994 / AOC / M • Erotic Zones #2 / 1985 / CA / M • Euro Extremities #27 / 199? / SVE / C • Euro Extremities #48 / 199? / SVE / C • Fantasy Nights / 1990 / VC / M • Fortune Cookie Nookie / 1986 / VCS / C • Friendly Persuasion / 1988 / NAP / B • Girlz N The Hood #1 / 1991 / HW / M • Girlz Towne #09 / 1995 / FC / F • Golden Girls #18 / 1984 / CA / M • Golden Girls #25 / 1984 / CA / M • Guess Who Came At Dinner? / 1987 / FAN / M • Hard Core Cafe / 1988 / VD / M • Harlem Honies #2: Nasty In New York / 1994 / CC / M • Helpless Coeds / 1987 / BIZ / B • Hill Street Blacks #1 / 1985 / 4R / M • Hot Chocolate #2 / 1986 / PLY / M • Hot Gypsy Love / 1985 / CDI / M • Hot Seat / 1986 / AVC / M • Hotter Chocolate / 1986 / AVC / M • Hyapatia Lee's Secret Dreams / 1986 / SE / M • In And Out Of Africa / 1986 / AVC / M • Interracial Sex / 1987 / M&M / M • Just Pepper / 1988 / NAP / F • Karate Girls / 1987 / VCR / M • Let Me Tell Ya 'Bout Black Chicks / 1985 / VC / M • Lurid Trios / 1994 / CA / C • The Luscious Baker Girls / 1990 / VD / M • Lusty Layout / 1986 / PV / M • The Luv Game / 1988 / VCX / M • Madame P In Hamburg / 199? / SVE / M • Magma: Splash Of Sperm / 1990 / MET / M • Maid For Pain / 1991 / PL / B • Maverdick / 1995 / WV / M • Max Bedroom / 1987 / ZA / M • Mixing It Up / 1991 / LV / C • Mo' Booty #1 / 1992 / HW / C • Nudes At Eleven #1 / 1986 / AVC / M • Paris Models / 1987 / CDI / M • Parliament: Sultry Black Dolls / 1986 / PM / F • Prescription For Pleasure / 1993 / HW / M • The Price Was Right / 1994 / PAE / M • Pussyman #06: House Of Games / 1994 / SNA / M • Red Hot Pepper / 1986 / V99 / M • Rock 'n' Roll Heaven / 1989 / EA / M • Rump-Shaker #2 / 1993 / HW / M • Salt And Pepper Blues / 1988 / NAP / B • Sex About Town / 1990 / LV / M • Sex Charades / 1990 / VEX / M • The Shaving / 1989 / SO / M • Sherlock Homie / 1995 / IN / M • Sleeping With Everybody / 1992 / MID / C • Soul Kiss This / 1988 / VCR / C • Spies / 1986 / PL / M • Strange Bedfellows / 1985 / PL / M • Suzy's Birth-

day Bang / 1985 / CDI / M • A Taste Of Purple Passion / 1990 / CA / C • Tit Tales #3 / 1991 / FC / M • Toppers #04 / 1993 / TV / M • Toppers #06 / 1993 / TV / M • Toppers #09 / 1993 / TV / M • Tough Girls Don't Dance / 1987 / SEV / M • Toys, Not Boys #3 / 1991 / FC / C • True Sin / 1990 / PP / M • Undress To Thrill / 1994 / VI / M • Wanda Does Transylvania / 1990 / V99 / M • The Wedding / 1986 / VC / M • Wet & Slippery / 1995 / WV / M • What Are Friends For? / 1985 / MAP / M • Where There's Smoke There's Fire / 1987 / FAN / M • White Trash, Black Splash / 1988 / WET / M • The Whore / 1989 / CA / M • Woman To Woman / 1989 / ZA / C • X-TV #1 / 1986 / PL / C • [Black Beauties / 1986 / ... / M

JEANNY
Dirty Stories #5 / 1996 / PE / M
JEANY JOSE
Venture Into The Bizarre / cr78 / VHL / M
JEFF
100% Amateur #18: / 1995 / OD / M • Amateur Nights #10 / 1990 / HO / M • Bobby Hollander's Sweet Cheeks #102 / 1992 / WV / M • Bondage Magic / 1996 / JAM / B • Bondage Models #1 / 1996 / JAM / B • Bondage Models #2 / 1996 / JAM / B • Breast Worx #13 / 1992 / LBO / M • Cindy Puts Out / 1996 / OLL / M • Gigi Gives It Away / 1995 / FRF / M • HomeGrown Video #434: Forrest Hump / 1994 / HOV / M • How To Make Love To A Black Woman #1: You Gotta Have Rhythm / 1996 / VCX / M • Jacklyn's Attitude Adjustment / 1995 / JAM / B • Pearl Necklace: Amorous Amateurs #07 / 1992 / SEE / M • Pearl Necklace: Amorous Amateurs #09 / 1992 / SEE / M • Pearl Necklace: Amorous Amateurs #41 / 1994 / SEE / M • Pearl Necklace: Premier Sessions #03 / 1994 / SEE / M • Reel Life Video #03: Julie, Sheldon and Jeff / 1994 / RLF / M • Revenge! / 1996 / JAM / B • Victim / 1996 / JAM / B • The Whitney Challenge / 1996 / JAM / B • Who's In Charge / 1995 / JAM / B • Xxxanadu / 1994 / HW / M
JEFF AMARON
Punished Deception / 1996 / STM / B
JEFF AUCKY
Buttman's Inferno / 1993 / EA / M
JEFF BARCO
Foxholes / 1983 / SE / M
JEFF BLOOM see Star Index I
JEFF CANDER
Elodie Does The U.S.A. / 1995 / PPR / M
JEFF CHAMBERLAIN see Star Index I
JEFF CHAZZ
Double Cross (Wicked) / 1995 / WP / M
JEFF COLDWATER see Geoff Coldwater
JEFF CONNER
Cafe Flesh / 1982 / VC / M
JEFF CONRAD see Star Index I
JEFF DEHARD see Star Index I
JEFF DILLON
Pom Pom She-Males / 1994 / HEA / G • Where The Bi's Are / 1994 / BIN / G
JEFF EAGLE
Hollywood Hot Tubs / 1984 / VES / S • The Honeymooners / 1978 / CV / M • Loose Threads / 1979 / S&L / M • Ms. Woman Of The Year / 1980 / BL / M • The Night Of The Spanish Fly / 1978 / CV / M • R.S.V.P. / 1983 / VES / S • Sex Appeal / 1986 / VES / S • Showgirl #04: Tina Russell Classics / 1981 / VCR / M • Slammer Girls / 1987 /

LIV / S
JEFF FOXE
Produce Or Suffer / 1994 / STM / B
JEFF FREE see Star Index I
JEFF GILLOOLY
Tonya & Jeff's Wedding Night / 1994 / PET / M
JEFF GOLDEN
Backdoor To Hollywood #10 / 1989 / CIN / M • Backdoor To Hollywood #11 / 1990 / CIN / M • Bad Mama Jama Busts Out / 1989 / VT / M • Bare Essence / 1989 / EA / M • Bright Lights, Big Titties / 1989 / CA / M • Bung-Ho Babes / 1991 / FC / M • Bush League #1 / 1990 / CC / M • Deep Inside Charli / 1990 / CDI / C • Double Jeopardy / 1990 / HO / M • The Eye Of The Needle / 1991 / CIN / M • Facial Attraction / 1988 / BEE / C • Fat Ends / 1989 / 4P / M • Girls Of The Double D #10 / 1989 / CDI / M • Hardbreak Ridge / 1990 / WV / M • Heart Breaker / 1989 / LE / M • Imagination X-Posed / 1989 / 4P / M • Innocent Obsession / 1989 / FC / M • Introducing Charli / 1989 / CIN / M • Let Me Tell Ya 'Bout Fat Chicks #1 / 1986 / 4P / C • Life In The Fat Lane #1 / 1990 / FC / M • Life In The Fat Lane #2 / 1990 / FC / M • Make Me Sweat / 1989 / CIN / M • National Pornographic #2: Orientals / 1987 / 4P / C • Raquel On Fire / 1990 / VC / M • Raw Sewage / 1989 / FC / M • Some Like It Hot / 1989 / CDI / M • Stiff Magnolias / 1990 / HO / M • Sunstroke Beach / 1990 / WV / M • Super Tramp / 1989 / VD / M • A Taste Of Genie / 1986 / 4P / M • Tit Tales #2 / 1990 / FC / M • Tons Of Buns / 1986 / 4P / M • Tons Of Fun #3: Abondonza / 1987 / 4P / M • Top Heavy / 1988 / VD / M • Two Tons Of Fun #1 / 1985 / 4P / C • Weird And Bizarre Bondage / 1991 / FC / C
JEFF HARDY see Star Index I
JEFF HARRIS
Dungeon Humiliation / 1996 / STM / B
JEFF HERBICK see Star Index I
JEFF HICKEY
Crew Sluts / 1996 / NOT / M
JEFF JACOBS see Mike Davis
JEFF JAGGER
Courting Libido / 1995 / HIV / G
JEFF JAMES (Jess James, Jeff West)
The A Chronicles / 1992 / CC / M • Anal Storm / 1991 / ZA / M • The Aroused / 1989 / IN / M • Babes With Attitudes / 1990 / EVN / M • Beach Bum Amateur's #02 / 1992 / MID / M • Blame It On The Heat / 1989 / VC / M • Bratgirl / 1989 / VI / M • Butt's Motel #1 / 1989 / EX / M • Cum On Line / 1991 / XPI / M • Cumming Clean / 1991 / FL / M • Deep Throat #5 / 1990 / AR / M • Diver Down / 1992 / CC / M • Dyno-Mite / 1992 / IF / M • Erectnophobia #1 / 1991 / MID / M • Gangbang Girl #01 / 1992 / ANA / M • Gangbang Girl #02 / 1992 / ANA / M • Gangbang Girl #03 / 1992 / ANA / M • Gangbang Girl #04 / 1992 / ANA / M • Gangbang Girl #06 / 1992 / ANA / M • Gangbang Girl #08 / 1992 / ANA / M • Grandma Does Dallas / 1990 / FC / M • Harry Horndog #05: Sex Hungry Couples #1 / 1992 / ZA / M • Head Talk / 1991 / ZA / M • Hot Box / 1995 / V99 / C • I Do #1 / 1989 / VI / M • L.A.D.P. / 1991 / PL / M • Masquerade (1992-Usa) / 1992 / SC / M • Midsummer Love Story / 1993 / WV / M • Mr. Peepers Amateur Home Videos #01:

Hot And Nasty / 1991 / LBO / M • Mr. Peepers Amateur Home Videos #02: Bachelorette Party / 1991 / LBO / M • Mr. Peepers Amateur Home Videos #15: When Company Comes / 1991 / LBO / M • Odyssey Amateur #67: Lascivious Lynette / 1991 / OD / M • Sex In A Singles Bar / 1992 / VC / M • Spellbound / 1989 / LV / M • Stairway To Paradise / 1990 / VC / M • Summer Lovers / 1991 / VEX / M • A Tall Dark Stranger / 1990 / LV / M • Taylor Made / 1989 / DR / M • Tickets To Paradise / 1992 / XPI / M • True Love / 1989 / VI / M • Young Buns #2 / 1990 / WV / M

JEFF JONES see Star Index I

JEFF LAWSON

Changing Places / 1984 / AVC / M

JEFF LYLE

The Spirit Of Seventy Six / 1976 / NGV / M

JEFF MEDUID

Love At First Sight / 1987 / SE / C

JEFF MILLER see Star Index I

JEFF MOORE see Star Index I

JEFF PARKER

Bucky Beaver's XXX Dragon Art Theatre Double Feature #01 / 1996 / SOW / M • Hitler's Harlots / cr73 / SOW / M • Pink Champagne / 1979 / CV / M

JEFF PETERS

Erotic Animation Festival / 1980 / VC / M

JEFF QUINN

Innocence Lost / 1987 / CAT / G • The Switch Is On / 1985 / CAT / G • Triple Play / 1983 / HO / M

JEFF RAE see Jeffrey Ray

JEFF ROBERTS

Bucky Beaver's Double Softies #04 / 1996 / SOW / S • Bucky Beaver's Double Softies #05 / 1996 / SOW / S • Bulls Market / 1970 / SOW / S • Harvey Swings / cr72 / SOW / S • Weekend Convention / cr71 / SOW / M

JEFF SCOTT *(Darby Double)*

Fat male who has difficulty getting it up.

Alex Jordan's First Timers #03 / 1993 / OD / M • America's Raunchiest Home Videos #39: Like A Hurricane / 1992 / ZA / M • America's Raunchiest Home Videos #76: / 1993 / ZA / M • Anal Camera #01 / 1994 / EVN / M • Anal Camera #02 / 1994 / EVN / M • Anal Camera #03 / 1994 / EVN / M • Beach Bum Amateur's #36 / 1993 / MID / M • Beach Bum Amateur's #37 / 1993 / MID / M • Behind The Blinds / 1992 / VIM / M • Blow Job Blvd #1 / 1993 / SC / M • Bobby Hollander's Maneaters #10 / 1993 / SFP / M • Bobby Hollander's Maneaters #11 / 1994 / SFP / M • Bobby Hollander's Sweet Cheeks #101 / 1992 / WV / M • Bra Busters #05 / 1993 / LBO / M • Bubble Butts #21 / 1993 / LBO / M • Bubble Butts #28 / 1993 / LBO / M • Bubble Butts Gold #1 / 1994 / LBO / M • Bun Busters #05 / 1993 / LBO / M • Bun Busters #10 / 1993 / LBO / M • Bun Busters #18 / 1994 / LBO / M • Bun Busters #20 / 1994 / LBO / M • Camp Beaverlake #1 / 1984 / AR / M • Cheap Thrills / 1984 / RLV / M • Colossal Orgy #1 / 1993 / HW / M • Colossal Orgy #3 / 1994 / HW / M • The Dragon Lady #4: Tales From The Bed #3 / 1992 / WV / M • Drainman / 1989 / BIZ / B • A Few Good Rears / 1993 / IN / M • Foot Mistress / 1986 / BIZ / B • Gang Bang Bitches #04 / 1995 / PP / M • Gang Bang Diaries #1 / 1993 / SFP / M • Girls Of The Third Reich / 1985 / FC / M • Hidden Camera #11 / 1993 / JMP

/ M • Hidden Camera #14 / 1994 / JMP / M • Hollywood Ho' House / 1994 / VC / M • Hollywood Swingers #05 / 1992 / LBO / M • Hot Seat / 1986 / AVC / M • Joanna Storm On Fire / 1985 / VIV / M • Ladies Of The Knight / 1984 / GO / M • Lust In America / 1985 / VCX / M • M Series #09 / 1993 / LBO / M • M Series #12 / 1993 / LBO / M • Mellon Man #02 / 1994 / AVI / M • Mitzi's Honor / 1987 / TAM / M • Mr. Peepers Amateur Home Videos #61: Four Play For Four / 1992 / LBO / M • Mr. Peepers Amateur Home Videos #66: Ready In Red / z993 / LBO / M • Mr. Peepers Amateur Home Videos #69: Love Tunnel / 1993 / LBO / M • Mr. Peepers Amateur Home Videos #84: She Put the Bra in Braz / 1994 / LBO / M • Mr. Peepers Amateur Home Videos #86: Tit A Ton / 1994 / LBO / M • My Favorite Rear / 1993 / PEP / M • Nasty Newcummers #03 / 1994 / MET / M • Odyssey 30 Min: #268: / 1992 / OD / M • Odyssey Triple Play #53: Butt-Fuck Bash / 1993 / OD / M • Oh My Gush / 1995 / OD / M • Orgy Attack / 1993 / DRP / M • Pearl Necklace: Amorous Amateurs #19 / 1992 / SEE / M • A Reason To Die / 1994 / PEP / M • Revenge Of The Babes #1 / 1985 / LA / M • Rising Buns / 1993 / HW / M • Royally Flushed / 1987 / BIZ / B • Rump Humpers #17 / 1994 / GLI / M • Secret Services / 1993 / PEP / M • Sex-O-Gram / 1986 / LA / M • Shear Ecstasy / 1993 / PEP / M • Starbangers #02 / 1993 / BIG / M • Straight A Students / 1993 / MET / M • Superstar Sex Challenge #1 / 1994 / VC / M • Teenage Games / 1985 / HO / M • Thighs & Dolls / 1993 / PEP / M • Tight Tushies #2 / 1994 / MET / M • Tit In A Wringer / 1993 / FC / M • Unfaithful Entry / 1992 / DR / M • Wendy Whoppers: Razorwoman / 1993 / PEP / M

JEFF SCOTT (80'S)

Sissy's Hot Summer / 1979 / CA / M • Taboo #01 / 1980 / VCX / M

JEFF SIMON

Back Down / 1996 / RB / B

JEFF SMOTHERS

Still The Brat / 1988 / VI / M

JEFF STEINMAN see Star Index I

JEFF STERLING see Star Index I

JEFF STRYKER

Gay, occasional bisexual, performer.

Cummin' Together / 1991 / JEF / M • Every Which Way / 1990 / V10 / G • Heartless / 1989 / REB / M • The Heiress / 1988 / VI / M • In Your Wildest Dreams / 1993 / STY / M • Jamie Loves Jeff #1 / 1987 / VI / M • Jamie Loves Jeff #2 / 1991 / VI / M • Jeff Stryker's Favorite Sexual Positions / 1993 / STY / C • Jeff Stryker's How to Enlarge Your Penis / 1990 / VC / M • Ladies Man / 1990 / REB / M • Milk 'n' Honey / 1991 / STY / M • Strykin' It Deep / 1989 / V10 / M • The Switch Is On / 1985 / CAT / G • Take Me / 1991 / NLE / M • Wild Buck / 1993 / STY / M

JEFF TALEY see Star Index I

JEFF WALLACH

Dirty Laundry #2 / 1994 / CV / M • Young Nurses In Love / 1986 / VES / S

JEFF WEST see Jeff James

JEFF WILLRIGHT

I Dream Of Ginger / 1985 / VI / M

JEFFERY MEDVID see Star Index I

JEFFREY COFFIN

Playthings / 1980 / VC / M

JEFFREY HURST *(Jeffrey Hyrst, Howard Humper)*

Standard seventies type male with moustache and black hair.

Babylon Gold / 1983 / COM / C • Bang Bang You Got It / 1975 / VXP / M • Barbie's Fantasies / 1974 / VHL / M • Bone Up My Hole / 1994 / MET / M • Call Me Angel, Sir / 1976 / ALP / M • Come With Me, My Love / 1976 / PVX / M • Couples / 1976 / VHL / M • Dear Pam / 1976 / CA / M • Dirty Looks / 1982 / VC / C • Ecstasy In Blue / 1976 / ALP / M • Erotic Animation Festival / 1980 / VC / M • Erotic Fantasies #4 / 1983 / CV / C • Fantasex / 1976 / COM / M • French Kittens / 1985 / VC / C • From Holly With Love / 1977 / CA / M • Georgia Peach / 1977 / COM / M • Heavy Load / 1975 / COM / M • Hot Nurses / 1977 / CA / M • Inside Georgina Spelvin / 1974 / VC / M • Love In Strange Places / 1977 / CA / M • The Night Of The Spanish Fly / 1978 / CV / M • Saturday Matinee Series #2 / 1996 / VCX / C • Saturday Night Special / 1980 / CV / M • Slippery When Wet / 1976 / VXP / M • Sweet Punkin...I Love You / 1975 / VC / M • Sweet, Sweet Freedom / 19?? / BL / M • Through The Looking Glass / 1976 / ALP / M • The Tiffany Minx / 1981 / SAT / M • Virgin Snow / 1976 / VXP / M • A Woman's Torment / 1977 / VC / M

JEFFREY HYRST see Jeffrey Hurst

JEFFREY IAN MELLAR

Breaker Beauties / 1977 / VHL / M

JEFFREY MORGAN see Star Index I

JEFFREY RAY *(Jeff Rae)*

Black male who looks like a homeless person with his hair all over the place.

Black To Basics / 1992 / ZA / M • Do The White Thing / 1992 / ZA / M

JEFFREY STERN see Jon Martin

JEFFREY WALLICH see Star Index I

JELLY

Anal Assault / 1995 / PEV / C

JEN

The Show / 1995 / VI / M

JEN FRIEDMAN

Rampaging Nurses / 1971 / MIT / M

JEN TEAL *(Teal (Jen))*

Blonde with long straight hair, very pretty face, medium firm natural tits, tight waist, nice butt, green eyes and creamy good skin. 18 years old in 1994.

Amateur Dreams #4 / 1994 / DR / M • American Pie / 1995 / WAV / M • Animal Instincts #3: The Seductress / 1996 / APE / S • Attitude / 1995 / VC / M • Babes Illustrated #3 / 1995 / IN / F • Bedlam / 1995 / WAV / M • Best Butt(e) In The West #2 / 1995 / CC / M • Blindfold / 1994 / SC / M • Bloopers & Boners / 1996 / VI / M • Bobby Sox / 1996 / VI / S • Born Bad / 1996 / WAV / M • Captured Beauty / 1995 / SAE / B • Cheap Shot / 1995 / WAV / M • Comeback / 1995 / VI / M • Cross Cuntry Vacation / 1995 / CC / M • Dangerous Games / 1995 / VI / M • Dirty Little Secrets / 1995 / WAV / M • The Doll House / 1995 / CV / M • Encore / 1995 / VI / M • Erotic Visions / 1995 / ULI / M • Fantasy Chamber / 1994 / ULI / M • Fashion Plate / 1995 / WAV / M • Fresh Meat (John Leslie) #1 / 1994 / EA / M • Gangland Bangers / 1995 / VC / M • Heat / 1995 / WAV / M • Jenteal Loves Rocco / 1996 / VI / M • The Naked Truth / 1995 / VI / M • New Faces, Hot Bodies #15 / 1994 /

STP / M • New Faces, Hot Bodies #17 / 1995 / STP / M • Night Play / 1995 / WAV / M • No Tell Motel / 1995 / CV / M • Ona Zee's Doll House #1 / 1995 / ONA / F • Paradise Found / 1995 / LE / M • Party House / 1995 / WAV / M • Penthouse: Miami Hot Talk / 1996 / PET / S • Private Eyes / 1995 / LE / M • Red Hot Lover / 1995 / CV / M • Sex Academy #4: The Art Of Anal / 1994 / ONA / M • Sex Gallery / 1995 / WAV / M • The Show / 1995 / VI / M • Smoke Screen / 1995 / WAV / M • Sodomania #11: In Your Face / 1994 / EL / M • Stardust #1 / 1996 / VI / M • Stardust #2 / 1996 / VI / M • Stardust #3 / 1996 / VI / M • Stardust #4 / 1996 / VI / M • Stardust #5 / 1996 / VI / M • Suggestive Behavior / 1996 / VI / M • Taboo #15 / 1995 / IN / M • This Year's Model / 1996 / WAV / M • Toy Time #3: / 1995 / STP / F • Video Virgins #18 / 1994 / NS / M • The Voyeur #3 / 1995 / EA / M • Where The Boys Aren't #8 / 1996 / VI / F • Where The Boys Aren't #9 / 1996 / VI / F • Wildfire: Wildgirl's Cleaning Service / 1994 / WIF / F

JENA
Amateur Hours #01 / 1989 / AFI / M

JENA COLLINS
Lady By Night / 1987 / CA / M

JENETTE
Filthy First Timers #4 / 1996 / EL / M

JENIFER
Lesbian Pros And Amateurs #03 / 1992 / GO / F

JENNA
Painless Steel #3 / 1996 / FLV / M • Toe Tales #26 / 1995 / GOT / B

JENNA (DIJANA) see Dijana

JENNA (JAMESON) see Jenna Jameson

JENNA CARRERA see Gina Carrera

JENNA JAMESON *(Daisy (Jenna J.), Jenna (Jameson))*
Very pretty blonde with long straight hair, lithe tight body, tight waist and nice butt. 19 years old in 1994. Medium sized tits which look natural. By early 1995 she had had her tits enhanced to gross watermelon size and had a tattoo (the words "Heart Breaker" encircling two broken hearts) put on her right butt. In December 1996 she married Brad Armstrong.
13th Annual Adult Video News Awards / 1996 / VC / S • Baby Doll / 1994 / SC / M • Betrayed / 1996 / WP / M • Blue Movie / 1995 / WP / M • Cherry Pie / 1994 / SC / M • Conquest / 1996 / WP / M • Cover To Cover / 1995 / WP / M • The Dinner Party #1 / 1994 / ULI / M • Dirty Bob's #23: Tampa Teasers / 1995 / FLP / S • Dirty Bob's #27: Laid Back In L.A.! / 1996 / FLP / S • Elements Of Desire / 1994 / ULI / M • Exposure / 1995 / WAV / M • The F Zone / 1995 / WP / M • Hard Evidence / 1996 / WP / M • I Love Lesbians / 1995 / ERW / F • Jenna Ink / 1996 / WP / M • Jenna Loves Rocco / 1996 / WAV / M • Jenna's Built For Speed / 1997 / WP / F • Jinx / 1996 / WP / M • The Kiss / 1995 / WP / M • Lip Service / 1995 / WP / M • N.Y. Video Magazine #09 / 1996 / OUP / M • On Her Back / 1994 / VI / M • Once In A Lifetime / 1996 / VC / C • Phantasm / 1995 / WP / M • Photo Play / 1995 / VI / M • Priceless / 1995 / WP / M • Pure / 1996 / WP / M • Satyr / 1996 / WP / M • Sex On The Strip: The Lusty Ladies Of Las Vegas / 1993 / CPG / F • Silk Stock-

ings: The Black Widow / 1994 / SPI / M • Silver Screen Confidential / 1996 / WP / M • Smells Like...Sex / 1995 / VC / M • Starting Over / 1995 / WAV / M • Up And Cummers #10 / 1994 / 4P / M • Up And Cummers #11 / 1994 / 4P / M • Up And Cummers #17 / 1994 / 4P / M • Virtual Reality Sixty Nine / 1995 / WP / M • Where The Boys Aren't #7 / 1995 / VI / F • The Wicked One / 1995 / WP / M

JENNA TALLIA
Tender And Wild / 1989 / MTP / M

JENNA WELLS *(Marlena Riche, Jana (Wells), Corrina (J. Wells), Corvina, Kristall, Karinna)*
Cute but teutonic blonde with nice body and an acceptable face. German. Drives a Yamaha.
3 Wives / 1993 / VT / M • Anal Extasy / 1992 / ROB / M • Anal Inferno / 1992 / ROB / M • Anal Madness / 1992 / ROB / M • Arabian Nights / 1993 / WP / M • As Time Goes Bi / 1993 / WMG / G • B-Witched / 1994 / PEP / G • Between The Bars / 1992 / FH / M • Bi Anonymous / 1993 / BIL / G • Bi-Athelon / 1993 / BIL / G • The Big E #10 / 1992 / PRE / B • Biker Chicks In Love / 1991 / LE / M • Black Detail #2 / 1994 / VT / M • Black In The Saddle Again / 1991 / ZA / M • Blue Angel / 1992 / AFV / M • Blue Angel / 1992 / AFV / M • Brainteasers / 1991 / ZA / M • Breast Worx #16 / 1991 / LBO / M • Breastman's Anal Adventure / 1993 / EVN / M • Buffy Malibu's Totally Nasty All-Girl Home Videos #04 / 1993 / ANA / F • Business And Pleasure / 1992 / AFV / M • Cape Rear / 1992 / WV / M • Catfighting Students / 1995 / PRE / C • Cheeks #5: The Ultimate Butt / 1991 / CC / M • Chug-A-Lug Girls #2 / 1993 / VT / M • City Of Sin / 1991 / LV / M • Close Quarters / 1992 / ME / M • Deep Inside Nikki Dial / 1994 / VC / C • The Dirty Little Mind of Martin Fink / 1991 / ME / M • The Dragon Lady #2: Tales From the Bed / 1992 / WV / M • Enemates #06 / 1992 / BIZ / B • The Fantasy Booth / 1993 / ONA / M • Gilligan's Bi-Land / 1994 / PL / G • Girls Just Wanna Have Toys / 1993 / PL / F • How To Love Your Lover / 1992 / XII / S • I Wanna Be A Lesbian / 1993 / HSV / F • Jail Babes #2: Bustin' Out / 1992 / PL / F • Ladies Lovin' Ladies #1 / 1990 / AR / F • Ladies Lovin' Ladies #2 / 1992 / AR / F • Ladies Lovin' Ladies #4 / 1992 / AFV / F • Leg...Ends #06 / 1992 / PRE / F • Lethal Passion / 1991 / PL / M • Little Secrets / 1991 / LE / M • Moist To The Touch / 1991 / DR / M • More Dirty Debutantes #12 / 1991 / 4P / M • Mummy Dearest #3: The Parting / 1991 / LV / M • Naked Buns 8 1/2 / 1992 / CC / M • Neighborhood Watch #12 / 1991 / LBO / M • Nikki's Bon Voyage / 1993 / VC / M • No Man's Land #05 / 1992 / VT / F • No Man's Land #07 / 1993 / VT / F • No Man's Land #08: Eight Women Who Ate Women / 1993 / VT / F • No Men 4 Miles / 1992 / LV / F • Odds 'n' Ends / 1992 / PRE / B • The Oval Office / 1991 / LV / M • The Pink Persuader / 1992 / LBO / M • Popped Tarts / 1992 / RB / B • Rainbows / 1992 / VT / F • Real Tickets #1 / 1994 / VC / M • Real Tickets #2 / 1994 / VC / M • The Screamer / 1991 / CA / M • Sexual Healing / 1992 / LV / M • The Sexual Limits / 1992 / VC / M • She's The Boss / 1992 / VIM / M • Slip Of The Tongue / 1993

/ DR / M • Spread Sheets / 1991 / DR / M • Student Fetish Videos: Catfighting #03 / 1991 / PRE / B • Student Fetish Videos: Catfighting #04 / 1992 / PRE / B • Student Fetish Videos: The Enema #07 / 1992 / PRE / B • Student Fetish Videos: Tickling #04 / 1992 / SFV / B • Student Nurses / 1991 / CA / M • Surfside Sex #1 / 1991 / LV / F • Tinseltown Wives / 1992 / AFV / M • Transparent Desires / 1991 / LV / M • Wendy's Bi Adventure / 1994 / STA / M

JENNEFER (HAZE) see Jennefer Haze

JENNEFER HAZE *(Jennefer (Haze), Jennefer Tee)*
Pretty, brown hair, medium tits, young curvaceous body, slightly flat on the butt. 21 years old in 1995.
Debutante Dreams / 1995 / 4P / M • More Dirty Debutantes #41 / 1995 / 4P / M • More Dirty Debutantes #43 / 1995 / 4P / M • More Dirty Debutantes #46 / 1995 / 4P / M • More Dirty Debutantes #48 / 1995 / 4P / M • World Famous Dirty Debutantes / 1995 / 4P / S

JENNEFER TEE see Jennefer Haze

JENNI (VERONICA LANE see Veronica Lane

JENNI LEWIS
Butt Bangers Ball #1 / 1996 / TTV / M • The Fabulous 50's Girls #1 / 1994 / EMC / M

JENNIE
Young And Anal #2 / 1995 / JMP / M

JENNIE (RUBY) see Ruby (1996)

JENNIE ATOLL
Swedish Erotica #48 / 1983 / CA / M

JENNIE ATTOL
Lusty Ladies #05 / 1983 / 4P / M

JENNIE FRAUNK see Star Index I

JENNIE JOYCE
Aged To Perfection #1 / 1994 / TTV / M • Aged To Perfection #2 / 1995 / TTV / M • Golden Oldies #3 / 1995 / TTV / M • Older Women Younger Men #3 / 1993 / CC / M

JENNIE LEE
Blue Vanities #115 / 1988 / FFL / M • Blue Vanities #556 / 1994 / FFL / M • Blue Vanities #580 / 1996 / FFL / M • Ding Dong: A Night At The Moulin Rouge / 1995 / SOW / S • French Follies / 1951 / SOW / S • Peek-A-Boo / 1953 / SOW / S

JENNIFE G.
Foreign Exchange Sluts / 1995 / TNT / M

JENNIFER
A&B AB#267: Lingerie Party / 1991 / A&B / S • A&B AB#269: Red Asses / 1991 / A&B / M • A&B AB#273: The Sexiest Home-Made Videos #3 / 1991 / A&B / C • A&B FL#01 /]995 / A&B / S • A&B FL#03: More Flashing Fun / 1995 / A&B / S • The Adventures Of Peeping Tom #4 / 1997 / OD / M • Alex Jordan's First Timers #05 / 1994 / OD / M • The Betrayal Of Innocence #1: The Awakening Of Marika / 1993 / CC / M • The Betrayal Of Innocence #2: The Decadence / 1993 / CC / M • The Betrayal Of Innocence #3: The Choice / 1993 / CC / M • Bitch Queendom / 1987 / BIZ / B • Black Fantasies #04 / 1995 / HW / M • Blue Vanities #541 / 1994 / FFL / M • Bun Busters #12 / 1993 / LBO / M • Cool Water / 1995 / DBM / M • Czech Mate / 1996 / BAC / M • Dynamite Dominator / 1993 / STM / B • Ebony Ecstacy / 1988 / HIO / C • For Love Or Money / 1994 / AFI / M • Girls With Curves #1 / 1985 / CV / M • HomeGrown Video #462: Motion In The Backfield / 1995

/ HOV / M • HomeGrown Video #463: Cum And Get It / 1995 / HOV / M • Hot Body Video Magazine: Southern Belle / 1994 / CG / F • Liquid Lips #2 / 1994 / MAV / M • Lovers, An Intimate Portrait #2: Jennifer & Steve / 1994 / FEM / M • Making Of The "Carousel Girls" Calendar / 1994 / DGD / S • Neighborhood Watch #39: / 1993 / LBO / M • Nu-West Screen Test #1 / 1988 / NUV / F • Ona Z's Star Search #02 / 1993 / GLI / M • Penthouse: Great Pet Hunt #1 / 1992 / PET / F • Photo Duo / 1987 / BON / B • Playboy's Girls Of Hooters / 1995 / PLA / S • Shades Of Passion / 1985 / CA / M • She-Male Friends #3 / cr94 / TTV / G • Sidone Bi / 1995 / FRF / G • Southern: Jennifer's Day Off / 1994 / SSH / F • Stevi's: Amy's First Time Bi / 1994 / SSV / F • Stevi's: At Home With Jennifer & Mac / 1995 / SSV / S • Stevi's: Oral Lover's Delight / 1992 / SSV / M • The Submissive Instinct / 1993 / STM / B • Teasedance Masturbation #3 / 1994 / MAV / F • Totally Ona: The Best Of Ona Zee / 1996 / ONA / C • Two Trained For Obedience / 1993 / STM / B • The Ultimate Master / cr87 / BIZ / B • VGA: Bureau Of Discipline #1 / 1993 / VGA / B • VGA: Bureau Of Discipline #3 / 1993 / VGA / B • Women On Women #2 / 1994 / MAV / F

JENNIFER (CRYSTAL K) see Crystal Knight

JENNIFER (HUNGARY)
Cumback Pussy #3: Coast To Coast Rump Romp / 1996 / EL / M

JENNIFER (J. TAYLOR) see Josalynn Taylor

JENNIFER (STEWART) see Jennifer Stewart

JENNIFER ANTONE
4 Of A Kind / 1995 / BON / B • Bound To Like It / 1995 / IBN / B • The Computer Date / 1994 / ATO / B • Corporal Affair #1 / 1995 / IBN / B • Corporal Affair #2 / 1995 / IBN / B • Full House / 1995 / BON / B • Jennifer's Revenge / 1995 / IBN / B • Knotty Nurse Domination / 1995 / IBN / B • Leather Obsession / 1996 / BON / B • Lessons From The Mistress / 1994 / BON / B • Magical Mistresses: Jennifer And Artemis / 1993 / RSV / B • Mother & Daughter From Hell / 1996 / ATO / B • Overruled / 1995 / IBN / B • Right On Track / 1995 / IBN / B • Taped, Tied & Tormented / 1996 / ATO / B • Transformed / 1995 / BON / B

JENNIFER BLOC
Stevi's: Dildo Duet / 1994 / SSV / F

JENNIFER BLOWDRYER
Dark Angel / 1983 / VC / M • Kamikaze Hearts / 1986 / FAC / S

JENNIFER BLUE
Bobby Hollander's Rookie Nookie #07 / 1993 / SFP / M • Stevi's: Jennifer Blue Pregnant / 1995 / SSV / F • Stevi's: Jennifer's Anal Lover / 1994 / SSV / M • Stevi's: Jennifer's Cream Pie / 1996 / SSV / M • Stevi's: Kiss My Feet / 1993 / SSV / M

JENNIFER BRAZEN see Star Index I

JENNIFER BROOKS
The Adult Version Of Dr Jekyll And Mr Hyde / 1971 / SOW / S • Girls Next Door / 1995 / SHL / B • Triple Cross / 198? / CS / B

JENNIFER CARTIER
Drop Sex: Wipe The Floor / 1997 / JLP / M

JENNIFER CHANG

The Dragon Lady #1 / 1988 / WV / C

JENNIFER CORY
Kym Wilde's On The Edge #38 / 1996 / RB / B

JENNIFER DEVROU see Star Index I

JENNIFER DIOR
Betty Bleu / 1996 / IP / M

JENNIFER EASLEY see Star Index I

JENNIFER GOLD see Brigitte Aime

JENNIFER GORDON see Jennifer Jordan

JENNIFER HALL see Star Index I

JENNIFER HAMILTON see Jennifer Stewart

JENNIFER HOLMES see Sharon Kane

JENNIFER HORN
Erotic Dimensions #7: Fulfilled / 1982 / NSV / M

JENNIFER HOYT see Jennifer Noxt

JENNIFER HURST see Star Index I

JENNIFER HURT see Star Index I

JENNIFER HUSS see Tricia Deveraux

JENNIFER IRWIN see Missy Warner

JENNIFER JAMES see Angel (1984)

JENNIFER JANSEN see Star Index I

JENNIFER JO SMITH see Scarlet Fever (96)

JENNIFER JOHN see Star Index I

JENNIFER JONES
Infidel / 1996 / WV / M • Juggs / 1984 / VCR / M

JENNIFER JORDAN (Sara Nicholson, *Jennifer Gordon, Sarah Nicholson*)
Hard personality with a thick body, short brown/blonde hair, not too pretty, flat ass.
Abigail Leslie Is Back In Town / 1974 / HOE / S • American Sex Fantasy / 1975 / IHV / M • Angel On Fire / 1974 / ALP / M • Angela, The Fireworks Woman / 1975 / VC / M • Anyone But My Husband / 1975 / VC / M • Bang Bang You Got It / 1975 / VXP / M • Beach House / 1981 / CA / C • The Bite / 1975 / SVE / M • Blonde Velvet / 1976 / COL / M • Bound And Punished / 1984 / BIZ / B • The Budding Of Brie / 1980 / TVX / M • Cherry Hustlers / 1977 / VEN / M • Dear Pam / 1976 / CA / M • Fantasex / 1976 / COM / M • Farewell Scarlett / 1976 / COM / M • Fire In Francesca / cr77 / ASR / M • Girls In Passion / 1979 / VHL / M • Heavenly Desire / 1979 / WV / M • Hot Shots / 1974 / COM / M • Invasion Of The Love Drones / 1977 / ALP / M • Little Orphan Sammy / 1976 / VC / M • The Love Bus / 1974 / OSC / M • The Naughty Victorians / 1975 / VC / M • The New York City Woman / 1979 / VC / C • The Night Of The Spanish Fly / 1978 / CV / M • Powerbone / 1976 / VC / M • Sexteen / 1975 / VC / M • Sometime Sweet Susan / 1974 / ALP / M • Sticky Wagons / cr70 / IVP / S • Sugar Britches / 1980 / VCX / C • Sweet Punkin...I Love You / 1975 / VC / M • Sweet Wet Lips / 1974 / PVX / M • They Shall Overcome / 1974 / VST / M • Tied, Trained And Transformed / 19?? / BIZ / B • The Tiffany Minx / 1981 / SAT / M • The Wetter The Better / 1975 / VST / M • A Woman's Torment / 1977 / VC / M

JENNIFER JOST see Star Index I

JENNIFER JUICE
Jennifer In Bondage / 1993 / BON / B • Jennifer's Mistake / 1993 / BON / B

JENNIFER KINGSLEY
Desire / 1990 / VC / M

JENNIFER KNOX see Jennifer Noxt

JENNIFER LANE see Jenny Lane

JENNIFER LANGDON
[No More Dirty Deals / 1994 / V-I / S

JENNIFER LEE
Streets Of New York #04 / 1995 / PL / M

JENNIFER LEIGH (Jennifer May)
Petite blonde with small to medium droopy tits and bad skin. Quite pretty but not a tight waist.
Alone / 1993 / OD / F • Field Of Wet Dreams / 1992 / EVN / M • Lialeh / 1973 / ALP / M

JENNIFER LOVE
The Hitch-Hiker #15: Cat & Mouse / 1995 / VIM / M

JENNIFER LOVE (JONE) see Jenny Jones

JENNIFER MASON see Helen Madigan

JENNIFER MAUSMAN
Visions Of Lust / 1983 / GO / M

JENNIFER MAY see Jennifer Leigh

JENNIFER MILES see April West

JENNIFER NOBLE see Jennifer Stewart

JENNIFER NOXT (Jennifer Knox, Jenny (J. Noxt), Cindy Arrgh, Jennifer Hoyt, Peggy L'More, Janet Trent, Cindy Arhh)
Slim pretty brunette who seemed to specialize in anals. Nice personality. Aged 19 in 1985 and was de-virginized at 15. First movie was **C-Hunt**. Is not Penny LaMore. May also be Cindy Rigdon (**Black On White** (1987)).
1001 Erotic Nights #2 / 1987 / VC / M • Age Of Consent / 1985 / AVC / M • All In The Family / 1985 / VCR / M • Black On White / 1987 / PL / C • Blacks & Blondes #13 / 1986 / WV / M • C-Hunt / 1985 / PL / M • Caught From Behind #04: Nasty Young Girls / 1985 / HO / M • Cheerleader Academy / 1986 / PL / M • Chocolate Kisses / 1986 / CA / M • Cram Session / 1986 / V99 / M • Dangerous Curves / 1985 / CV / M • Deliveries In The Rear #1 / 1985 / AVC / M • Devil In Miss Jones #3: A New Beginning / 1986 / VC / M • Double Penetration #2 / 1986 / WV / C • The Girls Of The A Team #1 / 1985 / WV / M • Head & Tails / 1988 / VD / M • The Heat Is On / 1985 / WV / M • Honeybuns #1 / 1987 / WV / C • Honeybuns #2: Grecian Formula / 1987 / WV / C • Hot Cars, Nasty Women / 1985 / WV / M • Immoral Majority / 1986 / HTV / M • The Layout / 1986 / CDI / M • The Lust Detector / 1986 / PIN / M • Miami Spice #2 / 1988 / CA / M • Nasty Habits Are Hard To Break / 1986 / 4P / M • Oral Majority #01 / 1986 / WV / C • Project Ginger / 1985 / VI / M • Rump Humpers / 1985 / WET / M • Sex The Hard Way / 1985 / CV / M • Shaved Pink / 1986 / WET / M • She Comes Undone / 1987 / AIR / C • Snatchbuckler / 1985 / DR / M • Soul Kiss This / 1988 / VCR / C • A Star Is Porn / 1985 / PL / M • Swedish Erotica #68 / 1985 / CA / M • Traci Who? / 1987 / AVC / C • The Wacky World Of X-Rated Bloopers / 1989 / GO / M • White Bun Busters / 1985 / VC / M • Wicked Whispers / 1985 / VD / M • Woman In The Window / 1986 / TEM / M • X-TV #1 / 1986 / PL / C

JENNIFER O'BRYAN see Jennifer Stewart

JENNIFER OAKLAND
Young Sluts In Heat #1 / 1996 / PL / M • Young Sluts In Heat #2 / 1996 / PL / M

JENNIFER PEACE see Devon Shire

JENNIFER PRIMM *see Star Index I*
JENNIFER RICHARDS
C.O.D. / 1981 / VES / S • The China Cat / 1978 / CA / M
JENNIFER ROSE *see* Dominique Simone
JENNIFER ROYCE *see Star Index I*
JENNIFER RUSSELL *see* Chrissy Beauchamp
JENNIFER SANDS
April Love / cr73 / CV / M • Whole Buncha Fucking / 1994 / MET / M
JENNIFER SAX
Bankok Connection / 1979 / CA / M
JENNIFER SCALLONE *see Star Index I*
JENNIFER STEEL *see* Jennifer Steele
JENNIFER STEELE *(Jennifer Steel)*
Behind Blue Eyes #2 / 1988 / ZA / M • The Beverly Thrillbillies / 1987 / EVN / M • Club Head (EVN) #2 / 1989 / EVN / C • The Girls Of Ball Street / 1988 / VEX / M • The Master Of Pleasure / 1988 / VD / M • Nasty Newshounds / 1988 / ME / M
JENNIFER STEWART *(Jennifer Noble, Jennifer Hamilton, Jennifer O'Bryan, Jennifer (Stewart), Simon (Jennifer St))*
Too tall "gee whiz" type blonde with small, slightly droopy tits. Jennifer Noble in **Torrid Without a Cause #2**. She says her first on screen appearence was **Out for Blood** (non sex role—credits: Jennifer O'Bryan). Her porn cherry was popped in **Tall Dark Stranger** (credits: Simon (sic)) by Racquel Darrien in a g/g and then Jeff James. 5'10" tall and 34-23-36. Worked on the **Solid Gold** TV show and then for Disneyland. Supposedly 22 years old in 1991.
Adult Video News 1991 Awards / 1991 / VC / M • Babes With Attitudes / 1990 / EVN / M • Beat The Heat / 1990 / VI / M • Blackballed / 1994 / VI / C • Designer Genes / 1990 / VI / M • Dreams Of Candace Hart / 1991 / VI / M • Jamie Loves Jeff #2 / 1991 / VI / M • Killer / 1991 / SC / M • Lifeguard / 1990 / VI / M • No Time For Love / 1991 / VI / M • Out For Blood / 1990 / VI / M • Pajama Party / 1993 / CV / C • Passages #1 / 1991 / VI / M • Passages #2 / 1991 / VI / M • Passages #3 / 1991 / VI / M • Passages #4 / 1991 / VI / M • Positions Wanted / 1990 / VI / M • Scarlet Fantasy / 1990 / VI / M • The Swap #1 / 1990 / VI / M • A Tall Dark Stranger / 1990 / LV / M • Torrid Without A Cause #2 / 1990 / VI / M • Veil / 1990 / VI / M
JENNIFER STEWART(OR) *see Star Index I*
JENNIFER STONE *see* Dallas St Claire
JENNIFER SUMMERS *see Star Index I*
JENNIFER THOMAS
The Outrageous Nurse / 1981 / VD / G • She-Male Encounters #03: Juicy Jennifer / 1981 / MET / G • She-Male Encounters #04: Jaded Jennifer / 1981 / MET / G • She-Male Encounters #05: Orgy At The Poysinberry Bar #1 / 1987 / MET / G • Sulka's Wedding / 1983 / MET / M
JENNIFER WALKER *see* Sharon Kane
JENNIFER WALTERS
Finger Pleasures #5 / 1996 / PL / F • Old Guys & Dolls #1 / 1995 / PL / M • Old Guys & Dolls #2 / 1995 / PL / M
JENNIFER WELLES *(Liza Duran)*
Old (about 45) in the mid-seventies when she was popular. Blonde with large tits—a maneater.

Blonde Velvet / 1976 / COL / M • Career Bed / 1969 / SOW / S • Confessions Of A Young American Housewife / 1973 / ALP / S • Expose Me, Lovely / 1976 / QX / M • The Groove Tube / 1972 / MED / S • Honeypie / 1975 / VC / M • Inside Jennifer Welles / 1977 / VXP / M • Is There Sex After Death? / 1970 / … / S • The Little Blue Box / 1978 / BL / M • Little Orphan Sammy / 1976 / VC / M • Love After Death / 1968 / SOW / S • Mrs. Barrington / 1974 / IHV / S • Only The Very Best On Film / 1992 / VC / C • Sugar Cookies / 1973 / VAM / S • Sweet Cakes / 1976 / VC / M • Temptations / 1976 / VXP / M • Thunderbuns / 1976 / VCX / C • True Legends Of Adult Cinema: The Cult Superstars / 1993 / VC / C • VCA Previews #2 / 1988 / VC / C • Virgin And The Lover / 1973 / ALP / M
JENNIFER WEST *(Cece Malone, C.C. Malone, Tina Ross (J. West), Sally Swift)*
Older, getting pudgy, shoulder length curly dark brown hair, medium tits.
3 Beauties And A Maid / cr82 / LIP / F • Auditions / 1978 / MEA / S • Ball Game / 1980 / CA / M • The Bitch Goddess / cr82 / BIZ / B • Blonde Velvet / 1976 / COL / M • Blue Confessions / 1983 / VCR / M • Blue Vanities #220 / 1994 / FFL / M • Blue Vanities #535 / 1993 / FFL / M • Blue Vanities #560 / 1994 / FFL / M • Bondage-Gram / 1983 / BIZ / B • Carnal Carnival / cr78 / VCX / M • Carnal Competition / 1985 / WV / C • College Lesbians / 1983 / JAN / F • Come Get Me / 1983 / VEL / M • Cover Girl Fantasies #2 / 1983 / VCR / C • Fantasy Peeps: Sensuous Delights / 1984 / 4P / M • Free And Foxy / 1986 / VCX / C • French Erotica: Love Story / 1980 / AR / M • Go For It / 1984 / VC / M • Goodbye My Love / 1980 / CA / M • Happy Birthday Bondage Gram / 1983 / BIZ / B • Heat Of The Moment / 1983 / S&L / M • Hell Squad / 1984 / MGM / S • Is The Dr In? / 1979 / AXV / M • Limited Edition #03 / 1979 / AVC / M • Lingerie / 1983 / CDI / M • Little Girls Lost / 1982 / VC / M • Love Goddesses / 1981 / VC / M • Love Letters (Now Showing) / 1983 / NSV / M • The Master And Mrs. Johnson / 1980 / SAT / M • Mrs. Smith's Erotic Holiday / 1982 / VCX / M • My Sister Seka / 1981 / CA / M • Nightdreams #1 / 1981 / CA / M • One Page Of Love / 1980 / VCX / M • Passion Play / 1984 / WV / C • Pink Champagne / 1979 / CV / M • Pleasure Dome / 1982 / SE / M • Porno Screentests / 1982 / VC / M • Pro Ball Cheerleaders / 1979 / AVC / M • Ring Of Desire / 1981 / SE / M • The Secrets Of Jennifer / 1982 / NSV / M • Sexcalibur / 1982 / SE / M • Stephanie's Lust Story / 1983 / VC / M • Super-Ware Party / 1979 / AR / M • Tangerine / 1979 / CXV / M • Tinsel Town / 1980 / VC / M • VCA Previews #2 / 1988 / VC / C • The Velvet Edge / cr76 / SE / M • Weekend Fantasy / 1980 / VCX / M • The Wetter The Better / 1975 / VST / M • The Younger The Better / 1982 / CA / M
JENNIFER WONG
National Pornographic #2: Orientals / 1987 / 4P / C • Sex On The Orient Express / 1991 / VC / C • You Turn Me On / 1986 / LIM / M • Young And Restless / 1983 / VIV / M
JENNIFER WORTHINGTON

Angel Eyes / 1995 / IN / M • British Cunts Are Cumming! / 1996 / SPL / M • Cumming Unscrewed / 1995 / TEG / F • Marilyn Chambers: Wet And Wild Fantasies / 1996 / PS / S • Splato: Sexual Fantasies #08 / 1996 / SPL / F • Up Close & Personal: Jennifer Worthington / 1996 / SPL / F
JENNIFER WREN *see* Loni Sanders
JENNIFER WRIGHT *see Star Index I*
JENNY
Blue Vanities #513 / 1992 / FFL / M • Blue Vanities #534 / 1993 / FFL / M • Blue Vanities #549 / 1994 / FFL / M • Dirty Bob's #23: Tampa Teasers / 1995 / FLP / S • Down And Out #2 / 1992 / CDP / B • Dutch Treat (1992-Video Team) / 1992 / VT / M • Full Moon Video #30: Rainy Day Lays / 1994 / FAP / M • Limited Edition #14 / 1980 / AVC / M • Northwest Pecker Trek #1 / 1994 / LBO / M • She-Male Encounters #22: She-Male Mystique / 1995 / MET / G • Sperm Injection / 1995 / PL / M • Triple X Video Magazine #13 / 1996 / OD / M • Up And Cummers #16 / 1994 / 4P / M • Voluptuous #4 / 199? / H&S / M
JENNY (J. NOXT) *see* Jennifer Noxt
JENNY BAXTER *(Janet Baldwin, Karen Regis, Laura Hunt, Sarah Barnes, Rene Verlaine, Joanne Iverson, Jenny Wexler)*
Pixieish sort of face with short black hair, small tits and a reasonably tight body. Maybe slightly too big on the butt. Sarah Barnes is from **The Trouble With Young Stuff**. Rene Verlaine is from **Secret Dreams Of Mona Q** (spelling may be off). Joanne Iverson is from **Jail Bait**.
Blow Some My Way / 1977 / VHL / M • Classic Erotica #5 / 1985 / SVE / M • Fury In Alice / 1976 / SVE / M • The Honey Cup / cr76 / VXP / M • Jail Bait / 1976 / VC / M • Kinky Potpourri #33 / 1997 / SVE / C • Magic Girls / 1983 / SVE / M • Maraschino Cherry / 1978 / QX / M • Midnight Desires / 1976 / VXP / M • The Opening Of Misty Beethoven / 1976 / VC / M • Secret Dreams Of Mona Q / 1977 / AR / M • Summer Of Suzanne / cr76 / VHL / M • That Lady From Rio / 1976 / VXP / M • The Travails Of June / 1976 / VHL / M • The Trouble With Young Stuff / 1976 / VC / M • Vanessa's Bed Of Pleasure / 1983 / SVE / M • Vanessa's Hot Nights / 1984 / SVE / M • Virgin Snow / 1976 / VXP / M • The Vixens Of Kung Fu: A Tale Of Yin Yang / 1975 / VC / M
JENNY BECKER
The Family Jewels / cr76 / GO / M
JENNY BLADE
Fangs Of Steel / Sexual Cutting / 1996 / FLV / M
JENNY BLAIR
Analtown USA #06 / 1995 / NIT / M • Buffy Malibu's Nasty Girls #09 / 1995 / ANA / F • Cockpit / 1996 / SC / M • Fashion Sluts #3 / 1995 / ABS / M • Latex #2 / 1995 / VC / M • Nasty Nymphos #14 / 1996 / ANA / M • The New Ass Masters #07 / 1996 / LEI / C • Pro-Am Jam / 1996 / GLI / M • Wildfire: Shaving Beauties / 1996 / WIF / F
JENNY BLAKE *see Star Index I*
JENNY BLUE *see* Sheila Kelly
JENNY COLE *see Star Index I*
JENNY CROWN
Bedtime Video #03 / 1984 / GO / M
JENNY D'MORNAY

The Girls Of Summer / 1995 / VT / M
JENNY FEELING *see Star Index I*
JENNY FEELINGS *see Star Index I*
JENNY GILLIAN *see Star Index I*
JENNY GOODE *see Star Index I*
JENNY JONES *(Jennifer Love (Jone), Little Jenny Jones)*
Brunette with small emaciated body and a slightly too big nose.
Magic Pool / 1988 / VD / M • The Secret Diaries / 1990 / V99 / M • Shaved Sinners #2 / 1987 / VT / M
JENNY JOYCE
The Fabulous 50's Girls #1 / 1994 / EMC / M • Golden Oldies #4 / 1996 / TTV / M • Golden Oldies #5 / 1996 / TTV / M • Lips / 1994 / FC / M • More To Love #1 / 1994 / TTV / M • Positively Pagan #11 / 1993 / ATA / M
JENNY LANE *(Jennifer Lane, Lisa Young, Cindy Lane)*
A little pudgy around the waist but passable face and long dark hair tied in a ponytail or braids depending on the movie. Small tits. Can well pass for a teenager.
Barbie's Fantasies / 1974 / VHL / M • Couples / 1976 / VHL / M • Pleasure Productions #11 / 1985 / VCR / M • Sexteen / 1975 / VC / M • Thunderbuns / 1976 / VCX / C • Winter Heat / 1975 / AVC / M
JENNY LASALLE
Campus Girl / 1972 / VXP / M
JENNY LIND
Maraschino Cherry / 1978 / QX / M
JENNY OLSEN *see Star Index I*
JENNY QUICK
The Nurses Are Coming / 1985 / VCR / C • Yummy Nymphs / 1983 / TGA / C
JENNY REYNOLDS
Inside Desiree Cousteau / 1979 / VCX / M
JENNY SAND
Erotic Dimensions: Aggressive Women / 1982 / NSV / M
JENNY ST. JAMES
Girly Video Magazine #2 / 1995 / BEP / M • Here Comes Jenny St. James / 1996 / HOV / M • Southern Belles #2 / 1995 / HOV / M • Southern Belles: Sugar Magnolias / 1996 / XPR / M • Strap-On Sally #09: / 1996 / PL / F • Strap-On Sally #10: / 1996 / PL / F • Sunset In Paradise / 1996 / PL / M
JENNY SUE LOGAN
Ecstasy / 1979 / SE / M
JENNY UPTON *see Star Index I*
JENNY WEXLER *see Jenny Baxter*
JENNY WILSON
Erotic Interlude / 1981 / CA / M • The World's Biggest Gang Bang #1 / 1995 / FPI / M
JENNYFER
Impulse #01: Memories Of An Italian Slut / 1995 / MBP / M
JEPH WILSON
Anal Therapy #2 / 1993 / FD / M • Anal Vision #15 / 1993 / LBO / M • Bra Busters #03 / 1993 / LBO / M • Bun Busters #03 / 1993 / LBO / M • Hidden Camera #06 / 1993 / JMP / M • Pearl Necklace: Amorous Amateurs #08 / 1992 / SEE / M • Pearl Necklace: Amorous Amateurs #13 / 1992 / SEE / M • Pearl Necklace: Amorous Amateurs #23 / 1993 / SEE / M • Pearl Necklace: Amorous Amateurs #25 / 1993 / SEE / M • Pearl Necklace: Amorous Amateurs #26 / 1993 / SEE / M • Pearl Necklace:

Amorous Amateurs #27 / 1993 / SEE / M • Pearl Necklace: Amorous Amateurs #30 / 1993 / SEE / M • Pearl Necklace: Amorous Amateurs #33 / 1992 / SEE / M • Pearl Necklace: Amorous Amateurs #34 / 1992 / SEE / M • Pearl Necklace: Amorous Amateurs #37 / 1993 / SEE / M • Pearl Necklace: Thee Bush League #30 / 1994 / SEE / M • Suburban Nymphos / 1994 / ATL / M
JEREMEY
Pet Hotel #1 / 1988 / BON / B • Pet Hotel #2 / 1988 / BON / B
JEREMIA LOGAN *see Jesse Eastern*
JEREMIAH JONES
Taboo #01 / 1980 / VCX / M
JEREMIAH LOGAN *see Jesse Eastern*
JEREMY
Black Video Virgins #1 / 1996 / NS / M
JEREMY AARONS
Slut Safari #1 / 1994 / FC / M
JEREMY BLUNT
Pink Lips / 1977 / VCX / M
JEREMY FOXX *see Star Index I*
JEREMY HAPNER *see Jesse Eastern*
JEREMY HAPPENER
A Private Love Affair / 1996 / IP / M
JEREMY HARDWOOD *see Jeremy Joshua*
JEREMY HARPER *see Star Index I*
JEREMY JOSHUA *(Jeromey, Jeremy Hardwood)*
SO of Kiss in her 1995/6 return. Kris Newz seems to have gone the way of all flesh.
Anal Witness #2: No Prisoners / 1996 / LBO / M • The Cable Girl / 1996 / NIT / M • Carnival Of Flesh / 1996 / NIT / M • Catch Of The Day #4 / 1996 / VG0 / M • Flexxx #3 / 1995 / VT / M • Friendly Fire / 1996 / EDP / M • From The Heart / 1996 / XCI / M • Girly Video Magazine #5 / 1996 / BEP / M • Jizz Glazed Goo Guzzlers #2 / 1996 / NIT / C • Make Me Over, Baby / 1996 / LOF / M • Nineteen #4 / 1996 / FOR / M • Profiles #07: Sexworld / 1996 / XPR / M • Sodomania #16: Sexxy Pistols / 1996 / EL / M • Sue / 1995 / VC / M
JEREMY KENT *see Star Index I*
JEREMY LOGAN *see Jesse Eastern*
JEREMY SCOTT *see Star Index I*
JEREMY SLADE *see Star Index I*
JEREMY STEELE
Adam & Eve's House Party #4 / 1996 / VC / M • The Adventures Of Peeping Tom #4 / 1997 / OD / M • Amazing Hardcore #1: Blow Jobs / 1997 / MET / M • Bedtime Stories / 1996 / VC / M • Burlesxxx / 1996 / VT / M • Decadence / 1996 / VC / M • Domination Nation / 1996 / VI / M • The Fanny Farm / 1996 / NIT / M • Friendly Fire / 1996 / EDP / M • Gazongas Galore #1 / 1996 / NIT / C • Here Comes Elska / 1997 / XPR / M • Incorrigible / 1996 / MET / M • Legs / 1996 / ZA / M • Lisa / 1997 / SC / M • The Other Woman / 1996 / VC / M • Passions Of Sin / 1996 / NIT / M • Pick Up Lines #05 / 1996 / OD / M • Pick Up Lines #06 / 1996 / OD / M • Pick Up Lines #07 / 1996 / OD / M • Pick Up Lines #10 / 1997 / OD / M • Pick Up Lines #12 / 1997 / OD / M • Rumpman In And Out Of Africa / 1996 / HW / M • Sexhibition #2 / 1996 / SUF / M • The Shocking Truth #2 / 1996 / DWO / M • Snake Pit / 1996 / DWO / M • Starbangers #09 / 1996 / ZA / M • Tight Fit #15 / 1996 / GO / M • Unchained Marylin / 1996 / VT / M • Valley Cooze / 1996 / SC / M • War

Whores / 1996 / EL / M
JEREMY STONE *see Dick Howard*
JEREMY WELLS
Hustler Video Magazine #1 / 1983 / SE / M • Hustler Video Magazine #2 / 1984 / SE / M
JEREMY WHITMAN
Betrayed / 1985 / CAL / B • Caught! / 1985 / BIZ / B • Curiosity Excited The Kat / 1984 / BIZ / B • The Experiment / 1983 / BIZ / B • Tourist Trap / 1984 / CS / B
JEREMY WYATT *see Rick Iverson*
JERICA FOX *see Jerrika Foxxx*
JERID (R. MASTERS) *see Rick Masters*
JERID STORM *see Rick Masters*
JERILYN HIRSCH
Ultraflesh / 1980 / GO / M
JEROME BRONSON
The Love Scene / 1985 / CDI / M
JEROME BRYSON
Classical Romance / 1984 / MAP / M • One Last Score / 1978 / CDI / M
JEROME DEEDS *see Star Index I*
JEROME JUICE *see Star Index I*
JEROME TANNER
Born To Run / 1985 / WV / M
JEROMEY *see Jeremy Joshua*
JERRII SINCLAIRE *see Barbie Doll*
JERRIKA FOXXX *(Jerica Fox, Erika Foxx)*
5'1" tall, 19 years old (but looks 39) 40F-22-36 supposedly a virgin (**Virgin Tales**) and looks hard as nails. Tits are, of course, enhanced. Started dancing at 16 and had her first boob job at 17 (she was "only" a B cup before). Supposedly sister to Jessica Foxxx.
2 For .89 / 1994 / SV / B • Battle Of The Boobsy Twins / 1994 / NAP / B • Battlecat #3 / 1996 / CAW / B • Battlecat #4 / 1996 / CAW / B • Busty Babes / 1995 / NAP / F • The Busty Foxxxes Of Napali Video / 1994 / NAP / F • Dick & Jane Big Breast Adventure / 1993 / AVI / M • The End Zone / 1993 / PRE / B • Fantasy Flings #01 / 1993 / WP / M • Frightmare On Elm Street / 1993 / ... / B • The Girls From Hootersville #02 / 1993 / SFP / M • Housewife From Hell / 1994 / TRI / S • How To Make A Model #04: Facial Cream Girls / 1994 / LBO / M • Lilli Chronicles #2 / 1994 / CAW / B • Moon Rivers / 1994 / PRE / B • One Million Heels B.C. / 1993 / SVE / S • Pearl Necklace: Amorous Amateurs #17 / 1992 / SEE / M • Schoolgirls In Disgrace / 1993 / SV / B • Sensual Solos #01 / 1993 / AVI / F • Tip Tap Toe / 1995 / PRE / C • Virgin Tales #01 / 1993 / 4P / M • Xhibitions: Jerika Fox / 1994 / XHI / F
JERRY
Amateur Hours #02 / 1989 / AFI / M • AVP #9126: Photo Finish / 1991 / AVP / M • Big Murray's New-Cummers #29: Tools Of The Trade / 1995 / FD / M • Breast Wishes #07 / 1992 / LBO / M • Dirty Dancers #4 / 1995 / 4P / M • Dirty Hairy's Amateurs #04: Black Dicks White Lips / 1995 / GOT / M • Hollywood Amateurs #05 / 1994 / MID / M • Mr. Peepers Amateur Home Videos #94: Calendar Cleavage / 1994 / LBO / M • Streets Of New York #06 / 1996 / PL / M
JERRY ABEL *see Star Index I*
JERRY BARR *see Jon Martin*
JERRY BEE
Skin #5: The 5th Column / 1996 / ERQ / M
JERRY BILT *see Star Index I*
JERRY BROWER *see Star Index I*
JERRY BUTLER *(Arthur West, Paul Sei-*

derman, Paul Ford, Jerry Rillios)
Paul Seiderman is his real name. As of late 1993 he was supposedly driving a bus for the handicapped in Brooklyn. In 1996 this was upgraded (?) to Staten Island and then further rumor said he had moved to upstate NY. Jerry Rillios is from the closing credits to **Little Darlings**.
10 1/2 Weeks / 1986 / SE / M • The Adventures Of Buttgirl & Wonder Wench / 1991 / AFV / M • Ali Boobie & The 40 D's / 1988 / 3DV / M • Alien Lust / 1985 / AVC / M • Amber's Desires / 1985 / CA / M • Amberella / 1986 / GO / M • America's Most Wanted Girl / 1989 / IN / M • The Amorous Adventures Of Janette Littledove / 1988 / AR / M • Anal Attraction #2 / 1993 / AFV / C • Angel Buns / 1981 / QX / M • Angel Gets Even / 1987 / FAN / M • Angel's Gotta Have It / 1988 / FAN / M • Angela Baron Series #1 / 1988 / VD / C • Angela Baron Series #2 / 1988 / VD / C • Angela Baron Series #3 / 1988 / VD / C • Angela Baron Series #4 / 1988 / VD / C • Angela Baron Series #5 / 1988 / VD / C • The Animal In Me / 1985 / IN / M • Another Dirty Western / 1992 / AFV / M • The Aroused / 1989 / IN / M • Baby Face #2 / 1987 / VC / M • Babylon Pink #2 / 1988 / COM / M • Babylon Pink #3 / 1988 / COM / M • Baccarat #1 / 1991 / FH / M • Baccarat #2 / 1991 / FH / M • Back On Top / 1988 / FAZ / M • Bad Girls #3 / 1984 / COL / M • Bad Girls #4 / 1984 / GO / M • Barbara Dare's Prime Choice / 1987 / SE / C • Barflies / 1990 / ZA / M • Beauty And The Beast #1 / 1988 / VC / M • Behind The Scenes With Angela Baron / 1988 / FAZ / C • Best Butt(e) In The West #1 / 1992 / CC / M • The Best Little Whorehouse In San Francisco / 1984 / LA / M • Best Of Atom / 1984 / AT / C • The Better Sex Video Series #6: Acting Out Your Fantasies / 1992 / LEA / M • Beverly Hills Cox / 1986 / CA / M • Beverly Hills Exposed / 1985 / SE / M • Big Bust Babes #10 / 1992 / AFI / M • The Big One / 1992 / GO / M • The Big Rock / 1988 / FOV / M • The Bimbo #2 / 1992 / AFV / M • Black Beauties #1 / 1992 / VIM / M • Blazing Matresses / 1986 / AVC / M • Blue Angel / 1992 / AFV / M • Blue Jeans / 1982 / VXP / M • Blue Moon / 1992 / AFV / M • Bobby Hollander's Maneaters #04 / 1993 / SFP / M • Bodies In Heat #2 / 1989 / DR / M • Body Heat / 1990 / CDI / M • Boobs, Butts And Bloopers #1 / 1990 / HO / M • Bootsie / 1984 / CC / M • Bordello...House Of The Rising Sun / 1985 / SE / M • Born To Run / 1985 / WV / M • The Boss / 1987 / FAN / M • Both Ends Burning / 1987 / VC / M • The Bottom Line / 1986 / WV / M • The Brat / 1986 / VI / M • Breaking It #2 / 1989 / GO / M • Breaststroke #1 / 1988 / EX / M • Broadway Fannie Rose / 1986 / CA / M • Bubble Butts #18 / 1992 / LBO / M • Built For Sex (Angela Baron's) / 1988 / FAZ / C • Bun For The Money / 1990 / FH / M • Burlexxx / 1984 / VC / M • Business And Pleasure / 1992 / AFV / M • But...Can She Type? / 1989 / CDI / M • Butt Woman #2 / 1992 / FH / M • Butt Woman #3 / 1992 / FH / M • Butt's Motel #1 / 1989 / EX / M • Butt's Motel #2 / 1989 / EX / M • Call Girl / 1991 / AFV / M • Can't Get Enough / 1985 / CA / M • Careena #1 / 1987 / WV / C • Careena

#2: A Star On The Rise / 1988 / WV / C • The Case Of The Cockney Cupcake / 1989 / ME / M • Cat Alley / 1986 / AVC / M • Caught From Behind #11 / 1989 / HO / M • Cheating American Style / 1988 / WV / M • Club Josephine / 1991 / AR / F • The Coach's Daughter / 1991 / AR / M • Confessions #1 / 1992 / OD / M • Confessions #2 / 1992 / OD / M • Confessions Of A Middle Aged Nympho / 1986 / WET / M • Cream Puff / 1986 / VSE / M • Cummin' Alive / 1984 / VC / M • Dangerous When Wet (Amber Lynn Is) / 1987 / VCX / M • Date With The Devil / 1989 / FAZ / M • Debbie Class Of '88 / 1987 / CC / M • Debbie Does Dallas #3 / 1985 / VC / M • Debbie Does Dishes #1 / 1985 / AVC / M • Debbie Does Dishes #3 / 1987 / AVC / M • Debbie Goes To College / 1986 / ELH / M • The Debutante / 1986 / BEA / M • Deep Inside Nikki Dial / 1994 / VC / C • Deep Inside Tyffany Million / 1995 / VC / C • Delicious / 1981 / VXP / M • Deranged / 1987 / REP / S • Despicable Dames / 1986 / CC / M • Devil's Agenda & Miss Jones / 1991 / AR / M • Dial A Dick / 1986 / AVC / M • Dial N Again / 1993 / PEP / M • Diamond In The Rough / 1989 / EX / M • Dick Of Death / 1985 / VCR / M • Dirty 30's Cinema: Ginger Lynn / 1986 / PV / C • Dirty Dreams / 1987 / CA / M • Divorce Court Expose #1 / 1986 / VD / M • Don't Get Them Wet / 1987 / VD / M • Don't Tell Daddy #1 / 1985 / PL / C • Dorm Girls / 1992 / VC / M • Double Dare / 1986 / SE / M • Double Heat / 1986 / LA / M • Double Penetration Fever / 1989 / MIR / C • Dr Lust / 1987 / VC / M • Dr Strange Sex / 1985 / CA / M • Dynamic Vices / 1987 / VC / M • Earth Girls Are Sleazy / 1990 / SO / M • Electric Blue #011 / 1983 / CA / S • Endless Passion / 1987 / LIM / C • Erotic Encounters / 1985 / LIM / C • Erotic Zones #2 / 1985 / CA / M • Escort Girls #1 / 198? / LVI / C • Evils Of The Night / 1985 / LIV / S • Exposure / 1988 / VD / M • Famous Ta-Ta's #1 / 1986 / VCS / C • Fantasy Nights / 1990 / VC / M • Femme / 1984 / VC / M • The Fire Inside / 1988 / VC / C • Firm / 1993 / MID / M • The First Of April / 1988 / VI / M • First Time At Cherry High / 1984 / VC / M • Flash Pants / 1983 / VC / M • Flash Trance / 1985 / IVP / M • Flashpoint / 1991 / AFV / M • Flesh In Ecstasy #06: Elle Rio / 1987 / GO / C • The Flirt / 1992 / EVN / M • Foolish Pleasures / 1989 / ME / M • Four X Feeling / 1986 / QX / M • Foxxxy Lady / 1992 / HW / M • The French Connexxxion / 1991 / VC / M • From Sweden With Love / 1989 / ZA / M • Fun In The Sun / 1988 / EVN / C • Future Lust / 1989 / ME / M • Gangbang Girl #06 / 1992 / ANA / M • Gangbang Girl #07 / 1992 / ANA / M • Gangbang Girl #08 / 1992 / ANA / M • Getting LA'd / 1986 / PV / M • Getting Lucky / 1983 / CA / M • The Ginger Effect / 1985 / VI / M • Ginger In Ecstasy / 1987 / GO / C • Ginger Then And Now / 1990 / VI / C • Ginger's Hawaiian Scrapbook / 1988 / GO / C • Girl Toys / 1986 / DR / M • Girls Of Silicone Valley / 1991 / FC / M • The Girls On F Street / 1986 / AVC / M • Glitter / 1983 / CA / M • The God Daughter #3 / 1992 / AFV / M • The God Daughter #4 / 1992 / AFV / M • Gold Diggers / 1993 / IN / M • Good Enough To Eat / 1988 / FAZ / M • Good Evening Vietnam / 1987 / WV / M • Good

Girl, Bad Girl / 1984 / SE / M • Good Morning Taija Rae / 1988 / VCX / M • Gourmet Quickies: Christy Canyon / Ellie Rio #730 / 1985 / GO / C • Gourmet Quickies: Erica Boyer / Rikki Blake #727 / 1985 / GO / C • Gourmet Quickies: Heather Wayne #722 / 1985 / GO / C • The Great Sex Contest #2 / 1989 / LV / M • Great Sexpectations / 1984 / VC / M • Groupies / 1993 / AFV / F • Hard Deck / 1991 / XPI / M • The Harder Way / 1991 / AR / M • Head Again / 1992 / AFV / M • The Hind-Lick Maneuver / 1991 / GO / C • Honey, I Blew Everybody #1 / 1992 / MID / M • Honeymoon Harlots / 1986 / AVC / M • Hostage Girls / 1984 / VC / M • The Hot Box Invasion / 1987 / AMB / M • Hot Gun / 1986 / CA / M • Hot Licks At The Pussycat Club / 1990 / WV / C • Hot Meat / 1990 / V99 / M • Hot Nights And Hard Bodies / 1986 / VD / M • Hot Rocks / 1986 / WET / M • Hot Shorts: Danielle / 1987 / VCR / C • Hotel California / 1986 / WV / M • Hotel Sex / 1992 / AFV / M • Hottest Ticket / 1987 / WV / C • Hush...My Mother Might Hear Us / 1993 / FL / M • Hyapatia Lee's Sexy / 1986 / SE / M • I Remember When / 1992 / ATL / M • I Wanna Be A Bad Girl / 1986 / PP / M • Ice Cream #4: Touch Of Mischief / 1984 / VC / M • If Dreams Come True / 1991 / AFV / M • Immorals #2: The Good, The Bad, And The Banged / 1990 / AR / M • In And Out (In Beverly Hills) / 1986 / WV / M • In And Out Of Africa / 1986 / EVN / M • In Love / 1983 / VC / M • The Initiation Of Cynthia / 1985 / VXP / M • Inner Blues / 1987 / VD / M • Irresistible #2 / 1986 / SE / M • Jack 'n' Jill #2 / 1984 / VC / M • Jack Hammer / 1987 / ZA / M • Jailhouse Blue / 1990 / SO / M • Joanna Storm On Fire / 1985 / VIV / M • Just Friends / 1991 / AFV / M • Just The Two Of Us / 1985 / WV / M • Karate Girls / 1987 / VCR / M • Keisha / 1987 / VD / M • King Tung Is The Egyptian Lover / 1990 / LA / M • Kinky Business #1 / 1984 / DR / M • Kinky Business #2 / 1989 / DR / M • Kinky Sluts / 1988 / MIR / C • Kinkyvision #2 / 1988 / VC / M • The Ladies Room / 1987 / CA / M • Lady Lust / 1984 / CA / M • Late After Dark / 1985 / BAN / M • Lay Down And Deliver / 1989 / VWA / M • Laying Down The Law #1 / 1992 / AFV / M • Laying Down The Law #2 / 1992 / AFV / M • Leave It To Cleavage #1 / 1988 / GO / M • Legacy Of Lust / 1985 / CA / M • Legal Tender (1990-X) / 1990 / VC / M • Legs / 1986 / AMB / M • Les Be Friends / 1988 / WV / C • Lethal Woman #1 / 1988 / SEV / M • Lethal Woman #2 / 1988 / SEV / M • Little American Maid / 1987 / VCX / M • A Little Bit Of Hanky Panky / 1984 / GO / M • Little Darlings / 1981 / VEP / M • Little Red Riding Hood / 1988 / WV / M • Live Bait / 1990 / IN / M • Living In A Wet Dream / 1986 / PEN / C • The Long Ranger / 1987 / VCX / M • Looking For Mr Goodsex / 1984 / CC / M • Low Blows: The Private Collection / 1989 / ME / M • Lucky Charm / 1986 / AVC / C • Lucky In Love #1 / 1985 / BAN / M • Lucky In Love #2 / 1988 / SEV / M • Lust At Sea / 1986 / VD / M • Lust Tango In Paris / 1987 / PEN / M • Mad About You / 1987 / VC / M • Mad Maxine / 1992 / AFV / M • Made In Germany / 1988 / FAZ / M • Made In Hollywood / 1990 / VEX / M • The Maltese Phallus / 1990 / V99 / M • Mama's Boy

/ 1984 / VD / M • Manhattan Mistress / 1980 / VBM / M • Manwiched / 1992 / FPI / M • The Many Shades Of Amber / 1986 / LIM / M • Mardi Gras / 1986 / SE / M • Mardi Gras Passions / 1987 / MET / M • Marilyn Chambers' Private Fantasies #5 / 1985 / CA / M • Marilyn Chambers' Private Fantasies #6 / 1985 / CA / M • Masquerade (1992-Usa) / 1992 / SC / M • Material Girl / 1986 / VD / M • Meat Market / 1992 / SEX / C • Moonlusting #1 / 1986 / WV / M • Moonlusting #2 / 1987 / WV / M • More Than A Handful #1 / 1985 / CV / C • Murder By Sex / 1993 / LAP / M • My Wife Is A Call Girl / 1989 / FAZ / M • Naked Scents / 1984 / VC / M • Naughty Girls Like It Big / 1986 / ELH / M • Night Cap / 1990 / EX / M • Night Hunger / 1983 / AVC / M • Nikki At Night / 1993 / LE / M • Nikki's Nightlife / 1992 / IN / M • Nina's Knockouts / 1987 / AVC / C • No One To Love / 1987 / PP / M • No Tell Motel / 1990 / ZA / M • No Way In / 1988 / EVN / M • Nookie Court / 1992 / AFV / M • Nudes At Eleven #1 / 1986 / AVC / M • Nymphette #1 / 1986 / WV / M • On Stage And In Color / 1991 / VIP / M • Once Upon A Secretary / 1983 / GO / M • One Night In Bangkok / 1985 / CA / M • One Of Our Porn Stars Is Missing / 1993 / OD / M • Only The Best #1 / 1986 / CV / C • Only The Best #3 / 1990 / CV / C • Only The Best Of Anal / 1992 / MET / C • Oral Majority #03 / 1986 / WV / C • Oral Majority #06 / 1988 / WV / C • Oriental Sorority Secrets / 1992 / VIM / M • Oriental Treatment #3: The Lost Empress / 1991 / AFV / M • Oriental Treatment #4: The Demon Lover / 1992 / AFV / M • Pandora's Mirror / 1981 / CA / M • Panty Raid / 1984 / GO / M • Paris Burning / 1989 / CC / M • Parliament: Shauna Grant #1 / 1988 / PM / C • Partners In Sex / 1988 / FAN / M • Passages #4 / 1991 / VI / M • Passion Chain / 1987 / ZA / M • Passionate Lee / 1984 / CRE / M • Peep Land / 1992 / FH / M • Peeping Tom / 1986 / CV / M • Piggies / 1984 / VC / M • The Pink Lagoon: A Sex Romp In Paradise / 1984 / GO / M • Play Me Again, Vanessa / 1986 / VC / M • Playpen / 1987 / VC / M • Pleasure Channel / 1984 / VC / M • Pleasure Chest / 1993 / IF / M • Pleasure Island / 1984 / AR / M • The Pleasure Maze / 1986 / PL / M • Porn Star's Day Off / 1990 / FAZ / M • Port Holes / 1988 / AVC / M • Pretty As You Feel / 1984 / PV / M • The Price Was Right / 1994 / PAE / M • Pubic Eye / 1992 / HW / M • Puppy Love / 1992 / AFV / M • Pure Sex / 1988 / FAN / C • Pussycat Galore / 1984 / VC / M • Quickies / 1992 / AFV / M • Rachel Ryan / 1988 / WV / C • Radioactive / 1990 / VIP / M • Raging Hormones / 1992 / LE / M • Rainwoman #01 / 1989 / CC / M • Ramb-Ohh #2 / 1988 / PV / M • Raquel Untamed / 1990 / CIN / M • Rated Sex / 1986 / SE / M • Raw #1 / 1994 / AFV / M • Raw #2 / 1994 / AFV / M • Raw Talent #1 / 1984 / VC / M • Raw Talent #2 / 1987 / VC / M • Raw Talent #3 / 1988 / VC / M • Ready, Willing & Anal / 1992 / OD / M • Ready, Willing & Anal (Cv) / 1993 / CV / C • Real Men Eat Keisha / 1986 / VC / M • Rear Admiral / 1990 / ZA / M • Rear Burner / 1990 / IN / M • Rears / 1987 / VI / M • Red Hot Pepper / 1986 / V99 / M • The Red Room And Other Places / 1992 / COM / C • Return To Alpha Blue / 1984 / AVC / M • Rock

Hard / 1985 / CV / M • Rocky-X #1 / 1986 / PEN / M • Rocky-X #2 / 1988 / PEN / M • Romeo And Juliet #1 / 1987 / WV / M • Roommates / 1982 / VXP / M • Rubdown / 1985 / VCX / M • Ruthless Women / 1988 / SE / M • Sam's Fantasy / 1990 / CIN / M • Satin Dolls / 1985 / CV / M • Satisfaction / 1992 / LE / M • Savannah Superstar / 1992 / VI / M • Say Something Nasty / 1989 / CC / M • Scenes They Wouldn't Let Me Shoot / 1984 / VC / M • Screw / 1985 / CV / M • Screwballs / 1991 / AFV / M • Sex About Town / 1990 / LV / M • The Sex Detective / 1987 / GO / M • Sex F/X / 1986 / VPE / M • Sex In Dangerous Places / 1988 / VI / M • Sex Life Of A Porn Star / 1986 / ELH / M • Sex Spa USA / 1984 / VC / M • Sexual Odyssey / 1985 / VC / M • Sexy Delights #2 / 1987 / CLV / M • Shacking Up / 1985 / VXP / M • Shades Of Blue / 1992 / VC / M • She Comes In Colors / 1987 / AMB / M • She's So Fine #1 / 1985 / VC / M • Silk, Satin & Sex / 1983 / SE / M • Simply Irresistible / 1988 / CC / M • Sinners #1 / 1988 / COM / M • Sinners #2 / 1988 / COM / M • Sinners #3 / 1989 / COM / M • The Sins Of Angel Kelly / 1987 / FAN / C • Sinset Boulevard / 1987 / WV / M • Sleazy Rider / 1990 / FOV / M • The Smart Ass Vacation / 1990 / VT / M • Snake Eyes #1 / 1984 / COM / M • Snake Eyes #2 / 1987 / COM / M • Snow White And The Seven Weenies / 1989 / FAN / M • Sodom & Gomorrah / 1992 / OD / M • Something New / 1991 / FH / M • Sorority Pink #3 / 1992 / SP / M • Space Virgins / 1984 / CRE / M • Special Treatment / 1991 / AFV / M • Spellbound / 1989 / LV / M • The Sperminator / 1985 / VXP / M • Spoiled / 1987 / VD / M • The Squirt / 1988 / AR / M • St. X-Where #1 / 1986 / VD / M • Stairway To Heaven / 1989 / ME / M • Star Angel / 1986 / COM / M • Star Gazers / 1986 / CA / M • Starved For Affection / 1985 / AVC / M • Steal Breeze / 1990 / SO / M • Strange Bedfellows / 1985 / PL / M • Strip Search / 1987 / SEV / M • Strong Language / 1989 / IN / M • Succulent / 1983 / VXP / M • Sun Bunnies #2: The Pink Cheek Tales / 1992 / SC / M • Super Models Do LA / 1986 / AT / M • Supertung / 1990 / LA / M • Surrender In Paradise / 1984 / GO / M • The Swap #1 / 1990 / VI / M • Sweat #1 / 1986 / PP / M • Swedish Erotica Superstar #4: Shauna Grant / 1984 / CA / C • Sweet Angel Ass / 1990 / FH / M • The Sweet Spurt Of Youth / 1988 / WV / M • Sweet Summer / 1986 / AMO / M • The T & A Team / 1984 / VC / M • Taboo #03 / 1983 / IN / M • Tail Of The Scorpion / 1990 / ELP / M • Tails From The Tower / 1993 / AFI / M • A Taste Of Cherry / 1985 / CV / M • A Taste Of Taija Rae / 1989 / PIN / C • A Taste Of Viper / 1990 / PIN / C • A Tasty Kind Of Love / 1987 / LV / M • This Stud's For You / 1986 / MAP / C • Those Lynn Girls / 1989 / WV / C • Three Men And A Barbi / 1989 / FAN / M • The Thrill Of It / 1986 / CAT / M • Throat...12 Years After / 1984 / VC / M • Ticket To Ride / 1990 / LV / M • Tiffany Minx Wildcat / 1993 / MID / C • Tinseltown Wives / 1992 / AFV / M • Tit Tales #1 / 1989 / 4P / M • Tongue Twisters / 1986 / VXP / M • Torrid House / 1989 / VI / M • Torrid Without A Cause #2 / 1990 / VI / M • Toying Around / 1992 / FL / M • Traci Who? / 1987 / AVC / C • Traci's Big Trick /

1987 / VAS / M • True Confessions Of Tori Welles / 1989 / VI / M • Twentysomething #1 / 1988 / VI / M • Twentysomething #2 / 1988 / VI / M • Twentysomething #3 / 1989 / VI / M • Twins / 1986 / WV / M • Two Times A Virgin / 1991 / AR / M • Unchain My Heart / 1990 / CC / M • Uncut Diamond / 1989 / IN / M • Under The Law / 1989 / AFV / M • Unnatural Act #2 / 1986 / DR / M • Unnatural Phenomenon #1 / 1985 / WV / M • Unnatural Phenomenon #2 / 1986 / WV / M • Up The Ying Yang / 1991 / EVN / C • Up Up And Away / 1984 / CA / M • V.I.C.E. #2 / 1991 / AFV / M • Vanessa...Maid In Manhattan / 1984 / VC / M • VCA Previews #2 / 1988 / VC / C • VCA Previews #4 / 1988 / VC / C • Velvet High / 1980 / VC / M • Video Voyeur #1 / 1988 / VT / C • Visions Of Jeannie / 1986 / VD / M • Viva Vanessa The Undresser / 1984 / VC / M • Vixens In Heat / 1984 / ECS / M • The Wacky World Of X-Rated Bloopers / 1989 / GO / M • Wanda Does Transylvania / 1990 / V99 / M • Wanda Whips The Dragon Lady / 1990 / V99 / M • Wee Wee's Big Misadventure / 1991 / FH / M • Wendy Is Watching / 1993 / ELP / M • Wet Dreams 2001 / 1987 / VD / M • Wet, Wild And Wicked / 1984 / SE / M • What Are Friends For? / 1985 / MAP / M • When Larry Ate Sally / 1989 / EX / M • When Love Came To Town / 1989 / EVN / M • The Whore Of The Worlds / 1985 / PV / M • Whose Fantasy Is It, Anyway? / 1983 / AVC / M • The Wild Brat / 1988 / VI / M • Wild Flower #2 / 1992 / VI / M • Wild In The Sheets / 1984 / WET / M • Wild Nurses In Lust / 1986 / PLY / M • The Wild One / 1990 / LE / M • Wild Oral Erotica / 1988 / VD / C • Wild Things #3 / 1992 / MET / M • Wildheart / 1989 / IN / M • With Love, Littledove / 1988 / AR / M • Women At Play / 1984 / SE / M • Women In Love / 1980 / CA / M • WPINK-TV #2 / 1986 / PV / M • The Wright Stuff / 1991 / AFV / M • X-TV #1 / 1986 / PL / C • Xstasy / 1986 / NSV / M • Young, Wild And Wonderful / 1980 / VCX / M • [Centerfolds & Covergirls #1 / 19?? / ... / M

JERRY CORBIN
Bedtime Video #09 / 1984 / GO / M

JERRY DAVIS
The Best Little Cathouse In Las Vegas / 1982 / HO / M • The Big Thrill / 1984 / ECS / M • Corrupt Desires / 1984 / MET / M • Cunning Coeds / 1985 / IVP / M • Cupid's Arrow / 1984 / VCR / M • Dear Fanny / 1984 / CV / M • The Divorce / 1986 / VC / G • The Erotic World Of Cody Nicole / 1984 / VCR / C • Fever / 1982 / EVI / C • Going Both Ways / 1984 / LIP / G • Hot Shorts: Laurie Smith / 1986 / VCR / C • The House / cr86 / TEM / G • House Of Pleasure / 1984 / CA / M • I Wanna Be Teased / 1984 / SE / M • Indian Lady / 1983 / VC / M • Interlude Of Lust / cr79 / HO / M • Lessons With My Aunt / 1986 / SHO / M • Little American Maid / 1987 / VCX / M • Love Button / 1985 / AVC / M • Making It Big / 1984 / CV / M • Many Faces Of Shannon / 1988 / VC / C • The Midnight Zone / 1986 / IN / M • Passionate Lee / 1984 / CRE / M • Personal Touch #3 / 1983 / AR / M • Samurai Dick / 1984 / VC / M • The Scam / 1986 / TEM / G • Sensuous Tales / 1984 / VCR / C • Sheer Delight / 1984 / VC / M • Sweet Surrender / 1985 / AVC / M • Traci Who? / 1987 / AVC / C • Twice A Virgin / 1984 / PL

/ G • Unthinkable / 1984 / SE / M • The Younger The Better / 1982 / CA / M

JERRY DELLA *see Star Index I*

JERRY GERARD *see Gerard Damiano*

JERRY GROVER *see Star Index I*

JERRY HALL *see Jon Martin*

JERRY HEATH *see Jon Martin*

JERRY HEFNER
The Black Anal-ist #1 / 1988 / VEX / M

JERRY HESS
Inside Desiree Cousteau / 1979 / VCX / M

JERRY JONES
Gorilla-Gram / 1993 / VAL / M • Homegrown Video #402 / 1993 / HOV / M • Mr. Peepers Amateur Home Videos #83: Roni And The Private's / 1994 / LBO / M • Nasty Fuckin' Movies #13: Nurse Roni / 1993 / RUM / M • Nasty Fuckin' Movies #15: Sink The Pink / 1993 / RUM / M • Pearl Necklace: Thee Bush League #22 / 1993 / SEE / M • SVE: Tales From The Lewd Library #3 / 1994 / SVE / M

JERRY KANE
Flipside: A Backdoor Adventure / 1985 / CV / M

JERRY KELLAR
Tied, Trained And Transformed / 19?? / BIZ / B

JERRY LEE
Dane's Surprise / 1991 / IF / G

JERRY MILLS
Moonshine Girls / 19?? / WWV / M

JERRY NICHOLS *see Star Index I*

JERRY PARIS
Little Girls Of The Streets / 1984 / CV / M

JERRY PIKE *see Gerry Pike*

JERRY PINE *see Gerry Pike*

JERRY PUTZ *see Jon Martin*

JERRY REYNOLDS
Curiosity Excited The Kat / 1984 / BIZ / B

JERRY RILLIOS *see Jerry Butler*

JERRY SALES
Chrome Wheel Circus / 1975 / CA / M

JERRY SCHNEIDERMAN
Highway Hookers / 1976 / SVE / M • Rollerbabies / 1976 / VC / M

JERRY SMITH *see Jon Martin*

JERRY SOKORSKI
Teenage Cruisers / 1977 / VCX / M

JERRY STYLES
Slave Quarters / 1995 / PRE / B • Tailz From Da Hood #3 / 1996 / AVI / M • Takin' It To The Limit #3 / 1994 / BS / M • Wet Mask / 1995 / SC / M

JERRY VALENTINE
[Bizarre Sex Bazaar / 197? / ... / M

JERRY WAD *see Star Index I*

JERRY WARD
Resurrection Of Eve / 1973 / MIT / M

JESEE
Fantasy In Oil #2 / 1996 / CAW / B

JESS FRANCO
[The Loves Of Irina / 1973 / PS / S

JESS JAMES *see Jeff James*

JESSE
Bi-Bi Love Amateurs #4 / 1994 / QUA / C • C-Hunt #03: Sunny Delights / 1995 / PEV / M

JESSE ADAMS *(Jessie Harper, Jesse Atlanta)*
11 / 1980 / VCX / M • 8 To 4 / 1981 / CA / M • Anticipation / 1982 / HIF / M • Any Time, Any Place / 1981 / CA0 / M • Ball Game / 1980 / CA / M • Bare Waves / 1986 / VD / M • Battle Of The Stars #2: East Versus West / 1985 / NSV / M • The Beat Goes On

/ 1987 / VCR / C • Best Of Buttman #2 / 1993 / EA / C • Beyond Shame / 1980 / VEP / M • Big Butts Of The Wild West / 1993 / BTO / M • Bionic Babes / 1986 / 4P / M • Black, White & Red All Over / 1984 / EXF / C • The Blonde Next Door / 1982 / GO / M • Blue Vanities #089 / 1988 / FFL / M • Blue's Velvet / 1979 / ECV / M • Boiling Point / 1978 / SE / M • Chastity Johnson / 1985 / AVC / M • Cracked Ice / 1977 / PVX / M • Daisy May / 1979 / VC / M • Dark Passions / 1984 / VCR / C • Deep Rub / 1979 / VC / M • Desire For Men / 1981 / MIT / M • Double Pleasure / 1985 / VCR / M • Erotic Dimensions #8: Just For Me / 1982 / NSV / M • Erotic Dimensions: Bold Fantasies / 1982 / NSV / M • Erotic Dimensions: The Wild Life / 1982 / NSV / M • Erotic Radio WSEX / 1983 / VC / M • The Erotic World Of Crystal Lake (#4) / 1984 / VCR / C • The Erotic World Of Sylvia Benedict (#5) / 1983 / VCR / C • The Executive Lady / 1980 / TOT / M • Facial Attraction / 1988 / BEE / C • Fantasy Girls / 1988 / CA / M • Fantasy World / 1979 / WWV / M • Fat Ends / 1989 / 4P / M • Female Athletes / 1977 / VXP / M • Fleshdance Fever / 1984 / SAT / M • Forbidden Desire / 1983 / NSV / M • From Russia With Lust / 1984 / VC / M • Girls U.S.A. / 1980 / AIR / M • The Godmother #1 / 1987 / VC / M • The Handyman And The Stepdaughter / cr80 / ASR / M • Hot Country / cr83 / WV / M • Hot Property (AVC) / 1975 / AVC / M • Hot Shorts: Sylvia Benedict / 1986 / VCR / C • The House Of Strange Desires / 1985 / NSV / M • I Love LA #1 / 1986 / PEN / C • I Love LA #2 / 1989 / PEN / C • I'm Yours / 1983 / AIR / C • Inflamed / 1984 / NSV / M • Inside Desiree Cousteau / 1979 / VCX / M • Intimate Realities #2 / 1983 / VC / M • Ladies Nights / 1980 / VC / M • Ladies Of The 80's / 1985 / PV / M • The Legend Of King Karl / 1986 / AR / M • Life, Love And Divorce / 1990 / LV / M • Limited Edition #03 / 1979 / AVC / M • Little Girls Talking Dirty / 1984 / VCX / M • Little Kimmi Johnson / 1983 / VEP / M • The Live Show / 1979 / SVE / M • Looking For Love / 1985 / VCX / M • Love Button / 1985 / AVC / M • Mai Lin Vs Serena / 1982 / HIF / M • Marathon / 1982 / CA / M • The Mistress #2 / 1990 / CV / M • Moments Of Love / 1983 / MID / M • Mrs. Rodger's Neighborhood / 1988 / EVN / C • National Pornographic #2: Orientals / 1987 / 4P / C • Never So Deep / 1981 / VCX / M • Nightfire / 1987 / LA / M • Nightlife / 1983 / CA / M • Nina Does 'em All / 1988 / 3HV / C • October Silk / 1980 / COM / M • Only The Very Best On Film / 1992 / VC / C • Oriental Hawaii / 1982 / CA / M • Peaches And Cream / 1982 / SE / M • Personal Touch #2 / 1983 / AR / M • Physical #1 / 1981 / SUP / M • The Pink Ladies / 1980 / VC / M • Please, Mr Postman / 1981 / VC / M • Princess Charming / 1987 / AVC / C • Private Moments / 1983 / CV / M • Pro Ball Cheerleaders / 1979 / AVC / M • Pumpkin Farm / 1983 / WV / M • Radio K-KUM / 1984 / HO / M • Rock 'n' Roll Heaven / 1989 / EA / M • Rubdown / 1985 / VCX / M • Scorching Secrets / 1988 / IN / M • Sensual Seduction / 1986 / LBO / M • The Sexaholic / 1988 / VC / M • Sexercise Girls / 1982 / CA / M • The Sleazy Detective / 1988 / VD / M • Small Town Girls / 1979 /

CXV / M • Smooth Operator / 1986 / AR / M • Soaking Wet / 1985 / CV / M • Summer In Heat / 1979 / VEP / M • Sweet Savage / 1978 / ALP / M • Sweet Surrender / 1985 / AVC / M • Taboo #01 / 1980 / VCX / M • Taboo #07 / 1980 / IN / M • Tales Of The Backside / 1985 / VCR / C • Top Heavy / 1988 / VD / M • Traci Who? / 1987 / AVC / C • Treasure Box / 1986 / PEN / M • Tricks Of The Trade / 1988 / CA / M • Type Cast / 1986 / AR / M • Ultraflesh / 1980 / GO / M • The Vanessa Obsession / 1987 / VCX / C • Video Guide To Sexual Positions / 1984 / JVV / M • Videobone / 1988 / WET / M • X-Rated Bloopers #1 / 1984 / AR / M

JESSE ATLANTA *see Jesse Adams*

JESSE CHACAN
Deep Roots / 1980 / XTR / M • Seka In Heat / 1988 / BMV / C • Starlet Nights / 1982 / XTR / M • Ultraflesh / 1980 / GO / M

JESSE EASTERN *(Jeremia Logan, Jesse Easton, Jeremy Logan, Jessie Easton, Jeremiah Logan, Jeremy Hapner, Jessie Hapner)*
Sleazy blonde male.
The $50,000,000 Cherry / 1987 / VD / M • AHV #40: Whole Lotta Love / 1993 / EVN / C • Amber Lynn's Peter Meter / 1988 / 3HV / C • Anal Camera #06 / 1995 / EVN / M • Anal Camera #07 / 1995 / EVN / M • Anal Camera #08 / 1995 / EVN / M • Anal Camera #10 / 1995 / EVN / M • Anal Camera #14 / 1996 / EVN / M • Around The World With Samantha Strong / 1989 / V99 / M • Babes With Attitudes / 1990 / EVN / M • The Best Of Hot Heels / 1992 / BIZ / B • The Beverly Thrillbillies / 1987 / EVN / M • Big Murray's New-Cummers #18: Crazy Cuties / 1993 / FD / M • Blonde Butt Babes / 1994 / LV / M • Blowing In Style / 1989 / EA / M • Book Of Love / 1992 / VC / M • The Call Girl / 1986 / VD / M • Campus Cuties / 1986 / CA / M • Captain Bob's Lust Boat #1 / 1993 / FCP / M • Cheeks #1 / 1988 / CC / M • Cherry Cheerleaders / 1987 / VEX / M • City Of Rage / 1989 / EVN / M • Country & Western Cuties #2: Naked Pie Eating Contest / 1996 / EVN / M • Creatures Of The Night / 1987 / FAN / M • De Blond / 1989 / EA / M • Debbie Does Dallas #4 / 1988 / VEX / M • Depraved Innocent / 1986 / VD / M • Dialing For Desires / 1988 / 4P / M • Dirty Movies / 1989 / VD / M • Doin' The Harlem Shuffle / 1986 / CA / M • Double D Roommates / 1989 / BTO / M • Dr Feelgood Sex Psychiatrist / 1994 / LV / M • Dream Jeans / 1987 / CA / M • Dreams Of Natasha / 1985 / AAH / M • Dreams Of The Everyday Housewife / 1990 / FAZ / M • East Vs West: Battle Of The Gang Bangs / 1994 / TTV / M • Easy Cum...Easy Go / 1985 / BAN / M • Enema Diary / 1989 / BIZ / B • Erotic Angel / 1994 / ERA / M • The Eyes Of Eddie Mars / 1984 / CV / M • Fantasy Confidential / 1988 / GO / M • Flash Trance / 1985 / IVP / M • For The Fun Of It / 1986 / SEV / M • Forbidden Pleasures / 1995 / ERA / M • The French Connexxxion / 1991 / VC / M • Fresh Faces #01 / 1994 / EVN / M • Fresh Faces #02 / 1994 / EVN / M • Fresh Faces #03 / 1995 / EVN / M • Fresh Faces #04 / 1995 / EVN / M • Fresh Faces #05 / 1995 / EVN / M • Fresh Faces #06 / 1995 / EVN / M • Fresh Faces #07 / 1995 / EVN / M • Fresh Faces #08 / 1995 / EVN / M • Fresh Faces #10 / 1996 / EVN /

M • The Fun House / 1988 / SEV / C • Fun In A Bun / 1990 / LV / M • Future Sodom / 1988 / VD / M • Gang Bangs #2 / 1989 / EA / M • Garter Charter Tours / 1986 / AVC / M • Getting Off On Broadway / 1989 / IN / M • A Girl Named Sam / 1988 / CC / M • Girl Toys / 1986 / DR / M • Girls Around The World #03 / 1990 / BTO / M • Glitz Tits #02 / 1992 / GLI / M • The Go-Go Girls / 1994 / EVN / M • The Great Sex Contest #1 / 1988 / LV / M • Hard Ride / 1986 / VT / M • Hard Talk / 1992 / VC / M • Head Trips / cr88 / EXH / C • Heavenly Hooters / 1994 / IF / M • Home Runs / 1995 / PRE / C • Hooter Ho-Down / 1994 / LV / M • The Hot Lunch Club / 1985 / WV / M • Huge Grant On The Sunset Strip / 1995 / EVN / M • I Dream Of Tiffany / 1993 / IF / M • In A Crystal Fantasy / 1988 / VD / M • In The Flesh / 1990 / IN / M • Indecent Wives / 1985 / HO / M • Jane Bond Meets Thunderballs / 1986 / VD / M • The Joy Of Sec's / 1989 / VEX / M • Late After Dark / 1985 / BAN / M • The Legend Of King Karl / 1986 / AR / M • Lip Service / 1988 / LV / C • The Load Warriors #1 / 1987 / VD / M • Lucky In Love #1 / 1985 / BAN / M • Lust In Bloom / 1988 / LV / M • Lust Letters / 1988 / CA / M • Maximum Head / 1987 / SE / M • Midnight Fire / 1990 / HU / M • Monkey Business / 1987 / SEV / M • Moonglow / 1989 / IN / M • More Unbelievable Orgies / 1989 / EVN / C • Motel Sweets / 1987 / VD / M • Naughty Nymphs / 1986 / VEX / M • Naughty Nymphs / 1991 / VEX / C • The Night Temptress / 1989 / HU / M • Nightfire / 1987 / LA / M • One Wife To Give / 1989 / ZA / M • Only The Best Of Barbara Dare / 1990 / CV / C • Oral Hijinx / 1990 / ERU / M • Orgy Camera #1 / 1995 / EVN / M • Orgy Camera #2 / 1996 / EVN / M • Oriental Gang Bang Fantasy / 1994 / FC / M • Oriental Oddballs #1 / 1994 / FH / M • Our Dinner With Andrea / 1988 / CA / M • The Out Of Towner / 1987 / CDI / M • Pai Gow Video #04: Tails Of The Town / 1994 / EVN / M • Pai Gow Video #06: New Wave Orientals / 1994 / EVN / M • Passion's Prisoners / 1994 / LV / M • Peepers / 1988 / CV / M • Peeping Passions / 1989 / CAE / M • Perils Of Paula / 1989 / CA / M • Plumpers Of Sundance Spa / 1993 / BTO / M • Pumping Irene #1 / 1986 / FAN / M • Raging Weekend / 1988 / GO / M • Revenge By Lust / 1986 / VCR / M • The Ribald Tales Of Canterbury / 1986 / CA / M • Screwing Around / 1988 / LV / M • Secret Of My Sex-Cess / 1988 / CV / M • Secrets Behind The Green Door / 1987 / SE / M • Sensual Seduction / 1986 / LBO / M • Sex F/X / 1986 / VPE / M • The Sex Game / 1987 / SE / C • Sex Search / 1988 / IN / S • Sex Sluts From Beyond The Galaxy / 1991 / LBO / C • Sex-A-Fari / 1994 / LV / M • She-Male Desires / 1989 / VC / C • Sins Of The Wealthy #2 / 1986 / CLV / M • The Sleazy Detective / 1988 / VD / M • Smoke Screen / 1990 / CA / M • Soaked To The Bone / 1989 / IN / M • Someone Else / 1992 / VC / M • Sophisticated Women / 1986 / BAN / M • Sound F/X / 1989 / V99 / M • Spanish Fly / 1993 / VEX / M • St. X-Where #1 / 1986 / VD / M • St. X-Where #2 / 1988 / VD / M • A Sticky Situation / 1987 / CA / M • Stolen Kisses / 1989 / VD / M • Sweet Chastity / 1990 / EVN / M • Taija Is Sizzling Hot / 1986 / VT / M • A Tall Dark

Stranger / 1990 / LV / M • Tangled / 1994 / PL / M • A Taste Of Angel / 1989 / PIN / C • A Taste Of Black / 1987 / WET / M • A Taste Of Nikki Charm / 1989 / PIN / C • A Taste Of White / 1987 / WET / M • Tasty / 1985 / CA / M • The Therapist / 1992 / VC / M • These Buns For Hire / 1990 / LV / M • Three By Three / 1989 / LV / C • Through The Walls / 1990 / FAZ / M • Tight Fit (Foot Fet) / 1988 / BIZ / B • Tracy Dick / 1985 / WV / M • Tres Riche / 1986 / CLV / M • Tropical Lust / 1987 / MET / M • Uniform Behavior / 1989 / ZA / M • Unnatural Act #2 / 1986 / DR / M • The Wacky World Of X-Rated Bloopers / 1989 / GO / M • Watersports Spree #2 / 1994 / BIZ / C • Wet 'n' Bare With Barbara Dare / 1988 / NEO / C • With Love From Susan / 1988 / HO / C

JESSE EASTON *see* **Jesse Eastern**

JESSE LANG *see* **Candy Vegas**

JESSE LANGE *see* **Candy Vegas**

JESSE LOWE *see* **Star Index I**

JESSE PRIDE
More Than Friends / 1995 / KDP / G

JESSE ROBERTS
Anal Auditions / 1995 / VMX / M • Mickey Ray's Sex Search #05: Deep Inside / 1995 / WIV / M

JESSE RONALD *see* **Star Index I**

JESSE TAYLOR
Married Men With Men On The Side / 1996 / BHE / G

JESSE THROTTLE *see* **Star Index I**

JESSE TYLER
More Than Friends / 1995 / KDP / G

JESSI *see* **Star Index I**

JESSI VENTURA
Dream Strokes / 1994 / WIV / M

JESSICA
Afternoon Delights / 1995 / FC / M • Amateur Nights #10 / 1990 / HO / M • Anal Camera #12 / 1995 / EVN / M • Asses Galore #6: Fallen Angels / 1996 / DFI / M • Beaver Hunt #03 / 1994 / LEI / M • Bend Over Brazilian Babes #2 / 1993 / EA / M • Blue Vanities #542 / 1994 / FFL / M • Contract / 1995 / LON / B • Eurotica #06 / 1996 / XC / M • Eurotica #12 / 1996 / XC / M • The Girls Of Fantasex #1 / 1996 / NIT / M • Hollywood Amateurs #27 / 1996 / MID / M • HomeGrown Video #461: Splendor In The Grasp / 1995 / HOV / M • Hot Body Video Magazine: Brunette Power / 1994 / CG / F • Hot Body Video Magazine: Southern Belle / 1994 / CG / F • The Janitor / 1995 / CS / B • Limited Edition #15 / 1980 / AVC / M • Mike Hott: #347 Bonus Cunt: Jessica / 1995 / MHV / M • Mike Hott: #348 Lesbian Sluts #23 / 1996 / MHV / F • Nostalgic Stockinged Maidens / 1994 / VER / F • Odyssey 30 Min: #155: Pregnant Jessica / 1991 / OD / M • Odyssey Triple Play #07: Anal Addictions / 1992 / OD / M • Private Film #18 / 1994 / OD / M • Pussy Hunt #03 / 1994 / LEI / M • Reel Life Video: Brunettes In Heat / 1995 / RLF / F • Slut Safari #1 / 1994 / FC / M • Super Sampler #5 / 1994 / LOD / C • Sweet Brown Sugar / 1994 / AVI / M • TV Birdcage Rage #2 / 1996 / GLI / G • Viva Viviana / 1994 / PME / F

JESSICA (BISHARD) *see* **Jessica Bishard**

JESSICA (ITAL) *see* **Star Index I**

JESSICA (SELINA ST) *see* **Selina St Clair**

JESSICA BAJAREK *see* **Star Index I**

JESSICA BENNETT *see* **Asia Carrera**

JESSICA BISHARD *(Jessica Bogard, Jessica (Bishard), Jessica Pashard, Jessica Vishard, Jessica Bogart, Jessica Law, Jessica Pachard, Jessica Harn)*
Small breasted tight bodied blonde with a vulnerable face believing her personality.
Bi And Beyond #3 / 1989 / INH / G • Bo-Dacious / 1989 / V99 / M • Breaking It #2 / 1989 / GO / M • Bun For The Money / 1990 / FH / M • De Blond / 1989 / EA / M • Dirty Diane / 1989 / V99 / M • Dump Site / 1989 / BIZ / C • The Fantasy Realm #1 / 1990 / RUM / M • The Fire Down Below / 1990 / IN / M • I Love X / 1992 / FC / C • Innocent Obsession / 1989 / FC / M • Jaded / 1989 / 4P / M • Lost Lovers / 1990 / VEX / M • The Love Mistress / 1989 / WV / M • Night Lessons / 1990 / V99 / M • Night Watch / 1990 / VEX / M • No Man's Land #03 / 1989 / VT / F • One More Time / 1990 / VEX / M • Only The Best Of Barbara Dare / 1990 / CV / C • Rock 'n' Roll Heaven / 1989 / EA / M • The Squirt Bunny / 1989 / ERU / M • Squirt On The Hunt / 1989 / ERU / M • Suzie Superstar #3 / 1989 / CV / M • Sweet Angel Ass / 1990 / FH / M • Tequilla Sunset / 1989 / V99 / M • Tit Tales #1 / 1989 / 4P / M • Undercover Carol / 1990 / FAN / M • Undressed For Success / 1990 / V99 / M • Wet Fingers / 1990 / HIO / M • Wetness For The Prosecution / 1989 / LV / M • Who Reamed Rosie Rabbit? #1 / 1989 / FAN / M

JESSICA BOGARD *see* **Jessica Bishard**

JESSICA BOGART *see* **Jessica Bishard**

JESSICA BRAZEN
Chatsworth Hall / 1989 / BIZ / B

JESSICA BRITTIAN *see* **Jessica Longe**

JESSICA CANDY
Anal Camera #14 / 1996 / EVN / M

JESSICA CASEY *see* **Star Index I**

JESSICA CRAIG-MARTIN
Hardcore: The Films Of Richard Kern #1 / 1991 / FTV / M

JESSICA DALTON
Painful Mistake (Dungeon) / 1993 / PL / B • Roommate Humiliation / 1993 / PL / B

JESSICA DEVILLE
Pearl Necklace: Facial #01 / 1994 / SEE / C • Pearl Necklace: Thee Bush League #11 / 1993 / SEE / M

JESSICA FAME
Amateur Models For Hire / 1996 / MP0 / M • The Butt Sisters Do New Orleans / 1995 / MID / M • Latin Fever #2 / 1996 / C69 / M • Lil' Latin Cutie Pies / 1996 / CDI / M • Vortex / 1995 / MET / M

JESSICA FOXXX
23 years old in 1992, 5'2", blue eyes, 38DD-20-32, weighs 102lbs. Lost her virginity at 19. Tits were enlarged from a C to a DD. First video was **America's Raunchiest #38**. Supposed sister to Jerrika Foxxx.
2 For .89 / 1994 / SV / B • Amateur Lesbians #25: International Budapest / 1992 / GO / F • Amateur Lesbians #35: Meo / 1993 / GO / F • Amateur Lesbians #36: Candi / 1993 / GO / F • Amateur Lesbians #38: Jessica / 1993 / GO / F • America's Raunchiest Home Videos #38: Fantasy Beach / 1992 / ZA / M • America's Raunchiest Home Videos #39: Like A Hurricane / 1992 / ZA / M • Anal Vision #02 / 1992 / LBO / M • Battle Of The Boobsy Twins / 1994 / NAP / B • Battlecat #3 / 1996 / CAW / B • Battlecat #4 / 1996 / CAW / B • Big

Bust Babes #14 / 1993 / AFI / M • Big Murray's New-Cummers #08: Blondes Have More #2 / 1993 / FD / M • Blonde Justice #1 / 1993 / VI / M • Blonde Justice #2 / 1993 / VI / M • Breast Collection #04 / 1995 / LBO / C • Breast Wishes #09 / 1992 / LBO / M • Breast Wishes #11 / 1993 / LBO / M • Breast Worx #41 / 1993 / LBO / M • Breastman Goes To Breastland #1 / 1993 / EVN / M • The Bust Blondes In The USA / 1995 / NAP / F • The Busty Foxxxes Of Napali Video / 1994 / NAP / F • Camera Shy / 1993 / FOR / M • Dick & Jane Big Breast Adventure / 1993 / AVI / M • Dirty Bob's #07: DanCES With OrifiCES / 1992 / FLP / S • Double D Amateurs #02 / 1993 / JMP / M • Double D Dykes #10 / 1993 / GO / F • Double Load #1 / 1993 / HW / M • Falling In Love Again / 1993 / PMV / M • Forget Me Not / 1994 / FH / M • Frat Girls Of Double D / 1993 / PP / M • Freaks Of Leather #1 / 1993 / IF / M • Gazonga Goddess #1 / 1993 / IF / M • The Girls From Hootersville #02 / 1993 / SFP / M • The Good, The Bed, And The Snuggly / 1993 / ZA / M • Hometown Honeys #4 / 1993 / VEX / M • How To Make A Model #03: Sunshine & Melons / 1994 / QUA / M • I Love Juicy / 1993 / ZA / M • Indecent Offer / 1993 / AFV / M • Ladies Lovin' Ladies #3 / 1993 / AFV / F • Little Magicians / 1993 / ANA / M • Lust For Leather / 1993 / IF / M • Maiden Heaven #2 / 1992 / MID / F • Odyssey Triple Play #79: Dildos Dykes & Dicks / 1994 / OD / M • Pearl Necklace: Amorous Amateurs #15 / 1992 / SEE / M • Pearl Necklace: Amorous Amateurs #16 / 1992 / SEE / M • Pearl Necklace: Amorous Amateurs #17 / 1992 / SEE / M • Pearl Necklace: Amorous Amateurs #18 / 1992 / SEE / M • The Pick Up / 1993 / MID / M • Positively Pagan #06 / 1993 / ATA / M • Read My Lips: No More Bush / 1992 / HW / M • Saturday Night Porn #2 / 1993 / AFV / M • Schoolgirls In Disgrace / 1993 / SV / B • Sensual Solos #02 / 1993 / AVI / F • Seymore Butts Is Blown Away / 1993 / FH / M • Seymore Butts: Bustin' Out My Best Anal / 1995 / FH / C • Streets Of New York #01 / 1994 / PL / M • This Could Be The Night / 1993 / IF / M • Tit For Tat / 1994 / PEP / M • Toe Biz / 1993 / PRE / S • Toppers #06 / 1993 / TV / M • Watersgate / 1994 / PRE / C

JESSICA GABRIEL
Toredo / 1996 / ROX / M

JESSICA GRABBIT
Decadent Dreams / 1996 / ME / M • Video Virgins #33 / 1996 / NS / M

JESSICA HAHN see Star Index I
JESSICA HARN see Jessica Bishard
JESSICA HAWN
Undercover Carol / 1990 / FAN / M

JESSICA HUNTER see Star Index I
JESSICA JAMES *(Sashia Lene)*
Blonde with small tits, tattoo on left shoulder back, pretty face, bubbly personality, creamy skin. Appeared on Jerry Springer Oct 1994 where she says she has done 100 movies and also bares her tits (not shown except to the audience). Supposedly she has a college degree. As of late 1994 has had her tits enhanced to large rock solid semi-watermelons. A write-off.

Babenet / 1995 / VC / M • Backhand / 1995 / SC / M • Beaver & Buttface / 1995 / SC / M • Big & Busty Superstars / 1996 / DGD /

F • Big Knockers #15 / 1995 / TV / M • Big Knockers #17 / 1995 / TV / M • Big Knockers #20 / 1995 / TV / C • Big Knockers #21: Best Of Lesbian #2 / 1995 / TV / C • Busty Babes In Heat #4 / 1995 / BTO / M • Carnal Garden / 1996 / KLP / M • Chug-A-Lug Girls #6 / 1995 / VT / M • Cybersex / 1996 / WAV / M • Cynthia And The Pocket Rocket / 1995 / CV / M • Desperate / 1995 / WP / M • Dildo Debutantes / 1995 / CA / F • Dream Lover / 1995 / SC / M • The Edge / 1995 / SC / M • Erotic Visions / 1995 / ULI / M • Fever Pitch / 1995 / ONA / M • Forever / 1995 / SC / M • Full Moon Madness / 1995 / CA / M • Gangbusters / 1995 / VC / M • The Girl With The Heart-Shaped Tattoo / 1995 / WAV / M • Hellriders / 1995 / SC / M • Hienie's Heroes / 1995 / VC / M • Hootersville (Legend) / 1995 / LE / M • Impact / 1995 / SC / M • Induced Pleasure / 1995 / ERA / M • Island Of Lust / 1995 / XCI / M • Little Girl Lost / 1995 / SC / M • Love Dancers / 1995 / ME / M • Mistress Of The Whip / 1996 / GOT / C • The New Babysitter / 1995 / GO / M • No Man's Land #12 / 1995 / VT / F • Nothing Like A Dame #1 / 1995 / IN / M • The Oh! Zone / 1995 / VC / M • Oral Addiction / 1995 / VI / M • The Passion Potion / 1995 / WP / M • The Player / 1995 / VI / M • Plaything #1 / 1995 / VI / M • The Portrait Of Dorie Grey / 1996 / KLP / M • The Reel World #3: Trouble In Paradise / 1995 / FOR / M • The Reel World #4 / 1995 / FOR / M • Return Engagement #01: New York City / 1994 / OUP / F • Road Trippin' #02: New York City / 1994 / OUP / F • Road Trippin' #03: New York City / 1994 / OUP / M • Rock Groupies In Heat / 1995 / LV / M • Rolling Thunder / 1995 / VI / M • The Romeo Syndrome / 1995 / SC / M • Scandal / 1995 / VI / M • Sex Alert / 1995 / PV / M • Sexual Trilogy #04 / 1994 / SFP / M • The Starlet / 1995 / SC / M • Strap-On Sally #03: Thigh Harness Terror / 1994 / PL / F • Strap-On Sally #04: Double Penetration Dykes / 1994 / PL / F • Streets Of New York #02 / 1994 / PL / M • Swedish Erotica #85 / 1995 / CA / M • Swing Into...Spring / 1995 / KWP / M • Toe Tales #19 / 1994 / GOT / B • Toe Tales #20 / 1995 / GOT / B • Toe Tales #24 / 1995 / GOT / C • Topless Stewardesses / 1995 / PV / M • Torrid Tales / 1995 / VI / M • The Voyeur #4 / 1995 / EA / M • Weekend At Joey's / 1995 / ERA / M • Wild Dreams / 1995 / V99 / M • Wildfire: #14 Jessica Solo / 1995 / WIF / F • Women Of Color #2 / 1994 / ANA / M • Work Of Art / 1995 / LE / M

JESSICA JONES
Creme De La Face #07 / 1995 / OD / M • Cum Tv / 1996 / NIT / M • Nothing Like Nurse Nookie #3 / 1996 / NIT / M

JESSICA JUGGS
Big Bust Strippers #03 / 1991 / BTO / F • Big Busty #47 / 1994 / BTO / S • Double D-Cup Dates / 1994 / BTO / M • Girls Around The World #25 / 1995 / BTO / S

JESSICA KANE
The Cellar Dweller / 1996 / EL / M

JESSICA LAINE
Journey Into Latex / 1992 / STM / B • Nasty Dancers #1 / 1996 / STM / B • Private Showings / 1992 / STM / B • Secret Retreat #1 / 1991 / STM / B • Secret Retreat #2 / 1991 / STM / B • Sissy Spanked In Red

Panties / 1992 / STM / B • Toe-Tally Foot-Age / 1992 / STM / C

JESSICA LANE
Nasty Dancers #2 / 1996 / STM / B

JESSICA LANGE (X) see Candy Vegas
JESSICA LAW see Jessica Bishard
JESSICA LEIGH see Star Index I
JESSICA LONDON see Star Index I
JESSICA LONGE *(Andrea Britton, Andrea Roland, Andrea Brittian, Jessica Brittian)*
Ball In The Family / 1988 / VWA / M • Blonde Temptation / 1995 / IF / M • Breaking It #2 / 1989 / GO / M • Broadcast Nudes / 1988 / EVN / M • Cab-O-Lay / 1988 / PL / M • Caught From Behind #03 / 1985 / HO / M • Come As You Are / 1985 / SUV / M • Down The Drain / 1986 / 4P / M • E Three / 1985 / GO / M • Feel The Heat / 1989 / VEX / M • Firefoxes / 1985 / PLY / M • Flesh Fire / 1985 / AVC / M • Future Voyeur / 1985 / SUV / M • Gourmet Premier: Heather & The Hitchhiker / Jessica's Joy903 / cr85 / GO / M • Inner Pink #1 / 1988 / LIP / F • Inner Pink #2 / 1989 / LIP / F • Just Like Sisters / 1988 / VEX / M • K.U.N.T.-TV / 1988 / WV / M • The Love Scene / 1985 / CDI / M • Lust In Space / 1985 / PV / M • Midnight Lady / 1985 / AA / C • No Man's Land #02 / 1988 / VT / F • No More Mr Nice Guy / 1989 / GO / M • Parting Shots / 1990 / VD / M • Perfection / 1985 / VD / M • Pipe Dreams / 1985 / 4P / M • The Pornbirds / 1985 / VC / M • The Pussywillows / 1985 / SUV / M • Satin Dolls / 1985 / CV / M • The Scent Of Samantha / 1988 / VEX / C • Sex Shoot / 1985 / AT / M • Snapshots: Confessions Of A Video Voyeur / 1988 / CC / M • Soft Caresses / 1988 / VEX / M • Spermbusters / 1984 / AT / M • Spooked / 1989 / VEX / M • Stand-In Studs / 1989 / V99 / M • Super Models Do LA / 1986 / AT / M • Sweet Addiction / 1988 / CIN / M • Two Women & A Man / 1988 / VEX / M • Two Women & A Man / 1991 / VEX / C • Weekend Delights / 1992 / V99 / M • The Whore Of The Worlds / 1985 / PV / M • Wild Oats / 1988 / CV / M • The Woman In Pink / 1984 / SE / M

JESSICA MOORE
The Tender Trap / 1978 / IHV / M

JESSICA MORALES
Private Film #12 / 1994 / OD / M

JESSICA PACHARD *see* **Jessica Bishard**
JESSICA PASHARD *see* **Jessica Bishard**
JESSICA PEELOFSKA
More Dirty Debutantes #49 / 1995 / 4P / M

JESSICA POLLEN see Star Index I
JESSICA RABBIT
Battle Of The Busty Foxxes / 1994 / NAP / B • Butthead Dreams / 1994 / FH / M • Heavenly Bodies / 1993 / NAP / B • Humiliating Defeat / 1996 / NAP / B • Let's Talk Anal / 1996 / ESF / M • Tongues On Fire / 1994 / NAP / B

JESSICA RAMIREZ
Immortal Desire / 1993 / VI / M

JESSICA RAVAGE
Desire Kills / 1996 / SUM / M

JESSICA SAVAGE see Star Index I
JESSICA STEHL see Star Index I
JESSICA STONE see Steavie Stone
JESSICA TEAL see Christine de Shaeffr
JESSICA TEMPLE-SMITH

The Jade Pussycat / 1977 / CA / M

JESSICA VERONICA

Is this the same as Skye Ryder (they both have tight bodies and a nipple ring in the right tit but Skye is a blonde and Jessica is a brunette)?

Amateur Lesbians #38: Jessica / 1993 / GO / F • Caught In The Act / 1993 / BS / B • Cherry Redder / 1993 / RB / B • Dominating Girlfriends #1 / 1992 / PL / B • House Of Torture / 1993 / PL / B • Kym Wilde's On The Edge #22 / 1995 / RB / B • Kym Wilde's On The Edge #24 / 1995 / RB / B • Openhanded Girlfriends / 1992 / RB / B • Pretty Cheeks / 1994 / RB / B • Scared Stiff / 1992 / PL / B • The Story Of Pain / 1992 / PL / B

JESSICA VISHARD see Jessica Bishard

JESSICA WILDE *(Jessica Wylde, Jessica Wilder, Jessy Wylde)*

Passable track, brunette, large enhanced tits but a lithe body otherwise. Nice personality. Was a dancer in Las Vegas for five years before getting into porno movies. In 1985, she had a five year old daughter. Supposedly has very poor eyesight.

Amber Lynn's Personal Best / 1986 / VD / M • The Angel In Mr. Holmes / 1988 / WV / C • Angels Of Passion / 1986 / CDI / M • Animal Impulse / 1985 / AA / M • Bedtime Stories / 1989 / WV / M • Best Of Foot Worship #2 / 1989 / BIZ / C • Best Of Hot Shorts #01 / 1987 / VCR / C • Black Valley Girls #2 / 1989 / DR / M • California Reaming / 1985 / WV / M • Changing Places / 1984 / AVC / M • Chastity And The Starlets / 1986 / RAV / M • Club Taboo / 1987 / MET / G • Country Girl / 1985 / AVC / M • Creamy Cheeks / 1986 / VEX / M • Creatures Of The Night / 1987 / FAN / M • Dance Fever / 1985 / VCR / M • Dangerous Curves / 1985 / CV / M • Deep Inside Tracey / 1987 / CDI / C • Deeper! Harder! Faster! / 1986 / VCS / C • Desperately Seeking Suzie / 1985 / VD / M • Dickman & Throbbin / 1985 / WV / M • Dirty Dreams / 1987 / CA / M • E Three / 1985 / GO / M • Extreme Heat / 1987 / ME / M • Fantasy Chamber / 1987 / VT / M • Flesh Fire / 1985 / AVC / M • Foot Lights / 1988 / BIZ / B • Gang Bangs #1 / 1985 / VCR / M • Garter Charter Tours / 1986 / AVC / M • Gazongas #01 / 1987 / VEX / M • Gettin' Ready / 1985 / CDI / M • The Girls Of The A Team #1 / 1985 / WV / M • The Girls On F Street / 1986 / AVC / M • Girls Together / 1985 / GO / C • Go For It / 1984 / VC / M • Goin' Down / 1985 / VC / M • Golddiggers #1 / 1985 / VC / M • Gourmet Premier: Heather & Bunny / Around the World #906 / cr85 / GO / M • Greek Lady / 1985 / TGA / M • Guess Who Came At Dinner? / 1987 / FAN / M • Happy Birthday Bondage Gram / 1983 / BIZ / B • Hard Choices / 1987 / CA / M • High Rollers / 1987 / VEX / M • Holiday For Angels / 1987 / IN / M • Honeybuns #2: Grecian Formula / 1987 / WV / C • Honeymoon Harlots / 1986 / AVC / M • Hot And Nasty! / 1986 / V99 / C • Hot Shorts: Susan Hart / 1986 / VCR / C • Hyapatia Lee's Secret Dreams / 1986 / SE / M • Hypnotic Sensations / 1985 / GO / M • The Insatiable Hyapatia Lee / 1987 / SE / C • Inside Candy Samples / 1984 / CV / M • Just Another Pretty Face / 1985 / AVC / M • Le Sex De Femme #4 / 1989 / AFI / C • Living In A

Wet Dream / 1986 / PEN / C • Loose Ends #3 / 1987 / BS / M • Mad Sex / 1986 / VD / M • Mix-N-Match / 1989 / LV / G • Mouth-watering / 1986 / BRA / M • Naked Lust / 1985 / SE / M • Nice 'n' Tight / 1985 / AIR / M • No Man's Land #01 / 1988 / VT / C • Nudes At Eleven #2 / 1987 / AVC / M • Obsession / 1985 / HO / M • On The Loose & Hot To Trot / 1987 / CA / M • Orifice Party / 1985 / GOM / M • The Perfect Brat / 1989 / VI / M • Pleasure Productions #11 / 1985 / VCR / M • The Pornbirds / 1985 / VC / M • Pornocchio / 1987 / ME / M • Portrait Of Lust / 1984 / CC / M • Princess Of Penetration / 1988 / VXP / M • Rear Ended / 1985 / WV / M • Rough Draft / 1986 / VEN / M • Science Friction / 1986 / AXT / M • Sex 5th Avenue / 1985 / WV / M • Sex Academy / 1985 / PLY / M • Sex Lives Of The Rich And Beautiful / 1988 / CA / M • Sex-O-Gram / 1986 / LA / M • Sexaholic / 1985 / AVC / M • Sexline You're On The Air / 1986 / CAT / M • Showgirls / 1985 / SE / M • Sin City / 1986 / WET / M • Smear My Ass With Cum / 1993 / EX / C • Sole Kisses / 1987 / BIZ / S • Sore Throat / 1985 / GO / M • A Sticky Situation / 1987 / CA / M • Suzie Superstar #2 / 1985 / CV / M • Switch Hitters #1 / 1987 / IN / G • Tarot Temptress / 1985 / AA / M • The Teacher's Pet / 1985 / WV / M • Teenage Games / 1985 / HO / M • Throbbin' Hood / 1987 / VD / M • Tickled! / 1989 / BIZ / C • Tight End / 1988 / VXP / M • The Trouble With Traci / 1984 / CHA / C • The Ultimate Lover / 1986 / VD / M • Unnatural Act #2 / 1986 / DR / M • Video Tramp #1 / 1985 / AA / M • Voyeur's Delight / 1986 / VCS / C • The Wacky World Of X-Rated Bloopers / 1989 / GO / M • Where There's Smoke There's Fire / 1987 / FAN / M • The Woman In Pink / 1984 / SE / M • You're The Boss / 1985 / VD / M

JESSICA WILDER see Jessica Wilde

JESSICA WYLDE see Jessica Wilde

JESSICA/MACY

Black Street Hookers #5: The Mean Streets Of Washington D.C. / 1997 / DFI / M

JESSIE

America's Raunchiest Home Videos #12: Bimbo Ballers From Brt / 1992 / ZA / M • Assford Wives / 1992 / ATL / M • Beach Bum Amateur's #03 / 1992 / MID / M • Blue Vanities #530 / 1993 / FFL / M • Bubble Butts #04 / 1992 / LBO / M • Full Moon Video #21: Me, You, And Your Brother Too! / 1994 / FAP / M • Girls Around The World #22: Letha Weapons & Friends / 1995 / BTO / M • Jessie's Audition / 1995 / DIP / M • Naughty Nanny / 1995 / DIP / F • Pearl Necklace: Thee Bush League #19 / 1993 / SEE / M • Quebec Perversity #5 / 1996 / INO / M • Rocco Unleashed / 1994 / SC / M • The Stand-Up / 1994 / VC / M

JESSIE ADAMS

Kate And The Indians / 1980 / SE / M

JESSIE BAE

Sabrina Starlet / 1994 / SC / M • Shades Of Erotica #02 / 1994 / GLI / M

JESSIE BLU see Debbie Northrup

JESSIE C. DANIELS see Star Index I

JESSIE CHANDLER see Jessie St James

JESSIE DALTON see Star Index I

JESSIE EASTON see Jesse Eastern

JESSIE HAPNER see Jesse Eastern

JESSIE HARPER see Jesse Adams

JESSIE JAMES

Slim, pretty girl with long dark blonde hair and tiny tits, tight body and waist and long legs. Maybe slightly flat on the butt. Nice personality. In early 1994 she had her tits expanded to a medium size and seems to have something done to her eyes with the result that her face is not nearly as attractive. 23 years old in 1994 and was 12 when de-virginized. Comes from Tampa, FL. Married to a guy named Dave Roach.

Anal Knights In Hollywood #2 / 1993 / MET / M • Bel Air Babes / 1996 / SUF / M • Big Knockers #16 / 1995 / TV / M • Buffy Malibu's Nasty Girls #06 / 1994 / ANA / F • Buffy Malibu's Nasty Girls #07 / 1994 / ANA / F • The Butt Sisters Do Sturgis / 1994 / MID / M • C-Hunt #01: Pandemonium / 1995 / PEV / M • Caribbean Sunset / 1996 / PL / M • The Couch Trap / 1993 / ELP / M • Cumback Pussy #3: Coast To Coast Rump Romp / 1996 / EL / M • Cunthunt / 1995 / AB / F • Desert Island Buttwatch / 1996 / SUF / M • Dirty Bob's #03: Xplicit Interviews / 1992 / FLP / S • Dirty Bob's #17: Tampa Teasers! / 1994 / FLP / S • Dirty Bob's #18: Under The Boardwalk! / 1995 / FLP / S • Dirty Bob's #19: Over The Boardwalk! / 1995 / FLP / S • Dirty Bob's #23: Tampa Teasers / 1995 / FLP / S • Dirty Bob's #25: Porn Never Sleeps! / 1996 / FLP / S • East Coast Sluts #07: Tampa Bay / 1995 / PL / M • East Coast Sluts #08: Atlantic City / 1995 / PL / M • East Coast Sluts #09: / 1995 / PL / M • First Time Lesbians #11 / 1993 / JMP / F • Hollywood '94: Butts Abound / 1993 / ELP / M • Interracial Anal #06 / 1995 / AFI / M • Love Potion 69 / 1994 / VC / M • Nasty Nymphos #03 / 1994 / ANA / M • Nasty Nymphos #13 / 1996 / ANA / M • No Man's Land #09 / 1994 / VT / F • Pearl Necklace: Amorous Amateurs #35 / 1993 / SEE / M • Pearl Necklace: Amorous Amateurs #37 / 1993 / SEE / M • Pearl Necklace: Amorous Amateurs #38 / 1993 / SEE / M • Pearl Necklace: Amorous Amateurs #39 / 1993 / SEE / M • Pearl Necklace: Premier Sessions #01 / 1993 / SEE / M • Pearl Necklace: Premier Sessions #02 / 1993 / SEE / M • Pearl Necklace: Thee Bush League #27 / 1993 / SEE / M • Philmore Butts Spring Break / 1996 / SUF / M • Private Video Magazine #09 / 1994 / OD / M • Reckless / 1995 / NOT / M • Shades Of Passion / 1995 / NOT / M • Strap-On Sally #07: Face Dildo Frenzy / 1995 / PL / F • Strap-On Sally #08: Strap-On Cock Fight / 1995 / PL / F • Strap-On Sally #09: / 1996 / PL / F • Streets Of New York #07 / 1996 / PL / M • Summer Vacation #1 / 1996 / RAS / M • Summer Vacation #2 / 1996 / RAS / M • Sunset In Paradise / 1996 / PL / M • Tampa Spice / 1996 / SUF / M • Up And Cummers #09 / 1994 / 4P / M • Video Virgins #15 / 1994 / NS / M • Wet In The Saddle / 1994 / ME / M • Xhibitions: Jessie James / 1995 / XHI / F • Xhibitions: Kissin' Kuzzins / 1995 / XHI / F

JESSIE JAY

Vivid Raw #1 / 1996 / VI / M

JESSIE JEAN see C.J. Bennett

JESSIE LAND see Candy Vegas

JESSIE LANGE see Candy Vegas

JESSIE SAVAGE see C.J. Laing

JESSIE ST CROIX

More Dirty Debutantes #37 / 1995 / 4P / M • More Dirty Debutantes #38 / 1995 / 4P / M • More Dirty Debutantes #39 / 1995 / 4P / M • More Dirty Debutantes #43 / 1995 / 4P / M

JESSIE ST JAMES *(Jessie Chandler)*
Blonde with mid-length fine hair, tiny tits, lithe body, marginal face. A little flat on the butt and not a tight waist.
The 8th Annual Erotic Film Awards / 1984 / SE / C • Behind The Brown Door / 1986 / VCR / C • Behind The Scenes Of An Adult Movie / 1983 / CV / M • The Best Of Gail Palmer / 1981 / WWV / C • Between Lovers / 1983 / CA / M • Blonde Fire / 1979 / EVI / M • Blondes Have More Fun / 1980 / SE / M • Blue Confessions / 1983 / VCR / M • Blue Heat / 1975 / IVP / M • Blue Vanities #055 / 1988 / FFL / M • Blue Vanities #090 / 1988 / FFL / M • Caballero Preview Tape #2 / 1983 / CA / C • Caballero Preview Tape #3 / 1984 / CA / C • Caballero Preview Tape #4 / 1985 / CA / C • Casanova #2 / 1976 / CA / M • Centerspread Girls / 1982 / CA / M • Charli / 1981 / VCX / M • Chopstix / 1979 / TVX / M • Easy / 1978 / CV / M • Erotic Fantasies #2 / 1983 / CV / C • Erotic Fantasies #4 / 1983 / CV / C • Erotic Fantasies: Women With Women / 1984 / CV / C • Exhausted / 1981 / CA / C • Extremes / 1981 / CA / M • Fantasy World / 1979 / WWV / M • Feels Like Silk / 1983 / SE / M • Female Athletes / 1977 / VXP / M • The Filthy Rich / 1981 / CA / M • Going Wild / 1983 / ... / M • The Gypsy Ball / 1979 / ENC / M • Her Wicked Ways / 1983 / CA / M • Hot Legs / 1979 / VCX / M • Hot Line / 1980 / CA / M • Indecent Exposure / 1981 / CA / M • Indecent Pleasures / 1984 / CA/ M • Insane Desires / cr78 / ... / M • Insatiable #1 / 1980 / CA / M • Le Sex De Femme #3 / 1989 / AFI / C • Legends Of Porn #1 / 1987 / CV / C • Matinee Idol / 1984 / VC / M • Ms. Magnificent / 1979 / SE / M • Nurses Of The 407th / 1982 / CA / M • Only The Best #1 / 1986 / CV / C • Only The Best Of Men's And Women's Fantasies / 1988 / CV / C • Only The Best Of Peepers / 1992 / CV / C • Oriental Hawaii / 1982 / CA / M • Randy, The Electric Lady / 1978 / VC / M • Sensual Fire / 1979 / HIF / M • The Sensuous Detective / 1979 / VC / M • Showgirl #09: Jessie St James' Fantasies / 1981 / VCR / M • Silk, Satin & Sex / 1983 / SE / M • Snow Honeys / 1983 / VC / M • Sound Of Love / 1981 / CA / M • Swedish Erotica #43 / 1982 / CA / M • Swedish Erotica #44 / 1982 / CA / M • Swedish Erotica #46 / 1983 / CA / M • Swedish Erotica Hard #31: Jessie's Wild Women / 1992 / OD / C • Sweethearts / 1986 / SE / C • Talk Dirty To Me #01 / 1980 / CA / M • Talk Dirty To Me #05 / 1987 / DR / M • A Taste Of Vanessa De Rio / 1990 / PIN / C • That's Porno / 1979 / CV / C • Tropic Of Desire / 1979 / WWV / M • True Legends Of Adult Cinema: The Golden Age / 1992 / VC / C • Vista Valley PTA / 1980 / CV / M • Yuppies In Heat / 1988 / CHA / C

JESSIE STEWART
The Taming Of Rebecca / 1982 / SVE / B

JESSIE TURNER
Sex Off The Runway / 1991 / GMI / M

JESSIE VEGAS
Bang City #6: Bugger's Banquet / 1995 /

SC / M

JESSIKA LANGES
Flamenco Ecstasy / 1996 / UEF / M

JESSY GORY see Star Index I

JESSY JOY
The Girls Of Fantasex #2 / 1996 / NIT / M

JESSY LANG see C.J. Laing

JESSY LORENZ
Take Me #8: For The Night / 1995 / VIO / M

JESSY WYLDE see Jessica Wilde

JESUS FRANCO
Sadisterotica / 1967 / ... / S • [Le Journal Intime D'Une Nymphomane / 1972 / ... / M

JESY GRANT
Jiggly Queens #3 / 1996 / LE / M

JETHRO
Sexual Trilogy #01 / 1993 / SFP / M

JETTE MONTERY see Cheri Monterey

JEUN MEI LING
Chinese Blue / 1976 / ... / M

JEWEL (NIGHT) see Veronica Lake

JEWEL NIGHT see Veronica Lake

JEWELL see Star Index I

JEWELL GOLDEN
Savage Lessons #1 / 1995 / BON / B • Streets Of New York #03 / 1994 / PL / M

JEWELS
New Faces, Hot Bodies #22 / 1996 / STP / M • Shane's World #6: Slumber Party / 1996 / OD / F

JEY see Star Index I

JEZEBEL
Goldilocks And The 3 Bares / 1996 / LBO / B • The Reunion / 1996 / CS / B

JEZEBEL (KIKI) see Kiki

JEZEBEL FLAIR
Filthy First Timers #1 / 1996 / EL / M • Solo Adventures / 1996 / AB / F

JEZEBEL TARTINI see Star Index I

JEZEBELLE see Lil Lee

JHANAE see Jhane Nickols

JHANE NICKOLS *(Jhanae)*
Not too pretty black girl with small droopy tits and a sloppy belly.
Dark Room / 1994 / VT / M • The Hitch-Hiker #06: Salty Dog / 1994 / WMG / M • My Baby Got Back #04 / 1994 / VT / M

JHANE PHILLIPE
Extraterrestrial Virgins / 1995 / VIT / M

JIANNI
Breastman's Triple X Cellent Adventure / 1995 / EVN / M • Jingle Balls / 1996 / EVN / M

JILANNA GALLEY see Star Index I

JILL
America's Raunchiest Home Videos #27: Here Cums Ginger! / 1992 / ZA / M • AVP #4005: The Ball Street Journal / 1991 / AVP / M • Biff Malibu's Totally Nasty Home Videos #09 / 1992 / ANA / M • Blue Vanities #169 (New) / 1996 / FFL / M • Blue Vanities #169 (Old) / 1991 / FFL / M • Blue Vanities #503 / 1992 / FFL / M • Blue Vanities #517 / 1992 / FFL / M • Blue Vanities #549 / 1994 / FFL / M • Blue Vanities #564 / 1994 / FFL / M • Blue Vanities #579 / 1995 / FFL / M • British Butt Search / 1995 / VC / M • Bubble Butts #26 / 1993 / LBO / M • Cherry Poppers #05: Playtime / 1994 / ZA / M • Lesbian Pros And Amateurs #07 / 1992 / GO / F • Letters From A Slave / 1995 / AOC / M • Mr. Peepers Amateur Home Videos #59: The Ball Of The Wild / 1992 / LBO / M • Profiles #02 / 1995 / XPR / M • Ron Hightower's White Chicks #12 / 1994 / LBO / M • Uncle Roy's Amateur Home Video #14 /

1992 / VIM / M • Uncle Roy's Amateur Home Video #15 / 1992 / VIM / M

JILL AMBER
Horny Henry's Peeping Adventures / 1994 / TTV / M • Prime Cuts #1 / 1994 / FOR / M • Prime Cuts #2 / 1994 / FOR / M

JILL BECK
Heat Wave / 1977 / COM / M

JILL CUMER
Deranged / 1987 / REP / S • If Looks Could Kill / 1987 / REP / S • Jailhouse Girls / 1984 / VC / M • Sex Appeal / 1986 / VES / S

JILL FELTON
The Virgin Forest / 1975 / AXV / M • Weekend Lovers / 1975 / AVC / M

JILL FERRAR see Jill Ferrari

JILL FERRARI *(Jill Jason, Jill Ferrar)*
Blonde Heat (VCA) / 1985 / VC / M • A Coming Of Angels, The Sequel / 1985 / CA / M • Future Sex / 1984 / NSV / M • The House Of Strange Desires / 1985 / NSV / M • Missing Pieces / 1985 / IN / M • Playing For Passion / 1987 / IN / M • Wild Things #1 / 1985 / CV / M

JILL FLAXON see Star Index I

JILL HAVEN
Visions / 1977 / QX / M

JILL HUNTER see Heather Mansfield

JILL JACKOFF
Sin City Cycle Sluts #2 / 1995 / SC / F

JILL JACKSON see Kay Parker

JILL JAMESON
Bottom Busters / 1973 / BLT / M

JILL JASON see Jill Ferrari

JILL JOHNS see Connie Peterson

JILL KELLY *(Calista J., Seth Damian, Jill Kennedy, Adrian (Jill Kelly), Jill Roberts)*
Tight bodied blonde with small tits, groucho eyebrows, pretty if a bit haughty face, good tan lines, tight waist, nice skin. Was married to Cal Jammer at the time of his suicide and appeared under the name of Calista J. in some movies with him. 22 years old in 1995. In 1996 she had her tits enhanced to rock solid cantaloupes.
100% Amateur #11: / 1995 / OD / M • 13th Annual Adult Video News Awards / 1996 / VC / S • Adam & Eve's House Party #2: Bachelor Party / 1996 / VC / M • Anal Island #1 / 1996 / VC / M • Anal Plaything #2 / 1995 / ROB / M • Anal Princess #1 / 1996 / VC / M • Anal Senorita #2 / 1995 / ROB / M • Arizona Gold / 1996 / KLP / M • Badgirls #5: Maximum Babes / 1995 / VI / M • Bar Bizarre / 1996 / WP / B • Best Butt(e) In The West #2 / 1995 / CC / M • The Best Of Strippers Inc / 1996 / ONA / C • Beverly Hills Sex Party / 1993 / EX / M • Blaze / 1996 / WAV / M • Bloopers & Boners / 1996 / VI / M • Blue Dreams / 1996 / SC / M • Body Language / 1995 / VI / M • Borderline (Vivid) / 1995 / VI / M • Bruce Seven: A Compendium Of His Most Graphic Scenes Vol 6 / 1994 / BS / C • Buffy Malibu's Nasty Girls #10 / 1996 / ANA / F • Butt Jammers #01 / 1995 / SC / F • Butt Jammers #02 / 1995 / SC / F • The Butt Sisters Do Boston / 1995 / MID / M • The Butt Sisters Do Hawaii / 1995 / MID / M • The Butt Sisters Do Philadelphia / 1995 / MID / M • Buttslammers #09: Fade To Anal / 1995 / BS / F • Buttslammers #10: Lust On The Internet / 1995 / BS / F • Buttslammers #13: The Madness Continues / 1996 / BS / F • Car Wash Angels / 1995 / VC / M • Carni-

val / 1995 / PV / M • Chained / 1995 / SC / M • Chasey Saves The World / 1996 / VI / M • The Cheater / 1994 / XCI / M • Cheerleader Strippers / 1996 / PE / M • Chronicles Of Submission / 1995 / BON / B • Club Erotica / 1996 / IN / M • The Comix / 1995 / VI / M • Concrete Heat / 1996 / XCI / M • Corporate Affairs / 1996 / CC / M • Cover To Cover / 1995 / WP / M • Crystal Images / 1995 / INB / M • Dare You / 1995 / CA / M • Daydreams, Nightdreams / 1996 / VC / M • Debbie Class Of '95 / 1995 / CC / M • Deception (1995-Executive) / 1995 / EX / M • Deep Cheeks #5 / 1995 / ROB / M • Deep Focus / 1995 / VC / M • Deep Inside Ariana / 1995 / VC / C • Deep Inside Jill Kelly / 1996 / VC / C • Deep Inside Juli Ashton / 1996 / VC / C • Deep Inside Kaitlyn Ashley / 1995 / VC / C • Deep Inside Misty Rain / 1995 / VC / C • Delaid Delivery / 1995 / EX / M • The Deviant Doctor / 1996 / NS / M • Dirty Stories #1 / 1995 / PE / M • Diva #2: Deep In Glamour / 1996 / VC / F • Double Cross (Wicked) / 1995 / WP / M • Double Penetration Virgins: DP Therapy / 1996 / JMP / M • Dr Finger's House Of Lesbians / 1996 / SC / M • Dreams Of Desires / 1995 / ONA / M • Everybody Wants Some / 1996 / EXQ / F • Extreme Close-Up / 1996 / VI / M • EXXXtra Parts: Interview With A Hermaphrodite / 1995 / PL / M • Fantasies Of Marylin / 1995 / VT / M • Fantasy Lover / 1995 / V99 / C • Fashion Plate / 1995 / WAV / M • Finger Pleasures #6 / 1996 / PL / F • The Finishing Touch / 1994 / DR / M • Fire & Ice: Caught In The Act / 1995 / WP / M • Firecrackers / 1994 / HW / M • Flipside / 1996 / VI / M • Fluff Dreams / 1995 / SUF / M • Forbidden Cravings / 1996 / VC / M • Getting Personal / 1995 / PE / M • Ghost Town / 1995 / WAV / M • A Girl's Affair #03 / 1993 / FD / F • A Girl's Affair #07 / 1995 / FD / F • Girls Of Sorority Row / 1994 / VT / M • Golddiggers #2 / 1995 / VC / M • Hard Core Beginners #10 / 1995 / LEI / M • Hard Feelings / 1995 / VI / M • Harder, She Craved / 1995 / VC / M • Head Shots / 1995/ VI / M • Head Trip / 1995 / VC / M • Heat / 1995 / WAV / M • Heatseekers / 1996 / PE / M • The Heist / 1996 / WAV / M • Hollywood Confidential / 1995 / TWP / B • Hollywood Confidential / 1996 / SC / M • I Touch Myself / 1994 / IP / F • Illicit Entry/ 1995 / WAV / M • In Your Face #4 / 1996 / PL / M • Intense Perversions #1 / 1995 / PL / M • Interview With A Vibrator / 1996 / WAV / M • Introducing Alexis / 1996 / VI / M • Jailhouse Nurses / 1995 / SC / M • Jenna's Built For Speed / 1997 / WP / F • Julia Ann: Superstar / 1995 / WAV / M • Kym Wilde's On The Edge #32 / 1996 / RB / B • Latex #2 / 1995 / VC / M • Leather / 1995 / LE / M • Leg Tease #1 / 1995 / VT / M • Lesbian Bitches #2 / 1994 / ROB / F • Lesbian Social Club / 1995 / ROB / F • Lip Service / 1995 / WP / M • Living On The Edge / 1997 / DWO / M • Love Exchange / 1995 / DR / M • Maneater / 1995 / ERA / M • Masque / 1995 / VC / M • Mickey Ray's Sex Search #04: Long And Hard / 1994 / WIV / M • Motel Sex #2 / 1995 / FAP / M • Motel Sex #3 / 1995 / RAP / M • My Surrender / 1996 / A&E / M • Mystique / 1996 / SC / M • The Naked Truth / 1995 / VI / M • Nasty Nymphos #15 / 1996 / ANA / M • Nature Girls #2: Get Wet / 1995 / WIV / F • The

New Ass Masters #11 / 1996 / LEI / C • The Night Shift / 1995 / LE / M • Night Tales / 1996 / VC / M • Nightbreed / 1995 / VI / M • Nightshift Nurses #2 / 1996 / VC / M • No Fear / 1996 / IN / F • No Man's Land #12 / 1995 / VT / F • No Man's Land #13 / 1996 / VT / F • Ona Zee's Doll House #3 / 1995 / ONA / F • Ona Zee's Learning The Ropes #11: Chains Required / 1994 / ONA / B • Oral Obsession #2 / 1995 / VI / M • Out Of Love / 1995 / VI / M • Painful Madness / 1995 / BS / B • Party House / 1995 / WAV / M • Peach Pit / 1995 / GLI / M • Perverted Women / 1995 / SC / M • Pick Up Lines #01 / 1995 / 4P / M • Pick Up Lines #02 / 1995 / 4P / M • Pick Up Lines #03 / 1995 / 4P / M • Pick Up Lines #07 / 1996 / OD / M • Playboy: Stripsearch: San Francisco / 1996 / UNI / S • Promises And Lies / 1996 / NIT / M • Punishing The Sluts / 1996 / RB / B • Pussyman #12: Sticky Fingers / 1995 / SNA / M • Pussyman Auditions #12 / 1995 / SNA / M • Rainwoman #09: Wetlands / 1995 / CC / M • Reckless Encounters / 1995 / LE / M • Reel People #08 / 1995 / PP / M • Return Engagement / 1995 / VI / M • The Right Connection / 1995 / VC / M • Rock Groupies In Heat / 1995 / LV / M • Scrue / 1995 / VI / M • Secret Seductions #1 / 1995 / LV / M • Secret Seductions #2 / 1995 / ULP / M • Selena Under Siege / 1995 / XCI / M • Sensations #1 / 1996 / SC / M • Sensuous Torture / 1996 / BS / B • Sex Academy #2: The Art Of Talking Dirty / 1994 / ONA / M • Sex Academy #3: The Art Of Real Sex / 1994 / ONA / M • Sex Gallery / 1995 / WAV / M • Sex Machine / 1995 / VI / M • Sex Raiders / 1996 / WAV / M • Sex Secrets Of A Mistress / 1995 / VI / M • Sex Suites / 1995 / TP / M • The Sexual Solution #1 / 1995 / LE / M • Shameless / 1995 / VC / M • Shave Tails #2 / 1994 / SO / M • The Sin-A-Bun Girls / 1995 / OD / M • Smooth Ride / 1996 / WP / M • Snatch Masters #11 / 1995 / LEI / M • Snow Bunnies #1 / 1995 / SC / M • Sorority Sex Kittens #3 / 1996 / VC / M • Stardust #1 / 1996 / VI / M • Stories Of Seduction / 1996 / MID / M • Street Legal / 1995 / WAV / M • Strippers Inc. #3 / 1994 / ONA / M • Strippers Inc. #4 / 1995 / ONA / M • Suburban Butnicks Forever / 1995 / CC / M • Sweet Things / 1996 / FF / C • Tainted Love / 1996 / VC / M • Takin' It To The Limit #5 / 1995 / BS / M • Takin' It To The Limit #6 / 1995 / BS / M • Takin' It To The Limit #8: Hooked On Crack / 1996 / BS / M • Telephone Expose / 1995 / VC / M • The Temple Of Poon / 1996 / PE / M • Thin Ice / 1996 / ONA / M • This Year's Model / 1996 / WAV / M • Treacherous / 1995 / VD / M • A Trip Through Pain / 1995 / BS / B • Unbridled Lust / 1995 / NOT / F • Virtual Encounters / 1996 / SCI / S • Voyeur Strippers / 1996 / PL / F • Wacky Weekend / 1995 / SUF / M • Waves Of Passion / 1996 / ERA / M • The Way They Wuz / 1996 / SHS / C • Whispered Secrets Of The Call Girls / 1995 / TVE / F • White Shadow / 1994 / VC / M • White Wedding / 1995 / VI / M • Wicked At Heart / 1995 / WP / M • Wicked Moments / 1996 / BS / B • The Wicked One / 1995 / WP / M • Wicked Ways #1: Interview With The Anal Queen / 1994 / WP / M • X-Tales / 1995 / VIM / M • The XXX Files: Lust In Space / 1995 / IMV / M

JILL KENNEDY see Jill Kelly
JILL MCMAHON
Blue Vanities #204 / 1993 / FFL / M
JILL MOREHEAD see Jillian Moorehead
JILL MORGAN
Cover Girl Fantasies #1 / 1983 / VCR / C • Cover Girl Fantasies #2 / 1983 / VCR / C
JILL MUNRO see Jill Munroe
JILL MUNROE (Jill Munro)
Post-op she-male, popular in the late seventies, who died of AIDS in late 1982. Ugly with rock solid large tits, tall, long black hair, hairy pussy so you can't tell about the quality of the surgery. Another story has her comitting suicide and a further has her dying of a drug overdose. Either way she/he's dead. Allegedly married to Marc Stevens at one point.
Centerfold Fever / 1981 / VXP / M • Consenting Adults / 1981 / VXP / M • Double Your Pleasure / 1978 / CV / M • Sensuous Caterer / 197? / HAV / S • Skin Flicks / 1978 / AVC / M • Tigresses...And Other Man-Eaters / 1979 / VXP / M • White Fire / 1980 / VC / M
JILL PETTINGTON
The Big Thing / 1973 / VHL / M
JILL ROBERTS see Jill Kelly
JILL SHEPHARD
Pleasure Fair / 19?? / ASR / M
JILL TUTTLE see Lauren Brice
JILL WENZ
Take Me #8: For The Night / 1995 / VIO / M
JILLIAN AMORE see Kym Wilde
JILLIAN GOODYEAR see Star Index I
JILLIAN JAMES see Star Index I
JILLIAN JOY
The Inseminator #1 / 1994 / LBO / M
JILLIAN LADD see Star Index I
JILLIAN MOOREHEAD (Juliana Moorehead, Jill Morehead)
Chocolate Candy #3 / 1986 / VD / M • Hot Lips / 1984 / VC / M • Inside Everybody / 1984 / AVC / M • Our Naked Eyes / 1988 / TME / M • Return To Alpha Blue / 1984 / AVC / M • Rimshot / 1987 / CDI / M • White Hot / 1984 / VXP / M
JILLIAN NICHOLS see Star Index I
JILLIAN SHELL see Star Index I
JILLIAN ST JAMES see Star Index I
JIM
100% Amateur #18: / 1995 / OD / M • AVP #7010: Get It In The Rear / 1991 / AVP / M • Blue Vanities #539 / 1993 / FFL / M • Bobby Hollander's Rookie Nookie #09 / 1993 / SFP / M • Bun Busters #21 / 1994 / LBO / M • The Good Stuff / 1989 / BON / C • Hollywood Amateurs #07 / 1994 / MID / M • HomeGrown Video #455 / 1995 / HOV / M • Journey Into Pain #1 / 1984 / BIZ / B • Mr. Peepers Amateur Home Videos #76: Sixty Nine Plus Seven / 1993 / LBO / M • She-Males Behind Closed Doors / 1991 / RSV / G • Uncle Roy's Amateur Home Video #16 / 1992 / VIM / M
JIM ANDREWS
Fantasy Chamber / 1994 / ULI / M • Gangland Bangers / 1995 / VC / M • Hard For The Money / 1984 / CV / M
JIM BALLS
Dickin' Around / 1994 / VEX / M
JIM BENTLEY
Bi Day...Bi Night / 1988 / PV / G • Bi Night / 1989 / PL / G • Bi-Surprise / 1988 / MET/ G • By Day Bi Night / 1989 / LV / G • Haulin' 'n' Ballin' / 1988 / MET / G • Moonlusting #2

/ 1987 / WV / M • Swing Shift / 1989 / PL / G • Switch Hitters #2: Swinging Both Ways / 1987 / IN / G • Switch Hitters #9 / 1995 / IN / G

JIM BOWMAN
Young Angel / cr75 / CLX / M

JIM BROWN
Inside Desiree Cousteau / 1979 / VCX / M

JIM BUCKLEY
All About Sex / 1970 / AR / M • It Happened In Hollywood / 1973 / WWV / M • S.O.S. / 1975 / QX / M

JIM CARDESIS see Star Index I

JIM CASSIDY see Rick Cassidy

JIM CRANE
A Girl Like That / 1979 / CDC / M • The Sexpert / 1975 / VEP / M

JIM DAVEY see Star Index I

JIM DEAN see Star Index I

JIM ED see Star Index I

JIM ENRIGHT *(Jay Shanahan)*
Director with a crew cut who appears in a dramatic role in some of his movies.
Ace Mulholland / 1995 / ERA / M • Allure / 1996 / WP / M • Always / 1993 / XCI / M • Arabian Nights / 1993 / WP / M • Beaver & Buttcheeks / 1993 / DR / M • Black Flava / 1994 / EX / M • Blindfold / 1994 / SC / M • Booty In The House / 1993 / WP / M • Carnival Of Knowledge / 1992 / XCI / M • Chinatown / 1994 / SC / M • Coming Of Fortune / 1994 / EX / M • Eleventh Annual AVN Awards / 1994 / VC / M • En Garde / 1993 / DR / M • The Erotic Adventures Of The Three Musketeers / 1992 / CEL / S • Exit In Rear / 1993 / XCI / M • Facesitter #1 / 1992 / CC / M • Flesh For Fantasy / 1994 / CV / M • The Fluffer #2 / 1993 / FD / M • Ghosts / 1994 / EMC / M • Hienie's Heroes / 1995 / VC / M • Mind Set / 1996 / VI / M • NYDP Blue / 1996 / WP / M • Pulse / 1994 / EX / M • Switched With Honors / 1993 / DR / M • Western Nights / 1994 / WP / M

JIM FRANK
Erotic Fantasies #1 / 1983 / CV / C

JIM GORDON
The Taking Of Christina / 1975 / NGV / M

JIM GRIFFITH see Star Index I

JIM GUNN
Love Doll Lucy #2 / 1994 / PL / F • Red Tails #1 / 1993 / STM / B • Red Tails #2 / 1993 / STM / B • Slave Girls' Agony / 1993 / PL / B

JIM HARDY
Bi This! / 1995 / BIL / G

JIM HARKER
Saturday Night Beaver / 1986 / EVN / M

JIM HENSON see Star Index I

JIM HOLLIDAY *(Jack Nash, Arthur Fenton, The Golden Ghost, Clay Hyde (Holliday), Amanda Hunter (Hol), Martin Brimmer)*
Industry blowhard.
Adult Video Nudes / 1993 / VC / M • The Angel In Mr. Holmes / 1988 / WV / C • Candy Factory / 1994 / PE / M • Car Wash Angels / 1995 / VC / M • Cheerleader Nurses #2 / 1993 / VC / M • The Cockateer #2 / 1992 / LE / M • Cumback Pussy #3: Coast To Coast Rump Romp / 1996 / EL / M • Dirty Little Lies / 1993 / VT / M • First Time Ever #1 / 1995 / PE / F • First Time Ever #2 / 1996 / PE / F • The Good Time Girls / 1985 / VEX / M • It's Your Move / 1990 / TAO / B • Latex #1 / 1994 / VC / M • Legend #4: Critic's Choice / 1992 / LE / M

• Legends Of Porn #1 / 1987 / CV / C • Legends Of Porn #2 / 1989 / CV / C • Love Scenes For Loving Couples / 1987 / CV / C • Only The Best #1 / 1986 / CV / C • Only The Best #2 / 1989 / CV / C • Only The Best #3 / 1990 / CV / C • Only The Best From Europe / 1989 / CV / C • Only The Best Of Barbara Dare / 1990 / CV / C • Only The Best Of Breasts / 1987 / CV / C • Only The Best Of The Erotic Eighties / 1992 / VC / C • Only The Very Best On Film / 1992 / VC / C • Only The Very Best On Video / 1992 / VC / C • Pajama Party X #1 / 1994 / VC / M • Pajama Party X #2 / 1994 / VC / M • Pajama Party X #3 / 1994 / VC / M • Sloppy Seconds / 1994 / PE / M • Sore Throat / 1985 / GO / M • Sorority Sex Kittens #2 / 1993 / VC / M • Sorority Sex Kittens #3 / 1996 / VC / M • Sorority Stewardesses #2 / 1995 / PE / M • Stripper Nurses / 1994 / PE / M • True Legends Of Adult Cinema: The Cult Superstars / 1993 / VC / C • True Legends Of Adult Cinema: The Erotic Eighties / 1992 / VC / C • True Legends Of Adult Cinema: The Golden Age / 1992 / VC / C • True Legends Of Adult Cinema: The Modern Era / 1992 / VC / C • True Legends Of Adult Cinema: Unsung Superstars / 1993 / VC / C

JIM HOPSON
Lusty Ladies #04 / 1983 / 4P / M

JIM JONES
Bare Essentials / 1987 / VEX / M • Hillary Vamp's Private Collection #06 / 1992 / HVD / M

JIM LAPH
Dungeon De Sade / 1993 / FC / B

JIM LEGMEN
Alana: A Gang Bang Fantasy / 1993 / FC / M • Bobby Hollander's Rookie Nookie #12 / 1993 / SFP / M • The Crackster / 1996 / OUP / M • East Vs West: Battle Of The Gang Bangs / 1994 / TTV / M • Gang Bang Bitches #02 / 1994 / PP / M • Gang Bang Bitches #03 / 1994 / PP / M • Gang Bang Diaries #4 / 1994 / SFP / M • Gangbang In The Fat Lane / 1996 / FC / M • High Heel Harlots #01 / 1993 / SFP / M • Mistress Elle's Golden Cuffs / 1993 / RSV / B • Mistress Elle's Transgression Of Reality / 1993 / RSV / B • Muffmania / 1995 / TTV / M • Oriental Gang Bang Fantasy / 1994 / FC / M • Shaving Mr. One Eye / 1996 / FC / M • Silk 'n' Spanking / 1994 / VER / M • Totally Tasteless Video #01 / 1994 / TTV / M

JIM LEWIS see Star Index I

JIM MACREADING see Star Index I

JIM MALIBU see Star Index I

JIM MATHESON see Star Index I

JIM MESSINA
Dracula Exotica / 1980 / TVX / M • Women In Love / 1980 / CA / M

JIM METROPOLE
Mystique / 1996 / SC / M

JIM MICHAELS see Star Index I

JIM MITCHELL see Star Index I

JIM MOORE
Bucky Beaver's XXX Dragon Art Theatre Double Feature #02 / 1996 / SOW / M • More / 1973 / BL / M • The Rites Of Uranus / 1975 / SOW / M

JIM MORALS see Star Index I

JIM MOUN
Scandanavian Double Features #3 / 1996 / PL / M

JIM PARKER

Frank Henenlotter's XXX Hardcore Horrors: Mad Love... / 1996 / SOW / M • The Mad Love Of The Red Hot Vampire / 1971 / SOW / M

JIM POWERS
Beach Bum Amateur's #18 / 1992 / MID / M • Beach Bum Amateur's #33 / 1993 / MID / M • Blue Angel / 1992 / AFV / M • Hellriders / 1995 / SC / M • Monkey Gang Bang / 1996 / NOT / M • Perverted Stories #05 / 1995 / JMP / M • Safari Jane / 1995 / ERA / M

JIM RAUSCH
Inside Georgina Spelvin / 1974 / VC / M • Saturday Matinee Series #2 / 1996 / VCX / C

JIM RAWLINGS see Star Index I

JIM RILEY see Star Index I

JIM SAVAGE see Star Index I

JIM SCHIFFER see Star Index I

JIM SIMS
The Erotic World Of Angel Cash / 1983 / VXP / M

JIM SLADE
Dirty Dating Service #04 / 1994 / WP / M

JIM SMITH see Star Index I

JIM SOUTH
Not generally a performer. The owner of *World Modeling*, one of the two major talent agencies in the porno business.
Fallen Angels / 1983 / VES / M • Macin' #2: Macadocious / 1996 / SMP / M • Up And Cummers: The Movie / 1994 / 4P / M • X Factor: The Next Generation / 1991 / HO / M

JIM SPARKS *(Sam Johnson)*
Husband of Danyel Cheeks..
A Is For Anal / 1993 / LV / M • Bend Over Babes #3 / 1992 / EA / M • Bring On The Night / 1994 / VEX / M • Butt Freak #1 / 1992 / EA / M • Butt Watch #03 / 1994 / FH / M • Desire Kills / 1996 / SUM / M • A Few Good Women / 1993 / CC / M • Infamous Crimes Against Nature / 1993 / SUM / M • Ready And Willing / 1993 / VEX / M • Split Decision / 1993 / FD / M

JIM STEEL
Conquest / 1996 / WP / M • Lost In Vegas / 1996 / AWV / G

JIM STEFFE
The Second Coming Of Eva / 1974 / ALP / M • [Justine Och Juliette / 1975 / ... / S

JIM SWAIN
Ring Of Desire / 1981 / SE / M

JIM TAYLOR
Devil In Miss Jones #4: The Final Outrage / 1987 / VC / M

JIM THOMPSON see Star Index I

JIM TODD
The Big Thing / 1973 / VHL / M

JIM TRAVERS
Boiling Point / 1978 / SE / M

JIM UZI see Marc DeBruin

JIM WARD
Erotic Tattooing And Piercing #1 / 1986 / FLV / M

JIM YATES
Treasure Chest / 1985 / GO / M

JIMI DARK
Kitty Foxx's Kinky Kapers #01 / 1995 / TTV / M

JIMM GUNN
Bump 'n' Grind / 1994 / HW / M

JIMM MAC see Star Index I

JIMM STUDD see Star Index I

JIMMIE NORTON see Star Index I

JIMMY
In Loving Color #4 / 1993 / VT / M • Intimate Interviews #3 / 1996 / NIT / M • Veronica The Screenwriting Hooker / 1996 / LE / M
JIMMY BOYD see Star Index I
JIMMY CAPP
Bottom Dweller: The Final Voyage / 1996 / EL / M
JIMMY DAVIS see Star Index I
JIMMY DIXX
Pretty Young Things Escort Service / 1995 / ZA / M
JIMMY DOE
Tobianna: A Gang Bang Fantasy / 1993 / FC / M
JIMMY FOX
Bright Lights, Big Titties / 1989 / CA / M
JIMMY GEORGE
The Rose And The Bee / 19?? / VST / M
JIMMY HOLLOSY
Marianne Bouquet / 1979 / VCX / M
JIMMY HOWARD
Bucky Beaver's XXX Dragon Art Theatre Double Feature #06 / 1996 / SOW / M • Finishing School / 1975 / SOW / M
JIMMY JACK
In Your Face #4 / 1996 / PL / M
JIMMY JOHNSON
The 8th Annual Erotic Film Awards / 1984 / SE / C
JIMMY JUICE
She-Male Loves Me / 1995 / VC / G • Spring Trannie / 1995 / VC / G • Super Bi Bowl / 1995 / BIL / G
JIMMY LAWRENCE see Star Index I
JIMMY MALTA see Star Index I
JIMMY MOON
Kink: Police Chronicles / 1995 / ROB / M
JIMMY PIKE see Star Index I
JIMMY RAY
Feelings / 1977 / VC / M
JIMMY REB see Star Index I
JIMMY SANDS see Star Index I
JIMMY SLICK
Sluts, Butts And Pussy / 1996 / DFI / M
JIMMY STARR
Girls Just Want To...Have Fun / 1984 / SE / M • Hot Flashes / 1984 / VC / M • Inside China Lee / 1984 / VC / M • The Loves Of Lolita / 1984 / VC / M • Mouthful Of Love / 1984 / VC / M • Naughty Nanette / 1984 / VC / M • Sizzling Summer / 1984 / VC / M • Spreading Joy / 1988 / VC / M • Up Desiree Lane / 1984 / VC / M • Young Nurses In Love / 1987 / VC / M
JIMMY TURF
The Best Little Whorehouse In Tijuana / 1995 / HBE / M • Ho Duzzit Model Agency #1 / 1993 / AFV / M
JIMMY Z.
8-Ball: Westside Gang Bang / 1995 / PL / M • Adventures Of The DP Boys: Backyard Boogie / 1994 / HW / M • Adventures Of The DP Boys: The Blacks Are Back / 1994 / HW / M • Anal Camera #01 / 1994 / EVN / M • Anal Oriental Sorority / 1994 / LBO / M • Anna Amore's Fantasy Gang Bang / 1996 / FC / M • Bang City #1: Kelly's Anal Gang Bang / 1995 / SC / M • Beach Bum Amateur's #28 / 1993 / MID / M • Beach Bum Amateur's #36 / 1993 / MID / M • Behind The Blackout / 1993 / HW / M • Big Black Bang / 1996 / HW / M • Big Murray's New-Cummers #11: Willing & Able / 1993 / FD / M • Big Murray's New-Cummers #15:

Rump Humpers / 1993 / FD / M • Big Murray's New-Cummers #16: Frat Boys #2 / 1993 / FD / M • Black Beauty (Coast To Coast) / 1994 / CC / M • The Black Butt Sisters Do Los Angeles / 1995 / MID / M • The Black Butt Sisters Do New Orleans / 1996 / MID / M • The Black Butt Sisters Do New York / 1995 / MID / M • Black Centerfold Celebrities / 1993 / MID / M • Black Cheerleader Search #02 / 1996 / ROB / M • Black Fire / 1993 / VIM / M • Black Gangbangers #02 / 1995 / HW / M • Black Gangbangers #04 / 1995 / HW / M • Black Gangbangers #05 / 1995 / HW / M • Black Gangbangers #06 / 1995 / HW / M • Black Hollywood Amateurs #01 / 1995 / MID / M • Black Hollywood Amateurs #02 / 1995 / MID / M • Black Hollywood Amateurs #04 / 1995 / MID / M • Black Hollywood Amateurs #06 / 1995 / MID / M • Black Hollywood Amateurs #24 / 1996 / MID / M • Black Jack City #3 / 1993 / HW / M • Black Jack City #4 / 1994 / HW / M • Black On Black (1994-Midnight) / 1994 / MID / C • Black Orgies #01 / 1993 / AFI / M • Black Orgies #05 / 1993 / AFI / M • Black Orgies #08 / 1993 / AFI / M • Black Orgies #14 / 1993 / AFI / M • Black Orgies #15 / 1993 / AFI / M • Black Orgies #16 / 1993 / AFI / M • Black Orgies #26 / 1994 / GO / M • Black Power / 1996 / LEI / C • Blackdoor Babes / 1994 / TIW / M • Bobby Hollander's Maneaters #05 / 1993 / SFP / M • Boomerwang / 1992 / MID / M • Bootylicious: It's A Butt Thang / 1994 / JMP / M • Brown Sugar From The Hood / 1996 / MID / M • California Blacks / 1994 / V99 / M • Champagne's House Party / 1996 / HW / M • China's House Party / 1996 / HW / M • Cinderella Society / 1993 / GO / M • Danger-Ass / 1992 / MID / M • Dark Alleys #01 / 1992 / FC / M • Dark Alleys #02 / 1992 / FC / M • Dark Alleys #07 / 1992 / FC / M • Dark Alleys #08 / 1992 / FC / M • Dark Alleys #28 / 1994 / FC / M • Dark Passions #02 / 1993 / AFV / M • East Vs West: Battle Of The Gang Bangs / 1994 / TTV / M • Ebony Erotica #01: Black Narcissys / 1993 / GO / M • Ebony Erotica #02: Midnight Madness / 1993 / GO / M • Ebony Erotica #03: Black Adonis / 1993 / GO / M • Ebony Erotica #04: Ebony Gods / 1993 / GO / M • Ebony Erotica #05: Black Obsessions / 1993 / GO / M • Ebony Erotica #06: Black Essence / 1993 / GO / M • Ebony Erotica #07: Sepia Salute / 1993 / GO / M • Ebony Erotica #08: Indigo Moods / 1993 / GO / M • Ebony Erotica #09: Bronze Thrills / 1993 / GO / M • Ebony Erotica #11: Harlem Knights / 1993 / GO / M • Ebony Erotica #12: Pussy Posse / 1993 / GO / M • Ebony Erotica #13: Dusky Beauties / 1994 / GO / M • Ebony Erotica #15: Chocolate Kisses / 1994 / GO / M • Ebony Erotica #16: Dark & Sweet / 1994 / GO / M • Ebony Erotica #17: Black Power / 1994 / GO / M • Ebony Erotica #18: Soul Kiss / 1994 / GO / M • Ebony Erotica #23: Black Betty / 1994 / GO / M • Ebony Erotica #24: Hot Chocolate / 1994 / GO / M • Ebony Erotica #25: Java Jive / 1994 / GO / M • Ebony Erotica #28: / 1994 / GO / M • Ebony Erotica #29: Dark Dreams / 1994 / GO / M • Ebony Erotica #30: Night Train / 1994 / GO / M • Ebony Erotica #31: Creme De Cocoa / 1995 / GO / M • Eskimo Gang Bang / 1994 / HW / M • Forbidden Subjects #4 / 1995 / FC / M •

Gang Bang Diaries #1 / 1993 / SFP / M • Gangbang Girl #15 / 1995 / ANA / M • Gimme Some Head / 1994 / VT / M • Hidden Camera #12 / 1993 / JMP / M • Hidden Camera: Interracial Special / 1994 / JMP / M • Hollywood Amateurs #11 / 1994 / MID / M • Honey, I Blew Everybody #2 / 1992 / MID / M • Hooter Tutor / 1996 / APP / M • Hooters In The 'hood / 1995 / TTV / M • I Dream Of Tiffany / 1993 / IF / M • Lessons In Love / 1995 / SPI / M • M Series #03 / 1993 / LBO / M • M Series #17 / 1993 / LBO / M • Malcolm XXX / 1992 / OD / M • Mickey Ray's Sex Search #05: Deep Inside / 1995 / WIV / M • More To Love #1 / 1994 / TTV / M • More To Love #2 / 1995 / TTV / M • Much More Than A Mouthful #3/ 1993 / VEX / M • My Baby Got Back #01 / 1992 / VT / M • My Baby Got Back #02 / 1993 / VT / M • The New Snatch Masters #21 / 1996 / LEI / C • Outcall Outlaws / 1995 / CC / M • Perverted Stories #06 / 1996 / JMP / M • The Players Club / 1994 / HW / M • Primal Rear / 1996 / TIW / M • Pumps In Da Rump #1 / 1994 / HW / M • Q Balls #1 / 1996 / TTV / M • Q Balls #2 / 1996 / TTV / M • Raw Talent: Deep Inside Lydia's Ass / 1993 / FH / M • Ready To Drop #03 / 1994 / FC / M • Ready To Drop #05 / 1995 / FC / M • Ready To Drop #09 / 1995 / FC / M • Ron Hightower's White Chicks #01 / 1993 / LBO / M • Ron Hightower's White Chicks #03 / 1993 / LBO / M • Ron Hightower's White Chicks #04 / 1993 / LBO / M • Ron Hightower's White Chicks #13 / 1994 / LBO / M • Ron Hightower's White Chicks #14 / 1994 / LBO / M • Ron Hightower's White Chicks #15 / 1994 / LBO / M • Ron Hightower's White Chicks #16 / 1994 / LBO / M • Rump-Shaker #1 / 1993 / HW / M • Rump-Shaker #2 / 1993 / HW / M • Rump-Shaker #4 / 1995 / HW / M • Sex In Dangerous Places / 1994 / OD / M • Stuff Your Ass #3 / 1996 / JMP / M • Takin' It To The Limit #2 / 1994 / BS / M • Toyz / 1993 / MID / M • Up The Ying Yang #1 / 1994 / CC / M • Video Virgins #03 / 1993 / NS / M
JINGER JAYE see Ginger Jaye
JINGLE
AVP #4002: Her Ding-A-Ling / 1990 / AVP / M
JINNY LYNNE see Stephanie Page
JINNY SING see Star Index I
JO AMARIZ
Eager Beaver / 1975 / AVC / M • Pleasure Island / 1975 / TGA / M • Sex Museum / 1976 / AXV / M • Y-All Come / 1975 / CDC / M
JO ANN FISCHER
Midnight Hustle / 1978 / VC / M
JO ANNA STEPHEN see Star Index I
JO ANNE HARRIS see Joanna Storm
JO BOB LENGTH see Star Index I
JO BOYCE see Star Index I
JO CAROL see Star Index I
JO FELDSEE see Star Index I
JO JO
Buffy Malibu's Totally Nasty All-Girl Home Videos #02 / 1992 / ANA / F • Honey Drippers / 1992 / ROB / F • Kittens & Vamps #1 / 1993 / ROB / F • Lesbian Lockup / 1993 / ROB / F • Sideshow Freaks / 1996 / ZA / M
JO JO SMITH
Babes Of The Bay #1 / 1994 / LIP / F • More Bad Girl Handling / 1994 / RB / B

JO JO STRONG
Climax At The Melting Pot #2 / 1996 / AVS / M

JO JONES
Kate And The Indians / 1980 / SE / M

JO KIDD see Star Index I

JO LAROCH see Star Index I

JO PETTY
A Party In My Tight Pussy / 1994 / MET / M • Revenge Of A Motorcycle Mama / 1972 / ALP / M

JO SCORPIO
San Francisco Lesbians #2 / 1992 / PL / F

JO-ANNE HEATHER
Resurrection Of Eve / 1973 / MIT / M

JOAN
A&B AB#391: Sexy Blondes / 1991 / A&B / M • A&B AB#431: Cum Dripping Orgy / 1994 / A&B / M • Blue Vanities #522 / 1993 / FFL / M • Blue Vanities #539 / 1993 / FFL / M • Blue Vanities #554 / 1994 / FFL / M • SVE: Swing Time / 1993 / SVE / M • World Sex Tour #4 / 1996 / ANA / M • Wrestling Classics #4 / 1993 / CDP / B

JOAN BEATTIE
Waterpower / 1975 / VHL / M

JOAN BENTON
Hungry Eyed Woman / cr71 / VCX / M

JOAN BERRY see Star Index I

JOAN BRAKEMAN
Reel Classics #2 / 1996 / H&S / M

JOAN BRINKMAN
Blue Vanities #514 / 1992 / FFL / M

JOAN COHN see Star Index I

JOAN DEVLON (Joan Manning, Giovan-ina, Linda Brooks)
If this is the girl who is credited as Linda Brooks in **Night Caller**, as I am assured she is, then she's ugly with black curly hair, medium tits and a womanly body.
Classic Erotica #5 / 1985 / SVE / M • Desires Within Young Girls / 1977 / CA / M • Hard Soap, Hard Soap / 1977 / EVI / M • Hardgore / 1973 / ALP / M • Lacey Bodine (The Decline And Fall Of) / 1975 / VCX / M • Legends Of Porn #2 / 1989 / CV / C • Little Angel Puss / cr76 / SVE / M • Melanie's Hot Line / 1975 / CDC / M • Night Caller / 1975 / ALP / M • Night Pleasures / 1975 / WWV / M • Sodom & Gomorrah / 1974 / MIT / M • Strange Experiences Cockfucking / 1994 / MET / M • Tell Them Johnny Wadd Is Here / 1975 / QX / M

JOAN EROTICA
Magma: Showtime Cunts / 1994 / MET / M

JOAN HOLMES
Deep Throat Girls / cr75 / ... / M

JOAN J.
Bucky Beaver's XXX Dragon Art Theatre Double Feature #04 / 1996 / SOW / M • Revelations / 1974 / SOW / M

JOAN KELLER see Star Index I

JOAN KERRY
Personals / 1972 / COM / M

JOAN LASGLOW
Sheila's Payoff / 1977 / VCX / M

JOAN LESLIE see Star Index I

JOAN MANNING see Joan Devlon

JOAN MILLS see Star Index I

JOAN MIQUEL see Beth Anna

JOAN MOORE
Debutante Training / 1995 / PL / B

JOAN NELSON
Ancient Secrets Of Sexual Ecstasy / 1996 / HIG / M

JOAN SAAR

Slip Of The Tongue (Vxp) / 19?? / VXP / M

JOAN TURNER see Star Index I

JOAN VICTORIA see Brooke Bennett

JOAN WALLACE see Star Index I

JOANIE WILSON
Blue Vanities #553 / 1994 / FFL / M

JOANN WOODS
Blue Vanities #165 (New) / 1996 / FFL / M

JOANNA
The Best Of Trained Transvestites / 1990 / BIZ / G • Joanna's In A Bind / 1993 / BON / B • Magma: Hot Shots / 1995 / MET / M • Southern Belles: Sugar Magnolias / 1996 / XPR / M

JOANNA (GRECO) see Alex Greco

JOANNA (T. WAYNE) see Taylor Wayne

JOANNA BELL see Star Index I

JOANNA COLLINS see Ona Zee

JOANNA FIRESTONE
Debbie's Love Spell / 1988 / STM / M • Sugar Tongues / 1992 / STM / C • Vanilla & Fudge / 1988 / JAN / M

JOANNA G. see Taylor Wayne

JOANNA GEE see Taylor Wayne

JOANNA HAU
That Lady From Rio / 1976 / VXP / M

JOANNA HILDEN see Star Index I

JOANNA JOY see Star Index I

JOANNA KNIGHT see Star Index I

JOANNA MIQUEL see Beth Anna

JOANNA NICHOLS see Star Index I

JOANNA REDFORD (Tizania Redford, Titzianna Redford)
Brunette with pudgy body, big butt, and huge enhanced tits. German.
Euro-Snatch / 1996 / SNA / M • Take Me #8: For The Night / 1995 / VIO / M • [Deep In Love / 1996 / PRE / M

JOANNA SAVAGE see Sharon Thorpe

JOANNA STEVENS
Backdoor Club / 1986 / CA / M • Backdoor Lust / 1987 / CV / C • Double Desires / 1988 / PIN / C

JOANNA STEWART see Fallon

JOANNA STORM (Johanna Storm, Jo Anne Harris)
Passable blonde with medium tits.
Alexandra / 1984 / VC / M • All American Girls #1 / 1982 / CA / M • Anything Goes / 1993 / VD / C • Aphrodesia's Diary / 1984 / CA / M • Babylon Blue / 1983 / VXP / M • Ball Busters / 1984 / CV / M • Bedtime Tales / 1985 / SE / M • The Bizarre World Of F.J. Lincoln / 19?? / VHL / C • Burlexxx / 1984 / VC / M • Caballero Preview Tape #4 / 1985 / CA / C • California Blondes #03 / 1991 / VD / C • The Casting Couch / 1983 / GO / M • Chastity And The Starlets / 1986 / RAV / M • Crazy With The Heat #1 / 1986 / CV / M • Debbie Does Dallas #3 / 1985 / VC / M • Devil In Miss Jones #2 / 1983 / VC / M • Diamond Collection #77 / 1986 / CDI / M • Dickman & Throbbin / 1985 / WV / M • Dirty Girls / 1984 / MIT / M • Dream Girls #3 / 1984 / CA / C • The Ecstasy Girls #2 / 1986 / CA / M • Erotic City / 1985 / CV / M • The Erotic World Of Angel Cash / 1983 / VXP / M • Every Man's Fancy / 1983 / BIZ / B • Firestorm #1 / 1984 / COM / M • Firestorm #2: The Angel Blade / 1986 / COM / M • Firestorm #3 / 1986 / COM / M • First Annual XRCO Awards / 1984 / AVC / C • First Time Lesbians (Gourmet) / 1987 / GO / F • Flaming Tongues #2 / 1988 / MET / F • Fowl Play / 1983 / ... / S • GM #108: The Privacy Of Joanna / 1985 / GMV

/ F • Golden Girls #32 / 1988 / CA / M • Great Sexpectations / 1984 / VC / M • GVC: Companions #122 / 1983 / GO / F • GVC: Family Affair / 1983 / GO / M • Heaven's Touch / 1983 / CA / M • Her Wicked Ways / 1983 / CA / M • Hot Dreams / 1983 / CA / M • Hot Gypsy Love / 1985 / CDI / M • Hot Stuff / 1984 / VXP / M • Hottest Ticket / 1987 / WV / C • In Love / 1983 / VC / M • In The Pink / 1983 / CA / M • Inches For Keisha / 1988 / WV / C • Indecent Itch / 1985 / VCR / M • Joanna Storm On Fire / 1985 / VIV / M • Joanna Storm Works Out / 1985 / GMV / F • Joint Effort / 1992 / SEX / C • Legends Of Porn #2 / 1989 / CV / C • Limited Edition #34 / 1984 / AVC / M • Looking For Mr Goodsex / 1984 / CC / M • Love Scenes For Loving Couples / 1987 / CV / C • Lucky Charm / 1986 / AVC / C • Maneaters / 1983 / VC / M • Nasty Girls (1983-VCX) / 1983 / VCX / M • Never Sleep Alone / 1984 / CA / M • Older Men With Young Girls / 1985 / CC / M • Only The Best #1 / 1986 / CV / C • Only The Best Of Men's And Women's Fantasies / 1988 / CV / C • Only The Best Of Peepers / 1992 / CV / C • Only The Best Of The Erotic Eighties / 1992 / VC / C • Only The Best Of Women With Women / 1988 / CV / C • Only The Very Best On Film / 1992 / VC / C • Personal Touch #2 / 1983 / AR / M • The Pleasure Maze / 1986 / PL / M • Private Teacher / 1983 / CA / M • Puss 'n' Boots / 1982 / VXP / M • Reel People #02 / 1984 / AR / M • Screaming Rage / 1988 / LV / C • The Sex Game / 1987 / SE / C • Sexcapades / 1983 / VC / M • Sexual Odyssey / 1985 / VC / M • Show Your Love / 1984 / VC / M • Showgirls / 1985 / SE / M • Silk, Satin & Sex / 1983 / SE / M • Slit Skirts / 1983 / VXP / M • Smoker / 1983 / VC / M • Snake Eyes #1 / 1984 / COM / M • Some Kind Of Woman / 1985 / CA / M • Splashing / 1986 / VCS / C • Starved For Affection / 1985 / AVC / M • Stephanie's Outrageous / 1988 / LV / C • Stud Hunters / 1984 / CA / M • Studs 'n' Stars / 1989 / VC / C • Summer Camp Girls / 1983 / CA / M • Suzy's Birthday Bang / 1985 / CDI / M • The T & A Team / 1984 / VC / M • A Taste Of Taija Rae / 1989 / PIN / C • Thrill Street Blues / 1985 / WV / M • Throat...12 Years After / 1984 / VC / M • True Legends Of Adult Cinema: The Cult Superstars / 1993 / VC / C • True Legends Of Adult Cinema: The Erotic Eighties / 1992 / VC / C • Two On The Tongue / 1988 / TAM / C • Up All Night / 1986 / CC / M • VCA Previews #1 / 1988 / VC / C • VCA Previews #2 / 1988 / VC / C • Why Gentlemen Prefer Blondes / 1983 / HO / C • The Widespread Scandals Of Lydia Lace / 1983 / CA / M • Wild Things #2 / 1986 / CV / M • Women Who Love Girls / 1989 / CLV / C • Working It Out / 1983 / CA / M • X-Rated Bloopers #1 /1984 / AR / M • Yiddish Erotica #1 / 1986 / SE / C

JOANNA T. see Taylor Wayne

JOANNA WALLER
Spanking Video #2: Naval Discipline / 1995 / MET / B

JOANNE
Big Boobs Around The World #2 / 1990 / BTO / M • Mike Hott: Older Girls #13 / 1996 / MHV / C • Real People Real Bondage #1 / 1995 / BON / C

JOANNE AKEWELL
The Girls In The Band / 1976 / SVE / M
JOANNE BARKER *see Star Index I*
JOANNE BECK
Family Affair / 1979 / MIT / M
JOANNE BISHOP *see Star Index I*
JOANNE GARVEY
Talk Dirty To Me #02 / 1982 / CA / M
JOANNE GRECO *see Alex Greco*
JOANNE IVERSON *see Jenny Baxter*
JOANNE PETERS
Fantasy Club Of America / 1980 / BL / M
JOANNE SMITH *see Star Index I*
JOANNI BLACK *see Johnnie Black*
JOANNIE JENKINS *see Star Index I*
JOANTHAN JOHN
Virgin And The Lover / 1973 / ALP / M
JOBETH DEE
Bedtime Video #09 / 1984 / GO / M
JOCELYN
Angel Hard / 1996 / STV / M • Impulse #05: When I Was 20... / 1995 / MBP / M
JOCELYN CLOUSEAU
Private Film #10 / 1994 / OD / M
JOCELYN JOYCE
Douce Penetrations / 1975 / LUM / M
JOCELYN MARTIN
The Analyst / 1975 / ALP / M
JOCELYNE CLARRIS *see Star Index I*
JOCHEN
Magma: Anal Teenies / 1994 / MET / M
JOCKO
Bedtime Stories / 1989 / WV / M • Jailhouse Girls / 1984 / VC / M • Rough Draft / 1986 / VEN / M • Silence Of The G.A.M.S. / 1992 / CA / M • Video Store Vixens / 1986 / PL / M
JODI
Dirty Bob's #22: Lube! / 1995 / FLP / S • Mr. Peepers Nastiest #5 / 1995 / LBO / C • Odyssey Amateur #07: Jodi's Sex Slaves / 1991 / OD / M • Odyssey Amateur #45: Head Nurse Jodi / 1991 / OD / M • Odyssey Amateur #56: Nurse Jodi Gets A Bum Rap / 1991 / OD / M
JODI (NIKKI KNIGHTS) *see Nikki Knights*
JODI DEE *see Nikki Knights*
JODI SWAFFORD
Collection #08 / 1984 / CA / M • Evils Of The Night / 1985 / LIV / S • Hot Shorts: Jodi Swafford / 1986 / VCR / C • Penthouse: The Girls Of Penthouse #1 / 1984 / VES / S
JODI THORPE
The Girls In The Band / 1976 / SVE / M
JODIE
Mr. Peepers Amateur Home Videos #41: Getting Off For Bad Beh / 1992 / LBO / M
JODIE PRESTON
All American Girls #2: In Heat / 1983 / CA / M
JODY
Biff Malibu's Totally Nasty Home Videos #37 / 1993 / ANA / M • Bitter She-Males / 1992 / BIZ / G • Pantyhose Teasers #1 / 1991 / JBV / S • Pretty Soles And Toes / 1993 / JBV / B
JODY BAXTER *see Star Index I*
JODY BRIGHT *see Star Index I*
JODY BURNS
Bondage Pleasures #1 / 1981 / 4P / B
JODY DONAHUE
Jezebel / 1979 / CV / M
JODY HOOPER *see Star Index I*
JODY JOY

Dirty Stories #4 / 1995 / PE / M
JODY LEVINE
Director's Punishment / 1996 / GOT / B
JODY MAXWELL
Reddish brunette, older, thick body, not too pretty, medium droopy tits.
The Devil Inside Her / 1977 / ALP / M • Expose Me, Lovely / 1976 / QX / M • Frank Henenlotter's XXX Hardcore Horrors #05 / 1996 / SOW / M • A Girl's Best Friend / 1981 / QX / M • Gums / 1976 / AVC / M • Kinky Potpourri #33 / 1997 / SVE / C • Neon Nights / 1981 / COM / M • Only The Best #2 / 1989 / CV / C • Outlaw Ladies #1 / 1981 / VC / M • Portrait / 1974 / SE / M • The Red Room And Other Places / 1992 / COM / C • S.O.S. / 1975 / QX / M • The Satisfiers Of Alpha Blue / 1980 / AVC / M • Snow Man / 1980 / BL / M • Teenage Cousins / cr76 / SOW / M • Thrilling Drilling / 1974 / SVE / M • Unwilling Lovers / 197? / SVE / M
JODY MILLER *see Star Index I*
JODY ROSE
Two Sides Of A Lady / 1994 / HDE / M
JODY SILVER
Angel Buns / 1981 / QX / M
JODY TUSSY
Most Valuable Slut / 1973 / HLV / M
JOE
America's Raunchiest Home Videos #28: Anal Aerobics / 1992 / ZA / M • Beach Bum Amateur's #09 / 1992 / MID / M • Between My Breasts #15 / 1991 / BTO / M • Foxx Tales / 1996 / TTV / M • FTV #07: DD Destroyer / 1996 / FT / B • Full Moon Video #21: Me, You, And Your Brother Too! / 1994 / FAP / M • Hollywood Amateurs #06 / 1994 / MID / M • Homegrown Video #112 / 1990 / HOV / M • Mr. Peepers Amateur Home Videos #59: The Ball Of The Wild / 1992 / LBO / M • New Faces, Hot Bodies #03 / 1992 / STP / M • New Faces, Hot Bodies #09 / 1993 / STP / M • Ona Zee's Date With Dallas / 1992 / ONA / M • Pearl Necklace: Amorous Amateurs #34 / 1992 / SEE / M • Pearl Necklace: Thee Bush League #01 / 1992 / SEE / M
JOE APONTE
Vanilla & Fudge / 1988 / JAN / M
JOE ARNOLD *see Joey Silvera*
JOE BLOWME
Motel Sex #2 / 1995 / FAP / M
JOE BRADLEY
Master Plan / 198? / BON / B • Next Door Neighbors #08 / 1990 / BON / M
JOE C. WILLIAMS
[Chicks Who Dig Ball Sweat / 1984 / ... / M
JOE CADE *see Star Index I*
JOE CAINE *see Herschel Savage*
JOE CALZONE
Midnight Obsession / 1995 / XC / M
JOE CLAUSSEN
Tinsel Town / 1980 / VC / M
JOE COLLEGE *see Joe College Boy*
JOE COLLEGE BOY *(Joe College, Joe Lewis (College), Joe Louis)*
Ariana's Domain / 1996 / GOT / B • Bedroom Slaves / 1994 / GOT / B • Beg For It / 1995 / GOT / B • The Best Of East Coast Sluts / 1995 / PL / C • Blow Below The Belt / 1995 / GOT / B • Caught! / 1994 / GOT / B • The Challenge / 1995 / GOT / B • East Coast Sluts #04: New York City / 1995 / PL / M • East Coast Sluts #06: Philadelphia / 1995 / PL / M • Final Test / 1993 / GOT / B

• The Golden Rule / 1993 / GOT / B • Jaded Mistress / 1993 / GOT / B • Marquesa's Dungeon / 1994 / GOT / B • Master's Frenzy / 1994 / GOT / B • Mistress For Bad Boys / 1993 / GOT / B • Mistress Of Depravity / 1993 / GOT / B • N.Y. Video Magazine #03 / 1995 / OUP / M • N.Y. Video Magazine #04 / 1995 / OUP / M • Rusty Boner's Late Night Videos #1 / 1995 / RHV / M • Streets Of New York #05 / 1995 / PL / M • Streets Of New York #06 / 1996 / PL / M • Striptease #1 / 1995 / PL / M • Striptease #2 / 1995 / PL / M • Toe Tales #05 / 1993 / GOT / B • Toe Tales #06 / 1993 / GOT / B • Toe Tales #08 / 1993 / GOT / B • Toe Tales #09 / 1993 / GOT / B • Toe Tales #11 / 1993 / GOT / B • Toe Tales #12 / 1994 / GOT / C • Toe Tales #14 / 1994 / GOT / B • Toe Tales #15 / 1994 / GOT / B • Toe Tales #18 / 1994 / GOT / B • Toe Tales #19 / 1994 / GOT / B • Toe Tales #24 / 1995 / GOT / C • Toe Tales #25 / 1995 / GOT / B • Toe Tales #27 / 1995 / GOT / B • Toe Tales #28 / 1995 / GOT / B • Toe Tales #31 / 1995 / GOT / B • Toe Tales #36 / 1996 / GOT / B • Toe Tales #37 / 1996 / GOT / B • Unforgiving Mistress / 1995 / GOT / B
JOE D'AMATO *(Aristide Massaccesi)*
Italian director of seventies sexploitation movies and later of porno movies.
Hamlet: For The Love Of Ophelia #2 / 1996 / IP / M
JOE DERRINGER
Pearl Necklace: Amorous Amateurs #24 / 1993 / SEE / M • Pearl Necklace: Amorous Amateurs #28 / 1993 / SEE / M • Pearl Necklace: Amorous Amateurs #30 / 1993 / SEE / M • Pearl Necklace: Amorous Amateurs #39 / 1993 / SEE / M
JOE DIPALO *see Joe Verducci*
JOE DUKE
FTV #09: Cast Iron Bitch #1 / 1996 / FT / B
JOE ELLIOT *(Joel Elliot)*
Army Brat #1 / 1987 / VI / M • College Video Virgins #04 / 1996 / AOC / M • College Video Virgins #07 / 1996 / AOC / M • Confessions Of A Candystriper / 1984 / VC / M • Inspiration / 1981 / CHX / M • Jane Bond Meets Thunderthighs / 1988 / VD / M • Joe Elliot's Asian College Girls #01 / 1995 / JOE / C • Joe Elliot's Asian College Girls #02 / 1995 / JOE / M • Joe Elliot's Black College Girls #01 / 1995 / JOE / M • Joe Elliot's College Girls #26 / 1994 / JOE / M • Joe Elliot's College Girls #27 / 1994 / JOE / M • Joe Elliot's College Girls #28 / 1994 / JOE / M • Joe Elliot's College Girls #29 / 1994 / JOE / M • Joe Elliot's College Girls #30 / 1994 / JOE / M • Joe Elliot's College Girls #31 / 1994 / JOE / M • Joe Elliot's College Girls #32 / 1994 / JOE / M • Joe Elliot's College Girls #33 / 1994 / JOE / M • Joe Elliot's College Girls #34 / 1994 / JOE / M • Joe Elliot's College Girls #35 / 1994 / JOE / M • Joe Elliot's College Girls #36 / 1994 / JOE / M • Joe Elliot's College Girls #37 / 1994 / JOE / M • Joe Elliot's College Girls #38 / 1994 / JOE / M • Joe Elliot's College Girls #39 / 1994 / JOE / F • Joe Elliot's College Girls #40 / 1995 / JOE / F • Joe Elliot's College Girls #41 / 1996 / JOE / M • Joe Elliot's College Girls #42 / 1995 / JOE / M • Joe Elliot's College Girls #43 / 1996 / JOE / M • Joe Elliot's College Girls #44 / 1996 / JOE / M • Joe Elliot's College Girls #45 / 1996 / JOE / M • Joe Elliot's College Girls

#46 / 1996 / JOE / M • Joe Elliot's College Girls: Brenda Uncut / 1994 / JOE / M • Joe Elliot's College Girls: Deven Uncut / 1994 / JOE / M • Joe Elliot's College Girls: Jamie Uncut / 1994 / JOE / M • Joe Elliot's Latin College Girls #01 / 1995 / JOE / M • Kinky College Cunts #15 / 1993 / NS / M • The Nicole Stanton Story #2 / 1989 / CA / M • Radio K-KUM / 1984 / HO / M • Rhinestone Cowgirls / 1981 / SE / M • Wild In The Wilderness / 1984 / GO / M

JOE ENGLISH
Beauty And The Biker / 1993 / GOT / B • Bondage Seduction / 1992 / STM / B • Bunnie's Bondage Land / 1994 / STM / C • The Chamber Maids / 1993 / GOT / B • Leather Lair #3 / 1993 / STM / B • Masters Of Dominance / 1996 / GOT / C • Savage Discipline / 1993 / STM / C • Wild Girls / 1994 / GOT / B

JOE FISHER see Star Index I

JOE GAGE
L.A. Tool & Die / 1979 / TMX / G

JOE GIBBONS see Star Index I

JOE HILL see Star Index I

JOE JAMES see Star Index I

JOE JONES see Star Index I

JOE JULIANS
Oriental Treatment #1 / 1978 / AR / M • Star Of The Orient / 1978 / VIP / M • Wild River Girls / 1977 / IVP / M

JOE KADO
Hot Property (AVC) / 1975 / AVC / M • Secret Desire / 1975 / CA / B • Sugar In The Raw / 1975 / AVC / M • The Velvet Hustle / 1975 / CA / M

JOE LEWIS (COLLEGE) see Joe College Boy

JOE LIMPETT
The Starmaker / 1982 / VC / M

JOE LOOMBARDI
Puritan Video Magazine #07 / 1996 / LE / M

JOE LOUIS see Joe College Boy

JOE LUGO
Bobby Hollander's Rookie Nookie #07 / 1993 / SFP / M • House Play (Bon Vue) / 1994 / BON / B • Mr. Peepers Amateur Home Videos #68: A Tough Load To Swallow / 1993 / LBO / M • Neighborhood Watch #39: / 1993 / LBO / M • Stevi's: All Butts About It / 1993 / SSV / M • Stevi's: Good Vibrations / 1994 / SSV / M • Stevi's: I'm Sorry, Daddy / 1993 / SSV / B • Upper Class Bondage / 1993 / BON / B • VGA: Bureau Of Discipline #1 / 1993 / VGA / B • VGA: Bureau Of Discipline #2 / 1993 / VGA / B • VGA: Bureau Of Discipline #3 / 1993 / VGA / B

JOE MAMA
Gangbang Girl #01 / 1992 / ANA / M • Gangbang Girl #02 / 1992 / ANA / M

JOE MASSERIA see Joey Silvera

JOE MASSEY see Star Index I

JOE MORGAN
Secrets Of A Willing Wife / 1979 / VXP / M

JOE MORRIS see Star Index I

JOE O'BRIEN see Star Index I

JOE PAN
My Brother's Girl / 1996 / AVV / M

JOE POWELL
Mean Ass Bitch / 1996 / RB / B

JOE RICH
Princess Seka / 1980 / VC / M

JOE ROBERTS
Old Guys & Dolls #2 / 1995 / PL / M • Ti-gresses...And Other Man-Eaters / 1979 / VXP / M

JOE ROMANO
The Rod Garetto Story / 1995 / FC / C

JOE ROMERO
Courting Libido / 1995 / HIV / G • Driven Home / 1995 / CSP / G

JOE SANTINO
The Bimbo #1 / 1985 / VXP / M • Hot Dreams / 1983 / CA / M • Inside Little Oral Annie / 1984 / VXP / M • Lady Madonna / 1985 / RLV / M • Little Oral Annie Takes Manhattan / 1985 / VXP / M • Miami Vice Girls / 1984 / RLV / M

JOE SARNO
Karla / 19?? / ... / M

JOE SAVAGE
Tight Tushies #1 / 1994 / SFP / M

JOE SCALZONE
Paprika / 1995 / XC / M

JOE SCHLUETER see Star Index I

JOE SCHMOE see Star Index I

JOE SIMMONS see Star Index I

JOE SKEG see Joey Silvera

JOE SPEARS
Bi-Conflict / 1994 / FST / G • Conflict Of Interest / 1994 / FST / G • Remembering Times Gone Bi / 1995 / AWV / G

JOE STEVENS see Star Index I

JOE STUD
The Adventures of Marilyn Ohno / 1996 / GLI / M • Denni O' #4: Beach Ballin' / 1996 / SP / M

JOE VALIACHI see Star Index I

JOE VEDUCCI see Joe Verducci

JOE VENTURI see Star Index I

JOE VERDUCCI *(Joe Veducci, Joe Veroucca, Frank Verducci, Joe DiPalo, Cowboy Joe, Mack Reynolds)*
Young Italian looking male. Also does gay movies.
Above And Beyond / 1990 / PNP / G • All About Teri Weigel / 1996 / XCI / M • American Garter / 1993 / VC / M • Anal Takeover / 1993 / PEP / M • Battle Of The Superstars / 1993 / VI / M • Bi And Beyond #5 / 1990 / INH / G • Biff Malibu's Totally Nasty Home Videos #36 / 1993 / ANA / M • Big Murray's New-Cummers #09: Oriental Lovers / 1993 / FD / M • The Big Shave / 1993 / PEP / M • Black & Beyond: The Darker Sid / 1990 / INH / G • Black Butt Jungle / 1993 / ME / M • Black Is Back / 1993 / HW / M • Blue Balls / 1995 / VEX / C • Butt Hole Boulevard / 1993 / CA / M • Butt Woman #4 / 1993 / FH / M • Butt Woman #5 / 1993 / FH / M • California Pizza Girls / 1992 / EVN / M • Cumming Clean / 1991 / FL / M • Dickin' Around / 1994 / VEX / M • Dirty Dominique / 1994 / V99 / M • Eleventh Annual AVN Awards / 1994 / VC / M • Erotica Optique / 1994 / SUF / M • Every Man Should Have One / 1991 / VEX / M • Forget Me Not / 1994 / FH / M • G Squad / 1990 / SO / G • Gangbang Girl #12 / 1993 / ANA / M • Gangbang Girl #13 / 1994 / ANA / M • The Hard Line / 1993 / PEP / M • The Hitch-Hiker #02: Dangerous Curves / 1994 / WMG / M • If Looks Could Kill / 1992 / V99 / M • A Kiss Before Dying / 1993 / CDI / M • Knockout / 1994 / VEX / M • The Living End / 1992 / OD / M • Mr. Peepers Amateur Home Videos #59: The Ball Of The Wild / 1992 / LBO / M • My Favorite Rear / 1993 / PEP / M • N.Y.D.P. / 1994 / PEP / M • Night And Day #1 / 1993 / VT / M • The Night Of The Coyote / 1993 / MED / M • Night Walk / 1995 / HIV / G • One In A Million / 1992 / HW / M • Party Doll / 1990 / VC / M • Passion Prescription / 1990 / V99 / M • Pearl Necklace: Thee Bush League #11 / 1993 / SEE / M • Private Film #12 / 1994 / OD / M • Private Film #13 / 1994 / OD / M • Private Film #14 / 1994 / OD / M • Private Film #18 / 1994 / OD / M • Private Video Magazine #09 / 1994 / OD / M • Private Video Magazine #11 / 1994 / OD / M • Private Video Magazine #12 / 1994 / OD / M • Private Video Magazine #15 / 1994 / OD / M • Private Video Magazine #17 / 1994 / OD / M • Private Video Magazine #19 / 1994 / OD / M • Private Video Magazine #22 / 1995 / OD / M • Rainwoman #07: In The Rainforest / 1993 / CC / M • A Reason To Die / 1994 / PEP / M • Scent Of A Wild Woman / 1993 / EVN / C • Secret Dreams / 1991 / VEX / M • Secret Services / 1993 / PEP / M • Sensual Exposure / 1993 / ULI / M • She's No Angel #2 / 1995 / V99 / M • Soap Me Up! / 1993 / FD / M • The Tattle Tail / 1993 / ME / M • Taxi Girls #3: Killer On The Loose / 1993 / MED / M • Top Debs #1: Prom Night / 1992 / GO / M • Unsolved Double Penetration / 1993 / PEP / M • The Uptown Girl / 1992 / ZA / M • Washington D.P. / 1993 / PEP / M • Wendy Whoppers: Psychic Healer / 1994 / PEP / M • Wendy Whoppers: Razorwoman / 1993 / PEP / M • Wild Thing / 1994 / IF / M

JOE VEROUCCA see Joe Verducci

JOE WALSH
L.A. Tool & Die / 1979 / TMX / G

JOE ZEE see Star Index I

JOEL
Dick & Jane Go To Hong Kong / 1995 / AVI / M • Pearl Necklace: Thee Bush League #03 / 1992 / SEE / M

JOEL BLACK see Herschel Savage

JOEL CAINE see Herschel Savage

JOEL CLUPPER see Joel Lawrence

JOEL CURRY see Star Index I

JOEL ELLIOT see Joe Elliot

JOEL KANE see Herschel Savage

JOEL L. HOLZMAN
Never So Deep / 1981 / VCX / M

JOEL LAITER see Herschel Savage

JOEL LAWRENCE *(Joel Clupper, Max Steed (Joel L.), Joel Schultz, Max Stryde, Max Stryce)*
Joel Clupper is from **Anything That Moves**.
1-800-TIME / 1990 / IF / M • Anal Adventures #3: Can Her! / 1991 / VC / M • Anal Adventures (Dragon) / 1992 / DRP / M • Anal Avenue / 1992 / LV / M • Anal Orgasms / 1992 / DRP / M • Anything That Moves / 1992 / VC / M • Burning Desire / 1992 / CDI / M • Carnival Of Knowledge / 1992 / XCI / M • Checkmate / 1992 / CDI / M • Dr Peter Proctor's House Of Anal Delights / 1996 / HO / M • Dreams Of The Everyday Housewife / 1990 / FAZ / M • Full Moon Fever / 1992 / PEP / M • Glitz Tits #04 / 1992 / GLI / M • Guttman's Paris Vacation / 1993 / PL / M • Hardcore Copy / 1993 / PL / M • Internal Affairs / 1992 / CDI / M • Lethal Love / 1990 / DAY / M • Looks Like A Million / 1992 / LV / M • Main Street, U.S.A. / 1992 / PP / M • The Makeup Room #1 / 1992 / VC / M • Maneater (1992-Las Vegas) / 1992 / LV / M • Mr. Peepers Amateur Home Videos #59: The Ball Of The Wild / 1992 / LBO / M • New Faces, Hot

Bodies #12 / 1993 / STP / M • New Faces, Hot Bodies #17 / 1995 / STP / M • Organic Facials / cr91 / GLI / M • The Party / 1992 / CDI / M • Phone Fantasy #2 / 1992 / ATL / M • Princess Of The Night / 1990 / VD / M • Professor Sticky's Anatomy 3X #01 / 1992 / FC / M • Raw Talent: Deep Inside Lydia's Ass / 1993 / FH / M • Raw Talent: Deep Inside Shana's Ass / 1993 / FH / M • Senior Sexcapades #1 / 1995 / PL / M • The Servants Of Midnight / 1992 / CDI / M • Sexual Olympics #1: The Trials / 1992 / VT / M • Shipwrecked / 1992 / CDI / M • Sinderella #1 / 1992 / VI / M • Sinderella #2 / 1992 / VI / M • Sunrise Mystery / 1992 / FD / M • Supermarket Babes In Heat / 1992 / OD / M • The Swap #1 / 1990 / VI / M • Tails From The Tower / 1993 / AFI / M • Telesex #1 / 1992 / VI / M • Through The Walls / 1990 / FAZ / M • Vienna's Place / 1996 / VCX / M • White Men Can Hump / 1992 / EVN / M • The Worst Porno Ever Made With The Best Sex / 1993 / PL / M

JOEL MURPHY *see* **Joey Murphy**

JOEL SCHULTZ *see* **Joel Lawrence**

JOEL SUMMERS
Too Much Too Soon / 1983 / VCX / M

JOELLE *see* **Star Index I**

JOELLE PETINOT
Skin #1 / 1994 / EUR / M

JOEY
HomeGrown Video #446: Slam Bam Thank You Ma'am! / 1995 / HOV / M • Hometown Girl / 1994 / VEX / M • Hot Body Competition: Lusty Lingerie Contest / 1996 / CG / F • Lunch / 1972 / VC / M • Make Me Over, Baby / 1996 / LOF / M • Pussy Hunt #04 / 1994 / LEI / M

JOEY ALLMAN *see* **Star Index I**

JOEY CARR
Mixed Apples / 1996 / APP / G

JOEY CARSON *(Joey Karson)*
Blonde female with very white hair that looks like it was cut short with a pair of hedge-clippers. Not too pretty, big tits.
Angel In Distress / 1982 / AVO / B • Hump Joey Carson / 199? / H&S / M • Midnight Heat / 1982 / VC / M • The Story Of Prunella / 1982 / AVO / M • The Widespread Scandals Of Lydia Lace / 1983 / CA / M

JOEY CEVERA *see* **Joey Silvera**

JOEY CILVERA *see* **Joey Silvera**

JOEY CIVERA *see* **Joey Silvera**

JOEY CUVERA *see* **Joey Silvera**

JOEY DEE
Hot Tight Asses #02 / 1993 / TCK / M

JOEY DELANO
Pleasure Dome: The Genesis Chamber / 1994 / AFV / M

JOEY EDWARDS
2 Thumbs Up / 1996 / ZA / M • Anal League / 1996 / IN / M • The Blowjob Adventures Of Doctor Fellatio / 1997 / EL / M • Booty And The Ho' Fish / 1996 / RAS / M • Compulsion (Fat Dog) / 1996 / FD / M • Delinquents On Butt Row / 1996 / EA / M • Dirty Tails / 1996 / SC / M • Heavy Breathing / 1996 / NIT / M • Mickey Ray's Sex Search #06 / 1996 / WIV / M • Mike Hott: #380 Girls Who Lap Cum From Cunts #03 / 1996 / MHV / C • More Dirty Debutantes #53 / 1996 / 4P / M • My First Time #6 / 1996 / NS / M • Nineteen #8 / 1997 / FOR / M • Pick Up Lines #07 / 1996 / OD / M • Prime Choice #6 / 1996 / RAS / M • Puritan

Video Magazine #03 / 1996 / LE / M • Santa Is Coming All Over Town / 1996 / EVN / M • Thunder And Lightning / 1996 / MID / M • Titty Slickers #3 / 1996 / LE / M • Video Virgins #30 / 1996 / NS / M • Young And Anal #5 / 1996 / JMP / M • Young Tails / 1996 / LV / M

JOEY EPINESSEO *see* **Star Index I**

JOEY GERADO
Campus Girl / 1972 / VXP / M

JOEY JOCOBI
50 And Still Pumping! / 1994 / EMC / M • Indiscreet! Video Magazine #1 / 1995 / FH / M

JOEY KARSON *see* **Joey Carson**

JOEY KARSTON
Palm Springs Or Bust / 1994 / BTO / M

JOEY KING *see* **Star Index I**

JOEY LENNON *see* **Star Index I**

JOEY LONG *see* **Joey Silvera**

JOEY LOVE *see* **Star Index I**

JOEY MORGAN
Bi-Ology: The Making Of Mr Right / 1992 / CAT / G • Down Bi Law / 1992 / CAT / G

JOEY MURPHY *(Joel Murphy, Johnny (Joey Murphy), Yoyo)*
From **More Dirty Debutantes #8**, this male is German, despite the name. He also speaks flawless English.
40 The Hard Way / 1991 / OD / M • Anal Encounters #1 / 1991 / VC / M • Angels / 1992 / VC / M • Big Titted Tarts / 1994 / PL / C • Blonde Forces #1 / 1991 / CC / M • Bonfire Of The Panties / 1990 / CC / M • Catalina: Tiger Shark / 1991 / CDI / M • Cyrano / 1991 / PL / M • Deep Inside Savannah / 1993 / VC / C • The Dragon Lady #3: Tales From The Bed #2 / 1992 / WV / M • Friends & Lovers #1 / 1991 / VT / M • The Housewife In Heat / 1991 / PL / M • In Too Deep / 1992 / AFD / M • Indiscretions / 1991 / PP / M • Inferno / 1991 / XCI / M • The Journey: Oral Majority / 1991 / WV / M • Kiss It Goodbye / 1991 / SE / M • Laying The Ghost / 1991 / VC / M • Lingerie Busters / 1991 / FH / M • More Dirty Debutantes #08 / 1991 / 4P / M • Mr. Peepers Amateur Home Videos #05: Hot To Trot / 1991 / LBO / M • Mr. Peepers Amateur Home Videos #07: Venus Butterfly / 1991 / LBO / M • Mr. Peepers Amateur Home Videos #38: Bringing Up the Rear / 1991 / LBO / M • Pink Card / 1991 / FH / M • Put It In Gere / 1991 / CA / M • Some Like It Big / 1991 / LE / M • The Stranger Beside Me / 1991 / WV / M • Three Men And A Hooker / 1991 / WV / M • Zara's Revenge / 1991 / XCI / M

JOEY NASSIVERA *see* **Joey Silvera**

JOEY RAY
New Faces, Hot Bodies #10 / 1993 / STP / M

JOEY RENADA *see* **Steven St. Croix**

JOEY SANTINI
Bad Attitude / 1987 / CC / M • Black Girls In Heat / 1985 / PL / M • Climax / 1985 / CA / M • Down & Out In New York City / 1986 / SE / M • Getting Ahead / 1983 / PL / M • Girl Busters / 1985 / VC / M • Harem Girls / 1986 / SE / M • The Honeydrippers / 1987 / VXP / M • Hot Lips / 1984 / VC / M • Night Hunger / 1983 / AVC / M • A Passage Thru Pamela / 1985 / VC / G • Sex Styles Of The Rich & Famous / 1986 / VXP / M • Slit Skirts / 1983 / VXP / M • Tongue 'n Cheek (Red Light) / 1984 / RLV / M • Wet Dreams

/ 1984 / CA / M

JOEY SCOTT *see* **Joey Silvera**

JOEY SHORT *see* **Joey Silvera**

JOEY SILVERA *(Joey Long, Joey Short, Joey Scott, Joe Arnold, Joe Skeg, Joe Masseria, Joseph Nassi, Joey Cevera, Joey Civera, Neil Long, Joey Cuvera, Joey Nassivera, Joey Silvora, Joseph Land, Joey Cilvera, Tony Nacivers)*
10 1/2 Weeks / 1986 / SE / M • 1001 Erotic Nights #1 / 1982 / VC / M • 1001 Erotic Nights #2 / 1987 / VC / M • 4F Dating Service / 1989 / AR / M • The 8th Annual Erotic Film Awards / 1984 / SE / C • 9 1/2 Weeks / 1986 / MGM / S • Acts Of Confession / 1991 / PP / M • Acts Of Love / 1989 / ... / M • Addicted To Love / 1988 / WAV / M • Adultery / 1986 / DR / M • The Adventures Of Billy Blues / 1990 / HO / M • The Adventures Of Major Morehead / 1994 / SC / M • The Adventures Of Mikki Finn / 1991 / CA / M • Alice In Whiteland / 1988 / VC / M • Alien Lust / 1985 / AVC / M • All About Annette / 1982 / SE / C • All For His Ladies / 1987 / PP / C • All I Want For Christmas Is A Gangbang / 1994 / AMP / M • All That Jism / 1994 / VD / M • Always / 1993 / XCI / M • Amber's Desires / 1985 / CA / M • American Garter / 1993 / VC / M • Americans Most Wanted / 1991 / HO / M • Anal Addiction #3 / 1991 / SO / M • Anal Addicts / 1994 / KWP / M • Anal Adventures #1: Anal Executive / 1991 / VC / M • Anal Adventures #3: Can Her! / 1991 / VC / M • The Anal Adventures Of Suzy Super Slut #1 / 1994 / AFV / M • Anal All Stars / 1994 / CA / M • Anal Analysis (Heatwave) / 1992 / HW / M • Anal Analysis / 1992 / ZA / M • Anal Breakdown / 1994 / ROB / M • Anal Candy Ass / 1994 / ROB / M • Anal Deep Rider / 1994 / ROB / M • Anal Delights #2 / 1992 / ROB / M • Anal Delights #3 / 1993 / ROB / M • Anal Delinquent #1 / 1993 / ROB / M • Anal Delinquent #2 / 1994 / ROB / M • Anal Hounds & Bitches / 1994 / ROB / M • Anal Hunger / 1994 / ROB / M • Anal Idol / 1994 / ROB / M • Anal Innocence #2 / 1993 / ROB / M • Anal International / 1992 / HW / M • Anal Intruder #04 / 1990 / CC / M • Anal Intruder #10 / 1995 / CC / M • Anal Justice / 1994 / ROB / M • Anal Kitten / 1992 / ROB / M • Anal Lover #3 / 1994 / ROB / M • Anal Misconduct / 1995 / VD / M • Anal Orgasms / 1992 / DRP / M • Anal Plaything #1 / 1994 / ROB / M • Anal Rampage #2 / 1993 / ROB / M • Anal Savage #1 / 1992 / ROB / M • Anal Savage #2 / 1994 / ROB / M • Anal Siege / 1993 / ROB / M • Anal Thrills / 1992 / ROB / M • Anal Thunder #1 / 1993 / ROB / M • Anal Thunder #2 / 1993 / ROB / M • Anal Urge / 1993 / ROB / M • The Anal-Europe Series #01: The Fisherman's Wife / 1992 / LV / M • And I Do Windows Too / 1986 / PP / M • Angel Gets Even / 1987 / FAN / M • Angel Puss / 1988 / VC / M • Angel's Back / 1988 / IN / M • Angels / 1992 / VC / M • Another Secret / 1990 / SO / M • Army Brat #1 / 1987 / VI / M • The Art Of Passion / 1987 / CA / M • Assault With A Friendly Weapon / 1990 / DAY / M • Assent Of A Woman / 1993 / DR / M • Attitude / 1995 / VC / M • Aussie Vice / 1989 / PM / M • Australian Connection / 1989 / PM / M • Babewatch #1 / 1993 / CC / M • Babewatch #2 / 1994 / CC / M • Baby Face #1 / 1977 / VC / M • Babylon Blue / 1983 / VXP

/ M • Babylon Pink #2 / 1988 / COM / M • Babylon Pink #3 / 1988 / COM / M • Back In The Pen / 1992 / FH / M • Back To Rears / 1988 / VI / M • Backdoor Brides #4 / 1993 / PV / M • Backdoor To Taiwan / 1994 / LV / M • Backside To The Future #2 / 1988 / ZA / M • Bad / 1990 / VC / M • Bad Attitude / 1992 / CDI / M • Bad Side Of Town / 1993 / AFD / M • Ball Street / 1988 / CA / M •Barbara Dare's Roman Holiday / 1987 / SE / M • Barby's On Butt Row / 1996 / ABS / M • Barflies / 1990 / ZA / M • Beach Ballerina Brat / 1989 / VI / M • Bedtime Stories / 1992 / CDI / M • Behind Blue Eyes #2 / 1988 / ZA / M • Behind The Scenes Of An Adult Movie / 1983 / CV / M • Behind The Scenes With Angela Baron / 1988 / FAZ / C • Behind You All The Way #2 / 1990 / SO / M • Bend Over Babes #4 / 1996 / EA / M • Bend Over Brazilian Babes #2 / 1993 / EA / M • Best Gang Bangs / 1996 / DFI / C • The Best Little Whorehouse In Hong Kong / 1987 / SE / M • The Best Little Whorehouse In San Francisco / 1984 / LA / M • The Best Of Alex De Renzy #1 / 1983 / VC / C • The Best Of Black Anal #1 / 1995 / ROB / C • The Best Of Oriental Anal #1 / 1994 / ROB / C • The Better Sex Video Series #5: Sharing Fantasies / 1992 / LEA / M • Between Lovers / 1983 / CA / M • Between The Sheets / 1982 / CA / M • Beyond Desire / 1986 / VC / M • Bi Cycling / 1989 / FC / G • Bi-Guy / 1990 / LA / G • Big Gulp #1 / 1986 / VIP / C • The Big Thrill / 1989 / VD / M • Biloxi Babes / 1988 / WV / M • The Bitches Of Westwood / 1987 / CA / M • Black Bottom Girlz / 1994 / CA / M • Black In The Saddle / 1990 / ZA / M • Black Is Back / 1993 / HW / M • Black Satin / 1994 / IN / M • Black Silk Stockings / 1978 / SE / C • Black Sister, White Brother / 1987 / AT / M • Black Stockings / 1990 / VD / M • Black, White & Red All Over / 1984 / EXF / C • Blame It On Ginger / 1986 / VI / M • Blazing Bedrooms / 1987 / LA / M • Blonde Butt Babes / 1994 / LV / M • Bloopers & Boners / 1996 / VI / M • Blue Vanities #042 (Old) / 1988 / FFL / M • Blue Vanities #064 / 1988 / FFL / M • Blue Vanities #067 / 1988 / FFL / M • Blue Vanities #069 / 1988 / FFL / M • Blue Vanities #072 / 1988 / FFL / M • Blue Vanities #105 / 1988 / FFL / M • Blue Vanities #209 / 1993 / FFL / M • Blue Vanities #248 / 1995 / FFL / M • Blue Voodoo / 1983 / VD / M • Bodies In Heat #2 / 1989 / DR / M • Body Heat / 1990 / CDI / M • Body Magic / 1982 / SE / M • Boobs, Butts And Bloopers #1 / 1990 / HO / M • Boobs, Butts And Bloopers #2 / 1990 / HO / M • Book Of Love / 1992 / VC / M • Boom Boom Valdez / 1988 / CA / M • Booty Ho #1 / 1993 / ROB / M • Booty Sister #1 / 1993 / ROB / M • Born For Love / 1987 / … / M • Born To Be Maid / 1987 / … / M • Born To Run / 1985 / WV / M • The Bottom Dweller 33 1/3 / 1995 / EL / M • Boxed Lunches / 1989 / … / M • The Brat / 1986 / VI / M • Brat Force / 1989 / VI / M • Brat On The Run / 1987 / VI / M • Breakin' In / 1986 / WV / M • The Breast Of Breastmen / 1995 / EVN / C • The Breast Things In Life Are Free / 1991 / LV / M • Breastman Does The Twin Towers / 1993 / EVN / M • Breastman's Wet T-Shirt Contest / 1994 / EVN / M • A Brief Affair / 1982 / CA / M • Bring On The Virgins / 1989 / CA / M • Broadcast Nudes / 1988 / EVN / M •

Brooke Does College / 1984 / VC / M • Bubbles / 1991 / IF / M • Bucky Beaver's XXX Dragon Art Theatre Double Feature #06 / 1996 / SOW / M • Buffy The Vamp / 1992 / FD / M • Bunny's Office Fantasies / 1984 / VC / M • Bunz-Eye / 1992 / ROB / M • Bush Pilots #1 / 1990 / VC / M • Bushwackers / 1990 / PM / M • Busted / 1992 / HO / M • Bustline / 1993 / LE / M • Butt Bangers Ball / 1994 / FPI / M • Butt Freak #1 / 1992 / EA / M • Butt Freak #2 / 1996 / EA / M • Butt Row Unplugged / 1996 / ABS / M • The Butt Sisters Do Las Vegas / 1994 / MID / M • Buttman Goes To Rio #4 / 1993 / EA / M • Buttman In The Crack / 1996 / EA / M • Buttman's Big Butt Backdoor Babes / 1995 / EA / M • Buttman's Big Tit Adventure #3 / 1995 / EA / M • Buttman's Bouncin' British Babes / 1994 / EA / M • Buttman's British Moderately Big Tit Adventure / 1994 / EA / M • Buttman's Double Adventure / 1993 / EA / M • Buttman's Orgies / 1996 / EA / M • Buttman's Wet Dream / 1994 / EA / M • Butts Up / 1994 / CA / M • Caballero Preview Tape #4 / 1985 / CA / C • California Taboo / 1986 / VC / M • The Call Girl / 1986 / VD / M • Call Girls In Action / 1989 / CV / M • Campus Capers / 1982 / VC / M • Can't Get Enough / 1985 / CA / M • Candy Stripers #1/ 1978 / ALP / M • Car Wash Angels / 1995 / VC / M • Careena #1 / 1987 / WV / C • Careena #2: A Star On The Rise / 1988 / WV / C • Carlita's Backway / 1993 / OD / M • Carnal Haven / 1976 / SVE / M • Carnival / 1995 / PV / M • Casanova #2 / 1993 / SC / M • Casual Sex / 1991 / GO / M • Cat Fight / 1992 / ONH / M • Catalina Five-O: White Coral, Blue Death / 1990 / CIN / M • Catalina Sixty-Nine / 1991 / AR / M • Catalina: Sabotage / 1991 / CDI / M • Catalina: Treasure Island / 1991 / CDI / M • The Catwoman / 1988 / VC / M • Caught From Behind #14 / 1990 / HO / M • Caught From Behind #16: The Reunion / 1992 / HO / M • Caught In The Act / 1987 / WV / M • Caught In The Act (1995-Wave) / 1995 / WAV / M • CB Mamas / 1976 / MIT / M • Cells Of Passion / 1981 / VD / M • Centerfold Fever / 1981 / VXP / M • Ceremony, The Ritual Of Love / 1976 / AVC / M • Certifiably Anal / 1993 / ROB / M • Chained / 1995 / SC / M • The Chameleon / 1989 / VC / M • Charlie's Girls #3 / 1990 / CC / M • Charm School / 1993 / PEP / M • Charmed Again / 1989 / VI / M • Cheap Thrills / 1984 / RLV / M • Cheeks #4: A Backstreet Affair / 1991 / CC / M • Cheeks #8 / 1995 / CC / M • Cheerleader Nurses #1 / 1993 / VC / M • Cheerleader Nurses #2 / 1993 / VC / M • Cherry Cheesecake / 1984 / AR / M • Cherry Tricks / 1985 / VPE / M • Cheryl Hanson: Cover Girl / 1981 / SE / M • Chicks In Black Leather / 1989 / VC / C • China White / 1986 / WV / M • Chorus Call / 1978 / TVX / M • Christine's Secret / 1986 / FEM / M • Circus Sluts / 1995 / LV / M • City Of Sin / 1991 / LV / M • Classic Erotica #1 / 1980 / SVE / M • Classic Pics / 1988 / PP / C • Classic Swedish Erotica #07 / 1986 / CA / C • Classic Swedish Erotica #23 / 1986 / CA / C • Classic Swedish Erotica #29 / 1987 / CA / C • Clean And Dirty / 1990 / ME / M • Climax / 1985 / CA / M • The Clock Strikes Bizarre On Butt Row / 1996 / ABS / M • Club DV8 #1 / 1993

/ SC / M • Club Ecstasy / 1987 / CA / M • Club Exotica #1 / 1985 / WV / M • Club Exotica #2 / 1985 / WV / M • Club Head (EVN) #2 / 1989 / EVN / C • Coming Of Age /1989 / CA / M • Coming Of Age / 1995 / VEX / C • Confessions Of A Middle Aged Nympho / 1986 / WET / M • Confessions Of A Woman / 1976 / SE / M • Confessions Of Christy / 1991 / CAY / M • Conflict / 1988 / VD / M • Consenting Adults / 1981 / VXP / M • Constant Craving / 1992 / VD / M • Corruption / 1990 / CC / M • The Corruption Of Christina / 1993 / WP / M • Count The Ways / 1976 / CA / M • County Line / 1993 / PEP / M • Cozy Cool / 1971 / WWV / M • The Crack Of Dawn / 1989 / GLE / M • Crazy Love / 1995 / VI / M • Cream Dream / 1991 / ZA / M • Crossing Over / 1990 / IN / M • Crude / 1991 / IN / M • The Cumming Of Sarah Jane #2 / 1993 / AFV / M • Cybersex / 1996 / WAV / M • D-Cup Dating Service / 1991 / ME / M • Daddy's Little Girl / 1977 / VCI / M • The Damp Spot / 1993 / AFD / C • Dance Naked / 1995 / PEP / M • The Dancers / 1981 / VCX / M • Dangerous Women / 1987 / WET / M • Daughters Of Darkness / 1975 / ASR / M • The De Renzy Tapes / 1990 / CA / C • Dear Bridgette / 1992 / ZA / M • Debbie 4 Hire / 1988 / AVC / M • Debbie Class Of '89 / 1989 / CC / M • Debbie Does Dishes #3 / 1987 / AVC / M • Debbie For President / 1988 / CC / M • Decadence / 1986 / VD / M • Decadent / 1991 / WV / M • Deep & Wet / 1986 / VD / M • Deep Cheeks #4 / 1993 / ROB / M • Deep Inside Brittany O'connell / 1996 / VC / C • Deep Inside Deidre Holland / 1993 / VC / C • Deep Inside Juli Ashton / 1996 / VC / C • Deep Inside Nicole London / 1995 / VC / C • Deep Inside Selena Steele / 1993 / VC / C • Deep Inside Shanna Mccullough / 1992 / VC / C • Defending Your Soul / 1995 / EX / M • Defenseless / 1992 / CDI / M • Delinquents On Butt Row / 1996 / EA / M • Designer Genes / 1990 / VI / M • Despicable Dames / 1986 / CC / M • Devil In Miss Jones #2 / 1983 / VC / M • The Devil In Miss Jones #5: The Inferno / 1994 / VC / M • Devil's Agenda & Miss Jones / 1991 / AR / M • Diamond Collection #06 / 1979 / CDI / M • Diamond Head / 1987 / AVC / M • Dick Tracer / 1990 / PM / M • The Dickheads #2 / 1993 / MID / M • Dirty 30's Cinema: Patti Petite / 1986 / PV / C • Dirty Blonde / 1984 / VXP / M • Dirty Business / 1992 / CV / M • Dirty Laundry / 1988 / PP / M • Diva / 1993 / XCI / M • Divine Decadence / 1988 / CA / M • Do You Wanna Be Loved? / 1977 / AR / M • Dog Walker / 1994 / EA / M • Doin' The Harlem Shuffle / 1986 / CA / M • Dollface / 1987 / CV / M • Double Crossed / 1994 / MID / M • Double Penetration #3 / 1986 / WV / C • Double Standards / 1988 / BIL / G • Doubletake / 1989 / CC / M • Down 4 Busine$$ / 1989 / GMI / M • Dr Blacklove #1 / 1987 / CC / M • Dr Juice's Lust Potion / 1986 / TEM / M • Dream Lover / 1995 / SC / M • Dream Lust / 1995 / NIT / M • The Dream Machine / 1992 / CDI / M • The Dream Merchants / 1990 / CDI / M • Dreams / 1995 / VC / M • Drop Sex: Wipe The Floor / 1997 / JLP / M • Earthquake Girls / 1990 / CC / M • Easy Alice / 1976 / VC / M • Eclipse / 1993 / SC / M • Ejacula #1 / 1992 / VC / M • Ejacula #2 / 1992 / VC / M • The Elixir / 1992 / CDI

CV / M • Sorority Sex Kittens #1 / 1992 / VC / M • Sorority Sex Kittens #2 / 1993 / VC/ M • Sorority Sex Kittens #3 / 1996 / VC / M • Sorority Stewardesses #1 / 1995 / PE / M • Sorority Stewardesses #2 / 1995 / PE / M • The Sperminator / 1985 / VXP / M • Spitfire / 1984 / COM / M • Splendor In The Ass #2 / 1992 / CA / M • Spoiled / 1987 / VD / M • Spoiled Rich / 1989 / CC / M • Spread Sheets / 1991 / DR / M • St. X-Where #1 / 1986 / VD / M • Stairway To Paradise / 1990 / VC / M • Stake Out / 1991 / CIN / M • Star 90 / 1990 / CAY / M • Star Struck / 1991 / AFV / M • Starbangers #01 / 1993 / BIG / M • Starbangers #03 / 1993 / ZA / M • The Starlet / 1991 / PP / M • Starship Intercourse / 1987 / DR / M • Steal Breeze / 1990 / SO / M • Steamy Windows / 1990 / VC / M • Stormy / 1980 / CV / M • Strange Behavior / 1991 / VD / M • Strange Curves / 1989 / VC / M • Strange Diary / 1976 / AXV / M • Stray Cats / 1985 / VXP / M • Street Angels / 1992 / LV / M • Street Heat / 1992 / CDI / M • Street Legal / 1995 / WAV / M • Student Bodies / 1975 / VC / M • Student Nurses / 1991 / CA / M • Suburban Swingers / 1993 / IF / M • Sugar Britches / 1980 / VCX / C • Summer Lovers / 1987 / WET / M • Super Chic / 1985 / VC / M • Superboobs / 1994 / LE / M • Supergirls Do General Hospital / 1984 / VC / M • Supergirls Do The Navy / 1984 / VC / M • Supertung / 1990 / LA / M • Suzie Superstar #1 / 1983 / CV / M • Suzie Superstar #2 / 1985 / CV / M • Suzie Superstar...The Search Continues / 1988 / CV / M • Sweat 'n' Bullets / 1995 / MID / M • Swedish Erotica #09 / 1980 / CA / M • Swedish Erotica #15 / 1980 / CA / M • Swedish Erotica #29 / 1980 / CA / M • Swedish Erotica #47 / 1983 / CA / M • Swedish Erotica #49 / 1983 / CA / M • Swedish Erotica #74 / 1994 / CA / M • Swedish Erotica #75 / 1994 / CA / M • Swedish Erotica #76 / 1994 / CA / M • Swedish Erotica #79 / 1994 / CA / M • Swedish Erotica #82 / 1995 / CA / M • Swedish Erotica Featurettes #2 / 1989 / CA / M • Swedish Erotica Featurettes #3 / 1989 / CA / M • Swedish Erotica Featurettes #4 / 1990 / CA / M • Swedish Sorority Girls / 1978 / CV / M • Sweet Poison / 1991 / CDI / M • Sweet Secrets / 1977 / VCS / M • Sweet Surrender / 1985 / AVC / M • Swing Into...Spring / 1995 / KWP / M • Taboo #02 / 1982 / IN / M • Taboo #04 / 1985 / IN / M • Taboo #05 / 1986 / IN / M • Taboo #06 / 1988 / IN / M • Taboo #08 / 1990 / IN / M • Taboo #12 / 1994 / MET / M • Taboo #15 / 1995 / IN / M • Taboo American Style #3: Nina Becomes An Actress / 1985 / VC / M • Taboo American Style #4: The Exciting Conclusion / 1985 / VC / M • Tactical Sex Force / 1994 / IN / M • Tailgate Party / 1990 / HO / M • Tailiens #2 / 1992 / FD / M • Tailspin #2 / 1991 / VT / M • Tales Of Taija Rae / 1989 / DR / M • Tales Of The Uncensored / 1987 / FAN / M • Talk Dirty To Me #04 / 1986 / DR / M • Talk Dirty To Me #05 / 1987 / DR / M • Talk Dirty To Me #06 / 1989 / DR / M • A Taste Of Alexa / 1989 / PIN / C • A Taste Of Cheri / 1990 / PIN / C • A Taste Of Madison / 1992 / VD / C • A Taste Of Pink / 1985 / VXP / M • A Taste Of Porsche / 1988 / PIN / C • A Taste Of Sahara / 1990 / PIN / C • A Taste Of Sugar / 1978 / AR / M • A Taste Of Tami Monroe /

1990 / PIN / C • Taste Of The Best #2 / 1988 / PIN / C • A Taste Of Tori Welles / 1990 / PIN / C • Teasers: Champagne Reunion / 1988 / MET / M • Teasers: Porno Princess / 1988 / MET / M • Teenage Birthday Ball / 19?? / SIL / M • Teenage Pony Girls / 1977 / VCX / M • Teenage Runaway / 1973 / AXV / M • Teenage Surfer Girls / 1976 / VCS / M • The Temple Of Poon / 1996 / PE / M • Temptations Of The Flesh / 1986 / VD / M • Tenth Annual Adult Video News Awards / 1993 / VC / M • That's Outrageous / 1983 / CA / M • That's Porno / 1979 / CV / C • The Theory Of Relativity / 1994 / EL / M • Thighs & Dolls / 1993 / PEP / M • This Year's Model / 1996 / WAV / M • Three For All / 1988 / PL / M • Three Men And A Geisha / 1990 / HO / M • The Three Muskatits / 1994 / PL / M • Throat...12 Years After / 1984 / VC / M • Thunderbuns / 1976 / VCX / C • The Tiffany Minx Affair / 1992 / FOR / M • Tit Tales #3 / 1991 / FC / M • Titty Bar #1 / 1993 / LE / M • Titty Bar #2 / 1994 / LE / M • The Titty Committee / 1986 / SE / C • Titty-Titty Bang-Bang / 1992 / FC / C • To Snatch A Thief / 1989 / PLD / M • Tongue Twisters / 1986 / VXP / M • Top It Off / 1990 / VC / M • Topless Stewardesses / 1995 / PV / M • Torrid / 1989 / VI / M • Totally Naked / 1994 / VC / M • Touched / 1990 / VI / M • Toys 4 Us #1 / 1987 / WV / C • Traci Who? / 1987 / AVC / C • Trading Places / 1985 / DR / M • Trampire / 1987 / FAN / M • Transformed / 1991 / MET / M • Trashi / 1980 / CA / M • Treasure Chest / 1994 / LV / M • Trick Or Treat / 1985 / ELH / M • Trick Shots / 1995 / PV / M • Trick Tracey #1 / 1990 / CC / M • Trinity Brown / 1984 / CV / M • Triple Xposure / 1986 / VD / M • Truck Stop Angel / 1994 / CC / M • True Blue / 1989 / PM / M • True Legends Of Adult Cinema: The Cult Superstars / 1993 / VC / C • True Legends Of Adult Cinema: The Erotic Eighties / 1992 / VC / C • True Legends Of Adult Cinema: The Golden Age / 1992 / VC / C • True Legends Of Adult Cinema: The Modern Era / 1992 / VC / C • True Legends Of Adult Cinema: Unsung Superstars / 1993 / VC / C • Tuff Stuff / 1987 / WET / M • Tush / 1992 / ZA / M • Twin Cheeks #1 / 1990 / CIN / M • Twin Cheeks #2 / 1991 / CIN / M • Twin Cheeks #4 / 1991 / CIN / M • Twisted / 1990 / VI / M • Two Of A Kind / 1991 / ZA / M • Two Women / 1992 / ROB / M • Ultimate Orgy #1 / 1992 / GLI / M • Unchain My Heart / 1990 / CC / M • Unnatural Phenomenon / 1985 / WV / M • Unnatural Phenomenon #2 / 1986 / WV / M • Unrefined / 1993 / CC / M • Untamed Passions / 1987 / CV / C • Urban Cowgirls / 1980 / CA / M • Urges In Young Girls / 1984 / VC / M • Used Cars / 1990 / CDI / M • V—The Hot One / 1978 / CV / M • Venus: Wings Of Seduction / 1991 / CDI / M • Victoria's Secret / 1989 / SO / M • Viper's Place / 1988 / VD / M • Virgin Spring / 1991 / FAZ / M • Vogue / 1994 / VD / C • The Voyeur #2 / 1994 / EA / M • The Voyeur #3 / 1995 / EA / M • The Wacky World Of X-Rated Bloopers / 1989 / GO / M • Wacs / 1992 / PP / M • Warm To The Touch / 1990 / CDI / M • Way Down Deep / cr78 / PYR / M • We're No Angels / 1990 / CIN / M • Wendy Whoppers: Brain Surgeon / 1993 / PEP / M • Wendy Whoppers: Park Ranger / 1993 /

PEP / M • Wendy Whoppers: Prison Love Doll / 1994 / PEP / M • Wet & Wild Tami Monroe / 1991 / CA / C • Wet Dreams / 1984 / CA / M • Wet Dreams 2001 / 1987 / VD / M • Wet Kink / 1989 / CDI / M • Wet Paint / 1990 / DR / M • The Wetter The Better / 1975 / VST / M • What Are Friends For? / 1985 / MAP / M • When Love Came To Town / 1989 / EVN / M • When She Was Bad / 1983 / CA / M • Where The Boys Aren't #1 / 1989 / VI / F • Where There's Smoke There's Fire / 1987 / FAN / M • White Boys & Black Bitches / 1995 / ROB / M • White Chicks Can't Hump / 1992 / FD / M • White Hot / 1984 / VXP / M • White Men Can't Iron On Butt Row / 1997 / ABS / M • White Women / 1986 / CC / M • Who Came In The Backdoor? / 1987 / PV / M • Who Shaved Lynn Lemay? / 1989 / EX / M • The Whore / 1989 / CA / M • Whore House / 1995 / IPI / M • Whose Fantasy Is It, Anyway? / 1983 / AVC / M • Wicked Sensations #2 / 1989 / DR / M • The Widespread Scandals Of Lydia Lace / 1983 / CA / M • Wild At Heart / 1990 / CDI / M • Wild Goose Chase / 1990 / EA / M • Wild In The Sheets / 1984 / WET / M • Wild Things #2 / 1986 / CV / M • Wild Things #4 / 1994 / CV / M • Wildheart / 1989 / IN / M • Willie Wanker And The Fun Factory / 1994 / FD / M • Willing Women / 1993 / VD / C • Winter Heat / 1994 / MID / M • Wire Desire / 1991 / XCI / M • The Witching Hour / 1992 / FOR / M • With Love, Loni / 1985 / CA / C • Witness For The Penetration / 1994 / PEP / M • Woman In The Window / 1986 / TEM / M • Working Stiffs / 1993 / FD / M • Wrapped Up / 1992 / VD / C • Yiddish Erotica #1 / 1986 / SE / C • Young And Abused / 19?? / ASR / M • The Young Like It Hot / 1983 / CA / M • Young, Hot And Nasty / cr88 / BWV / C • [Masquerade (1992-Italy) / 1992 / ... / S • [Porno Provini Bagnati Per Milli / 19?? / ... / M • [Two Horny Sisters / 1988 / ... / M

JOEY SILVORA *see* **Joey Silvera**

JOEY STEFANO (Nicholas A. Iocona)
Gay video actor. Born January 1, 1968 (according to one source it was 1967) as Nicholas Anthony Iacona. Died November 21, 1994 in Hollywood CA of a drug overdose. HIV positive at time of death.
Bi-Golly / 1993 / BIL / G • G Squad / 1990 / SO / G • Innocence Found / 1991 / PAL / G • Karen's Bi-Line / 1989 / MET / G • Sharon And Karen / 1989 / LV / G • The Stroke / 1990 / SO / M

JOEY THE MAGICIAN *see* **Star Index I**

JOEY VALENTE
Bi Bi Banjee Boyz / 1994 / PL / G

JOEY VAUGHAN
The Girls Of Spring Break / 1995 / VT / M • Mickey Ray's Sex Search #01: Sliding In / 1994 / WIV / M • Mickey Ray's Sex Search #06 / 1996 / WIV / M • Nature Girls #2: Get Wet / 1995 / WIV / F • Pussyman Auditions #11 / 1995 / SNA / M • The Sexual Solution #2 / 1995 / LE / M • Sinnocence / 1995 / CDI / M • Wicked Ways #3: An All-Anal Slutfest / 1995 / WP / M

JOHAN
S&M On The Ranch: Training The New Pony Girl / 1994 / VER / B

JOHANAN STEIN
MASH'ed / cr75 / ALP / M

JOHANN GUMPINGER
[Schulmadchen-Report 4: Was Eltern Oft

Verzweifeln LaBt / 1972 / ... / M

JOHANNA
A&B AB#441: Johanna's Kinky Adventure / 1994 / A&B / B • A&B AB#442: Kinky Submissive / 1994 / A&B / B • Come With Me / 1995 / GOT / M • Eurotica #11 / 1996 / XC / M • Private Gold #04: Amazonas / 1996 / OD / M • Private Stories #06 / 1995 / OD / M

JOHANNA CONSTANTINE
P.L.O.W.: Punk Ladies Of Wrestling / 1996 / GOT / B

JOHANNA STIRLING see Star Index I

JOHANNA STORM see Joanna Storm

JOHN
100% Amateur #09: Asians & Latinas / 1995 / OD / M • All Pain, No Gain / 1991 / NEP / B • Big Boob Bikini Bash / 1995 / BTO / M • Big Boob Celebration / 1994 / BTO / M • Breast Worx #03 / 1991 / LBO / M • Breast Worx #23 / 1992 / LBO / M • Homegrown Video #241 / 1990 / HOV / M • Homegrown Video #245 / 1990 / HOV / M • Homegrown Video #344 / 1991 / HOV / M • HomeGrown Video #452: Make Me Cum! / 1995 / HOV / M • HomeGrown Video #458: Cream Pie For Dessert / 1995 / HOV / C • Jus' Knockin' Boots #1: Fade To Black / 1996 / NIT / M • Jus' Knockin' Boots #2: Black On Line / 1996 / NIT / M • Mistress Manuela From Club Dom / 1993 / VER / B • Mr. Peepers Amateur Home Videos #45: Coming From Behind / 1992 / LBO / M • Nothing Butt Amateurs #01 / 1993 / AFI / M • Ona Z's Star Search #03 / 1993 / GLI / M • Ona Zee's Date With Dallas / 1992 / ONA / M • Pearl Necklace: Amorous Amateurs #41 / 1994 / SEE / M • Pearl Necklace: Premier Sessions #03 / 1994 / SEE / M • Pearl Necklace: Thee Bush League #02 / 1992 / SEE / M • A Sundae Kinda Love / 1995 / TVI / M • Swingers Confidential #1 / 1995 / FC / M

JOHN (STEVE HOUSTON) see Steve Houston

JOHN A. MOZZER see Alan Adrian

JOHN ANTHONY BAILEY see Jack Baker

JOHN ASHTON
Birds And Beads / 1974 / VC / M • Invasion Of The Love Drones / 1977 / ALP / M • Revenge Of The Rope Masters / 1979 / ... / B • Tina Makes A Deal / 1974 / TGA / M • The Tommyknockers / 1993 / VMA / S

JOHN BAILEY
Tight Spot / 1996 / WV / M

JOHN BANKS
Hot Property (AVC) / 1975 / AVC / M • Last Of The Wild / 1975 / CA / M

JOHN BANNER see Star Index I

JOHN BENNETT *(Johnny Jam)*
SO of Renee Bennett.
The Adventures Of Peeping Tom #1 / 1996 / OD / M • Eye On You: Rene / 1996 / EOY / M • Fresh Faces #08 / 1995 / EVN / M • Hollywood Amateurs #20 / 1995 / MID / M • House Of Hoochies / 1996 / DDP / M • Innocence Lost / 1995 / GO / M • Kym Wilde's On The Edge #26 / 1995 / RB / B • Kym Wilde's On The Edge #36 / 1996 / RB / B • My First Time #1 / 1995 / NS / M

JOHN BLACK
Erotic Dimensions #2: Black Desire / 1982 / NSV / M • Primal She-Male / 1996 / HSV / G • She Male Devil / 1996 / HSV / G • Showgirl She-Male / 1996 / HSV / G •

Sweetheart / 1976 / SVE / M • Texas Towers / 1993 / IF / M • Trannie Love / 1995 / HSV / G • Virtual She-Male / 1995 / HSV / G

JOHN BOWEN see John T. Bone

JOHN BOY
Prisoner Of Love / 1995 / CV / M

JOHN BRIGHTON
One Last Fling / cr76 / CPL / M

JOHN BROWN
Night Crawlers / 1994 / SC / M

JOHN BUCHANAN
Love Lips / 1976 / VC / M

JOHN BUCO
Waterpower / 1975 / VHL / M

JOHN BURGESS
Erotic Fantasies #5 / 1983 / CV / C

JOHN BUSCHE see Star Index I

JOHN BYRD
The Final Test / 197? / RLV / B

JOHN BYRON see Star Index I

JOHN C. HOLMES *(John Curtis Holmes, Big Jon Fallus, Johnny Wadd, John Rey, Long John Wadd)*
Died March 13, 1988 of AIDS in Sepulveda CA at age 43. Born John Curtis Estes, August 8, 1944 in Pickaway County, OH. Arrested for the "Four On The Floor" murders that occurred in July 1981 at Wonderland Drive and jailed for 110 days for refusing to identify the perpertrators. Divorced from his first wife, Sharon Gebenini, a nurse, in 1984 after 16 years of marriage. Second wife was Misty Dawn (Laurie Rose).
All Night Long / 1975 / SE / M • Anal Ultra Vixens / 197? / ALP / M • The Angel In Mr. Holmes / 1988 / WV / C • Around The World With Johnny Wadd / 1975 / ALP / C • Aunt Peg / 1980 / CV / M • Aunt Peg's Fulfillment / 1980 / CV / M • The Autobiography Of A Flea / 1976 / MIT / M • The Baby Sister / 1972 / ... / M • Backdoor Romance / 1984 / VIV / M • Backing In #1 / 1990 / WV / C • Balling For Dollars / 1980 / CA / M • Bedtime Video #01 / 1984 / GO / M • Bedtime Video #03 / 1984 / GO / M • Bedtime Video #04 / 1984 / GO / M • The Best Of Gail Palmer / 1981 / WWV / C • Beyond Fulfillment / 1975 / SE / M • Big Beaver Splits The Scene / 1972 / ALP / S • The Bigger The Better / 1986 / SE / C • Black Beauties / 1987 / SE / C • Black Silk Stockings / 1978 / SE / C • Black Widow's Nest / 1976 / ... / M • Blonde Fire / 1979 / EVI / M • Blonde In Black Lace / 1975 / VCX / M • Blue Vanities #005 / 1987 / FFL / M • Blue Vanities #010 / 1988 / FFL / M • Blue Vanities #011 (Old) / 1988 / FFL / M • Blue Vanities #014 / 1988 / FFL / M • Blue Vanities #015 (New) / 1988 / FFL / M • Blue Vanities #015 (Old) / 1988 / FFL / M • Blue Vanities #016 (New) / 1988 / FFL / M • Blue Vanities #016 (Old) / 1988 / FFL / M • Blue Vanities #017 (New) / 1988 / FFL / M • Blue Vanities #017 (Old) / 1988 / FFL / M • Blue Vanities #018 (New) / 1988 / FFL / M • Blue Vanities #034 / 1988 / FFL / M • Blue Vanities #039 (New) / 1988 / FFL / M • Blue Vanities #042 (New) / 1988 / FFL / M • Blue Vanities #042 (Old) / 1988 / FFL / M • Blue Vanities #043 / 1988 / FFL / M • Blue Vanities #044 (New) / 1988 / FFL / M • Blue Vanities #045 (New) / 1988 / FFL / M • Blue Vanities #045 (Old) / 1988 / FFL / M • Blue Vanities #046 (New) / 1988 / FFL / M • Blue Vanities #048 / 1988 / FFL / M • Blue Vanities #049 / 1988 / FFL

/ M • Blue Vanities #052 / 1988 / FFL / M • Blue Vanities #057 / 1988 / FFL / M • Blue Vanities #058 / 1988 / FFL / M • Blue Vanities #065 / 1988 / FFL / M • Blue Vanities #068 / 1988 / FFL / M • Blue Vanities #087 / 1988 / FFL / M • Blue Vanities #089 / 1988 / FFL / M • Blue Vanities #091 / 1988 / FFL / M • Blue Vanities #117 / 1989 / FFL / M • Blue Vanities #125 / 1990 / FFL / M • Blue Vanities #243 / 1996 / FFL / M • Blue Vanities #244 / 1995 / FFL / M • Blue Vanities #254 / 1996 / FFL / M • Blue Vanities #255 / 1996 / FFL / M • Body Candy / 1980 / VIS / M • Body Shop / 1984 / VCX / M • Bottoms Up #02 / 1983 / AVC / C • Bottoms Up #04 / 1983 / AVC / C • Bucky Beaver's XXX Dragon Art Theatre Double Feature #07 / 1996 / SOW / M • Caballero Preview Tape #3 / 1984 / CA / C • Caballero Preview Tape #4 / 1985 / CA / C • California Gigolo / 1979 / WWV / M • California Girls / 1980 / CA / M • California Valley Girls / 1983 / HO / M • Candi Girl / 1979 / PVX / M • Candy Samples' Video Review / 1984 / 4P / M • Candy's Candy / 1976 / BL / M • Carnal Encounters Of The Barest Kind / 1978 / VOY / C • Carnal Knowledge / 1970 / SOW / S • Casanova #2 / 1976 / CA / M • The Champ / 1984 / WV / M • Chastity And The Starlets / 1986 / RAV / M • Chastity Johnson / 1985 / AVC / M • Cheri / 1971 / VCX / M • The China Cat / 1978 / CA / M • Classic Erotica #1 / 1980 / SVE / M • Classic Erotica #4 / 1980 / SVE / M • Classic Erotica #5 / 1985 / SVE / M • Classic Erotica #7 / 1985 / SVE / M • Classic Swedish Erotica #04 / 1986 / CA / C • Classic Swedish Erotica #05 / 1986 / CA / C • Classic Swedish Erotica #06 / 1986 / CA / C • Classic Swedish Erotica #08 / 1986 / CA / C • Classic Swedish Erotica #11 / 1986 / CA / C • Classic Swedish Erotica #13 / 1986 / CA / C • Classic Swedish Erotica #14 / 1986 / CA / C • Classic Swedish Erotica #15 / 1986 / CA / C • Classic Swedish Erotica #16 / 1986 / CA / C • Classic Swedish Erotica #19 / 1986 / CA / C • Classic Swedish Erotica #21 / 1986 / CA / C • Classic Swedish Erotica #22 / 1986 / CA / C • Classic Swedish Erotica #26 / 1987 / CA / C • Classic Swedish Erotica #32 / 1987 / CA / C • Cock Robin / 1989 / SUE / M • Collection #08 / 1984 / CA / M • Coming Holmes / 1985 / VD / M • Confessions Of A Teenage Peanut Butter Freak / 1974 / LIM / M • Connection Live #1 / 1986 / VD / C • Country Girls / 197? / ... / M • Creme Rinse / 1976 / AXV / M • Critics' Choice #2 / 1984 / SE / C • Dallas School Girls / 1981 / VCX / M • Danish And Blue / 1970 / SOW / S • The Danish Connection / 1970 / SOW / S • Dear Pam / 1976 / CA / M • Deep Rub / 1979 / VC / M • The Devil In Mr Holmes / 1988 / PV / M • Dickman & Throbbin / 1985 / WV / M • Doctor I'm Coming / 1970 / SOW / M • Door To Door Salesman / cr70 / ... / M • Double Exposure / 1972 / VCX / M • Double Penetration #3 / 1986 / WV / C • Double Penetration #8 / 1994 / WV / C • Down And Dirty / 1985 / LBO / M • Dreams Of Misty / 1984 / VCX / M • Ecstasy / 1979 / SE / M • Electric Blue #005 / 1982 / CA / S • The Erotic Adventures Of Candy / 1978 / VCX / M • Erotic Fantasies #1 / 1983 / CV / C • Erotic Fantasies #5 / 1983 / CV / C • Eruption / 1977 / VCX / M • Evil Come Evil Go / 1972

/ ST0 / S • Executive Secretary / 1975 / CA / M • Exhausted / 1981 / CA / C • Exotic French Fantasies / 1974 / PVX / M • Extreme Close-Up / 1981 / VC / M • Extremes / 1981 / CA / M • Fantasm / 1976 / VS / S • Fantasm Cums Again / 1977 / VS / S • Fantastic Orgy / 197? / ... / M • Female Athletes / 1977 / VXP / M • Fire In Francesca / cr77 / ASR / M • First Annual XRCO Awards / 1984 / AVC / C • Flesh & Laces #2 / 1983 / CA / M • Flesh Of The Lotus / 1971 / VCX / M • Flight Sensations / 1983 / VC / C • Four Women In Trouble / 1973 / AXV / M • French Kiss / 1979 / PVX / M • French Schoolgirls / 1973 / AVC / M • Fulfillment / 1973 / SE / M • Garters And Lace / 1975 / SE / M • Ginger: The Movie / 1988 / PV / C • The Girls In The Band / 1976 / SVE / M • Girls On Fire / 1985 / VCX / M • Good To The Last Drop / 1986 / VCS / C • The Good, The Bad, And The Horny / 1985 / VCX / M • The Grafenberg Spot / 1985 / MIT / M • Hard Candy / 1977 / ... / M • Hard Soap, Hard Soap / 1977 / EVI / M • Heat Of The Moment / 1983 / S&L / M • Helen Bedd / cr73 / IHV / M • Here Comes Johnny Wadd / 197? / ... / C • Homecoming / 1981 / CA / M • Honey Throat / 1980 / CV / M • Honeybuns #1 / 1987 / WV / C • Honeysuckle Rose / 1979 / CA / M • Hot Child In The City / 1979 / PVX / M • Hot Nurses / 1977 / CA / M • Hot Skin In 3D / 1977 / ... / M • Hot Teenage Lovers / cr73 / VBM / M • I Am Always Ready / 1978 / HIF / M • I Love LA #1 / 1986 / PEN / C • I Love LA #2 / 1989 / PEN / C • I Want You / 1970 / ALP / M • Ice House / 1969 / SOW / S • The Idol / 1985 / WV / M • In Memory Of Connie / 197? / ... / M • Inches For Keisha / 1988 / WV / C • Insatiable #1 / 1980 / CA / M • Inside Desiree Cousteau / 1979 / VCX / M • The Jade Pussycat / 1977 / CA / M • John Holmes And The All-Star Sex Queens / 1984 / AMB / M • John Holmes Classic Series #1 / 1994 / CA / C • John Holmes Classic Series #2 / 1994 / CA / C • John Holmes Classic Series #3 / 1994 / CA / C • John Holmes Classic Series #4 / 1994 / CA / C • John Holmes Classic Series #5 / 1994 / CA / C • John Holmes Exposed / 1978 / AVC / C • John Holmes, King Of X / 1988 / LVI / C • John Holmes, The Lost Films / 1988 / PEN / C • John Holmes, The Man, The Legend / 1995 / EVN / C • Johnny Wadd / 1973 / ALP / M • The Kowloon Connection / 1973 / VCX / M • Lady's Bed Companion / 19?? / AXV / M • Legends Of Porn #1 / 1987 / CV / C • Let Me Count The Lays / 19?? / KOV / C • The Life And Times Of Xavier Hollander / 1973 / VXP / M • Limited Edition #09 / 1980 / AVC / M • Limited Edition #10 / 1980 / AVC / M • Limited Edition #17 / 1980 / AVC / M • Limited Edition #18 / 1980 / AVC / M • Lingerie / 1983 / CDI / M • Lipps & Mccain / 1978 / VC / M • Liquid Lips / 1976 / EVI / M • The Little French Maid / 1981 / VCX / M • Little Me & Marla Strangelove / 1979 / ALP / M • Little Orphan Dusty #1 / 1978 / ALP / M • Lollipop Palace / 1973 / VCX / M • Long Horns / 198? / ... / M • Looking For Mr Goodsex / 1984 / CC / M • Lottery Lust / 1986 / PEN / M • Love Boccaccio Style / 1970 / SOW / S • Love Goddesses / 1981 / VC / M • Love In Strange Places / 1977 / CA / M • Love Match / 198? / ... / G • Love Notes / 1986 /

HO / C • Love Scenes For Loving Couples / 1987 / CV / C • Love With A Proper Stranger / 1973 / VCX / M • The Loves Of Mary Jane / 1989 / BWV / C • Lucky Charm / 1986 / AVC / C • Lust At First Bite / 1978 / VC / M • Lust In America / 1985 / VCX / M • Lusty Princess / 1978 / HIF / M • Marilyn Chambers' Private Fantasies #1 / 1983 / CA / M • Marina Vice / 1985 / PEN / M • Masked Ball / 1975 / VCX / M • Moments Of Love / 1983 / MID / M • Mrs. Rodger's Neighborhood / 1988 / EVN / C • My Tongue Is Quick / cr73 / AXV / M • Nasty Nights / 1988 / PL / C • Nasty Nurses / 1983 / CA / M • Naughty Girls Like It Big / 1986 / ELH / M • The New York City Woman / 1979 / VC / C • A Night On The Wild Side / 1986 / VC / M • Nudes At Eleven #2 / 1987 / AVC / M • Ole / 1971 / KIT / M • One Way At A Time / 1979 / CA / M • Only The Best #1 / 1986 / CV / C • Only The Best Of Barbara Dare / 1990 / CV / C • Only The Best Of Oral / 1989 / CV / C • Open For Business / 1983 / AMB / M • Oral Majority #02 / 1987 / WV / C • Oral Majority #03 / 1986 / WV / C • Orgies / 1987 / WV / C • The Orgy Machine / 197? / AXV / M • Oriental Ecstasy Girls / 1974 / ... / M • Oriental Kitten / 1973 / VCX / M • Panorama Blue / 1974 / ALP / S • Passion Pit / 1985 / SE / M • Passion Play / 1984 / WV / C • The Passion Seekers / cr78 / SIL / S • Passions / 1985 / MIT / M • Personal Services / 1975 / CV / M • Pizza Girls (We Deliver) / 1978 / VCX / M • Playmate #11 / 1984 / VC / M • Princess Charming / 1987 / AVC / C • Prisoner Of Paradise / 1980 / VCX / M • The Private Pleasures Of John C. Holmes / 1983 / ... / G • Private Thighs / 1987 / AVC / C • Remember Connie / 1984 / MAP / M • The Return Of Johnny Wadd / 1986 / PEN / M • Ride A Cocked Horse / 1973 / VEP / M • Rings Of Passion / 1976 / VXP / G • The Rise Of The Roman Empress #1 / 1986 / PV / M • Rockin' With Seka / 1980 / WV / M • Rocky-X #1 / 1986 / PEN / M • Rubdown / 1985 / VCX / M • Salt & Pepper / 1986 / VCS / C • Saturday Night Beaver / 1986 / EVN / M • Scandal In The Mansion / 1985 / CDI / M • Scriptease / 1984 / WV / C • Secret Seduction / 1991 / FLA / C • Seka The Platinum Goddess / 1987 / WV / C • Self Service / cr85 / ... / G • The Senator's Daughter / 1978 / CV / M • Sex And The Single Vampire / 1970 / ALP / S • Sex As You Like It / 1972 / SVE / M • The Sex Machine / 1971 / SOW / M • Sex Psycho / 1971 / SOW / M • Sexual Heights / 1981 / ... / M • The Sexual Secrets Of Marijuana / 1971 / SOW / S • Sheer Panties / 1979 / SE / C • Singlehanded / cr80 / ... / M • Sissy's Hot Summer / 1979 / CA / M • Smash Or How To Get Hung / cr71 / SOW / M • Softie / 19?? / AVC / M • The Spirit Of Seventy Six / 1976 / NGV / M • Stormy / 1980 / CV / M • Studio Of Lust / 1984 / HO / C • Summertime Blue / 1979 / VCX / M • Sunset Strip Girls / 1975 / TGA / M • Superstar John Holmes / 1979 / AVC / M • Swedish Erotica #01 / 1980 / CA / M • Swedish Erotica #02 / 1980 / CA / M • Swedish Erotica #05 / 1980 / CA / M • Swedish Erotica #06 / 1980 / CA / M • Swedish Erotica #07 / 1980 / CA / M • Swedish Erotica #08 / 1980 / CA / M • Swedish Erotica #09 / 1980 / CA / M •

Swedish Erotica #10 / 1980 / CA / M • Swedish Erotica #11 / 1980 / CA / M • Swedish Erotica #12 / 1980 / CA / M • Swedish Erotica #13 / 1980 / CA / M • Swedish Erotica #15 / 1980 / CA / M • Swedish Erotica #16 / 1980 / CA / M • Swedish Erotica #18 / 1980 / CA / M • Swedish Erotica #31 / 1980 / CA / M • Swedish Erotica #44 / 1982 / CA / M • Swedish Erotica #65 / 1985 / CA / M • Swedish Erotica Hard #16: John Holmes Cum Facial / 1992 / OD / C • Swedish Erotica Hard #35: John Holmes Cum Facial #2 / 1992 / OD / C • Swedish Erotica Superstar #1: Seka / 1983 / CA / C • Swedish Erotica Superstar #2: Brigette Monet / 1983 / CA / C • Sweet Alice / 1983 / VCX / M • Sweet Captive / 1979 / EVI / M • Sweet Cheeks / 1980 / VCX / M • Sweet Julie / 1975 / CA / M • Sweet Punkin...I Love You / 1975 / VC / M • Sweet, Sweet Freedom / 19?? / BL / M • The Swing Thing / 1973 / TGA / M • Tapestry Of Passion / 1976 / SE / M • Taxi Girls #1 / 1980 / WV / M • Teenage Cowgirls / 1973 / ALP / M • Teenage Cruisers / 1977 / VCX / M • Teenage Fantasies #2 / 1980 / AR / M • Teenage Madam / 1979 / CXV / M • Tell Them Johnny Wadd Is Here / 1975 / QX / M • That's Erotic / 1979 / CV / C • That's Porno / 1979 / CV / C • This Stud's For You / 1986 / MAP / C • Those Lynn Girls / 1989 / WV / C • Those Young Girls / 1984 / PV / M • Three Came Running / 1974 / AVC / M • The Touch / 19?? / AXV / M • Tough Cookie / cr78 / M$M / C • Treasure Box / 1986 / PEN / M • A Tribute To The King / 1985 / VCX / C • Tropic Of Passion / 1971 / NGV / M • True Legends Of Adult Cinema: The Cult Superstars / 1993 / VC / C • True Legends Of Adult Cinema: The Golden Age / 1992 / VC / C • True Legends Of Adult Cinema: Unsung Superstars / 1993 / VC / C • The Ultimate Pleasure / 1977 / HIF / M • Undulations / 1980 / VC / M • Up 'n' Coming / 1983 / CA / M • VCA Previews #2 / 1988 / VC / C • Virgins In Heat / 1976 / SOW / M • Wait Till He Comes In Me! / 1994 / MET / M • The Whore Of The Worlds / 1985 / PV / M • The Winning Stroke / 1975 / VIS / M • WPINK-TV #1 / 1985 / PV / M • Zolotia / 1973 / AVC / M • [Ginger Lynn Meets John Holmes / 1991 / ... / C • [Inside Amy / 1975 / ... / S • [Over Easy / 19?? / ... / M • [Suburban Satanist / 1974 / ALP / M

JOHN CANNON
East Coast Sluts #06: Philadelphia / 1995 / PL / M

JOHN CHRISTIAN
What About Jane? / 1971 / ALP / M

JOHN CHRISTOPHER
Bang Bang You Got It / 1975 / VXP / M • Hot Dreams / 1983 / CA / M • The Love Syndrome / 1978 / CV / M • Roommates / 1982 / VXP / M • Sharon In The Roughhouse / 1976 / LA / M

JOHN CLEMENS
Devil In Miss Jones #1 / 1972 / VC / M • High Rise / 1973 / QX / M • Saturday Matinee Series #1 / 1996 / VCX / C

JOHN COCKSWELL
Inside Seka / 1980 / VXP / M

JOHN COLLINS *see Star Index I*

JOHN COLT
Fever / 1982 / EVI / C • Las Vegas Erotica

/ 1983 / MVI / M • Marilyn Chambers' Private Fantasies #3 / 1983 / CA / M • The Younger The Better / 1982 / CA / M

JOHN CORLEONE *see Star Index I*

JOHN CURTIS HOLMES *see* John C. Holmes

JOHN D. PLAYER
The Butt, The Boobs, The Lips / 1996 / C69 / M • The Crackster / 1996 / OUP / M • Dirty And Kinky Mature Women #3 / 1995 / C69 / M • Dirty And Kinky Mature Women #4 / 1995 / C69 / M • Gangbang Girl #04 / 1992 / ANA / M • Girlz In The Hood #3: Erotic Justice / 1993 / HW / M • Grateful Grandma's Gang Bang / 1994 / FC / M • Into The Fire / 1994 / ZA / M • Older And Anal #2 / 1995 / FC / M • Positively Pagan #03 / 1991 / ATA / M • Positively Pagan #11 / 1993 / ATA / M • Positively Pagan #12 / 1993 / ATA / M • Star Struck / 1991 / AFV / M

JOHN DALTON
Hong Kong Hookers / 1984 / AMB / M

JOHN DAVENPORT *see Star Index I*

JOHN DAVIDS *see Star Index I*

JOHN DAVIS *see Star Index I*

JOHN DECKER *(Adam Voughan, Adam Voughn)*
As of December 1996 was married to Roxanne Hall.
Adam & Eve's House Party #3: Swing Party / 1996 / VC / M • Addicted To Lust / 1996 / NIT / M • Airotica / 1996 / SC / M • Altered Paradise / 1995 / LE / M • Anal Hellraiser #2 / 1995 / ROB / M • Anal Nurses / 1996 / LBO / M • Ass Busters / 1995 / VMX / C • Babe Watch #5 / 1996 / VC / M • Backdoor Diaries / 1995 / BBE / M • Bareback / 1996 / LE / M • Bodywaves / 1994 / ELP / M • Boobwatch #2 / 1997 / SC / M • Buffy's New Boobs / 1996 / CIN / M • Burlesxxx / 1996 / VT / M • The Butt Sisters Do Houston / 1996 / MID / M • The Butt Sisters Do The Twin Cities / 1996 / MID / M • The Butt Sisters Do Washington D.C. / 1995 / MID / M • Butthead & Beaver / 1993 / HW / M • Carnival / 1995 / PV / M • Centerfold Celebrities '94 #1 / 1994 / SFP / M • Chronicles Of Pain #2 / 1996 / BIZ / B • Chronicles Of Pain #3: Slave Traders / 1996 / BIZ / B • Chronicles Of Pain #4: Tools Of The Trade / 1996 / BIZ / B • The Clock Strikes Bizarre On Butt Row / 1996 / ABS / M • Cloud 900 / 1996 / EYE / M • Colossal Orgy #3 / 1994 / HW / M • Cumback Pussy #3: Coast To Coast Rump Romp / 1996 / EL / M • Cyber-Sex Love Junkies / 1996 / BBE / M • Decadence / 1996 / VC / M • Deep Inside Nikki Sinn / 1996 / VC / C • Deep Seven / 1996 / VC / M • Defiance: The Art Of Spanking / 1996 / BIZ / B • The Desert Cafe / 1996 / NIT / M • Designer Bodies / 1993 / VI / M • The Deviant Doctor / 1996 / NS / M • Devil In A Wet T-Shirt / 1995 / SPI / M • Dick & Jane Big Breast Adventure / 1993 / AVI / M • Dirty Minds / 1996 / NIT / M • A Dirty Western #2: Smoking Guns / 1994 / CV / M • Domina #5: Whipper Snapper / 1996 / LBO / B • Domina #7 / 1996 / LBO / B • Dresden Diary #16: / 1996 / BIZ / B • Eclipse / 1993 / SC / M • Erotic Newcummers Vol 1 #5 / 1996 / DR / M • Erotica Optique / 1994 / SUF / M • Final Obsession / 1996 / LE / M • Flesh / 1996 / EA / M • Fresh Meat (John Leslie) #3 / 1996 / EA / M • Freshness

Counts / 1996 / EL / M • Future Doms #1 / 1996 / BIZ / B • Future Doms #2 / 1996 / BIZ / B • Gang Bang Bitches #08 / 1995 / PP / M • Gang Bang Bitches #11 / 1995 / PP / M • Gang Bang Jizz Queen / 1995 / ROB / M • Generation Sex #2: Nature's Revenge / 1996 / VT / M • Get Lucky / 1996 / NIT / M • Getting Personal / 1995 / PE / M • The Girls From Hootersville #06 / 1994 / SFP / M • Glory Days / 1996 / IN / M • Gold Coast / 1996 / FD / M • Golddiggers #2 / 1995 / VC / M • Golddiggers #3 / 1995 / VC / M • Gun Runner / 1996 / CIN / M • Hollywood Hookers / 1996 / DWV / M • Hollywood Spa / 1996 / WP / M • Hypnotic Hookers #1 / 1996 / NIT / M • In The Line Of Desire / 1996 / MID / M • Indecent Exposures / 1996 / MID / M • Indiscreet! Video Magazine #3 / 1995 / FH / M • Intense Perversions #2 / 1996 / PL / M • Jinx / 1996 / WP / M • Jizz Glazed Goo Guzzlers #1 / 1996 / NIT / C • Joanie Pneumatic / 1996 / PL / M • Kink Show / 1997 / BON / B • Ladies In Leather / 1995 / GO / M • Latex #2 / 1995 / VC / M • Latex And Lace / 1996 / BBE / M • Legend #6: / 1996 / LE / M • Lollipop Shoppe #2 / 1996 / SC / M • Made For A Gangbang / 1995 / ZA / M • The Many Faces Of P.J. Sparxx / 1996 / WP / M • Mistress Kane: Lessons In Terror / 1996 / BIZ / B • More Than A Handful #6: Life Under The Big Top / 1994 / MET / M • Nasty Nymphos #01 / 1993 / ANA / M • Night Stalker / 1995 / BBE / M • Nina Hartley's Guide To Anal Sex / 1996 / A&E / M • One Night In The Valley / 1996 / CA / M • The Orgy #2 / 1993 / EMC / M • The Other Woman / 1996 / VC / M • Phantasm / 1995 / WP / M • Please Take A Number / 1996 / CDI / M • Pounding Ass / 1995 / VMX / M • Prescription For Pleasure / 1993 / HW / M • Profiles #05: Planet Lust / 1995 / XPR / M • Promises And Lies / 1996 / NIT / M • Raincoat Fantasies / 1993 / ELP / M • Rainwoman #10: The Tenth Anniversary Edition / 1996 / CC / M • Raunchy Remedy / 1993 / ELP / M • Rebel Without A Condom / 1996 / ERA / M • Reckless / 1995 / NOT / M • Reckless Encounters / 1995 / LE / M • Reel People #04 / 1994 / PP / M • The Return Of Dr Blacklove / 1996 / CC / M • Road Kill / 1995 / CA / M • Sex Academy #2: The Art Of Talking Dirty / 1994 / ONA / M • Sex For Hire / 1996 / ONA / M • Sex Freaks / 1995 / EA / M • The Shocking Truth #1 / 1996 / DWO / M • A Shot In The Pink / 1995 / BBE / M • Sisters / 1993 / ZA / M • Snake Pit / 1996 / DWO / M • Sodomania #06: Gangs And Bangs And Other Thangs / 1993 / EL / M • Sodomania #21: Degenerate Lifestyles! / 1997 / EL / M • Sodomania: Slop Shots / 1996 / EL / C • Southern Comfort #1 / 1995 / DWV / M • Southern Comfort #2 / 1995 / DWV / M • Spazm #1: Point Blank / 1996 / LBO / M • Stalking Of Slave Laura / 1996 / BIZ / B • Steamy Sins / 1996 / IN / M • Strip Show / 1996 / CA / M • The Strippers / 1995 / GO / M • Strippers Inc. #5 / 1995 / ONA / M • The Submission Of Alicia Rio / 1996 / BIZ / B • Sweet As Honey / 1996 / NIT / M • Taboo #16 / 1996 / CV / M • Tainted Love / 1996 / VC / M • Takin' It To The Limit #9: Rear Action View / 1996 / BS / M • Tight Spot / 1996 / WV / M • Titty Slickers #3 / 1996 / LE / M • Trading Partners / 1995 / GO / M • The Ultimate Fantasy /

1995 / CV / M • Ultimate Sensations / 1996 / NIT / M • Undercover / 1996 / VC / M • Underground #1 / 1996 / SC / M • Underground #2: Subway To Sodom / 1996 / SC / M • Underground #3: Sit On This / 1996 / SC / M • Unleashed / 1996 / SAE / M • Up And Cummers #33 / 1996 / 4P / M • The Usual Anal Suspects / 1996 / CC / M • Valley Cooze / 1996 / SC / M • Venom #1 / 1995 / VD / M • Venom #2 / 1996 / VD / M • Venom #6 / 1996 / CA / M • Wet & Wicked / 1995 / PRK / M • White Men Can't Iron On Butt Row / 1997 / ABS / M • The Wicked Web / 1996 / WP / M • The Wild Ones / 1996 / CC / M • Women Of Color #1 / 1994 / ANA / M • The X-Rated OJ Truth... / 1995 / MID / M • XXX Channel / 1996 / VT / M

JOHN DILLON *see Star Index I*

JOHN DOUGLAS *see* Jon Dough

JOHN DRAGON
Girlz N The Hood #2 / 1992 / HW / M • Hard Core Cafe / 1988 / VD / M • Paris Models / 1987 / CDI / M • Rumpman In And Out Of Africa / 1996 / HW / M • The Wedding / 1986 / VC / M

JOHN DUGAN
Postgraduate Course In Sexual Love / 1975 / QX / M • The Texas Chainsaw Massacre / 1974 / WIZ / S

JOHN DURGESS *see Star Index I*

JOHN DUVAL
Blonde In Black Lace / 1975 / VCX / M

JOHN DUVAL (JOSE) *see* Jose Duval

JOHN EDWARDS *see Star Index I*

JOHN ENGLANDER
Private Film #13 / 1994 / OD / M

JOHN EVERSON
Love Lips / 1976 / VC / M

JOHN EWBANKS
Agony Of Love, Lace And Lash / cr73 / SOW / M • Bucky Beaver's XXX Dragon Art Theatre Double Feature #14 / 1996 / SOW / M

JOHN FIELGUD
Undercovers / 1982 / CA / M

JOHN FORREST
The Black Mystique / 1986 / CV / M

JOHN FOXX
Bad Company / 1978 / CV / M • Sexual Ecstasy Of The Macumba / 1975 / ... / M

JOHN FRANCIS
The Experience / 1988 / LON / B • Legacy Of Satan / 19?? / APB / S • Strange Days / 1995 / FXV / S

JOHN FRANKS
Beyond The Blue / cr78 / SVE / M • Sexual Communication / 19?? / HIF / M

JOHN FRASER
American Sex Fantasy / 1975 / IHV / M

JOHN G. *see Star Index I*

JOHN GATT *see Star Index I*

JOHN GIANNELLI
Overnight Sensation / 1976 / AR / M

JOHN GOLD
Inside Seka / 1980 / VXP / M • Seka Is Tara / 1981 / VC / M

JOHN GOODBAR *see Star Index I*

JOHN GRAHAM
Pony Girl #2: At The Ranch / 1986 / CS / B

JOHN HAMMER *see* Johnny Warner

JOHN HANDLER
Bad Girls #1 / 1981 / GO / M • Bad Girls #2 / 1983 / GO / M

JOHN HART
Blackenstein / 1973 / MED / S • Day Of The Nightmare / 1965 / SOW / S • Princess

Seka / 1980 / VC / M

JOHN HENDERSON
Blazing Zippers / 1974 / SE / M • Jail Bait / 1976 / VC / M

JOHN HERDE
Private Film #04 / 1993 / OD / M

JOHN HILLIOUS
Resurrection Of Eve / 1973 / MIT / M

JOHN HIRES see Star Index I

JOHN HOLLABAUGH
Sweet Savage / 1978 / ALP / M

JOHN HOLLYFIELD
Endless Lust / 1983 / VC / M • Little Girls Lost / 1982 / VC / M • A Little More Than Love / 1977 / SE / M • The Master And Mrs. Johnson / 1980 / SAT / M • Porno Screentests / 1982 / VC / M • Ring Of Desire / 1981 / SE / M • Scandalous Simone / 1985 / SE / M • Stephanie's Lust Story / 1983 / VC / M • VCA Previews #2 / 1988 / VC / C • A Very Small Case Of Rape / 1977 / TRP / M

JOHN HOLT see Star Index I
JOHN HOOKER see Star Index I
JOHN HYDE see Star Index I
JOHN JACKSON see Star Index I

JOHN JAMIESON
The Girls In The Band / 1976 / SVE / M

JOHN JANEIRO see Alex San Paolo
JOHN JANIERO see Alex San Paolo

JOHN JEAN
Teenage Deviates / 1975 / SVE / M

JOHN JOHNSON
Bedtime Video #07 / 1984 / GO / M • Leave It To Cleavage #1 / 1988 / GO / M • Vixens In Heat / 1984 / ECS / M

JOHN JONES
Magma: Spezial: Black & White #3 / 1995 / MET / M

JOHN KEATE
The Sex Machine / 1971 / SOW / M

JOHN KOVEN see Star Index I
JOHN LABETE see Star Index I

JOHN LANDER
The Desirous Wife / 1988 / PL / M

JOHN LAWRENCE
Alice In Wonderland / 1976 / CA / M • The Seven Minutes / 1971 / ST0 / S

JOHN LAZAR
Attack Of The 60 Foot Centerfold / 1995 / NEH / S • Beyond The Valley Of The Dolls / 1970 / CBS / S • Supervixens / 1975 / RMV / S • Up 'n' Coming / 1983 / CA / M

JOHN LEE
Bouncin' In The U.S.A. / 1986 / H&S / S • Deep Inside Ginger Lynn / 1986 / SE / C • Hidden Obsessions / 1992 / BFP / M

JOHN LENIN
Anita / 1996 / BLC / M • The Voyeur #8: Live In Europe #2 / 1996 / JLP / M

JOHN LESLIE *(John Leslie Dupree, John Lestor, Lenny Kent, John Nuzzo)*
Started as a worker in an Ohio steel mill and then moved to NYC in the early sixties to pursue a career as a painter. Worked for several pulp magazines as an illustrator, took up the blue's harmonica and moved to SFO in 1974. First movie was **Coming Attractions** where he is credited as John Nuzzo.
The $50,000,000 Cherry / 1987 / VD / M • 10 1/2 Weeks / 1986 / SE / M • 1001 Erotic Nights #1 / 1982 / VC / M • The 8th Annual Erotic Film Awards / 1984 / SE / C • A.S.S.(Anal Security Squad) / 1988 / VD / M • Addicted To Love / 1988 / WAV / M •

Adult 45 #01 / 1985 / DR / C • All For His Ladies / 1987 / PP / C • Amazing Sex Stories #2 / 1987 / SUV / C • And I Do Windows Too / 1986 / PP / M • Angel Of The Island / 1988 / IN / M • Angela Baron Series #1 / 1988 / VD / C • Angela Baron Series #2 / 1988 / VD / C • Angela Baron Series #3 / 1988 / VD / C • Angela Baron Series #4 / 1988 / VD / C • Angela Baron Series #5 / 1988 / VD / C • Angela Baron Series #6 / 1988 / VD / C • Anna Obsessed / 1978 / ALP / M • The Art Of Passion / 1987 / CA / M • Aunt Peg's Fulfillment / 1980 / CV / M • The Autobiography Of A Flea / 1976 / MIT / M • Baby Face #1 / 1977 / VC / M • Baby Rosemary / 1975 / SE / M • Babylon Gold/ 1983 / COM / C • Bad Girls #1 / 1981 / GO / M • Ball Busters / 1984 / CV / M • Barbara Dare's Bad / 1988 / SE / C • Barbara Dare's Roman Holiday / 1987 / SE / M • Beauty And The Beast #1 / 1988 / VC / M • Beauty And The Beast #2 / 1990 / VC / M • Bedtime Tales / 1985 / SE / M • Bedtime Video #01 / 1984 / GO / M • Bedtime Video #04 / 1984 / GO / M • Behind The Scenes Of An Adult Movie / 1983 / CV / M • The Best Little Whorehouse In Hong Kong / 1987 / SE / M • The Best Of Alex De Renzy #1 / 1983 / VC / C • The Best Of Gail Palmer / 1981 / WWV / C • Best Of Talk Dirty To Me #01 / 1991 / DR / C • Between Lovers / 1983 / CA / M • Between The Sheets / 1982 / CA / M • Beyond Desire / 1986 / VC / M • Big House Babes / 19?? / VC / M • The Bitches Of Westwood / 1987 / CA / M • Black Beauty (Ebony & Ivory) / 1989 / E&I / M • Black Silk Stockings / 1978 / SE / C • Black Widow's Nest / 1976 / ... / M • Blonde Heat (VCA) / 1985 / VC / M • The Blonde Next Door / 1982 / GO / M • Blondes Have More Fun / 1980 / SE / M • Blondes On Fire / 1987 / VCR / C • Blue Confessions / 1983 / VCR / M • Blue Movie / 1989 / VD / M • Blue Vanities #016 (New) / 1988 / FFL / M • Blue Vanities #090 / 1988 / FFL / M • Blue's Velvet / 1979 / ECV / M • Body Games / 1987 / DR / M • Boiling Point / 1978 / SE / M • Boom Boom Valdez / 1988 / CA / M • Born For Love / 1987 / ... / M • Born To Be Bad / 1987 / CV / M • Born To Run / 1985 / WV / M • Breakin' In / 1986 / WV / M • Breaking It #1 / 1984 / COL / M • Built For Sex (Angela Baron's) / 1988 / FAZ / C • Caballero Preview Tape #2 / 1983 / CA / C • Caballero Preview Tape #4 / 1985 / CA / C • California Blondes #03 / 1991 / VD / C • The Call Girl / 1986 / VD / M • Candy Goes To Hollywood / 1979 / VCX / M • Candy's Little Sister Sugar / 1988 / VD / M • Careena #1 / 1987 / WV / C • Careena #2: A Star On The Rise / 1988 / WV / C • Carnal Games / 1978 / BL / M • Carnal Haven / 1976 / SVE / M • The Case Of The Sensuous Sinners / 1988 / ME / M • The Catwoman / 1988 / VC / M • Celebrity Presents Celebrity / 1986 / VEP / C • Cells Of Passion / 1981 / VD / M • Centerfold Celebrities #4 / 1983 / VC / M • Centerfold Celebrities #5 / 1983 / VC / M • Champagne For Breakfast / 1980 / SE / M • Chastity And The Starlets / 1986 / RAV / M • Cherry Tricks / 1985 / VPE / M • Cheryl Hanson: Cover Girl / 1981 / SE / M • China Sisters / 1978 / SE / M • Cinderella / 1985 / VEL / M • Classic Erotica #1 / 1980 / SVE / M • Classic Pics / 1988 / PP / C • Classic

Swedish Erotica #05 / 1986 / CA / C • Classic Swedish Erotica #11 / 1986 / CA / C • Classic Swedish Erotica #14 / 1986 / CA / C • Classic Swedish Erotica #18 / 1986 / CA / C • Classic Swedish Erotica #29 / 1987 / CA / C • Classic Swedish Erotica #33 / 1987 / CA / C • Club Ecstasy / 1987 / CA / M • Coed Fever / 1980 / CA / M • Coming Attractions / 1976 / VEP / M • A Coming Of Angels / 1977 / CA / M • Coming On Strong / 1989 / CA / C • Confessions Of A Woman / 1976 / SE / M • Conflict / 1988 / VD / M • Cottontail Club / 1985 / HO / M • Critics' Choice #2 / 1984 / SE / C • Cry For Cindy / 1976 / AR / M • Dames / 1985 / SE / M • The Dancers / 1981 / VCX / M • Debbie Does Dishes #3 / 1987 / AVC / M • Debbie For President / 1988 / CC / M • Debbie Goes To Hawaii / 1988 / VD / C • Deep Inside Brittany O'connell / 1996 / VC / C • Deep Inside Ona Zee / 1992 / VC / C • Deep Inside Shanna Mccullough / 1992 / VC / C • Desires Within Young Girls / 1977 / CA / M • Diamond Collection #05 / 1979 / CDI / M • Diamond Head / 1987 / AVC / M • Dixie / 1976 / VHL / M • Dixie Ray Hollywood Star / 1983 / CA / M • Dog Walker / 1994 / EA / M • Dominatrix Without Mercy / 1976 / ALP / B • Double Desires / 1988 / PIN / C • Double Penetration #3 / 1986 / WV / C • Double Pleasure / 1985 / VCR / M • Dy-Nasty / 1988 / SE / M • Easy Alice / 1976 / VC / M • Ebony Love / 1992 / VT / C • Ecstasy / 1986 / PP / M • The Ecstasy Girls #1 / 1979 / CA / M • The Ecstasy Girls #2 / 1986 / CA / M • Electric Blue: World Nudes Tonight / 1985 / CA / C • The Erotic Adventures Of Candy / 1978 / VCX / M • Erotic City / 1985 / CV / M • Erotic Fantasies #1 / 1983 / CV / C • Erotic Fantasies #2 / 1983 / CV / C • Erotic Fantasies #3 / 1983 / CV / C • Erotic Fantasies #4 / 1983 / CV / C • Erotic Fantasies: John Leslie / 1985 / CV / C • The Erotic World Of Crystal Dawn (#3) / 1983 / VCR / C • Erotic Zones #1 / 1985 / CA / M • Every Woman Has A Fantasy #1 / 1984 / VC / M • Every Woman Has A Fantasy #2 / 1986 / VC / M • Expensive Taste / 1978 / VCX / M • Expert Tease / 1988 / CC / M • Exploring Young Girls / 1978 / ALP / M • Exposed / 1980 / SE / M • Exposure / 1988 / VD / M • Extremes / 1981 / CA / M • F / 1980 / GO / M • F...It / 1987 / SE / C • Famous Ta-Ta's #1 / 1986 / VCS / C • Fantasex Island / 1983 / NSV / M • Fantasies Of Jennifer Faye / 1983 / GO / M • Fantasy Peeps: Black On White / 1985 / 4P / M • Fantasy Peeps: Sensuous Delights / 1984 / 4P / M • Farmers Daughters / 1985 / WV / M • Femmes De Sade / 1976 / ALP / M • The Final Taboo / 1988 / CA / M • Fiona On Fire / 1978 / VC / M • Firestorm #1 / 1984 / COM / M • Firestorm #2: The Angel Blade / 1986 / COM / M • Firestorm #3 / 1986 / COM / M • First Annual XRCO Awards / 1984 / AVC / C • Fleshdance / 1983 / SE / M • For Your Love / 1988 / IN / M • Forbidden Worlds / 1988 / GO / C • Four X Feeling / 1986 / QX / M • Foxy Lady / 1978 / CV / M • Fresh Meat (John Leslie) #3 / 1996 / EA / M • Friday The 13th #1: A Nude Beginning / 1987 / VD / M • Frisky Business / 1984 / VC / M • Fury In Alice / 1976 / SVE / M • Garage Girls / 1981 / CV / M • Getting Off / 1979 / VIP / M • Girl Scout Cookies / 197? / SVE

JOHN LIVERMORE
Come With Me, My Love / 1976 / PVX / M
JOHN LONG
Black Beauty (Ebony & Ivory) / 1989 / E&I / M
JOHN LOPEZ
Latin Plump Humpers #1 / 1995 / TTV / M
JOHN LOURDES
Girls With Curves #1 / 1985 / CV / M
JOHN MADDOX *see* **Henri Pachard**
JOHN MANN
Hot Pursuit / 1983 / VC / M
JOHN MARK
Just One Look / 1993 / V99 / M • Make Me Sweat / 1994 / V99 / M
JOHN MARSHALL
Whatever Happened To Miss September? / 1973 / ALP / M
JOHN MARTIN *see* **Jon Martin**
JOHN MARTINEZ
Inside Desiree Cousteau / 1979 / VCX / M
JOHN MCDUFFY *see* **Star Index I**
JOHN MCGUIRE
Hardcore: The Films Of Richard Kern #1 / 1991 / FTV / M
JOHN MCKINNIS
Gettin' Ready / 1985 / CDI / M
JOHN MCKNIGHT *see* **Ric Lutz**
JOHN MORE *see* **Star Index I**
JOHN MORGAN *see* **Jonathan Morgan**
JOHN MORTON *see* **Jon Martin**
JOHN MOSER
Dark Discipline / 1994 / STM / B • Submissive Exposure Profile #5: Keli Thomas / 1996 / STM / C • Women Who Control The Family Jewels #4 / 1995 / STM / B
JOHN MURPHY
Reel People #04 / 1994 / PP / M
JOHN NICHOLS *see* **Star Index I**
JOHN NORMAN
Temptations / 1976 / VXP / M
JOHN NUZZO *see* **John Leslie**
JOHN O'CONNELL
The Orgy #2 / 1993 / EMC / M • The Portrait Of Dorie Grey / 1996 / KLP / M • Silver Screen Confidential / 1996 / WP / M • Student Fetish Videos: Bondage #02 / 1996 / PRE / B • Student Fetish Videos: Tickling #12 / 1995 / SFV / B • The Time Machine / 1996 / WP / M • Voices In My Bed / 1993 / VI / M • Wilder At Heart / 1993 / ANA / M
JOHN O'KEEFE *see* **Star Index I**
JOHN OCEAN *see* **John Seeman**
JOHN OGDEN
The Girl From S.E.X. / 1982 / CA / M • Let's Talk Sex / 1982 / CA / M • Lips: The Passage To Pleasure / 1981 / CA / M
JOHN OURY
Clarissa / 1978 / LUM / S • Flying Skirts / 1985 / HO / M • House Of 1001 Pleasures / 1985 / VC / M • Mobile Home Girls / 1985 / VC / M • Perverse / 1984 / CA / M • Take My Body / 1984 / SE / M
JOHN PACWOOD
Nineteen #2 / 1996 / FOR / M • Nineteen #3 / 1996 / FOR / M • Nineteen #4 / 1996 / FOR / M
JOHN PAISE *see* **Star Index I**
JOHN PAUL ANTHONY *see* **J.P. Anthony**
JOHN PAUL JONES
The Loves Of Mary Jane / 1989 / BWV / C • Resurrection Of Eve / 1973 / MIT / M • A Touch Of Sex / 1972 / AR / M
JOHN PECKER
Tripper Stripper / 1995 / VMX / M
JOHN PETERS *see* **Star Index I**

JOHN PIERCE
Adultery For Fun And Profit / 1971 / SOW / M • Ego Trip / 1969 / SOW / S • This Gun Is Loaded / 1970 / SOW / S
JOHN PLAYER
Older Women Younger Men #3 / 1993 / CC / M
JOHN POTTS
The Loves Of Mary Jane / 1989 / BWV / C • A Touch Of Sex / 1972 / AR / M
JOHN PRESSMAN *see* **Star Index I**
JOHN PRINCE
Bondage Memories #03 / 1994 / BON / C • Cindy Prince #1 / 1993 / BON / B • Cindy Prince #2 / 1993 / BON / B • Cindy Prince #3 / 1993 / BON / B • Cindy Prince #4 / 1993 / BON / B
JOHN RAGE *see* **John Wright**
JOHN RAMMER
Big Black Bang / 1996 / HW / M • Black Playhouse / 1995 / HBE / M • Ho Duzzit Model Agency #2 / 1993 / AFV / M • Rump Humpers #05 / 1992 / GLI / M
JOHN RAND *see* **Star Index I**
JOHN REESE
All The Way / 1980 / CDC / M • Fastlane Fuck-Holes! / 1994 / MET / M
JOHN RENSEN
Jungle Heat / 1995 / LUM / M
JOHN REY *see* **John C. Holmes**
JOHN REYNOLDS *see* **John Seeman**
JOHN ROBE
Romance & Fantasy / 1995 / VEX / M
JOHN ROCKLIN *see* **Star Index I**
JOHN ROLLING
Seven Into Snowy / 1977 / VC / M • The Untamed / 1978 / VCX / M • Visions Of Clair / 1977 / WWV / M
JOHN ROMPS *see* **Star Index I**
JOHN RUSSELL *see* **Jason Russell**
JOHN SAGE *see* **Star Index I**
JOHN SANBORN
Fan Fuxxx #2 / 1997 / DWV / M
JOHN SARDI
Looking Good / 1984 / ABV / M
JOHN SAUNDERS
Naughty Nurses / 1982 / VCR / M
JOHN SAVAGE
Bondage Classix #01: Making Danielle Talk / 1987 / BON / B • Bondage Classix #10: Painful Mistake / 1993 / BON / B • Bondage Memories #01 / 1993 / BON / C • The Dangerous / 1994 / ORI / S • John Savage: Bondage Master / 1991 / BON / B • The Killing Kind / 1973 / NEO / S • Killing Obsession / 1994 / TRI / S • Maria's Lovers / 1984 / MGM / S
JOHN SEEMAN *(John Toland, Jay Seemon, John Simon, John Ocean, John Reynolds, Roy Stells, John Shipley, Nag Analf, John Semany)*
All The Way In / 1984 / VC / M • Baby Rosemary / 1975 / SE / M • Baroness De Nica / 1972 / ALP / M • Black Beauty (Playtime) / 19?? / PLY / C • Blazing Zippers / 1974 / SE / M • Blonde Fire / 1979 / EVI / M • Blondes Have More Fun / 1980 / SE / M • Blue Vanities #017 (New) / 1988 / FFL / M • Blue Vanities #048 / 1988 / FFL / M • Blue Vanities #251 / 1996 / FFL / M • Body Candy / 1980 / VIS / M • Boiling Point / 1978 / SE / M • Bottoms Up #02 / 1983 / AVC / C • Bucky Beaver's XXX Dragon Art Theatre Double Feature #09 / 1996 / SOW / M • Carnal Highways / 1980 / HIF / M • Casanova #2 / 1976 / CA / M • Caught In

The Act / 1978 / MAP / M • Ceremony, The Ritual Of Love / 1976 / AVC / M • Champagne For Breakfast / 1980 / SE / M • The China Cat / 1978 / CA / M • Chopstix / 1979 / TVX / M • Classic Swedish Erotica #35 / 1987 / CA / C • Cry For Cindy / 1976 / AR / M • Deep Rub / 1979 / VC / M • Dental Nurse / 1973 / VXP / M • Desires Within Young Girls / 1977 / CA / M • Dixie / 1976 / VHL / M • Dream Girl / 1974 / AVC / M • Erotic Fantasies #3 / 1983 / CV / C • Erotic Fantasies #5 / 1983 / CV / C • Erotic Fortune Cookies / 1975 / VCX / M • Expensive Taste / 1978 / VCX / M • Exposed / 1980 / SE / M • Fantasex Island / 1983 / NSV / M • Fantasy In Blue / 1975 / IHV / M • Female Athletes / 1977 / VXP / M • The First Time I Ever... / cr75 / AR / M • For The Love Of Pleasure / 1979 / SE / M • Forbidden Desire / 1983 / NSV / M • A Formal Faucett / 1978 / VC / M • Garage Girls / 1981 / CV / M • Good To The Last Drop / 1986 / VCS / C • The Gypsy Ball / 1979 / ENC / M • Hardgore / 1973 / ALP / M • The Health Spa / 1978 / SE / M • House of Kinky Pleasures / 1975 / VCX / C • The House Of Strange Desires / 1985 / NSV / M • Inside Desiree Cousteau / 1979 / VCX / M • Island Of Dr Love / 1977 / S&L / M • The Journey Of O / 1975 / TVX / M • The Joy Of Letting Go / 1976 / SE / M • Judgement Day / 1976 / CV / M • Limited Edition #04 / 1979 / AVC / M • Little Girls Blue #1 / 1977 / VCX / M • The Live Show / 1979 / SVE / M • Long Hard Summer / 1989 / BMV / C • Love Secrets / 1976 / VIP / M • The Loves Of Mary Jane / 1989 / BWV / C • Midnight Hustle / 1978 / VC / M • Milk Chocolate / cr75 / VIS / M • Most Valuable Slut / 1973 / HLV / M • Ms. Magnificent / 1979 / SE / M • Night Pleasures / 1975 / WWV / M • Pizza Girls (We Deliver) / 1978 / VCX / M • Please Me! / cr86 / LIM / M • The Pleasure Hunt #1 / 1984 / NSV / M • Ready When You Are, CB / 19?? / BL / M • Rendezvous With Anne / 1973 / BL / M • Satisfaction / 1974 / CDC / M • Saturday Matinee Series #1 / 1996 / VCX / C • Screwples / 1979 / CA / M • Seka In Heat / 1988 / BMV / C • Service Entrance / 1979 / REG / C • Small Town Girls / 1979 / CXV / M • The Spirit Of Seventy Six / 1976 / NGV / M • The Starlets / 1976 / RAV / M • Steamy Sirens / 1984 / AIR / C • Stormy / 1980 / CV / M • Sweet Folds Of Flesh / 19?? / AST / M • Sweet Savage / 1978 / ALP / M • A Taste Of Sugar / 1978 / AR / M • Taxi Girls #1 / 1980 / WV / M • Teenage Desires / 1975 / IVP / M • Teenage Madam / 1979 / CXV / M • Teenage Runaway / 1973 / AXV / M • Teeny Buns / 1977 / VC / M • The Tender Trap / 1978 / IHV / M • That's Porno / 1979 / CV / C • Too Hot To Touch #1 / 1985 / CV / M • Triple Play / 1983 / HO / M • Ultraflesh / 1980 / GO / M • The Untamed / 1978 / VCX / M • Up In Flames / 1973 / SOW / M • V—The Hot One / 1978 / CV / M • Young Girls Do / 1984 / ELH / M • Yuppies In Heat / 1988 / CHA / C • [Fuck Me, Suck Me, Eat Me / 1990 / ... / M • [Wolf / 197? / ... / M
JOHN SEMANY *see* **John Seeman**
JOHN SHERIDAN
[Sorority Suck Sisters / 197? / ... / M
JOHN SHIPLEY *see* **John Seeman**
JOHN SIGLIONE
The Girl From S.E.X. / 1982 / CA / M

JOHN SILKWOOD
Frenzy / 1992 / SC / M • Worshipping Goddess Sondra / 1993 / VER / B • WPINK-TV #5 / 1993 / PV / M

JOHN SIMMONS *see* Chris Reed

JOHN SIMON *see* John Seeman

JOHN SIMPLE *see* Star Index I

JOHN SLUG
Every Man Should Have One / 1991 / VEX / M

JOHN SMITH
The Legend Of Lady Blue / 1978 / VCX / M • Take Off / 1978 / VXP / M

JOHN SMITH (1996)
Fame Is A Whore On Butt Row / 1996 / ABS / M

JOHN ST VINCENT
Switch Hitters #3: Squeeze Play / 1988 / IN / G

JOHN STAG *see* John Stagliano

JOHN STAGLIANO *(John Stag, John Staglione, Buttman)*
Male actor/dancer turned director. 38 years old in 1990. Took dance classes at UCLA and then a job in the first show of Chippendale's in LA in 1979. In early 1997 tested positive for HIV due (according to him) to a previously undisclosed homosexual relationship.
The Adventures Of Buttman / 1989 / EA / M • American Buttman In London / 1991 / EA / M • Amos & Candy / 1987 / VCR / C • Anatomy Of A Male Stripper / 1990 / 4P / S • Awesome #01 / 1986 / 4P / C • Backdoor To Hollywood #04 / 1988 / CDI / M • Bend Over Babes #1 / 1990 / EA / M • Bend Over Babes #2 / 1991 / EA / M • Bend Over Babes #3 / 1992 / EA / M • Bend Over Babes #4 / 1996 / EA / M • Bend Over Brazilian Babes #1 / 1993 / EA / M • Bend Over Brazilian Babes #2 / 1993 / EA / M • Best Of Buttman #1 / 1991 / EA / C • Best Of Buttman #2 / 1993 / EA / C • The Big Tease #1 / 1990 / VC / M • The Big Tease #2 / 1990 / VC / M • Blame It On Bambi / 1992 / BS / B • Blondes On Fire / 1987 / VCR / C • Bondage Interludes #1 / 1983 / BIZ / B • Bondage Interludes #2 / 1983 / BIZ / B • Bound For Slavery / 1983 / BLB / B • Bruce Seven: A Compendium Of His Most Graphic Scenes Vol 1 / 1991 / BS / C • Butt Banged Bicycle Babes / 1994 / ANA / M • Butt Banged Cycle Sluts / 1995 / ANA / M • Butt Freak #1 / 1992 / EA / M • Butt Freak #2 / 1996 / EA / M • Butt Row Unplugged / 1996 / ABS / M • Buttman At Nudes A Poppin' #1 / 1992 / EA / S • Buttman At Nudes A Poppin' #3 / 1996 / EA / S • Buttman Goes To Rio #1 / 1990 / EA / M • Buttman Goes To Rio #2 / 1991 / EA / M • Buttman Goes To Rio #3 / 1992 / EA / M • Buttman Goes To Rio #4 / 1993 / EA / M • Buttman In Barcelona / 1996 / EA / M • Buttman Vs Buttwoman / 1992 / EL / M • Buttman's Big Tit Adventure #1 / 1992 / EA / M • Buttman's Big Tit Adventure #3 / 1995 / EA / M • Buttman's British Moderately Big Tit Adventure / 1994 / EA / M • Buttman's Bubble Butt Babes / 1996 / EA / M • Buttman's European Vacation #1 / 1991 / EA / M • Buttman's European Vacation #2 / 1992 / EA / M • Buttman's Inferno / 1993 / EA / M • Buttman's Orgies / 1996 / EA / M • Buttman's Revenge / 1992 / EA / M • Buttman's Ultimate Workout / 1990 / EA / M • Buttman's Wet Dream / 1994 / EA / M •

Cheeks #5: The Ultimate Butt / 1991 / CC / M • The Clock Strikes Bizarre On Butt Row / 1996 / ABS / M • Coming Attractions / 1976 / VEP / M • D-Cup Delights / 1987 / VCR / M • Dance Fire / 1989 / EA / M • Delinquents On Butt Row / 1996 / EA / M • Dirty Stories #4 / 1995 / PE / M • English Class / 1995 / VC / M • Erotic Aerobics / 1984 / VC / M • Eye Of The Tigress / 1988 / VD / M • Face Dance #1 / 1992 / EA / M • Face Dance #2 / 1992 / EA / M • The Fear Zone / 1991 / BS / B • Flesh & Laces #1 / 1983 / CA / M • Flesh & Laces #2 / 1983 / CA / M • Girls Of The Double D #08 / 1989 / CDI / M • The Good Time Girls / 1985 / VEX / M • Hot Shorts: Sandy Taylor / 1986 / VCR / C • Impulse #07: / 1996 / MBP / M • Indecent Itch / 1985 / VCR / M • A Journey Into Darkness / 1991 / BS / B • Just Another Pretty Face / 1985 / AVC / M • Just For The Hell Of It / 1991 / CA / M • The Legend Of Reggie D. / 1989 / EA / M • Lovin' Spoonfuls #7 / 1996 / 4P / C • More Dirty Debutantes #32 / 1994 / 4P / M • Mystic Pieces / 1989 / EA / M • Party Of Payne / 1993 / BS / B • Power Play (Bruce Seven) / 1990 / BS / B • Prague By Night #1 / 1996 / EA / M • Prague By Night #2 / 1996 / EA/ M • Shadow Dancers #1 / 1989 / EA / M • Shadow Dancers #2 / 1989 / EA / M • Sodomania #05: Euro-American Style / 1993 / EL / M • Sodomania #14: C**t Lickin', C*m Drinkin' Bitches / 1995 / EL / M • Sodomania: The Baddest Of The Best...And Then Some / 1994 / EL / C • Striptease / 1983 / VC / M • Takin' It To The Limit #6 / 1995 / BS / M • The Teacher's Pet / 1985 / WV / M • Traci's Big Trick / 1987 / VAS / M • Undercovers / 1982 / CA / M • Very Sexy Ballet / 1988 / CA / M • Wild Goose Chase / 1990 / EA / M • World Sex Tour #6 / 1996 / ANA / M • Young And Restless / 1983 / VIV / M

JOHN STAGLIONE *see* John Stagliano

JOHN STALLION
Object(s) Of My Desire / 1988 / V99 / M

JOHN T. BONE *(Harry Horndog, Naomi Goldsmith, John Bowen)*
British (Manchester, England) porno director and star. Aged 49 in 1996. The Naomi Goldsmith name was used as a director.
America's Raunchiest Home Videos #43: Cum Blow My Horn / 1992 / ZA / M • America's Raunchiest Home Videos #44: Interracial Orgy Relay / 1992 / ZA / M • America's Raunchiest Home Videos #45: The Bigger They Cum / 1992 / ZA / M • American Connection Video Magazine #01 / 1992 / ZA / M • American Connection Video Magazine #02 / 1992 / ZA / M • American Connection Video Magazine #03 / 1993 / ZA / M • American Swinger Video Magazine #04 / 1993 / ZA / M • American Swinger Video Magazine #05 / 1993 / ZA / M • American Swinger Video Magazine #06 / 1993 / ZA / M • American Swinger Video Magazine #07 / 1993 / ZA / M • The British Are Coming / 1993 / ZA / M • Dark Secrets / 1995 / MID / S • Dirty Old Men #1 / 1995 / FPI / M • The Goddess / 1993 / ZA / M • Harry Horndog #04: Amateur Anal Orgies #1 / 1992 / ZA / M • Harry Horndog #09: Anal Orgy #2 / 1992 / ZA / M • Harry Horndog #10: Love Puppies #1 / 1992 / ZA / M • Harry Horndog #11: Love Puppies #2 / 1992 / ZA / M • Harry Horndog #14: Love

Puppies #3 / 1992 / ZA / M • Harry Horndog #16: Love Puppies #4 / 1992 / ZA / M • Harry Horndog #17: Love Puppies #5 / 1993 / ZA / M • Harry Horndog #19: Anal Lovers #3 / 1993 / ZA / M • Harry Horndog #20: Love Puppies #6 / 1993 / ZA / M • Harry Horndog #22: Huge Hooters / 1993 / ZA / M • Harry Horndog #28: Fabulous Squirt Queens / 1994 / FPI / M • Harry Horndog #29: Anal Lovers #5 / 1995 / FPI / M • Harry Horndog #30: Love Puppies #7 / 1995 / FPI / M • Horny Old Broads / 1995 / FPI / M • Laying Down The Law #1 / 1992 / AFV / M • Laying Down The Law #2 / 1992 / AFV / M • Outback Assignment / 1991 / VD / M • Songbird / 1993 / AMP / M • Starbangers #04 / 1993 / FPI / M • Starbangers #05 / 1993 / FPI / M • Who Killed Holly Hollywood? / 1993 / VC / M • The World's Biggest Gang Bang #1 / 1995 / FPI / M • The World's Biggest Gang Bang #2 / 1996 / FPI / M

JOHN TAYLOR *see* Star Index I

JOHN THOMAS
America's Raunchiest Home Videos #42: Swimsuit Sherrie / 1992 / ZA / M • Anal Camera #06 / 1995 / EVN / M • AVP #9103: The Ball Street Journal, PM Edition / 1991 / AVP / M • AVP #9105: Rude Awakening / 1991 / AVP / M • AVP #9106: The Dare / 1991 / AVP / M • Awakening In Blue / 1991 / PL / M • Hollywood Amateurs #14 / 1995 / MID / M • Nina Hartley's Professional Amateur Tournament #2 / 1990 / BKD / M • Positively Pagan #03 / 1991 / ATA / M • Thundercrack! / 1974 / LUM / M • Vixens Of Bandelero / 1995 / BVG / S

JOHN THOMAS GALT *see* Star Index I

JOHN TODD *see* J.T. Denver

JOHN TOLAND *see* John Seeman

JOHN VINCENT
The Exotic Dreams Of Casanova / 1970 / SOW / S • Experiments In Blue / 1982 / CA / M

JOHN VON FAUST
At The Mistress' Mercy / 1996 / OUP / B

JOHN W.
Erotic Dimensions #1: Ripe / 1982 / NSV / M

JOHN WADE
Candy Goes To Hollywood / 1979 / VCX / M

JOHN WALTON
Angel's Vengeance / 1995 / VMX / M • The Coming Of Nikita / 1995 / EL / M • Erika Bella: Euroslut / 1995 / EL / M • Penetration (Anabolic) #2 / 1995 / ANA / M • Sexhibtion #3 / 1996 / SUF / M • Sodomania #21: Degenerate Lifestyles! / 1997 / EL / M • The Voyeur #7: Live In Europe #1 / 1996 / JLP / M • The Voyeur #8: Live In Europe #2 / 1996 / JLP / M

JOHN WAYNE BOBBITT
Bloopers & Behind The Scenes / 1995 / LEI / M • Buttman At Nudes A Poppin' #2 / 1995 / EA / S • Frankenpenis / 1995 / LEI / M • John Wayne Bobbitt Uncut / 1994 / LEI / M • Kym Wilde's On The Edge #33 / 1996 / RB / B • Kym Wilde's On The Edge #37 / 1996 / RB / B • Miss Nude Galaxy #1 / 1995 / VOY / S • Miss Nude Galaxy #2 / 1995 / VOY / S

JOHN WEST
The Attendant / 1996 / SC / M • Beverly Hills Bikini Company / 1996 / NIT / M • Casting Couch Tips / 1996 / MPO / M •

Fuck Jasmin / 1997 / MET / M • Kool Ass / 1996 / BOT / M • Promises And Lies / 1996 / NIT / M • Pussyman's Nite Club Party #1 / 1996 / SNA / M • Pussyman's Nite Club Party #2 / 1997 / SNA / M • Sin-A-Matic / 1996 / VI / M • Starbangers #01 / 1993 / BIG / M • Starbangers #09 / 1996 / ZA / M • Starbangers #10 / 1997 / ZA / M • Venom #7 / 1996 / VD / M • Wet & Wicked / 1995 / PRK / M

JOHN WESTHEIMER *see Star Index I*
JOHN WILLIAMS
Taboo American Style #4: The Exciting Conclusion / 1985 / VC / M
JOHN WILSON *see Star Index I*
JOHN WINSTON
Triple Play (Vh) / cr75 / VC / M
JOHN WOODCOCK
Tina Makes A Deal / 1974 / TGA / M
JOHN WRIGHT *(John Rage)*
Crocodile Blondee #2 / 1988 / VCX / M • The Days Of Our Wives / 1988 / GO / M • I Dream Of Tiffany / 1993 / IF / M • Loose Lifestyles / 1988 / CA / M • Lucy Makes It Big / 1987 / ME / M • Raging Hormones / 1988 / VXP / M • Stephanie's Outrageous / 1988 / LV / C • Three By Three / 1989 / LV / C • Very Sexy Ballet / 1988 / CA / M • The Wacky World Of X-Rated Bloopers / 1989 / GO / M • The Way They Were / 1990 / CDI / M
JOHN ZEPPELIN
Kinky Villa / 1995 / PL / M
JOHN-ANTHONY BAILEY *see Star Index I*
JOHNATHAN LESTER
Anal In The Alps / 1996 / P69 / M
JOHNATHON YOUNGER *see Jonathan Younger*
JOHNNI BLACK *see Johnnie Black*
JOHNNIE BLACK *(Joanni Black, Johnnie Black)*
Female, despite name. Older, slutty looking, medium to large enhanced tits, womanly body, blonde with stringy hair, marginal face. You can see her with her natural (small) set in **Anal Maniacs #4** (much better then but still not good in other respects).
Anal Maniacs #4 / 1995 / WP / M • Bad Luck For Bad Girls / 1996 / EXQ / B • Beyond Reality #3: Stand Erect! / 1996 / EXQ / M • Butthole Bunnies / 1996 / ROB / F • Buttslammers #13: The Madness Continues / 1996 / BS / F • Career Girls / 1996 / OUP / M • Caught & Punished / 1996 / EXQ / B • The Complete & Total Anal Workout #1 / 1995 / ZA / M • Cumback Pussy #2: Crawling Back For More / 1996 / EL / M • Decadent Dreams / 1996 / ME / M • Deep Dippin' Anal Babes / 1996 / ROB / F • Dirty Tricks #2: This Ain't Love / 1996 / EA / M • Eighteen #2 / 1996 / SC / M • Fashion Sluts #8 / 1996 / ABS / M • Golddiggers #3 / 1995 / VC / M • The Happy Office / 1996 / NIT / M • Hot Wired / 1996 / VC / M • Hotwired / 1996 / VC / M • Let's Talk Anal / 1996 / ESF / M • Perverted Stories #09 / 1996 / JMP / M • Pocahotass #2 / 1996 / FD / M • Pussyman #15: The Bone Voyage Bash / 1997 / SNA / M • Sex After 50: A Guide To Life Long Sexual Pleasure / 1991 / BSI / M • Shane's World #5 / 1996 / OD / M • Sodomania #18: Shame Based / 1996 / EL / M • Spazm #1: Point Blank / 1996 / LBO / M • Takin' It To The Limit #8: Hooked On Crack / 1996 / BS / M • This Girl Is

Freaky / 1996 / NIT / M • Up Your Ass #3 / 1996 / ANA / M • Valentino's Euro-Invasion / 1997 / SC / M • The Voyeur #6 / 1996 / EA / M
JOHNNIE DEAN *see Star Index I*
JOHNNIE KEYES *see Johnny Keyes*
JOHNNY
America's Raunchiest Home Videos #56: Primed For A Party / 1993 / ZA / M • Big Murray's New-Cummers #03: Orgy 'Til Dawn / 1992 / FD / M • Harry Horndog #01: Amateur Double Penetration #1 / 1992 / ZA / M • Harry Horndog #11: Love Puppies #2 / 1992 / ZA / M • Harry Horndog #13: Anal Lovers #2 / 1992 / ZA / M • Hot Body Competition: Hot Pants Contest / 1996 / CG / F • Magma: Insatiable Lust / 1995 / MET / M • Pearl Necklace: Thee Bush League #01 / 1992 / SEE / M • Score 4 Me / 1991 / XPI / M • Screwed On The Job / 1991 / XPI / M • Swinging Couples #04 / 1994 / GO / M • Titan's Amateur Video Magazine #03 / 1995 / TEG / M
JOHNNY (JOEY MURPHY) *see Joey Murphy*
JOHNNY (MARC DEBRUI) *see Marc De-Bruin*
JOHNNY (WARNER) *see Johnny Warner*
JOHNNY ACE
Backdoor To Harley-Wood #1 / 1990 / AFV / M • Gang Bangs #2 / 1989 / EA / M • Hard Bodies / 1989 / CDI / M • Hot In The City / 1989 / VEX / M • Icy Hot / 1990 / MID / M • The Pillowman / 1988 / VC / M
JOHNNY ANGEL *(Miles Melon)*
Anal Angels / 1996 / PRE / B • Assinine / 1990 / CC / M • Bum Rap / 1990 / PLV / B • Fantasy Lover / 1995 / V99 / C • Flash Floods / 1991 / PRE / C • Head Nurse / 1990 / V99 / M • Hot Amber Nights / 1987 / CC / M • In Charm's Way / 1987 / IN / M • Party Animals / 1987 / VEX / M • Party Animals / 1994 / VEX / C • The Pawnbroker / 1990 / IF / M • Playing The Field / 1990 / VEX / M • Sexual Persuasion / 1991 / V99 / M • Suite Sensations / 1988 / SEX / M • Summer Dreams / 1990 / VEX / M • Wet Workout / 1987 / VEX / M
JOHNNY APOLLO
The Naked Truth / 1995 / VI / M • Smoke Screen / 1995 / WAV / M
JOHNNY ARMANI
Nightclub / 1996 / SC / M
JOHNNY B.
Sodomania #18: Shame Based / 1996 / EL / M • Wild In The Wilderness / 1984 / GO / M
JOHNNY B. BUTTS
Euro-Max #3: / 1995 / SC / M • Euro-Max #4: / 1995 / SC / M
JOHNNY B. GOODE *see Star Index I*
JOHNNY BLACKEAGLE
Caught From Behind #05: Blondes & Blacks / 1986 / HO / M • Hot Rocks / 1986 / WET / M • Mad About You / 1987 / VC / M
JOHNNY BOY
Midget On Milligan's Island / 1995 / FC / M
JOHNNY BUTT
Private Film #25 / 1995 / OD / M
JOHNNY CANADA
Corrupt Desires / 1984 / MET / M • She-Male Encounters #07: Divine Atrocities #1 / 1981 / MET / G • True Crimes Of Passion / 1983 / CA / G
JOHNNY COOL
Black Fox / 1988 / CC / M • Charlie's Girls

#1 / 1988 / CC / M • Ebony Humpers #4 / 1988 / VEX / M • The Legend Of Reggie D. / 1989 / EA / M • Let Me Tell Ya 'Bout Fat Chicks #2 / 1988 / 4P / M • Weekend Delights / 1992 / V99 / M
JOHNNY CUM LATELY
Big Boob Boat Ride #1 / 1992 / FC / M
JOHNNY DAWES *see Star Index I*
JOHNNY DEE
Dick Of Death / 1985 / VCR / M • Nineteen #1 / 1996 / FOR / M
JOHNNY DEEP
In Your Face #3 / 1995 / PL / M • In Your Face #4 / 1996 / PL / M
JOHNNY DOUGH *see Jon Dough*
JOHNNY DRAGON
American Nympho In London / 1987 / VD / M
JOHNNY FALCONBERG
L.A. Tool & Die / 1979 / TMX / G
JOHNNY GITAUR
The Best Of Both Worlds #2 / 1986 / MID / G • Bi 'n' Large / 1994 / PL / G • Bi Claudius / 1994 / BIL / G • Bi George / 1994 / BIL / G • Bi On The Fourth Of July / 1994 / BIL / G • Bi The Book / 1996 / MID / G • Bi The Rear Window / 1994 / BIL / G • The Bi Valley / 1994 / BIL / G • Bi-Nanza / 1994 / BIL / G • Cocks In Frocks #2 / 1996 / TTV / G • Corporate Bi Out / 1994 / BIL / G • Drive Bi / 1994 / BIL / G • Dungeons & Drag Queens / 1994 / HSV / G • Good Bi Girl / 1994 / BIL / G • Hot Bi Summer / 1994 / BIL / G • Las Vegas She-Males / 1995 / BCP / G • Melrose Trannie / 1995 / HEA / G • Transister Act / 1994 / HSV / G • Transsexual Prostitutes #1 / 1996 / DFI / G
JOHNNY HAMMER *see Star Index I*
JOHNNY HARDON
Inside Desiree Cousteau / 1979 / VCX / M • One Way At A Time / 1979 / CA / M • Sissy's Hot Summer / 1979 / CA / M • Star Virgin / 1979 / CXV / M
JOHNNY HOLIDAY *see Star Index I*
JOHNNY IDLE
Fresh Meat #2 / 1996 / PL / M
JOHNNY IDOL
East Coast Sluts #08: Atlantic City / 1995 / PL / M
JOHNNY JAM *see John Bennett*
JOHNNY JANAIRO *see Alex San Paolo*
JOHNNY JANIERO *see Alex San Paolo*
JOHNNY JAY
Switch Hitters #5: The Night Games / 1990 / IN / G
JOHNNY KEYES *(Johnnie Keyes)*
Black boxer whose main claim to fame was his appearence in **Behinf The Green Door**.
6 To 9 Black Style / 1987 / LIM / C • Aunt Peg's Fulfillment / 1980 / CV / M • Behind The Green Door #1 / 1972 / MIT / M • Black Heat / 1986 / VCR / C • Blue Vanities #015 (New) / 1988 / FFL / M • Blue Vanities #018 (New) / 1988 / FFL / M • Blue Vanities #044 (New) / 1988 / FFL / M • Blue Vanities #050 / 1988 / FFL / M • Blue Vanities #088 / 1988 / FFL / M • Classic Swedish Erotica #06 / 1986 / CA / C • Classic Swedish Erotica #08 / 1986 / CA / C • Classic Swedish Erotica #09 / 1986 / CA / C • Classic Swedish Erotica #12 / 1986 / CA / C • Classic Swedish Erotica #36 / 1987 / CA / C • Dark Passions / 1984 / VCR / C • Ebony Lust / 19?? / HOR / C • Femmes De Sade / 1976 / ALP / M • Flight Sensations / 1983 / VC / C • Heavenly Desire / 1979 / WV / M • In-

side Marilyn Chambers / 1975 / MIT / M •
John Holmes And The All-Star Sex Queens
/ 1984 / AMB / M • Legends Of Porn #1 /
1987 / CV / C • The Little French Maid /
1981 / VCX / M • Lust At First Bite / 1978 /
VC / M • Only The Best #2 / 1989 / CV / C
• Open For Business / 1983 / AMB / M • Pro
Ball Cheerleaders / 1979 / AVC / M •
Randy, The Electric Lady / 1978 / VC / M •
Resurrection Of Eve / 1973 / MIT / M • Sex
World / 1978 / SE / M • Sodom & Gomor-
rah / 1974 / MIT / M • Swedish Erotica #01
/ 1980 / CA / M • Swedish Erotica #04 /
1980 / CA / M • Swedish Erotica #05 / 1980
/ CA / M • Swedish Erotica #09 / 1980 / CA
/ M • Swedish Erotica #10 / 1980 / CA / M
• Swedish Erotica #11 / 1980 / CA / M •
Swedish Erotica #12 / 1980 / CA / M •
That's Porno / 1979 / CV / C • Triple
Header / 1987 / AIR / C • Wet Shots (Vcr) /
1983 / VCR / C
JOHNNY KING *see Star Index I*
JOHNNY LEGEND
Cheeks #2: The Bitter End / 1989 / CC / M
• Fantasm Cums Again / 1977 / VS / S •
Teenage Cruisers / 1977 / VCX / M
JOHNNY LIGHTNING *see Star Index I*
JOHNNY LINCOLN
Genital Hospital / 1987 / SE / M
JOHNNY LOVE
Adventures In Paradise / 1992 / VEX / M •
All In The Name Of Love / 1992 / IF / M •
America's Dirtiest Home Videos #01 / 1991
/ VEX / M • America's Dirtiest Home Videos
#03 / 1991 / VEX / M • America's Dirtiest
Home Videos #04 / 1991 / VEX / M • Amer-
ica's Dirtiest Home Videos #07 / 1991 /
VEX / M • America's Dirtiest Home Videos
#08 / 1992 / VEX / M • America's Dirtiest
Home Videos #09 / 1992 / VEX / M • Amer-
ica's Dirtiest Home Videos #14 / 1992 /
VEX / M • American Dream Girls #2 / 1994
/ LEI / M • Back To Black #2 / 1992 / VEX /
C • Beaver Hunt #03 / 1994 / LEI / M • Bev-
erly Hills Geisha / 1992 / V99 / M • Big Mur-
ray's New-Cummers #09: Oriental Lovers /
1993 / FD / M • Bring On The Night / 1994
/ VEX / M • Butt Hunt #11 / 1995 / LEI / M
• Casting Call (Venus 99) / 1993 / V99 / M
• Crazy On You / 1991 / IF / M • Executive
Positions / 1991 / V99 / M • Freaks Of
Leather #2 / 1994 / IF / C • Gazonga God-
dess #1 / 1993 / IF / M • Heartbreaker /
1991 / IF / M • Heavenly Hooters / 1994 /
IF / M • Hometown Girl / 1994 / VEX / M •
It's Only Love / 1992 / VEX / M • Lust For
Leather / 1993 / IF / M • Masked Ball / 1992
/ IF / M • Mix Up / 1992 / IF / M • Mr. Peep-
ers Amateur Home Videos #24: The Sleazy
Riders / 1991 / LBO / M • Nasty Jack's
Homemade Vid. #29 / 1991 / CDI / M •
Naughty By Nature / 1992 / IF / M • Neigh-
borhood Watch #28 / 1992 / LBO / M • One
Of A Kind / 1992 / VEX / M • Our Bang #05
/ 1992 / GLI / M • Petite & Sweet / 1994 /
V99 / M • Physically Fit / 1991 / V99 / C •
Pleasure Chest / 1993 / IF / M • Pussy Hunt
#13 / 1995 / LEI / M • Ripe & Ready (Infin-
ity) / 1995 / IF / M • Sheer Ecstasy / 1993 /
IF / M • Southern Accents / 1992 / VEX / M
• Sweet Cheeks (1991-Vid Excl) / 1991 /
VEX / C • Sweet Things / 1992 / VEX / M •
Take It Like A Man / 1994 / IF / M • To-
bianna: A Gang Bang Fantasy / 1993 / FC
/ M • Torrid Tonisha / 1992 / VEX / M
JOHNNY MAKE

Black Playhouse / 1995 / HBE / M
JOHNNY MARINO *see Star Index I*
JOHNNY MERCURY
Alana: A Gang Bang Fantasy / 1993 / FC /
M • Amateur Orgies #15 / 1992 / AFI / M •
Amateur Orgies #20 / 1992 / AFI / M • Am-
ateur Orgies #24 / 1993 / AFI / M • Amateur
Orgies #36 / 1993 / AFI / M • Anal Angel /
1994 / EX / M • Anal Gang Bangers #02 /
1993 / GLI / M • Asian Angel / 1993 / VEX
/ C • The Backway Inn #3 / 1993 / FD / M •
Big Murray's New-Cummers #04: Booty
Love / 1992 / FD / M • Big Murray's New-
Cummers #12: In The Pink / 1993 / FD / M
• Bone Alone / 1993 / MID / M • The Butt
Sisters Do The Twin Cities / 1996 / MID / M
• Candy Snacker / 1993 / WIV / M • Club
DV8 #1 / 1993 / SC / M • Dickin' Around /
1994 / VEX / M • Frathouse Sexcapades /
1993 / SFP / M • Gang Bang Party / 1994 /
HW / M • Hispanic Orgies #01 / 1993 / GO
/ M • Hole In One / 1993 / IF / M • Holly-
wood Swingers #03 / 1992 / LBO / M •
Hometown Honeys #4 / 1993 / VEX / M •
Hometown Honeys #5 / 1993 / VEX / M •
Hose Jobs / 1995 / VEX / M • I Dream Of
Tiffany / 1993 / IF / M • Incocknito / 1993 /
VIM / M • Much More Than A Mouthful #4 /
1994 / VEX / M • Nothing Else Matters /
1992 / V99 / C • One Of Our Porn Stars Is
Missing / 1993 / OD / M • Pleasure Chest /
1993 / IF / M • Raw Talent: Deep Inside
Gabriella's Ass (#4) / 1993 / FH / M •
Ready And Willing / 1993 / VEX / M • Red
Hot Honeys / 1994 / IF / M • Russian Se-
duction / 1993 / IP / M • Savage Fury #3 /
1994 / VEX / M • Spanish Fly / 1993 / VEX
/ M • Star Struck / 1992 / VEX / M • Sunset
Rides Again / 1995 / VC / M • Swing Rave
/ 1993 / EVN / M • Swinging Couples #03 /
1994 / GO / M • This Could Be The Night /
1993 / IF / M • Top Heavy / 1993 / IF / M •
Wet, Wild And Willing / 1993 / V99 / M •
Wild Dreams / 1995 / V99 / M
JOHNNY MORRIS
Deep Rub / 1979 / VC / M
JOHNNY NINETEEN
Supposedly owner of Mezzaluna (of O.J. Simp-
son fame).
Afrodisiac #1 / 1987 / CC / M • Black An-
gels / 1985 / VC / M • Blowing The Whistle
/ 1986 / VIP / M • Both Ends Burning / 1987
/ VC / M • Broadway Fannie Rose / 1986 /
CA / M • Brooke Does College / 1984 / VC
/ M • Candy Stripers #2 / 1985 / AR / M •
City Of Sin / 1991 / LV / M • Cocktales /
1985 / AT / M • Cravings / 1987 / VC / M •
Deep Throat #2 / 1986 / AR / M • Deep
Throat Girls / 1986 / ELH / M • Dream
Jeans / 1987 / CA / M • Flipside: A Back-
door Adventure / 1985 / CV / M • The God
Daughter #4 / 1992 / AFV / M • Good Golly,
Miss Molly / 1987 / CDI / M • Hot Rockers /
1985 / IVP / M • Hot Stuff / 1984 / VXP /
M • In All The Right Places / 1986 / VD / M
• Inside Little Oral Annie / 1984 / VXP / M •
Keisha / 1987 / VD / M • Merry X Miss /
1986 / VIP / M • Nudes At Eleven #1 / 1986
/ AVC / M • A Passage Thru Pamela / 1985
/ VC / G • Pleasure Channel / 1984 / VC /
M • Pleasure Island / 1984 / AR / M • Pretty
In Black / 1986 / WET / M • Return To Alpha
Blue / 1984 / AVC / M • Samantha, I Love
You / 1988 / WV / C • Sex Appeal / 1986 /
VES / S • Sex World Girls / 1987 / AR / M •
She's So Fine #1 / 1985 / VC / M • Sky

Foxes / 1987 / VC / M • Slumber Party Re-
union / 1987 / AR / M • Stray Cats / 1985 /
VXP / M • Street Angels / 1992 / LV / M •
Three Daughters / 1986 / FEM / M • Tick-
led Pink / 1985 / VC / M • Tracey's Love
Chamber / 1987 / AR / M • White Hot /
1984 / VXP / M
JOHNNY PAGE *see Star Index I*
JOHNNY PRINCE *see Star Index I*
JOHNNY PROBER
A&B GB#072: Chessie Does It / 1990 /
A&B / M • Alana: A Gang Bang Fantasy /
1993 / FC / M • Amateur Orgies #22 / 1993
/ AFI / M • America's Raunchiest Home
Videos #59: / 1993 / ZA / M • Anal Asian /
1994 / VEX / M • Anal Gang Bangers #02 /
1993 / GLI / M • Backdoor Boogie / 1994 /
TEG / M • Bareback Riders / 1992 / VEX /
M • Beach Bum Amateur's #13 / 1992 /
MID / M • Big Bad Biker Bitches / 1994 /
TTV / M • The Big Bang #1 / 1993 / LV / M
• The Big Bang #2 / 1994 / LV / M • Big
Black Bang / 1996 / HW / M • Big Boob Ball
/ 1995 / IF / C • Big Murray's New-Cum-
mers #19: The Ass Grabber / 1993 / FD / M
• Big Murray's New-Cummers #23:
Naughty Nymphettes / 1993 / FD / M •
Birthday Bash / 1995 / BOT / M • Black
Gangbangers #11 / 1996 / HW / M • Black
Gangbangers #12 / 1996 / HW / M • Breast
Worx #40 / 1992 / LBO / M • The Butt Sis-
ters Do Cleveland / 1994 / MID / M • Climax
At The Melting Pot #1 / 1996 / AVS / M •
Club DV8 #1 / 1993 / SC / M • Colossal
Orgy #1 / 1993 / HW / M • Colossal Orgy
#2 / 1994 / HW / M • Colossal Orgy #3 /
1994 / HW / M • Dangerous Behinds #1 /
1995 / HW / M • The Doll House / 1995 /
CV / M • Freaks Of Leather #2 / 1994 / IF /
C • Gang Bang Bitches #03 / 1994 / PP / M
• Gang Bang Bitches #04 / 1995 / PP / M •
Gang Bang Diaries #3 / 1994 / SFP / M •
Gonzo Groups & Gang Bangs / 1994 / GLI
/ M • Hedonism #01 / 1993 / FH / M • Hid-
den Camera #01 / 1993 / JMP / M • Hidden
Camera #03 / 1993 / JMP / M • Hidden
Camera #20 / 1994 / JMP / M • Hometown
Honeys #5 / 1993 / VEX / M • House Of
Sex #01: Banging Cumisha / 1994 / RTP /
M • House Of Sex #02: Banging Debbett /
1994 / RTP / M • Illusions #2 / 1992 / IF / M
• Kinky Debutante Interviews #01 / 1994 /
IP / M • Kinky Debutante Interviews #02 /
1994 / IP / M • Kinky Orientals / 1994 / FH
/ M • Knockout / 1994 / VEX / M • The Last
Temptation Of Teri / 1991 / IF / M • Lust /
1993 / FH / M • Nothing Else Matters / 1992
/ V99 / C • Odyssey Triple Play #75: Inter-
racial Anal Threesome / 1994 / OD / M •
One Lay At A Time / 1992 / V99 / M • Ori-
ental Gang Bang Fantasy / 1994 / FC / M •
Positively Pagan #04 / 1991 / ATA / M •
Positively Pagan #11 / 1993 / ATA / M •
Positively Pagan #12 / 1993 / ATA / M • R
& R / 1994 / VC / M • Raw Talent: Bang 'er
45 Times / 1993 / RTP / M • Raw Talent:
Deep Inside Lydia's Ass / 1993 / FH / M •
Raw Talent: Deep Inside Meo's Ass / 1993
/ RTP / M • Ready To Drop #04 / 1994 / FC
/ M • Ready To Drop #05 / 1995 / FC / M •
Rump Humpers #13 / 1993 / GLI / M •
Rump Humpers #14 / 1993 / GLI / M • Sat-
urday Night Porn #2 / 1993 / AFV / M • Six
Plus One #2 / 1993 / VEX / C • Star Struck
/ 1992 / VEX / M • Stiff Competition #2 /
1994 / CA / M • Stuff Your Face #1 / 1994 /

JMP / M • Stuff Your Face #2 / 1995 / JMP / M • Sugar Mommies / 1995 / FPI / M • Sweet Things / 1992 / VEX / M • Swing Rave / 1993 / EVN / M • This Could Be The Night / 1993 / IF / M • Tobianna: A Gang Bang Fantasy / 1993 / FC / M • U Witness: Video Three-Pak #3 / 1995 / MSP / M • Ultimate Anal Gang Bang #3 / 1995 / HW / M • Ultimate Gang Bang #1 / 1994 / HW / M • Voyeurism #1 / 1993 / FH / M • Wet & Wicked / 1992 / VEX / M • White Wedding / 1994 / V99 / M • WPINK-TV #5 / 1993 / PV / M

JOHNNY RABBIT *see Star Index I*

JOHNNY RAHM
Anything You Ever Wanted To Know About Sex / 1993 / VEX / M • Bi-Sex Pleasures / 1993 / PL / G • Big Switch #3: Bachelor Party / 1991 / CAT / G • Coming Out Bi / 1995 / IN / G • Dominique Goes Bi / 1994 / STA / G

JOHNNY REY
Bi Love Lucy / 1994 / PL / G • Inside Karl Thomas / 1994 / STA / G • More Than Friends / 1995 / KDP / G • Score Of Sex / 1995 / BAC / G

JOHNNY RINGO
Coming Out Bi / 1995 / IN / G • Lady & The Champ / 1991 / AFV / M

JOHNNY ROCCO
The Exotic Dreams Of Casanova / 1970 / SOW / S • The Notorious Cleopatra / 1970 / SOW / S • Tabacco Roody / 1970 / SOW / S • Wide Open / 1994 / GLI / M

JOHNNY ROCKET
Anal Gang Bangers #01 / 1992 / GLI / M • Anything You Ever Wanted To Know About Sex / 1993 / VEX / M • As Sweet As They Come / 1992 / V99 / M • Asian Heat #03: Tales Of The Golden Lotus / 1993 / SC / M • Bareback Riders / 1992 / VEX / M • Bobby Hollander's Rookie Nookie #01 / 1993 / SFP / M • Bubble Butts #20 / 1992 / LBO / M • The Burma Road #1 / 1994 / LBO / C • The Burma Road #2 / 1994 / LBO / C • Confessions #2 / 1992 / OD / M • Deliciously Teri / 1993 / IF / M • Dirty Dating Service #02 / 1993 / WP / M • Full Service Woman / 1992 / V99 / M • Gang Bang Diaries #2 / 1993 / SFP / M • Hometown Honeys #5 / 1993 / VEX / M • Hose Jobs / 1995 / VEX / M • House Of Spartacus #2 / 1993 / IF / M • Illusions #2 / 1992 / IF / M • The Last Temptation Of Teri / 1991 / IF / M • Long Dan Silver / 1992 / IF / M • Lust For Leather / 1993 / IF / M • Nasty Fuckin' Movies #09: Saki's Six Man Sexation #1 / 1992 / RUM / M • Neighborhood Watch #35 / 1992 / LBO / M • Nothing Else Matters / 1992 / V99 / C • Odyssey 30 Min: #282: / 1992 / OD / M • Opposite Attraction / 1992 / VEX / M • Party Dolls / 1992 / VEX / M • Pleasure Chest / 1993 / IF / M • Rump Humpers #13 / 1993 / GLI / M • Six Plus One #2 / 1993 / VEX / C • Southern Accents / 1992 / VEX / M • Star Struck / 1992 / VEX / M • Summertime Boobs / 1994 / LEI / M • This Could Be The Night / 1993 / IF / M • Tonight's The Night / 1992 / V99 / M • Udderly Fantastic / 1993 / IF / M • Uncle Roy's Amateur Home Video #04 / 1992 / VIM / M

JOHNNY ROOT
Raunchy Reggae / 1995 / SP / M

JOHNNY ROXX *see Star Index I*

JOHNNY RUBBER *see Star Index I*

JOHNNY SAILOR *see Star Index I*

JOHNNY SHARP
Backdoor Lambada / 1990 / GO / M • Tricky Business / 1995 / AFI / M

JOHNNY SOIREE
The Erotic Adventures Of Johnny Soiree / 1995 / LBO / M

JOHNNY SWEET
Kitty Foxx's Kinky Kapers #02 / 1995 / TTV / M

JOHNNY THRUST
Anal Reunion / 1996 / EVN / M • Covergirl / 1996 / LE / M • The Cumm Brothers #13: Rump Rangers / 1996 / OD / M • Dirty Dancers #5 / 1995 / 4P / M • Hollywood Amateurs #30 / 1996 / MID / M • Hollywood Amateurs #31 / 1996 / MID / M • Hollywood Amateurs #32 / 1996 / MID / M • Mike Hott: #345 Cum In My Cunt #07 / 1995 / MHV / C • Mike Hott: #349 Girls Who Swallow Cum #03 / 1996 / MHV / C • Mike Hott: #353 Bonus Cunt: April Lee / 1996 / MHV / M • Mike Hott: #364 Cunt Of The Month: Roxy Rider / 1996 / MHV / M • Mike Hott: #371 Horny Couples #19 / 1996 / MHV / M • Mike Hott: #386 / 1996 / MHV / M • Perverted Stories #06 / 1996 / JMP / M • Sorority Sluts Passed Out / 1995 / ZA / M • Stuff Your Ass #3 / 1996 / JMP / M • Tripper Stripper / 1995 / VMX / M • Young And Anal #4 / 1996 / JMP / M

JOHNNY TONE
The Best Little Whorehouse In Tijuana / 1995 / HBE / M

JOHNNY TURF
Ed Woody / 1995 / HBE / M

JOHNNY UTAH
Bi-Ology: The Making Of Mr Right / 1992 / CAT / G

JOHNNY WADD *see John C. Holmes*

JOHNNY WARNER *(Johnny (Warner), John Hammer, Frankie Donut)*
Missy Warner's boyfriend.
Anal Encounters #3: Back In The Dark One / 1991 / VC / M • Bob Lyons: Big Tits, Nude Slits, and a Six Foot Snake / 1992 / BLY / M • Bonfire Of The Panties / 1990 / CC / M • Breast Worx #02 / 1991 / LBO / M • Cheesecake / 1991 / VC / M • Dr Hooters / 1991 / PL / M • Mamm's The Word / 1991 / ZA / M • Mr. Peepers Amateur Home Videos #02: Bachelorette Party / 1991 / LBO / M • Mr. Peepers Amateur Home Videos #09: Western Panty Party / 1991 / LBO / M • A New Girlfriend / 1991 / XPI / M • Next Door Neighbors #33 / 1990 / BON / M • Raunchy Porno Picture Show / 1992 / FC / M • Sneek Peeks #1 / 1993 / FL / M • Someone Sent Me A Girl / 1991 / FH / M • Speedtrap / 1992 / VC / M • A Vision In Heather / 1991 / VI / M • Voodoo Vixens / 1991 / IF / M

JOHNNY WEST
Butthead Dreams: Big Boating Bonanza / 1994 / FH / M

JOHNNY WILSON *see Mike Horner*

JOHNNY ZIEHM *see Star Index I*

JOHNSON DIGGS
The Black Butt Sisters Do Boston / 1995 / MID / M • Black Hollywood Amateurs #21 / 1996 / MID / M

JOI (BLACK) *see Star Index I*

JOI LANSING
Blue Vanities #131 / 1991 / FFL / M • Blue Vanities #553 / 1994 / FFL / M

JOI RENO *(Whitney Prescott)*

Blonde with passable face and large enhanced tits.
Audition For Pain / 1996 / VTF / B • Big Bad Breasts Of Zina / 1995 / NAP / B • Big Bust Bikini Battle / 199? / NAP / B • Big Bust Fantasies / 1995 / PME / F • Big Busty Major Babes / 1996 / NAP / F • Bikini Brats / 199? / NAP / B • Binding Experience / 1994 / CS / B • Bip Shoots #2 / 1994 / BON / B • Body Locked / 1996 / NAP / B • Bondage Is My Pleasure #4 / 1994 / CS / B • Bound To Tease #5 / 1990 / BON / C • Breast Friends, Breast Enemies / 1994 / NAP / B • Busty Babes Milking Duel / 1996 / NAP / B • The Challenge Of Tushima / 1994 / NAP / B • Desert Starm (030 Min) / 1993 / NAP / B • Desert Starm (120 Min) / 1993 / NAP / B • The Enforcer / 199? / NAP / B • Face To Face #1 / 1994 / NAP / B • Face To Face #2: The Domination / 1994 / NAP / B • Fantasy Duel / 1996 / NAP / B • Girls And Guns / 1992 / KBR / M • Gringa / 1996 / NAP / B • Heels & Toes #2 / 1994 / BON / F • Kiss Of Domination / 1996 / NAP / B • The Kitten And The Foxxx / 1993 / NAP / B • Magnificent Seven / 1991 / NAP / F • Micki's Big Bust / 199? / NAP / B • The Mistress And The Wife / 1994 / NAP / B • The Model And The Showgirl / 1995 / NAP / B • Nancy Crew Meets Dr. Freidastein / cr90 / BON / B • Night Watch Woman / 199? / NAP / B • No Quarter Given / 199? / NAP / B • Over-Matched / 199? / NAP / B • Real People Real Bondage #1 / 1995 / BON / C • Satan's Mistress / 1993 / NAP / B • Slapped Senseless / 1993 / NAP / B • Survival Of The Fullest / 199? / NAP / B • This Time We Fight / 1996 / NAP / B • Tied & Tickled #14: Count Tickula / 1986 / CS / B • Trial Of The Tits / 1994 / NAP / B • The Whitney Challenge / 1996 / JAM / B • Whitney's Way / 1993 / HAV / B

JOI TOI *see Joie Wylde*

JOIE D'VISION *see Star Index I*

JOIE WYLDE *(Joi Toi)*
Pudgy brunette with short hair and large (36D) natural tits. OK facially. 5'0" tall and 25 in 1994. De-virginized at 17.
Adults Only / 1995 / BOT / M • All That Jism / 1994 / VD / M • Different Strokes / 1994 / PRE / B • Gas Works / 1994 / PRE / B • Kinky Debutante Interviews #04 / 1994 / IP / M • Lessons 'n' Love / 1994 / LBO / M • Lusty Lawyers / 1995 / PRK / M • New Girls In Town #7 / 1994 / CC / M • Perverted #1: The Babysitters / 1994 / ZA / M • Positions Wanted: Experienced Only / 1993 / PV / M • The Real Deal #1 / 1994 / FC / M • Swedish Erotica #74 / 1994 / CA / M • Tight Fit #03 / 1994 / GO / M • Tight Fit #06 / 1994 / GO / M • Triple Flay / 1995 / PRE / B • Triple Play / 1994 / PRE / B • Video Virgins #12 / 1994 / NS / M • Wet & Wicked / 1995 / PRK / M

JOJO (TONY MONTANA) *see Tony Montana*

JOJO HELMET
Dangerous Pleasures / 1995 / WIV / M

JOLIE POITRING
Juice / 19?? / COM / M

JOLT
Prima #09: ASSassins / 1995 / MBP / M • Prima #14: Hotel Europa / 1996 / MBP / M

JOLT GABER
Flamenco Ecstasy / 1996 / UEF / M

JOLT WALTON

Private Gold #11: The Pyramid #1 / 1996 / OD / M

JOLTE
Deep Behind The Scenes With Seymore Butts #2 / 1995 / ULI / M

JON
Zazel / 1996 / CV / M

JON BLACK see Star Index I

JON BLANSON see Star Index I

JON BRAZIL see Star Index I

JON BUOY
Up And Cummers #14 / 1994 / 4P / M

JON DAVIDS see Star Index I

JON DOUGH *(Carlos Chet, Chet Aznivour, Jan Sanders, Chad Sanders, Chet Sanders, Jay Sanders, Rock Taylor, John Douglas, Chet Anuszez, Gregory Phillips, Johnny Dough)*
Soft spoken male who is allegedly married to Diedre Holland (1992). Divorced in 1994. Carlos Chet (**Backdoor to Hollywood #3**). Jay Sanders (**Kascha's Blues**). Rock Taylor (**Who Shaved Trinity Loren?**). Gregory Phillips (**Deep Throat #3**).
13th Annual Adult Video News Awards / 1996 / VC / S • A.S.S.(Anal Security Squad) / 1988 / VD / M • Adult Video News 1992 Awards / 1992 / VC / M • The Adventures Of Mikki Finn / 1991 / CA / M • Affairs Of The Heart / 1993 / VI / M • The All American Girl / 1989 / FAN / M • All For One / 1988 / CIN / M • All Inside Eva / 1991 / PL / M • Alone And Dripping / 1991 / LV / M • Amazing Tails #5 / 1990 / CA / M • Anal Addict / 1995 / ROB / M • The Anal Adventures Of Bruce Seven / 1996 / BS / C • Anal Asian #2: The Won-Ton Woman / 1994 / IN / M • Anal Blues / 1994 / PEP / M • Anal Breakdown / 1994 / ROB / M • Anal Carnival / 1992 / ROB / M • Anal Centerfold / 1995 / ROB / M • Anal Climax #2 / 1991 / ROB / M • Anal Deep Rider / 1994 / ROB / M • Anal Delights #1 / 1992 / ROB / M • Anal Delights #2 / 1992 / ROB / M • Anal Delinquent #3 / 1995 / ROB / M • Anal Fury / 1992 / ROB / M • Anal Hunger / 1994 / ROB / M • Anal Innocence #1 / 1991 / ROB / M • Anal Innocence #3 / 1994 / ROB / M • Anal Insatiable / 1995 / ROB / M • Anal Intruder #03 / 1989 / CC / M • Anal Intruder #04 / 1990 / CC / M • Anal Justice / 1994 / ROB / M • Anal Legend / 1994 / ROB / M • Anal Lover #3 / 1994 / ROB / M • Anal Plaything #1 / 1994 / ROB / M • Anal Plaything #2 / 1995 / ROB / M • Anal Pleasures / 1988 / AVC / M • Anal Senorita #2 / 1995 / ROB / M • Anal Spitfire / 1994 / ROB / M • Anal Summer / 1994 / ROB / M • Anal Sweetheart / 1994 / ROB / M • Anal Thrills / 1992 / ROB / M • Anal Tight Ass / 1995 / ROB / M • Anal Trashy Ass / 1995 / ROB / M • Anal Woman #2 / 1993 / PL / M • Angel Eyes / 1995 / IN / M • Angela Takes A Dare / 1988 / FAZ / M • Angels In Flight / 1995 / NIT / M • Anniversary / 1992 / FOR / M • Another Secret / 1990 / SO / M • Army Brat #2 / 1989 / VI / M • As The Spirit Moves You / 1990 / LV / M • Attitude / 1995 / VC / M • Aussie Bloopers / 1993 / OD / M • Aussie Vice / 1989 / PM / M • Australian Connection / 1989 / PM / M • Babe Patrol / 1993 / FOR / M • Babe Watch #1 / 1994 / SC / M • Babenet / 1995 / VC / M • Babewatch #2 / 1994 / CC / M • Back On Top / 1988 / FAZ / M • Backdoor To Hollywood #03 / 1987 / CDI / M • Backdoor To Hollywood #04 /

1988 / CDI / M • Backdoor To Hollywood #09 / 1989 / CIN / M • Bad Habits / 1993 / VC / M • Badgirls #2: Strip Search / 1994 / VI / M • Badlands #1 / 1994 / PEP / M • Badlands #2: Back Into Hell / 1994 / PEP / M • The Bashful Blonde From Beautiful Bendover / 1993 / PEP / M • Batteries Included / 1988 / 3HV / M • Beach Blanket Brat / 1989 / VI / M • Beat The Heat / 1990 / VI / M • Beauty And The Beast #2 / 1990 / VC / M • The Beaverly Hillbillies / 1993 / IP / M • Bed & Breakfast / 1995 / WAV / M • Behind Blue Eyes #3 / 1989 / ME / M • Behind Closed Doors / 1990 / VI / M • Behind You All The Way #1 / 1990 / SO / M • Bend Over Babes #1 / 1990 / EA / M • Best Body In Town / 1989 / FAZ / F • Best Butt(e) In The West #2 / 1995 / CC / M • Best Gang Bangs / 1996 / DFI / C • The Best Of Andrew Blake / 1993 / CA / C • The Best Of Black Anal #1 / 1995 / ROB / C • Best Of Caught From Behind #5 / 1991 / HO / C • The Best Of Oriental Anal #1 / 1994 / ROB / C • The Best Of Strippers Inc / 1996 / ONA / C • Betrayal / 1992 / XCI / M • The Better Sex Video Series #1: The Better Sex Basics / 1991 / LEA / M • The Better Sex Video Series #2: Advanced Sex Techniques / 1991 / LEA / M • The Better Sex Video Series #6: Acting Out Your Fantasies / 1992 / LEA / M • The Better Sex Video Series #7: Advanced Sexual Fantasies / 1992 / LEA / M • Beverly Hills 90269 / 1992 / LV / M • Bi-Sex Pleasures / 1993 / PL / G • The Big Rock / 1988 / FOV / M • Big Town / 1993 / PP / M • The Bigger They Come / 1993 / VD / C • Bikini Beach #4 / 1996 / CC / M • Bionca On Fire / 1988 / 4P / M • Black By Popular Demand / 1992 / ZA / M • Black Cheerleader Search #02 / 1996 / ROB / M • Black Cheerleader Search #03 / 1996 / ROB / M • Blackman & Anal Woman #1 / 1990 / PL / M • Blonde Angel / 1994 / VI / M • Bloopers & Boners / 1996 / VI / M • Blue Bayou / 1993 / VC / M • Blue Fox / 1991 / VI / M • Bobby Sox / 1996 / VI / S • Body Music #1 / 1989 / DR / M • Bonnie & Clyde #3 / 1994 / VI / M • Bonnie & Clyde #4 / 1994 / VI / M • The Boob Tube / 1993 / MET / M • Booty Ho #3 / 1995 / ROB / M • Booty Mistress / 1994 / ROB / M • Booty Queen / 1995 / ROB / M • Brandy & Alexander / 1991 / VC / M • Bratgirl / 1989 / VI / M • The Breast Of Breastmen / 1995 / EVN / C • Breastman Does The Twin Towers / 1993 / EVN / M • Breastman Goes To Breastland #2 / 1993 / EVN / M • Breasts And Beyond #1 / 1991 / ME / M • Breasts And Beyond #2 / 1991 / ME / M • Breaststroke #1 / 1988 / EX / M • Breathless / 1989 / CIN / M • Bunmasters / 1995 / VC / M • Busen #03 / 1989 / BTO / M • Busen Extra #1 / 1991 / BTO / M • Busen Extra #3 / 1987 / BTO / M • Bushwackers / 1990 / PM / M • Busted / 1992 / HO / M • Butt Banged Bicycle Babes / 1994 / ANA / M • Butt Banged Cycle Sluts / 1995 / ANA / M • The Butt Detective / 1994 / VC / M • Butt Motors / 1995 / VC / M • Butt Woman #1 / 1990 / FH / M • Buttman's European Vacation #3 / 1995 / EA / M • Buttman's Orgies / 1996 / EA / M • Camera Shy / 1993 / FOR / M • Careless / 1993 / PP / M • Casanova #2 / 1993 / SC / M • Cat & Mouse #2 / 1993 / XCI / M • Cat Scratch Fever / 1989 / FAZ / M • Caught From Behind #09 / 1988 / HO

/ M • Caught From Behind #10 / 1989 / HO / M • Caught Looking / 1995 / CC / M • Chameleons: Not The Sequel / 1991 / VC / M • Chasey Saves The World / 1996 / VI / M • Cheerleader Nurses #1 / 1993 / VC / M • Cheerleader Nurses #2 / 1993 / VC / M • Christy In The Wild / 1992 / VI / M • City Of Sin / 1991 / LV / M • Climax 2000 #1 / 1994 / CC / M • Climax 2000 #2 / 1994 / CC / M • Clinique / 1989 / VC / M • A Clockwork Orgy / 1995 / PL / M • Club Bed / 1987 / CIX / M • Confessions Of A Slutty Nurse / 1994 / VIM / M • Conflict / 1988 / VD / M • The Contessa / 1989 / VC / M • County Line / 1993 / PEP / M • Crossing Over / 1990 / IN / M • Cry Baby / 1995 / CV / M • Cum Rain, Cum Shine / 1989 / FAZ / M • Cyberanal / 1995 / VC / M • Dancing Angels / 1989 / PL / M • Day Dreams / 1993 / CV / M • The Days Of Our Wives / 1988 / GO / M • De Sade / 1994 / SC / M • Dead Aim / 1994 / PEP / M • Debbie Class Of '89 / 1989 / CC / M • Debbie Does Dallas #4 / 1988 / VEX / M • Deception / 1991 / XCI / M • Deep Cheeks #5 / 1995 / ROB / M • Deep Inside Brittany O'connell / 1996 / VC / C • Deep Inside Charli / 1990 / CDI / C • Deep Inside Crystal Wilder / 1995 / VC / C • Deep Inside Deidre Holland / 1993 / VC / C • Deep Inside Jeanna Fine / 1992 / VC / C • Deep Inside Kaitlyn Ashley / 1995 / VC / C • Deep Inside Misty Rain / 1995 / VC / C • Deep Inside P.J. Sparxx / 1995 / VC / C • Deep Inside Samantha Strong / 1992 / CDI / C • Deep Inside Victoria / 1992 / CDI / C • Deep Inside Victoria Paris / 1993 / VC / C • Deep Throat #3 / 1989 / AR / M • Deep Throat #6 / 1992 / AFV / M • Denim / 1991 / LE / M • Der Champion / 1995 / BTO / M • Desert Moon / 1994 / SPI / M • Desire / 1990 / VC / M • The Devil In Miss Jones #5: The Inferno / 1994 / VC / M • Diary Of A Porn Star / 1993 / FOR / M • Dick At Nite / 1993 / MET / M • Dick Tracer / 1990 / PM / M • Diedre In Danger / 1990 / VI / M • The Dinner Party / 1995 / ERA / M • Dirty Laundry #2 / 1994 / CV / M • Dirty Lingerie / 1990 / VD / M • Dirty Stories #1 / 1995 / PE / M • Dirty Stories #2 / 1995 / PE / M • Dirty Stories #3 / 1995 / PE / M • Dirty Stories #4 / 1995 / PE / M • Doctor Feelgood / 1988 / CDI / M • Dog Walker / 1994 / EA / M • The Doll House / 1995 / CV / M • Domination Nation / 1996 / VI / M • Door To Door / 1990 / EX / M • Double Jeopardy / 1990 / HO / M • Double Load #2 / 1994 / HW / M • Double Trouble / 1988 / V99 / M • Doubletake / 1989 / CC / M • Dp #2: The Mighty Fhucks / 1994 / FC / M • Dr Butts #3 / 1993 / 4P / M • Dream Lover / 1995 / SC / M • Dripping With Desire / 1992 / DR / M • Earthquake Girls / 1990 / CC / M • Easy Way Out / 1989 / OD / M • Ebony Princess / 1994 / IN / M • Edward Penishands #1 / 1991 / VT / M • Eleventh Annual AVN Awards / 1994 / VC / M • Endangered / 1992 / PP / M • The Erotic Adventures Of The Three Musketeers / 1992 / CEL / S • Erotic Appetites / 1995 / IN / M • Euroflesh: Dentro Il Vulcano / 1996 / SC / M • Every Woman Has A Fantasy #3 / 1995 / VC / M • Everybody's Playmates / 1992 / CA / C • Everything Is Not Relative / 1994 / EL / M • Evil Woman / 1990 / LE / M • Executive Suites / 1990 / VEX / M • Executive Suites / 1993 / PL / M • Extreme Close-Up / 1996 / VI / M • Ex-

treme Sex #2: The Dungeon / 1994 / VI / M
• Eye Of The Tigress / 1988 / VD / M • The
Face / 1994 / PP / M • Facial Attraction /
1988 / BEE / C • Family Affairs / 1990 / VD
/ M • Famous Anus #1 / 1990 / EX / M •
Fantasy Du Jour / 1995 / FH / M • Fantasy
Girls / 1988 / CA / M • Fantasy Nights /
1990 / VC / M • Fashion Sluts #8 / 1996 /
ABS / M • Fat Ends / 1989 / 4P / M • Fire-
ball / 1988 / IN / M • Firm Offer / 1995 / SC
/ M • Fleshmates / 1994 / ERA / M • Forced
Love / 1990 / LV / M • Foreign Affairs / 1991
/ LE / M • Frankie And Joanie / 1991 / HW
/ M • The French Connexxxion / 1991 / VC
/ M • French Doll / 1994 / ME / M • Fresh
Meat (John Leslie) #1 / 1994 / EA / M •
Fresh Meat (John Leslie) #3 / 1996 / EA /
M • Freshness Counts / 1996 / EL / M •
From Kascha With Love / 1988 / CDI / M •
Full Metal Bikini / 1988 / PEN / M • Full
Throttle Girls: Boredom Pulled The Trigger
/ 1993 / VIM / M • Gang Bang Face Bath #3
/ 1994 / ROB / M • Gang Bang Nymphette
/ 1994 / ROB / M • Gang Bang Wild Style
#2 / 1994 / ROB / M • Gangbang Girl #13 /
1994 / ANA / M • Gangbang Girl #15 / 1995
/ ANA / M • Gere Up / 1991 / LV / C •
Gerein' Up / 1992 / VC / M • Ghosts / 1995
/ WV / M • The Girl In Room 69 / 1994 / VC
/ M • The Girl With The Blue Jeans Off /
1989 / FAZ / M • Girls In The Night / 1990 /
LE / M • Girls Of Silicone Valley / 1991 / FC
/ M • Girls Of The Double D #06 / 1989 /
CIN / M • Girls Of The Double D #07 / 1989
/ CIN / M • Girls Of The Double D #08 /
1989 / CDI / M • Girls Of The Double D #10
/ 1989 / CDI / M • Girls Of The Double D
#11 / 1990 / CIN / M • Girls With Curves #2
/ 1994 / CV / M • The Godmother #1 / 1987
/ VC / M • Good Vibrations #2: A Couples
Guide To Vibrator Use / 1991 / VT / M • The
Good, The Bed, And The Snuggly / 1993 /
ZA / M • Goodtime Charli / 1989 / CIN / M
• The Great American Boobs To Kill For
Dance Contest / 1995 / PEP / C • The
Great Sex Contest #1 / 1988 / LV / M •
Handle With Care / 1989 / FAZ / M • Hard
Sell / 1990 / VC / M • Hard Squeeze / 1994
/ EMC / M • Hate To See You Go / 1990 /
VC / M • Haunted Passions / 1990 / FC / M
• Haunting Dreams #1 / 1993 / LV / M •
Haunting Dreams #2 / 1993 / LV / M •
Hawaii Vice #7 / 1989 / CDI / M • Hawaii
Vice #8 / 1990 / CIN / M • Head First / 1993
/ LE / M • Head Lock / 1989 / VD / M • Head
Trip / 1995 / VC / M • Heart Breaker / 1989
/ LE / M • Heartbeat / 1995 / PP / M • The
Heat Of The Moment / 1990 / IN / M •
Heatwaves / 1994 / LE / M • Heavenly
Yours / 1995 / CV / M • Hidden Obsessions
/ 1992 / BFP / M • Hollywood Scandal: The
Heidi Flesh Story / 1993 / IP / M • Home-
town Honeys #3 / 1989 / VEX / M • Hooter-
mania / 1994 / VC / M • Hot Licks / 1990 /
CDI / M • Hot Property / 1993 / PEP / M •
Hot Shots / 1992 / VD / C • Hot Sweet 'n'
Sticky / 1992 / CA / C • Hothouse Rose #1
/ 1991 / VC / M • Hothouse Rose #2 / 1992
/ VC / M • How To Deep Throat Your Lover
/ 1994 / A&E / M • The Hunger / 1993 /
FOR / M • Hungry #1 / 1992 / SC / M • I Do
#1 / 1989 / VI / M • I Do #3 / 1992 / VI / M
• I'm No Brat / 1990 / FAZ / M • I'm Too
Sexy / 1992 / CA / M • Illicit Affairs / 1989 /
VD / M • Images Of Desire / 1990 / PM / M
• Imagine / 1991 / LV / M • In Cold Sweat /

1996 / VI / M • In The Bush / 1994 / PP / M
• The Initiation / 1995 / FD / M • Intense
Perversions #1 / 1995 / PL / M • Internal Affairs / 1995 / VI / M • Interview With A Milkman / 1996 / VI / M • Introducing Kascha /
1988 / CDI / M • Introducing Tracey Wynn
/ 1991 / PL / M • Invitation To The Blues /
1994 / LE / M • Jaded / 1989 / 4P / M • Jet-
stream / 1993 / AMP / M • Jezebel #1 /
1993 / SC / M • Jezebel #2 / 1993 / SC / M
• Joined: The Siamese Twins / 1989 / PL /
M • The Joy Of Sec's / 1989 / VEX / M •
Juggernaut / 1990 / EX / M • Just For The
Hell Of It / 1991 / CA / M • Just For Tonight
/ 1992 / VC / M • Kascha & Friends / 1988
/ CIN / M • Kascha's Blues / 1988 / CDI / M
• Kascha's Days & Nights / 1989 / CDI / M
• Kelly Jaye Close-Up / 1994 / VI / M • Kelly
Looks / 1991 / VI / M • Kink #1 / 1995 /
ROB / M • Kinky Roommates / 1992 / TP /
M • Kinkyvision #2 / 1988 / VC / M • Kiss
My Grits / 1989 / CA / M • Kisses Don't Lie
/ 1989 / PL / M • The Last Act / 1995 / VI /
M • Last Rumba In Paris / 1989 / VC / M •
Latex #1 / 1994 / VC / M • Latex #2 / 1995
/ VC / M • Laze / 1990 / ZA / M • Leena
Meets Frankenstein / 1993 / OD / M •
Legacy Of Love / 1992 / LE / M • Let's
Party / 1993 / VC / M • Lethal Affairs / 1996
/ VI / M • Lethal Lolita / 1993 / LE / M • Li-
censed To Thrill / 1990 / VC / M • Lifeguard
/ 1990 / VI / M • Little Big Dong / 1992 / ZA
/ M • Little Miss Anal / 1994 / ROB / M • A
Little Nookie / 1991 / VD / M • Live Bait /
1990 / IN / M • Lonely Hearts / 1995 / VC /
M • Loose Ends #4 / 1988 / 4P / M • Loose
Ends #5: The New Generation / 1988 / 4P
/ M • The Lottery / 1989 / CIN / M • Lotus /
1996 / VI / M • The Love Nest / 1989 / CA
/ M • Love Shack / 1990 / CC / M • Lover's
Trance / 1990 / LE / M • Lunachick / 1995 /
VI / M • Lust In Bloom / 1988 / LV / M •
Lusty Dusty / 1990 / VI / M • Mad Love /
1988 / VC / M • Madame X / 1990 / EX / M
• The Maddams Family / 1991 / XCI / M •
The Magic Box / 1993 / TP / M • Main
Street, U.S.A. / 1992 / PP / M • Make Me
Watch / 1994 / PV / M • Making Charli /
1989 / CDI / M • Malibu Spice / 1991 / VC
/ M • Mandii's Magic / 1988 / CDI / M •
Mask / 1993 / VI / M • Masterpiece / 1990 /
VI / M • Matched Pairs / 1988 / VEX / M •
Mind Games / 1995 / IMV / M • Mind Set /
1996 / VI / M • Mind Trips / 1992 / FH / M •
Mischief In The Mansion / 1989 / LE / M •
Misfits / 1994 / CV / M • Miss Nude Inter-
national / 1993 / LE / M • Mixed-Up Marriage / 1995 / CV / M • Monaco Falcon /
1990 / VC / M • Moonstroked / 1988 / 3HV
/ M • More Than Friends / 1989 / FAZ / M •
The Mountie / 1994 / PP / M • Mystic
Pieces / 1989 / EA / M • Nasty Dreams /
1994 / PRK / M • Nasty Nymphos #05 /
1994 / ANA / M • Nasty Nymphos #06 /
1994 / ANA / M • Nasty Nymphos #09 /
1995 / ANA / M • Nasty Nymphos #10 /
1995 / ANA / M • Nasty Nymphos #12 /
1996 / ANA / M • Nasty Nymphos #14 /
1996 / ANA / M • Nasty Nymphos #15 /
1996 / ANA / M • Naughty Neighbors / 1989
/ CA / M • Never Say Never / 1994 / SC / M
• Never Say Never, Again / 1994 / SC / M •
The New Barbarians #1 / 1990 / VC / M •
The New Barbarians #2 / 1990 / VC / M •
New Wave Hookers #3 / 1993 / VC / M •
New Wave Hookers #4 / 1994 / VC / M •

Night And Day #1 / 1993 / VT / M • Night
And Day #2 / 1993 / VT / M • Night Nurses
/ 1995 / WAV / M • Night Of Seduction /
1994 / VC / M • Night Seduction / 1995 /
VC / M • Night Trips #2 / 1990 / CA / M •
Night Walk / 1995 / HIV / G • Nightvision /
1993 / TP / M • Nikki Loves Rocco / 1996 /
VI / M • No More Mr Nice Guy / 1989 / GO
/ M • Nurse Tails / 1994 / VC / M • The Oh!
Zone / 1995 / VC / M • Oh, What A Night! /
1990 / VC / M • On The Make / 1988 / V99
/ M • On Trial #1: In Defense Of Savannah
/ 1991 / VI / M • On Trial #2: Oral Argu-
ments / 1991 / VI / M • Ona Zee's Black
Label #1: Sex Hunger / 1996 / ONA / C •
One Wife To Give / 1989 / ZA / M • Only In
Your Dreams / 1988 / VEX / M • Only The
Strong Survive / 1988 / ZA / M • Only The
Very Best On Video / 1992 / VC / C • Out-
call Outlaws / 1995 / CC / M • Overexposed
/ 1988 / VEX / M • Pajama Party X #1 /
1994 / VC / M • Pajama Party X #3 / 1994
/ VC / M • Paradise Found / 1995 / LE / M
• Paris By Night / 1990 / IN / M • Parting
Shots / 1990 / VD / M • The Party / 1992 /
CDI / M • Party Wives / 1988 / CDI / M •
Passages #4 / 1991 / VI / M • The Perfect
Brat / 1989 / VI / M • The Perfect Pair /
1991 / LE / M • Performance / 1990 / VI / M
• The Phoenix #1 / 1992 / VI / M • The
Phoenix #2 / 1992 / VI / M • Phone Sex
Girls: Australia / 1989 / PM / M • Play Me /
1989 / VI / M • Play School / 1990 / SO / M
• Plaything #2 / 1995 / VI / M • Playtime /
1996 / VI / M • Pleasure Is My Business /
1989 / EX / M • The Poetry Of The Flesh /
1993 / PEP / M • Pool Party / 1991 / CIN /
M • Poor Little Rich Girl #1 / 1992 / XCI / M
• Poor Little Rich Girl #2 / 1992 / XCI / M •
Prague By Night #1 / 1996 / EA / M •
Prague By Night #2 / 1996 / EA / M • The
Price Was Right / 1994 / PAE / M •
Princess Orgasma #1 / 1991 / PP / M • Pri-
vate Film #12 / 1994 / OD / M • Private Film
#14 / 1994 / OD / M • Private Film #18 /
1994 / OD / M • Private Film #24 / 1995 /
OD / M • Private Film #25 / 1995 / OD / M
• Private Film #26 / 1995 / OD / M • A Pri-
vate Love Affair / 1996 / IP / M • Private
Stories #01 / 1995 / OD / M • Private Sto-
ries #02 / 1995 / OD / M • Private Video
Magazine #26 / 1995 / OD / M • Pro Ball /
1991 / VD / M • Public Access / 1995 / VC
/ M • A Pussy Called Wanda #1 / 1992 / DR
/ M • A Pussy Called Wanda #2 / 1992 / DR
/ M • Pussyman #03: The Search Contin-
ues / 1993 / SNA / M • Pussyman #04: The
Celebration / 1993 / SNA / M • Pussyman
#08: The Squirt Queens / 1994 / SNA / M •
Pussyman #11: Prime Cuts / 1995 / SNA /
C • Pussyman #12: Sticky Fingers / 1995 /
SNA / M • Pussyman Auditions #21 / 1996
/ SNA / M • Pussywoman #3 / 1995 / CC /
M • Pyromaniac / 1990 / SO / M • Queen Of
Hearts #3: Heartless / 1992 / PL / M • Rac-
quel In Paradise / 1990 / VC / M • Racquel
In The Wild / 1992 / VI / M • Racquel's Ad-
diction / 1991 / VC / M • Rainwoman #02 /
1990 / CC / M • Raquel Released / 1991 / VI / M •
Raunch #01 / 1990 / CC / M • Raunch #02
/ 1990 / CC / M • Raunch #04: Silver Melts
/ 1991 / CC / M • Ravaged / 1990 / CIN / M
• Rear Burner / 1990 / IN / M • Rebel / 1991
/ ZA / M • The Red Baron / 1989 / FAN / M
• Red Hot Fire Girls / 1989 / VD / M • Red

Hot Lover / 1995 / CV / M • Restless Passion / 1987 / HO / M • Rhapsody / 1993 / VT / M • Ride 'em Hard / 1992 / LV / M • The Rise Of The Roman Empress #2 / 1990 / PV / M • Rising Buns / 1993 / HW / M • Rockin' The Boat / 1990 / VI / M • Ruthless Affairs / 1995 / LE / M • Rxx For A Gangbang / 1994 / ZA / M • Sam's Fantasy / 1990 / CIN / M • Satin & Lace / 1994 / WP / M • The Scent Of Samantha / 1988 / VEX / C • Scented Secrets / 1990 / CIN / M • The Screamer / 1991 / CA / M • Secret Diary #1 / 1994 / TAW / M • Secret Diary #2 / 1995 / MID / M • Secrets / 1990 / CA / M • The Seduction Of Mary / 1992 / VC / M • Sensual Recluse / 1994 / EX / M • Separated / 1989 / INH / M • Seriously Anal / 1996 / ONA / M • The Serpent's Dream / 1993 / VC / M • Sex #1 (Vca) / 1994 / VC / M • Sex #2: Fate (Vca) / 1995 / VC / M • Sex 4 Life / 1995 / XPR / M • Sex Bi-Lex / 1993 / CAT / G • Sex Circus / 1994 / VIM / M • Sex Crazy / 1989 / FAN / C • Sex Lives Of Clowns / 1994 / VC / M • Sex Pistol / 1990 / CDI / M • Sex Scenes / 1992 / VD / C • Sex Toy / 1993 / CA / C • Sex Under Glass / 1992 / VC / M • Sexmares / 1993 / FH / M • Sexual Fantasies / 1993 / ... / C • Sexual Healing / 1994 / VI / M • Sexual Instinct #1 / 1992 / DR / M • Sexy Country Girl / 1991 / PL / M • Shadow Dancers #1 / 1989 / EA / M • Shadow Dancers #2 / 1989 / EA / M • Shanna's Final Fling / 1991 / ME / M • She's America's Most Wanted / 1990 / VEX / M • Silky Thighs / 1994 / ERA / M • Silver Tongue / 1989 / CA / M • Simply Kia / 1994 / LE / M • Sin City: The Movie / 1992 / SC / M • Sin-A-Matic / 1996 / VI / M • Sins Of Tami Monroe / 1991 / CA / C • Sister Snatch #2 / 1995 / SNA / M • Sittin' Pretty #1 / 1990 / DR / M • Sittin' Pretty #2 / 1992 / DR / M • Sleeping Around / 1991 / CA / M • Sloppy Seconds / 1994 / PE / M • Smeers / 1992 / PL / M • Smells Like...Sex / 1995 / VC / M • Snakedance / 1992 / VI / M • Sodomania #03: Foreign Objects / 1993 / EL / M • Sodomania #06: Gangs And Bangs And Other Thangs / 1993 / EL / M • Sodomania #09: Doin' Time / 1994 / EL / M • Sodomania #12: Raw Filth / 1995 / EL / M • Sodomania #15: Warning! / 1996 / EL / M • Sodomania: The Baddest Of The Best...And Then Some / 1994 / EL / C • Some Like It Big / 1991 / LE / M • Sorority Pink #1 / 1989 / CV / M • Sorority Pink #2 / 1989 / CV / M • Sorority Sex Kittens #1 / 1992 / VC / M • Sorority Sex Kittens #2 / 1993 / VC / M • Sound F/X / 1989 / V99 / M • Spin For Sex / 1994 / IN / M • St. Tropez Lust / 1990 / VC / M • Star Attraction / 1995 / VT / M • Star Spangled Banner / 1990 / FAZ / M • Starbangers #03 / 1993 / ZA / M • Stardust #1 / 1996 / VI / M • The Starlet / 1991 / PP / M • Sterling Silver / 1992 / CC / M • Stick It In The Rear #2 / 1993 / PL / M • The Stiff / 1995 / WAV / M • Stiff Competition #2 / 1994 / CA / M • Street Angels / 1992 / LV / M • Strippers Inc. #1 / 1994 / ONA / M • Strippers Inc. #2 / 1994 / ONA / M • Strippers Inc. #3 / 1994 / ONA / M • Strippers Inc. #4 / 1995 / ONA / M • Student Nurses / 1991 / CA / M • Submission / 1994 / WP / M • Surfside Sex #2 / 1992 / LV / M • Surfside Sex / 1988 / CA / M • Surrogate Lover / 1992 / TP / M • Swallow / 1994 / VI / M • The Swap #2 / 1994 / VI / M • Swedish

Erotica Featurettes #3 / 1989 / CA / M • Swedish Erotica Featurettes #5 / 1990 / CA / M • Sweet Addiction / 1988 / CIN / M • Sweet As Honey / 1992 / LV / M • Sweet Miss Fortune / 1990 / LE / M • Sweet Seduction / 1990 / LV / M • Sweet Tease / 1990 / VEX / M • Swingers Ink / 1990 / VC / M • Taboo #14: Kissing Cousins / 1995 / IN / M • Tailiens #1 / 1992 / FD / M • Tailiens #2 / 1992 / FD / M • Tailiens #3 / 1992 / FD / M • Takin' It To The Limit #2 / 1994 / BS / M • Takin' It To The Limit #7: Debauched / 1996 / BS / M • The Tantric Guide To Sexual Potency And Extended Orgasm / 1994 / A&E / M • Temptations / 1989 / DR / M • The Thief / 1994 / SC / M • Things Change / 1992 / MET / M • Things Change #1: My First Time / 1992 / CV / M • Things Change #2: Letting Go / 1992 / CV / M • This Year's Blonde / 1990 / LE / M • Three Hearts / 1995 / CC / M • The Three Musketeers #1 / 1992 / FD / M • The Three Musketeers #2 / 1992 / FD / M • Titty City #1 / 1995 / TIW / M • Torch #1 / 1990 / VI / M • Torch #2 / 1990 / VI / M • Torrid Tales / 1995 / VI / M • Totally Naked / 1994 / VC / M • A Touch Of Gold / 1990 / IN / M • Transaction #1 / 1986 / WET / M • Triangle / 1989 / VI / M • Trick Tracey #1 / 1990 / CC / M • Trick Tracy #2: Tracy Loves Dick / 1990 / CC / M • Tricky Business / 1995 / AFI / M • Triple X Video Magazine #01 / 1995 / OD / M • Triple X Video Magazine #02 / 1995 / OD / M • Triple X Video Magazine #04 / 1995 / OD / M • Truck Stop Angel / 1994 / CC / M • True Blue / 1989 / PM / M • True Confessions Of Hyapatia Lee / 1989 / VI / M • True Confessions Of Tori Welles / 1989 / VI / M • Twentysomething #3 / 1989 / VI / M • Twin Action / 1993 / LE / M • Twin Peeks / 1990 / DR / M • Two Sides Of A Lady / 1994 / HDE / M • The Ultimate Fantasy / 1995 / CV / M • Ultimate Orgy #1 / 1992 / GLI / M • Undercover Angel / 1988 / IN / M • Uniform Behavior / 1989 / ZA / M • Unplugged / 1995 / CC / M • Unrefined / 1993 / CC / M • Up And Cummers #18 / 1995 / 4P / M • Vagablonde / 1994 / VI / M • Veil / 1990 / VI / M • Venom #1 / 1995 / VD / M • Venom #3 / 1996 / VD / M • Visions #2 / 1995 / ERA / M • Vivid Raw #3: Double Header / 1996 / VI / M • The Voyeur #2 / 1994 / EA / M • The Voyeur #3 / 1995 / EA / M • The Voyeur #4 / 1995 / EA / M • The Wacky World Of X-Rated Bloopers / 1989 / GO / M • Wanderlust / 1992 / LE / M • We're No Angels / 1990 / CIN / M • Wendy Whoppers: Environmental Attorney / 1993 / PEP / M • Wendy Whoppers: Ninja CPA / 1993 / PEP / M • Wendy Whoppers: Ufo Tracker / 1994 / PEP / M • Wet Faces #1 / 1997 / SC / C • Wet Fingers / 1990 / HIO / M • Where The Sun Never Shines / 1990 / IN / C • White Boys & Black Bitches / 1995 / ROB / M • White Chicks Can't Hump / 1992 / FD / M • Who Framed Ginger Grant? / 1989 / CC / M • Who Reamed Rosie Rabbit? #1 / 1989 / FAN / M • Who Shaved Trinity Loren? / 1988 / EX / M • The Wicked One / 1995 / WP / M • Wild At Heart / 1990 / CDI / M • Wild Oats / 1988 / CV / M • Wild Roomies / 1994 / VC / M • Wild Things #4 / 1994 / CV / M • Wishful Thinking / 1992 / VC / M • Witness For The Penetration / 1994 / PEP / M • Working Girls / 1995 / FH / M • World Sex Tour #3 / 1995 / ANA / M • World Sex

Tour #4 / 1996 / ANA / M • X Dreams / 1989 / CA / M • X Factor: The Next Generation / 1991 / HO / M • Young And Innocent / 1987 / HO / M • Young Nurses In Lust / 1994 / LBO / M • [Berlin Caper / 1989 / ... / M

JON ELDER
The Girls In The Band / 1976 / SVE / M

JON FOUL *see Star Index I*

JON GIMBEL
The Jade Pussycat / 1977 / CA / M

JON GREGORY *see Star Index I*

JON HALL *see Star Index I*

JON JONSON
Jubilee Of Eroticism / 1985 / GO / M

JON KEITH *see Jon Severini*

JON MARLIN *see Jon Martin*

JON MARTIN *(Jeffrey Stern, Jerry Barr, Jerry Smith, Fred Anton, Eric Marin, Eric Martin, Jerry Heath, Richard (Jon Martin), John Martin, Lyle Stewart, Jon Marlin, Robert Metz, Jon Martinstein, Lyle Stuart, John Morton, Jerry Putz, Jerry Hall)*

Lyle Stewart is from **The Jade Pussycat**.
10 1/2 Weeks / 1986 / SE / M • 1001 Erotic Nights #1 / 1982 / VC / M • 1001 Erotic Nights #2 / 1987 / VC / M • 11 / 1980 / VCX / M • Adultery / 1986 / DR / M • All The King's Ladies / 1981 / SUP / M • Amanda By Night #1 / 1981 / CA / M • Amber & Sharon Do Paris #1 / 1985 / PAA / M • Amber & Sharon Do Paris #2 / 1985 / PAA / M • American Pie / 1980 / SE / M • Anal Annie Just Can't Say No / 1984 / LIP / M • Angel's Back / 1988 / IN / M • Anticipation / 1982 / HIF / M • Back To Rears / 1988 / VI / M • Backdoor Romance / 1984 / VIV / M • Backing In #2 / 1990 / WV / C • Barbara Dare's Bad / 1988 / SE / C • Behind The Green Door #1 / 1972 / MIT / M • The Best Little Whorehouse In Hong Kong / 1987 / SE / M • Beyond Desire / 1986 / VC / M • Beyond Shame / 1980 / VEP / M • Beyond Taboo / 1984 / VIV / M • Beyond Your Wildest Dreams / 1980 / CAT / M • Bi-Dacious / 1989 / PL / G • The Big Bang / 1988 / WET / M • Big, Bad & Beautiful / 1988 / MIR / C • The Bitch / 1988 / FAN / M • The Bitches Of Westwood / 1987 / CA / M • Black Bimbos In Heat / 1989 / MIR / C • Blazing Matresses / 1986 / AVC / M • Blonde Fire / 1979 / EVI / M • Blonde Heat (VCA) / 1985 / VC / M • The Blonde Next Door / 1982 / GO / M • Body Games / 1987 / DR / M • Boiling Point / 1978 / SE / M • Bold Obsession / 1983 / NSV / M • Bon Appetite / 1985 / TGA / C • Boom Boom Valdez / 1988 / CA / M • The Boss / 1987 / FAN / M • Breakin' All The Rules / 1987 / SE / M • Butter Me Up / 1984 / CHX / M • Campus Capers / 1982 / VC / M • Careena #2: A Star On The Rise / 1988 / WV / C • Careful, He May Be Watching / 1986 / CA / M • The Case Of The Cockney Cupcake / 1989 / ME / M • The Case Of The Crooked Cathouse / 1989 / ME / M • The Case Of The Mad Tickler / 1988 / ME / M • The Case Of The Sensuous Sinners / 1988 / ME / M • The Catwoman / 1988 / VC / M • Caught In The Act / 1987 / WV / M • Cells Of Passion / 1981 / VD / M • Centerspread Girls / 1982 / CA / M • Challenge Of Desire / 1983 / NSV / M • Champagne For Breakfast / 1980 / SE / M • Cheating Wives / 1983 / PAC / M • Chicks In Black Leather / 1989 / VC / C • China Bitch / 1989 / PV / C

• China De Sade / 1977 / ALP / M • China White / 1986 / WV / M • Cinderella / 1985 / VEL / M • Circus Acts / 1987 / SE / C • Club Sex / 1989 / GO / M • Cock Robin / 1989 / SUE / M • Coed Fever / 1980 / CA / M • Coffee, Tea Or Me / 1984 / CV / M • Come Get Me / 1983 / VEL / M • A Coming Of Angels, The Sequel / 1985 / CA / M • Cool Sheets / 1989 / PP / M • Corporate Affairs / 1986 / SE / M • Cottontail Club / 1985 / HO / M • Critics' Choice #2 / 1984 / SE / C • The Dancers / 1981 / VCX / M • Dangerous Women / 1987 / WET / M • Dark Angel / 1983 / VC / M • Debbie 4 Hire / 1988 / AVC / M • Debbie Class Of '88 / 1987 / CC / M • Debbie Does Dishes #1 / 1985 / AVC / M • Debbie Does Dishes #3 / 1987 / AVC / M • Debbie For President / 1988 / CC / M • Debbie Goes To College / 1986 / ELH / M • Debbie Goes To Hawaii / 1988 / VD / C • Deep Inside Keisha / 1994 / VC / C • Deep Inside Ona Zee / 1992 / VC / C • Desires Within Young Girls / 1977 / CA / M • Diamond Head / 1987 / AVC / M • Disobedient Nancy / 1992 / RB / B • Doctor Blacklove / 1987 / CC / M • Doing It / 1982 / SE / M • Double Pleasure / 1985 / VCR / M • Down And Dirty / 1985 / LBO / M • Dr Juice's Lust Potion / 1986 / TEM / M • Dr Lust / 1987 / VC / M • Dream Lovers / 1987 / CA / M • Dreams In The Forbidden Zone / 1989 / PCP / M • Dreams Of Natasha / 1985 / AAH / M • Dynamic Vices / 1987 / VC / M • The Erotic Adventures Of Bonnie & Clyde / 1988 / GO / M • Erotic Dimensions #4: The Exhibitionist / 1982 / NSV / M • Erotic Dimensions: The Wild Life / 1982 / NSV / M • The Erotic World Of Linda Wong / 1985 / VIV / M • Exposed / 1980 / SE / M • Extra Sensual Pleasure / 1983 / PAC / M • F...It / 1987 / SE / C • Fantasy / 1978 / VCX / M • Fantasy World / 1979 / WWV / M • Female Athletes / 1977 / VXP / M • The First Time I Ever... / cr75 / AR / M • Flesh In Ecstasy #08: Traci Adams / 1987 / GO / C • Forbidden Desire / 1983 / NSV / M • From Paris With Lust / 1985 / PEN / M • Garage Girls / 1981 / CV / M • Getting Personal / 1986 / CA / M • Ginger Does Them All / 1988 / CV / M • Girl On The Run / 1985 / VC / M • Go For It / 1984 / VC / M • Grafenberg Girls Go Fishing / 1987 / MIT / M • Grind / 1988 / CV / M • Heavenly Desire / 1979 / WV / M • Her Wicked Ways / 1983 / CA / M • High School Memories / 1980 / VCX / M • Hitler Sucks / 1988 / GO / M • Homecoming / 1981 / CA / M • Hot And Nasty! / 1986 / V99 / C • Hot Flashes / 1984 / VC / M • Hot Legs / 1979 / VCX / M • Hot Line / 1980 / CA / M • Hot Lunch / 1978 / SE / M • Hot Number / 1987 / WET / M • Hot Ones / 1982 / SUP / C • Hot Rackets / 1979 / CV / M • Hot Rocks / 1986 / WET / M • Hot School Reunion / 1984 / CHX / F • Hyapatia Lee's Sexy / 1986 / SE / M • I Want To Be Bad / 1984 / CV / M • Illusions Of Ecstasy / 1985 / NSV / M • Indecent Pleasures / 1984 / CA / M • Inflamed / 1984 / NSV / M • The Jade Pussycat / 1977 / CA / M • Kamikaze Hearts / 1986 / FAC / S • Kinky Sluts / 1988 / MIR / C • The Last Condom / 1988 / PP / M • The Last Taboo / 1984 / VIV / M • The Legend Of King Karl / 1986 / AR / M • Legends Of Porn #1 / 1987 / CV / C • Let's Get Wet / 1987 / WV / M • Lifestyles Of The Blonde And Dirty / 1987 / WET / M • Liquid Love / 1988 / CA / M • A Little Bit Of Honey / 1987 / WET / M • Little Girls Blue #1 / 1977 / VCX / M • Lover's Lane / 1986 / SE / M • Mad Love / 1988 / VC / M • Mai Lin Vs Serena / 1982 / HIF / M • The Main Attraction / 1988 / 4P / M • Mardi Gras / 1986 / SE / M • Mardi Gras Passions / 1987 / MET / M • Mary! Mary! / 1977 / SE / M • Meat Market / 1992 / SEX / C • Memphis Cathouse Blues / 1982 / CA / M • Midnight Baller / 1989 / PL / M • Midnight Hustle / 1978 / VC / M • Midnight Pink / 1987 / WV / M • The Mile High Girls / 1987 / CA / M • Missing Pieces / 1985 / IN / M • Motel Sweets / 1987 / VD / M • Mouthwatering / 1986 / BRA / M • My Bare Lady / 1989 / ME / M • Mystery Of The Golden Lotus / 1989 / HU / M • Nasty Lovers / 1987 / SE / C • Nasty Newshounds / 1988 / ME / M • Nasty Nights / 1988 / PL / C • Never So Deep / 1981 / VCX / M • The Nicole Stanton Story #1 / 1989 / CA / M • The Nicole Stanton Story #2 / 1989 / CA / M • Night Of The Living Debbies / 1989 / EX / M • A Night On The Wild Side / 1986 / VC / M • Nudes At Eleven #2 / 1987 / AVC / M • Nurses Of The 407th / 1982 / CA / M • Nymphette #2 / 1986 / WV / M • Obsession / 1985 / HO / M • Oh, What A Night! / 1990 / VC / M • On The Loose & Hot To Trot / 1987 / CA / M • On White Satin / 1980 / VCX / M • Only The Best #3 / 1990 / CV / C • Only The Best Of Barbara Dare / 1990 / CV / C • Only The Best Of Breasts / 1987 / CV / C • Only The Best Of Oral / 1989 / CV / C • Oral Majority #05 / 1987 / WV / C • Oriental Babysitter / 1976 / SE / M • Oriental Hawaii / 1982 / CA / M • Oriental Temptations / 1984 / CV / C • Party Doll / 1990 / VC / M • Passion Pit / 1985 / SE / M • The Passion Within / 1986 / MAP / M • Peaches And Cream / 1982 / SE / M • Peeping Tom / 1986 / CV / M • The Penthouse / 1989 / PP / M • Perfect Partners / 1986 / CV / M • Physical #1 / 1981 / SUP / M • Play Me Again, Vanessa / 1986 / VC / M • Please Don't Stop / 1986 / CV / M • The Pleasure Game / 1988 / CA / M • The Pleasure Hunt #1 / 1984 / NSV / M • The Pleasure Maze / 1986 / PL / M • Pleasure Zone / 1984 / SE / M • Porno Screentests / 1982 / VC / M • Portrait Of A Nymph / 1988 / PP / M • Portrait Of Seduction / 1976 / SE / M • Postcards From Abroad / 1991 / CA / C • Power Blonde / 1988 / AVC / M • Pretty Peaches #3 / 1989 / VC / M • The Price Was Right / 1994 / PAE / M • Private Encounters / 1987 / SE / M • Private Moments / 1983 / CV / M • The PTX Club / 1988 / GO / M • Rachel Ryan Exposed / 1990 / WV / C • Rebecca's / 1983 / AVC / M • Red Hot Fire Girls / 1989 / VD / M • Red Hot Pepper / 1986 / V99 / M • Resurrection Of Eve / 1973 / MIT / M • Revenge By Lust / 1986 / VCR / M • The Ribald Tales Of Canterbury / 1986 / CA / M • Satisfactions / 1983 / CA / M • Saturday Night Special / 1989 / DR / M • Screwdriver / 1988 / CC / C • Screwples / 1979 / CA / M • Sensual Encounters Of Every Kind / 1978 / SE / M • Sex Academy / 1985 / PLY / M • Sex And Dreams On Maple Street / 1985 / WV / M • Sex Life Of A Porn Star / 1986 / ELH / M • The Sex Life Of Mata Hari / 1989 / GO / M • Sex Lives Of The Rich And Famous #1 / 1988 / VC / M • Sex Lives Of The Rich And Famous #2 / 1989 / VC / M • Sex Lives Of The Rich And Beautiful / 1988 / CA / M • Sex Loose / 1982 / VC / M • Sextrology / 1987 / CA / M • The Sexual Zone / 1989 / EX / M • Sexy Delights #2 / 1987 / CLV / M • Sheila's Payoff / 1977 / VCX / M • Showgirl #01: Leslie Bovee's Fantasies / 1981 / VCR / M • Showgirls / 1985 / SE / M • Sin City / 1986 / WET / M • Skin On Skin / 1981 / CV / M • The Sleazy Detective / 1988 / VD / M • Sleepless Nights / 1984 / VIV / M • Small Town Girls / 1979 / CXV / M • Soft As Silk...Sweet As Honey / 1984 / SE / M • Some Kind Of Woman / 1985 / CA / M • Spectators / 1984 / AVC / M • The Spirit Of Seventy Six / 1976 / NGV / M • St. X-Where #2 / 1988 / VD / M • Summer School / 1979 / VCX / M • Suzie Superstar #1 / 1983 / CV / M • Suzie Superstar...The Search Continues / 1988 / CV / M • Swedish Erotica #15 / 1980 / CA / M • Swedish Erotica #41 / 1982 / CA / M • Swedish Erotica #59 / 1984 / CA / M • Sweet Dreams Suzan / 1980 / CA / M • Sweet Things / 1987 / VC / M • Tail For Sale / 1988 / VD / M • Talk Dirty To Me #05 / 1987 / DR / M • Talk Dirty to Me One More Time #2 / 1988 / PP / C • A Taste Of Alexa / 1989 / PIN / C • A Taste Of Janey / 1990 / PIN / C • A Taste Of Sugar / 1978 / AR / M • A Taste Of Tawnee / 1988 / LV / C • Tawnee...Be Good! / 1988 / LV / M • Taxi Girls #2: In Search Of Toni / 1986 / ELD / M • Teeny Buns / 1977 / VC / M • Tell Me Something Dirty / 1991 / NWV / M • Temptation: The Story Of A Lustful Bride / 1983 / NSV / M • That's Porno / 1979 / CV / C • Torrid Zone / 1987 / MIR / M • Trans Europe Express / 1989 / VC / G • Trashi / 1980 / CA / M • Triple Header / 1987 / AIR / C • Tropic Of Desire / 1979 / WWV / M • Tuff Stuff / 1987 / WET / M • The Ultimate Lover / 1986 / VD / M • Unnatural Phenomenon #1 / 1985 / WV / M • Unnatural Phenomenon #2 / 1986 / WV / M • The Untamed / 1978 / VCX / M • Untamed Passions / 1987 / CV / C • VCA Previews #4 / 1988 / VC / C • Victoria's Secret Desires / 1983 / S&L / C • Voodoo Lust: The Possession / 1989 / PCP / M • Water Nymph / 1987 / LIM / M • Who Shaved Aja? / 1989 / EX / M • Wild Things #1 / 1985 / CV / M • The Wizard Of AHH's / 1985 / SE / M • Woman In The Window / 1986 / TEM / M • Working It Out / 1983 / CA / M • You Bring Out The Animal In Me / 1987 / MIR / M • You Turn Me On / 1986 / LIM / M • Young Girls Do / 1984 / ELH / M

JON MARTINSTEIN *see* **Jon Martin**
JON O'BRIEN
Blunt Trauma #3: Whiteslave / 1996 / ZFX / B • Voodoo Dolls / 1996 / ZFX / B • War Pigs #1 / 1996 / ZFX / B • War Pigs #2 / 1996 / ZFX / B
JON REEVES *see* **Star Index I**
JON ROY JONES *see* **Star Index I**
JON SEVERINI *(Jon Keith)*
Diseased-looking guy with tattoos all over. SO of Gina LaMarca.
Breeders / 1996 / MET / M
JON SILKWOOD
Masquerade (1992-Usa) / 1992 / SC / M
JON SIMMONS *see* **Chris Reed**
JON STALLION
Dirty Dr. Feelgood / 1988 / VEX / M • The Girls Of Cooze / 1992 / V99 / C • Holly

Does Hollywood #4 / 1990 / CAY / M •
Suite Sensations / 1988 / SEX / M • Suzie
Superstar #3 / 1989 / CV / M • Wet Kisses
/ 1988 / V99 / M

JON STEELE see Star Index I

JON TIFFANY see Cody Adams

JON TODD
Sex #1 (Vca) / 1994 / VC / M

JON VINCENT
Autobiography Of A Slave / 1993 / PL / B •
Bi Intruder / 1991 / STA / G • The Bi-Analyst / 1991 / STA / G • Chains Of Passion /
1993 / PL / B

JONAS
Eat At Daves #4: Condo Cummers / 1995 /
SP / M

JONATHAN
Ash Prod: We Aim To Tease / 1995 / ASH /
M • C-Hunt #03: Sunny Delights / 1995 /
PEV / M • Fresh Meat #1 / 1996 / PL / M •
The Gypsy / 1996 / NIT / M • HomeGrown
Video #446: Slam Bam Thank You Ma'am!
/ 1995 / HOV / M • Intimate Interviews #4 /
1996 / NIT / M • LA Nasty / 1995 / SP / M •
Pearl Necklace: Premier Sessions #04 /
1994 / SEE / M • Pearl Necklace: Premier
Sessions #05 / 1994 / SEE / M • Pussyman
Auditions #06 / 1995 / SNA / M

JONATHAN CHURCH
Society Affairs / 1982 / CA / M

JONATHAN FORD
The Blonde Goddess / 1982 / VXP / M •
Hot Stuff / 1984 / VXP / M

JONATHAN HILL
Hard To Swallow / 1985 / PV / M

JONATHAN KENT
Big Breast Beach / 1995 / LV / M • Nasty
Newcummers #08 / 1995 / MET / M

JONATHAN LEE
Color Me Amber / 1985 / VC / M • Don't Get
Them Wet / 1987 / VD / M • Hard To Swal-
low / 1985 / PV / M • House Of Sexual Fan-
tasies / 1987 / GO / M • Inn Of Sin / 1988 /
VT / M • Inner Blues / 1987 / VD / M •
Lover's Lane / 1986 / SE / M • Max Bed-
room / 1987 / ZA / M • Nasty Nights / 1988
/ PL / C • Only The Best #1 / 1986 / CV / C
• Passion Pit / 1985 / SE / M • Wild Things
#2 / 1986 / CV / M

JONATHAN LINDERO see J.P. Anthony

JONATHAN LINDERS see J.P. Anthony

JONATHAN MORGAN (John Morgan,
Jonathon Morgan, Scott Gallegos)
Young male who usually does a good acting job
and seems a cut above the usual porn studs.
During May 1993 he screwed a new actress
(Carrie Morgan) including an anal and later
it turned out she was HIV positive. In the
usual chickens-with-their-heads-cut-off
perfformance, the industry quarantined him
for six months, but then it was discovered
she wasn't HIV positive after all. Scott Gal-
legos is from **The Erotic Adventures Of
The Three Musketeers**.
'Ho! 'Ho! 'Ho! / 1993 / WP / M • 1-900-
FUCK / 1995 / SO / M • 113 Cherry
Lane / 1994 / FOR / M • 2 Hung 2 Tung /
1992 / MID / M • The 4th Vixxen / 1995 /
EMC / M • A Is For Asia / 1996 / 4P / M •
Ace Mulholland / 1995 / ERA / M • Adult
Video Nudes / 1993 / VC / M • Allure / 1996
/ WP / M • Always / 1993 / XCI / M • Amer-
ica's Raunchiest Home Videos #18: Anal
Crunch / 1992 / ZA / M • America's
Raunchiest Home Videos #19: Bedroom
Farce / 1992 / ZA / M • American Beauty #2

/ 1994 / FOR / M • American Built / 1992 /
LE / M • American Garter / 1993 / VC / M •
Anal Academy / 1996 / ZA / M • Anal
Anonymous / 1995 / SO / M • Anal Asian
#2: The Won-Ton Woman / 1994 / IN / M •
Anal Attitude / 1993 / HO / M • Anal Babes
/ 1995 / PPR / M • Anal Blues / 1994 / PEP
/ M • Anal Connection / 1996 / ZA / M • Anal
Disciples #2: The Anal Conflict / 1996 / ZA
/ M • Anal Exchange / 1995 / C69 / M • Anal
Freaks / 1994 / KWP / M • Anal Health Club
Babes / 1995 / EVN / M • Anal Inquisition /
1996 / ZA / M • Anal Institution #1 1996 /
ZA / M • Anal Institution #3 / 1996 / ZA / M
• Anal Interrogation / 1995 / ZA / M • Anal
Maniacs #1 / 1994 / WP / M • Anal Maniacs
#2 / 1994 / WP / M • Anal Maniacs #3 /
1995 / WP / M • Anal Planet / 1994 / CC /
M • Anal Professor / 1996 / ZA / M • Anal
Rippers #2: The Unveiling / 1996 / ZA / M •
Anal Virgins Of America #06 / 1994 / FOR
/ M • Anal Webb / 1995 / ZA / M • The Anal-
izer / 1994 / VD / M • The Anals Of History
#2 / 1992 / MID / M • Anals, Inc / 1995 / ZA
/ M • Animal Instinct / 1993 / VI / M • Animal
Instinct / 1996 / DTV / M • Anonymous /
1993 / VI / M • Arabian Nights / 1993 / WP
/ M • Assent Of A Woman / 1993 / DR / M •
Assford Wives / 1992 / ATL / M • The At-
tendant / 1996 / SC / M • Attic Toys / 1994
/ ERA / M • Attitude / 1995 / VC / M • The
Awakening / 1992 / SC / M • The Babe /
1992 / EX / M • Babes / 1993 / HO / M •
Backdoor To Harley-Wood #3 / 1993 / AFV
/ M • Backdoor To The City Of Sin / 1993 /
ANA / M • Badgirls #3: Cell Block 69 / 1994
/ VI / M • Badlands #1 / 1994 / PEP / M •
Badlands #2: Back Into Hell / 1994 / PEP /
M • Bangkok Boobarella / 1996 / BTO / M •
Beach Bum Amateur's #21 / 1993 / MID / F
• Beaver & Buttcheeks / 1993 / DR / M •
The Beaverly Hillbillies / 1993 / IP / M • Be-
dazzled / 1993 / OD / M • Beeping Miss
Buffy / 1995 / CDI / M • Behind The Back-
door #6 / 1993 / EVN / M • Best Butt(e) In
The West #1 / 1992 / CC / M • The Best Of
Strippers Inc / 1996 / ONA / C • The Best
Rears Of Our Lives / 1992 / OD / M • The
Beverly Thrillbillies / 1993 / ZA / M • The
Big Shave / 1993 / PEP / M • Big Titted
Tarts / 1994 / PL / C • Bigger / 1991 / PL /
M • Bikini Beach #1 / 1993 / CC / M • Bikini
Beach #2 / 1993 / CC / M • Biography: Kait-
lyn Ashley / 1996 / SC / C • Black Flava /
1994 / EX / M • Black Is Back / 1993 / HW
/ M • Black Jack City #2: Black's Revenge
/ 1992 / HW / M • Black Orchid / 1993 / WV
/ M • Black Tie Affair / 1993 / VEX / M •
Blonde City / 1992 / IN / M • Bloopers /
Boners / 1996 / VI / M • Bloopers (Video
Team) / 1994 / VT / M • Blow For Blow /
1992 / ZA / M • Blue Dreams / 1996 / SC /
M • The Blues #1 / 1992 / VT / M • Body Of
Love / 1994 / ERA / M • Bonnie & Clyde #1
/ 1992 / VI / M • Bonnie & Clyde #2 / 1992
/ VI / M • Boob-O-Rama #3 / 1995 / WNW
/ M • Booty In The House / 1993 / WP / M
• The Boss / 1993 / VT / M • The Breast
Files #2 / 1994 / AVI / M • The Breast Of
Breastmen / 1995 / EVN / C • Breastman
Does The Twin Towers / 1993 / EVN / M •
Breastman Goes To Breastland #1 / 1993 /
EVN / M • Breastman Goes To Breastland
#2 / 1993 / EVN / M • Breastman's Bikini
Pool Party / 1995 / EVN / M • Breastman's
Wet T-Shirt Contest / 1994 / EVN / M •

Breastman's Wild West Adventure / 1995 /
EVN / M • Bringing Up The Rear / 1993 /
VD / C • Bronco Millie / 1992 / ZA / M • The
Brothel / 1993 / OD / M • Bruise Control /
1993 / PRE / B • Brunette Roulette / 1996 /
LE / M • Buck Naked In The 21st Century /
1993 / EVN / M • Buffy's Anal Adventure /
1996 / CDI / M • Buffy's Malibu Adventure /
1995 / CDI / M • Buffy's Nude Camera-
Party / 1996 / CIN / M • Burbank Sperm
Bank / 1996 / CIN / M • Bush League #2 /
1992 / CC / M • Bush Wacked / 1991 / ZA
/ M • Butt Camp / 1993 / HW / C • Butt
Naked #2 / 1994 / OD / M • Butterfly / 1993
/ OD / M • Buttmasters / 1994 / AMP / M •
Buttsizer, King Of Rears #1 / 1992 / EVN /
M • Caged Beauty / 1994 / FD / M • Cap-
tain Butt's Beach / 1992 / LV / M • Charm
School / 1993 / PEP / M • Cheating / 1994
/ VI / M • Checkmate / 1996 / SNA / M •
Cherry Pie / 1994 / SC / M • Chinatown /
1994 / SC / M • Chug-A-Lug Girls #1 / 1993
/ VT / M • Chug-A-Lug Girls #5 / 1994 / VT
/ M • Cliff Banger / 1993 / HW / M • A Clock-
work Orgy / 1995 / PL / M • Close Quarters
/ 1992 / ME / M • Collectible / 1991 / LE / M
• The Come On / 1995 / EX / M • Coming
Of Fortune / 1994 / EX / M • The Complete
& Total Anal Workout #1 / 1995 / ZA / M •
The Complete & Total Anal Workout #2 /
1996 / ZA / M • Corporate Justice / 1996 /
TEP / M • The Couch Trap / 1993 / ELP / M
• Country Girl / 1996 / VC / M • County Line
/ 1993 / PEP / M • Covergirl / 1994 / WP /
M • Crazed #1 / 1992 / VI / M • Crazed #2
/ 1992 / VI / M • Crazy Love / 1995 / VI / M
• The Creasemaster / 1993 / VC / M • The
Creasemaster's Wife / 1993 / VC / M •
Cumming Clean (1996—Caballero) / 1996
/ CA / M • The Cumming Of Sarah Jane #1
/ 1993 / AFV / M • The D.P. Man #1 / 1992
/ FD / M • The D.P. Man #2 / 1992 / FD / M
• Deep Behind The Scenes With Seymore
Butts #1 / 1995 / ULI / M • Deep Inside
Crystal Wilder / 1995 / VC / C • Deep Inside
Misty Rain / 1995 / VC / C • Deep Inside
Tiffany Mynx / 1994 / VC / C • Demolition
Woman #1 / 1994 / IP / M • Demolition
Woman #2 / 1994 / IP / M • Depraved Fan-
tasies #3 / 1994 / FPI / M • Desperate /
1995 / WP / M • Dial N Again / 1993 / PEP
/ M • Dial N For Nikki / 1993 / PEP / M •
Dick & Jane Go To Hollywood #2 / 1993 /
AVI / M • Dick At Nite / 1993 / MET / M • Di-
rector's Wet Dreams / 1996 / BBE / M •
Dirty Books / 1992 / VC / M • Dirty Laundry
#1 / 1994 / CV / M • The Dirty Little Mind of
Martin Fink / 1991 / ME / M • Dirty
Thoughts / 1992 / LE / M • Dirty Work /
1995 / VC / M • Disoriented / 1992 / VI / M
• Doggie Style / 1994 / CA / M • Dominant
Jean / 1996 / CC / M • Double Detail / 1992
/ SO / M • Double Load #2 / 1994 / HW / M
• Dp #2: The Mighty Fhucks / 1994 / FC / M
• The Drifter / 1995 / CV / M • Eleventh An-
nual AVN Awards / 1994 / VC / M • Elvis
Slept Here / 1992 / LE / M • Employee's
Entrance In The Rear / 1996 / CC / M •
Endlessly / 1993 / VI / M • Erectnophobia
#2 / 1992 / MID / M • The Erotic Adventures
Of The Three Musketeers / 1992 / CEL / S
• Erotic Escape / 1995 / FH / M • Erotic
Newcummers Vol 1 #2: Texas Twisters /
1993 / DR / M • Erotic Visions / 1995 / ULI
/ M • Erotika / 1994 / WV / M • Eternal Lust
/ 1996 / VC / M • Euphoria / 1993 / CA / M

• Euroslut #2 / 1994 / CC / M • Exit In Rear / 1993 / XCI / M • The Face / 1994 / PP / M • Face Jam / 1996 / VC / M • Facesitter #1 / 1992 / CC / M • The Fantasy Booth / 1993 / ONA / M • Fantasy Inc. / 1995 / CV / M • Father Of The Babe / 1993 / ZA / M • Feds In Bed / 1993 / HO / M • Femme Fatale / 1996 / CIN / M • Film Buff / 1994 / WP / M • The Final Secret / 1992 / SO / M • Flesh For Fantasy / 1994 / CV / M • Fleshmates / 1994 / ERA / M • Flexxx #4 / 1995 / VT / M • The Fluffer #1 / 1993 / FD / M • Flying High #1 / 1992 / HO / M • Flying High #2 / 1992 / HO / M • Freak Dat Booty / 1994 / WP / M • Frendz? #1 / 1996 / RAS / M • Full Blown / 1992 / GO / M • The Fury / 1993 / WIV / M • Gang Bang Bitches #03 / 1994 / PP / M • Gang Bang Bitches #04 / 1995 / PP / M • Gang Bang Bitches #10 / 1995 / PP / M • Ghosts / 1994 / EMC / M • The Girl In Room 69 / 1994 / VC / M • A Girl Like You / 1995 / LE / M • Girls Of Sorority Row / 1994 / VT / M • The Girls Of Spring Break / 1995 / VT / M • Girls Of The Athletic Department / 1995 / VT / M • Girls Of The Ivy Leagues / 1994 / VT / M • Girls Of The Packed Ten / 1994 / VT / M • Girls Of The Very Big Eight / 1994 / VT / M • The Go-Go Girls / 1994 / EVN / M • The Golden Touch / 1995 / WP / M • The Great Pretenders / 1994 / FD / M • Greek Week / 1994 / CV / M • Group Therapy / 1992 / TP / M • Guilty By Seduction / 1993 / PI / M • Gun Runner / 1996 / CIN / M • Happy Endings / 1994 / WP / M • The Hard Line / 1993 / PEP / M • Hard To Stop #1 / 1992 / VC / M • Hard To Stop #2 / 1992 / VC / M • Haunted Nights / 1993 / WP / M • Heart Breaker / 1994 / CA / M • Heartbeats / 1992 / LE / M • Heel's Angels / 1995 / PRE / B • Hell Hole / 1996 / ZA / M • Her Name Is Asia / 1996 / SUF / M • Herman's Bed / 1992 / HO / M • Hienie's Heroes / 1995 / VC / M • Hillbilly Honeys / 1996 / WP / M • Hindfeld / 1993 / PI / M • Hole In One / 1994 / HO / M • Hollywood Boulevard / 1995 / CV / M • Hollywood Connection / 1992 / ... / M • Hollywood Scandal: The Heidi Flesh Story / 1993 / IP / M • Hooked / 1992 / SC / M • Hootermania / 1994 / VC / M • Hot Blooded / 1994 / ERA / M • Hot Box / 1995 / V99 / C • Hot Wishes / 1995 / LE / M • Howard Sperm's Private Parties / 1994 / LBO / M • I Made Marian / 1993 / PEP / M • I Touch Myself / 1992 / IN / M • The Illustrated Woman / 1995 / CA / M • In Loving Color #1 / 1992 / VT / M • In Loving Color #3 / 1992 / VT / M • Indecent Offer / 1993 / AFV / M • Induced Pleasure / 1995 / ERA / M • Inside Job / 1992 / ZA / M • Invitation For Lust / 1995 / C69 / M • Invitation To The Blues / 1994 / LE / M • Jack The Stripper / 1992 / ME / M • Jiggly Queens #1 / 1993 / LE / M • Juranal Park / 1993 / OD / M • Just A Gigolo / 1992 / SC / M • Just My Imagination / 1993 / WP / M • Kadillac & Devell / 1993 / ZA / M • KBBS: Weekend With Alicia Rio & Sheila Stone / 1992 / KBB / M • Kelly Eighteen #1 / 1993 / LE / M • Kelly Eighteen #2 / 1993 / LE / M • Kept Women / 1995 / LE / M • The Key to Love / 1992 / ZA / M • Kym Wilde Sessions #4 / 1993 / RB / B • Kym Wilde's On The Edge #04 / 1993 / RB / B • Kym Wilde's On The Edge #08 / 1994 / RB / B • Kym Wilde's On The

Edge #26 / 1995 / RB / B • La Femme Vanessa / 1995 / SC / M • Lap Of Luxury / 1994 / WIV / M • Latex #1 / 1994 / VC / M • Latex And Lace / 1996 / BBE / M • Layover / 1994 / VI / M • Leather For Lovers #1 / 1992 / LFL / M • Leena's Early Experiences / 1995 / OD / C • Leena's Favorite Studs / 1995 / OD / C • Leena's Oral Extravaganza / 1995 / OD / C • Leg Tease #1 / 1995 / VT / M • Let's Dream On / 1994 / FD / M • Let's Party / 1993 / VC / M • Lethal Passion / 1991 / PL / M • The Living End / 1992 / OD / M • Loopholes / 1993 / TP / M • Loose Jeans / 1996 / GO / M • Love Potion 69 / 1994 / VC / M • Love Tryst / 1995 / VPN / M • Lover Under Cover / 1995 / ERA / M • The Lovers / 1993 / HO / M • Malcolm XXX / 1992 / OD / M • Malibu Blue / 1992 / LE / M • Masquerade (1992-Usa) / 1992 / SC / M • Memories / 1992 / LE / M • Midnight Confessions / 1992 / XCI / M • The Mistress (1993-Caballero) / 1993 / CA / M • The Money Hole / 1993 / VD / M • More Than A Handful #2 / 1993 / MET / M • More Than A Handful #3 / 1993 / MET / M • More Than A Handful #4 / 1994 / MET / M • More Than A Handful #5: California Or Bust / 1994 / MET / M • Motel Matches / 1996 / LE / M • The Mountie / 1994 / PP / M • Ms. Behaved / 1994 / SC / M • My Favorite Rear / 1993 / PEP / M • My Generation / 1994 / HO / M • My Secret Lover / 1992 / XCI / M • Mystery Of The Maletease Dildo / 1992 / STR / M • N.Y.D.P. / 1994 / PEP / M • Naked Ambition / 1995 / VC / M • Naked Goddess #1 / 1991 / VC / M • Naked Goddess #2 / 1991 / VC / M • Nasty Backdoor Nurses / 1994 / LBO / M • Nasty Cracks / 1992 / PRE / B • Neutron Man / 1993 / HO / M • Never Never Land / 1992 / PL / M • Never Say Never / 1994 / SC / M • Never Say Never, Again / 1994 / SC / M • The New Ass Masters #07 / 1996 / LEI / C • The New Ass Masters #14 / 1996 / LEI / C • New Pussy Hunt #24 / 1996 / LEI / C • New Pussy Hunt #25 / 1996 / LEI / C • The New Snatch Masters #16 / 1995 / LEI / C • Nikki At Night / 1993 / LE / M • Nikki Never Says No / 1992 / LE / M • Nipples / 1994 / FOR / F • No Motive / 1994 / MID / M • Nude Awakenings / 1996 / PP / M • NYDP Blue / 1996 / WP / M • Objective: D.P. / 1993 / PEP / M • Obsexxed / 1992 / VD / M • On Her Back / 1994 / VI / M • Oral Majority #10 / 1993 / WV / C • The Orgy #3 / 1993 / EMC / M • Orgy Attack / 1993 / DRP / M • The Other Side / 1995 / ERA / M • Paging Betty / 1994 / VC / M • The Palace Of Pleasure / 1995 / ULI / M • The Party / 1992 / CDI / M • Passenger 69 #1 / 1994 / IP / M • Patriot X / 1995 / LE / M • The Pawn Shop / 1996 / MID / M • Penetrator #2: Grudge Day / 1995 / PL / M • Perfect Endings / 1994 / PLV / B • Performer Of The Year / 1994 / WP / M • Perplexed / 1994 / FD / M • Persuasion / 1995 / LE / M • The Pink Pussycat / 1992 / CA / M • Plumb And Dumber / 1995 / PP / M • The Poetry Of The Flesh / 1993 / PEP / M • Poor Little Rich Girl #1 / 1992 / XCI / M • Poor Little Rich Girl #2 / 1992 / XCI / M • A Portrait Of Dorian / 1992 / OD / M • The Power & The Passion / 1993 / CDI / M • Priceless / 1995 / WP / M • Primal Instinct / 1996 / SNA / M • Primarily Yours / 1996 / CA / M • Principles Of Lust / 1992 / WV / M

• Prisoner Of Love / 1995 / CV / M • Pristine #1 / 1996 / CA / M • Pristine #2 / 1996 / CA / M • Private Gold #16: Summer Wind / 1997 / OD / M • Private Stories #02 / 1995 / OD / M • Private Stories #11 / 1996 / OD / M • Private Video Magazine #05 / 1993 / M • Private Video Magazine #16 / 1994 / OD / M • Provocative / 1994 / LE / M • Pulp Friction / 1994 / PP / M • Pulse / 1994 / EX / M • Pumphouse Sluts / 1996 / CC / M • Puritan Video Magazine #07 / 1996 / LE / M • Puritan Video Magazine #09 / 1997 / LE / M • A Pussy To Die For / 1992 / CA / M • Pussy Whipped / 1994 / FOR / M • Pussywoman #1: Sisters In Sin / 1994 / CC / M • Pussywoman #2 / 1994 / CC / M • Raging Hormones / 1992 / LE / M • Raincoat Fantasies / 1993 / ELP / M • Rainwoman #06 / 1993 / CC / M • Raunch #05 / 1992 / CC / M • Raunchy Remedy / 1993 / ELP / M • A Rear And Pleasant Danger / 1995 / PP / M • A Reason To Die / 1994 / PEP / M • Rebecca Lord's World Tour #1: French Edition / 1995 / WP / M • Red Door Diaries #2 / 1996 / ZA / M • Red Hots / 1996 / PL / M • Reel Life / 1993 / ZA / M • Reel People #05 / 1994 / PP / M • Reel People #07 / 1995 / PP / M • Reel People #08 / 1995 / PP / M • Reel People #09 / 1995 / PP / M • Reel People #11 / 1995 / PP / M • The Reel Sex World #01 / 1993 / WP / M • The Reel Sex World #02 / 1994 / WP / M • The Reel Sex World #03 / 1994 / WP / M • The Reel Sex World #04: Laid In Hawaii / 1994 / WP / M • Reel Sex World #05 / 1994 / WP / M • The Reel World #1 / 1994 / FOR / M • The Reel World #2 / 1994 / FOR / M • Rhapsody / 1993 / VT / M • Rim Job Rita / 1994 / SC / M • Ring Of Passion / 1994 / ERA / M • Risque Burlesque #1 / 1994 / IN / M • Risque Burlesque #2 / 1996 / IN / M • Rockhard (Sin City) / 1996 / SC / M • The Romeo Syndrome / 1995 / SC / M • Samantha's Private Fantasies / 1994 / WV / M • Saturday Night Porn #3 / 1993 / AFV / M • The Secret Garden #1 / 1992 / XCI / M • The Secret Garden #2 / 1992 / XCI / M • Secret Services / 1995 / CV / M • Seduced / 1992 / VD / M • Seeing Red / 1993 / VI / M • Selina / 1993 / XCI / M • The Serpent's Dream / 1993 / VC / M • Sex Bandits / 1992 / ZA / M • Sex Lives Of Clowns / 1994 / VC / M • Sex Sting / 1992 / FD / M • Sex Trek #4: The Next Orgasm / 1994 / ME / M • Sex Trek #5: Deep Space Sex / 1994 / ME / M • Sexdrive #1: Topdown Girl / 1993 / OD / M • Sexed / 1993 / HO / M • Sexual Olympics #1: The Trials / 1992 / VT / M • Sexual Olympics #2: The Finals / 1992 / VT / M • Sexual Overdrive / 1996 / LE / M • Shave Tails #1 / 1994 / SO / M • Shave Tails #2 / 1994 / SO / M • Shave Tails #3 / 1994 / SO / M • Shave Tails #4 / 1995 / SO / M • A Shaver Among Us / 1992 / ZA / M • Shaving Grace / 1996 / GO / M • She Quest / 1994 / OD / M • She-Male Sex Clinic / 1991 / VC / G • Shear Ecstasy / 1993 / PEP / M • Show & Tell / 1994 / ELP / M • Silky Thighs / 1994 / ERA / M • Silver Screen Confidential / 1996 / WP / M • Sinnocence / 1995 / CDI / M • Sisters Of Sin / 1991 / VIM / G • Six Degrees Of Penetration / 1996 / PP / M • Sleeping Single / 1994 / CC / M • Slow Dancing / 1990 / VI / M • Smart Ass Delinquent / 1993 / VT / M •

The Smart Ass Returns / 1993 / VT / M • Smooth As Silk / 1994 / EMC / M • Snatch Masters #04 / 1995 / LEI / M • So I Married A Lesbian / 9993 / WV / M • Soap Opera Sluts / 1996 / AFI / M • Sodomania #03: Foreign Objects / 1993 / EL / M • Sodomania #07: Deep Down Inside / 1993 / EL / M • Sodomania: Slop Shots / 1996 / EL / C • Sole Search / 1996 / PRE / B • Southern Exposure / 1991 / LE / M • The Spa / 1993 / VC / M • Splendor In The Ass #2 / 1992 / CA / M • Stacked Deck / 1994 / IN / M • The Stand-Up / 1994 / VC / M • The Starlet / 1995 / SC / M • Steal This Heart #1 / 1993 / CV / M • Steal This Heart #2 / 1993 / CV / M • Steal This Heart (Director's) / 1993 / CV / M • Sterling Silver / 1992 / CC / M • Stretchin' The Rear / 1995 / PE / M • The Strip / 1992 / SC / M • Strippers Inc. #3 / 1994 / ONA / M • Stupid And Stupider / 1995 / SO / M • Style #1 / 1992 / VT / M • Summer Games / 1992 / HW / M • Supermodel #1 / 1994 / VI / M • Superstar Sex Challenge #1 / 1994 / VC / M • Superstar Sex Challenge #2 / 1994 / VC / M • Superstar Sex Challenge #3 / 1994 / VC / M • Sweet Smell Of Excess / 1996 / CIN / M • Taboo #10 / 1992 / IN / M • Taboo #11: Crazy On You / 1993 / IN / M • Taboo #13 / 1994 / IN / M • Tails Of Tribeca / 1993 / HW / M • Tailspin #3 / 1992 / VT / M • Take The A Train / 1993 / MID / M • The Tantric Guide To Sexual Potency And Extended Orgasm / 1994 / A&E / M • Telephone Expose / 1995 / VC / M • The Tempest / 1993 / SC / M • Temptation Of Serenity / 1994 / WP / M • Tender Loving Care / 1995 / WP / M • Teri Diver's Bedtime Tales / 1993 / FD / M • Thighs & Dolls / 1993 / PEP / M • Thin Ice / 1996 / ONA / M • The Three Musketeers #1 / 1992 / FD / M • The Three Musketeers #2 / 1992 / FD / M • The Tiffany Minx Affair / 1992 / FOR / M • Tiffany Minx Wildcat / 1993 / MID / C • The Time Machine / 1996 / WP / M • Tip Tap Toe / 1995 / PRE / C • Tit For Tat / 1994 / PEP / M • Tit Tease #1 / 1995 / VT / M • Titty City #1 / 1995 / TIW / M • To Shave And Shave Not / 1994 / PEP / M • Toe Nuts / 1994 / PRE / B • Tommyknockers / 1994 / CC / M • Tonya's List / 1994 / FD / M • Tori Welles Goes Behind The Scenes / 1992 / FD / M • Totally Depraved / 1996 / SC / M • Totally Real / 1996 / CA / M • The Truth Laid Bare / 1993 / ZA / M • Two Of A Kind / 1993 / PL / M • Two Sisters / 1992 / WV / M • Two Women / 1992 / ROB / M • Ultimate Orgy #1 / 1992 / GLI / M • Ultra Head / 1992 / CA / M • Unchained Melanie / 1992 / VC / M • Unfaithful Entry / 1992 / DR / M • Unforgettable / 1992 / HO / M • Uninhibited Love / 1994 / VPN / M • Unplugged / 1995 / CC / M • Unsolved Double Penetration / 1993 / PEP / M • Up Against It / 1993 / ZA / M • Use It Or Lose It / 1994 / CA / M • User Friendly / 1992 / VT / M • Vampire's Kiss / 1993 / AVI / M • Victoria's Secret Life / 1992 / WV / M • Visions Of Desire / 1993 / HO / M • The Wanderer #1: Road Tails / 1995 / CDI / M • The Wanderer #2: Slippery When Wet / 1995 / CDI / M • Wanderlust / 1992 / LE / M • Waves Of Passion / 1996 / ERA / M • Wendy Whoppers: Brain Surgeon / 1993 / PEP / M • Wendy Whoppers: Environmental Attorney / 1993 / PEP / M • Wendy Whoppers: Ninja CPA / 1993 / PEP / M •

Wendy Whoppers: Prison Love Doll / 1994 / PEP / M • Wendy Whoppers: Psychic Healer / 1994 / PEP / M • Wendy Whoppers: Razorwoman / 1993 / PEP / M • Wendy Whoppers: Ufo Tracker / 1994 / PEP / M • Western Nights / 1994 / WP / M • Wet Faces #1 / 1997 / SC / C • What's A Nice Girl Like You Doing In An Anal Movie? / 1995 / AMP / M • Whispers / 1992 / HO / M • White Shadow / 1994 / VC / M • Who Killed Holly Hollywood? / 1993 / VC / M • Whore House / 1995 / IPI / M • Wicked Ways #1: Interview With The Anal Queen / 1994 / WP / M • Wicked Ways #2: Education Of A D.P. Virgin / 1995 / WP / M • Wicked Ways #3: An All-Anal Slutfest / 1995 / WP / M • Wicked Woman / 1994 / HO / M • Wild & Wicked #4 / 1994 / VT / M • Wild Hearts / 1992 / SC / M • Wild Roomies / 1994 / VC / M • Within & Without You / 1993 / WP / M • Women On Fire / 1995 / LBO / M • XXX / 1996 / TEP / M • The XXX Files: Lust In Space / 1995 / IMV / M • You Bet Your Buns / 1992 / ZA / M

JONATHAN PAYNE
Pleasure And Company / 19?? / VHL / B

JONATHAN SHAW
Erotic Tattooing And Piercing #1 / 1986 / FLV / M

JONATHAN STEEL
Secret Sex #3: The Takeover / 1994 / CAT / G

JONATHAN WILDE
Born For Love / 1987 / ... / M

JONATHAN YOUNGER (Charlie Buck, Johnathon Younger)
Black male and therefore not the same as Jonathan Lee.
Battle Of The Stars #2: East Versus West / 1985 / NSV / M • Black Baby Dolls / 1985 / TAG / M • Blazing Matresses / 1986 / AVC / M • Champagne For Breakfast / 1980 / SE / M • Ebony Ecstacy / 1988 / HIO / C • Ebony Orgies / 1987 / SE / C • Forbidden Desire / 1983 / NSV / M • Future Sex / 1984 / NSV / M • The Hot Lunch Club / 1985 / WV / M • The House Of Strange Desires / 1985 / NSV / M • Illusions Of Ecstasy / 1985 / NSV / M • Inflamed / 1984 / NSV / M • Nasty / 1985 / NSV / M • The Sex Dancer / 1986 / NSV / M • Taboo #05 / 1986 / IN / M • Young Doctors In Lust / 1979 / NSV / M

JONATHON
She-Male Encounters #22: She-Male Mystique / 1995 / MET / G

JONATHON BLACKEAGLE see Star Index I

JONATHON KIND see Star Index I

JONATHON MORGAN see Jonathan Morgan

JONATHON X see Star Index I

JONI PIRO
Bucky Beaver's XXX Dragon Art Theatre Double Feature #11 / 1996 / SOW / M • San Francisco Ball / 1971 / SOW / S

JONI ROBERTS see Star Index I

JONI SON DOVI
Dirty Business / 1995 / WIV / M

JONNA
Buttman's Bubble Butt Babes / 1996 / EA / M

JONNY CANUUK see Dave Ruby

JONOI
Sexual Awareness / cr72 / CDC / M

JOO MIN LEE

Private Film #21 / 1995 / OD / M • Private Film #23 / 1995 / OD / M

JORDAN
Girls Games Of Summer #4 / 1994 / NIV / S • Joe Elliot's Black College Girls #01 / 1995 / JOE / M

JORDAN COXX
Decadent Dreams / 1996 / ME / M • Video Virgins #33 / 1996 / NS / M

JORDAN HART
Ash Prod: We Aim To Tease / 1995 / ASH / M • Big Breast Beach / 1995 / LV / M • Busty Babes In Heat #5 / 1995 / BTO / M • Dirty Old Men #1 / 1995 / FPI / M • GRG: Fuck My Eager Beaver / 1995 / GRG / M • Mellon Man #06 / 1995 / AVI / M • Mike Hott: #284 Cunt of the Month: Jordan Hart / 1995 / MHV / M • Mike Hott: #285 Fuck The Boss #05 / 1995 / MHV / M • Mike Hott: #296 Jordan Hart & Friends #1 / 1995 / MHV / M • Mike Hott: #299 Jordan Hart & Friends #2 / 1995 / MHV / M • Mike Hott: #312 Lesbian Sluts #19 / 1995 / MHV / F • Mike Hott: #330 Three-Sum Sluts #08 / 1995 / MHV / M • Mike Hott: #331 Lesbian Sluts #21 / 1996 / MHV / F • Nasty Newcummers #08 / 1995 / MET / M • Pussyman Auditions #06 / 1995 / SNA / M • Snatch Masters #04 / 1995 / LEI / M • Sugar Daddies / 1995 / FPI / M • Titan's Gonzo Video Magazine #02 / 1996 / TEG / M • Titty Troop / 1995 / CC / M

JORDAN JUSTICE
Nasty Nymphos #04 / 1994 / ANA / M • Nasty Nymphos #06 / 1994 / ANA / M

JORDAN LEE (Samantha (Jord. Lee), Nikki Lee (Jordan), Samantha Sweet)
Big tits, hard face and attitude, Southern accent, lithe body, tattoo on left belly and another (supposedly a swastika although she denies it) on her ankle, dark blonde long curly hair. Ex cop from Dallas TX and supposedly married to a cop. Born October 6, 1959 in East Prarie, MI, de-virginized at 13. (Must be wrong—she doesn't look 36.) 5'8" tall, 38-20-32 according to her (the 20 is with a heavy cannister of salt).
1-900-FUCK #2 / 1995 / SO / M • 10,000 Anal Maniacs #2 / 1994 / FOR / M • Addictive Desires / 1994 / OD / M • Anal All Stars / 1994 / CA / M • Anal Alley / 1996 / FD / M • Anal Anarchy / 1995 / VC / M • Anal Angels #5 / 1996 / VEX / C • Anal Disciples #1 / 1996 / ZA / M • Anal Disciples #2: The Anal Conflict / 1996 / ZA / M • Anal Institution #1 / 1996 / ZA / M • Anal Intruder #09: The Butt From Another Planet / 1995 / CC / M • Anal Island #1 / 1996 / VC / M • Anal Rippers #1: The Beginning / 1995 / ZA / M • Anal, Facial & Interracial / 1996 / FC / M • Anals, Inc / 1995 / ZA / M • The Artist / 1994 / HO / M • Back Door Mistress / 1994 / GO / M • Backdoor Play / 1996 / AVI / M • Backfield In Motion / 1995 / VT / M • Backing In #7 / 1995 / WV / C • Bare Ass In The Park / 1995 / PEP / M • Beach Mistress / 1994 / XCI / M • Bed & Breakfast / 1995 / WAV / M • Bi Stander / 1995 / BIN / G • Big & Busty Superstars / 1996 / DGD / F • The Big Pink / 1995 / MID / M • The Big Stick-Up / 1994 / WV / M • Black And White Revisited / 1995 / VT / F • Black Satin / 1994 / IN / M • Blue Collar Bootie / 1994 / BUT / M • The Body System / 1996 / FD / M • The Butt Detective / 1994 / VC / M • Butts Up / 1994 / CA / M • Canned Heat / 1995 / IN /

M • Car Wash Angels / 1995 / VC / M • Casting Couch #1 / 1994 / KV / M • Chained / 1995 / SC / M • Chasin' The Fifties / 1994 / WP / M • Cirque Du Sex #1 / 1996 / VT / M • Cockpit / 1996 / SC / M • Coming Attractions / 1995 / WHP / M • Cynthia And The Pocket Rocket / 1995 / CV / M • Decadence / 1994 / WHP / M • Decadence / 1995 / AMP / M • Dick & Jane Look For Pussy In The Park / 1995 / AVI / M • Dirty Bob's #21: Squeaky-Clean / 1995 / FLP / S • Doin' The Rounds / 1995 / VC / M • Don't Try This At Home / 1994 / FPI / M • Double D Amateurs #20 / 1994 / JMP / M • Dream Lover / 1995 / SC / M • Dreams / 1995 / VC / M • The Edge / 1995 / SC / M • Every Nerd Has A Fantasy / 1996 / FC / M • EXXXtra Parts: Interview With a Hermaphrodite / 1995 / PL / M • Fantasy Chamber / 1994 / ULI / M • Flesh Shopping Network #1 / 1995 / MID / M • Flexxx #1 / 1994 / VT / M • Four Weddings And A Honeymoon / 1995 / PL / M • Gang Bang Bitches #09 / 1995 / PP / M • Gangbang At The O.K. Corral / 1994 / FPI / M • Ghosts / 1995 / WV / M • The Girl Next Door #1 / 1994 / VT / M • The Girl Next Door #2 / 1994 / VT / M • Girl's School / 1994 / ERA / M • Girls Of The Packed Ten / 1994 / VT / M • Golddiggers #3 / 1995 / VC / M • The Hardwood Chronicles / 1995 / XCI / M • Harry Horndog #28: Fabulous Squirt Queens / 1994 / FPI / M • Here Comes Magoof #1 / 1995 / VC / M • Hot Tight Asses #08 / 1994 / TCK / M • Hot Tight Asses #10 / 1995 / TCK / M • Hot Tight Asses #14 / 1995 / TCK / M • Hotel Sodom #03 / 1995 / SNA / M • Hotel Sodom #09 / 1996 / SNA / M • Hourman Is Here / 1994 / CC / M • House Of Anal / 1995 / NOT / M • I Cream On Jeannie / 1995 / AVI / M • Impact / 1995 / SC / M • In The Fast Lane / 1995 / LE / M • In Your Face #3 / 1995 / PL / M • Interview: Doin' The Butt / 1995 / LV / M • Irresistible / 1995 / LV / M • Jenna Loves Rocco / 1996 / WAV / M • Jordan Lee: Anal Queen / 1997 / SC / C • Kinky Debutante Interviews #06 / 1994 / IP / M • La Femme Vanessa / 1995 / SC / M • Lady M's Anything Nasty #01: Pink Pussy Party / 1996 / AVI / F • Latex #1 / 1994 / VC / M • Legal Briefs / 1996 / EX / M • Lesbian Connection / 1996 / SUF / F • Lipstick Lesbians #1: Massage Parlor Dykes / 1994 / ZA / F • Lonely Hearts / 1995 / VC / M • Love Spice / 1995 / ERA / M • Lover Under Cover / 1995 / ERA / M • Lust & Desire / 1996 / WV / M • Lustful Obsessions / 1996 / NOT / M • Mickey Ray's Sex Search #03: Deep Heat / 1994 / WIV / M • Midget Goes Hawaiian / 1995 / FC / M • Mutual Consent / 1995 / VC / M • The New Ass Masters #09 / 1996 / LEI / C • The New Butt Hunt #19 / 1996 / LEI / C • Nurses Do It With Care / 1995 / EVN / M • Odyssey Triple Play #99: Hail, Hail, The Gang-Bang's Here #2 / 1995 / OD / M • On The Rise / 1994 / EX / M • On The Run / 1995 / SC / M • Ona Zee's Learning The Ropes #10: Chains Of Love / 1994 / ONA / B • One For The Gusher / 1995 / AMP / M • Orgies Orgies Orgies / 1994 / WV / M • Out Of My Mind / 1995 / PL / M • Party House / 1995 / WAV / M • Passenger 69 #1 / 1994 / IP / M • Perverted #1: The Babysitters / 1994 / ZA / M • Perverted Stories #05 / 1995 / JMP / M •

Philmore Butts Meets The Palm Beach Nymphomaniac Kathy Wille / 1995 / SUF / M • Philmore Butts On The Prowl / 1995 / SUF / M • Pizza Sluts: They Deliver / 1995 / XCI / M • Pussyclips #06 / 1995 / SNA / M • A Rear And Pleasant Danger / 1995 / PP / M • Reckless Passion / 1995 / WAV / M • Renegades #1 / 1994 / SC / M • Revenge Of The Pussy Suckers From Mars / 1994 / PP / M • Sex Academy #2: The Art Of Talking Dirty / 1994 / ONA / M • Sex Academy #4: The Art Of Anal / 1994 / ONA / M • Sgt. Peckers Lonely Hearts Club Gang Bang / 1995 / AMP / M • Shave Tails #1 / 1994 / SO / M • Silk Stockings: The Black Widow / 1994 / SPI / M • Sin Asylum / 1995 / CV / M • Sinnocence / 1995 / CDI / M • Snatch Motors / 1995 / VC / M • Sordid Stories / 1994 / AMP / M • The Star / 1994 / HO / M • The Starlet / 1995 / SC / M • Straight A's / 1994 / AMP / M • Strip Poker / 1995 / PEP / M • Strippers Inc. #1 / 1994 / ONA / M • Strippers Inc. #3 / 1994 / ONA / M • Strippers Inc. #4 / 1995 / ONA / M • Stripping / 1995 / NIT / M • Swedish Erotica #75 / 1994 / CA / M • Sweet A$ Money / 1994 / MID / M • Tail Taggers #126 / 1994 / WV / M • Titanic Orgy / 1995 / PEP / M • Tits A Wonderful Life / 1994 / CV / M • Titties 'n Cream #2 / 1995 / FC / M • Titty City #1 / 1995 / TIW / M • Titty Town #1 / 1994 / HW / M • The Tongue / 1995 / OD / M • The Ultimate Squirting Machine / 1994 / FPI / M • The Violation Of Felecia / 1995 / JMP / F • Western Nights / 1994 / WP / M • What You Are In The Dark / 1995 / KLP / M • Wild Breed / 1995 / SC / M • Willie Wanker At The Sushi Bar / 1995 / FD / M • Working Girl Gang-Bang / 1995 / GLI / M • The World's Biggest Gang Bang #1 / 1995 / FPI / M

JORDAN MCKNIGHT
Marginally pretty black girl with a lithe body, tight waist, very nice boy-like butt, medium to large natural tits, 20-something years old in 1994. In 1995 she has filled out to a womanly body. She says she comes from Windsor, Ont. As of 1997 she has had her tits expanded to huge size and become even more womanly and as of May 1997 she was allegedly found to be HIV positive.

Asses Galore #7: Lunatic Fringe / 1996 / DFI / M • Bad Girls / 1994 / VT / M • Black Bottom Girls / 1994 / ME / M • Black Cheerleader Search #11 / 1997 / IVC / M • Black Jack City #4 / 1994 / HW / M • Black Mystique #09 / 1994 / VT / F • Black Satin / 1994 / IN / M • Black Street Hookers #5: The Mean Streets Of Washington D.C. / 1997 / DFI / M • Butt Watch #06 / 1994 / FH / M • Cracklyn / 1994 / HW / M • Creme De Femme / 1994 / 4P / F • Dark Room / 1994 / VT / M • Ebony Dancer / 1994 / HBE / M • Florence Hump / 1994 / AFI / M • Frontin' Da Booty / 1994 / WP / M • Gang Bang Party / 1994 / HW / M • Gimme Some Head / 1994 / VT / M • Hard Core Beginners #09 / 1995 / LEI / M • Ho The Man Down / 1994 / WIV / M • Home Nurses Anal Adventure / 1994 / LBO / M • Mickey Ray's Sex Search #02: Tight Spots / 1994 / WIV / M • More Black Dirty Debutantes / 1994 / 4P / M • More Black Dirty Debutantes #4 / 1995 / 4P / M • My Baby Got Back #04 / 1994 / VT / M • My Baby Got Back #05 / 1995 / VT / M • Picture Perfect (Cal Vista) / 1995 / CV

/ M • Pumps In Da Rump #1 / 1994 / HW / M • Pussy Hunt #06 / 1994 / LEI / M • Pussyman #07: On The Dark Side / 1994 / SNA / M • Put 'em On Da Glass / 1994 / VT / M • Raw Sex #02 / 1995 / ERW / M • Sex Trek #4: The Next Orgasm / 1994 / ME / M • Sex Trek #5: Deep Space Sex / 1994 / ME / M • Sista! #2 / 1994 / VT / F • Sleaze Please!—October Edition / 1994 / FH / M • A Taste Of Fanny / 1994 / FH / M • Up And Cummers #12 / 1994 / 4P / M • Up And Cummers #18 / 1995 / 4P / M • Wet & Slippery / 1995 / WV / M • Women Of Color #2 / 1994 / ANA / M • Yankee Rose / 1994 / LE / M • Yo Yo Yo: A Very Black Christmas Tale! / 1994 / HW / M

JORDAN MICHAELS
Lifepod / 1980 / VC1 / S • Seymore & Shane Live On Tour / 1995 / ULI / M

JORDAN RUGGER
Filthy First Timers #6 / 1997 / EL / M

JORDAN SMITH *(Jordan Smythe, Jorden Smith, Todd (Jor. Smith), Bret Sting, Dick Gorby, Cole Stevens, Todd E.)*
SO of Candice Hart.

Anal Addiction #3 / 1991 / SO / M • Anal Adventures (Dragon) / 1992 / DRP / M • Anal Nation #2 / 1990 / CC / M • Anal Revolution / 1991 / ROB / M • The Back Doors (Executive) / 1991 / EX / M • Backdoor To Russia #1 / 1992 / VC / M • Backdoor To Russia #3 / 1993 / VC / M • Backfire / 1991 / GO / M • Backing In #4 / 1993 / WV / C • Beyond It All / 1991 / PAL / G • Bi & Large / 1994 / STA / G • Bi Madness / 1991 / STA / G • Bi-Inferno / 1992 / VEX / G • Biff Malibu's Totally Nasty Home Videos #07 / 1992 / ANA / M • Black & White In Living Color / 1992 / WV / M • Blonde Riders / 1991 / CC / M • Butt Woman #2 / 1992 / FH / M • Butt Woman #3 / 1992 / FH / M • Dr Butts #1 / 1991 / 4P / M • Dr Butts #2 / 1992 / 4P / M • Dream Date / 1992 / HO / M • Dreams Of Candace Hart / 1991 / VI / M • Everybody's Playmates / 1992 / CA / C • Fever / 1992 / CA / M • French Open / 1990 / OD / M • Heads Or Tails? / 1993 / PL / M • Hothouse Rose #2 / 1992 / VC / M • Internal Affairs / 1992 / CDI / M • The Last Blonde / 1991 / IN / M • Made In Heaven / 1991 / PP / M • Mind Trips / 1992 / FH / M • Mischief / 1991 / WV / M • The Newcummers / 1990 / 4P / M • Nothing Else Matters / 1992 / V99 / C • Once In A Blue Moon / 1991 / CC / M • One Million Years DD / 1992 / CC / M • Oral Majority #10 / 1993 / WV / C • The Pink Pussycat / 1992 / CA / M • Regarding Hiney / 1991 / CC / M • Shameless / 1991 / SC / M • Shoot To Thrill / 1992 / WV / M • To The Rear / 1992 / VC / M • Voyeur Video / 1992 / ZA / M • White Men Can Hump / 1992 / EVN / M • You Bet Your Butt / 1992 / VC / M

JORDAN SMYTHE *see* **Jordan Smith**
JORDAN ST. JAMES
Amateur Gay Girls / 1995 / LEI / C • Babe Watch #3 / 1995 / SC / M • Babe Watch #4 / 1995 / SC / M • Beverly Hills Blondes #2 / 1995 / LV / M • Big Busted Goddesses Of Beverly Hills / 1996 / NAP / S • Big Thingiees / 1996 / BEP / M • Bloopers & Behind The Scenes / 1995 / LEI / M • Blue Movie / 1995 / WP / M • Busty Porno Stars #2 / 1996 / H&S / M • Chained / 1995 / SC / M • Dear Diary / 1995 / WP / M • Deep Throat Girls #14 / 1995 / GO / M • Double

D Amateurs #22 / 1994 / JMP / M • Double D Dreams / 1996 / NAP / S • Electropussy / 1995 / CC / M • Every Woman Has A Fantasy #3 / 1995 / VC / M • Freak Of The Week / 1996 / LIP / F • Full Metal Babes / 1995 / LE / M • Girly Video Magazine #5 / 1996 / BEP / M • Hootersville (Legend) / 1995 / LE / M • Hot Leather #1 / 1995 / GO / M • Hot Tight Asses #11 / 1995 / TCK / M • Humpkin Pie / 1995 / HW / M • Interview's Blonde Bombshells / 1995 / LV / M • John Wayne Bobbitt Uncut / 1994 / LEI / M • Juicy Cheerleaders / 1995 / LE / M • Lolita / 1995 / SC / M • Lust Runner / 1995 / VC / M • Nightmare On Lesbian Street / 1995 / LIP / F • Picture Perfect (Big) / 1995 / BIP / F • Pussy Hunt #05 / 1994 / LEI / M • Pussy Hunt #10 / 1995 / LEI / M • Pussyman #10: Butts, Butts & More Butts / 1995 / SNA / M • Pussyman Auditions #01 / 1995 / SNA / M • Racially Motivated / 1994 / LV / M • Rear Entry / 1995 / LEI / M • Reminiscing / 1995 / LE / M • Satyriasis / 1995 / PL / M • The Sexual Solution #1 / 1995 / LE / M • Sluthunt #3 / 1996 / BIP / F • Southern Possession / 1995 / DEN / M • Sweet Sunshine / 1995 / IF / M • Thunder Boobs / 1995 / BTO / M • Work Of Art / 1995 / LE / M

JORDAN YOUNG
Lost In Vegas / 1996 / AWV / G • Our Trespasses / 1996 / AWV / G

JORDEN SMITH *see* Jordan Smith

JORDON
AVP #9509: Cum On Over / 1991 / AVP / M

JORDON ROBERTS
Sinderella She-Males / 1994 / HEA / G

JORGE
Private Video Magazine #01 / 1993 / OD / M

JORGEN HOLMBERG
Screamers / 1994 / HW / M

JOSALYNN TAYLOR *(Devan, Lynn York, Coreena Taylor, Jennifer (J. Taylor))*
Small breasted blonde first seen in **The Booby-Guard**. Tight waist, slightly too large hips, long straight hair, mole half-way down her back next to her spine and a pattern of dots on her left hip. Pretty. Not the same as Alison Parrish.
America's Raunchiest Home Videos #65: / 1993 / ZA / M • The Bitches / 1993 / LIP / F • The BoobyGuard / 1993 / FOR / M • Camera Shy / 1993 / FOR / M • Captain Bob's Pussy Patrol / 1993 / FCP / M • Dirty Dating Service #02 / 1993 / WP / M • Fantasy Flings #01 / 1993 / WP / M • First Time Lesbians #01 / 1993 / JMP / F • Hairy Horndog #17: Love Puppies #5 / 1993 / ZA / M • Joe Elliot's College Girls #28 / 1994 / JOE / M • Kiss Is A Rebel With A Cause / 1993 / WV / M • Mind Shadows #2 / 1993 / FD / M • Mr. Peepers Amateur Home Videos #72: Dirty Diary / 1993 / LBO / M • Mr. Peepers Amateur Home Videos #75: Trio In Rio / 1993 / LBO / M • Nasty Newcummers #02 / 1993 / MET / M • New Faces, Hot Bodies #07 / 1993 / STP / M • New Faces, Hot Bodies #21 / 1996 / STP / C • Odyssey 30 Min: #306: / 1993 / OD / M • Odyssey 30 Min: #328: / 1993 / OD / M • Odyssey Triple Play #66: Cum-Crazed Couples / 1994 / OD / M • Odyssey Triple Play #70: Three By Threeway / 1994 / OD / M • Odyssey Triple Play #79: Dildos Dykes & Dicks / 1994 / OD / M • The Orgy #2 / 1993 / EMC / M • Pearl Necklace: Thee Bush League

#16 / 1993 / SEE / M • Pearl Necklace: Thee Bush League #18 / 1993 / SEE / M • Slave To Love / 1993 / ROB / M • Wad Gobblers #09 / 1993 / GLI / M

JOSE
Dirty Hairy's Over 50 Meets Mr. Black 18 Inches / 1996 / GOT / M

JOSE ALVANAREZ *see* Star Index I

JOSE DUNO
Undulations / 1980 / VC / M

JOSE DUVAL *(John Duval (Jose), Jose Duvall, Josey Duval)*
Bi Bi American Style / cr85 / MET / G • Bi-Heat #03 / 1987 / ZA / G • Black Widow / 1988 / WV / M • Blowing Your Mind / 1984 / RSV / M • Burlexxx / 1984 / VC / M • Can't Get Enough / 1985 / CA / M • Deep & Wet / 1986 / VD / M • Deep Inside Keisha / 1994 / VC / C • Flesh Of The Lotus / 1971 / VCX / M • Flipside: A Backdoor Adventure / 1985 / CV / M • Freedom Of Choice / 1984 / VHL / M • Hot Fudge / 1984 / VC / M • Hot Girls In Love / 1985 / VXP / M • Hot Rockers / 1985 / IVP / M • Hot Service / 19?? / CDI / M • I Creme With Genie / 1991 / PL / M • Long Hard Nights / 1984 / ELH / M • Mature Women #01 / 1991 / BTO / M • Mature Women #02 / 1991 / BTO / M • New York's Finest / 1988 / AE / S • Nightshift Nurses #1 / 1988 / VC / M • Nightshift Nurses #2 / 1996 / VC / M • Oh, What A Night! / 1990 / VC / M • Only The Best Of Breasts / 1987 / CV / C • The Pillowman / 1988 / VC / M • Pussy Power #04 / 1992 / BTO / M • R.S.V.P. / 1983 / VES / S • Raw Talent #1 / 1984 / VC / M • Samantha, I Love You / 1988 / WV / C • Sex Spa USA / 1984 / VC / M • Silence Of The G.A.M.S. / 1992 / CA / M • Silk, Satin & Sex / 1983 / SE / M • The South Bronx Story / 1986 / CC / M • Star Angel / 1986 / COM / M • Succulent / 1983 / VXP / M • Supergirls Do General Hospital / 1984 / VC / M • Taboo American Style #4: The Exciting Conclusion / 1985 / VC / M • Teasers: Watch Me Sparkle / 1988 / MET / M • This Babe's For You / 1984 / TAR / M • Throbbin' Hood / 1987 / VD / M • Thunderstorm / 1987 / VC / M • Times Square Comes Alive / 1984 / VC / M • Tongue Twisters / 1986 / VXP / M • Turn On With Kelly Nichols / 1984 / CA / M • Viva Vanessa The Undresser / 1984 / VC / M • Young Nympho's / 1986 / VD / M

JOSE DUVALL *see* Jose Duval

JOSE FERRARO
Jungle Blue / 1978 / HIF / M

JOSE FINCH
Hungry Eyed Woman / cr71 / VCX / M

JOSE MONTERO
Private Film #12 / 1994 / OD / M

JOSE MORALES *see* Star Index I

JOSE RICCO
Ready To Drop #04 / 1994 / FC / M

JOSE SOLICA
L.A. Tool & Die / 1979 / TMX / G

JOSEF MOOSHOLZER
Confessions Of A Sexy Photographer / 1969 / SOW / S • [Die Madchenhandler / 1972 / ... / M • [Schulmadchen-Report 4: Was Eltern Oft Verzweifeln LaBt / 1972 / ... / M

JOSEF RABL
The Doll House / 1995 / CV / M

JOSEFINA
More Dirty Debutantes #56 / 1996 / 4P / M

JOSELYN

She-Male Call Girls / 1996 / BIZ / G • TV Dildo Fantasy #2 / 1996 / BIZ / G

JOSEPH
House Of Pleasure / 1984 / CA / M • Joe Elliot's College Girls #28 / 1994 / JOE / M • Mr. Peepers Amateur Home Videos #56: Hindsight Is Brownish / 1992 / LBO / M • Mr. Peepers Amateur Home Videos #64: Proposition 69 / 1992 / LBO / M • Neighborhood Watch #38: Pearlie's Curlie's / 1993 / LBO / M

JOSEPH BLACK
Can't Get Enough / 1985 / CA / M • Farmers Daughters / 1975 / VC / M • Inside Little Oral Annie / 1984 / VXP / M • Little Oral Annie Takes Manhattan / 1985 / VXP / M • Shacking Up / 1985 / VXP / M • Stray Cats / 1985 / VXP / M • A Taste Of Pink / 1985 / VXP / M • Tight Delight / 1985 / VXP / M

JOSEPH DARLING *see* Star Index I

JOSEPH ELLIOT
American Pie / 1980 / SE / M

JOSEPH HERTIGINE
Bi Bi European Style / 1990 / PL / G • Get Bi Tonight / 1991 / PL / G

JOSEPH JAMES *see* Star Index I

JOSEPH KEARNS
L.A. Tool & Die / 1979 / TMX / G

JOSEPH LAND *see* Joey Silvera

JOSEPH LOPEZ
Eruption / 1977 / VCX / M

JOSEPH MARKS
Bi-Conflict / 1994 / FST / G • Conflict Of Interest / 1994 / FST / G

JOSEPH NASSI *see* Joey Silvera

JOSEPH STRYKER
Black Voodoo / 1987 / FOV / M • Carnal College / 1987 / VT / M • Good Girl, Bad Girl / 1984 / SE / M • The Good Time Girls / 1985 / VEX / M • Pretty In Black / 1986 / WET / M • Quicksilver / 1987 / CDI / M • Thunderstorm / 1987 / VC / M

JOSEPH WHALES *see* Star Index I

JOSEPH YALE
The Private Pleasures Of John C. Holmes / 1983 / ... / G

JOSEPHE
Tania's Lustexzesse / 1994 / MET / M

JOSEPHINA
Reel Life Video #01: Josephina, Lisa & Julia / 1994 / RLF / F

JOSEPHINE
A Merry Widow / 1996 / SPI / M • Quest For Pleasure / 1996 / DIP / F

JOSEPHINE CARRINGTON
Dirty Letters / 1984 / VD / M • Fantasies Unltd. / 1985 / CDI / M • Firefoxes / 1985 / PLY / M • Flesh Fire / 1985 / AVC / M • The Girls Of The A Team #1 / 1985 / WV / M • Loose Morals / 1987 / HO / M • Love Bites / 1985 / CA / M • The Love Scene / 1985 / CDI / M • The Lover Girls / 1985 / VEX / M • Naked Lust / 1985 / SE / M • Naughty Nurses / 1986 / VEX / M • A Passage To Ecstasy / 1985 / CDI / M • The Ribald Tales Of Canterbury / 1986 / CA / M • Savage Fury #1 / 1985 / VEX / M • Summer Break / 1985 / VEX / M • Surfside Sex / 1985 / PV / M • Tailhouse Rock / 1985 / WV / M • Tracy Dick / 1985 / WV / M

JOSEPHINE COX *see* Star Index I

JOSEPHINE FARMER
Flight Sensations / 1983 / VC / C

JOSEY
Blue Vanities #540 / 1994 / FFL / M

JOSEY DUVAL *see* Jose Duval

JOSH
HomeGrown Video #470: Heroes, Torpedoes & Grinders / 1996 / HOV / M • HomeGrown Video #472: Everyday People / 1996 / HOV / M • New Faces, Hot Bodies #10 / 1993 / STP / M • New Faces, Hot Bodies #11 / 1993 / STP / M • New Faces, Hot Bodies #15 / 1994 / STP / M

JOSH ANDREWS
Blue Magic / 1981 / QX / M • Playpen / 1987 / VC / M • Sex Appeal / 1986 / VES / S

JOSH RAMSEY
Captain Bob's Lust Boat #2 / 1993 / FCP / M

JOSH STERLING
Lost In Vegas / 1996 / AWV / G

JOSH WAY see Star Index I

JOSI EMERSON see Debi Diamond

JOSIANNE CARTIER see Star Index I

JOSIE
Ben Dover's 9th / 1996 / VC / M • Chocolate Bunnies #06 / 1996 / LBO / C • Neighborhood Watch #17: Burning The Sausage / 1992 / LBO / M • Pearl Necklace: Thee Bush League #17 / 1993 / SEE / M

JOSIE FARMER see Star Index I

JOSIE JONES
Blue Magic / 1981 / QX / M

JOSIE KATS
The Bitch Biker #1: The Long Road Home / 1994 / RBP / F • The Whipped Voyeur's Lesbian Sex Show / 1994 / PL / F

JOSIE MOORE
Kitty Foxx's Kinky Kapers #02 / 1995 / TTV / M

JOURDAN ALEXANDER see Star Index I

JOVAN
Santa Is Coming All Over Town / 1996 / EVN / M

JOVANNA SILK
Black Trisexual Encounters #4 / 1986 / LA / G • Breast Of Britain #2 / 1987 / BTO / M • Forbidden Fruit #1 / 1987 / MET / G • She Studs #01 / 1990 / BIZ / G • Trisexual Encounters #04 / 1986 / PL / G

JOY
Blue Vanities #547 / 1994 / FFL / M • Blue Vanities #558 / 1994 / FFL / M • Crazy Lust / 1994 / ORE / C • Global Girls / 1996 / GO / F • Liquid Lips #2 / 1994 / MAV / M • Teasedance Masturbation #3 / 1994 / MAV / F

JOY (DORIAN GRANT) see Dorian Grant

JOY BLISS
Bottom Busters / 1973 / BLT / M

JOY BRAZIL
Most Valuable Slut / 1973 / HLV / M

JOY CUMMINGS
Blonde Heat (VCA) / 1985 / VC / M • Video Girls / 1984 / LIP / F

JOY FOX
Marginally pretty with long straight light brown hair, nicely shaped medium tits, slightly flabby body, fresh disposition, 19 years old in 1994, comes from CA.
Leg...Ends #16 / 1996 / PRE / F • Student Fetish Videos: Best of Catfighting #03 / 1995 / PRE / C • Student Fetish Videos: Best Of Foot Worship #03 / 1995 / PRE / C • Student Fetish Videos: The Enema #17 / 1995 / PRE / B • Student Fetish Videos: Foot Worship #13 / 1994 / PRE / B • Up And Cummers #12 / 1994 / 4P / M

JOY KAEL

The Unholy Child / 1972 / AVC / M

JOY KARINS
Big Busty #45 / 1994 / BTO / S • Buttman's European Vacation #1 / 1991 / EA / M • Buttman's European Vacation #2 / 1992 / EA / M • Cherry Busters / 1995 / WIV / M • Erotic Games / 1992 / PL / M • Impulse #06: / 1996 / MBP / M • Skin #3 / 1995 / ERQ / M

JOY KELLY see Dorothy Oh

JOY KING
John Holmes Exposed / 1978 / AVC / C • Tales Of A High Class Hooker / 19?? / VXP / M

JOY KISS
Private Film #27 / 1995 / OD / M • Private Film #28 / 1995 / OD / M • Triple X Video Magazine #01 / 1995 / OD / M • Triple X Video Magazine #02 / 1995 / OD / M • Triple X Video Magazine #04 / 1995 / OD / M

JOY KRENEK see Star Index I

JOY LAROCH see Star Index I

JOY LARSEN
Let's Talk Sex / 1982 / CA / M

JOY MADISON
Catfighting Students / 1995 / PRE / C • Student Fetish Videos: Best Of Foot Worship #02 / 1994 / PRE / C • Student Fetish Videos: Spanking #05 / 1991 / SFV / B

JOY MARCHANT see Dorothy Oh

JOY MERCHANT see Dorothy Oh

JOY RIDER
D.P. Party Tonite / 1995 / JMP / M

JOY RYDER see Star Index I

JOY STICK
Flash Pants / 1983 / VC / M

JOYCE
The All-Conference Nude Workout / 1995 / NIV / S • Blue Vanities #509 / 1992 / FFL / M • Blue Vanities #512 / 1992 / FFL / M • Blue Vanities #538 / 1993 / FFL / M • Blue Vanities #545 / 1994 / FFL / M • Blue Vanities #570 / 1995 / FFL / M • Blue Vanities #573 / 1996 / FFL / M • HomeGrown Video #456 / 1995 / HOV / M • HomeGrown Video #463: Cum And Get It / 1995 / HOV / M • Tempting Tianna / 1992 / V99 / M

JOYCE ANN
Bedtime Video #06 / 1984 / GO / M

JOYCE DELISIO see Star Index I

JOYCE FELICITY see Star Index I

JOYCE JAW
The Coming Of Angie / cr73 / TGA / M

JOYCE MCCLAY see Star Index I

JOYCE MORTON see Star Index I

JOYCE PATRICK
D-Cup Delights / 1987 / VCR / M

JOYCE PAYNE
Afrodisiac #1 / 1987 / CC / M

JOYCE RANDAL see Star Index I

JOYCE SEEMIA
Flight Sensations / 1983 / VC / C

JOYCE SNYDER see Star Index I

JOYCE WAGNER
Blue Vanities #514 / 1992 / FFL / M

JOYCE WITHERS see Star Index I

JOZSI
The Witch's Tail / 1994 / GOU / M

JR THE CAT
The Computer Date / 1994 / ATO / B

JUAN
Amazon Heat #1 / 1996 / CC / M • Naughty Senorita / 1994 / WIV / M • VGA: Spanking Sampler #2 / 1992 / VGA / B

JUAN HERNANDEZ

Full Moon Video #34: Wild Side Couples—From Head To Toe / 1995 / FAP / M • VGA: Cutting Room Floor #1 / 1993 / VGA / M • VGA: Sorry Salesman / 1993 / VGA / B

JUAN MARTINEZ
Ho The Man Down / 1994 / WIV / M • Pussy Showdown / 1994 / WIV / M

JUAN PEDOS see Star Index I

JUAN RICCARDO see Star Index I

JUAN SPIERS see Star Index I

JUANITA
Anal Auditions #4 / 1996 / LE / M • The Decadent Adventures Of Generation XXX / 1994 / MAX / M • Erotic Desires / 1994 / MAX / M

JUANITA DEL SOL
Teeny Talk / 1995 / DBM / M

JUANITA MARTI see Star Index I

JUANITA SLUSHER see Candy Barr

JUANITA VERANO see Star Index I

JUCELYN EON
The Thief, The Girl & The Detective / 1996 / HDE / M

JUDAH
GRG: Judah / 1995 / GRG / M

JUDD see Star Index I

JUDET see Star Index I

JUDGEE SEVILLE
Amateur Black: Starlets / 1995 / SUF / M • Interracial Affairs / 1996 / FC / M • The Real Deal #2 / 1995 / FC / M

JUDI (LITTLE ORAL A) see Little Oral Annie

JUDI KAY
Pornocopia Sensual / 1976 / VHL / M

JUDIT
Buttwoman In Budapest / 1992 / EA / M • Prague By Night #1 / 1996 / EA / M • Private Gold #02: Friends In Sex / 1995 / OD / M • The Witch's Tail / 1994 / GOU / M • World Sex Tour #3 / 1995 / ANA / M

JUDIT BRANDO
Anabolic Import #03: Oral X / 1994 / ANA / M

JUDITH
Lee Nover: The Search For The Perfect Butt / 1996 / IP / M • Prague By Night #2 / 1996 / EA / M • Private Gold #10: Sins / 1996 / OD / M • Private Gold #13: The Pyramid #3 / 1996 / OD / M • Private Gold #14: Sweet Lady #1 / 1997 / OD / M • Private Stories #14 / 1996 / OD / M

JUDITH ANDERSON see Juliet Anderson

JUDITH ARMBRUESTER
[Junge Madchen Mogen's HeiB, Hausfrauen Noch HeiBer / 1973 / ... / M

JUDITH BIZI
Prima #14: Hotel Europa / 1996 / MBP / M

JUDITH FLOREZ see Star Index I

JUDITH HAMILTON *(Penny Ashcroft, Clair Lumiere)*
Pretty brunette, medium tits, lithe firm body, unshaven armpits. Allegedly Georgina Spelvin's real life lesbian lover.
3 A.M. / 1975 / ALP / M • Badge 69 / cr74 / SVE / M • Devil In Miss Jones #1 / 1972 / VC / M • The Journey Of O / 1975 / TVX / M • Lip Service / 1974 / VHL / M • The Love Bus / 1974 / OSC / M • Only The Best #1 / 1986 / CV / C • Saturday Matinee Series #1 / 1996 / VCX / C • Sexual Witchcraft / 1973 / IHV / M • Sleepyhead / 1973 / VXP / M

JUDITH SMITH
Erotic Dimensions: Bold Fantasies / 1982 / NSV / M

JUDITH WILSON
Maids In Bondage /The Bondage Girls / 1985 / 4P / B
JUDITH Z.
Hotel Sodom #08 / 1995 / SNA / M
JUDY
ABA: Double Feature #2 / 1996 / ALP / M • Blue Vanities #522 / 1993 / FFL / M • Blue Vanities #525 / 1993 / FFL / M • Blue Vanities #545 / 1994 / FFL / M • Blue Vanities #554 / 1994 / FFL / M • Blue Vanities #565 / 1995 / FFL / M • HomeGrown Video #435: Seasoned To Perfection / 1994 / HOV / M • Kinky College Cunts #01 / 1993 / NS / F • Pussyman #08: The Squirt Queens / 1994 / SNA / M • Pussyman #10: Butts, Butts & More Butts / 1995 / SNA / M • Pussyman #11: Prime Cuts / 1995 / SNA / C • Rip-Off Of Millie / cr78 / VHL / M
JUDY (C.J. BENNETT) see C.J. Bennett
JUDY ABERNATHY see Star Index I
JUDY ANGEL
Mona The Virgin Nymph / 1970 / ALP / M • Southern Comforts / 1971 / SOW / S
JUDY BILODEAU see Star Index I
JUDY BLACK see Star Index I
JUDY BLUE
No Man's Land #04 / 1990 / VT / F • True Love / 1989 / VI / M
JUDY BLUE (P.THOMAS) see Paul Thomas
JUDY BLUE(A.SPRINGS) see Alice Springs
JUDY BURNS
Romeo And Juliet #2 / 1988 / WV / M
JUDY CALLENDER
The Older Women's Sperm Bank #6 / 1996 / SUF / M
JUDY CARR see Juliet Anderson
JUDY CINDERS see Star Index I
JUDY CRAVEN see Star Index I
JUDY DEE
Hindsight / 1985 / IN / M
JUDY DEWITT see Star Index I
JUDY EGOR see Star Index I
JUDY ELLIS
Loose Times At Ridley High / 1984 / VCX / M • Saturday Matinee Series #4 / 1996 / VCX / C
JUDY FAIRBANKS
Bondage Playmates / Taut Adventure / 1987 / BIZ / B • Tickle Time / 1987 / BIZ / B
JUDY FALLBROOK see Juliet Anderson
JUDY FATIMA
The Rise Of The Roman Empress #1 / 1986 / PV / M
JUDY FOX
Blue Vanities #578 / 1995 / FFL / M
JUDY GILLIS see Star Index I
JUDY GRINGER
1001 Danish Delights / cr68 / AR / M • Sexual Customs In Scandinavia / cr73 / QX / M
JUDY GROSS
Blue Vanities #500 / 1992 / FFL / M
JUDY HARRIS see Nancy Hoffman
JUDY HUTCHESON
Love Lips / 1976 / VC / M
JUDY JONES see Brittany Stryker
JUDY JORDAN
Toys, Not Boys #1 / 1991 / FC / C
JUDY KEHRLEIN
Sodom & Gomorrah / 1974 / MIT / M
JUDY KELLY
Once...And For All / 1979 / HLV / M • The Peek Snatchers / 1965 / SOW / S
JUDY LA ROCHE see Star Index I

JUDY LYNN see Valhalla
JUDY MARLAND see Star Index I
JUDY MEDFORD see Terri Johnson
JUDY MICHAELS
Quick Turnover / 19?? / VXP / M • Round Robin / 19?? / VXP / M
JUDY NOVA see Star Index I
JUDY POWERS see Lana Burner
JUDY SAMPLES
Inside Of Me / 1975 / NAT / M
JUDY WATT see Susan Sloan
JUDY WEST
All The Loving Couples / 1979 / KIT / M
JUDY ZEE see Star Index I
JUICE
Joe Elliot's College Girls #42 / 1995 / JOE / M
JUICY
Back Rent / 1996 / MP0 / M • Black Fantasies #09 / 1995 / HW / M • Black Fantasies #10 / 1995 / HW / M • Black Knockers #02 / 1995 / TV / M • Black Knockers #10 / 1995 / TV / M • Black Knockers #12 / 1995 / TV / M • Black Knockers #14 / 1995 / TV / M • Booty And The Ho' Bitch / 1995 / JMP / M • Bootylicious: Booty & The Ho Bitch / 1996 / JMP / M • Bow Down Backstreet / 1996 / HW / M • Chocolate Bunnies #06 / 1996 / LBO / C • Dangerous Behinds #2 / 1996 / HW / M • Heavyweight Contenders / 1996 / HW / M • Hooter Tutor / 1996 / APP / M • Juicy's Houseparty / 1995 / HW / M • Ron Hightower's Casting Couch #1 / 1995 / FC / M • Snatch Shot / 1996 / LBO / M • Sweet Black Cherries #1 / 1996 / TTV / M • Sweet Black Cherries #6 / 1996 / TTV / M • Waiting 2 XX Hale / 1996 / APP / M
JULE LOCKES see Star Index I
JULES PARIS see Star Index I
JULES ST CLOUD see Star Index I
JULI see Star Index I
JULI ASHTON *(Juli Austin, Juli Astin)*
Tall dark blonde with a so-so face, medium tits (possibly inflated but if so it was a good job), tattoo on belly just to the right of midline, a little flat on the ass. Looks a bit like Teddi Austin but has a much tighter body. 5'9" tall; 36-24-36; born Colorado Springs CO.
Adult Affairs / 1994 / VC / M • Anal Anarchy / 1995 / VC / M • Anal Candy Ass / 1994 / ROB / M • Anal Deep Rider / 1994 / ROB / M • Anal Island #1 / 1996 / VC / M • Anal Island #2 / 1996 / VC / M • Attitude / 1995 / VC / M • Bare Essentials / 1995 / NIV / F • Brassiere To Eternity / 1994 / PEP / F • The Butt Detective / 1994 / VC / M • Butt Motors / 1995 / VC / M • Car Wash Angels / 1995 / VC / M • The Complete Guide To Sexual Positions / 1996 / PME / S • Conquest / 1996 / WP / M • Cuntrol / 1994 / MID / F • Cyberanal / 1995 / VC / M • Daydreams, Nightdreams / 1996 / VC / M • Deep Inside Juli Ashton / 1996 / VC / C • Deep Inside Misty Rain / 1995 / VC / C • Deep Seven / 1996 / VC / M • The Devil In Miss Jones #5: The Inferno / 1994 / VC / M • The Dinner Party #1 / 1994 / ULI / M • Diva #1: Caught In The Act / 1996 / VC / F • Every Woman Has A Fantasy #3 / 1995 / VC / M • Film Buff / 1994 / WP / M • Gangland Bangers / 1995 / VC / M • Happy Ass Lesbians / 1994 / ROB / F • Head Trip / 1995 / VC / M • Latex #1 / 1994 / VC / M • Latex #2 / 1995 / VC / M • Lesbian Bitches #1 / 1994 / ROB

/ F • Masque / 1995 / VC / M • Mutual Consent / 1995 / VC / M • Naked Ambition / 1995 / VC / M • Naked Dolls / 1995 / NIV / F • New Wave Hookers #4 / 1994 / VC / M • Nightshift Nurses #2 / 1996 / VC / M • Once In A Lifetime / 1996 / VC / C • The Other Woman / 1996 / VC / M • Pajama Party X #3 / 1994 / VC / M • Passion In Venice / 1995 / ULI / M • Playboy: Stripsearch: Atlanta / 1996 / UNI / S • Playboy: Stripsearch: San Francisco / 1996 / UNI / S • Public Access / 1995 / VC / M • The Scarlet Woman / 1994 / WP / M • Scotty's X-Rated Adventure / 1996 / WP / M • Smells Like...Sex / 1995 / VC / M • Sorority Sex Kittens #3 / 1996 / VC / M • Stripping For Your Lover / 1995 / NIV / F • Twist Of Fate / 1996 / WP / M • Under The Pink / 1994 / ROB / F • Wide Open Spaces / 1995 / VC / F
JULI ASTIN see Juli Ashton
JULI AUSTIN see Juli Ashton
JULIA
A&B AB#477: Tina / 1994 / A&B / M • Anal Savage #3 / 1996 / ROB / M • Analtown USA #06 / 1995 / NIT / M • Another Fuckin' Anal Movie / 1996 / ROB / M • Behind The Backdoor #7 / 1995 / EVN / M • Black Hose Bag / 1996 / ROB / M • Blue Vanities #569 / 1996 / FFL / M • Booty Sister #2 / 1996 / ROB / M • Butt Bangers Ball #2 / 1996 / TTV / M • California Sluts / 1995 / ZA / M • Casting Call #15 / 1995 / SO / M • Catching Snapper / 1995 / XCI / M • Caught In The Act (1995-Lv) / 1995 / LV / M • Caught Looking / 1995 / CC / M • Dirty Stories #4 / 1995 / PE / M • Enemates #12 / 1996 / BIZ / B • Eurotica #01 / 1995 / XC / M • Forbidden Fantasies #2 / 1995 / ZA / M • Forbidden Fantasies #3 / 1995 / ZA / M • Fresh Faces #07 / 1995 / EVN / M • Hard Cum Cafe / 1996 / BCP / M • Hardcore Debutantes #02 / 1996 / TEP / M • Hardcore Schoolgirls #3: Legal And Eager / 1995 / XPR / M • Hidden Camera #21 / 1994 / JMP / M • Hit Parade / 1996 / PRE / B • Mike Hott: #341 Bonus Cunt: Julia / 1995 / MHV / M • Penetration (Anabolic) #2 / 1995 / ANA / M • Private Gold #13: The Pyramid #3 / 1996 / OD / M • Private Gold #14: Sweet Lady #1 / 1997 / OD / M • Reel Life Video #01: Josephina, Lisa & Julia / 1994 / RLF / F • RSK: Julia's Teenage Spanking / 1995 / RSK / B • Russian Champagne / 1993 / GOU / M • Salsa & Spice #3 / 1996 / TTV / M • Slave Julia / 1995 / VP0 / B • Sleeping Booty / 1995 / EL / M • Sodomania #15: Warning! / 1996 / EL / M • Sodomania: Slop Shots / 1996 / EL / C • Sole Search / 1996 / PRE / B • Swingers Confidential #1 / 1995 / FC / M • Triple X Video Magazine #11 / 1995 / OD / M
JULIA (L. CHANEL) see Lydia Chanel
JULIA ANN
13th Annual Adult Video News Awards / 1996 / VC / S • Adult Affairs / 1994 / VC / M • Casanova #3 / 1993 / SC / M • Casanova #4 / 1993 / SC / M • Elements Of Desire / 1994 / ULI / M • Eleventh Annual AVN Awards / 1994 / VC / M • Ginger Lynn Allen's Lingerie Gallery #1 / 1994 / UNI / F • The Heist / 1996 / WAV / M • Hidden Obsessions / 1992 / BFP / M • It's Blondage, The Video / 1994 / VI / M • Julia Ann: Superstar / 1995 / WAV / M • Les Femmes Erotiques / 1993 / BFP / M • Penthouse:

25th Anniversary Swimsuit Video / 1994 / A*V / F • Penthouse: Forum Letters #2 / 1994 / A*V / S • Penthouse: Women In & Out Of Uniform / 1994 / A*V / S • The Pink Lady Detective Agency: Case Of The Twisted Sister / 1994 / IN / M • Pussyman #03: The Search Continues / 1993 / SNA / M • Pussyman #04: The Celebration / 1993 / SNA / M • Raunch #09 / 1993 / CC / M • Return Engagement / 1995 / VI / M • The Seduction Of Julia Ann / 1993 / VT / M • Sex And Money / 1994 / DGD / S • Stiff Competition #2 / 1994 / CA / M • Stripping For Your Lover / 1995 / NIV / F • Taboo #13 / 1994 / IN / M • Where The Boys Aren't #6 / 1995 / VI / F • Where The Boys Aren't #7 / 1995 / VI / F • Wild Things #4 / 1994 / CV / M

JULIA BENULTI
Lil' Women: Vacation / 1996 / EUR / M
JULIA CHANEL *see* **Lydia Chanel**
JULIA COLT *see* **Gina Carrera**
JULIA FRANKLIN *see* **Star Index I**
JULIA HAVEN *see* **Star Index I**
JULIA JAMESON *see* **Star Index I**
JULIA LAROT
The Sex Clinic / 1995 / WIV / M • World Sex Tour #4 / 1996 / ANA / M
JULIA LODGE *see* **Star Index I**
JULIA MEANS *see* **Star Index I**
JULIA MURE
The Swing Thing / 1973 / TGA / M
JULIA PARTON *see* **Nina Alexander**
JULIA PERRIER *see* **Star Index I**
JULIA SNOW
Skin #1 / 1994 / EUR / M
JULIA SOREL
Virgin And The Lover / 1973 / ALP / M
JULIA SOUGH *see* **Lydia Chanel**
JULIA SOW *see* **Lydia Chanel**
JULIA SPAIN
Private Gold #05: Cape Town #1 / 1996 / OD / M • Private Gold #06: Cape Town #2 / 1996 / OD / M • Private Gold #07: Kruger Park / 1996 / OD / M • Triple X Video Magazine #14 / 1996 / OD / M
JULIAN *see* **Star Index I**
JULIAN JAMES *see* **Star Index I**
JULIAN MANN *see* **Star Index I**
JULIAN MARSH *see* **Michael Findlay**
JULIAN OTT
Russian Roulette / 1995 / NIT / M
JULIAN PAUL *see* **Julian St Jox**
JULIAN SPITZER
Kisses From Romania / 1995 / NIT / M
JULIAN ST JACQUES *see* **Julian St Jox**
JULIAN ST JOHN *see* **Julian St Jox**
JULIAN ST JOX *(Julian Paul, Julian St Jacques, Julian St John, Paul McCoy)*
Black male with a small moustache and a small beer gut. Paul McCoy is from **Realities #1** and others.
'Ho! 'Ho! 'Ho! / 1993 / WP / M • Adam & Eve's House Party #4 / 1996 / VC / M • The Adventures Of Peeping Tom #4 / 1997 / OD / M • Adventures Of The DP Boys: Janet And Da Boyz / 1994 / HW / M • Adventures Of The DP Boys: The Blacks Are Back / 1994 / HW / M • Adventures Of The DP Boys: The Blacks Are Cumming / 1994 / HW / M • Amateur Orgies #11 / 1992 / AFI / M • Amateur Orgies #18 / 1992 / AFI / M • Amateurs Exposed #02 / 1993 / CV / M • America's Raunchiest Home Videos #30: Hot Afternoon / 1992 / ZA / M • America's Raunchiest Home Videos #44: Interracial

Orgy Relay / 1992 / ZA / M • America's Raunchiest Home Videos #62: / 1993 / ZA / M • America's Raunchiest Home Videos #67: / 1993 / ZA / M • Anal Alien / 1994 / CC / M • Anal Angels #3 / 1995 / VEX / C • Anal Cannibals / 1996 / ZA / M • Anal Carnival / 1992 / ROB / M • Anal Delights #3 / 1993 / ROB / M • Anal Generation / 1995 / PE / M • Anal Hunger / 1994 / ROB / M • Anal Innocence #1 / 1991 / ROB / M • Anal International / 1992 / HW / M • Anal Legend / 1994 / ROB / M • Anal Lover #3 / 1994 / ROB / M • Anal Pandemonium / 1994 / TTV / M • Anal Pussycat / 1995 / ROB / M • Anal Rookies #2 / 1994 / ROB / M • Anal Savage #2 / 1994 / ROB / M • Anal Secrets (After Dark) / 1994 / AFD / M • Anal Senorita #1 / 1994 / ROB / M • Anal Sexual Silence / 1993 / IP / M • Anal Spitfire / 1994 / ROB / M • Anal Summer / 1994 / ROB / M • Anna Amore's Fantasy Gang Bang / 1996 / FC / M • Anus & Andy / 1993 / ZA / M • Arabian Nights / 1993 / WP / M • As Sweet As They Come / 1992 / V99 / M • Ass Masters (Leisure) #05 / 1995 / LEI / M • Ass-Capades / 1992 / HW / M • Asses Galore #6: Fallen Angels / 1996 / DFI / M • Bachelor Party #1 / 1993 / FPI / M • Back Rent / 1996 / MP0 / M • Backdoor Black #2 / 1993 / WV / C • Backdoor Ebony / 1995 / WV / M • Backdoor Play / 1996 / AVI / M • The Backline Reporter / 1996 / ZA / M • Behind The Blackout / 1993 / HW / M • Behind The Scenes: The Making Of The Wil & Ed Movies / 1992 / MID / M • The Best Of Black Anal #1 / 1995 / ROB / C • Beverly Hills Geisha / 1992 / V99 / M • Beyond Passion / 1993 / IF / M • Beyond Reality #2: Anal Expedition / 1996 / EXQ / M • Beyond Reality #3: Stand Erect! / 1996 / EXQ / M • Biff Malibu's Totally Nasty Home Videos #23 / 1992 / ANA / M • Big Bust Bangers #2 / 1994 / AMP / M • Bite The Black Bullets / 1995 / ME / M • Black Anal Dreams / 1995 / WV / M • Black Analyst #2 / 1995 / VEX / M • Black Beauties #2 / 1992 / VIM / M • Black Beauty (Coast To Coast) / 1994 / CC / M • Black Bottom Girls / 1994 / ME / M • Black Bottom Girlz / 1994 / CA / M • Black Buttman #01 / 1993 / CC / M • Black Buttman #02 / 1994 / CC / M • Black By Popular Demand / 1992 / ZA / M • Black Cheerleader Search #05 / 1996 / IVC / M • Black Cheerleader Search #06 / 1996 / IVC / M • Black Cheerleader Search #07 / 1996 / IVC / M • Black Cheerleader Search #08 / 1996 / IVC / M • Black Cheerleader Search #09 / 1996 / IVC / M • Black Fire / 1993 / VIM / M • Black Flava / 1994 / EX / M • Black For More / 1993 / ZA / M • Black Gangbangers #01 / 1994 / HW / M • Black Gangbangers #03 / 1995 / HW / M • Black Gangbangers #11 / 1996 / HW / M • Black Hollywood Amateurs #03 / 1995 / MID / M • Black Is Back / 1993 / HW / M • Black Jack City #1 / 1991 / VT / M • Black Knockers #05 / 1995 / TV / M • Black Magic #1 / 1993 / VIM / M • Black Magic #2 / 1994 / VIM / M • Black Mariah / 1991 / FC / M • Black On Black (1994-Midnight) / 1994 / MID / C • Black Orgies #03 / 1993 / AFI / M • Black Orgies #04 / 1993 / AFI / M • Black Orgies #21 / 1994 / GO / M • Black Orgies #25 / 1994 / GO / M • Black Orgies #26 / 1994 / GO / M • Black Orgies #27 / 1994 / GO / M • Black Orgies #35 / 1995 / GO / M

• Black Playhouse / 1995 / HBE / M • Black Power / 1996 / LEI / C • Black Satin / 1994 / IN / M • Black Street Hookers #5: The Mean Streets Of Washington D.C. / 1997 / DFI / M • Black Streets / 1994 / LE / M • Black Studs & Little White Trash / 1995 / ROB / M • Black Velvet #1 / 1992 / CC / M • Black Velvet #2 / 1993 / CC / M • Black Velvet #3 / 1994 / CC / M • Blackbroad Jungle / 1994 / IN / M • Blackdoor Babes / 1994 / TIW / M • The Blues #1 / 1992 / VT / M • The Blues #2 / 1994 / VT / M • Bobby Hollander's Maneaters #01 / 1993 / SFP / M • Bobby Hollander's Maneaters #03 / 1993 / SFP / M • The Bodacious Boat Orgy #1 / 1993 / GLI / M • The Bodacious Boat Orgy #2 / 1993 / GLI / M • Boomerwang / 1992 / MID / M • Booty By Nature / 1994 / WP / M • Booty Ho #1 / 1993 / ROB / M • Booty Ho #2 / 1995 / ROB / M • Booty In The House / 1993 / WP / M • Booty Mistress / 1994 / ROB / M • Booty Sister #1 / 1993 / ROB / M • Bootylicious: Yo Bitch / 1996 / JMP / M • The Breast Files #3 / 1994 / AVI / M • Brooklyn Nights / 1994 / OD / M • Brothers Bangin' / 1995 / ANA / M • Brown Sugar From The Hood / 1996 / MID / M • Bubble Butts #19 / 1992 / LBO / M • Bubbles / 1991 / IF / M • Bump 'n' Grind / 1994 / HW / M • Butt Camp / 1993 / HW / C • Butt Jammers / 1994 / WIV / M • The Buttnicks #4: The Black Buttnicks / 1993 / CC / M • Buttwiser / 1992 / HW / M • Can't Touch This / 1991 / PL / M • Casey At The Bat / 1991 / LV / M • Colossal Orgy #2 / 1994 / HW / M • Contrast / 1995 / CA / M • Cracklyn / 1994 / HW / M • Cumback Pussy #3: Coast To Coast Rump Romp / 1996 / EL / M • Da Booty Call / 1994 / HW / M • Danger-Ass / 1992 / MID / M • Dangerous / 1996 / SNA / M • Dark Alleys #01 / 1992 / FC / M • Dark Alleys #02 / 1992 / FC / M • Dark Alleys #03 / 1992 / FC / M • Dark Alleys #04 / 1992 / FC / M • Dark Alleys #07 / 1992 / FC / M • Dark Alleys #08 / 1992 / FC / M • Dark Alleys #09 / 1993 / FC / M • Dark Alleys #10 / 1993 / FC / M • Dark Alleys #11 / 1993 / FC / M • Dark Alleys #12 / 1993 / FC / M • Dark Alleys #25 / 1994 / FC / M • Dark Alleys #26 / 1994 / FC / M • Dark Alleys #28 / 1994 / FC / M • Dark Dreams / 1992 / WV / M • Dark Justice / 1992 / ZA / M • Dark Room / 1994 / VT / M • Deep Cheeks #4 / 1993 / ROB / M • Deep Cheeks #5 / 1995 / ROB / M • Deep Inside Dirty Debutantes #08 / 1993 / 4P / M • Defying The Odds / 1995 / OD / M • Deliciously Teri / 1993 / IF / M • Depraved Fantasies #3 / 1994 / FPI / M • Dick & Jane Look For Pussy In The Park / 1995 / AVI / M • Dick & Jane Sneak On The Set / 1993 / AVI / M • Dick & Jane's Video Mail: From Virginville (#4) / 1996 / AVI / M • Director's Wet Dreams / 1996 / BBE / M • Dirty Stories #2 / 1995 / PE / M • Dog Walker / 1994 / EA / M • Double Anal Alternatives / 1996 / EL / M • Double Penetration Virgins #02: The Second Cumming / 1994 / LE / M • Dr Freckle & Mr Jive / 1995 / IN / M • Dr Rear / 1995 / CC / M • Dream House / 1995 / XPR / M • Dreams Of A Gigolo / 1996 / SNA / M • Ebony Dancer / 1994 / HBE / M • Ebony Erotica #20: Brown Sugar / 1994 / GO / M • Ebony Erotica #21: Cordon Negro / 1994 / GO / M • Ebony Erotica #22: Fade To Black / 1994 / GO / M • Ebony Erotica

#25: Java Jive / 1994 / GO / M • Ebony Erotica #26: Night Shift / 1994 / GO / M • Eleventh Annual AVN Awards / 1994 / VC / M • Erotic Visions / 1995 / ULI / M • Erotica / 1992 / CC / M • Essence / 1996 / SO / M • European Debutantes #01 / 1995 / IP / M • Executive Positions / 1991 / V99 / M • Exit In Rear / 1993 / XCI / M • Face Jam / 1996 / VC / M • A Few Good Rears / 1993 / IN / M • Foreign Bodies / 1991 / IN / M • Freaknic / 1996 / IN / M • Freaky Tailz / 1996 / AVI / M • The French Invasion / 1993 / LBO / M • Fresh Meat (John Leslie) #1 / 1994 / EA / M • Frontin' Da Booty / 1994 / WP / M • Gang Bang Butthole Surfin' / 1996 / ROB / M • Gang Bang Dollies / 1996 / ROB / M • Gang Bang Party / 1994 / HW / M • Gangbang Girl #07 / 1992 / ANA / M • Gangbang Girl #08 / 1992 / ANA / M • Gangbang Girl #11 / 1993 / ANA / M • Gangbang Girl #13 / 1994 / ANA / M • Gangbang Girl #14 / 1994 / ANA / M • Gangbang Girl #15 / 1995 / ANA / M • Gangbang Girl #16 / 1995 / ANA / M • Gangbang Girl #17 / 1995 / ANA / M • Gangbang Girl #18 / 1996 / ANA / M • Gangbang Sluts / 1994 / VMX / M • Gimme Some Head / 1994 / VT / M • The Girls From Hootersville #01 / 1993 / SFP / M • Girls II Women / 1996 / AVI / M • Girlz N The Hood #1 / 1991 / HW / M • Girlz N The Hood #2 / 1992 / HW / M • Girlz In The Hood #3: Erotic Justice / 1993 / HW / M • Heartbreaker / 1991 / IF / M • Hidden Camera #09 / 1993 / JMP / M • Hidden Camera #14 / 1994 / JMP / M • Hidden Camera: Interracial Special / 1994 / JMP / M • Ho The Man Down / 1994 / WIV / M • Hollywood Swingers #05 / 1992 / LBO / M • Hollywood Swingers #06 / 1992 / LBO / M • Hollywood Swingers #07 / 1993 / LBO / M • Honey, I Blew Everybody #1 / 1992 / MID / M • The Hooker / 1995 / LOT / M • House Pet / 1992 / V99 / M • I Am Desire / 1992 / WV / M • I Can't Believe I Did The Whole Team! / 1994 / FPI / M • In Loving Color #1 / 1992 / VT / M • In Loving Color #2 / 1992 / VT / M • In Loving Color #3 / 1992 / VT / M • Janet's House Party / 1995 / HW / M • Jugsy (Western) / 1992 / WV / M • Jugsy (X-Citement) / 1992 / XCI / M • Jungle Jive / 1992 / VD / M • Just For The Hell Of It / 1991 / CA / M • Kimberly Kupps Gets Black Balled / 1996 / NIT / M • Kinky Fantasies / 1994 / KWP / M • Knockin' Da Booty / 1993 / WP / M • Koko Is Cumin' At Cha / 1994 / AVI / M • Lethal Passion / 1991 / PL / M • Little Miss Anal / 1994 / ROB / M • M Series #03 / 1993 / LBO / M • M Series #05 / 1993 / LBO / M • M Series #07 / 1993 / LBO / M • M Series #08 / 1993 / LBO / M • M Series #10 / 1993 / LBO / M • M Series #11 / 1993 / LBO / M • M Series #12 / 1993 / LBO / M • M Series #14 / 1993 / LBO / M • M Series #16 / 1993 / LBO / M • Macin' #1 / 1996 / SMP / M • Macin' #2: Macadocious / 1996 / SMP / M • Maverdick / 1995 / WV / M • Miss Judge / 1997 / VI / M • Mo' Booty #1 / 1992 / HW / C • Mo' Honey / 1993 / FH / M • Mocha Magic / 1992 / FH / M • Moment To Moment / 1996 / ONA / M • Mona Lisa / 1992 / LV / M • Money, Money, Money / 1993 / FD / M • More Than A Handful #5: California Or Bust / 1994 / MET / M • My Baby Got Back #01 / 1992 / VT / M • My Baby Got Back #02 / 1993 / VT

/ M • My Baby Got Back #03 / 1993 / VT / M • My Baby Got Back #04 / 1994 / VT / M • My Baby Got Back #05 / 1995 / VT / M • My Baby Got Back #06 / 1995 / VT / M • My Baby Got Back #08 / 1996 / VT / M • Naked Goddess #1 / 1991 / VC / M • Nasty Nymphos #02 / 1994 / ANA / M • Nasty Nymphos #06 / 1994 / ANA / M • Nasty Nymphos #13 / 1996 / ANA / M • Nba: Nuttin' Butt Ass / 1996 / SMP / M • Neighborhood Watch #26: / 1992 / LBO / M • The New Ass Masters #08 / 1996 / LEI / C • Nightlife / 1997 / CA / M • Odyssey 30 Min: #271: / 1992 / OD / M • Odyssey Triple Play #88: Candid Couples / 1995 / OD / M • Open Window #13 / 1990 / FAN / M • Oral Majority #11 / 1994 / WV / C • Oral Majority #12 / 1994 / WV / C • Oreo A Go-Go #1 / 1992 / FH / M • Our Bang #06 / 1992 / GLI / M • Our Bang #07 / 1992 / GLI / M • Paint It Black / 1995 / EVN / M • Pops / 1994 / PL / M • Principles Of Lust / 1992 / WV / M • Private Diaries #1: Christina / 1995 / AVI / M • Private Video Magazine #08 / 1994 / OD / M • Profiles #03: House Dick / 1995 / XPR / M • Pumps In Da Rump #1 / 1994 / HW / M • Pure Filth / 1995 / RV / M • Pussy-clips #09 / 1995 / SNA / M • Pussyman Auditions #18 / 1996 / SNA / M • Pussyman's House Party #1 / 1996 / SNA / M • Pussyman's House Party #2 / 1996 / SNA / M • Pussyman's Nite Club Party #1 / 1996 / SNA / M • Pussyman's Nite Club Party #2 / 1997 / SNA / M • Put 'em On Da Glass / 1994 / VT / M • Raunch #03 / 1991 / CC / M • Raw Sex #02 / 1995 / ERW / M • Realities #1 / 1991 / ZA / M • Rebecca Lord's World Tour #1: French Edition / 1995 / WP / M • Reel Sex #02: Splash Party / 1994 / SPP / M • Return To Melrose Place / 1993 / HW / M • Roman Goddess / 1992 / HW / M • Ron Hightower's White Chicks #07 / 1993 / LBO / M • Ron Hightower's White Chicks #08 / 1994 / LBO / M • Ron Hightower's White Chicks #09 / 1994 / LBO / M • Ron Hightower's White Chicks #15 / 1994 / LBO / M • Rump-Shaker #1 / 1993 / HW / M • Rump-Shaker #3 / 1994 / HW / M • Sean Michaels On The Road #01: The Barrio / 1993 / VT / M • Sean Michaels On The Road #02: Da Hood / 1993 / VT / M • Sean Michaels On The Road #10: Seattle / 1994 / VT / M • Secret Diary #2 / 1995 / MID / M • Seoul Train / 1991 / IN / M • Sex Machine / 1994 / VT / M • Sex Police 2000 / 1992 / AFV / M • Sex Secrets Of High Priced Call Girls / 1995 / MID / M • Sex Trek #4: The Next Orgasm / 1994 / ME / M • Sex Trek #5: Deep Space Sex / 1994 / ME / M • Sexual Misconduct / 1994 / VD / C • Sexual Trilogy #02 / 1993 / SFP / M • Sherlock Homie / 1995 / IN / M • Showtime / 1996 / VT / M • Silence Of The Buns / 1992 / WV / M • Sluts In Suburbia / 1994 / GLI / M • Snatch Shot / 1996 / LBO / M • Sniff Doggy Style / 1994 / PL / M • Sodomania #19: Sweet Cream / 1996 / EL / M • Sodomania #21: Degenerate Lifestyles! / 1997 / EL / M • Spanish Fly / 1993 / VEX / M • Sparkling Champagne / 1994 / FH / M • Star Spangled Blacks / 1994 / VEX / M • Starbangers #04 / 1993 / FPI / M • Starbangers #06 / 1994 / FPI / M • Starbangers #08 / 1996 / FPI / M • Straight A Students / 1993 / MET / M • Stylin' / 1994 / FD / M • Summer Dreams / 1996 / TEP / M • Sushi

Butts / 1994 / SCL / M • Sweet Brown Sugar / 1994 / AVI / M • The Sweet Sweet Back's Big Bone (#1) / 1994 / FH / M • The Sweet Sweet Back #2: Double Thaanng Dat Black Hole / 1994 / FH / M • The Sweet Sweet Back #3: Sho' Nuff Got Dat Woodski / 1994 / FH / M • Tailz From Da Hood #4 / 1996 / AVI / M • Tailz From Da Hood #5 / 1996 / AVI / M • Takin' It To The Limit #2 / 1994 / BS / M • Takin' It To The Limit #3 / 1994 / BS / M • Takin' It To The Limit #4 / 1995 / BS / M • Takin' It To The Limit #7: Debauched / 1996 / BS / M • Takin' It To The Limit #8: Hooked On Crack / 1996 / BS / M • Takin' It To The Limit #9: Rear Action View / 1996 / BS / M • Tight Fit #12 / 1995 / GO / M • Tight Pucker / 1992 / WV / M • Tit In A Wringer / 1993 / FC / M • Titanic Orgy / 1995 / PEP / M • Toyz / 1993 / MID / M • Two Of A Kind / 1993 / PL / M • Two Pac / 1996 / VT / M • Two-Pac / 1996 / VT / M • The Ultimate Squirting Machine / 1994 / FPI / M • Uncle Roy's Amateur Home Video #03 / 1992 / VIM / M • Uncle Roy's Amateur Home Video #04 / 1992 / VIM / M • Uncle Roy's Best Of The Best: Brazen Brunettes / 1993 / VIM / C • Up Your Ass #1 / 1996 / ANA / M • Up Your Ass #3 / 1996 / ANA / M • Venom #6 / 1996 / CA / M • The Voyeur #1 / 1994 / EA / M • Waiting To XXX-Hale / 1996 / MET / M • Welcome To Bondage: Rebecca And Julian / 1993 / BON / B • Wet & Slippery / 1995 / WV / M • Wet & Wicked / 1992 / VEX / M • What's Butt Got To Do With It? / 1993 / HW / M • White Trash Whore / 1996 / JMP / M • Whoomp! There She Is / 1993 / AVI / M • Whoreo / 1995 / BIP / M • Whoreos' / 1996 / BEP / M • Women Of Color #1 / 1994 / ANA / M • Yo Yo Yo: A Very Black Christmas Tale! / 1994 / HW / M • Yo' Where's Homey? / 1996 / SUF / M • You Go Girl! (Video Team) / 1995 / VT / M

JULIAN STARR
Bedroom Slaves / 1994 / GOT / B • Beg For It / 1995 / GOT / B • Beyond Domination / 1996 / GOT / B • Borderline / 1996 / GOT / B • No Pain, No Gain / 1992 / GOT / B • Respect And Obey / 1993 / GOT / B • Shame On You / 1995 / GOT / B • Toe Tales #02 / 1992 / GOT / B • Toe Tales #03 / 1992 / GOT / B • Toe Tales #07 / 1993 / GOT / B • Toe Tales #08 / 1993 / GOT / B • Toe Tales #22 / 1995 / GOT / B • Toe Tales #23 / 1995 / GOT / B • TV's And The Houseboy / 1993 / GOT / G

JULIAN STONE
Ona Zee's Learning The Ropes #08: Slaves In Training / 1992 / ONA / B • Ona Zee's Learning The Ropes #09: The Training Continues / 1992 / ONA / B

JULIANA DOMINGUEZ
Cheeky Response / 1995 / RB / B • Shaved #08 / 1995 / RB / F

JULIANA MOOREHEAD *see* **Jillian Moorehead**

JULIANNA A'MORE *see* **Kym Wilde**

JULIANNA DOMINGUEZ
Ass Thrashing / 1995 / RB / B • Finger Pleasures #2 / 1995 / PL / F • Kym Wilde's On The Edge #23 / 1995 / RB / B • The Submission Of Johns / 1995 / RB / B

JULIANNE
Pussy Fest Of The Northwest #5 / 1995 / NIT / M

JULIANNE JAMES

Anal Brat / 1993 / FL / M • Anal Vision #23 / 1994 / LBO / M • Anal Vision #25 / 1994 / LBO / M • Army Brat #2 / 1989 / VI / M • Beach Blanket Brat / 1989 / VI / M • Biff Malibu's Totally Nasty Home Videos #38 / 1993 / ANA / M • Blonde Forces #2 / 1994 / CC / M • Bloopers & Boners / 1996 / VI / M • Body English / 1993 / PL / M • Brat Force / 1989 / VI / M • The Brat Pack / 1989 / VWA / M • Bratgirl / 1989 / VI / M • Buffy Malibu's Totally Nasty All-Girl Home Videos #05 / 1993 / ANA / F • Cherry Poppers #02: Barely Legal / 1994 / ZA / M • Doubletake / 1989 / CC / M • Dream House / 1995 / XPR / M • Nymphobrat / 1989 / VI / M • The Perfect Brat / 1989 / VI / M • Pink To Pink / 1993 / VI / C • Pumping It Up / 1993 / ... / M • The Real Story Of Tonya & Nancy / 1994 / EX / M • Say Something Nasty / 1989 / CC / M • Screw The Right Thing / 1990 / VWA / M • Sexual Fantasies / 1993 / ... / C • Seymore Butts Meets The Cumback Brat / 1993 / FH / M • Victoria With An "A" / 1994 / PL / M • Who Framed Ginger Grant? / 1989 / CC / M • Wild Goose Chase / 1990 / EA / M

JULIE
The Best Of Hot Body Video Magazine / 1994 / CG / C • The Best Of Trained Transvestites / 1990 / BIZ / G • Black Cheerleader Search #05 / 1996 / IVC / M • Blue Vanities #130 / 1990 / FFL / M • Blue Vanities #515 / 1992 / FFL / M • Bosoms Triple X / 1990 / BTO / M • Bottoms Up #04 / 1983 / AVC / C • Casting Couch Cuties #1 / 1994 / WP / M • Creme De La Face #05 / 1994 / OD / M • Eurotica #12 / 1996 / XC / M • Homegrown Video #408: Hot Anal Action! / 1993 / HOV / C • Horny Henry's Strange Adventure / 1995 / TTV / M • J.E.G.: Maidens Of Masturbation #8 / 1995 / JEG / F • Joe Elliot's College Girls #31 / 1994 / JOE / M • Julie: Bondage Virgin / 1995 / GAL / B • Lesbian Pros And Amateurs #25 / 1993 / GO / F • Max World #2: Europa Issue / 1995 / XPR / M • New Busom Brits / 199? / H&S / S • The New Butt Hunt #14 / 1995 / LEI / C • Pearl Necklace: Premier Sessions #03 / 1994 / SEE / M • Private Film #15 / 1994 / OD / M • Reel Life Video #02: Becky, Julie & Amy / 1994 / RLF / M • Reel Life Video #03: Julie, Sheldon and Jeff / 1994 / RLF / M • The Royal Court Collection / 1993 / VER / S • Shaved #02 / 1992 / RB / F • She-Male Salsa / 1987 / VC / G • Stevi's: Black & White Anal / 1995 / SSV / M • Stevi's: Cum Together / 1994 / SSV / F • Stevi's: Julie's Big Toy / 1994 / SSV / M

JULIE (TRACEY P) see Tracey Prince
JULIE ANN
Anal Explosions #2 / 1996 / NIT / M • FTV #51: Amazon Queen / 1996 / FT / B • FTV #52: Busty Blood Bath / 1996 / FT / B • FTV #55: Fight Time Fiesta / 1996 / FT / B • Under The Cum Cum Tree / 1996 / BCP / M

JULIE BOND
Bondage Thrills / cr85 / STM / B • Days Gone Bi / 1988 / ZA / G • Dresden Mistress #1 / 1988 / BIZ / B • Gidget Goes Bi / 1990 / STA / G • Journey Into Submission / 1990 / BIZ / B • Matters In Hand / 1989 / STA / G • Painful Secrets Of A TV / 1996 / BIZ / G • Punished Crossdressers / cr85 / STM / B • Queens Behind Bars / 1990 / STA / G • Se-

cret Life Of Transvestites / cr89 / STM / G • She Males Enslaved / 1996 / BIZ / G • She Studs #04 / 1991 / BIZ / G • She-Male Encounters #19: Toga Party / 1989 / MET / G • She-Male Sex Toys / 1993 / SC / G • She-Male Solos: Julie / 1991 / LEO / G • She-Male Tales / 1990 / MET / G • She-Male Undercover / 1990 / STA / G • She-Males In Torment #3 / 1995 / BIZ / G • Sulka's Nightclub / 1989 / VT / G • Transitory States / 1989 / STA / G • Transvestites Ruled By Desire / cr88 / STM / G • Trisexual Encounters #07 / 1988 / PL / G • Trisexual Encounters #08 / 1988 / PL / G • TVs In Leather And Pain / 1996 / BIZ / G

JULIE BRYANT see Star Index I
JULIE BURGANDY
Caballero Preview Tape #2 / 1983 / CA / C • Heavenly Nurse / 1984 / CA / M

JULIE C. THOMPSON see Meo
JULIE COLT see Gina Carrera
JULIE COOMBS see Star Index I
JULIE DESMOND see Star Index I
JULIE DUREE see Star Index I
JULIE FLETCHER see Star Index I
JULIE HARRIS see Star Index I
JULIE HOLMES see Star Index I
JULIE HOPKINS
Bucky Beaver's XXX Dragon Art Theatre Double Feature #02 / 1996 / SOW / M • The Rites Of Uranus / 1975 / SOW / M

JULIE JOHNSON
Just Deserts / 1991 / BIZ / B

JULIE JONES
Bunbusters / 1984 / VCR / M

JULIE JUGGS see Alexis Gold
JULIE LAMBERT
Flesh Fever / 1978 / CV / M

JULIE MARTINO see Star Index I
JULIE OVERTON
San Francisco Lesbians #5 / 1994 / PL / F

JULIE PARTON see Nina Alexander
JULIE PRINCE
Bedtime Video #04 / 1984 / GO / M

JULIE RAGE
Blonde with short hair, cantaloupes, slim tight body, nice butt, striking but not very pretty face. 36D-22-32, 5'5" tall, 108lbs, and 26 years old in 1996. De-virginized at 13. SO of director Greg Steele.
Abducted / 1996 / ZA / M • Adam & Eve's House Party #1 / 1995 / VC / M • Al Borda's Brazilian Adventures / 1996 / BEP / M • Anal Academy / 1996 / ZA / M • Anal Bandits / 1996 / SO / M • Anal League / 1996 / IN / M • Anything Goes / 1996 / OUP / M • As Easy As A Bunch Of Cunts / 1996 / ROB / F • Burlesxxx / 1996 / VT / M • Butthole Bunnies / 1996 / ROB / F • Buttman In The Crack / 1996 / EA / M • Cheerleader Strippers / 1996 / PE / M • The Complete & Total Anal Workout #2 / 1996 / ZA / M • Corn Hole Kittens / 1996 / ROB / F • Corporate Justice / 1996 / TEP / M • Country Girl / 1996 / VC / M • Decadence / 1996 / VC / M • Deceit / 1996 / ZA / M • Deep Dippin' Anal Babes / 1996 / ROB / F • The Desert Cafe / 1996 / NIT / M • Domination Nation / 1996 / VI / M • Dukes Of Anal / 1996 / VC / M • Escape From Anal Lost Angels / 1996 / HO / M • Frendz? #2 / 1996 / RAS / M • Girly Video Magazine #6 / 1996 / AB / M • Golden Rod / 1996 / SPI / M • Gun Runner / 1996 / CIN / M • Hardcore Fantasies #1 / 1996 / LV / M • Hardcore Fantasies #4 / 1996 / LV / M • The Heart Breaker / 1996 /

MID / M • Hot Tight Asses #16 / 1996 / TCK / M • House On Paradise Beach / 1996 / VC / M • The Hunt / 1996 / ULP / M • In The Line Of Desire / 1996 / MID / M • Jinx / 1996 / WP / M • Jizz Glazed Goo Guzzlers #1 / 1996 / NIT / C • Jizz Glazed Goo Guzzlers #2 / 1996 / NIT / C • Kink: Police Chronicles / 1995 / ROB / M • Kym Wilde's On The Edge #33 / 1996 / RB / B • Kym Wilde's On The Edge #34 / 1996 / RB / B • Latex And Lace / 1996 / BBE / M • Lesbian Debutante #03 / 1996 / IP / F • Lollipop Shoppe #2 / 1996 / SC / M • Million Dollar Buns / 1996 / MYS / M • My Ass #3 / 1996 / NOT / M • Nektar / 1996 / BAC / M • New Pussy Hunt #21 / 1996 / LEI / C • Ona Zee's Doll House #3 / 1995 / ONA / F • Perverted Stories #04 / 1995 / JMP / M • Perverted Stories #07 / 1996 / JMP / M • Point Of Entry / 1996 / WP / M • Prime Choice #6 / 1996 / RAS / M • Pure / 1996 / WP / M • Puritan Video Magazine #02 / 1996 / LE / M • Puritan Video Magazine #04 / 1996 / LE / M • Pussyclips #09 / 1995 / SNA / M • Pussyman #13: Lips / 1996 / SNA / M • Pussyman Auditions #16 / 1995 / SNA / M • Pussyman Auditions #17 / 1995 / SNA / M • Rice Burners / 1996 / NOT / M • Rollover / 1996 / NIT / M • Sexual Overdrive / 1996 / LE / M • Show & Tell / 1996 / VI / M • Six Degrees Of Penetration / 1996 / PP / M • Sorority Sex Kittens #3 / 1996 / VC / M • Squirters / 1996 / ULI / M • Tainted Love / 1996 / VC / M • Totally Depraved / 1996 / SC / M • Trapped / 1996 / VI / M • Trouble In Paradise / 1996 / ULP / M • The Usual Anal Suspects / 1996 / CC / M • Venom #5 / 1996 / VD / M • Video Virgins #26 / 1996 / NS / M • View Point / 1995 / VI / M • Virgin Dreams / 1996 / EA / M • The Wild Ones / 1996 / CC / M • Women Behaving Badly / 1996 / RAS / M • XXX Channel / 1996 / VT / M

JULIE RICHARDSON
Triple Play (Vh) / cr75 / VC / M

JULIE SCOTT see Star Index I
JULIE SHINE see Laurel Canyon
JULIE SNOW
Doctor DeAngelo / 1994 / CS / B

JULIE ST. GERMAINE
Twilight Pink #2 / 1982 / VC / M

JULIE TAYLOR see Laurel Canyon
JULIE THOMPSON see Laurel Canyon
JULIE TOPPER see Star Index I
JULIE WEBSTER
Stinging Stewardesses / 1996 / BIZ / B

JULIE WINCHESTER see Gina Carrera
JULIEN AYRES
Bucky Beaver's XXX Dragon Art Theatre Double Feature #11 / 1996 / SOW / M • San Francisco Ball / 1971 / SOW / S

JULIEN ST JOX see Star Index I
JULIENE NICHOLS
Foreplay / 1982 / VC / M

JULIET
Prima #01: Anal Poker / 1995 / MBP / M

JULIET ANDERSON (Ruby Sapphire, Aunt Peg, Judith Anderson, Judy Fallbrook, Judy Carr, Aunt Peg Norton, Gigi (Juliet Ander.))
A real ball buster with short blonde hair, ugly face, aged body and medium tits.
8 To 4 / 1981 / CA / M • All About Angel Cash / 1982 / VXP / M • All The King's Ladies / 1981 / SUP / M • Aunt Peg / 1980 / CV / M • Aunt Peg Goes To Hollywood /

Swallow / 1985 / PV / M • A History Of Corsets / 1987 / VER / S • Huge Ladies #02 / cr90 / BTO / M • On The Wet Side / 1987 / V99 / M • Passion Pit / 1985 / SE / M • Smothering Tits And Pussy #3 / 199? / H&S / M • [Justice For All / 19?? / ... / M • [More Than A Handful / 1991 / ... / M

JUSTIN
AVP #9012: Slow & Easy, Long & Hard / 1990 / AVP / M • Blue Vanities #530 / 1993 / FFL / M • Far East Fantasy / 1995 / SUF / M • Mickey Ray's Sex Search #01: Sliding In / 1994 / WIV / M

JUSTIN CASE *(Michael Hughes)*
Husband of Alex Jordan.
1-900-FUCK #1 / 1995 / SO / M • Alex Jordan's First Timers #03 / 1993 / OD / M • Alex Jordan's First Timers #05 / 1994 / OD / M • Alex Jordan's First Timers #06 / 1994 / OD / M • Alex On My Mind / 1992 / VAL / M • Beach Bum Amateur's #03 / 1992 / MID / M • Beach Bum Amateur's #04 / 1992 / MID / M • Bend Over Babes #3 / 1992 / EA / M • Best Butt(e) In The West #1 / 1992 / CC / M • Biff Malibu's Totally Nasty Home Videos #07 / 1992 / ANA / M • Biff Malibu's Totally Nasty Home Videos #14 / 1992 / ANA / M • Big Murray's New-Cummers #03: Orgy 'Til Dawn / 1992 / FD / M • Bondage Memories #04 / 1994 / BON / C • Butt Freak #2 / 1996 / EA / M • Cheerleader Nurses #2 / 1993 / VC / M • The D.J. / 1992 / VC / M • Dirty Doc's Housecalls #16 / 1994 / LV / M • Dream Teams / 1992 / VAL / M • The Good, The Bad & The Nasty / 1992 / VC / M • Kym Wilde's Ocean View / 1993 / BON / B • Mike Hott: #198 Horny Couples #01 / 1992 / MHV / M • Mike Hott: #202 Horny Couples #02 / 1992 / MHV / M • Mr. Peepers Amateur Home Videos #55: Anal Antics / 1992 / LBO / M • Neighbors / 1994 / LE / M • Odyssey 30 Min: #159: Blonde Beauty And The Beast / 1991 / OD / M • Odyssey 30 Min: #190: The Other Fucking Roommate / 1991 / OD / M • Odyssey 30 Min: #263: Carmel's 4-Way Dating Game / 1992 / OD / M • Odyssey 30 Min: #318: Kitty Kitty Bang Bang / 1993 / OD / M • Odyssey Triple Play #29: Spontaneous & Raw 3-Ways / 1993 / OD / M • Odyssey Triple Play #58: Anal Insanity / 1994 / OD / M • Odyssey Triple Play #63: Orient Express / 1994 / OD / M • Odyssey Triple Play #94: Triple Decker Sex Sandwich / 1995 / OD / M • Ona Zee's Black Label #1: Sex Hunger / 1996 / ONA / C • Pudsucker / 1994 / MID / M • Roto-Rammer / 1993 / LV / M • Rump Humpers #01 / 1992 / GLI / M • Seymore Butts & The Honeymooners / 1992 / FH / M • Seymore Butts Rides Again / 1992 / FH / M • Seymore Butts: Bustin' Out My Best Anal / 1995 / FH / C • SVE: The Fun Bunch / 1992 / SVE / M • Tight Tushies #1 / 1994 / SFP / M • Uncle Roy's Amateur Home Video #07 / 1992 / VIM / M • Uncle Roy's Amateur Home Video #08 / 1992 / VIM / M • Uncle Roy's Amateur Home Video #10 / 1992 / VIM / M • Uncle Roy's Best Of The Best: Brazen Brunettes / 1993 / VIM / C • Welcome To Bondage: Alex Jordan With Justin Case / 1992 / BON / B • Welcome To Bondage: Starlets #1 / 1993 / BON / C • Wilder At Heart / 1993 / ANA / M

JUSTIN CASE (1975)
MASH'ed / cr75 / ALP / M

JUSTIN COOPER *see Star Index I*
JUSTIN FLETCHER
Sharon In The Rough-House / 1976 / LA / M
JUSTIN MALLORY
Eruption / 1977 / VCX / M
JUSTIN MYERS
Adam & Eve's House Party #1 / 1995 / VC / M • Bangkok Dreams / 1996 / SUF / M • Interview's Southern Cumfort / 1996 / LV / M • Interviews At The Hard Wok Cafe / 1996 / LOF / M • Lust In Time / 1996 / ONA / M • Perverted Stories #06 / 1996 / JMP / M • Pick Up Lines #04 / 1995 / 4P / M • Private Desires / 1995 / LE / M • Raw Footage / 1996 / VC / M • Yin Yang Oriental Love Bang #3: Bangkok Dreams / 1996 / SUF / M
JUSTIN NIN
Dirty Work / 1995 / VC / M
JUSTIN SIMON *see Star Index I*
JUSTIN STERLING
Sorority Sex Kittens #3 / 1996 / VC / M
JUSTIN THYME
[So Many Men, So Little Time / 19?? / BL / G
JUSTIN TYME *see Star Index I*
JUSTINA LYNN *(Stephanie Young, Candy Mason)*
Candy is from **Baby Doll**.
Baby Doll / 1975 / AR / M • Count The Ways / 1976 / CA / M • Femmes De Sade / 1976 / ALP / M • French Erotica: My Wife The Hooker / 1980 / AR / M • Hardcore / 1973 / ALP / M • The Joy Of Letting Go / 1976 / SE / M • Melanie's Hot Line / 1975 / CDC / M • The Pleasure Masters / 1975 / AST / M • Strange Experiences Cockfucking / 1994 / MET / M • Teenage Surfer Girls / 1976 / VCS / M
JUSTINE
Beneath The Cane / 1992 / BON / B • Best Butt(e) In The West #1 / 1992 / CC / M • The Bondage Club #4 / 1990 / LON / B • Cheek Busters / 1990 / FH / M • Final Exam #2 / 1988 / BON / B • Odyssey Amateur #27: Justine's Sandwich / 1991 / OD / M • Plumpers Of Sundance Spa / 1993 / BTO / M • Sweet Things / 1992 / VEX / M • Tempting Tianna / 1992 / V99 / M • Tit To Tit #1 / 1994 / BTO / M
JUSTINE (1985)
The House Of Strange Desires / 1985 / NSV / M • Missing Pieces / 1985 / IN / M • Sex Dreams On Maple Street / 1985 / WV / M
JUSTINE (1994)
Anal Camera #01 / 1994 / EVN / M • Babe Watch #1 / 1994 / SC / M • Bi George / 1994 / BIL / G • Bi On The Fourth Of July / 1994 / BIL / G • Bi The Rear Window / 1994 / BIL / G • Bi-Nanza / 1994 / BIL / G • Big Busty #45 / 1994 / BTO / S • Bubble Butts Gold #1 / 1994 / LBO / M • Corporate Bi Out / 1994 / BIL / G • The Cumm Brothers #04: Laid Off & Laid / 1994 / OD / M • Dirty Dating Service #05 / 1994 / WP / M • Fresh Faces #01 / 1994 / EVN / M • Full Moon Video #02: Justine's Hard Homework / 1994 / FAP / F • Full Moon Video #10: Squat City / 1994 / FAP / F • A Girl's Affair #05 / 1994 / FD / F • The Hitch-Hiker #09: Back Road Detour / 1994 / WMG / M • Mr. Peepers Amateur Home Videos #90: Back Door Bonanza / 1994 / LBO / M • Odyssey Triple Play #90: Black & White In Loving

Color / 1995 / OD / M • Tootsies & Footsies / 1994 / LBO / M
JUSTINE (1995)
Creme De La Face #07 / 1995 / OD / M • Fantasy Flings #03 / 1995 / WP / M • Hollywood Starlets Adventure #03 / 1995 / AVS / M • More Dirty Debutantes #38 / 1995 / 4P / M
JUSTINE (B&D)
Bondage Boot Camp / 1988 / TAN / B • The Bondage Club #1 / 1987 / LON / B • The Bondage Club #2 / 1987 / LON / B • The Bondage Club #5 / 1990 / LON / B • Bondage Memories #03 / 1994 / BON / C • I'll Take The Whip / 1993 / BON / B
JUSTINE FLETCHER
Captain Lust And The Amorous Contessa / 1977 / IHV / M • GVC: Strange Family / 1977 / GO / M
JUSTINE LOVE *see Jacy Allen*
JUTKA GOZ
Blue Vanities #517 / 1992 / FFL / M
JUTTA DAVID *see Star Index I*
JUVO STUD
Anal Palace / 1995 / VC / M
JYMES O. *see Star Index I*
K. COTTON
Nightclub / 1996 / SC / M
K. GEE BEE
Butt Hole In-One / 1994 / AFV / M
K. PHILLIP ANTHONY
Under Lock And Key / 1994 / IMP / S
K.C.
Puritan Video Magazine #10 / 1997 / LE / M • The Sodomizer #6 / 1996 / SC / M
K.C. COOL *(Casey Cool)*
Black With Sugar / 1989 / CIN / M • Blind Date / 1989 / E&I / M • The Hustler / 1989 / CDI / M • Stormi / 1988 / LV / M
K.C. DYLAN *see Kelli Dylan*
K.C. HALL *see Krista*
K.C. HARLEY
The Pain Connection / 1994 / BS / B
K.C. JAMES *see Star Index I*
K.C. KERRINGTON *see P.J. Sparxx*
K.C. KING *see Star Index I*
K.C. VALENTINE
All American Girls #1 / 1982 / CA / M • Behind The Scenes Of An Adult Movie / 1983 / CV / M • Bloopers #2 / 1991 / GO / C • Blue Interview / 1983 / VCR / M • Expose Me Now / 1982 / CV / M • Foreplay / 1982 / VC / M • Gourmet Premier: Broker's Esctacy / Student Fantasies / cr83 / GO / M • GVC: Real Estate #109 / 198? / GO / M • GVC: Women Who Love Women #115 / cr83 / GO / F • GVC: Women's Fantasies #108 / 1983 / GO / F • Intimate Lessons / 1982 / VC / M • Jawbreakers / 1985 / VEN / C • A Lacy Affair #1 / 1983 / HO / F • Parliament: Super Head #1 / 1989 / PM / C • Shaved / 1984 / VCR / M • Swedish Erotica #39 / 1981 / CA / M • Triangle Of Lust / 1983 / VCR / M • The Wacky World Of X-Rated Bloopers / 1989 / GO / M • Why Gentlemen Prefer Blondes / 1983 / HO / C
K.C. WILLIAMS *see Casey Williams*
K.T. *see King Tung*
K.T. (FEMALE)
Alex Jordan's First Timers #05 / 1994 / OD / M
K.Y. LEE *see Star Index I*
KABAL TURANI
Ejacula #1 / 1992 / VC / M • Ejacula #2 / 1992 / VC / M
KADINA *see Zumira*

KAELYNN ROBERTS
Hopeless Romantic / 1992 / LE / M •
Neighborhood Watch #30 / 1992 / LBO / M
• New Girls In Town #2 / 1992 / CC / M •
Radical Affairs Video Magazine #02 / 1992
/ ME / M

KAHLIA *(Fiona (Kahlia), Dana Star, Latisha Lani, Kahlua)*
Brunette who resembles a younger and smaller version of Bionca. Tight waist and dilated asshole. Fiona in **Passages #3**. This is not to imply that she is not attractive. Not the same as Lorraine Day (they both appear in **MDD #10**).
AHV #16: Let It Loose / 1992 / EVN / M •
Amateur A Cuppers / 1993 / VEX / C • Anal
Annie's All-Girl Escort Service / 1990 / LIP
/ F • Bardot / 1991 / VI / M • Biff Malibu's
Totally Nasty Home Videos #07 / 1992 /
ANA / M • More Dirty Debutantes #10 /
1991 / 4P / M • Oriental Temptations / 1992
/ WV / M • Passages #3 / 1991 / VI / M •
Rayne Storm / 1991 / VI / M • Tropic Of
Kahlia / 1991 / VI / M

KAHLUA *see* **Kahlia**

KAHUNA WONG
Cat And Bound Tickle Fest / 1996 / VTF / B
• Tricked & Tied / 1996 / VTF / B

KAI
Hong Kong Hookers / 1984 / AMB / M

KAI NOBEL
Private Film #07 / 1994 / OD / M • Private
Film #08 / 1994 / OD / M • Private Film #10
/ 1994 / OD / M • Private Video Magazine
#07 / 1994 / OD / M • Private Video Maga-
zine #09 / 1994 / OD / M • Private Video
Magazine #18 / 1994 / OD / M

KAI QUAN
Shang-Hai Slits / 1994 / ORE / C

KAI YING
100% Amateur #04: Oriental Orientation /
1995 / OD / M

KAIKO *(Keiko (Oriental), Kay (Kaiko))*
Oriental girl with a very tight body and quite a pretty face.
Buttman's Big Butt Backdoor Babes / 1995
/ EA / M • Dr Butts #2 / 1992 / 4P / M • For-
tune Cookie / 1992 / VI / M • Homegrown
Video #189 / 1990 / HOV / M • Home-
Grown Video #468: Lust American Style /
1996 / HOV / C • More Dirty Debutantes
#13 / 1992 / 4P / M • More Dirty Debu-
tantes #24 / 1993 / 4P / M • Odyssey 30
Min: #179: This Japanese Girl Loves A
Hard Dick / 1992 / OD / M

KAITLAN
Stalker's Punishment / 1995 / IBN / B

KAITLAND DOWN *see* **Kaitlyn Ashley**

KAITLYN ASHLEY *(Kaitlyn Down, Kait-
lynn (Ashley), Kaitland Down, Kelly (K.
Ashley), Kaitlynn Kelly, Cherry Stone,
Catlyn Ashley, Misty (Kaitlyn A))*
Ash blonde with small natural slightly droopy tits, not too good very white skin, Groucho eyebrows, pixieish face. 22 years old in 1993. Kelly is her real name. 36-24-34 and comes from Fort Lauderdale, Florida. As of early 1994 she seems to have had her breasts enhanced but they're still rather droopy. This must have been an interim job because in mid-1994 they are now rock hard.
1-900-FUCK #3 / 1995 / SO / M • 13th An-
nual Adult Video News Awards / 1996 / VC
/ S • Above The Knee / 1994 / WAV / M •
The Adventures Of Studman #1 / 1994 /

AFV / M • All Amateur Perfect 10's / 1995 /
LEI / M • All-Star Anal Interviews #1 / 1995
/ LEI / M • Amateur Orgies #31 / 1993 / AFI
/ M • Amazon Heat #1 / 1996 / CC / M •
American Beauty #1 / 1993 / FOR / M •
American Beauty #2 / 1994 / FOR / M •
American Blonde / 1993 / VI / M • The Anal
Adventures Of Bruce Seven / 1996 / BS / C
• The Anal Adventures Of Max Hardcore:
Video Games / 1994 / ZA / M • Anal Angels
#4 / 1995 / VEX / C • Anal Connection /
1996 / ZA / M • Anal Innocence #2 / 1993 /
ROB / M • Anal Inquisition / 1996 / ZA / M •
Anal Maniacs #1 / 1994 / WP / M • Anal
Maniacs #5 / 1996 / WP / M • Anal Over-
tures / 1993 / AFD / M • Anal Portrait / 1996
/ ZA / M • Anal Rampage #2 / 1993 / ROB
/ M • Anal Sex / 1996 / ZA / M • Anal Talis-
man / 1996 / ZA / M • Anal Virgins Of Amer-
ica #01 / 1993 / FOR / M • Anal Vision #16
/ 1993 / LBO / M • The Analizer / 1994 / VD
/ M • Ass Openers! #2 / 1995 / TCK / C •
Ass Ventura: Crack Detective / 1996 / PL /
M • The Attendant / 1996 / SC / M • Babes
Illustrated #2 / 1994 / IN / F • Babes Illus-
trated #5 / 1996 / IN / F • Back In Style /
1993 / VI / M • Back To Anal Alley / 1994 /
ME / M • The Backdoor Bradys / 1995 / PL
/ M • Badgirls #2: Strip Search / 1994 / VI /
M • Badgirls #3: Cell Block 69 / 1994 / VI /
M • Badgirls #5: Maximum Babes / 1995 /
VI / M • Badlands #1 / 1994 / PEP / M •
Badlands #2: Back Into Hell / 1994 / PEP /
M • The Basket Trick / 1993 / PL / M • Bat-
babe / 1995 / PL / M • Beach Bum Ama-
teur's #30 / 1993 / MID / M • The Best Of
Strippers Inc / 1996 / ONA / C • Bi-Bi Love
Amateurs #3 / 1993 / QUA / G • Big &
Busty Superstars / 1996 / DGD / F • Big
Knockers #02 / 1994 / TV / M • Big Knock-
ers #03 / 1994 / TV / M • Big Knockers #04
/ 1994 / TV / M • Big Knockers #12 / 1995
/ TV / C • The Big One / 1995 / HO / M • Bi-
ography: Kaitlyn Ashley / 1996 / SC / C •
Blonde Forces #2 / 1994 / CC / M • Boiling
Point / 1994 / WAV / M • Boogie In The Butt
/ 1993 / WIV / M • Born 2 B Wild / 1995 /
PL / M • Brassiere To Eternity / 1994 / PEP
/ F • Breastman's Wet T-Shirt Contest /
1994 / EVN / M • Breeders / 1996 / MET /
M • Bubble Butts #27 / 1993 / LBO / M •
Buffy's Malibu Adventure / 1995 / CDI / M •
Buffy's New Boobs / 1996 / CIN / M • Burn-
ing Desires / 1994 / BS / B • Butt Jammers
#04 / 1995 / SC / F • Buttslammers #06:
Over The Edge / 1994 / BS / F • Buttslam-
mers #07: Indecent Decadence / 1994 / BS
/ F • Buttslammers #08: The Ultimate Inva-
sion / 1994 / BS / F • Caged Beauty / 1994
/ FD / M • Carlita's Backway / 1993 / OD /
M • Carnal Country / 1996 / NIT / M • Cat
Lickers #2 / 1994 / ME / F • Certifiably Anal
/ 1993 / ROB / M • Checkmate / 1995 /
WAV / M • Cherry Cheeks / 1993 / CA / M
• Cinesex #2 / 1994 / CV / M • Climax 2000
#1 / 1994 / CC / M • Climax 2000 #2 / 1994
/ CC / M • A Clockwork Orgy / 1995 / PL /
M • Club Kiss / 1995 / ONA / M • The Come
On / 1995 / EX / M • Coming Attractions /
1995 / WHP / M • Cover To Cover / 1995 /
WP / M • Cumback Pussy #6: All-Star Poop
Chute Salute / 1997 / EL / M • Dear Diary /
1995 / WP / M • Deep Inside Kaitlyn Ashley
/ 1995 / VC / C • Deep Throat Girls #10 /
1995 / GO / M • Desert Moon / 1994 / SPI
/ M • Dick & Jane In The Mountains / 1994

/ AVI / M • Dirty Doc's Housecalls #05 /
1993 / LV / M • Dreams / 1995 / VC / M •
Dreams Of A Gigolo / 1996 / SNA / M •
Erotic Escape / 1995 / FH / M • Erotic New-
cummers Vol 1 #1: Capitol Desires / 1993 /
DR / M • Euro-Max #2: Cream n' Euro Sluts
/ 1995 / SC / M • Exit In Rear / 1993 / XCI
/ M • Extreme Sex #3: Wired / 1994 / VI / M
• The Face / 1994 / PP / M • Facesitter #3
/ 1994 / CC / M • Fever Pitch / 1995 / ONA
/ M • Filthy Sleazy Scoundrels / 1994 / HW
/ M • Finger Pleasures #3 / 1995 / PL / F •
Flexxx #2 / 1995 / VT / M • The Flirt / 1995
/ GO / M • For Your Mouth Only / 1995 / GO
/ M • Foreskin Gump / 1994 / LE / M • Four
Weddings And A Honeymoon / 1995 / PL /
M • The Freak Club / 1994 / VMX / M •
Ghosts / 1995 / WV / M • The Girl In Room
69 / 1994 / VC / M • A Girl's Affair #08 /
1995 / FD / F • Girl's School / 1994 / ERA /
M • Girls Off Duty / 1994 / LE / M • Glen
And Glenda / 1994 / CA / M • Hard Headed
/ 1994 / LE / M • Hardcore / 1994 / VI / M •
Harder, She Craved / 1995 / VC / M • Head
First / 1995 / OD / M • Head Shots / 1995 /
VI / M • Head Trip / 1995 / VC / M • The
Heart Breaker / 1996 / MID / M • Heartbeat
/ 1995 / PP / M • Helen & Louise / 1996 /
HDE / M • Hexxxed / 1994 / VT / M • Holly-
wood Boulevard / 1995 / CV / M • Holly-
wood In Your Face / 1993 / VC / M • Holly-
wood Scandal: The Heidi Flesh Story /
1993 / IP / M • Hollywood Sex Tour / 1995
/ VC / M • Hot Tight Asses #06 / 1994 / TCK
/ M • Hot Tight Asses #07 / 1994 / TCK / M
• Hot Wired / 1996 / VC / M • Hotel Fantasy
/ 1995 / IN / M • Hotel Sodom #04: Free
Parking In Rear / 1995 / SNA / M • Hotel
Sodom #09 / 1996 / SNA / M • Hotwired /
1996 / VC / M • Jaded Love / 1994 / CA / M
• Jailhouse Nurses / 1995 / SC / M • Junkyard Dykes #01 / 1994 / ZA / F • Junkyard
Dykes #03 / 1994 / ZA / F • Kittens #5 /
1994 / CC / F • Leena Is Nasty / 1994 / OD
/ M • Let's Dream On / 1994 / FD / M • Let's
Play Doctor / 1994 / PV / M • Lipstick Lesbians #1: Massage Parlor Dykes / 1994 /
ZA / F • Lonely Hearts / 1995 / VC / M •
Loose Morals / 1995 / EX / M • Lust Runner / 1995 / VC / M • Lust What The Doctor Ordered / 1994 / WIV / M • Makin' It /
1994 / A&E / M • More Dirty Debutantes
#24 / 1993 / 4P / M • Natural Born Thrillers
/ 1994 / LV / M • Never Say Never, Again /
1994 / SC / M • The New Ass Masters #15
/ 1996 / LEI / C • New Positions / 1994 / PV
/ M • New Pussy Hunt #24 / 1996 / LEI / C
• Night And Day #2 / 1993 / VT / M • No
Man's Land #11 / 1995 / VT / F • No Man's
Land #12 / 1995 / VT / F • NYDP Blue /
1996 / WP / M • Obsession / 1994 / BS / B
• Oral Obsession #1 / 1994 / VI / M • Pen-
etrator #2: Grudge Day / 1995 / PL / M •
Perverted Women / 1995 / SC / M • Power
Butt / 1994 / VI / C • Primal Instinct / 1996
/ SNA / M • Private Places / 1995 / IF / M •
Private Video Magazine #16 / 1994 / OD /
M • Provocative / 1994 / LE / M • Punished
Innocence / 1994 / BS / B • Pure Smut /
1996 / GO / M • Pussy Whipped / 1994 /
FOR / M • Pussyman #05: Captive Audi-
ence / 1994 / SNA / M • Pussyman #06:
House Of Games / 1994 / SNA / M •
Pussyman #11: Prime Cuts / 1995 / SNA /
C • Pussyman #14: Dreams Of A Gigolo /
1996 / SNA / M • The Quest / 1994 / SC /

M • Raunch Ranch / 1995 / LE / M • Razor's Edge / 1995 / ONA / M • Reality & Fantasy / 1994 / DR / M • A Rear And Pleasant Danger / 1995 / PP / M • Rear Window / 1996 / NIT / M • Reel Sex #02: Splash Party / 1994 / SPP / M • The Reel Sex World #04: Laid In Hawaii / 1994 / WP / M • Reflections / 1996 / ZA / M • Ride 'em Cow Girl / 1995 / VI / C • Ring Of Passion / 1994 / ERA / M • Riot Grrrls / 1994 / SC / M • Rituals / 1993 / SC / M • Rockhard (Sin City) / 1996 / SC / M • Rxx For A Gangbang / 1994 / ZA / M • Secret Urges (Vidco) / 1994 / VD / C • Seriously Anal / 1996 / ONA / M • Sex #1 (Vca) / 1994 / VC / M • Sex Alert / 1995 / PV / M • Sex Bandits / 1995 / VC / M • Sex Detective / 1994 / LV / M • Sex Lives Of Clowns / 1994 / VC / M • Sexual Healing / 1996 / SC / M • Shame / 1994 / VI / M • Shane's World #1 / 1996 / OD / M • Shave Tails #2 / 1994 / SO / M • Show Business / 1995 / LV / M • Sideshow Freaks / 1996 / ZA / M • The Sin-A-Bun Girls / 1995 / OD / M • Sindy Does Anal Again / 1994 / AFV / M • Sinnocence / 1995 / CDI / M • Sleeping Single / 1994 / CC / M • Sodomania #06: Gangs And Bangs And Other Thangs / 1993 / EL / M • Sodomania...And Then Some!!! A Compendium / 1995 / EL / C • Sodomania: Slop Shots / 1996 / EL / C • Sorority Cheerleaders / 1996 / PL / M • Southern Comfort #1 / 1995 / DWV / M • Southern Comfort #2 / 1995 / DWV / M • Stacked Deck / 1994 / IN / M • Starbangers #07 / 1995 / FPI / M • Starlet / 1994 / VI / M • The Starlet / 1995 / SC / M • Stowaway / 1995 / LE / M • Strippers Inc. #2 / 1994 / ONA / M • Suite 18 / 1994 / VI / M • Super Groupie / 1993 / PL / M • Supermodel #2 / 1994 / VI / M • Superstar Sex Challenge #1 / 1994 / VC / M • Surprise!!! / 1994 / VI / M • Sweet Revenge / 1996 / WAV / M • Tail Taggers #113: Behind The Scenes / 1994 / WV / M • Takin' It To The Limit #1 / 1994 / BS / M • Takin' It To The Limit #4 / 1995 / BS / M • Tales From The Clit / 1993 / OD / M • The Temple Of Poon / 1996 / PE / M • Tight Lips / 1994 / CA / M • Titty City #1 / 1995 / TIW / M • Tonya's List / 1994 / FD / M • Top Debs #4: Sex Boat / 1993 / GO / M • Topless Stewardesses / 1995 / PV / M • Topless Window Washers / 1996 / LE / M • Totally Naked / 1994 / VC / M • Uninhibited Love / 1994 / VPN / M • Up And Cummers #05 / 1993 / 4P / M • Use It Or Lose It / 1994 / CA / M • Vagina Town / 1993 / CA / M • Venom #5 / 1996 / VD / M • Video Virgins #05 / 1993 / NS / M • Video Virgins #06 / 1993 / NS / M • Violation / 1996 / LE / M • Visions Of Desire / 1993 / HO / M • Visions Of Seduction / 1994 / SC / M • A Week And A Half In The Life Of A Prostitute / 1997 / EL / M • What's Up, Tiger Pussy? / 1995 / VC / M • Wicked As She Seems / 1993 / WP / M • Wicked Fantasies / 1996 / CO2 / M • Wicked Ways #3: An All-Anal Slutfest / 1995 / WP / M • Women On Fire / 1995 / LBO / M • Young Girls Do #2: Sweet Meat / 1995 / CDI / M

KAITLYN DOWN see Kaitlyn Ashley

KAITLYN HILL *(Pandora (Kaitlyn H))*
Reddish-black hair, piggy eyes, small tits, big butt, out-of-condition body, not pretty but not ugly either. She has a tattoo on her right belly at the bikini line, another small one on her right shoulder back and a mole on the top of her left breast.

Beach Bum Amateur's #35 / 1993 / MID / M • Creme De La Face #06 / 1995 / OD / M • More Dirty Debutantes #27 / 1993 / 4P / M • Mr. Peepers Amateur Home Videos #85: Hand Puppet Job / 1994 / LBO / M • New Faces, Hot Bodies #10 / 1993 / STP / M • New Faces, Hot Bodies #13 / 1994 / STP / M • New Girls In Town #5 / 1994 / CC / M • Pussy Tails #01 / 1993 / CDY / M • Video Virgins #08 / 1993 / NS / M • The Voyeur #1 / 1994 / EA / M

KAITLYNN (ASHLEY) see Kaitlyn Ashley

KAITLYNN KELLY see Kaitlyn Ashley

KAJSA-LOTTA
Swedish Vip Magazine #1 / 1995 / PL / M • Swedish Vip Magazine #2 / 1995 / PL / M

KAL JAMMER see Cal Jammer

KALANI
Hot Body Competition: Bikinis & Bikes Contest / 1996 / CG / F • Hot Body Video Magazine: Sweet Dreams / 1996 / CG / F • New Ends #09 / 1994 / 4P / M • Sex On The Saddle: Wicked Women Of The Wild West / 1994 / CPG / S • Sex On The Strip: The Lusty Ladies Of Las Vagas / 1993 / CPG / F

KALANTAN
Blue Vanities #580 / 1996 / FFL / M

KALI
Bright Tails #2 / 1994 / STP / B • Creme De La Face #17: Semen For Seven / 1996 / OD / M • New Faces, Hot Bodies #10 / 1993 / STP / M

KALI HANSA
[Le Journal Intime D'Une Nymphomane / 1972 / ... / M

KALINA LYNX *(Kelly G'Raffe)*
Blonde, emaciated, marginal face, tall, tiny tits, shaven pussy, labia rings, unkempt hair, white not-too-good skin.

100% Amateur #26: / 1996 / OD / M • Butt Wackers / 1995 / FH / M • Conjugal Visits / 1995 / EVN / M • Creme De La Face #10: Cum Dome / 1995 / OD / M • Cry Babies #1: Anal Scream / 1995 / ZA / M • Debauchery / 1995 / MET / M • Dragxina, Queen Of The Underworld / 1995 / MET / G • Enemates #11 / 1995 / BIZ / B • Forbidden Fantasies #1 / 1995 / ZA / M • Innocence Lost / 1995 / GO / M • Leg...Ends #17 / 1996 / PRE / F • Little Shop Of Tickle / 1995 / SBP / B • Mike Hott: #311 Bonus Cunt: Kalina / 1995 / MHV / M • Mike Hott: #314 Cum In My Cunt #05 / 1995 / MHV / M • Mike Hott: #315 Cum In My Mouth #02 / 1995 / MHV / M • Mike Hott: #323 Three-Sum Sluts #07 / 1995 / MHV / M • Odyssey 30 Min: #538: / 1995 / OD / M • Shockers / 1996 / SBP / B • Student Fetish Videos: Bondage #01 / 1995 / PRE / B • Student Fetish Videos: Tickling #12 / 1995 / SFV / B • Suspend Thy Slaves / 1996 / VTF / B • Wild Orgies #19 / 1995 / AFI / M • Young & Natural #15 / 1996 / TV / F

KALLIE see Star Index I

KALMAN
Dick & Jane In Budapest / 1993 / AVI / M • Dick & Jane Return To Hungary / 1993 / OAP / M • Dirty Stories #4 / 1995 / PE / M • Love Slave / 1995 / WIV / M • Private Film #19 / 1994 / OD / M

KAMA SUTRA see Ricky Lee

KAMALI
Black Mystique #01 / 1993 / VT / F

KAMELA

Black Street Hookers #1 / 1996 / DFI / M

KAMEO see Cameo

KAMERA
Black Cheerleader Search #06 / 1996 / IVC / M

KAMILA (BLACK) see Star Index I

KAMIO YUDA
A Widow's Affair / 1996 / AVV / M

KAMISHA
HomeGrown Video #466: Loot The Booty / 1996 / HOV / M

KAMISHA (NIKKI SINN) see Nikki Sinn

KAMRY WOOD see Cory Wolf

KAN MIKAMI see Star Index I

KANDACE see Candace Berg

KANDACE BUNN see Candace Berg

KANDI
New Faces, Hot Bodies #20 / 1996 / STP / M • The Rookies / 1991 / VC / M • Toy Time #5: / 1996 / STP / F

KANDI BARBEAU see Kandy Barbour

KANDI BERBER see Kandy Barbour

KANDI CONNOR *(Candy Connor, Candy Connors, Cindi Connor, Carol Conners (Kand), Kandi Kisses, Candi Cash, Candy Cash)*
Not too pretty lithe blonde with small tits. Tattoo on back of left hand, another on left bicep and a third on chest above left tit that looks like tit tac toe. Twenty years old in 1994 and de-virginized at 12. Comes from New York and sounds German.

19 & Naughty #1 / 1994 / SKV / M • The 4th Vixxen / 1995 / EMC / M • The Anal Adventures Of Max Hardcore: High Voltage / 1994 / ZA / M • Anal Angels #3 / 1995 / VEX / C • Anal Chiropractor / 1995 / PEP / M • Anal Deep Rider / 1994 / ROB / M • Anal Destroyer / 1994 / ZA / M • Anal Torture / 1994 / ZA / M • Anal Virgins Of America #09 / 1994 / FOR / M • Analtown USA #02 / 1995 / NIT / M • Ass Ventura: Crack Detective / 1996 / PL / M • The Backdoor Bandit / 1994 / LV / M • The Backway Inn #5 / 1993 / FD / M • Beverly Hills Blondes #2 / 1995 / LV / M • Brothers Bangin' / 1995 / ANA / M • Butt Hunt #11 / 1995 / LEI / M • Casting Call #08 / 1994 / SO / M • Casting Call #18 / 1996 / SO / M • Cherry Poppers #06: Pretty And Pink / 1994 / ZA / M • Cherry Poppers #07: Li'l Darlin's / 1994 / ZA / M • Cum Buttered Corn Holes #3 / 1996 / NIT / C • D.P. Party Tonite / 1995 / JMP / M • Every Woman Has A Fantasy #3 / 1995 / VC / M • Exotic Car Models #1 / 1996 / INO / F • Fast Forward / 1995 / CA / M • The Fat, The Bald & The Ugly / 1995 / JMP / M • Hardcore Schoolgirls #2: Perverted Playmates / 1995 / XPR / M • The Hitch-Hiker #08: On The Trail / 1994 / WMG / M • Hollywood Amateurs #09 / 1994 / MID / M • Hotel Fantasy / 1995 / IN / M • Hotel Sodom #02 / 1995 / SNA / M • In Your Face #4 / 1996 / PL / M • Indiscreet! Video Magazine #1 / 1995 / FH / M • Itty Bitty Blonde Committee / 1995 / V99 / M • Juicy Cheerleaders / 1995 / LE / M • Lucky Lady / 1995 / CV / M • Max #03 / 1995 / FWE / M • Max #06: Going South / 1995 / FRM / M • Max World #1 / 1995 / FRM / M • Mike Hott: #298 Bonus Cunt: Candy Connor / 1995 / MHV / M • Orgies Orgies Orgies / 1994 / WV / M • Perverted #2: The Virgins / 1995 / ZA / M • Perverted Stories #01 / 1995 / JMP / M • Pizzas, Hot Tubs & Bimbos / 1995 / SUF / M • Rectal Rodeo /

1994 / ZA / M • Rumpman: Caught In An Anal Avalanche / 1995 / HW / M • Screamers (Ona Zee) / 1995 / ONA / M • Seriously Anal / 1996 / ONA / M • The Sexual Solution #2 / 1995 / LE / M • Snatch Masters #11 / 1995 / LEI / M • Sorority Stewardesses #1 / 1995 / PE / M • Sunset And Divine: The British Experience / 1996 / LEI / M • Taboo #14: Kissing Cousins / 1995 / IN / M • Tail Taggers #127: / 1994 / WV / M • Tails Of Desire / 1995 / GO / M • Tight Fit #14 / 1995 / GO / M • Video Virgins #15 / 1994 / NS / M • The World's Biggest Gang Bang #1 / 1995 / FPI / M

KANDI FYNE *see Star Index I*

KANDI JONES *(Cheranne Case)*
Pretty face, tight body, small tits, narrow hips, shoulder length black hair, tight waist, nice butt, small tattoo on her left hip.
Bottom Busters / 1973 / BLT / M • Dental Nurse / 1973 / VXP / M • Most Valuable Slut / 1973 / HLV / M • Resurrection Of Eve / 1973 / MIT / M

KANDI KISSES *see* Kandi Connor

KANDI KREME
C-Hunt #02: Hot Pockets / 1995 / PEV / M • Dirty Dirty Debutantes #6 / 1996 / 4P / M • Full Moon Video #36: Home Delivery / 1996 / FAP / M • Jus' Knockin' Boots #2: Black On Line / 1996 / NIT / M • Pearl Necklace: Premier Sessions #02 / 1993 / SEE / M • Pearl Necklace: Premier Sessions #03 / 1994 / SEE / M • Pearl Necklace: Thee Bush League #28 / 1994 / SEE / M • Pearl Necklace: Thee Bush League #29 / 1994 / SEE / M • Stevi's: Candi's First Time Bi / 1996 / SSV / F

KANDI VALENTINE *(Cindi Valentine, Tia De Angelo)*
Girls Will Be Boys #1 / 1990 / PL / F • In The Can / 1990 / EX / M • Laid In Heaven / 1991 / VC / M • More Dirty Debutantes #03 / 1990 / 4P / M • Nasty Girls #2 (1990-CDI) / 1990 / CDI / M • Rock Me / 1990 / LE / F

KANDICE
AVP #9122: Good Morning America / 1990 / AVP / F

KANDY
Aurora's Secret Diary / 1985 / LA / M • Dirty And Kinky Mature Women #1 / 1995 / C69 / M

KANDY BARBOUR *(Candy Barbour, Cindi Barbour, Kandi Berber, Kandi Barbeau)*
Shoulder length straight black hair, very pretty facially, medium tits, and soft plush body. Started in 1976 and stopped in 1984. Visible bodily deterioration over time. Not the same as Candi Barbo.
All The Loving Couples / 1979 / KIT / M • Babylon Gold / 1983 / COM / C • Blowing Your Mind / 1984 / RSV / M • Blue Shorts / cr83 / COM / C • Blue Vanities #017 (New) / 1988 / FFL / M • Blue Vanities #017 (Old) / 1988 / FFL / M • Blue Vanities #037 / 1988 / FFL / M • Blue Vanities #063 / 1988 / FFL / M • Blue Vanities #065 / 1988 / FFL / M • Blue Vanities #560 / 1994 / FFL / M • Bon Appetit / 1980 / QX / M • The Budding Of Brie / 1980 / TVX / M • California Gigolo / 1979 / WWV / M • Centerfold Fever / 1981 / VXP / M • Champagne For Breakfast / 1980 / SE / M • Chopstix / 1979 / TVX / M • Classic Swedish Erotica #22 / 1986 / CA / C • Classic Swedish Erotica #27 / 1987 /

CA / C • Classic Swedish Erotica #31 / 1987 / CA / C • Come Get Me / 1983 / VEL / M • Creme De Femme #1 / 1981 / AVC / C • Creme De Femme #2 / 1981 / AVC / C • Cum Shot Revue #2 / 1985 / HO / C • Erotic Gold #2 / 1985 / VEN / M • F / 1980 / GO / M • Forbidden Worlds / 1988 / GO / C • The Goodbye Girls / 1979 / CDI / M • Kate And The Indians / 1980 / SE / M • Love-In Arrangement / 1981 / VXP / M • Mrs. Rodger's Neighborhood / 1988 / EVN / C • Nanci Blue / 1979 / SE / M • Neon Nights / 1981 / COM / M • Odds And Ends / 1981 / TGA / M • Pandora's Mirror / 1981 / CA / M • Party #1 / 1979 / NAT / M • Party #2 / 1979 / NAT / M • The Pink Ladies / 1980 / VC / M • Platinum Paradise / 1980 / COM / M • R.S.V.P. / 1983 / VES / S • Regency #41: Jambo / cr81 / RHV / M • Rolls Royce #01 / 1980 / ... / C • Screwples / 1979 / CA / M • Seka In Heat / 1988 / BMV / C • Sex Boat / 1980 / VCX / M • Sizzle / 1979 / QX / M • Small Town Girls / 1979 / CXV / M • Snow Honeys / 1983 / VC / M • Stranger In Town / 1980 / FAN / M • Swedish Erotica #14 / 1980 / CA / M • Sweet Cheeks / 1980 / VCX / M • That Lucky Stiff / 1979 / QX / M • Twilight Pink #1 / 1980 / AR / M • Ultraflesh / 1980 / GO / M • VCA Previews #2 / 1988 / VC / C • Young, Wild And Wonderful / 1980 / VCX / M

KANDY KANE *see* Candy Kane

KANOS ROOEB
Pink Lips / 1977 / VCX / M

KAORI KAWAGUCHI *see Star Index I*

KAORI SHIMOKAWA
Desire & Pleasure / 1996 / AVE / M

KAR TAN JAI
Game Instructor / 1996 / AVV / M

KARA LOTT *see* Cara Lott

KARA NILE
Creme De La Face #07 / 1995 / OD / M • Creme De La Face #15: Showroom Sex / 1996 / OD / M • The Doctor Is In #3: Achy Breaky Tarts / 1995 / NIT / M • High Heeled & Horny #3 / 1995 / LBO / M • How To Make A Model #05: Back To Innocence / 1994 / LBO / M

KARAL BRODERICK *see* Isabella Rovetti

KARE *see Star Index I*

KAREN
A&B AB#375: I Love Cum / 1991 / A&B / M • A&B AB#453: Karen's Family Fun #1 / 1994 / A&B / M • A&B AB#454: Karen's Family Fun #2 / 1994 / A&B / M • A&B AB#455: Auntie's Gang Bang / 1994 / A&B / M • A&B AB#457: The Cum Eating Contest / 1994 / A&B / M • A&B AB#471: Sexy Ladies / 1994 / A&B / M • A&B AB#565: Bi-Sexual Gang Bang / 1995 / A&B / G • A&B AB#569: Sex Club Initiation / 1995 / A&B / M • America's Raunchiest Home Videos #64: / 1993 / ZA / M • Ben Dover's 9th / 1996 / VC / M • Between My Breasts #13 / 1990 / BTO / S • Beyond Passion / 1993 / IF / M • Big Bust Babes #15 / 1993 / AFI / M • Black Hollywood Amateurs #08 / 1995 / MID / M • Blue Vanities #129 / 1990 / FFL / M • Blue Vanities #169 (New) / 1996 / FFL / M • Blue Vanities #169 (Old) / 1991 / FFL / M • Blue Vanities #500 / 1992 / FFL / M • Blue Vanities #503 / 1992 / FFL / M • Blue Vanities #516 / 1992 / FFL / M • Blue Vanities #520 / 1993 / FFL / M • Blue Vanities

#521 / 1993 / FFL / M • Blue Vanities #557 / 1994 / FFL / M • Blue Vanities #570 / 1995 / FFL / M • Bondage Classix #11: Karen's B&D Phone Sex / 1984 / BON / B • Bondage Classix #17: The Millionaire / 198? / BON / B • Breast Of Britain #1 / 1986 / BTO / M • Breast Of Britain #2 / 1987 / BTO / M • Breast Of Britain #6 / 1990 / BTO / S • The Doorman Always Comes Twice / cr84 / AIR / C • GRG: Buzz & Karen / 1993 / GRG / M • Hole In One / 1993 / IF / M • Mr. Peepers Amateur Home Videos #70: New Tits On The Block / 1993 / LBO / M • New Faces, Hot Bodies #03 / 1992 / STP / M • Skintight / 1991 / VER / F • Suburban Swingers / 1993 / IF / M • Summertime Boobs / 1994 / LEI / M • SVE: Swing Time / 1993 / SVE / M • SVE: Tales From The Lewd Library #3 / 1994 / SVE / M • Under The Skirt #1 / 1995 / KAE / F

KAREN ALLEN
Outrageous Games / 1988 / VD / B • Two At Once / 1978 / CV / M

KAREN BARKER
Dial A Sailor / 1990 / PM / M • Singles Holiday / 1990 / PM / M

KAREN BLACK
Auntie Lee's Meat Pies / 1992 / C3S / S • Bad Manners / 1984 / STM / S • Bound And Gagged: A Love Story / 1993 / TRI / S • Candy Goes To Hollywood / 1979 / VCX / M • Haunting Fear / 1990 / ... / S • Her Name Was Lisa / 1979 / VC / M • The Primetime / 1960 / SOW / S • Suzie's Take Out Service / 1975 / CDC / M • [Drive, He Said / 1970 / ... / S

KAREN BLAKE
Undulations / 1980 / VC / M

KAREN BLUE
11 / 1980 / VCX / M • Beyond Your Wildest Dreams / 1980 / CAT / M

KAREN BOSTON
Inside Desiree Cousteau / 1979 / VCX / M

KAREN BREE
1001 Erotic Nights #2 / 1987 / VC / M • Blacks & Blondes #21 / 1986 / WV / M • Oral Majority #02 / 1987 / WV / C • Oral Majority Black #1 / 1987 / WV / C • Oral Majority Black #2 / 1988 / WV / C • Return To Sex 5th Avenue / 1985 / WV / M • VCA Previews #4 / 1988 / VC / C

KAREN CASTLE
Breast Collection #04 / 1995 / LBO / C • Breast Wishes #13 / 1993 / LBO / M

KAREN CHANDLER *see Star Index I*

KAREN CLARK
Bottoms Up / 1974 / SOW / M • Bucky Beaver's XXX Dragon Art Theatre Double Feature #05 / 1996 / SOW / M • Too Many Cocks In Me! / 1992 / MET / M

KAREN COOKNELL *see Star Index I*

KAREN CRAIG
The Bite / 1975 / SVE / M • A Touch Of Genie / 1974 / ... / M

KAREN CUMMINGS
Bucky Beaver's XXX Dragon Art Theatre Double Feature #02 / 1996 / SOW / M • The Rites Of Uranus / 1975 / SOW / M

KAREN CUSICK *see* Christine Heller

KAREN CUSTER *see* Christine Heller

KAREN D'OR *see* Karen Dior

KAREN DEE *see Star Index I*

KAREN DELAAR *see Star Index I*

KAREN DEVIN
That's Porno / 1979 / CV / C

KAREN DIOR *(Karen D'or, Rick Van,*

Geoff Gann)
She-Male.
All-Star Softball Game / 1995 / SAB / G • Auction #1 / 1992 / BIZ / B • Auction #2 / 1992 / BIZ / B • Be Careful What You Wish For / 1993 / VC / G • Bi And Busty / 1991 / STA / G • Bi Anonymous / 1993 / BIL / G • Bi Bi Birdie / 1993 / BIL / G • Bi Intruder / 1991 / STA / G • Bi Love Lucy / 1994 / PL / G • Bi-Golly / 1993 / BIL / G • Bimbo Boys / 1995 / PL / C • Bone Appetit: A She-Male Seduction / 1994 / BIZ / G • Creation Of Karen: Tormented & Transformed / 1993 / BIZ / B • Crossing Over / 1990 / IN / M • The Crying Flame / 1993 / HSV / G • A Decent Proposal / 1993 / BIL / G • Defiant TV's / 1994 / BIZ / G • The Education Of Karen / 1993 / BIZ / B • Fag Hags / 1991 / FC / G • Gilligan's Bi-Land / 1994 / PL / G • How To Impersonate A Woman #1 / 1993 / STM / G • How To Impersonate A Woman #2 / 1993 / STM / G • Incredible Dreams #2 / 1992 / BIZ / B • Karen's Bi-Line / 1989 / MET / G • Malibu She Males / 1994 / MET / G • Married With She-Males / 1993 / PL / G • More Than Friends / 1995 / KDP / G • Mystery Date / 1992 / CDI / G • Night Walk / 1995 / HIV / G • Painted / 1990 / INH / G • A Peek Over The Wall / 1995 / STM / G • The Prize Package / 1993 / HSV / G • Queens From Outer Space / 1993 / HSV / G • Rainwoman #03 / 1990 / CC / M • Secret Sex #3: The Takeover / 1994 / CAT / G • Sex Starved She-Males / 1995 / MET / G • Sharon And Karen / 1989 / LV / G • Sharon Kane's TV Tamer / 1993 / BIZ / G • Shaved She-Males / 1994 / PL / G • She Male Goddesses / 1994 / MET / G • She Male Sex Kittens / 1995 / MET / G • She Studs #07 / 1991 / BIZ / G • She's The Boss / 1993 / BIL / G • She-Mails / 1993 / PL / G • She-Male Mistress / 1992 / BIZ / G • She-Male Nymphos / 1995 / MET / G • She-Male Seduction / 1995 / MET / G • She-Male Sex Clinic / 1991 / VC / G • She-Male Slut House / 1994 / HEA / G • She Male Spirits Of The Night / 1991 / VC / G • She-Male Vacation / 1993 / HSV / G • Single White She-Male / 1993 / PL / G • Sisters Of Sin / 1991 / VIM / G • Sizzling She Males / 1995 / MET / G • SM TV #2 / 1995 / FC / G • Split Personality / 1991 / CIN / G • Steel Garters / 1992 / CAT / G • Stick Pussy / 1992 / HSV / G • Surprise Package / 1993 / HSV / G • Tranny Jerk-Fest / 1995 / VC / G • Transexual Blvd / 1994 / PL / G • Transfigured / 1993 / HSV / G • Transformed / 1991 / MET / M • Transitions (TV) / 1993 / HSV / G • Transsexual Passions #2 / 1994 / BIZ / G • Transvestite Secrets Revealed / 1993 / STM / G • Transvestite Tour Guide / 1993 / HSV / G • Trisexual Encounters #12 / 1990 / PL / C • Trisexual Encounters #14 / 1992 / PL / G • TV Dildo Fantasy #2 / 1996 / BIZ / G • TV Dungeon / 1992 / BIZ / G • TV Evangelist / 1993 / HSV / G • TV Nation #1 / 1995 / HW / G • TV Panty Party / 1994 / BIZ / G • TV Room / 1993 / BIZ / G • TV Shaved Pink / 1992 / BIZ / G • TV Toilet Challenge / 1993 / BIZ / G • TV Training Center / 1993 / LEO / G • TVs Teased And Tormented / 1995 / BIZ / G • The Ultimate Pleasure / 1991 / MET / G • The Ultimate Sex / 1992 / MET / G • [The River Made To Drown In / 1996 / ... / M

KAREN FIELDS

Big Titted Tarts / 1994 / PL / C

KAREN FINLEY
Hardcore: The Films Of Richard Kern #1 / 1991 / FTV / M

KAREN FLACH
Private Film #25 / 1995 / OD / M

KAREN GOLANS
18 And Anxious / cr78 / CDI / M • Insane Lovers / 1978 / VIS / M • Small Change / 1978 / CDC / M

KAREN HALL *see Star Index I*
KAREN HAPSBURG *see Star Index I*
KAREN HARLOW *see* Jeanette Harlow
KAREN HAVENS *see* Erica Havens
KAREN HORNELL *see Star Index I*
KAREN HUGHES *see* Alex Jordan
KAREN JEFFRIES *see Star Index I*
KAREN KARLSSON *see Star Index I*
KAREN KASTLE
Mr. Peepers Nastiest #1 / 1995 / LBO / C
KAREN KLEIN *see Star Index I*
KAREN KLINE
The Return Of Johnny Wadd / 1986 / PEN / M
KAREN KUSHMAN *see* Christine Heller
KAREN KUSICK (HELLR) *see* Christine Heller
KAREN KUSICK (MQ) *see* Mary Quint
KAREN LYNN *see Star Index I*
KAREN MANE
Hillary Vamp's Private Collection #06 / 1992 / HVD / M
KAREN MARSHALL *see Star Index I*
KAREN MAYO *see Star Index I*
KAREN MILLER
Free Love Confidential / 1967 / SOW / S • Passion Toys / 1985 / VCR / C
KAREN MOORE
A Decent Proposal / 1993 / BIL / G
KAREN NATIVIDAD
Still The Brat / 1988 / VI / M
KAREN POSEY *see Star Index I*
KAREN REGIS *see* Jenny Baxter
KAREN SANDERS
Sacred Doll / 1995 / FRF / M
KAREN SCHUBERT
Black Emmanuelle #1 / 1975 / TZV / S • Black Venus / 1983 / PLA / S • Bluebeard / 1972 / LIV / S • Born For Love / 1987 / ... / M • The Desirous Wife / 1988 / PL / M • The Devil In Mr Holmes / 1988 / PV / M • Emmanuelle Around The World / 1977 / WIZ / S • The Girl In Room 2A / 1976 / PRS / S • Karin & Barbara Superstars / 1988 / PL / M • Kiss Me With Lust / cr75 / ... / M • Panther Squad / 1984 / VES / S • The Rise Of The Roman Empress #1 / 1986 / PV / M • Till Marriage Do Us Part / 1974 / VES / S • [Cora / 19?? / PUB / M • [Gin Fizz #12: Moana & Karin / 19?? / ... / M • [Sex And Voodoo / 197? / ... / S • [Supermaschio Per Mogli Viziose / 19?? / ... / M
KAREN ST JOY *see* Erica Havens
KAREN STACY *see Star Index I*
KAREN STRIKER *see Star Index I*
KAREN SUMMER *(Ricky Lane, Michel Lee, Michelle Lee)*
Dark blonde or light brown hair, petite, small tits, sounds 50c on the dollar, de-virginized at age 14. Michel Lee (sic) in **Shades Of Ecstasy**.
All American Girls #2: In Heat / 1983 / CA / M • Amazing Sex Stories #1 / 1986 / SUV / M • Anal Annie And The Willing Husbands / 1984 / LIP / M • Anal Annie Just Can't Say No / 1984 / LIP / M • The Animal In Me /

1985 / IN / M • Backdoor Bandits / 1989 / MIR / C • Backstage Pass / 1983 / VC / M • Bad Attitude / 1987 / CC / M • Bad Girls #4 / 1984 / GO / M • Bare Elegance / 1984 / MAP / M • The Beat Goes On / 1987 / VCR / C • Bedtime Tales / 1985 / SE / M • Before She Says I Do / 1984 / MAP / M • Breastography, Lesson #1 / 1987 / VCR / M • Can't Get Enough / 1985 / CA / M • Candy Stripers #2 / 1985 / AR / M • Casino Of Lust / 1984 / AT / M • Celebrity Presents Celebrity / 1986 / VEP / C • Centerfold Celebrities #1 / 1982 / VC / M • Centerfold Celebrities #2 / 1983 / VC / M • Centerfold Celebrities #5 / 1983 / VC / M • Circus Acts / 1987 / SE / C • Club Head (EVN) #1 / 1987 / EVN / C • Confessions Of A Candystriper / 1984 / VC / M • Confessions Of Candy / 1984 / VC / M • Cupid's Arrow / 1984 / VCR / M • Daddy Doesn't Know / 1984 / HO / M • Daisy Chain / 1984 / IN / M • Dames / 1985 / SE / M • Dance Fever / 1985 / VCR / M • Dream Jeans / 1987 / CA / M • Educating Eva / 1984 / VC / M • Educating Nina / 1984 / AT / M • Electric Blue: Search For A Star / 1985 / CA / M • The Erotic Adventures Of Dr Storm / 1983 / XTR / M • Europe On Two Guys A Day / 1987 / PV / M • Every Man's Fantasy / 1985 / IN / M • The Fine Art Of Cunnilingus / 1985 / VCR / M • Foxy Boxing / 1982 / AVC / M • Gang Bangs #1 / 1985 / VCR / M • Girl Games / 1987 / PL / C • Head Waitress / 1984 / VC / M • Headgames / 1985 / WV / M • Headhunters / 1984 / VC / M • Hollywood Undercover / 1989 / BWV / C • Home Movies Ltd #2 / 1985 / SE / M • Hot Blooded / 1983 / CA / M • Hot Flashes / 1984 / VC / M • Hot Spa / 1984 / CA / M • Hot Wire / 1985 / VXP / M • How To Perform Fellatio / 1985 / VCR / M • Hustler #17 / 1984 / CA0 / M • I Never Say No / 1983 / VC / M • In All The Right Places / 1986 / VD / M • Inside China Lee / 1984 / VC / M • Intimate Realities #1 / 1983 / VC / M • John Holmes, The Man, The Legend / 1995 / EVN / C • Joys Of Erotica #112 / 1984 / VCR / C • A Little Dynasty / 1985 / CIV / M • Little Muffy Johnson / 1985 / VEP / M • Little Often Annie / 1984 / VC / M • Looking For Love / 1985 / VCX / M • Looking For Lust / 1984 / VEL / M • Loose Ends #1 / 1984 / 4P / M • The Lost Angel / 1989 / KIS / C • The Loves Of Lolita / 1984 / VC / M • Loving Spoonfulls / 1987 / 4P / C • Lust In America / 1985 / VCX / M • The Midnight Zone / 1986 / IN / M • Miss American Dream / 1985 / CIV / M • Mouthful Of Love / 1984 / VC / M • Naughty Angels / 1984 / VC / M • Naughty Nanette / 1984 / VC / M • One Night At A Time / 1984 / PV / M • Oriental Lesbian Fantasies / 1984 / PL / F • Our Major Is Sex / 1984 / VD / M • Perfection / 1985 / VD / M • Phone Sex Fantasies / 1984 / QX / M • Playing With Fire / 1983 / IN / M • Portrait Of Desire / 1985 / IVP / M • Raffles / 1988 / VC / M • The Rocky Porno Video Show / 1986 / 4P / M • Rocky-X #1 / 1986 / PEN / M • Saturday Night Beaver / 1986 / EVN / M • Sensuous Singles: Sandi Taylor / 1987 / VCR / F • Sex Busters / 1984 / PLY / M • Sex For Hire / 1989 / HOE / C • Sexual Odyssey / 1985 / VC / M • Shacking Up / 1985 / VXP / M • Shades Of Ecstasy / 1983 / HO / M • Shauna: Every Man's Fantasy / 1985 / CA / C • Sizzling

Summer / 1984 / VC / M • Soft As Silk...Sweet As Honey / 1984 / SE / M • Sounds Of Sex / 1985 / CA / M • The Sperminator / 1985 / VXP / M • Spreading Joy / 1988 / VC / M • Starlets / 1985 / 4P / M • Stephanie's Outrageous / 1988 / LV / C • Taboo #04 / 1985 / IN / M • Taboo #05 / 1986 / IN / M • A Taste Of Pink / 1985 / VXP / M • Taste Of The Best #1 / 1988 / PIN / C • Tasty / 1985 / CA / M • Tight Delight / 1985 / VXP / M • Tomboy / 1983 / VCX / M • Tongue Twisters / 1986 / VXP / M • Toys 4 Us #2 / 1987 / WV / C • Treasure Box / 1986 / PEN / M • Unbelievable Orgies #1 / 1987 / EVN / C • Wet Science / 1986 / PLY / M • What Are Friends For? / 1985 / MAP / M • Wicked Wenches / 1988 / LA / M • Wild Orgies / 1986 / SE / C • The Woman Who Loved Men / 1984 / SE / M • Women Without Men #1 / 1985 / VXP / F • X Factor / 1984 / HO / M • Young Nurses In Love / 1987 / VC / M

KAREN SWAIN
Flesh...And The Fantasies / 1991 / BIZ / B

KAREN SWEET *see Star Index I*

KAREN TRAVER
Hot Properties / 1975 / CA / M

KAREN WING
10 Years Of Big Busts #1 / 1989 / BTO / C • The Best Of Big Busty / 1986 / L&W / C • Breast Of Britain #3 / 1987 / BTO / M • The Kiss-O-Gram Girls / 1986 / L&W / S • The Very Best Of Breasts #1 / 1996 / H&S / S

KAREN WINTER
American Nympho In London / 1987 / VD / M • The Baroness / 1987 / VD / M • Playboy's Playmate Workout / 1983 / PLA / S

KAREN ZELAT
The Hottest Show In Town / 1974 / ... / M

KARENA
Blue Vanities #503 / 1992 / FFL / M

KARENE BERG *see Lana Woods*

KARESS *see Melody Midnight*

KARESSA CHANG *see Connie Yung*

KARESSE
Hidden Camera #17 / 1994 / JMP / M • More Black Dirty Debutantes #3 / 1994 / 4P / M • New Faces, Hot Bodies #14 / 1994 / STP / M

KARI DEE *see Star Index I*

KARI FOX *(Cari Fox, Carrie Fox, Lissi Fox, Keri Fox)*
1001 Erotic Nights #2 / 1987 / VC / M • Age Of Consent / 1985 / AVC / M • Amber Pays The Rent / 1986 / VT / M • The Anal-ist #2 / 1986 / VEX / M • Another Kind Of Love / 1985 / CV / M • Best Of Caught From Behind #1 / 1987 / HO / C • Blonde On The Run / 1985 / PV / M • Busty Wrestling Babes / 1986 / VD / M • California Reaming / 1985 / WV / M • Caught From Behind #06 / 1986 / HO / M • Caught In The Middle / 1985 / CDI / M • Corporate Affairs / 1986 / SE / M • Crystal Balls / 1986 / DR / M • Deep Inside Vanessa Del Rio / 1986 / VC / M • Devil In Miss Jones #3: A New Beginning / 1986 / VC / M • Devil In Miss Jones #4: The Final Outrage / 1987 / VC / M • Dickman & Throbbin / 1985 / WV / M • Dirty 30's Cinema: Kari Foxx / 1986 / PV / C • Double Messages / 1987 / MOV / M • The Ecstasy Girls #2 / 1986 / CA / M • Every Woman Has A Fantasy #2 / 1986 / VC / M • Family Heat / 1985 / AT / M • The Fine Art Of Cunnilingus / 1985 / VCR / M • For Your Thighs Only / 1985 / WV / M •

Genie's Dirty Girls / 1987 / VCX / M • Getting LA'd / 1986 / PV / M • Goddess Of Love / 1986 / CDI / M • Head & Tails / 1988 / VD / M • Hollywood Vice / 1985 / VD / M • Hometown Honeys #1 / 1986 / VEX / M • Hot Nights At The Blue Note Cafe / 1985 / WV / M • Hottest Parties / 1988 / VC / C • Indecent Itch / 1985 / VCR / M • Kiss Of The Dragon Lady / 1986 / SEV / M • License To Thrill / 1985 / VD / M • A Little Romance / 1986 / HO / M • The Magic Touch / 1985 / CV / M • Make My Night / 1985 / CIN / M • Mantrap / 1986 / BAN / M • Only The Best Of Oral / 1989 / CV / C • Oral Majority #02 / 1987 / WV / C • Orgies / 1987 / WV / C • Porn In The USA #1 / 1986 / WV / C • Project Ginger / 1985 / VI / M • Rambone The Destroyer / 1985 / WET / M • Rated Sex / 1986 / SE / M • Ready, Willing & Anal (Cv) / 1993 / CV / C • Rears / 1987 / VI / M • The Red Garter / 1986 / SE / M • Screaming Rage / 1988 / LV / C • Secret Lessons #1 / 1986 / BIZ / B • Sensuous Singles: Sandi Taylor / 1987 / VCR / F • Sexpertease / 1985 / VD / M • Sinful Sisters / 1986 / VEX / M • Skin Games / 1986 / VEX / M • Skin Games / 1991 / VEX / C • Star 85: Kari Fox / 1985 / VEX / M • Sweet Cheeks / 1987 / VCR / C • Taxi Girls #2: In Search Of Toni / 1986 / ELD / M • Teasers: Saturday Lovers / 1988 / MET / M • Teasers: The Inheritance / 1988 / MET / M • Two Into One #1 / 1988 / PIN / C • VCA Previews #4 / 1988 / VC / C • Wild Things #2 / 1986 / CV / M • WPINK-TV #2 / 1986 / PV / M • The X-Terminator / 1986 / PV / M

KARI KLARK *see Star Index I*

KARI SIMS *see Krista Lane*

KARIE STEVENS
The Adventures Of Peeping Tom #4 / 1997 / OD / M

KARIN
Magma: Old And Young / 1995 / MET / M • More Dirty Debutantes #40 / 1995 / 4P / M • More Dirty Debutantes #42 / 1995 / 4P / M

KARIN (S/M) *see Star Index I*

KARIN BOTTCHER
[Schulmadchen-Report 4: Was Eltern Oft Verzweifeln LaBt / 1972 / ... / M

KARIN EAST *see Kristarrah Knight*

KARIN GRUAS
[S.S. Bordello / 1978 / ... / M

KARIN HESKE
[Krankenschwestern-Report / 1972 / ... / M

KARIN LORSON
[Junge Madchen Mogen's HeiB, Hausfrauen Noch HeiBer / 1973 / ... / M

KARINA
Doing It / 1982 / SE / M • Girls Gone Bad #5: Mexican Justice / 1991 / GO / F • Private Film #05 / 1993 / OD / M • Private Film #09 / 1994 / OD / M

KARINA KALAN
The Bimbo #2: The Homecoming / 1986 / RLV / M • Sleazy Susan / 1986 / VXP / M • The Vamp / 1986 / AVC / M

KARINA KORTBEIN *see Jenna Wells*

KARINE GAMBIER *(Brigette Lanning)*
Come Play With Me #1 / 1979 / PS / S • European Sex Vacation / 1986 / VC / M • Island Women / 1976 / LUM / S • Professional Janine / 1984 / CA / M • Sexual Circles / 1977 / VD / M • Shocking / 1984 / SE / M • Swedish Nympho Slaves / 1977 / LUM / S • Sweet Taste Of Honey / 1977 /

ALP / M

KARINE STEPHAN
Two At Once / 1978 / CV / M

KARINNA *see Jenna Wells*

KARISMA *see Charisma*

KARL BLAKE
Happy Holiday / 1978 / CA / M

KARL MURDOCH
Bad Penny / 1978 / QX / M

KARL RADCLIFF *see Karl Redford*

KARL RADFORD *see Karl Redford*

KARL REDFORD *(Karl Radford, Karl Radcliff)*
Handsome blonde male who does look something like a young Robert Redford and who seems to swing both ways sexually.
Anal Queen / 1994 / FPI / M • Bi Love Lucy / 1994 / PL / G • Bi-Laddin / 1994 / BIN / G • Contrast / 1995 / CA / M • Cuntz #3 / 1994 / RTP / M • Depraved Fantasies #3 / 1994 / FPI / M • Dirt Bags / 1994 / FPI / M • Don't Try This At Home / 1994 / FPI / M • Electro Sex / 1994 / FPI / M • End Of Innocence / 1994 / WIV / M • Geisha To Go / 1994 / PPP / M • Guess Again / 1994 / FPI / G • Guess What? / 1994 / FPI / G • Man Made Pussy / 1994 / HEA / G • The Masseuse #2 / 1994 / VI / M • Mr. Madonna / 1994 / FPI / G • Oral Majority #12 / 1994 / WV / C • Queen Of The Bizarre / 1994 / AMP / G • Ridin' The Big One / 1994 / TEG / M • Score Of Sex / 1995 / BAC / G • A Step Beyond / 1994 / AMP / G • Treacherous / 1995 / VD / M

KARL THOMAS
Inside Karl Thomas / 1994 / STA / G • Party Partners / 1994 / STA / G

KARL-HEINZ OTTO
[Krankenschwestern-Report / 1972 / ... / M

KARLA
Blue Vanities #510 / 1992 / FFL / M • Creme De La Face #02 / 1994 / OD / M • Dick & Jane Go To Mexico / 1994 / AVI / M • Dreamgirls: Fort Lauderdale / 1996 / DR / M • Mr. Peepers Amateur Home Videos #55: Anal Antics / 1992 / LBO / M • Neighborhood Watch #33 / 1992 / LBO / M • Odyssey Triple Play #31: Double Penetration Babes / 1993 / OD / M • Sodomania...And Then Some!!! A Compendium / 1995 / EL / C • Sweet Secrets / 1977 / VCS / M

KARLA POLITANO *see Star Index I*

KARLA SEROZKY
Horny Henry's Euro Adventure / 1995 / TTV / M

KARMA
Private Film #16 / 1994 / OD / M

KARMA SUTRA *see Ricky Lee*

KARMEN KRUISE
Sex On The Strip: The Lusty Ladies Of Las Vagas / 1993 / CPG / F

KARO KAMOTO *see Star Index I*

KAROL
GVC: Sweet Dominance #127 / 1983 / GO / B

KARRE
Snatch Masters #07 / 1995 / LEI / M

KARRIE
A&B AB#207: Anal Gang Bang / 1990 / A&B / M • A&B AB#215: Anal Sex Session / 1990 / A&B / M • A&B AB#220: Karrie's Anal Show / 1990 / A&B / M

KARYL CARLYN *see Star Index I*

KARYN
AVP #7031: Working It Out Again / 1991 /

AVP / M • Backdoor Ebony / 1995 / WV / M • Bang City #2: China's Anal Gang Bang / 1995 / SC / M • Black Knockers #04 / 1995 / TV / M • Girlz Towne #10 / 1995 / FC / F • Maverdick / 1995 / WV / M • Reverse Gang Bang / 1995 / JMP / M • Snatch Shot / 1996 / LBO / M

KARYN BURCH *see Star Index I*

KARYN KENNEDY
N.Y. Video Magazine #10 / 1996 / OUP / M

KASA
AVP #9152: Three Man Slut / 1991 / AVP / M

KASCHA *(Alison LePriol)*
Alison LePriol is from **Caged Fury**.
Backdoor To Hollywood #05 / 1988 / CDI / M • Backdoor To Hollywood #06 / 1989 / CIN / M • Backdoor To Hollywood #07 / 1989 / CIN / M • The Bashful Blonde From Beautiful Bendover / 1993 / PEP / M • The Best Of Backdoor To Hollywood / 1990 / CIN / C • Bet Black / 1989 / CDI / M • Caged Fury / 1990 / C3S / S • Charlie's Girls #1 / 1988 / CC / M • Deep Inside Kascha / 1992 / CDI / C • Educating Kascha / 1989 / CIN / M • Fade To Black / 1988 / CDI / M • Fatal Seduction / 1988 / CDI / M • From Kascha With Love / 1988 / CDI / M • Girls Of The Double D #05 / 1988 / CIN / M • Girls Of The Double D #07 / 1989 / CIN / M • Girls Of The Double D #08 / 1989 / CDI / M • Girls Of Treasure Island / 1988 / CV / M • Good Morning Saigon / 1988 / ZA / M • Hawaii Vice #1 / 1988 / CIN / M • Hawaii Vice #2 / 1989 / CDI / M • Hawaii Vice #3 / 1988 / CIN / M • Hawaii Vice #4 / 1989 / CIN / M • Hawaii Vice #5 / 1989 / CDI / M • Hawaii Vice #6 / 1989 / CDI / M • Hawaii Vice #7 / 1989 / CDI / M • Hawaii Vice #8 / 1990 / CIN / M • Hawaii Vice: Reflections / 1990 / CIN / C • Hot Property / 1993 / PEP / M • Introducing Kascha / 1988 / CDI / C • Island Girls #1 / 1990 / CDI / C • Island Girls #2: Fun In The Sun / 1990 / CDI / C • Island Girls #3: Rip Tide / 1991 / CDI / C • Jealous Lovers / 1989 / CDI / M • Kascha & Friends / 1988 / CIN / M • Kascha's Blues / 1988 / CDI / M • Kascha's Days & Nights / 1989 / CDI / M • Mandii's Magic / 1988 / CDI / M • Nina's Toys And Boys / 1991 / LV / C • That Ole Black Magic / 1988 / CDI / M

KASEY
Splato: Sexual Fantasies #07 / 1996 / SPL / M

KASEY RODGERS
Blonde In Black Silk / 1979 / QX / M • Debbie Does Dallas #1 / 1978 / VC / M • Dirty Susan / 1979 / CPL / M • For Richer, For Poorer / 1979 / CXV / M • People / 1978 / QX / M • Satin Suite / 1979 / QX / M

KASHA
The Search For Canadian Beaver / 1995 / LIP / F • Sex On The Run #2 / 1994 / TTV / M

KASHARA
Black Casting Couch #1 / 1993 / WP / M • The New Butt Hunt #14 / 1995 / LEI / C

KASHMIR
Dr Bondo / 1995 / BON / B • Snared For Submission / 1995 / BON / B

KASMERE ROSE
Aggressive Lesbians / 1995 / STM / C • Deck His Balls With Holly / 1992 / STM / B • Matronly Stern Spankings / 1994 / STM / B • Sexy Ties & Videotape / 1992 / STM /

B • Spanked By Santa / 1992 / STM / B • Stern Auditor / 1992 / STM / B • Strictly Heels And Toes / 1992 / STM / B • Toe-Tally Foot-Age / 1992 / STM / C • Trained Transvestites / 1995 / STM / B • Transvestite Academy / 1991 / PL / G

KASSANDRA
Leg...Ends #03 / 1991 / BIZ / F • The Other Side Of Debbie / 1991 / CC / M • Robin Head / 1991 / CC / M

KASSANDRA DEL RIO *see* **Cassandra del Rio**

KASSANDRA JONES
The Black Butt Sisters Do New Orleans / 1996 / MID / M • The Black Butt Sisters Do Seattle / 1995 / MID / M • Fashion Sluts #7 / 1996 / ABS / M • Hollywood Amateurs #28 / 1996 / MID / M • Interview's Foreign Affair / 1996 / LV / M • My First Time #3 / 1996 / NS / M • Nothing Like Nurse Nookie #3 / 1996 / NIT / M • Video Virgins #26 / 1996 / NS / M

KASSI NOVA *(Cassie Nova, Yasmine (Kassi Nova), Jasmin (Kassi Nova), Tara Nova, Jasmine (Kassi Nova), Cassinova, Tera Nova)*
Ugly big-titted supposedly Turkish girl.
18 Candles / 1989 / LA / M • 4F Dating Service / 1989 / AR / M • Anal Attraction #1 / 1988 / 3HV / M • Angels Bi Day, Devils Bi Night / 1990 / FC / G • Backdoor Black #1 / 1992 / WV / C • Backdoor Summer #2 / 1989 / PV / C • Backdoor To Harley-Wood #1 / 1990 / AFV / M • Backdoor To Hollywood #08 / 1989 / CIN / M • Backdoor To Hollywood #10 / 1989 / CIN / M • Backing In 3 / 1991 / WV / C • Bad Mama Jama And The Fat Ladies Of The Evening / 1989 / VT / M • Bad Mama Jama Busts Out / 1989 / VT / M • Best Of Caught From Behind #5 / 1991 / HO / C • Bi And Beyond #2 / 1989 / CAT / G • Bi Dream Of Genie / 1990 / BIN / G • Bi Mistake / 1989 / VI / G • The Big Tease #1 / 1990 / VC / M • The Big Tease #2 / 1990 / VC / M • Black, White And Blue / 1989 / E&I / M • Blazing Nova / 1989 / LV / M • Blow Bi Blow / 1988 / MET / G • Breaststroke #1 / 1988 / EX / M • Butt's Motel #1 / 1989 / EX / M • Butt's Motel #3 / 1989 / EX / M • The Buttnicks #1 / 1990 / VEX / M • Can't Beat The Feeling / 1988 / VEX / M • Cat On A Hot Sin Roof / 1989 / LV / M • Caught From Behind #11 / 1989 / HO / M • Cheek-A-Boo / 1988 / LV / M • City Of Rage / 1989 / EVN / M • Club Lez / 1990 / PL / F • Devil In Vanity / 1990 / CC / M • Diamond For Sale / 1990 / EVN / M • Dirty Movies / 1989 / VD / M • Double Take / 1991 / BIZ / B • Double Trouble / 1988 / V99 / M • Frat Brats / 1990 / VC / M • Fun In A Bun / 1990 / LV / M • Gidget Goes Bi / 1990 / STA / G • Girls Will Be Girls / 1988 / LV / F • Good Morning Saigon / 1988 / ZA / M • The Great Sex Contest #2 / 1989 / LV / M • Hawaii Vice #2 / 1989 / CDI / M • Hawaii Vice #3 / 1988 / CIN / M • Heather's Secrets / 1990 / VEX / M • Hershe Highway #2 / 1989 / HO / M • Hot Dreams / 1989 / VEX / M • Hot Dreams / 1991 / VEX / M • Hot To Swap / 1988 / VEX / M • Hung Guns / 1988 / STA / G • The Hustler / 1989 / CDI / M • I Love X / 1992 / FC / C • Innocent Obsession / 1989 / FC / M • Juice Box / 1990 / AFV / M • The Kink / 1988 / WV / M • Leave It To Cleavage #2 / 1989 / EVN / M

• Lesbian Lingerie Fantasy #5 / 1991 / ESP / F • Life Is Butt A Dream / 1989 / V99 / M • The Lottery / 1989 / CIN / M • More Than Friends / 1989 / FAZ / M • My Sensual Body / 1989 / WET / M • Mystery Of The Golden Lotus / 1989 / HU / M • Naughty Neighbors / 1989 / CA / M • The Night Temptress / 1989 / HU / M • Nina's Toys And Boys / 1991 / LV / C • Oral Majority #07 / 1989 / WV / C • Passion From Behind / 1990 / LV / M • Perils Of Paula / 1989 / CA / M • Personal Touch #4 / 1989 / AR / M • Porn In The Pen / 1993 / LE / F • Positive Positions / 1989 / VEX / M • Raw Sewage / 1989 / FC / M • Red Velvet / 1988 / PV / M • The Rod Garetto Story / 1995 / FC / C • Sea Of Desire / 1990 / AR / M • Search For An Angel / 1988 / WV / M • Sex Crazy / 1989 / FAN / C • Sex On The Town 1989 / V99 / M • Simply Irresistible / 1988 / CC / M • Single Girl Masturbation #5 / 1991 / ESP / F • Some Like It Hot / 1989 / CDI / M • Splash Shots / 1989 / CC / M • A Taste Of Victoria Paris / 1990 / PIN / C • Telemates / 1988 / STA / M • Telemates / 1991 / V99 / M • This One's For You / 1989 / AR / M • Tit Tales #2 / 1990 / FC / M • Tit Tales #3 / 1991 / FC / M • Titty-Titty Bang-Bang / 1992 / FC / C • Toys, Not Boys #3 / 1991 / FC / C • Two Women & A Man / 1988 / VEX / M • Two Women & A Man / 1991 / VEX / C • The Ultimate Climax / 1989 / V99 / M • Undressed For Success / 1990 / V99 / M • Voodoo Lust: The Possession / 1989 / PCP / M • Weird And Bizarre Bondage / 1991 / FC / C • Wet Tails / 1989 / PL / M • Who Shaved Cassi Nova? / 1989 / EX / M

KASSIE
Amateur Models For Hire / 1996 / MP0 / M

KASSIE SHELDON
Anal Load Lickers / 1996 / ROB / M • Bootylicious: China Town / 1995 / JMP / M • Cute Cuddly Bubbly Butts / 1996 / TTV / M • Forbidden Fantasies #2 / 1995 / ZA / M • Fresh Faces #07 / 1995 / EVN / M • Gang Bang Face Bath #4 / 1995 / ROB / M • Hollywood Amateurs #22 / 1995 / MID / M • Hollywood Starlets Adventure #06 / 1995 / AVS / M • Leather Unleashed / 1995 / GO / M • The Real Deal #2 / 1995 / FC / M • The Seductive Secretary / 1995 / GO / M • Virgin Killers: The Killing Spree / 1995 / PEP / M

KAT
100% Amateur #18: / 1995 / OD / M • Black Snatch #1 / 1996 / DFI / F • Student Fetish Videos: Best Of Foot Worship #03 / 1995 / PRE / C • Student Fetish Videos: The Enema #18 / 1995 / PRE / B • Student Fetish Videos: Spanking #18 / 1995 / PRE / B

KAT COBI
Glory Days / 1996 / IN / M

KAT HARLOW *see* **Melissa Melendez**

KAT KARLSON *(Lisa (K. Karlson), Kate (K. Karlson))*
Small blonde with medium tits and a slutty attitude.
Babewatch #1 / 1993 / CC / M • Bobby Hollander's Rookie Nookie #08 / 1993 / SFP / M • Bondage Slut / 1994 / HOM / B • Breastman Goes To Breastland #1 / 1993 / EVN / M • First Time Lesbians #04 / 1993 / JMP / F • Mike Hott: #244 Horny Couples #14 / 1993 / MHV / M • Mike Hott: #257 Cunt of the Month: Selina / 1993 / MHV / M

• Mr. Peepers Amateur Home Videos #67: Backdoor Fantasy / 1993 / LBO / M • Positively Pagan #07 / 1993 / ATA / M • Positively Pagan #08 / 1993 / ATA / M • Sneek Peeks #2 / 1993 / OCV / M • Spell Of The Whip / 1994 / HOM / B

KAT MANDU
Bun Busters #14 / 1994 / LBO / M • Odyssey 30 Min: #382: Dildo Dykes / 1993 / OD / M

KATA
Triple X Video Magazine #11 / 1995 / OD / M

KATALIN
Eurotica #05 / 1996 / XC / M • Fashion Sluts #8 / 1996 / ABS / M • Private Gold #10: Sins / 1996 / OD / M • Pussyman Auditions #16 / 1995 / SNA / M • The Voyeur #7: Live In Europe #1 / 1996 / JLP / M

KATALIN HORVARTH
Screamers / 1994 / HW / M

KATALIN IVANKI
True Stories #1 / 1993 / SC / M • True Stories #2 / 1993 / SC / M

KATALIN LENGYEL
True Stories #1 / 1993 / SC / M • True Stories #2 / 1993 / SC / M

KATALIN LENIN
Private Gold #01: Study In Sex / 1995 / OD / M • Private Gold #02: Friends In Sex / 1995 / OD / M

KATALINA
More Dirty Debutantes #52 / 1996 / 4P / M

KATALYN
Checkmate / 1996 / SNA / M • Dreams Of A Gigolo / 1996 / SNA / M • Private Gold #12: The Pyramid #2 / 1996 / OD / M • Pussyman #14: Dreams Of A Gigolo / 1996 / SNA / M

KATANA
Stevi's: Mistress Katana / 1995 / SSV / B

KATARA JOY
Easy Binder / 1994 / VTF / B • Kane Video #1: The Riding Crop / 1993 / VTF / B • Kane Video #2 / 1994 / VTF / B • The Magnificent 7 / 1994 / VTF / B • Mistress Of The Dungeon / 1994 / VTF / B • Mr. Wilkes' Caning Academy / 1994 / VTF / B • The Rack / 1994 / SBP / B • The Rock / 1994 / SBP / B • Ropeburn / 1994 / VTF / B • Rubber Me Butt! / 1994 / SBP / B

KATARINA
Ass Lover's Special / 1996 / PE / M • Buttman's Bubble Butt Babes / 1996 / EA / M • Deep Behind The Scenes With Seymore Butts #2 / 1995 / ULI / M • Rock 'n' Roll Rocco / 1997 / EA / M • The Sodomizer #1 / 1995 / SC / M • World Sex Tour #6 / 1996 / ANA / M

KATARINA MENDEZ
Up And Cummers #10 / 1994 / 4P / M

KATE
Bootylicious: It's A Butt Thang / 1994 / JMP / M • Bound To Be Cute / 1994 / VIG / B • Green Piece Of Ass #3 / 1994 / RTP / M • Horny Henry's London Adventure / 1995 / TTV / M • Mr. Peepers Amateur Home Videos #86: Tit A Ton / 1994 / LBO / M

KATE (K. KARLSON) see Kat Karlson

KATE ADAMS
Caught! / 1985 / BIZ / B

KATE BUFFER
Erotic Fantasies #4 / 1983 / CV / C

KATE CASSIDY
Bright Tails #8 / 1996 / STP / B • New Faces, Hot Bodies #20 / 1996 / STP / M •

New Faces, Hot Bodies #22 / 1996 / STP / M • Toy Time #3: / 1995 / STP / F • Toy Time #5: / 1996 / STP / F

KATE COLEMAN *(Kate Little)*
Blonde tiny girl (4'10") but not petite in terms of body which is a bit womanly. Medium tits, good tan lines, marginal face, 23 years old in 1995, bit flat on the butt, hairy ass crack.
Cry Babies #1: Anal Scream / 1995 / ZA / M • More Dirty Debutantes #40 / 1995 / 4P / M • Muffmania / 1995 / TTV / M

KATE KATYE
The Cumm Brothers #05: These Nuts For Hire / 1994 / OD / M • Nasty Newcummers #05 / 1994 / MET / M

KATE LITTLE see Kate Coleman

KATE LYNN
Lovin' Spoonfuls #4 / 1995 / 4P / C

KATE MICHAELS
Anal Virgins Of America #06 / 1994 / FOR / M

KATE MILLET see Star Index I

KATE MINX see Star Index I

KATE MONTAINE
Bun Busters #20 / 1994 / LBO / M • Dick & Jane Do The Slopes In Ass Spin / 1994 / AVI / M • Dirty Doc's Housecalls #15 / 1994 / LV / M

KATE POST
MASH'ed / cr75 / ALP / M

KATE RUCH
Private Video Magazine #11 / 1994 / OD / M • Private Video Magazine #12 / 1994 / OD / M • Private Video Magazine #15 / 1994 / OD / M • Private Video Magazine #17 / 1994 / OD / M

KATE TAYLER
My Sister's Husband / 1996 / AWV / G

KATERINA
Rocco Goes To Prague / 1995 / EA / M

KATHERINE
Eric Kroll's Bondage #1 / 1994 / ERK / M • Eric Kroll's Fetish #1 / 1994 / ERK / M • Magma: Sperma / 1994 / MET / M • Mixed-Up Marriage / 1995 / CV / M • Neighbor Girls T21 / 1990 / NEI / F • New Faces, Hot Bodies #22 / 1996 / STP / M • Strange Diary / 1976 / AXV / M

KATHERINE GAMBIER see Star Index I

KATHERINE KINCAID
Latent Image: Katherine "Kitty" Kincaid / 1995 / LAT / F

KATHERINE MILES see Star Index I

KATHERINE RADCLIFFE
The Psychiatrist / 1978 / VC / M

KATHI ADAIR
Screwples / 1979 / CA / M

KATHI GATI
Angel Buns / 1981 / QX / M

KATHI HARCOURT see Kathy Harcourt

KATHIE
Blue Vanities #556 / 1994 / FFL / M • Onanie #2 / 1995 / MET / F

KATHLEEN
Blue Vanities #529 / 1993 / FFL / M • Dirty Dirty Debutantes #5 / 1996 / 4P / M • More Dirty Debutantes #40 / 1995 / 4P / M • More Dirty Debutantes #42 / 1995 / 4P / M • More Dirty Debutantes #49 / 1996 / 4P / M • Painless Steel #3 / 1996 / FLV / M • Private Stories #01 / 1995 / OD / M • Triple X Video Magazine #13 / 1996 / OD / M

KATHLEEN BARRY see Star Index I

KATHLEEN CLARK
Never Enough / 1971 / VCX / M • Saturday

Matinee Series #3 / 1996 / VCX / C

KATHLEEN COLLINS see Bo Derek

KATHLEEN FABERJIE see Star Index I

KATHLEEN GENTRY see Kathleen Jentry

KATHLEEN JENTRY *(Kathleen Gentry)*
69 Pump Street / 1988 / ZA / M • Adventures Of Buttwoman #1 / 1991 / EL / F • Aerobisex Girls #2 / 1989 / LIP / F • Bare Essence / 1989 / EA / M • Best Of Buttman #1 / 1991 / EA / C • Campfire Girls / 1988 / SE / M • The Catwoman / 1988 / VC / M • Dance Fire / 1989 / EA / M • Dy-Nasty / 1988 / SE / M • Erotic Rendezvous / 1988 / VEX / M • Eye Of The Tigress / 1988 / VD / M • Falcon Breast / 1987 / CDI / M • Fantasy Confidential / 1988 / GO / M • Fantasy Girls / 1988 / CA / M • Fatal Seduction / 1988 / CDI / M • From Rags To Riches / 1988 / CDI / M • Fuck This / 1988 / BEV / C • Goin' Down Slow / 1988 / VC / M • The Greatest American Blonde / 1987 / WV / C • A Hard Act To Swallow / 1988 / VT / M • Hot Scalding / 1989 / VC / M • I Can't Get No...Satisfaction / 1988 / CDI / M • Lays Of Our Lives / 1988 / ZA / M • Lethal Woman #1 / 1988 / SEV / M • Lethal Woman #2 / 1988 / SEV / M • Nasty Newshounds / 1988 / ME / M • Parliament: Sweethearts #1 / 1988 / PM / F • Peek-A-Boo / 1987 / VEX / M • Port Holes / 1988 / AVC / M • Spend The Holidays With Barbii / 1987 / CDI / M • Strong Rays / 1988 / IN / M • Super Blondes / 1989 / VEX / M • Swedish Erotica #70 / 1985 / CA / M • Switch Hitters #3: Squeeze Play / 1989 / IN / G • A Taste Of Tawnee / 1988 / LV / C • Three By Three / 1989 / LV / C • Tough Girls Don't Dance / 1987 / SEV / M • Tricks Of The Trade / 1988 / CA / M • The Way They Were / 1990 / CDI / M • Where The Girls Sweat #2 / 1991 / EL / F • Wild In The Wilderness / 1988 / SE / M • A Woman's Touch / 1988 / ZA / F • [Berlin Caper / 1989 / ... / M

KATHLEEN KELLY see Kathlyn Kelly

KATHLEEN KINSKI see Star Index I

KATHLEEN KRISTEL *(Sharon McIntyre, Kristin (K. Kristel))*
Body Magic / 1982 / SE / M • Little Girls Blue #2 / 1983 / VCX / M • Nurses Of The 407th / 1982 / CA / M

KATHLEEN LAJOIE
The Girls Of Fantasex #1 / 1996 / NIT / M

KATHLEEN MAZZOTTA see Leena

KATHLEEN STONE
Sex #1 (Vca) / 1994 / VC / M

KATHLYN KELLY *(Kathleen Kelly)*
Dirty 30's Cinema: Patti Petite / 1986 / PV / C • Hard To Swallow / 1985 / PV / M • Hollywood Pink / 1985 / HO / M • Once Upon A Madonna / 1985 / PV / M • Sexpertease / 1985 / VD / M

KATHLYN MOORE see Cher Delight

KATHRYN see Star Index I

KATHRYN GLEN see Star Index I

KATHRYN MOORE see Cher Delight

KATHRYN REED see Star Index I

KATHY
Blue Vanities #570 / 1995 / FFL / M • Bottoms Up #02 / 1983 / AVC / C • Breast Worx #14 / 1992 / LBO / M • Cumback Pussy #5: Groopin' / 1996 / EL / M • Donna Young: Ann & Kathy's First Lesbian Video #1 / 1995 / DY / F • Kathy's Bike Bondage / 1995 / GAL / B • Le Parfum De Mathilde / 1994 / VI / M • Limited Edition #22 / 1981 /

AVC / M • New Faces, Hot Bodies #05 / 1992 / STP / M • Triple X Video Magazine #01 / 1995 / OD / M

KATHY CARLTON *see* **Christine Heller**

KATHY CHRISTIAN *see* **Christine Heller**

KATHY CLARK
Cover Girl Fantasies #1 / 1983 / VCR / C

KATHY COLLINS (CH) *see* **Christine Heller**

KATHY DAVIS *see* **Star Index I**

KATHY DIVINE
Gangbang Girl #19 / 1996 / ANA / M

KATHY HARCOURT *(Kathy Marcourt, Kathy Harton, Kathi Harcourt)*
Beauty / 1981 / VC / M • Centerfold Fever / 1981 / VXP / M • Lips: The Passage To Pleasure / 1981 / CA / M • Little Darlings / 1981 / VEP / M • Mistress Electra / 1983 / AVO / B • Same Time Every Year / 1981 / VHL / M • The Seductress / 1982 / VC / M

KATHY HARTON *see* **Kathy Harcourt**

KATHY HESUN
Sex Boat / 1980 / VCX / M

KATHY HICKMAN
Draws / 1976 / VIG / S • Erotic Animation Festival / 1980 / VC / M

KATHY JONES
Golden Oldies #6 / 1996 / TTV / M • The Real Deal #4 / 1996 / FC / M

KATHY KANE *see* **Christine Heller**

KATHY KASH
The Voyeur #8: Live In Europe #2 / 1996 / JLP / M

KATHY KAUFMAN
Blue's Velvet / 1979 / ECV / M • Erotic Fantasies: John Leslie / 1985 / CV / C • Getting Off / 1979 / VIP / M

KATHY KAY
Blondes Like It Hot / 1984 / ELH / M • Doing It / 1982 / SE / M • Erotic Dimensions #1: Ripe / 1982 / NSV / M • Erotic Dimensions #2: Black Desire / 1982 / NSV / M • Erotic Dimensions #4: The Exhibitionist / 1982 / NSV / M • Erotic Dimensions: I Want To Watch / 1982 / NSV / M • Flying Skirts / 1985 / HO / M • Nightlife / 1983 / CA / M • [Erotic Dimensions Vols 1 To 8 / 1983 / NSV / C

KATHY KIRK *see* **Christine Heller**

KATHY KISSES
Bedtime Video #06 / 1984 / GO / M

KATHY KLINE *see* **Christine Heller**

KATHY KONNERS *see* **Star Index I**

KATHY KUSICK *see* **Christine Heller**

KATHY LANE *see* **Star Index I**

KATHY LAWRENCE
Midnight Hustle / 1978 / VC / M

KATHY LINGER
Casanova #2 / 1976 / CA / M

KATHY LYPPS
N.Y. Video Magazine #01 / 1994 / OUP / M • N.Y. Video Magazine #08 / 1996 / OUP / M • Sanctuary Of Sin / 1995 / OUP / B

KATHY MALWIN *see* **Star Index I**

KATHY MARCEAU
Anal Taboo / 1993 / ROB / M • Top Model / 1995 / SC / M

KATHY MARCOURT *see* **Kathy Harcourt**

KATHY MARSH *see* **Christine Heller**

KATHY MAY *see* **Star Index I**

KATHY REILLY *see* **Kathy Riley**

KATHY RILEY *(Kathy Reilly, Sarah Mills)*
Ecstasy / 1979 / SE / M • Naked Afternoon / 1976 / CV / M

KATHY ROBERTSON *see* **Star Index I**

KATHY RONDELL *see* **Star Index I**

KATHY STAR
Erotic Dimensions: Explode / 1982 / NSV / M

KATHY STEIN *see* **Star Index I**

KATHY STRENGE
Jail Bait / 1976 / VC / M

KATHY THOMAS *see* **Christine Heller**

KATHY WEST *see* **Star Index I**

KATHY WILLETS
The Babes Of Boneville / 1995 / VEX / C • GM #152: Oh Kathy Willet / 1994 / GMV / F • Naked Scandal #1 / 1995 / SPI / M • Naked Scandal #2 / 1996 / SPI / M • Philmore Butts Meets The Palm Beach Nymphomaniac Kathy Wille / 1995 / SUF / M • Seymore & Shane Live On Tour / 1995 / ULI / M • Seymore & Shane Meet Kathy Willets, The Naughty Nymph / 1994 / ULI / M • Snatch Masters #11 / 1995 / LEI / M • What's The Lesbian Doing In My Pirate Movie? / 1995 / LIP / F • [Creep / 1996 / … / S

KATHY YUNG *see* **Kitty Yung**

KATI
The Betrayal Of Innocence #1: The Awakening Of Marika / 1993 / CC / M • The Betrayal Of Innocence #2: The Decadence / 1993 / CC / M • The Betrayal Of Innocence #3: The Choice / 1993 / CC / M • Dick & Jane Return To Hungary / 1993 / OAP / M • Sperm Injection / 1995 / PL / M

KATI MIRAMBA *see* **Star Index I**

KATIA
Bend Over Brazilian Babes #1 / 1993 / EA / M • Bend Over Brazilian Babes #2 / 1993 / EA / M • Everything Is Not Relative / 1994 / EL / M • Jamie's French Debutantes / 1992 / SC / M • Triple X Video Magazine #08 / 1995 / OD / M • Triple X Video Magazine #09 / 1995 / OD / M

KATIA CARGO
Hamlet: For The Love Of Ophelia #1 / 1996 / IP / M

KATIA MARA
Farewell Scarlett / 1976 / COM / M

KATIE
Black Juice Bombs / 1996 / NIT / C • Blue Vanities #546 / 1994 / FFL / M • Cherry Poppers #08: Tender And Tight / 1994 / ZA / M • Georgie's Ordeal / 1993 / LED / B • Home Movie Production #05 / 1990 / DR / M • Jus' Knockin' Boots #1: Fade To Black / 1996 / NIT / M • Ron Hightower's White Chicks #11 / 1994 / LBO / M • Student Fetish Videos: Catfighting #11 / 1994 / PRE / B • Student Fetish Videos: Foot Worship #12 / 1994 / PRE / B • Student Fetish Videos: Spanking #15 / 1994 / PRE / B

KATIE AKIN
Resurrection Of Eve / 1973 / MIT / M

KATIE BERGMANN
Private Film #11 / 1994 / OD / M

KATIE GOLD
More Dirty Debutantes #64 / 1997 / SBV / M

KATIE KEAN
Erotic Fantasies: Women With Women / 1984 / CV / C • Honey Throat / 1980 / CV / M • Only The Best Of Women With Women / 1988 / CV / C

KATIE LANE
Butt Hunt #05 / 1995 / LEI / M • Pussy Hunt #10 / 1995 / LEI / M

KATIE LYNN
Wildfire: Shaving Beauties / 1996 / WIF / F

KATIE O'BRIAN *see* **Star Index I**

KATIE RICHARDS
Ron Hightower's White Chicks #08 / 1994 / LBO / M

KATIE THOMAS *(Kim Tatum)*
Ecstasy / 1986 / PP / M • Hill Street Blacks #1 / 1985 / 4R / M • The Layout / 1986 / CDI / M • Let's Get It On With Amber Lynn / 1986 / VC / M

KATIE WELCH *see* **Star Index I**

KATIEDID *see* **Star Index I**

KATJA
Chateau Duval / 1996 / HDE / M • Magma: Chateau Extreme / 1995 / MET / M • Skirts & Flirts #02 / 1997 / XPR / F

KATJA (TANYA FOX) *see* **Tanya Fox**

KATJA ECK *see* **Star Index I**

KATJA GILLISSEN *see* **Star Index I**

KATLAN
Green Piece Of Ass #4 / 1994 / RTP / M

KATLIN
Dick & Jane Return To Hungary / 1993 / OAP / M

KATMANDU *see* **Blu-Silk**

KATRIN
Penetration (Anabolic) #1 / 1995 / ANA / M

KATRIN S.
Private Gold #09: Private Dancer / 1996 / OD / M

KATRINA
Dirty Dancers #3 / 1995 / 4P / M • Odyssey Amateur #85: Katrina's Free For All / 1992 / OD / M • Porno X-Treme #2: Club Bizarre / 1995 / SC / M • Porno X-Treme #4: Wet Dream / 1995 / SC / M • Wildfire: Shaving Beauties / 1996 / WIF / F

KATRINA (CAMEO) *see* **Cameo**

KATRINA DEME
Live Sex Net / 1996 / SPR / M

KATRINA LEE
Resurrection Of Eve / 1973 / MIT / M

KATRINA REXFORD
Valerie / 1975 / VCX / M • Young, Hot And Nasty / cr88 / BWV / C

KATRINA TAYLOR
Beneath The Cane / 1992 / BON / B • Bondage Memories #01 / 1993 / BON / C • Canyon Capers / 1991 / BON / B • Capturing Katrina / 1994 / BON / B • Home Maid Memories #2 / 1994 / BON / C • Hot Daze #01: An Afternoon With Katrina / 1991 / BON / B • Hot Daze #02: The Trip / 1991 / BON / B • Hot Daze #03: Touch Me! / 1992 / BON / B • Hot Daze #04: Timid Feelings / 1993 / BON / B • Katrina And The Pros / 1992 / BON / B • Katrina's Awakening #1 / 1994 / BON / B • Katrina's Awakening #2 / 1994 / BON / B • Katrina's Awakening #3 / 1994 / BON / B • Katrina's Bondage Memories #1 / 1994 / BON / C • Katrina's Old Fashioned Spankings / 1991 / BON / B • Overtime / 1993 / BON / B • Real Breasts Real Torment / 1995 / BON / C • Red Bottom Blues / 199? / BON / B • Reel Domination Series #1: Mistress Katrina / 1995 / IBN / B • Switch / 1992 / BON / B • Tied & Teased / 1993 / BON / B

KATRINA VALENTINA *see* **Star Index I**

KATRINA WAVE *see* **Paisley Hunter**

KATRINE ENSKA *see* **Star Index I**

KATT
A Special Lesson / 1996 / GAL / B

KATT WILDER
Every Granny Has A Fantasy / 1996 / GLI / M

KATTIE HAYS *see Star Index I*

KATY
The Best Of Hot Body Video Magazine / 1994 / CG / C • The Betrayal Of Innocence #1: The Awakening Of Marika / 1993 / CC / M • The Betrayal Of Innocence #2: The Decadence / 1993 / CC / M • The Betrayal Of Innocence #3: The Choice / 1993 / CC / M • Blue Vanities #539 / 1993 / FFL / M • Private Gold #12: The Pyramid #2 / 1996 / OD / M

KATY JANOZ
Private Film #13 / 1994 / OD / M

KATYA
Anal Magic / 1995 / XC / M • Ron Hightower's White Chicks #13 / 1994 / LBO / M

KAURI *see* Pamela Dee

KAVIAR *see* Debi Diamond

KAY
Blue Vanities #544 / 1994 / FFL / M • Blue Vanities #557 / 1994 / FFL / M • Porn Store Whore / 1996 / VG0 / M • The Show / 1995 / VI / M • The Taming Of Kay / 1993 / SSP / B

KAY (KAIKO) *see* Kaiko

KAY FIGA *see Star Index I*

KAY LANI
Lovin' Spoonfuls #5 / 1996 / 4P / C

KAY LAYMAN
Bondage Brothel / 1996 / LBO / B • Innocent's Initiation / 1996 / BON / B • Pain Is The Price / 1996 / LBO / B • Student Fetish Videos: Spanking #22 / 1996 / PRE / B • Student Fetish Videos: Tickling #13 / 1996 / SFV / B • Tied Temptations / 1996 / BON / B

KAY LEIGH *see* Kayleigh Klein

KAY LONDON
Shoulder length blonde fine hair, not too pretty face, womanly body, rock solid cantaloupes, belly button ring. Comes from New Orleans and was de-virginized at 17.
Asses Galore #6: Fallen Angels / 1996 / DFI / M • The Attendant / 1996 / SC / M • Butt Row Unplugged / 1996 / ABS / M • Th Fanny / 1997 / WP / M • Living On The Edge / 1997 / DWO / M • Pussyman's Nite Club Party #1 / 1996 / SNA / M • Pussyman's Nite Club Party #2 / 1997 / SNA / M • Repression / 1996 / ZA / M • Up And Cummers #37 / 1996 / 4P / M • Women Behaving Badly / 1996 / RAS / M

KAY LOUIS *see Star Index I*

KAY MARLOW
Bound & Shaved / 1994 / BON / B • The XYZ Rope & Tape Company / 1993 / BON / B

KAY MARTIN *see Star Index I*

KAY NACEY
Video Virgins #14 / 1994 / NS / M

KAY O
Creme De La Face #11: Cum Plasterers / 1995 / OD / M • The Cumm Brothers #11: Oh Cum On Ye Faces / 1995 / OD / M • The Cumm Brothers #12: Two GOOS For Every Girl / 1995 / OD / M • The Cumm Brothers #13: Rump Rangers / 1996 / OD / M • Rodney's Rookies #1 / 1996 / NIT / M

KAY PARKER *(Kay Taylor, Jill Jackson)*
English big breasted brunette with a passable face and not-too-pudgy body. Born 8/28/44 in Birmingham, England. Jill Jackson is from **Untamed**. As of 1996 she was working at some sort of new age counseling job (you know: holding hands and running around the maypole in the nude).

The 8th Annual Erotic Film Awards / 1984 / SE / C • Big, Bad & Beautiful / 1988 / MIR / C • Blue Vanities #062 / 1988 / FFL / M • Blue Vanities #064 / 1988 / FFL / M • Body Talk / 1982 / VCX / M • Caballero Preview Tape #3 / 1984 / CA / C • Caballero Preview Tape #4 / 1985 / CA / C • Careful, He May Be Watching / 1986 / CA / M • Champagne For Breakfast / 1980 / SE / M • Chorus Call / 1978 / TVX / M • Connection Live #2 / 1986 / VD / C • The Dancers / 1981 / VCX / M • Desire / 1983 / VCX / M • Downstairs, Upstairs / 1980 / SE / M • Electric Blue: Nurse Fever / 1985 / CA / M • Erotic Radio WSEX / 1983 / VC / M • Fantasy Follies #1 / 1983 / VC / M • Fantasy Follies #2 / 1983 / VC / M • Fast Cars, Fast Women / 1979 / SE / M • Fire In The Hole / 1989 / ... / C • Firestorm #1 / 1984 / COM / M • Firestorm #2: The Angel Blade / 1986 / COM / M • Firestorm #3 / 1986 / COM / M • First Annual XRCO Awards / 1984 / AVC / C • Free And Foxy / 1986 / VCX / C • Good To The Last Drop / 1986 / VCS / C • The Health Spa / 1978 / SE / M • Hot Blooded / 1983 / CA / M • Hustler Video Magazine #1 / 1983 / SE / M • I Want To Be Bad / 1984 / CV / M • Intimate Lessons / 1982 / VC / M • Intimate Realities #2 / 1983 / VC / M • Kate And The Indians / 1980 / SE / M • L'Amour / 1984 / CA / M • Ladies Of The 80's / 1985 / PV / M • Legends Of Porn #1 / 1987 / CV / C • Lorelei / 1984 / CV / M • Lust At First Bite / 1978 / VC / M • Matinee Idol / 1984 / VC / M • Me, Myself & I / 1987 / SE / C • Memphis Cathouse Blues / 1982 / CA / M • Men's Video Magazine / 1984 / VCX / S • Nasty Nurses / 1983 / CA / M • Nice 'n' Tight / 1985 / AIR / M • A Night On The Wild Side / 1986 / VC / M • Only The Best #3 / 1990 / CV / C • Only The Best Of Breasts / 1987 / CV / C • Only The Best Of Women With Women / 1988 / CV / C • Private Teacher / 1983 / CA / M • Satisfactions / 1983 / CA / M • Screw / 1985 / CV / M • Seven Into Snowy / 1977 / VC / M • The Seven Seductions Of Madame Lau / 1981 / EVI / M • Sex Games / 1983 / CA / M • Sex Play / 1984 / SE / M • Sex World / 1978 / SE / M • Spectators / 1984 / AVC / M • Stairway To Paradise / 1990 / VC / M • Swedish Erotica #45 / 1983 / CA / M • Sweet Young Foxes / 1984 / VCX / M • Sweethearts / 1986 / SE / C • Taboo #01 / 1980 / VCX / M • Taboo #02 / 1982 / IN / M • Taboo #03 / 1983 / IN / M • Taboo #04 / 1985 / IN / M • Taboo #09 / 1991 / IN / M • Taboo #11: Crazy On You / 1993 / IN / M • Tales From The Chateau / 1987 / BON / B • The Tantric Guide To Sexual Potency And Extended Orgasm / 1994 / A&E / M • Three Faces Of Angel / 1987 / CV / M • The Titty Committee / 1986 / SE / C • Tomboy / 1983 / VCX / M • Too Hot To Touch #1 / 1985 / CV / M • Traci Lords' Fantasies / 1986 / CA / C • True Legends Of Adult Cinema: The Golden Age / 1992 / VC / C • Two On The Tongue / 1988 / TAM / C • The Untamed / 1978 / VCX / M • V—The Hot One / 1978 / CV / M • VCA Previews #2 / 1988 / VC / C • Vista Valley PTA / 1980 / CV / M • The Young Like It Hot / 1983 / CA / M • [High Yellow / 1965 / ... / S

KAY RUSSELL *see Star Index I*

KAY SERA *see Star Index I*

KAY TAYLOR *see* Kay Parker

KAYCEE
Spankology 101b / 1994 / BON / B

KAYE BUCKLEY *see Star Index I*

KAYE D'ANCE *see* Rayne D'Ance

KAYE DUNAWAYE
Dirty Dave's #1 / 1996 / VG0 / M • Dirty Dave's #3 / 1996 / XPR / M • Fashion Sluts #7 / 1996 / ABS / M • The Hunt / 1996 / ULP / M • Mike Hott: #391 / 1996 / MHV / M • Mike Hott: #393 / 1996 / MHV / M • Sticky Fingers / 1996 / WV / M

KAYLA
AVP #7025: Cum Specialist / 1991 / AVP / M • AVP #7026: Samantha Scores Again—The Playoffs / 1991 / AVP / M • Buffy Malibu's Nasty Girls #07 / 1994 / ANA / F • Dirty Dancers #2 / 1994 / 4P / M • Hard Core Beginners #05 / 1995 / LEI / M • Hot Body Video Magazine: Wild Thing / 1996 / CG / F • Love Chunks / 1996 / TTV / M • Western Whores Hotel / 1996 / VG0 / M • When The Fat Lady Sings / 1996 / EX / M

KAYLA KLEEVAGE
Big Boob Celebration / 1994 / BTO / M • Big Boob Lottery / 1993 / BTO / M • Big Boob Pajama Party / 1993 / BTO / F • Bodies In Motion / 1994 / IF / M • Duke Of Knockers #1 / 1992 / BTO / M • Gazongas #06 / 1996 / LEI / C • Girls Around The World #13: Lynn LeMay And Friends / 1994 / BTO / M • Girls Around The World #22: Letha Weapons & Friends / 1995 / BTO / M • Hot To Trot / 1994 / IF / M • Jugs Of Joy / 1994 / LEI / C • Party Animals / 1994 / VEX / C • Tit To Tit #2 / 1994 / BTO / M

KAYLA KUPCAKES
Girls Around The World #29 / 1995 / BTO / M

KAYLAN NICOLE
Blonde with medium tits and black eyebrows. Reasonably trim but not outstanding body. Tattoo of lips in red on her right buttock and another tattoo (the family crest?) on her right outside calf. 36-24-35 and 20 years old in 1993. Was originally a dancer from Wisconsin and got into the business courtesy of Alexis DeVell. Last movie was in June 1995 when she retired to Chicago to get married.
13th Annual Adult Video News Awards / 1996 / VC / S • Anal Crack Master / 1994 / ROB / M • Anal Ecstacy Girls #2 / 1993 / ROB / F • Anal Hounds & Bitches / 1994 / ROB / M • Anal Idol / 1994 / ROB / M • Anal Innocence #2 / 1993 / ROB / M • Assy Sassy #1 / 1994 / ROB / F • Big Busted Dream Girls / 1995 / PME / S • Brassiere To Eternity / 1994 / PEP / F • Butt Sluts #2 / 1993 / ROB / F • Candy Factory / 1994 / PE / M • Caught Looking / 1995 / CC / M • Certifiably Anal / 1993 / ROB / M • County Line / 1993 / PEP / M • Cry Baby / 1995 / CV / M • Dead Aim / 1994 / PEP / M • The Dinner Party #1 / 1994 / ULI / M • Dirty Laundry #1 / 1994 / CV / M • Dirty Laundry #2 / 1994 / CV / M • The Drifter / 1995 / CV / M • Gorgeous / 1995 / MET / M • The Gypsy Queen / 1996 / CC / M • House Arrest / 1995 / CV / M • Kissing Kaylan / 1995 / CC / M • Legend #5: The Legend Continues / 1994 / LE / M • Lucky Lady / 1995 / CV / M • Misfits / 1994 / CV / M • Picture Perfect (Cal Vista) / 1995 / CV / M • Politix / 1995 / CC / M • Prisoner Of Love / 1995 / CV / M • Red Hot Lover / 1995 / CV / M • Restrained By Desire / 1994 / NTP / B • Se-

cret Services / 1995 / CV / M • Sex And Money / 1994 / DGD / S • Something Blue / 1995 / CC / M • Split Tail Lovers / 1994 / ROB / F • Stand By Your Man / 1994 / CV / M • Strip Search / 1995 / CV / M • Stripper Nurses / 1994 / PE / M • Sure Bet / 1995 / CV / M • Three Hearts / 1995 / CC / M • Timepiece / 1994 / CV / M • Unmistakably You / 1995 / CV / M • Upbeat Love #1 / 1994 / CV / M • Upbeat Love #2 / 1995 / CV / M • Wicked As She Seems / 1993 / WP / M

KAYLEIGH see Kayleigh Klein

KAYLEIGH KLEIN *(Kay Leigh, Kayleigh)*
This may also be Amey Mour or Renee Summers (**Love In An Elevator**).
Making It Big / 1990 / TOR / M • Money Honey / 1994 / TOR / M • The Passion Of Heather Lear / 1990 / AFV / M

KAYMEN STUART
The Secret Life Of Nina Hartley / 1994 / VC / M

KAYOKA TATAKI see Star Index I

KAZUHIKO MURATA
Love Melody / 1983 / ORC / M

KAZUI TISHIKO
A Widow's Affair / 1996 / AVV / M

KAZUKO SATO
Erotic Nurses / 1996 / AVE / M

KEA
Cummin' 'round The Mountain / 1996 / BCP / M • Mr. Peepers Amateur Home Videos #92: M-Ass-terpieces / 1994 / LBO / M

KEANNA *(Keanna Reyes, Keanna Lee, Amy (Keanna), Keanna Jones, Terri Lee)*
Uncle Roy says this girl is Hispanic but I she looks like she has some Asian genes. Lovely body but I think she's had her tits enhanced (scar under right one) but not so that they look like watermelons. According to her in **America's Raunchiest #36** she comes from Hawaii which is a much more likely idea. She's 5'3" 105lbs and was 21 in 1992. In **Undercover Lover (1994)** she is credited on the box as Terri Lee.
America's Raunchiest Home Videos #36: Milky Way / 1992 / ZA / M • America's Raunchiest Home Videos #38: Fantasy Beach / 1992 / ZA / M • America's Raunchiest Home Videos #72: / 1993 / ZA / M • Anal Vision #03 / 1992 / LBO / M • As Sweet As Can Be / 1993 / V99 / M • Asian Angel / 1993 / VEX / C • Asian Appetite / 1993 / HO / M • Asian Heat #01: Cherry Blossom Tales / 1993 / SC / M • Asian Heat #02: Satin Angels / 1993 / SC / M • Asian Persuasion / 1993 / WV / M • The Ass Master #02 / 1993 / GLI / M • Beach Bum Amateur's #21 / 1993 / MID / F • Biff Malibu's Totally Nasty Home Videos #24 / 1992 / ANA / M • Big Murray's New-Cummers #09: Oriental Lovers / 1993 / FD / M • Big Murray's New-Cummers #11: Willing & Able / 1993 / FD / M • The Big One / 1992 / GO / M • Biography: Max Steiner / 1995 / SC / C • Bobby Hollander's Rookie Nookie #14 / 1993 / SFP / M • Buffy Malibu's Totally Nasty All-Girl Home Videos #04 / 1993 / ANA / F • The Burma Road #1 / 1994 / LBO / C • The Burma Road #2 / 1994 / LBO / C • The Burma Road #3 / 1996 / LBO / C • The Burma Road #4 / 1996 / LBO / C • Cheap Shots / 1994 / PRE / B • Confessions / 1992 / PL / M • Deep Inside The Ori-

ent / 1993 / LV / M • The Dragon Lady #5: Tales From The Bed #4 / 1993 / WV / M • Erotic Dripping Orientals / 1993 / WV / M • Erotic Oddities / 1993 / LEI / C • Foot Hold / 1994 / PRE / B • Fringe Benefits / 1992 / IF / M • Gazongas #04 / 1993 / LEI / C • Harry Horndog #09: Anal Orgy #2 / 1992 / ZA / M • Ho' Style Takeover / 1993 / FH / M • Hollywood Swingers #05 / 1992 / LBO / M • House Of Spartacus #1 / 1993 / IF / M • House Of Spartacus #2 / 1993 / IF / M • It's Only Love / 1992 / VEX / M • Just One Look / 1993 / V99 / M • Living For Love / 1993 / V99 / M • M Series #09 / 1993 / LBO / M • Mainstream / 1993 / PRE / B • More Dirty Debutantes #28 / 1994 / 4P / M • More Dirty Debutantes #43 / 1995 / 4P / M • Night Mare / 1995 / VTF / B • Nothing Else Matters / 1992 / V99 / C • Odyssey 30 Min: #220: / 1992 / OD / M • Odyssey Triple Play #26: Asian Delights / 1993 / OD / M • Oriental Girls In Heat / 1995 / IF / M • Pai Gow Video #03: Egg Foo Kitty Yung / 1993 / EVN / M • Pai Gow Video #04: Tails Of The Town / 1994 / EVN / M • Party Favors / 1993 / VEX / M • Phone Fantasy #1 / 1992 / ATL / M • Phone Fantasy #2 / 1992 / ATL / M • Pleasure Chest / 1993 / IF / M • Sean Michaels On The Road #04: Chinatown / 1993 / VT / M • The Seductress / 1992 / ZA / M • Single Girl Masturbation #6 / 1991 / ESP / F • Slave Wages / 1995 / PRE / B • Smokin' Buns / 1993 / PRE / B • Student Fetish Videos: Best of Catfighting #02 / 1994 / PRE / C • Student Fetish Videos: Catfighting #06 / 1992 / PRE / B • Student Fetish Videos: Foot Worship #16 / 1995 / PRE / B • Student Fetish Videos: Spanking #09 / 1993 / PRE / B • Student Fetish Videos: Tickling #07 / 1992 / SFV / B • Student Fetish Videos: Tickling #11 / 1995 / SFV / B • Suburban Swingers / 1993 / IF / M • Tip Tap Toe / 1995 / PRE / C • Twin Freaks / 1992 / ZA / M • Two Tied For Tickling / 1995 / SBP / B • Uncle Roy's Amateur Home Video #13 / 1992 / VIM / M • Undercover Lover / 1992 / CV / M • Wet & Wicked / 1992 / VEX / M

KEANNA JONES see Keanna

KEANNA LEE see Keanna

KEANNA REYES see Keanna

KEBB LIESER see Star Index I

KECIA KANE
Like Mother, Like Daughter / cr73 / VCX / M

KEDINA see Zumira

KEEKEE see Kiki

KEELY THOMAS see Star Index I

KEIARI LYNN see Krysti Lynn

KEIKO (ORIENTAL) see Kaiko

KEIKO KAZUMI see Star Index I

KEIKO NITTAKE *(Nikko (Keiko))*
Brunette with a womanly body—nah, fatbody, and droopy large tits. Supposedly of French/Filipino extraction.
Forgive Me, I Have Sinned / 1982 / ALP / B • House Of Pleasure / 1984 / CA / M • Kneel Before Me! / 1983 / ALP / B • Oriental Techniques Of Pain And Pleasure / 1983 / ALP / B • Sex Appeal / 1984 / ABV / M • The Stimulators / 1983 / VC / M • The Story Of O Continues: Fruits Of Passion / 1981 / MAE / B • The Story Of Prunella / 1982 / AVO / M • The Taming Of Rebecca / 1982 / SVE / B

KEIKO TSUCHIDA

The Sex Specialist / 1996 / AVV / M

KEIOKO HAMADA
Tonight / 1985 / ORC / M

KEIRA ASHTON
Casting Call #01 / 1993 / SO / M • Deep Inside Dirty Debutantes #04 / 1992 / 4P / M

KEISHA *(Raquel Rios, Rachel Rios, Quiche, Quisha)*
Hispanic looking with big tits and a marginal face. Later put on excessive poundage.
10 1/2 Weeks / 1986 / SE / M • 12 Steps To Domination / 1995 / IBN / B • 40 Plus / 1987 / MFM / M • The Adultress / 1987 / CA / M • Ali Boobie & The 40 D's / 1988 / 3DV / M • Alice In Whiteland / 1988 / VC / M • All The Right Motions / 1990 / DR / M • Angels In Flight / 1995 / NIT / M • Battling Mistresses / 1995 / IBN / B • The Beat Goes On / 1987 / VCR / C • Beauty & The Body Builder / 199? / NAP / B • Behavior Modification / 1995 / IBN / B • Beyond The Senses / 1986 / AVC / M • Big Bust Babes #09 / 1992 / AFI / M • Big Bust Casting Call / 1993 / PME / S • Big Busted Goddesses Of L.A. / 1991 / NAP / S • Big Knockers #01 / 1994 / TV / M • Big Knockers #02 / 1994 / TV / M • Big Knockers #12 / 1995 / TV / C • Bimbo Bowlers From Buffalo / 1989 / ZA / M • Body Music #1 / 1989 / DR / M • Body Music #2 / 1990 / DR / M • The Bondage Club #1 / 1987 / LON / B • The Bondage Club #2 / 1987 / LON / B • The Bondage Club #3 / 1990 / LON / B • Boobs, Butts And Bloopers #1 / 1990 / HO / M • Boom Boom Valdez / 1988 / CA / M • The Brazilian Connection / 1988 / CA / M • Breast Worx #21 / 1992 / LBO / M • Bubble Butts #09 / 1992 / LBO / M • Cabaret Sin / 1987 / IN / M • California Native / 1988 / CDI / M • Candy Factory / 1994 / PE / M • Caught By Surprise / 1987 / CDI / M • Cheating / 1986 / SEV / M • Classic Pics / 1988 / PP / C • Collection #09 / 1985 / CA / M • Confessions #1 / 1992 / OD / M • Convenience Store Girls / 1986 / VD / M • Dancing Angels / 1989 / PL / M • De Blond / 1989 / EA / M • Deep Inside Keisha / 1994 / VC / C • Deep Throat Fantasies / 1989 / VD / M • Defying The Odds / 1995 / OD / M • Diaries Of Fire And Ice #1 / 1989 / VC / M • Diaries Of Fire And Ice #2 / 1989 / VC / M • Dirty Laundry / 1988 / PP / M • Double D Dykes #03 / 1992 / GO / F • Down And Out #1 / 1990 / CDP / B • Dr Truth's Great Sex / 1986 / VD / M • Empire Of The Sins / 1988 / IN / M • Erotic Television Video / 1988 / VD / M • F...It / 1987 / SE / C • Fatal Erection / 1988 / SEV / M • Female Fury / 199? / NAP / B • Femmes On Fire / 1988 / VC / F • First Time Ever #1 / 1995 / PE / F • Forbidden Bodies / 1986 / HU / M • From Sweden With Love / 1989 / ZA / M • Furburgers / 1987 / VD / M • Games Couples Play / 1987 / HO / M • Get Me While I'm Hot / 1988 / PV / M • Girls Of The Double D #02 / 1987 / CDI / M • The Girls Of Tuxedo: Swimsuit Edition / 1989 / TUX / S • Gold Diggers / 1993 / IN / M • Hands Off / 1988 / PP / M • Harem Girls / 1986 / SE / M • Having It All / 1985 / IN / M • Head Talk / 1991 / ZA / M • Heavenly Bodies / 1993 / NAP / B • HHHHot! TV #2 / 1988 / CDI / M • Hollywood Halloween Sex Ball / 1996 / EUR / M • The Honeymooners / 1986 / CDI / M • Hustler Honeys #3 / 1988 / VC / S • Hyapatia Lee's Arcade Series #01 / 1988 /

ZA / C • In Loving Color #1 / 1992 / VT / M
• Inches For Keisha / 1988 / WV / C • In-
nocent Taboo / 1986 / VD / M • Keisha /
1987 / VD / M • The Ladies Room / 1987 /
CA / M • Last Tango In Rio / 1991 / DR / M
• Laze / 1990 / ZA / M • Lesbian Lovers /
1988 / GO / F • Let's Get It On With Amber
Lynn / 1986 / VC / M • The Long Ranger /
1987 / VCX / M • Love On The Borderline /
1987 / IN / M • Lucy Makes It Big / 1987 /
ME / M • Luscious Lucy In Love / 1986 /
AVC / M • Lust Tango In Paris / 1987 / PEN
/ M • Magic Fingers / 1987 / ME / M • Mag-
nificent Seven / 1991 / NAP / F • Making
Ends Meet / 1988 / VT / M • Mammary
Lane / 1988 / VT / C • The Million Dollar
Screw / 1987 / VT / M • The Mistake / 1989
/ CDP / B • Monkey Business / 1987 / SEV
/ M • Moonlusting #1 / 1986 / WV / M •
More Than A Handful / 1993 / CA / C • Mov-
ing In / 1986 / CV / M • Much More Than A
Mouthful #1 / 1987 / VEX / M • Mysteria /
1995 / NIT / M • Nasty Nurse / 1990 / TAO
/ B • A Natural Woman / 1989 / IN / M • The
Night Before / 1987 / WV / M • Nightshift
Nurses #1 / 1988 / VC / M • Nooner / 1986
/ AVC / M • Oh! You Beautiful Doll / 1990 /
ZA / M • Once Upon A Temptress / 1988 /
CA / M • One Wife To Give / 1989 / ZA / M
• Only The Best Of Breasts / 1987 / CV / C
• Out Of Control / 1987 / SE / M • The Out
Of Towner / 1987 / CDI / M • Outrageous
Foreplay / 1987 / WV / M • Pacific Intrigue
/ 1987 / AMB / M • Parliament: Hanging
Breasts #1 / 1986 / PM / F • Parliament:
Hard TV #1 / 1988 / PM / G • Parliament:
Lesbian Lovers #1 / 1986 / PM / F • Pent-
house: Satin & Lace #1 / 1992 / PET / F •
Phantom Of The Cabaret #1 / 1989 / VC /
M • Phantom Of The Cabaret #2 / 1989 /
VC / M • Philmore Butts Meets The Freak /
1995 / SUF / M • Piece Of Heaven / 1988 /
CDI / M • Playing For Passion / 1987 / IN /
M • Pretty Peaches #3 / 1989 / VC / M •
Pussyman #03: The Search Continues /
1993 / SNA / M • Pussyman #04: The Cel-
ebration / 1993 / SNA / M • Pussyman #11:
Prime Cuts / 1995 / SNA / C • Pussyman
#12: Sticky Fingers / 1995 / SNA / M •
Quadruple Trample / 1995 / IBN / B •
Queen Of Hearts #1 / 1987 / PL / M • Rais-
ing Hell / 1987 / VD / M • Ready, Willing &
Anal / 1992 / OD / M • Real Men Eat
Keisha / 1986 / VC / M • Real Tickets #1 /
1994 / VC / M • Real Tickets #2 / 1994 / VC
/ M • Rears / 1987 / VI / M • Reckless Pas-
sion / 1986 / ME / M • Red Hot Fire Girls /
1989 / VD / M • Reservoir Doms / 1995 /
IBN / B • Restless Nights / 1987 / SEV / M
• Restless Passion / 1987 / HO / M • Ride
A Pink Lady / 1986 / SE / M • The Rising /
1987 / SUV / M • Rock 'n' Roll Heaven /
1989 / EA / M • Romeo And Juliet #1 / 1987
/ WV / M • Russian Roulette / 1995 / NIT /
M • The Search For Canadian Beaver /
1995 / LIP / F • Secret Diary #1 / 1994 /
TAW / M • Seduction Of Jennifer / 1986 /
HO / M • The Sensual Massage Video /
1993 / ... / M • Sensuous Singles: Keisha /
1987 / VCR / F • Sex With A Stranger /
1986 / AVC / M • Sexaholics / 1987 / VCX
/ M • Seymore Butts Rides Again / 1992 /
FH / M • Skin #3 / 1995 / ERQ / M • Sleeping With Everybody / 1992 / MID / C • Soft
Warm Rain / 1987 / VD / M • Sorority Pink
#1 / 1989 / CV / M • Sorority Pink #2 / 1989

/ CV / M • Spanish Fly / 1987 / CA / M • St.
X-Where #2 / 1988 / VD / M • Strange Love
/ 1987 / WV / M • Stripper Nurses / 1994 /
PE / M • Strong-Willed / 1995 / NAP / B •
Sugarpussy Jeans / 1986 / TEM / M • Surf,
Sand And Sex / 1987 / SE / M • Swedish
Erotica #69 / 1985 / CA / M • The Sweeper
/ 1996 / PME / S • Sweet Cheeks / 1987 /
VCR / C • Sweet Nothings / 1987 / HO / M
• Tail For Sale / 1988 / VD / M • Talk Dirty
to Me One More Time #2 / 1988 / PP / C •
A Taste Of Tiffanie / 1990 / PIN / C • Teasin'
& Pleasin' / 1988 / LBO / F • Tell Me Some-
thing Dirty / 1991 / NWV / M • Texas Crude
/ 1995 / NIT / M • Three For All / 1988 / PL
/ M • To Serve Keisha / 1995 / IBN / B • Top
Heavy / 1988 / VD / M • Toppers #05 / 1993
/ TV / M • Toppers #06 / 1993 / TV / M •
Toppers #08 / 1993 / TV / M • Toppers #12
/ 1993 / TV / C • Toppers #29 / 1994 / TV /
M • Trisexual Encounters #06 / 1987 / PL /
G • The Trouble With Traci / 1984 / CHA /
C • Twin Peeks / 1990 / DR / M • Twisted
Sisters / 1995 / IBN / B • Two To Tango /
1987 / TEM / M • Uniform Behavior / 1989
/ ZA / M • Video Voyeur #1 / 1988 / VT / C
• Virgin Heat / 1986 / TEM / M • Warehouse
Domination / 1995 / IBN / B • Wet 'n' Bare
With Barbara Dare / 1988 / NEO / C • Wet
Kisses / 1986 / SE / M • Wet Nurses #1 /
1994 / LE / M • What A Country / 1989 / PL
/ M • Whispered Lies / 1993 / LBO / M •
White Trash / 1986 / PV / M • A Whole Lotta
Crushin' Going On / 1995 / IBN / B • Wild
Fire / 1990 / WV / C • Woman To Woman /
1989 / ZA / C • Wrestling Queen Of The
Nile / 1993 / NAP / B • The Young And The
Wrestling #2 / 1989 / PL / M

KEISHA (BLACK)
Backdoor Ebony / 1995 / WV / M • You Go
Girl! (Video Team) / 1995 / VT / M

KEISHA LYNN
Lovin' Spoonfuls #7 / 1996 / 4P / C • More
Dirty Debutantes #24 / 1993 / 4P / M • New
Ends #01 / 1993 / 4P / M • Up And Cum-
mers: The Movie / 1994 / 4P / M

KEITH
Beyond Reality #3: Stand Erect! / 1996 /
EXQ / M • Bobby Hollander's Rookie
Nookie #10 / 1993 / MET / M • Sodomania
#19: Sweet Cream / 1996 / EL / M

KEITH AGAIN see Star Index I

KEITH BLADE
Bi-Conflict / 1994 / FST / G • Conflict Of Interest / 1994 / FST / G

KEITH CASANOVA
Beach Bum Amateur's #10 / 1992 / MID /
M • C-Hunt #02: Hot Pockets / 1995 / PEV
/ M • Pearl Necklace: Amorous Amateurs
#10 / 1992 / SEE / M • Pearl Necklace:
Amorous Amateurs #11 / 1992 / SEE / M •
Pearl Necklace: Amorous Amateurs #12 /
1992 / SEE / M • Pearl Necklace: Amorous
Amateurs #17 / 1992 / SEE / M • Pearl
Necklace: Amorous Amateurs #18 / 1992 /
SEE / M • Pearl Necklace: Amorous Ama-
teurs #28 / 1993 / SEE / M • Pearl Neck-
lace: Amorous Amateurs #30 / 1993 / SEE
/ M • Pearl Necklace: Thee Bush League
#01 / 1992 / SEE / M • Pearl Necklace:
Thee Bush League #12 / 1993 / SEE / M •
Pearl Necklace: Thee Bush League #29 /
1994 / SEE / M

KEITH DONALDSON
Blue Confessions / 1983 / VCR / M

KEITH EDWARDS

Valley Girls Ferr Shurr / cr85 / EXF / M
KEITH ERICKSON *(Keith Nicholson, Rick
Powell)*
Balding guy with a moustache. Rick Powell is
from **An Act Of Confession**.
An Act Of Confession / 1972 / ALP / M •
The Cheaters / 1973 / ALP / M • The Life
And Times Of Xavier Hollander / 1973 /
VXP / M • Marriage And Other Four Letter
Words / 1974 / VC / M • Sex-O-Phrenia /
1970 / ALP / S • Swinging Genie / 1970 /
ALP / M
KEITH JAMES
Blue Vanities #198 / 1993 / FFL / M
KEITH JOHNSON see Star Index I
KEITH JONES
Heidi & Elke / 1995 / SHL / B • Poor Little
Rich Girls / 1994 / SHL / B
KEITH KING see Star Index I
KEITH LORD see Star Index I
KEITH LOWERY
I Know What Girls Like / 1986 / WET / G
KEITH MICHAELS
Chicks With Dicks #1: A Slick And Slippery
Oil Orgy / 1992 / BIZ / B • Shopping With A
Transvestite: In A Boy, Out A Girl / 1992 /
BIZ / G • TV Phone Sex / 1992 / BIZ / G •
TV Shaved Pink / 1992 / BIZ / G
KEITH NICHOLSON see Keith Erickson
KEITH VINCI
C-Hunt #05: Wett Worx / 1996 / PEV / M
KEITH WEBSTER
K-Sex / 1976 / VCR / M
KEITH WILSON see Star Index I
KEKE KANER see Kiss
KELAINE KVALE see Star Index I
KELANI
Anal Oriental Sorority / 1994 / LBO / M
KELD REX HOLM
Bel Ami / 1976 / VXP / M • Bordello / 1973
/ AR / M • [Justine Och Juliette / 1975 / ...
/ S
KELEMEN
True Stories #1 / 1993 / SC / M • True Sto-
ries #2 / 1993 / SC / M
KELI STEWART *(Kim Watson, Kelly Stu-
art, Kelli Stewart, Kelly Stewart)*
10 Years Of Big Busts #1 / 1989 / BTO / C
• 40 Plus / 1987 / MFM / M • Bedroom Dis-
pute / 1988 / NAP / B • Bedroom Show-
down / 1988 / NAP / B • The Best Of Big
Busty / 1986 / L&W / C • Best Of Richard
Rank #1 / 1987 / GO / F • Between My
Breasts #01 / 1986 / BTO / S • Big Bust
Babes #02 / 1984 / AFI / M • Big Bust Vix-
ens / 1984 / BTO / S • Big Busted God-
desses Of L.A. / 1991 / NAP / S • Biggest
And The Best / 1988 / NAP / B • Black On
White / 1988 / NAP / B • Blue Vanities #125
/ 1990 / FFL / M • Blue Vanities #579 / 1995
/ FFL / M • Boss Lady / 1988 / NAP / B •
Bouncin' In The U.S.A. / 1986 / H&S / S •
Brabusters #2 / 1982 / CA / S • Breast To
Breast / 1996 / H&S / S • Competition For
A Man / 1988 / NAP / B • Competition For
A Part / 1988 / NAP / B • Confrontation Of
The Cats / 1989 / NAP / B • Dance Chal-
lenge / 1988 / NAP / B • Detective Framed
/ 1988 / NAP / B • Duel Of The Bustlines /
1988 / NAP / B • Exposed / 1980 / SE / M
• The Final Match / 1988 / NAP / B • Home
For Unwed Mothers / 1984 / AMB / F •
Hypnotized / 1988 / NAP / B • Introducing
Cindy Kramer / 1989 / NAP / F • John
Holmes And The All-Star Sex Queens /
1984 / AMB / M • Just Kim / 1988 / NAP / F

• Kim Meets Reno / 1988 / NAP / B • Lingerie Kittens / 1989 / NAP / B • Medicated Madness / 1989 / NAP / B • Only The Best (Napali) / 1990 / NAP / B • Post Party Mayhem / 1988 / NAP / B • Sweet Revenge / 1989 / NAP / B • The Taming Of Teri #1 / 1988 / NAP / B • The Taming Of Teri #2 / 1988 / NAP / B • Top Cat / 1989 / NAP / B • Topless Trio / 1988 / NAP / B • Vampire Cats / 1994 / NAP / B

KELLEI
Bangkok Boobarella / 1996 / BTO / M • Big Bust Fantasies / 1995 / PME / F

KELLEY
Interview: New And Natural / 1995 / LV / M

KELLEY EVANS
Ball Game / 1980 / CA / M

KELLEY GRANT
Bubblegum / 1982 / VC / M • Foxholes / 1983 / SE / M

KELLEY O'DAY *see* **Paula Wain**

KELLI
Bang City #2: China's Anal Gang Bang / 1995 / SC / M • Bang City #3: Fallon's Anal Gang Bang / 1995 / SC / M • Big Bust Black Legends / 1991 / BTO / C • Blue Vanities #130 / 1990 / FFL / M • Student Fetish Videos: Best Of Foot Worship #02 / 1994 / PRE / C

KELLI (DYLAN) *see* **Kelli Dylan**

KELLI BUTTERCUP
Fat blonde with long straight hair, not too pretty face, medium (proportionately) tits.
Big Boob Bangeroo #5 / 1996 / TTV / M • Fresh Faces #03 / 1995 / EVN / M • Home-Grown Video #448: Look Who's Cumming For Dinner / 1995 / HOV / M • Latin Plump Humpers #2 / 1995 / TTV / M • Pussy Hunt #13 / 1995 / LEI / M • Reverse Gang Bang / 1995 / JMP / M

KELLI DILLON *see* **Kelli Dylan**

KELLI DYLAN *(Kelli (Dylan), Kelli Dillon, Tracy Kittridge, Kelli Thomas (Dylan), Kelly Thomas (Dylan), Kelli Star (Dylan), K.C. Dylan, Candy (Kelli Dylan))*
Blonde (sometimes brunette or dark blonde) with thickish body but quite a pretty face who only seems to do g/gs or act in the bondage movies. Medium droopy tits. Tracy Kittridge is from **New Ends #01**.
Amateur Lesbians #37: Gretta / 1993 / GO / F • Amateur Lesbians #41: Kelli / 1993 / GO / F • Auto Bound / 1995 / VTF / B • B.L.O.W. / 1992 / LV / M • Beach Bum Amateur's #31 / 1993 / MID / M • Blow Job Baby / 1993 / CC / M • Bondage Asylum / 1995 / LON / B • Bondage Brothel / 1996 / LBO / B • Bondage Slut / 1994 / HOM / B • Bone Therapy / 1992 / LV / M • Bruise Control / 1993 / PRE / B • Buffy Malibu's Totally Nasty All-Girl Home Videos #02 / 1992 / ANA / F • Cinderella In Chains #3 / 1996 / LBO / B • Club Midnight / 1992 / LV / M • Crunch Bunch / 1995 / PRE / C • Dr Dominatrix / 1996 / LBO / B • Dr Whacks Treatment / 1996 / VTF / B • Dracula's Dungeon / 1995 / HOM / B • Dungeon Brats / 1994 / STM / B • Dungeon Punishment / 1995 / STM / B • Enemates #07 / 1992 / PRE / B • First Time Lesbians #01 / 1993 / JMP / F • A Girl's Affair #02 / 1993 / FD / F • Girls Just Wanna Have Girls #3 / 1994 / HIO / F • Hard Hand Luc / 1994 / STM / B • Honeymooned / 1992 / PRE / B • Kittens #6 / 1994 / CC / F • Ladies Lovin' Ladies #3 /

1993 / AFV / F • Leg...Ends #09 / 1994 / PRE / F • Lesbian Castle: No Kings Allowed / 1994 / LIP / F • Lesbian Sex, Power & Money / 1994 / STM / F • Maidens Of Servitude #2: Obeisance / 1994 / STM / B • Maidens Of Servitude #3: A Jealous Bind / 1994 / STM / B • Major Exposure / 1995 / PL / F • Mike Hott: #219 Lesbian Sluts #09 / 1992 / MHV / F • Mistress Misery / 1996 / VTF / B • Mistress Rules / 1995 / STM / B • Mistress Sharon's Girl Toy / 1995 / STM / B • Moon Rivers / 1994 / PRE / B • Mr. Peepers Amateur Home Videos #62: Private Pussy Party / 1992 / LBO / M • The Natural / 1993 / VT / M • New Ends #01 / 1993 / 4P / M • Odyssey 30 Min: #296: / 1992 / OD / M • Odyssey Triple Play #68: Threesomes And Moresomes / 1994 / OD / M • Pleasure Dome: The Genesis Chamber / 1994 / AFV / M • Raging Waters / 1992 / PRE / B • Revolt Of The Slaves / 1996 / LBO / B • Running Mates / 1993 / PRE / B • Secret Urges (Starmaker) / 1994 / STM / F • Slave Exchange / 1995 / STM / B • The Spa / 1993 / VC / M • Student Fetish Videos: Catfighting #07 / 1993 / PRE / B • Student Fetish Videos: Catfighting #08 / 1993 / PRE / B • Student Fetish Videos: Catfighting #13 / 1994 / PRE / B • Student Fetish Videos: The Enema #09 / 1992 / PRE / B • Student Fetish Videos: Foot Worship #09 / 1993 / PRE / B • Student Fetish Videos: Foot Worship #13 / 1994 / PRE / B • Student Fetish Videos: Foot Worship #17 / 1995 / PRE / B • Student Fetish Videos: Spanking #08 / 1992 / PRE / B • Student Fetish Videos: Spanking #10 / 1993 / PRE / B • Student Fetish Videos: Spanking #11 / 1993 / PRE / B • Student Fetish Videos: Spanking #17 / 1994 / PRE / B • Student Fetish Videos: Spanking #20 / 1995 / PRE / B • Student Fetish Videos: Tickling #06 / 1992 / SFV / B • Submissive Exposure Profile #5: Keli Thomas / 1996 / STM / B • Succulent Toes / 1995 / STM / B • A Taste For Candy / 1995 / VTF / B • Taunted, Tied & Tickled / 1995 / SBP / B • Things Change #2: Letting Go / 1992 / CV / M • Virgin Tales #01 / 1993 / 4P / M • Welcome To Bondage: Kelli & Sharp / 1993 / BON / B • Where The Boys Aren't #4 / 1992 / VI / F • Where The Boys Aren't #5 / 1992 / VI / F • Women Of Influence / 1993 / LV / F

KELLI KEM
Sarah's Inheritance / 1995 / WIV / M

KELLI KLASS
Bad Attitude #1 / 1995 / LV / M • Nasty Newcummers #09 / 1995 / MET / M • Ripe & Ready (Infinity) / 1995 / IF / M

KELLI MAY
Jiggly Queens #1 / 1993 / LE / M

KELLI RICHARDS *(Kelly Fitzpatrick)*
1001 Erotic Nights #2 / 1987 / VC / M • Adult Video News Magazine / 1985 / ZEB / M • The Anal-ist #2 / 1986 / VEX / M • The Angel In Mr. Holmes / 1988 / WV / C • Angels Of Mercy / 1985 / HO / M • Back To Back #1 / 1987 / 4P / C • Backdoor Brides #1 / 1985 / PV / M • Backdoor Summer #1 / 1988 / PV / C • Backdoor To Hollywood #01 / 1986 / CDI / M • Best Of Caught From Behind #1 / 1987 / HO / C • Black Lava / 1986 / WET / M • Black On Black / 1987 / CDI / M • Blazing Matresses / 1986 / AVC / M • Boobs, Butts And Bloopers #1 / 1990 /

HO / M • Cagney & Stacey / 1984 / AT / M • Caught From Behind #04: Nasty Young Girls / 1985 / HO / M • Caught From Behind #06 / 1986 / HO / M • Debbie Does Dishes #1 / 1985 / AVC / M • Devil In Miss Jones #4: The Final Outrage / 1987 / VC / M • Dial A Dick / 1986 / AVC / M • Dickman & Throbbin / 1985 / WV / M • Double Penetration #1 / 1985 / WV / M • Double Penetration #2 / 1986 / WV / C • Double Penetration #3 / 1986 / WV / C • Double Whammy / 1986 / LA / M • Dr Lust / 1987 / VC / M • Dynamic Vices / 1987 / VC / M • Erica Boyer: Non-Stop / 1988 / VD / C • Erotic Penetration / 1987 / HO / C • Every Woman Has A Fantasy #2 / 1986 / VC / M • For Your Thighs Only / 1985 / WV / M • Ginger Lynn—Non-Stop / 1988 / VD / C • The Hind-Lick Maneuver / 1991 / GO / C • Hollywood Vice / 1985 / VD / M • Honeybuns #1 / 1987 / WV / C • Honeybuns #2: Grecian Formula / 1987 / WV / C • Hottest Parties / 1988 / VC / C • Hottest Ticket / 1987 / WV / C • Inches For Keisha / 1988 / WV / C • Legs / 1986 / AMB / M • Like A Virgin #2 / 1986 / AT / M • A Little Dove-Tale / 1987 / IN / M • Loose Ends #2 / 1986 / 4P / M • Love Lessons / 1986 / HO / M • Loving Spoonfulls / 1987 / 4P / C • Lust On The Orient X-Press / 1986 / CA / M • Lusty / 1986 / CDI / M • Mad Jack Beyond Thunderdome / 1986 / WET / M • Mad Sex / 1986 / VD / M • Nasty Habits Are Hard To Break / 1986 / 4P / M • Oral Majority #02 / 1987 / WV / C • Oral Majority Black #2 / 1988 / WV / C • Rambone The Destroyer / 1985 / WET / M • Rambone Meets The Double Penetrators / 1987 / WET / M • Rump Humpers / 1985 / WET / M • Scent Of A Woman / 1985 / GO / M • Sex The Hard Way / 1985 / CV / M • Sexscape / 1986 / CA / M • Sinful Sisters / 1986 / VEX / M • Skin Games / 1986 / VEX / M • Skin Games / 1991 / VEX / C • Stiff Competition #1 / 1984 / CA / M • This Butt's For You / 1986 / PME / M • Tip Of The Tongue / 1985 / V20 / M • Toys 4 Us #2 / 1987 / WV / C • Ubangis On Uranus / 1987 / WV / M • Unnatural Act #2 / 1986 / DR / M • Up All Night / 1986 / CC / M • VCA Previews #4 / 1988 / VC / C • Virgin Cheeks / 1986 / VD / M • The Wacky World Of X-Rated Bloopers / 1989 / GO / M • White Bun Busters / 1985 / VC / M

KELLI STAR *see* **Star Index I**

KELLI STAR (DYLAN) *see* **Kelli Dylan**

KELLI STEWART *see* **Keli Stewart**

KELLI THOMAS (DYLAN) *see* **Kelli Dylan**

KELLI WARNER
Long lanky brunette similar to Racquel Darrian. See **Strange Curves**.
Strange Curves / 1989 / VC / M

KELLIE EVERTS
Blue Vanities #518 / 1993 / FFL / M • Fashion Strip Date / 1989 / KEE / F • Full Service Butler / 1993 / KEE / B • Kellie Everts #035 / 1995 / KEE / B • Kellie Everts #036 / 1989 / KEE / B • Kellie Everts #045 / 1989 / KEE / B • Kellie Everts #078 / 1990 / KEE / B • Kellie Everts #081 / 1990 / KEE / B • Kellie Everts #083 / 1990 / KEE / B • Kellie Everts #089 / 1993 / KEE / B • Kellie Everts #118 / 1992 / KEE / B • Kellie Everts 196-204-207 / 1994 / KEE / B • Lesbian Love Slave / 1989 / KEE / B • Moon Goddess / 1993 / KEE / B • Mystical Fetish / 1989 /

KEE / B • Rich Bitches / 1993 / KEE / B • Stand On Your Man / 1989 / KEE / B

KELLY
AHV #40: Whole Lotta Love / 1993 / EVN / M • The Binding Of Kelly / 1995 / GAL / B • Blue Vanities #519 / 1993 / FFL / M • Blue Vanities #532 / 1993 / FFL / M • Breakfast At Tiffany's / 1994 / IF / M • British Babe Hunt / 1996 / VC / M • California Girl: Amateur Nude Auditions / 1995 / PME / S • Casting Call #12 / 1995 / MET / M • Creme De La Face #10: Cum Dome / 1995 / OD / M • Cutie Pies / 1995 / TTV / M • Dirty Blue Movies #03 / 1992 / JTV / M • Eurotica #01 / 1995 / XC / M • Fresh Cheeks / 1995 / VC / M • Full Moon Video #21: Me, You, And Your Brother Too! / 1994 / FAP / M • Girls Games Of Summer #4 / 1994 / NIV / S • The Gypsy / 1996 / NIT / M • Hard Core Beginners #03 / 1995 / LEI / M • Hard Core Beginners #07 / 1995 / LEI / M • Hidden Camera #19 / 1994 / JMP / M • Hollywood Amateurs #03 / 1994 / MID / M • Hollywood Amateurs #16 / 1995 / MID / M • Lesbian Pros And Amateurs #03 / 1992 / GO / F • Lesbian Pros And Amateurs #04 / 1992 / GO / F • Limited Edition #12 / 1980 / AVC / M • Mr. Peepers Amateur Home Videos #46: A Schnitzel In The Bush / 1992 / LBO / M • Nookie Professor #1 / 1996 / AVS / M • Pearl Necklace: Thee Bush League: The Best Of Oral #01 / 1993 / SEE / C • Pearl Necklace: Premier Sessions #04 / 1994 / SEE / M • Pearl Necklace: Thee Bush League #01 / 1992 / SEE / M • Safari Jane / 1995 / ERA / M • SM TV #2 / 1995 / FC / G • Stretchin' The Rear / 1995 / PE / M • SVE: Sexy Salesmanship / 1992 / SVE / M • Video Virgins #19 / 1994 / NS / M • Wrestling Classics #2 / 1984 / CDP / B

KELLY (K. ASHLEY) see Kaitlyn Ashley

KELLY (MALE)
Pearl Necklace: Amorous Amateurs #26 / 1993 / SEE / M • Pearl Necklace: Thee Bush League #13 / 1993 / SEE / M • Video Virgins #28 / 1996 / NS / M

KELLY ADAMS
Blue Vanities #555 / 1994 / FFL / M

KELLY ANN
Knocked-Up Nymphos #1 / 1996 / GLI / M

KELLY ANN CROZIER see Star Index I

KELLY BLUE
Big breasted blonde Australian girl who has been deported.
Anal Nation #2 / 1990 / CC / M • Aussie Bloopers / 1993 / OD / M • Aussie Exchange Girls / 1990 / PM / M • Aussie Maid In America / 1990 / PM / M • Aussie Vice / 1989 / PM / M • Australian Connection / 1989 / PM / M • Bikini City / 1991 / CC / M • Blue Fox / 1991 / VI / M • Blue Heaven / 1990 / IF / M • Bushwackers / 1990 / PM / M • Dane's Party / 1991 / IF / G • Dick Tracer / 1990 / PM / M • Images Of Desire / 1990 / PM / M • Jungle Beaver / 1991 / HIO / M • Once In A Blue Moon / 1991 / CC / M • Outback Assignment / 1991 / VD / M • Phone Sex Girls: Australia / 1989 / PM / M • Reflections Of Innocence / 1991 / VEX / C • Regarding Hiney / 1991 / CC / M • Sex Nurses / 1991 / VIR / M • Sexual Healer / 1991 / CA / M • Too Blue To Be True / 1991 / ... / M • True Blue / 1989 / PM / M • Two Women & A Man / 1991 / VEX / C

KELLY COLE
Body Magic / 1982 / SE / M • Perfect Gift / 1994 / BRI / S

KELLY COOK see Kelly Jaye

KELLY DEL RIO
Anal Nymphettes / 1995 / LIP / F • Babes Of The Bay #2 / 1995 / LIP / F

KELLY FITZPATRICK see Kelli Richards

KELLY G'RAFFE see Kalina Lynx

KELLY GREEN
How To Make A Model #01 / 1992 / MET / M • Sex Toys / 1985 / CA / M

KELLY GREON
People / 1978 / QX / M

KELLY GUTHRIE
Cherry Truckers / 1979 / ALP / M • The Devil's Playground / 1974 / VC / M • Sexorcist Devil / 1974 / CXV / M

KELLY HAMILTON
Sex Boat / 1980 / VCX / M

KELLY HEDLUND
Mile High Club / 1983 / CV / M

KELLY HOWE see Stacey Donovan

KELLY HOWELL see Stacey Donovan

KELLY JACKSON (JAYE) see Kelly Jaye

KELLY JACKSON (RACQ) see Racquel Darrian

KELLY JAYE *(Kelly Jackson (Jaye), Kelly Cook)*
Blonde with large enhanced tits. Dead from the neck up. Note the conflict with an alternate name of Racquel Darrien. De-virginized at 19.
Anthony's Desire / 1993 / ... / S • Babe Watch #5 / 1996 / VC / M • Backhand / 1995 / SC / M • Badgirls #4: Jayebird / 1995 / VI / M • Beaver & Buttface / 1995 / SC / M • Bel Air Babes / 1995 / PL / F • Blonde Angel / 1994 / VI / M • Centerfold / 1995 / SC / M • Channel Blonde / 1994 / VI / M • Circus Of Lesbians / 1995 / VI / C • Close To The Edge / 1994 / VI / M • Forever / 1995 / SC / M • Hellriders / 1995 / SC / M • Hollywood Dreams / 1993 / ... / S • Kelly Jaye Close-Up / 1994 / VI / M • Love Scenes #3 / 1993 / B/F / S • Malibu Dreams / 1993 / PHV / S • Malibu Hardbodies #2 / 1994 / PHV / F • Man Killer / 1996 / SC / M • My Wildest Date / 1995 / HO / M • Penthouse: Passport To Paradise / 1991 / PET / F • Sexual Healing / 1994 / VI / M • Snow Bunnies #1 / 1995 / SC / M • Snow Bunnies #2 / 1995 / SC / M • [Alexander's Dreams / 199? / ... / M • [Nude Daydreams / 1993 / ... / S

KELLY JEAN
Large enhanced tits, long curly reddish-brown hair, womanly body, big butt. Comes from Las Vegas, 25 years old in 1995 and de-virginized at 15. Nice personality but her body has had it.
$ex 4 Fun & Profit / 1996 / SPR / M • Anal Bandits / 1996 / SO / M • Anal Camera #08 / 1995 / EVN / M • Anal Princess #2 / 1996 / VC / M • Anal Virgins #02 / 1996 / NS / M • Attack Of The Killer Dildos / 1996 / RAS / M • Babe Wire / 1996 / HW / M • Babes Behind Bars / 1996 / CNP / F • Bedtime Stories / 1996 / VC / M • Big Boob Bangeroo #5 / 1996 / TTV / M • Big Boob Boat Butt Ride / 1996 / FC / M • Black & Booty-Full / 1996 / ROB / M • Bushwoman: She Takes Two / 1996 / RAS / M • The Cumm Brothers #12: Two GOOS For Every Girl / 1995 / OD / M • Cummin' 'round The Mountain / 1996 / BCP / M • The Delegate / 1996 / RAS / M • Erotic Newcummers Vol 1 #4 / 1996 / DR / M • Every Nerd's Big Boob Boat Butt Ride / 1996 / FC / M • The Fanny Farm / 1996 / NIT / M • Gazongas Galore #1 / 1996 / NIT / C • Incorrigible / 1996 / MET / M • Just Do It! / 1996 / RAS / M • Lady M's Anything Nasty #01: Pink Pussy Party / 1996 / AVI / F • Lust Behind Bars / 1996 / GO / M • Mutiny On The Booty / 1996 / FC / M • Mystique / 1996 / SC / M • Pay 4 Play / 1996 / RAS / M • Pocahotass #1 / 1996 / FD / M • Prime Choice #7 / 1996 / RAS / M • Pussyman Auditions #21 / 1996 / SNA / M • The Real Deal #3 / 1996 / FC / M • Salsa & Spice #2: Latin Lust / 1996 / TTV / M • Seymore Butts: Big Boobs In Buttsville / 1996 / FH / M • The Sodomizer #1 / 1995 / SC / M • Stevi's: Kelly Jean's Spreads / 1992 / SSV / M • Stevi's: Naughty Girls / 1993 / SSV / F • Stevi's: Pantyhose Seduction / 1995 / SSV / F • Stevi's: Vibrolust / 1994 / SSV / F • Strip Show / 1996 / CA / M • Suzi Bungholeo / 1995 / ROB / M • The Toy Box / 1996 / ONA / M • Video Virgins #28 / 1996 / NS / M

KELLY KANE see Star Index I

KELLY KLASS
Butt Alley / 1995 / VMX / M

KELLY LANE see Star Index I

KELLY LEE
Fashion Fantasy / 1972 / GO / M

KELLY MANCUSO
Hollywood She Males / 1995 / MET / G • Pom Pom She-Males / 1994 / HEA / G • She Male Sluts / 1995 / KDP / G • Sizzling She Males / 1995 / MET / G • Transexual Blvd / 1994 / PL / G

KELLY MARS see Kelly O'Dell

KELLY MATHEWS see Star Index I

KELLY MAUZ see Kelly O'Dell

KELLY MCDONALD see Star Index I

KELLY MCKAY
Night Prowler #3: Master Of Reality / 1995 / ZFX / B • Night Prowler #5 / 1995 / ZFX / B • Video Pirates #5: A Bullet To Bite / 1995 / ZFX / B

KELLY MICHAELS
Be Careful What You Wish For / 1993 / VC / G • Debauchery / 1995 / MET / M • Depraved Fantasies #3 / 1994 / FPI / M • Dragxina, Queen Of The Underworld / 1995 / MET / G • Fantasies Of A Transsexual / 1991 / BIZ / G • French-Pumped Femmes #4 / 1991 / RSV / G • Guess Again / 1994 / FPI / G • Guess What? / 1994 / FPI / G • Homegrown Video: Fallon #2 / 1990 / HOV / G • Las Vegas She-Males / 1995 / BCP / G • Mr. Madonna / 1994 / FPI / G • Nydp Trannie / 1996 / WP / G • Queen Goddess Of The Nile / 1990 / BIZ / G • Queen Of The Bizarre / 1994 / AMP / G • She-Male Sex Clinic / 1991 / VC / G • She Male Spirits Of The Night / 1991 / VC / G • A Step Beyond / 1994 / AMP / G • Transsexual Prostitutes #1 / 1996 / DFI / G • Trisexual Encounters #13 / 1992 / PL / G • Trisexual Encounters #14 / 1992 / PL / G • TV Birdcage Rage #1 / 1996 / GLI / G • TV Birdcage Rage #2 / 1996 / GLI / G • TVs Plaything / 1992 / BIZ / G • The Ultimate Pleasure / 1991 / MET / G • Your TS Princess / 1990 / CAB / G

KELLY MINT see Heather Young

KELLY NICHOLS *(Marianne Walter, Marian Walter)*
Ball busting brunette with reasonable acting skills, medium nicely-shaped tits, marginal face.

6000 Lash Lane / 1994 / LON / B • The 8th Annual Erotic Film Awards / 1984 / SE / C • Ball Busters / 1984 / CV / M • Be Careful What You Wish For / 1993 / VC / G • Blowing Your Mind / 1984 / RSV / M • Blue Vanities #117 / 1989 / FFL / M • Bon Appetit / 1980 / QX / M • Brats In Bondage / 1993 / LON / B • C.H.U.D. Cannibalistic Humanoid Underground Dwellers / 1983 / MED / S • Caballero Preview Tape #4 / 1985 / CA / C • Cherry Red / 1993 / RB / B • Cherry Redder / 1993 / RB / B • Climax / 1985 / CA / M • A Coming Of Angels, The Sequel / 1985 / CA / M • The Corner / 1994 / VT / M • Corruption / 1983 / VC / M • Covergirl / 1994 / WP / M • Deathmask / 1983 / PRS / S • Deep Inside Crystal Wilder / 1995 / VC / C • Delivery Boys / 1984 / NWW / S • Dirty Girls / 1984 / MIT / M • Dirty Looks / 1982 / VC / C • Dixie Ray Hollywood Star / 1983 / CA / M • Dominant's Dilemma / 1993 / LON / B • Dominating Girlfriends #1 / 1992 / PL / B • Dominating Girlfriends #2 / 1992 / PL / B • Double Trouble / 1986 / DRV / M • Down Under / 1986 / VIP / M • Exstasy / 1995 / WV / M • First Annual XRCO Awards / 1984 / AVC / C • Formula 69 / 1984 / JVV / M • G-Strings / 1984 / COM / M • Games Women Play #1 / 1980 / CA / M • A Gift Of Sam / 1992 / YOE / M • Girls On Girls / 1987 / SE / C • Girls That Talk Dirty / 1986 / VCS / C • Girls Will Be Boys #3 / 1991 / PL / F • Glitter / 1983 / CA / M • Great Sexpectations / 1984 / VC / M • Heart Breaker / 1985 / TAR / C • Heaven's Touch / 1983 / CA / M • Hellfire Society / 19?? / HOM / B • Hot Licks / 1984 / SE / M • In Love / 1983 / VC / M • The Interrogation / 1994 / HOM / B • Jailhouse Girls / 1984 / VC / M • Jane Bondage Is Captured / 1993 / LON / B • Joint Effort / 1992 / SEX / C • Latex #1 / 1994 / VC / M • The Legend And The Legacy / 1992 / BRE / F • Love Scenes For Loving Couples / 1987 / CV / C • Maid For Bondage / 1993 / LBO / B • Make Me Feel It / 1984 / SE / M • Maneaters / 1983 / VC / M • The Mistress #1 / 1983 / CV / M • Model Behavior / 1983 / LIV / S • Nasty Girls (1983-VCX) / 1983 / VCX / M • Night And Day #2 / 1993 / VT / M • Night Of Seduction / 1994 / VC / M • Night Seduction / 1995 / VC / M • No Man's Land #10 / 1994 / VT / F • No Mercy For The Witches / 1992 / HOM / B • Once Upon A Secretary / 1983 / GO / M • Painful Mistake (Dungeon) / 1993 / PL / B • Passions / 1985 / MIT / M • Pleasure Island / 1984 / AR / M • Public Affairs / 1984 / CA / M • Puss 'n' Boots / 1982 / VXP / M • R.S.V.P. / 1983 / VES / S • Reel People #02 / 1984 / AR / M • Roommate Humiliation / 1993 / PL / B • Roommates / 1982 / VXP / M • Secluded Passion / 1983 / VHL / M • Seka In Heat / 1988 / BMV / C • Sex Boat / 1980 / VCX / M • Sexcapades / 1983 / VC / M • Sheer Rapture / 1984 / ... / M • Show Your Love / 1984 / VC / M • Slip Into Silk / 1985 / CA / M • SM TV #1 / 1995 / FC / G • Sno-Line / 1985 / LIV / S • Society Affairs / 1982 / CA / M • Spanking Dreams / 1992 / RB / B • Splashing / 1986 / VCS / C • Strictly Enforced / 1992 / RB / B • Succulent / 1983 / VXP / M • Supergirls Do General Hospital / 1984 / VC / M • Supergirls Do The Navy / 1984 / VC / M • Suze's Centerfolds #5 / 1981 / CA / M • Swedish Erotica Superstar

#4: Shauna Grant / 1984 / CA / C • Taboo American Style #4: The Exciting Conclusion / 1985 / VC / M • Taste Of The Best #1 / 1988 / PIN / C • That Lucky Stiff / 1979 / QX / M • Thirst For Passion / 1988 / TRB / M • The Toolbox Murders / 1978 / VTR / S • Turn On With Kelly Nichols / 1984 / CA / M • Ultraflesh / 1980 / GO / M • VCA Previews #2 / 1988 / VC / C • VCA Previews #4 / 1988 / VC / C • Wet Dreams / 1984 / CA / M

KELLY NIELSON see Star Index I
KELLY O'DAY see Paula Wain
KELLY O'DELL *(Kelly Royal, Kelly Mars, Kelly Mauz)*
Tight bodied blonde with a nice smile and extra good quality skin. She came from Philadelphia and did bachelor parties before getting into the porno business. Born Aug 13 and was 18 in 1991, 5'5" 105 lbs 35-24-34 (pre-enhancement). A few of her earlier movies have her not using a condom. In **MDD #14** she sounds like she's on something and says her name is Kelly Mars (or something similar—it's hard to hear). In May 1994, she gave birth to a baby girl. In 1996 had her tits enlarged to cantaloupe size. Did her first on-screen anal in **The Bottom Dweller: The Final Voyage**.
Adult Video Nudes / 1993 / VC / M • Anal Avenue / 1992 / LV / M • Bedazzled / 1993 / OD / M • Bondage Memories #04 / 1994 / BON / C • Bone Therapy / 1992 / LV / M • Bottom Dweller: The Final Voyage / 1996 / EL / M • Bubble Butts #11 / 1992 / LBO / M • Candy Snacker / 1993 / WIV / M • Christy In The Wild / 1992 / VI / M • Circus Of Lesbians / 1995 / VI / C • Dark Destiny / 1992 / BS / B • Deep Inside Juli Ashton / 1996 / VC / C • Deep Inside Kelly O'Dell / 1994 / VC / C • Deep Inside Nicole London / 1995 / VC / C • Defending Your Sex Life / 1992 / LE / M • The Devil In Miss Jones #5: The Inferno / 1994 / VC / M • Dirty Books / 1992 / VC / M • Dirty Work / 1995 / VC / M • Dominoes / 1993 / VI / M • Dr Dominatrix / 1996 / LBO / B • Dream Bound / 1995 / BON / B • Erotique / 1992 / VC / M • Facesitter #1 / 1992 / CC / M • The Girls Of Mardi Gras / 1994 / P10 / S • The Horny Hiker / 1995 / LE / M • Kelly Eighteen #1 / 1993 / LE / M • Kelly Eighteen #2 / 1993 / LE / M • Kym Wilde's Ocean View / 1993 / BON / B • Latent Image: Kelly O'dell / 1992 / LAT / F • Legacy Of Love / 1992 / LE / M • Legend #4: Critic's Choice / 1992 / LE / M • Les Femmes Erotiques / 1993 / BFP / M • Lesbian Love Connection / 1992 / LIP / F • Little Shop Of Tortures / 1996 / LBO / B • Lovin' Spoonfuls #3 / 1995 / 4P / C • Lovin' Spoonfuls #6 / 1996 / 4P / C • Make My Wife Please... / 1993 / VC / M • Mike Hott: #274 Kelly / 1994 / MHV / M • More Dirty Debutantes #14 / 1992 / 4P / M • Mr. Peepers Amateur Home Videos #54: Cooking With Cum!! / 1992 / LBO / M • New Girls In Town #2 / 1992 / CC / M • Nightmare Of Discipline / 1993 / NTP / B • No Man's Land #06 / 1992 / VT / F • Nobody's Looking / 1993 / VC / M • One Of Our Porn Stars Is Missing / 1993 / OD / M • Out Of The Blue #2 / 1992 / VI / M • The Phoenix #1 / 1992 / VI / M • The Phoenix #2 / 1992 / VI / M • Picture Me Naked / 1993 / LE / M • Possessions / 1992 / HW / M • Private Desires / 1995 / LE / M • Racquel In The Wild /

1992 / VI / M • Radical Affairs Video Magazine #01 / 1992 / ME / M • Raw Footage / 1996 / VC / M • Rugburn / 1993 / LE / M • Seeing Red / 1993 / VI / M • Sensual Exposure / 1993 / ULI / M • Seymore Butts In The Love Shack / 1992 / FH / M • Skin To Skin / 1993 / LE / M • Sorority Sex Kittens #1 / 1992 / VC / M • Sorority Sex Kittens #2 / 1993 / VC / M • A Taste Of Torment / 1995 / NIT / B • Telesex #1 / 1992 / VI / M • Twister / 1992 / CC / M • Venom #6 / 1996 / CA / M • Virtual Sex / 1993 / VC / M • Warm Pink / 1992 / LE / M • Whiplash / 1996 / DFI / M • Wide Open Spaces / 1995 / VC / F • Wild & Wicked #3 / 1993 / VT / M • Wild Flower #1 / 1992 / VI / M

KELLY PAGE see Cameo
KELLY PUTTA see Star Index I
KELLY RAINY see Kelly Royce
KELLY ROYAL see Kelly O'Dell
KELLY ROYCE *(Kelly Rainy)*
Small dirty blonde with medium natural tits and a body that is getting pudgy. Canadian. As of her return in 1994 she has now has long dark blonde hair, her breasts look smaller, and she unaccountably looks prettier.
Amazing Tails #5 / 1990 / CA / M • Anal Secrets (After Dark) / 1994 / AFD / M • The Analizer / 1990 / LV / M • Backstage Pass / 1994 / SC / M • Barflies / 1990 / ZA / M • Between The Cheeks #2 / 1990 / VC / M • Blackbroad Jungle / 1994 / IN / M • Body Of Love / 1994 / ERA / M • Brassiere To Eternity / 1994 / PEP / F • Buck Naked In The 21st Century / 1993 / EVN / M • Caged Beauty / 1994 / FD / M • Confessions Of A Chauffeur / 1990 / DR / M • The Crack Of Dawn / 1989 / GLE / M • Deep Inside Raquel / 1992 / CDI / C • Down 4 Busine$$ / 1989 / GMI / M • Dream Girls / 1990 / CIN / M • Dreams Of The Everyday Housewife / 1990 / FAZ / M • Earth Girls Are Sleazy / 1990 / SO / M • The Face / 1994 / PP / M • Family Affairs / 1990 / VD / M • Fleshmates / 1994 / ERA / M • Forbidden Games / 1990 / CDI / M • Forced Love / 1990 / LV / M • The Girl Has Assets / 1990 / LV / M • The Girl In Room 69 / 1994 / VC / M • The Great Pretenders / 1994 / FD / M • Greek Week / 1994 / CV / M • Hot Blooded / 1994 / ERA / M • Hot Cherries / 1990 / CC / F • Hot Spot / 1990 / PL / F • Invitation To The Blues / 1994 / LE / M • Juicy Lucy / 1990 / VC / M • Laze / 1990 / ZA / M • Lethal Love / 1990 / DAY / M • Life, Love And Divorce / 1990 / LV / M • Naughty By Night / 1995 / DR / M • Nightdreams #2 / 1990 / VC / M • Ona Zee's Learning The Ropes #08: Slaves In Training / 1992 / ONA / B • Out For Blood / 1990 / VI / M • Paris By Night / 1990 / IN / M • Party Doll / 1990 / VC / M • Performance / 1990 / VI / M • Provocative / 1994 / LE / M • Pyromaniac / 1990 / SO / M • Roadgirls / 1990 / DR / M • Sea Of Love / 1990 / CIN / M • The Search For Pink October / 1990 / EX / M • Sexual Relations / 1990 / PP / M • The Taming Of Tami / 1990 / CA / M • Through The Walls / 1990 / FAZ / M • Tug O' Love / 1990 / CC / M • Wet Paint / 1990 / DR / M • Where The Boys Aren't #2 / 1989 / VI / F • Where The Boys Aren't #3 / 1990 / VI / F • Wild Roomies / 1994 / VC / M

KELLY SANDERS
Salsa & Spice #3 / 1996 / TTV / M

KELLY SAVAGE
Attitude Adjustment / 1993 / BS / B • Bruce Seven: A Compendium Of His Most Graphic Scenes Vol 5 / 1994 / BS / C • Dangerous Assignment / 1993 / BS / B

KELLY SHAW *see Star Index I*

KELLY SIENNA
Black Knockers #06 / 1995 / TV / M

KELLY SMITH
Maid For Pain / 1991 / PL / B • Naked Horror / 1995 / ... / S • One Of Our Porn Stars Is Missing / 1993 / OD / M

KELLY ST. JOHN
Sex On The Strip: The Lusty Ladies Of Las Vagas / 1993 / CPG / F

KELLY STEWART *see Keli Stewart*

KELLY STUART *see Keli Stewart*

KELLY THOMAS
Snatch Masters #07 / 1995 / LEI / M

KELLY THOMAS (DYLAN) *see Kelli Dylan*

KELLY TRUBB *see Kelly Trump*

KELLY TRUMP *(Kelly Trubb, Yvonne (Kelly Trump))*
German blonde. Born 8/27/70.
100% Amateur #25: / 1996 / OD / M • Adventures Of The DP Boys: D.P. Nurses / 1995 / HW / M • Amadeus Mozart / 1996 / XC / M • Amsterdam Nights #1 / 1996 / BLC / M • Amsterdam Nights #2 / 1996 / VC / M • Anal Palace / 1995 / VC / M • Anal Pussycat / 1995 / ROB / M • Angel Eyes / 1995 / IN / M • Ass Masters (Leisure) #02 / 1995 / LEI / M • Bang City #1: Kelly's Anal Gang Bang / 1995 / SC / M • Buttman's European Vacation #3 / 1995 / EA / M • Cyberanal / 1995 / VC / M • The Dinner Party #2: The Buffet / 1996 / ULI / M • Dirty Business / 1995 / WIV / M • Girls With Big Jugs / 1995 / V99 / M • Nasty Nymphos #08 / 1995 / ANA / M • Passion In Venice / 1995 / ULI / M • Point Of Entry / 1996 / WP / M • Snatch Masters #07 / 1995 / LEI / M • Video Virgins #18 / 1994 / NS / M • Video Virgins #19 / 1994 / NS / M • The Voyeur #3 / 1995 / EA / M • Wild Orgies #17 / 1995 / AFI / M

KELLY VAN DYKE *see Nancy Kelly*

KELLY VARNER *see Star Index I*

KELLY WEBB
Striptease #1 / 1995 / PL / M • Striptease #2 / 1995 / PL / M

KELLY WEST *see Star Index I*

KELLY WINSTON
Bondage Pleasures #1 / 1981 / 4P / B

KELLY WOODS *see Star Index I*

KELLY YOUNG *see Star Index I*

KELLY ZEE
New Girls In Town #6 / 1994 / CC / M

KELSEY KANE
Dirty Stories #2 / 1995 / PE / M • Fashion Sluts #6 / 1995 / ABS / M • Sex, Truth & Videotape #1 / 1995 / DOC / M

KELSIE CHAMBERS
Up And Cummers #36 / 1996 / 4P / M

KELSIE SHEEN
Casting Call #02 / 1993 / SO / M • Casting Call #03 / 1993 / SO / M • Deep Inside Dirty Debutantes #07 / 1993 / 4P / M • Hollywood Swingers #09 / 1993 / LBO / M • Rugburn / 1993 / LE / M

KEMBRA
Cheerleaders In Bondage #2 / 1995 / GOT / B • Crack Up / 1994 / GOT / B

KEMBRA PHAFLER
P.L.O.W.: Punk Ladies Of Wrestling / 1996

/ GOT / B • [War Is Menstrual Envy / 1991 / ... / S

KEN
Fresh Meat #1 / 1996 / PL / M • Fresh Meat #2 / 1996 / PL / M • SVE: Swing Time / 1993 / SVE / M

KEN B.
Bucky Beaver's XXX Dragon Art Theatre Double Feature #04 / 1996 / SOW / M • Revelations / 1974 / SOW / M

KEN BANGER *see Star Index I*

KEN BLAKE *see Ken Scudder*

KEN BURNS
Take Off / 1978 / VXP / M

KEN CASS
The Bite / 1975 / SVE / M

KEN CONARD
Ultraflesh / 1980 / GO / M

KEN COTTEN *see Ken Scudder*

KEN COTTON *see Ken Scudder*

KEN DAHL *(Ken Draper)*
All That: Black Women's Fantasies / 1996 / VT / M • Candy Stripers #3 / 1986 / AR / M • Dirty Dancers #7 / 1996 / 4P / M • In Your Face #4 / 1996 / PL / M • Kym Wilde's On The Edge #29 / 1995 / RB / B • My Ass #1 / 1996 / NOT / M • Mystique / 1979 / CA / M • The Shocking Truth #1 / 1996 / DWO / M • The Voyeur #6 / 1996 / EA / M

KEN DARWIN *see Ken Scudder*

KEN DAVIS
The Best Of Both Worlds #1 / 1986 / LA / G • Bi-Ceps / 1986 / LA / C • She-Male Encounters #14: She-Male Wrestlers / 1987 / MET / G

KEN DELUCIA *see Al Terego*

KEN DIOR *see Star Index I*

KEN DRAPER *see Ken Dahl*

KEN GARRETT *see Star Index I*

KEN GRANDON *see Star Index I*

KEN J. MIDI *see Star Index I*

KEN JACKSON *see Ken Scudder*

KEN KENNEDY
Bubble Butts #24 / 1993 / LBO / M • Old Wave Hookers #1 / 1995 / PL / M

KEN KITABAYASHI
Ken Chan, The Laundry Man / 1984 / ORC / M

KEN MARKUS
Captured On Camera / 1997 / BON / B

KEN MARSH *see Star Index I*

KEN MCCORMICK
The Girls On F Street / 1966 / AVC / B

KEN MICHAELS
Lust At First Bite / 1978 / VC / M • The Starmaker / 1982 / VC / M

KEN MILO
Ultraflesh / 1980 / GO / M

KEN MOORE
Frank Henenlotter's XXX Hardcore Horrors: Mad Love... / 1996 / SOW / M • The Mad Love Of The Red Hot Vampire / 1971 / SOW / M

KEN NICHOLS *see Star Index I*

KEN REDD *see Ken Scudder*

KEN ROXOFF
The Beauty Pageant / 1981 / AVC / M

KEN S. (SCUDDER) *see Ken Scudder*

KEN SCOTT *see Ken Scudder*

KEN SCUDDER *(Ken Cotton, Ken Cotten, Ken Struders, Stuart Hempole, Terence Scanlon (Ken, Ken Scott, Ken Darwin, Ken Redd, Grant Lombard, Grant Stockton, Kenny Cotton, Ken Jackson, Ken S. (Scudder), Stuart Hemple, Rick Jackson (Scud), Ken Scutter, Ken*

Blake)
11 / 1980 / VCX / M • Any Time, Any Place / 1981 / CA0 / M • Artful Lover / cr75 / BOC / M • Baby Face #1 / 1977 / VC / M • Baby Rosemary / 1975 / SE / M • The Best Of Alex De Renzy #1 / 1983 / VC / C • Beyond Shame / 1980 / VEP / M • Black, White & Red All Over / 1984 / EXF / C • Blazing Zippers / 1974 / SE / M • Blondes Have More Fun / 1980 / SE / M • Blue Confessions / 1983 / VCR / M • Blue Vanities #005 / 1987 / FFL / M • Blue Vanities #048 / 1988 / FFL / M • Blue Vanities #065 / 1988 / FFL / M • Blue Vanities #066 / 1988 / FFL / M • Blue's Velvet / 1979 / ECV / M • Bottom Busters / 1973 / BLT / M • Bucky Beaver's XXX Dragon Art Theatre Double Feature #04 / 1996 / SOW / M • Bucky Beaver's XXX Dragon Art Theatre Double Feature #17 / 1996 / SOW / M • Budding Blondes / 1979 / TGA / C • Ceremony, The Ritual Of Love / 1976 / AVC / M • Challenge Of Desire / 1983 / NSV / M • Champagne For Breakfast / 1980 / SE / M • China Bitch / 1989 / PV / C • China Lust / 1976 / VC / M • Classic Swedish Erotica #33 / 1987 / CA / C • Classic Swedish Erotica #34 / 1987 / CA / C • Classic Swedish Erotica #35 / 1987 / CA / C • Cry For Cindy / 1976 / AR / M • Cum Shot Revue #1 / 1985 / HO / C • Daddy / 1978 / BL / M • Dental Nurse / 1973 / VXP / M • Deviations / 1983 / SE / M • Dixie / 1976 / VHL / M • Do You Wanna Be Loved? / 1977 / AR / M • Easy / 1978 / CV / M • Erotic Dimensions #1: Ripe / 1982 / NSV / M • Erotic Dimensions #4: The Exhibitionist / 1982 / NSV / M • Erotic Dimensions: I Want To Watch / 1982 / NSV / M • Erotic Dimensions: A Woman's Lust / 1982 / NSV / M • Erotic Fantasies #2 / 1983 / CV / C • Erotic Fortune Cookies / 1975 / VCX / C • Expensive Taste / 1978 / VCX / M • Forbidden Desires / 1984 / BIZ / G • A Formal Faucett / 1978 / VC / M • Getting Off / 1979 / VIP / M • The Girls In The Band / 1976 / SVE / M • The Gypsy Ball / 1979 / ENC / M • Hard Soap, Hard Soap / 1977 / EVI / M • Hot Cookies / 1977 / WWV / M • Hot Line / 1980 / CA / M • House Of Green Desire / cr78 / CPL / M • House Of Kristina / cr78 / VCX / B • The House Of Strange Desires / 1985 / NSV / M • I Am Always Ready / 1978 / HIF / M • Inside Desiree Cousteau / 1979 / VCX / M • Intimate Explosions / 1982 / ... / C • Jawbreakers / 1985 / VEN / C • Lacey Bodine (The Decline And Fall Of) / 1975 / VCX / M • Ladies Nights / 1980 / VC / M • The Legend Of Lady Blue / 1978 / VCX / M • Limited Edition #16 / 1980 / AVC / M • Little Girls Blue #1 / 1977 / VCX / M • Love Lips / 1976 / VC / M • Love Slaves / 1976 / VCR / M • Make Mine Milk / 1974 / SOW / M • Mary! Mary! / 1977 / SE / M • Masterpiece / cr78 / VEP / M • Meter Maids / 1974 / SIL / M • Midnight Hustle / 1978 / VC / M • Milk Chocolate / cr75 / VIS / M • My First Time / 1976 / GO / M • Naked Afternoon / 1976 / CV / M • Night Caller / 1975 / ALP / M • Night Pleasures / 1975 / WWV / M • Odalisque / 19?? / ASR / M • Only The Best #1 / 1986 / CV / C • Pink Lips / 1977 / VCX / M • Porn In The USA #1 / 1986 / WV / C • The Power of Nicole / 1983 / BIZ / M • Pretty Peaches #1 / 1978 / MIT / M • Rendezvous With Anne / 1973 / BL / M • Resurrection Of Eve / 1973

/ MIT / M • Revelations / 1974 / SOW / M • Rolls Royce #01 / 1980 / ... / C • Saturday Matinee Series #1 / 1996 / VCX / C • The School Teachers / cr69 / HO / S • Screwples / 1979 / CA / M • The Secrets Of Jennifer / 1982 / NSV / M • Sex Ed With Lil' Red / 1983 / TGA / M • Sex For Secrets / 1987 / VCR / M • Shameless / 1982 / SVE / M • Sheila's Payoff / 1977 / VCX / M • Shiela's Deep Desires / 1986 / HO / M • Shoppe Of Temptation / 1979 / AR / M • Showgirl #14: Kitty Shane's Fantasies / 1983 / VCR / M • The Sinful Pleasures Of Reverend Star / 1976 / ... / M • Ski Hustlers / 1976 / SE / M • Snack Time / 1983 / HO / M • Sodom & Gomorrah / 1974 / MIT / M • Spank Me Daddy / cr74 / VDS / B • The Starlets / 1976 / RAV / M • Stormy / 1980 / CV / M • Strange Diary / 1976 / AXV / M • Studio Of Lust / 1984 / HO / C • Summer School / 1979 / VCX / M • Summer Session / cr75 / BL / M • Swedish Erotica #10 / 1980 / CA / M • Swedish Erotica #47 / 1983 / CA / M • Sweet Cakes / 1976 / VC / M • Taboo #01 / 1980 / VCX / M • Taboo #02 / 1982 / IN / M • Tangerine / 1979 / CXV / M • Temptation: The Story Of A Lustful Bride / 1983 / NSV / M • The Tender Trap / 1978 / IHV / M • That's Porno / 1979 / CV / C • Three Shades Of Flesh / 1976 / IVP / M • Thundercrack! / 1974 / LUM / M • Tropic Of Desire / 1979 / WWV / M • True Legends Of Adult Cinema: Unsung Superstars / 1993 / VC / C • Vista Valley PTA / 1980 / CV / M • Winter Of 1849 / cr73 / BL / M • [Cat Tails / 1976 / CVX / M • [Chain Letter / 1978 / ... / M

KEN SCUTTER *see* Ken Scudder
KEN SMITH *see Star Index I*
KEN STAR *see* Ken Starbuck
KEN STARBUCH *see* Ken Starbuck
KEN STARBUCK *(Starbuck (Ken), Ken Starbuck, Ken Star)*
All American Girls #1 / 1982 / CA / M • All American Girls #2: In Heat / 1983 / CA / M • A Brief Affair / 1982 / CA / M • Cafe Flesh / 1982 / VC / M • Caught From Behind #01 / 1982 / HO / M • Centerfold Celebrities #5 / 1983 / VC / M • Daughters Of Emmanuelle / 1982 / VCX / M • Dream Lover / 1985 / CDI / M • Educating Mandy / 1985 / CDI / M • Foreplay / 1982 / VC / M • Free And Foxy / 1986 / VCX / C • Ginger (1984-Vivid) / 1984 / VI / M • Ginger's Hawaiian Scrapbook / 1988 / GO / C • Gourmet Quickies: Marie Sharp / Christy Canyon #729 / 1985 / GO / C • GVC: Anything Goes #119 / 1983 / GO / M • Hyapatia Lee's Secret Dreams / 1986 / SE / M • In The Pink / 1983 / CA / M • In Your Face #2 / 1992 / PL / M • The Insatiable Hyapatia Lee / 1987 / SE / C • Intimate Realities #1 / 1983 / VC / M • Jean Genie / 1985 / CA / M • Little Girls Of The Streets / 1984 / CV / M • Lust Letters / 1988 / CA / M • Mrs. Smith's Erotic Holiday / 1982 / VCX / M • Nasty Romances / 1985 / HO / C • Nightdreams #1 / 1981 / CA / M • The Oui Girls / 1981 / VHL / M • Panty Raid / 1984 / GO / M • The Pink Lagoon: A Sex Romp In Paradise / 1984 / GO / M • Pleasure Dome / 1982 / SE / M • Ring Of Desire / 1981 / SE / M • Samurai Dick / 1984 / VC / M • Sex Waves / 1984 / EXF / M • Sexcalibur / 1982 / SE / M • Sizzling Suburbia / 1985 / CDI / M • Snow Honeys / 1983 / VC / M •

Swedish Erotica #46 / 1983 / CA / M • Terms Of Endowment / 1986 / PV / M • Undercovers / 1982 / CA / M
KEN STRUDERS *see* Ken Scudder
KEN TURNER
The Best Of Alex De Renzy #1 / 1983 / VC / C • Femmes De Sade / 1976 / ALP / M • Sodom & Gomorrah / 1974 / MIT / M
KEN WILLIAMS
Just Deserts / 1991 / BIZ / B
KEN YONTZ
Dr Bizarro / 1978 / ALP / B • Inside Seka / 1980 / VXP / M • Legends Of Porn #2 / 1989 / CV / C • Never Sleep Alone / 1984 / CA / M • Tales Of The Bizarre / 1983 / ALP / B
KENCHANA *see Star Index I*
KENDAL KOAS *see Star Index I*
KENDALL
Interview: Bun Busters / 1995 / LV / M • Nothing Like Nurse Nookie #1 / 1995 / NIT / M
KENDALL MARX *see* Isabella Rovetti
KENDRA
Hot Body Competition: Beverly Hill's Miniskirt Madness Cont. / 1996 / CG / F • More Dirty Debutantes #58 / 1996 / 4P / M
KENNA
The Case Of The Missing Seka Master / 1993 / VCX / C
KENNETH ACRES
The Girls In The Band / 1976 / SVE / M
KENNETH BRIGGS
The Goodbye Girls / 1979 / CDI / M • One Last Score / 1978 / CDI / M
KENNETH KALLENBACH
East Coast Sluts #01: New Jersey / 1995 / PL / M • Pussyman #09: Feeding Frenzy / 1995 / SNA / M
KENNETH WATLEY
Headmaster's Study Part I & Ii / 1993 / CS / B
KENNI MANN *see Star Index I*
KENNY
The Gang Bang Story / 1993 / IP / M • Mistress Brigit's Footsteps / 1993 / NEP / B
KENNY COTTON *see* Ken Scudder
KENNY DEE
Brooke Does College / 1984 / VC / M • Daddy's Little Girls / 1983 / CA / M • Hot Dreams / 1983 / CA / M • Inside Everybody / 1984 / AVC / M • Lady Lust / 1984 / CA / M • Piggies / 1984 / VC / M
KENNY DINO *see Star Index I*
KENNY DOOER *see Star Index I*
KENNY PINKHAM *see Star Index I*
KENNY SMITH
Dynamic Duo / 1992 / BIZ / B
KENT BOLTON
Double Trouble: Spanking English Style / 1996 / BIZ / B
KENT HALL *see Star Index I*
KERI
Hard Core Beginners #02 / 1995 / LEI / M
KERI CARPENTER *see Star Index I*
KERI DOVER *see* Kerri Downs
KERI FOX *see* Kari Fox
KERINE ELKINS
[More Than A Handful / 1991 / ... / M
KERRI DOWNS *(Keri Dover, Carrie (Downs))*
Blonde with a marginal face and small tits. Born March 20, 1968 in Frondulac, WI. De-virginized at 12.
Alien Probe #2 / 1994 / ZFX / B • Alien Probe #3 / 1994 / ZFX / B • All I Want For

Christmas Is A Gangbang / 1994 / AMP / M • Bondage "Sybian" Rides / 1994 / PSE / B • The Bottom Line / 1995 / NIT / M • Bun Busters #19 / 1994 / LBO / M • Butt Watch #06 / 1994 / FH / M • The Captive / 1995 / BIZ / B • Creme De La Face #03 / 1994 / OD / M • Dark Secrets / 1995 / MID / S • Detention Cell #101 / 1995 / VTF / B • Dirty Bob's #18: Under The Boardwalk! / 1995 / FLP / S • Dirty Bob's #19: Over The Boardwalk! / 1995 / FLP / S • Dirty Doc's Housecalls #16 / 1994 / LV / M • Don't Try This At Home / 1994 / FPI / M • Double Teamed / 1995 / PSE / B • Employee Of The Month / 1994 / PSE / B • Gangbang At The O.K. Corral / 1994 / FPI / M • Gangland #2: Mob Rules / 1994 / ZFX / B • Gangland #5 / 1995 / ZFX / B • Gypsy Queen / 1995 / CC / M • Harry Horndog #28: Fabulous Squirt Queens / 1994 / FPI / M • Hollywood Amateurs #02 / 1994 / MID / M • The Hollywood Starlet Search / 1995 / SC / M • Hot Parts / 1996 / NIT / M • Jizz Glazed Goo Guzzlers #1 / 1996 / NIT / C • Jizz Glazed Goo Guzzlers #2 / 1996 / NIT / C • Kink #2 / 1995 / ROB / M • Kinky Debutante Interviews #04 / 1994 / IP / M • Lipstick Lesbians #1: Massage Parlor Dykes / 1994 / ZA / F • Love Bunnies #10 / 1994 / FPI / F • The Maid / 1995 / VTF / B • Maid To Beat / 1994 / PL / B • Milli Vanilla / 1994 / TP / M • Nasty Newcummers #06 / 1995 / MET / M • The Necklace #1 / 1994 / ZFX / B • New Pussy Hunt #26 / 1996 / LEI / C • No Mercy / 1996 / VTF / B • Oh My Gush / 1995 / OD / M • One For The Gusher / 1995 / AMP / M • Project 69 / 1994 / VTF / B • Pussy Hunt #04 / 1994 / LEI / M • Pussyclips #04 / 1994 / SNA / M • Queen Of The Bizarre / 1994 / AMP / G • Rainwoman #09: Wetlands / 1995 / CC / M • Rxx For A Gangbang / 1994 / ZA / M • S&M Pet Control / 1995 / SBP / B • S&M Playtime / 1995 / SBP / B • S&M Pleasure Series: The Assistant / 1994 / VTF / B • S&M Pleasure Series: The Contract / 1994 / VTF / B • S&M Pleasure Series: The Gift / 1994 / VTF / B • S&M Pleasure Series: The Tomb / 1994 / VTF / B • Sgt. Peckers Lonely Hearts Club Gang Bang / 1995 / AMP / M • Shades Of Passion / 1995 / NOT / M • Slave Julia / 1995 / VP0 / B • Slaves Of Passion / 1995 / HOM / B • Sordid Stories / 1994 / AMP / M • Specter / 1994 / ZFX / B • Spotlight: Hot Sybian Orgasms / 1994 / SPV / F • Spotlight: Poke Her / 1994 / SPV / M • Spotlight: Sybian Overload / 1994 / SPV / F • Squirt Squad / 1995 / AMP / M • Straight A's / 1994 / AMP / M • Surgical Strike / 1994 / ZFX / B • Suspend Thy Slaves / 1996 / VTF / B • Suspended / 1995 / VTF / B • Tail Taggers #124 / 1994 / WV / M • A Taste For Candy / 1995 / VTF / B • Tickle Thy Slaves / 1995 / SBP / B • Tight Fit #04 / 1994 / GO / M • Titanic Orgy / 1995 / PEP / M • The Ultimate Squirting Machine / 1994 / FPI / M • Unbridled / 1995 / PPI / M • Video Pirates #1 / 1995 / ZFX / B • Video Pirates #2 / 1995 / ZFX / B • Voo Doo / 1995 / VTF / B • The World's Biggest Gang Bang #1 / 1995 / FPI / M
KERRI HART *see Star Index I*
KERRY KELLY *see* Kiri Kelly
KESHA
AVP #7034: Hard Days, Harder Nights / 1991 / AVP / M

KETHRIN BRUT
Sodomania #17: Simply Makes U Tingle / 1996 / EL / M • Thermonuclear Sex / 1996 / EL / M

KEVIN
American Connection Video Magazine #03 / 1993 / ZA / M • Beach Bum Amateur's #35 / 1993 / MID / M • Bizarre Mistress Series: Sharon Mitchell / 1992 / BIZ / C • Inch Bi Inch / 1989 / STA / G • Pearl Necklace: Amorous Amateurs #02 / 1992 / SEE / M • A Sundae Kinda Love / 1995 / TVI / M • Whipped Cream / 1995 / TVI / M

KEVIN (DICK NASTY) see Dick Nasty (Brit)

KEVIN ABALON
Tight Assets / cr80 / VC / M

KEVIN ABOWN
Limo Connection / 1983 / VC / M

KEVIN ANDRE
American Sex Fantasy / 1975 / IHV / M • Come Fly With Us / 1974 / QX / M • Defiance / 1974 / ALP / B • Fringe Benefits / 1975 / IHV / M • Invasion Of The Love Drones / 1977 / ALP / M • The Love Bus / 1974 / OSC / M • Naked Came The Stranger / 1975 / VC / M • The Passions Of Carol / 1975 / VXP / M • The Private Afternoons Of Pamela Mann / 1974 / TVX / M

KEVIN COOK
New Faces, Hot Bodies #04 / 1992 / STP / M • New Faces, Hot Bodies #06 / 1993 / STP / M • New Faces, Hot Bodies #07 / 1993 / STP / M • New Faces, Hot Bodies #21 / 1996 / STP / C

KEVIN CUCKER see Star Index I

KEVIN CURTIN
N.Y. Video Magazine #01 / 1994 / OUP / M

KEVIN DEAN
Night Walk / 1995 / HIV / G

KEVIN DONOVAN see Star Index I

KEVIN DOOR
Medically Bound Tickle Team / 1996 / VTF / B

KEVIN GIBBONS see Kevin James

KEVIN GIBSON see Kevin James

KEVIN GLADSTONE see Star Index I

KEVIN GLOVER
Bi-Ways / 1991 / PL / C • Dreams Bi-Night / 1989 / PL / G • Get Bi Tonight / 1991 / PL / G • Split Decision / 1989 / MET / G

KEVIN JAMES *(Kevin Jay, Kevin Gibson, Chris Parker (KJ), Kevin Gibbons)*
Died of cancer in 1987.
The $50,000,000 Cherry / 1987 / VD / M • All In The Family / 1985 / VCR / M • All The Action / 1980 / TVX / M • Amber Lynn's Peter Meter / 1988 / 3HV / C • Amber's Desires / 1985 / CA / M • Another Kind Of Love / 1985 / Any Time, Any Place / 1981 / CA0 / M • Aphrodesia's Diary / 1984 / CA / M • Aunt Peg Goes To Hollywood / 1982 / CA / M • Baby Face #2 / 1987 / VC / M • Bad Girls #1 / 1981 / GO / M • Black Throat / 1985 / VC / M • Bloopers #2 / 1991 / GO / C • Blue Interview / 1983 / VCR / M • Blue Vanities #090 / 1988 / FFL / M • Bottoms Up #04 / 1983 / AVC / C • Burning Desire / 1983 / HO / M • Cabaret Sin / 1987 / IN / M • Cafe Flesh / 1982 / VC / M • California Reaming / 1985 / WV / M • Campus Cuties / 1986 / CA / M • Chuck & Di In Heat / 1986 / DR / M • Daisy Chain / 1984 / IN / M • Daughters Of Emmanuelle / 1982 / VCX / M • Deep Inside Traci / 1986 / CDI / C • Deliveries In

The Rear #1 / 1985 / AVC / M • Devil In Miss Jones #3: A New Beginning / 1986 / VC / M • Devil In Miss Jones #4: The Final Outrage / 1987 / VC / M • Diamond Collection #70 / 1985 / CDI / M • Dixie Ray Hollywood Star / 1983 / CA / M • Double Penetration #3 / 1986 / WV / C • Dr Strange Sex / 1985 / CA / M • Ebony & Ivory Fantasies / 1988 / VD / C • Empire Of The Sins / 1988 / IN / M • Erica Boyer: Non-Stop / 1988 / VD / C • Erotic Encounters / 1985 / LIM / C • Erotic Interlude / 1981 / CA / M • Erotic Zones #3 / 1986 / CA / M • Fast Cars, Fast Women / 1979 / SE / M • Female Aggressors / 1986 / LAV / M • Free And Foxy / 1986 / VCX / C • Gentlemen Prefer Ginger / 1985 / VI / M • The Gentlemen's Club / 1986 / WV / M • Gimme An X / 1993 / VD / C • Ginger's Greatest Boy/Girl Hits / 1987 / VI / C • The Girl From S.E.X. / 1982 / CA / M • Girls Of Cell Block F / 1985 / WV / M • Girls Of The Hollywood Hills / 1983 / VD / M • Golden Girls #05 / 1982 / SVE / M • Golden Girls #06 / 1983 / SVE / M • Golden Girls #08 / 1983 / CA / M • Gourmet Premier: Sex School / Centerfold Layout #909 / cr84 / GO / M • Gourmet Premier: Side Pocket / Headline Sex #910 / cr85 / GO / M • Gourmet Premier: Swinging Singles / Sizzling Stripper #907 / cr85 / GO / M • Gourmet Quickies: Rhonda Jo Petty #711 / 1985 / GO / C • Grand Opening / 1985 / AT / M • GVC: The Babysitter #107 / 1983 / GO / M • GVC: Blonde Heat #136 / 1985 / GO / M • GVC: Danielle, Blonde Superstar #131 / 1983 / GO / C • GVC: Family Affair / 1983 / GO / M • GVC: The Therapist #101 / 1986 / GO / M • The Heat Is On / 1985 / WV / M • Heidi A / 1985 / PL / M • Hooters / 1986 / AVC / M • Hot Merchandise / 1985 / AVC / M • The Hottest Show In Town / 1987 / VIP / M • I Like To Watch / 1982 / CA / M • I've Never Done This Before / 1985 / NSV / M • In Search Of The Wild Beaver / 1986 / DR / M • Intimate Realities #1 / 1983 / VC / M • It's My Body / 1985 / CDI / M • Jewels Of The Night / 1986 / SE / M • Joy Toys / 1985 / WET / M • Kinkyvision #1 / 1986 / 3HV / M • Kiss Of The Gypsy / 1986 / WV / M • Legacy Of Lust / 1985 / CA / M • Legs / 1986 / AMB / M • Let's Talk Sex / 1982 / CA / M • Little Girls Blue #2 / 1983 / VCX / M • Little Orphan Dusty #2 / 1981 / VIS / M • Love Bites / 1985 / CA / M • Love Lessons / 1986 / HO / M • Loving Lips / 1987 / AMB / C • Luscious / 1980 / VXP / M • Lust American Style / 1985 / WV / M • Lust In Space / 1985 / PV / M • Lust Vegas Joyride / 1986 / LIM / M • Lusty Ladies #11 / 1984 / 4P / M • The Magic Touch / 1985 / CV / M • Marilyn Chambers' Private Fantasies #5 / 1985 / CA / M • Marilyn Chambers' Private Fantasies #6 / 1985 / CA / M • Mitzi's Honor / 1987 / TAM / M • Mrs. Smith's Erotic Holiday / 1982 / VCX / M • Nasty Romances / 1985 / HO / C • Naughty Girls In Heat / 1986 / SE / M • Naughty Network / 1981 / CA / M • Night Prowlers / 1985 / MAP / M • Nightdreams #1 / 1981 / CA / M • One Hot Night Of Passion / 1985 / COL / C • One Night In Bangkok / 1985 / CA / M • Only The Very Best On Film / 1992 / VC / C • The Performers / 1986 / NSV / M • Phone Sex Girls #1 / 1987 / VT / M • Pleasure Spot / 1986 / CA / M • The Poonies / 1985 / VI / M • Rated Sex / 1986 / SE / M •

Reckless Passion / 1986 / ME / M • Ring Of Desire / 1981 / SE / M • Rio Heat / 1986 / VD / M • Sailing Into Ecstasy / 1986 / VCX / M • Scent Of A Woman / 1985 / GO / M • Secret Dreams Of Mona Q / 1977 / AR / M • Sensuous Moments / 1983 / VIV / M • Sex Boat / 1980 / VCX / M • Sex Games / 1983 / CA / M • Sexline You're On The Air / 1986 / CAT / M • Sheets Of San Francisco / 1986 / AVC / M • Sheri's Gotta Have It / 1985 / LIM / C • Snow Honeys / 1983 / VC / M • Soul Kiss This / 1988 / VCR / C • Stiff Competition #1 / 1984 / CA / M • Strange Bedfellows / 1985 / PL / M • Suze's Centerfolds #2 / 1980 / CA / M • Swedish Erotica #21 / 1980 / CA / M • Swedish Erotica #25 / 1980 / CA / M • Swedish Erotica #29 / 1980 / CA / M • Swedish Erotica #32 / 1980 / CA / M • Swedish Erotica #39 / 1981 / CA / M • Swedish Erotica #51 / 1983 / CA / M • Swedish Erotica #58 / 1984 / CA / M • Swedish Erotica #62 / 1984 / CA / M • Swedish Erotica #63 / 1985 / CA / M • Swedish Erotica #66 / 1985 / CA / M • Swedish Erotica #68 / 1985 / CA / M • Swedish Erotica #70 / 1985 / CA / M • Swedish Erotica #73 / 1986 / CA / M • Swedish Erotica Superstar #4: Shauna Grant / 1984 / CA / C • Sweet Alice / 1983 / VCX / M • Sweet Cheeks / 1980 / VCX / M • Taboo #02 / 1982 / IN / M • Taboo #04 / 1985 / IN / M • Taboo #05 / 1986 / IN / M • Taija's Tasty Treats / 1988 / EXP / C • A Taste Of Julia Parton / 1992 / VD / C • Tawnee...Be Good! / 1988 / LV / M • Thanks For The Mammaries / 1987 / CA / M • Three By Three / 1989 / LV / C • Trashi / 1980 / CA / M • Triple Xposure / 1986 / VD / M • The Twilight Moan / 1985 / WV / M • Two Timing Tracie / 1985 / V20 / M • VCA Previews #4 / 1988 / VC / C • Visions Of Jeannie / 1986 / VD / M • The Wacky World Of X-Rated Bloopers / 1989 / GO / M • We Love To Tease / 1985 / VD / M • The Whore Of The Worlds / 1985 / PV / M • Why Gentlemen Prefer Blondes / 1983 / HO / C

KEVIN JAMES (1996)
Zazel / 1996 / CV / M

KEVIN JAY see Kevin James

KEVIN KANE
Double Anal Alternatives / 1996 / EL / M

KEVIN MEYERS
The Rod Garetto Story / 1995 / FC / C

KEVIN OLSEN see Steve Powers

KEVIN PATRICK
Bi George / 1994 / BIL / G • Fresh Meat (John Leslie) #1 / 1994 / EA / M • New Faces, Hot Bodies #15 / 1994 / STP / M • The Voyeur #3 / 1995 / EA / M

KEVIN RAYMOND see Star Index I

KEVIN RICHARDS see Star Index I

KEVIN SLEE see Star Index I

KEVIN THOMPSON see Star Index I

KEVIN WILLIAMS see Star Index I

KEVIN WOLF see Star Index I

KEY KEY
Ebony Assets / 1994 / VBE / M

KEY MACHINELLI see Star Index I

KEY O'NEIL see Star Index I

KEYA
Biff Malibu's Totally Nasty Home Videos #27 / 1992 / ANA / M • Filthy First Timers #3: Tearing Down The Walls Of Shame / 1996 / EL / M

KEYNAN see Star Index I

KI KI YOUNG

The Nite Bird / 1978 / BL / M

KIA (ORIENTAL)
2 Wongs Make A White / 1996 / FC / M • Adam & Eve's House Party #1 / 1995 / VC / M • Amazon Heat #1 / 1996 / CC / M • Anal Romp / 1995 / LIP / F • Anal Tramps / 1996 / LIP / F • Asian Pussyman Auditions / 1996 / SNA / M • Babes Behind Bars / 1996 / CNP / F • Bangkok Boobarella / 1996 / BTO / M • Bangkok Dreams / 1996 / SUF / M • Batbabe / 1995 / PL / M • Betty & Juice Possessed / 1995 / CA / M • Big & Busty Centerfolds / 1996 / DGD / F • Black Bamboo / 1995 / IN / M • Born 2 B Wild / 1995 / PL / M • Butthead Dreams: Down In The Bush / 1995 / FH / M • Carnival Of Flesh / 1996 / NIT / M • Concrete Heat / 1996 / XCI / M • Conquest / 1996 / WP / M • Cover To Cover / 1995 / WP / M • Dick & Jane Go To Hong Kong / 1995 / AVI / M • Dim Sum (Eating Chinese) / 1996 / SUF / M • DPTV: Double Penetration Television / 1996 / SUF / M • Erotic Fiction / 1995 / LE / M • Erotic Visions / 1995 / ULI / M • Every Woman Has A Fantasy #3 / 1995 / VC / M • Far East Fantasy / 1995 / SUF / M • Finger Pleasures #5 / 1996 / PL / F • Frankenpenis / 1995 / LEI / M • Generation X / 1995 / WAV / M • A Girl's Affair #09 / 1996 / FD / F • Heatseekers / 1996 / PE / M • Illicit Entry / 1995 / WAV / M • The Illustrated Woman / 1995 / CA / M • Intense Perversions #3 / 1996 / PL / M • Jenna Ink / 1996 / WP / M • Juliette's Desires / 1996 / LE / M • Kia Unmasked / 1995 / LE / M • Kym Wilde's On The Edge #29 / 1995 / RB / B • Latex #2 / 1995 / VC / M • Lay Of The Land / 1995 / LE / M • Leather / 1995 / LE / M • Miss Nude International / 1996 / LE / M • Mission Phenomenal / 1996 / HIP / M • New Pussy Hunt #17 / 1995 / LEI / M • The New Snatch Masters #13 / 1995 / LEI / C • Nothing Like A Dame / 1995 / IN / M • Paradise Found / 1995 / LE / M • Paradise Lost / 1995 / LE / M • Pearl Of The Orient / 1995 / IN / M • Private Eyes / 1995 / LE / M • Promises & Lies / 1995 / SS / M • The Right Connection / 1995 / VC / M • Rod Wood / 1995 / LE / M • Secret Games / 1995 / BON / B • Selena Under Siege / 1995 / XCI / M • Simply Kia / 1994 / LE / M • Smoke & Mirrors / 1996 / PL / M • Studio Girls / 1995 / SUF / F • Submission To Ecstasy / 1995 / NTP / B • Telephone Expose / 1995 / VC / M • Temple Of Love / 1995 / SUF / M • Titty Troop / 1995 / CC / M • The Twin Peaks Of Mount Fuji / 1996 / SUF / M • Undercover / 1996 / VC / M • Up The Ying Yang #2 / 1995 / CC / M • The Violation Of Kia / 1995 / JMP / F • Wacky Weekend / 1995 / SUF / M • Yin Yang Oriental Love Bang #3: Bangkok Dreams / 1996 / SUF / M

KIA DELAO *(Kiayah Delao)*
Adorable, exceptionally pretty, 21 years old in 1993, de-virginized at 15, 5'3 1/3", 105lbs, 34B-24-34, beautiful skin, little girl voice (annoying sometimes), nice smile, hairy pussy. Originally I thought this might be the same as Kelly Green in **How To Make A Model #01** but now I'm pretty sure it isn't. Kelly has trimmed pussy, whiter skin, red hair and larger tits. This girl was a *Penthouse* pet in April 1996 issue. Kiayah is from **Venus' Playhouse**.
Deep Inside Dirty Debutantes #07 / 1993 /

4P / M • Lovin' Spoonfuls #3 / 1995 / 4P / C • More Dirty Debutantes #21 / 1993 / 4P / M • Sex On The Beach!: Spring Break Texas Style / 1994 / CPG / F • Venus' Playhouse / 1994 / VDL / S

KIA LINDSTROME
Revenge Of The Brat / 1995 / NAP / B • Tame The Wild Brat / 1995 / NAP / B

KIA STERLING
Lusty Ladies / 1994 / MET / F • Sexual Trilogy #05 / 1994 / SFP / M

KIANA
Hot Body Competition: Beverly Hill's Miniskirt Madness Cont. / 1996 / CG / F • More Dirty Debutantes #65 / 1997 / SBV / M

KIANE LEE
Anal House Party / 1993 / IP / M • The Gang Bang Story / 1993 / IP / M • Lesbian Castle: No Kings Allowed / 1994 / LIP / F • More Than A Woman / 1994 / H&S / M

KIANNA
Desert Island Buttwatch / 1996 / SUF / M • East Coast Sluts #09: / 1995 / PL / M • Fresh Meat #2 / 1996 / PL / M

KIANNA BRADLEY
Butt Row Unplugged / 1996 / ABS / M • Up And Cummers #32 / 1996 / 4P / M

KIANNA MILAN
Butt Row Unplugged / 1996 / ABS / M

KIANNE *see Star Index I*

KIARA
Butt Hunt #04 / 1995 / LEI / M • Pussy Hunt #06 / 1994 / LEI / M

KIAYAH DELAO *see Kia Delao*

KIKI *(Keekee, Jezebel (Kiki))*
Small tight bodied red/brown hair white girl.
  The Jezebel is from **Bus Stop Tales #09**.
AC/DC #1 / 1991 / LA / G • Bi-Guy / 1990 / LA / G • Bus Stop Tales #09 / 1990 / PRI / M • Butt Woman #1 / 1990 / FH / M • The Enchantress / 1990 / VI / M • Hard On The Press / 1991 / AWV / M • Hot Licks / 1990 / CDI / M • King Tung Is The Egyptian Lover / 1990 / LA / M • Pajama Party / 1993 / CV / C • Sex Asylum #4 / 1991 / VI / M • Shadow Dancers #1 / 1989 / EA / M • Shadow Dancers #2 / 1989 / EA / M • Studio Sex / 1990 / FH / M • Supertung / 1990 / LA / M • Trisexual Encounters #14 / 1992 / PL / G • We're No Angels / 1990 / CIN / M • Wild At Heart / 1990 / CDI / M • Worthy Women / 1990 / AWV / M

KIKI (1982)
Porno Screentests / 1982 / VC / M

KIKI (1996)
Anal Honeypie / 1996 / ROB / M • Another Fuckin' Anal Movie / 1996 / ROB / M • Asses Galore #2: No Remorse...No Repent / 1996 / DFI / M • Club Deb #4 / 1996 / MET / M • Dick & Jane's Video Mail: From Virginville (#4) / 1996 / AVI / M • Dirty Dirty Debutantes #5 / 1996 / 4P / M • Gang Bang Butthole Surfin' / 1996 / ROB / M • Hardcore Fantasies #3 / 1996 / LV / M • Numba 1 Ass Fucka / 1996 / ROB / M • Over Exposed / 1996 / ULP / M • Pick Up Lines #05 / 1996 / OD / M • Sabrina The Booty Queen / 1997 / ROB / M • Up And Cummers #30 / 1996 / 4P / M • Valentino's Asian Invasion / 1997 / SC / M • Yin Yang Oriental Love Bang #5: Lotus Blossoms / 1996 / SUF / M

KIKI (BLACK)
Black Street Hookers #5: The Mean Streets Of Washington D.C. / 1997 / DFI / M

KIKI (BLONDE) *(Salina (Kiki))*
Blonde, curly shoulder length hair, very white body, thin, passable face, small tits.
Anal 247 / 1995 / CC / M • The Cumm Brothers #03: Go To Traffic School / 1994 / OD / M • Dirty Dating Service #06 / 1994 / WP / M • Mr. Peepers Amateur Home Videos #87: Groupie Therapy / 1994 / LBO / M • New Faces, Hot Bodies #13 / 1994 / STP / M

KIKI MAYER
The Hitch-Hiker #05: Traffic Jam / 1994 / WMG / M

KIKI MORGAN
Kiki Tree Bound #1 / 1993 / BON / B • Kiki Tree Bound #2 / 1993 / BON / B • Kiki's Backyard Bondage / 1994 / BON / B • Kiki's Bondage Desires / 1993 / BON / B • Real People Real Bondage #2 / 1996 / BON / C • Tormented Teaser #1 / 1994 / BON / B • Tormented Teaser #2 / 1994 / BON / B • Virgin On The Rack / cr90 / BON / B

KIKIKU MIKUTO *see Star Index I*

KIKKO
The Best Of Alex De Renzy #1 / 1983 / VC / C • Big Bust Babes #05 / 1990 / AFI / F • Femmes De Sade / 1976 / ALP / M • The Pleasure Masters / 1975 / AST / M

KIKO
Hong Kong Hookers / 1984 / AMB / M

KIKO SAMURAI
Tight Shots #1 / 1994 / VI / M

KILEY *see Kylie Channel*

KILIAN *(Norma (Kilian), Norma Walker, Kilian Rodriguez, Killian)*
Hispanic girl with pear shaped tits, a nice smile and a little mound of a belly, boy-like butt and big dark eyes. 34-24-34, 5' tall, 22 years old in 1993. In 1994 her body has totally gone to seed. De-virginized at 17.
America's Raunchiest Home Videos #45: The Bigger They Cum / 1992 / ZA / M • Biff Malibu's Totally Nasty Home Videos #23 / 1992 / ANA / M • Black Beauties #2 / 1992 / VIM / M • The Blues #1 / 1992 / VT / M • The Blues #2 / 1994 / VT / M • Creme De La Face #02 / 1994 / OD / M • Dirty Dating Service #04 / 1994 / WP / M • Dirty Doc's Housecalls #06 / 1993 / LV / M • First Time Lesbians #16 / 1994 / JMP / F • Harry Horndog #16: Love Puppies #4 / 1992 / ZA / M • Harry Horndog #24: The Lost Tapes / 1993 / ZA / M • M Series #20 / 1994 / LBO / M • Mistress (1993-HOM) / 1994 / HOM / B • More Dirty Debutantes #23 / 1993 / 4P / M • Mr. Peepers Amateur Home Videos #61: Four Play For Four / 1992 / LBO / M • New Ends #06 / 1994 / 4P / M • Oriental Sorority Secrets / 1992 / VIM / M • Shades Of Erotica #03 / 1994 / GLI / M • Up And Cummers #23 / 1995 / 4P / M • Video Virgins #13 / 1994 / NS / M

KILIAN RODRIGUEZ *see Kilian*

KILLIAN *see Kilian*

KIM
America's Raunchiest Home Videos #07: A Fucking Beauty / 1991 / ZA / M • Black Hollywood Amateurs #09 / 1995 / MID / M • Blue Vanities #194 / 1993 / FFL / M • Blue Vanities #522 / 1993 / FFL / M • Blue Vanities #528 / 1993 / FFL / M • Blue Vanities #532 / 1993 / FFL / M • Blue Vanities #571 / 1995 / FFL / M • Blue Vanities #573 / 1996 / FFL / M • Bobby Hollander's Rookie Nookie #09 / 1993 / SFP / M • Breast Wishes #07 / 1992 / LBO / M • Club Doma

M • Tail Taggers #107 / 1993 / WV / M • Tail Taggers #109 / 1993 / WV / M • Tail Taggers #110 / 1993 / WV / M • Tail Taggers #119 / 1994 / WV / M • Tales From Sodom / 1994 / BLC / M • Tommyknockers / 1994 / CC / M • Toppers #23 / 1994 / TV / M • Toppers #25 / 1994 / TV / M • Toppers #26 / 1994 / TV / M • Toppers #31 / 1994 / TV / C • Toppers #32 / 1994 / TV / C • Vagina Town / 1993 / CA / M • Wad Gobblers #11 / 1994 / GLI / M • Whoomp! There She Is / 1993 / AVI / M • Witness For The Penetration / 1994 / PEP / M

KIM CHANG *see Star Index I*
KIM CHI *see* Kim Saunders
KIM COLLIER
Cafe Flesh / 1982 / VC / M
KIM CUMMINGS *see* Kimberly Kummings
KIM DAHL
Erotic Fantasies #1 / 1983 / CV / C
KIM DUREY *see Star Index I*
KIM E.
Barby's On Butt Row / 1996 / ABS / M
KIM EDDIE *see Star Index I*
KIM ETERNITY *(Eternity, Kim Hines)*
Reasonably pretty black girl with humongous hooters (look natural).
Afro American Dream Girls #1 / 1996 / DR / M • Big Boob Bangeroo #1 / 1995 / TTV / M • Big Boob Bangeroo #2 / 1995 / TTV / M • The Black Butt Sisters Do Chicago / 1995 / MID / M • The Black Butt Sisters Do New Orleans / 1996 / MID / M • Black Gangbangers #08 / 1995 / HW / M • Black Hollywood Amateurs #12 / 1995 / MID / M • Black Hollywood Amateurs #17 / 1995 / MID / M • Black Jack City #5 / 1995 / HW / M • Black Knockers #02 / 1995 / TV / M • Black Knockers #13 / 1995 / TV / M • Black Women, White Men #7 / 1995 / FC / M • Bootylicious: Ghetto Booty / 1996 / JMP / M • Bow Down Backstreet / 1996 / HW / M • Busty Babes In Heat #5 / 1995 / BTO / M • Busty Porno Stars #1 / 1995 / H&S / M • Cindy's House Party / 1996 / HW / M • Fashion Sluts #7 / 1996 / ABS / M • Git Yo' Ass On Da Bus! / 1996 / HW / M • Henry's Big Boob Adventure / 1996 / HO / M • Kim's House Party / 1995 / HW / M • Muff Divers #2 / 1996 / TV / F • The New Snatch Masters #16 / 1995 / LEI / C • Pussy Hunt #08 / 1995 / LEI / M • Span's Garden Party / 1996 / HW / M • Toot Z Roll / 1995 / WP / M • Voluptuous #2 / 199? / H&S / M • Voluptuous #3 / 199? / H&S / M • Waiting 2 XX Hale / 1996 / APP / M • Young & Natural #20 / 1996 / TV / F • Young & Natural #22 / 1996 / TV / F
KIM EVANS
The Coming Of Angie / cr73 / TGA / M
KIM FRANK *see Star Index I*
KIM GARLING
Too Hot To Handle / 1975 / CDC / M
KIM GEE *see* Kimi Gee
KIM HINES *see* Kim Eternity
KIM JACOBS *see Star Index I*
KIM JADE
Nineteen #7 / 1996 / FOR / M
KIM KAFKALOFF *see* Sheri St Clair
KIM KATAIN *(Kimberly Kitaine, Kim Kitaine)*
Tight bodied brunette with small, slightly droopy breasts and a look (facially) of Ali Moore. Her first feature was **Dial 666 For Lust**. Appeared in the December 1991

issue of *Playboy* in the Grapevine section. Kimberly Lynn in **Killer**. Returned in late 1994/early 1995 with a small butterfly tattoo on her belly. Late 1995 / early 1996 had her tits enhanced to rock solid cantaloupes.
Anal Addict / 1995 / ROB / M • Anal Asian #1 / 1992 / IN / M • Anal Bad Girls / 1994 / ROB / F • Anal Maniacs #4 / 1995 / WP / M • Attitude / 1995 / VC / M • Booty Ho #3 / 1995 / ROB / M • Brenda: Back To Beverly Hills 9021A / 1994 / CA / M • Bubble Butts #01 / 1992 / LBO / M • Buffy Malibu's Nasty Girls #11 / 1996 / ANA / F • Burlesxxx / 1996 / VT / M • Butt Sluts #4 / 1995 / ROB / F • Buttsizer #3: Return Of The King Of Rears / 1995 / EVN / M • By Myself / 1996 / PL / F • Catfighting Students / 1995 / PRE / C • Cheerleader Strippers / 1996 / PE / M • Close Quarters / 1992 / ME / M • Crack Attack! / 1996 / PE / M • Debi Diamond's Dirty Dykes #2 / 1995 / FD / F • Decadence / 1996 / VC / M • Deep Focus / 1995 / VC / M • Deep Inside Juli Ashton / 1996 / VC / C • Deep Inside Kaitlyn Ashley / 1995 / VC / C • Deep Seven / 1996 / VC / M • The Deviant Doctor / 1996 / NS / M • Dial 666 For Lust / 1991 / AFV / M • Dirty Thoughts / 1992 / LE / M • Dirty Tricks #1: Just A Bunch Of Whores / 1995 / EA / M • The Distress Factor / 1992 / BS / B • Diva #1: Caught In The Act / 1996 / VC / F • Dreams Of A Gigolo / 1996 / SNA / M • Dreams Of Desires / 1995 / ONA / M • The F Zone / 1995 / WP / M • Flesh / 1996 / EA / M • For Your Mouth Only / 1995 / GO / M • Friendly Fire / 1996 / EDP / M • Ghost Writer / 1992 / LE / M • Girly Video Magazine #1 / 1995 / BEP / M • Hard Core Beginners #12 / 1995 / LEI / M • Heartbeats / 1992 / LE / M • Hollywood Hillbillies / 1996 / LE / M • Hot Tight Asses #13 / 1995 / TCK / M • Hunchback Of Notre Dame / 1991 / PL / M • The Illustrated Woman / 1995 / CA / M • Indiscreet! Video Magazine #3 / 1995 / FH / M • Insatiable Dreams / 1996 / CC / M • Interview: Naturals / 1995 / LV / M • Irresistible / 1995 / LV / M • Journal Of O #1: Servant Slave / 1994 / ONA / B • Julia Ann: Superstar / 1995 / WAV / M • Killer / 1991 / SC / M • Ladies In Leather / 1995 / GO / M • Leg Show #1 / 1995 / NIT / M • Legend #6: / 1996 / LE / M • Lollipops #1 / 1996 / SC / M • Lustful Obsessions / 1996 / NOT / M • Memories / 1992 / LE / M • Miss Nude International / 1996 / LE / M • Mission Phenomenal / 1996 / HIP / M • Mr. Peepers Amateur Home Videos #39: Cumming In Colors / 1992 / LBO / M • Muff Divers #1 / 1996 / TV / F • Muff Divers #2 / 1996 / TV / F • New Pussy Hunt #19 / 1996 / LEI / C • New Pussy Hunt #20 / 1996 / LEI / C • Nightshift Nurses #2 / 1996 / VC / M • No Man's Land #13 / 1996 / VT / F • Ona Zee's Doll House #2 / 1995 / ONA / F • Only The Very Best On Video / 1992 / VC / C • Penetrator #2: Grudge Day / 1995 / PL / M • Pick Up Lines #02 / 1995 / 4P / M • Prisoner Of Love / 1995 / CV / M • Profiles #04: Lust Lessons / 1995 / XPR / M • Profiles #07: Sexworld / 1996 / XPR / M • Puritan Video Magazine #10 / 1997 / LE / M • Pussyclips #07 / 1995 / SNA / M • Pussyman #14: Dreams Of A Gigolo / 1996 / SNA / M • Rainwoman #10: The Tenth Anniversary Edition / 1996 / CC / M • Red Hots / 1996 / PL / M • Return Engagement / 1995

/ VI / M • The Return Of Dr Blacklove / 1996 / CC / M • Samantha & Company / 1996 / PL / M • Screamers (Ona Zee) / 1995 / ONA / M • Seriously Anal / 1996 / ONA / M • Snake Pit / 1996 / DWO / M • Snatch Masters #03 / 1994 / LEI / M • Star Flash / 1996 / VT / M • Striptease / 1995 / SPI / M • Strong Sensations / 1996 / PL / M • Stud Finders / 1995 / ONA / M • Student Fetish Videos: Best of Catfighting #03 / 1995 / PRE / C • Student Fetish Videos: Catfighting #03 / 1991 / PRE / B • Student Fetish Videos: Catfighting #04 / 1992 / PRE / B • Style #2 / 1994 / VT / M • Sunset And Divine: The British Experience / 1996 / LEI / M • Taboo #16 / 1996 / CV / M • Unchained Marylin / 1996 / VT / M • Vanity / 1992 / HO / M • Venom #1 / 1995 / VD / M • Weird Sex / 1995 / GO / M • Whore D'erves / 1996 / OUP / F • Whore'n / 1996 / AB / M • XXX / 1996 / TEP / M • Young & Natural #03 / 1995 / PRE / F • Young & Natural #04 / 1995 / PRE / F • Young & Natural #05 / 1995 / PRE / F • Young & Natural #08 / 1995 / PRE / F • Young & Natural #09 / 1995 / PRE / C
KIM KELLY
Breast Worx #04 / 1991 / LBO / M • Hollywood Teasers #03 / 1992 / LBO / M
KIM KIM
Frank Henenlotter's XXX Hardcore Horrors: Mad Love... / 1996 / SOW / M • The Mad Love Of The Red Hot Vampire / 1971 / SOW / M
KIM KITAINE *see* Kim Katain
KIM KUMMINGS *see* Kimberly Kummings
KIM KWAN *see* Kristara Barrington
KIM LEE
Battling Bruisers / 1993 / SBP / B • The Burma Road #1 / 1994 / LBO / C • The Burma Road #2 / 1994 / LBO / C • Three For The Whip / 1995 / VTF / B
KIM LOWE
Dreams Bi-Night / 1989 / PL / G
KIM LUV *see Star Index I*
KIM MCKAMY *see* Ashlyn Gere
KIM MCKAY *see* Sunny McKay
KIM MOLINEAUX *see Star Index I*
KIM MORGAN *see* Kristara Barrington
KIM NELSON *see Star Index I*
KIM ODESSA
Creme De La Face #03 / 1994 / OD / M • Creme De La Face #04 / 1994 / OD / M • Northwest Pecker Trek #3: Ducks & Dicks / 1994 / LBO / M • Teacher's Pet #3 / 1995 / APP / M
KIM PARE *see* Tanya Fox
KIM PARKER *see* Tanya Fox
KIM PARKLAND *see Star Index I*
KIM POKE *see* Kim Pope
KIM POPE *(Kim Poke)*
Passable face, blonde short hair, white body, small tits, pleasant personality.
All About Sex / 1970 / AR / M • The Amazing Transplant / 1969 / SOW / S • Beneath The Mermaids / 1975 / ... / M • The Collegiates / 1971 / BL / M • Deep Sleep / cr72 / ... / M • Every Inch A Lady / 1975 / QX / M • Farewell Scarlett / 1976 / COM / M • French Shampoo / 1978 / VXP / M • Heavy Load / 1975 / COM / M • Intimate Teenagers / 1974 / BL / M • Intrusion / 1975 / CV / M • Little Orphan Sammy / 1976 / VC / M • Love Object / 1969 / SOW / S • Memories Within Miss Aggie / 1974 / VHL / M •

Mount Of Venus / 1975 / ... / M • Mrs. Barrington / 1974 / IHV / S • Night After Night / 1973 / BL / M • Oriental Blue / 1975 / ALP / M • The Passions Of Carol / 1975 / VXP / M • Penetration / 1976 / MV1 / S • Pleasure Plantation / 1970 / SOW / S • Practice Makes Perfect / 1975 / QX / M • Schoolgirl's Reunion / 1975 / VHL / M • Steam Heat / 1980 / COM / M • Summer Of Laura / 1975 / CXV / M • Through The Looking Glass / 1976 / ALP / M • The Whistle Blowers / cr72 / ... / M • The Young Nymphs / 1973 / ... / M • [White Slavery: New York City / cr72 / ... / M

KIM REED *see* **Trinity Lane**

KIM ROUGE
Magma: Showtime Cunts / 1994 / MET / M

KIM SAUNDERS *(Kim Chi, Kim Thomas, Sandy (K. Saunders), Miyoko)*
Oriental, not too pretty with a womanly body. Looks a bit like a young version of Imelda Marcos. Works with boyfriend, Mark Saunders or Chris Thomas (same person).
Anal Vision #09 / 1993 / LBO / M • Anal Vision #12 / 1993 / LBO / M • The Ass Master #04 / 1993 / GLI / M • Bun Busters #01 / 1993 / LBO / M • Bun Busters #02 / 1993 / LBO / M • The Burma Road #1 / 1994 / LBO / C • The Burma Road #2 / 1994 / LBO / C • The Burma Road #4 / 1996 / LBO / C • Hidden Camera #05 / 1993 / JMP / M • More Dirty Debutantes #22 / 1993 / 4P / M • Odyssey Triple Play #63: Orient Express / 1994 / OD / M • Vivid Raw #2 / 1996 / VI / M

KIM SCOTT
Daydreams / 1990 / VAL / M • H.H. Productions: Fantasy Fest '96 / 1996 / HH / S • In The Dark / 1996 / VAL / M • Kim's Convention Couples / 1995 / VAL / M • Kim's Party Cove / 1996 / VAL / M • Meet Me In St. Louis / 1996 / VAL / M

KIM SONG
Alm Bums / 1995 / DBM / M • Roman Orgy / 1991 / PL / M

KIM STONE
My Generation / 1994 / HO / M

KIM STRATON
Maids In Bondage /The Bondage Girls / 1985 / 4P / B

KIM SU
Headmaster's Study Part I & Ii / 1993 / CS / B

KIM TATUM *see* **Katie Thomas**

KIM THOMAS *see* **Kim Saunders**

KIM TURNER
Donna Young: Kim & Molly's Lesbian Video #1 / 1995 / DY / F • Donna Young: Kim Turner #1 / 1995 / DY / F

KIM VOGUE *see* **Star Index I**

KIM WARNER *see* **Bunny Bleu**

KIM WATSON *see* **Keli Stewart**

KIM WILDE (B. DARE) *see* **Barbara Dare**

KIM WILLIAMS
The Black Mystique / 1986 / CV / M

KIM WONG *see* **Siobhan Hunter**

KIM WYLDE *see* **Kym Wilde**

KIM WYLDE (B. DARE) *see* **Barbara Dare**

KIM YEE
Kinky College Cunts #01 / 1993 / NS / F

KIMBER ALLEN
The Necklace #3 / 1994 / ZFX / B

KIMBERLY
Bi-Bi Love Amateurs #1 / 1993 / SFP / G • California Girl: Amateur Nude Auditions /

1995 / PME / S • HomeGrown Video #434: Forrest Hump / 1994 / HOV / M • Hot Body Competition: Beverly Hill's Miniskirt Madness Cont. / 1996 / CG / F • Memphis Cathouse Blues / 1982 / CA / M • OUTS: Kimberly #1 / 1994 / OUT / F • OUTS: Kimberly #2 / 1994 / OUT / F • Playboy's Girls Of Hooters / 1995 / PLA / S • Reel People #02 / 1984 / AR / M

KIMBERLY (JADE) *see* **Kimberly Jade**

KIMBERLY (KANE) *see* **Kimberly Kane**

KIMBERLY ALLEN
Chamber Of Horrors / 1994 / ZFX / B • Dance Macabre / 1993 / ZFX / B • Guinea Pigs #3 / 1993 / ZFX / B

KIMBERLY ASHLEY
GVC: Party Stripper #130 / 1983 / GO / M

KIMBERLY BERN *see* **Kim Bernard**

KIMBERLY CARSON *(Star Weatherly, Holly Carson)*
Pretty, long dark curly hair, small tits, tight waist, nice skin, good personality. Star Weatherly is from **Bodies In Heat**. Holly Carson is from **Loose Times At Ridley High**. 21 in 1984.
Adult 45 #01 / 1985 / DR / C • The Beat Goes On / 1987 / VCR / C • Black On White / 1987 / PL / C • Blue Vanities #056 / 1988 / FFL / M • Bodies In Heat #1 / 1983 / CA / M • Caballero Preview Tape #4 / 1985 / CA / C • California Valley Girls / 1983 / HO / M • Channel 69 / 1986 / LA / M • Collection #10 / 1987 / CA / M • Coming In Style / 1986 / CA / M • Coming Together / 1984 / CA / M • Cotton Candy / 1987 / CV / C • Cover Girls / 1985 / VEX / C • Diamond Collection #59 / 1984 / CDI / M • The Doctor's In / 1986 / CDI / M • Double Heat / 1986 / LA / M • Dr Truth's Great Sex / 1986 / VD / M • Eat At The Blue Fox / 1983 / VC / M • The Ecstasy Girls #2 / 1986 / CA / M • The Erotic World Of Cody Nicole / 1984 / VCR / C • The Erotic World Of Crystal Lake (#4) / 1984 / VCR / C • Ex-Connection / 1986 / SEV / M • First Annual XRCO Awards / 1984 / AVC / C • Flesh And Ecstasy / 1985 / VD / M • Fleshdance / 1983 / SE / M • Frisky Business / 1984 / VC / M • Girl On The Run / 1985 / VC / M • Girls On Fire / 1985 / VCX / M • Girls On Girls / 1983 / VC / F • Glamour Girl #2 / 1984 / CDI / M • Glamour Girl #4 / 1984 / CDI / M • Golden Girls #15 / 1984 / CA / M • Golden Girls #16 / 1984 / CA / M • Golden Girls #20 / 1984 / CA / M • Golden Girls #28 / 1985 / CA / M • H.O.T.S. / 1979 / VES / S • Home Movies Ltd #1 / 1983 / SE / M • Hot Girls In Love / 1984 / VIV / C • I Love LA #1 / 1986 / PEN / C • I Love LA #2 / 1989 / PEN / C • I've Never Done This Before / 1985 / NSV / M • Ice Cream #1: Tuesday's Lover / 1983 / VC / M • John Holmes, The Man, The Legend / 1995 / EVN / C • The Ladies In Lace Party / 1985 / MAP / M • Lady Lust / 1984 / CA / M • Le Sex De Femme #3 / 1989 / AFI / C • Looking For Love / 1985 / VCX / M • Loose Times At Ridley High / 1984 / VCX / M • Losing Control / 1985 / CDI / M • Love Scenes For Loving Couples / 1987 / CV / C • The Lover Girls / 1985 / VEX / M • Marina Vice / 1985 / PEN / M • Maximum #6 / 1983 / CA / M • Midnight Lady / 1985 / AA / C • Mother's Pride / 1985 / DIM / M • Naked Lust / 1985 / SE / M • Nasty Nurses / 1983 / CA / M • New Wave Hookers #1 / 1984 / VC / M • Only The Best

Of Men's And Women's Fantasies / 1988 / CV / C • Only The Best Of Peepers / 1992 / CV / C • Only The Best Of Women With Women / 1988 / CV / C • Oriental Temptations / 1984 / CV / C • Party Girls / 1988 / MAP / M • A Passage Thru Pamela / 1985 / VC / G • Passionate Lee / 1984 / CRE / M • Peeping Tom / 1986 / CV / M • The Perfect Weekend / 1984 / AVC / M • The Pink Panties / 1985 / NSV / M • Pleasure Island / 1984 / AR / M • Red On The Noodle Like A Swance On A Poodle / 1990 / FC / C • The Return Of Johnny Wadd / 1986 / PEN / M • Rising Star / 1985 / CA / M • Rockin' Erotica / 1987 / SE / C • Rubdown / 1985 / VCX / M • Satin Finish / 1985 / SUV / M • Saturday Matinee Series #4 / 1996 / VCX / C • Scandalous Simone / 1985 / SE / M • Sensuous Tales / 1984 / VCR / C • Sex Play / 1984 / SE / M • Sex Star / 1983 / CA / M • Sex Toys / 1985 / CA / M • Shame On Shanna / 1989 / DR / C • Sheer Haven / 1989 / DR / C • Sheri's Gotta Have It / 1985 / LIM / C • Sinners #1 / 1988 / COM / M • Sinners #2 / 1988 / COM / M • Sinners #3 / 1989 / COM / M • Snatchbuckler / 1985 / DR / M • Space Virgins / 1984 / CRE / M • Strange Bedfellows / 1985 / PL / M • Stripteaser / 1986 / LA / M • Summer Camp Girls / 1983 / CA / M • Swedish Erotica #58 / 1984 / CA / M • The Sweetest Taboo / 1986 / SE / M • Tales Of Taija Rae / 1989 / DR / M • Talk Dirty To Me #04 / 1986 / DR / M • Temperatures Rising / 1986 / VT / M • Thy Neighbour's Wife / 1986 / DR / M • Treasure Box / 1986 / PEN / M • Triangle Of Lust / 1983 / VCR / M • Trinity Brown / 1984 / CV / M • An Unnatural Act #1 / 1984 / DR / M • VCA Previews #4 / 1988 / VC / C • Wet Panties / 1989 / MIR / C • Wild Nurses In Lust / 1986 / PLY / M • Wild Things #1 / 1985 / CV / M • Winner Take All / 1986 / SEV / M • Xstasy / 1986 / NSV / M • Yiddish Erotica #1 / 1986 / SE / C • You Turn Me On / 1986 / LIM / M • Young And Restless / 1983 / VIV / M

KIMBERLY CHAMBERS *see* **Kim Chambers**

KIMBERLY CUMMINGS *see* **Kimberly Kummings**

KIMBERLY CURTIS *see* **Kimberly Kummings**

KIMBERLY DARE *see* **Barbara Dare**

KIMBERLY DAWN
Tall big-boned girl with tight ass, brown hair and small breasts.
The Adventures Of Buttgirl & Wonder Wench / 1991 / AFV / M • AHV #13: Some Girls / 1991 / EVN / M • All The Way Down / 1991 / ZA / M • Amateur Lesbians #12: Kimberly / 1991 / GO / F • Amateur Lesbians #33: Mackala / 1992 / GO / F • Anal Heat / 1990 / ZA / M • The Back Doors (Western) / 1991 / WV / M • Backdoor Black #1 / 1992 / WV / C • The Backpackers #3 / 1991 / IN / M • Bedtime For Byron / 1991 / ME / M • Blonde Riders / 1991 / CC / M • Body Fire / 1991 / LV / M • Clean Out / 1991 / PRE / B • Cum To Dinner / 1991 / HO / M • Erectnophobia #2 / 1992 / MID / M • Foreign Bodies / 1991 / IN / M • The Harder Way / 1991 / AR / M • Her Obsession / 1991 / MID / M • High Fives / 1991 / PRE / B • Hit Parade / 1996 / PRE / B • Home But Not Alone / 1991 / WV / M • The Last Blonde / 1991 / IN / M • Leg...Ends

#05 / 1991 / PRE / F • Midnight Angel / 1992 / CDI / M • Mr. Peepers Amateur Home Videos #13: Backdoor Doctor / 1991 / LBO / M • Mr. Peepers Amateur Home Videos #15: When Company Comes / 1991 / LBO / M • Nasty Jack's Homemade Vid. #40 / 1991 / CDI / M • Odyssey Amateur #67: Lascivious Lynette / 1991 / OD / M • Rump Roasts / 1991 / PRE / B • Sole Goal / 1996 / PRE / B • Student Fetish Videos: The Enema #05 / 1991 / PRE / B • Wild Cats / 1991 / PRE / B

KIMBERLY JADE *(Kimberly (Jade))*
Shoulder length curly dark blonde hair, small tits, erect nipples, lithe body reminiscent of Alex Jordan, passable face, large multicolored tattoo (flowers) on right shoulder back, mole on right forehead, a little wide on the butt. Has a female child.
Anal Booty Burner / 1996 / ROB / M • Anal Lickers And Cummers / 1996 / ROB / M • Borsky's Back Door Bitches / 1996 / ROB / M • Caught From Behind #24 / 1996 / HO / M • Cumback Pussy #4: Get Some!!! / 1996 / EL / M • Drop Sex: Wipe The Floor / 1997 / JLP / M • Eighteen & Easy / 1996 / SC / M • Fashion Passion / 1997 / TEP / M • Hardcore Debutantes #01 / 1996 / TEP / M • I'm So Horny, Baby / 1997 / ROB / M • Lady Sterling Takes It Up The Arse / 1997 / ROB / M • More Dirty Debutantes #57 / 1996 / 4P / M • Nice Fuckin' Movie / 1997 / EL / M • Nightlife / 1997 / CA / M • Pocahotass #2 / 1996 / FD / M • Pussyman's Nite Club Party #1 / 1996 / SNA / M • Pussyman's Nite Club Party #2 / 1997 / SNA / M • Sexual Atrocities / 1996 / EL / M • Up Your Ass #3 / 1996 / ANA / M • Wild Assed Pooper Slut / 1996 / ROB / M

KIMBERLY JAY
Why Gentlemen Prefer Blondes / 1983 / HO / C

KIMBERLY KANE *(Debbie Foley, Kimberly (Kane))*
Debbie Foley is from **Holly Does Hollywood #4**.
50 Ways To Lick Your Lover / 1989 / ZA / M • Anal Angels #2 / 1990 / VEX / C • Aussie Maid In America / 1990 / PM / M • Backdoor To Hollywood #11 / 1990 / CIN / M • Backdoor To Hollywood #12 / 1990 / CIN / M • Bad Medicine / 1990 / VEX / M • Beauties And The Beast / 1990 / AFV / M • Behind You All The Way #1 / 1990 / SO / M • Bi-Bi-Baby / 1990 / CDI / G • Blacks & Blondes: The Movie / 1989 / WV / M • Blue Fire / 1991 / V99 / M • Breast Side Story / 1990 / LE / M • Candy Ass / 1990 / V99 / M • College Girl / 1990 / VEX / M • Con Jobs / 1990 / V99 / M • Drink Of Love / 1990 / V99 / M • The End Of The Innocence / 1989 / IN / M • Girls Don't Lie / 1990 / IN / F • Girls Of The Double D #10 / 1989 / CDI / M • Girls Of The Double D #11 / 1990 / CIN / M • Girls Of The Double D #13 / 1990 / CDI / M • Great Expectations / 1990 / V99 / M • Great Expectations / 1992 / VEX / C • Having It All / 1991 / VEX / M • Heavenly Hyapatia / 1990 / VI / M • Hidden Pleasures / 1990 / VEX / M • Holly Does Hollywood #4 / 1990 / CAY / M • Hollywood Knights #3 / 1991 / PCP / M • Intimate Affairs / 1990 / VEX / M • It Happened At Midnight / 1990 / IN / M • King Tongue Meets Anal Woman / 1990 / PL / M • Living In Sin / 1990 / VEX / M • The Luscious Baker Girls / 1990 / VD /

M • The New Ass Masters #10 / 1996 / LEI / C • One Of These Nights / 1991 / V99 / M • Only The Best Of Girls With Curves / 1992 / CV / C • Passion Princess / 1991 / VEX / M • Purple Haze / 1991 / WV / M • Raquel On Fire / 1990 / VC / M • Rear Entry / 1995 / LEI / M • Rear View / 1989 / LE / M • The Rebel / 1990 / CIN / M • Savage Fury #2 / 1989 / CAY / M • Scandalous / 1989 / CC / M • Secret Dreams / 1991 / VEX / M • Sex Kittens / 1990 / VEX / F • Sexual Persuasion / 1991 / V99 / M • Sexy Nurses #1 On And Off Duty / 1990 / CV / M • Some Like It Hot / 1989 / CDI / M • Stiff Magnolias / 1990 / HO / M • Suzanne's Grand Affair / 1990 / CV / M • Tailgunners / 1990 / CDI / M • A Tale Of Two Titties #1 / 1990 / AR / M • Teach Me Tonight / 1990 / VEX / M • Weekend Blues / 1990 / IN / M

KIMBERLY KILGORE *see* **Kimberly Kummings**

KIMBERLY KISS
Creme De Femme / 1994 / 4P / F

KIMBERLY KITAINE *see* **Kim Katain**

KIMBERLY KUMMINGS *(Kim Cummings, Kimberly Cummings, Kim Kummings, Kimberly Curtis, Kimberly Kurtis, Kimberly Summing, Kimberly Kilgore)*
Passable face (pretty in some movies), shoulder length dark hair, small slightly droopy tits with the right one looking slightly bigger than the left, lithe body except for a slightly flabby belly, very long nipples. Wonderful personality and actually seems to like sex (the professional movies should be able to beat that out of her, eh!). De-virginized at 15 and 27 years old in 1995. As of mid-1995 she has had her tits enhanced (scars under areola visible) but only to a medium size. Comes from Santa Maria, CA. Kimberly Kilgore is from **Rimmers #2**.
$ex 4 Fun & Profit / 1996 / SPR / M • Altered Paradise / 1995 / LE / M • Amateur Models For Hire / 1996 / MP0 / M • Anal Angels #3 / 1995 / VEX / C • Anal Angels #5 / 1996 / VEX / C • Anal Anonymous / 1995 / SO / M • Anal Auditions / 1995 / VMX / M • Anal Camera #09 / 1995 / EVN / M • Anal Institution #1 / 1996 / ZA / M • Anal Interrogation / 1995 / ZA / M • Anal Invader / 1995 / PEP / M • Anal Misconduct / 1995 / VD / M • The Anal Nurse Scam / 1995 / CA / M • Anal Nurses / 1996 / LBO / M • Anal Party Girls / 1996 / GV / M • Anal Pool Party / 1996 / PE / M • Anal Receivers / 3996 / MP0 / M • Anal Senorita #1 / 1994 / ROB / M • Anal Territory / 1996 / AVD / M • Anal, Facial & Interracial / 1996 / FC / M • Anna Malle Exposed / 1996 / WV / M • Babe Wire / 1996 / HW / M • Babes Behind Bars / 1996 / CNP / F • Backdoor Diaries / 1995 / BBE / M • Big Bust Babes #33 / 1995 / AFI / M • Big Bust Babes #35 / 1996 / AFI / M • Bimbette: Adventures In Anal Land / 1996 / TEP / M • Bobby Sox / 1996 / VI / S • The Body System / 1996 / FD / M • Booty And The Ho' Bitch / 1995 / JMP / M • Bootylicious: Booty & The Ho Bitch / 1996 / JMP / M • Broken Vows / 1996 / ULP / M • Bushwoman: She Takes Two / 1996 / RAS / M • The Butt Sisters Do New Orleans / 1995 / MID / M • Butt X Files #2: Anal Abduction / 1995 / WIV / M • California Covet / 1995 / CA / M • Camp Fire Tramps / 1995 / LOT / M • Casting Call #11 / 1995 / MET / M • Casting Couch Tips /

1996 / MP0 / M • Checkmate / 1996 / SNA / M • Compulsion (Amazing) / 1996 / MET / M • Conjugal Visits / 1995 / EVN / M • Creme De La Face #05 / 1994 / OD / M • The Cumm Brothers #07: Honeymoon On Uranus / 1995 / OD / M • The Cumm Brothers #11: Oh Cum On Ye Faces / 1995 / OD / M • Cumm For Dinner / 1995 / BCP / M • Dare You / 1995 / CA / M • Devil In A Wet T-Shirt / 1995 / SPI / M • Dick & Jane In San Francisco / 1996 / AVI / M • The Dinner Party #2: The Buffet / 1996 / ULI / M • Dirty Minds / 1996 / NIT / M • Double D Dykes #19 / 1995 / GO / F • Double D Dykes #20 / 1995 / GO / F • Double D Dykes #21 / 1995 / GO / F • Double D Dykes #22 / 1995 / GO / F • Double D Dykes #24 / 1995 / GO / F • Double Dicked #2 / 1996 / RAS / M • Double Penetration Virgins #06: DP Diner / 1995 / JMP / M • Dream House / 1995 / XPR / M • Dream Lust / 1995 / NIT / M • Dreams Of A Gigolo / 1996 / SNA / M • Dukes Of Anal / 1996 / VC / M • Employee's Entrance In The Rear / 1996 / CC / M • The Erotic Adventures Of Johnny Soiree / 1995 / LBO / M • Erotic Newcummers Vol 1 #4 / 1996 / DR / M • Fixing A Hole / 1995 / XCI / M • Flesh / 1996 / EA / M • Flesh Palace / 1995 / LBO / M • Gangbang Girl #15 / 1995 / ANA / M • Ganggstas Paradise / 1995 / AVI / M • Get Lucky / 1996 / NIT / M • Girly Video Magazine #2 / 1995 / BEP / M • Gold Coast / 1996 / FD / M • Goldenbush / 1996 / AVI / M • Hardcore Confidential #2 / 1996 / TEP / M • Hardcore Schoolgirls #2: Perverted Playmates / 1995 / XPR / M • The Hardwood Chronicles / 1995 / XCI / M • Here Comes Magoof #2 / 1995 / VC / M • Hollywood Amateurs #17 / 1995 / MID / M • Hollywood Hillbillies / 1996 / LE / M • Hollywood Starlets Adventure #06 / 1995 / AVS / M • Hot Tight Asses #17 / 1996 / TCK / M • House Of Anal / 1995 / NOT / M • House On Paradise Beach / 1996 / VC / M • In The Scope / 1996 / VI / M • Indiscreet! Video Magazine #2 / 1995 / FH / M • Innocence Lost / 1995 / GO / M • Interracial Escorts / 1995 / GO / M • Interview With A Milkman / 1996 / VI / M • Interview: Bun Busters / 1995 / LV / M • Jiggly Queens #3 / 1996 / LE / M • Kink #1 / 1995 / ROB / M • Kinky Debutante Interviews #10 / 1995 / IP / M • Kool Ass / 1996 / BOT / M • Ladies In Leather / 1995 / GO / M • A Lady / 1995 / FD / M • Lady M's Anything Nasty #01: Pink Pussy Party / 1996 / AVI / F • Leather Unleashed / 1995 / GO / M • Leg Show #1 / 1995 / NIT / M • Legend #6: / 1996 / LE / M • Lesbian Connection / 1996 / SUF / F • Lil' Latin Cutie Pies / 1996 / CDI / M • Lingerie / 1996 / RAS / M • Lust & Desire / 1996 / WV / M • Mall Slut / 1997 / SC / M • Max World #1 / 1995 / FRM / M • Mickey Ray's Sex Search #05: Deep Inside / 1995 / WIV / M • Mike Hott: #346 Cunt Of The Month: Kimberly Kummings / 1996 / MHV / M • Mike Hott: #349 Girls Who Swallow Cum #03 / 1996 / MHV / C • Mike Hott: #355 Lesbian Sluts #24 / 1996 / MHV / F • Mike Hott: #356 Girls Who Lap Cum From Cunts #01 / 1996 / MHV / M • Mike Hott: #369 Cum In My Mouth #05 / 1996 / MHV / C • Mike Hott: #373 Three-Sum Sluts #14 / 1996 / MHV / M • Mike Hott: #386 / 1996 / MHV / M • Mission Phenomenal / 1996 /

HIP / M • More Dirty Debutantes #39 / 1995 / 4P / M • Mrs. Buttfire / 1995 / SUF / M • The New Babysitter / 1995 / GO / M • The New Snatch Masters #18 / 1996 / LEI / C • Night Stalker / 1995 / BBE / M • No Man's Land #15 / 1996 / VT / F • Nookie Ranch / 1996 / NIT / M • The Other Woman / 1996 / VC / M • Outlaw Sluts / 1996 / RAS / M • Party Girl / 1995 / LV / M • Philmore Butts Las Vegas Vacation / 1995 / SUF / M • Philmore Butts Strikes Gold / 1996 / SUF / M • Pizza Sluts: They Deliver / 1995 / XCI / M • Pretty Young Things Escort Service / 1995 / ZA / M • Primal / 1995 / MET / M • Public Enemy / 1995 / GO / M • Pussyman #14: Dreams Of A Gigolo / 1996 / SNA / M • Pussyman Auditions #01 / 1995 / SNA / M • Red Door Diaries #2 / 1996 / ZA / M • Rimmers #2 / 1996 / MP0 / M • Ring Of Desire / 1995 / LBO / M • Salsa & Spice #2: Latin Lust / 1996 / TTV / M • Salsa & Spice #3 / 1996 / TTV / M • Samantha & Company / 1996 / PL / M • The Seduction Of Sabrina / 1996 / AVD / M • Sex For Hire / 1996 / ONA / M • Sexhibition #2 / 1996 / SUF / M • Seymore Butts: Big Boobs In Buttsville / 1996 / FH / M • Shaving Mr. One Eye / 1996 / FC / M • A Shot In The Pants / 1995 / HO / M • A Shot In The Pink / 1995 / BBE / M • Snatch Masters #12 / 1995 / LEI / M • Sodom Chronicles / 1995 / FH / M • Sperm Bitches / 1995 / ZA / M • Stripping / 1995 / NIT / M • Strong Sensations / 1996 / PL / M • Stuff Your Ass #1 / 1995 / JMP / M • Stuff Your Face #3 / 1995 / JMP / M • Suburban Buttnicks Forever / 1995 / CC / M • Tainted Love / 1996 / VC / M • Talking Trash #2 / 1995 / HW / M • Top Debs #6: Rear Entry Girls / 1995 / GO / M • Trapped / 1996 / VI / M • Treacherous / 1995 / VD / M • Triple Penetration Debutante Sluts #2 / 1996 / BAC / M • Up The Ying Yang #2 / 1995 / CC / M • The Usual Anal Suspects / 1996 / CC / M • Video Virgins #20 / 1995 / NS / M • Vortex / 1995 / MET / M • The Wanderer #2: Slippery When Wet / 1995 / CDI / M • What Women Want / 1996 / SUF / M • While The Cat's Away / 1996 / NIT / M

KIMBERLY KUPPS
976-76DD / 1993 / VI / M • Anal Explosions #1 / 1996 / NIT / M • Animal Instinct / 1996 / DTV / M • Arch Villains / 1994 / PRE / B • Arch Worship / 1995 / PRE / B • The Battle Of The Busty Blondes / 1994 / NAP / B • Big & Busty Centerfolds / 1996 / DGD / F • Big Boob Bikini Bash / 1995 / BTO / M • Big Bust Babes #13 / 1993 / AFI / M • Big Bust Blondes / 1992 / BTO / F • Big, Bad Bulging Bazooms / 1993 / NAP / F • Black Orchid / 1993 / WV / M • Bobby Hollander's Sweet Cheeks #103 / 1992 / QUA / M • Bobby Hollander's Sweet Cheeks #105 / 1993 / SFP / M • The Boob Tube / 1993 / MET / M • Born 2 B Wild / 1995 / PL / M • Bra Busters #01 / 1993 / LBO / M • Breast Collection #04 / 1995 / LBO / C • The Breast Files #3 / 1994 / AVI / M • Bustline / 1993 / LE / M • The Butt, The Boobs, The Lips / 1996 / C69 / M • Dick & Jane Look For Pussy In The Park / 1995 / AVI / M • Dirty Bob's #07: DanCES With OrifiCES / 1992 / FLP / S • Dirty Bob's #23: Tampa Teasers / 1995 / FLP / S • Double D Housewives / 1994 / PV / M • Double D Nurses / 1994 / PV / M • Double-D Reunion / 1995 / BTO / M • Dream Lust / 1995 / NIT / M • The

Ebony Connection #1 / 1994 / LBO / C • FTV #34: Kimberly Kupps Konquest #1 / 1996 / FT / B • FTV #35: Kimberly Kupps Konquest #2 / 1996 / FT / B • FTV #73: Killer Kupps / 1996 / FT / B • Gazongas Galore #1 / 1996 / NIT / C • The Girls From Hootersville #01 / 1993 / SFP / M • The Girls From Hootersville #03 / 1993 / SFP / M • Hollywood Swingers #03 / 1992 / LBO / M • How To Make A Model #02: Got Her In Bed / 1993 / QUA / M • Hump Chessie & Kimberly / 199? / H&S / M • Jus' Knockin' Boots #2: Black On Line / 1996 / NIT / M • Just Do It! / 1996 / RAS / M • Kimberly Kupps Gets 5 A's / 1996 / NIT / M • Kimberly Kupps Gets Black Balled / 1996 / NIT / M • The Knocker Room / 1993 / GO / M • Kym Wilde's On The Edge #25 / 1995 / RB / B • Lesbian Lust Bust / 1995 / GLI / F • Love Seats / 1994 / PRE / C • Lube Job / 1994 / PRE / B • M Series #12 / 1993 / LBO / M • Mellon Man #03 / 1994 / AVI / M • Micki Meets Her Match / 1992 / NAP / B • More Than A Mouthful / 1995 / LBO / C • The Mountainous Mams Of Alyssa Alps / 1993 / NAP / S • Natural Wonders / 1993 / VI / M • The New Butt Hunt #12 / 1995 / LEI / C • The Nympho Files / 1995 / NIT / M • The Panty Parlor / 1996 / VIM / M • Pearl Necklace: Amorous Amateurs #24 / 1993 / SEE / M • Pearl Necklace: Thee Bush League #12 / 1993 / SEE / M • Pearl Necklace: Thee Bush League #16 / 1993 / SEE / M • Pearl Necklace: Thee Bush League #21 / 1993 / SEE / M • Perverted Stories #02 / 1995 / JMP / M • Plumb And Dumber / 1995 / PP / M • Positions Wanted: Experienced Only / 1993 / PV / M • Reel Life Video #41: Lust In The Country / 1996 / RLF / F • Slap Happy / 1994 / PRE / B • Slummin' Hood Girlz / 1993 / CA / M • Southern: Kimberly Kupps / 1993 / SSH / F • Straight A Students / 1993 / MET / M • Stroke Play / 1994 / PLV / B • Summer Vacation #1 / 1996 / RAS / M • Summer Vacation #2 / 1996 / RAS / M • Super Enemates #2 / 1996 / PRE / C • Tails From The Tower / 1993 / AFI / M • Tech: Kimberly Kups #1 / 1994 / TWA / F • Tech: Kimberly Kups #2 / 1994 / TWA / F • Tip Tap Toe / 1995 / PRE / C • Tit To Tit #3 / 1995 / BTO / M • Titty Bar #1 / 1993 / LE / M • Toppers #11 / 1993 / TV / C • Toppers #13 / 1993 / TV / M • Toppers #14 / 1993 / TV / M • Toppers #16 / 1993 / TV / M • Toppers #22 / 1993 / TV / C • Toppers #30 / 1994 / TV / C • Toppers & Whoppers #1 / 1994 / PRE / C • Watersgate / 1994 / PRE / C

KIMBERLY KURTIS see Kimberly Kummings

KIMBERLY KYLE
Marginal blonde with large enhanced tits, slutty attitude, 26 years old in 1995.
1-900-FUCK #2 / 1995 / SO / M • All Amateur Perfect 10's / 1995 / LEI / M • Amateur Gay Girls / 1995 / LEI / C • Anal Anarchy / 1995 / VC / M • Anal Climax #4 / 1996 / ROB / M • Anal Hellraiser #2 / 1995 / ROB / M • Anal Nymphettes / 1995 / LIP / F • Anal Princess #2 / 1996 / VC / M • Anal Savage #3 / 1996 / ROB / M • Ass Ventura: Crack Detective / 1996 / PL / M • Babes Of The Bay #2 / 1995 / LIP / F • Batbabe / 1995 / PL / M • The Best Of Fabulous Flashers / 1996 / DGD / F • The Best Of Strippers Inc / 1996 / ONA / C • Black

Beach / 1995 / LV / M • Blonde Temptation / 1995 / IF / M • Born 2 B Wild / 1995 / PL / M • Buffy Malibu's Nasty Girls #09 / 1995 / ANA / F • Butt Banged Cycle Sluts / 1995 / ANA / M • Butt Jammers #03 / 1995 / SC / F • Butt Motors / 1995 / VC / M • Buttman In The Crack / 1996 / EA / M • Carnival / 1995 / PV / M • Creme De La Face #04 / 1994 / OD / M • Creme De La Face #06 / 1995 / OD / M • The Cumm Brothers #06: Hook, Line And Sphincter / 1995 / OD / M • The Cumm Brothers #08: Escape From Uranus / 1995 / OD / M • Dirty Stories #2 / 1995 / PE / M • The Dream Team / 1995 / VT / M • Fabulous Flashers #2 / 1996 / DGD / F • Fashion Sluts #1 / 1995 / ABS / M • Finger Pleasures #3 / 1995 / PL / F • Gang Bang Face Bath #4 / 1995 / ROB / M • Gang Bang Jizz Queen / 1995 / ROB / M • Getting Personal / 1995 / PE / M • Girls Just Wanna Have Cum / 1995 / HO / M • Girls Of The Athletic Department / 1995 / VT / M • Helen & Louise / 1996 / HDE / M • High Heeled & Horny #1 / 1994 / LBO / M • How To Make A Model #05: Back To Innocence / 1994 / LBO / M • Jailhouse Nurses / 1995 / SC / M • Journal Of O #2 / 1994 / ONA / B • Leg Tease #1 / 1995 / VT / M • Lusty Lap Dancers #2 / 1994 / HO / M • Malibu Heat / 1995 / HO / M • More Than A Whore / 1995 / OD / M • Nasty Nymphos #10 / 1995 / ANA / M • No Man's Land #12 / 1995 / VT / F • Northwest Pecker Trek #4: Laid In Latte Land / 1994 / LBO / M • Nothing Like A Dame #2 / 1995 / IN / M • Perverted Women / 1995 / SC / M • Prisoner Of Love / 1995 / CV / M • Private Matters / 1995 / EMC / M • Private Places / 1995 / IF / M • Pussyman #10: Butts, Butts & More Butts / 1995 / SNA / M • Pussyman Auditions #03 / 1995 / SNA / M • Pussyman Auditions #04 / 1995 / SNA / M • Razor's Edge / 1995 / ONA / M • Sluthunt #2 / 1995 / BIP / F • Snatch Masters #03 / 1994 / LEI / M • Strippers Inc. #3 / 1994 / ONA / M • Strippers Inc. #4 / 1995 / ONA / M • Teacher's Pet #2 / 1994 / WMG / M • The Temple Of Poon / 1996 / PE / M • Throbbing Threesomes / 1996 / NIT / M • Trading Partners / 1995 / GO / M • Trick Shots / 1995 / PV / M • Video Virgins #15 / 1994 / NS / M • Virgin Killers: Second Rampage / 1995 / PEP / M • The Voyeur #5 / 1995 / EA / M • Water Worked / 1995 / AB / F • Wet 'n' Wicked / 1995 / BEP / F • Wet Faces #1 / 1997 / SC / C • Wicked Ways #2: Education Of A D.P. Virgin / 1995 / WP / M • Wildfire: Wildgirl's Cleaning Service / 1994 / WIF / F

KIMBERLY LYNN see Lynn Francis

KIMBERLY MARSHALL see Ashlyn Gere

KIMBERLY MORGAN see Kristara Barrington

KIMBERLY O'NEAL see Star Index I

KIMBERLY PARE see Barbara Dare

KIMBERLY PATTON see Ashlyn Gere

KIMBERLY RULE
Triple Play (Vh) / cr75 / VC / M

KIMBERLY SUMMING see Kimberly Kummings

KIMBERLY WARNER see Bunny Bleu

KIMBERLY WONG see Kristara Barrington

KIMI see Star Index I

KIMI (GEE) see Kimi Gee

KIMI BEE see Kimi Gee

KIMI GEE *(Kim Gee, Kimmy Jee, Kimi Toyota, Kimi (Gee), Kimmi Ji, Kimi Ji, Kimi Bee)*
In her original appearence she was Oriental with long black hair, small tits, small areola, lithe body, tight waist, passable face, and a horrible little girl whiney voice. In 1997 she reappeared and looks and sounds the same except that she now has red hair.
Amazing Sex Stories #1 / 1986 / SUV / M • Asses Galore #6: Fallen Angels / 1996 / DFI / M • Bachelor's Paradise / 1986 / VEX / M • The Burma Road #3 / 1996 / LBO / C • The Burma Road #4 / 1996 / LBO / C • Cheek-A-Boo / 1988 / LV / M • China Girl / 1989 / V99 / M • Dirty Tricks / 1986 / 4P / M • Female Aggressors / 1986 / LAV / M • Girls Of The Bamboo Palace / 1989 / VEX / M • Girls Will Be Girls / 1988 / LV / F • Hospitality Sweet / 1988 / WV / M • Hot Chocolate #2 / 1986 / PLY / M • I'm So Horny, Baby / 1997 / ROB / M • In Search Of The Golden Bone / 1986 / CA / M • In Search Of The Wild Beaver / 1986 / DR / M • Karate Girls / 1987 / VCR / M • Keyhole #167: Ass Eaters / 1989 / KEH / M • Let Me Tell Ya 'Bout Fat Chicks #1 / 1986 / 4P / C • Lip Service / 1988 / LV / C • Loving Spoonfulls / 1987 / 4P / C • Madame X / 1989 / EVN / M • Mall Slut / 1997 / SC / M • Nasty Nymphos #16 / 1996 / ANA / M • National Pornographic #2: Orientals / 1987 / 4P / C • Over Eighteen #02 / 1997 / HW / M • Positive Positions / 1989 / VEX / M • Puritan Video Magazine #09 / 1997 / LE / M • Revenge Of The Babes #1 / 1985 / LA / M • Roll-X Girls / 1989 / DYV / M • Tons Of Fun #4: Hard And Lard / 1987 / 4P / M • The Ultimate Lover / 1986 / VD / M • Up The Ying Yang / 1991 / EVN / C • Valentino's Asian Invasion / 1997 / SC / M • Valentino's Euro-Invasion / 1997 / SC / M • White Men Can't Iron On Butt Row / 1997 / ABS / M

KIMI JI see Kimi Gee

KIMI LEE see Anisa

KIMI TOYOTA see Kimi Gee

KIMMI JI see Kimi Gee

KIMMI JOHNSON see Star Index I

KIMMY JEE see Kimi Gee

KIN
Sweet Dreams / 1994 / ORE / C

KIN KI
The Dragon Lady #1 / 1988 / WV / C • Oriental Sexpress / 1984 / WV / M

KINDRA
Filthy First Timers #5 / 1997 / EL / M

KINDRA TALENT
New York City Lesbian Gang Bang / 1995 / OUP / F

KING DONG
Ebony Dancer / 1994 / HBE / M

KING PAUL
Blacks & Big Boobs / 1986 / L&W / C • Blacks & Blondes #01 / 1986 / WV / M • Diamond Collection #01 / 1979 / SVE / M • Diamond Collection #76 / 1985 / CDI / M • Miss Twin Towers / 198? / BTO / M • Oriental Sexpress / 1984 / WV / M • Oriental Taboo / 1985 / CDI / M • San Francisco Original 200s Special / 1980 / SVE / C • The Twin Pyramids / 1988 / L&W / M

KING RAY
Jane Bond Meets Thunderthighs / 1988 / VD⁴/ M

KING TONGUE see King Tung

KING TUNG *(King Tongue, Al Thornton, K.T.)*
Black male with a very long tongue which he (sometimes) uses to good effect.
Anal Encounters #3: Back In The Dark One / 1991 / VC / M • Asian Pussyman Auditions / 1996 / SNA / M • Black Pussyman Auditions #1 / 1996 / SNA / M • The First Taboo / 1989 / LA / M • King Tongue Meets Anal Woman / 1990 / PL / M • King Tung: Bustin' The Royal Hienies / 1990 / LA / M • King Tung Is The Egyptian Lover / 1990 / LA / M • Pussyclips #09 / 1995 / SNA / M • Pussyclips #10 / 1995 / SNA / M • Pussyman #15: The Bone Voyage Bash / 1997 / SNA / M • Pussyman Auditions #05 / 1995 / SNA / M • Pussyman Auditions #06 / 1995 / SNA / M • Pussyman Auditions #10 / 1995 / SNA / M • Pussyman Auditions #11 / 1995 / SNA / M • Pussyman Auditions #12 / 1995 / SNA / M • Pussyman Auditions #14 / 1995 / SNA / M • Pussyman Auditions #15 / 1995 / SNA / M • Pussyman Auditions #19 / 1996 / SNA / M • Pussyman Auditions #22 / 1996 / SNA / M • Pussyman's House Party #2 / 1996 / SNA / M • Pussyman's Nite Club Party #1 / 1996 / SNA / M • Supertung / 1990 / LA / M

KINKO see Star Index I

KINZO TATSUNO see Star Index I

KIOKO see Star Index I

KIP COCHRAN
Sodom & Gomorrah / 1974 / MIT / M

KIP KASEY
Mr. Blue / 1996 / JSP / G

KIP SANBORN
Switch Hitters #8 / 1995 / IN / G

KIP TYLER
The Mating Game / 1992 / PL / G

KIRA *(Marisol)*
Black with...you don't want to know.
Adventures Of The DP Boys: Janet And Da Boyz / 1994 / HW / M • Adventures Of The DP Boys: South Of The Border / 1995 / HW / M • Adventures Of The DP Boys: Blacks Are Back / 1994 / HW / M • Anal Asian / 1994 / VEX / M • Anal Invader / 1995 / PEP / M • Ass Busters / 1995 / VMX / C • Battle Of The Glands / 1994 / LV / F • Big Bust Babes #15 / 1993 / AFI / M • Big Murray's New-Cummers #16: Frat Boys #2 / 1993 / FD / M • Black Beauty (Coast To Coast) / 1994 / CC / M • Black Buttwatch / 1995 / FH / M • Black Centerfold Celebrities / 1993 / MID / M • Black Fire / 1993 / VIM / M • Black Gangbangers #3 / 1995 / HW / M • Black Hollywood Amateurs #05 / 1995 / MID / M • Black Hollywood Amateurs #13 / 1995 / MID / M • Black Hollywood Amateurs #14 / 1995 / MID / M • Black Jack City #3 / 1993 / HW / M • Black Orgies #34 / 1995 / GO / M • Black Women, White Men #6 / 1995 / FC / M • Bootin' Up / 1995 / VT / B • Booty In Da House / 1995 / EVN / M • Booty In The House / 1993 / WP / M • Bra Busters #02 / 1993 / LBO / M • Breastman Does The Himalayas / 1993 / EVN / M • Bump 'n' Grind / 1994 / HW / M • Byron Long At Large / 1995 / VC / M • Cracklyn / 1994 / HW / M • Da Booty Call / 1994 / HW / M • Dirty Dating Service #03 / 1994 / WP / M • Dirty Dating Service #04 / 1994 / WP / M • Dirty Doc's Housecalls #14 / 1994 / LV / M •

Double D Dykes #17 / 1995 / GO / F • Ebony Erotica #04: Ebony Gods / 1993 / GO / M • Ebony Erotica #05: Black Obsessions / 1993 / GO / M • Ebony Erotica #11: Harlem Knights / 1993 / GO / M • Ebony Erotica #14: Black & Tan / 1994 / GO / M • Every Nerd Has A Fantasy / 1996 / FC / M • First Time Lesbians #13 / 1994 / JMP / F • Girl's Towne #1 / 1994 / FC / F • The Girls From Hootersville #04 / 1993 / SFP / M • The Girls From Hootersville #05 / 1994 / SFP / M • Girlz Towne #01 / 1995 / FC / F • Hollywood Amateurs #08 / 1994 / MID / M • Hot Tight Asses #04 / 1993 / TCK / M • Lips / 1994 / FC / M • M Series #09 / 1993 / LBO / M • M Series #12 / 1993 / LBO / M • Nasty Newcummers #02 / 1993 / MET / M • Opie Goes To South Central / 1995 / PP / M • Paint It Black / 1995 / EVN / M • Pussy Hunt #12 / 1995 / LEI / M • Rump-Shaker #2 / 1993 / HW / M • San Francisco Lesbians #4 / 1993 / PL / F • Sean Michaels On The Road #09: St. Louis / 1994 / VT / M • Shades Of Erotica #01 / 1994 / GLI / M • Sista! #1 / 1993 / VT / F • Sleazy Streets / 1995 / PEP / M • Sniff Doggy Style / 1994 / PL / M • Take All Cummers / 1996 / HO / M • Tight Fit #12 / 1995 / GO / M • Treacherous / 1995 / VD / M • Valentine's Challenge / 1992 / LIP / F • Whoopin' Her Behind / 1995 / VT / B • Winter Heat / 1994 / MID / M

KIRA RODRIGUEZ see Star Index I

KIRDY STEVENS *(Dave Arthur)*
Normally a director.

KIRI KELLY *(Kerry Kelly)*
Tall, slim, quite attractive girl who only seems to do B&D and sounds English.
Bondage Fantasia / 199? / CS / B • Bondage Is My Pleasure #4 / 1994 / CS / B • Bondage Memories #04 / 1994 / BON / C • Bondage Photo Session / 1990 / BIZ / B • Bound Tickled Tied / cr90 / BON / B • Bound To Tease #5 / 1990 / BON / C • The Bride Stripped Bare / 1994 / BON / B • Captured Cop #1: Deadly Explosion / 1991 / BON / B • Captured Cop #2: The Stakeout / 1991 / BON / B • Captured Cop #3: Double Cross / 1991 / BON / B • Five Card Stud / 1990 / BIZ / B • Hard Discipline #1 / 1993 / SHL / B • Her First Time / cr90 / BON / B • Home Maid Memories #2 / 1994 / BON / C • Jay Dee's Bondage Notebook #1 / cr90 / BON / B • Jay Dee's Bondage Notebook #2 / cr90 / BON / B • A Journey Into Darkness / 1991 / BS / B • Kiri Bound / 1988 / BON / B • Kiri Kelly Bondage Centerfold / 1993 / BON / B • Krystle's Surrender / 1988 / BON / B • Latex Slaves Discipline / 1990 / BIZ / B • Mistress Sondra's Playthings / 1990 / BON / B • More Dirty Debutantes #05 / 1990 / 4P / M • Nancy Crew Meets Dr. Freidastein / cr90 / BON / B • Our Sorority / 1993 / SHL / B • Rainy Days #1 / 1991 / BON / B • Rainy Days #2 / 1991 / BON / B • Real People Real Bondage #1 / 1995 / BON / C • The Riding Master / 1989 / BON / B • Spanking, Spanking And More / 1990 / BON / B • Tails From The Whip / 1991 / HOM / B • Tied & Tickled #18 / 1992 / CS / B • Wild Thing / 1989 / BON / B

KIRIAN MINELLI
Is probably the elder sister of Lei Lani.
The Amorous Adventures Of Janette Littledove / 1988 / AR / M • With Love, Littledove

/ 1988 / AR / M
KIRK
Homegrown Video #094 / 1990 / HOV / M
• Rusty Boner's Late Night Videos #1 / 1995 / RHV / M
KIRK REYNOLDS *see* **Sasha Gabor**
KIRK STONE
Catch Of The Day #5 / 1996 / VG0 / M • Catch Of The Day #6 / 1996 / VG0 / M • Dirty Dave's #2 / 1996 / XPR / M
KIRK WILDER
San Francisco Cosmopolitan Club Amateur Night / 1983 / WV / M • Ball Busters / 1984 / CV / M • Beyond Taboo / 1984 / VIV / M • Hard Times / 1985 / WV / M • Hot Close-Ups / 1984 / WV / M • Hot Country / cr83 / WV / M • Hot Heads / 1985 / WV / M • The Last Taboo / 1984 / VIV / M • A Night On The Wild Side / 1986 / VC / M • Sophisticated Pleasure / 1984 / WV / M
KIROSMI OKAMURA
Hot Spa Sex / 1996 / AVE / M
KIRSTEN
Ejacula #1 / 1992 / VC / M • Ejacula #2 / 1992 / VC / M • Triple Flay / 1995 / PRE / B
KIRSTEN BRADLEY
Just Deserts / 1991 / BIZ / B
KIRSTI ALLIN *see* **Star Index I**
KIRSTI WAY *see* **Kursti Way**
KIRSTLE *see* **Star Index I**
KIRSTYN LONDON
Different Strokes / 1996 / VC / M • Family Affair / 1996 / XC / M • Las Vegas Big Boob Hospitality Sweet / 1997 / HO / M • Real Big Tits / 1996 / P69 / M
KIRT KENT *see* **Star Index I**
KIS
Sodomania: Slop Shots / 1996 / EL / C
KISHA *see* **Cumisha Amado**
KISS *(Keke Kaner, Tamara Wild)*
Blonde with marginal face, husky voice, big butt. Born Jun 20, 1970 in Birmingham England. The Keke Kaner is from **Anal Vision #1**. She says her first video was **Radical Affairs #3**. Is this the same as Sharon Brady (**Licking Legends #1**)? Returned in 1996 but now looks like a blimp.
The Adventures Of Breastman / 1992 / EVN / M • The All Girl Anal Orgy / 1996 / BAC / F • Anal Crybabies / 1996 / BAC / M • Anal Vision #01 / 1992 / LBO / M • Anal Witness #2: No Prisoners / 1996 / LBO / M • Anything Goes / 1993 / VD / C • Ass Openers! #2 / 1995 / TCK / C • Big Bust Babes #11 / 1992 / AFI / M • Big Bust Platinum: Superstar Strip Tease / 1993 / PME / F • Big Knockers #05 / 1994 / TV / M • Big Knockers #06 / 1994 / TV / M • Big Knockers #07 / 1994 / TV / M • The Big One / 1992 / GO / M • Blonde Beaver Bonanza / 1992 / TCP / M • Breast Worx #29 / 1992 / LBO / M • Bringing Up The Rear / 1993 / VD / C • The British Are Coming / 1993 / ZA / M • Bronco Millie / 1992 / ZA / M • Brother Act / 1992 / PL / M • Bush League #2 / 1992 / CC / M • Butt Bongo Babes / 1993 / VD / M • Butt Jammers #04 / 1995 / SC / F • The Cable Girl / 1996 / NIT / M • California Pizza Girls / 1992 / EVN / M • Carnival Of Flesh / 1996 / NIT / M • Catch Of The Day #4 / 1996 / VG0 / M • Charm School / 1993 / PEP / M • Cheeks #6 / 1992 / CC / M • Cheerleader Nurses #1 / 1993 / VC / M • Cheerleader Nurses #2 / 1993 / VC / M • Deep Inside Nikki Sinn / 1996 / VC / C •

Double D Dykes #07 / 1992 / GO / F • Double Impact / 1992 / CDI / G • Dripping With Desire / 1992 / DR / M • End Of Innocence / 1994 / WIV / M • Face Dance #1 / 1992 / EA / M • Face Dance #2 / 1992 / EA / M • Feature Speciale: The Ultimate Squirt / 1996 / ANE / M • Finger Pleasures #4 / 1995 / PL / F • Flesh For Fantasy / 1994 / CV / M • Flexxx #3 / 1995 / VT / M • Flying High #2 / 1992 / HO / M • Foolish Pleasure / 1992 / VD / M • Friendly Fire / 1996 / EDP / M • From Brazil With Love / 1992 / ZA / M • From The Heart / 1996 / XCI / M • The Girls' Club / 1993 / VD / C • Girly Video Magazine #5 / 1996 / BEP / M • Girly Video Magazine #6 / 1996 / AB / M • Gland Slam / 1995 / PRE / B • The Goddess / 1993 / ZA / M • Harness Hannah At The Strap-On Ho Down / 1994 / WIV / F • Head Lines / 1992 / SC / M • Hot Tight Asses #02 / 1993 / TCK / M • Jennifer Ate / 1993 / XCI / F • Jizz Glazed Goo Guzzlers #2 / 1996 / NIT / C • Kiss Is A Rebel With A Cause / 1993 / WV / M • Leg...Ends #10 / 1994 / PRE / F • Lesbian Mystery Theatre: The Case Of The Deadly Dyke / 1994 / LIP / F • Licking Legends #1 / 1992 / LE / F • Licking Legends #2 / 1992 / LE / F • Lover Under Cover / 1995 / ERA / M • Make Me Over, Baby / 1996 / LOF / M • Maliboobies / 1993 / CDI / F • Miss Matches / 1996 / PRE / C • More Than A Handful #2 / 1993 / MET / M • Neutron Man / 1993 / HO / M • Nikki Never Says No / 1992 / LE / M • Nineteen #4 / 1996 / FOR / M • No Man's Land #12 / 1995 / VT / F • Nookie Cookies / 1993 / CDI / F • Obsexxed / 1992 / VD / M • Odyssey Triple Play #43: Anal Creaming & Reaming / 1993 / OD / M • One In A Million / 1992 / HW / M • Orgy Attack / 1993 / DRP / M • Outrageous Sex / 1995 / BIP / F • Profiles #07: Sexworld / 1996 / XPR / M • Puritan Video Magazine #07 / 1996 / LE / M • A Pussy Called Wanda #2 / 1992 / DR / M • The Queen Of Mean / 1992 / FC / M • Radical Affairs Video Magazine #03 / 1992 / ME / M • Revealed / 1992 / VT / M • The Serpent's Dream / 1993 / VC / M • The Sex Connection / 1993 / VC / M • Sexcalibur / 1992 / FD / M • A Shaver Among Us / 1992 / ZA / M • Sodomania #01: Tales Of Perversity / 1992 / EL / M • Sodomania #16: Sexxy Pistols / 1996 / EL / M • The Spa / 1993 / VC / M • Splendor In The Ass #2 / 1992 / CA / M • Student Fetish Videos: Best Of Spanking #02 / 1993 / PRE / C • Student Fetish Videos: The Enema #09 / 1992 / PRE / B • Student Fetish Videos: Spanking #08 / 1992 / PRE / B • Student Fetish Videos: Tickling #06 / 1992 / SFV / B • Sue / 1995 / VC / M • Surrogate Lover / 1992 / TP / M • Tailspin #3 / 1992 / VT / M • Tales From The Zipper #1 / 1993 / ME / M • Tiffany Lords Straps One On #1 / 1994 / WIV / F • Toe Biz / 1993 / PRE / S • Toe Hold / 1992 / PRE / B • Toppers #01 / 1992 / TV / F • Toppers #03 / 1993 / TV / M • Toppers #07 / 1993 / TV / M • Toppers #09 / 1993 / TV / M • Toppers #12 / 1993 / TV / C • Unchained Melanie / 1992 / VC / M • The Violation Of Juliette / 1996 / JMP / F • Waves Of Passion / 1996 / ERA / M • Whispers / 1992 / HO / M • Wicked Wish / 1992 / LE / M • Wild In Motion / 1992 / PL / M • X-Rated Blondes / 1992 / VD / C • You Assed For It / 1996 / NOT / M

KISS (OTHER)
Nineteen #5 / 1996 / FOR / M
KIT FOX *see* **Star Index I**
KIT HOLIDAY *see* **Star Index I**
KIT MARSEILLES *see* **Star Index I**
KITARO BABA *see* **Star Index I**
KITRA
Blue Vanities #512 / 1992 / FFL / M
KITSY STORME
The Good Girls Of Godiva High / 1979 / VCX / M
KITTEN
Black Cheerleader Search #09 / 1996 / IVC / M • Black Snatch #1 / 1996 / DFI / F • Booty Babes / 1993 / ROB / F • Butt Sluts #1 / 1993 / ROB / F • Dirty Girls / 1984 / MIT / M • Love Thrust / 1995 / ERA / M • Mistress Cherri's Basic (Slave) Training / 1992 / CAS / B • More Dirty Debutantes #61 / 1997 / SBV / M • Sex Stalker / 1983 / MPP / M • She-Male Friends #4 / cr94 / TTV / G • Student Fetish Videos: Bondage #03 / 1996 / PRE / B • Student Fetish Videos: Spanking #22 / 1996 / PRE / B • Student Fetish Videos: Tickling #13 / 1996 / SFV / B • Young & Natural #15 / 1996 / TV / F • Young & Natural #16 / 1996 / TV / F • Young & Natural #18 / 1996 / TV / C • Young & Natural #20 / 1996 / TV / F
KITTEN CREOLE
Cherry Poppin #01 / 1994 / CDY / M • Chocolate & Vanilla Twist / 1992 / PL / F • Debi Does Girls / 1992 / PL / F • Honey Drippers / 1992 / ROB / F • Kittens & Vamps #1 / 1993 / ROB / F • Lesbian Lockup / 1993 / ROB / F
KITTEN LOVE
Limited Edition #07 / 1979 / AVC / M
KITTEN NATIVIDAD *(Francesca Natividad, Frances Natividad, Lola Langusta, Kitty Nativy)*
Reasonably pretty face with humongous tits (natural). Fat in her later movies. Turns out in 1995 that her tits were not natural but "paid for" in 1979 by Russ Meyer with whom she lived for 15 years. Also, 47 years old in 1995 and started as a Hollywood stripper in the early seventies.
10 Years Of Big Busts #2 / 1990 / BTO / C • 40 The Hard Way / 1991 / OD / M • Airplane #2: The Sequel / 1982 / PAR / S • Another 48 Hours / 1990 / PAR / S • Bad Girls #4 / 1984 / GO / M • Bare-Chested, Bare-Breasted, Big-Busted, Wet T-Shirt Video / 1990 / NAP / B • Beneath The Valley Of The Ultra-Vixens / 1979 / RMV / S • The Best Little Whorehouse In Texas / 1982 / MCA / S • The Best Of Big Busty / 1986 / L&W / C • The Best Of The Big Boob Battles / 1993 / CDP / C • Big Boob Lottery / 1993 / BTO / M • Big Bust Babes #07 / 1991 / AFI / M • Big Bust Loops #15 / 1994 / SOW / M • Big Busty #03 / 1985 / CPL / S • Blue Vanities #125 / 1990 / FFL / M • Bodacious Ta Ta's / 1984 / CA / M • Breast Collection #01 / 1995 / LBO / C • Breast Worx #11 / 1991 / LBO / M • Breast Worx #30 / 1992 / LBO / M • Buford's Beach Bunnies / 1992 / IMP / S • Busen #01 / 1988 / L&W / M • Caballero Preview Tape #4 / 1985 / CA / C • Cum To Dinner / 1991 / HO / M • Deep Jaws / 1976 / SOW / S • Doin' Time / 1985 / WAR / S • Double D Dykes #01 / 1992 / GO / F • Eat At The Blue Fox / 1983 / VC / M • Electric Blue #005 / 1982 / CA / S • Enemates #07 /

1992 / PRE / B • Eroticise / 1982 / VES / S • An Evening With Kitten / 1993 / RHI / S • Exposure Images #04: Patty Plenty / 1992 / EXI / F • Famous Ta-Ta's #1 / 1986 / VCS / C • Faster, Kitten Natividad, Kill Kill! / 1995 / LCS / S • Fresh Tits Of Bel Air / 1992 / OD / M • The Girl I Want / 1990 / ... / S • Girls On Girls / 1983 / VC / F • The Gong Show Movie / 1980 / ... / S • Heel's Angels / 1995 / PRE / B • Honeymooned / 1992 / PRE / B • John Holmes And The All-Star Sex Queens / 1984 / AMB / M • Kitten Cums Back / 1995 / ... / M • La Cage Aux Zombies / 1995 / LCS / S • The Lady In Red / 1979 / VES / S • Leg...Ends #08 / 1993 / PRE / F • Let's Talk Sex / 1982 / CA / M • My Tutor / 1982 / MCA / S • Night Patrol / 1985 / NWW / S • Playboy: Inside Out #2 / 1992 / PLA / S • Raging Waters / 1992 / PRE / B • Red Lips / 1995 / VV1 / S • Seven Into Snowy / 1977 / VC / M • Sizzle / 1982 / JLT / S • The Slice / 1994 / ... / S • Spanking Scenes #01 / 1983 / TAO / C • Stiff Competition #1 / 1984 / CA / M • Stripper Of The Year / 1991 / MP / S • Super Enemates #1 / 1994 / PRE / C • Takin' It All Off / 1987 / VES / S • Takin' It Off / 1984 / VES / S • Taking Off / 1984 / VC / M • Talk Dirty To Me #02 / 1982 / CA / M • A Taste Of Julia Parton / 1992 / VD / C • Ten Little Maidens / 1985 / EXF / M • Thanks For The Mammaries / 1987 / CA / M • Titillation #1 / 1982 / SE / M • Titillation #3 / 1991 / SE / M • The Tomb / 1986 / TRW / S • Toppers #01 / 1992 / TV / F • Toppers #12 / 1993 / TV / C • Up! / 1976 / RMV / S • The Wild Life / 1984 / MCA / S • The Wild Wild Chest #3 / 1996 / HO / C • Wrestling Classics #2 / 1984 / CDP / B • [Body Shop / 1982 / ... / M • [Die Spalte / 1995 / ... / S • [Miss Burlesque U.S.A. / 19?? / ACV / M

KITTRA BERNSTEIN
Blue Vanities #581 / 1996 / FFL / M

KITTY
Anal Blues / 1994 / PEP / M • AVP #4000: Kitty's Bachelor Bang / 1990 / AVP / M • AVP #4001: Kitty Kitty Bang Bang / 1990 / AVP / M • AVP #4006: Any Cock'll Do / 1991 / AVP / M • AVP #4011: Dial-A-Dick / 1990 / AVP / M • AVP #6002: Bossed Around / 1990 / AVP / M • AVP #9107: Lust At First Sight / 1991 / AVP / M • Beach Bum Amateur's #39 / 1993 / MID / M • Blue Vanities #531 / 1993 / FFL / M • Brassiere To Eternity / 1994 / PEP / F • Bucky Beaver's XXX Dragon Art Theatre Double Feature #03 / 1996 / SOW / M • C-Hunt #03: Sunny Delights / 1995 / PEV / M • Dead Aim / 1994 / PEP / M • Dick & Jane In The Mountains / 1994 / AVI / M • Erotic Escape / 1995 / FH / M • Fresh Meat #1 / 1996 / PL / M • Invitation For Lust / 1995 / C69 / M • Kinky College Cunts #10 / 1993 / NS / M • Kitty's Bachelor Bang / 1990 / VAL / M • Lesbian Mystery Theatre: The Case Of The Deadly Dyke / 1994 / LIP / F • Neighbor Girls T35 / 1991 / NEI / F • Neighbor Girls T65 / 1993 / NEI / F • Pearl Necklace: Thee Bush League: The Best Of Oral #01 / 1993 / SEE / C • Pearl Necklace: Thee Bush League #09 / 1993 / SEE / M • School For Hookers / 1974 / SOW / M • So Bad / 1995 / VT / M • The Taming Of Kitty / 1996 / BON / B • Top Secret / 1995 / XHE / M • Up And Cummers: The Movie / 1994 / 4P / M • Wrasslin She-Babes #08 / 1996 / SOW / M •

Wrasslin She-Babes #09 / 1996 / SOW / M
KITTY (RHIANNON) *see* **Rhiannon**
KITTY (SAKI) *see* **Saki**
KITTY BLACK *see* **Star Index I**
KITTY BOXY
Final Exam #1 / 1987 / BON / B • Final Exam #2 / 1988 / BON / B
KITTY CARR *see* **Star Index I**
KITTY CAT
A&B AB#402: Cream Lovers / 1993 / A&B / C • Black Snatch #2 / 1996 / DFI / F • Dark Dreams / 1971 / ALP / M
KITTY CHANG *see* **Star Index I**
KITTY CREME *see* **Star Index I**
KITTY FOXX
50 And Still Gangbangin'! / 1995 / EMC / M • 50 And Still Pumping! / 1994 / EMC / M • A&B AB#484: Kitty's Desire #1 / 1995 / A&B / M • A&B AB#485: Kitty's Desire #2 / 1995 / A&B / M • A&B AB#486: Kitty Gets A Reaming #1 / 1995 / A&B / M • A&B AB#487: Kitty Gets A Reaming #2 / 1995 / A&B / M • Aged To Perfection #1 / 1994 / TTV / M • Aged To Perfection #2 / 1995 / TTV / M • Aged To Perfection #3 / 1995 / TTV / M • Anal Pandemonium / 1994 / TTV / M • Big Murray's New-Cummers #02: Las Vegas Swingers / 1992 / FD / M • Blue Bayou / 1993 / VC / M • Depraved Fantasies #3 / 1994 / FPI / M • Dirty Dating Service #05 / 1994 / WP / M • The Fabulous 50's Girls #1 / 1994 / EMC / M • The Fabulous 50's Girls Ride Again / 1994 / EMC / M • Fox Holes / 1995 / GLI / M • Foxx Tales / 1996 / TTV / M • Freaky Flix / 1995 / TTV / C • Golden Oldies #2 / 1995 / TTV / M • Horny Henry's Swinging Adventures / 1994 / TTV / M • House Of Sex #06: Banging Wendy, Kitty, Corby and Connie / 1994 / RTP / M • Kitty Foxx's Kinky Kapers #01 / 1995 / TTV / M • Kitty Foxx's Kinky Kapers #02 / 1995 / TTV / M • Kitty Foxx's Kinky Kapers #03 / 1995 / TTV / M • Kitty's Kinky Capers / 1996 / TTV / M • Meet Me In St. Louis / 1996 / VAL / M • Mike Hott: #276 Older Gals #5 / 1994 / MHV / M • Old Wives' Tails / 1995 / EMC / M • Older Women With Younger Men #2 / 1993 / CC / M • The Older Women's Sperm Bank #3: Red Hot Grandmas / 1996 / SUF / M • The Older Women's Sperm Bank #4 / 1996 / SUF / M • Oldies But Goodies / 1995 / WIV / M • Ooze: Cum Inside Kitty Fox / 1994 / RTP / M • Over 50 / 1994 / GLI / M • Positively Pagan #05 / 1993 / ATA / M • Raw Talent: Bang Kitty Foxx / 1994 / RTP / M • Sugar Mommies / 1995 / FPI / M • The Ultimate Climax / 1996 / EMC / M • The Ultimate Fantasy / 1995 / CV / M
KITTY KAT
Private School Girls / 1983 / CA / M
KITTY KELLY
Tight Tushies #1 / 1994 / SFP / M
KITTY KERBBY
Major Submission / 1996 / BON / B
KITTY KWAI
Tokohama Mamma / 1994 / ORE / C
KITTY LITTER
Toys, Not Boys #3 / 1991 / FC / C
KITTY LOREN
More To Love #1 / 1994 / TTV / M
KITTY LOVE *see* **Charisma**
KITTY LUV *see* **Charisma**
KITTY LYNN *see* **Star Index I**
KITTY MALONE *see* **Star Index I**
KITTY MONROE *(Verona Lake)*

Small pretty blonde with shoulder length platinum hair, 20 years old in 1995, de-virginized at 16, very tight waist, white body, nose ring in the left nostril, bubbly personality, nice laugh, small to medium slightly droopy tits, nice boy-like butt, shaven pussy, good skin. On reflection her tits are not that small in relation to the rest of her body.

Anal Angels / 1996 / PRE / B • Anal Delinquent #3 / 1995 / ROB / M • Anal Rippers #2: The Unveiling / 1996 / ZA / M • Anal Tight Ass / 1995 / ROB / M • Anal Virgins #01 / 1996 / NS / M • Ass Openers! #1 / 1995 / TCK / C • Bikini Beach #4 / 1996 / CC / M • Buttslammers #12: Anal Madness / 1996 / BS / F • Crunch Bunch / 1995 / PRE / C • Enemates #11 / 1995 / BIZ / B • Fashion Sluts #7 / 1996 / ABS / M • Flesh / 1996 / EA / M • Head To Head / 1996 / VI / M • Hot Tight Asses #14 / 1995 / TCK / M • Interview's Blonde Bombshells / 1995 / LV / M • Leg...Ends #16 / 1996 / PRE / F • More Dirty Debutantes #47 / 1995 / 4P / M • Nikki Loves Rocco / 1996 / VI / M • No Fear / 1996 / IN / F • Oral Addiction / 1995 / VI / M • Red Door Diaries #2 / 1996 / ZA / M • Sensations #2 / 1996 / SC / M • The Show / 1995 / VI / M • Spazm #1: Point Blank / 1996 / LBO / M • Toes 'n' Cons / 1996 / PRE / S • Video Virgins #24 / 1996 / NS / M • The Wicked Web / 1996 / WP / M • Young Girls Do #1: Troublemakers / 1995 / CDI / M
KITTY MOORE *see* **Star Index I**
KITTY NATIVY *see* **Kitten Natividad**
KITTY REYNOLDS *see* **Star Index I**
KITTY ROXY
Bondage Memories #03 / 1994 / BON / C
KITTY RYAN
The Farmer's Daughter / 1995 / TEG / M
KITTY SEEGER *see* **Star Index I**
KITTY SHANE *(Nicole O'Neal)*
Ugly and fat with huge enhanced tits, reddish-blonde hair and a very white body.

American Pie / 1980 / SE / M • Black 'n' White In Color / 1987 / VCR / C • Black Heat / 1986 / VCR / C • Blonde Fire / 1979 / EVI / M • Blue Confessions / 1983 / VCR / M • Blue Vanities #042 (New) / 1988 / FFL / M • California Gigolo / 1979 / WWV / M • Exhausted / 1981 / CA / C • Exposed / 1980 / SE / M • Extremes / 1981 / CA / M • Fantasy / 1978 / VCX / M • G...They're Big / 1981 / TGA / C • Only The Very Best On Film / 1992 / VC / C • Purely Physical / 1982 / SE / M • Ring Of Desire / 1981 / SE / M • Showgirl #14: Kitty Shane's Fantasies / 1983 / VCR / M • Three Ripening Cherries / 1979 / HIF / M • Tropic Of Desire / 1979 / WWV / M • Undulations / 1980 / VC / M
KITTY SINISI
How To Make A Model #01 / 1992 / MET / M
KITTY SUCKERMAN *(Deborah Kare)*
White blonde stringy hair, liquid eyes, hard boiled attitude, not so nice grin, medium tits, very white body. Deborah Kare comes from **High School Bunnies** but this could be her mother.

Breaker Beauties / 1977 / VHL / M • High School Bunnies / 1978 / VC / M
KITTY VICTUM
Delivered For Discipline / 1995 / BON / B • Mr. Parvo's Neighborhood / 1995 / BON / B • Orgy Of Cruelty / 1995 / BON / B • Orgy

Of Pain / 1995 / BON / B • Vagabondage / 1996 / B&D / B

KITTY WEST
Kat Fight At The Ok Korral / 199? / NAP / B

KITTY WILDCAT
A&B GB#047: Studs Party / 1992 / A&B / M • A&B GB#048: TV Repair / 1992 / A&B / M • Positively Pagan #11 / 1993 / ATA / M • Positively Pagan #12 / 1993 / ATA / M • Rump Humpers #06 / 1992 / GLI / M

KITTY YOUNG see Kitty Yung

KITTY YUN see Kitty Yung

KITTY YUNG *(Kitty Young, Ashley Young, Ashley Yung, Kitty Yun, Kathy Yung, Zana Que)*
Oriental looking with a flat face and tiny tits. Her rear end is also flat. 23 years old in 1993 and from Korea. Her nipples are inverted but pop out after a while. Supposedly de-virginized at 19. As of mid-1994 she has had her tits expanded to rock-hard cantaloupes.
A Is For Anal / 1993 / LV / M • America's Raunchiest Home Videos #63: / 1993 / ZA / M • American Swinger Video Magazine #05 / 1993 / ZA / M • Anal Alien / 1994 / CC / M • Anal Arsenal / 1994 / OD / M • Anal Asian #2: The Won-Ton Woman / 1994 / IN / M • Anal Delinquent #1 / 1993 / ROB / M • Anal Ecstacy Girls #2 / 1993 / ROB / F • Anal Hunger / 1994 / ROB / M • Anal Savage #2 / 1994 / ROB / M • Anal Secrets (After Dark) / 1994 / AFD / M • Anal Secrets (Metro) / 1994 / IN / M • Anal Vision #15 / 1993 / LBO / M • Anal Vision #18 / 1993 / LBO / M • Asian Appetite / 1993 / HO / M • Asian Heat #03: Tales Of The Golden Lotus / 1993 / SC / M • Asian Invasion / 1993 / IP / M • Ass Dweller / 1994 / WIV / M • Ass Freaks #1 / 1993 / ROB / F • The Ass Master #06 / 1994 / GLI / M • Ass Openers! #1 / 1995 / TCK / C • Backdoor To Taiwan / 1994 / LV / M • The Best Of Black Anal #1 / 1995 / ROB / C • The Best Of Buttslammers / 1995 / BS / C • The Best Of Oriental Anal #1 / 1994 / ROB / C • Biff Malibu's Totally Nasty Home Videos #40 / 1993 / ANA / M • Black Buttman #01 / 1993 / CC / M • Booty Ho #1 / 1993 / ROB / M • Brassiere To Eternity / 1994 / PEP / F • The Breast Of Breastmen / 1995 / EVN / C • Breastman Does The Twin Towers / 1993 / EVN / M • The Burma Road #1 / 1994 / LBO / C • The Burma Road #2 / 1994 / LBO / C • The Burma Road #3 / 1996 / LBO / C • Butt Sluts #2 / 1993 / ROB / F • Butt Whore / 1994 / WIV / M • Buttslammers #03: The Ultimate Dream / 1993 / BS / F • Cherry Poppers #03: School's Out / 1994 / ZA / M • Chow Down / 1994 / VI / M • A Clockwork Orgy / 1995 / PL / M • Coming Out / 1993 / VD / M • Crew Sluts / 1994 / KWP / M • Deep Cheeks #4 / 1993 / ROB / M • Deep Inside The Orient / 1993 / LV / M • Diary Of A Geisha / 1995 / WV / C • Double D Dykes #10 / 1993 / GO / F • Dr Rear / 1995 / CC / M • The Dragon Lady #6: Tales From The Bed #5 / 1993 / WV / M • Foolproof / 1994 / VC / M • Fortune Nookie / 1994 / PPP / M • Freak Dat Booty / 1994 / WP / M • From China With Love / 1993 / ZA / M • Gang Bang Bitches #04 / 1995 / PP / M • Gangbang Girl #12 / 1993 / ANA / M • Geranalmo / 1994 / PL / M • Go Ahead...Eat Me! / 1995 / KWP / M • Harry Horndog #20: Love Puppies #6 / 1993 / ZA

/ M • Hidden Camera #14 / 1994 / JMP / M • The Hitch-Hiker #04: Max Overdrive / 1994 / WMG / M • Hot Tight Asses #07 / 1994 / TCK / M • Hot Tight Asses #12 / 1995 / TCK / M • House Of The Rising Sun / 1993 / VT / M • In The Bush / 1994 / PP / M • Indecent Proposition / 1993 / LV / M • Jetstream / 1993 / AMP / M • Kinky Fantasies / 1994 / KWP / M • Kym Wilde's On The Edge #15 / 1994 / RB / B • The Last Action Whore / 1993 / LV / M • Let's Play Doctor / 1994 / PV / M • Lipstick Lesbians #1: Massage Parlor Dykes / 1994 / ZA / F • Luscious Lickin' Lesbians / 1995 / TIE / F • M Series #09 / 1993 / LBO / M • Midnight Angels #03 / 1993 / MID / F • Misty Rain's Anal Orgy / 1994 / FRM / M • Nasty Backdoor Nurses / 1994 / LBO / M • New Ends #02 / 1993 / 4P / M • The Nurses Are Cumming #1 / 1996 / LBO / C • Odyssey 30 Min: #318: Kitty Kitty Bang Bang / 1993 / OD / M • Odyssey 30 Min: #322: Oriental Pin Up Session / 1993 / OD / M • Odyssey 30 Min: #346: Kitty, Silky, and Studz / 1993 / OD / M • Odyssey Triple Play #63: Orient Express / 1994 / OD / M • Odyssey Triple Play #73: Oriental Sexpress / 1994 / OD / M • Odyssey Triple Play #95: Conjugal Couples #2 / 1995 / OD / M • Older Men With Younger Women #2 / 1994 / CC / M • Once Upon An Anus / 1993 / LV / M • Other People's Pussy / 1993 / LV / M • Pai Gow Video #03: Egg Foo Kitty Yung / 1993 / EVN / M • Pearl Necklace: Thee Bush League #25 / 1993 / SEE / M • Private Film #11 / 1994 / OD / M • Private Film #12 / 1994 / OD / M • Private Film #13 / 1994 / OD / M • Private Film #14 / 1994 / OD / M • Private Film #16 / 1994 / OD / M • Private Film #18 / 1994 / OD / M • Private Video Magazine #09 / 1994 / OD / M • Private Video Magazine #10 / 1994 / OD / M • Private Video Magazine #11 / 1994 / OD / M • Private Video Magazine #12 / 1994 / OD / M • Private Video Magazine #14 / 1994 / OD / M • Private Video Magazine #15 / 1994 / OD / M • Private Video Magazine #17 / 1994 / OD / M • Pussyman #07: On The Dark Side / 1994 / SNA / M • Racially Motivated / 1994 / LV / M • Rainwoman #07: In The Rainforest / 1993 / CC / M • Rainwoman #08 / 1994 / CC / M • The Real Story Of Tonya & Nancy / 1994 / EX / M • The Reel Sex World #02 / 1994 / WP / M • Rising Buns / 1993 / HW / M • Sarah Jane's Love Bunnies #03 / 1993 / FPI / F • Sex Machine / 1994 / VT / M • Sex Party / 1995 / KWP / M • Slave To Love / 1993 / ROB / M • Sleeping With Seattle / 1993 / LV / M • Smooth As Silk / 1994 / EMC / M • Sniff Doggy Style / 1994 / PL / M • Sodomania #05: Euro-American Style / 1993 / EL / M • Sodomania: The Baddest Of The Best...And Then Some / 1994 / EL / C • Split Decision / 1993 / FD / M • Sticky Lips / 1993 / EX / M • Super Hornio Brothers #1 / 1993 / MID / M • Sushi Butts / 1994 / SCL / M • SVE: Screentest Sex #4 / 1993 / SVE / M • Up And Cummers #01 / 1993 / 4P / M • Wet Silk #1 / 1995 / SC / C • What's Butt Got To Do With It? / 1993 / HW / M

KIVA
Bright Tails #2 / 1994 / STP / B • Colours De Kiva / 1995 / KPC / F • Completely Kiva / 1994 / KPC / F • Confidentially Kiva / 1994 / KPC / F • Dark Alleys #28 / 1994 / FC / M

• Hidden Camera #13 / 1994 / JMP / M • Kiva Corrected / 1994 / KPC / B • Kiva Vision / 1995 / KPC / M • Kiva's Creme A La Mode / 1994 / XPR / M • Let's Talk Anal / 1996 / ESF / M • New Faces, Hot Bodies #12 / 1993 / STP / M • New Faces, Hot Bodies #16 / 1994 / STP / M • The New Snatch Masters #21 / 1996 / LEI / C • Porn Star Confidential / 1996 / ESF / M • Toy Time #2: Nasty Solos / 1994 / STP / F

KJIRSTY OLSEN
Sex Over 40 #1 / 1994 / PL / M • Sex Over 40 #2 / 1994 / PL / M

KLARA BOROCZAY
True Stories #1 / 1993 / SC / M • True Stories #2 / 1993 / SC / M

KLARA KINOSKI
Casting Call #12 / 1995 / MET / M • Max #05: The Harder They Fall / 1995 / FRM / M

KLAUS BONZO
Take Me #8: For The Night / 1995 / VIO / M

KLAUS BRANDT see Star Index I

KLAUS DORTMUND see Star Index I

KLAUS JURICHS
The Young Seducers / 1971 / BL / M

KLAUS KLASSEN see Star Index I

KLAUS MULTIA
Dirty Blonde / 1984 / VXP / M • Femme / 1984 / VC / M • Good Girl, Bad Girl / 1984 / SE / M • Hostage Girls / 1984 / VC / M • Inside Little Oral Annie / 1984 / VXP / M • Little Oral Annie Takes Manhattan / 1985 / VXP / M • Make Me Feel It / 1984 / SE / M • Sex Spa USA / 1984 / VC / M • Turn On With Kelly Nichols / 1984 / CA / M • Urban Heat / 1985 / FEM / M

KLAUS MUNSTER
[Junge Madchen Mogen's HeiB, Hausfrauen Noch HeiBer / 1973 / ... / M

KLYN TAME
Kym Wilde's On The Edge #21 / 1995 / RB / B

KNAH-KNAH
Whatever Happened To Miss September? / 1973 / ALP / M

KNICK HOLIDAY
Internal Affairs / 1995 / VI / M

KNUD JORGENSEN
Practice Makes Perfect / 1975 / QX / M • The Second Coming Of Eva / 1974 / ALP / M

KNUD JORGENSON
Erotic Fantasies #1 / 1983 / CV / C

KNUMA SHIGCKI
The Sex Specialist / 1996 / AVV / M

KOBE TAI see Blake Young

KODA YOUKO
Lustful Angel / 1996 / AVV / M

KOHL MYNA
Black Talez N Da Hood / 1996 / APP / M

KOKO
The Black Butt Sisters Do Philadelphia / 1995 / MID / M • Koko Is Cumin' At Cha / 1994 / AVI / M

KOKO MOTION see Star Index I

KOKOA
Black Analyst #2 / 1995 / VEX / M

KOLTAI OLIVER
Sirens / 1995 / GOU / M

KONG see Darryl Edwards

KOPPANY LAZAR
Sirens / 1995 / GOU / M

KORA see Alicia Rio

KORLOVSZKY TAMAS
Sirens / 1995 / GOU / M

KOURTNEY VAN WALES
Chicks With Dicks #2 / 1996 / BIZ / B • She-Males In Torment #2 / 1992 / BIZ / G • Steel Garters / 1992 / CAT / G • Stick Pussy / 1992 / HSV / G • Transsexual Dynasty / 1996 / BIZ / G • TV Blondes Do It Best / 1992 / BIZ / G • TV Dildo Fantasy #1 / 1992 / BIZ / G • TV Ladies Room / 1993 / BIZ / G • TV Reform School / 1992 / BIZ / G • TV Room / 1993 / BIZ / G • TVs Teased And Tormented / 1995 / BIZ / G

KRATE W.
Foreign Exchange Sluts / 1995 / TNT / M

KRAYOLA BLUE *see* **Crayola Blue**

KRESTEN BOYD *see* **Tina Ross**

KRIMSON
Dream's House Party / 1995 / HW / M • Forbidden Subjects #2 / 1994 / FC / M • Latin Plump Humpers #1 / 1995 / TTV / M • Latin Plump Humpers #2 / 1995 / TTV / M • Muffmania / 1995 / TTV / M • Shades Of Color #2 / 1995 / LBO / M

KRIS
Girls Next Door / 1996 / ANE / M • Home-Grown Video #462: Motion In The Backfield / 1995 / HOV / M

KRIS AGUILAR
Marco Polo / 1995 / SC / M

KRIS KLARK *see* **Christophe Clark**

KRIS MONROE
Sex Boat / 1980 / VCX / M

KRIS NEWZ *(Peter Newz, Peter House, Chris News, Chris Knews)*
Spindly English male who started appearing at the same time as Kiss and was presumably her SO but in her 1995/6 appearance seems to have been replaced by Jeremy Joshua.
Anal Vision #01 / 1992 / LBO / M • Anal Vision #12 / 1993 / LBO / M • Bare Market / 1993 / VC / M • Beach Bum Amateur's #19 / 1992 / MID / M • The Big One / 1992 / GO / M • Bringing Up The Rear / 1993 / VD / C • The British Are Coming / 1993 / ZA / M • Brother Act / 1992 / PL / M • Butt Bongo Babes / 1993 / VD / M • Casting Call #01 / 1993 / SO / M • Charm School / 1993 / PEP / M • Cheeks #6 / 1992 / CC / M • Deep Inside Nicole London / 1995 / VC / C • The Dirtiest Girl In The World / 1992 / ZA / M • Double Impact / 1992 / CDI / G • Double Penetration #5 / 1992 / WV / C • Dripping With Desire / 1992 / DR / M • Face Dance #1 / 1992 / EA / M • Face Dance #2 / 1992 / EA / M • Faithless Companions / 1992 / WV / M • A Few Good Rears / 1993 / IN / M • Group Therapy / 1992 / TP / M • Harry Horndog #08: Anal Lovers #1 / 1992 / ZA / M • Harry Horndog #11: Love Puppies / 1992 / ZA / M • Head Lines / 1992 / SC / M • I Made Marian / 1993 / PEP / M • Kiss Is A Rebel With A Cause / 1993 / WV / M • More Than A Handful #2 / 1993 / MET / M • My Secret Lover / 1992 / XCI / M • Nobody's Looking / 1993 / VC / M • Odyssey Triple Play #43: Anal Creaming & Reaming / 1993 / OD / M • On The Come Line / 1993 / MID / M • Oral Majority #12 / 1994 / WV / C • Outlaws / 1993 / SC / M • Private Stories #05 / 1995 / OD / M • Private Video Magazine #21 / 1995 / OD / M • Private Video Magazine #22 / 1995 / OD / M • A Pussy Called Wanda #2 / 1992 / DR / M • The Queen Of Mean / 1992 / FC / M • Radical Affairs Video Magazine #03 / 1992 / ME / M • Realities #2 / 1992 / ZA / M • Revealed / 1992 / VT / M • The Sex Connec-

tion / 1993 / VC / M • Sex Heist / 1992 / WV / M • Sexcalibur / 1992 / FD / M • A Shaver Among Us / 1992 / ZA / M • The Spa / 1993 / VC / M • Tailspin #3 / 1992 / VT / M • Talk Dirty To Me #09 / 1992 / DR / M • Tight Pucker / 1992 / WV / M • Twin Freaks / 1992 / ZA / M • Unfaithful Entry / 1992 / DR / M • Working Stiffs / 1993 / FD / M

KRIS SMITH
Pleasure Productions #07 / 1984 / VCR / M

KRIS TAYLOR
Please Don't Tell / 1995 / CEN / G

KRIS WARE
Baby Doll / 1975 / AR / M

KRISS KLARK *see* **Christophe Clark**

KRISSE ORCHIDE *see* **Star Index I**

KRISSY
A&B AB#192: Home Shopping Club / 1990 / A&B / M • A&B AB#230: Krissy / 1990 / A&B / M • Hot Body Video Magazine #08 / 1994 / CG / S

KRISTA *(H.C., Casey (Krista), K.C. Hall, Krista Hall)*
Blonde with enhanced hard cantaloupes (see below) but otherwise nice, if big, body. Facially has a resemblence to Nikki Dial. Born Aug 10, 1971 (22 in 1993), 5'3" tall, 104lbs, 36C-24-34. Industry sources say she has natural tits and is short and small. Without actually touching, feeling, squeezing and checking for minute scars and doing a mammogram this is unverifiable—you can't rely on her word, and she's hardly likely to allow yours truly to do this probing much as I would enjoy it. The reason for the difference is that big and enhanced is how she appears ON SCREEN in relation to the other actresses (maybe they're all midgets) and, after all, that's what counts to you the viewer. Further the "big" indicates a fleshy body rather than height—you'll notice I give the height and weight—but I'll agree that perhaps the statement was rash. Married to a guy named Roy, 23 years old, with a four year old child (as of 1995).
10,000 Anal Maniacs #1 / 1993 / FOR / M • The Adventures Of Mr. Tootsie Pole #2 / 1995 / LBO / M • All The President's Women / 1994 / LV / M • Anal Asian #2: The Won-Ton Woman / 1994 / IN / M • The Best Of Sean Michaels / 1994 / VT / C • The Bet / 1993 / VT / M • Big Knockers #01 / 1994 / TV / M • The Big Pink / 1995 / MID / M • Black Detail #1 / 1994 / VT / M • Black Detail #2 / 1994 / VT / M • Blinded By Love / 1993 / OD / M • Blow Job Baby / 1993 / CC / M • Bob's Video #101: City Of Angels / 1996 / BOV / F • Bra Busters #03 / 1993 / LBO / M • Brassiere To Eternity / 1994 / PEP / F • Breast Collection #04 / 1995 / LBO / C • The Butt Sisters Do Las Vegas / 1994 / MID / M • C-Hunt #02: Hot Pockets / 1995 / PEV / M • Caged Beauty / 1994 / FD / M • Caged Fury / 1993 / DR / M • Cherry Cheeks / 1993 / CA / M • Chug-A-Lug Girls #2 / 1993 / VT / M • Chug-A-Lug Girls #3 / 1993 / VT / M • Chug-A-Lug Girls #4 / 1994 / VT / M • Chug-A-Lug Girls #5 / 1994 / VT / M • Cinesex #1 / 1995 / CV / M • Cinesex #2 / 1994 / CV / M • Club Anal #2 / 1993 / ROB / F • Coming Of Age / 1995 / VEX / C • Controlled / 1994 / FD / M • The Corner / 1994 / VT / M • Delicious Passions / 1993 / ROB / F • Dick & Jane Go To Hollywood #1 / 1993 / AVI / M • Dick & Jane Go To Hollywood #2 / 1993 / AVI / M • Dirty

Bob's #11: Vegas Blues #1 / 1994 / FLP / S • Dirty Bob's #12: Vegas Blues #2 / 1994 / FLP / S • Dirty Bob's #17: Tampa Teasers! / 1994 / FLP / S • Dirty Bob's #18: Under The Boardwalk! / 1995 / FLP / S • Dirty Bob's #19: Over The Boardwalk! / 1995 / FLP / S • Dirty Bob's #23: Tampa Teasers / 1995 / FLP / S • Dirty Doc's Housecalls #13 / 1994 / LV / M • Double Crossed / 1994 / MID / M • Dr Feelgood Sex Psychiatrist / 1994 / LV / M • Eight Is Never Enough / 1993 / ZA / M • Erotic Newcummers Vol 1 #2: Texas Twisters / 1993 / DR / M • The Farmer's Daughters / 1994 / LV / M • The Finishing Touch / 1994 / DR / M • Flesh Shopping Network #1 / 1995 / MID / M • Full Moon Fever / 1994 / LBO / M • Fundgeon Of The Mind #1 / 1994 / BON / B • Gangbang Sluts / 1994 / VMX / M • The Great Pretenders / 1994 / FD / M • Hexxxed / 1994 / VT / M • Horny Henry's Peeping Adventures / 1994 / TTV / M • Hot Wishes / 1995 / LE / M • Hotel Sodom #04: Free Parking In Rear / 1995 / SNA / M • Hotel Sodom #10 / 1996 / SNA / M • In The Bush / 1994 / PP / M • Kittens #5 / 1994 / CC / F • Love Doll Lucy #1 / 1994 / PL / F • Love Doll Lucy #2 / 1994 / PL / F • M Series #14 / 1993 / LBO / M • Mike Hott: #243 Cunt of the Month: Krista / 1993 / MHV / M • The Mistress (1993-Caballero) / 1993 / CA / M • Molly B-Goode / 1994 / FH / M • Naked Scandal #1 / 1995 / SPI / M • Naked Scandal #2 / 1996 / SPI / M • Nasty Fuckin' Movies #21 / 1994 / RUM / F • Nasty Nymphos #01 / 1993 / ANA / M • Nasty Thoughts / 1994 / ... / M • The Natural / 1993 / VT / M • Neighbor Girls T66 / 1993 / NEI / F • No Man's Land #07 / 1993 / VT / F • No Man's Land #09 / 1994 / VT / F • No Man's Land #10 / 1994 / VT / F • Pajama Party X #3 / 1994 / VC / M • Paradise Found / 1995 / LE / M • Paradise Lost / 1995 / LE / M • Pearl Necklace: Amorous Amateurs #39 / 1993 / SEE / M • Pearl Necklace: Thee Bush League #26 / 1993 / SEE / M • Photo Opportunity / 1994 / VC / M • The Pleasure Girl / 1994 / GO / M • Pussy Hunt #05 / 1994 / LEI / M • Raw Sex #01 / 1994 / ERW / M • Reel Life Video #11 / 1994 / RLF / M • Reel Life Video #16 / 1994 / RLF / M • Selina / 1993 / XCI / M • Sex Detective / 1994 / LV / M • Sexual Healing / 1994 / VI / M • Seymore & Shane On The Loose / 1994 / ULI / M • Shades Of Lust / 1993 / TP / M • Simply Kia / 1994 / LE / M • Sleaze Please!—August Edition / 1994 / FH / M • Sleaze Please!—September Edition / 1994 / FH / M • Soft Bodies: Pillow Talk / 1992 / SB / F • The Star / 1994 / HO / M • The Star / 1995 / CC / M • Superstar Sex Challenge #3 / 1994 / VC / M • Tales From The Clit / 1993 / OD / M • Tech: Krista #1 / 1994 / TWA / F • Tech: Krista #2 / 1994 / TWA / F • Titanic Orgy / 1995 / PEP / M • Toppers #28 / 1994 / TV / M • Toppers #29 / 1994 / TV / M • Toppers #31 / 1994 / TV / C • Toppers #32 / 1994 / TV / C • Uninhibited Love / 1994 / VPN / M • Up And Cummers #03 / 1993 / 4P / M • Up And Cummers: The Movie / 1994 / 4P / M • Vagablonde / 1994 / VI / M • The Wacky World Of Ed Powers / 1996 / 4P / C • Whispered Lies / 1993 / LBO / M • White Shadow / 1994 / VC / M • Wild & Wicked #4 / 1994 / VT / M

KRISTA HALL see **Krista**

KRISTA HUBER
Viola Video #105: / 1995 / PEV / M

KRISTA LANE (Cameron, Rebecca Lynn, Cameron Sims, Crystal Lane (KL), Kari Sims)
The Adultress / 1987 / CA / M • All For His Ladies / 1987 / PP / C • Amanda By Night #2 / 1987 / CA / M • And I Do Windows Too / 1986 / PP / M • The Art Of Passion / 1987 / CA / M • The Bare Truth / 1994 / FD / C • Behind Blue Eyes #1 / 1986 / ME / M • The Best Little Whorehouse In Hong Kong / 1987 / SE / M • Bi-Heat #06 / 1987 / ZA / G • Bi-Heat #08 / 1988 / ZA / G • Bi-Heat #08 To #10 / 1988 / ZA / G • Bi-Heat #09 / 1988 / ZA / G • Bi-Heat #10 / 1988 / ZA / G • The Bitches Of Westwood / 1987 / CA / M • Blame It On Ginger / 1986 / VI / M • Born To Burn / 1987 / HOT / M • Born To Run / 1985 / WV / M • The Boss / 1987 / FAN / M • The Brat / 1986 / VI / M • Breakin' All The Rules / 1987 / SE / M • Cabaret Sin / 1987 / IN / M • Caddy Shack-Up / 1986 / VD / M • Captain Hooker & Peter Porn / 1987 / VD / M • Careena #1 / 1987 / WV / C • Careena #2: A Star On The Rise / 1988 / WV / C • Cat Alley / 1986 / AVC / M • Charmed Forces / 1987 / VI / M • Classic Pics / 1988 / PP / C • Club Bed / 1987 / CIX / M • Club Ginger / 1986 / VI / M • Days Gone Bi / 1988 / ZA / G • Debbie Goes To Hawaii / 1988 / VD / C • Deep Inside Trading / 1986 / AR / M • Deep Inside Vanessa Del Rio / 1986 / VC / M • Deep Throat #2 / 1986 / AR / M • Devil In Miss Jones #4: The Final Outrage / 1987 / VC / M • Dial A Dick / 1986 / AVC / M • Diamond Head / 1987 / AVC / M • Dirty Harriet / 1986 / SAT / M • Dirty Pictures / 1988 / CA / M • Double Penetration #1 / 1985 / WV / M • Dressed To Thrill / 1986 / CDI / M • Easy Lovers / 1987 / SE / M • The Eleventh Commandment / 1987 / WAV / M • Empire Of The Sins / 1988 / IN / M • Erotic Therapy / 1987 / CDI / M • Escort To Ecstasy / 1987 / 3HV / M • Fantasy Chamber / 1987 / VT / M • Farmers Daughters / 1985 / WV / M • Fatal Erection 1988 / SEV / M • Forbidden Bodies / 1986 / HU / M • Free Ride / 1986 / LIV / S • Ginger Does Them All / 1988 / CV / M • The Girls Of Rodeo Drive / 1987 / BAD / M • Girls On Girls / 1987 / SE / C • The Greatest American Blonde / 1987 / WV / C • Grind / 1988 / CV / M • Hard Choices / 1987 / CA / M • Head Clinic / 1987 / AVC / M • Honeybuns #1 / 1987 / WV / C • Hot Gun / 1986 / CA / M • Hottest Ticket / 1987 / WV / C • In Search Of The Golden Bone / 1986 / CA / M • In Search Of The Perfect 10 / 1987 / MAE / S • In Search Of The Wild Beaver / 1986 / DR / M • Jane Bond Meets The Man With The Golden Rod / 1987 / VD / M • Jane Bond Meets Thunderballs / 1986 / VD / M • Kinky / 1987 / SE / M • L.A. Raw / 1986 / SE / M • The Ladies Room / 1987 / CA / M • Les Be Friends / 1988 / WV / C • Lethal Woman #1 / 1988 / SEV / M • Lethal Woman #2 / 1988 / SEV / M • Lingerie Party / 1987 / SE / C • The Load Warriors #1 / 1987 / VD / M • Love On The Borderline / 1987 / IN / M • Lucky Charm / 1986 / AVC / C • Lust At Sea / 1986 / VD / M • The Lust Potion Of Doctor F / 1985 / WV / M • Mad Jack Beyond Thunderdome / 1986 / WET / M • Mammary Lane / 1988 / VT / C

• Mantrap / 1986 / BAN / M • Memoirs Of A Chambermaid / 1987 / FIR / M • Nasty Dancing / 1989 / VEX / M • Nasty Girls #1 (1989-Plum) / 1989 / PP / C • Naughty Ninja Girls / 1987 / LA / M • Nina Does 'em All / 1988 / 3HV / C • No Man's Land #01 / 1988 / VT / C • Nudes At Eleven #2 / 1987 / AVC / M • On The Loose & Hot To Trot / 1987 / CA / M • Only The Best Of Girls With Curves / 1992 / CV / C • Oral Majority #03 / 1986 / WV / C • The Other Side Of Pleasure / 1987 / SEV / M • Parliament: Dildo Babes #1 / 1986 / PM / F • Parliament: Finger Friggin' #1 / 1986 / PM / F • Parliament: Lesbian Lovers #1 / 1986 / PM / F • Parliament: Lonesome Ladies #2 / 1985 / PM / F • Parliament: Three Way Lust / 1988 / PM / M • Parliament: Tip Top #1 / 1986 / PM / F • Portrait Of An Affair / 1988 / VD / M • Princess Of Penetration / 1988 / VXP / M • Raging Hormones / 1988 / VXP / M • Ramb-Ohh #1 / 1986 / PV / M • The Right Tool For The Job / 1988 / VXP / M • Robofox #1 / 1987 / FAN / M • Rubber Reamed Fuckholes / 1994 / MET / C • Screwdriver / 1988 / CC / C • Seduction By Fire / 1987 / VD / M • Sensations / 1987 / AE / S • Sex Beat / 1985 / WV / M • Sextrology / 1987 / CA / M • Sexy And 18 / 1987 / SE / M • Sexy Delights #2 / 1987 / CLV / M • Sins Of The Wealthy #1 / 1986 / CLV / M • Sins Of The Wealthy #2 / 1986 / CLV / M • Sky Foxes / 1987 / VC / M • Sophisticated Women / 1986 / BAN / M • Spies / 1986 / PL / M • A Sticky Situation / 1987 / CA / M • Strictly Business / 1987 / VD / M • Submissive Women / 1989 / ... / C • Sunset Strip / 1991 / PME / S • Suzie Superstar...The Search Continues / 1988 / CV / M • Sweat #2 / 1988 / PP / M • Taboo #06 / 1988 / IN / M • Take It Off / 1986 / TIF / M • Tales Of Taija Rae / 1989 / DR / M • Talk Dirty to Me One More Time #2 / 1988 / PP / C • A Taste Of Alexa / 1989 / PIN / C • A Tasty Kind Of Love / 1987 / LV / M • Thrilled To Death / 1988 / REP / S • Tight End / 1988 / VXP / M • Toys 4 Us #2 / 1987 / WV / C • Traci Who? / 1987 / AVC / C • Tunnel Of Love / 1986 / CLV / M • Two To Tango / 1987 / TEM / M • Unveiled / 1987 / VC / M • VCA Previews #4 / 1988 / VC / C • Wet 'n' Bare With Barbara Dare / 1988 / NEO / C • Wet Wonderland / 1988 / VEX / M • Whatever Turns You On / 1987 / CA / M • Wishbone / 1988 / VXP / M • [T&A #01 / 1989 / ... / C

KRISTA MAYES see **Krista Maze**
KRISTA MAYS see **Krista Maze**
KRISTA MAZE (Krista Mays, Krista Mayes, Krysta White)
Pretty dark blonde with reddish overtones, long straight hair, small to medium natural tits, tight waist, belly button ring, bit flat on the butt. 22 years old and 34-24-34 in 1995. Has had tits enhanced to medium size and put on some weight in late 1996.
Babenet / 1995 / VC / M • Body Language / 1995 / VI / M • The Butt Sisters Do Philadelphia / 1995 / MID / M • The Comix / 1995 / VI / M • Country Girl / 1996 / VC / M • Dangerous Games / 1995 / VI / M • Dear Diary / 1995 / WP / M • Diary Of A Mistress / 1995 / HOM / B • Director's Wet Dreams / 1996 / BBE / M • Domination Nation / 1996 / VI / M • Erotic Visions / 1995 / ULI / M • Eternal Lust / 1996 / VC / M •

Every Woman Has A Fantasy #3 / 1995 / VC / M • Face Jam / 1996 / VC / M • Hotel Fantasy / 1995 / IN / M • The House On Chasey Lane / 1995 / VI / M • Irresistible / 1995 / LV / M • Island Of Lust / 1995 / XCI / M • More Dirty Debutantes #34 / 1994 / 4P / M • Muff Divers #3 / 1996 / TV / F • Nothing Like A Dame #2 / 1995 / IN / M • Party Girl / 1995 / LV / M • The Passion Potion / 1995 / WP / M • Priceless / 1995 / WP / M • Raw Footage / 1996 / VC / M • The Show / 1995 / VI / M • Show & Tell / 1996 / VI / M • Sinister Sister / 1997 / WP / M • Sorority Sex Kittens #3 / 1996 / VC / M • The Superhawk Girls...And Their Fabulous Toys / 1996 / GLI / F • Sweet Revenge / 1997 / KBE / M • Takin' It To The Limit #9: Rear Action View / 1996 / BS / M • Vibrating Vixens #1 / 1996 / TV / F • Young & Natural #03 / 1995 / PRE / F • Young & Natural #05 / 1995 / PRE / F • Young & Natural #07 / 1995 / PRE / F • Young & Natural #08 / 1995 / PRE / F • Young & Natural #09 / 1995 / PRE / C

KRISTA RAIN see **Christa Rain**

KRISTA TAYLOR
Bound For Cash / 1994 / SBP / B

KRISTAL ROSE see **Star Index I**

KRISTALL see **Jenna Wells**

KRISTARA BARRINGTON (Kim Barrington, China Lee, Kim Morgan, Kim Kwan, Cristara Barrington, Christie Barrington, Kimberly Morgan, Kimberly Wong)
Not too pretty, hard Oriental. First movie was **Every Woman Has A Fantasy.**
1001 Erotic Nights #2 / 1987 / VC / M • All In The Family / 1985 / VCR / M • Another Kind Of Love / 1985 / CV / M • Aroused / 1985 / VIV / M • B.Y.O.B. / 1984 / VD / M • Baby Face #2 / 1987 / VC / M • Bachelor's Paradise / 1986 / VEX / M • Backing In #2 / 1990 / WV / C • Bad Girls #3 / 1984 / COL / M • Battle Of The Stars #2: East Versus West / 1985 / NSV / M • Battle Of The Stars #3: Stud Wars / 1985 / NSV / M • Beaverly Hills Cop / 1985 / SE / M • Best Of Caught From Behind #1 / 1987 / HO / C • Beverly Hills Copulator / 1986 / ... / M • Beyond Desire / 1986 / VC / M • The Big Bang / 1988 / WET / M • Big Gulp #2 / 1987 / VIP / C • Billionaire Girls Club / 1988 / LVI / C • Bionic Babes / 1986 / 4P / M • Black To The Future / 1986 / VD / M • Black Valley Girls #1 / 1986 / 4R / M • Blacks & Blondes #15 / 1986 / WV / M • Blue Vanities #195 / 1993 / FFL / M • Boobs, Butts And Bloopers #2 / 1990 / HO / M • Broadcast Nudes / 1988 / EVN / M • Cabaret Sin / 1987 / IN / M • Caught From Behind #03 / 1985 / HO / M • Chicks In Black Leather / 1989 / VC / C • China & Silk / 1984 / MAP / M • Circus Acts / 1987 / SE / C • Coming Together / 1984 / CA / M • Country Girl / 1985 / AVC / M • Crazy With The Heat #1 / 1986 / CV / M • Cum Shot Revue #2 / 1985 / HO / C • Cum Shot Revue #3 / 1988 / HO / C • Cum Shot Revue #5 / 1988 / HO / C • Dark Side Of The Moon / 1986 / VD / M • Debbie Does Dallas #3 / 1985 / VC / M • Deep & Wet / 1986 / VD / M • Deep Chill / cr85 / AT / M • Deliveries In The Rear #1 / 1985 / AVC / M • Detroit Dames / 1988 / DR / C • Devil In Miss Jones #4: The Final Outrage / 1987 / VC / M • Dirty Dreams / 1987 / CA / M • Double Standards / 1986 / VC / M • Double

Trouble / 1986 / DRV / M • Dr Strange Sex / 1985 / CA / M • The Dragon Lady #1 / 1988 / WV / C • Dream Girls / 1986 / VC / M • Dressed To Thrill / 1986 / CDI / M • The Ecstasy Girls #2 / 1986 / CA / M • Educating Eva / 1984 / VC / M • Electric Blue #011 / 1983 / CA / S • Electric Blue: World Nudes Tonight / 1985 / CA / C • Empire Of The Sins / 1988 / IN / M • Erotic Aerobics / 1984 / VC / M • Every Man's Fantasy / 1985 / IN / M • Every Woman Has A Fantasy #1 / 1984 / VC / M • Fallen Angels / 1983 / VES / M • Fire In The Hole / 1989 / ... / C • Firefoxes / 1985 / PLY / M • Flash Trance / 1985 / IVP / M • Flesh For Fantasies / 1986 / TAM / M • Formula 69 / 1984 / JVV / M • Fortune Cookie Nookie / 1986 / VCS / C • Free And Foxy / 1986 / VCX / C • Getting LA'd / 1986 / PV / M • Ginger (1984-Vivid) / 1984 / VI / M • The Ginger Effect / 1985 / VI / M • Girl Games / 1987 / PL / C • Girls On Girls / 1987 / SE / C • Girls That Love Girls / 1984 / CA / F • Give It To Me / 1984 / SE / M • Glamour Girl #1 / 1984 / CDI / M • Golden Girls #29 / 1985 / CA / M • Golden Girls #30 / 1985 / CA / M • Grand Opening / 1985 / AT / M • Headhunters / 1984 / VC / M • The Heat Is On / 1985 / WV / M • Hidden Fantasies / 1986 / VD / M • Hill Street Blacks #1 / 1985 / 4R / M • Hooters / 1986 / AVC / M • Hot Bodies (Ventura) / 1984 / VEN / C • Hot Flashes / 1984 / VC / M • Hot Licks / 1984 / SE / M • Hot Sweet Honey / 1985 / VEP / M • Hottest Parties / 1988 / VC / C • The Hottest Show In Town / 1987 / VIP / M • House Of Lust / 1984 / VD / M • I Know What Girls Like / 1986 / WET / G • I Love A Girl In A Uniform / 1989 / VC / C • Inside China Lee / 1984 / VC / M • Jailhouse Girls / 1984 / VC / M • Jane Bond Meets Octopussy / 1986 / VD / M • Jawbreakers / 1985 / VEN / C • The Joy-Stick Girls / 1986 / CLV / M • Jubilee Of Eroticism / 1985 / GO / M • Kinky Business #1 / 1984 / DR / M • Kiss Of The Married Woman / 1986 / WV / M • Legends Of Porn #2 / 1989 / CV / C • Lessons With My Aunt / 1986 / SHO / M • Limited Edition #27 / 1984 / AVC / M • Limited Edition #28 / 1984 / AVC / M • Lip Service / 1987 / BIK / C • Little Girls Talking Dirty / 1984 / VCX / M • Little Often Annie / 1984 / VC / M • Long Hard Nights / 1984 / ELH / M • Loose Morals / 1987 / HO / M • Losing Control / 1985 / CDI / M • The Loves Of Lolita / 1984 / VC / M • Loving Spoonfulls / 1987 / 4P / C • Lust Bug / 1985 / HO / M • Lust With The Stranger / 1986 / MAP / M • Lusty Adventurer / 1985 / GO / M • Make Me Feel It / 1984 / SE / M • New Wave Hookers #1 / 1984 / VC / M • Nice 'n' Tight / 1985 / AIR / M • One Night In Bangkok / 1985 / CA / M • Oral Majority #07 / 1987 / WV / C • Oriental Jade / 1985 / VC / M • Oriental Lesbian Fantasies / 1984 / PL / F • Oriental Lust / 1983 / GO / M • Parliament: Dildo Babes #1 / 1986 / PM / F • Parliament: Finger Friggin' #1 / 1986 / PM / F • Parliament: Geisha Girls #1 / 1986 / PM / F • Parliament: Lesbian Lovers #2 / 1988 / PM / F • Parliament: Lonesome Ladies #2 / 1985 / PM / F • Parliament: Teasers #2 / 1988 / PM / F • Parliament: Woman's Touch / 1988 / PM / F • A Passage To Ecstasy / 1985 / CDI / M • Peeping Tom / 1986 / CV / M • Perfect Fit / 1985 / DR / M • Pleasure Productions #07 / 1984

/ VCR / M • The Pleasure Seekers / 1985 / AT / M • Postcards From Abroad / 1991 / CA / C • Prescription For Passion / 1984 / VD / M • Raffles / 1988 / VC / M • Rambone Does Hollywood / 1986 / WET / M • Real Men Eat Keisha / 1986 / VC / M • Rearbusters / 1988 / LVI / C • Rich & Sassy / 1986 / VSE / M • The Rocky Porno Video Show / 1986 / 4P / M • Samurai Dick / 1984 / VC / M • Screaming Rage / 1988 / LV / C • Screw / 1985 / CV / M • Secret Mistress / 1986 / VD / M • Sex Academy / 1985 / PLY / M • Sex For Hire / 1989 / HOE / C • Sex Maniacs / 1987 / JOY / C • Sex Toys / 1985 / CA / M • Sexual Pursuit / 1985 / AT / M • Sheets Of San Francisco / 1986 / AVC / M • Slave Exchange / 1985 / BIZ / B • The Sleazy Detective / 1988 / VD / M • Stephanie's Outrageous / 1988 / LV / C • Stiff Competition #1 / 1984 / CA / M • Submissive Women / 1989 / ... / C • Super Chic / 1985 / VC / M • Supergirls Do General Hospital / 1984 / VC / M • Supergirls Do The Navy / 1984 / VC / M • Surfside Sex / 1985 / PV / M • Swinging Shift / 1985 / CDI / M • Taboo #03 / 1983 / IN / M • Tailenders / 1985 / WET / M • Tailhouse Rock / 1985 / WV / M • Taking Off / 1984 / VC / M • Talk Dirty To Me #04 / 1986 / DR / M • A Taste Of Paradise / 1984 / HO / M • A Taste Of Taija Rae / 1989 / PIN / C • Tasty / 1985 / CA / M • Tawnee...Be Good! / 1988 / LV / M • Tease Me / 1986 / VC / M • Teasers: Heavenly Bodies / 1988 / MET / M • Teasers: Hot Pursuit / 1988 / MET / M • Teenage Games / 1985 / HO / M • Tongue 'n Cheek (Vca) / 1984 / VC / M • Triple Play / 1983 / HO / M • Two Timing Tracie / 1985 / V20 / M • An Unnatural Act #1 / 1984 / DR / M • Up In The Air / 1984 / CDI / M • VCA Previews #4 / 1988 / VC / C • Wicked Wenches / 1988 / LA / M • Wicked Whispers / 1985 / VD / M • Wild Orgies / 1986 / SE / C • Women's Secret Desires / 1983 / LIP / F • WPINK-TV #2 / 1986 / PV / M • X Factor / 1984 / HO / M • Yankee Seduction / 1984 / WV / M • The Year Of The Sex Dragon / 1986 / PV / M • Yellow Fever / 1984 / PL / M • Young Nympho's / 1986 / VD / M

KRISTARRAH KNIGHT *(Christy Knights, Heather (K. Knight), Christarrah Knight, Karin East)*

Pudgy blonde with a smiling face.

The Adventures Of Billy Blues / 1990 / HO / M • All Over Me / 1991 / VC / M • Anal Addiction #1 / 1990 / SO / M • Anal Dawn / 1991 / AMB / M • Anal Rescue 811 / 1992 / PL / M • Backdoor Lambada / 1990 / GO / M • Backdoor To Brooklyn / 1992 / PL / M • The Backpackers #1 / 1990 / IN / M • Bed, Butts & Breakfast / 1990 / LV / M • Best Of Buttman #2 / 1993 / EA / C • Between The Cheeks #2 / 1990 / VC / M • Beyond Innocence / 1990 / VCR / F • Breast Worx #14 / 1992 / LBO / M • Bunny's Lesson In Pain / 1992 / PL / B • Butt Woman #1 / 1990 / FH / M • Call Girl Academy / 1990 / V99 / M • Club Head / 1990 / CA / M • The Coming Of Christy / 1990 / CAY / M • Deep Throat #4 / 1990 / AR / M • Dirty Books / 1990 / V99 / M • Girls Will Be Boys #1 / 1990 / PL / F • Girls Will Be Boys #2 / 1990 / PL / F • The Hind-Lick Maneuver / 1991 / GO / C • Hot Talk Radio / 1989 / VWA / M • I Said A Butt Light #1 / 1990 / LV / M • Introducing

Danielle / 1990 / CDI / M • It Happened At Midnight / 1990 / IN / M • Juicy Lips / 1991 / PL / F • King Tung: The Tongue Squad / 1990 / LA / M • Leading Lady / 1991 / V99 / M • The Magic Box / 1990 / SO / M • A Night At The Waxworks / 1990 / IF / M • On Stage And In Color / 1991 / VIP / M • Only With A Married Woman / 1990 / LE / M • Oral Majority #08 / 1990 / WV / C • Passion From Behind / 1990 / LV / M • The Pawnbroker / 1990 / IF / M • Punished Lesbians / 1992 / PL / B • Pussy Power #04 / 1992 / BTO / M • Radioactive / 1990 / VIP / M • Roadgirls / 1990 / DR / M • The Seduction Formula / 1990 / FAN / M • Sexual Persuasion / 1991 / V99 / M • Shadow Dancers #1 / 1989 / EA / M • Shadow Dancers #2 / 1989 / EA / M • Silence Of The G.A.M.S. / 1992 / CA / M • Sweet Miss Fortune / 1990 / LE / M • This Year's Blonde / 1990 / LE / M • Through The Walls / 1990 / FAZ / M • A Tongue Is Born / 1990 / ERU / M • Tools Of The Trade / 1990 / WV / M • Where The Girls Sweat #1 / 1990 / EA / F • White Lies / 1990 / VEX / M • Whore Of The Roses / 1990 / AFV / M • Wise Ass! / 1990 / FH / M

KRISTEN

Amateurs Exposed #07 / 1995 / CV / M • Big Knockers #21: Best Of Lesbian #2 / 1995 / TV / C • Big Reward / 1995 / CS / B • Bound By Design / 1995 / BON / B • The Convict / 1995 / TAO / B • Different Strokes / 1994 / PRE / B • The Fetish Files / 1995 / IBN / B • Housewife Lust #1 / 1995 / TV / F • Leg...Ends #14 / 1995 / PRE / F • Spank & Spank Again / 1995 / BON / B • Student Fetish Videos: Best of Catfighting #03 / 1995 / PRE / C • Student Fetish Videos: Best Of Foot Worship #03 / 1995 / PRE / C • Student Fetish Videos: Catfighting #13 / 1994 / PRE / B • Student Fetish Videos: Foot Worship #13 / 1994 / PRE / B • Student Fetish Videos: Spanking #17 / 1994 / PRE / B • Titan's Gonzo Video Magazine #02 / 1996 / TEG / M • Triple Play / 1994 / PRE / B • Wasted / 1995 / PRE / B

KRISTEN (A. LAUREN) see Ashley Lauren

KRISTEN BLUE

Caribbean Sunset / 1996 / PL / M • East Coast Sluts #07: Tampa Bay / 1995 / PL / M • Fresh Meat #1 / 1996 / PL / M • Fresh Meat #2 / 1996 / PL / M • Incident Images: First Time Shavers #1 / 1996 / II / F

KRISTEN GILMOUR

The Spanking Pact / 1995 / CAA / B

KRISTEN KARR

Foxy Boxing / 1982 / AVC / M

KRISTEN WEST see Kristina West

KRISTI

AVP #9135: The Big Move / 1991 / AVP / M • The Best Of Fabulous Flashers / 1996 / DGD / F • Blue Vanities #197 / 1993 / FFL / M • Dr Bondo / 1995 / BON / B • Pain In The Rent / 1996 / BON / B • Sold Into Slavery / 1996 / BON / B • Spy Trap / 1995 / BON / B • Whip Therapy / 1995 / BON / B

KRISTI BEY see Star Index I

KRISTI BRYANT see Ali Moore

KRISTI FLETCHER see Star Index I

KRISTI KEITH see Star Index I

KRISTI LYNN see Krysti Lynn

KRISTI MYST *(Tina Harlow, Pamela Sanderson)*

Pretty face, long straight blonde hair, tight waist, medium firm tits (later enhanced), good tan lines, small flower or Aztec sun symbol tattoo on her right belly/groin just beside her pubic hair and another (snake) on her ankle. Scar (burn) just below her belly button. 20 years old in 1995 and used to be a dental assistant.

Beeping Miss Buffy / 1995 / CDI / M • Buffy's Anal Adventure / 1996 / CDI / M • Buffy's Bare Ass Barbecue / 1996 / CDI / M • Buffy's First Encounter / 1995 / CIN / M • Buffy's Malibu Adventure / 1995 / CDI / M • Buffy's New Boobs / 1996 / CIN / M • The Girls Of Summer / 1995 / VT / M • Hit And Run / 1996 / CDI / M • More Dirty Debutantes #42 / 1995 / 4P / M • More Dirty Debutantes #43 / 1995 / 4P / M • Sweet Smell Of Excess / 1996 / CIN / M • Up And Cummers #20 / 1995 / 4P / M

KRISTI NICOLS see Star Index I

KRISTI WAAY see Kursti Way

KRISTI WARNER see Bunny Bleu

KRISTIAN SUMMERS see Star Index I

KRISTIANA CEA see Kristine Sea

KRISTIE

Penetration (Anabolic) #3 / 1995 / ANA / M • Raunch #10: Uncut Jewel / 1994 / CC / M

KRISTIE ALLEN

Up And Cummers #20 / 1995 / 4P / M • Up And Cummers #21 / 1995 / RWP / M

KRISTIE DEVEREAUX see Star Index I

KRISTIE IMBOCH

Boy Spanks Girl / 1995 / SHL / B

KRISTIE KISS

Blue Vanities #198 / 1993 / FFL / M

KRISTIE LEIGH (Christie Leigh, Christy Lane, Christie Lane, Christy Leigh, Christy Lee, Christi Lane)

Tall, pretty blonde with a fleshy but not chunky body, small/medium tits, and tattoos on her left belly and right shoulder back.

900 Desert Strip / 1991 / XPI / M • After The Lights Go Out / 1989 / VEX / M • Anal Encounters #4: Tales From The Crack / 1992 / VC / M • Anal Encounters #5: Deliveries In The Rear / 1992 / VC / M • Anal Encounters #6 / 1992 / VC / M • Anal Encounters #7: Enter Through The Rear / 1992 / VC / M • At The Pornies / 1989 / VC / M • Backdoor Suite / 1992 / EX / M • Bedside Brat / 1988 / VI / M • Bend Over Babes #1 / 1990 / EA / M • Blonde Temptation / 1995 / IF / M • The Box / 1992 / EX / M • Broadway Brat / 1988 / VI / M • Carnal Possessions / 1988 / VEX / M • Carnal Possessions / 1991 / VEX / M • The Case Of The Crooked Cathouse / 1989 / ME / M • Chance Meetings / 1988 / VEX / M • Debbie Does 'em All #2 / 1988 / CV / M • Debbie Does Dallas #5 / 1988 / VEX / M • Every Man's Fancy / 1988 / SEX / M • Every Man's Fancy / 1991 / V99 / M • A Fistful Of Bimbos / 1988 / FAZ / M • The Girls Of Cooze / 1992 / V99 / C • Guess Who? / 1991 / EX / M • Hot Summer Nites / 1988 / VEX / M • Indecent Proposals / 1988 / SEX / M • Just Like Sisters / 1988 / VEX / M • The Last Temptation Of Kristi / 1988 / ME / M • The Legend Of Reggie D. / 1989 / EA / M • Moonstroked / 1988 / 3HV / M • Mr. Peepers Amateur Home Videos #13: Backdoor Doctor / 1991 / LBO / M • Out Of The Blue #1 / 1991 / VI / M • The Oval Office / 1991 / LV / M • Phantom X / 1989 / VC / M • Porn Star Home Video Series 2 / 1990 / HOV / M • Porn Star's Day

Off / 1990 / FAZ / M • Rocky-X #2 / 1988 / PEN / M • Salsa Break / 1989 / EA / M • The Scent Of Samantha / 1988 / VEX / C • Stand-In Studs / 1989 / V99 / M • Telemates / 1988 / STA / M • Telemates / 1991 / V99 / M • Tight Squeeze / 1992 / SC / M

KRISTIE LOWE

Joys Of Erotica #110 / 1984 / VCR / C

KRISTIE NUSSMAN see Traci Lords

KRISTIN

Big Knockers #14 / 1995 / TV / M • Home-Grown Video #464: Liza, We Love You / 1995 / HOV / M • Housewife Lust #2 / 1995 / TV / F

KRISTIN (K. KRISTEL) see Kathleen Kristel

KRISTIN (L. SMITH) see Laurie Smith

KRISTIN SNAPP see Star Index I

KRISTIN STEEN see Star Index I

KRISTINA

Ancient Amateurs #1 / 1996 / LOF / M • The Coming Of Nikita / 1995 / EL / M • Erika Bella: Euroslut / 1995 / EL / M • Feuchte Muschies / 1995 / KRM / M • Jus' Knockin' Boots #1: Fade To Black / 1996 / NIT / M • Just Do It! / 1996 / RAS / M • Mr. Peepers Nastiest #1 / 1995 / LBO / C • Private Gold #03: The Chase / 1996 / OD / M • Private Gold #14: Sweet Lady #1 / 1997 / OD / M • Private Stories #05 / 1995 / OD / M • Quebec Perversity #5 / 1996 / IN0 / M • Russian Model Magazine #1 / 1996 / IP / M • Russian Model Magazine #2 / 1996 / IP / M • Sluts 'n' Angels In Budapest / 1994 / EL / M

KRISTINA (B&D) see Star Index I

KRISTINA (HOOKER)

Black Street Hookers #1 / 1996 / DFI / M

KRISTINA (KING) see Krystina King

KRISTINA (S/M) see Star Index I

KRISTINA BELANOVA

Sex-A-Holic Lady / 1995 / PL / M

KRISTINA DE BELL

Alice In Wonderland / 1976 / CA / M • The Big Brawl / 1980 / WAR / S • Cheerleaders' Wild Weekend / cr77 / VES / S • Club Life / 1986 / PRS / S • Emmanuelle Around The World / 1977 / WIZ / S • Lifepod / 1980 / VC1 / S • Meatballs #1 / 1979 / PAR / S • Rooster: Spurs Of Death! / 1983 / ... / S • T.A.G.: The Assassination Game / 1982 / SUL / S • Willie & Phil / 1980 / FOX / S

KRISTINA EVOL see Christina Evol

KRISTINA MAFALDA

Private Gold #11: The Pyramid #1 / 1996 / OD / M

KRISTINA RHAY see Star Index I

KRISTINA ST. JAMES

Not too pretty older woman, curly blonde hair, cantaloupes, small tattoo on left breast, womanly body. Part of the Stagliano AIDS controversy in that she apparently performed some oral sex on him (just licking and similar) after he knew he was HIV+.

Hardcore Debutantes #02 / 1996 / TEP / M • White Men Can't Iron On Butt Row / 1997 / ABS / M

KRISTINA WEST (Christina West, Kristen West)

Quite pretty lithe blonde with a delicious little rear end, small tits and a birthmark half way up her back to the left of her spine. Born December 25, 1969 in Canoga Park, CA.

1-900-FUCK #3 / 1995 / SO / M • Anal Addicts / 1994 / KWP / M • The Anal Adventures of Max Hardcore: The Resurrection /

1995 / ZA / M • Anal Justice / 1994 / ROB / M • Anal Misconduct / 1995 / VD / M • Anal Secrets (Metro) / 1994 / IN / M • Angel Baby / 1995 / SC / M • Assy Sassy #2 / 1994 / ROB / F • Babe Magnet / 1994 / IN / M • Bad Slaves / 1995 / HOM / B • Blonde In Blue Flannel / 1995 / CA / M • Bun Busters #16 / 1994 / LBO / M • Butt Hunt #08 / 1995 / LEI / M • Butt Sluts #3 / 1994 / ROB / F • Butthead Dreams / 1994 / FH / M • Buttslammers #10: Lust On The Internet / 1995 / BS / F • Captive In Sumanka / 1996 / LON / B • Circus Sluts / 1995 / LV / M • Club Kiss / 1995 / ONA / M • Crazy With The Heat #3 / 1994 / CV / M • Cross Cuntry Vacation / 1995 / CC / M • Cult Of The Whip / 1995 / LON / B • Deep Throat Girls #13 / 1995 / GO / M • Dollars And Yen / 1994 / FH / M • Dynamite Brat / 1995 / LV / M • Fantasies Of Alicia / 1995 / VT / M • Fantasies Of Persia / 1995 / VT / M • Fire & Ice / 1995 / LV / M • First Time Lesbians #18 / 1994 / JMP / F • Gang Bang Face Bath #3 / 1994 / ROB / M • Gemini / 1994 / SC / M • Hollywood Sex Tour / 1995 / VC / M • Hookers Of Hollywood / 1994 / LE / M • Housewife Lust #1 / 1995 / TV / F • Itty Bitty Blonde Committee / 1995 / V99 / M • Jaded Love / 1994 / CA / M • Ladies Room / 1994 / SC / F • Make Me Watch / 1994 / PV / M • Malibu Heat / 1995 / HO / M • The Masseuse #2 / 1994 / VI / M • The Meatman / 1995 / OUP / M • Mike Hott: #262 Cunt Of The Month: Christina West 4-94 / 1994 / MHV / M • Mike Hott: #263 Lesbian Sluts #16 / 1994 / MHV / F • Mistress Of The Mansion / 1994 / CV / M • Mr. Peepers Amateur Home Videos #85: Hand Puppet Job / 1994 / LBO / M • Naughty By Night / 1995 / DR / M • The Night Shift / 1995 / LE / M • No Tell Motel / 1995 / CV / M • The Nurses Are Cumming #2 / 1996 / LBO / C • Ona Zee's Black Label #1: Sex Hunger / 1996 / ONA / C • Peach Pit / 1995 / GLI / M • Persia's Back / 1994 / VT / M • The Perversionist / 1995 / HOM / B • Prime Cuts #1 / 1994 / FOR / M • Prime Cuts #2 / 1994 / FOR / M • Private Diaries #1: Christina / 1995 / AVI / M • Psychoanal Therapy / 1994 / CA / M • Public Places #2 / 1995 / SC / M • Pure Filth / 1995 / RV / M • Pussy Hunt #12 / 1995 / LEI / M • Red Light / 1994 / SC / S • Ring Of Passion / 1994 / ERA / M • Secret Seductions #1 / 1995 / LV / M • Secret Urges (Vidco) / 1994 / VD / C • Sex Therapy Ward / 1995 / LBO / M • Sexual Healing / 1994 / VI / M • Sexy Nurses #2 / 1994 / CV / M • Ski Sluts / 1995 / LV / M • Skid Row / 1994 / SC / M • Slave Sisters / 1995 / LON / B • Slavegirl Of Zor / 1996 / LON / B • The Starlet / 1995 / SC / M • Streetwalkers / 1995 / HO / M • Strippers Inc. #3 / 1994 / ONA / M • Superboobs / 1994 / LE / M • Swedish Erotica #85 / 1995 / CA / M • Swing Into...Spring / 1995 / KWP / M • Takin' It To The Limit #5 / 1995 / BS / M • Unbridled Lust / 1995 / NOT / F • Wet Faces #1 / 1997 / SC / C • Wicked Pleasures / 1995 / BS / B • Wild Orgies #15 / 1995 / AFI / M

KRISTINE APPLE see Christine Apple-lay

KRISTINE CHIREIX see Star Index I

KRISTINE HELLER see Christine Heller

KRISTINE IMBOCH

Detective Covergirls / 1996 / CUC / B •

Lessons Learned / 1994 / HAC / B

KRISTINE SEA *(Christina Sea, Kristiana Cea)*
Very small breasted redhead with a tight petite body.
Anal Illusions / 1991 / LV / M • Big Murray's New-Cummers #05: Luscious Lesbos / 1993 / FD / F • Bubble Butts #01 / 1992 / LBO / M • The Flirt / 1992 / EVN / M • Foxxxy Lady / 1992 / HW / M • Mr. Peepers Amateur Home Videos #39: Cumming In Colors / 1992 / LBO / M • The Oval Office / 1991 / LV / M • Wendy Is Watching / 1993 / ELP / M

KRISTINE SIMON
Juicy Virgins / 1995 / WIV / M

KRISTY
Full Service Woman / 1992 / V99 / M • Kim's Convention Couples / 1995 / VAL / M

KRISTY BOND *see* **Tina Ross**
KRISTY BOYD *see* **Tina Ross**
KRISTY DUVALL *see* **Star Index I**
KRISTY HORON *see* **Star Index I**
KRISTY LINDALL *see* **Star Index I**
KRISTY LOVE *see* **Kursti Way**
KRISTY NICHOLS *see* **Star Index I**
KRISTY WAY *see* **Kursti Way**
KRISTY WHY *see* **Kursti Way**

KRISZTI
Love Slave / 1995 / WIV / M

KRISZTINA
Keep On Fucking / 1995 / XHE / M

KRISZTINA HIUMAN
True Stories #2 / 1993 / SC / M

KRISZTINA SCHWARTZ
Private Gold #16: Summer Wind / 1997 / OD / M

KRYSTA
Bondage Classix #02: Krysta's Nightmare #1 / 1987 / BON / B

KRYSTA WHITE *see* **Krista Maze**
KRYSTAL CAY *see* **Star Index I**
KRYSTAL DAWN *see* **Star Index I**
KRYSTAL DESIRE
Freaky Flix / 1995 / TTV / C • Totally Tasteless Video #01 / 1994 / TTV / M

KRYSTAL DREAM
Black Mystique #04 / 1994 / VT / F • Date Night / 1992 / V99 / M

KRYSTAL KRAVIN *see* **Star Index I**
KRYSTAL LOVE *see* **Crystal Lovin**
KRYSTAL WILDER *see* **Crystal Wilder**
KRYSTALL
Gilligan's Bi-Land / 1994 / PL / G • She Male Jail / 1994 / HSV / G

KRYSTEN
Limited Edition #26 / 1984 / AVC / M

KRYSTI LYNN *(Christy (Krysti)Lynn, Harley (Krysti Lynn), Kristi Lynn, Keiari Lynn, Shawna Yager)*
22 year old (in 1993) blonde with smallish but not tiny tits. Not pretty but not ugly either. She seems to have a hard personality (see **New Ends #01**). According to her she was de-virginized at 12. Died December 3, 1995 in an auto accident.
Ace In The Hole / 1995 / PL / M • Anal Blues / 1994 / PEP / M • Anal Crack Master / 1994 / ROB / M • Anal Hounds & Bitches / 1994 / ROB / M • Anal Idol / 1994 / ROB / M • Anal Lover #3 / 1994 / ROB / M • Anal Spitfire / 1994 / ROB / M • Assy Sassy #1 / 1994 / ROB / F • Buffy Malibu's Nasty Girls #08 / 1995 / ANA / F • Butt Freak #2 / 1996 / EA / M • The Butt Sisters Do New York / 1994 / MID / M • Butt Sluts

#4 / 1995 / ROB / F • Buttman's Big Butt Backdoor Babes / 1995 / EA / M • Buttman's Inferno / 1993 / EA / M • Buttman's Wet Dream / 1994 / EA / M • Buttslammers #06: Over The Edge / 1994 / BS / F • Buttslammers #09: Fade To Anal / 1995 / BS / F • County Line / 1993 / PEP / M • The Coven #1 / 1993 / VI / M • The Coven #2 / 1993 / VI / M • Covergirl / 1994 / WP / M • Cum & Get Me / 1995 / PL / F • Deep Inside Dirty Debutantes #07 / 1993 / 4P / M • Dog Walker / 1994 / EA / M • The Ecstasy Of Payne / 1994 / BS / B • Fantasy Exchange / 1993 / VI / M • Fresh Meat (John Leslie) #1 / 1994 / EA / M • Heatwaves / 1994 / LE / M • Hollywood Lesbians / 1995 / ROB / F • Hot Blooded / 1994 / ERA / M • I Love Juicy / 1993 / ZA / M • Ice Woman #1 / 1993 / VI / M • Ice Woman #2 / 1993 / VI / M • Indecent / 1993 / XCI / M • Kink #1 / 1995 / ROB / M • Little Miss Anal / 1994 / ROB / M • Love Me, Love My Butt #1 / 1994 / ROB / F • Lovin' Spoonfuls #4 / 1995 / 4P / C • Nasty Nymphos #06 / 1994 / ANA / M • New Ends #01 / 1993 / 4P / M • The Night Of The Coyote / 1993 / MED / M • Ona Zee's Doll House #2 / 1995 / ONA / F • The Other Side Of Chelsea / 1993 / XCI / M • Pussyman #05: Captive Audience / 1994 / SNA / M • Pussyman #06: House Of Games / 1994 / SNA / M • Pussyman #11: Prime Cuts / 1995 / SNA / C • Sensual Exposure / 1993 / ULI / M • Sensual Recluse / 1994 / EX / M • Shooting Star / 1993 / XCI / M • Snow Bunnies #1 / 1995 / SC / M • Snow Bunnies #2 / 1995 / SC / M • Sodomania #09: Doin' Time / 1994 / EL / M • Sodomania: Slop Shots / 1996 / EL / C • Steal This Heart #2 / 1993 / CV / M • Super Hornio Brothers #1 / 1993 / MID / M • Super Hornio Brothers #2 / 1993 / MID / M • Takin' It To The Limit #2 / 1994 / BS / M • Up And Cummers #11 / 1994 / 4P / M • Up And Cummers #13 / 1994 / 4P / M • Visual Fantasies / 1995 / LE / M • The Voyeur #1 / 1994 / EA / M

KRYSTINA
Private Gold #04: Amazonas / 1996 / OD / M • Private Stories #03 / 1995 / OD / M • Private Stories #06 / 1995 / OD / M • Private Stories #07 / 1996 / OD / M • Triple X Video Magazine #09 / 1995 / OD / M • Triple X Video Magazine #15 / 1996 / OD / M

KRYSTINA KING *(Kristina (King), Christina (King), Heather White, Felicia (K. King), Cristina (King), Suzy St James)*
Lean older blonde with small tits.
Amazing Tails #4 / 1990 / CA / M • Anal Intruder #04 / 1990 / CC / M • Beach Blanket Brat / 1989 / VI / M • Breakfast With Tiffany / 1990 / HO / M • Butt Woman #1 / 1990 / FH / M • Butt's Motel #4 / 1989 / EX / M • Door To Door / 1990 / EX / M • The End Of The Innocence / 1989 / IN / M • Everything Goes / 1990 / SE / M • Girls Will Be Boys #1 / 1990 / PL / F • Girls Will Be Boys #2 / 1990 / PL / F • Good Things Come In Small Packages / 1989 / CA / M • In The Jeans / 1990 / ME / M • Jail Babes #1 / 1990 / PL / F • Juicy Lips / 1991 / PL / F • Kinky Potpourri #27 / 199? / SVE / C • The Lethal Squirt / 1990 / AR / M • Lickety Pink / 1990 / ME / M • The Naked Truth / 1990 / SE / M

• The Pleasure Seekers / 1990 / VD / M • Rear View / 1989 / LE / M • Secrets / 1990 / CA / M • Sex Acts & Video Tape / 1990 / AFV / M • Sex Flex / 1989 / CDI / M • The Smart Ass #1 / 1990 / VT / M • The Smart Ass #2: Rusty's Revenge / 1990 / VT / M • Smart Ass Delinquent / 1993 / VT / M • The Smart Ass Enquirer / 1990 / VT / M • The Smart Ass Returns / 1993 / VT / M • The Smart Ass Vacation / 1990 / VT / M • Swedish Erotica Featurettes #3 / 1989 / CA / M • Tailgunners / 1990 / CDI / M • A Tale Of Two Titties #1 / 1990 / AR / M • Undercover Angel / 1988 / IN / M • Where The Sun Never Shines / 1990 / IN / C

KRYSTINA LION
Private Film #27 / 1995 / OD / M • Private Film #28 / 1995 / OD / M • Triple X Video Magazine #01 / 1995 / OD / M • Triple X Video Magazine #04 / 1995 / OD / M • Triple X Video Magazine #06 / 1995 / OD / M • Triple X Video Magazine #07 / 1995 / OD / M

KRYSTLE
Krystle's Surrender / 1988 / BON / B

KRYSTLE LEE *see* **Star Index I**
KUMISHA *see* **Cumisha Amado**
KURNIE
New Pussy Hunt #17 / 1995 / LEI / M

KURSTI WAY *(Kirsti Way, Kristy Way, Christy Way, Kristi Waay, Christy Waay, Kristy Love, Kristy Why)*
Brunette with shoulder length hair, reasonable but slighly mannish face, good skin, nice butt, tight body, small tits, nice smile. Very tight washboard-flat belly. Was 21 years old in 1994 and was de-virginized at 17. Late 1995 she dyed her hair blonde; she looked better as a brunette.
19 & Naughty #1 / 1994 / SKV / M • Ace Mulholland / 1995 / ERA / M • Adult Affairs / 1994 / VC / M • Adults Only / 1995 / BOT / M • Alice In Analand / 1994 / SC / M • All Amateur Perfect 10's / 1995 / LEI / M • Amateur Gay Girls / 1995 / LEI / C • Anal Angels #4 / 1995 / VEX / C • Anal Misconduct / 1995 / VD / M • The Anal Nurse Scam / 1995 / CA / M • Anal Webb / 1995 / ZA / M • As Easy As A Bunch Of Cunts / 1996 / ROB / F • Ass Masters (Leisure) #02 / 1995 / LEI / M • Babenet / 1995 / VC / M • Badgirls #5: Maximum Babes / 1995 / VI / M • The Best Of Strippers Inc / 1996 / ONA / C • Big Murray's New-Cummers #26: Real Tits / 1994 / FD / M • Bizarre Desires / 1995 / ROB / F • Blindfold / 1994 / SC / M • Bobby Hollander's Sweet Cheeks #109 / 1994 / WV / M • The Booty Bandit / 1994 / FC / M • Bun Busters #17 / 1994 / LBO / M • Butt Watch #06 / 1994 / FH / M • Carnal Interludes / 1995 / NOT / M • Cherry Poppers #12: Playing Nookie / 1995 / ZA / M • Cluster Fuck #05 / 1994 / MAX / M • Cockpit / 1996 / SC / M • Cocksuckers #1 / 1994 / MET / M • College Cuties / 1995 / LE / M • Cynthia And The Pocket Rocket / 1995 / CV / M • The Decadent Adventures Of Generation XXX / 1994 / MAX / M • Deception (1995-Executive) / 1995 / EX / M • Dirty Stories #2 / 1995 / PE / M • Dirty Tricks #1: Just A Bunch Of Whores / 1995 / EA / M • Dirty Work / 1995 / VC / M • The Dragon Lady #7: Tales From The Bed #6 / 1994 / WV / M • The Dream Team / 1995 / VT / M • Erotic Fiction / 1995 / LE / M • Exotic Car Models #2 / 1996 / IN0 / F • Fan-

tasies Of Marilyn / 1995 / VT / M • Fantasy Du Jour / 1995 / FH / M • Fantasy Inc. / 1995 / CV / M • Fazano's Student Bodies / 1995 / EL / M • Firm Offer / 1995 / SC / M • First Time Lesbians #15 / 1994 / JMP / F • Fluff Dreams / 1995 / SUF / M • Freeway Love / 1994 / FD / M • Fresh Meat (John Leslie) #1 / 1994 / EA / M • The Girl Next Door #1 / 1994 / VT / M • A Girl's Affair #05 / 1994 / FD / F • Girls Of The Packed Ten / 1994 / VT / M • Girls With Curves #2 / 1994 / CV / M • Green Piece Of Ass #1 / 1994 / RTP / M • Harder, She Craved / 1995 / VC / M • Hawaiian Heat #1 / 1995 / CC / M • Hawaiian Heat #2 / 1995 / CC / M • Hidden Camera #16 / 1994 / JMP / M • Home Nurses Anal Adventure / 1994 / LBO / M • Hotel California / 1995 / MID / M • Hotel Fantasy / 1995 / IN / M • Initiation Of Kylie / 1995 / VT / M • Kinky Orientals / 1994 / FH / M • Lady's Choice / 1995 / VD / M • Laguna Nights / 1995 / FH / M • The Legend Of Barbi-Q And Little Fawn / 1994 / CA / M • Lesbian Bitches #2 / 1994 / ROB / F • Lesbian C*Nt Whores / 1996 / ROB / F • Lesbian Workout #1 / 1994 / GO / F • Lesbian Workout #2 / 1994 / GO / F • Lessons In Love / 1995 / SPI / M • Lingerie / 1995 / SC / M • Love Spice / 1995 / ERA / M • Mickey Ray's Sex Search #04: Long And Hard / 1994 / WIV / M • Ms. Behaved / 1994 / SC / M • Muff Divers #1 / 1996 / TV / F • Naked Ambition / 1995 / VC / M • The Naked Truth / 1995 / VI / M • Nasty Newcummers #04 / 1994 / MET / M • Natural Born Thrillers / 1994 / LV / M • Naughty / 1996 / LV / M • The New Butt Hunt #15 / 1995 / LEI / C • Nightmare On Lesbian Street / 1995 / LIP / F • No Man's Land #12 / 1995 / VT / F • Nothing Like A Dame #1 / 1995 / IN / M • Nothing Sacred / 1995 / LE / M • The Nurses Are Cumming #2 / 1996 / LBO / C • The Oh! Zone / 1995 / VC / M • Ona Zee's Doll House #2 / 1995 / ONA / F • Oral Addiction / 1995 / VI / M • Oriental Oddballs #2 / 1994 / FH / M • Out Of Love / 1995 / VI / M • Persia's Back / 1994 / VT / M • The Pleasure Girl / 1994 / GO / M • Private Matters / 1995 / EMC / M • Private Places / 1995 / IF / M • Private Video Magazine #16 / 1994 / OD / M • Pump Fiction / 1995 / VT / M • Putting It All Behind #2: Star Treatment / 1994 / IN / M • Rear Entry / 1995 / LEI / M • Reckless / 1995 / NOT / M • The Reel World #3: Trouble In Paradise / 1995 / FOR / M • The Reel World #4 / 1995 / FOR / M • Risque Burlesque #1 / 1994 / IN / M • Rocco Unleashed / 1994 / SC / M • The Romeo Syndrome / 1995 / SC / M • Ron Hightower's White Chicks #09 / 1994 / LBO / M • Ruthless Affairs / 1995 / LE / M • The Savage / 1994 / SC / M • The Scarlet Woman / 1994 / WP / M • Scorched / 1995 / ONA / M • Screamers (Gourmet) / 1995 / ONA / M • Sexual Healing / 1996 / SC / M • Shades Of Passion / 1995 / NOT / M • Shameless / 1995 / VC / M • Skin Hunger / 1995 / MET / M • Sleaze Please!—November Edition / 1994 / FH / M • Sluts In Suburbia / 1994 / GLI / M • Smoke Screen / 1995 / WAV / M • Snatch Masters #02 / 1994 / LEI / M • Snatch Masters #03 / 1994 / LEI / M • Sodomania: Slop Shots / 1996 / EL / C • Sodomize Me!!! / 1996 / SPR / M • Sorority Stewardesses #1 / 1995 / PE / M • Sorority Stewardesses #2

/ 1995 / PE / M • Spirit Guide / 1995 / IN / M • Splattered / 1996 / MET / M • Stacked Deck / 1994 / IN / M • Strippers Inc. #5 / 1995 / ONA / M • Student Fetish Videos: Bondage #01 / 1995 / PRE / B • Student Fetish Videos: Tickling #12 / 1995 / SFV / B • Style #2 / 1994 / VT / M • Sweat 'n' Bullets / 1995 / MID / M • Swedish Erotica #82 / 1995 / CA / M • Take It Inside / 1995 / PEP / M • The Tongue / 1995 / OD / M • Unbalanced Chemicals / 1996 / SUF / M • Unbridled Lust / 1995 / NOT / F • Velvet / 1995 / SPI / M • Vibrating Vixens #2 / 1996 / TV / F • Video Virgins #09 / 1993 / NS / M • View Point / 1995 / VI / M • Virtual Reality Sixty Nine / 1995 / WP / M • The Voyeur #4 / 1995 / EA / M • Wet Faces #1 / 1997 / SC / C • What You Are In The Dark / 1995 / KLP / M • Where The Girls Sweat...Not The Sequel / 1996 / EL / F • Wide Open / 1994 / GLI / M • Wild & Wicked #5 / 1995 / VT / M • Winter Heat / 1994 / MID / M • Young & Natural #03 / 1995 / PRE / F • Young & Natural #05 / 1995 / PRE / F • Young & Natural #09 / 1995 / PRE / C • Young & Natural #11 / 1995 / PRE / F

KURT
Back East Babes #2 / 1996 / NIT / M • The Gypsy / 1996 / NIT / M • Intimate Interviews #4 / 1996 / NIT / M • Up And Cummers #06 / 1993 / 4P / M

KURT BAUER
Bi And Beyond #1 / 1988 / LAV / G

KURT BLANKMEYER
Amour / 1978 / VC / M

KURT HARMON see Star Index I

KURT HOUSTON
Night Walk / 1995 / HIV / G

KURT HURST
Big Reward / 1995 / CS / B • Tied & Tickled #23: Tickling Dick / 1994 / CS / B

KURT LOVE see Star Index I
KURT LOVELL see Star Index I
KURT MANN
Bad Penny / 1978 / QX / M • Blonde Ambition / 1981 / QX / M • Bon Appetit / 1980 / QX / M • C.O.D. / 1981 / VES / S • Devil In Miss Jones #2 / 1983 / VC / M • Dirty Lilly / 1975 / VXP / M • Every Inch A Lady / 1975 / QX / M • Firestorm #1 / 1984 / COM / M • Games Women Play #1 / 1980 / CA / M • In Love / 1983 / VC / M • Jack 'n' Jill #1 / 1979 / VXP / M • Misbehavin' / 1979 / VXP / M • Roommates / 1982 / VXP / M • This Lady Is A Tramp / 1980 / CV / M • Visions / 1977 / QX / M

KURT SJOBERG
Lust At First Bite / 1978 / VC / M

KYLE
Hot Body Competition: The Beverly Hill's Naughty Nightie C. / 1995 / CG / F • Pearl Necklace: Amorous Amateurs #13 / 1992 / SEE / M

KYLE HOUSTON
The Creasemaster / 1993 / VC / M • Nikki At Night / 1993 / LE / M • Nikki Never Says No / 1992 / LE / M

KYLE KRAMMER
Catch Of The Day #1 / 1995 / VG0 / M

KYLE LONGLEY
Every Body / 1992 / LAP / M

KYLE PHILLIPS
Addictive Desires / 1994 / OD / M • Anal Camera #06 / 1995 / EVN / M • Anal Camera #08 / 1995 / EVN / M • Anal Territory / 1996 / AVD / M • Bad Girls #5 / 1994 / GO

/ M • Bang City #1: Kelly's Anal Gang Bang / 1995 / SC / M • Big Murray's New-Cummers #25: / 1994 / FD / M • Breastman's Triple X Cellent Adventure / 1995 / EVN / M • Bushwoman: She Takes Two / 1996 / RAS / M • Emerald: Princess Of The Night / 1996 / FC / M • Fantasy Chamber / 1994 / ULI / M • In Through The Out Door / 1995 / PE / M • Jingle Balls / 1996 / EVN / M • Jug Humpers / 1995 / V99 / C • Mike Hott: #339 Cum In My Mouth #04 / 1996 / MHV / C • Mike Hott: #349 Girls Who Swallow Cum #03 / 1996 / MHV / C • Night Stalker / 1995 / BBE / M • Orgy Camera #2 / 1996 / EVN / M • Oriental Gang Bang / 1995 / HO / M • Pro-Am Jam / 1996 / GLI / M • The Secret Life Of Nina Hartley / 1994 / VC / M • The Seduction Of Sabrina / 1996 / AVD / M • Seekers / 1994 / CA / M • Starbangers #08 / 1996 / FPI / M • Tail Taggers #121: Behind The Lens / 1994 / WV / M

KYLE POWERS
To Bi For / 1996 / PL / G
KYLE RICHARDS
The Best Of Both Worlds #2 / 1986 / MID / G

KYLE STONE *(Mark Hynes)*
Mark Hynes is from **Party Club**.
1-900-FUCK #1 / 1995 / SO / M • 1-900-FUCK #2 / 1995 / SO / M • 100% Amateur #02: Back Door And More / 1995 / OD / M • 100% Amateur #10: / 1995 / OD / M • 100% Amateur #27: / 1996 / OD / M • 113 Cherry Lane / 1994 / FOR / M • A List / 1996 / SO / M • Abducted / 1996 / ZA / M • Alice In Analand / 1994 / SC / M • All "A" / 1994 / SFP / C • Alpine Affairs / 1995 / LE / M • Amazing Nympho Stories / 1995 / TEG / M • Anal & 3-Way Play / 1995 / GLI / M • Anal Alley Cat / 1996 / KWP / M • Anal Angel / 1994 / EX / M • Anal Chiropractor / 1995 / PEP / M • Anal Connection / 1996 / ZA / M • Anal Dynomite / 1995 / ROB / M • Anal Freaks / 1994 / KWP / M • Anal Health Club Babes / 1995 / EVN / M • Anal Institution #3 / 1996 / ZA / M • Anal Plaything #2 / 1995 / ROB / M • Anal Senorita #2 / 1995 / ROB / M • Anal Sex / 1996 / ZA / M • Anals, Inc / 1995 / ZA / M • Analtown USA #01 / 1995 / NIT / M • Analtown USA #04 / 1995 / NIT / M • Analtown USA #09 / 1995 / NIT / M • Analtown USA #10 / 1996 / NIT / M • Animal Instinct / 1996 / DTV / M • Assy #2 / 1996 / JMP / M • Backing In #6 / 1994 / WV / C • The Backway Inn #5 / 1993 / FD / M • Batbabe / 1995 / PL / M • Big Bust Babes #25 / 1995 / AFI / M • Big Bust Babes #35 / 1996 / AFI / M • Big Bust Babes #38 / 1996 / AFI / M • Big Bust Babes #39 / 1996 / AFI / M • Black Women, White Men #6 / 1995 / FC / M • Bobby Hollander's Maneaters #11 / 1994 / SFP / M • Bobby Hollander's Sweet Cheeks #109 / 1994 / WV / M • Bobby Hollander's Sweet Cheeks #111 / 1994 / WV / M • Bobby Hollander's Sweet Cheeks #112 / 1994 / QUA / M • Boob Tube Lube / 1996 / RAS / M • Born 2 B Wild / 1995 / PL / M • The Breast Files #1 / 1994 / AVI / M • The Breast Files #2 / 1994 / AVI / M • Buffy's Bare Ass Barbecue / 1996 / CDI / M • Buffy's Nude Camera-Party / 1996 / CIN / M • Butthead Dreams: Exposed / 1995 / FH / M • Butthead Dreams: Mission Impenetrable / 1994 / FH / M • Cabin Fever / 1995 / ERA / M • California Swingers / 1996 / LV / M •

Candy's Custom Car Wash / 1995 / FC / M • Carnal Country / 1996 / NIT / M • Casting Couch #1 / 1994 / KV / M • Caught From Behind #23 / 1995 / HO / M • Caught From Behind #24 / 1996 / HO / M • Chained / 1995 / SC / M • Chained Heat / 1996 / APP / M • Cheeks #8 / 1995 / CC / M • Chemical Reaction / 1995 / CC / M • Cirque Du Sex #1 / 1996 / VT / M • A Clockwork Orgy / 1995 / PL / M • Compulsion (Fat Dog) / 1996 / FD / M • Concrete Heat / 1996 / XCI / M • Crazy With The Heat #3 / 1994 / CV / M • Cry Babies #1: Anal Scream / 1995 / ZA / M • Cum Buttered Corn Holes #2 / 1996 / NIT / C • Cum Buttered Corn Holes #3 / 1996 / NIT / C • Cyber-Sex Love Junkies / 1996 / BBE / M • Debbie Class Of '95 / 1995 / CC / M • Deceit / 1996 / ZA / M • Deep Cheeks #5 / 1995 / ROB / M • Devil In A Wet T-Shirt / 1995 / SPI / M • Dick & Jane Look For Pussy In The Park / 1995 / AVI / M • Dim Sum (Eating Chinese) / 1996 / SUF / M • Director's Wet Dreams / 1996 / BBE / M • Dirty Dancers #9 / 1996 / HO / M • Dirty Dating Service #04 / 1994 / WP / M • Dirty Laundry / 1994 / HOH / M • Dirty Tricks #1: Just A Bunch Of Whores / 1995 / EA / M • Diva / 1993 / XCI / M • Doin' The Rounds / 1995 / VC / M • Double D Housewives / 1994 / PV / M • DPTV: Double Penetration Television / 1996 / SUF / M • Dream Strokes / 1994 / WIV / M • Dreams Of Desires / 1995 / ONA / M • Dukes Of Anal / 1996 / VC / M • Eighteen #2 / 1996 / SC / M • Employee's Entrance In The Rear / 1996 / CC / M • Erotic Newcummers Vol 1 #1: Capitol Desires / 1993 / DR / M • Erotic Newcummers Vol 1 #2: Texas Twisters / 1993 / DR / M • Escape From Anal Lost Angels / 1996 / HO / M • Eurotica #05 / 1996 / XC / M • Every Nerd Has A Fantasy / 1996 / FC / M • The Fanny Farm / 1996 / NIT / M • Fast Forward / 1995 / CA / M • Femme Fatale / 1996 / CIN / M • For Your Mouth Only / 1995 / GO / M • Forbidden Pleasures / 1995 / ERA / M • Fortune Nookie / 1994 / PPP / M • Four Weddings And A Honeymoon / 1995 / PL / M • Fuck U: Girls Of The Packed-10 / 1995 / ZA / M • Full Metal Babes / 1995 / LE / M • Gang Bang Bitches #11 / 1995 / PP / M • Gangbang Girl #14 / 1994 / ANA / M • Gangland Bangers / 1995 / VC / M • Gazongas Galore #1 / 1996 / NIT / C • A Girl Like You / 1995 / LE / M • The Girls Of Spring Break / 1995 / VT / M • The Happy Office / 1996 / NIT / M • Hardcore Fantasies #2 / 1996 / LV / M • Hardcore Fantasies #4 / 1996 / LV / M • Her Name Is Asia / 1996 / SUF / M • Hidden Camera #18 / 1994 / JMP / M • Hollywood Amateurs #02 / 1994 / MID / M • Hollywood Amateurs #08 / 1994 / MID / M • Hollywood Amateurs #13 / 1994 / MID / M • Hollywood Amateurs #14 / 1995 / MID / M • Hollywood Amateurs #15 / 1995 / MID / M • Hollywood Amateurs #18 / 1995 / MID / M • Hooters And The Blowjobs / 1996 / HW / M • Hot Amateur Nights / 1996 / WV / M • The Hunt / 1996 / ULP / M • Hypnotic Hookers #2 / 1996 / NIT / M • In The Fast Lane / 1995 / LE / M • In Your Face #3 / 1995 / PL / M • In Your Face #4 / 1996 / PL / M • Inspector Croissant: The Case Of The Missing Pinky / 1995 / FC / M • Interracial 247 / 1995 / CC / M • Interview's Hard Bodied Harlots / 1996 / LV / M • Interview's

Southern Cumfort / 1996 / LV / M • Jailhouse Nurses / 1995 / SC / M • Jiggly Queens #3 / 1996 / LE / M • Juliette's Desires / 1996 / LE / M • A Lady / 1995 / FD / M • Laguna Nights / 1995 / FH / M • Leather / 1995 / LE / M • Legal Briefs / 1996 / EX / M • Lolita / 1995 / SC / M • Look What I Found On The Street #01 / 1996 / CC / M • Lost Angels / 1997 / WP / M • Lotus Blossoms / 1996 / SUF / M • Lust Behind Bars / 1996 / GO / M • Lusty Lap Dancers #2 / 1994 / HO / M • Lusty Lawyers / 1995 / PRK / M • M Series #22 / 1994 / LBO / M • M Series #25 / 1994 / LBO / M • Make Me Watch / 1994 / PV / M • Mellon Man #02 / 1994 / AVI / M • Mellon Man #03 / 1994 / AVI / M • Mellon Man #06 / 1995 / AVI / M • Mellon Man #07 / 1996 / AVI / M • Middle Aged Sex Maniacs / 1995 / SUF / M • Mike Hott: #317 Girls Who Swallow Cum #01 / 1995 / MHV / C • Mike Hott: #330 Three-Sum Sluts #08 / 1995 / MHV / M • Mike Hott: #354 Three-Sum Sluts #12 / 1996 / MHV / M • Mike Hott: #367 Girls Who Lap Cum From Cunts #02 / 1996 / MHV / M • Mike Hott: #368 Three-Sum Sluts #13 / 1996 / MHV / M • Mike Hott: #373 Three-Sum Sluts #14 / 1996 / MHV / M • Mile High Thrills / 1995 / VIM / M • Million Dollar Buns / 1996 / MYS / M • Miss Nude International / 1996 / LE / M • Mission Phenomenal / 1996 / HIP / M • Motel Matches / 1996 / LE / M • Mystic Tales Of The Orient / 1994 / PRK / M • Nasty Newcummers #07 / 1995 / MET / M • Nasty Newcummers #09 / 1995 / MET / M • Nasty Newcummers #10 / 1995 / MET / M • Nasty Newcummers #13 / 1995 / MET / M • Nasty Newcummers #14 / 1995 / MET / M • Nasty Pants / 1995 / SUF / M • Natural Born Thriller / 1994 / CC / M • Nektar / 1996 / BAC / M • New Hardcore Beginners #20 / 1996 / LEI / C • Night Stalker / 1995 / BBE / M • Nookie Ranch / 1996 / NIT / M • Nothing Like Nurse Nookie #1 / 1995 / NIT / M • Nurses Do It With Care / 1995 / EVN / M • Odyssey 30 Min: #552: / 1995 / OD / M • Odyssey Triple Play #67: Girls Who Love It Up The Ass / 1994 / OD / M • Off Duty Porn Stars / 1994 / VC / M • Oh My Gush / 1995 / OD / M • On The Run / 1995 / SC / M • Open Lips / 1994 / WV / M • Orgies Orgies Orgies / 1994 / WV / M • The Other Side Of Chelsea / 1993 / XCI / M • The Panty Parlor / 1996 / VIM / M • Party Club / 1996 / C69 / M • Patriot X / 1995 / LE / M • The Pawn Shop / 1996 / MID / M • Pay 4 Play / 1996 / RAS / M • Penetrator #2: Grudge Day / 1995 / PL / M • Perverted #2: The Virgins / 1995 / ZA / M • Perverted Women / 1995 / SC / M • The Phantom Of The Montague Stage / 1997 / HO / M • Pierced Punctured And Perverted / 1995 / FC / M • Pizzas, Hot Tubs & Bimbos / 1995 / SUF / M • Planet X #1 / 1996 / HW / M • Playmates Of The Rich And Famous / 1995 / BBE / M • Please Take A Number / 1996 / CDI / M • Positions Wanted: Experienced Only / 1993 / PV / M • Power Of The Pussy / 1995 / LEI / M • Pretty Anal Ladies / 1996 / ANE / M • Prisoner Of Love / 1995 / CV / M • Pristine #1 / 1996 / CA / M • Pristine #2 / 1996 / CA / M • Private Film #24 / 1995 / OD / M • Private Film #25 / 1995 / OD / M • Private Film #26 / 1995 / OD / M • Public Enemy / 1995 / GO / M • Puritan Video

Magazine #05 / 1996 / LE / M • Puritan Video Magazine #10 / 1997 / LE / M • Pussyman #06: House Of Games / 1994 / SNA / M • Pussyman Auditions #08 / 1995 / SNA / M • Pussyman Auditions #11 / 1995 / SNA / M • Pussyman Auditions #16 / 1995 / SNA / M • Raunch Ranch / 1995 / LE / M • Red Door Diaries #1 / 1995 / ZA / M • Reflections / 1996 / ZA / M • Reminiscing / 1995 / LE / M • Rollover / 1996 / NIT / M • Roxy Rider Is In Control / 1996 / NIT / M • Rump Humpers #17 / 1994 / GLI / M • Safari Jane / 1995 / ERA / M • Saki's Private Party / 1995 / TTV / M • Sapphire / 1995 / ERA / M • The Seduction Of Marylin Star / 1995 / VT / M • Selena Under Siege / 1995 / XCI / M • Senior Stimulation / 1996 / CC / M • Sex Drivers / 1996 / VMX / M • Sex Therapy Ward / 1995 / LBO / M • Sexual Overdrive / 1996 / LE / M • Sexual Trilogy #04 / 1994 / SFP / M • Shades Of Erotica #03 / 1994 / GLI / M • Shave Tails #4 / 1995 / SO / M • Shock / 1995 / LE / M • The Shocking Truth #1 / 1996 / DWO / M • A Shot In The Pink / 1995 / BBE / M • Show & Tell / 1994 / ELP / M • Sideshow Freaks / 1996 / ZA / M • Six Degrees Of Penetration / 1996 / PP / M • Sleeping Single / 1994 / CC / M • Smoke & Mirrors / 1996 / PL / M • Soap Opera Sluts / 1996 / AFI / M • The Social Club / 1995 / LE / M • Sodom Chronicles / 1995 / FH / M • The Sodomizer #1 / 1995 / SC / M • Some Like It Wet / 1995 / LE / M • Split Decision / 1993 / FD / M • Starbangers #07 / 1995 / FPI / M • Starbangers #08 / 1996 / FPI / M • Steam / 1996 / ULP / M • Sticky Fingers / 1996 / WV / M • Striptease / 1995 / SPI / M • Surf Babes / 1995 / LE / M • The Swing / 1996 / VI / M • Tailz From Da Hood #1 / 1995 / AVI / M • Tailz From Da Hood #3 / 1996 / AVI / M • The Temple Of Poon / 1996 / PE / M • Throbbing Threesomes / 1996 / NIT / M • Tickling Vamps / 1995 / SBP / B • Tight Fit #08 / 1994 / GO / M • Tight Fit #10 / 1994 / GO / M • Tight Fit #11 / 1995 / GO / M • Tight Tushies #2 / 1994 / MET / M • Tinsel Town Tales / 1995 / NOT / M • Tits / 1995 / AVI / M • Topless Window Washers / 1996 / LE / M • Totally Real / 1996 / CA / M • Trick Shots / 1995 / PV / M • Truck Stop Angel / 1994 / CC / M • The Twin Peaks Of Mount Fuji / 1996 / SUF / M • Twists Of The Heart / 1995 / NIT / M • The Usual Anal Suspects / 1996 / CC / M • Violation / 1996 / LE / M • Virgin Bar Maids / 1996 / VMX / M • The Voyeur #2 / 1994 / EA / M • A Week And A Half In The Life Of A Prostitute / 1997 / EL / M • Wet Faces #1 / 1997 / SC / C • Whackers / 1995 / PP / M • What's In It 4 Me / 1995 / TEG / M • Wicked Ways #1: Interview With The Anal Queen / 1994 / WP / M • Wicked Ways #3: An All-Anal Slutfest / 1995 / WP / M • Wild Orgies #08 / 1994 / AFI / M • Wild Orgies #15 / 1995 / AFI / M • Witches are Bitches / 1996 / NIT / M • Working Girls / 1995 / FH / M • Xcitement: The Movie / 1993 / XCI / M • Yin Yang Oriental Love Bang #5: Lotus Blossoms / 1996 / SUF / M

KYLE TABER
Bedtime Video #04 / 1984 / GO / M

KYLIE CHANNEL *(Kiley, Sabina (Kylie Ch.))*
Dumb brunette with droopy boobs who chews gum all the time. Has a shaven pussy in

MDD #9.
Against All Bods / 1991 / VEX / M • America's Raunchiest Home Videos #02: Cooking with Hot Sauce / 1991 / ZA / M • Beverly Hills Geisha / 1992 / V99 / M • Cheatin' Hearts / 1991 / VEX / M • Dreams Of Candace Hart / 1991 / VI / M • Heartbreaker / 1991 / IF / M • Jamie Loves Jeff #2 / 1991 / VI / M • Long Dan Silver / 1992 / IF / M • More Dirty Debutantes #09 / 1991 / 4P / M • Physically Fit / 1991 / V99 / C • Queen Of Midnight / 1991 / V99 / M • Sweet Stuff / 1991 / V99 / M • Sweet Sunshine / 1995 / IF / M • Tomboy / 1991 / V99 / M • Voodoo Vixens / 1991 / IF / M

KYLIE IRELAND
Tall, large enhanced tits (36D) but a trim body otherwise. Pretty face. 23 years old in 1994 and comes from Colorado. De-virginized at 13 or 14 and married to a male named Nick. 5'5" tall, 118lbs, 36D-24-34, born May 26.
The 4th Vixxen / 1995 / EMC / M • A Is For Asia / 1996 / 4P / M • Ace Mulholland / 1995 / ERA / M • The Adventures Of Studman #2 / 1994 / AFV / M • The Adventures Of Studman #3 / 1994 / AFV / M • Anal Persuasion / 1994 / EX / M • Babe Watch #1 / 1994 / SC / M • Babe Watch #2 / 1994 / SC / M • Backdoor Diaries / 1995 / BBE / M • Bad Company / 1994 / VI / M • Big Knockers #08 / 1994 / TV / M • Big Knockers #09 / 1995 / TV / M • Big Knockers #10 / 1995 / TV / M • Big Knockers #20 / 1995 / TV / C • Big Knockers #21: Best Of Lesbian #2 / 1995 / TV / C • The Big Pink / 1995 / MID / M • Blindfold / 1994 / SC / M • Blonde Justice #3 / 1994 / VI / M • Car Wash Angels / 1995 / VC / M • Cat Lickers #4 / 1995 / ME / F • The Cheater / 1994 / XCI / M • Cheerleader Strippers / 1996 / PE / M • Cherry Pie / 1994 / SC / M • Chug-A-Lug Girls #5 / 1994 / VT / M • Crazy Love / 1995 / VI / M • Crazy With The Heat #3 / 1994 / CV / M • Crew Sluts / 1994 / KWP / M • Daydreams, Nightdreams / 1996 / VC / M • Decadent Obsession / 1995 / OD / M • The Dinner Party #1 / 1994 / ULI / M • Dirty Bob's #23: Tampa Teasers / 1995 / FLP / S • The Drifter / 1995 / CV / M • Erotic Escape / 1995 / FH / M • The F Zone / 1995 / WP / M • Face Jam / 1996 / VC / M • Fantasy Chamber / 1994 / ULI / M • First Time Ever #1 / 1995 / PE / F • Flesh Shopping Network #1 / 1995 / MID / M • Ghosts / 1994 / EMC / M • A Girl's Affair #07 / 1995 / FD / F • The Girls From Hootersville #07 / 1994 / SFP / M • Go Ahead...Eat Me! / 1995 / KWP / M • Heart Breaker / 1994 / CA / M • High Heel Harlots #04 / 1994 / SFP / M • Immortal Lust / 1996 / KLP / M • Initiation Of Kylie / 1995 / VT / M • Jiggly Queens #2 / 1994 / LE / M • Kinky Fantasies / 1994 / KWP / M • Leena Is Nasty / 1994 / OD / M • Legend #5: The Legend Continues / 1994 / LE / M • Lusty Ladies / 1994 / MET / F • Mighty Man #1: Virgins In The Forest / 1994 / LE / M • Ms. Behaved / 1994 / SC / M • Naked Desert / 1995 / VI / M • Never Say Never / 1994 / SC / M • Never Say Never, Again / 1994 / SC / M • New Ends #08 / 1994 / 4P / M • Night Crawlers / 1994 / SC / M • Nightshift Nurses #2 / 1996 / VC / M • Pajama Party X #1 / 1994 / VC / M • Pajama Party X #2 / 1994 / VC / M • Pajama Party X #3 / 1994 / VC / M • The Passion / 1995 / IP / M •

Peepshow / 1994 / OD / M • Picture Perfect (Cal Vista) / 1995 / CV / M • Playmates Of The Rich And Famous / 1995 / BBE / M • Poison / 1994 / VI / M • Private Performance / 1994 / EX / M • Provocative / 1994 / LE / M • Pussyclips #06 / 1995 / SNA / M • Rainwoman #08 / 1994 / CC / M • Reality & Fantasy / 1994 / DR / M • Risque Burlesque #1 / 1994 / IN / M • Sex Party / 1995 / KWP / M • Sexual Healing / 1994 / VI / M • Sexy Nurses #2 / 1994 / CV / M • Seymore & Shane Do Ireland / 1994 / ULI / M • Shave Tails #1 / 1994 / SO / M • Skin Dive / 1996 / SC / M • Smells Like...Sex / 1995 / VC / M • Smooth Ride / 1996 / WP / M • Sorority Sex Kittens #3 / 1996 / VC / M • Sorority Stewardesses #1 / 1995 / PE / M • Sorority Stewardesses #2 / 1995 / PE / M • The Stand-Up / 1994 / VC / M • The Star / 1994 / HO / M • Stiff Competition #2 / 1994 / CA / M • Strange Days / 1995 / FXV / S • Submission / 1994 / WP / M • Talk Dirty To Me #10 / 1996 / DR / M • Telephone Expose / 1995 / VC / M • Tender Loving Care / 1995 / WP / M • Titty Slickers #2 / 1994 / LE / M • Tongue In Cheek / 1994 / LE / M • Twist Of Fate / 1996 / WP / M • Up And Cummers #10 / 1994 / 4P / M • Up And Cummers #18 / 1995 / 4P / M • The Valley Girl Connection / 1994 / IN / M • Visions Of Seduction / 1994 / SC / M • The Voyeur #2 / 1994 / EA / M • Western Nights / 1994 / WP / M • Wet Faces #1 / 1997 / SC / C • Yankee Rose / 1994 / LE / M

KYLIE JAMES
Cocks In Frocks #1 / 1996 / TTV / G

KYM
Girls Around The World #22: Letha Weapons & Friends / 1995 / BTO / M • Video Virgins #17 / 1994 / NS / M

KYM PASSINGER
Ante Up / 1995 / CZV / M

KYM WILDE *(Kim Wylde, Jillian Amore, Julianna A'more, Regina Gielser, Victoria Starr (Kym))*
After Hours Bondage / 1993 / BON / B • All That: Black Women's Fantasies / 1996 / VT / M • Amateur Hours #45 / 1992 / AFI / M • Amateur Nights #06 / 1990 / HO / M • Anal Alley / 1990 / ME / M • Anal Climax #1 / 1991 / ROB / M • Ariana's Torment / 1995 / BON / B • Asian Silk / 1992 / VI / M • Ass Backwards / 1991 / ME / M • B&D Sorority / 1991 / BON / B • Baccarat #1 / 1991 / FH / M • Baccarat #2 / 1991 / FH / M • Backing In #2 / 1990 / WV / C • Backing In #3 / 1991 / WV / C • Bend Over Babes #2 / 1991 / EA / M • Beneath The Cane / 1992 / BON / B • The Big E #09 / 1990 / BIZ / B • Bondage Academy #1 / 1991 / BON / B • Bondage Academy #2 / 1991 / BON / B • Bondage Across The Border / 1993 / B&D / B • Bondage Memories #01 / 1993 / BON / C • Bondage Memories #04 / 1994 / BON / C • Bondage Shoots / 1993 / BON / B • Book Of Love / 1992 / VC / M • Bottoms Up (1993-Bon Vue) / 1993 / BON / B • Catfighting Students / 1995 / PRE / C • Cheatin' Hearts / 1991 / VEX / M • Cherry Redder / 1993 / RB / B • Chicks, Licks And Dirty Tricks / 1993 / ME / F • Collected Spankings #1 / 1992 / BON / C • Criss-Cross / 1993 / BON / B • Desert Heat / 1992 / BON / B • Don't Bother To Knock / 1991 / FAZ / M • Double Take / 1991 / BIZ / B • Dr F #2: Bad Medicine / 1990 / WV /

M • Dream Caller Bondage / 1993 / BON / B • Driving Miss Daisy Crazy #1 / 1990 / WV / M • Easy Pussy / 1991 / ROB / M • Enemates #08 / 1993 / BIZ / B • Erotic Heights / 1991 / AR / M • Flash Floods / 1991 / PRE / C • Flashpoint / 1991 / AFV / M • Flow Job / 1992 / PLV / B • Forbidden Fantasies / 1991 / BON / B • Formal Affair / 1991 / ... / M • Giggles / 1992 / PRE / B • Girls Will Be Boys #3 / 1991 / PL / F • Girls Will Be Boys #4 / 1991 / PL / F • Girls Will Be Boys #5 / 1993 / PL / F • Girls Will Be Boys #6 / 1993 / PL / F • Girls With Big Jugs / 1995 / V99 / M • Grand Slam / 1993 / ... / B • Hidden Obsessions / 1992 / BFP / M • Home Maid Memories #2 / 1994 / BON / C • I Do #3 / 1992 / VI / M • I'll Take The Whip / 1993 / BON / B • If Dreams Come True / 1991 / AFV / M • Joint Effort / 1992 / SEX / C • Just For The Hell Of It / 1991 / CA / M • Katrina And The Pros / 1992 / BON / B • Katrina's Bondage Memories #1 / 1994 / BON / C • Kym Wilde Bound On Stage #1 / 1993 / BON / B • Kym Wilde Bound On Stage #2 / 1993 / BON / B • Kym Wilde Bound On Stage #3 / 1993 / BON / B • Kym Wilde Remembered #1 / 1995 / BON / C • Kym Wilde Remembered #2 / 1995 / BON / C • Kym Wilde Sessions #1 / 1991 / B&D / B • Kym Wilde Sessions #2 / 1993 / BON / B • Kym Wilde Sessions #3 / 1993 / RB / B • Kym Wilde Sessions #4 / 1993 / RB / B • Kym Wilde's Bondage House Party #1 / cr92 / BON / B • Kym Wilde's Bondage House Party #2 / 1993 / BON / B • Kym Wilde's Ocean View / 1993 / BON / B • Kym Wilde's On The Edge #01 / 1993 / RB / B • Kym Wilde's On The Edge #02 / 1993 / RB / B • Kym Wilde's On The Edge #03 / 1993 / RB / B • Kym Wilde's On The Edge #04 / 1993 / RB / B • Kym Wilde's On The Edge #05 / 1993 / RB / B • Kym Wilde's On The Edge #06 / 1993 / RB / B • Kym Wilde's On The Edge #07 / 1994 / RB / B • Kym Wilde's On The Edge #08 / 1994 / RB / B • Kym Wilde's On The Edge #09 / 1994 / RB / B • Kym Wilde's On The Edge #10 / 1994 / RB / B • Kym Wilde's On The Edge #11 / 1994 / RB / B • Kym Wilde's On The Edge #12 / 1994 / RB / B • Kym Wilde's On The Edge #13 / 1994 / RB / B • Kym Wilde's On The Edge #16 / 1994 / RB / B • Kym Wilde's On The Edge #17 / 1995 / RB / B • Kym Wilde's On The Edge #18 / 1995 / RB / B • Kym Wilde's On The Edge #19 / 1995 / RB / B • Kym Wilde's On The Edge #21 / 1995 / RB / B • Kym Wilde's On The Edge #22 / 1995 / RB / B • Kym Wilde's On The Edge #23 / 1995 / RB / B • Kym Wilde's On The Edge #24 / 1995 / RB / B • Kym Wilde's On The Edge #25 / 1995 / RB / B • Kym Wilde's On The Edge #26 / 1995 / RB / B • Kym Wilde's On The Edge #27 / 1995 / RB / B • Kym Wilde's On The Edge #28 / 1995 / RB / B • Kym Wilde's On The Edge #29 / 1995 / RB / B • Kym Wilde's On The Edge #30 / 1995 / RB / B • Kym Wilde's On The Edge #31 / 1996 / RB / B • Kym Wilde's On The Edge #32 / 1996 / RB / B • Kym Wilde's On The Edge #33 / 1996 / RB / B • Kym Wilde's On The Edge #34 / 1996 / RB / B • Kym Wilde's On The Edge #35 / 1996 / RB / B • Kym Wilde's On The Edge #36 / 1996 / RB / B • Kym Wilde's On The Edge #37 / 1996 / RB / B • Kym Wilde's On The Edge #38 / 1996

/ RB / B • Kym Wilde's On The Edge #39 / 1996 / RB / B • Kym Wilde's Spanking Fantasies / 1995 / BON / C • Last Tango In Rio / 1991 / DR / M • Laugh Factory / 1995 / PRE / C • Leg...Ends #10 / 1994 / PRE / F • Legs And Lingerie #2 / 1990 / BEB / F • Life, Love And Divorce / 1990 / LV / M • The Mauling / 1995 / NAP / B • Moist To The Touch / 1991 / DR / M • More Dirty Debutantes / 1990 / PRI / M • Mr. Peepers Amateur Home Videos #21: Home Style Humpin' / 1991 / LBO / M • Old Fashioned Spankings / 1991 / BON / B • On The Job Training / 1991 / RB / B • On Trial #3: Takin' It To The Jury / 1992 / VI / M • On Trial #4: The Verdict / 1992 / VI / M • Oral Majority #08 / 1990 / WV / C • The Other Woman / 1992 / IMP / S • Painful Initiation / 1992 / PL / B • Painful Mistake (Dungeon) / 1993 / PL / B • Pajama Party / 1993 / CV / C • The Pamela Principle #1 / 1992 / IMP / S • Peep Land / 1992 / FH / M • Pink To Pink / 1993 / VI / C • Prescription For Pain #2: The Ultimate Pain / 1993 / BON / B • Profiles #03: House Dick / 1995 / XPR / M • Puttin' Her Ass On The Line / 1991 / DR / M • Queen Of Midnight / 1991 / V99 / M • Red Bottom Blues / 199? / BON / B • Roommate Humiliation / 1993 / PL / B • Running Mates / 1993 / PRE / B • Sexual Relations / 1990 / PP / M • Shot From Behind / 1992 / FAZ / M • Spanked Shopper & Other Tales / 1991 / BON / C • Spies Get Trashed / 1995 / NAP / B • Spread Sheets / 1991 / DR / M • Stepsister's Discipline / 1992 / RB / B • Student Fetish Videos: Best of Enema #02 / 1992 / PRE / C • Student Fetish Videos: Best Of Foot Worship #02 / 1994 / PRE / C • Student Fetish Videos: Catfighting #05 / 1992 / PRE / B • Student Fetish Videos: The Enema #10 / 1993 / PRE / B • Student Fetish Videos: Foot Worship #08 / 1992 / PRE / B • Super Enemates #2 / 1996 / PRE / C • Sweet Licks / 1991 / MID / M • Sweet Stuff / 1991 / V99 / M • Taboo #09 / 1991 / IN / M • Talk Dirty To Me #08 / 1990 / DR / M • Things Change / 1992 / MET / M • Things Change #2: Letting Go / 1992 / CV / M • Tied & Teased / 1993 / BON / B • To Taste The Strap / 199? / BON / B • Tools Of The Trade / 1990 / WV / M • Tug O' Love / 1990 / CC / M • Two Hearts / 1991 / VI / M • The Two Janes / 1990 / WV / M • Unfaithful Entry / 1992 / DR / M • Up For Grabs / 1991 / FH / M • Victim Of Love #1 / 1992 / VI / M • Victim Of Love #2 / 1992 / VI / M • Where The Boys Aren't #4 / 1992 / VI / F • Where The Boys Aren't #5 / 1992 / VI / F • The Wild One / 1990 / LE / M • Wishful Thinking / 1992 / VC / M • Women In Need / 1990 / HO / M • Young Cheeks / 1990 / BEB / B
KYOTO GEE see Kyoto Sun
KYOTO SUN *(Miko Yani-Kyoto, Miko Yama, Kyoto Gee)*
Ugly looking Oriental with a standard body. The Awakening Of Sally / 1984 / VCR / M • The China Cat / 1978 / CA / M • Deep Passage / 1984 / VCR / C • Exhausted / 1981 / CA / C • Fantasy / 1978 / VCX / M • For The Love Of Pleasure / 1979 / SE / M • Oriental Lust / 1983 / GO / M • Oriental Treatment #1 / 1978 / AR / M • Passion Toys / 1985 / VCR / C • Screwples / 1979 / CA / M • Star Of The Orient / 1978 / VIP / M • Taboo #01 / 1980 / VCX / M

KYRA
Russian Model Magazine #1 / 1996 / IP / M
KYRIE
Eye On You: Kyrie And Friend / 1996 / EOY / M
KYTANA
Anal Vision #22 / 1993 / LBO / M • Big Bust Babes #29 / 1995 / AFI / M • The Booty Bandit / 1994 / FC / M • Casting Call #04 / 1993 / SO / M • Dirty Doc's Housecalls #10 / 1994 / LV / M • Double D Dykes #18 / 1995 / GO / F • Hard Core Beginners #01 / 1995 / LEI / M • House Of Leather / 1995 / GO / M • M Series #16 / 1993 / LBO / M • Ron Hightower's White Chicks #08 / 1994 / LBO / M • Snatch Masters #07 / 1995 / LEI / M • Snatch Motors / 1995 / VC / M • Spinners #1 (Wicked) / 1995 / WP / M • Video Virgins #16 / 1994 / NS / M • Video Virgins #18 / 1994 / NS / M
L
Bondage "Sybian" Rides / 1994 / PSE / B • Mistress Justine #2 / 1995 / VP0 / B
L'IL ANNIE
Certified Mail / 1975 / CDC / M
L'ORIELE
ABA: Double Feature #2 / 1996 / ALP / M • Candi Girl / 1979 / PVX / M • Hot Child In The City / 1979 / PVX / M • Rip-Off Of Millie / cr78 / VHL / M
L. BAILEY
Love Office Style / 19?? / BOC / M
L. BROWNING see Kim Alexis
L. FLANAGAN see Star Index I
L. LEMAY
Garage Girls / 1981 / CV / M
L.A. ROCK see Star Index I
L.A. ROYALS
Adventures Of The DP Boys: Backyard Boogie / 1994 / HW / M • The Booty Bandit / 1994 / FC / M
L.C.
The Savage / 1994 / SC / M
L.C. CHERRY
Adventures Of The DP Boys: Big Black Booty / 1994 / HW / M • The Hitch-Hiker #09: Back Road Detour / 1994 / WMG / M • Star Spangled Blacks / 1994 / VEX / M
L.J. see Star Index I
L.P. RONNOCCO
Velvet / 1995 / SPI / M
L.S. TALBOT
Adult Video Nudes / 1993 / VC / M • Body And Soul / 1992 / OD / M • Confessions #1 / 1992 / OD / M • Juranal Park / 1993 / OD / M • The Living End / 1992 / OD / M • One Of Our Porn Stars Is Missing / 1993 / OD / M • Sodom & Gomorrah / 1992 / OD / M • Wilder At Heart / 1993 / ANA / M
L.T. DEE
Anna Amore's Fantasy Gang Bang / 1996 / FC / M • Back Rent / 1996 / MP0 / M • Best Gang Bangs / 1996 / DFI / C • Black Knockers #13 / 1995 / TV / M • Black Lube Job Girls / 1995 / SUF / M • Black Sensations: Models In Heat / 1995 / SUF / M • Bow Down Backstreet / 1996 / HW / M • Casting Couch Tips / 1996 / MP0 / M • Dreamgirls: Fort Lauderdale / 1996 / DR / M • Essence / 1996 / SO / M • Git Yo' Ass On Da Bus! / 1996 / HW / M • In Da Booty / 1996 / LV / M • Live Sex Net / 1996 / SPR / M • Sodomize Me!!! / 1996 / SPR / M • Toot Z Roll / 1995 / WP / M
LA DAWN see Le Dawn
LA TIERGA see Letigre

LA TIGRE see Letigre
LA TOYA
Fucking Pregnant Babes #3: La Toya'a Office Visit / 1995 / AVS / M
LA WANDA
Blue Vanities #548 / 1994 / FFL / M
LABIA LATEX
Senior Sexcapades #1 / 1995 / PL / M
LACE
AVP #9123: Oops...My Boyfriend's Home / 1991 / AVP / M • Nasty Newcummers #05 / 1994 / MET / M • Prime Cuts #1 / 1994 / FOR / M • Prime Cuts #2 / 1994 / FOR / M • Pussyclips #02 / 1994 / SNA / M
LACEE
AVP #8010: Bi-Bi Shannon / 1990 / AVP / F • AVP #9010: Lustful Lacee / 1990 / AVP / F • AVP #9012: Slow & Easy, Long & Hard / 1990 / AVP / M
LACEY
Up And Cummers #21 / 1995 / RWP / M • Very Bad Girls / 1995 / GOT / B
LACEY LANCE see Star Index I
LACEY LOGAN *(Lacy Logan, Dina Rice)*
Dina Rice is from **Dialing For Desires**.
Backstage / 1988 / CDI / M • Born To Be Wild / 1987 / SE / M • The Color of Honey / 1987 / SUV / M • Debbie Does The Devil In Dallas / 1987 / SE / M • Dialing For Desires / 1988 / 4P / M • Fantasy Chamber / 1987 / VT / M • Hot Amber Nights / 1987 / CC / M • Hot Yachts / 1987 / VEX / M • Hyapatia Lee's Arcade Series #02 / 1988 / ZA / C • Interracial Sex / 1987 / M&M / M • The Joys Of Masturbation / 1988 / M&M / M • Lust Of Blacula / 1987 / VEX / M • No Man's Land #01 / 1988 / VT / C • Shipwrecked / 1991 / VEX / C • Strictly Business / 1987 / VD / M • Wet Workout / 1987 / VEX / M
LACEY LUV see Lana Burner
LACEY PLEASURE
10 Years Of Big Busts #3 / 199? / BTO / C • Big Bust Blondes / 1992 / BTO / F • Big Bust Strippers / 1992 / BTO / F • Exposure Images #01: Lacey Pleasure / 1992 / EXI / F • Score Busty Covergirls #3 / 1995 / BTO / S
LACEY RIVERS
Bizarre Styles / 1981 / ALP / B
LACEY ROSE see Lacy Rose
LACEY SMITH
Pandora's Mirror / 1981 / CA / M
LACONTESSA see Star Index I
LACTALLICA see Star Index I
LACY
The Ass Master #01 / 1993 / GLI / M • Biography: Max Steiner / 1995 / SC / C • Bubble Butts Gold #2 / 1994 / LBO / M • Creme De La Face #12: Pretty Faces To Cum On / 1995 / OD / M • Dirty Doc's Housecalls #07 / 1994 / LV / M • Mike Hott: #106 Dusty And Lacy / 1990 / MHV / F • Swinging Shift / 1985 / CDI / M
LACY ADAMS see Lacy Rose
LACY ANDREWS
The Girls From Butthole Ridge / 1994 / ZA / M • The Hitch-Hiker #02: Dangerous Curves / 1994 / WMG / M • Take This Wad And Shove It! / 1994 / ZA / M
LACY DIAMOND
More Dirty Debutantes #42 / 1995 / 4P / M
LACY LACE
Male Domination #14 / 1990 / BIZ / C • Punished By Two / 1990 / BIZ / B
LACY LOGAN see Lacey Logan

LACY LOVE
Breastman's Hot Legs Contest / 1996 / ... / M • Domina #5: Whipper Snapper / 1996 / LBO / B • Domina #7 / 1996 / LBO / B • Innocent Little Girls #2 / 1996 / MP0 / M • Macin' #1 / 1996 / SMP / M • My First Time #4 / 1996 / NS / M • Underground #1 / 1996 / SC / M • The Violation Of Paisley Hunter / 1996 / JMP / F • Young And Anal #6 / 1996 / JMP / M

LACY LUV see Lana Burner

LACY ROSE *(Lacy Adams, Scarlet Rose, Lacey Rose)*
Medium sized blonde/redhead with small breasts and a so so but not pretty face. Wavy long hair. Elephant ears pussy. Has had her tits inflated (from an A to a C) as of late 1992. First feature movie was **Hidden Agenda**. 5'8" and 120 lbs—she has a 6 year old child. Born Mar 4 1969 in Laguna Beach CA (21 in 1992). Started in the business in April 1992. First pro-am movie was **Bubble Butts #11** but says in **MDD #29** that that was her first movie.
Ace Mulholland / 1995 / ERA / M • Always Anal / 1995 / AVI / C • Amateur Lesbians #31: Lacy / 1992 / GO / F • Amateurs Exposed #01 / 1993 / CV / M • The Anal Adventures Of Bruce Seven / 1996 / BS / C • Anal Kitten / 1992 / ROB / M • Anal Orgy / 1993 / DRP / M • Anal Savage #1 / 1992 / ROB / M • Anal Siege / 1993 / ROB / M • Anal Squeeze / 1993 / FOR / M • Anal Taboo / 1993 / ROB / M • Anal Thunder #1 / 1993 / ROB / M • Anal Vision #21 / 1993 / LBO / M • Anal With An Oriental Slant / 1993 / ROB / M • The Anal-Europe Series #02: Fantasies / 1992 / LV / M • Animal Instinct / 1996 / DTV / M • Anus & Andy / 1993 / ZA / M • Anus The Menace / 1993 / CC / M • Arabian Nights / 1993 / WP / M • Assent Of A Woman / 1993 / DR / M • The Awakening / 1992 / SC / M • Babes / 1993 / HO / M • Behind The Backdoor #6 / 1993 / EVN / M • Behind The Blinds / 1992 / VIM / M • Between The Cheeks #3 / 1993 / VC / M • The Big Bang #2 / 1994 / LV / M • Big Boob Boat Ride #1 / 1992 / FC / M • Big Knockers #05 / 1994 / TV / M • Big Knockers #06 / 1994 / TV / M • Big Knockers #07 / 1994 / TV / M • Bikini Beach #1 / 1993 / CC / M • Bikini Beach #2 / 1993 / CC / M • Bikini Beach #3 / 1993 / CC / F • Black Booty / 1993 / ZA / M • Black For More / 1993 / ZA / M • Black Orchid / 1993 / WV / M • Blind Spot / 1993 / VI / M • Blonde Justice #2 / 1993 / VI / M • Body English / 1993 / PL / M • Body Of Innocence / 1993 / WP / M • The Bottom Dweller / 1993 / EL / M • The Bottom Dweller Part Deux / 1994 / EL / M • Bottoms Up (1993-Hollywood) / 1993 / HO / M • Breastman Does The Himalayas / 1993 / EVN / M • Bringing Up The Rear / 1993 / VD / C • Bubble Butts #11 / 1992 / LBO / M • Bubble Butts #16 / 1992 / LBO / M • Butt Bandits #4 / 1996 / VD / C • Butt Bongo Babes / 1993 / VD / M • Butt Hole Boulevard / 1993 / CA / M • Butt's Up, Doc #2 / 1992 / GO / M • Butt's Up, Doc #3 / 1992 / GO / M • Buttslammers #01 / 1993 / BS / F • Buttslammers #05: Quake, Rattle & Roll! / 1994 / BS / F • Captain Butt's Beach / 1992 / LV / M • Caught From Behind #19 / 1994 / HO / M • Cheerleader Nurses #1 / 1993 / VC / M • Cheerleader Nurses #2 / 1993 / VC / M • Coming Of For-

tune / 1994 / EX / M • The Creasemaster / 1993 / VC / M • Cumming Of Ass / 1995 / TP / M • The Cumming Of Sarah Jane #1 / 1993 / AFV / M • Dick & Jane Do The Strip / 1994 / AVI / M • Dick & Jane In San Francisco / 1996 / AVI / M • Dick & Jane Up, Down And All Around / 1994 / AVI / M • Dirty Bob's #12: Vegas Blues #2 / 1994 / FLP / S • Eleventh Annual AVN Awards / 1994 / VC / M • Extreme Passion / 1993 / WP / M • Facesitter #1 / 1992 / CC / M • Facesitter #2 / 1993 / CC / M • Gang Bang Face Bath #1 / 1993 / ROB / M • Ghosts / 1994 / EMC / M • Gimme An X / 1993 / VD / C • A Girl's Affair #01 / 1992 / FD / F • The Governess / 1993 / WP / M • Gypsy Queen / 1995 / CC / M • Hidden Agenda / 1992 / XCI / M • Hollywood Swingers #04 / 1992 / LBO / M • Hopeless Romantic / 1992 / LE / M • Hot For Teacher / 1993 / VD / M • Hot Tight Asses #03 / 1993 / TCK / M • In Your Wildest Dreams / 1993 / STY / M • International Analists / 1994 / AFD / M • Junkyard Dykes #01 / 1994 / ZA / F • Junkyard Dykes #02 / 1994 / ZA / F • Junkyard Dykes #03 / 1994 / ZA / F • Kinky Cameraman #2 / 1994 / LEI / C • Kittens #4: Bodybuilding Bitches / 1993 / CC / F • Lacy's Hot Anal Summer / 1992 / LV / M • Latex #1 / 1994 / VC / M • Legacy Of Love / 1992 / LE / M • Living Doll / 1992 / CDI / M • Love Me, Love My Butt #1 / 1994 / ROB / F • The Lovers / 1993 / HO / M • Madame Hiney: The Beverly Hills Butt Broker / 1993 / STR / M • Mask / 1993 / VI / M • Midnight Confessions / 1992 / XCI / M • More Dirty Debutantes #29 / 1994 / 4P / M • Muffy The Vampire Layer / 1992 / LV / M • Native Tongue / 1993 / VI / M • New Wave Hookers #3 / 1993 / VC / M • Night And Day #1 / 1993 / VT / M • Nightvision / 1993 / TP / M • Nikki's Nightlife / 1992 / IN / M • Nobody's Looking / 1993 / VC / M • Nothing To Hide #2 / 1993 / CV / M • Odyssey Triple Play #50: Rainbow Coition! / 1993 / OD / M • The Orgy #1 / 1993 / EMC / M • The Orgy #2 / 1993 / EMC / M • The Orgy #3 / 1993 / EMC / M • Orgy Attack / 1993 / DRP / M • Pussyman #01: The Search / 1993 / CC / M • Pussyman #05: Captive Audience / 1994 / SNA / M • Rainbird / 1994 / EMC / M • Rainwoman #06 / 1993 / CC / M • Raunch #07 / 1993 / CC / M • Reel Life / 1993 / ZA / M • The Reel World #1 / 1994 / FOR / M • The Reel World #2 / 1994 / FOR / M • Rhapsody / 1993 / VT / M • Satin & Lace / 1994 / WP / M • Satisfaction / 1992 / LE / M • Seven Good Women / 1993 / HO / F • Seymore Butts In The Love Shack / 1992 / FH / M • Seymore Butts: Bustin' Out My Best Anal / 1995 / FH / C • Sista Act / 1994 / AVI / M • Sister Snatch #2 / 1995 / SNA / M • Slip Of The Tongue / 1993 / DR / M • Sodom & Gomorrah / 1992 / OD / M • Sodomania #01: Tales Of Perversity / 1992 / EL / M • Sodomania: The Baddest Of The Best...And Then Some / 1994 / EL / C • Sorority Sex Kittens #1 / 1992 / VC / M • Sorority Sex Kittens #2 / 1993 / VC / M • Southern Cumfort / 1993 / HO / M • The Spa / 1993 / VC / M • Split Tail Lovers / 1994 / ROB / M • Steamy Windows / 1993 / VI / M • Stocking Stuffers / 1992 / LV / M • The Sweeper / 1996 / PME / S • Sweet Target / 1992 / CDI / M • Tales From Sodom / 1994 / BLC / M • Talk Dirty To Me

#09 / 1992 / DR / M • Tell Me...Dr Bumpers / 1994 / MV / S • Tight Ends In Motion / 1993 / TP / M • The Truth Laid Bare / 1993 / ZA / M • Unfaithful Entry / 1992 / DR / M • Unsolved Double Penetration / 1993 / PEP / M • Vampire's Kiss / 1993 / AVI / M • Visions Of Seduction / 1994 / SC / M • Wicked Woman / 1994 / HO / M • Wild Flower #2 / 1992 / VI / M • Wild Things #3 / 1992 / MET / M • Women Of Influence / 1993 / LV / F

LACY SOUTHERN see Star Index I

LADONNA see Star Index I

LADY A see Lady Antoinette

LADY ADEE see Star Index I

LADY AMANDA
Skin #4: The 4th Rite / 1995 / ERQ / M

LADY ANDREA see Star Index I

LADY ANTOINETTE *(Lady A)*
Ugly black girl with a two-seater butt, empty sacs for tits when not pregnant, tree trunk thighs and a fat belly.
Adventures Of The DP Boys: The Blacks Are Back / 1994 / HW / M • Anal Delinquent #2 / 1994 / ROB / M • Beach Bum Amateur's #38 / 1993 / MID / M • Black Beauty (Coast To Coast) / 1994 / CC / M • Black Centerfold Celebrities / 1993 / MID / M • Black Fantasies #12 / 1996 / HW / M • Black Fire / 1993 / VIM / M • Black Gangbangers #01 / 1994 / HW / M • Black Hollywood Amateurs #02 / 1995 / MID / M • Black Hollywood Amateurs #04 / 1995 / MID / M • Black Hollywood Amateurs #06 / 1995 / MID / M • Black Hollywood Amateurs #10 / 1995 / MID / M • Black Hollywood Amateurs #13 / 1995 / MID / M • Black Hollywood Amateurs #21 / 1996 / MID / M • Black Jack City #3 / 1993 / HW / M • Black Knockers #01 / 1995 / TV / M • Black On Black (1994-Evn) / 1994 / EVN / M • Black Streets / 1994 / LE / M • Brown Sugar From The Hood / 1996 / MID / M • Chocolate Bunnies #02 / 1995 / LBO / C • Chocolate Bunnies #03 / 1995 / LBO / C • Chocolate Bunnies #04 / 1995 / LBO / C • Da Booty Call / 1994 / HW / M • Ebony Anal Gang Bang #1 / 1994 / RTP / M • Ebony Erotica #11: Harlem Knights / 1993 / GO / M • Girl's Towne #2 / 1994 / FC / F • Hooters In The 'hood / 1995 / TTV / M • Lactamania #3 / 1995 / TTV / M • Lactamania #4 / 1996 / TTV / M • A Little Bit Pregnant / 1995 / SO / M • M Series #01 / 1993 / LBO / M • M Series #18 / 1994 / LBO / M • M Series #27 / 1994 / LBO / M • Mo' Honey / 1993 / FH / M • My Baby Got Back #02 / 1993 / VT / M • Odyssey Triple Play #31: Double Penetration Babes / 1993 / OD / M • Pumps In Da Rump #1 / 1994 / HW / M • Ready To Drop #09 / 1995 / FC / M • Ready To Drop #10 / 1996 / FC / M • Shades Of Erotica #02 / 1994 / GLI / M • Sista! #1 / 1993 / VT / F • Sparkling Champagne / 1994 / FH / M • Ultimate Gang Bang #1 / 1994 / HW / M • Up The Ying Yang #1 / 1994 / CC / M

LADY ASHLEY LIBERTY *(Ashley Liberty, Pamela Liberty, Liberty (Lady Ashl))*
The Bimbo #2: The Homecoming / 1986 / RLV / M • Black Licorice / 1985 / CDI / M • Cherry Cheesecake / 1984 / AR / M • Down & Out In New York City / 1986 / SE / M • Our Naked Eyes / 1988 / TME / M • Sex Crimes 2084 / 1985 / SE / M • Sinners #1 / 1988 / COM / M • Sinners #2 / 1988 / COM

/ M • Sinners #3 / 1989 / COM / M • Sleazy Susan / 1986 / VXP / M • Techsex / 1988 / VXP / M

LADY BERLIN see Berlin

LADY BOUNTIFUL
Blue Vanities #580 / 1996 / FFL / M

LADY CARLA
Learn Your Lessons / 1992 / BIZ / B

LADY CRYSTAL
The Bondage File / 19?? / BIZ / C • Kinky Couples / 1980 / BIZ / B • A Lady At Last / cr80 / BIZ / G

LADY D see Star Index I

LADY DIANA see Star Index I

LADY GABRIELLE
The Unsuspecting Repairman #2 / 1995 / TVI / B

LADY GODIVA
A Very Debauched Girl / 1988 / PL / M

LADY GREEN
Welcome To SM / 1996 / ESF / B

LADY HEATHER see Star Index I

LADY JESSICA
Revenge & Punishment / 1995 / GOT / B

LADY K.
Caught, Punished And Caged / 1991 / BIZ / B • A Slave For The Bride / 1991 / BIZ / B • Sweet Surrender / 1991 / BIZ / B • Sweet Surrender / 1991 / BIZ / B

LADY LAUREN
She-Males In Torment #3 / 1995 / BIZ / G • TVs In Leather And Pain / 1996 / BIZ / G

LADY LEATHER see Star Index I

LADY M. see Emily Hill

LADY MAGIC
Porked / 1986 / VXP / M • Sweet Revenge / 1986 / ZA / M • There's Magic In The Air / 1987 / AR / M • [Trailer Park Twats / 1986 / ... / M

LADY MARILYN
She-Male Slut House / 1994 / HEA / G

LADY MARTHA
Painful Mistake (Blowfish) / 1994 / BLP / B

LADY MYSTERIA see Star Index I

LADY NATASHA
Always Bet On Blond / 1995 / IBN / B

LADY NESBITT see Star Index I

LADY NICOLE
The Fantasy World Of Nicole / cr87 / BIZ / B • Mistress Sarona's School Of Discipline / 1987 / BIZ / B

LADY PAREE see Paree

LADY ROXANNE
The Piercing Of Jamie / 1983 / BIZ / B

LADY ROZANNE see Star Index I

LADY SABRINA SNOW
After The Party / 1993 / AMF / B • Bedroom Slaves / 1994 / GOT / B • Caught! / 1994 / GOT / B • Dangerous Desires (Gotham) / 1994 / GOT / B

LADY SAMANTHA see Velvet Touch

LADY SHANNE see Lydia Chanel

LADY SHARON see Star Index I

LADY STEPHANIE (Steph)
Bedtime Tales / 1985 / SE / M • Bi 'n' Large / 1992 / VD / C • Black Baby Dolls / 1985 / TAG / M • Black Bad Girls / 1985 / PLY / M • Black Bunbusters / 1985 / VC / M • Black Fox / 1988 / CC / M • Black Magic / 1985 / WET / M • Black On White / 1987 / PL / C • Black Throat / 1985 / VC / M • Blonde On Black / 1986 / CC / F • Chocolate Delights #1 / 1985 / TAG / C • Dark Brothers, Dark Sisters / 1986 / VCS / C • Ebony Ecstasy / 1988 / HIO / C • Ebony Orgies / 1987 / SE / C • Ebony Superstars / 1988 / VC / C • Hill

Street Blacks #1 / 1985 / 4R / M • Hot Cars, Nasty Women / 1985 / WV / M • Let Me Tell Ya 'Bout Black Chicks / 1985 / VC / M • Let Me Tell Ya 'Bout White Chicks / 1985 / VC / M • VCA Previews #4 / 1988 / VC / C

LADY THORN see Star Index I

LADY VICTORIA
Toe Tales #13 / 1994 / GOT / B • Toe Tales #18 / 1994 / GOT / B

LAETITIA
Adultress / 1995 / WIV / M

LAGINA VALENTINA see Gina Valentino

LAILANI see Laurien Dominique

LAINE
She-Male Encounters #06: Trilogy Of The Bizarre / 1981 / MET / G

LAINE CARLIN
Blue Vanities #544 / 1994 / FFL / M • House On Bare Mountain / 1962 / SOW / S

LAKE GENEVA GREG
Erotic Tattooing And Piercing #1 / 1986 / FLV / M

LAL HARDY
Erotic Tattooing And Piercing #1 / 1986 / FLV / M

LAMAR GILBERT see Star Index I

LAMAR JOHNSON
Love Airlines / 1978 / SE / M

LANA
100% Amateur #01: Double Penetration Sensation / 1995 / OD / M • East Coast Sluts #10: Ohio / 1996 / PL / M • Filthy First Timers #7 / 1997 / EL / M • GRG: Pretty And Perverted / 1996 / GRG / M • Jamie And Lana / 1992 / JBV / B • Mr. Peepers Nastiest #2 / 1995 / LBO / C • Pantyhose Teasers #1 / 1991 / JBV / S • Pantyhose Teasers #2 / 1992 / JBV / S • Prague By Night #1 / 1996 / EA / M

LANA ALBERTS
Pony Girl #2: At The Ranch / 1986 / CS / B

LANA BURNER (Lacy Luv, Judy Powers, Lacey Luv)
Blonde with black roots, large enhanced (seem to be) tits, reasonably pretty, tight body, too much make up.
Cover Girls / 1985 / VEX / C • Desperately Seeking Suzie / 1985 / VD / M • E Three / 1985 / GO / M • Ginger's Private Party / 1985 / VI / M • Girls Of Paradise #1 / 1986 / PV / C • Jean Genie / 1985 / CA / M • Jubilee Of Eroticism / 1985 / GO / M • Just Another Pretty Face / 1985 / AVC / M • Ladies Of The 80's / 1985 / PV / M • Like A Virgin #1 / 1985 / AT / M • The Lover Girls / 1985 / VEX / M • Lust In Space / 1985 / PV / M • Marilyn Chambers' Private Fantasies #6 / 1985 / CA / M • One Hot Night Of Passion / 1985 / COL / C • Oral Majority #01 / 1986 / WV / C • Savage Fury #1 / 1985 / VEX / M • Summer Break / 1985 / VEX / M • Thrill Street Blues / 1985 / WV / M • The Whore Of The Worlds / 1985 / PV / M • Wicked Whispers / 1985 / VD / M

LANA CAZAR
Man To Maiden / 1984 / BIZ / B • The Story of Bobby / cr80 / BIZ / B

LANA COX
Private Film #07 / 1994 / OD / M

LANA D'ANGELO
Erotic Dimensions: Explicit / 1982 / NSV / M

LANA EMERSON see Star Index I

LANA FLOWER
[Assmasters / 197? / ... / M

LANA GEMSER see Laura Gemser

LANA KARENINA
Russian Girls / 1996 / WV / M

LANA LUST see Star Index I

LANA LUSTER
The Best Little He/She House In Texas / 1993 / HSV / G • The Bi Valley / 1994 / BIL / G • Driven Home / 1995 / CSP / G • Lady Dick / 1993 / HSV / G • The Princess With A Penis / 1994 / HSV / G • Queens From Outer Space / 1993 / HSV / G • She Male Dicktation / 1994 / HEA / G • She's The Boss / 1993 / BIL / G • She-Male Instinct / 1995 / BCP / G • She-Male Vacation / 1993 / HSV / G • Trans America / 1993 / TSS / G • Transexual Blvd / 1994 / PL / G • TV Evangelist / 1993 / HSV / G

LANA PRESTON
In-Flight Service / 19?? / BL / M

LANA SANDS (Makayla, Leisha Chang Mai, Makayla Leigh, Alina, Makaya Leigh, Makayluh Leigh, Lana Starr, Lona Sands, Lana Stone, Elanna, Alina Kovalenco, Alina Kovelenco, Alina Kovaienco)
Hispanic young girl who may have Oriental overtones (especially when you look at the alternate names) 34-24-36, 5'6 1/2" tall with a small mole under her left nostril, tiny tits, pointed ears and long lobes. Nice smile. Wears a wedding ring. 21 years old in 1993.
The Adventures Of Buck Naked / 1994 / OD / M • The Adventures Of Peeping Tom #1 / 1996 / OD / M • Anal Climax #4 / 1996 / ROB / M • Anal Crash Test Dummies / 1997 / ROB / M • Anal Delinquent #1 / 1993 / ROB / M • The Anal Diary Of Misty Rain / 1993 / EL / M • Anal Heartbreaker / 1995 / ROB / M • Anal Lover #3 / 1994 / ROB / M • Anal Pussycat / 1995 / ROB / M • Anal Secrets (Metro) / 1994 / IN / M • Anal Sluts & Sweethearts #3 / 1995 / ROB / M • Anal Spitfire / 1994 / ROB / M • Asian Appetite / 1993 / HO / M • Asian Heat #03: Tales Of The Golden Lotus / 1993 / SC / M • Backfield In Motion / 1995 / VT / M • Backing In #5 / 1995 / WV / C • The Best Of Black Anal #1 / 1995 / ROB / C • Bikini Beach #4 / 1996 / CC / M • Black And White Revisited / 1995 / VT / F • Black Buttman #01 / 1993 / CC / M • Black Dirty Debutantes / 1993 / 4P / M • Black Jack City #4 / 1994 / HW / M • Black On White Revisited / 1995 / VT / M • Black Orgies #04 / 1993 / AFI / M • Black Velvet #3 / 1994 / CC / M • Bloopers & Behind The Scenes / 1995 / LEI / M • Blue Movie / 1995 / WP / M • Blue Saloon / 1996 / ME / M • The Blues #2 / 1994 / VT / M • Bobby Hollander's Rookie Nookie #04 / 1993 / SFP / M • Bobby Hollander's Rookie Nookie #13 / 1993 / SFP / M • Body Of Innocence / 1993 / WP / M • Boiling Point / 1994 / WAV / M • Booty Ho #1 / 1993 / ROB / M • Brassiere To Eternity / 1994 / PEP / F • Brooklyn Nights / 1994 / OD / M • Brothers Bangin' / 1995 / ANA / M • Bump 'n' Grind / 1994 / HW / M • Butthead Dreams / 1994 / FH / M • The Buttnicks #4: The Black Buttnicks / 1993 / CC / M • Caged Fury / 1993 / DR / M • Carnal College #2 / 1993 / AFV / M • Cloud 900 / 1996 / EYE / M • Club Decca / 1996 / BAC / F • Cracklyn / 1994 / HW / M • Creme De La Face #01 / 1994 / OD / M • Cumback Pussy #3: Coast To Coast Rump Romp / 1996 / EL / M • The Cumming Of Sarah Jane #1 / 1993 / AFV / M • Dark Alleys #12

/ 1993 / FC / M • Deadly Sin / 1996 / ONA / M • The Decadent Adventures Of Generation XXX / 1994 / MAX / M • Deep Cheeks #4 / 1993 / ROB / M • Deep Cheeks #5 / 1995 / ROB / M • Deep Focus / 1995 / VC / M • Deep Space 69 / 1994 / HW / M • Defying The Odds / 1995 / OD / M • Desert Moon / 1994 / SPI / M • Diary Of A Geisha / 1995 / WV / C • Dick & Jane Sneak On The Set / 1993 / AVI / M • Dirty Tricks #1: Just A Bunch Of Whores / 1995 / EA / M • Dog Walker / 1994 / EA / M • The Dragon Lady #5: Tales From The Bed #4 / 1993 / WV / M • The Dragon Lady #6: Tales From The Bed #5 / 1993 / WV / M • The Dream Team / 1995 / VT / M • Dreams Of A Gigolo / 1996 / SNA / M • Ebony Erotica #05: Black Obsessions / 1993 / GO / M • Every Nerd Has A Fantasy / 1996 / FC / M • Fantasy Flings #01 / 1993 / WP / M • The Finishing Touch / 1994 / DR / M • Fishbone / 1994 / WIV / F • Flexxx #4 / 1995 / VT / M • The French Invasion / 1993 / LBO / M • The Fury / 1993 / WIV / M • Gang Bang Face Bath #1 / 1993 / ROB / M • Gang Bang Wild Style #1 / 1993 / ROB / M • Girls Of The Athletic Department / 1995 / VT / M • Golddiggers #2 / 1995 / VC / M • Heart Breaker / 1994 / CA / M • Heat / 1995 / WAV / M • Heavenscent / 1993 / ZA / M • Hollywood On Ice / 1995 / VT / M • Hollywood Swingers #10 / 1993 / LBO / M • Hot Tight Asses #08 / 1994 / TCK / M • Hot Tight Asses #09 / 1994 / TCK / M • Hot Tight Asses #16 / 1996 / TCK / M • Immortal Desire / 1993 / VI / M • Jetstream / 1993 / AMP / M • John Wayne Bobbitt Uncut / 1994 / LEI / M • Kink World: The Seduction Of Nena / 1993 / PL / M • Kinky Cameraman #4 / 1996 / LEI / C • Lana Exposed / 1995 / VT / M • Little Miss Anal / 1994 / ROB / M • Lovin' Spoonfuls #3 / 1995 / 4P / C • M Series #01 / 1993 / LBO / M • Madame Hollywood / 1993 / LE / M • The Man Who Loves Women / 1994 / VC / M • Margarita On The Rocks / 1994 / SFP / M • My Baby Got Back #03 / 1993 / VT / M • My Baby Got Back #04 / 1994 / VT / M • My Baby Got Back #05 / 1995 / VT / M • My Baby Got Back #06 / 1995 / VT / M • My Baby Got Back #07 / 1995 / VT / M • My Baby Got Back #08 / 1996 / VT / M • My Baby Got Back #09 / 1996 / VT / M • The New Butt Hunt #19 / 1996 / LEI / C • No Man's Land #07 / 1993 / VT / F • No Man's Land #12 / 1995 / VT / F • Ona Zee's Doll House #3 / 1995 / ONA / F • Ona Zee's Doll House / 1996 / ONA / F • The Orgy #1 / 1993 / EMC / M • The Orgy #2 / 1993 / EMC / M • The Orgy #3 / 1993 / EMC / M • Outlaws / 1993 / SC / M • Perfect Gift / 1994 / BRI / S • Photo Opportunity / 1994 / VC / M • Pick Up Lines #03 / 1995 / 4P / M • Pick Up Lines #04 / 1995 / 4P / M • Pick Up Lines #12 / 1997 / OD / M • Profiles #03: House Dick / 1995 / XPR / M • Profiles #07: Sexworld / 1996 / XPR / M • Pussyman #07: On The Dark Side / 1994 / SNA / M • Pussyman #10: Butts, Butts & More Butts / 1995 / SNA / M • Pussyman #14: Dreams Of A Gigolo / 1996 / SNA / M • Pussyman Auditions #03 / 1995 / SNA / M • Pussyman's House Party #1 / 1996 / SNA / M • Pussyman's House Party #2 / 1996 / SNA / M • The Reel World #1 / 1994 / FOR / M • Rump-Shaker #3 / 1994 / HW / M •

Sarah Jane's Love Bunnies #02 / 1993 / FPI / F • Sarah Jane's Love Bunnies #03 / 1993 / FPI / F • Saturday Night Porn #1 / 1993 / AFV / M • Sean Michaels On The Road #02: Da Hood / 1993 / VT / M • The Search For Canadian Beaver / 1995 / LIP / F • Secret Of Her Suckcess / 1994 / VC / M • Secret Urges (Vidco) / 1994 / VD / C • Sensual Exposure / 1993 / ULI / M • Sex Academy #3: The Art Of Real Sex / 1994 / ONA / M • Sex Academy #4: The Art Of Anal / 1994 / ONA / M • Sex Fugitives / 1993 / LE / M • Sex On The Run #1 / 1994 / TTV / M • Sex On The Run #2 / 1994 / TTV / M • Sex Secrets Of A Mistress / 1995 / VI / M • Sexhibition #2 / 1996 / SUF / M • Seymore & Shane On The Loose / 1994 / ULI / M • Shane's World #2 / 1996 / OD / M • Sherlock Homie / 1995 / IN / M • Sista! #2 / 1994 / VT / F • Sista! #3 / 1995 / VT / F • Sista! #4 / 1996 / VT / F • Skin Hunger / 1995 / MET / M • Slammin! / 1994 / CA / C • Sleeping Booty / 1995 / EL / M • Slip Of The Tongue / 1993 / DR / M • Sloppy Seconds / 1994 / PE / M • Smells Like...Sex / 1995 / VC / M • Smooth As Silk / 1994 / EMC / M • Sodomania #13: Your Lucky Number / 1995 / EL / M • Sodomania #16: Sexxy Pistols / 1996 / EL / M • Sodomania: Slop Shots / 1996 / EL / C • Southern Comfort / 1993 / HO / M • Sparkling Champagne / 1994 / FH / M • Stacked With Honors / 1993 / DR / M • Strippers Inc. #1 / 1994 / ONA / M • Superstar Sex Challenge #2 / 1994 / VC / M • Sure Bet / 1995 / CV / M • The Sweet Sweet Back's Big Bone (#1) / 1994 / FH / M • Tail Taggers #103 / 1993 / WV / M • Take The A Train / 1993 / MID / M • The Tempest / 1993 / SC / M • Tender Loving Care / 1994 / BRI / S • The Tongue / 1995 / OD / M • Top Debs #3: Riding Academy / 1993 / GO / M • Trashy Ladies / 1993 / LIP / F • Up And Cummers #03 / 1993 / 4P / M • Up Your Ass #3 / 1996 / ANA / M • Valentino's Asian Invasion / 1997 / SC / M • The Voyeur #2 / 1994 / EA / M • Waiting For The Man / 1996 / VT / M • Whiplash / 1996 / DFI / M • White Wedding / 1995 / VI / M • Whoomp! There She Is / 1993 / AVI / M • Wild & Wicked #3 / 1993 / VT / M • Within & Without You / 1993 / WP / M • Women Of Color #1 / 1994 / ANA / M • [Sun Drenched She Males / 1994 / ... / G

LANA STARR see Lana Sands

LANA STONE see Lana Sands

LANA SWIFT see Star Index I

LANA TERRY see Star Index I

LANA TYME

Erotic Dimensions #8: Just For Me / 1982 / NSV / M

LANA WOODS *(Teddy (Lana Woods), Karene Berg)*

A post-op transsexual who could easily pass for a girl and in practice seems to make no effort to disclose or emphasize she has a Y on her 23rd pair of chromosones. Not ugly (no mannish facial characteristics), medium natural looking tits with large areola, blue eyes, lithe body, a little too tall, bad skin, female type butt (it's not a boy-like butt), big tattoo on her left shoulder, another of 2 birds in flight on her right shoulder and a third on her left hip, 24 years old in 1993. Her pussy doesn't have the standard female butterfly shape but is more like a fold of flesh and inside it's not pink but normal skin like you would find on an outside part of the body. Judging from the sexual encounters, her vagina is of normal depth although she does seem to prefer anal sex. This is really minutae; you wouldn't notice any difference if you weren't advised in advance. Karene is the credit from a European movie, **Hot To The Core**.

A&B AB#458: Dr. Dick From Man To Woman #1 / 1994 / A&B / M • A&B AB#459: Dr. Dick From Man To Woman #2 / 1994 / A&B / M • Amateur Orgies #35 / 1993 / AFI / M • Anal Camera #01 / 1994 / EVN / M • Angel Wolf / 1995 / WIV / M • Behind The Mask / 1995 / XC / M • Beverly She-Males / 1994 / PL / G • Bi Love Lucy / 1994 / PL / G • Bi-Laddin / 1994 / BIN / G • Bi-Sexual Anal #1 / 1994 / RTP / G • Chain Gang / 1994 / OD / F • Come Back Little She-Male / 1994 / HSV / G • Cuntz #1 / 1994 / RTP / M • Days Gone Bi / 1994 / BIN / G • Dick No More / 1994 / HEA / G • Dirty Dating Service #04 / 1994 / WP / M • Dirty Doc's Housecalls #04 / 1993 / LV / M • Dirty Doc's Housecalls #09 / 1994 / LV / M • Double Butts / 1994 / RTP / M • Double Penetration Virgins #01 / 1993 / LE / M • Electro Sex / 1994 / FPI / M • Felicia's Fantasies / 1995 / HOM / B • Gang Bang Diaries #4 / 1994 / SFP / M • Hot To The Core / 199? / SVE / M • House Of Sex #09: Dirty Anal / 1994 / RTP / M • Immortal Desire / 1993 / VI / M • Kinky Debutante Interviews #01 / 1994 / IP / M • Man Made Pussy / 1994 / HEA / G • Motel Sex #2 / 1995 / FAP / M • Odyssey Triple Play #9: The Anal Game / 1995 / OD / M • Ooze: Cum Inside Lana Woods / 1994 / RTP / M • The Other Side Of Melinda / 1995 / LON / B • Ron Hightower's White Chicks #07 / 1993 / LBO / M • Shaved She-Males / 1994 / PL / G • She-Male Trouble / 1994 / HEA / G • Sinderella She-Males / 1994 / HEA / G • Strap On Anal Attitude / 1994 / SCL / M • Video Virgins #08 / 1993 / NS / M • Where The Bi's Are / 1994 / BIN / G

LANCE

Bun Busters #09 / 1993 / LBO / M • Little Big Hole #1 / 199? / SVE / M • Little Big Hole #2 / 199? / SVE / M • Little Big Hole #3 / 199? / SVE / M • Sex Slave / 1995 / FGV / B

LANCE BOYLE *(Raymond Harmstorf)*
The Long Swift Sword Of Siegfried / 1971 / SOW / S

LANCE CARRINGTON see Lance Heywood

LANCE DEWHITE
Flash / 1980 / CA / M

LANCE HARDMAN see David Hardman

LANCE HEYWOOD *(Lance Carrington, Lance Viceroy, Mark Wood, Mark Woods, Rex King, Max King)*
Adventures In Paradise / 1992 / VEX / M • All In The Name Of Love / 1992 / IF / M • Amateur A Cuppers / 1993 / VEX / C • Amateur American Style #27 / 1992 / AR / M • Amateur American Style #30 / 1992 / AR / F • America's Dirtiest Home Videos #01 / 1991 / VEX / M • America's Dirtiest Home Videos #03 / 1991 / VEX / M • America's Dirtiest Home Videos #06 / 1991 / AMA / M • America's Dirtiest Home Videos #07 / 1991 / VEX / M • America's Dirtiest Home Videos #08 / 1992 / VEX / M • America's Dirtiest Home Videos #09 / 1992 / VEX / M

• American Dream Girls #2 / 1994 / LEI / M • The Anal Adventures Of Max Hardcore: The Resurrection / 1995 / ZA / M • Anal Asian / 1994 / VEX / M • Animal Instincts / 1991 / VEX / M • The Babes Of Bonerville / 1995 / VEX / C • Bareback Riders / 1992 / VEX / M • Beat The Heat / 1990 / VI / M • Beaver Hunt #01 / 1994 / LEI / M • Beaver Hunt #02 / 1994 / LEI / M • Ben Dover & Barbie / 1995 / SUF / M • Beyond Passion / 1993 / IF / M • Big Boob Ball / 1995 / IF / C • Blue Balls / 1995 / VEX / C • Burn It Up / 1994 / VEX / M • Butt Hunt #01 / 1994 / LEI / M • Butt Hunt #02 / 1994 / LEI / M • Butt Hunt #04 / 1995 / LEI / M • Butt Hunt #05 / 1995 / LEI / M • Butt Hunt #06 / 1995 / LEI / M • Butt Hunt #08 / 1995 / LEI / M • Butt Hunt #09 / 1995 / LEI / M • Butt Hunt #10 / 1995 / LEI / M • Butt Hunt #11 / 1995 / LEI / M • California Sluts / 1995 / ZA / M • Dickin' Around / 1994 / VEX / M • Dirty Deeds / 1992 / IF / M • Dirty Dominique / 1994 / V99 / M • Dyno-Mite / 1992 / IF / M • The Eliminators / 1991 / BIZ / B • Excitable / 1992 / IF / M • Flash Floods / 1991 / PRE / C • Flying High With Rikki Lee / 1992 / VEX / C • Forbidden Fantasies #1 / 1995 / ZA / M • Hangin' Out / 1992 / IF / M • Happy Endings / 1990 / BIZ / B • Hard Core Beginners #11 / 1995 / LEI / M • Hawaii Vice: Reflections / 1990 / CIN / C • Hose Jobs / 1995 / VEX / M • Hot Box / 1995 / V99 / C • If Looks Could Kill / 1992 / V99 / M • Illusions #1 / 1992 / IF / M • Just One Look / 1993 / V99 / M • The Last Temptation Of Teri / 1991 / IF / M • Lay Lady Lay / 1991 / VEX / M • Leading Lady / 1991 / V99 / M • Lifeguard / 1990 / VI / M • Lovin' Every Minute Of It / 1994 / VEX / C • Make Me Sweat / 1994 / V99 / M • Man Of Steel / 1992 / IF / M • More Dirty Debutantes #04 / 1990 / 4P / M • More Dirty Debutantes #05 / 1990 / 4P / M • Mr. Peepers Amateur Home Videos #17: No Holes Barred / 1991 / LBO / M • Mr. Peepers Amateur Home Videos #21: Home Style Humpin' / 1991 / LBO / M • Mr. Peepers Amateur Home Videos #22: Emergency Lip Service / 1991 / LBO / M • Nasty Girls #3 (1990-CDI) / 1990 / CDI / M • Nasty Jack's Homemade Vid. #04 / 1990 / CDI / M • Nasty Jack's Homemade Vid. #08 / 1990 / CDI / M • Nasty Jack's Homemade Vid. #09 / 1991 / CDI / M • Nasty Jack's Homemade Vid. #11 / 1990 / CDI / M • Nasty Jack's Homemade Vid. #12 / 1991 / CDI / M • Nasty Jack's Homemade Vid. #15 / 1991 / CDI / M • Nasty Jack's Homemade Vid. #16 / 1991 / CDI / M • Nasty Jack's Homemade Vid. #22 / 1991 / CDI / M • Nasty Jack's Homemade Vid. #26 / 1991 / CDI / M • Nasty Jack's Homemade Vid. #27 / 1991 / CDI / M • Nasty Jack's Homemade Vid. #29 / 1991 / CDI / M • Nasty Jack's Homemade Vid. #31 / 1991 / CDI / M • Nasty Jack's Kloset Klassics #04 / 1991 / CDI / M • One Lay At A Time / 1992 / V99 / M • One Of A Kind / 1992 / VEX / M • The Perfect Pet / 1991 / VEX / C • Pussy Hunt #04 / 1994 / LEI / M • Pussy Hunt #05 / 1994 / LEI / M • Pussy Hunt #07 / 1994 / LEI / M • Pussy Hunt #08 / 1995 / LEI / M • Pussy Hunt #09 / 1995 / LEI / M • Pussy Hunt #10 / 1995 / LEI / M • Pussy Hunt #11 / 1995 / LEI / M • Pussy Hunt #13 / 1995 / LEI / M • Pussy Hunt #15 / 1995 / LEI / M •

Rear Entry / 1995 / LEI / M • Red Hot Honeys / 1994 / IF / M • A Scent Of Leather / 1992 / IF / M • Sexual Persuasion / 1991 / V99 / M • She's My Cherry Pie / 1992 / V99 / M • She's No Angel #2 / 1995 / V99 / M • Skippy, Jiff & Jam / 1990 / CIA / M • Smarty Pants / 1992 / VEX / M • Surf City Sex / 1991 / CIA / M • The Swap #1 / 1990 / VI / M • Sweet Sunshine / 1995 / IF / M • Take It Like A Man / 1994 / IF / M • Too Cute For Words / 1992 / V99 / M • Welcome To Paradise / 1994 / IF / M

LANCE HOWARD
The Ultimate She-Male / 1995 / LEO / G

LANCE HUBBEL
Auction #1 / 1992 / BIZ / B • Auction #2 / 1992 / BIZ / B • The Best Of Hot Heels / 1992 / BIZ / B • Creation Of Karen: Tormented & Transformed / 1993 / BIZ / B • Hot Shoes / 1992 / BIZ / B • Latex Submission #1 / 1992 / BIZ / B • Latex Submission #2 / 1992 / BIZ / B • Obey Me Bitch #1 / 1992 / BIZ / B • Obey Me Bitch #4 / 1993 / BIZ / B • Office Heels / 1992 / BIZ / B

LANCE LOTT
Sounds Of Sex / 1985 / CA / M

LANCE MANYON
The Fantasy Booth / 1993 / ONA / M • Sex Academy #1 / 1993 / ONA / M • Totally Ona: The Best Of Ona Zee / 1996 / ONA / C

LANCE STEVENS
Where The Bi's Are / 1994 / BIN / G

LANCE THRUST
Naughty Network / 1981 / CA / M

LANCE VICEROY see Lance Heywood

LANDON see Paul Morgan

LANE MCGARTER see Star Index I

LANGDON see Star Index I

LANIQUE LOPE see Star Index I

LANKEY TOOTU see Star Index I

LANKY FLATCHER see Lysa Thatcher

LANNA
Filthy First Timers #3: Tearing Down The Walls Of Shame / 1996 / EL / M

LANNA CHRISTI
ABA: Double Feature #5 / 1996 / ALP / M • Night Of Submission / 1976 / BIZ / M

LANNY ROTH see Star Index I

LARA
HomeGrown Video #456 / 1995 / HOV / M

LARA CHRISTIE
Blow Some My Way / 1977 / VHL / M

LARA LAMBKIN
Buttwoman Back In Budapest / 1993 / EL / M • Buttwoman In Budapest / 1992 / EA / M • Depravity On The Danube / 1993 / EL / M • The Hungarian Connection / 1992 / EA / M • Sodomania #05: Euro-American Style / 1993 / EL / M • Sodomania #06: Gangs And Bangs And Other Thangs / 1993 / EL / M

LARK SCARLET
Sex Lessons / 1996 / NIT / M

LARRY
A&B AB#308: Bi-Sexual Playtime / 1991 / A&B / G • HomeGrown Video #461: Splendor In The Grasp / 1995 / HOV / M • Pussy Hunt #15 / 1995 / LEI / M

LARRY (BILLY DEE) see Billy Dee

LARRY BARNES
Double Trouble: Spanking English Style / 1996 / BIZ / B

LARRY BARNHOUSE
Beach Blanket Bango / 1975 / EVI / M • High School Fantasies / 1974 / EVI / M •

Legends Of Porn #1 / 1987 / CV / C • Teenage Throat / 1974 / ... / M

LARRY BEAVER
Romance & Fantasy / 1995 / VEX / M

LARRY CARR
Love Roots / 1987 / LIM / M • Love Under 16 / cr75 / VST / M

LARRY COLE
Strange Diary / 1976 / AXV / M

LARRY COX
Long Hard Summer / 1989 / BMV / C • Raw Footage / 1977 / CA / M • Virgin Dreams / 1976 / BMV / M

LARRY DAVIS see Star Index I

LARRY FIELD see Star Index I

LARRY FRADY
One Page Of Love / 1980 / VCX / M

LARRY FREDERICK
Deep Rub / 1979 / VC / M

LARRY GAMES see Star Index I

LARRY GELMAN see Star Index I

LARRY GREYTHORPE
Schoolgirl Fannies On Fire / 1994 / BIZ / B

LARRY HARDWOOD
Casino Of Lust / 1984 / AT / M • Erotic Express / 1983 / CV / M • GVC: Hot Numbers #133 / 1984 / GO / M • GVC: Olympix Affair #137 / 1985 / GO / M • Hershe Highway #1 / 1989 / HO / M • Up Up And Away / 1984 / CA / M

LARRY HUNTER
All About Sex / 1970 / AR / M • Come On Baby, Light My Fire / 1969 / SOW / S • Sock It To Me Baby / 1968 / SOW / S

LARRY KIEBASA
Love Theatre / cr80 / VC / M

LARRY KIRK
Lady On Top / cr73 / BL / M

LARRY LE
The New Ass Masters #10 / 1996 / LEI / C

LARRY LEVINSON
The Starmaker / 1982 / VC / M

LARRY LONG see Star Index I

LARRY MOORE see Star Index I

LARRY MORGAN
Old Wave Hookers #2 / 1995 / PL / M

LARRY O'BRIEN see Star Index I

LARRY PACIOTTI see Chi Chi La Rue

LARRY PARTS see Star Index I

LARRY POWERS see Star Index I

LARRY PRICE see Star Index I

LARRY REVENE see Chuck Vincent

LARRY ROTH
Hungry Eyed Woman / cr71 / VCX / M

LARRY ROTHSTEIN
Tongue 'n Cheek (Red Light) / 1984 / RLV / M

LARRY ROW
Bad Girls #2 / 1983 / GO / M

LARRY SHIPPS
The Outrageous Nurse / 1981 / VD / G • She-Male Encounters #05: Orgy At The Poysinberry Bar #1 / 1987 / MET / G

LARRY STRANGE see Star Index I

LARRY STRONG
Coed Fever / 1980 / CA / M

LARRY T see Star Index I

LARRY THOMAS
Apartment Girls / cr72 / CV / M • Bottom Busters / 1973 / BLT / M • Whole Buncha Fucking / 1994 / MET / M

LARRY TRASK
The Playgirl / 1982 / CA / M

LARRY WHITE see Terry Thomas

LARRY WILSON
Blue Vanities #042 (New) / 1988 / FFL / M

LARRY WINTERS
Bucky Beaver's XXX Dragon Art Theatre Double Feature #06 / 1996 / SOW / M • The Color of Honey / 1987 / SUV / M • Finishing School / 1975 / SOW / M

LARRY WOOD
AC/DC #2 / 1994 / HP / G

LARRY ZENON *see Star Index I*

LARS *see Star Index I*

LARS LENNARTSSON
Bel Ami / 1976 / VXP / M

LARS LIND
The Second Coming Of Eva / 1974 / ALP / M

LARTHITIA GAINSBORO
Dirty Business / 1995 / WIV / M

LASHER *see Star Index I*

LASSALLE MAKKE
Blue Vanities #198 / 1993 / FFL / M

LASSE BRAUN *(Alberto Ferro)*
European porno film maker of the seventies.
The Porn Brokers / 1977 / VAE / M

LASZLO
The Betrayal Of Innocence #1: The Awakening Of Marika / 1993 / CC / M • The Betrayal Of Innocence #2: The Decadence / 1993 / CC / M • The Betrayal Of Innocence #3: The Choice / 1993 / CC / M • Dirty Harriet / 1986 / SAT / M

LATASHA STARR *see Star Index I*

LATELLE OLAY *see Star Index I*

LATICE CHEVRON
Chocolate Cherries #1 / 1984 / LA / M

LATINA
Double D Dreams / 1996 / NAP / S • Voluptuous #2 / 199? / H&S / M • Voluptuous #3 / 199? / H&S / M

LATISHA *see Letigre*

LATISHA LANI *see Kahlia*

LATUSCH
The Ebony Connection #2 / 1994 / LBO / C

LATUSCHE *see Star Index I*

LAUDE
Liquid Lips #2 / 1994 / MAV / M

LAUINI DOMINIQUE *see Laurien Dominique*

LAUNA CHASS *see Monique Gabrielle*

LAURA
Alex Jordan's First Timers #05 / 1994 / OD / M • The All-Conference Nude Workout / 1995 / NIV / S • The Best Of Big Busty / 1986 / L&W / C • Blue Vanities #529 / 1993 / FFL / M • Bus Stop Tales #07 / 1989 / PRI / M • Bus Stop Tales #10 / 1990 / PRI / M • California Sluts / 1995 / ZA / M • Homegrown Video #221 / 1990 / HOV / M • HomeGrown Video #468: Lust American Style / 1996 / HOV / C • The Horny Housewife / 1996 / HO / M • KBBS: Weekend With Laurel Canyon / 1992 / KBB / M • Ladyfair Presents Laura / 1990 / LAD / F • Magma: Horny & Greedy / 1993 / MET / M • The Piercing Of Laura / 1980 / BIZ / B • Private Collection: #130: Key To Pleasure / 1992 / TOP / M • Sophisticated Pleasure / 1984 / WV / M • Triple X Video Magazine #15 / 1996 / OD / M • Veronica The Screenwriting Hooker / 1996 / LE / M

LAURA (STEP. PAGE) *see Stephanie Page*

LAURA ANN
Les Chaleurs De La Gyneco / 1996 / FAP / F

LAURA BACALLE *see Star Index I*

LAURA BENTLY
Round Robin / 19?? / VXP / M

LAURA BIRCH *see Star Index I*

LAURA BOND *see Star Index I*

LAURA BOURBON *see Star Index I*

LAURA BRADLEY *see Star Index I*

LAURA CANNON
Forced Entry / 1972 / ALP / M • Selling It / 1971 / BL / M

LAURA CATWOMAN
Private Film #09 / 1994 / OD / M • Private Film #27 / 1995 / OD / M • Private Film #28 / 1995 / OD / M • Triple X Video Magazine #04 / 1995 / OD / M

LAURA CHRISTINE *see Star Index I*

LAURA CHRISTY *see Star Index I*

LAURA CLAIR *see Star Index I*

LAURA DEAN *see Candice Hart*

LAURA ESSEX *see Star Index I*

LAURA FORSMAN
Call Girl / 1984 / CV / M

LAURA FUJIYAMA *(Tessie Lynn)*
Fantasy Girls / 1974 / VC / M • The Pleasure Masters / 1975 / AST / M

LAURA GARDENER *see Star Index I*

LAURA GEMSER *(Lana Gemser, Moira Chen)*
Pretty tight-bodied slightly Oriental looking girl who took over the **Emmanuelle** roles from Sylvia Kristel.
The Alcove / 1984 / LUM / S • The Best Of Sex And Violence / 1981 / WIZ / C • Black Emmanuelle #1 / 1975 / TZV / S • Caligula #2 / 1981 / LUM / S • Emmanuelle Around The World / 1977 / WIZ / S • Emmanuelle In America / 1977 / VAM / S • Emmanuelle In Bangkok / 1976 / VAM / S • Emmanuelle In Egypt / 1977 / CO1 / S • Emmanuelle In Hell / 1984 / VS / S • Emmanuelle In Prison / 1976 / LUM / S • Emmanuelle In The Country / 1978 / LUM / S • Emmanuelle On Taboo Island / 1976 / PAV / S • Emmanuelle's Amazon Adventure / 1977 / TWI / S • Emmanuelle, The Joys Of A Woman / 1976 / PAR / S • Emmanuelle, The Queen Of Sados / 1979 / VAM / S • Erotic Eva / 1976 / VIG / S • Famous T & A / 1982 / WIZ / C • Love Camp / 1976 / ACV / S • Lust / 1985 / … / S • [The Dirty Seven / 1976 / LUM / S • [Midnight Gigolo / 1986 / … / S • [The Pleasure / 1985 / … / S

LAURA HART *see Star Index I*

LAURA HUNT *see Jenny Baxter*

LAURA JO DEAN
Blunt Trauma #3: Whiteslave / 1996 / ZFX / B

LAURA KING *see Stacey Nichols*

LAURA LAKE
A Girl's Affair #06 / 1995 / FD / F • Reflections / 1995 / FD / M

LAURA LAMOUR *see Star Index I*

LAURA LANDERS
GVC: Anything Goes #119 / 1983 / GO / M

LAURA LAY *see Laurie Lay*

LAURA LAZARRE
1001 Erotic Nights #1 / 1982 / VC / M • All American Girls #1 / 1982 / CA / M • Blue Vanities #229 / 1994 / FFL / M • Cells Of Passion / 1981 / VD / M • Ladies Nights / 1980 / VC / M • Legends Of Porn #1 / 1987 / CV / C • Little Orphan Dusty #2 / 1981 / VIS / M • Pleasure Zone / 1984 / SE / M • Private Moments / 1983 / CV / M • Purely Physical / 1982 / SE / M • Satisfactions / 1983 / CA / M • Seka's Fantasies / 1981 / CA / M • The Seven Seductions Of Madame Lau / 1981 / EVI / M • Suzie Superstar #1 / 1983 / CV / M • Triplets / 1985

/ VCR / M

LAURA LECHE
Home For Unwed Mothers / 1984 / AMB / F

LAURA LEE *see Star Index I*

LAURA LEE (H. WAYNE) *see Heather Wayne*

LAURA LEI *see Laurie Lay*

LAURA LENZ *see Star Index I*

LAURA LITTLE *see Star Index I*

LAURA MANCHE
Skintight / 1981 / CA / M

LAURA MARTINE *see Star Index I*

LAURA NICHOLSON *see Star Index I*

LAURA PALMER *(Petra (Laura Palmer))*
Tall blonde (6'0") with small/medium tits, marginal face, womanly body, European, probably Hungarian or Czech.
Adult Affairs / 1994 / VC / M • The Anal-Europe Series #08: / 1995 / LV / M • Angel Baby / 1995 / SC / M • Babes Illustrated #4 / 1995 / IN / F • Ben Dover & Barbie / 1995 / SUF / M • Bondage Check-Up / 1996 / VTF / B • The Bottom Dweller 33 1/3 / 1995 / EL / M • The Butt Sisters Do Baltimore / 1995 / MID / M • The Butt Sisters Do Chicago / 1995 / MID / M • Casting Call #11 / 1995 / MET / M • Casting Call #16 / 1995 / SO / M • Chronicles Of Pain #3: Slave Traders / 1996 / BIZ / B • The Contessa De Sade / 1996 / LBO / B • Decadence / 1996 / VC / M • Deep Throat Girls #15 / 1995 / GO / M • Defiance: The Art Of Spanking / 1996 / BIZ / B • Diva #1: Caught In The Act / 1996 / VC / F • The Divine Marquis / 1995 / ONA / B • Double D Dykes #25 / 1995 / GO / F • Dr Freckle & Mr Jive / 1995 / IN / M • Electropussy / 1995 / CC / M • Flesh / 1996 / EA / M • French Twist / 1996 / HO / M • Get Lucky / 1996 / NIT / M • A Girl's Affair #08 / 1995 / FD / F • A Girl's Affair #09 / 1996 / FD / F • The Gypsy Queen / 1996 / CC / M • High Heeled & Horny #4 / 1995 / LBO / M • Hollywood Confidential / 1996 / SC / M • Hollywood Legs / 1996 / NIT / M • Horny Henry's Euro Adventure / 1995 / TTV / M • In Cold Sweat / 1996 / VI / M • Inspector Croissant: The Case Of The Missing Pinky / 1995 / FC / M • Interview With A Milkman / 1996 / VI / M • Kink #2 / 1995 / ROB / M • The Last Act / 1995 / VI / M • Latex And Lace / 1996 / BBE / M • Leather Bound Dykes From Hell #8 / 1996 / BIZ / B • Leg Tease #1 / 1995 / VT / M • Lesbian Debutante #02 / 1996 / IP / F • Lethal Affairs / 1996 / VI / M • Male Order Brides / 1996 / RAS / M • Maliboob Beach / 1995 / FH / M • Mistress Kane: Lessons In Terror / 1996 / BIZ / B • Mistress Kane: Town In Torment / 1996 / BIZ / B • Muff Divers #1 / 1996 / TV / F • Mystique / 1996 / SC / M • Nothing Like Nurse Nookie #2 / 1996 / NIT / M • Nylon / 1995 / VI / M • Pick Up Lines #06 / 1996 / OD / M • Pleasureland / 1996 / VI / M • Private Film #22 / 1995 / OD / M • Private Film #24 / 1995 / OD / M • Private Film #25 / 1995 / OD / M • Private Film #26 / 1995 / OD / M • Private Video Magazine #26 / 1995 / OD / M • Puritan Video Magazine #02 / 1996 / LE / M • Pussyclips #09 / 1995 / SNA / M • Pussyman's House Party #1 / 1996 / SNA / M • Pussyman's House Party #2 / 1996 / SNA / M • Pussywoman #3 / 1995 / CC / M • Rainwoman #10: The Tenth Anniversary Edition / 1996 / CC / M • Sadistic Sisters / 1996 / BON / B • Sarah's

Inheritance / 1995 / WIV / M • The Seduction Of Annah Marie / 1996 / VT / M • Sexual Overdrive / 1996 / LE / M • The Sexual Solution #1 / 1995 / LE / M • Six Degrees Of Penetration / 1996 / PP / M • Smoke & Mirrors / 1996 / PL / M • Snake Pit / 1996 / DWO / M • Sodomania: Slop Shots / 1996 / EL / C • Spazm #1: Point Blank / 1996 / LBO / M • Stalking Of Slave Laura / 1996 / BIZ / B • Stripping / 1995 / NIT / M • Student Fetish Videos: Bondage #03 / 1996 / PRE / B • Student Fetish Videos: Spanking #22 / 1996 / PRE / B • Student Fetish Videos: Tickling #13 / 1996 / SFV / B • Sue / 1995 / VC / M • Sweet As Honey / 1996 / NIT / M • Taboo #14: Kissing Cousins / 1995 / IN / M • Tied Temptations / 1996 / BON / B • Triple X Video Magazine #01 / 1995 / OD / M • Triple X Video Magazine #02 / 1995 / OD / M • Triple X Video Magazine #04 / 1995 / OD / M • Trouble Maker / 1995 / VI / M • Unleashed / 1996 / SAE / M • Up Close & Personal #2 / 1996 / IPI / M • Upbeat Love #2 / 1995 / CV / M • Violation / 1996 / LE / M • The Voyeur #4 / 1995 / EA / M • Wheel Of Obsession / 1996 / TWP / B • Whore D'erves / 1996 / OUP / F • X-Tales / 1995 / VIM / M • Young & Natural #19 / 1996 / TV / F • Young & Natural #22 / 1996 / TV / F

LAURA PAOUCK
Private Gold #05: Cape Town #1 / 1996 / OD / M

LAURA PRIMEUR *see Star Index I*
LAURA SANDS *see Star Index I*
LAURA SHAWN *see Star Index I*
LAURA SOTO
Behind The Brown Door / 1986 / VCR / C • Dark Passions / 1984 / VCR / C • Sex Ed With Lil' Red / 1983 / TGA / M

LAURA TOLEDO *see Star Index I*
LAURA TURNER
Bend Over Babes #4 / 1996 / EA / M

LAURA VALERIE *see Star Index I*
LAURA VALLERIES
Les Chaleurs De La Gyneco / 1996 / FAP / F

LAURA WENCH
French Erotica: Inside Hollywood / 1980 / AR / M

LAURA WEST *see Star Index I*
LAURA WINTERS
The Caning Of The Shrews / 1991 / BIZ / B

LAURA WREN *see Star Index I*
LAURA YOUNG *see Star Index I*
LAURA ZRAKE *see Nikki Sinn*
LAURALIE
Captive Coeds / 1996 / LON / B

LAURE
Cindy Puts Out / 1996 / OLL / M

LAURE VALERIE
Impulse #02: The Film / 1995 / MBP / M

LAURE VALOIS
Della Borsa / 1995 / WIV / M

LAUREL BLAKE *see Laurie Blue*
LAUREL CANTON *see Laurel Canyon*
LAUREL CANYN *see Laurel Canyon*
LAUREL CANYON *(Mandy (Laurel Can), Mandii, Laurel Canyn, Julie Taylor, Derin, Devon Delight, Candy Cruize, Suzy Q, Julie Shine, Derin Delight, Laurel Canton, Laurel Kanyon, Laurel Cayn, Julie Thompson)*
Not the same as Melinda Lee. Supposedly she did a DP in **Loose Ends #6** and was scheduled to do one in **Backdoor to Hollywood**

#5 but got her asshole torn and retired.
The Amorous Adventures Of Janette Littledove / 1988 / AR / M • Anal Pleasures / 1988 / AVC / M • Angel Kelly Raw / 1987 / FAN / M • Backdoor To Hollywood #04 / 1988 / CDI / M • Backdoor To Hollywood #05 / 1988 / CDI / M • Batteries Included / 1988 / 3HV / M • Best Of Caught From Behind #2 / 1988 / HO / C • The Bitch / 1988 / FAN / M • Black Dreams / 1988 / CDI / M • Blonde Fantasy / 1988 / CC / M • Blue Angel / 1992 / AFV / M • Blue Angel / 1992 / AFV / M • Bound To Tease #1 / 1988 / BON / C • Bound To Tease #2 / 1989 / BON / C • California Cherries / 1987 / EVN / M • Campfire Girls / 1988 / SE / M • Candy's Little Sister Sugar / 1988 / VD / M • The Case Of The Mad Tickler / 1988 / ME / M • The Catwoman / 1988 / VC / M • Caught From Behind #08 / 1988 / HO / M • Charlie's Girls #1 / 1988 / CC / M • Cheeks #1 / 1988 / CC / M • Club Head (EVN) #2 / 1989 / EVN / C • Deep Inside Laurel Canyon / 1989 / CDI / C • Deep Inside Samantha Strong / 1992 / CDI / C • Dirty Prancing / 1987 / EVN / M • Dreams / 1987 / AR / M • Educating Laurel / 1988 / BON / B • Enema Diary / 1989 / BIZ / B • Exposure / 1988 / VD / M • Facial Attraction / 1988 / BEE / C • Fade To Black / 1988 / CDI / M • Fatal Erection / 1988 / SEV / M • Fatal Seduction / 1988 / CDI / M • Frenzy / 1992 / SC / M • From Kascha With Love / 1988 / CDI / M • From Rags To Riches / 1988 / CDI / M • Future Sodom / 1988 / VD / M • Get It Straight / 1989 / CDI / M • Ginger Rides Again / 1988 / KIS / C • Girls Of The Double D #03 / 1988 / CDI / M • Hawaii Vice #8 / 1990 / CIN / M • Hidden Obsessions / 1992 / BFP / M • Home Runs / 1995 / PRE / C • Hot Blondes / 1988 / VEX / M • Hot Licks At The Pussycat Club / 1990 / WV / C • Hot Women / 1989 / E&I / C • Hyapatia Lee's Arcade Series #02 / 1988 / ZA / C • I Can't Get No...Satisfaction / 1988 / CDI / M • Introducing Barbii / 1987 / CDI / M • Kascha & Friends / 1988 / CIN / M • KBBS: Weekend With Laurel Canyon / 1992 / KBB / M • La Bimbo / 1987 / PEN / M • Laurel's Continuing Education / 1988 / BON / B • Lick Bush / 1992 / VD / C • Loose Ends #1 / 1984 / 4P / M • Loose Ends #4 / 1988 / 4P / M • Lust Connection / 1988 / VT / M • Lusty Desires / 1988 / CDI / M • Lusty Detective / 1988 / VEX / M • The Main Attraction / 1988 / 4P / M • Mandii's Magic / 1988 / CDI / M • Megasex / 1988 / EVN / M • Misadventures Of The Bang Gang / 1987 / AR / M • The Moon Girls / 1990 / ME / C • Nasty Newshounds / 1988 / ME / M • No Man's Land #02 / 1988 / VT / F • Nothing But Girls, Girls, Girls / 1988 / CDI / M • Party Wives / 1988 / CDI / M • Radio-Active / 1992 / SC / M • Rapture Girls #2: Ona & Stephanie / 1991 / OD / M • A Rare Starlet / 1987 / ME / M • Scorching Secrets / 1988 / IN / M • Sex Asylum #3 / 1988 / VI / M • Sex Sluts From Beyond The Galaxy / 1991 / LBO / C • The Sexaholic / 1988 / VC / M • Seymore Butts In The Love Shack / 1992 / FH / M • Seymore Butts: Bustin' Out My Best Anal / 1995 / FH / C • Shaved Sinners #1 / 1988 / VT / M • Shaved Sinners #2 / 1987 / VT / M • Spend The Holidays With Barbii / 1987 / CDI / M • Spoiled / 1987 / VD / M • St. X-Where #2 / 1988 / VD / M • Surf,

Sand And Sex / 1987 / SE / M • A Taste Of Ariel / 1989 / PIN / C • A Taste Of Laurel / 1990 / PIN / C • A Taste Of Viper / 1990 / PIN / C • That Ole Black Magic / 1988 / CDI / M • Tight Fit (Foot Fet) / 1988 / BIZ / B • Toys 4 Us #1 / 1987 / WV / C • Ubangis On Uranus / 1987 / WV / M • Watersports Spree #2 / 1994 / BIZ / C • Where The Girls Play / 1992 / CC / F • White Chocolate / 1987 / PEN / M • Who's Dat Girl / 1987 / VEX / M • Wild In The Wilderness / 1988 / SE / M • With Love, Littledove / 1988 / AR / M

LAUREL CAYN *see Laurel Canyon*
LAUREL COOMBES
Bucky Beaver's XXX Dragon Art Theatre Double Feature #02 / 1996 / SOW / M • The Rites Of Uranus / 1975 / SOW / M

LAUREL KANYON *see Laurel Canyon*
LAUREN
Amateurs Exposed #07 / 1995 / CV / M • Between My Breasts #14 / 1991 / BTO / S • Between My Breasts #15 / 1991 / BTO / M • C-Hunt #05: Wett Worx / 1996 / PEV / M • Dirty Doc's Housecalls #04 / 1993 / LV / M • Look What I Found On The Street #01 / 1996 / CC / M • Sex Starved She-Males / 1995 / MET / G • She-Male Nymphos / 1995 / MET / G • Southern Belles #8 / 1997 / XPR / M

LAUREN (S/M)
Transsexual Prostitutes #1 / 1996 / DFI / G

LAUREN BATES
Bi Stander / 1995 / BIN / G • Butt Hunt #04 / 1995 / LEI / M • Casting Call #08 / 1994 / SO / M • Double Dicked #2 / 1996 / RAS / M • The Erotic Adventures Of Johnny Soiree / 1995 / LBO / M • For Your Mouth Only / 1995 / GO / M • Hollywood Starlets Adventure #04 / 1995 / AVS / M • Nasty Newcummers #08 / 1995 / MET / M • The Real Deal #3 / 1996 / FC / M

LAUREN BEATTY
Attack Of The Killer Dildos / 1996 / RAS / M • Cum Swappers / 1995 / ZA / M • Fishin' For Lust / 1996 / WST / M • Hollywood Amateurs #14 / 1995 / MID / M • Inspector Croissant: The Case Of The Missing Pinky / 1995 / FC / M • Lady M's Anything Nasty #01: Pink Pussy Party / 1996 / AVI / F • Lesbian Debutante #02 / 1996 / IP / F • Live Sex Net / 1996 / SPR / M • Naughty / 1996 / LV / M • Pussy Lotto / 1995 / WIV / M • Swedish Erotica #74 / 1994 / CA / M

LAUREN BLACK *see Star Index I*
LAUREN BRICE *(Markeeta, Markita, Jill Tuttle, Demonic)*
Markeeta is from **Purple Haze**. Jill Tuttle is from **Toe Tales #09**. 5'11" tall.
All Inside Eva / 1991 / PL / M • Amazing Tails #5 / 1990 / CA / M • Ashley Renee In Jeopardy / 1991 / HOM / B • Assumed Innocence / 1990 / AR / M • Aussie Exchange Girls / 1990 / PM / M • Back To Nature / 1990 / CA / M • Bat Bitch #1 / 1989 / FAZ / M • Bat Bitch #2 / 1990 / FAZ / M • Beauties And The Beast / 1990 / AFV / M • Bend Over Babes #1 / 1990 / EA / M • Best Of Buttman #1 / 1991 / EA / C • Beyond Innocence / 1990 / VCR / F • Body Heat / 1990 / CDI / M • The Book / 1990 / IF / M • Bush Pilots #1 / 1990 / VC / M • Charlie's Girls #3 / 1990 / CC / M • Confessions Of A Chauffeur / 1990 / DR / M • Deep Inside Raquel / 1992 / CDI / C • Deep Throat #5 / 1990 / AR / M • Dirty Tricks / 1990 / VEX / M • Do

It In The Road / 1990 / LV / M • The Dream Merchants / 1990 / CDI / M • Dreams Of The Everyday Housewife / 1990 / FAZ / M • Dungeon Mistress / 198? / LON / B • Farmer's Daughter / 1989 / FAZ / M • Hate To See You Go / 1990 / VC / M • Hollywood Hustle #1 / 1990 / V99 / M • Hot Spot / 1990 / PL / F • I Said A Butt Light #1 / 1990 / LV / M • Insatiable Immigrants / 1989 / VT / M • Kinky Couples / 1990 / VD / M • Lady In Blue / 1990 / CIN / M • Lambody / 1990 / CDI / M • Lesbian Liasons / 1990 / SO / F • Married Women / 1990 / PP / M • The Mistress #2 / 1990 / CV / M • Mortal Passions / 1990 / CDI / M • Night Shift Latex Slaves / 1991 / GOT / B • The Night Temptress / 1989 / HU / M • Nightdreams #2 / 1990 / VC / M • Nightdreams #3 / 1991 / VC / M • Only The Very Best On Video / 1992 / VC / C • Oral Majority #08 / 1990 / WV / C • Oriental Spice / 1990 / SE / M • Prisoner Of Lust / 1991 / VC / F • Private & Confidential / 1990 / AR / M • Purple Haze / 1991 / WV / M • Rainwoman #02 / 1990 / CC / M • Raunchy Ranch / 1991 / AFV / M • Sam's Fantasy / 1990 / CIN / M • Scented Secrets / 1990 / CIN / M • Sex Appraisals / 1990 / HO / M • Sex Lives On Porno Tape / 1992 / VC / C • Sexy Country Girl / 1991 / PL / M • Shadow Dancers #1 / 1989 / EA / M • Shadow Dancers #2 / 1989 / EA / M • She's Got The Juice / 1990 / CDI / M • A Shot In The Mouth #1 / 1990 / ME / M • Sleepwalker / 1990 / XCI / M • The Smart Ass #2: Rusty's Revenge / 1990 / VT / M • Smooth And Easy / 1990 / XCV / M • Strangers When We Meet / 1990 / VCR / M • Sunstroke Beach / 1990 / WV / M • The Taming Of Tami / 1990 / CA / M • Through The Walls / 1990 / FAZ / M • Toe Tales #09 / 1993 / GOT / B • True Legends Of Adult Cinema: The Modern Era / 1992 / VC / C • True Sin / 1990 / PP / M • Truth And Bare / 1991 / LV / M • The Unauthorized Biography Of Rob Blow / 1990 / LV / M • War Of The Tulips / 1990 / IN / M • Warm To The Touch / 1990 / CDI / M • We're No Angels / 1990 / CIN / M • [Kiss My Whip / 19?? / LON / B

LAUREN DIKARLO
Cocks In Frocks #2 / 1996 / TTV / G • She Male Devil / 1996 / HSV / G • She Males Enslaved / 1996 / BIZ / G • Showgirl She-Male / 1996 / HSV / G

LAUREN DUBOIS
Pearl Necklace: Amorous Amateurs #19 / 1992 / SEE / M • Pearl Necklace: Amorous Amateurs #20 / 1992 / SEE / M • Pearl Necklace: Amorous Amateurs #22 / 1993 / SEE / M • Pearl Necklace: Amorous Amateurs #24 / 1993 / SEE / M • Pearl Necklace: Amorous Amateurs #27 / 1993 / SEE / M • Pearl Necklace: Thee Bush League #10 / 1993 / SEE / M • Pearl Necklace: Thee Bush League #13 / 1993 / SEE / M

LAUREN FAIRCHILD
3 Mistresses Of The Mansion / 1994 / STM / B • Dr Discipline #2: Appointment With Pain / 1994 / STM / B • Lauren's Adventures In Bondageland #1: Mistress Lauren / 1994 / STM / C • Lauren's Adventures In Bondageland #2: Mistress Shane / 1994 / STM / C • Matronly Stern Spankings / 1994 / STM / B • A Peek Over The Wall / 1995 / STM / G • Punished Deception / 1996 / STM / B • Sentence Of Pain / 1994 / STM

/ B • Spanking Tea Party / 1994 / STM / B • Trained Transvestites / 1995 / STM / B • Tricia's Painful Pleasure / 1995 / STM / B

LAUREN FELDREN *see Star Index I*

LAUREN HALL
Good looking brunette with nice firm medium sized tits. First movie was **Legend #1**. Supposedly left the business in July 1990 and was last seen working in a furniture store.
19 And Nasty / 1990 / ME / M • Bad / 1990 / VC / M • Breast Side Story / 1990 / LE / M • Dangerous Assignment / 1993 / BS / B • Deep Throat #5 / 1990 / AR / M • Forced Love / 1990 / LV / M • Ghost Lusters / 1990 / EL / F • Great Expectations / 1990 / V99 / M • Great Expectations / 1992 / VEX / C • The Last Resort / 1990 / VC / M • Legend #1 / 1990 / LE / M • Legend #2 / 1990 / LE / M • The New Barbarians #1 / 1990 / VC / M • The New Barbarians #2 / 1990 / VC / M • Night Trips #2 / 1990 / CA / M • Not So Innocent / 1989 / VEX / M • Princess Of The Night / 1990 / VD / M • Smooth And Easy / 1990 / XCV / M • Teach Me Tonight / 1990 / VEX / M • The Tease / 1990 / VC / M • Trick Tracey #1 / 1990 / CC / M • Trick Tracy #2: Tracy Loves Dick / 1990 / CC / M • True Legends Of Adult Cinema: The Modern Era / 1992 / VC / C

LAUREN HALL (FALLON) *see Fallon*
LAUREN HART *see Star Index I*
LAUREN HAZE
Crazy Times / 1995 / BS / B

LAUREN LANCEFORD *see Sheena Horne*

LAUREN MACK *see Lorrin Mick*
LAUREN MCCAUL
Perfect Endings / 1994 / PLV / B • Tip Tap Toe / 1995 / PRE / C • Toe Nuts / 1994 / PRE / B

LAUREN MONTGOMERY
Passable face, long blonde curly hair, enhanced scarred medium tits, passable but not lithe body, looks a little on the old side.
Diva #1: Caught In The Act / 1996 / VC / F • Drop Sex: Wipe The Floor / 1997 / JLP / M • Hypnotic Hookers #2 / 1996 / NIT / M • Sodomania #19: Sweet Cream / 1996 / EL / M • Sweet Revenge / 1997 / KBE / M

LAUREN QUIM
Hong Kong Hookers / 1984 / AMB / M • A Touch Of Desire / 1983 / VCR / C

LAUREN STEWART *see Star Index I*
LAUREN SUMMERS *see Tina Ross*
LAUREN SWEET
Married Men With Men On The Side / 1996 / BHE / G

LAUREN TAYLOR
Dixie Debutantes #1 / 1996 / MYS / M

LAUREN TRACEY
Burlesxxx / 1996 / VT / M • The Delegate / 1996 / RAS / M • Filthy First Timers #2: Innocence Lost / 1996 / EL / M

LAUREN WALDEN *see Rene Summers*
LAUREN WILDE *see Tina Ross*
LAURENT
Gigi Gives It Away / 1995 / FRF / M • Private Film #27 / 1995 / OD / M • Private Film #28 / 1995 / OD / M • Veronica The Screenwriting Hooker / 1996 / LE / M

LAURENT DEGAULLE *see Star Index I*
LAURI *see Star Index I*
LAURI LANDRY *see Lori Landry*
LAURI LAY *see Laurie Lay*
LAURI PEARL *see Tawny Pearl*
LAURIE

The Dong Show #03 / 1990 / AMB / M • Lesbian Pros And Amateurs #26 / 1993 / GO / F • Odyssey Triple Play #62: Gang Bangs All Around / 1994 / OD / M

LAURIE AMBROSIA *see Ambrosia Fox*
LAURIE ANDERSON
Sheila's Payoff / 1977 / VCX / M
LAURIE ARDEN *see Layla LaShell*
LAURIE BLUE *(Shirley Duke, Lisa Rush, Lori Blue, Lorri Blue, Laurel Blake, Lori Rhodes)*
Attractive tight bodied blonde with reddish overtones and small tits. Pretty face.
Beyond Shame / 1980 / VEP / M • Bondage Pleasures #1 / 1981 / 4P / B • Fantasy / 1978 / VCX / M • A Formal Faucett / 1978 / VC / M • Hot Bodies (Ventura) / 1984 / VEN / C • Legends Of Porn #2 / 1989 / CV / C • Lipps & Mccain / 1978 / VC / M • Little Girls Blue #1 / 1977 / VCX / M • Little Girls Blue #2 / 1983 / VCX / M • The Other Side Of Julie / 1978 / CV / M • Randy, The Electric Lady / 1978 / VC / M • Saturday Matinee Series #1 / 1996 / VCX / C • Sensual Encounters Of Every Kind / 1978 / SE / M • Tangerine / 1979 / CXV / M

LAURIE CAMERON *(Tana Tamlin, Tana, Lori Cameron)*
White skinned pretty redhead/brunette with small tits, nice tight body and waist and small ass. Came into the industry with SO Paul Morgan but in 1994 they separated.
3 Wives / 1993 / VT / M • Alex Jordan's First Timers #01 / 1993 / OD / M • All "A" / 1994 / SFP / C • Amateur Lesbians #41: Kelli / 1993 / GO / F • Amateur Lesbians #42: Rosie Lee / 1993 / GO / F • Amateur Orgies #32 / 1993 / AFI / M • Anal Delights #3 / 1993 / ROB / M • Anal House Party / 1993 / IP / M • Anal Thunder #2 / 1993 / ROB / M • Anal Virgins Of America #02 / 1993 / FOR / M • Anal Vision #03 / 1992 / LBO / M • Anal-Holics / 1993 / AFV / M • Beach Bum Amateur's #23 / 1993 / MID / M • Biff Malibu's Totally Nasty Home Videos #29 / 1993 / ANA / M • Big Murray's New-Cummers #20: Hot Honies In Heat / 1993 / FD / M • Blind Spot / 1993 / VI / M • Bobby Hollander's Rookie Nookie #02 / 1993 / SFP / M • Bobby Hollander's Sweet Cheeks #103 / 1992 / QUA / M • Bobby Hollander's Sweet Cheeks #105 / 1993 / SFP / M • Bone Alone / 1993 / MID / M • Bubble Butts #22 / 1993 / LBO / M • Bun Busters #06 / 1993 / LBO / M • Bun Busters #13 / 1994 / LBO / M • Butterfly / 1993 / OD / M • Camera Shy / 1993 / FOR / M • Casting Call #02 / 1993 / SO / M • Colossal Orgy #1 / 1993 / HW / M • Colossal Orgy #3 / 1994 / HW / M • Confessions Of A Slutty Nurse / 1994 / VIM / M • The Coven #1 / 1993 / VI / M • The Coven #2 / 1993 / VI / M • Dangerous Curves / 1995 / VC / M • Designs On Women / 1994 / IN / F • Dirty Bob's #06: NiCESt NoviCES / 1992 / FLP / S • Dirty Dating Service #02 / 1993 / WP / M • Double Load #2 / 1994 / HW / M • A Girl's Affair #03 / 1993 / FD / F • Girls Will Be Boys #6 / 1993 / PL / F • Heidi Does Hollywood / 1993 / AFV / M • Hollywood Swingers #09 / 1993 / LBO / M • How To Make A Model #02: Got Her In Bed / 1993 / QUA / M • Kym Wilde's On The Edge #03 / 1993 / RB / B • Ladies Lovin' Ladies #3 / 1993 / AFV / F • Latent Image: Laurie's Lust Unleashed / 1994 / LAT / F • Let's

Dream On / 1994 / FD / M • The Man Who Loved Women / 1993 / SC / M • Midnight Angels #03 / 1993 / MID / F • Mike Hott: #218 Cunt Of The Month: Laurie / 1993 / MHV / M • Nikki's Bon Voyage / 1993 / VC / M • Northwest Pecker Trek #1 / 1994 / LBO / M • Northwest Pecker Trek #4: Laid In Latte Land / 1994 / LBO / M • Nympho Zombie Coeds / 1993 / VIM / M • Odyssey 30 Min: #247: / 1992 / OD / M • Odyssey 30 Min: #262: / 1992 / OD / M • Odyssey 30 Min: #296: / 1992 / OD / M • Odyssey Triple Play #46: Ass-Splitting Sex / 1993 / OD / M • Odyssey Triple Play #68: Threesomes And Moresomes / 1994 / OD / M • Ona Z's Star Search #01 / 1993 / GLI / M • Ona Zee's Black Label #1: Sex Hunger / 1996 / ONA / C • Pearl Necklace: Amorous Amateurs #20 / 1992 / SEE / M • Pearl Necklace: Amorous Amateurs #24 / 1993 / SEE / M • Perplexed / 1994 / FD / M • The Pink Lady Detective Agency: Case Of The Twisted Sister / 1994 / IN / M • Positively Pagan #06 / 1993 / ATA / M • Private Label / 1993 / GLI / M • Raunch #09 / 1993 / CC / M • Rump Humpers #13 / 1993 / GLI / M • Sassy Pleasures / 1993 / RB / B • Sensual Solos #01 / 1993 / AVI / F • Seymore Butts Is Blown Away / 1993 / FH / M • Seymore Butts Meets The Cumback Brat / 1993 / FH / M • She Quest / 1994 / OD / M • Stevi's: Laurie & Paul / 1993 / SSV / M • Stevi's: The Casting Couch / 1993 / SSV / F • SVE: Anal Homecoming / 1992 / SVE / M • Tangled / 1994 / PL / M • The Tantric Guide To Sexual Potency And Extended Orgasm / 1994 / A&E / M • Totally Ona: The Best Of Ona Zee / 1996 / ONA / C • Uncle Roy's Amateur Home Video #16 / 1992 / VIM / M • Up And Cummers #06 / 1993 / 4P / M • Video Virgins #01 / 1992 / NS / M • Virtual Sex / 1993 / VC / M • Web Of Desire / 1993 / OD / M

LAURIE FOXX
Seka's Teenage Diary / 1984 / HO / C
LAURIE FRIEDMAN see Star Index I
LAURIE HAMMER see Star Index I
LAURIE HARRIS see Star Index I
LAURIE HENDRICKS
Thundercrack! / 1974 / LUM / M
LAURIE JACKOV
Alley Cat / 1983 / VC / M • Consenting Adults / 1981 / VXP / M • The Erotic World Of Angel Cash / 1983 / VXP / M • Intimate Realities #1 / 1983 / VC / M
LAURIE JONES
Bedtime Video #09 / 1984 / GO / M
LAURIE LAMARR
The Beat Goes On / 1987 / VCR / C
LAURIE LAY *(Lauri Lay, Lori Lay, Laura Lay, Laura Lei, Lora Lei, Loreli (Laurie Lay))*
Fat blonde with big tits and short hair.
The Battle Of The Breast Queens / 1989 / INS / C • Chance Meetings / 1988 / VEX / M • Chestmates / 1988 / VEX / M • Feel The Heat / 1989 / VEX / M • G Spot Girls / 1988 / V99 / M • Gazongas #02 / 1988 / VEX / M • Golden Globes / 1989 / VEX / M • Home Bodies / 1988 / VEX / M • Hot Dreams / 1989 / VEX / M • Hot Dreams / 1991 / VEX / M • Indecent Proposals / 1988 / SEX / M • Indecent Proposals / 1991 / V99 / M • Much More Than A Mouthful #2 / 1988 / VEX / M • Only The Strong Survive / 1988 / ZA / M • Push It To The Limit / 1988

/ EVN / M • Red Velvet / 1988 / PV / M • Sex On The Town / 1989 / V99 / M • Shaved Sinners #1 / 1988 / VT / M • Super Blondes / 1989 / VEX / M • Two Women & A Man / 1988 / VEX / M • Two Women & A Man / 1991 / VEX / C • Weekend Delights / 1992 / V99 / M
LAURIE LEIGH see Star Index I
LAURIE LOVETT see Lorrie Lovett
LAURIE MICHAELS *(Lori Michaels)*
Very pretty with long dark blonde or light brown hair with streaks of gray, looks like a blonde version of Nikole Lace but taller, medium enhanced tits (she says they're natural but I doubt it), narrow hips but not a tight waist. Supposedly married, comes from Kansas, and was 27 years old in 1995.
A Is For Asia / 1996 / 4P / M • Badgirls #7: Lust Confined / 1995 / VI / M • Cheap Shot / 1995 / WAV / M • Ghost Town / 1995 / WAV / M • More Dirty Debutantes #48 / 1995 / 4P / M • Pick Up Lines #02 / 1995 / 4P / M • Pick Up Lines #03 / 1995 / 4P / M • Pick Up Lines #04 / 1995 / 4P / M • Pick Up Lines #08 / 1996 / OD / M
LAURIE MOUTH
Anal Boat / 1996 / P69 / M
LAURIE NEWTON
Dreams Are Forever / cr72 / AVC / M • Oh Doctor / cr72 / ADU / M
LAURIE NIGHT
Erotic Dimensions #1: Ripe / 1982 / NSV / M
LAURIE NOEL
GVC: Summer Beach House #106 / 1980 / GO / M
LAURIE P. see Fallon
LAURIE PEACOCK see Fallon
LAURIE PIERSON
Resurrection Of Eve / 1973 / MIT / M
LAURIE POWELL see Star Index I
LAURIE ROSE see Misty Dawn
LAURIE SAINT see Star Index I
LAURIE SMITH *(Cherri Hill (ls), Stephanie Taylor, Lorri Smith, Kristin (L. Smith))*
Passable face, black short hair, small tits, lithe body, enthusiastic performer. Cherri Hill is from **Bad Girls 4**. Kristin is from **Olympic Fever**. Stephanie Taylor is from **Daughters Of Emmanuelle**. Started in 1978. Aged 25 in 1982. Originally from Huntington Beach CA.
All American Girls #2: In Heat / 1983 / CA / M • Amber Lynn: She's Back / 1995 / TTV / C • Anything Goes / 1993 / VD / C • The Awakening Of Sally / 1984 / VCR / M • Bad Girls #4 / 1984 / GO / M • Best Of Talk Dirty To Me #01 / 1991 / DR / C • Between The Cheeks #1 / 1985 / VC / M • Black Sensations / 1987 / VEX / M • Blonde Heat (VCA) / 1985 / VC / M • Brooke Does College / 1984 / VC / M • Bunbusters / 1984 / VCR / M • Caballero Preview Tape #4 / 1985 / CA / C • Centerfold Celebrities #1 / 1982 / VC / M • Cover Girl Fantasies #3 / 1983 / VCR / C • Daughters Of Emmanuelle / 1982 / VCX / M • Deep Inside Ginger Lynn / 1986 / SE / C • Electric Blue: Wickedly Wild West / 1985 / CA / C • Erotic City / 1985 / CV / M • The Erotic World Of Crystal Lake (#4) / 1984 / VCR / C • Exhausted / 1981 / CA / C • F / 1980 / GO / M • A Family Affair / 1984 / AVC / M • Fleshdance / 1983 / SE / M • Forbidden Worlds / 1988 / GO / C • Gang-Way / 1984 / ECO / C • Girls Of The Ice Cream Parlor / 19?? / REG / M • Girls

On Girls / 1983 / VC / F • Girls! Girls! Girls! #1 / 1986 / VCS / C • Golden Girls #02 / 1981 / SVE / M • Golden Girls #09 / 1983 / CA / M • Golden Girls #12 / 1984 / CA / M • Golden Girls #23 / 1984 / CA / M • Golden Girls #24 / 1984 / CA / M • The Good Time Girls / 1985 / VEX / M • Gourmet Quickies: Laurie Smith #717 / 1985 / GO / C • Heartthrobs / 1985 / CA / M • Heidi A / 1985 / PL / M • High Price Spread / 1986 / PV / C • Holly Does Hollywood #1 / 1985 / VEX / M • Hot Shorts: Laurie Smith / 1986 / VCR / C • Hypersexuals / 1984 / VC / M • I Dream Of Ginger / 1985 / VI / M • I Want To Be Bad / 1984 / CV / M • In The Pink / 1983 / CA / M • Indecent Pleasures / 1984 / CA / M • Intimate Realities #1 / 1983 / VC / M • Joys Of Erotica / 1984 / VCR / M • Joys Of Erotica #107 / 1984 / VCR / C • Kinky Business #1 / 1984 / DR / M • Let's Get Naked / 1987 / VEX / M • Limo Connection / 1983 / VC / M • Matinee Idol / 1984 / VC / M • Maximum #5 / 1983 / CA / M • Mistresses And Slaves: The Best Of Bruce Seven / 1991 / BEB / C • Nasty Romances / 1985 / HO / C • Naughty Network / 1981 / CA / M • Night Magic / 1984 / SE / M • Nudes In Limbo / 1983 / MCA / S • Olympic Fever / 1979 / AR / M • Only The Best #3 / 1990 / CV / C • Only The Best Of Girls With Curves / 1992 / CV / C • Oriental Jade / 1985 / VC / M • Paradise Motel / 1984 / FOX / S • Passion Toys / 1985 / VCR / C • Perfect Fit / 1985 / DR / M • The Perfect Weekend / 1984 / AVC / M • Piggies / 1984 / VC / M • Pleasure Channel / 1984 / VC / M • Private Teacher / 1983 / CA / M • The Seduction Of Lana Shore / 1984 / PL / M • Seka In Heat / 1988 / BMV / C • Sex Appeal / 1984 / ABV / M • Sex Play / 1984 / SE / M • Sex Wars / 1984 / EXF / M • Sexperiences / 1987 / VEX / M • She-Male Encounters #07: Divine Atrocities #1 / 1981 / MET / G • Sinners #1 / 1988 / COM / M • Sinners #2 / 1988 / COM / M • Sinners #3 / 1989 / COM / M • Slip Into Silk / 1985 / CA / M • Snake Eyes #1 / 1984 / COM / M • Snake Eyes #2 / 1987 / COM / M • Society Affairs / 1982 / CA / M • Soft As Silk...Sweet As Honey / 1984 / SE / M • Star 84: Tina Marie / 1984 / VEX / M • Starlets / 1985 / 4P / M • Suze's Centerfolds #9 / 1985 / CA / M • Suzie Superstar #1 / 1983 / CV / M • Suzie Superstar #2 / 1985 / CV / M • The Sweetest Taboo / 1986 / SE / M • A Taste For Passion / 1983 / AMB / M • A Taste Of Money / 1983 / AT / M • Terms Of Endowment / 1986 / PV / M • Throat...12 Years After / 1984 / VC / M • Ultraflesh / 1980 / GO / M • Up Up And Away / 1984 / CA / M • VCA Previews #3 / 1988 / VC / C • The Wacky World Of X-Rated Bloopers / 1989 / GO / M • Wet And Wild #1 / 1986 / VEX / M • Wet Kisses / 1986 / SE / M • Wet Panties / 1989 / MIR / C • Where The Girls Are / 1984 / VEX / M • X-Rated Bloopers #1 / 1984 / AR / M • X-TV #1 / 1986 / PL / C • The Young Like It Hot / 1983 / CA / M
LAURIE SUESAN
Lickity Split / 1974 / COM / M
LAURIE TOLEDO see Star Index I
LAURIE WHITMORE
Josephine / 1974 / VC / M
LAURIEL DION
Las Vegas Big Boob Hospitality Sweet / 1997 / HO / M

LAURIEN DOMINIQUE *(Dorothy Newkirk, Sharlyn Alexander, LaiLani, Sharon Alexander, Lauini Dominique)*
Passable face with short brown hair cut in an old-fashioned style. In later movies appeared with a hat even while screwing probaly due to chemotherapy. Medium tits, passable body. Died in June 1986 (cancer).
Beauty / 1981 / VC / M • The Best Of Gail Palmer / 1981 / WWV / C • The Budding Of Brie / 1980 / TVX / M • Calendar Girl '83 / 1983 / CXV / M • Doing It / 1982 / SE / M • Easy / 1978 / CV / M • The Ecstasy Girls #1 / 1979 / CA / M • Erotic Fantasies #4 / 1983 / CV / C • Erotic Fantasies: Women With Women / 1984 / CV / C • Exhausted / 1981 / CA / C • Fantasy World / 1979 / WWV / M • Hard Soap, Hard Soap / 1977 / EVI / M • Hot Legs / 1979 / VCX / M • Hot Rackets / 1979 / CV / M • Legends Of Porn #1 / 1987 / CV / C • Love Lips / 1976 / VC / M • Night Hunger / 1983 / AVC / M • One Way At A Time / 1979 / CA / M • Only The Best Of Women With Women / 1988 / CV / C • Pizza Girls (We Deliver) / 1978 / VCX / M • Porn In The USA #1 / 1986 / WV / C • Screwples / 1979 / CA / M • The Sensuous Detective / 1979 / VC / M • Sissy's Hot Summer / 1979 / CA / M • The Starlets / 1976 / RAV / M • Summer School / 1979 / VCX / M • Superstar John Holmes / 1979 / AVC / M • Sweet Dreams Suzan / 1980 / CA / M • Sweet Secrets / 1977 / VCS / M • V—The Hot One / 1978 / CV / M • Women In Love / 1980 / CA / M

LAURIEN ST GERMAIN
Pleasure So Deep / 1983 / AT / M • Rx For Sex / 1983 / AT / M

LAURN HALL see Tanya Fox
LAURY DAVIS see Star Index I
LAUTREC see Debbie Northrup
LAVONN
Limited Edition #24 / 1984 / AVC / M
LAWANDA PEABODY see Toy
LAWRENCE COOK
[No More Dirty Deals / 1994 / V-I / S
LAWRENCE EDWARDS
The Devil's Garden / 1970 / SOW / S • Yacht Orgy / 1984 / CA / M
LAWRENCE EYEMARD
Breaking And Entering / 1984 / CA / M • The Whore's Port / 1984 / CA / M
LAWRENCE JARRY
Perverse / 1984 / CA / M
LAWRENCE JOHNSON
Dementia / 1995 / IP / M • Stuff Your Ass #2 / 1995 / JMP / M
LAWRENCE PERTILLAH see Star Index I
LAWRENCE PIPER
Flesh...And The Fantasies / 1991 / BIZ / B
LAWRENCE ROTHSCHILD
Ball Game / 1980 / CA / M • Mrs. Smith's Erotic Holiday / 1982 / VCX / M • Undercovers / 1982 / CA / M
LAWRENCE SELDEN
Boy Spanks Girl / 1995 / SHL / B
LAWRENCE T. COLE *(Bob Wolf)*
Loop-maker, notorious for **Dogarama**.
LAWRENCE ZENON see Star Index I
LAYA
Oriental Sexpress / 1984 / WV / M
LAYA DOWNE see Star Index I
LAYDE MCCORMICK see Star Index I
LAYLA
Bedside Brat / 1988 / VI / M

LAYLA ANTHONY see Layla LaShell
LAYLA LASHELL *(Layla Anthony, Lela Leshell, Bertha (Layla), Laurie Arden)*
Ugly fatso, supposedly 350 to 450lbs. Layla Anthony is from **Hefty Mamas #1**. Real name is Laurie Arden and in 1994 was convicted of a sex offence concerning a 14 year old boy and sentenced to two years in jail.
Bad Mama Jama And The Fat Ladies Of The Evening / 1989 / VT / M • Bad Mama Jama Busts Out / 1989 / VT / M • Big Bad Bertha #1 / 1985 / UNQ / M • Big Bad Bertha #2 / 1985 / UNQ / M • Blind Date / 1989 / E&I / M • Fat Ends / 1989 / 4P / M • Fatliners #2 / 1991 / EX / M • Jane Bond Meets Thunderthighs / 1988 / VD / M • Let Me Tell Ya 'Bout Fat Chicks #1 / 1986 / 4P / C • Let Me Tell Ya 'Bout Fat Chicks #2 / 1988 / 4P / M • Parliament: Hefty Mamas #1 / 1987 / PM / F • Parliament: Kingsize / 1987 / PM / F • Sumo Sue And The Fat Ladies Of Wrestling / 1988 / FAN / M • Tantala's Fat Rack / 1990 / FC / B • Tons Of Buns / 1986 / 4P / M • Tons Of Fun #4: Hard And Lard / 1987 / 4P / M
LAYLITA
Exotic Tastes / 1995 / VEX / C • The New Ass Masters #10 / 1996 / LEI / C • Pussy Hunt #10 / 1995 / LEI / M
LAYNE see Star Index I
LAYNE PARKER
Drop Sex: Wipe The Floor / 1997 / JLP / M
LAYNEY
Very young looking with long blonde hair, pretty face but lots of acne, small tits, clit ring, two tongue pins, small tits. Says she comes from Montana.
Hard Core Beginners #09 / 1995 / LEI / M • The Reunion / 1996 / CS / B • Snatch Masters #09 / 1995 / LEI / M
LAZARUS LONG
Pearl Necklace: Amorous Amateurs #16 / 1992 / SEE / M • Pearl Necklace: Thee Bush League #09 / 1993 / SEE / M
LAZZLO LANDONI see Star Index I
LE DAWN *(La Dawn, Le Donna)*
Arches Of Triumph / 1995 / PRE / S • B*A*S*H / 1989 / BIZ / C • Best Exotic Dancers In The Usa / 1995 / PME / S • Big Busty#24 / 198? / H&S / S • The Big E #08 / 1988 / BIZ / B • Blonde Fantasy / 1988 / CC / M • Blows Job / 1989 / BIZ / B • Bound To Tease #1 / 1988 / BON / C • Bound To Tease #2 / 1989 / BON / C • Breast Wishes #02 / 1991 / LBO / M • Breast Worx #01 / 1991 / LBO / M • Confrontation Of The Cats / 1989 / NAP / B • Cramped Spaces / 1989 / PLV / B • Ebony Boxes / 1988 / NAP / B • Educating Laurel / 1988 / BON / B • Enemates #02 / 1989 / BIZ / B • Feet First / 1988 / BIZ / S • Flash Floods / 1991 / PRE / C • Fun In The Sun / 1988 / EVN / C • Girls Of The Double D #01 / 1986 / CDI / M • Introducing Barbii / 1987 / CDI / M • Laurel's Continuing Education / 1988 / BON / B • Leave It To Cleavage #1 / 1988 / GO / M • Leg...Ends #01 / 1988 / BIZ / F • Megasex / 1988 / EVN / M • Parliament: Licking Lesbians #1 / 1988 / PM / F • Pet Hotel #1 / 1988 / BON / B • Pet Hotel #2 / 1988 / BON / B • Rachel Arrives / 1989 / NAP / B • Rip Off #1 / 1988 / BIZ / B • Rip Off #2 / 1988 / PLV / B • Rumble-Cats / 1989 / NAP / B • Scorching Secrets / 1988 / IN / M • Sex Sluts From Beyond The Galaxy / 1991 / LBO / C • Slap Shots / 1991 / PRE / B •

Special Massage / 1989 / NAP / B • Super Leg-Ends / 1992 / PRE / C • Sweet Revenge / 1989 / NAP / B • Taken By Surprise / 1989 / NAP / B • Toed Off / 1989 / PLV / B • Top Heavy / 1988 / VD / M • [T&A #01 / 1989 / ... / C
LE DONNA see Le Dawn
LE LE see Le Le Adams
LE LE ADAMS *(Le Le, Lele, Vicki Meilleur, Alicia Adams)*
Huge falling apart body and too big teeth.
Amateur Lesbians #21: Daphne / 1992 / GO / F • Amateur Lesbians #23: Sherri / 1992 / GO / F • America's Dirtiest Home Videos #09 / 1992 / VEX / M • Beverly Hills Geisha / 1992 / V99 / M • Big Bust Babes #08 / 1991 / AFI / M • Breast Worx #34 / 1992 / LBO / M • Bruise Control / 1993 / PRE / B • Cannes Heat / 1992 / FD / M • The Come On: Skip's Video Guide To Scoring Chicks / 1991 / LE / M • Crunch Bunch / 1995 / PRE / C • Enemates #07 / 1992 / PRE / B • First Time Lesbians #09 / 1993 / JMP / F • Glitter Girls / 1992 / V99 / M • Hollywood Teasers #01 / 1992 / LBO / F • Honeymooned / 1992 / PRE / B • Hot Savannah Nights / 1991 / VEX / M • House Pet / 1992 / V99 / M • Leg...Ends #09 / 1994 / PRE / F • Long Dan Silver / 1992 / IF / M • Looking For Love / 1991 / VEX / M • Maid For Service / 1990 / LV / M • Nasty Jack's Kloset Klassics #04 / 1991 / CDI / M • Naughty Butt Nice / 1993 / IF / M • The Perfect Pet / 1991 / VEX / C • Raging Waters / 1992 / PRE / B • Riviera Heat / 1993 / FD / M • Running Mates / 1993 / PRE / B • Student Fetish Videos: Best of Enema #02 / 1992 / PRE / C • Student Fetish Videos: The Enema #08 / 1992 / PRE / B • Student Fetish Videos: Tickling #05 / 1992 / SFV / B • Suburban Seduction / 1991 / HO / M • SVE: Cheap Thrills #3: Self-Satisfaction / 1992 / SVE / F • SVE: Cheap Thrills #4: Woman To Woman / 1992 / SVE / F • Toppers #02 / 1992 / TV / M • Victoria's Amateurs #03 / 1992 / VGA / M • Virgin Spring / 1991 / FAZ / M • You Said A Mouthful / 1992 / IF / M
LEA *(Sinammon)*
Not too pretty blonde with huge tits and a diseased looking pussy. Originally a make-up artist.
Club Exotica #1 / 1985 / WV / M • Club Exotica #2 / 1985 / WV / M • Dirty Dancers #8 / 1996 / 4P / M • Lesbian Submission / 1994 / PL / B • Love Doll Lucy #1 / 1994 / PL / F • Love Doll Lucy #2 / 1994 / PL / F • Savage Torture / 1994 / PL / B • Strap-On Sally #01: Strap-On Psycho / 1993 / PL / F • Strap-On Sally #02: Ariana Bottoms Out / 1993 / PL / F • Sunset Rides Again / 1995 / VC / M
LEA (1996)
Executions On Butt Row / 1996 / EA / M • FTV #06: The Intruder / 1996 / FT / B • Video Virgins #27 / 1996 / NS / M
LEA MARTINI
Anal Virgins #01 / 1996 / NS / M • Betty Bleu / 1996 / IP / M • Buttman In The Crack / 1996 / EA / M • Executions On Butt Row / 1996 / EA / M • Family Affair / 1996 / XC / M • Illicit Affairs / 1996 / XC / M • Introducing Alexis / 1996 / VI / M • Miss Anal #3 / 1995 / C69 / M • Paris Chic / 1996 / SAE / M • Snake Pit / 1996 / DWO / M • Unleashed / 1996 / SAE / M • Video Virgins

THE X-RATED VIDEOTAPE STAR INDEX **391**

#26 / 1996 / NS / M
LEA MCCLOUD *see Star Index I*
LEA STONE
Erotic Dimensions: Aggressive Women / 1982 / NSV / M
LEA VALENTINE
Skin #5: The 5th Column / 1996 / ERQ / M
LEAH
Homegrown Video #358 / 1991 / HOV / M
LEAH (S/M)
Chicks With Dicks #2 / 1996 / BIZ / B • Kink: Police Chronicles / 1995 / ROB / M • Transsexual Dynasty / 1996 / BIZ / G
LEAH ANNE *see Star Index I*
LEAH DAWN
Butt Row Unplugged / 1996 / ABS / M • Cumback Pussy #4: Get Some!!! / 1996 / EL / M • More Dirty Debutantes #59 / 1996 / SBV / M • More Dirty Debutantes #61 / 1997 / SBV / M
LEAH GRANT *see Paula Wain*
LEAH LAMARR *see Star Index I*
LEAH LEFLEUR
The Agony Of D'Feet / 1993 / SOR / B • The Analyst / 1990 / SOR / B • Playing At Leah's / 1994 / LLF / B • Smothered / 1995 / LLF / B
LEAH LYONS *(Shelby (Leah Lyons))*
Bare Essentials / 1987 / VEX / M • Primal Urge / 1992 / VEX / M • Space Vixens / 1987 / V99 / M
LEAH MARLON
Virgin And The Lover / 1973 / ALP / M
LEAH MULLER
Little Angels In Pain / 1975 / ASR / B
LEANA GRANT
Society Affairs / 1982 / CA / M
LEANN
A&B AB#145: Wet Pussies / 1990 / A&B / F • A&B AB#182: Watch Me Spank Me / 1990 / A&B / M • A&B AB#226: Bondage Girls #1 / 1990 / A&B / C • A&B AB#226: Bondage Girls #2 / 1990 / A&B / C • A&B AB#530: Masters / 1995 / A&B / B • Amateurs In Action #2 / 1994 / MET / M • Oh My Gush / 1995 / OD / M
LEANN
A&B AB#145: Wet Pussies / 1990 / A&B / F • A&B AB#182: Watch Me Spank Me / 1990 / A&B / M • A&B AB#226: Bondage Girls #1 / 1990 / A&B / C • A&B AB#226: Bondage Girls #2 / 1990 / A&B / C • A&B AB#530: Masters / 1995 / A&B / B • Amateurs In Action #2 / 1994 / MET / M • Oh My Gush / 1995 / OD / M
LEANN (TERA HEART) *see Tera Heart*
LEANN LAMAR
Mr. Peepers Nastiest #1 / 1995 / LBO / C
LEANNA FOXXX *(Wendy (Leanna Foxxx), Lianna Foxxx, Chantaine, Lenna Fox, Leona Fox, Rene (Leanna) Foxx, Dixie Dynamite)*
Wendy is from **Love Shack**. Brain dead white skinned brunette with half cantelopes stuck on her chest of which she is inordinately proud. Chantaine is from **Dougie Hoser MD**. Is not Chantal LeMaire (Brigitte Aime is). Born 8/14/64 in Albuquerque NM (but an interview in 1995 says she's 26 years old—please yourself). 34EEE-23-36.
Adult Video Nudes / 1993 / VC / M • Amateur Lesbians #01: Leanna / 1991 / GO / F • Ambushed / 1990 / SE / M • America's Dirtiest Home Videos #03 / 1991 / VEX / M • America's Dirtiest Home Videos #20: Hot Sex / 1992 / VEX / M • Anal Attack / 1991 /

ZA / M • Anal Heat / 1990 / ZA / M • Anal Therapy #2 / 1993 / FD / M • Anal Therapy #4 / 1996 / FD / M • Another Dirty Western / 1992 / AFV / M • Asian Tit-Queen / 1996 / NAP / B • Ass Openers! #2 / 1995 / TCK / C • The Back Doors (Western) / 1991 / WV / M • Backfire / 1991 / GO / M • Ball Busters / 1991 / FH / M • Battle Of The Busty Foxxes / 1994 / NAP / B • Beeping Miss Buffy / 1995 / CDI / M • Behind The Scenes / 1996 / GO / M • Bi-Sex Pleasures / 1993 / PL / G • Biff Malibu's Totally Nasty Home Videos #10 / 1992 / ANA / M • Big Bust Babes #10 / 1992 / AFI / M • Big Bust Babes #14 / 1993 / AFI / M • Big Bust Babes #33 / 1995 / AFI / M • Big Bust Bangers #1 / 1994 / AMP / M • Big Bust Fantasies / 1995 / PME / F • Big Knockers #17 / 1995 / TV / M • Big Knockers #18 / 1995 / TV / M • Big Knockers #22 / 1995 / TV / M • The Bimbo #1 / 1992 / AFV / M • The Bimbo #2 / 1992 / AFV / M • Black & Blue / 1990 / SO / M • Black Obsession / 1991 / ZA / M • Bloopers #2 / 1991 / GO / C • Blow Out / 1991 / IF / M • Body Locked / 1996 / NAP / B • Boobytrap...The Next Generation / 1992 / HW / M • Breastman Goes To Breastland #1 / 1993 / EVN / M • Breasts And Beyond #1 / 1991 / ME / M • Broadway Babes / 1993 / FH / F • Bulging Babes At War / 1994 / NAP / B • Bus Stop Tales #13 / 1990 / 4P / M • Business And Pleasure / 1992 / AFV / M • Bust A Move / 1993 / SC / M • Busting Out / 199? / NAP / F • Bustline / 1993 / LE / M • The Butt Sisters Do Houston / 1996 / MID / M • Butt Woman #5 / 1993 / FH / M • Butt's Up, Doc #2 / 1992 / GO / M • The Buttnicks #2 / 1991 / HIO / M • The Buttnicks #3 / 1992 / CC / M • Carnal Carnival / 1992 / FC / M • Casual Sex / 1991 / GO / M • Chameleons: Not The Sequel / 1991 / VC / M • Cheatin' Hearts / 1991 / VEX / M • Club Josephine / 1991 / AR / F • Cooler Girls / 1994 / MID / C • The Creasemaster's Wife / 1993 / VC / M • Crotch To Crotch: Latex Madness / 1996 / NAP / B • The Danger Zone / 1990 / SO / M • Desert Starm (030 Min) / 1993 / NAP / B • Desert Starm (120 Min) / 1993 / NAP / C • Dirty Dixie / 1992 / IF / M • Dixie Dynamite / 1992 / IF / C • Dorm Girls / 1992 / VC / M • Double D Domination / 1993 / BIZ / B • Double D Dykes #04 / 1992 / GO / F • Double D Dykes #10 / 1993 / GO / F • Double D Dykes #22 / 1995 / GO / F • Dougie Hoser: The World's Youngest Gynaecologist / 1990 / VT / M • Duel Of The Show-Mates / 199? / NAP / B • Dyno-Mite / 1992 / IF / M • Facesitter #2 / 1993 / CC / M • Fixing A Hole / 1995 / XCI / M • Flying High #1 / 1992 / HO / M • Formal Affair / 1991 / … / M • Fortysomething #2 / 1991 / LE / M • Fox Fever / 1991 / LV / M • Foxx Hunt / 1991 / GO / M • Foxxxy Lady / 1992 / HW / M • Frat Girls / 1993 / VC / M • Fun & Games / 1994 / FD / C • Girl Lovers / 1990 / BIZ / F • A Girl's Affair #02 / 1993 / FD / F • Girls Gone Bad #3: Back To The Slammer / 1991 / GO / F • Girls In Heat / 1991 / ZA / F • Girls, Girls, Girls, Girls / 1993 / FD / C • Girlz N The Hood #1 / 1991 / HW / M • Glitz Tits #06 / 1993 / GLI / M • The Goddess / 1993 / ZA / M • Group Therapy / 1992 / TP / M • Guess Who Came To Dinner / 1992 / AFV / M • Hangin' Out / 1992 / IF / M • The Harley Girls / 1991 / AR

/ F • Have I Got A Girl For You / 1989 / VEX / M • Heatwave #2 / 1993 / FH / F • Heavy Petting / 1991 / SE / M • Hidden Agenda / 1992 / XCI / M • Home But Not Alone / 1991 / WV / M • Hootermania / 1994 / VC / M • Hot Property / 1993 / PEP / M • Hot Tight Asses #01 / 1992 / TCK / M • Immoral Support / 1992 / AFV / M • In Too Deep / 1992 / AFD / M • Jiggly Queens #1 / 1993 / LE / M • The Joi Of Tit Fighting / 199? / NAP / B • The Journey: Oral Majority / 1991 / WV / M • Just My Imagination / 1993 / WP / M • Kiss And Tell / 1992 / AFV / M • Kiss Of Domination / 1996 / NAP / B • The Kitten And The Foxxx / 1993 / NAP / B • Kym Wilde Sessions #3 / 1993 / RB / B • Kym Wilde's On The Edge #01 / 1993 / RB / B • Ladies Lovin' Ladies #1 / 1990 / AR / F • Ladies Lovin' Ladies #2 / 1992 / AR / F • Ladies Lovin' Ladies #4 / 1992 / AFV / F • Latex Lioness / 1996 / NAP / B • Laying Down The Law #2 / 1992 / AFV / M • Lesbian Pros And Amateurs #13 / 1992 / GO / F • Lesbians In Tight Shorts / 1992 / LV / F • Lingerie Vixens / 199? / NAP / B • Love Shack / 1990 / CC / M • Mad Maxine / 1992 / AFV / M • The Magnificence Of Minka / 1996 / NAP / S • Maiden Heaven #2 / 1992 / MID / F • Mamm's The Word / 1991 / ZA / M • Manbait #1 / 1991 / VC / M • Manbait #2 / 1992 / VC / M • The Many Loves Of Jennifer / 1991 / VC0 / S • The Mistress And The Wife / 1994 / NAP / B • Mo' Booty #1 / 1992 / HW / C • More Than A Handful #2 / 1993 / MET / M • More Than A Handful #3 / 1993 / MET / M • Mr. Peepers Amateur Home Videos #11: Fur Pie Smorgasbord / 1991 / LBO / M • Mystified / 1991 / V99 / M • New Wave Hookers #3 / 1993 / VC / M • Nothing Butt The Truth / 1993 / AFV / M • Nothing Else Matters / 1992 / V99 / C • The One And Only / 1993 / FD / M • Oreo A Go-Go #1 / 1992 / FH / M • Oreo A Go-Go #2 / 1992 / FH / M • Oriental Treatment #4: The Demon Lover / 1992 / AFV / M • The Outlaw / 1991 / WV / M • Pick Up Lines #01 / 1995 / 4P / M • Pink Card / 1991 / FH / M • Playin' Hard To Get / 1994 / VEX / M • Puppy Love / 1992 / AFV / M • Pussyman #01: The Search / 1993 / CC / M • Quantum Deep / 1993 / HW / M • The Queen Of Mean / 1992 / FC / M • Queen Of The Harem / 1993 / NAP / B • Quickies / 1992 / AFV / M • The Rage Meets The Foxxx / 1994 / NAP / B • Rainbwoman #05 / 1992 / CC / M • Red Hot Coeds / 1993 / VIM / M • Rock & Roll Fantasies / 1992 / FL / M • Rocky Mountains / 1991 / IF / M • Rumors / 1992 / FL / M • Satan's Mistress / 1993 / NAP / B • A Scent Of Leather / 1992 / IF / M • The Seductress / 1992 / ZA / M • Sex Asylum #4 / 1991 / VI / M • Sex Police 2000 / 1992 / AFV / M • Sex Under Glass / 1992 / VC / M • Sexual Instinct #1 / 1992 / DR / M • Soft Tail / 1991 / IN / M • Some Like It Big / 1991 / LE / M • Someone Sent Me A Girl / 1991 / FH / M • Steele Butt / 1993 / AFV / M • The Stranger Beside Me / 1991 / WV / M • A Stripper Named Desire / 1993 / CC / M • Sunrise Mystery / 1992 / FD / M • Survival Of The Fullest / 199? / NAP / B • Sweet Stuff / 1991 / V99 / M • A Tale Of Two Titties #2 / 1992 / AFV / M • The Taming Of Ciera / 1993 / NAP / B • The Taming Of Tushima / 1994 / NAP / B • This Time We

Fight / 1996 / NAP / B • Tit City #1 / 1993 / SC / M • Tit For Tat / 1994 / PEP / M • Tit In A Wringer / 1993 / FC / M • Tit Tales #3 / 1991 / FC / M • Tit Tales #4 / 1993 / FC / M • Titty Bar #1 / 1993 / LE / M • Tongues On Fire / 1994 / NAP / B • Toying Around / 1992 / FL / M • Transformation / 1996 / XCI / M • Transsexual 6900 / 1990 / LV / G • Tropic Of Kahlia / 1991 / VI / M • Two Of A Kind / 1990 / LV / M • A Vision In Heather / 1991 / VI / M • W.A.S.P. / 1992 / CC / M • Wet Nurses #2 / 1995 / LE / M • Whoppers #3 / 1993 / VEX / F • Wild Things #3 / 1992 / MET / M • Will & Ed's Keister Easter / 1992 / MID / M • The Women / 1993 / CAT / F • Women On Top / 1995 / BON / B • The Wonder Rears / 1990 / SO / M • Wrestling Queens / 1996 / NAP / B • You Said A Mouthful / 1992 / IF / M

LEANNA HEART

Adorable brunette with a very tight body. You can see her in **Up And Cummers #35** with her original perky small firm tits but according to her that was the eve of her tit surgery and sure enough she got large rock solid cantaloupes glued on for her later movies. 22 years old in 1996 and supposedly de-virginized at 18.

Cumback Pussy #5: Groopin' / 1996 / EL / M • I Wanna Be A Porn Star #2 / 1996 / 4P / M • Look What I Found On The Street #01 / 1996 / CC / M • Pick Up Lines #09 / 1996 / OD / M • Pick Up Lines #10 / 1997 / OD / M • Pick Up Lines #11 / 1997 / OD / M • Pick Up Lines #12 / 1997 / OD / M • Rebel Without A Condom / 1996 / ERA / M • She's No Angel / 1996 / ERA / S • Sodomania #20: For Members Only / 1997 / EL / M • The Swing / 1996 / VI / M • Up And Cummers #35 / 1996 / 4P / M • Video Virgins #33 / 1996 / NS / M

LEANNA RAI see Star Index I
LEANNE CRUZ
Immortal Desire / 1993 / VI / M
LEANNE LIZAMMA
Immortal Desire / 1993 / VI / M
LEANNE LOVELACE *(Leosha)*

As Leanne she's a blonde; as Leosha, a red-head.

Big Boob Celebration / 1994 / BTO / M • Big Busty #31 / 1989 / BTO / S • Big Busty #32 / 1989 / BTO / S • Biggest Sexiest Boobs In The USA Contest / 1989 / NAP / F • Busen Extra #3 / 1987 / BTO / M • Double D Amateurs #03 / 1993 / JMP / M • Duke Of Knockers #1 / 1992 / BTO / M • Duke Of Knockers #2 / 1995 / BTO / M • EE 7 / 1991 / NAP / S • Girls Around The World #22: Letha Weapons & Friends / 1995 / BTO / M • Glitz Tits #06 / 1993 / GLI / M • Glitz Tits #07 / 1993 / GLI / M • M Series #07 / 1993 / LBO / M • Mega-Tits / 1990 / NAP / F • Much More Than A Mouthful #4 / 1994 / VEX / M • Pussy Power #04 / 1992 / BTO / M • Pussy Power #05 / 1992 / BTO / M • Toppers #11 / 1993 / TV / C • Toppers #13 / 1993 / TV / M

LEATHER TRACY see Star Index I
LEE

AVP #7035: Not Hard-Lee In Vegas / 1991 / AVP / M • Beach Bum Amateur's #22 / 1993 / MID / M • Body Tease / 1992 / VER / F • Buffy Malibu's Totally Nasty All-Girl Home Videos #03 / 1992 / ANA / F • Girls Around The World #21: Tawny Peaks & Friends / 1995 / BTO / M • Hollywood Am-

ateurs #12 / 1994 / MID / M • Joe Elliot's Asian College Girls #02 / 1995 / JOE / M • New Faces, Hot Bodies #02 / 1992 / STP / M • New Faces, Hot Bodies #03 / 1992 / STP / M • New Faces, Hot Bodies #21 / 1996 / STP / C • New Girls In Town #3 / 1993 / CC / M • Raw Talent: Fetish of the Month #02 / 1992 / RTP / M • Swedish Erotica #37 / 1981 / CA / M • Swedish Erotica #40 / 1981 / CA / M • Wrasslin She-Babes #12 / 1996 / SOW / M

LEE (TAWNY DOWNS) see Tawny Downs
LEE ANN MORGAN see Star Index I
LEE BALDWIN

Bi-Heat #08 To #10 / 1988 / ZA / G • Days Gone Bi / 1988 / ZA / G • Sex Bi-Lex / 1993 / CAT / G • Sex World Girls / 1987 / AR / M • She Studs #03 / 1991 / BIZ / G • Slumber Party Reunion / 1987 / AR / M • Trisexual Encounters #07 / 1988 / PL / G

LEE CARROLL *(Leslie Barris)*

Ugly aged foul-mouthed blonde. Leslie Barris is from **Skintight**.

8 To 4 / 1981 / CA / M • The 8th Annual Erotic Film Awards / 1984 / SE / C • Amanda By Night #1 / 1981 / CA / M • American Pie / 1980 / SE / M • Any Time, Any Place / 1981 / CA0 / M • Aunt Peg Goes To Hollywood / 1982 / CA / M • Back In The Pen / 1992 / FH / M • Bad Girls #1 / 1981 / GO / M • Blue Ribbon Blue / 1984 / CA / C • Blue Vanities #048 / 1988 / FFL / M • Blue Vanities #090 / 1988 / FFL / M • Blue Vanities #091 / 1988 / FFL / M • Breast Worx #11 / 1991 / LBO / M • Breast Worx #15 / 1992 / LBO / M • Bums Away / 1995 / PRE / C • Caballero Preview Tape #3 / 1984 / CA / C • Candy Stripers #2 / 1990 / AR / M • Charli / 1981 / VCX / M • Clean Out / 1991 / PRE / B • Cover Girl Fantasies #1 / 1983 / VCR / C • Cover Girl Fantasies #2 / 1983 / VCR / C • Daughters Of Discipline / 1993 / GOT / B • Double D Dykes #01 / 1992 / GO / F • Dungeon Humiliation / 1996 / STM / B • Enemates #04 / 1992 / BIZ / B • Enemates #07 / 1992 / PRE / B • Erotic Heights / 1991 / AR / M • Famous Ta-Ta's #1 / 1986 / VCS / C • First Annual XRCO Awards / 1984 / AVC / C • The Flirt / 1992 / EVN / M • Flogged For His Sins / 1993 / STM / B • Foxholes / 1983 / SE / M • Girls That Talk Dirty / 1986 / VCS / C • Heart Breaker / 1985 / TAR / C • Heel's Angels / 1995 / PRE / B • High Fives / 1991 / PRE / B • Honeymooned / 1992 / PRE / B • Hot Buns / 1983 / VCX / M • Hot Girls In Love / 1984 / VIV / C • Immorals #1: Broken Hearts / 1989 / AR / M • Immorals #2: The Good, The Bad, And The Banged / 1990 / AR / M • Immorals #3: Stroked / 1991 / SC / M • Immorals #4: Choice Cuts / 1991 / SC / M • Killer / 1991 / SC / M • Kinky Couples / 1990 / VD / M • Ladies Lovin' Ladies #2 / 1992 / AR / F • Ladyfair Presents Lee / 1990 / LAD / F • Latex, Leather & Lace / 1993 / STM / B • Le Sex De Femme #1 / 1989 / AFI / C • Leg...Ends #06 / 1992 / PRE / F • Leg...Ends #08 / 1993 / PRE / F • Lipstick Lesbians / 1993 / STM / F • Mandy's Executive Sweet / 1982 / AVC / M • Mascara / 1982 / CA / M • Mature Women #01 / 1991 / BTO / M • Mike Hott: #17X Lee Caroll Queen Slut #1 / 1990 / MHV / F • Mike Hott: #18X Lee Caroll Queen Slut #2 /

1990 / MHV / F • Mike Hott: Cum Cocktails #2 / 1995 / MHV / C • Miss Matches / 1996 / PRE / C • Mommie Severest / 1992 / STM / B • Mr. Fun's Mondo Adventure / 1993 / VC / M • Nasty Dancers #1 / 1996 / STM / B • Nasty Dancers #2 / 1996 / STM / B • The Night Temptress / 1989 / HU / M • Only The Best #2 / 1989 / CV / C • Only The Very Best On Film / 1992 / VC / C • Oriental Treatment #2: The Pearl Divers / 1989 / AR / M • Perversion / 1984 / AVC / M • Pleasure Dome / 1982 / SE / M • Profiles In Discipline #02: Naughty Angel / 1994 / STM / C • Punished Deception / 1996 / STM / B • Pussy Power #03 / 1992 / BTO / M • Raging Waters / 1992 / PRE / B • Raw #2 / 1994 / AFV / M • Rump Roasts / 1991 / PRE / B • Sailor Beware / 1993 / GOT / B • Same Time Every Year / 1981 / VHL / M • The Satisfiers Of Alpha Blue / 1980 / AVC / C • The Seductress / 1982 / VC / M • Sexcalibur / 1982 / SE / M • Sexcapades / 1983 / VC / M • Skintight / 1981 / CA / M • Stairway To Paradise / 1990 / VC / M • Star Struck / 1991 / AFV / M • Super Enemates #1 / 1994 / PRE / C • Terms Of Endowment / 1986 / PV / M • Toe Tales #04 / 1992 / GOT / B • Toes 'n' Cons / 1996 / PRE / S • Toppers #01 / 1992 / TV / F • Toppers #12 / 1993 / TV / C • The Trouble With Traci / 1984 / CHA / C • Urban Cowgirls / 1980 / CA / M • Valley Of The Sluts / 1991 / OD / M • Video Tramp #2 / 1988 / TME / M • Way Inside Lee Caroll / 1992 / VIM / M • Wet Dreams / 1980 / WWV / M • The Widespread Scandals Of Lydia Lace / 1983 / CA / M • Wild Cats / 1991 / PRE / B

LEE CHANDLER see Star Index I
LEE COLT
Erotic Fantasies #6 / 1984 / CV / C
LEE COOPER see Dan T. Mann
LEE DONOVAN see Star Index I
LEE DUPREE
Feelings / 1977 / VC / M
LEE FOREST see Star Index I
LEE FOSTER
Erotic Fantasies #4 / 1983 / CV / C • Foxy Lady / 1978 / CV / M
LEE FRANCIS
Horny Henry's London Adventure / 1995 / TTV / M • The Inseminator #1 / 1994 / LBO / M • The Inseminator #2: Domination Day / 1994 / LBO / M • Lusting, London Style / 1992 / VC / M
LEE GARLAND
Conquest / 1996 / WP / M
LEE GERMAIN
Blue Vanities #132 / 1991 / FFL / M • Reel Classics #3 / 1996 / H&S / M
LEE GORDON
Fan Fuxxx #1 / 1996 / DWV / M
LEE GRIFFIN
ABA: Double Feature #5 / 1996 / ALP / M • Night Of Submission / 1976 / BIZ / M
LEE J. O'DONNELL
A Dirty Western #1 / 1973 / AR / M • The Erotic Adventures Of Peter Galore / 1973 / ALP / M • Saturday Matinee Series #3 / 1996 / VCX / C
LEE JAY see Star Index I
LEE JENNINGS
Bi And Busty / 1991 / STA / G • Bi Cycling / 1989 / FC / G • Bi Mistake / 1989 / VI / G • The Bi-Analyst / 1991 / STA / G • Matters In Hand / 1989 / STA / G • The Perfect Girl / 1992 / CDI / G • Switch Hitters #4: The

Grand Slam / 1989 / IN / G • Uninhibited / 1989 / VC / G

LEE LANE
Memories / 1996 / ZA / M

LEE LANZO *see Star Index I*

LEE LE MAY
Taboo #01 / 1980 / VCX / M

LEE MAJORS
Ice Cream Man / 1995 / APE / S • Pussy Showdown / 1994 / WIV / M

LEE MITCHELL
San Francisco Lesbians #4 / 1993 / PL / F • San Francisco Lesbians #5 / 1994 / PL / F • San Francisco Lesbians #6 / 1994 / PL / F

LEE MOORE
Eager Beaver / 1975 / AVC / M • Fantasy Fever / 1975 / AVC / M • Mortgage Of Sin / 1975 / CA / M • Night Of The Zombies / 1981 / PRS / S • Y-All Come / 1975 / CDC / M

LEE PARSONS
What About Jane? / 1971 / ALP / M

LEE PRICE
FTV #03: Queen Boxer & Mixed Fist / 1996 / FT / B

LEE ROTHERMUND
Where There's Smoke / 1986 / TIG / F

LEE SANCHO
Little Girl Lost / 1995 / SC / M

LEE STARR
Deep Inside Annie Sprinkle / 1981 / VXP / M

LEE STEVENS *see Star Index I*

LEE TREE
Old Guys & Dolls #2 / 1995 / PL / M

LEE VALENTINE
Amsterdam Nights #1 / 1996 / BLC / M • Amsterdam Nights #2 / 1996 / VC / M • Helen Does Holland / 1996 / VC / M

LEE WINSTON
The Shoe Store / 1985 / BIZ / B

LEEANN *see Star Index I*

LEENA *(Leena La Bianca, Kathleen Mazzotta)*
Started off in the Odyssey amateur series. Had her tits inflated before turning pro. Originally a drug-using topless dancer in Denver. As of 1993 wrote a column for *Looking Glass* magazine. Supposedly born in 1969 of Italian ancestry. Retired in 1995 and has appeared since in some infomercials, commercials and TV series.
The Anal Adventures Of Suzy Super Slut #1 / 1994 / AFV / M • Ass Openers! #1 / 1995 / TCK / C • Attack Of The 50 Foot Hooker / 1994 / OD / M • Backdoor Pleasures #1 / 1993 / MAV / M • Bedazzled / 1993 / OD / M • The Best Of Oriental Anal #1 / 1994 / ROB / C • Big Busted Dream Girls / 1995 / PME / S • Blinded By Love / 1993 / OD / M • Booty Ho #1 / 1993 / ROB / M • The Brothel / 1993 / OD / M • Butt Naked #2 / 1994 / OD / M • Buzzzz! / 1993 / OD / M • Carlita's Backway / 1993 / OD / M • Cheating / 1994 / VI / M • Cinesex #1 / 1995 / CV / M • Cinesex #2 / 1994 / CV / M • Cinnamon Twist / 1993 / OD / M • Climax 2000 #1 / 1994 / CC / M • The Corner / 1994 / VT / M • The Darker Side / 1994 / HO / M • Dirty Bob's #05: Vegas MasterpieCES / 1992 / FLP / S • Dirty Bob's #07: DanCES With OrifiCES / 1992 / FLP / S • Dirty Bob's #13: Getting Lucky In Vegas / 1994 / FLP / S • Dirty Bob's #18: Under The Boardwalk! / 1995 / FLP / S • Dirty Bob's

#19: Over The Boardwalk! / 1995 / FLP / S • Dirty Bob's #20: Back To Vegas! / 1995 / FLP / S • Dream Teams / 1992 / VAL / M • Eight Is Never Enough / 1993 / ZA / M • Eleventh Annual AVN Awards / 1994 / VC / M • Erotic Angel / 1994 / ERA / M • Euphoria / 1993 / CA / M • Fantasy Girls / 1994 / PME / F • Femalien / 1996 / SCI / S • Fetish Fever / 1993 / CA / C • Foolproof / 1994 / VC / M • From China With Love / 1993 / ZA / M • The Go-Go Girls / 1994 / EVN / M • Guilty By Seduction / 1993 / PI / M • Hindfeld / 1993 / PI / M • Hot Tight Asses #05 / 1994 / TCK / M • I Love Juicy / 1993 / ZA / M • I Love Lesbians / 1995 / ERW / F • Intimate Journey / 1993 / VI / M • It's Blondage, The Video / 1994 / VI / M • Juranal Park / 1993 / OD / M • Leena / 1992 / VT / M • Leena Goes Pro / 1992 / VT / M • Leena Is Nasty / 1994 / OD / M • Leena Meets Frankenstein / 1993 / OD / M • Leena's Early Experiences / 1995 / OD / C • Leena's Favorite Studs / 1995 / OD / C • Leena's Oral Extravaganza / 1995 / OD / C • Liquid Lips #1 / 1994 / MAV / M • The Living End / 1992 / OD / M • The Masseuse #2 / 1994 / VI / M • Mini Masterpiece #3 / 1994 / MAV / M • New Pussy Hunt #24 / 1996 / LEI / C • Odyssey 30 Min: #024: Fill 'Er Up / 1991 / OD / F • Odyssey 30 Min: #033: The Larger The Better / 1991 / OD / F • Odyssey 30 Min: #038: For Your Eyes Only / 1991 / OD / M • Odyssey 30 Min: #054: Leena's Big Dream / 1991 / OD / M • Odyssey Amateur #11: The Larger The Better / 1991 / OD / M • Odyssey Amateur #36: Leena's Big Dream / 1991 / OD / M • Odyssey Amateur #54: Leena's Lads / 1991 / OD / M • Odyssey Triple Play #04: Leena & Stacee / 1992 / OD / F • Oral Obsession #1 / 1994 / VI / M • Paging Betty / 1994 / VC / M • Pajama Party X #1 / 1994 / VC / M • Pajama Party X #2 / 1994 / VC / M • A Portrait Of Dorian / 1992 / OD / M • Pretending / 1993 / CV / M • Pussyclips #03 / 1994 / SNA / M • Pussyman #05: Captive Audience / 1994 / SNA / M • Pussyman #06: House Of Games / 1994 / SNA / M • Pussyman #11: Prime Cuts / 1995 / SNA / C • The Reel Sex World #01 / 1993 / WP / M • The Reel Sex World #03 / 1994 / WP / M • The Reel Sex World #04 / 1994 / WP / M • The Reel Sex World #04: Laid In Hawaii / 1994 / WP / M • Ride 'em Cow Girl / 1995 / VI / C • Sex #3: After Seven (Vivid) / 1994 / VI / M • Sex On The Saddle: Wicked Women Of The Wild West / 1994 / CPG / S • Shame / 1994 / VI / M • She Quest / 1994 / OD / M • Sister Snatch #1 / 1994 / SNA / M • Sister Snatch #2 / 1995 / SNA / M • Supermodel #1 / 1994 / VI / M • Supermodel #2 / 1994 / VI / M • The Swap #2 / 1994 / VI / M • Tales From The Clit / 1993 / OD / M • Up And Cummers #12 / 1994 / 4P / M • Web Of Desire / 1993 / OD / M • Whispered Lies / 1993 / LBO / M

LEENA (OTHER)
Joe Elliot's College Girls #30 / 1994 / JOE / M

LEENA LA BIANCA *see Leena*

LEESI FOX
Desperately Seeking Suzie / 1985 / VD / M

LEEZA HARPER *see Liza Rose Harper*

LEFTY COOPER *see Star Index I*

LEI DIM
Fantasy Club: Luau Orgy / 1980 / WV / M

LEI LANI *(Deann Gandeza)*
Sweet looking small breasted girl of Hawaiian ancestry. First movie was **Jaded**. There is another actress called Leilani (one word) who starred in **Flight Sensations** and **Classic Swedish Erotica #7** but is not the same person. Also not the same as the transsexual who starred in such movies as **She's a Boy**. Her elder sister is probably Kirian Minelli. Supposedly had some mental instability and died in 1993 after getting stuck inside a wall in a building in Florida. (Another story says a trailer park in California but the other details are the same.) Deann Rochelle Gandeza was her real name.
A&B GB#009: Cum Drenched / 1992 / A&B / M • A&B GB#029: Sex-A-Holics The Sequel / 1992 / A&B / M • A&B GB#068: Lani / 1992 / A&B / C • Amateur Hours #02 / 1989 / AFI / M • Amateur Hours #03 / 1989 / AFI / M • Amateur Lesbians #01: Leanna / 1991 / GO / F • Amateur Lesbians #02: Dominique / 1991 / GO / F • Amateur Lesbians #03: April / 1991 / GO / F • Amateur Lesbians #04: Tera / 1991 / GO / F • Amateur Lesbians #06: Taylor / 1991 / GO / F • Amateur Lesbians #08: Trixie / 1991 / GO / F • Any Port In The Storm / 1991 / LV / M • AVP #9113: Men...Who Needs 'em? / 1991 / AVP / F • AVP #9117: A Girl's Night In / 1990 / AVP / F • Bloopers #2 / 1991 / GO / C • Blow Out / 1991 / IF / M • Bus Stop Tales #09 / 1990 / PRI / M • Butt Naked #1 / 1990 / OD / M • Caught From Behind #14 / 1990 / HO / M • Date Night / 1992 / V99 / M • Double The Pleasure / 1990 / SE / M • Executive Positions / 1991 / V99 / M • First Time Bi-Ers #2 / 1991 / AWV / G • Gazonga Goddess #2 / 1994 / IF / M • Girls In Heat / 1991 / ZA / F • Girls Will Be Boys #4 / 1991 / PL / F • Glamour Girl / 1991 / VEX / M • Glitter Girls / 1992 / V99 / M • Hard Core Cafe Revisited / 1991 / PL / M • Hard On The Press / 1991 / AWV / M • Heartbreaker / 1991 / IF / M • Heavy Petting / 1991 / SE / M • I Said A Butt Light #2 / 1990 / LV / M • In Excess / 1991 / CA / M • Jaded / 1989 / 4P / M • Kiss It Goodbye / 1991 / SE / M • Lesbian Lingerie Fantasy #5 / 1991 / ESP / F • Lesbian Pros And Amateurs #03 / 1992 / GO / F • Letters From The Heart / 1991 / AWV / M • Love Letters / 1992 / ELP / F • Maiden Heaven #2 / 1992 / MID / F • Main Course / 1992 / FL / M • Most Wanted / 1991 / GO / M • Mr. Peepers Casting Couch / 1991 / LBO / M • Mystified / 1991 / V99 / M • Nasty Jack's Homemade Vid. #40 / 1991 / CDI / M • Nasty Jack's Kloset Klassics #02 / 1991 / CDI / M • Night With A Vampire / 1992 / MID / M • Physically Fit / 1991 / V99 / C • Rear Entry / 1995 / LEI / M • Safecracker / 1991 / CC / M • Single Girl Masturbation #5 / 1991 / ESP / F • Spanish Rose / 1991 / VEX / M • Star Struck / 1991 / AFV / M • Step To The Rear / 1991 / VD / M • Suburban Seduction / 1991 / HO / M • Sweat Shop / 1991 / EVN / M • Sweet Cheeks (1991-Vid Excl) / 1991 / VEX / C • Tomboy / 1991 / V99 / M • Transsexual 6900 / 1990 / LV / G • The Ultimate Sex / 1992 / MET / G • Viviana's Dude Ranch / 1992 / IF / M • Wicked Thoughts / 1991 / AFV / M • Wild & Wicked #1 / 1991 / VT / M • The Wonder Rears / 1990 / SO / M • The X-Producers / 1991 / XPI / M

LEI LANI (1992)
New Faces, Hot Bodies #03 / 1992 / STP / M • New Faces, Hot Bodies #05 / 1992 / STP / M

LEI LANI (S/M)
Buck's Excellent Transsexual Adventure / 1989 / STA / G • Hotel Transylvania #1 / 1990 / LIP / G • Hotel Transylvania #2 / 1990 / LIP / G • Inch Bi Inch / 1989 / STA / G • Queens Behind Bars / 1990 / STA / G • She's A Boy / 1989 / LV / G • She-Male Nurse / 1989 / LV / G • She-Male Undercover / 1990 / STA / G • Trans Europe Express / 1989 / VC / G

LEI PETITE
Tight bodied dark haired very pretty small breasted white girl.
Daddy Doesn't Know / 1984 / HO / M • Make Me Want It / 1986 / CA / M

LEI QUAN
Mrs. Smith's Erotic Holiday / 1982 / VCX / M

LEIA
New Faces, Hot Bodies #17 / 1995 / STP / M

LEIA NICOLES see Star Index I

LEIF STRATHAGEN
Detained / 1996 / PL / M • Scandanavian Double Features #3 / 1996 / PL / M • Scandanavian Double Features #4 / 1996 / PL / M • Upstairs And Downstairs / 1995 / PL / M

LEIGH
Casting Couch Cuties #1 / 1994 / WP / M • HomeGrown Video #452: Make Me Cum! / 1995 / HOV / M

LEIGH FRANK see Star Index I

LEIGH HOPE
Dracula Exotica / 1980 / TVX / M

LEIGH-ANN
RSK: Candy #1 / 1992 / RSK / F • RSK: Candy #2 / 1993 / RSK / F • RSK: Leigh-Ann #3: Office Spanking / 1992 / RSK / B

LEILA
Butt Watch #01 / 1993 / FH / M • Classic Swedish Erotica #07 / 1986 / CA / C • Flight Sensations / 1983 / VC / C • The Taking Of Christina / 1975 / NGV / M

LEILA HARRIS
Like Mother, Like Daughter / cr73 / VCX / M

LEILA LAVEAU see Cumisha Amado
LEILA VIGSO see Star Index I
LEISHA CHANG MAI see Lana Sands
LEITA see Greta Carlson

LEKILI
Bound To Be Punk / 1990 / BON / B • The Snoopy Niece / 1991 / BON / B

LELA JEAN
Young Sluts In Heat #2 / 1996 / PL / M

LELA LESHELL see Layla LaShell

LELDE
Private Gold #12: The Pyramid #2 / 1996 / OD / M

LELE see Le Le Adams
LEMIEUVRE JONES see Star Index I
LEMMON YELLOW see Heather Young
LEMON YOUNG see Heather Young
LEN FLEX see Star Index I

LENA
Blue Vanities #519 / 1993 / FFL / M • Blue Vanities #542 / 1994 / FFL / M • Full Moon Video #23: Lena's Oral And Anal Afternoon / 1994 / FAP / M

LENA ALANV
Immortal Desire / 1993 / VI / M

LENA DEL RIO see Star Index I

LENA HOLLIDAY
Bubble Butts #27 / 1993 / LBO / M • Gemini: Sex Packs #04 / 1993 / FAP / M • L.H.: Lena Solo / 1992 / LHI / M • Odyssey 30 Min: #193: Anal Lena Returns / 1991 / OD / M • Odyssey 30 Min: #214: Anal Holliday #2 / 1992 / OD / M • Odyssey 30 Min: #321: Lena Holliday's Oral Extravaganza #2 / 1993 / OD / M • Odyssey 30 Min: Anal Holliday / 1992 / OD / M • Odyssey Triple Play #21: Rear End Reaming / 1992 / OD / M • Odyssey Triple Play #28: Anally, Lena / 1993 / OD / M • Odyssey Triple Play #35: Anal Almanac / 1993 / OD / M • Odyssey Triple Play #56: Lena Holliday's 3-Way Fuck-A-Thon / 1994 / OD / M • Odyssey Triple Play #83: Three-Way Hollidays / 1994 / OD / M • Odyssey Triple Play #96: Anal Option #2 / 1995 / OD / M

LENE HEFNER
Enhanced titted pretty blonde. Professional cheerleader before coming (in 1988) a *Playboy* centerfold and entering the dance business. Started in March 1993 in **The Mask** and **Blind Spot**. De-virginized at 20 (yikes!). Married in 1995 to a guy named Rob.
Affairs Of The Heart / 1993 / VI / M • Badgirls #2: Strip Search / 1994 / VI / M • Blind Spot / 1993 / VI / M • Eleventh Annual AVN Awards / 1994 / VC / M • The Girls Of Mardi Gras / 1994 / P10 / S • Killer Looks / 1994 / IMP / S • Mask / 1993 / VI / M • Naked Reunion / 1993 / VI / M • Supermodel #1 / 1994 / VI / M • Supermodel #2 / 1994 / VI / M • The Swap #2 / 1994 / VI / M • Tempted / 1994 / VI / M • Zazel / 1996 / CV / M

LENE NYMAN
I Am Curious (Yellow) / 1967 / HTV / M

LENI KJELLANDER
Bordello / 1973 / AR / M

LENKA
Buttman's Orgies / 1996 / EA / M • Rock 'n' Roll Rocco / 1997 / EA / M

LENKA VEBOROVA
Dirty Stories #4 / 1995 / PE / M

LENNA FOX see Leanna Foxxx
LENNOX (LISA) see Lisa Lennox
LENNY CURTMAN see Leon Gucci
LENNY KENT see John Leslie
LENNY STRONG see Star Index I
LENORA BRUCE see Jacqueline Brooks

LENORE DUPREE (Lenore Poe)
The Honeydrippers / 1987 / VXP / M • Tongue 'n Cheek (Red Light) / 1984 / RLV / M

LENORE GRANT see Star Index I
LENORE POE see Lenore Dupree
LENSK see Star Index I

LENZI
The Black Butt Sisters Do Houston / 1996 / MID / M • The Black Butt Sisters Do Philadelphia / 1995 / MID / M • Black Fantasies #09 / 1995 / HW / M • Black Fantasies #10 / 1995 / HW / M

LEO FORD
Primarily gay actor who died in a motorcycle accident July 15, 1991.
Passion By Fire / 1986 / LAV / G • True Crimes Of Passion / 1983 / CA / G

LEO GAMBOA
Marco Polo / 1995 / SC / M

LEO LA RUE see Star Index I
LEO LOVELACE see Leo Lovemore

LEO LOVEMORE (Leo Lovelace)
Pudgy, curly-haired male.
ABA: Double Feature #3 / 1996 / ALP / M • China Doll / 1976 / VC / M • Doctor Yes / 1978 / VIS / M • Highway Hookers / 1976 / SVE / M • Lickity Split / 1974 / COM / M • The Love Couch / 1977 / VC / M • Saturday Matinee Series #2 / 1996 / VCX / C • Teenage Twins / 1976 / VCX / M

LEO LYONS see Star Index I
LEO MARTIN see Star Index I
LEO ZORBA see Star Index I

LEOKAVDIA OISZEWSKI
Lickity Split / 1974 / COM / M

LEON GUCCI (Lenny Curtman)
A director.

LEON MARLOW
Interlude Of Lust / 1981 / CA / M

LEON SPHINCTER see Star Index I

LEONA
Blue Vanities #544 / 1994 / FFL / M

LEONA FOX see Leanna Foxxx
LEONA SWIFT see Star Index I

LEONARD BELKAIEI
The Voyeur #3 / 1995 / EA / M

LEONARD COOPER
Midnight Desires / 1976 / VXP / M

LEONARDO
Bang City #1: Kelly's Anal Gang Bang / 1995 / SC / M • Dirty Tricks #2: This Ain't Love / 1996 / EA / M • Hard Core Beginners #07 / 1995 / LEI / M • Heavenly / 1995 / IF / M • The Voyeur #6 / 1996 / EA / M

LEONDRA SILVER
Teach Me / 1984 / VD / M

LEONIE MARS
Odyssey / 1977 / VC / M

LEONORA
World Sex Tour #7 / 1996 / ANA / M

LEONORA MORINA
A Merry Widow / 1996 / SPI / M

LEORA LYNCH see Star Index I

LEORA VAN HOKE
Shape Up For Sensational Sex / 1985 / SE / M

LEOSHA see Leanne Lovelace

LEROY
Porno Screentests / 1982 / VC / M

LES see Star Index I

LES HASSEL
Meatball / 1972 / VCX / M

LES KATZ
Centerfold Fever / 1981 / VXP / M

LES NICHOLS see Star Index I
LES SEK see David Book
LES STEIN see Star Index I

LESA
Blue Vanities #555 / 1994 / FFL / M

LESHA see lesha

LESLEY
Blue Vanities #543 / 1994 / FFL / M

LESLIE
100% Amateur #24: Dildos And Toys / 1996 / OD / M • A&B GB#012: Ona Z And Leslie / 1992 / A&B / M • A&B GB#013: Cumming Out Party #1 / 1992 / A&B / M • A&B GB#014: Cumming Out Party #2 / 1992 / A&B / M • A&B GB#015: Cumming Out Party #3 / 1992 / A&B / M • A&B GB#067: Leslie / 1992 / A&B / C • America's Raunchiest Home Videos #12: Bimbo Ballers From Brt / 1992 / ZA / M • Bizarre Mistress Series: Mistress Destiny / 1992 / BIZ / C • Black On Black (1994-Evn) / 1994 / EVN / M • Blue Vanities #584 / 1996 / FFL / M • Buffy Malibu's Totally Nasty All-Girl

Home Videos #03 / 1992 / ANA / F • Buffy Malibu's Totally Nasty All-Girl Home Videos #04 / 1993 / ANA / F • European Sex TV / 1996 / EL / M • Fuckin' Reamin' Screamin' / 1995 / TIE / M • Hidden Camera #17 / 1994 / JMP / M • Hidden Camera #18 / 1994 / JMP / M • Homegrown Video #350 / 1991 / HOV / M • HomeGrown Video #473: Furpie Feast #3 / 1997 / HOV / C • Latin Plump Humpers #3 / 1995 / TTV / M • Mr. Peepers Amateur Home Videos #89: Stiffy Stuffer / 1994 / LBO / M • Pearl Necklace: Amorous Amateurs #36 / 1993 / SEE / M • Sorority Lingerie Party / 1995 / NIV / F • Southern Belles #5 / 1995 / XPR / M • The Voyeur #8: Live In Europe #2 / 1996 / JLP / M

LESLIE ADAMS

Pleasure Productions #04 / 1984 / VCR / M

LESLIE ASH *see Star Index I*

LESLIE BARRIS *see Lee Carroll*

LESLIE BOVEE

Brunette with shoulder length hair, nice smile, small to medium tits, firm lithe body, big eyes.

Baby Rosemary / 1975 / SE / M • The Best Of Raffaelli #1 / 1980 / DIM / M • The Best Of Raffaelli #2 / 1980 / DIM / M • Blue Ecstasy / 1980 / CA / M • Blue Vanities #058 / 1988 / FFL / M • Blue Vanities #066 / 1988 / FFL / M • Blue Vanities #091 / 1988 / FFL / M • Carnal Haven / 1976 / SVE / M • CB Mamas / 1976 / MIT / M • Champagne For Breakfast / 1980 / SE / M • Classic Erotica #2 / 1980 / SVE / M • Classic Erotica Special / 1985 / SVE / M • Collection #02 / 1982 / CA / M • Collection #03 / 1983 / SVE / M • A Coming Of Angels / 1977 / CA / M • Critics' Choice #1 / 19?? / SE / C • Critics' Choice #2 / 1984 / SE / C • Dirty Looks / 1982 / VC / C • Double Pleasure / 1985 / VCR / M • Easy Alice / 1976 / VC / M • The Ecstasy Girls #1 / 1979 / CA / M • Erotic Fantasies #1 / 1983 / CV / C • Erotic Fantasies #4 / 1983 / CV / C • Eruption / 1977 / VCX / M • Fantastic Orgy / 197? / ... / M • Feelings / 1977 / VC / M • Femmes De Sade / 1976 / ALP / M • Games Women Play #1 / 1980 / CA / M • Garters And Lace / 1975 / SE / M • Girls That Talk Dirty / 1986 / VCS / C • Hot Pink / 1983 / VC / C • Hot Shorts: Vanessa Del Rio / 1986 / VCR / C • Hot Skin In 3D / 1977 / ... / M • John Holmes, The Lost Films / 1988 / PEN / C • Legends Of Porn #1 / 1987 / CV / C • The Little Blue Box / 1978 / BL / M • Love Scenes For Loving Couples / 1987 / CV / C • Love You / 1980 / CA / M • Maraschino Cherry / 1978 / QX / M • Misbehavin' / 1979 / VXP / M • Naughty Nurses / 1982 / VCR / M • The Nurses Are Coming / 1985 / VCR / C • One Of A Kind / 1976 / SVE / M • Only The Best #1 / 1986 / CV / C • The Senator's Daughter / 1978 / CV / M • Sensual Encounters Of Every Kind / 1978 / SE / M • Sex World / 1978 / SE / M • Showgirl #01: Leslie Bovee's Fantasies / 1981 / VCR / M • Showgirl #03: Vanessa Del Rio's Fantasies / 1981 / VCR / M • Showgirl #13: Chris Cassidy's Fantasies / 1983 / SVE / M • Showgirl #16: Samantha Fox's Fantasies / 1983 / VCR / M • Starlet Nights / 1982 / XTR / M • Sugar Britches / 1980 / VCX / C • Swinging Sorority / 1976 / VCX / S • Take Off / 1978 / VXP / M • Tapestry Of Passion / 1976 / SE / M • Too Young To Care / cr73

/ BOC / M • True Legends Of Adult Cinema: The Golden Age / 1992 / VC / C • VCA Previews #2 / 1988 / VC / C • With Love, Annette / 1985 / CA / C • [Bizarre Thunder / 19?? / ... / M

LESLIE CONNERS

Kitty's Pleasure Palace / 1971 / ALP / M

LESLIE CUNNINGHAM

Tina Makes A Deal / 1974 / TGA / M

LESLIE DUNCAN *see Star Index I*

LESLIE FORBES

The Devil In Miss Jones #5: The Inferno / 1994 / VC / M • New Wave Hookers #4 / 1994 / VC / M

LESLIE GLASS

Blonde Justice #3 / 1994 / VI / M • Penthouse: 1993 Pet Of The Year Playoff / 1993 / PET / F • Penthouse: 1994 Pet Of The Year Winners / 1994 / PET / F • Penthouse: All-Pet Workout / 1993 / NIV / F • Penthouse: Behind The Scenes / 1995 / PET / F • Penthouse: Great Pet Hunt #2 / 1993 / NIV / F • Penthouse: Party With The Pets / 1994 / PET / S • Penthouse: The Ultimate Pet Games / 1996 / PET / S • Vagablonde / 1994 / VI / M • Vampire Vixens From Venus / 1994 / SE0 / S

LESLIE JACKSON *see Star Index I*

LESLIE KING

Heaven's Touch / 1983 / CA / M

LESLIE L'AMOUR

GVC: Private Nurses #126 / cr84 / GO / M

LESLIE LAINE

The Handyman And The Stepdaughter / cr80 / ASR / M • Playthings / 1980 / VC / M

LESLIE LEIGH

[Sexy Twins / 19?? / ... / M

LESLIE LIXX

Babes Illustrated #1 / 1994 / IN / F • Ona Zee's Learning The Ropes #09: The Training Continues / 1992 / ONA / B • Sleaze Please!—October Edition / 1994 / FH / M • Sleaze Please!—November Edition / 1994 / FH / M • Student Fetish Videos: Best of Catfighting #03 / 1995 / PRE / C • Student Fetish Videos: Best Of Foot Worship #03 / 1995 / PRE / C • Student Fetish Videos: Catfighting #11 / 1994 / PRE / B • Student Fetish Videos: Foot Worship #12 / 1994 / PRE / B • Student Fetish Videos: Spanking #14 / 1994 / PRE / B

LESLIE MURRAY *(Lynn Stevens, Linda L'Amour)*

Looks very like Annette Haven with the same hair style and almost as white skin but her tits are not as big. She also sounds very similar. I've been told that they are not the same but the source is the usual suspect protect-the-cronies-real-name at all costs.

Badge 69 / cr74 / SVE / M • Certified Mail / 1975 / CDC / M • Dance Of Love / cr70 / BL / M • Lady On The Couch / 1978 / SVE / M • The Maids / 1973 / ... / M • More Than Sisters / 1978 / VC / M • The Sorceress / 1974 / BL / M • Special Order / cr75 / BL / M • A Taste For Passion / 1983 / AMB / M • Teenage Stepmother / cr74 / SVE / M • Thrilling Drilling / 1974 / SVE / M • A Touch Of Genie / 1974 / ... / M

LESLIE PARKER *see Star Index I*

LESLIE PHILLIPS *see Star Index I*

LESLIE SAVAGE *see Star Index I*

LESLIE SHARP

Depraved Innocent / 1986 / VD / M

LESLIE SPENCER

[Chicks Who Dig Ball Sweat / 1984 / ... / M

LESLIE THANE *see Star Index I*

LESLIE WALKER *see Leslie Winston*

LESLIE WHITE

Loveland / 1973 / VST / M

LESLIE WINSTON *(Leslie Walker)*

This is not Lorelei Winston.

2002: A Sex Odyssey / 1985 / DR / M • Alien Lust / 1985 / AVC / M • B*A*S*H / 1989 / BIZ / C • Bad Girls #1 / 1981 / GO / M • Best Of Foot Worship #3 / 1992 / BIZ / C • Beyond The Valley Of The Ultra Milkmaids / 1984 / 4P / F • Bodies By Jackie / 1985 / IVP / M • Body And Sole / 1990 / BIZ / B • The Bondage Club #2 / 1987 / LON / B • Bums Away / 1995 / PRE / C • Cabaret Sin / 1987 / IN / M • Club Exotica #1 / 1985 / WV / M • Club Exotica #2 / 1985 / WV / M • Convenience Store Girls / 1986 / VD / M • Crocodile Blondee #1 / 1987 / CA0 / M • Crunch Bunch / 1995 / PRE / C • Dangerous When Wet (Amber Lynn Is) / 1987 / VCX / M • Empire Of The Sins / 1988 / IN / M • Foot Mistress / 1986 / BIZ / B • Foot Show / 1989 / BIZ / B • Girl Games / 1987 / PL / C • Golden Girls #06 / 1983 / SVE / M • Grand Slam / 1990 / PRE / B • GVC: Suburban Lust #128 / 1983 / GO / M • I Like To Be Watched / 1984 / VD / M • John Holmes, The Man, The Legend / 1995 / EVN / C • Late After Dark / 1985 / BAN / M • Legs And Lingerie #1 / 1990 / BIZ / F • Lesbian Passion / 1985 / PL / F • Lucky In Love #1 / 1985 / BAN / M • Marina Vice / 1985 / PEN / M • Mother's Pride / 1985 / DIM / M • My Pretty Go Between / 1985 / VC / M • Oral Majority #04 / 1987 / WV / C • Peeping Tom / 1986 / CV / M • Playpen / 1987 / VC / M • Portrait Of Desire / 1985 / IVP / M • Red On The Noodle Like A Swance On A Poodle / 1990 / FC / C • Rio Heat / 1986 / VD / M • Sailing Into Ecstasy / 1986 / VCX / M • Sex-O-Gram / 1986 / LA / M • Showdown / 1985 / BON / B • Slave Exchange / 1985 / BIZ / B • Sole Kisses / 1987 / BIZ / S • Swedish Erotica #69 / 1985 / CA / M • Sweet Surrender / 1985 / AVC / M • Tickle Time / 1987 / BIZ / B • Toys, Not Boys #3 / 1991 / FC / C • Traci Who? / 1987 / AVC / C • Video Store Vixens / 1986 / PL / M • Wacked Waitresses / 1986 / CS / B • Wicked Wenches / 1988 / LA / M • Young Cheeks / 1990 / BEB / B

LESTER GOLDFINE

The Bottom Dweller Part Deux / 1994 / EL / M • Dr Butts #3 / 1993 / 4P / M • Escape From Anal Lost Angels / 1996 / HO / M • Junk Yard Dogs / 1991 / FC / M • The Phantom Of The Montague Stage / 1997 / HO / M • Ready To Drop #02 / 1992 / FC / M • The Secret Life Of Herbert Dingle / 1994 / TTV / M • Tit In A Wringer / 1993 / FC / M

LETHA WEAPONS

Passable face, long brown hair, huge tits, slim body otherwise.

Big Boob Bangeroo #8 / 1996 / TTV / M • Big Boob Bikini Bash / 1995 / BTO / M • Big Bust Babes #23 / 1994 / AFI / M • Big Bust Babes #24 / 1994 / AFI / M • Big Bust Babes #39 / 1996 / AFI / M • Big Bust Bangers #2 / 1994 / AMP / M • Big Knockers #05 / 1994 / TV / M • Big Knockers #11 / 1995 / TV / C • Big Knockers #12 / 1995 / TV / C • Big Tit Racket / 1995 / PEP / M • Bigggum's / 1995 / GLI / C • Bloopers & Behind The Scenes / 1995 / LEI / M • Blue

Balls / 1995 / VEX / C • Blueballs / 1995 / IF / C • Body Of Love / 1994 / ERA / M • Boob Tube Lube / 1996 / RAS / M • Boobs A Poppin' / 1994 / TTV / M • Booby Prize / 1995 / PEP / M • The Breast Of Breastmen / 1995 / EVN / C • Breastman's Wet T-Shirt Contest / 1994 / EVN / M • The Busty Kittens / 1995 / NAP / F • Coming Out Bi / 1995 / IN / G • Der Champion / 1995 / BTO / M • Dick & Jane Do The Strip / 1994 / AVI / M • Double D Dykes #27 / 1995 / GO / F • Double-D Reunion / 1995 / BTO / M • Duke Of Knockers #2 / 1995 / BTO / M • Fantasy Lover / 1995 / V99 / C • Freaky Flix / 1995 / TTV / C • Freeway Love / 1994 / FD / M • Girls Around The World #15 / 1994 / BTO / S • Girls Around The World #22: Letha Weapons & Friends / 1995 / BTO / M • Glitz Tits #08 / 1994 / GLI / M • Harlots From Hootersville / 1994 / BLC / M • The Hollywood Starlet Search / 1995 / SC / M • How To Make A Model #04: Facial Cream Girls / 1994 / LBO / M • Humongous Hooters / 1995 / PME / F • John Wayne Bobbitt Uncut / 1994 / LEI / M • Lesbian Castle: No Kings Allowed / 1994 / LIP / F • Mellon Man #01 / 1994 / AVI / M • The Mountie / 1994 / PP / M • Mystique / 1996 / SC / M • On Location In Palm Springs / 1996 / H&S / S • On Location In The Bahamas / 1996 / H&S / S • Philmore Butts Strikes Gold / 1996 / SUF / M • Savage Fury #3 / 1994 / VEX / M • Score Busty Covergirls #8 / 1995 / BTO / S • Seymore Butts: Big Boobs In Buttsville / 1996 / FH / M • She's No Angel #2 / 1995 / V99 / M • Switch Hitters #8 / 1995 / IN / G • Tit To Tit #3 / 1995 / BTO / M • The Way They Wuz / 1996 / SHS / C

LETICIA
J.E.G.: Amateurs Only #10 / 1996 / JEG / M

LETIGRE *(La Tigre, Latisha, La Tierga)*
Gorgeous little girl with square shoulders, small firm tits, tight waist, lovely little butt, short black hair, good quality white skin, shaven pussy except for a vertical pubic hair line, completely closed labia with no protruding labia minora, tattoo on her left calf. Only passable face, however, but with a nice smile. The above was written during her 1995 appearance but in late 1996 she returned with a thickened body and the usual sex worker attitude. Such a pity.
Anal Centerfold / 1995 / ROB / M • Anal Hellraiser #1 / 1995 / ROB / M • Anal Insatiable / 1995 / ROB / M • Anal Maniacs #5 / 1996 / WP / M • Anal Pussycat / 1995 / ROB / M • Anal Sluts & Sweethearts #3 / 1995 / ROB / M • Babes Of The Bay #2 / 1995 / LIP / F • Bizarre Desires / 1995 / ROB / F • Booty Ho #2 / 1995 / ROB / M • Butt Jammers #01 / 1995 / SC / F • Butt Jammers #02 / 1995 / SC / F • Hardcore Debutantes #03 / 1997 / TEP / M • Hot Tight Asses #18 / 1996 / TCK / M • Kink #2 / 1995 / ROB / M • Lesbian Bitches #2 / 1994 / ROB / F • Lesbian Social Club / 1995 / ROB / F • Living On The Edge / 1997 / DWO / M • Pick Up Lines #10 / 1997 / OD / M • Up Your Ass #3 / 1996 / ANA / M • The Voyeur #4 / 1995 / EA / M

LETIZIA BISSET *see* **Shalimar**
LETIZIA SHALIMAR *see* **Shalimar**
LEVI GREY
Devil In A Wet T-Shirt / 1995 / SPI / M

LEVI RICHARDS
China Doll / 1976 / VC / M • Devil In Miss Jones #1 / 1972 / VC / M • A Dirty Western #1 / 1973 / AR / M • Divine Obsession / 1976 / TVX / M • Dr Love And His House Of Perversions / 1978 / VC / M • Intrusion / 1975 / CV / M • The Love Bus / 1974 / OSC / M • Naked Came The Stranger / 1975 / VC / M • The Private Afternoons Of Pamela Mann / 1974 / TVX / M • Saturday Matinee Series #1 / 1996 / VCX / C • Saturday Matinee Series #3 / 1996 / VCX / C • Sensuous Flygirls / cr72 / VHL / M • Sexual Witchcraft / 1973 / IHV / M • Sleepyhead / 1973 / VXP / M • That's Erotic / 1979 / CV / C

LEVIN
Hollywood Amateurs #02 / 1994 / MID / M
LEVON
Dirty Hairy's Over 50 Meets Mr. Black 18 Inches / 1996 / GOT / M
LEW
The Dong Show #03 / 1990 / AMB / M
LEW MANN *see* **Star Index I**
LEW PETERS
Bottom Busters / 1973 / BLT / M
LEWIS AVERY
Devil's Ecstasy / 1974 / VCX / M
LEWIS CHARLES WOLFE *see* **Star Index I**
LEX CARRADINE *see* **Star Index I**
LEXI
Bi-Bi Love Amateurs #4 / 1994 / QUA / G • How To Make A Model #02: Got Her In Bed / 1993 / QUA / M • M Series #21 / 1994 / LBO / M
LEXI ERICKSON
Adorable petite blonde with small tits, long nipples, small tattoo on her left belly and a larger one on her left calf/ankle, very pretty face, long blonde hair, washboard flat belly. De-virginized at 13 (but she's not quite sure as she was drunk at time). 5'2" tall, 32-23-32, and 23 years old in 1996 (looks 15). Has been married but is now (1996) divorced. Originally from Wisconsin.
Adam & Eve's House Party #5 / 1996 / VC / M • Allure / 1996 / WP / M • Anal Party Girls / 1996 / GV / M • Anal Witness #1 / 1996 / LBO / M • California Swingers / 1996 / LV / M • Cheerleader Strippers / 1996 / PE / M • The Clock Strikes Bizarre On Butt Row / 1996 / ABS / M • Cumback Pussy #2: Crawling Back For More / 1996 / EL / M • Cumback Pussy #3: Coast To Coast Rump Romp / 1996 / EL / M • Dirty Diner #3 / 1996 / SC / M • Eighteen & Easy / 1996 / SC / M • I Wanna Be A Porn Star #1 / 1996 / 4P / M • Lollipop Shoppe #1 / 1996 / SC / M • Lollipop Shoppe #2 / 1996 / SC / M • More Dirty Debutantes #54 / 1996 / 4P / M • Nineteen #2 / 1996 / FOR / M • Pick Up Lines #05 / 1996 / OD / M • Shayla's Swim Party / 1997 / VC / M • Smoke & Mirrors / 1996 / PL / M • Strip Show / 1996 / CA / M • Summer Dreams / 1996 / TEP / M • Venom #7 / 1996 / VD / M • Waterbabies #3 / 1996 / CC / M • Young & Natural #21 / 1996 / TV / F • Young & Natural #22 / 1996 / TV / F
LEXI LEIGH *see* **Angel Snow**
LEXIE LOVE
Primal She-Male / 1996 / HSV / G
LEXIS DEE *see* **Star Index I**
LEXUS *(Lexus Locklear, Brandy Summerville)*
Pretty blonde with small tits and a nice tight

body. Unfortunately she seems to always insist on a condom. Born Mar 5, 1976; 36-24-34. De-virginized at 17. Appeared on **Hard Copy** where she used the name Brandy Summerville. Later had her tits enhanced to medium/large and acquired a tattoo on the top of the right one.
Black And White Revisited / 1995 / VT / F • Black On White Revisited / 1995 / VT / M • Dirty Bob's #11: Vegas Blues #1 / 1994 / FLP / S • Dirty Bob's #14: Can Hams! / 1994 / FLP / S • Dirty Bob's #15: The Contest! / 1994 / FLP / S • Eleventh Annual AVN Awards / 1994 / VC / M • The Girl Next Door #1 / 1994 / VT / M • The Girl Next Door #2 / 1994 / VT / M • Pearl Necklace: Amorous Amateurs #41 / 1994 / SEE / M • Pearl Necklace: Premier Sessions #03 / 1994 / SEE / M • Pearl Necklace: Thee Bush League #30 / 1994 / SEE / M • Pleasureland / 1996 / VI / M • Style #2 / 1994 / VT / M • Tech: Lexus #1 / 1994 / TWA / F • Tech: Lexus #2 / 1994 / TWA / F
LEXUS (BLACK)
Black Street Hookers #4: The Streets Of San Francisco / 1996 / DFI / M
LEXUS (OTHER)
Back East Babes #2 / 1996 / NIT / M
LEXUS LOCKLEAR *see* **Lexus**
LEXY CRUZ *see* **Star Index I**
LEYLA
Twisted Sisters / 1995 / IBN / B
LEYOSHA BLACK
Donna Young: Interracial Lesbians #1 / 1995 / DY / F
LEZA CRUZ
Busen Extra #2 / 1990 / BTO / M
LIA BAREN
The Adventures Of Buttwoman #2: Behind Bars / 1992 / EL / F • The Best Of Buttslammers / 1995 / BS / C • Blame It On Bambi / 1992 / BS / B • Blind Innocence / 1993 / BS / B • Bruce Seven: A Compendium Of His Most Graphic Scenes Vol 3 / 1992 / BS / C • Bruce Seven: A Compendium Of His Most Graphic Scenes Vol 4 / 1993 / BS / C • Bruce Seven: A Compendium Of His Most Graphic Scenes Vol 5 / 1994 / BS / C • Bruce Seven: A Compendium Of His Most Graphic Scenes Vol 6 / 1994 / BS / C • Buttman Vs Buttwoman / 1992 / EL / M • Buttslammers #01 / 1993 / BS / F • Buttslammers #02: The Awakening Of Felicia / 1993 / BS / F • Buttslammers #05: Quake, Rattle & Roll! / 1994 / BS / F • Buttslammers #09: Fade To Anal / 1995 / BS / F • Buttslammers #12: Anal Madness / 1996 / BS / F • Buttslammers #13: The Madness Continues / 1996 / BS / F • Cruel Passions / 1992 / BS / B • Dances With Pain / 1992 / BS / B • The Distress Factor / 1992 / BS / B • Double A Dykes / 1992 / GO / F • The Dungeon Master / 1992 / BS / B • Enemates #06 / 1992 / BIZ / B • Felecia's Folly / 1993 / BS / B • For The Hell Of It / 1992 / BS / B • Hot Rod To Hell #2 / 1992 / BS / B • Jane Bondage Is Captured / 1993 / LON / B • Odds 'n' Ends / 1992 / PRE / B • Painful Lessons (Bruce Seven) / 1992 / BS / B • The Power Of Summer #1: Revenge / 1992 / BS / B • The Power Of Summer #2: Reward / 1992 / BS / B • Shane's Ultimate Fantasy / 1994 / BS / B • Web Of Darkness / 1993 / BS / B
LIA SOUL *see* **Star Index I**
LIAM MULHALL

The Doll House / 1995 / CV / M

LIANNA FOXXX *see* **Leanna Foxxx**

LIBBY CURTIS
Bondage Pleasures #1 / 1981 / 4P / B • A
Loving Bind / 1986 / 4P / B

LIBBY HAYES *see* **Star Index I**

LIBERO GUIDI
[Die Madchenhandler / 1972 / ... / M

LIBERTY (1995)
6969 Mel'hose Place / 1995 / VG0 / M •
How To Make A College Co-Ed / 1995 /
VG0 / M

LIBERTY (LADY ASHL) *see* **Lady Ashley**
Liberty

LIBERTY JAY
Just Deserts / 1994 / BON / B

LIBERTY REIGNS *see* **Star Index I**

LIBRA
Neighborhood Nookie #1 / 1996 / RAS / M

LICA
Triple X Video Magazine #11 / 1995 / OD /
M

LICIA *see* **Star Index I**

LICORICE
Dark Passions #03 / 1995 / AFV / M

LIDO *see* **Star Index I**

LIGE CLARK
All About Sex / 1970 / AR / M

LIGIA
Private Gold #12: The Pyramid #2 / 1996 /
OD / M

LIL LEE *(Lisa Lee, Xouizit, Jezebelle)*
Ugly Hispanic with long black hair, rock solid
large cantaloupes, womanly body, large
mole (one of many) on right cheek. 21
years old in 1996 and was de-virginized at
19. Says she's originally from Brooklyn.
The Clock Strikes Bizarre On Butt Row /
1996 / ABS / M • Creme De La Face #17:
Semen For Seven / 1996 / OD / M • Mike
Hott: #384 Three-Sum Sluts #16 / 1996 /
MHV / M • Mike Hott: #385 Lesbian Sluts
#29 / 1996 / MHV / F • Mike Hott: #386 /
1996 / MHV / M • Mike Hott: #388 Cunt Of
The Month: Lil Lee / 1996 / MHV / M • Mike
Hott: #389 Jamie Lee Pregnant / 1996 /
MHV / F • Mike Hott: #390 / 1996 / MHV /
M • My First Time #6 / 1996 / NS / M • Nine-
teen #2 / 1996 / FOR / M • Puritan Video
Magazine #09 / 1997 / LE / M • Shadows
Of Lust / 1996 / NIT / M • The Sodomizer
#6 / 1996 / SC / M • Titty Slickers #3 / 1996
/ LE / M • Video Virgins #30 / 1996 / NS / M

LIL SQUEEZE
Daughters Of Darkness / 1975 / ASR / M

LIL' ASS
Raw Naked In Your Face / 1997 / ROB / M
• Suzi's Wild Anal Ride / 1997 / ROB / M

LIL' BITT *(Rainahh, Shayla (Lil' Bitt),*
Reyna)
Very young looking with long or shoulder
length dark red hair, small conical tits,
tongue pin, belly button ring, clit post,
shaven pussy, 19 years old in 1996, 5'2"
tall, very white skin in some movies, pass-
able face. Poor dentition especially on the
right side upper.
Anal Hanky-Panky / 1997 / ROB / M • Butt
Row Unplugged / 1996 / ABS / M • Cherry
Poppers: The College Years #01 / 1997 /
ZA / M • Cumback Pussy #2: Crawling
Back For More / 1996 / EL / M • Cumback
Pussy #4: Get Some!!! / 1996 / EL / M •
Cumback Pussy #5: Groopin' / 1996 / EL /
M • Dangerous Behinds #1 / 1995 / HW / M
• Decadent Dreams / 1996 / ME / M • Dirty

Dirty Debutantes #8 / 1996 / 4P / M • Filthy
First Timers #2: Innocence Lost / 1996 / EL
/ M • Horny Brits Take It In The Bum / 1997
/ ROB / M • Interracial Affairs / 1996 / FC /
M • More Dirty Debutantes #62 / 1997 /
SBV / M • Pick Up Lines #10 / 1997 / OD /
M • Raw Naked In Your Face / 1997 / ROB
/ M • Sodomania #19: Sweet Cream / 1996
/ EL / M • Suzi's Wild Anal Ride / 1997 /
ROB / M • Up And Cummers #37 / 1996 /
4P / M • Up And Cummers #39 / 1996 /
RWP / M

LIL' MAMA JAMA *see* **Star Index I**

LIL' RED
Anal Camera #10 / 1995 / EVN / M • Anal
Camera #11 / 1995 / EVN / M • Behind The
Backdoor #7 / 1995 / EVN / M • Fresh
Faces #07 / 1995 / EVN / M • Hot Box /
1995 / V99 / C • Innocence Lost / 1995 /
GO / M • Living On The Edge / 1997 / DWO
/ M • Mile High Thrills / 1995 / VIM / M • My
First Time #1 / 1995 / NS / M • My First
Time #5 / 1996 / NS / M • My First Time #6
/ 1996 / NS / M • Nudist Colony Vacation /
1996 / NIT / M • Old Wives' Tails / 1995 /
EMC / M • Perverted Stories #08 / 1996 /
JMP / M • The Seductive Secretary / 1995
/ GO / M • A Tall Tail / 1996 / FC / M

LIL' RED HOOD *see* **Lisa de Leeuw**

LIL' SINDERELLA *see* **Little Sinderella**

LILA
A&B AB#254: Dr. Ruthie's Grandma / 1991
/ A&B / M

LILA COUTARD *see* **Star Index I**

LILA HAMPTEY
Blue Vanities #556 / 1994 / FFL / M

LILA REGAN *see* **Star Index I**

LILA SHORT
Elodie Does The U.S.A. / 1995 / PPR / M

LILA TENNYSON *see* **Star Index I**

LILA TOUA
American Pie / 1980 / SE / M

LILAH GLASS *see* **Star Index I**

LILI
Penetration (Anabolic) #1 / 1995 / ANA / M

LILI CARATI *(Lilli Carati, Lilly Karat, Ileana*
Carenati)
Italian early eighties sexploitation performer.
Born September 23, 1956 in Varese, Italy.
Miss Italy 1975.
The Alcove / 1984 / LUM / S • Copenhagen
Nights / cr83 / MED / S • Lust / 1985 / ... /
S • On My Lips / 1989 / PV / M • Sexual
Freedom / cr76 / CO1 / S • Skin Deep /
1979 / ... / S • To Be Twenty / 1978 / ... / S
• A Very Debauched Girl / 1988 / PL / M •
The Whore / 1989 / CA / M • [Highway
Racer / 1977 / ... / S • [Il Marito In Vacanza
/ 1981 / ... / S • [L'Avvocato Della Mala /
1977 / ... / S • [L'Incredible Moglie Insazia-
bile / 19?? / HOB / M • [Le Super Scatenate
/ 19?? / PUB / M • [Look At Me / 1977 / ...
/ S • [Midnight Gigolo / 1986 / ... / S • [Pelle
Conro Pelle / 19?? / ... / M • [The Pleasure
/ 1985 / ... / S

LILI MARLENE *(Monerica, Marlene*
Justin)
Marlene Justin is from **Sex Dreams On Maple**
Street; Monerica is from **Nightlife**.
Anal Annie And The Backdoor Housewives
/ 1984 / LIP / F • Backdoor Bandits / 1989 /
MIR / C • Backdoor Romance / 1984 / VIV
/ M • Backing In #1 / 1990 / WV / C • Back-
ing In #2 / 1990 / WV / C • Bare Waves /
1986 / VD / M • The Beat Goes On / 1987
/ VCR / C • The Best Of Anal Annie: The

Girl-Girl Adventures / 1993 / LIP / C • The
Best Of Black White & Pink Inside / 1996 /
CV / C • Best Of Hot Shorts #01 / 1987 /
VCR / C • The Best Of Ron Jeremy / 1990
/ WET / C • Beyond Taboo / 1984 / VIV / M
• The Big Bang / 1988 / WET / M • Blacks
& Blondes #01 / 1986 / WV / M • Blondes!
Blondes! Blondes! / 1986 / VCS / C • But-
ter Me Up / 1984 / CHX / M • Challenge Of
Desire / 1983 / NSV / M • Cheating Wives
/ 1983 / PAC / M • Cheri's On Fire / 1986 /
V99 / M • Chicks In Black Leather / 1989 /
VC / C • Cinderella / 1985 / VEL / M • Cot-
tontail Club / 1985 / HO / M • Debbie Class
Of '88 / 1987 / CC / M • Debbie Does 'em
All #1 / 1985 / CV / M • Debbie Goes To
Hawaii / 1988 / VD / C • Deeper! Harder!
Faster! / 1986 / VCS / C • Deviations / 1983
/ SE / M • Diamond Collection #76 / 1985 /
CDI / M • Diary Of A Bad Girl / 1986 / SUP
/ M • Doing It / 1982 / SE / M • Dollface /
1987 / CV / M • Down And Dirty / 1985 /
LBO / M • Dr Lust / 1987 / VC / M • Dreams
Of Natasha / 1985 / AAH / M • E.X. / 1986
/ SUP / M • Educating Nina / 1984 / AT / M
• Erotic Encounters / 1985 / LIM / C • The
Erotic World Of Linda Wong / 1985 / VIV /
M • Farmers Daughters / 1985 / WV / M •
Fashion Fantasies / 1986 / VC / M • Flesh
In Ecstasy #08: Traci Adams / 1987 / GO /
C • For Love And Lust / 1985 / AVC / M •
Forbidden Desire / 1983 / NSV / M •
French Letters / 1984 / CA / M • Future Sex
/ 1984 / NSV / M • Girl On The Run / 1985
/ VC / M • Girlfriends / 1983 / MIT / M • Girl-
friends Of Candy Wong / 1984 / LIP / F •
Girls On Girls / 1987 / SE / C • Glamour
Girls / 1987 / SE / M • The Grafenberg Spot
/ 1985 / MIT / M • Hard Times / 1985 / WV
/ M • Hot And Nasty! / 1986 / V99 / C • Hot
Girls In Love / 1984 / VIV / C • Hot Heads /
1985 / WV / M • Hot Rocks / 1986 / WET /
M • Hot School Reunion / 1984 / CHX / F •
Hyapatia Lee's Arcade Series #02 / 1988 /
ZA / C • I've Never Done This Before / 1985
/ NSV / M • Illusions Of Ecstasy / 1985 /
NSV / M • It's Incredible / 1985 / SE / M •
Kinky Sluts / 1988 / MIR / C • Lady Dyna-
mite / 1983 / VC / M • The Legend Of King
Karl / 1986 / AR / M • Little Showoffs / 1984
/ VC / M • Looking For Lust / 1984 / VEL /
M • Love At First Sight / 1987 / SE / C •
Love Champions / 1987 / VC / M • Love
Letters (Now Showing) / 1983 / NSV / M •
Mardi Gras / 1986 / SE / M • Missing
Pieces / 1985 / IN / M • Moving In / 1986 /
CV / M • Nasty / 1985 / NSV / M • Nasty
Nights / 1988 / PL / C • Naughty Girls Like
It Big / 1986 / ELH / M • Night Moves / 1983
/ SUP / M • A Night On The Wild Side /
1986 / VC / M • Nightfire / 1987 / LA / M •
Nightlife / 1983 / CA / M • Obsession / 1985
/ HO / M • Only The Best Of Anal / 1992 /
MET / C • Oral Majority #01 / 1986 / WV /
C • Oral Majority #04 / 1987 / WV / C • Ori-
ental Sexpress / 1984 / WV / M • Oriental
Taboo / 1985 / CDI / M • Passion Pit / 1985
/ SE / M • Passions / 1985 / MIT / M • Per-
fect Partners / 1986 / CV / M • The Per-
formers / 1986 / NSV / M • The Pink
Panties / 1985 / NSV / M • Play Me Again,
Vanessa / 1986 / VC / M • Please Don't
Stop / 1986 / CV / M • The Pleasure Hunt
#1 / 1984 / NSV / M • The Pleasure Maze /
1986 / PL / M • Rear Action Girls #2 / 1985
/ LIP / F • Revenge By Lust / 1986 / VCR /

M • Rock Hard / 1985 / CV / M • Screwdriver / 1988 / CC / C • Sensual Seduction / 1986 / LBO / M • Sex Appeal / 1984 / ABV / M • Sex Dreams On Maple Street / 1985 / WV / M • Sex Life Of A Porn Star / 1986 / ELH / M • Sexually Altered States / 1986 / VC / M • Shameless / 1982 / SVE / M • She-Male Encounters #06: Trilogy Of The Bizarre / 1981 / MET / G • She-Male Encounters #07: Divine Atrocities #1 / 1981 / MET / G • Sheri's Gotta Have It / 1985 / LIM / C • Sin City / 1986 / WET / M • Sinderotica / 1985 / HO / M • Sleepless Nights / 1984 / VIV / M • Smooth Operator / 1986 / AR / M • Soft As Silk...Sweet As Honey / 1984 / SE / M • Sophisticated Pleasure / 1984 / WV / M • Sweet Summer / 1986 / AMO / M • Tales Of The Backside / 1985 / VCR / C • Taste Of The Best #3 / 1988 / PIN / C • Taxi Girls #2: In Search Of Toni / 1986 / ELD / M • Temptation: The Story Of A Lustful Bride / 1983 / NSV / M • Three Faces Of Angel / 1987 / CV / M • Tight Fit / 1987 / V99 / M • Tight Fit / 1991 / VEX / C • Too Hot To Touch #1 / 1985 / CV / M • Trading Partners / 1983 / AIR / M • Triple Header / 1986 / SE / C • Type Cast / 1986 / AR / M • Ubangis On Uranus / 1987 / WV / M • The Ultimate O / 1985 / NSV / M • Unnatural Phenomenon #1 / 1985 / WV / M • Up 'n' Coming / 1983 / CA / M • Victoria's Secret Desires / 1983 / S&L / C • Video Girls / 1984 / LIP / F • Virginia / 1983 / CA / M • Voyeur's Delight / 1986 / VCS / C • Woman To Woman / 1989 / ZA / C • You Turn Me On / 1986 / LIM / M • Young Girls Do / 1984 / ELH / M • The Young Like It Hot / 1983 / CA / M

LILI RODGERS
Centerspread Girls / 1982 / CA / M
LILI XIANG see Dallas D'Amour
LILIANE
Eurotica #04 / 1996 / XC / M
LILITH
Absolute Anal / 1996 / XC / M • Intimate Interviews #2 / 1996 / NIT / M
LILLA
Puritan Video Magazine #09 / 1997 / LE / M
LILLI CARATI see Lili Carati
LILLI DARC
French Heat / 1975 / VC / M
LILLI DIAMOND
Little Girls Lost / 1982 / VC / M
LILLI EXENE see Lilli Xene
LILLI ST. CYR
Blue Vanities #115 / 1988 / FFL / M • Buxom Beautease / 19?? / SOW / S • Grindhouse Follies: First Row #01 / 1993 / SOW / M • Kiss Me, Baby / 1957 / SOW / S • Striporama #1 / 1952 / SOW / S • Teaserama / 1954 / SOW / S • Varietease / 1955 / SOW / S
LILLI XENE (Lilli Exene)
Rather ugly girl with a going-to-seed body and large enhanced tits. Brunette, big butt. As of first quarter 1994 she has has them enhanced again to grotesque proportions (34G).
$exce$$ / 1993 / CA / M • Action In Black / 1993 / FD / M • Adam & Eve's Guide To A G-Spot Orgasm / 1994 / VI / M • The Adventures Of Buck Naked / 1994 / OD / M • Anal Intruder #07 / 1993 / CC / M • Anal Island / 1992 / LV / M • Anal Orgy / 1993 / DRP / M • The Backway Inn #3 / 1993 / FD

/ M • Bare Bottom Treatment / 1993 / RB / B • Batwoman & Catgirl / 1992 / HW / M • Behind The Blackout / 1993 / HW / M • Big Bust Babes #11 / 1992 / AFI / M • Big Knockers #05 / 1994 / TV / M • Big Knockers #06 / 1994 / TV / M • Big Knockers #07 / 1994 / TV / M • Big Knockers #17 / 1995 / TV / M • Big Knockers #18 / 1995 / TV / M • Big Knockers #22 / 1995 / TV / M • Black & White In Living Color / 1992 / WV / M • Blonde Bombshells / 1992 / VER / B • Breast Collection #02 / 1995 / LBO / C • Breast Worx #42 / 1993 / LBO / M • Breastman's Anal Adventure / 1993 / EVN / M • Buffy Malibu's Totally Nasty All-Girl Home Videos #05 / 1993 / ANA / F • Busty Nymphos / 1996 / H&S / M • Busty Porno Queens / 1996 / H&S / M • Busty Porno Stars #2 / 1996 / H&S / M • Butt Camp / 1993 / HW / C • Butt Seriously Folks / 1994 / AFV / M • Butt Woman #5 / 1993 / FH / M • California Pizza Girls / 1992 / EVN / M • Chug-A-Lug Girls #1 / 1993 / VT / M • Chug-A-Lug Girls #2 / 1993 / VT / M • Club DV8 #1 / 1993 / SC / M • Confessions / 1992 / PL / M • Crazy With The Heat #2 / 1993 / MET / M • Deep C Diver / 1992 / LV / M • Depths Of Domination / 1993 / NAP / B • Dirty Bob's #04: SliCES Of ViCES / 1992 / FLP / S • Double D Domination / 1993 / BIZ / B • Double D Dykes #07 / 1992 / GO / F • Dripping With Desire / 1992 / DR / M • Euphoria / 1993 / CA / M • F-Channel / 1994 / AFV / F • Feathermates / 1992 / PRE / B • Fetish Finishing School / 1995 / HOM / B • Flood Control / 1992 / PRE / B • Forget Me Not / 1994 / FH / M • Full Service / 1993 / GO / M • A Girl's Affair #01 / 1992 / FD / F • Girlie: Man In Training / 1993 / LEO / B • Girls Around The World #24 / 1995 / BTO / S • Girls Will Be Boys #5 / 1993 / PL / F • Glittering Gartered Girls / 1993 / RSV / B • Greek Week / 1994 / CV / M • Heatwave #2 / 1993 / FH / F • Herman's Other Head / 1992 / LV / M • Hits & Misses / 1992 / PRE / B • Hollywood's Hills / 1992 / LV / M • Hot Tight Asses #10 / 1995 / TCK / M • Hotel Sodom #08 / 1995 / SNA / M • Humongous Hooters / 1995 / PME / F • Ice Woman #2 / 1993 / VI / M • If These Walls Could Talk (Director's Cut) / 1993 / MET / M • If These Walls Could Talk #1: Wicked Whispers / 1993 / MET / M • Jennifer 69 / 1992 / PL / M • The Joi Fuk Club / 1993 / WV / M • Junkyard Dykes #03 / 1994 / ZA / F • Kym Wilde's Bondage House Party #1 / cr92 / BON / B • LA, Citadel Of The Busty Angels / 1995 / NAP / S • Laugh Factory / 1995 / PRE / C • Lilli Chronicles #2 / 1994 / CAW / B • Lilli Xene And Tanya Fox's Espionage Interrogation / 1993 / RSV / B • Looks Like A Million / 1992 / LV / M • The Love Doctor / 1992 / HIP / M • Maid For Punishment / 1993 / ... / B • Mellon Man #01 / 1994 / AVI / M • Mellon Man #05 / 1995 / AVI / M • Murphie's Brown / 1992 / LV / M • Nasty Cracks / 1992 / PRE / B • Neighborhood Watch #35 / 1992 / LBO / M • Nookie Cookies / 1993 / CDI / F • Open Lips / 1994 / WV / M • Playtoys For Mistress Artemis / 1992 / RSV / B • Pussyman #01: The Search / 1993 / CC / M • Pussyman #04: The Celebration / 1993 / SNA / M • Pussyman #08: The Squirt Queens / 1994 / SNA / M • Pussyman #11: Prime Cuts / 1995 / SNA / C • Queen Dom-

inatrix / 1993 / NAP / B • Rainwoman #07: In The Rainforest / 1993 / CC / M • Read My Lips: No More Bush / 1992 / HW / M • Return To Melrose Place / 1993 / HW / M • Roto-Rammer / 1993 / LV / M • Sex Fantasy / 1993 / PPR / M • Sexorcist / 1994 / HW / M • Shaved #07 / 1995 / RB / F • Shear Ecstasy / 1993 / PEP / M • Sodomania #04: Further On Down The Road / 1993 / EL / M • Split Decision / 1993 / FD / M • Student Fetish Videos: Best of Enema #02 / 1992 / PRE / C • Student Fetish Videos: Best Of Foot Worship #02 / 1994 / PRE / C • Student Fetish Videos: The Enema #08 / 1992 / PRE / B • Student Fetish Videos: Foot Worship #06 / 1992 / PRE / B • Student Fetish Videos: Tickling #05 / 1992 / SFV / B • Summer Games / 1992 / HW / M • Taxi Girls #4: Daughter Of Lust / 1994 / CA / M • Things Change #2: Letting Go / 1992 / CV / M • The Three Muskatits / 1994 / PL / M • Tit To Tit #4 / 1996 / BTO / S • Titillator / 1994 / HW / C • Toppers #10 / 1993 / TV / M • Toppers #14 / 1993 / TV / M • Toppers #15 / 1993 / TV / M • Toppers #16 / 1993 / TV / M • Toppers #22 / 1993 / TV / C • Tracey Adams' Girls School / 1993 / BIZ / B • Two Women / 1992 / ROB / M • Up And Coming Executive / 1993 / TP / M • Warehouse Wenches #1 / 1994 / BIZ / B • Warehouse Wenches #2 / 1994 / BIZ / B • Web Of Desire / 1993 / OD / M • Wendy Whoppers: Park Ranger / 1993 / PEP / M • Wicked Thoughts / 1992 / PL / M • Wild Girls / 1993 / LV / F • Xene's TV Tenant / 1992 / RSV / G
LILLIAN
Blue Vanities #545 / 1994 / FFL / M • Homegrown Video #355 / 1991 / HOV / M
LILLIAN ALAN
Flesh Fever / 1978 / CV / M
LILLIAN PARKER
Blue Vanities #559 / 1994 / FFL / M
LILLIAN SCHROEDER see Star Index I
LILLIAN WILCZKOWSKY see Chesty Morgan
LILLIE
Innocent Little Girls #2 / 1996 / MP0 / M • Neighborhood Nookie #1 / 1996 / RAS / M
LILLY
Bizarre Fantasies / 1983 / BIZ / B • Blue Vanities #170 (New) / 1996 / FFL / M • Blue Vanities #170 (Old) / 1991 / FFL / M • Blue Vanities #503 / 1992 / FFL / M • Blue Vanities #520 / 1993 / FFL / M • Blue Vanities #578 / 1995 / FFL / M • Kym Wilde's On The Edge #29 / 1995 / RB / B
LILLY FOSTER
Bucky Beaver's XXX Dragon Art Theatre Double Feature #26 / 1996 / SOW / M • Bucky Beaver's XXX Dragon Art Theatre Double Feature #27 / 1996 / SOW / M • Inside Pussycat / cr75 / SOW / M • Liz: Mama's Little Girl / cr73 / SOW / M
LILLY KARAT see Lili Carati
LILLY LAMARR
Sexorcist Devil / 1974 / CXV / M • Underage / 1974 / IHV / M
LILLY LOVETREE see Rene Bond
LILO
Magma: Fuck Me Diana / 1994 / MET / M
LILY see Star Index I
LILY BRAINDROP
Fangs Of Steel / Sexual Cutting / 1996 / FLV / M
LILY DAWN

Blue Vanities #556 / 1994 / FFL / M
LILY LABOUCHE *see Star Index I*
LILY LACEDALE
Overnight Sensation / 1976 / AR / M
LILY OVERSTREET
Irresistible #1 / 1982 / SE / M
LILY ST. CYR
Blue Vanities #552 / 1994 / FFL / M
LILY VERDE *see Star Index I*
LILY WONG *see Mai Lin*
LIN CHAN
High Heel Harlots #05 / 1994 / SFP / M
LIN CHEN FU
The Vixens Of Kung Fu: A Tale Of Yin Yang / 1975 / VC / M
LIN DIANNO
Elodie Does The U.S.A. / 1995 / PPR / M
LIN DOG
Big Black Bang / 1996 / HW / M • Black Fantasies #15 / 1996 / HW / M • Black Gangbangers #09 / 1995 / HW / M • Black Knockers #06 / 1995 / TV / M • Black Knockers #09 / 1995 / TV / M • Black Knockers #10 / 1995 / TV / M • Black Knockers #13 / 1995 / TV / M • Black Knockers #14 / 1995 / TV / M • Black Lube Job Girls / 1995 / SUF / M • Bootylicious: It's A Bootyful Thing / 1996 / JMP / M • Bootylicious: Trailer Trash / 1996 / JMP / M • Bow Down Backstreet / 1996 / HW / M • Double Penetration Virgins: DP Therapy / 1996 / JMP / M • My Ass #1 / 1996 / NOT / M • Perverted Stories #07 / 1996 / JMP / M • Perverted Stories #08 / 1996 / JMP / M • Shake Your Booty / 1996 / EVN / M • Triple Penetration Debutante Sluts #1 / 1996 / BAC / M • White Trash Whore / 1996 / JMP / M
LIN SHIA
Hidden Camera #17 / 1994 / JMP / M • Horny Henry's Oriental Adventure / 1994 / TTV / M • Mike Hott: #110 Lin Shia And Charlene / 1990 / MHV / F • Mike Hott: #111 Lin Shia, Charlene And Paul / 1990 / MHV / M • Pai Gow Video #09: Naked Asians / 1995 / EVN / M
LIN SHIN *see Jade East*
LIN WONG *see Star Index I*
LINA
Blue Vanities #579 / 1995 / FFL / M
LINA LEWIS
Ebony Erotica / 1985 / SVE / C
LINA ROMAY
[The Loves Of Irina / 1973 / PS / S
LINA SPENCER *see Star Index I*
LINCOLN REGAN *see Star Index I*
LINDA
Angie, Trish, Linda, Samantha / 1990 / PLV / B • Ateball: Linda & Friends #1 / 1995 / ATE / M • Ateball: Linda & Friends #2 / 1995 / ATE / M • Ateball: Linda's West Coast Talent Search / 1996 / ATE / M • Ateball: Massage Me / 1996 / ATE / M • AVP #9164: The Voyeur / 1990 / AVP / F • Banned In Britain / 1995 / VC / M • Big Tit Roundup #1 / 199? / H&S / S • Blue Vanities #112 / 1988 / FFL / M • Blue Vanities #228 / 1994 / FFL / M • Blue Vanities #509 / 1992 / FFL / M • Blue Vanities #514 / 1992 / FFL / M • Blue Vanities #528 / 1993 / FFL / M • Blue Vanities #538 / 1993 / FFL / M • Bottoms Up #03 / 1983 / AVC / C • Breast Of Britain #9 / 1990 / BTO / M • College Video Virgins #07 / 1996 / AOC / M • Double D Amateurs #08 / 1993 / JMP / M • Eric Kroll's Bondage #1 / 1994 / ERK / M • Eric

Kroll's Fetish #1 / 1994 / ERK / M • Eurotica #08 / 1996 / XC / M • Hot Legs #1 / 1990 / PLV / B • House Play (California Star) / 1994 / CS / B • Joe Elliot's College Girls #33 / 1994 / JOE / M • Joe Elliot's College Girls #39 / 1994 / JOE / F • Lesbian Pros And Amateurs #08 / 1992 / GO / F • Magma: Fuck Me Diana / 1994 / MET / M • Magma: Insatiable Lust / 1995 / MET / M • Magma: Shopping Anal / 1994 / MET / M • Mike Hott: #216 Linda / 1993 / MHV / M • Mike Hott: #231 Linda Special / 1994 / MHV / F • Mike Hott: #256 Linda And Georgia / 1994 / MHV / F • Odyssey Amateur #64: Linda Takes It Black / 1991 / OD / M • Private Film #15 / 1994 / OD / M • Private Film #24 / 1995 / OD / M • Swedish Sex / 1996 / PL / M • Tit To Tit #3 / 1995 / BTO / M
LINDA (STEVI) *see Stevi*
LINDA ASCOR *see Star Index I*
LINDA BAILE
Meter Maids / 1974 / SIL / M
LINDA BAILEY
Satisfaction Guaranteed / 1972 / AXV / M
LINDA BARRETT *see Star Index I*
LINDA BLANE
Sheila's Payoff / 1977 / VCX / M
LINDA BOREMAN *see Linda Lovelace*
LINDA BROOKS *see Joan Devlon*
LINDA BROWN *see Star Index I*
LINDA BYRD *see Lynn Francis*
LINDA CHU
The Bimbo #1 / 1985 / VXP / M • The Bimbo #2: The Homecoming / 1986 / RLV / M • Sleazy Susan / 1986 / VXP / M
LINDA CORSICA *see Star Index I*
LINDA DANIEL *see Star Index I*
LINDA DEL RAY
Interracial 247 / 1995 / CC / M
LINDA DEL TORRO
The Love Witch / 1973 / AR / M
LINDA DELOVE
Bucky Beaver's XXX Dragon Art Theatre Double Feature #26 / 1996 / SOW / M • Inside Pussycat / cr75 / SOW / M
LINDA DIGEONE
Casanova #2 / 1976 / CA / M
LINDA DONG
Toys, Not Boys #3 / 1991 / FC / C
LINDA DOYLE *see Star Index I*
LINDA ELSTRO *see Linda Shaw*
LINDA ESTRELLA *see Star Index I*
LINDA FILLER
Little Girls Blue #2 / 1983 / VCX / M
LINDA FRENCH *see Star Index I*
LINDA GORDON
Blue Vanities #029 / 1988 / FFL / M • Blue Vanities #524 / 1993 / FFL / M
LINDA GRANT
Behind The Green Door #1 / 1972 / MIT / M
LINDA GRAZIER
Bucky Beaver's XXX Dragon Art Theatre Double Feature #06 / 1996 / SOW / M • Finishing School / 1975 / SOW / M
LINDA HANSON
Spank Me, Spank Me, Spank Me / 199? / BON / B
LINDA HARRIS
A Climax Of Blue Power / 1974 / EVI / M
LINDA JADE
Bankok Connection / 1979 / CA / M
LINDA JAMES
Girls In Passion / 1979 / VHL / M • Tender Loving Care / 1994 / BRI / S

LINDA JENSEN
Rabin's Revenge / 1971 / MIT / M
LINDA JOHNSON
Pink Champagne / 1979 / CV / M • Video Kixs Magazine #6 / 1983 / GLD / M
LINDA JOY *see Star Index I*
LINDA KATZ
Vanessa's Hot Nights / 1984 / SVE / M
LINDA KAY *see Star Index I*
LINDA L'AMOUR *see Leslie Murray*
LINDA LEE (JASMINE) *see Jasmine*
LINDA LEE TRACY *see Star Index I*
LINDA LICKS *see Star Index I*
LINDA LIPPS
1001 Erotic Nights #2 / 1987 / VC / M
LINDA LONDON
The Nurses / 1971 / SOW / M
LINDA LOU *see Star Index I*
LINDA LOU (TESS N.) *see Tess Newhart*
LINDA LOVEALL
More Ways Than One / 1973 / ALP / M
LINDA LOVELACE *(Linda Boreman, Linda Marchiano, Linda Marciano)*
Not too pretty, medium tits, frizzy hair, brunette. You shouldn't need a description of Linda.
Blue Vanities #057 / 1988 / FFL / M • Blue Vanities #093 / 1988 / FFL / M • Blue Vanities #563 / 1994 / FFL / M • The Confessions Of Linda Lovelace / 1974 / AR / C • Deep Throat #1 / 1972 / AR / M • Dog Fucker / 1969 / ... / M • Dogarama / 1969 / ... / M • Exotic French Fantasies / 1974 / PVX / M • Linda Lovelace For President / 1975 / ... / C • Lovelace Meets Miss Jones / 1975 / AVC / M • Midnight Blue #2 / 1980 / VXP / M • [Classics Of Porn / 19?? / ... / M
LINDA LOVELIPS
More Than A Voyeur / cr73 / SEP / M
LINDA LOVELL *see Star Index I*
LINDA LOVEMORE *(Rita Davis, Rhonda Blake)*
Passable face, long brown hair, thin body, small tits.
Airport Girls / 1975 / VXP / M • The Bite / 1975 / SVE / M • Emmanuelle: Black And White / 197? / WIZ / S • Highway Hookers / 1976 / SVE / M • Joy Riders / 1975 / SAT / M • Lickity Split / 1974 / COM / M • The Love Bus / 1974 / OSC / M • Midnight Desires / 1976 / VXP / M • Mount Of Venus / 1975 / ... / M • Naked Came The Stranger / 1975 / VC / M • They Shall Overcome / 1974 / VST / M
LINDA LOWE *see Star Index I*
LINDA MAIDSTONE *see Star Index I*
LINDA MARCHIANO *see Linda Lovelace*
LINDA MARCIANO *see Linda Lovelace*
LINDA MCDOWELL *(Claudia Grayson, Linda Powell, Claudine Grayson)*
The Adult Version Of Dr Jekyll And Mr Hyde / 1971 / SOW / M • Beyond Fulfillment / 197? / ALP / M • Blue Vanities #039 (New) / 1988 / FFL / M • Blue Vanities #043 / 1988 / FFL / M • Blue Vanities #057 / 1988 / FFL / M • City Of Sin / 1971 / CLX / M • Classic Erotica #4 / 1980 / SVE / M • Fulfillment / 1973 / SE / M • Garters And Lace / 1975 / SE / M • Helen Bedd / cr73 / IHV / M • Playmate #11 / 1984 / VC / M • Sweet, Sweet Busty / 1979 / ALP / M
LINDA MCGILL
Shape Up For Sensational Sex / 1985 / SE / M

LINDA MOOR
Private Film #25 / 1995 / OD / M • Private Film #26 / 1995 / OD / M

LINDA MOORE
The Bottom Line / 1990 / AMB / M • Triple X Video Magazine #01 / 1995 / OD / M • Triple X Video Magazine #02 / 1995 / OD / M

LINDA MORGAN *see Star Index I*

LINDA O'BRYANT
Sensual Encounters Of Every Kind / 1978 / SE / M

LINDA POWELL *see Linda McDowell*

LINDA PRIEST
Oriental Hawaii / 1982 / CA / M

LINDA REEVES
Sex Boat / 1980 / VCX / M

LINDA ROCK *see Star Index I*

LINDA ROGERS *see Star Index I*

LINDA ROSE KIMBALL *(Rose-Linda Kimball, Rose Lynn, Rose Kimball, Rose Kindal, Rose Brandon)*
Too tall blonde with small tits, tattoo on right butt, not a tight waist and a passable face.
All American Girls #2: In Heat / 1983 / CA / M • Coffee, Tea Or Me / 1984 / CV / M • Feels Like Silk / 1983 / SE / M • Flesh & Laces #1 / 1983 / CA / M • Flesh & Laces #2 / 1983 / CA / M • Golden Girls, The Movie / 1984 / SE / M • The Young Like It Hot / 1983 / CA / M

LINDA S.
Up And Cummers #32 / 1996 / 4P / M

LINDA SANDERSON *see Tina Russell*

LINDA SANSAMOOR *see Star Index I*

LINDA SHALL *see Star Index I*

LINDA SHAW *(Lindy Shaw, Nancy Garcia, Lindy Show, Anna Pierce, Lorna Wills, Lorna Mills, Linda Elstro)*
Anna Pierce is from **I Like To Watch**. Lorna Wills is from **Suze's Centerfolds #6**. Blonde with the black growing out, large sloppy tits, a little chunky, older, quite pretty, small tattoo on back just above right butt.
Aunt Peg Goes To Hollywood / 1982 / CA / M • Body Double / 1984 / C3S / S • Bold Obsession / 1983 / NSV / M • Caballero Preview Tape #2 / 1983 / CA / C • Challenge Of Desire / 1983 / NSV / M • Daughters Of Emmanuelle / 1982 / VCX / M • Diamond Collection #52 / 1984 / CIN / M • Diamond Collection #56 / 1984 / CIN / M • Dinner With Samantha / 1983 / PTV / M • Dream Girls #1 / 1983 / CA / C • Erotic Dimensions #9: The Fantasy Trade / 1982 / NSV / M • Erotic Encounters / 1985 / LIM / C • Erotic Interlude / 1981 / CA / M • A Family Affair / 1984 / AVC / M • First Time Lesbians (Gourmet) / 1987 / GO / F • Foot Show / 1989 / BIZ / B • Gimme An X / 1993 / VD / C • Golden Girls #33 / 1988 / CA / M • Golden Girls #35 / 1988 / CA / M • Gourmet Quickies: Danielle #709 / 1985 / GO / C • GVC: Paper Dolls #117 / 1983 / GO / F • GVC: Real Estate #109 / 1983 / GO / M • GVC: Women Who Love Women #115 / cr83 / GO / F • GVC: Women's Fantasies #108 / 1983 / GO / F • Hot Girls In Love / 1984 / VIV / C • I Like To Watch / 1982 / CA / M • Keyhole #109: Linda Shaw Sucks / 198? / KEH / M • Let's Talk Sex / 1982 / CA / M • Linda Shaw Sucks / 19?? / ... / M • Lingerie / 1983 / CDI / M • Parliament: Super Head #1 / 1989 / PM / C • Passion Flowers / 1987 / CDI / C • Physi-

cal #1 / 1981 / SUP / M • Physical #2 / 1985 / SUP / M • Playing With Fire / 1983 / IN / M • Pussy Galore / 1993 / VD / C • Scared Stiff / 1984 / PV / M • Shameless / 1982 / SVE / M • Sheri's Gotta Have It / 1985 / LIM / C • Sorority Sweethearts / 1983 / CA / M • Suze's Centerfolds #6 / 1981 / CA / M • Swedish Erotica #36 / 1980 / CA / M • Too Much Too Soon / 1983 / VCX / M • The Wacky World Of X-Rated Bloopers / 1989 / GO / M • Where The Girls Are / 1984 / VEX / M • Woman Times Four / 1983 / LIP / F • Young And Restless / 1983 / VIV / M • The Young Like It Hot / 1983 / CA / M

LINDA SOFT
Blue Vanities #121 / 1990 / FFL / M

LINDA SOUTHERN
The Amazing Transplant / 1969 / SOW / S • Hungry Mouth / 19?? / VXP / M

LINDA STRONG
Erotic Dimensions #7: Fulfilled / 1982 / NSV / M

LINDA TALLEY
Apartment Girls / cr72 / CV / M • Whole Buncha Fucking / 1994 / MET / M

LINDA TEMPLETON
Body Magic / 1982 / SE / M

LINDA TERRY
Inside Georgina Spelvin / 1974 / VC / M • Saturday Matinee Series #2 / 1996 / VCX / C • Steamy Sirens / 1984 / AIR / C

LINDA THOMAS *see Linda Thorens*

LINDA THOMPSON *see Purple Passion*

LINDA THOMPSON (78) *see Star Index I*

LINDA THORENS *(Linda Thomas)*
Swedish blonde with long hair parted in the middle, 18 years old in 1996 and still in the Swedish equivalent of high school, tight waist, lots of freckles, medium tits with very large areola, marginal face.
Dirty Dirty Debutantes #4 / 1996 / 4P / M • Dirty Dirty Debutantes #8 / 1996 / 4P / M • I Wanna Be A Porn Star #1 / 1996 / 4P / M • Lollipops #1 / 1996 / SC / M • More Dirty Debutantes #50 / 1996 / 4P / M • Nasty Nymphos #15 / 1996 / ANA / M • Rock 'n' Roll Rocco / 1997 / EA / M • Up And Cummers #29 / 1996 / ERW / M • Up And Cummers #30 / 1996 / 4P / M

LINDA TRAN
Pai Gow Video #08: Asian Fantasies / 1995 / EVN / M

LINDA TRUSSELL
The Vixens Of Kung Fu: A Tale Of Yin Yang / 1975 / VC / M

LINDA VALE *(Ultra Max, Ultra Maxine)*
Older blonde, small tits, womanly body, cronelike hands, marginal face, hard personality, mole on her right cheek.
Call Me Angel, Sir / 1976 / ALP / M • Certified Mail / 1975 / CDC / M • Dominatrix Without Mercy / 1976 / ALP / B • Foxtrot / 1982 / COM / M • A Girl's Best Friend / 1981 / QX / M • Neon Nights / 1981 / COM / M • One Last Fling / cr76 / CPL / M • Platinum Paradise / 1980 / COM / M • Referral Service / cr71 / BL / M • A Scream In The Streets / 1971 / SOW / S • Through The Looking Glass / 1976 / ALP / M • Whatever Happened To Miss September? / 1973 / ALP / M

LINDA VAN IMP
Violated / 1973 / PVX / M

LINDA VISTA
Backing In #1 / 1990 / WV / C • Desire In The Night / 1983 / VC / M

LINDA WEST
Reel Classics #1 / 1996 / H&S / M • Reel Classics #2 / 1996 / H&S / M • The Senator's Daughter / 1978 / CV / M

LINDA WIESMEIER
Malibu Express / 1984 / MCA / S • Playboy Video Magazine #02 / 1983 / PLA / S • Playboy Video Magazine #05 / 1983 / PLA / S • Playboy's Playmate Review #1 / 1983 / PLA / S • Playboy's Playmate Workout / 1983 / PLA / S • Playboy: Playmates At Play / 1990 / HBO / S • Playboy: Wet & Wild #1 / 1989 / HBO / S • Preppies / 1982 / VES / S • R.S.V.P. / 1983 / VES / S • Shape Up For Sensational Sex / 1985 / SE / M

LINDA WILLIAMS
Resurrection Of Eve / 1973 / MIT / M

LINDA WOGOMAN
Sex Boat / 1980 / VCX / M

LINDA WONG
Died of a drug overdose.
Baby Face #1 / 1977 / VC / M • The Best Of Alex De Renzy #1 / 1983 / VC / C • Black Silk Stockings / 1978 / SE / C • China De Sade / 1977 / ALP / M • China Lust / 1976 / VC / M • Classic Erotica #1 / 1980 / SVE / M • Classic Swedish Erotica #32 / 1987 / CA / C • The Dragon Lady #1 / 1988 / WV / C • Easy Alice / 1976 / VC / M • Erotic Fantasies #5 / 1983 / CV / C • The Erotic World Of Linda Wong / 1985 / VIV / M • Exhausted / 1981 / CA / C • Femmes De Sade / 1976 / ALP / M • Fortune Cookie Nookie / 1986 / VCS / C • Good To The Last Drop / 1986 / VCS / C • The Jade Pussycat / 1977 / CA / M • Legends Of Porn #1 / 1987 / CV / C • Love Secrets / 1976 / VIP / M • One Of A Kind / 1976 / SVE / M • Oriental Babysitter / 1976 / SE / M • Oriental Temptations / 1984 / CV / C • Postcards From Abroad / 1991 / CA / C • Private Thighs / 1987 / AVC / C • Rebecca's / 1983 / AVC / M • Reflections / 1977 / VCX / M • Rollerbabies / 1976 / VC / M • Salt & Pepper / 1986 / VCS / C • San Francisco Original 200s #9 / 1980 / SVE / M • Sex On The Orient Express / 1991 / VC / C • Sexsations / 1984 / NSV / M • Sheer Panties / 1979 / SE / C • Stormy / 1980 / CV / M • Student Bodies / 1975 / VC / M • Swedish Erotica #02 / 1980 / CA / M • Swedish Erotica #10 / 1980 / CA / M • Swedish Erotica #12 / 1980 / CA / M • Sweet Cakes / 1976 / VC / M • Sweet Folds Of Flesh / 19?? / AST / M • Tenderloins / 19?? / ... / M • Thunderbuns / 1976 / VCX / C • True Legends Of Adult Cinema: Unsung Superstars / 1993 / VC / C

LINDA YORK *(Brittany Laine, Brittany Lane)*
The Adult Version Of Dr Jekyll And Mr Hyde / 1971 / SOW / S • Angel Above, Devil Below / 1974 / CV / M • Chain Gang Women / 1971 / AE / S • Fantasm / 1976 / VS / S • Love Garden / 1971 / SOW / S • Marriage And Other Four Letter Words / 1974 / VC / M • Panorama Blue / 1974 / ALP / S • A Scream In The Streets / 1971 / SOW / S • Video Vixens / 1972 / VES / S

LINDI *see Star Index I*

LINDI STARR
Slave Training (Vid Tech) / 1994 / VTF / B

LINDSAY LOOKS
Black Knockers #03 / 1995 / TV / M • Black Knockers #04 / 1995 / TV / M • Bootyli-

Alex Sanders (*Conquest*)

Nici Sterling (*Wicked Weapons*)*

* All photographs in insert courtesy of Wicked Pictures

Rebecca Bardoux (*Body of Innocence*)

P.J. Sparxx (*The Corruption of Christina*)

Chasey Laine (*The Original Wicked Woman*)

Tom Byron (*Conquest*)

Kelly Trump (*Point of Entry*)

Missy (*Fatyr*)

cious: Big Badd Booty / 1995 / JMP / M •
Bootylicious: Booty & The Ho Bitch / 1996
/ JMP / M • Interracial 247 / 1995 / CC / M

LINDSAY MAY
Chasin' The Fifties / 1994 / WP / M

LINDSAY TAINE
An Editor's Nightmare / 1995 / LON / B

LINDSEY
Black Fantasies #13 / 1996 / HW / M •
Black Fantasies #16 / 1996 / HW / M •
Cindy's House Party / 1996 / HW / M •
Coco's House Party / 1995 / HW / M •
Kinky College Cunts #09 / 1993 / NS / M

LINDSEY ALLEN
Butt Row Unplugged / 1996 / ABS / M •
Filthy First Timers #3: Tearing Down The
Walls Of Shame / 1996 / EL / M • Filthy
First Timers #4 / 1996 / EL / M • Sodoma-
nia #19: Sweet Cream / 1996 / EL / M

LINDSEY DAY
Donna Young: Lindsey Day #1 / 1995 / DY
/ F

LINDY
The Satisfiers Of Alpha Blue / 1980 / AVC /
M

LINDY DORN
That's Porno / 1979 / CV / C

LINDY JACKOV *see Star Index I*

LINDY LABARE *see Cindy LaBare*

LINDY MCPHEARSON
Undulations / 1980 / VC / M

LINDY SHAW *see Linda Shaw*

LINDY SHOW *see Linda Shaw*

LINETTE
Big Bust Babes #12 / 1993 / AFI / M •
Magma: Party Extreme / 1995 / MET / M

LINETTE NARAWAY
The Joy Of Fooling Around / 1978 / CV / M

LING FAT
The Vixens Of Kung Fu: A Tale Of Yin Yang
/ 1975 / VC / M

LINKA
Rocco Goes To Prague / 1995 / EA / M

LINNEA QUIGLEY
Adult Fairytales / 1979 / WIZ / S • Assault
Of The Party Nerds #1 / 1989 / PRS / S •
Assault Of The Party Nerds #2: The Heavy
Petting Detective / 1993 / PRS / S • Audi-
tions / 1978 / MEA / S • Beach Babes From
Beyond #1 / 1993 / BRI / S • Beverly Hills
Girls / 1985 / HID / S • Creepozoids / 1987
/ UCV / S • Deadly Embrace / 1989 / PRS
/ S • Dr Alien / 1989 / PAR / S • The Girl I
Want / 1990 / ... / S • Hollywood Chainsaw
Hookers / 1988 / CAM / S • Innocent Blood
/ 1992 / WAR / S • Kidnapped Girls Agency
/ cr86 / HOM / S • Murder Weapon / 1989 /
CHV / S • Nightmare Sisters / 1987 / TRW
/ S • Savage Streets / 1983 / LIV / S •
Sorority Babes In The Slimeball Bowl-O-
Rama / 1988 / UCV / S • Summer Camp /
1980 / MED / S • Vice Academy #1 / 1988
/ PRS / S • Vice Academy #2 / 1990 / PRS
/ S • Virgin High / 1990 / C3S / S

LINNEA STEVENS
Home For Unwed Mothers / 1984 / AMB /
F • Valley Girls Ferr Shurr / cr85 / EXF / M

LINNY *see Star Index I*

LINSHIA *see Star Index I*

LINWOOD HILL
Bi Love Lucy / 1994 / PL / G • Transexual
Blvd / 1994 / PL / G

LINZI DREW
American Buttman In London / 1991 / EA /
M • An American Werewolf In London /
1981 / VES / S • Aria / 1987 / AE / S •

Buttman's Bouncin' British Babes / 1994 /
EA / M • Electric Blue #017 / 1984 / CA / S
• Emmanuelle In Soho / 1978 / PRS / S •
The Lair Of The White Worm / 1988 / VES
/ S • Pussy Woman #1 (H&S) / 199? / H&S
/ F • Salome's Last Dance / 1988 / VES / S
• Thunder Boobs / 1995 / BTO / M

LINZI HONEY
Buttman's Bouncin' British Babes / 1994 /
EA / M

LIONA
Private Video Magazine #03 / 1993 / OD /
M

LIONEL BRAGDON
Sex The Hard Way / 1985 / CV / M

LIONEL NORBERRY
The Swing Thing / 1973 / TGA / M

LIQUID SLATER
The Voyeur #2 / 1994 / EA / M

LIRA CASTLE
Captive In Sumanka / 1996 / LON / B • The
Interrogation / 1994 / HOM / B

LIRA LEE
Sex Over 40 #1 / 1994 / PL / M • Sex Over
40 #2 / 1994 / PL / M

LIRA ROSS
Education Of The Dominatrix / 1993 / HOM
/ B • The Golden Dagger / 1993 / LON / B
• Harem Nights / 1996 / SHL / B • The
Spanking Pact / 1995 / CAA / B

LISA
A&B AB#071: Blonde And Beautiful / 1990
/ A&B / F • A&B AB#081: Sucking Contest
/ 1990 / A&B / M • A&B AB#086: Dolly's
Surprise / 1990 / A&B / M • A&B AB#103: A
Couples Fantasy / 1990 / A&B / M • A&B
AB#139: Inside Lisa / 1990 / A&B / M • A&B
AB#191: She's Back / 1990 / A&B / M •
A&B AB#221: Young Lovers / 1990 / A&B /
M • A&B AB#343: Foot Lovers And How To
Stuff A Wild Pussy / 1991 / A&B / M • A&B
AB#402: Cream Lovers / 1993 / A&B / C •
A&B Dr. Lisa #1: Oh Doctor Put It In / 1990
/ A&B / M • A&B Dr. Lisa #2: The Condom
Video / 1990 / A&B / M • A&B Dr. Lisa #3:
The Facial / 1990 / A&B / M • A&B GB#050:
The Interview #1 / 1992 / A&B / M • A&B
GB#051: The Interview #2 / 1992 / A&B / M
• A&B GB#054: Love Doctor / 1992 / A&B /
M • America's Raunchiest Home Videos
#06: Fuck Frenzy / 1992 / ZA / M • AVP
#9122: Good Morning America / 1990 /
AVP / F • AVP #9137: Sunshine Sexplay /
1990 / AVP / F • Beach Bum Amateur's #32
/ 1993 / MID / M • The Best Of Hot Body
Video Magazine / 1994 / CG / C • Between
My Breasts #14 / 1991 / BTO / S • Big
Boobs Around The World #2 / 1990 / BTO
/ M • Bikini Seasons / 1993 / PHV / F • The
Black Anal-ist #1 / 1988 / VEX / M • Blue
Vanities #112 / 1988 / FFL / M • Blue Vani-
ties #167 (New) / 1996 / FFL / M • Blue
Vanities #167 (Old) / 1991 / FFL / M • Blue
Vanities #577 / 1995 / FFL / M • Body
Tease / 1992 / VER / F • Bottoms Up #02 /
1983 / AVC / C • Breast Wishes #02 / 1991
/ LBO / M • Bus Stop Tales #01 / 1989 / PRI
/ M • Bus Stop Tales #07 / 1989 / PRI / M •
Bus Stop Tales #08 / 1990 / PRI / M •
Creme De Femme #2 / 1981 / AVC / C •
Creme De Femme #4 / 1981 / AVC / C •
Dick & Jane Penetrate Paris / 1994 / AVI /
M • Dirty Blue Movies #02 / 1992 / JTV / M
• English Class / 1995 / VC / M • English
Muffins / 1995 / VC / M • Fresh Cheeks /
1995 / VC / M • FTV #01: Muscle Brawl /

1996 / FT / B • FTV #31: Trio Of Terror /
1996 / FT / B • Gourmet Premier: Side
Pocket / Headline Sex #910 / cr85 / GO / M
• Green Piece Of Ass #5 / 1994 / RTP / M
• Hirsute Lovers #2 / 1995 / BTO / M •
HomeGrown Video #455 / 1995 / HOV / M
• Hot Body Video Magazine #08 / 1994 /
CG / S • Hot Body Video Magazine:
Brunette Power / 1994 / CG / F • Joe El-
liot's College Girls #35 / 1994 / JOE / M •
Joe Elliot's College Girls #36 / 1994 / JOE
/ M • Joe Elliot's College Girls #44 / 1996 /
JOE / M • Kinky College Cunts #08 / 1993
/ NS / F • Knocked-Up Nymphos #1 / 1996
/ GLI / M • Limited Edition #13 / 1980 / AVC
/ M • Limited Edition #20 / 1980 / AVC / M
• Lisa And Sandy: East Meets West / 1992
/ LOD / F • Lisa: Hot Shorts & Miniskirt /
1990 / LOD / F • Lisa: In Trouble Again /
1994 / VIG / B • Lisa: Shaved Pink / 1992 /
LOD / F • Living For Love / 1993 / V99 / M
• More Dirty Debutantes #19 / 1993 / 4P /
M • Moving Violations / 1992 / BON / B •
Neighborhood Watch #22: In The Pink And
Wet / 1992 / LBO / M • Nest Of Joy / 19??
/ GO / M • New Faces, Hot Bodies #13 /
1994 / STP / M • Next Door Neighbors #04
/ 1989 / BON / M • Odyssey Triple Play
#25: Consenting Threesomes / 1993 / OD
/ M • Pearl Necklace: Amorous Amateurs
#36 / 1993 / SEE / M • Pearl Necklace:
Amorous Amateurs #37 / 1993 / SEE / M •
Pearl Necklace: Facial #01 / 1994 / SEE /
C • Penetration (Flash) #1 / 1995 / FLV / M
• Perversity In Paris / 1994 / AVI / M •
Porno Screentests / 1982 / VC / M • Raw
Talent: Bang 'er 31 Times / 1992 / RTP / M
• Rebecca's Dream / cr83 / VD / B • Reel
Life Video #01: Josephina, Lisa & Julia /
1994 / RLF / F • Reel Life Video #31: An-
other Hairy Girl Special / 1995 / RLF / F •
Reel Life Video #46: Roommates / 1996 /
RLF / F • Reel Life Video #55: Lisa & Missy
/ 1996 / RLF / F • Score 4 Me / 1991 / XPI
/ M • Soda Jerk / 1992 / ZA / M • Starlet
Screen Test / 1990 / NST / S • Super Sam-
pler #5 / 1994 / LOD / C • Trans America /
1993 / TSS / G • Two Bitches From Hell /
1994 / CAW / B • Uncle Roy's Amateur
Home Video #17 / 1993 / VIM / M • Up And
Cummers #10 / 1994 / 4P / M • Wet Work-
out: Shape Up, Then Strip Down / 1995 /
PME / S • Wrasslin She-Babes #05 / 1996
/ SOW / M

LISA (FALLON) *see Fallon*

LISA (K. KARLSON) *see Kat Karlson*

LISA (S/M)
Interview With A She-Male / 1995 / PL / G

LISA (SHANE) *see Shane*

LISA (STEVI) *see Stevi*

LISA (SUKOYA) *see Sukoya*

LISA ADAMS *see Lysa Thatcher*

LISA ANDERSON
Blondes Like It Hot / 1984 / ELH / M • Marilyn, My Love / 1985 / ELH / M

LISA ANN *(Zina Sunshine, Zina (Lisa
Ann), Lisa Picotte)*
Comes from Pennsylvania and in 1994 was
38DD-20-34 (inflated) and 5'2" tall. I
doubt the "20"—her waist looks thick.
Danced under the name "Sunshine" before
getting into the porno movies. De-virginized at 13. Hangs around with a man-
ager/boyfriend/p... called Sledge.
13th Annual Adult Video News Awards /
1996 / VC / S • Airotica / 1996 / SC / M •

Angel Eyes / 1995 / IN / M • Bar Bizarre / 1996 / WP / B • Big Bad Breasts Of Zina / 1995 / NAP / B • Big Bust Fantasies / 1995 / PME / F • Big Busty Major Babes / 1996 / NAP / F • Cinesex #2 / 1994 / CV / M • The Dinner Party #2: The Buffet / 1996 / ULI / M • Dirty Bob's #23: Tampa Teasers / 1995 / FLP / S • A Dirty Western #2: Smoking Guns / 1994 / CV / M • The Doll House / 1995 / CV / M • Dresden Diary #16: / 1996 / BIZ / B • Entangled / 1996 / KLP / M • Flesh / 1996 / EA / M • Flesh For Fantasy / 1994 / CV / M • Heavenly Yours / 1995 / CV / M • House On Paradise Beach / 1996 / VC / M • Invisible: The Chronicles Of Benjamin Knight / 1995 / PAR / S • LA, Citadel Of The Busty Angels / 1995 / NAP / S • Loving You Always / 1994 / IN / M • Mixed-Up Marriage / 1995 / CV / M • Molina / 1996 / KLP / M • More Than A Handful #5: California Or Bust / 1994 / MET / M • New Pussy Hunt #24 / 1996 / LEI / C • No Tell Motel / 1995 / CV / M • Pussyman Auditions #16 / 1995 / SNA / M • Say Anything / 1989 / 2CF / S • Sin Asylum / 1995 / CV / M • Skin Hunger / 1995 / MET / M • Strange Days / 1995 / FXV / S • Tits A Wonderful Life / 1994 / CV / M • Trained By Payne / 1994 / ONA / B • The Ultimate Fantasy / 1995 / CV / M • The Wicked Web / 1996 / WP / M

LISA ANN (1988)
Erotic Rendezvous / 1988 / VEX / M
LISA ANNE
HomeGrown Video #453: / 1995 / HOV / M
LISA BAKER *see* **Star Index I**
LISA BARONE *see* **Star Index I**
LISA BE *(Lisa Beth)*
Short haired brunette with a mannish body and medium droopy tits. Ugly face and sounds like a hooker.
Angel Buns / 1981 / QX / M • Babe / 1982 / AR / M • Centerfold Fever / 1981 / VXP / M • Classic Swedish Erotica #14 / 1986 / CA / C • The Cosmopolitan Girls / 1982 / VC / M • Debbie Does Dallas #2 / 1980 / VC / M • Deep Inside Annie Sprinkle / 1981 / VXP / M • The Erotic World Of Angel Cash / 1983 / VXP / M • French Kiss / 1979 / PVX / M • Liquid A$$ets / 1982 / CA / M • Loop Hole / cr80 / … / M • A Scent Of Heather / 1981 / VXP / M • Scoundrels / 1982 / COM / M • The Starmaker / 1982 / VC / M • Teach Me / 1984 / VD / M • That's Outrageous / 1983 / CA / M • Wanda Whips Wall Street / 1982 / VXP / M • The Widespread Scandals Of Lydia Lace / 1983 / CA / M • Wild Innocents / 1982 / VCX / M • Women In Love / 1980 / CA / M • Young, Wild And Wonderful / 1980 / VCX / M
LISA BELLA
Barbara Dare's Roman Holiday / 1987 / SE / M • Double Desires / 1988 / PIN / C • Double Play / 1993 / CA / C • Grand Prixxx / 1987 / CA / M • Lust Italian Style / 1987 / CA / M
LISA BERENGER
Girl With The Million $ Legs / 1987 / PL / M • Mimi / 1987 / CA / M • Private Film #22 / 1995 / OD / M
LISA BERNIE *see* **Star Index I**
LISA BETH *see* **Lisa Be**
LISA BLOSSOM
Love Doll Lucy #1 / 1994 / PL / F • Love Doll Lucy #2 / 1994 / PL / F • New York City Lesbian Gang Bang / 1995 / OUP / F •

Sapphire Unleashed / 1996 / OUP / B
LISA BOND *see* **Star Index I**
LISA BREEZE *see* **Crystal Breeze**
LISA BRIGHT *see* **Isabella Rovetti**
LISA BUNN *see* **Star Index I**
LISA CANARY *see* **Bella Donna**
LISA CARRINGTON *see* **Isabella Rovetti**
LISA CINTRICE *(Julie Shine, Derin Delight, Laurel Canton)*
Fairly tall golden blonde with not-too-pretty face, tattoo on right shoulder back, large tits, not a tight waist, a bit big on the butt.
Alley Cat / 1983 / VC / M • Aphrodesia's Diary / 1984 / CA / M • Debbie Does Dallas #2 / 1980 / VC / M • Mascara / 1982 / CA / M • Society Affairs / 1982 / CA / M • The Starmaker / 1982 / VC / M • That's Outrageous / 1983 / CA / M • Twilight Pink #2 / 1982 / VC / M • The Widespread Scandals Of Lydia Lace / 1983 / CA / M
LISA CLARKE
Bedtime Video #07 / 1984 / GO / M
LISA COLLERA
Resurrection Of Eve / 1973 / MIT / M
LISA COLLINS (CJL) *see* **C.J. Laing**
LISA COMSHAW
Almost Pregnant / 1991 / VII / S • Bob's Video #101: City Of Angels / 1996 / BOV / F • Bob's Video #104: Mood Pieces / 1996 / BOV / F • The Girls Of Mardi Gras / 1996 / P10 / S • Hot Body Video Magazine #09: Bikini Ski Trip / 1994 / CG / S • Housewife From Hell / 1994 / TRI / S • Laugh Factory / 1995 / PRE / C • Torturer's Apprentice / 1996 / LBO / B
LISA CONROY *see* **Star Index I**
LISA CROWN
Erotic Dimensions #7: Fulfilled / 1982 / NSV / M
LISA D'AMONA *see* **Tiffany Storm**
LISA D'AMONE *see* **Tiffany Storm**
LISA D. *see* **Tiffany Storm**
LISA DARLING
Creme De La Face #10: Cum Dome / 1995 / OD / M • The Devil In Grandma Jones / 1994 / FC / M • How To Make A Model #01 / 1992 / MET / M
LISA DE ANGELO *see* **Tiffany Storm**
LISA DE LEEUW *(Lil' Red Hood, Lisa DeLeeue, Lisa Leeua, Lisa Trego, Lisa Trigot, Lisa Woods)*
Incredibly ugly big titted female with the personality of Andrea Dworkin. Lisa Trego is from the soft core version of **Dixie Ray, Hollywood Star**. Supposedly married to porn actor Billy Thornberg. Comes from Moline, IL. Rumor (unconfirmed) has it that she died of AIDS.
1001 Erotic Nights #1 / 1982 / VC / M • 8 To 4 / 1981 / CA / M • 800 Fantasy Lane / 1979 / GO / M • All The Way In / 1984 / VC / M • Amanda By Night #1 / 1981 / CA / M • Anal Ultra Vixens / 197? / ALP / M • Aunt Peg Goes To Hollywood / 1982 / CA / M • Babylon Gold / 1983 / COM / C • Bad Girl / 1984 / LIM / M • Ball Game / 1980 / CA / M • Behind The Scenes Of An Adult Movie / 1983 / CV / M • Best Of Caught From Behind #2 / 1988 / HO / C • Best Of Richard Rank #1 / 1987 / GO / F • Best Of Talk Dirty To Me #01 / 1991 / DR / C • Beverly Hills Cox / 1986 / CA / M • Beverly Hills Exposed / 1985 / SE / M • Big Busty #05 / 198? / BTO / M • Big Mamas / 1981 / … / C • Black & White Affair / 1984 / VD / M • Blacks & Blondes #09 / 1986 / WV / M • The Blonde

Next Door / 1982 / GO / M • Blowoff / 1985 / CA / M • Blue Ribbon Blue / 1984 / CA / C • Blue Vanities #003 / 1987 / FFL / M • Blue Vanities #065 / 1988 / FFL / M • Blue Vanities #080 / 1988 / FFL / M • Blue Vanities #091 / 1988 / FFL / M • Blue Vanities #105 / 1988 / FFL / M • Blue Vanities #176 / 1992 / FFL / M • Blue Vanities #534 / 1993 / FFL / M • Blue Vanities #535 / 1993 / FFL / M • Blue Vanities #576 / 1995 / FFL / M • Bodies In Heat #1 / 1983 / CA / M • Bound And Punished / 1984 / BIZ / B • A Brief Affair / 1982 / CA / M • Caballero Preview Tape #2 / 1983 / CA / C • Caballero Preview Tape #3 / 1984 / CA / C • Caballero Preview Tape #4 / 1985 / CA / C • Carnal Encounters Of The Barest Kind / 1978 / VOY / C • Caught From Behind #07 / 1987 / HO / M • Centerspread Girls / 1982 / CA / M • Chocolate Cream / 1984 / SUP / M • Coed Fever / 1980 / CA / M • Collection #01 / 1982 / CA / M • Collection #02 / 1982 / CA / M • Collection #05 / 1984 / CA / M • Cupid's Arrow / 1984 / VCR / M • Diamond Collection #60 / 1984 / CDI / M • Diamond Collection #65 / 1984 / CDI / M • Diamond Collection #79 / 1986 / CDI / M • Dixie Ray Hollywood Star / 1983 / CA / M • Downstairs, Upstairs / 1980 / SE / M • Electric Blue: Cosmic Coeds / 1985 / CA / M • Erotic Dimensions: Bold Fantasies / 1982 / NSV / M • Erotic Fantasies: John Leslie / 1985 / CV / C • Every Which Way She Can / 1981 / CA / M • Fantasy Peeps: Untamed Desires / 1985 / 4P / M • Fantasy Peeps: Women In Love / 1985 / 4P / M • The Filthy Rich / 1981 / CA / M • Flaming Tongues #1 / 1984 / MET / F • Forbidden Worlds / 1988 / GO / C • Foxholes / 1983 / SE / M • Frat House / 1979 / NGV / M • Garage Girls / 1981 / CV / M • Ginger (1984-Vivid) / 1984 / VI / M • The Girl From S.E.X. / 1982 / CA / M • Girls On Girls / 1987 / SE / C • Girls That Love Girls / 1984 / CA / F • Glamour Girl #1 / 1984 / CDI / M • Glamour Girl #3 / 1984 / CDI / M • Glamour Girl #4 / 1984 / CDI / M • The Good, The Bad, And The D-Cup / 1991 / GO / C • Homecoming / 1981 / CA / M • I Dream Of Ginger / 1985 / VI / M • I Like To Watch / 1982 / CA / M • Inspiration / 1981 / CHX / M • Intimate Entry / 1988 / V99 / C • Joys Of Erotica / 1984 / VCR / M • Joys Of Erotica #107 / 1984 / VCR / C • Ladies In Love / 19?? / PLY / C • Ladies Nights / 1980 / VC / M • Legends Of Porn #1 / 1987 / CV / C • Limited Edition #07 / 1979 / AVC / M • Limited Edition #09 / 1980 / AVC / M • Limited Edition #10 / 1980 / AVC / M • Lips: The Passage To Pleasure / 1981 / CA / M • Luscious / 1980 / VXP / M • Lusty Ladies #12 / 1984 / 4P / M • Making Of A Star / 19?? / … / M • Mascara / 1982 / CA / M • Memphis Cathouse Blues / 1982 / CA / M • The Midnight Zone / 1986 / IN / M • Miss Passion / 1984 / VD / M • Moments Of Love / 1983 / MID / M • Mondo Topless #2 / 1966 / RMV / S • Mrs. Rodger's Neighborhood / 1988 / EVN / C • Nanci Blue / 1979 / SE / M • Never Enough / 1983 / SE / M • Night Magic / 1984 / SE / M • October Silk / 1980 / COM / M • Olympic Fever / 1979 / AR / M • On White Satin / 1980 / VCX / M • Only The Best Of Breasts / 1987 / CV / C • Only The Best Of Oral / 1989 / CV / C • The Other Side Of Lianna / 1984 / LA / M • The Oui Girls /

1981 / VHL / M • Passion Play / 1984 / WV / C • Penetration #1 / 1984 / AVC / M • Penetration #2 / 1984 / AVC / M • Personal Touch #3 / 1983 / AR / M • Physical #2 / 1985 / SUP / M • Pink Champagne / 1979 / CV / M • Plato's, The Movie / 1980 / SE / M • Pleasure #1 / 1985 / LA / M • Pleasure Productions #06 / 1984 / VCR / M • Pro Ball Cheerleaders / 1979 / AVC / M • Pussy Power #03 / 1992 / BTO / M • Raw Talent #1 / 1984 / VC / M • Rebecca's / 1983 / AVC / M • Rolls Royce #01 / 1980 / ... / C • Scandal In The Mansion / 1985 / CDI / M • Scared Stiff / 1984 / PV / M • The Seduction Of Cindy / 1980 / VC / M • The Seductress / 1982 / VC / M • Seka In Heat / 1988 / BMV / C • Sex Ed With Lil' Red / 1983 / TGA / M • Sex Loose / 1982 / VC / M • Sheer Haven / 1989 / DR / C • Skintight / 1981 / CA / M • Sorority Sweethearts / 1983 / CA / M • Splashing / 1986 / VCS / C • Springtime In The Rockies / 1984 / CIN / M • Squalor Motel / 1985 / SE / M • Steamy Dreams / cr70 / CVX / M • Stranger In Town / 1980 / FAN / M • Sulka's Daughter / 1984 / MET / G • Summer Of '72 / 1982 / CA / M • Swedish Erotica #20 / 1980 / CA / M • Swedish Erotica #25 / 1980 / CA / M • Swedish Erotica #28 / 1980 / CA / M • Swedish Erotica #29 / 1980 / CA / M • Swedish Erotica #31 / 1980 / CA / M • Swedish Erotica #32 / 1980 / CA / M • Swedish Erotica #33 / 1980 / CA / M • Swedish Erotica #36 / 1980 / CA / M • Swedish Erotica #38 / 1981 / CA / M • Swedish Erotica #39 / 1981 / CA / M • Swedish Erotica #41 / 1982 / CA / M • Swedish Erotica #42 / 1982 / CA / M • Swedish Erotica #43 / 1982 / CA / M • Swedish Erotica #44 / 1982 / CA / M • Swedish Erotica #45 / 1983 / CA / M • Swedish Erotica #46 / 1983 / CA / M • Swedish Erotica Hard #14: Outdoor Anal / Other Fantasies / 1992 / OD / C • Swedish Erotica Superstar #1: Seka / 1983 / CA / C • Swedish Erotica Superstar #3: Janey Robbins / 1984 / CA / C • Swinging Shift / 1985 / CDI / M • Tales Of Taija Rae / 1989 / DR / M • Talk Dirty To Me #03 / 1986 / DR / M • Taste Of The Best #3 / 1988 / PIN / C • Ten Little Maidens / 1985 / EXF / M • That's My Daughter / 1982 / NGV / M • The Titty Committee / 1986 / SE / C • Too Naughty To Say No / 1984 / CA / M • Touch Me In The Morning / 1982 / CA / M • Trashi / 1980 / CA / M • Triple Header / 1986 / SE / C • Ultraflesh / 1980 / GO / M • Up 'n' Coming / 1983 / CA / M • VCA Previews #4 / 1988 / VC / C • Watermelon Babes / 1984 / VCR / M • With Love, Lisa / 1985 / CA / C • With Love, Loni / 1985 / CA / C • [Can't Stop Coming / 1984 / ... / M • [Lisa's Girls / 1980 / ... / M • [Small Guage Shotgun / 19?? / PEY / M

LISA DEL RIO *see Star Index I*

LISA DELEEUE *see Lisa de Leeuw*

LISA DESIRE
All The Senator's Girls / 1977 / CA / M

LISA DONOVAN
A Girl's Affair #08 / 1995 / FD / F

LISA DORN
Big Titted Tarts / 1994 / PL / C

LISA ELAINE *see Star Index I*

LISA EVANS *see Star Index I*

LISA FIELDS
Bitches In Heat / 1994 / PL / C

LISA FIRESTONE *see Star Index I*

LISA FREDERICKS *see Star Index I*

LISA GABRIELLE
Double Agents / 1988 / VXP / M • Panting At The Opera / 1988 / VXP / M • Twisted Sisters / 1988 / ZA / M • Wrong Arm Of The Law / 1987 / ZA / M

LISA GEORGE *see Lisa Lake*

LISA GRANT *see Phaedra Grant*

LISA GREEN *see Lisa Sue Corey*

LISA HARPER *see Liza Rose Harper*

LISA HARRIS
Bedtime Video #07 / 1984 / GO / M

LISA HENDRICKS
Penetration #1 / 1984 / AVC / M

LISA HESS
Temptation: The Story Of A Lustful Bride / 1983 / NSV / M

LISA HOLLAND
Where The Bi's Are / 1994 / BIN / G

LISA JOVAN
Peek-A-Boo / 1987 / VEX / M

LISA K. LORING *(Adele Charts)*
Pretty with small tits, petite body and long black hair. Not the same as the girl who was married to Jerry Butler and appeared in **Laying Down The Law #1** (see Lisa Loring) but apparently a big fan of **The Addams Family** hence the confusion. The "K" stands for "Kamela". Was a dancer at the Mitchell Brothers' O'Farrell Theatre in SFO for seven years and as of 1991 was married to an sound technician and lives in Oakland.

Beyond Your Wildest Dreams / 1980 / CAT / M • Blondes Have More Fun / 1980 / SE / M • Chopstix / 1979 / TVX / M • Coed Fever / 1980 / CA / M • Daisy May / 1979 / VC / M • Fantasy World / 1979 / WWV / M • Female Athletes / 1977 / VXP / M • Garage Girls / 1981 / CV / M • Girlfriends / 1983 / MIT / M • Inside Desiree Cousteau / 1979 / VCX / M • One Way At A Time / 1979 / CA / M • Sadie / 1980 / EVI / M • Sissy's Hot Summer / 1979 / CA / M • Summer School / 1979 / VCX / M • Taboo #01 / 1980 / VCX / M • [Prisoner Of The Green Slime / cr80 / ... / S

LISA KING *see Star Index I*

LISA KINKAID
The Art Of Darkness / 1996 / ZFX / B • Beyond Driven #3 / 1996 / ZFX / B • Blunt Trauma #2 / 1996 / ZFX / B • Blunt Trauma #3: Whiteslave / 1996 / ZFX / B • Mincemeat Pie / 1996 / ZFX / B • Voodoo Dolls / 1996 / ZFX / B • War Pigs #1 / 1996 / ZFX / B • War Pigs #2 / 1996 / ZFX / B

LISA KITCHEN *see Star Index I*

LISA KOSS *see Star Index I*

LISA LA MORE *see Bella Donna*

LISA LACE *see Lisa Lake*

LISA LAKE *(Lisa George, Ashley St John, Lisa Laroo, Lisa Larue, Lisa Lace, Jean Cine, Cheri Roberts, Lissu Lake)*
Pretty blonde with Marilyn Monroe style hair, good tan lines, small tits, lithe body. She was a *Hustler* centerfold in November 1983.

The Best Of Blondes / 1986 / VCR / C • Breast Collection #01 / 1995 / LBO / C • Centerfold Celebrities #3 / 1983 / VC / M • Centerfold Screen Test #1 / 1986 / ACV / S • Classical Romance / 1984 / MAP / M • Daisy Chain / 1984 / IN / M • Diamond Collection #77 / 1986 / CDI / M • Educating Eva / 1984 / VC / M • Eroticise / 1982 / VES

/ S • Every Man's Fantasy / 1985 / IN / M • Every Woman Has A Fantasy #1 / 1984 / VC / M • Female Sensations / 1984 / VC / M • Flesh And Ecstasy / 1985 / VD / M • Going Both Ways / 1984 / LIP / G • Golden Girls #20 / 1984 / CA / M • Golden Girls #25 / 1984 / CA / M • Golden Girls #30 / 1985 / CA / M • GVC: Hot Numbers #133 / 1984 / GO / M • GVC: Party Stripper #130 / 1983 / GO / M • Holiday For Passion / 1988 / VCR / M • Hot Flashes / 1984 / VC / M • Hottest Parties / 1988 / VC / C • Hustler Video Magazine #2 / 1984 / SE / M • I Never Say No / 1983 / VC / M • Intimate Realities #2 / 1983 / VC / M • Island Of Love / 1983 / CV / M • Limited Edition #26 / 1984 / AVC / M • Lingerie / 1983 / CDI / M • Physical Attraction / 1984 / MAP / M • Raffles / 1988 / VC / M • The Red Hot Roadrunner / 1987 / VD / M • Sex Play / 1984 / SE / M • Stiff Competition #1 / 1984 / CA / M • Stripper Of The Year / 1991 / MP / S • Stud Hunters / 1984 / CA / M • Taboo #03 / 1983 / IN / M • Takin' It Off / 1984 / VES / S • Tongue 'n Cheek (Vca) / 1984 / VC / M • Undressed Rehearsal / 1984 / VD / M • Weekend Pass / 1984 / VES / S • The Wild Life / 1984 / MCA / S • Women's Secret Desires / 1983 / LIP / F

LISA LAMBORGHINI *see* **Tabitha Stevens**

LISA LAMONTE *see Star Index I*

LISA LAMORE *see Bella Donna*

LISA LANE
Fast Cars, Fast Women / 1979 / SE / M • Striptease / 1983 / VC / M

LISA LANG *see Sylvia Benedict*

LISA LAROO *see Lisa Lake*

LISA LARUE *see Lisa Lake*

LISA LATORE *see Mila Shegol*

LISA LAWRENCE
Transsexual Prostitutes #2 / 1997 / DFI / G

LISA LAZZARRO
Blue Vanities #537 / 1993 / FFL / M

LISA LEATHER *see Star Index I*

LISA LEE *see Lil Lee*

LISA LEEUA *see Lisa de Leeuw*

LISA LENNOX *(Lennox (Lisa))*
Not too pretty girl with long wavy (or curly) black hair (occasionally blonde), marginal face, womanly body, enhanced medium tits but not too rock solid, nose pin, belly button ring, tattoo on her right belly, pushy personality. She says she's from NY, is 24 years old (in 1995) and was de-virginized at age 11 or 12.

Anal Aristocrat / 1995 / KWP / M • Anal Chiropractor / 1995 / PEP / M • Anal Hellraiser #2 / 1995 / ROB / M • Ass Freaks #2 / 1995 / ROB / M • Ass Masters (Leisure) #03 / 1995 / LEI / M • Backdoor Diaries / 1995 / BBE / M • Bang City #5: Lennox's Anal Gang Bang / 1995 / SC / M • Best Butt(e) In The West #2 / 1995 / CC / M • Big Bust Babes #29 / 1995 / AFI / M • Bizarre Desires / 1995 / ROB / F • Black Knockers #05 / 1995 / TV / M • Booty Ho #3 / 1995 / ROB / M • Call Of The Wild / 1995 / AFI / M • Caught Looking / 1995 / CC / M • Debi Diamond's Dirty Dykes #2 / 1995 / FD / F • Dirty Little Secrets / 1995 / WAV / M • Double D Dykes #18 / 1995 / GO / F • Double D Dykes #21 / 1995 / GO / F • Double D Dykes #22 / 1995 / GO / F • Exotic Car Models #2 / 1996 / IN0 / F • For Your Mouth Only / 1995 / GO / M • Gangbusters / 1995

/ VC / M • A Girl Like You / 1995 / LE / M • Hard Core Beginners #10 / 1995 / LEI / M • Hollywood On Ice / 1995 / VT / M • Humpkin Pie / 1995 / HW / M • Jailhouse Nurses / 1995 / SC / M • Kittens & Vamps #2 / 1995 / ROB / F • Lesbian Debutante #02 / 1996 / IP / F • Lesbian Social Club / 1995 / ROB / F • The New Butt Hunt #19 / 1996 / LEI / C • New Pussy Hunt #18 / 1995 / LEI / C • Philmore Butts Meets The Freak / 1995 / SUF / M • Pussyman Auditions #08 / 1995 / SNA / M • Ready To Drop #11 / 1996 / FC / M • A Round Behind / 1995 / PEP / M • Rump Man: Forever / 1995 / HW / M • Sex Freaks / 1995 / EA / M • Snatch Masters #06 / 1995 / LEI / M • Snatch Masters #10 / 1995 / LEI / M • Striptease / 1995 / SPI / M • Tails From The Crack / 1995 / HW / M • Tight Fit #13 / 1995 / GO / M • Tinsel Town Tales / 1995 / NOT / M • Trading Partners / 1995 / GO / M • Tricky Business / 1995 / AFI / M • Video Virgins #22 / 1995 / NS / M

LISA LIPPS
Big Boob Ball / 1995 / IF / C • Big Boob Bikini Bash / 1995 / BTO / M • Big Busty #51 / 1994 / BTO / S • Boob-O-Rama #3 / 1995 / WNW / M • Booberella / 1992 / BTO / M • The Breast Of Breastmen / 1995 / EVN / C • Breastman Goes To Breastland #2 / 1993 / EVN / M • Busty Debutantes / 1996 / H&S / M • Busty Porno Queens / 1996 / H&S / M • Dickin' Around / 1994 / VEX / M • Dirty Bob's #17: Tampa Teasers! / 1994 / FLP / S • Double Load #2 / 1994 / HW / M • Freaks Of Leather #1 / 1993 / IF / M • Gazonga Goddess #1 / 1993 / IF / M • Gazongas #05 / 1993 / VEX / C • Girls Around The World #27 / 1995 / BTO / M • Hard To Hold / 1993 / IF / M • Housewife From Hell / 1994 / TRI / S • Humongous Hooters / 1993 / IF / M • Mellon Man #07 / 1996 / AVI / M • More Than A Woman / 1994 / H&S / M • On Location In The Bahamas / 1996 / H&S / S • On Location: Boob Cruise / 1996 / H&S / S • Playin' Hard To Get / 1994 / VEX / M • Pleasure Chest / 1993 / IF / M • Score Busty Covergirls #6 / 1995 / BTO / S • Tit To Tit #2 / 1994 / BTO / M • Tit To Tit #3 / 1995 / BTO / M • Titillator / 1994 / HW / C • Whoppers #3 / 1993 / VEX / F

LISA LISA
Tranny Claus / 1994 / HEA / G

LISA LORING
Main claim to fame was the part of Wednesday in the TV series **The Addams Family** and then a role in the TV soap **As The World Turns**. Born February 16, 1958 somewhere in the South Pacific. Married in succession Farrell Foumberg, Doug Stevenson, and then Jerry Butler but later got divorced from him. Has two daughters, Vanessa and Marianne. Not to be confused with Lisa K. Loring.
Blood Frenzy / 1987 / VES / S • Death Feud / 1989 / HHV / S • Iced / 1988 / PRS / S • Laying Down The Law #1 / 1992 / AFV / M

LISA LOVE *see Star Index I*

LISA LYONS
All About Annette / 1982 / SE / C • Hollywood Erotic Film Festival / 1987 / PAR / S

LISA MANNING
Triple Play (Vh) / cr75 / VC / M

LISA MARIE
Hot Body Hall Of Fame: Angela Dawn /

1995 / CG / F • Strangers / 1972 / SE / M

LISA MARIE (CRYS B) *see* **Crystal Breeze**

LISA MARIE ABATO *see* **Holly Ryder**

LISA MARIE STAGNO *see* **Crystal Breeze**

LISA MARKS
Her Total Response / 1975 / SVE / M • Honeymoon Haven / 1977 / QX / M • Jackpot / 1979 / VCX / M • Teenage Stepmother / cr74 / SVE / M • White Fire / 1980 / VC / M

LISA MELENDEZ *(Raquel (L.Melendez), Racquel (L.Melendez))*
Sister of Melissa Melendez.
American Dream Girls #1 / 1986 / VEX / M • Cab-O-Lay / 1988 / PL / M • Charmed Forces / 1987 / VI / M • Flesh In Ecstasy #06: Elle Rio / 1987 / GO / C • Flesh In Ecstasy #08: Traci Adams / 1987 / GO / C • Flying High With Rikki Lee / 1992 / VEX / C • Flying High With Tracey Adams / 1987 / VEX / M • Games Couples Play / 1987 / HO / M • Grafenberg Girls Go Fishing / 1987 / MIT / M • Parliament: Hanging Breasts #1 / 1986 / PM / F • Parliament: Lesbian Lovers #1 / 1986 / PM / F • Quicksilver / 1987 / CDI / M • Secret Loves / 1986 / CDI / M • Sexperiences / 1987 / VEX / M • Swedish Erotica #69 / 1985 / CA / M • Sweet Nothings / 1987 / HO / M • Tailspin / 1987 / AVC / M • Talk Dirty To Me #04 / 1986 / DR / M • Warm Bodies, Hot Nights / 1988 / PV / M • Wet Workout / 1987 / VEX / M

LISA MILLER
Voluptuous #4 / 199? / H&S / M

LISA MONROE
Captured On Camera / 1997 / BON / B

LISA MONTEL *see* **Star Index I**

LISA MOORE
Harrad Summer / 1974 / WIZ / S • The Pick Up / 1993 / MID / M

LISA MORE *(Lisa Moreau, Liza Morceau, Liza Moore)*
Gangly blonde with frizzy hair and a nose like (worse than?) Barbara Streisand. Also has projecting teeth. Not too pretty. Medium tits.
Bad Girls #1 / 1981 / GO / M • Beverly Hills Seduction / 1988 / WV / M • Caught In The Act / 1978 / MAP / M • Fantasy / 1978 / VCX / M • Ms. Magnificent / 1979 / SE / M

LISA MOREAU *see* **Lisa More**

LISA NUYGEN *see* **Star Index I**

LISA PENNY *see* **Star Index I**

LISA PERRY
Deep Dreams / 1990 / IN / M • It Happened At Midnight / 1990 / IN / M • Queens In Danger / 1990 / STA / G

LISA PHILLIPS
Big Busty #31 / 1989 / BTO / S • Big Busty #37 / 198? / H&S / S • Girls Around The World #06 / 1992 / BTO / M • H&S: Lisa Phillips / 199? / H&S / S • Studio Bust Out / 1994 / BTO / M

LISA PICOTTE *see* **Lisa Ann**

LISA PINSON *see* **Star Index I**

LISA PLUSH
Red Riding She Male / 1995 / PL / G

LISA POPE
Buttsizer, King Of Rears #1 / 1992 / EVN / M

LISA RISTINA
Bare Bottom Treatment / 1993 / RB / B • Dominating Girlfriends #2 / 1992 / PL / B •

Kym Wilde's On The Edge #07 / 1994 / RB / B • More On The Job Training / 1994 / RB / B • Openhanded Girlfriends / 1992 / RB / B • Pretty Cheeks / 1994 / RB / B • Roommate Humiliation / 1993 / PL / B

LISA ROCHE *see* **Star Index I**

LISA RUBIO
Blue Vanities #191 / 1993 / FFL / M

LISA RUE *see* **Star Index I**

LISA RUSH *see* **Laurie Blue**

LISA SANDERS *see* **Alice Noland**

LISA SAVAGE
Charming Cheapies #4: Duelling Dildos / 1985 / 4P / F

LISA SHINE *see* **Star Index I**

LISA SHORE *see* **Star Index I**

LISA SMITH *see* **Star Index I**

LISA SOSERIOUS
Made In The Hood / 1995 / HBE / M

LISA SUE COREY *(Melissa Jennings, Lisa Green)*
Pretty with light brown or dark blonde hair, small tits, very white body.
The Best Of Gail Palmer / 1981 / WWV / C • Blazing Zippers / 1974 / SE / M • Boiling Point / 1978 / SE / M • A Formal Faucett / 1978 / VC / M • Hot Legs / 1979 / VCX / M • Saturday Matinee Series #1 / 1996 / VCX / C • Telefantasy / 1978 / AR / M

LISA TERE
Salsa & Spice #5 / 1997 / TTV / M

LISA THOMAS
Enemates #06 / 1992 / BIZ / B • Kneel Before Me! / 1983 / ALP / B • Up Up And Away / 1984 / CA / M

LISA TODD
Taboo #07 / 1980 / IN / M

LISA TREGO *see* **Lisa de Leeuw**

LISA TRIGOT *see* **Lisa de Leeuw**

LISA TROY *see* **Star Index I**

LISA VANNILAN
Golden Girls, The Movie / 1984 / SE / M

LISA WALLER
Little Girls Blue #2 / 1983 / VCX / M

LISA WARD
Buttman's British Moderately Big Tit Adventure / 1994 / EA / M

LISA WARNER
African Angels #1 / 1996 / NIT / M

LISA WATANABI
Triple Sex Play / 1985 / ORC / M

LISA WICKED
Fresh Faces #08 / 1995 / EVN / M

LISA WILSON
Amateur Lesbians #02: Dominique / 1991 / GO / F • Amateur Lesbians #03: April / 1991 / GO / F • B.K. #4: Lesbian Clean Up / 1991 / BKD / F • Dirty Bob's #01: Xcellent Adventure / 1991 / FLP / S • Every Man Should Have One / 1991 / VEX / M • First Time Bi-Ers #1 / 1991 / AWV / G • First Time Bi-Ers #2 / 1991 / AWV / G • Glamour Girl / 1991 / VEX / M • Hot Savannah Nights / 1991 / VEX / M • Lady & The Champ / 1991 / AFV / M • Leading Lady / 1991 / V99 / M • Leg...Ends #04 / 1991 / PRE / F • Leg...Ends #05 / 1991 / PRE / F • Mike Hott: #167 Holly Ryder And Lisa Wilson #1 / 1991 / MHV / F • Mike Hott: #168 Holly Ryder And Lisa Wilson #2 / 1991 / MHV / F • Mike Hott: #176 Terry And Lisa / 1990 / MHV / M • Mike Hott: Cum Cocktails #1 / 1995 / MHV / C • Mr. Peepers Amateur Home Videos #08: Heavy Load / 1991 / LBO / M • Next Door Neighbors #29 / 1990 / BON / M • P.S.: Back Alley Cats #02 /

1992 / PSP / F • P.S.: Back Alley Cats #04 / 1992 / PSP / F • The Perfect Pet / 1991 / VEX / C • Positively Pagan #02 / 1991 / ATA / M • Positively Pagan #03 / 1991 / ATA / M • Positively Pagan #04 / 1991 / ATA / M • Pump It Up / 1990 / LV / M • Redliners / 1980 / VXP / M • Sneek Peeks #1 / 1993 / FL / M • Sole Food / 1992 / PRE / B • Student Fetish Videos: Foot Worship #03 / 1991 / PRE / B • Sweet Cheeks (1991-Prestige) / 1991 / PRE / B • Taste For Submission / 1991 / LON / C • Things That Go Hump in the Night / 1991 / LV / M • The Ultimate Pleasure / 1991 / MET / G

LISA WINDSOR *see Star Index I*
LISA WOODS *see Lisa de Leeuw*
LISA YOUNG *see Jenny Lane*
LISBET SIMMS *see Star Index I*
LISBETH OLSEN
Bel Ami / 1976 / VXP / M • The Blue Balloon / cr72 / VHL / M • The Sinful Dwarf / 1972 / BPI / S • [Justine Och Juliette / 1975 / ... / S

LISIA
More Dirty Debutantes #44 / 1995 / 4P / M • More Dirty Debutantes #45 / 1995 / 4P / M

LISSA ANDERS *see Star Index I*
LISSI FOX *see Kari Fox*
LISSU LAKE *see Lisa Lake*
LITA
Bright Tails #1 / 1993 / STP / B • Harlem Honies #1 / 1993 / CC / M • New Faces, Hot Bodies #11 / 1993 / STP / M • Tied & Tickled #23: Tickling Dick / 1994 / CS / B • Toy Time #2: Nasty Solos / 1994 / STP / F
LITA DODGE *see Sunny Ray*
LITA WU *see Star Index I*
LITTL' SWEET HEART
Itsy Bitsy Gang Bang / 1996 / HW / M • Somewhere Under The Rainbow #2 / 1995 / HW / M
LITTLE ANTHONY
Toe Tales #13 / 1994 / GOT / B
LITTLE CINDERELLA *see Little Sinderella*
LITTLE DEBBIE *see Star Index I*
LITTLE DOVE *see Janette Littledove*
LITTLE J.
Done In The Desert Sun / 1995 / OUP / M
LITTLE JENNY JONES *see Jenny Jones*
LITTLE JOE
The Voyeur #7: Live In Europe #1 / 1996 / JLP / M
LITTLE LOUIE *see Short Stud*
LITTLE MICHAEL
Cruel Lessons / 1996 / GOT / B • No Respect / 1995 / GOT / B
LITTLE ORAL ANNIE *(Judi (Little Oral A), Annie Owen, Annie Owens)*
Not too pretty brunette with large droopy tits and a womanly body. In 1980 was 5'6" tall, 125lbs, 40D-24-34 and supposedly 22 years old.
69 Park Avenue / 1985 / ELH / M • Aunt Peg Goes To Hollywood / 1982 / CA / M • Battle Of The Stars #3: Stud Wars / 1985 / NSV / M • The Best Of Anal Annie: The Girl-Girl Adventures / 1993 / LIP / C • The Best Of Big Busty / 1986 / L&W / C • The Best Of The Big Boob Battles / 1993 / CDP / C • Beyond Desire / 1986 / VC / M • Big Busty #03 / 1985 / CPL / S • Bondage Classix #09: Andrea's Fault / 1987 / BON / B • Bondage Memories #02 / 1993 / BON / C • Caballero Preview Tape #2 / 1983 / CA / C

• Caballero Preview Tape #3 / 1984 / CA / C • Classic Erotica #2 / 1980 / SVE / M • Debbie Class Of '88 / 1987 / CC / M • Debbie Goes To College / 1986 / ELH / M • Deep Inside Little Oral Annie / 19?? / VXP / C • Dirty 30's Cinema: Oral Annie / 1986 / PV / C • Dirty Looks / 1982 / VC / C • F / 1980 / GO / M • Forbidden Worlds / 1988 / GO / C • French Lessons / 1985 / VD / M • Girls Of Paradise #1 / 1986 / PV / C • Girls That Love Girls / 1984 / CA / F • GVC: Danielle's Girlfriends #116 / cr83 / GO / F • GVC: Women's Fantasies #108 / 1983 / GO / F • Hard To Swallow / 1985 / PV / M • I Like To Watch / 1982 / CA / M • Inside Little Oral Annie / 1984 / VXP / M • Judi's B&D Slave School / 1980 / BON / B • Kinky Potpourri #29 / 199? / SVE / C • Legacy Of Lust / 1985 / CA / M • Little Oral Annie Takes Manhattan / 1985 / VXP / M • Lusty Ladies #02 / 1983 / 4P / M • Nasty Nights / 1988 / PL / C • New York Vice / 1984 / CC / M • Once Upon A Madonna / 1985 / PV / M • Passion Pit / 1985 / SE / M • Real Breasts Real Torment / 1995 / BON / C • Rear Action Girls #2 / 1985 / LIP / F • School Dayze / 1987 / BON / B • Screwdriver / 1988 / CC / C • Sex Boat / 1980 / VCX / M • Sinderotica / 1985 / HO / M • Spanking Scenes #01 / 1983 / TAO / C • Splashing / 1986 / VCS / C • Succulent / 1983 / VXP / M • Swedish Erotica #39 / 1981 / CA / M • Swedish Erotica #41 / 1982 / CA / M • Swedish Erotica #42 / 1982 / CA / M • Swedish Erotica #53 / 1984 / CA / M • Swedish Erotica #62 / 1984 / CA / M • Swedish Erotica Superstar #3: Janey Robbins / 1984 / CA / C • Sweet Summer / 1986 / AMO / M • Tales From The Chateau / 1987 / BON / B • Tickling Scenes / 1991 / TAO / C • The Ultimate Thrill / 1988 / PIN / C • Ultraflesh / 1980 / GO / M • The Wacky World Of X-Rated Bloopers / 1989 / GO / M • Whatever Turns You On / 1987 / CA / M • White Women / 1986 / CC / M
LITTLE RED
Erotic Dimensions: Bold Fantasies / 1982 / NSV / M
LITTLE SINDERELLA *(Little Cinderella, Lil' Sinderella)*
Blonde, ugly, very petite, 19 years old, 4'11" and 84lbs in 1996, small tits, Caesarian scar, emaciated. Supposedly a dancer from Texas.
Anal Sex Freaks / 1996 / ZA / M • Anal Virgins #02 / 1996 / NS / M • Casting Call #17 / 1996 / SO / M • Casting Call #18 / 1996 / SO / M • Caught From Behind #22 / 1995 / HO / M • Cherry Poppers #15: Mischievous Maidens / 1996 / ZA / M • Deceit / 1996 / ZA / M • Dukes Of Anal / 1996 / VC / M • Eighteen #1 / 1996 / SC / M • Hillbilly Honeys / 1996 / WP / M • Indecent Exposures / 1996 / MID / M • Lollipop Shoppe #1 / 1996 / SC / M • Max #09: Where Danger Lurks / 1996 / XPR / M • Max #11: Tunnel Of Lust / 1996 / LE / M • Million Dollar Buns / 1996 / MYS / M • More Dirty Debutantes #56 / 1996 / 4P / M • New Pussy Hunt #26 / 1996 / LEI / C • Nineteen #7 / 1996 / FOR / M • Nineteen #8 / 1997 / FOR / M • Nothing Like Nurse Nookie #3 / 1996 / NIT / M • Passion / 1996 / SC / M • Pussyman Auditions #18 / 1996 / SNA / M • Shooting Gallery / 1996 / EL / M • Sinboy #2: Yo' Ass Is Mine / 1996 / SC / M • Slippery Slopes /

1995 / ME / M • Sluts, Butts And Pussy / 1996 / DFI / M • Solo Adventures / 1996 / AB / F • Sorority Sex Kittens #3 / 1996 / VC / M • Strip Show / 1996 / CA / M • Underground #1 / 1996 / SC / M • Underground #2: Subway To Sodom / 1996 / SC / M • Underground #3: Sit On This / 1996 / SC / M • Up And Cummers #29 / 1996 / ERW / M • Video Virgins #29 / 1996 / NS / M • War Whores / 1996 / EL / M • Whiplash / 1996 / DFI / M • Wild & Wicked #7 / 1996 / VT / M
LITTLE SWEET HEART
Somewhere Under The Rainbow #1 / 1995 / HW / M
LITTLE VELVET SUMMER *see Velvet Summers*
LIZ
HomeGrown Video #472: Everyday People / 1996 / HOV / M • Joe Elliot's College Girls #27 / 1994 / JOE / M • Limited Edition #25 / 1984 / AVC / M • Plumpers Of Sundance Spa / 1993 / BTO / M • Pregnant Mamas / 1984 / CPL / M • Shaved #01 / 1991 / RB / F • Spanked Senseless / 1995 / BIZ / B
LIZ ALEXANDER *(Stormi)*
Black girl with droopy boobs.
Black Voodoo / 1987 / FOV / M • Carnal College / 1987 / VT / M • Endless Nights / 1988 / CDI / M • Girls Just Wanna Have Girls #2 / 1990 / HIO / F • Lesbian Fantasies / 1990 / BIZ / F • A Little Dove-Tale / 1987 / IN / M • No Man's Land #01 / 1988 / VT / C • Raw Talent #3 / 1988 / VC / M • The Return Of Indiana Joan / 1989 / PL / M • Stormi / 1988 / LV / M • Toothless People / 1988 / SUV / M • Video Tramp #2 / 1988 / TME / M
LIZ ANNE *see Star Index I*
LIZ DINIRO
More Dirty Debutantes #46 / 1995 / 4P / M
LIZ GOLDEN *see Avalone*
LIZ LEATHER *see Star Index I*
LIZ LEE JUNG
Carnal Carnival / cr78 / VCX / M
LIZ MURPHY *see Star Index I*
LIZ ORIANNA *see Star Index I*
LIZ RAKEY
Venture Into The Bizarre / cr78 / VHL / M
LIZ RANDALL *(Maggie Randall)*
Another Kind Of Love / 1985 / CV / M • Backdoor To Hollywood #01 / 1986 / CDI / M • Busty Wrestling Babes / 1986 / VD / M • City Of Sin / 1971 / CLX / M • Daddy's Darling Daughters / 1986 / PL / M • Deep Inside Vanessa Del Rio / 1986 / VC / M • Devil In Miss Jones #4: The Final Outrage / 1987 / VC / M • Dollface / 1987 / CV / M • Double Penetration #3 / 1986 / WV / C • Dressed To Thrill / 1986 / CDI / M • Ex-Connection / 1986 / SEV / M • House Of Blue Dreams / 1985 / WV / M • In Search Of The Golden Bone / 1986 / CA / M • Monkey Business / 1987 / SEV / M • Rated Sex / 1986 / SE / M • Return To Sex 5th Avenue / 1985 / WV / M • Sacrificed To Love / 1986 / CDI / M • Shaved Pink / 1986 / WET / M • Showgirls / 1985 / SE / M • Top Buns / 1986 / HO / M • Winner Take All / 1986 / SEV / M • Yiddish Erotica #1 / 1986 / SE / C
LIZ RENAY
Big titted blonde stripper born in 1927 who was mixed up with the mob. She performed frequently with her daughter.
Blackenstein / 1973 / MED / S • A Date With Death / 1959 / ... / S • Day Of The

Nightmare / 1965 / SOW / S • Deep Roots / 1980 / XTR / M • Desperate Living / 1977 / NLH / S • The Divorcee / 1969 / PS / S • Frank Henenlotter's XXX Hardcore Horrors: Mad Love... / 1996 / SOW / M • The Hard Road / 1970 / SOW / S • Interlude Of Lust / 1981 / CA / M • Lady Godiva Rides / 1968 / VDM / S • Las Vegas Girls / 1983 / HIF / M • The Mad Love Of The Red Hot Vampire / 1971 / SOW / M • Refinements In Love / 19?? / HIF / M • Saturday Night Sleazies #2 / 1995 / RHI / C • The Thrill Killers / 1965 / CAM / S • Tonight I Love You / 19?? / HIF / M • The Virgin Cowboy / 1975 / ALP / S • [Body Fever / 1969 / ... / S • [Eat The Scabs Of Dracula / 19?? / ACV / M

LIZ STANLEY *see Star Index I*

LIZ STREET
Private Film #23 / 1995 / OD / M

LIZ THOMAS
Bedtime Video #05 / 1984 / GO / M

LIZ TORRES *see Star Index I*

LIZ TURNER *see Tawni Lee*

LIZ WILSON *see Star Index I*

LIZA
The All-Conference Nude Workout / 1995 / NIV / S • Homegrown Video #432: Beach Blanket Bang-O / 1994 / HOV / M • Home-Grown Video #435: Seasoned To Perfection / 1994 / HOV / M • HomeGrown Video #461: Splendor In The Grasp / 1995 / HOV / M • Homegrown Video #464: Liza, We Love You / 1995 / HOV / M • HomeGrown Video #473: Furpie Feast #3 / 1997 / HOV / C • The New Snatch Masters #14 / 1995 / LEI / C • On White Satin / 1980 / VCX / M • Screwples / 1979 / CA / M

LIZA (BRAZILIAN)
Asses Galore #7: Lunatic Fringe / 1996 / DFI / M

LIZA ADAMS *see Lysa Thatcher*

LIZA ANNE
California Blondes #02 / 1987 / VEX / M • Ebony Humpers #3 / 1987 / VEX / M • Naughty Neighbors / 1986 / VEX / M • Princess Of Darkness / 1987 / VEX / M

LIZA BERTINI
Prisoners Of Love / 19?? / BL / M

LIZA CRUZ *see Star Index I*

LIZA DURAN *see Jennifer Welles*

LIZA DWYER
California Gigolo / 1979 / WWV / M • Classic Erotica #6 / 1985 / SVE / M • Classic Erotica #9 / 1996 / SVE / M • Pretty Peaches #1 / 1978 / MIT / M • Rockin' With Seka / 1980 / WV / M • Swedish Erotica #06 / 1980 / CA / M • Tangerine / 1979 / CXV / M

LIZA KITCHEN
She-Male Encounters #09: She-Male Confidential / 1984 / MET / G

LIZA LINELLI *see Star Index I*

LIZA MOORE *see Lisa More*

LIZA MORCEAU *see Lisa More*

LIZA ROSE *see Liza Rose Harper*

LIZA ROSE HARPER *(Lisa Harper, Liza Rose, Leeza Harper)*
French despite the name, black hair, dark freckles, medium ttits, tight waist, narrow hips, good tan lines, nice smile, tattoo on her right hip/butt.
$ex 4 Fun & Profit / 1996 / SPR / M • Anal Cannibals / 1996 / ZA / M • Anal Institution #1 / 1996 / ZA / M • Anal Therapy #4 / 1996 / FD / M • Beyond Reality #1 / 1995 / EXQ

/ M • Beyond Reality #3: Stand Erect! / 1996 / EXQ / M • Black & Booty-Full / 1996 / ROB / M • Brunette Roulette / 1996 / LE / M • Buffy Malibu's Nasty Girls #09 / 1995 / ANA / F • Casting Call #15 / 1995 / SO / M • Caught From Behind #22 / 1995 / HO / M • Caught From Behind #23 / 1995 / HO / M • Caught From Behind #24 / 1996 / HO / M • Double Anal Alternatives / 1996 / EL / M • Double Cross (Wicked) / 1995 / WP / M • DPTV: Double Penetration Television / 1996 / SUF / M • Eighteen #2 / 1996 / SC / M • Erotic Newcummers Vol 1 #5 / 1996 / DR / M • Euro-Max #4: / 1995 / SC / M • The Fanny Farm / 1996 / NIT / M • Fashion Sluts #4 / 1995 / ABS / M • Flesh / 1996 / EA / M • Foreign Asses / 1996 / MP0 / M • Foreign Fucks / 1995 / FOR / M • Fresh Meat (John Leslie) #2 / 1995 / EA / M • The Hitch-Hiker #16: Dirty Low Down / 1996 / VIM / M • Hollywood Hillbillies / 1996 / LE / M • House Of Anal / 1995 / NOT / M • Illicit Affairs / 1996 / XC / M • Interview: Doin' The Butt / 1995 / LV / M • Ladies In Leather / 1995 / GO / M • Lesbian Pooper Sluts / 1996 / ROB / F • Lisa / 1997 / SC / M • Live Sex Net / 1996 / SPR / M • Malibu Butt Sluts / 1996 / ROB / F • Mike Hott: #316 Cunt Of The Month: Liza Harper / 1995 / MHV / M • Mike Hott: #323 Three-Sum Sluts #07 / 1995 / MHV / M • Mike Hott: #324 Cum In My Cunt #06 / 1995 / MHV / C • Mike Hott: #326 Cum In My Mouth #03 / 1995 / MHV / C • Miss Anal #1 / 1995 / C69 / M • The Most Dangerous Game / 1996 / HO / M • Mystique / 1996 / SC / M • Nasty Nymphos #11 / 1995 / ANA / M • New Pussy Hunt #24 / 1996 / LEI / C • Nookie Ranch / 1996 / NIT / M • Party Club / 1996 / C69 / M • Perverted Stories #07 / 1996 / JMP / M • Pick Up Lines #09 / 1996 / OD / M • Pick Up Lines #11 / 1997 / OD / M • Pretty Anal Ladies / 1996 / ANE / M • Private Film #23 / 1995 / OD / M • Private Stories #01 / 1995 / OD / M • Pure / 1996 / WP / M • Pure Anal / 1996 / MET / M • Rebecca Lord's World Tour #1: French Edition / 1995 / WP / M • Rumpman's Backdoor Sailing / 1996 / HW / M • Sam Gets Shafted / 1996 / MP0 / M • Sexhibition #1 / 1996 / SUF / M • The Streets Of Paris / 1996 / SC / M • Surfin' The Net / 1996 / RAS / M • Takin' It To The Limit #7: Debauched / 1996 / BS / M • Triple X Video Magazine #01 / 1995 / OD / M • Valentino's Euro-Invasion / 1997 / SC / M • Where The Girls Sweat...Not The Sequel / 1996 / EL / F • Young And Anal #1 / 1995 / JMP / M

LIZA TURNER
Big Babies In Budapest / 1996 / EL / M

LIZA WIGAN
Schoolgirl Fannies On Fire / 1994 / BIZ / B

LIZZIE
Raw Talent: Bang 'er 26 Times / 1992 / RTP / M

LLOYD ALLEN
Flash / 1980 / CA / M • Gunblast / 1974 / ... / S • Hollywood Babylon / 1972 / AIR / S

LLUVIA *see Star Index I*

LO WOK KONG
Wild Cherry / 1983 / ORC / M

LOCITA
Lesbian Lust Bust / 1995 / GLI / F

LOCKEBDE TITTEN
Take Me #8: For The Night / 1995 / VIO / M

LOGAN REED

Lost In Vegas / 1996 / AWV / G

LOIC
The French Canal / 1995 / DVP / G

LOIS
Blue Vanities #500 / 1992 / FFL / M

LOIS ALLEY
Creme De La Face #03 / 1994 / OD / M • Fantasy Flings #03 / 1995 / WP / M

LOIS ANGEL
Absolute Anal / 1996 / XC / M

LOIS AYER *see Lois Ayers*

LOIS AYERS *(Sondra Stillman, Lonnie Harris, Lois Ayer)*
Tall blonde with small/medium tits, not too pretty, started with a weird punk hairstyle. Occasionally a brunette. Lonnie Harris is from **What's My Punishment**.
Adult Video News Magazine / 1985 / ZEB / M • Aerobics Girls Club / 1986 / 4P / F • Anal Angels #1 / 1986 / VEX / M • Ariana's Dirty Dancers: The Professionals / 1996 / 4P / M • Babewatch #1 / 1993 / CC / M • Baby Face #2 / 1987 / VC / M • Bad Habits / 1990 / WV / M • Ball Busters / 1984 / CV / M • The Best Little Whorehouse In San Francisco / 1984 / LA / M • The Best Of Both Worlds #1 / 1986 / LA / G • Beyond The Senses / 1986 / AVC / M • Bi Bi Love / 1986 / LAV / G • Bi-Ceps / 1986 / LA / C • Bi-Ology: The Making Of Mr Right / 1992 / CAT / G • The Black Chill / 1986 / WET / M • Black On White / 1987 / PL / C • Black Trisexual Encounters #2 / 1985 / LA / G • Black Trisexual Encounters #4 / 1986 / LA / G • Blacks & Blondes #18 / 1986 / WV / M • Blame It On Ginger / 1986 / VI / M • Blazing Matresses / 1986 / AVC / M • Bodies By Jackie / 1985 / IVP / M • Bootsie / 1984 / CC / M • Bound And Punished / 1984 / BIZ / B • Bruce Seven: A Compendium Of His Most Graphic Scenes Vol 1 / 1991 / BS / C • Bruise Control / 1993 / PRE / B • The Butt Sisters Do The Twin Cities / 1996 / MID / M • Buttslammers #07: Indecent Decadence / 1994 / BS / F • Buttslammers #08: The Ultimate Invasion / 1994 / BS / C • Cherry Tricks / 1985 / VPE / M • Chicks In Black Leather / 1989 / VC / C • The Color Black / 1986 / WET / M • Coming Of Fortune / 1994 / EX / M • Controlled / 1990 / BS / B • Cummin' Alive / 1984 / VC / M • Dancing Angels / 1989 / PL / M • Dear Fanny / 1984 / CV / M • Debbie Class Of '88 / 1987 / CC / M • Debbie Goes To College / 1986 / ELH / M • Deep Inside Vanessa Del Rio / 1986 / VC / M • Devil In Miss Dare / 1986 / AVC / C • Devil In Miss Jones #3: A New Beginning / 1986 / VC / M • Devil In Miss Jones #4: The Final Outrage / 1987 / VC / M • The Dinner Party / 1986 / WV / M • Double Heat / 1986 / LA / M • Down Bi Law / 1992 / CAT / G • Dr Penetration / 1986 / WET / M • Dr Strange Sex / 1985 / CA / M • Ebony Humpers #1 / 1986 / VEX / M • Ejacula #1 / 1992 / VC / M • Ejacula #2 / 1992 / VC / M • Electric Blue: Nurse Fever / 1985 / CA / M • Erotica / 1992 / CC / M • Every Woman Has A Fantasy #2 / 1986 / VC / M • The Exhibitionist / 1991 / VD / M • Fantasy Mansion / 1983 / BIZ / B • Fever Pitch / 1995 / ONA / M • The Finer Things In Life / 1990 / PL / F • The Fire Inside / 1988 / VC / C • Firecrackers / 1994 / HW / M • Flaming Tongues #1 / 1984 / MET / F • Forbidden Fruit #1 / 1987 / MET / G • Forbidden Fruit #2 / 1987 / MET / G • Friends &

Lovers #2 / 1991 / VT / M • Ginger And Spice / 1986 / VI / M • Ginger's Hawaiian Scrapbook / 1988 / GO / C • Girls Of The Chorus Line / 1986 / CLV / M • Go For It / 1984 / VC / M • The Good, The Bad, And The Horny / 1985 / VCX / M • Hard Ride / 1986 / VT / M • Harlem Candy / 1987 / WET / M • Heartthrobs / 1985 / CA / M • The Hindlick Maneuver / 1991 / CC / M • Honeymooned / 1992 / PRE / B • Hot And Nasty! / 1986 / V99 / C • Hottest Parties / 1988 / VC / C • Hung Jury / 1989 / VWA / M • Hyperkink / 1989 / VWA / M • I Am Curious Black / 1986 / WET / M • In Search Of The Perfect 10 / 1987 / MAE / S • In Too Deep / 1992 / AFD / M • Irresistible #2 / 1986 / SE / M • It's Incredible / 1985 / SE / M • The Journey: Oral Majority / 1991 / WV / M • Kinky Business #1 / 1984 / DR / M • Kiss Of The Dragon Lady / 1986 / SEV / M • The Kitty Kat Club / 1990 / PL / F • L.A. Stories / 1990 / VI / M • Lace / 1989 / VT / F • Ladies Lovin' Ladies #3 / 1993 / AFV / F • Le Sex De Femme #3 / 1989 / AFI / C • Leather / 1989 / VT / F • Leather And Lace / 1989 / VT / F • Legends Of Porn #2 / 1989 / CV / C • Legs / 1986 / AMB / M • Lesbian Liasons / 1990 / SO / F • Let Me Tell Ya 'Bout White Chicks / 1985 / VC / M • Let's Get Naked / 1987 / VEX / M • A Little Bit Of Hanky Panky / 1984 / GO / M • Little Miss Curious / 1991 / CA / M • The Load Warriors #1 / 1987 / VD / M • Looking For Mr Goodsex / 1984 / CC / M • Lorelei / 1984 / CV / M • Love On The Line / 1990 / SO / M • Loving Lips / 1987 / AMB / C • Lustfully Seeking Susan / 1985 / PLY / M • Mammary Lane / 1988 / VT / C • Mardi Gras / 1986 / SE / M • Mardi Gras Passions / 1987 / MET / M • Merry X Miss / 1986 / VIP / M • Midnight Pink / 1987 / WV / M • Money, Money, Money / 1993 / FD / M • Mrs. Rodger's Neighborhood / 1988 / EVN / C • Nasty Habits Are Hard To Break / 1986 / 4P / M • The National Transsexual / 1990 / GO / G • Night Creatures / 1992 / PL / M • Night Deposit / 1991 / VC / M • Nightshift Nurses #1 / 1988 / VC / M • Nightshift Nurses #2 / 1996 / VC / M • No Man's Land #01 / 1988 / VT / C • Only The Best Of Anal / 1992 / MET / C • Only The Best Of Women With Women / 1988 / CV / C • Only The Very Best On Video / 1992 / VC / C • Panty Raid / 1984 / GO / M • Parliament: Blonde Dominas #1 / 1988 / PM / F • Parliament: Dildo Babes #2 / 1988 / PM / F • Parliament: Finger Friggin' #2 / 1988 / PM / F • Parliament: Hard TV #1 / 1988 / PM / G • Parliament: Samantha Strong #1 / 1986 / PM / M • Parliament: Three Way Lust / 1988 / PM / M • Peggy Sue / 1987 / VT / M • Phone Sex Girls #1 / 1987 / VT / M • The Pink Lagoon: A Sex Romp In Paradise / 1984 / GO / M • Poor Little Rich Girl #1 / 1992 / XCI / M • Poor Little Rich Girl #2 / 1992 / XCI / M • A Portrait Of Christy / 1990 / VI / M • Prince Of Beverly Hills #1 / 1987 / VEX / M • Princess Charming / 1987 / AVC / C • Provocative Pleasures / 1988 / VC / C • Pumping Flesh / 1985 / CA / M • Pumping Irene #1 / 1986 / FAN / M • Pumping Irene #2 / 1986 / FAN / M • Raging Waters / 1992 / PRE / B • Rainwoman #04 / 1990 / CC / M • Rambone The Destroyer / 1985 / WET / M • The Riding Mistress / 1983 / BIZ / B • Samantha, I Love You / 1988 / WV / C •

Screw / 1985 / CV / M • Screwdriver / 1988 / CC / C • Secret Recipe / 1990 / PL / F • Sexplorations / 1991 / VC / C • She Studs #01 / 1990 / BIZ / G • She Studs #02 / 1991 / BIZ / G • She's A Boy Toy / 1985 / DR / M • She-Male Desires / 1989 / VC / C • She-Male Encounters #10: She-Male Vacation / 1986 / MET / G • She-Male Whorehouse / 1988 / VD / G • Sin City / 1986 / WET / M • Sinful Sisters / 1986 / VEX / M • The Sins Of Angel Kelly / 1987 / FAN / C • Sins Of The Wealthy #2 / 1986 / CLV / M • Sister Dearest / 1984 / DR / M • Sisters Of Sin / 1991 / VIM / G • The Slutty Professor / 1989 / VWA / M • Starship Intercourse / 1987 / DR / M • The Stranger Beside Me / 1991 / WV / M • Stripteaser / 1986 / LA / M • Surrender In Paradise / 1984 / GO / M • Swedish Erotica #65 / 1985 / CA / M • Swedish Erotica #66 / 1985 / CA / M • Sweet Brown Sugar / 1994 / AVI / M • A Taste Of Angel / 1989 / PIN / C • Taste Of The Best #3 / 1988 / PIN / C • Terms Of Endowment / 1986 / PV / M • To Snatch A Thief / 1989 / PLD / M • Toe Hold / 1992 / PRE / B • Too Naughty To Say No / 1984 / CA / M • Toppers #01 / 1992 / TV / F • Tougher Than Leather / 1988 / C3S / S • Transaction #1 / 1986 / WET / M • Transformation #2 / 199? / BIZ / G • Trisexual Encounters #01 / 1985 / PL / G • Trisexual Encounters #02 / 1985 / PL / G • Trisexual Encounters #03 / 1986 / PL / G • Trisexual Encounters #04 / 1986 / PL / G • TV Training Center / 1993 / LEO / G • Two Into One #1 / 1988 / PIN / C • Unforgettable / 1992 / HO / M • Untamed Passions / 1987 / CV / C • VCA Previews #3 / 1988 / VC / C • VCA Previews #4 / 1988 / VC / C • Video Paradise / 1988 / ZA / M • Virgin Heat / 1986 / TEM / M • What's My Punishment / 1983 / BIZ / B • Whore D'erves / 1996 / OUP / F • World Of Good, Safe & Unusual Sex / 1987 / ... / M • The X-Team / 1984 / CV / M • Zara's Revenge / 1991 / XCI / M • [Wet Water T's / 1987 / ... / S

LOIS BOUTON see Star Index I
LOIS ESTER see Star Index I
LOIS GRANT see April Grant
LOIS HUNTLEY see Star Index I
LOIS KLINGER
Fanny Hill / 1975 / TGA / M
LOIS LANE
ABA: Double Feature #1 / 1996 / ALP / M • A Bride For Brenda / 1968 / SOW / S • Teenage Deviates / 1975 / SVE / M
LOIS LUV see Star Index I
LOIS OVERDRIP see Star Index I
LOIS SLOANE see Star Index I
LOIS TURKAN
Waterpower / 1975 / VHL / M
LOKI
Cherry Poppers: The College Years #01 / 1997 / ZA / M • Sweet Revenge / 1997 / KBE / M
LOLA
Black And Horny / 1994 / MET / M • Magma: Olympus Of Lust / 1994 / MET / M • Magma: Spezial: Black & White #3 / 1995 / MET / M • Magma: Tanja's Horny Nights / 1994 / MET / M • Nasty Travel Tails #02 / 1993 / CC / M • Odyssey Amateur #24: Whatever Lola Wants / 1991 / OD / M • Rump Man: Forever / 1995 / HW / M • The T & A Team / 1984 / VC / M • [No More Dirty Deals / 1994 / V-I / S

LOLA (ASHLEY WINGER) see Ashley Winger
LOLA (TANYA DEVRIES) see Tanya De-Vries
LOLA FERRARI
Big DD / 1996 / C69 / M • Double Air Bags / 1996 / C69 / M • Planet Boobs / 1996 / C69 / M
LOLA JAMES see Star Index I
LOLA LAGARCE see Star Index I
LOLA LANGUSTA see Kitten Natividad
LOLA ROYCE see Star Index I
LOLA STAR see Star Index I
LOLA SUMMERS see Star Index I
LOLA TRENT
Anal Squeeze / 1993 / FOR / M
LOLAH SHORES
Filthy First Timers #1 / 1996 / EL / M • Here Comes Elska / 1997 / XPR / M
LOLIPOP
Blue Vanities #170 (New) / 1996 / FFL / M • Blue Vanities #170 (Old) / 1991 / FFL / M • Blue Vanities #504 / 1992 / FFL / M
LOLITA
Absolute Anal / 1996 / XC / M • Blue Vanities #504 / 1992 / FFL / M • David Friedman's Road Show Shorts #06 / 1994 / SOW / S • David Friedman's Road Show Shorts #07 / 1994 / SOW / S • Hot New Imports / 1996 / XC / M • Private Film #15 / 1994 / OD / M • Private Video Magazine #06 / 1993 / OD / M
LOLITA (S/M)
Parliament: Hard TV #1 / 1988 / PM / G • She-Male Desires / 1989 / VC / C • Trisexual Encounters #03 / 1986 / PL / G • Trisexual Encounters #06 / 1987 / PL / G
LOLITA DANOVA
Body Love / 1976 / CA / M • Caballero Preview Tape #3 / 1984 / CA / C
LOLITA GRANT
Sexual Heights / 1981 / ... / M
LOLLI POPP
Dirty Dancers #4 / 1995 / 4P / M • Finger Pleasures #3 / 1995 / PL / F • Kym Wilde's On The Edge #24 / 1995 / RB / B • Vibrating Vixens #1 / 1996 / TV / F • Young & Natural #01 / 1995 / PRE / F • Young & Natural #02 / 1995 / PRE / F • Young & Natural #06 / 1995 / PRE / F • Young & Natural #08 / 1995 / PRE / F • Young & Natural #09 / 1995 / PRE / C
LOLLI POPP (HUNGARY)
Big Babies In Budapest / 1996 / EL / M
LOLLIPOP
Blue Vanities #584 / 1996 / FFL / M
LOLLY
Painless Steel #3 / 1996 / FLV / M
LONA
New Faces, Hot Bodies #16 / 1994 / STP / M
LONA SANDS see Lana Sands
LONDON see Paul Morgan
LONDON MOORE see Paul Morgan
LONDON RENE
Deep Dish Booty Pie / 1996 / ROB / M • Dirty Video #1 / 1996 / AB / M • More Dirty Debutantes #56 / 1996 / 4P / M • Solo Adventures / 1996 / AB / F
LONDON TAMLIN see Paul Morgan
LONE HELMER see Star Index I
LONE HIRTZ
1001 Danish Delights / cr68 / AR / M
LONG CHAINY see Star Index I
LONG DONG SILVER
Black guy with a two foot long dick of

Clarence Thomas fame. Never actually been seen in use.

Beauty And The Beast / 1982 / KEN / S • Blue Vanities #053 / 1988 / FFL / M • Blue Vanities #243 / 1996 / FFL / M • Electric Blue #001 (Marilyn Chambers) / 1983 / CA / S • Electric Blue #003 / 1981 / CA / S • Electric Blue #004 / 1981 / CA / S • Erotography / 1971 / SOW / M • Porno Bizarro / 1995 / GLI / M • Sex Freaks / 1991 / TAB / M • [Long Dong Silver: The Legend Returns / 19?? / ... / M

LONG JEAN SILVER *(Jean Silver, Jeanne Silver)*

Lithe body, medium tits, overbite, left leg amputated half way down the shin leaving a stump that can and is used as an artifical dick. Passable face, tattoo (looks like a bird in flight) on her left outside shoulder. Comes from Tempe, AZ.

The Bizarre World Of F.J. Lincoln / 19?? / VHL / C • Brooke Does College / 1984 / VC / M • Debbie Does Dallas #2 / 1980 / VC / M • Desire For Men / 1981 / MIT / M • Every Man's Fancy / 1983 / BIZ / B • Fashion Dolls / 1985 / LA / M • Freedom Of Choice / 1984 / VHL / M • Hot Pink / 1983 / VC / C • House Of Sin / 1982 / AVO / M • Hypersexuals / 1984 / VC / M • Intimate Action #2 / 1983 / INP / M • Kinky Potpourri #33 / 1997 / SVE / C • Lady Lust / 1984 / CA / M • Long Jeanne Silver / 1977 / VC / M • Maneaters / 1983 / VC / M • Mistress Electra / 1983 / AVO / B • Peepholes / 1982 / AVC / M • Piggies / 1984 / VC / M • Pleasure Channel / 1984 / VC / M • Prisoner Of Pleasure / 1981 / ALP / B • Taboo American Style #3: Nina Becomes An Actress / 1985 / VC / M • The Violation Of Claudia / 1977 / QX / M • Waterpower / 1975 / VHL / M

LONG JOHN *see Star Index I*
LONG JOHN WADD *see John C. Holmes*
LONG PETER
The Coming Of Angie / cr73 / TGA / M
LONI (ALEX DANE) *see Alex Dane*
LONI HENDERSON *see Tawny Pearl*
LONI JAMES *see Toni James*
LONI MORGAN
AHV #23: Hidden Charms / 1992 / EVN / M • Amateur Lesbians #39: Tiffany / 1993 / GO / F • Amateur Lesbians #40: Sunset / 1993 / GO / F • America's Raunchiest Home Videos #09: Orgasmic Oriental / 1992 / ZA / M • Anal Asian / 1994 / VEX / M • Backdoor Suite / 1992 / EX / M • Date Night / 1992 / V99 / M • Dirty Deeds / 1992 / IF / M • Executive Positions / 1991 / V99 / M • Hillary Vamp's Private Collection #03 / 1992 / HVD / M • Hillary Vamp's Private Collection #04 / 1992 / HVD / M • Hillary Vamp's Private Collection #06 / 1992 / HVD / M • Hillary Vamp's Private Collection #06 / 1992 / HOV / M • Looking For Love / 1991 / VEX / M • Midnight Caller / 1992 / MID / M • Neighborhood Watch #11 / 1991 / LBO / M • Neighborhood Watch #23: Sinsational Sex / 1992 / LBO / M • Odyssey Amateur #82: Loni's 5 Stud Gang Bang / 1991 / OD / M • One Night Love Affair / 1991 / IF / M • Opposite Attraction / 1992 / VEX / M • Rump Humpers #18 / 1994 / GLI / M • Six Plus One #2 / 1993 / VEX / C • Viviana's Dude Ranch / 1992 / IF / M

LONI NELSON
Diary Of A Bed / 1979 / HOE / M
LONI SANDERS *(Sarah Harris, Terry*

Galko, Dominique (Loni S), Jennifer Wren, Teri Galko, Haiku)
Ex-*Penthouse* Pet brunette with a pretty face, medium tits, and a reasonable body. Terry Galko is from **Sex Boat** and Teri Galko is from **All The Action**. Rumor has it that as of 1996 she was married to Steven Hirsch, the owner of Vivid Video.

8 To 4 / 1981 / CA / M • All The Action / 1980 / TVX / M • Beauty / 1981 / VC / M • The Blonde Goddess / 1982 / VXP / M • Blue Confessions / 1983 / VCR / M • Blue Vanities #042 (Old) / 1988 / FFL / M • Blue Vanities #061 / 1988 / FFL / M • Blue Vanities #064 / 1988 / FFL / M • Blue Vanities #066 / 1988 / FFL / M • Blue Vanities #067 / 1988 / FFL / M • Blue Vanities #080 / 1988 / FFL / M • Blue Vanities #090 / 1988 / FFL / M • Body Double / 1984 / C3S / S • Bondage Pleasures #2 / 1981 / 4P / B • A Brief Affair / 1982 / CA / M • Caballero Preview Tape #2 / 1983 / CA / C • Caballero Preview Tape #3 / 1984 / CA / C • Classic Erotica #9 / 1996 / SVE / M • Cover Girl Fantasies #2 / 1983 / VCR / C • Dream Lovers / 1980 / MET / G • Electric Blue: Cosmic Coeds / 1985 / CA / M • An Erotic Trilogy / cr81 / GO / M • Every Which Way She Can / 1981 / CA / M • Fetish Fever / 1993 / CA / C • Forbidden Dreams / 1984 / BIZ / G • Ginger (1984-Vivid) / 1984 / VI / M • Ginger On The Rocks / 1985 / VI / M • Girls Just Wanna Have Boys / 1986 / AMB / M • Golden Girls #01 / 1981 / CA / M • Golden Girls #02 / 1981 / SVE / M • Golden Girls #05 / 1982 / SVE / M • Hustler Video Magazine #2 / 1984 / SE / M • I Dream Of Ginger / 1985 / VI / M • Kiss And Tell / 1980 / CA / M • Ladies Three / cr81 / GO / F • Lusty Ladies #02 / 1983 / 4P / M • Lusty Ladies #07 / 1984 / 4P / M • Lusty Ladies #12 / 1984 / 4P / M • Maximum #6 / 1983 / CA / M • Nasty Romances / 1985 / HO / C • Naughty Network / 1981 / CA / M • Never So Deep / 1981 / VCX / M • Nightdreams #1 / 1981 / CA / M • Nightlife / 1983 / CA / M • Please, Mr Postman / 1981 / VC / M • Same Time Every Year / 1981 / VHL / M • Sensuous Moments / 1983 / VIV / M • Sex Boat / 1980 / VCX / M • Sheri's Gotta Have It / 1985 / LIM / C • Sound Of Love / 1981 / CA / M • Summer Of '72 / 1982 / CA / M • Swedish Erotica #31 / 1980 / CA / M • Swedish Erotica #32 / 1980 / CA / M • Taboo #01 / 1980 / VCX / M • Tight Assets / cr80 / VC / M • To Man From Woman / 19?? / BL / M • Trashi / 1980 / CA / M • True Legends Of Adult Cinema: The Cult Superstars / 1993 / VC / C • Twice A Virgin / 1984 / PL / G • Up 'n' Coming / 1983 / CA / M • What Would Your Mother Say? / 1981 / HAV / M • With Love, Lisa / 1985 / CA / C • With Love, Loni / 1985 / CA / C

LONIE
Liquid Lips #2 / 1994 / MAV / M
LONNA EMERSON *see Star Index I*
LONNIE (ALEX DANE) *see Alex Dane*
LONNIE HARRIS *see Lois Ayers*
LONNIE LABELLE *see Lorrie Lovett*
LONNIE LEE *see Star Index I*
LONNIE LOVE *see Star Index I*
LONNIE RICH *see Star Index I*
LONNIE STILLS *see Star Index I*
LONNIE TAYLOR *see Star Index I*
LONNY FEDDERSEN
Bordello / 1973 / AR / M

LONY BROWN
The Best Little He/She House In Texas / 1993 / HSV / G • Charade / 1993 / HSV / G • Come Back Little She-Male / 1994 / HSV / G • Crossing The Line / 1993 / STA / G • Dragula: Queen Of Darkness / 1996 / HSV / G • Dragxina, Queen Of The Underworld / 1995 / MET / G • Dungeon Queens / 1995 / BIZ / G • Gentlemen Prefer She-Males / 1995 / CDI / G • He-She Hangout / 1995 / HSV / G • I'm A Curious She-Male / 1993 / HSV / G • Lady Dick / 1993 / HSV / G • Little Shop Of She-Males / 1994 / HSV / G • Married With She-Males / 1993 / PL / G • Melrose Trannie / 1995 / HEA / G • Mr. Madonna / 1994 / FPI / G • My She-Male Valentine / 1994 / HSV / G • Painful Secrets Of A TV / 1996 / BIZ / G • The Princess With A Penis / 1994 / HSV / G • The Prize Package / 1993 / HSV / G • Queens From Outer Space / 1993 / HSV / G • Samurai She-Males / 1994 / HSV / G • Shaved She-Males / 1992 / STA / G • She Male Jail / 1994 / HSV / G • She Male Service / 1994 / HEA / G • She Males Enslaved / 1996 / BIZ / G • She-Male Encounters #21: Psychic She Males / 1994 / MET / G • She-Male Encounters #22: She-Male Mystique / 1995 / MET / G • She-Male Instinct / 1995 / BCP / G • She-Male Nymphos / 1995 / MET / G • She-Male Seduction / 1995 / MET / G • She-Male She Devils / 1996 / BIZ / G • She-Male Shenanigans / 1994 / HSV / G • She-Male Showgirls / 1992 / STA / G • She-Male Surprise / 1995 / CDI / G • She-Male Swish Bucklers / 1994 / HSV / G • She-Male Valentine / 1996 / HSV / G • The She-Male Who Stole Christmas / 1993 / HSV / G • She-Males In Torment #3 / 1995 / BIZ / G • SM TV #1 / 1995 / FC / G • Surprise Package / 1993 / HSV / G • Trans America / 1993 / TSS / G • Transitions (TV) / 1993 / HSV / G • Transsexual Try Outs / 1993 / HSV / G • Transvestite Tour Guide / 1993 / HSV / G • TV Dinner / 1993 / HSV / G • TV Evangelist / 1993 / HSV / G • TVs In Leather And Pain / 1996 / BIZ / G • Virtual She-Male / 1995 / HSV / G • Wings Of Change / 1993 / HSV / G

LOOSE BRUCE
Blue Vanities #204 / 1993 / FFL / M
LOOSE LATUE *see Star Index I*
LORA
Penetration (Anabolic) #1 / 1995 / ANA / M
LORA ANN *see Star Index I*
LORA BURST
Paris Taxis / 1995 / XYS / M
LORA LAMBKIN
Cool Water / 1995 / DBM / M
LORA LEI *see Laurie Lay*
LORA LIMPINI
Prima #01: Anal Poker / 1995 / MBP / M
LORAINE
Blue Vanities #506 / 1992 / FFL / M • Blue Vanities #541 / 1994 / FFL / M
LORAINE BURRETT
Blue Vanities #514 / 1992 / FFL / M
LORALI HART
Big Busty #40 / 1991 / BTO / S • Mature Women #01 / 1991 / BTO / M
LORANE
Raw Talent: Bang 'er 06 Times / 1991 / RTP / M • Raw Talent: Bang 'er 09 Times / 1992 / RTP / M
LORD MATHEUX
Hot Crimson Buns / 1996 / STM / B

LORD ORION
The Boy Toy / 1995 / BON / B • Greta's Ultimate Penalty #1 / 1995 / BON / B
LORD PARVO
Mr. Parvo's Neighborhood / 1995 / BON / B
LOREAL
Hardcore Debutantes #03 / 1997 / TEP / M
LORELEI ADAMS
No Man's Land #02 / 1988 / VT / F
LORELEI RAND *see Star Index I*
LORELEI WINSTON
Petite, tight bodied blonde.
Pink Champagne / 1979 / CV / M • Sex Boat / 1980 / VCX / M
LORELI (LAURIE LAY) *see Laurie Lay*
LORELL BROWNELL
Erotic Animation Festival / 1980 / VC / M
LORELLE
Three Girl Tickle #2 / 1996 / SY / B
LOREN
Eurotica #10 / 1996 / XC / M • Nasty Newcummers #13 / 1995 / MET / M
LOREN LOVING *see Star Index I*
LOREN MICHAELS
Barbara Broadcast / 1977 / VC / M • Maraschino Cherry / 1978 / QX / M
LOREN SANDS *see Regina Bardot*
LORENA
HomeGrown Video #452: Make Me Cum! / 1995 / HOV / M • Real Sex Magazine #02 / 1997 / HO / M • Sharon Mitchell's Sex Clinic #02 / 1993 / FC / M
LORENA MINER *see Star Index I*
LORENNA
Toy Time #2: Nasty Solos / 1994 / STP / F • Wildfire: Solos #3 / 1994 / WIF / F
LORENZO
The Booty Bandit / 1994 / FC / M
LORENZO HIGHTOWER
Stuff Your Ass #3 / 1996 / JMP / M • Vivid Raw #1 / 1996 / VI / M • Vivid Raw #4 / 1996 / VI / M
LORETTA
Blue Vanities #523 / 1993 / FFL / M • Blue Vanities #550 / 1994 / FFL / M • Magma: Anal Wedding / 1995 / MET / M
LORETTA JAGGERS
Overnight Sensation / 1976 / AR / M
LORETTA STERLING *see Candice Hart*
LORETTA STERLING (M) *(Ed de Roo)*
This is a male director.
Aged To Perfection #1 / 1994 / TTV / M • Aged To Perfection #2 / 1995 / TTV / M • Aged To Perfection #3 / 1995 / TTV / M • Big Boob Boat Ride #1 / 1992 / FC / M • The Bottom Dweller Part Deux / 1994 / EL / M • Butt Bongo Bonanza / 1993 / FC / M • Dr Butts #3 / 1993 / 4P / M • Dresden Diary #03 / 1989 / BIZ / B • Dresden Diary #04 / 1989 / BIZ / B • East Vs West: Battle Of The Gang Bangs / 1994 / TTV / M • Escape From Anal Lost Angels / 1996 / HO / M • Freak Show / 1991 / FC / M • Hooters In The 'hood / 1995 / TTV / M • Junk Yard Dogs / 1991 / FC / M • Lactamania #2: The Squirt Fest / 1995 / TTV / M • Life In The Fat Lane #1 / 1990 / FC / M • Life In The Fat Lane #2 / 1990 / FC / M • Life In The Fat Lane #3 / 1990 / FC / M • More To Love #1 / 1994 / TTV / M • The Phantom Of The Montague Stage / 1997 / HO / M • Prime Offender / 1993 / PEP / M • Ready To Drop #05 / 1995 / FC / M • Ready To Drop #06 / 1995 / FC / M • Ready To Drop #07 / 1995 / FC / M • Ready To Drop #08 / 1995 / FC

/ M • Salsa & Spice #1 / 1995 / TTV / M • The Sex Change Girls / 1987 / 4P / G • Sexual Harassment / 1996 / TTV / M • Sweet Black Cherries #1 / 1996 / TTV / M • Tit In A Wringer / 1993 / FC / M • Tit Tales #4 / 1993 / FC / M • Totally Tasteless Video #02 / 1994 / TTV / M • A Trip Down Mammary Lane / 1991 / FC / M • Up And Cummers: The Movie / 1994 / 4P / M
LORI
AVP #7012: Sex Collections / 1991 / AVP / M • Big Bust Vixens / 1984 / BTO / S • Black Casting Couch #1 / 1993 / WP / M • Blue Vanities #556 / 1994 / FFL / M • Creme De Femme #3 / 1981 / AVC / C • Golden Moments / 1985 / BAK / F • Hollywood Swingers #05 / 1992 / LBO / M • HomeGrown Video #466: Loot The Booty / 1996 / HOV / M • Hot Body Video Magazine: Sweet Dreams / 1996 / CG / F • Hot Legs #2 / 1990 / PLV / B • Lesbian Dildo Fever #1 / 1989 / BIZ / F • Limited Edition #06 / 1979 / AVC / M • More Dirty Debutantes #41 / 1995 / 4P / M • Mr. Peepers Amateur Home Videos #63: Sexual Soiree / 1992 / LBO / M • Mr. Peepers Nastiest #2 / 1995 / LBO / C • Nancy Vs Lori / 1993 / VVO / B • Neighborhood Watch #37: Pelvic Thrusters / 1993 / LBO / M • Raw Talent: Motel Room Fantasies / 1992 / RTP / M • Wrasslin She-Babes #10 / 1996 / SOW / M • Yellow Waters #1 / 1985 / BAK / F • Yellow Waters #2 / 1985 / BAK / F • Yellow Waters Vol 72-S / 1985 / BAK / F
LORI (STACEY NICH.) *see Stacey Nichols*
LORI AMBROSIA *see Ambrosia Fox*
LORI BLUE *see Laurie Blue*
LORI CAMERON *see Laurie Cameron*
LORI DAWN
Foxy Boxing / 1982 / AVC / M
LORI GILLETTE *see Star Index I*
LORI GRACE
Ancient Secrets Of Sexual Ecstasy / 1996 / HIG / M
LORI HAZAN *see Star Index I*
LORI KAYE
Lori Kaye Bondage Model / 1993 / BON / B
LORI LAKE *see Star Index I*
LORI LANDRY *(Lauri Landry)*
Charlie's Girls #3 / 1990 / CC / M • Digital Lust / 1990 / SE / M • Down And Out / 1995 / PRE / B • Easy Pickin's / 1990 / LV / M • The Eliminators / 1991 / BIZ / B • Happy Endings / 1990 / BIZ / B • Love Is ... / 1990 / EVN / M • Mortal Passions / 1990 / CDI / M • Prisoner Of Lust / 1991 / VC / F • Read My Lips / 1990 / FH / M • Red On The Noodle Like A Swance On A Poodle / 1990 / FC / C • Steal Breeze / 1990 / SO / M
LORI LANG *see Star Index I*
LORI LAY *see Laurie Lay*
LORI LEVELL
Angel Of The Night / 1985 / IN / M
LORI LEWIS *see Star Index I*
LORI LOVE *see Star Index I*
LORI LOVETT *see Lorrie Lovett*
LORI LUST
Anal Hanky-Panky / 1997 / ROB / M • Raw Naked In Your Face / 1997 / ROB / M • Suzi's Wild Anal Ride / 1997 / ROB / M
LORI MARJON *see Star Index I*
LORI MARR *see Star Index I*
LORI MICHAELS *see Laurie Michaels*
LORI PALMER
Little Darlings / 1981 / VEP / M • Undula-

tions / 1980 / VC / M
LORI PEACOCK *see Fallon*
LORI RHODES *see Laurie Blue*
LORI ROGERS
Golden Girls #02 / 1981 / SVE / M • Lusty Ladies #03 / 1983 / SVE / M • Starship Eros / 1980 / SE / M
LORI SAMS *see Star Index I*
LORI WAGNER
Big Busty Major Babes / 1996 / NAP / F • Buttman At Nudes A Poppin' #2 / 1995 / EA / S • Caligula #1 / 1979 / VES / S • Dark Secrets / 1995 / MID / S • Frankenpenis / 1995 / LEI / M • Miss Nude Galaxy #1 / 1995 / VOY / S • Miss Nude Galaxy #2 / 1995 / VOY / S • Penthouse: On The Wild Side / 1988 / A*V / S • Pussyman Auditions #22 / 1996 / SNA / M • Trained To Kill / 1988 / PRS / S • Uhf / 1989 / ORI / S
LORIE *see Star Index I*
LORIN MACK *see Lorrin Mick*
LORISSA MCCOMAS
The Anal Adventures Of Max Hardcore: The Resurrection / 1995 / ZA / M • Bare Essentials / 1995 / NIV / F • Droid Gunner / 1995 / NEH / S • Forbidden Fantasies #3 / 1995 / ZA / M • Nookie Professor #1 / 1996 / AVS / M • Vamps: Deadly Dreamgirls / 1996 / EJF / S
LORISSA ROCKETS
Mike Hott: #352 Cunt Of The Month: Lorissa Rockit / 1996 / MHV / M • Mike Hott: #355 Lesbian Sluts #24 / 1996 / MHV / M
LORNA
Blue Vanities #539 / 1993 / FFL / M
LORNA DEE
Chocolate Bunnies #03 / 1995 / LBO / C • M Series #02 / 1993 / LBO / M • Murphie's Brown / 1992 / LV / M • My Baby Got Back #01 / 1992 / VT / M
LORNA LAKE *see Star Index I*
LORNA MAITLAND *(Barbara Joy)*
Hip, Hot & 21 / 1967 / SOW / S • Hot Thrills And Warm Chills / 1966 / SOW / S • Lorna / 1964 / RMV / S • Mondo Topless #1 / 1966 / RMV / S • Mudhoney / 1965 / RMV / S
LORNA MAY
The Caning Of The Shrews / 1991 / BIZ / B
LORNA MILLS *see Linda Shaw*
LORNA NUYGEN
Joys Of Erotica / 1984 / VCR / M • Oriental Lust / 1983 / GO / M
LORNA WILLS *see Linda Shaw*
LORNI *see Star Index I*
LORRAINE
Hollywood Amateurs #07 / 1994 / MID / M • Neighborhood Watch #28 / 1992 / LBO / M • Nu-West Screen Test #1 / 1988 / NUV / F
LORRAINE ADAMS
Chocolate Candy #1 / 1984 / VD / M
LORRAINE ALRAUNE
Highway Hookers / 1976 / SVE / M • In Sarah's Eyes / 1975 / VHL / M
LORRAINE BERNETT
Blue Vanities #581 / 1996 / FFL / M
LORRAINE DAY *(Shayne Lee)*
The Shayne Lee is from **Queen Of Midnight** and is by no means solid. This is not the same as Kahlia but she has a very similar body style. Lorraine has a tattoo on her left arm just above the elbow and a tattoo of lips in red on her right buttock.
Amateur Lesbians #15: Courtney / 1991 /

GO / F • Amateur Lesbians #16: Lorraine / 1991 / GO / F • Amateur Lesbians #33: Mackala / 1992 / GO / F • Amateur Lesbians #34: Honey / 1991 / GO / F • As Sweet As Can Be / 1993 / V99 / M • Biff Malibu's Totally Nasty Home Videos #19 / 1992 / ANA / M • Bite / 1991 / LE / M • Bobby Hollander's Sweet Cheeks #101 / 1992 / WV / M • Breathless / 1991 / WV / M • Decadent / 1991 / WV / M • Girls Will Be Boys #3 / 1991 / PL / F • Harry Horndog #13: Anal Lovers #2 / 1992 / ZA / M • In Loving Color #4 / 1993 / VT / M • More Dirty Debutantes #10 / 1991 / 4P / M • Mr. Peepers Amateur Home Videos #58: Penthouse Pussy Power / 1992 / LBO / M • Mr. Peepers Amateur Home Videos #60: The Backdoor Is Open / 1992 / V99 / M • Mystified / 1991 / V99 / M • Pearl Necklace: Thee Bush League #08 / 1992 / SEE / M • Pubic Eye / 1992 / HW / M • Queen Of Midnight / 1991 / V99 / M • Rocks / 1993 / VT / M • Sweet Cheeks (1991-Vid Excl) / 1991 / VEX / C • Tomboy / 1991 / V99 / M • We're Having A Party / 1991 / EVN / M

LORRAINE L. VIOLI see Sasha Strange
LORRAINE WADE
Her Total Response / 1975 / SVE / M
LORRI BLUE see Laurie Blue
LORRI PARIEER see Star Index I
LORRI SMITH see Laurie Smith
LORRIE
Odyssey Triple Play #94: Triple Decker Sex Sandwich / 1995 / OD / M • Wrasslin She-Babes #12 / 1996 / SOW / M
LORRIE LOVETT *(Lonnie LaBelle, Lori Lovett, Laurie Lovett)*
Amber Lynn's Peter Meter / 1988 / 3HV / C • Anal Angels #1 / 1986 / VEX / M • Backdoor Brides #2: The Honeymoon / 1986 / PV / M • The Best Little Whorehouse In Beverly Hills / 1986 / CDI / M • Black 'n' White In Color / 1987 / VCR / C • Black Lava / 1986 / WET / M • Broadway Fannie Rose / 1986 / CA / M • Cabaret Sin / 1987 / IN / M • Caddy Shack-Up / 1986 / VD / M • Dark Side Of The Moon / 1986 / VD / M • Empire Of The Sins / 1988 / IN / M • French Cleaners / 1986 / VCR / M • Hard Ride / 1986 / VT / M • Helpless Coeds / 1987 / BIZ / B • Humongous Squirting Knockers / 1992 / CA / C • Interracial Anal Bonanza / 1993 / CA / C • Jane Bond Meets Octopussy / 1986 / VD / M • Kinkyvision #1 / 1986 / 3HV / M • Luscious Lucy In Love / 1986 / AVC / M • The Lust Detector / 1986 / PIN / M • Lusty Layout / 1986 / PV / M • National Pornographic #1: Lesbians / 1987 / 4P / C • National Pornographic #2: Orientals / 1987 / 4P / C • No Man's Land #01 / 1988 / VT / C • Oral Majority Black #2 / 1988 / WV / C • Parliament: Dirty Blondes #1 / 1991 / PM / F • Parliament: Eating Pussy #1 / 1989 / PM / C • Sex Aliens / 1987 / CA / M • Star Gazers / 1986 / CA / M • Taboo #05 / 1986 / IN / M • Taija Is Sizzling Hot / 1986 / VT / M • A Taste Of Purple Passion / 1990 / CA / C • WIse Girls / 1989 / IN / C
LORRIE LUNDEN
Southern Belles #4 / 1995 / HOV / M
LORRIN
A&B GB#043: How To Pick Up Girls / 1992 / A&B / M
LORRIN MCCEE see Lorrin Mick
LORRIN MICK *(Carlotta (Lorrin M), Lorin*

Mack, Lauren Mack, Lorrin McCee)
Very thin ugly brunette with big inflated tits. Seems brain dead.
Amateur Orgies #05 / 1992 / AFI / M • Amateur Orgies #11 / 1992 / AFI / M • America's Raunchiest Home Videos #23: Video Virgin / 1992 / ZA / M • The Anal Adventures Of Max Hardcore: Adventures In Shopping / 1992 / ZA / M • Anal International / 1992 / HW / M • Anal Therapy #1 / 1992 / FD / M • Art Of Sex / 1992 / FD / M • Backdoor To Russia #2 / 1993 / VC / M • The Backway Inn #2 / 1992 / FD / M • Beach Bum Amateur's #05 / 1992 / MID / M • Beverly Hills 90269 / 1992 / LV / M • Body And Soul / 1992 / OD / M • Bubble Butts #06 / 1992 / LBO / M • Bubble Butts #22 / 1993 / LBO / M • Buttman's Revenge / 1992 / EA / M • Checkmate / 1992 / CDI / M • Confessions #1 / 1992 / OD / M • The Dragon Lady #3: Tales From The Bed #2 / 1992 / WV / M • Eat My Cherry / 1994 / BHS / M • Elegant Bargain / 1994 / FD / C • The Flintbones / 1992 / FR / M • GRG: Sensuous Lorrin Mick / 1994 / GRG / M • L.A. Rear / 1992 / FD / M • Lesbian Pros And Amateurs #12 / 1992 / GO / F • Maid Service / 1993 / FL / M • Manwiched / 1992 / FPI / M • Mo' Booty #1 / 1992 / HW / C • Motel Hell / 1992 / PL / M • Mr. Peepers Amateur Home Videos #44: A Royal Reaming / 1992 / LBO / M • Nasty Fuckin' Movies #12: Rub My Twat / 1992 / RUM / F • Neighborhood Watch #25: / 1992 / LBO / M • Neighborhood Watch #26: / 1992 / LBO / M • Our Bang #01 / 1992 / GLI / M • Our Bang #02 / 1992 / GLI / M • Our Bang #05 / 1992 / GLI / M • Our Bang #08 / 1992 / GLI / M • Parlor Games / 1992 / VT / M • Peekers / 1993 / MID / M • Raw Talent: Bang 'er 18 Times / 1992 / RTP / M • Ripe And Ready #02 / 1994 / BTO / M • Rump Humpers #04 / 1992 / GLI / M • Rump Humpers #05 / 1992 / GLI / M • Sam Shaft's Anal Thrusts #2 / 1992 / RTP / M • Sex Police 2000 / 1992 / AFV / M • Shoot To Thrill / 1992 / WV / M • Soda Jerk / 1992 / ZA / M • Spring Break / 1992 / PL / M • Student Fetish Videos: Foot Worship #07 / 1992 / PRE / B • Student Fetish Videos: Foot Worship #08 / 1992 / PRE / B • Student Fetish Videos: Spanking #07 / 1992 / PRE / B • SVE: Cheap Thrills #4: Woman To Woman / 1992 / SVE / F • Tailiens #1 / 1992 / FD / M • Tailiens #2 / 1992 / FD / M • Tailiens #3 / 1992 / FD / M • Twin Peaks / 1993 / PL / M • Ultimate Orgy #3 / 1992 / GLI / M • Uncle Roy's Amateur Home Video #04 / 1992 / VIM / M • Uncle Roy's Amateur Home Video #06 / 1992 / VIM / M • Uncle Roy's Best Of The Best: Cornhole Classics / 1992 / VIM / C • Victoria's Amateurs #04 / 1992 / VGA / M • Welcome To Bondage: Lorrin Mick / 1993 / BON / B • Welcome To Bondage: Starlets #2 / 1994 / BON / C • Wicked Stepmother / 1993 / NAP / B
LOTTA GUE
The Breast Files #3 / 1994 / AVI / M
LOTTA LAIG
Twilight Pink #1 / 1980 / AR / M
LOTTA LEGGS see Valerie Darlyn
LOTTA LOVE
Bad Mama Jama And The Fat Ladies Of The Evening / 1989 / VT / M • Bad Mama Jama Busts Out / 1989 / VT / M • Fat Ends

/ 1989 / 4P / M • Fatliners #2 / 1991 / EX / M • Freak Show / 1991 / FC / M • Freaky Flix / 1995 / TTV / C • Let Me Tell Ya 'Bout Fat Chicks #2 / 1988 / 4P / M • Totally Tasteless Video #01 / 1994 / TTV / M • Weird And Bizarre Bondage / 1991 / FC / C
LOTTA SEMEN
Meatball / 1972 / VCX / M
LOTTA TOP
Anal Intruder #01 / 1986 / CC / M • Basic Desire / cr85 / STM / B • Between My Breasts #03 / 1986 / L&W / S • Between My Breasts #06 / 1989 / BTO / M • Between My Breasts #09 / 1990 / BTO / M • Big Busty #17 / 198? / H&S / M • Big Tit Hookers / 1989 / BTO / M • Big Tit Orgy #01 / 1987 / H&S / M • Big Top Cabaret #1 / 1986 / BTO / M • Big Top Cabaret #2 / 1989 / BTO / M • Bizarre Dildo Obsession / 1989 / BIZ / B • Bra Busting Mistress / 1989 / BIZ / B • Bursting Bras / 1990 / BTO / C • Busen Extra #1 / 1991 / BTO / M • Bust Lust / cr83 / BIZ / B • Busty Bitches / 1990 / BIZ / S • Chocolate Bon-Bons / 1985 / PL / M • Dildoe Action / cr85 / STM / B • Erotic Moments / 1985 / CDI / C • Flesh Mountain / 1994 / VI / C • Flipside: A Backdoor Adventure / 1985 / CV / M • Forbidden Dildo Taboos / 1992 / STM / F • The Full Treatment / cr85 / STM / B • Girls Of The Double D #01 / 1986 / CDI / M • Humiliated Husband / cr83 / BIZ / B • Lotta Top Is The Collector / 19?? / BIZ / B • Only The Best Of Breasts / 1987 / CV / C • Pleasure #4 / 1990 / BTO / M • Porked / 1986 / VXP / M • Punished Crossdressers / cr85 / STM / B • Smothering Boobs / cr83 / BIZ / B • Top Control / cr85 / JAN / B
LOTTE CARDY
Bel Ami / 1976 / VXP / M
LOTTIE HAYWORTH
Vista Valley PTA / 1980 / CV / M
LOTTIE RUMBLE see Madelyn Knight
LOTUS
Blue Vanities #170 (New) / 1996 / FFL / M • Blue Vanities #170 (Old) / 1991 / FFL / M • Blue Vanities #503 / 1992 / FFL / M
LOTUS BLOSSOM see Star Index I
LOTUS WING see Star Index I
LOU see Star Index I
LOU BEHR
Telefantasy / 1978 / AR / M
LOU CAS see Star Index I
LOU DEAN *(Lou Denny)*
Frat House / 1979 / NGV / M
LOU DENNY see Lou Dean
LOU FALCO
The Nite Bird / 1978 / BL / M
LOU FARREL
Let's Talk Sex / 1982 / CA / M
LOU GANAPOLER see Star Index I
LOU MANN see Star Index I
LOU MORGAN see Star Index I
LOU PERRY *(Anthony Perraino)*
One of the original backers of **Deep Throat** and a principal in Arrow.
LOU SHERRY see Star Index I
LOU STERN see Star Index I
LOUIE
Dirty Dancers #3 / 1995 / 4P / M • Play Me Again, Vanessa / 1986 / VC / M
LOUIE HERSTEIN
Old Guys & Dolls #1 / 1995 / PL / M
LOUIS
Bi-Bi Love Amateurs #3 / 1993 / QUA / G • Taxi Girls #2: In Search Of Toni / 1986 /

ELD / M

LOUIS G.
Devil In A Wet T-Shirt / 1995 / SPI / M • Foreskin Gump / 1994 / LE / M • In The Bush / 1994 / PP / M • The Mountie / 1994 / PP / M • Next...! / 1996 / CDI / M • Revenge Of The Pussy Suckers From Mars / 1994 / PP / M • Sinnocence / 1995 / CDI / M

LOUIS GRECO *see Star Index I*

LOUIS LOVE
Bitch School / 1996 / BON / B • Delivered For Discipline / 1995 / BON / B • Final Orgy / 1996 / BON / B • Orgy Of Cruelty / 1995 / BON / B • Orgy Of Pain / 1995 / BON / B • Vagabondage / 1996 / B&D / B

LOUIS PAUL
69 Pump Street / 1988 / ZA / M • The Naked Stranger / 1988 / VI / M • Sex In Dangerous Places / 1988 / VI / M • The Sweet Spurt Of Youth / 1988 / WV / M

LOUIS PRIMO *see Luis Primo*

LOUIS RUPERT *see Star Index I*

LOUIS SHORTSTUD *see Short Stud*

LOUIS VALENCIA *see Star Index I*

LOUISE
Big Boobs Around The World #2 / 1990 / BTO / M • Blue Vanities #501 / 1992 / FFL / M • Blue Vanities #518 / 1993 / FFL / M • Blue Vanities #551 / 1994 / FFL / M • Blue Vanities #572 / 1995 / FFL / M • Climax At The Melting Pot #2 / 1996 / AVS / M • Georgie's Ordeal / 1993 / LED / B • Homegrown Video #373 / 1991 / HOV / M • In Your Face #3 / 1995 / PL / M • Lesbian Pros And Amateurs #07 / 1992 / GO / F • Penetration (Flash) #2 / 1995 / FLV / M • Porno Screentests / 1982 / VC / M • Private Film #02 / 1993 / OD / M • Private Film #16 / 1994 / OD / M • The World Of Double-D #2 / 199? / H&S / S

LOUISE ARMANI *(Angelica (L. Armani), Louise Drysden, Louise Looker)*
Pretty English blonde with a nice personality, hard body and a tight waist, small tits. Louise Drysden comes from **Mr. Peepers #43**, Louise Looker from **Star Struck**.
America's Raunchiest Home Videos #12: Bimbo Ballers From Brt / 1992 / ZA / M • American Buttman In London / 1991 / EA / M • Bubble Butts #01 / 1992 / LBO / M • Butt's Up, Doc #1 / 1992 / GO / M • Buttman's European Vacation #2 / 1992 / EA / M • The Cannes Sex Fest / 1992 / SFP / M • Destination Moon / 1992 / GO / C • Mike Hott: #251 Cunt of the Month: Veronica / 1993 / MHV / M • Mike Hott: Apple Asses #13 / 1992 / MHV / F • Mr. Peepers Amateur Home Videos #39: Cumming In Colors / 1992 / LBO / M • Mr. Peepers Amateur Home Videos #43: Gym-Nastiness / 1992 / LBO / M • Neighborhood Watch #13: Teasers and Crumpets / 1991 / LBO / M • The Pink Persuader / 1992 / LBO / M • Pudsucker / 1994 / MID / M • Star Struck / 1991 / AFV / M

LOUISE BARNET *see Star Index I*

LOUISE DRAKE *see Star Index I*

LOUISE DRYSDEN *see Louise Armani*

LOUISE HASLER
A Scent Of Heather / 1981 / VXP / M

LOUISE JACKSON
Talk Dirty To Me #02 / 1982 / CA / M

LOUISE LAMBERT
Blue Vanities #551 / 1994 / FFL / M

LOUISE LOOKER *see Louise Armani*

LOUISE MAIER
Body Love / 1976 / CA / M

LOUISE MONTGOMERY
Voluptuous #5 / 1996 / H&S / M

LOUISE PARSONS
C.T. Coed Teasers / 1978 / VXP / M • The Erotic Aventures Of Lolita / 1982 / VXP / M

LOUISE PIKE *see Star Index I*

LOUISE SHERRY
Large tits, pudgy, long reddish black hair, not too pretty.
Amateur Models For Hire / 1996 / MP0 / M • Anal Camera #12 / 1995 / EVN / M • Breastman's Triple X Cellent Adventure / 1995 / EVN / M • The Cumm Brothers #12: Two GOOS For Every Girl / 1995 / OD / M • Dirty Hairy's Shove It Up My Ass / 1996 / GOT / M • Girls Of The Panty Raid / 1995 / VT / M • Gothic / 1995 / MET / M • Jiggly Queens #3 / 1996 / LE / M • Lesbian Debutante #01 / 1996 / IP / F • Lesbian Nights / 1996 / AVI / F • Lil' Latin Cutie Pies / 1996 / CDI / M • Orgy Camera #2 / 1996 / EVN / M • Pizza Sluts: They Deliver / 1995 / XCI / M • Salsa & Spice #2: Latin Lust / 1996 / TTV / M • The Spa / 1996 / RAS / M • Squirt Flirts / 1996 / RAS / M • Underground #1 / 1996 / SC / M • Vortex / 1995 / MET / M

LOUISE TECHEKAN
Private Film #20 / 1995 / OD / M • Private Film #21 / 1995 / OD / M

LOUISE WILSHIRE
Spanking Video #3: Cambridge Blues / 1995 / MET / B

LOUISI (VERONICA) *see* **Veronica (Louisi)**

LOUISON BOUTIN
Body Love / 1976 / CA / M • Erotic Pleasures / 1976 / CA / M

LOUSIE LABOCA
Bound And Gagged #05 / 1992 / RB / B

LOVE *see Tracy Love*

LOVE (CHARISMA) *see Charisma*

LOVE HANSON *see Tracy Love*

LOVELA HARRIS
Love Mexican Style / cr75 / BLT / M

LOVETTE
Beefy blonde with large inflated tits, marginal face and an unpleasant pushy disposition. Started as a dancer in Indiana. 5'2" 36DD-24-34 in 1995. De-virginized at 16.
The All Girl Anal Orgy / 1996 / BAC / F • American Tushy! / 1996 / ULI / M • Anal Camera #12 / 1995 / EVN / M • Anal Crybabies / 1996 / BAC / M • Anal Island #2 / 1996 / VC / M • Anal Jeopardy / 1996 / ZA / M • Anal Rippers #1: The Beginning / 1995 / ZA / M • Anal Webb / 1995 / ZA / M • Anals, Inc / 1995 / ZA / M • Analtown USA #03 / 1995 / NIT / M • Analtown USA #04 / 1995 / NIT / M • Ass Angels / 1996 / PAL / F • Asses Galore #6: Fallen Angels / 1996 / DFI / M • Big & Busty Centerfolds / 1996 / DGD / F • Big Boob Boat Ride #2 / 1995 / FC / M • Big Bust Babes #36 / 1996 / AFI / M • Bimbette: Adventures In Anal Land / 1996 / TEP / M • The Blowjob Adventures Of Doctor Fellatio / 1997 / EL / M • Brian Sparks: Virtually Unreal #1 / 1996 / ALD / M • Buffy Malibu's Nasty Girls #11 / 1996 / ANA / F • Casting Call #15 / 1995 / SO / M • Casting Call #16 / 1995 / SO / M • Club Anal #3 / 1995 / ROB / F • Cum Buttered Corn Holes #1 / 1996 / NIT / C • Double D Dykes #21 / 1995 / GO / F • Double D Dykes #25 / 1995 / GO / F • Dresden Diary

#16: / 1996 / BIZ / B • Employee's Entrance In The Rear / 1996 / CC / M • Erotic Newcummers Vol 1 #3: Anal Adventures / 1996 / DR / M • EXXXtra Parts: Interview With a Hermaphrodite / 1995 / PL / M • Fashion Sluts #4 / 1995 / ABS / M • Friendly Fire / 1996 / EDP / M • Fuck U: Girls Of The Packed-10 / 1995 / ZA / M • Gang Bang Fury #2 / 1996 / ROB / M • Get Lucky / 1996 / NIT / M • Hardcore Schoolgirls #3: Legal And Eager / 1995 / XPR / M • Hardcore Schoolgirls #4: Little Kittens / 1996 / XPR / M • Hawaiian Buttwatch / 1995 / SUF / M • Head To Head / 1996 / VI / M • Henry's Big Boob Adventure / 1996 / HO / M • The Hitch-Hiker #15: Cat & Mouse / 1995 / VIM / M • Hollywood Halloween Sex Ball / 1996 / EUR / M • Hooters And The Blowjobs / 1996 / HW / M • House Of Hoochies / 1996 / DDP / M • The Hungry Heart / 1996 / AOP / M • In Your Face #3 / 1995 / PL / M • Interview: Doin' The Butt / 1995 / LV / M • Kittens & Vamps #2 / 1995 / ROB / F • Leg Show #2 / 1996 / NIT / M • Lesbian Debutante #01 / 1996 / IP / F • Lingerie / 1996 / RAS / M • Love Exchange / 1995 / DR / M • Max #08: The Fugitive / 1995 / XPR / M • Max #09: Where Danger Lurks / 1996 / XPR / M • Max World #2: Europa Issue / 1995 / XPR / M • Mellon Man #07 / 1996 / AVI / M • Naked Scandal #1 / 1995 / SPI / M • Naked Scandal #2 / 1996 / SPI / M • Nasty Nymphos #09 / 1995 / ANA / M • Naughty / 1996 / LV / M • New Hardcore Beginners #20 / 1996 / LEI / C • Ona Zee's Doll House #2 / 1995 / ONA / F • Paradise / 1995 / FD / M • Penetrator #2: Grudge Day / 1995 / PL / M • Perverted Stories #03 / 1995 / JMP / M • The Phantom Of The Montague Stage / 1997 / HO / M • Philmore Butts Goes Hollyweird / 1996 / SUF / M • Philmore Butts Hawaiian Anal Adventure / 1995 / SUF / M • The Portrait Of Dorie Grey / 1996 / KLP / M • Private Dancers / 1996 / RAS / M • Pumphouse Sluts / 1996 / CC / M • Pure / 1996 / WP / M • Pussyman Auditions #12 / 1995 / SNA / M • Pussyman's House Party #1 / 1996 / SNA / M • Pussyman's House Party #2 / 1996 / SNA / M • Pussyman's Nite Club Party #1 / 1996 / SNA / M • Pussyman's Nite Club Party #2 / 1997 / SNA / M • Rockhard (Sin City) / 1996 / SC / M • Sex Freaks / 1995 / EA / M • Sex On The Beach Hawaiian Style #1 / 1995 / ULP / M • Sex On The Beach Hawaiian Style #2 / 1995 / ULP / M • Sex On The Beach Hawaiian Style #3 / 1995 / ULP / M • Sex Raiders / 1996 / WAV / M • Sexual Atrocities / 1996 / EL / M • Sodomania #16: Sexxy Pistols / 1996 / EL / M • Sodomania: Slop Shots / 1996 / EL / C • Sorority Sluts Passed Out / 1995 / ZA / M • Spinners #2 (Wicked) / 1996 / WP / M • Strange Lesbian Tales / 1996 / BAC / F • Street Workers / 1995 / ME / M • Streets Of New York #08 / 1996 / PL / M • Striptease / 1995 / SPI / M • Suzi Bungholeo / 1995 / ROB / M • Talk Dirty To Me #10 / 1996 / DR / M • Tinsel Town Tales / 1995 / NOT / M • Topless Brain Surgeons / 1995 / LE / M • Topless Window Washers / 1996 / LE / M • Tropical Taboo / 1995 / HO / M • Trouble In Paradise / 1996 / ULP / M • Ultimate Sensations / 1996 / NIT / M • Unbalanced Chemicals / 1996 / SUF / M • Up And Cummers #23 / 1995 / 4P / M • Up And Cummers #26 / 1996 / 4P / M • Up Your Ass #3 / 1996 / ANA / M • Valley Cooze / 1996 / SC / M • Venom #2 / 1996 / VD / M • Venom #7 / 1996 / VD / M • Video Virgins #24 / 1996 / NS / M • Violation / 1996 / LE / M • The Voyeur #6 / 1996 / EA / M • Voyeur Strippers / 1996 / PL / F • The Wanderer #1: Road Tails / 1995 / CDI / M • The Wicked Web / 1996 / WP / M

LOVIE BENSON
Bedtime Video #04 / 1984 / GO / M

LOVING MORE *(Tamisha, Tamisha Allure)*
Black girl with medium natural tits and small frame.
Anal Camera #02 / 1994 / EVN / M • The Black Butt Sisters Do Los Angeles / 1995 / MID / M • Black Hollywood Amateurs #03 / 1995 / MID / M • Black Hollywood Amateurs #05 / 1995 / MID / M • Black Hollywood Amateurs #06 / 1995 / MID / M • Bootyville / 1994 / EVN / M • Chocolate Bunnies #02 / 1995 / LBO / C • Chocolate Bunnies #04 / 1995 / LBO / C • Girlz Towne #08 / 1995 / FC / F • Liar's Poke Her / 1995 / NIW / M • M Series #24 / 1994 / LBO / M • M Series #25 / 1994 / LBO / M • M Series #28 / 1994 / LBO / M • Tail Taggers #119 / 1994 / WV / M

LOWELL
ABA: Double Feature #2 / 1996 / ALP / M • Rip-Off Of Millie / cr78 / VHL / M

LUA MIZUNO
Tokyo Dreams #03: Touch Me / 1995 / XCI / M

LUANA BORGIA
Erotic Dreams / 1992 / VTV / M • Euroflesh: Dentro Il Vulcano / 1996 / SC / M • Rosa / Francesca / 1995 / XC / M • Selen / 1996 / HW / M

LUANNE
A&B AB#301: Fruit Dildos / 1991 / A&B / F • Odyssey Amateur #23: Luanne Cums To The Big City / 1991 / OD / M • Odyssey Amateur #42: Luanne's Oral Odyssey / 1991 / OD / M • Odyssey Triple Play #32: Cum-Loving Nasty Girls / 1993 / OD / M • Odyssey Triple Play #93: Satisfaction Via Gang Bang / 1995 / OD / M

LUC WILDER *(Luc Wylder)*
Tall male who used to be the SO of Ariana. She apparently found him screwing some other girls and they broke up.
Agony & Extacy / 1993 / GOT / B • Anal Virgins Of America #06 / 1994 / FOR / M • Ariana's Bondage / 1993 / BON / B • Ariana's Torment / 1995 / BON / B • The Attendant / 1996 / SC / M • Backlash / 1992 / GOT / B • Beauty's Punishment / 1996 / BIZ / B • Bizarre Master Series: Luc Wylder / 1995 / BIZ / C • Bizarre's Dracula #1 / 1995 / BIZ / B • Bizarre's Dracula #2 / 1995 / BIZ / B • Bondage Journey / 1995 / STM / B • The Breast Of Breastmen / 1995 / EVN / C • Buffy The Vamp / 1992 / FD / M • Butt Bandits #4 / 1996 / VD / C • Captive #1 / 1995 / BON / B • Casting Call #01 / 1993 / SO / M • Chasey Revealed / 1994 / WP / M • Chateau Of Torment / 1995 / STM / B • Cheerleaders In Bondage #1 / 1994 / GOT / B • Cheerleaders In Bondage #2 / 1995 / GOT / B • Chronicles Of Pain #3: Slave Traders / 1996 / BIZ / B • Chug-A-Lug Girls #4 / 1994 / VT / M • Cinderella Society / 1993 / GO / M • Club Midnight / 1992 / LV / M • Colossal Orgy #1 / 1993 / HW / M • Colossal Orgy #3 / 1994 / HW / M • Com-

ing Attractions / 1995 / WHP / M • Corporate Affairs / 1996 / CC / M • Crazy Times / 1995 / BS / B • Debi's Darkest Desires / 1996 / BIZ / B • Deep Inside Ariana / 1995 / VC / C • Defiance: Spanking And Beyond / 1993 / PRE / B • Defiance: The Art Of Spanking / 1996 / BIZ / B • Defiance: The Ultimate Spanking / 1993 / BIZ / B • The Devil In Miss Jones #5: The Inferno / 1994 / VC / M • Diamond Likes It Rough / 1995 / BON / B • Dirty Dancers #1 / 1994 / 4P / M • Dirty Dancers #3 / 1995 / 4P / M • Dirty Dancers #4 / 1995 / 4P / M • Dirty Dancers #5 / 1995 / 4P / M • Dirty Dancers #6 / 1995 / 4P / M • Dirty Dancers #7 / 1996 / 4P / M • Dirty Dancers #9 / 1996 / HO / M • Dirty Laundry #1 / 1994 / CV / M • Dirty Laundry #2 / 1994 / CV / M • Doctors Of Pain / 1995 / BIZ / B • The Domination Of Summer #1 / 1994 / BIZ / B • The Domination Of Summer #2 / 1994 / BIZ / B • Dr Of Pain / 1995 / BIZ / B • Dresden Diary #09 / 1993 / BIZ / B • Dresden Diary #10: Punishment For Their Sins / 1993 / BIZ / B • Dresden Diary #11: Endangered Secrets / 1994 / BIZ / B • Dresden Diary #12: / 1995 / BIZ / B • Dresden Diary #13: / 1995 / BIZ / B • Dresden Diary #14: Ecstasy In Hell / 1996 / BIZ / B • Dresden Diary #15: / 1996 / BIZ / B • Dungeon Discipline / 1996 / STM / B • Dungeon Punishment / 1995 / STM / B • Eighteen #1 / 1996 / SC / M • The Enema Bandit / 1994 / BIZ / B • The Enema Bandit Returns / 1995 / BIZ / B • The Enema Bandit Strikes Again / 1995 / BIZ / B • Enema Obedience #2 / 1994 / BIZ / B • Enema Obedience #3: The Ultimate Punishment / 1994 / BIZ / B • Erotica / 1992 / CC / M • Fundgeon Of The Mind #1 / 1994 / BON / B • Happy Endings / 1994 / WP / M • Hard Hand Luc / 1994 / STM / B • Hard Licks / 1993 / GOT / B • Herman's Other Head / 1992 / LV / M • Hostile Takeover: Bitch Bosses / 1995 / BIZ / B • Hot Tight Asses #10 / 1995 / TCK / M • Hourman Is Here / 1994 / CC / M • The Illustrated Woman / 1995 / CA / M • Inhuman Bondage / 1993 / GOT / B • The Initiation / 1995 / FD / M • International Analists / 1994 / AFD / M • Judgement / 1994 / GOT / B • Kinky Cameraman #1 / 1996 / LEI / C • Kym Wilde's On The Edge #20 / 1995 / RB / B • Masquerade (1992-Usa) / 1992 / SC / M • Masquerade / 1995 / HO / M • The Master And The Mistress / 1993 / GOT / B • Masters Of Dominance / 1996 / GOT / C • Mistress Kane: Town In Torment / 1996 / BIZ / B • Mistress Rules / 1995 / STM / B • Misty Rain: Wrestling Terror / 1995 / BIZ / B • More Dirty Debutantes #34 / 1994 / 4P / M • More Than A Handful / 1995 / VC / M • Mr. Peepers Amateur Home Videos #51: Bun Burners / 1992 / LBO / M • Mr. Peepers Amateur Home Videos #73: Carnal Capture / 1993 / LBO / M • Night Calls / 1993 / GOT / B • Night Of Seduction / 1994 / VC / M • Night Seduction / 1995 / VC / M • Nina Hartley's Guide To Swinging / 1996 / A&E / M • Nurses 30 Min: #187: She Loves the Two Cock System / 1991 / OD / M • Odyssey 30 Min: #201: / 1992 / OD / M • The Orgy #2 / 1993 / EMC / M • The Orgy #3 / 1993 / EMC / M • P.K. & Company / 1995 / CV / M • Pitfalls Of Sasha / 1995 / GOT / B • Porsche Lynn, Vault Mistress #1 / 1994 / BIZ / B • Porsche

Lynn, Vault Mistress #2 / 1994 / BIZ / B • The Princess Slave / 1994 / BIZ / B • Profiles #03: House Dick / 1995 / XPR / M • Public Enemy / 1995 / GO / M • Pussy Tamer #1 / 1993 / BIZ / B • Pussy Tamer #2 / 1993 / BIZ / B • Reckless Passion / 1995 / WAV / M • Rough Games / 1994 / GOT / B • S&M Sessions / 1996 / VTF / B • Sex Scientist / 1992 / FD / M • Shelby's Forbidden Fears / 1995 / BIZ / B • Slave Girls' Agony / 1993 / PL / B • Sleeping Booty / 1995 / EL / M • Sodomania: Slop Shots / 1996 / EL / C • The Spirit Of My Master / 1994 / BIZ / B • Stalking Of Slave Laura / 1996 / BIZ / B • Steady As She Blows / 1993 / LV / M • Strip Search / 1995 / CV / M • Submission Of Ariana / 1995 / BIZ / B • Take Me...Use Me...Make Me Your Slave / 1994 / BIZ / B • Takin' It To The Limit #5 / 1995 / BS / M • Tangled / 1994 / PL / M • Telephone Expose / 1995 / VC / M • Third Degree / 1992 / GOT / B • Titanic Orgy / 1995 / PEP / M • To Serve...Protect...And Submit / 1994 / BIZ / B • The Training #2 / 1994 / BIZ / B • Ultimate Orgy #1 / 1992 / GLI / M • Ultimate Submissives #3: Best of Tanya Fox / 1995 / BIZ / C • Undeniable Urge / 1996 / HAC / B • Valley Cooze / 1996 / SC / M • Waterworld: The Enema Movie / 1996 / BIZ / B • Whore House / 1995 / IPI / M • Willing & Wilder / 1995 / BON / B • Without Pity / 1995 / GOT / B • A World Of Hurt / 1994 / BS / B • Wylder Nights / 1996 / BON / B

LUC WYLDER *see* **Luc Wilder**

LUCA
The Big E #08 / 1988 / BIZ / B • Cramped Spaces / 1989 / PLV / B • Toed Off / 1989 / PLV / B

LUCA CAMILLETT
Robin Thief Of Wives / 1996 / XC / M

LUCA VALENTINI
Anal Pow Wow / 1995 / XC / M • Essence Of A Woman / 1995 / ONA / M • Hot Diamond / 1995 / LE / M

LUCERO
Private Film #18 / 1994 / OD / M

LUCI DOLL
Two At Once / 1978 / CV / M

LUCIA
Buttwoman In Budapest / 1992 / EA / M • J.E.G.: Amateurs Only #10 / 1996 / JEG / M • More Dirty Debutantes #15 / 1992 / 4P / M • Prima #01: Anal Poker / 1995 / MBP / M • Prima #08: Sex Camping / 1995 / MBP / M

LUCIA CAMILIETTI
Juliet & Romeo / 1996 / XC / M

LUCIA LUCIANO *see* **Aja**

LUCIANA *see* **Star Index I**

LUCIE
Buttman In Barcelona / 1996 / EA / M • Rocco Goes To Prague / 1995 / EA / M • Triple X Video Magazine #09 / 1995 / OD / M

LUCIE DOLL *see* **Star Index I**

LUCIE MAY
Pussy Fest Of The Northwest #1 / 1995 / NIT / M • Teacher's Pet #4 / 1995 / APP / M

LUCIENNE CAMILLE *see* **Star Index I**

LUCILLE
Magma: Dirty Diana / 1994 / MET / M

LUCILLE BRAGG *see* **Star Index I**

LUCILLE GRANT *see* **Star Index I**

LUCINDA
Kinky College Cunts #07 / 1993 / NS / F •

Kinky College Cunts #12 / 1993 / NS / F •
Kinky College Cunts #13 / 1993 / NS / F •
Kinky College Cunts #15 / 1993 / NS / M •
Lunch / 1972 / VC / M
LUCINDA (C. DARK) see Cassandra Dark
LUCINDA CHIN see Star Index I
LUCKII CHARMM
Forbidden Session / 1996 / VTF / B
LUCKY
The Cockateer #2 / 1992 / LE / M • Home-Grown Video #434: Forrest Hump / 1994 / HOV / M • Meltin' The Burgh / 1996 / DGD / F • Southern Exposure / 1991 / LE / M
LUCKY (HARLEY) see Harley (male)
LUCKY (MALE)
Bottom Dweller: The Final Voyage / 1996 / EL / M • Video Virgins #28 / 1996 / NS / M
LUCKY GREENHOG see Star Index I
LUCKY SMITH
Nightshift Nurses #2 / 1996 / VC / M
LUCKY STARR
Lovin' Spoonfuls #4 / 1995 / 4P / C
LUCKY STRIKER see Star Index I
LUCY
A&B GB#031: Spoon Lover #1 / 1992 / A&B / M • A&B GB#069: Licky Lucy / 1992 / A&B / C • Ben Dover's 9th / 1996 / VC / M • The Best Of The Big Boob Battles / 1993 / CDP / C • Bi-Bi Love Amateurs #4 / 1994 / QUA / G • Blue Vanities #510 / 1992 / FFL / M • Blue Vanities #527 / 1993 / FFL / M • Blue Vanities #531 / 1993 / FFL / M • Dirty Stories #1 / 1995 / PE / M • Dominique Goes Bi / 1994 / STA / G • English Class / 1995 / VC / M • Harry Horndog #16: Love Puppies #4 / 1992 / ZA / M • Homegrown Video #404 / 1993 / HOV / M • Homegrown Video #409 / 1993 / HOV / M • International Leg...Ends #03 / 1991 / BIZ / F • Limited Edition #16 / 1980 / AVC / M
LUCY ANGEL
K-Sex / 1976 / VCR / M
LUCY BARDOT see Star Index I
LUCY BUSH
Sex Boat / 1980 / VCX / M
LUCY DELIGHT
Dyke's Discipline / 1994 / PL / F
LUCY DULAC
Bucky Beaver's XXX Dragon Art Theatre Double Feature #02 / 1996 / SOW / M • The Rites Of Uranus / 1975 / SOW / M
LUCY DUVALL see Star Index I
LUCY FINE
Ridin' The Big One / 1994 / TEG / M
LUCY GILL see Star Index I
LUCY HANDY
Big Mamas / 1981 / ... / C
LUCY LOVE see Berlin
LUCY MCMILLAN see Star Index I
LUCY RELAPPA
Blue Vanities #192 / 1993 / FFL / M • Blue Vanities #589 / 1996 / FFL / M
LUCY TELLERMAN
Sensual Fire / 1979 / HIF / M
LUCY WOODS see Star Index I
LUCYFER
Lesbian Sleaze / 1994 / PL / F
LUCYNDA
Thief Of Passion / 1996 / P69 / M
LUDA
Buttman's Orgies / 1996 / EA / M • The Coming Of Nikita / 1995 / EL / M • Prague By Night #1 / 1996 / EA / M
LUDMILLA

Buttman's Orgies / 1996 / EA / M
LUDMILLA HERNSCHULTZ
Private Film #08 / 1994 / OD / M
LUIGI
Prague By Night #1 / 1996 / EA / M
LUIS BARBOO
La Coda Dello Scorpione / 1971 / LUM / S • [Le Journal Intime D'Une Nymphomane / 1972 / ... / M • [The Loves Of Irina / 1973 / PS / S
LUIS PRIMO *(Louis Primo)*
Carrie...Sex On Wheels / 1985 / AA / M • Treasure Chest / 1985 / GO / M
LUIS RODRIQUEZ see Star Index I
LUISEA see Star Index I
LUKE
Alex Jordan's First Timers #05 / 1994 / OD / M
LUKE JOHNSON see Star Index I
LUKE ROPEWACKER
Take Off / 1978 / VXP / M
LULU
Fazano's Student Bodies / 1995 / EL / M • Sodomania #10: Euro/American Again / 1994 / EL / M • Sodomania: Slop Shots / 1996 / EL / C
LULU BONNEL
Pink Lips / 1977 / VCX / M
LULU BRACE *(De Ju, Deju)*
Young looking blonde with straggly crimped long hair, bands on teeth, small droopy tits, lithe tight body, quite pretty.
Dark Star / 1991 / VI / M • Dreams Of Candace Hart / 1991 / VI / M • Every Woman Has A Secret / 1991 / ROB / M • Hurts So Good / 1991 / VEX / M • Organic Facials / cr91 / GLI / M
LULU CHANG *(Lulu Tang, Cindy Shinn, Cherry Chen)*
Tall(er) Oriental girl with a standard body and a doll-like (i.e., impassive, expressionless) face.
Casting Call #07 / 1994 / SO / M • Cherry Poppers #04: Ripe 'n' Ready / 1994 / ZA / M • The Cumm Brothers #04: Laid Off & Laid / 1994 / OD / M • The Hitch-Hiker #04: Max Overdrive / 1994 / WMG / M • More Dirty Debutantes #34 / 1994 / 4P / M • Nasty Backdoor Nurses / 1994 / LBO / M • Pai Gow Video #06: New Wave Orientals / 1994 / EVN / M
LULU DIVINE
The Amazing Lulu Divine / 1993 / BTO / S • D-Cup Holiday / 1991 / BTO / M • Girls Around The World #03 / 1990 / BTO / M • Girls Of Sundance Spa: Hardcore Plumpers #1 / 1992 / BTO / M • The Incredible Sisters / 199? / H&S / S • On Location In Palm Springs / 1996 / H&S / S • Pussy Power #06 / 1992 / BTO / M
LULU REED see Star Index I
LULU TANG see Lulu Chang
LUMA CARIOCA
Private Film #22 / 1995 / OD / M
LUMA TROPICAL
The Seduction Of Marylin Star / 1995 / VT / M • You Go Girl! (Video Team) / 1995 / VT / M
LUNA see Alex Dane
LUNA PARKER
Rumpman In And Out Of Africa / 1996 / HW / M • Sinboy #3: The Island Of Dr. Moron / 1996 / SC / M
LUNA PARKS
Cherry Poppers #11: California Co-Eds / 1995 / ZA / M • Creme De La Face #08:

Wanna Blow Job / 1995 / OD / M • Cumm For Dinner / 1995 / BCP / M • Fresh Faces #06 / 1995 / EVN / M • Tails Of Desire / 1995 / GO / M
LUNA STARR see Star Index I
LUNETTE
Magma: Showtime Cunts / 1994 / MET / M
LUNG LEG
Hardcore: The Films Of Richard Kern #1 / 1991 / FTV / M
LUNI CHIA LUCERO
Ready To Drop #04 / 1994 / FC / M
LUPE
Blue Vanities #167 (New) / 1996 / FFL / M • Blue Vanities #167 (Old) / 1991 / FFL / M • Blue Vanities #565 / 1995 / FFL / M • Blue Vanities #577 / 1995 / FFL / M
LUPE LABOCA
Blush: Burlez Live! #1 / 1993 / FAT / F • San Francisco Lesbians #1 / 1992 / PL / F
LUPE LOPEZ
Blue Vanities #558 / 1994 / FFL / M
LUSCIOUS
Black Cheerleader Search #10 / 1997 / IVC / M • Hard Core Beginners #05 / 1995 / LEI / M • Interracial 247 / 1995 / CC / M • My Baby Got Back #07 / 1995 / VT / M • Shake Your Booty / 1996 / EVN / M
LUSCIOUS LYNN
She-Male Encounters #02: Carnal Candy / 1981 / MET / G
LUSITA DUARTE
Paprika / 1995 / XC / M
LUSTY LIANE
Harry Horndog #28: Fabulous Squirt Queens / 1994 / FPI / M
LUTHER
Anal Virgins Of America #08 / 1994 / FOR / M
LUTHER WORTH
Blue Vanities #017 (New) / 1988 / FFL / M • Blue Vanities #045 (New) / 1988 / FFL / M • Blue Vanities #045 (Old) / 1988 / FFL / M • Disco Madness / cr80 / VST / S • Sexual Therapist / cr71 / CLX / M
LUVI see Star Index I
LUVLEE
Amateur Black: Honeys / 1995 / SUF / M
LUWANDA
Mo' Better Ho' Movies #41 / 1995 / MID / M
LYDA
Buttman's Orgies / 1996 / EA / M
LYDIA
Homegrown Video #371 / 1991 / HOV / M • Magma: Test Fuck / 1995 / MET / M • Playtex / 1996 / GLI / M
LYDIA (BLACK) see Star Index I
LYDIA BURKE see Star Index I
LYDIA CASSELL
[Voices Of Desire / 1973 / ... / M
LYDIA CHANEL *(Julia (L. Chanel), Lady Shanne, Julia Sow, Julia Chanel, Julia Sough)*
French girl whose father was Egyptian and mother, Thai. Adorable body with black hair, large natural tits, tight waist and great butt. She exudes sex. Was 19 in 1993. Has a boyfriend, Jean LeCastel. Medium slightly droopy tits. Born Nov 3, 1973 in Paris, France. Danced for 10 years. Got de-virginized at 15. (That would make her 9 when she started!)
1001 Nights / 1996 / IP / M • America's Raunchiest Home Videos #52: / 1993 / ZA / M • Anal Vision #08 / 1993 / LBO / M • Angel Wolf / 1995 / WIV / M • Boys R' Us /

1995 / WIV / M • Butt Bongo Bonanza / 1993 / FC / M • Dangerous Pleasure / 1995 / WIV / M • Deep Inside Debi Diamond / 1995 / VC / C • Deep Inside Dirty Debutantes #07 / 1993 / 4P / M • The Erotic Adventures Of Alladin X / 1995 / IP / M • Euro-Max #1: Frisky In France / 1995 / SC / M • Filthy Sleazy Scoundrels / 1994 / HW / M • Full Moon Bay / 1993 / VI / M • Gangbang Girl #10 / 1993 / ANA / M • Harry Horndog #17: Love Puppies #5 / 1993 / ZA / M • Harry Horndog #18: Double Penetration #3 / 1993 / ZA / M • Horny Henry's French Adventure / 1994 / TTV / M • The Husband / 1995 / WIV / M • International Affairs / 1994 / PL / M • Le Parfum De Mathilde / 1994 / VI / M • Lovin' Spoonfuls #3 / 1995 / 4P / C • Lovin' Spoonfuls #4 / 1995 / 4P / C • Marco Polo / 1995 / SC / M • More Dirty Debutantes #21 / 1993 / 4P / M • More Dirty Debutantes #22 / 1993 / 4P / M • More Dirty Debutantes #26 / 1993 / 4P / M • Odyssey 30 Min: #295: / 1992 / OD / M • Odyssey Triple Play #58: Anal Insanity / 1994 / OD / M • Odyssey Triple Play #67: Girls Who Love It Up The Ass / 1994 / OD / M • Prime Offender / 1993 / PEP / M • Private Film #03 / 1993 / OD / M • Private Film #07 / 1994 / OD / M • Raw Talent: Deep Inside Lydia's Ass / 1993 / FH / M • The Rehearsal / 1993 / VC / M • Sex Scandals / 1995 / XC / M • Totally Tasteless Video #02 / 1994 / TTV / M • Whore'n / 1996 / AB / M

LYDIA JAZZ
Lovin' Spoonfuls #4 / 1995 / 4P / C

LYDIA LANGUISH
The Girls In The Band / 1976 / SVE / M

LYDIA LORING see Star Index I

LYDIA LUNCH
Hardcore: The Films Of Richard Kern #1 / 1991 / FTV / M

LYDIA MAJORS
Lovin' Spoonfuls #7 / 1996 / 4P / C • New Ends #09 / 1994 / 4P / M

LYDIA SPLITZ
Anal Camera #14 / 1996 / EVN / M • Dirty & Kinky Mature Women #06 / 1995 / C69 / M • Lactamania #2: The Squirt Fest / 1995 / TTV / M • More To Love #2 / 1995 / TTV / M • The Older Women's Sperm Bank #3: Red Hot Grandmas / 1996 / SUF / M • Salsa & Spice #1 / 1995 / TTV / M • The Ultimate Climax / 1996 / EMC / M

LYDIA STEEL see Star Index I

LYDIA STONE
Anal Vision #17 / 1993 / LBO / M • The Backway Inn #3 / 1993 / FD / M • Bun Busters #07 / 1993 / LBO / M • A Girl's Affair #02 / 1993 / FD / F • Rump Humpers #16 / 1993 / GLI / M

LYDIE BEGGY see Star Index I

LYLA CHERRY
Fishbone / 1994 / WIV / F

LYLA PICCOLO see Star Index I

LYLAN BROWNING see Kim Alexis

LYLE STEWART see Jon Martin

LYLE STUART see Jon Martin

LYLE TUTTLE
Erotic Tattooing And Piercing #1 / 1986 / FLV / M • Tattoo San Francisco / 1996 / FLV / M

LYN
Blue Vanities #554 / 1994 / FFL / M

LYN CHAN
Oh My Gush / 1995 / OD / M

LYN MANSTONE

Long Hard Summer / 1989 / BMV / C • Raw Footage / 1977 / CA / M

LYN MARTIN
The Love Couch / 1977 / VC / M

LYN RICHARDS see Victoria Jackson

LYN TARS
Rumor has it that she committed suicide. Crazy On You / 1991 / IF / M • Decadent Delights / 1992 / IF / M • Executive Positions / 1991 / V99 / M • Looking For Love / 1991 / VEX / M

LYNDA
Blue Vanities #546 / 1994 / FFL / M • HomeGrown Video #473: Furpie Feast #3 / 1997 / HOV / C

LYNDA GRASSER see Seka

LYNDA MANTZ see Jean Jennings

LYNDA ST JAMES
Matinee Idol / 1984 / VC / M

LYNDEE MITCHELL see Star Index I

LYNDEN GREY see Lynden Johnson

LYNDEN JOHNSON (*Lynden Grey*)
Fat blonde with huge natural (I think) tits. 976-76DD / 1993 / VI / M • All Over Me / 1991 / VC / M • Big Bust Babes #14 / 1993 / AFI / M • Big Bust Babes #23 / 1994 / AFI / M • Big Bust Bangers #2 / 1994 / AMP / M • Big Busty #51 / 1994 / BTO / S • Big Knockers #02 / 1994 / TV / M • Big Knockers #03 / 1994 / TV / M • Big Knockers #04 / 1994 / TV / M • The Boob Tube / 1993 / MET / M • Boobies / 1995 / RTP / M • Bra Busters #02 / 1993 / LBO / M • Breast Collection #02 / 1995 / LBO / C • Breastman Goes To Breastland #2 / 1993 / EVN / M • The Bust Things In Life Are Free / 1994 / NAP / S • Bustline / 1993 / LE / M • Busty Babes / 1995 / NAP / F • The Butt Sisters Do New York / 1994 / MID / M • The Cumm Brothers #03: Go To Traffic School / 1994 / OD / M • Dark Interludes / 1991 / BS / B • Desire Kills / 1996 / SUM / M • Double D Dykes #10 / 1993 / GO / F • Dun-Hur #1 / 1994 / SC / M • The Ebony Connection #4 / 1994 / LBO / C • Erotic Angel / 1994 / ERA / M • Exposure Images #13: Lynden Johnson / 1992 / EXI / F • The Face Of Fear / 1990 / BS / B • The Fantasy Realm #1 / 1990 / RUM / M • Flashback / 1993 / SC / M • Glitz Tits #05 / 1993 / GLI / M • I Love Juicy / 1993 / ZA / M • Kittens #3 / 1992 / CC / F • Leg...Ends #11 / 1994 / PRE / F • Lesbian Castle: No Kings Allowed / 1994 / LIP / F • M Series #06 / 1993 / LBO / M • M Series #21 / 1994 / LBO / M • Mellon Man #01 / 1994 / AVI / M • Miss Nude International / 1993 / LE / M • Model's Memoirs / 1993 / IP / M • More Than A Handful #3 / 1993 / MET / M • More Than A Handful #4 / 1994 / MET / M • More Than A Mouthful / 1995 / LBO / C • My Generation / 1994 / HO / M • Natural Wonders / 1993 / VI / M • Pajama Party X #1 / 1994 / VC / M • Pajama Party X #2 / 1994 / VC / M • Perplexed / 1994 / FD / M • Pouring It On / 1993 / CV / M • The Proposal / 1993 / HO / M • Raincoat Fantasies / 1993 / ELP / M • Rainwoman #08 / 1994 / CC / M • Saturday Night Porn #2 / 1993 / AFV / M • Sex Circus / 1994 / VIM / M • Sex In Abissi / 1993 / WIV / M • Sexorcist / 1994 / HW / M • Sexual Trilogy #05 / 1994 / SFP / M • Shades Of Lust / 1993 / TP / M • Shayla's Home Repair / 1993 / EVN / M • Sodomania #04: Further On Down The Road / 1993 / EL / M • Superboobs / 1994 / LE / M • Tail Taggers

#116 / 1993 / WV / M • Titties 'n Cream #1 / 1994 / FC / M • Titty Bar #1 / 1993 / LE / M • Titty Bar #2 / 1994 / LE / M • Titty Slickers #2 / 1994 / LE / M • Too Hot To Touch #2 / 1993 / CV / M • Toppers #16 / 1993 / TV / M • Toppers #17 / 1993 / TV / M • Toppers #18 / 1993 / TV / M • Toppers #21 / 1993 / TV / C • Toppers #22 / 1993 / TV / C • Twin Action / 1993 / LE / M • Wendy Whoppers: Environmental Attorney / 1993 / PEP / M • What About Boob? / 1993 / CV / M • What's Butt Got To Do With It? / 1993 / HW / M • X-Net: Interactive Phone Sex / 1995 / RTP / M

LYNDON BRIDGES see Star Index I

LYNDON RYDER see Star Index I

LYNETTE
Big Bust Babes #05 / 1990 / AFI / F • Neighborhood Watch #28 / 1992 / LBO / M • Rent-A-Butt / 1992 / VC / M • You Bet Your Butt / 1992 / VC / M

LYNETTE SHELDON
Bloodsucking Freaks / 1975 / VES / B • C.O.D. / 1981 / VES / S • Let My Puppets Come / 1975 / CA / M

LYNETTE STERLING see Alicyn Sterling

LYNKA see Star Index I

LYNN
AVP #6003: Lynn's Desire / 1991 / AVP / M • AVP #7014: Dealin' With Dicks / 1991 / AVP / M • Blue Vanities #051 / 1988 / FFL / M • Blue Vanities #509 / 1992 / FFL / M • Lynn: Red-Head Passion / 1990 / LOD / F • Mike Hott: #188 Lynn / 1992 / MHV / M • Mike Hott: #188 Lynn Solo / 1991 / MHV / F • Mike Hott: #377 Lesbian Sluts #28 / 1996 / MHV / F • Odyssey Amateur #81: Lynn's Oral Kaleidoscope / 1991 / OD / M • Odyssey Triple Play #27: Black & White Adventures / 1993 / OD / M • Odyssey Triple Play #31: Double Penetration Babes / 1993 / OD / M • Swedish Erotica #18 / 1980 / CA / M

LYNN (ORIENTAL) see Lynn Isosu

LYNN ANN CARVER
[Voices Of Desire / 1973 / ... / M

LYNN ANN NEWTON see Star Index I

LYNN ANN WILCOX see Star Index I

LYNN ANNE
Beyond The Valley Of The Ultra Milkmaids / 1984 / ZA / M • Big Bust Babes #05 / 1990 / AFI / F • Charming Cheapies #5: Fancy Flesh / 1985 / 4P / M

LYNN ANNE WILSON
Transsexual Secretary / 19?? / BIZ / G

LYNN ARMITAGE see Star Index I

LYNN ASHLEY see Star Index I

LYNN BISHOP see Star Index I

LYNN BODICA see Star Index I

LYNN CARLIN
Blue Vanities #566 / 1995 / FFL / M

LYNN CARTIER
Club Head (EVN) #1 / 1987 / EVN / C • Ice Cream #3: Naked Eyes / 1984 / VC / M • Ice Cream #4: Touch Of Mischief / 1984 / VC / M • Unbelievable Orgies #1 / 1987 / EVN / C

LYNN CASEY
Bedtime Video #03 / 1984 / GO / M

LYNN CONNELLY see Champagne

LYNN COSTAN
Pleasure Productions #01 / 1984 / VCR / M

LYNN CUDDLES MALONE
Baby Face #1 / 1977 / VC / M • The Best Of Alex De Renzy #1 / 1983 / VC / C

LYNN FRANCIE see Lynn Francis

416   THE X-RATED VIDEOTAPE STAR INDEX

/ MID / M • Working Girl / 1993 / VI / M •
The Worst Porno Ever Made With The
Best Sex / 1993 / PL / M
LYNN LUCAS
Blondes Have More Fun / 1980 / SE / M •
Exposed / 1980 / SE / M • Wild Orgies /
1986 / SE / C
LYNN MARGUILES
Teenage Cruisers / 1977 / VCX / M
LYNN MOORE see Star Index I
LYNN RAE
[Home From The Sea / 19?? / ... / M
LYNN RAY (Sandy Taylor, Eselle Ferrand)
Supposedly married to Jean Pierre Ferrand. Pe-
tite blonde (dark) with passable face, curly
hair and small tits. Eselle Ferrand is the
name used as a director.
The Beat Goes On / 1987 / VCR / C •
Blowoff / 1985 / CA / M • Daddy Doesn't
Know / 1984 / HO / M • Dance Fever / 1985
/ VCR / M • Dirty 30's Cinema: Ginger Lynn
/ 1986 / PV / C • The Erotic World Of Candy
Shields / 1984 / VCR / C • Fantasy Peeps:
Sensuous Delights / 1984 / 4P / M • Girls
That Love Girls / 1984 / CA / F • Hot
Shorts: Sandy Taylor / 1986 / VCR / C • Hot
Spa / 1984 / CA / M • I Never Say No / 1983
/ VC / M • Joys Of Erotica #108 / 1984 /
VCR / C • Joys Of Erotica #111 / 1984 /
VCR / C • Pretty As You Feel / 1984 / PV /
M • Rear Action Girls #1 / 1984 / LIP / F •
Sensuous Singles: Sandi Taylor / 1987 /
VCR / F • Sweet Cheeks / 1987 / VCR / C
• Teasers / 1984 / HO / M • Weird And
Bizarre Bondage / 1991 / FC / C • Where
The Girls Are / 1984 / VEX / M • [House Of
Kinky Pleasures / 19?? / ... / M
LYNN SHEA see Star Index I
LYNN STAR
Erotic Dimensions #8: Just For Me / 1982 /
NSV / M
LYNN STEVENS see Leslie Murray
LYNN SUZU see Lynn Isosu
LYNN THATCHER see Lysa Thatcher
LYNN TRUE
Swap Meet / 1984 / VD / M
LYNN WARLAUMONT
Sex Boat / 1980 / VCX / M
LYNN WOODS see Star Index I
LYNN YORK see Josalynn Taylor
LYNN ZAMORA see Mina
LYNNE
Hillary Vamp's Private Collection #06 /
1992 / HVD / M
LYNNE ANNE see Star Index I
LYNNE FRANCIS see Lynn Francis
LYNNE RIO
Lesbian Castle: No Kings Allowed / 1994 /
LIP / F
LYNNETTE ASHLEY
Double Trouble: Spanking English Style /
1996 / BIZ / B
LYNNZ see Star Index I
LYNX
Cute Cuddly Bubbly Butts / 1996 / TTV / M
• Cutie Pies / 1995 / TTV / M • Interstate 95
Amateurs #1 / 1995 / RHV / M
LYNX (CHELSEA) see Chelsea Lynx
LYNX CANNON (Jean Damage, Susan
Kaye, Gene Damage, Della Damage,
Zenia Damage, Gean Damage, Susan
Kuchinski)
Quite pretty older woman with a sloppy waist
and a big butt. Small tits, blonde.
All American Girls #1 / 1982 / CA / M • All
The King's Ladies / 1981 / SUP / M • Anal

Annie And The Backdoor Housewives /
1984 / LIP / F • Anal Annie Just Can't Say
No / 1984 / LIP / M • The Best Of Anal
Annie: The Girl-Girl Adventures / 1993 /
LIP / C • Body Magic / 1982 / SE / M • Bun-
busters / 1984 / VCR / M • Butter Me Up /
1984 / CHX / M • Campus Capers / 1982 /
VC / M • Carnal Olympics / 1983 / CA / M •
China Bitch / 1989 / PV / C • Coffee, Tea Or
Me / 1984 / CV / M • Color Me Amber /
1985 / VC / M • Dark Angel / 1983 / VC / M
• Debbie Does 'em All #1 / 1985 / CV / M •
The Erotic World Of Crystal Dawn (#3) /
1983 / VCR / C • Expose Me Now / 1982 /
CV / M • Inflamed / 1984 / NSV / M • Leg-
ends Of Porn #1 / 1987 / CV / C • Legends
Of Porn #2 / 1989 / CV / C • Love At First
Sight / 1987 / SE / C • Lust Inferno / 1982 /
CA / M • Nasty / 1985 / NSV / M • Nasty
Lady / 1984 / CV / M • Never So Deep /
1981 / VCX / M • Nooner / 1985 / AMB / M
• Nurses Of The 407th / 1982 / CA / M • On
White Satin / 1980 / VCX / M • Only The
Best Of Anal / 1992 / MET / C • Only The
Best Of Men's And Women's Fantasies /
1988 / CV / C • Please, Mr Postman / 1981
/ VC / M • The Pleasure Hunt #1 / 1984 /
NSV / M • The Right Stiff / 1983 / AMB / M
• Same Time Every Year / 1981 / VHL / M •
The Satisfiers Of Alpha Blue / 1980 / AVC /
M • Screwdriver / 1988 / CC / C • Sex Over
40 #1 / 1994 / PL / M • Sex Over 40 #2 /
1994 / PL / M • Sweet Cream / 1991 / VC /
C • Temptation: The Story Of A Lustful
Bride / 1983 / NSV / M • Too Hot To Touch
#1 / 1985 / CV / M • United We Fall / 19??
/ REG / C • Wet 'n' Bare With Barbara Dare
/ 1988 / NEO / C
LYNX DYAN
100% Amateur #15: / 1995 / OD / M • Back
East Babes #1 / 1996 / NIT / M • The Best
Of Fabulous Flashers / 1996 / DGD / F •
Bright Tails #7 / 1995 / STP / B • Cumm For
Dinner / 1995 / BCP / M • Eternal Bonds /
1995 / RHV / B • Fabulous Flashers #2 /
1996 / DGD / F • High Heeled & Horny #2
/ 1995 / LBO / M • New Faces, Hot Bodies
#17 / 1995 / STP / M • New Faces, Hot
Bodies #18 / 1995 / STP / M • New Faces,
Hot Bodies #22 / 1996 / STP / M • North-
west Pecker Trek #2: Evergreen, Ever
Horny / 1994 / LBO / M • Northwest Pecker
Trek #3: Ducks & Dicks / 1994 / LBO / M •
Northwest Pecker Trek #4: Laid In Latte
Land / 1994 / LBO / M • Northwest Pecker
Trek #5: Cumming In King County / 1995 /
LBO / M • Northwest Pecker Trek #6: Two
Girls For Every Boy / 1995 / LBO / M • Out-
rageous Sex / 1995 / BIP / F • Pearl Neck-
lace: Premier Sessions #04 / 1994 / SEE /
M • Profiles #03: House Dick / 1995 / XPR
/ M • Puritan Video Magazine #07 / 1996 /
LE / M • Pussy Fest Of The Northwest #1 /
1995 / NIT / M • Pussy Fest Of The North-
west #2 / 1995 / NIT / M • Rusty Boner's
Late Night Videos #1 / 1995 / RHV / M •
Sorority Slumber Sluts / 1995 / WIV / F •
Spanked In Spades / 1995 / STM / B •
Teacher's Pet #1 / 1994 / WMG / M •
Teacher's Pet #3 / 1995 / APP / M • Toy
Time #3: / 1995 / STP / F • Under The Cum
Cum Tree / 1996 / BCP / M • Wildfire:
Shaving Beauties / 1996 / WIF / F
LYSA THATCHER (Lisa Adams, Liza
Adams, Lynn Thatcher, Lanky Flatcher)
Blonde with small tits, marginal but striking

face, not-so-tight body, and poor skin.
1001 Erotic Nights #1 / 1982 / VC / M •
American Desire / 1981 / CA / M • Ameri-
can Pie / 1980 / SE / M • Babes In Toyland
/ 1988 / COM / C • Babylon Gold / 1983 /
COM / C • Backdoor Girls / 1983 / VCR / C
• Backing In #2 / 1990 / WV / C • Beyond
Shame / 1980 / VEP / M • Beyond Your
Wildest Dreams / 1980 / CAT / M • Blondes
Have More Fun / 1980 / SE / M • Blue
Shorts / cr83 / COM / C • Blue Vanities
#533 / 1993 / FFL / M • Budding Blondes /
1979 / TGA / C • Coed Fever / 1980 / CA /
M • Daisy May / 1979 / VC / M • Double
Pleasure / 1985 / VCR / M • The Erotic
World Of Seka / 1983 / VCR / C • Every
Which Way She Can / 1981 / CA / M • Ex-
posed / 1980 / SE / M • Fantasy / 1978 /
VCX / M • For The Love Of Pleasure / 1979
/ SE / M • Gold Or Bust / 1977 / BL / M •
High School Memories / 1980 / VCX / M •
Hot Ones / 1982 / SUP / C • Jawbreakers /
1985 / VEN / C • Kid Stuff / 1981 / ... / M •
Le Sex De Femme #3 / 1989 / AFI / C • Lit-
tle Darlings / 1981 / VEP / M • Loving Les-
bos / 1983 / VCR / C • Lusty Ladies #01 /
1983 / 4P / M • Midnight Blue #2 / 1980 /
VXP / M • Neon Nights / 1981 / COM / M •
Never So Deep / 1981 / VCX / M • Oh
Those Nurses / 1982 / VC / M • On White
Satin / 1980 / VCX / M • Peach Fuzz / 1976
/ CDI / M • Pink Punk / 19?? / ECO / C •
Playthings / 1980 / VC / M • The Red Room
And Other Places / 1992 / COM / C • The
Satisfiers Of Alpha Blue / 1980 / AVC / M •
Showgirl #12: Lisa Thatcher's Fantasies /
1983 / VCR / M • Steamy Sirens / 1984 /
AIR / C • Summer School / 1979 / VCX / M
• Taboo #07 / 1980 / IN / M • Touch Me In
The Morning / 1982 / CA / M • Trashi / 1980
/ CA / M • True Legends Of Adult Cinema:
Unsung Superstars / 1993 / VC / C •
Yummy Nymphs / 1983 / TGA / C
M see Emily Hill
M. BORTOLONI
A Very Debauched Girl / 1988 / PL / M
M. DAMICK see Star Index I
M. MATISSE see Mimi Morgan
M. MURREY
Girls On Fire / 1985 / VCX / M
M.C.
Sleeping Booty / 1995 / EL / M
M.E. TATARSAL see Star Index I
M.L. PARKS
Ropemasters / cr90 / BON / B
MABEL
Homegrown Video #359 / 1991 / HOV / M
MAC JOSEPHS
Little Darlings / 1981 / VEP / M
MAC MACGOWAN
Is The Dr In? / 1979 / AXV / M
MACHI TAKABARA
Lust In Old Edo / 1978 / ORC / M
MACHI TAKEI
Honey Sex / 1996 / AVE / M
MACHINE
Heavy Breathing / 1996 / NIT / M • Rice
Burners / 1996 / NOT / M • Whammin' &
Jammin' At The Hard Cock Ole / 1996 / GLI
/ M
MACHO MALE see Star Index I
MACI
Black Cheerleader Search #11 / 1997 / IVC
/ M • Black Snatch #2 / 1996 / DFI / F •
More Dirty Debutantes #63 / 1997 / SBV /
M

MACK HOWARD *see* **Dick Howard**
MACK REYNOLDS *see* **Joe Verducci**
MACK STEAD *see* **Jake Steed**
MACKALA *see* **Mikala**
MAD DAN DAN *see* **Star Index I**
MAD MAX
Euro-Max #1: Frisky In France / 1995 / SC / M • Euro-Max #2: Cream n' Euro Sluts / 1995 / SC / M • Euro-Max #4: / 1995 / SC / M

MADAM BUTTERFLY
All That: Black Women's Fantasies / 1996 / VT / M • Black Cheerleader Jungle Jerk-Off / 1996 / WIC / F • Black Cheerleader Search #03 / 1996 / ROB / M • Black Cheerleader Search #07 / 1996 / IVC / M • Black Cheerleader Search #10 / 1997 / IVC / M • Black Snatch #2 / 1996 / DFI / F • How To Make Love To A Black Woman #1: You Gotta Have Rhythm / 1996 / VCX / M

MADAM WONG
Oriental Treatment / 1995 / GOT / B
MADAME NICOLE *see* **Star Index I**
MADAME SCUTT
The Training #1 / 1984 / BIZ / B
MADAME WALEWSKA
Itsy Bitsy Gang Bang / 1996 / HW / M
MADAME WONG
Toe Tales #25 / 1995 / GOT / B • Toe Tales #30 / 1995 / GOT / C
MADAME X
Chicks With Dicks #1: A Slick And Slippery Oil Orgy / 1992 / BIZ / B • Secrets Of Madame X #1 / 1995 / WIV / M • Secrets Of Madame X #2 / 1995 / WIV / M • Shopping With A Transvestite: In A Boy, Out A Girl / 1992 / BIZ / G • TV Dungeon / 1992 / BIZ / G • TV Phone Sex / 1992 / BIZ / G
MADDY
Perversity In Paris / 1994 / AVI / M
MADELAINE LAFORET *see* **Jacqueline Laurent**
MADELAINE MILLS
Blue Vanities #581 / 1996 / FFL / M
MADELEINE
Erotica S.F. / 1994 / ORP / M • Let's Talk Anal / 1996 / ESF / M • Magma: Live And Learn / 1995 / MET / M • Porn Star Confidential / 1996 / ESF / M • Private Video Magazine #06 / 1993 / OD / M
MADELEINE ARMAND
Born For Love / 1987 / ... / M
MADELEINE KNIGHT *see* **Madelyn Knight**
MADELINE JACK
White Hot / 1984 / VXP / M
MADELINE KNIGHT *see* **Madelyn Knight**
MADELYN KNIGHT (*Madeline Knight, Madeleine Knight, Lottie Rumble, Brice*)
Pretty brunette with long straight hair, very nice smile, shaven pussy, very tight body but inflated canteloupes (how sad). 24 years old in 1996.
Arizona Gold / 1996 / KLP / M • Black Masters: Hidden Fear / 1996 / GOT / B • Black Masters: Red Flesh / 1996 / GOT / B • Borderline (Vivid) / 1995 / VI / M • Buffy Malibu's Nasty Girls #09 / 1995 / ANA / F • The Comix / 1995 / VI / M • Deep Behind The Scenes With Seymore Butts #1 / 1995 / ULI / M • Deep Focus / 1995 / VC / M • Dirty Work / 1995 / VC / M • Fresh Meat (John Leslie) #2 / 1995 / EA / M • A Girl's Affair #06 / 1995 / FD / F • Head To Head / 1996 / VI / M • In The Scope / 1996 / VI / M • In-

terview With A Milkman / 1996 / VI / M • The Naked Fugitive / 1995 / CA / M • Nightclub / 1996 / SC / M • The Palace Of Pleasure / 1995 / ULI / M • A Pool Party At Seymores #1 / 1995 / ULI / M • A Pool Party At Seymores #2 / 1995 / ULI / M • Pristine #1 / 1996 / CA / M • Return Engagement / 1995 / VI / M • Suburban Buttnicks Forever / 1995 / CC / M • Sweet Revenge / 1996 / WAV / M • Toe Tales #25 / 1995 / GOT / B • Torrid Tales / 1995 / VI / M • The Toy Box / 1996 / ONA / M • The Voyeur #5 / 1995 / EA / M

MADGE ALOTTA
The Best Little Whorehouse In Hong Kong / 1987 / SE / M • Hot Property / 1989 / EXH / C

MADGE TRILUST
Positively Pagan #06 / 1993 / ATA / M
MADINA *see* **Nikki King**
MADISON (*Madison Stone*)
Madison Stone is from **Evil Toons**. Apparently Madison is her middle name. She was 25 in 1991.
1-800-TIME / 1990 / IF / M • The Adventures Of Buttwoman #2: Behind Bars / 1992 / EL / F • Aerienne's Surprise / 1995 / WIV / M • All That Sex / 1990 / LE / M • All The Way Down / 1991 / ZA / M • Anal Addiction #2 / 1990 / SO / M • Anal Climax #1 / 1991 / ROB / M • Anal Ecstacy Girls #1 / 1993 / ROB / F • Anal Revolution / 1991 / ROB / M • The Anus Family / 1991 / CC / M • Ariana's Dirty Dancers: The Professionals / 1996 / 4P / M • Bad / 1990 / VC / M • Bardot / 1991 / VI / M • Batwoman & Catgirl / 1992 / HW / M • Bedtime For Byron / 1991 / ME / M • Beverly Hills Geisha / 1992 / V99 / M • Bi Bi Birdie / 1993 / BIL / G • Bi-Golly / 1993 / BIL / G • Bi-Ology: The Making Of Mr Right / 1992 / CAT / G • Big Game / 1990 / LV / M • Black In The Saddle Again / 1991 / ZA / M • Black On White / 1991 / VT / F • Black Stockings / 1990 / VD / M • Boobs, Butts And Bloopers #1 / 1990 / HO / M • Bruce Seven's Favorite Endings #1 / 1991 / EL / C • Bubbles / 1991 / IF / M • Buffy Malibu's Totally Nasty All-Girl Home Videos #03 / 1992 / ANA / F • Bustline / 1993 / LE / M • Butt Sluts #1 / 1993 / ROB / F • Buttman's Ultimate Workout / 1990 / EA / M • Buttslammers #01 / 1993 / BS / F • Cat Lickers #1 / 1990 / ME / F • City Girls / 1991 / VC / M • Club Anal #1 / 1993 / ROB / F • The Cockateer #1 / 1991 / LE / M • The Coming Of Christy / 1990 / CAY / M • Cyrano / 1991 / PL / M • Deep Cheeks #1 / 1991 / ROB / M • Deep Inside Jeanna Fine / 1992 / VC / C • Deep Inside Racquel Darrian / 1994 / VC / C • Depraved / 1993 / BS / B • Desert Fox / 1990 / VD / M • Designer Genes / 1990 / VI / M • Dirty Bob's #27: Laid Back In L.A.! / 1996 / FLP / S • Dirty Looks / 1990 / IN / M • The Distress Factor / 1992 / BS / B • Dr Jeckel & Ms Hide / 1990 / LV / M • Ebony Love / 1992 / VT / C • Edward Penishands #2 / 1991 / VT / M • Edward Penishands #3 / 1991 / VT / M • The Erotic Adventures Of The Three Musketeers / 1992 / CEL / S • Evil Toons / 1990 / PRS / S • Executive Suites / 1993 / PL / M • The Exhibitionist / 1991 / VD / M • Eyewitness Nudes / 1990 / VC / M • Fast Track / 1992 / LIP / F • Femme Fatale / 1993 / SC / M • The Finer Things In Life / 1990 / PL / F • Formal Affair

/ 1991 / ... / M • Genie In A Bikini / 1991 / ZA / M • Gettin' Wet / 1990 / VC / M • A Girl's Best Friend (Madison Is) / 1990 / PL / F • Girls Just Wanna Have Toys / 1993 / PL / F • The Girls' Club / 1990 / VC / F • The Girls' Club / 1993 / VD / C • Girls, Girls And More Girls / 1990 / LV / F • The Harley Girls / 1991 / AR / F • Headbangers Balls / 1991 / PL / M • Heather Hunted / 1990 / VI / M • Hot Body Competition: The Beverly Hill's Naughty Nightie C. / 1995 / CG / F • Hot Dreams / 1991 / VEX / M • Hot On Her Tail / 1990 / CA / M • House Of Sleeping Beauties #1 / 1992 / VI / M • House Of Sleeping Beauties #2 / 1992 / VI / M • I Love X / 1992 / FC / C • If These Walls Could Talk (Director's Cut) / 1993 / MET / M • If These Walls Could Talk #1: Wicked Whispers / 1993 / MET / M • Images Of Desire / 1990 / PM / M • Indian Summer #1 / 1991 / VI / M • Indian Summer #2: Sandstorm / 1991 / VI / M • Innocence Found / 1991 / PAL / G • Introducing Danielle / 1990 / CDI / M • Jail Babes #1 / 1990 / PL / F • Jail Babes #2: Bustin' Out / 1992 / PL / F • The Journey: Oral Majority / 1991 / WV / M • Jugsy (X-Citement) / 1992 / XCI / M • Juicy Lips / 1991 / PL / F • Juicy Sex Scandals / 1991 / VD / M • Junk Yard Dogs / 1991 / FC / M • Kelly Eighteen #2 / 1993 / LE / M • Lady Of The House / 1990 / VEX / M • Laid Off / 1990 / CA / M • The Landlady / 1990 / VI / M • The Last Girl Scout / 1992 / PL / M • The Last Resort / 1990 / VC / M • Leather And Lace Revisited / 1991 / VT / F • Leena Meets Frankenstein / 1993 / OD / M • The Legend Of The Kama Sutra / 1990 / A&E / M • Lesbian Dating Game / 1993 / LIP / F • Little Magicians / 1993 / ANA / M • Lucky Break / 1991 / SE / M • Lusting, London Style / 1992 / VC / M • Magma: Intimate Anal Games / 1994 / MET / M • Maneaters (1992-Vidco) / 1992 / VD / C • Marked #1 / 1993 / FD / M • The Mistress #2 / 1990 / CV / M • Modern Torture / 1992 / PL / B • Naked Obsession / 1992 / VES / S • Naked Truth #2 / 1993 / FH / M • The New Kid On The Block / 1991 / VD / M • New Wave Hookers #2 / 1991 / VC / M • No Boys Allowed / 1991 / VC / F • No Man's Land #04 / 1990 / VT / F • The Only Game In Town / 1991 / VC / M • Only The Best Of Girls With Curves / 1992 / CV / C • Pajama Party / 1993 / CV / C • Parlor Games / 1992 / VT / M • Party Doll A Go-Go #1 / 1991 / VC / M • Party Doll A Go-Go #2 / 1991 / VC / M • The Perfect Pet / 1991 / VEX / C • Personalities / 1991 / PL / M • Play School / 1990 / SO / M • Pointers / 1990 / LV / M • Princess Of The Night / 1990 / VD / M • Private Dancer (Caballero) / 1992 / CA / M • Pussyman #02: The Prize / 1993 / CC / M • Queen Of Hearts #2: Hearts On Fire / 1990 / PL / M • Queen Of Hearts #3: Heartless / 1992 / PL / M • Racquel's Addiction / 1991 / VC / M • Radioactive / 1990 / VIP / M • Red Hot And Ready / 1990 / V99 / M • Scared Stiff / 1992 / PL / B • Secret Recipe / 1990 / PL / F • Secretaries / 1990 / PL / F • Sex Appraisals / 1990 / HO / M • Sex Scientist / 1992 / FD / M • Shameless / 1991 / SC / M • Silver Elegance / 1992 / VT / M • Silver Seduction / 1992 / VT / M • Sno Bunnies / 1990 / PL / F • So Fine / 1992 / VT / C • Sorority Sex Kittens #1 / 1992 / VC / M • Sorority Sex Kittens #2 / 1993 / VC / M •

Splatman / 1992 / FR / M • Surfer Girl / 1992 / PP / M • The Swap #1 / 1990 / VI / M • A Taste Of Madison / 1992 / VD / C • The Three Musketeers #1 / 1992 / FD / M • The Three Musketeers #2 / 1992 / FD / M • Top It Off / 1990 / VC / M • Tori Welles Goes Behind The Scenes / 1992 / FD / M • Torrid Without A Cause #2 / 1990 / VI / M • Total Reball / 1990 / CC / M • Tropic Of Kahlia / 1991 / VI / M • Up Against It / 1993 / ZA / M • Vampirass / 1992 / VC / M • Voodoo Vixens / 1991 / IF / M • Waterbabies #2 / 1992 / CC / M • Wedding Rituals / 1995 / DVP / M • Wenches / 1991 / VT / F • Where The Girls Play / 1992 / CC / F • Where The Girls Sweat #1 / 1990 / EA / F • Where The Girls Sweat #2 / 1991 / EL / F • Who Killed Holly Hollywood? / 1993 / VC / M • Wicked / 1991 / XCI / M • Willing Women / 1993 / VD / C • Zane's World / 1992 / ZA / M

MADISON (1996)
Hell Cats / 1996 / HO / F

MADISON HUGHES
African Angels #2 / 1996 / NIT / M • Amateur Black: Hot Flesh / 1996 / SUF / M • Black Cool / 1996 / EVN / M • Innocent Little Girls #2 / 1996 / MP0 / M

MADISON STONE see Madison

MADONNA
Baring It All / 1995 / PEK / S • Body Of Evidence / 1993 / MGM / S • A Certain Sacrifice / 1980 / WHV / S • Crossing Over / 1990 / IN / M • Playboy Video Magazine #08 / 1985 / PLA / S

MAE BIRD
Erotic Dimensions: Macho Women / 1982 / NSV / M

MAEVA *(Marva, Mava, Maheva Dream)*
Tall, big French blonde.
The Adventures Of Mr. Tootsie Pole #2 / 1995 / LBO / M • Anal Arsenal / 1994 / OD / M • Anal Planet / 1994 / CC / M • Anal Pow Wow / 1995 / XC / M • Anal Virgins Of America #06 / 1994 / FOR / M • Angel Hard / 1996 / STV / M • Bachelor Party #2 / 1993 / FPI / M • Bastille Erotica / 1996 / P69 / M • Blonde Forces #2 / 1994 / CC / M • Chain Gang / 1994 / OD / F • Circus Of Lesbians / 1995 / VI / C • The Cross Of Lust / 1995 / CL0 / M • Della Borsa / 1995 / WIV / M • Dirty Doc's Housecalls #12 / 1994 / LV / M • Dog Walker / 1994 / EA / M • Draghixa With An X / 1994 / EX / M • The Ebony Connection #1 / 1994 / LBO / C • Elements Of Desire / 1994 / ULI / M • Euro-Max #1: Frisky In France / 1995 / SC / M • Euroslut #2 / 1994 / CC / M • French Ed. #2 / 1995 / C69 / M • Games Women Play / 1995 / XC / M • Gangbang Girl #13 / 1994 / ANA / M • Geranalmo / 1994 / PL / M • Girls Off Duty / 1994 / LE / M • The Grind / 1995 / XC / M • Hamlet: For The Love Of Ophelia #1 / 1996 / IP / M • Hamlet: For The Love Of Ophelia #2 / 1996 / IP / M • Hot Tight Asses #06 / 1994 / TCK / M • The Husband / 1995 / WIV / M • International Analists / 1994 / AFD / M • Le Parfum De Mathilde / 1994 / VI / M • M Series #22 / 1994 / LBO / M • Nymphos: They Can't Help It...Really! / 1996 / P69 / M • Off Duty Porn Stars / 1994 / VC / M • Perversity In Paris / 1994 / AVI / M • Rump Man: Goes To Cannes / 1995 / HW / M • Rumpman In And Out Of Africa / 1996 / HW / M • Skin #2 / 1995 / ERQ / M • Sniff Doggy Style / 1994 / PL / M

• Sperm Injection / 1995 / PL / M • Tales From Sodom / 1994 / BLC / M • Up And Cummers #15 / 1994 / 4P / M • Victoria With An "A" / 1994 / PL / M

MAEVA (BRUNETTE)
Anal Explosions #2 / 1996 / NIT / M

MAGANDA see Alex Dane

MAGDA
Tit To Tit #3 / 1995 / BTO / M

MAGDA CORBITT
She-Male Encounters #07: Divine Atrocities #1 / 1981 / MET / G • She-Male Encounters #08: Divine Atrocities #2 / 1981 / MET / G

MAGDA DOLLMA
[Pussy Photographer / 197? / ... / M

MAGDA MONS see Star Index I

MAGDALENA
Dirty Dave's #4 / 1996 / XPR / M • Magma: Puszta Teenies / 1995 / MET / M • Solo Adventures / 1996 / AB / F

MAGELLA
Chateau Duval / 1996 / HDE / M • Frank Thring's Double Penetration #3 / 1996 / XPR / M • The Streets Of Paris / 1996 / SC / M

MAGELLA BRUNO
Miss Anal #3 / 1995 / C69 / M

MAGENTA
Cottontail Club / 1985 / HO / M • Dream Lover / 1985 / CDI / M • Triple X Video Magazine #10 / 1995 / OD / M • Whip Therapy / 1995 / BON / B

MAGGEN MORRIS
Limited Edition #04 / 1979 / AVC / M

MAGGIE
Blue Vanities #130 / 1990 / FFL / M • Blue Vanities #197 / 1993 / FFL / M • FTV #39: Balls In A Bunch / 1996 / FT / B • FTV #40: Triple Terror / 1996 / FT / B • J.E.G.: Just The Way You Like It #29 / 1995 / JEG / M • K-Sex / 1976 / VCR / M • Lesbian Sex, Power & Money / 1994 / STM / F • Mellon Man #05 / 1995 / AVI / M • Mondo Extreme / 1996 / SHS / M • Rev #101a: Rev World / 1990 / REV / M • Rev #221: Inside Maggie / 1990 / REV / M • Spanked In Spades / 1995 / STM / B

MAGGIE (MAY) see Maggie May

MAGGIE BEST see Star Index I

MAGGIE JONES
Flesh...And The Fantasies / 1991 / BIZ / B • Tongue Of Velvet / 1985 / VCR / M

MAGGIE MAE see Maggie May

MAGGIE MATSON
The Nurses / 1971 / SOW / M

MAGGIE MAY *(Maggie (May), Maggie Mae)*
Lithe body, small tits, tight waist, narrow hips, brown/blonde hair, good tan lines, sounds hard and comes from Toronto, Canada where she was a nude dancer. Facially quite pretty but with a slight double chin. This is not the same as the English redhead who was called "Can Can Maggie" and appeared in the **Dirty Diner** series.
The Anal-Europe Series #05: Anal European Vacation / 1993 / LV / M • Butt Seriously Folks / 1994 / AFV / M • Controlled / 1994 / FD / M • F-Channel / 1994 / AFV / F • More Dirty Debutantes #27 / 1993 / 4P / M • The Pink Lady Detective Agency: Case Of The Twisted Sister / 1994 / IN / M • Raw Sex #01 / 1994 / ERW / M • Superstar Sex Challenge #1 / 1994 / VC / M • The Tattle Tail / 1993 / ME / M • Up And Cummers #08

/ 1994 / 4P / M • Whorelock / 1993 / LV / M

MAGGIE PEARSON see Star Index I

MAGGIE PYLE
Thundercrack! / 1974 / LUM / M

MAGGIE RANDALL see Liz Randall

MAGGIE RAY
Matinee Idol / 1984 / VC / M

MAGGIE SINCLAIR
Little Girls Blue #2 / 1983 / VCX / M

MAGGIE SMITH
Black Bad Girls / 1985 / PLY / M • Bordello...House Of The Rising Sun / 1985 / SE / M • Ebony Ecstacy / 1988 / HIO / C • Woman Of The Night / 1971 / SVE / M

MAGGIE SNATCHER see Taylor Wayne

MAGGIE THAMES see Star Index I

MAGGIE WILLIAMS
Hungry Eyed Woman / cr71 / VCX / M

MAGGIE WILSON *(Margaret Smith)*
Note that Maggie Smith is a different person (probably black).
Fantasies Of Jennifer Faye / 1983 / GO / M • In Love / 1983 / VC / M

MAGIC see Star Index I

MAGIC LADY see Star Index I

MAGIC MARK see Star Index I

MAGIC PASSION see Star Index I

MAGICK see Star Index I

MAGNIFICENT MARGO
Dream Lovers / 1980 / MET / G • Dude Looks Like A Lady / 1993 / SC / G • She-Male Encounters #01: Tanatalizing Toni / 1981 / MET / G • She-Male Encounters #04: Jaded Jennifer / 1981 / MET / G • She-Male Encounters #09: She-Male Confidential / 1984 / MET / G • Squalor Motel / 1985 / SE / M • Sulka's Daughter / 1984 / MET / G

MAGNOLIA LANKERSHIM see Star Index I

MAGNOLIA THUNDER see Star Index I

MAGNUM
Amadeus Mozart / 1996 / XC / M • Dirty Dancers #1 / 1994 / 4P / M • Dirty Dancers #5 / 1995 / 4P / M • East Coast Sluts #03: South Florida / 1995 / PL / M

MAGNUM D.
8-Ball: Westside Gang Bang / 1995 / PL / M • Abused / 1996 / ZA / M • Black Babes / 1995 / LV / M • Black Gangbangers #03 / 1995 / HW / M • Booty In Da House / 1995 / EVN / M • Call Of The Wild / 1995 / AFI / M • The Case Of The Black Booty / 1996 / LV / M • Contrast / 1995 / CA / M • Ebony Princess / 1994 / IN / M • Forbidden Subjects #3 / 1995 / FC / M • Gang Bang Party / 1994 / HW / M • Gangbang Girl #15 / 1995 / ANA / M • Girlz N The Hood #5 / 1995 / HW / M • Interview: Chocolate Treats / 1995 / LV / M • Interview: New And Natural / 1995 / LV / M • The Kiss / 1995 / WP / M • Lady's Choice / 1995 / VD / M • Maverdick / 1995 / WV / M • Persia's Back / 1994 / VT / M • Playmates Of The Rich And Famous / 1995 / BBE / M • Ready To Drop #06 / 1995 / FC / M • Rump-Shaker #4 / 1995 / HW / M • Sex Secrets Of A Mistress / 1995 / VI / M • Shake Your Booty / 1996 / EVN / M • So Bad / 1995 / VT / M • Toot Z Roll / 1995 / WP / M • Video Virgins #13 / 1994 / NS / M • Video Virgins #17 / 1994 / NS / M

MAHALIA
Erotic Westernscapes / 1994 / PHV / S • Penthouse: 1993 Pet Of The Year Winners / 1993 / PET / F • Primal / 1994 / PHV / S •

Sex Off The Runway / 1991 / GMI / M

MAHAMMAD CADILLAC *see Star Index I*

MAHEVA DREAM *see* **Maeva**

MAHOGANY
The Adventures Of Peeping Tom #1 / 1996 / OD / M • Bite The Black Bullets / 1995 / ME / M • Black Cheerleader Search #08 / 1996 / IVC / M • Fashion sluts #5: Ethnic Ecstasy / 1995 / ABS / M • How To Make Love To A Black Woman #1: You Gotta Have Rhythm / 1996 / VCX / M • My Baby Got Back #08 / 1996 / VT / M • My Baby Got Back #09 / 1996 / VT / M • My Baby Got Back #10 / 1996 / VT / M • Sista! #4 / 1996 / VT / F • Sista! #5 / 1996 / VT / F • Up And Cummers #31 / 1996 / 4P / M • Video Virgins #25 / 1995 / NS / M • Waiting For The Man / 1996 / VT / M

MAI
Sweet Dreams / 1994 / ORE / C

MAI LIN *(Miko Moto, Lily Wong, Mai Tai)*
Miki Moto is ex **Prisoner Of Paradise**. Marginal looking, hard, small tits.
1001 Erotic Nights #1 / 1982 / VC / M • All About Annette / 1982 / SE / C • All The King's Ladies / 1981 / SUP / M • All The Way In / 1984 / VC / M • Amanda By Night #1 / 1981 / CA / M • Amber's Desires / 1985 / CA / M • American Desire / 1981 / CA / M • Anal Asians / 1991 / PL / F • Anal Delights #2 / 1992 / ROB / M • Anal Thrills / 1992 / ROB / M • The Awakening Of Sally / 1984 / VCR / M • Battle Of The Stars #1 / 1985 / NSV / M • Beauty / 1981 / VC / M • The Best Little Whorehouse In San Francisco / 1984 / LA / M • The Best Of Oriental Anal #1 / 1994 / ROB / C • Between Lovers / 1983 / CA / M • Beyond Shame / 1980 / VEP / M • Black 'n' White In Color / 1987 / VCR / C • Black In The Saddle / 1990 / ZA / M • The Black Mystique / 1986 / CV / M • Black Silk Secrets / 1989 / VC / C • The Blonde / 1980 / VCX / M • The Blonde Next Door / 1982 / GO / M • Blue Vanities #042 (Old) / 1988 / FFL / M • Blue Vanities #065 / 1988 / FFL / M • Blue Vanities #505 / 1992 / FFL / M • Boobs, Butts And Bloopers #2 / 1990 / HO / M • Bunz-Eye / 1992 / ROB / M • Campus Capers / 1982 / VC / M • Chills / 1989 / LV / M • China Bitch / 1989 / PV / C • China Girl / 1989 / V99 / M • Cracked Ice / 1977 / PVX / M • The Dancers / 1981 / VCX / M • Debi Does Girls / 1992 / PL / F • Deep Throat #5 / 1990 / AR / M • Desire / 1983 / VCX / M • Disoriented / 1992 / VI / M • Double Dare / 1986 / SE / M • The Dragon Lady #1 / 1988 / WV / C • Endless Passion / 1987 / LIM / C • Erotic Dimensions #7: Fulfilled / 1982 / NSV / M • Erotic Dimensions: Explicit / 1982 / NSV / M • Erotic Dimensions: Macho Women / 1982 / NSV / M • Femme Fatale / 1984 / VIV / M • Fortune Cookie Nookie / 1986 / VCS / C • Girl Games / 1987 / PL / C • Girlfriends / 1983 / MIT / M • Going Wild / 1983 / ... / M • Gourmet Quickies: Mai Lin #724 / 1985 / GO / C • GVC: Olympix Affair #137 / 1985 / GO / M • The Heat Is On / 1985 / WV / M • Hot Cargo / 1990 / MID / M • Hot Ones / 1982 / SUP / C • Hyapatia Lee's Secret Dreams / 1986 / SE / M • I Love A Girl In A Uniform / 1989 / VC / C • Inspiration / 1981 / CHX / M • Interlude Of Lust / 1981 / CA / M • Irresistible #1 / 1982 / SE / M • Karate Girls / 1987 / VCR / M • Lip Service / 1987

/ BIK / C • Lottery Fever / 1985 / BEA / M • Love From The Backside / 1989 / FAZ / M • Lusty Ladies #07 / 1984 / 4P / M • Mai Lin Vs Serena / 1982 / HIF / M • Mai Lin's Anal Asians / 1992 / PL / C • The Many Shades Of Amber / 1986 / LIM / M • Marathon / 1982 / CA / M • Moments Of Love / 1983 / MID / M • Nasty Lady / 1984 / CV / M • National Pornographic #2: Orientals / 1987 / 4P / C • Object Of Desire / 1979 / GO / B • One Night At A Time / 1984 / PV / M • One Night In Bangkok / 1985 / CA / M • Only The Best Of Barbara Dare / 1990 / CV / C • Only The Best Of Debbie / 1992 / MET / C • Oriental Hawaii / 1982 / CA / M • Oriental Lesbian Fantasies / 1984 / PL / F • Oriental Madam / 1981 / TGA / M • Oriental Obsession / 1993 / HO / C • Oriental Spice / 1990 / SE / M • Oriental Temptations / 1984 / CV / C • Oriental Treatment #2: The Pearl Divers / 1989 / AR / M • Parliament: Super Head #1 / 1989 / PM / C • Peepholes / 1982 / AVC / M • Physical #2 / 1985 / SUP / M • The Pleasure Hunt #2 / 1985 / NSV / M • Pleasure Zone / 1984 / SE / M • Prisoner Of Paradise / 1980 / VCX / M • Queen Of Hearts #3: Heartless / 1992 / PL / M • Rambone: The First Time / 1985 / JOH / M • Rated Sex / 1986 / SE / M • Regency #01 / 1981 / RHV / M • The Return Of Johnny Wadd / 1986 / PEN / M • Rock Hard / 1985 / CV / M • Sex Life Of A Porn Star / 1986 / ELH / M • Sex On The Orient Express / 1991 / VC / C • Sex Wars / 1984 / EXF / M • Sex-O-Gram / 1986 / LA / M • Sexcapades / 1983 / VC / M • Sexual Heights / 1981 / ... / M • Sexual Odyssey / 1985 / VC / M • Silk, Satin & Sex / 1983 / SE / M • Skin On Skin / 1981 / CV / M • Skintight / 1981 / CA / M • Sorority Pink #2 / 1989 / CV / M • The Specialist / 1990 / HO / M • Spoiled Rich / 1989 / CC / M • Street Heat / 1984 / VC / M • Suzie Superstar #1 / 1983 / CV / M • Swedish Erotica #15 / 1980 / CA / M • Swedish Erotica #30 / 1980 / CA / M • Swedish Erotica #57 / 1984 / CA / M • Taboo #07 / 1980 / IN / M • A Taste Of Taija Rae / 1989 / PIN / C • That's Outrageous / 1983 / CA / M • Three Men And A Geisha / 1990 / HO / M • To Man From Woman / 19?? / BL / M • Triple Xposure / 1986 / VD / M • Undulations / 1980 / VC / M • Up The Ying Yang / 1991 / EVN / C • VCA Previews #1 / 1988 / VC / C • Video Girls / 1984 / LIP / F • The Wacky World Of X-Rated Bloopers / 1989 / GO / M • Wet Panties / 1989 / MIR / C • Wet Pink / 1989 / PL / F • When Love Came To Town / 1989 / EVN / M • Wicked Sensations #1 / 1981 / CA / M • Yamamaha Mamas / 1983 / TGA / C • Yellow Fever / 1984 / PL / M

MAI LING *see* **Jasmine**

MAI TAI *see* **Mai Lin**

MAIKO KAZAMA
The Toy Woman / 1984 / ... / S • [Love Thy Neighbor's Wife / 19?? / ... / M

MAILE *(Mei-Lin)*
Small breasted Asian girl with a bad overbite and very bad teeth but quite a nice personality. 5'2" tall and 19 years old in 1993.
Euroslut #1: French Tart / 1993 / CC / M • A Geisha's Secret / 1993 / VI / M • The Golden Dagger / 1993 / LON / B • Her Darkest Desire / 1993 / HOM / B • The Interrogation / 1994 / HOM / B • Molly B-Goode / 1994 / FH / M • New Ends #03 /

1993 / 4P / M • Pai Gow Video #01: Asian Beauties / 1993 / EVN / M • Pai Gow Video #02: Wok & Roll / 1993 / EVN / M • The Price Of Curiosity / 1993 / LON / B • Rising Buns / 1993 / HW / M • Up And Cummers #02 / 1993 / 4P / M • Up And Cummers #08 / 1994 / 4P / M

MAIR SIMON
Ancient Secrets Of Sexual Ecstasy / 1996 / HIG / M

MAIZIE
Blue Vanities #565 / 1995 / FFL / M

MAJENTA
Joe Elliot's College Girls #35 / 1994 / JOE / M

MAJORIE
Odyssey Amateur #84: Majorie's First 3-Way / 1991 / OD / M

MAJORIE MILLER *see* **Blondi**

MAKALA *see* **Mikala**

MAKALA (1994)
Hole In One / 1994 / HO / M

MAKAYA LEIGH *see* **Lana Sands**

MAKAYLA *see* **Lana Sands**

MAKAYLA LEIGH *see* **Lana Sands**

MAKAYLUH LEIGH *see* **Lana Sands**

MAKETA
Amsterdam Nights #2 / 1996 / VC / M

MAL CROSS
Heat Wave / 1977 / COM / M

MAL O'RAE *see* **Scott Mallory**

MAL O'REE *see* **Scott Mallory**

MAL WOROB *see* **Carter Stevens**

MALCOLM (RICK O'S) *see* **Rick O'Shea**

MALCOLM DOVE *see Star Index I*

MALCOLM S. WOROB *see* **Carter Stevens**

MALCOLM SANDS *see* **Dave Cummings**

MALCOLM ZEE *see Star Index I*

MALCOMB DAY *see Star Index I*

MALE TOY
Petticoat Therapy / 1994 / LEO / G

MALEKA MOUR
Irresistible #1 / 1982 / SE / M

MALIA *(Shawnee (Malia), Shawnee Cates, Shawnee E. Cates, Malika, Shawn Lee, Talia (Malia))*
Medium titted but quite pretty white/slightly oriental girl. Good skin. Born Jul 12, 1970 in Seoul, Korea. Came to the US when she was 18. Friend of Mimi Miyagi. First appearance was probably **MDD #09**. Supposedly she has retired and will be dancing and going to UCLA.
Almost Home Alone / 1993 / SFP / M • Amateur Lesbians #25: International Budapest / 1992 / GO / F • Amateur Lesbians #35: Meo / 1993 / GO / F • Amateur Lesbians #36: Candi / 1993 / GO / F • Anal Asians / 1991 / PL / F • Anal Cuties #3 / 1992 / ROB / M • Anal Ski Vacation / 1993 / ANA / M • The Anal-Europe Series #01: The Fisherman's Wife / 1992 / LV / M • Asian Angel / 1993 / VEX / C • Asian Heat #01: Cherry Blossom Tales / 1993 / SC / M • Asian Heat #02: Satin Angels / 1993 / SC / M • Asian Heat #03: Tales Of The Golden Lotus / 1993 / SC / M • Asian Silk / 1992 / VI / M • Ass-Capades / 1992 / HW / M • Back To The Orient / 1992 / HW / M • Backstage Entrance #1 / 1992 / FH / M • Bad To The Bone / 1992 / LE / M • Beach Bum Amateur's #21 / 1993 / MID / F • Bedrooms And Boardrooms / 1992 / DR / M • The Best Of Oriental Anal #1 / 1994 / ROB / C • Big Murray's New-Cummers #09: Orien-

tal Lovers / 1993 / FD / M • Black By Popular Demand / 1992 / ZA / M • Black Jack City #2: Black's Revenge / 1992 / HW / M • Blonde City / 1992 / IN / M • Blue Angel / 1992 / AFV / M • Blue Angel / 1992 / AFV / M • Buffy Malibu's Totally Nasty All-Girl Home Videos #01 / 1992 / ANA / F • Buffy Malibu's Nasty Girls #08 / 1995 / ANA / F • Buffy Malibu's Nasty Girls #09 / 1995 / ANA / F • Buttman Vs Buttwoman / 1992 / EL / M • Buttwiser / 1992 / HW / M • Captain Butt's Beach / 1992 / LV / M • Cheerleader Nurses #1 / 1993 / VC / M • Cheerleader Nurses #2 / 1993 / VC / M • China Black / 1992 / IN / M • Chocolate & Vanilla Twist / 1992 / PL / F • Club DV8 #1 / 1993 / SC / M • Committed / 1992 / LE / M • Crash In The Rear / 1992 / HW / C • Deep C Diver / 1992 / LV / M • Deep Inside Jeanna Fine / 1992 / VC / C • Deep Inside Nikki Sinn / 1996 / VC / C • Dial A Nurse / 1992 / VD / M • The Dragon Lady #3: Tales From The Bed #2 / 1992 / WV / M • Driving Miss Daisy Crazy #2 / 1992 / WV / M • Dyno-Mite / 1992 / IF / M • The Erotic Adventures Of The Three Musketeers / 1992 / CEL / S • Erotic Dripping Orientals / 1993 / WV / M • Fast Track / 1992 / LIP / F • Final Anal Tease / 1992 / MID / M • Gazongas #04 / 1993 / LEI / C • Girls And Guns / 1992 / KBR / M • Girls Just Wanna Have Toys / 1993 / PL / F • Girlz N The Hood #2 / 1992 / HW / M • Gold LeMay / 1991 / VIM / M • Gone Wild / 1993 / LV / M • Guttman's Paris Vacation / 1993 / PL / M • Hardcore Copy / 1993 / PL / M • Heads Or Tails? / 1993 / PL / M • Heartbeats / 1992 / LE / M • Heatwave #1 / 1992 / FH / F • Ho' Style Takeover / 1993 / FH / M • Hollywood's Hills / 1992 / LV / M • Hometown Honeys #4 / 1993 / VEX / M • Hot Body Video Magazine: Naughty But Nice / 1994 / CG / F • House Of Spartacus #1 / 1993 / IF / M • Hyapatia Obsessed / 1993 / EX / M • In Loving Color #3 / 1992 / VT / M • In Your Face #1 / 1992 / PL / M • Just One Look / 1993 / V99 / M • Lesbian Pros And Amateurs #22 / 1993 / GO / F • Little Magicians / 1993 / ANA / M • Living Doll / 1992 / CDI / M • M Series #02 / 1993 / LBO / M • Madam X / 1992 / HO / M • Made In Japan / 1992 / VI / M • Major Slut / 1993 / LV / M • Married With Hormones #2 / 1992 / PL / M • The Merry Widows / 1993 / VC / M • Mike Hott: #198 Horny Couples #01 / 1992 / MHV / M • Mike Hott: #201 Lesbian Sluts #04 / 1992 / MHV / F • Mike Hott: Apple Asses #01 / 1992 / MHV / F • More Dirty Debutantes #09 / 1991 / 4P / M • More Dirty Debutantes #23 / 1993 / 4P / M • More Dirty Debutantes #28 / 1994 / 4P / M • Mr. Peepers Amateur Home Videos #25: The 25th Anniversary Ed / 1991 / LBO / M • Naked Goddess #1 / 1991 / VC / M • Nasty Nymphos #06 / 1994 / ANA / M • Naughty Nurses / 1992 / VD / C • Night Of Passion / 1993 / BIA / C • Nothing Else Matters / 1992 / V99 / C • Oral Madness #2 / 1992 / OD / M • Oriental Anal Sluts / 1993 / WV / C • Oriental Treatment #3: The Lost Empress / 1991 / AFV / M • Oriental Treatment #4: The Demon Lover / 1992 / AFV / M • Pajama Party / 1993 / CV / C • Penthouse: Satin & Lace #1 / 1992 / PET / F • Phone Fantasy #2 / 1992 / ATL / M • The Pick Up / 1993 / MID / M • Puttin' Out /

1992 / VD / M • Raunch #04: Silver Melts / 1991 / CC / M • Ready And Willing / 1993 / VEX / M • Sexual Olympics #1: The Trials / 1992 / VT / M • Sexual Olympics #2: The Finals / 1992 / VT / M • Seymore Butts Rides Again / 1992 / FH / M • Silver Seduction / 1992 / VT / M • Snakedance / 1992 / VI / M • Sorority Sex Kittens #1 / 1992 / VC / M • Sorority Sex Kittens #2 / 1993 / VC / M • Spanish Fly / 1992 / LE / M • Sweet Things / 1992 / VEX / M • Take My Wife, Please / 1993 / WP / M • Too Cute For Words / 1992 / V99 / M • Tori Welles Goes Behind The Scenes / 1992 / FD / M • Voyeur Video / 1992 / ZA / M • Walking Small / 1992 / ZA / M • Web Of Darkness / 1993 / BS / B • Wet & Wicked / 1992 / VEX / M • Wet Silk #1 / 1995 / SC / C • Wild Fire / 1990 / WV / C • The Worst Porno Ever Made With The Best Sex / 1993 / PL / M

MALIBU
AVP #9153: The Monday Night Game / 1991 / AVP / M • Behind The Backdoor #7 / 1995 / EVN / M • Sex Search / 1988 / IN / S • Spanking Debutantes / 1992 / RB / B

MALIBU BARBI see *Star Index I*
MALIBU ROSE see *Star Index I*
MALICCIA see Malitia
MALIKA see Malia
MALINE see *Star Index I*
MALISHA
Ass Angels / 1996 / PAL / F • Butt Jammers #05 / 1996 / SC / F

MALITIA *(Maliccia, Melicia)*
Too tall (5'11"/6'00") reddish blonde with shoulder length fine hair, not too pretty face, lithe but large body, rock solid cantaloupes, and a pushy attitude. She says (in 1996) she's 23 years old, was de-virginized at 16 and comes from Glendale, CA. In **More Dirty Debutantes #48** she had tiny tits and said she was 22 years old. Melicia is from **Nineteen #1**.
Ass Freaks #2 / 1995 / ROB / F • Asses Galore #7: Lunatic Fringe / 1996 / DFI / M • Barby's On Butt Row / 1996 / ABS / M • Club Anal #3 / 1995 / ROB / F • Eighteen #3 / 1996 / SC / M • Eighteen & Easy / 1996 / SC / M • Frendz? #2 / 1996 / RAS / M • Interview: New And Natural / 1995 / LV / M • More Dirty Debutantes #48 / 1995 / 4P / M • Nineteen #1 / 1996 / FOR / M • Pick Up Lines #08 / 1996 / OD / M • Pussyman's Nite Club Party #1 / 1996 / SNA / M • Pussyman's Nite Club Party #2 / 1997 / SNA / M • Raw Footage / 1996 / VC / M • Rockhard (Sin City) / 1996 / SC / M • Video Virgins #32 / 1996 / NS / M

MALMO
Swedish Sex / 1996 / PL / M
MAME GROVES see *Star Index I*
MAME YONG
Private Film #15 / 1994 / OD / M
MANA LA FANTUNA
Frat House / 1979 / NGV / M
MANAMI NISHI
Unchained Instinct / 1996 / AVE / M
MANCHILD
It Could Happen To You / 1996 / HW / M
MANCOW
Shane's World #3 / 1996 / OD / M
MANDI
Tight Ties / 1994 / BON / B
MANDI WINE *(Mandi Wyne)*
Anal Angels #2 / 1990 / VEX / C • The Babes Of Bonerville / 1995 / VEX / C •

Backstage Pass / 1992 / VEX / M • Black Valley Girls #2 / 1989 / DR / M • Blue Heaven / 1990 / IF / M • Buns And Roses (V9) / 1990 / V99 / M • Caught From Behind #09 / 1988 / HO / M • Chills / 1989 / LV / M • Coming Of Age / 1989 / CA / M • Coming On America / 1989 / VWA / M • Con Jobs / 1990 / V99 / M • Dane's Surprise / 1991 / IF / G • Dirty Books / 1990 / V99 / M • Dirty Tricks / 1990 / VEX / M • Double Trouble / 1988 / V99 / M • Easy Lover / 1989 / EX / M • Easy Pickin's / 1990 / LV / M • Fantasy Drive / 1990 / VEX / M • Fun In A Bun / 1990 / LV / M • Having It All / 1991 / VEX / M • Heraldo: Streetwalkers Of NY / 1990 / GOT / M • Hollywood Hustle #2 / 1990 / V99 / M • Hungry / 1990 / GLE / M • I Dream Of Christy / 1989 / CAY / M • If Looks Could Kill / 1992 / V99 / M • Internal Affair / 1990 / V99 / M • Intimate Affairs / 1990 / VEX / M • Jug Humpers / 1995 / V99 / C • Keep It Cumming / 1990 / V99 / M • Leading Lady / 1991 / V99 / M • Legal Tender (1990-X) / 1990 / VC / M • The Life Of The Party / 1991 / ZA / M • A Live Nude Girl / 1989 / VWA / M • Monday Nite Ball / 1990 / VT / M • Naturally Sweet / 1989 / VEX / M • Naughty Neighbors / 1989 / CA / M • A Night At The Waxworks / 1990 / IF / M • One Flew Over The Cuckoo's Breast / 1989 / FAZ / M • Party Dolls / 1992 / VEX / M • Passion Princess / 1991 / VEX / M • Playing Dirty / 1989 / VEX / M • Pleasure Is My Business / 1989 / EX / M • Plenty Of Pleasure / 1990 / WET / M • Retail Slut / 1989 / LV / M • Riding Miss Daisy / 1990 / VEX / M • Rituals / 1989 / V99 / M • Santa Comes Again / 1990 / GLE / M • Savage Fury #2 / 1989 / CAY / M • Say Something Nasty / 1989 / CC / M • Scent Of A Wild Woman / 1993 / EVN / C • Seduction / 1990 / VEX / M • Sex About Town / 1990 / LV / M • Sex Crazed / 1989 / VEX / M • Sins Of Tami Monroe / 1991 / CA / C • Slumber Party / 1990 / LV / M • The Slutty Professor / 1989 / VWA / M • Storm Warning / 1989 / LV / M • Super Ball / 1989 / VWA / M • Suzie Superstar #3 / 1989 / CV / M • Swedish Erotica Featurettes #3 / 1989 / CA / M • Switch Hitters #4: The Grand Slam / 1989 / IN / G • Tales Of The Golden Pussy / 1989 / RUM / M • Teach Me Tonight / 1990 / VEX / M • These Buns For Hire / 1990 / LV / M • Ticket To Ride / 1990 / LV / M • Toppers #19 / 1993 / TV / M • Toppers #20 / 1993 / TV / M • Toppers #21 / 1993 / TV / C • Toppers #22 / 1993 / TV / C • Toppers #24 / 1994 / TV / M • Toppers #30 / 1994 / TV / C • Uncut Diamond / 1989 / IN / M • Vixens / 1989 / LV / F • Wet Fingers / 1990 / HIO / M • White Satin Nights / 1991 / V99 / M • Who Reamed Rosie Rabbit? #1 / 1989 / FAN / M • Wives Of The Rich And Famous / 1989 / V99 / M • Words Of Love / 1989 / LE / M

MANDI WYNE see Mandi Wine
MANDII see Laurel Canyon
MANDY
Blue Vanities #574 / 1996 / FFL / M • Blue Vanities #578 / 1995 / FFL / M • Joe Elliot's Black College Girls #01 / 1995 / JOE / M • Northwest Pecker Trek #5: Cumming In King County / 1995 / LBO / M • Royal Ass Force / 1996 / VC / M • Suze's Centerfolds #6 / 1981 / CA / M
MANDY (LAUREL CAN) see Laurel

Canyon

MANDY ALISON
Huge Grant On The Sunset Strip / 1995 / EVN / M

MANDY ASHLEY see Star Index I

MANDY FOXXX
Small lithe-bodied (except for tits which are medium-enhanced) blonde with a large tattoo of what looks like a dog's head on her right shoulder back. Says she's married. Tight waist and small hips, not too pretty facially but sounds like she wants to please.
The Beaverly Hillbillies / 1993 / IP / M • Dr Butts #3 / 1993 / 4P / M • Lovin' Spoonfuls #6 / 1996 / 4P / C • More Dirty Debutantes #29 / 1994 / 4P / M • Up And Cummers: The Movie / 1994 / 4P / M

MANDY JAMES
Charming Cheapies #5: Fancy Flesh / 1985 / 4P / M

MANDY JONES
Just Deserts / 1991 / BIZ / B

MANDY KING
The Inseminator #2: Domination Day / 1994 / LBO / M

MANDY LANE see Star Index I

MANDY MONROE see Star Index I

MANDY SPARKS
Golden Girls, The Movie / 1984 / SE / M

MANDY ST JOHN
Steamy Dreams / cr70 / CVX / M

MANDY STARR see Mindy Rae

MANDY WHITE see Alicyn Sterling

MANFRED SPIES
[Junge Madchen Mogen's HeiB, Hausfrauen Noch HeiBer / 1973 / ... / M

MAGNUM
The Best Of East Coast Sluts / 1995 / PL / C

MANIA
Prima #01: Anal Poker / 1995 / MBP / M

MANIE MEITER
Get Bi Tonight / 1991 / PL / G

MANLEY MANN see Star Index I

MANNIE CLAYTON
Two Way Mirror / 1985 / CV / M

MANNIE HARDING
School Teacher's Weekend Vacation / cr72 / SVE / M

MANNY SPEIGEL
Hungry Eyed Woman / cr71 / VCX / M

MANNY WIERDMANN
Purely Physical / 1982 / SE / M

MANON
Private Film #21 / 1995 / OD / M

MANTRA STARK
Little Showoffs / 1984 / VC / M • Nurses Of The 407th / 1982 / CA / M

MANUEL CRUZ see Star Index I

MANUEL PEREIRO
[Le Journal Intime D'Une Nymphomane / 1972 / ... / M

MANUELLE PHALLE
Skin #1 / 1994 / EUR / M

MANYA *(Cristina Colecchia)*
Italian, 29 years old in 1995, ugly face, hairy ass crack, womanly body, big tits.
N.Y. Video Magazine #06 / 1995 / OUP / M • New York City Lesbian Gang Bang / 1995 / OUP / F • Streets Of New York #06 / 1996 / PL / M • Western Whores Hotel / 1996 / VG0 / M

MAO see Meo

MAO (ASIAN) see Star Index I

MARA
Blue Vanities #511 / 1992 / FFL / M

MARA AMADO see Cumisha Amado

MARA SOL see Star Index I

MARARA DUNN see Star Index I

MARC
Honeypie / 1975 / VC / M • Sugar Britches / 1980 / VCX / C • Uncle Roy's Amateur Home Video #16 / 1992 / VIM / M

MARC ALEXIS
Gangbang Girl #04 / 1992 / ANA / M

MARC BARROW
Family Affair / 1996 / XC / M

MARC BROCK
The Love Witch / 1973 / AR / M

MARC BROWN see Marc DeBruin

MARC CURTIS see Mark Carriere

MARC DAVID see Star Index I

MARC DEBRUIN *(Marc Brown, Jim Uzi, Mark Brown, Johnny (Marc DeBrui))*
The Adventures Of Buttman / 1989 / EA / M • The Best Of Andrew Blake / 1993 / CA / C • Best Of Caught From Behind #5 / 1991 / HO / C • Caught From Behind #12 / 1989 / HO / M • Double Jeopardy / 1990 / HO / M • Dutch Masters / 1990 / IN / M • Dutch Treat / 1989 / BON / B • Hidden Desire / 1989 / HO / M • Insatiable Immigrants / 1989 / VT / M • Kiss My Grits / 1989 / CA / M • Lust In The Woods / 1990 / VI / M • Night Trips #1 / 1989 / CA / M • Postcards From Abroad / 1991 / CA / C • Rainwoman #02 / 1990 / CC / M • Swedish Erotica Featurettes #3 / 1989 / CA / M

MARC FRANCIS
Desire / 1990 / VC / M

MARC GOLD see Marc Wallice

MARC GREENE
Hot Properties / 1975 / CA / M • Little Orphan Sammy / 1976 / VC / M

MARC HOWARD see Richard Pacheco

MARC LEBEAU see Star Index I

MARC LUKATHER
Private Film #10 / 1994 / OD / M

MARC RADCLIFFE see Star Index I

MARC ROBERTS see Star Index I

MARC ROSS
Angel Pays Her Bill / 1994 / VIG / B • Asking For Bondage / 1994 / VIG / B • The Binding Of Kelly / 1995 / GAL / B • Bound Seductress / 1994 / VIG / B • Bunny's Bind / 1994 / GAL / B • Cassandra's Punishment #1 / 1994 / GAL / B • Gina Learns The Ropes / 1994 / VIG / B • Master's Delight / 1994 / VIG / B • Rope Dance / 1994 / VIG / B • Stevie's Bondage Seduction #1 / 1995 / IBN / B • Stevie's Bondage Seduction #2 / 1995 / GAL / B

MARC RYDER see Star Index I

MARC SABER
Conflict Of Interest / 1994 / FST / G

MARC SKOVRAS see Star Index I

MARC SLATER
My Sister Seka / 1981 / CA / M

MARC STEVENS *(Mick Allman, Dave Longshlong)*
Young blonde male also know as Mr Ten-and-a-half referring to the length of his dick. Died 1989 of AIDS (one story). Story #2: died in 1989 all right but of a heart attack brought on by excessive drug use. I prefer the AIDS version because it's a NY source and it details much of his past history; the other is remote hearsay (someone told me that they were told, etc).
The $50,000 Climax Show / 1975 / ... / M • ABA: Double Feature #3 / 1996 / ALP / M • All About Gloria Leonard / 1978 / VXP / M

• Angel On Fire / 1974 / ALP / M • Angela, The Fireworks Woman / 1975 / VC / M • Assault Of Innocence / cr78 / VHL / M • Badge 69 / cr74 / SVE / M • The Big Thing / 1973 / VHL / M • Black Licorice / 1985 / CDI / M • Blow Some My Way / 1977 / VHL / M • Blue Vanities #229 / 1994 / FFL / M • Blue Vanities #239 / 1995 / FFL / M • Blue Vanities #256 / 1996 / FFL / M • Bottoms Up #01 / 1983 / AVC / C • Bottoms Up / 1974 / SOW / M • Bridal Intrigue / 1975 / VHL / M • Bucky Beaver's XXX Dragon Art Theatre Double Feature #05 / 1996 / SOW / M • Campus Girl / 1972 / VXP / M • Centerfold Fever / 1981 / VXP / M • Certified Mail / 1975 / CDC / M • Cherry Blossom / 1972 / VXP / M • Christy / 1975 / CA / M • Cocktales / 1985 / AT / M • Consenting Adults / 1981 / VXP / M • Contact / 1975 / VC / M • Deep Sleep / cr72 / ... / M • Defiance / 1974 / ALP / B • Devil In Miss Jones #1 / 1972 / VC / M • Devil's Due / 1974 / ALP / M • Dominatrix Without Mercy / 1976 / ALP / B • Dr Teen Dilemma / 1973 / VHL / M • Drills And Frills / cr75 / BOC / M • Ecstasy In Blue / 1976 / ALP / M • Employee Benefits / 1983 / AMB / M • Every Inch A Lady / 1975 / QX / M • Fantasy Club Of America / 1980 / BL / M • Fantasy Peeps: Sensuous Delights / 1984 / 4P / M • French Kiss / 1979 / PVX / M • French Shampoo / 1978 / VXP / M • French Wives / 1970 / VC / M • Gourmet Quickies: Vanessa Del Rio #710 / 1984 / GO / C • GVC: Forbidden Ways #114 / 1978 / GO / M • GVC: Hotel Hooker #113 / 1975 / GO / M • GVC: Strange Family / 1977 / GO / M • Head Nurse / cr74 / VXP / M • High Rise / 1973 / QX / M • Historic Erotica #2: Hippies In Heat / 1992 / GMI / M • Honeymoon Suite / 1974 / VHL / M • Hypnorotica / 1972 / EVI / M • In Sarah's Eyes / 1975 / VHL / M • Inside Georgina Spelvin / 1974 / VC / M • International Intrigue / 1983 / AMB / M • Intimate Teenagers / 1974 / BL / M • It Happened In Hollywood / 1973 / WWV / M • Joe Rock Superstar / cr76 / ALP / M • Joy Riders / 1975 / SAT / M • Keep On Truckin' / cr73 / BL / M • Lady On The Couch / 1978 / SVE / M • Lip Service / 1974 / VHL / M • The Love Bus / 1974 / OSC / M • Meatball / 1972 / VCX / M • The Millionairess / cr74 / CDC / M • Naked Came The Stranger / 1975 / VC / M • The Newcomers / 1973 / VSH / M • Not A Love Story / 1980 / ... / M • Not Just Another Woman / 1974 / ... / M • Over Sexposure / 1974 / VHL / M • The Passions Of Carol / 1975 / VXP / M • Powerbone / 1976 / VC / M • The Private Afternoons Of Pamela Mann / 1974 / TVX / M • Prurient Interest / 1974 / BL / M • Psyched For Sex / cr73 / BL / M • Purely Physical / 1982 / SE / M • Revolving Teens / 1974 / SEP / M • Road Service / cr73 / VHL / M • Saturday Matinee Series #1 / 1996 / VCX / C • Saturday Matinee Series #2 / 1996 / VCX / C • Sensuous Caterer / 197? / HAV / S • Sensuous Flygirls / cr72 / VHL / M • Sexual Witchcraft / 1973 / IHV / M • Sexually Altered States / 1986 / VC / M • Sleepyhead / 1973 / VXP / M • Slip Up / 1974 / ALP / M • Sophie Says No / 1975 / VHL / M • Special Order / cr75 / BL / M • The Starmaker / 1982 / VC / M • Steamy Sirens / 1984 / AIR / C • Street Girls Of Ny / 19?? / SIL / M • Sweet Wet Lips / 1974 /

PVX / M • Switchcraft / 1975 / VHL / M • Sylvia / 1976 / VCX / M • Teenage Beauties / cr73 / SEP / M • Teenage Cheerleader / 1978 / VXP / M • Teenage Stepmother / cr74 / SVE / M • That's Erotic / 1979 / CV / C • That's Porno / 1979 / CV / C • Thrilling Drilling / 1974 / SVE / M • Throat...12 Years After / 1984 / VC / M • Too Many Cocks In Me! / 1992 / MET / M • A Touch Of Genie / 1974 / ... / M • True Legends Of Adult Cinema: The Golden Age / 1992 / VC / C • Two Senoritas / 197? / VHL / M • Tycoon's Daughter / cr73 / SVE / M • Ultrasex / 1987 / VC / M • Veronica's Kiss / 1979 / VCI / M • Virgin And The Lover / 1973 / ALP / M • Whatever Happened To Miss September? / 1973 / ALP / M • The Whistle Blowers / cr72 / ... / M • Women In Uniform / 1977 / VHL / M • [Diary Of A High Class Hooker / 1973 / ... / M • [Flesh Fantasy / 1981 / ... / M • [Grant Takes Richmond / 1981 / ... / M • [Wild Girls / cr73 / ... / M

MARC TAYLOR *see Star Index I*
MARC THE JEW *see Star Index I*
MARC TREVOR *see Star Index I*
MARC UBELL *see* **Chuck Vincent**
MARC VALENTINE
Deep Inside Annie Sprinkle / 1981 / VXP / M • Dracula Exotica / 1980 / TVX / M • Girls U.S.A. / 1980 / AIR / M • Inside Seka / 1980 / VXP / M • Misbehavin' / 1979 / VXP / M • Pandora's Mirror / 1981 / CA / M • Platinum Paradise / 1980 / COM / M • Silky / 1980 / VXP / M • Sizzle / 1979 / QX / M • Sunny / 1979 / VC / M • Sweet Surrender / 1980 / VCX / M • Tigresses...And Other Man-Eaters / 1979 / VXP / M • Twilight Pink #1 / 1980 / AR / M

MARC VERLAINE
Pussyman #09: Feeding Frenzy / 1995 / SNA / M • Pussyman #10: Butts, Butts & More Butts / 1995 / SNA / M

MARC WALLICE *(Marc Gold, Mark Goldberg, Marc Wallis, Mark Gold, Don Webber, Mark Butler)*
150lbs, 5'10" tall. Don Webber is Marc's name from the gay movies. As of mid 1995 he was caught forging AIDS certificates but supposedly he's not infected, just cheap. 36 years old in 1996.
$exce$$ / 1993 / CA / M • 1-800-934-BOOB / 1992 / VD / C • 10,000 Anal Maniacs #1 / 1993 / FOR / M • 10,000 Anal Maniacs #2 / 1994 / FOR / M • 40 The Hard Way / 1991 / OD / M • 4F Dating Service / 1989 / AR / M • The 4th Vixxen / 1995 / EMC / M • 976-76DD / 1993 / VI / M • A Is For Asia / 1996 / 4P / M • Above The Knee / 1994 / WAV / M • Adam & Eve's Guide To A G-Spot Orgasm / 1994 / VI / M • Adult Video News 1992 Awards / 1992 / VC / M • Adultery / 1989 / PP / M • The Adventures Of Billy Blues / 1990 / HO / M • The Adventures Of Breastman / 1992 / EVN / M • The Adventures Of Seymore Butts / 1992 / FH / M • The Adventures Of Studman #1 / 1994 / AFV / M • The Adventures Of Studman #2 / 1994 / AFV / M • After Midnight / 1994 / IN / M • Aja / 1988 / PL / M • Alice In Hollywierd / 1992 / ZA / M • The All American Girl / 1989 / FAN / M • All American Girls #2: In Heat / 1983 / CA / M • All For One / 1988 / CIN / M • All That Sex / 1990 / LE / M • All The Way Down / 1991 / ZA / M • Amazing Tails #1 / 1987 / CA / M • Amazing Tails #2 / 1987 / CA / M • Amaz-

ing Tails #3 / 1987 / CA / M • Amazing Tails #4 / 1990 / CA / M • Amber Lynn's Peter Meter / 1988 / 3HV / C • American Beauty #1 / 1993 / FOR / M • American Pie / 1995 / WAV / M • American Sweethearts / 1996 / PL / M • The Amorous Adventures Of Cissy / 1982 / WWV / M • The Anal Adventures Of Bruce Seven / 1996 / BS / C • The Anal Adventures Of Suzy Super Slut #1 / 1994 / AFV / M • The Anal Adventures Of Suzy Super Slut #3 / 1994 / IPI / M • Anal All Stars / 1994 / CA / M • Anal Analysis / 1992 / ZA / M • Anal Anarchy / 1995 / VC / M • Anal Angels #6 / 1996 / VEX / C • Anal Attitude / 1993 / HO / M • Anal Blitz / 1991 / MID / M • Anal Booty Burner / 1996 / ROB / M • Anal Centerfold / 1995 / ROB / M • Anal Climax #3 / 1993 / ROB / M • Anal Co-Ed / 1993 / ROB / M • Anal Commander / 1990 / ZA / M • Anal Cuties #1 / 1992 / ROB / M • Anal Cuties #2 / 1992 / ROB / M • Anal Cuties #3 / 1992 / ROB / M • Anal Deep Rider / 1994 / ROB / M • Anal Delinquent #2 / 1994 / ROB / M • Anal Delinquent #3 / 1995 / ROB / M • The Anal Diary Of Misty Rain / 1993 / EL / M • Anal Encounters #1 / 1991 / VC / M • Anal Encounters #2 / 1991 / VC / M • Anal Encounters #3: Back In The Dark One / 1991 / VC / M • Anal Extasy / 1992 / ROB / M • Anal Hanky-Panky / 1997 / ROB / M • Anal Hellraiser #1 / 1995 / ROB / M • Anal Hellraiser #2 / 1995 / ROB / M • Anal Hunger / 1994 / ROB / M • Anal Inferno / 1992 / ROB / M • Anal Innocence #3 / 1994 / ROB / M • Anal Insatiable / 1995 / ROB / M • Anal Intruder #02 / 1988 / CC / M • Anal Intruder #04 / 1990 / CC / M • Anal Intruder #05: The Final Outrage / 1990 / CC / M • Anal Intruder #06: The Anal Twins / 1992 / CC / M • Anal Jammin' & Slammin' / 1996 / ROB / M • Anal Lover #2 / 1993 / ROB / M • Anal Mystique / 1994 / EMC / M • Anal Nation #1 / 1990 / CC / M • Anal Orgy / 1993 / DRP / M • Anal Pleasures / 1988 / AVC / M • Anal Princess #1 / 1996 / VC / M • Anal Queen / 1994 / FPI / M • Anal Rampage #1 / 1992 / ROB / M • Anal Revolution / 1991 / ROB / M • Anal Savage #1 / 1992 / ROB / M • Anal Savage #2 / 1994 / ROB / M • Anal Savage #3 / 1996 / ROB / M • Anal Secrets (Metro) / 1994 / IN / M • Anal Sensation / 1993 / ROB / M • Anal Sluts & Sweethearts #1 / 1992 / ROB / M • Anal Sweetheart / 1994 / ROB / M • Anal Thrills / 1992 / ROB / M • Anal Tight Ass / 1995 / ROB / M • Anal Trashy Ass / 1995 / ROB / M • Anal Urge / 1993 / ROB / M • Anal With An Oriental Slant / 1993 / ROB / M • The Anal-ist #2 / 1986 / VEX / M • The Analizer / 1994 / VD / M • Angela Takes A Dare / 1988 / FAZ / M • Angelica / 1989 / ARG / M • Angels Of Mercy / 1985 / HO / M • Another Fuckin' Anal Movie / 1996 / ROB / M • Another Rear View / 1990 / LE / M • Anything Goes / 1993 / VD / C • The Aroused / 1989 / IN / M • Ass Openers! #1 / 1995 / TCK / C • Ass Openers! #2 / 1995 / TCK / C • Assault With A Friendly Weapon / 1990 / DAY / M • Asses Galore #7: Lunatic Fringe / 1996 / DFI / M • Asspiring Actresses / 1989 / CA / M • Aussie Exchange Girls / 1990 / PM / M • Aussie Maid In America / 1990 / PM / M • Babe Magnet / 1994 / IN / M • Babewatch #1 / 1993 / CC / M • Baby Doll / 1994 / SC / M • Baby Face #2 / 1987 / VC / M • Bachelor Party #1 /

1993 / FPI / M • Bachelorette Party / 1984 / JVV / M • Back In The Pen / 1992 / FH / M • Back On Top / 1988 / FAZ / M • Back Road To Paradise / 1984 / CDI / M • Back To Back #2 / 1992 / FC / C • Back To Class #1 / 1984 / DR / M • Backdoor Babes / 1985 / WET / M • Backdoor Brides #1 / 1985 / PV / M • Backdoor Brides #2: The Honeymoon / 1986 / PV / M • Backdoor Brides #4 / 1993 / PV / M • Backdoor Romance / 1984 / VIV / M • Backdoor To Hollywood #04 / 1988 / CDI / M • Backdoor To Hollywood #05 / 1988 / CDI / M • Backdoor To Hollywood #07 / 1989 / CIN / M • Backdoor To Hollywood #08 / 1989 / CIN / M • Backdoor To Hollywood #09 / 1989 / CIN / M • Backdoor To Hollywood #10 / 1989 / CIN / M • Backdoor To Hollywood #11 / 1990 / CIN / M • Backdoor To Hollywood #12 / 1990 / CIN / M • Backdoor To Hollywood #13 / 1990 / CDI / M • Backfield In Motion / 1990 / PV / M • Backing In #3 / 1991 / WV / C • Backing In #5 / 1994 / WV / C • Bad / 1990 / VC / M • Bad Company / 1994 / VI / M • Bad Girls #5 / 1994 / GO / M • Bad Habits / 1990 / WV / M • Bad Influence / 1991 / CDI / M • The Bad News Brat / 1991 / VI / M • Badgirls #2: Strip Search / 1994 / VI / M • Bangkok Nights / 1994 / VI / M • Bare Elegance / 1984 / MAP / M • The Barlow Affairs / 1991 / XCI / M • Bat Bitch #2 / 1990 / FAZ / M • Battle Of The Superstars / 1993 / VI / M • Battle Of The Titans / 1986 / AVC / M • Bazooka County #3 / 1991 / CC / M • The Beat Goes On / 1987 / VCR / C • Beaver & Buttcheeks / 1993 / DR / M • Beaverly Hills Cop / 1985 / SE / M • Bed, Butts & Breakfast / 1990 / LV / M • Bedtime Video #09 / 1984 / GO / M • Before She Says I Do / 1984 / MAP / M • Behind The Backdoor #2 / 1989 / EVN / M • Behind The Brown Door / 1994 / PE / M • Best Butt(e) In The West #1 / 1992 / CC / M • Best Gang Bangs / 1996 / DFI / C • The Best Little Whorehouse In Hong Kong / 1987 / SE / M • Best Of Bruce Seven #1 / 1990 / BIZ / C • Best Of Caught From Behind #1 / 1987 / HO / C • Best Of Caught From Behind #5 / 1991 / HO / C • Best Of Hot Shorts #01 / 1987 / VCR / C • The Best Of Oriental Anal #1 / 1994 / ROB / C • The Best Rears Of Our Lives / 1992 / OD / M • Bet Black / 1989 / CDI / M • The Better Sex Video Series #5: Sharing Fantasies / 1992 / LEA / M • Between My Breasts #11 / 1990 / BTO / M • Between The Cheeks #1 / 1985 / VC / M • Between The Cheeks #2 / 1990 / VC / M • Between The Cheeks #3 / 1993 / VC / M • Biff Malibu's Totally Nasty Home Videos #40 / 1993 / ANA / M • Billionaire Girls Club / 1988 / LVI / C • Bionca On Fire / 1988 / 4P / M • Black Beauties / 1987 / SE / C • Black Bunbusters / 1985 / VC / M • Black Hose Bag / 1996 / ROB / M • Black Lava / 1986 / WET / M • Black Lust / 1983 / VCR / C • The Black Mystique / 1986 / CV / M • Black Stockings / 1990 / VD / M • Black Throat / 1985 / VC / M • Black Tie Affair / 1993 / VEX / M • Black Valley Girls #1 / 1986 / 4R / M • Black Valley Girls #2 / 1989 / DR / M • Blacks & Blondes #21 / 1986 / WV / M • Blacks & Blondes #26 / 1986 / WV / M • The Blonde & The Beautiful #1 / 1993 / LV / M • The Blonde & The Beautiful #2 / 1993 / LV / M • Blonde / 1995 / LE / M • Blonde

Ambition / 1991 / CIN / M • Blonde Angel / 1994 / VI / M • Blonde On The Run / 1985 / PV / M • Blonde Savage / 1991 / CDI / M • Blondie / 1985 / TAR / M • Blow Job Baby / 1993 / CC / M • Blue Angel / 1991 / SE / M • Blue Interview / 1983 / VCR / M • Blue Vanities #030 / 1988 / FFL / M • Blue Views / 1990 / CDI / M • Bobby Hollander's Maneaters #03 / 1993 / SFP / M • Body And Soul / 1992 / OD / M • Body Of Innocence / 1993 / WP / M • Boiling Desires / 1986 / VC / M • Boiling Point / 1994 / WAV / M • The Boneheads / 1992 / PL / M • Boobs, Butts And Bloopers #1 / 1990 / HO / M • Boobs, Butts And Bloopers #2 / 1990 / HO / M • Booty Bitch / 1995 / ROB / M • Booty Ho #3 / 1995 / ROB / M • Booty In The House / 1993 / WP / M • Booty Queen / 1995 / ROB / M • Booty Sister #2 / 1996 / ROB / M • Born To Burn / 1987 / HOT / M • Borsky's Back Door Bitches / 1996 / ROB / M • The Bottom Dweller Part Deux / 1994 / EL / M • The Bottom Line / 1990 / AMB / M • The Bottom Line / 1995 / NIT / M • Bottoms Up #07 / 1986 / AVC / C • Bottoms Up #08 / 1986 / AVC / C • The Brazilian Connection / 1988 / CA / M • Breaking It #1 / 1984 / COL / M • Breaking It #2 / 1989 / GO / M • The Breast Things In Life Are Free / 1991 / LV / M • Breathless / 1989 / CIN / M • Bright Lights, Big Titties / 1989 / CA / M • Bringing Up The Rear / 1993 / VD / C • The British Are Coming / 1993 / ZA / M • Broad Of Directors / 1992 / PEP / M • Bubblegum / 1982 / VC / M • Bun For The Money / 1990 / FH / M • Bunbusters / 1984 / VCR / M • Burgundy Blues / 1993 / MET / M • Busted / 1989 / CA / M • Butt Bandits #4 / 1996 / VD / C • Butt Banged Bicycle Babes / 1994 / ANA / M • Butt Banged Cycle Sluts / 1995 / ANA / M • Butt Bongo Babes / 1993 / VD / M • The Butt Boss / 1993 / VD / M • Butt Darling / 1994 / WIV / M • Butt Hole Boulevard / 1993 / CA / M • The Butt Stops Here / 1991 / LV / M • Butt's Motel #1 / 1989 / EX / M • Butt's Motel #3 / 1989 / EX / M • Butt's Motel #4 / 1989 / EX / M • Butt's Motel #5 / 1990 / EX / M • Butthole Sweetheart / 1996 / ROB / M • Butts Of Steel / 1994 / BLC / M • Butts Up / 1994 / CA / M • Cajun Heat / 1993 / SC / M • California Fever / 1987 / CV / M • Campfire Girls / 1988 / SE / M • Candy Factory / 1994 / PE / M • Candy's Bedtime Story / 1983 / CA / M • Canned Heat / 1995 / IN / M • Captain Butt's Beach / 1992 / LV / M • Casual Lies / 1992 / CA / M • Cat Scratch Fever / 1989 / FAZ / M • Catalina: Sabotage / 1991 / CDI / M • Catalina: Tiger Shark / 1991 / CDI / M • The Cathouse / 1994 / VI / M • Catwalk #1 / 1995 / SC / M • Catwalk #2 / 1995 / SC / M • Caught From Behind #02: The Sequel / 1983 / HO / M • Caught From Behind #03 / 1985 / HO / M • Caught From Behind #04: Nasty Young Girls / 1985 / HO / M • Caught From Behind #06 / 1986 / HO / M • Caught From Behind #08 / 1988 / HO / M • Caught From Behind #09 / 1988 / HO / M • Caught From Behind #10 / 1989 / HO / M • Caught From Behind #11 / 1989 / HO / M • Caught From Behind #14 / 1990 / HO / M • Caught From Behind #16: The Reunion / 1992 / HO / M • Caught From Behind #17 / 1992 / HO / M • Caught From Behind #18 / 1993 / HO / M • Caught From Behind #19 / 1994 / HO / M • Caught In The Act (1995-Wave) /

1995 / WAV / M • Caught In The Middle / 1985 / CDI / M • Cavalcade Of Stars / 1985 / VCR / C • Celebrity Presents Celebrity / 1986 / VEP / C • Centerfold / 1992 / VC / M • Centerfold Celebrities #1 / 1982 / VC / M • Centerfold Celebrities '94 #2 / 1994 / SFP / M • Chance Meetings / 1988 / VEX / M • Charm School / 1993 / PEP / M • Chasey Loves Rocco / 1996 / VI / M • Checkmate / 1995 / WAV / M • Cheek To Cheek / 1997 / EL / M • Cheeks #3 / 1990 / CC / M • Cherry Cheeks / 1993 / CA / M • Chocolate Bunnies #02 / 1995 / LBO / C • Chow Down / 1994 / VI / M • Club DV8 #1 / 1993 / SC / M • Club DV8 #2 / 1993 / SC / M • Coffee & Cream / 1984 / AVC / M • Come As You Are / 1985 / SUV / M • Coming Together / 1984 / CA / M • Con Jobs / 1990 / V99 / M • The Corner / 1994 / VT / M • Corrupt Desires / 1984 / MET / M • The Corruption Of Christina / 1993 / WP / M • Country Girl / 1985 / AVC / M • Covergirl / 1994 / WP / M • Crazed #2 / 1992 / VI / M • Crazy With The Heat #2 / 1993 / MET / M • The Creasemaster / 1993 / VC / M • Cum Rain, Cum Shine / 1989 / FAZ / M • Cum Shot Revue #2 / 1985 / HO / C • Cumback Pussy #6: All-Star Poop Chute Salute / 1997 / EL / M • Cumming Of Ass / 1995 / TP / M • Curse Of The Catwoman / 1990 / VC / M • Cybersex / 1996 / WAV / M • Daddy Doesn't Know / 1984 / HO / M • Dances With Foxes / 1991 / CC / M • Dangerous Debi / 1993 / HO / C • Dark Corners / 1991 / LV / M • Debbie Class Of '88 / 1987 / CC / M • Debbie Does 'em All #1 / 1985 / CV / M • Debbie Does 'em All #2 / 1988 / CV / M • Debbie Does Wall Street / 1991 / VC / M • The Debutante / 1986 / BEA / M • Deception (1995-Executive) / 1995 / EX / M • Deep Cheeks #1 / 1991 / ROB / M • Deep Cheeks #2 / 1991 / ROB / M • Deep Chill / cr85 / AT / M • Deep Cover / 1993 / WP / M • Deep Dish Booty Pie / 1996 / ROB / M • Deep Inside Ariana / 1995 / VC / C • Deep Inside Barbie / 1989 / CDI / C • Deep Inside Brittany O'connell / 1996 / VC / C • Deep Inside Centerfold Girls / 1991 / VC / M • Deep Inside Crystal Wilder / 1995 / VC / C • Deep Inside Nikki Dial / 1994 / VC / C • Deep Inside Nina Hartley / 1993 / VC / M • Deep Inside P.J. Sparxx / 1995 / VC / C • Deep Inside Racquel Darrian / 1994 / VC / C • Deep Inside Shanna Mccullough / 1992 / VC / C • Deep Inside Tracey / 1987 / CDI / C • Deep Inside Traci / 1986 / CDI / C • Deep Inside Vanessa Del Rio / 1986 / VC / M • Deep Throat Girls #10 / 1995 / GO / M • Deja Vu / 1993 / XCI / M • Delusions / 1983 / PRC / M • Denim Dolls #2 / 1990 / CDI / M • Desire / 1990 / VC / M • Desire Kills / 1996 / SUM / M • The Determinator #2 / 1991 / VIM / M • Devil In Miss Jones #3: A New Beginning / 1986 / VC / M • Devil In Miss Jones #4: The Final Outrage / 1987 / VC / M • The Devil In Miss Jones #5: The Inferno / 1994 / VC / M • The Devil Made Her Do It / 1992 / HO / M • Dial A For Anal / 1994 / CA / M • Dial A Nurse / 1992 / VD / M • Dial F For Fantasy / 1984 / PL / M • Diamond Collection #59 / 1984 / CDI / M • Diamond Collection #60 / 1984 / CDI / M • Diamond Collection #61 / 1984 / CDI / M • Diamond Collection #66 / 1985 / CDI / M • Diamond Collection #67 / 1985 / CDI / M • Diamond Collection #68 / 1985 /

CDI / M • Diamond Collection #79 / 1986 / CDI / M • Diamond Collection #80 / 1986 / CDI / M • Diamond In The Rough / 1989 / EX / M • Dickman & Throbbin / 1985 / WV / M • The Dinner Party #1 / 1994 / ULI / M • The Dinner Party / 1986 / WV / M • The Dirtiest Girl In The World / 1992 / ZA / M • Dirty Blondes / 1986 / CDI / M • Dirty Letters / 1984 / VD / M • Dirty Looks / 1994 / VI / M • Dirty Pictures / 1985 / SUP / M • Domination Of Tammy / 1983 / JAN / B • Don't Bother To Knock / 1991 / FAZ / M • Don't Tell Daddy #1 / 1985 / PL / C • Double Crossing / 1991 / IN / M • Double D Roommates / 1989 / BTO / M • Double Desires / 1988 / PIN / C • Double Detail / 1992 / SO / M • Double Penetration #1 / 1985 / WV / M • Double Penetration #2 / 1986 / WV / C • Double Penetration #3 / 1986 / WV / C • Double Penetration #4 / 1991 / WV / C • Double Penetration #5 / 1992 / WV / C • Double Penetration Fever / 1989 / MIR / C • Double Whammy / 1986 / LA / M • Double Your Pleasure / 1989 / VEX / M • Dougie Hoser: The World's Youngest Gynaecologist / 1990 / VT / M • Dp #2: The Mighty Fhucks / 1994 / FC / M • Dr Butts #2 / 1992 / 4P / M • The Dragon Lady #1 / 1988 / WV / C • The Dragon Lady #4: Tales From The Bed #3 / 1992 / WV / M • Dream Lust / 1995 / NIT / M • The Dream Machine / 1992 / CDI / M • Dreams Of Candace Hart / 1991 / VI / M • Dreams Of Misty / 1984 / VCX / M • The Drifter / 1995 / CV / M • Easy Lover / 1989 / EX / M • Easy Pussy / 1991 / ROB / M • Ebony Erotica / 1985 / SVE / C • Electric Blue: Caribbean Cruise / 1984 / CA / S • Electric Blue: Search For A Star / 1985 / CA / M • Eleventh Annual AVN Awards / 1994 / VC / M • The Enchantress / 1985 / 4P / M • Encore / 1995 / VI / M • The End Of The Innocence / 1989 / IN / M • Endless Passion / 1987 / LIM / C • Endlessly / 1993 / VI / M • Entertainment L.A. Style / 1990 / HO / M • The Erotic Adventures Of The Three Musketeers / 1992 / CEL / S • Erotic Express / 1983 / CV / M • Erotic Therapy / 1987 / CDI / M • The Erotic World Of Cody Nicole / 1984 / VCR / C • The Erotic World Of Crystal Lake (#4) / 1984 / VCR / C • Erotica Jones / 1985 / AVC / M • Essence Of A Woman / 1993 / FOR / M • The Eternal Idol / 1992 / CDI / M • Eternity / 1991 / CDI / M • Eve Of Seduction / 1991 / CDI / M • Every Woman Has A Secret / 1991 / ROB / M • Everybody's Playmates / 1992 / CA / C • Executions On Butt Row / 1996 / EA / M • The Exhibitionist / 1991 / VD / M • Exit In Rear / 1993 / XCI / M • Extreme Sex #1: The Club / 1994 / VI / M • Extreme Sex #2: The Dungeon / 1994 / VI / M • Extreme Sex #4: The Experiment / 1995 / VI / M • Eyewitness Nudes / 1990 / VC / M • Facesitter #1 / 1992 / CC / M • Faithless Companions / 1992 / WV / M • Fantasy Peeps: Three For Love / 1985 / 4P / M • Fantasy World / 1991 / NWV / C • Fashion sluts #5: Ethnic Ecstasy / 1995 / ABS / M • Fashion Sluts #6 / 1995 / ABS / M • Fashion Sluts #8 / 1996 / ABS / M • Fast Girls #1 / 1987 / GBX / M • Fast Girls #2 / 1988 / DIS / M • Fat Ends / 1989 / 4P / M • Father Of The Babe / 1993 / ZA / M • Fatliners #1 / 1990 / EX / M • Fatliners #2 / 1991 / EX / M • Feds In Bed / 1993 / HO / M • Female Sensations / 1984

/ VC / M • Femme Fatale / 1984 / VIV / M • Femme Fatale / 1993 / SC / M • Filet-O-Breast / 1988 / AVC / M • Filthy First Timers #2: Innocence Lost / 1996 / EL / M • The Fine Art Of Anal Intercourse / 1985 / VCR / M • The Fine Art Of Cunnilingus / 1985 / VCR / M • The Fire Inside / 1988 / VC / C • Firefoxes / 1985 / PLY / M • Flame / 1989 / ARG / M • Flashback / 1993 / SC / M • Flesh Palace / 1995 / LBO / M • Flesh Shopping Network #1 / 1995 / MID / M • Fleshdance Fever / 1984 / SAT / M • Florence Hump / 1994 / AFI / M • The Fluffer #2 / 1993 / FD / M • Flying High #1 / 1992 / HO / M • Flying High #2 / 1992 / HO / M • Foolish Pleasure / 1992 / VD / M • For Love Or Money / 1994 / AFI / M • For Your Lips Only / 1989 / FAZ / M • Forbidden / 1992 / FOR / M • Forbidden Bodies / 1986 / HU / M • Forbidden Dreams / 1984 / BIZ / G • Forbidden Entry / 1984 / VCR / M • Forever Young / 1994 / VI / M • Fortysomething #1 / 1990 / LE / M • Freak Dat Booty / 1994 / WP / M • French Doll / 1994 / ME / M • French Open / 1990 / OD / M • Frenzy / 1992 / SC / M • Fresh Meat (John Leslie) #1 / 1994 / EA / M • Friends & Lovers #2 / 1991 / VT / M • From Japan With Love / 1990 / SLV / M • Full Moon Bay / 1993 / VI / M • Full Moon Fever / 1992 / PEP / M • Full Moon Fever / 1994 / LBO / M • Full Throttle Girls: Boredom Pulled The Trigger / 1993 / VIM / M • Future Voyeur / 1985 / SUV / M • Games Couples Play / 1987 / HO / M • Gang Bang Butthole Surfin' / 1996 / ROB / M • Gang Bang Cummers / 1993 / ROB / M • Gang Bang Dollies / 1996 / ROB / M • Gang Bang Face Bath #2 / 1994 / ROB / M • Gang Bang Face Bath #3 / 1994 / ROB / M • Gang Bang Face Bath #4 / 1995 / ROB / M • Gang Bang Jizz Jammers / 1994 / ROB / M • Gang Bang Jizz Queen / 1995 / ROB / M • Gang Bang Nymphette / 1994 / ROB / M • Gang Bang Pussycat / 1992 / ROB / M • Gang Bang Thrills / 1992 / ROB / M • Gang Bang Wild Style #2 / 1994 / ROB / M • Gang Bangs #1 / 1985 / VCR / M • Gang Bangs #2 / 1989 / EA / M • Gangbang Girl #03 / 1992 / ANA / M • Gangbang Girl #12 / 1993 / ANA / M • Gangbang Girl #13 / 1994 / ANA / M • Gangbang Girl #17 / 1995 / ANA / M • Gazongas #03 / 1991 / VEX / M • A Geisha's Secret / 1993 / VI / M • Genital Hospital / 1987 / SE / M • Gettin' Ready / 1985 / CDI / M • Gettin' Wet / 1990 / VC / M • Getting Lucky / 1983 / CA / M • Ghost To Ghost / 1991 / CC / M • Ginger Lynn—Non-Stop / 1988 / VD / C • Ginger On The Rocks / 1985 / VI / M • Ginger's Private Party / 1985 / VI / M • Ginger: The Movie / 1988 / PV / C • The Girl With The Blue Jeans Off / 1989 / FAZ / M • The Girl With The Heart-Shaped Tattoo / 1995 / WAV / M • The Girls From Hootersville #07 / 1994 / SFP / M • The Girls Next Door / 1990 / LE / F • Girls Of Cell Block F / 1985 / WV / M • The Girls Of Rodeo Drive / 1987 / BAD / M • Girls Of Silicone Valley / 1991 / FC / M • The Girls Of The A Team #1 / 1985 / WV / M • Girls Of The Chorus Line / 1986 / CLV / M • Girls Of The Double D #04 / 1989 / CDI / M • Girls Of The Double D #06 / 1989 / CIN / M • Girls Of The Double D #08 / 1989 / CDI / M • Girls Of The Double D #09 / 1989 / CDI / M • Girls Of The Double D

#11 / 1990 / CIN / M • Girls Of The Double D #12 / 1990 / CDI / M • Girls Of The Double D #13 / 1990 / CDI / M • Girls With Curves #2 / 1994 / CV / M • The Girls' Club / 1993 / VD / C • Glamour Girl #2 / 1984 / CDI / M • Glamour Girl #5 / 1985 / CDI / M • Glen And Glenda / 1994 / CA / M • The God Daughter #1 / 1991 / AFV / M • The God Daughter #2 / 1991 / AFV / M • The God Daughter #3 / 1992 / AFV / M • The God Daughter #4 / 1992 / AFV / M • Goddess Of Love / 1986 / CDI / M • Golddiggers #1 / 1985 / VC / M • Golden Girls #19 / 1984 / CA / M • Golden Girls #22 / 1984 / CA / M • Golden Girls #26 / 1985 / CA / M • Golden Girls #28 / 1985 / CA / M • Golden Girls #30 / 1985 / CA / M • Good Girls Do / 1984 / HO / M • Gorgeous / 1990 / CA / M • Gourmet Premier: Throbbing Threesome / Hot Wife's Hunger 902 / cr86 / GO / M • The Governess / 1993 / WP / M • Graduation Ball / 1989 / CAE / M • Graduation From F.U. / 1992 / FOR / M • The Great American Boobs To Kill For Dance Contest / 1995 / PEP / C • The Greatest American Blonde / 1987 / WV / C • Groupies Galore / 1983 / VC / M • Guilty By Seduction / 1993 / PI / M • GVC: Blonde Heat #136 / 1985 / GO / M • GVC: Lost In Lust #134 / 1984 / GO / M • Handle With Care / 1989 / FAZ / M • Happy Endings / 1994 / WP / M • Hard As A Rock / 1992 / ZA / M • Hard Headed / 1994 / LE / M • Hard Rider / 1992 / IN / M • Hard To Thrill / 1991 / CIN / M • Harlequin Affair / 1985 / CIX / M • Hate To See You Go / 1990 / VC / M • Haunted Nights / 1993 / WP / M • Hawaii / 1995 / VI / M • Hawaii Vice #2 / 1989 / CDI / M • Hawaii Vice #4 / 1989 / CIN / M • Hawaii Vice #5 / 1989 / CDI / M • Hawaii Vice #6 / 1989 / CDI / M • Head & Tails / 1988 / VD / M • Head Lines / 1992 / SC / M • Head Talk / 1991 / ZA / M • Headgames / 1985 / WV / M • Heart To Heart / 1990 / LE / M • Heat Of The Moment / 1983 / S&L / M • Heavy Petting / 1991 / SE / M • Heidi's Girls / 1995 / GO / M • Hello Molly / 1989 / CA / M • Hello Norma Jeane / 1994 / VT / M • Her Obsession / 1991 / MID / M • Herman's Bed / 1992 / HO / M • Hershe Highway #1 / 1989 / HO / M • Hershe Highway #2 / 1989 / HO / M • Hershe Highway #3 / 1990 / HO / M • Hershe Highway #4 / 1991 / HO / M • Hidden Agenda / 1992 / XCI / M • Hidden Obsessions / 1992 / BFP / M • The Hindlick Maneuver / 1991 / CC / M • Holiday For Angels / 1987 / IN / M • Holly Does Hollywood #1 / 1985 / VEX / M • Holly Does Hollywood #4 / 1990 / CAY / M • Hollywood Bikini Party Girls / 1989 / VC / M • Hollywood Knights #3 / 1991 / PCP / M • Honeybuns #1 / 1987 / WV / C • Honeybuns #2: Grecian Formula / 1987 / WV / C • Hooter Heaven / 1992 / CA / M • Hootermania / 1994 / VC / M • Hospitality Sweet / 1988 / WV / M • Hot And Nasty! / 1986 / V99 / C • Hot In The Saddle / 1994 / ERA / M • Hot Line / 1991 / VC / M • Hot Palms / 1989 / GO / M • Hot Shorts: Ginger Lynn / 1986 / VCR / C • Hot Shots / 1992 / VD / C • Hot Spa / 1984 / CA / M • Hot Sweet 'n' Sticky / 1992 / CA / C • Hot Sweet Honey / 1985 / VEP / M • Hot Tails / 1984 / VEN / M • Hot Tight Asses #05 / 1994 / TCK / M • Hot Tight Asses #06 / 1994 / TCK / M • Hot Tight Asses #07 / 1994 / TCK / M • Hot

Tight Asses #08 / 1994 / TCK / M • Hot Tight Asses #09 / 1994 / TCK / M • Hotel Paradise / 1989 / CA / M • Hotel Sodom #02 / 1995 / SNA / M • Hotel Sodom #05: Tammi Ann Bends Over / 1995 / SNA / M • Hothouse Rose #1 / 1991 / VC / M • House Of Pleasure / 1984 / CA / M • House Of Sleeping Beauties #1 / 1992 / VI / M • House Of Sleeping Beauties #2 / 1992 / VI / M • House Of The Rising Sun / 1993 / VT / M • The House On Chasey Lane / 1995 / VI / M • How To Have Oral Sex / 1993 / A&E / M • How To Perform Fellatio / 1985 / VCR / M • The Hunger / 1993 / FOR / M • Hyapatia Obsessed / 1993 / EX / M • I Can't Get No...Satisfaction / 1988 / CDI / M • I Dream Of Christy / 1989 / CAY / M • I Like To Be Watched / 1984 / VD / M • I Made Marian / 1993 / PEP / M • I Never Say No / 1983 / VC / M • I Remember When / 1992 / ATL / M • I Touch Myself / 1992 / IN / M • I Want It All / 1984 / VD / M • I Want To Be Bad / 1984 / CV / M • I'm Too Sexy / 1992 / CA / M • The Idol / 1985 / WV / M • If These Walls Could Talk (Director's Cut) / 1993 / MET / M • If These Walls Could Talk #1: Wicked Whispers / 1993 / MET / M • If These Walls Could Talk #2: Burning Secrets / 1993 / CV / M • Illusions Of Ecstasy / 1985 / NSV / M • Images Of Desire / 1990 / PM / M • Imagination X-Posed / 1989 / 4P / M • Immaculate Erection / 1992 / VD / M • The Immoral Miss Teeze / 1987 / CV / M • In The Jeans Again / 1990 / ME / M • In The Scope / 1996 / VI / M • In Your Face #1 / 1992 / PL / M • In-N-Out With John Leslie / 1988 / WV / C • Indecent Itch / 1985 / VCR / M • Indiscretions / 1991 / PP / M • Inferno #2 / 1993 / SC / M • Inferno / 1991 / XCI / M • An Innocent Woman / 1991 / FAZ / M • Internal Affairs / 1992 / CDI / M • Interview With A Vamp / 1994 / ANA / M • Intimate Realities #1 / 1983 / VC / M • Introducing Charli / 1989 / CIN / M • It's Blondage, The Video / 1994 / VI / M • It's My Body / 1985 / CDI / M • Jealous Lovers / 1989 / CDI / M • Jezebel #1 / 1993 / SC / M • Joy Toys / 1985 / WET / M • Juicy Lucy / 1990 / VC / M • Juicy Sex Scandals / 1991 / VD / M • Julia Ann: Superstar / 1995 / WAV / M • Just For The Thrill Of It / 1989 / V99 / M • Kadillac & Devell / 1993 / ZA / M • Kascha & Friends / 1988 / CIN / M • Kascha's Days & Nights / 1989 / CDI / M • Keyhole #109: Linda Shaw Sucks / 198? / KEH / M • Kinky Fantasies / 1994 / KWP / M • Kinkyvision #2 / 1988 / VC / M • Kiss My Asp / 1989 / EXH / M • Kisses Don't Lie / 1989 / PL / M • L.A. Fantasies / 1990 / WV / C • The Lady In Red / 1993 / VC / M • Lady Sterling Takes It Up The Arse / 1997 / ROB / M • Laid In Heaven / 1991 / VC / M • The Lascivious Ladies Of Dr Lipo / 1991 / OD / M • The Last Resort / 1990 / VC / M • Layover / 1985 / HO / M • Leather & Lace / 1987 / SE / C • Leather / 1995 / LE / M • Leather Revenge / 1983 / BIZ / B • Leena / 1992 / VT / M • Leena Goes Pro / 1992 / VT / M • The Legend Of Barbi-Q And Little Fawn / 1994 / CA / M • Les Femmes Erotiques / 1993 / BFP / M • Let Me Tell Ya 'Bout Black Chicks / 1985 / VC / M • Let Me Tell Ya 'Bout White Chicks / 1985 / VC / M • Let's Play Doctor / 1994 / PV / M • Like A Virgin #1 / 1985 / AT / M • Limited Edition #27 /

1984 / AVC / M • Linda Shaw Sucks / 19?? / ... / M • Lingerie Busters / 1991 / FH / M • Little Girl Blue / 1995 / RHS / M • Little Girls Talking Dirty / 1984 / VCX / M • Little Girls, Dirty Desires / 1984 / JVV / M • A Little Irresistible / 1991 / ZA / M • Little Miss Curious / 1991 / CA / M • Little Muffy Johnson / 1985 / VEP / M • Lonely Lady / 1984 / VC / M • Loose Ends #1 / 1984 / 4P / M • Loose Ends #2 / 1986 / 4P / M • Loose Ends #6 / 1989 / 4P / M • Loose Morals / 1987 / HO / M • Love Champions / 1987 / VC / M • Love Ghost / 1990 / WV / M • Love Lessons / 1986 / HO / M • The Love Mistress / 1989 / WV / M • The Love Scene / 1985 / CDI / M • Love Triangle / 1986 / PLY / C • Lovin' USA / 1989 / EXH / C • Loving Lips / 1987 / AMB / C • Loving You Always / 1994 / IN / M • Lucky Break / 1991 / SE / M • Luscious Lucy In Love / 1986 / AVC / M • Lust American Style / 1985 / WV / M • Lust At The Top / 1985 / CDI / M • Lust Bug / 1985 / HO / M • The Lust Detector / 1986 / PIN / M • Lust In The Fast Lane / 1984 / PV / M • Lust Never Sleeps / 1991 / FAZ / M • Lusty Ladies #05 / 1983 / 4P / M • Lusty Layout / 1986 / PV / M • The Luv Game / 1988 / VCX / M • M Series #18 / 1994 / LBO / M • Mad Jack Beyond Thunderdome / 1986 / WET / M • Made In Heaven / 1991 / PP / M • The Magic Shower / 1989 / CDI / M • Major Slut / 1993 / LV / M • Make Me Sweat / 1989 / CIN / M • Make Me Want It / 1986 / CA / M • Make My Night / 1985 / CIN / M • Make My Wife Please... / 1993 / VC / M • Makin' It / 1994 / A&E / M • Making It Big / 1984 / CV / M • Malibu Spice / 1991 / VC / M • Manbait #1 / 1991 / VC / M • Maneaters (1992-Vidco) / 1992 / VD / C • Manwiched / 1992 / FPI / M • The Many Shades Of Amber / 1986 / LIM / M • Mardi Gras / 1986 / SE / M • Marilyn Chambers' Private Fantasies #2 / 1983 / CA / M • The Mark Of Zara / 1990 / XCI / M • The Mating Pot / 1994 / LBO / M • The Mating Season / 1984 / VC / M • Maximum #4 / 1983 / CA / M • Meat Market / 1992 / SEX / C • The Merry Widows / 1993 / VC / M • A Mid-Slumber's Night Dream / 1985 / 4P / M • Midnight Angel / 1992 / CDI / M • Midnight Confessions / 1992 / XCI / M • The Midnight Hour / 1991 / VT / M • Midnight Pink / 1987 / WV / M • Mighty Man #1: Virgins In The Forest / 1994 / LE / M • Mile High Club / 1983 / CV / M • Mind Shadows #1 / 1993 / FD / M • Mind Shadows #2 / 1993 / FD / M • Mirage #1 / 1991 / VC / M • Miss 21st Century / 1991 / ZA / M • Miss Anal America / 1993 / LV / M • Miss Nude International / 1996 / LE / M • Mission Phenomenal / 1996 / HIP / M • Mistress Of The Mansion / 1994 / CV / M • Mistresses And Slaves: The Best Of Bruce Seven / 1991 / BEB / C • Model Wife / 1991 / CA / M • The Modelling Studio / 1984 / GO / M • Modern Love / 1991 / FAZ / M • Moon Godesses #1 / 1992 / VIM / M • Moondance / 1991 / WV / M • Moonstroked / 1988 / 3HV / M • More Than Friends / 1989 / FAZ / M • Mr. Peepers Amateur Home Videos #87: Groupie Therapy / 1994 / LBO / M • Muff 'n' Jeff / 1992 / ZA / M • My 500 Pound Vibrator / 1991 / LV / C • My Boyfriend's Black / 1994 / FD / M • My Way / 1993 / CA / M • Mystery Of The Golden Lotus / 1989 / HU / M • Naked & Nasty / 1995 / WP / M • Naked

Desert / 1995 / VI / M • Naked Lust / 1985 / SE / M • Naked Night / 1985 / VCR / M • Naked Truth #1 / 1993 / FH / M • The Naked Truth / 1990 / SE / M • Native Tongue / 1993 / VI / M • Natural Wonders / 1993 / VI / M • Naughty Nurses / 1986 / VEX / M • Naughty Nurses / 1992 / VD / C • Never Never Land / 1992 / PL / M • The New Ass Masters #14 / 1996 / LEI / C • The New Kid On The Block / 1991 / VD / M • New Positions / 1994 / PV / M • New Wave Hookers #2 / 1991 / VC / M • New Wave Hookers #3 / 1993 / VC / M • New Wave Hookers #4 / 1994 / VC / M • Nice 'n' Tight / 1985 / AIR / M • Nice Fuckin' Movie / 1997 / EL / M • Night Creatures / 1992 / PL / M • Night Deposit / 1991 / VC / M • The Night Temptress / 1989 / HU / M • Night Vibes / 1990 / KNI / M • Nightbreed / 1995 / VI / M • Nightfire / 1991 / CIN / M • Nina Hartley: Wild Thing / 1991 / CIN / M • No Tell Motel / 1990 / ZA / M • Nothing But Trouble / 1991 / CIN / M • Nothing Personal / 1993 / CA / M • Notorious / 1992 / SC / M • Numba 1 Ass Fucka / 1996 / ROB / M • Nurse Nancy / 1991 / CA / M • The Nympho Files / 1995 / NIT / M • Object Of Desire / 1991 / FAZ / M • Obsession / 1991 / CDI / M • Oh, What A Night! / 1990 / VC / M • Older Women With Young Boys / 1984 / CC / M • On Golden Blonde / 1984 / PV / M • On Her Back / 1994 / VI / M • Once In A Blue Moon / 1991 / CC / M • Only The Best Of Anal / 1992 / MET / C • Only The Best Of Breasts / 1987 / CV / C • Only The Best Of The Erotic Eighties / 1992 / VC / C • Only The Very Best On Video / 1992 / VC / C • Open Up Tracy / 1984 / VD / M • Oral Majority #01 / 1986 / WV / C • Oral Majority #04 / 1987 / WV / C • Oral Majority #06 / 1988 / WV / C • Oral Majority #07 / 1989 / WV / C • Oral Majority #08 / 1990 / WV / C • Orgies / 1987 / WV / C • Oriental Treatment #2: The Pearl Divers / 1989 / AR / M • Our Major Is Sex / 1984 / VD / M • The Outlaw / 1991 / WV / M • Overnight Sensation / 1991 / XCI / M • A Paler Shade Of Blue / 1991 / CC / M • Paradise Found / 1995 / LE / M • Paradise Lost / 1995 / LE / M • Parliament: Three Way Lust / 1988 / PM / M • Party Doll / 1990 / VC / M • Party Wives / 1988 / CDI / M • Passages #1 / 1991 / VI / M • Passages #2 / 1991 / VI / M • Passenger 69 #1 / 1994 / IP / M • Peepshow / 1994 / OD / M • Peggy Sue / 1987 / VT / M • Penetration #1 / 1984 / AVC / M • Penetration #3 / 1984 / AVC / M • The Penetration Of Elle Rio / 1987 / GO / M • The Penetrator #1 / 1991 / PL / M • Perfect Fit / 1985 / DR / M • Perks / 1992 / ZA / M • Phone Sex Girls #1 / 1987 / VT / M • Photoflesh / 1984 / HO / M • Physical #2 / 1985 / SUP / M • Picture Perfect (Cal Vista) / 1995 / CV / M • The Pink Lady Detective Agency: Case Of The Twisted Sister / 1994 / IN / M • Play Me Again, Vanessa / 1986 / VC / M • Playin' Dirty / 1990 / VC / M • Playing With A Full Dick / 1988 / PL / M • Plaything #1 / 1995 / VI / M • Plaything #2 / 1995 / VI / M • Pleasure Dome: The Genesis Chamber / 1994 / AFV / M • The Pleasure Hunt #2 / 1985 / NSV / M • Pleasure Party (Gourmet) / 1985 / GO / M • Pleasure Productions #11 / 1985 / VCR / M • The Pleasure Seekers / 1985 / AT / M • The Pleasure Seekers / 1990 / VD / M • The Poetry Of The Flesh /

1993 / PEP / M • Poison / 1994 / VI / M • Pool Party / 1991 / CIN / M • The Poonies / 1985 / VI / M • The Pornbirds / 1985 / VC / M • A Portrait Of Dorian / 1992 / OD / M • Pouring It On / 1993 / CV / M • Precious Peaks / 1990 / ZA / M • Prescription For Lust / 1995 / NIT / M • Pretty As You Feel / 1984 / PV / M • Pretty Peaches #3 / 1989 / VC / M • The Price Was Right / 1994 / PAE / M • Prince Of Beverly Hills #2 / 1988 / VEX / M • Princess Charming / 1987 / AVC / C • Private Dancer (CDI) / 1992 / CDI / M • Private Love Affairs / 1985 / VCR / C • Private Stuff / 1994 / FD / M • Private Teacher / 1983 / CA / M • Pro Ball / 1991 / VD / M • Project Ginger / 1985 / VI / M • Public Places #1 / 1994 / SC / M • Public Places #2 / 1995 / SC / M • Pure Filth / 1995 / RV / M • Purple Haze / 1991 / WV / M • A Pussy To Die For / 1992 / CA / M • Pussyclips #04 / 1994 / SNA / M • Pussyman #01: The Search / 1993 / CC / M • Pussyman #02: The Prize / 1993 / CC / M • The Pussywillows / 1985 / SUV / M • Putting It All Behind #2: Star Treatment / 1994 / IN / M • Queen Of Hearts #3: Heartless / 1992 / PL / M • Radical Affairs Video Magazine #08 / 1994 / ME / M • Radio K-KUM / 1984 / HO / M • Rainbird / 1994 / EMC / M • Rainwoman #04 / 1990 / CC / M • Rambone The Destroyer / 1985 / WET / M • Rambone Meets The Double Penetrators / 1987 / WET / M • Raunch #01 / 1990 / CC / M • Raunch #02 / 1990 / CC / M • Raunch #05 / 1992 / CC / M • Raunch #07 / 1993 / CC / M • Raunchy Ranch / 1991 / AFV / M • Raven / 1985 / VCR / M • Rayne Storm / 1991 / VI / M • Realities #1 / 1991 / ZA / M • Realities #2 / 1992 / ZA / M • Rear Ended / 1985 / WV / M • Rear View / 1989 / LE / M • Rearbusters / 1988 / LVI / C • Rearing Rachel / 1990 / ZA / M • The Rebel / 1990 / CIN / M • Rectal Raiders / 1997 / ROB / M • The Red Baron / 1989 / FAN / M • Red Beaver Bonanza / 1992 / TCP / M • Reflections Of Rio / 1993 / WP / M • The Ribald Tales Of Canterbury / 1986 / CA / M • Rich Bitch / 1985 / HO / M • Ring Of Desire / 1995 / LBO / M • The Rise Of The Roman Empress #2 / 1990 / PV / M • The Rising / 1987 / SUV / M • The Rocky Porno Video Show / 1986 / 4P / M • Roll-X Girls / 1989 / DYV / M • Romancing The Butt / 1992 / ATL / M • The Rookies / 1991 / VC / M • Roxy / 1991 / VC / M • Rump Humpers #02 / 1992 / GLI / M • Rump Reamers / 1994 / TTV / M • Russian Roulette / 1995 / NIT / M • Rxx For A Gangbang / 1994 / ZA / M • Sabrina The Booty Queen / 1997 / ROB / M • Saints & Sinners / 1992 / PEP / M • Salt & Pepper / 1986 / VCS / C • Satin Shadows / 1991 / CIN / M • Saturday Night Porn #1 / 1993 / AFV / M • Saturday Night Porn #2 / 1993 / AFV / M • Savannah R.N. / 1992 / HW / M • Savannah's Last Stand / 1993 / VI / M • Scandal In The Mansion / 1985 / CDI / M • The Scarlet Woman / 1994 / WP / M • Scent Of A Woman / 1985 / GO / M • Science Friction / 1986 / AXT / M • Score 4 Me / 1991 / XPI / M • Screaming Rage / 1988 / LV / C • Screen Play / 1984 / XTR / M • Secret Diary #1 / 1994 / TAW / M • The Secret Life Of Nina Hartley / 1994 / VC / M • Secrets / 1984 / HO / M • The Seducers / 1992 / ZA / M • Seeing Red / 1993 / VI / M • Sensual Exposure / 1993 / ULI / M • Sex

#3: After Seven (Vivid) / 1994 / VI / M • Sex 5th Avenue / 1985 / WV / M • Sex Appraisals / 1990 / HO / M • Sex Beat / 1985 / WV / M • Sex Busters / 1984 / PLY / M • Sex Crazy / 1989 / FAN / C • Sex For Hire / 1989 / HOE / C • The Sex Game / 1987 / SE / C • Sex In Strange Places: The Sphincter Zone / 1994 / FPI / M • Sex In The Great Outdoors / 1987 / SE / C • Sex Lives On Porno Tape / 1992 / VC / C • Sex Maniacs / 1987 / JOY / C • Sex Play / 1984 / SE / M • Sex Sting / 1992 / FD / M • Sex Toys / 1985 / CA / M • Sex Waves / 1984 / EXF / M • Sexpertease / 1985 / VD / M • Sexual Olympics #1: The Trials / 1992 / VT / M • Sexual Olympics #2: The Finals / 1992 / VT / M • Sexy Delights #1 / 1986 / CLV / M • Sexy Nurses #2 / 1994 / CV / M • Shades Of Ecstasy / 1983 / HO / M • Shades Of Lust / 1993 / TP / M • Shadow Dancers #1 / 1989 / EA / M • Shadow Dancers #2 / 1989 / EA / M • Shameless / 1991 / SC / M • Shaved / 1984 / VCR / M • Shaved Pink / 1986 / WET / M • Shayla's Gang / 1994 / WP / M • She's Got The Juice / 1990 / CDI / M • She's Ready / 1990 / CDI / M • Sheri's Gotta Have It / 1985 / LIM / C • Shiver / 1993 / FOR / M • Shot From Behind / 1992 / FAZ / M • Silent Women / 1995 / ERA / M • Silver Sensations / 1992 / VT / M • Simply Blue / 1995 / WAV / M • Simply Kia / 1994 / LE / M • Sin City / 1986 / WET / M • Sindy Does Anal Again / 1994 / AFV / M • Sindy's Sexercise Workout / 1994 / AFV / M • Sinful Pleasures / 1987 / HO / C • Sinful Sisters / 1986 / VEX / M • Sinfully Yours / 1984 / HO / M • Sisters / 1993 / ZA / M • Six Faces Of Samantha / 1984 / AA / M • Skin Games / 1986 / VEX / M • Skin Games / 1991 / VEX / C • Sky Pies / 1985 / GO / M • Slave To Love / 1993 / ROB / M • Sleeping With Everybody / 1992 / MID / C • Sleepless / 1993 / VD / M • Slick Honey / 1989 / VC / M • Slip Of The Tongue / 1993 / DR / M • Slippery When Wet / 1986 / PL / M • Sloppy Seconds / 1994 / PE / M • Slow Dancing / 1990 / VI / M • Slumber Party / 1984 / HO / M • The Smart Ass Returns / 1993 / VT / M • Smoke Screen / 1995 / WAV / M • Sodomania #13: Your Lucky Number / 1995 / EL / M • Sodomania #17: Simply Makes U Tingle / 1996 / EL / M • Some Like It Hot / 1989 / CDI / M • Sordid Stories / 1994 / AMP / M • Sorority Sweethearts / 1983 / CA / M • Sounds Of Sex / 1985 / CA / M • Southern Comfort / 1991 / CIN / M • Speedster / 1992 / VI / M • Spin For Sex / 1994 / IN / M • Splash Shots / 1989 / CC / M • Spooked / 1989 / VEX / M • The Star / 1994 / HO / M • Star 84: Tina Marie / 1984 / VEX / M • Star 85: Kari Fox / 1985 / VEX / M • Star 88: Dana Lynn / 1988 / VEX / C • Star 90 / 1990 / CAY / M • Starbangers #01 / 1993 / BIG / M • Starbangers #06 / 1994 / FPI / M • Starr / 1991 / CA / M • Starship Intercourse / 1987 / DR / M • Starting Over / 1995 / WAV / M • Steam / 1993 / AMP / M • Step To The Rear / 1991 / VD / M • Stephanie's Outrageous / 1988 / LV / C • Stiletto / 1994 / WAV / M • Strange Behavior / 1991 / VD / M • Strange Sex In Strange Places / 1994 / ZA / M • Stranger At The Backdoor / 1994 / CC / M • Street Legal / 1995 / WAV / M • Street Walkers / 1990 / PL / M • A Stroke At Midnight / 1993

/ LBO / M • Stud Hunters / 1984 / CA / M • Studio Sex / 1990 / FH / M • Style #1 / 1992 / VT / M • Stylin' / 1994 / FD / M • Sugarpussy Jeans / 1986 / TEM / M • Suite 18 / 1994 / VI / M • Summer Break / 1985 / VEX / M • Summer Camp Girls / 1983 / CA / M • Summer Heat / 1991 / CIN / M • Sumo Sue And The Fat Ladies Of Wrestling / 1988 / FAN / M • Sunny After Dark / 1990 / WV / M • Super Tramp / 1989 / VD / M • Surfside Sex / 1985 / PV / M • Surprise!!! / 1994 / VI / M • Suzi's Wild Anal Ride / 1997 / ROB / M • Swallow / 1994 / VI / M • The Swap #2 / 1994 / VI / M • Swedish Erotica #53 / 1984 / CA / M • Swedish Erotica #54 / 1984 / CA / M • Swedish Erotica #56 / 1984 / CA / M • Swedish Erotica #57 / 1984 / CA / M • Swedish Erotica #74 / 1994 / CA / M • Sweet Angel Ass / 1990 / FH / M • Sweet Little Things / 1985 / COL / M • Sweet Nothings / 1987 / HO / M • The Sweetest Taboo / 1986 / SE / M • Taboo #03 / 1983 / IN / M • Taboo #10 / 1992 / IN / M • Taboo #11: Crazy On You / 1993 / IN / M • Tactical Sex Force / 1994 / IN / M • Taija / 1986 / WV / C • Tail Taggers #125 / 1994 / WV / M • Tailenders / 1985 / WET / M • Tailgunners / 1990 / CDI / M • Tailhouse Rock / 1985 / WV / M • Tailiens #1 / 1992 / FD / M • Tailiens #2 / 1992 / FD / M • Tailspin #1 / 1991 / VT / M • Tailspin #2 / 1991 / VT / M • Takin' It To The Limit #2 / 1994 / BS / M • Takin' It Up The Butt / 1995 / IF / C • Tales By Taylor / 1989 / AMB / M • Tales Of The Backside / 1985 / VCR / C • Talk Dirty To Me #03 / 1986 / DR / M • Talk Dirty To Me #09 / 1992 / DR / M • The Taming Of Savannah / 1993 / VI / M • A Taste Of Ecstasy / 1991 / CIN / M • A Taste Of Madison / 1992 / VD / C • A Taste Of Patricia Kennedy / 1992 / VD / C • A Taste Of Rachel / 1990 / PIN / C • A Taste Of Tawnee / 1988 / LV / C • Taste Of The Best #2 / 1988 / PIN / C • Taste Of The Best #3 / 1988 / PIN / C • The Teacher's Pet / 1985 / WV / M • The Tease / 1990 / VC / M • Teasers / 1984 / HO / M • Telesex #1 / 1992 / VI / M • Temple Of Lust / 1992 / VC / M • Temptation Eyes / 1991 / VT / M • Tenth Annual Adult Video News Awards / 1993 / VC / M • Terri Gets Her Wish / 1983 / BIZ / B • Texas Crude / 1995 / NIT / M • This Butt Lite Is For You / 1992 / ATL / M • Those Lynn Girls / 1989 / WV / C • Three By Three / 1989 / LV / C • The Three Musketeers #1 / 1992 / FD / M • The Three Musketeers #2 / 1992 / FD / M • Three's A Crowd / 1990 / HO / M • Thrill Street Blues / 1985 / WV / M • Tickets To Paradise / 1992 / XPI / M • Tight And Tender / 1985 / CA / M • Tight Ends In Motion / 1993 / TP / M • Tight Spot / 1992 / VD / M • Tip Of The Tongue / 1985 / V20 / M • Titillation #3 / 1991 / SE / M • Tomboy / 1983 / VCX / M • The Tongue / 1995 / OD / M • Tongue In Cheek / 1994 / LE / M • Too Good To Be True / 1984 / MAP / M • Too Hot To Touch #2 / 1993 / CV / M • Too Young To Know / 1984 / CC / M • Tools Of The Trade / 1990 / WV / M • Top Buns / 1986 / HO / M • Top It Off / 1990 / VC / M • Topless Brain Surgeons / 1995 / LE / M • Tori Welles Goes Behind The Scenes / 1992 / FD / M • Torrid Without A Cause #1 / 1989 / VI / M • Toys 4 Us #2 / 1987 / WV / C • Tracie Lords / 1984 / CIT / M • Tracy Dick / 1985 / WV / M • Tracy In Heaven

(Orig 1985) / 1985 / WV / M • Tracy In Heaven (Rewrite) / 1986 / WV / M • Trashy Lady / 1985 / MAP / M • Trick Or Treat / 1985 / ELH / M • Triple Header / 1990 / KNI / M • True Legends Of Adult Cinema: The Erotic Eighties / 1992 / VC / C • The Truth Laid Bare / 1993 / ZA / M • Truth Or Dare / 1993 / VI / M • Twice A Virgin / 1984 / PL / G • Twin Cheeks #1 / 1990 / CIN / M • Twin Cheeks #2 / 1991 / CIN / M • Twin Cheeks (Arrow) / 1991 / AR / M • Twins / 1986 / WV / M • Two In The Bush / 1991 / EX / M • Two Timing Tracie / 1985 / V20 / M • Two Women & A Man / 1988 / VEX / M • Two Women & A Man / 1991 / VEX / C • The Ultimate Fantasy / 1995 / CV / M • The Ultimate Thrill / 1988 / PIN / C • Ultra Head / 1992 / CA / M • The Unashamed / 1993 / FD / M • The Unauthorized Biography Of Rob Blow / 1990 / LV / M • Under The Law / 1989 / AFV / M • Undercover Lover / 1993 / VC / M • Undress To Thrill / 1994 / VI / M • Unforgivable / 1989 / IN / M • Uninhibited Love / 1994 / VPN / M • Up Against It / 1993 / ZA / M • Up And Cummers #17 / 1994 / 4P / M • Up The Ying Yang / 1991 / EVN / C • Used And Abused #1 / 1994 / SFP / M • User Friendly / 1992 / VT / M • Vagina Town / 1993 / CA / M • VCA Previews #4 / 1988 / VC / C • Vegas #5: Blackjack / 1991 / CIN / M • Vice / 1994 / WAV / M • Video Paradise / 1988 / ZA / M • Video Tramp #1 / 1985 / AA / M • A Vision In Heather / 1991 / VI / M • Visions Of Desire / 1993 / HO / M • Vivid Raw #2 / 1996 / VI / M • Voluptuous / 1993 / CA / M • Voodoo Lust: The Possession / 1989 / PCP / M • The Voyeur #1 / 1994 / EA / M • The Wacky World Of X-Rated Bloopers / 1989 / GO / M • The Way They Were / 1990 / CDI / M • We Love To Tease / 1985 / VD / M • We're Having A Party / 1991 / EVN / M • A Week And A Half In The Life Of A Prostitute / 1997 / EL / M • Welcome To The House Of Fur Pi / 1989 / GO / M • Wet Faces #1 / 1997 / SC / C • Wet Nurses #2 / 1995 / LE / M • Wet Science / 1986 / PLY / M • Wet Sex / 1984 / CA / M • What Gets Me Hot / 1984 / ISV / M • What's Love Got To Do With It / 1989 / WV / M • Where The Girls Are / 1984 / VEX / M • Where The Sun Never Shines / 1990 / IN / C • Whispered Lies / 1993 / LBO / M • Whispers / 1992 / HO / M • White Boys & Black Bitches / 1995 / ROB / M • White Bun Busters / 1985 / VC / M • White Wedding / 1995 / VI / M • Whitey's On The Moon / 1996 / ROB / M • Who Framed Ginger Grant? / 1989 / CC / M • Who Killed Holly Hollywood? / 1993 / VC / M • Who Reamed Rosie Rabbit? #2 / 1989 / FAN / M • The Whore / 1989 / CA / M • Why Things Burn / 1994 / LBO / M • Wicked / 1991 / XCI / M • Wicked Fascination / 1991 / CIN / M • Wicked Whispers / 1985 / VD / M • Wild Assed Pooper Slut / 1996 / ROB / M • Wild Flower #2 / 1992 / VI / M • Wild In The Wilderness / 1988 / SE / M • Wild In The Woods / 1988 / VEX / M • Wild Thing / 1994 / IF / M • Wild Weekend / 1984 / HO / M • Will & Ed Are Geeks In Heat / 1994 / MID / M • Will & Ed's Back To Class / 1992 / MID / M • Will And Ed: The Curse Of Poona / 1994 / MID / C • Willie Wanker And The Fun Factory / 1994 / FD / M • Wings Of Passion / 1984 / HO / M • Wire Desire / 1991 / XCI / M • With A Wiggle In Her Walk

/ 1989 / WV / M • With Love From Ginger /
1986 / HO / C • With Love From Susan /
1988 / HO / C • With The Devil In Her Rear
/ 1992 / WV / M • The Woman In Pink /
1984 / SE / M • Women On Fire / 1995 /
LBO / M • Working Girl / 1993 / VI / M •
WPINK-TV #1 / 1985 / PV / M • X Dreams
/ 1989 / CA / M • X Factor: The Next Generation / 1991 / HO / M • X-Rated Blondes
/ 1992 / VD / C • The X-Terminator / 1986 /
PV / M • You're The Boss / 1985 / VD / M •
Young And Naughty / 1984 / HO / M •
Young And Restless / 1983 / VIV / M •
Young Nurses In Lust / 1994 / LBO / M •
[Berlin Caper / 1989 / ... / M

MARC WALLIS see Marc Wallice
MARC WOLFE
Dr Bondo / 1995 / BON / B • Gallery Of
Pain / 1995 / BON / B • Pain In The Rent /
1996 / BON / B • Portraits Of Pain / 1995 /
B&D / B • Snared For Submission / 1995 /
BON / B • Sold Into Slavery / 1996 / BON /
B • Spy Trap / 1995 / BON / B • The Tam-
ing Of Kitty / 1996 / BON / B • Unruly
Slaves #1 / 1995 / BON / B • Unruly Slaves
#2 / 1995 / BON / B • Whip Therapy / 1995
/ BON / B

MARC WYANDI see Star Index I
MARCEA BLACKMAN
All About Sex / 1970 / AR / M
MARCEL
Amazon Heat #1 / 1996 / CC / M
MARCELLA
Blue Vanities #545 / 1994 / FFL / M • Les-
bian Pros And Amateurs #02 / 1992 / GO /
F • Magma: Hot Shots / 1995 / MET / M •
Prague By Night #1 / 1996 / EA / M • Stu-
dent Fetish Videos: Best Of Spanking #02
/ 1993 / PRE / C • TV Birdcage Rage #2 /
1996 / GLI / G

MARCELLA JOHNS
Pony Girl #2: At The Ranch / 1986 / CS / B
MARCELLA LEROY see Star Index I
MARCELLE DUPUE see Star Index I
MARCELLE LETIG see Star Index I
**MARCELLO (V.CORREA) see Vladimir
Correa**
MARCELLO BONINO
Whatever Happened To Miss September?
/ 1973 / ALP / M
MARCELLO FUSI
Impulse #05: When I Was 20... / 1995 /
MBP / M • Impulse #07: / 1996 / MBP / M
**MARCELO MATTER see Vladimir Cor-
rea**
MARCI DAMON
How To Make Love To A Woman / 19?? /
VVO / M
MARCI HOLLANDER see Star Index I
MARCI STERN
Dianna's Destiny / 19?? / BIZ / B
MARCIA see Star Index I
MARCIA ALLEN
Boiling Point / 1978 / SE / M
MARCIA BACALL
Marine Code Of Silence: Don't Ask Don't
Tell / 1996 / BHE / G
MARCIA BRADY
San Francisco Lesbians #1 / 1992 / PL / F
MARCIA EDDINGTON see Star Index I
MARCIA GRAY see Shanna McCullough
MARCIA JORDAN see Marsha Jordan
MARCIA MAJOR
Take Off / 1978 / VXP / M
MARCIA MINOR
Venture Into The Bizarre / cr78 / VHL / M

MARCIA MORENO
Terri Gets Her Wish / 1983 / BIZ / B
MARCIE CARTER see Star Index I
MARCIE LOPEZ
Rodney's Rookies #1 / 1996 / NIT / M
MARCO
AVP #9153: The Monday Night Game /
1991 / AVP / M • Rebecca Lord's World
Tour #1: French Edition / 1995 / WP / M •
When In L.A. / 1991 / ... / M
MARCO ROSSI
Lana Exposed / 1995 / VT / M • Long Play
/ 1995 / 3XP / G • The Search For Cana-
dian Beaver / 1995 / LIP / F • Smooth As
Silk / 1994 / EMC / M
MARCO ROY
Club Privado / 1995 / KP / M
MARCO SOLO
Anita / 1996 / BLC / M
MARCUM MCDOWEL
How To Make A College Co-Ed / 1995 /
VG0 / M
MARCUS
Euromania #2 / 1996 / AOC / M
MARCUS ALSTON see Mr. Marcus
MARCUS JOHNSON see Star Index I
MARCUS POLE
Midnight Fantasies / 1992 / VIM / M
MARCUS VALENTINO
The Nite Bird / 1978 / BL / M
MARCY DAVIS see Star Index I
MARCY LOPEZ
Creme De La Face #06 / 1995 / OD / M •
Latin Plump Humpers #1 / 1995 / TTV / M
• Latin Plump Humpers #2 / 1995 / TTV / M
• Makin' Bacon / 1994 / WIV / M • Rollie
Pollie Chicks / 1996 / TTV / M
MARCY ST CLAIRE
Undulations / 1980 / VC / M
MAREE
Blue Vanities #130 / 1990 / FFL / M
MAREECE
Black Gangbangers #03 / 1995 / HW / M
MAREK
Prague By Night #1 / 1996 / EA / M •
Prague By Night #2 / 1996 / EA / M
MARELLA INARI
Sex-A-Holic Lady / 1995 / PL / M
MARGA EUER
Erotic Fantasies #2 / 1983 / CV / C • The
Joy Of Fooling Around / 1978 / CV / M
MARGARET
Blue Vanities #509 / 1992 / FFL / M •
Mondo Extreme / 1996 / SHS / M
MARGARET GATES
The Psychiatrist / 1978 / VC / M
MARGARET MIDDLETON
Blue Vanities #517 / 1992 / FFL / M • Reel
Classics #3 / 1996 / H&S / M
MARGARET NOLAN
Blue Vanities #582 / 1996 / FFL / M
MARGARET PETERS
Homegrown Video: Special #1 / 1991 /
HOV / M
MARGARET RAINES
Up 'n' Coming / 1983 / CA / M
MARGARET SILVERMAN
Bucky Beaver's XXX Dragon Art Theatre
Double Feature #06 / 1996 / SOW / M •
Finishing School / 1975 / SOW / M
MARGARET SMITH see Maggie Wilson
MARGARETTE
Reel Life Video #31: Another Hairy Girl
Special / 1995 / RLF / F
MARGARITA
Drop Sex: Wipe The Floor / 1997 / JLP / M

MARGARITA ESPANA see Zumira
MARGE see Star Index I
MARGE ATWOOD see Star Index I
MARGE PILLARS see Star Index I
MARGE STEWART
GVC: Hotel Hooker #113 / 1975 / GO / M
MARGERY ARCHER
Lipps & Mccain / 1978 / VC / M • Yuppies
In Heat / 1988 / CHA / C
MARGIA MELLON
The Joy Of Fooling Around / 1978 / CV / M
MARGIE
Hardcore: The Films Of Richard Kern #1 /
1991 / FTV / M
MARGIE HILLS see Star Index I
MARGIT
Dick & Jane In Budapest / 1993 / AVI / M •
Magma: Dreams Of Lust / 1994 / MET / M
• Private Gold #12: The Pyramid #2 / 1996
/ OD / M
MARGIT SZOPOS
True Stories #1 / 1993 / SC / M • True Sto-
ries #2 / 1993 / SC / M
MARGO
Best Butt(e) In The West #1 / 1992 / CC /
M • Dirty Dancers #8 / 1996 / 4P / M • Eric
Kroll's Bondage #1 / 1994 / ERK / M • Glitz
Clits #01 / 1992 / GLI / F • Global Girls /
1996 / GO / F • Porno Bizarro / 1995 / GLI
/ M • Tongue / 1974 / ALP / M • Wrasslin
She-Babes #05 / 1996 / SOW / M
MARGO ALABASTER see Star Index I
MARGO ANAND
Ancient Secrets Of Sexual Ecstasy / 1996
/ HIG / M
MARGO BENNETT see Star Index I
MARGO DAY
Hardcore: The Films Of Richard Kern #1 /
1991 / FTV / M
MARGO FELLER see Star Index I
MARGO MULLER
Viola Video #102: Anal #8 / 1995 / PEV / M
MARGO NEAL see Star Index I
MARGO O'CONNOR
Thundercrack! / 1974 / LUM / M
MARGO STEVENS
Executions On Butt Row / 1996 / EA / M •
Introducing Alexis / 1996 / VI / M • Pick Up
Lines #13 / 1997 / OD / M • Pussyman Au-
ditions #21 / 1996 / SNA / M • Video Virgins
#28 / 1996 / NS / M
MARGO WATLEY
Headmaster's Study Part I & Ii / 1993 / CS
/ B
MARGO YOUNGER
Have Blower Will Travel / 1975 / SOW / M
MARGOT
Big Babies In Budapest / 1996 / EL / M •
Cherry Busters / 1995 / WIV / M • Private
Film #16 / 1994 / OD / M • Sodomania #17:
Simply Makes U Tingle / 1996 / EL / M
MARGRET CICEK
The Young Seducers / 1971 / BL / M
MARGRIT SIEGEL
[Die Madchenhandler / 1972 / ... / M
MARGUERITE
Old Wave Hookers #1 / 1995 / PL / M • Old
Wave Hookers #2 / 1995 / PL / M
**MARGUERITE NUIT see Roxanne Rol-
land**
MARGUERITE PARTEE see Star Index I
MARI LEWIS
Gift Of Love / 1979 / ... / M
MARI MONROE see Star Index I
MARI PENKOVA
Sex-A-Holic Lady / 1995 / PL / M

MARI-ANGE
Hardcore Debutantes #02 / 1996 / TEP / M • Nineteen #7 / 1996 / FOR / M

MARIA
100% Amateur #01: Double Penetration Sensation / 1995 / OD / M • Back East Babes #2 / 1996 / NIT / M • The Baroness / 1987 / VD / M • Big Babies In Budapest / 1996 / EL / M • Blue Vanities #569 / 1996 / FFL / M • Buttman Goes To Rio #3 / 1992 / EA / M • Drop Sex: Wipe The Floor / 1997 / JLP / M • HomeGrown Video #448: Look Who's Cumming For Dinner / 1995 / HOV / M • Intimate Interviews #4 / 1996 / NIT / M • Limited Edition #15 / 1980 / AVC / M • Max World #6: Rolling + Reaming! / 1996 / LE / M • Nu-West Screen Test #1 / 1988 / NUV / F • Onanie #2 / 1995 / MET / F • OUTS: Maria / 1995 / OUT / F • Prague By Night #1 / 1996 / EA / M • Prague By Night #2 / 1996 / EA / M • Private Stories #10 / 1996 / OD / M • Private Video Magazine #01 / 1993 / OD / M • Screwed On The Job / 1991 / XPI / M • Tickling Scenes / 1991 / TAO / C • Triple X Video Magazine #12 / 1996 / OD / M • The Voyeur #8: Live In Europe #2 / 1996 / JLP / M • Wrasslin She-Babes #04 / 1996 / SOW / M • Wrestling Classics #4 / 1993 / CDP / B

MARIA (H. LEE) *see* **Heather Lee**
MARIA (ZUMIRA) *see* **Zumira**
MARIA ARNOLD
Country Hooker / 1970 / BPI / S • Cozy Cool / 1971 / WWV / M • The Godson / 1971 / BPI / S • The Hand Of Pleasure / 1971 / SOW / S • Hollywood Babylon / 1972 / AIR / S • The Magic Mirror / 1970 / ALP / S • Necromania / 1971 / SOW / S • The Toy Box / 1971 / BPI / S • Wham Bam Thank You Spaceman / 1973 / BPI / S • [The Liberated Lady / 1972 / ... / S

MARIA AVELENS
The House Of Strange Desires / 1985 / NSV / M

MARIA BIANCO
Club Privado / 1995 / KP / M
MARIA CHRISTI *see* **Star Index I**
MARIA CHRISTINA
Eurotica #03 / 1995 / XC / M
MARIA CHRISTINE
Eurotica #04 / 1996 / XC / M

MARIA DAMARIS
Cheerleader Bondage Hell / 1995 / OUP / B • N.Y. Video Magazine #07 / 1996 / OUP / M • N.Y. Video Magazine #09 / 1996 / OUP / M • New York City Lesbian Gang Bang / 1995 / OUP / F • Streets Of New York #06 / 1996 / PL / M

MARIA DE SANCHEZ
Pretty Spanish girl supposedly from Barcelona. English not too good. Long black hair, lithe body, nice butt, tight waist, narrow hips, and medium tits. 27 years old in 1996.
Amateur Lusty Latins #2 / 1997 / SUF / M • Asses Galore #6: Fallen Angels / 1996 / DFI / M • Betty Bleu / 1996 / IP / M • Buttman In Barcelona / 1996 / EA / M • Flamenco Ecstasy / 1996 / UEF / M • More Dirty Debutantes #63 / 1997 / SBV / M • Pick Up Lines #12 / 1997 / OD / M • Pick Up Lines #13 / 1997 / OD / M • Private Gold #15: Sweet Lady #2 / 1997 / OD / M • The Voyeur #7: Live In Europe #1 / 1996 / JLP / M

MARIA DIABLO
Enter Into Slavery / 1996 / GOT / B • Toe

Tales #29 / 1995 / GOT / B • Toe Tales #32 / 1996 / GOT / B • Toe Tales #33 / 1996 / GOT / B • Toe Tales #34 / 1996 / GOT / B • Toe Tales #36 / 1996 / GOT / B

MARIA DOMINIQUE *see* **Star Index I**
MARIA DONADA
Creme De Femme / 1994 / 4P / F
MARIA DUYADARE
Canadian Beaver Hunt #2 / 1996 / PL / M
MARIA ESTOBAN *see* **Star Index I**
MARIA FORSA *see* **Maria Lynn**
MARIA FROST
Blue Vanities #567 / 1995 / FFL / M
MARIA GARCIA *see* **Star Index I**
MARIA GASKET
San Francisco Lesbians #5 / 1994 / PL / F
MARIA GRANADA *see* **Star Index I**
MARIA JAMES *see* **Star Index I**
MARIA KARINA *see* **Star Index I**
MARIA LONGO
The Rise Of The Roman Empress #1 / 1986 / PV / M
MARIA LYNN *(Maria Forsa)*
Bel Ami / 1976 / VXP / M • Butterflies / 1974 / CA / M • Immoral Tales / 1974 / LUM / S • Veil Of Lust / 1973 / BL / M • [Justine Och Juliette / 1975 / ... / S • [Molly / 1977 / ... / S

MARIA MOORE
Strap-On Sally #01: Strap-On Psycho / 1993 / PL / F • Strap-On Sally #02: Ariana Bottoms Out / 1993 / PL / F
MARIA PERON
Josephine / 1974 / VC / M
MARIA PFEFFER *see* **Star Index I**
MARIA PIA
Casanova #2 / 1976 / CA / M • I Am Curious (Tahiti) / 1970 / ... / S
MARIA PROKANE *see* **Star Index I**
MARIA RATTI
Hotel Fear / 1996 / ONA / M
MARIA REINA
[Kansas City Trucking Company / 1976 / TMX / G
MARIA ROSENTHAL *see* **Star Index I**
MARIA SAVARESE *see* **Star Index I**
MARIA SCHELL
Bucky Beaver's XXX Dragon Art Theatre Double Feature #01 / 1996 / SOW / M • Hitler's Harlots / cr73 / SOW / M
MARIA SENTRY
The Stimulators / 1983 / VC / M
MARIA SPYDEL *see* **Star Index I**
MARIA SZASZ
Diamonds / 1996 / HDE / M
MARIA TORRES *see* **Maria Tortuga**
MARIA TORTUGA *(Mary Christian, Irene Best, Maria Torres)*
Not too pretty with black hair and small tits. Mary Christian is from **Skintight**. Irene Best is from **Lust At First Bite**.
3 Beauties And A Maid / cr82 / LIP / F • Bad Girl / 1984 / LIM / M • Ball Game / 1980 / CA / M • Bi-Sexual Fantasies / 1984 / LAV / G • Blue Vanities #537 / 1993 / FFL / M • Burning Desire / 1983 / HO / M • Carnal Encounters Of The Barest Kind / 1978 / VOY / C • Cherry-Ettes For Hire / 1984 / 4P / M • Confessions Of A Nymph / 1985 / VCR / M • Creme De Femme #1 / 1981 / AVC / C • Deep Throat #1 / 1972 / AR / M • Delusions Of Grandeur / cr85 / DRV / B • Erotic Encounters / 1985 / LIM / C • The Erotic World Of Rene Summers / 1984 / VCR / C • The Erotic World Of Seka / 1983 / VCR / C • First Annual XRCO Awards /

1984 / AVC / C • For Services Rendered / 1984 / CA / M • Foreplay / 1982 / VC / M • Free And Foxy / 1986 / VCX / C • Girls And Their Toys / 1983 / LIP / F • GVC: Reincarnation Of Serena #121 / 1983 / GO / M • Heat Of The Moment / 1983 / S&L / M • Hot Bodies (Ventura) / 1984 / VEN / C • Hot Girls In Love / 1984 / VIV / C • Hot Love / 1981 / SAT / M • Hot Skin In 3D / 1977 / ... / M • I Wanna Be Teased / 1984 / SE / M • Inspiration / 1981 / CHX / M • Intimate Lessons / 1982 / VC / M • John Holmes Exposed / 1978 / AVC / C • John Holmes, The Lost Films / 1988 / PEN / C • Joys Of Erotica / 1984 / VCR / M • Joys Of Erotica #108 / 1984 / VCR / C • Joys Of Erotica #114 / 1984 / VCR / C • A Lacy Affair #1 / 1983 / HO / F • Let Me Tell Ya 'Bout White Chicks / 1985 / VC / M • Limited Edition #04 / 1979 / AVC / M • Limited Edition #14 / 1980 / AVC / M • Love Goddesses / 1981 / VC / M • Love To Mother / 1984 / VIV / M • Lust At First Bite / 1978 / VC / M • Mrs. Rodger's Neighborhood / 1988 / EVN / C • Mrs. Smith's Erotic Holiday / 1982 / VCX / M • National Pornographic #1: Lesbians / 1987 / 4P / C • Never So Deep / 1981 / VCX / M • Night Flight / cr80 / CRE / M • Oriental Temptations / 1984 / CV / C • Pink Champagne / 1979 / CV / M • Plato's, The Movie / 1980 / SE / M • Pleasure Dome / 1982 / SE / M • Pleasure Productions #08 / 1984 / VCR / M • Remember Connie / 1984 / MAP / M • The Satisfiers Of Alpha Blue / 1980 / AVC / M • Scared Stiff / 1984 / PV / M • The Sensuous Detective / 1979 / VC / M • Sexcalibur / 1982 / SE / M • Sheri's Gotta Have It / 1985 / LIM / C • Showgirl #15: Taylor Evans' Fantasies / 1983 / VCR / M • Skintight / 1981 / CA / M • Sounds Of Sex / 1985 / CA / M • Splashing / 1986 / VCS / C • Stranger In Town / 1980 / FAN / M • Swedish Erotica #27 / 1980 / CA / M • Taxi Girls #2: In Search Of Toni / 1986 / ELD / M • Trouble Down Below / 1981 / CA / M • The Trouble With Traci / 1984 / CHA / C • The Vanessa Obsession / 1987 / VCX / C • Voyeur's Delight / 1986 / VCS / C • Weekend Fantasy / 1980 / VCX / M • Weekend Lovers / 1975 / AVC / M • Wet Dreams / 1980 / WWV / M • What Would Your Mother Say? / 1981 / HAV / M • Why Gentlemen Prefer Blondes / 1983 / HO / C • Young And Restless / 1983 / VIV / M • [Carnal Cuties / 1979 / ... / M • [Romeo And Juliet / 1984 / ... / M • [Three For Love / 1983 / ... / M

MARIA VOMTIEF *see* **Star Index I**
MARIA WOOLF
Pink Champagne / 1979 / CV / M
MARIAH
Score 4 Me / 1991 / XPI / M • Tales From The Chateau / 1987 / BON / B • Weird And Bizarre Bondage / 1991 / FC / C • Women On Women #2 / 1994 / MAV / F
MARIAH BONET
Sin City Cycle Sluts #1 / 1995 / SC / F • Sin City Cycle Sluts #2 / 1995 / SC / F
MARIAN
Painless Steel #3 / 1996 / FLV / M
MARIAN WALTER *see* **Kelly Nichols**
MARIANA *see* **Star Index I**
MARIANNA *see* **Star Index I**
MARIANNA ARENSBAK
Resurrection Of Eve / 1973 / MIT / M
MARIANNA AUBERT *see* **Star Index I**

MARIANNA KISS
Dirty Stories #5 / 1996 / PE / M
MARIANNE
The Last Vamp / 1996 / IP / M • Magma:
Anita #2 / 1996 / MET / M • Magma: Old
And Young / 1995 / MET / M • Magma:
Sperm Dreams / 1990 / MET / M • Private
Stories #04 / 1995 / OD / M
MARIANNE DE MANILLA see Star Index
I
MARIANNE DUPONT
Strip For Action / 1982 / MED / S • [Mad-
chen, Die Sich Selbst, Bedienen / 1974 / ...
/ M
MARIANNE FLOWERS
Aphrodesia's Diary / 1984 / CA / M • Sex-
tasy / 1978 / COM / M • The Tale Of Tiffany
Lust / 1981 / CA / M
MARIANNE FOURNIER see Star Index I
MARIANNE LAMONTE
Private Film #01 / 1993 / OD / M
MARIANNE NILSSON
Bordello / 1973 / AR / M
MARIANNE WALTER see Kelly Nichols
MARIE
The Best Of The Big Boob Battles / 1993 /
CDP / C • Blue Vanities #194 / 1993 / FFL
/ M • Blue Vanities #522 / 1993 / FFL / M •
English Class / 1995 / VC / M • High Heels
In Heat #1 / 1988 / RSV / F • High Heels In
Heat #3 / 1989 / RSV / F • Hot Legs #2 /
1990 / PLV / B • Joe Elliot's College Girls
#36 / 1994 / JOE / M • Joe Elliot's Latin
College Girls #01 / 1995 / JOE / M •
Magma: Bizarre Games / 1996 / MET / M •
Magma: Claudine In Action / 1996 / MET /
M • Magma: Dirty Diana / 1994 / MET / M •
Magma: Horny For Cock / 1990 / MET / M
• Magma: Sperma / 1994 / MET / M • Pri-
vate Gold #14: Sweet Lady #1 / 1997 / OD
/ M • Rev #107: Marie's Debut / 1990 / REV
/ M • Rev #119: Marie Plays / 1990 / REV /
M • Rev #120: Gang Bang / 1990 / REV /
M • Student Fetish Videos: Foot Worship
#14 / 1995 / PRE / B • Valentine's Chal-
lenge / 1992 / LIP / B • Valentine's Won-
derland / 1992 / LIP / F
MARIE ANN see Star Index I
MARIE ANTOINETTE
Letters From A Slave / 1995 / AOC / M
MARIE BOTBOL see Star Index I
MARIE CAPET
Chateau Duval / 1996 / HDE / M
MARIE CHRISTINE
Skin #4: The 4th Rite / 1995 / ERQ / M
MARIE CORY
The Horny Housewife / 1996 / HO / M
MARIE DANSEN see Star Index I
MARIE DE MUIR see Star Index I
MARIE EKKORE
Keyhole / 1977 / SE / M
MARIE FAITIER see Star Index I
MARIE FLASCHSK see Star Index I
MARIE GRUBER
Blackmail For Daddy / 1976 / VCX / M
MARIE JAMES
Frat House Frolics / cr78 / CPL / M
MARIE LAPUTA
Erotic Fantasies #3 / 1983 / CV / C
MARIE LAVAR see Star Index I
MARIE LAWRENCE
Beyond Desire / 1986 / VC / M
MARIE LUCETTE see Star Index I
MARIE MAIDEN see Star Index I
MARIE MASON (Cougar, Inca, Buffy Mal-
ibu, Suzette Alexander, Suzanne

Alexander)
Hispanic looking with small tits but a bit pudgy
around the middle. Married to Biff Malibu
(Christopher Alexander). Tattoo of a scor-
pion on her left butt.
The Anal Adventures Of Max Hardcore:
Animalistic Urge / 1992 / ZA / M • Anal Vi-
sion #02 / 1992 / LBO / M • Gangbang Girl
#17 / 1995 / ANA / M • L.A. Rear / 1992 /
FD / M • Mr. Peepers Amateur Home
Videos #53: Dirty Laundry / 1992 / LBO / M
• Odyssey 30 Min: Clarissa's 4-Way Return
/ 1992 / OD / M • Uncle Roy's Amateur
Home Video #12 / 1992 / VIM / M
MARIE MATOUX see Star Index I
MARIE METIER see Star Index I
MARIE MONELLE see Sydney Dance
MARIE MONET see Heather Lere
MARIE NICKERSON
May also be the same as Natalie Taylor.
Knights In Black Satin / 1990 / VEX / M •
Living In Sin / 1990 / VEX / M • Perfect Girl
/ 1991 / VEX / M
MARIE NOEL see Star Index I
MARIE NOELLY
Skin #3 / 1995 / ERQ / M
MARIE NOVEAU
Canadian Beaver Hunt #1 / 1996 / PL / M
MARIE PASCAL
Five Kittens / 19?? / ... / M
MARIE REDD
Black On Black / 1987 / CDI / M
MARIE SAVAGE see Star Index I
MARIE SHARP (Gina Carnali, Mercedes
Perez, Trina (Marie Sharp))
Adorable brunette with long black hair, tight
petite body, tight waist, nice butt, small tits,
wonderful smile, overbite, big eyes and a
pretty face. Does not appear in **Golden
Girls #35** despite box. Trina is the name
she used in a centerfold in *Hustler*, Sep-
tember 1982.
Blue Interview / 1983 / VCR / M • Breezy /
1985 / VCR / M • Cafe Flesh / 1982 / VC /
M • Diamond Collection #39 / 1983 / CDI /
M • Foreplay / 1982 / VC / M • Glamour Girl
#2 / 1984 / CDI / M • Gourmet Quickies:
Marie Sharp / Christy Canyon #729 / 1985
/ GO / C • GVC: Anything Goes #119 / 1983
/ GO / M • GVC: Companions #122 / 1983
/ GO / F • In The Pink / 1983 / CA / M •
Lusty Ladies #03 / 1983 / SVE / M • Orien-
tal Lust / 1983 / GO / M • Pleasure Pro-
ductions #08 / 1984 / VCR / M • Pleasure
Productions #10 / 1985 / VCR / M • The
Vanessa Obsession / 1987 / VCX / C •
VCA Previews #1 / 1988 / VC / C
MARIE SHAY
Golden Girls #35 / 1988 / CA / M
MARIE ST. CLAIRE
Bedtime Stories / 1996 / VC / M
MARIE TAYLOR see Star Index I
MARIE VOE
Blue Vanities #556 / 1994 / FFL / M
MARIE WESTBROOK see Star Index I
MARIE WILDER see Star Index I
MARIE-CHRISTINE
Girls Of France / 1991 / BTO / M
MARIE-CLAUDE
White Heat / 1981 / CA / M
MARIELLE RENAUD see Star Index I
MARIENNELLE
Eurotica #09 / 1996 / XC / M
MARIKO (Tara Mariko, Mariko Kemo)
Asia Blue #04: Mariko / 1993 / AOC / S •
Blush: Private Pleasures / 1993 / FAT / F •

China Bitch / 1989 / PV / C • For Love And
Lust / 1985 / AVC / M • Geisha Slave / 1985
/ BIZ / B • Hustler #17 / 1984 / CA0 / M • A
Lacy Affair #1 / 1983 / HO / F • One Night
In Bangkok / 1985 / CA / M • Oriental Taboo
/ 1985 / CDI / M • Private Pleasures / 1985
/ FAT / C • Reel People #02 / 1984 / AR / M
• Sex Appeal / 1984 / ABV / M • Sex Wars
/ 1984 / EXF / M • A Taste Of Money / 1983
/ AT / M
MARIKO KEMO see Mariko
MARILENA RAMANA
Intimate Secrets Of Sex & Spirit / 1995 /
TMM / M
MARILYN
100% Amateur #05: Threesomes & Group
Scenes / 1995 / OD / M • A&B AB#492:
Marilyn's Kinky Dreams #1 / 1995 / A&B /
M • A&B AB#493: Marilyn's Kinky Dreams
#2 / 1995 / A&B / M • A&B AB#494: Mari-
lyn's Kinky Dreams #3 / 1995 / A&B / M •
A&B AB#524: Dr. Lisa's Cum Soaked Girls
#3 / 1995 / A&B / M • A&B AB#540: Cum
Girl Cum / 1995 / A&B / M • Blue Vanities
#512 / 1992 / FFL / M • Chicks With Dicks
#2 / 1996 / BIZ / B • Creme De La Face
#12: Pretty Faces To Cum On / 1995 / OD
/ M • G-Strings / 1984 / COM / M • Rick's
Bondage Playmate #2 / 1993 / HMV / B •
Transsexual Dynasty / 1996 / BIZ / G • TV
Birdcage Rage #1 / 1996 / GLI / G
MARILYN BERG see Serena
MARILYN BLAKE
Was 26 in 1993 and comes from Flint Michican
where she was an exotic dancer in a club.
Saggy medium tits, blonde, slutty looking.
A Is For Anal / 1993 / LV / M • Anal Nature
/ 1993 / AFD / M • Deep Inside Dirty Debu-
tantes #08 / 1993 / 4P / M • Falling In Love
Again / 1993 / PMV / M • Harry Horndog
#20: Love Puppies #6 / 1993 / ZA / M • In-
decent Proposition / 1993 / LV / M • Precious Cargo / 1993 / VIM / M
**MARILYN BRIGGS see Marilyn Cham-
bers**
MARILYN CHAMBERS (Marilyn Briggs)
Blonde ice princess (medium firm tits) whose
claim to fame was her appearence on soap
boxes as the Ivory Snow girl prior to star-
ring in **Behind The Green Door**. Born
1952. Comes from Westport CT. In 1991
had first child. First married to a guy called
Doug prior to making **Behind**. Later mar-
ried to Chuck Traynor (of Linda Lovelace
fame).
Angel Of H.E.A.T. / 1981 / VES / S • Behind
The Green Door #1 / 1972 / MIT / M • Be-
yond De Sade / 1979 / MIT / M • Bikini
Bistro / 1995 / 3SR / S • Blue Vanities #090
/ 1988 / FFL / M • Breakfast In Bed / 1990
/ PS / S • Collection #08 / 1984 / CA / M •
Deadly Force / 1983 / NLH / S • Electric
Blue #001 (Marilyn Chambers) / 1983 / CA
/ S • Electric Blue #008 / 1983 / CA / S •
First Annual XRCO Awards / 1984 / AVC /
C • Insatiable #1 / 1980 / CA / M • Insa-
tiable #2 / 1984 / CA / M • Inside Marilyn
Chambers / 1975 / MIT / M • Legends Of
Porn #1 / 1987 / CV / C • Legends Of Porn
#2 / 1989 / CV / C • Marilyn Chambers'
Bedtime Fantasies / 1996 / PS / S • Mari-
lyn Chambers' Bedtime Stories / 1993 / PS
/ S • Marilyn Chambers' Private Fantasies
#1 / 1983 / CA / M • Marilyn Chambers' Pri-
vate Fantasies #2 / 1983 / CA / M • Marilyn
Chambers' Private Fantasies #3 / 1983 /

CA / M • Marilyn Chambers' Private Fantasies #4 / 1983 / CA / M • Marilyn Chambers' Private Fantasies #5 / 1985 / CA / M • Marilyn Chambers' Private Fantasies #6 / 1985 / CA / M • Marilyn Chambers: Wet And Wild Fantasies / 1996 / PS / S • The Marilyn Diaries / 1990 / 3SR / S • Mitchell Brothers Ultra Core Collection / 1996 / SVE / C • My Therapist / 1983 / MED / S • Never A Tender Moment / 1979 / MIT / B • New York Nights / 1994 / … / S • Night On The Town / 1982 / KEN / S • The Owl And The Pussycat / 1970 / GTE / S • Party Girls / 1989 / NWW / S • Playboy Video Magazine #04 / 1983 / PLA / S • Rabid / 1977 / WAR / S • Resurrection Of Eve / 1973 / MIT / M • Sex Surrogate / 1990 / NST / S • Together / 1971 / … / S • Up 'n' Coming / 1983 / CA / M • [Classics Of Porn / 19?? / … / M • [Marilyn Chambers' Great Sexual Outdoors / 1995 / … / S • [Marilyn Chambers' Lusty Busty Fantasies / 1996 / … / S • [Marilyn Chambers' Sex On The Set / 1996 / … / S

MARILYN DOWLING
The Bride Stripped Bare / 1994 / BON / B
MARILYN DU PRE see Star Index I
MARILYN GEE
The Satisfiers Of Alpha Blue / 1980 / AVC / M
MARILYN GULE
Everything Goes / 1975 / CA / M
MARILYN JESS *(Dominique Troyes, Dominique Humbert, Marilyn Wild, Platinette)*
The Arrangement / 1984 / CV / M • Bachelor Party / 1987 / VCX / M • Barbara Dare's Roman Holiday / 1987 / SE / M • The Comeback Of Marilyn / 1986 / VC / M • Coming On Strong / 1989 / CA / C • For Love And Money / 1987 / CV / S • Forbidden Pleasures / 1987 / VC / M • Girl With The Million $ Legs / 1987 / PL / M • Grand Prixxx / 1987 / CA / M • Honeymoon In Paradise / 1985 / VC / M • Hotel Lesbos / 1986 / LIP / F • Looking Good / 1984 / ABV / M • Lust Italian Style / 1987 / CA / M • Mimi / 1987 / CA / M • Open Nightly / 1982 / CA / M • Paris Models / 1987 / CDI / M • Postcards From Abroad / 1991 / CA / C • Programmed For Pleasure / 1984 / VD / M • Sex Sleuth / cr80 / … / M • Sweet Dreams / 1978 / CON / M • Taste Of The Best #2 / 1988 / PIN / C • Traci, I Love You / 1987 / CA / M
MARILYN KENNEDY
Bedtime Video #04 / 1984 / GO / M
MARILYN LAMOUR see Olinka
MARILYN MALONE
The Worm / 1995 / ZFX / B
MARILYN MANSFIELD
Blue Vanities #552 / 1994 / FFL / M • The Outlaw / 1991 / WV / M
MARILYN MARTIN *(Marilyn Martyr, Martina Martin)*
Blue eyed blonde with very bad skin and medium hard tits which look enhanced but you can't see any scars. Was 21 years old in 1993 but looks much, much older. Supposedly only devirginized at 20 (but given her type of movies I doubt this). About September 1995 she had had her tits made large and even more rock solid.
A&B AB#415: Sex Club #2 / 1993 / A&B / M • The Adventures Of Mr. Tootsie Pole #1 / 1995 / LBO / M • Amateur Orgies #26 /

1993 / AFI / M • America's Raunchiest Home Videos #74: / 1993 / ZA / M • The Anal Adventures Of Max Hardcore: Video Games / 1994 / ZA / M • The Anal Adventures Of Max Hardcore: Wildlife / 1994 / ZA / M • Anal Anonymous / 1995 / SO / M • Anal Auditions / 1995 / VMX / M • Anal Health Club Babes / 1995 / EVN / M • Anal Legend / 1994 / ROB / M • Anal Maniacs #1 / 1994 / WP / M • Anal Queen / 1994 / FPI / M • Anal Sluts & Sweethearts #3 / 1995 / ROB / M • Anal Summer / 1994 / ROB / M • Anal Therapy #3 / 1994 / FD / M • Anal Virgins Of America #04 / 1993 / FOR / M • Anal Vision #10 / 1993 / LBO / M • Anal Vision #21 / 1993 / LBO / M • Anal Vision #24 / 1994 / LBO / M • Anal Woman #3 / 1995 / PL / M • The Artist / 1994 / HO / M • The Ass Master #02 / 1993 / GLI / M • Bachelor Party #2 / 1993 / FPI / M • Backdoor Smugglers / 1994 / JAV / M • Beach Bum Amateur's #40 / 1993 / MID / M • Biography: Max Steiner / 1995 / SC / C • Black Beauty (Las Vegas) / 1995 / LV / M • Blonde Butt Babes / 1994 / LV / M • Bobby Hollander's Maneaters #06 / 1993 / SFP / M • Booty Mistress / 1994 / ROB / M • The Bottom Dweller 33 1/3 / 1995 / EL / M • Brassiere To Eternity / 1994 / PEP / F • The Breast Of Breastmen / 1995 / EVN / C • Bubble Butts #26 / 1993 / LBO / M • Bun Busters #22 / 1994 / LBO / M • Butt Bangers Ball / 1994 / FPI / M • The Butt Sisters Do Denver / 1994 / MID / M • Butt Whore / 1994 / WIV / M • Buttmasters / 1994 / AMP / M • Buttslammers #10: Lust On The Internet / 1995 / BS / F • Casting Call #05 / 1994 / SO / M • The Crack / 1994 / LV / M • The Cumm Brothers #02: Goin' To A Ho' Down / 1994 / OD / M • The Cumm Brothers #03: Go To Traffic School / 1994 / OD / M • Cunthunt / 1995 / AB / F • Cyberanal / 1995 / VC / M • Dick & Jane Go To Northridge / 1994 / AVI / M • Dirty Dating Service #06 / 1994 / WP / M • Dungeon Dykes #2 / 1994 / FPI / F • Fantasy Du Jour / 1995 / FH / M • Fantasy Flings #02 / 1994 / WP / M • Filthy Sleazy Scoundrels / 1994 / HW / M • Fire & Ice / 1995 / LV / M • Flappers / 1995 / EMC / M • Gang Bang Bitches #04 / 1995 / PP / M • Head First / 1995 / OD / M • Hollywood Amateurs #07 / 1994 / MID / M • Hotel Sodom #01 / 1995 / SNA / M • Hotel Sodom #04: Free Parking In Rear / 1995 / SNA / M • Hotel Sodom #08 / 1995 / SNA / M • Hotel Sodom #10 / 1996 / SNA / M • Howard Sperm's Private Parties / 1994 / LBO / M • Intense Perversions #1 / 1995 / PL / M • Intersextion / 1994 / HO / M • Just Eat Me, Damn It! / 1995 / BVW / F • Kink #1 / 1995 / ROB / M • Lesbian Castle: No Kings Allowed / 1994 / LIP / F • Lesbian Mystery Theatre: The Case Of The Deadly Dyke / 1994 / LIP / F • Lust What The Doctor Ordered / 1994 / WIV / M • M Series #03 / 1993 / LBO / M • Make Me Watch / 1994 / PV / M • Mike Hott: #264 Cunt Of The Month: Marilyn Martin / 1994 / MHV / M • Mike Hott: #279 Fuck The Boss #4 / 1995 / MHV / M • Mike Hott: #298 Bonus Cunt: Candy Connor / 1995 / MHV / M • Mike Hott: #302 Lesbian Sluts #17 / 1995 / MHV / F • Mike Hott: #366 Lactating Lesbians / 1996 / MHV / F • Misfits / 1994 / CV / M • Missed You / 1995 / RTP / M • Mr. Peepers Nastiest #3 / 1995 / LBO / C • Mu-

tual Consent / 1995 / VC / M • New Wave Hookers #4 / 1994 / VC / M • Paisley Hunter: The Girl Just Can't Help It / 1996 / BEP / M • Pearl Necklace: Thee Bush League #25 / 1993 / SEE / M • Picture Perfect (Big) / 1995 / BIP / F • Positions Wanted: Experienced Only / 1993 / PV / M • Private Film #12 / 1994 / OD / M • Private Film #14 / 1994 / OD / M • Private Matters / 1995 / EMC / M • Private Video Magazine #02 / 1993 / OD / M • Pussyclips #05 / 1994 / SNA / M • Pussyman #13: Lips / 1996 / SNA / M • Putting It All Behind #2: Star Treatment / 1994 / IN / M • Reel People #05 / 1994 / PP / M • Ridin' The Big One / 1994 / TEG / M • Ring Of Passion / 1994 / ERA / M • Rock Groupies In Heat / 1995 / LV / M • The Room Mate / 1995 / EX / M • Sabrina Starlet / 1994 / SC / M • Sensual Recluse / 1994 / EX / M • Shave Tails #3 / 1994 / SO / M • Show Business / 1995 / LV / M • Sluthunt #1 / 1995 / BIP / F • Sluthunt #2 / 1995 / BIP / F • Sodomania: Slop Shots / 1996 / EL / C • Solo Adventures / 1996 / AB / F • Spirit Guide / 1995 / IN / M • Star Struck / 1994 / ERA / M • Stewardesses Behind Bars / 1994 / HW / M • Stupid And Stupider / 1995 / SO / M • Summer Of '69 / 1994 / MID / M • Take This Wad And Shove It! / 1994 / ZA / M • Tiffany Lords Straps One On #2 / 1994 / WIV / F • Titanic Orgy / 1995 / PEP / M • The Tonya Hard-On Story / 1994 / GO / M • Video Virgins #09 / 1993 / NS / M • Vivid At Home #01 / 1994 / VI / M • Water Worked / 1995 / AB / F • Wedding Vows / 1994 / ZA / M • What's Up, Tiger Pussy? / 1995 / VC / M • Wild Orgies #01 / 1994 / AFI / M
MARILYN MARTIN (1977
The Ultimate Pleasure / 1977 / HIF / M
MARILYN MARTYR see Marilyn Martin
MARILYN MCKAY see Star Index I
MARILYN MELLONS
Heavenly Bodies / 1993 / NAP / B • Million Dollar Mellons / 199? / NAP / F
MARILYN OHNO
The Adventures of Marilyn Ohno / 1996 / GLI / M • Seven Year Bitch / 1996 / GLI / M
MARILYN PALMER
Prince Of Beverly Hills #1 / 1987 / VEX / M • Sex Slaves / 1986 / VEX / M
MARILYN ROBERTS see Star Index I
MARILYN ROSE *(Cheri (Marilyn Rose), Mindy Rose)*
Pretty blonde with medium slightly droopy tits and blue eyes. Very white smooth skin. Supposedly had her tits enhanced one time and then by 1996 she had had her tits inflated to large rock-solid cantaloupes. Has one child.
Amateur Lesbians #17: Sharise / 1992 / GO / F • Amateur Lesbians #19: Sophia / 1992 / GO / F • As Cute As They Cum / 1990 / VEX / M • As Dirty As She Wants To Be / 1990 / ME / M • Avenging Angeli / 1990 / CC / M • B&D Sorority / 1991 / BON / B • Bad Side Of Town / 1993 / AFD / M • Behind You All The Way #2 / 1990 / SO / M • Boobs, Butts And Bloopers #1 / 1990 / HO / M • Camp Beaverlake #2 / 1991 / AFV / M • Carnal College #1 / 1991 / AFV / F • Cream Pies #01 / 1993 / ZA / M • Crossing Over / 1990 / IN / M • Denim Dolls #2 / 1990 / CDI / M • Dirty Looks / 1990 / IN / M • Driving Miss Daisy Crazy #1 / 1990 / WV / M • Female Persuasion / 1990 / SO / F •

The Fire Down Below / 1990 / IN / M • Great Expectations / 1990 / V99 / M • Great Expectations / 1992 / VEX / C • Hawaii Vice: Reflections / 1990 / CIN / C • Hillary Vamp's Private Collection #23 / 1992 / HOV / M • Hollywood Hustle #2 / 1990 / V99 / M • I'm No Brat / 1990 / FAZ / M • If Looks Could Kill / 1992 / V99 / M • Immorals #4: Choice Cuts / 1991 / SC / M • It Happened At Midnight / 1990 / IN / M • Jane Bondage Is Captured / 1993 / LON / B • The Journey: Oral Majority / 1991 / WV / M • Lesbian Lingerie Fantasy #4 / 1990 / ESP / F • Live Bait / 1990 / IN / M • Love Thirsty / 1990 / IN / M • Lunar Lust / 2990 / HO / M • Masterpiece / 1990 / VI / M • The Mistress #2 / 1990 / CV / M • Mortal Passions / 1990 / CDI / M • Mr. Peepers Amateur Home Videos #02: Bachelorette Party / 1991 / LBO / M • Nasty Jack's Homemade Vid. #02 / 1990 / CDI / M • Not So Innocent / 1989 / VEX / M • Not So Innocent / 1990 / HO / M • Nothing Personal / 1990 / IN / M • Odyssey Amateur #63: Pussy, Pussy Everywhere! / 1991 / OD / M • One Of These Nights / 1991 / V99 / M • Oral Clinic / 1990 / DAY / M • Passionate Angels / 1990 / HO / M • Punished Princess / 1992 / HOM / B • A Reason To Die / 1994 / PEP / M • Sex Kittens / 1990 / VEX / F • Sex Liners / 1991 / CIN / M • Sex Trek #1: The Next Peneration / 1990 / ME / M • Shaved Sinners #3 / 1990 / VT / M • Single Girl Masturbation #4 / 1990 / ESP / F • Sizzle / 1990 / PP / M • Star Spangled Banner / 1990 / FAZ / M • Sweet Darlin' / 1990 / VEX / M • Terrors Of The Inquisition / 1992 / HOM / B • Three Men And A Hooker / 1991 / WV / M • Trial By Bondage / 1991 / LON / B • V.I.C.E. #1 / 1991 / AFV / M • Vegas #1: Royal Flush / 1990 / CIN / M • Welcum To My Place / 1990 / ZA / M • White Satin Nights / 1991 / V99 / M • Women In Charge / 1990 / VEX / M

MARILYN SEYERS
Juice / 19?? / COM / M

MARILYN SIMMONS *see Star Index I*
MARILYN STAPERT *see Star Index I*
MARILYN TYLER *see Star Index I*
MARILYN WARD *see Star Index I*
MARILYN WEST *see Star Index I*
MARILYN WILD *see Marilyn Jess*
MARILYN ZUKOR *see Star Index I*
MARINA
AVP #7035: Not Hard-Lee In Vegas / 1991 / AVP / M • Barby's On Butt Row / 1996 / ABS / M • Command Performance / 1996 / ZA / M • Creme De La Face #16: Ladies Licking / 1996 / OD / M • Joe Elliot's College Girls #32 / 1994 / JOE / M • Joe Elliot's Latin College Girls #01 / 1995 / JOE / M • Lovin' Spoonfuls #6 / 1996 / 4P / C • Magma: Old And Young / 1995 / MET / M • Magma: Swinger / 1995 / MET / M • More Dirty Debutantes #14 / 1992 / 4P / M • More Dirty Debutantes #16 / 1992 / 4P / M • Nasty Nurses / 1983 / CA / M • Reflections / 1996 / ZA / M • Toy Time #5: / 1996 / STP / F

MARINA BLUMEL
[Schulmadchen-Report 4: Was Eltern Oft Verzweifeln LaBt / 1972 / ... / M

MARINA HEDMAN *see Star Index I*
MARINA PERLA
The Joy Club / 1996 / XC / M • Paprika / 1995 / XC / M • Sex Penitentiary / 1996 /

XC / M
MARINA SAMPSON *see Star Index I*
MARINA SIERRA
New Ends #06 / 1994 / 4P / M
MARINA SWALLONA
Toredo / 1996 / ROX / M
MARINE CARTIER
Anal Magic / 1995 / XC / M • Anal Nitrate / 1995 / PE / M • Buttman's European Vacation #3 / 1995 / EA / M • Buttslammers #10: Lust On The Internet / 1995 / BS / F • Cannes 93: Broads Abroad / 1993 / ELP / M • Chug-A-Lug Girls #6 / 1995 / VT / M • Deep Focus / 1995 / VC / M • Dr Max And The Oral Girls / 1995 / VIT / M • French Open / 1993 / PV / M • French Open Part Deux / 1993 / MET / M • Hotel Guard / 1995 / WIV / M • Latex #2 / 1995 / VC / M • The Naked Fugitive / 1995 / CA / M • Nasty Nymphos #08 / 1995 / ANA / M • Nightbreed / 1995 / VI / M • Pick Up Lines #01 / 1995 / 4P / M • Pick Up Lines #03 / 1995 / 4P / M • Pick Up Lines #04 / 1995 / 4P / M • Profiles #05: Planet Lust / 1995 / XPR / M • Pussyman Auditions #09 / 1995 / SNA / M • Sarah's Inheritance / 1995 / WIV / M • Sex Scandals / 1995 / XC / M • Strap-On Sally #05: Chantilly's French Kiss / 1995 / PL / F • Strap-On Sally #06: Triple Penetration Trollop / 1995 / PL / F • Takin' It To The Limit #6 / 1995 / BS / M • Venom #1 / 1995 / VD / M

MARINE GRIMAUD *see Star Index I*
MARINO (MARIO) *see Mario (English)*
MARINO FRANCHI
The Statesman's Wife / 1996 / PAL / M
MARINO PINAFARINA *see Mario (English)*
MARIO
Intimate Interviews #1 / 1996 / NIT / M • Odyssey Amateur #80: Good Bi Mario / 1991 / OD / G
MARIO (ENGLISH) *(Marino (Mario), Super Mario, Marino Pinafarina)*
Handsome English guy who generally appears with Steve Perry.
Alley Cats / 1995 / VC / M • Bangkok Boobarella / 1996 / BTO / M • Ben Dover's 9th / 1996 / VC / M • British Babe Hunt / 1996 / VC / M • British Butt Search / 1995 / VC / M • Different Strokes / 1996 / VC / M • English Class / 1995 / VC / M • English Muffins / 1995 / VC / M • Fresh Cheeks / 1995 / VC / M • Jenteal Loves Rocco / 1996 / VI / M • Little Big Girls / 1996 / VC / M • Royal Ass Force / 1996 / VC / M • Star Girl / 1996 / ERA / M
MARIO ANTONELLI *see Star Index I*
MARIO BEDORF
Dangerous Pleasure / 1995 / WIV / M
MARIO DENIDI
The Joy Of Fooling Around / 1978 / CV / M
MARIO FERELLI *see Star Index I*
MARIO GRANDE
ABA: Double Feature #5 / 1996 / ALP / M • Night Of Submission / 1976 / BIZ / M
MARIO LUCCA
[Krankenschwestern-Report / 1972 / ... / M
MARIO STEVENS
Fresh Faces #12 / 1996 / EVN / M
MARION EATON
Sip The Wine / 1974 / SVE / M • Thundercrack! / 1974 / LUM / M • [Sparkles Tavern / 1976 / ... / S
MARION MADRAS
Plastic Workshop / 1995 / LAF / M

MARION MALONE
Hot Teenage Lovers / cr73 / VBM / M
MARISA
Afrodisiac #2 / 1989 / CC / M • Hardcore Male/Female Oil Wrestling / 1996 / JSP / M
MARISA BETANCOURT
Black Voodoo / 1987 / FOV / M • Extreme Heat / 1987 / ME / M • Little House Of Pleasure / 1987 / WDD / S • Love Hammer / 1988 / VXP / M • N.Y. Video Magazine #01 / 1994 / OUP / M • Sex World Girls / 1987 / AR / M • Tight End / 1988 / VXP / M • Toothless People / 1988 / SUV / M • Tracey's Love Chamber / 1987 / AR / M
MARISA MALIBU *see Marissa Malibu*
MARISELLA
Dirty Dirty Debutantes #7 / 1996 / 4P / M
MARISOL *see Kira*
MARISSA
Lesbian Pros And Amateurs #09 / 1992 / GO / F • Lesbian Pros And Amateurs #10 / 1992 / GO / F • Marissa's Wedding Bells #1 / 1989 / LOD / F • Marissa's Wedding Bells #2 / 1989 / LOD / F
MARISSA CONSTANTINE
Corruption / 1983 / VC / M • Foxtrot / 1982 / COM / M • Scoundrels / 1982 / COM / M • Show Your Love / 1984 / VC / M
MARISSA FUJI
Creme De La Face #13: Nine Nasty Nymphs / 1995 / OD / M
MARISSA LYNN *see Star Index I*
MARISSA MALIBU *(Marisa Malibu)*
Dyed blonde with small breasts, a tattoo on her right hip on the side and cunt rings. Small body. Has had her tits enhanced in mid 1992.
2 Hung 2 Tung / 1992 / MID / M • Ambitious Blondes / 1992 / VIM / M • America's Raunchiest Home Videos #24: Suck My Thumb / 1992 / ZA / M • Backdoor To Cannes / 1993 / VC / M • Backstage Entrance #1 / 1992 / FH / M • Backstage Entrance #2 / 1992 / FH / M • The Backway Inn #2 / 1992 / FD / M • Beaverjuice / 1992 / LV / M • Behind The Scenes: The Making Of The Wil & Ed Movies / 1992 / MID / M • Bi-Ology: The Making Of Mr Right / 1992 / CAT / G • Blonde Beaver Bonanza / 1992 / TCP / M • Bubble Butts #03 / 1992 / LBO / M • Butt Woman #2 / 1992 / FH / M • Butt's Up, Doc #1 / 1992 / GO / M • Carnal Carnival / 1992 / FC / M • Christy In The Wild / 1992 / VI / M • Committed / 1992 / LE / M • Cookie 'n' Cream / 1992 / ME / M • Dig It / 1994 / FD / C • Down Bi Law / 1992 / CAT / G • The Dungeon Master / 1992 / BS / B • Fast Girls #3 / 1992 / XPI / M • Fast Track / 1992 / LIP / F • Herman's Bed / 1992 / HO / M • Hidden Obsessions / 1992 / BFP / M • Hot Pie Delivery / 1993 / AFV / M • I Remember When / 1992 / ATL / M • L.A.D.P. / 1991 / PL / M • Lawnmower Woman / 1992 / MID / M • Laying Down The Law #1 / 1992 / AFV / M • Lesbian Love Connection / 1992 / LIP / F • Maiden Heaven #1 / 1992 / MID / F • Married With Hormones #2 / 1992 / PL / M • Mummy Dearest #3: The Parting / 1991 / LV / M • Musical Bedrooms / 1993 / AFV / M • Mystery Of The Maletease Dildo / 1992 / STR / M • Nightmare On Dyke Street / 1992 / PL / M • Obsexxed / 1992 / VD / M • Penetrating Thoughts / 1992 / LV / M • Poor Little Rich Girl #1 / 1992 / XCI / M • Poor Little Rich Girl #2 / 1992 / XCI / M • The Power & The

Passion / 1993 / CDI / M • Professor Sticky's Anatomy 3X #02 / 1992 / FC / M • Pussy Galore / 1993 / VD / C • A Pussy To Die For / 1992 / CA / M • Racquel In The Wild / 1992 / VI / M • Rhapsody / 1993 / VT / M • Servin' It Up / 1993 / VC / M • Sexual Olympics #1: The Trials / 1992 / VT / M • Sexual Olympics #2: The Finals / 1992 / VT / M • Silver Elegance / 1992 / VT / M • Slipping It In / 1992 / FD / M • Temple Of Lust / 1992 / VC / M • This Butt Lite Is For You / 1992 / ATL / M • Tori Welles Goes Behind The Scenes / 1992 / FD / M • Whispers / 1992 / HO / M • Wil And Ed's Excellent Boner Christmas / 1991 / MID / M • Wild Hearts / 1992 / SC / M • Will & Ed Are Geeks In Heat / 1994 / MID / M • Will & Ed's Keister Easter / 1992 / MID / M • Will And Ed's Bogus Gang Bang / 1992 / MID / M

MARISSA MONTEIL *see Star Index I*
MARISSA STEVENS *see Star Index I*
MARITA EKBERG
Black Girls In Heat / 1985 / PL / M • Bordello...House Of The Rising Sun / 1985 / SE / M • Cheap Thrills / 1984 / RLV / M • Christine's Secret / 1986 / FEM / M • Coming In Style / 1986 / CA / M • Dick Of Death / 1985 / VCR / M • Ebony & Ivory Sisters / 1985 / PL / C • Flesh And Fantasy / 1985 / VC / M • Freedom Of Choice / 1984 / VHL / M • Hot Rockers / 1985 / IVP / M • Ladies Of The Knight / 1984 / GO / M • Sinners #1 / 1988 / COM / M • Sinners #2 / 1988 / COM / M • Sinners #3 / 1989 / COM / M • Snake Eyes #2 / 1987 / COM / M • Star Angel / 1986 / COM / M • Urban Heat / 1985 / FEM / M

MARITZA HERNANDEZ
Future Sodom / 1988 / VD / M
MARIUCHA *see Star Index I*
MARIUS AICHER
Butterflies / 1974 / CA / M
MARIWAN ROBERTS *see* **Mariwin Roberts**
MARIWIN ROBERTS *(Michelle Roberts, Mariwan Roberts)*
Erroneous credit for the same movie, **Pet Of The Month**.
The Beach Bunnies / 1975 / ... / S • Cinderella / 1977 / VAM / S • Pet Of The Month / 1978 / VC / M
MARJOLAINE
Eurotica #07 / 1996 / XC / M
MARK
Amateurs In Action #4 / 1995 / MET / M • Ancient Secrets Of Sexual Ecstasy / 1996 / HIG / M • AVP #9133: Plunger Power / 1991 / AVP / M • Backdoor Club #1 / 1996 / VEX / C • Bi-Bi Love Amateurs #3 / 1993 / QUA / G • Big Bust Babes #10 / 1992 / AFI / M • Bubble Butts #21 / 1993 / LBO / M • Bubble Butts #27 / 1993 / LBO / M • Double Butts / 1994 / RTP / M • Duke Of Knockers #2 / 1995 / BTO / M • The French Canal / 1995 / DVP / G • The Gypsy / 1996 / NIT / M • Hollywood Amateurs #05 / 1994 / MID / M • Kinky Ladies Of London / 1995 / VC / M • New Faces, Hot Bodies #07 / 1993 / STP / M • New Faces, Hot Bodies #20 / 1996 / STP / M • New Faces, Hot Bodies #21 / 1996 / STP / C • Spectator Sport / 1993 / VVO / B • Trample Goddess #2 / 1994 / VVO / B
MARK (HANK ROSE) *see* Hank Rose
MARK ALLEN

More Than Friends / 1995 / KDP / G
MARK ANDREWS
Anal Pandemonium / 1994 / TTV / M • Bad Side Of Town / 1993 / AFD / M • Be Careful What You Wish For / 1993 / VC / G • The Best Little He/She House In Texas / 1993 / HSV / G • Beverly She-Males / 1994 / PL / G • Bi & Large / 1994 / STA / G • Bi Bi Birdie / 1993 / BIL / G • The Bi-Linguist / 1993 / BIL / G • The Bi Spy / 1991 / STA / G • The Bi Valley / 1994 / BIL / G • The Bi-Analyst / 1991 / STA / G • Bi-Golly / 1993 / BIL / G • Bi-Inferno / 1992 / VEX / G • Bi-Sex Pleasures / 1993 / PL / G • Big Switch #3: Bachelor Party / 1991 / CAT / G • Charade / 1993 / HSV / G • The Collegiates / 1971 / BL / M • Come Back Little She-Male / 1994 / HSV / G • Crossing The Line / 1993 / STA / G • Dominique Goes Bi / 1994 / STA / G • Fire & Ice / 1992 / CDI / G • Gentlemen Prefer She-Males / 1995 / CDI / G • Guess What? / 1994 / FPI / G • Hollywood She Males / 1995 / MET / G • I'm A Curious She-Male / 1993 / HSV / G • The Journey: Oral Majority / 1991 / WV / M • Lady Dick / 1993 / HSV / G • Lickity Split / 1974 / COM / M • Man Made Pussy / 1994 / HEA / G • Mr. Madonna / 1994 / FPI / G • My She-Male Valentine / 1994 / HSV / G • Night Breed / 1992 / CDI / G • The Outlaw / 1991 / WV / M • Promises In The Dark / 1991 / CIN / G • Samurai She-Males / 1994 / HSV / G • She Male Goddesses / 1994 / MET / G • She Male Jail / 1994 / HSV / G • She Male Sluts / 1995 / KDP / G • She-Male Sex Stories / 1996 / STA / G • She-Male Shenanigans / 1994 / HSV / G • She-Male Showgirls / 1992 / STA / G • She-Male Vacation / 1993 / HSV / G • She-Male Valentine / 1996 / HSV / G • Sizzling She Males / 1995 / MET / G • SM TV #1 / 1995 / FC / G • Strange Night On Earth / 1993 / PEP / G • Switch Hitters #6: Back In The Bull Pen / 1991 / IN / G • Switch Hitters #7 / 1994 / IN / G • Trannie Get Your Gun / 1994 / HSV / G • Transexual Blvd / 1994 / PL / G • Transvestite Tour Guide / 1993 / HSV / G
MARK ANSARA *see Star Index I*
MARK ANTHONY
Bi Bi Banjee Boyz / 1994 / PL / G • Black Hollywood Amateurs #07 / 1995 / MID / M • Black Hollywood Amateurs #08 / 1995 / MID / M • Black Knockers #02 / 1995 / TV / M • Dream's House Party / 1995 / HW / M • Liar's Poke Her / 1995 / NIW / M • My Baby Got Back #07 / 1995 / VT / M
MARK ANTHONY (70'S)
Dominatrix Without Mercy / 1976 / ALP / B • Dr Love And His House Of Perversions / 1978 / VC / M • The Final Sin / 1977 / COM / M • Lickity Split / 1974 / COM / M
MARK ARNOLD *see* Ed Powers
MARK BARAMY *see Star Index I*
MARK BARRETT
Buttman's Bubble Butt Babes / 1996 / EA / M
MARK BOLIN *see Star Index I*
MARK BRANDON *see Star Index I*
MARK BROCK
The Bride's Initiation / 1976 / VIP / M
MARK BRODEY
Courting Libido / 1995 / HIV / G
MARK BRONSON
Shaved She-Males / 1994 / PL / G
MARK BROWN *see* Marc DeBruin
MARK BUTLER *see* Marc Wallice

MARK CARRIERE *(Marc Curtis)*
CEO of Video Exclusives who pleaded guilty to tax evasion in 1991. His income was substantially greater than $800,000. Now head of Multi Media Distributing which owns Video Exclusives, Venus 99, and Infinity. This is either owned by or owns Leisure Time Entertainment. Annual gross is estimated a $30M. Also convicted of violation of federal obscenity laws and fined $3.5M and sentenced to four months house detention in 1992. In 1995 was again convicted of obscenity and fined $1.5M and sentenced to six months in prison. In 1996 he was sentenced to 2400 hours of community service, a fine of $850,000, a compulsory donation of $250,000 and three years probation for something similar.
Lady In Blue / 1990 / CIN / M
MARK CHESTER
Erotic Tattooing And Piercing #1 / 1986 / FLV / M
MARK CHRISTOPHER
Seymore & Shane Do Ireland / 1994 / ULI / M
MARK CLOVER *see Star Index I*
MARK COOPER
Bedtime Video #03 / 1984 / GO / M
MARK CORDONE
Filthy First Timers #2: Innocence Lost / 1996 / EL / M • Filthy First Timers #3: Tearing Down The Walls Of Shame / 1996 / EL / M • Slave Boy / 1996 / VTF / B
MARK CUMMINGS
Naughty Nights / 1996 / PLP / C
MARK DANIELS
Heidi & Elke / 1995 / SHL / B
MARK DAVIS *(Scott James (Davis))*
Supposedly a British male model. 6'2" tall. In April 1996 married Blake Young aka Kobe Tai.
13th Annual Adult Video News Awards / 1996 / VC / S • 3 Wives / 1993 / VT / M • Adam & Eve's House Party #1 / 1995 / VC / M • Affairs Of The Heart / 1993 / VI / M • American Pie / 1995 / WAV / M • Anal Alice / 1992 / AFV / M • Anal Distraction / 1993 / PEP / M • Anal Fever / 1996 / ROB / M • Anal Island #1 / 1996 / VC / M • Anal Island #2 / 1996 / VC / M • Anal Lovebud / 1996 / ROB / M • Anal Palace / 1995 / VC / M • Anal Ski Vacation / 1993 / ANA / M • Anal Takeover / 1993 / PEP / M • Angel Eyes / 1995 / IN / M • Ashlyn Rising / 1995 / VI / M • Asses Galore #2: No Remorse...No Repent / 1996 / DFI / M • Asses Galore #3: Pure Evil / 1996 / DFI / M • Asses Galore #4: Extreme Noise Terror / 1996 / DFI / M • Asses Galore #5: T.T. Vs The World / 1996 / DFI / M • Backdoor To The City Of Sin / 1993 / ANA / M • Bad Habits / 1993 / VC / M • Badgirls #7: Lust Confined / 1995 / VI / M • Barby's On Butt Row / 1996 / ABS / M • Bedlam / 1995 / WAV / M • Beyond Reality #1 / 1995 / EXQ / M • The Big Shave / 1993 / PEP / M • Big Tit Racket / 1995 / PEP / M • Black & Booty-Full / 1996 / ROB / M • Black Cheerleader Search #09 / 1996 / IVC / M • Blind Spot / 1993 / VI / M • Bloopers (Video Team) / 1994 / VT / M • Body English / 1993 / PL / M • Boiling Point / 1994 / WAV / M • Booby Prize / 1995 / PEP / M • Borderline (Vivid) / 1995 / VI / M • Born Bad / 1996 / WAV / M • Breastman Goes To Breastland #1 / 1993 / EVN / M • Busty Backdoor Nurses / 1996 / PL / M •

Butt Banged Bicycle Babes / 1994 / ANA / M • Butt Banged Cycle Sluts / 1995 / ANA / M • Butt Motors / 1995 / VC / M • Butt Row Unplugged / 1996 / ABS / M • The Butt Sisters Do Denver / 1994 / MID / M • Butt Watch #03 / 1994 / FH / M • Butt Watch #04 / 1994 / FH / M • Buttman's European Vacation #3 / 1995 / EA / M • Buttman's Orgies / 1996 / EA / M • Candy Snacker / 1993 / WIV / M • Caribbean Sunset / 1996 / PL / M • Carnal College #2 / 1993 / AFV / M • Cheap Shot / 1995 / WAV / M • Checkmate / 1995 / WAV / M • Checkmate / 1996 / SNA / M • Cherry Poppers #08: Tender And Tight / 1994 / ZA / M • The Clock Strikes Bizarre On Butt Row / 1996 / ABS / M • Close To The Edge / 1994 / VI / M • Conquest / 1996 / WP / M • The Coven #1 / 1993 / VI / M • The Coven #2 / 1993 / VI / M • Cover To Cover / 1995 / WP / M • Cumback Pussy #1 / 1996 / EL / M • Cumback Pussy #4: Get Some!!! / 1996 / EL / M • Cumback Pussy #5: Groopin' / 1996 / EL / M • Cumback Pussy #6: All-Star Poop Chute Salute / 1997 / EL / M • Dangerous / 1996 / SNA / M • Deadly Sin / 1996 / ONA / M • Decadence / 1996 / VC / M • Deep Focus / 1995 / VC / M • Deep Inside Brittany O'connell / 1996 / VC / C • Deep Inside Debi Diamond / 1995 / VC / C • Deep Inside Juli Ashton / 1996 / VC / C • Deep Seven / 1996 / VC / M • Delinquents On Butt Row / 1996 / EA / M • Der Champion / 1995 / BTO / M • The Devil In Miss Jones #5: The Inferno / 1994 / VC / M • The Dinner Party #1 / 1994 / ULI / M • Dirty Stories #1 / 1995 / PE / M • Dirty Stories #4 / 1995 / PE / M • Dirty Stories #5 / 1996 / PE / M • Double Anal Alternatives / 1996 / EL / M • Elements Of Desire / 1994 / ULI / M • The End / 1995 / VI / M • Erotic Obsession / 1994 / IN / M • Fantasy Chamber / 1994 / ULI / M • Foreskin Gump / 1994 / LE / M • Frat Girls Of Double D / 1993 / PP / M • Freaks Of Leather #2 / 1994 / IF / C • Full Moon Madness / 1995 / CA / M • Gang Bang Butthole Surfin' / 1996 / ROB / M • Gang Bang Dollies / 1996 / ROB / M • Gang Bang Fury #2 / 1996 / ROB / M • Gangbang Girl #09 / 1993 / ANA / M • Gangbang Girl #10 / 1993 / ANA / M • Gangbang Girl #11 / 1993 / ANA / M • Gangbang Girl #13 / 1994 / ANA / M • Gangbang Girl #14 / 1994 / ANA / M • Gangbang Girl #15 / 1995 / ANA / M • Gangbang Girl #16 / 1995 / ANA / M • Gangbang Girl #17 / 1995 / ANA / M • Gangbang Girl #18 / 1996 / ANA / M • Gangland Bangers / 1995 / VC / M • Gazongas Galore #1 / 1996 / NIT / C • The Gift / 1996 / FEM / M • The Go-Go Girls / 1994 / EVN / M • Golddiggers #2 / 1995 / VC / M • Golddiggers #3 / 1995 / VC / M • Gone Wild / 1993 / LV / M • The Good, The Bed, And The Snuggly / 1993 / ZA / M • Guttman's Paris Vacation / 1993 / PL / M • Hard Evidence / 1996 / WP / M • Hard Feelings / 1995 / VI / M • Hardcore Copy / 1993 / PL / M • Heatseekers / 1996 / PE / M • Heavenly Hooters / 1994 / IF / M • Hornet's Nest / 1996 / ONA / M • House On Paradise Beach / 1996 / VC / M • The Hungry Heart / 1996 / AOP / M • Hypnotic Hookers #1 / 1996 / NIT / M • I Dream Of Tiffany / 1993 / IF / M • In Cold Sweat / 1996 / VI / M • Intense Perversions #1 /

1995 / PL / M • Intense Perversions #3 / 1996 / PL / M • Intimate Journey / 1993 / VI / M • Introducing Alexis / 1996 / VI / M • Jenteal Loves Rocco / 1996 / VI / M • Jiggly Queens #2 / 1994 / LE / M • Julia Ann: Superstar / 1995 / WAV / M • Juliet & Romeo / 1996 / XC / M • Kelly Eighteen #1 / 1993 / LE / M • The Last Act / 1995 / VI / M • Legend #5: The Legend Continues / 1994 / LE / M • Lethal Affairs / 1996 / VI / M • Lip Service / 1995 / WP / M • Lotus / 1996 / VI / M • Mask / 1993 / VI / M • Ms. Behaved / 1994 / SC / M • Much More Than A Mouthful #3 / 1993 / VEX / M • Mutual Consent / 1995 / VC / M • My Desire / 1996 / NIT / M • My Surrender / 1996 / A&E / M • The Naked Fugitive / 1995 / CA / M • Naked Reunion / 1993 / VI / M • Naked Scandal #1 / 1995 / SPI / M • Naked Scandal #2 / 1996 / SPI / M • Nasty Nymphos #02 / 1994 / ANA / M • Nasty Nymphos #03 / 1994 / ANA / M • Nasty Nymphos #04 / 1994 / ANA / M • Nasty Nymphos #05 / 1994 / ANA / M • Nasty Nymphos #06 / 1994 / ANA / M • Nasty Nymphos #07 / 1994 / ANA / M • Nasty Nymphos #08 / 1994 / ANA / M • Nasty Nymphos #09 / 1995 / ANA / M • Nasty Nymphos #10 / 1995 / ANA / M • Nasty Nymphos #11 / 1995 / ANA / M • Nasty Nymphos #12 / 1995 / ANA / M • Nasty Nymphos #13 / 1996 / ANA / M • Nasty Nymphos #14 / 1996 / ANA / M • Nasty Nymphos #15 / 1996 / ANA / M • Nasty Nymphos #16 / 1996 / ANA / M • New Wave Hookers #4 / 1994 / VC / M • Nightshift Nurses #2 / 1996 / VC / M • Nurse Tails / 1994 / VC / M • Once In A Lifetime / 1996 / VC / C • Oral Addiction / 1995 / VI / M • Passenger 69 #1 / 1994 / IP / M • Passenger 69 #2 / 1994 / IP / M • The Passion / 1995 / IP / M • Passion In Venice / 1995 / ULI / M • Philmore Butts All American Butt Search / 1996 / SUF / M • Philmore Butts Meets The Palm Beach Nymphomaniac Kathy Wille / 1995 / SUF / M • Philmore Butts On The Prowl / 1995 / SUF / M • Pick Up Lines #07 / 1996 / OD / M • The Player / 1995 / VI / M • Playtime / 1996 / VI / M • The Portrait Of Dorie Grey / 1996 / KLP / M • Pretending / 1993 / CV / M • Pure / 1996 / WP / M • Puritan Video Magazine #01 / 1996 / LE / M • Rainwoman #07: In The Rainforest / 1993 / CC / M • Rainwoman #08 / 1994 / CC / M • Raw Sex #01 / 1994 / ERW / M • The Rehearsal / 1993 / VC / M • Robin Thief Of Wives / 1996 / XC / M • Rugburn / 1993 / LE / M • Samantha & Company / 1996 / PL / M • Satyr / 1996 / WP / M • A Scent Of A Girl / 1993 / LV / M • Sensations #1 / 1996 / SC / M • Sensations #2 / 1996 / SC / M • Sensual Exposure / 1993 / ULI / M • The Serpent's Dream / 1993 / VC / M • Sex And Money / 1994 / DGD / S • The Sex Clinic / 1995 / WIV / M • Sex For Hire / 1996 / ONA / M • Sex Hungry Butthole Sluts / 1996 / ROB / M • Sex Raiders / 1996 / WAV / M • Sex Secrets Of A Mistress / 1995 / VI / M • Sex Therapy Ward / 1995 / LBO / M • Seymore & Shane Mount Tiffany / 1994 / FH / M • Seymore & Shane On The Loose / 1994 / ULI / M • Seymore Butts Goes Nuts / 1994 / FH / M • Seymore Butts: Big Boobs In Buttsville / 1996 / FH / M • Seymore Butts: Slippin' In Through The Out Door / 1996 / FH / M • Shane's World #1 / 1996 /

OD / M • Shane's World #2 / 1996 / OD / M • Shane's World #5 / 1996 / OD / M • Sinboy #2: Yo' Ass Is Mine / 1996 / SC / M • Skin Hunger / 1995 / MET / M • Sleaze Please!—August Edition / 1994 / FH / M • Sleaze Please!—September Edition / 1994 / FH / M • Sleaze Please!—October Edition / 1994 / FH / M • Smells Like...Sex / 1995 / VC / M • Snatch Motors / 1995 / VC / M • Sodomania #03: Foreign Objects / 1993 / EL / M • Sodomania #09: Doin' Time / 1994 / EL / M • Sodomania #15: Warning! / 1996 / EL / M • Sodomania #16: Sexxy Pistols / 1996 / EL / M • Sodomania: The Baddest Of The Best...And Then Some / 1994 / EL / C • Sorority Sex Kittens #3 / 1996 / VC / M • Stacked Deck / 1994 / IN / M • Star Crossed / 1995 / VC / M • Star Struck / 1991 / AFV / M • Steele Butt / 1993 / AFV / M • Stiletto / 1994 / WAV / M • Stories Of Seduction / 1996 / MID / M • Strong Sensations / 1996 / PL / M • Sunset And Divine: The British Experience / 1996 / LEI / M • Sunset In Paradise / 1996 / PL / M • Sunset's Anal & D.P. Gangbang / 1996 / PL / M • Supermodel #2 / 1994 / VI / M • Swedish Erotica #79 / 1994 / CA / M • Tainted Love / 1996 / VC / M • Takin' It To The Limit #5 / 1995 / BS / M • Takin' It To The Limit #6 / 1995 / BS / M • Takin' It To The Limit #7: Debauched / 1996 / BS / M • Takin' It To The Limit #8: Hooked On Crack / 1996 / BS / M • Takin' It To The Limit #9: Rear Action View / 1996 / BS / M • Temptation / 1994 / VC / M • Tempted / 1994 / VI / M • The Theory Of Relativity / 1994 / EL / M • Thin Ice / 1996 / ONA / M • Tit For Tat / 1994 / PEP / M • The Toy Box / 1996 / ONA / M • Trapped / 1996 / VI / M • Trouble Maker / 1995 / VI / M • Unleashed / 1996 / SAE / M • Up And Cummers #03 / 1993 / 4P / M • Up And Cummers #07 / 1994 / 4P / M • Venom #6 / 1996 / CA / M • Virtual Sex / 1993 / VC / M • The Voyeur #4 / 1995 / EA / M • The Voyeur #6 / 1996 / EA / M • Washington D.P. / 1993 / PEP / M • Weird Sex / 1995 / GO / M • Wendy Whoppers: Brain Surgeon / 1993 / PEP / M • White Men Can't Iron On Butt Row / 1997 / ABS / M • The Wicked One / 1995 / WP / M • Wildcats / 1995 / WP / M • World Sex Tour #1 / 1995 / ANA / M • World Sex Tour #2 / 1995 / ANA / M • World Sex Tour #3 / 1995 / ANA / M • World Sex Tour #4 / 1996 / ANA / M • World Sex Tour #6 / 1996 / ANA / M • World Sex Tour #7 / 1996 / ANA / M • The Worst Porno Ever Made With The Best Sex / 1993 / PL / M • Yankee Rose / 1994 / LE / M

MARK DEMARCO see Mike DeMarco
MARK DICKERSON
She-Male Encounters #19: Toga Party / 1989 / MET / G • Sulka's Nightclub / 1989 / VT / G
MARK EDWARDS
Too Much Too Soon / 1983 / VCX / M
MARK ELLINGER
Lunch / 1972 / VC / M • Resurrection Of Eve / 1973 / MIT / M • Thundercrack! / 1974 / LUM / M
MARK FROST see Star Index I
MARK GOLD see Marc Wallice
MARK GOLDBERG see Marc Wallice
MARK GOLDEN see Star Index I
MARK HARDER see Star Index I
MARK HARRIS
The Bitch Goddess / cr82 / BIZ / B • Erotic

Aerobics / 1984 / VC / M • Erotic Radio WSEX / 1983 / VC / M • Ginger (1984-Vivid) / 1984 / VI / M • Girls Of The Third Reich / 1985 / FC / M • I Wanna Be Teased / 1984 / SE / M • Lessons With My Aunt / 1986 / SHO / M • Sheer Delight / 1984 / VC / M • Unthinkable / 1984 / SE / M

MARK HODSON see Star Index I

MARK HOPKINS see Star Index I

MARK HOWARD see Richard Pacheco

MARK HUNTER
Temptations / 1989 / DR / M

MARK HYNES see Kyle Stone

MARK JAY BERNSTEIN
Heat Wave / 1977 / COM / M

MARK JENNINGS
Diamond Collection #77 / 1986 / CDI / M • Driven Home / 1995 / CSP / G • Little Girls Of The Streets / 1984 / CV / M • Nice 'n' Tight / 1985 / AIR / M • SM TV #2 / 1995 / FC / G • Soaking Wet / 1985 / CV / M

MARK JOVE
While The Cat's Away / 1996 / NIT / M

MARK JOWETT
Private Gold #16: Summer Wind / 1997 / OD / M

MARK KEARNS see Mark Kernes

MARK KERNES (Bobby Neuwave, Mark Kearns, Bobby Newwave)
Fat guy with a moustache and reasonable disposition who works for the industry advertising magazine (as of 1994). The "Newwave" and "Kearns" are *Hustler's* misspellings (presumably some inside joke).
Eclipse / 1993 / SC / M • The Fantasy Booth / 1993 / ONA / M • Prescription For Pleasure / 1993 / HW / M • The Secret Life Of Herbert Dingle / 1994 / TTV / M

MARK KOVAK
The Rod Garetto Story / 1995 / FC / C

MARK LEWIS
A Scent Of Heather / 1981 / VXP / M

MARK LOWE see Star Index I

MARK LUKATHER
Private Film #06 / 1994 / OD / M

MARK MACGREGORY see Star Index I

MARK MCDONOUGH see Star Index I

MARK MCGUIRE see Jack Wright

MARK MCINTYRE see Jack Wright

MARK MILLER see Star Index I

MARK MONROE see Star Index I

MARK RAMJET
Going Down Under / 1993 / OD / M

MARK RANGER see Star Index I

MARK RAYMOND
Hot Pursuit / 1983 / VC / M

MARK RICHARDS
Intimate Realities #1 / 1983 / VC / M

MARK RIDNER see Star Index I

MARK ROSS
The Jade Pussycat / 1977 / CA / M

MARK SAND see Mark Saunders

MARK SAUNDERS (Chris Thomas, Skip Jones, Mark Sand, Art Saunders, Chris (Mark Saunder))
Emaciated male who is the boyfriend of Kim Saunders.
Anal Camera #04 / 1995 / EVN / M • Anal Knights In Hollywood #1 / 1993 / MET / M • Anal Knights In Hollywood #2 / 1993 / MET / M • Anal Vision #09 / 1993 / LBO / M • Anal Vision #11 / 1993 / LBO / M • Asian Heat #05: The Joy Suck Club / 1994 / SC / M • Bachelor Party #2 / 1993 / FPI / M • Big Bust Bangers #1 / 1994 / AMP / M • Big

Murray's New-Cummers #19: The Ass Grabber / 1993 / FD / M • Bobby Hollander's Maneaters #09 / 1993 / SFP / M • Bobby Hollander's Maneaters #10 / 1993 / SFP / M • Bobby Hollander's Rookie Nookie #14 / 1993 / SFP / M • Bun Busters #01 / 1993 / LBO / M • The Burma Road #1 / 1994 / LBO / C • The Burma Road #2 / 1994 / LBO / C • The Catburglar / 1994 / PL / M • Chocolate Bunnies #02 / 1995 / LBO / C • Fresh Faces #02 / 1994 / EVN / M • Gang Bang Diaries #2 / 1993 / SFP / M • Hidden Camera #05 / 1993 / JMP / M • Hot Tight Asses #04 / 1993 / TCK / M • More Dirty Debutantes #22 / 1993 / 4P / M • Mr. Peepers Amateur Home Videos #88: A For Effort / 1994 / LBO / M • Odyssey Triple Play #63: Orient Express / 1994 / OD / M • Pai Gow Video #03: Egg Foo Kitty Yung / 1993 / EVN / M • Sexual Trilogy #02 / 1993 / SFP / M • Special Reserve / 1994 / VC / M • Super Groupie / 1993 / PL / M

MARK SHERATON
The Clinic / cr71 / GO / M

MARK SIERRA see Star Index I

MARK STEEL see Star Index I

MARK STEPHENSON
Amateur Dreams #4 / 1994 / DR / M

MARK STILLETO see Star Index I

MARK VISCIOUS
Sexhibition #2 / 1996 / SUF / M

MARK WALTERS
She-Male Encounters #03: Juicy Jennifer / 1981 / MET / G

MARK WEISS see Star Index I

MARK WEST
Like Father Like Son / 1996 / AWV / G • Lost In Vegas / 1996 / AWV / G

MARK WISE see Steve Austin

MARK WOOD see Lance Heywood

MARK WOODS see Lance Heywood

MARK ZORRO see Star Index I

MARKEETA see Lauren Brice

MARKETA
Prague By Night #1 / 1996 / EA / M

MARKETTA
Prague By Night #2 / 1996 / EA / M

MARKEY JOHN see Star Index I

MARKI
American Tushy! / 1996 / ULI / M • Anal Reunion / 1996 / EVN / M • As Easy As A Bunch Of Cunts / 1996 / ROB / F • Bend Over Babes #4 / 1996 / EA / M • Beverly Hills Bikini Company / 1996 / NIT / M • Busted-D-D In Las Vegas / 1996 / LV / M • Butt Love / 1995 / AB / M • Buttman In The Crack / 1996 / EA / M • Corn Hole Kittens / 1996 / ROB / F • The Cumm Brothers #13: Rump Rangers / 1996 / OD / M • Debi Diamond's Dirty Dykes #2 / 1995 / FD / F • Dirty Dancers #5 / 1995 / 4P / M • Frendz? #1 / 1996 / RAS / M • A Girl's Affair #08 / 1995 / FD / F • Hollywood Amateurs #30 / 1996 / MID / M • Hot Tight Asses #14 / 1995 / TCK / M • Interview: New And Natural / 1995 / LV / M • Lesbian Debutante #01 / 1996 / IP / F • Mike Hott: #286 Fuck The Boss #06 / 1996 / MHV / M • Mike Hott: #312 Lesbian Sluts #19 / 1995 / MHV / F • Mike Hott: #317 Girls Who Swallow Cum #01 / 1995 / MHV / C • Mike Hott: #319 Bonus Cunt: Marki / 1995 / MHV / M • Mike Hott: #324 Cum In My Cunt #06 / 1995 / MHV / C • Mike Hott: #326 Cum In My Mouth #03 / 1995 / MHV / C • Mike Hott: #342 Three-Sum Sluts #10 / 1995 /

MHV / M • Mike Hott: #365 Lesbian Sluts #26 / 1996 / MHV / F • Mike Hott: #371 Horny Couples #19 / 1996 / MHV / M • Nasty Newcummers #12 / 1995 / MET / M • Nightclub / 1996 / SC / M • No Man's Land #13 / 1996 / VT / F • Pussyman Auditions #08 / 1995 / SNA / M • The Right Connection / 1995 / VC / M • Screamers (Ona Zee) / 1995 / ONA / M • Sorority Sluts Passed Out / 1995 / ZA / M • Strange Lesbian Tales / 1996 / BAC / F • Stripping / 1995 / NIT / M • Student Fetish Videos: Bondage #02 / 1996 / PRE / B • Student Fetish Videos: Tickling #12 / 1995 / SFV / B • Underground #2: Subway To Sodom / 1996 / SC / M • Up Your Ass #1 / 1996 / ANA / M • Video Virgins #23 / 1995 / NS / M • The Violation Of Paisley Hunter / 1996 / JMP / F • Virgin Bar Maids / 1996 / VMX / M

MARKIE DEE
Black Knockers #12 / 1995 / TV / M

MARKITA see Lauren Brice

MARLA see Star Index I

MARLA FRANKS see Star Index I

MARLA MONROE see Star Index I

MARLA RAY
Blue Vanities #192 / 1993 / FFL / M • Blue Vanities #560 / 1994 / FFL / M

MARLA RENEE see Star Index I

MARLENA
Eurotica #03 / 1995 / XC / M • Eurotica #04 / 1996 / XC / M

MARLENA BOND see Eva Allen

MARLENA RICHE see Jenna Wells

MARLENE
Bikini Watch / 1996 / PHV / F • Blue Vanities #511 / 1992 / FFL / M • Hot Babes / cr78 / CIG / M • On The Prowl In Paris / 1992 / SC / M • Wrasslin She-Babes #11 / 1996 / SOW / M

MARLENE BOA see Star Index I

MARLENE CIPHER see Marlene Monroe

MARLENE DUVAL
Her Total Response / 1975 / SVE / M

MARLENE FOSTER
The Bite / 1975 / SVE / M

MARLENE GIL
Bankok Connection / 1979 / CA / M

MARLENE JANSSEN see Star Index I

MARLENE JUSTIN see Lili Marlene

MARLENE MATHEWS see Melanie Scott

MARLENE MONROE (Marlene Cipher)
Brunette with curly hair, passable face, white skin, womanly body, small/medium tits, and a hairy pussy.
Bad Company / 1978 / CV / M • Blue Confessions / 1983 / VCR / M • Bunbusters / 1984 / VCR / M • Carnal Encounters Of The Barest Kind / 1978 / VOY / C • Carnal Highways / 1980 / HIF / M • Come Under My Spell / cr78 / HIF / M • Fantasy World / 1979 / WWV / M • House Of Desires / cr78 / BL / M • House Of Green Desire / cr78 / CPL / M • I Am Always Ready / 1978 / HIF / M • The Live Show / 1979 / SVE / M • Serena, An Adult Fairy Tale / 1979 / VEN / M • Swedish Erotica #07 / 1980 / CA / M • A Taste Of Sugar / 1978 / AR / M

MARLENE MYLLER see Star Index I

MARLENE OURY
Sex Roulette / 1979 / CA / M

MARLENE ROSS
The Girls Of Mr X / 1978 / CA / M

MARLENE STEVENS
Inside Desiree Cousteau / 1979 / VCX / M

MARLENE TAYLOR
Analtown USA #07 / 1995 / NIT / M • Cum Buttered Corn Holes #2 / 1996 / NIT / C
MARLENE WILLOUGHBY *(Rena Vane, Terry Maxwell, Rena Vale)*
Pretty (sometimes) brunette with a nice tight body and small tits. Very hard to ID as she constantly changes her appearance, in some movies looking very young and in others looking like a well used female. Supposedly married to Sonny Landham at one time.
ABA: Double Feature #4 / 1996 / ALP / M • Angel In Distress / 1982 / AVO / B • The Anger In Jennie / 1975 / VHL / M • Auto-Erotic Practices / 1980 / VCR / F • Bang Bang You Got It / 1975 / VXP / M • Beach House / 1981 / CA / C • Betrayed Teens / 1974 / VHL / M • Blue Vanities #057 / 1988 / FFL / M • The Burning Sensation / cr78 / ASR / B • Candy Lips / 1975 / CXV / M • Come Softly / 1977 / TVX / M • Dear Pam / 1976 / CA / M • Dirty Lilly / 1975 / VXP / M • Dixie Ray Hollywood Star / 1983 / CA / M • Dominatrix Without Mercy / 1976 / ALP / B • Dracula Exotica / 1980 / TVX / M • Fantasy Peeps: Solo Girls / 1985 / 4P / M • Farmers Daughters / 1975 / VC / M • Fascination / 1980 / QX / M • Fiona On Fire / 1978 / VC / M • Foxtrot / 1982 / COM / M • Frat House Frolics / cr78 / CPL / M • From Holly With Love / 1977 / CA / M • Fulfilling Young Cups / 1978 / ... / M • The Fur Trap / 1973 / AVC / M • A Girl Like That / 1979 / CDC / M • Girls In Passion / 1979 / VHL / M • Girls U.S.A. / 1980 / AIR / M • Glitter / 1983 / CA / M • The Honey Cup / cr76 / VXP / M • Honeymoon Haven / 1977 / QX / M • Hot Dreams / 1983 / CA / M • Hot Nurses / 1977 / CA / M • Inside Jennifer Welles / 1977 / VXP / M • Intimate Desires / 1978 / VEP / M • Kinky Potpourri #31 / 199? / SVE / C • Kinky Potpourri #33 / 1997 / SVE / C • The Lady Vanessa / 1985 / HOR / C • Legends Of Porn #2 / 1989 / CV / C • Lisa Meets Mr Big / cr75 / VHL / M • Long Hard Summer / 1989 / BMV / C • Love In Strange Places / 1977 / CA / M • The Love Tapes / 1980 / BL / M • Magic Girls / 1983 / SVE / M • Midnight Blue #2 / 1980 / VXP / M • Mistress Electra / 1983 / AVO / B • More Than Sisters / 1978 / VC / M • Murder By Sex / 1993 / LAP / M • Nasty Girls (1983-VCX) / 1983 / VCX / M • Naughty Nurses / 1982 / VCR / M • New York Babes / 1979 / AR / M • The New York City Woman / 1979 / VC / C • The Nite Bird / 1978 / BL / M • The Nurses Are Coming / 1985 / VCR / C • The Opening Of Misty Beethoven / 1976 / VC / M • Oriental Techniques Of Pain And Pleasure / 1983 / ALP / B • Outlaw Ladies #1 / 1981 / VC / M • Painmania / 1983 / AVO / B • Pandora's Mirror / 1981 / CA / M • The Passion Seekers / cr78 / SIL / S • People / 1978 / QX / M • The Pink Ladies / 1980 / VC / M • The Pitfalls Of Bunny / cr76 / SVE / M • Pop-Porn: Safari Club / 1992 / 4P / M • Prized Possession / cr80 / ... / M • Raw Footage / 1977 / CA / M • Reunion (Vanessa Del Rio's) / 1977 / LIM / M • Safari Club / 1977 / 4P / M • The Sexpert / 1975 / VEP / M • Sharon In The Rough-House / 1976 / LA / M • She's No Angel / cr75 / AXV / M • Solo Girls / 19?? / 4P / F • Steamy Sirens / 1984 / AIR / C • Sunny / 1979 / VC / M • Swedish

Erotica #14 / 1980 / CA / M • Swedish Erotica #34 / 1980 / CA / M • Swedish Erotica #35 / 1980 / CA / M • Sweet Punkin...I Love You / 1975 / VC / M • Sweet, Sweet Freedom / 19?? / BL / M • A Taste Of Bette / 1978 / VHL / M • Temptations / 1976 / VXP / M • That Lady From Rio / 1976 / VXP / M • The Tiffany Minx / 1981 / SAT / M • Triple Header / 1987 / AIR / C • The Trouble With Young Stuff / 1976 / VC / M • Twilight Pink #2 / 1982 / VC / M • Underage / 1974 / IHV / M • The Untamed Vixens / 1976 / VHL / M • Vanessa's Bed Of Pleasure / 1983 / SVE / M • VCA Previews #2 / 1988 / VC / C • Venture Into The Bizarre / cr78 / VHL / M • Waterpower / 1975 / VHL / M • Way Down Deep / cr78 / PYR / M • Wet Shots (Vcr) / 1983 / VCR / C • What's Behind Love / 1979 / ... / M • While The Cat's Away / 1972 / SOW / S • A Woman's Torment / 1977 / VC / M • [Bizarre Thunder / 19?? / ... / M • [Dark Side Of Danielle / 1976 / VCI / M • [Gulp / cr75 / ... / M • [Intimidation / 199? / ... / M • [Lust Fire / 1984 / ... / M • [Voices Of Desire / 1973 / ... / M

MARLINE
Blue Vanities #508 / 1992 / FFL / M
MARLO
Blue Vanities #521 / 1993 / FFL / M • FTV #41: Fight To The Finish / 1996 / FT / B • FTV #45: Mother Knows Best / 1996 / FT / B
MARLOW FERGUSON
Dirty Lilly / 1975 / VXP / M • Draws / 1976 / VIG / S
MARNI *see Uschi Digart*
MARNIE *see Star Index I*
MAROLIN
Butt Banged Bicycle Babes / 1994 / ANA / M
MARQUESA DE SADE
Marquesa's Dungeon / 1994 / GOT / B • Mistress Of The Whip / 1996 / GOT / C • Rough Games / 1994 / GOT / B
MARQUISE MARIE
Corporal Collectors #5: Breeders / 1984 / LA / B • Exquisite Agony / 1988 / BIZ / B • Master, Mistress And Slaves / cr85 / BIZ / B • Taught To Obey / 1988 / BIZ / B
MARS BONFIRE *see Star Index I*
MARSHA
Blue Vanities #516 / 1992 / FFL / M • Shaved #03 / 1992 / RB / F
MARSHA ALLEN *see Star Index I*
MARSHA BACALL
Married Men With Men On The Side / 1996 / BHE / G
MARSHA COBBEL
Like Mother, Like Daughter / cr73 / VCX / M
MARSHA HART
More Than Friends / 1973 / AXV / M
MARSHA JORDAN *(Marcia Jordan, Marsha Jorden, Marsha Kopete)*
Big-titted blonde who was Queen of the softcore back in the sixties.
Big Bust Loops #15 / 1994 / SOW / M • The Black Alley Cats / 1971 / SOW / S • Blue Vanities #514 / 1992 / FFL / M • Brand Of Shame / 1986 / SOW / S • Class Reunion / 1972 / PS / S • College Girl Confidential / 1968 / ... / S • Count Yorga, Vampire / 1970 / ORI / S • The Divorcee / 1969 / PS / S • Dr Sex / 1964 / SOW / S • Everybody Goes Ape / 1970 / ALP / S • From Woman To Woman To Woman / 1966 / SOW / S • The

Golden Box / 1970 / SOW / S • The Head Mistress / 1968 / SOW / S • Her Odd Tastes / 1969 / SOW / S • I Want More / 1970 / SOW / S • Ice House / 1969 / SOW / S • Lady Godiva Rides / 1968 / VDM / S • Love Boccaccio Style / 1970 / SOW / S • Marsha, The Erotic Housewife / 1970 / SOW / S • The Muthers / 1968 / SOW / S • Nudie Cuties #025 / 1993 / SOW / S • The Ramrodder / 1969 / SOW / S • Saturday Night Sleazies #1 / 1995 / RHI / C • Saturday Night Sleazies #2 / 1995 / RHI / C • Saturday Night Sleazies #3 / 1995 / RHI / C • Snow Bunnies / 1970 / NFV / S • Sticky Wagons / cr70 / IVP / S • Sweet Georgia / 1970 / SOW / S • Swingers Massacre / 1975 / SVE / S • The Toy Box / 1971 / BPI / S • [The Daisy Chain / cr68 / ... / S • [Diary Of A Madam / cr68 / ... / M • [The House Near The Prado / 1969 / ... / M • [Inside Amy / 1975 / ... / S • [Last Sundown / cr71 / ... / S • [Office Love-In / 1968 / ... / S • [S.M.U.T. / 197? / ... / S • [Six Women / 1975 / ... / S • [The Wild Females / 1971 / ... / S
MARSHA JORDEN *see Marsha Jordan*
MARSHA JUDD
Oriental Treatment #1 / 1978 / AR / M • Star Of The Orient / 1978 / VIP / M
MARSHA KOPETE *see Marsha Jordan*
MARSHA LAMONTE
Pleasure Fair / 19?? / ASR / M
MARSHA MALONE
Bedtime Video #09 / 1984 / GO / M
MARSHA MOON *see Star Index I*
MARSHA MOORE *see Star Index I*
MARSHA WOLFE *see Star Index I*
MARSHALL EFRON *(Victor Alter)*
Is There Sex After Death? / 1970 / ... / S • Roseland / 1970 / SOW / S
MARSHALL O'BOY
Interview With A She-Male / 1995 / PL / G
MARSIE BARDOT *see Star Index I*
MARTA
Spanking Tea Party / 1994 / STM / B • Trained Transvestites / 1995 / STM / B
MARTA GITANA
San Francisco Lesbians #6 / 1994 / PL / F
MARTA NILLSEN *see Star Index I*
MARTHA
Blue Vanities #529 / 1993 / FFL / M • Hollywood Amateurs #17 / 1995 / MID / M • Magma: Spezial: Anal Ii / 1994 / MET / M • Penetration (Flash) #1 / 1995 / FLV / M
MARTHA (REG. BARDOT) *see Regina Bardot*
MARTHA BAHAN *see Star Index I*
MARTHA MASON
Melanie's Hot Line / 1975 / CDC / M • Strange Experiences Cockfucking / 1994 / MET / M
MARTHA MITCHELL *see Star Index I*
MARTHA STRAWBERRY
Behind The Green Door #1 / 1972 / MIT / M • What About Jane? / 1971 / ALP / M
MARTHA TYLER *see Star Index I*
MARTHA UBELL *see Chuck Vincent*
MARTIA SCHILLER *see Star Index I*
MARTIKA DANE *see Star Index I*
MARTIN
AVP #9101: Caught In The Act—Almost / 1991 / AVP / M • AVP #9130: Tailor Made / 1991 / AVP / M • Wrasslin She-Babes #09 / 1996 / SOW / M
MARTIN (BLACK)
More Black Dirty Debutantes / 1994 / 4P /

M • More Black Dirty Debutantes #3 / 1994 / 4P / M • More Black Dirty Debutantes #5 / 1995 / 4P / M • More Dirty Debutantes #34 / 1994 / 4P / M

MARTIN ANDERSON
Sex U.S.A / 1970 / SEP / M

MARTIN BRIMMER *see* **Jim Holliday**

MARTIN BURROWES
[Sex With Stars / 19?? / ... / M

MARTIN DANIELLES *see Star Index I*

MARTIN DANIELS *see Star Index I*

MARTIN DIETERMAN
Bi Bi European Style / 1990 / PL / G • Get Bi Tonight / 1991 / PL / G

MARTIN GARDENER *see Star Index I*

MARTIN JONES
The Untamed Vixens / 1976 / VHL / M

MARTIN L. DORF
Lust At First Bite / 1978 / VC / M

MARTIN LONDON *see* **Anthony Crane**

MARTIN MAJORS *see Star Index I*

MARTIN MARKLEY *see Star Index I*

MARTIN MORGAN
Masquerade (1992-Usa) / 1992 / SC / M

MARTIN NOBLE
Hungry Eyed Woman / cr71 / VCX / M

MARTIN PATTON *see Star Index I*

MARTIN STONE
Bottom Dweller: The Final Voyage / 1996 / EL / M • European Sex TV / 1996 / EL / M • Sodomania #17: Simply Makes U Tingle / 1996 / EL / M • Thermonuclear Sex / 1996 / EL / M

MARTIN TAYLOR *see Star Index I*

MARTIN TWEEBAL *see Star Index I*

MARTINA
Magma: Dreams Of Lust / 1994 / MET / M • Magma: Puszta Teenies / 1995 / MET / M • Prague By Night #1 / 1996 / EA / M • Prague By Night #2 / 1996 / EA / M

MARTINA (BRANDT) *see* **Martina Brandt**

MARTINA ALBERTI
White Heat / 1981 / CA / M

MARTINA BOOT
Viola Video #101: Anal #7 / 1995 / PEV / M

MARTINA BRANDT *(Martina (Brandt), Martina Nation, Martina Panzer)*
An Abigail Clayton look-alike with small breasts. First seen in **Dark Angel** where she does a genial anal. Not in **Let's Get Physical**.
All The Way In / 1984 / VC / M • Come Get Me / 1983 / VEL / M • Dark Angel / 1983 / VC / M • Every Woman Has A Fantasy #1 / 1984 / VC / M • Extra Sensual Pleasure / 1983 / PAC / M • Girlfriends / 1983 / MIT / M • The Good Time Girls / 1985 / VEX / M • Trading Partners / 1983 / AIR / M • VCA Previews #3 / 1988 / VC / C

MARTINA DOMINGO
Girls Without Lovers / 1985 / LUN / S • [Madchen, Die Sich Selbst, Bedienen / 1974 / ... / M

MARTINA HOLLAND *see* **Cris Cassidy**

MARTINA MARTIN *see* **Marilyn Martin**

MARTINA NATION *see* **Martina Brandt**

MARTINA PANZER *see* **Martina Brandt**

MARTINE
Hot Body Competition: Lusty Lingerie Contest / 1996 / CG / F • Magma: Spezial: Black & White #3 / 1995 / MET / M • Magma: Swinger / 1995 / MET / M

MARTINE ANUSZEK *see* **Diedre Holland**

MARTINE DUBOIS *see Star Index I*

MARTINE GERRAULT *see Star Index I*

MARTINE GRIMAUD

House Of Love / cr77 / VC / M • Love Play / 1977 / CA / M • [Jouissances / 1976 / ... / M

MARTINE HELENE *see* **Diedre Holland**

MARTINE REUNION *see Star Index I*

MARTINE SEMA *see Star Index I*

MARTINE SEMOT
[S.S. Bordello / 1978 / ... / M

MARTY *see Star Index I*

MARTY ADLER
All About Sex / 1970 / AR / M

MARTY NEWMAR
Enemarathon / 1987 / BIZ / B • Facial Attraction / 1988 / BEE / C • Naughty Girls In Heat / 1986 / SE / M • Three Wishes #1 / 1991 / CDP / B • Three Wishes #2 / 1991 / CDP / B • Top Heavy / 1988 / VD / M

MARUSSIA *see Star Index I*

MARV
Seymore & Shane Playing With Fire / 1994 / ULI / M

MARVA *see* **Maeva**

MARVIN BATES *see Star Index I*

MARVIN HEMPSTEAD
Inside Little Oral Annie / 1984 / VXP / M • Little Oral Annie Takes Manhattan / 1985 / VXP / M

MARVIN MICHAELSON *see Star Index I*

MARY
A&B GB#060: Mary, Janet & Stacey / 1992 / A&B / M • Blue Vanities #512 / 1992 / FFL / M • Blue Vanities #522 / 1993 / FFL / M • Blue Vanities #532 / 1993 / FFL / M • Blue Vanities #583 / 1996 / FFL / M • Hollywood Amateurs #06 / 1994 / MID / M • Lesbian Pros And Amateurs #08 / 1992 / GO / F • Little Big Girls / 1996 / VC / M • Mary's Lakeside Ordeal #1 / 1993 / BON / B • Mary's Lakeside Ordeal #2 / 1993 / BON / B • A Merry Widow / 1996 / SPI / M • Reel People #02 / 1984 / AR / M • Royal Ass Force / 1996 / VC / M • She Babes Cavalcade Of Sports #01 / 1996 / SOW / M • Sleeping Booty / 1995 / EL / M • Sodomania #14: C**t Lickin', C*m Drinkin' Bitches / 1995 / EL / M • Sorority Lingerie Party / 1995 / NIV / F • Wrestling Classics #4 / 1993 / CDP / B

MARY ANDERSON
Call Girl / 1984 / CV / M

MARY ANDREWS
The Nurses / 1971 / SOW / M

MARY ANN
Ancient Amateurs #2 / 1996 / LOF / M • Blue Vanities #558 / 1994 / FFL / M • Joe Elliot's College Girls #40 / 1995 / JOE / F • Joe Elliot's College Girls #43 / 1996 / JOE / M

MARY ANN BARDET *see Star Index I*

MARY ANN EVANS *see* **Eileen Welles**

MARY ANN LABELLE
N.Y. Video Magazine #05 / 1995 / OUP / M

MARY ANN MOORE *see Star Index I*

MARY ANN PAGE
Curiosity Excited The Kat / 1984 / BIZ / B

MARY ANN RICHARD
Getting Lucky / 1983 / CA / M

MARY ANN SWEET
Long Hard Summer / 1989 / BMV / C • Raw Footage / 1977 / CA / M

MARY ARNOLD *see* **Breanna Malloy**

MARY BETH *see Star Index I*

MARY BETH HOLLIDAY *see Star Index I*

MARY BETH JOHNSON *see* **Crystal Sync**

MARY CARTER

Valley Girls Ferr Shurr / cr85 / EXF / M

MARY CHRISTIAN *see* **Maria Tortuga**

MARY CRAVAT *see Star Index I*

MARY CRUISER *see* **Holly McCall**

MARY DANTE
Bullwhip: Art Of The Single-Tail Whip / 1996 / BN / B

MARY DARLING
F / 1980 / GO / M

MARY DEGRYS *see Star Index I*

MARY FLEMING
Sex For Sale / 1972 / BWV / M

MARY GAVIN *see* **Candy Samples**

MARY GEE *see Star Index I*

MARY GOLLISH
A Taste Of Pleasure / 1988 / AVC / M

MARY HADDA *see Star Index I*

MARY JACKSON
Bucky Beaver's XXX Dragon Art Theatre Double Feature #04 / 1996 / SOW / M • Revelations / 1974 / SOW / M

MARY JANE *see Star Index I*

MARY JANE MIZE
Angel Buns / 1981 / QX / M

MARY JEAN
Dirty Old Men #1 / 1995 / FPI / M

MARY JESUS
Painless Steel #3 / 1996 / FLV / M

MARY JO ANNE *see Star Index I*

MARY KATHLEEN COLLIN *see* **Bo Derek**

MARY KAY *see Star Index I*

MARY LAMB *see Star Index I*

MARY LANE
Worksex / 1980 / ... / M

MARY LAUREE *see Star Index I*

MARY LEE *see Star Index I*

MARY LOU
A'Mature: Missy, Mary Lou & Nine Inches / 1990 / AVP / M • A'mature: Sex In The Smokies / 1991 / AVP / M • A'mature: Snatching Sasha / 1991 / AVP / M • Homegrown Video #152 / 1990 / HOV / F • Ripe And Ready #02 / 1994 / BTO / M

MARY LOU MORRIS
Bucky Beaver's XXX Dragon Art Theatre Double Feature #15 / 1996 / SOW / M • Left At The Altar / 1974 / SOW / M

MARY LOUP *see Star Index I*

MARY LOVE
Bedtime Video #03 / 1984 / GO / M • Fantasy Fulfilled / 1975 / AVC / M

MARY LU
Attention: Ropes & Gags / 1994 / BON / B • Fetish Competition / 1993 / BON / B • Home Maid Memories #1 / 1994 / BON / C • Pajama Party Bondage / 1993 / BON / B • Service Call Bondage / 199? / BON / B • Shanna McCullough's College Bound / 1992 / BON / B • Trained To Heel / 1993 / BON / B

MARY MADIGAN *see* **Helen Madigan**

MARY MARGET *see Star Index I*

MARY MARTIN
Moonshine Girls / 19?? / WWV / M

MARY MCALLISTER *see Star Index I*

MARY MCMURPHY *see Star Index I*

MARY MENDUM *see* **Rebecca Brooke**

MARY MILLINGTON
Come Play With Me / 1977 / ... / S • Intimate Games / 1976 / ... / S • The Playbirds / 1978 / ... / S

MARY MONROE
The Bimbo #1 / 1985 / VXP / M • Miami Vice Girls / 1984 / RLV / M • Teenage Hustler / 1975 / VD / M

MARY MONROE (OLINKA) *see* Olinka
MARY MOONS *see* Tiffany Storm
MARY MUFKIN
The Beauty Pageant / 1981 / AVC / M •
[The Raw Report / 1978 / ... / M
MARY PEARSON *see Star Index I*
MARY PHILLIPS
All About Sex / 1970 / AR / M
MARY PICO
Blue Vanities #121 / 1990 / FFL / M
MARY QUINT *(Karen Kusick (MQ))*
Karen Kusick could be either Mary Quint or
Kristine Heller.
Fortune Cookie Nookie / 1986 / VCS / C •
Oriental Babysitter / 1976 / SE / M
MARY RYAN *see Star Index I*
MARY SCHAFER
Daddy's Rich / 1972 / ALP / M
MARY SIMON *see Star Index I*
MARY STUART *(Merrie Holiday)*
Not too pretty brunette with short hair, lithe
body, medium tits.
Classic Erotica #3 / 1980 / SVE / M • Cou-
ples / 1976 / VHL / M • Dr Love And His
House Of Perversions / 1978 / VC / M •
Honeypie / 1975 / VC / M • Intensive Care
/ 1974 / BL / M • Lady On The Couch / 1978
/ SVE / M • Lickity Split / 1974 / COM / M •
Memories Within Miss Aggie / 1974 / VHL /
M • The Mind Blowers / 1968 / SOW / S •
Naked Came The Stranger / 1975 / VC / M
• The Opening Of Misty Beethoven / 1976
/ VC / M • The Passions Of Carol / 1975 /
VXP / M • Rollerbabies / 1976 / VC / M •
Sensuous Flygirls / cr72 / VHL / M • Thun-
derbuns / 1976 / VCX / C • Tina Makes A
Deal / 1974 / TGA / M • True Legends Of
Adult Cinema: Unsung Superstars / 1993 /
VC / C • Tycoon's Daughter / cr73 / SVE /
M • Wet Rainbow / 1973 / AR / M • The
World Of Henry Paris / 1981 / VC / C
MARY SWAN *see Star Index I*
MARY TIERNEY *see Star Index I*
MARY TYLER *see Star Index I*
MARY WALKER *see Star Index I*
MARY WORTH *see Star Index I*
MARY-LOU
The Girls Of Fantasex #2 / 1996 / NIT / M
MARYA TAYLOR
Lesbian Pros And Amateurs #01 / 1992 /
GO / F • Lesbian Pros And Amateurs #04 /
1992 / GO / F • San Francisco Lesbians #5
/ 1994 / PL / F
MARYANN
Tania's Lustexzesse / 1994 / MET / M
MARYANNE FISHER
Cry For Cindy / 1976 / AR / M
MARYLIN
A Merry Widow / 1996 / SPI / M
MARYLIN COUSKOS
Angel Buns / 1981 / QX / M
MARYLIN STARR
Blonde with a pretty face, long hair, can-
taloupes, nice tight butt, not a particularly
tight waist, too pushy. Was 24 in 1993,
comes from Edmonton, Canada, and stud-
ied pre-med before becoming a stripper.
Married to an Oriental guy.
Babe Watch #3 / 1995 / SC / M • Babe
Watch #4 / 1995 / SC / M • Best Exotic
Dancers In The Usa / 1995 / PME / S • The
Best Of Fabulous Flashers / 1996 / DGD /
F • Cirque Du Sex #2 / 1996 / VT / M •
Coming Of Age / 1995 / VEX / C • The
Dream Team / 1995 / VT / M • Fantasies Of
Marylin / 1995 / VT / M • More Dirty Debu-

tantes #30 / 1994 / 4P / M • No Man's Land
#12 / 1995 / VT / F • Once In A Lifetime /
1996 / VC / C • The Passion Potion / 1995
/ WP / M • The Seduction Of Marylin Star /
1995 / VT / M • Sex On The Strip: The
Lusty Ladies Of Las Vagas / 1993 / CPG /
F • Smells Like...Sex / 1995 / VC / M • Star
Attraction / 1995 / VT / M • Star Flash /
1996 / VT / M • Unchained Marylin / 1996 /
VT / M • XXX Channel / 1996 / VT / M
MARYLINE GUILLAUME
Erotic Pleasures / 1976 / CA / M
MARYNA
Buttman's Orgies / 1996 / EA / M • Prague
By Night #1 / 1996 / EA / M • Prague By
Night #2 / 1996 / EA / M
MASAHIKO SHIMADA *see Star Index I*
MASAHITO NOMURA
Private Escort / 1996 / AVE / M
MASAMI MATSUSHITA
Honey Sex / 1996 / AVE / M
MASKED MAN
The Adventures of Marilyn Ohno / 1996 /
GLI / M
MASKED SAVAGE
New Pussy Hunt #19 / 1996 / LEI / C •
Snatch Masters #12 / 1995 / LEI / M
MASKED SLAVE *see Star Index I*
MASONORI OJAMA
The Kimono / 1983 / ORC / M
MASSIMO DEL ARTE *see Star Index I*
MASTAH MEAT
Slut Safari #1 / 1994 / FC / M • Slut Safari
#2 / 1994 / FC / M • Slut Safari #3 / 1994 /
FC / M
MASTER ALEX
Bunny Tails / 1994 / SV / B
MASTER ARYN
Master Of Ecstasy / 1997 / BON / B •
Painful Desire / 1996 / BON / B
MASTER BILL
Painful Employment / 1996 / OUP / B
MASTER D
Tight Ties / 1994 / BON / B
MASTER DAVE
Bondage Classix #05: Painful Lesson /
1987 / BON / B
MASTER DON *see Star Index I*
MASTER DRAGON
The Bondage Club #1 / 1987 / LON / B •
The Bondage Club #2 / 1987 / LON / B •
Party Of The Dammed / 1996 / BON / B
MASTER DREW *see Star Index I*
MASTER FRED
I Command! You Obey! / 1994 / TVI / B •
Painful Overtime / 1995 / TVI / B
MASTER G.P. *see* George Payne
MASTER GREG *see* Greg Wilcocks
MASTER HANS
Enter Into Slavery / 1996 / GOT / B •
Worthless Wives / 1996 / GOT / B
MASTER JAMES
Gwyn's Lakeside Ordeal / 1994 / BON / B
• The Imprisonment Of Sheena / 1994 /
BON / B • Mary's Lakeside Ordeal #1 /
1993 / BON / B • Mary's Lakeside Ordeal
#2 / 1993 / BON / B • Real People Real
Bondage #1 / 1995 / BON / C • Sandy In
The Woods / 1993 / BON / B • Sandy's
Lakeside Ordeal #1 / 1993 / BON / B •
Sandy's Lakeside Ordeal #2 / 1993 / BON
/ B • Sheena's Bondage Dreams / 1994 /
BON / B
MASTER JIM
Bondage Memories #03 / 1994 / BON / C •
Taught To Obey / 1988 / BIZ / B

MASTER LEW
Slapped Around Sluts / 1995 / PL / B
MASTER LOCK *see Star Index I*
MASTER LOGAN
Bondage Classix #02: Krysta's Nightmare
#1 / 1987 / BON / B
MASTER MANTIX
Leather Master / 1996 / STM / B
MASTER MARCUS
Black Masters: Hidden Fear / 1996 / GOT /
B
MASTER MAT
Housekeeper's Mistake / 1993 / BON / B •
Real People Real Bondage #1 / 1995 /
BON / C
MASTER MAX
Master Of Masters #1 / 1995 / BBB / B
MASTER MICHAEL
Slapped Around Sluts / 1995 / PL / B
MASTER RENE
Club Doma Global #4 / 1994 / VER / B
MASTER RON
Bizarre Master Series: Sir Michael / 1992 /
BIZ / C • Female Domination #2 / 1991 /
BIZ / B • Male Domination #16 / 1990 / BIZ
/ C • Punished By The Latex Mistress /
1992 / BIZ / B • Submission Of Susie /
1993 / BIZ / B • The Ultimate Master / cr87
/ BIZ / B • Working Girls In Bondage / 1991
/ BIZ / B
MASTER SPIKE
Chain Of Command / 1991 / GOT / B • The
Dominator / 1992 / GOT / B • A Lesson
Well Taut / 1994 / GOT / B • Masters Of
Dominance / 1996 / GOT / C • Night Calls
/ 1993 / GOT / B • No Pain, No Gain / 1992
/ GOT / B • The Shah Of Pain / 1993 / JOB
/ B
MASTER T.
Bondage Classix #10: Painful Mistake /
1993 / BON / B • Bondage Classix #12: No
Trespassing / 1991 / BON / B • Bondage
Memories #03 / 1994 / BON / C • Bondage
Photo Session / 1990 / BIZ / B • Cry Misty
For Me / 1994 / BON / B • Five Card Stud /
1990 / BIZ / B • Latex Slaves / cr87 / GOT
/ B • Misty Bound At Home / 1991 / BON /
B • Misty Returns / 1991 / BON / B • Misty,
Down And Dirty / 1990 / BON / B • Molding
Misty / 1986 / BON / B • Night Shift Latex
Slaves / 1991 / GOT / B
MASTER WING
Raw Talent #2 / 1987 / VC / M
MASTEREX *see Star Index I*
MASUGANA ROY *see Star Index I*
MAT MERRICK *see Star Index I*
MATHEW ARMON
Pretty Baby / 1978 / PAR / S • Resurrection
Of Eve / 1973 / MIT / M
MATHEW COLE
Punished #1 / 19?? / BIZ / B
MATHEW DANIELS *see* Rob Tyler
MATHEW FORDE
L.A. Tool & Die / 1979 / TMX / G
MATHEW WILD *see Star Index I*
MATHEW WINDSOR *see Star Index I*
MATS NILSSON
The Wild Women / 1996 / PL / M
MATSUURA TAIICHI
Virgin Cover Girl / 1996 / AVE / M
MATT
New Faces, Hot Bodies #22 / 1996 / STP /
M
MATT BRADY
Adventures Of The DP Boys: The Pool
Service / 1993 / HW / M • Almost Home

Alone / 1993 / SFP / M • Bimbonese 101 / 1993 / PL / M • Confessions / 1992 / PL / M • Lovebone Invasion / 1993 / PL / M • Rears In Windows / 1993 / FH / M • Secret Services / 1993 / PEP / M • The Spa / 1993 / VC / M • Top Debs #1: Prom Night / 1992 / GO / M • Top Debs #2: The Reunion / 1993 / GO / M • Torrid Tonisha / 1992 / VEX / M

MATT CRUISE see Star Index I
MATT DANIELS see Rob Tyler
MATT ELLIS see Star Index I
MATT FOREST see Star Index I
MATT GREENE
Dreams Of Desires / 1983 / PAV / M
MATT GUNTHER
Long Play / 1995 / 3XP / G
MATT JADE
Dirty Diner #3 / 1996 / SC / M • Dirty Tails / 1996 / SC / M • Eighteen #2 / 1996 / SC / M • Eighteen & Easy / 1996 / SC / M • Fresh Faces #12 / 1996 / EVN / M • Interviews At The Hard Wok Cafe / 1996 / LOF / M
MATT JORDAN
The Submission Of Johns / 1995 / RB / B
MATT LANSING
Black & Gold / 1990 / CIN / M • Cumming Clean / 1991 / FL / M • Driving Miss Daisy Crazy #1 / 1990 / WV / M • Grandma Does Dallas / 1990 / FC / M • Life, Love And Divorce / 1990 / LV / M • Vegas #2: Snake Eyes / 1990 / CIN / M
MATT LARGO see Star Index I
MATT MITCHELL see Star Index I
MATT NILSSON
Scandanavian Double Features #1 / 1996 / PL / M
MATT RAMSEY see Peter North
MATT STEVENS
The Decadent Adventures Of Generation XXX / 1994 / MAX / M
MATT SWAN
Going Down Under / 1993 / OD / M
MATT WEST
The Blonde Goddess / 1982 / VXP / M • The Cosmopolitan Girls / 1982 / VC / M • Wild Innocents / 1982 / VCX / M
MATT WINDSOR
Bi Bi Birdie / 1993 / BIL / G • Bi This! / 1995 / BIL / G • Bi-Sex Pleasures / 1993 / PL / G • Cocks In Frocks #2 / 1996 / TTV / G • Dane's Party / 1991 / IF / G • Stasha's Last Kiss / 1993 / VEX / G
MATT YORK
Filthy First Timers #7 / 1997 / EL / M
MATTHEW SEBASTIAN see Star Index I
MATTHYS
Summertime Boobs / 1994 / LEI / M
MATTMAN
Sorority Stewardesses #1 / 1995 / PE / M • Tight Shots #1 / 1994 / VI / M
MAUDE CAROLLE
[Vibrations Sensuelles / 1976 / ... / M
MAUDE MORGAN
Sex, Truth & Videotape #2 / 1996 / DOC / M
MAUREEN
Blue Vanities #509 / 1992 / FFL / M
MAUREEN ANDERSON see Star Index I
MAUREEN BRADLEY
Dear Throat / 1979 / HLV / M
MAUREEN KELLY see Star Index I
MAUREEN RYAN
[Wolf / 197? / ... / M
MAUREEN SPRING see Star Index I

MAURICE TYRONE see Star Index I
MAURICE WILSON see Star Index I
MAURY HERTZ see Star Index I
MAUVAIS see Mauvais DeNoire
MAUVAIS DENOIRE *(Mauve, Mauvais, Mavois DeNoire, Mauve Noir, Asheya)*
Anal Annie And The Backdoor Housewives / 1984 / LIP / F • Anal Carnival / 1992 / ROB / M • Anal Innocence #1 / 1991 / ROB / M • The Best Little Whorehouse In Beverly Hills / 1986 / CDI / M • The Best Little Whorehouse In Hong Kong / 1987 / SE / M • The Best Of Black Anal #1 / 1995 / ROB / C • The Best Of Oriental Anal #1 / 1994 / ROB / C • Black 'n' White In Color / 1987 / VCR / C • Black Magic / 1985 / WET / M • Black Magic / 1986 / DR / M • Black Magic Sex Clinic / 1987 / DOX / M • Black On Black / 1987 / CDI / M • Black Taboo #2 / 1986 / SE / M • Black Velvet #1 / 1992 / CC / M • Blazing Matresses / 1986 / AVC / M • Blue Lace / 1986 / SE / M • Campus Cuties / 1986 / CA / M • Chocolate Cream / 1984 / SUP / M • Chocolate Delights #2 / 1985 / TAG / C • Club Josephine / 1991 / AR / F • The Color Black / 1986 / WET / M • Color Me Amber / 1985 / VC / M • Cottontail Club / 1985 / HO / M • Debbie Class Of '88 / 1987 / CC / M • Diary Of A Bad Girl / 1986 / SUP / M • Doin' The Harlem Shuffle / 1986 / CA / M • Dr Blacklove #1 / 1987 / CC / M • Dr Lust / 1987 / VC / M • Ebony & Ivory Fantasies / 1988 / VD / C • Ebony Humpers #1 / 1986 / VEX / M • French Cleaners / 1986 / VCR / M • Girlfriends Of Candy Wong / 1984 / LIP / F • Girls On Girls / 1987 / SE / C • Hot Close-Ups / 1984 / WV / M • Hot Property / 1989 / EXH / C • Hot School Reunion / 1984 / CHX / F • House Of The Rising Moon / 1986 / VD / M • Humiliated White Boy #1 / 1992 / RB / B • Illusions Of Ecstasy / 1985 / NSV / M • Jane Bond Meets Octopussy / 1986 / VD / M • Kinkyvision #1 / 1986 / 3HV / M • The Layout / 1986 / CDI / M • Let's Get It On With Amber Lynn / 1986 / VC / M • The Lust Detector / 1986 / PIN / M • Mardi Gras / 1986 / SE / M • Missing Pieces / 1985 / IN / M • Modern Torture / 1992 / PL / B • More Chocolate Candy / 1986 / VD / M • The More the Merrier / 1989 / VC / C • On The Wet Side / 1987 / V99 / M • Oral Majority Black #1 / 1987 / WV / C • Parliament: Lonesome Ladies #1 / 1987 / PM / F • Parliament: Sultry Black Dolls / 1986 / PM / F • Passions / 1985 / MIT / M • The Red Garter / 1986 / SE / M • Rent-A-Butt / 1992 / VC / M • Scared Stiff / 1992 / PL / B • Screwdriver / 1988 / CC / C • Shaved Bunnies / 1985 / LIP / F • Sleeping With Everybody / 1992 / MID / C • Soft As Silk...Sweet As Honey / 1984 / SE / M • Soul Games / 1988 / PV / C • Swedish Erotica #68 / 1985 / CA / M • Swedish Erotica #70 / 1985 / CA / M • Swedish Erotica #71 / 1986 / CA / M • Tales From The Backside / 1993 / VC / M • White Trash / 1986 / PV / M • Wil And Ed's Excellent Boner Christmas / 1991 / MID / M • Wild Things #1 / 1985 / CV / M • Young Nurses In Love / 1987 / VC / M
MAUVE see Mauvais DeNoire
MAUVE NOIR see Mauvais DeNoire
MAVA see Maeva
MAVERICK see Star Index I
MAVIS ENGEL see Star Index I
MAVOIS DENOIRE see Mauvais DeNoire

MAX
Black Beauties #2 / 1992 / VIM / M • Boss Lady / 1988 / NAP / B • Mr. Peepers Amateur Home Videos #88: A For Effort / 1994 / LBO / M
MAX BELLOCCHIO
Dr Max And The Anal Girls / 1994 / WIV / M • Ejacula #1 / 1992 / VC / M • Ejacula #2 / 1992 / VC / M • Impulse #02: The Film / 1995 / MBP / M • Prima #01: Anal Poker / 1995 / MBP / M • Prima #13: Dr. Max Back To Budapest / 1995 / MBP / M
MAX BIRNBAUM see Beerbohm Tree
MAX CADDY
50 And Still Gangbangin'! / 1995 / EMC / M • Addictive Desires / 1994 / OD / M • Anal Camera #03 / 1994 / EVN / M • Anal Rippers #2: The Unveiling / 1996 / ZA / M • Bar-B-Que Gang Bang / 1994 / JMP / M • Beach Bunny / 1994 / V99 / M • Bushwoman: She Takes Two / 1996 / RAS / M • Butt Hole In-One / 1994 / AFV / M • The Cheater / 1994 / XCI / M • Come And Get It! / 1995 / LBO / M • Cuntz #4 / 1994 / RTP / M • Dick & Jane's Video Mail: From Virginville (#4) / 1996 / AVI / M • Dirty & Kinky Mature Women #10 / 1996 / C69 / M • Dixie Downes Gang Bang / 1996 / FC / M • Fishin' For Lust / 1996 / WST / M • Gang Bang Bitches #04 / 1995 / PP / M • Gang Bang Bitches #06 / 1995 / PP / M • Gang Bang Bitches #07 / 1995 / PP / M • Gang Bang Bitches #09 / 1995 / PP / M • Gang Bang Bitches #10 / 1995 / PP / M • Gang Bang Diaries #4 / 1994 / SFP / M • Gang Bang Diaries #5 / 1994 / SFP / M • Gang Bang Virgin #2 / 1995 / HO / M • Horny Henry's Peeping Adventures / 1994 / TTV / M • Junkyard Anal / 1994 / JAV / M • Kinky Debutante Interviews #01 / 1994 / IP / M • Kinky Debutante Interviews #02 / 1994 / IP / M • Kinky Debutante Interviews #03 / 1994 / IP / M • Legs / 1996 / ZA / M • The Line Up / 1996 / CDI / M • Lusty Lawyers / 1995 / PRK / M • Memories / 1996 / ZA / M • Mystic Tales Of The Orient / 1994 / PRK / M • The New Babysitter / 1995 / GO / M • New Girls In Town #7 / 1994 / CC / M • Next...! / 1996 / CDI / M • Nici Sterling's DP Gang Bang / 1996 / FC / M • Nineteen #2 / 1996 / FOR / M • Orgies Orgies Orgies / 1994 / WV / M • Outcall Outlaws / 1995 / CC / M • Please Take A Number / 1996 / CDI / M • Sgt. Peckers Lonely Hearts Club Gang Bang / 1995 / AMP / M • Snatch Masters #02 / 1994 / LEI / M • Southern Possession / 1995 / DEN / M • Sperm Bitches / 1995 / ZA / M • Starbangers #09 / 1996 / ZA / M • Stuff Your Ass #3 / 1996 / JMP / M • Stuff Your Face #1 / 1994 / JMP / M • Super Ball Sunday / 1994 / LBO / M • Wicked Ways #1: Interview With The Anal Queen / 1994 / WP / M • Wild Orgies #09 / 1994 / AFI / M • Zena's Gang Bang / 1995 / HO / M
MAX CASH see T.T. Boy
MAX DE LONGUE see Max DeLong
MAX DELONG *(Max De Longue)*
The Big E #08 / 1988 / BIZ / B • Cramped Spaces / 1989 / PLV / B • Deep Inside Barbie / 1989 / CDI / C • From Rags To Riches / 1988 / CDI / M • Inches For Keisha / 1988 / WV / C • Shaved Sinners #1 / 1988 / VT / M • Shaved Sinners #2 / 1987 / VT / M • Toed Off / 1989 / PLV / B
MAX DENIRO *(Israel Gonzalez)*

American Dream Girls #2 / 1994 / LEI / M • Beaver Hunt #01 / 1994 / LEI / M • Beaver Hunt #02 / 1994 / LEI / M • Beaver Hunt #03 / 1994 / LEI / M • Black Beauties #1 / 1992 / VIM / M • Blue Balls / 1995 / VEX / C • Boobytrap...The Next Generation / 1992 / HW / M • Butt Hunt #01 / 1994 / LEI / M • Butt Hunt #02 / 1994 / LEI / M • Butt Hunt #05 / 1995 / LEI / M • Dirty Dominique / 1994 / V99 / M • From Brazil With Love / 1992 / ZA / M • Gazonga Goddess #2 / 1994 / IF / M • Jug Humpers / 1995 / V99 / C • Kinky Orientals / 1994 / FH / M • Lovin' Every Minute Of It / 1994 / VEX / C • Midnight Fantasies / 1992 / VIM / M • No Bust Babes / 1992 / AFI / M • Pussy Hunt #04 / 1994 / LEI / M • Pussy Hunt #05 / 1994 / LEI / M • Pussy Hunt #06 / 1994 / LEI / M • Pussy Hunt #07 / 1994 / LEI / M • Pussy Hunt #09 / 1995 / LEI / M • Pussyclips #03 / 1994 / SNA / M • Rear Entry / 1995 / LEI / M • She's No Angel #2 / 1995 / V99 / M • The Ultimate Pleasure / 1995 / LEI / M • Victoria's Amateurs #04 / 1992 / VGA / M • Welcome To Paradise / 1994 / IF / M

MAX DEVO see Star Index I

MAX HARDCORE *(Video Paul, Paul (Max Hardcore), Sam (Max Hardcore), Max Steiner, Sam Smythe, Paul Max, Max Stiener, Max West, Paul Little, Rex Reamer)*

Sleazy looking and sounding sandy haired male who never gets fully hard. The Paul Little ID was confirmed by advertisements by Zane in December 1995 and by the 2257 statements.

2 For .89 / 1994 / SV / B • Al Borda's Brazilian Adventures / 1996 / BEP / M • Alana: A Gang Bang Fantasy / 1993 / FC / M • America's Raunchiest Home Videos #17: This Butt's For You / 1992 / ZA / M • America's Raunchiest Home Videos #24: Suck My Thumb / 1992 / ZA / M • America's Raunchiest Home Videos #28: Anal Aerobics / 1992 / ZA / M • America's Raunchiest Home Videos #29: Love Box / 1992 / ZA / M • America's Raunchiest Home Videos #30: Hot Afternoon / 1992 / ZA / M • America's Raunchiest Home Videos #35: Nothing Butt / 1992 / ZA / M • America's Raunchiest Home Videos #36: Milky Way / 1992 / ZA / M • America's Raunchiest Home Videos #37: Learning Her Lesson / 1992 / ZA / M • America's Raunchiest Home Videos #38: Fantasy Beach / 1992 / ZA / M • America's Raunchiest Home Videos #39: Like A Hurricane / 1992 / ZA / M • America's Raunchiest Home Videos #40: Anal Lady / 1992 / ZA / M • America's Raunchiest Home Videos #41: Welcum Neighbor / 1992 / ZA / M • America's Raunchiest Home Videos #42: Swimsuit Sherrie / 1992 / ZA / M • America's Raunchiest Home Videos #46: / 1993 / ZA / M • America's Raunchiest Home Videos #58: / 1993 / ZA / M • America's Raunchiest Home Videos #77: / 1993 / ZA / M • American Blonde / 1993 / VI / M • The Anal Adventures Of Max Hardcore: Adventures In Shopping / 1992 / ZA / M • The Anal Adventures Of Max Hardcore: Animalistic Urge / 1992 / ZA / M • The Anal Adventures Of Max Hardcore: Between The Lines / 1993 / ZA / M • The Anal Adventures Of Max Hardcore: Cafe Life / 1994 / ZA / M • The Anal Adventures Of Max Hardcore:

Full Throttle / 1994 / ZA / M • The Anal Adventures Of Max Hardcore: Grand Prix / 1994 / ZA / M • The Anal Adventures Of Max Hardcore: High Voltage / 1994 / ZA / M • The Anal Adventures Of Max Hardcore: Hombre / 1995 / ZA / M • The Anal Adventures Of Max Hardcore: Love Hurts / 1994 / ZA / M • The Anal Adventures Of Max Hardcore: The Resurrection / 1995 / ZA / M • The Anal Adventures Of Max Hardcore: Sunset Boulevard / 1992 / ZA / M • The Anal Adventures Of Max Hardcore: Suzy Superslut / 1992 / ZA / M • The Anal Adventures Of Max Hardcore: Video Games / 1994 / ZA / M • The Anal Adventures Of Max Hardcore: Wildlife / 1994 / ZA / M • Anal Anonymous / 1994 / ZA / M • Anal Auditions #1 / 1996 / XPR / M • Anal Auditions #2 / 1996 / LE / M • Anal Auditions #3 / 1996 / LE / M • Anal Cum Queens / 1995 / ZA / M • Anal Destroyer / 1994 / ZA / M • Anal Explosions #1 / 1996 / NIT / M • Anal Explosions #2 / 1996 / NIT / M • Anal Injury / 1994 / ZA / M • Anal Torture / 1994 / ZA / M • Anal Virgins Of America #09 / 1994 / FOR / M • Anal Vision #01 / 1992 / LBO / M • Anal Vision #02 / 1992 / LBO / M • Anal Vision #03 / 1992 / LBO / M • Anal Vision #04 / 1992 / LBO / M • Anal Vision #05 / 1993 / LBO / M • Anal Vision #06 / 1992 / LBO / M • Anal Vision #08 / 1993 / LBO / M • Anal Vision #09 / 1993 / LBO / M • Anal Vision #10 / 1993 / LBO / M • Anal Vision #11 / 1993 / LBO / M • Anal Vision #14 / 1993 / LBO / M • Anal Vision #15 / 1993 / LBO / M • Anal Vision #16 / 1993 / LBO / M • Anal Vision #17 / 1993 / LBO / M • Anal Vision #18 / 1993 / LBO / M • Anal Vision #19 / 1993 / LBO / M • Anal Vision #20 / 1993 / LBO / M • Anal Vision #21 / 1993 / LBO / M • Anal Vision #23 / 1994 / LBO / M • Anal Vision #24 / 1994 / LBO / M • Anal Vision #26 / 1994 / LBO / M • Anal Vision #28 / 1994 / LBO / M • Analtown USA #01 / 1995 / NIT / M • Analtown USA #02 / 1995 / NIT / M • Analtown USA #03 / 1995 / NIT / M • Analtown USA #04 / 1995 / NIT / M • Analtown USA #05 / 1995 / NIT / M • Analtown USA #06 / 1995 / NIT / M • Analtown USA #07 / 1995 / NIT / M • Analtown USA #08 / 1995 / NIT / M • Analtown USA #09 / 1995 / NIT / M • Analtown USA #10 / 1996 / NIT / M • Analtown USA #11 / 1996 / NIT / M • Analtown USA #12 / 1996 / NIT / M • The Ass Master #01 / 1993 / GLI / M • The Ass Master #02 / 1993 / GLI / M • The Ass Master #03 / 1993 / GLI / M • The Ass Master #04 / 1993 / GLI / M • The Ass Master #05 / 1994 / GLI / M • The Ass Master #06 / 1994 / GLI / M • Ass Openers! #1 / 1995 / TCK / C • Ass Openers! #2 / 1995 / TCK / C • Biography: Max Steiner / 1995 / SC / C • Blonde Justice #2 / 1993 / VI / M • Bobby Hollander's Maneaters #07 / 1993 / SFP / M • Bra Busters #05 / 1993 / LBO / M • Bubble Butts #03 / 1992 / LBO / M • Bubble Butts #17 / 1992 / LBO / M • Bubble Butts #22 / 1993 / LBO / M • Bubble Butts #24 / 1993 / LBO / M • Bubble Butts #25 / 1993 / LBO / M • Bubble Butts #26 / 1993 / LBO / M • Bun Busters #02 / 1993 / LBO / M • Bun Busters #10 / 1993 / LBO / M • Bun Busters #13 / 1994 / LBO / M • Bun Busters #14 / 1994 / LBO / M • Bun Busters #15 / 1994 / LBO / M • Bun Busters #19 / 1994 / LBO / M • The Burma Road #1 / 1994 /

LBO / C • The Burma Road #2 / 1994 / LBO / C • Butt Banged Cycle Sluts / 1995 / ANA / M • Casting Call #01 / 1993 / SO / M • Casting Call #02 / 1993 / SO / M • Casting Call #03 / 1993 / SO / M • Casting Call #04 / 1993 / SO / M • Casting Call #05 / 1994 / SO / M • Casting Call #06 / 1994 / SO / M • Casting Call #07 / 1994 / SO / M • Casting Call #08 / 1994 / SO / M • Casting Call #09 / 1995 / SO / M • Casting Call #10 / 1994 / MET / M • Casting Call #11 / 1995 / MET / M • Casting Call #12 / 1995 / MET / M • Casting Call #13 / 1995 / SO / M • Casting Call #14 / 1995 / SO / M • Casting Call #15 / 1995 / SO / M • Casting Call #16 / 1995 / SO / M • Casting Call #17 / 1996 / SO / M • Casting Call #18 / 1996 / SO / M • Cherry Poppers #01 / 1993 / ZA / M • Cherry Poppers #02: Barely Legal / 1994 / ZA / M • Cherry Poppers #03: School's Out / 1994 / ZA / M • Cherry Poppers #04: Ripe 'n' Ready / 1994 / ZA / M • Cherry Poppers #05: Playtime / 1994 / ZA / M • Cherry Poppers #06: Pretty And Pink / 1994 / ZA / M • Cherry Poppers #07: Li'l Darlin's / 1994 / ZA / M • Cherry Poppers #08: Tender And Tight / 1994 / ZA / M • Cherry Poppers #09: Misbehavin' / 1995 / ZA / M • Cherry Poppers #10: Sweet And Sassy / 1995 / ZA / M • The Coven #1 / 1993 / VI / M • The Coven #2 / 1993 / VI / M • Cum Buttered Corn Holes #1 / 1996 / NIT / C • Cum Buttered Corn Holes #2 / 1996 / NIT / C • Cum Buttered Corn Holes #3 / 1996 / NIT / C • Deep Throat Girls #10 / 1995 / GO / M • Dirty Diner #03 / 1993 / GLI / M • Feet And Head / 1994 / SV / M • Forever Young / 1994 / VI / M • Frightmare On Elm Street / 1993 / ... / B • Gangbang Girl #13 / 1994 / ANA / M • The Girls From Butthole Ridge / 1994 / ZA / M • The Girls From Hootersville #03 / 1993 / SFP / M • Hardcore Schoolgirls #1: Sweet Young Things / 1995 / XPR / M • Hardcore Schoolgirls #2: Perverted Playmates / 1995 / XPR / M • Hardcore Schoolgirls #3: Legal And Eager / 1995 / XPR / M • Hardcore Schoolgirls #4: Little Kittens / 1996 / XPR / M • Hardcore Schoolgirls #5: Virgin Killers / 1996 / XPR / M • Hidden Camera #10 / 1993 / JMP / M • Hidden Camera #11 / 1993 / JMP / M • Hidden Camera #13 / 1994 / JMP / M • The Hitch-Hiker #01: Wide Open Spaces / 1993 / WMG / M • The Hitch-Hiker #02: Dangerous Curves / 1994 / WMG / M • The Hitch-Hiker #03: No Exit / 1994 / WMG / M • The Hitch-Hiker #04: Max Overdrive / 1994 / WMG / M • The Hitch-Hiker #05: Traffic Jam / 1994 / WMG / M • The Hitch-Hiker #06: Salty Dog / 1994 / WMG / M • The Hitch-Hiker #07: Life In The Fast Lane / 1994 / WMG / M • The Hitch-Hiker #10: Rolling & Reaming / 1995 / WMG / M • The Hitch-Hiker #11: / 1995 / WMG / M • The Hitch-Hiker #12: Southern Exposure / 1995 / VIM / M • The Hitch-Hiker #13: Highway To Hell / 1995 / VIM / M • The Hitch-Hiker #15: Cat & Mouse / 1995 / VIM / M • The Hitch-Hiker #16: Dirty Low Down / 1996 / VIM / M • The Hitch-Hiker #17: Dead End / 1996 / VIM / M • Hollywood Swingers #05 / 1992 / LBO / M • Hollywood Swingers #06 / 1992 / LBO / M • Homegrown Video: Here Comes Anna Malle / 1994 / HOV / M • Hot Tight Asses #12 / 1995 / TCK / M • Hot Tight Asses #13 / 1995 / TCK / M • Hot

Tight Asses #14 / 1995 / TCK / M • Hot Tight Asses #15 / 1996 / TCK / M • Major Fucking Whore / 1995 / BEP / M • Max #01 / 1994 / FWE / M • Max #02 / 1994 / FWE / M • Max #03 / 1995 / FWE / M • Max #04: The Harder They Come / 1995 / FWE / M • Max #05: The Harder They Fall / 1995 / FRM / M • Max #06: Going South / 1995 / FRM / M • Max #07: French Kiss / 1995 / XPR / M • Max #08: The Fugitive / 1995 / XPR / M • Max #09: Where Danger Lurks / 1996 / XPR / M • Max #10: Dirty Deeds / 1996 / XPR / M • Max #11: Tunnel Of Lust / 1996 / LE / M • Max #12: Spread Eagle / 1996 / LE / M • Max Gold #1 / 1996 / XPR / C • Max World #1 / 1995 / FRM / M • Max World #2: Europa Issue / 1995 / XPR / M • Max World #3: Formula 1 / 1996 / XPR / M • Max World #4: Let's Party / 1996 / XPR / M • Mr. Peepers Amateur Home Videos #34: Bed Bait / 1991 / LBO / M • Mr. Peepers Amateur Home Videos #39: Cumming In Colors / 1992 / LBO / M • Mr. Peepers Amateur Home Videos #41: Getting Off For Bad Beh / 1992 / LBO / M • Mr. Peepers Amateur Home Videos #56: Hindsight Is Brownish / 1992 / LBO / M • Mr. Peepers Amateur Home Videos #60: The Backdoor Is Open / 1992 / LBO / M • Mr. Peepers Amateur Home Videos #83: Roni And The Private's / 1994 / LBO / M • Nasty Backdoor Nurses / 1994 / LBO / M • Neighborhood Watch #07: Made Up To Go Down / 1991 / LBO / M • Neighborhood Watch #09: Dial-A-Slut / 1991 / LBO / M • Neighborhood Watch #13: Teasers and Crumpets / 1991 / LBO / M • Neighborhood Watch #15: All Worked Up / 1992 / LBO / M • Neighborhood Watch #16: Dirty Laundry / 1992 / LBO / M • The New Ass Masters #14 / 1996 / LEI / C • Odyssey Triple Play #32: Cum-Loving Nasty Girls / 1993 / OD / M • Odyssey Triple Play #47: Backdoor Bingers / 1993 / OD / M • Odyssey Triple Play #67: Girls Who Love It Up The Ass / 1994 / OD / M • Ona Zee's Black Label #1: Sex Hunger / 1996 / ONA / C • Oral Obsession #1 / 1994 / VI / M • Pearl Necklace: Thee Bush League #25 / 1993 / SEE / M • Pearl Necklace: Thee Bush League #27 / 1993 / SEE / M • Philmore Butts Meets The Palm Beach Nymphomaniac Kathy Wille / 1995 / SUF / M • The Pink Persuader / 1992 / LBO / M • Private Film #12 / 1994 / OD / M • Private Video Magazine #04 / 1993 / OD / M • Private Video Magazine #09 / 1994 / OD / M • Private Video Magazine #14 / 1994 / OD / M • Private Video Magazine #15 / 1994 / OD / M • Puritan Video Magazine #03 / 1996 / LE / M • Puritan Video Magazine #04 / 1996 / LE / M • Puritan Video Magazine #05 / 1996 / LE / M • Rectal Rodeo / 1994 / ZA / M • Rump Humpers #5 / 1992 / GLI / M • Satyriasis / 1995 / PL / M • Screamers (Ona Zee) / 1995 / ONA / M • Seriously Anal / 1996 / ONA / M • Sex 4 Life / 1995 / XPR / M • Sinboy #1 / 1996 / SC / M • Spazm #1 / 1996 / SC / M • Take This Wad And Shove It! / 1994 / ZA / M • Uncle Roy's Amateur Home Video #03 / 1992 / VIM / M • Video Virgins #15 / 1994 / NS / M • The Way They Wuz / 1996 / SHS / C

MAX HORN
Keyhole / 1977 / SE / M
MAX JAXOPH

Bon Appetite / 1985 / TGA / C
MAX KING *see* **Lance Heywood**
MAX MAGNUM
Juliet & Romeo / 1996 / XC / M • Robin Thief Of Wives / 1996 / XC / M
MAX MAHONEY
Let's Talk Sex / 1982 / CA / M
MAX MIDORI
Chow Down / 1994 / VI / M
MAX OSTERHAUT
L.A. Tool & Die / 1979 / TMX / G
MAX PACKS
Lickity Split / 1974 / COM / M
MAX PARDOS
Bored Games / 1988 / ALF / M • The Devil In Mr Holmes / 1988 / PV / M • For Services Rendered / 1986 / VD / M • Hot Babes / cr78 / CIG / M • Sweet Paradise / 1980 / ELV / M
MAX REN
Balling Instinct / 1992 / FH / M • Black Beauties #1 / 1992 / VIM / M • Confessions #1 / 1992 / OD / M • The Flirt / 1992 / EVN / M • Foxxxy Lady / 1992 / HW / M • Hush...My Mother Might Hear Us / 1993 / FL / M • Interracial Affairs / 1996 / FC / M • Main Course / 1992 / FL / M • Mr. Peepers Amateur Home Videos #58: Penthouse Pussy Power / 1992 / LBO / M • Nasty Calendar / 1991 / XPI / M • Peekers / 1993 / MID / M • Pubic Eye / 1992 / HW / M • Star Struck / 1991 / AFV / M • Suck Channel / 1991 / VIM / M • Uncle Roy's Amateur Home Video #10 / 1992 / VIM / M • Way Inside Lee Caroll / 1992 / VIM / M
MAX RENNA
Angel Hard / 1996 / STV / M • Rosa / Francesca / 1995 / XC / M
MAX REYNOLDS *see* **T.T. Boy**
MAX SAVAGE
The Velvet Edge / cr76 / SE / M
MAX STEAD *see* **Jake Steed**
MAX STEED *see* **Jake Steed**
MAX STEED (JOEL L.) *see* **Joel Lawrence**
MAX STEINER *see* **Max Hardcore**
MAX STIENER *see* **Max Hardcore**
MAX STONE
Night Walk / 1995 / HIV / G
MAX STRYCE *see* **Joel Lawrence**
MAX STRYDE *see* **Joel Lawrence**
MAX WEIGHT
Domination In Black & White / 19?? / BIZ / B
MAX WEST *see* **Max Hardcore**
MAX ZAKS
Starlet Nights / 1982 / XTR / M
MAXINE
Anal Future / 1992 / VC / M • Between The Bars / 1992 / FH / M • Black Cheerleader Search #08 / 1996 / IVC / M • Girl Gone Bad #6: On Parole / 1992 / GO / F • Girls Of France / 1991 / BTO / M • Lesbian Pros And Amateurs #07 / 1992 / GO / F • The Pink Persuader / 1992 / LBO / M • Something New / 1991 / FH / M • Squirt Flirts / 1996 / RAS / M • Stevi's: Maxine Spreads / 1996 / SSV / F
MAXINE CARAT *see* **Star Index I**
MAXINE CHARMIN
Platinum Paradise / 1980 / COM / M
MAXINE VON BRAUN *see* **Star Index I**
MAXWELL MAXIMUM
Bad Penny / 1978 / QX / M • Visions / 1977 / QX / M
MAXX *see* **Star Index I**

MAY BELFORT
The Swing Thing / 1973 / TGA / M
MAY LAWRENCE
The Openings / 1975 / BL / M
MAY MAGNUM
Anal Palace / 1995 / VC / M
MAYA (1992)
Hollywood Teasers #02 / 1992 / LBO / F
MAYA LAYA
Tokohama Mamma / 1994 / ORE / C
MAYA SOULS
Pretty/passable face, very nice tight body, small tits, some exotic blend of races which makes her look slightly Oriental, lips tattoo on her right butt and a woman symbol on her right belly, long blonde hair with a fringe. 24 years old in 1996, was de-virginized at 16 and comes from SFO.
The Adventures Of Peeping Tom #4 / 1997 / OD / M • Cumback Pussy #4: Get Some!!! / 1996 / EL / M • Cumback Pussy #5: Groopin' / 1996 / EL / M • Interracial Video Virgins #01 / 1996 / NS / M • More Dirty Debutantes #59 / 1996 / SBV / M • Pick Up Lines #10 / 1997 / OD / M • Pick Up Lines #11 / 1997 / OD / M • Profiles #10: / 1997 / XPR / M • Pussyman's Nite Club Party #1 / 1996 / SNA / M • Pussyman's Nite Club Party #2 / 1997 / SNA / M • Shane's World #7 / 1996 / OD / M • Up Your Ass #3 / 1996 / ANA / M • Video Virgins #33 / 1996 / NS / M
MAYARA *see* **Star Index I**
MAYLAY
New York City Lesbian Gang Bang / 1995 / OUP / F
MAZDA LEE
The Secret Life Of Nina Hartley / 1994 / VC / M
MAZEL RUMAN *see* **Star Index I**
MCGOOGLE SCHLEPPER
Lust At First Bite / 1978 / VC / M
ME ME JUNG LAO
Viet Tran / 1996 / LBO / G
MEA TUE
The Kowloon Connection / 1973 / VCX / M
MEAGAN
Girl's Towne #1 / 1994 / FC / F • Master's Delight / 1994 / VIG / B • More Dirty Debutantes #58 / 1996 / 4P / M
MEAGAN BARKER *see* **Star Index I**
MEAGEN *see* **Star Index I**
MEDEA *see* **Tracey Prince**
MEDINE *see* **Nikki King**
MEECAH *see* **Meekah**
MEEKA (1997)
Filthy First Timers #7 / 1997 / EL / M
MEEKAH *(Francescia, Meecah)*
Francesia is from **The Anals Of History #2**. Born Nov 3, 1971 in Los Angeles.
American Built / 1992 / LE / M • Anal Lover #1 / 1992 / ROB / M • The Anals Of History #2 / 1992 / MID / M • Ass Openers! #1 / 1995 / TCK / C • Biff Malibu's Totally Nasty Home Videos #39 / 1993 / ANA / M • Bubble Butts #10 / 1992 / LBO / M • Bubble Butts #17 / 1992 / LBO / M • Buffy Malibu's Totally Nasty All-Girl Home Videos #02 / 1992 / ANA / F • The Buttnicks #3 / 1992 / CC / M • Carnal Carnival / 1992 / FC / M • Casual Lies / 1992 / CA / M • Deep Cheeks #3 / 1992 / ROB / M • The Devil Made Her Do It / 1992 / HO / M • Dial A Nurse / 1992 / VD / M • Dial N For Nikki / 1993 / PEP / M • Do The White Thing / 1992 / ZA / M • Double Crossing / 1991 / IN / M • Elvis Slept

Here / 1992 / LE / M • Frat Girls / 1993 / VC / M • The Girls Of Summer / 1992 / FOR / M • Girls, Girls, Girls, Girls / 1993 / FD / C • Hannibal Lickter / 1992 / MID / M • Hard Rider / 1992 / IN / M • Hooter Heaven / 1992 / CA / M • Hot Tight Asses #01 / 1992 / TCK / M • Immaculate Erection / 1992 / VD / M • The Lady In Red / 1993 / VC / M • Lesbian Lingerie Fantasy #6 / 1991 / ESP / F • The Makeup Room #1 / 1992 / VC / M • The Makeup Room #2 / 1992 / VC / M • Mike Hott: #212 Cunt of the Month: Meekah / 1992 / MHV / M • Mike Hott: #214 Lesbian Sluts #07 / 1992 / MHV / F • Naughty Nurses / 1992 / VD / C • Passion For Fashion / 1992 / PEP / G • Patriot Dames / 1992 / ZA / M • Raising Kane / 1992 / FD / M • Revealed / 1992 / VT / M • Seymore Butts Meets The Cumback Brat / 1993 / FH / M • A Shaver Among Us / 1992 / ZA / M • Sin City: The Movie / 1992 / SC / M • Single Girl Masturbation #6 / 1991 / ESP / F • Sittin' Pretty #2 / 1992 / DR / M • Student Fetish Videos: The Enema #09 / 1992 / PRE / B • Student Fetish Videos: Spanking #08 / 1992 / PRE / B • Summer Games / 1992 / HW / M • Taboo #10 / 1992 / IN / M • The Tiffany Minx Affair / 1992 / FOR / M • Unforgettable / 1992 / HO / M • User Friendly / 1992 / VT / M • Women Who Love Men, Men Who Love Women / 1993 / FD / C • X-Rated Blondes / 1992 / VD / C

MEESHA
Titan's Amateur Video Magazine #03 / 1995 / TEG / M

MEESHA (STEFFI) see Steffi

MEESHA LYNN
Ugly redhead with humongous watermelons.
Big Boob Bangeroo #8 / 1996 / TTV / M • The Butt Sisters Do Washington D.C. / 1995 / MID / M • Catch Of The Day #4 / 1996 / VG0 / M • Cum Tv / 1996 / NIT / M • Dirty Dave's #2 / 1996 / XPR / M • Girly Video Magazine #6 / 1996 / AB / M • Home-Grown Video #471: Heads I Win / 1996 / HOV / M • Joe Elliot's College Girls #44 / 1996 / JOE / M • More Dirty Debutantes #53 / 1996 / 4P / M • The Night Of The Living Bed / 1996 / LE / M • Pussyman Auditions #23 / 1996 / SNA / M • Titty Slickers #3 / 1996 / LE / M • Video Virgins #30 / 1996 / NS / M

MEG
All About Meg: The Interview / 1994 / VIG / B • Asking For Bondage / 1994 / VIG / B • Blue Vanities #511 / 1992 / FFL / M • Meg's First Time / 1994 / VIG / B

MEG FERGUS
Shape Up For Sensational Sex / 1985 / SE / M

MEGAN
Amateur Lesbians #27: Megan / 1992 / GO / F • Amateur Nights #14 / 1996 / HO / M • Breast Worx #19 / 1992 / LBO / M • Breast Worx #26 / 1992 / LBO / M • Breast Worx #27 / 1992 / LBO / M • Dead Ends / 1992 / PRE / B • Enemates #06 / 1992 / BIZ / B • Green Piece Of Ass #5 / 1994 / RTP / M • Hits & Misses / 1992 / PRE / B • Hollywood Amateurs #23 / 1995 / MID / M • Hot Body Competition: Bikinis & Bikes Contest / 1996 / CG / F • Leg...Ends #07 / 1993 / PRE / F • Lesbian Kink Trilogy #1 / 1992 / STM / F • Return To Leather Lair / 1993 / STM / B • Student Fetish Videos: The

Enema #07 / 1992 / PRE / B • Student Fetish Videos: Tickling #04 / 1992 / SFV / B • Tales From Leather Lair: The Leather Master / 1992 / STM / B

MEGAN BRADLEY see Scarlet Windsor

MEGAN DANIELS
The Hot Box Invasion / 1987 / AMB / M • Soft Warm Rain / 1987 / VD / M • The Switch Is On / 1985 / CAT / G

MEGAN GIVERS see Star Index I

MEGAN HOFFMAN
Dirty Bob's #03: Xplicit Interviews / 1992 / FLP / S • First Time Lesbians #01 / 1993 / JMP / F • First Time Lesbians #02 / 1993 / JMP / F • First Time Lesbians #05 / 1993 / JMP / F • GRG: Dripping Wet Dykes / 1994 / GRG / B • GRG: Fighting Mad Hussies / 1994 / GRG / F • GRG: Finger Fucking Females / 1994 / GRG / F • GRG: Kinky Kunts / 1994 / GRG / F • GRG: Ladies Only Affair / 1995 / GRG / F • GRG: Megan's Fantasy / 1995 / GRG / M • GRG: Solo & Sexy / 1993 / GRG / F • GRG: Windy City Wenches / 1995 / GRG / F • Nasty Jack's Homemade Vid. #17 / 1991 / CDI / M • Next Door Neighbors #02 / 1989 / BON / M • Next Door Neighbors #06 / 1989 / BON / M • Positively Pagan #07 / 1993 / ATA / M • SVE: Cheap Thrills #2: The More The Merrier / 1992 / SVE / M • SVE: Cheap Thrills #4: Woman To Woman / 1992 / SVE / F • SVE: Mardi Gras Mystery Couple / 1992 / SVE / M • SVE: The Audition / 1992 / SVE / M • SVE: Three On A Couch / 1992 / SVE / M • Victoria's Amateurs #01 / 1992 / VGA / M • Victoria's Amateurs #03 / 1992 / VGA / M

MEGAN LEE see Megan Leigh

MEGAN LEIGH (Caroline Chambers, Carolyn Chambers, Heather Newman, Megan Lee, Michelle Schei, Megan Teigh)
First movie was **Secrets Behind the Green (Censored) Door**. She was born Michelle Schei on 3-2-64, grew up in Oakland and ran away from home when 14. By 17, was working in a massage parlor in Guam. Had been employed by the Mitchell Bros as the house stripper. Last feature was **Jail Babes** (released posthumously). On 6-16-90 she put a gun in her mouth and blew her brains out.
Afrodisiac #2 / 1989 / CC / M • Ali Boobie & The 40 D's / 1988 / 3DV / M • Asspiring Actresses / 1989 / CA / M • Beauty And The Beast #1 / 1988 / VC / M • Bi And Beyond #2 / 1989 / CAT / G • Bi Cycling / 1989 / FC / G • The Black Anal-ist #1 / 1988 / VEX / M • Black Rage / 1988 / ZA / M • Blue Movie / 1989 / VD / M • Breakin' All The Rules / 1987 / SE / M • California Native / 1988 / CDI / M • The Case Of The Cockney Cupcake / 1989 / ME / M • The Case Of The Mad Tickler / 1988 / ME / M • The Catwoman / 1988 / VC / M • Caught In The Act / 1987 / WV / M • Debbie Class Of '88 / 1987 / CC / M • Deep Throat #3 / 1989 / AR / M • Dildoe Action / cr85 / STM / B • Dirty Laundry / 1988 / PP / M • Dirty Pictures / 1988 / CA / M • The Ebony Garden / 1988 / ZA / M • The Eleventh Commandment / 1987 / WAV / M • Expert Tease / 1988 / CC / M • First Time Lesbians (Gourmet) / 1987 / GO / F • For His Eyes Only / 1989 / PL / M • Friday The 13th #2 / 1989 / VD / M • Girls Just Wanna Have Girls #1 / 1988 /

HIO / F • The Girls Of Porn / 1989 / FRV / F • Girlworld #1 / 1987 / LIP / F • Girlworld #2 / 1988 / LIP / F • Goin' Down Slow / 1988 / VC / M • Hawaii Vice #4 / 1989 / CIN / M • Heavenly Hyapatia / 1990 / VI / M • Hello Molly / 1989 / CA / M • HHHHot! TV #1 / 1988 / CDI / M • Hitler Sucks / 1988 / GO / M • Hot Amber Nights / 1987 / CC / M • Hot Black Moon Rising Forever / 1988 / ZA / M • Hot Scalding / 1989 / VC / M • House Of Sexual Fantasies / 1987 / GO / M • In-N-Out With John Leslie / 1988 / WV / C • Inn Of Sin / 1988 / VT / M • Inner Pink #1 / 1988 / LIP / F • Jail Babes #1 / 1990 / PL / F • Jamie Loves Jeff #1 / 1987 / VI / M • Jane Bond Meets Thunderthighs / 1988 / VD / M • Kinky Lesbians #01 / 1992 / BIZ / B • The Last Condom / 1988 / PP / M • Lesbian Dildo Fever #2 / 1989 / BIZ / F • Lesbian Fantasies / 1990 / BIZ / F • Let's Get Naked / 1987 / VEX / M • Lips On Lips / 1989 / LIP / F • Loose Ends #6 / 1989 / 4P / M • Love Lies / 1988 / IN / M • Love On The Run / 1989 / CA / M • Lust In The Woods / 1990 / VI / M • Made In Germany / 1988 / FAZ / M • Magic Pool / 1988 / VD / M • The Magic Shower / 1989 / CDI / M • The Main Attraction / 1988 / 4P / M • Makeout / 1988 / VT / M • Making Charli / 1989 / CDI / M • Mischief In The Mansion / 1989 / LE / M • The Mischief Maker / 1987 / SE / M • Nasty Newshounds / 1988 / ME / M • A Natural Woman / 1989 / IN / M • The Nicole Stanton Story #1 / 1989 / CA / M • The Nicole Stanton Story #2 / 1989 / CA / M • No Man's Land #01 / 1988 / VT / C • On Your Honor / 1989 / LE / M • One Wife To Give / 1989 / ZA / M • Only The Best Of Barbara Dare / 1990 / CV / C • Only The Best Of Girls With Curves / 1992 / CV / C • Only The Best Of The Erotic Eighties / 1992 / VC / C • Oral Majority #05 / 1987 / WV / C • Out Of Control / 1987 / SE / M • Outrageous Foreplay / 1987 / WV / M • Parliament: Bare Assets / 1988 / PM / F • Parliament: Sweethearts #1 / 1988 / PM / F • Phone Mates / 1988 / CA / M • Piece Of Heaven / 1988 / CDI / M • Portrait Of A Nymph / 1988 / PP / M • Private Lessons / 1989 / STM / B • Prom Girls / 1988 / CA / M • Ramb-Ohh #2 / 1988 / PV / M • The Right Tool For The Job / 1988 / VXP / M • Romeo And Juliet #1 / 1987 / WV / M • Rubber Reamed Fuckholes / 1994 / MET / C • Screwdriver / 1988 / CC / C • Secrets Behind The Green Door / 1987 / SE / M • The Sex Life Of Mata Hari / 1989 / GO / M • Sex Lives Of The Rich And Famous #1 / 1988 / VC / M • Sex Lives Of The Rich And Famous #2 / 1989 / VC / M • Sexperiences / 1987 / VEX / M • She-Male Whorehouse / 1988 / VD / G • The Sleazy Detective / 1988 / VD / M • The Slut / 1988 / FAN / M • Smoke Screen / 1990 / CA / M • Sorority Pink #1 / 1989 / CV / M • Sorority Pink #2 / 1989 / CV / M • Spanked Students / 1989 / PLV / B • Sugar Tongues / 1992 / STM / C • Switch Hitters #2: Swinging Both Ways / 1987 / IN / G • A Taste Of Black / 1987 / WET / M • A Taste Of White / 1987 / WET / M • Tell Me Something Dirty / 1991 / NWV / M • Tropical Lust / 1987 / MET / M • True Legends Of Adult Cinema: The Erotic Eighties / 1992 / VC / C • Uniform Behavior / 1989 / ZA / M • Wet Kink / 1989 / CDI / M • Wet Workout / 1987 / VEX / M • The Wild

Brat / 1988 / VI / M • Wishbone / 1988 / VXP / M • Woman To Woman / 1989 / ZA / C

MEGAN MARIE *(Megan Roxxi)*
Tiny droopy tits, thin (ribs showing) but muscular body, long wavy dark blonde hair, pretty face, belly button ring, tight waist, and narrow hips.
The Best Of East Coast Sluts / 1995 / PL / C • Dirty Dancers #4 / 1995 / 4P / M • East Coast Sluts #02: Syracuse, NY / 1995 / PL / M • The Making Of Mistress Megan / 1996 / ... / B • Strap-On Sally #07: Face Dildo Frenzy / 1995 / PL / F • Strap-On Sally #08: Strap-On Cock Fight / 1995 / PL / F • Strap-On Sally #10: / 1996 / PL / F • Streets Of New York #06 / 1996 / PL / M • Striptease #1 / 1995 / PL / M • Striptease #2 / 1995 / PL / M

MEGAN MEGATITS
The Best Of Wild Bill's Big Ladies / 1996 / H&S / C

MEGAN MOORE
Streets Of New York #02 / 1994 / PL / M

MEGAN MORRIS see Star Index I

MEGAN ROSS see Star Index I

MEGAN ROXXI see Megan Marie

MEGAN SMITH
Black Booty / 1995 / UBP / M • Black Bottom Girlz / 1994 / CA / M • Black Buttman #02 / 1994 / CC / M • Black Hollywood Amateurs #22 / 1996 / MID / M • Fishbone / 1994 / WIV / F • Ho The Man Down / 1994 / WIV / M • Outcall Outlaws / 1995 / CC / M

MEGAN TEIGH see Megan Leigh

MEGAN WELLES see Star Index I

MEGAS see Star Index I

MEGUMI HORI
G-String Geisha / 1978 / ORC / M

MEI LING see Jasmine

MEI LING CHAN
The Girls In The Band / 1976 / SVE / M

MEI-LIN see Maile

MEL see Star Index I

MEL BLANCO
Dirty Hairy's Back To Black / 1996 / GOT / M

MEL BOURNE see Star Index I

MEL CURTIS see Star Index I

MEL JUFFE
Take Off / 1978 / VXP / M

MEL MACK see Star Index I

MEL MORAN see Star Index I

MEL SIMPSON
Up And Cummers #22 / 1995 / RWP / M

MEL STARSKY
Schoolgirl Fannies On Fire / 1994 / BIZ / B

MEL WHITE see Star Index I

MELANE see Melinda Masglow

MELANIE
Best Butt(e) In The West #1 / 1992 / CC / M • Biff Malibu's Totally Nasty Home Videos #04 / 1992 / ANA / M • Breast Worx #02 / 1991 / LBO / M • Debi Diamond's Dirty Dykes #1 / 1995 / FD / F • English Class / 1995 / VC / M • English Muffins / 1995 / VC / M • Fresh Cheeks / 1995 / VC / M • Little Big Girls / 1996 / VC / M • Ona Zee's Doll House #2 / 1995 / ONA / F • Penetration (Anabolic) #1 / 1995 / ANA / M • The Perfect Pet / 1991 / VEX / C • Queens In Danger / 1990 / STA / G • Skin #5: The 5th Column / 1996 / ERQ / M • Student Fetish Videos: Spanking #14 / 1994 / PRE / B

MELANIE (MASGLOW) see Melinda Masglow

MELANIE ANTON
Big Bust Babes #08 / 1991 / AFI / M • Flesh / 1996 / EA / M • H&S: Roberta Smallwood / 1996 / H&S / S • Hard Core Beginners #05 / 1995 / LEI / M • Hardcore Plumpers / 1991 / BTO / M • Paradise Of Plumpers / 1996 / H&S / S • Plumpers Of Sundance Spa / 1993 / BTO / M • Roly Poly Gang Bang / 1995 / HW / M • Sex Freaks / 1995 / EA / M • The Very Best Of Breasts #3 / 1996 / H&S / S • Voluptuous #1 / 199? / H&S / S

MELANIE BROOKS see Melinda Masglow

MELANIE DANIELS see Star Index I

MELANIE HILL see Melissa Hill

MELANIE LEE see Star Index I

MELANIE MOORE *(Angela Davis)*
Angela Davis (**The Strip**). Tall blonde with crinkly hair and lithe body. 5'9", 125 lbs, born in Oklahoma. In 1993 was five years out of high school. That would make her about 23. **Midnight Hour** was her first movie.
$exce$$ / 1993 / CA / M • 'Ho! 'Ho! 'Ho! / 1993 / WP / M • The 900 Club / 1993 / BON / B • The Adventures Of Buttwoman #2: Behind Bars / 1992 / EL / F • Alone And Dripping / 1991 / LV / M • American Garter / 1993 / VC / M • Americans Most Wanted / 1991 / HO / M • Anal Addiction #3 / 1991 / SO / M • Anal Adventures #2: Bodacious Buns / 1991 / VC / M • Anal Adventures #3: Can Her! / 1991 / VC / M • Anal Adventures #4: Doin' Her Up! / 1992 / VC / M • Anal Analysis (Heatwave) / 1992 / HW / M • Anal Analysis / 1992 / ZA / M • Anal Blitz / 1991 / MID / M • Anal Climax #1 / 1991 / ROB / M • The Anal Diary Of Misty Rain / 1993 / EL / M • Anal Encounters #4: Tales From The Crack / 1992 / VC / M • Anal Fever / 1991 / AMB / M • Anal Future / 1992 / VC / M • Anal Intruder #06: The Anal Twins / 1992 / CC / M • Anal Mystique / 1994 / EMC / M • Anal Queen / 1994 / FPI / M • Arabian Nights / 1993 / WP / M • Arsenal Of Fear / 1993 / BS / B • Assford Wives / 1992 / ATL / M • Assy Sassy #2 / 1994 / ROB / F • Babes / 1993 / HO / M • Babes Illustrated #2 / 1994 / IN / F • Baccarat #1 / 1991 / FH / M • Baccarat #2 / 1991 / FH / M • Backing In #4 / 1993 / WV / C • The Bare Truth / 1994 / FD / C • Battlestar Orgasmica / 1992 / EVN / M • Bed & Breakfast / 1992 / VC / M • Bedazzled / 1993 / OD / M • Bedrooms And Boardrooms / 1992 / DR / M • Behind The Backdoor #5 / 1992 / EVN / M • Behind The Blackout / 1993 / HW / M • The Bigger They Come / 1993 / VD / C • The Bitches / 1993 / LIP / F • Black Encounters / 1992 / ZA / M • Black In The Saddle Again / 1991 / ZA / M • Black Jack City #1 / 1991 / VT / M • Black Tie Affair / 1993 / VEX / M • Black To Basics / 1992 / ZA / M • Blonde City / 1992 / IN / M • Body Work / 1993 / MET / M • Bondage Shoots / 1993 / BON / B • Bronco Millie / 1992 / ZA / M • Brother Act / 1992 / PL / M • Burgundy Blues / 1993 / MET / M • Bush Wacked / 1991 / ZA / M • Busted / 1992 / HO / M • Butt Camp / 1993 / HW / C • The Butt Sisters Do Detroit / 1993 / MID / M • Butt Sluts #3 / 1994 / ROB / F • Buttman's Revenge / 1992 / EA / M • Buttsizer, King Of Rears #2 / 1992 / EVN / M • Buttslammers #01 / 1993 / BS / F •

Buttslammers #03: The Ultimate Dream / 1993 / BS / F • Buttslammers #05: Quake, Rattle & Roll! / 1994 / BS / F • A Cameo Appearence / 1992 / VI / M • Cape Lere / 1992 / CC / M • Captain Butt's Beach / 1992 / LV / M • Carnal College #2 / 1993 / AFV / M • Casanova #3 / 1993 / SC / M • Cat Lickers #2 / 1994 / ME / F • Caught From Behind #16: The Reunion / 1992 / HO / M • Centerfold Celebrities '94 #2 / 1994 / SFP / M • Cheerleader Nurses #1 / 1993 / VC / M • Cheerleader Nurses #2 / 1993 / VC / M • Cherry Cheeks / 1993 / CA / M • Cherry Redder / 1993 / RB / B • China Black / 1992 / IN / M • Clit Cleaners / 1994 / CA / C • Club DV8 #1 / 1993 / SC / M • Collectible / 1991 / LE / M • Constant Craving / 1992 / VD / M • Contract For Service / 1994 / NTP / B • Crash In The Rear / 1992 / HW / C • Crazed #1 / 1992 / VI / M • Crazed #2 / 1992 / VI / M • Cream Dream / 1991 / ZA / M • Cuntrol / 1994 / MID / F • Dark Justice / 1992 / ZA / M • Dark Obsessions / 1993 / WV / M • Deep Cheeks #1 / 1991 / ROB / M • Deep Cheeks #2 / 1991 / ROB / M • Deep Cover / 1993 / WP / M • Deep Inside Deidre Holland / 1993 / VC / C • Deep Inside Nicole London / 1995 / VC / C • Deep Inside Nikki Dial / 1994 / VC / C • Deep Inside Nikki Sinn / 1996 / VC / C • Deep Inside P.J. Sparxx / 1995 / VC / C • Deep Inside Tiffany Mynx / 1994 / VC / C • Defenseless / 1992 / CDI / M • Depraved / 1993 / BS / B • Depraved Fantasies #2 / 1994 / FPI / M • The Determinator #2 / 1991 / VIM / M • The Devil Made Her Do It / 1992 / HO / M • Diamond In The Rough / 1993 / BIA / C • Diary Of A Porn Star / 1993 / FOR / M • Dick At Nite / 1993 / MET / M • The Dickheads #2 / 1993 / MID / M • Double Detail / 1992 / SO / M • Double Down / 1993 / LBO / M • The Dragon Lady #3: Tales From The Bed #2 / 1992 / WV / M • The Dream Machine / 1992 / CDI / M • Dungeon Dykes #1 / 1994 / FPI / F • Dungeon Dykes #2 / 1994 / FPI / F • Easy Pussy / 1991 / ROB / M • Eat My Cherry / 1994 / BHS / M • The Elixir / 1992 / CDI / M • En Garde / 1993 / DR / M • The End / 1992 / SC / M • Endangered / 1992 / PP / M • Erotic Angel / 1994 / ERA / M • Euphoria / 1993 / CA / M • Euro Studs / 1996 / SC / C • Everybody's Playmates / 1992 / CA / C • Facesitter #3 / 1994 / CC / M • The Fantasy Booth / 1993 / ONA / M • Fever / 1992 / CA / M • The Fire Down Below / 1992 / CDI / M • First Time Ever #1 / 1995 / PE / F • Flying High #1 / 1992 / HO / M • Flying High #2 / 1992 / HO / M • Foreign Affairs / 1991 / LE / M • Frat Girls Of Double D / 1993 / PP / M • French Open Part Deux / 1993 / MET / M • A Girl's Affair #04 / 1994 / FD / F • Girls Gone Bad #7: Misfits Of Society / 1992 / GO / F • Girls Just Wanna Have Toys / 1993 / PL / F • Girls Off Duty / 1994 / LE / M • Girls Will Be Boys #5 / 1993 / PL / F • The Girls' Club / 1993 / VD / C • Good Vibrations #1: Self Satisfaction With A Vibrator / 1991 / VT / M • Group Therapy / 1992 / TP / M • Hard Drive / 1994 / TRI / S • Hard Talk / 1992 / VC / M • Hard To Stop #1 / 1992 / VC / M • Hard To Stop #2 / 1992 / VC / M • Heads Or Tails? / 1993 / PL / M • Heatseekers / 1991 / IN / M • Herman's Bed / 1992 / HO / M • Hidden Desires / 1992 / CDI / M • Hidden Obsessions

/ 1992 / BFP / M • Honey, I Blew Everybody #1 / 1992 / MID / M • Hot Bodies In Bondage / 1993 / LBO / B • Hot Sweet 'n' Sticky / 1992 / CA / C • Hot Tight Asses #06 / 1994 / TCK / M • I Touch Myself / 1992 / IN / M • I Touch Myself / 1994 / IP / F • I Want A Divorce / 1993 / ZA / M • I'm Too Sexy / 1992 / CA / M • If These Walls Could Talk (Director's Cut) / 1993 / MET / M • If These Walls Could Talk #1: Wicked Whispers / 1993 / MET / M • If These Walls Could Talk #2: Burning Secrets / 1993 / CV / M • In Loving Color #2 / 1992 / VT / M • In Loving Color #3 / 1992 / VT / M • In Your Face #1 / 1992 / PL / M • It's Blondage, The Video / 1994 / VI / M • Jennifer Ate / 1993 / XCI / F • Jezebel #1 / 1993 / SC / M • John Holmes, The Lost Films / 1988 / PEN / C • Jungle Jive / 1992 / VD / M • Junkyard Dykes #02 / 1994 / ZA / F • Just For The Hell Of It / 1991 / CA / M • Kinky Roommates / 1992 / TP / M • Kittens #5 / 1994 / CC / F • Kym Wilde's On The Edge #06 / 1993 / RB / B • Kym Wilde's On The Edge #13 / 1994 / RB / B • The Lady In Red / 1993 / VC / M • Lesbian Workout #1 / 1994 / GO / F • Lesbian Workout #2 / 1994 / GO / F • Lethal Lolita / 1993 / LE / M • Lez Go Crazy / 1992 / HW / C • Licking Legends #1 / 1992 / LE / F • A Little Irresistible / 1991 / ZA / M • Love Me, Love My Butt #2 / 1994 / ROB / F • Lust Crimes / 1992 / WV / M • Madam X / 1992 / HO / M • Main Street, U.S.A. / 1992 / PP / M • Maliboobies / 1993 / CDI / F • The Merry Widows / 1993 / VC / M • The Midnight Hour / 1991 / VT / M • Midsummer Love Story / 1993 / WV / M • Mind Shadows #2 / 1993 / FD / M • Mindsex / 1993 / MPA / M • The Mistress (1993-Caballero) / 1993 / CA / M • Model's Memoirs / 1993 / IP / M • Molly B-Goode / 1994 / FH / M • The Money Hole / 1993 / VD / M • Moon Godesses #2 / 1993 / VIM / M • Moore, Moore, Moore: An Anal Explosion / 1992 / IN / M • My Cousin Ginny / 1993 / MET / M • Mystery Date / 1992 / CDI / G • The Naked Pen / 1992 / VC / M • Neutron Man / 1993 / HO / M • A Night Of Hell / 1993 / LBO / B • Nighttime Stories / 1991 / LE / M • No Fly Zone / 1993 / LE / F • No Man's Land #05 / 1992 / VT / F • No Man's Land #06 / 1992 / VT / F • No Man's Land #07 / 1993 / VT / F • No Man's Land #08: Eight Women Who Ate Women / 1993 / VT / F • No Men 4 Miles / 1992 / LV / F • Nookie Cookies / 1993 / CDI / F • Obsexxed / 1992 / VD / M • Oral Majority #10 / 1993 / WV / C • Oral Majority #11 / 1994 / WV / C • The Orgy #3 / 1993 / EMC / M • Other People's Honey / 1991 / HW / M • Out Of The Blue #1 / 1991 / VI / M • The Oval Office / 1991 / LV / M • Pajama Party / 1993 / CV / C • The Party / 1992 / CDI / M • Party Of Payne / 1993 / BS / B • The Perfect Stranger / 1991 / IN / M • Picture Me Naked / 1993 / LE / M • The Pink Pussycat / 1992 / CA / M • The Poetry Of The Flesh / 1993 / PEP / M • Porn In The Pen / 1993 / LE / F • Pornographic Priestess / 1992 / CA / M • Portrait Of Lust / 1992 / WV / M • Positively Pagan #06 / 1993 / ATA / M • Possessions / 1992 / HW / M • The Power Of Summer #1: Revenge / 1992 / BS / B • Prelude / 1992 / VT / M • Prisoner Of Lust / 1991 / VC / F • Private & Perverse / 1994 / CA / C • Private Dancer (Caballero) / 1992

/ CA / M • Private Stuff / 1994 / FD / M • Professor Sticky's Anatomy 3X #03 / 1992 / FC / M • The Psychic / 1993 / CC / M • Pulse / 1994 / EX / M • A Pussy Called Wanda #1 / 1992 / DR / M • Pussy Galore / 1993 / VD / C • Pussyman #01: The Search / 1993 / CC / M • Pussyman #02: The Prize / 1993 / CC / M • Pussyman #03: The Search Continues / 1993 / SNA / M • Pussyman #04: The Celebration / 1993 / SNA / M • Rainwoman #06 / 1993 / CC / M • Realities #2 / 1992 / ZA / M • Rebel / 1991 / ZA / M • Return To Melrose Place / 1993 / HW / M • Rhapsody / 1993 / VT / M • Romancing The Butt / 1992 / ATL / M • Roommate Humiliation / 1993 / PL / B • Saturday Night Porn #1 / 1993 / AFV / M • Saturday Night Porn #2 / 1993 / AFV / M • Scenes From A Crystal Ball / 1992 / ZA / M • The Screamer / 1991 / CA / M • The Secret Garden #1 / 1992 / XCI / M • The Secret Garden #2 / 1992 / XCI / M • Secret Lives / 1994 / SC / F • Seduced / 1992 / VD / M • The Seducers / 1992 / ZA / M • Sensual Exposure / 1993 / ULI / M • Seven Good Women / 1993 / HO / F • Sex On The Run #1 / 1994 / TTV / M • Sex Under Glass / 1992 / VC / M • Sexmares / 1993 / FH / M • Sexual Instinct #1 / 1992 / DR / M • The Sexual Limits / 1992 / VC / M • Seymore Butts Rides Again / 1992 / FH / M • Shanna's Final Fling / 1991 / ME / M • Sharon Starlet / 1993 / WIV / M • She Likes To Watch / 1992 / EVN / M • Shiver / 1993 / FOR / M • A Shot In The Mouth #2 / 1991 / ME / M • Sinderella #1 / 1992 / VI / M • Sinderella #2 / 1992 / VI / M • Slammin! / 1994 / CA / C • Slow Dancing / 1990 / VI / M • Slurp 'n' Gag / 1994 / CA / C • So You Want To Be In The Movies? / 1994 / VC / M • Something New / 1991 / FH / M • Sorority Sex Kittens #1 / 1992 / VC / M • Sorority Sex Kittens #2 / 1993 / VC / M • Southern Exposure / 1991 / LE / M • The Spa / 1993 / VC / M • Sterling Silver / 1992 / CC / M • The Strip / 1992 / SC / M • Stripper Nurses / 1994 / PE / M • Student Fetish Videos: Best of Catfighting #02 / 1994 / PRE / C • Student Fetish Videos: Best Of Spanking #02 / 1993 / PRE / C • Student Fetish Videos: Catfighting #06 / 1992 / PRE / B • Student Fetish Videos: Spanking #09 / 1993 / PRE / B • Student Fetish Videos: Tickling #07 / 1992 / SFV / B • Student Fetish Videos: Tickling #09 / 1994 / SFV / B • Student Nurses / 1991 / CA / M • Superstar Sex Challenge #1 / 1994 / VC / M • Superstar Sex Challenge #2 / 1994 / VC / M • Superstar Sex Challenge #3 / 1994 / VC / M • Surfside Sex #1 / 1991 / LV / F • Surfside Sex #2 / 1992 / LV / M • Swallow / 1994 / VI / M • Sweet As Honey / 1992 / LV / M • Taboo #10 / 1992 / IN / M • Taboo #11: Crazy On You / 1993 / IN / M • Tailiens #2 / 1992 / FD / M • The Taming Of Savannah / 1993 / VI / M • Temple Of Lust / 1992 / VC / M • Temptation Of Serenity / 1994 / WP / M • Tenth Annual Adult Video News Awards / 1993 / VC / M • The Therapist / 1992 / VC / M • This Butt Lite Is For You / 1992 / ATL / M • Tickled Pink / 1993 / LE / F • Tight Squeeze / 1992 / SC / M • Total Exposure / 1992 / CDI / M • Twilight / 1991 / ZA / M • Twin Cheeks #3 / 1991 / CIN / M • Twin Cheeks #4 / 1991 / CIN / M • Two Of A Kind / 1991 / ZA / M • Unchained Melanie

/ 1992 / VC / M • Undercover Lover / 1993 / VC / M • Unforgettable / 1992 / HO / M • Unlike A Virgin / 1991 / HO / M • Unrefined / 1993 / CC / M • Untamed Cowgirls Of The Wild West #01: The Pillow Biters / 1992 / ZA / M • Vanity / 1992 / HO / M • The Visualizer / 1992 / VC / M • Voices In My Bed / 1993 / VI / M • Voyeur Video / 1992 / ZA / M • W.A.S.P. / 1992 / CC / M • Wacs / 1992 / PP / M • Walking Small / 1992 / ZA / M • Waterbabies #1 / 1992 / CC / M • Whispered Lies / 1993 / LBO / M • White Chicks Can't Hump / 1992 / FD / M • Wild & Wicked #2 / 1992 / VT / M • Wild Dreams / 1995 / V99 / M • The Wild Thing / 1992 / HO / M • Willie Wanker And The Fun Factory / 1994 / FD / M • The Women / 1993 / CAT / F • X-Rated Blondes / 1992 / VD / C • X-TV / 1992 / CA / C

MELANIE RAMEL
Samantha And The Deep Throat Girls / 1988 / CV / M

MELANIE RIMMER
Harry Horndog #23: The Final Flick / 1993 / ZA / M

MELANIE ROSE
Not the same a Marilyn Rose. This is a blonde with medium large tits and a pretty face. Rather speckled skin on rear end.
Buns And Roses (LV) / 1990 / LV / M • The Harley Girls / 1991 / AR / F • Hump Up The Volume / 1991 / AR / M • Maiden Heaven #1 / 1992 / MID / F • Shake Well Before Using / 9990 / LV / M • Twin Cheeks (Arrow) / 1991 / AR / M

MELANIE ROWAN
Private Film #01 / 1993 / OD / M

MELANIE SCOTT (Marlene Mathews, Melissa Walker, Melody Scott, Melissa Christian)
Blonde with young looking but chunky body, passable face, small tits. Marlene Mathews is from **Let's Talk Sex** and Melissa Walker is from **Tomboy**.
Body Double / 1984 / C3S / S • Bondage-Gram / 1983 / BIZ / B • Can't Get Enough / 1985 / CA / M • Chastity And The Starlets / 1986 / RAV / M • Cherry Busters / 1984 / VIV / M • Cherry Cheesecake / 1984 / AR / M • Commando Lovers / 1986 / SUV / M • Cravings / 1987 / VC / M • Dear Fanny / 1984 / CV / M • Delusions / 1983 / PRC / M • Double Standards / 1986 / VC / M • Dr Strange Sex / 1985 / CA / M • Easy Cum...Easy Go / 1985 / BAN / M • Endless Passion / 1987 / LIM / C • Free And Foxy / 1986 / VCX / C • Ginger Snaps / 1987 / VI / M • Girls And Their Toys / 1983 / LIP / F • Golden Girls #09 / 1983 / CA / M • GVC: Hot Numbers #133 / 1984 / GO / M • Happy Birthday Bondage Gram / 1983 / BIZ / B • Hot Rockers / 1985 / IVP / M • Hot Tails / 1984 / VEN / M • How Do You Like It? / 1985 / CA / M • I Wanna Be Teased / 1984 / SE / M • Jane Bonda's Bizarre Workout / 1984 / BIZ / B • Let's Talk Sex / 1982 / CA / M • Lucky In Love #1 / 1985 / BAN / M • The Many Shades Of Amber / 1986 / LIM / M • My Pretty Go Between / 1985 / VC / M • Porn In The USA #1 / 1986 / WV / C • Sex Drive / 1984 / VXP / M • Sex Games / 1983 / CA / M • Sex In The Great Outdoors / 1987 / SE / C • Sexplorations / 1991 / VC / C • Shacking Up / 1985 / VXP / M • Shades Of Ecstasy / 1983 / HO / M • Shape Up For Sensational Sex / 1985 / SE / M • She's So

Fine #1 / 1985 / VC / M • Sinners #1 / 1988 / COM / M • Sinners #2 / 1988 / COM / M • Sinners #3 / 1989 / COM / M • Snack Time / 1983 / HO / M • Snake Eyes #2 / 1987 / COM / M • Sophisticated Women / 1986 / BAN / M • Swedish Erotica Featurettes #4 / 1990 / CA / M • Thought You'd Never Ask / 1986 / CA / M • Tickled Pink / 1985 / VC / M • Tight Delight / 1985 / VXP / M • Tomboy / 1983 / VCX / M • Tower Of Power / 1985 / CV / M • Treasure Box / 1986 / PEN / M • Trinity Brown / 1984 / CV / M • The X-Team / 1984 / CV / M

MELANIE SMITH *see Star Index I*

MELANIE STARR *see Star Index I*

MELANIE SUMMERS *see Star Index I*

MELANIE WONG

Two Can Chew / 1995 / FD / M

MELBA BRUCE *(Melba Peach, Melba Raye, Melba Peche, Melba May, Melba Walsh)*

Very pretty girl with long straight blonde hair parted in the middle and a very tight body. Small tits and nice little butt. Unfortunately the word is that she committed suicide in 1977.

Baby Rosemary / 1975 / SE / M • China Lust / 1976 / VC / M • Erotic Fantasies #3 / 1983 / CV / C • Femmes De Sade / 1976 / ALP / M • The Final Sin / 1977 / COM / M • The Girls In The Band / 1976 / SVE / M • Honeypie / 1975 / VC / M • Liquid Lips / 1976 / EVI / M • Night Pleasures / 1975 / WWV / M • Private Thighs / 1987 / AVC / C • The Sinful Pleasures Of Reverend Star / 1976 / ... / M • The Starlets / 1976 / RAV / M • Teenage Surfer Girls / 1976 / VCS / M • [Sorority Suck Sisters / 197? / ... / M

MELBA CRUISE *see Melba Cruz*

MELBA CRUZ *(Melba Cruise, Carmella (Melba C.), Cheryl Sunset)*

The Adventures Of Dick Black, Black Dick / 1987 / DR / M • Backstage / 1988 / CDI / M • The Bride / 1986 / WV / M • The Color of Honey / 1987 / SUV / M • Deep Inside Rachel Ashley / 1987 / VEX / M • Deep Inside Viviana / 1992 / VEX / C • Deep Obsession / 1987 / WV / M • First Time Lesbians (Gourmet) / 1987 / GO / F • Flesh In Ecstasy #06: Elle Rio / 1987 / GO / C • Flesh In Ecstasy #07: Brittany Stryker / 1987 / GO / C • Flesh In Ecstasy #08: Traci Adams / 1987 / GO / C • Naughty Ninja Girls / 1987 / LA / M • Night Games / 1986 / WV / M • Parliament: Three Way Lust / 1988 / PM / M

MELBA MAY *see Melba Bruce*

MELBA PEACH *see Melba Bruce*

MELBA PECHE *see Melba Bruce*

MELBA RAYE *see Melba Bruce*

MELBA TEA

The Black Anal-ist #1 / 1988 / VEX / M

MELENDEZ *see Star Index I*

MELICIA *see Malitia*

MELINA

Bizarre Mistress Series: Mistress Jacqueline / 1992 / BIZ / C • Dresden Mistress #2 / 1989 / BIZ / B • Emmanuelle #6 / 1992 / NEH / S • Magma: Tanja's Horny Nights / 1994 / MET / M

MELINA (M.MASGLOW) *see Melinda Masglow*

MELINA DEVORA

Dirty Dirty Debutantes #6 / 1996 / 4P / M • Dirty Dirty Debutantes #7 / 1996 / 4P / M • Dirty Dirty Debutantes #8 / 1996 / 4P / M •

Lollipop Shoppe #1 / 1996 / SC / M • More Dirty Debutantes #53 / 1996 / 4P / M • More Dirty Debutantes #61 / 1997 / SBV / M • Up And Cummers #30 / 1996 / 4P / M • Up And Cummers #34 / 1996 / 4P / M • Valentina: Princess Of The Forest / 1996 / SC / M

MELINA MILIANI

Bare-Chested, Bare-Breasted, Big-Busted, Wet T-Shirt Video / 1990 / NAP / B • Scratch And Claw / 1990 / NAP / B • Wet T-Shirt Wildcats / 1990 / NAP / B

MELINDA

Blue Vanities #578 / 1995 / FFL / M • House Of Correction / 1991 / HOM / B • The Last Vamp / 1996 / IP / M • Mr. Peepers Amateur Home Videos #45: Coming From Behind / 1992 / LBO / M • Private Stories #01 / 1995 / OD / M • Punished Princess / 1992 / HOM / B

MELINDA K.

Private Gold #09: Private Dancer / 1996 / OD / M

MELINDA LEE

Black Heat / 1986 / VC / M • The Gentlemen's Club / 1986 / WV / M • Get Me While I'm Hot / 1988 / PV / M • Loose Caboose / 1987 / 4P / M • Parliament: Blonde Dominas #1 / 1988 / PM / F • Parliament: Dildo Babes #2 / 1988 / PM / F • The Rising / 1987 / SUV / M • Twin Cheeks (Arrow) / 1991 / AR / M

MELINDA MARLOW

Joy / 1977 / QX / M

MELINDA MASGLOW *(Melina (M.Masglow), Melanie (Masglow), Isabel (M.Masglow), Meline (M.Masglow), Sheila (M. Masglow), Cookie (M. Masglow), Meline Brooks, Melanie Brooks, Melane, Melissa Ashley, Chop Shop)*

Small bodied oriental with tiny tits who doesn't look like she likes any sex.

19 & Naughty #2 / 1995 / SKV / M • Alex Jordan's First Timers #01 / 1993 / OD / M • Anal Asian #2: The Won-Ton Woman / 1994 / IN / M • Anal Vision #03 / 1992 / LBO / M • Asian Appetite / 1993 / HO / M • Beach Bum Amateur's #23 / 1993 / MID / M • Bi-Laddin / 1994 / BIN / G • Bobby Hollander's Rookie Nookie #01 / 1993 / SFP / M • The Bold, The Bald & The Beautiful / 1993 / VIM / M • Brassiere To Eternity / 1994 / PEP / F • The Burma Road #1 / 1994 / LBO / C • The Burma Road #2 / 1994 / LBO / C • Chinatown / 1994 / SC / M • Chow Down / 1994 / VI / M • Crazy Lust / 1994 / ORE / C • The Cumm Brothers #02: Goin' To A Ho' Down / 1994 / OD / M • Cuntz #3 / 1994 / RTP / M • Cuntz #4 / 1994 / RTP / M • Deep Inside Dirty Debutantes #05 / 1993 / 4P / M • Dominique's Bi Adventure / 1995 / STA / G • From China With Love / 1993 / ZA / M • Gang Bang Bitches #03 / 1994 / PP / M • Geisha To Go / 1994 / PPP / M • A Geisha's Secret / 1993 / VI / M • Harry Horndog #13: Anal Lovers #2 / 1992 / ZA / M • Ho' Style Takeover / 1993 / FH / M • Hollywood Amateurs #12 / 1994 / MID / M • Hollywood Swingers #09 / 1993 / LBO / M • House Of The Rising Sun / 1993 / VT / M • In The Bush / 1994 / PP / M • Intercourse With The Vampyre #2 / 1994 / SC / M • Maid To Beat / 1994 / PL / B • More Dirty Debutantes #20 / 1993 / 4P / M • Oriental Sorority Secrets / 1992 / VIM / M • Pom Pom She-Males / 1994 / HEA /

G • R & R / 1994 / VC / M • Sensual Solos #03 / 1994 / AVI / F • Stripper Nurses / 1994 / PE / M • Student Fetish Videos: Best of Enema #03 / 1994 / PRE / C • Student Fetish Videos: The Enema #14 / 1994 / PRE / B • Student Fetish Videos: The Enema #16 / 1994 / PRE / B • Student Fetish Videos: Spanking #17 / 1994 / PRE / B • Student Fetish Videos: Tickling #10 / 1994 / SFV / B • Top Debs #1: Prom Night / 1992 / GO / M • Ultimate Anal Gang Bang #3 / 1995 / HW / M • Uncle Roy's Amateur Home Video #18 / 1993 / VIM / M • Video Virgins #02 / 1992 / NS / M • Wet Memories / 1993 / WV / M • Wild Orgies #04 / 1994 / AFI / M • Women Of Color #2 / 1994 / ANA / M

MELINDA MATYNS

True Stories #1 / 1993 / SC / M • True Stories #2 / 1993 / SC / M

MELINDA MCDOWELL

Thundercrack! / 1974 / LUM / M • [Sparkles Tavern / 1976 / ... / S

MELINDA ROBERTS

Volunteer Victim #1 / 1993 / BON / B • Volunteer Victim #2 / 1994 / BON / B

MELINDA ROUGH

Private Gold #01: Study In Sex / 1995 / OD / M • Private Gold #02: Friends In Sex / 1995 / OD / M

MELINDA RUSSEL

Private Gold #01: Study In Sex / 1995 / OD / M • Private Gold #02: Friends In Sex / 1995 / OD / M

MELINDA SHELBY

The Whips & Chains Affair / 1994 / HOM / B

MELINDA STEVENS

Twilight Pink #2 / 1982 / VC / M

MELINE *see Star Index I*

MELINE (M.MASGLOW) *see Melinda Masglow*

MELINE BROOKS *see Melinda Masglow*

MELISA (MELENDEZ) *see Melissa Melendez*

MELISSA

A&B AB#404: Milk Filled Tits / 1993 / A&B / M • A&B AB#405: Cum Explosion / 1993 / A&B / M • A&B FL#20: 4 Girl Flashing / 1995 / A&B / M • A&B FL#21: Melissa Is Back / 1995 / A&B / S • AVP #7000: Service By A Stud / 1990 / AVP / M • Blue Vanities #542 / 1994 / FFL / M • Collectors Series #01 / 1991 / TAO / B • Eric Kroll's Fetish #1 / 1994 / ERK / M • Eric Kroll's Fetish #2 / 1994 / ERK / M • Eric Kroll's Fetish #3: Female Hygiene / 1994 / ERK / M • Eurotica #07 / 1996 / XC / M • Funky Brewster / 1986 / DR / M • Ginger Lynn Allen's Lingerie Gallery #1 / 1994 / UNI / F • High Heel Harlots #01 / 1993 / SFP / M • Homegrown Video #418: Looks As Good As It Feels / 1994 / HOV / M • Limited Edition #26 / 1984 / AVC / M • Neighbor Girls T83 / 1995 / NEI / F • Neighborhood Watch #37: Pelvic Thrusters / 1993 / LBO / M • Pearl Necklace: Premier Sessions #07 / 1996 / SEE / M • Penthouse: Great Pet Hunt #1 / 1992 / PET / F • Private Video Magazine #01 / 1993 / OD / M • Rusty Boner's Late Night Videos #1 / 1995 / RHV / M • SVE: Screentest Sex #2 / 1992 / SVE / M • Sweet Cheeks / 1987 / VCR / C • Wet Workout: Shape Up, Then Strip Down / 1995 / PME / S • Whipped And Shaved / 1995 / FLV / B

MELISSA (M. RAIN) *see* **Misty Rain**
MELISSA (MELENDEZ) *see* **Melissa Melendez**
MELISSA ADAMS
How To Make A Model #02: Got Her In Bed / 1993 / QUA / M
MELISSA ASHLEY *see* **Melinda Masglow**
MELISSA BONSARDO *see* **Star Index I**
MELISSA CHRISTIAN *see* **Melanie Scott**
MELISSA COLLIER *see* **Star Index I**
MELISSA DAYE
Irresistible #1 / 1982 / SE / M
MELISSA DUBOIS
The Erotic Adventures Of Dr Storm / 1983 / XTR / M
MELISSA GEE *see* **Melissa Melendez**
MELISSA HALL *see* **Star Index I**
MELISSA HILL *(Melanie Hill)*
Reddish black curly hair, 23 years old in 1993, large tits, out-of-shape body, very white skin, quite pretty, blue eyes. 5'4" tall, 36C-24-36 in 1994. De-virginized at 17.
The Adventures Of Studman #1 / 1994 / AFV / M • The Adventures Of Studman #2 / 1994 / AFV / M • The Adventures Of Studman #3 / 1994 / AFV / M • Amateur Dreams #4 / 1994 / DR / M • American Pie / 1995 / WAV / M • The Anal Adventures Of Suzy Super Slut #2 / 1994 / AFV / M • Babewatch #2 / 1994 / CC / M • Beach Bum Amateur's #36 / 1993 / MID / M • Bed & Breakfast / 1995 / WAV / M • Bedlam / 1995 / WAV / M • Blaze / 1996 / WAV / M • Blonde / 1995 / LE / M • Bloopers & Boners / 1996 / VI / M • Brassiere To Eternity / 1994 / PEP / F • The Butt Sisters Do Boston / 1995 / MID / M • The Butt Sisters Do New York / 1994 / MID / M • The Butt Sisters Do Seattle / 1995 / MID / M • Cherry Poppin #02 / 1994 / CDY / M • Creme De La Face #03 / 1994 / OD / M • Cry Baby / 1995 / CV / M • Dangerous Games / 1995 / VI / M • De Sade / 1994 / SC / M • Deadly Sin / 1996 / ONA / M • Deep Behind The Scenes With Seymore Butts #1 / 1995 / ULI / M • Dick & Jane Go To Northridge / 1994 / AVI / M • Dirty Dating Service #05 / 1994 / WP / M • Dirty Dating Service #06 / 1994 / WP / M • Dirty Doc's Housecalls #20 / 1994 / LV / M • Dirty Laundry #2 / 1994 / CV / M • Dirty Little Secrets / 1995 / WAV / M • Dreams / 1995 / VC / M • Dreams Of Desires / 1995 / ONA / M • Euro-Max #3: / 1995 / SC / M • Every Woman Has A Fantasy #3 / 1995 / VC / M • Exposure / 1995 / WAV / M • Fabulous Flashers #1 / 1995 / DGD / F • Fantasy Flings #02 / 1994 / WP / M • Four Weddings And A Honeymoon / 1995 / PL / M • Ghost Town / 1995 / WAV / M • The Girl With The Heart-Shaped Tattoo / 1995 / WAV / M • Hard Squeeze / 1994 / EMC / M • Harder, She Craved / 1995 / VC / M • Hawaiian Heat #1 / 1995 / CC / M • Hawaiian Heat #2 / 1995 / CC / M • Hornet's Nest / 1996 / ONA / M • Hot Wishes / 1995 / LE / M • Invitation For Lust / 1995 / C69 / M • Jenna Loves Rocco / 1996 / WAV / M • Latex And Lace / 1996 / BBE / M • Lay Of The Land / 1995 / LE / M • Little Girl Lost / 1995 / SC / M • Loose Morals / 1995 / EX / M • M Series #23 / 1994 / LBO / M • Make Me Watch / 1994 / PV / M • Midnight Snacks / 1995 / KLP / M • The Mile High Club / 1995 / PL / M • Milli Vanilla / 1994 / TP / M • Mind Set / 1996 / VI / M • Mixed-

Up Marriage / 1995 / CV / M • Mr. Peepers Amateur Home Videos #90: Back Door Bonanza / 1994 / LBO / M • Nasty Nymphos #05 / 1994 / ANA / M • Natural Born Thriller / 1994 / CC / M • New Faces, Hot Bodies #10 / 1993 / STP / M • New Faces, Hot Bodies #11 / 1993 / STP / M • New Faces, Hot Bodies #12 / 1993 / STP / M • New Faces, Hot Bodies #13 / 1994 / STP / M • New Faces, Hot Bodies #20 / 1996 / STP / M • New Pussy Hunt #16 / 1995 / LEI / M • The New Snatch Masters #14 / 1995 / LEI / C • Nightclub / 1996 / SC / M • Nikki Loves Rocco / 1996 / VI / M • On The Rise / 1994 / EX / M • Ona Zee's Learning The Ropes #08: Slaves In Training / 1992 / ONA / B • Outcall Outlaws / 1995 / CC / M • The Palace Of Pleasure / 1995 / ULI / M • Penetrator #2: Grudge Day / 1995 / PL / M • Pristine #2 / 1996 / CA / M • Private Eyes / 1995 / LE / M • Private Film #24 / 1995 / OD / M • Private Film #25 / 1995 / OD / M • Private Film #26 / 1995 / OD / M • Reckless Passion / 1995 / WAV / M • Red Hot Lover / 1995 / CV / M • Rock Me / 1994 / CC / M • Rod Wood / 1995 / LE / M • Rump Man: Goes To Cannes / 1995 / HW / M • Secret Rendez-Vous / 1994 / XCI / M • Sex Academy #2: The Art Of Talking Dirty / 1994 / ONA / M • Sex Academy #3: The Art Of Real Sex / 1994 / ONA / M • Sex Academy #4: The Art Of Anal / 1994 / ONA / M • Sex Machine / 1995 / VI / M • Shave Tails #1 / 1994 / SO / M • Shaved #06 / 1993 / RB / F • The Show / 1995 / VI / M • Skin Hunger / 1995 / MET / M • Smoke Screen / 1995 / WAV / M • Something Blue / 1995 / CC / M • Southern Belles #4 / 1995 / HOV / M • The Star / 1995 / CC / M • Street Legal / 1995 / WAV / M • Strippers Inc. #1 / 1994 / ONA / M • Strippers Inc. #2 / 1994 / ONA / M • Strippers Inc. #3 / 1994 / ONA / M • Striptease / 1995 / SPI / M • Style #3 / 1996 / VT / M • Suggestive Behavior / 1996 / VI / M • Surprise!!! / 1994 / VI / M • Sweet Revenge / 1996 / WAV / M • Taboo #14: Kissing Cousins / 1995 / IN / M • Teacher's Pet #1 / 1994 / WMG / M • The Thief / 1994 / SC / M • The Tongue / 1995 / OD / M • Torrid Tales / 1995 / VI / M • The Toy Box / 1996 / ONA / M • Triple X Video Magazine #01 / 1995 / OD / M • Triple X Video Magazine #02 / 1995 / OD / M • Triple X Video Magazine #03 / 1995 / OD / M • Triple X Video Magazine #06 / 1995 / OD / M • Video Virgins #08 / 1993 / NS / M • Video Virgins #09 / 1993 / NS / M • Visions #1 / 1995 / ERA / M • Visions #2 / 1995 / ERA / M • Vivid Raw #3: Double Header / 1996 / VI / M • The Voyeur #2 / 1994 / EA / M • Wet Faces #1 / 1997 / SC / C • Wildfire: #04 Melissa Hill / 1994 / WIF / F • Wildfire: Wildgirl's Cleaning Service / 1994 / WIF / F • Wildfire: Wildgirls #1 / 1994 / WIF / F • XXX / 1996 / TEP / M
MELISSA JENNINGS *see* **Lisa Sue Corey**
MELISSA MAGONAN *see* **Star Index I**
MELISSA MANCHESTER *see* **Star Index I**
MELISSA MARCUS *see* **Star Index I**
MELISSA MELENDEZ *(Melisa (Melendez), Steffine Stone, Melissa Gee, Ava Maria, Melissa Mellon, Elisa (M. Melendez), Melissa (Melendez), Kat Harlow)*
Brunette with curly hair and Hispanic over-

tones. A little bit on the flabby side with medium tits but a nice personality.
Alien Lust / 1985 / AVC / M • Amber Lynn's Peter Meter / 1988 / 3HV / C • Anal Encounters #2 / 1991 / VC / M • Anal Encounters #3: Back In The Dark One / 1991 / VC / M • Baby Face #2 / 1987 / VC / M • Bad Attitude / 1987 / CC / M • The Beat Goes On / 1987 / VCR / C • The Best Of Both Worlds #1 / 1986 / LA / G • Bi Bi Love / 1986 / LAV / G • Bi-Ceps / 1986 / LA / C • Black To The Future / 1986 / VD / M • Bootsie / 1984 / CC / M • Breastography, Lesson #1 / 1987 / VCR / M • Debbie Class Of '88 / 1987 / CC / M • Deep Throat #2 / 1986 / AR / M • The Dinner Party / 1986 / WV / M • Double Play / 1993 / CA / C • Dr Juice's Lust Potion / 1986 / TEM / M • Dr Lust / 1987 / VC / M • Dr Penetration / 1986 / WET / M • Dream Girls / 1986 / VC / M • Eaten Alive / 1985 / VXP / M • Escort To Ecstasy / 1987 / 3HV / M • The Girls Of Rodeo Drive / 1987 / BAD / M • Grafenberg Girls Go Fishing / 1987 / MIT / M • I Wanna Be A Bad Girl / 1986 / PP / M • The Immoral Miss Teeze / 1987 / CV / M • Innocent Taboo / 1986 / VD / M • Kiss My Asp / 1989 / EXH / M • Let's Get It On With Amber Lynn / 1986 / VC / M • Lottery Fever / 1985 / BEA / M • Lottery Lust / 1986 / PEN / M • Lover's Lane / 1986 / SE / M • Lust With The Stranger / 1986 / MAP / M • Mardi Gras / 1986 / SE / M • Marina Vice / 1985 / PEN / M • My Party Doll / 1987 / VXP / M • Nasty Girls #2 (1990-Plum) / 1990 / PP / M • Nasty Nights / 1988 / PL / C • Naughty By Nature / 1992 / IF / M • No Man's Land #01 / 1988 / VT / C • No Man's Land #04 / 1990 / VT / F • One Night In Bangkok / 1985 / CA / M • Only The Very Best On Video / 1992 / VC / C • Parliament: Fuckin' Superstars #1 / 1990 / PM / C • Peggy Sue / 1987 / VT / M • Play Me Again, Vanessa / 1986 / VC / M • The Pleasure Machine / 1987 / VXP / M • Pretty Peaches #2 / 1987 / VC / M • Prince Of Beverly Hills #1 / 1987 / VEX / M • Quicksilver / 1987 / CDI / M • The Return Of Johnny Wadd / 1986 / PEN / M • Revenge Of The Babes #1 / 1985 / LA / M • Rich & Sassy / 1986 / VSE / M • Rocky-X #1 / 1986 / PEN / M • Seduction By Fire / 1987 / VD / M • Sensuous Singles: Whitney Prince / 1987 / VCR / F • Sex Styles Of The Rich & Famous / 1986 / VXP / M • Sex-A-Vision / 1985 / DR / M • Shame On Shanna / 1989 / DR / C • She's A Boy Toy / 1985 / DR / M • Starship Intercourse / 1987 / DR / M • Super Sex / 1986 / MAP / M • Sweat Shop / 1991 / EVN / M • Swedish Erotica #66 / 1985 / CA / M • Taxi Girls #2: In Search Of Toni / 1986 / ELD / M • Teasin' & Pleasin' / 1988 / LBO / F • Tight Squeeze / 1986 / AVC / M • Traci's Big Trick / 1987 / VAS / M • Two Handfuls / 1986 / ... / G • The Ultimate Thrill / 1988 / PIN / C • VCA Previews #4 / 1988 / VC / C • Video Store Vixens / 1986 / PL / M • Welcome To Paradise / 1994 / IF / M • Woman In The Window / 1986 / TEM / M • Women In Uniform / 1986 / TEM / M • Yank My Doodle, It's A Dandy / 1985 / GOM / M
MELISSA MELLON *see* **Melissa Melendez**
MELISSA MERCOUR *see* **Star Index I**
MELISSA MILO
Erotic Dimensions: Aggressive Women /

1982 / NSV / M
MELISSA MONET *(Clarissa (M. Monet))*
Not too pretty brunette with small droopy tits, petite body and narrow hips. Tattoos on her right ankle and right hip.
1-900-FUCK #1 / 1995 / SO / M • 113 Cherry Lane / 1994 / FOR / M • 3 Mistresses Of The Chateau / 1995 / STM / B • The 4th Vixxen / 1995 / EMC / M • The Adventures Of Studman #2 / 1994 / AFV / M • The Anal Adventures Of Suzy Super Slut #3 / 1994 / IPI / M • Anal Alien / 1994 / CC / M • Anal Nitrate / 1995 / PE / M • Badgirls #3: Cell Block 69 / 1994 / VI / M • Badgirls #5: Maximum Babes / 1995 / VI / M • Badgirls #6: Ridin' Into Town / 1995 / VI / M • The Butt Sisters Do Baltimore / 1995 / MID / M • The Butt Sisters Do Chicago / 1995 / MID / M • The Butt Sisters Do Daytona / 1995 / MID / M • The Butt Sisters Do Hawaii / 1995 / MID / M • Butthole Dreams: Big Boating Bonanza / 1994 / FH / M • Caught In The Act (1995-Lv) / 1995 / LV / M • Cinesex #2 / 1994 / CV / M • Dance Naked / 1995 / PEP / M • Deep Inside Brittany O'connell / 1996 / VC / C • Dirty Laundry #1 / 1994 / CV / M • Dirty Work / 1995 / VC / M • Dr Finger's House Of Lesbians / 1996 / SC / M • The Drifter / 1995 / CV / M • Dungeon Training / 1995 / STM / B • Erotic World Of Anne Spice / 1995 / WV / M • Explicit Entry / 1995 / LE / M • Extreme Sex #4: The Experiment / 1995 / VI / M • Fazano's Student Bodies / 1995 / EL / M • Firm Offer / 1995 / SC / M • Fluff Dreams / 1995 / SUF / M • A Girl's Affair #06 / 1995 / FD / F • Girls Of The Packed Ten / 1994 / VT / M • The Go-Go Girls / 1994 / EVN / M • Gorgeous / 1995 / MET / M • Hang 'em High / 1995 / BS / B • Harder, She Craved / 1995 / VC / M • Hotel California / 1995 / MID / M • In Search Of The Perfect Blow Job / 1995 / OD / M • In Your Face #3 / 1995 / PL / M • Kept Women / 1995 / LE / M • Kym Wilde's On The Edge #28 / 1995 / RB / B • Life's A Beach, Then You're Fucked / 1995 / FRM / M • Long Dark Shadow / 1994 / LE / M • Loving You Always / 1994 / IN / M • Mistress Rules / 1995 / STM / B • The Night Shift / 1995 / LE / M • Nutts About Butts / 1994 / LE / M • Obsessions In Lace / 1994 / PL / M • Oh My Gush / 1995 / OD / M • Painful Madness / 1995 / BS / B • Peepshow / 1994 / OD / M • Pussy Whipped / 1994 / FOR / M • Pussyman #08: The Squirt Queens / 1994 / SNA / M • Pussyman #13: Lips / 1996 / SNA / M • Pussyman Auditions #01 / 1995 / SNA / M • Rainwoman #09: Wetlands / 1995 / CC / M • Rainwoman #10: The Tenth Anniversary Edition / 1996 / CC / M • The Romeo Syndrome / 1995 / SC / M • Scorched / 1995 / ONA / M • Sex Alert / 1995 / PV / M • Sex Suites / 1995 / TP / M • Shameless / 1995 / VC / M • Sin Asylum / 1995 / CV / M • Slave Quarters / 1995 / PRE / B • Sodomania #11: In Your Face / 1994 / EL / M • The Star / 1994 / HO / M • Strap-On Sally #05: Chantilly's French Kiss / 1995 / PL / F • Strap-On Sally #06: Triple Penetration Trollop / 1995 / PL / F • Strip Poker / 1995 / PEP / M • Student Fetish Videos: Best of Catfighting #03 / 1995 / PRE / C • Student Fetish Videos: Catfighting #14 / 1994 / PRE / B • Student Fetish Videos: The Enema #18 / 1995 / PRE / B • Student

Fetish Videos: Foot Worship #15 / 1995 / PRE / B • Swedish Erotica #76 / 1994 / CA / M • Taboo #14: Kissing Cousins / 1995 / IN / M • Takin' It To The Limit #3 / 1994 / BS / M • A Trip Through Pain / 1995 / BS / B • True Sex / 1994 / EMC / M • Unbridled Lust / 1995 / NOT / F • Voyeur Strippers / 1996 / PL / F • Where The Girls Sweat...Not The Sequel / 1996 / EL / F • While You Were Dreaming / 1995 / WV / M • Wicked Ways #1: Interview With The Anal Queen / 1994 / WP / M • Women On Fire / 1995 / LBO / M • [Black & White & Brutal #1 / 1996 / ... / S • [Black & White & Brutal #2 / 1996 / ... / S
MELISSA MOUNDS
Best In Bed / 1988 / NAP / B • Between My Breasts #12 / 1990 / BTO / M • Biggest Sexiest Boobs In The USA Contest / 1989 / NAP / F • Breast Wishes #03 / 1991 / LBO / M • Busen Extra #2 / 1990 / BTO / M • Cat-Fight Queen / 1988 / NAP / B • Cats Will Be Cats / 1988 / NAP / B • Closet Nazi / 1989 / NAP / B • EL 7 / 1991 / NAP / S • Flesh Gordon #2: Flesh Gordon Meets The Cosmic Cheerleaders / 1993 / NEH / S • The Girls Of Daytona / 1993 / BTO / S • Hollywood Teasers #04 / 1992 / LBO / F • Introducing Gina Gianetti / 1989 / NAP / F • Introducing Melissa Mounds / 1989 / NAP / F • Mega-Tits / 1990 / NAP / F • Only The Best (Napali) / 1990 / NAP / B • Purr Of The Cats / 1988 / NAP / B • Pussy Power #01 / 1991 / BTO / M • The Trainee / 1989 / NAP / B • The Very Best Of Breasts #3 / 1996 / H&S / S • Working Girls / 1988 / NAP / B • Wrestling Queens / 1989 / NAP / B
MELISSA MURRAY see Star Index I
MELISSA PISANO see Star Index I
MELISSA POPE
Disciplz Of Pain / 1995 / ZFX / B • Innocent Exile / 1995 / ZFX / B • Video Pirates #1 / 1995 / ZFX / B • Video Pirates #2 / 1995 / ZFX / B • Video Pirates #5: A Bullet To Bite / 1995 / ZFX / B
MELISSA RIO see Star Index I
MELISSA RYAN
Bondage Pleasures #1 / 1981 / 4P / B
MELISSA SANDS see Star Index I
MELISSA WALKER see Melanie Scott
MELITTA TEGELER
[Krankenschwestern-Report / 1972 / ... / M
MELIZA
Private Video Magazine #23 / 1995 / OD / M
MELLISSA SADE see Sade
MELODIE
Magma: Fuck Me Diana / 1994 / MET / M
MELODIE KISS
Les Chaleurs De La Gyneco / 1996 / FAP / F
MELODY
Blue Vanities #512 / 1992 / FFL / M • Blue Vanities #540 / 1994 / FFL / M • Good Girl, Bad Girl / 1984 / SE / M • Housekeeper's Mistake / 1993 / BON / B • Ona Zee's Learning The Ropes #12: Couples / 1995 / ONA / B • Ona Zee's Learning The Ropes #13: Best Of Male Submission / 1996 / ONA / C • Real People Real Bondage #1 / 1995 / BON / C
MELODY ANTON see Star Index I
MELODY C. ROGERS
Sound Of Love / 1981 / CA / M
MELODY GORDON see Star Index I
MELODY HART

Summer Girls / 1986 / HO / C
MELODY KISS
Girls Around The World #05 / 1992 / BTO / S • Girls Around The World #21: Tawny Peaks & Friends / 1995 / BTO / M • Mammary Manor / 1992 / BTO / M
MELODY MIDNIGHT *(Karess)*
Brunette, with curly black hair. Only OK facially, small tits.
C-Hunt #02: Hot Pockets / 1995 / PEV / M • Pearl Necklace: Amorous Amateurs #09 / 1992 / SEE / M • Pearl Necklace: Amorous Amateurs #10 / 1992 / SEE / M • Pearl Necklace: Amorous Amateurs #11 / 1992 / SEE / M • Pearl Necklace: Amorous Amateurs #12 / 1992 / SEE / M • Pearl Necklace: Amorous Amateurs #13 / 1992 / SEE / M • Pearl Necklace: Amorous Amateurs #23 / 1993 / SEE / M • Pearl Necklace: Amorous Amateurs #28 / 1993 / SEE / M • Pearl Necklace: Amorous Amateurs #30 / 1993 / SEE / M • Pearl Necklace: Amorous Amateurs #32 / 1993 / SEE / F • Pearl Necklace: Thee Bush League: The Best Of Oral #01 / 1993 / SEE / C • Pearl Necklace: Facial #01 / 1994 / SEE / C • Pearl Necklace: Thee Bush League #01 / 1992 / SEE / M • Pearl Necklace: Thee Bush League #03 / 1992 / SEE / M • Pearl Necklace: Thee Bush League #12 / 1993 / SEE / M • Pearl Necklace: Thee Bush League #18 / 1993 / SEE / M • Pearl Necklace: Thee Bush League #29 / 1994 / SEE / M
MELODY MOORE see Star Index I
MELODY PHILLIPS see Star Index I
MELODY SCOTT see Melanie Scott
MELONIE
Jamie Gillis: The Private Collection Vol #1 / 1991 / SC / F • Jamie Gillis: The Private Collection Vol #2 / 1991 / SC / F • Orient Sexpress / 1996 / AVI / M • Seymore & Shane Live On Tour / 1995 / ULI / M • Shane's World #6: Slumber Party / 1996 / OD / F
MELVA JACKSON
Too Hot To Handle / 1975 / CDC / M
MELVIN
Back East Babes #3 / 1996 / NIT / M
MELVIN MUSHMOUTH see Star Index I
MELVIN WARD
Indiana Joan In The Black Hole Of Mammoo / 1984 / VC / M
MENAGE TROIS *(Menaja Twa, Tamika (Menage))*
Black, passable face, small tits, nice butt, tight waist, protruding belly button, long straight hair, light skin, tattoo on left shoulder back.
$ex 4 Fun & Profit / 1996 / SPR / M • Anal Receivers / 3996 / MP0 / M • Analtown USA #12 / 1996 / NIT / M • Another Fuckin' Anal Movie / 1996 / ROB / M • Asses Galore #2: No Remorse...No Repent / 1996 / DFI / M • Best Gang Bangs / 1996 / DFI / C • Big Man's Ebony Dreams / 1996 / LOK / M • Black Babes / 1995 / LV / M • The Black Butt Sisters Do Boston / 1995 / MID / M • The Black Butt Sisters Do New Orleans / 1996 / MID / M • Black Cheerleader Search #02 / 1996 / ROB / M • Black Fantasies #09 / 1995 / HW / M • Black Fantasies #10 / 1995 / HW / M • Black Fantasies #11 / 1996 / HW / M • Black Fantasies #12 / 1996 / HW / M • Black Fantasies #13 / 1996 / HW / M • Black Fantasies #14 / 1996 / HW / M • Black Gangbangers #11 / 1996 / HW / M • Black Hollywood Amateurs #21 / 1996 /

MID / M • Black Hollywood Amateurs #23 / 1996 / MID / M • Black Hose Bag / 1996 / ROB / M • Black Jack City #5 / 1995 / HW / M • Black Juice Bombs / 1996 / NIT / C • Black Snatch #2 / 1996 / DFI / F • Black Talez N Da Hood / 1996 / APP / M • Booty Bang #1 / 1996 / HW / M • Booty Bang #2 / 1996 / HW / M • Bootylicious: Big Badd Booty / 1995 / JMP / M • Bootylicious: Bitches & Ho's / 1996 / JMP / M • Bootylicious: Yo Bitch / 1996 / JMP / M • Bow Down Backstreet / 1996 / HW / M • Butt-hole Sweetheart / 1996 / ROB / M • China's House Party / 1996 / HW / M • Chocolate Bunnies #06 / 1996 / LBO / C • Climax At The Melting Pot #2 / 1996 / AVS / M • Coochie's Under Fire / 1996 / HW / F • Da Booty Bang #2 / 1996 / HW / M • Danger-ous Behinds #2 / 1996 / HW / M • Dark Eyes / 1995 / FC / M • Devil In A Wet T-Shirt / 1995 / SPI / M • Dirty Hairy's Back To Black / 1996 / GOT / M • Gang Bang Butthole Surfin' / 1996 / ROB / M • Gang Bang Dollies / 1996 / ROB / M • Girlz N The Hood #5 / 1995 / HW / M • Golden Rod / 1996 / SPI / M • Hardcore Confidential #2 / 1996 / TEP / M • Harlem Harlots #3 / 1996 / AVS / M • Hollywood Legs / 1996 / NIT / M • How To Make Love To A Black Woman #1: You Gotta Have Rhythm / 1996 / VCX / M • Kink Inc. / 1996 / MP0 / M • Kink: Po-lice Chronicles / 1995 / ROB / M • Lock-down / 1996 / NIT / M • A Lowdown Dirty Game / 1996 / LBO / M • Macin' #1 / 1996 / SMP / M • Menaja's House Party / 1996 / HW / M • Nba: Nuttin' Butt Ass / 1996 / SMP / M • Primal Rear / 1996 / TIW / M • Pumps In Da Rump #2 / 1996 / HW / M • The Return Of Dr Blacklove / 1996 / CC / M • Rump-Shaker #5 / 1996 / HW / M • Shake Your Booty / 1996 / EVN / M • Sluts, Butts And Pussy / 1996 / DFI / M • Small Top Bitches / 1996 / AVI / M • Snatch Shot / 1996 / LBO / M • Sweet Black Cherries #3 / 1996 / TTV / M • Sweet Black Cherries #3 / 1996 / TTV / M • Sweet Black Cherries #4 / 1996 / TTV / M • Two-Pac / 1996 / VT / M • Virgin Dreams / 1996 / EA / M

MENAJA TWA *see* **Menage Trois**

MENDALAINA
Catch Of The Day #6 / 1996 / VG0 / M

MENETTE *see* **Stephanie DuValle**

MENO *see* **Star Index I**

MEO *(Cris Collins, Chris Collins, Mao, Mio, Julie C. Thompson)*
Older female. Started as blonde and has since become a brunette, enhanced tits but not too big, very energetic and seems to like sex.
Adventures Of The DP Boys: Back In The Bush / 1993 / HW / M • Adventures Of The DP Boys: Down At The Sunset Grill / 1993 / HW / M • AHV #34: Ring My Bell / 1993 / EVN / M • AHV #35: Odds And Ends / 1993 / EVN / M • Amateur Lesbians #25: Inter-national Budapest / 1992 / GO / F • Ama-teur Lesbians #35: Meo / 1993 / GO / F • Amateur Lesbians #37: Gretta / 1993 / GO / F • Amateur Lesbians #38: Jessica / 1993 / GO / F • Amateur Orgies #22 / 1993 / AFI / M • America's Raunchiest Home Videos #56: Primed For A Party / 1993 / ZA / M • Anal Vision #05 / 1993 / LBO / M • Asian Heat #02: Satin Angels / 1993 / SC / M • Ass Openers! #1 / 1995 / TCK / C • Back In Style / 1993 / VI / M • Backdoor Black #2 /

1993 / WV / C • Backing In #6 / 1994 / WV / C • Behind The Blackout / 1993 / HW / M • Between The Cheeks #3 / 1993 / VC / M • Bi-Sex Pleasures / 1993 / PL / G • Big Murray's New-Cummers #05: Luscious Lesbos / 1993 / FD / F • Big Murray's New-Cummers #12: In The Pink / 1993 / FD / M • Big Murray's New-Cummers #13: Hot Tight Ladies / 1993 / FD / M • Bimbonese 101 / 1993 / PL / M • Bitch / 1993 / VIM / M • Blonde Ice #2 / 1993 / EX / M • Bobby Hollander's Maneaters #02 / 1993 / SFP / M • Bobby Hollander's Sweet Cheeks #103 / 1992 / QUA / M • Bobby Hollander's Sweet Cheeks #105 / 1993 / SFP / M • Bubble Butts #22 / 1993 / LBO / M • The Butt Boss / 1993 / VD / M • Butt Watch #01 / 1993 / FH / M • Casanova #2 / 1993 / SC & Mouse #2 / 1993 / XCI / M • Coming Out / 1993 / VD / M • The Damp Spot / 1993 / AFD / C • The Darker Side Of Shayla #2 / 1993 / PL / M • Deja Vu / 1993 / XCI / M • Double D Domination / 1993 / BIZ / B • Dresden Diary #09 / 1993 / BIZ / B • Dres-den Diary #10: Punishment For Their Sins / 1993 / BIZ / B • The Ebony Connection #4 / 1994 / LBO / C • Femme Fatale / 1993 / SC / M • First Time Lesbians #02 / 1993 / JMP / F • The Fluffer #1 / 1993 / FD / M • Girls Will Be Boys #6 / 1993 / PL / F • He-donism #01 / 1993 / FH / M • Horny Orgy / 1993 / GOU / M • Hot Tight Asses #03 / 1993 / TCK / M • Hungarian Dp Birthday / 1993 / HW / M • The Hunger / 1993 / FOR / M • I Dream Of Teri / 1993 / IF / M • I Was An Undercover Slave / 1994 / HOM / B • In-ferno #1 / 1993 / SC / M • It's Only Love / 1992 / VEX / M • The Joy Dick Club / 1994 / MID / M • Just My Imagination / 1993 / WP / M • Just One Look / 1993 / V99 / M • Kink World: The Seduction Of Nena / 1993 / PL / M • The Love Doctor / 1992 / HIP / M • Lovebone Invasion / 1993 / PL / M • Lust / 1993 / FH / M • Lusty Lesbos / 1994 / CA / C • M Series #11 / 1993 / LBO / M • Maiden Heaven #1 / 1992 / MID / F • Maiden Heaven #2 / 1992 / MID / F • Make My Wife Please... / 1993 / VC / M • Marked #2 / 1993 / FD / M • Midnight Angels #02 / 1993 / MID / F • Mr. Peepers Amateur Home Videos #65: Suckateral Skills / 1993 / LBO / M • Mr. Peepers Nastiest #3 / 1995 / LBO / C • My Way / 1993 / CA / M • N.Y.D.P. / 1994 / PEP / M • Needful Sins / 1993 / WV / M • Night Shade Video #2 / 1992 / ... / M • Night Shade Video #4 / 1992 / ... / M • Nothing Else Matters / 1992 / V99 / C • Nothing Personal / 1993 / CA / M • Odyssey Triple Play #53: Butt-Fuck Bash / 1993 / OD / M • Party Favors / 1993 / VEX / M • Pearl Necklace: Amorous Am-ateurs #22 / 1993 / SEE / M • The Pick Up / 1993 / MID / M • The Princess Slave / 1994 / BIZ / B • Pussy Tamer #1 / 1993 / BIZ / B • Pussy Tamer #2 / 1993 / BIZ / B • The Queens Of Mean / 1994 / NTP / B • Raw Talent: Deep Inside Meo's Ass / 1993 / RTP / M • Raw Talent: Lust / 1993 / FH / M • Raw Talent: Swing Rave / 1993 / FH / M • Reflections Of Rio / 1993 / WP / M • Russian Champagne / 1993 / GOU / M • Saturday Night Porn #1 / 1993 / AFV / M • Saturday Night Porn #1 / 1993 / AFV / M • Sex Fantasy / 1993 / PPR / M • Slaves Bound For Passion / 1994 / BIZ / B • Slip

Of The Tongue / 1993 / DR / M • The Spirit Of My Master / 1994 / BIZ / B • Straight A's / 1993 / VC / M • Student Fetish Videos: Best of Catfighting #02 / 1994 / PRE / C • Student Fetish Videos: Best of Enema #03 / 1994 / PRE / C • Student Fetish Videos: Best Of Foot Worship #02 / 1994 / PRE / C • Student Fetish Videos: Catfighting #07 / 1993 / PRE / B • Student Fetish Videos: The Enema #11 / 1994 / PRE / B • Student Fetish Videos: Foot Worship #09 / 1993 / PRE / B • Swing Rave / 1993 / EVN / M • Tail Taggers #101 / 1993 / WV / M • Tail Taggers #106 / 1993 / WV / M • Tail Tag-gers #108: Vibro Love / 1993 / WV / M • Tails From The Tower / 1993 / AFI / M • Tarts In Torment / 1993 / LBO / B • This Could Be The Night / 1993 / IF / M • To Serve...Protect...And Submit / 1994 / BIZ / B • To Shave And Shave Not / 1994 / PEP / M • Tonight's The Night / 1992 / V99 / M • Tracey's Academy Of DD Dominance / 1993 / BIZ / B • Voluptuous / 1993 / CA / M • Voyeurism #1 / 1993 / FH / M • Ware-house Wenches #1 / 1994 / BIZ / B • Ware-house Wenches #2 / 1994 / BIZ / B • Wet Event / 1992 / IF / M • Wet Faces #1 / 1997 / SC / C • Whoppers #3 / 1993 / VEX / F • WPINK-TV #4 / 1993 / PV / M • Xcitement: The Movie / 1993 / XCI / M

MEPHISTO
Behind The Mask / 1995 / XC / M • Frank Thring's Double Penetration #3 / 1996 / XPR / M • French Roommate / 1995 / C69 / M • Fresh Meat (John Leslie) #3 / 1996 / EA / M • Nymphos: They Can't Help It...Re-ally! / 1996 / P69 / M • Rebecca Lord's World Tour #1: French Edition / 1995 / WP / M • The Voyeur #3 / 1995 / EA / M

MERCADO
Computer Girls / 1983 / LIP / F • The Girls Of Klit House / 1984 / LIP / F • Lusty Cou-ples (Come To) / cr85 / CHX / M

MERCEDES
Hot Body Video Magazine: Wild Thing / 1996 / CG / F • Little Shop Of She-Males / 1994 / HSV / G • M Series #03 / 1993 / LBO / M • Miss Bondwell's Reformatory / 1994 / LON / B • Misty's First Whipping / 1994 / LON / B • Sean Michaels On The Road #08: Chicago / 1993 / VT / M • The Watering Hole / 1994 / HO / M

MERCEDES (1996)
The Adventures Of Peeping Tom #2 / 1996 / OD / M • Anal Fantasy / 1996 / SUF / M • Anal Honeypie / 1996 / ROB / M • Anal Jammin' & Slammin' / 1996 / ROB / M • Anal Runaway / 1996 / ZA / M • Anal Vir-gins #02 / 1996 / NS / M • Borsky's Back Door Bitches / 1996 / ROB / M • Corporate Justice / 1996 / TEP / M • The Cumm Brothers #16: Deja Goo / 1996 / OD / M • Hot Tight Asses #17 / 1996 / TCK / M • Manhandled! / 1997 / BON / B • Monkey Gang Bang / 1996 / NOT / M • More Dirty Debutantes #54 / 1996 / 4P / M • Naked Mockey-Rayna / 1996 / EVN / M • Nba: Nuttin' Butt Ass / 1996 / SMP / M • Nine-teen #4 / 1996 / FOR / M • One Night In The Valley / 1996 / CA / M • Philmore Butts Lake Poontang / 1996 / SUF / M • Planet X #1 / 1996 / HW / M • Prime Choice #8 / 1996 / RAS / M • Roller Babes / 1996 / ERA / M • Strip Show / 1996 / CA / M • Summer Dreams / 1996 / TEP / M • You Assed For It / 1996 / NOT / M

MERCEDES (GERMAN) *see Star Index I*
MERCEDES (HUNGARY)
Big Babies In Budapest / 1996 / EL / M •
Thermonuclear Sex / 1996 / EL / M
MERCEDES (LYNN) *see Mercedes Lynn*
MERCEDES ALEXANDER
Bullwhip: Art Of The Single-Tail Whip /
1996 / BN / B
MERCEDES ALLEN
Cheeky Response / 1995 / RB / B •
Housemother's Discipline #6 / 1994 / RB /
B • Shaved #07 / 1995 / RB / F
MERCEDES COY (BLACK) *see Star*
Index I
MERCEDES HART *see Star Index I*
MERCEDES LYNN *(Mercedes (Lynn),*
Mercedez (Lynn))
Ugly dark haired girl with a flabby body and
masses of curly hair.
America's Dirtiest Home Videos #01 / 1991
/ VEX / M • Ass Backwards / 1991 / ME / M
• The Back Doors (Western) / 1991 / WV /
M • Bad Side Of Town / 1993 / AFD / M •
Blonde Bombshell / 1991 / CC / M • Breath-
less / 1991 / WV / M • The Butt Stops Here
/ 1991 / LV / M • Camp Beaverlake #2 /
1991 / AFV / M • Catalina Sixty-Nine / 1991
/ AR / M • Catalina: Tiger Shark / 1991 /
CDI / M • Cheeks #4: A Backstreet Affair /
1991 / CC / M • Decadent / 1991 / WV / M
• Double Penetration #5 / 1992 / WV / C •
East L.A. Law / 1991 / WV / M • Edward
Penishands #2 / 1991 / VT / M • The Erotic
Adventures Of Fanny Annie / 1991 / WV /
M • Ghost To Ghost / 1991 / CC / M • Girls
Of Sin / 1994 / PL / C • Hard To Thrill / 1991
/ CIN / M • I Want To Be Nasty / 1991 / XCV
/ M • Immorals #4: Choice Cuts / 1991 / SC
/ M • Interactive / 1994 / SC / M • The Jour-
ney: Oral Majority / 1991 / WV / M •
Leg...Ends #04 / 1991 / PRE / F •
Leg...Ends #05 / 1991 / PRE / F • A Little
Nookie / 1991 / VD / M • Lust Never Sleeps
/ 1991 / FAZ / M • Married With Hormones
#1 / 1991 / PL / M • The Midas Touch /
1991 / VT / M • Modern Love / 1991 / FAZ
/ M • Mr. Peepers Casting Couch / 1991 /
LBO / M • Put It In Gere / 1991 / CA / M •
Putting It All Behind #1 / 1991 / IN / M •
Skin Deep / 1991 / CIN / M • Sleeping
Around / 1991 / CA / M • Sole Food / 1992
/ PRE / B • The Spectacle / 1991 / IN / M •
Summer Heat / 1991 / CIN / M • Super En-
emates #1 / 1994 / PRE / C • Sweet
Cheeks (1991-Prestige) / 1991 / PRE / B •
Tailgate Party / 1990 / HO / M • Tailspin #2
/ 1991 / VT / M • Toy Box Lingerie Show /
1991 / ESP / S • Twin Cheeks #1 / 1990 /
CIN / M • Twin Cheeks #2 / 1991 / CIN / M
MERCEDES PEREZ *see Marie Sharp*
MERCEDESZ
The Voyeur #8: Live In Europe #2 / 1996 /
JLP / M
MERCEDEZ
The Black Butt Sisters Do Los Angeles /
1995 / MID / M • The Black Butt Sisters Do
New York / 1995 / MID / M
MERCEDEZ (LYNN) *see Mercedes Lynn*
MERCURY BLUE *see Star Index I*
MERCY
Maid For Bondage / 1993 / LBO / B •
Piglitz: Pudgy Porkers / 1996 / GLI / M •
Student Fetish Videos: Catfighting #08 /
1993 / PRE / B • Student Fetish Videos:
Spanking #11 / 1993 / PRE / B
MEREDITH LUCY *see Star Index I*

MERI CASH
Finger Pleasures #2 / 1995 / PL / F •
Shaved #09 / 1995 / RB / F
MERIDIAN
Adam & Eve's House Party #4 / 1996 / VC
/ M • Amazing Hardcore #1: Blow Jobs /
1997 / MET / M • Anal Party Girls / 1996 /
GV / M • Anal Rippers #1: The Beginning /
1995 / ZA / M • Anal Toy Story / 1996 / MP0
/ M • Anal Webb / 1995 / ZA / M • Anything
Goes / 1996 / OUP / M • As Easy As A
Bunch Of Cunts / 1996 / ROB / F • Ass
Lover's Special / 1996 / PE / M • Black
Hose Bag / 1996 / ROB / M • The Butt Sis-
ters Do The Twin Cities / 1996 / MID / M •
Carnal Invasions / 1996 / NIT / M • Corn
Hole Kittens / 1996 / ROB / F • Dirty Dirty
Debutantes #6 / 1996 / 4P / M • Double D
Dykes #25 / 1995 / GO / F • Head To Head
/ 1996 / VI / M • Hollywood Amateurs #30 /
1996 / MID / M • In The Fast Lane / 1995 /
LE / M • Jizz Glazed Goo Guzzlers #1 /
1996 / NIT / C • Kool Ass / 1996 / BOT / M
• Kym Wilde's On The Edge #34 / 1996 /
RB / B • Leg Show #1 / 1995 / NIT / M •
Lesbian C*Nt Whores / 1996 / ROB / F •
My First Time #2 / 1996 / NS / M • Nasty
Nymphos #12 / 1996 / ANA / M • New
Pussy Hunt #16 / 1995 / LEI / M • Next...! /
1996 / CDI / M • Prime Choice #5 / 1996 /
RAS / M • Private Desires / 1995 / LE / M •
Pumphouse Sluts / 1996 / CC / M • Pure
Anal / 1996 / MET / M • Pussyman Audi-
tions #15 / 1995 / SNA / M • Sideshow
Freaks / 1996 / ZA / M • Underground #3:
Sit On This / 1996 / SC / M • Video Virgins
#23 / 1995 / NS / M • Whitey's On The
Moon / 1996 / ROB / M • Wild Cherries /
1996 / SC / F • Young & Natural #13 / 1996
/ TV / F • Young & Natural #14 / 1996 / TV
/ F • Young & Natural #18 / 1996 / TV / C •
Young & Natural #19 / 1996 / TV / F
MERIEA DANCE *(Neira)*
Long blonde sandy hair, not too pretty, young
looking, 19 years old in 1997,
small/medium tits, shaven pussy, good tan
lines, very small areola. In **White Men**
Can't Iron she says she has a non-func-
tioning arm due to the removal of a brain
tumor but whether this is the usual horsing
around or true I don't know.
More Dirty Debutantes #62 / 1997 / SBV /
M • White Men Can't Iron On Butt Row /
1997 / ABS / M
MERILYN *see Star Index I*
MERLE LAKE
[Rear End Crashes / 197? / ... / M
MERLE MICHAELS *(Merrill Townsend,*
Barbi Svenson)
Shoulder length blonde hair, small tits, very
white skin, tight waist but a bit big on the
butt, very distinctive passable face. Barbi
Svenson is from **Sweet Surrender**.
Afternoon Delights / 1981 / CA / M • Baby-
lon Pink #1 / 1979 / COM / M • Backdoor
Girls / 1983 / VCR / C • Behind The Brown
Door / 1986 / VCR / C • Blonde In Black
Silk / 1979 / QX / M • Blue Magic / 1981 /
QX / M • Bon Appetit / 1980 / QX / M • Clas-
sic Swedish Erotica #36 / 1987 / CA / C •
Debbie Does Dallas #1 / 1978 / VC / M •
Devil In Miss Jones #2 / 1983 / VC / M •
Dirty Looks / 1982 / VC / C • Double Plea-
sure / 1985 / VCR / M • Double Your Plea-
sure / 1978 / CV / M • The Erotic World Of
Vanessa #1 / 1983 / VCR / C • The Erotic

World Of Vanessa #2 / 1984 / VCR / C •
Fascination / 1980 / QX / M • Games
Women Play #1 / 1980 / CA / M • A Girl Like
That / 1979 / CDC / M • A Girl's Best Friend
/ 1981 / QX / M • The Good Girls Of Godiva
High / 1979 / VCX / M • Inside Seka / 1980
/ VXP / M • Jack 'n' Jill #1 / 1979 / VXP / M
• Justine: A Matter Of Innocence / 1980 /
SAT / M • The Love Syndrome / 1978 / CV
/ M • The Love Tapes / 1980 / BL / M •
Love-In Arrangement / 1981 / VXP / M •
Manhattan Mistress / 1980 / VBM / M •
Mystique / 1979 / CA / M • Naughty Nurses
/ 1982 / VCR / M • The Nurses Are Coming
/ 1985 / VCR / C • October Silk / 1980 /
COM / M • Oh Those Nurses / 1982 / VC /
M • Outlaw Ladies #1 / 1981 / VC / M •
Pandora's Mirror / 1981 / CA / M • Platinum
Paradise / 1980 / COM / M • The Playgirl /
1982 / CA / M • Potpourri / 1981 / TGA / M
• Roommates / 1982 / VXP / M • Secrets Of
A Willing Wife / 1979 / VXP / M • Seka Is
Tara / 1981 / VC / M • Showgirl #03:
Vanessa Del Rio's Fantasies / 1981 / VCR
/ M • Showgirl #11: Merle Michaels' Fan-
tasies / 1983 / VCR / M • Showgirl #16:
Samantha Fox's Fantasies / 1983 / VCR /
M • Silky / 1980 / VXP / M • Sizzle / 1979 /
QX / M • Steamy Sirens / 1984 / AIR / C •
Sunny / 1979 / VC / M • Sweet Surrender /
1980 / VCX / M • The Tale Of Tiffany Lust /
1981 / CA / M • That Lucky Stiff / 1979 / QX
/ M • That's Porno / 1979 / CV / C • This
Lady Is A Tramp / 1980 / CV / M • The
Tiffany Minx / 1981 / SAT / M • Velvet High
/ 1980 / VC / M • Wild & Wicked #2 / 1977
/ ADU / C • Young, Wild And Wonderful /
1980 / VCX / M • [Vanessa's Dirty Deeds /
19?? / SVE / M
MERLINA FROELICH
Streets Of New York #02 / 1994 / PL / M
MERRI
Blue Vanities #508 / 1992 / FFL / M
MERRI EVE
Blue Vanities #548 / 1994 / FFL / M
MERRICK FLINT
Centerfold Celebrities #1 / 1982 / VC / M
MERRICK MATHEWS *see Star Index I*
MERRIE HOLIDAY *see Mary Stuart*
MERRIE WOLFSON
Resurrection Of Eve / 1973 / MIT / M
MERRILL TOWNSEND *see Merle*
Michaels
MERRY SUN *see Star Index I*
MERRY WIDOW *see Star Index I*
MESCHEL
Amateur Lesbians #09: Meschel / 1991 /
GO / F • Interview: Bun Busters / 1995 / LV
/ M • Wicked / 1991 / XCI / M
METRO
New Faces, Hot Bodies #05 / 1992 / STP /
M
MEVIA MONTOYA
SM TV #1 / 1995 / FC / G
MEYIA *see Star Index I*
MHYSTIE BLACKMORE
Ginger (1984-Vivid) / 1984 / VI / M
MIA
Black Snatch #2 / 1996 / DFI / F • Blue
Vanities #520 / 1993 / FFL / M • Hot Body
Video Magazine: Brunette Power / 1994 /
CG / F • The Statesman's Wife / 1996 / PAL
/ M • Stilettos And Spikes / 1991 / JBV / S
MIA (BLACK)
Black Cheerleader Search #10 / 1997 / IVC
/ M • European Sex TV / 1996 / EL / M •

More Dirty Debutantes #63 / 1997 / SBV / M

MIA CICCERO
Canadian Beaver Hunt #2 / 1996 / PL / M • Carnal Invasions / 1996 / NIT / M • Daydreams, Nightdreams / 1996 / VC / M • Essence / 1996 / SO / M • Jizz Glazed Goo Guzzlers #2 / 1996 / NIT / C • Macin' #2: Macadocious / 1996 / SMP / M • Nasty Nymphos #13 / 1996 / ANA / M • Profiles #06: Super Model Orgy / 1996 / XPR / M • Pussyclips #09 / 1995 / SNA / M • Shaving Mr. One Eye / 1996 / FC / M • Snake Pit / 1996 / DWO / M • Soap Opera Sluts / 1996 / AFI / M • Sodomania #21: Degenerate Lifestyles! / 1997 / EL / M • Sweet Revenge / 1996 / WAV / M • A Tall Tail / 1996 / FC / M • Video Virgins #28 / 1996 / NS / M

MIA LEE
The Whips & Chains Affair / 1994 / HOM / B

MIA MATZ
A Peek Over The Wall / 1995 / STM / G

MIA POWERS *(Mia Sterling, Stacy (Mia Powers))*
Black haired girl with very pretty face, overbite, small tits and a nice personality.
Blackman & Anal Woman #1 / 1990 / PL / M • Blackman & Anal Woman #2 / 1990 / PL / M • Bush League #1 / 1990 / CC / M • Deep In The Bush / 1990 / KIS / M • Dirty Debutantes / 1990 / 4P / M • Earthquake Girls / 1990 / CC / M • The Girls' Club / 1990 / VC / F • Hot Cargo / 1990 / MID / M • Juicy Lips / 1991 / PL / F • Juicy Lucy / 1990 / VC / M • The Luscious Baker Girls / 1990 / VD / M • More Dirty Debutantes / 1990 / PRI / M • More Dirty Debutantes #03 / 1990 / 4P / M • More Dirty Debutantes #08 / 1991 / 4P / M • The New Barbarians #1 / 1990 / VC / M • The New Barbarians #2 / 1990 / VC / M • No Man's Land #04 / 1990 / VT / F • Passionate Lips / 1990 / OD / M • Public Enemy / 1990 / VIP / M • Sea Of Love / 1990 / CIN / M • Sea Of Lust / 1990 / FAN / M • Sex & Other Games / 1990 / CIN / M • The Smart Aleck / 1990 / PM / M • Talk Dirty To Me #07 / 1990 / DR / M • The Whole Diamond / 1990 / EVN / M

MIA SERENE *(Mia Sonata)*
Hispanic, 18 years old in 1994, de-virginized at 16, pretty, long dark blonde hair, tight waist, good skin, tight little butt, medium natural tits with large areola hung a little low on her chest, nice smile and seemingly a good sense of humor.
Lovin' Spoonfuls #3 / 1995 / 4P / C • Lovin' Spoonfuls #5 / 1996 / 4P / C • More Dirty Debutantes #31 / 1994 / 4P / M • More Dirty Debutantes #33 / 1994 / 4P / M • New Ends #07 / 1994 / 4P / M

MIA SMILES
More Dirty Debutantes #58 / 1996 / 4P / M • More Dirty Debutantes #59 / 1996 / SBV / M • More Dirty Debutantes #60 / 1997 / SBV / M • More Dirty Debutantes #61 / 1997 / SBV / M

MIA SONATA *see* **Mia Serene**

MIA SOPHIA
Honey Drippers / 1992 / ROB / F • Kittens & Vamps #1 / 1993 / ROB / F

MIA STERLING *see* **Mia Powers**

MIANDA JOY *see Star Index I*

MIAYAH
African Angels #2 / 1996 / NIT / M • Black Cheerleader Search #03 / 1996 / ROB / M • Black Juice Bombs / 1996 / NIT / C • Macin' #1 / 1996 / SMP / M

MIBI NEST
Tied, Trained And Transformed / 19?? / BIZ / B

MIC FREEZE *see Star Index I*

MICH IGAN *(Scott St James, Scott Preston)*
Scott Preston is from **Smoke Screen**.
Amateur Orgies #07 / 1992 / AFI / M • Amateur Orgies #08 / 1992 / AFI / M • Amateur Orgies #10 / 1992 / AFI / M • Amateur Orgies #11 / 1992 / AFI / M • Assuming The Position / 1989 / V99 / M • Belle Of The Ball / 1989 / V99 / M • Biff Malibu's Totally Nasty Home Videos #14 / 1992 / ANA / M • Bimbonese 101 / 1993 / PL / M • Breast Side Story / 1990 / LE / M • Covergirl / 1994 / WP / M • Dallas Does Debbie / 1992 / PL / M • Deep Throat #4 / 1990 / AR / M • Depraved / 1990 / IN / M • Dream Dates / 1990 / V99 / M • Eclipse / 1993 / SC / M • Fashion Fantasies / 1986 / VC / M • Fuck U: Girls Of The Packed-10 / 1995 / ZA / M • Gangbang Girl #07 / 1992 / ANA / M • Gangbang Girl #08 / 1992 / ANA / M • Giving It To Barbii / 1990 / TOR / M • Heavenly Hyapatia / 1990 / VI / M • Hollywood Swingers #04 / 1992 / LBO / M • Hypersexuals / 1984 / VC / M • I Do #1 / 1989 / VI / M • Insatiable Nurses / 1992 / VIM / M • KBBS: Weekend With Alicia Rio & Sheila Stone / 1992 / KBB / M • No Motive / 1994 / MID / M • Oral Support / 1989 / V99 / M • Private Film #12 / 1994 / OD / M • Private Video Magazine #25 / 1995 / OD / M • Raising Kane / 1992 / FD / M • Realities #1 / 1991 / ZA / M • Rears In Windows / 1993 / FH / M • Riding Miss Daisy / 1990 / VEX / M • Smoke Screen / 1990 / CA / M • Soda Jerk / 1992 / ZA / M • Sudden Urge / 1990 / IN / M • Swedish Erotica Featurettes #2 / 1989 / CA / M • Swingers Ink / 1990 / VC / M • Tailiens #2 / 1992 / FD / M • Tailiens #3 / 1992 / FD / M • Tattle Tales / 1989 / SE / M • Uncle Roy's Amateur Home Video #13 / 1992 / VIM / M • Untamed Passion / 1991 / VEX / M • Willie Wanker And The Fun Factory / 1994 / FD / M • Wives Of The Rich And Famous / 1989 / V99 / M • The World's Biggest Gang Bang #1 / 1995 / FPI / M

MICHAEL
Breast Wishes #07 / 1992 / LBO / M • Breast Worx #24 / 1992 / LBO / M • Deep Throat Girls #03 / 1994 / GO / M • Dick & Jane Big Breast Adventure / 1993 / AVI / M • Domino's Dungeon / 1993 / COC / B • Journey Into Servitude: The Pleasures Of Ultimate Humil... / 1992 / BIZ / B • On The Prowl #2 / 1991 / SC / M • Prague By Night #1 / 1996 / EA / M • Satisfaction Guaranteed / 1972 / AXV / M • Striptease #2 / 1995 / PL / M • VGA: Spanks-A-Lot / 1993 / VGA / B

MICHAEL ANDERSON
Dog Walker / 1994 / EA / M

MICHAEL ANTHONY *see Star Index I*

MICHAEL ASHLEY
Bi Anonymous / 1993 / BIL / G • Charade / 1993 / HSV / G • The Crying Flame / 1993 / HSV / G • The Prize Package / 1993 / HSV / G • Stick Pussy / 1992 / HSV / G • Surprise Package / 1993 / HSV / G • Wings Of Change / 1993 / HSV / G

MICHAEL BAIE *see Star Index I*

MICHAEL BEAN
Innocence Found / 1991 / PAL / G

MICHAEL BLACK
Beyond Reality #3: Stand Erect! / 1996 / EXQ / M • Eighteen #2 / 1996 / SC / M • The Happy Office / 1996 / NIT / M • Pussyman #15: The Bone Voyage Bash / 1997 / SNA / M • Up Your Ass #3 / 1996 / ANA / M

MICHAEL BLANDON *see Star Index I*

MICHAEL BLODGETT *(Mike Blodgett)*
Was married to or was the lover of Patti Davis (Reagan's daughter) at one time. Rumor has it that this is the same as Mike Ranger.
Beyond The Valley Of The Dolls / 1970 / CBS / S • The Carey Treatment / 1972 / ... / S • There Was A Crooked Man / 1970 / WAR / S • The Trip / 1967 / VES / S • The Ultimate Thrill / 1974 / VIG / S • The Velvet Vampire / 1971 / EHE / S • [Catalina Caper / 1968 / ... / S

MICHAEL BRUCE
Boyfriend of Sharon Kane. Died of testicular cancer.
Babylon Blue / 1983 / VXP / M • Blue Jeans / 1982 / VXP / M • Brooke Does College / 1984 / VC / M • Daddy's Little Girls / 1983 / CA / M • Devil In Miss Jones #2 / 1983 / VC / M • Firestorm #1 / 1984 / COM / M • Hot Dreams / 1983 / CA / M • Hypersexuals / 1984 / VC / M • In Love / 1983 / VC / M • Midnight Heat / 1982 / VC / M • Nasty Girls (1983-VCX) / 1983 / VCX / M • Night Hunger / 1983 / AVC / M • The Pink Ladies / 1980 / VC / M • Private School Girls / 1983 / CA / M • Sexcapades / 1983 / VC / M • Slit Skirts / 1983 / VXP / M • That's Outrageous / 1983 / CA / M • True Legends Of Adult Cinema: The Cult Superstars / 1993 / VC / C • Yes, My Lady / 1984 / VHL / B

MICHAEL CALVENCIA *see Star Index I*

MICHAEL CATTORE *see* **Michael Gaunt**

MICHAEL CHRISTOPHER *see Star Index I*

MICHAEL COLA
Cafe Flesh / 1982 / VC / M

MICHAEL D'AMOURS
Lost In Vegas / 1996 / AWV / G

MICHAEL DALY *see Star Index I*

MICHAEL DANZE
Latex #1 / 1994 / VC / M

MICHAEL DATTORRE *see* **Michael Gaunt**

MICHAEL DAYTON *see* **Michael Gaunt**

MICHAEL DELONG *(Mike DeLong)*
Is this the same as Max DeLong?
Anal Intruder #01 / 1986 / CC / M • Angela In Wonderland / 1986 / VD / M • Black Flesh / 1986 / LA / M • Blow By Blow / 1984 / QX / M • Moans & Groans / 1987 / 4P / M • Oversexed / 1986 / VXP / M • Seven Minutes In Heaven / 1986 / VXP / M • Sweet Spread / 1986 / VXP / M

MICHAEL DESHANE
Anal Nurses / 1996 / LBO / M • The Bottom Dweller 33 1/3 / 1995 / EL / M

MICHAEL DEVON
Body Talk / 1982 / VCX / M

MICHAEL DUSHANE *see* **Santino Lee**

MICHAEL DUSK *see Star Index I*

MICHAEL FINDLAY *(Julian Marsh, Robert West, Robert Wuesterwurst)*
Sexploitation film maker of the late sixties/early seventies. Married to and worked with another director, Roberta Findlay. Decapitated by a helicopter on top of the Pan-Am building in NYC in 1974.

Bacchanale / 1972 / ALP / M • Bucky Beaver's XXX Dragon Art Theatre Double Feature #07 / 1996 / SOW / M • The Curse Of Her Flesh / 1967 / SOW / S • The Kiss Of Her Flesh / 1968 / SOW / S • Mnasidika / 1969 / ALP / S • Take Me Naked / 1966 / SOW / S • A Thousand Pleasures / 1968 / SOW / S • The Touch Of Her Flesh / 1967 / SOW / S • The Ultimate Degenerate / 1969 / SOW / S • Virgins In Heat / 1976 / SOW / M

MICHAEL GABINCERA
Reel People #03 / 1989 / PP / M

MICHAEL GANT
Twist Of Fate / 1996 / WP / M

MICHAEL GARRETT
The Stewardesses / 1969 / SOW / S • The Stewardesses / 1981 / CA / M

MICHAEL GAUNT *(Michael Grant, Mike Reed (Gaunt), Michael Dayton, Michael Dattorre, Michael Martin, Michael Cattore)*
Michael Grant is from **A Woman's Torment**. Michael Dayton in **Sweet Surrender**. Michael Dattorre from **Teenage Pajama Party**. Michael Martin is from **Blue Ecstasy**. Michael Cattore is from **Intrusion**.
69th Street Vice / 1984 / VC / M • Alexandra / 1984 / VC / M • American Babylon / 1985 / PV / M • Angela In Wonderland / 1986 / VD / M • Babylon Blue / 1983 / VXP / M • Bang Bang You Got It / 1975 / VXP / M • Beach House / 1981 / CA / C • Blow Dry / 1977 / SVE / M • Blue Ecstasy / 1980 / CA / M • The Budding Of Brie / 1980 / TVX / M • Candy Stripers #2 / 1985 / AR / M • Chocolate Bon-Bons / 1985 / PL / M • Come With Me, My Love / 1976 / PVX / M • Corruption / 1983 / VC / M • Cravings / 1987 / VC / M • Deep Inside Annie Sprinkle / 1981 / VXP / M • Delicious / 1981 / VXP / M • Dirty Looks / 1982 / VC / C • Draws / 1976 / VIG / S • Fashion Fantasies / 1986 / VC / M • Firestorm #2: The Angel Blade / 1986 / COM / M • Firestorm #3 / 1986 / COM / M • First Time At Cherry High / 1984 / VC / M • Flasher / 1986 / VD / M • From Holly With Love / 1977 / CA / M • The Fur Trap / 1973 / AVC / M • Hidden Fantasies / 1986 / VD / M • Honeymoon Haven / 1977 / QX / M • Hot Lips / 1984 / VC / M • Intrusion / 1975 / CV / M • Joint Venture / 1977 / ELV / M • Lenny's Comeback / cr78 / CIN / M • Maraschino Cherry / 1978 / QX / M • Naughty Nurses / 1982 / VCR / M • The Nite Bird / 1978 / BL / M • Odyssey / 1977 / VC / M • Only The Very Best On Film / 1992 / VC / C • The Pink Ladies / 1980 / VC / M • Shauna: Every Man's Fantasy / 1985 / CA / C • Succulent / 1983 / VXP / M • Sweet Surrender / 1980 / VCX / M • Teenage Pajama Party / 1977 / VC / M • Tigresses...And Other Man-Eaters / 1979 / VXP / M • Ultrasex / 1983 / VC / M • Wet Shots (Vcr) / 1983 / VCR / C • White Hot / 1984 / VXP / M • A Woman's Torment / 1977 / VC / M • [Best Of Annette Haven / 1986 / ... / C

MICHAEL GRANT *see* **Michael Gaunt**
MICHAEL GRAY *see* **Star Index I**
MICHAEL HARRIS
Ole / 1971 / KIT / M

MICHAEL HART
Dirty & Kinky Mature Women #10 / 1996 / C69 / M

MICHAEL HUGHES *see* **Justin Case**

MICHAEL HUNT
55 And Still Bangin' / 1995 / HW / M
MICHAEL HURT
Airotica / 1996 / SC / M • Brunette Roulette / 1996 / LE / M • The Butt Sisters Do Washington D.C. / 1995 / MID / M • Cloud 900 / 1996 / EYE / M • Dirty Diner #3 / 1996 / SC / M • Fellatio Fanatics / 1996 / NIT / M • Friendly Fire / 1996 / EDP / M • The Letter X #2 / 1996 / MID / M • My First Time #7 / 1996 / NS / M • Pick Up Lines #07 / 1996 / OD / M • Rebel Without A Condom / 1996 / ERA / M • She's No Angel / 1996 / ERA / S • Strip Show / 1996 / CA / M • Venom #7 / 1996 / VD / M

MICHAEL J. COX *(Ted Craig, Mikey (J. Cox), Troy (Michael J Cox))*
Young male who bears some resemblence to the similarly named mainstream actor. In 1994 he was 24 years old. In 1995 he acquired a tattoo on his right belly.
100% Amateur #27: / 1996 / OD / M • Adam & Eve's House Party #1 / 1995 / VC / M • Adam & Eve's House Party #2: Bachelor Party / 1996 / VC / M • The Adventures Of Peeping Tom #4 / 1997 / OD / M • Adventures Of The DP Boys: The Golden Girls / 1995 / HW / M • All The President's Women / 1994 / LV / M • Amateur Orgies #26 / 1993 / AFI / M • Amateur Orgies #27 / 1993 / AFI / M • Amateur Orgies #28 / 1993 / AFI / M • Amateur Orgies #31 / 1993 / AFI / M • Amateur Orgies #32 / 1993 / AFI / M • Amateur Orgies #33 / 1993 / AFI / M • Amateur Orgies #35 / 1993 / AFI / M • Amateur Orgies #36 / 1993 / AFI / M • Anal Academy / 1996 / ZA / M • Anal Alley Cat / 1996 / KWP / M • Anal Angel / 1994 / EX / M • Anal Auditions / 1995 / VMX / M • Anal Brat / 1993 / FL / M • Anal Fugitive / 1995 / PEP / M • Anal Inquisition / 1996 / ZA / M • Anal Invader / 1995 / PEP / M • Anal Jeopardy / 1996 / ZA / M • Anal Sex Freaks / 1996 / ZA / M • Anal Therapy #3 / 1994 / FD / M • Anal Therapy #4 / 1996 / FD / M • Anal Virgins Of America #04 / 1993 / FOR / M • Anal Vision #24 / 1994 / LBO / M • Anal-Holics / 1993 / AFV / M • Ass Busters / 1995 / VMX / C • Ass Kisser: A Love Story / 1995 / PEP / M • Ass Poppers / 1995 / VMX / M • Baby Doll / 1994 / SC / M • The Backdoor Bradys / 1995 / PL / M • The Backway Inn #5 / 1993 / FD / M • Bad Habits / 1993 / VC / M • Barby's On Butt Row / 1996 / ABS / M • Beach Bum Amateur's #36 / 1993 / MID / M • Behind The Scenes / 1996 / GO / M • Bel Air Babes / 1996 / SUF / M • Big Bust Babes #16 / 1993 / AFI / M • Big Bust Babes #17 / 1993 / AFI / M • Big Bust Bangers #2 / 1994 / AMP / M • Big Murray's New-Cummers #24: / 1993 / FD / M • Big Murray's New-Cummers #26: Real Tits / 1994 / FD / M • Black Cheerleader Search #01 / 1996 / ROB / M • Black Cheerleader Search #10 / 1997 / IVC / M • Boudoir Babe / 1996 / VMX / M • The Breast Files #3 / 1994 / AVI / M • British Babe Hunt / 1996 / VC / M • Buffy's New Boobs / 1996 / CIN / M • Bun Busters #21 / 1994 / LBO / M • The Burma Road #1 / 1994 / LBO / C • The Burma Road #2 / 1994 / LBO / C • Butt Alley / 1995 / VMX / M • Butt Bangers Ball / 1994 / FPI / M • Butt Row Unplugged / 1996 / ABS / M • The Butt Sisters Do New Orleans / 1995 / MID / M • The Butt Sisters Do Philadelphia / 1995 / MID / M • The Butt

Sisters Do Washington D.C. / 1995 / MID / M • Buttman In The Crack / 1996 / EA / M • Buttman's Bubble Butt Babes / 1996 / EA / M • Candy's Custom Car Wash / 1995 / FC / M • Captain Bob's Lust Boat #2 / 1993 / FCP / M • Centerfold Celebrities '94 #1 / 1994 / SFP / M • Centerfold Celebrities '94 #2 / 1994 / SFP / M • Cheatin' / 1994 / FD / M • Cluster Fuck #01 / 1993 / MAX / M • The Come On / 1995 / EX / M • Comeback / 1995 / VI / M • Cousin Bubba Country Corn Porn #01 / 1994 / VIM / M • Cuntz #4 / 1994 / RTP / M • Deep Inside Crystal Wilder / 1995 / VC / C • Deliciously Teri / 1993 / IF / M • Delinquents On Butt Row / 1996 / EA / M • The Devil In Miss Jones #5: The Inferno / 1994 / VC / M • Dick & Jane Go To Northridge / 1994 / AVI / M • Dirty Doc's Housecalls #02 / 1993 / LV / M • The Doll House / 1995 / CV / M • Double D Housewives / 1994 / PV / M • Double D Nurses / 1994 / PV / M • Drop Sex: Wipe The Floor / 1997 / JLP / M • Dun-Hur #1 / 1994 / SC / M • Every Woman Has A Fantasy #3 / 1995 / VC / M • The Fabulous 50's Girls #1 / 1994 / EMC / M • The Fantasy Booth / 1993 / ONA / M • Fashion Sluts #7 / 1996 / ABS / M • Final Obsession / 1996 / LE / M • Flesh / 1996 / EA / M • Frathouse Sexcapades / 1993 / SFP / M • From A Whisper To A Scream / 1993 / GO / M • The Fucking Elvises / 1994 / GLI / M • Full Throttle Girls: Boredom Pulled The Trigger / 1993 / VIM / M • Gang Bang Bitches #04 / 1995 / PP / M • Gang Bang Bitches #07 / 1995 / PP / M • Gang Bang Bitches #10 / 1995 / PP / M • Gang Bang Diaries #1 / 1993 / SFP / M • Gangbang Girl #16 / 1995 / ANA / M • Gangbang In The Fat Lane / 1996 / FC / M • Gazongo / 1995 / PEP / M • A Girl's Affair #04 / 1994 / FD / F • Girls II Women / 1996 / AVI / M • Gold Coast / 1996 / FD / M • Goldenbush / 1996 / AVI / M • Gun Runner / 1996 / CIN / M • Gypsy Queen / 1995 / CC / M • Hard Core Beginners #01 / 1995 / LEI / M • Hard Core Beginners #02 / 1995 / LEI / M • Hard Core Beginners #03 / 1995 / LEI / M • Hard Core Beginners #04 / 1995 / LEI / M • Hard Core Beginners #06 / 1995 / LEI / M • Hard Core Beginners #09 / 1995 / LEI / M • Hard Core Beginners #12 / 1995 / LEI / M • Hard-On Copy / 1994 / WV / M • Heatseekers / 1996 / PE / M • Hedonism #01 / 1993 / FH / M • Hell Hole / 1996 / ZA / M • Hidden Camera #09 / 1993 / JMP / M • High Heel Harlots #03 / 1994 / SFP / M • Hispanic Orgies #02 / 1993 / GO / M • Hollywood Boulevard / 1995 / CV / M • Hollywood Hillbillies / 1996 / LE / M • The Hollywood Starlet Search / 1995 / SC / M • Hootermania / 1994 / VC / M • The Horny Hiker / 1995 / LE / M • House Of Leather / 1995 / GO / M • In The Crack / 1995 / VMX / M • Incantation / 1996 / FC / M • Induced Pleasure / 1995 / ERA / M • Interracial 247 / 1995 / CC / M • Introducing Alexis / 1996 / VI / M • Jenteal Loves Rocco / 1996 / VI / M • Jiggly Queens #3 / 1996 / LE / M • The Knocker Room / 1993 / GO / M • Leather Unleashed / 1995 / GO / M • Leg Show #1 / 1995 / NIT / M • Leg Show #2 / 1996 / NIT / M • Legal Briefs / 1996 / EX / M • Lethal Affairs / 1996 / VI / M • Lisa / 1997 / SC / M • Living On The Edge / 1997 / DWO / M • Lust / 1993 / FH / M • M Series #20 / 1994 / LBO / M •

Masque / 1995 / VC / M • Mickey Ray's Sex Search #02: Tight Spots / 1994 / WIV / M • Milli Vanilla / 1994 / TP / M • Mistress Of The Mansion / 1994 / CV / M • Mixed-Up Marriage / 1995 / CV / M • My Desire / 1996 / NIT / M • My First Time #1 / 1995 / NS / M • My First Time #2 / 1996 / NS / M • My First Time #3 / 1996 / NS / M • My First Time #4 / 1996 / NS / M • My First Time #5 / 1996 / NS / M • My First Time #7 / 1996 / NS / M • Nasty Newcummers #02 / 1993 / MET / M • Nasty Newcummers #04 / 1994 / MET / M • Nasty Newcummers #06 / 1995 / MET / M • Naughty / 1996 / LV / M • The New Ass Masters #08 / 1996 / LEI / C • The New Babysitter / 1995 / GO / M • New Girls In Town #3 / 1993 / CC / M • New Girls In Town #4 / 1993 / CC / M • New Girls In Town #5 / 1994 / CC / M • New Pussy Hunt #18 / 1995 / LEI / C • Odyssey 30 Min: #332: / 1993 / OD / M • Odyssey Triple Play #70: Three By Threeway / 1994 / OD / M • Odyssey Triple Play #94: Triple Decker Sex Sandwich / 1995 / OD / M • Open Lips / 1994 / WV / M • Oral Majority #12 / 1994 / WV / C • Pajama Party X #2 / 1994 / VC / M • Passions Of Sin / 1996 / NIT / M • The Pawn Shop / 1996 / MID / M • Pearl Of The Orient / 1995 / IN / M • Pick Up Lines #03 / 1995 / 4P / M • Pick Up Lines #09 / 1996 / OD / M • Positions Wanted: Experienced Only / 1993 / PV / M • Primal Desires / 1993 / EX / M • Private Audition / 1995 / EVN / M • Private Desires / 1995 / LE / M • Private Film #12 / 1994 / OD / M • Private Film #14 / 1994 / OD / M • Private Gold #16: Summer Wind / 1997 / OD / M • Raw Footage / 1996 / VC / M • Rebel Without A Condom / 1996 / ERA / M • Ride The Pink Lady / 1993 / WV / M • Royal Ass Force / 1996 / VC / M • Saturday Night Porn #2 / 1993 / AFV / M • Scotty's X-Rated Adventure / 1996 / WP / M • Senior Stimulation / 1996 / CC / M • Sensations #2 / 1996 / SC / M • Sensual Spirits / 1995 / LE / M • Sex Academy #1 / 1993 / ONA / M • Sex Freaks / 1995 / EA / M • Sex In Dangerous Places / 1994 / OD / M • Sex In Strange Places: The Sphincter Zone / 1994 / FPI / M • Sexhibition #1 / 1996 / SUF / M • Sexual Trilogy #03 / 1994 / SFP / M • She's No Angel / 1996 / ERA / S • Shock / 1995 / LE / M • The Shocking Truth #2 / 1996 / DWO / M • Sleaze Please!—November Edition / 1994 / FH / M • Small Top Bitches / 1996 / AVI / M • Snake Pit / 1996 / DWO / M • So I Married A Lesbian / 9993 / WV / M • Sodomania #21: Degenerate Lifestyles! / 1997 / EL / M • Star Girl / 1996 / ERA / M • Starbangers #08 / 1996 / FPI / M • Steady As She Blows / 1993 / LV / M • Stewardesses Behind Bars / 1994 / HW / M • Stories Of Seduction / 1996 / MID / M • Surprise!!! / 1994 / VI / M • Sweet As Honey / 1996 / NIT / M • Swing Rave / 1993 / EVN / M • Swinging Couples #01 / 1993 / GO / M • Swinging Couples #02 / 1993 / GO / M • Swinging Couples #03 / 1994 / GO / M • Swinging Couples #04 / 1994 / GO / M • Taboo #15 / 1995 / IN / M • Tail Taggers #109 / 1993 / WV / M • Tails From The Crack / 1995 / HW / M • Tailz From Da Hood #4 / 1996 / AVI / M • Three Hearts / 1995 / CC / M • Thunder Boobs / 1995 / BTO / M • Tight Fit #06 / 1994 / GO / M • The Tigress / 1995 / VIM / M • Timepiece /

1994 / CV / M • Totally Ona: The Best Of Ona Zee / 1996 / ONA / C • Transformation / 1996 / XCI / M • Tripper Stripper / 1995 / VMX / M • Turnabout / 1996 / CTP / M • The Ultimate Pleasure / 1995 / LEI / M • Up The Ying Yang #2 / 1995 / CC / M • Upbeat Love #2 / 1995 / CV / M • Vagabonds / 1996 / ERA / M • Valley Cooze / 1996 / SC / M • Video Virgins #03 / 1993 / NS / M • Video Virgins #04 / 1993 / NS / M • Video Virgins #05 / 1993 / NS / M • Video Virgins #07 / 1993 / NS / M • Video Virgins #09 / 1993 / NS / M • Video Virgins #15 / 1994 / NS / M • Video Virgins #18 / 1994 / NS / M • Video Virgins #19 / 1994 / NS / M • Video Virgins #21 / 1995 / NS / M • Video Virgins #23 / 1995 / NS / M • Video Virgins #33 / 1996 / NS / M • View Point / 1995 / VI / M • Virgins / 1995 / ERA / M • Vivid Raw #3: Double Header / 1996 / VI / M • The Voyeur #6 / 1996 / EA / M • Wanted / 1995 / DR / M • Wedding Vows / 1994 / ZA / M • Wild Orgies #01 / 1994 / AFI / M • Wild Orgies #10 / 1994 / AFI / M

MICHAEL JACOT *see Star Index I*

MICHAEL JAMES
Little Girls Blue #2 / 1983 / VCX / M • Transsexual Prostitutes #1 / 1996 / DFI / G

MICHAEL JEFFRIES
Beverly Hills Heat / 1985 / VEP / M • The Ladies In Lace Party / 1985 / MAP / M • Party Girls / 1988 / MAP / M • Soaking Wet / 1985 / CV / M

MICHAEL JOHN
Long Play / 1995 / 3XP / G

MICHAEL KEARNS
L.A. Tool & Die / 1979 / TMX / G

MICHAEL KEYE
4 Of A Kind / 1995 / BON / B • Bev's Bondage Torment / 1994 / BON / B • Bondage Fantasy #1 / 1995 / BON / B • Bondage Fantasy #2 / 1995 / BON / B • Bondage Fantasy #3 / 1995 / BON / B • Bondage Is Our Pleasure / 1996 / BON / B • Bound & Shaved / 1994 / BON / B • Bound Brats / 1994 / BON / B • The Boy Toy / 1995 / BON / B • Director Dilemma #1 / 1995 / BON / B • Director Dilemma #2 / 1995 / BON / B • Dressed For Bondage / 1993 / BON / B • Fantasy Abduction / 1997 / BON / B • Full House / 1995 / BON / B • Greta Carlson Sessions #1 / 1994 / BON / B • Greta Carlson Sessions #4 / 1995 / BON / B • Just Deserts / 1994 / BON / B • Katrina's Awakening #3 / 1994 / BON / B • Leather Obsession / 1996 / BON / B • Lessons From The Mistress / 1994 / BON / B • The Luxury Of Servitude / 1994 / BON / B • Real People Real Bondage #2 / 1996 / BON / C • Spank & Spank Again / 1995 / BON / B • Spankology 101a / 1994 / BON / B • Sparxx Fly / 1995 / B&D / B • Threshold Of Fear / 1993 / BON / B • Transformed / 1995 / BON / B • The XYZ Rope & Tape Company / 1993 / BON / B • Your Cheatin' Butt / 1996 / BON / B

MICHAEL KNIGHT
Adam & Eve's House Party #1 / 1995 / VC / M • Ball In The Family / 1988 / VWA / M • Bedroom Thighs / 1986 / VXP / M • The Big Pink / 1989 / VWA / M • Blow By Blow / 1984 / QX / M • Brooke Does College / 1984 / VC / M • Can't Get Enough / 1985 / CA / M • Coming On America / 1989 / VWA / M • Deep Throat #2 / 1986 / AR / M • Dirty Blonde / 1984 / VXP / M • Dirty Girls / 1984

/ MIT / M • Eaten Alive / 1985 / VXP / M • The Erotic Adventures Of Bedman And Throbbin / 1989 / VWA / M • The Erotic Adventures Of Chi Chi Chan / 1988 / VWA / M • Femme / 1984 / VC / M • Firebox / 1986 / VXP / M • Frankenhunter, Queen Of The Porno Zombies / 1989 / GMI / M • Fresh! / 1987 / VXP / M • Glitter / 1983 / CA / M • Harem Girls / 1986 / SE / M • Head Trip / 1995 / VC / M • Heather / 1989 / VWA / M • Heather Hunter On Fire / 1988 / VWA / M • Heather Hunter's Bedtime Stories / 1991 / GLE / C • Heaven's Touch / 1983 / CA / M • The Heist / 1996 / WAV / M • Hot Stuff / 1984 / VXP / M • The Hot Tip / 1986 / VXP / M • Hot Wire / 1985 / VXP / M • Hypersexuals / 1984 / VC / M • I Ream A Jeannie / 1990 / GLE / M • In Love / 1983 / VC / M • Inside Little Oral Annie / 1984 / VXP / M • Lady Lust / 1984 / CA / M • Luscious / 1980 / VXP / M • The Naked Bun / 1989 / VWA / M • Never Sleep Alone / 1984 / CA / M • Oral Addiction / 1995 / VI / M • Oversexed / 1986 / VXP / M • Parted Lips / 1986 / QX / M • Party House / 1995 / WAV / M • Passions / 1985 / MIT / M • Phone Sex Fantasies / 1984 / QX / M • Piggies / 1984 / VC / M • Pink Baroness / 1988 / VWA / M • Pink Clam / 1986 / RLV / M • Playpen / 1987 / VC / M • Pleasure Channel / 1984 / VC / M • The Pleasure Chest / 1988 / VWA / M • Porked / 1986 / VXP / M • Private School Girls / 1983 / CA / M • Puss 'n' Boots / 1982 / VXP / M • Pussyman #13: Lips / 1996 / SNA / M • Seven Minutes In Heaven / 1986 / VXP / M • Sex Drive / 1984 / VXP / M • Sex Styles Of The Rich & Famous / 1986 / VXP / M • Shacking Up / 1985 / VXP / M • Shauna: Every Man's Fantasy / 1985 / CA / C • The Show / 1995 / VI / M • Slammer Girls / 1987 / LIV / S • Stray Cats / 1985 / VXP / M • Sucker / 1988 / VWA / M • Suzie Creamcheese / 1988 / VWA / M • Sweet Spread / 1986 / VXP / M • A Taste Of Pink / 1985 / VXP / M • Teaser / 1986 / RLV / M • Tight Delight / 1985 / VXP / M • Twice As Nice / 1989 / VWA / M • The Voyeur / 1985 / VC / M • When She Was Bad / 1983 / CA / M

MICHAEL LAWN
A Girl Like That / 1979 / CDC / M

MICHAEL LAWRENCE
Behind Closed Doors / 1969 / SOW / S • A Taste Of Flesh / 1967 / SOW / S • White Hot / 1984 / VXP / M

MICHAEL LEBOEUF
Indiana Joan In The Black Hole Of Mammoo / 1984 / VC / M

MICHAEL LEE
ABA: Double Feature #5 / 1996 / ALP / M • Beyond The Senses / 1986 / AVC / M • Chuck & Di In Heat / 1986 / DR / M • The Honeymooners / 1986 / CDI / M • Hooters / 1986 / AVC / M • I Obey You / 1993 / VTF / B • Irresistible #2 / 1986 / SE / M • Night Of Submission / 1976 / BIZ / M • A Scream In The Streets / 1971 / SOW / S

MICHAEL LEMOINE
Castle Of The Creeping Flesh / 1967 / LUM / S • Chambermaid's Dream / 1986 / PS / S • Frustration / 1970 / ... / S • Je Suis Une Nymphomane / 1970 / ... / S • Kiss Me, Monster / 1967 / LUM / S • Marianne Bouquet / 1979 / VCX / M • Sadisterotica / 1967 / ... / S • Sin On The Beach / 1963 / SOW / S • Succubus / 1967 / ... / S

MICHAEL LOMBARDI
World Class Ass / 1995 / FC / M
MICHAEL MANN
Bi Bi Love / 1986 / LAV / G • Bi-Coastal / 1985 / LAV / G • Close Friends / 1987 / CC / G • Forbidden Fruit #2 / 1987 / MET / G • The National Transsexual / 1990 / GO / G • Parliament: Hard TV #1 / 1988 / PM / G • Passion Chain / 1987 / ZA / M • Sex Tips For Modern Women / 1987 / VXP / M • Sexpot / 1987 / VXP / M • Trisexual Encounters #01 / 1985 / PL / G
MICHAEL MANOS see Star Index I
MICHAEL MARTIN see Michael Gaunt
MICHAEL MAXWELL
Venture Into The Bizarre / cr78 / VHL / M
MICHAEL MENCH see Star Index I
MICHAEL MOORE
50 And Still Pumping! / 1994 / EMC / M • More Dirty Debutantes #31 / 1994 / 4P / M
MICHAEL MORRISON *(Milt Ingley, Milton Ingersoll, Uncle Miltie, Mike Morrison, Milt Ingersoll, Milton Englie, Chuck Morrison)*
Started in 1977 with **Tangerine**. Was 45 in 1992. Milton Ingley is the name he uses as a director.
6 To 9 Black Style / 1987 / LIM / C • All The King's Ladies / 1981 / SUP / M • Amanda By Night #1 / 1981 / CA / M • Anal Intruder #05: The Final Outrage / 1990 / CC / M • The Anals Of History #1 / 1991 / MID / M • Aunt Peg / 1980 / CV / M • The Awakening Of Emily / 1976 / CDI / M • Backstage Pass / 1994 / SC / M • The Bare-Assed Naked Gun / 1992 / MID / M • Beach Bum Amateur's #02 / 1992 / MID / M • Beauty / 1981 / VC / M • Bedlam / 1995 / WAV / M • Behind The Scenes: The Making Of The Wil & Ed Movies / 1992 / MID / M • Beyond Shame / 1980 / VEP / M • Beyond Your Wildest Dreams / 1980 / CAT / M • Black, White & Red All Over / 1984 / EXF / C • The Blonde / 1980 / VCX / M • The Blonde Next Door / 1982 / GO / M • Blow Job Blvd #1 / 1993 / SC / M • Blue Vanities #064 / 1988 / FFL / M • Blue Vanities #095 / 1988 / FFL / M • Body Candy 1980 / VIS / M • Budding Blondes / 1979 / TGA / C • Buttman Vs Buttwoman / 1992 / EL / M • Campus Capers / 1982 / VC / M • Captives / 1983 / BIZ / B • Carnal Interludes / 1995 / NOT / M • Centerspread Girls / 1982 / CA / M • Chained / cr76 / BIZ / B • Champagne For Breakfast / 1980 / SE / M • Cheryl Hanson: Cover Girl / 1981 / SE / M • Coed Fever / 1980 / CA / M • Confessions Of A Nymph / 1985 / VCR / M • Corruption / 1983 / VC / M • Cream / 1993 / SC / M • Daisy May / 1979 / VC / M • Deep Rub / 1979 / VC / M • Diamond Collection #39 / 1983 / CDI / M • The Doorman Always Comes Twice / cr84 / AIR / C • Double Pleasure / 1985 / VCR / M • Ebony Erotica #01: Black Narcissys / 1993 / GO / M • Ebony Erotica #02: Midnight Madness / 1993 / GO / M • Erotic Angel / 1994 / ERA / M • The Erotic World Of Candy Shields / 1984 / VCR / C • The Erotic World Of Crystal Lake (#4) / 1984 / VCR / C • The Erotic World Of Rene Summers / 1984 / VCR / C • The Erotic World Of Seka / 1983 / VCR / C • Expose Me Now / 1982 / CV / M • Fantasy / 1978 / VCX / M • Fantasy World / 1979 / WWV / M • Female Athletes / 1977 / VXP / M • Fetish Fever / 1993 / CA / C •

Fox Fever / 1991 / LV / M • Getting Ahead / 1983 / PL / M • The Girl From S.E.X. / 1982 / CA / M • Go For It / 1984 / VC / M • Heavenly Hooters / 1994 / IF / M • Hot Ones / 1982 / SUP / C • I'm Yours / 1983 / AIR / C • Jacuzzi Girls / cr75 / HOR / C • K-Sex / 1976 / VCR / M • L.A.D.P. / 1991 / PL / M • Love Bites / 1985 / CA / M • Meatballs #2 / 1984 / PAR / S • Memphis Cathouse Blues / 1982 / CA / M • Miracle On 69th Street / 1992 / HW / M • Mistress Electra / 1983 / AVO / B • Nasty Habits Are Hard To Break / 1986 / 4P / M • Nightlife / 1983 / CA / M • Nylon / 1995 / VI / M • The Other Side Of Julie / 1978 / CV / M • The Oui Girls / 1981 / VHL / M • Parliament: Fuckin' Superstars #1 / 1990 / PM / C • Peach Fuzz / 1976 / CDI / M • Playthings / 1980 / VC / M • Please Me! / cr86 / LIM / M • Please, Mr Postman / 1981 / VC / M • Purely Physical / 1982 / SE / M • Raven / 1985 / VCR / M • Raw Talent #3 / 1988 / VC / M • Rear Entry / 1985 / VCR / C • Rocco Unleashed / 1994 / SC / M • Same Time Every Year / 1981 / VHL / M • The Satisfiers Of Alpha Blue / 1980 / AVC / M • Seka's Fantasies / 1981 / CA / M • Skintight / 1981 / CA / M • Slipping It In / 1992 / FD / M • Small Town Girls / 1979 / CXV / M • Spitfire / 1984 / COM / M • Spreading Joy / 1984 / IN / M • Stand By Your Woman / cr80 / HOR / M • Stiff Competition #2 / 1994 / CA / M • Stud Hunters / 1984 / CA / M • Sweet Dreams Suzan / 1980 / CA / M • Taboo #01 / 1980 / VCX / M • Taboo #07 / 1980 / IN / M • Tangerine / 1979 / CXV / M • A Taste Of Vanessa De Rio / 1990 / PIN / C • Too Much Too Soon / 1983 / VCX / M • Too Naughty To Say No / 1984 / CA / M • Touch Me In The Morning / 1982 / CA / M • Trashi / 1980 / CA / M • Triangle Of Lust / 1983 / VCR / M • Triplets / 1985 / VCR / M • The Ultimate Fantasy / 1995 / CV / M • V—The Hot One / 1978 / CV / M • Visions Of Clair / 1977 / WWV / M • Water Nymph / 1987 / LIM / M • Wicked Sensations #1 / 1981 / CA / M • Willie Wanker And The Fun Factory / 1994 / FD / M • X-Rated Bloopers #2 / 1986 / AR / M
MICHAEL MUIR
Like Mother, Like Daughter / cr73 / VCX / M
MICHAEL NORRIS see Star Index I
MICHAEL O'LEARY see Star Index I
MICHAEL PATAKI
All American Hustler / cr73 / SOW / M • The Black Bunch / 1970 / SOW / S • Bucky Beaver's XXX Dragon Art Theatre Double Feature #28 / 1996 / SOW / M • R.S.V.P. / 1983 / VES / S
MICHAEL PERSICO
Street Workers / 1995 / ME / M
MICHAEL PHILLIPS
Once Upon A Madonna / 1985 / PV / M
MICHAEL PLATT see Star Index I
MICHAEL PONY
Taboo American Style #4: The Exciting Conclusion / 1985 / VC / M
MICHAEL POWERS
Deep Throat #1 / 1972 / AR / M • The Fabulous 50's Girls #1 / 1994 / EMC / M
MICHAEL REZNICK
Sexhibition #3 / 1996 / SUF / M
MICHAEL RUBINSTEIN
Asses Galore #1: From L.A. To Brazil / 1996 / DFI / M • Asses Galore #3: Pure Evil / 1996 / DFI / M • Asses Galore #4: Ex-

treme Noise Terror / 1996 / DFI / M • Asses Galore #5: T.T. Vs The World / 1996 / DFI / M • Asses Galore #6: Fallen Angels / 1996 / DFI / M • Asses Galore #7: Lunatic Fringe / 1996 / DFI / M • Kink: Police Chronicles / 1995 / ROB / M • Whiplash / 1996 / DFI / M
MICHAEL RUSH
Mutiny On The Booty / 1996 / FC / M
MICHAEL SALEM
How To Impersonate A Woman #1 / 1993 / STM / G • How To Impersonate A Woman #2 / 1993 / STM / G • A Peek Over The Wall / 1995 / STM / G • Transvestite Secrets Revealed / 1993 / STM / G
MICHAEL SANDS
She Studs #01 / 1990 / BIZ / G • Trisexual Encounters #03 / 1986 / PL / G
MICHAEL SANTINO see Santino Lee
MICHAEL SHAW see Sikki Nixx
MICHAEL SHEA see Star Index I
MICHAEL SIMON see Star Index I
MICHAEL SLOTA see Star Index I
MICHAEL SMALL
Family Affair / 1979 / MIT / M
MICHAEL SNOW see Star Index I
MICHAEL STEPP see Mike Ranger
MICHAEL SULLIVAN see Star Index I
MICHAEL THORN see Star Index I
MICHAEL THORPE
High School Bunnies / 1978 / VC / M
MICHAEL VINCENT see Star Index I
MICHAEL WARREN
Bad Girls #2 / 1983 / GO / M
MICHAEL WAYNE
Alley Cat / 1984 / LIV / S • Bi-Sexual Fantasies / 1984 / LAV / G
MICHAEL WHEATLEY
Conquest / 1996 / WP / M
MICHAEL WILDE
Genital Hospital / 1987 / SE / M
MICHAEL WILKINS see Mickey (Missy)
MICHAEL ZARILLA see Star Index I
MICHAEL ZEN
Lost In Vegas / 1996 / AWV / G
MICHAELA (ADKINS) see Michaela Adkins
MICHAELA ADKINS *(Michaela (Adkins), Mikala (Adkins), Mikala Adkins, Mikalah)*
Very hard ID here as to the alternates. In **Tight Shots #2** she has long black straight hair, medium natural tits, tight waist, very bad teeth, marginal face, and glasses and is credited as Mikala. She also says she's 18 years old. In **Anal Candy Ass** she's blonde and has a tattoo on her belly. In **Sodomania #9** she looks like she has small tits but she doesn't look like she's had a tit job at any time. In **Up And Cummers #13** she says she comes from CA and was thrown out by her parents but she also says she doesn't like sex. First video was **Hidden Camera #20**.
All That Jism / 1994 / VD / M • Anal All Stars / 1994 / CA / M • Anal Candy Ass / 1994 / ROB / M • Black Bottom Girlz / 1994 / CA / M • Crystal Images / 1995 / INB / M • Girls Of The Very Big Eight / 1994 / VT / M • Hidden Camera #20 / 1994 / JMP / M • Hot Tight Asses #08 / 1994 / TCK / M • Nutts About Butts / 1994 / LE / M • Sex In Black & White / 1995 / OD / M • Sexual Misconduct / 1994 / VD / C • Sista! #2 / 1994 / VT / F • Sleaze Please!—December Edition / 1994 / FH / M • Snatch Masters #01 / 1994 / LEI / M • Sodomania #09:

Doin' Time / 1994 / EL / M • Southern Possession / 1995 / DEN / M • Swedish Erotica #79 / 1994 / CA / M • Tight Shots #2 / 1994 / VI / M • Up And Cummers #13 / 1994 / 4P / M

MICHAELA JAMES

Long straight blonde hair parted in the middle, thin, pretty, small/medium tits, tight waist, belly button jewel. 18 years old in 1997 and de-virginized at 13.

More Dirty Debutantes #63 / 1997 / SBV / M • Pick Up Lines #13 / 1997 / OD / M

MICHAELA REGIUS

San Francisco Lesbians #1 / 1992 / PL / F • San Francisco Lesbians #2 / 1992 / PL / F

MICHEAL D. SADE

Double Teamed / 1995 / PSE / B

MICHEL

Anabolic Import #01: Anal X / 1994 / ANA / M • Veronica The Screenwriting Hooker / 1996 / LE / M

MICHEL BRETON

Rebecca Lord's World Tour #1: French Edition / 1995 / WP / M

MICHEL JACOT

[Madchen, Die Sich Selbst, Bedienen / 1974 / … / M

MICHEL KITTY

Saturday Matinee Series #4 / 1996 / VCX / C

MICHEL LEE *see* **Karen Summer**

MICHELE

A&B AB#356: Submissive Lady / 1991 / A&B / M • House Of Love / cr77 / VC / M

MICHELE CAPOZZI *see Star Index I*

MICHELE D'AGRO

Body Love / 1976 / CA / M

MICHELE DAVY *see Star Index I*

MICHELE GROSS

Thundercrack! / 1974 / LUM / M

MICHELE MARCELLE

[Madchen, Die Sich Selbst, Bedienen / 1974 / … / M

MICHELE MARTIN *see* **Barbie Doll**

MICHELE WELCH

Debutante Training / 1995 / PL / B

MICHELINE AVENTI *see Star Index I*

MICHELLE

A&B AB#354: All Day Cock / 1991 / A&B / M • A&B AB#366: Banana Boat / 1991 / A&B / F • Ben Dover's 9th / 1996 / VC / M • Betty Bleu / 1996 / IP / M • Blue Vanities #583 / 1996 / FFL / M • Bubble Butts #04 / 1992 / LBO / M • Bucky Beaver's XXX Dragon Art Theatre Double Feature #03 / 1996 / SOW / M • Cherry Poppers #05: Playtime / 1994 / ZA / M • Eric Kroll's Fetish #2 / 1994 / ERK / M • Eric Kroll's Fetish #4: Michelle / 1994 / ERK / M • Euro-Snatch / 1996 / SNA / M • European Cleavage Queens / 199? / H&S / S • Eye On You: Michelle Meets Anna Malle / 1995 / EOY / M • FTV #40: Triple Terror / 1996 / FT / B • Girls Around The World #11 / 199? / BTO / S • Homegrown Video #359 / 1991 / HOV / M • Homegrown Video #402 / 1993 / HOV / M • Hot Body Competition: Beverly Hill's Miniskirt Madness Cont. / 1996 / CG / F • Hot Body Video Magazine: Naughty But Nice / 1994 / CG / F • Illusions Of A Lady / 1972 / VSH / M • Limited Edition #13 / 1980 / AVC / M • Michelle's Silver Bullet / 1995 / DIP / F • Mike Hott: #351 Three-Sum Sluts #11 / 1996 / MHV / M • Mismatch / 1995 / TVI / M • Mr. Peepers Nastiest #2 / 1995 /

LBO / C • Neighborhood Watch #17: Burning The Sausage / 1992 / LBO / M • New Faces, Hot Bodies #16 / 1994 / STP / M • Out Of The Closet / 1989 / NUV / B • Pearl Necklace: Thee Bush League: The Best Of Oral #01 / 1993 / SEE / C • Pearl Necklace: Thee Bush League #02 / 1992 / SEE / M • Photo Duo / 1987 / BON / B • Private Gold #03: The Chase / 1996 / OD / M • Promises And Lies / 1996 / NIT / M • School For Hookers / 1974 / SOW / PL / M • Swedish Vip Magazine #2 / 1995 / PL / M • Toe Tales #06 / 1993 / GOT / B • TV Terrorists: Hostage Sluts / 1993 / BIZ / G • The Universal Ball / 1989 / LEO / G • The Very Best Of Breasts #3 / 1996 / H&S / S • Wet & Willing Co-Eds #103 / 1994 / PEI / F

MICHELLE (S/M) *see Star Index I*

MICHELLE (SCARLETT) *see* **Scarlett**

MICHELLE (T. RIVERS) *see* **Tanya Rivers**

MICHELLE ADAMS *see Star Index I*

MICHELLE AMBER

Blue Vanities #537 / 1993 / FFL / M

MICHELLE ANDERSON

Deep Inside Dirty Debutantes #09 / 1993 / 4P / M • Lovin' Spoonful #7 / 1996 / 4P / C

MICHELLE ANGELO

Blue Vanities #131 / 1991 / FFL / M • Blue Vanities #519 / 1993 / FFL / M • Blue Vanities #548 / 1994 / FFL / M • Blue Vanities #571 / 1995 / FFL / M • For Love And Money / 1967 / SOW / S • Street Of 1000 Pleasures / 1970 / SOW / S

MICHELLE ARIAS

Sin City Cycle Sluts #1 / 1995 / SC / F

MICHELLE BAUER *see* **Pia Snow**

MICHELLE BAYER

18 And Anxious / cr78 / CDI / M

MICHELLE BELLE *see Star Index I*

MICHELLE BLANCA *see Star Index I*

MICHELLE CHAN

Creme De La Face #15: Showroom Sex / 1996 / OD / M • Jizz Glazed Goo Guzzlers #2 / 1996 / NIT / C • Nothing Like Nurse Nookie #4 / 1996 / NIT / M • The Sodomizer #3 / 1996 / SC / M • Witches Are Bitches / 1996 / NIT / M

MICHELLE COHN-BENDIT *see Star Index I*

MICHELLE COLE

Blue Vanities #560 / 1994 / FFL / M

MICHELLE D. *see Star Index I*

MICHELLE DAMON *see Star Index I*

MICHELLE DIOR

Amsterdam Nights #1 / 1996 / BLC / M • Amsterdam Nights #2 / 1996 / VC / M

MICHELLE DUBOIS *see* **Georgette Sanders**

MICHELLE DUMEE

French Classmates / 1977 / PVI / M

MICHELLE ESCOBAR *see* **Pia Snow**

MICHELLE GABRIEL *see* **Michelle Gabrielle**

MICHELLE GABRIELLE (Michelle Gabriel, Michelle Garielle)

Agony & Extacy / 1993 / GOT / B • Anal Amateurs / 1992 / VD / M • Backdoor To Brooklyn / 1992 / PL / M • Big Busted Lesbians At Play / 1991 / BIZ / F • Catfighting Lesbians / 1991 / BIZ / F • The Chamber Maids / 1993 / GOT / B • Dildo Fantasy Party / 1990 / BIZ / F • The Dominator / 1992 / GOT / B • Double Agents / 1988 / VXP / M • Every Body / 1992 / LAP / M •

Final Test / 1993 / GOT / B • Girl Lovers / 1990 / BIZ / F • Girls Don't Lie / 1990 / IN / F • Girls Just Wanna Have Girls #2 / 1990 / HIO / F • Hog Tied And Spanked / 1991 / BIZ / B • Inhuman Bondage / 1993 / GOT / B • Lesbian Catfights / 1990 / BIZ / F • N.Y. Video Magazine #02 / 1995 / OUP / M • No Pain, No Gain / 1992 / GOT / B • Panting At The Opera / 1988 / VXP / M • Rock 'n' Roll Bondage Sluts / 1992 / STM / B • Sex Between The Scenes / 1994 / LAP / M • Silence Of The G.A.M.S. / 1992 / CA / M • Spanked Ecstasy / 1991 / BIZ / B • Streets Of New York #02 / 1994 / PL / M • Superstar Masturbation / 1990 / BIZ / F • Toe Tales #08 / 1993 / GOT / B • Twisted Sisters / 1988 / ZA / M • Wild Girls / 1994 / GOT / B • Wrong Arm Of The Law / 1987 / ZA / M

MICHELLE GARIELLE *see* **Michelle Gabrielle**

MICHELLE GILLIS *see Star Index I*

MICHELLE J. FOX *see Star Index I*

MICHELLE JEFFRIES

Small tight little black girl with small breasts.

Tight Squeeze / 1986 / AVC / M

MICHELLE JENNET

Older & Bolder In San Francisco / 1996 / TEP / M

MICHELLE LAKE

Insane Lovers / 1978 / VIS / M • Loose Threads / 1979 / S&L / M • The Pink Ladies / 1980 / VC / M

MICHELLE LEE *see* **Karen Summer**

MICHELLE LESKA *see Star Index I*

MICHELLE LOUDER *see Star Index I*

MICHELLE MAGAZINE

Coming Through The Window / cr75 / VXP / F • Fringe Benefits / 1975 / IHV / M

MICHELLE MAREN

Flash Pants / 1983 / VC / M • Piggies / 1984 / VC / M • Throat...12 Years After / 1984 / VC / M

MICHELLE MATELL *see* **Barbie Doll**

MICHELLE MCCLENNAN *see* **Pia Snow**

MICHELLE MCLENNAN *see* **Pia Snow**

MICHELLE MICHAELS *see Star Index I*

MICHELLE MONROE

Abducted For Pleasure / 1990 / BIZ / B • Auction #1 / 1992 / BIZ / B • Auction #2 / 1992 / BIZ / B • The Awakening Of Sally / 1984 / VCR / M • Babes In Bondage / 1991 / BIZ / B • Bad / 1990 / VC / M • Black In The Saddle / 1990 / ZA / M • The Book / 1990 / IF / M • Chain Of Command / 1991 / GOT / B • Club Head / 1990 / CA / M • Con Jobs / 1990 / V99 / M • Cruel Passions / 1992 / BS / B • Dresden Diary #06: The Hellfire Legend / 1992 / BIZ / B • Dresden Diary #07 / 1992 / BIZ / B • Dresden Diary #08 / 1992 / BIZ / B • Drink Of Love / 1990 / V99 / M • Every Body / 1992 / LAP / M • Fantasy Drive / 1990 / VEX / M • Female Domination #1: Babes In Bondage / 1991 / BEB / B • Female Domination #2 / 1991 / BIZ / B • The French Connexxxion / 1991 / VC / M • Holly Does Hollywood #4 / 1990 / CAY / M • Internal Affair / 1990 / V99 / M • It Happened At Midnight / 1990 / IN / M • The Last Resort / 1990 / VC / M • Laze / 1990 / ZA / M • A Lesson Well Taut / 1994 / GOT / B • Lover's Trance / 1990 / LE / M • Made In Hollywood / 1990 / VEX / M • Male Domination #16 / 1990 / BIZ / C • Michelle Monroe Star Bound / 1990 / BON / B • The New Barbarians #1 / 1990 / VC /

M • The New Barbarians #2 / 1990 / VC / M • Next Door Neighbors #14 / 1990 / BON / M • Next Door Neighbors #41 / 1993 / BON / M • Pointers / 1990 / LV / M • Saki's House Party / 1990 / KNI / M • Sea Of Love / 1990 / CIN / M • Secret Admirer / 1992 / VEX / M • Southern Side Up / 1992 / LV / M • Submission Of Susie / 1993 / BIZ / B • Taboo #08 / 1990 / IN / M • Tail Of The Scorpion / 1990 / ELP / M • Tanya Foxx Star Bound / 1989 / BON / B • Tied For The Master / 1991 / BIZ / B • Toe Tales #01 / 1992 / GOT / B • Toe Tales #38 / 1996 / GOT / B • A Touch Of Gold / 1990 / IN / M • Warehouse Slaves Discipline / 1990 / BIZ / B • White Lies / 1990 / VEX / M • Working Girls In Bondage / 1991 / BIZ / B

MICHELLE MOORE *see* **Mimi Morgan**

MICHELLE NORRIS *see Star Index I*

MICHELLE O'HAIR

Creme De La Face #15: Showroom Sex / 1996 / OD / M • The Cumm Brothers #16: Deja Goo / 1996 / OD / M • The Sodomizer #5: Destination Moon / 1996 / SC / M

MICHELLE PAGE

Bondage Pleasures #1 / 1981 / 4P / B

MICHELLE PARR *see Star Index I*

MICHELLE ROBERTS *see* **Mariwin Roberts**

MICHELLE ROBINSON

Blue Vanities #514 / 1992 / FFL / M

MICHELLE SCHEI *see* **Megan Leigh**

MICHELLE SCHOONVER

Coming Of Fortune / 1994 / EX / M • Girls Of The Packed Ten / 1994 / VT / M

MICHELLE SHADE

Finger Pleasures #5 / 1996 / PL / F • Old Guys & Dolls #2 / 1995 / PL / M • Shaved #09 / 1995 / RB / F

MICHELLE SIMON

The Erotic Adventures Of Zorro / 1969 / SOW / S • Strangers / 1972 / SE / M

MICHELLE SMALL *see Star Index I*

MICHELLE THOMAS *see Star Index I*

MICHELLE THOMPSON

Fantasy Exotic Dancers / 1995 / PME / S • Southern: Previews #1 / 1992 / SSH / C

MICHELLE VALENTIN

The Making Of A Porno Movie / 1984 / CA / M • Naughty Fantasy / 1986 / CA / M • The Whore's Port / 1984 / CA / M

MICHELLE VENCE *see Star Index I*

MICHELLE VERRAN *see* **Barbii**

MICHELLE VISION

Hollywood Starlets Adventure #01 / 1995 / AVS / M

MICHELLE WATLEY *see* **Midori**

MICHELLE WILLINGS

Girls Around The World #20: Deena Duos & Friends / 1994 / BTO / M • Tit To Tit #3 / 1995 / BTO / M • The Very Best Of Breasts #1 / 1996 / H&S / S

MICK ALLMAN *see* **Marc Stevens**

MICK DAVIS

Strange Diary / 1976 / AXV / M

MICK E. POP *see Star Index I*

MICK FLAIR *see Star Index I*

MICK FLEET *see* **Mickey (Missy)**

MICK HANDLE *see Star Index I*

MICK JONES *see* **Miguel Jones**

MICK RILEY *see* **Mickey Ray**

MICK SOFT

Depraved Fantasies #1 / 1993 / FPI / M

MICK SOUTH

Blondes Have More Fun / 1980 / SE / M • High School Memories / 1980 / VCX / M •

Sweet Dreams Suzan / 1980 / CA / M

MICK SPUNKMEYER

Filthy First Timers #6 / 1997 / EL / M

MICK STONE *see Star Index I*

MICKAELA

Private Film #05 / 1993 / OD / M • Private Film #09 / 1994 / OD / M

MICKALA *see* **Mikala**

MICKEY

AVP #9121: The Date / 1991 / AVP / M • Blue Vanities #554 / 1994 / FFL / M • Bound Fantasies / 1994 / VIG / B • Home-Grown Video #434: Forrest Hump / 1994 / HOV / M • Julie: A First Time Submissive In A Dungeon / 1996 / DHP / B • Midnite Follies / cr65 / SOW / S • Pearl Necklace: Thee Bush League #26 / 1993 / SEE / M

MICKEY (MISSY) *(Mickey G., Mick Fleet, Ed Oaks, Michael Wilkins)*

Husband of Missy. Michael Wilkins is from May 97 *GQ* article. 37 years old in 1996.

The Adventures Of Peeping Tom #1 / 1996 / OD / M • Airotica / 1996 / SC / M • Allure / 1996 / WP / M • American Fan Club Prowl / 1996 / VT / M • Anal Academy / 1996 / ZA / M • Anal Inquisition / 1996 / ZA / M • Anal Island #2 / 1996 / VC / M • Anal Jeopardy / 1996 / ZA / M • Anal Portrait / 1996 / ZA / M • Anal Professor / 1996 / ZA / M • Anal Runaway / 1996 / ZA / M • Anal Sex / 1996 / ZA / M • Anal Talisman / 1996 / ZA / M • Asses Galore #1: From L.A. To Brazil / 1996 / DFI / M • The Attendant / 1996 / SC / M • Babe Watch Beach / 1996 / SC / M • Beyond Reality #2: Anal Expedition / 1996 / EXQ / M • Beyond Reality #3: Stand Erect! / 1996 / EXQ / M • Bitches In Heat #1: Locked In the Basement / 1995 / ZA / M • The Cellar Dweller / 1996 / EL / M • Cherry Poppers #13: Anal Pajama Party / 1996 / ZA / M • Cirque Du Sex #2 / 1996 / VT / M • The Complete & Total Anal Workout #1 / 1995 / ZA / M • Conquest / 1996 / WP / M • Daydreams, Nightdreams / 1996 / VC / M • Eternal Lust / 1996 / VC / M • Gangbang Girl #18 / 1996 / ANA / M • Girly Video Magazine #5 / 1996 / BEP / M • House On Paradise Beach / 1996 / VC / M • The Hungry Heart / 1996 / AOP / M • Intense Perversions #3 / 1996 / PL / M • Jenna Ink / 1996 / WP / M • Lethal Affairs / 1996 / VI / M • Living On The Edge / 1997 / DWO / M • Lollipops #2 / 1996 / SC / M • Masque / 1995 / VC / M • My Ass #1 / 1996 / NOT / M • Nektar / 1996 / BAC / M • Planet X #1 / 1996 / HW / M • Prime Choice #4 / 1995 / RAS / M • Prime Choice #8 / 1996 / RAS / M • Puritan Video Magazine #01 / 1996 / LE / M • Roller Babes / 1996 / ERA / M • Satyr / 1996 / WP / M • Sex, Truth & Videotape #1 / 1995 / DOC / M • The Shocking Truth #2 / 1996 / DWO / M • Shooting Gallery / 1996 / EL / M • Sinboy #1 / 1996 / SC / M • Smoke & Mirrors / 1996 / PL / M • The Stranger / 1996 / BEP / M • Takin' It To The Limit #6 / 1995 / BS / M • Tender Loins / 1996 / PE / M • Tight Spot / 1996 / WV / M • Ultimate Sensations / 1996 / NIT / M • Venom #4 / 1996 / VD / M • Vivid Raw #3: Double Header / 1996 / VI / M

MICKEY CALLAHAN *see Star Index I*

MICKEY DEE

Granada Affair / 1984 / JAN / B

MICKEY G. *see* **Mickey (Missy)**

MICKEY HUMM

American Sex Fantasy / 1975 / IHV / M • Sexteen / 1975 / VC / M • Thunderbuns / 1976 / VCX / C • Winter Heat / 1975 / AVC / M

MICKEY JINES

Blue Vanities #514 / 1992 / FFL / M • The Secret Sex Lives Of Romeo And Juliet / 1968 / PS / S

MICKEY KAY

Angel Rising / 1988 / IN / M

MICKEY KIDWELL *see Star Index I*

MICKEY O

Caught! / 1994 / GOT / B • Flames Of Submission / 1995 / GOT / B • Marquesa's Dungeon / 1994 / GOT / B • Toe Tales #11 / 1993 / GOT / B • Toe Tales #13 / 1994 / GOT / B • Toe Tales #15 / 1994 / GOT / B • Toe Tales #18 / 1994 / GOT / B • Toe Tales #20 / 1995 / GOT / B • Trial And Error / 1994 / GOT / B • Twisted Rage / 1995 / GOT / B

MICKEY RAY *(Mick Riley, Mike Riley, Micky Ray, Mickey Rey)*

Adam & Eve's House Party #2: Bachelor Party / 1996 / VC / M • Anal Planet / 1994 / CC / M • Asian Silk / 1992 / VI / M • Babe Watch #5 / 1996 / VC / M • Bachelor Party #1 / 1993 / FPI / M • Backing In #6 / 1994 / WV / C • The Bad News Brat / 1991 / VI / M • Batteries Included / 1988 / 3HV / M • Beauty And The Beach / 1991 / CC / M • Big Bust Bangers #2 / 1994 / AMP / M • Bonnie & Clyde #1 / 1992 / VI / M • Bonnie & Clyde #2 / 1992 / VI / M • Brandy & Alexander / 1991 / VC / M • Bunny Bleu: A Gang Bang Fantasy / 1994 / FC / M • Chameleons: Not The Sequel / 1991 / VC / M • Collectible / 1991 / LE / M • Coming Clean / 1992 / ME / M • The Complete Guide To Sexual Positions / 1996 / PME / S • Cum On Line / 1991 / XPI / M • Deep Behind The Scenes With Seymore Butts #1 / 1995 / ULI / M • Deep Inside Savannah / 1993 / VC / C • Deep Seven / 1996 / VC / M • Dick & Jane Up, Down And All Around / 1994 / AVI / M • The Dirty Little Mind of Martin Fink / 1991 / ME / M • Dream Date / 1992 / HO / M • Gangbang Girl #16 / 1995 / ANA / M • Gangbang Girl #17 / 1995 / ANA / M • The Girls Of Spring Break / 1995 / VT / M • The God Daughter #2 / 1991 / AFV / M • In Deep With The Devil / 1991 / ME / M • Jamie Loves Jeff #2 / 1991 / VI / M • Killer Looks / 1991 / VI / M • Kym Wilde's On The Edge #10 / 1994 / RB / B • Kym Wilde's On The Edge #14 / 1994 / RB / B • Kym Wilde's On The Edge #24 / 1995 / RB / B • Leather For Lovers #1 / 1992 / LFL / M • Leather For Lovers #2 / 1995 / VEG / M • Lust & Desire / 1996 / WV / M • Mickey Ray's Sex Search #01: Sliding In / 1994 / WIV / M • Mickey Ray's Sex Search #02: Tight Spots / 1994 / WIV / M • Mickey Ray's Sex Search #03: Deep Heat / 1994 / WIV / M • Mickey Ray's Sex Search #04: Long And Hard / 1994 / WIV / M • Mickey Ray's Sex Search #05: Deep Inside / 1995 / WIV / M • Mickey Ray's Sex Search #06 / 1996 / WIV / M • Micky Ray's Hot Shots #01 / 1996 / DIG / M • Needful Sins / 1993 / WV / M • Nothing Serious / 1990 / EX / M • On Trial #2: Oral Arguments / 1991 / VI / M • The Palace Of Pleasure / 1995 / ULI / M • Passages #3 / 1991 / VI / M • The Passion / 1995 / IP / M • Philmore Butts All American Butt Search / 1996 / SUF / M •

The Phoenix #1 / 1992 / VI / M • The Phoenix #2 / 1992 / VI / M • Playing With A Full Dick / 1988 / PL / M • Racquel's Addiction / 1991 / VC / M • Rainbird / 1994 / EMC / M • Rayne Storm / 1991 / VI / M • Red Line / 1991 / PL / M • The Reel World #1 / 1994 / FOR / M • The Reel World #2 / 1994 / FOR / M • Ride 'em Cow Girl / 1995 / VI / C • Screamers (Gourmet) / 1995 / ONA / M • Southern Exposure / 1991 / LE / M • Star Attraction / 1995 / VT / M • Starbangers #03 / 1993 / ZA / M • Starbangers #05 / 1993 / FPI / M • Starbangers #06 / 1994 / FPI / M • Starbangers #10 / 1997 / ZA / M • Surprise!!! / 1994 / VI / M • Things Change / 1992 / MET / M • Things Change #1: My First Time / 1992 / CV / M • Thunder And Lightning / 1996 / MID / M • Tight Spot / 1996 / WV / M • Tommyknockers / 1994 / CC / M • Top Debs #4: Sex Boat / 1993 / GO / M • Up The Middle / 1995 / V99 / M • Victim Of Love #1 / 1992 / VI / M • Victim Of Love #2 / 1992 / VI / M • The Wanderer #1: Road Tails / 1995 / CDI / M

MICKEY REILLY
The Bride Stripped Bare / 1994 / BON / B • Sex Toy / 1993 / CA / C • Swedish Erotica Featurettes #4 / 1990 / CA / M
MICKEY REY *see* **Mickey Ray**
MICKEY ROYCE
Sulka's Wedding / 1983 / MET / G
MICKEY STORM
Binding Intruder / 1993 / VTF / B • Hitched And Bound! / 1994 / VTF / B • Obey Thy Feet / 1994 / SBP / B • Ropeburn / 1994 / VTF / B • Rubber Bondage Asylum / 1994 / VTF / B • Rubber Me Butt! / 1994 / SBP / B
MICKEY VARTAN
Bootsie / 1984 / CC / M
MICKI
A&B GB#113: Micki's Gang Bang / 1994 / A&B / M • Amateur Hours #04 / 1989 / AFI / M • Amateur Night #03 / 1990 / HME / F • Anabolic Import #07: Anal X / 1995 / ANA / M • Stevi's: Oral Lover's Delight / 1992 / SSV / M
MICKI LYNN *(Micky Lynn, Mikky Lynn)*
Blonde with an adorable body but a hard and not very pretty face. Born Mar 10, 1973 in Englewood NJ. Started working at Show World in NY and then moved to CA and Jim South.
Always / 1993 / XCI / M • Amateur Gay Girls / 1995 / LEI / C • America's Raunchiest Home Videos #46: / 1993 / ZA / M • American Connection Video Magazine #01 / 1992 / ZA / M • Anal Angels #6 / 1996 / VEX / C • Anal Intruder #07 / 1993 / CC / M • Anal Knights In Hollywood #1 / 1993 / MET / M • Anus The Menace / 1993 / CC / M • Arches Of Triumph / 1995 / PRE / S • Ass Openers! #2 / 1995 / TCK / C • Babes Illustrated #2 / 1994 / IN / F • Barrio Bitches / 1994 / SC / F • Beaver & Buttcheeks / 1993 / DR / M • Big Murray's New-Cummers #19: The Ass Grabber / 1993 / FD / M • Black For More / 1993 / ZA / M • Bush League #2 / 1992 / CC / M • Butt Busters / 1995 / EX / M • Butt Hunt #01 / 1994 / LEI / M • The Butt Sisters Do Hawaii / 1995 / MID / M • Car Wash Angels / 1995 / VC / M • The Catburglar / 1994 / PL / M • Caught From Behind #21 / 1995 / HO / M • Caught In The Act / 1993 / BS / B • Chained / 1995 / SC / M • Chateau Du Cheeks / 1994 / VC

/ M • Cheeks #7: Mirror Image / 1994 / CC / M • Cherry Cheeks / 1993 / CA / M • Cherry Poppers #15: Mischievous Maidens / 1996 / ZA / M • Coming Of Age / 1995 / VEX / C • Covergirl / 1996 / LE / M • Cumback Pussy #6: All-Star Poop Chute Salute / 1997 / EL / M • Cunthunt / 1995 / AB / F • Deception (1995-Executive) / 1995 / EX / M • Desire Kills / 1996 / SUM / M • Ding Dung School / 1994 / PLV / B • Dr Butts #3 / 1993 / 4P / M • Dream Reamin' / 1995 / LV / M • Dream Strokes / 1994 / WIV / M • Dynasty's S&M Initiation / 1994 / OUP / B • East Coast Sluts #06: Philadelphia / 1995 / PL / M • Eternal Lust / 1996 / VC / M • Fantasy Fuchs / 1996 / PLP / C • Fantasy Inc. / 1995 / CV / M • Forbidden Obsessions / 1993 / BS / B • Freak Dat Booty / 1994 / WP / M • Fresh Meat (John Leslie) #2 / 1995 / EA / M • Fun "4" All / 1994 / PRE / B • The Fury / 1993 / WIV / M • Generation Sex #2: Nature's Revenge / 1996 / VT / M • The Gift / 1996 / FEM / M • Harry Horndog #14: Love Puppies #3 / 1992 / ZA / M • Head First / 1995 / OD / M • Heidigate / 1993 / HO / M • Hienie's Heroes / 1995 / VC / M • Hit Ladies / 1995 / PRE / B • Hollywood Ho' House / 1994 / VC / M • Hollywood Sex Tour / 1995 / VC / M • Hot Tight Asses #02 / 1993 / TCK / M • Hot Tight Asses #07 / 1994 / TCK / M • Hot Tight Asses #11 / 1995 / TCK / M • Jaded Love / 1994 / CA / M • Juicy Cheerleaders / 1995 / LE / M • Lesbian Submission / 1994 / PL / B • Lolita / 1995 / SC / M • Lollipop Shoppe #1 / 1996 / SC / M • Love Doll Lucy #1 / 1994 / PL / F • Love Doll Lucy #2 / 1994 / PL / F • Make Me Watch / 1994 / PV / M • Malcolm XXX / 1992 / OD / M • Milli Vanilla / 1994 / TP / M • Muff Divers #3 / 1996 / TV / F • N.Y. Video Magazine #02 / 1995 / OUP / M • N.Y. Video Magazine #07 / 1996 / OUP / M • The New Ass Masters #07 / 1996 / LEI / C • The New Ass Masters #11 / 1996 / LEI / C • The New Butt Hunt #12 / 1995 / LEI / C • Night Vision / 1996 / WP / M • No Fly Zone / 1993 / LE / F • The Oh! Zone / 1995 / VC / M • Perverted #2: The Virgins / 1995 / ZA / M • Picture Perfect (Big) / 1995 / BIP / F • Pump Fiction / 1995 / VT / M • Pussy Galore / 1993 / VD / C • Pussyman #09: Feeding Frenzy / 1995 / SNA / M • Radical Affairs Video Magazine #03 / 1992 / ME / M • Raunch #06: French Kiss / 1992 / CC / M • Real Tickets #1 / 1994 / VC / M • Real Tickets #2 / 1994 / VC / M • Reckless Encounters / 1995 / LE / M • Reflections / 1996 / ZA / M • Reminiscing / 1995 / LE / M • Risque Burlesque #2 / 1996 / IN / M • Secret Urges (Vidco) / 1994 / VD / C • The Seduction Of Marylin Star / 1995 / VT / M • Sex Bandits / 1995 / VC / M • Sex Punk 2000 / 1993 / FOR / M • Sexdrive #1: Topdown Girl / 1993 / OD / M • Sharon Starlet / 1993 / WIV / M • Sheepless In Montana / 1993 / FOR / M • Sindy Does Anal / 1993 / AFV / M • Smoke & Mirrors / 1996 / PL / M • Snatch Masters #05 / 1995 / LEI / M • Sodomania #12: Raw Filth / 1995 / EL / M • Sodomania #13: Your Lucky Number / 1995 / EL / M • Sodomania: Slop Shots / 1996 / EL / C • Sorority Sex Kittens #3 / 1996 / VC / M • Sorority Stewardesses #1 / 1995 / PE / M • Sorority Stewardesses #2 / 1995 / PE / M • Special Reserve / 1994 / VC / M • Splattered / 1996

/ MET / M • The Stand-Up / 1994 / VC / M • Subway / 1994 / SC / M • Super Groupie / 1993 / PL / M • Swat Team / 1995 / PRE / B • Sweet Things / 1996 / FF / C • Take The A Train / 1993 / MID / M • Tight Lips / 1994 / CA / M • Top Debs #1: Prom Night / 1992 / GO / M • Trashy Ladies / 1993 / LIP / F • Ultimate Orgy #1 / 1992 / GLI / M • Ultra Head / 1992 / CA / M • Undercover / 1996 / VC / M • Up And Coming Executive / 1993 / TP / M • Up And Cummers: The Movie / 1994 / 4P / M • The Uptown Girl / 1992 / ZA / M • Using Your Assets To Get A Head / 1996 / OUP / F • Vibrating Vixens #1 / 1996 / TV / F • Virgin / 1993 / HW / M • What's Up, Tiger Pussy? / 1995 / VC / M • Whiplash / 1996 / DFI / M • Whoomp! There She Is / 1993 / AVI / M • Wicked At Heart / 1995 / WP / M • Young & Natural #01 / 1995 / PRE / F • Young & Natural #02 / 1995 / PRE / C • Young & Natural #04 / 1995 / PRE / F • Young & Natural #08 / 1995 / PRE / F • Young & Natural #09 / 1995 / PRE / C
MICKI MANOS
18 And Anxious / cr78 / CDI / M • Insane Lovers / 1978 / VIS / M • Small Change / 1978 / CDC / M
MICKI MARSAILLE *see* **Ashley Rene**
MICKI SNOW *(Mikki Snow)*
Has a pimply, pasty body with small tits and curly black hair.
AHV #04: Checkerboard Cherries / 1991 / EVN / M • Amateur Hours #49 / 1992 / AFI / M • Amateur Orgies #01 / 1992 / AFI / M • Amateur Orgies #03 / 1992 / AFI / M • Beach Bum Amateur's #14 / 1992 / MID / M • Dirty Bob's #01: Xcellent Adventure / 1991 / FLP / S • The End / 1992 / SC / M • Glitter Girls / 1992 / V99 / M • Gold: A Roommate's Best Friend / 1993 / GCG / F • Love From The Backside / 1989 / FAZ / M • Lyons: Micki's Nine Real Cums / 1992 / LDV / F • Mike Hott: #197 Lesbian Sluts #02 / 1992 / MHV / F • Mike Hott: #203 Horny Couples #03 / 1992 / MHV / M • Mike Hott: #248 Fuck The Boss #03 / 1993 / MHV / M • Mike Hott: Cum Cocktails #3 / 1995 / MHV / C • Mr. Peepers Amateur Home Videos #51: Bun Burners / 1992 / LBO / M • Odyssey 30 Min: #240: Micki Snow's Outdoor Menage-A-Trois / 1992 / OD / M • Our Bang #07 / 1992 / GLI / M • P.S.: Back Alley Cats #03 / 1992 / PSP / F • Positively Pagan #02 / 1991 / ATA / M • Positively Pagan #03 / 1991 / ATA / M • Positively Pagan #04 / 1991 / ATA / M • Sin City: The Movie / 1992 / SC / M • Single Girl Masturbation #2 / 1989 / ESP / F • Spoiled Rich / 1989 / CC / M • SVE: Cheap Thrills #2: The More The Merrier / 1992 / SVE / M • SVE: Cheap Thrills #3: Self-Satisfaction / 1992 / SVE / F • SVE: Micki And The Movers / 1992 / SVE / M • Uncle Roy's Amateur Home Video #06 / 1992 / VIM / M • User Friendly #1 / 1990 / LV / M • User Friendly #2 / 1990 / LV / M
MICKI WANTASHI *see* **Star Index I**
MICKIE LYNN (73)
All American Hustler / cr73 / SOW / M • Bucky Beaver's XXX Dragon Art Theatre Double Feature #28 / 1996 / SOW / M
MICKY LYNN *see* **Micki Lynn**
MICKY RAY *see* **Mickey Ray**
MIDNIGHT
Mike Hott: #156 Alexandra And Midnight

#1 / 1991 / MHV / F • Mike Hott: #157 Alexandra And Midnight #2 / 1991 / MHV / F • Mike Hott: #159 Midnight Solo / 1991 / MHV / F • Mike Hott: #169 Midnight Solo / 1991 / MHV / F

MIDNIGHT SNACK
We Be Bangin' 24/7 / 1996 / FD / M

MIDORI *(Michelle Watley)*
Black, quite pretty but a little toothy when she smiles, straight hair, medium tits, tight waist, nice little butt, 20 years old in 1996 and de-virginized at 17. Real name is Michelle Watley. Sister of singer Jody Watley. Has a child. As of 1997 has had her tits made into rock solid cantaloupes.
The Adventures Of Peeping Tom #2 / 1996 / OD / M • The Adventures Of Peeping Tom #4 / 1997 / OD / M • All That: Black Women's Fantasies / 1996 / VT / M • Anal Fever / 1996 / ROB / M • Anal Honeypie / 1996 / ROB / M • Anal Lovebud / 1996 / ROB / M • Anal Virgins #03 / 1996 / NS / M • Asses Galore #2: No Remorse...No Repent / 1996 / DFI / M • Backdoor Play / 1996 / AVI / M • Black Cheerleader Search #06 / 1996 / IVC / M • Cumback Pussy #2: Crawling Back For More / 1996 / EL / M • The Dinner Party #2: The Buffet / 1996 / ULI / M • Freaky Tailz / 1996 / AVI / M • Gang Bang Butthole Surfin' / 1996 / ROB / M • Gang Bang Dollies / 1996 / ROB / M • I'm So Horny, Baby / 1997 / ROB / M • Lady Sterling Takes It Up The Arse / 1997 / ROB / M • Macin' #1 / 1996 / SMP / M • My Baby Got Back #09 / 1996 / VT / M • Nba: Nuttin' Butt Ass / 1996 / SMP / M • Pick Up Lines #06 / 1996 / OD / M • Pick Up Lines #09 / 1996 / OD / M • Pussyman Auditions #03 / 1995 / SNA / M • Pussyman's Nite Club Party #1 / 1996 / SNA / M • Pussyman's Nite Club Party #2 / 1997 / SNA / M • Rectal Raiders / 1997 / ROB / M • Sabrina The Booty Queen / 1997 / ROB / M • Sex Hungry Butthole Sluts / 1996 / ROB / M • Showtime / 1996 / VT / M • Sin-A-Matic / 1996 / VI / M • Sista! #5 / 1996 / VT / F • Southern Belles #7 / 1996 / XPR / M • Southern Belles: Sugar Magnolias / 1996 / XPR / M • Up And Cummers #35 / 1996 / 4P / M • Up Your Ass #1 / 1996 / ANA / M • Video Virgins #34 / 1996 / NS / M

MIDORI LIN
Debutante Training / 1995 / PL / B

MIEKI SUZUKI
Honey Sex / 1996 / AVE / M

MIEKO MIZUTANI
Ken Chan, The Laundry Man / 1984 / ORC / M

MIG LE BRIG
Dangerous Pleasure / 1995 / WIV / M

MIGUEL *see Star Index I*

MIGUEL GUIDES
Private Film #12 / 1994 / OD / M

MIGUEL JONES *(Mick Jones)*
Small black/Hispanic male.
Agony Of Love, Lace And Lash / cr73 / SOW / M • Bucky Beaver's XXX Dragon Art Theatre Double Feature #14 / 1996 / SOW / M • Carnal Haven / 1976 / SVE / M • Count The Ways / 1976 / CA / M • Dark Angel / 1983 / VC / M • Do You Wanna Be Loved? / 1977 / AR / M • The Final Sin / 1977 / COM / M • Once Upon A Time/Cave Woman / 1978 / VI / M • Robofox #1 / 1987 / FAN / M • Tapestry Of Passion / 1976 / SE

/ M

MIGUEL LOPEZ
Inside Karl Thomas / 1994 / STA / G

MIGUEL MONTOYA
Tight Spot / 1996 / WV / M

MIGUEL ROMERO *see Star Index I*

MIHALY ILCSIK
Private Gold #02: Friends In Sex / 1995 / OD / M • Private Stories #07 / 1996 / OD / M • True Stories #1 / 1993 / SC / M • True Stories #2 / 1993 / SC / M

MIHO NIKAIDO *see Star Index I*

MIJE D'MARCO *see Mike DeMarco*

MIKA
Bored Games / 1988 / ALF / M • Bus Stop Tales #09 / 1990 / PRI / M • Private Film #16 / 1994 / OD / M • Red Hot Coeds / 1993 / VIM / M • Women Of Color #2 / 1994 / ANA / M

MIKA BARTEL *see Star Index I*

MIKAL KARR *see Star Index I*

MIKALA *(Mickala, Makala, Mackala)*
Blonde, medium sized natural tits, quite pretty but a horrible actress.
The Adventures Of Buttwoman #2: Behind Bars / 1992 / EL / F • Amateur Lesbians #33: Mackala / 1992 / GO / F • Beach Bum Amateur's #22 / 1993 / MID / M • Facesitter #1 / 1992 / CC / M • Hopeless Romantic / 1992 / LE / M • I Made Marian / 1993 / PEP / M • Living Doll / 1992 / CDI / M • The Makeup Room #1 / 1992 / VC / M • The Makeup Room #2 / 1992 / VC / M • Midnight Confessions / 1992 / XCI / M • Nikki At Night / 1993 / LE / M • No Man's Land #06 / 1992 / VT / F • Odyssey 30 Min: #204: / 1992 / OD / M • Odyssey Triple Play #25: Consenting Threesomes / 1993 / OD / M • Out Of The Blue #2 / 1992 / VI / M • Raging Hormones / 1992 / LE / M • Sorority Sex Kittens #2 / 1993 / VC / M • Video Virgins #02 / 1992 / NS / M • Video Virgins #04 / 1993 / NS / M • Wild Flower #1 / 1992 / VI / M • Wild Flower #2 / 1992 / VI / M

MIKALA (ADKINS) *see Michaela Adkins*

MIKALA ADKINS *see Michaela Adkins*

MIKALAH *see Michaela Adkins*

MIKE
AVP #9131: Kelly Doubles Up / 1991 / AVP / M • Back East Babes #1 / 1996 / NIT / M • Beach Bum Amateur's #32 / 1993 / MID / M • Bi-Bi Love Amateurs #3 / 1993 / QUA / G • Bondage Classix #17: The Millionaire / 198? / BON / B • Breast Wishes #09 / 1992 / LBO / M • British Butt Search / 1995 / VC / M • Buttwoman In Budapest / 1992 / EA / M • Depravity On The Danube / 1993 / EL / M • Fan Fuxxx #1 / 1996 / DWV / M • FTV #03: Queen Boxer & Mixed Fist / 1996 / FT / B • FTV #18: Lump Lovers Liason / 1996 / FT / B • FTV #27: Secretaries' Revenge & Twist & Shout / 1996 / FT / B • FTV #44: Tight Tamali And Bam Jam / 1996 / FT / B • FTV #46: One Lump Or Two? / 1996 / FT / B • FTV #53: Topless Boxing Terror / 1996 / FT / B • FTV #57: Birthday Boxing Bash! / 1996 / FT / B • FTV #60: Big Bust Punch Out / 1996 / FT / B • Homegrown Video #419: Reigning Pussycats And Horndogs / 1994 / HOV / M • Hot New Imports / 1996 / XC / M • The Hungarian Connection / 1992 / EA / M • Lunch / 1972 / VC / M • Mammary Manor / 1992 / BTO / M • Nightclub / 1996 / SC / M • Pearl Necklace: Amorous Amateurs #01 / 1992 / SEE / M • Pearl Necklace: Amorous Amateurs #22 / 1993 / SEE

/ M • Pearl Necklace: Thee Bush League #02 / 1992 / SEE / M • Uncle Roy's Amateur Home Video #18 / 1993 / VIM / M

MIKE AHOLE *see Star Index I*

MIKE ALBO
Hot Tight Asses #09 / 1994 / TCK / M • Hot Tight Asses #17 / 1996 / TCK / M • Pussyman #08: The Squirt Queens / 1994 / SNA / M • Pussyman #10: Butts, Butts & More Butts / 1995 / SNA / M • Pussyman #13: Lips / 1996 / SNA / M • Pussyman Auditions #22 / 1996 / SNA / M • Pussyman's House Party #2 / 1996 / SNA / M • Pussyman's Nite Club Party #1 / 1996 / SNA / M • Rainwoman #09: Wetlands / 1995 / CC / M • Rainwoman #10: The Tenth Anniversary Edition / 1996 / CC / M

MIKE ASHLEY *see Star Index I*

MIKE BLATTERMAN
Bedtime Video #09 / 1984 / GO / M

MIKE BLODGETT *see Michael Blodgett*

MIKE BLUE *see Star Index I*

MIKE BRADFORD
Resurrection Of Eve / 1973 / MIT / M

MIKE BRADLEY *see Star Index I*

MIKE CAPONE *see Star Index I*

MIKE CLAXRON *see Star Index I*

MIKE CONE *see Star Index I*

MIKE DALY *see Star Index I*

MIKE DANI
Private Stories #03 / 1995 / OD / M • Sodomania #05: Euro-American Style / 1993 / EL / M • Sodomania #06: Gangs And Bangs And Other Thangs / 1993 / EL / M

MIKE DAVIS *(Jeff Jacobs, Mr. Lucky)*
SO of Avalon (1996). You never see his face on camera.
The Adventures Of Peeping Tom #3 / 1996 / OD / M • Pick Up Lines #09 / 1996 / OD / M • Pick Up Lines #10 / 1997 / OD / M • Pick Up Lines #11 / 1997 / OD / M

MIKE DEAN
Chronicles Of Pain #3: Slave Traders / 1996 / BIZ / B • Debi's Darkest Desires / 1996 / BIZ / B • Dresden Diary #11: Endangered Secrets / 1994 / BIZ / B • Dresden Diary #12: / 1995 / BIZ / B • Flame's Bondage Bash / 1994 / BIZ / B • Hostile Takeover: Bitch Bosses / 1995 / BIZ / B • Mistress Kane: Lessons In Terror / 1996 / BIZ / B • Mistress Kane: Town In Torment / 1996 / BIZ / B • Prisoners Of Pain / 1994 / BIZ / B • Spiked Heel Diaries #1 / 1994 / BIZ / B • Spiked Heel Diaries #2 / 1994 / BIZ / B • Spiked Heel Diaries #3 / 1995 / BIZ / B • Stalking Of Slave Laura / 1996 / BIZ / B • Submission Of Ariana / 1995 / BIZ / B • The Training #3 / 1995 / BIZ / B • A Weekend In Bondage / 1994 / BIZ / B

MIKE DELONG *see Michael DeLong*

MIKE DEMARCO *(Mike DiMarco, Mije D'Marco, Mark DeMarco)*
Amberella / 1986 / GO / M • Backdoor To Hollywood #01 / 1986 / CDI / M • Broadway Fannie Rose / 1986 / CA / M • Chuck & Di In Heat / 1986 / DR / M • Club Exotica #1 / 1985 / WV / M • Club Exotica #2 / 1985 / WV / M • Deep Throat Girls / 1986 / ELH / M • Double Dare / 1986 / SE / M • Ex-Connection / 1986 / SEV / M • Irresistible #2 / 1986 / SE / M • Leather & Lace / 1987 / SE / C • Miami Spice #1 / 1987 / CA / M • Miami Spice #2 / 1988 / CA / M • Pornocopia Sensual / 1976 / VHL / M • Sex Asylum #2 / 1986 / VI / M • Sheets Of San Francisco / 1986 / AVC / M • The South

Bronx Story / 1986 / CC / M • Stripteaser / 1986 / LA / M • Sweat #1 / 1986 / PP / M • Winner Take All / 1986 / SEV / M
MIKE DEVINCI
Flamenco Ecstasy / 1996 / UEF / M
MIKE DIMARCO see Mike DeMarco
MIKE EPPS see Star Index I
MIKE EYRE
Flash / 1980 / CA / M • Kiss And Tell / 1980 / CA / M • Snow Honeys / 1983 / VC / M • Sweet Alice / 1983 / VCX / M • Sweet Cheeks / 1980 / VCX / M
MIKE FAIRMONT see Star Index I
MIKE FELINE
Bad Girls #1 / 1981 / GO / M • The Blonde Goddess / 1982 / VXP / M • Deep Inside Annie Sprinkle / 1981 / VXP / M • Fascination / 1980 / QX / M • Inside Seka / 1980 / VXP / M • Manhattan Mistress / 1980 / VBM / M • Seka Is Tara / 1981 / VC / M
MIKE FONTANA
Dirty Stories #5 / 1996 / PE / M
MIKE FOSTER
1001 Nights / 1996 / IP / M • Angel's Vengeance / 1995 / VMX / M • Bedtime Story Italiano / 1995 / UGO / M • Behind The Mask / 1995 / XC / M • The Coming Of Nikita / 1995 / EL / M • Deep Behind The Scenes With Seymore Butts #2 / 1995 / ULI / M • Erika Bella: Euroslut / 1995 / EL / M • Hot Diamond / 1995 / LE / M • Lee Nover: The Search For The Perfect Butt / 1996 / IP / M • Marquis De Sade / 1995 / IP / M • Private Gold #10: Sins / 1996 / OD / M • The Sex Clinic / 1995 / WIV / M • Sleeping Booty / 1995 / EL / M • Sodomania #14: C**t Lickin', C*m Drinkin' Bitches / 1995 / EL / M • Sodomania: Slop Shots / 1996 / EL / C • The Thief, The Girl & The Detective / 1996 / HDE / M
MIKE GREGORY see Star Index I
MIKE HADLEY
Dianna's Destiny / 19?? / BIZ / B
MIKE HAMMER
Filthy First Timers #6 / 1997 / EL / M • How To Make A College Co-Ed / 1995 / VG0 / M
MIKE HAVEN
Softie / 19?? / AVC / M
MIKE HENRISSON
Bucky Beaver's XXX Dragon Art Theatre Double Feature #11 / 1996 / SOW / M • Teenage Fantasies #1 / 1972 / SOW / M
MIKE HORNER *(Don Hart, Don Horner, Johnny Wilson)*
19 And Nasty / 1990 / ME / M • 3 Wives / 1993 / VT / M • 69 Park Avenue / 1985 / ELH / M • 8 To 4 / 1981 / CA / M • Acts Of Love / 1989 / ... / M • Adam & Eve's House Party #5 / 1996 / VC / M • Adult Video News 1992 Awards / 1992 / VC / M • Adultery / 1986 / DR / M • Adultery / 1989 / PP / M • The Adventures Of Breastman / 1992 / EVN / M • The Adventures Of Buttman / 1989 / EA / M • The Adventures Of Dick Black, Black Dick / 1987 / DR / M • The Adventures Of Major Morehead / 1994 / SC / M • The Adventures Of Studman #1 / 1994 / AFV / M • The Adventures Of Studman #3 / 1994 / AFV / M • Aged To Perfection #1 / 1994 / TTV / M • Airotica / 1996 / SC / M • Alexandria, I Love You / 1993 / AFV / M • Ali Boobie & The 40 D's / 1988 / 3DV / M • Alice In Whiteland / 1988 / VC / M • All The King's Ladies / 1981 / SUP / M • All The President's Women / 1994 / LV / M • All The Way In / 1984 / VC / M • Amanda By Night

#2 / 1987 / CA / M • Amber's Desires / 1985 / CA / M • American Garter / 1993 / VC / M • The Anal Adventures Of Suzy Super Slut #2 / 1994 / AFV / M • Anal Alien / 1994 / CC / M • Anal Alley / 1990 / ME / M • Anal Attraction #2 / 1993 / AFV / C • Anal Avenue / 1992 / LV / M • Anal Fever / 1991 / AMB / M • Anal Freaks / 1994 / KWP / M • Anal Intruder #08: Rich Girls Gone Bad / 1993 / CC / M • Anal Island / 1992 / LV / M • Anal Romance / 1993 / LV / M • Anal Storm / 1991 / ZA / M • The Anal-Europe Series #03: The Museum Of The Living Art / 1993 / LV / M • The Anal-Europe Series #04: Anal Recall / 1993 / LV / M • Angel Gets Even / 1987 / FAN / M • Angel Kelly Raw / 1987 / FAN / M • Angel Of The Island / 1988 / IN / M • Angel's Back / 1988 / IN / M • Angela Baron Series #1 / 1988 / VD / C • Angela Baron Series #2 / 1988 / VD / C • Angela Baron Series #3 / 1988 / VD / C • Angela Baron Series #4 / 1988 / VD / C • Angela Baron Series #5 / 1988 / VD / C • Angela Baron Series #6 / 1988 / VD / C • Any Port In The Storm / 1991 / LV / M • Ass Ventura: Crack Detective / 1996 / PL / M • At The Pornies / 1989 / VC / M • The Attendant / 1996 / SC / M • Autoerotica #1 / 1991 / EX / M • Autoerotica #2 / 1991 / EX / M • Baby Cakes / 1982 / SE / M • Back To Nature / 1990 / CA / M • The Backdoor Club / 1992 / LV / M • Backdoor To The City Of Sin / 1993 / ANA / M • Bad Influence / 1991 / CDI / M • Bad Side Of Town / 1993 / AFD / M • Badlands #1 / 1994 / PEP / M • Badlands #2: Back Into Hell / 1994 / PEP / M • Ball Street / 1988 / CA / M • Bare Waves / 1986 / VD / M • Barflies / 1990 / ZA / M • Batbabe / 1995 / PL / M • Battle Of The Stars #1 / 1985 / NSV / M • Bazooka County #5: The Jugs / 1993 / CC / M • Beauty And The Beast #1 / 1988 / VC / M • Beaver Ridge / 1991 / VC / M • Beaverjuice / 1992 / LV / M • The Beaverly Hillbillies / 1993 / IP / M • Bed & Breakfast / 1992 / VC / M • Bedazzled / 1993 / OD / M • Bedside Brat / 1988 / VI / M • Bedtime Stories / 1996 / VC / M • Beefeaters / 1989 / PV / M • Behind Blue Eyes #3 / 1989 / ME / M • Behind The Scenes With Angela Baron / 1988 / FAZ / C • Best Butt(e) In The West #1 / 1992 / CC / M • The Best Little Whorehouse In Hong Kong / 1987 / SE / M • Betrayal / 1992 / XCI / M • Beverly Hills 90269 / 1992 / LV / M • Beyond Desire / 1986 / VC / M • Beyond Shame / 1980 / VEP / M • Biff Malibu's Totally Nasty Home Videos #22 / 1992 / ANA / M • Biff Malibu's Totally Nasty Home Videos #25 / 1992 / ANA / M • Biff Malibu's Totally Nasty Home Videos #34 / 1993 / ANA / M • Big Boob Babys / 1982 / ... / M • The Big One / 1995 / HO / M • Big, Bad & Beautiful / 1988 / MIR / C • Biloxi Babes / 1988 / WV / M • Bimbo Bowlers From Boston / 1990 / ZA / M • Bimbo Bowlers From Buffalo / 1989 / ZA / M • The Bitch / 1988 / FAN / M • Bite / 1991 / LE / M • Blame It On The Heat / 1989 / VC / M • Blazing Matresses / 1986 / AVC / M • Blinded By Love / 1993 / OD / M • The Blonde & The Beautiful #1 / 1993 / LV / M • The Blonde & The Beautiful #2 / 1993 / LV / M • Blonde Forces #1 / 1991 / CC / M • Blonde Ice #1 / 1990 / EX / M • Blonde Ice #2 / 1993 / EX / M • The Blonde Next Door / 1982 / GO / M • Bloopers (Video Team) /

1994 / VT / M • Blue Confessions / 1983 / VCR / M • Blue Dreams / 1996 / SC / M • Blue Movie / 1989 / VD / M • Blue Vanities #016 (Old) / 1988 / FFL / M • Blue Vanities #017 (Old) / 1988 / FFL / M • Blue Vanities #042 (Old) / 1988 / FFL / M • Blue Vanities #055 / 1988 / FFL / M • Blue Vanities #056 / 1988 / FFL / M • Blue Vanities #062 / 1988 / FFL / M • Blue Vanities #066 / 1988 / FFL / M • Blue Vanities #067 / 1988 / FFL / M • Blue Vanities #071 / 1988 / FFL / M • Blue Vanities #103 / 1988 / FFL / M • Blue Vanities #108 / 1988 / FFL / M • Blue Vanities #120 / 1990 / FFL / M • Blue Vanities #193 / 1993 / FFL / M • Blue Vanities #195 / 1993 / FFL / M • Blue Vanities #204 / 1993 / FFL / M • Bodies In Heat #2 / 1989 / DR / M • Body And Soul / 1992 / OD / M • Body Girls / 1983 / SE / M • Body Music #2 / 1990 / DR / M • Body Of Love / 1994 / ERA / M • Body Talk / 1982 / VCX / M • Bold Obsession / 1983 / NSV / M • Boobs A Poppin' / 1994 / TTV / M • Boobwatch #1 / 1996 / SC / M • Boobwatch #2 / 1997 / SC / M • Born 2 B Wild / 1995 / PL / M • Born To Be Bad / 1987 / CV / M • Born To Be Wild / 1987 / SE / M • Born To Run / 1985 / WV / M • The Boss / 1987 / FAN / M • The Boss / 1993 / VT / M • Brat On The Run / 1987 / VI / M • The Breast Files #1 / 1994 / AVI / M • Breast Worx #26 / 1992 / LBO / M • Breastman Does The Himalayas / 1993 / EVN / M • Breastman's Anal Adventure / 1993 / EVN / M • Breastman's Wet T-Shirt Contest / 1994 / EVN / M • Breaststroke #3 / 1989 / EX / M • The Bride / 1986 / WV / M • A Brief Affair / 1982 / CA / M • Bring On The Virgins / 1989 / CA / M • Broadway Brat / 1988 / VI / M • Broadway Fannie Rose / 1986 / CA / M • The Brothel / 1993 / OD / M • Buck Naked In The 21st Century / 1993 / EVN / M • Built For Sex (Angela Baron's) / 1988 / FAZ / C • Burgundy Blues / 1993 / MET / M • Burn / 1991 / LE / M • Bush Pilots #1 / 1990 / VC / M • Bush Pilots #2 / 1991 / VC / M • The Butt Detective / 1994 / VC / M • The Butt Sisters Do Las Vegas / 1994 / MID / M • Butt Woman #4 / 1993 / FH / M • Butt Woman #5 / 1993 / FH / M • Buzzzz! / 1993 / OD / M • A Cameo Appearence / 1992 / VI / M • Camera Shy / 1993 / FOR / M • The Can Can / 1993 / LV / M • Candy Factory / 1994 / PE / M • Candy's Little Sister Sugar / 1988 / VD / M • Cape Lere / 1992 / CC / M • Careena #1 / 1987 / WV / C • Careena #2: A Star On The Rise / 1988 / WV / C • Careful, He May Be Watching / 1986 / CA / M • Carlita's Backway / 1993 / OD / M • Carnal Carnival / 1992 / FC / M • Carnal Interludes / 1995 / NOT / M • Carnal Invasions / 1996 / NIT / M • The Case Of The Cockney Cupcake / 1989 / ME / M • The Case Of The Mad Tickler / 1988 / ME / M • The Case Of The Sensuous Sinners / 1988 / ME / M • Casual Sex / 1991 / GO / M • Cat & Mouse #1 / 1992 / XCI / M • Cat & Mouse #2 / 1993 / XCI / M • Catwalk #1 / 1995 / SC / M • Catwalk #2 / 1995 / SC / M • Caught & Bound / 1993 / BON / B • Caught In The Act / 1987 / WV / M • Centerspread Girls / 1982 / CA / M • Chained / 1995 / SC / M • Challenge Of Desire / 1983 / NSV / M • Charlie's Girls #3 / 1990 / CC / M • Cheaters / 1990 / LE / M • Cheating Hearts / 1994 / AFI / M • Cheating Wives / 1983 / PAC / M • Cheeks #4: A Backstreet

side Desiree Cousteau / 1979 / VCX / M • Inspiration / 1981 / CHX / M • International Affairs / 1994 / PL / M • Intersextion / 1994 / HO / M • Interview With A Vamp / 1994 / ANA / M • Intimate Explosions / 1982 / ... / C • Jack The Stripper / 1992 / ME / M • Jane Bond Meets Thunderthighs / 1988 / VD / M • Jewel Of The Nite / 1986 / WV / M • Jiggly Queens #1 / 1993 / LE / M • Jiggly Queens #2 / 1994 / LE / M • Jiggly Queens #3 / 1996 / LE / M • Joys Of Erotica #102 / 1980 / VCR / C • Jugsy (X-Citement) / 1992 / XCI / M • Just For Tonight / 1992 / VC / M • K-Sex / 1976 / VCR / M • K.U.N.T.-TV / 1988 / WV / M • Kelly Eighteen #1 / 1993 / LE / M • Kinky Fantasies / 1994 / KWP / M • The Kiss / 1995 / WP / M • L.A. Topless / 1994 / LE / M • Ladies Nights / 1980 / VC / M • Lambody / 1990 / CDI / M • The Landlady / 1990 / VI / M • Lap Of Luxury / 1994 / WIV / M • The Last Anal Hero / 1993 / OD / M • Last Rumba In Paris / 1989 / VC / M • Last Tango In Paradise / 1995 / ERA / M • The Last Temptation Of Kristi / 1988 / ME / M • Latex #1 / 1994 / VC / M • Lay Of The Land / 1995 / LE / M • Le Hot Club / 1987 / WV / M • Leather / 1995 / LE / M • Leena Meets Frankenstein / 1993 / OD / M • Leena's Oral Extravaganza / 1995 / OD / C • Legend #2 / 1990 / LE / M • Legend #3 / 1991 / LE / M • Legend #6: / 1996 / LE / M • Lessons In Love / 1995 / SPI / M • Let's Get Physical (Hyapatia Lee's) / 1984 / CA / M • Let's Get Wet / 1987 / WV / M • Let's Talk Sex / 1982 / CA / M • Lethal Love / 1990 / DAY / M • Lethal Woman #1 / 1988 / SEV / M • Lethal Woman #2 / 1988 / SEV / M • Licensed To Thrill / 1990 / VC / M • Lickety Pink / 1990 / ME / M • Lies Of Passion / 1992 / LV / M • Limited Edition #15 / 1980 / AVC / M • Liquid Love / 1988 / CA / M • A Little Bit Of Honey / 1987 / WET / M • The Little French Maid / 1981 / VCX / M • Little Shop Of Whores / 1987 / VI / M • Live Sex / 1994 / LE / M • The Living End / 1992 / OD / M • Lollipop Lickers / 1996 / V99 / C • The Lost Angel / 1989 / KIS / C • Love Letters (Now Showing) / 1983 / NSV / M • Love Lies / 1988 / IN / M • Love On The Run / 1989 / CA / M • Love Shack / 1990 / CC / M • A Lover For Susan / 1987 / CLV / M • The Loves Of Mary Jane / 1989 / BWV / C • The Luscious Baker Girls / 1990 / VD / M • Lust & Desire / 1996 / WV / M • Lust At First Bite / 1978 / VC / M • Lust In The Woods / 1990 / VI / M • Lust In Time / 1996 / ONA / M • Lust Never Sleeps / 1991 / FAZ / M • The Lust Potion Of Doctor F / 1985 / WV / M • Lusty Ladies #12 / 1984 / 4P / M • The Maddams Family / 1991 / XCI / M • Made In Germany / 1988 / FAZ / M • The Main Attraction / 1988 / 4P / M • Makeout / 1988 / VT / M • The Makeup Room #1 / 1992 / VC / M • The Makeup Room #2 / 1992 / VC / M • Maneater / 1995 / ERA / M • Mardi Gras Passions / 1987 / MET / M • Married Women / 1990 / PP / M • The Master Of Pleasure / 1988 / VD / M • Mellon Man #04 / 1995 / AVI / M • Memphis Cathouse Blues / 1982 / CA / M • Midnight Baller / 1989 / PL / M • Midnight Fire / 1990 / HU / M • Mighty Man #1: Virgins In The Forest / 1994 / LE / M • The Mile High Club / 1995 / PL / M • Mirage #1 / 1991 / VC / M • Mirage #2 / 1992 / VC / M • The Mischief Maker / 1987 / SE / M • Miss 21st Century

/ 1991 / ZA / M • Miss Nude International / 1993 / LE / M • Miss Nude International / 1996 / LE / M • Missing Pieces / 1985 / IN / M • The Mistress #1 / 1983 / CV / M • Mistress To Sin / 1994 / LV / M • Molly B-Goode / 1994 / FH / M • Moments Of Love / 1983 / MID / M • Monaco Falcon / 1990 / VC / M • Moonlusting #2 / 1987 / WV / M • More Than A Handful #3 / 1993 / MET / M • More Than A Whore / 1995 / OD / M • Mortal Passions / 1990 / CDI / M • Motel Sweets / 1987 / VD / M • Moving In / 1986 / CV / M • Mr. Peepers Amateur Home Videos #38: Bringing Up the Rear / 1991 / LBO / M • Ms. Magnificent / 1979 / SE / M • Mummy Dearest #1 / 1990 / LV / M • Mummy Dearest #2: The Unwrapping / 1990 / LV / M • Mummy Dearest #3: The Parting / 1991 / LV / M • My Bare Lady / 1989 / ME / M • My First Time #4 / 1996 / NS / M • My Secret Lover / 1992 / XCI / M • My Way / 1993 / CA / M • Mystery Of The Maletease Dildo / 1992 / STR / M • The Naked Pen / 1992 / VC / M • Naked Scandal #1 / 1995 / SPI / M • Naked Scandal #2 / 1996 / SPI / M • Naked Stranger / 1987 / CDI / M • Nasty / 1985 / NSV / M • Nasty Nymphos #05 / 1994 / ANA / M • Nasty Nymphos #06 / 1994 / ANA / M • Natural Born Thriller / 1994 / CC / M • Natural Born Thrillers / 1994 / LV / M • Naughty Cheerleaders / 1985 / HO / M • Naughty Girls Like It Big / 1986 / ELH / M • Needful Sins / 1993 / WV / M • Never So Deep / 1981 / VCX / M • The Night Before / 1987 / WV / M • Night Games / 1986 / WV / M • Night Moves / 1983 / SUP / M • Night Of Seduction / 1994 / VC / M • The Night Of The Living Bed / 1996 / LE / M • Night Seduction / 1995 / VC / M • Nightlife / 1983 / CA / M • Nightmare On Porn Street / 1988 / ME / M • Nightvision / 1993 / TP / M • Nookie Court / 1992 / AFV / M • Nookie Ranch / 1996 / NIT / M • Nothing Personal / 1993 / CA / M • Nothing To Hide #2 / 1993 / CV / M • Nudes At Eleven #2 / 1987 / AVC / M • Nymphette #1 / 1986 / WV / M • Nymphette #2 / 1986 / WV / M • Obsession / 1985 / HO / M • Odds And Ends / 1981 / TGA / M • Oh! You Beautiful Doll / 1990 / ZA / M • Older Men With Younger Women #2 / 1994 / CC / M • On My Lips / 1989 / PV / M • On The Loose & Hot To Trot / 1987 / CA / M • Ona Zee's Date With Dallas / 1992 / ONA / M • One In A Million / 1992 / HW / M • One Of Our Porn Stars Is Missing / 1993 / OD / M • The Only Game In Town / 1991 / VC / M • Only The Best Of Breasts / 1987 / CV / C • Opening Night / 1991 / AR / M • Oral Clinic / 1990 / DAY / M • Oral Majority #01 / 1986 / WV / C • Oral Majority #03 / 1986 / WV / C • Oral Majority #08 / 1990 / WV / C • Oral Majority Black #1 / 1987 / WV / C • The Orgy #1 / 1993 / EMC / M • The Orgy #2 / 1993 / EMC / M • The Orgy #3 / 1993 / EMC / M • Oriental Madam / 1981 / TGA / M • Other People's Honey / 1991 / HW / M • The Other Side Of Debbie / 1991 / CC / M • Our Dinner With Andrea / 1988 / CA / M • Out Of The Blue #2 / 1992 / VI / M • Outrageous Foreplay / 1987 / WV / M • Overnight Sensation / 1991 / XCI / M • Panties / 1993 / VD / M • Paper Tiger / 1992 / VI / M • Paris Blues / 1990 / WV / C • Parliament: Fuckin' Superstars #1 / 1990 / PM / C • Parliament: Three Way Lust /

1988 / PM / M • Passenger 69 #2 / 1994 / IP / M • Passion's Prisoners / 1994 / LV / M • Passions Of Sin / 1996 / NIT / M • Peaches And Cream / 1982 / SE / M • The Penthouse / 1989 / PP / M • The Perfect Pair / 1991 / LE / M • Perfect Partners / 1986 / CV / M • The Performers / 1986 / NSV / M • Perils Of Paula / 1989 / CA / M • Perverted Women / 1995 / SC / M • Phantom X / 1989 / VC / M • Phone Fantasy #1 / 1992 / ATL / M • Phone Fantasy #2 / 1992 / ATL / M • Phone Sex Girls #2 / 1987 / VT / M • Physical #1 / 1981 / SUP / M • Physical #2 / 1985 / SUP / M • Piece Of Heaven / 1988 / CDI / M • The Pink Panties / 1985 / NSV / M • Play Me Again, Vanessa / 1986 / VC / M • Playin' With Fire / 1993 / LV / M • Please, Mr Postman / 1981 / VC / M • Pleasure Dome: The Genesis Chamber / 1994 / AFV / M • The Pleasure Game / 1988 / CA / M • The Pleasure Hunt #1 / 1984 / NSV / M • The Pleasure Hunt #2 / 1985 / NSV / M • Point Of Entry / 1996 / WP / M • Poison / 1994 / VI / M • Portrait Of An Affair / 1988 / VD / M • Potpourri / 1981 / TGA / M • The Power of Nicole / 1983 / BIZ / M • Pretty Peaches #3 / 1989 / VC / M • Primal Desires / 1993 / EX / M • The Prince Of Lies / 1992 / LE / M • Private Eyes / 1995 / LE / M • Promises & Lies / 1995 / SS / M • The PTX Club / 1988 / GO / M • Public Places #1 / 1994 / SC / M • Pure / 1996 / WP / M • Pure Sex / 1988 / FAN / C • A Pussy Called Wanda #1 / 1992 / DR / M • Pussywoman #3 / 1995 / CC / M • The Queen Of Mean / 1992 / FC / M • The Quest / 1994 / SC / M • Rachel Ryan / 1988 / WV / C • Rachel Ryan Exposed / 1990 / WV / C • Rainwoman #07: In The Rainforest / 1993 / CC / M • Rainwoman #08 / 1994 / CC / M • Ramb-Ohh #2 / 1988 / PV / M • Rated Sex / 1986 / SE / M • Raw Footage / 1996 / VC / M • Reamin' Reunion / 1988 / CC / M • Reckless Encounters / 1995 / LE / M • Red Hot Coeds / 1993 / VIM / M • Red Hot Fire Girls / 1989 / VD / M • Red Hots / 1996 / PL / M • Red Light / 1994 / SC / S • Reel People #03 / 1989 / PP / M • The Return Of The A Team / 1988 / WV / M • Return To Melrose Place / 1993 / HW / M • Return To Sex 5th Avenue / 1985 / WV / M • The Ribald Tales Of Canterbury / 1986 / CA / M • Ring Of Desire / 1995 / LBO / M • Robin Head / 1991 / CC / M • Robofox #1 / 1987 / FAN / M • Rock Me / 1994 / CC / M • Rocket Girls / 1993 / VC / M • Rod Wood / 1995 / LE / M • Roxy / 1991 / VC / M • Rugburn / 1993 / LE / M • Runnin' Hot / 1992 / LV / M • Russian Roulette / 1995 / NIT / M • Ruthless Women / 1988 / SE / M • Salt & Pepper / 1986 / VCS / C • San Fernando Valley Girls / 1983 / CA / M • Saturday Night Porn #1 / 1993 / AFV / M • Scarlet Fantasy / 1990 / VI / M • A Scent Of A Girl / 1993 / LV / M • Screwdriver / 1988 / CC / C • Second Skin / 1989 / VC / M • The Secret Garden #1 / 1992 / XCI / M • The Secret Garden #2 / 1992 / XCI / M • Secret Seductions #1 / 1995 / LV / M • Secret Seductions #2 / 1995 / ULP / M • Secret Services / 1995 / CV / M • The Secrets Of Jennifer / 1982 / NSV / M • Seduction By Fire / 1987 / VD / M • The Seduction Formula / 1990 / FAN / M • The Seduction Of Annah Marie / 1996 / VT / M • The Seduction Of Mary / 1992 /

VC / M • Seka's Fantasies / 1981 / CA / M • Sensual Seduction / 1986 / LBO / M • Servin' It Up / 1993 / VC / M • Sex #1 (Vivid) / 1993 / VI / M • Sex #2 (Vivid) / 1993 / VI / M • Sex Academy #3: The Art Of Real Sex / 1994 / ONA / M • Sex Academy / 1985 / PLY / M • Sex Alert / 1995 / PV / M • Sex And The Secretary / 1988 / PP / M • Sex Asylum #3 / 1988 / VI / M • The Sex Detective / 1987 / GO / M • Sex Dreams On Maple Street / 1985 / WV / M • Sex Gallery / 1995 / WAV / M • The Sex Game / 1987 / SE / C • The Sex Life Of Mata Hari / 1989 / GO / M • Sex Lives Of Clowns / 1994 / VC / M • Sex Lives Of The Rich And Famous #1 / 1988 / VC / M • Sex Lives Of The Rich And Famous #2 / 1989 / VC / M • Sex Loose / 1982 / VC / M • Sex Machine / 1986 / LA / M • Sex Party / 1995 / KWP / M • Sex Ranch / 1993 / VC / M • Sex Trek #1: The Next Peneration / 1990 / ME / M • Sex Trek #2: The Search For Sperm / 1991 / ME / M • Sex Trek #3: The Wrath Of Bob / 1992 / ME / M • Sex Under Glass / 1992 / VC / M • Sex Wars / 1984 / EXF / M • Sexual Harassment / 1996 / TTV / M • Sexual Instinct #1 / 1992 / DR / M • Sexual Instinct #2 / 1994 / DR / M • Sexually Altered States / 1986 / VC / M • Sexy Delights #2 / 1987 / CLV / M • Shades Of Blue / 1992 / VC / M • Shadows Of Lust / 1996 / NIT / M • Shame / 1994 / VI / M • Shameless / 1982 / SVE / M • Shanna's Final Fling / 1991 / ME / M • Sharon Starlet / 1993 / WIV / M • Shayla's Swim Party / 1997 / VC / M • She Likes To Watch / 1992 / EVN / M • She's No Angel / 1996 / ERA / S • She's The Boss / 1992 / VIM / M • She-Male Encounters #18: Murder She-Male Wrote / 1987 / MET / G • Shipwrecked / 1992 / CDI / M • Showdown / 1986 / CA / M • Showgirl #01: Leslie Bovee's Fantasies / 1981 / VCR / M • Showgirl #08: Serena's Fantasies / 1983 / VCR / M • Showgirl #09: Jessie St James' Fantasies / 1981 / VCR / M • Showgirl #13: Chris Cassidy's Fantasies / 1983 / SVE / M • Showgirl #17: Phaedra Grant's Fantasies / 1983 / VCR / M • Showgirls / 1985 / SE / M • Sin City / 1986 / WET / M • Sin City: The Movie / 1992 / SC / M • Sinderella #1 / 1992 / VI / M • Sinderotica / 1985 / HO / M • The Sins Of Angel Kelly / 1987 / FAN / C • Sins Of Tami Monroe / 1991 / CA / C • Sinset Boulevard / 1987 / WV / M • Sirens / 1991 / VC / M • Skin To Skin / 1993 / LE / M • Skintight / 1981 / CA / M • Sky Foxes / 1987 / VC / M • The Sleazy Detective / 1988 / VD / M • Sleeping With Seattle / 1993 / LV / M • Slick Honey / 1989 / VC / M • Slow Burn / 1991 / VC / M • Slow Dancing / 1990 / VI / M • A Slow Hand / 1992 / FD / M • The Smart Ass #2: Rusty's Revenge / 1990 / VT / M • Smart Ass Delinquent / 1993 / VT / M • Smoke & Mirrors / 1996 / PL / M • Snakedance / 1992 / VI / M • Snow Honeys / 1983 / VC / M • Society Affairs / 1982 / CA / M • Some Like It Big / 1991 / LE / M • Someone Else / 1992 / VC / M • Sorority Sex Kittens #1 / 1992 / VC / M • Sorority Sweethearts / 1983 / CA / M • Sound Of Love / 1981 / CA / M • Southern Comfort #1 / 1995 / DWV / M • Southern Comfort #2 / 1995 / DWV / M • Spanish Fly / 1992 / LE / M • Spermacus / 1993 / PI / M • Splash / 1990 / WV / C • Spread The Wealth / 1993 / DR / M • St. Tropez Lust /

1990 / VC / M • Stairway To Heaven / 1989 / ME / M • Star Tricks / 1988 / WV / M • Starbangers #10 / 1997 / ZA / M • Stardust #1 / 1996 / VI / M • Stardust #2 / 1996 / VI / M • Starship Intercourse / 1987 / DR / M • Stiletto / 1994 / WAV / M • Strange Love / 1987 / WV / M • Strippers Inc. #2 / 1994 / ONA / M • Strippers Inc. #3 / 1994 / ONA / M • Strippers Inc. #4 / 1995 / ONA / M • Strong Rays / 1988 / IN / M • Summer Of '72 / 1982 / CA / M • Sunrise Mystery / 1992 / FD / M • Surrogate Lover / 1992 / TP / M • Sweat 'n' Bullets / 1995 / MID / M • Swedish Erotica #06 / 1980 / CA / M • Swedish Erotica #08 / 1980 / CA / M • Swedish Erotica #14 / 1980 / CA / M • Swedish Erotica #15 / 1980 / CA / M • Swedish Erotica #33 / 1980 / CA / M • Swedish Erotica #38 / 1981 / CA / M • Swedish Erotica #39 / 1981 / CA / M • Swedish Erotica #45 / 1983 / CA / M • Swedish Erotica #57 / 1984 / CA / M • Swedish Erotica #58 / 1984 / CA / M • Swedish Erotica #59 / 1984 / CA / M • Swedish Erotica #71 / 1986 / CA / M • Swedish Erotica Featurettes #5 / 1990 / CA / M • Swedish Erotica Letters #2 / 1989 / CA / C • Swedish Erotica Superstar #3: Janey Robbins / 1984 / CA / C • Switch Hitters #2: Swinging Both Ways / 1987 / IN / G • Switch Hitters #3: Squeeze Play / 1988 / IN / G • Taboo #08 / 1990 / IN / M • Taboo #14: Kissing Cousins / 1995 / IN / M • Tailiens #2 / 1992 / FD / M • Tailiens #3 / 1992 / FD / M • Tales From The Clit / 1993 / OD / M • Talk Dirty To Me #09 / 1992 / DR / M • Tangerine / 1979 / CXV / M • Tangled / 1994 / PL / M • The Tantric Guide To Sexual Potency And Extended Orgasm / 1994 / A&E / M • A Taste Of Ariel / 1989 / PIN / C • A Taste Of Janey / 1990 / PIN / C • A Taste Of Julia Parton / 1992 / VD / C • A Taste Of Money / 1983 / AT / M • A Taste Of Rachel / 1990 / PIN / C • Tasty / 1985 / CA / M • Teasers: Poor Little Rich Girl / 1988 / MET / M • Teasers: Watch Me Sparkle / 1988 / MET / M • Tell Me What To Do / 1991 / CA / M • Temple Of Lust / 1992 / VC / M • The Temple Of Poon / 1996 / PE / M • Temptation: The Story Of A Lustful Bride / 1983 / NSV / M • Tender And Wild / 1989 / MTP / M • Teri Diver's Bedtime Tales / 1993 / FD / M • Texas Crude / 1995 / NIT / M • The Therapist / 1992 / VC / M • This Is Your Sex Life / 1987 / VD / M • Tight Fit / 1987 / V99 / M • Tight Fit / 1991 / VEX / C • Tight Spot / 1996 / WV / M • Titillation #1 / 1982 / SE / M • Titty Slickers #2 / 1994 / LE / M • Titty Slickers #3 / 1996 / LE / M • Topless Brain Surgeons / 1995 / LE / M • Topless Stewardesses / 1995 / PV / M • Topless Window Washers / 1996 / LE / M • Totally Ona: The Best Of Ona Zee / 1996 / ONA / C • Touch Me In The Morning / 1982 / CA / M • The Touchables / 1988 / CC / M • Toys 4 Us #1 / 1987 / WV / C • Trampire / 1987 / FAN / M • Tropical Lust / 1987 / MET / M • True Sin / 1990 / PP / M • The Ultimate Lover / 1986 / VD / M • Undercover / 1996 / VC / M • Undercover Angel / 1988 / IN / M • Unnatural Phenomenon #2 / 1986 / WV / M • Unplugged / 1995 / CC / M • Unveiled / 1987 / VC / M • Up And Coming Executive / 1993 / TP / M • Upbeat Love #1 / 1994 / CV / M • V.I.C.E. #1 / 1991 / AFV / M • V.I.C.E. #2 / 1991 / AFV / M • Valley Of The

Sluts / 1991 / OD / M • VCA Previews #4 / 1988 / VC / C • Velvet / 1995 / SPI / M • Vice / 1994 / WAV / M • Victoria's Secret Desires / 1983 / S&L / C • Videobone / 1988 / WET / M • Violation / 1996 / LE / M • Viper's Place / 1988 / VD / M • The Vision / 1991 / LE / M • The Visualizer / 1992 / VC / M • Voluptuous / 1993 / CA / M • Warm To The Touch / 1990 / CDI / M • Waterbabies #1 / 1992 / CC / M • Waves Of Passion / 1996 / ERA / M • Web Of Desire / 1993 / OD / M • Wet Nurses #1 / 1994 / LE / M • Wet Nurses #2 / 1995 / LE / M • What A Country / 1989 / PL / M • What About Boob? / 1993 / CV / M • What's In It 4 Me / 1995 / TEG / M • What's Up Doc / 1988 / SEV / M • What's Up, Tiger Pussy? / 1995 / VC / M • Where There's Smoke There's Fire / 1987 / FAN / M • Whispered Lies / 1993 / LBO / M • Who Shaved Aja? / 1989 / EX / M • Who's In Charge (Titan) / 1995 / TEG / M • The Whore / 1989 / CA / M • Whorelock / 1993 / LV / M • Why Things Burn / 1994 / LBO / M • Wicked Thoughts / 1992 / PL / M • Wildcats / 1995 / WP / M • Winter Heat / 1994 / MID / M • Wishful Thinking / 1992 / VC / M • With Love, Annette / 1985 / CA / C • With Love, Lisa / 1985 / CA / C • With Love, Loni / 1985 / CA / C • The Wizard Of AHH's / 1985 / SE / M • Women In Uniform / 1986 / TEM / M • Working Girls / 1985 / CA / M • Working It Out / 1983 / CA / M • WPINK-TV #2 / 1986 / PV / M • WPINK-TV #3 / 1988 / PV / M • X-TV / 1992 / CA / C • Xstasy / 1986 / NSV / M • Yankee Rose / 1994 / LE / M • The Young And The Wrestling #2 / 1989 / PL / M • Young Doctors In Lust / 1979 / NSV / M • The Young Like It Hot / 1983 / CA / M • Yuppies In Heat / 1988 / CHA / C • [Grant Takes Richmond / 1981 / … / M • [Men In Control / 1988 / … / B • [O.Z. Productions / 1979 / … / M

MIKE HOTT
Mike Hott: #120 Dildo Debbie, Dusty, Mike And Steve / 1990 / MHV / M • Mike Hott: #298 Bonus Cunt: Candy Connor / 1995 / MHV / M • Mike Hott: #324 Bonus Cunt: Brandie Rio / 1996 / MHV / M • Mike Hott: #325 Bonus Cunt: Shonna Lynn / 1995 / MHV / M • Mike Hott: #340 Cunt Of The Month: Westin Chase / 1996 / MHV / M • Mike Hott: #341 Bonus Cunt: Julia / 1995 / MHV / M • Mike Hott: #356 Girls Who Lap Cum From Cunts #01 / 1996 / MHV / M • Mike Hott: #359 Bonus Cunt: Sophia Rio / 1996 / MHV / M • Mike Hott: #362 Fuck The Boss #7 / 1996 / MHV / M

MIKE HOWARD see Star Index I
MIKE HUFFMAN
Is The Dr In? / 1979 / AXV / M
MIKE HUNGARY
Private Film #08 / 1994 / OD / M
MIKE HUNT
Daddy's Little Girls / 1983 / CA / M • Let's Talk Sex / 1982 / CA / M • Private Film #10 / 1994 / OD / M
MIKE JEFFERSON see Roger Caine
MIKE JEFFRIES see Roger Caine
MIKE JONES see Star Index I
MIKE JONES (T.CHAP.) see Tom Chapman
MIKE JORDAN see Star Index I
MIKE KHUNTER
Prima #01: Anal Poker / 1995 / MBP / M
MIKE KLEM

Naked Prey / 1996 / GOT / B • Toe Tales #39 / 1996 / GOT / B

MIKE KNIGHT *see Star Index I*

MIKE LAMAS
No Reservations / 1995 / MN0 / G • Switch Hitters #9 / 1995 / IN / G

MIKE LAWRENCE
The Starmaker / 1982 / VC / M

MIKE LENNART
Body Love / 1976 / CA / M

MIKE LEONARD *see Star Index I*

MIKE LEVINSON
American Pie / 1980 / SE / M

MIKE LEWIS *see Star Index I*

MIKE LIVERPOOL
Buttman's Inferno / 1993 / EA / M

MIKE LONDON *see Star Index I*

MIKE LUCKY
Kym Wilde's On The Edge #33 / 1996 / RB / B

MIKE MANN *see Star Index I*

MIKE MARSH
The Coming Of Angie / cr73 / TGA / M

MIKE MASON
Hot Pursuit / 1983 / VC / M

MIKE MCGUFFIN
Amazon Island / 1984 / VHL / B

MIKE MILLER
I, The Jury / 1982 / 2CF / S • The Switch Is On / 1985 / CAT / G

MIKE MITCHELL
Camp Beaverlake #1 / 1984 / AR / M • Killer / 1991 / SC / M • Party #1 / 1979 / NAT / M

MIKE MOORE *see Star Index I*

MIKE MORRISON *see Michael Morrison*

MIKE NICHOLS
My Sister's Husband / 1996 / AWV / G

MIKE O'DONG *see Star Index I*

MIKE O'HAIRA
Next Door Neighbors #15 / 1990 / BON / M • Office Ties / 1992 / BON / B

MIKE ORFEN
Ejacula #1 / 1992 / VC / M • Ejacula #2 / 1992 / VC / M

MIKE ORTEGA *see Star Index I*

MIKE PARKER *see Biff Parker*

MIKE PAYNE *see George Payne*

MIKE PAYNE (OTHER)
Bon Appetite / 1985 / TGA / C

MIKE POWER
Lusty Lawyers / 1995 / PRK / M

MIKE PRESCOTT
Ebony Erotica / 1995 / VT / M • Gang Bang Diaries #5 / 1994 / SFP / M • Sushi Butts / 1994 / SCL / M

MIKE PRESTON
Anal Oriental Sorority / 1994 / LBO / M • Home Nurses Anal Adventure / 1994 / LBO / M

MIKE RABINO
My Pleasure / 1992 / CS / B

MIKE RANGER *(Mike Wrangler, Mike Stephan, Mike Stapp, Mike Stephfen, Rick Ranger, Mike Stepp, Michael Stepp, Mike Strong)*
SO of Loni Sanders at one time. Rumor has it that this is the same as Michael Blodgett.
All About Annette / 1982 / SE / C • All The Action / 1980 / TVX / M • And Four To Go / cr70 / REG / M • Any Time, Any Place / 1981 / CA0 / M • Aunt Peg / 1980 / CV / M • Aunt Peg's Fulfillment / 1980 / CV / M • Bad Girls #1 / 1981 / GO / M • Ball Game / 1980 / CA / M • Balling For Dollars / 1980 / CA / M • The Best Of Raffaelli #1 / 1980 /

DIM / M • Beyond The Valley Of The Ultra Milkmaids / 1984 / 4P / F • Big Mamas / 1981 / ... / C • Black Garters / 19?? / VIS / C • Blue Confessions / 1983 / VCR / M • Blue Vanities #013 / 1988 / FFL / M • Blue Vanities #016 (New) / 1988 / FFL / M • Blue Vanities #017 (Old) / 1988 / FFL / M • Blue Vanities #031 / 1988 / FFL / M • Blue Vanities #037 / 1988 / FFL / M • Blue Vanities #042 (New) / 1988 / FFL / M • Blue Vanities #042 (Old) / 1988 / FFL / M • Blue Vanities #046 (New) / 1988 / FFL / M • Blue Vanities #046 (Old) / 1988 / FFL / M • Blue Vanities #047 (New) / 1988 / FFL / M • Blue Vanities #053 / 1988 / FFL / M • Blue Vanities #061 / 1988 / FFL / M • Blue Vanities #066 / 1988 / FFL / M • Blue Vanities #069 / 1988 / FFL / M • Blue Vanities #070 / 1988 / FFL / M • Blue Vanities #087 / 1988 / FFL / M • Blue Vanities #088 / 1988 / FFL / M • Blue Vanities #090 / 1988 / FFL / M • Blue Vanities #092 / 1988 / FFL / M • Blue Vanities #097 / 1988 / FFL / M • Blue Vanities #104 / 1988 / FFL / M • Blue Vanities #176 / 1992 / FFL / M • Blue Vanities #193 / 1993 / FFL / M • Blue Vanities #204 / 1993 / FFL / M • Blue Vanities #205 / 1993 / FFL / M • Blue Vanities #221 / 1994 / FFL / M • Blue Vanities #246 / 1995 / FFL / M • Blue Vanities #252 / 1996 / FFL / M • Budding Blondes / 1979 / TGA / C • Candy Goes To Hollywood / 1979 / VCX / M • Carnal Encounters Of The Barest Kind / 1978 / VOY / C • Classic Seka #1 / 1988 / AR / C • Classic Seka #2 / 1988 / SUV / C • Classic Swedish Erotica #02 / 1986 / CA / C • Classic Swedish Erotica #03 / 1986 / CA / C • Classic Swedish Erotica #06 / 1986 / CA / C • Classic Swedish Erotica #09 / 1986 / CA / C • Classic Swedish Erotica #13 / 1986 / CA / C • Classic Swedish Erotica #17 / 1986 / CA / C • Classic Swedish Erotica #31 / 1987 / CA / C • Danish Erotica #2 / 1980 / CA / M • Disco Lady / 1978 / EVI / M • Dreams Are Forever / cr72 / AVC / M • Erotic Interlude / 1981 / CA / M • Fantasy Peeps: Sensuous Delights / 1984 / 4P / M • Flight Sensations / 1983 / VC / C • Free And Foxy / 1986 / VCX / C • French Erotica: Inside Hollywood / 1980 / AR / M • French Erotica: Love Story / 1980 / AR / M • French Erotica: Report Card / 1980 / AR / M • Girls Just Wanna Have Boys / 1986 / AMB / M • Golden Girls #02 / 1981 / SVE / M • Goodbye My Love / 1980 / CA / M • Heavenly Desire / 1979 / WV / M • High School Report Card / 1979 / CA / M • Hong Kong Hookers / 1984 / AMB / M • Hot Ones / 1982 / SUP / C • Hot Property (AVC) / 1975 / AVC / M • Hot Skin In 3D / 1977 / ... / M • Hustler Video Magazine #2 / 1984 / SE / M • Insatiable #1 / 1980 / CA / M • Kate And The Indians / 1980 / SE / M • Kiss And Tell / 1980 / CA / M • A Lacy Affair #2 / 1985 / HO / C • Las Vegas Lady / 1981 / VCX / M • Lights, Camera, Orgy / 1979 / LOV / M • Limited Edition #02 / 1979 / AVC / M • Limited Edition #07 / 1979 / AVC / M • The Little French Maid / 1981 / VCX / M • Little Orphan Dusty #1 / 1978 / ALP / M • Long Hard Summer / 1989 / BMV / C • Love Goddesses / 1981 / VC / M • Loving Lesbos / 1983 / VCR / C • Loving Lips / 1987 / AMB / C • Lust At First Bite / 1978 / VC / M • Lust Flight 2000 / 1978 / VHL / M • Lusty Ladies #02 / 1983 / 4P / M • Lusty Ladies

#03 / 1983 / SVE / M • Lusty Ladies #11 / 1984 / 4P / M • Mrs. Rodger's Neighborhood / 1988 / EVN / C • Nanci Blue / 1979 / SE / M • Nasty Romances / 1985 / HO / C • Naughty Network / 1981 / CA / M • Never So Deep / 1981 / VCX / M • Night Flight / cr80 / CRE / M • Odds And Ends / 1981 / TGA / M • Only The Best Of Breasts / 1987 / CV / C • The Perils Of Prunella #1 / 1980 / BIZ / B • Physical #1 / 1981 / SUP / M • Plato's Retreat West / 1983 / CRE / M • Plato's, The Movie / 1980 / SE / M • Porn In The USA #2 / 1987 / VEN / C • Remember Connie / 1984 / MAP / M • The Rites Of Uranus / 1975 / SOW / M • Same Time Every Year / 1981 / VHL / M • The Seduction Of Seka / 1981 / AVC / M • Seka's Teenage Diary / 1984 / HO / C • Sensual Encounters Of Every Kind / 1978 / SE / M • Sex Boat / 1980 / VCX / M • Sex Rink / 1976 / ALP / M • Shoppe Of Temptation / 1979 / AR / M • Showgirl #14: Kitty Shane's Fantasies / 1983 / VCR / M • Star Virgin / 1979 / CXV / M • Starship Eros / 1980 / SE / M • Sugar In The Raw / 1975 / AVC / M • Super-Ware Party / 1979 / AR / M • Swedish Erotica #02 / 1980 / CA / M • Swedish Erotica #05 / 1980 / CA / M • Swedish Erotica #13 / 1980 / CA / M • Swedish Erotica #14 / 1980 / CA / M • Swedish Erotica #20 / 1980 / CA / M • Swedish Erotica #21 / 1980 / CA / M • Swedish Erotica #27 / 1980 / CA / M • Swedish Erotica #31 / 1980 / CA / M • Swedish Erotica #32 / 1980 / CA / M • Swedish Erotica #33 / 1980 / CA / M • Swedish Erotica #35 / 1980 / CA / M • Sweet Cheeks / 1980 / VCX / M • Sweet Temptations / cr74 / AVC / M • Swing Club / 1975 / VC / M • Taboo #01 / 1980 / VCX / M • Taboo #04 / 1985 / IN / M • A Taste For Passion / 1983 / AMB / M • A Taste Of Sugar / 1978 / AR / M • Taxi Girls #1 / 1980 / WV / M • Teenage Dessert / 1976 / ALP / M • Teenage Playmates / 1979 / LOV / M • Telefantasy / 1978 / AR / M • That's Erotic / 1979 / CV / C • That's Porno / 1979 / CV / C • Tinsel Town / 1980 / VC / M • A Touch Of Love / cr70 / VC / C • Tough Cookie / cr78 / M$M / C • Triple Header / 1987 / AIR / C • Ultraflesh / 1980 / GO / M • The Velvet Edge / cr76 / SE / M • Wet Dreams / 1980 / WWV / M • Wet Shots (Vcr) / 1983 / VCR / C • What Would Your Mother Say? / 1981 / HAV / M • Yamahama Mamas / 1983 / TGA / C • Young And Foolish / 197? / IHV / M • Young Doctors In Lust / 1979 / NSV / M • Young, Hot And Nasty / cr88 / BWV / C • Yummy Nymphs / 1983 / TGA / C • [Fuck Me, Suck Me, Eat Me / 1990 / ... / M

MIKE RAY
Lactamania #1 / 1994 / TTV / M • Ready To Drop #03 / 1994 / FC / M

MIKE REED *see Star Index I*

MIKE REED (GAUNT) *see Michael Gaunt*

MIKE RILEY *see Mickey Ray*

MIKE ROGERS
Angela In Wonderland / 1986 / VD / M • Naughty Cheerleaders / 1985 / HO / M

MIKE RONDS
The Nite Bird / 1978 / BL / M

MIKE RYAN *see Star Index I*

MIKE SCHIFF *see Star Index I*

MIKE SCORPIO *see Star Index I*

MIKE SCORTINO *see Star Index I*

MIKE SEPULVEDA
Butt-Nanza / 1995 / WV / M
MIKE SHADOE *see Star Index I*
MIKE SHADOW
Western Nights / 1994 / WP / M
MIKE SHEA
Beneath The Mermaids / 1975 / ... / M
MIKE SHIGGS
Nightclub / 1996 / SC / M
MIKE SILVER
Family Affair / 1996 / XC / M
MIKE SOUTH
AVP #7004: Orgy 1 at Topside II / 1990 / AVP / M • Here Comes Jenny St. James / 1996 / HOV / M • More Black Dirty Debutantes / 1994 / 4P / M • Odyssey 30 Min: #303: / 1993 / OD / M • Southern Belles #1 / 1994 / HOV / M • Southern Belles #2 / 1995 / HOV / M • Southern Belles #3 / 1995 / HOV / M • Southern Belles #4 / 1995 / HOV / M • Southern Belles #5 / 1995 / XPR / M • Southern Belles #6 / 1996 / XPR / M • Southern Belles #7 / 1996 / XPR / M • Southern Belles #8 / 1997 / XPR / M • Southern Belles: Sugar Magnolias / 1996 / XPR / M
MIKE SPENCE
N.Y. Video Magazine #05 / 1995 / OUP / M
MIKE STANS
Employee Benefits / 1983 / AMB / M
MIKE STAPP *see Mike Ranger*
MIKE STEELE
Nasty Newcummers #13 / 1995 / MET / M
MIKE STEPHAN *see Mike Ranger*
MIKE STEPHANO *see Star Index I*
MIKE STEPHEN
Bon Appetite / 1985 / TGA / C • Service Entrance / 1979 / REG / C
MIKE STEPHFEN *see Mike Ranger*
MIKE STEPP *see Mike Ranger*
MIKE STRONG *see Mike Ranger*
MIKE THOMAS
Kym Wilde's On The Edge #17 / 1995 / RB / B
MIKE WILD *see Star Index I*
MIKE WINARD
Oriental Gang Bang Fantasy / 1994 / FC / M
MIKE WINNINGER *see Star Index I*
MIKE WRANGLER *see Mike Ranger*
MIKE YEAGER
Beach Bum Amateur's #10 / 1992 / MID / M • Pearl Necklace: Amorous Amateurs #18 / 1992 / SEE / M • Pearl Necklace: Amorous Amateurs #20 / 1992 / SEE / M
MIKELLA
She'll Take A Spanking / 199? / BON / B
MIKEY
All For His Ladies / 1987 / PP / C • Meat Market / 1992 / SEX / C • Reel People #02 / 1984 / AR / M
MIKEY (J. COX) *see Michael J. Cox*
MIKHAIL
100% Amateur #19: / 1996 / OD / M
MIKI
Rodney's Rookies #1 / 1996 / NIT / M • The Witch's Tail / 1994 / GOU / M
MIKI KUROSAWA *see Star Index I*
MIKI MARSALLI *see Ashley Rene*
MIKI MING *see Star Index I*
MIKI MURAKAMI
Hot Spa Sex / 1996 / AVE / M • Jacuzzi Lust / 1996 / AVE / M
MIKI STAR *see Star Index I*
MIKKI
Fantasy Photography: Hot Date / 1995 /

FAP / F
MIKKI BRENNER
Penthouse: Paradise Revisited / 1992 / PET / F • Sex Off The Runway / 1991 / GMI / M
MIKKI DAVIDSON
Dream Jeans / 1987 / CA / M • Nudes At Eleven #1 / 1986 / AVC / M • Star Gazers / 1986 / CA / M
MIKKI LYNN *see Micki Lynn*
MIKKI MALONE
Not too pretty blonde with white skin, cantaloupes with a large tattoo on the left one, and a getting-womanly body. 21 years old in 1996 and de-virginized at 16.
Anal Crash Test Dummies / 1997 / ROB / M • Anal Jammin' & Slammin' / 1996 / ROB / M • The Blowjob Adventures Of Doctor Fellatio / 1997 / EL / M • Butt Row Unplugged / 1996 / ABS / M • Butthole Sweetheart / 1996 / ROB / M • Cumback Pussy #4: Get Some!!! / 1996 / EL / M • Drop Sex: Wipe The Floor / 1997 / JLP / M • Filthy First Timers #5 / 1997 / EL / M • Hot Tight Asses #18 / 1996 / TCK / M • Interracial Video Virgins #01 / 1996 / NS / M • Lady Sterling Takes It Up The Arse / 1997 / ROB / M
MIKKI SNOW *see Micki Snow*
MIKKI STAR *see Star Index I*
MIKLA
Mike Hott: #255 Cunt Of The Month: Mikla / 1994 / MHV / M • Reel People #04 / 1994 / PP / M
MIKO
Blue Vanities #548 / 1994 / FFL / M • Joe Elliot's Asian College Girls #01 / 1995 / JOE / F • Porno Screentests / 1982 / VC / M
MIKO MOTO *see Mai Lin*
MIKO NAMURA *see Star Index I*
MIKO YAMA *see Kyoto Sun*
MIKO YANI-KYOTO *see Kyoto Sun*
MIKOSCH
Sperm Injection / 1995 / PL / M
MILA SHEGOL *(Mishka (Mila), Lisa Latore)*
Supposedly Polish although some sources say Russian, this girl is petite with short blonde hair, passable face, small tits, and a tight little body.
The Adventures Of Peeping Tom #3 / 1996 / OD / M • Anal Booty Burner / 1996 / ROB / M • Anal Jammin' & Slammin' / 1996 / ROB / M • Anna Malle Exposed / 1996 / WV / M • Another White Trash Whore / 1996 / JMP / M • Badgirls #7: Lust Confined / 1995 / VI / M • Basix / 1996 / MET / M • Beyond Reality #2: Anal Expedition / 1996 / EXQ / M • Butthole Sweetheart / 1996 / ROB / M • Buttslammers #12: Anal Madness / 1996 / BS / F • By Myself / 1996 / PL / F • Casting Call #18 / 1996 / SO / M • Cherry Poppers #14: Teeny Tongues / 1996 / ZA / M • Cumback Pussy #4: Get Some!!! / 1996 / EL / M • Deadly Sin / 1996 / ONA / M • Erotic Newcummers Vol 1 #5 / 1996 / DR / M • Fashion Passion / 1997 / TEP / M • Hot Tight Asses #18 / 1996 / TCK / M • I'm So Horny, Baby / 1997 / ROB / M • Introducing Mishka / 1995 / H&S / S • Lockdown / 1996 / NIT / M • Lust Behind Bars / 1996 / GO / M • Macin' #1 / 1996 / SMP / M • Mall Slut / 1997 / SC / M • Max #10: Dirty Deeds / 1996 / XPR / M • Max World #4: Let's Party / 1996 / XPR / M •

Nymphos / 1995 / MET / M • Perverted Stories #11 / 1996 / JMP / M • The Phantom Of The Montague Stage / 1997 / HO / M • Pick Up Lines #09 / 1996 / OD / M • Promises And Lies / 1996 / NIT / M • Puritan Video Magazine #07 / 1996 / LE / M • Pussyman #15: The Bone Voyage Bash / 1997 / SNA / M • Rectal Raiders / 1997 / ROB / M • Rockhard (Sin City) / 1996 / SC / M • Rumpman In And Out Of Africa / 1996 / HW / M • Samantha & Company / 1996 / PL / M • The Shocking Truth #2 / 1996 / DWO / M • Sodomania #19: Sweet Cream / 1996 / EL / M • Triple X Video Magazine #02 / 1995 / OD / M • The Very Best Of Breasts #2 / 1996 / H&S / S • War Whores / 1996 / EL / M • Wild Assed Pooper Slut / 1996 / ROB / M
MILES
Gang Bangs #1 / 1985 / VCR / M • Headgames / 1985 / WV / M • Lust American Style / 1985 / WV / M
MILES LONG
Denni O' #5: / 1996 / SP / M • Eat At Dave's #7 / 1996 / SP / M • Heartthrobs / 1985 / CA / M • Oriental Jade / 1985 / VC / M • The Spectacular Denni O'Brien / 1995 / SP / M
MILES MELON *see Johnny Angel*
MILES MOODY *see Star Index I*
MILES WEST
Animal Impulse / 1985 / AA / M • New Girls In Town #5 / 1994 / CC / M • Sexaholic / 1985 / AVC / M
MILINDA
Slave Of Fashion / 1993 / LON / B
MILKMAID
Fantasy Peeps: Sensuous Delights / 1984 / 4P / M
MILKY DEMARIS
All About Sex / 1970 / AR / M
MILLER
HomeGrown Video #444: / 1995 / HOV / M • HomeGrown Video #458: Cream Pie For Dessert / 1995 / HOV / C
MILLICENT
Blue Vanities #130 / 1990 / FFL / M • Blue Vanities #579 / 1995 / FFL / M
MILLIE
A&B AB#252: Grandma Is In The Ali Again! / 1991 / A&B / F • Big British Plumpers / 1989 / BTO / M • Blue Vanities #512 / 1992 / FFL / M • Blue Vanities #558 / 1994 / FFL / M • Blue Vanities #568 / 1995 / FFL / M • New Busom Brits / 199? / H&S / S
MILLIE *see Texas Milly*
MILLIE MUSHMOUTH
Gum Me Bare #1 / 1994 / GLI / M
MILLIE SUTTON
Flipside: A Backdoor Adventure / 1985 / CV / M
MILLY MOON *see Star Index I*
MILO *see Star Index I*
MILT INGERSOLL *see Michael Morrison*
MILT INGLEY *see Michael Morrison*
MILTON BOIL
Teenage Pajama Party / 1977 / VC / M
MILTON BURLEY
N.Y. Video Magazine #03 / 1995 / OUP / M
MILTON CAMP *see Star Index I*
MILTON ENGLIE *see Michael Morrison*
MILTON INGERSOLL *see Michael Morrison*
MIMI
Blue Vanities #565 / 1995 / FFL / M • The Booty Bandit / 1994 / FC / M • I Obey You / 1993 / VTF / B • Sweet Dreams / 1994 /

ORE / C

MIMI DANIELS *see Star Index I*

MIMI GOODE *see Star Index I*

MIMI HALE
The Devil's Playground / 1974 / VC / M

MIMI LACROIX
Sex Off The Runway / 1991 / GMI / M

MIMI MIAGGI *see Mimi Miyagi*

MIMI MILLER *see Star Index I*

MIMI MIYAGI *(Myagi, Miyagi, Mimi Miaggi)*
Hard Oriental girl with inflated tits and a superiority attitude. Japanese extraction comes from Guam. She was born in Davao in the Phillipines and is half Chinese. Born Jul 3, 1973. She was born in Shinguki, Japan. Well, take your pick; she was probably hatched!
America's Raunchiest Home Videos #09: Orgasmic Oriental / 1992 / ZA / M • Anal Adventures #1: Anal Executive / 1991 / VC / M • Anal Asian #1 / 1992 / IN / M • Anal Asian / 1994 / VEX / M • Anal Asians / 1991 / PL / F • Anal Climax #2 / 1991 / ROB / M • Anal Delights #1 / 1992 / ROB / M • Anal Innocence #1 / 1991 / ROB / M • Asian Angel / 1993 / VEX / C • Bangkok Bangers / 1995 / BTO / M • Bardot / 1991 / VI / M • The Best Of Oriental Anal #1 / 1994 / ROB / C • Blow Job Betty / 1991 / CC / M • Blue Fox / 1991 / VI / M • Busty Bangkok Bangers / 1996 / H&S / M • Butthead Dreams: Exposed / 1995 / FH / M • Caught From Behind #17 / 1992 / HO / M • Chocolate & Vanilla Twist / 1992 / PL / F • The Cockateer #1 / 1991 / LE / M • Debi Does Girls / 1992 / PL / F • Deep Throat #6 / 1992 / AFV / M • The Dragon Lady #2: Tales From the Bed / 1992 / WV / M • The Dragon Lady #4: Tales From The Bed #3 / 1992 / WV / M • Girlz N The Hood #1 / 1991 / HW / M • Juicy Treats / 1991 / ROB / M • The Last Good Sex / 1992 / FD / M • Lather / 1991 / LE / M • Madam X / 1992 / HO / M • Made In Japan / 1992 / VI / M • Made To Order / 1994 / FD / C • Mai Lin's Anal Asians / 1992 / PL / C • More Dirty Debutantes #12 / 1991 / 4P / M • Oriental Anal Sluts / 1993 / WV / C • Oriental Girls In Heat / 1995 / IF / M • Oriental Obsession / 1993 / HO / C • Oriental Temptations / 1992 / WV / M • Paper Tiger / 1992 / VI / M • Penthouse: Satin & Lace #1 / 1992 / PET / F • Rainbows / 1992 / VT / F • Raquel Released / 1991 / VI / M • Reflections / 1995 / FD / M • Ripe & Ready (Infinity) / 1995 / IF / M • Secret Diary #2 / 1995 / MID / M • Sensual Exposure / 1993 / ULI / M • Seoul Train / 1991 / IN / M • Sex #1 (Vivid) / 1993 / VI / M • Sex Drive / 1993 / VEX / M • Sex Sting / 1992 / FD / M • Sex Symphony / 1992 / VC / M • Sex Trek #2: The Search For Sperm / 1991 / ME / M • She's The Boss / 1992 / VIM / M • Star Struck / 1992 / VEX / M • The Starlet / 1991 / PP / M • Whoppers #6 / 1993 / VEX / F • Women Of Color / 1991 / PL / F • The Wong Side Of Town / 1992 / LV / M

MIMI MORGAN *(Mimi Zuber, M. Matisse, Mimi Sanderson, Michelle Moore, Susan Smreker)*
Passable face, tiny tits, bit flat on butt, shoulder length brown hair, emaciated body. Michelle Moore is from **Sissy's Hot Summer** and **One Way At A Time**.
Assbusters / cr70 / WV / M • The Awakening Of Sally / 1984 / VCR / M • Black Heat

/ 1986 / VCR / C • Blue Confessions / 1983 / VCR / M • Blue Vanities #054 / 1988 / FFL / M • Candy Stripers #1 / 1978 / ALP / M • Coming Home Baby / 1975 / VEP / M • Dark Passions / 1984 / VCR / C • Dixie / 1976 / VHL / M • Fantastic Orgy / 197? / … / M • Fantasy In Blue / 1975 / IHV / M • Femmes De Sade / 1976 / ALP / M • Finishing School / 1975 / SOW / M • Foxy Lady / 1978 / CV / M • The Girls In The Band / 1976 / SVE / M • House Of Desires / cr78 / BL / M • Is The Dr In? / 1979 / AXV / M • Island Of Dr Love / 1977 / S&L / M • The Jade Pussycat / 1977 / CA / M • Judgement Day / 1976 / CV / M • Legends Of Porn #1 / 1987 / CV / C • My First Time / 1976 / GO / M • One Of A Kind / 1976 / SVE / M • One Way At A Time / 1979 / CA / M • Open For Business / 1983 / AMB / M • Pink Punk / 19?? / ECO / C • Pretty Peaches #1 / 1978 / MIT / M • Rear Entry / 1985 / VCR / C • Resurrection Of Eve / 1973 / MIT / M • Rollerbabies / 1976 / VC / M • Sally's Palace Of Delight / cr76 / CV / M • Savage Lust / 19?? / SIL / M • Screwples / 1979 / CA / M • Service Entrance / 1979 / REG / C • Sheila's Payoff / 1977 / VCX / M • Sissy's Hot Summer / 1979 / CA / M • Studio Of Lust / 1984 / HO / C • Telefantasy / 1978 / AR / M • Treasure Box / 1981 / VC / M • True Legends Of Adult Cinema: The Cult Superstars / 1993 / VC / C • The Ultimate Pleasure / 1977 / HIF / M • United We Fall / 19?? / REG / C • [Chain Letter / 1978 / … / M

MIMI SANDERSON *see Mimi Morgan*

MIMI VAN AENT
Close Up / 19?? / BOC / M

MIMI VAN ZANT *see Star Index I*

MIMI WONG *see Trisha Yin*

MIMI WOODSTOCK
School Teacher's Weekend Vacation / cr72 / SVE / M

MIMI YEN *see Trisha Yin*

MIMI ZUBER *see Mimi Morgan*

MINA *(Lynn Zamora)*
Short stocky Oriental with enhanced large tits and marginal face. May have some black overtones. Lynn Zamora is from **Shame**.
100% Amateur #09: Asians & Latinas / 1995 / OD / M • Anal Asian #2: The Wonton Woman / 1994 / IN / M • Creme De Femme / 1994 / 4P / F • Horny Henry's Oriental Adventure / 1994 / TTV / M • Invitation To The Blues / 1994 / LE / M • Makin' It / 1994 / A&E / M • More Dirty Debutantes #38 / 1995 / 4P / M • More Dirty Debutantes #40 / 1995 / 4P / M • More Dirty Debutantes #45 / 1995 / 4P / M • New Ends #10 / 1995 / 4P / M • Reel People #05 / 1994 / PP / M • Reel People #11 / 1995 / PP / M • Ride 'em Cow Girl / 1995 / VI / C • Shame / 1994 / VI / M • Sleeping Single / 1994 / CC / M

MINA BYRD
The End Zone / 1993 / PRE / B • Red Bottoms / 1988 / BIZ / B

MINA SOLE
The Comeback Of Marilyn / 1986 / VC / M • Hot Desires / 1986 / VC / M

MINDI
Rainwoman #07: In The Rainforest / 1993 / CC / M

MINDY
The Best Of Big Busty / 1986 / L&W / C • Classic Swedish Erotica #10 / 1986 / CA /

C • Hard Ball / 1991 / NAN / M • Hot Body Video Magazine: Beverly Hills Wet T-Shirt Contest / 1994 / CG / F • Midnight Angels #03 / 1993 / MID / F • The Nurses Are Cumming #2 / 1996 / LBO / C

MINDY BRANDT *see Rene Bond*

MINDY COLE
Sound Of Love / 1981 / CA / M

MINDY RAE *(Amanda Rae (Mindy), Mandy Starr, Dee Vine)*
Amanda Rae is from **Eyes of Eddie Mars**.
Amber Aroused / 1985 / CA / M • Backdoor Romance / 1984 / VIV / M • The Beat Goes On / 1987 / VCR / C • Between My Breasts #01 / 1986 / BTO / S • Beverly Hills Exposed / 1985 / SE / M • Beverly Hills Heat / 1985 / VEP / M • Big, Bad & Beautiful / 1988 / MIR / C • Bouncin' In The U.S.A. / 1986 / H&S / S • Breastography, Lesson #1 / 1987 / VCR / M • Bursting Bras / 1990 / BTO / C • Camp Beaverlake #1 / 1984 / AR / M • Cherry Busters / 1984 / VIV / M • Classic Swedish Erotica #16 / 1986 / CA / C • Cummin' Alive / 1984 / VC / M • Dear Fanny / 1984 / CV / M • Erotic Zones #1 / 1985 / CA / M • Erotic Zones #3 / 1986 / CA / M • The Eyes Of Eddie Mars / 1984 / CV / M • Famous Ta-Ta's #1 / 1986 / VCS / C • Fantasy Land / 1984 / LA / M • The Fire Inside / 1988 / VC / C • Gettin' Ready / 1985 / CDI / M • The Girl With The Hungry Eyes / 1984 / ECS / M • Girls Of Cell Block F / 1985 / WV / M • Girls Of The Third Reich / 1985 / FC / M • Hot Gypsy Love / 1985 / CDI / M • Hot Merchandise / 1985 / AVC / M • Hot Touch / 1984 / VCX / M • How To Perform Fellatio / 1985 / VCR / M • I Love LA #1 / 1986 / PEN / C • I Love LA #2 / 1989 / PEN / C • Indecent Itch / 1985 / VCR / M • Juggs / 1984 / VCR / M • Limited Edition #29 / 1984 / AVC / M • Looking For Love / 1985 / VCX / M • Make My Night / 1985 / CIN / M • Parliament: Dildo Babes #1 / 1986 / PM / F • Parliament: Kingsize / 1987 / PM / F • Parliament: Lonesome Ladies #1 / 1987 / PM / F • The Pornbirds / 1985 / VC / M • Pulsating Flesh / 1986 / VC / M • Rubdown / 1985 / VCX / M • Sensuous Singles: Trinity Loren / 1987 / VCR / F • The Sex Change Girls / 1987 / 4P / G • Sexpertease / 1985 / VD / M • Skin Games / 1986 / VEX / M • Skin Games / 1991 / VEX / C • Spring Fever / 1986 / FAN / C • Star 85: Kari Fox / 1985 / VEX / M • Swedish Erotica #59 / 1984 / CA / M • Sweet Cheeks / 1987 / VCR / C • A Taste Of Julia Parton / 1992 / VD / C • Voyeur's Delight / 1986 / VCS / C • Wet Panties / 1989 / MIR / C • Wild Toga Party / 1985 / VD / M • The Wizard Of AHH's / 1985 / SE / M • [Trailer Park Twats / 1986 / … / M

MINDY ROSE *see Marilyn Rose*

MINDY WEST *see Star Index I*

MINDY WILSON
ABA: Double Feature #2 / 1996 / ALP / M • Fannie / 1975 / ALP / M

MINERVA *see Evon Crawford*

MING JADE *see Star Index I*

MING SONG
Pleasure Productions #06 / 1984 / VCR / M

MING TOY *(Ming Toy Epstein)*
All About Gloria Leonard / 1978 / VXP / M • Captain Lust And The Amorous Contessa / 1977 / IHV / M • Erotic Fortune Cookies / 1975 / VCX / M • Heat Wave / 1977 / COM / M • The Little Blue Box / 1978 / BL / M •

Matinee Idol / 1984 / VC / M • Open For Business / 1983 / AMB / M • Oriental Lust / 1983 / GO / M • A Touch Of Desire / 1983 / VCR / C

MING TOY EPSTEIN *see* **Ming Toy**

MINK

Anal & 3-Way Play / 1995 / GLI / M • Black Ass Masters #1 / 1995 / GLI / M • Older Women With Younger Ideas / 1995 / GLI / M • Titan's Amateur Video Magazine #03 / 1995 / TEG / M • Wet Mask / 1995 / SC / M

MINKA

Asian Tit-Queen / 1996 / NAP / B • Bangkok Bangers / 1995 / BTO / M • Bangkok Boobarella / 1996 / BTO / M • Busty Bangkok Bangers / 1996 / H&S / M • Dim Sum (Eating Chinese) / 1996 / SUF / M • Duke Of Knockers #2 / 1995 / BTO / M • Girls Around The World #25 / 1995 / BTO / S • H&S: Minka / 199? / H&S / S • Lesbian Nights / 1996 / AVI / F • The Magnificence Of Minka / 1996 / NAP / S • Orient Sexpress / 1996 / AVI / M • The Twin Peaks Of Mount Fuji / 1996 / SUF / M

MINKY

100% Amateur #04: Oriental Orientation / 1995 / OD / M

MINNI CHAMP

Brollopsnatten / 1993 / RUM / M • Inter City 11.25 / 1993 / RUM / M

MINNIE BLACK *see* **Star Index I**

MINNIE CHAMP

Detained / 1996 / PL / M • Scandanavian Double Features #4 / 1996 / PL / M • Upstairs And Downstairs / 1995 / PL / M

MINNIE FORD

Flesh...And The Fantasies / 1991 / BIZ / B

MINNIE WHITE

Bad Black Beulah / 1975 / VCX / M

MINT PENNY *see* **Star Index I**

MINU MENAGE

Bizarre Styles / 1981 / ALP / B

MINX *see* **Chelsea Lynx**

MINX MANX

San Francisco Lesbians #1 / 1992 / PL / F

MINX ST CLAIR *see* **Star Index I**

MIO *see* **Meo**

MIORI YADAMI *see* **Star Index I**

MIOSHI *see* **Star Index I**

MIRANDA

Black Mystique #03 / 1994 / VT / F • Pearl Necklace: Amorous Amateurs #07 / 1992 / SEE / M • Pearl Necklace: Amorous Amateurs #08 / 1992 / SEE / M

MIRANDA CHANEY *see* **Star Index I**

MIRANDA PARKS *see* **Star Index I**

MIRANDA RIGHTS

Pearl Necklace: Amorous Amateurs #39 / 1993 / SEE / M • Pearl Necklace: Facial #01 / 1994 / SEE / C • Pearl Necklace: Premier Sessions #02 / 1993 / SEE / M • Pearl Necklace: Thee Bush League #26 / 1993 / SEE / M • Tech: Miranda Wright #1 / 1994 / TWA / F • Tech: Miranda Wright #2 / 1994 / TWA / F

MIRANDA STEVENS

The Cosmopolitan Girls / 1982 / VC / M • The Erotic World Of Angel Cash / 1983 / VXP / M • Twilight Pink #2 / 1982 / VC / M • VCA Previews #2 / 1988 / VC / C

MISA

Black Snatch #1 / 1996 / DFI / F

MISAKI

Anal Asians / 1991 / PL / F • Anal Cuties #1 / 1992 / ROB / M • Anal Cuties #2 / 1992 / ROB / M • Anal Cuties #3 / 1992 / ROB / M

• The Best Of Oriental Anal #1 / 1994 / ROB / C • Booty Babes / 1993 / ROB / F • Confessions #2 / 1992 / OD / M • Nikki's Nightlife / 1992 / IN / M • Tails From The Tower / 1993 / AFI / M

MISHA

Between My Breasts #10 / 1990 / BTO / M • Ebony Lust / 19?? / HOR / C • New Ends #10 / 1995 / 4P / M • New Faces, Hot Bodies #02 / 1992 / STP / M • New Faces, Hot Bodies #03 / 1992 / STP / M • New Faces, Hot Bodies #21 / 1996 / STP / C

MISHA BOYKO

Ultraflesh / 1980 / GO / M

MISHA GARR *see* **Star Index I**

MISHI

Cumback Pussy #7: NUGIRLZ / 1997 / EL / M

MISHKA (MILA) *see* **Mila Shegol**

MISKOLE GYOR

Blue Vanities #192 / 1993 / FFL / M

MISS C.

A&B AB#443: We Love Cock / 1994 / A&B / M

MISS CHELSEA

The New Snatch Masters #16 / 1995 / LEI / C

MISS CLEOPATRA *see* **Star Index I**

MISS D.D. *see* **Debi Diamond**

MISS DEE

Raw Deal / 1994 / GOT / B

MISS DIVA

She Males Enslaved / 1996 / BIZ / G • She-Males In Torment #3 / 1995 / BIZ / G

MISS HIGGENBOTTOM *see* **Star Index I**

MISS J. FOX *see* **Star Index I**

MISS JADE

Erotic Tattooing And Piercing #1 / 1986 / FLV / M

MISS JENNIFER *see* **Star Index I**

MISS M. *see* **Star Index I**

MISS PETERSON *see* **Star Index I**

MISS POMODORO

Beefy blonde from Hungary (not Italy) who looked like she had potential but turns out to have an inflated idea of her own importance. Medium tits, not too pretty face, flattish rear end.

All Inside Eva / 1991 / PL / M • Anal Assassins / 1991 / IN / M • Anal Commander / 1990 / ZA / M • The Backpackers #3 / 1991 / IN / M • Erotic Games / 1992 / PL / M • Foreign Bodies / 1991 / IN / M • Lovin' Spoonfuls #5 / 1996 / 4P / C • Malibu Spice / 1991 / VC / M • Model Wife / 1991 / CA / M • More Dirty Debutantes #26 / 1993 / 4P / M • Passionate Lovers / 1991 / PL / M • Sexy Country Girl / 1991 / PL / M • Strange Behavior / 1991 / VD / M • World Cup / 1990 / PL / M • [Baby Nata Per Godere / 19?? / ... / M • [Desideri Bestiali E Vuluttuosi / 19?? / ... / M • [Giochi & Follie Di Miss Pomodoro / 19?? / HOB / M • [H'perversioni Deglie Angeli / 19?? / HOB / M • [Piu' Di Sodoma E Gomorra / 19?? / HOB / M

MISS SCARLET

Hershe Highway #5: Backdoor Blues / 1996 / HO / M

MISS TWIN PYRAMIDS

Between My Breasts #07 / 1989 / L&W / M • Huge Ladies #07 / cr90 / H&S / M

MISS TWIN TOWERS

Ataack Of The Giant Mutant Tits / 1996 / H&S / S • Bad Mama Jama Busts Out / 1989 / VT / M • Between My Breasts #02 / 1986 / L&W / S • Big Busty #19 / 198? /

H&S / M • Big Tit Orgy #01 / 1987 / H&S / M • Big Top Cabaret #1 / 1986 / BTO / M • Breast Of Britain #2 / 1987 / BTO / M • Bursting Bras / 1990 / BTO / C • Fatliners #2 / 1991 / EX / M • Mega-Tits / 1990 / NAP / F • Miss Twin Towers / 198? / BTO / M • Underdog / 1990 / NAP / B

MISS TWIN VOLCANOS

The Best Of Wild Bill's Big Ladies / 1996 / H&S / C • Huge Ladies #06 / cr90 / L&W / S • Huge Ladies #07 / cr90 / H&S / M • Miss Twin Volcanos / 198? / H&S / M • The Twin Pyramids / 1988 / L&W / M

MISSOURI GUILT

Anal Virgins Of America #07 / 1994 / FOR / M • Video Virgins #17 / 1994 / NS / M

MISSY *(Natasha Marie)*

Pretty blonde with long curly hair, peaches and cream complexion, strong thighs, two moles on her left cheek, small tits, nice personality. Says she was 27 years old and 5'3" tall in 1995. Married to an older guy with a beard who is usually credited as just Mickey.

1-900-FUCK #3 / 1995 / SO / M • 100% Amateur #05: Threesomes & Group Scenes / 1995 / OD / M • Adam & Eve's House Party #2: Bachelor Party / 1996 / VC / M • Airotica / 1996 / SC / M • American Fan Club Prowl / 1996 / VT / M • American Tushy! / 1996 / ULI / M • Anal Academy / 1996 / ZA / M • Anal Alley / 1996 / FD / M • Anal Anarchy / 1995 / VC / M • Anal Fever / 1996 / ROB / M • Anal Inquisition / 1996 / ZA / M • Anal Interrogation / 1995 / ZA / M • Anal Island #2 / 1996 / VC / M • Anal Jeopardy / 1996 / ZA / M • Anal Maniacs #3 / 1995 / WP / M • Anal Nitrate / 1995 / PE / M • Anal Portrait / 1996 / ZA / M • Anal Professor / 1996 / ZA / M • Anal Runaway / 1996 / ZA / M • Anal Savage #3 / 1996 / ROB / M • Anal Sex / 1996 / ZA / M • Anal Talisman / 1996 / ZA / M • Ass Lover's Special / 1996 / PE / M • Asses Galore #1: From L.A. To Brazil / 1996 / DFI / M • Asses Galore #5: T.T. Vs The World / 1996 / DFI / M • Asst #01 / 1996 / JMP / M • Assy #1 / 1996 / JMP / M • The Attendant / 1996 / SC / M • Babe Watch Beach / 1996 / SC / M • Bad Influence / 1996 / ZA / M • Best Butt(e) In The West #2 / 1995 / CC / M • Beyond Reality #2: Anal Expedition / 1996 / EXQ / M • Beyond Reality #3: Stand Erect! / 1996 / EXQ / M • Bitches In Heat #1: Locked In The Basement / 1995 / ZA / M • Bite The Black Bullets / 1995 / ME / M • Bodyslammers / 1996 / ME / M • Bondage Of The Rising Sun / 1996 / BON / B • Borderline (Vivid) / 1995 / VI / M • Born 2 B Wild / 1995 / PL / M • Buffy Malibu's Nasty Girls #10 / 1996 / ANA / F • Busty Backdoor Nurses / 1996 / PL / M • The Butt Sisters Do Seattle / 1995 / MID / M • Buttslammers #10: Lust On The Internet / 1995 / BS / F • Buttslammers #11: / 1996 / BS / F • Buttslammers #13: The Madness Continues / 1996 / BS / F • Car Wash Angels / 1995 / VC / M • Caught From Behind #22 / 1995 / HO / M • Caught Looking / 1995 / CC / M • The Cellar Dweller / 1996 / EL / M • Chained Heat / 1996 / APP / M • Channel 69 / 1996 / CC / M • Chasey Saves The World / 1996 / VI / M • Cheerleader Strippers / 1996 / PE / M • Cherry Poppers #13: Anal Pajama Party / 1996 / ZA / M • Cirque Du Sex #1 / 1996 / VT / M • Cirque Du Sex

#2 / 1996 / VT / M • Coming Of Fortune / 1994 / EX / M • The Comix / 1995 / VI / M • The Complete & Total Anal Workout #1 / 1995 / ZA / M • Concrete Heat / 1996 / XCI / M • Conquest / 1996 / WP / M • Creme De Femme / 1994 / 4P / F • Cum Buttered Corn Holes #3 / 1996 / NIT / C • Cuntrol / 1994 / MID / F • Daydreams, Nightdreams / 1996 / VC / M • Decadent Dreams / 1996 / ME / M • Deep Inside Juli Ashton / 1996 / VC / C • Deep Inside Kaitlyn Ashley / 1995 / VC / C • Deep Inside Missy / 1996 / VC / C • Deep Seven / 1996 / VC / M • Dirty Stories #3 / 1995 / PE / M • Done In The Desert Sun / 1995 / OUP / M • Dreams Of A Gigolo / 1996 / SNA / M • English Class / 1995 / VC / M • Eternal Lust / 1996 / VC / M • Everybody Wants Some / 1996 / EXQ / F • Exotic Car Models #2 / 1996 / IN0 / F • Expose Me Again / 1996 / CV / M • Fashion Sluts #2 / 1995 / ABS / M • Filth / 1996 / SPI / M • Finger Pleasures #6 / 1996 / PL / F • Flipside / 1996 / VI / M • Florence Rump / 1995 / SUF / M • Forbidden Cravings / 1996 / VC / M • Frendz? #1 / 1996 / RAS / M • Gangbang Girl #17 / 1995 / ANA / M • Generation Sex #1 / 1996 / VT / M • Getting Personal / 1995 / PE / M • Girls Of The Very Big Eight / 1994 / VT / M • Girly Video Magazine #2 / 1995 / BEP / M • Girly Video Magazine #5 / 1996 / BEP / M • Girly Video Magazine #6 / 1996 / AB / M • Golddiggers #2 / 1995 / VC / M • GRG: Windy City Wenches / 1995 / GRG / F • Guilty As Sin / 1996 / KLP / M • Hard Core Beginners #11 / 1995 / LEI / M • Hard Evidence / 1996 / WP / M • Harder, She Craved / 1995 / VC / M • Head First / 1995 / OD / M • Heat / 1995 / WAV / M • Heatseekers / 1996 / PE / M • The Heist / 1996 / WAV / M • Hell Cats / 1996 / HO / F • Here Comes Jenny St. James / 1996 / HOV / M • House On Paradise Beach / 1996 / VC / M • The Hungry Heart / 1996 / AOP / M • Illicit Entry / 1995 / WAV / M • In Cold Sweat / 1996 / VI / M • In The Fast Lane / 1995 / LE / M • Independence Night / 1996 / SC / M • Intense Perversions #3 / 1996 / PL / M • Interview With A Vibrator / 1996 / WAV / M • Interview: Naturals / 1995 / LV / M • Introducing Alexis / 1996 / VI / M • Jenna Ink / 1996 / WP / M • Jenna's Built For Speed / 1997 / WP / F • Kink: Police Chronicles / 1995 / ROB / M • Kym Wilde's On The Edge #28 / 1995 / RB / B • Lesbian Connection / 1996 / SUF / F • Lethal Affairs / 1996 / VI / M • Live Sex Net / 1996 / SPR / M • Lollipops #2 / 1996 / SC / M • Love Exchange / 1995 / DR / M • Lust & Money / 1995 / SUF / M • Malibu Ass Blasters / 1996 / ROB / M • Malibu Heat / 1995 / HO / M • Malibu Madam / 1995 / CC / M • Masque / 1995 / VC / M • Mickey Ray's Sex Search #03: Deep Heat / 1994 / WIV / M • Mixed-Up Marriage / 1995 / CV / M • Muff Divers #1 / 1996 / TV / M • My Ass #1 / 1996 / NOT / M • N.Y. Video Magazine #06 / 1995 / OUP / M • N.Y. Video Magazine #09 / 1996 / OUP / M • Nasty Nymphos #10 / 1995 / ANA / M • Nba: Nuttin' Butt Ass / 1996 / SMP / M • Nektar / 1996 / BAC / M • Night Play / 1995 / WAV / M • Nightclub / 1996 / SC / M • No Fear / 1996 / IN / F • No Man's Land #13 / 1996 / VT / F • Nookie Ranch / 1996 / NIT / M • Ona Zee's Learning The Ropes #10: Chains Of Love / 1994 / ONA / B • The

Other Side / 1995 / ERA / M • Patent Leather / 1995 / CA / M • Perverted Stories #02 / 1995 / JMP / M • Perverted Stories #05 / 1995 / JMP / M • Philmore Butts Meets The Palm Beach Nymphomaniac Kathy Wille / 1995 / SUF / M • Pick Up Lines #01 / 1995 / 4P / M • Picture Perfect (Big) / 1995 / BIP / F • Planet X #1 / 1996 / HW / M • Planet X #2 / 1996 / HW / M • Prime Choice #4 / 1995 / RAS / M • Private Stories #09 / 1996 / OD / M • Puritan Video Magazine #01 / 1996 / LE / M • Pussyman #13: Lips / 1996 / SNA / M • Pussyman Auditions #13 / 1995 / SNA / M • Raw Footage / 1996 / VC / M • Reckless Encounters / 1995 / LE / M • Red Door Diaries #1 / 1995 / ZA / M • Release Me / 1996 / VT / M • Roller Babes / 1996 / ERA / M • Satyr / 1996 / WP / M • Selena Under Siege / 1995 / XCI / M • Sensations #1 / 1996 / SC / M • Sex Academy #2: The Art Of Talking Dirty / 1994 / ONA / M • Sex Academy #3: The Art Of Real Sex / 1994 / ONA / M • Sex Bandits / 1995 / VC / M • Sex Drives Of The Rich And Famous / 1996 / ERA / M • Sex Freaks / 1995 / EA / M • Sex Gallery / 1995 / WAV / M • Sex Hungry Butthole Sluts / 1996 / ROB / M • Sex, Truth & Videotape #1 / 1995 / DOC / M • The Sexual Solution #2 / 1995 / LE / M • Seymore & Shane Do Ireland / 1994 / ULI / M • Shameless / 1995 / VC / M • The Shocking Truth #2 / 1996 / DWO / M • Shooting Gallery / 1996 / EL / M • The Sin-A-Bun Girls / 1995 / OD / M • Sinboy #1 / 1996 / SC / M • Sinister Sister / 1997 / WP / M • Sinnocence / 1995 / CDI / M • Skin Dive / 1996 / SC / M • Slippery Slopes / 1995 / ME / M • Sluthunt #3 / 1996 / BIP / F • Smoke & Mirrors / 1996 / PL / M • Smoke Screen / 1995 / WAV / M • Sodomania #15: Warning! / 1996 / EL / M • Sorority Sex Kittens #3 / 1996 / VC / M • Southern Comfort #1 / 1995 / DWV / M • Southern Comfort / 1995 / DWV / M • The Stand-Up / 1994 / VC / M • Stardust #1 / 1996 / VI / M • The Stranger / 1996 / BEP / M • The Strippers / 1995 / GO / M • Submission To Ecstasy / 1995 / NTP / B • Tactical Sex Force / 1994 / IN / M • Takin' It To The Limit #6 / 1995 / BS / M • Talk Dirty To Me #10 / 1996 / DR / M • Tender Loins / 1996 / PE / M • Tight Spot / 1996 / WV / M • Titty Troop / 1995 / CC / M • Torrid Tales / 1995 / VI / M • The Toy Box / 1996 / ONA / M • Triple X Video Magazine #16 / 1996 / OD / M • Ultimate Sensations / 1996 / NIT / M • Up Your Ass #1 / 1996 / ANA / M • Venom #1 / 1995 / VD / M • Venom #4 / 1996 / VD / M • Vibrating Vixens #2 / 1996 / TV / F • The Violation Of Missy / 1996 / JMP / F • Vivid Raw #3: Double Header / 1996 / VI / M • The Voyeur #5 / 1995 / EA / M • Wacky Weekend / 1995 / SUF / M • What's Up, Tiger Pussy? / 1995 / VC / M • Where The Girls Sweat...Not The Sequel / 1996 / EL / F • Whore'n / 1996 / AB / M • Young & Natural #01 / 1995 / PRE / F • Young & Natural #02 / 1995 / PRE / F • Young & Natural #06 / 1995 / PRE / F • Young & Natural #08 / 1995 / PRE / F • Young & Natural #09 / 1995 / PRE / C • Young Girls Do #2: Sweet Meat / 1995 / CDI / M

MISSY (OTHER)
A'Mature: Missy, Mary Lou & Nine Inches / 1990 / AVP / M • Anal Freaks / 1994 / KWP

/ M • AVP #8004: Missy's Surprise / 1990 / AVP / F • AVP #8006: Missy's Caller / 1991 / AVP / M • AVP #8007: First Moves / 1991 / AVP / M • AVP #8010: Bi-Bi Shannon / 1990 / AVP / F • AVP #8011: Initiating Shannon / 1990 / AVP / M • AVP #9102: The Joys Of Toys / 1990 / AVP / F • AVP #9112: Double Booked / 1991 / AVP / M • AVP #9115: The Mysteries of Missy / 1991 / AVP / C • Reel Life Video #47: Hairy Pussy Chronicles / 1996 / RLF / F • Reel Life Video #55: Lisa & Missy / 1996 / RLF / F

MISSY (PHILIPPINES)
Anal Delights #1 / 1992 / ROB / M • Juicy Treats / 1991 / ROB / M • More Dirty Debutantes #13 / 1992 / 4P / M • On The Prowl #2 / 1991 / SC / M

MISSY LYNN *see Star Index I*
MISSY MANNERS *(Elisa Florez)*
Not too pretty girl who was an aide to Senator Orrin Hatch before becoming the drug-addicted girlfriend of Artie Mitchell and the lead in **Behind The Green Door #2**.
Behind The Green Door #2: The Sequel / 1985 / MIT / M

MISSY MCKINNEY
Hollywood Starlets Adventure #06 / 1995 / AVS / M • Kinky Debutante Interviews #08 / 1995 / IP / M

MISSY MEADOWS
Dressed For Bondage / 1993 / BON / B • Real People Real Bondage #2 / 1996 / BON / C

MISSY MORGAN
Fantasy Mansion / 1983 / BIZ / B • Vas-O-Line Alley / 1985 / VC / M • What's My Punishment / 1983 / BIZ / B

MISSY TAYLOR
My First Time #1 / 1995 / NS / M
MISSY TIGER *see Star Index I*
MISSY WAGNER *see* Missy Warner
MISSY WARNER *(Missy Wells, Janee, Jennifer Irwin, Missy Wagner)*
Blonde in the Stephanie Rage mold with a small tight body, rather large enhanced boobs and a nice but vapid disposition. Jennifer Irwin is from **Wild Child**.
Adventures Of Buttwoman #1 / 1991 / EL / F • Amateur Lesbians #05: Missy / 1991 / GO / F • Amateur Lesbians #13: Brandi / 1991 / GO / F • Amateur Lesbians #14: Avalon / 1991 / GO / F • Anal Encounters #3: Back In The Dark One / 1991 / VC / M • Anal Heat / 1990 / ZA / M • Angels / 1992 / VC / M • The Barlow Affairs / 1991 / XCI / M • Bedtime For Byron / 1991 / ME / M • Big Bust Casting Call / 1993 / PME / S • The Bikini Carwash Company #1 / 1990 / IMP / S • Bikini Summer #1 / 1991 / PME / S • Bob Lyons: Big Tits, Nude Slits, and Six Foot Snake / 1992 / BLY / M • Bonfire Of The Panties / 1990 / CC / M • Breast Worx #02 / 1991 / LBO / M • Bruce Seven: A Compendium Of His Most Graphic Scenes Vol 3 / 1992 / BS / C • Bruce Seven: A Compendium Of His Most Graphic Scenes Vol 4 / 1993 / BS / C • The Butler Did It / 1991 / FH / M • Cheesecake / 1991 / VC / M • Dark Corners / 1991 / LV / M • Dr Hooters / 1991 / PL / M • Ecstasy / 1991 / LE / M • The Gate / 1987 / VES / S • Girl Friends / 1990 / PL / F • Girls Gone Bad #4: Cell Block Riot / 1991 / GO / F • Godmother / 1991 / AWV / F • Hollywood Teasers #02 / 1992 / LBO / F • Imagine /

1991 / LV / M • Kat Fight At The Ok Korral / 199? / NAP / B • Kiss It Goodbye / 1991 / SE / M • Lesbians In Tight Shorts / 1992 / LV / F • Maid For Service / 1990 / LV / M • Mamm's The Word / 1991 / ZA / M • Mike Hott: #184 Cunt Of The Month: Missy / 1990 / MHV / M • Mike Hott: Apple Asses #08 / 1992 / MHV / F • Mr. Peepers Amateur Home Videos #02: Bachelorette Party / 1991 / LBO / M • Mr. Peepers Amateur Home Videos #09: Western Panty Party / 1991 / LBO / M • Nasty Jack's Kloset Klassics #02 / 1991 / CDI / M • Neighborhood Watch #03 / 1991 / LBO / M • A New Girlfriend / 1991 / XPI / M • Next Door Neighbors #33 / 1990 / BON / M • The Only Game In Town / 1991 / VC / M • Raunchy Porno Picture Show / 1992 / FC / M • Sneek Peeks #1 / 1993 / FL / M • Someone Sent Me A Girl / 1991 / FH / M • Southern: Previews #1 / 1992 / SSH / C • Speedtrap / 1992 / VC / M • The Sting Of Ecstasy / 1991 / BS / B • Till She Screams / 1992 / HOM / B • Too Fast For Love / 1992 / IF / M • A Vision In Heather / 1991 / VI / M • Voodoo Vixens / 1991 / IF / M • When Blondes Compete / 1993 / NAP / B • Where The Girls Sweat #2 / 1991 / EL / F • Wild Child / 1991 / BRU / S

MISSY WELLS *see* **Missy Warner**
MISTER MILLER *see Star Index I*
MISTER THORN *see Star Index I*
MISTER XXX *see Star Index I*
MISTI *see Star Index I*
MISTRESS ADRIANNA
Dark Reality #1 / 1995 / STM / B • Dark Reality #2 / 1995 / STM / B
MISTRESS AERIAL *see Star Index I*
MISTRESS ALEX
Welcome To SM / 1996 / ESF / B
MISTRESS AMANDA
Payne In Amsterdam / 1993 / STM / B • Spank You Very Much / 1995 / IBN / B • A Visit To Mistress Amanda's / 1993 / CAS / B
MISTRESS ANDREA
Welcome To SM / 1996 / ESF / B
MISTRESS ANGEL *see Star Index I*
MISTRESS ANGELA *see Star Index I*
MISTRESS ANGELINA
Corporal Collectors #5: Breeders / 1984 / LA / B • Shy Houseboy / 1985 / BIZ / B • World Of Male Torture / 1985 / BIZ / B
MISTRESS ANN MURRAY *see Star Index I*
MISTRESS ANN PIERCE *see Star Index I*
MISTRESS ANNE
Domination In Black & White / 19?? / BIZ / B • Training A New Dominant / 19?? / BIZ / B
MISTRESS ANTOINETTE
Angel In Bondage / 1983 / CA / B • Angel's Revenge / 1987 / VER / B • Annie Sprinkle's Fantasy Salon / 1990 / VER / B • Diane's Night Out / 1988 / VER / B • Doctor Drag / 1990 / VER / G • Fabulous Footwear / 1993 / LEO / B • Foot Worship #1 / 1992 / VER / B • A History Of Corsets / 1987 / VER / S • Interlude / 1983 / CA / B • The Lingerie Shop / 1987 / VER / G • The Mistress Of The Rubber Mask / 1993 / VER / B • Naughty Gabrielle / 1993 / VER / B • Night For Dressing / 1987 / VER / G • Nostalgic Stockinged Maidens / 1994 / VER / F • The Party / 1987 / VER / B • Queen An-

toinette At The Sex Maniacs' Ball 1992 / 1993 / VER / B • Rebecca's Dream / cr83 / VD / B • Sex Maniac's Ball / 1995 / AOC / S • Sizzling Latex / 1992 / VER / B • Skintight / 1991 / VER / F
MISTRESS BARBARA *see Star Index I*
MISTRESS BETTY *see Star Index I*
MISTRESS BEVERLY *see Star Index I*
MISTRESS BRADY *see Star Index I*
MISTRESS BRAZEN *see Star Index I*
MISTRESS BREANNA
No Justice...No Piece / 1995 / IBN / B
MISTRESS BRIGITTE
Mistress Brigit's Footsteps / 1993 / NEP / B
MISTRESS CANDICE *(Candice (Mistress), Candace Daley)*
Fat blonde with large tits and a marginal face.
ABA: Double Feature #4 / 1996 / ALP / M • Afrodisiac #1 / 1987 / CC / M • Amazon Island / 1992 / STM / B • American Desire / 1981 / CA / M • Anal Intruder #01 / 1986 / CC / M • Angel In Distress / 1982 / AVO / B • Bra Busting Mistress / 1989 / BIZ / B • Fashion Dolls / 1985 / LA / M • House Of Sin / 1982 / AVO / M • Isle Of The Amazon Women / 1992 / STM / B • Learn Your Lessons / 1992 / BIZ / B • Lesbian Dildo Fever #1 / 1989 / BIZ / F • Mascara / 1982 / CA / M • Officer's Discipline / 1985 / BIZ / B • Oriental Techniques Of Pain And Pleasure / 1983 / ALP / B • Painmania / 1983 / AVO / B • Rebecca's / 1983 / AVC / M • Romancing The Bone / 1984 / VC / M • Secluded Passion / 1983 / VHL / M • Secret Urges (Starmaker) / 1994 / STM / F • Sex Academy #4: The Art Of Anal / 1994 / ONA / M • Shameful Desires In Black & White Girls / 1984 / PL / M • The South Bronx Story / 1986 / CC / M • Twilight Pink #1 / 1980 / AR / M • Video Kixs Magazine #6 / 1983 / GLD / M
MISTRESS CARMEN
Mistress Of The Whip / 1996 / GOT / C • Twisted Rage / 1995 / GOT / B
MISTRESS CELINA
Domination Vacation / 1995 / COC / B
MISTRESS CHAMPAGNE
Dark Reality #1 / 1995 / STM / B • Dark Reality #2 / 1995 / STM / B
MISTRESS CHASTITY *see Star Index I*
MISTRESS CHERRI *see Star Index I*
MISTRESS CHERRY
Mistress Vs Mistress / 1991 / COC / B
MISTRESS CHEYENNE
Welcome To SM / 1996 / ESF / B
MISTRESS CHRISTIANA
Eternal Bonds / 1991 / RHV / B
MISTRESS CHRISTINA
Sw: Bound / 1994 / SWE / B • Sw: Consequences / 1994 / SWE / B
MISTRESS CINDY *see Star Index I*
MISTRESS COLINA *see Star Index I*
MISTRESS CONNIE *see Star Index I*
MISTRESS DANGER
Dangerous Lessons / 1994 / STM / C • Enslaved / 1995 / GOT / B • A Touch Of Danger / 1994 / STM / B
MISTRESS DANGEROUS
Last Resort / 1994 / GOT / B
MISTRESS DANIELLE *see Star Index I*
MISTRESS DEANNA
Red Boot Diaries / 1992 / STM / B • Secret Retreat #2 / 1991 / STM / B
MISTRESS DEBBIE
Visit To Mistress Debbie's / 1991 / COC / B
MISTRESS DEE

Agony & Extacy / 1993 / GOT / B • The Golden Rule / 1993 / GOT / B • Mistress Of Depravity / 1993 / GOT / B • Respect And Obey / 1993 / GOT / B • Toe Tales #05 / 1993 / GOT / B • Toe Tales #06 / 1993 / GOT / B • Toe Tales #21 / 1995 / GOT / B
MISTRESS DESI
MatboXer / 1995 / IBN / B
MISTRESS DESIRE
The Bondage File / 19?? / BIZ / C • Corporal Collectors #3: Night At Hellfire / cr85 / BIZ / B
MISTRESS DESTINY
The Best Of Trained Transvestites / 1990 / BIZ / G • Bizarre Mistress Series: Mistress Destiny / 1992 / BIZ / C • Bra Busting Mistress / 1989 / BIZ / B • Bunnie's Bondage Land / 1994 / STM / C • Caught, Punished And Caged / 1991 / BIZ / B • A Date With Destiny / 1992 / BIZ / B • Deeper Spikes / 1984 / BIZ / B • Demolition Dom / 1995 / IBN / B • Discipline Collectors #1: Deep Spikes / 1985 / BIZ / B • First Training / 1987 / BIZ / B • The Goddesses Must Be Crazy / 1995 / IBN / B • Mistress Destiny's Pets / 1991 / BIZ / B • Naughty TV's / cr85 / STM / G • Punished Crossdressers / cr85 / STM / B • Rendezvous With Destiny / 1984 / LA / B • Show Them No Mercy #2 / 1991 / STM / B • A Slave For The Bride / 1991 / BIZ / B • Sweet Surrender / 1991 / BIZ / B • Sweet Surrender / 1991 / BIZ / B • TV Husband, Submissive Wife / cr83 / BIZ / B • TVs By Choice / 19?? / BIZ / G • [S&M Club Tour / 19?? / ... / B
MISTRESS DEVYLYN
DOM And DOMer / 1995 / IBN / B • Dominant Neighbors From Hell / 1995 / IBN / B
MISTRESS DIAMOND
Fetish Phone Femmes / 1996 / STM / B • Humiliated White Boy #2 / 1995 / RB / B
MISTRESS DIANE
Box Of Slavegirls / 1995 / LON / B • An Editor's Nightmare / 1995 / LON / B • Gangbang Bitches / 1996 / LON / B • I Was An Undercover Slave / 1994 / HOM / B • Kym Wilde's On The Edge #11 / 1994 / RB / B • Lessons In Bondage / 1995 / HOM / B • The Other Side Of Melinda / 1995 / LON / B • The Story Of Ouch! / 1996 / LBO / B
MISTRESS DIANNA
Goddess Dianna's TV Transformation / 1993 / IPR / G • Mistress Kimbra's Island Of Hell / 1991 / BIZ / B
MISTRESS DOMINIQUE
Helpless Coeds / 1987 / BIZ / B • SVE: Mistress Dominique And Her Slave / 1994 / SVE / B
MISTRESS DOMINO
All Pain, No Gain / 1991 / NEP / B • Domino's Dungeon / 1993 / COC / B • An Evening At Mistress Dominos / 1990 / PL / B • Forgive Them Not #01 / 1993 / STM / B • Forgive Them Not #02 / 1993 / STM / B • Heel To Toe With Domino / 1993 / STM / B • Latex, Leather & Lace / 1993 / STM / B • The Painful World Of Moose Malloy / 1993 / AMF / B • Profiles In Discipline #04: Mistress Domino / 1994 / STM / C • VGA: Don't Defy Domino / 1991 / VGA / B • VGA: Spanks-A-Lot / 1993 / VGA / B
MISTRESS DOROTHY *see Star Index I*
MISTRESS DYNAMITE
Black And White And Red All Over / 1994 / STM / B • Corrected Deception / 1994 / STM / B • Dark Discipline / 1994 / STM / B

• Dynamite Dominator / 1993 / STM / B •
Punishment Playpen / 1995 / STM / B •
The Submissive Instinct / 1993 / STM / B
MISTRESS ELECTRA
Mistress Electra / 1983 / AVO / B
MISTRESS ELIZABETH
Bright Tails #7 / 1995 / STP / B
MISTRESS ELLE *see Star Index I*
MISTRESS ELSA
Mistress Elsa's Latex Sex Camp / 1994 /
PL / F
MISTRESS EVA *see Star Index I*
MISTRESS FLAXEN
Manhater / 1995 / IBN / B • Overruled /
1995 / IBN / B
MISTRESS FRANCESCA
Black Masters: Den Of Punishment / 1996
/ GOT / B • Blindfold / 1996 / GOT / B •
Chambers Of Discipline / 1992 / PL / B •
Extreme Guilt / 1996 / GOT / B • Home
Maid Transvestites / 1992 / STM / G •
Power Games / 1992 / STM / B • Profiles In
Discipline #02: Naughty Angel / 1994 /
STM / C • Profiles In Discipline #03: Mis-
tress Franchesca / 1994 / STM / C • Proper
Penance / 1992 / STM / B • Unforgiving
Mistress / 1995 / GOT / B
MISTRESS GINA
Battling Mistresses / 1995 / IBN / B • Ware-
house Domination / 1995 / IBN / B
MISTRESS GLAM DOOM
Feminine Brutality / 1995 / IBN / B • Inter-
rogation Dom #1 / 1995 / IBN / B • Interro-
gation Dom #2 / 1995 / IBN / B
MISTRESS GLORIA
Mean Ass Bitch / 1996 / RB / B
MISTRESS GRACE *see Star Index I*
MISTRESS GRETCHEN
DOM And DOMer / 1995 / IBN / B • Domi-
nant Neighbors From Hell / 1995 / IBN / B
MISTRESS GYPSY *see Star Index I*
MISTRESS HELGA *see Star Index I*
MISTRESS HELLA
Euro Bondage #1 / 1995 / ONA / B • Euro
Bondage #2 / 1995 / ONA / B
MISTRESS HOLIDAY
S&M Pet Control / 1995 / SBP / B
MISTRESS HOLLY
Bizarre Encounters / 1986 / 4P / B •
Bondage Classix #02: Krysta's Nightmare
#1 / 1987 / BON / B • Bound By Desire /
1983 / BIZ / B
MISTRESS ILSA *see Star Index I*
MISTRESS JACQUELINE
4 Of A Kind / 1995 / BON / B • Amazons
From Burbank / 1990 / PL / F • Bizarre Mis-
tress Series: Mistress Jacqueline / 1992 /
BIZ / C • Bondage Fantasies #1 / 1989 /
BIZ / B • Bondage Fantasies #2 / 1989 /
BIZ / B • Bondage Thrills / cr85 / STM / B •
Disciples Of Discipline / 1994 / STM / B •
Dresden Mistress #1 / 1988 / BIZ / B •
Dresden Mistress #2 / 1989 / BIZ / B • Dun-
geon Punishment / 1995 / STM / B •
Enema Bondage / 1992 / BIZ / B • Fire &
Ice / 1988 / BON / B • Full House / 1995 /
BON / B • Journey Into Servitude: The
Pleasures Of Ultimate Humil... / 1992 / BIZ
/ B • Learn Your Lessons / 1992 / BIZ / B •
Leather Clad Mistress / 19?? / STM / B •
The Many Faces of Mistress Jacqueline /
1990 / BIZ / B • Mistress Jacqueline's
Slave School / 1992 / BIZ / B • Mistresses
At War #01 / 1993 / BIZ / B • Mistresses At
War #02 / 1993 / BIZ / B • Naughty Boys #1
/ 1992 / RB / B • Naughty Boys #2 / 1992 /

RB / B • The Night Temptress / 1989 / HU /
M • Painted / 1990 / INH / G • Power Play
(Bruce Seven) / 1990 / BS / B • Rippin' 'n'
Strippin' #1 / 1987 / BON / B • Rippin' 'n'
Strippin' #2 / 1988 / BON / B • Slave Boy /
1996 / VTF / B • Slavegirls In Suspension /
19?? / STM / B • Spell Of The Whip / 1994
/ HOM / B • A Strict Affair...Lessons in Dis-
cipline and Obedience / 1992 / BIZ / B •
The Ultimate Mistress / 1989 / STM / B •
Wake-Up Call #1 / 1987 / BON / B • Wake-
Up Call #2 / 1987 / BON / B
MISTRESS JASMINE *see Star Index I*
MISTRESS JENNIFER
Mistress Jennifer / 1995 / IBN / B • Reel
Domination Series #2: Mistress Jennifer /
1995 / IBN / B • Spank You Very Much /
1995 / IBN / B
MISTRESS JESSICA
The Challenge / 1995 / GOT / B
MISTRESS JUSTINE
Mistress Justine #2 / 1995 / VPO / B
MISTRESS KAITLAN
Operation: Mistress / 1995 / IBN / B •
Quadruple Trample / 1995 / IBN / B
MISTRESS KARLA
She-Male Encounters #06: Trilogy Of The
Bizarre / 1981 / MET / G
MISTRESS KAT
House Of Pain / 1996 / OUP / B • Pain
Dance / cr82 / BIZ / B • That's My Daugh-
ter / 1982 / NGV / M
MISTRESS KATRINA
Dungeon Madness / 1995 / IBN / B • Mis-
tress Katrina / 1995 / IBN / B
MISTRESS KATT
Kickin' Ass / 1995 / IBN / B
MISTRESS KELLY *see Star Index I*
MISTRESS KEMBRA
Bossy Mistresses / 1993 / STM / B • Cor-
rected Deception / 1994 / STM / B • Dam-
aged Goods / 1995 / GOT / B • Dungeon
Builder's Pun-
ishment / 1994 / STM / B • Flames Of Sub-
mission / 1995 / GOT / B • Forbidden Ways
/ 1994 / GOT / B • The Fury Inside / 1994 /
GOT / B • Humiliating Bind / 1996 / STM /
B • I Love Pain / 1995 / GOT / B • Jaded
Mistress / 1993 / GOT / B • Kimbra's
Wimps / 1995 / STM / B • Kimbra, Slave
Trainer / 1993 / STM / B • Kiss My Ass /
1994 / GOT / B • Masked Mistress / 1994 /
STM / B • Master's Frenzy / 1994 / GOT /
B • Mistress In Training / 1996 / STM / B •
Mistress Kimbra's Island Of Hell / 1991 /
BIZ / B • Mistress Of The Whip / 1996 /
GOT / C • The Payoff / 1994 / GOT / B •
Playthings / 1995 / GOT / B • Ruling Meth-
ods / 1994 / GOT / B • Shame On You /
1995 / GOT / B • Slave Traders / 1995 /
GOT / B • The Taming Of Sable / 1995 /
OUP / B • Toe Tales #10 / 1993 / GOT / B •
Toe Tales #12 / 1994 / GOT / C • Toe Tales
#17 / 1994 / GOT / B • Toe Tales #18 / 1994
/ GOT / B • Toe Tales #24 / 1995 / GOT / C
• Torturess #2: Trained For Pleasure / 1996
/ STM / B • Trained Transvestites / 1995 /
STM / B • TV Trained To Perform / 1994 /
STM / G • Two Trained For Obedience /
1993 / STM / B • Web Of The Mistress /
1994 / GOT / B • Women Who Control The
Family Jewels #3 / 1995 / STM / C
MISTRESS KIM
Euro Bondage #1 / 1995 / ONA / B
MISTRESS KITTY
Beg For It / 1995 / GOT / B • Blindfold /

1996 / GOT / B • Cruel Lessons / 1996 /
GOT / B • Cry Babies (Gotham) / 1995 /
GOT / B • Mistress Of The Whip / 1996 /
GOT / C • No Respect / 1995 / GOT / B •
Toe Tales #29 / 1995 / GOT / B
MISTRESS KLARINS
Dominant Smoker / 1995 / IBN / B • Ger-
man Marks #1 / 1995 / IBN / B • German
Marks #2 / 1995 / IBN / B
MISTRESS KRISTEEN *see Star Index I*
MISTRESS LADY JADE
Sensuous Asian Dominance / 1995 / IBN /
B
MISTRESS LANA
Amazon Trample / 1995 / IBN / B • Pain By
Lana / 19?? / CS / B
MISTRESS LAUREN
Mistress Lauren's Bizarre Picnic / 1992 /
STM / B • Red Boot Diaries / 1992 / STM /
B • TS Trains TV Hubby / 1994 / STM / G •
Victim Of Her Thighs / 1993 / STM / B • Vir-
gil To Virginia / 1993 / STM / G
MISTRESS LEYLA
Behavior Modification / 1995 / IBN / B
MISTRESS LISA
Footgames In Bondage / 1992 / BIZ / C •
Housebreaking / 1995 / GOT / B
MISTRESS LONDON
Liquid Lips #2 / 1994 / MAV / M • Scumbag
Alley / 1993 / INN / B
MISTRESS LORI
Raw Talent: Fetish Of The Month #01 /
1994 / RTP / G
MISTRESS MADELEINE
Welcome To SM / 1996 / ESF / B
MISTRESS MALAY
Wrath Of The Dungeon Brats / 1996 / OUP
/ B
MISTRESS MANUELA *see Star Index I*
MISTRESS MARA *see Star Index I*
MISTRESS MARIANNE
Bondage Classix #04: Mistress Marianne's
Slave Of Love / 198? / BON / B
MISTRESS MARILYN *see Star Index I*
MISTRESS MAXINE
Club Doma Global #4 / 1994 / VER / B
MISTRESS MELINA *see Star Index I*
MISTRESS MICHELLE
The Bizarre World Of Mistress Michelle /
1985 / BIZ / B • The Bondage File / 19?? /
BIZ / C • Corporal Collectors #3: Night At
Hellfire / cr85 / BIZ / B • Philappetite / 19??
/ ... / M • The Piercing Of Jamie / 1983 /
BIZ / B
MISTRESS MINDY *see Star Index I*
MISTRESS MIR
Ebony Goddesses / 1985 / LON / B • Fe-
male Domination #2 / 1991 / BIZ / B • Mis-
tress Mir...At Her Wildest / 1984 / EPV / B
MISTRESS NATASHA
True Ties / 1995 / IBN / B
MISTRESS NICOLE *see Star Index I*
MISTRESS NICOLINA
Behind Closed Doors / 1996 / GOT / B
MISTRESS PAULA
Pleasure And Company / 19?? / VHL / B
MISTRESS PERSEPHONE
Compelled By Restraints / 1996 / VTF / B
MISTRESS PLEASURE
Pleasure And Company / 19?? / VHL / B
MISTRESS RACQUEL
Natural Born Dominants / 1995 / IBN / B
MISTRESS RAPTURE
The Bizarre World Of Mistress Michelle /
1985 / BIZ / B
MISTRESS RENE

Begging For Bondage / 1993 / PL / B • Euro Bondage #2 / 1995 / ONA / B • Fit To Be Tied / 1993 / PL / B • Mistress Memoirs #1 / 1993 / PL / C • Mistress Memoirs #2 / 1993 / PL / C • My Mistress...Her Slave / 1990 / PL / B

MISTRESS RHIANNON
Naked Prey / 1996 / GOT / B

MISTRESS ROBIN
Demolition Dom / 1995 / IBN / B • The Goddesses Must Be Crazy / 1995 / IBN / B • Ira's Ordeal / 198? / BON / B • Payback Time / 1995 / IBN / B • Reservoir Doms / 1995 / IBN / B • Spank You Very Much / 1995 / IBN / B • Tied, Trampled, Terminated / 1995 / IBN / B

MISTRESS SABINE *see Star Index I*

MISTRESS SAMANTHA
Bright Tails #5 / 1995 / STP / B

MISTRESS SANDRA
Housebreaking / 1995 / GOT / B

MISTRESS SAPPHIRE
At The Mistress' Mercy / 1996 / OUP / B • Muffs In Cuffs / 1995 / PL / B • Sapphire Unleashed / 1996 / OUP / B

MISTRESS SASHA *see Star Index I*

MISTRESS SEVERITY
Disciples Of Discipline / 1996 / BON / B • Labyrinth Of The Lash / 1996 / BON / B • Severity / 1996 / BON / B

MISTRESS SHADEE
Painful Desire / 1996 / BON / B • Rivals In Submission / 1996 / BON / B

MISTRESS SHALIMAR
Fetish Phone Femmes / 1996 / STM / B • I Command! You Obey! / 1994 / TVI / B

MISTRESS SHANE
Caught! / 1994 / GOT / B • Corrected Deception / 1994 / STM / B • Crack Up / 1994 / GOT / B • Hellfire Mistress / 1996 / OUP / B • Lauren's Adventures In Bondageland #2: Mistress Shane / 1994 / STM / C • Leather Master / 1996 / STM / B • Produce Or Suffer / 1994 / STM / B • Secrets In The Attic #1 / 1994 / STM / B • Secrets In The Attic #2: Extreme Measures / 1994 / STM / B • Secrets in the Attic #3: Trials Of Acceptance / 1994 / STM / B • Secrets in the Attic #4: Purchased And Punished / 1994 / STM / B

MISTRESS SHARON T.
Kneel Before Me / 1995 / BON / B

MISTRESS SHARP *see Star Index I*

MISTRESS SHENA *see Star Index I*

MISTRESS SHERRI
Bright Tails #1 / 1993 / STP / B

MISTRESS SIMONE
Below The Belt / 1993 / RB / B • Bright Tails #2 / 1994 / STP / B • The Building Of Mistress Simone's Dungeon Of Pleasure / 1991 / BIZ / B • Dominated Dudes / 1992 / PL / B • Dynamic Duo / 1992 / BIZ / B • Lesbians, Bondage & Blackjack / 1991 / BIZ / B • Trapped By The Mistress / 1991 / BIZ / B

MISTRESS SONDRA *see Sondra Rey*

MISTRESS SUPREME *see Star Index I*

MISTRESS SUZY *see Star Index I*

MISTRESS SYBIL
The Unsuspecting Repairman #1 / 1995 / TVI / B

MISTRESS SYLVIE *see Star Index I*

MISTRESS TANTALA *see Tantala Ray*

MISTRESS TANYA
Marlene Tanya's Private Chambers / 1989 / BIZ / B • Mistress Tanya's Private Cham-

bers / 1993 / BIZ / B

MISTRESS TERMINATRIX
Tied, Trampled, Terminated / 1995 / IBN / B

MISTRESS TIE TIE
Master's Touch #5: Slave Revolt / 1995 / FAP / B • Master's Touch #6: Dom's In Distress / 1995 / FAP / B

MISTRESS TYLER
No Justice...No Piece / 1995 / IBN / B

MISTRESS VENUS
Gallery Of Pain / 1995 / BON / B

MISTRESS VERA
Kym Wilde's On The Edge #33 / 1996 / RB / B • Kym Wilde's On The Edge #37 / 1996 / RB / B

MISTRESS VERA SADE
12 Steps To Domination / 1995 / IBN / B • The Controller / 1995 / IBN / B • Latex Goddess / 1995 / IBN / B • Obedience Training / 1995 / IBN / B • Operation: Mistress / 1995 / IBN / B • Quadruple Trample / 1995 / IBN / B

MISTRESS XANDRA *see Star Index I*

MISTY
A&B AB#070: Misty Play For Me / 1990 / A&B / F • America's Raunchiest Home Videos #08: Who Was That Masked Mn / 1991 / ZA / M • Blue Vanities #505 / 1992 / FFL / M • Blue Vanities #541 / 1994 / FFL / M • Blue Vanities #568 / 1995 / FFL / M • Bondage Classix #10: Painful Mistake / 1993 / BON / B • Bondage Classix #12: No Trespassing / 1991 / BON / B • Bondage Memories #03 / 1994 / BON / C • Bondage Photo Session / 1990 / BIZ / B • Breast Worx #16 / 1991 / LBO / M • Campus Capers / 1982 / VC / M • Cry Misty For Me / 1994 / BON / B • Five Card Stud / 1990 / BIZ / B • High School Memories / 1980 / VCX / M • Homegrown Video #241 / 1990 / HOV / M • HomeGrown Video #458: Cream Pie For Dessert / 1995 / HOV / C • Latex Slaves / cr87 / GOT / B • Latex Slaves Discipline / 1990 / BIZ / B • Misty Bound At Home / 1991 / BON / B • Misty Returns / 1991 / BON / B • Misty, Down And Dirty / 1990 / BON / B • Molding Misty / 1986 / BON / B • Mr. Peepers Amateur Home Videos #92: M-Ass-terpieces / 1994 / LBO / M • Night Shift Latex Slaves / 1991 / GOT / B • Odyssey Triple Play #21: Rear End Reaming / 1992 / OD / M • Private Quarters / 1987 / BIZ / B • Reel Life Video #50: Natural, Pregnant & Starting To Show / 1996 / RLF / M • Reel Life Video: Misty— A Natural Beauty / 1996 / RLF / F • Southern: Previews #1 / 1992 / SSH / C • Talk Dirty To Me #04 / 1986 / DR / M • Three Women / 1975 / IVP / M • Toppers #12 / 1993 / TV / C • Toy Time #3: / 1995 / STP / F • Up And Cummers #22 / 1995 / RWP / M • Wildfire: Solos #3 / 1994 / WIF / F • Wildfire: Wildgirls #1 / 1994 / WIF / F

MISTY (KAITLYN A) *see Kaitlyn Ashley*

MISTY (REGAN) *see Misty Regan*

MISTY ANDERSON
The Angel In Mr. Holmes / 1988 / WV / C • Dream Lover / 1985 / CDI / M • The Idol / 1985 / WV / M • Orgies / 1987 / WV / C • Swinging Shift / 1985 / CDI / M • Vote Pink / 1984 / VD / M

MISTY BARLOW
Anal Vision #07 / 1993 / LBO / M • The Ebony Connection #2 / 1994 / LBO / C • M Series #01 / 1993 / LBO / M

MISTY BLEAU *see Star Index I*

MISTY BLUE *see Misty Regan*

MISTY BRENTWOOD *see Star Index I*

MISTY DAWN *(Laurie Rose, Gypsy (Misty Dawn))*
Has a nasty Caesarian scar. Was John Holmes second wife "Laurie". Petite body, dark brown curly hair, passable face.
Aerobisex Girls #1 / 1983 / LIP / F • The Best Little Cathouse In Las Vegas / 1982 / HO / M • Caballero Preview Tape #4 / 1985 / CA / C • California Valley Girls / 1983 / HO / M • Centerfold Celebrities #5 / 1983 / VC / M • Desire / 1983 / VCX / M • Dreams Of Misty / 1984 / VCX / M • Freak Show / 1991 / FC / M • Getting Lucky / 1983 / CA / M • Girls On Fire / 1985 / VCX / M • Girls Together / 1985 / GO / C • Gourmet Quickies: Misty Dawn #703 / 1985 / GO / C • Gourmet Quickies: Shauna Grant #2 #718 / 1985 / GO / C • Greatest Cathouse In Las Vegas / 1983 / EVI / M • GVC: The Bad Bride #135 / 1985 / GO / M • GVC: Dreams Of Pleasure #120 / 1983 / GO / M • GVC: Lost In Lust #134 / 1984 / GO / M • GVC: Private Nurses #126 / cr84 / GO / M • Heat Of The Moment / 1983 / S&L / M • Intimate Entry / 1988 / V99 / C • Lingerie / 1983 / CDI / M • Marathon / 1982 / CA / M • Nasty Nurses / 1983 / CA / M • Naughty Cheerleaders / 1985 / HO / M • The Newcomers / 1983 / VCX / M • Personal Touch #1 / 1983 / AR / M • Shades Of Ecstasy / 1983 / HO / M • The Wacky World Of X-Rated Bloopers / 1989 / GO / M • X-Rated Bloopers #1 / 1984 / AR / M

MISTY DEE *see Star Index I*

MISTY GREY *see Star Index I*

MISTY KNIGHT
Anal Nymphettes / 1995 / LIP / F • Babes Of The Bay #2 / 1995 / LIP / F • Blue Vanities #204 / 1993 / FFL / M • Dirty Bob's #02: Xciting XperienCES / 1992 / FLP / S • Fantasy Flings #03 / 1995 / WP / M • Tootsies & Footsies / 1994 / LBO / M • Wildfire: Wildgirl's Cleaning Service / 1994 / WIF / F

MISTY LANE
Big Boys Toy / 1994 / SV / B • Binding Intruder / 1993 / VTF / B • Exposed / 1993 / HOM / B • Full Moon Video #35: Wild Side Couples: The School HeadMaste / 1995 / FAP / M • Kane Video #1: The Riding Crop / 1993 / VTF / B • Latex Bound #03 / 1993 / BON / B • Master's Touch #3: A Dream Or A Nightmare / 1995 / FAP / B • Medieval Whines / 1994 / SV / B • Monkee Business / 1994 / CS / B • Paint Balled / 1993 / SV / B • The Price Is Wrong / 1995 / SV / B • Student Fetish Videos: Catfighting #06 / 1992 / PRE / B • Toppers #04 / 1993 / TV / M • Toppers #06 / 1993 / TV / M • Toppers #07 / 1993 / TV / M

MISTY LEWIS
Creme De La Face #09: Princess Of Cream / 1995 / OD / M • The Princess Of Cream / 1995 / OD / M

MISTY LYNN *(Dorice, Deja)*
Strawberry sometime reddish blonde, passable face, large droopy boobs sometimes with a large mole just above and between them, very white skin, blue eyes, and the personality of a greasy spoon waitress.
American Dream Girls #2 / 1994 / LEI / M • The Anals Of History #1 / 1991 / MID / M • The Backway Inn #1 / 1992 / FD / M • The Bare-Assed Naked Gun / 1992 / MID / M •

Breast Wishes #07 / 1992 / LBO / M • Bubble Butts #03 / 1992 / LBO / M • Full Service Woman / 1992 / V99 / M • Hooked / 1992 / SC / M • Love Hurts / 1992 / VD / M • Nasty Fuckin' Movies #04: Neighborhood Slut Puppy / 1992 / RUM / M • Naughty By Nature / 1992 / IF / M • Odyssey 30 Min: #170: Blonde On Black / 1991 / OD / M • Slipping It In / 1992 / FD / M • Torrid Tonisha / 1992 / VEX / M • Uncle Roy's Amateur Home Video #02 / 1992 / VIM / M • Uncle Roy's Amateur Home Video #05 / 1992 / VIM / M

MISTY MALLORY *see* **Misty Regan**

MISTY MCCAINE *see* **Star Index I**

MISTY MIDDLETON *see* **Misty Regan**

MISTY MUNROE *see* **Misty Regan**

MISTY RAIN *(Misty Raines, Pierce Ringo, Melissa (M. Rain))*

Reasonably pretty gray/blonde with a lithe body, small slightly droopy tits, long nose, green eyes, pretty pussy, moles on the right buttock flank, right buttock back and left belly. Later movies she has both nipples with rings. Hangs around with Chad Thomas. Born August 10, 1969 in Long Beach, CA. 34B-24-34. 5'7" tall.

Ace In The Hole / 1995 / PL / M • Adam & Eve's House Party #2: Bachelor Party / 1996 / VC / M • Addictive Desires / 1994 / OD / M • America's Raunchiest Home Videos #59: / 1993 / ZA / M • American Blonde / 1993 / VI / M • The Anal Adventures Of Bruce Seven / 1996 / BS / C • The Anal Adventures Of Suzy Super Slut #1 / 1994 / AFV / M • The Anal Adventures Of Suzy Super Slut #2 / 1994 / AFV / M • The Anal Adventures Of Suzy Super Slut #3 / 1994 / IPI / M • Anal Al's Adventures / 1995 / PL / M • Anal Arsenal / 1994 / OD / M • The Anal Diary Of Misty Rain / 1993 / EL / M • Anal Intruder #10 / 1995 / CC / M • Anal Therapy #3 / 1994 / FD / M • Anal Vision #06 / 1992 / LBO / M • Attitude / 1995 / VC / M • Backdoor Magic / 1994 / LV / M • Battling Bitches #1 / 1995 / BIZ / B • Beach Bum Amateur's #26 / 1993 / MID / M • Beg For Mercy / 1993 / LBO / B • The Best Of Buttslammers / 1995 / BS / C • Bi-Athelon / 1993 / BIL / G • Bi-Golly / 1993 / BIL / G • Big Murray's New-Cummers #07: Swinging in the "A" / 1993 / FD / M • Black Buttman #02 / 1994 / CC / M • Black Satin / 1994 / IN / M • Blonde Butt Babes / 1994 / LV / M • Bobby Hollander's Rookie Nookie #03 / 1993 / SFP / M • Bondage Journey / 1995 / STM / B • Brassiere To Eternity / 1994 / PEP / F • Buffy Malibu's Nasty Girls #06 / 1994 / ANA / F • Buffy Malibu's Nasty Girls #07 / 1994 / ANA / F • Buffy Malibu's Nasty Girls #08 / 1995 / ANA / F • Buffy Malibu's Nasty Girls #09 / 1995 / ANA / F • Butt Banged Bicycle Babes / 1994 / ANA / M • Butt Banged Cycle Sluts / 1995 / ANA / M • Butthunt / 1994 / AFV / F • Buttslammers #01 / 1993 / BS / F • Buttslammers #02: The Awakening Of Felicia / 1993 / BS / F • Buttslammers #04: Down And Dirty / 1993 / BS / F • Buttslammers #09: Fade To Anal / 1995 / BS / F • Buttslammers #13: The Madness Continues / 1996 / BS / F • Captured Beauty / 1995 / SAE / B • Catfighting Cheerleaders / 1989 / BIZ / B • Chain Gang / 1994 / OD / F • Cheerleader Strippers / 1996 / PE / M • Cum & Get Me / 1995 / PL / F • Cuntrol / 1994 / MID / F • De Sade /

1994 / SC / M • Debbie Does Dallas Again / 1994 / AFV / M • Deep Inside Debi Diamond / 1995 / VC / C • Deep Inside Misty Rain / 1995 / VC / C • Deep Space 69 / 1994 / HW / M • The Dinner Party #1 / 1994 / ULI / M • Director's Wet Dreams / 1996 / BBE / M • Dirty Bob's #08: LAid Over In L.A. / 1993 / FLP / S • Dirty Bob's #27: Laid Back In L.A.! / 1996 / FLP / S • Diva #1: Caught In The Act / 1996 / VC / F • Doctors Of Pain / 1995 / BIZ / B • Dr Of Pain / 1995 / BIZ / B • The Edge / 1995 / SC / M • Elements Of Desire / 1994 / ULI / M • Eleventh Annual AVN Awards / 1994 / VC / M • The End Zone / 1993 / PRE / B • Erotic Appetites / 1995 / IN / M • Erotic Escape / 1995 / FH / M • Every Woman Has A Fantasy #3 / 1995 / VC / M • Everybody Wants Some / 1996 / EXQ / F • F-Channel / 1994 / AFV / F • Fantasy Chamber / 1994 / ULI / M • First Time Ever #2 / 1996 / PE / F • Floor Play / 1989 / PLV / B • Foot Teasers / 1988 / BIZ / C • Footgames In Bondage / 1992 / BIZ / C • The French Way / 1994 / HOV / M • Geranalmo / 1994 / PL / M • Giggles / 1992 / PRE / B • A Girl's Affair #05 / 1994 / FD / F • Gland Slam / 1995 / PRE / B • GM #173: Memorial Weekend T&A / 1995 / 1995 / GMV / S • Golden Rod / 1996 / SPI / M • Grand Slam / 1990 / PRE / B • Heat / 1997 / XPR / M • Here Comes Elska / 1997 / XPR / M • Hotel California / 1995 / MID / M • House Arrest / 1995 / CV / M • I Love Lesbians / 1995 / ERW / F • Indecent Interview / 1995 / PL / F • International Affairs / 1994 / PL / M • Invitation To The Blues / 1994 / LE / M • Junkyard Dykes #01 / 1994 / ZA / F • Kittens #6 / 1994 / CC / F • Kittens #7 / 1995 / CC / F • Latex #2 / 1995 / VC / M • Leather Bound Dykes From Hell #5 / 1995 / BIZ / B • Leena Is Nasty / 1994 / OD / M • Leg...Ends #01 / 1988 / BIZ / F • Leg...Ends #09 / 1994 / PRE / F • Lesbian Pros And Amateurs #04 / 1992 / GO / F • Lick-A-Thon #2 / 1996 / HW / C • Lovin' Spoonfuls #5 / 1996 / 4P / C • Lucky Lady / 1995 / CV / M • Masquerade / 1995 / HO / M • Mighty Man #1: Virgins In The Forest / 1994 / LE / M • Misty Rain's Anal Orgy / 1994 / FRM / M • Misty Rain: Wrestling Terror / 1995 / BIZ / B • Moist Thighs / 1995 / STM / F • Money, Money, Money / 1993 / FD / M • Moon Beads / 1995 / STM / F • The Mountie / 1994 / PP / M • N.Y. Video Magazine #03 / 1995 / OUP / M • N.Y. Video Magazine #09 / 1996 / OUP / M • Nasty Nymphos #05 / 1994 / ANA / M • Nasty Nymphos #11 / 1995 / ANA / M • Neighbors / 1994 / LE / M • New Ends #09 / 1994 / 4P / M • New Wave Hookers #4 / 1994 / VC / M • Nightshift Nurses #2 / 1996 / VC / M • No Man's Land #10 / 1994 / VT / F • The Nurses Are Cumming #1 / 1996 / LBO / C • Nurses Bound By Duty / 1996 / BIZ / B • Nylon / 1995 / VI / M • Odyssey Triple Play #61: Rump Humpers / 1994 / OD / M • Once A Slave / 1995 / HOM / B • Once In A Lifetime / 1996 / VC / C • Paisley Hunter: The Girl Just Can't Help It / 1996 / BEP / M • Pajama Party X #1 / 1994 / VC / M • Pajama Party X #2 / 1994 / VC / M • Picture Perfect (Big) / 1995 / BIP / F • The Pleasure Girl / 1994 / GO / M • Power Butt / 1994 / VI / C • Priceless / 1995 / WP / M • Prison World / 1994 / NTP / B • Profiles #02 / 1995 / XPR / M • Pure Filth /

1995 / RV / M • Pussyman #05: Captive Audience / 1994 / SNA / M • Pussyman #12: Sticky Fingers / 1995 / SNA / M • Pussywoman #2 / 1994 / CC / M • Pussywoman #3 / 1995 / CC / M • R.E.A.L. #2 / 1994 / LV / F • Radical Affairs Video Magazine #08 / 1994 / ME / M • Red Hot Lover / 1995 / CV / M • Reservoir Bitches / 1994 / BIP / M • Return Engagement / 1995 / VI / M • Revenge Of The Pussy Suckers From Mars / 1994 / PP / M • The Right Connection / 1995 / VC / M • Rip Off #1 / 1988 / BIZ / B • Secret Rendez-Vous / 1994 / XCI / M • Sex #1 (Vca) / 1994 / VC / M • Sex #2: Fate (Vca) / 1995 / VC / M • Sex 4 Life / 1995 / XPR / M • Sex And Money / 1994 / DGD / S • Sindy Does Anal Again / 1994 / AFV / M • Sindy's Sexercise Workout / 1994 / AFV / M • Sodom Chronicles / 1995 / FH / M • Sodomania #04: Further On Down The Road / 1993 / EL / M • Sodomania #06: Gangs And Bangs And Other Thangs / 1993 / EL / M • Sodomania...And Then Some!!! A Compendium / 1995 / EL / C • Sodomania: Slop Shots / 1996 / EL / C • Sorority Sex Kittens #3 / 1996 / VC / M • Southern: Misty Rain, Nasty Girl! / 1994 / SSH / F • Spiked Heel Diaries #3 / 1995 / BIZ / B • Stand By Your Man / 1994 / CV / M • Stardust #1 / 1996 / VI / M • Stiff Competition #2 / 1994 / CA / M • Strap-On Sally #05: Chantilly's French Kiss / 1995 / PL / F • Strap-On Sally #06: Triple Penetration Trollop / 1995 / PL / F • Student Fetish Videos: Best of Catfighting #02 / 1994 / PRE / C • Student Fetish Videos: Best of Enema #03 / 1994 / PRE / C • Student Fetish Videos: Best Of Foot Worship #02 / 1994 / PRE / C • Student Fetish Videos: Catfighting #07 / 1993 / PRE / B • Student Fetish Videos: The Enema #13 / 1994 / PRE / B • Student Fetish Videos: Foot Worship #09 / 1993 / PRE / B • Student Fetish Videos: Spanking #10 / 1993 / PRE / B • Student Fetish Videos: Spanking #12 / 1994 / PRE / B • Student Fetish Videos: Tickling #08 / 1994 / SFV / B • Submission Of Ariana / 1995 / BIZ / B • Super Leg-Ends / 1992 / PRE / C • The Swap #2 / 1994 / VI / M • Taboo #12 / 1994 / MET / M • Taboo #15 / 1995 / IN / M • Tactical Sex Force / 1994 / IN / M • Takin' It To The Limit #4 / 1995 / BS / M • Takin' It To The Limit #6 / 1995 / BS / M • Talking Dirty Video / 1990 / NAP / F • Telephone Expose / 1995 / VC / M • Tender Loving Care / 1995 / WP / M • Tickled In Pink / 1988 / BIZ / B • Truck Stop Angel / 1994 / CC / M • A Twist Of Payne / 1993 / BS / B • Undercover / 1996 / VC / M • Unleashed / 1996 / SAE / M • Untamed Cowgirls Of The Wild West #02: Jammy Glands... / 1993 / ZA / M • Up And Cummers #04 / 1993 / 4P / M • Up And Cummers #06 / 1993 / 4P / M • Up And Cummers #23 / 1995 / 4P / M • Up And Cummers #26 / 1996 / 4P / M • Video Virgins #03 / 1993 / NS / M • Video Virgins #18 / 1994 / NS / M • Wanted / 1995 / DR / M • Whispered Secrets Of The Call Girls / 1995 / TVE / F • Whoreo / 1995 / BIP / M • Wide Open Spaces / 1995 / VC / F • Working Girls / 1995 / FH / M • The XXX Files: Lust In Space / 1995 / IMV / M • Young Nurses In Lust / 1994 / LBO / M

MISTY RAINES *see* **Misty Rain**

MISTY REGAN *(Misty Blue, Misty*

(Regan), Misty Mallory, Misty Middleton, Misty Munroe)
Hard looking curly haired reddish blonde with a very white body. Medium tits. Married to John T. Bone at one stage. Note that Lovette used the name Misty Blue as a dancer. According to rumor in 1995 runs her own escort service in Denver CO.
Alexandra The Greatest / 1990 / NAP / F • All American Girls #2: In Heat / 1983 / CA / M • American Nympho In London / 1987 / VD / M • Aussie Vice / 1989 / PM / M • Baby Cakes / 1982 / SE / M • Backfire / 1991 / GO / M • The Baroness / 1987 / VD / M • Battling Bruisers / 1993 / SBP / B • The Big E #09 / 1990 / BIZ / B • The Big Rock / 1988 / FOV / M • The Black Avenger #1: The Titty Romp / 1996 / OUP / C • The Blonde Goddess / 1982 / VXP / M • Bloopers #2 / 1991 / GO / C • Blue Dream Lover / 1985 / TAR / M • The Breast Things In Life Are Free / 1991 / LV / M • Breast Worx #08 / 1991 / LBO / M • Bums Away / 1995 / PRE / C • Bushwackers / 1990 / PM / M • Cats Are Also Pets / 1990 / NAP / B • Cheryl Hanson: Cover Girl / 1981 / SE / M • Club Head (EVN) #1 / 1987 / EVN / C • Coming Holmes / 1985 / VD / M • Cuffed And Beaten / 1990 / NAP / B • D-Cup Delights / 1987 / VCR / M • Dallas School Girls / 1981 / VCX / M • Dance Fever / 1985 / VCR / M • The Danger Zone / 1990 / SO / M • Deep Throat Fantasies / 1989 / VD / M • Deep Throat Girls / 1986 / ELH / M • Destination Moon / 1992 / GO / C • Diamond Collection #80 / 1986 / CDI / M • Dick Tracer / 1990 / PM / M • Double D Delights / 1989 / VCR / C • Double Take / 1991 / BIZ / B • Easy Way Out / 1989 / OD / M • End Results / 1991 / PRE / C • Forbidden Fruit / 1985 / PV / M • Girl Games / 1987 / PL / C • Golddiggers #1 / 1985 / VC / M • Golden Girls #11 / 1983 / CA / M • The Good Time Girls / 1985 / VEX / M • Gourmet Quickies: Misty #705 / 1985 / GO / C • GVC: The Bad Bride #135 / 1985 / GO / M • GVC: Blonde Heat #136 / 1985 / GO / M • Hard Core Cafe / 1988 / VD / M • Hershe Highway #4 / 1991 / HO / M • Hollywood Knights #3 / 1991 / PCP / M • Hollywood X-Posed #1 / 1992 / VIM / C • Hot Licks At The Pussycat Club / 1990 / WV / C • Hot Nights And Dirty Days / 1988 / VD / M • Hot Shorts: Sandy Taylor / 1986 / VCR / C • I Love A Girl In A Uniform / 1989 / VC / C • Ice Cream #3: Naked Eyes / 1984 / VC / M • Ice Cream #4: Touch Of Mischief / 1984 / VC / M • Inflamed / 1984 / NSV / M • Inside Desiree Cousteau / 1979 / VCX / M • International Phone Sex Girls #1 / 1988 / VD / M • International Phone Sex Girls #5 / 1991 / PM / M • Kinky Business #1 / 1984 / DR / M • Kissin' Cousins / 1984 / PL / M • Leather & Lace / 1987 / SE / C • Legs And Lingerie #2 / 1990 / BEB / F • Lesbian Pros And Amateurs #01 / 1992 / GO / F • Lesbian Pros And Amateurs #03 / 1992 / GO / F • Little Girls Talking Dirty / 1984 / VCX / M • Little Muffy Johnson / 1985 / VEP / M • Lusty Adventurer / 1985 / GO / M • Lusty Ladies #01 / 1983 / 4P / M • Lusty Ladies #04 / 1983 / 4P / M • Mamm's The Word / 1991 / ZA / M • The Midnight Zone / 1986 / IN / M • Miss American Dream / 1985 / CIV / M • The Night Of The Headhunter / 1985 / WV / M • Nightmare On Lesbian Street / 1995 / LIP /

F • Nothing To Hide #1 / 1981 / CV / M • Nudity Required / 1989 / AE / S • Oral Majority #01 / 1986 / WV / C • Parliament: Eating Pussy #1 / 1989 / PM / C • Parliament: Lesbian Lovers #1 / 1986 / PM / F • Parliament: Lesbian Lovers #2 / 1988 / PM / F • Parliament: Sweethearts #1 / 1988 / PM / F • Parliament: Woman's Touch / 1988 / PM / F • Phone Sex Girls #5 / 1990 / TOR / M • Phone Sex Girls: Australia / 1989 / PM / M • Please, Mr Postman / 1981 / VC / M • The Pussywillows / 1985 / SUV / M • Rapture Girls #2: Ona & Stephanie / 1991 / OD / M • The Red Garter / 1986 / SE / M • Sacrificed To Love / 1986 / CDI / M • Satin Finish / 1985 / SUV / M • Showgirls / 1985 / SE / M • Sky Pies / 1985 / GO / M • Slap Shots / 1991 / PRE / B • Sound Of Love / 1981 / CA / M • Steamy Sirens / 1984 / AIR / C • Stiff Competition #1 / 1984 / CA / M • Stud Hunters / 1984 / CA / M • Sulka's Wedding / 1983 / MET / G • Suze's Centerfolds #8 / 1984 / CA / M • The Tale Of Tiffany Lust / 1981 / CA / M • A Taste Of Misty / 1990 / CA / C • A Taste Of Paradise / 1984 / HO / M • Tease Me / 1986 / VC / M • Teasers: Heavenly Bodies / 1988 / MET / M • Teasers: Porno Princess / 1988 / MET / M • Teasers: The Inheritance / 1988 / MET / M • Three Ripening Cherries / 1979 / HIF / M • Too Much Too Soon / 1983 / VCX / M • Toys 4 Us #1 / 1987 / WV / C • Toys 4 Us #2 / 1987 / WV / C • Unbelievable Orgies #1 / 1987 / EVN / C • An Unnatural Act #1 / 1984 / DR / M • Urban Cowgirls / 1980 / CA / M • Velvet High / 1980 / VC / M • The Wacky World Of X-Rated Bloopers / 1989 / GO / M • Water Nymph / 1987 / LIM / M • Wrestling Tongues / 1990 / NAP / B • Young Cheeks / 1990 / BEB / B • [T&A #01 / 1989 / … / C

MISTY RUSH
Student Fetish Videos: Best Of Foot Worship #03 / 1995 / PRE / C • Student Fetish Videos: The Enema #18 / 1995 / PRE / B • Student Fetish Videos: Spanking #18 / 1995 / PRE / B

MISTY WINTER *see* **Christie Ford**
MITCH DARK *see* **Mitch Powers**
MITCH IRON
Heat Wave / 1977 / COM / M
MITCH KNIGHT *see* **Mitch Powers**
MITCH MADISON
Service Call Bondage / 199? / BON / B
MITCH MANDELL *see* **Star Index I**
MITCH MORRILL
Lust At First Bite / 1978 / VC / M • [The Raw Report / 1978 / … / M
MITCH POWERS *(Mitch Knight, Mitch Dark)*
Boyfriend of Cassandra Dark.
Bus Stop Tales #05 / 1989 / PRI / M • Bus Stop Tales #07 / 1989 / PRI / M • Dr Butts #2 / 1992 / 4P / M • The Honeymoon: The Bride's Running Behind / 1990 / 4P / M • More Dirty Debutantes #12 / 1991 / 4P / M • Next Door Neighbors #08 / 1990 / BON / M

MITCH PRESTON
AC/DC #2 / 1994 / HP / G • Bi The Rear Window / 1994 / BIL / G
MITCH RABIDA
Battling Bitches #2 / 1995 / BIZ / B • Bizarre's Dracula #1 / 1995 / BIZ / B • Bizarre's Dracula #2 / 1995 / BIZ / B • Diary

Of A Tormented TV / 1995 / BIZ / G • Painful Secrets Of A TV / 1996 / BIZ / G • Switch Hitters #7 / 1994 / IN / G • TVs In Leather And Pain / 1996 / BIZ / G
MITCH RANIER
Most Valuable Slut / 1973 / HLV / M
MITCH RONSHARE
Gangbang Girl #02 / 1992 / ANA / M
MITCH TAYLOR
The Submission Of Johns / 1995 / RB / B
MITCHELL
Back East Babes #1 / 1996 / NIT / M
MITCHELL GANT *(Mitchell Grant)*
Most of the time this guy seems to be credited as Mitchell Gant.
Adam & Eve's House Party #3: Swing Party / 1996 / VC / M • Blue Saloon / 1996 / ME / M • Born Bad / 1996 / WAV / M • Burlesxxx / 1996 / VT / M • Cheerleader Strippers / 1996 / PE / M • Corporate Affairs / 1996 / CC / M • Director's Wet Dreams / 1996 / BBE / M • Eternal Lust / 1996 / VC / M • Expose Me Again / 1996 / CV / M • Golden Rod / 1996 / SPI / M • Head To Head / 1996 / VI / M • Hillbilly Honeys / 1996 / WP / M • Hollywood Hookers / 1996 / DWV / M • Introducing Alexis / 1996 / VI / M • Pick Up Lines #06 / 1996 / OD / M • Pick Up Lines #08 / 1996 / OD / M • Princess Of Pain / 1996 / LBO / B • Rainwoman #10: The Tenth Anniversary Edition / 1996 / CC / M • Shane's World #3 / 1996 / OD / M • Star Flash / 1996 / VT / M • The Story Of Ouch! / 1996 / LBO / B • The Time Machine / 1996 / WP / M • Vivid Raw #2 / 1996 / VI / M
MITCHELL GRANT *see* **Mitchell Gant**
MITCHELL ZAILLANT
Submission (Knight) / 1994 / KNF / B
MITICA *see* **Gidgette**
MITZI FRASER *see* **Star Index I**
MITZIE
Blue Vanities #566 / 1995 / FFL / M
MIYA
Dragula: Queen Of Darkness / 1996 / HSV / G
MIYAGI *see* **Mimi Miyagi**
MIYOKO *see* **Kim Saunders**
MIYOSHI
Welcome To Bondage: Miyoshi / 1992 / BON / B • Welcome To Bondage: Starlets #1 / 1993 / BON / C
MO RIVERS
Interview With A She-Male / 1995 / PL / G • TV Nation #2 / 1995 / HW / G
MO TWILLY
Tracy In Heaven (Orig 1985) / 1985 / WV / M • Yankee Seduction / 1984 / WV / M
MOANA LISA *see* **Mona Lisa**
MOANA POZZI *(Moanna Pozzi)*
Italian porno star who died mid-September 1994 of a liver tumor. 33 years old at time of death. Born in Genoa to a middle class family (father a nuclear engineer), raised in the convent, started in porno films aged 18. Blonde, tall, big body, large tits.
Backdoor Summer #2 / 1989 / PV / C • Backfield In Motion / 1990 / PV / M • Beefeaters / 1989 / PV / M • Crossing Over / 1990 / IN / M • Double Crossing / 1991 / IN / M • Euroflesh: Dentro Il Vulcano / 1996 / SC / M • Ginger & Fred / 1986 / MGM / S • Malibu Spice / 1991 / VC / M • Manbait #1 / 1991 / VC / M • Manbait #2 / 1992 / VC / M • Naked Goddess #1 / 1991 / VC / M • Naked Goddess #2 / 1991 / VC / M • Noth-

ing Personal / 1990 / IN / M • Passionate Lovers / 1991 / PL / M • Rear Burner / 1990 / IN / M • The Rise Of The Roman Empress #2 / 1990 / PV / M • World Cup / 1990 / PL / M • [Due Porno Diue Per Uomini / 19?? / HOB / M • [Eccitazione Fatale / cr93 / ... / M • [Gin Fizz #12: Moana & Karin / 19?? / ... / M • [Gola Profonda / 19?? / ... / M • [I Vizi Transsexual Di Moana / 19?? / BMA / M • [Il Castello Del Piacere / 19?? / ... / M • [La Chiave Porno / 19?? / PUB / M • [Palm Springs Weekend / 19?? / ... / M • [Pelle Conro Pelle / 19?? / ... / M • [Summer Temptations / 19?? / ... / S • [Supermen Special #22 / 19?? / ... / M • [Tocco Magico / 19?? / ... / M • [Vizi E Stravizi Di Moana E Cicciolina / 19?? / BMA / M

MOANNA POZZI *see* **Moana Pozzi**
MOCHA
Black Cheerleader Search #10 / 1997 / IVC / M

MODERN
Blue Vanities #569 / 1996 / FFL / M

MODESTY GOLD
Outlaw Women / 1983 / LIP / F

MOE BEAVER
Pussy Hunt #12 / 1995 / LEI / M • Romance & Fantasy / 1995 / VEX / M

MOE BIGGSLEY
As Sweet As Can Be / 1993 / V99 / M • Make Me Sweat / 1994 / V99 / M

MOE KATSURA *see* **Star Index I**
MOIRA BENSON
Judgement Day / 1976 / CV / M • Thundercrack! / 1974 / LUM / M

MOIRA CHEN *see* **Laura Gemser**
MOIRA CUMMINGS
Lactamania #2: The Squirt Fest / 1995 / TTV / M • More To Love #2 / 1995 / TTV / M

MOIRA DONOVAN *see* **Star Index I**
MOLLY
Corporal Affair #1 / 1995 / IBN / B • Corporal Affair #2 / 1995 / IBN / B • Donna Young: Kim & Molly's Lesbian Video #1 / 1995 / DY / F • HomeGrown Video #461: Splendor In The Grasp / 1995 / HOV / M • Rapture Girls #3: Molly & Renee / 1991 / OD / M

MOLLY DRAKER
Puritan Video Magazine #09 / 1997 / LE / M

MOLLY HAAG *see* **Star Index I**
MOLLY MALONE *see* **Paula Morton**
MOLLY MANNING
Ultraflesh / 1980 / GO / M

MOLLY MAXINE
Painful Desire / 1996 / BON / B • Rivals In Submission / 1996 / BON / B

MOLLY MCGUIRE *see* **Star Index I**
MOLLY MUNRO *see* **Star Index I**
MOLLY O'BRIEN
American Nympho In London / 1987 / VD / M • The Baroness / 1987 / VD / M • Double Penetration #3 / 1986 / WV / C • Hard Core Cafe / 1988 / VD / M • Hello Molly / 1989 / CA / M • Hot Nights And Dirty Days / 1988 / VD / M • Hottest Ticket / 1987 / WV / C • In-N-Out With John Leslie / 1988 / WV / C • International Phone Sex Girls #1 / 1988 / VD / M • Oral Majority #05 / 1987 / WV / C • Oral Majority #06 / 1988 / WV / C • Private Video Magazine #01 / 1993 / OD / M

MOLLY PETERS
Blue Vanities #517 / 1992 / FFL / M

MOLLY ROYLE *see* **Star Index I**
MOLLY SEAGRIM *see* **Star Index I**

MOMS MARGOLD *see* **William Margold**
MON CHERI JANVIER *see* **Cheri Janvier**
MONA
Amateur Nights #14 / 1996 / HO / M • The Best Of The Big Boob Battles / 1993 / CDP / C • Blue Vanities #130 / 1990 / FFL / M • Blue Vanities #530 / 1993 / FFL / M • Bubble Butts #04 / 1992 / LBO / M • The Cumm Brothers #17: Goo Guy Gone Bad / 1996 / OD / M • Every Woman Wants A Penis #2 / 1996 / MID / M • Golden Oldies #5 / 1996 / TTV / M • Hardcore Fantasies #5 / 1996 / LV / M • Harry Horndog #02: Amateur Oriental Orgasms #1 / 1992 / ZA / M • Home-Grown Video #464: Liza, We Love You / 1995 / HOV / M • Hustler Honeys #4 / 1988 / VC / S • Innocent Girls Of Legal Age #3 / 1996 / MP0 / M • Joe Elliot's College Girls #33 / 1994 / JOE / M • Love Theatre / cr80 / VC / M • Make Me Over, Baby / 1996 / LOF / M • Mike Hott: #386 / 1996 / MHV / M • Private Gold #08: The Longest Night / 1996 / OD / M • Profiles #07: Sexworld / 1996 / XPR / M • Santa Is Coming All Over Town / 1996 / EVN / M • Squirt Flirts / 1996 / RAS / M • Teasedance Masturbation #3 / 1994 / MAV / F • That's My Daughter / 1982 / NGV / M • Wrestling Classics #4 / 1993 / CDP / B • Yellow Fever / 1994 / ORE / C

MONA DONNA
Creme De Femme / 1994 / 4P / F • Tight Shots #2 / 1994 / VI / M

MONA EVANS
Snack Time / 1983 / HO / M

MONA JAMES *see* **Star Index I**
MONA JENKS
Fantasy Fever / 1975 / AVC / M • Mortgage Of Sin / 1975 / CA / M • Pleasure Island / 1975 / TGA / M • Sex Museum / 1976 / AXV / M

MONA LEASAH
Love With A Proper Stranger / 1973 / VCX / M

MONA LEE *see* **Star Index I**
MONA LIND
Lesbian Mystery Theatre: The Case Of The Deadly Dyke / 1994 / LIP / F

MONA LISA *(Moana Lisa, Talon, Barbara Woods (Mona))*
Auburn hair, tight firm body, small tits, valley girl voice, long nose. In Feb 1992 she had her breasts enlarged from a reasonable size to rock-solid large cantaloupes. Also same year she said she was 22 years old and came from Tacoma, Washington.
The Adventures Of Seymore Butts / 1992 / FH / M • Amateur Lesbians #21: Daphne / 1992 / GO / F • Ambitious Blondes / 1992 / VIM / M • America's Dirtiest Home Videos #07 / 1991 / VEX / M • America's Dirtiest Home Videos #08 / 1992 / VEX / M • America's Dirtiest Home Videos #09 / 1992 / VEX / M • America's Raunchiest Home Videos #26: Tiptoe Thru The 2 Lips / 1992 / ZA / M • Anal Delights #2 / 1992 / ROB / M • Anal Encounters #4: Tales From The Crack / 1992 / VC / M • Anal Encounters #5: Deliveries In The Rear / 1992 / VC / M • Anal International / 1992 / HW / M • Anal Lover #1 / 1992 / ROB / M • Anal Thrills / 1992 / ROB / M • The Anals Of History #2 / 1992 / MID / M • Autoerotica #1 / 1991 / EX / M • Autoerotica #2 / 1991 / EX / M • The Awakening / 1992 / SC / M • Back In The Pen / 1992 / FH / M • Beach Bum Amateur's #02 / 1992 / MID / M • Bend Over

Babes #3 / 1992 / EA / M • Big Bust Babes #09 / 1992 / AFI / M • Big Titted Tarts / 1994 / PL / C • Biker Chicks In Love / 1991 / LE / M • Blue Angel / 1992 / AFV / M • Blue Angel / 1992 / AFV / M • Breast Collection #03 / 1995 / LBO / C • Breast Wishes #05 / 1991 / LBO / M • Breast Wishes #08 / 1992 / LBO / M • Breast Worx #22 / 1992 / LBO / M • Breast Worx #24 / 1992 / LBO / M • Breast Worx #31 / 1992 / LBO / M • Bronco Millie / 1992 / ZA / M • Buffy Malibu's Totally Nasty All-Girl Home Videos #03 / 1992 / ANA / F • Business And Pleasure / 1992 / AFV / M • Butt Freak #2 / 1996 / EA / M • Butt Woman #2 / 1992 / FH / M • Butt Woman #3 / 1992 / FH / M • Buttsizer, King Of Rears #1 / 1992 / EVN / M • Buttsizer, King Of Rears #2 / 1992 / EVN / M • California Pony Girls / 1992 / STM / B • Captain Butt's Beach / 1992 / LV / M • Checkmate / 1992 / CDI / M • Coming Clean / 1992 / ME / M • Committed / 1992 / LE / M • Confessions #2 / 1992 / OD / M • The D.J. / 1992 / VC / M • The D.P. Man #2 / 1992 / FD / M • Dear Bridgette / 1992 / ZA / M • Deep Cheeks #3 / 1992 / ROB / M • The Devil Made Her Do It / 1992 / HO / M • Dial N Again / 1993 / PEP / M • Dial N For Nikki / 1993 / PEP / M • Diamond In The Rough / 1993 / BIA / C • Diary Of A Porn Star / 1993 / FOR / M • Dirty Thoughts / 1992 / LE / M • Do The White Thing / 1992 / ZA / M • Double D Dykes #03 / 1992 / GO / F • The Dragon Lady #2: Tales From the Bed / 1992 / WV / M • The Dragon Lady #3: Tales From The Bed #2 / 1992 / WV / M • Driving Miss Daisy Crazy #2 / 1992 / WV / M • Dyno-Mite / 1992 / IF / M • Edward Penishands #3 / 1991 / VT / M • Elvis Slept Here / 1992 / LE / M • Firm / 1993 / MID / M • Fringe Benefits / 1992 / IF / M • A Girl's Affair #01 / 1992 / FD / F • Gold LeMay / 1991 / VIM / M • The Good, The Bad & The Nasty / 1992 / VC / M • Herman's Bed / 1992 / HO / M • Hose Jobs / 1995 / VEX / M • How To Have Anal Sex / 1993 / A&E / M • How To Love Your Lover / 1992 / XII / S • I Touch Myself / 1992 / IN / M • In Your Face #1 / 1992 / PL / M • It's A Wonderful Sexlife / 1991 / LE / M • The Joy Dick Club / 1994 / MID / M • Just A Gigolo / 1992 / SC / M • The Key to Love / 1992 / ZA / M • Ladies Lovin' Ladies #2 / 1992 / AR / F • The Last Temptation Of Teri / 1991 / IF / M • Lethal Passion / 1991 / PL / M • Little Secrets / 1991 / LE / M • Lust Crimes / 1992 / WV / M • Malcolm XXX / 1992 / OD / M • Maliboobies / 1993 / CDI / F • Mo' Booty #1 / 1992 / HW / C • Mona Lisa / 1992 / LV / M • Mystery Date / 1992 / CDI / G • New Pussy Hunt #26 / 1996 / LEI / C • Night Cap / 1990 / EX / M • Night Of Passion / 1993 / BIA / C • Night Wish / 1992 / CDI / M • No Man's Land #06 / 1992 / VT / F • One Night Love Affair / 1991 / IF / M • Opposite Attraction / 1992 / VEX / M • Orgy Attack / 1993 / DRP / M • Oriental Anal Sluts / 1993 / WV / C • The Perfect Stranger / 1991 / IN / M • Poor Little Rich Girl #1 / 1992 / XCI / M • Poor Little Rich Girl #2 / 1992 / XCI / M • Prelude / 1992 / VT / M • The Prince Of Lies / 1992 / LE / M • Puppy Love / 1992 / AFV / M • Quickies / 1992 / AFV / M • Return To Leather Lair / 1993 / STM / B • Rocky Mountains / 1991 / IF / M • Saints & Sinners / 1992 / PEP / M • Seeing Red / 1993 / VI / M • Sex Bandits / 1992 / ZA / M • Sex Trek #2: The Search For Sperm / 1991 / ME / M • Sexvision / 1992 / HO / M • Seymore Butts & His Mystery Girl / 1993 / FH / M • Shipwrecked / 1992 / CDI / M • A Shot In The Mouth #2 / 1991 / ME / M • Someone Else / 1992 / VC / M • Spermacus / 1993 / PI / M • Split Personality / 1991 / CIN / G • The Strip / 1992 / SC / M • Taboo #10 / 1992 / IN / M • Taboo #11: Crazy On You / 1993 / IN / M • Tailspin #3 / 1992 / VT / M • A Tale Of Two Titties #2 / 1992 / AFV / M • Tales From Leather Lair: The Leather Master / 1992 / STM / B • Toppers #02 / 1992 / TV / M • Toppers #09 / 1993 / TV / M • Toppers #10 / 1993 / TV / M • Toppers #12 / 1993 / TV / C • Twilight / 1991 / ZA / M • Twin Freaks / 1992 / ZA / M • Unchained Melanie / 1992 / VC / M • Uncle Roy's Best Of The Best: Red Hots / 1993 / VIM / C • Undercover Lover / 1993 / VC / M • Welcome To Bondage: Mona Lisa / 1992 / BON / B • Whispers / 1992 / HO / M • White Men Can Hump / 1992 / EVN / M • Wicked Wenches / 1991 / LV / M

MONA LIZA
All About Sex / 1970 / AR / M

MONA MONTIGUE
School For Sex / cr72 / SOW / M

MONA MOUNDS
Black Knockers #09 / 1995 / TV / M • Black Knockers #12 / 1995 / TV / M

MONA PAGE (Alexandria (M. Page))
Brunette with shoulder length curly (sometimes straight) hair, passable face, large natural tits, slightly thick around the waist.
The Awakening Of Sally / 1984 / VCR / M • Candy's Bedtime Story / 1983 / CA / M • Collection #07 / 1984 / CA / M • Delusions / 1983 / PRC / M • Famous Ta-Ta's #1 / 1986 / VCS / C • Girls Together / 1985 / GO / C • Golden Girls #06 / 1983 / SVE / M • Golden Girls #11 / 1983 / CA / M • Golden Girls #24 / 1984 / CA / M • Gourmet Quickies: Mona Page #704 / 1985 / GO / C • GVC: Valley Vixens #124 / 1983 / GO / M • GVC: Women Who Seduce Men #123 / 1982 / GO / M • Maximum #4 / 1983 / CA / M • Naughty Girls Need Love Too / 1983 / SE / M • Sensuous Moments / 1983 / VIV / M • Shades Of Ecstasy / 1983 / HO / M • A Taste For Passion / 1983 / AMB / M • A Touch Of Desire / 1983 / VCR / C

MONA REED
Dirty & Kinky Mature Women #07 / 1996 / C69 / M • Golden Oldies #4 / 1996 / TTV / M • The Older Women's Sperm Bank #6 / 1996 / SUF / M

MONA VAN CAMP
Euro Extremities #54 / 199? / SVE / C

MONA WHINER
Erecter Sex #5: Oral Fantasies / cr72 / AR / M

MONDO SCENTI see Star Index I

MONERICA see Lili Marlene

MONET LUV
Come Back Little She-Male / 1994 / HSV / G • Dragula: Queen Of Darkness / 1996 / HSV / G • Dungeons & Drag Queens / 1994 / HSV / G • He-She Hangout / 1995 / HSV / G • I'm A Curious She-Male / 1993 / HSV / G • Lady Dick / 1993 / HSV / G • Little Shop Of She-Males / 1994 / HSV / G • My She-Male Valentine / 1994 / HSV / G • The Princess With A Penis / 1994 / HSV / G • She Male Sex Kittens / 1995 / MET / G

• She-Male Encounters #21: Psychic She Males / 1994 / MET / G • She-Male Loves Me / 1995 / VC / G • She-Male Seduction / 1995 / MET / G • She-Male Surprise / 1995 / CDI / G • She-Male Swish Bucklers / 1994 / HSV / G • The She-Male Who Stole Christmas / 1993 / HSV / G • Spring Trannie / 1995 / VC / G • Trannie Angel / 1995 / HSV / G • Trannie Get Your Gun / 1994 / HSV / G • Trannie Love / 1995 / HSV / G • Tranny Hill: Sweet Surrender / 1994 / HSV / G • Transister Act / 1994 / HSV / G • Transsexual Try Outs / 1993 / HSV / G

MONICA
The Betrayal Of Innocence #1: The Awakening Of Marika / 1993 / CC / M • The Betrayal Of Innocence #2: The Decadence / 1993 / CC / M • The Betrayal Of Innocence #3: The Choice / 1993 / CC / M • Big Girl Dildo Show / 1995 / BTO / F • Big Tits And Fat Fannies #10 / 1994 / BTO / M • Blue Vanities #526 / 1993 / FFL / M • Compulsion (Fat Dog) / 1996 / FD / M • Creme De Femme #3 / 1981 / AVC / C • Deep Behind The Scenes With Seymore Butts #2 / 1995 / ULI / M • Dick & Jane In Budapest / 1993 / AVI / M • Eurotica #10 / 1996 / XC / M • Frank Thring's Double Penetration #1 / 1995 / XPR / M • Home Maid Memories #1 / 1994 / BON / C • Intimate Interviews #1 / 1996 / NIT / M • Joe Elliot's College Girls #46 / 1996 / JOE / M • Lil' Women: Vacation / 1996 / EUR / M • Mistress Monica / 1996 / CVP / B • Private Film #18 / 1994 / OD / M • Private Film #20 / 1995 / OD / M • Private Film #21 / 1995 / OD / M • Private Film #23 / 1995 / OD / M • Private Stories #10 / 1996 / OD / M • Private Video Magazine #18 / 1994 / OD / M • Private Video Magazine #24 / 1995 / OD / M • Private Video Magazine #26 / 1995 / OD / M • Real People Real Bondage #1 / 1995 / BON / C • Shaved #02 / 1992 / RB / F • Triple X Video Magazine #01 / 1995 / OD / M • Triple X Video Magazine #03 / 1995 / OD / M • Triple X Video Magazine #15 / 1996 / OD / M

MONICA (HOPE RIS) see Hope Rising

MONICA (PRESHIA) see Preshia

MONICA ADAMS see Star Index I

MONICA ANDERSSON
Erotic Fantasies: Women With Women / 1984 / CV / C • The Second Coming Of Eva / 1974 / ALP / M

MONICA BAAL
Private Gold #02: Friends In Sex / 1995 / OD / M • Triple X Video Magazine #10 / 1995 / OD / M

MONICA BAM
Private Gold #01: Study In Sex / 1995 / OD / M

MONICA BENZ see Star Index I

MONICA BLISS see Star Index I

MONICA CAIRNS
Private Film #27 / 1995 / OD / M • Private Film #28 / 1995 / OD / M • Triple X Video Magazine #02 / 1995 / OD / M • Triple X Video Magazine #04 / 1995 / OD / M

MONICA CARMAN
Sex Over 40 #1 / 1994 / PL / M

MONICA COPELAND see Star Index I

MONICA DARE
Blue Vanities #514 / 1992 / FFL / M

MONICA DEVON see Star Index I

MONICA FLEISCHER
[Schulmadchen-Report 4: Was Eltern Oft

Verzweifeln LaBt / 1972 / ... / M

MONICA HARRISON see Star Index I

MONICA KABAY
A Merry Widow / 1996 / SPI / M

MONICA KITT see Star Index I

MONICA LUCAS see Star Index I

MONICA MARC
[Die Madchenhandler / 1972 / ... / M

MONICA MUNCH
Bi The Time You Get Back / 1995 / BIN / G

MONICA ORSINI
All Grown Up / 1996 / XC / M • Checkmate / 1996 / SNA / M • Don Salvatore: The Last Sicilian / 1995 / XC / M • Dreams Of A Gigolo / 1996 / SNA / M • Flamenco Ecstasy / 1996 / UEF / M • Primal Instinct / 1996 / SNA / M • Pussyman #14: Dreams Of A Gigolo / 1996 / SNA / M • Virility / 1996 / XC / M

MONICA PATTON see Star Index I

MONICA REGIUS
Bright Tails #1 / 1993 / STP / B • Trained To Heel / 1993 / BON / B

MONICA RIVERS see Star Index I

MONICA SANDS see Star Index I

MONICA ST. CLAIR
Catch Of The Day #3 / 1996 / VG0 / M

MONICA STRAND see Star Index I

MONICA SWINN
[The Loves Of Irina / 1973 / PS / S

MONICA TITE see Star Index I

MONICA TOBIAS
Blue Vanities #535 / 1993 / FFL / M

MONICA TROUT
Corsets & Cords / 1994 / BON / B • Fetish Competition / 1993 / BON / B • Service Call Bondage / 199? / BON / B

MONICA VICARE
Challenge Of Desire / 1983 / NSV / M • Love Letters (Now Showing) / 1983 / NSV / M • Shameless / 1982 / SVE / M

MONICA VINCI
Prima #09: ASSassins / 1995 / MBP / M • Prima #14: Hotel Europa / 1996 / MBP / M

MONICA WELLES see Nancy Hoffman

MONICA WHITE
Private Gold #01: Study In Sex / 1995 / OD / M

MONICA ZON
The House Of Strange Desires / 1985 / NSV / M

MONIKA
The Betrayal Of Innocence #1: The Awakening Of Marika / 1993 / CC / M • The Betrayal Of Innocence #2: The Decadence / 1993 / CC / M • The Betrayal Of Innocence #3: The Choice / 1993 / CC / M • Eurotica #07 / 1996 / XC / M • Fazano's Student Bodies / 1995 / EL / M • Frank Thring's Double Penetration #2 / 1996 / XPR / M • Frank Thring's Double Penetration #3 / 1996 / XPR / M • Magma: Puszta Teenies / 1995 / MET / M • Prima #13: Dr. Max Back To Budapest / 1995 / MBP / M • Private Stories #14 / 1996 / OD / M • Sluts 'n' Angels In Budapest / 1994 / EL / M • Sodomania #10: Euro/American Again / 1994 / EL / M • Sodomania #11: In Your Face / 1994 / EL / M • Sodomania: Slop Shots / 1996 / EL / C • Triple X Video Magazine #05 / 1995 / OD / M • Triple X Video Magazine #06 / 1995 / OD / M • Triple X Video Magazine #11 / 1995 / OD / M • Triple X Video Magazine #12 / 1996 / OD / M

MONIKA (BERLIN) see Berlin

MONIKA BELLA

Private Gold #05: Cape Town #1 / 1996 / OD / M

MONIKA CANCELLIERI
Never Say Never To Rocco Siffredi / 1995 / EA / M

MONIKA GARAI
True Stories #2 / 1993 / SC / M

MONIKA GOLOMBOEYS
True Stories #2 / 1993 / SC / M

MONIKA METZGER
Born Erect / cr80 / CA / M

MONIKA SPERMALOVER
Dirty Stories #4 / 1995 / PE / M • World Sex Tour #3 / 1995 / ANA / M

MONIKA TANNER
Private Film #20 / 1995 / OD / M • Private Film #21 / 1995 / OD / M

MONIKA WHITE
Private Gold #02: Friends In Sex / 1995 / OD / M

MONINA *see Star Index I*

MONIQUE
AVP #9120: The Therapist / 1991 / AVP / M • Bound By Desire / 1983 / BIZ / B • California Reaming / 1985 / WV / M • China Lee's Bachelorette Party / 1995 / RHV / M • Dirty Old Men #2 / 1995 / IP / M • Fantasy Exotic Dancers / 1995 / PME / S • L.A. Woman / 1990 / PHV / F • Magma: Bizarre Games / 1996 / MET / M • Monique's Weekend Bondage / cr90 / BON / B • Pearl Necklace: Amorous Amateurs #31 / 1993 / SEE / M • Pussyman Auditions #17 / 1995 / SNA / M • The Satisfiers Of Alpha Blue / 1980 / AVC / M • The Search For Canadian Beaver / 1995 / LIP / F • Sex On The Run #2 / 1994 / TTV / M • Tender Loins / 1996 / PE / M • Victoria's Amateurs #01 / 1992 / VGA / M

MONIQUE (BLACK)
All That: Black Women's Fantasies / 1996 / VT / M • Black Cheerleader Search #06 / 1996 / IVC / M • Black Cheerleader Search #11 / 1997 / IVC / M • Black Snatch #2 / 1996 / DFI / F • Cumback Pussy #2: Crawling Back For More / 1996 / EL / M • Cumback Pussy #5: Groopin' / 1996 / EL / M • Dick & Jane's Video Mail: From Virginville (#4) / 1996 / AVI / M • Dirty Dancers #9 / 1996 / HO / M • Miss Judge / 1997 / VI / M • Sista! #4 / 1996 / VT / F • Sista! #5 / 1996 / VT / F

MONIQUE (CARDIN) *see* Monique Cardin

MONIQUE (EAST)
Back East Babes #3 / 1996 / NIT / M • Intimate Interviews #3 / 1996 / NIT / M

MONIQUE (EUROPEAN)
Barby's On Butt Row / 1996 / ABS / M • Diamonds / 1996 / HDE / M • Fashion Sluts #8 / 1996 / ABS / M • Magma: Pussy Jobs / 1994 / MET / M • Magma: Young & Old / 1995 / MET / M • Naughty Butt Nice / 1993 / IF / M • Private Film #02 / 1993 / OD / M • Sheer Ecstasy / 1993 / IF / M • Video Virgins #33 / 1996 / NS / M • The Voyeur #7: Live In Europe #1 / 1996 / JLP / M

MONIQUE (H. NELSON) *see* Heidi Nelson

MONIQUE (S. DUVALLE) *see* Stephanie DuValle

MONIQUE AMORE
Blondes / 1995 / MET / M • Muffs In Cuffs / 1995 / PL / M • Striptease #1 / 1995 / PL / M • Striptease #2 / 1995 / PL / M

MONIQUE CARDIN *(Monique (Cardin),*

Debbie Hamilton, Samantha Cardin, Samantha King)
An adorable perfect body and face. First seen in **Ceremony, The Ritual Of Love** where she is credited as Debbie Hamilton. In the **Secret Dreams Of Mona Q** she has reddish hair as is not as attractive. Samantha King is the credit in **Baby Rosemary** and Samantha Cardin in **Sensual Encounters Of Every Kind**.
All About Annette / 1982 / SE / C • Baby Rosemary / 1975 / SE / M • Ceremony, The Ritual Of Love / 1976 / AVC / M • For The Love Of Pleasure / 1979 / SE / M • Portrait Of Seduction / 1976 / SE / M • Secret Dreams Of Mona Q / 1977 / AR / M • Sensual Encounters Of Every Kind / 1978 / SE / M • The Starlets / 1976 / RAV / M

MONIQUE COVET
Chateau Duval / 1996 / HDE / M

MONIQUE DEBARGE
Sin City Cycle Sluts #2 / 1995 / SC / F

MONIQUE DEMOAN *see* Monique De-Mone

MONIQUE DEMONE *(Monique DeMoan, Monique Pemean, Cheyenne (Monique))*
Reasonably pretty but tall (5'7 1/2") Hispanic looking girl with small to medium tits, washboard flat belly, thin legs, prominent rib cage, 21 years old in 1994, tattoo all around her right ankle. Self composed attitude. Supposedly worked in rock videos and as a model. De-virginized at age 13. Credited as Cheyenne in **A Lady**.
Anal Centerfold / 1995 / ROB / M • Anal Climax #4 / 1996 / ROB / M • Anal Cum Queens / 1995 / ZA / M • Anal Glamour Girls / 1995 / ME / M • Anal Hellraiser #1 / 1995 / ROB / M • Anal Island #1 / 1996 / VC / M • Anal Island #2 / 1996 / VC / M • Anal Romp / 1995 / LIP / F • Anal Savage #3 / 1996 / ROB / M • Anal Tramps / 1996 / LIP / F • Ass Masters (Leisure) #02 / 1995 / LEI / M • Assy Sassy #3 / 1995 / ROB / F • Babes Illustrated #5 / 1995 / IN / F • Backstage Pass / 1994 / SC / M • Bad Influence / 1996 / ZA / M • Bitches In Heat #1: Locked In the Basement / 1995 / ZA / M • Booty Sister #2 / 1996 / ROB / M • Buffy Malibu's Nasty Girls #09 / 1995 / ANA / F • Butt Banged Cycle Sluts / 1995 / ANA / M • Butt Jammers #03 / 1995 / SC / F • Butt Sluts #5 / 1995 / ROB / F • Casting Call #13 / 1995 / SO / M • Casting Call #16 / 1995 / SO / M • Dangerous Games / 1995 / VI / M • Diva #1: Caught In The Act / 1996 / VC / F • Dr Butts #3 / 1993 / 4P / M • The End / 1995 / VI / M • Finger Pleasures #4 / 1995 / PL / F • Fresh Meat (John Leslie) #1 / 1996 / EA / M • Hardcore Schoolgirls #1: Sweet Young Things / 1995 / XPR / M • The Hitch-Hiker #12: Southern Exposure / 1995 / VIM / M • Hotel Fantasy / 1995 / IN / M • I Want It All / 1995 / WAV / M • Illicit Entry / 1995 / WAV / M • In Cold Sweat / 1996 / VI / M • Interview With A Vibrator / 1996 / WAV / M • A Lady / 1995 / FD / M • Lethal Affairs / 1996 / VI / M • Lotus / 1996 / VI / M • Love Exchange / 1995 / DR / M • Max #06: Going South / 1995 / FRM / M • More Dirty Debutantes #23 / 1993 / 4P / M • More Dirty Debutantes #35 / 1994 / 4P / M • My Baby Got Back #06 / 1995 / VT / M • Nasty Nymphos #10 / 1995 / ANA / M • No Man's Land #14 / 1996 / VT / F • Nothing

Like A Dame #2 / 1995 / IN / M • Oral Obsession #2 / 1995 / VI / M • Pussyman Auditions #22 / 1996 / SNA / M • Raw Footage / 1996 / VC / M • Sin-A-Matic / 1996 / VI / M • Snatch Masters #10 / 1995 / LEI / M • So You Wanna Be A Porn Star #1: The Russians Are Cumming / 1994 / WHP / M • Style #3 / 1996 / VT / M • Sugar Daddies / 1995 / FPI / M • Suggestive Behavior / 1996 / VI / M • Ultimate Sensations / 1996 / NIT / M • Unleashed / 1996 / SAE / M • Up And Cummers #08 / 1994 / 4P / M • Up And Cummers: The Movie / 1994 / 4P / M • Video Virgins #21 / 1995 / NS / M • View Point / 1995 / VI / M • Virgin Dreams / 1996 / EA / M • Wild Thing / 1994 / IF / M

MONIQUE DESPARD
Private Film #08 / 1994 / OD / M

MONIQUE DEVERAUX
Blue Perfume / 1978 / HOE / M

MONIQUE DICHAMBERS
Chicks With Dicks #2 / 1996 / BIZ / B • He-She Hangout / 1995 / HSV / G • Malibu She Males / 1994 / MET / G • Sex Starved She-Males / 1995 / MET / G • She Male Goddesses / 1994 / MET / G • She Male Sluts / 1995 / KDP / G • Spring Trannie / 1995 / VC / G • Trannie Angel / 1995 / HSV / G • Trannie Love / 1995 / HSV / G • Transister Act / 1994 / HSV / G • Transsexual Dynasty / 1996 / BIZ / G • TV Dildo Fantasy #2 / 1996 / BIZ / G

MONIQUE DU PREZ
Erotic Fantasies: Women With Women / 1984 / CV / C • The Joy Of Fooling Around / 1978 / CV / M

MONIQUE DUBOIS *see* Eva Allen
MONIQUE DUBOIS (75) *see Star Index I*
MONIQUE FABRAGE
Bad Girls #2 / 1983 / GO / M • Endless Lust / 1983 / VC / M • Little Girls Lost / 1982 / VC / M • The Master And Mrs. Johnson / 1980 / SAT / M • Ring Of Desire / 1981 / SE / M

MONIQUE GABRIELLE *(Launa Chass)*
Dark blonde or brunette with a very lithe body and a very tight waist, narrow hips, reasonable butt, pretty face, large natural tits. Looks very like her co-star Tina Ross in **Bad Girls #4** where she is credited both as Monique and as Launa Chass.
Amazon Women On The Moon / 1987 / MCA / S • Angel Eyes / 1991 / ... / S • Bad Girls #4 / 1984 / GO / M • Black Venus / 1983 / PLA / S • Chained Heat #1 / 1983 / VES / S • Cleo/Leo / 1989 / NWW / S • Emmanuelle #5 / 1986 / LUM / S • Evil Toons / 1990 / PRS / S • Hollywood Erotic Film Festival / 1987 / PAR / S • Hollywood Scream Queen Hot Tub Party / 1992 / WRE / S • Leg Art / 1996 / PPO / S • Lingerie Dreams #1 / 1993 / PHV / F • Love Scenes / 1984 / MGM / S • Not Of This Earth / 1994 / MGM / S • Penthouse: Forum Letters #1 / 1993 / A*V / S • Penthouse: Love Stories / 1986 / A*V / S • Penthouse: Ready To Ride / 1992 / PET / F • Penthouse: Satin & Lace #1 / 1992 / PET / F • Playboy's Erotic Fantasies #1 / 1987 / UNI / S • Playboy's Erotic Fantasies #2 / 1990 / UNI / S • The Rosebud Beach Hotel / 1985 / VES / S • Screen Test / 1985 / C3S / S • Up 'n' Coming / 1983 / CA / M • Young Lady Chatterly #2 / 1985 / LIV / S

MONIQUE GABRIELLE-78
The Love Syndrome / 1978 / CV / M

MONIQUE GOSS *see* **Monique Hall**

MONIQUE GURU
Lust Boat / 1984 / NSV / M

MONIQUE HALL *(Elizabeth Marr, Monique Goss)*
Brunette with large watermelons.
America's Dirtiest Home Videos #05 / 1991 / VEX / M • Anal Angel / 1991 / ZA / M • Backstage Pass / 1992 / VEX / M • Biggies #04 / 1992 / XPI / M • Brainteasers / 1991 / ZA / M • Breast Worx #07 / 1991 / LBO / M • Breast Worx #13 / 1992 / LBO / M • Breast Worx #18 / 1992 / LBO / M • Bus Stop Tales #11 / 1990 / 4P / M • Edward Penishands #3 / 1991 / VT / M • Fever / 1992 / CA / M • Genie In A Bikini / 1991 / ZA / M • Just One Look / 1993 / V99 / M • Lather / 1991 / LE / M • Long Dan Silver / 1992 / IF / M • Make Me Sweat / 1994 / V99 / M • Man Of Steel / 1992 / IF / M • Mike Hott: #186 Monique Solo / 1991 / MHV / F • Mike Hott: Apple Asses #10 / 1992 / MHV / F • Moore, Moore, Moore: An Anal Explosion / 1992 / IN / M • Mr. Peepers Amateur Home Videos #17: No Holes Barred / 1991 / LBO / M • Nasty Calendar / 1991 / XPI / M • The Perfect Stranger / 1991 / IN / M • Score 4 Me / 1991 / XPI / M • Screwed On The Job / 1991 / XPI / M • Sexlock / 1992 / XPI / M • Shattered / 1991 / LE / M • Silver Sensations / 1992 / VT / M • Student Fetish Videos: The Enema #01 / 1990 / PRE / B • Student Fetish Videos: The Enema #02 / 1990 / SFV / B • Student Fetish Videos: Foot Worship #01 / 1990 / PRE / B • Student Fetish Videos: Foot Worship #02 / 1990 / PRE / B • Student Fetish Videos: Spanking #01 / 1990 / PLV / B • Student Fetish Videos: Spanking #02 / 1990 / SFV / B • Tickets To Paradise / 1992 / XPI / M • Two Of A Kind / 1991 / ZA / M • Valleys Of The Moon / 1991 / SC / M • Wee Wee's Big Misadventure / 1991 / FH / M • Women Of Color / 1991 / PL / F

MONIQUE HOCHEPIED
Whore'n / 1996 / AB / M

MONIQUE LARUE
N.Y. Video Magazine #09 / 1996 / OUP / M

MONIQUE LEBARE
Starlet Nights / 1982 / XTR / M

MONIQUE MOON
[Soul Sex / 197? / ... / M

MONIQUE PEMEAN *see* **Monique De-Mone**

MONIQUE PERRI *see* **Monique Perry (1992)**

MONIQUE PERRIJ *see Star Index I*

MONIQUE PERRY *see* **Jacqueline Lorians**

MONIQUE PERRY (1992) *(Monique St Paris, Monique Perri)*
Not to be confused with Jacqueline Lorians who used the name at one stage, this is an older girl with big natural tits. 5'10" tall, 37D-26-35 in 1994.
Amateurs Exposed #03 / 1993 / CV / M • Bobby Hollander's Maneaters #07 / 1993 / SFP / M • Bra Busters #03 / 1993 / LBO / M • Breast Worx #41 / 1993 / LBO / M • Bun Busters #04 / 1993 / LBO / M • Butt Light: Queen Of Rears / 1992 / STR / M • Dirty Dating Service #02 / 1993 / WP / M • Double D Amateurs #05 / 1993 / JMP / M • Fantasy Flings #01 / 1993 / WP / M • A Few Good Rears / 1993 / IN / M • M Series #01

/ 1993 / LBO / M • Masquerade (1992-Usa) / 1992 / SC / M • Neighborhood Watch #33 / 1992 / LBO / M • Odyssey 30 Min: #269: / 1992 / OD / M • Odyssey 30 Min: #282: / 1992 / OD / M • Odyssey Triple Play #74: Conjugal Couples / 1994 / OD / M • Odyssey Triple Play #77: Hail Hail The Gang Bangs Here / 1994 / OD / M • Older Women With Younger Men #2 / 1993 / CC / M • SVE: Screentest Sex #5 / 1994 / SVE / M

MONIQUE PINA
Pussy Hunt #09 / 1995 / LEI / M

MONIQUE SEABROOK *see* **Yasmine Pendarvis**

MONIQUE SIMON *see* **Dominique Simone**

MONIQUE SIMONE *see* **Dominique Simone**

MONIQUE ST PARIS *see* **Monique Perry (1992)**

MONIQUE STARR *see Star Index I*

MONIQUE SWEET
The Sodomizer #6 / 1996 / SC / M

MONIQUE WHITE *see Star Index I*

MONROE (TOBIANNA) *see* **Tobianna**

MONROE TOBIANA *see* **Tobianna**

MONROE ZEENA
50 And Still Pumping! / 1994 / EMC / M

MONTAGUE HORTON
The Crackster / 1996 / OUP / M

MONTANA
Hispanic looking with long black hair. 5'3" tall, 34D-26-33, weighs 116lbs as of June 1994. Born April 8, 1970.
Anal Hunger / 1994 / ROB / M • Anal Rookies #2 / 1994 / ROB / M • Anal Savage #2 / 1994 / ROB / M • Anal Takeover / 1993 / PEP / M • Assy Sassy #2 / 1994 / ROB / F • Battle Of The Glands / 1994 / LV / F • Beach Bum Amateur's #21 / 1993 / MID / F • The Big Bang #3 / 1994 / LV / M • Butt Sluts #3 / 1994 / ROB / F • Cheatin' / 1994 / FD / M • Club DV8 #1 / 1993 / SC / M • Club DV8 #2 / 1993 / SC / M • Desire Kills / 1996 / SUM / M • Dickin' Around / 1994 / VEX / M • Exposure Images #24: Montana / 1995 / EXI / F • Filthy Sleazy Scoundrels / 1994 / HW / M • First Time Lesbians #14 / 1994 / JMP / F • FTV #65: DD Domination #2 / 1996 / FT / B • A Girl's Affair #04 / 1994 / FD / F • A Girl's Affair #05 / 1994 / FD / F • Girls Around The World #20: Deena Duos & Friends / 1994 / BTO / M • Girls Around The World #27 / 1995 / BTO / M • Lesbian Workout #2 / 1994 / GO / F • Lipstick Lesbians / 1993 / STM / F • Love Me, Love My Butt #2 / 1994 / ROB / F • More Dirty Debutantes #23 / 1993 / 4P / M • New Ends #07 / 1994 / 4P / M • Odyssey 30 Min: #285: / 1992 / OD / M • Odyssey Triple Play #60: Interracial Facial / 1994 / OD / M • A Reason To Die / 1994 / PEP / M • Sex On The Beach!: Spring Break Texas Style / 1994 / CPG / F • Sleaze Please!—August Edition / 1994 / FH / M • Taxi Girls #4: Daughter Of Lust / 1994 / CA / M • To Shave And Shave Not / 1994 / PEP / M • The Tonya Hard-On Story / 1994 / GO / M • Video Virgins #10 / 1993 / NS / M • Video Virgins #12 / 1994 / NS / M • White Wedding / 1994 / V99 / M

MONTANA (C. CASSIDY) *see* **Cris Cassidy**

MONTANA BRENT *see* **Cris Cassidy**

MONTANA GREY *see Star Index I*

MONTANA GUNN

Anal Bandits / 1996 / SO / M • The Blowjob Adventures Of Doctor Fellatio / 1997 / EL / M • Booty And The Ho' Fish / 1996 / RAS / M • Buffy's Anal Adventure / 1996 / CDI / M • Butt Sluts #6 / 1996 / ROB / F • The Clock Strikes Bizarre On Butt Row / 1996 / ABS / M • Crack Attack! / 1996 / PE / M • The Dinner Party #2: The Buffet / 1996 / ULI / M • Domina #5: Whipper Snapper / 1996 / LBO / B • Domina #7 / 1996 / LBO / B • Double D Dykes #27 / 1995 / GO / F • Girls Of The Panty Raid / 1995 / VT / M • Golddiggers #3 / 1995 / VC / M • Gutter Mouths / 1996 / JMP / M • Hardcore Debutantes #03 / 1997 / TEP / M • Intense Perversions #2 / 1996 / PL / M • Lesbian Pooper Sluts / 1996 / ROB / F • Malibu Butt Sluts / 1996 / ROB / F • Mickey Ray's Sex Search #01: Sliding In / 1994 / WIV / M • Neighborhood Slut / 1996 / LV / M • Over Exposed / 1996 / ULP / M • Passions Of Sin / 1996 / NIT / M • Prime Choice #8 / 1996 / RAS / M • Pussyman #15: The Bone Voyage Bash / 1997 / SNA / M • Rockhard (Coast) / 1996 / CC / M • Scotty's X-Rated Adventure / 1996 / WP / M • Shadows Of Lust / 1996 / NIT / M • Shayla's Swim Party / 1997 / VC / M • Spazm #1: Point Blank / 1996 / LBO / M • Spinners #2 (Wicked) / 1996 / WP / M • Topless Window Washers / 1996 / LE / M • Underground #1 / 1996 / SC / M • Violation / 1996 / LE / M • Virgin Killers: Second Rampage / 1995 / PEP / M

MONTANA STATION *see* **Cris Cassidy**

MONTANA WOLF
Tender Loins / 1996 / PE / M

MONTANNA HOUSTON
Hardcore: The Films Of Richard Kern #1 / 1991 / FTV / M

MONTE MARANO
Inside Seka / 1980 / VXP / M

MONTE MOUNT
Heat Wave / 1977 / COM / M

MONTGOMERY WILDE
Another Day, Another Million / 1993 / BON / B • The Audition / 1992 / BON / B • Beach Blanket Bondage / 1993 / BON / B • Bondage Outcall / 1994 / BON / B • Control / 1993 / BON / B • Kathryn's Maid / 1993 / BON / B • Maid For Bondage / 1993 / BON / B • Two For The Price Of One / 1993 / BON / B • Two Tied & Tormented / 1993 / BON / B

MONTI
Blonde hair with, in some movies, reddish overtones, passable face, slim body, belly button ring, small tits, tattoo of a dolphin on her left belly, and slightly big on the butt. In 1996 she said she was 18 years old and was de-virginized at 15 but sounds querelous and difficult and said she was going to get implants. To date (March 1997) this has not occurred and she seems to have mellowed.
Butt Row Unplugged / 1996 / ABS / M • Drop Sex: Wipe The Floor / 1997 / JLP / M • More Dirty Debutantes #59 / 1996 / SBV / M • More Dirty Debutantes #61 / 1997 / SBV / M • More Dirty Debutantes #65 / 1997 / SBV / M • Puritan Video Magazine #10 / 1997 / LE / M • Real Sex Magazine #01 / 1996 / HO / M

MONTI STEVENS *see* **Cris Cassidy**

MONTSERRAT PROUST
[Le Journal Intime D'Une Nymphomane / 1972 / ... / M

MONTY HOFFMAN *see Star Index I*

MOOKIE BLODGET *(Phil Heffernan)*
Thundercrack! / 1974 / LUM / M

MOON MAN
Private Film #12 / 1994 / OD / M

MOONSHINE see Star Index I

MOOSE
Attack Of The 50 Foot Hooker / 1994 / OD / M • Black Gangbangers #01 / 1994 / HW / M • California Blacks / 1994 / V99 / M • The Freak Club / 1994 / VMX / M • Girlz In The Hood #3: Erotic Justice / 1993 / HW / M • The Joi Fuk Club / 1993 / WV / M • Koko Is Cumin' At Cha / 1994 / AVI / M • Naughty Nicole / 1994 / SC / M • Savage Fury #3 / 1994 / VEX / M • Stiff Competition #2 / 1994 / CA / M • Superstar Sex Challenge #3 / 1994 / VC / M • The Sweet Sweet Back #2: Double Thaanng Dat Black Hole / 1994 / FH / M • Tail Taggers #112 / 1993 / WV / M • Tail Taggers #114: Booty Brunch / 1994 / WV / M • Under The Hood: Nina Hartley's Guide To Better Cunnilingus / 1994 / A&E / M • Wild Orgies #04 / 1994 / AFI / M

MOOSE MALLOY
Mistress Cherri's Basic (Slave) Training / 1992 / CAS / B • The Painful World Of Moose Malloy / 1993 / AMF / B • Payne In The Behind / 1993 / AMF / C • VGA: Down In Dorothy's Dungeon / 1993 / VGA / B • The World Of Payne / 1991 / STM / B

MOOSE MARTIN see Star Index I

MORA
Big Murray's New-Cummers #29: Tools Of The Trade / 1995 / FD / M

MORELLE DE KEISH see Morelle DeKeith

MORELLE DEKEIGH see Morelle DeKeith

MORELLE DEKEITH *(Morelle DeKeigh, Morelle De Keish, Morrelle DeKeigh)*
Pudgy transsexual.
Aunty V's Panty Boy / 1991 / LEO / B • Black Orchid / 1993 / WV / M • Charade / 1993 / HSV / G • Good Boy, Bad Girl / 1990 / VT / G • Petticoat Therapy / 1994 / LEO / G • Queens Are Wild #1 / 1992 / VIM / G • Shaved She-Males / 1992 / STA / G • She-Male Encounters #13: She-Male Reformatory / 1987 / MET / G • She-Male Encounters #14: She-Male Wrestlers / 1987 / MET / G • She-Male Salsa / 1987 / VC / G • She-Male Sex Clinic / 1991 / VC / G • She-Male Showgirls / 1992 / STA / G • She-Male Solos #05 / 1990 / LEO / G • She Male Spirits Of The Night / 1991 / VC / G • She-Male Whorehouse / 1988 / VD / G • Sin City: The Movie / 1992 / SC / M • Sisters Of Sin / 1991 / VIM / G • Taboo #09 / 1991 / IN / M • Transformed / 1991 / MET / M • Transsexual 6900 / 1990 / LV / G • The Ultimate Sex / 1992 / MET / G • The Ultimate She-Male / 1995 / LEO / G

MORGAN
3 Mistresses Of The Chateau / 1995 / STM / B • Anal Camera #11 / 1995 / EVN / M • Best Exotic Dancers In The Usa / 1995 / PME / S • Bondage Imagination Unlimited / 1994 / BON / B • Crimson Thighs / 1995 / HW / M • The Cumm Brothers #17: Goo Guy Gone Bad / 1996 / OD / M • Deep Inside Anal Camera / 1996 / EVN / C • Filthy First Timers #2: Innocence Lost / 1996 / EL / M • More Dirty Debutantes #38 / 1995 / 4P / M • More Dirty Debutantes #39 / 1995 / 4P / M • Northwest Pecker Trek #2: Ever-

green, Ever Horny / 1994 / LBO / M • Northwest Pecker Trek #4: Laid In Latte Land / 1994 / LBO / M • Northwest Pecker Trek #6: Two Girls For Every Boy / 1995 / LBO / M • Rump Man: Sex On The Beach / 1995 / HW / M • Strictly For Ladies Only /]983 / CAT / S • Three Girl Tickle #2 / 1996 / SY / B

MORGAN ASHLEY see Star Index I

MORGAN BRITTANY
Secrets Behind The Green Door / 1987 / SE / M

MORGAN DANIELS
The Anal Nurse Scam / 1995 / CA / M • Bare Ass In The Park / 1995 / PEP / M • Blonde In Blue Flannel / 1995 / CA / M • The Butt Sisters Do Daytona / 1995 / MID / M • Double D Dykes #17 / 1995 / GO / F • Erotic Visions / 1995 / ULI / M • Layover / 1994 / VI / M • N.Y. Video Magazine #02 / 1995 / OUP / M • Sexual Impulse / 1995 / VD / M

MORGAN FAIRLANE
Short haired blonde with small/medium tits, passable (sometimes pretty) face, large tattoo on left shoulder and another very small one on her right pussy, and pleasant but strong personality. Devirginized at 17 and was 30 years old in 1996. Comes from Utah by way of Denver CO.
The Adventures Of Peeping Tom #2 / 1996 / OD / M • American Tushy! / 1996 / ULI / M • Anal Cornhole Cutie / 1996 / ROB / M • Anal Fireball / 1996 / ROB / M • Craze Du Sex #2 / 1996 / VT / M • Dr Peter Proctor's House Of Anal Delights / 1996 / HO / M • Face Jam / 1996 / VC / M • First Whores Club / 1996 / ERA / M • Frendz? #2 / 1996 / RAS / M • Macin' #1 / 1996 / SMP / M • One Night In The Valley / 1996 / CA / M • Philmore Butts Lake Poontang / 1996 / SUF / M • Pretty Anal Ladies / 1996 / ANE / M • Seymore Butts: Slippin' In Through The Out Door / 1996 / FH / M • Shane's World #7 / 1996 / OD / M • Sorority Sex Kittens #3 / 1996 / VC / M • Star Flash / 1996 / VT / M • Strip Show / 1996 / CA / M • This Girl Is Freaky / 1996 / NIT / M • Up And Cummers #32 / 1996 / 4P / M • Venom #7 / 1996 / VD / M • Video Virgins #31 / 1996 / NS / M • Wild Widow / 1996 / NIT / M

MORGAN GRANT see Star Index I

MORGAN JONES see Star Index I

MORGAN LANE
Heartthrobs / 1985 / CA / M

MORGAN LEE see Taylor Evans

MORGAN LEFAY
Amazing Nympho Stories / 1995 / TEG / M • Anal Anonymous / 1995 / SO / M • Anal Interrogation / 1995 / ZA / M • Anal Webb / 1995 / ZA / M • Ass Poppers / 1995 / VMX / M • Butt Hunt #08 / 1995 / LEI / M • The Butt Sisters Do Chicago / 1995 / MID / M • Cover To Cover / 1995 / WP / M • Decadent Obsession / 1995 / OD / M • Dream House / 1995 / XPR / M • The Girls Of Spring Break / 1995 / VT / M • Kym Wilde's On The Edge #25 / 1995 / RB / B • Leather / 1995 / LE / M • Mike Hott: #312 Lesbian Sluts #19 / 1995 / MHV / F • Mike Hott: #317 Girls Who Swallow Cum #01 / 1995 / MHV / C • Mike Hott: #324 Cum In My Cunt #06 / 1995 / MHV / C • Mike Hott: #326 Cum In My Mouth #03 / 1995 / MHV / C • Mike Hott: #336 Three-Sum Sluts #09 / 1995 / MHV / M • Miss Nude International /

1996 / LE / M • The New Snatch Masters #16 / 1995 / LEI / C • Profiles #04: Lust Lessons / 1995 / XPR / M • Pussy Hunt #15 / 1995 / LEI / M • Sex Bandits / 1995 / VC / M • Sex On The Beach Hawaiian Style #1 / 1995 / ULP / M • Sinnocence / 1995 / CDI / M • Sodomize Me!!! / 1996 / SPR / M • Some Like It Wet / 1995 / LE / M • Surf Babes / 1995 / LE / M • Tailz From Da Hood #1 / 1995 / AVI / M • Video Virgins #23 / 1995 / NS / M • The Wanderer #1: Road Tails / 1995 / CDI / M • What's Up, Tiger Pussy? / 1995 / VC / M • Wicked Ways #3: An All-Anal Slutfest / 1995 / WP / M

MORGAN MCCLOUD *(Morgan McLeod)*
Long red hair, very white body, small tits, flat butt, marginal face.
Butt Wackers / 1995 / FH / M • Fashion Sluts #2 / 1995 / ABS / M • Hollywood Amateurs #11 / 1994 / MID / M • Interracial Escorts / 1995 / GO / M • Mile High Thrills / 1995 / VIM / M • Reverse Gang Bang / 1995 / JMP / M • The Tigress / 1995 / VIM / M

MORGAN MCLEOD see Morgan McCloud

MORGAN MONROE
Transsexual Secretary / 19?? / BIZ / G

MORGAN NAVARRO
The Ambassador File / 1995 / HOM / B • Cat And Bound Tickle Fest / 1996 / VTF / B • Dungeon Training / 1995 / STM / B • Filthy First Timers #4 / 1996 / EL / M • More Dirty Debutantes #45 / 1995 / 4P / M • More Dirty Debutantes #49 / 1995 / 4P / M • New Pussy Hunt #18 / 1995 / LEI / C • The New Snatch Masters #14 / 1995 / LEI / C • Sex Freaks / 1995 / EA / M • Slave Wages / 1995 / PRE / B • Student Fetish Videos: Best of Catfighting #03 / 1995 / PRE / C • Student Fetish Videos: Foot Worship #16 / 1995 / PRE / B • Student Fetish Videos: Spanking #20 / 1995 / PRE / B • Summer Dreams / 1996 / TEP / M • Taxi Girls #4: Daughter Of Lust / 1994 / CA / M • Video Virgins #28 / 1996 / NS / M

MORGAN PHOENIX
A Dirty Western #2: Smoking Guns / 1994 / CV / M

MORGAN RAY see Star Index I

MORGAN STEEL
Anal Intruder #01 / 1986 / CC / M • Bitch Queendom / 1987 / BIZ / B • Cocktales / 1985 / AT / M • She's The Boss (B&D) / 19?? / LON / B • Top Control / cr85 / JAN / B

MORGAN UPTON
Body Talk / 1982 / VCX / M

MORGANA
Cherry Busters / 1995 / WIV / M

MORGANA DUNDEE
Dirty Business / 1995 / WIV / M

MORGANE
Eurotica #09 / 1996 / XC / M

MORGANNA
Girls Come Too / 1963 / SOW / S • Indian Raid, Indian Made / 1969 / SOW / S • Painless Steel #3 / 1996 / FLV / M • Riverboat Mama / 1969 / SOW / S • Swamp Girl / cr70 / SOW / S

MORGONA
Under The Skirt #2 / 1995 / KAE / F

MORIAH WILLIAMS see Star Index I

MORNING STAR
Erotic Fantasies #4 / 1983 / CV / C • Judgement Day / 1976 / CV / M

MORRELLE DEKEIGH *see* **Morelle DeKeith**

MORRIS ELEGANT *see Star Index I*

MORY MORRIS *see Star Index I*

MOTH
Blue Vanities #555 / 1994 / FFL / M

MOUNTAIN MARY *see Star Index I*

MOURA
Dirty & Kinky Mature Women #05 / 1995 / C69 / M

MOUSIENDI
Hot Nurses / 1977 / CA / M • Love In Strange Places / 1977 / CA / M • Odyssey / 1977 / VC / M

MR. 18
Dirty Hairy's Over 50 Meets Mr. Black 18 Inches / 1996 / GOT / M

MR. BLACK
Beaverly Hills Cop / 1985 / SE / M • Bedtime For Byron / 1991 / ME / M • Big Sister Substitute / 1990 / LEO / G • Sex Busters / 1984 / PLY / M • The Woman In Pink / 1984 / SE / M

MR. BLUE
Mr. Blue / 1996 / JSP / G

MR. CANE
Bitch / 1993 / VIM / M

MR. CHEEKS
Crack Attack! / 1996 / PE / M

MR. DICK
Big Tits And Fat Fannies #03 / 1990 / BTO / M

MR. DOO DOO *see* **Hank Rose**

MR. ED
The Spectacular Denni O'Brien / 1995 / SP / M

MR. EMMANUEL *(Emmanuel)*
Transaction #2 / 1987 / WV / G • Transverse Tail / 1987 / CDI / M • Trisexual Encounters #13 / 1992 / PL / G • Unexpected Encounter / 1989 / WV / G • [Mr. Emmanuelle / 19?? / ... / M

MR. HANKS
Orient Sexpress / 1996 / AVI / M

MR. IRON ROD
More Dirty Debutantes #13 / 1992 / 4P / M

MR. J
Diane's Night Out / 1988 / VER / B • Video Virgins #05 / 1993 / NS / M

MR. JOHNSON
Hollywood On Ice / 1995 / VT / M

MR. JONES
Neighborhood Watch #22: In The Pink And Wet / 1992 / LBO / M • Stevi's: How Short Do You Want It? / 1994 / SSV / F • VGA: Bureau Of Discipline #1 / 1993 / VGA / B

MR. LEWIS
Kitty's Kinky Capers / 1996 / TTV / M

MR. LUCKY *see* **Mike Davis**

MR. MACK
Itsy Bitsy Gang Bang / 1996 / HW / M • Somewhere Under The Rainbow #1 / 1995 / HW / M • Somewhere Under The Rainbow #2 / 1995 / HW / M

MR. MARCUS *(Marcus Alston)*
Quite pleasant big black guy.
8-Ball: Westside Gang Bang / 1995 / PL / M • The Adventures Of Peeping Tom #4 / 1997 / OD / M • Amateur Black: Honeys / 1995 / SUF / M • Anal Alley Cat / 1996 / KWP / M • Anal Anarchy / 1995 / VC / M • Anal Cannibals / 1996 / ZA / M • Anal Fantasy / 1996 / SUF / M • Anal Heartbreaker / 1995 / ROB / M • Anal Pool Party / 1996 / PE / M • Anal Pussycat / 1995 / ROB / M • Anal Savage #3 / 1996 / ROB / M • Anal

Senorita #1 / 1994 / ROB / M • Anal Toy Story / 1996 / MP0 / M • Ass Lover's Special / 1996 / PE / M • Asses Galore #1: From L.A. To Brazil / 1996 / DFI / M • Asses Galore #3: Pure Evil / 1996 / DFI / M • Asses Galore #4: Extreme Noise Terror / 1996 / DFI / M • Backdoor Ebony / 1995 / WV / M • Barby's On Butt Row / 1996 / ABS / M • Best Gang Bangs / 1996 / DFI / C • Beyond Reality #3: Stand Erect! / 1996 / EXQ / M • The Black Avenger #1: The Titty Romp / 1996 / OUP / C • Black Bamboo / 1995 / IN / M • Black Bush Bashers / 1996 / LOK / M • The Black Butt Sisters Do New Orleans / 1996 / MID / M • The Black Butt Sisters Do Seattle / 1995 / MID / M • Black Cheerleader Search #01 / 1996 / ROB / M • Black Cheerleader Search #02 / 1996 / ROB / M • Black Cheerleader Search #03 / 1996 / ROB / M • Black Cheerleader Search #04 / 1996 / ROB / M • Black Cheerleader Search #05 / 1996 / IVC / M • Black Cheerleader Search #07 / 1996 / IVC / M • Black Cheerleader Search #09 / 1996 / IVC / M • Black Cheerleader Search #11 / 1997 / IVC / M • Black Hollywood Amateurs #09 / 1995 / MID / M • Black Hollywood Amateurs #18 / 1995 / MID / M • Black Hollywood Amateurs #20 / 1995 / MID / M • Black Jack City #5 / 1995 / HW / M • Black Lube Job Girls / 1995 / SUF / M • Black Power / 1996 / LEI / C • Black Sensations: Models In Heat / 1995 / SUF / M • Black Street Hookers #2 / 1996 / DFI / M • Black Studs & Little White Trash / 1995 / ROB / M • Black Talez N Da Hood / 1996 / APP / M • Booty Sister #2 / 1996 / ROB / M • Brothers Bangin' / 1995 / ANA / M • Buffy's Bare Ass Barbecue / 1996 / CDI / M • Butthead Dreams: Down In The Bush / 1995 / FH / M • The Case Of The Black Booty / 1996 / LV / M • Cheek To Cheek / 1997 / EL / M • Crack Attack! / 1996 / PE / M • Cumback Pussy #3: Coast To Coast Rump Romp / 1996 / EL / M • Dark Eyes / 1995 / FC / M • Decadent Dreams / 1996 / ME / M • Defying The Odds / 1995 / OD / M • The Dinner Party #2: The Buffet / 1996 / ULI / M • Dirty Stories #2 / 1995 / PE / M • Dirty Tricks #1: Just A Bunch Of Whores / 1995 / EA / M • Doin' The Nasty / 1996 / AVI / M • Double Anal Alternatives / 1996 / EL / M • Dr Freckle & Mr Jive / 1995 / IN / M • Drop Sex: Wipe The Floor / 1997 / JLP / M • East Vs West: Battle Of The Gang Bangs / 1994 / TTV / M • Ebony Erotica / 1995 / VT / M • Essence / 1996 / SO / M • Ethnic Cheerleader Search #1 / 1996 / WIC / M • Extreme Sex #3: Wired / 1994 / VI / M • Fantasies Of Persia / 1995 / VT / M • Fashion Sluts #3 / 1995 / ABS / M • Fashion sluts #5: Ethnic Ecstasy / 1995 / ABS / M • Freaknic / 1996 / IN / M • Freaky Tailz / 1996 / AVI / M • Fresh Meat (John Leslie) #1 / 1994 / EA / M • Fresh Meat (John Leslie) #2 / 1995 / EA / M • Fresh Meat (John Leslie) #3 / 1996 / EA / M • Gangbang Girl #15 / 1995 / ANA / M • Gangbang Girl #16 / 1995 / ANA / M • Gangbang Girl #17 / 1995 / ANA / M • Gangbang Girl #18 / 1996 / ANA / M • Ganggstas Paradise / 1995 / AVI / M • Generation Sex #1 / 1996 / VT / M • Gimme Some Head / 1994 / VT / M • The Girls From Hootersville #08 / 1994 / SFP / M • Hollywood On Ice / 1995 / VT / M • The Horny Housewife / 1996 /

HO / M • I Want It All / 1995 / WAV / M • Indiscreet! Video Magazine #1 / 1995 / FH / M • Interracial Anal #06 / 1995 / AFI / M • Interracial Escorts / 1995 / GO / M • Interracial Video Virgins #01 / 1996 / NS / M • Lana Exposed / 1995 / VT / M • Macin' #1 / 1996 / SMP / M • Mall Slut / 1997 / SC / M • Maverdick / 1995 / WV / M • Middle Aged Sex Maniacs / 1995 / SUF / M • Miss Anal #2 / 1995 / C69 / M • Miss Judge / 1997 / VI / M • More Than A Whore / 1995 / OD / M • My Baby Got Back #05 / 1995 / VT / M • My Baby Got Back #06 / 1995 / VT / M • My Baby Got Back #07 / 1995 / VT / M • My Baby Got Back #08 / 1996 / VT / M • My Baby Got Back #09 / 1996 / VT / M • Naked Juice / 1995 / OD / G • Nasty Nymphos #06 / 1994 / ANA / M • Nasty Nymphos #07 / 1994 / ANA / M • Nasty Nymphos #11 / 1995 / ANA / M • Nasty Nymphos #12 / 1996 / ANA / M • Nasty Nymphos #13 / 1996 / ANA / M • Nasty Nymphos #15 / 1996 / ANA / M • Nasty Nymphos #16 / 1996 / ANA / M • Nba: Nuttin' Butt Ass / 1996 / SMP / M • Nightlife / 1997 / CA / M • Once In A Lifetime / 1996 / VC / C • Party Club / 1996 / C69 / M • Persia's Back / 1994 / VT / M • Puritan Video Magazine #04 / 1996 / LE / M • Pussyman #15: The Bone Voyage Bash / 1997 / SNA / M • Pussyman Auditions #09 / 1995 / SNA / M • Pussyman Auditions #15 / 1995 / SNA / M • Pussyman's House Party #1 / 1996 / SNA / M • Pussyman's House Party #2 / 1996 / SNA / M • Pussyman's Nite Club Party #1 / 1996 / SNA / M • Pussyman's Nite Club Party #2 / 1997 / SNA / M • Put 'em On Da Glass / 1994 / VT / M • Rump-Shaker #5 / 1996 / HW / M • Shades Of Color #1 / 1995 / LBO / M • Sharon's House Party / 1995 / HW / M • Sherlock Homie / 1995 / IN / M • The Shocking Truth #1 / 1996 / DWO / M • The Shocking Truth #2 / 1996 / DWO / M • Showtime / 1996 / VT / M • Sin-A-Matic / 1996 / VI / M • Sleazy Streets / 1995 / PEP / M • So Bad / 1995 / VT / M • The Stiff / 1995 / WAV / M • Sweet Brown Sugar / 1994 / AVI / M • Tails From The Hood / 1995 / FH / M • Tailz From Da Hood #2 / 1995 / AVI / M • Tailz From Da Hood #3 / 1996 / AVI / M • Takin' It To The Limit #2 / 1994 / BS / M • Takin' It To The Limit #3 / 1994 / BS / M • Takin' It To The Limit #4 / 1995 / BS / M • Takin' It To The Limit #7: Debauched / 1996 / BS / M • Toot Z Roll / 1995 / WP / M • Two-Pac / 1996 / VT / M • Up And Cummers #32 / 1996 / 4P / M • Up And Cummers #36 / 1996 / 4P / M • Up The Ying Yang #2 / 1995 / CC / M • Up Your Ass #1 / 1996 / ANA / M • Venom #4 / 1996 / VD / M • Venom #6 / 1996 / CA / M • Vivid Raw #1 / 1996 / VI / M • The Voyeur #5 / 1995 / EA / M • The Voyeur #6 / 1996 / EA / M • The Voyeur #7: Live In Europe #1 / 1996 / JLP / M • Waiting For The Man / 1996 / VT / M • Whiplash / 1996 / DFI / M • Whoreo / 1995 / BIP / M • Whoreos' / 1996 / BEP / M • You Go Girl! (Video Team) / 1995 / VT / M

MR. MARQUIS
Bootylicious: Booty & The Ho Bitch / 1996 / JMP / M

MR. MEANS
Punished Embezzler / 1993 / BON / B

MR. PENN
Delinquent Renter / 1994 / BON / B

MR. SCOTT
Kitty's Kinky Capers / 1996 / TTV / M
MR. SEBASTIAN
Painless Steel #1 / 1991 / AOC / M
MR. TIM
Catching Snapper / 1995 / XCI / M
MR. WILKES
Mr. Wilkes' Caning Academy / 1994 / VTF / B
MR. X
Bun Busters #11 / 1993 / LBO / M • More Dirty Debutantes #10 / 1991 / 4P / M • Spooky Night / 1993 / BON / B
MR. XX
More Dirty Debutantes #12 / 1991 / 4P / M
MS. ANGIE
She-Male Salsa / 1987 / VC / G
MS. SEXXY
Black Cheerleader Search #11 / 1997 / IVC / M
MS. SHAPE see Star Index I
MS. X
Wet Mask / 1995 / SC / M
MUCH MARY
The Coming Of Angie / cr73 / TGA / M
MUFFIN
Menaja's House Party / 1996 / HW / M
MUFFIN MCINTOSH see Star Index I
MUFFY see Star Index I
MUFFY FIELDS see Star Index I
MUFFY MORGAN see Star Index I
MULE JOHNSON see Star Index I
MURAY WORK see Star Index I
MURIEL
Magma: Anita #2 / 1996 / MET / M • Magma: Huge Cum Shots / 1995 / MET / M
MURRAY BUKOFSKI
Dracula Exotica / 1980 / TVX / M
MURRILL MAGLIO
Deliciously Teri / 1993 / IF / M • Illusions #1 / 1992 / IF / M • Illusions #2 / 1992 / IF / M • Inferno / 1991 / XCI / M • More Dirty Debutantes #09 / 1991 / 4P / M • Spellbound / 1991 / CDI / M • Starr / 1991 / CA / M • Totally Teri / 1992 / IF / M • Wicked / 1991 / XCI / M
MUS
Gigi Gives It Away / 1995 / FRF / M
MUSTANG SALLY LAYD see Sally Layd
MUSTAPHA
Cindy Puts Out / 1996 / OLL / M • Veronica The Screenwriting Hooker / 1996 / LE / M
MY MAN
Crazy Times / 1995 / BS / B
MYA LUVV
Delinquents On Butt Row / 1996 / EA / M • Desert Island Buttwatch / 1996 / SUF / M • Dirty Bob's #23: Tampa Teasers / 1995 / FLP / S • East Coast Sluts #07: Tampa Bay / 1995 / PL / M • Fresh Meat #1 / 1996 / PL / M • Philmore Butts Spring Break / 1996 / SUF / M • Strap-On Sally #07: Face Dildo Frenzy / 1995 / PL / F • Strap-On Sally #08: Strap-On Cock Fight / 1995 / PL / F • Tampa Spice / 1996 / SUF / M • Up And Cummers #18 / 1995 / 4P / M • Xhibitions: Kissin' Kuzzins / 1995 / XHI / F • Xhibitions: Mya Luvv / 1995 / XHI / F
MYAGI see Mimi Miyagi
MYAKI
Pai Gow Video #04: Tails Of The Town / 1994 / EVN / M
MYKA see Star Index I
MYLAND BYRON see Star Index I
MYLENE
Euro-Max #4: / 1995 / SC / M • Family Af-

fair / 1996 / XC / M • World Sex Tour #2 / 1995 / ANA / M
MYLINDA
Hirsute Lovers #2 / 1995 / BTO / M
MYNDI
Decadent Dreams / 1996 / ME / M • Up And Cummers #37 / 1996 / 4P / M
MYRA
Blue Vanities #550 / 1994 / FFL / M • Score 4 Me / 1991 / XPI / M • Screwed On The Job / 1991 / XPI / M
MYRA AMADO see Cumisha Amado
MYRA SONTAG
Strange Diary / 1976 / AXV / M
MYREE MAMBO see Star Index I
MYRIA see Star Index I
MYRIAH see Star Index I
MYSTERY LANE see Star Index I
MYSTERY MAN see Star Index I
MYSTIC
Odyssey Triple Play #88: Candid Couples / 1995 / OD / M
MYSTIC GREY
San Francisco Lesbians #3 / 1993 / PL / F
MYSTIC SOMMERS see Star Index I
MYSTICA see Star Index I
MYSTIQUE
Backdoor Boogie / 1994 / TEG / M • Titan's Gonzo Video Magazine #02 / 1996 / TEG / M
N'J DEBAHIA
Foreign Tongues #1: Going Down / 1995 / VI / M • Foreign Tongues #2: Mesmerized / 1995 / VI / M
N. COOPER
Hardcore: The Films Of Richard Kern #1 / 1991 / FTV / M
NADA
Voluptuous #4 / 199? / H&S / M
NADECHE
Magma: Horny For Cock / 1990 / MET / M
NADIA
The Best Of Fabulous Flashers / 1996 / DGD / F • Deep Inside Dirty Debutantes #10 / 1993 / 4P / M • Prima #13: Dr. Max Back To Budapest / 1995 / MBP / M • Thrill Seekers / 1993 / ROB / F • Triple X Video Magazine #15 / 1996 / OD / M
NADIA HENKOWA
Butterflies / 1974 / CA / M • Veil Of Lust / 1973 / BL / M
NADIA LINDEN
Penetration (Anabolic) #2 / 1995 / ANA / M
NADIA MOORE (Nadjia Moore)
Tall (about 5'7") brunette, long curly dark brown hair, medium inflated tits (they look too rigid to be real but no scars are visible), tight waist, toally shaven pussy, passable face, tattoo of a circle enclosing three large dots at the top of her ass crack. 20 years old in 1996. Seems to have a pleasant personality. Comes from Texas and was de-virginized at 16.
Asses Galore #3: Pure Evil / 1996 / DFI / M • The Attendant / 1996 / SC / M • Betrayed / 1996 / WP / M • Bottom Dweller: The Final Voyage / 1996 / EL / M • Breeders / 1996 / MET / M • Delinquents On Butt Row / 1996 / EA / M • Eighteen #1 / 1996 / SC / M • Indecent Exposures / 1996 / MID / M • Jenna's Built For Speed / 1997 / WP / F • More Dirty Debutantes #51 / 1996 / 4P / M • Muff Divers #3 / 1996 / TV / F • Passion / 1996 / SC / M • Pick Up Lines #05 / 1996 / OD / M • Up And Cummers #33 / 1996 / 4P / M • Video Virgins #31 / 1996 / NS / M •

The Voyeur #8: Live In Europe #2 / 1996 / JLP / M • Wild & Wicked #7 / 1996 / VT / M • Young & Natural #21 / 1996 / TV / F • Young & Natural #22 / 1996 / TV / F
NADIA NYCE
Creme De La Face #05 / 1994 / OD / M • Creme De La Face #06 / 1995 / OD / M • Creme De La Face #07 / 1995 / OD / M • Creme De La Face #08: Wanna Blow Job / 1995 / OD / M • Creme De La Face #09: Princess Of Cream / 1995 / OD / M • Creme De La Face #12: Pretty Faces To Cum On / 1995 / OD / M • Creme De La Face #13: Nine Nasty Nymphs / 1995 / OD / M • Creme De La Face #14: Kiss My Cum / 1996 / OD / M • Cum To Drink Of It / 1996 / BCP / M • Cum Tv / 1996 / NIT / M • The Cumm Brothers #07: Honeymoon On Uranus / 1995 / OD / M • The Cumm Brothers #08: Escape From Uranus / 1995 / OD / M • Cumm For Dinner / 1995 / BCP / M • Debutante Dreams / 1995 / 4P / M • Dirty Bob's #22: Lube! / 1995 / FLP / S • The Doctor Is In #1 / 1995 / NIT / M • The Doctor Is In #2: Pussy Pox / 1995 / NIT / M • The Doctor Is In #3: Achy Breaky Tarts / 1995 / NIT / M • Fabulous Flashers #2 / 1996 / DGD / F • Girls Just Wanna Have Cum / 1995 / HO / M • High Heeled & Horny #2 / 1995 / LBO / M • High Heeled & Horny #3 / 1995 / LBO / M • High Heeled & Horny #4 / 1995 / LBO / M • How To Make A Model #05: Back To Innocence / 1994 / LBO / M • How To Make A Model #06: Many Happy Returns / 1995 / LBO / M • Lusty Lap Dancers #1 / 1994 / HO / M • Lusty Lap Dancers #2 / 1994 / HO / M • More Dirty Debutantes #43 / 1995 / 4P / M • The New Snatch Masters #18 / 1996 / LEI / C • Northwest Pecker Trek #6: Two Girls For Every Boy / 1995 / LBO / M • The Princess Of Cream / 1995 / OD / M • Puritan Video Magazine #07 / 1996 / LE / M • Pussy Fest Of The Northwest #5 / 1995 / NIT / M • Teacher's Pet #2 / 1994 / WMG / M • Teacher's Pet #3 / 1995 / APP / M • Teacher's Pet #4 / 1995 / APP / M • Throbbing Threesomes / 1996 / NIT / M • Up And Cummers #15 / 1994 / 4P / M
NADINE
A&B GB#010: Double Creamer / 1992 / A&B / M • A&B GB#014: Cumming Out Party #2 / 1992 / A&B / M • A&B GB#015: Cumming Out Party #3 / 1992 / A&B / M • A&B GB#016: Nadine's New Job / 1992 / A&B / M • A&B GBG#04: Cum Sluts / 1995 / A&B / M • A&B GBG#08: Nadine And Friends / 1995 / A&B / M • Big Boob Ball / 1995 / IF / C • Big Busted Lesbians At Play / 1991 / BIZ / F • A Geisha's Secret / 1993 / VI / M • Hard Core Beginners #02 / 1995 / LEI / M • J.E.G.: Nadine / 1995 / JEG / M • Magma: Sperm Dreams / 1990 / MET / M • Magma: Sperm-Crazy / 1994 / MET / M • Magma: Swinger / 1995 / MET / M • Nature Girls #2: Get Wet / 1995 / WIV / F • Private Video Magazine #04 / 1993 / OD / M • Profiles #01 / 1995 / XPR / M • Raw Talent Compilations: Gang Bang #1 / 1995 / RTP / C • Raw Talent: Bang 'er 08 Times / 1992 / RTP / M • Raw Talent: Bang 'er 09 Times / 1992 / RTP / M • Raw Talent: Bang 'er Megamix 1 / 1994 / RTP / C • Raw Talent: Nadine's Pregnant Gang Bang #1 / 1996 / RTP / M • Wet Daydreams / 1996 / XCI / M
NADINE (TABITHA) see Tabitha (1995)

NADINE BLEU
Viola Video #104: Miss France To Visit / 1995 / PEV / M
NADINE BRONX
Skin #1 / 1994 / EUR / M
NADINE BURR
Private Film #05 / 1993 / OD / M
NADINE DERANGOT
[Die Madchenhandler / 1972 / ... / M
NADINE RUSSELL see Star Index I
NADJA
Magma: Dreams Of Lust / 1994 / MET / M
NADJA KERN
Sex Mountain / cr80 / VCX / M
NADJA MOORE see Nadia Moore
NADJII
Video Virgins #27 / 1996 / NS / M
NAG ANALF see John Seeman
NAIROBI KNIGHT see Nyrobi Knight
NAKEETA LANE
Harlem Harlots #2 / 1995 / AVS / M
NAKIMA
Ready To Drop #05 / 1995 / FC / M
NALA GREBLOC
Sissy's Hot Summer / 1979 / CA / M
NAN
Blue Vanities #527 / 1993 / FFL / M • Blue Vanities #543 / 1994 / FFL / M
NANA
Made In The Hood / 1995 / HBE / M
NANA FLACK
Flesh Factory / 1970 / AVC / M
NANAH
The Best Little Whorehouse In Tijuana / 1995 / HBE / M • Ebony Dancer / 1994 / HBE / M • Ed Woody / 1995 / HBE / M
NANCY
ABA: Double Feature #2 / 1996 / ALP / M • Afternoon Delights / 1995 / FC / M • All About Sex / 1970 / AR / M • Blue Vanities #502 / 1992 / FFL / M • Blue Vanities #505 / 1992 / FFL / M • Blue Vanities #522 / 1993 / FFL / M • Blue Vanities #574 / 1996 / FFL / M • Bottoms Up #03 / 1983 / AVC / C • Bus Stop Tales #04 / 1989 / PRI / M • Different Strokes / 1996 / VC / M • Fantasy Escorts / 1993 / FOR / M • FTV #03: Queen Boxer & Mixed Fist / 1996 / FT / B • Hollywood Confidential #2 / 1983 / PRC / M • Hollywood Swingers #03 / 1992 / LBO / M • Homegrown Video #152 / 1990 / HOV / F • HomeGrown Video #473: Furpie Feast #3 / 1997 / HOV / C • The Hunt Is On / 1994 / HU / F • Limited Edition #16 / 1980 / AVC / M • Limited Edition #25 / 1984 / AVC / M • Lunch / 1972 / VC / M • Match #3: Battling Babes / 1995 / NPA / B • Match #4: Hellcats / 1995 / NPA / B • Nancy Vs Robin / 1994 / VSL / B • Rip-Off Of Millie / cr78 / VHL / M • She Babes Cavalcade Of Sports #01 / 1996 / SOW / M • Two Bitches From Hell / 1994 / CAW / B • Wrasslin She-Babes #08 / 1996 / SOW / M
NANCY (BROOKE DUNN) see Brooke Dunn
NANCY (CUM. AMADO) see Cumisha Amado
NANCY (DESTINY LANE) see Destini Lane
NANCY (VANESSA) see Vanessa (French)
NANCY AVNER see Star Index I
NANCY BINGHAMPTON see Rene Bond
NANCY BOUGAULT
The Girls Of Fantasex #1 / 1996 / NIT / M • The Girls Of Fantasex #2 / 1996 / NIT / M

• Julie's Diary / 1995 / LBO / M
NANCY BROWN
Reel Classics #2 / 1996 / H&S / M
NANCY COX
The Psychiatrist / 1978 / VC / M
NANCY DARE *(Suzie Sparkle, Nancy Drake, Honey Bare, Nancy Love)*
Ugly foul-mouthed blonde with a getting pudgy body and medium to large tits. Very white skin with a mole just below her belly button. Nancy Drake is from **The Trouble with Young Stuff**. Nancy Love is from **Reunion**.
Alice In Wonderland / 1976 / CA / M • Captain Lust And The Amorous Contessa / 1977 / IHV / M • Come With Me, My Love / 1976 / PVX / M • The Devil Inside Her / 1977 / ALP / M • Farmers Daughters / 1975 / VC / M • Feelings / 1977 / VC / M • Frank Henenlotter's XXX Hardcore Horrors #05 / 1996 / SOW / M • The Honey Cup / cr76 / VXP / M • Legends Of Porn #2 / 1989 / CV / C • The Felines / 1975 / VCX / M • My Master, My Love / 1975 / BL / B • Odyssey / 1977 / VC / M • The Opening Of Misty Beethoven / 1976 / VC / M • Reunion (Vanessa Del Rio's) / 1977 / LIM / M • Through The Looking Glass / 1976 / ALP / M • The Trouble With Young Stuff / 1976 / VC / M • Vanessa's Hot Nights / 1984 / SVE / M
NANCY DRAKE see Nancy Dare
NANCY FRANKLIN
Like Mother, Like Daughter / cr73 / VCX / M
NANCY GARCIA see Linda Shaw
NANCY GRAHAM
Aunt Peg's Fulfillment / 1980 / CV / M
NANCY HERBIE
Softie / 19?? / AVC / M
NANCY HOFFMAN *(Judy Harris, Monica Welles)*
Judy Harris is from **Teeny Buns**.
The Beauty Pageant / 1981 / AVC / M • Black Silk Stockings / 1978 / SE / C • Candy Goes To Hollywood / 1979 / VCX / M • Candy Stripers #1 / 1978 / ALP / M • A Formal Faucett / 1978 / VC / M • Gold Or Bust / 1977 / BL / M • Legends Of Porn #2 / 1989 / CV / C • Little Girls Blue #1 / 1977 / VCX / M • Little Me & Marla Strangelove / 1979 / ALP / M • Lust At First Bite / 1978 / VC / M • One Page Of Love / 1980 / VCX / M • The Other Side Of Julie / 1978 / CV / M • Pink Lips / 1977 / VCX / M • Pretty Peaches #1 / 1978 / MIT / M • Saturday Matinee Series #1 / 1996 / VCX / C • Superstar John Holmes / 1979 / AVC / M • Swinging Sorority / 1976 / VCX / S • Taxi Girls #1 / 1980 / WV / M • Teenage Housewife / 1976 / BL / M • Teeny Buns / 1977 / VC / M • Treasure Box / 1981 / VC / M • True Legends Of Adult Cinema: Unsung Superstars / 1993 / VC / C • The Untamed / 1978 / VCX / M
NANCY KELLER
Like Mother, Like Daughter / cr73 / VCX / M • Take Off / 1978 / VXP / M
NANCY KELLY *(Kelly Van Dyke)*
Daughter of the star of **Coach**, Jerry Van Dyke. Born in 1958 and hanged herself in 1991, aged 33.
Anal Adventures #2: Bodacious Buns / 1991 / VC / M • Anal Adventures #3: Can Her! / 1991 / VC / M • Catfighting Students / 1995 / PRE / C • Clean Out / 1991 / PRE

/ B • Club Josephine / 1991 / AR / F • The Coach's Daughter / 1991 / AR / M • Harry Horndog #06: Girls On Girls #2 / 1992 / ZA / F • High Fives / 1991 / PRE / B • Hillary Vamp's Private Collection #15 / 1992 / HVD / M • Hollywood X-Posed #1 / 1992 / VIM / C • Leg...Ends #05 / 1991 / PRE / F • Neighborhood Watch #14: The Beaver Cleaver / 1991 / LBO / M • Positively Pagan #02 / 1991 / ATA / M • Positively Pagan #04 / 1991 / ATA / M • Rump Roasts / 1991 / PRE / B • Student Fetish Videos: Best Of Spanking #02 / 1993 / PRE / C • Student Fetish Videos: The Enema #05 / 1991 / PRE / B • Student Fetish Videos: Spanking #06 / 1991 / PRE / B • Super Enemates #1 / 1994 / PRE / C • Wild Cats / 1991 / PRE / B
NANCY KNIBB see Star Index I
NANCY LEE
Teenage Party People / 19?? / ... / M
NANCY LOVE see Nancy Dare
NANCY MAE
Blue Vanities #030 / 1988 / FFL / M • Blue Vanities #560 / 1994 / FFL / M • Dream Girls #2 / 1983 / CA / C
NANCY MARSHALL see Star Index I
NANCY MEND
Erotic Dimensions #8: Just For Me / 1982 / NSV / M
NANCY MYERS
Juggs / 1984 / VCR / M
NANCY NICHOLS see Star Index I
NANCY NORTON
Blue Vanities #552 / 1994 / FFL / M
NANCY NOVAK
Demolition Derriere / 1990 / VVO / B • Down With Wimps / 1990 / VVO / B • Facesitting / 1994 / VVO / B • How To Worship Mistress Nancy / 1990 / VVO / B • Mistress Commands / 1990 / VVO / B • Mixed Titty Tumbles / 1990 / NPA / B • Nancy Vs Lori / 1993 / VVO / B • Nancy's Workout / 1993 / VVO / B • Wrestling Sluts #3 / 1990 / NPA / B
NANCY NUKEE
The Beauty Pageant / 1981 / AVC / M
NANCY NYMPHO
Prime Choice #1 / 1995 / RAS / M • Stuff Your Ass #2 / 1995 / JMP / M • Trading Partners / 1995 / GO / M
NANCY PEARSON
Housemother's Discipline #4 / 1992 / RB / B
NANCY PERELMANN
The Girls In The Band / 1976 / SVE / M
NANCY PETERS
Triple Cross / 198? / CS / B
NANCY RACETOR see Angel Cash
NANCY RHODES see Star Index I
NANCY RIVERS
Adorable brunette with long hair with a reddish tinge, small tits, a very white body, tight waist, exquisite butt, pretty face, and a beautiful smile.
Bad Girls #3 / 1984 / COL / M • Breaking It #1 / 1984 / COL / M
NANCY ROSS see Star Index I
NANCY SCHWARTZ see Star Index I
NANCY SHANNON see Star Index I
NANCY STRONG
Erotic Dimensions: Explicit / 1982 / NSV / M
NANCY SUITER *(Nancy Sutter)*
800 Fantasy Lane / 1979 / GO / M • The Angel In Mr. Holmes / 1988 / WV / C • The

Beauty Pageant / 1981 / AVC / M • Best Of
Richard Rank #1 / 1987 / GO / F • Blue
Vanities #016 (New) / 1988 / FFL / M • Blue
Vanities #029 / 1988 / FFL / M • Blue Van-
ities #059 / 1988 / FFL / M • The Ecstasy
Girls #1 / 1979 / CA / M • Taxi Girls #1 /
1980 / WV / M • True Legends Of Adult Cin-
ema: The Cult Superstars / 1993 / VC / C •
Wine Me, Dine Me, 69 Me / 1989 / COL / C

NANCY SUTTER see Nancy Suiter

NANCY TALMADGE
Bucky Beaver's XXX Dragon Art Theatre
Double Feature #11 / 1996 / SOW / M •
Teenage Fantasies #1 / 1972 / SOW / M

NANCY TROUP
Twilight / 1996 / ESN / M

NANCY TULLEY
Penitent Wife / Miss Armstrong / 1993 / CS
/ B

NANCY VEE
Amateur Gay Girls / 1995 / LEI / C • Back-
hand / 1995 / SC / M • Batbabe / 1995 / PL
/ M • Battling Bitches #1 / 1995 / BIZ / B •
Battling Bitches #2 / 1995 / BIZ / B • The
Best Of Buttslammers / 1995 / BS / C •
Black Masters: Den Of Punishment / 1996
/ GOT / B • Black Masters: Restrained /
1995 / GOT / B • Blindfold / 1996 / GOT / B
• Buffy Malibu's Nasty Girls #09 / 1995 /
ANA / F • Buttslammers #10: Lust On The
Internet / 1995 / BS / F • Carnival / 1995 /
PV / M • Caught In The Act (1995-Wave) /
1995 / WAV / M • Chained / 1995 / SC / M
• College Cruelty / 1995 / FFE / B • Crunch
Bunch / 1995 / PRE / C • Cry Babies
(Gotham) / 1995 / GOT / B • Debi Dia-
mond: Mega Mistress / 1995 / BIZ / B •
Deep Focus / 1995 / VC / M • Diamond In
The Raw / 1996 / XCI / M • Dildo Debu-
tantes / 1995 / CA / F • Dirty Dancers #3 /
1995 / 4P / M • Doctors Of Pain / 1995 / BIZ
/ B • Dr Of Pain / 1995 / BIZ / B • Dream
House / 1995 / XPR / M • Dresden Diary
#11: Endangered Secrets / 1994 / BIZ / B •
Dresden Diary #12: / 1995 / BIZ / B • Dy-
nasty's Anal Brat Pack / 1996 / OUP / F •
East Coast Sluts #01: New Jersey / 1995 /
PL / M • Electropussy / 1995 / CC / M • Ex-
otic Car Models #1 / 1996 / INO / F • Flush
Dance / 1996 / PRE / C • Foreign Tongues
#1: Going Down / 1995 / VI / M • Getting
Personal / 1995 / PE / M • The Girl With
The Heart-Shaped Tattoo / 1995 / WAV / M
• Girly Video Magazine #2 / 1995 / BEP / M
• Hard Core Beginners #12 / 1995 / LEI / M
• Hot Crimson Buns / 1996 / STM / B • Hot
Tight Asses #12 / 1995 / TCK / M • House
Of Leather / 1995 / GO / M • The Kiss /
1995 / WP / M • Last Resort / 1994 / GOT
/ B • Leather Bound Dykes From Hell #5 /
1995 / BIZ / B • Lolita / 1995 / SC / M • Love
Doll Lucy #1 / 1994 / PL / F • Love Doll
Lucy #2 / 1994 / PL / F • Masters Of Dom-
inance / 1996 / GOT / C • Muff Divers #1 /
1996 / TV / F • N.Y. Video Magazine #07 /
1996 / OUP / M • Nasty Dancers #1 / 1996
/ STM / B • Nasty Nymphos #09 / 1995 /
ANA / M • Nasty Nymphos #10 / 1995 /
ANA / M • The New Butt Hunt #14 / 1995 /
LEI / C • Nurses Bound By Duty / 1996 /
BIZ / B • Nylon / 1995 / VI / M • Ona Zee's
Doll House #1 / 1995 / ONA / F • Painful
Employment / 1996 / OUP / B • Perverted
Women / 1995 / SC / M • Pick Up Lines #01
/ 1995 / 4P / M • Pizzas, Hot Tubs & Bim-
bos / 1995 / SUF / M • Private Audition /

1995 / EVN / M • Profiles #04: Lust
Lessons / 1995 / XPR / M • Pussyman Auditions #02 / 1995 / SNA / M • Reel People
#09 / 1995 / PP / M • Revenge & Punish-
ment / 1995 / GOT / B • Road Trippin' #01:
New York City / 1994 / OUP / F • Road Trip-
pin' #02: New York City / 1994 / OUP / F •
Savage Liasons / 1995 / BEP / F • The
Sexual Solution #1 / 1995 / LE / M • Skye's
The Limit / 1995 / BON / B • Sluthunt #2 /
1995 / BIP / F • Snatch Masters #05 / 1995
/ LEI / M • Sodomania #12: Raw Filth /
1995 / EL / M • Sodomania: Slop Shots /
1996 / EL / C • Sodomania: Smokin' Sex-
tions / 1996 / EL / C • Sole Goal / 1996 /
PRE / B • Strange Lesbian Tales / 1996 /
BAC / F • Student Fetish Videos: Catfight-
ing #17 / 1996 / PRE / B • Student Fetish
Videos: The Enema #20 / 1996 / PRE / B •
Student Fetish Videos: Foot Worship #18 /
1995 / PRE / B • Submission Of Ariana /
1995 / BIZ / B • Swat Team / 1995 / PRE /
B • Takin' It To The Limit #4 / 1995 / BS / M
• Talking Trash #2 / 1995 / HW / M • The
Temple Of Poon / 1996 / PE / M • Toe Tales
#21 / 1995 / GOT / B • Toe Tales #22 / 1995
/ GOT / B • Toe Tales #24 / 1995 / GOT / C
• The Training #2 / 1994 / BIZ / B • The
Training #3 / 1995 / BIZ / B • Trick Shots /
1995 / PV / M • TV Sorority Sister / 1996 /
STM / G • Twisted Rage / 1995 / GOT / B •
Upbeat Love #2 / 1995 / CV / M • Using
Your Assets To Get A Head / 1996 / OUP /
F • The Wanderer #1: Road Tails / 1995 /
CDI / M • Water Worked / 1995 / AB / F •
What's In It 4 Me / 1995 / TEG / M • Wicked
Moments / 1996 / BS / B • Without Pity /
1995 / GOT / B • Wrath Of The Dungeon
Brats / 1996 / OUP / B • Young & Natural
#01 / 1995 / PRE / F • Young & Natural #02
/ 1995 / PRE / F • Young & Natural #04 /
1995 / PRE / F • Young & Natural #08 /
1995 / PRE / F • Young & Natural #09 /
1995 / PRE / C • Young Lips / 1996 / STM
/ F

NANCY WANG see Star Index I

NANCY WELCH
Resurrection Of Eve / 1973 / MIT / M

NANDO ROCCA
Ejacula #1 / 1992 / VC / M • Ejacula #2 /
1992 / VC / M

NANDO RONCHI
Selen / 1996 / HW / M

NANETTE
Blue Vanities #531 / 1993 / FFL / M •
Magma: Horny For Cock / 1990 / MET / M

NANETTE HEAVEN
Baby Blue / 1978 / CIG / M

NANETTE PETERS
All The Senator's Girls / 1977 / CA / M

NANGNOI see Star Index I

NANNA
The Dinner Party #2: The Buffet / 1996 /
ULI / M

NANNY BLAZE
Great Grandma Gets Her Cookies / 1995 /
FC / M

NAOMI
Blue Vanities #167 (New) / 1996 / FFL / M
• Blue Vanities #167 (Old) / 1991 / FFL / M
• Blue Vanities #538 / 1993 / FFL / M

NAOMI (BLACK)
The Adventures Of Peeping Tom #2 / 1996
/ OD / M • Black Cheerleader Jungle Jerk-
Off / 1996 / WIC / F • Black Cheerleader
Search #06 / 1996 / IVC / M • Black Snatch

#2 / 1996 / DFI / F • Black Street Hookers
#3 / 1996 / DFI / M • Cumback Pussy #1 /
1996 / EL / M • Cumback Pussy #4: Get
Some!!! / 1996 / EL / M • Latex And Lace /
1996 / BBE / M • Loose Jeans / 1996 / GO
/ M • My Baby Got Back #09 / 1996 / VT /
M • Pick Up Lines #05 / 1996 / OD / M •
Sista! #4 / 1996 / VT / F • Sodomania #18:
Shame Based / 1996 / EL / M • Up And
Cummers #33 / 1996 / 4P / M • Up And
Cummers #34 / 1996 / 4P / M • Up Close &
Personal #3 / 1996 / IPI / M • Waiting For
The Man / 1996 / VT / M

NAOMI CLEMENS see Star Index I
NAOMI GOLDSMITH see John T. Bone
NAOMI JASON see Star Index I
NAOMI JENSEN see Star Index I
NAOMI LEGG see Star Index I

NAOMI LOVE
Debutante Dreams / 1995 / 4P / M

NAOMI WANG see Anisa

NAOMI WOLFE
Nightlife / 1997 / CA / M

NAOMIE
Filthy First Timers #6 / 1997 / EL / M

NAPOLEON
Flesh For Fantasy / 1994 / CV / M • Little
Big Dong / 1992 / ZA / M • A Little Christ-
mas Tail / 1991 / ZA / M • A Little Irresistible
/ 1991 / ZA / M • Made For A Gangbang /
1995 / ZA / M • Muff 'n' Jeff / 1992 / ZA / M
• Perverted Stories #02 / 1995 / JMP / M •
Perverted Stories #03 / 1995 / JMP / M •
Porno Bizarro / 1995 / GLI / M • Shane's
World #3 / 1996 / OD / M • Sin City: The
Movie / 1992 / SC / M • Twin Freaks / 1992
/ ZA / M • Two Of A Kind / 1991 / ZA / M •
Walking Small / 1992 / ZA / M • You Assed
For It / 1996 / NOT / M

NASTASCHA VERELL
Butterflies / 1974 / CA / M

NASTASSIA KINKEL
Paris Taxis / 1995 / XYS / M

NASTASSIA KINSKI *(Nastassja Kinski,
Nastassia Nakzsynski)*
Born 1961. In early movies such as **To The
Devil A Daughter** adorable slim bodied
brunette with a sex kitten type face. As she
aged her hips seemed to spread and and her
waist fattened but she's still (1995) within
reasonable limits. In 1984 married Ibrahim
Moussa and had two kids; then got rid of
him in 1992 and married Quincy Jones and
had another kid (must be pretty sloppy by
now).
Baring It All / 1995 / PEK / S • Boarding
School / 1977 / VES / S • Cat People /
1982 / MCA / S • Crackerjack / 1994 / ... /
S • Exposed / 1983 / MGM / S • Faraway,
So Close / 1993 / C3S / S • For Your Love
Only / 1976 / ALP / S • Harem / 1985 / VES
/ S • Hotel New Hampshire / 1984 / VES /
S • Il Segreto / 1990 / ... / S • Magdelene /
1988 / PAR / S • Maria's Lovers / 1984 /
MGM / S • The Moon In The Gutter / 1983
/ C3S / S • Night Sun / 1990 / ... / S • One
From The Heart / 1982 / C3S / S • Paris,
Texas / 1984 / FOX / S • Revolution / 1985
/ WAR / S • Spring Symphony / 1983 / LIV
/ S • Stay As You Are / 1978 / WAR / S •
Terminal Velocity / 1994 / NYF / S • Tess /
1979 / C3S / S • To The Devil A Daughter /
1976 / REP / S • Torrents Of Spring / 1989
/ ... / S • Unfaithfully Yours / 1983 / FOX /
S • The Wrong Movement / 1974 / FAC / S

NASTASSIA NAKZSYNSKI see Nastas-

sia Kinski
NASTASSJA
A Merry Widow / 1996 / SPI / M
NASTASSJA KINSKI see Nastassia Kinski
NASTIA
Triple X Video Magazine #08 / 1995 / OD / M • Triple X Video Magazine #09 / 1995 / OD / M
NASTIQUE
Black Street Hookers #3 / 1996 / DFI / M
NASTY DAN see Woody Long
NASTY NATASIA see Courtney
NASTY REGAN
Ready To Drop #11 / 1996 / FC / M • Ready To Drop #12 / 1996 / FC / M
NASTYA
Russian Model Magazine #2 / 1996 / IP / M
NAT COOPERMAN see Star Index I
NATACHA
Eurotica #05 / 1996 / XC / M • Private Film #15 / 1994 / OD / M • Private Film #17 / 1994 / OD / M • The Psychiatrist / 1978 / VC / M • Russian Model Magazine #1 / 1996 / IP / M • Russian Model Magazine #2 / 1996 / IP / M • Sappho Connection / 19?? / LIP / F
NATACHA BAREBUSH see Star Index I
NATACHA NIKKOLS
Anal Boat / 1996 / P69 / M
NATALI
Love Slave / 1995 / WIV / M
NATALIA
Eurotica #03 / 1995 / XC / M • Girls Around The World #24 / 1995 / BTO / S • Prague By Night #1 / 1996 / EA / M • Soft Bodies: Invitational / 1990 / SB / F • Tit To Tit #4 / 1996 / BTO / S
NATALIA HARRIS see Natalie Harris
NATALIA MULHAUSEN see Star Index I
NATALIA SALLAI
True Stories #1 / 1993 / SC / M • True Stories #2 / 1993 / SC / M
NATALIA ST JAMES see Natalie Harris
NATALIE
Babewatch Video Magazine #2 / 1994 / ERI / F • Blue Vanities #548 / 1994 / FFL / M • Dick & Jane In Budapest / 1993 / AVI / M • Finger Pleasures #4 / 1995 / PL / F • Hot Body Competition: The Beverly Hill's Naughty Nightie C. / 1995 / CG / F • Joe Elliot's College Girls #38 / 1994 / JOE / M • Lovin' Spoonfuls #5 / 1996 / 4P / C • My Baby Got Back #05 / 1995 / VT / M • Nasty Newcummers #10 / 1995 / MET / M • Neighborhood Watch #10 / 1991 / LBO / M • Penthouse: All-Pet Workout / 1993 / NIV / F • Private Video Magazine #12 / 1994 / OD / M • Student Fetish Videos: Best of Enema #03 / 1994 / PRE / C • Student Fetish Videos: The Enema #14 / 1994 / PRE / B • Student Fetish Videos: Spanking #14 / 1994 / PRE / B • Toy Time #2: Nasty Solos / 1994 / STP / F
NATALIE BLACKAW
Sweet Black Cherries #6 / 1996 / TTV / M
NATALIE BOET
Private Film #04 / 1993 / OD / M
NATALIE BRADSHAW
Black Fantasies #16 / 1996 / HW / M • Black Knockers #12 / 1995 / TV / M • Dirty Dirty Debutantes #7 / 1996 / 4P / M
NATALIE HARRIS *(Corby Wells, Natalia Harris, Natasia (N. Harris), Shannon Hurts, Shannon Hurtz, Natalia St James)*

Slutty but nice bodied brunette or dark blonde with medium firm tits and a tattoo on the right one. As of early 1995 she has had her tits enhanced to canteloupe size.
Amateur Lesbians #35: Meo / 1993 / GO / F • Amateur Orgies #26 / 1993 / AFI / M • Amateurs Exposed #05 / 1995 / CV / M • Anal Alice / 1992 / AFV / M • Anal Vision #12 / 1993 / LBO / M • The Ass Master #03 / 1993 / GLI / M • Ateball: More Than A Mouthful / 1995 / ATE / F • Beach Bum Amateur's #22 / 1993 / MID / M • Biff Malibu's Totally Nasty Home Videos #35 / 1993 / ANA / M • Big Murray's New-Cummers #11: Willing & Able / 1993 / FD / M • Big Murray's New-Cummers #13: Hot Tight Ladies / 1993 / FD / M • Bobby Hollander's Maneaters #04 / 1993 / SFP / M • Casting Call #03 / 1993 / SO / M • Cinderella Society / 1993 / GO / M • Club DV8 #2 / 1993 / SC / M • Crime Doesn't Pay / 1993 / BS / B • The Cumm Brothers #06: Hook, Line And Sphincter / 1995 / OD / M • Dick & Jane Go To Hollywood #1 / 1993 / AVI / M • Dick & Jane Go To Hollywood #2 / 1993 / AVI / M • Dirty Doc's Housecalls #08 / 1994 / LV / M • Dr Butts #3 / 1993 / 4P / M • Erotic Newcummers Vol 1 #1: Capitol Desires / 1993 / DR / M • First Time Lesbians #08 / 1993 / JMP / F • Harry Horndog #16: Love Puppies #4 / 1992 / ZA / M • Heaven Scent (Las Vegas) / 1993 / LV / M • House Of Sex #05: Banging Corby And Tanya / 1994 / RTP / M • House Of Sex #06: Banging Wendy, Kitty, Corby and Connie / 1994 / RTP / M • Hungry Humpers / 1996 / SP / M • Just Eat Me, Damn It! / 1995 / BVW / F • Just One Look / 1993 / V99 / M • Ladies Lovin' Ladies #3 / 1993 / AFV / F • The Last American Sex Goddess / 1993 / IF / M • Maliboob Beach / 1995 / FH / M • Moon Godesses #2 / 1993 / VIM / M • More Than A Mouthful #1 / 1995 / VEX / F • Motel Sex #1 / 1995 / FAP / M • Mr. Peepers Amateur Home Videos #67: Backdoor Fantasy / 1993 / LBO / M • New Girls In Town #3 / 1993 / CC / M • Odyssey Triple Play #56: Lena Holliday's 3-Way Fuck-A-Thon / 1994 / OD / M • Odyssey Triple Play #57: Hot Coupling Couples / 1994 / OD / M • Odyssey Triple Play #68: Threesomes And Moresomes / 1994 / OD / M • Private Request / 1994 / GLI / M • Pussy Tales / 1993 / SC / F • Reel Sex #05: Lesbian Toy Part / 1994 / SPP / F • Ron Hightower's White Chicks #04 / 1993 / LBO / M • Rump Humpers #15 / 1993 / GLI / M • Shades Of Lust / 1993 / TP / M • Squirt Squad / 1995 / AMP / M • Swedish Erotica #82 / 1995 / CA / M • To Shave And Shave Not / 1994 / PEP / M • Two Can Chew / 1995 / FD / M • Video Virgins #01 / 1992 / NS / M • Vivid At Home #02 / 1994 / VI / M • Wild Orgies #19 / 1995 / AFI / M
NATALIE IDOUX see Star Index I
NATALIE KANE
Bucky Beaver's XXX Dragon Art Theatre Double Feature #01 / 1996 / SOW / M • Hitler's Harlots / cr73 / SOW / M
NATALIE POLANSKI
Deep Inside Dirty Debutantes #11 / 1996 / 4P / M • Dirty Dirty Debutantes #7 / 1996 / 4P / M • More Dirty Debutantes #50 / 1996 / 4P / M
NATALIE ROSE
Young Sluts In Heat #2 / 1996 / PL / M

NATALIE STREB see Star Index I
NATALIE TAYLOR
This girl may also be Marie Nickerson. Blonde with an emaciated body and a sweet smiling face. Hair is curly.
Queens Behind Bars / 1990 / STA / G • Queens In Danger / 1990 / STA / G
NATALIE TIZARA *(Natalte Tizara)*
Black hair, petite frame, muscular and beefy, ugly face.
Bad Attitude #1 / 1995 / LV / M • The Breast Files #3 / 1994 / AVI / M • Butt Jammers #03 / 1995 / SC / F • Camp Fire Tramps / 1995 / LOT / M • Deep Inside Dirty Debutantes #06 / 1993 / 4P / M • Dirty Stories #2 / 1995 / PE / M • Fashion Sluts #4 / 1995 / ABS / M • Ganggstas Paradise / 1995 / AVI / M • Mellon Man #06 / 1995 / AVI / M • More Dirty Debutantes #41 / 1995 / 4P / M • Small Top Bitches / 1996 / AVI / M • Sunset Rides Again / 1995 / VC / M • Tailz From Da Hood #2 / 1995 / AVI / M • Takin' It To The Limit #5 / 1995 / BS / M • The Voyeur #5 / 1995 / EA / M
NATALTE TIZARA see Natalie Tizara
NATALY
Private Video Magazine #24 / 1995 / OD / M
NATALY WOULD
Up And Cummers #25 / 1995 / 4P / M
NATASCHA
Magma: Spezial: Black & White #3 / 1995 / MET / M
NATASCHA BEBE
Dangerous Pleasure / 1995 / WIV / M
NATASCHA HUBER
Viola Video #107: Private Party / 1995 / PEV / M
NATASHA
Ace In The Hole / 1995 / PL / M • Afternoon Delights / 1995 / FC / M • Creme De La Face #08: Wanna Blow Job / 1995 / OD / M • The Cumm Brothers #08: Escape From Uranus / 1995 / OD / M • Cumm For Dinner / 1995 / BCP / M • FTV #05: Spy Vs. Spy / 1996 / FT / B • High Heeled & Horny #3 / 1995 / LBO / M • International Love And The Dancer / 1995 / PME / S • Kiss Me Quick / 1964 / SOW / S • Latex Slaves / cr87 / GOT / B • Night Shift Latex Slaves / 1991 / GOT / B • Northwest Pecker Trek #2: Evergreen, Ever Horny / 1994 / LBO / M • Northwest Pecker Trek #5: Cumming In King County / 1995 / LBO / M • Pussy Fest Of The Northwest #2 / 1995 / NIT / M • Pussy Fest Of The Northwest #5 / 1995 / NIT / M • Russian Champagne / 1993 / GOU / M • Sorority Slumber Sluts / 1995 / WIV / F • Spanking Video #3: Cambridge Blues / 1995 / MET / B • That's Outrageous / 1983 / CA / M • Triple X Video Magazine #01 / 1995 / OD / M • Trisexual Encounters #07 / 1988 / PL / G • TVs By Choice / 19?? / BIZ / G
NATASHA (COURTNEY) see Courtney
NATASHA (R. MORGAN) see Rene Morgan
NATASHA (TEXAS M) see Texas Milly
NATASHA COLE see Star Index I
NATASHA DAHLING
Matinee Idol / 1984 / VC / M
NATASHA DESIRE
The Girls Of Fantasex #1 / 1996 / NIT / M
NATASHA MARIE see Missy
NATASHA NASH see Eva Allen
NATASHA PULINAKOVA see Star Index

I

NATASHA RAPHAEL *see Star Index I*
NATASHA ROSE *see Star Index I*
NATASHA SKYLER *(Tasha (N. Skyler), Natasha Star)*
Started with small tits and then returned in mid 1995 with rock solid cantaloupes. Natasha Star is from **Pumping Ethel**.
Amazing Tails #1 / 1987 / CA / M • Amazing Tails #3 / 1987 / CA / M • Assmania!! #2 / 1995 / ME / M • Barbara Dare's Prime Choice / 1987 / SE / C • Barflies / 1990 / ZA / M • Bet Black / 1989 / CDI / M • Blue Balls / 1995 / VEX / C • Candy Ass / 1990 / V99 / M • Cheatin' Hearts / 1991 / VEX / M • Con Jobs / 1990 / V99 / M • Deep Dreams / 1990 / IN / M • Deep Throat Girls / 1986 / ELH / M • Desert Foxes / 1989 / SE / M • Dirty Lingerie / 1990 / VD / M • Even More Dangerous / 1990 / SO / M • Every Man Should Have One / 1991 / VEX / M • Finely Back / 1990 / PL / F • The Finer Things In Life / 1990 / PL / F • First Time At Cherry High / 1984 / VC / M • For Her Pleasure Only / 1989 / FAZ / M • Girls Gone Bad #1 / 1990 / GO / F • Head Co-Ed Society / 1989 / VT / M • Hot Palms / 1989 / GO / M • Hot To Swap / 1988 / VEX / M • Jailhouse Blue / 1990 / SO / M • Lace / 1989 / VT / F • Laze / 1990 / ZA / M • Leather & Lace / 1987 / SE / C • Leather / 1989 / VT / F • Leather And Lace / 1989 / VT / F • Lesbian Liasons / 1990 / SO / F • Love Shack / 1990 / CC / M • The New Barbarians #2 / 1990 / VC / M • No Man's Land #04 / 1990 / VT / F • Paris By Night / 1990 / IN / M • Parliament: Dirty Blondes #1 / 1991 / PM / F • Parliament: Teasers #1 / 1986 / PM / F • Positive Positions / 1989 / VEX / M • Public Enemy / 1990 / VIP / M • Pumping Ethel / 1988 / PV / M • Pumping Irene #1 / 1986 / FAN / M • Pyromaniac / 1990 / SO / M • Queen Of Spades / 1986 / VD / M • The Secret (USA) / 1990 / SO / M • Secret Dreams / 1991 / VEX / M • Send Me An Angel / 1990 / V99 / M • Sex Kittens / 1990 / VEX / F • Shameless Desire / 1989 / VEX / M • Silver Tongue / 1989 / CA / M • Sophisticated Lady / 1988 / SEX / M • Sweat Out / 1991 / CIN / M • Sweet Darlin' / 1990 / VEX / M • The T & A Team / 1984 / VC / M • Taija Is Sizzling Hot / 1986 / VT / M • Telemates / 1988 / STA / M • Telemates / 1991 / V99 / M • An Unnatural Act #1 / 1984 / DR / M • Up All Night / 1986 / CC / M • Used Cars / 1990 / CDI / M • Victoria's Secret / 1989 / SO / M • What Kind of Girls Do You Think We Are? / 1991 / VEX / C • Who Framed Ginger Grant? / 1989 / CC / M • Wild Fire / 1990 / VIV / C
NATASHA STAR *see Natasha Skyler*
NATASHA TESO
Bi Madness / 1991 / STA / G
NATASHA ZIMMERMAN *see Courtney*
NATASIA
Girls, Girls, Girls, Girls / 1993 / FD / C • Sex Bi-Lex / 1993 / CAT / G • She Studs #03 / 1991 / BIZ / G • Tell Me What To Do / 1991 / CA / M
NATASIA (COURTNEY) *see Courtney*
NATASIA (N. HARRIS) *see Natalie Harris*
NATHALIE
Afternoon Delights / 1995 / FC / M • Bedside Manor / 1986 / CA / M • Diva #2: Deep In Glamour / 1996 / VC / F • Magma: Chateau Extreme / 1995 / MET / M •

Magma: Horny For Cock / 1990 / MET / M • Private Film #16 / 1994 / OD / M • Private Video Magazine #07 / 1994 / OD / M • Sharp Shooters / 1984 / CA / M • Snow Honeys / 1983 / VC / M
NATHALIE IDOUX *see Star Index I*
NATHALIE L'HERMITE *see Star Index I*
NATHALIE MORIN
Sensations / 1975 / ALP / M
NATHALIE PAUL *see Star Index I*
NATHALIE ROSE
The Girls Of Fantasex #1 / 1996 / NIT / M • The Girls Of Fantasex #2 / 1996 / NIT / M
NATHALIE TUSSOT *see Star Index I*
NATHALIE ZEIGER
The Felines / 1975 / VCX / M • [Playing With Fire (French) / 1975 / ... / S
NATHALY *see Star Index I*
NATHAN
C-Hunt #03: Sunny Delights / 1995 / PEV / M • The Sodomizer #5: Destination Moon / 1996 / SC / M
NATHAN GILLETTE *see Star Index I*
NATHAN NIX *see Star Index I*
NATICE *see Star Index I*
NATIELLI
Amazon Heat #1 / 1996 / CC / M
NATIONAL VELVET *see Terri Hall*
NATO ERIKA
Sexy Doctress / 1996 / AVV / M
NATSUICO OXUDA
A Soldier's Desire / 1985 / ORC / M
NATZ *see Star Index I*
NAUGHTY ANGEL
Banana Slits / 1993 / STM / F • Lipstick Lesbians / 1993 / STM / F • Nasty Dancers #2 / 1996 / STM / B • Profiles In Discipline #02: Naughty Angel / 1994 / STM / C • Toe Tales #08 / 1993 / GOT / B • Torturess #2: Trained For Pleasure / 1996 / STM / B
NAUGHTY DREAD
Creme De La Face #05 / 1994 / OD / M • Creme De La Face #06 / 1995 / OD / M • Girls Just Wanna Have Cum / 1995 / HO / M
NAUGHTY NANCY *see Star Index I*
NAUGHTY NIKKO *see Star Index I*
NAUTICA
Black Street Hookers #5: The Mean Streets Of Washington D.C. / 1997 / DFI / M
NAZARRA
Limited Edition #08 / 1979 / AVC / M • Wild Innocents / 1982 / VCX / M
NEAL
Amateur Hours #01 / 1989 / AFI / M
NEAL DEVERO
Lusty Ladies #04 / 1983 / 4P / M
NEAL GRACE
Peaches And Cream / 1982 / SE / M
NED BEAUMONT
American Pie / 1980 / SE / M
NEDDA SHORES
[Dawn Patrol / 197? / ... / M
NEIL
Fresh Cheeks / 1995 / VC / M • Pearl Necklace: Amorous Amateurs #12 / 1992 / SEE / M
NEIL ALMABOR
Sexual Customs In Scandinavia / cr73 / QX / M
NEIL CHAMBERS *see Star Index I*
NEIL FLANAGAN
Sometime Sweet Susan / 1974 / ALP / M • [Bloodthirsty Butchers / 1970 / SOW / S
NEIL KELTON *see Star Index I*

NEIL LONG *see Joey Silvera*
NEIL OAKLEY *see Star Index I*
NEIL PETERS *see Star Index I*
NEIL PODORECKI *see Star Index I*
NEIL RHODES
Satan Was A Lady / 1977 / ALP / M
NEIL RICHARDS *see Star Index I*
NEIL RONDS *see Star Index I*
NEIL THOMAS *see Star Index I*
NEIL TUCKER
The Art Of Intimate Love: Ecstasy And Peace / 1994 / PME / M
NEIRA *see Meriea Dance*
NEJLA *see Nikki King*
NELL
HomeGrown Video #455 / 1995 / HOV / M
NELL GALE
Too Hot To Handle / 1975 / CDC / M
NELL SUNSHINE
Motel Sex #1 / 1995 / FAP / M
NELLI
Bedtime Story Italiano / 1995 / UGO / M
NELLIE GOLD
Night Hunger / 1983 / AVC / M • The Starmaker / 1982 / VC / M
NELLIE MARIE VICKERS *see Raven*
NELLIE PIERCE
Long straight brown hair, medium slightly droopy tits, nice butt, lithe tight body, and nice skin. According to her she's 18 years old (in 1996) and comes from Las Vegas.
Ass, Gas & The Mystical GLOP / 1997 / EL / M • Cumback Pussy #7: NUGIRLZ / 1997 / EL / M • Filthy First Timers #7 / 1997 / EL / M • Real Sex Magazine #02 / 1997 / HO / M • Sodomania #21: Degenerate Lifestyles! / 1997 / EL / M
NELLIE THOMPSON
Odyssey / 1977 / VC / M
NELS STENSGAARD
L.A. Tool & Die / 1979 / TMX / G
NENA
More Dirty Debutantes #57 / 1996 / 4P / M
NENA ANDERSON *(Nena Cherry, Nina Anderson, Nina Richard, Nina Cherry)*
Black hair done in Oriental style which looks like a wig or platinum blonde shoulder length hair depending on the movie, not too pretty, pudgy body, large enhanced tits, looks a little like an uglier version of Victoria Lee with the black hair. Tattoo of a lightening strike on the right shoulder outside and a mole on her right chin. 25 years old in 1996, comes from Houston TX and de-virginized at 17. As early as September 1996 tested positive for HIV but this was not disclosed until around February 1997. According to rumor she either contracted the disease from alleged IV drug activities or from too much partying (?). There's something perculiar about the whole affair as it was reported that although testing positive on the ELISA and Western Blot tests she had tested negative on the supposedly more accurate DNA test and she herself claims inconclusivity; on the other hand, I wouldn't want to risk screwing her. Someone who presumably was or is is Dale Weinberg, her husband.
Adam & Eve's House Party #2: Bachelor Party / 1996 / VC / M • Addicted To Lust / 1996 / NIT / M • Anal Climax #4 / 1996 / ROB / M • Anal Connection / 1996 / ZA / M • Anal Cornhole Cutie / 1996 / ROB / M • Anal Delinquent #3 / 1995 / ROB / M • Anal Fantasy / 1996 / SUF / M • Anal Inquisition

/ 1996 / ZA / M • Anal Jeopardy / 1996 / ZA / M • Anal Maniacs #4 / 1995 / WP / M • Anal Professor / 1996 / ZA / M • Anal Rippers #2: The Unveiling / 1996 / ZA / M • Anal Savage #3 / 1996 / ROB / M • Anal Territory / 1996 / AVD / M • Anal Trashy Ass / 1995 / ROB / M • Anal Virgins #01 / 1996 / NS / M • Babe Wire / 1996 / HW / M • Backfield In Motion / 1995 / VT / M • Bedtime Stories / 1996 / VC / M • Big Boob Boat Butt Ride / 1996 / FC / M • Blondes / 1995 / MET / M • Boob Acres / 1996 / HW / M • Breastman's Hot Legs Contest / 1996 / … / M • The Butt Sisters Do New Orleans / 1995 / MID / M • By Myself / 1996 / PL / F • Career Girls / 1996 / OUP / M • Caught In The Act (1995-Lv) / 1995 / LV / M • Cock Busters #3 / 1996 / GWV / C • Dirty Tails / 1996 / SC / M • Double Dicked #1 / 1996 / RAS / M • DPTV: Double Penetration Television / 1996 / SUF / M • Dr Peter Proctor's House Of Anal Delights / 1996 / HO / M • Dukes Of Anal / 1996 / VC / M • Erotic Newcummers Vol 1 #3: Anal Adventures / 1996 / DR / M • Every Nerd's Big Boob Boat Butt Ride / 1996 / FC / M • Exotic Car Models #2 / 1996 / INO / F • Frankenpenis / 1995 / LEI / M • Friendly Fire / 1996 / EDP / M • Girls Of The Panty Raid / 1995 / VT / M • Gutter Mouths / 1996 / JMP / M • Hardcore Debutantes #02 / 1996 / TEP / M • Hardcore Fantasies #2 / 1996 / LV / M • Hell Hole / 1996 / ZA / M • Hellfire / 1995 / MET / M • Hollywood Legs / 1996 / NIT / M • Hooters And The Blowjobs / 1996 / HW / M • Hot Tight Asses #15 / 1996 / TCK / M • Hot Tight Asses #16 / 1996 / TCK / M • House Of Anal / 1995 / NOT / M • The Hunt / 1996 / ULP / M • Illicit Affairs / 1996 / XC / M • In Your Face #3 / 1995 / PL / M • Intense Perversions #3 / 1996 / PL / M • Ir4: Inrearendence Day / 1996 / HW / M • Juliette's Desires / 1996 / LE / M • Lady M's Anything Nasty #01: Pink Pussy Party / 1996 / AVI / F • Legal Briefs / 1996 / EX / M • Love Dancers / 1995 / ME / M • Love Exchange / 1995 / DR / M • The Most Dangerous Game / 1996 / HO / M • My Ass #1 / 1996 / NOT / M • Nektar / 1996 / BAC / M • Nena Cherry's Dp Gang Bang / 1996 / NIT / M • The New Butt Hunt #14 / 1995 / LEI / C • New Pussy Hunt #19 / 1996 / LEI / C • New Pussy Hunt #24 / 1996 / LEI / C • Night Tales / 1996 / VC / M • Odyssey 30 Min: #553: / 1995 / OD / M • Philmore Butts On The Prowl / 1995 / SUF / M • Pizza Sluts: They Deliver / 1995 / XCI / M • Planet X #1 / 1996 / HW / M • Pocahotass #1 / 1996 / FD / M • Prime Choice #7 / 1996 / RAS / M • Puritan Video Magazine #04 / 1996 / LE / M • Pussyman Auditions #20 / 1996 / SNA / M • Pussyman's House Party #1 / 1996 / SNA / M • Pussyman's House Party #2 / 1996 / SNA / M • Rumpman In And Out Of Africa / 1996 / HW / M • Rumpman's Backdoor Sailing / 1996 / HW / M • Samantha & Company / 1996 / PL / M • Under The Covers / 1996 / GO / M • Velvet / 1995 / SPI / M • Video Virgins #23 / 1995 / NS / M • Voyeur Strippers / 1996 / PL / F • Young And Anal #2 / 1995 / JMP / M • Young And Anal #5 / 1996 / JMP / M • Young Girls Do #1: Troublemakers / 1995 / CDI / M • Young Girls Do #2: Sweet Meat / 1995 / CDI / M

NENA CHERRY *see* **Nena Anderson**

NEOLA GRASS *see Star Index I*
NEOMI
Private Gold #08: The Longest Night / 1996 / OD / M
NERO ST JAMES *see Star Index I*
NESSA TRUDU *see Star Index I*
NEVILLE CHAMBERS
Love Doll Lucy #1 / 1994 / PL / F • The Maltese Bimbo / 1993 / FD / M
NEVILLE FRANCIS *see Star Index I*
NEW JACK
Juicy's Houseparty / 1995 / HW / M
NIA
GRG: Nia's Nasty Interview / 1995 / GRG / M
NIC COLLINS
Like Father Like Son / 1996 / AWV / G • Married Men With Men On The Side / 1996 / BHE / G
NIC CREAM
Confessions / 1992 / PL / M • Hardcore / 1994 / VI / M • Starlet / 1994 / VI / M
NICCKI PINK *see* **Nikki Pink**
NICHOL PARK *see Star Index I*
NICHOLAS A. IOCONA *see* **Joey Stefano**
NICHOLAS FOXE
Bone Appetit: A She-Male Seduction / 1994 / BIZ / G • Chronicles Of Pain #2 / 1996 / BIZ / B • Date With A Mistress / 1995 / BIZ / B • Defiant TV's / 1994 / BIZ / G • Dresden Diary #13: / 1995 / BIZ / B • Spiked Heel Diaries #4 / 1995 / BIZ / B • The Submission Of Alicia Rio / 1996 / BIZ / B • Transsexual Passions #2 / 1994 / BIZ / G • TV Panty Party / 1994 / BIZ / G • TVs Teased And Tormented / 1995 / BIZ / G • Waterworld: The Enema Club / 1996 / BIZ / B
NICHOLAS GEORGE *see Star Index I*
NICHOLAS JACKSON *see Star Index I*
NICHOLAS JANES
Dr Max And The Oral Girls / 1995 / VIT / M
NICHOLAS PAGE *see* **Nick Rage**
NICHOLAS PERA *see* **Ron Jeremy**
NICHOLAS RAGE *see* **Nick Rage**
NICHOLE (NOT WEST)
Show Them No Mercy #1 / 1991 / STM / B
NICHOLE (WEST) *see* **Nichole West**
NICHOLE HART
Bondage Is My Pleasure #3 / 1994 / CS / B • Bondage Is My Pleasure #4 / 1994 / CS / B
NICHOLE WEST *(Nichole (West), Nicole (West), Susan Lion (N. West))*
Adorable tiny brunette with an overbite, small tits, nice personality and smile. Probably Susan Lion in **Dirty Letters.** Not in **Up Desiree Lane** (despite credits) nor **Blacks & Blondes #12** (despite credits) nor **Times Square Comes Alive** nor **French Postcards** nor **French Tarts** nor **Beverly Hills Heat.** First movie was **Nice 'n' Tight.** Not the same as the Nicole West who appeared in 1992 and is taller and does not have the same overbite. Was sighted at the 1993 VSDA.
Backdoor Romance / 1984 / VIV / M • Backing In #2 / 1990 / WV / C • Come As You Are / 1985 / SUV / M • Fantasy Club #41: Luscious Lolita / 1984 / WV / M • Flesh And Ecstasy / 1985 / VD / M • Flesh For Fantasies / 1986 / TAM / M • Future Voyeur / 1985 / SUV / M • Ginger On The Rocks / 1985 / VI / M • Hindsight / 1985 / IN / M • Holiday For

Angels / 1987 / IN / M • Hollywood Heartbreakers / 1985 / VEX / M • Hot Sweet Honey / 1985 / VEP / M • House Of Lust / 1984 / VD / M • Lick Bush / 1992 / VD / C • Love Bites / 1985 / CA / M • The Love Scene / 1985 / CDI / M • Loving Spoonfulls / 1987 / 4P / C • Lust American Style / 1985 / WV / M • Lust At The Top / 1985 / CDI / M • A Mid-Slumber's Night Dream / 1985 / 4P / M • Nice 'n' Tight / 1985 / AIR / M • Perfect Fit / 1985 / DR / M • Portrait Of Lust / 1984 / CC / M • Sex 5th Avenue / 1985 / WV / M • Sky Pies / 1985 / GO / M • Sore Throat / 1985 / GO / M • Tease Me / 1986 / VC / M • Teenage Games / 1985 / HO / M • Wicked Whispers / 1985 / VD / M • You're The Boss / 1985 / VD / M
NICHOLETTE
AVP #7032: Just Drop On Bi / 1990 / AVP / F
NICI NORMAN *see* **Nici Sterling**
NICI STERLING *(Nici Norman, Nikki Sterling, Nikki Norman, Nikki Teen, Nicyteen)*
Reaonably pretty face, far too tall, medium (originally natural but later it seems firmed-up artificially) tits, narrow hips, nice butt, long light brown hair. 24 years old in 1995, de-virginized at 14, married to Wilde Oscar, English.
The Adventures Of Peeping Tom #1 / 1996 / OD / M • American Fan Club Prowl / 1996 / VT / M • Anal Centerfold / 1995 / ROB / M • Anal Dynomito / 1005 / ROB / M • Anal Glamour Girls / 1995 / ME / M • Anal Insatiable / 1995 / ROB / M • Anal Portrait / 1996 / ZA / M • Anal Therapy #4 / 1996 / FD / M • Backdoor Club #1 / 1996 / VEX / C • Backdoor Imports / 1995 / LV / M • Best Butt(e) In The West #2 / 1995 / CC / M • Beyond Reality #1 / 1995 / EXQ / M • Big Knockers #19 / 1995 / TV / M • Big Knockers #22 / 1995 / TV / M • Bloopers & Boners / 1996 / VI / M • Blue Dreams / 1996 / SC / M • Boobwatch #2 / 1997 / SC / M • Borderline (Vivid) / 1995 / VI / M • Borrowed Bodies / 1996 / CC / M • The Bottom Dweller 33 1/3 / 1995 / EL / M • British Butt Search / 1995 / VC / M • Buffy's Bare Ass Barbecue / 1996 / CDI / M • Bushwoman: She Takes Two / 1996 / RAS / M • Busty Backdoor Nurses / 1996 / PL / M • Busty Brittany Takes London / 1996 / H&S / M • The Butt Sisters Do The Twin Cities / 1996 / MID / M • Buttman's Bouncin' British Babes / 1994 / EA / M • Cat Lickers #3 / 1995 / ME / F • Caught From Behind #22 / 1995 / HO / M • Centerfold / 1995 / SC / M • Cirque Du Sex #1 / 1996 / VT / M • Cumback Pussy #4: Get Some!!! / 1996 / EL / M • Cumback Pussy #6: All-Star Poop Chute Salute / 1997 / EL / M • Dark Eyes / 1995 / FC / M • Deep Behind The Scenes With Seymore Butts #1 / 1995 / ULI / M • Devil In A Wet T-Shirt / 1995 / SPI / M • Dirty Stories #1 / 1995 / PE / M • Double Cross (Wicked) / 1995 / WP / M • Drilling For Gold / 1995 / ME / M • Escape From Anal Lost Angels / 1996 / HO / M • The F Zone / 1995 / WP / M • Face Jaam / 1996 / VC / M • Face To Face / 1995 / ME / M • Flesh / 1996 / EA / M • Foreign Tongues #2: Mesmerized / 1995 / VI / M • Freaknic / 1996 / IN / M • Gangbang Girl #15 / 1995 / ANA / M • A Girl's Affair #09 / 1996 / FD / F • Golden Rod / 1996 / SPI / M • Hollywood On Ice /

1995 / VT / M • Hornet's Nest / 1996 / ONA / M • House Of Anal / 1995 / NOT / M • The Hungry Heart / 1996 / AOP / M • Indiscreet! Video Magazine #2 / 1995 / FH / M • Intense Perversions #1 / 1995 / PL / M • Interview: Backdoor Imports / 1996 / LV / M • Ir4: Inrearendence Day / 1996 / HW / M • Kissing Kaylan / 1995 / CC / M • Kym Wilde's On The Edge #35 / 1996 / RB / B • Lady Sterling Takes It Up The Arse / 1997 / ROB / M • The Last Act / 1995 / VI / M • Lesbian Connection / 1996 / SUF / F • Lip Service / 1995 / WP / M • Love Exchange / 1995 / DR / M • Lust Runner / 1995 / VC / M • Malibu Madam / 1995 / CC / M • Man Killer / 1996 / SC / M • Mile High Thrills / 1995 / VIM / M • Moondance / 1996 / VT / M • My Desire / 1996 / NIT / M • My Surrender / 1996 / A&E / M • Nasty Nymphos #09 / 1995 / ANA / M • Nici Sterling's DP Gang Bang / 1996 / FC / M • Night Nurses / 1995 / WAV / M • Night Tales / 1996 / VC / M • Nightbreed / 1995 / VI / M • No Fear / 1996 / IN / F • No Man's Land #13 / 1996 / VT / F • Ona Zee's Doll House #4 / 1996 / ONA / F • One Night In The Valley / 1996 / CA / M • The Palace Of Pleasure / 1995 / ULI / M • Philmore Butts Las Vegas Vacation / 1995 / SUF / M • Philmore Butts On The Prowl / 1995 / SUF / M • Pick Up Lines #02 / 1995 / 4P / M • Pick Up Lines #04 / 1995 / 4P / M • Pick Up Lines #07 / 1996 / OD / M • Pick Up Lines #10 / 1997 / OD / M • A Pool Party At Seymores #1 / 1995 / ULI / M • Prime Choice #2 / 1995 / RAS / M • Prime Time / 1995 / CA / M • Private Video Magazine #16 / 1994 / OD / M • Puritan Video Magazine #02 / 1996 / LE / M • Pussyman #10: Butts, Butts & More Butts / 1995 / SNA / M • Pussyman Auditions #03 / 1995 / SNA / M • Rainwoman #09: Wetlands / 1995 / CC / M • Rainwoman #10: The Tenth Anniversary Edition / 1996 / CC / M • Raw Silk / 1996 / RAS / M • Right Up Her Alley / 1996 / CA / M • Royal Ass Force / 1996 / VC / M • Sabrina The Booty Queen / 1997 / ROB / M • Sensations #2 / 1996 / SC / M • Sex Freaks / 1995 / EA / M • The Sex Therapist / 1995 / GO / M • Sinboy #3: The Island Of Dr. Moron / 1996 / SC / M • Six Degrees Of Penetration / 1996 / PP / M • Smells Like...Sex / 1995 / VC / M • Sodomania #12: Raw Filth / 1995 / EL / M • Sodomania #13: Your Lucky Number / 1995 / EL / M • Sodomania #15: Warning! / 1996 / EL / M • Sodomania: Slop Shots / 1996 / EL / C • Sodomania: Smokin' Sextions / 1996 / EL / C • Something Blue / 1995 / CC / M • Squirters / 1996 / ULI / M • Star Attraction / 1995 / VT / M • Starbangers #08 / 1996 / FPI / M • Steamy Sins / 1996 / IN / M • The Stiff / 1995 / WAV / M • Street Workers / 1995 / ME / M • Striptease / 1995 / SPI / M • Taboo #16 / 1996 / CV / M • Talk Dirty To Me #10 / 1996 / DR / M • The Theory Of Relativity / 1994 / EL / M • Thin Ice / 1996 / ONA / M • The Tigress / 1996 / VIM / M • To Bi For / 1996 / PL / G • Totally Real / 1996 / CA / M • Up And Cummers #24 / 1995 / 4P / M • Up Close & Personal #2 / 1996 / IPI / M • Valentina: Princess Of The Forest / 1996 / SC / M • Venom #4 / 1996 / VD / M • Venom #5 / 1996 / VD / M • Video Virgins #20 / 1995 / NS / M • Video Virgins #21 / 1995 / NS / M • Virgin Dreams / 1996 / EA / M •

Vivid Raw #3: Double Header / 1996 / VI / M • The Voyeur #3 / 1995 / EA / M • The Voyeur #5 / 1995 / EA / M • Wet Faces #1 / 1997 / SC / C • Wild & Wicked #6 / 1995 / VT / M • Wild Cherries / 1996 / SC / F • The Wild Ones / 1996 / CC / M

NICK
AVP #7024: Bodyguard Bang / 1991 / AVP / M • Nothing Butt Amateurs #01 / 1993 / AFI / M • Odyssey Triple Play #94: Triple Decker Sex Sandwich / 1995 / OD / M • Pearl Necklace: Premier Sessions #03 / 1994 / SEE / M

NICK ADAMS *see* **Nick Random**
NICK ADAMS (1980)
Games Women Play #1 / 1980 / CA / M
NICK BAKER
Stinging Stewardesses / 1996 / BIZ / B
NICK BAKERS
Spanked Young Tails / 1996 / BIZ / B
NICK BARRIS *see* **Herschel Savage**
NICK CASTRO *see* **Star Index I**
NICK COLLINS
Bi The Book / 1996 / MID / G
NICK COUGAR
Switch Hitters #5: The Night Games / 1990 / IN / G
NICK DALTON *see* **Star Index I**
NICK DANE
America's Raunchiest Home Videos #41: Welcum Neighbor / 1992 / ZA / M • Bubble Butts #13 / 1992 / LBO / M • Odyssey Triple Play #43: Anal Creaming & Reaming / 1993 / OD / M
NICK DEAN *see* **Star Index I**
NICK E. *see* **Nick East**
NICK EAST *(Nick E., Scott Turner, Scott Tazer)*
10,000 Anal Maniacs #2 / 1994 / FOR / M • The A Chronicles / 1992 / CC / M • Adam & Eve's House Party #2: Bachelor Party / 1996 / VC / M • Adult Video Nudes / 1993 / VC / M • The Adventures Of Breastman / 1992 / EVN / M • The Adventures Of Studman #2 / 1994 / AFV / M • The Adventures Of Studman #3 / 1994 / AFV / M • Affairs Of The Heart / 1993 / VI / M • After Midnight / 1994 / IN / M • America's Dirtiest Home Videos #08 / 1992 / VEX / M • America's Raunchiest Home Videos #22: City Lites / 1992 / ZA / M • America's Raunchiest Home Videos #24: Suck My Thumb / 1992 / ZA / M • American Garter / 1993 / VC / M • Anal Adventures #1: Anal Executive / 1991 / VC / M • The Anal Adventures Of Bruce Seven / 1996 / BS / C • Anal Angel / 1991 / ZA / M • Anal Angels #6 / 1996 / VEX / C • Anal Fever / 1996 / ROB / M • Anal Honeypie / 1996 / ROB / M • Anal Lovebud / 1996 / ROB / M • Anal Orgy / 1993 / DRP / M • Anal Squeeze / 1993 / FOR / M • Anal Vision #10 / 1993 / LBO / M • Anal Woman #2 / 1993 / PL / M • Angel Baby / 1995 / SC / M • Angel Eyes / 1995 / IN / M • Anniversary / 1992 / FOR / M • Anything That Moves / 1992 / VC / M • Aroused #2 / 1995 / VI / M • Ass Openers! #1 / 1995 / TCK / C • Ass Openers! #2 / 1995 / TCK / C • Attack Of The 50 Foot Hooker / 1994 / OD / M • Babe Magnet / 1994 / IN / M • Babe Patrol / 1993 / FOR / M • Badgirls #1: Lockdown / 1994 / VI / M • Badgirls #3: Cell Block 69 / 1994 / VI / M • Badgirls #4: Jayebird / 1995 / VI / M • Barby's On Butt Row / 1996 / ABS / M • The Basket Trick / 1993 / PL / M • Battlestar Orgasmica / 1992

/ EVN / M • Beach Mistress / 1994 / XCI / M • Bedazzled / 1993 / OD / M • Bend Over Babes #3 / 1992 / EA / M • The Best Of Strippers Inc / 1996 / ONA / C • Betty & Juice Possessed / 1995 / CA / M • Black & Booty-Full / 1996 / ROB / M • Black Bottom Girlz / 1994 / CA / M • Black Cheerleader Search #07 / 1996 / IVC / M • Black Cheerleader Search #10 / 1997 / IVC / M • Black Detail #1 / 1994 / VT / M • Black Detail #2 / 1994 / VT / M • Black Pussyman Auditions #1 / 1996 / SNA / M • Blazing Butts / 1991 / LV / M • Blue Fox / 1991 / VI / M • Body And Soul / 1992 / OD / M • Bonnie & Clyde #1 / 1992 / VI / M • Bonnie & Clyde #2 / 1992 / VI / M • Bordello / 1995 / VI / M • The Bottom Dweller / 1993 / EL / M • The Bottom Dweller Part Deux / 1994 / EL / M • The Bottom Line / 1995 / NIT / M • The Breast Files #1 / 1994 / AVI / M • Bubble Butts #23 / 1992 / LBO / M • Bunny Bleu: A Gang Bang Fantasy / 1994 / FC / M • Burgundy Blues / 1993 / MET / M • Butt Busters / 1995 / EX / M • Butt Darling / 1994 / WIV / M • The Butt Detective / 1994 / VC / M • Butt Motors / 1995 / VC / M • Butt Naked #2 / 1994 / OD / M • Butt Row Unplugged / 1996 / ABS / M • Butt Woman #2 / 1992 / FH / M • Butt Woman #3 / 1992 / FH / M • Butthead Dreams: Exposed / 1995 / FH / M • Buttman In The Crack / 1996 / EA / M • Buttman's Bubble Butt Babes / 1996 / EA / M • Buttsizer #3: Return Of The King Of Rears / 1995 / EVN / M • Buzzzz! / 1993 / OD / M • California Pizza Girls / 1992 / EVN / M • Candy Factory / 1994 / PE / M • Cape Lere / 1992 / CC / M • Carnival Of Flesh / 1996 / NIT / M • Carnival Of Knowledge / 1992 / XCI / M • The Catburglar / 1994 / PL / M • The Cathouse / 1994 / VI / M • Catwalk #1 / 1995 / SC / M • Catwalk #2 / 1995 / SC / M • Caught From Behind #15 / 1991 / HO / M • Centerfold / 1992 / VC / M • Chameleons: Not The Sequel / 1991 / VC / M • Channel Blonde / 1994 / VI / M • Cheating / 1994 / VI / M • Cherry Pie / 1994 / SC / M • Chow Down / 1994 / VI / M • Christy In The Wild / 1992 / VI / M • Chug-A-Lug Girls #3 / 1993 / VT / M • Cinnamon Twist / 1993 / OD / M • Climax 2000 #1 / 1994 / CC / M • Climax 2000 #2 / 1994 / CC / M • Colossal Orgy #1 / 1993 / HW / M • Colossal Orgy #2 / 1994 / HW / M • Colossal Orgy #3 / 1994 / HW / M • Coming Clean / 1992 / ME / M • Controlled / 1994 / FD / M • The Corruption Of Christina / 1993 / WP / M • The Coven #1 / 1993 / VI / M • Crazy With The Heat #3 / 1994 / CV / M • Cumming Of Ass / 1995 / TP / M • Dallas Does Debbie / 1992 / PL / M • The Darker Side Of Shayla #2 / 1993 / PL / M • Deep Inside Brittany O'connell / 1996 / VC / C • Deep Inside Juli Ashton / 1996 / VC / C • Deep Inside Shanna Mccullough / 1992 / VC / C • Deep Inside Tyffany Million / 1995 / VC / C • Deep Seven / 1996 / VC / M • Derrier / 1991 / CC / M • The Deviant Doctor / 1996 / NS / M • The Devil In Miss Jones #5: The Inferno / 1994 / VC / M • Diamond In The Rough / 1993 / BIA / C • Diary Of A Porn Star / 1993 / FOR / M • The Dinner Party #1 / 1994 / ULI / M • Dirty Laundry #2 / 1994 / CV / M • Dirty Little Lies / 1993 / VT / M • Dirty Little Mind / 1994 / IP / M • Diver Down / 1992 / CC / M • Domination / 1994 / WP / M • Double

/ 1994 / ONA / M • A Stroke At Midnight /
1993 / LBO / M • Super Groupie / 1993 / PL
/ M • Superstar Sex Challenge #1 / 1994 /
VC / M • Superstar Sex Challenge #3 /
1994 / VC / M • Surprise!!! / 1994 / VI / M •
Taboo #13 / 1994 / IN / M • Tactical Sex
Force / 1994 / IN / M • Tails Of Desire /
1995 / GO / M • Take The A Train / 1993 /
MID / M • Takin' It To The Limit #3 / 1994 /
BS / M • Takin' It To The Limit #4 / 1995 /
BS / M • Takin' It Up The Butt / 1995 / IF /
C • Tales From Sodom / 1994 / BLC / M •
Telesex #2 / 1992 / VI / M • The Therapist /
1992 / VC / M • Thighs & Dolls / 1993 / PEP
/ M • The Three Musketeers #1 / 1992 / FD
/ M • The Three Musketeers #2 / 1992 / FD
/ M • Tight Ends In Motion / 1993 / TP / M •
Timepiece / 1994 / CV / M • Too Cute For
Words / 1992 / V99 / M • Tori Welles Goes
Behind The Scenes / 1992 / FD / M • Tran-
sitions: An Anal Adventure / 1993 / PL / M •
The Truth Laid Bare / 1993 / ZA / M • Twin
Cheeks #4 / 1991 / CIN / M • Twists Of The
Heart / 1995 / NIT / M • Unchained Marylin
/ 1996 / VT / M • Undress To Thrill / 1994 /
VI / M • Unlike A Virgin / 1991 / HO / M •
Unmistakably You / 1995 / CV / M • Un-
solved Double Penetration / 1993 / PEP /
M • Upbeat Love #1 / 1994 / CV / M •
Vagabonds / 1996 / ERA / M • The Valley
Girl Connection / 1994 / IN / M • Venom #1
/ 1995 / VD / M • Venus Of The Nile / 1991
/ WV / M • Virgin / 1993 / HW / M • Visions
#2 / 1995 / ERA / M • Visions Of Seduction
/ 1994 / SC / M • Vivid Raw #2 / 1996 / VI /
M • W.A.S.P. / 1992 / CC / M • Washington
D.P. / 1993 / PEP / M • Waves Of Passion
/ 1993 / PL / M • We're Having A Party /
1991 / EVN / M • Wet Nurses #2 / 1995 /
LE / M • White Wedding / 1995 / VI / M •
Why Things Burn / 1994 / LBO / M •
Wicked As She Seems / 1993 / WP / M •
Wicked At Heart / 1995 / WP / M • The
Wicked Web / 1996 / WP / M • Wild Buck /
1993 / STY / M • Wild Dreams / 1995 / V99
/ M • Wild Flower #1 / 1992 / VI / M • Wild
Flower #2 / 1992 / VI / M • Wild In Motion /
1992 / PL / M • Willie Wanker And The Fun
Factory / 1994 / FD / M • With The Devil In
Her Rear / 1992 / WV / M • The XXX Files:
Lust In Space / 1995 / IMV / M • Young And
Anal #1 / 1995 / JMP / M

NICK FERILLI
Nightshift Nurses #2 / 1996 / VC / M

NICK FERRARA see Star Index I

NICK FORRINI see Star Index I

NICK FRENAIRE
Back To Rears / 1988 / VI / M • The Bimbo
#1 / 1985 / VXP / M • The Bitch Is Back /
1988 / FAN / M • Black Voodoo / 1987 /
FOV / M • Cheating American Style / 1988
/ WV / M • The Deep Insiders / 1987 / VXP
/ M • The Heiress / 1988 / VI / M • Pretty In
Black / 1986 / WET / M • Robofox #2 / 1988
/ FAN / M • Tight End / 1988 / VXP / M •
Toothless People / 1988 / SUV / M •
Twisted Sisters / 1988 / ZA / M

NICK FRENCH
The Bimbo #2: The Homecoming / 1986 /
RLV / M • Sleazy Susan / 1986 / VXP / M

NICK HARLEY see Star Index I

NICK HARMON see Star Index I

NICK HENNING
Dreams Are Forever / cr72 / AVC / M • Oh
Doctor / cr72 / ADU / M

NICK IRELAND

Dirty Laundry #2 / 1994 / CV / M

NICK JACKSON see Star Index I

NICK JOHNSON
Russian Girls / 1996 / WV / M

NICK JONES see Star Index I

NICK KNIGHT
The Comix / 1995 / VI / M • Fire & Ice:
Caught In The Act / 1995 / WP / M • The
Voyeur #5 / 1995 / EA / M

NICK KNIGHT (RAGE) see Nick Rage

NICK LONG
Alien Probe #2 / 1994 / ZFX / B • Alien
Probe #3 / 1994 / ZFX / B • Arcade Slut /
1994 / PSE / B • Auto Bound / 1995 / VTF
/ B • Bondage "Sybian" Rides / 1994 / PSE
/ B • Bound Before Xmas / 1995 / VTF / B
• The Captive / 1995 / BIZ / B • Detention
Cell #101 / 1995 / VTF / B • Dirty Old Men
#1 / 1995 / FPI / M • Double Teamed / 1995
/ PSE / B • Employee Of The Month / 1994
/ PSE / B • Gangland #2: Mob Rules / 1994
/ ZFX / B • Gangland #5 / 1995 / ZFX / B •
Harry Horndog #28: Fabulous Squirt
Queens / 1994 / FPI / M • Kane Video #4:
Customer Satisfaction / 1995 / VTF / B •
Kink #2 / 1995 / ROB / M • Kinky Debutante
Interviews #04 / 1994 / IP / M • The Maid /
1995 / VTF / B • Maid To Beat / 1994 / PL /
B • Mis-Fortune / 1995 / VTF / B • Night
Mare / 1995 / VTF / B • Project 69 / 1994 /
VTF / B • S&M Pleasure Series: The As-
sistant / 1994 / VTF / B • S&M Pleasure Se-
ries: The Contract / 1994 / VTF / B • S&M
Pleasure Series: The Gift / 1994 / VTF / B
• S&M Pleasure Series: The Tomb / 1994 /
VTF / B • Specter / 1994 / ZFX / B • Surgi-
cal Strike / 1994 / ZFX / B • Suspend Thy
Slaves / 1996 / VTF / B • Suspended / 1995
/ VTF / B • Taunted, Tied & Tickled / 1995 /
SBP / B • Tickle Thy Slaves / 1995 / SBP /
B • Video Pirates #1 / 1995 / ZFX / B •
Video Pirates #2 / 1995 / ZFX / B • Voo Doo
/ 1995 / VTF / B • The World's Biggest
Gang Bang #1 / 1995 / FPI / M

NICK MANETTI
Bi-Wicked / 1994 / BIN / G • Inside Of Me /
1993 / PL / G • Trans America / 1993 / TSS
/ G

NICK MAURO
I Know What Girls Like / 1986 / WET / G

NICK NICKERSON
The Girls On F Street / 1966 / AVC / B

NICK NITER *(Randy Jane)*
Thin male with a full beard and moustache.
Randy Jane seems to be a perculiar name
for a guy but it's the obvious choice from
Hindsight.
Blue Dream Lover / 1985 / TAR / M • Body
Girls / 1983 / SE / M • Confessions Of A
Candystriper / 1984 / VC / M • Confessions
Of Candy / 1984 / VC / M • Dark Angel /
1983 / VC / M • Debbie Does 'em All #1 /
1985 / CV / M • Educating Eva / 1984 / VC
/ M • Educating Nina / 1984 / AT / M • Fan-
tasy Club #41: Luscious Lolita / 1984 / WV
/ M • Flesh And Ecstasy / 1985 / VD / M •
Gang Bangs #1 / 1985 / VCR / M • Go For
It / 1984 / VC / M • Head Waitress / 1984 /
VC / M • Headhunters / 1984 / VC / M •
Hindsight / 1985 / IN / M • Hot Flashes /
1984 / VC / M • House Of Lust / 1984 / VD
/ M • Hustler #17 / 1984 / CA0 / M • Inde-
cent Pleasures / 1984 / CA / M • Inflamed /
1984 / NSV / M • Inside China Lee / 1984 /
VC / M • Little Often Annie / 1984 / VC / M
• Looking For Lust / 1984 / VEL / M •

Mouthful Of Love / 1984 / VC / M • Naughty
Nanette / 1984 / VC / M • Nice 'n' Tight /
1985 / AIR / M • Passions / 1985 / MIT / M
• Playmate #01 / 1984 / VC / M • Prescrip-
tion For Passion / 1984 / VD / M • Radio K-
KUM / 1984 / HO / M • Raffles / 1988 / VC
/ M • Shape Up For Sensational Sex / 1985
/ SE / M • Sizzling Summer / 1984 / VC / M
• Spreading Joy / 1984 / IN / M • Tempta-
tion: The Story Of A Lustful Bride / 1983 /
NSV / M • Tongue 'n Cheek (Vca) / 1984 /
VC / M • Too Hot To Touch #1 / 1985 / CV
/ M • Too Naughty To Say No / 1984 / CA /
M • Tracy In Heaven (Orig 1985) / 1985 /
WV / M • Up Desiree Lane / 1984 / VC / M
• Up In The Air / 1984 / CDI / M • The
Wacky World Of X-Rated Bloopers / 1989 /
GO / M • Young Nurses In Love / 1987 / VC
/ M

NICK ORLEANS see Star Index I

NICK PHOENIX
Spanking Double Feature / 1994 / SHL / B

NICK PIERCE
Ass Masters (Leisure) #02 / 1995 / LEI / M
• Fire Down Below / 1994 / GO / M • Misty
Rain's Anal Orgy / 1994 / FRM / M • Nasty
Nymphos #06 / 1994 / ANA / M • Sgt. Peck-
ers Lonely Hearts Club Gang Bang / 1995
/ AMP / M • Snatch Patch / 1995 / LE / M •
Video Virgins #16 / 1994 / NS / M

NICK QUICK
Older Women Younger Men #3 / 1993 / CC
/ M

NICK RAGE *(Nick Knight (Rage), Nicholas
Rage, Nicholas Page, Chip Knights,
Rick Rage, Ben (Nick Rage))*
Husband or boyfriend of Summer Knight.
100% Amateur #02: Back Door And More /
1995 / OD / M • 100% Amateur #10: / 1995
/ OD / M • 100% Amateur #13: / 1995 / OD
/ M • Addicted To Lust / 1996 / NIT / M •
America's Raunchiest Home Videos #05:
Sasha Gets Stuffed / 1992 / ZA / M • Amer-
ica's Raunchiest Home Videos #15: Outra-
geous Reaming / 1992 / ZA / M • America's
Raunchiest Home Videos #72: / 1993 / ZA
/ M • America's Raunchiest Home Videos
#74: / 1993 / ZA / M • Anal Alley / 1996 / FD
/ M • Anal Interrogation / 1995 / ZA / M •
B.L.O.W. / 1992 / LV / M • Back Seat Bush
/ 1992 / LV / M • Bangin' With The Home
Girls / 1991 / AFV / M • Beach Bum Ama-
teur's #10 / 1992 / MID / M • Bend Over
Babes #3 / 1992 / EA / M • Biff Malibu's To-
tally Nasty Home Videos #04 / 1992 / ANA
/ M • Biff Malibu's Totally Nasty Home
Videos #14 / 1992 / ANA / M • Bikini Beach
#1 / 1993 / CC / M • Bikini Beach #2 / 1993
/ CC / M • Blonde Justice #1 / 1993 / VI / M
• Blonde Justice #2 / 1993 / VI / M • Born 2
B Wild / 1995 / PL / M • Breast Worx #38 /
1992 / LBO / M • Breast Worx #39 / 1992 /
LBO / M • Bubble Butts #22 / 1993 / LBO /
M • Bun Busters #16 / 1994 / LBO / M • Bun
Busters #17 / 1994 / LBO / M • Butthead
Dreams: Big Boating Bonanza / 1994 / FH
/ M • Caught Looking / 1995 / CC / M •
Chameleons: Not The Sequel / 1991 / VC /
M • Cirque Du Sex #1 / 1996 / VT / M •
Concrete Heat / 1996 / XCI / M • Crazed #1
/ 1992 / VI / M • Crazed #2 / 1992 / VI / M
• Deep C Diver / 1992 / LV / M • Deep
Seven / 1996 / VC / M • Dirty Doc's House-
calls #18 / 1994 / LV / M • Dirty Doc's
Housecalls #19 / 1994 / LV / M • Double D
Amateurs #21 / 1994 / JMP / M • Dr Feel-

good Sex Psychiatrist / 1994 / LV / M • Extreme Passion / 1993 / WP / M • The God Daughter #1 / 1991 / AFV / M • Hidden Camera #21 / 1994 / JMP / M • Hidden Camera #22 / 1994 / JMP / M • Hidden Desires / 1992 / CDI / M • Hot Summer Knights / 1991 / LV / M • Hotel Sex / 1992 / AFV / M • Insatiable Nurses / 1992 / VIM / M • Kinky Cameraman #1 / 1996 / LEI / C • Mortal Passions / 1995 / FD / M • Mr. Peepers Amateur Home Videos #48: Dialing For Services / 1992 / LBO / M • Mr. Peepers Amateur Home Videos #67: Backdoor Fantasy / 1993 / LBO / M • Mr. Peepers Amateur Home Videos #90: Back Door Bonanza / 1994 / LBO / M • Mr. Peepers Amateur Home Videos #92: M-Ass-terpieces / 1994 / LBO / M • Neighbors / 1994 / LE / M • Odyssey 30 Min: #190: The Other Fucking Roommate / 1991 / OD / M • Odyssey 30 Min: #232: / 1992 / OD / M • Odyssey 30 Min: #263: Carmel's 4-Way Dating Game / 1992 / OD / M • Odyssey 30 Min: #318: Kitty Kitty Bang Bang / 1993 / OD / M • Odyssey Triple Play #29: Spontaneous & Raw 3-Ways / 1993 / OD / M • Odyssey Triple Play #63: Orient Express / 1994 / OD / M • Odyssey Triple Play #94: Triple Decker Sex Sandwich / 1995 / OD / M • Odyssey Triple Play #98: Three Ways To Sunday / 1995 / OD / M • Odyssey Triple Play #99: Hail, Hail, The Gang-Bang's Here #2 / 1995 / OD / M • Painful Lessons (Bruce Seven) / 1992 / BS / B • Perverted Stories #02 / 1995 / JMP / M • Perverted Stories #05 / 1995 / JMP / M • Philmore Butts Meets The Palm Beach Nymphomaniac Kathy Wille / 1995 / SUF / M • The Phoenix #1 / 1992 / VI / M • Pretty In Peach / 1992 / VI / M • Private Stories #09 / 1996 / OD / M • Pussyman #03: The Search Continues / 1993 / SNA / M • Release Me / 1996 / VT / M • Shades Of Blue / 1992 / VC / M • Snatch Patch / 1995 / LE / M • Streetwalkers / 1995 / HO / M • SVE: Cheap Thrills #2: The More The Merrier / 1992 / SVE / M • Sweet As Honey / 1992 / LV / M • Tailiens #2 / 1992 / FD / M • Tight Tushies #1 / 1994 / SFP / M • Uncle Roy's Amateur Home Video #04 / 1992 / VIM / M • Uncle Roy's Amateur Home Video #11 / 1992 / VIM / M • Uncle Roy's Amateur Home Video #14 / 1992 / VIM / M • Unfaithful Entry / 1992 / DR / M • White Chicks Can't Hump / 1992 / FD / M

NICK RANDOM *(Nick Adams)*
Beverly Hills Cox / 1986 / CA / M • The Big Thrill / 1984 / ECS / M • Bizarre Encounters / 1986 / 4P / B • Blondie / 1985 / TAR / M • Celebrity Presents Celebrity / 1986 / VEP / C • Centerfold Celebrities #4 / 1983 / VC / M • Charm School / 1986 / VI / M • Charmed And Dangerous / 1987 / VI / M • Cheeks #2: The Bitter End / 1989 / CC / M • Cherry Tricks / 1985 / VPE / M • Cleopatra's Bondage Revenge / cr85 / BIZ / B • Corporate Assets / 1985 / SE / M • Daisy Chain / 1984 / IN / M • Dear Fanny / 1984 / CV / M • Desperate Women / 1986 / VD / M • Dirty Tricks / 1986 / 4P / M • Don't Tell Daddy #1 / 1985 / PL / C • Dr Strange Sex / 1985 / CA / M • Dreams Of Misty / 1984 / VCX / M • Erotic Zones #2 / 1985 / CA / M • Family Secrets / 1985 / AMB / M • Fantasy Mansion / 1983 / BIZ / B • Girls Of The Night / 1985 / CA / M • Hard Choices / 1987

/ CA / M • Heidi A / 1985 / PL / M • Hot Touch / 1984 / VCX / M • The Hottest Show In Town / 1987 / VIP / M • In A Crystal Fantasy / 1988 / VD / M • Jewel Of The Nite / 1986 / WV / M • Jewels Of The Night / 1986 / SE / M • K.U.N.T.-TV / 1988 / WV / M • Kinky Sluts / 1988 / MIR / C • Lusty Couples (Come To) / cr85 / CHX / M • Mad About You / 1987 / VC / M • The Magic Touch / 1985 / CV / M • Marilyn Chambers' Private Fantasies #3 / 1983 / CA / M • Marilyn Chambers' Private Fantasies #5 / 1985 / CA / M • Memoirs Of A Chambermaid / 1987 / FIR / M • Motel Sweets / 1987 / VD / M • Nasty Habits Are Hard To Break / 1986 / 4P / M • National Pornographic #2: Orientals / 1987 / 4P / C • Naughty Girls In Heat / 1986 / SE / M • Nudes At Eleven #2 / 1987 / AVC / M • Older Men With Young Girls / 1985 / CC / M • Only The Best Of Anal / 1992 / MET / C • Orifice Party / 1985 / GOM / M • Out For Blood / 1990 / VI / M • Pacific Intrigue / 1987 / AMB / M • Peeping Tom / 1986 / CV / M • The Return Of Johnny Wadd / 1986 / PEN / M • Schoolgirl By Day / 1985 / LA / M • Sexual Odyssey / 1985 / VC / M • Showdown / 1986 / CA / M • Soaking Wet / 1985 / CV / M • Squalor Motel / 1985 / SE / M • Stiff Competition #1 / 1984 / CA / M • Swedish Erotica #68 / 1985 / CA / M • Swedish Erotica #73 / 1986 / CA / M • A Taste Of Nikki Charm / 1989 / PIN / C • Thanks For The Mammaries / 1987 / CA / M • Triangle / 1980 / VI / M • True Love / 1989 / VI / M • What's My Punishment / 1983 / BIZ / B

NICK REDDY *see Star Index I*
NICK REMSY
Euro-Snatch / 1996 / SNA / M
NICK ROMANO
Blazing Nova / 1989 / LV / M • Bon Appetit / 1980 / QX / M • My Girl: Transaction #2 / 1993 / SC / G • The Prize Package / 1993 / HSV / G • Single White She-Male / 1993 / PL / G • Stick Pussy / 1992 / HSV / G • Surprise Package / 1993 / HSV / G • Transitions (TV) / 1993 / HSV / G
NICK RUSSELL *see Randy Spears*
NICK SANTEARO *see Star Index I*
NICK SANTIAGO *see Star Index I*
NICK STEEL
Man Made Pussy / 1994 / HEA / G
NICK STONE *see Star Index I*
NICK TATE
The Devil's Playground / 1976 / IFE / S • Hollywood Boulevard / 1995 / CV / M
NICK THE GREEK
Nikki Arizona's Tomboys / 1995 / GAL / M
NICK ZEDD
Hardcore: The Films Of Richard Kern #1 / 1991 / FTV / M • Whoregasm / cr87 / FTV / M • [War Is Menstrual Envy / 1991 / ... / S
NICKI
Harry Horndog #29: Anal Lovers #5 / 1995 / FPI / M • Scandanavian Double Features #1 / 1996 / PL / M
NICKI (COREY GATES) *see Corey Gates*
NICKI CHERRY *see Nikki Cherry*
NICKI CHRISTENSSON
Scandanavian Double Features #3 / 1996 / PL / M
NICKI DEE *see Nikki Knights*
NICKI DESIGN *see Star Index I*
NICKI FLYNN
The Pleasure Palace / 1978 / CV / M
NICKI GATES *see Corey Gates*

NICKI PARADISE
FTV #11: Tough Girl Boxing / 1996 / FT / B • FTV #13: Crotch Crunch / 1996 / FT / B • FTV #14: Big Bust Boxing / 1996 / FT / B • FTV #18: Lump Lovers Liason / 1996 / FT / B • FTV #19: Topless Lingerie Cat-Fight / 1996 / FT / B • FTV #36: Power Boxing / 1996 / FT / B • FTV #37: Power Wrestling / 1996 / FT / B • FTV #57: Birthday Boxing Bash / 1996 / FT / B • FTV #58: Jab-O-Rama / 1996 / FT / B • FTV #77: TV Fight / 1996 / FT / B
NICKI PHILLIPS
800 Fantasy Lane / 1979 / GO / M
NICKI RONSON
All The Way / 1980 / CDC / M • Fastlane Fuck-Holes! / 1994 / MET / M
NICKIE
Babe Watch Beach / 1996 / SC / M
NICKKI
FTV #06: The Intruder / 1996 / FT / B
NICKO *see Star Index I*
NICKOL
Titan's Gonzo Video Magazine #02 / 1996 / TEG / M
NICKY
Helen Does Holland / 1996 / VC / M • Swedish Sex / 1996 / PL / M
NICKY BRANT *see Nikki Brantz*
NICKY C. O'BRIEN
Between Lovers / 1983 / CA / M
NICKY DARBY
Bitches In Heat #2: On Vacation / 1995 / ZA / M
NICKY DEE *see Nikki Knights*
NICKY FOSTER
Buttman's Bouncin' British Babes / 1994 / EA / M
NICKY JAMES
Bright Tails #1 / 1993 / STP / B
NICKY KNIGHT *see Nikki Knights*
NICKY RANDALL *see Nikki Randall*
NICKY SLICK *see Star Index I*
NICKY WILD
Sex On The Run #2 / 1994 / TTV / M
NICKY WILDE *see Nikki Wylde*
NICO SAFIR
Anal Magic / 1995 / XC / M • Behind The Mask / 1995 / XC / M • Essence Of A Woman / 1995 / ONA / M • Prima #09: AS-Sassins / 1995 / MBP / M • Prima #14: Hotel Europa / 1996 / MBP / M
NICO TIELIER
French Blue / 1974 / ... / M
NICO TREASURES
Asses Galore #2: No Remorse...No Repent / 1996 / DFI / M • Bend Over Babes #4 / 1996 / EA / M • Cheek To Cheek / 1997 / EL / M • Cheerleader Strippers / 1996 / PE / M • Erotic Newcummers Vol 1 #5 / 1996 / DR / M • In The Line Of Desire / 1996 / MID / M • Indecent Exposures / 1996 / MID / M • Jinx / 1996 / WP / M • Maui Waui / 1996 / PE / M • No Man's Land #15 / 1996 / VT / F • No Man's Land #16 / 1996 / VT / F • Philmore Butts Adventures In Paradise / 1996 / SUF / M • Pure / 1996 / WP / M • Raw Footage / 1996 / VC / M • Sodomania #19: Sweet Cream / 1996 / EL / M • Sorority Sex Kittens #3 / 1996 / VC / M • Surfin' The Net / 1996 / RAS / M • Up And Cummers #26 / 1996 / 4P / M • Up Close & Personal #2 / 1996 / IPI / M • Virgin Dreams / 1996 / EA / M • Whiplash / 1996 / DFI / M • The Wild Ones / 1996 / CC / M
NICO WAGNER

Private Film #08 / 1994 / OD / M

NICOL
Blue Vanities #517 / 1992 / FFL / M

NICOLA
Bedtime Video #04 / 1984 / GO / M •
Leg...Ends #01 / 1988 / BIZ / F

NICOLA AUSTIN
Blue Vanities #582 / 1996 / FFL / M

NICOLA BAXTER *see* **Nikki Randall**

NICOLA RUSSELL
Spanking Video #2: Naval Discipline / 1995
/ MET / B

NICOLE
A&B AB#397: Cum Sisters / 1990 / A&B /
M • Amateur Hours #09 / 1990 / AFI / M •
Anabolic Import #01: Anal X / 1994 / ANA /
M • Anal Bandits / 1996 / SO / M • Bizarre
Dildo Obsession / 1989 / BIZ / B • Black
Women, White Men #8 / 1995 / FC / M •
Bond-Aid / 1992 / STM / B • Catch Of The
Day #3 / 1996 / VG0 / M • Cherry Poppers
#14: Teeny Tongues / 1996 / ZA / M • Dil-
ton: Dilton De002 / 1996 / DIL / F • Feuchte
Muschies / 1995 / KRM / M • Forbidden
Dildo Taboos / 1992 / STM / F • FTV #44:
Tight Tamali And Bam Jam / 1996 / FT / B
• Holly's Hollywood / 1992 / STM / F • Hot
New Imports / 1996 / XC / M • The Hunt Is
On / 1994 / HU / F • Ice Cream #2: French
Postcard / 1983 / VC / M • Intimate Inter-
views #1 / 1996 / NIT / M • Magma: Horny
Bulls / 1994 / MET / M • Magma: Insatiable
Lust / 1995 / MET / M • Nicole: Lady Ec-
stasy / 1990 / LOD / F • Ona Zee's Doll
House #3 / 1995 / ONA / F • Pearl Neck-
lace: Amorous Amateurs #35 / 1993 / SEE
/ M • Pearl Necklace: Premier Sessions
#01 / 1993 / SEE / M • Shaved Submission
/ 1996 / GAL / B • Southern Belles #3 /
1995 / HOV / M • Southern Belles: Sugar
Magnolias / 1996 / XPR / M • Student
Fetish Videos: Foot Worship #13 / 1994 /
PRE / B • Super Sampler #5 / 1994 / LOD
/ C

NICOLE (T. RIVERS) *see* **Tanya Rivers**

NICOLE (WEST) *see* **Nichole West**

NICOLE ADAMS *see* **Star Index I**

NICOLE ANDREA *see* **Star Index I**

NICOLE ANN
Caribbean Sunset / 1996 / PL / M • East
Coast Sluts #09: / 1995 / PL / M • Pearl
Necklace: Premier Sessions #07 / 1996 /
SEE / M • Philmore Butts Spring Break /
1996 / SUF / M • Southern Belles #7 / 1996
/ XPR / M • Summer Vacation #1 / 1996 /
RAS / M • Summer Vacation #2 / 1996 /
RAS / M • Tampa Spice / 1996 / SUF / M

NICOLE AVRIL
Love Play / 1977 / CA / M

NICOLE BARDOT
French Schoolgirls / 1973 / AVC / M • Plea-
sure Motel / 197? / CV / M • Wait Till He
Comes In Me! / 1994 / MET / M

NICOLE BERNARD
Afrodisiac #1 / 1987 / CC / M • Bizarre Sor-
ceress / 1979 / STM / B • Corruption / 1983
/ VC / M • Flash Pants / 1983 / VC / M •
Lesbian Dildo Fever #1 / 1989 / BIZ / F •
Secluded Passion / 1983 / VHL / M •
Shameful Desires In Black & White Girls /
1984 / PL / M • Snake Eyes #1 / 1984 /
COM / M

NICOLE BLACK *(Nicole Noir, Jeanette*
James)
Tall thin not-too-pretty brunette with small
droopy tits.

1001 Erotic Nights #1 / 1982 / VC / M •
Amanda By Night #1 / 1981 / CA / M • Any
Time, Any Place / 1981 / CA0 / M • Beauty
/ 1981 / VC / M • The Best Of Alex De
Renzy #1 / 1983 / VC / C • A Brief Affair /
1982 / CA / M • Caballero Preview Tape #2
/ 1983 / CA / C • Cheryl Hanson: Cover Girl
/ 1981 / SE / M • Confessions Of A Can-
dystriper / 1984 / VC / M • Daughters Of
Emmanuelle / 1982 / VCX / M • Desire For
Men / 1981 / MIT / M • Erotic Dimensions
#2: Black Desire / 1982 / NSV / M • Erotic
Dimensions: Bold Fantasies / 1982 / NSV /
M • The Erotic World Of Nicole Black /
1984 / VCR / C • Every Which Way She
Can / 1981 / CA / M • A Family Affair / 1984
/ AVC / M • The Girl From S.E.X. / 1982 /
CA / M • Holly Rolling / 1984 / AVC / M • Hot
Line / 1980 / CA / M • Hot Pink / 1983 / VC
/ C • Indecent Exposure / 1981 / CA / M •
Inspiration / 1981 / CHX / M • Irresistible #1
/ 1982 / SE / M • Ladies Nights / 1980 / VC
/ M • Mistress Electra / 1983 / AVO / B •
Moments Of Love / 1983 / MID / M •
Naughty Network / 1981 / CA / M • Nudes
In Limbo / 1983 / MCA / S • Please, Mr
Postman / 1981 / VC / M • The Power of
Nicole / 1983 / BIZ / M • Purely Physical /
1982 / SE / M • Sex Boat / 1980 / VCX / M
• Sex Games / 1983 / CA / M • Sex Loose
/ 1982 / VC / M • Stephanie's Lust Story /
1983 / VC / M • Summer Of '72 / 1982 / CA
/ M • Talk Dirty To Me #02 / 1982 / CA / M •
Touch Me In The Morning / 1982 / CA / M •
Trashi / 1980 / CA / M • [Erotic Dimensions
Vols 1 To 8 / 1983 / NSV / C

NICOLE BLANC *see* **Traci Duzit**

NICOLE BUDVAR *see* **Deborah Wells**

NICOLE CARRINGTON *see* **Star Index I**

NICOLE DAUDET *see* **Star Index I**

NICOLE GREINER *see* **Nikki Dial**

NICOLE GRENIER *see* **Nikki Dial**

NICOLE HOMELL
Immortal Desire / 1993 / VI / M

NICOLE JEFFERSON
Black girl with small tits, tight body, tight
waist, pretty face, narrow hips, and a nice
butt. 23 years old in 1995 and de-virginized
at 19. At first you get the idea she might
have an exploitative personality but this
concept disappeared over time.
African Angels #1 / 1996 / NIT / M • Amateur Black: Honeys / 1995 / SUF / M • Be-
hind The Backdoor #7 / 1995 / EVN / M •
Black Babes / 1995 / LV / M • The Black
Butt Sisters Do Boston / 1995 / MID / M •
Black Cheerleader Jungle Jerk-Off / 1996 /
WIC / F • Black Cheerleader Search #01 /
1996 / ROB / M • Black Cheerleader
Search #02 / 1996 / ROB / M • Black Fan-
tasies #16 / 1996 / HW / M • Black Holly-
wood Amateurs #17 / 1995 / MID / M •
Black Hollywood Amateurs #18 / 1995 /
MID / M • Butt-Nanza / 1995 / WV / M •
Chocolate Bunnies #06 / 1996 / LBO / C •
The Cumm Brothers #09: Chewin' The
Bush / 1995 / OD / M • The Cumm Broth-
ers #10: Night Of The Giving Head / 1995 /
OD / M • Dangerous Behinds #2 / 1996 /
HW / M • Dirty Tricks #2: This Ain't Love /
1996 / EA / M • The Doctor Is In #1 / 1995
/ NIT / M • Fashion sluts #5: Ethnic Ecstasy
/ 1995 / ABS / M • Here Comes Elska /
1997 / XPR / M • Here Comes Magoof #1 /
1995 / VC / M • Here Comes Magoof #2 /
1995 / VC / M • Jingle Balls / 1996 / EVN /

M • Life's A Beach, Then You're Fucked /
1995 / FRM / M • Look What I Found On
The Street #01 / 1996 / CC / M • A Low-
down Dirty Game / 1996 / LBO / M • Pick
Up Lines #02 / 1995 / 4P / M • Profiles #05:
Planet Lust / 1995 / XPR / M • Ron High-
tower's Casting Couch #2 / 1995 / FC / M •
Sweet Black Cherries #1 / 1996 / TTV / M
• Video Virgins #25 / 1995 / NS / M

NICOLE JOHNSON
Skintight / 1981 / CA / M

NICOLE K.
Private Gold #09: Private Dancer / 1996 /
OD / M

NICOLE KIDDER *see* **Star Index I**

NICOLE LACE *see* **Nikole Lace**

NICOLE LONDON *(Nicole Valiant)*
Tall medium titted blonde/redhead/brunette (it
changes) with a major rear-end acne problem in lots of her movies. In her first ones
she looked like a yupette but quickly deteriorated into a "nasty" girl. Born October
24, 1969 in South Amboy NJ (23 in 1992).
Lost her virginity at age 13. Nicole Valiant
is from **More Dirty Debutantes #8**.
Addictive Desires / 1994 / OD / M • Adven-
tures Of The DP Boys: The Pool Service /
1993 / HW / M • All That Jism / 1994 / VD /
M • America's Raunchiest Home Videos
#36: Milky Way / 1992 / ZA / M • America's
Raunchiest Home Videos #37: Learning
Her Lesson / 1992 / ZA / M • America's
Raunchiest Home Videos #43: Cum Blow
My Horn / 1992 / ZA / M • American Garter
/ 1993 / VC / M • The Anal Adventures Of
Max Hardcore: Suzy Superslut / 1992 / ZA
/ M • Anal Amateurs / 1992 / VD / M • Anal
Attitude / 1993 / HO / M • Anal Ecstacy
Girls #1 / 1993 / ROB / F • Anal Innocence
#2 / 1993 / ROB / M • Anal Island #2 / 1996
/ VC / M • Anal Mystique / 1994 / EMC / M
• Anal Planet / 1994 / CC / M • Anal Ram-
page #2 / 1993 / ROB / M • Anal Siege /
1993 / ROB / M • Anal Urge / 1993 / ROB /
M • Anal Vision #02 / 1992 / LBO / M • Anal
Vision #21 / 1993 / LBO / M • Anniversary /
1992 / FOR / M • The Artist / 1994 / HO / M
• Backing In #6 / 1994 / WV / C • Backing
In #7 / 1995 / WV / C • Badd Girls / 1994 /
SC / F • Badgirls #2: Strip Search / 1994 /
VI / M • Badgirls #3: Cell Block 69 / 1994 /
VI / M • Bare Market / 1993 / VC / M •
Beaver & Buttface / 1995 / SC / M • The
Bet / 1993 / VT / M • Between The Cheeks
#3 / 1993 / VC / M • Beyond Reality #1 /
1995 / EXQ / M • The Big Stick-Up / 1994 /
WV / M • Bizarre's Dracula #1 / 1995 / BIZ
/ B • Bizarre's Dracula #2 / 1995 / BIZ / B •
Black Booty / 1993 / ZA / M • Black
Buttman #02 / 1994 / CC / M • Black Detail
#1 / 1994 / VT / M • Black For More / 1993
/ ZA / M • Black Satin / 1994 / IN / M • Bon-
nie & Clyde #3 / 1994 / VI / M • Boobtown
/ 1995 / VC / M • The Boss / 1993 / VT / M
• Bottoms Up (1993-Hollywood) / 1993 /
HO / M • The Breast Files #1 / 1994 / AVI /
M • Breastman Goes To Breastland #2 /
1993 / EVN / M • Brooklyn Nights / 1994 /
OD / M • The Brothel / 1993 / OD / M • Butt
Alley / 1995 / VMX / M • Butt Bandits #4 /
1996 / VC / C • Butt Darling / 1994 / WIV /
M • Butt Sluts #1 / 1993 / ROB / F •
Buttslammers #10: Lust On The Internet /
1995 / BS / F • Buzzzz! / 1993 / OD / M •
Casanova #2 / 1993 / SC / M • Caught
From Behind #19 / 1994 / HO / M • Charm

School / 1993 / PEP / M • Chateau Of Torment / 1995 / STM / B • Cheek To Cheek / 1997 / EL / M • Chronicles Of Pain #4: Tools Of The Trade / 1996 / BIZ / B • Club Anal #1 / 1993 / ROB / F • Club Erotica / 1996 / IN / M • The Come On / 1995 / EX / M • Coming Of Fortune / 1994 / EX / M • The Corner / 1994 / VT / M • Covergirl / 1994 / WP / M • The Crimson Kiss / 1993 / WV / M • The Darker Side / 1994 / HO / M • Debi's Darkest Desires / 1996 / BIZ / B • Decadence / 1994 / WHP / M • Deep Inside Nicole London / 1995 / VC / C • Deep Inside P.J. Sparxx / 1995 / VC / C • Desert Moon / 1994 / SPI / M • The Dirtiest Girl In The World / 1992 / ZA / M • Dirty Laundry #1 / 1994 / CV / M • Dirty Little Mind / 1994 / IP / M • The Domination Of Summer #1 / 1994 / BIZ / B • Double D Domination / 1993 / BIZ / B • Dp #2: The Mighty Fhucks / 1994 / FC / M • Dresden Diary #13: / 1995 / BIZ / B • Dun-Hur #1 / 1994 / SC / M • Dungeon Discipline / 1996 / STM / B • Endlessly / 1993 / VI / M • The Enema Bandit / 1994 / BIZ / B • The Enema Bandit Returns / 1995 / BIZ / B • Enema Obedience #2 / 1994 / BIZ / B • Enema Obedience #3: The Ultimate Punishment / 1994 / BIZ / B • Extreme Sex #2: The Dungeon / 1994 / VI / M • Face Jams / 1996 / VC / M • Fast Forward / 1995 / CA / M • Feds In Bed / 1993 / HO / M • Flame's Bondage Bash / 1994 / BIZ / B • The Fluffer #1 / 1993 / FD / M • Foolish Pleasure / 1992 / VD / M • Forbidden Pleasures / 1995 / ERA / M • The Freak Club / 1994 / VMX / M • Frenzy / 1992 / SC / M • Games Women Play / 1995 / XC / M • Gang Bang Bitches #06 / 1995 / PP / M • Generation Sex #2: Nature's Revenge / 1996 / VT / M • Ghosts / 1994 / EMC / M • A Girl Like You / 1995 / LE / M • The Girls From Butthole Ridge / 1994 / ZA / M • Girls With Curves #2 / 1994 / CV / M • The Grind / 1995 / XC / M • The Hard Line / 1993 / PEP / M • Hard To Stop #1 / 1992 / VC / M • Hard To Stop #2 / 1992 / VC / M • Haunted Nights / 1993 / WP / M • Head First / 1993 / LE / M • Hostile Takeover: Bitch Bosses / 1995 / BIZ / B • Hot Tight Asses #05 / 1994 / TCK / M • Hotel Sodom #03 / 1995 / SNA / M • The Hypnotist / 1994 / SBP / B • Induced Pleasure / 1995 / ERA / M • Intercourse With The Vampyre #1 / 1994 / SC / M • Intersextion / 1994 / HO / M • Jaded Love / 1994 / CA / M • Joanie Pneumatic / 1996 / PL / M • Junkyard Dykes #01 / 1994 / ZA / F • Juranal Park / 1993 / OD / M • L.A. Topless / 1994 / LE / M • Lady Of The House / 1990 / VEX / M • Leather Bound Dykes From Hell #1 / 1994 / BIZ / F • Leather Bound Dykes From Hell #2 / 1994 / BIZ / F • Leather Bound Dykes From Hell #3 / 1994 / BIZ / F • Leather Bound Dykes From Hell #4 / 1995 / BIZ / F • Leather Bound Dykes From Hell #6 / 1995 / BIZ / B • Leena Meets Frankenstein / 1993 / OD / M • Les Wrestle / 1994 / SBP / B • Lethal Lolita / 1993 / LE / M • Licking Legends #1 / 1992 / LE / F • Licking Legends #2 / 1992 / LE / F • Lollipop Lickers / 1996 / V99 / C • Love Potion / 1993 / WV / M • Lover Under Cover / 1995 / ERA / M • Lust & Desire / 1996 / WV / M • The Magic Box / 1993 / TP / M • Maid For Punishment / 1993 / ... / B • Make My Wife Please... / 1993 / VC / M • Malibu Blue / 1992 / LE / M

• The Mating Pot / 1994 / LBO / M • Mistress Rules / 1995 / STM / B • Mo' White Trash / 1993 / MET / M • More Dirty Debutantes #08 / 1991 / 4P / M • More Than A Handful #4 / 1994 / MET / M • My Favorite Rear / 1993 / PEP / M • Naughty Nicole / 1994 / SC / M • The New Babysitter / 1995 / GO / M • The New Butt Hunt #19 / 1996 / LEI / C • Night Crawlers / 1994 / SC / M • Night Of Seduction / 1994 / VC / M • Night Seduction / 1995 / VC / M • No Man's Land #06 / 1992 / VT / F • No Man's Land #08: Eight Women Who Ate Women / 1993 / VT / F • No Man's Land #10 / 1994 / VT / F • No Man's Land #11 / 1995 / VT / F • Nobody's Looking / 1993 / VC / M • Obsexxed / 1992 / VD / M • Off Duty Porn Stars / 1994 / VC / M • The Older Women's Sperm Bank #2 / 1996 / SUF / M • One Of Our Porn Stars Is Missing / 1993 / OD / M • Oral Majority #13 / 1995 / WV / C • Pajama Party X #3 / 1994 / VC / M • Plaything #2 / 1995 / VI / M • Poison Ivory / 1993 / MID / F • Porsche Lynn, Vault Mistress #1 / 1994 / BIZ / B • Porsche Lynn, Vault Mistress #2 / 1994 / BIZ / B • Pounding Ass / 1995 / VMX / M • Prisoners Of Pain / 1994 / BIZ / B • Pussyman #03: The Search Continues / 1993 / SNA / M • Rainwoman #09: Wetlands / 1995 / CC / M • Ready, Willing & Anal (Vidco) / 1993 / VD / C • Revelations / 1993 / FEM / M • Ride The Pink Lady / 1993 / WV / M • Ring Of Passion / 1993 / WV / M • Rump Reamers / 1994 / TTV / M • Ruthless Affairs / 1995 / LE / M • Screamers (Gourmet) / 1995 / ONA / M • The Secret Life Of Herbert Dingle / 1994 / TTV / M • Secret Services / 1993 / PEP / M • The Seduction Of Annah Marie / 1996 / VT / M • Seven Good Women / 1993 / HO / F • The Sex Connection / 1993 / VC / M • Sex Heist / 1992 / WV / M • Sex Lives Of Clowns / 1994 / VC / M • Sex Stories / 1992 / VC / M • Sex Suites / 1995 / TP / M • Sexual Instinct #2 / 1994 / DR / M • Shelby's Forbidden Fears / 1995 / BIZ / B • Shooting Gallery / 1996 / EL / M • Silence Of My Dreams / 1993 / ... / B • Ski Bunnies #2 / 1994 / HW / M • Skin To Skin / 1993 / LE / M • Smoke Screen / 1995 / WAV / M • Sodomania #01: Tales Of Perversity / 1992 / EL / M • Sodomania #04: Further On Down The Road / 1993 / EL / M • Sodomania: The Baddest Of The Best...And Then Some / 1994 / EL / C • Sparxx / 1993 / MID / F • Spiked Heel Diaries #1 / 1994 / BIZ / B • Spiked Heel Diaries #2 / 1994 / BIZ / B • Spiked Heel Diaries #4 / 1995 / BIZ / B • Taboo #12 / 1994 / MET / M • Taboo #13 / 1994 / IN / M • Tail Taggers #102 / 1993 / WV / M • Tail Taggers #105 / 1993 / WV / M • Tail Taggers #106 / 1993 / WV / M • Tail Taggers #111 / 1993 / WV / M • Tail Taggers #126 / 1994 / WV / M • Tails Of Desire / 1995 / GO / M • Tales From The Clit / 1993 / OD / M • Teri Diver's Bedtime Tales / 1993 / FD / M • Thighs & Dolls / 1993 / PEP / M • Tight Ends In Motion / 1993 / TP / M • Tight Lips / 1994 / CA / M • Titanic Orgy / 1995 / PEP / M • Tommyknockers / 1994 / CC / M • Top Debs #2: The Reunion / 1993 / GO / M • The Training #2 / 1994 / BIZ / B • The Training #3 / 1995 / BIZ / B • The Truth Laid Bare / 1993 / ZA / M • Twin Freaks / 1992 / ZA / M • Unsolved Double Penetration / 1993 / PEP / M • Up The Ying

Yang #2 / 1995 / CC / M • Visions Of Desire / 1994 / DR / M • Warehouse Wenches #1 / 1994 / BIZ / B • Warehouse Wenches #2 / 1994 / BIZ / B • Washington D.P. / 1993 / PEP / M • A Weekend In Bondage / 1994 / BIZ / B • Wendy Whoppers: Ninja CPA / 1993 / PEP / M • Wet Faces #1 / 1997 / SC / C • Wet Memories / 1993 / WV / M • Wet Nurses #1 / 1994 / LE / M • Whipped And Waxed / 1993 / SBP / B • The Whips & Chains Affair / 1994 / HOM / B • Whispers / 1992 / HO / M • Wicked Wish / 1992 / LE / M • WPINK-TV #5 / 1993 / PV / M • You Bet Your Buns / 1992 / ZA / M • [The Couch Audition / 1992 / ... / M

NICOLE LOWE *see Star Index I*

NICOLE LUTTERBACH *see Star Index I*

NICOLE MICHELLE *see Star Index I*

NICOLE MITCHELL *(Nicole West (Mitch.))*
Not to be confused with the Nichole West of the mid eighties. This one is taller, doesn't have the overbite and is not as pretty. She's still very natural. Her first two movies were as West and then she changed her name to Mitchell.
American Swinger Video Magazine #04 / 1993 / ZA / M • Anal Distraction / 1993 / PEP / M • Anal Kitten / 1992 / ROB / M • Anal Lover #2 / 1993 / ROB / M • Anal Savage #1 / 1992 / ROB / M • Backdoor Brides #4 / 1993 / PV / M • Harry Horndog #17: Love Puppies #5 / 1993 / ZA / M • Harry Horndog #21: Birthday Orgy / 1993 / ZA / M

NICOLE NATTE
Flesh Fever / 1978 / CV / M

NICOLE NOIR *see Nicole Black*

NICOLE NUANCE
Venom #2 / 1996 / VD / M

NICOLE O'NEAL *see Kitty Shane*

NICOLE PATUREL *see Nina Preta*

NICOLE PRICE *see Star Index I*

NICOLE PRUDENCE *see Star Index I*

NICOLE RAM
Girly Video Magazine #6 / 1996 / AB / M

NICOLE REED
10 Years Of Big Busts #1 / 1989 / BTO / C • Between My Breasts #05 / 1988 / BTO / S • Big Busty #22 / 198? / H&S / S • Big Busty #24 / 198? / H&S / S

NICOLE RIDDELL *(Nicole Ridell)*
Beach Blanket Bango / 1975 / EVI / M • Five Loose Women / 1974 / NFV / S • High School Fantasies / 1974 / EVI / M • Ilsa, She Wolf Of The SS / 1974 / VID / S • Private Thighs / 1987 / AVC / C • Teenage Throat / 1974 / ... / M

NICOLE RIDELL *see Nicole Riddell*

NICOLE ROCHAMBEAU *see Star Index I*

NICOLE ROSE
Amateur Nights #16 / 1997 / HO / M

NICOLE SCENT
The Blonde Goddess / 1982 / VXP / M • Delicious / 1981 / VXP / M • A Scent Of Heather / 1981 / VXP / M

NICOLE SCHNEIDER
Worksex / 1980 / ... / M

NICOLE SIMPSON
Hard Core Beginners #06 / 1995 / LEI / M • New Pussy Hunt #18 / 1995 / LEI / C

NICOLE STANTON *see Star Index I*

NICOLE STARDUST
N.Y. Video Magazine #07 / 1996 / OUP / M

NICOLE SWEET *see Tanya Rivers*

NICOLE VALIANT *see Nicole London*

NICOLE VARTAN *see Star Index I*

NICOLE VERNA
Sensations / 1975 / ALP / M • [La Rabatteuse / 1977 / ... / M

NICOLE WEST (MITCH.) *see* Nicole Mitchell

NICOLE WEST (OTHER)
Up Desiree Lane / 1984 / VC / M

NICOLE WILD (NIKKI) *see* Nikki Wylde

NICOLE YELNA
Blue Vanities #567 / 1995 / FFL / M

NICOLET (BLACK)
The Adventures Of Peeping Tom #4 / 1997 / OD / M • Black Centerfolds #1 / 1996 / DR / M • Black Centerfolds #2 / 1996 / DR / M • Black Cheerleader Search #09 / 1996 / IVC / M • Pick Up Lines #11 / 1997 / OD / M

NICOLETTE
All Grown Up / 1996 / XC / M • Don Salvatore: The Last Sicilian / 1995 / XC / M • Erika Bella: Euroslut / 1995 / EL / M • Hot Body Competition: Hot Pants Contest / 1996 / CG / F • Juliet & Romeo / 1996 / XC / M • Private Gold #12: The Pyramid #2 / 1996 / OD / M • Private Gold #13: The Pyramid #3 / 1996 / OD / M • Private Stories #04 / 1995 / OD / M • Private Stories #06 / 1995 / OD / M • Robin Thief Of Wives / 1996 / XC / M • Virility / 1996 / XC / M

NICOLETTE FALUDI
Private Film #26 / 1995 / OD / M • Private Stories #01 / 1995 / OD / M • Private Video Magazine #25 / 1995 / OD / M • Triple X Video Magazine #01 / 1995 / OD / M • Triple X Video Magazine #02 / 1995 / OD / M • Triple X Video Magazine #05 / 1995 / OD / M

NICOLETTE ORSINI
Amadeus Mozart / 1996 / XC / M

NICOLETTE ROSE *see* Star Index I

NICOLETTE SHA
Photo Opportunity / 1994 / VC / M

NICOLLETTE
Blue Vanities #542 / 1994 / FFL / M

NICOLLINA FOX
Canadian Beaver Hunt #1 / 1996 / PL / M • Canadian Beaver Hunt #2 / 1996 / PL / M • Canadian Beaver Hunt #3 / 1996 / PL / M • Canadian Beaver Hunt #4 / 1996 / PL / M • East Coast Sluts #06: Philadelphia / 1995 / PL / M • East Coast Sluts #07: Tampa Bay / 1995 / PL / M • East Coast Sluts #08: Atlantic City / 1995 / PL / M • Love Doll Lucy #1 / 1994 / PL / F • Love Doll Lucy #2 / 1994 / PL / F • N.Y. Video Magazine #04 / 1995 / OUP / M • Strap-On Sally #07: Face Dildo Frenzy / 1995 / PL / F • Strap-On Sally #08: Strap-On Cock Fight / 1995 / PL / F • Streets Of New York #05 / 1995 / PL / M • Striptease #1 / 1995 / PL / M • Toe Tales #34 / 1996 / GOT / B • Toe Tales #36 / 1996 / GOT / B • Toe Tales #37 / 1996 / GOT / B • Toe Tales #38 / 1996 / GOT / B • Worthless Wives / 1996 / GOT / B

NICYTEEN *see* Nici Sterling

NIGEL EVANS *see* Star Index I

NIGEL GRANT
Great Grandma Gets Her Cookies / 1995 / FC / M

NIGEL WILD *see* E.Z. Ryder

NIGEL WORTHINGTON
American Nympho In London / 1987 / VD / M • The Baroness / 1987 / VD / M • Hard Core Cafe / 1988 / VD / M • Hot Nights And Dirty Days / 1988 / VD / M • International Phone Sex Girls #1 / 1988 / VD / M

NIIJIMA MAYUMI
Virgin Cover Girl / 1996 / AVE / M

NIK DOUGLAS
Ancient Secrets Of Sexual Ecstasy / 1996 / HIG / M

NIK-A-CHOIX
White Men Can't Iron On Butt Row / 1997 / ABS / M

NIKI
Blue Vanities #513 / 1992 / FFL / M • Blue Vanities #559 / 1994 / FFL / M • Depravity On The Danube / 1993 / EL / M

NIKI (ONE K) *see* Tanya Storm

NIKI DARLING *see* Nyrobi Knight

NIKI DICKERS *see* Raven

NIKI KNOCKERS
Between My Breasts #12 / 1990 / BTO / M • Big Bust Strippers #03 / 1991 / BTO / F • Bras And Panties #1 / 199? / H&S / S • Girls Around The World #15 / 1994 / BTO / S

NIKI STEVENS
F / 1980 / GO / M

NIKIE ST. GILES
Zazel / 1996 / CV / M

NIKITA
Bondage "Sybian" Rides / 1994 / PSE / B • Buffy Malibu's Totally Nasty All-Girl Home Videos #02 / 1992 / ANA / F • Dirty Stories #5 / 1996 / PE / M • Mission Hard / 1995 / XC / M • Up And Cummers #14 / 1994 / 4P / M

NIKITA (GROSS) *see* Nikita Gross

NIKITA GROSS *(Nikita (Gross))*
Tall, long hair, blonde, Hungarian, pretty face, large tits, voluptuous body, very nice pussy with closed labia majora and no protruding labia minora.

Angel's Vengeance / 1995 / VMX / M • Bottom Dweller: The Final Voyage / 1996 / EL / M • The Coming Of Nikita / 1995 / EL / M • Jungle Heat / 1995 / LUM / M • Sodomania: Slop Shots / 1996 / EL / C • Thermonuclear Sex / 1996 / EL / M

NIKKI
AVP #1002: Night Dreams With Nikki / 1991 / AVP / M • Backlash / 1992 / GOT / B • Blue Vanities #194 / 1993 / FFL / M • Blue Vanities #195 / 1993 / FFL / M • Bobby Hollander's Maneaters #03 / 1993 / SFP / M • Bobby Hollander's Rookie Nookie #09 / 1993 / SFP / M • Chocolate Bunnies #03 / 1995 / LBO / C • Creme De Femme #3 / 1981 / AVC / C • Dirty Bob's #25: Porn Never Sleeps! / 1996 / FLP / S • Dynasty's Anal Brat Pack / 1996 / OUP / F • English Muffins / 1995 / VC / M • Fashion Sluts #3 / 1995 / ABS / M • Green Piece Of Ass #2 / 1994 / RTP / M • Harry Horndog #10: Love Puppies #1 / 1994 / FPI / F • HomeGrown Video #462: Motion In The Backfield / 1995 / HOV / M • HomeGrown Video #463: Cum And Get It / 1995 / HOV / M • Horny Henry's Swinging Adventures / 1994 / TTV / M • Hot Bi Summer / 1994 / BIL / G • Indiscreet! Video Magazine #2 / 1995 / FH / M • Kitty Kat Club / 1994 / SC / F • Limited Edition #13 / 1980 / AVC / M • Love Bunnies #07 / 1994 / FPI / F • Mr. Peepers Amateur Home Videos #82: Born To Swing! / 1993 / LBO / M • My Cum Is Oozing From Nikki's Pussy / 1995 / RTP / M • Nasty Fuckin' Movies #22 / 1994 / RUM / M • Neighborhood Watch #31: Sticking It To The Neighbors / 1992 / LBO / M • Nikki's Playground / 1995 / GAL / B • Pearl Neck-

lace: Premier Sessions #02 / 1993 / SEE / M • Real Women...Real Fantasies! / 1996 / WSD / F • Reel People #05 / 1994 / PP / M • Rock And Roll Auditions / 1995 / CZV / M • Softouch: Nikki Flashing / 1994 / SOF / F • Southern Belles #6 / 1996 / XPR / M • Triple X Video Magazine #11 / 1995 / OD / M

NIKKI (J.JACKME) *see* Janet Jackme

NIKKI (SOFIA F.) *see* Sofia Ferrari

NIKKI ADAMS *see* Star Index I

NIKKI ALLISON *see* Star Index I

NIKKI ANDERSON
The Blonde / 1980 / VCX / M • Blue Vanities #537 / 1993 / FFL / M • Blue Vanities #586 / 1996 / FFL / M • Prisoner Of Paradise / 1980 / VCX / M

NIKKI ANDERSON (AZ) *see* Nikki Arizona

NIKKI ANDERSSON
Private Gold #13: The Pyramid #3 / 1996 / OD / M • Private Gold #14: Sweet Lady #1 / 1997 / OD / M • Private Gold #15: Sweet Lady #2 / 1997 / OD / M

NIKKI ARIZONA *(Nikki Anderson (AZ))*
Masses of long red curly hair, very white skin, rock solid medium to large tits, a little womanly body-wise, tattoo (looks like a head) on her left belly, marginal face. Supposedly a dancer from Arizona, hence the name. 30 years old in 1995 and de-virginized at 13. Nikki Anderson is from **Butt Hunt #11**.

Anal Health Club Babes / 1995 / EVN / M • Analtown USA #01 / 1995 / NIT / M • Ass Masters (Leisure) #06 / 1995 / LEI / M • Assy Sassy #3 / 1995 / ROB / F • The Best Of East Coast Sluts / 1995 / PL / C • Butt Hunt #11 / 1995 / LEI / M • Butt Sluts #5 / 1995 / ROB / F • Cum Buttered Corn Holes #1 / 1996 / NIT / C • Dirty Stories #3 / 1995 / PE / M • Double D Dykes #20 / 1995 / GO / F • Dream Butt / 1995 / VMX / M • East Coast Sluts #04: New York City / 1995 / PL / M • Fantasies Of Marylin / 1995 / VT / M • Fantasy Inc. / 1995 / CV / M • Fashion Sluts #2 / 1995 / ABS / M • The Hitch-Hiker #13: Highway To Hell / 1995 / VIM / M • Hollywood Amateurs #18 / 1995 / MID / M • Hot Tight Asses #11 / 1995 / TCK / M • Indiscreet! Video Magazine #3 / 1995 / FH / M • Lesbian Climax / 1995 / ROB / F • N.Y. Video Magazine #03 / 1995 / OUP / M • N.Y. Video Magazine #04 / 1995 / OUP / M • New Money / 1995 / ULP / M • Nikki Arizona's Tomboys / 1995 / GAL / M • Odyssey 30 Min: #507: / 1995 / OD / M • The Passion Potion / 1995 / WP / M • Patent Leather / 1995 / CA / M • Perverted Stories #01 / 1995 / JMP / M • Pizzas, Hot Tubs & Bimbos / 1995 / SUF / M • Poop Dreams / 1995 / ULP / M • Pounding Ass / 1995 / VMX / M • Prescription For Lust / 1995 / NIT / M • Pump Fiction / 1995 / VT / M • Pussyman Auditions #07 / 1995 / SNA / M • Rusty Boner's Late Night Videos #1 / 1995 / RHV / M • Shave Tails #4 / 1995 / SO / M • Snatch Masters #11 / 1995 / LEI / M • Sperm Bitches / 1995 / ZA / M • Video Virgins #22 / 1995 / NS / M • The Wanderer #1: Road Tails / 1995 / CDI / M • Wild & Wicked #5 / 1995 / VT / M

NIKKI BLAZE *see* Star Index I

NIKKI BRANTZ *(Nicky Brant)*
Adorable little brunette with reddish hair and white skin. 18 years old in 1995 (August

7th if you want to mail her a card or your right arm), tight body, tight waist, slightly protruding belly in some movies but generally flat and hard, pretty face reminiscent of Brigitte Monet, Italian/Danish ancestry, used to be a manicurist, small firm tits. De-virginized at 16.
Abducted / 1996 / ZA / M • Abused / 1996 / ZA / M • Anal Auditions #2 / 1996 / LE / M • Anal Delinquent #3 / 1995 / ROB / M • Anal Disciples #1 / 1996 / ZA / M • Anal Disciples #2: The Anal Conflict / 1996 / ZA / M • Anal Institution #1 / 1996 / ZA / M • Anal Institution #3 / 1996 / ZA / M • Anal Island #1 / 1996 / VC / M • Anal Island #2 / 1996 / VC / M • Anal Portrait / 1996 / ZA / M • Anal Runaway / 1996 / ZA / M • Anal Sex / 1996 / ZA / M • Anal Tight Ass / 1995 / ROB / M • Anal Trashy Ass / 1995 / ROB / M • Analtown USA #12 / 1996 / NIT / M • Ass Freaks #2 / 1995 / ROB / F • Ass Openers! #2 / 1995 / TCK / C • Babe Wire / 1996 / HW / M • Boot Camp / 1996 / PRE / B • Buffy Malibu's Nasty Girls #10 / 1996 / ANA / F • Butt Sluts #6 / 1996 / ROB / F • Casting Call #17 / 1996 / SO / M • Caught From Behind #21 / 1995 / HO / M • Cherry Poppers #12: Playing Nookie / 1995 / ZA / M • Corn Hole Kittens / 1996 / ROB / F • Corporate Justice / 1996 / TEP / M • Country Girl / 1996 / VC / M • Cum Buttered Corn Holes #3 / 1996 / NIT / C • Cumback Pussy #1 / 1996 / EL / M • Double Anal Alternatives / 1996 / EL / M • The Fanny Farm / 1996 / NIT / M • Fashion Sluts #0 / 1995 / ABS / M • Flipside / 1996 / VI / M • Fuck U: Girls Of The Packed-10 / 1995 / ZA / M • Gangbang Girl #18 / 1996 / ANA / M • Hardcore Confidential #1 / 1996 / TEP / M • Head Shots / 1995 / VI / M • The Hitch-Hiker #16: Dirty Low Down / 1996 / VIM / M • Hot Tight Asses #15 / 1996 / TCK / M • Hot Tight Asses #16 / 1996 / TCK / M • Intense Perversions #2 / 1996 / PL / M • Kittens & Vamps #2 / 1995 / ROB / F • Lesbian C*Nt Whores / 1996 / ROB / F • Lesbian Debutante #03 / 1996 / IP / F • Lesbian Pooper Sluts / 1996 / ROB / F • Malibu Ass Blasters / 1996 / ROB / M • Memories / 1996 / ZA / M • More Dirty Debutantes #47 / 1995 / 4P / M • Muff Divers #2 / 1996 / TV / F • Nasty Nymphos #14 / 1996 / ANA / M • Numba 1 Ass Fucka / 1996 / ROB / M • Nymphos / 1995 / MET / M • Ona Zee's Doll House #3 / 1995 / ONA / F • Puritan Video Magazine #01 / 1996 / LE / M • Pussyman #13: Lips / 1996 / SNA / M • Runaway / 1996 / ZA / M • Sodomania #17: Simply Makes U Tingle / 1996 / EL / M • Sodomania: Slop Shots / 1996 / EL / C • Squirters / 1996 / ULI / M • Sweet Smell Of Excess / 1996 / CIN / M • Tainted Love / 1996 / VC / M • Takin' It To The Limit #8: Hooked On Crack / 1996 / BS / M • Totally Depraved / 1996 / SC / M • Virgin Dreams / 1996 / EA / M • The Voyeur #6 / 1996 / EA / M • Wet Faces #1 / 1997 / SC / C • Young & Natural #09 / 1995 / PRE / C • Young & Natural #10 / 1995 / PRE / F • Young & Natural #11 / 1995 / PRE / F • Young & Natural #12 / 1996 / TV / F • Young Girls Do #1: Troublemakers / 1995 / CDI / M • Young Tails / 1996 / LV / M

NIKKI CHARM
Above And Beyond / 1990 / PNP / G • Adam & Eve's Guide To A G-Spot Orgasm / 1994 / VI / M • All For His Ladies / 1987 / PP / C • Bad Attitude / 1987 / CC / M • Bare Waves / 1986 / VD / M • Beverly Hills Wives / 1985 / CV / M • Cab-O-Lay / 1988 / PL / M • Calender Girls #5: May Flowers / 1986 / VC / C • Campus Cuties / 1986 / CA / M • Charm School / 1986 / VI / M • Charmed Again / 1989 / VI / M • Charmed And Dangerous / 1987 / VI / M • Charmed Forces / 1987 / VI / M • Chastity Johnson / 1985 / AVC / M • Cum Shot Revue #2 / 1985 / HO / C • Daddy's Darling Daughters / 1986 / PL / M • Dressed To Thrill / 1986 / CDI / M • Erotic Penetration / 1987 / HO / C • Flesh In Ecstasy #09: Nikki Charm / 1987 / GO / C • Gimme An X / 1993 / VD / C • Ginger And Spice / 1986 / VI / M • Good Girls Do / 1984 / HO / M • In Charm's Way / 1987 / IN / M • Jacqueline / 1986 / MAP / M • Legends Of Porn #1 / 1987 / CV / C • The Life & Loves Of Nikki Charm / 1986 / MAL / M • Little American Maid / 1987 / VCX / M • Lottery Lust / 1986 / PEN / M • Lucky Charm / 1986 / AVC / C • Lucky In Love #1 / 1985 / BAN / M • Lucky In Love #2 / 1988 / SEV / M • Marina Heat / 1985 / CV / M • Miss Directed / 1990 / VI / M • Mouthwatering / 1986 / BRA / M • Nicki / 1987 / VI / M • Nightfire / 1987 / LA / M • Nikki And The Pom-Pom Girls / 1987 / VEX / M • Only The Best Of Girls With Curves / 1992 / CV / C • Only The Best Of Oral / 1989 / CV / C • Pajama Party / 1993 / CV / C • Princess Charming / 1987 / AVC / C • The Scarlet Mistress / 1990 / VI / M • Sex In Dangerous Places / 1988 / VI / M • Sexual Odyssey / 1985 / VC / M • She's A Good Lust Charm / 1987 / LA / C • Sinful Pleasures / 1987 / HO / C • Smooth Operator / 1986 / AR / M • Soul Kiss This / 1988 / VCR / C • Starved For Affection / 1985 / AVC / M • Strip Search / 1987 / SEV / M • Swedish Erotica #67 / 1985 / CA / M • Swedish Erotica #68 / 1985 / CA / M • Swedish Erotica #69 / 1985 / CA / M • Talk Dirty To Me One More Time #1 / 1985 / PP / C • A Taste Of Nikki Charm / 1989 / PIN / C • Taste Of The Best #1 / 1988 / PIN / C • Touched / 1990 / VI / M • Traci Who? / 1987 / AVC / C • Triple Dare / 1989 / VC / C • Triple Xposure / 1986 / VD / M • Visions Of Jeannie / 1986 / VD / M • Walk On The Wild Side / 1987 / CDI / M • What Kind Of Girls Do You Think We Are? / 1986 / VEX / M • What Kind of Girls Do You Think We Are? / 1991 / VEX / C • The Wild And The Innocent / 1990 / CC / M • Wild Things #2 / 1986 / CV / M • X-TV #1 / 1986 / PL / C • Young And Naughty / 1984 / HO / M

NIKKI CHERRY *(Nicki Cherry, Pink Rio, Tabatha Paris)*
The Big E #08 / 1988 / BIZ / B • Crackdown / 1988 / BIZ / B • Cramped Spaces / 1989 / PLV / B • Dirty Dr. Feelgood / 1988 / VEX / M • Foot Teasers / 1988 / BIZ / B • Full Metal Bikini / 1988 / PEN / M • The Girls Of Ball Street / 1988 / VEX / M • On The Make / 1988 / V99 / M • Rip Off #1 / 1988 / BIZ / B • Rip Off #2 / 1988 / PLV / B • Rollover & Cell Blocks / 1988 / PLV / B • Steam Heat / 1989 / VEX / M • Wet Kisses / 1988 / V99 / M

NIKKI DARE *see Star Index I*
NIKKI DARLING *see Nyrobi Knight*
NIKKI DEE *see Nikki Knights*
NIKKI DIAL *(Nicole Greiner, Nicole*

Greiner)
Very tight body except for her large droopy tits, big eyes, very pretty face, nice smile, nice butt. Was 18 in 1992 and used to work in a B&D parlor. She was supposed to have left the business in mid to late 1993 to go back to college. There is a rumor that she is the same as Candice Bottoms.
American Built / 1992 / LE / M • Anonymous / 1993 / VI / M • Battle Of The Porno Queens / 1994 / NAP / B • Big Bust Casting Call / 1993 / PME / S • Bonnie & Clyde #1 / 1992 / VI / M • Bonnie & Clyde #2 / 1992 / VI / M • Brats In Bondage / 1993 / LON / B • Breast Wishes #07 / 1992 / LBO / M • Breast Worx #33 / 1992 / LBO / M • Bubble Butts #07 / 1992 / LBO / M • Bubble Butts #11 / 1992 / LBO / M • Clit Cleaners / 1994 / CA / C • Confessions #2 / 1992 / OD / M • Deep Inside Crystal Wilder / 1995 / VC / C • Deep Inside Nikki Dial / 1994 / VC / C • Deep Inside Tyffany Million / 1995 / VC / C • Designer Bodies / 1993 / VI / M • Dial N Again / 1993 / PEP / M • Dial N For Nikki / 1993 / PEP / M • Elvis Slept Here / 1992 / LE / M • Endlessly / 1993 / VI / M • The Fine Art Of Hairpulling / 1993 / NAP / B • Hard To Stop #1 / 1992 / VC / M • Hard To Stop #2 / 1992 / VC / M • Hard Whips For Soft Bodies / 1993 / NTP / B • Hardcore / 1994 / VI / M • Hopeless Romantic / 1992 / LE / M • House Of Correction / 1991 / HOM / B • Intimate Secrets / 1993 / PME / F • Latent Image: Nikki Dial / 1993 / LAT / F • Legacy Of Love / 1992 / LE / M • Legend #4: Critic's Choice / 1992 / LE / M • A Lover's Guide To Sexual Ecstasy / 1992 / PME / S • Mistress Of Hair Pulling / 1993 / NAP / B • More Dirty Debutantes #23 / 1993 / 4P / M • Mr. Peepers Amateur Home Videos #50: All That Glitters / 1992 / LBO / M • New Wave Hookers #3 / 1993 / VC / M • Nikki At Night / 1993 / LE / M • Nikki Never Says No / 1992 / LE / M • Nikki's Bon Voyage / 1993 / VC / M • Nikki's Last Stand / 1993 / VC / M • Nikki's Nightlife / 1992 / IN / M • Odyssey Triple Play #15: Cumming Together / 1992 / OD / M • Out Of The Blue #2 / 1992 / VI / M • Penthouse: 1993 Pet Of The Year Winners / 1993 / PET / F • Positively Pagan #06 / 1993 / ATA / M • Punishment Of Ashley Renee / 1993 / BON / B • Queen Of The Lash / 1993 / LON / B • Radical Affairs Video Magazine #01 / 1992 / ME / M • Rump Humpers #01 / 1992 / GLI / M • Rump Humpers #02 / 1992 / GLI / M • Sex #1 (Vivid) / 1993 / VI / M • Sex #2 (Vivid) / 1993 / VI / M • Shades Of Blue / 1992 / VC / M • Sodom & Gomorrah / 1992 / OD / M • Sorority Pink #3 / 1992 / SP / M • Southern: Nikki Dial / 1992 / SSH / F • Southern: Previews #2 / 1992 / SSH / C • Starlet / 1994 / VI / M • Surprise!!! / 1994 / VI / M • Things Change / 1992 / MET / M • Things Change #1: My First Time / 1992 / CV / M • Things Change #2: Letting Go / 1992 / CV / M • The Tower Of Lyndon / 1994 / LON / B • Vampire's Kiss / 1993 / AVI / M • The Way They Wuz / 1996 / SHS / C • White Men Can't Hump / 1992 / CC / M • Wild Flower #1 / 1992 / VI / M

NIKKI DOLL
Alex Jordan's First Timers #03 / 1993 / OD / M • America's Raunchiest Home Videos #66: / 1993 / ZA / M • Anal House Party /

1993 / IP / M • The Cumm. Brothers #01 / 1993 / OD / M • The Gang Bang Story / 1993 / IP / M • Mr. Peepers Amateur Home Videos #69: Love Tunnel / 1993 / LBO / M • Mr. Peepers Amateur Home Videos #71: I Dream Of Creamy / 1993 / LBO / M • Mr. Peepers Nastiest #2 / 1995 / LBO / C • SVE: Screentest Sex #4 / 1993 / SVE / M

NIKKI ENG
The Burma Road #1 / 1994 / LBO / C • The Burma Road #2 / 1994 / LBO / C

NIKKI FRAME
Nicole's Revenge / 1995 / MID / F

NIKKI HILTON *see Star Index I*

NIKKI HORN
Blue Vanities #030 / 1988 / FFL / M • Blue Vanities #534 / 1993 / FFL / M

NIKKI KENNEDY
The Wild Women / 1996 / PL / M

NIKKI KING *(Madina, Nejla, Medine, Arabian Treasure Cht)*
Fat and ugly.
10 Years Of Big Busts #1 / 1989 / BTO / C • The Arabian Treasure Chest / 1987 / L&W / C • Between My Breasts #01 / 1986 / BTO / S • Between My Breasts #07 / 1989 / L&W / M • Big Bust Babes #04 / 1988 / AFI / M • Big Busty #18 / 198? / H&S / M • Big Busty #21 / 198? / H&S / M • Big Tit Hookers / 1989 / BTO / M • Big Tit Orgy #01 / 1987 / H&S / M • Big Tit Orgy #03 / 1991 / BTO / C • Big Top Cabaret #1 / 1986 / BTO / M • Big Top Cabaret #2 / 1989 / BTO / M • Black Dreams / 1988 / CDI / M • Breast Of Britain #2 / 1987 / BTO / M • Bright Lights, Big Titties / 1989 / CA / M • Bun Runners / 1994 / PRE / B • Candy's Back / 199? / H&S / M • End Around / 1994 / PRE / B • The End Zone / 1993 / PRE / B • Girls Of The Double D #03 / 1988 / CDI / M • Girls Of The Double D #13 / 1990 / CDI / M • Leg...Ends #12 / 1994 / PRE / F • Much More Than A Mouthful #1 / 1987 / VEX / M • Red Bottoms / 1988 / BIZ / B • Rippin' 'n' Strippin' #1 / 1987 / BON / B • Rippin' 'n' Strippin' #2 / 1988 / BON / B • Rollover & Cell Blocks / 1988 / PLV / B • Sorority Bound / 1988 / BON / B • Supersluts Of Wrestling / 1986 / VD / M • Tit Tales #1 / 1989 / 4P / M • Toys, Not Boys #3 / 1991 / FC / C

NIKKI KNIGHTS *(Nicky Knight, Nikki Dee, Jodi Dee, Jodi (Nikki Knights), Nicky Dee, Nicki Dee, Nikki Nights, Nikki Nites)*
10 1/2 Weeks / 1986 / SE / M • All Night Long / 1990 / NWV / C • Amanda By Night #2 / 1987 / CA / M • American Dream Girls #1 / 1986 / VEX / M • Anal Angels #2 / 1990 / VEX / C • Anal Annie And The Magic Dildo / 1984 / LIP / F • Anal Intruder #02 / 1988 / CC / M • Angel's Gotta Have It / 1988 / FAN / M • Army Brat #1 / 1987 / VI / M • As Nasty As She Wants To Be / 1990 / IN / M • At The Pornies / 1989 / VC / M • Babes / 1991 / CIN / M • Babylon Pink #2 / 1988 / COM / M • Babylon Pink #3 / 1988 / COM / M • Barbara The Barbarian / 1987 / SE / M • Bare Essence / 1989 / EA / M • Beach Blanket Brat / 1989 / VI / M • Beauty And The Beast #1 / 1988 / VC / M • Beeches / 1990 / KIS / M • Behind The Scenes With Angela Baron / 1988 / FAZ / C • Bend Over Babes #1 / 1990 / EA / M • The Best Of Anal Annie: The Girl-Girl Adventures / 1993 / LIP / C • Between A Rock And A Hot Place

/ 1989 / VEX / M • The Big Bang / 1988 / WET / M • Black Bimbos In Heat / 1989 / MIR / C • Black Dreams / 1988 / CDI / M • Black Magic / 1986 / DR / M • Black Magic Sex Clinic / 1987 / DOX / M • Blue Fire / 1991 / V99 / M • Body Games / 1987 / DR / M • Boom Boom Valdez / 1988 / CA / M • Brat On The Run / 1987 / VI / M • Bringing Up Brat / 1987 / VI / M • Built For Sex (Angela Baron's) / 1988 / FAZ / C • California Blondes #01 / 1986 / VEX / M • The Call Girl / 1986 / VD / M • Call Girl Academy / 1990 / V99 / M • Captain Hooker & Peter Porn / 1987 / VD / M • Cat On A Hot Sin Roof / 1989 / LV / M • The Catwoman / 1988 / VC / M • Club Sex / 1989 / GO / M • Conflict / 1988 / VD / M • Corporate Affairs / 1986 / SE / M • Cream Dreams / 1986 / VEX / M • Dark Desires / 1989 / BMV / C • Deep In The Bush / 1990 / KIS / M • Deep Inside Samantha Strong / 1992 / CDI / C • Delicate Matters / 1989 / VEX / M • Deviled X / 1987 / 4P / M • Dirty Movies / 1989 / VD / M • Double Dare / 1986 / SE / M • Dream Dates / 1990 / V99 / M • Dream Lovers / 1987 / CA / M • Dreams Of Natasha / 1985 / AAH / M • Executive Suites / 1990 / VEX / M • Fantasy Land / 1984 / LA / M • Fatal Passion / 1988 / CC / M • The Final Taboo / 1988 / CA / M • Fireball / 1988 / IN / M • Flesh For Frankenstein / 1987 / VEX / M • Friday The 13th #1: A Nude Beginning / 1987 / VD / M • Full Nest / 1992 / WV / C • Getting Off On Broadway / 1989 / IN / M • Ginger Snaps / 1987 / VI / M • Girlworld #1 / 1987 / LIP / F • Girlworld #2 / 1988 / LIP / F • Good Vibrations / 1991 / PM / M • Grind / 1988 / CV / M • A Hard Act To Swallow / 1988 / VT / M • Hard At Work / 1989 / VEX / M • HHHHot! TV #1 / 1988 / CDI / M • Hitler Sucks / 1988 / GO / M • Hollywood Knights #3 / 1991 / PCP / M • The Hot Box Invasion / 1987 / AMB / M • Hot Fudge / 1984 / VC / M • The Hot Lunch Club / 1985 / WV / M • Hot Number / 1987 / WET / M • How To Get A "Head" / 1988 / CV / M • The Huntress / 1987 / IN / M • I Cream Of Genie / 1988 / SE / M • I Found My Thrill On Cheri Hill / 1988 / PL / M • Jamie Loves Jeff #1 / 1987 / VI / M • Joanna's Dreams / 1988 / SEV / M • Just For The Thrill Of It / 1989 / V99 / M • Keep It Cumming / 1990 / V99 / M • Krazy 4 You / 1987 / 4P / M • Lesbian Lingerie Fantasy #1 / 1988 / ESP / F • Let's Get Wet / 1987 / WV / M • Liquid Love / 1988 / CA / M • Little Shop Of Whores / 1987 / VI / M • The Load Warriors #2 / 1987 / VD / M • Lost Lovers / 1990 / VEX / M • Lust Connection / 1988 / VT / M • Mad About You / 1987 / VC / M • Makeout / 1988 / VT / M • Mammary Lane / 1988 / VT / C • Matched Pairs / 1988 / VEX / M • Midnight Fantasies / 1989 / VEX / M • Moonglow / 1989 / IN / M • Motel Sweets / 1987 / VD / M • A Natural Woman / 1989 / IN / M • Naughty Nurses / 1992 / VD / C • Naughty Nymphs / 1986 / VEX / M • Naughty Nymphs / 1991 / VEX / C • Night On The Town / 1990 / V99 / M • Nina Does 'em All / 1988 / 3HV / C • No Man's Land #01 / 1988 / VT / C • On The Loose & Hot To Trot / 1987 / CA / M • Once Upon A Temptress / 1988 / CA / M • One For The Road / 1989 / V99 / M • One More Time / 1990 / VEX / M • Out Of Control / 1987 / SE / M • Outlaw Ladies #2 / 1988 / VC / M • Outrageous

Foreplay / 1987 / WV / M • Parliament: Samantha Strong #1 / 1986 / PM / M • Passion Chain / 1987 / ZA / M • Peeping Passions / 1989 / CAE / M • Phantom X / 1989 / VC / M • Phone Sex Girls #2 / 1987 / VT / M • Platinum Princess / 1988 / VEX / M • Playing Dirty / 1989 / VEX / M • Playing The Field / 1990 / VEX / M • The Pleasure Game / 1988 / CA / M • Pleasure Principle / 1988 / VEX / M • Prince Of Beverly Hills #1 / 1987 / VEX / M • Purple Haze / 1991 / WV / M • Queen Of Hearts #1 / 1987 / PL / M • Rachel Ryan / 1988 / WV / C • Rachel Ryan Exposed / 1990 / WV / C • Raising Hell / 1987 / VD / M • Rubber Reamed Fuckholes / 1994 / MET / C • Sea Of Lust / 1990 / FAN / M • Secret Cravings / 1989 / V99 / M • Secret Dreams / 1991 / VEX / M • Sex Kittens / 1990 / VEX / F • Sex Lives Of The Rich And Famous #2 / 1989 / VC / M • Sex Pistol / 1990 / CDI / M • Sex Slaves / 1986 / VEX / M • Sextrology / 1987 / CA / M • She's America's Most Wanted / 1990 / VEX / M • She's So Fine #2 / 1988 / VC / M • Sinset Boulevard / 1987 / WV / M • Soul Games / 1988 / PV / C • Space Cadet / 1989 / IN / M • St. X-Where #2 / 1988 / VD / M • Star 88: Dana Lynn / 1988 / VEX / C • Swedish Erotica Featurettes #5 / 1990 / CA / M • Sweet Things / 1987 / VC / M • Tales Of The Uncensored / 1987 / FAN / M • Talk Dirty To Me #05 / 1987 / DR / M • Tell Me Something Dirty / 1991 / NWV / M • Trampire / 1987 / FAN / M • Unveiled / 1987 / VC / M • VCA Previews #4 / 1988 / VC / C • Videobone / 1988 / WET / M • Virgin Busters / 1989 / LV / M • Vixens / 1989 / LV / F • Wet Panties / 1989 / MIR / C • Where There's Smoke There's Fire / 1987 / FAN / M • The Wild Brat / 1988 / VI / M • Wild Stuff / 1987 / WET / M • Wildheart / 1989 / IN / M • Wrecked 'em / 1985 / CC / M • XXX Workout / 1987 / VEX / M • You Bring Out The Animal In Me / 1987 / MIR / M

NIKKI KNOX
Serviced With A Smile / 1985 / VD / M

NIKKI LAKE
Anal Camera #01 / 1994 / EVN / M

NIKKI LEE
Sinboy #4: Bareass Barbecue / 1996 / SC / M

NIKKI LEE (JORDAN) *see* **Jordan Lee**

NIKKI LIPS
Almost Home Alone / 1993 / SFP / M • Bi-Bi Love Amateurs #1 / 1993 / SFP / G

NIKKI MASTERS *see Star Index I*

NIKKI NIGHTS *see* **Nikki Knights**

NIKKI NITES *see* **Nikki Knights**

NIKKI NORMAN *see* **Nici Sterling**

NIKKI NYCE
Cumback Pussy #7: NUGIRLZ / 1997 / EL / M • Puritan Video Magazine #10 / 1997 / LE / M

NIKKI PEARCE *see Star Index I*

NIKKI PINK *(Pinky Rio, Cherry (Nikki Pink), Valentina (N. Pink), Niccki Pink)*
All For One / 1988 / CIN / M • My Wife Is A Call Girl / 1989 / FAZ / M • Porn Star's Day Off / 1990 / FAZ / M • Salsa Break / 1989 / EA / M • Three Men And A Barbi / 1989 / FAN / M • Very Sexy Ballet / 1988 / CA / M • Wet Dream On Maple Street / 1988 / FAN / M

NIKKI PRINCE
Prime Choice #1 / 1995 / RAS / M • The

Wild Wild Chest #3 / 1996 / HO / C

NIKKI PRINCE (TIARRA see Tiarra

NIKKI PRINCE (WEST) see Tiara West

NIKKI RANDALL *(Rachal Free, Nicola Baxter, Nicky Randall, Carol Frazier)*
Very pretty tight bodied brunette (a couple of movies she was blonde which didn't suit her) who, unfortunately, didn't seem to have a great personality. Either Janet Wheeler or Beverly (Woman/Loman/Homan) in **L'Amour**, Rachal Free in **Girls Just Want To Have Fun**, Nicola Baxter in **I Wanna Be Teased**. According to *Raw Talent* (the book) her real name is Carol... Not in **Pacific Intrigue**, **Transaction**, **Showdown**, nor **Black Analist** (despite credits). **Woman Of Frankenstein** does not exist. May also be in **Triple Tease**. Not in **Sexual Odyssey**. Returned after a hiatus of a few years for **John Wayne Bobbitt Uncut** with large enhanced tits. Carol Frazier is from **Keisha**.
Around The World With Samantha Strong / 1989 / V99 / M • As Cute As They Cum / 1990 / VEX / M • The Beat Goes On / 1987 / VCR / C • Bedside Brat / 1988 / VI / M • Best Of Bruce Seven #1 / 1990 / BIZ / C • Beverly Hills Copulator / 1986 / ... / M • Big Bust Babes #04 / 1988 / AFI / M • Big Titted Tarts / 1994 / PL / C • Black Sensations / 1987 / VEX / M • Black Widow / 1988 / WV / M • Bloopers & Behind The Scenes / 1995 / LEI / M • Bondage Interludes #1 / 1983 / BIZ / B • Bondage Interludes #2 / 1983 / BIZ / B • Bottoms Up #05 / 1986 / AVC / C • Broadway Brat / 1988 / VI / M • Candy's Custom Car Wash / 1995 / FC / M • Club Exotica #1 / 1985 / WV / M • Club Exotica #2 / 1985 / WV / M • Coming Alive / 1988 / LV / M • Dynamite Brat / 1995 / LV / M • Ebony Humpers #4 / 1988 / VEX / M • Erotic Dreams / 1990 / CEL / S • Europe On Two Guys A Day / 1987 / PV / M • Fast Girls #2 / 1988 / DIS / M • Female Aggressors / 1986 / LAV / M • Girl Toys / 1986 / DR / M • Girls Just Want To...Have Fun / 1984 / SE / M • The Girls Of Porn / 1989 / FRV / F • Heat Of The Nite / 1988 / VEX / M • Heatwaves / 1987 / LAV / G • Home Bodies / 1988 / VEX / M • Hot Summer Nites / 1988 / VEX / M • I Wanna Be Teased / 1984 / SE / M • I'm No Brat / 1990 / FAZ / M • In All The Right Places / 1986 / VD / M • Innocence Lost / 1987 / CAT / G • Jailhouse Nurses / 1995 / SC / M • Jane Bond Meets Thunderthighs / 1988 / VD / M • John Wayne Bobbitt Uncut / 1994 / LEI / M • Just Between Friends / 1988 / VEX / M • Just The Two Of Us / 1985 / WV / M • Keisha / 1987 / VD / M • Kiss Thy Mistress' Feet #2 / 1990 / BIZ / B • L'Amour / 1984 / CA / M • A Lady / 1995 / FD / M • Loose Ends #3 / 1987 / BS / M • Lucky In Love #2 / 1988 / SEV / M • The Mile High Club / 1995 / PL / M • Moonstroked / 1988 / 3HV / M • Nothing Like A Dame #1 / 1995 / IN / M • On Her Back / 1994 / VI / M • On The Make / 1988 / V99 / M • Only In Your Dreams / 1988 / VEX / M • Only The Best Of Peepers / 1992 / CV / C • Overexposed / 1988 / VEX / M • Passion By Fire / 1986 / LAV / G • Personal Touch #3 / 1983 / AR / M • Perverted Women / 1995 / SC / M • Pink To Pink / 1993 / VI / C • Reality & Fantasy / 1994 / DR / M • Reflections / 1995 / FD / M • Rocky-X #1 / 1986 / PEN / M •

Romeo And Juliet #2 / 1988 / WV / M • Sapphire / 1995 / ERA / M • Sensual Spirits / 1995 / LE / M • Sex Machine / 1986 / LA / M • Sexline You're On The Air / 1986 / CAT / M • Sluthunt #1 / 1995 / BIP / F • Soft Caresses / 1988 / VEX / M • Some Like It Hard / 1995 / VC / M • St. X-Where #1 / 1986 / VD / M • Star Spangled Banner / 1990 / FAZ / M • Steam Heat / 1989 / VEX / M • Still The Brat / 1988 / VI / M • Strip Search / 1987 / SEV / M • Talk Dirty To Me #04 / 1986 / DR / M • A Taste Of Ariel / 1989 / PIN / C • A Taste Of Black / 1987 / WET / M • A Taste Of White / 1987 / WET / M • Teasin' & Pleasin' / 1988 / LBO / F • Timepiece / 1994 / CV / M • Transitory States / 1989 / STA / G • The Ultimate Lover / 1986 / VD / M • Unmistakably You / 1995 / CV / M • Unnatural Act #2 / 1986 / DR / M • Wacked Waitresses / 1986 / CS / B • Weird Fantasy / 1986 / LA / M • Wet And Wild #1 / 1986 / VEX / M • Wild In The Woods / 1988 / VEX / M • The Woman Who Loved Men / 1984 / SE / M • X-Rated Bloopers #2 / 1986 / AR / M

NIKKI SATIN see Star Index I

NIKKI SCOTT
Perverted Stories #10 / 1996 / JMP / M

NIKKI SHANE *(Shane (Nikki))*
Sleazy looking blonde with a small body and small tits (in original movies); 5'6" tall, 117lbs, 34C-24-34 (after enhancement), plus a nasty Caesarian scar across her lower belly which she manages to keep covered most of the time. You can see it in the **Harry Horndog** segment. Born June 23, 1967. Has a tattoo that looks like a bunch of grapes on her back at shoulder level. In **Steady As She Blows** (about September 1993) she appears with new enhanced tits (medium sized—not too bad).
Anal Intruder #08: Rich Girls Gone Bad / 1993 / CC / M • Asian Persuasion / 1993 / WV / M • Asian Tigress / 1994 / NAP / B • Attitude Adjustment / 1993 / BS / B • Babe Patrol / 1993 / FOR / M • Babewatch #1 / 1993 / CC / M • Battlestar Orgasmica / 1992 / EVN / M • The Beverly Thrillbillies / 1993 / ZA / M • Big Murray's New-Cummers #06: Men & Women / 1993 / FD / M • The Bitches / 1993 / LIP / F • Blind Innocence / 1993 / BS / B • The Blonde & The Beautiful #1 / 1993 / LV / M • Blow Job Blvd #1 / 1993 / SC / M • Bobby Hollander's Maneaters #07 / 1993 / SFP / M • Bobby Hollander's Maneaters #08 / 1993 / SFP / M • Body Language / 1995 / VI / M • The Bottom Dweller / 1993 / EL / M • Breastman Does The Twin Towers / 1993 / EVN / M • Bringing Up The Rear / 1993 / VD / C • Bruce Seven: A Compendium Of His Most Graphic Scenes Vol 5 / 1994 / BS / C • Bubble Butts #23 / 1992 / LBO / M • Butt Bongo Babes / 1993 / VD / M • Butt's Up, Doc #4 / 1994 / GO / M • Buttslammers #01 / 1993 / BS / F • Buttslammers #04: Down And Dirty / 1993 / BS / F • Caught & Bound / 1993 / BON / B • Caught In The Act / 1993 / BS / B • Centerfold Celebrities '94 #1 / 1994 / SFP / M • Cheap Shots / 1994 / PRE / B • Chug-A-Lug Girls #3 / 1993 / VT / M • The Coven #1 / 1993 / VI / M • The Coven #2 / 1993 / VI / M • Deep Inside Kaitlyn Ashley / 1995 / VC / C • Designs On Women / 1994 / IN / F • Diary Of A Porn Star / 1993 / FOR / M • Fantasy Escorts /

1993 / FOR / M • Felecia's Folly / 1993 / BS / B • Flashback / 1993 / SC / M • The Fluffer #1 / 1993 / FD / M • The Fluffer #2 / 1993 / FD / M • Foot Hold / 1994 / PRE / B • Forbidden Obsessions / 1993 / BS / B • The French Invasion / 1993 / LBO / M • The Fury / 1993 / WIV / M • A Girl's Affair #04 / 1994 / FD / F • Girls Will Be Boys #6 / 1993 / PL / F • Harlots / 1993 / MID / M • Harry Horndog #04: Amateur Anal Orgies #1 / 1992 / ZA / M • Harry Horndog #14: Love Puppies #3 / 1992 / ZA / M • Hollywood Swingers #08 / 1993 / LBO / M • How To Deep Throat Your Lover / 1994 / A&E / M • The Hunger / 1993 / FOR / M • The Hustlers / 1993 / MID / M • I Married An Anal Queen / 1993 / MID / M • Intimate Spys / 1992 / FOR / M • L.A. Topless / 1994 / LE / M • The Last Anal Hero / 1993 / OD / M • Lesbian Dating Game / 1993 / LIP / F • Love Letters #1 / 1993 / SC / M • Love Letters #2 / 1993 / SC / M • Mainstream / 1993 / PRE / B • Midnight Angels #01 / 1993 / MID / F • Midnight Angels #02 / 1993 / MID / F • Mike Hott: #246 Cunt of the Month: Nikki 8-93 / 1993 / MHV / M • Mind Shadows #1 / 1993 / FD / M • Mind Shadows #2 / 1993 / FD / M • Molly B-Goode / 1994 / FH / M • Mr. Peepers Amateur Home Videos #71: I Dream Of Creamy / 1993 / LBO / M • Mr. Peepers Amateur Home Videos #74: C Foam Surfer / 1993 / LBO / M • My Way / 1993 / CA / M • Neighborhood Watch #39: / 1993 / LBO / M • Nikki's Bon Voyage / 1993 / VC / M • Nookie Of The Year / 1993 / HW / M • On The Come Line / 1993 / MID / M • The One And Only / 1993 / FD / M • Painful Pleasures / 1993 / BS / B • Princess Of Thieves / 1994 / SC / M • Private Stuff / 1994 / FD / M • Sexophrenia / 1993 / VC / M • Sexual Trilogy #03 / 1994 / SFP / M • Seymore Butts Swings / 1992 / FH / M • Ski Bunnies #1 / 1994 / HW / M • Skin To Skin / 1993 / LE / M • Sluts In Slavery / 1995 / LBO / B • Smokin' Buns / 1993 / PRE / B • Sodomania #06: Gangs And Bangs And Other Thangs / 1993 / EL / M • Spin For Sex / 1994 / IN / M • Steady As She Blows / 1993 / LV / M • Student Fetish Videos: Best of Enema #03 / 1994 / PRE / C • Stylin' / 1994 / FD / M • Superstar Sex Challenge #1 / 1994 / VC / M • Superstar Sex Challenge #2 / 1994 / VC / M • Swallow / 1994 / VI / M • Take The A Train / 1993 / MID / M • The Teacher's Pet / 1993 / LV / M • Trailer Trash / 1994 / VC / M • Trashy Ladies / 1993 / LIP / F • Two Of A Kind / 1993 / PL / M • Used And Abused #1 / 1994 / SFP / M • Welcome To Bondage: Nikki / 1993 / BON / B • Welcome To Bondage: Starlets #2 / 1994 / BON / C • Wendy Whoppers: Bomb Squad / 1993 / PEP / M • Wet Faces #1 / 1997 / SC / C • Whacked! / 1993 / BS / B • Working Stiffs / 1993 / FD / M

NIKKI SINN *(Laura Zrake, Kamisha (Nikki Sinn))*
Brunette with a hook nose and a large tattoo on her left breast. She is one who has seemingly inverted the function of ass and cunt. She was 25 in 1993 and was born in Des Moines, Iowa and grew up in the circus. Has been in jail on a drug charge. In late 1993 / early 1994 she had her nose fixed and some work on her tits. De-virginized at the age of 15. As of 1994 she is 36D-26-36,

5'3" tall and 127lbs.
3 Mistresses Of The Chateau / 1995 / STM / B • Addicted To Lust / 1996 / NIT / M • All "A" / 1994 / SFP / C • Altered Paradise / 1995 / LE / M • Anal Alley / 1996 / FD / M • Anal Alley Cat / 1996 / KWP / M • Anal Angels #4 / 1995 / VEX / C • Anal Arsenal / 1994 / OD / M • Anal Attitude / 1993 / HO / M • Anal Blues / 1994 / PEP / M • Anal Delights #2 / 1992 / ROB / M • Anal Encounters #4: Tales From The Crack / 1992 / VC / M • Anal Encounters #7: Enter Through The Rear / 1992 / VC / M • Anal Encounters #8 / 1992 / VC / M • Anal Fury / 1992 / ROB / M • Anal Intruder #09: The Butt From Another Planet / 1995 / CC / M • Anal Shame / 1995 / VD / M • Anal Takeover / 1993 / PEP / M • Anal Thrills / 1992 / ROB / M • Anal Woman #3 / 1995 / PL / M • Anally Insatiable / 1995 / KWP / M • Ass Busters / 1995 / VMX / C • Ass Freaks #2 / 1995 / ROB / F • Ass Openers! #1 / 1995 / TCK / C • Assmania!! #1 / 1994 / ME / M • Babes Illustrated #3 / 1995 / IN / F • Badlands #1 / 1994 / PEP / M • Badlands #2: Back Into Hell / 1994 / PEP / M • Bareback / 1996 / LE / M • The Bashful Blonde From Beautiful Bendover / 1993 / PEP / M • Behind The Backdoor #5 / 1992 / EVN / M • Behind The Backdoor #6 / 1993 / EVN / M • Behind The Brown Door / 1994 / PE / M • The Best Of Both Worlds #2 / 1986 / MID / G • The Best Of Hot Heels / 1992 / BIZ / B • The Best Of Strippers Inc / 1996 / ONA / C • Betty & Juice Possessed / 1995 / CA / M • Bianca Trump's Towers / 1992 / LV / M • Big Bust Babes #30 / 1995 / AFI / M • Big Bust Babes #38 / 1996 / AFI / M • The Big Shave / 1993 / PEP / M • Big Tit Racket / 1995 / PEP / M • Big Town / 1993 / PP / M • Black Flava / 1994 / EX / M • Blackbroad Jungle / 1994 / IN / M • Blackdoor Babes / 1994 / TIW / M • The Blowjob Adventures Of Doctor Fellatio / 1997 / EL / M • Bobby Hollander's Maneaters #11 / 1994 / SFP / M • The Booty Guard / 1993 / IP / M • Bossy Babes / 1993 / TCK / M • The Bottom Dweller Part Deux / 1994 / EL / M • Boudoir Babe / 1996 / VMX / M • Breastman's Anal Adventure / 1993 / EVN / M • Breastman's Wet T-Shirt Contest / 1994 / EVN / M • Bubble Butts #02 / 1992 / LBO / M • Bubble Butts #05 / 1992 / LBO / M • Buffy's New Boobs / 1996 / CIN / M • Bunz-Eye / 1992 / ROB / M • Butt Alley / 1995 / VMX / M • Butt Bandits #4 / 1996 / VD / C • Butt Busters / 1995 / EX / M • The Butt Connection / 1993 / TIW / M • Butt Darling / 1994 / WIV / M • Butt Hole Boulevard / 1993 / CA / M • The Butt Sisters Do Chicago / 1995 / MID / M • Butt's Motel #6 / 1994 / EX / M • Butthead & Beaver / 1993 / HW / M • Butthead Dreams: Mission Impenetrable / 1994 / FH / M • The Buttnicks #4: The Black Buttnicks / 1993 / CC / M • Butts Up / 1994 / CA / M • The Cable Girl / 1996 / NIT / M • Caged Beauty / 1994 / FD / M • California Covet / 1995 / CA / M • Careless / 1993 / PP / M • Carnal Country / 1996 / NIT / M • Carnival Of Flesh / 1996 / NIT / M • Casanova #3 / 1993 / SC / M • Cat Fight / 1992 / ONH / M • Caught From Behind #18 / 1993 / HO / M • Centerfold Celebrities '94 #1 / 1994 / SFP / M • Chain Gang / 1994 / OD / G • Chateau Duval / 1996 / HDE / M • Cheap Shots / 1994 /

PRE / B • Cheerleader Nurses #1 / 1993 / VC / M • Cheerleader Nurses #2 / 1993 / VC / M • Chinatown / 1994 / SC / M • Cliff Banger / 1993 / HW / M • Climax 2000 #1 / 1994 / CC / M • Climax 2000 #2 / 1994 / CC / M • Club Anal #3 / 1995 / ROB / F • Club Decca / 1996 / BAC / F • Cold As Ice / 1994 / IN / M • Colossal Orgy #1 / 1993 / HW / M • Colossal Orgy #2 / 1994 / HW / M • Coming Out / 1993 / VD / M • Coming Out Bi / 1995 / IN / G • Confessions Of A Slutty Nurse / 1994 / VIM / M • Corporate Justice / 1996 / TEP / M • Cum Buttered Corn Holes #3 / 1996 / NIT / C • Dance Naked / 1995 / PEP / M • Dark Dreams / 1992 / WV / M • Deep Inside Nikki Sinn / 1996 / VC / C • Deep Seven / 1996 / VC / M • Deja Vu / 1993 / XCI / M • The Desert Cafe / 1996 / NIT / M • Designer Bodies / 1993 / VI / M • Designs On Women / 1994 / IN / F • The Deviant Doctor / 1996 / NS / M • Devil In A Wet T-Shirt / 1995 / SPI / M • Dick & Jane Do The Strip / 1994 / AVI / M • Dick & Jane Go To Hollywood #1 / 1993 / AVI / M • Ding Dung School / 1994 / PLV / B • Dirty Bob's #27: Laid Back In L.A.! / 1996 / FLP / S • Dirty Little Ass Slut / 1995 / KWP / M • Diva / 1993 / XCI / M • Dominique's Bi Adventure / 1995 / STA / G • Double D Dykes #17 / 1995 / GO / F • Double D Dykes #19 / 1995 / GO / F • Double D Dykes #20 / 1995 / GO / F • Double D Dykes #21 / 1995 / GO / F • Double D Housewives / 1994 / PV / M • Double Load #2 / 1994 / HW / M • The Dragon Lady #7: Tales From The Bed #6 / 1994 / WV / M • Dragon Lady / 1995 / SP0 / G • Dream House / 1995 / XPR / M • Dreams Of A Gigolo / 1996 / SNA / M • Ebony Princess / 1994 / IN / M • Eclipse / 1993 / SC / M • Enema Bondage / 1992 / BIZ / B • Enema Obedience #1 / 1992 / BIZ / B • Enemates #08 / 1993 / BIZ / B • Erotika / 1994 / WV / M • Essence Of A Woman / 1993 / FOR / M • Euro Studs / 1996 / SC / C • Every Nerd Has A Fantasy / 1996 / FC / M • The Face / 1994 / PP / M • Fantasy Exchange / 1993 / VI / M • Fellatio Fanatics / 1996 / NIT / M • Final Obsession / 1996 / LE / M • Finger Pleasures #5 / 1996 / PL / F • Fireball #1 / 1994 / VI / C • Flexxx #1 / 1994 / VT / M • Foot Hold / 1994 / PRE / B • Foreskin Gump / 1994 / LE / M • Friendly Fire / 1996 / EDP / M • From A Whisper To A Scream / 1993 / GO / M • Frontin' Da Booty / 1994 / WP / M • Gazongo / 1995 / PEP / M • Geranalmo / 1994 / PL / M • A Girl's Affair #04 / 1994 / FD / F • Girl Gone Bad #6: On Parole / 1992 / GO / F • Girlz In The Hood #3: Erotic Justice / 1993 / HW / M • Goldenbush / 1996 / AVI / M • The Grunge Girl Chronicles / 1995 / MAX / M • The Hard Line / 1993 / PEP / M • Harlots / 1993 / MID / M • Head Nurse / 1996 / RAS / M • Heart Breaker / 1994 / CA / M • Heatwaves / 1994 / LE / M • The Horny Housewife / 1996 / HO / M • Hot Parts / 1996 / NIT / M • Hot Shoes / 1992 / BIZ / B • Hot Tight Asses #03 / 1993 / TCK / M • Hot Tight Asses #15 / 1996 / TCK / M • Hot Tight Asses #16 / 1996 / TCK / M • Infamous Crimes Against Nature / 1993 / SUM / M • Jam / 1993 / PL / M • Jizz Glazed Goo Guzzlers #2 / 1996 / NIT / C • Journal Of O #2 / 1994 / ONA / B • Jugsy (Western) / 1992 / WV / M • Kadillac & Devell / 1993 / ZA / M • Kittens & Vamps #2 /

1995 / ROB / F • Kym Wilde's On The Edge #28 / 1995 / RB / B • Kym Wilde's On The Edge #29 / 1995 / RB / B • Kym Wilde's On The Edge #32 / 1996 / RB / B • Lap Of Luxury / 1994 / WIV / M • The Last Anal Hero / 1993 / OD / M • Latex Submission #1 / 1992 / BIZ / B • Leg Show #2 / 1996 / NIT / M • Lick-A-Thon #2 / 1996 / HW / C • Love Seats / 1994 / PRE / C • Love Spice / 1995 / ERA / M • Lust Behind Bars / 1996 / GO / M • Lust In Time / 1996 / ONA / M • Lusty Ladies / 1994 / MET / F • Many Happy Returns / 1995 / NIT / M • Mellon Man #03 / 1994 / AVI / M • Midnight Caller / 1992 / MID / M • Midnight Fantasies / 1992 / VIM / M • Mind Shadows #2 / 1993 / FD / M • Mistress Jacqueline's Slave School / 1992 / BIZ / B • More Than A Handful #5: California Or Bust / 1994 / MET / M • More Than A Handful #6: Life Under The Big Top / 1994 / MET / M • Motel Sex #3 / 1995 / RAP / M • Mr. Peepers Amateur Home Videos #37: Stairway to Heaven / 1991 / LBO / M • Mr. Peepers Nastiest #6 / 1995 / LBO / C • My Way / 1993 / CA / M • N.Y. Video Magazine #08 / 1996 / OUP / M • N.Y.D.P. / 1994 / PEP / M • Naked Scandal #1 / 1995 / SPI / M • Naked Scandal #2 / 1996 / SPI / M • Neighborhood Watch #13: Teasers and Crumpets / 1991 / LBO / M • No Fly Zone / 1993 / LE / F • No Motive / 1994 / MID / M • Nookie Of The Year / 1993 / HW / M • Nude Awakenings / 1996 / PP / M • Obey Me Bitch #1 / 1992 / BIZ / B • Obey Me Bitch #2 / 1992 / BIZ / B • Obey Me Bitch #3 / 1992 / BIZ / B • Obey Me Bitch #4 / 1993 / BIZ / B • Objective: D.P. / 1993 / PEP / M • Office Heels / 1992 / BIZ / B • Orgies Orgies Orgies / 1994 / WV / M • The Orgy #1 / 1993 / EMC / M • The Orgy #2 / 1993 / EMC / M • The Orgy #3 / 1993 / EMC / M • The Other Side Of Chelsea / 1993 / XCI / M • The Other Woman / 1996 / VC / M • Outcall Outlaws / 1995 / CC / M • Panties / 1993 / VD / M • The Pawn Shop / 1996 / MID / M • Penitentiary / 1995 / HW / M • Perverted #3: The Parents / 1995 / ZA / M • Porn In The Pen / 1993 / LE / F • Psychoanal Therapy / 1994 / CA / M • Pudsucker / 1994 / MID / M • Punishing The Sluts / 1996 / RB / B • Pussyman #05: Captive Audience / 1994 / SNA / M • Pussyman #08: The Squirt Queens / 1994 / SNA / M • Pussyman #11: Prime Cuts / 1995 / SNA / C • Pussyman #14: Dreams Of A Gigolo / 1996 / SNA / M • Pussywoman #2 / 1994 / CC / M • Quantum Deep / 1993 / HW / M • The Quest / 1994 / SC / M • Rainwoman #06 / 1993 / CC / M • Raunch #07 / 1993 / CC / M • A Rear And Pleasant Danger / 1995 / PP / M • A Reason To Die / 1994 / PEP / M • Rent-A-Butt / 1992 / VC / M • The Return Of Dr Blacklove / 1996 / CC / M • Revenge Of The Pussy Suckers From Mars / 1994 / PP / M • Rim Job Rita / 1994 / SC / M • Rising Buns / 1993 / HW / M • Rituals / 1993 / SC / M • Rock Her / 1992 / LV / M • Rockhard (Coast) / 1996 / CC / M • Ron Hightower's White Chicks #01 / 1993 / LBO / M • Rxx For A Gangbang / 1994 / ZA / M • The Secret Garden #2 / 1992 / XCI / M • Secret Urges (Vidco) / 1994 / VD / C • Seekers / 1994 / CA / M • Sex Academy #1 / 1993 / ONA / M • Sex Academy #4: The Art Of Anal / 1994 / ONA / M • Sex Circus / 1994 / VIM / M • Sex In Dangerous

Places / 1994 / OD / M • Sex Machine / 1995 / VI / M • Sex On The Run #1 / 1994 / TTV / M • Shayla's Home Repair / 1993 / EVN / M • Shayla's Swim Party / 1997 / VC / M • A Shot In The Pants / 1995 / HO / M • Ski Bunnies #1 / 1994 / HW / M • Ski Bunnies #2 / 1994 / HW / M • Slammed / 1995 / PV / M • Slave Quarters / 1995 / PRE / B • Slutsville U.S.A. / 1995 / VMX / M • The Smart Ass Returns / 1993 / VT / M • Sodomania: Smokin' Sextions / 1996 / EL / C • Sparxx / 1993 / MID / F • Split Decision / 1993 / FD / M • Stacked Deck / 1994 / IN / M • The Star / 1995 / CC / M • Star Struck / 1991 / AFV / M • Sticky Lips / 1993 / EX / M • Stranger At The Backdoor / 1994 / CC / M • Strip Poker / 1995 / PEP / M • Strippers Inc. #1 / 1994 / ONA / M • Striptease / 1995 / SPI / M • Stroke Play / 1994 / PLV / B • Student Fetish Videos: Best of Catfighting #02 / 1994 / PRE / C • Student Fetish Videos: Best of Enema #03 / 1994 / PRE / C • Student Fetish Videos: Best Of Foot Worship #02 / 1994 / PRE / C • Student Fetish Videos: Catfighting #07 / 1993 / PRE / B • Student Fetish Videos: The Enema #11 / 1994 / PRE / B • Student Fetish Videos: Foot Worship #09 / 1993 / PRE / B • Super Enemates #2 / 1996 / PRE / C • Sweet As Honey / 1992 / LV / M • Switch Hitters #9 / 1995 / IN / G • Tail Taggers #111 / 1993 / WV / M • Tail Taggers #113: Behind The Scenes / 1994 / WV / M • Tail Taggers #115 / 1993 / WV / M • Tail Taggers #129: / 1994 / WV / M • Tails Of Tribeca / 1993 / HW / M • Tales From The Backside / 1993 / VC / M • Tight Fit #12 / 1995 / GO / M • Tight Spot / 1996 / WV / M • Tip Tap Toe / 1995 / PRE / C • Titanic Orgy / 1995 / PEP / M • Tits / 1995 / AVI / M • Tits A Wonderful Life / 1994 / CV / M • To The Rear / 1992 / VC / M • Trailer Trash / 1994 / VC / M • Twin Peaks / 1993 / PL / M • The Ultimate Fantasy / 1995 / CV / M • Ultimate Gang Bang #1 / 1994 / HW / M • Under The Covers / 1996 / GO / M • Undercover / 1996 / VC / M • Underground #3: Sit On This / 1996 / SC / M • Unplugged / 1995 / CC / M • Used And Abused #1 / 1994 / SFP / M • Used And Abused #2 / 1994 / SFP / M • The Usual Anal Suspects / 1996 / CC / M • Valentino's Asian Invasion / 1997 / SC / M • Velvet / 1995 / SPI / M • Venom #2 / 1996 / VD / M • Virtual Reality / 1993 / EX / M • Voices In My Bed / 1993 / VI / M • Voluptuous / 1993 / CA / M • Vow Of Passion / 1991 / VI / M • Wasted / 1995 / PRE / B • Watersgate / 1994 / PRE / C • Weird Sex / 1995 / GO / M • Whackers / 1995 / PP / M • Wild Cherries / 1996 / SC / F • Wild Roomies / 1994 / VC / M • Willie Wanker At The Sushi Bar / 1995 / FD / M • Witness For The Penetration / 1994 / PEP / M • You Bet Your Butt / 1992 / VC / M • [Black & White & Brutal #1 / 1996 / ... / S • [Black & White & Brutal #2 / 1996 / ... / S
NIKKI STERLING *see* Nici Sterling
NIKKI STONE
More Dirty Debutantes #55 / 1996 / 4P / M • Salsa & Spice #4 / 1996 / TTV / M
NIKKI TEE
Girls Of The Packed Ten / 1994 / VT / M • Mike Hott: #267 Cunt of the Month: Nikki Tee / 1994 / MHV / M • Show & Tell / 1994 / ELP / M
NIKKI TEEN *see* Nici Sterling

NIKKI TROY *see* Star Index I
NIKKI TYLER *(Christine Tyler)*
Shoulder length blonde hair, marginal face, small tattoo on right butt, a bit hefty on the hips, originally small to medium tits (pre-1995) then enhanced to rock-solid cantaloupes. Originally a *Penthouse* model and then a make-up girl for Vivid. Married. 22 years old in 1995 and comes from CA. Supposedly as of 1996 put on too much weight and retired.
American Garter / 1993 / VC / M • American Pie / 1995 / WAV / M • Bedlam / 1995 / WAV / M • Bloopers & Boners / 1996 / VI / M • Bobby Sox / 1996 / VI / S • Body Language / 1995 / VI / M • Flipside / 1996 / VI / M • Foreign Tongues #2: Mesmerized / 1995 / VI / M • Illicit Entry / 1995 / WAV / M • Latent Image: Christine & Susan / 1993 / LAT / F • Latent Image: Christine Tyler / 1993 / LAT / F • Les Femmes Erotiques / 1993 / BFP / M • Nikki Loves Rocco / 1996 / VI / M • Oral Obsession #2 / 1995 / VI / M • Out Of Love / 1995 / VI / M • Playboy: Stripsearch: San Francisco / 1996 / UNI / S • Plaything #1 / 1995 / VI / M • Plaything #2 / 1995 / VI / M • Playtime / 1996 / VI / M • Pleasureland / 1996 / VI / M • Rolling Thunder / 1995 / VI / M • Sensual Exposure / 1993 / ULI / M • Street Legal / 1995 / WAV / M • The Tale Of The Rope / 1993 / CS / B • Torrid Tales / 1995 / VI / M • Virtual Reality Sixty Nine / 1995 / WP / M • Where The Boys Aren't #8 / 1996 / VI / F • Where The Boys Aren't #9 / 1996 / VI / F
NIKKI VALENTINE *(Elise, Elise Aline)*
Petite brunette with short curly hair, with tattoos on right shoulder and right forearm.
Elise Aline is from **The Devil In Vanity**.
976-STUD / 1989 / LV / M • Bionca, Just For You / 1989 / BON / F • Buck's Excellent Transsexual Adventure / 1989 / STA / G • Cat Scratch Fever / 1989 / FAZ / M • Cum Rain, Cum Shine / 1989 / FAZ / M • Cum Shot Revue #5 / 1988 / HO / C • Depraved / 1990 / IN / M • Devil In Vanity / 1990 / CC / M • Dirty Books / 1990 / V99 / M • Dream Dates / 1990 / V99 / M • Erotic Tales / 1989 / V99 / M • Girl Crazy / 1989 / CDI / F • Heartless / 1989 / REB / M • Holly Does Hollywood #3 / 1989 / VEX / M • Inch Bi Inch / 1989 / STA / G • Miss Adventures / 1989 / VEX / M • More Than Friends / 1989 / FAZ / M • Night Watch / 1990 / VEX / M • Parliament: Lesbian Seduction #1 / 1990 / PM / F • Plenty Of Pleasure / 1990 / WET / M • Power Play (Venus 99) / 1990 / V99 / M • Pure Energy / 1990 / VEX / M • The Red Baron / 1989 / FAN / M • Secret Cravings / 1989 / V99 / M • Sex About Town / 1990 / LV / M • Sex And The Single Girl / 1990 / FAN / M • Sex On Location / 1989 / KIS / M • She-Male Nurse / 1989 / LV / G • Single She-Male Singles Bar / 1990 / STA / G • Slumber Party / 1990 / LV / M • The Squirt Bunny / 1989 / ERU / M • Squirt On The Hunt / 1989 / ERU / M • Stephanie, Just For You / 1989 / BON / F • Tales By Taylor / 1989 / AMB / M • Taylor Made / 1989 / DR / M • Tequilla Sunset / 1989 / V99 / M • A Tongue Is Born / 1990 / ERU / M • Untamed Passion / 1991 / VEX / M • Virgin Busters / 1989 / LV / M • The Way They Were / 1990 / CDI / M • Who Framed Ginger Grant? / 1989 / CC / M • [The Devil In Barbara Dare / 1990 / VEX / M

NIKKI WILDE *see* Nikki Wylde
NIKKI WRIGHT *see* Star Index I
NIKKI WYLDE *(Nicole Wild (Nikki), Nikki Wilde, Arrow Garrett, Honey Rose, Nicky Wilde, Sunny (Nikki Wylde), Carrie (Nikki Wylde), Susan Kool)*
With **Smart Ass Vacation** had breasts enhanced to grotesque proportions. Was married to Beau Michaels in 1987. As of August 1992 she was in process of filing for divorce. Credited as Susan Kool in **More Dirty Debutantes #8**.
Adventures Of Buttwoman #1 / 1991 / EL / F • All That Sex / 1990 / LE / M • Amateur Lesbians #15: Courtney / 1991 / GO / F • Amateur Lesbians #17: Sharise / 1992 / GO / F • Amateur Lesbians #20: Flame / 1992 / GO / F • Amazons From Burbank / 1990 / PL / F • Anal Intruder #05: The Final Outrage / 1990 / CC / M • Autoerotica #1 / 1991 / EX / M • The Back Doors (Executive) / 1991 / EX / M • Backfire / 1991 / GO / M • Bazooka County #3 / 1991 / CC / M • The Best Of Andrew Blake / 1993 / CA / C • Between The Cheeks #2 / 1990 / VC / M • Biff Malibu's Totally Nasty Home Videos #08 / 1992 / ANA / M • Blonde Bombshell / 1991 / CC / M • Blue Views / 1990 / CDI / M • Bonfire Of The Panties / 1990 / CC / M • Breasts And Beyond #2 / 1991 / ME / M • Bruce Seven's Favorite Endings #1 / 1991 / EL / C • Bruce Seven: A Compendium Of His Most Graphic Scenes Vol 3 / 1992 / BS / C • Bruce Seven: A Compendium Of His Most Graphic Scenes Vol 4 / 1993 / BS / C • Can't Touch This / 1991 / PL / M • The Chains Of Torment / 1991 / BS / B • Cheek Busters / 1990 / FH / M • Cheesecake / 1991 / VC / M • Club Head / 1990 / CA / M • Confessions Of Christy / 1991 / CAY / M • Destination Moon / 1992 / GO / C • Eve Of Seduction / 1991 / CDI / M • Famous Anus #1 / 1990 / EX / M • The Fear Zone / 1991 / BS / B • Ghost To Ghost / 1991 / CC / M • Headbangers Balls / 1991 / PL / M • The Hindlick Maneuver / 1991 / CC / M • Hollywood Studs / 1993 / FD / M • House Of Dreams / 1990 / CA / M • Intimate Secrets / 1993 / PME / F • Kittens #1 / 1990 / CC / F • Lesbian Lingerie Fantasy #4 / 1990 / ESP / F • The Lethal Squirt / 1990 / AR / M • Maiden Heaven #1 / 1992 / MID / F • Married With Hormones #1 / 1991 / PL / M • More Dirty Debutantes #08 / 1991 / 4P / M • Naughty By Nature / 1992 / IF / M • New Pussy Hunt #25 / 1996 / LEI / C • A Night At The Waxworks / 1990 / IF / M • Once In A Blue Moon / 1991 / CC / M • One Night Love Affair / 1991 / IF / M • Oral Clinic / 1990 / DAY / M • Party Doll A Go-Go #1 / 1991 / VC / M • Party Doll A Go-Go #2 / 1991 / VC / M • The Passion Of Heather Lear / 1990 / AFV / M • The Pawnbroker / 1990 / IF / M • The Penetrator #1 / 1991 / PL / M • The Perfect Pair / 1991 / LE / M • Private & Confidential / 1990 / AR / M • Rainwoman #04 / 1990 / CC / M • Rear Estates / 1991 / ... / M • Secretaries / 1990 / PL / F • Secrets / 1990 / CA / M • Shaved Sinners #3 / 1990 / VT / M • Single Girl Masturbation #4 / 1990 / ESP / F • The Smart Ass Vacation / 1990 / VT / M • Sno Bunnies / 1990 / PL / F • Soft And Wild / 1991 / LV / M • Some Like It Big / 1991 / LE / M • The Sting Of Ecstasy / 1991 / BS / B • Swing & Swap #02 / 1990 / CDI / M • The

Tasting / 1991 / EX / M • Total Reball / 1990 / CC / M • Twin Peeks / 1990 / DR / M • Val Girls / 1990 / PL / F • Wet 'n' Working / 1990 / EA / F • Where The Girls Play / 1992 / CC • Where The Girls Sweat #2 / 1991 / EL / F • Who Shaved Cassi Nova? / 1989 / EX / M • The Wild And The Innocent / 1990 / CC / M • Wilde At Heart / 1992 / VEX / M

NIKKO (KEIKO) see Keiko Nittake

NIKKO DOLLA
Class Reunion / cr77 / BL / F

NIKKO DULEY see Star Index I

NIKKO LENNOX
Sex Off The Runway / 1991 / GMI / M

NIKKO MICKI see Star Index I

NIKKY
Bondage Models #1 / 1996 / JAM / B • Bondage Models #2 / 1996 / JAM / B • Revenge! / 1996 / JAM / B

NIKOLE LACE (Nicole Lace)
Quite pretty brunette, lithe body, good skin, medium natural tits, 24 years old in 1994 but looks younger, too pushy and takes a flippant attitude to sex. Attempted suicide (pills) in early 1995. Later married Patrick Collins (of Elegant Angel) and as of early 1997 was expecting.

100% Amateur #22: / 1996 / OD / M • After Midnight / 1994 / IN / M • Anal Bad Girls / 1994 / ROB / F • Anal Heartbreaker / 1995 / ROB / M • Anal Intruder #10 / 1995 / CC / M • Anal Persuasion / 1994 / EX / M • Anal Plaything #2 / 1995 / ROB / M • Anal Pussycat / 1995 / ROB / M • Anal Senorita #1 / 1994 / ROB / M • Anal Senorita #2 / 1995 / ROB / M • Anal Sluts & Sweethearts #3 / 1995 / ROB / M • Attitude / 1995 / VC / M • Babewatch #2 / 1994 / CC / M • Backdoor Club #1 / 1996 / VEX / C • Badgirls #3: Cell Block 69 / 1994 / VI / M • Badgirls #4: Jayebird / 1995 / VI / M • Bed & Breakfast / 1995 / WAV / M • Booty Ho #2 / 1995 / ROB / M • Bordello / 1995 / VI / M • Bottom Dweller: The Final Voyage / 1996 / EL / M • The Butt Detective / 1994 / VC / M • Butt Freak #2 / 1996 / EA / M • Call Me / 1995 / CV / M • Caught In The Act (1995-Wave) / 1995 / WAV / M • A Clockwork Orgy / 1995 / PL / M • Cum Soaked And Loaded / 1994 / BCP / M • Cunthunt / 1995 / AB / F • Cyberanal / 1995 / VC / M • Deep Cheeks #5 / 1995 / ROB / M • The Devil In Miss Jones #5: The Inferno / 1994 / VC / M • Dirty Bob's #20: Back To Vegas! / 1995 / FLP / S • Dirty Doc's Housecalls #19 / 1994 / LV / M • Domination / 1994 / WP / M • Dresden Diary #11: Endangered Secrets / 1994 / BIZ / B • Dresden Diary #12: / 1995 / BIZ / B • The Erotic Artist / 1995 / VC / M • Fantasy Chamber / 1994 / ULI / M • Fantasy Du Jour / 1995 / FH / M • First Time Lesbians #20 / 1994 / JMP / F • Forever / 1995 / SC / M • Generation X / 1995 / WAV / M • The Girl With The Heart-Shaped Tattoo / 1995 / WAV / M • Girls Of The Athletic Department / 1995 / VT / M • Gorgeous / 1995 / MET / M • Gypsy Queen / 1995 / CC / M • Hellriders / 1995 / SC / M • Hollywood Lesbians / 1995 / ROB / F • Hotel Sodom #03 / 1995 / SNA / M • Just Lesbians 1995 / NOT / F • Kinky Cameraman #2 / 1996 / LEI / C • Kinky Cameraman #4 / 1996 / LEI / C • The Last Act / 1995 / VI / M • Little Girl Blue / 1995 / RHS / M • Lovin' Spoonfuls #5 / 1996 / 4P / C • Loving You Always / 1994

/ IN / M • Lusty Lawyers / 1995 / PRK / M • More Dirty Debutantes #35 / 1994 / 4P / M • The New Butt Hunt #14 / 1995 / LEI / C • New Wave Hookers #4 / 1994 / VC / M • Ona Zee's Learning The Ropes #08: Slaves In Training / 1992 / ONA / B • Outrageous Sex / 1995 / BIP / F • Pick Up Lines #01 / 1995 / 4P / M • Picture Perfect (Big) / 1995 / BIP / F • Raunch #10: Uncut Jewel / 1994 / CC / M • Ride 'em Cow Girl / 1995 / VI / C • Seymore & Shane Do Ireland / 1994 / ULI / M • Shelby's Forbidden Fears / 1995 / BIZ / B • Silk Stockings: The Black Widow / 1994 / SPI / M • Sleaze Please!—December Edition / 1994 / FH / M • Sodomania #12: Raw Filth / 1995 / EL / M • Sodomania: Slop Shots / 1996 / EL / C • Sodomania: Smokin' Sextions / 1996 / EL / C • The Starlet / 1995 / SC / M • Strap-On Sally #05: Chantilly's French Kiss / 1995 / PL / F • Strap-On Sally #06: Triple Penetration Trollop / 1995 / PL / F • Streetwalkers / 1995 / HO / M • Summer Of '69 / 1994 / MID / M • Swedish Erotica #84 / 1995 / CA / M • Tailz From Da Hood #2 / 1995 / AVI / M • Takin' It Up The Butt / 1995 / IF / C • Three Hearts / 1995 / CC / M • The Training #3 / 1995 / BIZ / B • Unmistakably You / 1995 / CV / M • Up And Cummers #14 / 1994 / 4P / M • Up And Cummers #17 / 1994 / 4P / M • Video Virgins #14 / 1994 / NS / M • Visual Fantasies / 1995 / LE / M • Wet & Wicked / 1995 / PRK / M • Where The Girls Sweat...Not The Sequel / 1996 / EL / F • Whore House / 1995 / IPI / M • Xhibitions: Nicole Lace / 1994 / XHI / F

NIKOLETTA
Nasty Travel Tails #01 / 1993 / CC / M • Penetration (Anabolic) #2 / 1995 / ANA / M

NILLI WILLIS
Big Boob Celebration / 1994 / BTO / M • Duke Of Knockers #1 / 1992 / BTO / M • Girls Around The World #05 / 1992 / BTO / S • H&S: Nilli Willis / 199? / H&S / S • The Nilli Special / 1993 / BTO / M • Plumper Therapy / 1995 / BTO / M • Tit To Tit #2 / 1994 / BTO / M

NILS HORTZ see Star Index I

NILS-ERIK JOHANSSON
Brollopsnatten / 1993 / RUM / M • Inter City 11.25 / 1993 / RUM / M

NINA
Blue Vanities #502 / 1992 / FFL / M • Bobby Hollander's Rookie Nookie #09 / 1993 / SFP / M • Captain Bob's Lust Boat #1 / 1993 / FCP / M • Creme De La Face #11: Cum Plasterers / 1995 / OD / M • Deep Behind The Scenes With Seymore Butts #2 / 1995 / ULI / M • The Dong Show #03 / 1990 / AMB / M • Eurotica #07 / 1996 / XC / M • FTV #16: He's Mine / 1996 / FT / B • FTV #17: Double Trouble / 1996 / FT / B • FTV #27: Secretaries' Revenge & Twist & Shout / 1996 / FT / B • FTV #28: Femme Fatale / Black & Blue / 1996 / FT / B • FTV #29: Boss Lady And Black & Blue / 1996 / FT / B • FTV #31: Trio Of Terror / 1996 / FT / B • GRG: Your Ass Is Mine / 1996 / GRG / M • HomeGrown Video #470: Heroes, Torpedoes & Grinders / 1996 / HOV / M • Joe Elliot's College Girls #38 / 1994 / JOE / M • Master Of Masters #1 / 1995 / BBB / B • Mr. Peepers Amateur Home Videos #52: Tail Wackers / 1992 / LBO / M • Mr. Peepers Nastiest #2 / 1995 / LBO / C • Nasty Travel Tails #01 / 1993 / CC / M • New Faces, Hot

Bodies #19 / 1995 / STP / M • Seymore Butts In Paradise / 1993 / FH / M • Shaved #03 / 1992 / RB / F

NINA (ALEXANDRIA) see Alexandria (1976)

NINA ALEXANDER (Julie Parton, Julia Parton)
Arches Of Triumph / 1995 / PRE / S • Babewatch Video Magazine #1 / 1994 / ERI / F • Bel Air Babes / 1995 / PL / F • Big Busted Goddesses Of L.A. / 1991 / NAP / S • Big Tit Orgy #03 / 1991 / BTO / C • Black Mail / 1990 / TAO / C • Blows Job / 1989 / BIZ / B • Body And Sole / 1990 / BIZ / B • Breast To Breast / 1996 / H&S / S • Bums Away / 1995 / PRE / C • Club Head / 1990 / CA / M • Desire / 1990 / VC / M • Double D Roommates / 1989 / BTO / M • Down Mammary Lane #4 / 1989 / BTO / F • Electric Blue #015 / 1984 / CA / S • End Results / 1991 / PRE / C • Enemates #02 / 1989 / BIZ / B • Erotic Images / 1983 / VES / S • Golden Girls #06 / 1983 / SVE / M • Hot Seats / 1989 / PLV / B • Let's Talk Sex / 1982 / CA / M • Love Skills: A Guide To The Pleasures Of Sex / 1984 / MCA / S • Miss Matches / 1996 / PRE / C • Models In Dispute / 1989 / NAP / B • Modern Love #1 / 1991 / HOP / S • Mr. Peepers Amateur Home Videos #16: Julie Parton / 1991 / LBO / M • New York Nights / 1994 / ... / S • Night Trips #2 / 1990 / CA / M • Penthouse: Love Stories / 1986 / A*V / S • Penthouse: On The Wild Side / 1988 / A*V / S • Raunch #01 / 1990 / CC / M • Reform School Girls / 1986 / NWW / S • The Rosebud Beach Hotel / 1985 / VES / S • Scratch And Claw / 1990 / NAP / B • Secrets / 1990 / CA / M • Sex Games / 1983 / CA / M • Sex On The Saddle: Wicked Women Of The Wild West / 1994 / CPG / S • Sex On The Strip: The Lusty Ladies Of Las Vegas / 1993 / CPG / F • Sex Sluts From Beyond The Galaxy / 1991 / LBO / C • Shoe Horny / 1989 / BIZ / B • Slap Shots / 1991 / PRE / B • Soft Bodies: Double Exposure / 1994 / SB / F • Soft Bodies: Invitational / 1990 / SB / F • Soft Bodies: Pleasure Island / 1990 / SB / F • Sole-Ohs / 1989 / BIZ / F • Super Enemates #1 / 1994 / PRE / C • A Taste Of Julia Parton / 1992 / VD / C • Theatre Of Seduction #1 / 1990 / BON / B • To Tame A Burglar / 1990 / NAP / B • Tongue Kissing Duel / 1989 / NAP / B • Trick Tracey #1 / 1990 / CC / M • Venus' Playhouse / 1994 / VDL / S • Vice Academy #3 / 1991 / PRS / S • Vice Academy #4 / 1994 / PRS / S • Wet T-Shirt Wildcats / 1990 / NAP / B • Young Cheeks / 1990 / BEB / B • [Good Girls Don't / 1993 / ... / S

NINA ANDERSON see Nena Anderson

NINA CHAREESE
She-Male Loves Me / 1995 / VC / G • She-Male Nymphos / 1995 / MET / G • Spring Trannie / 1995 / VC / G • Viet Tran / 1996 / LBO / G

NINA CHERRY see Nena Anderson

NINA CHONG
Bon Appetite / 1985 / TGA / C • Service Entrance / 1979 / REG / C

NINA DAPONCO see Nina DePonca

NINA DE POMP see Star Index I

NINA DE PONKA see Nina DePonca

NINA DEPONCA (Jane Deville, Vera Butler, Jane Davil, Nina DaPonco, Jane Daniels, Felene, Jane Daniel, Nina de

Ponka, Feline)
Dina Deville is white and not the same person. In 1989 was 5'3", 106 lbs, 34B-22-34, 21 years old.
20th Century Fox / 1989 / FAZ / M • A.S.S.(Anal Security Squad) / 1988 / VD / M • The Adventures Of Dick Black, Black Dick / 1987 / DR / M • Aerobisex Girls #2 / 1989 / LIP / F • Amber Lynn's Peter Meter / 1988 / 3HV / C • Anal Pleasures / 1988 / AVC / M • Army Brat #2 / 1989 / VI / M • Aspiring Actresses / 1989 / CA / M • Back To Black #1 / 1988 / VEX / M • Backdoor Brides #2: The Honeymoon / 1986 / PV / M • Backdoor Brides #3 / 1988 / PV / M • Backdoor To Hollywood #05 / 1988 / CDI / M • Backdoor To Hollywood #06 / 1989 / CIN / M • Backdoor To Hollywood #07 / 1989 / CIN / M • Backdoor To Hollywood #09 / 1989 / CIN / M • Banana Splits / 1987 / 3HV / M • Barbii Unleashed / 1988 / 4P / M • Beefeaters / 1989 / PV / M • Behind Blue Eyes #2 / 1988 / ZA / M • Bet Black / 1989 / CDI / M • Beverly Hills Seduction / 1988 / WV / M • Bimbo Cheerleaders From Outer Space / 1988 / FAN / M • The Black Anal-ist #1 / 1988 / VEX / M • Black Beauty (Ebony & Ivory) / 1989 / E&I / M • Black Bimbos In Heat / 1989 / MIR / C • Black Cobra / 1989 / WV / M • Black Dreams / 1988 / CDI / M • Black Fox / 1988 / CC / M • Black Heat / 1986 / VC / M • Black Valley Girls #2 / 1989 / DR / M • Black With Sugar / 1989 / CIN / M • Blackballed / 1994 / VI / C • Blacks & Blondes #57 / 1989 / WV / M • Blame It On The Heat / 1989 / VC / M • Blind Date / 1989 / E&I / M • The Bod Squad / 1989 / VT / M • Brat Force / 1989 / VI / M • The Bride / 1986 / WV / M • Busted / 1989 / CA / M • Butt's Motel #3 / 1989 / EX / M • California Gigolo / 1987 / VD / M • Call Girls In Action / 1989 / CV / M • Charlie's Girls #1 / 1988 / CC / M • Charlie's Girls #2 / 1989 / CC / M • Cheeks #2: The Bitter End / 1989 / CC / M • Club Bed / 1987 / CIX / M • Crossover / 1989 / STA / G • Dance Fire / 1989 / EA / M • Debbie Class Of '89 / 1989 / CC / M • Deep Undercover / 1989 / PV / M • Detroit Dames / 1988 / DR / C • Dialing For Desires / 1988 / 4P / M • Double Black Fantasy / 1987 / CC / C • Dreams In The Forbidden Zone / 1989 / PCP / M • Fade To Black / 1988 / CDI / M • A Fistful Of Bimbos / 1988 / FAZ / M • Full Metal Bikini / 1988 / PEN / M • Girl Crazy / 1989 / CDI / F • Girls Don't Lie / 1990 / IN / F • Good Golly, Miss Molly / 1987 / CDI / M • Hard Bodies / 1989 / CDI / M • Harlem Candy / 1987 / WET / M • Hawaii Vice #1 / 1988 / CIN / M • Hawaii Vice #2 / 1989 / CDI / M • Hawaii Vice #3 / 1988 / CIN / M • Hawaii Vice #4 / 1989 / CIN / M • Hawaii Vice #7 / 1989 / CDI / M • Heat Of The Nite / 1988 / VEX / M • Hospitality Sweet / 1988 / WV / M • Hot Licks At The Pussycat Club / 1990 / WV / C • Hot Pink And Chocolate Brown / 1988 / PV / M • Hot Services / 1989 / WET / M • Hot Women / 1989 / E&I / C • House Of Sexual Fantasies / 1987 / GO / M • Icy Hot / 1990 / MID / M • Imagination X-Posed / 1989 / 4P / M • Innocence Lost / 1988 / CA / M • Introducing Charli / 1989 / CIN / M • Invasion Of The Samurai Sluts From Hell / 1988 / FAZ / M • Island Girls #2: Fun In The Sun / 1990 / CDI / C • Island Girls #3: Rip

Tide / 1991 / CDI / C • Jaded / 1989 / 4P / M • Jewel Of The Nite / 1986 / WV / M • Kinkyvision #2 / 1988 / VC / M • Love In Reverse / 1988 / FAZ / M • Lust Letters / 1988 / CA / M • Lust Of Blacula / 1987 / VEX / M • Madame X / 1989 / EVN / M • The Maltese Phallus / 1990 / V99 / M • A New Girlfriend / 1991 / XPI / M • Nikki And The Pom-Pom Girls / 1987 / VEX / M • No Man's Land #01 / 1988 / VT / C • Nothing But Girls, Girls, Girls / 1988 / CDI / M • Only The Best Of Girls With Curves / 1992 / CV / C • Open House (Vid Exc) / 1989 / VEX / M • Oral Majority #07 / 1989 / WV / C • Oral Majority Black #2 / 1988 / WV / C • Pajama Party / 1993 / CV / C • Paris Blues / 1990 / WV / C • Precious Gems / 1988 / CV / M • Ready, Willing & Anal (Vidco) / 1993 / VD / C • The Red Baron / 1989 / FAN / M • Reflections Of Innocence / 1988 / SEX / M • Reflections Of Innocence / 1991 / VEX / C • Roll-X Girls / 1989 / DYV / M • Samantha, I Love You / 1988 / WV / C • Satin Angels / 1986 / WV / M • The Scarlet Bride / 1989 / VI / M • Sex Lies / 1988 / FAN / M • Sex Sluts In The Slammer / 1988 / FAN / M • Smooth As Silk / 1987 / VIP / M • Snatched / 1989 / VI / M • Soul Games / 1988 / PV / C • Storm Warning / 1989 / LV / M • Stormi / 1988 / LV / M • Taija's Tasty Treats / 1988 / EXP / C • Tails Of The Town / 1988 / WV / M • A Taste Of Black / 1987 / WET / M • A Taste Of White / 1987 / WET / M • Teasers: Poor Little Rich Girl / 1988 / MET / M • Teasers: Watch Me Sparkle / 1988 / MET / M • That Ole Black Magic / 1988 / CDI / M • This Is Your Sex Life / 1987 / VD / M • Toys 4 Us #3: Follow The Leader / 1990 / WV / C • True Confessions Of Hyapatia Lee / 1989 / VI / M • Turn Up The Heat / 1988 / SEX / M • Turn Up The Heat / 1991 / VEX / C • Voodoo Lust: The Possession / 1989 / PCP / M • Warm Bodies, Hot Nights / 1988 / PV / M • Wet Dream On Maple Street / 1988 / FAN / M • Wet Panties / 1989 / MIR / C • What A Country / 1989 / PL / M • What Kind Of Girls Do You Think We Are? / 1986 / VEX / M • What Kind of Girls Do You Think We Are? / 1991 / VEX / C • Wild Fire / 1990 / WV / C • Wild Oats / 1988 / CV / M • Wild Stuff / 1987 / WET / M • Winning Score / 1989 / E&I / C • WPINK-TV #3 / 1988 / PV / M • You Bring Out The Animal In Me / 1987 / MIR / M • The Young And The Wrestling #2 / 1989 / PL / M

NINA DEW
Maximum Desade / 1995 / ZFX / B

NINA FAUSSE
Avalon Calling / cr72 / AXV / M • Diary Of A Bed / 1979 / HOE / M • Don't Tell Mama / 1974 / VIP / M • Guess Who's Coming This Weekend / 1973 / CLX / M • Jungle Blue / 1978 / HIF / M • Marilyn And The Senator / 1974 / HIF / M • Rings Of Passion / 1976 / VXP / G • Sex Prophet / 1973 / ALP / M • Sexual Ecstasy Of The Macumba / 1975 / ... / M • South Of The Border / 1977 / VC / M • Three Came Running / 1974 / AVC / M • The True Way / 1975 / SVE / M • The Ultimate Pleasure / 1977 / HIF / M

NINA FAWCETT see Star Index I

NINA GENOH
Bon Appetite / 1985 / TGA / C • Showgirl #14: Kitty Shane's Fantasies / 1983 / VCR / M • Torch Of Desire / 1983 / REG / M

NINA HARTLEY (Nina Hartwell, Anal

Annie, Nina Hartman)
First movie: **Educating Nina**. According to *Raw Talent* her real name is Debbie (something) but there seems to be some doubt as to the veracity of this statement. Has had breasts enhanced but only very slightly in end-1989. Started in Mar 1984. Husband is called David Hartley and wife is Bobby Lilly. Was 29 in 1991 and has a BS in nursing—36-24-36, 5'4" tall. In 1995 went whole-hog on the breast enhancement and now has rock solid large cantaloupes. Also seems to have developed a beer belly.
1001 Erotic Nights #2 / 1987 / VC / M • A&B NINA#1: A Special Video / 1995 / A&B / M • Acts Of Love / 1989 / ... / M • Adam & Eve's House Party #1 / 1995 / VC / M • Adult Affairs / 1994 / VC / M • Adult Video News 1991 Awards / 1991 / VC / M • Adultery / 1986 / DR / M • Adultery / 1989 / PP / M • Alice In Whiteland / 1988 / VC / M • All Night Long / 1990 / NWV / C • Amanda By Night #2 / 1987 / CA / M • Amazing Tails #4 / 1990 / CA / M • Amber Lynn's Personal Best / 1986 / VD / M • Anal Annie And The Backdoor Housewives / 1984 / LIP / F • Anal Annie And The Magic Dildo / 1984 / LIP / F • Anal Annie And The Willing Husbands / 1984 / LIP / M • Anal Annie Just Can't Say No / 1984 / LIP / M • Anal Annie's All-Girl Escort Service / 1990 / LIP / F • Angel's Back / 1988 / IN / M • As The Spirit Moves You / 1990 / LV / M • Ashlyn Rising / 1995 / VI / M • The Backdoor Bradys / 1995 / PL / M • Backdoor Brides #3 / 1988 / PV / M • Backdoor Summer #2 / 1989 / PV / C • Ball Busters / 1984 / CV / M • Barbara Dare's Prime Choice / 1987 / SE / C • Barbara The Barbarian / 1987 / SE / M • Battle Of The Stars #1 / 1985 / NSV / M • Battle Of The Stars #2: East Versus West / 1985 / NSV / M • Battle Of The Stars #3: Stud Wars / 1985 / NSV / M • Battle Of The Titans / 1986 / AVC / M • Beaver Ridge / 1991 / VC / M • Behind Blue Eyes #3 / 1989 / ME / M • The Best Of Anal Annie: The Girl-Girl Adventures / 1993 / LIP / C • Best Of Buttman #2 / 1993 / EA / C • Best Of Caught From Behind #5 / 1991 / HO / C • Best Of Hot Shorts #01 / 1987 / VCR / C • The Better Sex Video Series #7: Advanced Sexual Fantasies / 1992 / LEA / M • Betty & Juice Possessed / 1995 / CA / M • Beyond Desire / 1986 / VC / M • The Big Bang / 1988 / WET / M • The Big Thrill / 1989 / VD / M • Billionaire Girls Club / 1988 / LVI / C • Biloxi Babes / 1988 / WV / M • Black Magic / 1985 / WET / M • Blacks & Blondes #22 / 1986 / WV / M • Blazing Bedrooms / 1987 / LA / M • Blazing Matresses / 1986 / AVC / M • The Blonde & The Beautiful #1 / 1993 / LV / M • The Blonde & The Beautiful #2 / 1993 / LV / M • Blondes! Blondes! Blondes! / 1986 / VCS / C • Bloopers & Boners / 1996 / VI / M • Blue Cabaret / 1989 / VTO / M • Blue Movie / 1989 / VD / M • Blush: Suburban Dykes / 1991 / BLV / F • The Bod Squad / 1989 / VT / M • Body Games / 1987 / DR / M • Body Music #2 / 1990 / DR / M • Body Of Love / 1994 / ERA / M • Boobs, Butts And Bloopers #2 / 1990 / HO / M • Book Of Love / 1992 / VC / M • Born To Be Bad / 1987 / CV / M • Born To Be Wild / 1987 / SE / M • Born To Suck Cock / 1994 / MET / C • Breakin' All The Rules / 1987 / SE / M • Breakin' In

/ 1986 / WV / M • Bring On The Virgins / 1989 / CA / M • Bubbles / 1991 / IF / M • Buns And Roses (LV) / 1990 / LV / M • Butt Freak #1 / 1992 / EA / M • Butt Freak #2 / 1996 / EA / M • Butter Me Up / 1984 / CHX / M • Buttman's Revenge / 1992 / EA / M • California Taboo / 1986 / VC / M • Call Girls In Action / 1989 / CV / M • Candy's Little Sister Sugar / 1988 / VD / M • The Case Of The Cockney Cupcake / 1989 / ME / M • Caught From Behind #14 / 1990 / HO / M • Caught From Behind #16: The Reunion / 1992 / HO / M • Caught In The Act (1995-Wave) / 1995 / WAV / M • Cheap Shot / 1995 / WAV / M • Cheating / 1986 / SEV / M • Chicks In Black Leather / 1989 / VC / C • China Bitch / 1989 / PV / C • Club Ecstasy / 1987 / CA / M • Coming On Strong / 1989 / CA / C • Conflict / 1988 / VD / M • Corporate Affairs / 1986 / SE / M • Cum Shot Revue #5 / 1988 / HO / C • Dancing Angels / 1989 / PL / M • Dangerous Desire / 1986 / NSV / M • Dangerous Women / 1987 / WET / M • The De Renzy Tapes / 1990 / CA / C • Debbie 4 Hire / 1988 / AVC / M • Debbie Class Of '89 / 1989 / CC / M • Debbie Does Dishes #1 / 1985 / AVC / M • Debbie Does Dishes #3 / 1987 / AVC / M • Debbie Does Wall Street / 1991 / VC / M • Debbie For President / 1988 / CC / M • Debbie Goes To Hawaii / 1988 / VD / C • Deep Desires / 1989 / VC / C • Deep Inside Juli Ashton / 1996 / VC / C • Deep Inside Nina Hartley / 1993 / VC / M • Deep Inside Selena Steele / 1993 / VC / C • Diamond In The Rough / 1999 / EX / M • Dirty Bob's #27: Laid Back In L.A.! / 1996 / FLP / S • Dirty Lingerie / 1990 / VD / M • Dirty Little Mind / 1994 / IP / M • Dirty Little Secrets / 1995 / WAV / M • Dirty Minds / 1996 / NIT / M • Dirty Pictures / 1988 / CA / M • Dirty Tricks / 1993 / CC / M • Divine Decadence / 1988 / CA / M • Doctor Blacklove / 1987 / CC / M • Dollface / 1987 / CV / M • Dominique's Inheritance / 1990 / CVC / M • Dr Blacklove #1 / 1987 / CC / M • Dream Girls / 1986 / VC / M • Dream Lovers / 1987 / CA / M • Dreams Of Natasha / 1985 / AAH / M • Dreamwalk / 1989 / COM / M • Dy-Nasty / 1988 / SE / M • Dyke Bar / 1991 / PL / F • Dynamic Vices / 1987 / VC / M • E.X. / 1986 / SUP / M • Educating Nina / 1984 / AT / M • The End Zone / 1987 / LA / C • The Erotic Adventures Of The Three Musketeers / 1992 / CEL / S • Erotica S.F. / 1994 / ORP / M • Every Man's Dream, Every Woman's Nightmare / 1988 / CC / C • Every Woman Has A Fantasy #2 / 1986 / VC / M • Exposure / 1988 / VD / M • Extreme Passion / 1993 / WP / M • Falcon Breast / 1987 / CDI / M • Family Affairs / 1990 / VD / M • Fantasy Confidential / 1988 / GO / M • Fashion Fantasies / 1986 / VC / M • Fashion Passion / 1985 / VD / M • Fatal Erection / 1988 / SEV / M • Female Aggressors / 1986 / LAV / M • The Final Taboo / 1988 / CA / M • Finely Back / 1990 / PL / F • Firestorm #3 / 1986 / COM / M • The First Taboo / 1989 / LA / M • First Time Ever #1 / 1995 / PE / F • For His Eyes Only / 1989 / PL / M • For Love And Lust / 1985 / AVC / M • For Your Love / 1988 / IN / M • Frankie And Joanie / 1991 / HW / M • Friday The 13th #1: A Nude Beginning / 1987 / VD / M • Full Moon Bay / 1993 / VI / M • The Fun House / 1988 / SEV / C • Future Lust / 1989 / ME / M • Gang Bangs #1 / 1985 / VCR / M • Getting LA'd / 1986 / PV / M • Getting Personal / 1986 / CA / M • Ginger Does Them All / 1988 / CV / M • Ginger Snaps / 1987 / VI / M • Girl Games / 1987 / PL / C • Girl Toys / 1986 / DR / M • Girls Don't Lie / 1990 / IN / F • Girls Like Us / cr88 / IN / C • Girls On Girls / 1987 / SE / C • Girls Will Be Boys #3 / 1991 / PL / F • Girls Will Be Boys #4 / 1991 / PL / F • Girlworld #1 / 1987 / LIP / F • Girlworld #2 / 1988 / LIP / F • Girlworld #4 / 1989 / LIP / F • Girlz N The Hood #1 / 1991 / HW / M • The Grafenberg Spot / 1985 / MIT / M • The Greatest American Blonde / 1987 / WV / C • Group Therapy / 1992 / TP / M • Hard Choices / 1987 / CA / M • Hate To See You Go / 1990 / VC / M • Hay Fever / 1988 / TIG / F • Head Trips / cr88 / EXH / C • Here...Eat This! / 1990 / FAZ / M • HHHHot! TV #1 / 1988 / CDI / M • Holiday For Angels / 1987 / IN / M • Hollywood Halloween Sex Ball / 1996 / EUR / M • Honkytonk Angels / 1988 / IN / C • Hot And Nasty! / 1986 / V99 / C • The Hot Box Invasion / 1987 / AMB / M • Hot Line / 1991 / VC / M • Hot Nights And Hard Bodies / 1986 / VD / M • Hot Nights At The Blue Note Cafe / 1985 / WV / M • Hot Number / 1987 / WET / M • Hot Pink And Chocolate Brown / 1988 / PV / M • Hot Rocks / 1986 / WET / M • Hot Shorts: Gabriella / 1986 / VCR / C • Hot Shorts: Susan Hart / 1986 / VCR / C • Hot Shorts: Tracey Adams / 1986 / VCR / C • Hotel California / 1995 / MID / M • Hothouse Rose #1 / 1991 / VC / M • Hothouse Rose #2 / 1992 / VC / M • Hottest Parties / 1988 / VC / C • House Of Blue Dreams / 1985 / WV / M • How To Achieve Multiple Orgasms / 1994 / A&E / M • Hump Up The Volume / 1991 / AR / M • Hungry / 1990 / GLE / M • Hustler #17 / 1984 / CA0 / M • Hyapatia Lee's Arcade Series #01 / 1988 / ZA / C • I Cream Of Genie / 1988 / SE / M • I've Never Done This Before / 1985 / NSV / M • In And Out Of Africa / 1986 / EVN / M • In Excess / 1991 / CA / M • In Search Of The Golden Bone / 1986 / CA / M • In The Scope / 1996 / VI / M • Infamous Crimes Against Nature / 1993 / SUM / M • Introducing Tracey Wynn / 1991 / PL / M • It's Incredible / 1985 / SE / M • Jack Hammer / 1987 / ZA / M • Jan B: Jan & Nina Hartley / 1995 / JB0 / F • Juicy Lucy / 1990 / VC / M • Kinkyvision #2 / 1988 / VC / M • The Kiss / 1986 / SC / M • Lady By Night / 1987 / CA / M • The Last Temptation Of Kristi / 1988 / ME / M • The Last X-Rated Movie #1 / 1990 / COM / M • The Last X-Rated Movie #2 / 1990 / COM / M • The Last X-Rated Movie #3 / 1990 / COM / M • The Last X-Rated Movie #4 / 1990 / COM / M • Late After Dark / 1985 / BAN / M • The Legend Of King Karl / 1986 / AR / M • Legends Of Porn #2 / 1989 / CV / C • Les Be Friends / 1988 / WV / C • Let's Talk Anal / 1996 / ESF / M • Lethal Passion / 1991 / PL / M • The Life Of The Party / 1991 / ZA / M • Lifestyles Of The Blonde And Dirty / 1987 / WET / M • Lingerie Girls / 1987 / ... / F • A Little Bit Of Honey / 1987 / WET / M • Living Doll / 1987 / WV / M • Looking For Lust / 1984 / VEL / M • The Lost Angel / 1989 / KIS / C • The Love Nest / 1989 / CA / M • A Lover For Susan / 1987 / CLV / M • Lucky In Love #1 / 1985 / BAN / M • Maiden Heaven #1 / 1992 / MID / F • Manbait #1 / 1991 / VC / M • Material Girl / 1986 / VD / M • Meat Market / 1992 / SEX / C • Mermaid / 1991 / BAD / C • Mirage #1 / 1991 / VC / M • Mirage #2 / 1992 / VC / M • The Mischief Maker / 1987 / SE / M • Missing Pieces / 1985 / IN / M • Monkey Business / 1987 / SEV / M • Mouthwatering / 1986 / BRA / M • Moving In / 1986 / CV / M • Mummy Dearest #1 / 1990 / LV / M • Mummy Dearest #2: The Unwrapping / 1990 / LV / M • Mummy Dearest #3: The Parting / 1991 / LV / M • My Bare Lady / 1989 / ME / M • N.Y. Video Magazine #09 / 1996 / OUP / M • Naked Reunion / 1993 / VI / M • Naked Stranger / 1987 / CDI / M • Nasty Girls #2 (1990-Plum) / 1990 / PP / M • A Natural Woman / 1989 / IN / M • Naughty Girls Like It Big / 1986 / ELH / M • The New Barbarians #1 / 1990 / VC / M • The New Barbarians #2 / 1990 / VC / M • The Nicole Stanton Story #1 / 1989 / CA / M • The Nicole Stanton Story #2 / 1989 / CA / M • Night Nurses / 1995 / WAV / M • Night Of The Living Debbies / 1989 / EX / M • Night Play / 1995 / WAV / M • Nina Does 'em All / 1988 / 3HV / C • Nina Hartley's Guide To Anal Sex / 1996 / A&E / M • Nina Hartley's Guide To Swinging / 1996 / A&E / M • Nina Hartley's Lifestyles Party / 1995 / FRM / M • Nina Hartley's Professional Amateur Tournament #1 / 1990 / RUM / M • Nina Hartley's Professional Amateur Tournament #2 / 1990 / BKD / M • Nina Hartley's Real-Deal Swinger's Video / 1994 / BKD / M • Nina Hartley: Wild Thing / 1991 / CIN / M • Nina's Knockouts / 1987 / AVC / C • Nina's Toys And Boys / 1991 / LV / C • Nina, Just For You / 1989 / BON / F • No Man's Land #10 / 1994 / VT / F • No One To Love / 1987 / PP / M • Nooner / 1986 / AVC / M • Nudes At Eleven #1 / 1986 / AVC / M • Nudes At Eleven #2 / 1987 / AVC / M • Oh, What A Night! / 1990 / VC / M • On The Loose & Hot To Trot / 1987 / CA / M • Once In A Lifetime / 1996 / VC / C • One Wife To Give / 1989 / ZA / M • Only The Best #1 / 1986 / CV / C • Only The Best #3 / 1990 / CV / C • Only The Best Of Barbara Dare / 1990 / CV / C • Only The Best Of Girls With Curves / 1992 / CV / C • Only The Best Of Men's And Women's Fantasies / 1988 / CV / C • Only The Best Of Oral / 1989 / CV / C • Only The Best Of Peepers / 1992 / CV / C • Oral Majority #02 / 1987 / WV / C • Oral Majority #03 / 1986 / WV / C • Oral Majority #07 / 1989 / WV / C • The Other Side Of Pleasure / 1987 / SEV / M • Outlaw Ladies #2 / 1988 / VC / M • Outrageous Foreplay / 1987 / WV / M • P.S.: Back Alley Cats #02 / 1992 / PSP / F • P.S.: Back Alley Cats #06 / 1992 / PSP / F • Pajama Party X #1 / 1994 / VC / M • Pajama Party X #2 / 1994 / VC / M • Parliament: Samantha Strong #1 / 1986 / PM / M • Passion Chain / 1987 / ZA / M • The Passion Within / 1986 / MAP / M • Peeping Tom / 1986 / CV / M • The Penthouse / 1989 / PP / M • The Performers / 1986 / NSV / M • Phone Sex Girls #2 / 1987 / VT / M • Pin-Up / 1991 / BAD / C • The Pink Panties / 1985 / NSV / M • Play It Again, Samantha / 1986 / EVN / M • Play Me Again, Vanessa / 1986 / VC / M • Plaything #1 / 1995 / VI / M • The Pleasure Maze / 1986 / PL / M • Porn Star Confidential / 1996 / ESF / M • Porsche Lynn, Every

Man's Dream / 1988 / CC / C • Portrait Of A Nymph / 1988 / PP / M • Portrait Of An Affair / 1988 / VD / M • Positively Pagan #04 / 1991 / ATA / M • Power Blonde / 1988 / AVC / M • The Price Was Right / 1994 / PAE / M • Princess Charming / 1987 / AVC / C • Princess Orgasma #1 / 1991 / PP / M • Private Encounters / 1987 / SE / M • Profiles #03: House Dick / 1995 / XPR / M • Pumping Flesh / 1985 / CA / M • Pussyman #03: The Search Continues / 1993 / SNA / M • Pussyman #11: Prime Cuts / 1995 / SNA / C • Pussyman #15: The Bone Voyage Bash / 1997 / SNA / M • Rachel Ryan Exposed / 1990 / WV / C • Rear Action Girls #2 / 1985 / LIP / F • The Red Garter / 1986 / SE / M • Red Hot Fire Girls / 1989 / VD / M • The Red Room And Other Places / 1992 / COM / C • Reel People #03 / 1989 / PP / M • Restless Nights / 1987 / SEV / M • The Return Of The A Team / 1988 / WV / M • Revenge By Lust / 1986 / VCR / M • Rising Buns / 1993 / HW / M • Rites Of Passion / 1988 / FEM / M • Rock Hard / 1985 / CV / M • Rockin' Erotica / 1987 / SE / C • Romeo And Juliet #1 / 1987 / WV / M • Ruthless Women / 1988 / SE / M • Saddletramp / 1988 / VD / M • Saki's Private Party / 1995 / TTV / M • Samantha And The Deep Throat Girls / 1988 / CV / M • Samantha, I Love You / 1988 / WV / C • Scarlet Fantasy / 1990 / VI / M • Screaming Rage / 1988 / LV / C • The Secret Life Of Nina Hartley / 1994 / VC / M • The Seduction Formula / 1990 / FAN / M • Selena's Secrets / 1991 / MIN / M • Sensual Escape / 1988 / FEM / M • Sensual Seduction / 1986 / LBO / M • Sex And The Secretary / 1988 / PP / M • The Sex Game / 1987 / SE / C • Sex Life Of A Porn Star / 1986 / ELH / M • Sex Professionals / 1994 / LIP / F • Sex With A Stranger / 1986 / AVC / M • Sex-A-Vision / 1985 / DR / M • Sexline You're On The Air / 1986 / CAT / M • Sexual Power / 1988 / CV / M • Sexually Altered States / 1986 / VC / M • Seymore Butts In The Love Shack / 1992 / FH / M • Seymore Butts Rides Again / 1992 / FH / M • Shadow Dancers #1 / 1989 / EA / M • Shadow Dancers #2 / 1989 / EA / M • Shake Well Before Using / 9990 / LV / M • Shameless / 1991 / SC / M • Shane's World #2 / 1996 / OD / M • Shaved Bunnies / 1985 / LIP / F • She's So Fine #2 / 1988 / VC / M • Showdown / 1986 / CA / M • Showgirls / 1985 / SE / M • Silver Tongue / 1989 / CA / M • Sin City / 1986 / WET / M • Sinful Sisters / 1986 / VEX / M • Sins Of Nina Hartley / 1989 / MIR / C • Slip Of The Tongue / 1990 / SE / M • The Smart Ass #2: Rusty's Revenge / 1990 / VT / M • Smoke Screen / 1990 / CA / M • So Deep, So Good / 1988 / NSV / M • Sorority Pink #1 / 1989 / CV / M • Sorority Pink #2 / 1989 / CV / M • Sorority Sex Kittens #2 / 1993 / VC / M • Sorority Sex Kittens #3 / 1996 / VC / M • Sorority Stewardesses #1 / 1995 / PE / M • Sorority Stewardesses #2 / 1995 / PE / M • Soul Games / 1988 / PV / C • Splendor In The Ass #1 / 1989 / CA / M • Spoiled / 1987 / VD / M • Spread It Wide / 1996 / AVI / M • Stairway To Heaven / 1989 / ME / M • Stairway To Paradise / 1990 / VC / M • The Stand-Up / 1994 / VC / M • Star Tricks / 1988 / WV / M • The Stiff / 1995 / WAV / M • Street Walkers / 1990 / PL / M • Strictly

Business / 1987 / VD / M • Stripper Nurses / 1994 / PE / M • Super Sex / 1986 / MAP / M • Suzie Superstar...The Search Continues / 1988 / CV / M • Sweat #1 / 1986 / PP / M • Swedish Erotica #68 / 1985 / CA / M • Sweet Cheeks / 1987 / VCR / C • Sweet Summer / 1986 / AMO / M • Sweet Things / 1987 / VC / M • Switch Hitters #2: Swinging Both Ways / 1987 / IN / G • Taboo #06 / 1988 / IN / M • Taija / 1986 / WV / C • Tailspin / 1987 / AVC / M • Talk Dirty To Me #06 / 1989 / DR / M • Tangled / 1994 / PL / M • A Taste Of Ariel / 1989 / PIN / C • A Taste Of Ecstasy / 1991 / CIN / M • A Taste Of Tawnee Laurel / 1990 / PIN / C • A Taste Of The Best #3 / 1988 / LV / C • Taste Of The Best #3 / 1988 / PIN / C • Ten Little Maidens / 1985 / EXF / M • Thought You'd Never Ask / 1986 / CA / M • Three For All / 1988 / PL / M • The Three Musketeers #1 / 1992 / FD / M • The Three Musketeers #2 / 1992 / FD / M • Toys 4 Us #1 / 1987 / WV / C • Tracy In Heaven (Rewrite) / 1986 / WV / M • Trick Or Treat / 1985 / ELH / M • Trinity, Just For You / 1989 / BON / F • True Legends Of Adult Cinema: The Erotic Eighties / 1992 / VC / C • True Legends Of Adult Cinema: The Modern Era / 1992 / VC / C • Tuff Stuff / 1987 / WET / M • Twins / 1986 / WV / M • Two Into One #2 / 1988 / PIN / C • Two To Tango / 1987 / TEM / M • The Tyffany Million Diaries / 1995 / IMV / C • The Ultimate Lover / 1986 / VD / M • The Ultimate O / 1985 / NSV / M • Ultimate Orgy #1 / 1992 / GLI / M • Under The Hood: Nina Hartley's Guide To Better Cunnilingus / 1994 / A&E / M • Uniform Behavior / 1989 / ZA / M • Unnatural Act #2 / 1986 / DR / M • Up And Cummers #08 / 1994 / 4P / M • The Valley Girl Connection / 1994 / IN / M • Vienna's Place / 1996 / VCX / M • Viper's Place / 1988 / VD / M • Virgin Hotline / 1996 / LVP / F • Visions Of Jeannie / 1986 / VD / M • Wendy Whoppers: Bomb Squad / 1993 / PEP / M • Wet Pink / 1989 / PL / F • Whatever Turns You On / 1987 / CA / M • Whispered Secrets Of The Call Girls / 1995 / TVE / F • Who Shaved Aja? / 1989 / EX / M • Who Shaved Lynn Lemay? / 1989 / EX / M • Wide Open Spaces / 1995 / VC / F • Wild Fire / 1990 / WV / C • Wild Stuff / 1987 / WET / M • The Wild Wild Chest #1 / 1990 / HO / M • Wildheart / 1989 / IN / M • Woodworking 101: Nina Hartley's Guide To Better Fellatio / 1994 / A&E / M • WPINK-TV #2 / 1986 / PV / M • Xstasy / 1986 / NSV / M • You Bring Out The Animal In Me / 1987 / MIR / M • Young Girls In Tight Jeans / 1989 / VD / M • [Nina Hartley's Guide To Alternative Sex / 199? / ... / M • [Nina Hartley's Guide To Anal Sex / 199? / ... / M • [Nina Hartley's Guide To Swinging / 199? / ... / M

NINA HARTMAN *see* **Nina Hartley**
NINA HARTWELL *see* **Nina Hartley**
NINA LAURIE
Sodom & Gomorrah / 1974 / MIT / M
NINA LOPEZ *see* **Star Index I**
NINA LUND *see* **Star Index I**
NINA MICHAELS
Barbie's Fantasies / 1974 / VHL / M
NINA PETA *see* **Nina Preta**
NINA PRETA *(Nina Reta, Nina Peta, Nicole Paturel)*
Shoulder length brown frizzy hair, tiny, almost non-existent tits, lithe body, marginal face.

Angela In Wonderland / 1986 / VD / M • Bi Bi American Style / cr85 / MET / G • Candy Stripers #3 / 1986 / AR / M • Down & Out In New York City / 1986 / SE / M • Firebox / 1986 / VXP / M • Oversexed / 1986 / VXP / M • Parted Lips / 1986 / QX / M • Pink Clam / 1986 / RLV / M • Porked / 1986 / VXP / M • Seven Minutes In Heaven / 1986 / VXP / M • Teaser / 1986 / RLV / M • Three Daughters / 1986 / FEM / M • Thunderstorm / 1987 / VC / M • Wimps / 1987 / LIV / S
NINA RETA *see* **Nina Preta**
NINA RICHARD *see* **Nena Anderson**
NINA RUSH
Fury In Alice / 1976 / SVE / M
NINA SUAVE
Amateurs Exposed #02 / 1993 / CV / M • Anal Avenue / 1992 / LV / M • Anal Island / 1992 / LV / M • Anal Lover #1 / 1992 / ROB / M • The Anal-Europe Series #04: Anal Recall / 1993 / LV / M • Breast Worx #39 / 1992 / LBO / M • Cinderella Society / 1993 / GO / M • Dark Tunnels / 1994 / LV / M • Junkyard Dykes #03 / 1994 / ZA / F • La Princesa Anal / 1993 / ROB / M • Lies Of Passion / 1992 / LV / M • Madame A / 1992 / LV / M • Maneater (1992-Las Vegas) / 1992 / LV / M • Pearl Necklace: Thee Bush League: The Best Of Oral #01 / 1993 / SEE / C • Pearl Necklace: Thee Bush League #09 / 1993 / SEE / M • R.E.A.L. #1 / 1994 / LV / F • Sex Sting / 1992 / FD / M • Sex Stories / 1992 / VC / M • Seymore Butts Swings / 1992 / FH / M • So I Married A Lesbian / 9993 / WV / M • Straight A's / 1993 / VC / M • Tail Taggers #108: Vibro Love / 1993 / WV / M
NINA TREAT *see* **Star Index I**
NINE MYLES
N.Y. Video Magazine #04 / 1995 / OUP / M
NINETY SIX
Big Murray's New-Cummers #15: Rump Humpers / 1993 / FD / M
NINI *see* **Hanaku**
NIOKA *see* **Star Index I**
NIROKO FUJIDO *see* **Star Index I**
NITA
Buttman's British Moderately Big Tit Adventure / 1994 / EA / M • Homegrown Video #358 / 1991 / HOV / M • Porno Bizarro / 1995 / GLI / M
NITA SIRNERE *see* **Star Index I**
NIVA *see* **Niva Styles**
NIVA STYLES *(Niva, Styles)*
Long dark brown hair, small/medium tits, loss of belly muscle tone, large tattoo on left shoulder back, marginal face, shaven pussy. 22 years old in 1996.
Dirty Dirty Debutantes #5 / 1996 / 4P / M • More Dirty Debutantes #53 / 1996 / 4P / M • Nineteen #4 / 1996 / FOR / M
NOAH RATTE *see* **Star Index I**
NOBU ICHIGAWA *see* **Star Index I**
NODA YASUHIRO
Lustful Angel / 1996 / AVV / M
NOEL
Wicked Waxxx Worxxx / 1995 / HW / M
NOEL HEMPHILL *see* **Franklin Anthony**
NOELLE
Anal 247 / 1995 / CC / M • Hot Body Competition: Bikinis & Bikes Contest / 1996 / CG / F • Hot Body Video Magazine: Sweet Dreams / 1996 / CG / F • Magma: Hot Business / 1995 / MET / M • Rough-House Room-Mates / 1996 / NAP / B • Snatch Masters #02 / 1994 / LEI / M • Thoroughly

Thrashed / 1996 / NAP / B
NOELLE BUDVAR *see Star Index I*
NOELLE RIDER
Princess Of Thieves / 1994 / SC / M
NOK
Global Girls / 1996 / GO / F
NOLAN *see Star Index I*
NOLAN STOWE
[Kink, Hollywood Style / 197? / ... / M
NOLAN VELOURS
Pleasure So Deep / 1983 / AT / M
NORA
International Love And The Dancer / 1995 / PME / S • Rev Eb #03 / 1990 / REV / B • Transsexual Trouble / 1991 / CIN / G
NORA BLACK
Black Fantasies #15 / 1996 / HW / M
NORA KUZMA *see Traci Lords*
NORA LOUISE KUZMA *see Traci Lords*
NORA WIETERNIK
Blue Vanities #007 / 1988 / FFL / M • Blue Vanities #240 / 1995 / FFL / M • Blue Vanities #241 / 1995 / FFL / M • Blue Vanities #250 / 1996 / FFL / M • Blue Vanities #588 / 1996 / FFL / M • Flesh Gordon #1 / 1974 / FAC / S
NORBERT
Magma: Perverse Games / 1995 / MET / M
NORBERT CIRET *see Star Index I*
NOREEN
Blue Vanities #526 / 1993 / FFL / M • Blue Vanities #539 / 1993 / FFL / M • Blue Vanities #554 / 1994 / FFL / M
NORI
Blue Vanities #129 / 1990 / FFL / M
NORICA TAKARASHI
The Kimono / 1983 / ORC / M
NORIKO TANAKA
Private Escort / 1996 / AVE / M
NORM NOEVENT
The Stand-Up / 1994 / VC / M
NORMA
Blue Vanities #509 / 1992 / FFL / M • Blue Vanities #516 / 1992 / FFL / M
NORMA (KILIAN) *see Kilian*
NORMA BAXTER *see Star Index I*
NORMA GENE *see Dorothy Le May*
NORMA JAMES *see Star Index I*
NORMA JEAN (D.LEMAY) *see Dorothy Le May*
NORMA JEANE
Anal Candy Ass / 1994 / ROB / M • Anal Legend / 1994 / ROB / M • Anal Summer / 1994 / ROB / M • As Easy As A Bunch Of Cunts / 1996 / ROB / F • Assy Sassy #1 / 1994 / ROB / F • Black & Booty-Full / 1996 / ROB / M • Cuntrol / 1994 / MID / F • The Dinner Party #1 / 1994 / ULI / M • Dr Rear / 1995 / CC / M • Extreme Sex #2: The Dungeon / 1994 / VI / M • Film Buff / 1994 / WP / M • Gang Bang Fury #2 / 1996 / ROB / M • Gang Bang Nymphette / 1994 / ROB / M • Happy Ass Lesbians / 1994 / ROB / F • Hello Norma Jeane / 1994 / VT / M • Lesbian C*Nt Whores / 1996 / ROB / F • Love Me, Love My Butt #1 / 1994 / ROB / F • Misfits / 1994 / CV / M • Misty @ Midnight / 1995 / LE / M • My Evil Twin / 1994 / LE / M • No Man's Land #14 / 1996 / VT / F • The Other Side / 1995 / ERA / M • Private Performance / 1994 / EX / M • Put 'em On Da Glass / 1994 / VT / M • Putting It All Behind #2: Star Treatment / 1994 / IN / M • Split Tail Lovers / 1994 / ROB / F • Under The Pink / 1994 / ROB / F
NORMA WALKER *see Kilian*

NORMA WILCOX
Total Sexual Power: Mastering Ejaculatory Control / 1994 / EPR / M • Total Sexual Power: The Ecstasy Of Female Orgasm / 1994 / EPR / M
NORMAN
Breast Worx #14 / 1992 / LBO / M • Juicy Virgins / 1995 / WIV / M
NORMAN APSTEIN *see Paul Norman*
NORMAN BATES
Overnight Sensation / 1976 / AR / M
NORMAN BEY
Angel Buns / 1981 / QX / M
NORMAN HAZZARD
F / 1980 / GO / M
NORMAN JACKSON
Intimate Action #1 / 1983 / INP / M
NORMAN MINCE *see Star Index I*
NORMAN OSAKA *see Star Index I*
NORMAN WESTBERG
Hardcore: The Films Of Richard Kern #1 / 1991 / FTV / M
NORRIS O'NEAL *see Star Index I*
NOVA
Lisa / 1997 / SC / M
NOVA KANE *see Susan Sloan*
NOVA X
Streets Of New York #06 / 1996 / PL / M
NOVITIA
Magma: Bizarre Lust / 1995 / MET / M
NUATY DRED
Northwest Pecker Trek #6: Two Girls For Every Boy / 1995 / LBO / M
NUKE ROCKEM *see Star Index I*
NUKE ROPKNEE *see Star Index I*
NUMBERS PERU
Resurrection Of Eve / 1973 / MIT / M
NUREA
Bosoms Triple X / 1990 / BTO / M • The World Of Double-D #1 / 199? / H&S / S
NURSE LAY
The Adventures Of Mr. Tootsie Pole #1 / 1995 / LBO / M • The Nurses Are Cumming #2 / 1996 / LBO / C
NUTE *see Star Index I*
NYOMI WATERS
More Dirty Debutantes #44 / 1995 / 4P / M
NYRIBI KALMAN
Skin #4: The 4th Rite / 1995 / ERQ / M
NYROBI KNIGHT *(Nikki Darling, Niki Darling, Nyrubi, Nairobi Knight)*
Black girl with long curly hair, large inflated tits, lithe body, birthmark or tattoo on right shoulder back, nice smile, passable face.
Anal Addict / 1995 / ROB / M • Anal Delinquent #3 / 1995 / ROB / M • Anal Hellraiser #2 / 1995 / ROB / M • Anal Load Lickers / 1996 / ROB / M • Anal Tight Ass / 1995 / ROB / M • Anal Trashy Ass / 1995 / ROB / M • Ass Angels / 1996 / PAL / F • Beverly Hills Bikini Company / 1996 / NIT / M • Bi Dream Of Genie / 1994 / BIL / G • Bi George / 1994 / BIL / G • Bikini Beach #4 / 1996 / CC / M • Bimbette: Adventures In Anal Land / 1996 / TEP / M • Black Juice Bombs / 1996 / NIT / C • Black Knockers #03 / 1995 / TV / M • Black Knockers #13 / 1995 / TV / M • Black Pussyman Auditions #1 / 1996 / SNA / M • Booty Bitch / 1995 / ROB / M • Booty Ho #3 / 1995 / ROB / M • Bootylicious: Ghetto Booty / 1996 / JMP / M • Born Bad / 1996 / WAV / M • Bow Down Backstreet / 1996 / HW / M • Butt Sluts #5 / 1995 / ROB / F • The Case Of The Black Booty / 1996 / LV / M • Casting Call #16 / 1995 / SO / M • Caught From Behind #23 /

1995 / HO / M • Caught From Behind #24 / 1996 / HO / M • Checkmate / 1996 / SNA / M • Club Anal #3 / 1995 / ROB / F • Cumback Pussy #1 / 1996 / EL / M • Cumback Pussy #2: Crawling Back For More / 1996 / EL / M • Debi Diamond's Dirty Dykes #2 / 1995 / FD / F • Dirty Minds / 1996 / NIT / M • Dirty Stories #4 / 1995 / PE / M • Dreams Of A Gigolo / 1996 / SNA / M • Entangled / 1996 / KLP / M • Escape From Anal Lost Angels / 1996 / HO / M • Fashion sluts #5: Ethnic Ecstasy / 1995 / ABS / M • Fire & Ice: Caught In The Act / 1995 / WP / M • Forbidden Cravings / 1996 / VC / M • Frankenpenis / 1995 / LEI / M • Gang Bang Face Bath #4 / 1995 / ROB / M • Gang Bang Jizz Queen / 1995 / ROB / M • Hot Tight Asses #14 / 1995 / TCK / M • The Illustrated Woman / 1995 / CA / M • Interview's Dark And Delicious / 1996 / LV / M • Interview: Dark And Delicious / 1996 / LV / M • Kittens & Vamps #2 / 1995 / ROB / F • Lesbian Climax / 1995 / ROB / F • Licorice Lollipops: Summer Break / 1996 / HW / M • Lockdown / 1996 / NIT / M • The Meatman / 1995 / OUP / M • Mister Stickypants / 1996 / LV / M • My Baby Got Back #08 / 1996 / VT / M • Nasty Pants / 1995 / SUF / M • The New Butt Hunt #12 / 1995 / LEI / C • Nightlife / 1997 / CA / M • Odyssey 30 Min: #547: / 1995 / OD / M • Pay 4 Play / 1996 / RAS / M • Perverted Stories #06 / 1996 / JMP / M • Philmore Butts Goes Wild! / 1996 / SUF / M • Pick Up Lines #01 / 1995 / 4P / M • Primal Instinct / 1996 / SNA / M • Puritan Video Magazine #01 / 1996 / LE / M • Pussyman #14: Dreams Of A Gigolo / 1996 / SNA / M • Pussyman's House Party #1 / 1996 / SNA / M • Pussyman's House Party #2 / 1996 / SNA / M • Rockhard (Sin City) / 1996 / SC / M • Roommates To Lovers / 1995 / LIP / F • Sex Freaks / 1995 / EA / M • Sodomania #18: Shame Based / 1996 / EL / M • Sodomize Me!!! / 1996 / SPR / M • Tender Box / 1996 / MP0 / M • Tinsel Town Tales / 1995 / NOT / M • Toot Z Roll / 1995 / WP / M • Two-Pac / 1996 / VT / M • Valentino's Euro-Invasion / 1997 / SC / M • Vienna's Place / 1996 / VCX / M • Virgin Dreams / 1996 / EA / M • Yo' Where's Homey? / 1996 / SUF / M
NYRUBI *see Nyrobi Knight*
O'BRYAN *see Star Index I*
O.B.D.
Final Orgy / 1996 / BON / B • Orgy Of Cruelty / 1995 / BON / B • Orgy Of Pain / 1995 / BON / B • Tight Security / 1995 / BON / B
OBI WAHN *see Billy Dee*
OBSESSION
Light skinned black girl with a pretty face, small tits, tight waist, narrow hips, nice tight butt, tattoo on top of her right breast and another on right bicep both of which are the names of her previous boyfriends, 20 years old and measures 34B-?-? Seems to have a nice but quiet and shy personality.
Black & Booty-Full / 1996 / ROB / M • The Black Butt Sisters Do Chicago / 1995 / MID / M • The Black Butt Sisters Do Seattle / 1995 / MID / M • Black Cheerleader Jerk-Off / 1996 / WIC / F • Black Cheerleader Search #01 / 1996 / ROB / M • Black Hollywood Amateurs #18 / 1995 / MID / M • Black Hollywood Amateurs #22 / 1996 / MID / M • Black Lube Job Girls / 1995 /

SUF / M • Black Sensations: Models In Heat / 1995 / SUF / M • Black Street Hookers #2 / 1996 / DFI / M • Dirty Dirty Debutantes #2 / 1996 / 4P / M • Dirty Tricks #2: This Ain't Love / 1996 / EA / M • Fashion sluts #5: Ethnic Ecstasy / 1995 / ABS / M • Freaknic / 1996 / IN / M • Hardcore Confidential #2 / 1996 / TEP / M • Kink: Police Chronicles / 1995 / ROB / M • My Baby Got Back #07 / 1995 / VT / M • Pick Up Lines #07 / 1996 / OD / M • Suzi Bungholeo / 1995 / ROB / M • Waiting To XXX-Hale / 1996 / MET / M

OCEANA
Hollywood Amateurs #22 / 1995 / MID / M
ODETTE BUREL
Diamond Snatch / 1977 / COM / M • The Making Of A Porno Movie / 1984 / CA / M • Vacation / 1984 / CA / M • Visions Of Lust / 1983 / GO / M
ODUS HAMLIN see Erik Anderson
OH SUSANNAH
Dr Juice's Lust Potion / 1986 / TEM / M
OLA
Hot New Imports / 1996 / XC / M
OLAE JULOVE
Dangerous Pleasure / 1995 / WIV / M
OLAF SACHENWEGER
Private Film #01 / 1993 / OD / M
OLE SOTTUPT see Star Index I
OLES
Perversity In Paris / 1994 / AVI / M
OLGA
Frank Thring's Double Penetration #2 / 1996 / XPR / M • Palomino Heat / 1985 / COM / F • Prague By Night #1 / 1996 / EA / M • Private Stories #05 / 1995 / OD / M • Russian Model Magazine #2 / 1996 / IP / M • Sodomania #11: In Your Face / 1994 / EL / M • Sorority Lingerie Party / 1995 / NIV / F • Triple X Video Magazine #15 / 1996 / OD / M
OLGA DAVIS
And Then Came Eve / cr72 / VCX / M • Fantastic Voyeur / 1975 / AVC / M
OLGA JOHANSON see Star Index I
OLGA KINSKY see Star Index I
OLGA KORNEL
Love Theatre / cr80 / VC / M
OLGA LARENCIN see Star Index I
OLGA LEWIS
Pleasure Productions #06 / 1984 / VCR / M
OLGA SINYAVSKA
Russian Girls / 1996 / WV / M
OLGA STERN
The Big E #08 / 1988 / BIZ / B • Cramped Spaces / 1989 / PLV / B • TV Dragnet / 1988 / BIZ / G
OLINKA *(Mary Monroe (Olinka), Olinka Podany, Marilyn Lamour, Olinka Hardiman, Olinka Johnson, Olinka Richter)*
Marilyn Lamour is from **Call Girl (1984)**. Olinka Podany is from **Virgin And The Lover**.
Almost Anything Goes / cr75 / ASR / M • Backing In #2 / 1990 / WV / C • Blondes Like It Hot / 1984 / ELH / M • Blondes! Blondes! Blondes! / 1986 / VCS / C • Burning Snow / 1984 / CA / M • Caballero Preview Tape #5 / 1986 / CA / C • Call Girl / 1984 / CV / M • The Comeback Of Marilyn / 1986 / VC / M • Emmanuelle Goes To Cannes / 1984 / ECV / S • Erotic Intruders / 1985 / CA / M • Flying Skirts / 1985 / HO / M • Hot Bodies (Caballero) / 1984 / CA / M • House Of 1001 Pleasures / 1985 / VC

/ M • Ingrid, The Whore Of Hamburg / 1984 / CA / M • Inside Marilyn / 1984 / CA / M • Inside Olinka / 1993 / CA / C • Marilyn, My Love / 1985 / ELH / M • Mobile Home Girls / 1985 / VC / M • Mrs. Winter's Lover / 1984 / CA / M • Olinka, Goddess Of Love / 1987 / CA / C • Olinka, Grand Priestess Of Love / 1985 / CA / M • Only The Best From Europe / 1989 / CV / C • Only The Best Of Men's And Women's Fantasies / 1988 / CV / C • Postcards From Abroad / 1991 / CA / C • Revolution / 1984 / CA / M • Secret Spankings / 198? / TLV / B • Secrets Of Marilyn / 19?? / ... / M • Spanish Fly / 1987 / CA / M • Take My Body / 1984 / SE / M • A Taste Of Olinka / 1990 / PIN / C • Tickle Time / 1987 / BIZ / B • The Titty Committee / 1986 / SE / C • Trashy Tourist / 1985 / CA / M • Vacation / 1984 / CA / M • Virgin And The Lover / 1973 / ALP / M • White Heat / 1981 / CA / M • Yiddish Erotica #1 / 1986 / SE / C
OLINKA FEROVA
Private Film #08 / 1994 / OD / M • Private Video Magazine #09 / 1994 / OD / M
OLINKA HARDIMAN see Olinka
OLINKA JOHNSON see Olinka
OLINKA JONSSON
Happy Holiday / 1978 / CA / M
OLINKA PODANY see Olinka
OLINKA RICHTER see Olinka
OLIVER HOLMES
Pussyman #10: Butts, Butts & More Butts / 1995 / SNA / M
OLIVER SANCHEZ *(Oliver Sansley)*
Presumably the SO of Maria De Sanchez as he always seems to appear with her.
Asses Galore #6: Fallen Angels / 1996 / DFI / M • Buttman In Barcelona / 1996 / EA / M • Flamenco Ecstasy / 1996 / UEF / M • Pick Up Lines #12 / 1997 / OD / M • Pick Up Lines #13 / 1997 / OD / M • The Voyeur #7: Live In Europe #1 / 1996 / JLP / M
OLIVER SANSLEY see Oliver Sanchez
OLIVER TATE
Bad Girls #4 / 1984 / GO / M
OLIVER THOMAS see Star Index I
OLIVIA
Large blonde with masses of curly hair, huge enhanced tits, not too pretty face, big butt, large tattoo on her left center belly, another on her ankle and a third on the back of her neck. Supposedly shot herself (not fatally) in mid-1995 however she says it was appendicitis. First movie was a g/g with Sara Jane Hamilton in **Erotique Optique**. Has a daughter.
Alpine Affairs / 1995 / LE / M • Anabolic Import #01: Anal X / 1994 / ANA / M • Anal Delinquent #2 / 1994 / ROB / M • The Anal-Europe Series #07: / 1994 / LV / M • Back Door Babewatch / 1995 / IF / C • Backdoor To Buttsville / 1995 / ULI / M • Big & Busty Superstars / 1996 / DGD / F • Big Bust Babes #26 / 1995 / AFI / M • Big Busted Goddesses Of Beverly Hills / 1996 / NAP / S • Big Knockers #16 / 1995 / TV / M • Big Knockers #18 / 1995 / TV / M • Big Knockers #21: Best Of Lesbian #2 / 1995 / TV / C • Blonde / 1995 / LE / M • Blonde In Blue Flannel / 1995 / CA / M • Bloopers & Behind The Scenes / 1995 / LEI / M • Blue Vanities #558 / 1994 / FFL / M • Boobtown / 1995 / VC / M • Burn It Up / 1994 / VEX / M • The Busty Kittens / 1995 / NAP / F • Butt Jammers #02 / 1995 / SC / F • Butt

Love / 1995 / AB / M • The Butt Sisters Do Baltimore / 1995 / MID / M • Butthead Dreams: Exposed / 1995 / FH / M • Cabin Fever / 1995 / ERA / M • Chained / 1995 / SC / M • Cheeks #8 / 1995 / CC / M • A Clockwork Orgy / 1995 / PL / M • Debbie Class Of '95 / 1995 / CC / M • Dirty Little Ass Slut / 1995 / KWP / M • Double D Amateurs #21 / 1994 / JMP / M • Dream House / 1995 / XPR / M • Erotic Visions / 1995 / ULI / M • Erotica Optique / 1994 / SUF / M • Eurotica #04 / 1996 / XC / M • Evil Temptations #1 / 1995 / ULP / M • Evil Temptations #2 / 1995 / ULP / M • Flexxx #3 / 1995 / VT / M • The Flirt / 1995 / GO / M • Frank Thring's Double Penetration #3 / 1996 / XPR / M • French Twist / 1996 / HO / M • Gang Bang Jizz Jammers / 1994 / ROB / M • Hawaiian Heat #1 / 1995 / CC / M • Hawaiian Heat #2 / 1995 / CC / M • Horny Henry's Euro Adventure / 1995 / TTV / M • Horny Henry's London Adventure / 1995 / TTV / M • Hotel California / 1995 / MID / M • House Arrest / 1995 / CV / M • John Wayne Bobbitt Uncut / 1994 / LEI / M • Kinky Nurses / 1995 / VEX / C • Living Legend / 1995 / V99 / M • Lucky Lady / 1995 / CV / M • Lusty Lawyers / 1995 / PRK / M • The Magnificence Of Minka / 1996 / NAP / S • Misty Rain's Anal Orgy / 1994 / FRM / M • Models Etc. / 1995 / LV / M • Nasty Nymphos #07 / 1994 / ANA / M • National Boom Boom's European Vacation / 1994 / HW / M • Private Gold #12: The Pyramid #2 / 1996 / OD / M • Profiles #01 / 1995 / XPR / M • Pump Fiction / 1995 / VT / M • Pussyclips #07 / 1995 / SNA / M • Rebel Cheerleaders / 1995 / VI / M • Romance & Fantasy / 1995 / VEX / M • A Round Behind / 1995 / PEP / M • Rump Man: Sex On The Beach / 1995 / HW / M • Satyriasis / 1995 / CA / M • Sensual Spirits / 1995 / LE / M • Silk Stockings: The Black Widow / 1994 / SPI / M • Sin City Cycle Sluts #1 / 1995 / SC / F • Spirit Guide / 1995 / IN / M • The Story Of Olivia / 1996 / MID / M • Thunder Boobs / 1995 / BTO / M • Titty Troop / 1995 / CC / M • Topless Brain Surgeons / 1995 / LE / M • Topless Stewardesses / 1995 / PV / M • Wanted / 1995 / DR / M • The Way They Wuz / 1996 / SHS / C • Wet Nurses #2 / 1995 / LE / M • White Wedding / 1994 / V99 / M • A Woman Scorned / 1995 / CA / M • Work Of Art / 1995 / LE / M • Xxxanadu / 1994 / HW / M • Young Nurses In Lust / 1994 / LBO / M
OLIVIA (ALEX DANE) see Alex Dane
OLIVIA BROWN
Bound To Pay / 1995 / CS / B
OLIVIA CHASE
1-900-SPANKME Ext.1 / 1994 / BON / B • 1-900-SPANKME Ext.2 / 1994 / BON / B • Prescription For Pain #3: Bad Medicine / 1993 / BON / B • Trainer's Turnabout / 1994 / BON / B
OLIVIA DEL RIO
Private Film #27 / 1995 / OD / M • Private Film #28 / 1995 / OD / M • Toredo / 1996 / ROX / M • Triple X Video Magazine #02 / 1995 / OD / M • Triple X Video Magazine #04 / 1995 / OD / M • The Voyeur #7: Live In Europe #1 / 1996 / JLP / M • World Sex Tour #6 / 1996 / ANA / M
OLIVIA DEVILLE
Busty Babes In Heat #2 / 1993 / BTO / M
OLIVIA FLEMING

The Psychiatrist / 1978 / VC / M
OLIVIA FLORES *see Star Index I*
OLIVIA OUTRE
Big Reward / 1995 / CS / B • Bondage Brothel / 1996 / LBO / B • Dance To The Whip / 1996 / LBO / B • The Dean Of Discipline / 1996 / HAC / B • Diary Of A Mistress / 1995 / HOM / B • Dr Dominatrix / 1996 / LBO / B • Forbidden Session / 1996 / VTF / B • Jasmine's Girls / 1995 / LON / B • Kym Wilde's On The Edge #22 / 1995 / RB / B • Mistress Of Shadows / 1995 / HOM / B • No Mercy For The Bitches / 1996 / LBO / B • Pain Is The Price / 1996 / LBO / B • Pain Puppets / 1996 / LBO / B • Porsche's Ordeal / 1996 / LBO / B • Punishment Of The Liars / 1996 / LBO / B • Sisters In Submission / 1996 / BON / B • Taste For Submission / 1996 / VTF / B
OLIVIER SANCHEZ
Betty Bleu / 1996 / IP / M
OLU ZILCH *see Star Index I*
OMAHA
Bright Tails #8 / 1996 / STP / B
OMAR
Back East Babes #3 / 1996 / NIT / M • Intimate Interviews #3 / 1996 / NIT / M • N.Y. Video Magazine #09 / 1996 / OUP / M
OMAR BOGG
Tale Of Bearded Clam / cr71 / PYR / M
OMAR CLAY
ABA: Double Feature #5 / 1996 / ALP / M • Night Of Submission / 1976 / BIZ / M
OMEGAMAN *see Star Index I*
ONA SIMMS *see Ona Zee*
ONA SIMMS WIEGERS *see Ona Zee*
ONA STORM *see Star Index I*
ONA ZEE *(Joanna Collins, Ona Simms, Ona Simms Wiegers)*
Older woman but quite pretty with black hair and medium tits. 5'6" tall and 120lbs in 1987 (a little more in 1994). Married to Frank Zee.
1-800-934-BOOB / 1992 / VD / C • A&B BD#01: Submissive Slaves / 1991 / A&B / B • A&B BD#02: Submissive Wife #1 / 1991 / A&B / B • A&B BD#03: Male Slave / 1991 / A&B / B • A&B BD#04: Submissive Ladies / 1991 / A&B / B • A&B BD#05: Submissive Slave #2 / 1991 / A&B / B • A&B BD#06: Submissive Wife #2 / 1991 / A&B / B • A&B BD#07: Submissive Husband / 1991 / A&B / B • A&B GB#012: Ona Z And Leslie / 1992 / A&B / M • A&B GB#013: Cumming Out Party #1 / 1992 / A&B / M • A&B GB#014: Cumming Out Party #2 / 1992 / A&B / M • A&B GB#015: Cumming Out Party #3 / 1992 / A&B / M • A&B GB#026: The Judgement / 1992 / A&B / M • Adult Video News 1992 Awards / 1992 / VC / M • Adult Video Therapist / 1987 / CLV / C • Adultery / 1989 / PP / M • Afternoon With Goddess Sondra / 1992 / SSP / B • The All American Girl / 1991 / PP / M • Alone And Dripping / 1991 / LV / M • Amanda By Night #2 / 1987 / CA / M • American Garter / 1993 / VC / M • Anal Adventures #4: Doin' Her Up! / 1992 / VC / M • Anal Analysis (Heatwave) / 1992 / HW / M • Angel Kelly Raw / 1987 / FAN / M • The Art Of Dying / 1990 / PME / S • Babylon Pink #2 / 1988 / COM / M • Babylon Pink #3 / 1988 / COM / M • Back To Rears / 1988 / VI / M • Backdoor Brides #4 / 1993 / PV / M • Backing In #4 / 1993 / WV / C • Bedtime Stories / 1992 / CDI / M • The Best

Of Strippers Inc / 1996 / ONA / C • Beyond The Denver Dynasty / 1988 / CA / M • Bi-Dacious / 1989 / PL / G • Birthday Surprise / 1988 / BON / B • The Bitch / 1988 / FAN / M • The Bitch Is Back / 1988 / FAN / M • The Bitches Of Westwood / 1987 / CA / M • Black Orchid / 1993 / WV / M • Bondage Boot Camp / 1988 / TAN / B • The Bondage Club #1 / 1987 / LON / B • The Bondage Club #2 / 1987 / LON / B • The Bondage Club #4 / 1990 / LON / B • The Bondage Club #5 / 1990 / LON / B • Bondage Landlord / 1989 / ... / B • Bondage Memories #03 / 1994 / BON / C • Boom Boom Valdez / 1988 / CA / M • Boy-Girl Spanking #606: The Therapist / 1988 / CTS / B • The Brazilian Connection / 1988 / CA / M • Bringing Up The Rear / 1993 / VD / C • Bubble Butts #21 / 1993 / LBO / M • Bush Pilots #2 / 1991 / VC / M • Buzzzz! / 1993 / OD / M • Careless / 1993 / PP / M • The Cat Club / 1987 / SE / M • Cheating American Style / 1988 / WV / M • Checkmate / 1992 / CDI / M • Cheeks #1 / 1988 / CC / M • Cherry Red / 1993 / RB / B • City Of Sin / 1991 / LV / M • Club Kiss / 1995 / ONA / M • Crazy With The Heat #2 / 1993 / MET / M • Dazzling Dominants / 1991 / RSV / B • Debbie 4 Hire / 1988 / AVC / M • Debbie's Lesson / 1988 / ... / B • Deep Inside Ariana / 1995 / VC / C • Deep Inside Ona Zee / 1992 / VC / C • Deep Inside Shanna Mccullough / 1992 / VC / C • Defenseless / 1992 / CDI / M • The Dinner Party / 1986 / WV / M • Dirty Books / 1992 / VC / M • Dominating Girlfriends #1 / 1992 / PL / B • Dominating Girlfriends #2 / 1992 / PL / B • Double Play / 1993 / CA / C • The Dream Machine / 1992 / CDI / M • Easy Pussy / 1991 / ROB / M • Ebony Love / 1992 / VT / C • Eclipse / 1993 / SC / M • Eleventh Annual AVN Awards / 1994 / VC / M • Enrapture / 1990 / ATL / S • Erectnophobia #2 / 1992 / MID / M • Erotique / 1992 / VC / M • Facial Attraction / 1988 / BEE / C • Fade To Black / 1988 / CDI / M • The Fantasy Booth / 1993 / ONA / M • Fatal Passion / 1988 / CC / M • Fever Pitch / 1995 / ONA / M • Final Exam #1 / 1987 / BON / B • Final Exam #2 / 1988 / BON / B • The Final Taboo / 1988 / CA / M • Flesh In Ecstasy #02: Samantha Strong / 1987 / GO / C • Flesh In Ecstasy #03: Purple Passion / 1987 / GO / C • Flesh In Ecstasy #04: Jeanna Fine / 1987 / GO / C • Forever Yours / 1992 / CDI / M • Frisky Fables / 1988 / LV / M • Full Moon Fever / 1992 / PEP / M • Get Bi Tonight / 1991 / PL / G • Girls Gone Bad #5: Mexican Justice / 1991 / GO / F • Goin' Down Slow / 1988 / VC / M • Good Enough To Eat / 1988 / FAZ / M • Good Evening Vietnam / 1987 / WV / M • The Good Stuff / 1989 / BON / C • Guilty By Seduction / 1993 / PI / M • Hard Ride / 1992 / WV / M • Head Clinic / 1987 / AVC / M • The Heiress / 1988 / VI / M • Hidden Desires / 1992 / CDI / M • High Heels In Heat #1 / 1988 / RSV / F • Hooked / 1992 / SC / M • Hornet's Nest / 1996 / ONA / M • House Of Sexual Fantasies / 1987 / GO / M • The Hunger / 1993 / FOR / M • I Remember When / 1992 / ATL / M • Immaculate Erection / 1992 / VD / M • In A Crystal Fantasy / 1988 / VD / M • Internal Affairs / 1992 / CDI / M • Joint Effort / 1992 / SEX / C • Journal Of O #1: Servant Slave / 1994 / ONA / B • Journal Of O #2 / 1994 /

ONA / B • Joy-Fm #06 / 1994 / BHS / M • Juicy Treats / 1991 / ROB / M • Kinky / 1987 / SE / M • A Kiss Before Dying / 1993 / CDI / M • The Last Condom / 1988 / PP / M • Latex #2 / 1995 / VC / M • Le Hot Club / 1987 / WV / M • Let's Talk Dirty / 1987 / SE / M • Lick-A-Thon #2 / 1996 / HW / C • Little Red Riding Hood / 1988 / WV / M • Long Hot Summer / 1992 / CDI / M • Love Potion / 1993 / WV / M • Lust Connection / 1988 / VT / M • The Luv Game / 1988 / VCX / M • The Maddams Family / 1991 / XCI / M • Maid Service / 1993 / FL / M • Making Ends Meet / 1988 / VT / M • Maximum Head / 1987 / SE / M • Memoirs Of A Chambermaid / 1987 / FIR / M • More Than A Handful #3 / 1993 / MET / M • Motel Sweets / 1987 / VD / M • My Favorite Rear / 1993 / PEP / M • Mystery Of The Maletease Dildo / 1992 / STR / M • Nikki's Last Stand / 1993 / VC / M • No One To Love / 1987 / PP / M • Ona & Stephanie / 1992 / OD / C • Ona Z's Star Search #01 / 1993 / GLI / M • Ona Z's Star Search #02 / 1993 / GLI / M • Ona Z's Star Search #03 / 1993 / GLI / M • Ona Zee's Black Label #1: Sex Hunger / 1996 / ONA / C • Ona Zee's Date With Dallas / 1992 / ONA / M • Ona Zee's Doll House #1 / 1995 / ONA / F • Ona Zee's Doll House #2 / 1995 / ONA / F • Ona Zee's Flesh Tease / 1991 / RSV / F • Ona Zee's Learning The Ropes #01: Male Submissive / 1992 / ONA / B • Ona Zee's Learning The Ropes #02: Male Submissive / 1992 / ONA / B • Ona Zee's Learning The Ropes #03: Male Submissive / 1992 / ONA / B • Ona Zee's Learning The Ropes #04: Female Submissive / 1992 / ONA / B • Ona Zee's Learning The Ropes #05: Female Submissive / 1992 / ONA / B • Ona Zee's Learning The Ropes #06: Lesbian Bondage / 1992 / ONA / B • Ona Zee's Learning The Ropes #07: At Lady Laura's / 1992 / ONA / B • Ona Zee's Learning The Ropes #08: Slaves In Training / 1992 / ONA / B • Ona Zee's Learning The Ropes #09: The Training Continues / 1992 / ONA / B • Ona Zee's Learning The Ropes #10: Chains Of Love / 1994 / ONA / B • Ona Zee's Learning The Ropes #11: Chains Required / 1994 / ONA / B • Ona Zee's Learning The Ropes #12: Couples / 1995 / ONA / B • Ona Zee's Learning The Ropes #13: Best Of Male Submission / 1996 / ONA / C • Ona's Dynamite D.P.'s / 1995 / ONA / C • Other People's Honey / 1991 / HW / M • Our Dinner With Andrea / 1988 / CA / M • Over 40 / 1989 / BIZ / B • Paging Betty / 1994 / VC / M • Parliament: Dark & Sweet #1 / 1991 / PM / C • Partners In Sex / 1988 / FAN / M • The Party / 1992 / CDI / M • Peggy Sue / 1987 / VT / M • Phone Mates / 1988 / CA / M • Phone Sex Girls #1 / 1987 / VT / M • Portrait Of An Affair / 1988 / VD / M • A Portrait Of Dorian / 1992 / OD / M • Power Blonde / 1988 / AVC / M • Prelude / 1992 / VT / M • Professor Butts / 1994 / SBP / F • Profiles #03: House Dick / 1995 / XPR / M • Pure Sex / 1988 / FAN / C • Rapture Girls #2: Ona & Stephanie / 1991 / OD / M • Raw Talent #3 / 1988 / VC / M • Razor's Edge / 1995 / ONA / M • Rippin' 'n' Strippin' #1 / 1987 / BON / B • Rippin' 'n' Strippin' #2 / 1988 / BON / B • Robofox #2 / 1988 / FAN / M • Satisfaction Jackson / 1988 / CA / M • Saturday Night

Special / 1989 / DR / M • The Savannah Affair / 1993 / CDI / M • Scorched / 1995 / ONA / M • Second Skin / 1989 / VC / M • The Secret Garden #1 / 1992 / XCI / M • The Secret Garden #2 / 1992 / XCI / M • Secret Services / 1993 / PEP / M • Seduction By Fire / 1987 / VD / M • The Servants Of Midnight / 1992 / CDI / M • Servin' It Up / 1993 / VC / M • Sex Academy #1 / 1993 / ONA / M • Sex Academy #2: The Art Of Talking Dirty / 1994 / ONA / M • Sex Academy #3: The Art Of Real Sex / 1994 / ONA / M • Sex Academy #4: The Art Of Anal / 1994 • ONA / M • Sex And The Secretary / 1988 / PP / M • Sex For Hire / 1996 / ONA / M • Sex Lives Of The Rich And Famous #1 / 1988 / VC / M • Sex Lives Of The Rich And Famous #2 / 1989 / VC / M • Sex Lives Of The Rich And Beautiful / 1988 / CA / M • Sex Ranch / 1993 / VC / M • Sex Wish / 1992 / WV / M • Sextrology /1987 / CA / M • Shame On Shanna / 1989 / DR / C • She Likes To Watch / 1992 / EVN / M • Sin City: The Movie / 1992 / SC / M • Sleeping Beauty Aroused / 1989 / VI / M • Slightly Used / 1987 / VD / M • The Slut / 1988 / FAN / M • Soap Me Up! / 1993 / FD / M • Splatman / 1992 / FR / M • The Starlet / 1991 / PP / M • Starship Intercourse / 1987 / DR / M • Street Angels / 1992 / LV / M • Street Heat / 1992 / CDI / M • Strippers Inc. #1 / 1994 / ONA / M • Strippers Inc. #2 / 1994 / ONA / M • Strippers Inc. #3 / 1994 / ONA / M • Strippers Inc. #4 / 1995 / ONA / M • Strippers Inc. #5 / 1995 / ONA / M • Surfside Sex #2 / 1992 / LV / M • Swedish Erotica Letters #1 / 1989 / CA / C • Swedish Erotica Letters #2 / 1989 / CA / C • Sweet Alicia Rio / 1992 / FH / M • The Sweet Spurt Of Youth / 1988 / WV / M • Talk Dirty To Me #05 / 1987 / DR / M • Talk Dirty To Me #06 / 1989 / DR / M • Tangled / 1994 / PL / M • Temple Of Lust / 1992 / VC / M • Tenth Annual Adult Video News Awards / 1993 / VC / M • The Therapist / 1992 / VC / M • This Butt Lite Is For You / 1992 / ATL / M • Too Sexy / 1992 / MID / M • Totally Ona: The Best Of Ona Zee / 1996 / ONA / C • The Toy Box / 1996 / ONA / M • Tropical Lust / 1987 / MET / M • Twentysomething #1 / 1988 / VI / M • Twentysomething #2 / 1988 / VI / M • Two Hearts / 1991 / VI / M • Velma And Clarice/What Are Friends For / 1994 / HAC / B • Wacs / 1992 / PP / M • Wendy Whoppers: Environmental Attorney / 1993 / PEP / M • Wendy Whoppers: Ninja CPA / 1993 / PEP / M • Wicked Sensations #2 / 1989 / DR / M • Wild Hearts / 1992 / SC / M • Working Stiffs / 1993 / FD / M • [Older Women Are Sexy #4 / 19?? / ... / M

ONNA BACQUE
Student Fetish Videos: Foot Worship #14 / 1995 / PRE / B

ONYX/VANITY
Asses Galore #3: Pure Evil / 1996 / DFI / M • The Black Butt Sisters Do Los Angeles / 1995 / MID / M • Black Cheerleader Search #06 / 1996 / IVC / M • Black Street Hookers #1 / 1996 / DFI / M • Fetish Phone Femmes / 1996 / STM / B • Lovin' Spoonfuls #7 / 1996 / 4P / C • More Black Dirty Debutantes / 1994 / 4P / M • More Black Dirty Debutantes #3 / 1994 / 4P / M • More Black Dirty Debutantes #4 / 1995 / 4P / M • My Baby Got Back #09 / 1996 / VT / M • My

First Time #5 / 1996 / NS / M • Sista! #3 / 1995 / VT / F • Valentina: Princess Of The Forest / 1996 / SC / M

OPAL
Raw Talent: Top Bang / 1994 / RTP / M
OPALAKA MIKE see Star Index I
OPHELIA RASS
They Shall Overcome / 1974 / VST / M
OPHELIA TOZZY
Anal Vision #07 / 1993 / LBO / M • The Anal-Europe Series #03: The Museum Of The Living Art / 1993 / LV / M • The Anal-Europe Series #04: Anal Recall / 1993 / LV / M • Backdoor To The City Of Sin / 1993 / ANA / M • Bright Tails #5 / 1995 / STP / B • Bright Tails #7 / 1995 / STP / B • New Faces, Hot Bodies #15 / 1994 / STP / M • Toy Time #3: / 1995 / STP / F
ORALEE S. WET see Star Index I
ORALIE
Eurotica #05 / 1996 / XC / M
ORCHID
Anal Asians / 1991 / PL / F • Butt Watch #03 / 1994 / FH / M
ORGIE GEORGIE see Beau Michaels
ORGY GEORGE see Beau Michaels
ORIANA
Private Gold #04: Amazonas / 1996 / OD / M • Triple X Video Magazine #10 / 1995 / OD / M
ORLAN
Thief Of Passion / 1996 / P69 / M
ORLANE
Triple X Video Magazine #12 / 1996 / OD / M
ORLY
FTV #01: Muscle Brawl / 1996 / FT / B
ORRIN NORTH
Mona The Virgin Nymph / 1970 / ALP / M
ORSANDA T.
Private Gold #09: Private Dancer / 1996 / OD / M
ORSOLYA
Frank Thring's Double Penetration #1 / 1995 / XPR / M
ORSON ROSEBUD see Star Index I
ORSYLA
Private Stories #10 / 1996 / OD / M
ORZSE
The Witch's Tail / 1994 / GOU / M
OSCAR
Batwoman & Catgirl / 1992 / HW / M • Shane's World #7 / 1996 / OD / M • Stinging Stewardesses / 1996 / BIZ / B
OSCAR TRIPE see Star Index I
OSCAR WILD (1976)
The Girls In The Band / 1976 / SVE / M
OSCAR WILDE see Wild Oscar
OSSIE OSBORNE
Sacred Doll / 1995 / FRF / M
OSTRICH MAN
Kneel Before Me / 1995 / BON / B
OSWALDO
Dirty Hairy's Over 50 Meets Mr. Black 18 Inches / 1996 / GOT / M
OSWALDO CIRILO see Star Index I
OTIS SISTRUNK
Baby Face #1 / 1977 / VC / M • The Best Of Alex De Renzy #1 / 1983 / VC / C
OTTO LOADER
Bi The Time You Get Back / 1995 / BIN / G
OTTO WRECK
The Operation / 1995 / 210 / M
OUMAR see Star Index I
OVID G. see Star Index I
OYCETTA

Black Playhouse / 1995 / HBE / M • Ed Woody / 1995 / HBE / M
OYGA VAULT see Colleen Brennan
OZZIE
Homegrown Video #168 / 1990 / HOV / M • HomeGrown Video #458: Cream Pie For Dessert / 1995 / HOV / C
P. HARLOW see Paula Harlow
P. KALBACH
Cheating Wives / 1983 / PAC / M
P. NEDEH see Paul Fishbein
P. ROBERT see Star Index I
P.J.
Dirty Dancers #3 / 1995 / 4P / M • East Coast Sluts #01: New Jersey / 1995 / PL / M • Striptease #1 / 1995 / PL / M
P.J. (PAISLEY H) see Paisley Hunter
P.J. (SPARXX) see P.J. Sparxx
P.J. CARRINGTON see P.J. Sparxx
P.J. HARRINGTON see P.J. Sparxx
P.J. KERRINGTON see P.J. Sparxx
P.J. SOMMERS
Horny Brits Take It In The Bum / 1997 / ROB / M
P.J. SPARXX *(P.J. Kerrington, P.J. Carrington, Peejay, P.J. (Sparxx), P.J. Harrington, R.J. Starx, K.C. Kerrington)*
Blonde with small breasts but little facial animation. Originally P. J. Carrington but now seems to have settled on Sparxx. Born in Colorado and moved to Arizona and then CA. Originally did some *Playboy* videos. By 1995 she has deteriorated facially to hard and worn out and she has put on lots of weight. You have to know when to quit.
3 Wives / 1993 / VT / M • 69th Street / 1993 / VIM / M • Adam & Eve's Guide To A G-Spot Orgasm / 1994 / VI / M • The Adventures Of Mikki Finn / 1991 / CA / M • Alone / 1993 / OD / F • Anal Climax #1 / 1991 / ROB / M • Anal Encounters #4: Tales From The Crack / 1992 / VC / M • Anal Encounters #5: Deliveries In The Rear / 1992 / VC / M • Anal Encounters #6 / 1992 / VC / M • Anal Encounters #8 / 1992 / VC / M • Anal Intruder #10 / 1995 / CC / M • Anal Madness / 1992 / ROB / M • Anal Revolution / 1991 / ROB / M • Backdoor To Cannes / 1993 / VC / M • Backdoor To Russia #1 / 1992 / VC / M • Backdoor To Russia #2 / 1993 / VC / M • Backing In #4 / 1993 / WV / C • The Bad News Brat / 1991 / VI / M • Balling Instinct / 1992 / FH / M • Bare Market / 1993 / VC / M • Bedrooms And Boardrooms / 1992 / DR / M • Big Titted Tarts / 1994 / PL / C • Bitches In Heat / 1994 / PL / C • Bite / 1991 / LE / M • Blazing Boners / 1992 / MID / M • Bloopers (Video Team) / 1994 / VT / M • Blue Bayou / 1993 / VC / M • Blue Fox / 1991 / VI / M • Body Work / 1993 / MET / M • Bondage Memories #04 / 1994 / BON / C • Bondage Shoots / 1993 / BON / B • Broadway Babes / 1993 / FH / F • Bubbles / 1991 / IF / M • Butt Camp / 1993 / HW / C • Butt Freak #2 / 1996 / EA / M • The Butt Sisters / 1993 / MID / M • The Butt Sisters Do Los Angeles / 1993 / MID / M • Butties / 1992 / VC / M • Buttman's Big Tit Adventure #3 / 1995 / EA / M • Buttsizer, King Of Rears #1 / 1992 / EVN / M • Buttsizer, King Of Rears #2 / 1992 / EVN / M • Carnal Garden / 1996 / KLP / M • Carnival Of Knowledge / 1992 / XCI / M • Chameleons: Not The Sequel / 1991 / VC / M • Chemical Reaction / 1995 / CC / M • Chicks, Licks And Dirty Tricks / 1993 / ME

/ F • Competent People / 1994 / FD / C • Cookie 'n' Cream / 1992 / ME / M • The Corruption Of Christina / 1993 / WP / M • Cover To Cover / 1995 / WP / M • Covergirl / 1996 / LE / M • Crude / 1991 / IN / M • The D.P. Man #1 / 1992 / FD / M • The D.P. Man #2 / 1992 / FD / M • Dark Obsessions / 1993 / WV / M • Decadence / 1996 / VC / M • Deep Cheeks #2 / 1991 / ROB / M • Deep Inside Nicole London / 1995 / VC / C • Deep Inside P.J. Sparxx / 1995 / VC / C • Deep Inside Tiffany Mynx / 1994 / VC / C • Diamond In The Rough / 1993 / BIA / C • Diary Of A Porn Star / 1993 / FOR / M • The Dinner Party / 1995 / ERA / M • Dirty Little Lies / 1993 / VT / M • Don't Bother To Knock / 1991 / FAZ / M • Double Load #1 / 1993 / HW / M • Dr Finger's House Of Lesbians / 1996 / SC / M • Dyno-Mite / 1992 / IF / M • Elements Of Desire / 1994 / ULI / M • The Eternal Idol / 1992 / CDI / M • Executive Suites / 1993 / PL / M • Explicit Entry / 1995 / LE / M • Facesitter #2 / 1993 / CC / M • Facesitter #3 / 1994 / CC / M • Finger Pleasures #6 / 1996 / PL / F • Fingers / 1993 / LE / M • Fire & Ice: Caught In The Act / 1995 / WP / M • Flesh Palace / 1995 / LBO / M • Florence Hump / 1994 / AFI / M • Forbidden Pleasures / 1995 / ERA / M • Foreign Affairs / 1992 / VT / C • French Open / 1993 / PV / M • French Open Part Deux / 1993 / MET / M • A Girl's Affair #07 / 1995 / FD / F • A Girl's Affair #08 / 1995 / FD / F • A Grand Obsession / 1992 / B&D / B • Hard Headed / 1994 / LE / M • Hard Ride / 1992 / WV / M • Harder, She Craved / 1995 / VC / M • Heatwave #1 / 1992 / FH / F • Heatwave #2 / 1993 / FH / F • Heels & Toes #1 / 1994 / BON / F • Hidden Obsessions / 1992 / BFP / M • Hollywood Temps / 1993 / ZA / M • Hot Box / 1995 / V99 / C • Hot In The Saddle / 1994 / ERA / M • Hot Rod To Hell #1 / 1991 / BS / B • Hot Shots / 1992 / VD / C • I Do #3 / 1992 / VI / M • Immortal Desire / 1993 / VI / M • In The Can With Oj / 1994 / HCV / M • Intense Perversions #1 / 1995 / PL / M • Interactive / 1994 / SC / M • Jamie Loves Jeff #2 / 1991 / VI / M • Jennifer Ate / 1993 / XCI / F • Jugsy (X-Citement) / 1992 / XCI / M • Juicy Treats / 1991 / ROB / M • Kym Wilde's On The Edge #03 / 1993 / RB / B • Kym Wilde's On The Edge #09 / 1994 / RB / B • Kym Wilde's On The Edge #10 / 1994 / RB / B • Kym Wilde's On The Edge #19 / 1995 / RB / B • Kym Wilde's On The Edge #31 / 1996 / RB / B • The Last Good Sex / 1992 / FD / M • Last Tango In Rio / 1991 / DR / M • Les Femmes Erotiques / 1993 / BFP / M • Lesbian Dating Game / 1993 / LIP / F • Lesbian Love Connection / 1992 / LIP / F • Loose Morals / 1995 / EX / M • Love Scenes #1 / 1991 / B/F / S • Lust & Money / 1995 / SUF / M • Lust Crimes / 1992 / WV / M • Manbait #1 / 1991 / VC / M • The Many Faces Of P.J. Sparxx / 1996 / WP / M • Marked #1 / 1993 / FD / M • Masquerade (1992-Usa) / 1992 / SC / M • The Merry Widows / 1993 / VC / M • Messy Mouth / 1994 / CA / C • Midsummer Love Story / 1993 / WV / M • Mind Games / 1995 / IMV / M • More On The Job Training / 1994 / RB / B • Muffy The Vampire Layer / 1992 / LV / M • Mysteria / 1995 / NIT / M • Nature Girls #2: Get Wet / 1995 / WIV / F • Never Say Never / 1994 / SC / M • New

Wave Hookers #3 / 1993 / VC / M • A Night Of Hell / 1993 / LBO / B • Nightfire / 1991 / CIN / M • Nightvision / 1993 / TP / M • No Fear / 1996 / IN / F • No Fly Zone / 1993 / LE / F • No Man's Land #10 / 1994 / VT / F • No Man's Land #11 / 1995 / VT / F • No Man's Land #12 / 1995 / VT / F • Nude Nurses / 1993 / EDE / S • The Nurses Are Cumming #2 / 1996 / LBO / C • On The Job Training / 1991 / RB / B • On Trial #3: Takin' It To The Jury / 1992 / VI / M • On Trial #4: The Verdict / 1992 / VI / M • On Your Bare Bottom / 1992 / BON / B • Oral Majority #10 / 1993 / WV / C • The Original Wicked Woman / 1993 / WP / M • P.J. Sparxx On Fire / 1992 / MID / C • Paddle Tales / 1992 / BON / B • Painful Initiation / 1992 / PL / B • Passages #4 / 1991 / VI / M • The Perils Of Prunella #2 / 1991 / BIZ / B • Phantom Pain / 1995 / BON / B • The Pink Pussycat / 1992 / CA / M • Prescription For Pleasure / 1993 / HW / M • Pretty Cheeks / 1994 / RB / B • Primal Desires / 1993 / EX / M • Prisoners Of Payne / 1995 / NIT / B • Profiles #03: House Dick / 1995 / XPR / M • Pussy Whipped / 1991 / PL / B • Pussyman #03: The Search Continues / 1993 / SNA / M • Pussyman #04: The Celebration / 1993 / SNA / M • Quantum Deep / 1993 / HW / M • Radical Affairs Video Magazine #01 / 1992 / ME / M • Radical Affairs Video Magazine #02 / 1992 / ME / M • Raunch Ranch / 1995 / LE / M • Reflections / 1995 / FD / M • Return To Melrose Place / 1993 / HW / M • Rocket Girls / 1993 / VC / M • Roman Goddess / 1992 / HW / M • Ruthless Affairs / 1995 / LE / M • The Secret Garden #1 / 1992 / XCI / M • Secret Lives / 1994 / SC / F • Secret Seductions #1 / 1995 / LV / M • Secret Seductions #2 / 1995 / ULP / M • Sensual Exposure / 1993 / ULI / M • Sex #1 (Vivid) / 1993 / VI / M • Sex #2 (Vivid) / 1993 / VI / M • Sex Drivers / 1996 / VMX / M • Sex For Hire / 1996 / ONA / M • Sex Stories / 1992 / VC / M • Sex Suites / 1995 / TP / M • Sex Wish / 1992 / WV / M • Sexual Instinct #1 / 1992 / DR / M • The Sexual Limits / 1992 / VC / M • Shameless / 1995 / VC / M • Sharon Starlet / 1993 / WIV / M • Shock / 1995 / LE / M • Sinderella #1 / 1992 / VI / M • Sinderella #2 / 1992 / VI / M • Single White Nympho / 1992 / MID / M • Slave's Revenge / cr94 / LON / B • Sleeping With Emily / 1991 / LE / M • Smart Ass / 1992 / RB / B • Smarty Pants / 1992 / VEX / M • Southern Comfort / 1991 / CIN / M • Spankology 101a / 1994 / BON / B • Spankology 101b / 1994 / BON / B • Sparxx / 1993 / MID / F • Sparxx Fly / 1995 / B&D / B • Sparxx Plug / 1993 / HW / C • Spread Sheets / 1991 / DR / M • Spring Break / 1992 / PL / M • Starlet / 1994 / VI / M • Steamy Windows / 1993 / VI / M • Stocking Stuffers / 1992 / LV / M • Strange Lesbian Tales / 1996 / BAC / F • Suite 18 / 1994 / VI / M • Sun Bunnies #2: The Pink Cheek Tales / 1992 / SC / M • Sunrise Mystery / 1992 / FD / M • Taboo #09 / 1991 / IN / M • Taboo #15 / 1995 / IN / M • Talk Dirty To Me #08 / 1990 / DR / M • Tender Loving Care / 1995 / WP / M • Tickled Pink / 1993 / LE / F • To The Rear / 1992 / VC / M • The Violation Of Missy / 1996 / JMP / F • The Violation Of Rachel Love / 1995 / JMP / F • Vow Of Passion / 1991 / VI / M • Waterbabies #1 / 1992 / CC / M • Where There's

Sparxx, There's Fire / 1991 / LV / M • Whispered Secrets Of The Call Girls / 1995 / TVE / F • Wicked At Heart / 1995 / WP / M • Wild & Wicked #3 / 1993 / VT / M • Wild Cherries / 1996 / SC / F • Wild Child / 1991 / BRU / S • Women On Top / 1995 / BON / B • Women Who Love Men, Men Who Love Women / 1993 / FD / C • X-TV / 1992 / CA / C • The XXX Files: Lust In Space / 1995 / IMV / M • You Bet Your Butt / 1992 / VC / M • Young Nurses In Lust / 1994 / LBO / M

P.J. WHIGHAM *see Star Index I*

P.K. SNYDER
Bobby Sox / 1996 / VI / S

P.L. MANN *see Star Index I*

P.T. MARTIN *see Star Index I*

PABLO
Latex #1 / 1994 / VC / M

PABLO R.
Private Gold #09: Private Dancer / 1996 / OD / M

PACE BARLOW *see Casey Williams*

PACO *see Star Index I*

PACO PASQUA
Dangerous Behinds #1 / 1995 / HW / M

PADDY COLONA
The Caning Of The Shrews / 1991 / BIZ / B

PAEGN FALKNER
Dick & Jane In The Mountains / 1994 / AVI / M

PAGE *see Star Index I*

PAGE POWERS *see Paige Powers*

PAGE TURNER *see Buffy Davis*

PAIGE ANTHONY *see Paige Powers*

PAIGE CARLSON *(Becky (P. Carlson))*
Brunette with small tits who sounds like she's retarded.
Adventures Of The DP Boys: The Pool Service / 1993 / HW / M • American Swinger Video Magazine #04 / 1993 / ZA / M • Anal Climax #3 / 1993 / ROB / M • Anal Co-Ed / 1993 / ROB / M • Anal Sensation / 1993 / ROB / M • Anal Vision #05 / 1993 / LBO / M • Anal Vision #08 / 1993 / LBO / M • Beach Bum Amateur's #24 / 1993 / MID / M • Bubble Butts #25 / 1993 / LBO / M • Casting Call #02 / 1993 / SO / M • Dirty Diner #02 / 1993 / GLI / M • Harry Horndog #17: Love Puppies #5 / 1993 / ZA / M • Harry Horndog #21: Birthday Orgy / 1993 / ZA / M • Kiss Is A Rebel With A Cause / 1993 / WV / M • Leena Meets Frankenstein / 1993 / OD / M • Odyssey 30 Min: #310: / 1993 / OD / M • Odyssey Triple Play #67: Girls Who Love It Up The Ass / 1994 / OD / M • Pearl Necklace: Thee Bush League #12 / 1993 / SEE / M • Poison Ivory / 1993 / MID / F • Private Video Magazine #02 / 1993 / OD / M • Sparxx / 1993 / MID / F • Top Debs #2: The Reunion / 1993 / GO / M

PAIGE HAMILTON
Butt Hunt #07 / 1995 / LEI / M • Conjugal Visits / 1995 / EVN / M • The Cumm Brothers #09: Chewin' The Bush / 1995 / OD / M • D.P. Grannies / 1995 / JMP / M • The Doctor Is In #1 / 1995 / NIT / M • Fresh Faces #06 / 1995 / EVN / M • Pussy Hunt #14 / 1995 / LEI / M • Small Top Bitches / 1996 / AVI / M • The Superhawk Girls...And Their Fabulous Toys / 1996 / GLI / F

PAIGE HART
Boob Acres / 1996 / HW / M • The Fanny Farm / 1996 / NIT / M

PAIGE JACKSON
Donna Young: Paige Jackson #1 / 1995 /

DY / F
PAIGE KANE
She-Male Slut House / 1994 / HEA / G
PAIGE NICHOLS *see Star Index I*
PAIGE PILAR *see Star Index I*
PAIGE POWERS *(Page Powers, Paige Anthony)*
Brunette with long black hair, marginal face, double chin, small tits, very white body, tongue pin, and not a tight body. She says she was 21 years old in 1995.
Bi And Beyond #6: Authentic / 1996 / FD / G • Buttsizer #3: Return Of The King Of Rears / 1995 / EVN / M • Entangled / 1996 / KLP / M • EXXXtra Parts: Interview With a Hermaphrodite / 1995 / PL / M • Hollywood Amateurs #23 / 1995 / MID / M • The Horny Hiker / 1995 / LE / M • In Your Face #4 / 1996 / PL / M • My First Time #2 / 1996 / NS / M • Private Desires / 1995 / LE / M • Pussyman Auditions #14 / 1995 / SNA / M • Sex Freaks / 1995 / EA / M • Twist Of Fate / 1996 / WP / M • Venom #3 / 1996 / VD / M • Venom #4 / 1996 / VD / M • Video Virgins #22 / 1995 / NS / M • Virgin Killers: Second Rampage / 1995 / PEP / M
PAIGE REYNOLDS *see Star Index I*
PAISLEY HUNTER *(Paisley Park, Paisley Venture, P.J. (Paisley H), Paisley Winter, Katrina Wave)*
Marginal face (squinty little eyes) with shoulder length brown hair, small tits, long trunk, lithe body, a bit flat on the ass. Seems to have a nice disposition however (depending on the movie) and could be worth following. Aged 26 in 1995 and comes from Seattle, WA. Spent some time in the US Air Force, stationed in Germany (she says in 1987 but that wouldn't jell with her reputed age), then worked as a waitress. Wasn't devirginized until 19. 5'7" tall.
100% Amateur #23: / 1996 / OD / M • Anal Addict / 1995 / ROB / M • Anal Cum Queens / 1995 / ZA / M • Anal Intruder #10 / 1995 / CC / M • Anal Romp / 1995 / LIP / F • Anal Tramps / 1996 / LIP / F • Beyond Reality #3: Stand Erect! / 1996 / EXQ / M • Bi The Book / 1996 / MID / G • Black Bamboo / 1995 / IN / M • Blonde Temptation / 1995 / IF / M • Bondage Watch #2 / 1996 / STM / B • Booty Bitch / 1995 / ROB / M • Booty Ho #3 / 1995 / ROB / M • Bruce Seven: A Compendium Of His Most Graphic Scenes Vol 6 / 1994 / BS / C • Buffy Malibu's Nasty Girls #08 / 1995 / ANA / F • Butt Hunt #06 / 1995 / LEI / M • Car Wash Angels / 1995 / VC / M • Casting Call #13 / 1995 / SO / M • Casting Call #18 / 1996 / SO / M • Cat And Bound Tickle Fest / 1996 / VTF / B • Cherry Poppers #12: Playing Nookie / 1995 / ZA / M • Crotch Tied / 1996 / STM / B • The Cumm Brothers #10: Night Of The Giving Head / 1995 / OD / M • Dirty Dirty Debutantes #1 / 1995 / 4P / M • Diva #2: Deep In Glamour / 1996 / VC / F • The Doctor Is In #3: Achy Breaky Tarts / 1995 / NIT / M • Eighteen #3 / 1996 / SC / M • The End / 1995 / VI / M • Everybody Wants Some / 1996 / EXQ / F • Fantasy Lover / 1995 / V99 / C • Hard Core Beginners #02 / 1995 / LEI / M • Hardcore Schoolgirls #2: Perverted Playmates / 1995 / XPR / M • Hit Parade / 1996 / PRE / B • The Hitch-Hiker #12: Southern Exposure / 1995 / VIM / M • Indiscreet! Video Magazine #1 / 1995 / FH / M • Interracial

Anal #03: Black And White All Over / 1995 / AFI / M • Interview With A Mistress / 1996 / BON / B • Kym Wilde's On The Edge #39 / 1996 / RB / B • Leather / 1995 / LE / M • Leg...Ends #17 / 1996 / PRE / F • Lollipop Shoppe #2 / 1996 / SC / M • My Desire / 1996 / NIT / M • Nasty Newcummers #11 / 1995 / MET / M • Nasty Nymphos #12 / 1996 / ANA / M • The New Babysitter / 1995 / GO / M • The New Butt Hunt #13 / 1995 / LEI / C • New Pussy Hunt #17 / 1995 / LEI / M • Night Blooms / 1997 / BON / B • Nothing Sacred / 1995 / LE / M • Paisley Hunter: The Girl Just Can't Help It / 1996 / BEP / M • Passage To Pleasure / 1995 / LE / M • Phantasm / 1995 / WP / M • Puritan Video Magazine #02 / 1996 / LE / M • Quality Control / 1996 / VTF / B • Sex Freaks / 1995 / EA / M • The Sex Therapist / 1995 / GO / M • Sinboy #1 / 1996 / SC / M • Sluthunt #1 / 1995 / BIP / F • Sluthunt #3 / 1996 / BIP / F • Snatch Masters #08 / 1995 / LEI / M • Sorority Sex Kittens #3 / 1996 / VC / M • Sticky Fingers / 1996 / WV / M • The Stranger / 1996 / BEP / M • Suggestive Behavior / 1996 / VI / M • Tailz From Da Hood #2 / 1995 / AVI / M • Takin' It To The Limit #8: Hooked On Crack / 1996 / BS / M • Toes 'n' Cons / 1996 / PRE / S • Up And Cummers #27 / 1996 / ERW / M • Up The Ying Yang #2 / 1995 / CC / M • Video Virgins #18 / 1994 / NS / M • The Violation Of Juliette / 1996 / JMP / F • The Violation Of Paisley Hunter / 1996 / JMP / F • The Voyeur #4 / 1995 / EA / M • The Voyeur #6 / 1996 / EA / M • Waves Of Passion / 1996 / ERA / M • Whoreo / 1995 / BIP / M • Young & Natural #14 / 1996 / TV / F • Young & Natural #18 / 1996 / TV / C • Young & Natural #19 / 1996 / TV / F • Young & Natural #22 / 1996 / TV / F
PAISLEY LICK *see Jacqueline Lick*
PAISLEY PARK *see Paisley Hunter*
PAISLEY VENTURE *see Paisley Hunter*
PAISLEY WINTER *see Paisley Hunter*
PAL KOVESI
True Stories #1 / 1993 / SC / M • True Stories #2 / 1993 / SC / M
PALEMA NIMO *see Pamela Jennings*
PALLE ARRESTRUP
Bordello / 1973 / AR / M
PALVA ITANO
Blue Vanities #514 / 1992 / FFL / M
PAM
A&B AB#502: Cherry / 1995 / A&B / M • Big Bust Black Legends / 1991 / BTO / C • Blue Vanities #505 / 1992 / FFL / M • Blue Vanities #542 / 1994 / FFL / M • Blue Vanities #570 / 1995 / FFL / M • Bottoms Up #03 / 1983 / AVC / C • Limited Edition #16 / 1980 / AVC / M • Limited Edition #20 / 1980 / AVC / M • Neighborhood Watch #10 / 1991 / LBO / M • School Dayze / 1987 / BON / B • Stevi's: Love And The Blade / 1994 / SSV / M • The Test #2 / 1989 / CDP / B • Wrasslin She-Babes #08 / 1996 / SOW / M
PAM BARRERA
Catch Of The Day #6 / 1996 / VG0 / M
PAM BOWMAN
Ultraflesh / 1980 / GO / M
PAM COX *see Star Index I*
PAM DASH *see Star Index I*
PAM DOBBINS *see Star Index I*
PAM EVANS
[Rear End Crashes / 197? / ... / M
PAM FRANCIS

Resurrection Of Eve / 1973 / MIT / M
PAM HOWER
The Unholy Child / 1972 / AVC / M
PAM JACKSON *see Star Index I*
PAM JALIMOV
Sex Boat / 1980 / VCX / M
PAM JENNINGS *see Pamela Jennings*
PAM LARSEN
Bedtime Video #05 / 1984 / GO / M
PAM MONDY
Fantasy Peeps: Solo Girls / 1985 / 4P / M
PAM NEMMO *see Pamela Jennings*
PAM NIMMO *see Pamela Jennings*
PAM OSAKA *see Star Index I*
PAM SANTINI
Shape Up For Sensational Sex / 1985 / SE / M
PAM SIMON
Matinee Idol / 1984 / VC / M
PAM WESTON *see Cara Lott*
PAM-ANN
Mike Hott: #116 Ali And Pam-Ann And Dusty And Paul / 1990 / MHV / M
PAMELA
Blue Vanities #554 / 1994 / FFL / M • Girl Busters / 1985 / VC / M • Joe Elliot's College Girls #46 / 1996 / JOE / M • College Cunts #06 / 1993 / NS / F • The New Submit To Me #1 / 1996 / SY / B • Pamela: Mini Skirt Madness / 1990 / LOD / F • A Passage Thru Pamela / 1985 / VC / G • Surprise Package / 1994 / BON / B • Three Girl Tickle #2 / 1996 / SY / B
PAMELA ANDERSON (84) *see Pamela Mann*
PAMELA ASHLEY *see Star Index I*
PAMELA BROWN
10 Years Of Big Busts #1 / 1989 / BTO / C • Big Busty #14 / 198? / H&S / S • Victims Of Love / 1975 / ALP / M • [The Night Digger / 1971 / ... / S
PAMELA CROWLEY
Triple Cross / 198? / CS / B
PAMELA DEE *(Kauri, Dee Lyte)*
Ugly but tight bodied Hawaiian girl. Brunette, small tits.
A&B GB#072: Chessie Does It / 1990 / A&B / M • All "A" / 1994 / SFP / C • Amateur Lesbians #43: Poppy / 1993 / GO / F • Anal Thunder #1 / 1993 / ROB / M • Anal Variations #01 / 1993 / FH / M • Arch Villains / 1994 / PRE / B • Arch Worship / 1995 / PRE / B • Ass Openers! #2 / 1995 / TCK / C • Beach Bum Amateur's #37 / 1993 / MID / M • Bedroom Bondage / 1994 / LON / B • Bi-Laddin / 1994 / BIN / G • Blue Bayou / 1993 / VC / M • Bobby Hollander's Maneaters #04 / 1993 / SFP / M • Bobby Hollander's Sweet Cheeks #106 / 1993 / QUA / M • Bubble Butts #17 / 1992 / LBO / M • Bubble Butts #18 / 1992 / LBO / M • Butt Bongo Bonanza / 1993 / FC / M • Chocolate Bunnies #03 / 1995 / LBO / C • Coming Out / 1993 / VD / M • The Cumm Brothers #02: Goin' To A Ho' Down / 1994 / OD / M • The Domination Of Summer #1 / 1994 / BIZ / B • The Domination Of Summer #2 / 1994 / BIZ / B • Double Penetration Virgins #03 / 1994 / LE / M • Dresden Diary #10: Punishment For Their Sins / 1993 / BIZ / B • The End Zone / 1993 / PRE / B • The Enema Bandit Returns / 1995 / BIZ / B • Enema Obedience #3: The Ultimate Punishment / 1994 / BIZ / B • Enemates #08 / 1993 / BIZ / B • Fettered Femmes / 1994 / BON / B • First Time Les-

bians #04 / 1993 / JMP / F • First Time Lesbians #05 / 1993 / JMP / F • Fresh Meat (John Leslie) #1 / 1994 / EA / M • Fun "4" All / 1994 / PRE / B • Giggles / 1992 / PRE / B • GRG: Forced Anal / 1994 / GRG / M • GRG: Nasty Naughty Nymphos / 1994 / GRG / F • GRG: Two Mistresses And A Slave / 1994 / GRG / B • Harry Horndog #12: Harry's Xmas Party / 1992 / ZA / M • Harry Horndog #13: Anal Lovers #2 / 1992 / ZA / M • Hollywood Swingers #08 / 1993 / LBO / M • Hot Tight Asses #02 / 1993 / TCK / M • Hot Tight Asses #03 / 1993 / TCK / M • House Of Slaves / 1995 / HOM / B • Kittens #4: Bodybuilding Bitches / 1993 / CC / F • La Princesa Anal / 1993 / ROB / M • Laugh Factory / 1995 / PRE / C • Leg...Ends #10 / 1994 / PRE / F • Lesbian Lingerie Fantasy #7 / 1991 / ESP / F • Licking Legends #2 / 1992 / LE / F • The Living End / 1992 / OD / M • Love Seats / 1994 / PRE / C • Lube Job / 1994 / PRE / B • Maliboobies / 1993 / CDI / F • Mr. Peepers Amateur Home Videos #77: Facial Coverage / 1993 / LBO / M • My Anal Valentine / 1993 / FD / M • My Favorite Rear / 1993 / PEP / M • Nookie Cookies / 1993 / CDI / F • Odyssey Triple Play #61: Rump Humpers / 1994 / OD / M • The Other Side Of Melinda / 1995 / LON / B • Pearl Necklace: Amorous Amateurs #35 / 1993 / SEE / M • Pearl Necklace: Thee Bush League #15 / 1993 / SEE / M • Porsche Lynn, Vault Mistress #1 / 1994 / BIZ / B • Porsche Lynn, Vault Mistress #2 / 1994 / BIZ / B • The Princess Slave / 1994 / BIZ / B • Reel Sex #02: Splash Party / 1994 / SPP / M • Rump Humpers #05 / 1992 / GLI / M • Running Mates / 1993 / PRE / B • Sexophrenia / 1993 / VC / M • Sharon Mitchell's Sex Clinic #01 / 1993 / FC / M • Slap Happy / 1994 / PRE / B • The Spirit Of My Master / 1994 / BIZ / B • Stiff Competition #2 / 1994 / CA / M • Storehouse Of Agony #1 / 1993 / BIZ / B • Storehouse Of Agony #2 / 1992 / BIZ / B • Straight A Students / 1993 / MET / M • Stroke Play / 1994 / PLV / B • Student Fetish Videos: Best of Catfighting #02 / 1994 / PRE / C • Student Fetish Videos: Best of Enema #02 / 1992 / PRE / C • Student Fetish Videos: The Enema #10 / 1993 / PRE / B • Student Fetish Videos: Spanking #10 / 1993 / PRE / B • Student Fetish Videos: Spanking #12 / 1994 / PRE / B • Student Fetish Videos: Tickling #07 / 1992 / SFV / B • SVE: Spanks For The Memories / 1994 / SVE / B • Taboo #12 / 1994 / MET / M • Taboo #13 / 1994 / IN / M • Take Me...Use Me...Make Me Your Slave / 1994 / BIZ / B • Tie Me, Tease Me / 1994 / CS / B • Title Shots / 1995 / PRE / B • To Serve...Protect...And Submit / 1994 / BIZ / B • Totally Tasteless Video #02 / 1994 / TTV / M • TV Terrorists: Hostage Sluts / 1993 / BIZ / G • TV Toilet Challenge / 1993 / BIZ / G • Video Virgins #02 / 1992 / NS / M • Weak-Ends / 1995 / PRE / B • White Stockings / 1994 / BHS / M • Willie Wanker And The Fun Factory / 1994 / FD / M • Xcitement: The Movie / 1993 / XCI / M

PAMELA DREGEZ
Buttman In Barcelona / 1996 / EA / M

PAMELA FIELD see Star Index I

PAMELA GREEN
As Nature Intended / 1958 / SOW / S • Blue Vanities #515 / 1992 / FFL / M • Blue Van-

ities #516 / 1992 / FFL / M • Blue Vanities #551 / 1994 / FFL / M • Cry Uncle / 1971 / VCX / S

PAMELA GRIFFIN
Switchcraft / 1975 / VHL / M

PAMELA GRIMES
French Teen / 1977 / CV / M • Teenage Pajama Party / 1977 / VC / M

PAMELA JENNINGS *(Pam Jennings, Pam Nimmo, Pam Nemmo, Pamela Nimmo, Palema Nimo)*
Amber Aroused / 1985 / CA / M • Animal Impulse / 1985 / AA / M • Blonde Desire / 1984 / AIR / M • Blue Dream Lover / 1985 / TAR / M • Blue Vanities #003 / 1987 / FFL / M • Body Shop / 1984 / VCX / M • Centerfold Celebrities #4 / 1983 / VC / M • Centerfold Celebrities #5 / 1983 / VC / M • Coffee & Cream / 1984 / AVC / M • D-Cup Delights / 1987 / VCR / M • Dear Fanny / 1984 / CV / M • Dirty Letters / 1984 / VD / M • Double D Delights / 1989 / VCR / C • Dream Lover / 1985 / CDI / M • Fantasies Unltd. / 1985 / CDI / M • Gourmet Quickies: Pam Jenning #714 / 1985 / GO / C • GVC: Broadcast Babes #138 / 1985 / GO / M • GVC: Lost In Lust #134 / 1984 / GO / M • Holly Does Hollywood #1 / 1985 / VEX / M • Hot Spa / 1984 / CA / M • How Do You Like It? / 1985 / CA / M • Intimate Couples / 1984 / VCX / M • Lady Cassanova / 1985 / AVC / M • Letters Of Love / 1985 / CA / M • Limited Edition #29 / 1984 / AVC / M • The Mating Season / 1984 / VC / M • Only The Best Of Men's And Women's Fantasies / 1988 / CV / C • Pretty As You Feel / 1984 / PV / M • Secrets / 1984 / HO / M • Sex Boat / 1980 / VCX / M • Sex Toys / 1985 / CA / M • The Sexaholic / 1988 / VC / M • The Shoe Store / 1985 / BIZ / B • Sinfully Yours / 1984 / HO / M • Six Faces Of Samantha / 1984 / AA / M • Sizzling Suburbia / 1985 / CDI / M • Slave Exchange / 1985 / BIZ / B • Sounds Of Sex / 1985 / CA / M • Springtime In The Rockies / 1984 / CIN / M • Sunny Side Up / 1984 / VC / M • Suzie Superstar #2 / 1985 / CV / M • This Side Up / 1987 / VSX / C • Thought You'd Never Ask / 1986 / CA / M • Tight And Tender / 1985 / CA / M • Treasure Chest / 1985 / GO / M • An Unnatural Act #1 / 1984 / DR / M • The Wacky World Of X-Rated Bloopers / 1989 / GO / M • Wings Of Passion / 1984 / HO / M • You Make Me Wet / 1985 / SVE / M

PAMELA JOY see Star Index I

PAMELA LIBERTY see Lady Ashley Liberty

PAMELA LOUISE (MANN) see Pamela Mann

PAMELA LYNN see Star Index I

PAMELA MANN *(Pamela Manning, Pamela Anderson (84), Pamela Louise (Mann))*
Older brunette with sloppy tits and a body that is going to seed. Marginal face.
Eat At The Blue Fox / 1983 / VC / M • Fleshdance Fever / 1984 / SAT / M • Once Upon A Secretary / 1983 / GO / M • Personal Touch #2 / 1983 / AR / M • Physical Attraction / 1984 / MAP / M • Taboo #03 / 1983 / IN / M • Unthinkable / 1984 / SE / M • X Factor / 1984 / HO / M • X-Rated Bloopers #1 / 1984 / AR / M

PAMELA MANNING see Pamela Mann

PAMELA MASON
ABA: Double Feature #5 / 1996 / ALP / M •

Night Of Submission / 1976 / BIZ / M

PAMELA NAUGHTLIE see Star Index I

PAMELA NIMMO see Pamela Jennings

PAMELA PAYNE
Mistress Vs Mistress / 1991 / COC / B • The Painful World Of Moose Malloy / 1993 / AMF / B • Payne In The Behind / 1993 / AMF / C • The Payne Principle / 1995 / COC / B • Princess Pamela Payne's Dutch Treat / 1992 / STM / B • VGA: Spanks-A-Lot / 1993 / VGA / B • A Visit To Mistress Amanda's / 1993 / CAS / B • The World Of Payne / 1991 / STM / B

PAMELA PECK see Star Index I

PAMELA PRESLEY see Star Index I

PAMELA ROSE *(Caitlyn Lewis)*
The Chameleon / 1989 / VC / M • Girls Just Want To...Have Fun / 1984 / SE / M • Girlworld #3 / 1989 / LIP / F • Girlworld #4 / 1989 / LIP / F • Hot Scalding / 1989 / VC / M • Phantom X / 1989 / VC / M • Pony Girls / 1993 / ROB / F • Saturday Night Special / 1989 / DR / M • Second Skin / 1989 / VC / M • Thrill Seekers / 1993 / ROB / F • Uniform Behavior / 1989 / ZA / M

PAMELA SANDERSON see Kristi Myst

PAMELA SELF see Tamara Lee

PAMELA STRASSER see Star Index I

PAMELA WESTON see Cara Lott

PAMELA YEN see Ramola Young

PAMMY see Star Index I

PANCHO see Star Index I

PANDORA
America's Raunchiest Home Videos #41: Welcum Neighbor / 1992 / ZA / M • Bubble Butts #13 / 1992 / LBO / M • Canadian Beaver Hunt #3 / 1996 / PL / M • Mr. Peepers Amateur Home Videos #52: Tail Wackers / 1992 / LBO / M • Odyssey Triple Play #43: Anal Creaming & Reaming / 1993 / OD / M

PANDORA (1993) see Star Index I

PANDORA (1996) see Pandora Rye

PANDORA (KAITLYN H) see Kaitlyn Hill

PANDORA PADILLA
Private Eyes / 1995 / LE / M

PANDORA PEAKS *(Stephanie Schick)*
Do Or Die / 1991 / C3S / S • Girls Around The World #24 / 1995 / BTO / S • H&S: Pandora Peaks / 199? / H&S / S • On Location In Palm Springs / 1996 / H&S / S • Score Busty Covergirls #2 / 1995 / BTO / S

PANDORA RYE *(Pandora (1996))*
Blonde with long straight hair, large cantaloupes, showgirl body, good tan lines, and marginal face. Comes from San Deigo and used to work "in construction".
Anal Crash Test Dummies / 1997 / ROB / M • Anal Jammin' & Slammin' / 1996 / ROB / M • Borsky's Back Door Bitches / 1996 / ROB / M • Butthole Sweetheart / 1996 / ROB / M • Canadian Beaver Hunt #4 / 1996 / PL / M • Cumback Pussy #1 / 1996 / EL / M • Dirty Dave's #2 / 1996 / XPR / M • Dirty Dave's #3 / 1996 / XPR / M • Filthy First Timers #1 / 1996 / EL / M • Filthy First Timers #2: Innocence Lost / 1996 / EL / M • Up And Cummers #36 / 1996 / 4P / M

PANTERA
Cheating Hearts / 1994 / AFI / M • Mellon Man #02 / 1994 / AVI / M • Welcome To Bondage: Pantera / 1994 / BON / B

PANTHER
Itsy Bitsy Gang Bang / 1996 / HW / M • Somewhere Under The Rainbow #1 / 1995 / HW / M • We Be Bangin' 24/7 / 1996 / FD

/ M
PAOLA
Hot Close-Ups / 1985 / CA / M • Magma: Swinger / 1995 / MET / M
PAOLO
Sunset Rides Again / 1995 / VC / M
PAPA SMURF
Foxx Tales / 1996 / TTV / M
PAPILLON
Not too pretty (or marginal depending on the movie) with black hair with a white streak in it, pushy personality, medium tits, clit ring, tongue pin, lithe body, and tattoos: in the shape of a butterfly as a replacement for her pubic hair (hence her name), around left bicep, and around both ankles. May be a slight mixture of black in her genetic background. In 1996 she said she was 20 years old and was de-virginized at 18 (yeah, sure!).

Adam & Eve's House Party #4 / 1996 / VC / M • The Adventures Of Peeping Tom #2 / 1996 / OD / M • Anal Virgins #03 / 1996 / NS / M • Asian Boom Boom Girls / 1997 / HO / M • Asses Galore #1: From L.A. To Brazil / 1996 / DFI / M • Bedtime Stories / 1996 / VC / M • Black Cheerleader Jungle Jerk-Off / 1996 / WIC / F • Black Cheerleader Search #05 / 1996 / IVC / M • Blue Saloon / 1996 / ME / M • California Swingers / 1996 / LV / M • Cirque Du Sex #2 / 1996 / VT / M • Cumback Pussy #2: Crawling Back For More / 1996 / EL / M • Deep Dish Booty Pie / 1996 / ROB / M • Dirty Dancers #9 / 1996 / HO / M • Dirty Debutantes #5 / 1996 / 4P / M • Eighteen #2 / 1996 / SC / M • Fame Is A Whore On Butt Row / 1996 / ABS / M • Freaky Tailz / 1996 / AVI / M • Hardcore Fantasies #3 / 1996 / LV / M • Hardcore Fantasies #5 / 1996 / LV / M • Hollywood Spa / 1996 / WP / M • Hot Tight Asses #17 / 1996 / TCK / M • Lesbian Debutante #03 / 1996 / IP / F • Lollipop Shoppe #1 / 1996 / SC / M • Lotus Blossoms / 1996 / SUF / M • Macin' #2: Macadocious / 1996 / SMP / M • Malibu Ass Blasters / 1996 / ROB / M • Mall Slut / 1997 / SC / M • More Dirty Debutantes #52 / 1996 / 4P / M • Naked Mockey-Rayna / 1996 / EVN / M • Nineteen #5 / 1996 / FOR / M • One Night In The Valley / 1996 / CA / M • Perverted Stories #11 / 1996 / JMP / M • Philmore Butts Lake Poontang / 1996 / SUF / M • Salsa & Spice #5 / 1997 / TTV / M • Showtime / 1996 / VT / M • Sin-A-Matic / 1996 / VI / M • Sinboy #4: Bareass Barbecue / 1996 / SC / M • Smoke & Mirrors / 1996 / PL / M • Up And Cummers #34 / 1996 / 4P / M • Up And Cummers #35 / 1996 / 4P / M • Valentina: Princess Of The Forest / 1996 / SC / M • Valentino's Asian Invasion / 1997 / SC / M • Vibrating Vixens #2 / 1996 / TV / F • Video Virgins #29 / 1996 / NS / M • Vivid Raw #2 / 1996 / VI / M • Yin Yang Oriental Love Bang #5: Lotus Blossoms / 1996 / SUF / M • Young & Natural #20 / 1996 / TV / F • Young & Natural #22 / 1996 / TV / F
PAPPILION see Francois Pappilion
PARA DICE see Star Index I
PARAMOUR
Real People Real Bondage #2 / 1996 / BON / C • Welcome To Bondage: Paramour & Quinn / 1993 / BON / B • Welcome To Bondage: Starlets #2 / 1994 / BON / C
PARATANA

Ancient Secrets Of Sexual Ecstasy / 1996 / HIG / M
PAREE *(Lady Paree, Parre, Paree Latiejira)*
Incredibly ugly black girl who looks like Wanda on **In Living Color**. Apparently someone suggested that she was originally a man and this has got her most upset (as of end 1993). Has humongous tits (artificial). Born March 19, 1971. Didn't get de-virinized until 18 (the ugly third grader syndrome).

Adventures Of The DP Boys: Backyard Boogie / 1994 / HW / M • Big Bust Babes #13 / 1993 / AFI / M • Big Bust Babes #20 / 1994 / AFI / M • Black Gangbangers #02 / 1995 / HW / M • Black Power / 1996 / LEI / C • Bobby Hollander's Maneaters #06 / 1993 / SFP / M • Bobby Hollander's Sweet Cheeks #108 / 1993 / QUA / M • Bra Busters #04 / 1993 / LBO / M • California Blacks / 1994 / V99 / M • Chocolate Bunnies #01 / 1995 / LBO / C • Chocolate Bunnies #02 / 1995 / LBO / C • Da Booty Call / 1994 / HW / M • Dark Passions #02 / 1993 / AFV / M • Depraved Fantasies #1 / 1993 / FPI / M • Double D Amateurs #08 / 1993 / JMP / M • The Dragon Lady #5: Tales From The Bed #4 / 1993 / WV / M • The Ebony Connection #1 / 1994 / LBO / C • The Ebony Connection #2 / 1994 / LBO / C • Gazongas #05 / 1993 / VEX / C • Harry Horndog #20: Love Puppies #6 / 1993 / ZA / M • Ho The Man Down / 1994 / WIV / M • Immortal Desire / 1993 / VI / M • The Knocker Room / 1993 / GO / M • Lady Paree Presents / 1993 / AVS / F • Leg...Ends #12 / 1994 / PRE / F • M Series #11 / 1993 / LBO / M • Pussy Showdown / 1994 / WIV / M • Sean Michaels On The Road #02: Da Hood / 1993 / VT / M • Seymore Butts In Paradise / 1993 / FH / M • Star Spangled Blacks / 1994 / VEX / M • Street Fantasies / 1993 / AFV / M • Tail Taggers #103 / 1993 / WV / M • Toppers #27 / 1994 / TV / M • Toppers #31 / 1994 / TV / C
PAREE LATIEJIRA see Paree
PARIS
Black Cheerleader Search #08 / 1996 / IVC / M • European Sex TV / 1996 / EL / M • New Faces, Hot Bodies #01 / 1992 / STP / M
PARIS FRANCISCO
Days Gone Bi / 1994 / BIN / G • She Male Dicktation / 1994 / HEA / G • She Male Service / 1994 / HEA / G
PARIS PHILLIPS see Star Index I
PARK RICHARDS
Debbie Does Dallas #2 / 1980 / VC / M • The Starmaker / 1982 / VC / M
PARKER GALLION
Glamour Girl / 1991 / VEX / M • The Perfect Pet / 1991 / VEX / C
PARKER SCHURMAN
The Bottom Dweller Part Deux / 1994 / EL / M
PARRE see Paree
PASCAL
Big Bust Babes #29 / 1995 / AFI / M • Family Affair / 1996 / XC / M
PASHA see Pasha Lee
PASHA LEE *(Pasha)*
She male.
Back To Back #1 / 1987 / 4P / C • Forbidden Fruit #2 / 1987 / MET / G • The Na-

tional Transsexual / 1990 / GO / G • Parliament: Hard TV #1 / 1988 / PM / G • The Sex Change Girls / 1987 / 4P / G • She Studs #02 / 1991 / BIZ / G • She-Male Tales / 1990 / MET / G • Transsexual Secretary / 19?? / BIZ / G • Trisexual Encounters #01 / 1985 / PL / G
PASSION
Black Mystique #11 / 1995 / VT / F • My Sensual Body / 1989 / WET / M • Sista! #2 / 1994 / VT / F
PASSION ROSE
Daughters Of Darkness / 1975 / ASR / M
PAT
AVP #1006: Candy's Debut / 1987 / AVP / M • Black Knockers #04 / 1995 / TV / M • Blue Vanities #509 / 1992 / FFL / M • Blue Vanities #516 / 1992 / FFL / M • Blue Vanities #520 / 1993 / FFL / M • Blue Vanities #527 / 1993 / FFL / M • Blue Vanities #538 / 1993 / FFL / M • Blue Vanities #554 / 1994 / FFL / M • Blue Vanities #555 / 1994 / FFL / M • Blue Vanities #557 / 1994 / FFL / M • HomeGrown Video #444: / 1995 / HOV / M • HomeGrown Video #458: Cream Pie For Dessert / 1995 / HOV / C • Leg...Ends #03 / 1991 / BIZ / F • Teasedance Masturbation #3 / 1994 / MAV / F
PAT BARRINGER see Pat Barrington
PAT BARRINGTON *(Pat Barringer)*
The Agony Of Love / 1965 / SOW / S • All The Way Down / 1968 / SOW / S • The Girl With The Hungry Eyes / 1967 / SOW / S • Hedonistic Pleasures / 1969 / SOW / S • Mantis In Lace / 1968 / BPI / S • Mondo Topless #1 / 1966 / RMV / S • Psychopathia Sexualis / 1966 / SOW / S • Sisters In Leather / 1969 / SOW / S
PAT BENCO
The Psychiatrist / 1978 / VC / M
PAT DORSEY see Star Index I
PAT FINLEY see Spring Finlay
PAT FINNEGAN
C.O.D. / 1981 / VES / S • Private School Girls / 1983 / CA / M
PAT FUCHS see Star Index I
PAT HARPER see Star Index I
PAT LEE see Desiree West
PAT LUIS see Star Index I
PAT LUNGI
The Psychiatrist / 1978 / VC / M
PAT MANNING *(Paula Prescott)*
Short haired older blonde with medium tits and a thick body.
Amanda By Night #1 / 1981 / CA / M • Bi-Coastal / 1985 / LAV / G • Blue Vanities #011 (New) / 1988 / FFL / M • Blue Vanities #011 (Old) / 1988 / FFL / M • Blue Vanities #204 / 1993 / FFL / M • Blue's Velvet / 1979 / ECV / M • Bodacious Ta Ta's / 1984 / CA / M • Carnal Encounters Of The Barest Kind / 1978 / VOY / C • College Lesbians / 1983 / JAN / F • Dial F For Fantasy / 1984 / PL / M • Dickman & Throbbin / 1985 / WV / M • Dreams Of Misty / 1984 / VCX / M • Erotic Dreams / 1987 / HO / M • Erotica Jones / 1985 / AVC / M • The Eyes Of Eddie Mars / 1984 / CV / M • Fantasy Peeps: Sensuous Delights / 1984 / 4P / M • Flight Sensations / 1983 / VC / C • Foxholes / 1983 / SE / M • French Erotica: Inside Hollywood / 1980 / AR / M • French Erotica: Report Card / 1980 / AR / M • Getting Off / 1979 / VIP / M • The Girls Of Klit House / 1984 / LIP / F • Heat Of The Moment / 1983 / S&L / M • High School Report

Card / 1979 / CA / M • Hot Line / 1980 / CA / M • I Like To Watch / 1982 / CA / M • I Love A Girl In A Uniform / 1989 / VC / C • Jezebel / 1979 / CV / M • Let Me Tell Ya 'Bout White Chicks / 1985 / VC / M • Let's Talk Sex / 1982 / CA / M • Looking For Love / 1985 / VCX / M • Love Bites / 1985 / CA / M • Love Probe / 1986 / VT / M • Lust At First Bite / 1978 / VC / M • Lust Flight 2000 / 1978 / VHL / M • Lust On The Orient X-Press / 1986 / CA / M • Maximum Head / 1987 / SE / M • Mrs. Rodger's Neighborhood / 1988 / EVN / C • Nasty Nurses / 1983 / CA / M • Nothing To Hide #1 / 1981 / CV / M • Older Women With Young Boys / 1984 / CC / M • Pink Champagne / 1979 / CV / M • Samurai Dick / 1984 / VC / M • Sheer Delight / 1984 / VC / M • Skin On Skin / 1981 / CV / M • Starship Intercourse / 1987 / DR / M • Summer School / 1979 / VCX / M • Swedish Erotica #53 / 1984 / CA / M • Sweet Young Foxes / 1984 / VCX / M • Taxi Girls #1 / 1980 / WV / M • Tinsel Town / 1980 / VC / M • The Ultimate Thrill / 1988 / PIN / C • The Young Like It Hot / 1983 / CA / M • [The Raw Report / 1978 / ... / M

PAT MOOREHEAD
That's My Daughter / 1982 / NGV / M

PAT RHEA *see Star Index I*

PAT RHOMBERG *see Star Index I*

PAT RICIAN
Motel Sex #1 / 1995 / FAP / M

PAT ROMANO *see Star Index I*

PAT SANTINI *see Star Index I*

PAT SMITH *see Star Index I*

PAT WINN *see Star Index I*

PATCHES
LA Nasty / 1995 / SP / M

PATER LINDGREN
I Am Curious (Yellow) / 1967 / HTV / M

PATIA *see Star Index I*

PATRIC HUTTON *see Star Index I*

PATRICE DE VEUR *see Star Index I*

PATRICE LAPERLE *see Patrice Trudeau*

PATRICE TRUDEAU *(Patrice LaPerle)*
In **Prisoner Of Pleasure** the credits say Patrice LaPerle but the voice over on the preview at the back of **House Of Sin** says Patrice Trudeau. The position in the credits make one believe that this is a girl (not too pretty, frizzy reddish blonde hair, pasty body, prominent overbite, large tits.)
Babe / 1982 / AR / M • Firestorm #2: The Angel Blade / 1986 / COM / M • Prisoner Of Pleasure / 1981 / ALP / B

PATRICE VALLE *see Beatrice Valle*

PATRICIA
6 To 9 Black Style / 1987 / LIM / C • Absolute Anal / 1996 / XC / M • Anal In The Alps / 1996 / P69 / M • Blue Vanities #195 / 1993 / FFL / M • Blue Vanities #522 / 1993 / FFL / M • Blue Vanities #529 / 1993 / FFL / M • Blue Vanities #574 / 1996 / FFL / M • Breast Of Britain #3 / 1987 / BTO / M • The Eliminators / 1991 / BIZ / B • HomeGrown Video #444: / 1995 / HOV / M • Home-Grown Video #458: Cream Pie For Dessert / 1995 / HOV / C • Magma: Chateau Extreme / 1995 / MET / M • Magma: Party Extreme / 1995 / MET / M • Magma: Sperm Dreams / 1990 / MET / M • More Dirty Debutantes #32 / 1994 / 4P / M • Sex Appeal / 1984 / ABV / M • Skirts & Flirts #02 / 1997 / XPR / F • Up And Cummers #27 / 1996 / ERW / M

PATRICIA BOWMAN
I Like To Watch / 1982 / CA / M

PATRICIA DALE
Blonde Ambition / 1981 / QX / M • Bon Appetit / 1980 / QX / M • Games Women Play #1 / 1980 / CA / M • Roommates / 1982 / VXP / M • This Lady Is A Tramp / 1980 / CV / M

PATRICIA FEIN
The Stewardesses / 1969 / SOW / S • The Stewardesses / 1981 / CA / M

PATRICIA JAY
Up And Cummers #39 / 1996 / RWP / M

PATRICIA KENNEDY
Born in San Francisco but has travelled a lot. Started in porn in May 1990 in **The Girls' Club**. Supposedly has retired as of September 1993. Resurfaced in late 1994/early 1995 with her enhanced tits, tongue pin, and tattoos on ring ankle and belly.
1-900-FUCK #3 / 1995 / SO / M • The Adventures Of Breastman / 1992 / EVN / M • All The Way Down / 1991 / ZA / M • Almost Home Alone / 1993 / SFP / M • Altered Paradise / 1995 / LE / M • Amateur Lesbians #04: Tera / 1991 / GO / F • Ambushed / 1990 / SE / M • Anal Ecstacy Girls #1 / 1993 / ROB / F • Anal Invader / 1995 / PEP / M • The Anal Nurse Scam / 1995 / CA / M • Anal Storm / 1991 / ZA / M • Anally Insatiable / 1995 / KWP / M • Another Secret / 1990 / SO / M • As Dirty As She Wants To Be / 1990 / ME / M • Ass Kisser: A Love Story / 1995 / PEP / M • Awakening In Blue / 1991 / PL / M • Babenet / 1995 / VC / M • Bad Habits / 1990 / WV / M • Beat The Heat / 1990 / VI / M • Beeping Miss Buffy / 1995 / CDI / M • Best Of Foot Worship #3 / 1992 / BIZ / C • Bi-Ology: The Making Of Mr Right / 1992 / CAT / G • Big Bust Platinum: Superstar Strip Tease / 1993 / PME / F • The Big Busteddd / 1993 / AFD / M • Big Game / 1990 / LV / M • The Big One / 1992 / GO / M • Black Beach / 1995 / LV / M • Bloopers #2 / 1991 / GO / C • Blow Job Bonnie / 1992 / CC / M • Body Heat / 1990 / CDI / M • Bondage Academy #1 / 1991 / BON / B • Bondage Academy #2 / 1991 / BON / B • Bondage Proposal / 1993 / STM / B • Broad Of Directors / 1992 / PEP / M • Bruce Seven: A Compendium Of His Most Graphic Scenes Vol 3 / 1992 / BS / C • Bruce Seven: A Compendium Of His Most Graphic Scenes Vol 4 / 1993 / BS / C • Bruise Control / 1993 / PRE / B • Bubble Butts #15 / 1992 / LBO / M • Buffy's First Encounter / 1995 / CIN / M • Butt Bandits #4 / 1996 / VD / C • The Butt Sisters Do Philadelphia / 1995 / MID / M • Buttman Vs Buttwoman / 1992 / EL / M • Buttman's Ultimate Workout / 1990 / EA / M • The Can Can / 1993 / LV / M • Carnal Interludes / 1995 / NOT / M • Carnival Of Knowledge / 1992 / XCI / M • Catalina Five-O: White Coral, Blue Death / 1990 / CIN / M • Catalina: Treasure Island / 1991 / CDI / M • Chronicles Of Submission / 1995 / BON / B • Club Anal #1 / 1993 / ROB / F • Concrete Heat / 1996 / XCI / M • Cooler Girls / 1994 / MID / C • Crunch Bunch / 1995 / PRE / C • Cum On Inn / 1995 / TEG / M • Curse Of The Catwoman / 1990 / VC / M • The D.P. Man #1 / 1992 / FD / M • The D.P. Man #2 / 1992 / FD / M • Dark Justice / 1992 / ZA / M • The Darker Side Of Shayla #1 / 1993 / PL / M • Deception (1995-Ex-

ecutive) / 1995 / EX / M • Deep Inside Jeanna Fine / 1992 / VC / C • Deep Inside Racquel Darrian / 1994 / VC / C • Deep Inside Selena Steele / 1993 / VC / C • Deep Throat Girls #12 / 1995 / GO / M • The Deviant Doctor / 1996 / NS / M • Dick At Nite / 1993 / MET / M • Dirty Looks / 1990 / IN / M • The Doll House / 1995 / CV / M • Dominant's Dilemma / 1993 / LON / B • Double D Dykes #17 / 1995 / GO / F • Down Bi Law / 1992 / CAT / G • Dynamite Brat / 1995 / LV / M • Easy Pickin's / 1990 / LV / M • The Edge / 1995 / SC / M • Education Of The Dominatrix / 1993 / HOM / B • Ejacula #1 / 1992 / VC / M • Ejacula #2 / 1992 / VC / M • Enemates #03 / 1991 / BIZ / B • Eyewitness Nudes / 1990 / VC / M • The Fear Zone / 1991 / BS / B • Female Persuasion / 1990 / SO / F • Fixing A Hole / 1995 / XCI / M • Flame's Bondage Bash / 1994 / BIZ / B • Flash Floods / 1991 / PRE / C • Flexxx #4 / 1995 / VT / M • Foxx Hunt / 1991 / GO / M • Full Blown / 1992 / GO / M • Gang Bang Bitches #10 / 1995 / PP / M • A Girl's Best Friend (Madison Is) / 1990 / PL / F • Girl Gone Bad #6: On Parole / 1992 / GO / F • Girls Gone Bad #7: Misfits Of Society / 1992 / GO / F • Girls In Heat / 1991 / ZA / F • Girls, Girls And More Girls / 1990 / LV / F • The Golden Dagger / 1993 / LON / B • Guttman's Hollywood Adventure / 1993 / PL / M • Guttman's Paris Vacation / 1993 / PL / M • Happy Endings / 1990 / BIZ / B • Hard Core Beginners #06 / 1995 / LEI / M • The Harley Girls / 1991 / AR / F • Head First / 1995 / OD / M • The Heart Breaker / 1996 / MID / M • Hellfire Society / 19?? / HOM / B • Her Obsession / 1991 / MID / M • Hollywood Swingers #04 / 1992 / LBO / M • Honeymooned / 1992 / PRE / B • The Horny Housewife / 1996 / HO / M • Hot On Her Tail / 1990 / CA / M • Hot Tight Asses #11 / 1995 / TCK / M • If You're Nasty / 1991 / PL / F • Impulse #05: When I Was 20... / 1995 / MBP / M • Impulse #07: / 1996 / MBP / M • In The Crack / 1995 / VMX / M • In Your Face #1 / 1992 / PL / M • Infamous Crimes Against Nature / 1993 / SUM / M • Inferno #1 / 1993 / SC / M • Jennifer 69 / 1992 / PL / M • Juicy Lips / 1991 / PL / F • Jungle Jive / 1992 / VD / M • Just A Gigolo / 1992 / SC / M • La Femme Vanessa / 1995 / SC / M • Ladies In Combat / 1991 / PRE / B • Lady Of The House / 1990 / VEX / M • The Landlady / 1990 / VI / M • Leather And Tether / 1993 / STM / C • Leather Bound Dykes From Hell #1 / 1994 / BIZ / F • Leather Bound Dykes From Hell #2 / 1994 / BIZ / F • Leather Bound Dykes From Hell #3 / 1994 / BIZ / F • Leather Bound Dykes From Hell #4 / 1995 / BIZ / F • Leg...Ends #09 / 1994 / PRE / F • The Legend Of The Kama Sutra / 1990 / A&E / M • Lesbian Love Connection / 1992 / LIP / F • Lesbian Pros And Amateurs #23 / 1993 / GO / F • Lesbo A Go-Go / 1990 / PL / F • The Love Doctor / 1992 / HIP / M • Love Is ... / 1990 / EVN / M • Love On The Line / 1990 / SO / M • Lucky Break / 1991 / SE / M • Lust & Desire / 1996 / WV / M • Lusty Dusty / 1990 / VI / M • Maiden Heaven #1 / 1992 / MID / F • Making Tracks / 1990 / DR / M • Messy Mouth / 1994 / CA / C • Miss Matches / 1996 / PRE / C • The Naked Fugitive / 1995 / CA / M • New Wave Hookers #2 / 1991 / VC / M •

Night Creatures / 1992 / PL / M • Night Wish / 1992 / CDI / M • Nightbreed / 1995 / VI / M • No Boys Allowed / 1991 / VC / F • No Man's Land #04 / 1990 / VT / F • Nothing Personal / 1990 / IN / M • P.K. & Company / 1995 / CV / M • Party Doll A Go-Go #1 / 1991 / VC / M • Party Doll A Go-Go #2 / 1991 / VC / M • The Pawn Shop / 1996 / MID / M • The Perfect Pet / 1991 / VEX / C • Perverted #2: The Virgins / 1995 / ZA / M • Play School / 1990 / SO / M • Plaything #1 / 1995 / VI / M • Plaything #2 / 1995 / VI / M • Pops / 1994 / PL / M • A Portrait Of Christy / 1990 / VI / M • The Power & The Passion / 1993 / CDI / M • Power Of The Pussy / 1995 / LEI / M • Private Matters / 1995 / EMC / M • Pro Ball / 1991 / VD / M • Pussyman #10: Butts, Butts & More Butts / 1995 / SNA / M • Racquel's Addiction / 1991 / VC / M • Raging Waters / 1992 / PRE / B • Rainwoman #04 / 1990 / CC / M • Rear Window / 1996 / NIT / M • Reckless Encounters / 1995 / LE / M • Red Hot And Ready / 1990 / V99 / M • Ride 'em Hard / 1992 / LV / M • Rock Her / 1992 / LV / M • A Round Behind / 1995 / PEP / M • Rump Man: Forever / 1995 / HW / M • Saturday Night Porn #1 / 1993 / AFV / M • Saturday Night Porn #2 / 1993 / AFV / M • Scented Secrets / 1990 / CIN / M • Secret Diary #2 / 1995 / MID / M • Secret Recipe / 1990 / PL / F • Secret Services / 1993 / PEP / M • The Seducers / 1992 / ZA / M • The Seduction Of Marylin Star / 1995 / VT / M • Sex Bandits / 1995 / VC / M • Sex Fantasy / 1993 / PPR / M • Sex Trek #1: The Next Peneration / 1990 / ME / M • Shameless / 1995 / VC / M • Shave Tails #4 / 1995 / SO / M • Silence Of The Buns / 1992 / WV / M • Slaves Of The Warrior Queen / 1993 / HOM / B • The Smart Ass Enquirer / 1990 / VT / M • Sole Goal / 1996 / PRE / B • Sorority Stewardesses #1 / 1995 / PE / M • Sorority Stewardesses #2 / 1995 / PE / M • Spell Of The Whip / 1994 / HOM / B • Spiked Heel Diaries #1 / 1994 / BIZ / B • Spiked Heel Diaries #2 / 1994 / BIZ / B • Splatman / 1992 / FR / M • Steal Breeze / 1990 / SO / M • Steele Butt / 1993 / AFV / M • Strange Behavior / 1991 / VD / M • Street Walkers / 1990 / PL / M • Style #1 / 1992 / VT / M • Submissive Flashbacks / 1995 / STM / C • Super Enemates #1 / 1994 / PRE / C • The Swap #1 / 1990 / VI / M • Swat Team / 1995 / PRE / B • Sweet Tarts / 1993 / STM / B • Tailspin #1 / 1991 / VT / M • Take Me / 1991 / NLE / M • A Taste Of K.C. Williams / 1992 / VD / C • A Taste Of Patricia Kennedy / 1992 / VD / C • Tender Loving Care / 1995 / WP / M • Toe Hold / 1992 / PRE / B • Top It Off / 1990 / VC / M • Torrid Without A Cause #2 / 1990 / VI / M • Trash In The Can / 1993 / LV / M • True Legends Of Adult Cinema: The Modern Era / 1992 / VC / C • Truth Or Dare / 1993 / VI / M • Two Of A Kind / 1990 / LV / M • The Ultimate / 1991 / BON / B • Unbridled Lust / 1995 / NOT / F • User Friendly / 1992 / VT / M • A Vision In Heather / 1991 / VI / M • Voodoo Vixens / 1991 / IF / M • Whackers / 1995 / PP / M • What's Up, Tiger Pussy? / 1995 / VC / M • The Wicked One / 1995 / WP / M • Wicked Thoughts / 1991 / AFV / M • Wild Goose Chase / 1990 / EA / M • Wild Innocence / 1992 / PL / M • The Women / 1993 / CAT / F • X-Tales /

1995 / VIM / M

PATRICIA LAURA *see Star Index I*

PATRICIA LEE *see* Desiree West

PATRICIA LOCKHART *see Star Index I*

PATRICIA LUCIUS
The Girls In The Band / 1976 / SVE / M

PATRICIA MASON *see* Patricia Morehead

PATRICIA MOREHEAD *(Patricia Mason)*
Not too pretty, medium tits, womanly body.
Girls U.S.A. / 1980 / AIR / M

PATRICIA RIVERS *see Star Index I*

PATRICIA TRUDEAU
Flipside: A Backdoor Adventure / 1985 / CV / M

PATRICIA VIOLET
Ladies Deluxe / 1978 / CON / M • Mobile Home Girls / 1985 / VC / M • The Seduction Of Tessa / cr86 / CA / M • Sex Sleuth / cr80 / ... / M

PATRICIA WEST *(Patty Weston)*
Passable face, small tits, red hair, very thin.
Mystique / 1979 / CA / M

PATRICK
The French Canal / 1995 / DVP / G • The Girls Of Fantasex #2 / 1996 / NIT / M • Julie's Diary / 1995 / LBO / M • VGA: Spanks-A-Lot / 1993 / VGA / B

PATRICK ANDERSON
Sensations / 1975 / ALP / M

PATRICK CHERONE *see Star Index I*

PATRICK COLLINS *see* Roscoe Bowltree

PATRICK DALY
Experiments In Blue / 1982 / CA / M • Model Behavior / 1983 / LIV / S

PATRICK FARRELLY *see Star Index I*

PATRICK GRAHAM
L.A. Tool & Die / 1979 / TMX / G

PATRICK IVES
Bi The Book / 1996 / MID / G

PATRICK LONG
Looking For Love / 1985 / VCX / M

PATRICK PARIS
Behind Closed Doors / 1996 / GOT / B • Toe Tales #34 / 1996 / GOT / B

PATRICK STAR
The Secret Diaries / 1990 / V99 / M

PATRICK VON BECK
Sex Magic / 1996 / CAW / B

PATRICK WRIGHT
Beneath The Valley Of The Ultra-Vixens / 1979 / RMV / S • Caged Heat #1 / 1974 / ST0 / S • Good Morning...And Goodbye / 1967 / RMV / S • If You Don't Stop It You'll Go Blind / 1977 / MED / S • Prison Babies / 1976 / ... / M

PATRIZIA
Magma: Sperm-Crazy / 1994 / MET / M

PATRIZIA CASAT
Selen / 1996 / HW / M

PATRIZIA ROVERSI
Impulse #06: / 1996 / MBP / M

PATSY
Domina #3 / 1996 / LBO / G

PATTI
Blue Vanities #129 / 1990 / FFL / M • Blue Vanities #559 / 1994 / FFL / M • Blue Vanities #570 / 1995 / FFL / M • Dirty Dating Service #04 / 1994 / WP / M • Mr. Peepers Nastiest #4 / 1995 / LBO / C • Peek-A-Boo / 1953 / SOW / S • When The Fat Lady Sings / 1996 / EX / M

PATTI BUCKNER
Fastlane Fuck-Holes! / 1994 / MET / M • Supercharger / cr75 / CV / M

PATTI CAKES *see* Patty Plenty

PATTI DIXON
Bad Black Beulah / 1975 / VCX / M

PATTI JONES
Talk Dirty To Me #02 / 1982 / CA / M

PATTI PERRIER *see Star Index I*

PATTI PETITE *(Petite Luv, Tracy Dione, Heather Vesper)*
Tracy Dione is from **Rambone Does Hollywood**. Heather Vesper in **Hindsight**. Was in the same accident as Tiffany Lane and had to have a leg amputated.
1001 Erotic Nights #2 / 1987 / VC / M • 69 Park Avenue / 1985 / ELH / M • Anal Annie And The Magic Dildo / 1984 / LIP / F • Angel's Revenge / 1985 / IN / M • Backdoor Lust / 1987 / CV / C • Backdoor Summer #1 / 1988 / PV / C • Bedtime Stories / 1989 / WV / M • Behind The Backdoor #1 / 1986 / EVN / M • The Best Of Anal Annie: The Girl-Girl Adventures / 1993 / LIP / C • The Best Of Black White & Pink Inside / 1996 / CV / C • Best Of Caught From Behind #1 / 1987 / HO / C • Beyond Desire / 1986 / VC / M • The Black Mystique / 1986 / CV / M • Blonde On The Run / 1985 / PV / M • Boobs, Butts And Bloopers #1 / 1990 / HO / M • Born To Be Wild / 1987 / SE / M • C-Hunt / 1985 / PL / M • Cagney & Stacey / 1984 / AT / M • Caught From Behind #04: Nasty Young Girls / 1985 / HO / M • Caught From Behind #05: Blondes & Blacks / 1986 / HO / M • Cheating / 1986 / SEV / M • Chocolate Delights #2 / 1985 / TAG / C • The Chocolate Fudge Factory / 1987 / PIN / M • Club Ginger / 1986 / VI / M • Club Taboo / 1987 / MET / G • Cottontail Club / 1985 / HO / M • Debbie Does The Devil In Dallas / 1987 / SE / M • Devil In Miss Jones #4: The Final Outrage / 1987 / VC / M • Dirty 30's Cinema: Patti Petite / 1986 / PV / C • Dirty Tricks / 1986 / 4P / M • Double Penetration #3 / 1986 / WV / C • Ebony Superstars / 1988 / VC / C • Erotic Penetration / 1987 / HO / C • For Your Thighs Only / 1985 / WV / M • Getting Personal / 1986 / CA / M • Ginger's Greatest Girl/Girl Hits / 1986 / VI / C • The Girls On F Street / 1986 / AVC / M • Hard To Swallow / 1985 / PV / M • Heidi A / 1985 / PL / M • Hindsight / 1985 / IN / M • Hollywood Undercover / 1989 / BWV / C • Honeymoon Harlots / 1986 / AVC / M • Hot Nights At The Blue Note Cafe / 1985 / WV / M • Hyapatia Lee's Arcade Series #01 / 1988 / ZA / C • Indecent Wives / 1985 / HO / M • Jewels Of The Night / 1986 / SE / M • Knights In White Satin / 1987 / SUV / C • Like A Virgin #2 / 1986 / AT / M • Losing Control / 1985 / CDI / M • The Lust Detector / 1986 / PIN / M • The Magic Touch / 1985 / CV / M • Nina's Knockouts / 1987 / AVC / C • Once Upon A Madonna / 1985 / PV / M • Oral Majority #03 / 1986 / WV / C • The Pleasure Game / 1988 / CA / M • Pleasure Spot / 1986 / CA / M • Rambone Does Hollywood / 1986 / WET / M • Rambone The Destroyer / 1985 / WET / M • Rambone Meets The Double Penetrators / 1987 / WET / M • Ready, Willing & Anal (Cv) / 1993 / CV / C • Restless Nights / 1987 / SEV / M • Rough Draft / 1986 / VEN / M • Sacrificed To Love / 1986 / CDI / M • Sailing Into Ecstasy / 1986 / VCX / M • Science Friction / 1986 / AXT / M • The Sex Dancer / 1986 / NSV / M • Sex For Hire / 1989 / HOE / C • Shaved Bun-

nies / 1985 / LIP / F • Showdown / 1986 / CA / M • Simply Outrageous / 1989 / VC / C • Sinderotica / 1985 / HO / M • Soul Kiss This / 1988 / VCR / C • A Star Is Porn / 1985 / PL / M • Sweat #1 / 1986 / PP / M • Swedish Erotica #62 / 1984 / CA / M • Taste Of The Best #3 / 1988 / PIN / C • Tasty / 1985 / CA / M • They Call My Sugar Candie / 1989 / SUE / M • The Thrill Of It / 1986 / CAT / M • Tip Of The Tongue / 1985 / V20 / M • Trisexual Encounters #03 / 1986 / PL / G • Ubangis On Uranus / 1987 / WV / M • Untamed Passions / 1987 / CV / C • Unveiled / 1987 / VC / M • Where The Sun Never Shines / 1990 / IN / C • Wild Things #1 / 1985 / CV / M • Wise Girls / 1989 / IN / C • The Wizard Of AHH's / 1985 / SE / M • Woman In The Window / 1986 / TEM / M • Working Girls / 1985 / CA / M • The World According To Ginger / 1985 / VI / M • The X-Terminator / 1986 / PV / M • X-TV #1 / 1986 / PL / C

PATTI PLENTY *see* **Patty Plenty**
PATTI RHODES *see* **Star Index I**
PATTI RICE
Dirty Dirty Debutantes #4 / 1996 / 4P / M
PATTI ROESCH
Big Bust Babes #05 / 1990 / AFI / F • Blue Vanities #524 / 1993 / FFL / M • Ladies With Big Boobs / 1984 / AMB / M
PATTI SEBRING *(Susan Moore, Patty Boyd)*
Short reddish blonde hair, tiny tits, pretty, very nice smile, lithe body, tight waist.
Beach House / 1981 / CA / C • Flesh Gordon #1 / 1974 / FAC / S • From Holly With Love / 1977 / CA / M • High School Bunnies / 1978 / VC / M • Take Off / 1978 / VXP / M
PATTI SEGAL
Flesh Factory / 1970 / AVC / M
PATTI SNYDER
Tropic Of Passion / 1971 / NGV / M
PATTI THOMAS *see* **Star Index I**
PATTI WRIGHT *see* **Patty Plenty**
PATTIE DOUGLAS *see* **Star Index I**
PATTIE LOVE *see* **Star Index I**
PATTIE PAULSON
Passionate Lovers / 1991 / PL / M
PATTY
Blue Vanities #506 / 1992 / FFL / M • Blue Vanities #579 / 1995 / FFL / M • Homegrown Video #402 / 1993 / HOV / M • Limited Edition #22 / 1981 / AVC / M • Paradise Of Plumpers / 1996 / H&S / S
PATTY BALL
My Sister Eileen / 19?? / HOE / M
PATTY BARNETT *see* **Star Index I**
PATTY BOYD *see* **Patti Sebring**
PATTY BRIDGES
Blue Confessions / 1983 / VCR / M
PATTY CAKES
Juicy Lucy / 1990 / VC / M
PATTY CLARK *see* **Star Index I**
PATTY DEBARE *see* **Star Index I**
PATTY DOUGLAS *see* **Star Index I**
PATTY GLADDEN
Mile High Club / 1983 / CV / M
PATTY KAKE
Tigresses...And Other Man-Eaters / 1979 / VXP / M
PATTY LESTER
Inside Desiree Cousteau / 1979 / VCX / M
PATTY O'FURNITURE *see* **Star Index I**
PATTY PARKER
Fatliners #1 / 1990 / EX / M • Heavyweight Contenders / 1996 / HW / M • Life In The

Fat Lane #1 / 1990 / FC / M
PATTY PLEASE *see* **Patty Plenty**
PATTY PLENTY *(Patti Plenty, Patty Wright, Patti Wright, Patti Cakes, Patty Please)*
Autobiography Of Patty Plenty / 1990 / PPV / F • Between My Breasts #12 / 1990 / BTO / M • Big Boob Bangeroo #2 / 1995 / TTV / M • Big Boob Bangeroo #4 / 1995 / TTV / M • Big Bust Strippers #01 / 1990 / BTO / F • Big Busty #32 / 1989 / BTO / S • Bodacious Ta Ta's / 1984 / CA / M • Breast Collection #01 / 1995 / LBO / C • Breast Worx #30 / 1992 / LBO / M • Creatures Of The Night / 1987 / FAN / M • Deep Desires / 1989 / VC / C • Dirty & Kinky Mature Women #09 / 1996 / C69 / M • Dirty And Kinky Mature Women #4 / 1995 / C69 / M • Dirty And Kinky Mature Women #9 / 1996 / C69 / M • Dynamic Vices / 1987 / VC / M • Exposure Images #04: Patty Plenty / 1992 / EXI / F • Fortysomething And Still Hot / 1995 / SUF / M • FTV #04: Tough Turf / 1996 / FT / B • Gazongas #01 / 1987 / VEX / M • Girls Around The World #13: Lynn LeMay And Friends / 1994 / BTO / M • Good 'n' Plenty / 1987 / AVC / M • Hedonism #01 / 1993 / FH / M • High Rollers / 1987 / VEX / M • Hot And Nasty! / 1986 / V99 / C • Hustler Honeys #1 / 1988 / VC / S • Hyapatia Lee's Arcade Series #02 / 1988 / ZA / C • La Boomba / 1987 / VCX / M • Lust / 1993 / FH / M • Masturbation Ages 20 To 45 / 1996 / C69 / F • Nightmare On Lesbian Street / 1995 / LIP / F • Older Women With Younger Men #2 / 1993 / CC / M • Older Women Younger Men #3 / 1993 / CC / M • Only The Best Of Oral / 1989 / CV / C • Passion Pit / 1985 / SE / M • Patty Plenty Live On Stage / 1990 / PPV / M • Patty Plenty Special / 199? / H&S / M • Patty Plenty's Gang Bang / 1995 / NIT / M • Patty Plenty's Home Video #01 / 1988 / PPV / F • Patty Plenty's Home Video #02 / 1988 / PPV / F • Patty Plenty's Home Video #03 / 1989 / PPV / F • Patty Plenty's Home Video #04 / 1989 / PPV / F • Patty Plenty's Home Video #05 / 1989 / PPV / F • Patty Plenty's Home Video #06 / 1989 / PPV / F • Patty Plenty's Pussy Power / 1991 / PPV / B • Pussy Hunt #06 / 1994 / LEI / M • Pussy Power #02 / 1989 / BTO / M • Raw Talent: Swing Rave / 1993 / FH / M • Rock Hard / 1985 / CV / M • Secrets Behind The Green Door / 1987 / SE / M • Sin City / 1986 / WET / M • Stiff Competition #1 / 1984 / CA / M • Swedish Erotica #73 / 1986 / CA / M • Sweet Summer / 1986 / AMO / M • Swing Rave / 1993 / EVN / M • Thanks For The Mammaries / 1987 / CA / M • Titties 'n Cream #3 / 1995 / FC / M • Voyeurism #1 / 1993 / FH / M
PATTY REDDING *see* **Clair James**
PATTY SEAGULL
Bucky Beaver's XXX Dragon Art Theatre Double Feature #01 / 1996 / SOW / M • Hitler's Harlots / cr73 / SOW / M
PATTY SHERWOOD
Bucky Beaver's XXX Dragon Art Theatre Double Feature #15 / 1996 / SOW / M • Left At The Altar / 1974 / SOW / M
PATTY SINGER
Teenage Party People / 19?? / ... / M
PATTY STEINBERG
Virgin And The Lover / 1973 / ALP / M
PATTY WESTON *see* **Patricia West**

PATTY WRIGHT *see* **Patty Plenty**
PATTY ZUMA *see* **Star Index I**
PAUL
100% Amateur #19: / 1996 / OD / M • A&B AB#258: Spanked Intruder / 1991 / A&B / M • Amateur Hours #01 / 1989 / AFI / M • Amateur Hours #04 / 1989 / AFI / M • Amateur Hours #05 / 1990 / AFI / M • Amateur Night #02 / 1990 / HME / M • AVP #9120: The Therapist / 1991 / AVP / M • AVP #9152: Three Man Slut / 1991 / AVP / M • The Betrayal Of Innocence #1: The Awakening Of Marika / 1993 / CC / M • The Betrayal Of Innocence #2: The Decadence / 1993 / CC / M • The Betrayal Of Innocence #3: The Choice / 1993 / CC / M • Classic Swedish Erotica #02 / 1986 / CA / C • Fresh Faces #07 / 1995 / EVN / M • Full Moon Video #30: Rainy Day Lays / 1994 / FAP / M • The Girls Of Fantasex #1 / 1996 / NIT / M • Mike Hott: #105 Dusty And Paul / 1990 / MHV / M • Mike Hott: #111 Lin Shia, Charlene And Paul / 1990 / MHV / M • Mike Hott: #114 Jan, Ali And Paul / 1990 / MHV / M • Mike Hott: #116 Ali And Pam-Ann And Dusty And Paul / 1990 / MHV / M • Neighborhood Watch #28 / 1992 / LBO / M • Ona Z's Star Search #03 / 1993 / GLI / M • Private Gold #08: The Longest Night / 1996 / OD / M • Swingers Confidential #1 / 1995 / FC / M • Victoria's Amateurs #01 / 1992 / VGA / M • Victoria's Amateurs #04 / 1992 / VGA / M
PAUL (MAX HARDCORE) *see* **Max Hardcore**
PAUL ALBA
Resurrection Of Eve / 1973 / MIT / M
PAUL BANION *see* **Star Index I**
PAUL BARESSI *(Paul Benson, Paul Beresski, Paul Barrsi, Paul Barresi)*
Black haired heavy (in the type of character sense) with a moustache. Also performed in gay movies in the late seventies/early eighties.
All American Girls #1 / 1982 / CA / M • All American Girls #2: In Heat / 1983 / CA / M • Amazing Sex Stories #1 / 1986 / SUV / M • Backdoor Girls / 1983 / VCR / C • Backstage Pass / 1983 / VC / M • Bad Girls #2 / 1983 / GO / M • China & Silk / 1984 / MAP / M • Club Head (EVN) #1 / 1987 / EVN / C • Diary Of A Sex Goddess / 1984 / VC / M • Ice Cream #4: Touch Of Mischief / 1984 / VC / M • Joanna Storm On Fire / 1985 / VIV / M • L.A. Tool & Die / 1979 / TMX / G • Lingerie / 1983 / CDI / M • The Love Scene / 1985 / CDI / M • Marine Code Of Silence: Don't Ask Don't Tell / 1996 / BHE / G • Miami Spice #2 / 1988 / CA / M • Miss Passion / 1984 / VD / M • Nasty Nurses / 1983 / CA / M • Shape Up For Sensational Sex / 1985 / SE / M • Spreading Joy / 1984 / IN / M • Stud Hunters / 1984 / CA / M • Sulka's Wedding / 1983 / MET / G • Too Naughty To Say No / 1984 / CA / M • Unbelievable Orgies #1 / 1987 / EVN / C • Why Gentlemen Prefer Blondes / 1983 / HO / C
PAUL BARRESI *see* **Paul Baressi**
PAUL BARRSI *see* **Paul Baressi**
PAUL BAUMGARTNER
Killer Looks / 1994 / IMP / S • The Masseuse #2 / 1994 / VI / M
PAUL BENSON *see* **Paul Baressi**
PAUL BERESSKI *see* **Paul Baressi**
PAUL BLACK
Long Dark Shadow / 1994 / LE / M

PAUL BORASKY see Star Index I
PAUL BRAZIL
Inside Karl Thomas / 1994 / STA / G • Night
Walk / 1995 / HIV / G
PAUL CARSON see Star Index I
PAUL CASTANO see Star Index I
PAUL CODER see Star Index I
PAUL COLBECK
Flesh & Laces #1 / 1983 / CA / M
PAUL COLLETI
Marine Code Of Silence: Don't Ask Don't
Tell / 1996 / BHE / G
PAUL COP see Star Index I
PAUL CORDELL
Sinister Servants / 1996 / CUC / B
PAUL COX
Adam & Eve's House Party #4 / 1996 / VC
/ M • Anal Institution #2 / 1996 / ZA / M •
Anal Squeeze / 1993 / FOR / M • Anal Wit-
ness #1 / 1996 / LBO / M • Anal Witness
#2: No Prisoners / 1996 / LBO / M • An-
niversary / 1992 / FOR / M • Ass, Gas &
The Mystical GLOP / 1997 / EL / M • Big
Boob Boat Butt Ride / 1996 / FC / M • Black
Pussyman Auditions #1 / 1996 / SNA / M •
Butt Bandits #4 / 1996 / VD / C • Caught
From Behind #23 / 1995 / HO / M • Caught
From Behind #24 / 1996 / HO / M • Coming
Of Age / 1995 / VEX / C • Cumming Of Ass
/ 1995 / TP / M • Dark Eyes / 1995 / FC / M
• Deadly Sin / 1996 / ONA / M • Delirium /
1996 / MET / M • Desperado / 1994 / SC /
M • Double Anal Alternatives / 1996 / EL /
M • Drop Sex: Wipe The Floor / 1997 / JLP
/ M • Erotic Newcummers Vol 1 #5 / 1996 /
DR / M • Escape From Anal Lost Angels /
1996 / HO / M • Every Nerd's Big Boob
Boat Butt Ride / 1996 / FC / M • Executions
On Butt Row / 1996 / EA / M • Fantasy Es-
corts / 1993 / FOR / M • Gang Bang
Bitches #11 / 1995 / PP / M • Gazongas
Galore #1 / 1996 / NIT / C • The Girl Grab-
bers / 1968 / SOW / S • Group Therapy /
1992 / TP / M • Hot Tight Asses #16 / 1996
/ TCK / M • Hypnotic Passions / 1993 /
FOR / M • Ir4: Inrearendence Day / 1996 /
HW / M • Kimberly Kupps Gets 5 A's / 1996
/ NIT / M • Kinky Roommates / 1992 / TP /
M • Leg Show #1 / 1995 / NIT / M • The
Line Up / 1996 / CDI / M • Lingerie / 1996 /
RAS / M • Living On The Edge / 1997 /
DWO / M • The Magic Box / 1993 / TP / M
• Major Fucking Whore / 1995 / BEP / M •
More Dirty Debutantes #58 / 1996 / AP / M
• More Dirty Debutantes #59 / 1996 / SBV
/ M • More Dirty Debutantes #61 / 1997 /
SBV / M • Nena Cherry's Dp Gang Bang /
1996 / NIT / M • Next...! / 1996 / CDI / M •
Nice Fuckin' Movie / 1997 / EL / M • Nudist
Colony Vacation / 1996 / NIT / M • Pay 4
Play / 1996 / RAS / M • Pocahotass #1 /
1996 / FD / M • Pocahotass #2 / 1996 / FD
/ M • Prime Choice #2 / 1995 / RAS / M •
Prime Choice #4 / 1995 / RAS / M • Prime
Cuts #1 / 1994 / FOR / M • Prime Cuts #2
/ 1994 / FOR / M • Princess Of Thieves /
1994 / SC / M • Profiles #06: Super Model
Orgy / 1996 / XPR / M • Pure Anal / 1996 /
MET / M • Pussyman Auditions #19 / 1996
/ SNA / M • Pussyman's House Party #1 /
1996 / SNA / M • Pussyman's House Party
#2 / 1996 / SNA / M • Raw Silk / 1996 / RAS
/ M • Release Me / 1996 / VT / M • Saman-
tha & Company / 1996 / PL / M • Selina /
1993 / XCI / M • Shades Of Lust / 1993 / TP
/ M • The Shocking Truth #1 / 1996 / DWO

/ M • The Shocking Truth #2 / 1996 / DWO
/ M • Silver Screen Confidential / 1996 /
WP / M • Sodomania #16: Sexxy Pistols /
1996 / EL / M • Sodomania: Slop Shots /
1996 / EL / C • Starbangers #08 / 1996 /
FPI / M • Surfin' The Net / 1996 / RAS / M
• Surrogate Lover / 1992 / TP / M • This Girl
Is Freaky / 1996 / NIT / M • Underground
#1 / 1996 / SC / M • Venom #3 / 1996 / VD
/ M • Venom #6 / 1996 / CA / M • Vienna's
Place / 1996 / VCX / M • Virgin Bar Maids
/ 1996 / VMX / M • Wet Faces #1 / 1997 /
SC / C
PAUL CRANDELL see Star Index I
PAUL FISHBEIN (P. Nedeh)
Publisher of the industry advertising magazine.
Layover / 1985 / HO / M • Radical Affairs
Video Magazine #08 / 1994 / ME / M
PAUL FISHMAN
The Girls From Hootersville #06 / 1994 /
SFP / M
PAUL FORD see Jerry Butler
PAUL FRENCH see Star Index I
PAUL GOTTI
Tight Spot / 1996 / WV / M
PAUL GRANT
Cocks In Frocks #2 / 1996 / TTV / G
PAUL GUILD
L.A. Tool & Die / 1979 / TMX / G
PAUL HARMAN
Love At First Sight / 1987 / SE / C
PAUL HARMON see Star Index I
PAUL HOFFMAN
Road Trippin' #03: New York City / 1994 /
OUP / M • SVE: Three On A Couch / 1992
/ SVE / M
PAUL HUES see Herschel Savage
PAUL HUG
Double Cross (Wicked) / 1995 / WP / M
PAUL HUGHS see Herschel Savage
PAUL IVORY
Angel Buns / 1981 / QX / M
PAUL JONES
Carnal Knowledge / 1970 / SOW / S • Fish-
erman's Luck / 1970 / SOW / S • Magic
Pool / 1988 / VD / M
PAUL LANG see Star Index I
PAUL LEE
Adventures In Paradise / 1992 / VEX / M •
Backdoor Lambada / 1990 / GO / M • Bub-
ble Butts #15 / 1992 / LBO / M • Double
Penetration Virgins #02: The Second Cum-
ming / 1994 / LE / M • Freaks Of Leather #1
/ 1993 / IF / M • The Hind-Lick Maneuver /
1991 / GO / C • House Pet / 1992 / V99 / M
• Hurts So Good / 1991 / VEX / M • Kinky
Debutante Interviews #01 / 1994 / IP / M •
Lay Lady Lay / 1991 / VEX / M • Spanish
Rose / 1991 / VEX / M • Starbangers #03 /
1993 / ZA / M • Super Ball Sunday / 1994 /
LBO / M • Sweet Things / 1992 / VEX / M •
Tonight's The Night / 1992 / V99 / M
PAUL LITTLE see Max Hardcore
PAUL LYLE
Chatsworth Hall / 1989 / BIZ / B
PAUL MAX see Max Hardcore
PAUL MCCOY see Julian St Jox
PAUL MCGIBBONEY
Cafe Flesh / 1982 / VC / M
PAUL MEYERSON see Star Index I
PAUL MICHAELS see Star Index I
PAUL MORGAN (London, London Tamlin,
Landon, London Moore).
Emaciated looking male who used to be mar-
ried to Laurie Cameron.
3 Wives / 1993 / VT / M • 55 And Still Ban-

gin' / 1995 / HW / M • Alex Jordan's First
Timers #01 / 1993 / OD / M • All "A" / 1994
/ SFP / C • Anal House Party / 1993 / IP /
M • Anal Virgins Of America #02 / 1993 /
FOR / M • Anal Vision #03 / 1992 / LBO / M
• Anal Vision #14 / 1993 / LBO / M • Anal
Vision #27 / 1994 / LBO / M • Anal-Holics /
1993 / AFV / M • Beach Bum Amateur's
#23 / 1993 / MID / M • Beach Bum Ama-
teur's #39 / 1993 / MID / M • Beach Bum
Amateur's #41 / 1995 / MID / M • Beach
Bum Amateur's #42 / 1995 / MID / M • The
Best Of Strippers Inc / 1996 / ONA / C • Biff
Malibu's Totally Nasty Home Videos #29 /
1993 / ANA / M • Big Black & Beautiful
Gang Bang / 1995 / HO / M • Big Bust
Babes #15 / 1993 / AFI / M • Big Murray's
New-Cummers #20: Hot Honies In Heat /
1993 / FD / M • The Big Stick-Up / 1994 /
WV / M • Bitches In Heat #1: Locked In the
Basement / 1995 / ZA / M • Black Women,
White Men #1 / 1995 / FC / M • Blind Spot
/ 1993 / VI / M • Bobby Hollander's Rookie
Nookie #02 / 1993 / SFP / M • Bobby Hol-
lander's Sweet Cheeks #103 / 1992 / QUA
/ M • Bobby Hollander's Sweet Cheeks
#105 / 1993 / SFP / M • Bobby Hollander's
Sweet Cheeks #111 / 1994 / WV / M • Bra
Busters #02 / 1993 / LBO / M • Breast Col-
lection #04 / 1995 / LBO / C • Bubble Butts
#28 / 1993 / LBO / M • Bun Busters #06 /
1993 / LBO / M • Bun Busters #08 / 1993 /
LBO / M • Bun Busters #17 / 1994 / LBO /
M • The Burma Road #1 / 1994 / LBO / C •
The Burma Road #2 / 1994 / LBO / C •
Casting Call #02 / 1993 / SO / M • Cousin
Bubba Country Corn Porn #02 / 1994 / VIM
/ M • The Coven #1 / 1993 / VI / M • The
Coven #2 / 1993 / VI / M • Creme De La
Face #14: Kiss My Cum / 1996 / OD / M •
Creme De La Face #15: Showroom Sex /
1996 / OD / M • Cum Tv / 1996 / NIT / M •
The Cumm Brothers #03: Go To Traffic
School / 1994 / OD / M • Dangerous
Curves / 1995 / VC / M • Dick & Jane Go
To Northridge / 1994 / AVI / M • Dick & Jane
Up, Down And All Around / 1994 / AVI / M •
Dirty Dating Service #02 / 1993 / WP / M •
Dirty Doc's Housecalls #16 / 1994 / LV / M
• Done In The Desert Sun / 1995 / OUP / M
• Double Penetration Virgins #03 / 1994 /
LE / M • Double Penetration Virgins #05:
Go To Hell / 1994 / BBO / M • Double Pen-
etration Virgins #06: DP Diner / 1995 / JMP
/ M • East Vs West: Battle Of The Gang
Bangs / 1994 / TTV / M • Fantasy Flings
#02 / 1994 / WP / M • Fantasy Flings #03 /
1995 / WP / M • The Fat, The Bald & The
Ugly / 1995 / JMP / M • For Love Or Money
/ 1994 / AFI / M • For Your Mouth Only /
1995 / GO / M • Gang Bang Diaries #1 /
1993 / SFP / M • Gang Bang Diaries #2 /
1993 / SFP / M • Gang Bang Diaries #3 /
1994 / SFP / M • Gang Bang Diaries #5 /
1994 / SFP / M • Gang Bang Party / 1994 /
HW / M • Gangbang Girl #12 / 1993 / ANA
/ M • The Girls From Hootersville #04 /
1993 / SFP / M • Glitz Tits #07 / 1993 / GLI
/ M • The Go-Go Girls / 1994 / EVN / M •
Gypsy Queen / 1995 / CC / M • Hidden
Camera #11 / 1993 / JMP / M • Hot In The
Saddle / 1994 / ERA / M • How To Make A
Model #02: Got Her In Bed / 1993 / QUA /
M • How To Make A Model #04: Facial
Cream Girls / 1994 / LBO / M • Inspector
Croissant: The Case Of The Missing Pinky

/ 1995 / FC / M • Jizz Glazed Goo Guzzlers #1 / 1996 / NIT / C • Kinky Debutante Interviews #04 / 1994 / IP / M • Kinky Debutante Interviews #06 / 1994 / IP / M • Koko Is Cumin' At Cha / 1994 / AVI / M • A Lady / 1995 / FD / M • Lady M's Anal Gang Bang / 1995 / FC / M • Layover / 1994 / VI / M • Lustful Obsessions / 1996 / NOT / M • Lusty Lap Dancers #2 / 1994 / HO / M • M Series #08 / 1993 / LBO / M • Madame Hollywood / 1993 / LE / M • Mellon Man #03 / 1994 / AVI / M • Mike Hott: #218 Cunt Of The Month: Laurie / 1993 / MHV / M • More Than A Mouthful / 1995 / LBO / C • Mr. Peepers Amateur Home Videos #72: Dirty Diary / 1993 / LBO / M • Mr. Peepers Amateur Home Videos #75: Trio In Rio / 1993 / LBO / M • Mr. Peepers Amateur Home Videos #84: She Put the Bra in Braz / 1994 / LBO / M • Mr. Peepers Amateur Home Videos #85: Hand Puppet Job / 1994 / LBO / M • Mr. Peepers Amateur Home Videos #93: Creative Fornication / 1994 / LBO / M • Nasty Backdoor Nurses / 1994 / LBO / M • Nasty Newcummers #04 / 1994 / MET / M • Nasty Newcummers #08 / 1995 / MET / M • New Pussy Hunt #26 / 1996 / LEI / C • Nikki's Bon Voyage / 1993 / VC / M • Nothing Like Nurse Nookie #4 / 1996 / NIT / M • Nympho Zombie Coeds / 1993 / VIM / M • Odyssey 30 Min: #247: / 1992 / OD / M • Odyssey 30 Min: #296: / 1992 / OD / M • Odyssey Triple Play #46: Ass-Splitting Sex / 1993 / OD / M • Odyssey Triple Play #59: Two On Two Fuckfest / 1994 / OD / M • Odyssey Triple Play #68: Threesomes And Moresomes / 1994 / OD / M • Ona Z's Star Search #01 / 1993 / GLI / M • Ona Zee's Black Label #1: Sex Hunger / 1996 / ONA / C • Organic Facials / cr91 / GLI / M • Pearl Necklace: Amorous Amateurs #20 / 1992 / SEE / M • Pearl Necklace: Amorous Amateurs #24 / 1993 / SEE / M • Perverted Stories #01 / 1995 / JMP / M • Positively Pagan #06 / 1993 / ATA / M • Private Diaries #1: Christina / 1995 / AVI / M • Private Label / 1993 / GLI / M • Private Video Magazine #04 / 1993 / OD / M • Private Video Magazine #13 / 1994 / OD / M • Roxy: A Gang Bang Fantasy / 1994 / FC / M • Rump Humpers #18 / 1994 / GLI / M • Sex Academy #2: The Art Of Talking Dirty / 1994 / ONA / M • Sex Academy #4: The Art Of Anal / 1994 / ONA / M • Sex Fugitives / 1993 / LE / M • Seymore Butts Is Blown Away / 1993 / FH / M • Sgt. Peckers Lonely Hearts Club Gang Bang / 1995 / AMP / M • Sodom Chronicles / 1995 / FH / M • Stevi's: Laurie & Paul / 1993 / SSV / M • Strippers Inc. #1 / 1994 / ONA / M • Stud Finders / 1995 / ONA / M • Stuff Your Face #3 / 1995 / JMP / M • Supermodel #2 / 1994 / VI / M • SVE: Anal Homecoming / 1992 / SVE / M • Tail Taggers #127: / 1994 / WV / M • Tail Taggers #129: / 1994 / WV / M • Tail Taggers #130 / 1994 / WV / M • Take This Wad And Shove It! / 1994 / ZA / M • Top Debs #6: Rear Entry Girls / 1995 / GO / M • Uncle Roy's Amateur Home Video #16 / 1992 / VIM / M • Video Virgins #01 / 1992 / NS / M • Web Of Desire / 1993 / OD / M • Wild Orgies #12 / 1994 / AFI / M • Wild Orgies #17 / 1995 / AFI / M • Witches Are Bitches / 1996 / NIT / M

PAUL NELSON *see Star Index I*

PAUL NEVITT *see Andrew Blake*

PAUL NEWMAN
Thermonuclear Sex / 1996 / EL / M

PAUL NORMAN *(Norman Apstein)*
Director. The Norman Apstein attribution is from **The Erotic Adventures Of The Three Musketeers**.
Controlled / 1994 / FD / M • The Erotic Adventures Of The Three Musketeers / 1992 / CEL / S • The Fluffer #1 / 1993 / FD / M • For The Money #1 / 1993 / FH / M • For The Money #2 / 1993 / FH / M • Inferno #1 / 1993 / SC / M • Inferno #2 / 1993 / SC / M • Naked Truth #2 / 1993 / FH / M • Stick It In The Rear #2 / 1993 / PL / M • Tori Welles Goes Behind The Scenes / 1992 / FD / M

PAUL ORBOIS *see Star Index I*

PAUL PIERSON
Resurrection Of Eve / 1973 / MIT / M

PAUL POUNDER
Animal Instincts / 1991 / VEX / M • Blue Fire / 1991 / V99 / M • Chocolate Cherries #2 / 1990 / CC / M • College Girl / 1990 / VEX / M • Con Jobs / 1990 / V99 / M • Exotic Tastes / 1995 / VEX / C • Glamour Girl / 1991 / VEX / M • Having It All / 1991 / VEX / M • Holly Does Hollywood #4 / 1990 / CAY / M • Hot Savannah Nights / 1991 / VEX / M • Lady Badass / 1990 / V99 / M • Living In Sin / 1990 / VEX / M • Nasty Reputation / 1991 / VEX / M • Orgy On The Ranch / 1991 / NLE / M • Ride 'em Cowgirl / 1991 / V99 / M • The Rock Hard Files / 1991 / VEX / M • Seduction / 1990 / VEX / M • The Ultimate Pleasure / 1995 / LEI / M • The War Of The Hoses / 1991 / NLE / M

PAUL RAMANA
Intimate Secrets Of Sex & Spirit / 1995 / TMM / M

PAUL RAMSWELL
Freshness Counts / 1996 / EL / M

PAUL ROBIN
AVP #1001: Candy's Fantasy—The Robbery / 1987 / AVP / M

PAUL SCHARF *(Andy Brown)*
The Analyst / 1975 / ALP / M • Ceremony, The Ritual Of Love / 1976 / AVC / M • Count The Ways / 1976 / CA / M • Easy Alice / 1976 / VC / M • Erotic Fortune Cookies / 1975 / VCX / M • Flight Sensations / 1983 / VC / C • House of Kinky Pleasures / 1975 / VCX / C • Night Pleasures / 1975 / WWV / M • Seven Into Snowy / 1977 / VC / M • The Starlets / 1976 / RAV / M • V—The Hot One / 1978 / CV / M

PAUL SEIDERMAN *see Jerry Butler*

PAUL SHELLEY
Hard Action / 1975 / AXV / M

PAUL SIMONE
The Tale Of Tiffany Lust / 1981 / CA / M

PAUL STRYDER
The Attendant / 1996 / SC / M • Dirty & Kinky Mature Women #10 / 1996 / C69 / M • Eighteen & Easy / 1996 / SC / M • Frendz? #2 / 1996 / RAS / M • Interviews At The Hard Wok Cafe / 1996 / LOF / M • Nineteen #8 / 1997 / FOR / M • Pussyman's Nite Club Party #1 / 1996 / SNA / M • Pussyman's Nite Club Party #2 / 1997 / SNA / M • Summer Dreams / 1996 / TEP / M

PAUL TANNER *see Paul Thomas*

PAUL TAYLOR *see Star Index I*

PAUL THOMAS *(Phil Tobis, Phil Tobias, Phil Tobus, Grady Sutton, Toby Phillips, Judy Blue (P.Thomas), Paul Tanner, Phil Toubes, Paul Tomas, Phil Toubus,*

Philip Toubus)
Toby Phillips is the director of **The Pamela Principle**.
1001 Erotic Nights #1 / 1982 / VC / M • 8 To 4 / 1981 / CA / M • The 8th Annual Erotic Film Awards / 1984 / SE / C • Addicted To Love / 1988 / WAV / M • Adult Video News Magazine / 1985 / ZEB / M • All About Annette / 1982 / SE / C • All American Girls #2: In Heat / 1983 / CA / M • Amazing Tails #5 / 1990 / CA / M • American Pie / 1980 / SE / M • Angel Kelly Raw / 1987 / FAN / M • Angel Of The Night / 1985 / IN / M • Another Roll In The Hay / 1985 / COL / M • Anything Goes / 1993 / VD / C • Aroused #2 / 1995 / VI / M • The Autobiography Of A Flea / 1976 / MIT / M • Baby Face #1 / 1977 / VC / M • Backdoor Girls / 1983 / VCR / C • Backdoor Lust / 1987 / CV / C • Backdoor Romance / 1984 / VIV / M • Backside To The Future #1 / 1986 / ZA / M • Bad Company / 1978 / CV / M • The Bad News Brat / 1991 / VI / M • Beach Blanket Brat / 1989 / VI / M • Beat The Heat / 1990 / VI / M • Beauty / 1981 / VC / M • Bedside Brat / 1988 / VI / M • Bedtime Tales / 1985 / SE / M • The Best Of Alex De Renzy #1 / 1983 / VC / C • Best Of Atom / 1984 / AT / C • The Best Of Blondes / 1986 / VCR / C • The Best Of Gail Palmer / 1981 / WWV / C • The Better Sex Video Series #6: Acting Out Your Fantasies / 1992 / LEA / M • Beyond Shame / 1980 / VEP / M • The Bigger The Better / 1986 / SE / C • Black Widow / 1988 / WV / M • Blazing Bedrooms / 1987 / LA / M • Blonde Justice #1 / 1993 / VI / M • Blonde Justice #2 / 1993 / VI / M • Blue Confessions / 1983 / VCR / M • Blue Ice / 1985 / CA / M • Blue Ribbon Blue / 1984 / CA / C • Blue Vanities #016 (New) / 1988 / FFL / M • Blue Vanities #018 (New) / 1988 / FFL / M • Blue Vanities #037 / 1988 / FFL / M • Blue Vanities #039 (New) / 1988 / FFL / M • Blue Vanities #046 (New) / 1988 / FFL / M • Blue Vanities #054 / 1988 / FFL / M • Blue Vanities #063 / 1988 / FFL / M • Blue Vanities #067 / 1988 / FFL / M • Blue Vanities #080 / 1988 / FFL / M • Blue Vanities #091 / 1988 / FFL / M • Blue Vanities #220 / 1994 / FFL / M • Blue Vanities #246 / 1995 / FFL / M • Bon Appetite / 1985 / TGA / C • Boobs, Butts And Bloopers #2 / 1990 / HO / M • Bordello...House Of The Rising Sun / 1985 / SE / M • The Brat / 1986 / VI / M • Brat Force / 1989 / VI / M • Brat On The Run / 1987 / VI / M • Breaking It #1 / 1984 / COL / M • Breezy / 1985 / VCR / A • A Brief Affair / 1982 / CA / M • Broadway Brat / 1988 / VI / M • Caballero Preview Tape #2 / 1983 / CA / C • Caballero Preview Tape #4 / 1985 / CA / C • California Blondes #03 / 1991 / VD / C • California Valley Girls / 1983 / HO / M • Camp Beaverlake #1 / 1984 / AR / M • Campus Capers / 1982 / VC / M • Can't Get Enough / 1985 / CA / M • Candy Stripers #1 / 1978 / ALP / M • Careena #1 / 1987 / WV / C • Caught From Behind #02: The Sequel / 1983 / HO / M • Caught From Behind #03 / 1985 / HO / M • Caught In The Act / 1987 / WV / M • CB Mamas / 1976 / MIT / M • Centerfold Celebrities #3 / 1983 / VC / M • Centerspread Girls / 1982 / CA / M • Champagne For Breakfast / 1980 / SE / M • Charm School / 1986 / VI / M • Cheating / 1986 / SEV / M • Cheating American Style / 1988

1986 / VC / M • Shacking Up / 1985 / VXP / M • Shauna: Every Man's Fantasy / 1985 / CA / C • She's So Fine #1 / 1985 / VC / M • Sheer Bedlam / 1986 / VI / M • Sheila's Payoff / 1977 / VCX / M • Sheri's Gotta Have It / 1985 / LIM / C • Shiela's Deep Desires / 1986 / HO / M • Show Your Love / 1984 / VC / M • Showgirl #06: Sue Nero's Fantasies / 1983 / VCR / M • Silk, Satin & Sex / 1983 / SE / M • Sinners #1 / 1988 / COM / M • Sinners #2 / 1988 / COM / M • Sinners #3 / 1989 / COM / M • Sins Of The Wealthy #2 / 1986 / CLV / M • Skintight / 1981 / CA / M • Snake Eyes #1 / 1984 / COM / M • Soft Places / 1978 / CXV / M • Some Kind Of Woman / 1985 / CA / M • Sore Throat / 1985 / GO / M • Space Virgins / 1984 / CRE / M • Speedster / 1992 / VI / M • Stiff Competition #1 / 1984 / CA / M • Still The Brat / 1988 / VI / M • Street Heat / 1984 / VC / M • Summer Camp Girls / 1983 / CA / M • Summer Of '72 / 1982 / CA / M • Super Chic / 1985 / VC / M • Supergirls Do General Hospital / 1984 / VC / M • Supergirls Do The Navy / 1984 / VC / M • Superstar John Holmes / 1979 / AVC / M • Surfside Sex / 1985 / PV / M • Suze's Centerfolds #5 / 1981 / CA / M • Suze's Centerfolds #6 / 1981 / CA / M • Suze's Centerfolds #8 / 1984 / CA / M • Swedish Erotica #01 / 1980 / CA / M • Swedish Erotica #02 / 1980 / CA / M • Swedish Erotica #03 / 1980 / CA / M • Swedish Erotica #04 / 1980 / CA / M • Swedish Erotica #05 / 1980 / CA / M • Swedish Erotica #08 / 1980 / CA / M • Swedish Erotica #11 / 1980 / CA / M • Swedish Erotica #13 / 1980 / CA / M • Swedish Erotica #14 / 1980 / CA / M • Swedish Erotica #17 / 1980 / CA / M • Swedish Erotica #22 / 1980 / CA / M • Swedish Erotica #25 / 1980 / CA / M • Swedish Erotica #28 / 1980 / CA / M • Swedish Erotica #29 / 1980 / CA / M • Swedish Erotica #40 / 1981 / CA / M • Swedish Erotica #41 / 1982 / CA / M • Swedish Erotica #43 / 1982 / CA / M • Swedish Erotica #50 / 1983 / CA / M • Swedish Erotica #63 / 1985 / CA / M • Swedish Erotica #64 / 1985 / CA / M • Swedish Erotica #67 / 1985 / CA / M • Swedish Erotica #68 / 1985 / CA / M • Swedish Erotica Superstar #1: Seka / 1983 / CA / C • Swedish Erotica Superstar #4: Shauna Grant / 1984 / CA / C • Sweet Alice / 1983 / VCX / M • Sweet Captive / 1979 / EVI / M • The Sweetest Taboo / 1986 / SE / M • Taboo American Style #1: The Ruthless Beginning / 1985 / VC / M • Taboo American Style #2: The Story Continues / 1985 / VC / M • Taboo American Style #3: Nina Becomes An Actress / 1985 / VC / M • Taboo American Style #4: The Exciting Conclusion / 1985 / VC / M • Taija Is Sizzling Hot / 1986 / VT / M • Tales Of The Uncensored / 1987 / FAN / M • A Taste Of Candy / 1985 / LA / M • A Taste Of Janey / 1990 / PIN / C • A Taste Of Money / 1983 / AT / M • A Taste Of Nikki Charm / 1989 / PIN / C • A Taste Of Pink / 1985 / VXP / M • A Taste Of Porsche / 1988 / PIN / C • A Taste Of Vanessa De Rio / 1990 / PIN / C • Teenage Madam / 1979 / CXV / M • Temptations Of The Flesh / 1986 / VD / M • Ten Little Maidens / 1985 / EXF / M • Things Change #1: My First Time / 1992 / CV / M • Things Change #2: Letting Go / 1992 / CV

/ M • This Stud's For You / 1986 / MAP / C • Thoroughly Amorous Amy / 1978 / VCX / M • Thrill Street Blues / 1985 / WV / M • Thy Neighbour's Wife / 1986 / DR / M • Too Much Too Soon / 1983 / VCX / M • Torch #1 / 1990 / VI / M • Torrid Without A Cause #1 / 1989 / VI / M • Touch Me In The Morning / 1982 / CA / M • Tracie Lords / 1984 / CIT / M • Trashi / 1980 / CA / M • Triple Xposure / 1986 / VD / M • The Trouble With Traci / 1984 / CHA / C • True Legends Of Adult Cinema: The Cult Superstars / 1993 / VC / C • True Legends Of Adult Cinema: The Golden Age / 1992 / VC / C • True Love / 1989 / VI / M • Twentysomething #1 / 1988 / VI / M • Twentysomething #2 / 1988 / VI / M • The Ultimate Lover / 1986 / VD / M • The Ultimate O / 1985 / NSV / M • The Ultimate Thrill / 1988 / PIN / C • Unnatural Phenomenon #1 / 1985 / WV / M • Unnatural Phenomenon #2 / 1986 / WV / M • The Untamed / 1978 / VCX / M • Untamed Passions / 1987 / CV / C • Up Up And Away / 1984 / CA / M • Urban Cowgirls / 1980 / CA / M • V—The Hot One / 1978 / CV / M • VCA Previews #4 / 1988 / VC / C • Virginia / 1983 / CA / M • Vow Of Passion / 1991 / VI / M • Where The Boys Aren't #1 / 1989 / VI / F • Where The Boys Aren't #3 / 1990 / VI / F • Where There's Smoke There's Fire / 1987 / FAN / M • White Women / 1986 / CC / M • Wicked Sensations #1 / 1981 / CA / M • The Wild Brat / 1988 / VI / M • Wild Dallas Honey / 1985 / VCX / M • With Love From Susan / 1988 / HO / C • With Love, Annette / 1985 / CA / C • With Love, Lisa / 1985 / CA / C • Women In Love / 1980 / CA / M • Working Girls / 1985 / CA / M • X Factor / 1984 / HO / M • Yank My Doodle, It's A Dandy / 1985 / GOM / M • Yellow Fever / 1984 / PL / M • Yiddish Erotica #1 / 1986 / SE / C • Young And Naughty / 1984 / HO / M • Young And Restless / 1983 / VIV / M • Young Doctors In Lust / 1979 / NSV / M • Young Girls Do / 1984 / ELH / M • The Young Like It Hot / 1983 / CA / M • Yuppies In Heat / 1988 / CHA / C • [Hotel Flesh / 1983 / CV / M

PAUL TOMAS see Paul Thomas
PAUL VATELLI
Doin' The Harlem Shuffle / 1986 / CA / M • The Girl From S.E.X. / 1982 / CA / M • Let's Talk Sex / 1982 / CA / M • Stiff Competition #1 / 1984 / CA / M
PAUL VEREL see Star Index I
PAUL WEST
All The King's Ladies / 1981 / SUP / M
PAUL WHITECOCK see Star Index I
PAUL WINDSOR see Star Index I
PAUL WRIGHT
Talk Dirty To Me #02 / 1982 / CA / M
PAUL Z.
Screamers / 1994 / HW / M
PAULA
Blue Vanities #501 / 1992 / FFL / M • Buttman Goes To Rio #3 / 1992 / EA / M • Buttman's European Vacation #3 / 1995 / EA / M • Hot Legs #2 / 1990 / PLV / B • Prague By Night #2 / 1996 / EA / M
PAULA ANGELESIS see Star Index I
PAULA BOND
Lacey Bodine (The Decline And Fall Of) / 1975 / VCX / M
PAULA BRASILE
World Sex Tour #6 / 1996 / ANA / M
PAULA BROWN see Star Index I

PAULA COX
Seka's Teenage Diary / 1984 / HO / C
PAULA DONNELLY see Paula Wain
PAULA GAINES
Lady On Top / cr73 / BL / M
PAULA GRAY
Boiling Point / 1978 / SE / M
PAULA HARLOW (Taylor Dane, Paula LaBelle, P. Harlow, Paula Marlow)
Behind Blue Eyes #1 / 1986 / ME / M • Caddy Shack-Up / 1986 / VD / M • Careena #2: A Star On The Rise / 1988 / WV / C • Charmed And Dangerous / 1987 / VI / M • Dominoes / 1993 / VI / M • Dream Girls / 1986 / VC / M • Ebony & Ivory Fantasies / 1988 / VD / C • Hometown Honeys #1 / 1986 / VEX / M • Hottest Parties / 1988 / VC / C • House Of Sleeping Beauties #2 / 1992 / VI / M • The Life & Loves Of Nikki Charm / 1986 / MAL / M • Long Hard Summer / 1989 / BMV / C • Lust At Sea / 1986 / VD / M • The Lust Detector / 1986 / PIN / M • New Lovers / 1993 / VI / M • Nicki / 1987 / VI / M • Nymphette #1 / 1986 / WV / M • Oral Majority #03 / 1986 / WV / C • Sky Foxes / 1987 / VC / M • Things Change / 1992 / MET / M • Things Change #1: My First Time / 1992 / CV / M • Things Change #2: Letting Go / 1992 / CV / M • Tunnel Of Love / 1986 / CLV / M
PAULA KINCHLOE see Star Index I
PAULA LABELLE see Paula Harlow
PAULA MARLOW see Paula Harlow
PAULA MASON
All American Hustler / cr73 / SOW / M • Bucky Beaver's XXX Dragon Art Theatre Double Feature #28 / 1996 / SOW / M
PAULA MEADOWS see Star Index I
PAULA MORTON (Paula Reis, Paula Reisenwitz, Molly Malone, Paula Reison, Paula Stewart)
Was the wife of Gerard Damiano at one time. Blonde with medium tits, lithe body and passable face.
Bad Penny / 1978 / QX / M • Beach House / 1981 / CA / C • Blonde Ambition / 1981 / QX / M • Bon Appetit / 1980 / QX / M • Bridal Intrigue / 1975 / VHL • Decendance Of Grace / 1977 / CA / M • Dirty Lilly / 1975 / VXP / M • Domination Blue / 1976 / SVE / B • The Double Exposure Of Holly / 1977 / TVX / M • Erotic Fantasies #3 / 1983 / CV / C • The Final Test / 197? / RLV / B • For Richer, For Poorer / 1979 / CXV / M • French Classmates / 1977 / PVI / M • French Teen / 1977 / CV / M • GVC: Strange Family / 1977 / GO / M • Here Comes The Bride / 1977 / CV / M • High School Bunnies / 1978 / VC / M • Honeymoon Haven / 1977 / QX / M • House Of DeSade / 1975 / ALP / B • Jail Bait / 1976 / VC / M • Joint Venture / 1977 / ELV / M • Joy / 1977 / QX / M • Legends Of Porn #1 / 1987 / CV / C • The Love Couch / 1977 / VC / M • Love Roots / 1987 / LIM / M • The Love Syndrome / 1978 / CV / M • Magic Girls / 1983 / SVE / M • Misbehavin' / 1979 / VXP / M • The Perfect Position / cr75 / SIL / M • Pop-Porn: Safari Club / 1992 / 4P / M • Pussycat Ranch / 1978 / CV / M • Safari Club / 1977 / 4P / M • Swedish Sorority Girls / 1978 / CV / M • Teenage Housewife / 1976 / BL / M • Teenage Runaways / 1977 / WWV / M • This Lady Is A Tramp / 1980 / CV / M • The Travails Of June / 1976 / VHL / M • Triple Header / 1987 / AIR / C • Un-

derage / 1974 / IHV / M • Visions / 1977 / QX / M • Voluptuous Predators / cr76 / VHL / M

PAULA PAGE
The Candy Store / cr71 / GO / M • Reel Classics #3 / 1996 / H&S / M • Reel Classics #4 / 1996 / H&S / M

PAULA PAIN
Master's Touch #6: Dom's In Distress / 1995 / FAP / B

PAULA PARK *see Star Index I*

PAULA PAYNE
Out-Foxed / 1995 / SV / B

PAULA PRESCOTT *see Pat Manning*

PAULA PRICE *(Raquel Gold)*
Not too pretty large brunette. Raquel Gold is from **Breaststroke #3**. Breasts were enhanced from a small C to 36DD. (They were too big to start with.) Supposedly lost her virginity at age 12. 5'9" tall, 115lbs 36DD-25-35 (all in 1991). At one stage married to (and may still be) Eric Price. Sister is in the business under the name Brittany.

All The Way Down / 1991 / ZA / M • Ambushed / 1990 / SE / M • Anal Addiction #1 / 1990 / SO / M • Anal Intruder #05: The Final Outrage / 1990 / CC / M • Anal Storm / 1991 / ZA / M • The Analizer / 1990 / LV / M • The Backpackers #2 / 1990 / IN / M • Bad Habits / 1990 / WV / M • Behind The Backdoor #4 / 1990 / EVN / M • Blue Views / 1990 / CDI / M • Boobs, Butts And Bloopers #1 / 1990 / HO / M • Breasts And Beyond #1 / 1991 / ME / M • Breaststroke #3 / 1989 / EX / M • Butt Naked #1 / 1990 / OD / M • Chasey Revealed / 1994 / WP / M • Cheek Busters / 1990 / FH / M • City Girls / 1991 / VC / M • D-Cup Dating Service / 1991 / ME / M • Deep In The Bush / 1990 / KIS / M • Delicious Passions / 1993 / ROB / F • Derrier / 1991 / CC / M • Do It In The Road / 1990 / LV / M • Door To Door / 1990 / EX / M • Double Detail / 1992 / SO / M • Double The Pleasure / 1990 / SE / M • Dr Hooters / 1991 / PL / M • Elements Of Desire / 1994 / ULI / M • Exiles / 1991 / VT / M • Falcon Head / 1990 / ARG / M • Famous Anus #1 / 1990 / EX / M • Fantasy In Blue / 1991 / VI / M • Fortysomething #1 / 1990 / LE / M • Gemini / 1994 / SC / M • Girls In The Night / 1990 / LE / M • Hard Core Cafe Revisited / 1991 / PL / M • Hidden Obsessions / 1992 / BFP / M • How To Love Your Lover / 1992 / XII / S • In The Can / 1990 / EX / M • Indian Summer #1 / 1991 / VI / M • Indian Summer #2: Sandstorm / 1991 / VI / M • Jennifer Ate / 1993 / XCI / F • Leather And Lace Revisited / 1991 / VT / F • The Legend Of The Kama Sutra / 1994 / A&E / M • Lover's Trance / 1990 / LE / M • Lunar Lust / 2990 / HO / M • Lust Fever / 1991 / FH / M • Madame X / 1990 / EX / M • Nasty Jack's Homemade Vid. #01 / 1990 / CDI / M • Naughty 90's / 1990 / HO / M • Night Trips #2 / 1990 / CA / M • Nightdreams #3 / 1991 / VC / M • One Million Years DD / 1992 / CC / M • Only With A Married Woman / 1990 / LE / M • Passionate Angels / 1990 / HO / M • The Price Is Right / 1992 / VT / C • Private & Confidential / 1994 / AR / M • Pussywoman #1: Sisters In Sin / 1994 / CC / M • Ready, Willing & Anal (Cv) / 1993 / CV / C • Robin Head / 1991 / CC / M • Rock Me / 1990 / LE / F • Scarlet Fantasy / 1990 / VI / M •

The Search For Pink October / 1990 / EX / M • Sensual Exposure / 1993 / ULI / M • Sex Symphony / 1992 / VC / M • A Shot In The Mouth #1 / 1990 / ME / M • Sirens / 1991 / VC / M • Stacked With Honors / 1993 / DR / M • Strangers When We Meet / 1990 / VCR / M • Style #1 / 1992 / VT / M • Sudden Urge / 1990 / IN / M • The Swap #1 / 1990 / VI / M • Tailspin #2 / 1991 / VT / M • Temptation Eyes / 1991 / VT / M • Titillation #3 / 1991 / SE / M • User Friendly / 1992 / VT / M • Vanity / 1992 / HO / M • Waterbabies #2 / 1992 / CC / M • Women In Need / 1990 / HO / M • The Wrong Woman / 1990 / LE / M

PAULA PRINCIPE
Hard Action / 1975 / AXV / M

PAULA REIS *see Paula Morton*

PAULA REISENWITZ *see Paula Morton*

PAULA REISON *see Paula Morton*

PAULA SCHNALL *see Rene Bond*

PAULA SHERWOOD *see Star Index I*

PAULA SMITH
Campus Capers / 1982 / VC / M • The Little French Maid / 1981 / VCX / M

PAULA STEWART *see Paula Morton*

PAULA STONE *see Star Index I*

PAULA THOMAS (CH HE) *see Christine Heller*

PAULA UCELLO
All About Annette / 1982 / SE / C

PAULA VANCE
Bucky Beaver's XXX Dragon Art Theatre Double Feature #26 / 1996 / SOW / M • Inside Pussycat / cr75 / SOW / M

PAULA WAIN *(Christian Sarner, Kelly O'Day, Leah Grant, Sally Mack, Paula Donnelly, Christian Sarver, Kelley O'Day, Christine Sarver)*
. Christine Sarver is from **The Jade Pussycat** box. Blonde with straight fine hair, medium tits, passable face.

Casanova #2 / 1976 / CA / M • The China Cat / 1978 / CA / M • China De Sade / 1977 / ALP / M • Classic Swedish Erotica #13 / 1986 / CA / C • Daddy / 1978 / BL / M • Do You Wanna Be Loved? / 1977 / AR / M • Exhausted / 1981 / CA / C • The Jade Pussycat / 1977 / CA / M • Masterpiece / cr78 / VEP / M • Only The Best #2 / 1989 / CV / C • The Other Side Of Julie / 1978 / CV / M • Private Thighs / 1987 / AVC / C • Sex Ed With Lil' Red / 1983 / TGA / M • That's Erotic / 1979 / CV / C • V—The Hot One / 1978 / CV / M

PAULA WINTERS *(Stacey Poole, Honey Malone, Stacey Devolin, Stacey Delavan, Stacy Pool)*
Not too bad looking. Brunette with breasts like Kari Fox.

Born To Be Wild / 1987 / SE / M • The Boss / 1987 / FAN / M • Debbie Does The Devil In Dallas / 1987 / SE / M • Don't Get Them Wet / 1987 / VD / M • Friday The 13th #1: A Nude Beginning / 1987 / VD / M • Girls On Fire / 1985 / VCX / M • Harlem Candy / 1987 / WET / M • Hottest Ticket / 1987 / WV / C • Hyapatia Lee's Arcade Series #01 / 1988 / ZA / C • Lingerie Party / 1987 / SE / C • Little Shop Of Whores / 1987 / VI / M • Oral Majority #05 / 1987 / WV / C • Sexy Delights #2 / 1987 / CLV / M • Sinset Boulevard / 1987 / WV / M

PAULINA (B. MONROE) *see Brigitte Monroe*

PAULINA DOWN *see Brigitte Monroe*

PAULINA DOWNS *see Brigitte Monroe*

PAULINA PETERS *see Zara Whites*

PAULINE
Blue Vanities #541 / 1994 / FFL / M • Blue Vanities #568 / 1995 / FFL / M • Busty Superstars #1 / 199? / H&S / S • Eat At Daves #4: Condo Cummers / 1995 / SP / M • European Cleavage Queens / 199? / H&S / S • Homegrown Video #409 / 1993 / HOV / M

PAULINE AITKINS
Love Airlines / 1978 / SE / M

PAULINE KRANTZ
Upstairs And Downstairs / 1995 / PL / M

PAULINE LAMONROE *see Star Index I*

PAULINE LARRIEU
Five Kittens / 19?? / … / M • The Felines / 1975 / VCX / M

PAULINE PEPPER *see Star Index I*

PAUNCHY GONZALEZ *see Star Index I*

PAVEL
Buttman's Orgies / 1996 / EA / M • Prague By Night #1 / 1996 / EA / M • Prague By Night #2 / 1996 / EA / M

PAYLESS SHOE SUE *see Star Index I*

PAYTON FOX
Freaky Flix / 1995 / TTV / C • Lactamania #1 / 1994 / TTV / M • Ready To Drop #03 / 1994 / FC / M

PEACH
Buttsizer #3: Return Of The King Of Rears / 1995 / EVN / M • Interview's Southern Cumfort / 1996 / LV / M • Nothing Like Nurse Nookie #1 / 1995 / NIT / M • The Sodomizer #1 / 1995 / SC / M • Under The Cum Cum Tree / 1996 / BCP / M

PEACH PUDDIN'
Anal Alley / 1996 / FD / M • Because I Can / 1995 / BEP / M • Behind The Backdoor #7 / 1995 / EVN / M • Fresh Faces #08 / 1995 / EVN / M • Middle Aged Sex Maniacs / 1995 / SUF / M • A Pool Party At Seymores #2 / 1995 / ULI / M • Pussyman Auditions #13 / 1995 / SNA / M

PEACHES
The Big E #08 / 1988 / BIZ / B • The Butt, The Boobs, The Lips / 1996 / C69 / M • Eat At Dave's #3 / 1995 / SP / M • Eat At Dave's #6 / 1996 / SP / M • Helpless Coeds / 1987 / BIZ / B • My First Time #3 / 1996 / NS / M • Reel Life Video #25: The Drip / 1995 / RLF / M • Student Fetish Videos: Catfighting #02 / 1991 / PLV / B • Student Fetish Videos: The Enema #02 / 1990 / SFV / B • Student Fetish Videos: Tickling #01 / 1991 / SFV / B

PEACHES FLAMBE
Lickity Split / 1974 / COM / M

PEACHES HARDIN *see Star Index I*

PEARL *(Crystal Pearl, Pearl Joyce)*
Brunette with quite a pretty face and medium to large natural tits. Her body is getting a little sloppy.

Amateurs Exposed #05 / 1995 / CV / M • Biff Malibu's Totally Nasty Home Videos #25 / 1992 / ANA / M • Big Murray's New-Cummers #13: Hot Tight Ladies / 1993 / FD / M • Blazing Boners / 1992 / MID / M • Bobby Hollander's Maneaters #02 / 1993 / SFP / M • Breast Worx #35 / 1992 / LBO / M • The D.P. Man #1 / 1992 / FD / M • The D.P. Man #2 / 1992 / FD / M • Dirty Blue Movies #04 / 1993 / JTV / F • Dirty Laundry / 1994 / HOH / M • A Few Good Women / 1993 / CC / M • First Time Lesbians #19 / 1994 / JMP / F • From A Whisper To A Scream / 1993 / GO / M • Head Lines /

1992 / SC / M • Hollywood Amateurs #02 / 1994 / MID / M • Hollywood Swingers #01 / 1992 / LBO / M • Hollywood Swingers #07 / 1993 / LBO / M • Kelly Eighteen #1 / 1993 / LE / M • Kelly Eighteen #2 / 1993 / LE / M • Lollipop Lickers / 1996 / V99 / C • Maneater (1992-Las Vegas) / 1992 / LV / M • Mr. Fun's Mondo Adventure / 1993 / VC / M • Neighborhood Watch #38: Pearlie's Curlie's / 1993 / LBO / M • New Girls In Town #3 / 1993 / CC / M • The One And Only / 1993 / FD / M • Pearl Necklace: Thee Bush League #11 / 1993 / SEE / M • Positions Wanted: Experienced Only / 1993 / PV / M • Sex Scientist / 1992 / FD / M • Single Tight Female / 1992 / LV / M • Sluts In Suburbia / 1994 / GLI / M • Smeers / 1992 / PL / M • Soap Me Up! / 1993 / FD / M • Street Girl Named Desire / 1992 / FD / M • Untamed Cowgirls Of The Wild West #01: The Pillow Biters / 1992 / ZA / M • Wild Desires / 1994 / MAX / M • Will & Ed's Back To Class / 1992 / MID / M

PEARL (BLONDE)
Bubble Butts Gold #1 / 1994 / LBO / M • Creme De La Face #01 / 1994 / OD / M • Creme De La Face #02 / 1994 / OD / M • Mr. Peepers Amateur Home Videos #88: A For Effort / 1994 / LBO / M • Northwest Pecker Trek #2: Evergreen, Ever Horny / 1994 / LBO / M • Odyssey Triple Play #96: Anal Option #2 / 1995 / OD / M

PEARL ESSENCE
Oriental overtones, long straight dark reddish blonde hair, small tits, belly button ring, passable face, black eyebrows, overbite, tattoo on left ankle, generally lithe body but a little thick around the waist and a little flat on the butt.
Asses Galore #7: Lunatic Fringe / 1996 / DFI / M • Cumback Pussy #7: NUGIRLZ / 1997 / EL / M • Filthy First Timers #7 / 1997 / EL / M

PEARL GREY
[The Last Virgin / 197? / … / M

PEARL HARBOR *see Star Index I*
PEARL HOUSTON *see Holly Ryder*
PEARL JOYCE *see Pearl*
PEBBLES *see Star Index I*
PEDRO MONTOYA *see Star Index I*
PEE WEE
In Loving Color #4 / 1993 / VT / M • My Baby Got Back #01 / 1992 / VT / M • Rocks / 1993 / VT / M

PEEJAY *see P.J. Sparxx*
PEEPERS THE ROBOT *see Star Index I*
PEG SOX
Bottom Busters / 1973 / BLT / M

PEGGY
Blue Vanities #500 / 1992 / FFL / M • Blue Vanities #528 / 1993 / FFL / M • Blue Vanities #538 / 1993 / FFL / M • Limited Edition #14 / 1980 / AVC / M • VGA: Cutting Room Floor #1 / 1993 / VGA / M

PEGGY BOND *see Star Index I*
PEGGY L'MORE *see Jennifer Noxt*
PEGGY SCOTT
The Girls Of Mr X / 1978 / CA / M

PEGGY SIMPSON
Hungry Mouth / 19?? / VXP / M

PEGGY SINGLETON
Blue Vanities #558 / 1994 / FFL / M

PEGGY SUE
Big Girl Dildo Show / 1995 / BTO / F • Blue Vanities #502 / 1992 / FFL / M • Itsy Bitsy Gang Bang / 1996 / HW / M • Somewhere

Under The Rainbow #2 / 1995 / HW / M
PENCIL SHARP *see Tyler Horne*
PENELOPE
Buffy Malibu's Nasty Girls #10 / 1996 / ANA / F • Dirty Dating Service #01 / 1993 / WP / M • French Taboo / 1985 / ABV / M • Nasty Nymphos #12 / 1996 / ANA / M • Rebecca Lord's World Tour #1: French Edition / 1995 / WP / M • Sodomania #14: C**t Lickin', C*m Drinkin' Bitches / 1995 / EL / M • Triple X Video Magazine #07 / 1995 / OD / M • World Sex Tour #1 / 1995 / ANA / M

PENELOPE DIXON
The Loves Of Mary Jane / 1989 / BWV / C • A Touch Of Sex / 1972 / AR / M

PENELOPE JONES *see Star Index I*
PENELOPE LAMOUR
Anal In The Alps / 1996 / P69 / M • Kinky Ladies Of Bourbon Street / 1976 / LUM / M • Pussy Talk #1 / 1975 / TVX / M

PENELOPE PACE
Blunt Trauma #2 / 1996 / ZFX / B • Blunt Trauma #3: Whiteslave / 1996 / ZFX / B • Hitchhiker / 1996 / ZFX / B • Mincemeat Pie / 1996 / ZFX / B • Phantacide Peepshow / 1996 / ZFX / B • Subject Nine / 1995 / ZFX / B

PENELOPE STEELE
Private School Girls / 1983 / CA / M
PENELOPE VALENTIN
Les Chaleurs De La Gyneco / 1996 / FAP / F

PENI BURK
Hot Property (AVC) / 1975 / AVC / M • Secret Desire / 1975 / CA / B • Sugar In The Raw / 1975 / AVC / M • The Velvet Hustle / 1975 / CA / M

PENNY
America's Raunchiest Home Videos #21: Pumping Pussy / 1992 / ZA / M • Blue Vanities #557 / 1994 / FFL / M

PENNY ANTINE *see Raven Touchstone*
PENNY ARCADE
Body Magic / 1982 / SE / M
PENNY ASHCROFT *see Judith Hamilton*
PENNY CASH
Audra's Ordeal / 1983 / BIZ / B • Taxi Girls #1 / 1980 / WV / M

PENNY CLAIRE *see Star Index I*
PENNY G. *see Star Index I*
PENNY LAMORE
Backdoor Babes / 1985 / WET / M
PENNY LANE *(Rene Hunter, Suzi J.)*
She started at age 18 in about 1986 with **Double Penetration**, directed by Ron Jeremy and then did a movie for Scotty Fox (probably **Chuck & Di In Heat**). She then left the business, returning in 1989.
Amateur Lesbians #10: Stephanie / 1991 / GO / F • Amateur Lesbians #16: Lorraine / 1991 / GO / F • Amateur Nights #02 / 1989 / HO / M • Amateur Nights #03 / 1990 / HO / M • Anal Attack / 1991 / ZA / M • Anal Intruder #03 / 1989 / CC / M • The Applicant / 1988 / BON / B • Babes In Bondage / 1991 / BIZ / B • Backdoor To Hollywood #10 / 1989 / CIN / M • The Best Of Both Worlds #1 / 1986 / LA / G • Bi-Ceps / 1986 / LA / C • Body Triple / 1991 / VC / M • Bound To Tease #5 / 1990 / BON / C • Butt Woman #1 / 1990 / FH / M • Cat Scratch Fever / 1989 / FAZ / M • Chuck & Di In Heat / 1986 / DR / M • Creatures Of The Night / 1987 / FAN / M • Date With The Devil / 1989 / FAZ / M • Double Penetration #1 / 1985 / WV / M • Dream Dates / 1990 / V99

/ M • Driving Miss Daisy Crazy #1 / 1990 / WV / M • East L.A. Law / 1991 / WV / M • Female Domination In Bondage / 1991 / BEB / B • Female Domination #2 / 1991 / BIZ / B • Flash Backs / 1990 / BON / B • Frat Brats / 1990 / VC / M • Girls In Heat / 1991 / ZA / F • Great Balls Of Fire / 1989 / FAZ / M • Handle With Care / 1989 / FAZ / M • Have I Got A Girl For You / 1989 / VEX / M • Head Lock / 1989 / VD / M • Hershe Highway #1 / 1989 / HO / M • Hollywood Bikini Party Girls / 1989 / VC / M • Innocent Bi Standers / 1989 / LV / G • Love From The Backside / 1989 / FAZ / M • Odyssey 30 Min: #102: / 1991 / OD / F • Paradise Road / 1990 / WV / M • Party In The Rear / 1989 / LV / M • Punished By The Latex Mistress / 1992 / BIZ / B • Riding Miss Daisy / 1990 / VEX / M • Seduction / 1990 / VEX / M • Sex And The Single Girl / 1990 / FAN / M • Sheets Of San Francisco / 1986 / AVC / M • Snow White And The Seven Weenies / 1989 / FAN / M • Space Cadet / 1989 / IN / M • Spoiled Rich / 1989 / CC / M • Temperatures Rising / 1986 / VT / M • Thy Neighbour's Wife / 1986 / DR / M • Working Girls In Bondage / 1991 / BIZ / B

PENNY LEE
Eat At Dave's #5 / 1996 / SP / M
PENNY LLOYD FOX
Banned In Britain / 1995 / VC / M
PENNY MICHAELS *see Star Index I*
PENNY MORGAN *see Rachel Ryan*
PENNY NICHOLS *see Star Index I*
PENNY NORRIS
Cover Girl Fantasies #1 / 1983 / VCR / C
PENNY SERVANT *see Star Index I*
PENNY SLINGER
Ancient Secrets Of Sexual Ecstasy / 1996 / HIG / M
PENNY YANG
Chinese Blue / 1976 / … / M
PEONIE *see Peonies Jong*
PEONIES JONG *(Peonie, Peonies Young, Peony Jones)*
Ugly old oriental woman. Peony Jones is from **American Sex Fantasy**.
American Sex Fantasy / 1975 / IHV / M • Blow Dry / 1977 / SVE / M • Classic Erotica #5 / 1985 / SVE / M • Oriental Blue / 1975 / ALP / M • The Vixens Of Kung Fu: A Tale Of Yin Yang / 1975 / VC / M

PEONIES YOUNG *see Peonies Jong*
PEONY JONES *see Peonies Jong*
PEPE
Blue Vanities #547 / 1994 / FFL / M • Fiona On Fire / 1978 / VC / M • Odyssey / 1977 / VC / M • SVE: Foxy's Audition / 1994 / SVE / M • Through The Looking Glass / 1976 / ALP / M

PEPE LEPEW
Beaver & Buttcheeks / 1993 / DR / M • Caught From Behind #18 / 1993 / HO / M • Flesh For Fantasy / 1994 / CV / M • Interactive / 1994 / SC / M • Private Film #12 / 1994 / OD / M • The Reel Sex World #03 / 1994 / WP / M • Risque Burlesque #1 / 1994 / IN / M

PEPE VALENTINE
Honeymoon Haven / 1977 / QX / M
PEPE VASQUEZ *see Star Index I*
PEPPER *see Star Index I*
PEPPER BOND
Big Bust Babes #02 / 1984 / AFI / M • Blue Vanities #004 / 1987 / FFL / M • Blue Van-

cent Exposures / 1996 / MID / M • Indecent Itch / 1985 / VCR / M • Indecent Wives / 1985 / HO / M • Independence Night / 1996 / SC / M • Indian Summer #1 / 1991 / VI / M • Indian Summer #2: Sandstorm / 1991 / VI / M • Infamous Crimes Against Nature / 1993 / SUM / M • Inferno #1 / 1993 / SC / M • Initiation Of Kylie / 1995 / VT / M • Inn Of Sin / 1988 / VT / M • Innocent Obsession / 1989 / FC / M • Innocent Taboo / 1986 / VD / M • Intense Perversions #2 / 1996 / PL / M • Interactive / 1993 / VD / M • Interactive / 1994 / SC / M • Introducing Barbii / 1987 / CDI / M • The Invisible Girl / 1989 / VI / M • Irresistible #2 / 1986 / SE / M • Island Girls #1 / 1990 / CDI / C • Island Girls #2: Fun In The Sun / 1990 / CDI / C • It's My Body / 1985 / CDI / M • Jaded Love / 1994 / CA / M • Jam / 1993 / PL / M • Jane Bond Meets The Man With The Golden Rod / 1987 / VD / M • Jetstream / 1993 / AMP / M • Jewel Of The Nite / 1986 / WV / M • Jezebel #1 / 1993 / SC / M • Juicy Cheerleaders / 1995 / LE / M • Just Another Pretty Face / 1985 / AVC / M • Kascha & Friends / 1988 / CIN / M • Kascha's Blues / 1988 / CDI / M • The Key to Love / 1992 / ZA / M • Kinky / 1987 / SE / M • Kinky Couples / 1990 / VD / M • Kinkyvision #2 / 1988 / VC / M • The Kiss / 1995 / WP / M • Kiss Of The Dragon Lady / 1986 / SEV / M • La Femme Vanessa / 1995 / SC / M • Lady In Blue / 1990 / CIN / M • Laid Off / 1990 / CA / M • The Lascivious Ladies Of Dr Lipo / 1991 / OD / M • The Last American Sex Goddess / 1993 / IF / M • The Last Good Sex / 1992 / FD / M • The Last Resort / 1990 / VC / M • The Last Temptation / 1988 / VD / M • Late Night For Lovers / 1989 / ME / M • Latex #2 / 1995 / VC / M • Laying The Ghost / 1991 / VC / M • Leena Goes Pro / 1992 / VT / M • Leena's Early Experiences / 1995 / OD / C • Leena's Oral Extravaganza / 1995 / OD / C • Legal Tender (1990-X) / 1990 / VC / M • Legend #2 / 1990 / LE / M • The Legend Of Barbi-Q And Little Fawn / 1994 / CA / M • Les Femmes Erotiques / 1993 / BFP / M • Let Me Tell Ya 'Bout Fat Chicks #1 / 1986 / 4P / C • Let's Talk Dirty / 1987 / SE / M • Lethal Woman #1 / 1988 / SEV / M • Lethal Woman #2 / 1988 / SEV / M • Lethal Woman / 1991 / CIN / M • Lick Bush / 1992 / VD / C • The Life & Loves Of Nikki Charm / 1986 / MAL / M • Like A Virgin #1 / 1985 / AT / M • Like A Virgin #2 / 1984 / AT / M • Lips / 1994 / FC / M • A Little Romance / 1986 / HO / M • Live In, Love In / 1989 / ME / M • The Load Warriors #1 / 1987 / VD / M • The Load Warriors #2 / 1987 / VD / M • Loopholes / 1993 / TP / M • Loose Ends #2 / 1986 / 4P / M • Loose Ends #3 / 1987 / BS / M • Loose Ends #4 / 1988 / 4P / M • Loose Morals / 1987 / HO / M • Love Bites / 1985 / CA / M • Love Button / 1989 / VD / M • Love Ghost / 1990 / WV / M • Love In Reverse / 1988 / FAZ / M • Love Lessons / 1986 / HO / M • The Love Nest / 1989 / CA / M • Love Tryst / 1995 / VPN / M • Lovin' USA / 1989 / EXH / C • Loving Lips / 1987 / AMB / C • Lucky Break / 1991 / SE / M • Lucy Has A Ball / 1987 / ME / M • Luscious Lucy In Love / 1986 / AVC / M • Lust American Style / 1985 / WV / M • Lust At The Top / 1985 / CDI / M • Lust Bug / 1985 / HO / M • Lust Connection / 1988 / VT / M • Lust

Crimes / 1992 / WV / M • Lust In The Fast Lane / 1984 / PV / M • Lust Runner / 1995 / VC / M • Lusty Layout / 1986 / PV / M • Mad Jack Beyond Thunderdome / 1986 / WET / M • The Magic Shower / 1989 / CDI / M • Make Me Watch / 1994 / PV / M • Make My Night / 1985 / CIN / M • Makeout / 1988 / VT / M • Making Charli / 1989 / CDI / M • Making Ends Meet / 1988 / VT / M • Malibu Madam / 1995 / CC / M • Malibu Spice / 1991 / VC / M • Mammary Lane / 1988 / VT / C • The Man Who Loves Women / 1994 / VC / M • Manbait #1 / 1991 / VC / M • Manbait #2 / 1992 / VC / M • Marilyn Chambers' Private Fantasies #4 / 1983 / CA / M • Masque / 1995 / VC / M • Megasex / 1988 / EVN / M • Meltdown / 1990 / LV / M • Mickey Ray's Sex Search #04: Long And Hard / 1994 / WIV / M • A Midslumber's Night Dream / 1985 / 4P / M • Midnight Fire / 1990 / HU / M • Midnight Madness / 1993 / DR / M • Midnight Pink / 1987 / WV / M • The Million Dollar Screw / 1987 / VT / M • Mind Shadows #1 / 1993 / FD / M • Mind Shadows #2 / 1993 / FD / M • Mirage #1 / 1991 / VC / M • Mirage #2 / 1992 / VC / M • The Mistress #2 / 1990 / CV / M • Molly B-Goode / 1994 / FH / M • The Money Hole / 1993 / VD / M • Moonstroked / 1988 / 3HV / M • More Than A Handful #1 / 1985 / CV / C • Muff 'n' Jeff / 1992 / ZA / M • My Sensual Body / 1989 / WET / M • My Wildest Dreams / 1988 / IN / C • Mystery Of The Golden Lotus / 1989 / HU / M • Mystic Pieces / 1989 / EA / M • Naked & Nasty / 1995 / WP / M • Naked Ambition / 1995 / VC / M • Naked Goddess #1 / 1991 / VC / M • Naked Juice / 1995 / OD / G • Naked Scandal #1 / 1995 / SPI / M • Naked Scandal #2 / 1996 / SPI / M • Naked Stranger / 1987 / CDI / M • The Naked Truth / 1995 / VI / M • Nasty Habits Are Hard To Break / 1986 / 4P / M • Nasty Lovers / 1987 / SE / C • Nasty Newshounds / 1988 / ME / M • Nasty Nymphos #03 / 1994 / ANA / M • Nasty Nymphos #06 / 1994 / ANA / M • National Poontang's Summer Vacation / 1990 / FC / M • The Natural / 1993 / VT / M • Naughty 90's / 1990 / HO / M • Naughty Nurses / 1986 / VEX / M • Naughty Nymphs / 1986 / VEX / M • Naughty Nymphs / 1991 / VEX / C • Neutron Man / 1993 / HO / M • Never Say Never / 1994 / SC / M • The New Butt Hunt #15 / 1995 / LEI / C • New Wave Hookers #1 / 1984 / VC / M • New Wave Hookers #2 / 1991 / VC / M • The Newcomers / 1983 / VCX / M • The Nicole Stanton Story #1 / 1989 / CA / M • The Nicole Stanton Story #2 / 1989 / CA / M • Night And Day #2 / 1993 / VT / M • A Night At The Waxworks / 1990 / IF / M • Night Deposit / 1991 / VC / M • Night Games / 1986 / WV / M • Night Of Loving Dangerously / 1984 / PV / M • Night Of Passion / 1993 / BIA / C • The Night Of The Headhunter / 1985 / WV / M • Night Tales / 1996 / VC / M • The Night Temptress / 1989 / HU / M • Night Trips #1 / 1989 / CA / M • Night Vision / 1996 / WP / M • Nightshift Nurses #1 / 1988 / VC / M • Nina's Knockouts / 1987 / AVC / C • Nobody's Looking / 1993 / VC / M • Not So Innocent / 1990 / HO / M • Nothing Like A Dame #1 / 1995 / IN / M • Nothing Like A Dame #2 / 1995 / IN / M • Nurse Nancy / 1991 / CA / M • Obsessions In Lace / 1994

/ PL / M • Office Girls / 1989 / CA / M • The Oh! Zone / 1995 / VC / M • On Golden Blonde / 1984 / PV / M • On The Loose / 1991 / LV / M • On Trial #1: In Defense Of Savannah / 1991 / VI / M • On Trial #4: The Verdict / 1992 / VI / M • Once In A Lifetime / 1996 / VC / C • One Million Years DD / 1992 / CC / M • One Night Stand / 1990 / LE / M • The Only Game In Town / 1991 / VC / M • Only The Best Of Barbara Dare / 1990 / CV / C • Only The Best Of The Erotic Eighties / 1992 / VC / C • Only The Very Best On Video / 1992 / VC / C • Oral Madness #1 / 1991 / OD / M • Oral Majority #01 / 1986 / WV / C • Oral Majority #03 / 1986 / WV / C • Oral Majority #04 / 1987 / WV / C • Oral Majority #07 / 1989 / WV / C • Oral Majority #09 / 1992 / WV / C • Oral Majority #10 / 1993 / WV / C • Oral Majority #11 / 1994 / WV / C • Orgies / 1987 / WV / C • Out Of Control / 1987 / SE / M • Out Of Love / 1995 / VI / M • Out Of The Blue #1 / 1991 / VI / M • The Outlaw / 1991 / WV / M • Outlaws / 1993 / SC / M • The Oval Office / 1991 / LV / M • The Palace Of Pleasure / 1995 / ULI / M • Paradise Lost / 1995 / LE / M • Parliament: Dirty Blondes #1 / 1991 / PM / F • Parliament: Fuckin' Superstars #1 / 1990 / PM / C • Parliament: Three Way Lust / 1988 / PM / M • Party Doll A Go-Go #1 / 1991 / VC / M • Party Doll A Go-Go #2 / 1991 / VC / M • A Passage To Ecstasy / 1985 / CDI / M • Passages #1 / 1991 / VI / M • Passages #2 / 1991 / VI / M • Passages #3 / 1991 / VI / M • Passages #4 / 1991 / VI / M • The Passion / 1995 / IP / M • Passion / 1996 / SC / M • The Passion Of Heather Lear / 1990 / AFV / M • Passionate Angels / 1990 / HO / M • Passionate Heiress / 1987 / CA / M • Patriot Dames / 1992 / ZA / M • Patriot X / 1995 / LE / M • Peggy Sue / 1987 / VT / M • Penetration #4 / 1984 / AVC / M • Penetration #5 / 1984 / AVC / M • Perfect Fit / 1985 / DR / M • The Perfect Pair / 1991 / LE / M • Performance / 1990 / VI / M • Perils Of Paula / 1989 / CA / M • Perks / 1992 / ZA / M • Perverted #1: The Babysitters / 1994 / ZA / M • Phone Sex Girls #2 / 1987 / VT / M • Photo Opportunity / 1994 / VC / M • Pick Up Lines #01 / 1995 / 4P / M • Pick Up Lines #02 / 1995 / 4P / M • Pick Up Lines #03 / 1995 / 4P / M • Pick Up Lines #04 / 1995 / 4P / M • Pick Up Lines #05 / 1996 / OD / M • Pick Up Lines #06 / 1996 / OD / M • Pick Up Lines #07 / 1996 / OD / M • Pick Up Lines #08 / 1996 / OD / M • Pick Up Lines #09 / 1996 / OD / M • Pick Up Lines #10 / 1997 / OD / M • Pick Up Lines #11 / 1997 / OD / M • Pick Up Lines #12 / 1997 / OD / M • Pick Up Lines #13 / 1997 / OD / M • Piece Of Heaven / 1988 / CDI / M • The Pillowman / 1988 / VC / M • The Pink Pussycat / 1992 / CA / M • Plan 69 From Outer Space / 1993 / CA / M • Play It Again, Samantha / 1986 / EVN / M • The Pleasure Hunt #2 / 1985 / NSV / M • Pleasureland / 1996 / VI / M • Pocahotass #1 / 1996 / FD / M • Pocahotass #2 / 1996 / FD / M • The Poonies / 1985 / VI / M • Porn On The 4th Of July / 1990 / IN / M • Pornographic Priestess / 1992 / CA / M • A Portrait Of Christy / 1990 / VI / M • A Portrait Of Dorian / 1992 / OD / M • Possessions / 1992 / HW / M • The Postman Always Comes Twice / 1986 / AMB / M • Power Of The Pussy / 1995 / LEI

THE X-RATED VIDEOTAPE STAR INDEX   521

Bang-Bang / 1992 / FC / C • To The Rear / 1992 / VC / M • Too Good To Be True / 1984 / MAP / M • Top It Off / 1990 / VC / M • Total Reball / 1990 / CC / M • Toys 4 Us #2 / 1987 / WV / C • Traci's Big Trick / 1987 / VAS / M • Tracy Dick / 1985 / WV / M • Tracy Takes Paris / 1987 / VIP / M • Tricks Of The Trade / 1988 / CA / M • A Trip Down Mammary Lane / 1991 / FC / M • True Legends Of Adult Cinema: The Erotic Eighties / 1992 / VC / C • True Legends Of Adult Cinema: The Modern Era / 1992 / VC / C • Twisted Sisters / 1988 / ZA / M • Two Handfuls / 1986 / ... / G • Two Sides Of A Lady / 1994 / HDE / M • Two Tons Of Fun #1 / 1985 / 4P / C • Unbelievable Orgies #1 / 1987 / EVN / C • Unchain My Heart / 1990 / CC / M • Unchained Melanie / 1992 / VC / M • Uncut Diamond / 1989 / IN / M • Unforgivable / 1992 / HO / M • Unforgivable / 1989 / IN / M • Unlike A Virgin / 1991 / HO / M • Up And Coming Executive / 1993 / TP / M • Up And Cummers #07 / 1994 / 4P / M • Up And Cummers: The Movie / 1994 / 4P / M • Up Close & Personal #1 / 1996 / IPI / M • The Uptown Girl / 1992 / ZA / M • Use It Or Lose It / 1994 / CA / M • Used And Abused #2 / 1994 / SFP / M • Vagina Town / 1993 / CA / M • The Valley Girl Connection / 1994 / IN / M • VCA Previews #4 / 1988 / VC / C • Vegas #2: Snake Eyes / 1990 / CIN / M • Vegas #3: Let It Ride / 1990 / CIN / M • Victoria's Secret / 1989 / SO / M • Video Paradise / 1988 / ZA / M • The Violation Of Tori Welles / 1990 / VD / C • Virgin Dreams / 1996 / EA / M • Virgin Heat / 1986 / TEM / M • Virtual Reality / 1993 / EX / M • Virtual Reality Sixty Nine / 1995 / WP / M • Visions #1 / 1995 / ERA / M • Visions Of Desire / 1993 / HO / M • Visions Of Desire / 1994 / DR / M • Vogue / 1994 / VD / C • Voodoo Lust: The Possession / 1989 / PCP / M • The Voyeur #5 / 1995 / EA / M • The Wacky World Of Ed Powers / 1996 / 4P / C • Warm Bodies, Hot Nights / 1988 / PV / M • Waterbabies #2 / 1992 / CC / M • The Way They Were / 1990 / CDI / M • We Love To Tease / 1985 / VD / M • Wet Deal / 1994 / FD / M • Wet Event / 1992 / IF / M • What A Country / 1989 / PL / M • What You Are In The Dark / 1995 / KLP / M • Whispered Lies / 1993 / LBO / M • White Bun Busters / 1985 / VC / M • Who Killed Holly Hollywood? / 1993 / VC / M • Whore House / 1995 / IPI / M • The Whore Of The Worlds / 1985 / PV / M • Wicked As She Seems / 1993 / WP / M • The Wicked One / 1995 / WP / M • Wicked Ways #2: Education Of A D.P. Virgin / 1995 / WP / M • Wicked Whispers / 1985 / VD / M • Wicked Women / 1993 / ME / M • Wide World Of Sex / 1987 / CLV / C • Wild & Wicked #1 / 1991 / VT / M • Wild & Wicked #2 / 1992 / VT / M • Wild & Wicked #3 / 1993 / VT / M • Wild & Wicked #4 / 1994 / VT / M • Wild & Wicked #5 / 1995 / VT / M • Wild & Wicked #7 / 1996 / VT / M • Wild Buck / 1993 / STY / M • Wild Flower #1 / 1992 / VI / M • Wild In The Wilderness / 1988 / SE / M • The Wild Ones / 1996 / CC / M • The Wild Thing / 1992 / HO / M • Wild Weekend / 1984 / HO / M • The Wild Wild Chest #3 / 1996 / HO / C • Willing Women / 1993 / VD / C • The Witching Hour / 1992 / FOR / M • With Love From Ginger / 1986 / HO / C • Within & Without You / 1993 / WP

/ M • Women In Need / 1990 / HO / M • Women Of Color #2 / 1994 / ANA / M • Women Who Love Men, Men Who Love Women / 1993 / FD / C • The World According To Ginger / 1985 / VI / M • WPINK-TV #3 / 1988 / PV / M • Wrapped Up / 1992 / VD / C • Wrong Arm Of The Law / 1987 / ZA / M • X Dreams / 1989 / CA / M • X-Rated Blondes / 1992 / VD / C • X-TV #1 / 1986 / PL / C • XXX Workout / 1987 / VEX / M • The Year Of The Sex Dragon / 1986 / PV / M • Yiddish Erotica #1 / 1986 / SE / C • You Bet Your Butt / 1992 / VC / M • Young And Naughty / 1984 / HO / M • The Young And The Wrestling #2 / 1989 / PL / M • Young Buns #2 / 1990 / WV / M • Young Girls In Tight Jeans / 1989 / VD / M • Young Nurses In Lust / 1994 / LBO / M • [Palm Springs Weekend / 19?? / ... / M

PETER OUTERBRIDGE
Paris France / 1993 / APE / G • [Replikator / 1994 / ... / S

PETER OXFORD see Star Index I
PETER PACKER see Star Index I
PETER PARKER
Master's Touch #6: Dom's In Distress / 1995 / FAP / B

PETER PIPER see Star Index I
PETER POLE see Star Index I
PETER PUMA see Star Index I
PETER RAMIZOV
Russian Girls / 1996 / WV / M

PETER RINGS
Bizarre Styles / 1981 / ALP / B

PETER ROCK see Star Index I
PETER ROSS
Bad Penny / 1978 / QX / M

PETER SCHUSTER
Inside Marilyn / 1984 / CA / M

PETER SHEPARD see Star Index I
PETER SMITH
ABA: Double Feature #3 / 1996 / ALP / M • Beyond The Blue / cr78 / SVE / M • Christy / 1975 / CA / M

PETER STRAUS
Born Erect / cr80 / CA / M

PETER SUTINOV see Carter Stevens
PETER VELO see Star Index I
PETER WHIGHAM see Star Index I
PETER WHITE see Star Index I
PETER YOUNG see Star Index I
PETEY BALLS
Headbangers Balls / 1991 / PL / M

PETITE LUV see Patti Petite
PETRA
Blue Vanities #539 / 1993 / FFL / M • Der Spritz-Treff / 1995 / KRM / M • Magma: Anal Teenies / 1994 / MET / M • Magma: Fucking Holidays / 1995 / MET / M • Magma: Spezial: Anal Ii / 1994 / MET / M

PETRA (LAURA PALMER) see Laura Palmer
PETRA BERGER
Teeny Talk / 1995 / DBM / M

PETRA PAUK
Viola Video #102: Anal #8 / 1995 / PEV / M

PETRA SCHNELL
Viola Video #105: / 1995 / PEV / M • Viola Video #107: Private Party / 1995 / PEV / M

PETTY
Fresh Meat (John Leslie) #3 / 1996 / EA / M

PETULA SMITH
ABA: Double Feature #5 / 1996 / ALP / M • Night Of Submission / 1976 / BIZ / M

PEYTON ALEXANDER

The Adventures Of Peeping Tom #3 / 1996 / OD / M • Compulsion (Fat Dog) / 1996 / FD / M • Diva #2: Deep In Glamour / 1996 / VC / F • Fame Is A Whore On Butt Row / 1996 / ABS / M • Hardcore Debutantes #01 / 1996 / TEP / M • Head Nurse / 1996 / RAS / M • Peyton's Place / 1996 / ULP / M • Pick Up Lines #08 / 1996 / OD / M • Puritan Video Magazine #05 / 1996 / LE / M • Whiplash / 1996 / DFI / M

PEZ D. SPENCER see Star Index I
PHAE BIRD see Fay Burd
PHAEDRA
Long straight red hair, pretty face reminiscent of Shauna Grant, very white skin, medium firm tits, a bit womanly and a big butt. Seems to associate with or be the SO of Loki who is much smaller than her.
Cherry Poppers: The College Years #01 / 1997 / ZA / M • Horny Brits Take It In The Bum / 1997 / ROB / M • Nice Fuckin' Movie / 1997 / EL / M • Sweet Revenge / 1997 / KBE / M

PHAEDRA (HEAVY)
Parliament: Hefty Mamas #1 / 1987 / PM / F

PHAEDRA GRANT (Lisa Grant)
Too tall redhead with medium droopy tits, marginal face, mole just to the right of her mouth at the lip line, tattoo in the small of her back, 6 foot tall and 24 years old in 1980 (don't believe that!).
Black Heat / 1986 / VCR / C • Boiling Point / 1978 / SE / M • Bottoms Up #02 / 1983 / AVC / C • Candy Stripers #1 / 1978 / ALP / M • Cheating Wives / 1983 / PAC / M • China Sisters / 1978 / SE / M • Classic Erotica #8 / 1985 / SVE / M • Contact / 1975 / VC / M • Dark Angel / 1983 / VC / M • Ebony & Ivory Sisters / 1985 / PL / C • The Executive's Wives / 1970 / ALP / S • Exhausted / 1981 / CA / C • Girls! Girls! Girls! #1 / 1986 / VCS / C • Head / 1985 / LA / M • Hot Fudge / 1984 / VC / M • Hot Line / 1980 / CA / M • Hot Pink / 1983 / VC / C • Joys Of Erotica / 1984 / VCR / M • The Legend Of Lady Blue / 1978 / VCX / M • Limited Edition #10 / 1980 / AVC / M • Oriental Lust / 1983 / GO / M • Pink Lips / 1977 / VCX / M • Pretty Peaches #1 / 1978 / MIT / M • Rolls Royce #01 / 1980 / ... / C • Rolls Royce #04 / 1980 / ... / C • Shameful Desires In Black & White Girls / 1984 / PL / M • Showgirl #06: Sue Nero's Fantasies / 1983 / VCR / M • Showgirl #17: Phaedra Grant's Fantasies / 1983 / VCR / M • Showgirl #18: Holly McCall's Fantasies / 1983 / VCR / M • Sophisticated Pleasure / 1984 / WV / M • Trader Hornee / 1994 / PS / S • Two Roses And A Golden Rod / 1969 / SOW / S • Urges In Young Girls / 1984 / VC / M • Wilbur And The Baby Factory / 1970 / SOW / S • [Grant Takes Richmond / 1981 / ... / M

PHAERY BURD see Fay Burd
PHARON AMOS
Little Angel Puss / cr76 / SVE / M

PHIL
Blue Vanities #538 / 1993 / FFL / M • Neighborhood Watch #10 / 1991 / LBO / M • Nymphos: They Can't Help It...Really! / 1996 / P69 / M • Ona Zee's Date With Dallas / 1992 / ONA / M

PHIL CAMPANERA
The Case Of The Sensuous Sinners / 1988 / ME / M • Slammer Girls / 1987 / LIV / S

PHIL FORREST
Hardcore: The Films Of Richard Kern #1 / 1991 / FTV / M

PHIL GAROE see Star Index I

PHIL HEFFERNAN see Mookie Blodget

PHIL HURRUP
Denni O' #5: / 1996 / SP / M

PHIL KING
Bucky Beaver's XXX Dragon Art Theatre Double Feature #10 / 1996 / SOW / M • Sins Of Sandra / cr72 / SOW / M

PHIL MARINO
Big Bust Babes #24 / 1994 / AFI / M • Seymore & Shane Mount Tiffany / 1994 / FH / M

PHIL MILANO see Star Index I

PHIL MOORE
Fleshdance Fever / 1984 / SAT / M

PHIL MORINI
Teenage Pajama Party / 1977 / VC / M • Waterpower / 1975 / VHL / M

PHIL MORSE see Star Index I

PHIL NOIR
Private Gold #11: The Pyramid #1 / 1996 / OD / M

PHIL PALADIN
Close Up / 19?? / BOC / M

PHIL RIVERA see Star Index I

PHIL SALAD see Star Index I

PHIL SMITH see Star Index I

PHIL TOBIAS see Paul Thomas

PHIL TOBIS see Paul Thomas

PHIL TOBUS see Paul Thomas

PHIL TOUBES see Paul Thomas

PHIL TOUBUS see Paul Thomas

PHIL WAXWOOD
The Ultimate She-Male / 1995 / LEO / G

PHILIP
Impulse #05: When I Was 20... / 1995 / MBP / M

PHILIP FORD
The National Transsexual / 1990 / GO / G • Trisexual Encounters #04 / 1986 / PL / G

PHILIP STEVENS
Pick Up Lines #13 / 1997 / OD / M

PHILIP TOUBUS see Paul Thomas

PHILIPE DEAN
Private Gold #15: Sweet Lady #2 / 1997 / OD / M • Sodomania #14: C**t Lickin', C*m Drinkin' Bitches / 1995 / EL / M

PHILIPPE
Magma: Bizarre Games / 1996 / MET / M • Magma: Claudine In Action / 1996 / MET / M

PHILIPPE DEAN
Private Gold #11: The Pyramid #1 / 1996 / OD / M • Private Gold #12: The Pyramid #2 / 1996 / OD / M • Private Gold #13: The Pyramid #3 / 1996 / OD / M • Triple X Video Magazine #09 / 1995 / OD / M

PHILIPPE JEAN
Helen Does Holland / 1996 / VC / M

PHILLIP
Breast Worx #20 / 1992 / LBO / M • Buttman's European Vacation #1 / 1991 / EA / M • Buttman's European Vacation #2 / 1992 / EA / M • Magma: Bizarre Lust / 1995 / MET / M

PHILLIP ABBOTT see Star Index I

PHILLIP ARMAND see Star Index I

PHILLIP CHILDES
Dungeon Of Lust / 197? / AVC / M

PHILLIP D.
Erotic Dimensions #2: Black Desire / 1982 / NSV / M

PHILLIP DE HAT

Rollerbabies / 1976 / VC / M

PHILLIP HART see Star Index I

PHILLIP KALOUGINE see Star Index I

PHILLIP MARLOW
The 8th Annual Erotic Film Awards / 1984 / SE / C • The Coming Of Joyce / 1977 / VIS / M • Farmers Daughters / 1975 / VC / M • Odyssey / 1977 / VC / M • Sweetheart / 1976 / SVE / M

PHILLIP MCCANN
Classical Romance / 1984 / MAP / M • Doogan's Woman / 1978 / S&L / M • Pop-Porn: Safari Club / 1992 / 4P / M • Safari Club / 1977 / 4P / M

PHILLIP SILVER
Angel Buns / 1981 / QX / M

PHILLIP TYLER
Heidi's High Heeled Hookers / 1995 / BBE / M

PHILLIPE
Different Strokes / 1996 / VC / M • Magma: Dirty Diana / 1994 / MET / M • Magma: Horny Bulls / 1994 / MET / M • Magma: Olympus Of Lust / 1994 / MET / M • Magma: Shopping Anal / 1994 / MET / M • Magma: Sperm Dreams / 1990 / MET / M • Rebecca Lord's World Tour #1: French Edition / 1995 / WP / M • Skin #2 / 1995 / ERQ / M

PHILLIPE ASTE
Five Kittens / 19?? / ... / M

PHILLIPE COUCHON
Dr Max And The Oral Girls / 1995 / VIT / M

PHILLIPE GASPARD
Two At Once / 1978 / CV / M

PHILLIPE SOINE
Amsterdam Nights #1 / 1996 / BLC / M • Amsterdam Nights #2 / 1996 / VC / M • Dirty Tricks #2: This Ain't Love / 1996 / EA / M • Hotel Fear / 1996 / ONA / M • Midnight Obsession / 1995 / XC / M • Paprika / 1995 / XC / M • Private Film #15 / 1994 / OD / M • Private Film #17 / 1994 / OD / M • Private Film #27 / 1995 / OD / M • Private Film #28 / 1995 / OD / M • Private Gold #05: Cape Town #1 / 1996 / OD / M • Private Gold #06: Cape Town #2 / 1996 / OD / M • Private Gold #07: Kruger Park / 1996 / OD / M • Private Gold #13: The Pyramid #3 / 1996 / OD / M • Private Gold #15: Sweet Lady #2 / 1997 / OD / M • Private Stories #03 / 1995 / OD / M • Private Stories #05 / 1995 / OD / M • Sperm Injection / 1995 / PL / M • Triple X Video Magazine #07 / 1995 / OD / M • Triple X Video Magazine #09 / 1995 / OD / M • Triple X Video Magazine #11 / 1995 / OD / M • The Voyeur #6 / 1996 / EA / M

PHILLIPE THE HAMMER see Star Index I

PHILMORE BUTTS see Tony Martino

PHILOU
Private Film #27 / 1995 / OD / M • Private Film #28 / 1995 / OD / M

PHOENIA
Bright Tails #8 / 1996 / STP / B

PHOENIX see Star Index I

PHYLIS ROBERTS see Ebony Ayes

PHYLISS WHITE
White Heat / 1981 / CA / M

PHYLLIS
A&B AB#453: Karen's Family Fun #1 / 1994 / A&B / M • A&B AB#454: Karen's Family Fun #2 / 1994 / A&B / M • A&B AB#455: Auntie's Gang Bang / 1994 / A&B / M • A&B AB#483: Kinky Grandma / 1995 / A&B / M • Blue Vanities #530 / 1993 / FFL

/ M • Homegrown Video #395 / 1993 / HOV / M • HomeGrown Video #458: Cream Pie For Dessert / 1995 / HOV / C

PHYLLIS TRUAX
Pink Champagne / 1979 / CV / M

PHYLLIS WOLF
Little Girls Blue #1 / 1977 / VCX / M • Teeny Buns / 1977 / VC / M

PHYSSISHA
Shane's World #6: Slumber Party / 1996 / OD / F

PIA AMORA see Star Index I

PIA CONNERS
Bedtime Video #03 / 1984 / GO / M

PIA OLSSON
Swedish Vip Magazine #1 / 1995 / PL / M • Swedish Vip Magazine #2 / 1995 / PL / M

PIA RYDBERG
Bel Ami / 1976 / VXP / M • [Justine Och Juliette / 1975 / ... / S • [Molly / 1977 / ... / S

PIA SANDS see Pia Snow

PIA SNOW *(Pia Sands, Michelle Bauer, Carmel Snow, Michelle McClennan, Michelle McLennan, Kim Bittner, Michelle Escobar, Jane Brandon, Emma Bovary)*
Born 1958 in Los Angeles CA and was *Penthouse* Pet of the Month in July 1981. Michelle Escobar, Jane Brandon and Emma Bovary are print credits.
The American Success Company / 1979 / C3S / S • Armed Response / 1986 / VES / S • Assault Of The Party Nerds #1 / 1989 / PRS / S • Assault Of The Party Nerds #2: The Heavy Petting Detective / 1993 / PRS / S • Attack Of The 60 Foot Centerfold / 1995 / NEH / S • Bad Girls #1 / 1981 / GO / M • Best Chest In The West / 1984 / ACV / S • Beverly Hills Girls / 1985 / HID / S • Beverly Hills Vamp / 1988 / VMA / S • Bikini Drive-In / 1995 / ... / S • Blonde Heaven / 1994 / TLE / S • Blue Cabaret / 1989 / VTO / M • Blue Vanities #176 / 1992 / FFL / M • Bondage Under The Bigtop / cr86 / BIZ / B • Breaking In Rachel / 1989 / NAP / B • Cafe Flesh / 1982 / VC / M • Candid Candid Camera #4 / 1985 / VES / S • Candid Candid Camera #5 / 1986 / VES / S • Cave Girl / 1985 / C3S / S • Centerfold Screen Test #2 / 1986 / ACV / S • Cheri And The Pirates / 1988 / CS / B • Cleopatra's Bondage Revenge / cr85 / BIZ / B • Commando Squad / 1987 / TRW / S • Cyclone / 1986 / C3S / S • Dancing Angels / 1989 / PL / M • Deadly Embrace / 1989 / PRS / S • Death Row Diner / 1988 / CAM / S • Demonwarp / 1988 / VMA / S • Dinosaur Island / 1993 / NEH / S • Dominated By Desire #1 / 1984 / 4P / B • Dr Alien / 1989 / PAR / S • Dresden Diary #01 / 1986 / BIZ / B • Evil Toons / 1990 / PRS / S • The Flesh Merchant / 1993 / TDH / S • Hollywood Chainsaw Hookers / 1988 / CAM / S • Hollywood Scream Queen Hot Tub Party / 1992 / WRE / S • Homework / 1982 / MCA / S • In Search Of The Perfect 10 / 1987 / MAE / S • Inner Sanctum / 1991 / C3S / S • Jane Bonda's Bizarre Workout / 1984 / BIZ / B • The Jigsaw Murders / 1988 / MGM / S • Kidnapped Girls Agency / cr86 / HOM / B • Lady Avenger / 1987 / ... / S • Love Skills: A Guide To The Pleasures Of Sex / 1984 / MCA / S • Lust For Freedom / 1987 / AIP / S • The Man Who Wasn't There / 1983 / PAR / S • Many Faces Of Shannon

/ 1988 / VC / C • Monaco Forever / 1983 / BRI / S • Murder Weapon / 1989 / CHV / S • Naked Instinct / 1993 / DHV / S • Night Of The Living Babes / 1987 / MAE / S • Nightmare Sisters / 1987 / TRW / S • Nudes In Limbo / 1983 / MCA / S • One Million Heels B.C. / 1993 / SVE / S • Penthouse: Love Stories / 1986 / A*V / S • Penthouse: On The Wild Side / 1988 / A*V / S • Phantom Empire / 1987 / PRS / S • Playboy Video Magazine #12 / 1987 / PLA / S • Playboy: Romantic Visions / 199? / UNI / S • Pony Girl #1: In Harness / 1985 / CS / B • Pony Girl #2: At The Ranch / 1986 / CS / B • Puppet Master #3: Toulon's Revenge / 1990 / PAR / S • The Real Test / 1989 / NAP / B • Red Lips / 1995 / VV1 / S • Reform School Girls / 1986 / NWW / S • Roller Blade / 1985 / NWW / S • Rope Burn / 1984 / 4P / B • Screen Test / 1985 / C3S / S • Shannon / 1982 / BIZ / G • Sorority Babes In The Slimeball Bowl-O-Rama / 1988 / UCV / S • Special Request #1 / 198? / HOM / B • Spirits / 1991 / VMA / S • Terminal Force / 1990 / PRS / S • Terror On Tape / cr85 / CO1 / S • The Tomb / 1986 / TRW / S • Tomboy / 1985 / VES / S • The Trap / 1985 / CS / B • Vampire Vixens From Venus / 1994 / SE0 / S • Virgin High / 1990 / C3S / S • Warlords / 1988 / VMA / S • What's My Punishment / 1983 / BIZ / B • Wild Man / 1988 / CEL / S • Wine Me, Dine Me, 69 Me / 1989 / COL / C • [Bi-Housewife / 19?? / ... / M • [Bimbo Penitentiary / 1992 / ... / S • [Brinke Stevens' Private Collection #1 / 1995 / ... / S • [Camp Fear / 1991 / ... / S • [Chickboxer / 1992 / CHV / S • [The Dwelling / 1991 / ... / S • [Hellroller / 1992 / ... / S • [Invasion Of The Scream Queens / 1993 / ... / S • [L.A. Pony Girls / 198? / ... / B • [Little Devils / 1991 / ... / S • [Mrs. Lambert Remembers Love / 1991 / ... / S • [Redneck County Fever / 19?? / CHV / S • [Scarlet Submission / 198? / ... / B • [Shock Cinema / 3 / 199? / ... / S • [Terror Night / 1991 / ... / S • [That's Outrageous / 199? / ... / S • [Witch Academy / 1992 / AIP / S • [Women In Trouble / 1986 / ... / B

PIA TIACOLODA
Shape Up For Sensational Sex / 1985 / SE / M

PIB
Orgy Of Cruelty / 1995 / BON / B

PICCOLO
Itsy Bitsy Gang Bang / 1996 / HW / M • Somewhere Under The Rainbow #1 / 1995 / HW / M • Somewhere Under The Rainbow #2 / 1995 / HW / M

PICO HARNEDEN
Too Hot To Handle / 1975 / CDC / M

PIER BANUS
Pony Girl #2: At The Ranch / 1986 / CS / B

PIERCE ADONNA
More Dirty Debutantes #08 / 1991 / 4P / M

PIERCE BENTLY
Dirty Dancers #7 / 1996 / 4P / M

PIERCE RINGO see Misty Rain

PIERCED BLONDE see Star Index I

PIERRE
Big Butt Babes #1 / 1994 / BTO / M • Dirty Stories #2 / 1995 / PE / M • Euromania #2 / 1996 / AOC / M • Fashion Sluts #6 / 1995 / ABS / M • The Girls Of Fantasex #1 / 1996 / NIT / M • Magma: Horny Bulls / 1994 / MET / M

PIERRE BELOT

[S.S. Bordello / 1978 / ... / M

PIERRE DANY see Star Index I

PIERRE DELON
Love Slaves / 1976 / VCR / M

PIERRE HAR DANN
Up And Cummers #15 / 1994 / 4P / M

PIERRE LADICK
Old Wave Hookers #1 / 1995 / PL / M • Old Wave Hookers #2 / 1995 / PL / M

PIERRE LAFLEUR
America's Raunchiest Home Videos #78: Stairway To Anal / 1993 / ZA / M • Bobby Hollander's Maneaters #11 / 1994 / SFP / M • Bobby Hollander's Rookie Nookie #14 / 1993 / SFP / M • Motel Sex #1 / 1995 / FAP / M

PIERRE LATOUR see Star Index I

PIERRE LOUIS
Gangland Bangers / 1995 / VC / M

PIERRE MARTINELLI see Star Index I

PIERRE MATAUX see Star Index I

PIERRE PHAGUAT
Naughty Network / 1981 / CA / M

PIERRE PULLIER
Up And Cummers #15 / 1994 / 4P / M

PIERRE RAYMOND
House Of Love / cr77 / VC / M • Salon D'amour / 19?? / IHV / M

PIERRE SWAMI see Star Index I

PIERRE WOODMAN
Private Film #27 / 1995 / OD / M • Private Film #28 / 1995 / OD / M • Private Gold #11: The Pyramid #1 / 1996 / OD / M

PIET PAULO
Mystique / 1996 / SC / M

PINK MINK
Anal Camera #10 / 1995 / EVN / M • Butt Bangers Ball #1 / 1996 / TTV / M • Deep Inside Anal Camera / 1996 / EVN / C • Dirty And Kinky Mature Women #4 / 1995 / C69 / M • Flappers / 1995 / EMC / M • Golden Oldies #1 / 1995 / TTV / M • Golden Oldies #2 / 1995 / TTV / M • Horny Old Broads / 1995 / FPI / M • Sugar Mommies / 1995 / FPI / M

PINK PEDDLES
Pearl Necklace: Premier Sessions #07 / 1996 / SEE / M

PINK RIO see Nikki Cherry

PINKY
Bimbo Cheerleaders From Outer Space / 1988 / FAN / M • Blue Vanities #572 / 1995 / FFL / M

PINKY RIO see Nikki Pink

PINKY STOLBACH see Star Index I

PINTO
Hollywood Amateurs #24 / 1995 / MID / M

PIOTR STANISLAS
Ingrid, The Whore Of Hamburg / 1984 / CA / M • Magma: Hot Service / 1995 / MET / M • Menage A Trois / 1981 / HLV / M • [Segrete Espereinze Di Luca E Fanny / 1980 / ... / S

PIP WARD
Spanking Video #2: Naval Discipline / 1995 / MET / B

PIPER see Star Index I

PIPER JO
Dirty & Kinky Mature Women #09 / 1996 / C69 / M

PIPER JO SPENTZ
Anal Witness #1 / 1996 / LBO / M • Domina #3 / 1996 / LBO / G

PIPER SMITH
F / 1980 / GO / M • Nighthawks / 1981 / MCA / S • Ultraflesh / 1980 / GO / M

PIPER SPENTZ
Domina #4 / 1996 / LBO / G

PIPPI ANDERSON
Stud Hunters / 1984 / CA / M

PIRAHNA see Star Index I

PIRO LEENA see Star Index I

PIROSIA K.
Private Gold #09: Private Dancer / 1996 / OD / M

PIROSKA HOFFMAN
Screamers / 1994 / HW / M

PIXIE
Blue Vanities #170 (New) / 1996 / FFL / M • Blue Vanities #170 (Old) / 1991 / FFL / M

PIXIE LEE
Blue Vanities #556 / 1994 / FFL / M • The Princess With A Penis / 1994 / HSV / G • She-Male Loves Me / 1995 / VC / G

PJOTER CIELINSKI see Star Index I

PJOTR STANISLAS see Star Index I

PLAIN BILL
Black Masters: Black Obsession / 1995 / GOT / B • Cry Babies (Gotham) / 1995 / GOT / B • Oriental Treatment / 1995 / GOT / B • Toe Tales #22 / 1995 / GOT / B • Toe Tales #23 / 1995 / GOT / B • Toe Tales #25 / 1995 / GOT / B

PLATINETTE see Marilyn Jess

PLAYER
Amateur Hours #19 / 1990 / AFI / M

PLEASURE
Black 'n' Blew / 1988 / VC / M • Black Knockers #06 / 1995 / TV / M • Knights In White Satin / 1987 / SUV / C • The Sexaholic / 1988 / VC / M • Sound F/X / 1989 / V99 / M

PLUCKY RENE see Rene LaPaz

POISON
Fetish Phone Femmes / 1996 / STM / B • N.Y. Video Magazine #07 / 1996 / OUP / M • Nasty Dancers #1 / 1996 / STM / B

POITRE
Magma: Huge Cum Shots / 1995 / MET / M

POLA BLACK
Powerbone / 1976 / VC / M

POLLY
Blue Vanities #538 / 1993 / FFL / M • Creme De Femme #4 / 1981 / AVC / C • Limited Edition #20 / 1980 / AVC / M

POLLY DUBOIS see Star Index I

POLLY ESTER
Cafe Flesh / 1982 / VC / M

POLLY HAMPTON see Star Index I

POLLY PERKINS
Bottoms Up #03 / 1983 / AVC / C

POLLY PRISM
Creme De Femme / 1994 / 4P / F • Dr Butts #2 / 1992 / 4P / M

POLLY VALE
Vixens (Avc) / 19?? / AVC / M

POLLY WAGNER
Taboo #07 / 1980 / IN / M

POLO see Star Index I

POOKIE THORN see Ricky Lee

POPPIA LOTTELA see Star Index I

POPPY *(Poppy Posveve)*
Tall (6 ft), rather big blonde with medium tits and a hard body. Nice smile and attitude.
Amateur Lesbians #43: Poppy / 1993 / GO / F • Anal Knights In Hollywood #1 / 1993 / MET / M • Bubble Butts #14 / 1992 / LBO / M • Cream / 1993 / SC / M • How To Make A Model #04: Facial Cream Girls / 1994 / LBO / M • Midnight Angels #03 / 1993 / MID / F • Mr. Peepers Amateur Home Videos #71: I Dream Of Creamy / 1993 / LBO / M

• Mr. Peepers Amateur Home Videos #78: She Dreams Of Weenie / 1993 / LBO / M
POPPY POSVEVE *see* **Poppy**
PORSCHE CARRINGTON *see* **Porsche Lynn**
PORSCHE LYNN *(Portia Lynn, Porsche Carrington, Porsche Lynne)*
21 Hump Street / 1988 / VWA / M • 3 Mistresses Of The Chateau / 1995 / STM / B • Adventures Of Buttwoman #1 / 1991 / EL / F • The Adventures Of Mikki Finn / 1991 / CA / M • Affair With Destiny / 1996 / STM / F • After Midnight / 1994 / IN / M • Against All Bods / 1988 / ZA / M • All For His Ladies / 1987 / PP / C • Andrew Blake's Girls / 1992 / CA / C • Arabian Nights / 1993 / WP / M • Ariana's Dirty Dancers: The Professionals / 1996 / 4P / M • Ashlyn Gere: The Savage Mistress / 1992 / BIZ / B • Auction #1 / 1992 / BIZ / B • Auction #2 / 1992 / BIZ / B • Autobiography Of A Slave / 1993 / PL / B • Bad Boy's Punishment / 1993 / BIZ / B • Bad Slaves / 1995 / HOM / B • Barbara Dare's Bad / 1988 / SE / C • Barbara Dare's Roman Holiday / 1987 / SE / M • The Barlow Affairs / 1991 / XCI / M • Battling Bitches #1 / 1995 / BIZ / B • Battling Bitches #2 / 1995 / BIZ / B • Beast Of Bondage / 199? / LON / B • Bend Over Babes #2 / 1991 / EA / M • The Best Of Andrew Blake / 1993 / CA / C • The Best Of Ashlyn Gere / 1995 / BIZ / C • The Best Of Porsche Lynn #1 / 1994 / BIZ / C • The Better Sex Video Series #5: Sharing Fantasies / 1992 / LEA / M • The Better Sex Video Series #6: Acting Out Your Fantasies / 1992 / LEA / M • Beverly Hills Madam / 1993 / FH / F • The Big Thrill / 1989 / VD / M • The Bigger The Better / 1986 / SE / C • Black Taboo #2 / 1986 / SE / M • Blazing Bedrooms / 1987 / LA / M • Bondage Slut / 1994 / HOM / B • Born To Be Bad / 1987 / CV / M • Born To Burn / 1987 / HOT / M • Bring On The Virgins / 1989 / CA / M • Bruce Seven's Favorite Endings #1 / 1991 / EL / C • Bruce Seven: A Compendium Of His Most Graphic Scenes Vol 1 / 1991 / BS / C • Bruce Seven: A Compendium Of His Most Graphic Scenes Vol 3 / 1992 / BS / C • Bruce Seven: A Compendium Of His Most Graphic Scenes Vol 4 / 1993 / BS / C • Bums Away / 1995 / PRE / C • Buttman's Revenge / 1992 / EA / M • Buttslammers #11: / 1996 / BS / F • California Blondes #03 / 1991 / VD / C • The Call Girl / 1986 / VD / M • Candy Snacker / 1993 / WIV / M • Captive In Sumanka / 1996 / LON / B • The Case Of The Crooked Cathouse / 1989 / ME / M • Centerfold / 1992 / VC / M • Chains Of Passion / 1993 / PL / B • The Chains Of Torment / 1991 / BS / B • Cherry Red / 1993 / RB / B • Chronicles Of Pain #3: Slave Traders / 1996 / BIZ / B • Clinique / 1989 / VC / M • Club DV8 #1 / 1993 / SC / M • Club Ecstasy / 1987 / CA / M • Coming Of Age / 1989 / CA / M • The Contessa / 1989 / VC / M • Corruption / 1990 / CC / M • Creation Of Karen: Tormented & Transformed / 1993 / BIZ / B • Date With A Mistress / 1995 / BIZ / B • The De Renzy Tapes / 1990 / CA / C • Debi Diamond: Mega Mistress / 1995 / BIZ / B • Deep Desires / 1989 / VC / C • Defiance: The Ultimate Spanking / 1993 / BIZ / B • Depraved Innocent / 1986 / VD / M • Designing Babes / 1990 / GOT / M • Destiny / 1996 / BON / B • The Distress

Factor / 1992 / BS / B • Dominating Girlfriends #1 / 1992 / PL / B • The Domination Of Summer #1 / 1994 / BIZ / B • The Domination Of Summer #2 / 1994 / BIZ / B • Down And Dirty In Beverly Hills / 1986 / CV / M • Dresden Diary #06: The Hellfire Legend / 1992 / BIZ / B • Dresden Diary #07 / 1992 / BIZ / B • Dresden Diary #08 / 1992 / BIZ / B • Dresden Diary #13: / 1995 / BIZ / B • Dressed To Tease / 1992 / RB / B • Dungeon Delight / 1995 / LON / B • Dungeon Training / 1995 / STM / B • Easy Access / 1988 / ZA / M • The Education Of Karen / 1993 / BIZ / B • Eleventh Annual AVN Awards / 1994 / VC / M • The Enchantress / 1990 / VI / M • The End Zone / 1987 / LA / C • The Enema Bandit / 1994 / BIZ / B • The Enema Bandit Returns / 1995 / BIZ / B • The Enema Bandit Strikes Again / 1995 / BIZ / B • Enema Obedience #3: The Ultimate Punishment / 1994 / BIZ / B • Erica Boyer: Non-Stop / 1988 / VD / C • Erotika / 1994 / WV / M • Every Man's Dream, Every Woman's Nightmare / 1988 / CC / C • The Exchange / 1995 / BON / B • A Family Affair / 1991 / AWV / G • Fantasy Doctor / 1993 / PL / B • Fantasy In Blue / 1991 / VI / M • Felicia's Fantasies / 1995 / HOM / B • The Filthy Rich / 1989 / LA / M • Fireball #1 / 1994 / VI / C • Flame's Bondage Bash / 1994 / BIZ / B • Friday The 13th #2 / 1989 / VD / M • Girl With The Million $ Legs / 1987 / PL / M • Girls Gone Bad #7: Misfits Of Society / 1992 / GO / F • Golden Arches / 1992 / PRE / B • Grand Prixxx / 1987 / CA / M • The Great Sex Contest #2 / 1989 / LV / M • Hard Rider / 1992 / IN / M • Hard Rockin' Babes / 1987 / VD / F • Hard Whips For Soft Bodies / 1993 / NTP / B • Hard-On Copy / 1994 / WV / M • Head Talk / 1991 / ZA / M • Hellfire Society / 19?? / HOM / B • Her Every Wish / 1988 / GO / M • Hot Flushes / 1992 / PRE / B • The Hot Lick Cafe / 1990 / AMB / M • The Hot Lunch Club / 1985 / WV / M • Hot Rod To Hell #2 / 1992 / BS / B • House Of Slaves / 1995 / HOM / B • I Love A Girl In A Uniform / 1989 / VC / C • I Wanna Be A Bad Girl / 1986 / PP / M • In A Crystal Fantasy / 1988 / VD / M • Innocent Taboo / 1986 / VD / M • Jamie Gillis: The Private Collection Vol #1 / 1991 / SC / F • Jamie Gillis: The Private Collection Vol #2 / 1991 / SC / F • Jane Bond Meets Octopussy / 1986 / VD / M • Jennifer Ate / 1993 / XCI / F • Just For You (Five K) / 1989 / 5KS / F • The Kink / 1988 / WV / M • Kinky Lesbians #02 / 1993 / BIZ / B • Kittens #7 / 1995 / CC / F • Kym Wilde's On The Edge #16 / 1994 / RB / B • Last Rumba In Paris / 1989 / VC / M • Leather Bound Dykes From Hell #2 / 1994 / BIZ / F • Leather Bound Dykes From Hell #3 / 1994 / BIZ / F • Leather Bound Dykes From Hell #4 / 1995 / BIZ / F • Leather Bound Dykes From Hell #5 / 1995 / BIZ / B • Leather Bound Dykes From Hell #6 / 1995 / BIZ / B • Leather Bound Dykes From Hell #8 / 1996 / BIZ / B • Legends Of Porn #2 / 1989 / CV / C • Legends Of Porn #3 / 1991 / MET / C • Lesbian Nymphos / 1988 / GO / C • Lessons In Lust / 1987 / LA / M • Living In A Wet Dream / 1986 / PEN / C • The Load Warriors #2 / 1987 / VD / M • Love On The Run / 1989 / CA / M • Lust Italian Style / 1987 / CA / M • Mad About You / 1987 / VC

/ M • The Masseuse #1 / 1990 / VI / M • Maxine / 1987 / EXF / M • Miami Spice #1 / 1987 / CA / M • The Mile High Girls / 1987 / CA / M • Mimi / 1987 / CA / M • Mistress Kane: Lessons In Terror / 1996 / BIZ / B • Mistresses At War #01 / 1993 / BIZ / B • Mistresses At War #02 / 1993 / BIZ / B • The More the Merrier / 1989 / VC / C • My Bare Lady / 1989 / ME / M • Naked Ambition / 1995 / VC / M • Nasty Girls #1 (1989-Plum) / 1989 / PP / C • Naughty Girls Like It Big / 1986 / ELH / M • Night Of The Living Debbies / 1989 / EX / M • Night Trips #1 / 1989 / CA / M • No Time For Love / 1991 / VI / M • Not A Normal Boy! / 1992 / LEO / B • Nurses Bound By Duty / 1996 / BIZ / B • On Your Honor / 1989 / LE / M • Only The Best Of Barbara Dare / 1990 / CV / C • Only The Best Of Girls With Curves / 1992 / CV / C • Oriental Temptations / 1992 / WV / M • Pajama Party / 1993 / CV / C • Pajama Party X #1 / 1994 / VC / M • Pajama Party X #2 / 1994 / VC / M • The Perversionist / 1995 / HOM / B • Pink And Pretty / 1986 / CA / M • Popped Tarts / 1992 / RB / B • Pornographic Priestess / 1992 / CA / M • Porsche / 1990 / NSV / M • Porsche Lynn, Every Man's Dream / 1988 / CC / C • Porsche Lynn, Vault Mistress #1 / 1994 / BIZ / B • Porsche Lynn, Vault Mistress #2 / 1994 / BIZ / B • Porsche's Ordeal / 1996 / LBO / B • The Power Dykes / 1993 / BIZ / B • Prison World / 1994 / NTP / B • Prisoners In The House From Hell / 1995 / LON / B • Pussy Tamer #1 / 1993 / BIZ / B • Pussy Tamer #2 / 1993 / BIZ / B • Pussyman #01: The Search / 1993 / CC / M • Pussywoman #3 / 1995 / CC / M • The Queen Of Mean / 1992 / FC / M • Radical Affairs Video Magazine #05 / 1993 / ME / M • Radical Affairs Video Magazine #06 / 1993 / ME / M • Raging Weekend / 1988 / GO / M • The Return Of Indiana Joan / 1989 / PL / M • Rocket Girls / 1993 / VC / M • Samantha's Private Fantasies / 1994 / WV / M • School For Wayward Wives / 1993 / BIZ / B • Selena's Secrets / 1991 / MIN / M • Servin' It Up / 1993 / VC / M • Sex Asylum #4 / 1991 / VI / M • Sex Heist / 1992 / WV / M • Sex In The Great Outdoors / 1987 / SE / C • Sex Professionals / 1994 / LIP / F • Sex Starved / 1986 / VWA / M • Sins Of Tami Monroe / 1991 / CA / C • Slave Sisters / 1995 / LON / B • Slaves Of Passion / 1995 / HOM / B • Sorority Pink #1 / 1989 / CV / M • Sorority Pink #2 / 1989 / CV / M • Sorority Sex Kittens #2 / 1993 / VC / M • Special Request #3 / 1993 / HOM / B • Spiked Heel Diaries #1 / 1994 / BIZ / B • Spiked Heel Diaries #2 / 1994 / BIZ / B • Spiked Heel Diaries #3 / 1995 / BIZ / B • Spiked Heel Diaries #4 / 1995 / BIZ / B • Splash / 1990 / WV / C • St. X-Where #1 / 1986 / VD / M • The Sting Of Ecstasy / 1991 / BS / B • Strip For The Whip / 1997 / BON / B • Studs 'n' Stars / 1989 / VC / C • Swedish Erotica Featurettes #2 / 1989 / CA / M • Swedish Erotica Featurettes #3 / 1989 / CA / M • Sweet Cheeks (1991-Prestige) / 1991 / PRE / B • Taboo #05 / 1986 / IN / M • Taboo #15 / 1995 / IN / M • Take Me...Use Me...Make Me Your Slave / 1994 / BIZ / B • Takin' It Off / 1994 / DGD / S • Takin' It To The Limit #7: Debauched / 1996 / BS / M • A Taste Of Angel / 1989 / PIN / C • A Taste Of Porsche / 1988 / PIN / C • Taste Of The Best #1 /

1988 / PIN / C • Temple Of Lust / 1992 / VC / M • Tempting Tianna / 1992 / V99 / M • Tenth Annual Adult Video News Awards / 1993 / VC / M • Those Lynn Girls / 1989 / WV / C • To Serve...Protect...And Submit / 1994 / BIZ / B • Tori Welles Exposed / 1990 / VD / C • Tortured Passions / 1994 / PL / B • The Torturous Infidel / 1994 / PL / B • Tropical Lust / 1987 / MET / M • The Ultimate Fantasy / 1995 / CV / M • User Friendly #1 / 1990 / LV / M • User Friendly #2 / 1990 / LV / M • Very Sexy Ballet / 1988 / CA / M • Voodoo Lust: The Possession / 1989 / PCP / M • The Wacky World Of X-Rated Bloopers / 1989 / GO / M • The Way They Were / 1990 / CDI / M • A Weekend In Bondage / 1994 / BIZ / B • Wet & Wild Tami Monroe / 1991 / CA / C • What A Country / 1989 / PL / M • When Love Came To Town / 1989 / EVN / M • When The Mistress Is Away... / 1995 / HAC / B • Where The Girls Play / 1992 / CC / F • Where The Girls Sweat #1 / 1990 / EA / F • Who Shaved Lynn Lemay? / 1989 / EX / M • Wicked Sensations #2 / 1989 / DR / M • The Wild And The Innocent / 1990 / CC / M • The Wild Wild West / 1986 / SE / M • Wishbone / 1988 / VXP / M • Wishful Thinking / 1992 / VC / M • Woman To Woman / 1989 / ZA / C • X-Rated Blondes / 1992 / VD / C • You Bet Your Ass / 1991 / EA / B • The Young And The Wrestling #2 / 1989 / PL / M

PORSCHE LYNNE see Porsche Lynn

PORSHA
Byron Long At Large / 1995 / VC / M • Girls Around The World #15 / 1994 / BTO / S • More Black Dirty Debutantes #4 / 1995 / 4P / M • More Black Dirty Debutantes #5 / 1995 / 4P / M • Tit To Tit #1 / 1994 / BTO / M

PORSIA
Black Snatch #1 / 1996 / DFI / F

PORTHOS
East Coast Sluts #02: Syracuse, NY / 1995 / PL / M

PORTIA see Star Index I

PORTIA LYNN see Porsche Lynn

PRAGITZA SPACK
Swedish Sex / 1996 / PL / M

PREBEN MAHRT
Bel Ami / 1976 / VXP / M

PRECIOUS
Anal Auditions #2 / 1996 / LE / M • Black Street Hookers #5: The Mean Streets Of Washington D.C. / 1997 / DFI / M • Dark Angel / 1983 / VC / M • Nineteen #8 / 1997 / FOR / M

PRECIOUS DIMAE
Filthy First Timers #4 / 1996 / EL / M

PRECIOUS PINK
Alley Cat Showdown / 1990 / NAP / B • Cat-Fight Audition / 1990 / NAP / B • The Cats Of Club Napali / 1990 / NAP / B • Claws And Fangs / 1990 / NAP / B • Down And Out #1 / 1990 / CDP / B • Drainman / 1989 / BIZ / B • Feet First / 1988 / BIZ / S • Fighting Mad / 1990 / NAP / B • Grand Slam / 1990 / PRE / B • Horny Toed / 1989 / BIZ / S • Hot Blood / 1990 / NAP / B • Introducing Micki Marsaille / 1990 / NAP / F • It's Your Move / 1990 / TAO / B • Models In Dispute / 1989 / NAP / B • Ring Revenge / 1990 / NAP / B • Super Leg-Ends / 1992 / PRE / C • Three Wishes #1 / 1991 / CDP / B • Three Wishes #2 / 1991 / CDP / B • Title

Shots / 1995 / PRE / B • Tongue Kissing Duel / 1989 / NAP / B • Triumph Of The Flesh / 1990 / NAP / B • Who's Teaching Who? / 1990 / NAP / B

PRECIOUS SILVER
A Week And A Half In The Life Of A Prostitute / 1997 / EL / M

PRESHA see Preshia

PRESHIA *(Monica (Preshia), Presha, Pershia)*
Brunette with long reddish brown hair or short black hair depending on the movie, pretty, overbite, totally shaven pussy, medium tits, lithe body, tight little butt, tight waist, good body skin but, depending on the movie, excessive facial acne. She either has a double belly button or has a very small ring in it. 21 years old in 1995 and de-virginized at 16.

Anal Playground / 1995 / CA / M • Fresh Meat (John Leslie) #2 / 1995 / EA / M • Hard Core Beginners #01 / 1995 / LEI / M • Hard Core Beginners #03 / 1995 / LEI / M • My First Time #3 / 1996 / NS / M • Nasty Nymphos #09 / 1995 / ANA / M • Nasty Nymphos #14 / 1996 / ANA / M • The New Butt Hunt #13 / 1995 / LEI / C • Video Virgins #16 / 1994 / NS / M

PRESLEY
Ona Zee's Learning The Ropes #12: Couples / 1995 / ONA / B • Ona Zee's Learning The Ropes #13: Best Of Male Submission / 1996 / ONA / C

PRICE X see Star Index I

PRICELLA SHIELDS
Reel People #01 / 1983 / AR / M

PRICILLA see Star Index I

PRINCESCA see Star Index I

PRINCESS
Black & Wet Private Parts / 1994 / STM / F • Black Street Hookers #5: The Mean Streets Of Washington D.C. / 1997 / DFI / M • Bondage Love Slave / 1994 / SBP / B • Bus Stop Tales #03 / 1989 / PRI / M • Candyman #03 / 1993 / GLI / M • Club DOM / 1994 / SBP / B • Dark Angels / 1996 / STM / F • Dream Slave / 199? / CS / B • Hoetown / 1994 / STM / F • Latex Bound #03 / 1993 / BON / B • Lesbian C*Nt Whores / 1996 / ROB / F • The Missing Report / 1992 / CS / B • Shared Moments With You / 1992 / CS / B

PRINCESS ALISE
Dancing Dominant Damsels / 1994 / RSV / B

PRINCESS LOVE see Star Index I

PRINCESS LTL. BEAVER
Motel Sex #1 / 1995 / FAP / M

PRINCESS PAULINA
The Unsuspecting Repairman #1 / 1995 / TVI / B • The Unsuspecting Repairman #2 / 1995 / TVI / B

PRIS TEEN see Star Index I

PRISCA
Eurotica #08 / 1996 / XC / M • Hotel Lesbos / 1986 / LIP / F

PRISCELLA POX
Final Orgy / 1996 / BON / B • Orgy Of Cruelty / 1995 / BON / B • Orgy Of Pain / 1995 / BON / B

PRISCILLA
AVP #6001: Priscilla's Prestige Pizza / 1990 / AVP / M • Bi-Bi Love Amateurs #2 / 1993 / SFP / G • Blue Vanities #540 / 1994 / FFL / M • Buttman Goes To Rio #4 / 1993 / EA / M • Tranny Claus / 1994 / HEA / G

PRISCILLA ALDEN
Loving Friends / 1975 / AXV / M • Made To Order / 1975 / AXV / M • Sodom & Gomorrah / 1974 / MIT / M

PRISCILLA LEE see Rene Bond

PRISCILLA LOVE see Star Index I

PRISCILLA MAJOR
French Teen / 1977 / CV / M • Teenage Pajama Party / 1977 / VC / M

PRISCILLA PONZI
School Teacher's Weekend Vacation / cr72 / SVE / M

PROFESSOR PERVO
N.Y. Video Magazine #10 / 1996 / OUP / M

PROMISE
More Dirty Debutantes #55 / 1996 / 4P / M

PRUDENCE MYERS see Tina Lindstrom

PRYCE LEIGH
Bottom Dweller: The Final Voyage / 1996 / EL / M • Canadian Beaver Hunt #2 / 1996 / PL / M • Skin Dive / 1996 / SC / M • Video Virgins #28 / 1996 / NS / M

PU PU see Short Stud

PUMA WEST see Star Index I

PUNCHY BARROWS
Let's Talk Sex / 1982 / CA / M

PURPLE PASSION *(Linda Thompson)*
Black girl with small droopy breasts and a tattoo on the left one.

Anal Angels #2 / 1990 / VEX / C • As Cute As They Cum / 1990 / VEX / M • The Beat Goes On / 1987 / VCR / C • Beeches / 1990 / KIS / M • Behind The Black Door / 1987 / VEX / M • Black 'n' Blew / 1988 / VC / M • Black Babes / 1995 / LV / M • Black Bad Girls / 1985 / PLY / M • Black Beauties / 1987 / SE / C • Black Chicks In Heat / 1988 / VC / M • Black Dynasty / 1985 / VD / M • Black Knockers #04 / 1995 / TV / M • Black Magic / 1985 / WET / M • Black Mariah / 1991 / FC / M • Black Mystique #12 / 1995 / VT / F • Black Power / 1996 / LEI / C • Black Throat / 1985 / VC / M • Black, White And Blue / 1989 / E&I / M • Blackman / 1989 / PL / M • Blackman & Anal Woman #1 / 1990 / PL / M • Blonde On Black / 1986 / CC / F • Buns And Roses (V9) / 1990 / V99 / M • Caddy Shack-Up / 1986 / VD / M • California Cherries / 1987 / EVN / M • Changing Partners / 1989 / FAZ / M • Cheek To Cheek / 1986 / VEX / M • Chocolate Delights #1 / 1985 / TAG / C • Chocolate Delights #2 / 1985 / TAG / C • Chocolate Dreams (Venus 99) / 1987 / V99 / M • Chocolate Kisses / 1986 / CA / M • Dark Side Of The Moon / 1986 / VD / M • Devil In Miss Jones #4: The Final Outrage / 1987 / VC / M • Dirty Pictures / 1985 / SUP / M • Ebony Dreams / 1988 / PIN / C • Ebony Humpers #1 / 1986 / VEX / M • Ebony Humpers #3 / 1987 / VEX / M • Ebony Orgies / 1987 / SE / C • Ebony Superstars / 1988 / VC / C • Fashion Passion / 1985 / VD / M • Flesh In Ecstasy #03: Purple Passion / 1987 / GO / C • Girlz N The Hood #5 / 1995 / HW / M • Great Expectations / 1992 / VEX / C • Heartless / 1989 / REB / M • Interracial Anal Bonanza / 1993 / CA / C • Interview: Black Babes / 1996 / LV / M • Intimate Affairs / 1990 / VEX / M • Let Me Tell Ya 'Bout Black Chicks / 1985 / VC / M • Let Me Tell Ya 'Bout White Chicks / 1985 / VC / M • Licorice Twists / 1985 / WET / M • Lost Lovers / 1990 / VEX / M • Love Thirsty / 1990 / IN / M • Lust With The Stranger / 1986 / MAP / M • Magic Pool /

1988 / VD / M • Nasty Blacks / 1988 / VEX / M • National Pornographic #1: Lesbians / 1987 / 4P / C • Naturally Sweet / 1989 / VEX / M • Not So Innocent / 1989 / VEX / M • Oral Addiction / 1989 / LV / M • Parliament: Dark & Sweet #1 / 1991 / PM / C • Playing Dirty / 1989 / VEX / M • Pumps In Da Rump #2 / 1996 / HW / M • Salt & Pepper / 1986 / VCS / C • The Secret Diaries / 1990 / V99 / M • Sex Kittens / 1990 / VEX / F • Sexy Nurses #1 On And Off Duty / 1990 / CV / M • Slumber Party / 1990 / LV / M • Spanish Fly / 1987 / CA / M • Stormi / 1988 / LV / M • Sweet Chocolate / 1987 / VD / M • Sweet Temptations / 1989 / V99 / M • A Taste Of Purple Passion / 1990 / CA / C • Taste Of The Best #1 / 1988 / PIN / C • Toys, Not Boys #1 / 1991 / FC / C • Toys, Not Boys #3 / 1991 / FC / C • Up & In / 1985 / AA / M • VCA Previews #4 / 1988 / VC / C • Virgin Busters / 1989 / LV / M • White Chocolate / 1987 / PEN / M • Woman In The Window / 1986 / TEM / M • The Zebra Club / 1986 / VSE / M

PUSSYCAT
1001 Nights / 1996 / IP / M • Angel Hard / 1996 / STV / M • Blue Vanities #505 / 1992 / FFL / M • The Erotic Adventures Of Alladin X / 1995 / IP / M • Rosa / Francesca / 1995 / XC / M • Wad Gobblers #09 / 1993 / GLI / M

PUSSYMAN *see* **David Christopher**

PUT BULL JONES
Hellfire Mistress / 1996 / OUP / B

PUTTIN' PETE *see* **Star Index I**

Q
Visions / 1977 / QX / M

QUEEN ADRENA *see* **Star Index I**

QUEEN VICTORIA *see* **Victoria Queen**

QUEENIE
Bi-Bi Love Amateurs #2 / 1993 / SFP / G • Warm Summer Rain / 1989 / C3S / S

QUENTIN JAMES *see* **Star Index I**

QUICHE *see* **Keisha**

QUICK STONE
Black Knockers #06 / 1995 / TV / M

QUINN
Real People Real Bondage #2 / 1996 / BON / C • Welcome To Bondage: Paramour & Quinn / 1993 / BON / B • Welcome To Bondage: Starlets #2 / 1994 / BON / C

QUISHA *see* **Keisha**

R. BEARDSLEY
Breaker Beauties / 1977 / VHL / M

R. BOLLA *see* **Robert Bolla**

R. DAID
A Very Debauched Girl / 1988 / PL / M

R. JEFFERSON
Pussyman's House Party #2 / 1996 / SNA / M

R. TOMY *see* **Tim Lake**

R.C. CUMMINGS *see* **Star Index I**

R.C. MILLER *see* **Arcie Miller**

R.D. WALKER
Kiva Corrected / 1994 / KPC / B • Kiva Vision / 1995 / KPC / M

R.J. *see* **Ron Jeremy**

R.J. LEONE
The Pleasures Of Innocence / 1985 / VC / M

R.J. REYNOLDS *(Randy Roteman, Zack (R.J. Reynolds))*
Randy Roteman is from **Skintight**, and Zack is from **Kiss And Tell**. Dead (AIDS), apparently bisexual.
American Pie / 1980 / SE / M • Baby Cakes

/ 1982 / SE / M • Ball Game / 1980 / CA / M • Behind The Brown Door / 1986 / VCR / C • Between The Sheets / 1982 / CA / M • Beyond Shame / 1980 / VEP / M • Blue Confessions / 1983 / VCR / M • Coed Fever / 1980 / CA / M • Cover Girl Fantasies #1 / 1983 / VCR / C • Cover Girl Fantasies #2 / 1983 / VCR / C • Downstairs, Upstairs / 1980 / SE / M • The Ecstasy Girls #1 / 1979 / CA / M • The Erotic Adventures Of Dr Storm / 1983 / XTR / M • The Filthy Rich / 1981 / CA / M • Foxholes / 1983 / SE / M • Hot Dallas Nights / 1981 / VCX / M • Kiss And Tell / 1980 / CA / M • The Master And Mrs. Johnson / 1980 / SAT / M • My Sister Seka / 1981 / CA / M • Plato's, The Movie / 1980 / SE / M • Seka's Fantasies / 1981 / CA / M • Sex Boat / 1980 / VCX / M • Showgirl #13: Chris Cassidy's Fantasies / 1983 / SVE / M • Skintight / 1981 / CA / M • Taxi Girls #1 / 1980 / WV / M • With Love, Lisa / 1985 / CA / C • [The Texas Hacksaw Melange / 1977 / .... / M

R.J. STARX *see* **P.J. Sparxx**

R.P. FRANK
Vivid At Home #02 / 1994 / VI / M

R.T. BRISBANE
The Night Shift / 1995 / LE / M

R.W. CRESSE *see* **Bob Cresse**

RA RICHARDS
B-Witched / 1994 / PEP / G • Bi-Athelon / 1993 / BIL / G • Wendy's Bi Adventure / 1994 / STA / M

RABBIT
Dirty And Kinky Mature Women #3 / 1995 / C69 / M • Dixie Debutantes #1 / 1996 / MYS / M • Older And Anal #2 / 1995 / FC / M

RACE MCCRORY *see* **Star Index I**

RACHAEL LIVINGSTONE
Ball Game / 1980 / CA / M

RACHAEL MANN *see* **Holly White**

RACHAEL STEPHENS
The Rock / 1994 / SBP / B

RACHAL FREE *see* **Nikki Randall**

RACHAL LOVE *see* **Rachel Love**

RACHEL
America's Raunchiest Home Videos #19: Bedroom Farce / 1992 / ZA / M • The Best Of Fabulous Flashers / 1996 / DGD / F • Black On Black (1994-Evn) / 1994 / EVN / M • Blue Vanities #548 / 1994 / FFL / M • Bound To Tease #4 / 1989 / BON / C • Dear Fanny / 1984 / CV / M • Fbi In Search Of Bondage #1 / 1991 / BON / B • Flesh Fever / 1978 / CV / M • Homegrown Video #193 / 1990 / HOV / M • Jus' Knockin' Boots #2: Black On Line / 1996 / NIT / M • Mike Hott: #226 Cunt Of The Month: Rachel / 1993 / MHV / M • Ona Zee's Black Label #1: Sex Hunger / 1996 / ONA / C • OUTS: Rachel #2 / 1994 / OUT / F • Pearl Necklace: Amorous Amateurs #41 / 1994 / SEE / M • Pearl Necklace: Premier Sessions #03 / 1994 / SEE / M • Pearl Necklace: Premier Sessions #07 / 1996 / SEE / M • Penitentiary / 1995 / HW / M • Roommates / 1989 / BON / B • The Sodomizer #6 / 1996 / SC / M • Sorority Lingerie Party / 1995 / NIV / F • Southern: Rachel / 1993 / SSH / F • Squalor Motel / 1985 / SE / M • Swimming Pool Orgy / 1995 / FRF / M • Uncle Roy's Amateur Home Video #20 / 1993 / VIM / M

RACHEL ASHLEY *(Ashley Summer, Rachel Orion, Rachel O'Rien, Rhonda Vandegriff)*

Big breasted brunette with a passable face.
Alexandra / 1984 / VC / M • All For One / 1988 / CIN / M • Another Roll In The Hay / 1985 / COL / M • Backdoor To Harley-Wood #1 / 1990 / AFV / M • Backstage / 1988 / CDI / M • Bad Girls #3 / 1984 / COL / M • Bad Girls #4 / 1984 / GO / M • Beaver Hunt #01 / 1994 / LEI / M • Breaking It #1 / 1984 / COL / M • Can't Get Enough / 1985 / CA / M • Cheeks #2: The Bitter End / 1989 / CC / M • Corporate Assets / 1985 / SE / M • Deep Inside Rachel Ashley / 1987 / VEX / M • Deep Inside Samantha Strong / 1992 / CDI / C • Deep Inside Viviana / 1992 / VEX / C • The Deep Insiders / 1987 / VXP / M • Every Woman Has A Fantasy #1 / 1984 / VC / M • Famous Ta-Ta's #1 / 1986 / VCS / C • Famous Ta-Ta's #2 / 1986 / SE / C • Flesh In Ecstasy #05: Rachel Ashley / 1987 / GO / C • Fleshdance / 1983 / SE / M • Golden Girls, The Movie / 1984 / SE / M • Good To The Last Drop / 1986 / VCS / C • Holly Does Hollywood #2 / 1987 / VEX / M • Hot Wire / 1985 / VXP / M • Hot Yachts / 1987 / VEX / M • Hottest Parties / 1988 / VC / C • I Wanna Be A Bad Girl / 1986 / PP / M • In Love / 1983 / VC / M • Lay Down And Deliver / 1989 / VWA / M • Love Lotion #9 / 1987 / VXP / M • Lucy Makes It Big / 1987 / ME / M • Magic Fingers / 1987 / ME / M • Mike Hott: #204 Lesbian Sluts #05 / 1992 / MHV / F • Mike Hott: #207 Cunt of the Month: Ashley / 1995 / MHV / M • Miss Passion / 1984 / VD / M • The Moon Girls / 1990 / ME / C • Naughty Girls Need Love Too / 1983 / SE / M • The Night Before / 1987 / WV / M • No Man's Land #02 / 1988 / VT / F • Pay The Lady / 1987 / VXP / M • Phone Sex Fantasies / 1984 / QX / M • Playin' Dirty / 1990 / VC / M • Pleasure Principle / 1988 / VEX / M • Precious Assets / cr87 / VEX / M • Rachel Ryan Exposed / 1990 / WV / C • Sex World Girls / 1987 / AR / M • Sexpionage / 1987 / VXP / M • Sexual Odyssey / 1985 / VC / M • Shacking Up / 1985 / VXP / M • Shauna: Every Man's Fantasy / 1985 / CA / C • Shaved Sinners #1 / 1988 / VT / M • Shaved Sinners #2 / 1987 / VT / M • She's So Fine #1 / 1985 / VC / M • Shipwrecked / 1991 / VEX / C • Slick Honey / 1989 / VC / M • Slit Skirts / 1983 / VXP / M • Slumber Party Reunion / 1987 / AR / M • The Sperminator / 1985 / VXP / M • Splashing / 1986 / VCS / C • Strange Love / 1987 / WV / M • Swedish Erotica #51 / 1983 / CA / M • The Titty Committee / 1986 / SE / C • Tongue Twisters / 1986 / VXP / M • Tracey's Love Chamber / 1987 / AR / M • Transverse Tail / 1987 / CDI / M • Wet Weekend / 1987 / MAC / M • Women Without Men #1 / 1985 / VXP / F

RACHEL DAVON *see* **Racquel Darrian**

RACHEL ELDERMAN
Final Exam #1 / 1987 / BON / B • Final Exam #2 / 1988 / BON / B

RACHEL FRANK
Redliners / 1980 / VXP / M

RACHEL HARMS
Quick Turnover / 19?? / VXP / M

RACHEL HARRIS
Headset / 19?? / VXP / M

RACHEL JENKINS
M Series #23 / 1994 / LBO / M

RACHEL KANE
Domestic Discipline / 1995 / HAC / B

RACHEL KUNTZ
Parliament: Anal Babes #1 / 1989 / PM / F
• Parliament: Finger Friggin' #2 / 1988 / PM
/ F • Parliament: Lonesome Ladies #1 /
1987 / PM / F • Parliament: Queens Of
Double Penetration #1 / 1991 / PM / F

RACHEL LANE
Picture Me Bound / 1995 / LON / B

RACHEL LEVINE see Star Index I

RACHEL LOVE *(Rachal Love)*
Not too pretty blonde with a falling-apart body,
large droopy tits and a flabby body. Born
November 22, 1973 in San Bernadino, CA.
All Amateur Perfect 10's / 1995 / LEI / M •
Amazing Nympho Stories / 1995 / TEG / M
• Anal Alley Cat / 1996 / KWP / M • Anal
Fugitive / 1995 / PEP / M • Ass Kisser: A
Love Story / 1995 / PEP / M • Ass Masters
(Leisure) #03 / 1995 / LEI / M • Assmania!!
#2 / 1995 / ME / M • Ateball: More Than A
Mouthful / 1995 / ATE / F • The Backdoor
Bradys / 1995 / PL / M • Bad Attitude #1 /
1995 / LV / M • Bad Attitude #2 / 1995 / LV
/ M • Beeping Miss Buffy / 1995 / CDI / M •
Beverly Hills Blondes #1 / 1995 / LV / M •
Big Boob Boat Ride #2 / 1995 / FC / M • Big
Bust Babes #25 / 1995 / AFI / M • Big
Knockers #07 / 1994 / TV / M • Big Knock-
ers #08 / 1994 / TV / M • Big Knockers #10
/ 1995 / TV / M • Big Knockers #20 / 1995
/ TV / C • Big Knockers #21: Best Of Les-
bian #2 / 1995 / TV / C • Black Bamboo /
1995 / IN / M • Blade / 1996 / MID / M •
Buffy's First Encounter / 1995 / CIN / M •
Buffy's Malibu Adventure / 1995 / CDI / M •
Busty Babes / 1995 / NAP / F • Busty
Babes In Heat #4 / 1995 / BTO / M • Busty
Porno Stars #1 / 1995 / H&S / M • Butt
Freak #2 / 1996 / EA / M • Buttman's Big Tit
Adventure #3 / 1995 / EA / M • Candy's
Custom Car Wash / 1995 / FC / M • Chug-
A-Lug Girls #6 / 1995 / VT / M • Dare You /
1995 / CA / M • Double D Amateurs #22 /
1994 / JMP / M • Double D Dykes #16 /
1995 / GO / F • Dream Lover / 1995 / SC /
M • Fast Forward / 1995 / CA / M •
Fazano's Student Bodies / 1995 / EL / M •
First Time Ever #1 / 1995 / PE / F • Flexxx
#2 / 1995 / VT / M • Flexxx #4 / 1995 / VT
/ M • Foot Masters / 1995 / PRE / B • For-
eign Tongues #1: Going Down / 1995 / VI /
M • Foreskin Gump / 1994 / LE / M • Full
Moon Madness / 1995 / CA / M • Gang
Bang Bitches #07 / 1995 / PP / M • A Girl's
Affair #08 / 1995 / FD / F • Girls Of Soror-
ity Row / 1994 / VT / M • Hit Ladies / 1995
/ PRE / B • Hollywood Boulevard / 1995 /
CV / M • Home Runs / 1995 / PRE / C •
Horny Henry's Snowballing Adventure /
1995 / TTV / M • The Horny Housewife /
1996 / HO / M • Hot Tight Asses #09 / 1994
/ TCK / M • LA, Citadel Of The Busty An-
gels / 1995 / NAP / S • Last Tango In Par-
adise / 1995 / ERA / M • Legal Briefs / 1996
/ EX / M • The Legend Of Barbi-Q And Lit-
tle Fawn / 1994 / CA / M • Lingerie / 1995 /
SC / M • Little Girl Lost / 1995 / SC / M •
Love Dancers / 1995 / ME / M • The Luv
Bang / 1994 / SC / M • Maneater / 1995 /
ERA / M • The Meatman / 1995 / OUP / M
• Mellon Man #05 / 1995 / AVI / M • Mike
Hott: #300 Cunto Of The Month: Rachel
Love / 1995 / MHV / M • Mike Hott: #314
Cum In My Cunt #05 / 1995 / MHV / M •
More Than A Handful #6: Life Under The
Big Top / 1994 / MET / M • More Than A

Mouthful #1 / 1995 / VEX / F • Nude Awak-
enings / 1996 / PP / M • Ona Zee's Doll
House #2 / 1995 / ONA / F • The Panty Par-
lor / 1996 / VIM / M • Patent Leather / 1995
/ CA / M • Plumb And Dumber / 1995 / PP
/ M • Prisoner Of Love / 1995 / CV / M •
Promises & Lies / 1995 / SS / M • Pussy-
clips #08 / 1995 / SNA / M • Pussyman #12:
Sticky Fingers / 1995 / SNA / M • Remi-
niscing / 1995 / LE / M • Rod Wood / 1995
/ LE / M • Sapphire / 1995 / ERA / M • Sav-
age Liasons / 1995 / BEP / F • The Scarlet
Woman / 1994 / WP / M • Secret Seduc-
tions #1 / 1995 / LV / M • Secret Seductions
#2 / 1995 / ULP / M • Sexual Harassment /
1996 / TTV / M • Snatch Masters #01 /
1994 / LEI / M • Snatch Masters #05 / 1995
/ LEI / M • The Social Club / 1995 / LE / M
• Sodomania: Slop Shots / 1996 / EL / C •
Sodomania: Smokin' Sextions / 1996 / EL /
C • Soft Bodies: Beyond Blonde / 1995 /
SB / F • Sorority Stewardesses #1 / 1995 /
PE / M • Sorority Stewardesses #2 / 1995 /
PE / M • Star Crossed / 1995 / VC / M •
Strippers Inc. #5 / 1995 / ONA / M • Student
Fetish Videos: Tickling #11 / 1995 / SFV / B
• Style #2 / 1994 / VT / M • Swat Team /
1995 / PRE / B • Tit Tease #1 / 1995 / VT /
M • Titty Town #2 / 1995 / HW / M • The Vi-
olation Of Rachel Love / 1995 / JMP / F •
Weird Sex / 1995 / GO / M • Whackers /
1995 / PP / M • Who's In Charge (Titan) /
1995 / TEG / M

RACHEL LYNN
Leg...Ends #14 / 1995 / PRE / F • Slave
Wages / 1995 / PRE / B • Student Fetish
Videos: Best Of Foot Worship #03 / 1995 /
PRE / C • Student Fetish Videos: The
Enema #18 / 1995 / PRE / B • Student
Fetish Videos: Foot Worship #14 / 1995 /
PRE / B • Student Fetish Videos: Spanking
#18 / 1995 / PRE / B

RACHEL MANN see Holly White

RACHEL MARIE see Star Index I

RACHEL MILLER see Arcie Miller

RACHEL MONTAND
Sex Roulette / 1979 / CA / M

RACHEL MORGAN
Lady M's Anything Nasty #01: Pink Pussy
Party / 1996 / AVI / F

RACHEL O'RIEN see Rachel Ashley

RACHEL ORION see Rachel Ashley

RACHEL RAMOS
M Series #10 / 1993 / LBO / M

RACHEL RIOS see Keisha

RACHEL ROBBINS see Star Index I

RACHEL ROCKETS
Score Busty Centerfolds #2 / 1995 / BTO /
M

RACHEL ROYCE see Star Index I

RACHEL RYAN *(Penny Morgan, Ingrid Elliott, Serina, Serena Robinson, Serina
Robinson)*
Pretty brunette (sometimes blonde) with a
going-to seed body and a penchant for anal
sex. In 1991, she had her siliconized boobs
returned to normal supposedly because of
the health risks! She married TV star
Richard Mulligan on April 27, 1992 but is
now (1994) either divorced or in process of
getting same. Her real name is Serena
Robinson.
4F Dating Service / 1989 / AR / M • 50
Ways To Lick Your Lover / 1989 / ZA / M •
Adult Video Therapist / 1987 / CLV / C •
Alone And Dripping / 1991 / LV / M • Anal

Adventures #3: Can Her! / 1991 / VC / M •
Anal Adventures #4: Doin' Her Up! / 1992 /
VC / M • Anal Angel / 1991 / ZA / M • Anal
Asian #1 / 1992 / IN / M • Anal Assassins /
1991 / IN / M • Anal Attraction #2 / 1993 /
AFV / C • Anal Commander / 1990 / ZA / M
• Anal Encounters #1 / 1991 / VC / M • Anal
Encounters #3: Back In The Dark One /
1991 / VC / M • Anal Intruder #02 / 1988 /
CC / M • Anal Intruder #04 / 1990 / CC / M
• Anal Storm / 1991 / ZA / M • The Anal-ist
#2 / 1986 / VEX / M • Angel's Revenge /
1985 / IN / M • Asspiring Actresses / 1989 /
CA / M • Backdoor Summer #2 / 1989 / PV
/ C • Backdoor To Hollywood #08 / 1989 /
CIN / M • Backdoor To Hollywood #09 /
1989 / CIN / M • Backdoor To Hollywood
#10 / 1989 / CIN / M • Backdoor To Holly-
wood #11 / 1990 / CIN / M • Backdoor To
Hollywood #12 / 1990 / CIN / M • Backing
In #1 / 1990 / WV / C • Beauty And The
Beast #2 / 1990 / VC / M • Beefeaters /
1989 / PV / M • The Best Of Backdoor To
Hollywood / 1990 / CIN / C • Best Of
Caught From Behind #1 / 1987 / HO / C •
Best Of Caught From Behind #2 / 1988 /
HO / C • Beyond The Casting Couch / 1986
/ VD / M • Beyond The Denver Dynasty /
1988 / CA / M • Bianca Trump's Towers /
1992 / LV / M • Black Beauty (Ebony &
Ivory) / 1989 / E&I / M • The Black Chill /
1986 / WET / M • Black Encounters / 1992
/ ZA / M • Black Magic / 1986 / DR / M •
Black Magic Sex Clinic / 1987 / DOX / M •
Blackman & Anal Woman #1 / 1990 / PL /
M • Blacks & Blondes #36 / 1986 / WV / M
• The Bod Squad / 1989 / VT / M • Boobs,
Butts And Bloopers #1 / 1990 / HO / M •
The Bride / 1986 / WV / M • Broadway Fan-
nie Rose / 1986 / CA / M • Butt's Motel #5
/ 1990 / EX / M • Call Girls In Action / 1989
/ CV / M • Can't Touch This / 1991 / PL / M
• Candy Stripers #4 / 1990 / AR / M • Casey
At The Bat / 1991 / LV / M • Caught From
Behind #05: Blondes & Blacks / 1986 / HO
/ M • Caught From Behind #06 / 1986 / HO
/ M • Caught From Behind #07 / 1987 / HO
/ M • Caught From Behind #16: The Re-
union / 1992 / HO / M • Charlie's Girls #2 /
1989 / CC / M • Cheeks #2: The Bitter End
/ 1989 / CC / M • China Black / 1992 / IN /
M • Clean And Sober / 1988 / FAC / S •
Club Bed / 1987 / CIX / M • Colossal Orgy
#3 / 1994 / HW / M • Crystal Balls / 1986 /
DR / M • Daddy's Girls / 1985 / LA / M •
Dear Bridgette / 1992 / ZA / M • The Debu-
tante / 1986 / BEA / M • Deep Inside Keisha
/ 1994 / VC / C • Deep Inside Savannah /
1993 / VC / C • Deep Inside Traci / 1986 /
CDI / C • Deep Obsession / 1987 / WV / M
• Deliveries In The Rear #1 / 1985 / AVC /
M • Denim Dolls #1 / 1989 / CDI / M •
Desert Foxes / 1989 / SE / M • Diamond
Collection #80 / 1986 / CDI / M • Diamond
In The Rough / 1993 / BIA / C • Dirty
Blondes / 1986 / CDI / M • Dirty Dreams /
1987 / CA / M • Dirty Tricks / 1986 / 4P / M
• Double Jeopardy / 1990 / HO / M • Dou-
ble Whammy / 1986 / LA / M • Doubletake
/ 1989 / CC / M • Easy Cum...Easy Go /
1985 / BAN / M • Family Heat / 1985 / AT /
M • Fantasy Nights / 1990 / VC / M • Find
Your Love / 1988 / CV / M • First Impres-
sions / 1989 / ... / C • For The Fun Of It /
1986 / SEV / M • Four Alarm / 1991 / SE /
M • From Japan With Love / 1990 / SLV / M

• Full Nest / 1992 / WV / C • The Fun House / 1988 / SEV / C • Games Couples Play / 1987 / HO / M • Genital Hospital / 1987 / SE / M • Girls Don't Lie / 1990 / IN / F • Girls Gone Bad #1 / 1990 / GO / F • Girls Gone Bad #2: The Breakout / 1990 / GO / F • The Girls Of Rodeo Drive / 1987 / BAD / M • Girls Of The Double D #09 / 1989 / CDI / M • Girls Of The Double D #12 / 1990 / CDI / M • Goodtime Charli / 1989 / CIN / M • Graduation Ball / 1989 / CAE / M • Grand Opening / 1985 / AT / M • GVC: Blonde Heat #136 / 1985 / GO / M • Haunted Passions / 1990 / FC / M • Head Talk / 1991 / ZA / M • Hershe Highway #2 / 1989 / HO / M • Hollywood Vice / 1985 / VD / M • Hollywood X-Posed #1 / 1992 / VIM / C • Hometown Honeys #1 / 1986 / VEX / M • Honeybuns #1 / 1987 / WV / C • Honeybuns #2: Grecian Formula / 1987 / WV / C • Hot Gun / 1986 / CA / M • Hot Nights And Hard Bodies / 1986 / VD / M • Hotel Paradise / 1989 / CA / M • Hottest Ticket / 1987 / WV / C • The Hustler / 1989 / CDI / M • In Search Of The Perfect 10 / 1987 / MAE / S • In The Flesh / 1990 / IN / M • In The Heat Of The Night / 1990 / CDI / M • In-N-Out With John Leslie / 1988 / WV / C • Inner Pink #2 / 1989 / LIP / F • Insatiable Immigrants / 1989 / VT / M • The Joy-Stick Girls / 1986 / CLV / M • King Tongue Meets Anal Woman / 1990 / PL / M • Kinky Business #2 / 1989 / DR / M • Kinkyvision #1 / 1990 / 3HV / M • L.A. Fantasies / 1990 / WV / C • Laid In The USA / 1988 / CC / M • The Layout / 1986 / CDI / M • Les Be Friends / 1988 / WV / C • Licorice Twists / 1985 / WET / M • Lifestyles Of The Black And Famous / 1986 / WET / M • A Little Romance / 1986 / HO / M • Loose Ends #2 / 1986 / 4P / M • Loose Ends #6 / 1989 / 4P / M • The Lottery / 1989 / CIN / M • The Love Mistress / 1989 / WV / M • The Love Nest / 1989 / CA / M • Loving Spoonfulls / 1987 / 4P / C • Lust At Sea / 1986 / VD / M • The Luv Game / 1988 / VCX / M • The Magic Touch / 1985 / CV / M • Make Me Sweat / 1989 / CIN / M • Making Charli / 1989 / CDI / M • Meltdown / 1990 / LV / M • Moon Godesses #1 / 1992 / VIM / M • Moondance / 1991 / WV / M • Moonlusting #2 / 1987 / WV / M • Moore, Moore, Moore: An Anal Explosion / 1992 / IN / M • National Poontang's Summer Vacation / 1990 / FC / M • Naughty 90's / 1990 / HO / M • Naughty Ninja Girls / 1987 / LA / M • The Night Before / 1987 / WV / M • No Men 4 Miles / 1992 / LV / F • Office Girls / 1989 / CA / M • Oral Majority #03 / 1986 / WV / C • Oral Majority #07 / 1989 / WV / C • Oral Majority Black #1 / 1987 / WV / C • Orgies / 1987 / WV / C • Part-Time Stewardesses / 1989 / VCR / M • Playboy: Inside Out #1 / 1992 / PLA / S • Playboy: Secrets Of Making Love To The Same Person Forever / 1991 / HBO / S • The Pleasure Seekers / 1990 / VD / M • Pool Party / 1991 / CIN / M • Porn On The 4th Of July / 1990 / IN / M • The Postman Always Comes Twice / 1986 / AMB / M • Pretty Peaches #3 / 1989 / VC / M • Private Eyes, Public Thighs / 1989 / DR / C • Private Places / 1992 / VC / M • Puttin' Out / 1992 / VD / M • Rachel Ryan / 1988 / WV / C • Rachel Ryan Exposed / 1990 / WV / C • Rachel's Fantasies / 1990 / LV / C • Rambone The Destroyer / 1985 / WET / M •

Ready, Willing & Anal (Vidco) / 1993 / VD / C • Rear View / 1989 / LE / M • Rearing Rachel / 1990 / ZA / M • The Rise Of The Roman Empress #2 / 1990 / PV / M • Route 69 / 1989 / OD / M • Roxy / 1991 / VC / M • Scandalous / 1989 / CC / M • Screaming Rage / 1988 / LV / C • Screwing Around / 1988 / LV / M • Sex & Other Games / 1990 / CIN / M • Sex Star Competition / 1985 / PL / M • Sex The Hard Way / 1985 / CV / M • A Sexual Obsession / 1989 / PP / M • Sins Of The Wealthy #1 / 1986 / CLV / M • Sinset Boulevard / 1987 / WV / M • The Smart Ass #1 / 1990 / VT / M • Smear My Ass With Cum / 1993 / EX / C • Soaked To The Bone / 1989 / IN / M • Some Like It Hot / 1989 / CDI / M • Sorceress / 1990 / GO / M • Splash / 1990 / WV / C • Splendor In The Ass #1 / 1989 / CA / M • Star 85: Kari Fox / 1985 / VEX / M • Star 88: Dana Lynn / 1988 / VEX / C • Star Gazers / 1986 / CA / M • Steamy Windows / 1990 / VC / M • Sterling Silver / 1992 / CC / M • Stiff Magnolias / 1990 / HO / M • Strange Love / 1987 / WV / M • Super Tramp / 1989 / VD / M • Surfside Sex #1 / 1991 / LV / F • Surfside Sex #2 / 1992 / LV / M • Suzy Cue / 1988 / VI / M • Swedish Erotica Featurettes #1 / 1989 / CA / M • Swedish Erotica Featurettes #2 / 1989 / CA / M • Taija / 1986 / WV / C • A Taste Of Rachel / 1990 / PIN / C • This Butt's For You / 1986 / PME / M • Tip Of The Tongue / 1985 / V20 / M • Tropical Temptations / 1989 / VEX / M • Tush / 1992 / ZA / M • Twin Cheeks (Arrow) / 1991 / AR / M • Two To Tango / 1987 / TEM / M • Ubangis On Uranus / 1987 / WV / M • Unchain My Heart / 1990 / CC / M • Unzipped / 1991 / WV / M • Venus Of The Nile / 1991 / WV / M • Voodoo Lust: The Possession / 1989 / PCP / M • Westside Tori / 1989 / ERO / M • Wet Paint / 1990 / DR / M • Whatever Turns You On / 1987 / CA / M • White Bun Busters / 1985 / VC / M • Wide World Of Sex / 1987 / CLV / C • Wild Fire / 1990 / WV / C • Young Girls In Tight Jeans / 1989 / VD / M • [Blonde Seduction / 1985 / ... / M

RACHEL SNOW
Wad Gobblers #11 / 1994 / GLI / M

RACHEL ST. MARIE
Anal Angels #3 / 1995 / VEX / C • Anal Heartbreaker / 1995 / ROB / M • Anal Senorita #1 / 1994 / ROB / M • Babes Of The Bay #2 / 1995 / LIP / F • The Best Of Black Anal #1 / 1995 / ROB / C • Black Analyst #2 / 1995 / VEX / M • Black Gangbangers #09 / 1995 / HW / M • Black Sensations: Models In Heat / 1995 / SUF / M • Booty Ho #2 / 1995 / ROB / M • Carnal Interludes / 1995 / NOT / M • Contrast / 1995 / CA / M • Crimson Thighs / 1995 / HW / M • Dare You / 1995 / CA / M • Finger Pleasures #2 / 1995 / PL / F • Horny Old Broads / 1995 / FPI / M • Interracial Escorts / 1995 / GO / M • Kink #2 / 1995 / ROB / M • The New Ass Masters #09 / 1996 / LEI / C • New Pussy Hunt #16 / 1995 / LEI / M • The New Snatch Masters #15 / 1995 / LEI / C • Old Guys & Dolls #1 / 1995 / PL / M • Rump-Shaker #4 / 1995 / HW / M • Shaved #08 / 1995 / RB / F • Tailz From Da Hood #1 / 1995 / AVI / M • White Boys & Black Bitches / 1995 / ROB / M • Young Sluts In Heat #1 / 1996 / PL / M

RACHEL STARR *see Star Index I*

RACHEL STEPHENS
The Rack / 1994 / SBP / B • Ropeburn / 1994 / VTF / B

RACHEL TEDMAN *see Star Index I*
RACHEL VICKERS *see Raven*
RACHEL WELLES *see Star Index I*
RACHEL WEST
Alexandra The Greatest / 1990 / NAP / F • Blonde Jail-Bait / 1989 / NAP / B • Breaking In Rachel / 1989 / NAP / B • Caught From Behind #12 / 1989 / HO / M • Confrontation Of The Cats / 1989 / NAP / B • Fight For Supremacy / 1989 / NAP / B • Medicated Madness / 1989 / NAP / B • Rachel Arrives / 1989 / NAP / B • The Real Test / 1989 / NAP / B • Sweet Revenge / 1989 / NAP / B • Taken By Surprise / 1989 / NAP / B • Top Cat / 1989 / NAP / B

RACHEL WHITE
More Dirty Debutantes #33 / 1994 / 4P / M
RACHELE
House Of Sex #14: All Black Gang Bang / 1994 / RTP / M • Sinboy #3: The Island Of Dr. Moron / 1996 / SC / M

RACHELLE
Blue Vanities #194 / 1993 / FFL / M • Blush: Suburban Dykes / 1991 / BLV / F • Rumpman In And Out Of Africa / 1996 / HW / M

RACHIDA
Magma: Deep Inside Janine / 1994 / MET / M • Russian Model Magazine #2 / 1996 / IP / M

RACQUEL
A&B AB#448: Girlfriends / 1996 / A&B / F
RACQUEL (DARRIAN) *see Racquel Darrian*
RACQUEL (L.MELENDEZ) *see Lisa Melendez*
RACQUEL DARRIAN *(Rachel Davon, Raquel Darian, Racquel (Darrian), Kelly Jackson (Racq))*
Fantastic bodied (except for her enhanced tits), very pretty girl whose butt is probably as close to perfection as you will ever get. Has a pest of a boyfriend, Derrick Lane, who is apparently ultra jealous. First movie was supposedly **Joined** but I'm not sure about this because in **Class Act** (credits: Rachel Davon) she only does a girl/girl with Champagne (very often a first role). Appeared on the front cover of October 1989's *Hustler*. 21 in 1989. As from **Welcum To My Place** she had grotesque enhanced tits. Kelly Jackson is from **Tall Dark Stranger** and conflicts with an alternate name of Kelly Jaye. Born 7/21/68 in Kansas; 5'8" tall, 34B-21-34 before enhancement; 36C-22-35 after. Small tattoo of a black panther on her right butt.

Above And Beyond / 1990 / PNP / G • Backdoor To Hollywood #13 / 1990 / CDI / M • Beauty And The Beach / 1991 / CC / M • Bitches In Heat / 1994 / PL / C • Bonnie & Clyde #1 / 1992 / VI / M • Bonnie & Clyde #2 / 1992 / VI / M • Bonnie & Clyde #3 / 1994 / VI / M • Bonnie & Clyde #4 / 1994 / VI / M • Boobs, Butts And Bloopers #1 / 1990 / HO / M • Bratgirl / 1989 / VI / M • Charlie's Girls #3 / 1990 / CC / M • Cheeks #3 / 1990 / CC / M • Christy In The Wild / 1992 / VI / M • Class Act / 1989 / WAV / M • Cloud 9 / 1995 / VI / M • Curse Of The Catwoman / 1990 / VC / M • Dangerous Debi / 1993 / HO / C • Deep Inside Racquel Darrian / 1994 / VC / C • Deep Inside Raquel / 1992 / CDI / C • Deep Inside

Samantha Strong / 1992 / CDI / C • Desire / 1990 / VC / M • Dream Girls / 1990 / CIN / M • The Dream Merchants / 1990 / CDI / M • Exiles / 1991 / VT / M • Hershe Highway #3 / 1990 / HO / M • In The Heat Of The Night / 1990 / CDI / M • Intimate Journey / 1993 / VI / M • Joined: The Siamese Twins / 1989 / PL / M • King Tongue Meets Anal Woman / 1990 / PL / M • Lace / 1989 / VT / F • Lambody / 1990 / CDI / M • Leather / 1989 / VT / F • Leather And Lace / 1989 / VT / F • Lunachick / 1995 / VI / M • Modern Love #1 / 1991 / HOP / S • More Dirty Debutantes #05 / 1990 / 4P / M • New Girls In Town #1 / 1990 / CC / M • Night Trips #2 / 1990 / CA / M • No Boys Allowed / 1991 / VC / F • Not So Innocent / 1990 / HO / M • Nymphobrat / 1989 / VI / M • On Trial #3: Takin' It To The Jury / 1992 / VI / M • On Trial #4: The Verdict / 1992 / VI / M • Out For Blood / 1990 / VI / M • Private Collection / 1990 / CEL / S • Racquel In Paradise / 1990 / VC / M • Racquel In The Wild / 1992 / VI / M • Racquel's Addiction / 1991 / VC / M • Racquel's Treasure Hunt / 1990 / VC / M • Raquel On Fire / 1990 / VC / M • Raquel Released / 1991 / VI / M • Raquel Untamed / 1990 / CIN / M • Raunch #02 / 1990 / CC / M • Ravaged / 1990 / CIN / M • Red Line / 1991 / PL / M • Renegade / 1990 / CIN / M • Ride 'em Cow Girl / 1995 / VI / C • Rolling Thunder / 1995 / VI / M • Sea Of Love / 1990 / CIN / M • Separated / 1989 / INH / M • Sexmares / 1993 / FH / M • Silent Stranger / 1992 / VI / M • Sinderella #1 / 1992 / VI / M • Sinderella #2 / 1992 / VI / M • Stake Out / 1991 / CIN / M • Student Fetish Videos: Tickling #04 / 1992 / SFV / B • A Tall Dark Stranger / 1990 / LV / M • Tenth Annual Adult Video News Awards / 1993 / VC / M • Top It Off / 1990 / VC / M • Torrid Tales / 1995 / VI / M • Tropic Of Kahlia / 1991 / VI / M • Two Hearts / 1991 / VI / M • Used Cars / 1990 / CDI / M • Vegas / 1993: Let It Ride / 1990 / CIN / M • Warm To The Touch / 1990 / CDI / M • Welcum To My Place / 1990 / ZA / M • Where The Boys Aren't #5 / 1992 / VI / F • Words Of Love / 1989 / LE / M • [101 Sex Positions / 199? / ... / M

RACQUEL LINNEAU
Anal Therapy #2 / 1993 / FD / M • Anal Vision #15 / 1993 / LBO / M • Bra Busters #03 / 1993 / LBO / M • Bun Busters #03 / 1993 / LBO / M • Delicious (Midnight-1993) / 1993 / MID / M • Hidden Camera #06 / 1993 / JMP / M • Marathon / 1994 / FD / C • Pearl Necklace: Amorous Amateurs #23 / 1993 / SEE / M • Pearl Necklace: Amorous Amateurs #25 / 1993 / SEE / M • Pearl Necklace: Amorous Amateurs #26 / 1993 / SEE / M • Pearl Necklace: Amorous Amateurs #27 / 1993 / SEE / M • Pearl Necklace: Amorous Amateurs #30 / 1993 / SEE / M • Pearl Necklace: Amorous Amateurs #32 / 1993 / SEE / M • Pearl Necklace: Amorous Amateurs #33 / 1992 / SEE / M • Pearl Necklace: Amorous Amateurs #34 / 1992 / SEE / M • Pearl Necklace: Amorous Amateurs #37 / 1993 / SEE / M • Pearl Necklace: Amorous Amateurs #39 / 1993 / SEE / M • Pearl Necklace: Thee Bush League #13 / 1993 / SEE / M • Pearl Necklace: Thee Bush League #30 / 1994 / SEE / M • Suburban Nymphos / 1994 / ATL / M • Tech: A Night At Big Daddies' / 1994 /

TWA / S • Tech: Racquel Linneau #1 / 1993 / TWA / F

RACQUEL TOWERS
Tall big girl with large droopy tits, long straight dark brown hair, passable face, shaven pussy, sagging belly, poor skin. 19 years old in 1996 and de-virginized as 16. She says she's of Spanish/Italian extraction, was born in Italy and measures 36E-24-33. She sounds very down-to-earth.
Legend #6: / 1996 / LE / M • My First Time #6 / 1996 / NS / M • The Night Of The Living Bed / 1996 / LE / M • Shadows Of Lust / 1996 / NIT / M

RAD TAD
Forbidden Fantasies #2 / 1995 / ZA / M

RADIO RAY WELLS *(Ray Randall)*
Thin male with full beard and moustache, sandy colored hair.
Body Candy / 1980 / VIS / M • Caught In The Act / 1978 / MAP / M • Ceremony, The Ritual Of Love / 1976 / AVC / M • Desires Within Young Girls / 1977 / CA / M • F / 1980 / GO / M • The Joy Of Letting Go / 1976 / SE / M • Seka In Heat / 1988 / BMV / C • The Spirit Of Seventy Six / 1976 / NGV / M • Teeny Buns / 1977 / VC / M • V—The Hot One / 1978 / CV / M • Young Doctors In Lust / 1979 / NSV / M

RADLEY METZGER see Henry Paris

RAE ANN LEE
Mother's Wishes / 1974 / GO / M

RAEVEN
Man In Chains / 1995 / HOM / B

RAEVIN NITE
Catch Of The Day #4 / 1996 / VG0 / M

RAFAEL
Mr. Peepers Amateur Home Videos #59: The Ball Of The Wild / 1992 / LBO / M

RAFAEL CALDERO
Bi Bi Banjee Boyz / 1994 / PL / G

RAFAEL SCHUMANN see Star Index I

RAFIAL RENTARIA
Score Of Sex / 1995 / BAC / G

RAGNE REBEL
Sex-A-Holic Lady / 1995 / PL / M

RAIN
Auction #2 / 1992 / BIZ / B

RAINA TAYLOR
GVC: Suburban Lust #128 / 1983 / GO / M

RAINAHH see Lil' Bitt

RAINBEAUX SMITH see Cheryl Smith

RAINBOW ROBBINS see Star Index I

RAINER FISCHER
[Junge Madchen Mogen's HeiB, Hausfrauen Noch HeiBer / 1973 / ... / M • [Schulmadchen-Report 4: Was Eltern Oft Verzweifeln LaBt / 1972 / ... / M

RAINEY DOUGLASS see Star Index I

RALF
Hot New Imports / 1996 / XC / M

RALF SCOTT
Ejacula #1 / 1992 / VC / M • Ejacula #2 / 1992 / VC / M • Impulse #05: When I Was 20... / 1995 / MBP / M • Private Film #28 / 1995 / OD / M

RALLY ESSEN
American Nympho In London / 1987 / VD / M • The Baroness / 1987 / VD / M • Hard Core Cafe / 1988 / VD / M • Hot Nights And Dirty Days / 1988 / VD / M • International Phone Sex Girls #1 / 1988 / VD / M

RALPH
Homegrown Video #241 / 1990 / HOV / M • Homegrown Video #291 / 1990 / HOV / M • HomeGrown Video #458: Cream Pie For

Dessert / 1995 / HOV / C

RALPH CARL see Star Index I

RALPH ENO
Resurrection Of Eve / 1973 / MIT / M

RALPH HARPER
The Erotic Aventures Of Lolita / 1982 / VXP / M

RALPH HERMAN see Star Index I

RALPH JENKINS
Desires Within Young Girls / 1977 / CA / M • [The Ribald Tales Of Robin Hood / 1968 / ... / S

RALPH JOHNSON
Baby Rosemary / 1975 / SE / M

RALPH LOREN see Star Index I

RALPH MARVELL
Poor Little Rich Girls / 1994 / SHL / B

RALPH PARFAIT
Supposedly the son of Henri Pachard.
Head First / 1995 / OD / M • Oral Addiction / 1995 / VI / M • What's Up, Tiger Pussy? / 1995 / VC / M • The Whore / 1989 / CA / M

RALPH QUAIL see Aaron Stuart

RALPH SHERWOOD see Star Index I

RALPH STEPHENS
Hard Action / 1975 / AXV / M

RALPH TOYO
ABA: Double Feature #5 / 1996 / ALP / M • Night Of Submission / 1976 / BIZ / M

RAMBONE
Self Service / cr85 / ... / G • Tonight's The Night / 1992 / V99 / M

RAMEL
Sexhibition #3 / 1996 / SUF / M

RAMO RICO
Bi Bi Banjee Boyz / 1994 / PL / G

RAMOLA YOUNG *(Pamela Yen)*
All About Annette / 1982 / SE / C • China Girl / 1974 / SE / M

RAMONA KASSEL see Star Index I

RAMONA MOON
Resurrection Of Eve / 1973 / MIT / M

RAMRY WORD see Star Index I

RAMSEY KARSON see Harold Lime

RANDALL SAVAGE
Flesh & Laces #1 / 1983 / CA / M

RANDEE LEE
Anal Hanky-Panky / 1997 / ROB / M • Nice Fuckin' Movie / 1997 / EL / M • Raw Naked In Your Face / 1997 / ROB / M • Suzi's Wild Anal Ride / 1997 / ROB / M • Women Behaving Badly / 1996 / RAS / M

RANDI
100% Amateur #01: Double Penetration Sensation / 1995 / OD / M • Amateur Hours #07 / 1990 / AFI / M • Amateur Hours #09 / 1990 / AFI / M • Amateur Hours #19 / 1990 / AFI / M • Big Busty #10 / 198? / H&S / M • Butt Hunt #05 / 1995 / LEI / M • GRG: Poppin' Fresh Buns / 1995 / GRG / M • Heavenly / 1995 / IF / M • Hollywood Amateurs #02 / 1994 / MID / M • Shaved #01 / 1991 / RB / F • Toy Time #2: Nasty Solos / 1994 / STP / F

RANDI HART
The Adventures Of Studman #3 / 1994 / AFV / M • America's Raunchiest Home Videos #75: / 1993 / ZA / M • The Anal Adventures Of Suzy Super Slut #1 / 1994 / AFV / M • Anal Camera #04 / 1995 / EVN / M • Anal Hellraiser #2 / 1995 / ROB / M • Babe Watch #2 / 1994 / SC / M • Bi Dream Of Genie / 1994 / BIL / G • The Bondage Adventures Of Randy Ranger / 1994 / SBP / B • Boot Camp / 1996 / PRE / B • The Bridges Of Anal County / 1996 / PV0 / C •

Bun Busters #20 / 1994 / LBO / M • Bus Stop Tales #09 / 1990 / PRI / M • Busted-D-D In Las Vegas / 1996 / LV / M • Butt Hunt #02 / 1994 / LEI / M • Cousin Bubba Country Corn Porn #02 / 1994 / VIM / M • Creme De La Face #04 / 1994 / OD / M • Desire Kills / 1996 / SUM / M • Dirty Doc's Housecalls #14 / 1994 / LV / M • Dirty Doc's Housecalls #18 / 1994 / LV / M • Drive Bi / 1994 / BIL / G • Girls Just Wanna Have Cum / 1995 / HO / M • Horny Henry's Peeping Adventures / 1994 / TTV / M • The Horny Housewife / 1996 / HO / M • M Series #26 / 1994 / LBO / M • M Series #28 / 1994 / LBO / M • Neighborhood Watch #32 / 1992 / LBO / M • Our Bang #12 / 1993 / GLI / M • Private Bound / 1994 / VTF / B • Pubic Eye / 1992 / HW / M • Pussyclips #03 / 1994 / SNA / M • Ron Hightower's White Chicks #09 / 1994 / LBO / M • She's No Angel #2 / 1995 / V99 / M • She-Male Nurse / 1989 / LV / G • Tail Taggers #123 / 1994 / WV / M • Tail Taggers #127: / 1994 / WV / M • Yankee Rose / 1994 / LE / M

RANDI JONES see Randy Jones

RANDI MACARTHUR see Star Index I

RANDI RAGE
Boobwatch #2 / 1997 / SC / M • Crew Sluts / 1996 / NOT / M • Frendz? #2 / 1996 / RAS / M • Living On The Edge / 1997 / DWO / M • Manhandled! / 1997 / BON / B • Profiles #10: / 1997 / XPR / M • Shane's World #7 / 1996 / OD / M • The Violation Of Juliette / 1996 / JMP / F

RANDI RANDI
Dancing Dominant Damsels / 1994 / RSV / B

RANDI RAVAGE
Puritan Video Magazine #10 / 1997 / LE / M

RANDI SABLOW
Postgraduate Course In Sexual Love / 1975 / QX / M

RANDI STORM
Blonde with shoulder length hair, marginal face, originally medium droopy tits later enhanced to 44DD, lithe body.
Amazing Nympho Stories / 1995 / TEG / M • Anal Institution #3 / 1996 / ZA / M • Anal Interrogation / 1995 / ZA / M • The Backway Inn #5 / 1993 / FD / M • The Blowjob Adventures Of Doctor Fellatio / 1997 / EL / M • The Butt Sisters Do Washington D.C. / 1995 / MID / M • Caught From Behind #24 / 1996 / HO / M • Cumming Unscrewed / 1995 / TEG / F • Devil In A Wet T-Shirt / 1995 / SPI / M • Dirty Bob's #23: Tampa Teasers / 1995 / FLP / S • Dirty Dancers #9 / 1996 / HO / M • Dukes Of Anal / 1996 / VC / M • The Farmer's Daughter / 1995 / TEG / M • Fashion Passion / 1997 / TEP / M • Horny Henry's Snowballing Adventure / 1995 / TTV / M • Interview's Southern Cumfort / 1996 / LV / M • It Could Happen To You / 1996 / HW / M • The Maid / 1995 / VTF / B • Medically Bound Tickle Team / 1996 / VTF / B • Mike Hott: #294 Cunt of the Month: Randi Storm / 1995 / MHV / M • Mike Hott: #301 Three-Sum Sluts #04 / 1995 / MHV / M • Mike Hott: #377 Lesbian Sluts #28 / 1996 / MHV / F • Mike Hott: #378 Fuck The Boss #8 / 1996 / MHV / M • Mike Hott: #387 Girls Who Lap Cum From Cunts #04 / 1996 / MHV / M • Mission Phenomenal / 1996 / HIP / M • Mistress Misery / 1996 / VTF / B • Nookie Ranch /

1996 / NIT / M • The Panty Parlor / 1996 / VIM / M • Passions Of Sin / 1996 / NIT / M • Perverted Stories #11 / 1996 / JMP / M • Pretty Anal Ladies / 1996 / ANE / M • Rebel Without A Condom / 1996 / ERA / M • Red Door Diaries #1 / 1995 / ZA / M • Reel Life Video #41: Lust In The Country / 1996 / RLF / F • Rumpman: Caught In An Anal Avalanche / 1995 / HW / M • Sinister Servants / 1996 / CUC / B • Summer Vacation #1 / 1996 / RAS / M • Summer Vacation #2 / 1996 / RAS / M • Tickling Vamps / 1995 / SBP / B • The Violation Of Juliette / 1996 / JMP / F • Who's In Charge (Titan) / 1995 / TEG / M

RANDI SUMMERS
Backdoor To Hollywood #13 / 1990 / CDI / M

RANDOLPH ROEBLING see Star Index I

RANDY
100% Amateur #09: Asians & Latinas / 1995 / OD / M • Amateur Nights #05 / 1990 / HO / M • America's Raunchiest Home Videos #45: The Bigger They Cum / 1992 / ZA / M • AVP #6969: Lights, Camera, Sexation / 1990 / AVP / M • Blue Vanities #502 / 1992 / FFL / M • Blue Vanities #570 / 1995 / FFL / M • Casting Couch Cuties #1 / 1994 / WP / M • Fantasy Peeps: Three For Love / 1985 / 4P / M • Harry Horndog #13: Anal Lovers #2 / 1992 / ZA / M • Harry Horndog #14: Love Puppies #3 / 1992 / ZA / M • Homegrown Video #260 / 1990 / HOV / M • Homegrown Video #350 / 1991 / HOV / M • Kinky College Cunts #08 / 1993 / NS / F • Neighborhood Watch #08: Extended Foreplay / 1991 / LBO / M • Northwest Pecker Trek #3: Ducks & Dicks / 1994 / LBO / M • SVE: Ho-Nuff / 1994 / SVE / M • Uncle Roy's Amateur Home Video #15 / 1992 / VIM / M

RANDY (FEMALE) see Star Index I

RANDY ALEXANDER see Star Index I

RANDY ALLEN
Frat House / 1979 / NGV / M • Limited Edition #03 / 1979 / AVC / M

RANDY BARSTOW see Star Index I

RANDY COCHRAN
Gidget Goes Bi / 1990 / STA / G • Haulin' 'n' Ballin' / 1988 / MET / G • Heatwaves / 1987 / LAV / G • Innocent Bi Standers / 1989 / LV / G • Let Me Tell Ya 'Bout Fat Chicks #2 / 1988 / 4P / M • Randy And Dane / 1991 / IF / G • She-Male Encounters #14: She-Male Wrestlers / 1987 / MET / G

RANDY DAMON see Star Index I

RANDY DETROIT
Climax At The Melting Pot #2 / 1996 / AVS / M • Fucking Pregnant Babes #1: Che-Ne's Pelvic Exam / 1995 / AVS / M • Fucking Pregnant Babes #2: I Re-Enter Mamma / 1995 / AVS / M • Harlem Harlots #1 / 1995 / AVS / M • Harlem Harlots #2 / 1995 / AVS / M • Harlem Harlots #3 / 1996 / AVS / M • Here Come Them Fat Girls #1 / 1995 / AVS / M • Here Come Them Fat Girls #2 / 1996 / AVS / M • Ho Duzzit Model Agency #1 / 1993 / AFV / M • Ho Duzzit Model Agency #2 / 1993 / AFV / M • Hollywood Amateurs #12 / 1994 / MID / M • Hollywood Starlets Adventure #01 / 1995 / AVS / M • Hollywood Starlets Adventure #03 / 1995 / AVS / M • Hollywood Starlets Adventure #04 / 1995 / AVS / M • Hollywood Starlets Adventure #05 / 1995 / AVS

/ M • Hollywood Starlets Adventure #06 / 1995 / AVS / M • Nookie Professor #1 / 1996 / AVS / M • Nookie Professor #2 / 1996 / AVS / M • Our Bang #06 / 1992 / GLI / M • Ready To Drop #05 / 1995 / FC / M • Ready To Drop #06 / 1995 / FC / M • Ready To Drop #07 / 1995 / FC / M • Slut Safari #3 / 1994 / FC / M • SVE: Black Magic Woman / 1992 / SVE / M • SVE: Cheap Thrills #1: Detroit's Dollies / 1992 / SVE / M • SVE: Whip My Cream / 1992 / SVE / M • Tails From The Crib #03 / 1996 / AVS / M • Tails From The Crib #04 / 1996 / AVS / M

RANDY DICKERSON see Star Index I

RANDY EAST see Randy Paul

RANDY ERIC see Star Index I

RANDY FRIDEN see Star Index I

RANDY FRUTH see Derek Lane

RANDY GREASE
Blue Vanities #121 / 1990 / FFL / M

RANDY JAMES see Star Index I

RANDY JANE see Nick Niter

RANDY JONES (Randi Jones)
Pretty black-haired, small breasted girl who was 27 in 1992.
Amateur Lesbians #30: Randi / 1992 / GO / F • Buffy Malibu's Totally Nasty All-Girl Home Videos #01 / 1992 / ANA / F • Double D Dykes #04 / 1992 / GO / F • First Time Lesbians #13 / 1994 / JMP / F • House Of Correction / 1991 / HOM / B • KBBS: Weekend With Laurel Canyon / 1992 / KBB / M • Lovin' Spoonfuls #6 / 1996 / 4P / C • More Dirty Debutantes #14 / 1992 / 4P / M • Mr. Peepers Amateur Home Videos #62: Private Pussy Party / 1992 / LBO / M • Out Of The Blue #2 / 1992 / VI / M • Penthouse: Ready To Ride / 1992 / PET / F • The Price Of Curiosity / 1993 / LON / B • Talk Dirty To Me #09 / 1992 / DR / M • Uncle Roy's Amateur Home Video #15 / 1992 / VIM / M • Wild Flower #1 / 1992 / VI / M • Wildfire: Solos #3 / 1994 / WIF / F

RANDY KRAMER
10 Years Of Big Busts #1 / 1989 / BTO / C • Between My Breasts #01 / 1986 / BTO / S • Big Busty #17 / 198? / H&S / M • Warm Summer Rain / 1989 / C3S / S

RANDY LANCE
Fashion Fantasy / 1972 / GO / M

RANDY LANE
The Master And Mrs. Johnson / 1980 / SAT / M

RANDY LONG see Star Index I

RANDY MIXER
Bi-Ology: The Making Of Mr Right / 1992 / CAT / G • Down Bi Law / 1992 / CAT / G

RANDY PAUL (Randy East)
Backdoor To Hollywood #04 / 1988 / CDI / M • Between My Breasts #09 / 1990 / BTO / M • Bi-Heat #03 / 1987 / ZA / G • Big Tit Hookers / 1989 / BTO / M • Blazing Bedrooms / 1987 / LA / M • Body Games / 1987 / DR / M • Breakin' In / 1986 / WV / M • Built For Sex (Angela Baron's) / 1988 / FAZ / C • Careena #1 / 1987 / WV / C • Careena #2: A Star On The Rise / 1988 / WV / C • Caught From Behind #08 / 1988 / HO / M • Charmed And Dangerous / 1987 / VI / M • Cheating American Style / 1988 / WV / M • Chicks With Dicks #2 / 1996 / BIZ / B • Close Friends / 1987 / CC / G • Crocodile Blondee #1 / 1987 / CA0 / M • Debbie's Love Spell / 1988 / STM / M • Deep Inside Trading / 1986 / AR / M • Divorce Court Ex-

pose #2 / 1987 / VD / M • Easy Access / 1988 / ZA / M • The End Zone / 1987 / LA / C • Every Man's Fancy / 1988 / SEX / M • Every Man's Fancy / 1991 / V99 / M • Firm Hands / 1996 / GOT / B • The Flirt / 1987 / VWA / M • Fresh! / 1987 / VXP / M • The Girls Of The B.L.O. / 1988 / VWA / M • Good Evening Vietnam / 1987 / WV / M • Heat Of The Nite / 1988 / VEX / M • The Heiress / 1988 / VI / M • Horneymooners #1 / 1988 / VXP / M • Horneymooners #2 / 1988 / VXP / M • House Of Pain / 1996 / OUP / B • Little Red Riding Hood / 1988 / WV / M • Living Doll / 1987 / WV / M • Lust Tango In Paris / 1987 / PEN / M • Much More Than A Mouthful #2 / 1988 / VEX / M • Oral Majority #03 / 1986 / WV / C • Oral Majority #06 / 1988 / WV / C • Pacific Intrigue / 1987 / AMB / M • Pay The Lady / 1987 / VXP / M • Pink Baroness / 1988 / VWA / M • Raging Hormones / 1988 / VXP / M • The Return Of Indiana Joan / 1989 / PL / M • Revenge Of The Babes #2 / 1987 / PL / M • The Right Tool For The Job / 1988 / VXP / M • The Scent Of Samantha / 1988 / VEX / C • Scorching Secrets / 1988 / IN / M • Sex Derby / 1986 / GO / M • Sex World Girls / 1987 / AR / M • She Males Enslaved / 1996 / BIZ / G • Shoot To Thrill / 1988 / VWA / M • Snapshots: Confessions Of A Video Voyeur / 1988 / CC / M • Spend The Holidays With Barbii / 1987 / CDI / M • Sweet Revenge / 1986 / ZA / M • Taija / 1986 / WV / C • A Taste Of Ambrosia / 1987 / FEM / M • A Taste Of Pleasure / 1988 / AVC / M • A Taste Of Porsche / 1988 / PIN / C • A Tasty Kind Of Love / 1987 / LV / M • Toe Tales #27 / 1995 / GOT / B • Toe Tales #31 / 1995 / GOT / B • Toe Tales #33 / 1996 / GOT / B • Toys 4 Us #1 / 1987 / WV / C • Transsexual Dynasty / 1996 / BIZ / G • TVs In Leather And Pain / 1996 / BIZ / G • Twentysomething #1 / 1988 / VI / M • Twentysomething #2 / 1988 / VI / M • Twins / 1986 / WV / M • Twisted Sisters / 1988 / ZA / M • Young And Innocent / 1987 / HO / M

RANDY POTES *see* **Cal Jammer**

RANDY QUINN
Mean Ass Bitch / 1996 / RB / B

RANDY RADISURE *see* **Star Index I**

RANDY RAVAGE
Las Vegas Big Boob Hospitality Sweet / 1997 / HO / M

RANDY ROD *see* **Star Index I**

RANDY ROTEMAN *see* **R.J. Reynolds**

RANDY SPEARS *(Nick Russell, Randy Sprars, Gregory Patrick, Greg Ory, Greg Slavin, Greg Patrick)*
Handsome and reasonably respectable male. Married to Danielle Rogers. As of mid 1994 he was supposedly operating a gym in Philadelphia.
19 And Nasty / 1990 / ME / M • 20th Century Fox / 1989 / FAZ / M • 50 Ways To Lick Your Lover / 1989 / ZA / M • A.S.S.(Anal Security Squad) / 1988 / VD / M • The Adventures Of Buttman / 1989 / EA / M • All That Sex / 1990 / LE / M • American Built / 1992 / LE / M • Anal Addiction #1 / 1990 / SO / M • Anal Alley / 1990 / ME / M • Anal Sluts & Sweethearts #2 / 1993 / ROB / M • Anal Taboo / 1993 / ROB / M • The Anals Of History #2 / 1992 / MID / M • Anything That Moves / 1992 / VC / M • Bad / 1990 / VC / M • Bad Blood / 1989 / AE / S • Bad

Habits / 1993 / VC / M • Bat Bitch #1 / 1989 / FAZ / M • Bat Bitch #2 / 1990 / FAZ / M • Beat The Heat / 1990 / VI / M • Beauty And The Beast #2 / 1990 / VC / M • Bedtime Tales / 1995 / IF / M • Behind Blue Eyes #2 / 1988 / ZA / M • Behind Blue Eyes #3 / 1989 / ME / M • Best Gang Bangs / 1996 / DFI / C • Best Of Buttman #2 / 1993 / EA / C • The Better Sex Video Series #7: Advanced Sexual Fantasies / 1992 / LEA / M • Bianca Trump's Towers / 1992 / LV / M • Bimbo Bowlers From Boston / 1990 / ZA / M • Bimbo Cheerleaders From Outer Space / 1988 / FAN / M • A Blaze Of Glory / 1993 / ME / M • Blowing In Style / 1989 / EA / M • The BoobyGuard / 1993 / FOR / M • Breaking And Entering / 1991 / AFV / M • Bust A Move / 1993 / SC / M • Buttman's Ultimate Workout / 1990 / EA / M • Call Girls In Action / 1989 / CV / M • Camera Shy / 1993 / FOR / M • Camp Beaverlake #2 / 1991 / AFV / M • Candy's Little Sister Sugar / 1988 / VD / M • Captain Butt's Beach / 1992 / LV / M • The Case Of The Sensuous Sinners / 1988 / ME / M • Centerfold / 1992 / VC / M • Cheerleader Nurses #1 / 1993 / VC / M • Cheerleader Nurses #2 / 1993 / VC / M • Chug-A-Lug Girls #2 / 1993 / VT / M • Class Act / 1989 / WAV / M • Collectible / 1991 / LE / M • The Come On: Skip's Video Guide To Scoring Chicks / 1991 / LE / M • The Creasemaster's Wife / 1993 / VC / M • Curious / 1992 / LE / M • Curse Of The Catwoman / 1990 / VC / M • Cycle Sluts / 1992 / CC / M • Dancing Angels / 1989 / PL / M • Dangerous Curves / 1995 / VC / M • Danielle's Dirty Deeds / 1991 / CC / M • De Blond / 1989 / EA / M • Deception / 1991 / XCI / M • Deep Inside Danielle / 1990 / CDI / C • Deep Inside Deidre Holland / 1993 / VC / C • Deep Inside Jeanna Fine / 1992 / VC / C • Deep Inside Nikki Sinn / 1996 / VC / C • Deep Inside Shanna Mccullough / 1992 / VC / C • Denim / 1991 / LE / M • Denim Dolls #1 / 1989 / CDI / M • Dial A Sailor / 1990 / PM / M • Diaries Of Fire And Ice #1 / 1989 / VC / M • Diaries Of Fire And Ice #2 / 1989 / VC / M • Dick-Tation / 1991 / AFV / M • Diedre In Danger / 1990 / VI / M • Dirty Lingerie / 1990 / VD / M • Dominoes / 1993 / VI / M • Earthquake Girls / 1990 / CC / M • The Easy Way / 1990 / VC / M • Edge Of Sensation / 1990 / LE / M • Eleventh Annual AVN Awards / 1994 / VC / M • Elvis Slept Here / 1992 / LE / M • Erectnophobia #1 / 1991 / MID / M • Erotic Tales / 1989 / V99 / M • Essence Of A Woman / 1993 / FOR / M • Fantasy Confidential / 1988 / GO / M • Fantasy Escorts / 1993 / FOR / M • Fantasy Exchange / 1993 / VI / M • Farmer's Daughter / 1989 / FAZ / M • Filet-O-Breast / 1988 / AVC / M • The Final Taboo / 1988 / CA / M • Flashpoint / 1991 / AFV / M • Flesh Mountain / 1994 / VI / C • For His Eyes Only / 1989 / PL / M • For Your Love / 1988 / IN / M • The French Connexxxion / 1991 / VC / M • Frisky Fables / 1988 / LV / M • Gang Bang Cummers / 1993 / ROB / M • Gang Bang Wild Style #1 / 1993 / ROB / M • Gang Bangs #2 / 1989 / EA / M • A Geisha's Secret / 1993 / VI / M • Ghost Writer / 1992 / LE / M • Ghostest With The Mostest / 1988 / CA / M • Girls In The Night / 1990 / LE / M • Girls Of The Double D #04 / 1989 / CDI / M •

Good Enough To Eat / 1988 / FAZ / M • Good Things Come In Small Packages / 1989 / CA / M • Good Vibrations #2: A Couples Guide To Vibrator Use / 1991 / VT / M • Hate To See You Go / 1990 / VC / M • Haunted Nights / 1993 / WP / M • Hawaii Vice #2 / 1989 / CDI / M • Hawaii Vice #4 / 1989 / CIN / M • Hawaii Vice #5 / 1989 / CDI / M • Hawaii Vice #6 / 1989 / CDI / M • Hawaii Vice #8 / 1990 / CIN / M • Head First / 1993 / LE / M • Heart To Heart / 1990 / LE / M • The Heat Of The Moment / 1990 / IN / M • Hollywood Assets / 1990 / FH / M • Hooray For Hineywood / 1991 / MID / M • Hopeless Romantic / 1992 / LE / M • House Of Dreams / 1990 / CA / M • Hyapatia Obsessed / 1993 / EX / M • I Creme With Genie / 1991 / PL / M • I Do #2 / 1990 / VI / M • If Dreams Come True / 1991 / AFV / M • Illicit Affairs / 1989 / VD / M • In The Jeans / 1990 / ME / M • Invasion Of The Samurai Sluts From Hell / 1988 / FAZ / M • Island Girls #3: Rip Tide / 1991 / CDI / C • Jane Bond Meets Thunderthighs / 1988 / VD / M • Jetstream / 1993 / AMP / M • Joined: The Siamese Twins / 1989 / PL / M • Juggernaut / 1990 / EX / M • Juice Box / 1990 / AFV / M • Just For The Hell Of It / 1991 / CA / M • KTSX-69 / 1988 / CA / M • The Last Resort / 1990 / VC / M • Lawyers In Heat / 1989 / CDI / M • Leena Meets Frankenstein / 1993 / OD / M • Leena's Favorite Studs / 1995 / OD / C • Legend #4: Critic's Choice / 1992 / LE / M • Licensed To Thrill / 1990 / VC / M • Lick Bush / 1992 / VD / C • Lickety Pink / 1990 / ME / M • Life, Love And Divorce / 1990 / LV / M • Lifeguard / 1990 / VI / M • Living Doll / 1992 / CDI / M • Loose Ends #5: The New Generation / 1988 / 4P / M • Lost In Paradise / 1990 / CA / M • The Love Nest / 1989 / CA / M • Lover's Trance / 1990 / LE / M • The Luv Game / 1988 / VCX / M • Made In Japan / 1992 / VI / M • The Masseuse #1 / 1990 / VI / M • Memories / 1992 / LE / M • Mind Trips / 1992 / FH / M • Monaco Falcon / 1990 / VC / M • Moonstroked / 1988 / 3HV / M • More Than A Handful / 1993 / CA / C • My Way / 1993 / CA / M • Naked Buns 8 1/2 / 1992 / CC / M • Naked Edge / 1992 / LE / M • The New Barbarians #1 / 1990 / VC / M • The New Barbarians #2 / 1990 / VC / M • New Lovers / 1993 / VI / M • New Wave Hookers #2 / 1991 / VC / M • Night Trips #1 / 1989 / CA / M • Night Trips #2 / 1990 / CA / M • Nightmare On Porn Street / 1988 / ME / M • Nighttime Stories / 1991 / LE / M • Nightvision / 1993 / TP / M • Nikki's Bon Voyage / 1993 / VC / M • Nikki's Last Stand / 1993 / VC / M • Nurse Tails / 1994 / VC / M • Nymphobrat / 1989 / VI / M • Oh, What A Night! / 1990 / VC / M • On Trial #3: Takin' It To The Jury / 1992 / VI / M • On Trial #4: The Verdict / 1992 / VI / M • One Night Stand / 1990 / LE / M • Open House (Vid Exc) / 1989 / VEX / M • Opening Night / 1991 / AR / M • The Orgy #2 / 1993 / EMC / M • The Orgy #3 / 1993 / EMC / M • Out For Blood / 1990 / VI / M • Outback Assignment / 1991 / VD / M • Panties / 1993 / VD / M • Paris By Night / 1990 / IN / M • Partners In Sex / 1988 / FAN / M • Party Doll A Go-Go #1 / 1991 / VC / M • Party Doll A Go-Go #2 / 1991 / VC / M • Phantom Of The Cabaret #1 / 1989 / VC / M • Phantom Of The Cabaret #2 / 1989 /

VC / M • Phone Mates / 1988 / CA / M • Play School / 1990 / SO / M • Porn On The 4th Of July / 1990 / IN / M • Porn Star's Day Off / 1990 / FAZ / M • Portrait Of A Nymph / 1988 / PP / M • Pouring It On / 1993 / CV / M • The Prince Of Lies / 1992 / LE / M • Prisoner Of Love / 1991 / ME / M • Private Eyes, Public Thighs / 1989 / DR / C • Private Places / 1992 / VC / M • Pure Sex / 1988 / FAN / C • Pyromaniac / 1990 / SO / M • Queen Of Hearts #1 / 1987 / PL / M • Radical Affairs Video Magazine #04 / 1992 / ME / M • Rapture / 1990 / SC / M • Ravaged / 1990 / CIN / M • The Red Baron / 1989 / FAN / M • Ringside Knockout / 1990 / DR / M • Roadgirls / 1990 / DR / M • Rock 'n' Roll Heaven / 1989 / EA / M • Route 69 / 1989 / OD / M • Runaway / 1992 / VI / M • Ruthless Women / 1988 / SE / M • Satisfaction / 1992 / LE / M • Satisfaction Jackson / 1988 / CA / M • Savannah Superstar / 1992 / VI / M • Sea Of Desire / 1990 / AR / M • The Secret Garden #1 / 1992 / XCI / M • The Secret Garden #2 / 1992 / XCI / M • The Seduction Formula / 1990 / FAN / M • See-Thru / 1992 / LE / M • Separated / 1989 / INH / M • Sex In A Singles Bar / 1992 / VC / M • Sex Sluts In The Slammer / 1988 / FAN / M • Sex Trek #1: The Next Peneration / 1990 / ME / M • Sex Trek #2: The Search For Sperm / 1991 / ME / M • Sex Trek #3: The Wrath Of Bob / 1992 / ME / M • Sexpot / 1988 / AE / S • Sexual Healer / 1991 / CA / M • The Sexual Zone / 1989 / EX / M • Shadow Dancers #1 / 1989 / EA / M • Shadow Dancers #2 / 1989 / EA / M • Shadows In The Dark / 1990 / 4P / M • A Shot In The Mouth #1 / 1990 / ME / M • A Shot In The Mouth #2 / 1991 / ME / M • Sinderella #1 / 1992 / VI / M • Sinderella #2 / 1992 / VI / M • Singles Holiday / 1990 / PM / M • Skin To Skin / 1993 / LE / M • Slave To Love / 1993 / ROB / M • The Slut / 1988 / FAN / M • The Smart Ass Enquirer / 1990 / VT / M • Snakedance / 1992 / VI / M • Sodomania #03: Foreign Objects / 1993 / EL / M • Sodomania: The Baddest Of The Best...And Then Some / 1994 / EL / C • Someone Else / 1992 / VC / M • Southern Exposure / 1991 / LE / M • Splendor In The Ass #1 / 1989 / CA / M • Stairway To Paradise / 1990 / VC / M • Steal Breeze / 1990 / SO / M • Steal This Heart #1 / 1993 / CV / M • Steal This Heart #2 / 1993 / CV / M • Steal This Heart (Director's) / 1993 / CV / M • Steamy Windows / 1990 / VC / M • Sticky Lips / 1993 / EX / M • Stolen Hearts / 1991 / AFV / M • Street Angels / 1992 / LV / M • Studio Sex / 1990 / FH / M • Summer Games / 1992 / HW / M • Sweet Dreams / 1994 / LEI / M • Sweet Dreams / 1991 / VC / M • Sweet Miss Fortune / 1990 / LE / M • Sweet Seduction / 1990 / LV / M • Sweet Target / 1992 / CDI / M • Swingers Ink / 1990 / VC / M • Tailiens #3 / 1992 / FD / M • Tailspin #2 / 1991 / VT / M • Tales From The Zipper #1 / 1993 / ME / M • The Tease / 1990 / VC / M • Temptations / 1989 / DR / M • Tenth Annual Adult Video News Awards / 1993 / VC / M • This Year's Blonde / 1990 / LE / M • Tit City #1 / 1993 / SC / M • Top It Off / 1990 / VC / M • Torch #1 / 1990 / VI / M • A Touch Of Gold / 1990 / IN / M • True Confessions Of Hyapatia Lee / 1989 / VI / M • True Legends Of Adult Cinema: The Modern Era / 1992 / VC / C •

Twin Action / 1993 / LE / M • Two Hearts / 1991 / VI / M • Two Women / 1992 / ROB / M • Unexpected Encounters #3 / 1990 / CPV / S • Up And Cummers #01 / 1993 / 4P / M • V.I.C.E. #1 / 1991 / AFV / M • V.I.C.E. #2 / 1991 / AFV / M • Veil / 1990 / VI / M • Victim Of Love #1 / 1992 / VI / M • Victim Of Love #2 / 1992 / VI / M • The Violation Of Tori Welles / 1990 / VD / C • Wet Dream On Maple Street / 1988 / FAN / M • Wet Paint / 1990 / DR / M • What About Boob? / 1993 / CV / M • The Wild One / 1990 / LE / M • The Wrong Woman / 1990 / LE / M • The Young And The Wrestling #1 / 1988 / PL / M • Young Girls In Tight Jeans / 1989 / VD / M

RANDY SPRARS *see* **Randy Spears**
RANDY STORM
Mr. Madonna / 1994 / FPI / G
RANDY STYLES *see* **Veronica Hart**
RANDY SUMMERS *see* **Wayne Summers**
RANDY WEST *(Andy Deer, Andy Abrams)*
Andy Deer is from **Kiss And Tell**. Andy Abrams is from **Pink And Pretty**.
2 Hung 2 Tung / 1992 / MID / M • 20th Century Fox / 1989 / FAZ / M • 50 Ways To Lick Your Lover / 1989 / ZA / M • The A Chronicles / 1992 / CC / M • A.S.S.(Anal Security Squad) / 1988 / VD / M • Acts Of Confession / 1991 / PP / M • Adult Affairs / 1994 / VC / M • Adult Video News 1991 Awards / 1991 / VC / M • Adult Video News 1992 Awards / 1992 / VC / M • Adult Video Therapist / 1987 / CLV / C • The Adventures Of Peeping Tom #1 / 1996 / OD / M • Age Of Consent / 1985 / AVC / M • The All American Girl / 1989 / FAN / M • All That Sex / 1990 / LE / M • Amazing Tails #5 / 1990 / CA / M • Amber Lynn's Hotline 976 / 1987 / VCR / M • Amber Lynn's Peter Meter / 1988 / 3HV / C • Amber Pays The Rent / 1986 / VT / M • American Fan Club Prowl / 1996 / VT / M • American Garter / 1993 / VC / M • American Pie / 1980 / SE / M • Americans Most Wanted / 1991 / HO / M • Anal Addiction #2 / 1990 / SO / M • Anal Analysis (Heatwave) / 1992 / HW / M • Anal Attraction #1 / 1988 / 3HV / M • Anal Climax #3 / 1993 / ROB / M • Anal Co-Ed / 1993 / ROB / M • Anal Cuties #1 / 1992 / ROB / M • Anal Cuties #3 / 1992 / ROB / M • Anal Encounters #1 / 1991 / VC / M • Anal Encounters #4: Tales From The Crack / 1992 / VC / M • Anal Encounters #8 / 1992 / VC / M • Anal Fever / 1991 / AMB / M • Anal Kitten / 1992 / ROB / M • Anal Lover #2 / 1993 / ROB / M • Anal Nation #1 / 1990 / CC / M • Anal Rampage #2 / 1993 / ROB / M • Anal Rookies #1 / 1992 / ROB / M • Anal Sensation / 1993 / ROB / M • Anal Sluts & Sweethearts #1 / 1992 / ROB / M • The Anal Team / 1993 / LV / M • The Anal-Europe Series #02: Fantasies / 1992 / LV / M • The Anal-Europe Series #03: The Museum Of The Living Art / 1993 / LV / M • The Anal-Europe Series #04: Anal Recall / 1993 / LV / M • The Analizer / 1990 / LV / M • The Anals Of History #2 / 1992 / MID / M • Angel Kelly Raw / 1987 / FAN / M • Angel Of H.E.A.T. / 1981 / VES / S • Angel Of The Island / 1988 / IN / M • Angel Rising / 1988 / IN / M • Angela Baron Series #1 / 1988 / VD / C • Angela Baron Series #2 / 1988 / VD / C • Angela Baron Series #3 / 1988 / VD / C • Angela Baron Series #4 / 1988 / VD / C •

Angela Baron Series #5 / 1988 / VD / C • Angela Baron Series #6 / 1988 / VD / C • Angels Of Passion / 1986 / CDI / M • Another Rear View / 1990 / LE / M • Anus The Menace / 1993 / CC / M • Aroused #2 / 1995 / VI / M • As Dirty As She Wants To Be / 1990 / ME / M • As The Spirit Moves You / 1990 / LV / M • Asian Invasion / 1993 / IP / M • Asian Silk / 1992 / VI / M • Ass Backwards / 1991 / ME / M • Asses Galore #3: Pure Evil / 1996 / DFI / M • Assford Wives / 1992 / ATL / M • At The Pornies / 1989 / VC / M • Aunt Peg Goes To Hollywood / 1982 / CA / M • Aussie Vice / 1989 / PM / M • Australian Connection / 1989 / PM / M • The Autobiography Of Herman Flogger / 1986 / AVC / M • Autoerotica #1 / 1991 / EX / M • Autoerotica #2 / 1991 / EX / M • Avenging Angeli / 1990 / CC / M • Baby Cakes / 1982 / SE / M • Bachelor's Paradise / 1986 / VEX / M • Bachelorette Party / 1986 / ACV / S • Back In Style / 1993 / VI / M • Back To Nature / 1990 / CA / M • Back To Rears / 1988 / VI / M • Backdoor Black #1 / 1992 / WV / C • Backdoor Brides #4 / 1993 / PV / M • Backdoor To Cannes / 1993 / VC / M • Backdoor To Hollywood #01 / 1986 / CDI / M • Backdoor To Hollywood #02 / 1986 / CDI / M • Backdoor To Hollywood #12 / 1990 / CIN / M • Backing In #3 / 1991 / WV / C • Backside To The Future #1 / 1986 / ZA / M • The Backway Inn #1 / 1992 / FD / M • Bad Girls #1 / 1981 / GO / M • Badgirls #4: Jayebird / 1995 / VI / M • Balling Instinct / 1992 / FH / M • Barbara The Barbarian / 1987 / SE / M • Barbii Unleashed / 1988 / 4P / M • The Bare-Assed Naked Gun / 1992 / MID / M • The Barlow Affairs / 1991 / XCI / M • Batteries Included / 1988 / 3HV / M • Battle Of The Titans / 1986 / AVC / M • Bazooka County #2 / 1989 / CC / M • Beach Blanket Brat / 1989 / VI / M • Beauty And The Beast #2 / 1990 / VC / M • Beaver Ridge / 1991 / VC / M • Bedrooms And Boardrooms / 1992 / DR / M • Bedtime For Byron / 1991 / ME / M • Bedtime Stories / 1989 / WV / M • Bedtime Tales / 1985 / SE / M • Beefeaters / 1989 / PV / M • Behind The Backdoor #6 / 1993 / EVN / M • Behind The Scenes With Angela Baron / 1988 / FAZ / C • Behind You All The Way #2 / 1990 / SO / M • Bend Over Backwards / 1993 / VIM / M • Best Butt(e) In The West #1 / 1992 / CC / M • The Best Of Doctor Butts / 1994 / 4P / C • The Best Of Oriental Anal #1 / 1994 / ROB / C • The Best Rears Of Our Lives / 1992 / OD / M • Betrayed / 1996 / WP / M • The Better Sex Video Series #7: Advanced Sexual Fantasies / 1992 / LEA / M • Between The Sheets / 1982 / CA / M • Beverly Hills Copulator / 1986 / … / M • Beverly Hills Cox / 1986 / CA / M • Beyond The Denver Dynasty / 1988 / CA / M • The Big Bang #2 / 1994 / LV / M • Big Game / 1990 / LV / M • The Big Thrill / 1989 / VD / M • Biker Chicks In Love / 1991 / LE / M • Bikini Beach #1 / 1993 / CC / M • Bikini Beach #2 / 1993 / CC / M • Bikini Beach #3 / 1992 / CC / F • The Bimbo #1 / 1992 / AFV / M • Bimbo Bowlers From Boston / 1990 / ZA / M • Bimbo Bowlers From Buffalo / 1989 / ZA / M • Bimbo Cheerleaders From Outer Space / 1988 / FAN / M • Bionca On Fire / 1988 / 4P / M • The Bitch Is Back / 1988 / FAN / M • Bite / 1991 / LE / M • Black Dirty

Debutantes / 1993 / 4P / M • Black Encounters / 1992 / ZA / M • Black Valley Girls #1 / 1986 / 4R / M • Blacks & Whites #2 / 1995 / GO / M • Blazing Bedrooms / 1987 / LA / M • Blazing Boners / 1992 / MID / M • The Blonde & The Beautiful #1 / 1993 / LV / M • The Blonde & The Beautiful #2 / 1993 / LV / M • Blonde Ice #1 / 1990 / EX / M • Blonde Ice #2 / 1993 / EX / M • Blonde Riders / 1991 / CC / M • Blonde Savage / 1991 / CDI / M • Blow Job Baby / 1993 / CC / M • Blow Job Betty / 1991 / CC / M • Blowing In Style / 1989 / EA / M • Blue Dreams / 1996 / SC / M • Blue Movie / 1989 / VD / M • Blue Vanities #055 / 1988 / FFL / M • The Bod Squad / 1989 / VT / M • Bodies By Jackie / 1985 / IVP / M • Body Music #1 / 1989 / DR / M • Body Talk / 1982 / VCX / M • Boiling Point / 1994 / WAV / M • Bon Appetit / 1980 / QX / M • Bonnie & Clyde #1 / 1992 / VI / M • Bonnie & Clyde #2 / 1992 / VI / M • Boobs, Butts And Bloopers #1 / 1990 / HO / M • Boomeranal / 1992 / CC / M • The Boss / 1993 / VT / M • Bottoms Up #08 / 1986 / AVC / C • Bottoms Up (1993-Hollywood) / 1993 / HO / M • The Breast Of Breastmen / 1995 / EVN / C • Breast Side Story / 1990 / LE / M • Breastman Goes To Breastland #1 / 1993 / EVN / M • Breaststroke #2 / 1989 / EX / M • Breathless / 1989 / CIN / M • Bring On The Virgins / 1989 / CA / M • Built For Sex (Angela Baron's) / 1988 / FAZ / C • Bung-Ho Babes / 1991 / FC / M • Burlesxxx / 1996 / VT / M • Burn / 1991 / LE / M • Burning Desire / 1983 / HO / M • Bush League #1 / 1990 / CC / M • Bush Pilots #2 / 1991 / VC / M • Bushwackers / 1990 / PM / M • Busted / 1989 / CA / M • The Butt Sisters Do Detroit / 1993 / MID / M • Butt Woman #1 / 1990 / FH / M • Butt's Up, Doc #3 / 1992 / GO / M • Caged Fury / 1993 / DR / M • Cagney & Stacey / 1984 / AT / M • California Gigolo / 1987 / VD / M • California Reaming / 1985 / WV / M • Casanova #1 / 1993 / SC / M • Casbah Fantasy / 1989 / BON / B • The Case Of The Crooked Cathouse / 1989 / ME / M • Casey At The Bat / 1991 / LV / M • Casing The Crack / 1987 / V99 / M • Cat Scratch Fever / 1989 / FAZ / M • Certifiably Anal / 1993 / ROB / M • Channel Blonde / 1994 / VI / M • Charli / 1981 / VCX / M • Charmed And Dangerous / 1987 / VI / M • Cheeks #5: The Ultimate Butt / 1991 / CC / M • Cheeks #7: Mirror Image / 1994 / CC / M • Cherry Cheeks / 1993 / CA / M • Chinatown / 1994 / SC / M • Clean And Dirty / 1990 / ME / M • The Clock Strikes Bizarre On Butt Row / 1996 / ABS / M • Close To The Edge / 1994 / VI / M • Club DV8 #1 / 1993 / SC / M • Club DV8 #2 / 1993 / SC / M • Club Exotica #1 / 1985 / WV / M • Club Exotica #2 / 1985 / WV / M • Club Ginger / 1986 / VI / M • Club Head / 1990 / CA / M • The Cockateer #1 / 1991 / LE / M • The Cockateer #2 / 1992 / LE / M • Coed Fantasy / 1979 / CDI / M • Collectible / 1991 / LE / M • Color Me Anal / 1995 / ME / M • Coming Clean / 1992 / ME / M • Coming Of Age / 1989 / CA / M • Confessions / 1992 / PL / M • Constant Craving / 1992 / VD / M • Convenience Store Girls / 1986 / VD / M • Cookie 'n' Cream / 1992 / ME / M • Cool Sheets / 1989 / PP / M • Corruption / 1990 / CC / M • Country Comfort / 1981 / SE / M • Crackdown / 1988 / BIZ / B • Cram Ses-

sion / 1986 / V99 / M • Crash In The Rear / 1992 / HW / C • Critics' Choice #2 / 1984 / SE / C • Crocodile Blondee #1 / 1987 / CA0 / M • Cum Rain, Cum Shine / 1989 / FAZ / M • Cum Shot Revue #2 / 1985 / HO / C • Cum To Dinner / 1991 / HO / M • Cumback Pussy #7: NUGIRLZ / 1997 / EL / M • Cumming Clean (1996—Caballero) / 1996 / CA / M • The Dancers / 1981 / VCX / M • Dark Side Of The Moon / 1986 / VD / M • Daydreams, Nightdreams / 1996 / VC / M • The De Renzy Tapes / 1990 / CA / C • Dear Bridgette / 1992 / ZA / M • Debbie 4 Hire / 1988 / AVC / M • Debbie Does 'em All #1 / 1985 / CV / M • Debbie Does 'em All #2 / 1988 / CV / M • Debbie Does Wall Street / 1991 / VC / M • Deception / 1991 / XCI / M • Deep Inside Barbie / 1989 / CDI / C • Deep Inside Charli / 1990 / CDI / C • Deep Inside Danielle / 1990 / CDI / C • Deep Inside Debi Diamond / 1995 / VC / C • Deep Inside Dirty Debutantes #01 / 1992 / 4P / M • Deep Inside Nina Hartley / 1993 / VC / M • Deep Inside Ona Zee / 1992 / VC / C • Deep Inside P.J. Sparxx / 1995 / VC / C • Deep Inside Selena Steele / 1993 / VC / C • Deep Inside The Orient / 1993 / LV / M • Deep Inside Tiffany Mynx / 1994 / VC / C • Deep Inside Victoria Paris / 1993 / VC / C • Desire / 1983 / VCX / M • Desire / 1990 / VC / M • Desperate Women / 1986 / VD / M • Devil In Miss Dare / 1986 / AVC / C • Devil In The Blue Dress / 1989 / ME / M • Devil's Agenda & Miss Jones / 1991 / AR / M • Dial F For Fantasy / 1984 / PL / M • Dial N For Nikki / 1993 / PEP / M • Dick Tracer / 1990 / PM / M • The Dinner Party #1 / 1994 / ULI / M • The Dinner Party / 1986 / WV / M • Dirty Bob's #17: Tampa Teasers! / 1994 / FLP / S • Dirty Bob's #23: Tampa Teasers / 1995 / FLP / S • Dirty Bob's #27: Laid Back In L.A.! / 1996 / FLP / S • Dirty Dreams / 1987 / CA / M • Dirty Harriet / 1986 / SAT / M • Dirty Laundry #1 / 1994 / CV / M • The Dirty Little Mind of Martin Fink / 1991 / ME / M • Dirty Looks / 1990 / IN / M • Dirty Movies / 1989 / VD / M • Disoriented / 1992 / VI / M • Door To Door / 1990 / EX / M • Double Detail / 1992 / SO / M • Double Standards / 1986 / VC / M • Doubletake / 1989 / CC / M • Dr Butts #1 / 1991 / 4P / M • Dr Butts #2 / 1992 / 4P / M • Dr Butts #3 / 1993 / 4P / M • Dr F #2: Bad Medicine / 1990 / WV / M • Dr Jeckel & Ms Hide / 1990 / LV / M • Dr Juice's Lust Potion / 1986 / TEM / M • Dr Truth's Great Sex / 1986 / VD / M • Dracula Exotica / 1980 / TVX / M • Dreams Of A Gigolo / 1996 / SNA / M • Earthquake Girls / 1990 / CC / M • The Easy Way / 1990 / VC / M • Easy Way Out / 1989 / OD / M • Eat 'em And Smile / 1990 / ME / M • Ebony & Ivory Fantasies / 1988 / VD / C • Eclipse / 1993 / SC / M • Ecstasy / 1991 / LE / M • Edge Of Sensation / 1990 / LE / M • Educating Kascha / 1989 / CIN / M • Eleventh Annual AVN Awards / 1994 / VC / M • The Eleventh Commandment / 1987 / WAV / M • Elvis Slept Here / 1992 / LE / M • Empire Of The Sins / 1988 / IN / M • The End Of The Innocence / 1989 / IN / M • The End Zone / 1987 / LA / C • Erotic Aerobics / 1984 / VC / M • Erotic Radio WSEX / 1983 / VC / M • The Erotic World Of Vanessa #1 / 1983 / VCR / C • The Erotic World Of Vanessa #2 / 1984 / VCR / C • Erotica / 1992 / CC / M • Eternity / 1990 /

SC / M • Even More Dangerous / 1990 / SO / M • Everybody's Playmates / 1992 / CA / C • Everything Goes / 1990 / SE / M • Excitable / 1992 / IF / M • Expose Me Again / 1996 / CV / M • The Eye Of The Needle / 1991 / CIN / M • Face To Face / 1995 / ME / M • Family Secrets / 1985 / AMB / M • Famous Anus #1 / 1990 / EX / M • Fantasy Exchange / 1993 / VI / M • Fast Girls #2 / 1988 / DIS / M • Feds In Bed / 1993 / HO / M • Fetish Fever / 1993 / CA / C • The Filthy Rich / 1981 / CA / M • Find Your Love / 1988 / CV / M • A Fistful Of Bimbos / 1988 / FAZ / M • Flashpoint / 1991 / AFV / M • Foolish Pleasures / 1989 / ME / M • Foolproof / 1994 / VC / M • For Her Pleasure Only / 1989 / FAZ / M • For Your Lips Only / 1989 / FAZ / M • Forbidden Bodies / 1986 / HU / M • Forbidden Games / 1990 / CDI / M • Forced Love / 1990 / LV / M • Forever / 1991 / LE / M • Fortysomething #2 / 1991 / LE / M • Four Alarm / 1991 / SE / M • Foxholes / 1983 / SE / M • Freak Dat Booty / 1994 / WP / M • Free And Foxy / 1986 / VCX / C • French Twist / 1995 / IN / M • Friends & Lovers #2 / 1991 / VT / M • Frisky Business / 1984 / VC / M • From A Whisper To A Scream / 1993 / GO / M • From Rags To Riches / 1988 / CDI / M • From Russia With Lust / 1984 / VC / M • Full Moon Bay / 1993 / VI / M • The Fun House / 1988 / SEV / C • Gang Bangs #2 / 1989 / EA / M • Gangbang Girl #01 / 1992 / ANA / M • Gangbang Girl #02 / 1992 / ANA / M • A Geisha's Secret / 1993 / VI / M • Gentlemen Prefer Ginger / 1985 / VI / M • Gere Up / 1991 / LV / C • Get Lucky / 1996 / NIT / M • Gettin' Ready / 1985 / CDI / M • Ghost Writer / 1992 / LE / M • Ginger Then And Now / 1990 / VI / C • The Girl With The Blue Jeans Off / 1989 / FAZ / M • Girls Of Silicone Valley / 1991 / FC / M • Girls Of The Double D #03 / 1988 / CDI / M • Girls Of The Double D #10 / 1989 / CDI / M • The Girls On F Street / 1986 / AVC / M • The God Daughter #1 / 1991 / AFV / M • The God Daughter #2 / 1991 / AFV / M • Gold LeMay / 1991 / VIM / M • Good Morning Saigon / 1988 / ZA / M • The Great American Boobs To Kill For Dance Contest / 1995 / PEP / C • Great Expectations / 1990 / V99 / M • Great Expectations / 1992 / VEX / C • Group Therapy / 1992 / TP / M • Halloweenie / 1991 / PL / M • A Handful Of Summers / 1991 / ME / M • Handle With Care / 1989 / FAZ / M • Hanna Does Her Sisters / 1986 / HUR / M • Hard To Stop #1 / 1992 / VC / M • Having It All / 1985 / IN / M • Hawaii Vice #3 / 1988 / CIN / M • Hawaii Vice #5 / 1989 / CDI / M • Heads Or Tails? / 1993 / PL / M • Heartbeats / 1992 / LE / M • Heat Of The Nite / 1988 / VEX / M • Heaven Scent (Las Vegas) / 1993 / LV / M • The Heiress / 1988 / VI / M • Hello Norma Jeane / 1994 / VT / M • Her Name Was Lisa / 1979 / VC / M • Here's Looking At You / 1988 / V99 / M • Hidden Desire / 1989 / HO / M • Hidden Obsessions / 1992 / BFP / M • Holiday For Angels / 1987 / IN / M • Holly Does Hollywood #3 / 1989 / VEX / M • Holly Does Hollywood #4 / 1990 / CAY / M • Hollywood Hustle #1 / 1990 / V99 / M • Hollywood Studs / 1993 / FD / M • Hollywood Swingers #10 / 1993 / LBO / M • Honey, I Blew Everybody #2 / 1992 / MID / M • Honeymoon Harlots / 1986 / AVC / M •

/ SNA / M • Pussywoman #3 / 1995 / CC / M • Put It In Gere / 1991 / CA / M • Puttin' Her Ass On The Line / 1991 / DR / M • Rachel Ryan / 1988 / WV / C • Rachel Ryan Exposed / 1990 / WV / C • Radical Affairs Video Magazine #03 / 1992 / ME / M • Radical Affairs Video Magazine #07 / 1994 / ME / M • Radical Affairs Video Magazine #09 / 1995 / ME / M • Raging Weekend / 1988 / GO / M • Rainwoman #01 / 1989 / CC / M • Rainwoman #02 / 1990 / CC / M • Rapture / 1990 / SC / M • Raunch #01 / 1990 / CC / M • Raunch #10: Uncut Jewel / 1994 / CC / M • Ravaged Rivalry / 1990 / HO / M • Raw Sex #01 / 1994 / ERW / M • Raw Sex #02 / 1995 / ERW / M • Read My Lips / 1990 / FH / M • Ready, Willing & Anal (Cv) / 1993 / CV / C • Ready, Willing & Anal (Vidco) / 1993 / VD / C • Real Men Eat Keisha / 1986 / VC / M • Real Sex Magazine #02 / 1997 / HO / M • Rear View / 1989 / LE / M • Rears In Windows / 1993 / FH / M • The Red Garter / 1986 / SE / M • Red Hot Fire Girls / 1989 / VD / M • Red Velvet / 1988 / PV / M • Reel People #02 / 1984 / AR / M • Revealed / 1992 / VT / M • Rich & Sassy / 1986 / VSE / M • Ride A Pink Lady / 1986 / SE / M • Roadgirls / 1990 / DR / M • Robofox #1 / 1987 / FAN / M • Robofox #2 / 1988 / FAN / M • Rocket Girls / 1993 / VC / M • Romancing The Butt / 1992 / ATL / M • Roto-Rammer / 1993 / LV / M • Rough Draft / 1986 / VEN / M • Sacrificed To Love / 1986 / CDI / M • Saddletramp / 1988 / VD / M • Saturday Night Special / 1989 / DR / M • Savage Fury #2 / 1989 / CAY / M • The Savannah Affair / 1993 / CDI / M • Savannah Superstar / 1992 / VI / M • Savannah's Last Stand / 1993 / VI / M • Scandalous / 1989 / CC / M • Scared Stiff / 1984 / PV / M • The Scarlet Mistress / 1990 / VI / M • A Scent Of A Girl / 1993 / LV / M • Science Friction / 1986 / AXT / M • Scotty's X-Rated Adventure / 1996 / WP / M • Scream In The Middle Of The Night / 1990 / CC / M • Sea Of Lust / 1990 / FAN / M • Search For An Angel / 1988 / WV / M • The Search For Pink October / 1990 / EX / M • Secret Cravings / 1989 / V99 / M • Secrets / 1990 / CA / M • Seduction By Fire / 1987 / VD / M • Seduction Of Jennifer / 1986 / HO / M • Seeing Red / 1993 / VI / M • Seka's Fantasies / 1981 / CA / M • Servin' It Up / 1993 / VC / M • Sex Asylum #3 / 1988 / VI / M • Sex Boat / 1980 / VCX / M • Sex Crazy / 1989 / FAN / C • Sex For Hire / 1989 / HOE / C • Sex In The Great Outdoors / 1987 / SE / C • Sex Lives Of The Rich And Famous #1 / 1988 / VC / M • Sex Lives Of The Rich And Famous #2 / 1989 / VC / M • Sex Ranch / 1993 / VC / M • Sex Scenes / 1992 / VD / C • Sex Search / 1988 / IN / S • Sex Trek #2: The Search For Sperm / 1991 / ME / M • Sex Trek #3: The Wrath Of Bob / 1992 / ME / M • Sex Under Glass / 1992 / VC / M • Sex With A Stranger / 1986 / AVC / M • The Sexpert / 1975 / VEP / M • Sextectives / 1989 / CIN / M • Sexual Intent / 1990 / PP / M • The Sexual Limits / 1992 / VC / M • A Sexual Obsession / 1989 / PP / M • Sexual Relations / 1990 / PP / M • Sexy Delights #1 / 1986 / CLV / M • Sexy Nurses #2 / 1994 / CV / M • Shadows In The Dark / 1990 / 4P / M • Shameless Lady / 1993 / ME / M • Shattered / 1991 / LE / M •

Shaved Sinners #2 / 1987 / VT / M • She Comes Undone / 1987 / AIR / C • She's A Good Lust Charm / 1987 / LA / C • Shifting Gere / 1990 / VT / M • A Shot In The Mouth #2 / 1991 / ME / M • Showgirl #16: Samantha Fox's Fantasies / 1983 / VCR / M • Silver Elegance / 1992 / VT / M • Silver Seduction / 1992 / VT / M • Sinderella #1 / 1992 / VI / M • Sinderella #2 / 1992 / VI / M • Single Tight Female / 1992 / LV / M • Single White Woman / 1992 / FD / M • The Sins Of Angel Kelly / 1987 / FAN / C • Sittin' Pretty #2 / 1992 / DR / M • Skin Dive / 1988 / AVC / M • Skintight / 1981 / CA / M • Slave To Love / 1993 / ROB / M • Sleeping Beauty Aroused / 1989 / VI / M • Sleeping With Emily / 1991 / LE / M • Slipping It In / 1992 / FD / M • The Smart Aleck / 1990 / PM / M • The Smart Ass #2: Rusty's Revenge / 1990 / VT / M • The Smart Ass Vacation / 1990 / VT / M • Smooth And Easy / 1990 / XCV / M • Snatchbuckler / 1985 / DR / M • Sodom & Gomorrah / 1992 / OD / M • Sodomania #01: Tales Of Perversity / 1992 / EL / M • Sodomania #02: More Tails / 1992 / EL / M • Sodomania #05: Euro-American Style / 1993 / EL / M • Sodomania: The Baddest Of The Best...And Then Some / 1994 / EL / C • Soft Tail / 1991 / IN / M • Soft Warm Rain / 1987 / VD / M • Someone Else / 1992 / VC / M • Songbird / 1993 / AMP / M • Sophisticated Women / 1986 / BAN / M • Sounds Of Sex / 1985 / CA / M • Spanish Fly / 1992 / LE / M • Speedtrap / 1992 / VC / M • Spellbound / 1991 / CDI / M • Splash Shots / 1989 / CC / M • Squalor Motel / 1985 / SE / M • Squirt On The Hunt / 1989 / ERU / M • Stacked With Honors / 1993 / DR / M • Stake Out / 1991 / CIN / M • Star Spangled Banner / 1990 / FAZ / M • Steamy Windows / 1990 / VC / M • Sterling Silver / 1992 / CC / M • Sticky Lips / 1993 / EX / M • A Sticky Situation / 1987 / CA / M • Stiff Competition #2 / 1994 / CA / M • Strange Love / 1987 / WV / M • Strictly Business / 1987 / VD / M • Strippers Inc. #1 / 1994 / ONA / M • Strippers Inc. #2 / 1994 / ONA / M • Strippers Inc. #3 / 1994 / ONA / M • Stud Hunters / 1984 / CA / M • Studio Sex / 1990 / FH / M • Submission / 1994 / WP / M • Summer Games / 1992 / HW / M • Summer Lovers / 1987 / WET / M • Sunny / 1979 / VC / M • Superstar Sex Challenge #1 / 1994 / VC / M • Suze's Centerfolds #2 / 1980 / CA / M • Swedish Erotica #28 / 1980 / CA / M • Swedish Erotica Featurettes #2 / 1989 / CA / M • Sweet Chastity / 1990 / EVN / M • Sweet Cheeks / 1980 / VCX / M • Sweet Dreams / 1991 / VC / M • Sweethearts / 1986 / SE / C • Switch Hitters #1 / 1987 / IN / G • Taboo #07 / 1980 / IN / M • Taboo #08 / 1990 / IN / M • Taboo #16 / 1996 / CV / M • Taija's Tasty Treats / 1988 / EXP / C • Tailiens #2 / 1992 / FD / M • Tailiens #3 / 1992 / FD / M • Takin' It To The Limit #1 / 1994 / BS / M • Taking It To The Streets / 1987 / CDI / M • A Tale Of Two Titties #1 / 1990 / AR / M • Tales By Taylor / 1989 / AMB / M • Tales From The Zipper #1 / 1993 / ME / M • Tales Of The Uncensored / 1987 / FAN / M • Talk Dirty To Me #06 / 1989 / DR / M • Talk Dirty To Me #07 / 1990 / DR / M • Talk Dirty To Me #08 / 1990 / DR / M • The Taming Of Tami / 1990 / CA / M • A Taste Of Ariel / 1989 / PIN / C • A Taste Of Porsche

/ 1988 / PIN / C • A Taste Of Purple Passion / 1990 / CA / C • A Taste Of Stephanie / 1990 / PIN / C • A Taste Of Tami Monroe / 1990 / PIN / C • A Taste Of Tori Welles / 1990 / PIN / C • The Tasting / 1991 / EX / M • The Tattle Tail / 1993 / ME / M • The Tease / 1990 / VC / M • Temperatures Rising / 1986 / VT / M • Tenth Annual Adult Video News Awards / 1993 / VC / M • Teri Diver's Bedtime Tales / 1993 / FD / M • That Lucky Stiff / 1979 / QX / M • Those Lynn Girls / 1989 / WV / C • Three Men And A Barbi / 1989 / FAN / M • Tiffany Minx Wildcat / 1993 / MID / C • Tinsel Town / 1980 / VC / M • Titillation #1 / 1982 / SE / M • Titty Slickers #1 / 1991 / LE / M • To Lust In LA / 1986 / LA / M • Too Hot To Stop / 1989 / V99 / M • Too Hot To Touch #2 / 1993 / CV / M • Tools Of The Trade / 1990 / WV / M • Torrid Without A Cause #1 / 1989 / VI / M • Torrid Without A Cause #2 / 1990 / VI / M • Total Reball / 1990 / CC / M • A Touch Of Gold / 1990 / IN / M • A Touch Of Mink / 1990 / V99 / M • Tracey And The Bandit / 1987 / LA / M • Trampire / 1987 / FAN / M • Transparent Desires / 1991 / LV / M • Trick Tracey #1 / 1990 / CC / M • Trick Tracy #2: Tracy Loves Dick / 1990 / CC / M • Trouble / 1989 / VD / M • True Blue / 1989 / PM / M • True Confessions Of Hyapatia Lee / 1989 / VI / M • True Confessions Of Tori Welles / 1989 / VI / M • True Legends Of Adult Cinema: The Modern Era / 1992 / VC / C • True Sin / 1990 / PP / M • Truth Or Dare / 1993 / VI / M • Tug O' Love / 1990 / CC / M • Tunnel Of Love / 1986 / CLV / M • Two Times A Virgin / 1991 / AR / M • Ultra Head / 1992 / CA / M • The Unashamed / 1993 / FD / M • Unchain My Heart / 1990 / CC / M • Unchained Melanie / 1992 / VC / M • Undercover Lover / 1992 / CV / M • Uniform Behavior / 1989 / ZA / M • Uninhibited Love / 1994 / VPN / M • Up All Night / 1986 / CC / M • Up And Cummers #01 / 1993 / 4P / M • Up And Cummers #02 / 1993 / 4P / M • Up And Cummers #03 / 1993 / 4P / M • Up And Cummers #04 / 1993 / 4P / M • Up And Cummers #05 / 1993 / 4P / M • Up And Cummers #06 / 1993 / 4P / M • Up And Cummers #07 / 1993 / 4P / M • Up And Cummers #08 / 1993 / 4P / M • Up And Cummers #09 / 1994 / 4P / M • Up And Cummers #10 / 1994 / 4P / M • Up And Cummers #11 / 1994 / 4P / M • Up And Cummers #12 / 1994 / 4P / M • Up And Cummers #13 / 1994 / 4P / M • Up And Cummers #14 / 1994 / 4P / M • Up And Cummers #15 / 1994 / 4P / M • Up And Cummers #16 / 1994 / 4P / M • Up And Cummers #17 / 1994 / 4P / M • Up And Cummers #18 / 1994 / 4P / M • Up And Cummers #19 / 1994 / 4P / M • Up And Cummers #20 / 1995 / 4P / M • Up And Cummers #21 / 1995 / 4P / M • Up And Cummers #22 / 1995 / RWP / M • Up And Cummers #23 / 1995 / RWP / M • Up And Cummers #24 / 1995 / 4P / M • Up And Cummers #25 / 1995 / 4P / M • Up And Cummers #26 / 1995 / 4P / M • Up And Cummers #27 / 1996 / 4P / M • Up And Cummers #28 / 1996 / ERW / M • Up And Cummers #29 / 1996 / ERW / M • Up And Cummers #30 / 1996 / 4P / M • Up And Cummers #31 / 1996 / 4P / M • Up And Cummers #32 / 1996 / 4P / M • Up And Cummers #33 / 1996 / 4P / M • Up And Cummers #33 /

1996 / 4P / M • Up And Cummers #34 / 1996 / 4P / M • Up And Cummers #35 / 1996 / 4P / M • Up And Cummers #36 / 1996 / 4P / M • Up And Cummers #37 / 1996 / 4P / M • Up And Cummers #38 / 1996 / RWP / M • Up And Cummers #39 / 1996 / RWP / M • Up And Cummers: The Movie / 1994 / 4P / M • Use It Or Lose It / 1994 / CA / M • Used Cars / 1990 / CDI / M • Vampire's Kiss / 1993 / AVI / M • Vanity / 1992 / HO / M • VCA Previews #2 / 1988 / VC / C • Vegas #1: Royal Flush / 1990 / CIN / M • Vegas #3: Let It Ride / 1990 / CIN / M • Vegas #4: Joker's Wild / 1990 / CDI / M • Vegas #5: Blackjack / 1991 / CIN / M • Venus: Wings Of Seduction / 1991 / CDI / M • Video Virgins #03 / 1993 / NS / M • The Violation Of Tori Welles / 1990 / VD / C • The Vision / 1991 / LE / M • The Wacky World Of X-Rated Bloopers / 1989 / GO / M • Warm Pink / 1992 / LE / M • Warm To The Touch / 1990 / CDI / M • Weekend At Joey's / 1995 / ERA / M • Westside Tori / 1989 / ERO / M • Wet 'n' Bare With Barbara Dare / 1988 / NEO / C • Wet Dream On Maple Street / 1988 / FAN / M • Wet Fingers / 1990 / HIO / M • Wet Paint / 1990 / DR / M • What's Up Doc / 1988 / SEV / M • Whiplash / 1996 / DFI / M • White Trash, Black Splash / 1988 / WET / M • Who Framed Ginger Grant? / 1989 / CC / M • Who Reamed Rosie Rabbit? #1 / 1989 / FAN / M • Who Reamed Rosie Rabbit? #2 / 1989 / FAN / M • Whore House / 1995 / IPI / M • Why Gentlemen Prefer Blondes / 1983 / HO / C • Wicked Sensations #2 / 1989 / DR / M • Wicked Wenches / 1991 / LV / M • Wicked Wish / 1992 / LE / M • Wide World Of Sex / 1987 / CLV / C • Wild Dallas Honey / 1985 / VCX / M • Wild Flower #1 / 1992 / VI / M • Wild Flower #2 / 1992 / VI / M • Wild Goose Chase / 1990 / EA / M • Wild In The Woods / 1988 / VEX / M • The Wild Wild Chest #1 / 1990 / HO / M • The Wild Wild West / 1986 / SE / M • Willing Women / 1993 / VD / C • The Witching Hour / 1992 / FOR / M • Women In Uniform / 1986 / TEM / M • The Wong Side Of Town / 1992 / LV / M • Words Of Love / 1989 / LE / M • The World According To Ginger / 1985 / VI / M • WPINK-TV #4 / 1993 / PV / M • WPINK-TV #5 / 1993 / PV / M • Wrapped Up / 1992 / VD / C • X Dreams / 1989 / CA / M • The X-Team / 1984 / CV / M • XXX / 1996 / TEP / M • The Year Of The Sex Dragon / 1986 / PV / M • You Bet Your Buns / 1992 / ZA / M • Young And Innocent / 1987 / HO / M • The Young And The Wrestling #1 / 1988 / PL / M • The Young And The Wrestling #2 / 1989 / PL / M • [European Invasion / cr93 / A&E / M

RANDY WHITE
Married Men With Men On The Side / 1996 / BHE / G

RANDY WOODS
Swing Club / 1975 / VC / M

RANIER ABERNOTH *see Star Index I*

RAOUL DISSART *see Star Index I*

RAPHAEL *see Star Index I*

RAPHAELLA
Euro-Max #4: / 1995 / SC / M • Rump Man: Goes To Cannes / 1995 / HW / M • World Sex Tour #2 / 1995 / ANA / M

RAPPALO *(Rappolo)*
Fifties looking rocker male with a ducktail hairstyle.

Bi 'n' Sell / 1990 / VC / G • Bi Cycling / 1989 / FC / G • Bi-Swingers / 1991 / PL / G • Jewel Of The Orient / 1991 / VEX / M • Live Bi-Me / 1990 / PL / G • Party Doll / 1990 / VC / M

RAPPOLO *see* **Rappalo**

RAQUEL
A&B AB#553: Girlfriends—Raquel And Her Girlfriends / 1995 / A&B / F • A&B AB#554: Gang Bang Raquel / 1995 / A&B / M • A&B AB#555: Gang Bang #2 / 1995 / A&B / M • Creme De La Face #17: Semen For Seven / 1996 / OD / M • Match #3: Battling Babes / 1995 / NPA / B • Match #4: Hellcats / 1995 / NPA / B • Mike Hott: #390 / 1996 / MHV / M • Skintight / 1991 / VER / F

RAQUEL (L.MELENDEZ) *see* Lisa Melendez

RAQUEL BLACKWELL *see Star Index I*

RAQUEL CHAN
Erotic Dimensions #1: Ripe / 1982 / NSV / M • Erotic Dimensions: Explicit / 1982 / NSV / M • Erotic Dimensions: The Wild Life / 1982 / NSV / M

RAQUEL DARIAN *see* **Racquel Darrian**

RAQUEL GOLD *see* **Paula Price**

RAQUEL JENKINS
The Ebony Connection #1 / 1994 / LBO / C

RAQUEL LACE
Addicted To Lust / 1996 / NIT / M • Anal Anarchy / 1995 / VC / M • Anal Camera #14 / 1996 / EVN / M • Anal Maidens Three / 1996 / BOT / M • Anal Party Girls / 1996 / GV / M • Backdoor Imports / 1995 / LV / M • Behind The Scenes / 1996 / GO / M • Bel Air Babes / 1996 / SUF / M • Booty And The Ho' Fish / 1996 / RAS / M • Bootylicious: It's A Bootyful Thing / 1996 / JMP / M • Breastman's Hot Legs Contest / 1996 / ... / M • The Cable Girl / 1996 / NIT / M • Cherry Poppers #12: Playing Nookie / 1995 / ZA / M • Dirty Dirty Debutantes #1 / 1995 / 4P / M • Dirty Minds / 1996 / NIT / M • Domina #5: Whipper Snapper / 1996 / LBO / B • Domina #7 / 1996 / LBO / B • Every Woman Wants A Penis #2 / 1996 / MID / M • Gutter Mouths / 1996 / JMP / M • The Hardwood Chronicles / 1995 / XCI / M • Heavy Breathing / 1996 / NIT / M • Here Comes Magoof #2 / 1995 / VC / M • Hollywood Amateurs #31 / 1996 / MID / M • Hungry Humpers / 1996 / SP / M • In The Fast Lane / 1995 / LE / M • Interview's Backdoor To The Orient / 1996 / LV / M • Interview: Backdoor Imports / 1996 / LV / M • Interviews At The Hard Wok Cafe / 1996 / LOF / M • Jizz Glazed Goo Guzzlers #2 / 1996 / NIT / C • Leather / 1996 / LE / M • Loose Jeans / 1996 / GO / M • Miss Nude International / 1996 / LE / M • Mister Stickypants / 1996 / LV / M • Motel Matches / 1996 / LE / M • Nudist Colony Vacation / 1996 / NIT / M • Over Eighteen #02 / 1997 / HW / M • Perverted Stories #03 / 1995 / JMP / M • Perverted Stories #04 / 1995 / JMP / M • Perverted Stories #08 / 1996 / JMP / M • Philmore Butts On The Prowl / 1995 / SUF / M • Planet X #1 / 1996 / HW / M • Pretty Anal Ladies / 1996 / ANE / M • Prime Choice #4 / 1995 / RAS / M • Puritan Video Magazine #03 / 1996 / LE / M • Red Hots / 1996 / PL / M • Rumpman's Backdoor Sailing / 1996 / HW / M • Salsa & Spice #3 / 1996 / TTV / M • Salsa & Spice #4 / 1996 / TTV / M • The Seductive Secretary / 1995 / GO / M • Sex Drives Of The

Rich And Famous / 1996 / ERA / M • Sodom Bottoms / 1996 / SP / M • Stuff Your Ass #3 / 1996 / JMP / M • Summer Dreams / 1996 / TEP / M • Underground #1 / 1996 / SC / M • Up And Cummers #24 / 1995 / 4P / M • The Violation Of Juliette / 1996 / JMP / F • The Violation Of Missy / 1996 / JMP / F • The Violation Of Paisley Hunter / 1996 / JMP / F • Virgin Killers: Second Rampage / 1995 / PEP / M • Yin Yang Oriental Love Bang #1 / 1996 / SUF / M • Yin Yang Oriental Love Bang #2 / 1996 / SUF / M • Yin Yang Oriental Love Bang #5: Lotus Blossoms / 1996 / SUF / M • Young And Anal #2 / 1995 / JMP / M • Young And Anal #4 / 1996 / JMP / M

RAQUEL MARTINE *see Star Index I*

RAQUEL MONET *see Star Index I*

RAQUEL RIOS *see* **Keisha**

RAS KEAN *(Ras King)*
Ras King is from **The Opening Of Misty Beethoven.**
The Affairs Of Janice / 1975 / ALP / M • Candy Lips / 1975 / CXV / M • Expose Me, Lovely / 1976 / QX / M • Feelings / 1977 / VC / M • Gums / 1976 / AVC / M • Only The Very Best On Film / 1992 / VC / C • The Opening Of Misty Beethoven / 1976 / VC / M • Pornocopia Sensual / 1976 / VHL / M • Sweet Cakes / 1976 / VC / M

RAS KING *see* **Ras Kean**

RASHA ROMANA *see* **Russia**

RASHNEEN KERIM-KORAM
Private Film #10 / 1994 / OD / M • Private Video Magazine #10 / 1994 / OD / M

RASTA
8-Ball: Westside Gang Bang / 1995 / PL / M • Black Ass Masters #1 / 1995 / GLI / M • Black Ass Masters #2 / 1995 / GLI / M • Black Ass Masters #3 / 1995 / GLI / M • Black Gangbangers #05 / 1995 / HW / M • Black Gangbangers #10 / 1996 / HW / M • Black Hollywood Amateurs #05 / 1995 / MID / M • Black Hollywood Amateurs #09 / 1995 / MID / M • Blonde Temptation / 1995 / IF / M • Bootylicious: Baby Got Booty / 1996 / JMP / M • Bootylicious: White Trash / 1995 / JMP / M • Ebony Erotica #31: Creme De Cocoa / 1995 / GO / M • Gangbang Girl #15 / 1995 / ANA / M • Gangbang Girl #16 / 1995 / ANA / M • Hard Core Beginners #07 / 1995 / LEI / M • Interracial Escorts / 1995 / GO / M • Nasty Newcummers: Black Edition / 1995 / MET / M • Opie Goes To South Central / 1995 / PP / M • Sex 4 Life / 1995 / XPR / M • Sleazy Streets / 1995 / PEP / M • Sticky Fingers / 1996 / WV / M • Tailz From Da Hood #2 / 1995 / AVI / M • Up The Ying Yang #2 / 1995 / CC / M • Wet Mask / 1995 / SC / M

RAUL
Buttman's Big Butt Backdoor Babes / 1995 / EA / M

RAUL FONGOOL
The Stand-Up / 1994 / VC / M

RAVAN RICHARDS *see* **Raven Richards**

RAVEN *(Niki Dickers, Vicki Vickers, Raven St James, Vicky Vickers, Nellie Marie Vickers, Rachel Vickers)*
Black hair, striking passable face, small tits later enhanced to rock-solid cantaloupes, lithe body.
Adult Video News 1991 Awards / 1991 / VC / M • All That Glitters / 1992 / LV / M • Amateur Lesbians #11: Rusty / 1991 / GO / F • Anal Encounters #1 / 1991 / VC / M • Anal

Island / 1992 / LV / M • Angel Eyes / 1991 / ... / S • Back Seat Bush / 1992 / LV / M • Bad Side Of Town / 1993 / AFD / M • The Bedford Wives / 1994 / LON / B • Big Game / 1990 / LV / M • Black Obsession / 1991 / ZA / M • Blue Views / 1990 / CDI / M • Bonfire Of The Panties / 1990 / CC / M • Breast Friends / 1991 / PL / M • The Breast Things In Life Are Free / 1991 / LV / M • Breast Worx #16 / 1991 / LBO / M • Breezy / 1985 / VCR / M • Catalina Five-O: White Coral, Blue Death / 1990 / CIN / M • Catalina: Sabotage / 1991 / CDI / M • Catalina: Tiger Shark / 1991 / CDI / M • Catalina: Treasure Island / 1991 / CDI / M • Catalina: Undercover / 1991 / CIN / M • City Of Sin / 1991 / LV / M • Crude / 1991 / IN / M • Curse Of The Catwoman / 1990 / VC / M • Debbie Does Wall Street / 1991 / VC / M • Decadent / 1991 / WV / M • Deep Inside Racquel Darrian / 1994 / VC / C • Digital Lust / 1990 / SE / M • Drainman / 1989 / BIZ / B • Dyke Bar / 1991 / PL / F • Eternity / 1991 / CDI / M • Eyewitness Nudes / 1990 / VC / M • Flash Floods / 1991 / PRE / C • Forbidden Desires / 1991 / CIN / F • Gettin' Wet / 1990 / VC / M • Ginger's Hawaiian Scrapbook / 1988 / GO / C • Girls On Fire / 1985 / VCX / M • Gourmet Premier: Lust X 4 / Raven's Rendezvous #901 / cr85 / GO / M • Hard Core Cafe / 1991 / PL / M • Hard Core Cafe Revisited / 1991 / PL / M • Haunted Passions / 1990 / FC / M • Heartthrobs / 1985 / CA / M • High Price Spread / 1986 / PV / C • Hot Pink / 1985 / VCR / F • Hot Shorts: Ginger Lynn / 1986 / VCR / C • Hot Shorts: Raven / 1986 / VCR / C • House Of Dreams / 1990 / CA / M • I Do #2 / 1990 / VI / M • Ice Cream #3: Naked Eyes / 1984 / VC / M • Images Of Desire / 1990 / PM / M • Imagine / 1991 / LV / M • Jailhouse Girls / 1984 / VC / M • Joys Of Erotica / 1984 / VCR / C • Joys Of Erotica #107 / 1984 / VCR / C • Joys Of Erotica #109 / 1984 / VCR / C • Joys Of Erotica #110 / 1984 / VCR / C • Joys Of Erotica #114 / 1984 / VCR / C • Kinky Business #1 / 1984 / DR / M • L.A.D.P. / 1991 / PL / M • Legend #3 / 1991 / LE / M • Legs And Lingerie #1 / 1990 / BIZ / F • Les Femmes Erotiques / 1993 / BFP / M • Lesbian Pros And Amateurs #07 / 1992 / GO / F • Lethal Passion / 1991 / PL / M • Lick My Lips / 1990 / LV / M • Lies Of Passion / 1992 / LV / M • Limited Edition #26 / 1984 / AVC / M • A Little Irresistible / 1991 / ZA / M • Lonely Lady / 1984 / VC / M • Loose Lips / 1990 / VC / M • Lucky Break / 1991 / SE / M • Lust And The Law / 1991 / GO / C • Madame X / 1990 / EX / M • Maid For Service / 1990 / LV / M • Mamm's The Word / 1991 / ZA / M • Married Women / 1990 / PP / M • Melts In Your Mouth / 1984 / ROY / M • More Dirty Debutantes #04 / 1990 / 4P / M • Mummy Dearest #2: The Unwrapping / 1990 / LV / M • Mummy Dearest #3: The Parting / 1991 / LV / M • No Men 4 Miles / 1992 / LV / F • On Stage And In Color / 1991 / VIP / M • On The Loose / 1991 / LV / M • Oriental Jade / 1985 / VC / M • A Paler Shade Of Blue / 1991 / CC / M • Panty Raid / 1984 / GO / M • Party Doll A Go-Go #1 / 1991 / VC / M • Party Doll A Go-Go #2 / 1991 / VC / M • Passionate Partners: The Guide For Daring Lovers / 1993 / PHV / S • Penthouse: The Girls Of Penthouse #1 / 1984 / VES /

S • Penthouse: Love Stories / 1986 / A*V / S • Photoflesh / 1984 / HO / M • The Pink Lagoon: A Sex Romp In Paradise / 1984 / GO / M • Pleasure Productions #06 / 1984 / VCR / M • Pleasure Productions #07 / 1984 / VCR / M • Pleasure Productions #12 / 1985 / VCR / M • Possession / 1990 / CIN / M • Precious Peaks / 1990 / ZA / M • Pretty As You Feel / 1984 / PV / M • Private Love Affairs / 1985 / VCR / C • The Pump / 1991 / CC / M • Purely Sexual / 1991 / HO / M • Radio K-KUM / 1984 / HO / M • Rainbows / 1992 / VT / F • Raunch #01 / 1990 / CC / M • Raven / 1985 / VCR / M • The Rookies / 1991 / VC / M • Sappho Sextet / 1983 / LIP / F • The Secret Dungeon / 1993 / HOM / B • Sensual Exposure / 1993 / ULI / M • Sensuous / 1991 / LV / M • Sex Liners / 1991 / CIN / M • Sexual Healing / 1992 / LV / M • Sexual Intent / 1990 / PP / M • Shattered / 1991 / LE / M • Sizzle / 1990 / PP / M • Sky Pies / 1985 / GO / M • Slumber Party / 1984 / HO / M • So Fine / 1992 / VT / C • Some Like It Big / 1991 / LE / M • Speedtrap / 1992 / VC / M • Splashing / 1986 / VCS / C • Stake Out / 1991 / CIN / M • Summer Break / 1991 / PP / C • Supergirls Do General Hospital / 1984 / VC / M • Supergirls Do The Navy / 1984 / VC / M • Surfside Sex #1 / 1991 / LV / F • Swinging Shift / 1985 / CDI / M • Taboo #09 / 1991 / IN / M • Taboo American Style #1: The Ruthless Beginning / 1985 / VC / M • Taboo American Style #2: The Story Continues / 1985 / VC / M • Taboo American Style #3: Nina Becomes An Actress / 1985 / VC / M • Taboo American Style #4: Exciting Conclusion / 1985 / VC / M • Teacher's Pets / 1985 / AVC / M • Teasers / 1984 / HO / M • Temptation Eyes / 1991 / VT / M • Too Naughty To Say No / 1984 / CA / M • Total Reball / 1990 / CC / M • Tracie Lords / 1984 / CIT / M • Triplets / 1985 / VCR / M • Used Cars / 1990 / CDI / M • Vegas #4: Joker's Wild / 1990 / CDI / M • Vegas #5: Blackjack / 1991 / CIN / M • Warm To The Touch / 1990 / CDI / M • Where The Girls Are / 1984 / VEX / M • Wild Attraction / 1992 / ... / S • With Love From Ginger / 1986 / HO / C • Women Of Color / 1991 / PL / F • [Centerfolds & Covergirls #1 / 19?? / ... / M • [Masquerade (1992-Italy) / 1992 / ... / S

RAVEN (OTHER)
Borderline / 1996 / GOT / B • Ginger Lynn Allen's Lingerie Gallery #1 / 1994 / UNI / F • Hard Core Beginners #08 / 1995 / LEI / M • HomeGrown Video #466: Loot The Booty / 1996 / HOV / M • Interracial Affairs / 1996 / FC / M • Joe Elliot's College Girls #47 / 1996 / JOE / F • Limited Edition #17 / 1980 / AVC / M • Northwest Pecker Trek #5: Cumming In King County / 1995 / LBO / M • Pearl Necklace: Facial #01 / 1994 / SEE / C • Raven (Anal Gang Bang Series) / 1993 / FH / M • Submission (Knight) / 1994 / KNF / B • Toe Tales #32 / 1996 / GOT / B • Toe Tales #33 / 1996 / GOT / B • Toe Tales #35 / 1996 / GOT / B • Toe Tales #39 / 1996 / GOT / B

RAVEN (T.TAYLOR) see Tianna Taylor
RAVEN ALEXANDER
American Garter / 1993 / VC / M • Anthony's Desire / 1993 / ... / S • Love Scenes #2 / 1992 / B/F / S • Witchcraft #5: Dance With The Devil / 1992 / AE / S

RAVEN BATES see Cassandra Dark
RAVEN BLACK
Casting Call (Venus 99) / 1993 / V99 / M • Club DV8 #2 / 1993 / SC / M • Hermaphrodites / 1996 / REB / C • Suburban Swingers / 1993 / IF / M • Top Heavy / 1993 / IF / M • Udderly Fantastic / 1993 / IF / M • Wet, Wild And Willing / 1993 / V99 / M

RAVEN DELACROIX
40 Plus / 1987 / MFM / M • Best Chest In The West / 1984 / ACV / S • Between My Breasts #05 / 1988 / BTO / S • Big Bust Vixens / 1984 / BTO / S • Boss Lady / 1988 / NAP / B • Competition For A Man / 1988 / NAP / B • Competition For A Part / 1988 / NAP / B • Detective Framed / 1988 / NAP / B • The Lost Empire / 1983 / LIV / S • Up! / 1976 / RMV / S

RAVEN MCCALL
Anal Crybabies / 1996 / BAC / M • Anal Sex / 1996 / ZA / M • Club Deb #4 / 1996 / MET / M • Cum TV / 1996 / NIT / M • Deep Throat Girls #15 / 1995 / GO / M • From The Heart / 1996 / XCI / M • Hardcore Debutantes #01 / 1996 / TEP / M • Legs / 1996 / ZA / M • Lesbian Pooper Sluts / 1996 / ROB / F • Male Order Brides / 1996 / RAS / M • Malibu Butt Sluts / 1996 / ROB / F • Nudist Colony Vacation / 1996 / NIT / M • Profiles #10: / 1997 / XPR / M • Rollover / 1996 / NIT / M • Sexual Atrocities / 1996 / EL / M • Shaving Grace / 1996 / GO / M • Sodomania #20: For Members Only / 1997 / EL / M • This Girl Is Freaky / 1996 / NIT / M • Wild Widow / 1996 / NIT / M

RAVEN RICHARDS (Ravan Richards, Raven Wells)
4F Dating Service / 1989 / AR / M • Acts Of Confession / 1991 / PP / M • Adult Video News 1992 Awards / 1992 / VC / M • Anal Addiction #1 / 1990 / SO / M • Anal Alley / 1990 / ME / M • Angelica / 1989 / ARG / M • Bat Bitch #2 / 1990 / FAZ / M • Bazooka County #2 / 1989 / CC / M • Beeches / 1990 / KIS / M • Best Of Caught From Behind #5 / 1991 / HO / C • Beyond Innocence / 1990 / VCR / F • The Big E #09 / 1990 / BIZ / B • Black Cobra / 1989 / WV / M • Black Mail / 1990 / TAO / C • Bloopers #2 / 1991 / GO / C • Blows Job / 1989 / BIZ / B • Boobs, Butts And Bloopers #1 / 1990 / HO / M • Boobs, Butts And Bloopers #2 / 1990 / HO / M • Breast Side Story / 1990 / LE / M • Breast Worx #40 / 1992 / LBO / M • Bruce Seven: A Compendium Of His Most Graphic Scenes Vol 1 / 1991 / BS / C • Burn / 1991 / LE / M • The Butt Stops Here / 1991 / LV / M • The Buttnicks #1 / 1990 / VEX / M • The Case Of The Cockney Cupcake / 1989 / ME / M • Cat On A Hot Sin Roof / 1989 / LV / M • Catalina: Treasure Island / 1991 / CDI / M • Caught From Behind #11 / 1989 / HO / M • Caught From Behind #12 / 1989 / HO / M • Caught From Behind #13 / 1990 / HO / M • Caught From Behind #15 / 1991 / HO / M • Cheaters / 1990 / LE / M • Cherry Red / 1993 / RB / B • Club Lez / 1990 / PL / F • Controlled / 1990 / BS / B • D-Cup Dating Service / 1991 / ME / M • Diamond In The Rough / 1989 / EX / M • Dominating Girlfriends #2 / 1992 / PL / B • Easy Lover / 1989 / EX / M • Easy Way Out / 1989 / OD / M • Entertainment L.A. Style / 1990 / HO / M • Farmer's Daughter / 1989 / FAZ / M • The Finer Things In Life / 1990 / PL / F •

Girl Crazy / 1989 / CDI • Girls Gone Bad #1 / 1990 / GO / F • Girls Gone Bad #2: The Breakout / 1990 / GO / F • Girls Gone Bad #3: Back To The Slammer / 1991 / GO / F • Girls Gone Bad #4: Cell Block Riot / 1991 / GO / F • Godmother / 1991 / AWV / F • Graduation Ball / 1989 / CAE / M • Hard Sell / 1990 / VC / M • Heather's Secrets / 1990 / VEX / M • Hershe Highway #4 / 1991 / HO / M • Hidden Desire / 1989 / HO / M • Hocus Poke-Us / 1991 / HO / M • Hot Sweet 'n' Sticky / 1992 / CA / C • I Want To Be Nasty / 1991 / XCV / M • It's Your Move / 1990 / TAO / B • Itty Bitty Titty Committee #1 / 1990 / PL / F • Joint Effort / 1992 / SEX / C • Juggernaut / 1990 / EX / M • The Kitty Kat Club / 1990 / PL / F • A Lacy Affair #4 / 1991 / HO / F • Laid In Heaven / 1991 / VC / M • Legal Tender (1990-X) / 1990 / VC / M • Lesbian Lingerie Fantasy #2 / 1989 / ESP / F • Lesbian Lingerie Fantasy #3 / 1989 / ESP / F • Letters From The Heart / 1991 / AWV / M • Lickety Pink / 1990 / ME / M • A Little Nookie / 1991 / VD / M • Lost Lovers / 1990 / VEX / M • Maiden Heaven #2 / 1992 / MID / F • Making The Grade / 1989 / IN / M • Midnight Fire / 1990 / HU / M • Moondance / 1991 / WV / M • Moonglow / 1989 / IN / M • My Sensual Body / 1989 / WET / M • Night On The Town / 1990 / V99 / M • Nightdreams #2 / 1990 / VC / M • Office Manners And Double Punishment / 1992 / TAO / B • Parliament: Lesbian Seduction #1 / 1990 / PM / F • Parliament: Lesbian Seduction #2 / 1990 / PM / C • Peeping Passions / 1989 / CAE / M • Pleasure Is My Business / 1989 / EX / M • Pool Party / 1991 / CIN / M • Raven Richards Star Bound / 1990 / BON / B • Raw Sewage / 1989 / FC / M • Rear View / 1989 / LE / M • Rearing Rachel / 1990 / ZA / M • Rene Summers Star Bound / 1990 / BON / B • Rituals / 1989 / V99 / M • The Rookies / 1991 / VC / M • Saki's House Party / 1990 / KNI / M • Say Something Nasty / 1989 / CC / M • Sex Liners / 1991 / CIN / M • A Shot In The Mouth #1 / 1990 / ME / M • Single Girl Masturbation #3 / 1989 / ESP / F • Sleeping With Emily / 1991 / LE / M • Sole-Ohs / 1989 / BIZ / F • Sweet Chastity / 1990 / EVN / M • Sweet Seduction / 1990 / LV / M • Tail Of The Scorpion / 1990 / ELP / M • Tailgate Party / 1990 / HO / M • Tell Me What To Do / 1991 / CA / M • Things That Go Hump in the Night / 1991 / LV / M • This Bun's For You / 1989 / FAN / M • This Year's Blonde / 1990 / LE / M • Titillation #2 / 1990 / SE / M • Undressed For Success / 1990 / V99 / M • Vixens / 1989 / LV / F • Welcome To The House Of Fur Pi / 1989 / GO / M • Wet 'n' Working / 1990 / EA / F • When Larry Ate Sally / 1989 / EX / M • The Whore / 1989 / CA / M • Why Do You Want To be In An Adult Video / 1990 / PM / F • Wicked Thoughts / 1991 / AFV / M • The Wild One / 1990 / LE / M • X Factor: The Next Generation / 1991 / HO / M • X-Rated Bloopers #2 / 1986 / AR / M • X-TV / 1992 / CA / C • Young Cheeks / 1990 / BEB / B

RAVEN ST JAMES *see* **Raven**

RAVEN TEAL
Cham Pain / 1991 / DCV / B • Cry Hard / 1990 / DOM / B • White Slavery / 1991 / DCV / B

RAVEN TOUCHSTONE *(Penny Antine)*
Photographer and sometimes scriptwriter.

RAVEN TURNER
Blue Vanities #589 / 1996 / FFL / M • Flash / 1980 / CA / M • Hot Dallas Nights / 1981 / VCX / M • Nothing To Hide #1 / 1981 / CV / M

RAVEN WELLS *see* **Raven Richards**
RAVENESS *see* **Rayveness**
RAVIN
Chocolate Silk: Ravin / 1995 / CHS / F • Maid For Bondage / 1993 / LBO / B

RAVON
Toe Tales #36 / 1996 / GOT / B • Toe Tales #37 / 1996 / GOT / B

RAY
AVP #5002: Naive And Naughty / 1990 / AVP / M • AVP #7018: Special Services / 1990 / AVP / M • Big Bust Babes #12 / 1993 / AFI / M • Big Bust Babes #15 / 1993 / AFI / M • Blue Vanities #538 / 1993 / FFL / M • Homegrown Video #418: Looks As Good As It Feels / 1994 / HOV / M • Intimate Interviews #2 / 1996 / NIT / M • Lovers, An Intimate Portrait #1: Sydney & Ray / 1993 / FEM / M • Streets Of New York #06 / 1996 / PL / M

RAY AGE
Shake Your Booty / 1996 / EVN / M

RAY ALDO
Pai Gow Video #06: New Wave Orientals / 1994 / EVN / M

RAY AUSTIN *see* **Star Index I**
RAY BAN *see* **Star Index I**
RAY BRADBURY
Flesh...And The Fantasies / 1991 / BIZ / B

RAY CARTER *see* **Star Index I**
RAY COOPER *see* **Ray Welles**
RAY DAVIES
The Family Jewels / cr76 / GO / M

RAY DAVIS *see* **Star Index I**
RAY DENNIS STECKLER *(Sven Christian)*
Late sixties/early seventies director who also made some explicit.
[Body Fever / 1969 / ... / S

RAY GUERRA
Mai Lin Vs Serena / 1982 / HIF / M • Tropic Of Desire / 1979 / WWV / M

RAY HARDIN *(Raymond Dandee)*
Blonde Desire / 1984 / AIR / M • California Fever / 1987 / CV / M • Chuck & Di In Heat / 1986 / DR / M • Daddy's Girls / 1985 / LA / M • Dirty Tricks / 1986 / 4P / M • GVC: The Therapist #101 / 1986 / GO / M • Heavy Breathing / 1986 / CV / M • Hollywood Pink / 1985 / HO / M • Irresistible #2 / 1986 / SE / M • Lady Cassanova / 1985 / AVC / M • Let Me Tell Ya 'Bout Black Chicks / 1985 / VC / M • Lust In America / 1985 / VCX / M • Lusty Ladies #05 / 1983 / 4P / M • Lusty Ladies #11 / 1984 / 4P / M • Midnight Lady / 1985 / AA / C • Porn Star's Day Off / 1990 / FAZ / M • Pulsating Flesh / 1986 / VC / M • The Pussywillows / 1985 / SUV / M • Ramb-Ohh #1 / 1986 / PV / M • The Red Garter / 1986 / SE / M • Sex Star Competition / 1985 / PL / M • Sexpertease / 1985 / VD / M • Sheets Of San Francisco / 1986 / AVC / M • Slippery When Wet / 1986 / PL / M • Spies / 1986 / PL / M • Tailenders / 1985 / WET / M • To Live & Shave In LA / 1986 / WET / M • The Trouble With Traci / 1984 / CHA / C • Up & In / 1985 / AA / M

RAY HARDON *see* **Ray Welles**
RAY HOLLIDAY
Gangbang Girl #14 / 1994 / ANA / M

RAY HORSCH

N.Y. Video Magazine #06 / 1995 / OUP / M • Streets Of New York #07 / 1996 / PL / M • Streets Of New York #08 / 1996 / PL / M

RAY JEFFRIES
Midnight Desires / 1976 / VXP / M

RAY LOVE
Big Top Cabaret #2 / 1989 / BTO / M • Easy Access / 1988 / ZA / M • Kiss Thy Mistress' Feet #1 / 1990 / BIZ / B • Scent Of A Wild Woman / 1993 / EVN / C • Tales Of The Golden Pussy / 1989 / RUM / M • This Dick For Hire / 1989 / ZA / M • Toe Tales #07 / 1993 / GOT / B • Twisted Sisters / 1988 / ZA / M

RAY MICHAELS
The Best Little Whorehouse In Hong Kong / 1987 / SE / M • Bootsie / 1984 / CC / M • Crazy With The Heat #1 / 1986 / CV / M • Hot Property / 1989 / EXH / C • Matinee Idol / 1984 / VC / M

RAY ORBITSIN *see* **Star Index I**
RAY OROZCO *see* **Star Index I**
RAY OWENS *see* **Star Index I**
RAY PREVET *see* **Star Index I**
RAY PRICE *see* **Star Index I**
RAY RANDALL *see* **Radio Ray Wells**
RAY SWAZE
Dirty Dirty Debutantes #8 / 1996 / 4P / M • Ethnic Cheerleader Search #1 / 1996 / WIC / M • Fame Is A Whore On Butt Row / 1996 / ABS / M • Hollywood Amateurs #18 / 1995 / MID / M • I Wanna Be A Porn Star #1 / 1996 / 4P / M • I Wanna Be A Porn Star #2 / 1996 / 4P / M • More Dirty Debutantes #52 / 1996 / 4P / M • More Dirty Debutantes #54 / 1996 / 4P / M • More Dirty Debutantes #62 / 1997 / SBV / M • Up And Cummers #36 / 1996 / 4P / M

RAY VAN *see* **Ray Victory**
RAY VICTOR *see* **Ray Victory**
RAY VICTORY *(Imperial Sugar, Ray Victor, Ray Van, Cole Fury, Ray Visor)*
Cole Fury is from **Cheeks #1**. Born in 1960 according to **Bloopers #2**. Got married to Jean Afrique and as of 1992 lives in Europe doing live sex shows.
After The Lights Go Out / 1989 / VEX / M • Alice In Blackland / 1988 / VC / M • All For One / 1988 / CIN / M • Anal Angels #1 / 1986 / VEX / M • Anal Attraction #2 / 1993 / AFV / C • Anal Intruder #02 / 1988 / CC / M • Angel Of The Island / 1988 / IN / M • Angel Rising / 1988 / IN / M • As Nasty As She Wants To Be / 1990 / IN / M • Assinine / 1990 / CC / M • Back To Black #1 / 1988 / VEX / M • Backdoor Black #1 / 1992 / WV / C • Backdoor Brides #3 / 1988 / PV / M • Backdoor To Hollywood #12 / 1990 / CIN / M • Backing In #2 / 1990 / WV / C • Backing In #3 / 1991 / WV / C • Bad Mama Jama Busts Out / 1989 / VT / M • Banana Splits / 1987 / 3HV / M • Barbii Unleashed / 1988 / 4P / M • The Battle Of The Breast Queens / 1989 / INS / C • Beauty And The Beast #2 / 1990 / VC / M • Beefeaters / 1989 / PV / M • Behind The Black Door / 1987 / VEX / M • The Best Of Andrew Blake / 1993 / CA / C • Bet Black / 1989 / CDI / M • Big Black Dicks / 1993 / GO / C • Big Bust Babes #04 / 1988 / AFI / M • Black & Gold / 1990 / CIN / M • Black 'n' Blew / 1988 / VC / M • The Black Anal-ist #1 / 1988 / VEX / M • Black Beauty (Ebony & Ivory) / 1989 / E&I / M • Black Chicks In Heat / 1988 / VC / M • Black Cobra / 1989 / WV / M • Black Dreams / 1988 / CDI / M • Black Fox / 1988

/ CC / M • Black Heat / 1986 / VC / M • Black In The Saddle / 1990 / ZA / M • Black Rage / 1988 / ZA / M • Black Sensations / 1987 / VEX / M • Black Studies / 1992 / GO / M • Black To Africa / 1987 / PL / C • Black With Sugar / 1989 / CIN / M • Black, White And Blue / 1989 / E&I / M • Blackballed / 1994 / VI / C • Blackman / 1989 / PL / M • Blackman & Anal Woman #1 / 1990 / PL / M • Blackman & Anal Woman #2 / 1990 / PL / M • Blacks & Blondes #58 / 1989 / WV / M • Blacks & Blondes: The Movie / 1989 / WV / M • Blind Date / 1989 / E&I / M • Bloopers #2 / 1991 / GO / C • Blow Job Babes / 1988 / BEV / C • The Bod Squad / 1989 / VT / M • Buns And Roses (V9) / 1990 / V99 / M • The Catwoman / 1988 / VC / M • The Chameleon / 1989 / VC / M • Charlie's Girls #1 / 1988 / CC / M • Charlie's Girls #2 / 1989 / CC / M • Cheeks #1 / 1988 / CC / M • Cheeks #2: The Bitter End / 1989 / CC / M • Cherry Cheerleaders / 1987 / VEX / M • Chocolate Cherries #2 / 1990 / CC / M • Chocolate Dreams (Venus 99) / 1987 / V99 / M • Coming In America / 1988 / VEX / M • Dangerous / 1989 / PV / M • Debbie Does Dallas #4 / 1988 / VEX / M • Debbie Does Dallas #5 / 1988 / VEX / M • Deep In The Bush / 1990 / KIS / M • Deep Undercover / 1989 / PV / M • Diamond For Sale / 1990 / EVN / M • Diedre In Danger / 1990 / VI / M • Dirty Dr. Feelgood / 1988 / VEX / M • Double Black Fantasy / 1987 / CC / C • Dr F #2: Bad Medicine / 1990 / WV / M • The Dragon Lady #1 / 1988 / WV / C • Dreams / 1987 / AR / M • Dreams In The Forbidden Zone / 1989 / PCP / M • Drink Of Love / 1990 / V99 / M • Driving Miss Daisy Crazy #1 / 1990 / WV / M • Easy Way Out / 1989 / OD / M • The Ebony Garden / 1988 / ZA / M • Ebony Humpers #1 / 1986 / VEX / M • Ebony Humpers #3 / 1987 / VEX / M • Ebony Humpers #4 / 1988 / VEX / M • Erotic Games / 1992 / PL / M • Executive Suites / 1990 / VEX / M • Eye Of The Tigress / 1988 / VD / M • Fade To Black / 1988 / CDI / M • Find Your Love / 1988 / CV / M • Fireball / 1988 / IN / M • Flesh For Frankenstein / 1987 / VEX / M • For Her Pleasure Only / 1989 / FAZ / M • Frat Brats / 1990 / VC / M • From Kascha With Love / 1988 / CDI / M • From Rags To Riches / 1988 / CDI / M • Full Metal Bikini / 1988 / PEN / M • Future Lust / 1989 / ME / M • Ginger Lynn—Non-Stop / 1988 / VD / C • A Girl Named Sam / 1988 / CC / M • The Girls Of Ball Street / 1988 / VEX / M • The Girls Of Cooze / 1992 / V99 / C • The Godmother #1 / 1987 / VC / M • The Godmother #2 / 1988 / VC / M • Good Morning Saigon / 1988 / ZA / M • Goodtime Charli / 1989 / CIN / M • Great Expectations / 1990 / V99 / M • Great Expectations / 1992 / VEX / C • The Great Sex Contest #1 / 1988 / LV / M • Hard Road To Victory / 1989 / WV / C • Hard Sell / 1990 / VC / M • Hardbreak Ridge / 1990 / WV / M • Harlem Candy / 1987 / WET / M • Haunted Passions / 1990 / FC / M • Hawaii Vice #4 / 1989 / CIN / M • Hawaii Vice #7 / 1989 / CDI / M • Hawaii Vice #8 / 1990 / CIN / M • Heat Of The Nite / 1988 / VEX / M • Heather's Home Movies / 1989 / VWA / M • Here...Eat This! / 1990 / FAZ / M • Hidden Pleasures / 1990 / VEX / M • Hometown Honeys #2 / 1988 / VEX / M •

Hospitality Sweet / 1988 / WV / M • Hot Black Moon Rising Forever / 1988 / ZA / M • Hot Pink And Chocolate Brown / 1988 / PV / M • Hot Services / 1989 / WET / M • Hot Talk Radio / 1989 / VWA / M • How To Get A "Head" / 1988 / CV / M • The Hustler / 1989 / CDI / M • Hyapatia Lee's Arcade Series #02 / 1988 / ZA / C • I Can't Get No...Satisfaction / 1988 / CDI / M • I Found My Thrill On Cheri Hill / 1988 / PL / M • Icy Hot / 1990 / MID / M • Images Of Desire / 1990 / PM / M • Immorals #1: Broken Hearts / 1989 / AR / M • In The Flesh / 1990 / IN / M • Intimate Affairs / 1990 / VEX / M • Introducing Kascha / 1988 / CDI / M • Island Girls #2: Fun In The Sun / 1990 / CDI / C • Jeanette Starion #1 / 1993 / RUM / M • Jeanette Starion #2 / 1993 / RUM / M • The Joy Of Sec's / 1989 / VEX / M • Juice Box / 1990 / AFV / M • Just For The Thrill Of It / 1989 / V99 / M • Keep It Cumming / 1990 / V99 / M • King Tongue Meets Anal Woman / 1990 / PL / M • The Kink / 1988 / WV / M • Kiss My Grits / 1989 / CA / M • Knights In White Satin / 1987 / SUV / C • Laid In The USA / 1988 / CC / M • The Last Good-Bi / 1990 / CDI / G • Lay Lady Lay / 1991 / VEX / M • Legal Tender (1990-X) / 1990 / VC / M • The Legend Of Reggie D. / 1989 / EA / M • Let Me Tell Ya 'Bout Fat Chicks #2 / 1988 / 4P / M • Life In The Fat Lane #1 / 1990 / FC / M • Life In The Fat Lane #2 / 1990 / FC / M • Little French Maids / 1988 / VEX / M • Living In Sin / 1990 / VEX / M • The Lottery / 1989 / CIN / M • Love Thirsty / 1990 / IN / M • Lust Of Blacula / 1987 / VEX / M • Lusty Detective / 1988 / VEX / M • Magic Pool / 1988 / VD / M • Mandii's Magic / 1988 / CDI / M • Masterpiece / 1990 / VI / M • Matched Pairs / 1988 / VEX / M • Maximum Head / 1987 / SE / M • Midnight Fantasies / 1989 / VEX / M • Misadventures Of The Bang Gang / 1987 / AR / M • Mixing It Up / 1991 / LV / C • Moon Rivers / 1994 / PRE / B • Mystery Of The Golden Lotus / 1989 / HU / M • Nasty Blacks / 1988 / VEX / M • Nasty Dancing / 1989 / VEX / M • Nasty Girls #2 (1990-CDI) / 1990 / CDI / M • National Poontang's Summer Vacation / 1990 / FC / M • Night Trips #1 / 1989 / CA / M • Night Watch / 1990 / VEX / M • One Flew Over The Cuckoo's Breast / 1989 / FAZ / M • One Of These Nights / 1991 / V99 / M • Only In Your Dreams / 1988 / VEX / M • Opposite Attraction / 1992 / VEX / M • Oral Majority #07 / 1989 / WV / C • Oral Majority #08 / 1990 / WV / C • Oral Majority Black #1 / 1987 / WV / C • Oral Majority Black #2 / 1988 / WV / C • Oriental Anal Sluts / 1993 / WV / C • Paris Blues / 1990 / WV / C • Party Wives / 1988 / CDI / M • Passion Princess / 1991 / VEX / M • Peepers / 1988 / CV / M • Perfect Girl / 1991 / VEX / M • Personal Touch #4 / 1989 / AR / M • Pleasure Principle / 1988 / VEX / M • Precious Gems / 1988 / CV / M • The Price Was Right / 1994 / PAE / M • Prince Of Beverly Hills #1 / 1987 / VEX / M • Prince Of Beverly Hills #2 / 1988 / VEX / M • Proposals / 1988 / CC / M • Public Enemy / 1990 / VIP / M • Queen Of Spades / 1986 / WV / M • Raunchy Ranch / 1991 / AFV / M • The Red Baron / 1989 / FAN / M • The Rise Of The Roman Empress #2 / 1990 / PV / M • The Rock Hard Files / 1991 / VEX / M • Salsa

Break / 1989 / EA / M • Scandanavian Double Features #1 / 1996 / PL / M • Scandanavian Double Features #2 / 1996 / PL / M • Screwing Around / 1988 / LV / M • Sea Of Desire / 1990 / AR / M • Search For An Angel / 1988 / WV / M • Secret Obsession / 1990 / V99 / M • Secret Of My Sex-Cess / 1988 / CV / M • Sex Contest / 1988 / LV / M • Sex Toy / 1993 / CA / C • The Sexaholic / 1988 / VC / M • Sexy Nurses #1 On And Off Duty / 1990 / CV / M • She's America's Most Wanted / 1990 / VEX / M • Six-Nine Love / 1990 / LV / M • Smooth And Easy / 1990 / XCV / M • Snapshots: Confessions Of A Video Voyeur / 1988 / CC / M • Snatched / 1989 / VI / M • Soft Caresses / 1988 / VEX / M • Soul Games / 1988 / PV / C • Splash Dance / 1987 / AR / M • Stairway To Heaven / 1989 / ME / M • Star 88: Dana Lynn / 1988 / VEX / C • Storm Warning / 1989 / LV / M • Stormi / 1988 / LV / M • Strange Curves / 1989 / VC / M • Suzy Cue / 1988 / VI / M • Swedish Erotica Featurettes #1 / 1989 / CA / M • Swedish Erotica Featurettes #5 / 1990 / CA / M • Sweet Addiction / 1988 / CIN / M • Sweet Chocolate / 1987 / VD / M • Tails Of The Town / 1988 / WV / M • A Taste Of Black / 1987 / WET / M • A Taste Of Cheri / 1990 / PIN / C • A Taste Of Purple Passion / 1990 / CA / C • A Taste Of Tami Monroe / 1990 / PIN / C • This One's For You / 1989 / AR / M • Titty-Titty Bang-Bang / 1992 / FC / C • Tomboy / 1991 / V99 / M • Tools Of The Trade / 1990 / WV / M • Torch #1 / 1990 / VI / M • Twin Cheeks (Arrow) / 1991 / AR / M • The Two Janes / 1990 / WV / M • Unclassified Carol / 1989 / FAN / C • Under The Law / 1989 / AFV / M • Undercover Carol / 1990 / FAN / M • Voodoo Lust: The Possession / 1989 / PCP / M • Weekend Blues / 1990 / IN / M • Weekend Delights / 1992 / V99 / M • Welcome To The House Of Fur Pi / 1989 / GO / M • What's Love Got To Do With It / 1989 / WV / M • White Trash, Black Splash / 1988 / WET / M • Who's Dat Girl / 1987 / VEX / M • The Whole Diamond / 1990 / EVN / M • Wise Ass! / 1990 / FH / M • With A Wiggle In Her Walk / 1989 / WV / M • The Young And The Wrestling #1 / 1988 / PL / M

RAY VISOR *see* **Ray Victory**

RAY WELLES *(Ray Hardon, Ben Dover)*
(R.Welles), Ray Cooper)
Is this the same as Ray Hardin?
Backdoor Brides #2: The Honeymoon / 1986 / PV / M • Behind The Backdoor #1 / 1986 / EVN / M • Blue Heat / 1975 / IVP / M • Bubblegum / 1982 / VC / M • Caddy Shack-Up / 1986 / VD / M • Carnal Carnival / cr78 / VCX / M • Dirty Harriet / 1986 / SAT / M • Do You Wanna Be Loved? / 1977 / AR / M • Eat At The Blue Fox / 1983 / VC / M • Foxholes / 1983 / SE / M • The Girls In The Band / 1976 / SVE / M • Limited Edition #23 / 1983 / AVC / M • Limo Connection / 1983 / VC / M • Lust In America / 1985 / VCX / M • Lusty Layout / 1986 / PV / M • Mandy's Executive Sweet / 1982 / AVC / M • Naughty Network / 1981 / CA / M • Pen Pals / 1973 / TGA / M • Porn In The USA #1 / 1986 / WV / C • The Pornbirds / 1985 / VC / M • The Pussywillows / 1985 / SUV / M • Slip Up / 1974 / ALP / M • Spies / 1986 / PL / M • Stormy / 1980 / CV / M • Up All Night / 1986 / CC / M • The Wacky

World Of X-Rated Bloopers / 1989 / GO / M • The Young Like It Hot / 1983 / CA / M • The Younger The Better / 1982 / CA / M

RAY WILLIAMS *see Star Index I*

RAYANN DREW *(Tammy Hart)*

Angel Of The Night / 1985 / IN / M • Angel's Revenge / 1985 / IN / M • California Reaming / 1985 / WV / M • Honkytonk Angels / 1988 / IN / C • Skin Games / 1986 / VEX / M • Skin Games / 1991 / VEX / C • Wise Girls / 1989 / IN / C

RAYANNE

Gourmet Premier: Between Rooms / Rear Entry #911 / cr85 / GO / M • Scent Of A Woman / 1985 / GO / M • Star 85: Kari Fox / 1985 / VEX / M

RAYE HARRIS *see Star Index I*

RAYLENE

Homegrown Video #291 / 1990 / HOV / M

RAYLIN

Intimate Interviews #3 / 1996 / NIT / M • Southern Belles #8 / 1997 / XPR / M

RAYMAN SHARQUE *see Star Index I*

RAYMOND

Beyond Passion / 1993 / IF / M • Humongous Hooters / 1993 / IF / M • Sheer Ecstasy / 1993 / IF / M • Wet, Wild And Willing / 1993 / V99 / M

RAYMOND ANDRES *see Star Index I*

RAYMOND BARR

Tight Assets / cr80 / VC / M

RAYMOND COURT-THOMAS *see Star Index I*

RAYMOND DANDEE *see Ray Hardin*

RAYMOND HARDY

[The Loves Of Irina / 1973 / PS / S

RAYMOND HARMSTORF *see Lance Boyle*

RAYMOND NORTH

Wet Wilderness / 1975 / VCX / B

RAYMOND ROBERTS

For Services Rendered / 1984 / CA / M • An Unnatural Act #1 / 1984 / DR / M

RAYMOND XIRNAY

Body Love / 1976 / CA / M

RAYNA LAFAYE

A Is For Asia / 1996 / 4P / M • More Dirty Debutantes #42 / 1995 / 4P / M • More Dirty Debutantes #43 / 1995 / 4P / M • More Dirty Debutantes #44 / 1995 / 4P / M • More Dirty Debutantes #45 / 1995 / 4P / M

RAYNA TERESEE

Most Valuable Slut / 1973 / HLV / M

RAYNE *(Rayne Dawn, Rayne Kayne, Simone Lash, Diane Rachel)*

Pretty blonde who often appears with her boyfriend, Rod Ryker (Buster Cheri—same guy). One movie in 1994 shows her with enhanced rock-solid large tits.

Bad / 1990 / VC / M • Beauty And The Beach / 1991 / CC / M • Behind You All The Way #2 / 1990 / SO / M • Biff Malibu's Totally Nasty Home Videos #03 / 1992 / ANA / M • Bloopers #2 / 1991 / GO / C • Bush Pilots #1 / 1990 / VC / M • Bush Pilots #2 / 1991 / VC / M • Crossing Over / 1990 / IN / M • Cum Blasted Cuties / 1993 / GO / C • Dresden Diary #06: The Hellfire Legend / 1992 / BIZ / B • Dresden Diary #08 / 1992 / BIZ / B • Eat 'em And Smile / 1990 / ME / M • Eternity / 1990 / SC / M • Everything Goes / 1990 / SE / M • The Girl Has Assets / 1990 / LV / M • Growing Up / 1990 / GO / M • Hard Deck / 1991 / XPI / M • Hot Diggity Dog / 1990 / ME / M • Hot Spot / 1990

/ PL / F • In The Can / 1990 / EX / M • The Last Resort / 1990 / VC / M • The Magic Box / 1990 / SO / M • Mickey Ray's Sex Search #03: Deep Heat / 1994 / WIV / M • Only With A Married Woman / 1990 / LE / M • Prisoner Of Love / 1991 / ME / M • The Pump / 1991 / CC / M • Racquel In Paradise / 1990 / VC / M • Read My Lips / 1990 / FH / M • Red Line / 1991 / PL / M • Ringside Knockout / 1990 / DR / M • Roadgirls / 1990 / DR / M • Slip Of The Tongue / 1990 / SE / M • Slow Burn / 1991 / VC / M • The Smart Ass #1 / 1990 / VT / M • Sweet Miss Fortune / 1990 / LE / M • Taboo #08 / 1990 / IN / M • The Tease / 1990 / VC / M • This Year's Blonde / 1990 / LE / M • Wet Paint / 1990 / DR / M

RAYNE D'ANCE *(Kaye D'Ance)*

Blonde with straight shoulder length hair, 25 years old in 1996, devirginized at 14, comes from Portland OR, rock solid cantaloupes, black eyebrows, shaven pussy, curvaceous body.

Fresh Meat (John Leslie) #3 / 1996 / EA / M • Hot Body Competition: Hot Pants Contest / 1996 / CG / F • The Many Faces Of P.J. Sparxx / 1996 / WP / M • Steamy Sins / 1996 / IN / M • Video Virgins #30 / 1996 / NS / M

RAYNE DAWN *see Rayne*

RAYNE KAYNE *see Rayne*

RAYSHEENA

Bodies In Heat #1 / 1983 / CA / M • Caught From Behind #01 / 1982 / HO / M • Caught From Behind #02: The Sequel / 1983 / HO / M • Collection #10 / 1987 / CA / M • Computer Girls / 1983 / LIP / F • Diary Of A Sex Goddess / 1984 / VC / M • Fallen Angels / 1983 / VES / M • The Girls Of Klit House / 1984 / LIP / F • Island Of Love / 1983 / CV / M • Lusty Couples (Come To) / cr85 / CHX / M • Malibu Summer / 1983 / VC / M • Sex And The Cheerleaders / 1983 / XTR / M • Stacey's Hot Rod / 1983 / CV / M

RAYVENESS *(Raveness)*

Long black hair, enhanced large tits (34D), marginal face, womanly body, very pushy, de-virginized at 16. Wife/girlfriend of Red Bone. Comes from North Carolina and an accent to match.

Ass Masters (Leisure) #01 / 1995 / LEI / M • Babes Illustrated #3 / 1995 / IN / F • Behind The Brown Door / 1994 / PE / M • Bi Stander / 1995 / BIN / G • Big Knockers #09 / 1995 / TV / M • Big Knockers #10 / 1995 / TV / M • Big Knockers #20 / 1995 / TV / C • Big Knockers #21: Best Of Lesbian #2 / 1995 / TV / C • Brenda: Back To Beverly Hills 9021A / 1994 / CA / M • Buffy Malibu's Nasty Girls #10 / 1996 / ANA / F • Buffy's New Boobs / 1996 / CIN / M • Call Me / 1995 / CV / M • Casting Couch #1 / 1994 / KV / M • Club Kiss / 1995 / ONA / M • Crazy Love / 1995 / VI / M • Dirty Bob's #20: Back To Vegas! / 1995 / FLP / S • Dirty Bob's #23: Tampa Teasers / 1995 / FLP / S • East Coast Sluts #05: North Carolina / 1995 / PL / M • East Coast Sluts #08: Atlantic City / 1995 / PL / M • Emerald: Princess Of The Night / 1996 / FC / M • Filthy Little Bitches / 1996 / APP / F • Hotel Sodom #07 / 1995 / SNA / M • Hotel Sodom #09 / 1996 / SNA / M • Housewife Lust #2 / 1995 / TV / F • Intense Perversions #4 / 1996 / PL / M • Kinky Cameraman #1 / 1996 / LEI / C • Lingerie / 1996 /

RAS / M • N.Y. Video Magazine #10 / 1996 / OUP / M • Nightvision / 1995 / VI / M • Ona Zee's Doll House #1 / 1995 / ONA / F • Ona Zee's Doll House #3 / 1995 / ONA / F • Pearl Necklace: Amorous Amateurs #02 / 1992 / SEE / M • Pearl Necklace: Amorous Amateurs #10 / 1992 / SEE / M • Pearl Necklace: Amorous Amateurs #11 / 1992 / SEE / M • Pearl Necklace: Amorous Amateurs #22 / 1993 / SEE / M • Prime Choice #5 / 1996 / RAS / M • Puritan Video Magazine #02 / 1996 / LE / M • Radical Affairs Video Magazine #09 / 1995 / ME / M • Raw Silk / 1996 / RAS / M • Razor's Edge / 1995 / ONA / M • Renegades #1 / 1994 / SC / M • Scorched / 1995 / ONA / M • Secret Services / 1995 / CV / M • Slippery Slopes / 1995 / ME / M • Southern Possession / 1995 / DEN / M • Strap-On Sally #09: / 1996 / PL / F • Streets Of New York #08 / 1996 / PL / M • Stretchin' The Rear / 1995 / PE / M • Strippers Inc. #5 / 1995 / ONA / M • Student Fetish Videos: Best of Catfighting #03 / 1995 / PRE / C • Student Fetish Videos: Catfighting #14 / 1994 / PRE / B • Student Fetish Videos: The Enema #18 / 1995 / PRE / B • Student Fetish Videos: Foot Worship #15 / 1995 / PRE / B • Temptation Eyes / 1996 / XCI / M • Totally Ona: The Best Of Ona Zee / 1996 / ONA / C • Turnabout / 1996 / CTP / M • Up And Cummers #13 / 1994 / 4P / M • Video Virgins #18 / 1994 / NS / M • Virgins / 1995 / ERA / M • Wedding Night Blues / 1995 / EMC / M • Where The Girls Sweat...Not The Sequel / 1996 / EL / F

RAZOR SHARP *see Star Index I*

REAL GOLDIE

Black Hollywood Amateurs #06 / 1995 / MID / M • Liar's Poke Her / 1995 / NIW / M

REAL STEEL

Backdoor To Harley-Wood #2 / 1990 / AFV / M • Gangbang Girl #01 / 1992 / ANA / M • Gangbang Girl #02 / 1992 / ANA / M

REANA CUMMINGS *see Star Index I*

REANNONA *see Rhiannon*

REB JAWITZ *see Reb Stout*

REB STOUT *(Reb Jawitz)*

The owner of *Pretty Girl International*, one of the two talent agencies in the porno industry.

REBECCA

Beach Bum Amateur's #09 / 1992 / MID / M • Bondage Models #2 / 1996 / JAM / B • Down And Out / 1995 / PRE / B • Girls Gone Bad #7: Misfits Of Society / 1992 / GO / F • Leg...Ends #05 / 1991 / PRE / F • Mike Hott: #219 Lesbian Sluts #09 / 1992 / MHV / F • Mike Hott: Apple Asses #02 / 1992 / MHV / F • New Busom Brits / 199? / H&S / S • Odyssey Amateur #18: Two Cocks For Rebecca / 1991 / OD / M • Odyssey Amateur #33: Rebecca Breaks New Ground / 1991 / OD / M • Reel Life Video #46: Roommates / 1996 / RLF / F • Student Fetish Videos: The Enema #16 / 1994 / PRE / B • Student Fetish Videos: The Enema #19 / 1995 / PRE / B • Student Fetish Videos: Spanking #16 / 1994 / PRE / B • Student Fetish Videos: Tickling #11 / 1995 / SFV / B • Wild Cats / 1991 / PRE / B

REBECCA (CASSIDY) *see Cassidy*

REBECCA (HONEY W) *see Honey Wells*

REBECCA BARDOUX *(Rebecca Bordaux, Becky Bardot, Rebecca Bor-*

deaux)
Ugly looking blonde with small natural tits. Facially looks like a cross between Lilli Marlene and Misty Regan. She says she comes from Pittsburgh and is 5'6" 126lbs 36B-25-35. **Brother Act** was her first video. What about a girl credited as Kay Martin in **Anal Attack**; she has dark hair but looks very similar body-wise and facially? She is supposedly married to Jake Ryder.

Above The Knee / 1994 / WAV / M • Adult Video Nudes / 1993 / VC / M • All "A" / 1994 / SFP / C • Always / 1993 / XCI / M • Always Anal / 1995 / AVI / C • The Anal Adventures Of Bruce Seven / 1996 / BS / C • The Anal Diary Of Misty Rain / 1993 / EL / M • Anal Distraction / 1993 / PEP / M • Anal Ecstasy Girls #1 / 1993 / ROB / F • Anal Intruder #07 / 1993 / CC / M • Anal Mystique / 1994 / EMC / M • Anal Sluts & Sweethearts #2 / 1993 / ROB / M • Anal Urge / 1993 / ROB / M • Anal Vision #09 / 1993 / LBO / M • Anything Goes / 1993 / VD / C • Back Door Babewatch / 1995 / IF / C • The Backdoor Bandit / 1994 / LV / M • Backdoor Black #2 / 1993 / WV / C • The Backway Inn #4 / 1993 / FD / M • Badd Girls / 1994 / SC / F • Badgirls #5: Maximum Babes / 1995 / VI / M • Bare Ass Beach / 1994 / TP / M • The Bashful Blonde From Beautiful Bendover / 1993 / PEP / M • Beaver & Buttcheeks / 1993 / DR / M • Beaver & Buttface / 1995 / SC / M • Bedazzled / 1993 / OD / M • Behind The Backdoor #6 / 1993 / EVN / M • Bendover / 1994 / ... / M • Between The Cheeks #3 / 1993 / VC / M • Big Knockers #03 / 1994 / TV / M • Big Knockers #04 / 1994 / TV / M • Big Knockers #06 / 1994 / TV / M • Big Knockers #12 / 1995 / TV / C • Big Town / 1993 / PP / M • Bikini Beach #1 / 1993 / CC / M • Bikini Beach #3 / 1993 / CC / F • Blonde Justice #3 / 1994 / VI / M • Bobby Hollander's Maneaters #03 / 1993 / SFP / M • Body Of Innocence / 1993 / WP / M • Boiling Point / 1994 / WAV / M • The Booty Guard / 1993 / IP / M • The Breast Files #1 / 1994 / AVI / M • The British Are Coming / 1993 / ZA / M • Brother Act / 1992 / PL / M • The Butt Detective / 1994 / VC / M • Butt Jammers / 1994 / WIV / M • The Butt Sisters / 1993 / MID / M • The Butt Sisters Do Detroit / 1993 / MID / M • The Butt Sisters Do Los Angeles / 1993 / MID / M • Butt Sluts #1 / 1993 / ROB / F • Buttslammers #01 / 1993 / BS / F • Caught & Punished / 1996 / EXQ / B • Caught From Behind #17 / 1992 / HO / M • Cheating Hearts / 1994 / AFI / M • Cheerleader Nurses #1 / 1993 / VC / M • Cheerleader Nurses #2 / 1993 / VC / M • Circus Of Lesbians / 1995 / VI / C • Club Anal #1 / 1993 / ROB / F • Constant Craving / 1992 / VD / M • The Corruption Of Christina / 1993 / WP / M • County Line / 1993 / PEP / M • Cumming Of Ass / 1995 / TP / M • Dick & Jane Do The Slopes In Ass Spin / 1994 / AVI / M • Dirty Little Lies / 1993 / VT / M • Double D Dykes #07 / 1992 / GO / F • Double Down / 1993 / LBO / M • Dun-Hur #1 / 1994 / SC / M • Eleventh Annual AVN Awards / 1994 / VC / M • Erotika / 1994 / WV / M • Euphoria / 1993 / CA / M • Every Woman Has A Fantasy #3 / 1995 / VC / M • Exposure / 1995 / WAV / M • Extreme Passion / 1993 / WP / M • Extreme Sex #1: The Club / 1994 / VI / M • Extreme Sex #4: The Ex-

periment / 1995 / VI / M • Face Dance #1 / 1992 / EA / M • Face Dance #2 / 1992 / EA / M • A Few Good Rears / 1993 / IN / M • Firm Offer / 1995 / SC / M • Flesh For Fantasy / 1994 / CV / M • For The Money #1 / 1993 / FH / M • Frat Girls Of Double D / 1993 / PP / M • The French Invasion / 1993 / LBO / M • Gang Bang Wild Style #1 / 1993 / ROB / M • Gazongas Galore #1 / 1996 / NIT / C • Generation X / 1995 / WAV / M • Ghosts / 1994 / EMC / M • Girl Gone Bad #6: On Parole / 1992 / GO / F • The Girls' Club / 1993 / VD / C • The Hard Line / 1993 / PEP / M • Harry Horndog #13: Anal Lovers #2 / 1992 / ZA / M • Heidigate / 1993 / HO / M • Hot Property / 1993 / PEP / M • Hot Tight Asses #02 / 1993 / TCK / M • Hotel California / 1995 / MID / M • Hotel Sodom #08 / 1995 / SNA / M • Hypnotic Passions / 1993 / FOR / M • I Love Juicy / 1993 / ZA / M • Jizz Glazed Goo Guzzlers #1 / 1996 / NIT / C • Junkyard Dykes #01 / 1994 / ZA / F • Junkyard Dykes #03 / 1994 / ZA / F • The Last Of The Muff Divers / 1992 / MID / M • Lessons In Love / 1995 / SPI / M • Let's Party / 1993 / VC / M • Licking Legends #1 / 1992 / LE / F • The Living End / 1992 / OD / M • Loopholes / 1993 / TP / M • Love Potion / 1993 / WV / M • Madame Hollywood / 1993 / LE / M • Malibu Blue / 1992 / LE / M • Model's Memoirs / 1993 / IP / M • The Money Hole / 1993 / VD / M • Mr. Peepers Amateur Home Videos #60: The Backdoor Is Open / 1992 / LBO / M • Mr. Peepers Nastiest #2 / 1995 / LBO / C • My Favorite Rear / 1993 / PEP / M • Neighborhood Watch #37: Pelvic Thrusters / 1993 / LBO / M • The New Butt Hunt #15 / 1995 / LEI / C • Nightclub / 1996 / SC / M • Odyssey Triple Play #47: Backdoor Bingers / 1993 / OD / M • Odyssey Triple Play #61: Rump Humpers / 1994 / OD / M • Pajama Party X #2 / 1994 / VC / M • Pajama Party X #3 / 1994 / VC / M • Pearl Necklace: Thee Bush League: The Best Of Oral #01 / 1993 / SEE / C • Pearl Necklace: Thee Bush League #07 / 1992 / SEE / M • Prescription For Lust / 1995 / NIT / M • Pussyman #01: The Search / 1993 / CC / M • Pussyman #05: Captive Audience / 1994 / SNA / M • Pussyman #06: House Of Games / 1994 / SNA / M • Pussyman #11: Prime Cuts / 1995 / SNA / C • Rainbird / 1994 / EMC / M • Ready, Willing & Anal (Vidco) / 1993 / VD / C • Rebel Cheerleaders / 1995 / VI / M • Reflections Of Rio / 1993 / WP / M • Ring Of Desire / 1995 / LBO / M • The Serpent's Dream / 1993 / VC / M • Seven Good Women / 1993 / HO / F • Sexed / 1993 / HO / M • Seymore Butts Goes Deep Inside Shane / 1994 / FH / M • Seymore Butts: Bustin' Out My Best Anal / 1995 / FH / C • Sleepless / 1993 / VD / M • Slip Of The Tongue / 1993 / DR / M • Slurp 'n' Gag / 1994 / CA / C • Smart Ass Delinquent / 1993 / VT / M • The Smart Ass Returns / 1993 / VT / M • Sodomania #02: More Tails / 1992 / EL / M • Sodomania: Slop Shots / 1996 / EL / C • Sodomania: The Baddest Of The Best...And Then Some / 1994 / EL / C • The Spa / 1993 / VC / M • Splendor In The Ass #2 / 1992 / CA / M • Stacked With Honors / 1993 / DR / M • Steal This Heart #1 / 1993 / CV / M • Steal This Heart (Director's) / 1993 / CV / M • A Stroke At Midnight / 1993 / LBO / M • Sur-

rogate Lover / 1992 / TP / M • Takin' It To The Limit #2 / 1994 / BS / M • The Tempest / 1993 / SC / M • Tempted / 1994 / VI / M • Tight Ends In Motion / 1993 / TP / M • Tight Pucker / 1992 / WV / M • Titty Bar #2 / 1994 / LE / M • Ultra Head / 1992 / CA / M • Uninhibited Love / 1994 / VPN / M • Unsolved Double Penetration / 1993 / PEP / M • Vampire's Kiss / 1993 / AVI / M • Video Virgins #02 / 1992 / NS / M • Voices In My Bed / 1993 / VI / M • Warm Pink / 1992 / LE / M • Washington D.P. / 1993 / PEP / M • Wedding Vows / 1994 / ZA / M • Whispered Lies / 1993 / LBO / M • Willing Women / 1993 / VD / C • X-Rated Blondes / 1992 / VD / C • You Bet Your Buns / 1992 / ZA / M

REBECCA BORDAUX see Rebecca Bardoux

REBECCA BORDEAUX see Rebecca Bardoux

REBECCA BROOKE *(Mary Mendum)*
Mary Mendum is from **The Punishment Of Anne**.

Bang Bang You Got It / 1975 / VXP / M • Confessions Of A Young American Housewife / 1973 / ALP / S • Felicia / 1975 / QX / M • Little Girl...Big Tease / 1975 / PAV / S • The Punishment Of Anne / 1975 / VC / B • [Laura's Toys / 1975 / ... / S

REBECCA CARRE
Private Film #10 / 1994 / OD / M

REBECCA DUPONT
30 Men For Sandy / 1995 / SC / M

REBECCA FRANCES see Rebekka Frances

REBECCA GRANGER see Star Index I

REBECCA H. HEELS
Angel's TV & TS Harlots / 1993 / RSV / G • Bound & Mastered #1 Thru #4 / 1986 / VER / B • Coco In Private / 1991 / RSV / G • The Escapades Of Marie Maiden / 1993 / RSV / G • Fetish High Heels And Corsets / 1987 / RSV / G • High Heels In Heat #3 / 1989 / RSV / F • High Heels In Heat #4 / 1989 / RSV / F • Ivana Lushbottom's Skyscrapers / 1990 / RSV / B • Rebecca's Dream / cr83 / VD / B • Rebecca's Private Moments / 1994 / RSV / G • Stockings & Stilettos #1 / 1989 / RSV / G

REBECCA LONDON
Girl On The Run / 1985 / VC / M • A Night On The Wild Side / 1986 / VC / M • Shaved Bunnies / 1985 / LIP / F • You Turn Me On / 1986 / LIM / M

REBECCA LORD
French brunette with elegant rather than pretty face, medium tits (which are allegedly enhanced but it was an excellent job), emaciated body, long black hair, tight waist. Devirginized at 17.

13th Annual Adult Video News Awards / 1996 / VC / S • Angel Baby / 1995 / SC / M • Angel Eyes / 1995 / IN / M • Angels In Flight / 1995 / NIT / M • Attitude / 1995 / VC / M • Bare Essentials / 1995 / NIV / F • Beaver & Buttface / 1995 / SC / M • Betty & Juice Possessed / 1995 / CA / M • Blue Dreams / 1996 / SC / M • Blue Movie / 1995 / WP / M • Body Language / 1995 / VI / M • Butt Hunt #02 / 1994 / LEI / M • Cat Lickers #4 / 1995 / ME / F • Catwalk #1 / 1995 / SC / M • Catwalk #2 / 1995 / SC / M • A Clockwork Orgy / 1995 / PL / M • Contrast / 1995 / CA / M • Cracklyn / 1994 / HW / M • Creme De Femme / 1994 / 4P / F • Dare You / 1995 / CA / M • Dark Encounters / 1996 / ME / M • De Sade / 1994 / SC / M • The Devil In Miss Jones #5: The Inferno / 1994 / VC / M • Erotic Obsession / 1994 / IN / M • Erotic Visions / 1995 / ULI / M • Euro Studs / 1996 / SC / C • Euro-Max #2: Cream n' Euro Sluts / 1995 / SC / M • Euro-Max #3: / 1995 / SC / M • Expose Me Again / 1996 / CV / M • The F Zone / 1995 / WP / M • Fantasy Chamber / 1994 / ULI / M • Finger Sluts #1 / 1996 / LV / F • The French Way / 1994 / HOV / M • Gangbang Girl #14 / 1994 / ANA / M • A Girl's Affair #09 / 1996 / FD / F • Head Shots / 1995 / VI / M • Heavenly Yours / 1995 / CV / M • Hollywood Confidential / 1996 / SC / M • Hollywood Halloween Sex Ball / 1996 / EUR / M • Horny Henry's French Adventure / 1994 / TTV / M • Kym Wilde's On The Edge #35 / 1996 / RB / B • Kym Wilde's On The Edge #39 / 1996 / RB / B • The Last Act / 1995 / VI / M • Latex #2 / 1995 / VC / M • Latex And Lace / 1996 / BBE / M • Lessons 'n' Love / 1994 / LBO / M • Lip Service / 1995 / WP / M • Lunachick / 1995 / VI / M • Mike Hott: #271 Cunt of the Month: Rebecca / 1994 / MHV / M • Mike Hott: #272 Jack Off On My Cunt #01 / 1994 / MHV / M • Mind Set / 1996 / VI / M • Mystique / 1996 / SC / M • Naked & Nasty / 1995 / WP / M • Naked Ambition / 1995 / VC / M • Naked Dolls / 1995 / NIV / F • The Naked Fugitive / 1995 / CA / M • Naked Scandal #1 / 1995 / SPI / M • Naked Scandal #2 / 1996 / SPI / M • Nasty Nymphos #05 / 1994 / ANA / M • Nasty Nymphos #11 / 1995 / ANA / M • No Man's Land #11 / 1995 / VT / F • Pristine #2 / 1996 / CA / M • Private Film #15 / 1994 / OD / M • Private Stories #01 / 1995 / OD / M • Private Video Magazine #16 / 1994 / OD / M • Profiles #03: House Dick / 1995 / XPR / M • Profiles #05: Planet Lust / 1995 / XPR / M • Public Access / 1995 / VC / M • Pussyman #08: The Squirt Queens / 1994 / SNA / M • Pussyman #09: Feeding Frenzy / 1995 / SNA / M • Pussyman #11: Prime Cuts / 1995 / SNA / C • Pussywoman #3 / 1995 / CC / M • Rebecca Lord's World Tour #1: French Edition / 1995 / WP / M • Scotty's X-Rated Adventure / 1996 / WP / M • Sensations #1 / 1996 / SC / M • Sensations #2 / 1996 / SC / M • Sex Kitten / 1995 / SC / M • Sex Raiders / 1996 / WAV / M • Sex Therapy Ward / 1995 / LBO / M • Stacked Deck / 1994 / IN / M • Star Girl / 1996 / ERA / M • Strap-On Sally #05: Chantilly's French Kiss / 1995 / PL / F • Strap-On Sally #06: Triple Penetration Trollop / 1995 / PL / F • Stripping For Your Lover / 1995 / NIV / F • Sure Bet / 1995 / CV / M • Sweat 'n' Bullets / 1995 / MID / M • Tight Shots #1 / 1994 / VI / M • Unleashed / 1996 / SAE / M • Up And Cummers #15 / 1994 / 4P / M • Up And Cummers #19 / 1995 / 4P / M • Vagabonds / 1996 / ERA / M • Venom #1 / 1995 / VD / M • Venom #4 / 1996 / VD / M • Virtual Reality Sixty Nine / 1995 / WP / M • The Wacky World Of Ed Powers / 1996 / 4P / C • Wet Faces #1 / 1997 / SC / C • Where The Girls Sweat...Not The Sequel / 1996 / EL / F • Wild Cherries / 1996 / SC / F

REBECCA LOVE *see Star Index I*
REBECCA LYNN *see Krista Lane*
REBECCA MANUEL *see Star Index I*
REBECCA MONET *see Rebecca Sloan*
REBECCA MONTGOMERY *see Star*

Index I
REBECCA RAGE *see Stephanie Rage*
REBECCA ROBINS *see Star Index I*
REBECCA ROCKET
Black Jack City #4 / 1994 / HW / M
REBECCA ROSE
Black Beauties #1 / 1992 / VIM / M • Collected Spankings #1 / 1992 / BON / C • Collected Spankings #2 / 1992 / BON / C • Lesbian Lingerie Fantasy #5 / 1991 / ESP / F • Maid Service / 1993 / FL / M • Main Course / 1992 / FL / M • Single Girl Masturbation #5 / 1991 / ESP / F • Student Fetish Videos: Catfighting #12 / 1994 / PRE / B • Suck Channel / 1991 / VIM / M
REBECCA SAVAGE *see Becky Savage*
REBECCA SIMMONS
Jezebel / 1979 / CV / M
REBECCA SLOAN *(Rebecca Monet, Rustee, Dana Woods)*
Very thin redhead with small but firm tits and a tight waist. Sounds like a runaway or drug user.
Big Murray's New-Cummers #04: Booty Love / 1992 / FD / M • Deep Inside Dirty Debutantes #02 / 1992 / 4P / M • Lovebone Invasion / 1993 / PL / M • Odyssey Triple Play #62: Gang Bangs All Around / 1994 / OD / M • Video Virgins #01 / 1992 / NS / M • Welcome To Bondage: Rebecca And Julian / 1993 / BON / B
REBECCA STEELE *(Deborah Steele)*
27 years old in 1990 and comes from Virginia. Was a call girl before becoming a porno star.
Adventures Of The DP Boys: Down At The Sunset Grill / 1993 / HW / M • Amateur Lesbians #37: Gretta / 1993 / GO / F • Amateur Lesbians #38: Jessica / 1993 / GO / F • Amazing Tails #4 / 1990 / CA / M • Anal Intruder #04 / 1990 / CC / M • Anal-Holics 1993 / AFV / M • Backdoor To Hollywood #11 / 1990 / CIN / M • Backdoor To Hollywood #12 / 1990 / CIN / M • The Best Of Backdoor To Hollywood / 1990 / CIN / C • Bi 'n' Sell / 1990 / VC / G • Bi-Bi-Baby / 1990 / CDI / G • Biff Malibu's Totally Nasty Home Videos #38 / 1993 / ANA / M • The Big E #09 / 1990 / BIZ / B • Black & Gold / 1990 / CIN / M • Buffy Malibu's Totally Nasty All-Girl Home Videos #03 / 1992 / ANA / F • Bums Away / 1995 / PRE / C • Butt's Motel #5 / 1990 / EX / M • Casting Call (Venus 99) / 1993 / V99 / M • Charmed Again / 1989 / VI / M • Deranged / 1994 / GOT / B • Diedre In Danger / 1990 / VI / M • Double Take / 1991 / BIZ / B • Driving Miss Daisy Crazy #1 / 1990 / WV / M • Dutch Masters / 1990 / IN / M • End Results / 1991 / PRE / C • Flash Floods / 1991 / PRE / C • Gazongas #04 / 1993 / LEI / C • The Hardriders / 1990 / 4P / M • Hershe Highway #3 / 1990 / HO / M • Juicy Lucy / 1990 / VC / M • Ladies Lovin' Ladies #3 / 1993 / AFV / F • Ladies Man / 1990 / REB / M • The Last Good-Bi / 1990 / CDI / G • Legs And Lingerie #2 / 1990 / BEB / F • Lunar Lust / 2990 / HO / M • Miss Directed / 1990 / VI / M • Mistress For Bad Boys / 1993 / GOT / B • Mistress Of The Whip / 1996 / GOT / C • Oral Majority #08 / 1990 / WV / C • Party Doll / 1990 / VC / M • The Rebel / 1990 / CIN / M • The Scarlet Mistress / 1990 / VI / M • Sex & Other Games / 1990 / CIN / M • Sex Lives On Porno Tape / 1992 / VC / C • Slap Shots / 1991 / PRE /

B • Tailgunners / 1990 / CDI / M • Taming Of Laura / 1994 / GOT / B • Toe Tales #09 / 1993 / GOT / B • Toe Tales #10 / 1993 / GOT / B • Toe Tales #12 / 1994 / GOT / C • Torch #1 / 1990 / VI / M • Touched / 1990 / VI / M • Udderly Fantastic / 1993 / IF / M • Vegas #2: Snake Eyes / 1990 / CIN / M • Young Cheeks / 1990 / BEB / B
REBECCA SYMONS
Erotic Fantasies: Women With Women / 1984 / CV / C
REBECCA WILD *(Christina Cruise)*
Pudgy redhead/blonde with inflated tits. Comes from South Carolina and in 1992 was 20 (one story). She came from Columbus OH and was 21 on April 4, 1993 (another story). She's 5'4" and has 34DD tits. Married Rob King on August 7, 1993 in Las Vegas, now (1996) divorced. As of the first quarter 1994 she looks as though she has had further breast enhancement going from too big to enormous (34EE).
Adam & Eve's House Party #4 / 1996 / VC / M • Adults Only / 1995 / BOT / M • The Adventures Of Buck Naked / 1994 / OD / M • The Adventures Of Major Morehead / 1994 / SC / M • Babe Watch #1 / 1994 / SC / M • Babe Watch #2 / 1994 / SC / M • Babe Wire / 1996 / HW / M • Babes Illustrated #3 / 1995 / IN / F • Babes Illustrated #4 / 1995 / IN / F • Backdoor To Taiwan / 1994 / LV / M • Bare Ass Beach / 1994 / TP / M • Barrio Bitches / 1994 / SC / F • Battle Of The Glands / 1994 / LV / F • Battle Of The Porno Queens / 1994 / NAP / B • Battlestar Orgasmica / 1992 / EVN / M • Beach Ball / 1994 / SC / M • Between The Cheeks #3 / 1993 / VC / M • Big & Busty Superstars / 1996 / DGD / F • The Big Bang #2 / 1994 / LV / M • Big Boob Boat Butt Ride / 1996 / FC / M • Big Breast Beach / 1995 / LV / M • Big Busted Dream Girls / 1995 / PME / S • Big Busty Whoppers / 1994 / PME / F • Bigggum's / 1995 / GLI / C • The Blonde & The Beautiful #2 / 1993 / LV / M • Blonde Butt Babes / 1994 / LV / M • Booty And The Ho' Fish / 1996 / RAS / M • The Bottom Dweller Part Deux / 1994 / EL / M • Bust A Move / 1993 / SC / M • Bustin' Thru / 1993 / LV / M • Bustline / 1993 / LE / M • Buttslammers #06: Over The Edge / 1994 / BS / F • Camera Shy / 1993 / FOR / M • The Can Can / 1993 / LV / M • Cheeks #8 / 1995 / CC / M • Cliff Banger / 1993 / HW / M • Corporate Justice / 1996 / TEP / M • Country Girl / 1996 / VC / M • Debbie Class Of '95 / 1995 / CC / M • Deep Inside Dirty Debutantes #01 / 1992 / 4P / M • Deep Inside Juli Ashton / 1996 / VC / C • Deep Inside Nikki Dial / 1994 / VC / C • Deep Throat Girls #04 / 1994 / GO / M • Demolition Woman #2 / 1994 / IP / M • Dick & Jane Do The Strip / 1994 / AVI / M • Dirty Little Mind / 1994 / IP / M • Double D Dreams / 1996 / NAP / S • Dripping Wet Video / 1993 / NAP / F • Every Nerd's Big Boob Boat Butt Ride / 1996 / FC / M • Every Woman Has A Fantasy #3 / 1995 / VC / M • Frankenstein / 1994 / LV / M • From China With Love / 1993 / ZA / M • Full Metal Babes / 1995 / LE / M • Golden Rod / 1996 / SPI / M • Gone Wild / 1993 / LV / M • The Great American Boobs To Kill For Dance Contest / 1995 / PEP / C • Hardcore Fantasies #3 / 1996 / LV / M • Haunting Dreams #1 / 1993 / LV / M • Haunting

Dreams #2 / 1993 / LV / M • The Heart Breaker / 1996 / MID / M • Heaven Scent (Las Vegas) / 1993 / LV / M • Hollywood Scandal: The Heidi Flesh Story / 1993 / IP / M • Hotel Sodom #02 / 1995 / SNA / M • Hotel Sodom #06 / 1995 / SNA / M • Hotel Sodom #10 / 1996 / SNA / M • The Howard Sperm Show / 1993 / LV / M • The Hunger / 1993 / FOR / M • The Hustlers / 1993 / MID / M • In X-Cess / 1994 / LV / M • Interactive / 1993 / VD / M • Kelly Eighteen #2 / 1993 / LE / M • L.A. Topless / 1994 / LE / M • The Last Action Whore / 1993 / LV / M • Lesbian Connection / 1996 / SUF / F • Let's Play Doctor / 1994 / PV / M • Little Girl Lost / 1995 / SC / M • Lovin' Every Minute Of It / 1994 / VEX / C • Micky Ray's Hot Shots #01 / 1996 / DIG / M • Mistress To Sin / 1994 / LV / M • Molly B-Goode / 1994 / FH / M • Motel Sex #2 / 1995 / FAP / M • My Way / 1993 / CA / M • Natural Born Thriller / 1994 / CC / M • New Positions / 1994 / PV / M • Nikki's Last Stand / 1993 / VC / M • Nipples / 1994 / FOR / F • No Motive / 1994 / MID / M • On The Run / 1995 / SC / M • Once Upon An Anus / 1993 / LV / M • Pajama Party X #3 / 1994 / VC / M • Passion's Prisoners / 1994 / LV / M • Peach Pit / 1995 / GLI / M • Philmore Butts All American Butt Search / 1996 / SUF / M • Philmore Butts Goes Wild! / 1996 / SUF / M • The Proposal / 1993 / HO / M • Public Access / 1995 / VC / M • Public Places #2 / 1995 / SC / M • R.E.A.L. #2 / 1994 / LV / F • Radical Affairs Video Magazine #04 / 1992 / ME / M • Red Beaver Bonanza / 1992 / TCP / M • Renegades #1 / 1994 / SC / M • Renegades #2 / 1995 / SC / M • Reservoir Bitches / 1994 / BIP / M • Ring Of Passion / 1994 / ERA / M • Rock Me / 1994 / CC / M • The Savage / 1994 / SC / M • A Scent Of A Girl / 1993 / LV / M • Sexperiment / 1996 / ULP / M • Sister Snatch #1 / 1994 / SNA / M • Ski Sluts / 1995 / LV / M • Skid Row / 1994 / SC / M • Sleeping With Seattle / 1993 / LV / M • Snow Bunnies #1 / 1995 / SC / M • Snow Bunnies #2 / 1995 / SC / M • Spermacus / 1993 / PI / M • Spread The Wealth / 1993 / DR / M • Subway / 1994 / SC / M • Superboobs / 1994 / LE / M • Supermodel #2 / 1994 / VI / M • The Swing / 1996 / VI / M • Taxi Girls #3: Killer On The Loose / 1993 / MED / M • The Three Muskatits / 1994 / PL / M • Thunder And Lightning / 1996 / MID / M • Thunder Road / 1995 / SC / M • Tit City #1 / 1993 / SC / M • Titty Bar #1 / 1993 / LE / M • Toppers #20 / 1993 / TV / M • Toppers #21 / 1993 / TV / C • Toppers #23 / 1994 / TV / M • Toppers #24 / 1994 / TV / M • Toppers #32 / 1994 / TV / C • The Toy Box / 1996 / ONA / M • Trash In The Can / 1993 / LV / M • Treasure Chest / 1994 / LV / M • Tunnel Of Lust / 1993 / LV / M • Twin Action / 1993 / LE / M • Under The Covers / 1996 / GO / M • The Valley Girl Connection / 1994 / IN / M • Vampire's Kiss / 1993 / AVI / M • The Violation Of Felecia / 1995 / JMP / F • Walk On The Wild Side / 1994 / VIM / M • Wet And Wild #2 / 1995 / VEX / M • Wet Nurses #1 / 1994 / LE / M • Wide Open / 1994 / GLI / M • Wild Desires / 1994 / MAX / M • Wilde Palms / 1994 / XCI / M • Young & Natural #15 / 1996 / TV / F • Young & Natural #16 / 1996 / TV / F • Young & Natural #18 / 1996 / TV / C • Young & Natural #20 / 1996 / TV / F

REBEKKA ARMSTRONG

Playboy centerfold for September 1986. Born 2/20/67 in Bakersfield CA. Dropped out of high school to live in a trailer with her boyfriend and believes she contracted HIV during this period in either a "fling with a bisexual model or as a result of a blood transfusion during minor surgery". At 19 became the *Playboy* centerfold and then in 1989 found out she was HIV positive. Went gay and then in 1994 made her condition public. Married to 25 year old male called Joe Shea. Still alive in 1997.

Angel #4: Undercover / 1994 / NLH / S • Hider In The House / 1989 / LIV / S • Instant Karma / 1990 / MGM / S • Playboy Video Calendar 1987 / 1986 / PLA / S • Playboy Video Centerfold: Kerri Kendall / 1990 / HBO / S • Playboy Video Centerfold: Rebekka Armstrong / 1986 / PLA / S • Playboy's Sexy Lingerie #3 / 1991 / HBO / S • Playboy: Wet & Wild #2 / 1990 / HBO / S • Playboy: Wet & Wild #3 / 1991 / HBO / S

REBEKKA FRANCES *(Rebecca Frances)*

Large framed girl but quite pretty with small tits. Looks foreign—maybe Russian—but isn't when you hear her speak.

Indecent Proposals / 1991 / V99 / M • Lonely And Blue / 1990 / VEX / M • More Dirty Debutantes / 1990 / PRI / M • A Touch Of Mink / 1990 / V99 / M • Trick Tracy #2: Tracy Loves Dick / 1990 / CC / M

REBEL DEAN *(Dawn Rebel)*

Short black hair, passable face, cunt ring, medium tits, womanly body, strong Southern accent.

Anal Camera #05 / 1995 / EVN / M • Ass Masters (Leisure) #03 / 1995 / LEI / M • Butt Hunt #11 / 1995 / LEI / M • Creme De La Face #06 / 1995 / OD / M • Deep Inside Anal Camera / 1996 / EVN / C • Designated Hitters / 1995 / PRE / B • Dirty Bob's #17: Tampa Teasers! / 1994 / FLP / S • Dirty Bob's #19: Over The Boardwalk! / 1995 / FLP / S • Dirty Bob's #23: Tampa Teasers / 1995 / FLP / S • Dirty Old Men #1 / 1995 / FPI / M • Drop Outs / 1995 / PRE / B • Leg...Ends #15 / 1995 / PRE / F • Nasty Dreams / 1994 / PRK / M • Old Guys & Dolls #2 / 1995 / PL / M • Reverse Gang Bang / 1995 / JMP / M • Snatch Masters #08 / 1995 / LEI / M • Swedish Erotica #79 / 1994 / CA / M • Tech: Teasing James T / 1994 / TWA / S • Transformation / 1996 / XCI / M • Triple Flay / 1995 / PRE / B • Triple Play / 1994 / PRE / B

REBEL ROUSER see *Star Index I*

RED

Big Bust Babes #30 / 1995 / AFI / M • Hollywood Amateurs #25 / 1995 / MID / M • Leather Unleashed / 1995 / GO / M • Leg...Ends #01 / 1988 / BIZ / F • Mike Hott: #330 Three-Sum Sluts #08 / 1995 / MHV / M • Mike Hott: #332 Girls Who Swallow Cum #02 / 1995 / MHV / C • Mike Hott: #339 Cum In My Mouth #04 / 1996 / MHV / C • Mike Hott: #342 Three-Sum Sluts #10 / 1995 / MHV / M • Mike Hott: #345 Cum In My Cunt #07 / 1995 / MHV / C • Mike Hott: #349 Girls Who Swallow Cum #03 / 1996 / MHV / C • Mike Hott: #354 Three-Sum Sluts #12 / 1996 / MHV / M • Mike Hott: #356 Girls Who Lap Cum From Cunts #01 / 1996 / MHV / M • Mike Hott: #358 Cunt Of The Month: Chardonnay / 1996 / MHV / M • Mike Hott: #360 Cum In My Cunt #08 /

1995 / MHV / C • Mike Hott: #364 Cunt Of The Month: Roxy Rider / 1996 / MHV / M • Mike Hott: #368 Three-Sum Sluts #13 / 1996 / MHV / M • Mike Hott: #372 Stacey Pregnant / 1996 / MHV / M • Mike Hott: #373 Three-Sum Sluts #14 / 1996 / MHV / M • Mike Hott: #375 Girls Who Swallow Cum #05 / 1996 / MHV / C • Mike Hott: #379 Three-Sum Sluts #15 / 1996 / MHV / M • Mike Hott: #380 Girls Who Lap Cum From Cunts #03 / 1996 / MHV / C • Mike Hott: #383 Bonus Cunt: Tameya Jewels / 1996 / MHV / M • My First Time #7 / 1996 / NS / M • Nothing Like Nurse Nookie #2 / 1996 / NIT / M • Orgy Camera #1 / 1995 / EVN / M • Over Eighteen #02 / 1997 / HW / M • Tailz From Da Hood #2 / 1995 / AVI / M

RED BARON

ABA: Double Feature #5 / 1996 / ALP / M • Appointment With Agony / cr80 / AVO / B • Night Of Submission / 1976 / BIZ / M • Pornocopia Sensual / 1976 / VHL / M • Sharon In The Rough-House / 1976 / LA / M

RED BOAN see Red Bone

RED BONE *(Red Boan)*

Perculiar looking rocker type boyfriend/husband of Rayveness.

Ass Masters (Leisure) #01 / 1995 / LEI / M • Behind The Brown Door / 1994 / PE / M • Brenda: Back To Beverly Hills 9021A / 1994 / CA / M • Call Me / 1995 / CV / M • Casting Couch #1 / 1994 / KV / M • Club Kiss / 1995 / ONA / M • East Coast Sluts #05: North Carolina / 1995 / PL / M • East Coast Sluts #07: Tampa Bay / 1995 / PL / M • East Coast Sluts #08: Atlantic City / 1995 / PL / M • Emerald: Princess Of The Night / 1996 / FC / M • Lingerie / 1996 / RAS / M • N.Y. Video Magazine #10 / 1996 / OUP / M • Nightvision / 1995 / VI / M • Pearl Necklace: Amorous Amateurs #02 / 1992 / SEE / M • Pearl Necklace: Amorous Amateurs #10 / 1992 / SEE / M • Pearl Necklace: Amorous Amateurs #11 / 1992 / SEE / M • Prime Choice #5 / 1996 / RAS / M • Puritan Video Magazine #02 / 1996 / LE / M • Radical Affairs Video Magazine #09 / 1995 / ME / M • Raw Silk / 1996 / RAS / M • Renegades #1 / 1994 / SC / M • Secret Services / 1995 / CV / M • Southern Possession / 1995 / DEN / M • Streets Of New York #08 / 1996 / PL / M • Turnabout / 1996 / CTP / M • Up And Cummers #13 / 1994 / 4P / M • Video Virgins #18 / 1994 / NS / M • Virgins / 1995 / ERA / M • Wedding Night Blues / 1995 / EMC / M

RED MADONNA see *Star Index I*
RED PEPPER see *Star Index I*
RED RIDING BOOTS

Lickin' Good / 1995 / TVI / F

RED RIDING HOOD

Aggressive Lesbians / 1995 / STM / C • Anal Angels / 1996 / PRE / B • Arch Villains / 1994 / PRE / B • Arch Worship / 1995 / PRE / B • Bun Runners / 1994 / PRE / B • The Captive / 1995 / BIZ / B • The Convict / 1995 / TAO / B • Double Cross (Vid Tech) / 1995 / VTF / B • Double Xx Cross / 1995 / VTF / B • Dr Discipline #1 / 1994 / STM / B • Dr Discipline #2: Appointment With Pain / 1994 / STM / B • Enemates #11 / 1995 / BIZ / B • Finger Pleasures #6 / 1996 / PL / F • Flush Dance / 1996 / PRE / C • Girls Just Wanna Have Girls #3 / 1994 /

HIO / F • Harsh Treatment / 1995 / RB / B • Kym Wilde's On The Edge #21 / 1995 / RB / B • Kym Wilde's On The Edge #31 / 1996 / RB / B • Leg...Ends #12 / 1994 / PRE / F • Leg...Ends #16 / 1996 / PRE / F • Maidens Of Servitude #1 / 1993 / STM / B • Maidens Of Servitude #2: Obeisance / 1994 / STM / B • Maidens Of Servitude #3: A Jealous Bind / 1994 / STM / B • Private Pleasures / 1994 / STM / F • The Punishment Of Red Riding Hood / 1996 / LBO / B • Shaved #08 / 1995 / RB / F • Slap Happy / 1994 / PRE / B • Slave Wages / 1995 / PRE / B • Smothered, Bound & Tickled / 1993 / STM / B • Spanking In Shining Armor / 1995 / IBN / B • Student Fetish Videos: Best of Catfighting #02 / 1994 / PRE / C • Student Fetish Videos: Best Of Foot Worship #03 / 1995 / PRE / C • Student Fetish Videos: Foot Worship #09 / 1994 / PRE / B • Student Fetish Videos: Foot Worship #16 / 1995 / PRE / B • Student Fetish Videos: Tickling #11 / 1995 / SFV / B • Submissive Exposure Profile #5: Keli Thomas / 1996 / STM / C • Succulent Toes / 1995 / STM / B • Suspend Thy Slaves / 1996 / VTF / B • A Taste Of Torment / 1995 / NIT / B • Toes 'n' Cons / 1996 / PRE / S • Torturer's Apprentice / 1996 / LBO / B • Two Tied For Tickling / 1995 / SBP / B

RED STARR
The Final Test / 197? / RLV / B
REECE MONTGOMERY see Star Index I
REED LOGGERHEAD
Curiosity Excited The Kat / 1984 / BIZ / B
REEL STEEL see Star Index I
REEVES see Star Index I
REG SMITH
Bucky Beaver's XXX Dragon Art Theatre Double Feature #10 / 1996 / SOW / M • Sins Of Sandra / cr72 / SOW / M
REG WEIL
A Taste Of Sugar / 1978 / AR / M
REG WILSON see Star Index I
REGAN SENTER
The Erotic Adventures Of Johnny Soiree / 1995 / LBO / M • Harlem Harlots #1 / 1995 / AVS / M • Harlem Harlots #2 / 1995 / AVS / M • Harlem Harlots #3 / 1996 / AVS / M • Hollywood Amateurs #12 / 1994 / MID / M • Hollywood Starlets Adventure #01 / 1995 / AVS / M • Hollywood Starlets Adventure #02 / 1995 / AVS / M • Hollywood Starlets Adventure #03 / 1995 / AVS / M • Hollywood Starlets Adventure #04 / 1995 / AVS / M • Hollywood Starlets Adventure #05 / 1995 / AVS / M • Hollywood Starlets Adventure #06 / 1995 / AVS / M • Nookie Professor #1 / 1996 / AVS / M • Nookie Professor #2 / 1996 / AVS / M
REGANIS BAKER
Valley Cooze / 1996 / SC / M
REGGAE
Creme De La Face #10: Cum Dome / 1995 / OD / M • The Cumm Brothers #01 / 1993 / OD / M
REGGIE
M Series #17 / 1993 / LBO / M • M Series #26 / 1994 / LBO / M • Mr. Peepers Amateur Home Videos #88: A For Effort / 1994 / LBO / M
REGGIE DEFOE
Virgin And The Lover / 1973 / ALP / M
REGGIE DEMORTON see Star Index I
REGGIE GUNN see Star Index I

REGGIE NALDER
Blue Ice / 1985 / CA / M • Lust At First Bite / 1978 / VC / M • Seven / 1979 / LIV / S
REGGIE SLACKSON
Black Lust / 1995 / UBP / M
REGIA
Lettre Da Rimini / 1995 / MID / M
REGIE see Star Index I
REGINA
Blue Vanities #505 / 1992 / FFL / M • Blue Vanities #510 / 1992 / FFL / M • Hustler Honeys #2 / 1988 / VC / S • M Series #25 / 1994 / LBO / M • Mr. Peepers Amateur Home Videos #91: Hole Lot'a Humping Goin / 1994 / LBO / M • My Baby Got Back #04 / 1994 / VT / M • Penetration (Anabolic) #3 / 1995 / ANA / M • Pet Hotel #1 / 1988 / BON / B • Pet Hotel #2 / 1988 / BON / B • Private Gold #11: The Pyramid #1 / 1996 / OD / M • Private Video Magazine #10 / 1994 / OD / M • Private Video Magazine #13 / 1994 / OD / M • SVE: Ho-Nuff / 1994 / SVE / M • The Voyeur #7: Live In Europe #1 / 1996 / JLP / M
REGINA BARDOT *(Brittany Bardot, Toy Sin, Martha (Reg. Bardot), Loren Sands, Brittany Barent, Doran O'Dare, Brittany Bardo)*
Petite girl with shoulder length reddish brown or blonde hair, medium tits, Oriental overtones, not an exceptionally tight body but passable, passable face and nice personality. Doran O'Dare is from **Genital Hospital** and Brittany Bardot from **Cram Session**.
Amazing Tails #2 / 1987 / CA / M • Amazing Tails #3 / 1987 / CA / M • Angels Of Mercy / 1985 / HO / M • Backdoor Lust / 1987 / CV / C • The Black Mystique / 1986 / CV / M • Careena #2: A Star On The Rise / 1988 / WV / C • Cram Session / 1986 / V99 / M • Dickman & Throbbin / 1985 / WV / M • Dressed To Thrill / 1986 / CDI / M • Genital Hospital / 1987 / SE / M • Hooters / 1986 / AVC / M • Hottest Ticket / 1987 / WV / C • Kinkyvision #1 / 1986 / 3HV / M • Les Be Friends / 1988 / WV / C • Loose Morals / 1987 / HO / M • Love Lessons / 1986 / HO / M • Mantrap / 1986 / BAN / M • Nymphette #1 / 1986 / WV / M • Only The Best Of Women With Women / 1988 / CV / C • Oral Majority #01 / 1986 / WV / C • Oral Majority #03 / 1986 / WV / C • Parliament: Bare Assets / 1988 / PM / F • Parliament: Dildo Babes #1 / 1986 / PM / F • Parliament: Shaved #1 / 1986 / PM / F • Return To Sex 5th Avenue / 1985 / WV / M • The Sex Change Girls / 1987 / 4P / G • Sexscape / 1986 / CA / M • Sophisticated Women / 1986 / BAN / M • A Sticky Situation / 1987 / CA / M • To Live & Shave In LA / 1986 / WET / M • VCA Previews #1 / 1988 / VC / C • Wild Things #2 / 1986 / CV / M
REGINA DOURADO
Al Borda's Brazilian Adventures / 1996 / BEP / M
REGINA GIELSER see Kym Wilde
REGINA JAX see William Margold
REGINA MOMSEY see Star Index I
REGINA RAMSEY
The Loves Of Mary Jane / 1989 / BWV / C • A Touch Of Sex / 1972 / AR / M
REGINA SANDERS
Love Slave / 1995 / WIV / M
REGINA WRIGHT see Star Index I
REGINE

Black Booty / 1995 / UBP / M • Black Hollywood Amateurs #02 / 1995 / MID / M • Black Mystique #13 / 1995 / VT / F • Chocolate Bunnies #01 / 1995 / LBO / C • Chocolate Bunnies #03 / 1995 / LBO / C • Girl's Towne #1 / 1994 / FC / F • Girl's Towne #2 / 1994 / FC / F • HomeGrown Video #465: Bong The Schlong / 1996 / HOV / M • M Series #21 / 1994 / LBO / M • Made In The Hood / 1995 / HBE / M • Magma: Anal Wedding / 1995 / MET / M
REGINE FELINE see Star Index I
REGIS STALLION see Star Index I
REGO
Buttman's Big Butt Backdoor Babes / 1995 / EA / M • Double Penetration Virgins #06: DP Diner / 1995 / JMP / M • Flappers / 1995 / EMC / M
REI KITHAAM
[Love Thy Neighbor's Wife / 19?? / ... / M
REINHARD HARD
Private Gold #02: Friends In Sex / 1995 / OD / M • Sodomania #20: For Members Only / 1997 / EL / M
REKA
European Sex TV / 1996 / EL / M
RELONDA LOVE
Between My Breasts #12 / 1990 / BTO / M • Big Bust Black Legends / 1991 / BTO / C • Bras And Panties #1 / 199? / H&S / S
REN ADAMS
B-Witched / 1994 / PEP / G • Bi-Athelon / 1993 / BIL / G
REN MICHAELS
Cluster Fuck #01 / 1993 / MAX / M • Pearl Necklace: Amorous Amateurs #33 / 1992 / SEE / M • Pearl Necklace: Thee Bush League #20 / 1993 / SEE / M • Pearl Necklace: Thee Bush League #23 / 1993 / SEE / M
RENA see Star Index I
RENA BERGEN
The Young Seducers / 1971 / BL / M • [Die Madchenhandler / 1972 / ... / M
RENA BROWN see Star Index I
RENA HARMON see Rena Horten
RENA HORTEN *(Renate Hutte, Rena Harmon)*
Cinderella 2000 / 1977 / SVI / S • Fanny Hill: Memoirs Of A Woman Of Pleasure / 1964 / PAV / S • Mudhoney / 1965 / RMV / S
RENA VALE see Marlene Willoughby
RENA VANE see Marlene Willoughby
RENATA
In Your Wildest Dreams / 1993 / STY / M • Playboy's Girls Of Hooters / 1995 / PLA / S
RENATA KOMYATHY
True Stories #1 / 1993 / SC / M • True Stories #2 / 1993 / SC / M
RENATE HUTTE see Rena Horten
RENATE KASCHE
[Junge Madchen Mogen's Heiß, Hausfrauen Noch HeiBer / 1973 / ... / M
RENATE PUTZ
Inside Marilyn / 1984 / CA / M
RENE
A&B AB#313: Sweet Pussy / 1991 / A&B / F • A&B AB#538: Sexy Swingers / 1995 / A&B / M • African Angels #3 / 1996 / NIT / M • America's Raunchiest Home Videos #63: / 1993 / ZA / M • Anabolic Import #01: Anal X / 1994 / ANA / M • Beach Bum Amateur's #18 / 1992 / MID / M • Big Murray's New-Cummers #28: Rump Humpers #2 / 1995 / FD / M • Blue Vanities #546 / 1994 /

FFL / M • Bob's Video #101: City Of Angels / 1996 / BOV / F • Candyman #01: 1-900-Fantasies / 1992 / GLI / M • Extra Sensual Pleasure / 1983 / PAC / M • HomeGrown Video #472: Everyday People / 1996 / HOV / M • N.Y. Video Magazine #02 / 1995 / OUP / M • Neighborhood Watch #17: Burning The Sausage / 1992 / LBO / M • Nothing Like Nurse Nookie #5 / 1996 / NIT / M • Old Fashioned Spankings / 1991 / BON / B • Purple Pain / 1995 / OUP / B • Rapture Girls #3: Molly & Renee / 1991 / OD / M • Swingers Confidential #1 / 1995 / FC / M • Wrasslin She-Babes #04 / 1996 / SOW / M • Wrasslin She-Babes #05 / 1996 / SOW / M • Wrasslin She-Babes #07 / 1996 / SOW / M • Wrasslin She-Babes #12 / 1996 / SOW / M

RENE (1997)
Marginal face, Hispanic, long fine brown hair, very young looking, small/medium firm tits, toothbrush pubic hair, braces, white but good skin. In **Amateur Lusty Latins #2** she says she's 19 years old and in **More Dirty Debutantes #63** she says 21; in both she says she was de-virginized at 16.
Amateur Lusty Latins #2 / 1997 / SUF / M • More Dirty Debutantes #63 / 1997 / SBV / M

RENE (LEANNA) FOXX *see* **Leanna Foxxx**

RENE BAKER *see* **Star Index I**

RENE BAR
The Thief, The Girl & The Detective / 1996 / HDE / M

RENE BLISS *see* **Rene Morgan**

RENE BOND *(Lilly Lovetree, Paula Schnall, Rene Lutz, Priscilla Lee, Nancy Binghampton, Mindy Brandt, Diane Lee, Annie Hall, Jane (Rene Bond))*
Passable face with good tan lines and large enhanced tits. Always seems to wear too long eyelashes in the style of the sixties.
ABA: Double Feature #5 / 1996 / ALP / M • The Adult Version Of Dr Jekyll And Mr Hyde / 1971 / SOW / S • Angel Above, Devil Below / 1974 / CV / M • Bad Bad Gang / 1972 / SOW / M • Beach Blanket Bango / 1975 / EVI / M • Below The Belt / 1971 / SOW / S • Betrayal / 1974 / JFF / S • Between My Breasts #06 / 1989 / BTO / M • Blue Heat / 1975 / IVP / M • Blue Vanities #018 (New) / 1988 / FFL / M • Blue Vanities #044 (Old) / 1988 / FFL / M • Blue Vanities #052 / 1988 / FFL / M • Blue Vanities #063 / 1988 / FFL / M • Blue Vanities #252 / 1996 / FFL / M • Blue Vanities #559 / 1994 / FFL / M • Blue Vanities #562 / 1994 / FFL / M • Blue Vanities #584 / 1996 / FFL / M • Brute Therapy / cr75 / ... / M • Bucky Beaver's Double Softies #04 / 1996 / SOW / S • Bucky Beaver's Double Softies #06 / 1996 / SOW / S • Bucky Beaver's XXX Dragon Art Theatre Double Feature #07 / 1996 / SOW / M • Bucky Beaver's XXX Dragon Art Theatre Double Feature #10 / 1996 / SOW / M • Bucky Beaver's XXX Dragon Art Theatre Double Feature #11 / 1996 / SOW / M • Bucky Beaver's XXX Dragon Art Theatre Double Feature #14 / 1996 / SOW / M • Bucky Beaver's XXX Dragon Art Theatre Double Feature #18 / 1996 / SOW / M • Bucky Beaver's XXX Dragon Art Theatre Double Feature #19 / 1996 / SOW / M • Bucky Beaver's XXX

Dragon Art Theatre Double Feature #20 / 1996 / SOW / M • City Women / 1972 / SVE / M • Class Reunion / 1972 / PS / S • The Cocktail Hostesses / 1972 / ... / S • Collection #03 / 1983 / SVE / M • Convict's Women / 1973 / SOW / S • Country Cuzzins / 1970 / SOW / S • Country Hooker / 1970 / BPI / S • Creme Rinse / 1976 / AXV / M • The Danish Connection / 1970 / SOW / S • The Daring French Touch / 1971 / ... / M • The Dicktator / 1974 / SOW / S • Disco Lady / 1978 / EVI / M • Do You Wanna Be Loved? / 1977 / AR / M • The Dominators #2 / 1979 / ALP / B • Fantasm / 1976 / VS / S • Five Loose Women / 1974 / NFV / S • Frank Henenlotter's XXX Hardcore Horrors: Mad Love... / 1996 / SOW / M • Girl In The Basket / 1972 / ALP / M • Guess Who's Coming This Weekend / 1973 / CLX / M • The Hawaiian Split / 1971 / SOW / S • High School Fantasies / 1974 / EVI / M • Hitchhiker's Hold-Up / cr71 / SOW / M • Hollywood Babylon / 1972 / AIR / S • Honey Buns / cr75 / BL / M • Hot Pistols / 1972 / CLX / M • Hot Teenage Lovers / cr73 / VBM / M • I'm No Virgin / 1971 / WWV / M • Invasion Of The Bee Girls / 1973 / EHE / S • The Jekyll And Hyde Portfolio / 1972 / ... / S • Journal Of Love / 1970 / ALP / M • Kim Comes Home / 1976 / SOW / M • Lash Of Lust / 1968 / ... / S • Legends Of Porn #1 / 1987 / CV / C • The Likes Of Louise / 197? / BL / M • The Loves Of Mary Jane / 1989 / BWV / C • The Mad Love Of The Red Hot Vampire / 1971 / SOW / M • Mary! Mary! / 1977 / SE / M • Naked Encounters / 1974 / SOW / M • Necromania / 1971 / SOW / S • Never Enough / 1971 / VCX / M • Panorama Blue / 1974 / ALP / S • Panty Girls / 1972 / BMV / M • The Partnership / 1973 / ALP / M • Peeping Camera / 1973 / SOW / M • Please Don't Eat My Mother / 1972 / BPI / S • Pleasure Unlimited / 1972 / PS / S • Private Private / 1971 / ALP / M • Private Thighs / 1987 / AVC / C • Rendezvous In Hell / cr72 / SOW / M • Saturday Matinee Series #3 / 1996 / VCX / C • Sex Asylum / cr72 / SOW / M • Sex Crazy Girls / cr71 / SAT / M • Sex, Love And Happiness / 1973 / ... / S • Sex-O-Phrenia / 1970 / ALP / S • Shot On Location / 1972 / ALP / S • Snow Bunnies / 1970 / NFV / S • Souzy's House / cr75 / BOC / M • Strangers / 1972 / SE / M • Swingers Massacre / 1975 / SVE / S • Teaser / 1973 / SOW / S • Teenage Fantasies #1 / 1972 / SOW / M • Teenage Fantasies #2 / 1980 / AR / M • Teenage Sex Kitten / 1972 / CA / M • Teenage Throat / 1974 / ... / M • Tender Flesh / cr72 / SOW / M • Touch Me / 1971 / SE / M • A Touch Of Sex / 1972 / AR / M • Tough Guns / 1972 / ALP / S • A World Of Peeping Toms / cr72 / SOW / M • [The Boob Tube Strikes Again / 1976 / ... / M • [Deep Love / 19?? / ... / M • [Devil's Little Acre / 19?? / ... / M • [Frankie And Johnny / 1973 / ... / M • [Good Morning Glory / 19?? / ... / M • [Heads Of Tails / 197? / ... / S • [Inside Amy / 1975 / ... / S • [The Miss Layed Genie / 1974 / ... / M • [Orgy American Style / 1975 / ... / M • [Runaway Hormones / 1973 / ... / S • [Satisfaction Guaranteed (2) / 1972 / ... / S • [Secret Fantasies / 1971 / ... / M • [Teenage Jailbait / 1973 / ... / M • [A Touch Of Death / 1972 / ... / M • [Welcome Home Johnny / 1972 /

... / M

RENE DOUGLAS *see* **Star Index I**

RENE EMERALD *see* **Star Index I**

RENE FOXX
1-800-TIME / 1990 / IF / M • Back To Nature / 1990 / CA / M • Behind Blue Eyes #3 / 1989 / ME / M • Best Of Caught From Behind #5 / 1991 / HO / C • Breaststroke #3 / 1989 / EX / M • Caught From Behind #13 / 1990 / HO / M • Cheaters / 1990 / LE / M • The Coming Of Christy / 1990 / CAY / M • Con Jobs / 1990 / V99 / M • Confessions Of Christy / 1991 / CAY / M • Digital Lust / 1990 / SE / M • Dildo Fantasy Party / 1990 / BIZ / F • Earth Girls Are Sleazy / 1990 / SO / M • Entertainment L.A. Style / 1990 / HO / M • Falcon Head / 1990 / ARG / M • Ghost Lusters / 1990 / EL / F • Girls In The Night / 1990 / LE / M • Girls Just Wanna Have Girls #2 / 1990 / HIO / F • Girls Will Be Boys #2 / 1990 / PL / F • The Girls' Club / 1990 / VC / F • Hot Spot / 1990 / PL / F • Juicy Lips / 1991 / PL / F • King Tung: The Tongue Squad / 1990 / LA / M • Legend #2 / 1990 / LE / M • Loose Lips / 1990 / VC / M • New Girls In Town #1 / 1990 / CC / M • P.S.: Back Alley Cats #03 / 1992 / PSP / F • P.S.: Back Alley Cats #05 / 1992 / PSP / F • The Pawnbroker / 1990 / IF / M • Rainwoman #03 / 1990 / CC / M • Rear Burner / 1990 / IN / M • The Smart Ass #1 / 1990 / VT / M • Superstar Masturbation / 1990 / BIZ / F • Welcum To My Place / 1990 / ZA / M

RENE HUNTER *see* **Penny Lane**

RENE LAFLEUR *see* **Star Index I**

RENE LAPAZ *(Plucky Rene)*
Indecent Exposure / 1981 / CA / M • Naughty Network / 1981 / CA / M • Sex Boat / 1980 / VCX / M

RENE LE VELLERS *see* **Danielle Rogers**

RENE LOVIN *see* **Rene Lovins**

RENE LOVING *see* **Rene Lovins**

RENE LOVINS *(Rene Lovions, Rene Lovin, Rene Loving)*
Reddish blonde with womanly body, small tits, marginal face.
Beyond Desire / 1986 / VC / M • Blonde Heat (VCA) / 1985 / VC / M • Bold Obsession / 1983 / NSV / M • China Bitch / 1989 / PV / C • Cream Puff / 1986 / VSE / M • It's Incredible / 1985 / SE / M • Legacy Of Lust / 1985 / CA / M • Little Showoffs / 1984 / VC / M • Naked Lust / 1985 / SE / M • Naughty Cheerleaders / 1985 / HO / M • One Night In Bangkok / 1985 / CA / M • Red Hot Pepper / 1986 / V99 / M • Working Girls / 1985 / CA / M • The Young Like It Hot / 1983 / CA / M

RENE LOVIONS *see* **Rene Lovins**

RENE LUTZ *see* **Rene Bond**

RENE MORGAN *(Rene Bliss, Natasha (R. Morgan))*
Rene Bliss is from **Inner Pink**.
A.S.S.(Anal Security Squad) / 1988 / VD / M • Ali Boobie & The 40 D's / 1988 / 3DV / M • Alice In Blackland / 1988 / VC / M • America's Most Wanted Girl / 1989 / IN / M • Anal Dawn / 1991 / AMB / M • Anal Intruder #03 / 1989 / CC / M • Angel Puss / 1988 / VC / M • Angel Rising / 1988 / IN / M • Angel's Back / 1988 / IN / M • Ball Street / 1988 / CA / M • Bedside Brat / 1988 / VI / M • Beeches / 1990 / KIS / M • Best Of Bi And Beyond / 1992 / PNP / C • Bi And Beyond #5 / 1990 / INH / G • The Big Gun

/ 1989 / FAN / M • The Big Thrill / 1989 / VD / M • Biloxi Babes / 1988 / WV / M • Binding Experience / 1994 / CS / B • Black & Beyond: The Darker Sid / 1990 / INH / G • Bloopers #2 / 1991 / GO / C • Bodies In Heat #2 / 1989 / DR / M • Bondage Fantasia / 199? / CS / B • Boobs, Butts And Bloopers #1 / 1990 / HO / M • Born For Porn / 1989 / FAZ / M • Brat Force / 1989 / VI / M • Caged Fury / 1990 / C3S / S • The Case Of The Sensuous Sinners / 1988 / ME / M • Caught From Behind #11 / 1989 / HO / M • De Blond / 1989 / EA / M • The De Renzy Tapes / 1990 / CA / C • Debbie 4 Hire / 1988 / AVC / M • Debbie For President / 1988 / CC / M • Debbie Goes To Hawaii / 1988 / VD / C • Deep Throat #3 / 1989 / AR / M • Fantasy Confidential / 1988 / GO / M • The Final Taboo / 1988 / CA / M • For Your Love / 1988 / IN / M • Getting Off On Broadway / 1989 / IN / M • Girl Country / 1990 / CC / F • Girlworld #4 / 1989 / LIP / F • Growing Up / 1990 / GO / M • Hard At Work / 1989 / VEX / M • Hardbreak Ridge / 1990 / WV / M • Having It All / 1991 / VEX / M • Hidden Pleasures / 1990 / VEX / M • Hollywood Hustle #2 / 1990 / V99 / M • I Want Your Sex / 1990 / FAZ / M • Inch Bi Inch / 1989 / STA / G • Inner Pink #1 / 1988 / LIP / F • Inner Pink #2 / 1989 / LIP / F • K.U.N.T.-TV / 1988 / WV / M • King Tung: Bustin' The Royal Hienies / 1990 / LA / M • The Kink / 1988 / WV / M • Kinky Business #2 / 1989 / DR / M • Lethal Love / 1990 / DAY / M • Lonely Is The Night / 1990 / V99 / M • Loose Ends #5: The New Generation / 1988 / 4P / M • Mad Love / 1988 / VC / M • Madame X / 1989 / EVN / M • Made In Hollywood / 1990 / VEX / M • The Maltese Phallus / 1990 / V99 / M • The Master Of Pleasure / 1988 / VD / M • Midnight Baller / 1989 / PL / M • My Friend, My Lover / 1990 / FIR / M • A Natural Woman / 1989 / IN / M • Next Door Neighbors #07 / 1989 / BON / M • The Nicole Stanton Story #2 / 1989 / CA / M • Night Of The Living Debbies / 1989 / EX / M • Night Shift Latex Slaves / 1991 / GOT / B • No More Mr Nice Guy / 1989 / GO / M • Oh! You Beautiful Doll / 1990 / ZA / M • On The Prowl #1 / 1989 / SC / M • Paradise Road / 1990 / WV / M • Parting Shots / 1990 / VD / M • Passion Princess / 1991 / VEX / M • Perfect Girl / 1991 / VEX / M • Phone Mates / 1988 / CA / M • The Pillowman / 1988 / VC / M • Playin' Dirty / 1990 / VC / M • Playing Dirty / 1989 / VEX / M • Power Blonde / 1988 / AVC / M • Prom Girls / 1988 / CA / M • Rock 'n' Roll Heaven / 1989 / EA / M • Ruthless Women / 1988 / SE / M • Satisfaction Jackson / 1988 / CA / M • Saturday Night Special / 1989 / DR / M • Scent Of A Wild Woman / 1993 / EVN / C • Search For An Angel / 1988 / WV / M • Secret Dreams / 1991 / VEX / M • Sex Lives Of The Rich And Famous #2 / 1989 / VC / M • She-Male Encounters #17: Sorority / 1987 / MET / C • She-Male Encounters #18: Murder She-Male Wrote / 1987 / MET / G • She-Male Sanitarium / 1988 / VD / G • The Slut / 1988 / FAN / M • Snatched / 1989 / VI / M • Split Decision / 1989 / MET / G • Strong Rays / 1988 / IN / M • Sulka's Nightclub / 1989 / VT / G • Sunstroke Beach / 1990 / WV / M • Suzanne's Grand Affair / 1990 / CV / M • Sweet Temptations / 1989 / V99 / M •

Switch Hitters #3: Squeeze Play / 1988 / IN / G • Tales Of The Golden Pussy / 1989 / RUM / M • Teach Me Tonight / 1990 / VEX / M • Three For All / 1988 / PL / M • Tied & Tickled #14: Count Tickula / 1986 / CS / B • Toe Tales #09 / 1993 / GOT / B • Tour De Trans / 1989 / STA / G • Trans Europe Express / 1989 / VC / G • The Ultimate Climax / 1989 / V99 / M • Unchain My Heart / 1990 / CC / M • Uninhibited / 1989 / VC / G • Wanda Does Transylvania / 1990 / V99 / M • Wanda Whips The Dragon Lady / 1990 / V99 / M • Weekend Blues / 1990 / IN / M • Wet Kink / 1989 / CDI / M • Wet Pink / 1989 / PL / F • What's Love Got To Do With It / 1989 / WV / M • What's Up Doc / 1988 / SEV / M • Wildheart / 1989 / IN / M • Wise Girls / 1989 / IN / C • [Masquerade (1992-Italy) / 1992 / … / S

RENE ROBERT
Fade To Rio / 1984 / VHL / M
RENE RODAS
Borderline (Vivid) / 1995 / VI / M
RENE ROSS
Squalor Motel / 1985 / SE / M
RENE ST CLAIR *see Star Index I*
RENE STANTON *see Star Index I*
RENE STERLING *see Star Index I*
RENE SUMMERS *(Cherri Summers, Lauren Walden)*
Pudgy not-too-pretty blonde who was married to Eric Edwards at one time.
2002: A Sex Odyssey / 1985 / DR / M • The Adventures Of Dick Black, Black Dick / 1987 / DR / M • The Analizer / 1990 / LV / M • The Applicant / 1988 / BON / B • Avenging Angeli / 1990 / CC / M • Backdoor To Paradise / 1990 / ELV / M • The Backpackers #1 / 1990 / IN / M • Best Of Bruce Seven #3 / 1990 / BIZ / C • Best Of Bruce Seven #4 / 1990 / BIZ / C • The Big Rock / 1988 / FOV / M • Bizarre Encounters / 1986 / 4P / B • Bondage Boot Camp / 1988 / TAN / B • The Bondage Club #4 / 1990 / LON / B • The Bondage Club #5 / 1990 / LON / B • Bouncing Buns / 1983 / VC / M • Bound For Slavery / 1983 / BLB / B • Bound To Tease #3 / 1989 / BON / C • Bound To Tease #4 / 1989 / BON / C • Bound To Tease #5 / 1990 / BON / C • The Bride / 1986 / WV / M • Burlexxx / 1984 / VC / M • Cherry Tricks / 1985 / VPE / M • Classical Romance / 1984 / MAP / M • Climax / 1985 / CA / M • Coming Together / 1984 / CA / M • Commando Lovers / 1986 / SUV / M • Competition / 1989 / BON / B • Confessions Of A Nymph / 1985 / VCR / M • Couples Club #1 / 1988 / BON / B • Couples Club #2 / 1989 / BON / B • Crazy With The Heat #1 / 1986 / CV / M • Cunning Coeds / 1985 / IVP / M • Dangerous Stuff / 1985 / COM / M • Deep Obsession / 1987 / WV / M • Detroit Dames / 1988 / DR / C • Dirty Blonde / 1984 / VXP / M • Don't Tell Daddy #1 / 1985 / PL / C • Driller / 1984 / VC / M • Dutch Masters / 1990 / IN / M • Easy Way Out / 1989 / OD / M • Erotic Aerobics / 1984 / VC / M • Erotic Express / 1983 / CV / M • Erotic Radio WSEX / 1983 / VC / M • The Erotic World Of Rene Summers / 1984 / VCR / C • Female Sensations / 1984 / VC / M • Firestorm #2: The Angel Blade / 1986 / COM / M • Firestorm #3 / 1986 / COM / M • First Time At Cherry High / 1984 / VC / M • Flame / 1989 / ARG / M • Flash Backs / 1990 / BON / B • For Your Lips Only / 1989

/ FAZ / M • Forced Love / 1990 / LV / M • Full Nest / 1992 / WV / C • Getting Lucky / 1983 / CA / M • Girls Gone Bad #1 / 1990 / GO / F • Girls On Girls / 1987 / SE / C • Good Girls Do / 1984 / HO / M • Graduation Ball / 1989 / CAE / M • Great Sexpectations / 1984 / VC / M • Here...Eat This! / 1990 / FAZ / M • Hocus Poke-Us / 1991 / HO / M • Hostage Girls / 1984 / VC / M • Hot Shorts: Rene Summers / 1986 / VCR / C • Hot Spa / 1984 / CA / M • I Never Say No / 1983 / VC / M • Immorals #2: The Good, The Bad, And The Banged / 1990 / AR / M • Joys Of Erotica #112 / 1984 / VCR / C • La Boomba / 1987 / VCX / M • The Last X-Rated Movie #1 / 1990 / COM / M • The Last X-Rated Movie #2 / 1990 / COM / M • The Last X-Rated Movie #3 / 1990 / COM / M • The Last X-Rated Movie #4 / 1990 / COM / M • Le Hot Club / 1987 / WV / M • Lingerie / 1983 / CDI / M • Loose Times At Ridley High / 1984 / VCX / M • Losing Control / 1985 / CDI / M • Lottery Lust / 1986 / PEN / M • Making It / 1990 / FH / M • Memoirs Of A Chambermaid / 1987 / FIR / M • Moondance / 1991 / WV / M • The Night Before / 1987 / WV / M • Night Games / 1986 / WV / M • Only The Best Of The Erotic Eighties / 1992 / VC / C • Oral Majority #08 / 1990 / WV / C • P.S.: Back Alley Cats #04 / 1992 / PSP / F • P.S.: Back Alley Cats #05 / 1992 / PSP / F • Parliament: Lesbian Seduction #1 / 1990 / PM / F • Parliament: Lesbian Seduction #2 / 1990 / PM / C • Peeping Passions / 1989 / CAE / M • Pleasure Island / 1984 / AR / M • Pleasure Productions #01 / 1984 / VCR / M • Pleasure Productions #02 / 1984 / VCR / M • Pleasure Productions #08 / 1984 / VCR / M • Porn Star Of The Year Contest / 1984 / VWA / M • Pulsating Flesh / 1986 / VC / M • Pussycat Galore / 1984 / VC / M • Rachel Ryan / 1988 / WV / C • Raven Richards Star Bound / 1990 / BON / B • Rebecca's / 1983 / AVC / M • Rene Summers Star Bound / 1990 / BON / B • Revenge Of The Babes #1 / 1985 / LA / M • Sailing Into Ecstasy / 1986 / VCX / M • Saturday Matinee Series #4 / 1996 / VCX / C • Scenes They Wouldn't Let Me Shoot / 1984 / VC / M • The Seduction Formula / 1990 / FAN / M • The Seduction Of Lana Shore / 1984 / PL / M • Sex In The Great Outdoors / 1987 / SE / C • Sex On The Set / 1984 / RLV / M • Sex Spa USA / 1984 / VC / M • Sex Waves / 1984 / EXF / M • Sinful Pleasures / 1987 / HO / C • Smoke Screen / 1990 / CA / M • Smooth And Easy / 1990 / XCV / M • Stiff Magnolias / 1990 / HO / M • Strange Love / 1987 / WV / M • Stray Cats / 1985 / VXP / M • Swingers Ink / 1990 / VC / M • The T & A Team / 1984 / VC / M • Teasers: Frustrated Housewife / 1988 / MET / M • Theatre Of Seduction #1 / 1990 / BON / B • Theatre Of Seduction #2 / 1990 / BON / B • Too Young To Know / 1984 / CC / M • Tools Of The Trade / 1990 / WV / M • Urges In Young Girls / 1984 / VC / M • Viva Vanessa The Undresser / 1984 / VC / M • Wet Dreams / 1984 / CA / M • When Larry Ate Sally / 1989 / EX / M • Who Reamed Rosie Rabbit? #2 / 1989 / FAN / M • Why Do You Want To be In An Adult Video / 1990 / PM / F • Wise Ass! / 1990 / FH / M • Young And Naughty / 1984 / HO / M
RENE TIFFANY *(Renee Tiffani, Tiffany*

Rene)
Judging by the accent this girl is actually French. She has a lithe body, small tits, tight waist, short curly reddish-blonde hair; unfortunately also a not too pretty face. Amber Aroused / 1985 / CA / M • Blondie / 1985 / TAR / M • Camp Beaverlake #1 / 1984 / AR / M • Endless Passion / 1987 / LIM / C • The Eyes Of Eddie Mars / 1984 / CV / M • The Girl With The Hungry Eyes / 1984 / ECS / M • Girls Of The Night / 1985 / CA / M • Hot Touch / 1984 / VCX / M • Inflamed / 1984 / NSV / M • Kinky Business #1 / 1984 / DR / M • Limited Edition #29 / 1984 / AVC / M • A Little Bit Of Hanky Panky / 1984 / GO / M • Mama's Boy / 1984 / VD / M • The Many Shades Of Amber / 1986 / LIM / M • The Mating Season / 1984 / VC / M • Palomino Heat / 1985 / COM / F • Passionate Lee / 1984 / CRE / M • Scandalous Simone / 1985 / SE / M • Surrender In Paradise / 1984 / GO / M • Teasers / 1984 / HO / M • Tight Squeeze / 1986 / AVC / M • Vixens In Heat / 1984 / ECS / M

RENE VERLAINE see Jenny Baxter

RENE-JEAN see Star Index I

RENEE
Bi-Bi Love Amateurs #4 / 1994 / QUA / G • Blue Vanities #545 / 1994 / FFL / M • Blue Vanities #553 / 1994 / FFL / M • Dixie Debutantes #1 / 1996 / MYS / M • Mike Hott: #393 / 1996 / MHV / M • The Perfect Woman #1: Renee, From Innocence To Not So Innoc. / 1992 / ERK / S • Southern: Previews #2 / 1992 / SSH / C • Wet & Willing Co-Eds #103 / 1994 / PEI / F

RENEE (GORDZILLA)
Kink #2 / 1995 / ROB / M

RENEE ANDREE
Blue Vanities #556 / 1994 / FFL / M • Lust At First Bite / 1978 / VC / M

RENEE BENNETT
The Adventures Of Peeping Tom #1 / 1996 / OD / M • Cyber-Sex Love Junkies / 1996 / BBE / M • Eye On You: Rene / 1996 / EOY / M • Fresh Faces #08 / 1995 / EVN / M • Hollywood Amateurs #20 / 1995 / MID / M • House Of Hoochies / 1996 / DDP / M • Innocence Lost / 1995 / GO / M • Interview's Blonde Bombshells / 1995 / LV / M • Kym Wilde's On The Edge #25 / 1995 / RB / B • Kym Wilde's On The Edge #26 / 1995 / RB / B • Kym Wilde's On The Edge #36 / 1996 / RB / B • My First Time #1 / 1995 / NS / M • Solo Adventures / 1996 / AB / F

RENEE DUBOIS see Star Index I

RENEE ROYALLE
The Casting Couch / 1983 / GO / M

RENEE SANZ
The Affairs Of Janice / 1975 / ALP / M • The Devil Inside Her / 1977 / ALP / M • Frank Henenlotter's XXX Hardcore Horrors #05 / 1996 / SOW / M

RENEE SUMMERS see Star Index I

RENEE TIFFANI see Rene Tiffany

RENIE see Star Index I

RENNIE
100% Amateur #24: Dildos And Toys / 1996 / OD / M

RENO FLAMES
N.Y. Video Magazine #10 / 1996 / OUP / M • Streets Of New York #06 / 1996 / PL / M

RENYA
Brunette Roulette / 1996 / LE / M

REO
Voyeur's Fantasies / 1996 / C69 / M

REO ROBERTO
Bi Bi Banjee Boyz / 1994 / PL / G

RETAMA HAAG see Star Index I

REV. ROBERT PETERSON see Star Index I

REVA WONDU see Star Index I

REVEREND PARSONS
County Line / 1993 / PEP / M • The Mountie / 1994 / PP / M • Revenge Of The Pussy Suckers From Mars / 1994 / PP / M • Sex Circus / 1994 / VIM / M • Surfer Girl / 1992 / PP / M • Unplugged / 1995 / CC / M

REX
Fresh Faces #03 / 1995 / EVN / M • Harry Horndog #19: Anal Lovers #3 / 1993 / ZA / M • Ona Zee's Date With Dallas / 1992 / ONA / M • Profiles #03: House Dick / 1995 / XPR / M

REX BLAZER
Latex #1 / 1994 / VC / M

REX BORSKY see Alex DeRenzy

REX BRUCE
Below The Belt / 1993 / RB / B

REX HONDO see Star Index I

REX HOUSTON see Steve Houston

REX KING see Lance Heywood

REX MORRISON
Biff Malibu's Totally Nasty Home Videos #32 / 1993 / ANA / M • Casting Call #02 / 1993 / SO / M • Casting Call (Venus 99) / 1993 / V99 / M • The Darker Side Of Shayla #2 / 1993 / PL / M • Femme Fatale / 1993 / SC / M • For The Money #2 / 1993 / FH / M • Hollywood Swingers #10 / 1993 / LBO / M • Inferno #2 / 1993 / SC / M • Private Film #04 / 1993 / OD / M • Raunch #06: French Kiss / 1992 / CC / M • WPINK-TV #4 / 1993 / PV / M

REX NEMO
And I Do Windows Too / 1986 / PP / M • The Best Little Whorehouse In Hong Kong / 1987 / SE / M • Born To Be Bad / 1987 / CV / M • Born To Be Wild / 1987 / SE / M • Cheri's On Fire / 1986 / V99 / M • Debbie Does The Devil In Dallas / 1987 / SE / M • Glamour Girls / 1987 / SE / M • Hands Off / 1988 / PP / M • Hot Property / 1989 / EXH / C • Hyapatia Lee's Arcade Series #01 / 1988 / ZA / C • Laid In The USA / 1988 / CC / M • Love At First Sight / 1987 / SE / C • The Mile High Girls / 1987 / CA / M • No One To Love / 1987 / PP / M

REX RAPPERS see Star Index I

REX REAMER see Max Hardcore

REX ROMAN
Confessions Of A Teenage Peanut Butter Freak / 1974 / LIM / M

REX SAYRE see Star Index I

REX TEX see Star Index I

REX THE WONDER HORSE see Star Index I

REYNA see Lil' Bitt

REYZIN INDASON
Harlem Harlots #1 / 1995 / AVS / M

RHAPSODY IN BRONZE
We Be Bangin' 24/7 / 1996 / FD / M

RHEA see Star Index I

RHEA ANN see Star Index I

RHEA LUCAS see Star Index I

RHEANNA see Rhiannon

RHEANON see Rhiannon

RHIANNA see Rhiannon

RHIANNON *(Rheanon, Rheanna, Rhianna, Kitty (Rhiannon), Reannona)*
Tall brunette with small to medium tits, small areola, husky male-like voice, flat ass, long

black curly hair, not too pretty. Barrio Bitches / 1994 / SC / F • First Time Lesbians #19 / 1994 / JMP / F • Gang Bang Bitches #04 / 1995 / PP / M • Harness Hannah At The Strap-On Palace / 1994 / WIV / F • High Heel Harlots #04 / 1994 / SFP / M • Love Thrust / 1995 / ERA / M • Mr. Peepers Amateur Home Videos #87: Groupie Therapy / 1994 / LBO / M • Nasty Newcummers #05 / 1994 / MET / M • Pussyclips #01 / 1994 / SNA / M • Subway / 1994 / SC / M • Tight Tushies #2 / 1994 / MET / M • Toe Tales #39 / 1996 / GOT / B • The Voyeur #2 / 1994 / EA / M • Witness For The Penetration / 1994 / PEP / M

RHIANNON KITAAEN
Love Tryst / 1995 / VPN / M

RHODA
Creme De La Face #16: Ladies Licking / 1996 / OD / M • Nothing Like Nurse Nookie #5 / 1996 / NIT / M

RHONDA
A&B AB#301: Fruit Dildos / 1991 / A&B / F • Blue Vanities #503 / 1992 / FFL / M • Blue Vanities #519 / 1993 / FFL / M • Blue Vanities #534 / 1993 / FFL / M • Blue Vanities #573 / 1996 / FFL / M • HomeGrown Video #472: Everyday People / 1996 / HOV / M • Odyssey 30 Min: #144: Rhonda's Cum Cocktail / 1991 / OD / M • Odyssey Amateur #53: Hump Me, Rhonda / 1991 / OD / M • Odyssey Triple Play #49: Intimate Couples / 1993 / OD / M • The Pawnbroker / 1990 / IF / M • Skirts & Flirts #01 / 1997 / XPR / F

RHONDA BARR
Pleasure Productions #12 / 1985 / VCR / M

RHONDA BAXTER
Girls Around The World #22: Letha Weapons & Friends / 1995 / BTO / M • Top Heavy: Rhonda Baxter / 1996 / H&S / S

RHONDA BLAKE see Linda Lovemore

RHONDA CHANTRELL see Star Index I

RHONDA CLARKE
Bedtime Video #09 / 1984 / GO / M

RHONDA GELLARD
3 A.M. / 1975 / ALP / M

RHONDA HISTED
Stinging Stewardesses / 1996 / BIZ / B

RHONDA JO PETTY *(Sarah Dawcett)*
Fleshy show girl type with large flabby tits. Marginal face. Acting ability of a rock. All The King's Ladies / 1981 / SUP / M • The Angel In Mr. Holmes / 1988 / WV / C • Auditions / 1978 / MEA / S • Aunt Peg Goes To Hollywood / 1982 / CA / M • Baby Cakes / 1982 / SE / M • Bedtime Video #02 / 1984 / GO / M • The Best Little Cathouse In Las Vegas / 1982 / HO / M • Big Bust Babes #01 / 1984 / AFI / M • Blonde At Both Ends / 1993 / TGA / M • Blue Vanities #042 (New) / 1988 / FFL / M • Blue Vanities #046 (New) / 1988 / FFL / M • Blue Vanities #046 (Old) / 1988 / FFL / M • Blue Vanities #047 (Old) / 1988 / FFL / M • Blue Vanities #129 / 1990 / FFL / M • Blue Vanities #176 / 1992 / FFL / M • Blue Vanities #560 / 1994 / FFL / M • Blue Vanities #561 / 1994 / FFL / M • Caballero Preview Tape #3 / 1984 / CA / C • California Girls / 1980 / CA / M • Candy Girls #3 / 19?? / AVC / M • Candy Goes To Hollywood / 1979 / VCX / M • Carnal Olympics / 1983 / CA / M • Casanova #2 / 1976 / CA / M • Cathouse Fever / 1984 / VC / M • Celebration / 1984 / GO / C • The Champ / 1984 / WV / M • Cheap Thrills /

1984 / RLV / M • Cherry Cheesecake / 1984 / AR / M • Classic Swedish Erotica #08 / 1986 / CA / C • Classic Swedish Erotica #31 / 1987 / CA / C • Climax / 1985 / CA / M • Collection #05 / 1984 / CA / M • Country Comfort / 1981 / SE / M • Cover Girl Fantasies #1 / 1983 / VCR / C • Cover Girl Fantasies #3 / 1983 / VCR / C • Creme De Femme #1 / 1981 / AVC / C • Critics' Choice #2 / 1984 / SE / C • Daughters Of Emmanuelle / 1982 / VCX / M • Diamond Collection #01 / 1979 / SVE / M • Disco Lady / 1978 / EVI / M • Down & Dirty Scooter Trash / 1988 / CA / M • Dreamwalk / 1989 / COM / M • Erotic Gold #2 / 1985 / VEN / M • Erotic Moments / 1985 / CDI / C • F / 1980 / GO / M • Fannie's Fantail / 1985 / VC / M • Femme / 1984 / VC / M • Fever / 1982 / EVI / C • Firestorm #2: The Angel Blade / 1986 / COM / M • Firestorm #3 / 1986 / COM / M • Forbidden Worlds / 1988 / GO / C • Glitter / 1983 / CA / M • Golden Girls #33 / 1988 / CA / M • Gourmet Quickies: Rhonda Jo Petty #711 / 1985 / GO / C • Greatest Cathouse In Las Vegas / 1983 / EVI / M • GVC: The Babysitter #107 / 1983 / GO / M • GVC: Lust Weekend #103 / 1980 / GO / M • GVC: Pool Service #105 / cr84 / GO / M • GVC: Women Who Love Women #115 / cr83 / GO / F • Hot Ones / 1982 / SUP / C • Hot Rackets / 1979 / CV / M • Hot Stuff / 1984 / VXP / M • I Know What Girls Like / 1986 / WET / G • Interlude Of Lust / cr79 / HO / M • John Holmes, The Lost Films / 1988 / PEN / C • Las Vegas Erotica / 1983 / MVI / M • The Last X-Rated Movie #1 / 1990 / COM / M • The Last X-Rated Movie #2 / 1990 / COM / M • The Last X-Rated Movie #3 / 1990 / COM / M • Little Orphan Dusty #1 / 1978 / ALP / M • Little Orphan Dusty #2 / 1981 / VIS / M • Love Notes / 1986 / HO / C • Memphis Cathouse Blues / 1982 / CA / M • Moments Of Love / 1983 / MID / M • Mrs. Rodger's Neighborhood / 1988 / EVN / C • Mud Madness / 1983 / AVC / M • National Pornographic #1: Lesbians / 1987 / 4P / C • Oriental Hawaii / 1982 / CA / M • Parliament: Super Head #1 / 1989 / PM / C • Physical #2 / 1985 / SUP / M • Pretty In Black / 1986 / WET / M • Raw Talent #1 / 1984 / VC / M • Rhinestone Cowgirls / 1981 / SE / M • Satisfactions / 1983 / CA / M • The Seduction Of Seka / 1981 / AVC / M • Seka In Heat / 1988 / BMV / C • Sex In The Great Outdoors / 1987 / SE / C • Sex Loose / 1982 / VC / M • Sex Rink / 1976 / ALP / M • Skin Deep / 1982 / CA / M • Snow Honeys / 1983 / VC / M • Succulent / 1983 / VXP / M • Swedish Erotica #03 / 1980 / CA / M • Swedish Erotica #15 / 1980 / CA / M • Swedish Erotica #36 / 1980 / CA / M • Sweet Captive / 1979 / EVI / M • Sweet Cheeks / 1980 / VCX / M • Sweet Dreams Suzan / 1980 / CA / M • Tickled Pink / 1985 / VC / M • Tinsel Town / 1980 / VC / M • Urban Heat / 1985 / FEM / M • VCA Previews #4 / 1988 / VC / C • Voyeur's Delight / 1986 / VCS / C • The Wacky World Of X-Rated Bloopers / 1989 / GO / M • White Women / 1986 / CC / M • Wish You Were Here / 1984 / VXP / M • [Censored Acts / 1983 / ... / M

RHONDA LEES
Lust American Style / 1985 / WV / M
RHONDA MOREY *see Star Index I*

RHONDA SHANTEL *see* **Shantell Day**
RHONDA VANDEGRIFF *see* **Rachel Ashley**
RIA
Club Doma Global #4 / 1994 / VER / B
RIA ASHLEY *see Star Index I*
RIA DE JANERIO
America's Raunchiest Home Videos #55: / 1993 / ZA / M • America's Raunchiest Home Videos #56: Primed For A Party / 1993 / ZA / M • Black Magic #1 / 1993 / VIM / M • The Bold, The Bald & The Beautiful / 1993 / VIM / M • Dark Passions #01 / 1993 / AFV / M • First Time Lesbians #08 / 1993 / JMP / F • Hidden Camera #10 / 1993 / JMP / M • Mr. Peepers Amateur Home Videos #75: Trio In Rio / 1993 / LBO / M • Nympho Zombie Coeds / 1993 / VIM / M • Pearl Necklace: Thee Bush League #17 / 1993 / SEE / M
RIC
Big Bust Babes #12 / 1993 / AFI / M
RIC LEE *(Rick Lee)*
AC/DC #1 / 1991 / LA / G • Black Masters: Trapped / 1995 / GOT / B • Caught! / 1994 / GOT / B • The Challenge / 1995 / GOT / B • Cry Babies (Gotham) / 1995 / GOT / B • Degraded / 1995 / GOT / B • The Fury Inside / 1994 / GOT / B • HomeGrown Video #448: Look Who's Cumming For Dinner / 1995 / HOV / M • I Love Pain / 1995 / GOT / B • Toe Tales #07 / 1993 / GOT / B • Toe Tales #11 / 1993 / GOT / B • Toe Tales #12 / 1994 / GOT / C • Toe Tales #14 / 1994 / GOT / B • Toe Tales #16 / 1994 / GOT / B • Toe Tales #20 / 1995 / GOT / B • Toe Tales #21 / 1995 / GOT / B • Toe Tales #22 / 1995 / GOT / B • Toe Tales #23 / 1995 / GOT / B • Toe Tales #25 / 1995 / GOT / B • Toe Tales #28 / 1995 / GOT / B • Toe Tales #33 / 1996 / GOT / B • Toe Tales #34 / 1996 / GOT / B • Toe Tales #35 / 1996 / GOT / B • Toe Tales #36 / 1996 / GOT / B • Toe Tales #38 / 1996 / GOT / B • Unforgiving Mistress / 1995 / GOT / B • Without Pity / 1995 / GOT / B
RIC LOOTS *see Ric Lutz*
RIC LUTZ *(Rick Lutz, Ric Lutze, Ric Loots, John McKnight, Rick Johns, Jack Livermore)*
Married to Rene Bond at one stage.
ABA: Double Feature #5 / 1996 / ALP / M • All Night Long / 1975 / SE / M • Auditions / 1978 / MEA / S • Bad Bad Gang / 1972 / SOW / M • Beach Blanket Bango / 1975 / EVI / M • Black Beauty (Playtime) / 19?? / PLY / C • Bottoms Up #02 / 1983 / AVC / C • Bottoms Up #05 / 1986 / AVC / C • Bucky Beaver's Double Softies #04 / 1996 / SOW / S • Bucky Beaver's XXX Dragon Art Theatre Double Feature #11 / 1996 / SOW / M • Caught From Behind #01 / 1982 / HO / M • Class Reunion / 1972 / PS / S • The Cocktail Hostesses / 1972 / ... / S • Country Hooker / 1970 / BPI / S • Devil's Ecstasy / 1974 / VCX / M • Disco Lady / 1978 / EVI / M • Flesh Gordon #1 / 1974 / FAC / S • Garters And Lace / 1975 / SE / M • Girl In The Basket / 1972 / ALP / M • High School Fantasies / 1974 / EVI / M • Jezebel / 1979 / CV / M • Lady Luck / 1975 / VCX / M • Legends Of Porn #2 / 1989 / CV / C • The Life And Times Of Xavier Hollander / 1973 / VXP / M • Lipps & Mccain / 1978 / VC / M • Little Angel Puss / cr76 / SVE / M • Little Me & Marla Strangelove / 1979 / ALP / M •

Little Orphan Dusty #1 / 1978 / ALP / M • Lollipop Palace / 1973 / VCX / M • The Loves Of Mary Jane / 1989 / BWV / C • Lust Flight 2000 / 1978 / VHL / M • The Mating Season / 1984 / VC / M • Midnight Hustler / 1972 / ALP / M • Mrs. Rodger's Neighborhood / 1988 / EVN / C • Necromania / 1971 / SOW / S • Panorama Blue / 1974 / ALP / S • Panty Girls / 1972 / BMV / M • The Partnership / 1973 / ALP / M • Please Don't Eat My Mother / 1972 / BPI / S • Pleasure Unlimited / 1972 / PS / S • Private Private / 1971 / ALP / M • Pro Ball Cheerleaders / 1979 / AVC / M • Service Entrance / 1979 / REG / C • Sex, Love And Happiness / 1973 / ... / S • Shot On Location / 1972 / ALP / S • Snow Bunnies / 1970 / NFV / S • Sunny Side Up / 1984 / VC / M • Taxi Girls #1 / 1980 / WV / M • Teaser / 1973 / SOW / S • Teenage Fantasies #1 / 1972 / SOW / M • Teenage Throat / 1974 / ... / M • That's Porno / 1979 / CV / C • Touch Me / 1971 / SE / M • A Touch Of Sex / 1972 / AR / M • True Legends Of Adult Cinema: The Golden Age / 1992 / VC / C • Where The Girls Are / 1984 / VEX / M • The Winning Stroke / 1975 / VIS / M • Yuppies In Heat / 1988 / CHA / C
RIC LUTZE *see Ric Lutz*
RIC MEYERS
Kidnapped Girls Agency / cr86 / HOM / B
RIC NAVARRO
She-Male Encounters #07: Divine Atrocities #1 / 1981 / MET / C
RICARDO ORTIZ *see Star Index I*
RICCI
Der Spritz-Treff / 1995 / KRM / M
RICCI HOHLT
[Junge Madchen Mogen's HeiB, Hausfrauen Noch HeiBer / 1973 / ... / M
RICE JAMES
Bedtime Video #03 / 1984 / GO / M
RICH
Thermonuclear Sex / 1996 / EL / M
RICH ALLSON *see Star Index I*
RICH CASSIDY *see* **Rick Cassidy**
RICH FRIEND
Toe Tales #19 / 1994 / GOT / B • Toe Tales #21 / 1995 / GOT / B
RICH LOAD
Bottom Busters / 1973 / BLT / M
RICH MACKOTA *see Star Index I*
RICH MAGUIRE *see Star Index I*
RICH PLADO *see Star Index I*
RICH ROBERTS *see* **Roland Neves**
RICH STUDMASTER
Great Grandma Gets Her Cookies / 1995 / FC / M
RICHARD
Della Borsa / 1995 / WIV / M • Denni O' #3: Fanta-Sea Of Cum / 1996 / SP / M • Dirty Dancers #1 / 1994 / 4P / M • Double Butts / 1994 / RTP / M • Extraterrestrial Virgins / 1995 / VIT / M • I Want What I See / 1985 / VC / M • Magma: Claudine In Action / 1996 / MET / M • Magma: Deep Inside Janine / 1994 / MET / M • Magma: Double Anal / 1994 / MET / M • Magma: Olympus Of Lust / 1994 / MET / M • Magma: Pussy Jobs / 1994 / MET / M • Magma: Shopping Anal / 1994 / MET / M • Magma: Sperm Dreams / 1990 / MET / M • Profiles In Discipline #04: Mistress Domino / 1994 / STM / C • Skin #2 / 1995 / ERQ / M • Video Virgins #23 / 1995 / NS / M
RICHARD (JON MARTIN) *see* **Jon Martin**

RICHARD ADAMS
Five Loose Women / 1974 / NFV / S • Flesh Factory / 1970 / AVC / M
RICHARD ALAN
Flesh Fever / 1978 / CV / M • Kinky Ladies Of Bourbon Street / 1976 / LUM / M • Two At Once / 1978 / CV / M
RICHARD ALBA *see Star Index I*
RICHARD ALDRICH *see Damon Christian*
RICHARD ALLAN *see Star Index I*
RICHARD ALLEN
Sexual Initiation Of A Married Woman / 1984 / VD / M
RICHARD ALSTON *see Star Index I*
RICHARD ANDERSON *see Star Index I*
RICHARD AUSTIN
[Ripoff / 1984 / ... / M
RICHARD BALLA *see Robert Bolla*
RICHARD BARNES
Rhinestone Cowgirls / 1981 / SE / M
RICHARD BELNICK *see Star Index I*
RICHARD BELZER
Cafe Flesh / 1982 / VC / M • The Groove Tube / 1972 / MED / S
RICHARD BERN *see Star Index I*
RICHARD BOCCA *see Robert Bolla*
RICHARD BOLLA *see Robert Bolla*
RICHARD BOLLAR *see Robert Bolla*
RICHARD BOOTH
One Page Of Love / 1980 / VCX / M
RICHARD BRANDT JR *see Star Index I*
RICHARD BUCKLER *see Star Index I*
RICHARD BULICK *see Robert Bullock*
RICHARD CALDER *see Star Index I*
RICHARD CAMPOS
The Phantom Of The Montague Stage / 1997 / HO / M
RICHARD DIXON *see Star Index I*
RICHARD DOUGLAS
Kiki Tree Bound #1 / 1993 / BON / B • Kiki Tree Bound #2 / 1993 / BON / B • Kiki's Backyard Bondage / 1994 / BON / B • Kiki's Bondage Desires / 1993 / BON / B • Tormented Teaser #1 / 1994 / BON / B • Tormented Teaser #2 / 1994 / BON / B • Trinity Brown / 1984 / CV / M • Virgin On The Rack / cr90 / BON / B
RICHARD DOVE *see Star Index I*
RICHARD DOWNS *see Star Index I*
RICHARD FELLOW
The Young Nymphs / 1973 / ... / M
RICHARD FRENCH *see Star Index I*
RICHARD GILMORE *see Star Index I*
RICHARD GOLD
Anal Connection / 1996 / ZA / M • Sinnocence / 1995 / CDI / M
RICHARD GRANT
Sticky Situation / 1975 / VXP / M
RICHARD HEMMINGWAY
Call Girl / 1984 / CV / M
RICHARD HILLER *see Dave Ruby*
RICHARD JACKSON
Please, Mr Postman / 1981 / VC / M
RICHARD KANTER *see Harold Lime*
RICHARD KARLE *see Star Index I*
RICHARD KERN
Hardcore: The Films Of Richard Kern #1 / 1991 / FTV / M
RICHARD LAIDLAW
The Seductress / 1982 / VC / M
RICHARD LANGIN
Anal Pow Wow / 1995 / XC / M • Dirty Tricks #2: This Ain't Love / 1996 / EA / M • Games Women Play / 1995 / XC / M • Hamlet: For The Love Of Ophelia #1 / 1996

/ IP / M • Hamlet: For The Love Of Ophelia #2 / 1996 / IP / M • Le Parfum De Mathilde / 1994 / VI / M • A Merry Widow / 1996 / SPI / M • Private Film #20 / 1995 / OD / M • Private Film #23 / 1995 / OD / M • Private Film #27 / 1995 / OD / M • Private Gold #05: Cape Town #1 / 1996 / OD / M • Private Gold #06: Cape Town #2 / 1996 / OD / M • Private Gold #07: Kruger Park / 1996 / OD / M • Private Gold #11: The Pyramid #1 / 1996 / OD / M • Private Gold #13: The Pyramid #3 / 1996 / OD / M • Private Gold #14: Sweet Lady #1 / 1997 / OD / M • Secrets Of Madame X #2 / 1995 / WIV / M • Sex Scandals / 1995 / XC / M • Skin #1 / 1994 / EUR / M
RICHARD LEMIEUVRE
Clarissa / 1978 / LUM / S • [Rentre C'est Bon / 1977 / ... / M
RICHARD LOCKE
L.A. Tool & Die / 1979 / TMX / G
RICHARD LOGAN *(Bill Crawford)*
Ceremony, The Ritual Of Love / 1976 / AVC / M • The Other Side Of Julie / 1978 / CV / M • Seven Into Snowy / 1977 / VC / M
RICHARD LONG
Black Booty / 1995 / UBP / M • Y-All Come / 1975 / CDC / M
RICHARD MARIS *see Rick Savage*
RICHARD MARS *see Star Index I*
RICHARD MASON
Josephine / 1974 / VC / M
RICHARD MASTIER *see Star Index I*
RICHARD MCCOY
Undercovers / 1982 / CA / M
RICHARD MILES
One Last Score / 1978 / CDI / M
RICHARD MILLER
The Starmaker / 1982 / VC / M
RICHARD O'NEAL
A Dirty Western #1 / 1973 / AR / M • Erotic Fantasies #1 / 1983 / CV / C • Saturday Matinee Series #3 / 1996 / VCX / C • That's Erotic / 1979 / CV / C
RICHARD PACHECO *(Dewey Alexander, Mark Howard, Richard Pecheko, Marc Howard, Mack Howard)*
The 8th Annual Erotic Film Awards / 1984 / SE / C • Anal Annie And The Willing Husbands / 1984 / LIP / M • Anal Annie Just Can't Say No / 1984 / LIP / M • Aunt Peg's Fulfillment / 1980 / CV / M • Baby Love & Beau / 1979 / TVX / M • Bad Girls #1 / 1981 / GO / M • Bad Girls #4 / 1984 / GO / M • The Best Of Gail Palmer / 1981 / WWV / C • Between The Sheets / 1982 / CA / M • Blonde Heat (VCA) / 1985 / VC / M • Boom Boom Valdez / 1988 / CA / M • Candy Goes To Hollywood / 1979 / VCX / M • Candy Stripers #1 / 1978 / ALP / M • Careful, He May Be Watching / 1986 / CA / M • The Chameleon / 1989 / VC / M • Critics' Choice #2 / 1984 / SE / C • The Dancers / 1981 / VCX / M • Debbie Does Dishes #3 / 1987 / AVC / M • Easy / 1978 / CV / M • Erotic Fantasies #2 / 1983 / CV / C • Erotic Fantasies #6 / 1984 / CV / C • The Erotic World Of Linda Wong / 1985 / VIV / M • Expose Me Now / 1982 / CV / M • Female Athletes / 1977 / VXP / M • The Final Taboo / 1988 / CA / M • For Love And Lust / 1985 / AVC / M • Garage Girls / 1981 / CV / M • Goin' Down Slow / 1988 / VC / M • High School Memories / 1980 / VCX / M • Honkytonk Angels / 1988 / IN / C • Hot Legs / 1979 / VCX / M • The Huntress /

1987 / IN / M • Insatiable #1 / 1980 / CA / M • The Insatiable Hyapatia Lee / 1987 / SE / C • Inside Desiree Cousteau / 1979 / VCX / M • Irresistible #1 / 1982 / SE / M • The Legend Of Lady Blue / 1978 / VCX / M • Legends Of Porn #1 / 1987 / CV / C • Lethal Woman #1 / 1988 / SEV / M • Lethal Woman #2 / 1988 / SEV / M • Love Scenes For Loving Couples / 1987 / CV / C • Mad Love / 1988 / VC / M • Naughty Girls Need Love Too / 1983 / SE / M • Never So Deep / 1981 / VCX / M • Nina's Knockouts / 1987 / AVC / C • Nothing To Hide #1 / 1981 / CV / M • Once Upon A Temptress / 1988 / CA / M • Only The Best Of Men's And Women's Fantasies / 1988 / CV / C • Our Dinner With Andrea / 1988 / CA / M • The Passion Within / 1986 / MAP / M • Passions / 1985 / MIT / M • Pizza Girls (We Deliver) / 1978 / VCX / M • Please, Mr Postman / 1981 / VC / M • Porn Star Confidential / 1996 / ESF / M • Portrait Of A Nymph / 1988 / PP / M • Portrait Of An Affair / 1988 / VD / M • Pretty Peaches #3 / 1989 / VC / M • Princess Charming / 1987 / AVC / C • Randy, The Electric Lady / 1978 / VC / M • The Red Garter / 1986 / SE / M • Reel People #01 / 1983 / AR / M • Rockin' Erotica / 1987 / SE / C • Screwples / 1979 / CA / M • Second Skin / 1989 / VC / M • Sensual Encounters Of Every Kind / 1978 / SE / M • Sensual Escape / 1988 / FEM / M • The Sensuous Detective / 1979 / VC / M • The Seven Seductions Of Madame Lau / 1981 / EVI / M • Sex Loose / 1982 / VC / M • Sex Play / 1984 / SE / M • Sex Wars / 1984 / EXF / M • Shauna Grant: The Early Years / 1988 / PV / C • Skin On Skin / 1981 / CV / M • Spectators / 1984 / AVC / M • Summer Of '72 / 1982 / CA / M • Sunny Days / cr80 / BOC / M • Sweat #2 / 1988 / PP / M • Swedish Erotica #46 / 1983 / CA / M • Sweethearts / 1986 / SE / C • Tailspin / 1987 / AVC / M • Talk Dirty To Me #01 / 1980 / CA / M • Talk Dirty to Me One More Time #2 / 1988 / PP / C • Telefantasy / 1978 / AR / M • Ten Little Maidens / 1985 / EXF / M • The Titty Committee / 1986 / SE / C • Up 'n' Coming / 1983 / CA / M • VCA Previews #4 / 1988 / VC / C • Vista Valley PTA / 1980 / CV / M • White Hot / 1984 / VXP / M • With Love, Annette / 1985 / CA / C • With Love, Loni / 1985 / CA / C
RICHARD PARNES *see Robert Bullock*
RICHARD PATRICK
Kitty's Pleasure Palace / 1971 / ALP / M
RICHARD PECHEKO *see Richard Pacheco*
RICHARD PHILLIPE
Lettre Da Rimini / 1995 / MID / M
RICHARD PORTA *see Star Index I*
RICHARD PORTER *see Star Index I*
RICHARD REYES
Goldilocks And The 3 Bi Bears / 1997 / TTV / G
RICHARD RIMMER
Secret Dreams Of Mona Q / 1977 / AR / M • Tigresses...And Other Man-Eaters / 1979 / VXP / M
RICHARD RUSSELL
Undercovers / 1982 / CA / M
RICHARD SAMSON
Nicole: The Story Of O / 1972 / CLX / M
RICHARD SEGAL *see Star Index I*
RICHARD SMEDLY
Come Ring My Chimes / 19?? / ... / M

RICHARD SMILES
Sodomania #08: The London Sessions / 1994 / EL / M
RICHARD STEELE *see Star Index I*
RICHARD STERNBERGER *see Star Index I*
RICHARD STEVENS
Here Comes The Bride / 1977 / CV / M • X Factor / 1984 / HO / M
RICHARD STRONG *see Star Index I*
RICHARD THORPE
Suburban Wives / 19?? / VST / M
RICHARD TRACY *see Star Index I*
RICHARD VICTOR
Bon Appetit / 1980 / QX / M
RICHARD VOISIN
Magma: Spezial: Black & White #3 / 1995 / MET / M • Private Film #04 / 1993 / OD / M • Private Film #06 / 1994 / OD / M
RICHARD VOISSIS
Ejacula #1 / 1992 / VC / M • Ejacula #2 / 1992 / VC / M • Impulse #06: / 1996 / MBP / M
RICHARD WILLIAMS
Sodom & Gomorrah / 1974 / MIT / M
RICHARD YOUNGBLOOD
L.A. Tool & Die / 1979 / TMX / G
RICHARD ZUFGER *see Star Index I*
RICHI CUMMINGS *see Star Index I*
RICHIE DAGGER *see Star Index I*
RICHIE MCWILLIAMS
Lady Zazu's Daughter / 1971 / ALP / M
RICHIE RAVENS
The Line Up / 1996 / CDI / M
RICHIE RAZOR *see Ritchie Razor*
RICK
Amateur Hours #02 / 1989 / AFI / M • AVP #7031: Working It Out Again / 1991 / AVP / M • Bobby Hollander's Rookie Nookie #01 / 1993 / SFP / M • Depravity On The Danube / 1993 / EL / M • Girls Around The World #21: Tawny Peaks & Friends / 1995 / BTO / M • Hidden Camera #21 / 1994 / JMP / M • Mondo Extreme / 1996 / SHS / M • Mr. Madonna / 1994 / FPI / G • On The Prowl #2 / 1991 / SC / M • Pearl Necklace: Amorous Amateurs #01 / 1992 / SEE / M • Pearl Necklace: Amorous Amateurs #03 / 1992 / SEE / M • Pearl Necklace: Amorous Amateurs #08 / 1992 / SEE / M • Pussy Tails #01 / 1993 / CDY / M • Rump Humpers #05 / 1992 / GLI / M • Sodomania #05: Euro-American Style / 1993 / EL / M • Sodomania #17: Simply Makes U Tingle / 1996 / EL / M • Torturess #2: Trained For Pleasure / 1996 / STM / B • Victoria's Amateurs #02 / 1992 / VGA / M • The Voyeur #8: Live In Europe #2 / 1996 / JLP / M
RICK ADAMS *see Star Index I*
RICK ARDO
Golden Girls, The Movie / 1984 / SE / M • Rhinestone Cowgirls / 1981 / SE / M • Sound Of Love / 1981 / CA / M
RICK ARDONNE *see Star Index I*
RICK BLAINE *(Rick Hudson, Harvey (Rick Blaine))*
Ugly, balding white male with a hook nose.
The A Chronicles / 1992 / CC / M • American Swinger Video Magazine #04 / 1993 / ZA / M • Anal Climax #2 / 1991 / ROB / M • As Sweet As Can Be / 1993 / V99 / M • Assford Wives / 1992 / ATL / M • Bareback Riders / 1992 / VEX / M • Beach Bum Amateur's #03 / 1992 / MID / M • Behind The Backdoor #5 / 1992 / EVN / M • Big Murray's New-Cummers #13: Hot Tight Ladies

/ 1993 / FD / M • Bubble Butts #11 / 1992 / LBO / M • Bubble Butts #23 / 1992 / LBO / M • The Burma Road #1 / 1994 / LBO / C • The Burma Road #2 / 1994 / LBO / C • Burn It Up / 1994 / VEX / M • Butt Light: Queen Of Rears / 1992 / STR / M • California Taxi Girls / 1991 / AFV / M • Casting Call (Venus 99) / 1993 / V99 / M • Dresden Diary #09 / 1993 / BIZ / B • Dresden Diary #10: Punishment For Their Sins / 1993 / BIZ / B • The Finishing Touch / 1994 / DR / M • Fringe Benefits / 1992 / IF / M • Gangbang Girl #06 / 1992 / ANA / M • Gangbang Girl #08 / 1992 / ANA / M • Gangbang Girl #11 / 1993 / ANA / M • It's Only Love / 1992 / VEX / M • Jennifer 69 / 1992 / PL / M • The Last Temptation Of Teri / 1991 / IF / M • Laying Down The Law #1 / 1992 / AFV / M • Laying Down The Law #2 / 1992 / AFV / M • Living For Love / 1993 / V99 / M • Musical Bedrooms / 1993 / AFV / M • Mystery Of The Maletease Dildo / 1992 / STR / M • Nookie Court / 1992 / AFV / M • One Lay At A Time / 1992 / V99 / M • One Of A Kind / 1992 / VEX / M • Party Favors / 1993 / VEX / M • Petite & Sweet / 1994 / V99 / M • The Princess Slave / 1994 / BIZ / B • Pussy Tamer #1 / 1993 / BIZ / B • Pussy Tamer #2 / 1993 / BIZ / B • Romancing The Butt / 1992 / ATL / M • Secret Admirer / 1992 / VEX / M • Sex In A Singles Bar / 1992 / VC / M • Six Plus One #2 / 1993 / VEX / C • So You Want To Be In The Movies? / 1994 / VC / M • The Spirit Of My Master / 1994 / BIZ / B • Star Struck / 1992 / VEX / M • Super Hornio Brothers #1 / 1993 / MID / M • Super Hornio Brothers #2 / 1993 / MID / M • The Sweet Sweet Back's Big Bone (#1) / 1994 / FH / M • Take Me...Use Me...Make Me Your Slave / 1994 / BIZ / B • Tempting Tianna / 1992 / V99 / M • To Serve...Protect...And Submit / 1994 / BIZ / B • Tonight's The Night / 1992 / V99 / M • Torrid Tonisha / 1992 / VEX / M • Unsolved Double Penetration / 1993 / PEP / M • Up For Grabs / 1991 / FH / M • Visions Of Desire / 1994 / DR / M • White Wedding / 1994 / V99 / M • Who Killed Holly Hollywood? / 1993 / VC / M
RICK BOLTON
Bi-Ology: The Making Of Mr Right / 1992 / CAT / G • Down Bi Law / 1992 / CAT / G
RICK BOWE *(T.C. (Rick Bowe), Vic Nixon)*
Young male with a moustache who first appeared with his wife Heather in **Deep Inside Dirty Debutantes #02**.
America's Raunchiest Home Videos #73: / 1993 / ZA / M • Anal Vision #19 / 1993 / LBO / M • Assmania!! #2 / 1995 / ME / M • Back In Style / 1993 / VI / M • The Big Bang #1 / 1993 / LV / M • The Bottom Dweller Part Deux / 1994 / EL / M • Bun Busters #05 / 1993 / LBO / M • Butthead & Beaver / 1993 / HW / M • Colossal Orgy #2 / 1994 / HW / M • Deep Inside Dirty Debutantes #02 / 1992 / 4P / M • The Flirt / 1995 / GO / M • Gangbang Girl #12 / 1993 / ANA / M • Gangbang Girl #13 / 1994 / ANA / M • Hidden Camera #06 / 1993 / JMP / M • Hidden Camera #08 / 1993 / JMP / M • Hollywood '94: Butts Abound / 1993 / ELP / M • Madame Hollywood / 1993 / LE / M • Nasty Nymphos #01 / 1993 / ANA / M • Odyssey Triple Play #71: Bodacious Blondes / 1994 / OD / M • Pearl Necklace: Thee Bush League #24 / 1993 / SEE / M • Private

Video Magazine #05 / 1993 / OD / M • The Quest / 1994 / SC / M • Rocks / 1993 / VT / M • Supermodel #2 / 1994 / VI / M • Tales From The Clit / 1993 / OD / M • Top Debs #5: Deb Of The Month / 1994 / GO / M • Up And Cummers #03 / 1993 / 4P / M
RICK BROCK
Bedtime Stories / 1996 / VC / M • Dominique's Inheritance / 1996 / CVC / M • Double Penetration Virgins: DP Therapy / 1996 / JMP / M • Naked Mockey-Rayna / 1996 / EVN / M
RICK CANON
Bobby Hollander's Maneaters #02 / 1993 / SFP / M • More Dirty Debutantes #20 / 1993 / 4P / M • Mr. Peepers Amateur Home Videos #65: Suckaterial Skills / 1993 / LBO / M • Uncle Roy's Amateur Home Video #09 / 1992 / VIM / M
RICK CASSIDY *(Jim Cassidy, Rich Cassidy, Cal Cassidy)*
Blonde bodybuilder type male who also appeared in lots of gay movies including **All American Boys in Heat** and **Thunderbolt #2**.
Auditions / 1978 / MEA / S • Audra's Ordeal / 1983 / BIZ / B • The Beach Bunnies / 1975 / ... / S • Bizarre People / 1982 / BIZ / G • Blue Vanities #046 (Old) / 1988 / FFL / M • Blue Vanities #244 / 1995 / FFL / M • Cathouse Fever / 1984 / VC / M • The Cheaters / 1973 / ALP / M • Cheri / 1971 / VCX / M • Classified Sex / 1975 / CPL / M • The Cocktail Hostesses / 1972 / ... / S • Come Ring My Chimes / 19?? / ... / M • Country Girls / 1977 / ... / M • The Danish Connection / 1970 / SOW / S • Desires Of Wendy / 1975 / CA / M • Diamond Collection #60 / 1984 / CDI / M • Divorce Court Expose #1 / 1986 / VD / M • Divorce Court Expose #2 / 1987 / VD / M • Don't Tell Mama / 1974 / VIP / M • The Erotic Adventures Of Peter Galore / 1973 / ALP / M • Evil Come Evil Go / 1972 / STO / S • Fantasm Cums Again / 1977 / VS / S • For Services Rendered / 1984 / CA / M • French Schoolgirls / 1973 / AVC / M • Ginger's Hawaiian Scrapbook / 1988 / GO / C • Girls & Guys & Girls Or Guys / 19?? / REG / M • Godmother / 1975 / ... / M • Gourmet Quickies: Ginger Lynn #720 / 1985 / GO / C • Gourmet Quickies: Mai Lin #724 / 1985 / GO / C • GVC: Olympix Affair #137 / 1985 / GO / M • Here Comes Johnny Wadd / 197? / ... / C • Hot Tails / 1984 / VEN / M • How Sweet It Is / 1974 / SE / M • Hypnotic Sensations / 1985 / GO / M • Juggs / 1984 / VCR / M • The Liars / cr71 / AXV / M • The Life And Times Of Xavier Hollander / 1973 / VXP / M • Lonely Lady / 1984 / VC / M • Love Skills: A Guide To The Pleasures Of Sex / 1984 / MCA / S • The Loves Of Mary Jane / 1989 / BWV / C • The Lumberjacks / 1971 / ALP / M • Marilyn Chambers' Private Fantasies #3 / 1983 / CA / M • Marriage And Other Four Letter Words / 1974 / VC / M • Mislaid Lovers / 1978 / ... / M • More Than Friends / 1973 / AXV / M • New Wave Hookers #1 / 1984 / VC / M • Panorama Blue / 1974 / ALP / S • Panty Girls / 1972 / BMV / M • Penthouse Passions / 1975 / BLT / M • The Perfect Weekend / 1984 / AVC / M • Please Me! / cr86 / LIM / M • Pleasure Productions #08 / 1984 / VCR / M • Pleasure Unlimited / 1972 / PS / S • Rich Quick, Private Dick / 1984 / CA /

M • Satan's Sex Slaves / 1971 / ALP / M • Sex Prophet / 1973 / ALP / M • Sex Psycho / 1971 / SOW / M • Swedish Erotica #53 / 1984 / CA / M • Swedish Erotica #55 / 1984 / CA / M • Swedish Erotica #60 / 1984 / CA / M • Swinging Ski Girls / 1981 / VCX / M • Swinging Sorority / 1976 / VCX / S • Teenage Cruisers / 1977 / VCX / M • Too Naughty To Say No / 1984 / CA / M • A Touch Of Sex / 1972 / AR / M • The Ultimate Kiss / 1984 / ZA / M • The Wacky World Of X-Rated Bloopers / 1989 / GO / M • Welcome Wagon / 1973 / VCX / M • The Winning Stroke / 1975 / VIS / M • [Hot Summer Night / 1972 / VCI / M • [Love For Sale / 1973 / VIP / M • [Love Hollywood Style / 1972 / ... / M • [Men In Control / 1988 / ... / B • [The Professionals / cr72 / ... / M • [The S&M Group / 197? / ... / M

RICK CHAMBERLAIN
Exploring Young Girls / 1978 / ALP / M

RICK CHRISTMAS
Dirty Dancers #4 / 1995 / 4P / M • Stiff Competition #2 / 1994 / CA / M

RICK COLEMAN
Fan Fuxxx #1 / 1996 / DWV / M

RICK DANIELS
The Adventures Of Buttman / 1989 / EA / M • Anal Attraction #1 / 1988 / 3HV / M • Backdoor To Harley-Wood #1 / 1990 / AFV / M • Backdoor To Hollywood #06 / 1989 / CIN / M • Backdoor To Hollywood #07 / 1989 / CIN / M • Backdoor To Hollywood #08 / 1989 / CIN / M • Bored Housewife / 1989 / CIN / M • Bush League #1 / 1990 / CC / M • Caught From Behind #10 / 1989 / HO / M • Champagne Bound At Home / cr90 / BON / B • Dance Fire / 1989 / EA / M • Do It In The Road / 1990 / LV / M • Don't Worry Be Sexy / 1989 / EVN / C • Double Trouble / 1988 / V99 / M • Dreams In The Forbidden Zone / 1989 / PCP / M • Dutch Masters / 1990 / IN / M • Gangbang Girl #03 / 1992 / ANA / M • Gangbang Girl #04 / 1992 / ANA / M • Girls Of The Double D #05 / 1988 / CIN / M • Girls Of The Double D #14 / 1990 / CIN / M • Hard Sell / 1990 / VC / M • Hot Cargo / 1990 / MID / M • I Said A Butt Light #1 / 1990 / LV / M • Insatiable Immigrants / 1989 / VT / M • L.A. Fantasies / 1990 / WV / C • Lawyers In Heat / 1989 / CDI / M • The Love Mistress / 1989 / WV / M • Miss Adventures / 1989 / VEX / M • Swingers Ink / 1990 / VC / M • The Whole Diamond / 1990 / EVN / M

RICK DEAN
Back Down / 1996 / RB / B • Naked Obsession / 1992 / VES / S • Saturday Night Special / 1994 / NEH / S

RICK DILLON
Female Chauvinists / 1975 / ... / M

RICK DONOVAN see Star Index I

RICK ESTEPHAN
Married Men With Men On The Side / 1996 / BHE / G • Mr. Blue / 1996 / JSP / G

RICK FLICK see Star Index I

RICK FONTE see Winston Fonte

RICK FRIEND
Toe Tales #20 / 1995 / GOT / B

RICK GOZINYA see Star Index I

RICK HAMMER see Star Index I

RICK HOLIDAY
Kym Wilde's On The Edge #33 / 1996 / RB / B

RICK HOLLAND see Star Index I

RICK HUDSON see Rick Blaine

RICK IVERSON *(Jeremy Wyatt)*
The Budding Of Brie / 1980 / TVX / M • The Cosmopolitan Girls / 1982 / VC / M • Dr Love And His House Of Perversions / 1978 / VC / M • Justine: A Matter Of Innocence / 1980 / SAT / M • Love-In Arrangement / 1981 / VXP / M • The Pink Ladies / 1980 / VC / M • Silky / 1980 / VXP / M • Sunny / 1979 / VC / M

RICK JACKSON see Star Index I

RICK JACKSON (SCUD) see Ken Scudder

RICK JAYES
Pai Gow Video #09: Naked Asians / 1995 / EVN / M

RICK JOHNS see Ric Lutz

RICK JOHNSON
All "A" / 1994 / SFP / C • America's Raunchiest Home Videos #57 / 1993 / ZA / M • Bikini Bistro / 1995 / 3SR / S • Bobby Hollander's Maneaters #05 / 1993 / SFP / M • Bobby Hollander's Rookie Nookie #06 / 1993 / SFP / M • Boob Tube Lube / 1996 / RAS / M • Fatal Instinct / 1992 / NLH / S • Princess Of Persia / 1993 / IP / M • Starbangers #01 / 1993 / BIG / M • Thundercrack! / 1974 / LUM / M

RICK JONES see Star Index I

RICK JOYCE
Taboo American Style #4: The Exciting Conclusion / 1985 / VC / M

RICK LAROCCO see Star Index I

RICK LAVERNE
The Pay-Off / cr70 / VHL / M

RICK LAW see Star Index I

RICK LEE see Ric Lee

RICK LIETER
Triple Play (Vh) / cr75 / VC / M

RICK LONG
Ho The Man Down / 1994 / WIV / M

RICK LUTZ see Ric Lutz

RICK LUV see Star Index I

RICK MAGUIRE
Amateur Dreams #3 / 1994 / DR / M • Colossal Orgy #1 / 1993 / HW / M • Colossal Orgy #2 / 1994 / HW / M • Double D Amateurs #13 / 1994 / JMP / M • Hillary Vamp's Private Collection #06 / 1992 / HOV / M • Next Door Neighbors #36 / 1991 / BON / M • The Other Side Of Debbie / 1991 / CC / M • Our Bang #09 / 1993 / GLI / M • Positively Pagan #01 / 1991 / ATA / M • Positively Pagan #02 / 1991 / ATA / M • Positively Pagan #04 / 1991 / ATA / M • Positively Pagan #05 / 1993 / ATA / M • Positively Pagan #07 / 1993 / ATA / M • Positively Pagan #08 / 1993 / ATA / M • Raw Talent: Bang 'er 14 Times / 1992 / RTP / M • Robin Head / 1991 / CC / M • Ultimate Gang Bang #1 / 1994 / HW / M • Wendy Is Watching / 1993 / ELP / M

RICK MARTINO see Star Index I

RICK MARX
The 8th Annual Erotic Film Awards / 1984 / SE / C • In Love / 1983 / VC / M

RICK MASTERS *(Jerid Storm, Jerid (R. Masters), Jarad (R. Masters), Dick Masters)*
50 And Still Gangbangin'! / 1995 / EMC / M • 50 And Still Pumping! / 1994 / EMC / M • 55 And Still Bangin' / 1995 / HW / M • Abducted / 1996 / ZA / M • Abused / 1996 / ZA / M • Addicted To Lust / 1996 / NIT / M • Adventures Of The DP Boys: At The French Riviera / 1994 / HW / M • Adventures Of The DP Boys: Back In Town / 1994 / HW /

M • Adventures Of The DP Boys: Berlin Butt Babes / 1993 / HW / M • Adventures Of The DP Boys: Big Black Booty / 1994 / HW / M • Adventures Of The DP Boys: Chocolate City / 1994 / HW / M • Adventures Of The DP Boys: Hooter County / 1995 / HW / M • Adventures Of The DP Boys: Sicilian Sluts / 1995 / HW / M • Adventures Of The DP Boys: South Of The Border / 1995 / HW / M • Adventures Of The DP Boys: The Blacks Are Back / 1994 / HW / M • Adventures Of The DP Boys: The Blacks Are Cumming / 1994 / HW / M • Adventures Of The DP Boys: The Golden Girls / 1995 / HW / M • Adventures Of The DP Boys: The Hollywood Bubble Butts / 1993 / HW / M • Adventures Of The DP Boys: Tokyo Tramps / 1994 / HW / M • Adventures Of The DP Boys: Triple Penetration Girls / 1993 / HW / M • Alice In Analand / 1994 / SC / M • All "A" / 1994 / SFP / C • Amateur Orgies #34 / 1993 / AFI / M • Amazing Hardcore #1: Blow Jobs / 1997 / MET / M • America's Raunchiest Home Videos #47: / 1993 / ZA / M • America's Raunchiest Home Videos #48: / 1993 / ZA / M • America's Raunchiest Home Videos #58: / 1993 / ZA / M • Anal Academy / 1996 / ZA / M • Anal Alien / 1994 / CC / M • Anal Connection / 1996 / ZA / M • The Anal Diary Of Misty Rain / 1993 / EL / M • Anal Disciples #1 / 1996 / ZA / M • Anal Disciples #2: The Anal Conflict / 1996 / ZA / M • Anal Gang Bangers #02 / 1993 / GLI / M • Anal Injury / 1994 / ZA / M • Anal Inquisition / 1996 / ZA / M • Anal Institution #1 / 1996 / ZA / M • Anal Institution #2 / 1996 / ZA / M • Anal Institution #3 / 1996 / ZA / M • Anal Jeopardy / 1996 / ZA / M • Anal Maidens Three / 1996 / BOT / M • Anal Misconduct / 1995 / VD / M • Anal Nurses / 1996 / LBO / M • Anal Pandemonium / 1994 / TTV / M • Anal Party Girls / 1996 / GV / M • Anal Pool Party / 1996 / PE / M • Anal Professor / 1996 / ZA / M • Anal Rippers #1: The Beginning / 1995 / ZA / M • Anal Rippers #2: The Unveiling / 1996 / ZA / M • Anal Runaway / 1996 / ZA / M • Anal Sex / 1996 / ZA / M • Anal Sex Freaks / 1996 / ZA / M • Anal Virgins #01 / 1996 / NS / M • Anal Virgins #02 / 1996 / NS / M • Anal Virgins #03 / 1996 / NS / M • Anal Virgins Of America #01 / 1993 / FOR / M • Anal Virgins Of America #02 / 1993 / FOR / M • Anal Virgins Of America #03 / 1993 / FOR / M • Anal Virgins Of America #05 / 1993 / FOR / M • Anal Virgins Of America #09 / 1994 / FOR / M • Anal Virgins Of America #10 / 1994 / FOR / M • Anal Webb / 1995 / ZA / M • Anal Witness #1 / 1996 / LBO / M • Anal-Holics / 1993 / AFV / M • Anals, Inc / 1995 / ZA / M • Ass Openers! #2 / 1995 / TCK / C • Ass Poppers / 1995 / VMX / M • Backdoor Play / 1996 / AVI / M • Backing In #5 / 1994 / WV / C • Backing In #7 / 1995 / WV / C • Backstage Pass / 1994 / SC / M • The Backway Inn #3 / 1993 / FD / M • Bad To The Bone / 1996 / ULP / M • Bang City #2: China's Anal Gang Bang / 1995 / SC / M • Bang City #3: Fallon's Anal Gang Bang / 1995 / SC / M • Bang City #6: Bugger's Banquet / 1995 / SC / M • Bar-B-Que Gang Bang / 1994 / JMP / M • Beach Bum Amateur's #33 / 1993 / MID / M • Beach Bum Amateur's #34 / 1993 / MID / M •

Beach Bum Amateur's #40 / 1993 / MID / M • Behind The Blinds / 1992 / VIM / M • Bi And Beyond #5 / 1990 / INH / G • The Big Bang #1 / 1993 / LV / M • Big Black & Beautiful Gang Bang / 1995 / HO / M • Big Bust Babes #29 / 1995 / AFI / M • Big Bust Babes #30 / 1995 / AFI / M • Big Bust Babes #33 / 1995 / AFI / M • Big Murray's New-Cummers #07: Swinging in the "A" / 1993 / FD / M • Big Murray's New-Cummers #09: Oriental Lovers / 1993 / FD / M • Big Murray's New-Cummers #11: Willing & Able / 1993 / FD / M • Big Murray's New-Cummers #13: Hot Tight Ladies / 1993 / FD / M • Big Murray's New-Cummers #17: Age Before Beauty / 1993 / FD / M • Big Murray's New-Cummers #25: / 1994 / FD / M • Big Murray's New-Cummers #26: Real Tits / 1994 / FD / M • Big Murray's New-Cummers #28: Rump Humpers #2 / 1995 / FD / M • The Big Stick-Up / 1994 / WV / M • Birthday Bash / 1995 / BOT / M • Bitches In Heat #1: Locked In the Basement / 1995 / ZA / M • Bitches In Heat #2: On Vacation / 1995 / ZA / M • Black & Beyond: The Darker Sid / 1990 / INH / G • Black Gang-bangers #04 / 1995 / HW / M • Black Gang-bangers #05 / 1995 / HW / M • Black Gang-bangers #06 / 1995 / HW / M • Black Gang-bangers #07 / 1995 / HW / M • Black Gangbangers #08 / 1995 / HW / M • Black Gangbangers #09 / 1995 / HW / M • Black Hollywood Amateurs #15 / 1995 / MID / M • Black Hollywood Amateurs #16 / 1995 / MID / M • Black Jack City #3 / 1993 / HW / M • Black Juice Bombs / 1996 / NIT / C • Black Video Virgins #1 / 1996 / NS / M • Black Women, White Men #1 / 1995 / FC / M • Black Women, White Men #6 / 1995 / FC / M • Blow Job Blvd #1 / 1993 / SC / M • Blue Saloon / 1996 / ME / M • Bobby Hollander's Maneaters #05 / 1993 / SFP / M • Bobby Hollander's Maneaters #06 / 1993 / SFP / M • Bobby Hollander's Rookie Nookie #03 / 1993 / SFP / M • Bobby Hollander's Sweet Cheeks #109 / 1994 / WV / M • The Booty Bandit / 1994 / FC / M • Bra Busters #04 / 1993 / LBO / M • Breast Worx #32 / 1992 / LBO / M • Breast Worx #34 / 1992 / LBO / M • Breast Worx #35 / 1992 / LBO / M • Breastman's Wild West Adventure / 1995 / EVN / M • Bun Busters #17 / 1994 / LBO / M • The Butt Detective / 1994 / VC / M • Butt Hole Boulevard / 1993 / CA / M • Butt Light: Queen Of Rears / 1992 / STR / M • Butt Seriously Folks / 1994 / AFV / M • Butt's Up, Doc #4 / 1994 / GO / M • Call Of The Wild / 1995 / AFI / M • Candy's Custom Car Wash / 1995 / FC / M • Carnal Country / 1996 / NIT / M • Caught From Behind #20 / 1995 / HO / M • Caught From Behind #22 / 1995 / HO / M • The Cellar Dweller / 1996 / EL / M • Chemical Reaction / 1995 / CC / M • Chocolate Bunnies #02 / 1995 / LBO / C • Cluster Fuck #05 / 1994 / MAX / M • Come And Get It! / 1995 / LBO / M • The Complete & Total Anal Workout #1 / 1995 / ZA / M • The Complete & Total Anal Workout #2 / 1996 / ZA / M • Compulsion (Amazing) / 1996 / MET / M • Compulsion (Fat Dog) / 1996 / FD / M • Cream / 1993 / SC / M • Cream Pies #01 / 1993 / ZA / M • Cry Babies #1: Anal Scream / 1995 / ZA / M • Cum Buttered Corn Holes #3 / 1996 / NIT / C • Cum On Inn / 1995 / TEG / M • D.P. Grannies / 1995

/ JMP / M • D.P. Party Tonite / 1995 / JMP / M • Dangerous Behinds #2 / 1996 / HW / M • Dangerous Curves / 1995 / VC / M • Deceit / 1996 / ZA / M • Deep Space 69 / 1994 / HW / M • Deliciously Teri / 1993 / IF / M • Delirium / 1996 / MET / M • Diary Of A Geisha / 1995 / WV / C • The Dickheads #1 / 1993 / MID / M • The Dickheads #2 / 1993 / MID / M • Dirt Bags / 1994 / FPI / M • The Dirtiest Girl In The World / 1992 / ZA / M • Dirty Doc's Housecalls #05 / 1993 / LV / M • Dirty Doc's Housecalls #18 / 1994 / LV / M • Dirty Minds / 1996 / NIT / M • Dirty Stories #1 / 1995 / PE / M • Dixie Downes Gang Bang / 1996 / FC / M • Don't Try This At Home / 1994 / FPI / M • Done In The Desert Sun / 1995 / OUP / M • Double D Housewives / 1994 / PV / M • Double D Nurses / 1994 / PV / M • Double Decadence / 1995 / NOT / M • Double Penetration #6 / 1993 / WV / C • Double Penetration Virgins #01 / 1993 / LE / M • Double Penetration Virgins #02: The Second Cumming / 1994 / LE / M • Double Penetration Virgins #03 / 1994 / LE / M • Double Penetration Virgins #05: Go To Hell / 1994 / BB0 / M • Double Penetration Virgins #06: DP Diner / 1995 / JMP / M • Dr Rear / 1995 / CC / M • The Dragon Lady #5: Tales From The Bed #4 / 1993 / WV / M • The Dragon Lady #6: Tales From The Bed #5 / 1993 / WV / M • The Dragon Lady #7: Tales From The Bed #6 / 1994 / WV / M • Dream Butt / 1995 / VMX / M • Dukes Of Anal / 1996 / VC / M • East Vs West: Battle Of The Gang Bangs / 1994 / TTV / M • Ebony Anal Gang Bang #2 / 1994 / RTP / M • Eighteen #1 / 1996 / SC / M • Eighteen & Easy / 1996 / SC / M • Enigma / 1995 / MET / M • Escape From Anal Lost Angels / 1996 / HO / M • Eskimo Gang Bang / 1994 / HW / M • The Fabulous 50's Girls Ride Again / 1994 / EMC / M • Fame Is A Whore On Butt Row / 1996 / ABS / M • Fashion sluts #5: Ethnic Ecstasy / 1995 / ABS / M • The Fat, The Bald & The Ugly / 1995 / JMP / M • A Few Good Women / 1993 / CC / M • Flesh And Boner / 1993 / WV / M • For Your Mouth Only / 1995 / GO / M • Forbidden Pleasures / 1995 / ERA / M • Forbidden Subjects #1 / 1994 / FC / M • Frathouse Sexcapades / 1993 / SFP / M • Freeway Love / 1994 / FD / M • Fresh Meat (John Leslie) #1 / 1994 / EA / M • Fuck Jasmin / 1997 / MET / M • Fuck U: Girls Of The Packed-10 / 1995 / ZA / M • Gang Bang Bitches #05 / 1995 / PP / M • Gang Bang Diaries #1 / 1993 / SFP / M • Gang Bang Diaries #4 / 1994 / SFP / M • Gang Bang Diaries #5 / 1994 / SFP / M • Gang Bang Party / 1994 / HW / M • Gang Bang Virgin #1 / 1994 / HO / M • Gang Bang Virgin #2 / 1995 / HO / M • Gangbang At The O.K. Corral / 1994 / FPI / M • Gangbang Girl #10 / 1993 / ANA / M • Gangbang Girl #11 / 1993 / ANA / M • Gangbang Girl #16 / 1995 / ANA / M • Gazongas Galore #1 / 1996 / NIT / C • Geriatric Valley Girls / 1995 / FC / M • The Girls From Hootersville #05 / 1994 / SFP / M • Glitz Tits #03 / 1992 / GLI / M • Glory Days / 1996 / IN / M • Goldenbush / 1996 / AVI / M • The Good The Fat & The Ugly / 1995 / OD / M • Granny Bangers / 1995 / MET / M • Grateful Grandma's Gang Bang / 1994 / FC / M • Green Piece Of Ass #1 / 1994 / RTP / M • Gypsy Queen / 1995 / CC

/ M • Hardcore Fantasies #1 / 1996 / LV / M • Hardcore Fantasies #2 / 1996 / LV / M • Hardcore Fantasies #4 / 1996 / LV / M • Harry Horndog #08: Anal Lovers #1 / 1992 / ZA / M • Harry Horndog #11: Love Puppies #2 / 1992 / ZA / M • Harry Horndog #13: Anal Lovers #2 / 1992 / ZA / M • Harry Horndog #24: The Lost Tapes / 1993 / ZA / M • Head Lines / 1992 / SC / M • Hedonism #01 / 1993 / FH / M • Hell Hole / 1996 / ZA / M • Her Name Is Asia / 1996 / SUF / M • Hidden Camera #05 / 1993 / JMP / M • Hidden Camera #07 / 1993 / JMP / M • Hidden Camera #16 / 1994 / JMP / M • High Heeled & Horny #2 / 1995 / LBO / M • Hollywood Amateurs #01 / 1994 / MID / M • Hollywood Amateurs #03 / 1994 / MID / M • Hollywood Amateurs #10 / 1994 / MID / M • Hollywood Amateurs #15 / 1995 / MID / M • Hollywood Amateurs #16 / 1995 / MID / M • Hollywood Amateurs #19 / 1995 / MID / M • Hollywood Amateurs #21 / 1995 / MID / M • Horny Henry's Strange Adventure / 1995 / TTV / M • Hot Parts / 1996 / NIT / M • Hot Pie Delivery / 1993 / AFV / M • Hot Tight Asses #01 / 1992 / TCK / M • House Of Leather / 1995 / GO / M • The Hungry Heart / 1996 / AOP / M • I Can't Believe I Did The Whole Team! / 1994 / FPI / M • I Cream On Jeannie / 1995 / AVI / M • Illicit Affairs / 1996 / XC / M • The Illustrated Woman / 1995 / CA / M • In Loving Color #4 / 1993 / VT / M • In Through The Out Door / 1995 / PE / M • In Your Face #2 / 1992 / PL / M • Incorrigible / 1996 / MET / M • Indiscreet! Video Magazine #1 / 1995 / FH / M • Innocence Lost / 1995 / GO / M • Intense / 1996 / MET / M • Interracial 247 / 1995 / CC / M • Interracial Escorts / 1995 / GO / M • Interview's Backdoor To The Orient / 1996 / LV / M • Interview's Hard Bodied Harlots / 1996 / LV / M • Into The Fire / 1994 / ZA / M • Jiggly Queens #3 / 1996 / LE / M • Jizz Glazed Goo Guzzlers #1 / 1996 / NIT / C • The Joi Fuk Club / 1993 / WV / M • Jordan Lee: Anal Queen / 1997 / SC / C • Kinky Orientals / 1994 / FH / M • The Knocker Room / 1993 / GO / M • La Femme Vanessa / 1995 / SC / M • Ladies In Leather / 1995 / GO / M • A Lady / 1995 / FD / M • Lady M's Anal Gang Bang / 1995 / FC / M • Lady's Choice / 1995 / VD / M • Laguna Nights / 1995 / FH / M • Leg Show #1 / 1995 / NIT / M • A Little Bit Pregnant / 1995 / SO / M • Living On The Edge / 1997 / DWO / M • Lockdown / 1996 / NIT / M • Long Dark Shadow / 1994 / LE / M • Lust / 1993 / FH / M • M Series #16 / 1993 / LBO / M • The Mad D.P. Tea Party / 1994 / FC / M • Made For A Gangbang / 1995 / ZA / M • Make Me Watch / 1994 / PV / M • Mellon Man #01 / 1994 / AVI / M • Memories / 1996 / ZA / M • Microslut / 1996 / TTV / M • Miss D.P. Butterfly / 1995 / TIW / M • Missed You / 1995 / RTP / M • Mo' Booty #4 / 1995 / TIW / M • More To Love #1 / 1994 / TTV / M • Mr. Peepers Amateur Home Videos #57: Super-Suckers Of Flight / 1992 / LBO / M • My Baby Got Back #01 / 1992 / VT / M • My Evil Twin / 1994 / LE / M • Nasty Newcummers #02 / 1993 / MET / M • Nasty Newcummers #04 / 1994 / MET / M • Nasty Newcummers #06 / 1995 / MET / M • Nasty Newcummers #07 / 1995 / MET / M • Nasty Newcummers #14 / 1995 / MET / M • Naughty Nicole / 1994 / SC / M • Neighborhood Watch #31: Sticking It To The Neighbors / 1992 / LBO / M • Nena Cherry's Dp Gang Bang / 1996 / NIT / M • New Girls In Town #2 / 1992 / CC / M • New Girls In Town #3 / 1993 / CC / M • The Night Of The Living Bed / 1996 / LE / M • Nothing Butt Amateurs #01 / 1993 / AFI / M • Nurses Do It With Care / 1995 / EVN / M • Nympho Zombie Coeds / 1993 / VIM / M • Odyssey 30 Min: #269: / 1992 / OD / M • Odyssey 30 Min: #282: / 1992 / OD / M • Odyssey 30 Min: #332: / 1993 / OD / M • Odyssey Triple Play #31: Double Penetration Babes / 1993 / OD / M • Odyssey Triple Play #70: Three By Threeway / 1994 / OD / M • Odyssey Triple Play #74: Conjugal Couples / 1994 / OD / M • Odyssey Triple Play #97: The Anal Game / 1995 / OD / M • Old Wives' Tails / 1995 / EMC / M • Older And Anal #2 / 1995 / FC / M • Older Women Younger Men #3 / 1993 / CC / M • Ona Zee's Black Label #1: Sex Hunger / 1996 / ONA / C • One Of Our Porn Stars Is Missing / 1993 / OD / M • Orgies Orgies Orgies / 1994 / WV / M • Oriental Oddballs #2 / 1994 / FH / M • Pai Gow Video #07: East Meets West / 1995 / EVN / M • Pearl Necklace: Amorous Amateurs #25 / 1993 / SEE / M • Pearl Necklace: Amorous Amateurs #26 / 1993 / SEE / M • Perverted #1: The Babysitters / 1994 / ZA / M • Perverted #2: The Virgins / 1995 / ZA / M • Perverted #3: The Parents / 1995 / ZA / M • Perverted Stories #01 / 1995 / JMP / M • Perverted Stories #02 / 1995 / JMP / M • Perverted Stories #07 / 1996 / JMP / M • Perverted Stories #11 / 1996 / JMP / M • Peyton's Place / 1996 / ULP / M • Pierced Punctured And Perverted / 1995 / FC / M • Positions Wanted: Experienced Only / 1993 / PV / M • Possessed / 1996 / MET / M • Primal Desires / 1993 / EX / M • Private Audition / 1995 / EVN / M • Private Video #1: Christina / 1995 / AVI / M • Public Enemy / 1995 / GO / M • Pure Anal / 1996 / MET / M • Q Balls #2 / 1996 / TTV / M • Raw Talent: Deep Inside Lydia's Ass / 1993 / FH / M • The Real Deal #1 / 1994 / FC / M • The Real Deal #3 / 1996 / FC / M • Real Sex Magazine #01 / 1996 / HO / M • Real Sex Magazine #02 / 1997 / HO / M • Realities #2 / 1992 / ZA / M • Red Door Diaries #1 / 1995 / ZA / M • Red Door Diaries #2 / 1996 / ZA / M • Reflections / 1996 / ZA / M • Rice Burners / 1996 / NOT / M • Rocco Unleashed / 1994 / SC / M • Rocks / 1993 / VT / M • Roly Poly Gang Bang / 1995 / WV / M • Ron Hightower's Casting Couch #1 / 1995 / FC / M • Roxy Rider Is In Control / 1996 / NIT / M • Roxy: A Gang Bang Fantasy / 1994 / FC / M • Rumpman's Backdoor Sailing / 1996 / HW / M • Safari Jane / 1995 / ERA / M • Saki's Private Party / 1995 / TTV / M • Samantha & Company / 1996 / PL / M • Samantha's Private Fantasies / 1994 / WV / M • Saturday Night Porn #2 / 1993 / AFV / M • Secrets in the Attic #3: Trials Of Acceptance / 1994 / STM / B • Secrets in the Attic #4: Purchased And Punished / 1994 / STM / B • The Seductive Secretary / 1995 / GO / M • Sex Fantasy / 1993 / PPR / M • Sex Freaks / 1995 / EA / M • Sex In Dangerous Places / 1994 / OD / M • Sex In Strange Places: The Sphincter Zone / 1994 / FPI / M • The Sex Therapist / 1995 / GO / M • Sexual Atrocities / 1996 /

EL / M • Sexual Trilogy #01 / 1993 / SFP / M • Sgt. Peckers Lonely Hearts Club Gang Bang / 1995 / AMP / M • Shock / 1995 / LE / M • The Shocking Truth #2 / 1996 / DWO / M • Shooting Gallery / 1996 / EL / M • Slammed / 1995 / PV / M • Slave Quarters / 1995 / PRE / B • Slut Safari #1 / 1994 / FC / M • Smooth As Silk / 1994 / EMC / M • Snake Pit / 1996 / DWO / M • So I Married A Lesbian / 9993 / WV / M • Sodom Chronicles / 1995 / FH / M • Sodomania #19: Sweet Cream / 1996 / EL / M • Sodomania: Tales Of Perversity / 1992 / EL / M • Sodomania #19: Sweet Cream / 1996 / EL / M • Sofia: A Gang Bang Fantasy / 1994 / FC / M • Sordid Stories / 1994 / AMP / M • Sorority Sluts Passed Out / 1995 / ZA / M • Squirt Squad / 1995 / AMP / M • Star Girl / 1996 / ERA / M • Starbangers #08 / 1996 / FPI / M • Starbangers #09 / 1996 / ZA / M • Starbangers #10 / 1997 / ZA / M • Steamy Sins / 1996 / IN / M • Stewardesses Behind Bars / 1994 / HW / M • Sticky Fingers / 1996 / WV / M • Strange Sex In Strange Places / 1994 / ZA / M • Stripping / 1995 / NIT / M • Strong Sensations / 1996 / PL / M • Stuff Your Ass #2 / 1995 / JMP / M • Stuff Your Face #1 / 1994 / JMP / M • Stuff Your Face #3 / 1995 / JMP / M • Sugar Mommies / 1995 / FPI / M • Swedish Erotica #80 / 1994 / CA / M • Swedish Erotica #84 / 1995 / CA / M • Sweet Black Cherries #1 / 1996 / TTV / M • Swinging Couples #03 / 1994 / GO / M • Tail Taggers #103 / 1993 / WV / M • Tail Taggers #108: Vibro Love / 1993 / WV / M • Tail Taggers #110 / 1993 / WV / M • Tail Taggers #112 / 1993 / WV / M • Tail Taggers #113: Behind The Scenes / 1994 / WV / M • Tail Taggers #115 / 1993 / WV / M • Tail Taggers #121: Behind The Lens / 1994 / WV / M • Tail Taggers #126 / 1994 / WV / M • Tail Taggers #129: / 1994 / WV / M • Tails Of Desire / 1995 / GO / M • Talking Trash #1 / 1995 / HW / M • This Girl Is Freaky / 1996 / NIT / M • Tia's Holiday Gang Bang / 1995 / HO / M • Tiffany Minx Wildcat / 1993 / MID / C • Tight Fit #01 / 1994 / GO / M • Tight Fit #02 / 1994 / GO / M • Tight Fit #04 / 1994 / GO / M • Tight Fit #09 / 1994 / GO / M • Tight Fit #11 / 1995 / GO / M • Tight Fit #14 / 1995 / GO / M • Titties 'n Cream #1 / 1994 / FC / M • Titty City #1 / 1995 / TIW / M • Top Heavy / 1993 / IF / M • Tricky Business / 1995 / AFI / M • Triple Penetration Debutante Sluts #1 / 1996 / BAC / M • Triple Penetration Debutante Sluts #2 / 1996 / BAC / M • Trouble In Paradise / 1996 / ULP / M • Two Too Much / 1996 / MET / M • Uncle Roy's Amateur Home Video #13 / 1992 / VIM / M • Vagabonds / 1996 / ERA / M • Video Virgins #02 / 1992 / NS / M • Video Virgins #04 / 1993 / NS / M • Video Virgins #06 / 1993 / NS / M • Video Virgins #07 / 1993 / NS / M • Video Virgins #08 / 1993 / NS / M • Video Virgins #09 / 1993 / NS / M • Video Virgins #10 / 1993 / NS / M • Video Virgins #11 / 1994 / NS / M • Video Virgins #14 / 1994 / NS / M • Video Virgins #16 / 1994 / NS / M • Video Virgins #17 / 1994 / NS / M • Video Virgins #21 / 1995 / NS / M • Video Virgins #22 / 1995 / NS / M • Video Virgins #24 / 1996 / NS / M • Video Virgins #25 / 1995 / NS / M • Video Virgins #28 / 1996 / NS / M • Video Virgins #29 / 1996 / NS / M • Video Virgins #32 / 1996 / NS / M • War Whores / 1996 / EL / M • Wasted / 1995 /

PRE / B • Wedding Vows / 1994 / ZA / M • Weird Sex / 1995 / GO / M • What Women Want / 1996 / SUF / M • When The Fat Lady Sings / 1996 / EX / M • Wild Orgies #04 / 1994 / AFI / M • Wild Orgies #12 / 1994 / AFI / M • Wild Orgies #16 / 1995 / AFI / M • Wild Orgies #17 / 1995 / AFI / M • Wild Widow / 1996 / NIT / M • Will & Ed's Back To Class / 1992 / MID / M • World Class Ass / 1995 / FC / M • Yo Yo Yo: A Very Black Christmas Tale! / 1994 / HW / M

RICK MASTERS (ZFX)
The Abduction Of Sweet Christine / 1993 / ZFX / B • Alien Probe #1 / 1993 / ZFX / B • Alien Probe #2 / 1994 / ZFX / B • Binding Contract / 1992 / ZFX / B • Bondage Imagination Unlimited / 1994 / BON / B • Chamber Of Horrors / 1994 / ZFX / B • Dance Macabre / 1993 / ZFX / B • Erotic Bondage Confessions / 1992 / ZFX / B • Fair Warning / 1995 / ZFX / B • Full Moon Video #24: Wild Side Couples / 1992 / FAP / M • Futureshock / 1993 / ZFX / B • Gangland #2: Mob Rules / 1994 / ZFX / B • Gangland #5 / 1995 / ZFX / B • Guinea Pigs #2 / 1993 / ZFX / B • Guinea Pigs #3 / 1993 / ZFX / B • Hitchhiker / 1996 / ZFX / B • Maximum Desade / 1995 / ZFX / B • Meanstreak / 1993 / ZFX / B • Mincemeat Pie / 1996 / ZFX / B • The Misadventures Of Lois Payne / 1995 / ZFX / B • The Necklace #3 / 1994 / ZFX / B • Phantacide Peepshow / 1996 / ZFX / B • Pretty Tied Up / 1993 / ZFX / B • Sorority Bondage Hazing / 1990 / BON / B • Southern Discomfort / 1992 / ZFX / B • Spellbound (Bizarre) / 1991 / BIZ / B • Spread Eagle / 1992 / ZFX / B • Story Of Sweet Nicole / 1992 / ZFX / B • Tiffany Twisted / 1993 / ZFX / B • Video Pirates #1 / 1995 / ZFX / B • Video Pirates #2 / 1995 / ZFX / B • Video Pirates #5: A Bullet To Bite / 1995 / ZFX / B • Voodoo Dolls / 1996 / ZFX / B • War Pigs #1 / 1996 / ZFX / B • War Pigs #2 / 1996 / ZFX / B • Z F/X #1 / cr92 / BON / B

RICK MICHEL
Thunder And Lightning / 1996 / MID / M

RICK MONTANA *see Star Index I*

RICK NERO
Rich & Sassy / 1986 / VSE / M

RICK O'SHEA *(Malcolm (Rick O'S), Guy (Rick O'S))*
Pretty short blonde male who usually has his long hair in a pony tail. Supposedly married to Carmel St. Clair, then to Trisha Yin and then to Brittany O'Connell.
50 And Still Gangbangin'! / 1995 / EMC / M • Adventures Of The DP Boys: South Of The Border / 1995 / HW / M • Amazing Nympho Stories / 1995 / TEG / M • America's Raunchiest Home Videos #75: / 1993 / ZA / M • American Swinger Video Magazine #06 / 1993 / ZA / M • American Swinger Video Magazine #07 / 1993 / ZA / M • Anal Camera #04 / 1995 / EVN / M • Anal Nitrate / 1995 / PE / M • Anal Queen / 1994 / FPI / M • Anything You Ever Wanted To Know About Sex / 1993 / VEX / M • Asian Heat #04: House Of The Rising Sun / 1993 / SC / M • Ass Dweller / 1994 / WIV / M • Bachelor Party #1 / 1993 / FPI / M • Bachelor Party #2 / 1993 / FPI / M • Backdoor Boogie / 1994 / TEG / M • Beach Bum Amateur's #39 / 1993 / MID / M • Big Bust Bangers #1 / 1994 / AMP / M • Big Bust Bangers #2 / 1994 / AMP / M • Big Murray's

New-Cummers #26: Real Tits / 1994 / FD / M • Blow Job Blvd #1 / 1993 / SC / M • Bobby Hollander's Rookie Nookie #10 / 1993 / MET / M • Bobby Hollander's Sweet Cheeks #110 / 1994 / WV / M • Bodywaves / 1994 / ELP / M • Breastman's Wild West Adventure / 1995 / EVN / M • Bun Busters #13 / 1994 / LBO / M • The Butt Connection / 1993 / TIW / M • Butt's Up, Doc #4 / 1994 / GO / M • Butthead Dreams / 1994 / FH / M • Butthead Dreams: Mission Impenetrable / 1994 / FH / M • Casting Couch #1 / 1994 / KV / M • Cheerleader Strippers / 1996 / PE / M • Colossal Orgy #1 / 1993 / HW / M • Colossal Orgy #3 / 1994 / HW / M • Cream / 1993 / SC / M • Depraved Fantasies #3 / 1994 / FPI / M • The Devil In Grandma Jones / 1994 / FC / M • Dirty Dating Service #02 / 1993 / WP / M • Dirty Doc's Housecalls #04 / 1993 / LV / M • A Dirty Western #2: Smoking Guns / 1994 / CV / M • Dollars And Yen / 1994 / FH / M • Double D Amateurs #15 / 1994 / JMP / M • Double D Amateurs #21 / 1994 / JMP / M • Double Decadence / 1995 / NOT / M • DPTV: Double Penetration Television / 1996 / SUF / M • Eclipse / 1993 / SC / M • Enigma / 1995 / MET / M • Erotica Optique / 1994 / SUF / M • Erotika / 1994 / WV / M • Escape To The Party / 1994 / ELP / M • The Farmer's Daughter / 1995 / TEG / M • Fresh Faces #09 / 1996 / EVN / M • Gang Bang Bitches #01 / 1994 / PP / M • Gang Bang Bitches #02 / 1994 / PP / M • Geisha To Go / 1994 / PPP / M • The Girls From Hootersville #04 / 1993 / SFP / M • The Girls From Hootersville #08 / 1994 / SFP / M • Girlz In The Hood #3: Erotic Justice / 1993 / HW / M • Hard-On Copy / 1994 / WV / M • Hedonism #01 / 1993 / FH / M • Hidden Camera #01 / 1993 / JMP / M • Horny Henry's Snowballing Adventure / 1995 / TTV / M • I Can't Believe I Did The Whole Team! / 1994 / FPI / M • Indecent Obsessions / 1995 / BBE / M • Love Letters #1 / 1993 / SC / M • Lust / 1993 / FH / M • Lust What The Doctor Ordered / 1994 / WIV / M • Margarita On The Rocks / 1994 / SFP / M • Mike Hott: #241 Cunt of the Month: Sabrina Bliss / 1993 / MHV / M • Mike Hott: #246 Cunt of the Month: Nikki 8-93 / 1993 / MHV / M • Mike Hott: #248 Fuck The Boss #03 / 1993 / MHV / M • Mike Hott: #251 Cunt of the Month: Veronica / 1993 / MHV / M • Mike Hott: #252 Horny Couples #15 / 1994 / MHV / M • Mike Hott: #254 Cunt of the Month: Uma 9-93 / 1993 / MHV / M • Mike Hott: #255 Cunt Of The Month: Mikla / 1994 / MHV / M • Mike Hott: #257 Cunt of the Month: Selina / 1993 / MHV / M • Mike Hott: #258 Horny Couples #16 / 1994 / MHV / M • Mike Hott: #259 Cunt Of The Month: C.J. Bennett 2-94 / 1994 / MHV / M • Mike Hott: #260 Cunt of the Month: Trinity / 1994 / MHV / M • Mike Hott: #261 Horny Couples #17 / 1994 / MHV / M • Mike Hott: #262 Cunt Of The Month: Christina West 4-94 / 1994 / MHV / M • Mike Hott: #268 Cum In My Mouth #01 / 1994 / MHV / C • Mike Hott: #269 Cunt Of The Month: Scarlett / 1994 / MHV / M • Mike Hott: #272 Jack Off On My Cunt #01 / 1994 / MHV / M • Mike Hott: #273 Cunt of the Month: Abby 10-94 / 1994 / MHV / M • Mike Hott: #275 Cunt of the Month: Amanda 1-95 / 1995 / MHV / M • Mike Hott:

#276 Older Gals #5 / 1994 / MHV / M • Mike Hott: #277 Cum In My Cunt #2 / 1994 / MHV / M • Mike Hott: #280 Horny Couples #18 / 1995 / MHV / M • Mike Hott: #281 Cunt of the Month: Anna Marie / 1995 / MHV / M • Mike Hott: #282 Three-Sum Sluts #01 / 1995 / MHV / M • Mike Hott: #284 Cunt of the Month: Jordan Hart / 1995 / MHV / M • Mike Hott: #289 Three-Sum Sluts #02 / 1995 / MHV / M • Mike Hott: #291 Cunt Of The Month: Satania / 1995 / MHV / M • Mike Hott: #292 Three-Sum Sluts #03 / 1995 / MHV / M • Mike Hott: #294 Cunt of the Month: Randi Storm / 1995 / MHV / M • Mike Hott: #297 Cunt of the Month: Blake / 1995 / MHV / M • Mike Hott: #300 Cunto Of The Month: Rachel Love / 1995 / MHV / M • Mike Hott: #301 Three-Sum Sluts #04 / 1995 / MHV / M • Mike Hott: #308 Bonus Cunt: Alabama / 1995 / MHV / M • Mike Hott: #310 Cunt Of The Month: Bobbi Soxx / 1995 / MHV / M • Mike Hott: #311 Bonus Cunt: Kalina / 1995 / MHV / M • Mike Hott: #313 Three-Sum Sluts #05 / 1995 / MHV / M • Mike Hott: #314 Cum In My Cunt #05 / 1995 / MHV / M • Mike Hott: #315 Cum In My Mouth #02 / 1995 / MHV / C • Mike Hott: #317 Girls Who Swallow Cum #01 / 1995 / MHV / C • Mike Hott: #319 Bonus Cunt: Marki / 1995 / MHV / M • Mike Hott: #323 Three-Sum Sluts #07 / 1995 / MHV / M • Mike Hott: #327 Older Gals #12 / 1995 / MHV / F • Mike Hott: #328 Cunt Of The Month: Calie / 1995 / MHV / M • Mike Hott: #329 Cunt Of The Month: Tia / 1995 / MHV / M • Mike Hott: #332 Girls Who Swallow Cum #02 / 1995 / MHV / C • Mike Hott: #333 Bonus Cunt: Serrena / 1995 / MHV / M • Mike Hott: #336 Three-Sum Sluts #09 / 1995 / MHV / M • Mike Hott: #342 Three-Sum Sluts #10 / 1995 / MHV / M • Mike Hott: #345 Cum In My Cunt #07 / 1995 / MHV / C • Mike Hott: #346 Cunt Of The Month: Kimberly Kummings / 1996 / MHV / M • Mike Hott: #349 Girls Who Swallow Cum #03 / 1996 / MHV / C • Mike Hott: #352 Cunt Of The Month: Lorissa Rockit / 1996 / MHV / M • Mike Hott: Cum Cocktails #3 / 1995 / MHV / C • Mr. Peepers Amateur Home Videos #69: Love Tunnel / 1993 / LBO / M • Odyssey Triple Play #70: Three By Threeway / 1994 / OD / M • One For The Gusher / 1995 / AMP / M • Pearl Necklace: Thee Bush League #07 / 1992 / SEE / M • Possessed / 1996 / MET / M • Prime Offender / 1993 / PEP / M • Pussy Posse / 1993 / CC / M • Reckless / 1995 / NOT / M • Reel People #04 / 1994 / PP / M • Ridin' The Big One / 1994 / TEG / M • Rumpman's Backdoor Sailing / 1996 / HW / M • Rumpman: Caught In An Anal Avalanche / 1995 / HW / M • Russian Seduction / 1993 / IP / M • Seekers / 1994 / CA / M • Sexual Trilogy #05 / 1994 / SFP / M • Sgt. Peckers Lonely Hearts Club Gang Bang / 1995 / AMP / M • Snatch Patch / 1995 / LE / M • So You Wanna Be A Porn Star #1: The Russians Are Cumming / 1994 / WHP / M • Sordid Stories / 1994 / AMP / M • Squirt Squad / 1995 / AMP / M • Starbangers #05 / 1993 / FPI / M • Starbangers #06 / 1994 / FPI / M • Starbangers #07 / 1995 / FPI / M • Starbangers #08 / 1996 / FPI / M • Stardust #4 / 1996 / VI / M • Streetwalkers / 1995 / HO / M • Sugar Mommies / 1995 /

FPI / M • Super Ball Sunday / 1994 / LBO / M • Swinging Couples #01 / 1993 / GO / M • Tail Taggers #122: Anal Delight / 1994 / WV / M • Tight Fit #08 / 1994 / GO / M • Titan's Amateur Video Magazine #03 / 1995 / TEG / M • Titan's Gonzo Video Magazine #02 / 1996 / TEG / M • Truck Stop Angel / 1994 / CC / M • The Twin Peaks Of Mount Fuji / 1996 / SUF / M • Ultimate Anal Gang Bang #3 / 1995 / HW / M • Unsolved Double Penetration / 1993 / PEP / M • Video Virgins #05 / 1993 / NS / M • Vortex / 1995 / MET / M • The Watering Hole / 1994 / HO / M • Who's In Charge (Titan) / 1995 / TEG / M • Xcitement: The Movie / 1993 / XCI / M

RICK POWELL *see* **Keith Erickson**

RICK RACER *see* **Star Index I**

RICK RAGE *see* **Nick Rage**

RICK RANGER *see* **Mike Ranger**

RICK RICHARD
Aerienne's Surprise / 1995 / WIV / M • Wedding Rituals / 1995 / DVP / M

RICK RIVERS *see* **Star Index I**

RICK ROBERTS
Starlet Nights / 1982 / XTR / M

RICK ROBERTS (1994) *see* **Roland Neves**

RICK ROC *see* **Star Index I**

RICK ROGUE
Bad She-Males / 1994 / HSV / G • The Best Little He/She House In Texas / 1993 / HSV / G • Bi On The Fourth Of July / 1994 / BIL / G • Bi-Nanza / 1994 / BIL / G • Cocks In Frocks #2 / 1996 / TTV / G • Come Back Little She-Male / 1994 / HSV / G • Dragon Lady / 1995 / SP0 / G • Drive Bi / 1994 / BIL / G • Dungeons & Drag Queens / 1994 / HSV / G • Good Bi Girl / 1994 / BIL / G • He-She Hangout / 1995 / HSV / G • He-She Haw / 1996 / HSV / G • Hot Bi Summer / 1994 / BIL / G • Las Vegas She-Males / 1995 / BCP / G • Malibu She Males / 1994 / MET / G • Mechanics Bi Day, Lube Job Bi Night / 1995 / SP0 / G • Melrose Trannie / 1995 / HEA / G • Nydp Trannie / 1996 / WP / G • The Princess With A Penis / 1994 / HSV / G • Red Riding She Male / 1995 / PL / G • She Male Devil / 1996 / HSV / G • She Male Dicktation / 1994 / HEA / G • She Male Sex Kittens / 1995 / MET / G • She-Male Encounters #21: Psychic She Males / 1994 / MET / G • She-Male Instinct / 1995 / BCP / G • She-Male Trouble / 1994 / HEA / G • Spring Trannie / 1995 / VC / G • Trannie Angel / 1995 / HSV / G • Transsexual Prostitutes #2 / 1997 / DFI / G • Virtual She-Male / 1995 / HSV / G • Wet And Wild #2 / 1995 / VEX / M • Wet Daydreams / 1996 / XCI / M

RICK ROPER *see* **Star Index I**

RICK RYDER
Body Girls / 1983 / SE / M • Yank My Doodle, It's A Dandy / 1985 / GOM / M

RICK SAVAGE *(Fred Savage, Richard Maris)*
Against All Bods / 1988 / ZA / M • All In The Family / 1985 / VCR / M • Anal Amateurs / 1992 / VD / M • Anal Dawn / 1991 / AMB / M • Anal Rescue 811 / 1992 / PL / M • Angel's Revenge / 1985 / IN / M • Angels Of Passion / 1986 / CDI / M • Angels With Sticky Faces / 1991 / VD / M • Army Brat #2 / 1989 / VI / M • Ass Tales / 1991 / PL / M • Awakening In Blue / 1991 / PL / M • Backdoor Babes / 1985 / WET / M • Backdoor

Brides #1 / 1985 / PV / M • Backdoor Lambada / 1990 / GO / M • Backdoor Summer #1 / 1988 / PV / C • Backdoor To Brooklyn / 1992 / PL / M • Backing In #2 / 1990 / WV / C • Ball In The Family / 1988 / VWA / M • Barbii's Painful Examination / 1995 / GAL / B • Bedside Brat / 1988 / VI / M • Beettlejizum / 1991 / PL / M • Behind Blue Eyes #1 / 1986 / ME / M • Behind The Backdoor #1 / 1986 / EVN / M • The Best Of Flame / 1994 / BIZ / C • The Better Sex Video Series #1: The Better Sex Basics / 1991 / LEA / M • The Better Sex Video Series #2: Advanced Sex Techniques / 1991 / LEA / M • Beyond The Senses / 1986 / AVC / M • The Big Pink / 1989 / VWA / M • Bizarre Master Series: Rick Savage / 1992 / BIZ / C • Bizarre Mistress Series: Mistress Jacqueline / 1992 / BIZ / C • Black Bound Beauty / 1995 / GAL / B • Black Widow / 1988 / WV / M • Bobby Hollander's Rookie Nookie #02 / 1993 / SFP / M • Bobby Hollander's Rookie Nookie #14 / 1993 / SFP / M • Bondage Academy #1 / 1991 / BON / B • Bondage Academy #2 / 1991 / BON / B • Bondage Fantasies #1 / 1989 / BIZ / B • Bondage Fantasies #2 / 1989 / BIZ / B • Bondage Games #1 / 1991 / BIZ / B • Bondage Games #2 / 1991 / BIZ / B • Bondage Memories #01 / 1993 / BON / C • Bondage Workout / 1995 / GAL / B • Boobs, Butts And Bloopers #1 / 1990 / HO / M • Bound And Suspended / 1996 / GAL / B • The Brat Pack / 1989 / VWA / M • The Brazilian Connection / 1988 / CA / M • Breaststroke #1 / 1988 / EX / M • Broadway Brat / 1988 / VI / M • The Building Of Mistress Simone's Dungeon Of Pleasure / 1991 / BIZ / B • Bunnie's Bondage Land / 1994 / STM / C • Bunny's Lesson In Pain / 1992 / PL / B • Bush Pilots #1 / 1990 / VC / M • C-Hunt / 1985 / PL / M • California Fever / 1987 / CV / M • Call Girl Academy / 1990 / V99 / M • Campus Cuties / 1986 / CA / M • The Case Of The Crooked Cathouse / 1989 / ME / M • Caught In The Middle / 1985 / CDI / M • Cavalcade Of Stars / 1985 / VCR / C • Channel 69 / 1986 / LA / M • Chatsworth Hall / 1989 / BIZ / B • Cheating American Style / 1988 / WV / M • Cheerleader Bondage Hell / 1995 / OUP / B • China Bitch / 1989 / PV / C • Chocolate Kisses / 1986 / CA / M • Class Ass / 1992 / PL / M • Cleo/Leo / 1989 / NWW / S • Co-Ed In Bondage / 1996 / GAL / B • Coming On America / 1989 / VWA / M • Competent People / 1994 / FD / C • The Crack Of Dawn / 1989 / GLE / M • Crossing Over / 1990 / IN / M • Dangerous Curves / 1985 / CV / M • Deep Chill / cr85 / AT / M • Deep Inside Tracey / 1987 / CDI / C • Deep Inside Trading / 1986 / AR / M • Defiance, The Spanking Saga / 1992 / BIZ / B • Designing Babes / 1990 / GOT / M • The Desk Top Dolls / 1990 / BAD / C • Diaries Of Fire And Ice #1 / 1989 / VC / M • Diaries Of Fire And Ice #2 / 1989 / VC / M • Dirty / 1993 / FD / C • Dirty 30's Cinema: Heather Wayne / 1985 / PV / C • Dirty Dreams / 1987 / CA / M • Dirty Lingerie / 1990 / VD / M • Disciples Of Bondage / 1992 / STM / B • Double Agents / 1988 / VXP / M • Double Messages / 1987 / MOV / M • Dr Discipline #1 / 1994 / STM / B • Dr Discipline #2: Appointment With Pain / 1994 / STM / B • Dresden Diary #05: Invasion of Privacy / 1992 / BIZ / B • Dresden Mistress #1 / 1988 / BIZ / B • Dresden Mistress #2 / 1989 / BIZ / B • Dresden Mistress #3 / 1989 / BIZ / B • Dynasty's S&M Initiation / 1994 / OUP / B • Easy Lover / 1989 / EX / M • The Erotic Adventures Of Bedman And Throbbin / 1989 / VWA / M • The Erotic Adventures Of Chi Chi Chan / 1988 / VWA / M • Every Body / 1992 / LAP / M • Extreme Heat / 1987 / ME / M • Family Thighs / 1989 / AR / M • Fantasy Nights / 1990 / VC / M • Flesh For Fantasies / 1986 / TAM / M • For Love And Lust / 1985 / AVC / M • Frankenhunter, Queen Of The Porno Zombies / 1989 / GMI / M • Gere Up / 1991 / LV / C • Gillie's Isle / 1990 / GOT / M • Ginger Snaps / 1987 / VI / M • The Girl Has Assets / 1990 / LV / M • The Girls Of The B.L.O. / 1988 / VWA / M • The Grafenberg Spot / 1985 / MIT / M • Head Co-Ed Society / 1989 / VT / M • The Heartbreak Girl / 1985 / GO / M • Heather / 1989 / VWA / M • Heather Hunter's Bedtime Stories / 1991 / GLE / C • Heraldo: Streetwalkers Of NY / 1990 / GOT / M • The Hind-Lick Maneuver / 1991 / GO / C • Hog Tied And Spanked / 1991 / BIZ / B • Hollywood Harlots / 1986 / VEX / C • Hollywood Heartbreakers / 1985 / VEX / M • Hollywood Vice / 1985 / VD / M • Hometown Honeys #1 / 1986 / VEX / M • Hooters / 1986 / AVC / M • Horneymooners #2 / 1988 / VXP / M • The Hot Lick Cafe / 1990 / AMB / M • Hot Merchandise / 1985 / AVC / M • Hot Talk Radio / 1989 / VWA / M • Hotel Paradise / 1989 / CA / M • The Hottest Show In Town / 1987 / VIP / M • The House Of Strange Desires / 1985 / NSV / M • Hung Jury / 1989 / VWA / M • Hyperkink / 1989 / VWA / M • I Said A Butt Light #1 / 1990 / LV / M • Indecent Itch / 1985 / VCR / M • Innocence Bound / 1995 / GAL / B • It's Incredible / 1985 / SE / M • Jailhouse Blue / 1990 / SO / M • Journey Into Hellfire / 1995 / GAL / B • Journey Into Latex / 1992 / STM / B • Journey Into Pain #2 / 1989 / BIZ / B • Journey Into Submission / 1990 / BIZ / B • Julie: Bondage Virgin / 1995 / GAL / B • Kathy's Bike Bondage / 1995 / GAL / B • Lauren's Adventures In Bondageland #2: Mistress Shane / 1994 / STM / C • Lays Of Our Lives / 1988 / ZA / M • Legend #1 / 1990 / LE / M • Lesbian Submission / 1994 / PL / B • Lessons In Humiliation / 1991 / BIZ / B • The Life & Loves Of Nikki Charm / 1986 / MAL / M • A Live Nude Girl / 1989 / VWA / M • Loose Morals / 1987 / HO / M • Love Bites / 1985 / CA / M • Love Doll Lucy #1 / 1994 / PL / F • The Love Scene / 1985 / CDI / M • The Lover Girls / 1985 / VEX / M • Lucky Charm / 1986 / AVC / C • Lucy Makes It Big / 1987 / ME / M • Lust In Space / 1985 / PV / M • Lusty Dusty / 1990 / VI / M • Magic Fingers / 1987 / ME / M • The Magic Touch / 1985 / CV / M • Make My Night / 1985 / CIN / M • Male Domination #14 / 1990 / BIZ / C • Male Domination #15: Women In Suspension / 1990 / BIZ / C • The Maltese Bimbo / 1993 / FD / M • Marilyn Chambers' Private Fantasies #4 / 1983 / CA / M • Matronly Stern Spankings / 1994 / STM / B • Midnight Pink / 1987 / WV / M • Missing Pieces / 1985 / IN / M • Missy Impossible / 1989 / CAR / M • The Mistress And The Prince / 1995 / STM / B • Mother's Pride / 1985 / DIM / M • Mr. Big / 1991 / PL / M • Mystery Of The Golden Lotus / 1989 / HU / M • N.Y. Video Magazine #01 / 1994 / OUP / M • N.Y. Video Magazine #02 / 1995 / OUP / M • N.Y. Video Magazine #03 / 1995 / OUP / M • N.Y. Video Magazine #04 / 1995 / OUP / M • N.Y. Video Magazine #05 / 1995 / OUP / M • N.Y. Video Magazine #06 / 1995 / OUP / M • N.Y. Video Magazine #07 / 1996 / OUP / M • N.Y. Video Magazine #08 / 1996 / OUP / M • N.Y. Video Magazine #09 / 1996 / OUP / M • N.Y. Video Magazine #10 / 1996 / OUP / M • The Naked Bun / 1989 / VWA / M • Naked Night / 1985 / VCR / M • Nasty Girls (1983-VCX) / 1983 / VCX / M • Neighborhood Watch #24: Nice Sticky Stuff / 1992 / LBO / M • Next Door Neighbors #39 / 1992 / BON / M • Night Of The Living Debbies / 1989 / EX / M • Nikki's Playground / 1995 / GAL / B • Nina's Knockouts / 1987 / AVC / C • One Hot Night Of Passion / 1985 / COL / C • Oral Majority #04 / 1987 / WV / C • Oral Majority #07 / 1989 / WV / C • Orgies / 1987 / WV / C • Over 40 / 1989 / BIZ / B • Pain Slut / 1995 / OUP / B • Panting At The Opera / 1988 / VXP / M • Pay The Lady / 1987 / VXP / M • The Pearl Divers / 1988 / VWA / M • Phantom Of The Cabaret #1 / 1989 / VC / M • Phantom Of The Cabaret #2 / 1989 / VC / M • Phantom X / 1989 / VC / M • Pink Baroness / 1988 / VWA / M • Play Me Again, Vanessa / 1986 / VC / M • Playing For Passion / 1987 / IN / M • Pointers / 1990 / LV / M • Political Party / 1985 / AVC / M • The Pornbirds / 1985 / VC / M • Pornocchio / 1987 / ME / M • A Portrait Of Christy / 1990 / VI / M • Primal Submission / A Glutton For Punishment / 1995 / OUP / B • Princess Of Penetration / 1988 / VXP / M • Project Ginger / 1985 / VI / M • Punished By Two / 1990 / BIZ / B • Punished Lesbians / 1992 / PL / B • The Punishment Of Dynasty / 1995 / OUP / B • Purple Pain / 1995 / OUP / B • Rambone Meets The Double Penetrators / 1987 / WET / M • Raquel Untamed / 1990 / CIN / M • Raw Talent #3 / 1988 / VC / M • Ready, Willing & Anal (Vidco) / 1993 / VD / C • Rearbusters / 1988 / LVI / C • The Red Head / 1989 / VWA / M • Red On The Noodle Like A Swance On A Poodle / 1990 / FC / C • Renegade / 1990 / CIN / M • The Return Of Indiana Joan / 1989 / PL / M • Rick's Bondage Playmate #1 / 1992 / BON / B • Rick's Bondage Playmate #2 / 1993 / HMV / B • Ride A Pink Lady / 1986 / SE / M • Robofox #2 / 1988 / FAN / M • Romeo And Juliet #2 / 1988 / WV / M • Rump Humpers / 1985 / WET / M • Sable Is Sorry / 1996 / GAL / B • Sacrificed To Love / 1986 / CDI / M • Sanctuary Of Sin / 1995 / OUP / B • Santa Comes Again / 1990 / GLE / M • Savage Delights / 1995 / OUP / B • Savage Discipline / 1993 / STM / C • Savage Fury #1 / 1985 / VEX / M • Savage Lessons #1 / 1995 / BON / B • Savage Lessons #2 / 1995 / BON / B • Savage Pain / 1995 / STM / C • Savage Torture / 1994 / PL / B • Say Something Nasty / 1989 / CC / M • The Scarlet Bride / 1989 / VI / M • Scent Of A Wild Woman / 1993 / EVN / C • Science Friction / 1986 / AXT / M • Screw The Right Thing / 1990 / VWA / M • The Secret (USA) / 1990 / SO / M • Secret Lessons #2 / 1989 / BIZ / B • Seductive TV / 1995 / GOT / G •

Sensations / 1987 / AE / S • Sessions With A Slave / cr90 / BON / B • Sex Asylum #2 / 1986 / VI / M • Sex Dreams On Maple Street / 1985 / WV / M • Sex For Hire / 1989 / HOE / C • Sex In Dangerous Places / 1988 / VI / M • Sex Lives Of The Rich And Beautiful / 1988 / CA / M • Sex Sluts From Beyond The Galaxy / 1991 / LBO / C • Sex Wars / 1984 / EXF / M • Sexeo / 1985 / PV / M • Sexpionage / 1987 / VXP / M • Sexual Pursuit / 1985 / AT / M • Sexual Trilogy #04 / 1994 / SFP / M • Sexy Delights #1 / 1986 / CLV / M • Sexy Ties & Videotape / 1992 / STM / B • Silver Tongue / 1989 / CA / M • Slave Slut Tied, Tickled, Spanked / 1993 / BON / B • Slavegirls In Suspension / 19?? / STM / B • The Slutty Professor / 1989 / VWA / M • Spanked Ecstasy / 1991 / BIZ / B • Spanked Geisha Girl / 1995 / STM / B • Spellbound / 1989 / LV / M • Steel Cage Bondage / 1995 / GAL / B • Stern Auditor / 1992 / STM / B • Stick It In The Rear #1 / 1991 / PL / M • Still The Brat / 1988 / VI / M • Streets Of New York #01 / 1994 / PL / M • Streets Of New York #02 / 1994 / PL / M • Streets Of New York #03 / 1994 / PL / M • Streets Of New York #04 / 1995 / PL / M • Sucker / 1988 / VWA / M • Summer Break / 1985 / VEX / M • Super Ball / 1989 / VWA / M • Surfside Sex / 1985 / PV / M • Suzie Creamcheese / 1988 / VWA / M • Sweet Cheeks / 1987 / VCR / C • The Sweet Spurt Of Youth / 1988 / WV / M • Tales Of Taija Rae / 1989 / DR / M • Tales Of The Golden Pussy / 1989 / RUM / M • Talk Dirty To Me #06 / 1989 / DR / M • Talk Dirty To Me #07 / 1990 / DR / M • The Taming Of Sable / 1995 / OUP / B • Taste Of The Best #1 / 1988 / PIN / C • Tattiana's Terror / 1996 / GAL / B • The Teacher's Pet / 1985 / WV / M • Teacher's Pets / 1985 / AVC / M • Tease Me / 1986 / VC / M • This Dick For Hire / 1989 / ZA / M • Thrilled To Death / 1988 • REP / S • Throbbin' Hood / 1987 / VD / M • Thy Neighbour's Wife / 1986 / DR / M • Tied & Tickled / 1996 / GAL / B • Tied And Taunted / 1992 / JAN / B • Tied And Tormented / 1995 / GAL / B • A Tongue Is Born / 1990 / ERU / M • Torrid / 1989 / VI / M • Totally Disgusting / 1995 / GAL / B • Traci Who? / 1987 / AVC / C • Trashy Lady / 1985 / MAP / M • Tricia's Painful Pleasure / 1995 / STM / B • The Trouble With Traci / 1984 / CHA / C • TV Encounter / 1992 / GOT / G • The Twilight Moan / 1985 / WV / M • The Ultimate / 1991 / BON / B • Uncut Diamond / 1989 / IN / M • Unforgivable / 1989 / IN / M • Unlaced / 1992 / PL / M • Victoria's Secret / 1989 / SO / M • Video Paradise / 1988 / ZA / M • Virgin Cheeks / 1986 / VD / M • Virgins / 1989 / CAR / M • Who Shaved Lynn Lemay? / 1989 / EX / M • Who Shaved Trinity Loren? / 1988 / EX / M • Whore Of The Roses / 1990 / AFV / M • The Whore Of The Worlds / 1985 / PV / M • Wicked Sensations #2 / 1989 / ZA / M • The Wizard Of AHH's / 1985 / SE / M • The World According To Ginger / 1985 / VI / M • X Factor / 1984 / HO / M • The X-Terminator / 1986 / PV / M

RICK SEEMAN
Kinky Debutante Interviews #05 / 1994 / IP / M

RICK SMEARS see Star Index I
RICK SMITH see Star Index I
RICK SNOW

Bobby Hollander's Sweet Cheeks #102 / 1992 / WV / M

RICK STAR see Star Index I
RICK STEARNS see Rock Steadie
RICK STEEL
Cheap Shot / 1995 / WAV / M
RICK STETSON
Sex, Truth & Videotape #1 / 1995 / DOC / M

RICK STICK see Star Index I
RICK STRYKER
Every Which Way / 1990 / V10 / G • Loose Ends #5: The New Generation / 1988 / 4P / M • Sex Lies / 1988 / FAN / M

RICK STUCCO see Star Index I
RICK THOMAS
Natural Response / 1996 / GPI / G
RICK TRICKLE
Nektar / 1996 / BAC / M
RICK VALENZIO see Star Index I
RICK VAN see Karen Dior
RICK WYNN see Star Index I
RICKEY P.
In Your Face #4 / 1996 / PL / M
RICKEY RAY see Rikki Rey
RICKI
Bound By Design / 1995 / BON / B • Director Dilemma #1 / 1995 / BON / B • Director Dilemma #2 / 1995 / BON / B • First Time Lesbians #07 / 1993 / JMP / F • Spank & Spank Again / 1995 / BON / B • Swinging Couples #03 / 1994 / GO / M
RICKI LANE
Intimate Realities #1 / 1983 / VC / M
RICKIE
1-900-SPANKME Ext.1 / 1994 / BON / B • 1-900-SPANKME Ext.2 / 1994 / BON / B • Rubber Me Butt! / 1994 / SBP / B • Spankology 101b / 1994 / BON / B
RICKIE HAMMER see Star Index I
RICKY
Blue Vanities #516 / 1992 / FFL / M • Blue Vanities #532 / 1993 / FFL / M
RICKY D. see Star Index I
RICKY JET
Geisha To Go / 1994 / PPP / M • I Dream Of Tiffany / 1993 / IF / M • Southern Accents / 1992 / VEX / M • Women Who Love Men, Men Who Love Women / 1993 / FD / C
RICKY LANE see Karen Summer
RICKY LEE *(Rikki Lee (Ricky), Kama Sutra, Karma Sutra, Pookie Thorn, Ricky Lynn, Sara (Ricky Lee))*
Thai girl but a bit plump in the magazines but adorable on the screen. Not to be confused with an unknown male in **Backpackers #2** and **Gorgeous**. She is called by mistake, Sara, in **MDD #7**. She did layouts in *Hustler* August 1991 and *Chic* June 1991.
Flying High With Rikki Lee / 1992 / VEX / C • Jewel Of The Orient / 1991 / VEX / M • More Dirty Debutantes #07 / 1991 / 4P / M • More Dirty Debutantes #08 / 1991 / 4P / M • Mystified / 1991 / V99 / M • Nasty Jack's Homemade Vid. #27 / 1991 / CDI / M • New Wave Hookers #2 / 1991 / VC / M • Positions Wanted / 1990 / VI / M
RICKY LEE (MALE)
The Backpackers #2 / 1990 / IN / M • Butt Naked #1 / 1990 / OD / M • Gorgeous / 1990 / CA / M • Mad Love / 1988 / VC / M • Painted / 1990 / INH / G • A Taste Of K.C. Williams / 1992 / VD / C
RICKY LYNN see Ricky Lee
RICKY MCCULLEN

Campus Girl / 1972 / VXP / M
RICKY NEWMAN see Star Index I
RICKY P.
In Your Face #3 / 1995 / PL / M
RICKY RACER
Four Screws And An Anal / 1994 / NEY / M • Swedish Erotica #80 / 1994 / CA / M
RICKY RICARDO
Anal Injury / 1994 / ZA / M • Bi-Wicked / 1994 / BIN / G • Ms. Fix-It / 1994 / PRK / M • Reel Sex #02: Splash Party / 1994 / SPP / M • The Voyeur #2 / 1994 / EA / M
RICKY STARR
Real Tickets #1 / 1994 / VC / M
RICKY TURNER
Bi-Coastal / 1985 / LAV / G • Bi-Sexual Fantasies / 1984 / LAV / G • Parliament: Hard TV #1 / 1988 / PM / G • The Scam / 1986 / TEM / G • She Studs #02 / 1991 / BIZ / G • Trisexual Encounters #02 / 1985 / PL / G
RICO
Jus' Knockin' Boots #1: Fade To Black / 1996 / NIT / M • Jus' Knockin' Boots #2: Black On Line / 1996 / NIT / M • Sweet Black Cherries #4 / 1996 / TTV / M
RICO ESTRADA see Star Index I
RICO GALLARZA
The Psychiatrist / 1978 / VC / M
RICO SUAVE
Canadian Beaver Hunt #3 / 1996 / PL / M
RICO VESPA
Star 84: Tina Marie / 1984 / VEX / M
RIE MURAKAMI
The Sex Exchange / 1996 / AVV / M
RIE YUKUMA
Desire & Pleasure / 1996 / AVE / M
RIFF LAKES see Star Index I
RIFF MILES see Star Index I
RIK ANGEL
Dark Reality #2 / 1995 / STM / B
RIKKI
The Magnificent 7 / 1994 / VTF / B • Mistress Of The Dungeon / 1994 / VTF / B • Mr. Wilkes' Caning Academy / 1994 / VTF / B
RIKKI ANDERSIN
Tight Ass / 1996 / AMP / M
RIKKI BLAKE
Gray blonde with a nice personality and small droopy tits but a slightly thickening body.
Aurora's Secret Diary / 1985 / LA / M • Bad Girls #3 / 1984 / COL / M • Bad Girls #4 / 1984 / COL / M • Bare Elegance / 1984 / MAP / M • Blondie / 1985 / TAR / M • Breaking It #1 / 1984 / COL / M • Doctor Desire / 1984 / VD / M • Gourmet Quickies: Rikki Boyer / Rikki Blake #727 / 1985 / GO / C • Gourmet Quickies: Rikki Blake #721 / 1985 / GO / C • Holly Does Hollywood #1 / 1985 / VEX / M • Hypnotic Sensations / 1985 / GO / M • I Like To Be Watched / 1984 / VD / M • Intimate Couples / 1984 / VCX / M • Loose Ends #1 / 1984 / 4P / M • Lorelei / 1984 / CV / M • Nice 'n' Tight / 1985 / AIR / M • Only The Best Of Women With Women / 1988 / CV / C • The Sex Goddess / 1984 / GO / M • The Shoe Store / 1985 / BIZ / B • Slave Exchange / 1985 / BIZ / B • Spreading Joy / 1984 / IN / M • Talk Dirty To Me #03 / 1986 / DR / M • A Taste Of Candy / 1985 / LA / M • Tracy In Heaven (Orig 1985) / 1985 / WV / M • Tracy In Heaven (Rewrite) / 1986 / WV / M • The Wacky World Of X-Rated Bloopers / 1989 / GO / M
RIKKI FOXX

Anal Virgins Of America #09 / 1994 / FOR / M • Backing In #5 / 1994 / WV / C • Tail Taggers #105 / 1993 / WV / M

RIKKI GAMBINO *see Star Index I*

RIKKI HARTE

Babylon Gold / 1983 / COM / C • Firestorm #1 / 1984 / COM / M • Firestorm #3 / 1986 / COM / M • The Red Room And Other Places / 1992 / COM / C • Snake Eyes #1 / 1984 / COM / M • Snake Eyes #2 / 1987 / COM / M • Spitfire / 1984 / COM / M

RIKKI LEE *see Star Index I*

RIKKI LEE (RICKY) *see Ricky Lee*

RIKKI LEIGH

The Best Little He/She House In Texas / 1993 / HSV / G • Charade / 1993 / HSV / G • She Male Jail / 1994 / HSV / G • She-Male Vacation / 1993 / HSV / G

RIKKI MONTEBANK

Fantasy Mansion / 1983 / BIZ / B

RIKKI O'NEAL *(Sherri Tart)*

Tall with large natural tits, black hair, passable face, very hairy pussy.

Debbie Does Dallas #1 / 1978 / VC / M • Double Your Pleasure / 1978 / CV / M • Erotic Fantasies #1 / 1983 / CV / C • Honeysuckle Rose / 1979 / CA / M • Jack 'n' Jill #1 / 1979 / VXP / M • Misbehavin' / 1979 / VXP / M • New York Babes / 1979 / AR / M • Satin Suite / 1979 / QX / M • Secrets Of A Willing Wife / 1979 / VXP / M • Tigresses...And Other Man-Eaters / 1979 / VXP / M

RIKKI PARKER *see Star Index I*

RIKKI RACER

Lady's Choice / 1995 / VD / M

RIKKI REY *(Rickey Ray, Rikki Strong)*

Small titted brunette with a pretty face and nice smile. Small areola and pencil eraser nipples. Has a small tattoo on her belly just to the right of her pubic hair which according to her is Chinese characters for "Trust In No Man". In **New Ends #08** she says it's "Trust In No One" but I suppose it could be interpreted both ways. In the same movie (1994) she says she's 30 years old and of Lebanese/Italian extraction. Note that this is not the same as Steffi.

Amateur Lesbians #41: Kelli / 1993 / GO / F • Amateur Lesbians #42: Rosie Lee / 1993 / GO / F • The Backway Inn #3 / 1993 / FD / M • Beach Bum Amateur's #31 / 1993 / MID / M • Big Murray's New-Cummers #20: Hot Honies In Heat / 1993 / FD / M • Big Murray's New-Cummers #21: Double Penetration One / 1993 / FD / M • Bobby Hollander's Maneaters #09 / 1993 / SFP / M • Delicious (Midnight-1993) / 1993 / MID / M • The Dickheads #1 / 1993 / MID / M • Erotic Newcummers Vol 1 #1: Capitol Desires / 1993 / DR / M • A Girl's Affair #02 / 1993 / FD / F • Haunting Dreams #1 / 1993 / LV / M • Haunting Dreams #2 / 1993 / LV / M • Hollywood In Your Face / 1993 / VC / M • Hot Tight Asses #04 / 1993 / TCK / M • Lovin' Spoonfuls #7 / 1996 / 4P / C • New Ends #08 / 1994 / 4P / M • Pearl Necklace: Amorous Amateurs #34 / 1992 / SEE / M • Pearl Necklace: Thee Bush League #20 / 1993 / SEE / M • Please, Mistress! / 1993 / SV / B • Prime Time Slime #01 / 1993 / GLI / M • Student Fetish Videos: Best of Enema #03 / 1994 / PRE / C • Student Fetish Videos: The Enema #13 / 1994 / PRE / B • Student Fetish Videos: Tickling #08 / 1994 / SFV / B • Super

Hornio Brothers #1 / 1993 / MID / M

RIKKI SAWYER

Whip Therapy / 1995 / BON / B

RIKKI STRONG *see Rikki Rey*

RIKKY DIX

Amsterdam Nights #1 / 1996 / BLC / M • Amsterdam Nights #2 / 1996 / VC / M

RINALDO TALAMONTI

Love 'n' Leather Pants / 1974 / LHV / S • [Schulmadchen-Report 4: Was Eltern Oft Verzweifeln LaBt / 1972 / ... / M

RINGMAN

Boobwatch #1 / 1996 / SC / M • Rockhard (Sin City) / 1996 / SC / M

RINI SENYA *see Star Index I*

RINO CELONTE

Matrimony Intrigue / 1995 / WIV / M

RINSE DREAM *(Steve Sayadian)*

Nightdreams #1 / 1981 / CA / M

RINY REY

Amsterdam Nights #1 / 1996 / BLC / M • Amsterdam Nights #2 / 1996 / VC / M • Chateau Duval / 1996 / HDE / M • Dirty Tricks #2: This Ain't Love / 1996 / EA / M • Private Gold #04: Amazonas / 1996 / OD / M • Private Gold #09: Private Dancer / 1996 / OD / M • Private Gold #10: Sins / 1996 / OD / M • Private Stories #06 / 1995 / OD / M • Private Stories #07 / 1996 / OD / M • The Voyeur #6 / 1996 / EA / M

RIP ENGEL

[Pussy Photographer / 197? / ... / M

RIP HYMAN

Between The Cheeks #2 / 1990 / VC / M • Deep Inside Centerfold Girls / 1991 / VC / M • The Devil In Miss Jones #5: The Inferno / 1994 / VC / M • Malibu Spice / 1991 / VC / M • New Wave Hookers #2 / 1991 / VC / M • Sex Freaks / 1995 / EA / M

RIP IVAN

Kitty Foxx's Kinky Kapers #02 / 1995 / TTV / M • Kitty's Kinky Capers / 1996 / TTV / M

RIP SOWN

Sloppy Seconds / 1994 / PE / M

RIP STONE

Bi And Beyond #6: Authentic / 1996 / FD / G • Bi This! / 1995 / BIL / G • Night Walk / 1995 / HIV / G • Score Of Sex / 1995 / BAC / G

RIP TYLER *see Star Index I*

RITA

Blue Vanities #500 / 1992 / FFL / M • Blue Vanities #506 / 1992 / FFL / M • Blue Vanities #550 / 1994 / FFL / M • Blue Vanities #583 / 1996 / FFL / M • GM #139: Raunchy Rita (Goldie) / 1993 / GMV / F • Homegrown Video #403 / 1993 / HOV / M • Inside Seka / 1980 / VXP / M

RITA (1997)

Filthy First Timers #7 / 1997 / EL / M

RITA BERLIN *see Star Index I*

RITA COUS

The Kowloon Connection / 1973 / VCX / M

RITA CRUZ

Bold Obsession / 1983 / NSV / M • Flesh & Laces #2 / 1983 / CA / M • Forbidden Desire / 1983 / NSV / M • Marathon / 1982 / CA / M

RITA DAVIS *see Linda Lovemore*

RITA EROTICA

Anal Annie And The Magic Dildo / 1984 / LIP / F • The Best Of Anal Annie: The Girl-Girl Adventures / 1993 / LIP / C • Big Tits And Fat Fannies #10 / 1994 / BTO / M • Cheri's On Fire / 1986 / V99 / M • Double Standards / 1988 / BIL / G • Fat Fannies

#10 / 1994 / BTO / M • Girlworld #2 / 1988 / LIP / F • Glamour Girls / 1987 / SE / M • The Grafenberg Spot / 1985 / MIT / M • Haulin' 'n' Ballin' / 1988 / MET / G • Hotel Transylvania #2 / 1990 / LIP / G • Love At First Sight / 1987 / SE / C

RITA GEORGE

Bad Company / 1978 / CV / M

RITA GONZOLES

All About Sex / 1970 / AR / M

RITA H. *see Kim Alexis*

RITA HEGEDUS

Juicy Virgins / 1995 / WIV / M

RITA JORDAN *see Star Index I*

RITA LANNING *see Star Index I*

RITA LUSTY

The Swing Thing / 1973 / TGA / M

RITA MAIDEN *see Star Index I*

RITA PAYNE *see Star Index I*

RITA RICARDO

The Best Of Hot Heels / 1992 / BIZ / B • Cheating Wives / 1983 / PAC / M • Cheri's On Fire / 1986 / V99 / M • Corporate Affairs / 1986 / SE / M • Crisp Bottoms / 1988 / PLV / B • Flesh Pond / 1983 / VC / M • Foot Mistress / 1986 / BIZ / B • Getting Personal / 1986 / CA / M • Girlfriends / 1983 / MIT / M • Girlfriends Of Candy Wong / 1984 / LIP / F • Glamour Girls / 1987 / SE / M • Hard To Swallow / 1985 / PV / M • Hot Girls In Love / 1985 / VXP / M • Kinky Sluts / 1988 / MIR / C • The Last Taboo / 1984 / VIV / M • Love At First Sight / 1987 / SE / C • Lust Inferno / 1982 / CA / M • Mad About You / 1987 / VC / M • Nasty Lady / 1984 / CV / M • Reel People #01 / 1983 / AR / M • She-Male Encounters #05: Orgy At The Poysinberry Bar #1 / 1987 / MET / G • She-Male Encounters #11: She-Male Roommates / 1986 / MET / G • She-Male Encounters #12: Orgy At The Poysinberry #2 / 1987 / MET / G • Sleepless Nights / 1984 / VIV / M • Trick Or Treat / 1985 / ELH / M • Video Girls / 1984 / LIP / F • The Wizard Of AHH's / 1985 / SE / M

RITA ROSA

Bi Bi Banjee Boyz / 1994 / PL / G

RITA STARLING

The Beauty Pageant / 1981 / AVC / M

RITA STONE *see Star Index I*

RITA WALDENBERG

[Madchen, Die Sich Selbst, Bedienen / 1974 / ... / M

RITA WEEMS *see Star Index I*

RITA ZISK *see Star Index I*

RITCHIE RAZOR *(Ingo, Richie Razor)*

Used to be husband of Tiffany Million.

Adult Affairs / 1994 / VC / M • The Beaverly Hillbillies / 1993 / IP / M • Deep Inside Tyffany Million / 1995 / VC / C • Dirty Little Mind / 1994 / IP / M • The Fantasy Booth / 1993 / ONA / M • Generally Horny Hospital / 1995 / IMV / M • Initiation Of Kylie / 1995 / VT / M • Jailhouse Cock / 1993 / IP / M • Latex #1 / 1994 / VC / M • Mind Games / 1995 / IMV / M • Nightbreed / 1995 / VI / M • Once In A Lifetime / 1996 / VC / C • Plaything #2 / 1995 / VI / M • The Right Connection / 1995 / VC / M • Sex #1 (Vca) / 1994 / VC / M • Sex #2: Fate (Vca) / 1995 / VC / M • The Tyffany Million Diaries / 1995 / IMV / C • The Voyeur #4 / 1995 / EA / M

RIVIERA

Under The Skirt #1 / 1995 / KAE / F

ROADBLOCK

Blue Movie / 1995 / WP / M

ROAHNE ALEXANDER *see Star Index I*

ROARY TAYLOR
Sex Over 40 #2 / 1994 / PL / M

ROB
AVP #9131: Kelly Doubles Up / 1991 / AVP / M • AVP #9135: The Big Move / 1991 / AVP / M • Bubble Butts #28 / 1993 / LBO / M • Frathouse Sexcapades / 1993 / SFP / M • Hard To Hold / 1993 / IF / M • Hidden Camera #17 / 1994 / JMP / M • Humongous Hooters / 1993 / IF / M • Living For Love / 1993 / V99 / M • Northwest Pecker Trek #2: Evergreen, Ever Horny / 1994 / LBO / M • Suburban Swingers / 1993 / IF / M • Swingers Confidential #1 / 1995 / FC / M

ROB BALDWIN
Road Trippin' #03: New York City / 1994 / OUP / M

ROB BARONE
Titanic Orgy / 1995 / PEP / M

ROB BARREN
Flexxx #1 / 1994 / VT / M • Revenge Of The Bi Dolls / 1994 / CAT / G • Smooth As Silk / 1994 / EMC / M

ROB COX
Club DV8 #1 / 1993 / SC / M • Firecrackers / 1994 / HW / M

ROB CRYSTON
Long Play / 1995 / 3XP / G • Marine Code Of Silence: Don't Ask Don't Tell / 1996 / BHE / G • Night Walk / 1995 / HIV / G • Secret Sex #2: The Sex Radicals / 1994 / CAT / G • Switch Hitters #7 / 1994 / IN / G

ROB EAST *see Star Index I*

ROB EASTMAN *see Rob Tyler*

ROB EMMETT *see Eric Edwards*

ROB EVERETT *see Eric Edwards*

ROB EVERT *see Eric Edwards*

ROB HARD
She-Male Instinct / 1995 / BCP / G

ROB JOHNSON
K-Sex / 1976 / VCR / M

ROB KING
Bimbette: Adventures In Anal Land / 1996 / TEP / M

ROB LONG *see Star Index I*

ROB LOWE
Hotel New Hampshire / 1984 / VES / S • Masquerade / 1988 / CBS / S • Midnight Blue: Rob Lowe, The Go-Go's, and Chuck Berry / 1990 / SVE / M • [Youngblood / 1986 / MGM / S

ROB MATHEWS
Up And Cummers #20 / 1995 / 4P / M • Up And Cummers #22 / 1995 / RWP / M

ROB Q BYRD *see Star Index I*

ROB SAVAGE
Anonymous / 1993 / VI / M • Endlessly / 1993 / VI / M • Hollywood Swingers #01 / 1992 / LBO / M • The XXX Files: Lust In Space / 1995 / IMV / M

ROB SMITH *see Star Index I*

ROB STEVENS
Kimbra's Wimps / 1995 / STM / B

ROB STONE
Marine Code Of Silence: Don't Ask Don't Tell / 1996 / BHE / G

ROB TERMINATOR
Private Film #05 / 1993 / OD / M • Private Film #09 / 1994 / OD / M

ROB TYLER *(Robert Jackson, Matt Daniels, Robert J., Rob Eastman, Robert Leer, Bob Tyler, Mathew Daniels, Rod Tyler)*
Heather Lere's boyfriend. Looks prettier than

she does. Has long dark blonde (sometimes brown) hair but a five o'clock shadow.
Cape Lere / 1992 / CC / M • Dear Bridgette / 1992 / ZA / M • Honey, I Blew Everybody #1 / 1992 / MID / M • I Touch Myself / 1992 / IN / M • Jugsy (X-Citement) / 1992 / XCI / M • The Last Girl Scout / 1992 / PL / M • Main Street, U.S.A. / 1992 / PP / M • More Dirty Debutantes #11 / 1991 / 4P / M • The Party / 1992 / CDI / M • Professor Sticky's Anatomy 3X #02 / 1992 / FC / M • Putting On The Ritz / 1990 / VEX / M • Ready Freddy? / 1992 / FH / M • Shipwrecked / 1992 / CDI / M • Sunrise Mystery / 1992 / FD / M • Taboo #10 / 1992 / IN / M • Twister / 1992 / CC / M • White Men Can't Hump / 1992 / CC / M • Women Who Love Men, Men Who Love Women / 1993 / FD / C

ROBBI ROBINSON *see Star Index I*

ROBBIE
The Betrayal Of Innocence #1: The Awakening Of Marika / 1993 / CC / M • The Betrayal Of Innocence #2: The Decadence / 1993 / CC / M • The Betrayal Of Innocence #3: The Choice / 1993 / CC / M • Nasty Travel Tails #02 / 1993 / CC / M

ROBBIE ANDERSON
Sex Bi-Lex / 1993 / CAT / G

ROBBIE DEE *(Robert Dee, Robby Dee, Bobby Dee, Robbie Watson)*
Bedtime Video #09 / 1984 / GO / M • Between My Breasts #02 / 1986 / L&W / S • Black Bad Girls / 1985 / PLY / M • The Black Chill / 1986 / WET / M • Black Encounters / 1992 / ZA / M • Black On Black / 1987 / CDI / M • Black Taboo #2 / 1986 / SE / M • Black To The Future / 1986 / VD / M • Black Valley Girls #1 / 1986 / 4R / M • Blonde City / 1992 / IN / M • Boobs, Butts And Bloopers #1 / 1990 / HO / M • Caught From Behind #05: Blondes & Blacks / 1986 / HO / M • Charming Cheapies #6: Red Tide / 1985 / 4P / M • Daddy's Darling Daughters / 1986 / PL / M • Deep Inside Tracey / 1987 / CDI / C • Detroit Dames / 1988 / DR / C • Devil In Miss Jones #4: The Final Outrage / 1987 / VC / M • Double Penetration #3 / 1986 / WV / C • Ebony Ecstacy / 1988 / HIO / C • Ebony Orgies / 1987 / SE / C • Hill Street Blacks #1 / 1985 / 4R / M • Hotter Chocolate / 1986 / AVC / M • I Am Curious Black / 1986 / WET / M • Insatiable #2 / 1984 / CA / M • Kate And The Indians / 1980 / SE / M • Lessons In Lust / 1987 / LA / M • Love On The Borderline / 1987 / IN / M • Marilyn Chambers' Private Fantasies #2 / 1983 / CA / M • The More the Merrier / 1989 / VC / C • Oral Majority Black #1 / 1987 / WV / C • Oral Majority Black #2 / 1988 / WV / C • Soul Kiss This / 1988 / VCR / C • A Taste Of Black / 1987 / WET / M • To Live & Shave In LA / 1986 / WET / M • Ubangis On Uranus / 1987 / WV / M • The Zebra Club / 1986 / VSE / M

ROBBIE HALL
Tight Spot / 1996 / WV / M

ROBBIE PARRISH *see Star Index I*

ROBBIE PERON
The Stand-Up / 1994 / VC / M

ROBBIE WATSON *see Robbie Dee*

ROBBY DEE *see Robbie Dee*

ROBBY SENSON
Stasha's Adult School / 1993 / CDI / G

ROBBY TAYLOR
Natural Response / 1996 / GPI / G

ROBERT
Amateur Hours #01 / 1989 / AFI / M • Big Babies In Budapest / 1996 / EL / M • Breast Wishes #06 / 1991 / LBO / M • Domino's Dungeon / 1993 / COC / B • Fresh Faces #04 / 1995 / EVN / M • Hollywood Amateurs #17 / 1995 / MID / M • Mr. Peepers Amateur Home Videos #68: A Tough Load To Swallow / 1993 / LBO / M • New Faces, Hot Bodies #15 / 1994 / STP / M • Pearl Necklace: Amorous Amateurs #02 / 1992 / SEE / M • Stevi's: Trish & Robert / 1993 / SSV / M

ROBERT ADAMS
The Coming Of Joyce / 1977 / VIS / M

ROBERT ALAIN COUTE *see Star Index I*

ROBERT ALBAN *see Star Index I*

ROBERT APONTE *see Star Index I*

ROBERT ARIA *see Star Index I*

ROBERT BALDER *see Star Index I*

ROBERT BEDFORD *see Star Index I*

ROBERT BELL *see Star Index I*

ROBERT BIGO *see Star Index I*

ROBERT BLACK
Ass, Gas & The Mystical GLOP / 1997 / EL / M • The Cellar Dweller / 1996 / EL / M • Nice Fuckin' Movie / 1997 / EL / M • Sexual Atrocities / 1996 / EL / M • A Week And A Half In The Life Of A Prostitute / 1997 / EL / M

ROBERT BOLLA *(R. Bolla, Richard Bolla, Richard Bocca, Robert Kerns, Richard Bollar, Robert Brown, Richard Balla, Sam Speed, Robert Kerman)*
Robert Kerns is from **Beach House**.
The 8th Annual Erotic Film Awards / 1984 / SE / C • The Adventures Of Dick Black, Black Dick / 1987 / DR / M • Alexandra / 1984 / VC / M • All About Gloria Leonard / 1978 / VXP / M • Amanda By Night #1 / 1981 / CA / M • Amazing Sex Stories #2 / 1987 / SUV / C • American Desire / 1981 / CA / M • Angel Buns / 1981 / QX / M • Anyone But My Husband / 1975 / VC / M • Babes In Toyland / 1988 / COM / C • Babylon Pink #1 / 1979 / COM / M • Bad Penny / 1978 / QX / M • Bare Elegance / 1984 / MAP / M • Beach House / 1981 / CA / C • Blonde Ambition / 1981 / QX / M • Blonde Velvet / 1976 / COL / M • Blow Dry / 1977 / SVE / M • Blue Ecstasy / 1980 / CA / M • Blue Voodoo / 1983 / VD / M • Body Shop / 1984 / VCX / M • Breaker Beauties / 1977 / VHL / M • The Budding Of Brie / 1980 / TVX / M • Bunny's Office Fantasies / 1984 / VC / M • Burlexxx / 1984 / VC / M • Caballero Preview Tape #4 / 1985 / CA / C • Cannibal Holocaust / 1979 / LUM / S • Carnal Games / 1978 / BL / M • Casino Of Lust / 1984 / AT / M • Celebrity Presents Celebrity / 1986 / VEP / C • Centerfold Celebrities #4 / 1983 / VC / M • Centerfold Celebrities #5 / 1983 / VC / M • Centerfold Fever / 1981 / VXP / M • Centerspread Girls / 1982 / CA / M • Cherry Cheesecake / 1984 / AR / M • Chorus Call / 1978 / TVX / M • Come With Me, My Love / 1976 / PVX / M • Command Performance / cr75 / LA / M • Corporate Assets / 1985 / SE / M • The Cosmopolitan Girls / 1982 / VC / M • Cover Girl Fantasies #1 / 1983 / VCR / C • Dangerous Stuff / 1985 / COM / M • Dear Fanny / 1984 / CV / M • Deathmask / 1983 / PRS / S • Debbie Does Dallas #1 / 1978 / VC / M • Debbie Does Dallas #2 / 1980 /

VC / M • Debbie Does Dallas #3 / 1985 / VC / M • Decendance Of Grace / 1977 / CA / M • Deep Inside Ginger Lynn / 1986 / SE / C • Delicious / 1981 / VXP / M • Devil In Miss Jones #2 / 1983 / VC / M • Dirty Lilly / 1975 / VXP / M • Dirty Looks / 1982 / VC / C • Doctor Desire / 1984 / VD / M • Eaten Alive / 1980 / CO1 / S • Electric Blue #013: Campus Fever / 1984 / CA / C • Electric Blue: Caribbean Cruise / 1984 / CA / S • Electric Blue: Cosmic Coeds / 1985 / CA / M • Feelings / 1977 / VC / M • Fiona On Fire / 1978 / VC / M • Flesh And Ecstasy / 1985 / VD / M • For Love And Money / 1987 / CV / S • For Richer, For Poorer / 1979 / CXV / M • Foxtrot / 1982 / COM / M • From Holly With Love / 1977 / CA / M • Fulfilling Young Cups / 1978 / … / M • The Fur Trap / 1973 / AVC / M • G-Strings / 1984 / COM / M • Ginger's Hawaiian Scrapbook / 1988 / GO / C • A Girl's Best Friend / 1981 / QX / M • Girls Of The Night / 1985 / CA / M • Girls On Fire / 1985 / VCX / M • Girls U.S.A. / 1980 / AIR / M • Give It To Me / 1984 / SE / M • The Good Girls Of Godiva High / 1979 / VCX / M • Gourmet Quickies: Christy Canyon #719 / 1985 / GO / C • Great Sexpectations / 1984 / VC / M • Gums / 1976 / AVC / M • Heat Wave / 1977 / COM / M • Hindsight / 1985 / IN / M • Holiday For Angels / 1987 / IN / M • Honeymoon Haven / 1977 / QX / M • Hot Blooded / 1983 / CA / M • Hot Licks / 1984 / SE / M • House Of Sin / 1982 / AVO / M • Hypnotic Sensations / 1985 / GO / M • I Love LA #1 / 1986 / PEN / C • I Love LA #2 / 1989 / PEN / C • In Love / 1983 / VC / M • Indecent Exposure / 1981 / CA / M • Inside Jennifer Welles / 1977 / VXP / M • Inside Seka / 1980 / VXP / M • Jawbreakers / 1985 / VEN / C • Joint Venture / 1977 / ELV / M • Joy / 1977 / QX / M • Kid Stuff / 1981 / … / M • Lenny's Comeback / cr78 / CIN / M • Limited Edition #01 / 1979 / AVC / M • Limited Edition #11 / 1980 / AVC / M • Lip Service / 1988 / LV / C • Liquid A$$ets / 1982 / CA / M • Little Darlings / 1981 / VEP / M • Long Hard Nights / 1984 / ELH / M • Looking For Love / 1985 / VCX / M • Lorelei / 1984 / CV / M • The Love Couch / 1977 / VC / M • Lust At The Top / 1985 / CDI / M • Lusty Adventurer / 1985 / GO / M • Make Me Feel It / 1984 / SE / M • Make Them Die Slowly / 1983 / IVE / S • Manhattan Mistress / 1980 / VBM / M • Mascara / 1982 / CA / M • More Than Sisters / 1978 / VC / M • Naked Scents / 1984 / VC / M • Nasty Girls (1983-VCX) / 1983 / VCX / M • Naughty Nurses / 1982 / VCR / M • The New York City Woman / 1979 / VC / C • The Nurses Are Coming / 1985 / VCR / C • Odyssey / 1977 / VC / M • Oh Those Nurses / 1982 / VC / M • Once Upon A Secretary / 1983 / GO / M • One Night At A Time / 1984 / PV / M • Oriental Madam / 1981 / TGA / M • Outlaw Ladies #1 / 1981 / VC / M • Passion Flowers / 1987 / CDI / C • Peepholes / 1982 / AVC / M • People / 1978 / QX / M • The Perfect Weekend / 1984 / AVC / M • Perfection / 1985 / VD / M • The Pink Ladies / 1980 / VC / M • The Playgirl / 1982 / CA / M • Pleasure Island / 1984 / AR / M • The Pleasure Palace / 1978 / CV / M • The Pleasures Of Innocence / 1985 / VC / M • Pop-Porn: Safari Club / 1992 / 4P / M • Prey Of A Call Girl / 1975 /

ALP / M • Public Affairs / 1984 / CA / M • Pussycat Ranch / 1978 / CV / M • Regency #01 / 1981 / RHV / M • Rich Quick, Private Dick / 1984 / CA / M • Safari Club / 1977 / 4P / M • Satin Suite / 1979 / QX / M • Satisfactions / 1983 / CA / M • The Satisfiers Of Alpha Blue / 1980 / AVC / M • A Scent Of Heather / 1981 / VXP / M • Scoundrels / 1982 / COM / M • Sex Play / 1984 / SE / M • Sharon In The Rough-House / 1976 / LA / M • Silky / 1980 / VXP / M • Skin Flicks / 1978 / AVC / M • Sky Pies / 1985 / GO / M • Slave Of Pleasure / 1978 / BL / M • Small Change / 1978 / CDC / M • Society Affairs / 1982 / CA / M • Spitfire / 1984 / COM / M • The Starmaker / 1982 / VC / M • Street Heat / 1984 / VC / M • Succulent / 1983 / VXP / M • The Sweetest Taboo / 1986 / SE / M • Taboo American Style #1: The Ruthless Beginning / 1985 / VC / M • Taboo American Style #2: The Story Continues / 1985 / VC / M • A Taste Of Tawnee / 1988 / LV / C • Teach Me / 1984 / VD / M • Teenage Pajama Party / 1977 / VC / M • Teenage Runaways / 1977 / WWV / M • This Lady Is A Tramp / 1980 / CV / M • Three Faces Of Angel / 1987 / CV / M • The Tiffany Minx / 1981 / SAT / M • Tower Of Power / 1985 / CV / M • Triangle Of Lust / 1983 / VCR / M • Trinity Brown / 1984 / CV / M • The Trouble With Young Stuff / 1976 / VC / M • Twilight Pink #1 / 1980 / AR / M • Twilight Pink #2 / 1982 / VC / M • VCA Previews #4 / 1988 / VC / C • Virgin Snow / 1976 / VXP / M • Viva Vanessa The Undresser / 1984 / VC / M • The Wacky World Of X-Rated Bloopers / 1989 / GO / M • Way Down Deep / cr78 / PYR / M • Wet Shots (Vcr) / 1983 / VCR / C • When She Was Bad / 1983 / CA / M • Where The Sun Never Shines / 1990 / IN / C • The Widespread Scandals Of Lydia Lace / 1983 / CA / M • The Woman Who Loved Men / 1984 / SE / M • Women In Love / 1980 / CA / M • Young, Wild And Wonderful / 1980 / VCX / M • [Vanessa's Dirty Deeds / 19?? / SVE / M

ROBERT BOSSI
Skin #5: The 5th Column / 1996 / ERQ / M
ROBERT BROWN *see* **Robert Bolla**
ROBERT BROWN JR *see* *Star Index I*
ROBERT BULLOCK *(Robert Burrows, Richard Bulick, Bobby Bullock, Richard Parnes, Anthony Richard, Chuck Cee)*
Ali Boobie & The 40 D's / 1988 / 3DV / M • Amanda By Night #2 / 1987 / CA / M • America's Most Wanted Girl / 1989 / IN / M • Babylon Pink #2 / 1988 / COM / M • Babylon Pink #3 / 1988 / COM / M • Backdoor Brides #3 / 1988 / PV / M • Ball Street / 1988 / CA / M • Barbara Dare's Bad / 1988 / SE / C • Behind Blue Eyes #2 / 1988 / ZA / M • Beverly Hills Seduction / 1988 / WV / M • Biloxi Babes / 1988 / WV / M • Bimbo Cheerleaders From Outer Space / 1988 / FAN / M • The Bitches Of Westwood / 1987 / CA / M • Blondie / 1985 / TAR / M • Blowing In Style / 1989 / EA / M • Bodies In Heat #2 / 1989 / DR / M • Boom Boom Valdez / 1988 / CA / M • Bound To Tease #1 / 1988 / BON / C • Bound To Tease #2 / 1989 / BON / C • Boxed Lunches / 1989 / … / M • Bringing Up The Rear / 1993 / VD / C • Butt's Motel #2 / 1989 / EX / M • Call Girls In Action / 1989 / CV / M • Campfire Girls / 1988 / SE / M • Candy's Little Sister Sugar

/ 1988 / VD / M • Carnal Encounters Of The Barest Kind / 1978 / VOY / C • The Cat Club / 1987 / SE / M • Coming In Style / 1986 / CA / M • Conflict / 1988 / VD / M • Couples Club #1 / 1988 / BON / B • Couples Club #2 / 1989 / BON / B • Cupid's Arrow / 1984 / VCR / M • Dear Fanny / 1984 / CV / M • Debbie 4 Hire / 1988 / AVC / M • Debbie Class Of '89 / 1989 / CC / M • Deep Throat #3 / 1989 / AR / M • The Desk Top Dolls / 1990 / BAD / C • Desperate Women / 1986 / VD / M • Diamond In The Rough / 1989 / EX / M • Double Heat / 1986 / LA / M • Dy-Nasty / 1988 / SE / M • Easy Lover / 1989 / EX / M • Easy Lovers / 1987 / SE / M • The Ecstasy Girls #1 / 1979 / CA / M • Educating Laurel / 1988 / BON / B • Enrapture / 1990 / ATL / S • Fashion Fantasies / 1986 / VC / M • Fatal Passion / 1988 / CC / M • The Final Taboo / 1988 / CA / M • A Fistful Of Bimbos / 1988 / FAZ / M • Foolish Pleasures / 1989 / ME / M • For Your Love / 1988 / IN / M • Forbidden Bodies / 1986 / HU / M • Frankenhunter, Queen Of The Porno Zombies / 1989 / GMI / M • Genital Hospital / 1987 / SE / M • Ghostly Estate / 1989 / BON / B • Girls On Fire / 1985 / VCX / M • Goin' Down Slow / 1988 / VC / M • Good Enough To Eat / 1988 / FAZ / M • A Hard Act To Swallow / 1988 / VT / M • Hawaii Vice #2 / 1989 / CDI / M • Hawaii Vice #3 / 1988 / CIN / M • Hawaii Vice #4 / 1989 / CIN / M • Hawaii Vice #5 / 1989 / CDI / M • Hot Buns / 1983 / VCX / M • Hot Cars, Nasty Women / 1985 / WV / M • I Do #1 / 1989 / VI / M • Illicit Affairs / 1989 / VD / M • Invasion Of The Samurai Sluts From Hell / 1988 / FAZ / M • Island Girls #3: Rip Tide / 1991 / CDI / C • Jane Bond Meets The Man With The Golden Rod / 1987 / VD / M • Jane Bond Meets Thunderballs / 1986 / VD / M • Jane Bond Meets Thunderthighs / 1988 / VD / M • Jean Genie / 1985 / CA / M • The Kink / 1988 / WV / M • KTSX-69 / 1988 / CA / M • The Last Condom / 1988 / PP / M • The Last Temptation Of Kristi / 1988 / ME / M • Late Night For Lovers / 1989 / ME / M • Laurel's Continuing Education / 1988 / BON / B • The Legend Of Sleepy Hollow / 1989 / LE / M • Let's Talk Dirty / 1987 / SE / M • Lilith Unleashed / 1986 / VC / M • Little Girls Lost / 1982 / VC / M • Live In, Love In / 1989 / ME / M • Love In Reverse / 1988 / FAZ / M • Lust At First Bite / 1978 / VC / M • Lust Connection / 1988 / VT / M • The Luv Game / 1988 / VCX / M • Makeout / 1988 / VT / M • Making Ends Meet / 1988 / VT / M • The Many Loves Of Jennifer / 1991 / VCO / S • The Master And Mrs. Johnson / 1980 / SAT / M • Maximum Head / 1987 / SE / M • Maxine / 1987 / EXF / M • Meat Market / 1992 / SEX / C • Melts In Your Mouth / 1984 / ROY / M • Memoirs Of A Chambermaid / 1987 / FIR / M • Miami Spice #1 / 1987 / CA / M • Miami Spice #2 / 1988 / CA / M • Motel Sweets / 1987 / VD / M • My Bare Lady / 1989 / ME / M • Nasty Lovers / 1987 / SE / C • A Natural Woman / 1989 / IN / M • Naughty Neighbors / 1989 / CA / M • Naughty Nurses / 1992 / VD / C • Nice 'n' Tight / 1985 / AIR / M • Night Of The Living Debbies / 1989 / EX / M • Nightmare On Porn Street / 1988 / ME / M • No One To Love / 1987 / PP / M • The Oddest Couple / 1986 / VC / M • Olympic Fever / 1979 / AR

/ M • Once Upon A Temptress / 1988 / CA /
M • One Page Of Love / 1980 / VCX / M •
One Wife To Give / 1989 / ZA / M • Oral
Majority #07 / 1989 / WV / C • Orgies /
1987 / WV / C • Orifice Party / 1985 / GOM
/ M • Our Dinner With Andrea / 1988 / CA /
M • Out Of Control / 1987 / SE / M • Outlaw
Ladies #2 / 1988 / VC / M • Outrageous
Foreplay / 1987 / WV / M • Partners In Sex
/ 1988 / FAN / M • Passionate Lee / 1984 /
CRE / M • Paul, Lisa And Caroline / 1976 /
SE / M • Peeping Tom / 1986 / CV / M • The
Penthouse / 1989 / PP / M • Phone Mates
/ 1988 / CA / M • Piece Of Heaven / 1988 /
CDI / M • Playpen / 1987 / VC / M • Portrait
Of An Affair / 1988 / VD / M • Portrait Of De-
sire / 1985 / IVP / M • Precious Gems /
1988 / CV / M • The Psychiatrist / 1978 /
VC / M • Pure Sex / 1988 / FAN / C • Queen
Of Hearts #1 / 1987 / PL / M • Real Men Eat
Keisha / 1986 / VC / M • The Red Head /
1989 / VWA / M • The Return Of The A
Team / 1988 / WV / M • Rites Of Passion /
1988 / FEM / M • Romeo And Juliet #1 /
1987 / WV / M • Ruthless Women / 1988 /
SE / M • Satisfaction Jackson / 1988 / CA /
M • Say Something Nasty / 1989 / CC / M
• Search For An Angel / 1988 / WV / M •
Secret Mistress / 1986 / VD / M • Sex
Crimes 2084 / 1985 / SE / M • Sex Drive /
1984 / VXP / M • Sex Lies / 1988 / FAN / M
• Sextrology / 1987 / CA / M • Sexually Al-
tered States / 1986 / VC / M • She's So
Fine #2 / 1988 / VC / M • She-Male Sani-
tarium / 1988 / VD / G • Simply Outrageous
/ 1989 / VC / C • Sleeping Beauty Aroused
/ 1989 / VI / M • Slightly Used / 1987 / VD /
M • The Slut / 1988 / FAN / M • Smoke
Screen / 1990 / CA / M • Space Virgins /
1984 / CRE / M • Strictly Business / 1987 /
VD / M • Super Sex / 1986 / MAP / M • Talk
Dirty To Me #05 / 1987 / DR / M • A Taste
Of Ariel / 1989 / PIN / C • A Taste Of Victo-
ria Paris / 1990 / PIN / C • Taylor Made /
1989 / DR / M • Temptations Of An Angel /
1989 / PEN / M • Those Lynn Girls / 1989 /
WV / C • Three Daughters / 1986 / FEM /
M • Torrid House / 1989 / VI / M • Triangle
/ 1989 / VI / M • Tropical Lust / 1987 / MET
/ M • True Confessions Of Hyapatia Lee /
1989 / VI / M • Twice As Nice / 1989 / VWA
/ M • Uncut Diamond / 1989 / IN / M • Un-
dressed Rehearsal / 1984 / VD / M • VCA
Previews #4 / 1988 / VC / C • Video Guide
To Sexual Positions / 1984 / JVV / M • The
Voyeur / 1985 / VC / M • Wet Dream On
Maple Street / 1988 / FAN / M • Wet Fin-
gers / 1990 / HIO / M • Wet Kisses / 1986 /
SE / M • What A Country / 1989 / PL / M •
Who Reamed Rosie Rabbit? #1 / 1989 /
FAN / M • Wicked Sensations #2 / 1989 /
DR / M • Wild In The Wilderness / 1988 /
SE / M • Wildheart / 1989 / IN / M • Work-
ing Girls / 1985 / CA / M • The X-Team /
1984 / CV / M • The Young And The
Wrestling #2 / 1989 / PL / M • Young
Nympho's / 1986 / VD / M • [Berlin Caper /
1989 / ... / M

ROBERT BURROWS *see* **Robert Bullock**

ROBERT BYRNE *see Star Index I*

ROBERT CARLSON *see Star Index I*

ROBERT COLE *see Star Index I*

ROBERT DANTE
Bullwhip: Art Of The Single-Tail Whip /
1996 / BN / B

ROBERT DE SIDNE *see Star Index I*

ROBERT DEE *see* **Robbie Dee**

ROBERT DENNIS *see Star Index I*

ROBERT DESIDNE *see Star Index I*

ROBERT DONAHUE *see Star Index I*

ROBERT DROTES
That Lady From Rio / 1976 / VXP / M

ROBERT DUNN
Resurrection Of Eve / 1973 / MIT / M • Wild
Hearts / 1992 / SC / M

ROBERT FRANKLIN
Bedtime Video #07 / 1984 / GO / M

ROBERT FREY
Ancient Secrets Of Sexual Ecstasy / 1996
/ HIG / M

ROBERT GIRARD *see Star Index I*

ROBERT HANNIE
Journal Of Love / 1970 / ALP / M

ROBERT HARRIS
Bi & Large / 1994 / STA / G • Close Friends
/ 1987 / CC / G • Crossing The Line / 1993
/ STA / G • Haulin' 'n' Ballin' / 1988 / MET /
G

ROBERT HILL *see Star Index I*

ROBERT IRONWOOD
Pink Champagne / 1979 / CV / M

ROBERT J. *see* **Rob Tyler**

ROBERT J. BOISVERT
Wild Goose Chase / 1990 / EA / M

ROBERT JACK
Back Down / 1996 / RB / B

ROBERT JACKSON *see* **Rob Tyler**

ROBERT JAY *see* **Scottie Schwartz**

ROBERT KERMAN *see* **Robert Bolla**

ROBERT KERNS *see* **Robert Bolla**

ROBERT KREMP
The Caning Of The Shrews / 1991 / BIZ / B

ROBERT LAKEWOOD *see Star Index I*

ROBERT LAZER *see Star Index I*

ROBERT LE RAY *see* **Jean Villroy**

ROBERT LEAR
Whatever Happened To Miss September?
/ 1973 / ALP / M

ROBERT LEE
Blacksnake! / 1973 / ST0 / S • Hot Close-
Ups / 1984 / WV / M • Oriental Sexpress /
1984 / WV / M • Playmate #01 / 1984 / VC
/ M • The Pregnant Babysitter / 1984 / WV
/ M

ROBERT LEER *see* **Rob Tyler**

ROBERT LERAY *see* **Jean Villroy**

ROBERT LERAY *see* **Jean Villroy**

ROBERT LERCY
Made In France / 1974 / VC / M • Sex
Roulette / 1979 / CA / M

ROBERT LEROY *see Star Index I*

ROBERT LONG
Bondage Memories #04 / 1994 / BON / C •
The Bondage Producer / 1991 / BON / B •
Shades Of Bondage / 1991 / BON / B

ROBERT LOURGE *see Star Index I*

ROBERT LUCAS
Sex #1 (Vca) / 1994 / VC / M

ROBERT LYON *see* **Turk Lyon**

ROBERT MAGATONEY *see* **Turk Lyon**

ROBERT MALONE
Angel Hard / 1996 / STV / M • Angel's
Vengeance / 1995 / VMX / M • Barbara
Dare's Roman Holiday / 1987 / SE / M •
Chateau Duval / 1996 / HDE / M • Clinique
/ 1989 / VC / M • The Contessa / 1989 / VC
/ M • Deep Blue / 1989 / PV / M • Dirty
Tricks #2: This Ain't Love / 1996 / EA / M •
Double Desires / 1988 / PIN / C • Eu-
roflesh: Dentro Il Vulcano / 1996 / SC / M •
Grand Prixxx / 1987 / CA / M • Hamlet: For

The Love Of Ophelia #1 / 1996 / IP / M •
Hamlet: For The Love Of Ophelia #2 / 1996
/ IP / M • Last Rumba In Paris / 1989 / VC
/ M • Licensed To Thrill / 1990 / VC / M •
Lust Italian Style / 1987 / CA / M • Paprika
/ 1995 / XC / M • Porsche / 1990 / NSV / M
• Private Film #27 / 1995 / OD / M • Private
Film #28 / 1995 / OD / M • Sex Penitentiary
/ 1996 / XC / M • St. Tropez Lust / 1990 /
VC / M • Thief Of Passion / 1996 / P69 / M
• The Thief, The Girl & The Detective /
1996 / HDE / M • Toredo / 1996 / ROX / M
• Triple X Video Magazine #02 / 1995 / OD
/ M • Triple X Video Magazine #10 / 1995 /
OD / M • Triple X Video Magazine #11 /
1995 / OD / M • World Cup / 1990 / PL / M

ROBERT MANNING *see Star Index I*

ROBERT MARKS *see Star Index I*

ROBERT MCCALLUM *(Gary Graver)*
McCallum is the name used for directing porno
movies.
Wild, Free And Hungry / 1970 / SOW / S

ROBERT MCDOWELL *see Star Index I*

ROBERT METZ *see* **Jon Martin**

ROBERT MILLS, JR
The Coming Of Joyce / 1977 / VIS / M

ROBERT MUSS
Viola Video #108: Sondra Love On Tour /
1995 / PEV / M

ROBERT NADI *see Star Index I*

ROBERT NEIL
Beaver & Buttcheeks / 1993 / DR / M

ROBERT NESKI *(Robert Ness)*
Hefty guy with long blonde hair.
Fantasy Land / 1984 / LA / M • One Last
Score / 1978 / CDI / M • Terms Of Employ-
ment / 1984 / LA / M

ROBERT NESS *see* **Robert Neski**

ROBERT NORMAN
Cry For Cindy / 1976 / AR / M

ROBERT NORTH *see Star Index I*

ROBERT PACE
A Party In My Tight Pussy / 1994 / MET / M
• Revenge Of A Motorcycle Mama / 1972 /
ALP / M

ROBERT POWERS *see Star Index I*

ROBERT RANDOM *see Star Index I*

ROBERT REDMAN *see Star Index I*

ROBERT RICHARD *see Star Index I*

ROBERT ROSE
Black Girls Do It Better / 1986 / CV / M •
Hot Chocolate #2 / 1986 / PLY / M •
Swedish Erotica #71 / 1986 / CA / M •
Swedish Erotica #72 / 1986 / CA / M • Taste
Of The Best #2 / 1988 / PIN / C

ROBERT SANFORD
Beverly She-Males / 1994 / PL / G • Red
Riding She Male / 1995 / PL / G

ROBERT SARGENT
The Love Witch / 1973 / AR / M

ROBERT SCOTT
Meet Me In St. Louis / 1996 / VAL / M

ROBERT SIMON
Sodom & Gomorrah / 1974 / MIT / M

ROBERT SPALLONE
Rollover / 1996 / NIT / M

ROBERT STEELE
Hard Feelings / 1991 / V99 / M

ROBERT STEWART *see Star Index I*

ROBERT TILL *see Star Index I*

ROBERT VAN RIGN
Bi Bi European Style / 1990 / PL / G • Get
Bi Tonight / 1991 / PL / G

ROBERT W. CRESSE *see* **Bob Cresse**

ROBERT WEST *see* **Michael Findlay**

ROBERT WILLIAMS *see Star Index I*

ROBERT WUESTERWURST *see* **Michael Findlay**

ROBERT ZELLIS
Love Theatre / cr80 / VC / M

ROBERTA
Blue Vanities #519 / 1993 / FFL / M • Blue Vanities #558 / 1994 / FFL / M • Shock-O-Rama / 1955 / SOW / S

ROBERTA DEDFORT *see Star Index I*

ROBERTA FINDLAY *(Anna Riva)*
Sixties and early seventies sexploitation film-maker along with her husband, Michael.
Bacchanale / 1972 / ALP / M • Dear Pam / 1976 / CA / M • Take Me Naked / 1966 / SOW / S • A Thousand Pleasures / 1968 / SOW / S • The Touch Of Her Flesh / 1967 / SOW / S

ROBERTA JONES *see Star Index I*

ROBERTA MARLOWE
Blue Confessions / 1983 / VCR / M

ROBERTA PEDON
Reel Classics #1 / 1996 / H&S / M

ROBERTA ROSE
Bedtime Video #07 / 1984 / GO / M

ROBERTA SHEPPS
Resurrection Of Eve / 1973 / MIT / M

ROBERTA SMALLWOOD
H&S: Roberta Smallwood / 1996 / H&S / S • Hardcore Plumpers / 1991 / BTO / M • Paradise Of Plumpers / 1996 / H&S / S • Plumpers Of Sundance Spa / 1993 / BTO / M • The Very Best Of Breasts #1 / 1996 / H&S / S

ROBERTO
Blanche / 1971 / LUM / S • Magma: Horny For Cock / 1990 / MET / M

ROBERTO (S/M) *see Star Index I*

ROBERTO ARIAS
Bi Day...Bi Night / 1988 / PV / G • Bi-Bi-Baby / 1990 / CDI / G • Blow Bi Blow / 1988 / MET / G • By Day Bi Night / 1989 / LV / G • She-Male Undercover / 1990 / STA / G • Switch Hitters #4: The Grand Slam / 1989 / IN / G • Tour De Trans / 1989 / STA / G • Transitory States / 1989 / STA / G

ROBERTO BIGO *see Star Index I*

ROBERTO FERRARA *see Star Index I*

ROBERTO RAMOS *see Star Index I*

ROBIN
Biff Malibu's Totally Nasty Home Videos #13 / 1992 / ANA / M • Biff Malibu's Totally Nasty Home Videos #35 / 1993 / ANA / M • Blue Vanities #528 / 1993 / FFL / M • Buffy Malibu's Totally Nasty All-Girl Home Videos #02 / 1992 / ANA / F • Facesitting Frenzy / 1995 / IBN / B • International Love And The Dancer / 1995 / PME / S • Limited Edition #14 / 1980 / AVC / M • Nancy Vs Robin / 1994 / VSL / B • Neighborhood Watch #40: / 1993 / LBO / M • New Faces, Hot Bodies #22 / 1996 / STP / M • Odyssey Triple Play #65: Black & White & Spread All Over / 1994 / OD / M • Over The Knee / 1996 / OUP / B • Penthouse: All-Pet Workout / 1993 / NIV / F • Penthouse: Great Pet Hunt #1 / 1992 / PET / F • Thrill Seekers / 1993 / ROB / F • Time For Action / 1993 / CS / B

ROBIN (CHES. MOORE) *see* **Chessie Moore**

ROBIN ALLISON *see Star Index I*

ROBIN BYRD
Affairs Of The Heart / 1993 / VI / M • Angie, Undercover Cop / 1980 / MSI / M • Bad Penny / 1978 / QX / M • Beyond The Blue / cr78 / SVE / M • Bon Appetit / 1980 / QX / M • Debbie Does Dallas #1 / 1978 / VC / M • Her Name Was Lisa / 1979 / VC / M • Hot Honey / 1977 / VXP / M • Kinky Pot-pourri #32 / 199? / SVE / C • Mystique / 1979 / CA / M • The Nurses Are Coming / 1985 / VCR / C • The Pink Ladies / 1980 / VC / M • Robin's Nest / 1979 / BL / M • Showgirl #10: Candida Royale's Fantasies / 1983 / VCR / M • Silky / 1980 / VXP / M • That Lucky Stiff / 1979 / QX / M • [Go On Your Own Way / 19?? / ASR / M

ROBIN BYRD (OTHER)
Bon Appetite / 1985 / TGA / C

ROBIN CANNES
Pretty, long black hair, large enhanced tits, tight body, nice smile.
All In The Family / 1985 / VCR / M • Beaverly Hills Cop / 1985 / SE / M • Bouncin' In The U.S.A. / 1986 / H&S / S • Busty Wrestling Babes / 1986 / VD / M • Dames / 1985 / SE / M • Diamond Collection #79 / 1986 / CDI / M • Dirty 30's Cinema: Heather Wayne / 1985 / PV / C • E Three / 1985 / GO / M • Erotic Zones #2 / 1985 / CA / M • The Eyes Of Eddie Mars / 1984 / CV / M • Firefoxes / 1985 / PLY / M • First Time Lesbians (Gourmet) / 1987 / GO / F • Girls Of Cell Block F / 1985 / WV / M • The Heat Is On / 1985 / WV / M • Hollywood Pink / 1985 / HO / M • Honeybuns #2: Grecian Formula / 1987 / WV / C • Hot Shorts: Robin Cannes / 1986 / VCR / C • How Do You Like It? / 1985 / CA / M • In And Out (In Beverly Hills) / 1986 / WV / M • Joy Toys / 1985 / WET / M • Jubilee Of Eroticism / 1985 / GO / M • Lady Cassanova / 1985 / AVC / M • Love Scenes For Loving Couples / 1987 / CV / C • Loving Lips / 1987 / AMB / C • Lusty / 1986 / CDI / M • Maximum #4 / 1983 / CA / M • Naked Night / 1985 / VCR / M • Naughty Nurses / 1986 / VEX / M • One Hot Night Of Passion / 1985 / COL / C • Political Party / 1985 / AVC / M • The Postman Always Comes Twice / 1986 / AMB / M • The Pussywillows / 1985 / SUV / M • Sex F/X / 1986 / VPR / M • Sex Wars / 1984 / EXF / M • Sexeo / 1985 / PV / M • Shape Up For Sensational Sex / 1985 / SE / M • Sore Throat / 1985 / GO / M • Summer Break / 1985 / VEX / M • Taboo #04 / 1985 / IN / M • Toys 4 Us #2 / 1987 / WV / C • Traci Who? / 1987 / AVC / C • The Trouble With Traci / 1984 / CHA / C • Two Timing Tracie / 1985 / V20 / M • The Ultimate Lover / 1986 / VD / M • Unnatural Act #2 / 1986 / DR / M • We Love To Tease / 1985 / VD / M • Wild Things #1 / 1985 / CV / M • [Centerfolds & Covergirls #1 / 19?? / ... / M

ROBIN CLAY
Leather Master / 1996 / STM / B

ROBIN COCK
ABA: Double Feature #5 / 1996 / ALP / M • Night Of Submission / 1976 / BIZ / M

ROBIN EVERETTE
American Pie / 1980 / SE / M • Body Girls / 1983 / SE / M • Body Magic / 1982 / SE / M • Dangerous Stuff / 1985 / COM / M • Deviations / 1983 / SE / M • Doing It / 1982 / SE / M • Good To The Last Drop / 1986 / VCS / C • Night Moves / 1983 / SUP / M • Parliament: Ass Masters #1 / 1987 / PM / M • The Pleasures Of Innocence / 1985 / VC / M • Porn Star Of The Year Contest / 1984 / VWA / M • Scenes They Wouldn't Let Me Shoot / 1984 / VC / M • Sex On The Set / 1984 / RLV / M • Wild Orgies / 1986 / SE /

C
ROBIN GOEBEL *see* **Holly White**

ROBIN HALL *see Star Index I*

ROBIN HARRIS *see* **Gail Harris**

ROBIN LANE
Mother's Wishes / 1974 / GO / M • Teenage Tramp / 1973 / SOW / S

ROBIN LEE *see* **Fallon**

ROBIN LEE FALLON *see* **Fallon**

ROBIN LUCKLEY *see Star Index I*

ROBIN MORGAN *see Star Index I*

ROBIN REDBREST
Borderline / 1996 / GOT / B • Toe Tales #31 / 1995 / GOT / B • Toe Tales #32 / 1996 / GOT / B • Toe Tales #35 / 1996 / GOT / B • Toe Tales #36 / 1996 / GOT / B • Toe Tales #37 / 1996 / GOT / B • Toe Tales #38 / 1996 / GOT / B • Toe Tales #39 / 1996 / GOT / B

ROBIN REDFORD *see Star Index I*

ROBIN RENZI
Hardcore: The Films Of Richard Kern #1 / 1991 / FTV / M

ROBIN ROUNDTREE *see Star Index I*

ROBIN SANE
Centerfold Fever / 1981 / VXP / M • Consenting Adults / 1981 / VXP / M • Dracula Exotica / 1980 / TVX / M • The Good Girls Of Godiva High / 1979 / VCX / M • Hot Dreams / 1983 / CA / M • Pandora's Mirror / 1981 / CA / M • Prisoner Of Pleasure / 1981 / ALP / B • Wicked Schoolgirls / 1981 / SVE / M • Wild Innocents / 1982 / VCX / M

ROBIN SAVAGE *see Star Index I*

ROBIN SELLERS *see Star Index I*

ROBIN STEIN *see Star Index I*

ROBIN STONE
Cheerleaders '85 / 1984 / VD / M

ROBIN STORRS *see Star Index I*

ROBIN THORN
ABA: Double Feature #4 / 1996 / ALP / M • Daughters Of Discipline #2 / 1983 / AVO / B • Painmania / 1983 / AVO / B

ROBIN TRAMP
6969 Mel'hose Place / 1995 / VG0 / M

ROBIN WILLIAMS
Can I Do It...Till I Need Glasses? / 1977 / MED / S • Softie / 19?? / AVC / M

ROBIN WINDSOR
Eat At Daves #4: Condo Cummers / 1995 / SP / M • Eat At Dave's #5 / 1996 / SP / M

ROBYN
Blue Vanities #116 / 1988 / FFL / M • The Inseminator #1 / 1994 / LBO / M • Odyssey Amateur #15: Robyn and Buddy's Backdoor Bash / 1991 / OD / M • Odyssey Amateur #17: The Full-fillment Of Robyn / 1991 / OD / M

ROBYN HARRIS *see* **Gail Harris**

ROC HARD *see Star Index I*

ROCCO
Caught From Behind #10 / 1989 / HO / M • Inspector Croissant: The Case Of The Missing Pinky / 1995 / FC / M

ROCCO CARLUCCI *see* **Rocco Siffredi**

ROCCO CARUCCI *see* **Rocco Siffredi**

ROCCO HAPER *see Star Index I*

ROCCO LORENZ *see* **Rocco Siffredi**

ROCCO MANUEL *see Star Index I*

ROCCO SAFRIDI *see* **Rocco Siffredi**

ROCCO SANDS
New Faces, Hot Bodies #01 / 1992 / STP / M • New Faces, Hot Bodies #08 / 1993 / STP / M • Take Out Torture / 1990 / PL / B

ROCCO SIFFREDI *(Rocco Tano, Rocco Safridi, Rock Sifferdy, Rocco Carlucci,*

Rocco Carucci, Rocco Lorenz, Dario, Tano Rocco)

Uncircumcized large Italian male who is very energetic (brutal?) in his sex scenes. Allegedly the women think he's handsome. Married to Rosa Caracciolo and as of mid 1996 had a boy, Lorenzo, by her.

13th Annual Adult Video News Awards / 1996 / VC / S • 30 Men For Sandy / 1995 / SC / M • Adult Affairs / 1994 / VC / M • Adult Video News 1992 Awards / 1992 / VC / M • The Adventures Of Mikki Finn / 1991 / CA / M • All Hands On Dick / 1988 / STA / G • All Inside Eva / 1991 / PL / M • American Buttman In London / 1991 / EA / M • Anal Delinquent #1 / 1993 / ROB / M • Anal Island #1 / 1996 / VC / M • Anal Island #2 / 1996 / VC / M • Anal Nation #1 / 1990 / CC / M • Anal Princess #1 / 1996 / VC / M • Anal Siege / 1993 / ROB / M • Anal Ski Vacation / 1993 / ANA / M • Anal Thunder #1 / 1993 / ROB / M • Anal With An Oriental Slant / 1993 / ROB / M • As Dirty As She Wants To Be / 1990 / ME / M • Ashlyn Rising / 1995 / VI / M • Backdoor To The City Of Sin / 1993 / ANA / M • Backstage Pass / 1994 / SC / M • Barbara Dare's Roman Holiday / 1987 / SE / M • Bed & Breakfast / 1995 / WAV / M • Bend Over Babes #2 / 1991 / EA / M • Bend Over Babes #4 / 1996 / EA / M • Bend Over Brazilian Babes #1 / 1993 / EA / M • Bend Over Brazilian Babes #2 / 1993 / EA / M • The Best Of Andrew Blake / 1993 / CA / C • The Best Of Oriental Anal #1 / 1994 / ROB / C • Biography: Rocco Siffredi / 1995 / SC / C • Bloopers & Boners / 1996 / VI / M • Blow Job Betty / 1991 / CC / M • The Bodyguard / 1995 / SC / M • Booty Ho #1 / 1993 / ROB / M • Butt Freak #1 / 1992 / EA / M • Butt Woman #5 / 1993 / FH / M • Buttman Goes To Rio #3 / 1992 / EA / M • Buttman Goes To Rio #4 / 1993 / EA / M • Buttman's Big Butt Backdoor Babes / 1995 / EA / M • Buttman's Big Tit Adventure #3 / 1995 / EA / M • Buttman's Bouncin' British Babes / 1994 / EA / M • Buttman's British Moderately Big Tit Adventure / 1994 / EA / M • Buttman's European Vacation #1 / 1991 / EA / M • Buttman's European Vacation #2 / 1992 / EA / M • Buttman's European Vacation #3 / 1995 / EA / M • Buttman's Orgies / 1996 / EA / M • Buttman's Ultimate Workout / 1990 / EA / M • Casanova #1 / 1993 / SC / M • Casanova #2 / 1993 / SC / M • Casanova #3 / 1993 / SC / M • Casanova #4 / 1993 / SC / M • Chameleons: Not The Sequel / 1991 / VC / M • Chasey Loves Rocco / 1996 / VI / M • Cheeks #5: The Ultimate Butt / 1991 / CC / M • Club DV8 #1 / 1993 / SC / M • Club DV8 #2 / 1993 / SC / M • County Line / 1993 / PEP / M • Crossing Over / 1990 / IN / M • Curse Of The Catwoman / 1990 / VC / M • Cyberanal / 1995 / VC / M • Deep Blue / 1989 / PV / M • Deep Cheeks #4 / 1993 / ROB / M • Deep Inside Brittany O'connell / 1996 / VC / C • Deep Inside Crystal Wilder / 1995 / VC / C • Deep Inside Deidre Holland / 1993 / VC / C • Deep Inside Dirty Debutantes #07 / 1993 / 4P / M • Deep Inside Juli Ashton / 1996 / VC / C • Deep Inside Racquel Darrian / 1994 / VC / C • Deep Inside Selena Steele / 1993 / VC / C • Dippy Longstocking / 1994 / GOU / M • Dirty Blue Movies #03 / 1992 / JTV / M • Double Desires /

1988 / PIN / C • Double Load #1 / 1993 / HW / M • Ejacula #1 / 1992 / VC / M • Ejacula #2 / 1992 / VC / M • Erotic Games / 1992 / PL / M • Euro Studs / 1996 / SC / C • Euroflesh: Dentro Il Vulcano / 1996 / SC / M • Exposure / 1995 / WAV / M • Face Dance #1 / 1992 / EA / M • Face Dance #2 / 1992 / EA / M • Facesitter #2 / 1993 / CC / M • A Few Good Women / 1993 / CC / M • Forget Me Not / 1994 / FH / M • Frat Girls Of Double D / 1993 / PP / M • Girl With The Million $ Legs / 1987 / PL / M • Grand Prixxx / 1987 / CA / M • Hot Shots / 1992 / VD / C • Hotel Sex / 1992 / AFV / M • House Of Dreams / 1990 / CA / M • The Housewife In Heat / 1991 / PL / M • I Do #2 / 1990 / VI / M • Impulse #09: / 1996 / MBP / M • Intercourse With The Vampyre #1 / 1994 / SC / M • Intercourse With The Vampyre #2 / 1994 / SC / M • Jenna Loves Rocco / 1996 / WAV / M • Jenteal Loves Rocco / 1996 / VI / M • Jungle Heat / 1995 / LUM / M • Karin & Barbara Superstars / 1988 / PL / M • Kink #1 / 1995 / ROB / M • Little Magicians / 1993 / ANA / M • Lust Italian Style / 1987 / CA / M • Magma: Anal Fever / 1994 / MET / M • Magma: Double Anal / 1994 / MET / M • Magma: Tits Practice / 1995 / MET / M • The Man Who Loved Women / 1993 / SC / M • Marco Polo / 1995 / SC / M • Marquis De Sade / 1995 / IP / M • Miss Liberty / 1996 / IP / M • More Dirty Debutantes #21 / 1993 / 4P / M • Nasty Nymphos #08 / 1995 / ANA / M • Never Say Never Ends To Rocco Siffredi / 1995 / EA / M • New Ends #01 / 1993 / 4P / M • New Wave Hookers #3 / 1993 / VC / M • Nikki Loves Rocco / 1996 / VI / M • Nothing Personal / 1990 / IN / M • Nylon / 1995 / VI / M • On My Lips / 1989 / PV / M • Personal Touch #4 / 1989 / AR / M • Porsche / 1990 / NSV / M • Positive Positions / 1989 / VEX / M • Prague By Night #1 / 1996 / EA / M • Prague By Night #2 / 1996 / EA / M • A Private Love Affair / 1996 / IP / M • The Pump / 1991 / CC / M • A Pussy Called Wanda #2 / 1992 / DR / M • Queen Of Hearts #3: Heartless / 1992 / PL / M • The Quest / 1994 / SC / M • Radical Affairs Video Magazine #05 / 1993 / ME / M • Rear Burner / 1990 / IN / M • Reckless Passion / 1995 / WAV / M • The Rehearsal / 1993 / VC / M • Rocco Goes To Prague / 1995 / EA / M • Rocco Unleashed / 1994 / SC / M • Rocco's Real Italian Swingers / 1996 / EA / M • Rock 'n' Roll Rocco / 1997 / EA / M • Roman Orgy / 1991 / PL / M • Sandy Insatiable / 1995 / EA / M • Secrets / 1990 / CA / M • The Serpent's Dream / 1993 / VC / M • Sex #1 (Vivid) / 1993 / VI / M • Sex #2 (Vivid) / 1993 / VI / M • Sex Alert / 1995 / PV / M • Sexophrenia / 1993 / VC / M • Sexy Country Girl / 1991 / PL / M • Seymore Butts & His Mystery Girl / 1993 / FH / M • Seymore Butts Is Blown Away / 1993 / FH / M • Seymore Butts Meets The Cumback Brat / 1993 / FH / M • Seymore Butts Swings / 1992 / FH / M • Seymore Butts: Bustin' Out My Best Anal / 1995 / FH / C • A Shot In The Mouth #2 / 1991 / ME / M • Snatch Shots / 1991 / AFV / M • Sodomania #02: More Tails / 1992 / EL / M • Sodomania: The Baddest Of The Best...And Then Some / 1994 / EL / C • Spread Sheets / 1991 / DR / M • The Starlet / 1991 / PP / M • Steamy Windows / 1990 / VC / M

• Steele Butt / 1993 / AFV / M • Taste Of The Best #1 / 1988 / PIN / C • Tenth Annual Adult Video News Awards / 1993 / VC / M • This One's For You / 1989 / AR / M • Top Model / 1995 / SC / M • Topless Stewardesses / 1995 / PV / M • Toredo / 1996 / ROX / M • Total Reball / 1990 / CC / M • Trouble Maker / 1995 / VI / M • True Legends Of Adult Cinema: The Modern Era / 1992 / VC / C • True Stories #1 / 1993 / SC / M • True Stories #2 / 1993 / SC / M • Uninhibited / 1993 / ANT / S • A Very Debauched Girl / 1988 / PL / M • The Voyeur #3 / 1995 / EA / M • Wet Faces #1 / 1997 / SC / C • Whipped Cream / 1996 / EA / M • Wild Attraction / 1992 / ... / S • WPINK-TV #4 / 1993 / PV / M • WPINK-TV #5 / 1993 / PV / M • Wrapped Up / 1992 / VD / C • X-TV / 1992 / CA / C • [Bizarr Interview / 1989 / ... / M • [In Due Di Dietro / 19?? / ... / M • [La Camionista / 19?? / ... / M • [Masquerade (1992-Italy) / 1992 / ... / S • [Porno Provini Bagnati Per Milli / 19?? / ... / M • [Scatenta P.R. / 19?? / ... / M

ROCCO TANO *see* **Rocco Siffredi**

ROCHELLE

East Coast Sluts #08: Atlantic City / 1995 / PL / M • Strap-On Sally #07: Face Dildo Frenzy / 1995 / PL / F • Strap-On Sally #08: Strap-On Cock Fight / 1995 / PL / F

ROCK ALLEN

East Coast Sluts #09: / 1995 / PL / M • Summer Vacation #1 / 1996 / RAS / M

ROCK HARD

Itsy Bitsy Gang Bang / 1996 / HW / M • Somewhere Under The Rainbow #1 / 1995 / HW / M • Somewhere Under The Rainbow #2 / 1995 / HW / M

ROCK HEINRICH

Frank Henenlotter's XXX Hardcore Horrors: Mad Love... / 1996 / SOW / M • The Mad Love Of The Red Hot Vampire / 1971 / SOW / M

ROCK LOVE *see* **Star Index I**

ROCK PETER

Bang City #6: Bugger's Banquet / 1995 / SC / M

ROCK ROMAN

Cheri's On Fire / 1986 / V99 / M • Glamour Girls / 1987 / SE / M • Love At First Sight / 1987 / SE / C

ROCK ROME *see* **Greg Rome**

ROCK ROSE

Busty Babes In Heat #5 / 1995 / BTO / M • Deep Throat #2 / 1986 / AR / M • N.Y. Video Magazine #02 / 1995 / OUP / M • N.Y. Video Magazine #03 / 1995 / OUP / M

ROCK SIFFERDY *see* **Rocco Siffredi**

ROCK STEADIE *(Rick Stearns)*

All American Girls #1 / 1982 / CA / M • Candy Stripers #1 / 1978 / ALP / M • Nurses Of The 407th / 1982 / CA / M

ROCK TAYLOR *see* **Jon Dough**

ROCKETMAN

Made In The Hood / 1995 / HBE / M

ROCKI DILORENZO *see* **Rocky DiLorenzo**

ROCKI ROADS

Boobwatch #1 / 1996 / SC / M • Boobwatch #2 / 1997 / SC / M • Cock Busters #1 / 1996 / GWV / C • Connections / 1996 / LEI / C • Miss Nude World International Pageant / 1996 / WAT / F • New Pussy Hunt #21 / 1996 / LEI / C • Philmore Butts Travels The Rocki Roads Of South Florida / 1996 / SUF / M • Rockhard (Sin City) / 1996 / SC / M

ROCKIN' ROBIN
When The Fat Lady Sings / 1996 / EX / M
ROCKO
Bang City #4: Gina's Anal Gang Bang / 1995 / SC / M • Bi-Bi Love Amateurs #1 / 1993 / SFP / G • Deep Inside Samantha Strong / 1992 / CDI / C • Reel Life Video #52: Crystal Fox & The Plumber / Barbarito / 1996 / RLF / M
ROCKY
All For One / 1988 / CIN / M • Hard Times / 1985 / WV / M • Hot On Her Tail / 1990 / CA / M • Las Vegas She-Males / 1995 / BCP / G • Midnight Dancers / 1993 / MID / S
ROCKY BALBOA
Backing In #1 / 1990 / WV / C • The Big Bang / 1988 / WET / M • The Erotic World Of Linda Wong / 1985 / VIV / M • Sleepless Nights / 1984 / VIV / M • Tuff Stuff / 1987 / WET / M
ROCKY COMPANO *see* **Rocky DiLorenzo**
ROCKY DILORENZO *(Rocki DiLorenzo, Rocky Compano)*
Rocky Compano is from **Nasty Dancing**.
21 Hump Street / 1988 / VWA / M • Big Tit Hookers / 1989 / BTO / M • Easy Access / 1988 / ZA / M • Family Thighs / 1989 / AR / M • The First of April / 1988 / VI / M • The Flirt / 1987 / VWA / M • The Great Sex Contest #2 / 1989 / LV / M • Hawaii Vice #2 / 1989 / CDI / M • Heather / 1989 / VWA / M • A Live Nude Girl / 1989 / VWA / M • Missy Impossible / 1989 / CAR / M • The Naked Stranger / 1988 / VI / M • Nasty Dancing / 1989 / VEX / M • The Pleasure Chest / 1988 / VWA / M • Primary Pleasure / 1987 / VXP / M • Raw Talent #3 / 1988 / VC / M • Sex Crimes 2084 / 1985 / SE / M • Sex Starved / 1986 / VWA / M • Sweat #2 / 1988 / PP / M • Virgins / 1989 / CAR / M • Wrong Arm Of The Law / 1987 / ZA / M
ROCKY FERRARI see Star Index I
ROCKY GRANT
Date Night / 1992 / V99 / M • Rear Entry / 1995 / LEI / M
ROCKY HAYNE
69 Park Avenue / 1985 / ELH / M • Beyond Desire / 1986 / VC / M • Reel People #02 / 1984 / AR / M • Spectators / 1984 / AVC / M
ROCKY JOHNSON see Star Index I
ROCKY MILLHOUSE *(Erik Von Serokhardt)*
Blonde nasty looking male.
Breaker Beauties / 1977 / VHL / M • Doctor Yes / 1978 / VIS / M • Honeypie / 1975 / VC / M • Only The Very Best On Film / 1992 / VC / C • Sugar Britches / 1980 / VCX / C
ROCKY MILLSTONE
Little Orphan Sammy / 1976 / VC / M • Temptations / 1976 / VXP / M
ROCKY RACOON
One Way At A Time / 1979 / CA / M
ROCKY REEME
Kitty Foxx's Kinky Kapers #02 / 1995 / TTV / M
ROCKY RHODES
A Formal Faucett / 1978 / VC / M • Saturday Matinee Series #1 / 1996 / VCX / C
ROCKY RIO see Star Index I
ROCKY ROCKHARD see Star Index I
ROCKY ROME see Greg Rome
ROCKY TORO
Bad She-Males / 1994 / HSV / G • Bi 'n'

Large / 1994 / PL / G • Bi Dream Of Genie / 1994 / BIL / G • Bi George / 1994 / BIL / G • Bi On The Fourth Of July / 1994 / BIL / G • Bi-Nanza / 1994 / BIL / G • Come Back Little She-Male / 1994 / HSV / G • Dragula: Queen Of Darkness / 1996 / HSV / G • Drive Bi / 1994 / BIL / G • Dungeons & Drag Queens / 1994 / HSV / G • Gentlemen Prefer She-Males / 1995 / CDI / G • Good Bi Girl / 1994 / BIL / G • Hot Bi Summer / 1994 / BIL / G • Little Shop Of She-Males / 1994 / HSV / G • The Princess With A Penis / 1994 / HSV / G • She Male Fuckathon #04 / 1995 / HSV / G • She-Male Loves Me / 1995 / VC / G • She-Male Sex Stories / 1996 / STA / G • She-Male Swish Bucklers / 1994 / HSV / G • Spring Trannie / 1995 / VC / G • Super Bi Bowl / 1995 / BIL / G
ROCKY VENTURA see Star Index I
ROD
AVP #7022: 1 + 2 = 3 Times The Fun / 1991 / AVP / M • Breast Worx #18 / 1992 / LBO / M • New Faces, Hot Bodies #14 / 1994 / STP / M • Ron Hightower's White Chicks #01 / 1993 / LBO / M • Ron Hightower's White Chicks #02 / 1993 / LBO / M • Uncle Roy's Amateur Home Video #09 / 1992 / VIM / M
ROD CHENKO
Full Throttle Girls: Boredom Pulled The Trigger / 1993 / VIM / M
ROD DUMONT
The Devil Inside Her / 1977 / ALP / M • Frank Henenlotter's XXX Hardcore Horrors #05 / 1996 / SOW / M
ROD DURELL
Ron Hightower's White Chicks #03 / 1993 / LBO / M • Ron Hightower's White Chicks #04 / 1993 / LBO / M
ROD FONTANA
2 Wongs Make A White / 1996 / FC / M • Anal Fantasy / 1996 / SUF / M • Anal Virgins #03 / 1996 / NS / M • Anal Witness #1 / 1996 / LBO / M • Anal Witness #2: No Prisoners / 1996 / LBO / M • Bang City #6: Bugger's Banquet / 1995 / SC / M • Bang City #7: Carolina's Anal Gang Bang / 1995 / SC / M • Bangkok Dreams / 1996 / SUF / M • Beyond Reality #3: Stage Erect! / 1996 / EXQ / M • Big Bust Babes #38 / 1996 / AFI / M • Big Bust Babes #39 / 1996 / AFI / M • Brian Sparks: Virtually Unreal #1 / 1996 / ALD / M • Bushwoman: She Takes Two / 1996 / RAS / M • Butt Busting / 1996 / RB / B • Career Girls / 1996 / OUP / M • Carnal Interludes / 1995 / NOT / M • Carolina's D.P. Anal Gangbang / 1996 / FC / M • Contrast / 1995 / CA / M • Delaid Delivery / 1995 / EX / M • Dirty & Kinky Mature Women #08 / 1996 / C69 / M • Dirty Dave's #1 / 1996 / VG0 / M • Dirty Dave's #2 / 1996 / XPR / M • Dirty Dave's #3 / 1996 / XPR / M • Dirty Old Men #1 / 1995 / FPI / M • Double Dicked #2 / 1996 / RAS / M • Eighteen #1 / 1996 / SC / M • Every Granny Has A Fantasy / 1996 / GLI / M • Fashion Passion / 1997 / TEP / M • Father Of The Babe / 1993 / ZA / M • Fellatio Fanatics / 1996 / NIT / M • Fresh Faces #12 / 1996 / EVN / M • Hardcore Confidential #1 / 1996 / TEP / M • Hardcore Debutantes #01 / 1996 / TEP / M • Hardcore Debutantes #02 / 1996 / TEP / M • Hardcore Debutantes #03 / 1997 / TEP / M • Her Name Is Asia / 1996 / SUF / M • Hidden Camera #19 / 1994 / JMP / M • Hollywood Amateurs #31

/ 1996 / MID / M • Hollywood Confidential / 1996 / SC / M • Hot Tight Asses #18 / 1996 / TCK / M • If These Walls Could Talk (Director's Cut) / 1993 / MET / M • If These Walls Could Talk #1: Wicked Whispers / 1993 / MET / M • If These Walls Could Talk #2: Burning Secrets / 1993 / CV / M • Jizz Glazed Goo Guzzlers #2 / 1996 / NIT / C • Juliette's Desires / 1996 / LE / M • Mike Hott: #392 / 1996 / MHV / M • Mutiny On The Booty / 1996 / FC / M • Mystique / 1996 / SC / M • Naked Mockey-Rayna / 1996 / EVN / M • Nineteen #3 / 1996 / FOR / M • Nineteen #4 / 1996 / FOR / M • Old Bitches / 1996 / GLI / M • Old Guys & Dolls #1 / 1995 / PL / M • Old Guys & Dolls #2 / 1995 / PL / M • Old Wave Hookers #2 / 1995 / PL / M • Older & Bolder In San Francisco / 1996 / TEP / M • The Older Women's Sperm Bank #3: Red Hot Grandmas / 1996 / SUF / M • The Older Women's Sperm Bank #5 / 1996 / SUF / M • Outlaw Sluts / 1996 / RAS / M • Passion / 1996 / SC / M • Perverted Stories #05 / 1995 / JMP / M • Piglitz: Pudgy Porkers / 1996 / GLI / M • Planet X #1 / 1996 / HW / M • Playtex / 1996 / GLI / M • Pro-Am Jam / 1996 / GLI / M • Santa Is Coming All Over Town / 1996 / EVN / M • Senior Sexcapades #1 / 1995 / PL / M • Senior Stimulation / 1996 / CC / M • Sex Over 40 #2 / 1994 / PL / M • Sex, Truth & Videotape #2 / 1996 / DOC / M • The Sodomizer #3 / 1996 / SC / M • Sugar Daddies / 1995 / FPI / M • Summer Dreams / 1996 / TEP / M • Triple Penetration Debutante Sluts #2 / 1996 / BAC / M • Under The Covers / 1996 / GO / M • Underground #1 / 1996 / SC / M • Venom #7 / 1996 / VD / M • Video Virgins #32 / 1996 / NS / M • The Voyeur #1 / 1994 / EA / M • White Boys & Black Bitches / 1995 / ROB / M • Witches Are Bitches / 1996 / NIT / M • Working Girl Gang-Bang / 1995 / GLI / M • Yin Yang Oriental Love Bang #3: Bangkok Dreams / 1996 / SUF / M • Yin Yang Oriental Love Bang #4: Yellow Orchid / 1996 / SUF / M • Young And Anal #4 / 1996 / JMP / M • Young And Anal #5 / 1996 / JMP / M • Young Sluts In Heat #1 / 1996 / PL / M
ROD GARETTO
All About Teri Weigel / 1996 / XCI / M • Angels Bi Day, Devils Bi Night / 1990 / FC / G • Bad Mama Jama Busts Out / 1989 / VT / M • Bi & Large / 1994 / STA / G • Bi Intruder / 1991 / STA / G • Bi Madness / 1991 / STA / G • Bi Mistake / 1989 / VI / G • The Bi Spy / 1991 / STA / G • Bi This! / 1995 / BIL / G • Bi-Inferno / 1992 / VEX / G • Bright Lights, Big Titties / 1993 / CA / M • The Clock Strikes Bizarre On Butt Row / 1996 / ABS / M • Crossing The Line / 1993 / STA / G • Dance Fire / 1989 / EA / M • Dirty Diane / 1989 / V99 / M • Dominique Goes Bi / 1994 / STA / G • Dominique's Bi Adventure / 1995 / STA / G • Fag Hags / 1991 / FC / G • Grandma Does Dallas / 1990 / FC / M • The Last Good-Bi / 1990 / CDI / G • Life In The Fat Lane #1 / 1990 / FC / M • Life In The Fat Lane #2 / 1990 / FC / M • Life In The Fat Lane #3 / 1990 / FC / M • More To Love #1 / 1994 / TTV / M • The Perfect Girl / 1992 / CDI / G • Promises In The Dark / 1991 / CIN / G • Queens Behind Bars / 1990 / STA / G • Queens In Danger / 1990 / STA / G • The Rod Garetto Story / 1995 /

FC / C • Shaved She-Males / 1992 / STA / G • She-Male Showgirls / 1992 / STA / G • Stasha: Portrait Of A Swinger / 1992 / CDI / G • Switch Hitters #6: Back In The Bull Pen / 1991 / IN / G • Switch Hitters #8 / 1995 / IN / G • Tit Tales #2 / 1990 / FC / M • Tit Tales #3 / 1991 / FC / M • Titty-Titty Bang-Bang / 1992 / FC / C • Totally Tasteless Video #01 / 1994 / TTV / M • Viet Tran / 1996 / LBO / G

ROD GRANT
Debbie Does 'em All #1 / 1985 / CV / M • Liquid A$$ets / 1982 / CA / M • Three Faces Of Angel / 1987 / CV / M • Too Hot To Touch #1 / 1985 / CV / M

ROD HARD
Mechanics Bi Day, Lube Job Bi Night / 1995 / SP0 / G

ROD HARDER
Here Comes Elska / 1997 / XPR / M

ROD HARRIS see Star Index I

ROD HUNT
Weekend Roulette / 1975 / VCX / M

ROD HUNTER
Triple Play / 1983 / HO / M

ROD JACOBI see Star Index I

ROD LONGER
Working Girls / 1995 / FH / M

ROD LOOMIS see Star Index I

ROD MAJORS
Bi-Conflict / 1994 / FST / G • Conflict Of Interest / 1994 / FST / G • Secret Sex #2: The Sex Radicals / 1994 / CAT / G

ROD NEWKIRK see Star Index I

ROD RAMMER
Canadian Beaver Hunt #2 / 1996 / PL / M

ROD RETTA
Extremly handsome dark haired male current around the mid eighties.
Bedroom Thighs / 1986 / VXP / M • The Bimbo #1 / 1985 / VXP / M • The Bimbo #2: The Homecoming / 1986 / RLV / M • Deep & Wet / 1986 / VD / M • Fannie's Fantail / 1985 / VC / M • Flasher / 1986 / VD / M • The Honeydrippers / 1987 / VXP / M • Lady Madonna / 1985 / RLV / M • Poltergash / 1987 / AVC / M • Secret Mistress / 1986 / VD / M • Sex Crimes 2084 / 1985 / SE / M • Sex Styles Of The Rich & Famous / 1986 / VXP / M • Sleazy Susan / 1986 / VXP / M • Tongue 'n Cheek (Red Light) / 1984 / RLV / M • The Vamp / 1986 / AVC / M • Young Nympho's / 1986 / VD / M

ROD RYKER see Buster Cheri

ROD SHORTENER
Diary Of A Bed / 1979 / HOE / M

ROD STERLING see Star Index I

ROD STROKER
N.Y. Video Magazine #05 / 1995 / OUP / M • N.Y. Video Magazine #06 / 1995 / OUP / M

ROD STRONG
Black Knockers #02 / 1995 / TV / M

ROD TOWERS
50 And Still Gangbangin'! / 1995 / EMC / M • Black Cheerleader Search #08 / 1996 / IVC / M • Black Women, White Men #7 / 1995 / FC / M • The Crackster / 1996 / OUP / M • D.P. Grannies / 1995 / JMP / M • The Desert Cafe / 1996 / NIT / M • Dirty Laundry / 1994 / HOH / M • Done In The Desert Sun / 1995 / OUP / M • Flappers / 1995 / EMC / M • Generation Sex #1 / 1996 / VT / M • My First Time #1 / 1995 / NS / M • My First Time #4 / 1996 / NS / M • My First Time #6 / 1996 / NS / M • Nurses Do It With

Care / 1995 / EVN / M • Old Wives' Tails / 1995 / EMC / M • Trading Partners / 1995 / GO / M

ROD TUIET
Girl Service / 1972 / CV / M • Strange Experiences Cockfucking / 1994 / MET / M

ROD TURNER see Star Index I

ROD TYLER see Rob Tyler

RODD
Filthy First Timers #3: Tearing Down The Walls Of Shame / 1996 / EL / M

RODERIC PIERCE
Babe / 1982 / AR / M

RODERICK USHER
Defiance / 1974 / ALP / B

RODGER
Ultimate Fantasy / 1993 / BON / B

RODNEY
GVC: Reincarnation Of Serena #121 / 1983 / GO / M • Homegrown Video #403 / 1993 / HOV / M • Pearl Necklace: Thee Bush League #02 / 1992 / SEE / M • Pearl Necklace: Thee Bush League #12 / 1993 / SEE / M

RODNEY FARRELL see Star Index I

RODNEY FUDDPUCKER
While The Cat's Away / 1996 / NIT / M

RODNEY LUCKY
Invasion Of The Lust Snatchers / 1988 / 4P / M

RODNEY MALTRAVERS
Spanked Young Tails / 1996 / BIZ / B

RODNEY MOORE *(Dr. Deacon, Dr. Dick)*
A&B AB#458: Dr. Dick From Man To Woman #1 / 1994 / A&B / M • A&B AB#459: Dr. Dick From Man To Woman #2 / 1994 / A&B / M • A&B AB#460: Dr. Dick's Black Fantasy / 1994 / A&B / M • A&B AB#461: Innocent Blonde #1 / 1994 / A&B / M • A&B AB#467: Dr. Dick's Skin Treatment #2 / 1994 / A&B / M • African Angels #1 / 1996 / NIT / M • African Angels #2 / 1996 / NIT / M • African Angels #3 / 1996 / NIT / M • America's Raunchiest Home Videos #65: / 1993 / ZA / M • Analtown USA #11 / 1996 / NIT / M • Black Casting Couch #1 / 1993 / WP / M • Black Casting Couch #2 / 1994 / WP / M • Black Juice Bombs / 1996 / NIT / C • Bobby Hollander's Maneaters #07 / 1993 / SFP / M • Breast Wishes #10 / 1992 / LBO / M • Breast Wishes #14 / 1993 / LBO / M • Breast Worx #31 / 1992 / LBO / M • Breast Worx #36 / 1992 / LBO / M • Breast Worx #38 / 1992 / LBO / M • Breast Worx #39 / 1992 / LBO / M • Breast Worx #41 / 1993 / LBO / M • Bubble Butts Gold #1 / 1994 / LBO / M • Bun Busters #03 / 1993 / LBO / M • Bun Busters #04 / 1993 / LBO / M • Bun Busters #07 / 1993 / LBO / M • Bun Busters #10 / 1993 / LBO / M • Bun Busters #18 / 1994 / LBO / M • Bun Busters #19 / 1994 / LBO / M • Bun Busters #21 / 1994 / LBO / M • Bun Busters #22 / 1994 / LBO / M • The Burma Road #1 / 1994 / LBO / C • The Burma Road #2 / 1994 / LBO / C • Casting Couch Cuties #1 / 1994 / WP / M • Chocolate Bunnies #02 / 1995 / LBO / C • Creme De La Face #01 / 1994 / OD / M • Creme De La Face #02 / 1994 / OD / M • Creme De La Face #03 / 1994 / OD / M • Creme De La Face #04 / 1994 / OD / M • Creme De La Face #05 / 1994 / OD / M • Creme De La Face #06 / 1995 / OD / M • Creme De La Face #07 / 1995 / OD / M • Creme De La Face #08: Wanna Blow Job / 1995 / OD / M • Creme De La Face

#09: Princess Of Cream / 1995 / OD / M • Creme De La Face #10: Cum Dome / 1995 / OD / M • Creme De La Face #11: Cum Plasterers / 1995 / OD / M • Creme De La Face #12: Pretty Faces To Cum On / 1995 / OD / M • Creme De La Face #13: Nine Nasty Nymphs / 1995 / OD / M • Creme De La Face #14: Kiss My Cum / 1996 / OD / M • Creme De La Face #15: Showroom Sex / 1996 / OD / M • Creme De La Face #16: Ladies Licking / 1996 / OD / M • Creme De La Face #17: Semen For Seven / 1996 / OD / M • Creme De La Face #18: Cum Mops / 1997 / OD / M • Cum To Drink Of It / 1996 / BCP / M • Cum Tv / 1996 / NIT / M • The Cumm Brothers #01 / 1993 / OD / M • The Cumm Brothers #02: Goin' To A Ho' Down / 1994 / OD / M • The Cumm Brothers #03: Go To Traffic School / 1994 / OD / M • The Cumm Brothers #04: Laid Off & Laid / 1994 / OD / M • The Cumm Brothers #05: These Nuts For Hire / 1994 / OD / M • The Cumm Brothers #06: Hook, Line And Sphincter / 1994 / OD / M • The Cumm Brothers #07: Honeymoon On Uranus / 1995 / OD / M • The Cumm Brothers #08: Escape From Uranus / 1995 / OD / M • The Cumm Brothers #09: Chewin' The Bush / 1995 / OD / M • The Cumm Brothers #10: Night Of The Giving Head / 1995 / OD / M • The Cumm Brothers #11: Oh Cum On Ye Faces / 1995 / OD / M • The Cumm Brothers #12: Two GOOS For Every Girl / 1995 / OD / M • The Cumm Brothers #13: Rump Rangers / 1996 / OD / M • The Cumm Brothers #14: Buttdraft / 1995 / OD / M • The Cumm Brothers #15: Hot Primal Sex / 1996 / OD / M • The Cumm Brothers #16: Deja Goo / 1996 / OD / M • The Cumm Brothers #17: Goo Guy Gone Bad / 1996 / OD / M • Cumm For Dinner / 1995 / BCP / M • Cummin' 'round The Mountain / 1996 / BCP / M • Dirty Dating Service #01 / 1993 / WP / M • Dirty Dating Service #02 / 1993 / WP / M • Dirty Dating Service #03 / 1994 / WP / M • Dirty Dating Service #04 / 1994 / WP / M • Dirty Dating Service #05 / 1994 / WP / M • Dirty Dating Service #06 / 1994 / WP / M • The Doctor Is In #1 / 1995 / NIT / M • The Doctor Is In #2: Pussy Pox / 1995 / NIT / M • The Doctor Is In #3: Achy Breaky Tarts / 1995 / NIT / M • Fantasy Flings #01 / 1993 / WP / M • Fantasy Flings #02 / 1994 / WP / M • Fantasy Flings #03 / 1995 / WP / M • Girls Just Wanna Have Cum / 1995 / HO / M • Hard Cum Cafe / 1996 / BCP / M • High Heeled & Horny #1 / 1994 / LBO / M • High Heeled & Horny #2 / 1995 / LBO / M • High Heeled & Horny #3 / 1995 / LBO / M • High Heeled & Horny #4 / 1995 / LBO / M • How To Make A Model #01 / 1992 / MET / M • How To Make A Model #02: Got Her In Bed / 1993 / QUA / M • How To Make A Model #03: Sunshine & Melons / 1994 / QUA / M • How To Make A Model #04: Facial Cream Girls / 1994 / LBO / M • How To Make A Model #05: Back To Innocence / 1994 / LBO / M • How To Make A Model #06: Many Happy Returns / 1995 / LBO / M • Jizz Glazed Goo Guzzlers #1 / 1996 / NIT / C • Jizz Glazed Goo Guzzlers #2 / 1996 / NIT / C • Kinky Cameraman #1 / 1996 / LEI / C • Kinky Potpourri #23 / 199? / SVE / C • Lusty Lap Dancers #1 / 1994 / HO / M • Lusty Lap Dancers #2 / 1994 / HO / M • M Series #18 / 1994 / LBO / M • M Series #20

/ 1994 / LBO / M • M Series #21 / 1994 / LBO / M • M Series #26 / 1994 / LBO / M • Mr. Peepers Amateur Home Videos #55: Anal Antics / 1992 / LBO / M • Mr. Peepers Amateur Home Videos #64: Proposition 69 / 1992 / LBO / M • Mr. Peepers Amateur Home Videos #74: C Foam Surfer / 1993 / LBO / M • Mr. Peepers Amateur Home Videos #85: Hand Puppet Job / 1994 / LBO / M • Mr. Peepers Amateur Home Videos #86: Tit A Ton / 1994 / LBO / M • Mr. Peepers Amateur Home Videos #88: A For Effort / 1994 / LBO / M • Mr. Peepers Amateur Home Videos #92: M-Ass-terpieces / 1994 / LBO / M • Mr. Peepers Amateur Home Videos #93: Creative Fornication / 1994 / LBO / M • Mr. Peepers Amateur Home Videos #94: Calendar Cleavage / 1994 / LBO / M • New Pussy Hunt #21 / 1996 / LEI / C • The New Snatch Masters #18 / 1996 / LEI / C • The New Snatch Masters #22 / 1996 / LEI / C • Northwest Pecker Trek #1 / 1994 / LBO / M • Northwest Pecker Trek #2: Evergreen, Ever Horny / 1994 / LBO / M • Northwest Pecker Trek #3: Ducks & Dicks / 1994 / LBO / M • Northwest Pecker Trek #4: Laid In Latte Land / 1994 / LBO / M • Northwest Pecker Trek #5: Cumming In King County / 1995 / LBO / M • Northwest Pecker Trek #6: Two Girls For Every Boy / 1995 / LBO / M • Nothing Like Nurse Nookie #1 / 1995 / NIT / M • Nothing Like Nurse Nookie #2 / 1996 / NIT / M • Nothing Like Nurse Nookie #3 / 1996 / NIT / M • Nothing Like Nurse Nookie #4 / 1996 / NIT / M • Nothing Like Nurse Nookie #5 / 1996 / NIT / M • Odyssey Triple Play #72: Backdoor Score / 1994 / OD / M • Odyssey Triple Play #79: Dildos Dykes & Dicks / 1994 / OD / M • Odyssey Triple Play #89: Group Sex Grab Bag / 1995 / OD / M • Odyssey Triple Play #96: Anal Option #2 / 1995 / OD / M • Pearl Necklace: Thee Bush League #03 / 1992 / SEE / M • Pearl Necklace: Thee Bush League #11 / 1993 / SEE / M • Pearl Necklace: Thee Bush League #14 / 1993 / SEE / M • Pearl Necklace: Thee Bush League #17 / 1993 / SEE / M • The Princess Of Cream / 1995 / OD / M • Puritan Video Magazine #07 / 1996 / LE / M • Puritan Video Magazine #10 / 1997 / LE / M • Pussy Fest Of The Northwest #1 / 1995 / NIT / M • Pussy Fest Of The Northwest #2 / 1995 / NIT / M • Pussy Fest Of The Northwest #3 / 1995 / NIT / M • Pussy Fest Of The Northwest #4 / 1995 / NIT / M • Pussy Fest Of The Northwest #5 / 1995 / NIT / M • Red Rumpers #01 / 1996 / LBO / B • Rodney's Rookies #1 / 1996 / NIT / M • Rump Humpers #06 / 1992 / GLI / M • Sex Lessons / 1996 / NIT / M • Sexual Trilogy #02 / 1993 / SFP / M • Six Stud Swingathon #01 / 1992 / VAL / M • The Sodomizer #1 / 1995 / SC / M • The Sodomizer #2 / 1995 / SC / M • The Sodomizer #3 / 1996 / SC / M • The Sodomizer #4 / 1996 / SC / M • The Sodomizer #5: Destination Moon / 1996 / SC / M • The Sodomizer #6 / 1996 / SC / M • The Spank Master / 1996 / PRE / B • SVE: Anally Made Jade / 1993 / SVE / M • SVE: Ho-Nuff / 1994 / SVE / M • SVE: Raunchy Rustie & Ready Roxanne / 1992 / SVE / M • SVE: Screentest Sex #2 / 1992 / SVE / M • SVE: Screentest Sex #3 / 1993 / SVE / M • SVE: Screentest Sex #4 / 1993 / SVE / M • SVE: Screentest Sex #5 / 1994

/ SVE / M • SVE: Spank'er Butt #2 / 1994 / SVE / B • SVE: Spanks For The Memories / 1994 / SVE / B • Tail Taggers #122: Anal Delight / 1994 / WV / M • Teacher's Pet #1 / 1994 / WMG / M • Teacher's Pet #2 / 1994 / WMG / M • Teacher's Pet #3 / 1995 / APP / M • Teacher's Pet #4 / 1995 / APP / M • Throbbing Threesomes / 1996 / NIT / M • Tootsies & Footsies / 1994 / LBO / M • Uncle Roy's Amateur Home Video #19 / 1993 / VIM / M • Uncle Roy's Amateur Home Video #22 / 1993 / VIM / M • Under The Cum Cum Tree / 1996 / BCP / M • Witches Are Bitches / 1996 / NIT / M

RODOLFO AGUILAR
Borderline (Vivid) / 1995 / VI / M

ROGER
Alex Jordan's First Timers #06 / 1994 / OD / M • Magma: Old And Young / 1995 / MET / M

ROGER ALLEN
The Starmaker / 1982 / VC / M

ROGER BLADE
Love Bites / 1985 / CA / M • Princess Charming / 1987 / AVC / C

ROGER BURNSIDE
Matinee Idol / 1984 / VC / M

ROGER CAINE *(Mike Jefferson, Mike Jeffries, Al Levinsky, Al Levitsky, Al Lavinsky, Alan Levitt)*
Alan Levitt is from **Sweet Surrender**.
ABA: Double Feature #2 / 1996 / ALP / M • Angie, Undercover Cop / 1980 / MSI / M • Bad Penny / 1978 / QX / M • Blonde Velvet / 1976 / COL / M • Bon Appetit / 1980 / QX / M • Cherry Hustlers / 1977 / VEN / M • Come With Me, My Love / 1976 / PVX / M • Dirty Lilly / 1975 / VXP / M • Dirty Looks / 1982 / VC / C • Dirty Susan / 1979 / CPL / M • Dominatrix Without Mercy / 1976 / ALP / B • Double Your Pleasure / 1978 / CV / M • Dracula Exotica / 1980 / TVX / M • Dutch Treat / 1977 / VHL / M • Erotic Fantasies #3 / 1983 / CV / C • Erotic Fantasies #6 / 1984 / CV / C • Fantasex / 1976 / COM / M • Farewell Scarlett / 1976 / COM / M • French Kittens / 1985 / VC / C • Funk / 1977 / … / M • Games Women Play #1 / 1980 / CA / M • Girls U.S.A. / 1980 / AIR / M • Here Comes The Bride / 1977 / CV / M • High School Bunnies / 1978 / VC / M • Highway Hookers / 1976 / SVE / M • Honeymoon Haven / 1977 / QX / M • The Immoral Three / 1973 / SOW / S • It Happened In Hollywood / 1973 / WWV / M • Jack 'n' Jill #1 / 1979 / VXP / M • Little Orphan Sammy / 1976 / VC / M • Martin / 1976 / THO / S • MASH'ed / cr75 / ALP / M • More Than Sisters / 1978 / VC / M • Naughty Nurses / 1982 / VCR / M • Nighthawks / 1981 / MCA / S • The Nite Bird / 1978 / BL / M • Playgirls Of Munich / 1977 / VC / M • The Pleasure Palace / 1978 / CV / M • Powerbone / 1976 / VC / M • Pussycat Ranch / 1978 / CV / M • Revenge & Punishment / 1996 / ALP / M • Rip-Off Of Millie / cr78 / VHL / M • Sexteen / 1975 / VC / M • Sizzle / 1979 / QX / M • Slave Of Pleasure / 1978 / BL / M • Slippery When Wet / 1976 / VXP / M • Sugar Britches / 1980 / VCX / C • Summertime Blue / 1979 / VCX / M • Swedish Sorority Girls / 1978 / CV / M • Sweet Surrender / 1980 / VCX / M • Sweet Throat / 1979 / CV / M • The Taking Of Christina / 1975 / NGV / M • Temptations / 1976 / VXP / M • That

Lady From Rio / 1976 / VXP / M • Through The Looking Glass / 1976 / ALP / M • The Trouble With Young Stuff / 1976 / VC / M • Victims Of Love / 1975 / ALP / M • Virgin Snow / 1976 / VXP / M • The Vixens Of Kung Fu: A Tale Of Yin Yang / 1975 / VC / M

ROGER CANDY
Euro-Snatch / 1996 / SNA / M

ROGER CARR *see Star Index I*

ROGER COTY *see Star Index I*

ROGER DEE
The Fury / 1993 / WIV / M • Princess Of Thieves / 1994 / SC / M

ROGER DICKSON *see Star Index I*

ROGER FOX
Feelings / 1977 / VC / M

ROGER FRAZIER *see Star Index I*

ROGER KARNS *see Austin Moore*

ROGER LEHMAN
Bedtime Video #09 / 1984 / GO / M

ROGER MILLER
Deep Butt / 1994 / MID / C

ROGER PLANT *see Star Index I*

ROGER RANDALL
Women's Penitentiary / 1992 / VIM / M

ROGER RIGEL
The Joy Of Fooling Around / 1978 / CV / M

ROGER ROLL
Daughters Of Darkness / 1975 / ASR / M

ROGER SCORPIO
Bare Waves / 1986 / VD / M • Bionic Babes / 1986 / 4P / M • Hot And Nasty! / 1986 / V99 / C • I've Never Done This Before / 1985 / NSV / M • Mouthwatering / 1986 / BRA / M

ROGER T. DODGER *see Star Index I*

ROLAND BOSS
Dirty Business / 1995 / WIV / M

ROLAND CHARBAUX *see Star Index I*

ROLAND NEVES *(Rick Roberts (1994), Rich Roberts)*
Male with long black hair and hairy body with lots of tattoos. Looks like a rocker type. Boyfriend or husband of Sindee Cox.
Babewatch #2 / 1994 / CC / M • Bad Girls #5 / 1994 / GO / M • Bun Busters #15 / 1994 / LBO / M • The Devil In Miss Jones #5: The Inferno / 1994 / VC / M • Dreams Of Desires / 1995 / ONA / M • The Initiation / 1995 / FD / M • Models Etc. / 1995 / LV / M • Pussyman Auditions #10 / 1995 / SNA / M • Sex Machine / 1995 / VI / M • Stowaway / 1995 / LE / M • Upbeat Love #2 / 1995 / CV / M

ROLF
Trans America / 1993 / TSS / G

ROLF BECK *see Star Index I*

ROLF HAEUBI
[Die Madchenhandler / 1972 / … / M

ROLF KRUGER *see Star Index I*

ROLF MEDUS *see Star Index I*

ROLLY EVANS *see Taylor Evans*

ROMAN HOLLIDAY
Borderline (Vivid) / 1995 / VI / M • Oral Addiction / 1995 / VI / M

ROMAN HUBER
Come Play With Me #2 / 1980 / PS / S • Untamed Sex / 1979 / … / S • [Madchen, Die Sich Selbst, Bedienen / 1974 / … / M

ROMANA
Prague By Night #1 / 1996 / EA / M • Prague By Night #2 / 1996 / EA / M • Rocco Goes To Prague / 1995 / EA / M

ROMANA ST. LEGER
One Page Of Love / 1980 / VCX / M

ROMEO
Bun Busters #13 / 1994 / LBO / M • Northwest Pecker Trek #4: Laid In Latte Land / 1994 / LBO / M
ROMEO VERDI *see Star Index I*
ROMI PANTERA
Dangerous Pleasure / 1995 / WIV / M • Double Pleasure / 1995 / XYS / M
RON
AVP #9132: Barbara Likes It Hard / 1991 / AVP / M • China Lee's Bachelorette Party / 1995 / RHV / M • Cousin Bubba Country Corn Porn #02 / 1994 / VIM / M • Homegrown Video #414: Pussy Hairstylist / 1994 / HOV / M • Pearl Necklace: Thee Bush League #23 / 1993 / SEE / M • Rusty Boner's Late Night Videos #1 / 1995 / RHV / M
RON ANDERS
Starlet Nights / 1982 / XTR / M
RON ANDERSON
Bedtime Video #09 / 1984 / GO / M • Frathouse Sexcapades / 1993 / SFP / M
RON BROWNE
The Case Of The Full Moon Murders / 1971 / SOW / M
RON DARYL
Limited Edition #07 / 1979 / AVC / M
RON DELANY *see Star Index I*
RON DYE *see Star Index I*
RON FEILEN *see Ron Filene*
RON FILENE *(Ron Feilen)*
Centerfold Fever / 1981 / VXP / M • The Starmaker / 1982 / VC / M • Twilight Pink #2 / 1982 / VC / M
RON FORE
All The Loving Couples / 1979 / KIT / M
RON GOMEZ *see Don Fernando*
RON HAMILTON
The Erotic Aventures Of Lolita / 1982 / VXP / M
RON HARDWAY
Slut Safari #3 / 1994 / FC / M
RON HARLEY *see Star Index I*
RON HEDGE *see Ron Jeremy*
RON HIGHTOWER
2 Hung 2 Tung / 1992 / MID / M • Anal International / 1992 / HW / M • Anal Kitten / 1992 / ROB / M • Anal Lover #2 / 1993 / ROB / M • Anal Rescue 811 / 1992 / PL / M • Anal Savage #1 / 1992 / ROB / M • Anal Vision #13 / 1993 / LBO / M • Anal With An Oriental Slant / 1993 / ROB / M • Angels With Sticky Faces / 1991 / VD / M • As Sweet As They Come / 1992 / V99 / M • Awakening In Blue / 1991 / PL / M • Babewatch #1 / 1993 / CC / M • The Backway Inn #2 / 1992 / FD / M • Beach Bum Amateur's #05 / 1992 / MID / M • Behind The Blackout / 1993 / HW / M • Best Gang Bangs / 1996 / DFI / C • Big Black Dicks / 1993 / GO / C • Black Centerfold Celebrities / 1993 / MID / M • Black Men Can Hump / 1992 / FH / M • Black Orgies #01 / 1993 / AFI / M • Black Orgies #02 / 1993 / AFI / M • Black Orgies #03 / 1993 / AFI / M • Black Orgies #04 / 1993 / AFI / M • Black Orgies #05 / 1993 / AFI / M • Black Orgies #08 / 1993 / AFI / M • Black Orgies #11 / 1993 / AFI / M • Black Orgies #15 / 1993 / AFI / M • Black Orgies #16 / 1993 / AFI / M • Black Studies / 1992 / GO / M • Black To Basics / 1992 / ZA / M • Black Velvet #1 / 1992 / CC / M • Black Velvet #2 / 1993 / CC / M • Boomerwang / 1992 / MID / M • The Booty Bandit / 1994 / FC / M • Breast

Wishes #05 / 1991 / LBO / M • Breast Wishes #14 / 1993 / LBO / M • Brother Act / 1992 / PL / M • Brown Sugar From The Hood / 1996 / MID / M • Bubble Butts #05 / 1992 / LBO / M • Bubble Butts #07 / 1992 / LBO / M • The Burma Road #1 / 1994 / LBO / C • The Burma Road #2 / 1994 / LBO / C • Burn It Up / 1994 / VEX / M • Busty Babes In Heat #1 / 1993 / BTO / M • The Butt Boss / 1993 / VD / M • Butt Light: Queen Of Rears / 1992 / STR / M • Butt's Up, Doc #2 / 1992 / GO / M • Buttman Vs Buttwoman / 1992 / EL / M • The Buttnicks #4: The Black Buttnicks / 1993 / CC / M • California Pony Girls / 1992 / STM / B • Danger-Ass / 1992 / MID / M • Dark Alleys #01 / 1992 / FC / M • Dark Alleys #02 / 1992 / FC / M • Dark Alleys #07 / 1992 / FC / M • Dark Alleys #08 / 1992 / FC / M • Dark Alleys #25 / 1994 / FC / M • Deep Throat #6 / 1992 / AFV / M • The Devil In Grandma Jones / 1994 / FC / M • Do The White Thing / 1992 / ZA / M • Ebony Erotica #01: Black Narcissys / 1993 / GO / M • Ebony Erotica #02: Midnight Madness / 1993 / GO / M • Ebony Erotica #03: Black Adonis / 1993 / GO / M • Ebony Erotica #04: Ebony Gods / 1993 / GO / M • Ebony Erotica #05: Black Obsessions / 1993 / GO / M • Ebony Erotica #06: Black Essence / 1993 / GO / M • Ebony Erotica #07: Sepia Salute / 1993 / GO / M • Ebony Erotica #08: Indigo Moods / 1993 / GO / M • Ebony Erotica #09: Bronze Thrills / 1993 / GO / M • Ebony Erotica #10: Dark Eyes / 1993 / GO / M • Ebony Erotica #11: Harlem Knights / 1993 / GO / M • Ebony Erotica #12: Pussy Posse / 1993 / GO / M • Ebony Erotica #13: Dusky Beauties / 1994 / GO / M • Ebony Erotica #14: Black & Tan / 1994 / GO / M • Ebony Erotica #15: Chocolate Kisses / 1994 / GO / M • Ebony Erotica #16: Dark & Sweet / 1994 / GO / M • Ebony Erotica #17: Black Power / 1994 / GO / M • Ebony Erotica #18: Soul Kiss / 1994 / GO / M • Ebony Erotica #19: Ebony Angels / 1994 / GO / M • Ebony Erotica #20: Brown Sugar / 1994 / GO / M • Ebony Erotica #21: Cordon Negro / 1994 / GO / M • Ebony Erotica #22: Fade To Black / 1994 / GO / M • Ebony Erotica #23: Black Betty / 1994 / GO / M • Ebony Erotica #24: Hot Chocolate / 1994 / GO / M • Ebony Erotica #28: / 1994 / GO / M • Encino Woman / 1992 / VIM / M • Full Blown / 1992 / GO / M • Gang Bang Face Bath #1 / 1993 / ROB / M • Gang Bang Pussycat / 1992 / ROB / M • Gang Bang Thrills / 1992 / ROB / M • Gang Bang Wild Style #1 / 1993 / ROB / M • The Girls Of Summer / 1992 / FOR / M • Girlz N The Hood #2 / 1992 / HW / M • Hannibal Lickter / 1992 / MID / M • Hooter Heaven / 1992 / CA / M • In Loving Color #1 / 1992 / VT / M • In Loving Color #2 / 1992 / VT / M • In Loving Color #3 / 1992 / VT / M • In Loving Color #4 / 1993 / VT / M • In Your Face #1 / 1992 / PL / M • In Your Face #2 / 1992 / PL / M • It's Only Love / 1992 / VEX / M • Jennifer 69 / 1992 / PL / M • Jezebel #2 / 1993 / SC / M • Kink World: The Seduction Of Nena / 1993 / PL / M • The Love Doctor / 1992 / HIP / M • Malcolm XXX / 1992 / OD / M • Mocha Magic / 1992 / FH / M • Molly B-Goode / 1994 / FH / M • Mr. Peepers Amateur Home Videos #43: Gym-Nastiness / 1992 / LBO / M • Mr. Peepers Amateur

Home Videos #52: Tail Wackers / 1992 / LBO / M • My Baby Got Back #01 / 1992 / VT / M • My Baby Got Back #02 / 1993 / VT / M • Neighborhood Watch #16: Dirty Laundry / 1992 / LBO / M • Neighborhood Watch #25: / 1992 / LBO / M • New Girls In Town #3 / 1993 / CC / M • Nothing Butt Amateurs #01 / 1993 / AFI / M • Odyssey Triple Play #55: Black & White & Up The Ass / 1994 / OD / M • Old Throat And D.P. / 1993 / FC / M • Oreo A Go-Go #1 / 1992 / FH / M • Oreo A Go-Go #2 / 1992 / FH / M • Pearl Necklace: Thee Bush League #12 / 1993 / SEE / M • The Pick Up / 1993 / MID / M • Pornographic Priestess / 1992 / CA / M • Pussy Posse / 1993 / CC / M • Rocks / 1993 / VT / M • Ron Hightower's White Chicks #01 / 1993 / LBO / M • Ron Hightower's White Chicks #02 / 1993 / LBO / M • Ron Hightower's White Chicks #03 / 1993 / LBO / M • Ron Hightower's White Chicks #04 / 1993 / LBO / M • Ron Hightower's White Chicks #05 / 1993 / LBO / M • Ron Hightower's White Chicks #07 / 1993 / LBO / M • Ron Hightower's White Chicks #08 / 1994 / LBO / M • Ron Hightower's White Chicks #10 / 1994 / LBO / M • Ron Hightower's White Chicks #11 / 1994 / LBO / M • Ron Hightower's White Chicks #12 / 1994 / LBO / M • Rump-Shaker #1 / 1993 / HW / M • Sexmares / 1993 / FH / M • Slipping It In / 1992 / FD / M • The Strip / 1992 / SC / M • Stud Puppy / 1992 / STM / B • Tailiens #2 / 1992 / FD / M • Tailiens #3 / 1992 / FD / M • Uncle Roy's Amateur Home Video #08 / 1992 / VIM / M • Up The Ying Yang #1 / 1994 / CC / M • Victoria's Amateurs #02 / 1992 / VGA / M • Video Virgins #01 / 1992 / NS / M • Video Virgins #02 / 1992 / NS / M • Vivid Raw #1 / 1996 / VI / M • Vivid Raw #4 / 1996 / VI / M • Wet & Wicked / 1992 / VEX / M • White Chicks Can't Hump / 1992 / FD / M • White Men Can't Hump / 1992 / CC / M • Will & Ed's Keister Easter / 1992 / MID / M • Will And Ed's Bogus Gang Bang / 1992 / MID / M • Will And Ed: The Curse Of Poona / 1994 / MID / C • Women's Penitentiary / 1992 / VIM / M • X-Rated Blondes / 1992 / VD / C
RON HOUSTON
Fade To Rio / 1984 / VHL / M
RON HUDD
Afternoon Delights / 1981 / CA / M • Beauty / 1981 / VC / M • The Bimbo #1 / 1985 / VXP / M • Bizarre Styles / 1981 / ALP / B • Blue Magic / 1981 / QX / M • Bon Appetit / 1980 / QX / M • Candi Girl / 1979 / PVX / M • Consenting Adults / 1981 / VXP / M • The Cosmopolitan Girls / 1982 / VC / M • Dallas School Girls / 1981 / VCX / M • Debbie Does Dallas #2 / 1980 / VC / M • Deep Inside Annie Sprinkle / 1981 / VXP / M • Double Your Pleasure / 1978 / CV / M • Dracula Exotica / 1980 / TVX / M • French Kiss / 1979 / PVX / M • Games Women Play #1 / 1980 / CA / M • A Girl Like That / 1979 / CDC / M • Her Name Was Lisa / 1979 / VC / M • Hollywood Erotic Film Festival / 1987 / PAR / S • Honey Throat / 1980 / CV / M • Hot Child In The City / 1979 / PVX / M • Inside Seka / 1980 / VXP / M • Jack 'n' Jill #1 / 1979 / VXP / M • Lady Madonna / 1985 / RLV / M • The Love Tapes / 1980 / BL / M • Miami Vice Girls / 1984 / RLV / M • Outlaw Ladies #1 / 1981 / VC / M • Pandora's Mirror / 1981 / CA / M • The Pink Ladies /

1980 / VC / M • Puss 'n' Boots / 1982 / VXP / M • Roommates / 1982 / VXP / M • Satin Suite / 1979 / QX / M • The Satisfiers Of Alpha Blue / 1980 / AVC / M • Scoundrels / 1982 / COM / M • Silky / 1980 / VXP / M • Sizzle / 1979 / QX / M • Summertime Blue / 1979 / VCX / M • Sunny / 1979 / VC / M • The Taming Of Rebecca / 1982 / SVE / B • That Lucky Stiff / 1979 / QX / M • Tigresses...And Other Man-Eaters / 1979 / VXP / M • Velvet High / 1980 / VC / M • Wanda Whips Wall Street / 1982 / VXP / M • Wicked Schoolgirls / 1981 / SVE / M • Wild Innocents / 1982 / VCX / M

RON HUNTER
Private School Girls / 1983 / CA / M

RON HYATT *see* Ron Jeremy

RON JABAR
Joanna Storm On Fire / 1985 / VIV / M

RON JEREMY *(David Elliot, Bill Blackman, Nicholas Pera, R.J., Ron Hyatt, Ron Jeremy Hyatt, Ron Hedge, Hedge)*
Known as the hedgehog because of his hairy back. Graduated class of 1971 from Cardoza High School in Brooklyn which is great except that Cardoza High School is in Queens. Born 3/12/53 which would make him 43 in 1996.
2 Baggers / 1994 / ZA / M • 21 Hump Street / 1988 / VWA / M • 52 Pick-Up / 1986 / MED / S • The 8th Annual Erotic Film Awards / 1984 / SE / C • 900 Desert Strip / 1991 / XPI / M • The Absolute Worst Of Amateur #1 / 1993 / VEX / M • Adam & Eve's House Party #5 / 1996 / VC / M • Adult Video Nudes / 1993 / VC / M • The Adventures Of Buttgirl & Wonder Wench / 1991 / AFV / M • Adventures Of The DP Boys: At The French Riviera / 1994 / HW / M • The Affairs Of Miss Roberts / 19?? / ... / M • Against All Bods / 1991 / VEX / M • All Amateur Kinky Couples #1 / 1995 / LEI / M • All Amateur Kinky Couples #2 / 1995 / LEI / M • All American Girls #2: In Heat / 1983 / CA / M • All For One / 1988 / CIN / M • All I Want For Christmas Is A Gangbang / 1994 / AMP / M • All The Action / 1980 / TVX / M • All The Way In / 1984 / VC / M • All-Star Anal Interviews #1 / 1995 / LEI / M • Alley Cat / 1983 / VC / M • Amanda By Night #1 / 1981 / CA / M • Amateur Dreams #3 / 1994 / DR / M • Amateur Hours #68 / 1994 / AFI / M • Amateur Orgies #19 / 1992 / AFI / M • Amateur Orgies #20 / 1992 / AFI / M • Amber Aroused / 1985 / CA / M • Ambushed / 1990 / SE / M • America's Dirtiest Home Videos #01 / 1991 / VEX / M • America's Dirtiest Home Videos #03 / 1991 / VEX / M • America's Dirtiest Home Videos #09 / 1992 / VEX / M • America's Raunchiest Home Videos #43: Cum Blow My Horn / 1992 / ZA / M • American Dream Girls #1 / 1986 / VEX / M • Americans Most Wanted / 1991 / HO / M • The Amorous Adventures Of Cissy / 1982 / WWV / M • Anal Addiction #2 / 1990 / SO / M • Anal Al's Adventures / 1995 / PL / M • Anal Angels #3 / 1995 / VEX / C • Anal Angels #4 / 1995 / VEX / C • Anal Angels #5 / 1996 / VEX / C • Anal Attraction #1 / 1988 / 3HV / M • Anal Attraction #2 / 1993 / AFV / C • Anal Jeopardy / 1996 / ZA / M • Anal Queen / 1994 / FPI / M • Anal Vision #25 / 1994 / LBO / M • Anal Vision #26 / 1994 / LBO / M • The Anals Of History #1 / 1991 / MID / M • Angel Buns / 1981 / QX / M • Angel In Distress / 1982 / AVO / B •

Angel Wolf / 1995 / WIV / M • The Anus Family / 1991 / CC / M • Anything Goes / 1996 / OUP / M • Aphrodesia's Diary / 1984 / CA / M • As Cute As They Cum / 1990 / VEX / M • Ass Masters (Leisure) #01 / 1995 / LEI / M • Ass Masters (Leisure) #02 / 1995 / LEI / M • Ass Masters (Leisure) #03 / 1995 / LEI / M • Ass Masters (Leisure) #04 / 1995 / LEI / M • Ass Masters (Leisure) #05 / 1995 / LEI / M • Ass Masters (Leisure) #06 / 1995 / LEI / M • Ass, Gas & The Mystical GLOP / 1997 / EL / M • At The Pornies / 1989 / VC / M • Attack Of The Monster Mammaries / 1987 / LA / C • Aunt Peg Goes To Hollywood / 1982 / CA / M • AVP #1003: Rendezvous With Ron / 1991 / AVP / M • Babe / 1982 / AR / M • Babes In Toyland / 1988 / COM / C • The Babes Of Bonerville / 1995 / VEX / C • Bachelor Party #1 / 1993 / FPI / M • Bachelor Party #2 / 1993 / FPI / M • Back Door Babewatch / 1995 / IF / C • The Backdoor Bandit / 1994 / LV / M • Backdoor Bandits / 1989 / MIR / C • Backdoor Brides #1 / 1985 / PV / M • Backdoor Brides #2: The Honeymoon / 1986 / PV / M • Backdoor Imports / 1995 / LV / M • Backdoor Lust / 1987 / CV / C • Backdoor To Hollywood #02 / 1986 / CDI / M • Backdoor To Hollywood #04 / 1988 / CDI / M • Backdoor To Hollywood #06 / 1989 / CIN / M • Backdoor To Hollywood #08 / 1989 / CIN / M • Backing In #1 / 1990 / WV / C • Backing In #2 / 1990 / WV / C • Backing In #4 / 1993 / WV / C • Backing In #6 / 1994 / WV / C • Backstage / 1988 / CDI / M • Backstage Pass / 1992 / VEX / M • Bad Girl / 1984 / LIM / M • Bad Girls #1 / 1981 / GO / M • Bad Girls #2 / 1983 / GO / M • Bad Girls #4 / 1984 / GO / M • Bad Mama Jama And The Fat Ladies Of The Evening / 1989 / VT / M • Bad Mama Jama Busts Out / 1989 / VT / M • Ball In The Family / 1988 / VWA / M • Bare Essentials / 1987 / VEX / M • Barely Legal / 1985 / CDI / M • The Battle Of The Breast Queens / 1989 / INS / C • Battle Of The Ultra Milkmaids / 1992 / LET / M • Beach Bum Amateur's #07 / 1992 / MID / M • Beauties And The Beast / 1990 / AFV / M • Beaver & Buttcheeks / 1993 / DR / M • Beaver Hunt #01 / 1994 / LEI / M • Beaver Hunt #02 / 1994 / LEI / M • Beaver Hunt #03 / 1994 / LEI / M • Because I Can / 1995 / BEP / M • Behind The Mask / 1995 / XC / M • Behind The Scenes Of An Adult Movie / 1983 / CV / M • Best Butt(e) In The West #2 / 1995 / CC / M • The Best Little Whorehouse In Beverly Hills / 1986 / CDI / M • Best Of Caught From Behind #1 / 1987 / HO / C • Best Of Caught From Behind #5 / 1991 / HO / C • The Best Of Ron Jeremy / 1990 / WET / C • The Better Sex Video Series #5: Sharing Fantasies / 1992 / LEA / M • Between A Rock And A Hot Place / 1989 / VEX / M • Between My Breasts #04 / 1986 / L&W / S • Beverly Hills Bikini Company / 1996 / NIT / M • Beverly Hills Seduction / 1988 / WV / M • Beyond The Casting Couch / 1986 / VD / M • The Bi-Analyst / 1991 / STA / G • Biff Malibu's Totally Nasty Home Videos #27 / 1992 / ANA / M • Biff Malibu's Totally Nasty Home Videos #38 / 1993 / ANA / M • The Big Bang #3 / 1994 / LV / M • The Big Bang / 1994 / FF / M • Big Bust Babes #26 / 1995 / AFI / M • Big Bust Babes #27 / 1995 / AFI / M • Big Bust Bangers #1 / 1994 / AMP / M • Big Busty

#20 / 198? / H&S / M • Big Mamas / 1981 / ... / C • Big Murray's New-Cummers #04: Booty Love / 1992 / FD / M • Big Tit Orgy #01 / 1987 / H&S / M • Big Top Cabaret #1 / 1986 / BTO / M • Big Top Cabaret #2 / 1989 / BTO / M • Bikini Beach Race / 1992 / BRU / S • Bimbonese 101 / 1993 / PL / M • Black & White In Living Color / 1992 / WV / M • Black 'n' Blew / 1988 / VC / M • Black Analyst #2 / 1995 / VEX / M • Black Angel / 1987 / CC / M • Black Angels / 1985 / VC / M • Black Babes / 1995 / LV / M • Black Babes In Heat / 1993 / VIM / M • Black Beauty (Playtime) / 19?? / PLY / C • Black Dreams / 1988 / CDI / M • Black Fox / 1988 / CC / M • Black Knockers #03 / 1995 / TV / M • Black Knockers #04 / 1995 / TV / M • Black Knockers #09 / 1995 / TV / M • Black Knockers #10 / 1995 / TV / M • Black Knockers #14 / 1995 / TV / M • Black On Black / 1987 / CDI / M • Black With Sugar / 1989 / CIN / M • Blacks & Blondes #15 / 1986 / WV / M • Blazing Boners / 1992 / MID / M • Blonde Angel / 1994 / VI / M • The Blonde Goddess / 1982 / VXP / M • Blonde In Black Silk / 1979 / QX / M • The Blonde Next Door / 1982 / GO / M • Blonde On The Run / 1985 / PV / M • Blonde Temptation / 1995 / IF / M • Blondes / 1995 / MET / M • Blondes! Blondes! Blondes! / 1986 / VCS / C • Blondie / 1985 / TAR / M • Bloopers #2 / 1991 / GO / C • Blow Job Baby / 1993 / CC / M • Blow Out / 1991 / IF / M • Blowoff / 1985 / CA / M • Blue Angel / 1991 / SE / M • Blue Angel / 1992 / AFV / M • Blue Angel / 1992 / AFV / M • Blue Ice / 1985 / CA / M • Blue Jeans / 1982 / VXP / M • Blue Vanities #014 / 1988 / FFL / M • Blue Vanities #017 (New) / 1988 / FFL / M • Blue Vanities #017 (Old) / 1988 / FFL / M • Blue Vanities #038 / 1988 / FFL / M • Blue Vanities #048 / 1988 / FFL / M • Blue Vanities #061 / 1988 / FFL / M • Blue Vanities #064 / 1988 / FFL / M • Blue Vanities #065 / 1988 / FFL / M • Blue Vanities #068 / 1988 / FFL / M • Blue Vanities #071 / 1988 / FFL / M • Blue Vanities #072 / 1988 / FFL / M • Blue Vanities #088 / 1988 / FFL / M • Blue Vanities #097 / 1988 / FFL / M • Blue Vanities #098 / 1988 / FFL / M • Blue Vanities #128 / 1990 / FFL / M • Blue Vanities #195 / 1993 / FFL / M • Blue Vanities #197 / 1993 / FFL / M • Blue Vanities #221 / 1994 / FFL / M • Blue Vanities #252 / 1996 / FFL / M • Bobby Hollander's Sweet Cheeks #112 / 1994 / QUA / M • Bodacious Ta Ta's / 1984 / CA / M • Bodies In Motion / 1994 / IF / M • Boiling Desires / 1986 / VC / M • Bon Appetit / 1980 / QX / M • Bone Alone / 1993 / MID / M • Boobs A Poppin' / 1994 / TTV / M • Boobs, Butts And Bloopers #1 / 1990 / HO / M • Boobs, Butts And Bloopers #2 / 1990 / HO / M • Born To Run / 1985 / WV / M • Bottoms Up #04 / 1983 / AVC / C • Boys R' Us / 1995 / WIV / M • Bra Busters #02 / 1993 / LBO / M • Breasts And Beyond #2 / 1991 / ME / M • Breathless / 1991 / WV / M • The Bridges Of Anal County / 1996 / PV0 / C • Bronco Millie / 1992 / ZA / M • The Budding Of Brie / 1980 / TVX / M • Bunny Bleu: A Gang Bang Fantasy / 1994 / FC / M • Burlexxx / 1984 / VC / M • Business And Pleasure / 1992 / AFV / M • Busted-D-D In Las Vegas / 1996 / LV / M • Butt Bandits #4 / 1996 / VD / C • Butt Bangers Ball / 1994 / FPI / M • Butt Hole Boulevard / 1993 / CA /

LV / M • Interview: Doin' The Butt / 1995 / LV / M • Interviews At The Hard Wok Cafe / 1996 / LOF / M • Intimate Affairs / 1990 / VEX / M • Intimate Realities #1 / 1983 / VC / M • Into The Fire / 1994 / ZA / M • Introducing Charli / 1989 / CIN / M • Invitation Only / 1989 / AMB / M • It's Incredible / 1985 / SE / M • Jailhouse Cock / 1993 / IP / M • Jennifer 69 / 1992 / PL / M • Jesus Christ, Superstar / 1972 / MCA / S • Jiggly Queens #3 / 1996 / LE / M • Jingle Balls / 1996 / EVN / M • Joanna Storm On Fire / 1985 / VIV / M • Joy-Fm #11 / 1994 / BHS / M • Joy-Fm #12 / 1994 / BHS / M • Joys Of Erotica #101 / 1980 / VCR / C • The Joy Of Sec's / 1989 / VEX / M • Jug Humpers / 1995 / V99 / C • Jugsy (X-Citement) / 1992 / XCI / M • Juice Box / 1990 / AFV / M • Junk Yard Dogs / 1991 / FC / M • Just For The Thrill Of It / 1989 / V99 / M • Just Friends / 1991 / AFV / M • Just Like Sisters / 1988 / VEX / M • KBBS: Weekend With Laurel Canyon / 1992 / KBB / M • Killing Zoe / 1994 / LIV / S • Kinky Business #1 / 1984 / DR / M • Kiss And Tell / 1992 / AFV / M • Kneel Before Me! / 1983 / ALP / B • Krazy 4 You / 1987 / 4P / M • Kym Wilde's On The Edge #33 / 1996 / RB / B • Ladies Lovin' Ladies #3 / 1993 / AFV / F • Lady Badass / 1990 / V99 / M • Lady Domina / 1989 / FC / B • Lady In Blue / 1990 / CIN / M • Lady Of The House / 1990 / VEX / M • The Last X-Rated Movie #1 / 1990 / COM / M • The Last X-Rated Movie #2 / 1990 / COM / M • The Last X-Rated Movie #3 / 1990 / COM / M • The Last X-Rated Movie #4 / 1990 / COM / M • Laugh Factory / 1995 / PRE / C • Lay Down And Deliver / 1989 / VWA / M • Laying Down The Law #1 / 1992 / AFV / M • Legends Of Porn #2 / 1989 / CV / C • Let Me Tell Ya 'Bout Fat Chicks #1 / 1986 / 4P / C • Let's Get Naked / 1987 / VEX / M • Lethal Passion / 1991 / PL / M • Lettre Da Rimini / 1995 / MID / M • Lilith Unleashed / 1986 / VC / M • Limited Edition #08 / 1979 / AVC / M • Limited Edition #14 / 1980 / AVC / M • Limited Edition #19 / 1980 / AVC / M • Limited Edition #20 / 1980 / AVC / M • Limited Edition #29 / 1984 / AVC / M • Lingerie / 1983 / CDI / M • Lips: The Passage To Pleasure / 1981 / CA / M • Liquid A$$ets / 1982 / CA / M • A Little American Maid / 1987 / VCX / M • A Little Bit Of Hanky Panky / 1984 / GO / M • Little French Maids / 1988 / VEX / M • Little Girl Blue / 1995 / RHS / M • Little Girls Lost / 1982 / VC / M • Little Magicians / 1993 / ANA / M • Little Red Riding Hood / 1988 / WV / M • A Little Romance / 1986 / HO / M • Living Legend / 1995 / V99 / M • Living On The Edge / 1997 / DWO / M • Lonely Is The Night / 1990 / V99 / M • Loose Jeans / 1996 / GO / M • Lotus Blossoms / 1996 / SUF / M • Love Champions / 1987 / VC / M • The Love Doctor / 1992 / HIP / M • Love Lotion #9 / 1987 / VXP / M • Love Potion / 1993 / WV / M • Love Potion 69 / 1994 / VC / M • Love-In Arrangement / 1981 / VXP / M • Lovebone Invasion / 1993 / PL / M • The Lover Girls / 1985 / VEX / M • Lucky Ladies #107 / 1992 / STI / M • Lust / 1993 / FH / M • Lust American Style / 1985 / WV / M • Lust And The Law / 1991 / GO / C • Lust Bug / 1985 / HO / M • Lust For Freedom / 1987 / AIP / S • Lust In Bloom / 1988 / LV / M • Lust In Space /

1985 / PV / M • Lust Of Blacula / 1987 / VEX / M • Lusty Adventurer / 1985 / GO / M • Lusty Detective / 1988 / VEX / M • Lusty Ladies #09 / 1984 / 4P / M • Lusty Ladies #11 / 1984 / 4P / M • M Series #12 / 1993 / LBO / M • Madame Hiney: The Beverly Hills Butt Broker / 1993 / STR / M • The Maddams Family / 1991 / XCI / M • Magic Pool / 1988 / VD / M • Malibu Summer / 1983 / VC / M • Mandy's Executive Sweet / 1982 / AVC / M • Manhattan Mistress / 1980 / VBM / M • Marathon / 1982 / CA / M • Marilyn Chambers' Private Fantasies #1 / 1983 / CA / M • Marilyn Chambers' Private Fantasies #3 / 1983 / CA / M • Mascara / 1982 / CA / M • Masquerade (1992-Usa) / 1992 / SC / M • Meet Wally Sparks / 1997 / … / S • Midnight Blue #1 / 1980 / VXP / M • Midwest: At The Ponderosa / 1992 / MV0 / S • Mike Hott: #317 Girls Who Swallow Cum #01 / 1995 / MHV / C • Mind Trips / 1992 / FH / M • Miss Adventures / 1989 / VEX / M • Miss Nude Galaxy #1 / 1995 / VOY / S • Miss Nude Galaxy #2 / 1995 / VOY / S • Miss Nude North America #1 / 1995 / VOY / S • Miss Nude North America #2 / 1995 / VOY / S • Miss Mix Up / 1992 / IF / M • Moans & Groans / 1987 / 4P / M • Modesty Gold / 19?? / MID / M • Moments Of Love / 1983 / MID / M • Money Honey / 1990 / TOR / M • Monkey Business / 1987 / SEV / M • More Than A Handful #1 / 1985 / CV / C • Motel Hell / 1992 / PL / M • Motel Sex #3 / 1995 / RAP / M • Mouth To Mouth / 1986 / CC / M • Moving In / 1986 / CV / M • Mr. Peepers Casting Couch / 1991 / LBO / M • Mrs. Rodger's Neighborhood / 1988 / EVN / C • Much More Than A Mouthful #2 / 1988 / VEX / M • Mud Madness / 1983 / AVC / M • Mutiny On The Booty / 1996 / FC / M • My Anal Valentine / 1993 / FD / M • My Party Doll / 1987 / VXP / M • Mystery Of The Maletease Dildo / 1992 / STR / M • Mystified / 1991 / V99 / M • Mystique / 1979 / CA / M • Naked Lust / 1985 / SE / M • Nanci Blue / 1979 / SE / M • Nasty / 1985 / NSV / M • Nasty Girls #1 (1990-CDI) / 1990 / CIN / M • Nasty Girls #2 (1990-CDI) / 1990 / CDI / M • Nasty Girls #3 (1990-CDI) / 1990 / CDI / M • Nasty Pants / 1995 / SUF / M • Natural Born Thrillers / 1994 / LV / M • Natural Pleasure / 1994 / … / M • Naughty By Nature / 1992 / IF / M • Naughty Cheerleaders / 1985 / HO / M • Naughty Girls Like It Big / 1986 / ELH / M • Naughty Girls Need Love Too / 1983 / SE / M • Naughty In Nature / 1994 / PL / M • Naughty Neighbors / 1986 / VEX / M • Naughty Nurses / 1982 / VCR / M • Needful Sins / 1993 / WV / M • Never Say Good Bi / 1989 / STA / G • Never Sleep Alone / 1984 / CA / M • The New Ass Masters #07 / 1996 / LEI / C • The New Ass Masters #08 / 1996 / LEI / C • The New Ass Masters #09 / 1996 / LEI / C • The New Ass Masters #11 / 1996 / LEI / C • The New Ass Masters #14 / 1996 / LEI / C • The New Butt Hunt #12 / 1995 / LEI / C • The New Butt Hunt #19 / 1996 / LEI / C • New Pussy Hunt #16 / 1995 / LEI / M • New Pussy Hunt #17 / 1995 / LEI / M • New Pussy Hunt #19 / 1996 / LEI / C • New Pussy Hunt #20 / 1996 / LEI / C • The New Snatch Masters #14 / 1995 / LEI / C • The New Snatch Masters #15 / 1995 / LEI / C • The New Snatch Masters #22 / 1996 / LEI

/ C • Night Crawlers / 1994 / SC / M • Night Of Passion / 1993 / BIA / C • The Night Of The Headhunter / 1985 / WV / M • The Night Of The Living Bed / 1996 / LE / M • Night Vibes / 1990 / KNI / M • Nikki And The Pom-Pom Girls / 1987 / VEX / M • Nikki Loves Rocco / 1996 / VI / M • Nikki's Nightlife / 1992 / IN / M • Nookie Court / 1992 / AFV / M • Nothing But Girls, Girls, Girls / 1988 / CDI / M • Nothing Else Matters / 1992 / V99 / C • Nymphette #1 / 1986 / WV / M • Nymphos / 1995 / MET / M • Oh Those Nurses / 1982 / VC / M • The Older Women's Sperm Bank #5 / 1996 / SUF / M • Olympic Fever / 1979 / AR / M • On The Wet Side / 1987 / V99 / M • Once Upon A Madonna / 1985 / PV / M • One Hot Night Of Passion / 1985 / COL / C • One Night Love Affair / 1991 / IF / M • The Only Game In Town / 1991 / VC / M • Only The Best Of Anal / 1992 / MET / C • Only The Best Of Men's And Women's Fantasies / 1988 / CV / C • Only The Best Of Oral / 1989 / CV / C • Only The Strong Survive / 1988 / ZA / M • Open Lips / 1983 / AVO / M • Opening Night / 1991 / AR / M • Opportunity Knocks / 1990 / HO / M • Oral Hijinx / 1990 / ERU / M • Oral Majority #01 / 1986 / WV / C • Oriental Anal Sluts / 1993 / WV / C • Oriental Gang Bang Fantasy / 1994 / FC / M • Oriental Jade / 1985 / VC / M • Oriental Techniques Of Pain And Pleasure / 1983 / ALP / B • Oriental Treatment #3: The Lost Empress / 1991 / AFV / M • The Other Side Of Lianna / 1984 / LA / M • Our Bang #08 / 1992 / GLI / M • Out Of My Mind / 1995 / PL / M • The Out Of Towner / 1987 / CDI / M • Outlaw Sluts / 1996 / RAS / M • Pandora's Mirror / 1981 / CA / M • Paradise / 1995 / FD / M • Parliament: Ass Masters #1 / 1987 / PM / M • Parliament: Dark & Sweet #1 / 1991 / PM / C • Parliament: Dirty Blondes #1 / 1991 / PM / F • Parliament: Eating Pussy #1 / 1989 / PM / C • Parliament: Shauna Grant #1 / 1988 / PM / C • Parliament: Three Way Lust / 1988 / PM / M • Party Animals / 1987 / VEX / M • Party Animals / 1994 / VEX / C • Party Doll / 1990 / VC / M • Party In The Rear / 1989 / LV / M • Party Wives / 1988 / CDI / M • The Passion Of Heather Lear / 1990 / AFV / M • Passionate Lee / 1984 / CRE / M • The Pearl Divers / 1988 / VWA / M • Pearl Necklace: Amorous Amateurs #36 / 1993 / SEE / M • Pearl Necklace: Amorous Amateurs #38 / 1993 / SEE / M • The Peek A Boo Gang / 1985 / COL / M • Peek-A-Boo / 1987 / VEX / M • Peepshow / 1994 / OD / M • Penetration #4 / 1984 / AVC / M • The Penetrator #1 / 1991 / PL / M • Penitentiary / 1995 / HW / M • The Perils Of Prunella #1 / 1980 / BIZ / B • Persia's Back / 1994 / VT / M • Personal Touch #1 / 1983 / AR / M • Perversion / 1984 / AVC / M • Perverted Stories #02 / 1995 / JMP / M • Perverted Stories #03 / 1995 / JMP / M • Perverted Stories #07 / 1996 / JMP / M • Perverted Stories #10 / 1996 / JMP / M • The Phantom Of The Montague Stage / 1997 / HO / M • Phantom X / 1989 / VC / M • Philmore Butts Goes Hollyweird / 1996 / SUF / M • Philmore Butts Hawaiian Anal Adventure / 1995 / SUF / M • Phone Sex Girls #1 / 1987 / VT / M • Physically Fit / 1991 / V99 / C • Pink Champagne / 1979 / CV / M • The Pink Ladies / 1980 / VC / M • The Pink La-

gers #118 / 1993 / WV / M • Tail Taggers #120 / 1994 / WV / M • Tailgunners / 1990 / CDI / M • Tailspin / 1987 / AVC / M • Take It Off / 1986 / TIF / M • The Tale Of Tiffany Lust / 1981 / CA / M • A Tale Of Two Titties #2 / 1992 / AFV / M • Tales By Taylor / 1989 / AMB / M • The Taming Of Savannah / 1993 / VI / M • A Taste Of Misty / 1990 / CA / C • A Taste Of Paradise / 1984 / HO / M • A Taste Of Purple Passion / 1990 / CA / C • A Taste Of Vanessa De Rio / 1990 / PIN / C • Taxi Girls #3: Killer On The Loose / 1993 / MED / M • Taylor Wayne's World / 1992 / AFV / M • Teaser / 1986 / RLV / M • Temptation: The Story Of A Lustful Bride / 1983 / NSV / M • Tender Loving Care / 1994 / BRI / S • Terms Of Endowment / 1986 / PV / M • That Lucky Stiff / 1979 / QX / M • That Ole Black Magic / 1988 / CDI / M • This Lady Is A Tramp / 1980 / CV / M • Three Men And A Geisha / 1990 / HO / M • The Three Musketeers #1 / 1992 / FD / M • The Three Musketeers #2 / 1992 / FD / M • Tight And Tender / 1985 / CA / M • Tight Fit #09 / 1994 / GO / M • Tigresses...And Other Man-Eaters / 1979 / VXP / M • Tip Of The Tongue / 1985 / V20 / M • Tit Tales #1 / 1989 / 4P / M • Titillation #2 / 1990 / SE / M • The Tongue / 1995 / OD / M • Tonight's The Night / 1992 / V99 / M • Tons Of Fun #3: Abondonza / 1987 / 4P / M • Too Hot / 1996 / LV / M • Too Much Too Soon / 1983 / VCX / M • Tough Girls Don't Dance / 1987 / SEV / M • Toys / 1982 / INF / M • Toys 4 Us #1 / 1987 / WV / C • Tracey's Love Chamber / 1987 / AR / M • Traci's Big Trick / 1987 / VAS / M • Transverse Tail / 1987 / CDI / M • Treasure Chest / 1985 / GO / M • Trick Or Treat / 1985 / ELH / M • Triple Header / 1986 / SE / C • Triple Penetration Debutante Sluts #1 / 1996 / BAC / M • Triple Penetration Debutante Sluts #2 / 1996 / BAC / M • Triple Play / 1983 / HO / M • Tropical Taboo / 1995 / HO / M • True Legends Of Adult Cinema: The Erotic Eighties / 1992 / VC / C • True Sex / 1994 / EMC / M • Turn Up The Heat / 1988 / SEX / M • Turn Up The Heat / 1991 / VEX / C • Twentysomething #1 / 1988 / VI / M • Twentysomething #2 / 1988 / VI / M • Twilight Pink #2 / 1982 / VC / M • Twin Cheeks (Arrow) / 1991 / AR / M • Twin Freaks / 1992 / ZA / M • Twister / 1992 / CC / M • Two Times A Virgin / 1991 / AR / M • Two Women / 1992 / ROB / M • Two Women & A Man / 1988 / VEX / M • Two Women & A Man / 1991 / VEX / C • Udderly Fantastic / 1983 / TGA / C • Udderly Fantastic / 1993 / IF / M • Ultimate Gang Bang #1 / 1994 / HW / M • The Ultimate Lover / 1986 / VD / M • The Ultimate Pleasure / 1995 / LEI / M • Ultraflesh / 1980 / GO / M • Undercover Lover / 1992 / CV / M • An Unnatural Act #1 / 1984 / DR / M • Unveil My Love / 1991 / HO / M • Up The Gulf / 1991 / AR / M • Valet Girls / 1987 / ... / S • The Vamp / 1986 / AVC / M • Vegas #1: Royal Flush / 1990 / CIN / M • Vice Versa / 1992 / FD / M • Victoria's Secret Life / 1992 / WV / M • Video Virgins #01 / 1992 / NS / M • Virgin Cheeks / 1986 / VD / M • Virgins / 1989 / CAR / M • Voodoo Vixens / 1991 / IF / M • Vortex / 1995 / MET / M • Vow Of Passion / 1991 / VI / M • Voyeurism #1 / 1993 / FH / M • The Wacky World Of X-Rated Bloopers / 1989 / GO / M • Wad Gobblers #11 / 1994 / GLI /

M • Walk On The Wild Side / 1987 / CDI / M • Walk On The Wild Side / 1994 / VIM / M • Wanda Whips Wall Street / 1982 / VXP / M • Warm Bodies, Hot Nights / 1988 / PV / M • Way Inside Lee Caroll / 1992 / VIM / M • The Way They Wuz / 1996 / SHS / C • We Love To Tease / 1985 / VD / M • Wedding Vows / 1994 / ZA / M • A Week And A Half In The Life Of A Prostitute / 1997 / EL / M • Wendy Is Watching / 1993 / ELP / M • Wet And Wild #1 / 1986 / VEX / M • Wet And Wild #2 / 1995 / VEX / M • Wet Sex / 1984 / CA / M • Wet Workout / 1987 / VEX / M • Wet, Wild And Wicked / 1984 / SE / M • What's A Nice Girl Like You Doing In An Anal Movie? / 1995 / AMP / M • What's Butt Got To Do With It? / 1993 / HW / M • What's The Lesbian Doing In My Pirate Movie? / 1995 / LIP / F • What's Up, Tiger Pussy? / 1995 / VC / M • When She Was Bad / 1983 / CA / M • Where The Girls Are / 1984 / VEX / M • White Trash / 1986 / PV / M • Who Killed Holly Hollywood? / 1993 / VC / M • Who's Dat Girl / 1987 / VEX / M • Whore'n / 1996 / AB / M • Whose Fantasy Is It, Anyway? / 1983 / AVC / M • Wicked Thoughts / 1992 / PL / M • Wide World Of Sex / 1987 / CLV / C • Wild & Wicked #7 / 1996 / VT / M • Wild Dreams / 1995 / V99 / M • Wild Innocents / 1982 / VCX / M • Wild Oats / 1988 / CV / M • The Wild Thing / 1992 / HO / M • Wild Thing / 1994 / IF / M • Wild Widow / 1996 / NIT / M • The Wild Wild Chest #1 / 1990 / HO / M • Will & Ed's Back To Class / 1992 / MID / M • Wine Me, Dine Me, 69 Me / 1989 / COL / C • Winner Take All / 1986 / SEV / M • Winning Score / 1989 / E&I / C • The Wizard Of AHH's / 1985 / SE / M • Women In Love / 1980 / CA / M • Women In Need / 1990 / HO / M • Women In Uniform / 1986 / TEM / M • Words Of Love / 1989 / LE / M • Working Girls / 1985 / CA / M • Working It Out / 1993 / CA / M • World Cup / 1990 / PL / M • The World's Biggest Gang Bang #1 / 1995 / FPI / M • The World's Biggest Gang Bang #2 / 1996 / FPI / M • The Worst Porno Ever Made With The Best Sex / 1993 / PL / M • WPINK-TV #1 / 1985 / PV / M • WPINK-TV #2 / 1986 / PV / M • X Factor: The Next Generation / 1991 / HO / M • X-Rated Bloopers #1 / 1984 / AR / M • X-TV #1 / 1986 / PL / C • X-TV #2 / 1989 / PL / C • The XXX Files: Lust In Space / 1995 / IMV / M • Yankee Seduction / 1984 / WV / M • Yin Yang Oriental Love Bang #1 / 1996 / SUF / M • Yin Yang Oriental Love Bang #5: Lotus Blossoms / 1996 / SUF / M • You Make Me Wet / 1985 / SVE / M • You Said A Mouthful / 1992 / IF / M • You're The Boss / 1985 / VD / M • Young And Anal #3 / 1995 / JMP / M • Young And Anal #4 / 1996 / JMP / M • Young And Innocent / 1987 / HO / M • [Lust Bug / 1991 / HO / M • [Older Women Are Sexy #4 / 19?? / ... / M • [They Bite / 1989 / ... / S

RON JEREMY HYATT *see* **Ron Jeremy**
RON JOHN
The Doll House / 1995 / CV / M
RON LONDON
Personal Trainer (Cs) / 1995 / CS / B
RON NELSON *see* **Star Index I**
RON RODGERS
Confessions Of A Woman / 1976 / SE / M • The Untamed / 1978 / VCX / M
RON SULLIVAN *see* **Henri Pachard**

RON THRASHER *see* **Star Index I**
RON TOWERS
Gangbang In The Fat Lane / 1996 / FC / M
RON VOGEL
Beauty And The Beast #2 / 1990 / VC / M • The Fury / 1993 / WIV / M • The Makeup Room #1 / 1992 / VC / M • The Makeup Room #2 / 1992 / VC / M • The Pink Pussycat / 1992 / CA / M • Take The A Train / 1993 / MID / M
RON WILLIAMS
Bucky Beaver's XXX Dragon Art Theatre Double Feature #15 / 1996 / SOW / M • Left At The Altar / 1974 / SOW / M
RON WIRTHHEIM
Sex U.S.A / 1970 / SEP / M
RON WORM *see* **Star Index I**
RON WOULD
Up And Cummers #21 / 1995 / RWP / M
RONA
A&B AB#304: Stripping Lesbians / 1991 / A&B / F
RONA LEE COHEN
A Guide To Making Love / 1973 / VES / M
RONALD DAVIS
Easy / 1978 / CV / M
RONALD DUNCAN
Bad Company / 1978 / CV / M
RONALD HOLDEN
One Of A Kind / 1976 / SVE / M
RONDA
My Baby Got Back #04 / 1994 / VT / M
RONDA FULLER *see* **Star Index I**
RONDA JONES *see* **Star Index I**
RONELL RANDALL *see* **Star Index I**
RONI
Lesbian Pros And Amateurs #09 / 1992 / GO / F
RONI BROOKES *see* **Star Index I**
RONI RAYE
Cousin Bubba Country Corn Porn #02 / 1994 / VIM / M • Dirty Bob's #15: The Contest! / 1994 / FLP / S • Gorilla-Gram / 1993 / VAL / M • Homegrown Video #402 / 1993 / HOV / M • Mr. Peepers Amateur Home Videos #83: Roni And The Private's / 1994 / LBO / M • Mr. Peepers Nastiest #1 / 1995 / LBO / C • Nasty Fuckin' Movies #13: Nurse Roni / 1993 / RUM / M • Nasty Fuckin' Movies #15: Sink The Pink / 1993 / RUM / M • Odyssey Triple Play #71: Bodacious Blondes / 1994 / OD / M • Pearl Necklace: Thee Bush League #22 / 1993 / SEE / M • Pearl Necklace: Thee Bush League #23 / 1993 / SEE / M • Roni Raye: Images Of Roni / 1995 / RR / F • Roni Raye: Playful Playmates / 1996 / RR / F • Roni Raye: Slippery Sex / 1994 / RR / F • Roni Raye: Toy Party / 1996 / RR / F • SVE: Tales From The Lewd Library #3 / 1994 / SVE / M
RONNIE
Blue Vanities #507 / 1992 / FFL / M • Blue Vanities #530 / 1993 / FFL / M • Lesbian Pros And Amateurs #06 / 1992 / GO / F
RONNIE CROWN
Bedtime Video #05 / 1984 / GO / M
RONNIE DICKENS *see* **Ronnie Dickson**
RONNIE DICKERSON *see* **Ronnie Dickson**
RONNIE DICKINSON *see* **Ronnie Dickson**
RONNIE DICKSON *(Ronnie Dixon, Ronnie Dickens, Ronnie Dickerson, Ronnie Dickinson)*
Ex Miss America contestant.

The Autobiography Of Herman Flogger / 1986 / AVC / M • Backdoor Brides #2: The Honeymoon / 1986 / PV / M • The Beat Goes On / 1987 / VCR / C • Beyond The Senses / 1986 / AVC / M • The Big E #08 / 1988 / BIZ / B • Broadcast Nudes / 1988 / EVN / M • Catfighting Cheerleaders / 1989 / BIZ / B • Catfights #3 / 1987 / OHV / B • Cheri And The Pirates / 1988 / CS / B • Crackdown / 1988 / BIZ / B • Devil In Miss Dare / 1986 / AVC / C • Dump Site / 1989 / BIZ / C • Floor Play / 1989 / PLV / B • Girls, Girls, Girls, Girls / 1993 / FD / C • Hanna Does Her Sisters / 1986 / HUR / M • The Immoral Miss Teeze / 1987 / CV / M • Leg...Ends #01 / 1988 / BIZ / F • Ride A Pink Lady / 1986 / SE / M • Rip Off #1 / 1988 / BIZ / B • Rollover & Cell Blocks / 1988 / PLV / B • Seduction Of Jennifer / 1986 / HO / M • Sensuous Singles: Keisha / 1987 / VCR / F • Sweet Cheeks / 1987 / VCR / C • Take It Off / 1986 / TIF / M • Teasin' & Pleasin' / 1988 / LBO / F • Tight Fit (Foot Fet) / 1988 / BIZ / B • The Trouble With Traci / 1984 / CHA / C • The Year Of The Sex Dragon / 1986 / PV / M

RONNIE DIXON see Ronnie Dickson

RONNIE LOVE
Anyone But My Husband / 1975 / VC / M • Too Hot To Handle / 1975 / CDC / M

RONNIE MICHELS see Star Index I

RONNIE ROSS
I Am Always Ready / 1978 / HIF / M • Lusty Princess / 1978 / HIF / M

RONNIE ROUNDHEELS see Uschi Digart

RONNIE SCOTT
Blue Vanities #110 / 1988 / FFL / M

RONNY FREY see Star Index I

RONNY MORGAN see Jamie Gillis

ROOT LOGGIN
Nightshift Nurses #2 / 1996 / VC / M • Sorority Sex Kittens #3 / 1996 / VC / M • Sorority Stewardesses #1 / 1995 / PE / M • Sorority Stewardesses #2 / 1995 / PE / M

ROPO ROSELLO
Bi Bi Banjee Boyz / 1994 / PL / G

RORY
GRG: Private Moments #312: Analize Me / 1996 / GRG / M

ROSA see Star Index I

ROSA (CARACCIOLO) see Rosa Caracciolo

ROSA CARACCIOLO *(Rossa, Rosa (Caracciolo), Rozsa Tassi)*
Adorable Hungarian (pretends to be Italian) brunette who seems to be the girlfriend or wife of Rocco Siffredi (as of 1993). Tight body, tight waist, small tits, very pretty, nice smile, boy-like butt, very passionate in her sex scenes. By 1995, she had had her tits enhanced to a medium/large size (very pancake shaped) and the passion, referred to above, seems to have disappeared. As of 1996 married to Rocco with a new son, Lorenzo.
Anal Delinquent #1 / 1993 / ROB / M • The Bodyguard / 1995 / SC / M • County Line / 1993 / PEP / M • Deep Cheeks #4 / 1993 / ROB / M • Jungle Heat / 1995 / LUM / M • Marquis De Sade / 1995 / IP / M • Top Model / 1995 / SC / M

ROSA DURAN see Star Index I

ROSA PEREZ
San Francisco Lesbians #4 / 1993 / PL / F

ROSA VOLARE see Star Index I

ROSALIE
Blue Vanities #533 / 1993 / FFL / M • Magma: Insatiable Lust / 1995 / MET / M

ROSALIE PASSION
Anal In The Alps / 1996 / P69 / M

ROSALIND NOLIAN
Personals / 1972 / COM / M

ROSALINE
Magma: Double Anal / 1994 / MET / M

ROSANNA
Fresh Cheeks / 1995 / VC / M

ROSANNA MELENDES
Buttman's Bouncin' British Babes / 1994 / EA / M • Private Film #06 / 1994 / OD / M • Private Film #07 / 1994 / OD / M • Private Video Magazine #07 / 1994 / OD / M

ROSCOE BOWLTREE *(Patrick Collins)*
Hefty male who, under the name Patrick Collins, is the owner of Elegant Angel. The Collins name is also used as director. Supposedly married to Tianna, then divorced, later married to Nikole Lace.
Bend Over Babes #3 / 1992 / EA / M • Bend Over Brazilian Babes #2 / 1993 / EA / M • The Bottom Dweller / 1993 / EL / M • The Bottom Dweller Part Deux / 1994 / EL / M • The Bottom Dweller 33 1/3 / 1995 / EL / M • Bottom Dweller: The Final Voyage / 1996 / EL / M • Butt Freak #1 / 1992 / EA / M • Buttman Goes To Rio #4 / 1993 / EA / M • Buttman Vs Buttwoman / 1992 / EL / M • Buttman's Big Butt Backdoor Babes / 1995 / EA / M • Buttman's Big Tit Adventure #1 / 1992 / EA / M • Buttman's Big Tit Adventure #3 / 1995 / EA / M • Buttman's Inferno / 1993 / EA / M • Buttman's Revenge / 1992 / EA / M • Buttman's Wet Dream / 1994 / EA / M • Buttwoman Back In Budapest / 1993 / EL / M • Buttwoman In Budapest / 1992 / EA / M • The Challenge / 1990 / EA / B • The Coming Of Nikita / 1995 / EL / M • Controlled / 1990 / BS / B • Cruel Passions / 1992 / BS / B • Dark Interludes / 1991 / BS / B • Depravity On The Danube / 1993 / EL / M • Dirty Stories #1 / 1995 / PE / M • Dresden Diary #03 / 1989 / BIZ / B • Eleventh Annual AVN Awards / 1994 / VC / M • Face Dance #1 / 1992 / EA / M • The Face Of Fear / 1990 / BS / B • Fazano's Student Bodies / 1995 / EL / M • Filthy First Timers #1 / 1996 / EL / M • House Of Dark Dreams #1 / 1990 / BS / B • House Of Dark Dreams #2 / 1990 / BS / B • The Power Of Summer #2: Reward / 1992 / BS / B • Route 69 / 1989 / OD / M • Sleeping Booty / 1995 / EL / M • Sodomania #01: Tales Of Perversity / 1992 / EL / M • Sodomania #03: Foreign Objects / 1993 / EL / M • Sodomania #04: Further On Down The Road / 1993 / EL / M • Sodomania #05: Euro-American Style / 1993 / EL / M • Sodomania #06: Gangs And Bangs And Other Thangs / 1993 / EL / M • Sodomania #07: Deep Down Inside / 1993 / EL / M • Sodomania #08: The London Sessions / 1994 / EL / M • Sodomania #09: Doin' Time / 1994 / EL / M • Sodomania #10: / 1994 / EL / M • Sodomania #11: In Your Face / 1994 / EL / M • Sodomania #12: Raw Filth / 1995 / EL / M • Sodomania #13: Your Lucky Number / 1995 / EL / M • Sodomania #14: C**t Lickin', C*m Drinkin' Bitches / 1995 / EL / M • Sodomania #15: Warning! / 1996 / EL / M • Sodomania #16: Sexxy Pistols / 1996 / EL / M • Sodomania #17: Simply Makes U

Tingle / 1996 / EL / M • Sodomania #18: Shame Based / 1996 / EL / M • Sodomania #19: Sweet Cream / 1996 / EL / M • Sodomania #20: For Members Only / 1997 / EL / M • Sodomania: Slop Shots / 1996 / EL / C • Sodomania: The Baddest Of The Best...And Then Some / 1994 / EL / C • Thermonuclear Sex / 1996 / EL / M • You Bet Your Ass / 1991 / EA / B

ROSE
A&B AB#226: Bondage Girls #1 / 1990 / A&B / C • A&B AB#226: Bondage Girls #2 / 1990 / A&B / C • Blue Vanities #527 / 1993 / FFL / M • Blue Vanities #583 / 1996 / FFL / M • Homegrown Video #260 / 1990 / HOV / M • Joe Elliot's College Girls #39 / 1994 / JOE / F • Kinky College Cunts #02 / 1993 / NS / M • Older Women With Younger Ideas #11 / 1995 / OD / M • Triple X Video Magazine #11 / 1995 / OD / M

ROSE BRANDON see Linda Rose Kimball

ROSE BUD
Mind Mirror / 1994 / LAP / M • Sex Between The Scenes / 1994 / LAP / M

ROSE BUSH
Honeypie / 1975 / VC / M

ROSE CRANSTON see Susan Sloan

ROSE GREER see Star Index I

ROSE HELLER see Star Index I

ROSE HUNTER see Rose Marie

ROSE KIMBALL see Linda Rose Kimball

ROSE KINDAL see Linda Rose Kimball

ROSE LASH see Star Index I

ROSE LYNN see Linda Rose Kimball

ROSE MARIE *(Ruby Belnap, Rose Hunter, Rosey Belinda, Rosey Marie)*
Reddish blonde (very curly hair and lots of it) with a sharp nose (marginal face) and droopy medium tits.
Best Of Caught From Behind #1 / 1987 / HO / C • Black By Popular Demand / 1992 / ZA / M • Blowing The Whistle / 1986 / VIP / M • Blowing Your Mind / 1984 / RSV / M • Blowoff / 1985 / CA / M • Bodacious Ta Ta's / 1984 / CA / M • Caught By Surprise / 1987 / CDI / M • Caught From Behind #02: The Sequel / 1983 / HO / M • Cupid's Arrow / 1984 / VCR / M • Delusions / 1983 / PRC / M • The Erotic World Of Sylvia Benedict (#5) / 1983 / VCR / C • Forbidden Entry / 1984 / VCR / M • Getting Lucky / 1983 / CA / M • Glamour Girl #3 / 1984 / CDI / M • Gourmet Premier: Throbbing Threesome / Hot Wife's Hunger 902 / cr86 / GO / M • Gourmet Quickies: Rose Marie #707 / 1985 / GO / C • GVC: Broadcast Babes #138 / 1985 / GO / M • GVC: Hot Numbers #133 / 1984 / GO / M • Hot Buns / 1983 / VCX / M • Hyapatia Lee's Sexy / 1986 / SE / M • Intimate Realities #2 / 1983 / VC / M • The Ladies Room / 1987 / CA / M • Lingerie / 1983 / CDI / M • Little Big Dong / 1992 / ZA / M • Merry X Miss / 1986 / VIP / M • Moist To The Touch / 1991 / DR / M • Parliament: Anal Babes #1 / 1989 / PM / F • Parliament: Ass Masters #1 / 1987 / PM / M • Parliament: Queens Of Double Penetration #1 / 1991 / PM / F • Photoflesh / 1984 / HO / M • Radio K-KUM / 1984 / HO / M • Scenes From A Crystal Ball / 1992 / ZA / M • Tales Of The Backside / 1985 / VCR / C • The Wacky World Of X-Rated Bloopers / 1989 / GO / M • The X-Team / 1984 / CV / M

ROSE MARMIN see Star Index I

ROSE MARY DILLON *see Star Index I*
ROSE O'NEAL
[Suburban Sex Fiends / 197? / ... / M
ROSE PEDAL *see Star Index I*
ROSE SANTANA
Young Sluts In Heat #1 / 1996 / PL / M •
Young Sluts In Heat #2 / 1996 / PL / M
ROSE SIMPSON *see Star Index I*
ROSE STEVENS
Round Robin / 19?? / VXP / M
ROSE TAFT
Secret Dreams Of Mona Q / 1977 / AR / M
ROSE TORRES
The Wacky World Of X-Rated Bloopers /
1989 / GO / M
ROSE WILDE *see Tiffany Lane*
ROSE-LINDA KIMBALL *see Linda Rose Kimball*
ROSEANNE FARROW *(Theodora Duncan)*
Slave Of Pleasure / 1978 / BL / M • Two
Lives Of Jennifer / 1979 / VHL / M
ROSEANNE LANG
The Vixens Of Kung Fu: A Tale Of Yin Yang
/ 1975 / VC / M
ROSEBUD *see Star Index I*
ROSEMARY
Blue Vanities #130 / 1990 / FFL / M • Blue
Vanities #528 / 1993 / FFL / M • Bras And
Panties #1 / 199? / H&S / S
ROSEMARY CAMELOT
The Loves Of Mary Jane / 1989 / BWV / C
• A Touch Of Sex / 1972 / AR / M
ROSEMARY MORLAN
Sexual Communication / 19?? / HIF / M
ROSEY BELINDA *see Rose Marie*
ROSI DELMI
Reel Classics #3 / 1996 / H&S / M
ROSIE
100% Amateur #09: Asians & Latinas /
1995 / OD / M • The Anal Adventures Of
Max Hardcore: Love Hurts / 1994 / ZA / M
• Black Hollywood Amateurs #13 / 1995 /
MID / M • Black Talez N Da Hood / 1996 /
APP / M • Breast Worx #14 / 1992 / LBO /
M • Casting Call #09 / 1995 / SO / M •
Cherry Poppers #08: Tender And Tight /
1994 / ZA / M • Dick & Jane In San Francisco / 1996 / AVI / M • Fan Fuxxx #1 / 1996
/ DWV / M • Female Mimics International:
Behind The Scenes / 1988 / LEO / G •
Fresh Faces #07 / 1995 / EVN / M • Home-
Grown Video #434: Forrest Hump / 1994 /
HOV / M • Jura Sexe / 1995 / JP / G • More
Dirty Debutantes #36 / 1994 / 4P / M •
More To Love #2 / 1995 / TTV / M • My
Baby Got Back #07 / 1995 / VT / M
ROSIE (EVON CRAWFOR) *see Evon Crawford*
ROSIE LEE *see Yvonne (Rosie Lee)*
ROSIE MARIE *see Rose Marie*
ROSIE ROSARIO
Erecter Sex #5: Oral Fantasies / cr72 / AR
/ M
ROSINE VANECK *see Star Index I*
ROSITA
Blue Vanities #506 / 1992 / FFL / M
ROSL MAYR
[Junge Madchen Mogen's HeiB, Hausfrauen Noch HeiBer / 1973 / ... / M
[Krankenschwestern-Report / 1972 / ... / M
• [Schulmadchen-Report 4: Was Eltern Oft
Verzweifeln LaBt / 1972 / ... / M
ROSS BENTON *see Star Index I*
ROSS FINK
Sodom & Gomorrah / 1974 / MIT / M

ROSS LOWELL
No Man's Land #02 / 1988 / VT / F
ROSS ROBERTS *see Star Index I*
ROSSA *see Rosa Caracciolo*
ROSSANA DOLL
A Merry Widow / 1996 / SPI / M
ROSSI *see Star Index I*
ROSSIE *see Star Index I*
ROSY ICING *see Star Index I*
ROSY PALM *see Star Index I*
ROTH ANITA
Sirens / 1995 / GOU / M
ROWAN FAIRMONT *see Rowan Lee*
ROWAN LEE *(Rowan Fairmont)*
Marginal face (looks a little like Madison),
medium enhanced tits, too much eye make-
up, long black curly hair, petite frame, tat-
toos on inside right forearm, right belly and
right shoulder back.
Buffy Malibu's Nasty Girls #08 / 1995 / ANA
/ F • The Devil In Miss Jones #5: The In-
ferno / 1994 / VC / M • Dirty Dancers #3 /
1995 / 4P / M • Hot Tight Asses #10 / 1995
/ TCK / M • Little Girl Blue / 1995 / RHS / M
• More Dirty Debutantes #34 / 1994 / 4P /
M • More Dirty Debutantes #37 / 1995 / 4P
/ M • Nasty Nymphos #12 / 1996 / ANA / M
• Profiles #03: House Dick / 1995 / XPR / M
• A Trip Through Pain / 1995 / BS / B • The
Voyeur #3 / 1995 / EA / M
ROWDY GALLAHAD
Hollywood Hookers / 1996 / DWV / M • The
Sex Therapist / 1995 / GO / M
ROWENNA
Blue Vanities #540 / 1994 / FFL / M
ROXANNE
Afternoon Delights / 1995 / FC / M • Bay
City Hot Licks / 1993 / ROB / F • Big Girl
Workout / 1991 / BTO / M • Big Tit
Roundup #1 / 199? / H&S / S • Blue Vani-
ties #557 / 1994 / FFL / M • Blue Vanities
#559 / 1994 / FFL / M • Bootyville / 1994 /
EVN / M • Bottoms Up #06 / 1986 / AVC /
C • Breast Wishes #02 / 1991 / LBO / M •
The Girls Of Malibu / 1986 / ACV / S • Hir-
sute Lovers #2 / 1995 / BTO / M • Home-
grown Video #035 / 1990 / HOV / M •
Homegrown Video #128 / 1990 / HOV / M
• HomeGrown Video #458: Cream Pie For
Dessert / 1995 / HOV / C • HomeGrown
Video #473: Furpie Feast #3 / 1997 / HOV
/ C • Huge Ladies #09 / 1991 / BTO / S •
Huge Ladies #10 / 1991 / BTO / M • Les-
bian Pros And Amateurs #25 / 1993 / GO /
F • Living In A Wet Dream / 1986 / PEN / C
• Painful Overtime / 1995 / TVI / B • Pony
Girls / 1993 / ROB / F • Private Film #16 /
1994 / OD / M • Singapore Sluts / 1994 /
ORE / C • Stevi's: Dressed For Wet / 1994
/ SSV / F • Super Sampler #5 / 1994 / LOD
/ C • SVE: Raunchy Rustie & Ready Rox-
anne / 1992 / SVE / M • VGA: Family Tie /
1993 / VGA / B • VGA: Spanking Sampler
#1 / 1991 / VGA / B • VGA: Taming Of
Tammy #2 / 1991 / VGA / B
ROXANNE (CODY N) *see Cody Nicole*
ROXANNE (HALL) *see Roxanne Hall*
ROXANNE (JALYNN) *see Jalynn*
ROXANNE (S/M)
Euro Extremities #50 / 199? / SVE / C
ROXANNE BLASE *see Roxanne Blaze*
ROXANNE BLAZE *(Blaze (Roxanne), Sarah Bellomo, Crystal Lea, Roxanne Blase)*
Tall blonde with long straight hair, a tight body
and small tits. Mole under her left armpit

and another halfway up her back just to the
right of her spine. Started at 18 and was 19
in September 1993. Born in Burbank CA
and lived there all her life. First on-screen
anal in **Up And Cummers #01**. As of No-
vember 1993 has left the business.
Beach Babes From Beyond #1 / 1993 / BRI
/ S • Bikini Drive-In / 1995 / ... / S • A Blaze
Of Glory / 1993 / ME / M • Burgundy Blues
/ 1993 / MET / M • Cavegirl Island / 1993 /
TLE / S • Crazy With The Heat #2 / 1993 /
MET / M • Eleventh Annual AVN Awards /
1994 / VC / M • Heavenscent / 1993 / ZA /
M • If These Walls Could Talk (Director's
Cut) / 1993 / MET / M • If These Walls
Could Talk #1: Wicked Whispers / 1993 /
MET / M • If These Walls Could Talk #2:
Burning Secrets / 1993 / CV / M • The In-
terrogation / 1994 / HOM / B • Lollipop Lick-
ers / 1996 / V99 / C • The Magic Box / 1993
/ TP / M • Nothing To Hide #2 / 1993 / CV /
M • The Pamela Principle #2: Seduce Me /
1994 / IMP / S • Parlor Games / 1993 / VI /
M • The Serpent's Dream / 1993 / VC / M •
Sleepless / 1993 / VD / M • Steamy Win-
dows / 1993 / VI / M • Sticky Lips / 1993 /
EX / M • A Stroke At Midnight / 1993 / LBO
/ M • Tina And The Professor / 1995 / BRI /
S • Up And Cummers #01 / 1993 / 4P / M •
Up And Cummers #03 / 1993 / 4P / M • Vi-
sions Of Desire / 1994 / DR / M
ROXANNE BREWER
Big Bust Babes #01 / 1984 / AFI / M • Blue
Vanities #125 / 1990 / FFL / M • Female
Chauvinists / 1975 / ... / M
ROXANNE CODY NICHOLE *see Cody Nicole*
ROXANNE HALL *(Roxanne (Hall), Cindy Stevens)*
Brunette, passable face, lithe body, medium
tits, English, 18 years old in 1994 and de-
virginized at 13. In Fall 1995, she tested
positive for HIV but later a more complex
test showed negative. As of 1996 rumor has
it that she's married to John Decker.
Adult Affairs / 1994 / VC / M • The Anal Ad-
ventures Of Max Hardcore: Grand Prix /
1994 / ZA / M • Anal Bad Girls / 1994 / ROB
/ F • Anal Intruder #10 / 1995 / CC / M •
Anal Jeopardy / 1996 / ZA / M • Anal
Nurses / 1996 / LBO / M • Anal Princess #1
/ 1996 / VC / M • Anal Rippers #2: The Un-
veiling / 1996 / ZA / M • Backdoor Boogie /
1994 / TEG / M • Black Bottom Girls / 1994
/ ME / M • Blaze / 1996 / WAV / M • British
Cunts Are Cumming! / 1996 / SPL / M •
Buffy Malibu's Nasty Girls #11 / 1996 / ANA
/ F • Bunmasters / 1995 / VC / M • The Butt
Sisters Do Hawaii / 1995 / MID / M • The
Butt Sisters Do Houston / 1996 / MID / M •
The Butt Sisters Do Washington D.C. /
1995 / MID / M • Butthead Dreams: Big
Boating Bonanza / 1994 / FH / M •
Buttman's Bouncin' British Babes / 1994 /
EA / M • Buttman's Wet Dream / 1994 / EA
/ M • Casting Call #09 / 1995 / SO / M •
Casting Call #16 / 1995 / SO / M • Catwalk
#1 / 1995 / SC / M • Catwalk #2 / 1995 / SC
/ M • Chasey Loves Rocco / 1996 / VI / M •
Cheeks #8 / 1995 / CC / M • Cherry Pop-
pers #06: Pretty And Pink / 1994 / ZA / M •
Cum Buttered Corn Holes #3 / 1996 / NIT /
C • Cumback Pussy #1 / 1996 / EL / M •
Cumback Pussy #4: Get Some!!! / 1996 /
EL / M • Debbie Class Of '95 / 1995 / CC /
M • Deep Inside Juli Ashton / 1996 / VC / C

• Dirty Tails / 1996 / SC / M • Dream Lover / 1995 / SC / M • Dreams / 1995 / VC / M • Dresden Diary #16: / 1996 / BIZ / B • Erotic Visions / 1995 / ULI / M • Fazano's Student Bodies / 1995 / EL / M • Firm Offer / 1995 / SC / M • Flesh Palace / 1995 / LBO / M • Four Weddings And A Honeymoon / 1995 / PL / M • Frank Thring's Double Penetration #3 / 1996 / XPR / M • Fresh Faces #02 / 1994 / EVN / M • Full Moon Fever / 1994 / LBO / M • Gangland Bangers / 1995 / VC / M • Generation X / 1995 / WAV / M • Girls Of Sorority Row / 1994 / VT / M • Glory Days / 1996 / IN / M • Heidi's Girls / 1995 / GO / M • Hell Hole / 1996 / ZA / M • Hienie's Heroes / 1995 / VC / M • The Hitch-Hiker #07: Life In The Fast Lane / 1994 / WMG / M • Hollywood Lesbians / 1995 / ROB / F • Hot Diamond / 1995 / LE / M • Hot Tight Asses #09 / 1994 / TCK / M • Impact / 1995 / SC / M • The Initiation / 1995 / FD / M • The Inseminator #2: Domination Day / 1994 / LBO / M • Interview's Foreign Affair / 1996 / LV / M • Jenna Loves Rocco / 1996 / WAV / M • Jinx / 1996 / WP / M • Jordan Lee: Anal Queen / 1997 / SC / C • Kink Show / 1997 / BON / B • La Femme Vanessa / 1995 / SC / M • Lana Exposed / 1995 / VT / M • The Line Up / 1996 / CDI / M • Lingerie / 1995 / SC / M • The Many Faces Of P.J. Sparxx / 1996 / WP / M • The Mile High Club / 1995 / PL / M • Muff Divers #3 / 1996 / TV / F • Mutual Consent / 1995 / VC / M • Naked Ambition / 1995 / VC / M • Nasty Nymphos #06 / 1994 / ANA / M • Nasty Nymphos #12 / 1996 / ANA / M • The New Snatch Masters #16 / 1995 / LEI / C • No Man's Land #14 / 1996 / VT / F • Nookie Ranch / 1996 / NIT / M • Nurses Do It With Care / 1995 / EVN / M • Patriot X / 1995 / LE / M • Priceless / 1995 / WP / M • Pristine #1 / 1996 / CA / M • Public Access / 1995 / VC / M • Pure Smut / 1996 / GO / M • Pussy Hunt #07 / 1994 / LEI / M • Pussyclips #08 / 1995 / SNA / M • Pussywoman #3 / 1995 / CC / M • Rebel Cheerleaders / 1995 / VI / M • Red Door Diaries #2 / 1996 / ZA / M • The Reel World #4 / 1995 / FOR / M • Ring Of Desire / 1995 / LBO / M • Sapphire / 1995 / ERA / M • Scrue / 1995 / VI / M • Sensations #1 / 1996 / SC / M • Sex Alert / 1995 / PV / M • Sex Kitten / 1995 / SC / M • Shave Tails #2 / 1994 / SO / M • Shock / 1995 / LE / M • Simply Blue / 1995 / WAV / M • Snake Pit / 1996 / DWO / M • Snatch Masters #09 / 1995 / LEI / M • Sodomania #08: The London Sessions / 1994 / EL / M • Sodomania #21: Degenerate Lifestyles! / 1997 / EL / M • Sodomania...And Then Some!!! A Compendium / 1995 / EL / C • Starting Over / 1995 / WAV / M • Steamy Sins / 1996 / IN / M • Stretchin' The Rear / 1995 / PE / M • Takin' It To The Limit #9: Rear Action View / 1996 / BS / M • Tiffany Lords Straps One On #1 / 1994 / WIV / F • Tiffany Lords Straps One On #2 / 1994 / WIV / F • Topless Stewardesses / 1995 / PV / M • Triple X Video Magazine #04 / 1995 / OD / M • Up And Cummers #18 / 1995 / 4P / M • Venom #2 / 1996 / VD / M • Venom #4 / 1996 / VD / M • Video Virgins #16 / 1994 / NS / M • Virgin Dreams / 1996 / EA / M • White Wedding / 1995 / VI / M • Why Things Burn / 1994 / LBO / M • Young & Natural #21 /

1996 / TV / F

ROXANNE HOLLAND see Roxanne Rolland

ROXANNE KLINKERT see Star Index I

ROXANNE LOUIS
That Lady From Rio / 1976 / VXP / M

ROXANNE NEUFELD
Hungry Eyed Woman / cr71 / VCX / M

ROXANNE POTTS see Cody Nicole

ROXANNE REYNOLDS
White Hot / 1984 / VXP / M

ROXANNE ROLLAND *(Marguerite Nuit, Christina Howard, Roxanne Holland)*
Christina Howard is from **Perfect Weekend**. She is not Roxanne Potts in **Girls On Fire** (it's Cody Nicole). Gray blonde with small very droopy tits but a nice personality. The Marguerite Nuit is from **Breaking It #1** but this could be an eroneous reference.

All The Way / 1989 / LIM / C • Animal Impulse / 1985 / AA / M • Bad Girls #4 / 1984 / GO / M • Breaking It #1 / 1984 / COL / M • Country Girl / 1985 / AVC / M • Don't Tell Daddy #1 / 1985 / PL / C • Ginger's Hawaiian Scrapbook / 1988 / GO / C • Holly Does Hollywood #1 / 1985 / VEX / M • Hot Spa / 1984 / CA / M • The Ladies In Lace Party / 1985 / MAP / M • The Modelling Studio / 1984 / GO / M • Our Major Is Sex / 1984 / VD / M • Panty Raid / 1984 / GO / M • Party Girls / 1988 / MAP / M • Passions / 1985 / MIT / M • The Perfect Weekend / 1984 / AVC / M • The Pink Lagoon: A Sex Romp In Paradise / 1984 / GO / M • Private Love Affairs / 1985 / VCR / C • Raven / 1985 / VCR / M • Secrets / 1984 / HO / M • Spreading Joy / 1984 / IN / M • This Babe's For You / 1984 / TAR / M • Too Young To Know / 1984 / CC / M • The Ultimate Thrill / 1988 / PIN / C • Vote Pink / 1984 / VD / M

ROXANNE SIMMONS see Star Index I

ROXY
Used And Abused #2 / 1994 / SFP / M

ROXIE
Blue Vanities #114 / 1988 / FFL / M • Creme De La Face #14: Kiss My Cum / 1996 / OD / M

ROXIE HIGH
The Girls Of Fantasex #1 / 1996 / NIT / M

ROXXI RAYE
Emaciated short-haired blonde with a pretty face and large tattoos on both her right and left upper arms. Small tits. De-virginized at 17. Says her mother is also a nudie bar dancer—is this perhaps Ronni Raye?

The Best Of East Coast Sluts / 1995 / PL / C • Dirty Dancers #2 / 1994 / 4P / M • East Coast Sluts #02: Syracuse, NY / 1995 / PL / M • Love Doll Lucy #1 / 1994 / PL / F • Love Doll Lucy #2 / 1994 / PL / F • Muffs In Cuffs / 1995 / PL / B • Strap-On Sally #03: Thigh Harness Terror / 1994 / PL / F • Strap-On Sally #04: Double Penetration Dykes / 1994 / PL / F • Strap-On Sally #09: / 1996 / PL / F • Streets Of New York #05 / 1995 / PL / M • Striptease #1 / 1995 / PL / M • Striptease #2 / 1995 / PL / M

ROXY
100% Amateur #02: Back Door And More / 1995 / OD / M • Anal Vision #04 / 1992 / LBO / M • Beaver Hunt #02 / 1994 / LEI / M • Bra Busters #02 / 1993 / LBO / M • Bun Busters #16 / 1994 / LBO / M • The Cumm Brothers #03: Go To Traffic School / 1994 / OD / M • Double D Amateurs #17 / 1994 / JMP / M • First Time Lesbians #17 / 1994 /

JMP / F • First Time Lesbians #19 / 1994 / JMP / F • Hollywood Amateurs #03 / 1994 / MID / M • Kinky Ladies Of London / 1995 / VC / M • M Series #24 / 1994 / LBO / M • Neighborhood Watch #21 / 1992 / LBO / M • Roxy #103 / 1990 / RSP / F

ROXY (FRANCESCA) *(Francesca (Roxy))*
Here's a nuisance person. Sometimes she's credited as Roxy and other times as Francesca but according to her in **MDD #30** and **Video Virgins #11**, she's a confirmed dyke. She says she's 28 years old in 1994 and was de-virginized at 16—that is by a woman—she has never had sex with a male. She has medium tits, is a little pudgy, and isn't too pretty. According to Ed, she's Chinese/Columbian.

First Time Lesbians #16 / 1994 / JMP / F • Honey Drippers / 1992 / ROB / F • More Dirty Debutantes #30 / 1994 / 4P / M • Video Virgins #11 / 1994 / NS / M

ROXY BODAY
Love Chunks / 1996 / TTV / M • Piglitz: Pudgy Porkers / 1996 / GLI / M • Salsa & Spice #5 / 1997 / TTV / M

ROXY BOURDONNAY
Big Boob Bangeroo #6 / 1996 / TTV / M

ROXY FOX
Explore With Coralie / 1996 / C69 / M

ROXY HARD see Star Index I

ROXY HART
The Box / 1992 / EX / M • The End / 1992 / SC / M • Guess Who? / 1991 / EX / M • Nasty Jack's Kloset Klassics #03 / 1991 / CDI / M • Tight Squeeze / 1992 / SC / M • Wee Wee's Big Misadventure / 1991 / FH / M

ROXY RIDER
Anal Explosions #1 / 1996 / NIT / M • Carnival Of Flesh / 1996 / NIT / M • Cum Buttered Corn Holes #1 / 1996 / NIT / C • DPTV: Double Penetration Television / 1996 / SUF / M • East Coast Sluts #09: / 1995 / PL / M • Gazongas Galore #1 / 1996 / NIT / C • Jizz Glazed Goo Guzzlers #1 / 1996 / NIT / C • Leg Show #2 / 1996 / NIT / M • Mike Hott: #360 Cum In My Cunt #08 / 1995 / MHV / C • Mike Hott: #363 Lesbian Sluts #25 / 1996 / MHV / F • Mike Hott: #364 Cunt Of The Month: Roxy Rider / 1996 / MHV / M • Mike Hott: #379 Three-Sum Sluts #15 / 1996 / MHV / M • Mike Hott: #380 Girls Who Lap Cum From Cunts #03 / 1996 / MHV / C • OUTS: Roxy / 1996 / OUT / F • Pussyman Auditions #19 / 1996 / SNA / M • Roxy Rider Is In Control / 1996 / NIT / M • Roxy: A Gang Bang Fantasy / 1994 / FC / M • Vibrating Vixens #1 / 1996 / TV / F • Young & Natural #19 / 1996 / TV / F • Young & Natural #21 / 1996 / TV / F

ROXY STONE
Cross Cuntry Vacation / 1995 / CC / M

ROY
Anal Vision #22 / 1993 / LBO / M • S&M On The Ranch: Training The New Pony Girl / 1994 / VER / B

ROY BOY
Lick My Ink #7 / 1994 / TWP / M

ROY BRIDGE
Seymore Butts: My Travels With The Tramp / 1994 / FH / M

ROY BRIDGES
Buttwoman Back In Budapest / 1993 / EL / M • Drop Sex: Wipe The Floor / 1997 / JLP / M

ROY CARLTON see Star Index I

ROY HARWOOD
L.A. Tool & Die / 1979 / TMX / G
ROY PHIPPS *see Star Index I*
ROY QUEST
Raunch #01 / 1990 / CC / M
ROY RAMSING
Thundercrack! / 1974 / LUM / M
ROY SIMPSON *see Star Index I*
ROY STELLS *see John Seeman*
ROY STUART *see Star Index I*
ROY THE SHIPPER
Face To Face / 1995 / ME / M • Radical Affairs Video Magazine #07 / 1994 / ME / M
ROY WILSON
Swinging Ski Girls / 1981 / VCX / M
ROY WINTER *see Star Index I*
ROYAL SINCLAIR
Blue Vanities #222 / 1994 / FFL / M
ROZ GREENWOOD
Classic Films Of Irving Klaw / 1984 / LON / M
ROZANA KHAN
Kiss Me With Lust / cr75 / ... / M
ROZSA TASSI *see Rosa Caracciolo*
RUBBER MAN *see Star Index I*
RUBEN OMAR
Conflict Of Interest / 1994 / FST / G
RUBI GRENADINE
Deep Inside Dirty Debutantes #11 / 1996 / 4P / M
RUBI MEDEL
Young And Anal #6 / 1996 / JMP / M
RUBIO
Bi Bi Banjee Boyz / 1994 / PL / G
RUBY
Hot Body Competition: Hot Pants Contest / 1996 / CG / F • Micro X Video #1 / 1992 / VIP / M
RUBY (1996) *(Jennie (Ruby))*
Large girl with big enhanced tits, short red hair, marginal face and womanly body.
A List / 1996 / SO / M • Asses Galore #5: T.T. Vs The World / 1996 / DFI / M • Assy #2 / 1996 / JMP / M • Babe Watch Beach / 1996 / SC / M • Bend Over Babes #4 / 1996 / EA / M • Betrayed / 1996 / WP / M • Blue Saloon / 1996 / ME / M • Boobwatch #1 / 1996 / SC / M • Breeders / 1996 / MET / M • Buffy Malibu's Nasty Girls #11 / 1996 / ANA / F • Burlesxxx / 1996 / VT / M • Buttman In The Crack / 1996 / EA / M • The Clock Strikes Bizarre On Butt Row / 1996 / ABS / M • Decadence / 1996 / VC / M • Dirty Dancers #9 / 1996 / HO / M • Dirty Minds / 1996 / NIT / M • Diva #2: Deep In Glamour / 1996 / VC / F • Fresh Meat (John Leslie) #3 / 1996 / EA / M • Friendly Fire / 1996 / EDP / M • Gazongas Galore #1 / 1996 / NIT / C • Hollywood Spa / 1996 / WP / M • Hypnotic Hookers #1 / 1996 / NIT / M • Indecent Exposures / 1996 / MID / M • Lollipop Shoppe #2 / 1996 / SC / M • The Many Faces Of P.J. Sparxx / 1996 / WP / M • No Man's Land #15 / 1996 / VT / F • One Night In The Valley / 1996 / CA / M • Roller Babes / 1996 / ERA / M • Scotty's X-Rated Adventure / 1996 / WP / M • Sex For Hire / 1996 / ONA / M • Shane's World #2 / 1996 / OD / M • Shane's World #3 / 1996 / OD / M • She's No Angel / 1996 / ERA / S • Sin-A-Matic / 1996 / VI / M • Squirters / 1996 / ULI / M • This Girl Is Freaky / 1996 / NIT / M • The Time Machine / 1996 / WP / M • XXX Channel / 1996 / VT / M
RUBY (HISPANIC)
Latin Fever #2 / 1996 / C69 / M • Salsa &

Spice #4 / 1996 / TTV / M • Salsa & Spice #5 / 1997 / TTV / M
RUBY BEGONIA
Papa's Got A Brand New Jag / 1995 / GOT / M
RUBY BELNAP *see Rose Marie*
RUBY FOXX
Lady Luck / 1975 / VCX / M
RUBY JEAN BAKER
Against All Bods / 1988 / ZA / M • Bi-Surprise / 1988 / MET / G • Double Standards / 1988 / BIL / G • Easy Access / 1988 / ZA / M • Woman To Woman / 1989 / ZA / C
RUBY MILLS
Matinee Idol / 1984 / VC / M
RUBY RED
Black Masters: Seduction In Bondage / 1996 / GOT / B • Toe Tales #27 / 1995 / GOT / B
RUBY RICHARDS *see Star Chandler*
RUBY RUNHOUSE *see Star Index I*
RUBY SAPPHIRE *see Juliet Anderson*
RUBY SMART *see Bunny Bleu*
RUDOLPH ECKMANN *see Star Index I*
RUDOLPH KRONK *see Star Index I*
RUDOLPH REGAL *see Star Index I*
RUDY
Amateur Hours #09 / 1990 / AFI / M
RUDY GRAHAM *see Star Index I*
RUDY JOHNSON
One Last Score / 1978 / CDI / M
RUDY KAZ *see Star Index I*
RUDY RHODES *see Rugby Rhodes*
RUE WIL
All The Loving Couples / 1979 / KIT / M
RUFUS JOHNSON
Black Heat / 1986 / VCR / C
RUGBY RHODES *(Rudy Rhodes)*
Deep Inside Trading / 1986 / AR / M • Love Hammer / 1988 / VXP / M • Sex World Girls / 1987 / AR / M • Slumber Party Reunion / 1987 / AR / M • A Taste Of Ambrosia / 1987 / FEM / M • Techsex / 1988 / VXP / M
RUNE HALLBERG
Bel Ami / 1976 / VXP / M • The Second Coming Of Eva / 1974 / ALP / M • [Justine Och Juliette / 1975 / ... / S • [Molly / 1977 / ... / S
RUPERT
Anal Rippers #2: The Unveiling / 1996 / ZA / M
RUPPERT *see Star Index I*
RUSH ADAMS *see Star Index I*
RUSS
GRG: Pretty And Perverted / 1996 / GRG / M • Homegrown Video #374 / 1992 / HOV / M
RUSS BATTLE
N.Y. Video Magazine #07 / 1996 / OUP / M
RUSS CARLSON *(Warren Evans, Shaun Costello, William Morini)*
Normally a director.
Forced Entry / 1972 / ALP / M • Fury In Alice / 1976 / SVE / M • Girl Scout Cookies / 197? / SVE / M • Joe Rock Superstar / cr76 / ALP / M • Kathy's Graduation Present / 1975 / SVE / M • The Love Bus / 1974 / OSC / M • More Than Sisters / 1978 / VC / M • The Passions Of Carol / 1975 / VXP / M • Sin Of Lust / 1976 / SVE / M • Slave Of Pleasure / 1978 / BL / M • The Story Of Eloise / 1976 / SVE / M • Sweet Sixteen / 1974 / SVE / M • A Taste Of Bette / 1978 / VHL / M • Two Lives Of Jennifer / 1979 / VHL / M • Tycoon's Daughter / cr73 / SVE / M

RUSS MEYER *(Adolph A. Schwartz)*
Director who is obviously fascinated with big boobs. Born in 1922.
All The Way In / 1984 / VC / M • Amazon Women On The Moon / 1987 / MCA / S • Beneath The Valley Of The Ultra-Vixens / 1979 / RMV / S • Finders Keepers...Lovers Weepers! / 1968 / RMV / S • Heavenly Bodies / 1963 / ... / S • The Immoral Mr. Teas / 1958 / RMV / S • Motor Psycho / 1965 / RMV / S • Mudhoney / 1965 / RMV / S • Supervixens / 1975 / RMV / S • Up! / 1976 / RMV / S • Vixen / 1968 / RMV / S • Wild Gals Of The Naked West / 1961 / RMV / S
RUSS NICHOLSON *see Star Index I*
RUSSELL
Amateurs In Action #2 / 1994 / MET / M
RUSSELL BLUE *see Star Index I*
RUSSELL ELLISON
Bad Company / 1978 / CV / M
RUSSELL GRAY *see Star Index I*
RUSSELL MOORE
Immortal Desire / 1993 / VI / M
RUSSELL STOVER *see Star Index I*
RUSSELL TYNAN *see Star Index I*
RUSSIA *(Rasha Romana)*
Tall blonde with a pretty face, small slightly droopy tits, tight waist and an excellent boy-like butt.
American Blonde / 1993 / VI / M • Blind Spot / 1993 / VI / M • Endlessly / 1993 / VI / M • New Lovers / 1993 / VI / M • Oral Obsession #1 / 1994 / VI / M • Sex #1 (Vivid) / 1993 / VI / M • Silent Stranger / 1992 / VI / M
RUSTEE *see Rebecca Sloan*
RUSTI RHODES *see Rusty Rhodes*
RUSTIE RHODES *see Rusty Rhodes*
RUSTY
Blue Vanities #527 / 1993 / FFL / M • Blue Vanities #539 / 1993 / FFL / M • Blue Vanities #573 / 1996 / FFL / M • Mike Hott: #280 Horny Couples #18 / 1995 / MHV / M • R/H Productions #5002: An Interview For A Roommate / 1995 / R/H / M • Wrasslin She-Babes #04 / 1996 / SOW / M • Wrasslin She-Babes #13 / 1996 / SOW / M
RUSTY BAKER
Bi-Laddin / 1994 / BIN / G
RUSTY BOLT
Denni O' #3: Fanta-Sea Of Cum / 1996 / SP / M
RUSTY BONER *(Cal Martin)*
Older guy who looks and sounds like a used car salesman.
Back East Babes #1 / 1996 / NIT / M • Back East Babes #2 / 1996 / NIT / M • Back East Babes #3 / 1996 / NIT / M
RUSTY BUSTY *see Rusty Rhodes*
RUSTY RED
Mr. Peepers Amateur Home Videos #64: Proposition 69 / 1992 / LBO / M
RUSTY RHOADS *see Rusty Rhodes*
RUSTY RHODES *(Rustie Rhodes, Rusti Rhodes, Rusty Rhoads, Rusty Busty)*
Ugly fatso with droopy natural big boobs and red hair.
Amateur Lesbians #11: Rusty / 1991 / GO / F • Autobiography Of A Slave / 1993 / PL / B • The Back Doors (Western) / 1991 / WV / M • Bi Madness / 1991 / STA / G • The Bi Spy / 1991 / STA / G • The Bi-Analyst / 1991 / STA / G • Bi-Inferno / 1992 / VEX / G • Black Masters: Black Obsession / 1995 / GOT / B • Blow Out / 1991 / IF / M •

Bondage Memories #04 / 1994 / BON / C • The Bondage Producer / 1991 / BON / B • Breakfast With Tiffany / 1990 / HO / M • Breast Worx #06 / 1991 / LBO / M • Breast Worx #15 / 1992 / LBO / M • Breast Worx #17 / 1991 / LBO / M • Breasts And Beyond #2 / 1991 / ME / M • Chains Of Passion / 1993 / PL / B • Cheesecake / 1991 / VC / M • Dirty Dixie / 1992 / IF / M • Double The Pleasure / 1990 / SE / M • East L.A. Law / 1991 / WV / M • Enslaved / 1995 / GOT / B • Glitter Girls / 1992 / V99 / M • Hard Deck / 1991 / XPI / M • Harlem Honies #2: Nasty In New York / 1994 / CC / M • Hillary Vamp's Private Collection #11 / 1992 / HVD / M • Hillary Vamp's Private Collection #20 / 1992 / HOV / M • Hillary Vamp's Private Collection #24 / 1992 / HOV / M • Hurts So Good / 1991 / VEX / M • L.A. Rear / 1992 / FD / M • Lay Lady Lay / 1991 / VEX / M • Long Dan Silver / 1992 / IF / M • Master's Frenzy / 1994 / GOT / B • Motel Hell / 1992 / PL / M • Mr. Fun's Mondo Adventure / 1993 / VC / M • Naked Bun 2 1/2 / 1991 / WV / M • Night Breed / 1992 / CDI / G • Night Deposit / 1991 / VC / M • Nina Hartley: Wild Thing / 1991 / CIN / M • Odyssey 30 Min: #161: Hush, Hush, Sweet Charlotte / 1991 / OD / M • Party Dolls / 1992 / VEX / M • Playthings / 1995 / GOT / B • Red Hot Honeys / 1994 / IF / M • Savage Delights / 1995 / OUP / B • Screwed On The Job / 1991 / XPI / M • Shades Of Bondage / 1991 / BON / B • Some Like It Big / 1991 / LE / M • Streets Of New York #03 / 1994 / PL / M • SVE: Raunchy Rustie & Ready Roxanne / 1992 / SVE / M • Titty-Titty Bang-Bang / 1992 / FC / C • Toe Tales #13 / 1994 / GOT / B • Toe Tales #17 / 1994 / GOT / B • Toe Tales #18 / 1994 / GOT / B • Toe Tales #22 / 1995 / GOT / B • A Trip Down Mammary Lane / 1991 / FC / M • Twin Peaks / 1993 / PL / M • Unveil My Love / 1991 / HO / M • Venus Of The Nile / 1991 / WV / M • Vice Versa / 1992 / FD / M • Viviana's Dude Ranch / 1992 / IF / M • The Wild Wild Chest #3 / 1996 / HO / C • The Wright Stuff / 1991 / AFV / M • The X-Producers / 1991 / XPI / M

RUSTY SHELDON
A Formal Faucett / 1978 / VC / M • Lust Inferno / 1982 / CA / M • Saturday Matinee Series #1 / 1996 / VCX / C

RUSTY THOMAS
Bi-Surprise / 1988 / MET / G • Haulin' 'n' Ballin' / 1988 / MET / G

RUSTY WATERS
A&B AB#541: Sexy Rusty Waters / 1995 / A&B / F • A&B AB#556: Rusty Waters Is Back / 1995 / A&B / M

RUSTY ZIPPER see Star Index I

RUTE MORGAN see Star Index I

RUTH
Blue Vanities #540 / 1994 / FFL / M • Blue Vanities #546 / 1994 / FFL / M • Wrasslin She-Babes #01 / 1995 / SOW / M

RUTH ANN LOTT
Sacrilege / 1971 / AXV / M

RUTH BANKS
Bucky Beaver's XXX Dragon Art Theatre Double Feature #01 / 1996 / SOW / M • Hitler's Harlots / cr73 / SOW / M

RUTH BLANK
Flesh Factory / 1970 / AVC / M

RUTH JOHNSON
Corsetry 101 / 1996 / ESF / B

RUTH JONES
Lesbian Orgy / 1980 / WID / F

RUTH KUELLENBERG
[Junge Madchen Mogen's HeiB, Hausfrauen Noch HeiBer / 1973 / ... / M • [Schulmadchen-Report 4: Was Eltern Oft Verzweifeln LaBt / 1972 / ... / M

RUTH MORRELL
Body Talk / 1982 / VCX / M

RUTH RAYMOND see Georgina Spelvin

RUTH ROSE
All The Loving Couples / 1979 / KIT / M

RUTH SIMS
Quick Turnover / 19?? / VXP / M • Redliners / 1980 / VXP / M

RUTH VERMOUTH
Teenage Beauties / cr73 / SEP / M

RYAN
HomeGrown Video #446: Slam Bam Thank You Ma'am! / 1995 / HOV / M

RYAN BLOCK
Bi Watch / 1994 / BIN / G • Bi-Laddin / 1994 / BIN / G • Bi-Sex Pleasures / 1993 / PL / G • The Crying Flame / 1993 / HSV / G • End Of Innocence / 1994 / WIV / M • Guess What? / 1994 / FPI / G • Night Walk / 1995 / HIV / G • She Male Service / 1994 / HEA / G • Switch Hitters #8 / 1995 / IN / G • Switch Hitters #9 / 1995 / IN / G • Trans America / 1993 / TSS / G

RYAN HELM
The Goodbye Girls / 1979 / CDI / M • One Last Score / 1978 / CDI / M

RYAN IDOL see Star Index I

RYAN KNIGHT see Star Index I

RYAN THOMAS
Naughty Ninja Girls / 1987 / LA / M

RYAN WAGNER
Like Father Like Son / 1996 / AWV / G

S. BUTTERWORTH
The Convict / 1995 / TAO / B

S. BUTZ see Star Index I

S. SCOTT
The Family Jewels / cr76 / GO / M

SABATHA
Slam Dunk / 1993 / NAP / B • Tina On Top / 1993 / NAP / B

SABATIER
Chateau Duval / 1996 / HDE / M

SABELLA see Star Index I

SABER (Sabre)
First movie was **Joined**. Not in **Class Act**. Breasts enhanced, had a baby, and put on lots of weight.
Big Boob Tease / 1993 / NAP / F • Big Busted Lesbians At Play / 1991 / BIZ / F • Breast Worx #26 / 1992 / LBO / M • Crossing Over / 1990 / IN / M • Good Vibrations #2: A Couples Guide To Vibrator Use / 1991 / VT / M • House Of Dreams / 1990 / CA / M • Joined: The Siamese Twins / 1989 / PL / M • Lace / 1989 / VT / F • Leather / 1989 / VT / F • Leather And Lace / 1989 / VT / F • Lesbian Lingerie Fantasy #6 / 1991 / ESP / F • More Dirty Debutantes / 1990 / PRI / M • More Dirty Debutantes #18 / 1992 / 4P / M • Nasty Calendar / 1991 / XPI / M • A New Girlfriend / 1991 / XPI / M • Ravaged / 1990 / CIN / M • Sabre's Last Stand / 1993 / NAP / B • Secrets / 1990 / CA / M • Separated / 1989 / INH / M • Single Girl Masturbation #6 / 1991 / ESP / F • The Smart Ass Vacation / 1990 / VT / M • Steal Breeze / 1990 / SO / M • Val Girls / 1990 / PL / F

SABINA

The Bad News Brat / 1991 / VI / M • Bus Stop Tales #05 / 1989 / PRI / M • Bus Stop Tales #08 / 1990 / PRI / M • Bus Stop Tales #09 / 1990 / PRI / M • Bus Stop Tales #11 / 1990 / 4P / M • Buttman's Bubble Butt Babes / 1996 / EA / M • Buttman's European Vacation #3 / 1995 / EA / M • Buttman's Orgies / 1996 / EA / M • Prague By Night #1 / 1996 / EA / M

SABINA (KYLIE CH.) see Kylie Channel

SABINA GENIE see Star Index I

SABINE
S&M On The Ranch: Training The New Pony Girl / 1994 / VER / B

SABINE JISSEN
Viola Video #101: Anal #7 / 1995 / PEV / M

SABINE SAUER
Viola Video #105: / 1995 / PEV / M • Viola Video #107: Private Party / 1995 / PEV / M

SABINE STACK
Viola Video #102: Anal #8 / 1995 / PEV / M

SABLE
Bootin' Up / 1995 / VT / B • Mistress 'n Da Hood / 1995 / VT / B • N.Y. Video Magazine #05 / 1995 / OUP / M • Sable Is Sorry / 1996 / GAL / B • Sistaz In Chains / 1995 / VT / B • The Taming Of Sable / 1995 / OUP / B

SABLE CRUISE
ABA: Double Feature #4 / 1996 / ALP / M • Daughters Of Discipline #2 / 1983 / AVO / B • Mature Women #02 / 1991 / BTO / M • Painmania / 1983 / AVO / B • Sexy Ties & Videotape / 1992 / STM / B • Stern Auditor / 1992 / STM / B

SABLE FUCHS
Hard Core Beginners #02 / 1995 / LEI / M • Naked Lunch / 1995 / LEI / M • Whoopin' Her Rind / 1995 / VT / B

SABOU
Skin #4: The 4th Rite / 1995 / ERQ / M

SABRE see Saber

SABRINA
Against All Bods / 1991 / VEX / M • Bend Over Brazilian Babes #2 / 1993 / EA / M • The Best Of Fabulous Flashers / 1996 / DGD / F • Bikini Watch / 1996 / PHV / F • Black Analyst #2 / 1995 / VEX / M • Blondes Like It Hot / 1984 / ELH / M • Breast Worx #28 / 1992 / LBO / M • Captive Sessions / 1994 / GOT / B • Chocolate & Vanilla Twist / 1992 / PL / F • Crazy On You / 1991 / IF / M • Decadent Delights / 1992 / IF / M • Desires Within Young Girls / 1977 / CA / M • Domina #2: Every Inch A Lady / 1996 / LBO / G • Eurotica #13 / 1996 / XC / M • Far East Fantasy / 1995 / SUF / M • Filthy First Timers #5 / 1997 / EL / M • Glitter Girls / 1992 / V99 / M • Hard Soap, Hard Soap / 1977 / EVI / M • Heartbreaker / 1991 / IF / M • Hot Licks / 1990 / CDI / M • Ice House / 1969 / SOW / S • In The Jeans / 1990 / ME / M • Interracial Sex / 1987 / M&M / M • Jane Bond Meets Thunderthighs / 1988 / VD / M • The Joys Of Masturbation / 1988 / M&M / M • Kinky College Cunts #03 / 1993 / NS / F • Lesbian Pros And Amateurs #25 / 1993 / GO / F • Lickety Pink / 1990 / ME / M • Lovin' Spoonfuls #6 / 1996 / 4P / C • More Dirty Debutantes #23 / 1993 / 4P / M • Neighbor Girls T24 / 1990 / NEI / F • New Faces, Hot Bodies #02 / 1992 / STP / M • Northwest Pecker Trek #6: Two Girls For Every Boy / 1995 / LBO / M • Peepers / 1988 / CV / M • Physically Fit / 1991 / V99 / C • Pussy

Fest Of The Northwest #3 / 1995 / NIT / M • Pussy Hunt #15 / 1995 / LEI / M • Reel Life Video #30: Welcome To The Bi World! / 1996 / RLF / F • Secrets Behind The Green Door / 1987 / SE / M • Sherlock Homie / 1995 / IN / M • Sorority Slumber Sluts / 1995 / WIV / F • Spanish Rose / 1991 / VEX / M • Stroke Of Nine / 1994 / GOT / B • Teacher's Pet #4 / 1995 / APP / M • Texas Towers / 1993 / IF / M • Thief Of Passion / 1996 / P69 / M • Tickling Scenes / 1991 / TAO / C • Toe Tales #09 / 1993 / GOT / B • Toe Tales #18 / 1994 / GOT / B • Twin Peaks / 1993 / PL / M • Web Of Darkness / 1993 / BS / B

SABRINA (BRAZIL)
Asses Galore #5: T.T. Vs The World / 1996 / DFI / M

SABRINA (DAWN) see Sabrina Dawn
SABRINA (GELATA) see Sabrina Gelata
SABRINA (H. LEE) see Heather Lee
SABRINA ASET
Club Head (EVN) #2 / 1989 / EVN / C • Our Bang #01 / 1992 / GLI / M • Our Bang #02 / 1992 / GLI / M • Our Bang #04 / 1992 / GLI / M • Our Bang #06 / 1992 / GLI / M • Over 50 / 1994 / GLI / M • Positively Pagan #01 / 1991 / ATA / M • Positively Pagan #03 / 1991 / ATA / M • Positively Pagan #04 / 1991 / ATA / M • Positively Pagan #06 / 1993 / ATA / M • Positively Pagan #08 / 1993 / ATA / M • When Love Came To Town / 1989 / EVN / M

SABRINA BLISS *(Vanya)*
Blonde (really white hair) with large frame and large natural tits. Not too pretty but some people think she looks like Bridgette Neilson. 24 years old in 1993, 5'7" tall, 38DD-26-36.
America's Raunchiest Home Videos #58: / 1993 / ZA / M • America's Raunchiest Home Videos #60: / 1993 / ZA / M • American Swinger Video Magazine #06 / 1993 / ZA / M • American Swinger Video Magazine #07 / 1993 / ZA / M • Another Secret / 1990 / SO / M • Anything You Ever Wanted To Know About Sex / 1993 / VEX / M • Buffy Malibu's Totally Nasty All-Girl Home Videos #05 / 1993 / ANA / F • Caught From Behind #12 / 1989 / HO / M • Double D Amateurs #08 / 1993 / JMP / M • First Time Lesbians #06 / 1993 / JMP / F • Forbidden Erotika / 1994 / GLI / M • GRG: Fighting Mad Hussies / 1994 / GRG / F • Hard-On Copy / 1994 / WV / M • Love Letters #2 / 1993 / SC / M • Margarita On The Rocks / 1994 / SFP / M • Mike Hott: #241 Cunt of the Month: Sabrina Bliss / 1993 / MHV / M • Mike Hott: #248 Fuck The Boss #03 / 1993 / MHV / M • Mike Hott: #285 Fuck The Boss #05 / 1995 / MHV / M • Mike Hott: #299 Jordan Hart & Friends #2 / 1995 / MHV / M • Mike Hott: #330 Three-Sum Sluts #08 / 1995 / MHV / M • Mike Hott: Cum Cocktails #3 / 1995 / MHV / C • Ron Hightower's White Chicks #01 / 1993 / LBO / M • Seymore Butts Goes Nuts / 1994 / FH / M • Supermodel #1 / 1994 / VI / M • Titillating Temptresses / 1993 / VER / F • Witchcraft 2000 / 1994 / GLI / M

SABRINA DAWN *(Sabrina (Dawn), Sabrina Scott (Dawn))*
Comes from CO and used to be a professional dancer. First movie was **Westside Tori**. Pretty but too big with large tits and a slightly too big butt; blonde hair; looks like

a showgirl.
19 And Nasty / 1990 / ME / M • All The Right Motions / 1990 / DR / M • Barflies / 1990 / ZA / M • Beauty And The Beast #2 / 1990 / VC / M • Behind Blue Eyes #3 / 1989 / ME / M • Behind You All The Way #1 / 1990 / SO / M • Bend Over Babes #1 / 1990 / EA / M • Best Of Buttman #1 / 1991 / EA / C • Best Of Foot Worship #3 / 1992 / BIZ / C • Bi-Swingers / 1991 / PL / G • Body Heat / 1990 / CDI / M • The Book / 1990 / IF / M • Bush League #1 / 1990 / CC / M • Butt's Motel #4 / 1989 / EX / M • Candy Stripers #4 / 1990 / AR / M • The Danger Zone / 1990 / SO / M • Deep Inside Victoria Paris / 1993 / VC / C • Double Jeopardy / 1990 / HO / M • Dr F #2: Bad Medicine / 1990 / WV / M • Earthquake Girls / 1990 / CC / M • Falcon Head / 1990 / ARG / M • First Impressions / 1989 / ... / C • Girls In The Night / 1990 / LE / M • Grand Slam / 1990 / PRE / B • Grandma Does Dallas / 1990 / FC / M • Hollywood Assets / 1990 / FH / M • Hollywood Bikini Party Girls / 1989 / VC / M • Hollywood Knights #3 / 1991 / PCP / M • Hot Cherries / 1990 / CC / F • Hot Scalding / 1989 / VC / M • In Pursuit Of Passion / 1990 / V99 / M • Juice Box / 1990 / AFV / M • Juicy Lucy / 1990 / VC / M • Kinky Couples / 1990 / VD / M • Kittens #1 / 1990 / CC / F • Legend #1 / 1990 / LE / M • The Legend Of Sleepy Hollow / 1989 / LE / M • Live Bi-Me / 1990 / PL / G • Love Shack / 1990 / CC / M • Miss Directed / 1990 / VI / M • Monday Nite Ball / 1990 / VT / M • Moondance / 1991 / WV / M • My Friend, My Lover / 1990 / FIR / M • Nasty Jack's Homemade Vid. #04 / 1990 / CDI / M • Never Enough / 1990 / PP / M • The New Barbarians #1 / 1990 / VC / M • The New Barbarians #2 / 1990 / VC / M • No Strings Attached / 1990 / ERO / M • Oral Majority #08 / 1990 / WV / C • Parting Shots / 1990 / VD / M • Passion Prescription / 1990 / V99 / M • Passionate Lips / 1990 / OD / M • The Pawnbroker / 1990 / IF / M • Prisoner Of Lust / 1991 / VC / F • Ready, Willing & Anal (Vidco) / 1993 / VD / C • Ringside Knockout / 1990 / DR / M • Sam's Fantasy / 1990 / CIN / M • The Scarlet Mistress / 1990 / VI / M • Sea Of Desire / 1990 / AR / M • The Search For Pink October / 1990 / EX / M • Sex Lives On Porno Tape / 1992 / VC / C • The Smart Aleck / 1990 / PM / M • Soft And Wild / 1991 / LV / M • Some Like It Hot / 1989 / CDI / M • Surf City Sex / 1991 / CIA / M • Swedish Erotica Featurettes #4 / 1990 / CA / M • Things Mommy Taught Me / 1990 / KNI / M • Tight Tushies #1 / 1994 / SFP / M • Trick Tracey #1 / 1990 / CC / M • War Of The Tulips / 1990 / IN / M • Westside Tori / 1989 / ERO / M • Wet 'n' Working / 1990 / EA / F • The Wrong Woman / 1990 / LE / M • [Blondes Like It Hot / 1990 / ... / M

SABRINA GELATA *(Sabrina (Gelata), Sabrina Maldano, Sabrina Malnero, Sabrina Heaven)*
Hispanic girl (she says half-Spanish, half-Italian) with reddish dark blonde hair and gray/blue eyes, medium tits, tight waist, good skin and good tan lines. Was 18 years old in 1994. Born Feb 20, 1975 in Cancun Mexico. As of the end of 1994 she got pregnant, popped, had her tits enhanced to large cantaloupe size and put on weight ruining a

nice little body.
100% Amateur #27: / 1996 / OD / M • The Anal Adventures Of Suzy Super Slut #1 / 1994 / AFV / M • Anal Al's Adventures / 1995 / PL / M • Anal Camera #10 / 1995 / EVN / M • Anal Fireball / 1996 / ROB / M • Anal Honeypie / 1996 / ROB / M • Anal Injury / 1994 / ZA / M • Anal Torture / 1994 / ZA / M • Anal Virgins Of America #10 / 1994 / FOR / M • Anal Vision #28 / 1994 / LBO / M • Analtown USA #01 / 1995 / NIT / M • Another Fuckin' Anal Movie / 1996 / ROB / M • Backdoor Smugglers / 1994 / JAV / M • Ben Dover & Barbie / 1995 / SUF / M • Black Hose Bag / 1996 / ROB / M • Butt Hunt #11 / 1995 / LEI / M • Butt Pumpers / 1995 / FH / M • Buttman In The Crack / 1996 / EA / M • Byron Long At Large / 1995 / VC / M • Casting Call #06 / 1994 / SO / M • Catching Snapper / 1995 / XCI / M • Cheating Hearts / 1994 / AFI / M • Cherry Poppers #05: Playtime / 1994 / ZA / M • Cherry Poppers #06: Pretty And Pink / 1994 / ZA / M • Cherry Poppers #11: California Co-Eds / 1995 / ZA / M • Chocolate Bunnies #04 / 1995 / LBO / C • Cry Babies #1: Anal Scream / 1995 / ZA / M • Cum Buttered Corn Holes #2 / 1996 / NIT / C • The Cumm Brothers #04: Laid Off & Laid / 1994 / OD / M • Decadent Dreams / 1996 / ME / M • Dick & Jane's Video Mail: From Virginville (#4) / 1996 / AVI / M • Dirty Doc's Housecalls #19 / 1994 / LV / M • Double D Dykes #14 / 1994 / GO / F • Explicit / 1995 / MET / M • Fashion Sluts #1 / 1995 / ABS / M • Gang Bang Butthole Surfin' / 1996 / ROB / M • Ganggstas Paradise / 1995 / AVI / M • Green Piece Of Ass #3 / 1994 / RTP / M • Hard Headed / 1994 / LE / M • Hardcore Schoolgirls #2: Perverted Playmates / 1995 / XPR / M • Hidden Camera #16 / 1994 / JMP / M • High Heeled & Horny #4 / 1995 / LBO / M • The Hitch-Hiker #05: Traffic Jam / 1994 / WMG / M • The Hitch-Hiker #07: Life In The Fast Lane / 1994 / WMG / M • Hollywood Amateurs #10 / 1994 / MID / M • Hot In The Saddle / 1994 / ERA / M • Indiscreet! Video Magazine #2 / 1995 / FH / M • International Affairs / 1994 / PL / M • Junkyard Anal / 1994 / JAV / M • Kinky Debutante Interviews #06 / 1994 / IP / M • Kinky Debutante Interviews #08 / 1995 / IP / M • The Kiss / 1995 / WP / M • Knocked-Up Nymphos #1 / 1996 / GLI / M • Lady Sterling Takes It Up The Arse / 1997 / ROB / M • A Little Bit Pregnant / 1995 / SO / M • Love Bunnies #09 / 1994 / FPI / F • Lovin' Spoonfuls #3 / 1995 / 4P / C • Lust What The Doctor Ordered / 1994 / WIV / M • M Series #19 / 1994 / LBO / M • M Series #27 / 1994 / LBO / M • Malibu Ass Blasters / 1996 / ROB / M • Max #01 / 1994 / FWE / M • Max Gold #1 / 1996 / XPR / C • The Meatman / 1995 / OUP / M • Mechanics Bi Day, Lube Job Bi Night / 1995 / SP0 / G • Mickey Ray's Sex Search #02: Tight Spots / 1994 / WIV / M • Mike Hott: #331 Lesbian Sluts #21 / 1996 / MHV / F • More Black Dirty Debutantes #3 / 1994 / 4P / M • More Dirty Debutantes #35 / 1994 / 4P / M • More Than A Whore / 1995 / OD / M • Mother Nature's Bulging Bellies / 1995 / LIP / F • Nasty Newcummers #12 / 1995 / MET / M • Nasty Newcummers #13 / 1995 / MET / M • Nasty Nymphos #04 / 1994 / ANA / M • Naughty Senorita / 1994 / WIV /

M • New Ends #06 / 1994 / 4P / M • The New Snatch Masters #14 / 1995 / LEI / C • Nightlife / 1997 / CA / M • Numba 1 Ass Fucka / 1996 / ROB / M • Odyssey Triple Play #98: Three Ways To Sunday / 1995 / OD / M • Orgies Orgies Orgies / 1994 / WV / M • Over Exposed / 1996 / ULP / M • Private Video Magazine #13 / 1994 / OD / M • Pussy Hunt #10 / 1995 / LEI / M • Ready To Drop #05 / 1995 / FC / M • Ready To Drop #06 / 1995 / FC / M • Ready To Drop #07 / 1995 / FC / M • Right To Life #2 / 1996 / AOC / M • Romance & Fantasy / 1995 / VEX / M • Sabrina Starlet / 1994 / SC / M • Sabrina The Booty Queen / 1997 / ROB / M • Salsa & Spice #1 / 1995 / TTV / M • The Seduction Of Sabrina / 1996 / AVD / M • Sexperiment / 1996 / ULP / M • Seymore Butts: My Travels With The Tramp / 1994 / FH / M • Sleaze Please!—August Edition / 1994 / FH / M • So Bad / 1995 / VT / M • Swinging Couples #03 / 1994 / GO / M • Tight Fit #03 / 1994 / GO / M • Tight Fit #06 / 1994 / GO / M • Tight Fit #07 / 1994 / GO / M • Tight Shots #2 / 1994 / VI / M • Triple Penetration Debutante Sluts #1 / 1996 / BAC / M • Video Virgins #12 / 1994 / NS / M • Whitey's On The Moon / 1996 / ROB / M • Wild Orgies #06 / 1994 / AFI / M

SABRINA GONZALEZ *see Star Index I*

SABRINA HEAVEN *see* **Sabrina Gelata**

SABRINA JOHNSON

Amsterdam Nights #1 / 1996 / BLC / M • Amsterdam Nights #2 / 1996 / VC / M • Buffy Malibu's Nasty Girls #11 / 1996 / ANA / F • Cumback Pussy #1 / 1996 / EL / M • Gangbang Girl #18 / 1996 / ANA / M • Helen Does Holland / 1996 / VC / M • Nasty Nymphos #14 / 1996 / ANA / M • World Sex Tour #7 / 1996 / ANA / M

SABRINA JURGENS

Both Ends Burning / 1987 / VC / M • Butt's Motel #3 / 1989 / EX / M • Casing The Crack / 1987 / V99 / M • A Girl Named Sam / 1988 / CC / M • The Red Hot Roadrunner / 1987 / VD / M • Tracey And The Bandit / 1987 / LA / M • Wild At Heart / 1990 / CDI / M

SABRINA K.

Up And Cummers #38 / 1996 / RWP / M

SABRINA LONDON

Night Stalker / 1995 / BBE / M

SABRINA MALDANO *see* **Sabrina Gelata**

SABRINA MALNERO *see* **Sabrina Gelata**

SABRINA RAE

Captive In Sumanka / 1996 / LON / B • Video Dominatrix / 1996 / LON / B

SABRINA SAVAGE *see Star Index I*

SABRINA SCOTT

Behind Blue Eyes #1 / 1986 / ME / M • Pajama Party X #2 / 1994 / VC / M

SABRINA SCOTT (DAWN) *see* **Sabrina Dawn**

SABRINA SNOW

Mistress Of The Whip / 1996 / GOT / C

SABRINA STONE

Anal Angels #3 / 1995 / VEX / C • Anal Health Club Babes / 1995 / EVN / M • Anal Maidens Three / 1996 / BOT / M • Butt Hunt #06 / 1995 / LEI / M • Foot Masters / 1995 / PRE / B • Fresh Faces #04 / 1995 / EVN / M • Hard Core Beginners #01 / 1995 / LEI / M • Hit Ladies / 1995 / PRE / B • Hollywood Amateurs #13 / 1994 / MID / M •

Home Runs / 1995 / PRE / C • Journal Of O #2 / 1994 / ONA / B • Snatch Masters #02 / 1994 / LEI / M • Snatch Masters #04 / 1995 / LEI / M • Swat Team / 1995 / PRE / B • The Violation Of Kia / 1995 / JMP / F • The Voyeur #4 / 1995 / EA / M • Wet And Wild #2 / 1995 / VEX / M

SABRINA VALE

Corruption / 1983 / VC / M • Getting Ahead / 1983 / PL / M

SABRINA WALKER *see Star Index I*

SABURO MORI

Snow Country / 1984 / ORC / M

SACHICA HIDE *see Star Index I*

SACHICA KIJOI *see Star Index I*

SACHIKO KOYAMA

Sex For Money / 1985 / ORC / M

SADE *(Elissa Vanderbilt, Aleisha Lashley, Mellissa Sade, Ebony Parks, Alisha Lashley, Alisha (Sade), Alicia Lashley, Elise Vanderbilt)*

Battle Of The Titans / 1986 / AVC / M • Black Angel / 1987 / CC / M • The Black Chill / 1986 / WET / M • Black Heat / 1986 / VC / M • Black Mystique #04 / 1994 / VT / F • Blowing The Whistle / 1986 / VIP / M • Caught By Surprise / 1987 / CDI / M • Changing Partners / 1989 / FAZ / M • Cheeks #1 / 1988 / CC / M • The Chocolate Fudge Factory / 1987 / PIN / M • Creatures Of The Night / 1987 / FAN / M • Depraved / 1990 / IN / M • Fast Girls #1 / 1987 / GBX / M • Future Lust / 1989 / ME / M • I Am Curious Black / 1986 / WET / M • Lust Letters / 1988 / CA / M • The Maltese Phallus / 1990 / V99 / M • Merry X Miss / 1986 / VIP / M • The Out Of Towner / 1987 / CDI / M • The Red Hot Roadrunner / 1987 / VD / M • Sugarpussy Jeans / 1986 / TEM / M • Sweet Chocolate / 1987 / VD / M • Wanda Whips The Dragon Lady / 1990 / V99 / M

SADIE

Blue Vanities #578 / 1995 / FFL / M • Ona Zee's Date With Dallas / 1992 / ONA / M • Orgy Of Cruelty / 1995 / BON / B

SADIE LYNN

Eat At Daves #4: Condo Cummers / 1995 / SP / M

SADIE MAE *see Star Index I*

SADIE SWEETHEART

Delivered For Discipline / 1995 / BON / B • Mr. Parvo's Neighborhood / 1995 / BON / B

SADIE THOMPSON

Toys, Not Boys #1 / 1991 / FC / C

SADISTIC SIDNEY

Julie: A First Time Submissive In A Dungeon / 1996 / DHP / B

SAFINA

Intimate Interviews #2 / 1996 / NIT / M

SAGE

Creme De La Face #12: Pretty Faces To Cum On / 1995 / OD / M • Sweet Black Cherries #5 / 1996 / TTV / M

SAGE HUGHES

Anal Reunion / 1996 / EVN / M • Fresh Faces #10 / 1996 / EVN / M • Hollywood Amateurs #29 / 1996 / MID / M • Mike Hott: #367 Girls Who Lap Cum From Cunts #02 / 1996 / MHV / M • Mike Hott: #369 Cum In My Mouth #05 / 1996 / MHV / C • Mike Hott: #379 Three-Sum Sluts #15 / 1996 / MHV / M • Nothing Like Nurse Nookie #2 / 1996 / NIT / M • The Sodomizer #1 / 1995 / SC / M

SAGE WINTERS

A Foot Story / 1996 / OUP / B • Over The

Knee / 1996 / OUP / B

SAHARA

Adorable black girl with small tits and quite a pretty face.Supposedly born and raised in Paris, France.

Bachelorette Party / 1984 / JVV / M • Back To Back #1 / 1987 / 4P / C • Back To Class #1 / 1984 / DR / M • Beaverly Hills Cop / 1985 / SE / M • The Best Of Black White & Pink Inside / 1996 / CV / C • Black Baby Dolls / 1985 / TAG / M • Black Beauties / 1987 / SE / C • Black Bunbusters / 1985 / VC / M • Black Dynasty / 1985 / VD / M • Black Girls Do It Better / 1986 / CV / M • Black Jailbait / 1984 / PL / M • Black On White / 1987 / PL / C • Black Reamers / 1986 / 4P / M • Black Satin Nights / 1988 / DR / C • Black Taboo #1 / 1984 / JVV / M • Black Throat / 1985 / CV / C • Black To Africa / 1987 / PL / C • Blonde On Black / 1986 / CC / F • Brown Sugar / 1984 / VC / M • California Reaming / 1985 / WV / M • Chocolate Cherries #1 / 1984 / LA / M • Chocolate Delights #1 / 1985 / TAG / C • Chocolate Delights #2 / 1985 / TAG / C • Cocktales / 1985 / AT / M • The Color Black / 1986 / WET / M • Cotton Candy / 1987 / CV / C • Dark Brothers, Dark Sisters / 1986 / VCS / C • The Doctor's In / 1986 / CDI / M • Doin' The Harlem Shuffle / 1986 / CA / M • Double Penetration #2 / 1986 / WV / C • Dream Girls / 1986 / VC / M • Ebony Dreams / 1988 / PIN / C • Ebony Ecstacy / 1988 / HIO / C • Ebony Orgies / 1987 / SE / C • Ebony Superstars / 1988 / VC / C • Ex-Connection / 1986 / SEV / M • Firefoxes / 1985 / PLY / M • Foxy Brown / 1984 / VC / M • The Girls Of The A Team #1 / 1985 / WV / M • Girls Of The Night / 1985 / CA / M • Harlequin Affair / 1985 / CIX / M • Honeybuns #1 / 1987 / WV / C • Honeybuns #2: Grecian Formula / 1987 / WV / C • Hot And Nasty! / 1986 / V99 / C • Hot Chocolate #2 / 1986 / PLY / M • Hotter Chocolate / 1986 / AVC / M • In And Out (In Beverly Hills) / 1986 / WV / M • In And Out Of Africa / 1986 / EVN / M • Let Me Tell Ya 'Bout Black Chicks / 1985 / VC / M • Loving Spoonfulls / 1987 / 4P / C • More Chocolate Candy / 1986 / VD / M • Orgies / 1987 / WV / C • Pipe Dreams / 1985 / 4P / M • Pleasure Productions #12 / 1985 / VCR / M • The Plumber Cometh / 1985 / 4P / M • Salt & Pepper / 1986 / VCS / C • Sex 5th Avenue / 1985 / WV / M • Sex In The Great Outdoors / 1987 / SE / C • Sister Dearest / 1984 / DR / M • Soul Kiss This / 1988 / VCR / C • Strange Bedfellows / 1985 / PL / M • Swedish Erotica #71 / 1986 / CA / M • Swedish Erotica #72 / 1986 / CA / M • Tailenders / 1985 / WET / M • A Taste Of Sahara / 1990 / PIN / C • Taste Of The Best #2 / 1988 / PIN / C • Toys 4 Us #1 / 1987 / WV / C • Two Timing Tracie / 1985 / V20 / M • VCA Previews #4 / 1988 / VC / C • Winner Take All / 1986 / SEV / M • X-TV #1 / 1986 / PL / C

SAHARA (SANDS) *see* **Sahara Sands**

SAHARA SANDS *(Sahara (Sands), Saharah Sands)*

Large-framed blonde with small breasts and not particularly pretty face, big rear end, not a tight waist but not fat, tattoo of a fish on her belly. 6' tall, 34C-24-34. Born December 27, 1972 in Long Beach CA. Got into the porn business by answering an ad

in the paper. Produced a daughter in December 1994 and by this stage (excluding pregnancy) had filled out to a womanly body. In 1996 had her tits enhanced to large rock solid cantaloupes.
30 Days In The Hole / 1993 / ZA / M • Adam & Eve's House Party #1 / 1995 / VC / M • Adam & Eve's House Party #5 / 1996 / VC / M • All "A" / 1994 / SFP / C • America's Raunchiest Home Videos #62: / 1993 / ZA / M • America's Raunchiest Home Videos #73: / 1993 / ZA / M • Anal Blues / 1994 / PEP / M • Anal Chiropractor / 1995 / PEP / M • Anal Cornhole Cutie / 1996 / ROB / M • Anal Delinquent #1 / 1993 / ROB / M • Anal Fireball / 1996 / ROB / M • Anal Intruder #08: Rich Girls Gone Bad / 1993 / CC / M • Anal Load Lickers / 1996 / ROB / M • Anal Pool Party / 1996 / PE / M • Anal Princess #1 / 1996 / VC / M • Anal Sexual Silence / 1993 / IP / M • Anal Vision #09 / 1993 / LBO / M • Anything Goes / 1996 / OUP / M • The Ass Master #03 / 1993 / GLI / M • Attack Of The 50 Foot Hooker / 1994 / OD / M • Baby Doll / 1994 / SC / M • Badd Girls / 1994 / SC / F • Badgirls #1: Lockdown / 1994 / VI / M • Badlands #1 / 1994 / PEP / M • Badlands #2: Back Into Hell / 1994 / PEP / M • Bareback / 1996 / LE / M • The Beaverly Hillbillies / 1993 / IP / M • Behind The Scenes / 1996 / GO / M • Beyond Reality #1 / 1995 / EXQ / M • The Black Avenger #1: The Titty Romp / 1996 / OUP / C • Black Detail #1 / 1994 / VT / M • Black Detail #2 / 1994 / VT / M • Black Tie Affair / 1993 / VEX / M • Blackbroad Jungle / 1994 / IN / M • Blow Job Blvd #1 / 1993 / SC / M • Bobby Hollander's Maneaters #09 / 1993 / SFP / M • Bobby Hollander's Sweet Cheeks #110 / 1994 / WV / M • Boogie In The Butt / 1993 / WIV / M • Both My Lovers / 1994 / ... / G • Brassiere To Eternity / 1994 / PEP / F • Breastman Does The Twin Towers / 1993 / EVN / M • Breastman's Anal Adventure / 1993 / EVN / M • Bubble Butts #26 / 1993 / LBO / M • Bubble Butts #28 / 1993 / LBO / M • Buck Naked In The 21st Century / 1993 / EVN / M • Buffy's Bare Ass Barbecue / 1996 / CDI / M • Buffy's First Encounter / 1995 / CIN / M • Burbank Sperm Bank / 1996 / CIN / M • Butt Bandits #4 / 1996 / VD / C • Butt Camp / 1993 / HW / C • Butt Jammers / 1994 / WIV / M • Butt Naked #2 / 1994 / OD / M • Butterfly / 1993 / OD / M • Buttslammers #05: Quake, Rattle & Roll! / 1994 / BS / F • Caged Fury / 1993 / DR / M • Carnal Garden / 1996 / KLP / M • Caught From Behind #18 / 1993 / HO / M • Caught From Behind #19 / 1994 / HO / M • Channel 69 / 1996 / CC / M • Cheap Shot / 1995 / WAV / M • Cheatin' / 1994 / FD / M • Chinatown / 1994 / SC / M • Cliff Banger / 1993 / HW / M • Colossal Orgy #1 / 1993 / HW / M • Colossal Orgy #2 / 1994 / HW / M • The Come On / 1995 / EX / M • Conquest / 1996 / WP / M • Crazy With The Heat #3 / 1994 / CV / M • Dead Aim / 1994 / PEP / M • Deadly Sin / 1996 / ONA / M • Defending Your Soul / 1995 / EX / M • Designs On Women / 1994 / IN / F • Devil In A Wet T-Shirt / 1995 / SPI / M • Double Penetration Virgins #01 / 1993 / LE / M • Dp #2: The Mighty Fhucks / 1994 / FC / M • The Dragon Lady #6: Tales From The Bed #5 / 1993 / WV / M • Dream Butt / 1995 / VMX

/ M • Eleventh Annual AVN Awards / 1994 / VC / M • En Garde / 1993 / DR / M • End Around / 1994 / PRE / B • Enemates #09 / 1994 / BIZ / B • Entangled / 1996 / KLP / M • Euroslut #1: French Tart / 1993 / CC / M • Exit In Rear / 1993 / XCI / M • Facesitter #3 / 1994 / CC / M • A Fairy's Tail / 1996 / TTV / M • The Fantasy Booth / 1993 / ONA / M • Femme Fatale / 1996 / CIN / M • Fleshmates / 1994 / ERA / M • Flexxx #4 / 1995 / VT / M • The Fluffer #2 / 1993 / FD / M • Foolproof / 1994 / VC / M • Forbidden Subjects #3 / 1995 / FC / M • The Freak Club / 1994 / VMX / M • French Open Part Deux / 1993 / MET / M • Fresh Tender Asses / 1994 / RB / B • Fun Zone / 1994 / PRE / B • Gang Bang Bitches #02 / 1994 / PP / M • Gang Bang Diaries #1 / 1993 / SFP / M • Gang Bang Dollies / 1996 / ROB / M • Gas Works / 1994 / PRE / B • Generation Sex #2: Nature's Revenge / 1996 / VT / M • Ghost Town / 1995 / WAV / M • The Girl In Room 69 / 1994 / VC / M • Girls Just Wanna Have Girls #3 / 1994 / HIO / F • Girls Off Duty / 1994 / LE / M • Good Vibrations / 1993 / ZA / M • Greek Week / 1994 / CV / M • Harry Horndog #21: Birthday Orgy / 1993 / ZA / M • Haunted Nights / 1993 / WP / M • Head First / 1995 / OD / M • Hindfeld / 1993 / PI / M • Hollywood Ho' House / 1994 / VC / M • Homegrown Video #426: Best Big Breasted Women / 1994 / HOV / C • Hot Tight Asses #17 / 1996 / TCK / M • Induced Pleasure / 1995 / ERA / M • Initiation Of Kylie / 1995 / VT / M • Jam / 1993 / PL / M • Jenteal Loves Rocco / 1996 / VI / M • The Joi Fuk Club / 1993 / WV / M • Juliette's Desires / 1996 / LE / M • Kym Wilde's On The Edge #08 / 1994 / RB / B • Kym Wilde's On The Edge #34 / 1996 / RB / B • Lactamania #2: The Squirt Fest / 1995 / TTV / M • Lactamania #3 / 1995 / TTV / M • Lactamania #4 / 1996 / TTV / M • Laguna Nights / 1995 / FH / M • The Last Anal Hero / 1993 / OD / M • Leg...Ends #13 / 1995 / PRE / F • Let's Dream On / 1994 / FD / M • Lethal Affairs / 1996 / VI / M • Lick-A-Thon #2 / 1996 / HW / C • A Little Bit Pregnant / 1995 / SO / M • The Mad D.P. Tea Party / 1994 / FC / M • Midget Goes Hawaiian / 1995 / FC / M • Midget On Milligan's Island / 1995 / FC / M • Mike Hott: #283 Sahara / 1994 / MHV / M • Mike Hott: #302 Lesbian Sluts #17 / 1995 / MHV / F • Mike Hott: #323 Three-Sum Sluts #07 / 1995 / MHV / M • Mike Hott: #331 Lesbian Sluts #21 / 1996 / MHV / F • Mike Hott: #366 Lactating Lesbians / 1996 / MHV / F • Mistress Of The Mansion / 1994 / CV / M • The Mountie / 1994 / PP / M • My Boyfriend's Black / 1994 / FD / M • N.Y.D.P. / 1994 / PEP / M • Naughty Nicole / 1994 / SC / M • Neighbors / 1994 / LE / M • Never Say Never / 1994 / SC / M • Nina Hartley's Guide To Swinging / 1996 / A&E / M • No Fear / 1996 / IN / F • No Man's Land #09 / 1994 / VT / F • No Man's Land #12 / 1995 / VT / F • No Man's Land #15 / 1996 / VT / F • Nude Awakenings / 1996 / PP / M • Odyssey 30 Min: #324: Slam Bam, Thank You Sam / 1993 / OD / M • Odyssey Triple Play #71: Bodacious Blondes / 1994 / OD / M • Old Throat And D.P. / 1993 / FC / M • Ona Zee's Doll House #4 / 1996 / ONA / F • Organic Facials / cr91 / GLI / M • The Original Wicked Woman / 1993 / WP / M •

Pajama Party X #1 / 1994 / VC / M • Pajama Party X #2 / 1994 / VC / M • The Panty Parlor / 1996 / VIM / M • Passion / 1996 / SC / M • Perplexed / 1994 / FD / M • Persuasion / 1995 / LE / M • Pocahotass #2 / 1996 / FD / M • Point Of Entry / 1996 / WP / M • Prescription For Pleasure / 1993 / HW / M • Private Pleasures / 1994 / STM / F • Pumphouse Sluts / 1996 / CC / M • Pure Filth / 1995 / RV / M • Pussy Tales / 1993 / SC / F • Pussyclips #10 / 1995 / SNA / M • Pussyman Auditions #20 / 1996 / SNA / M • Pussyman's House Party #1 / 1996 / SNA / M • Pussyman's House Party #2 / 1996 / SNA / M • Radical Affairs Video Magazine #07 / 1994 / ME / M • Ready To Drop #05 / 1995 / FC / M • Ready To Drop #06 / 1995 / FC / M • Ready To Drop #07 / 1995 / FC / M • Ready To Drop #08 / 1995 / FC / M • Real Tickets #1 / 1994 / VC / M • Real Tickets #2 / 1994 / VC / M • The Right Connection / 1995 / VC / M • Right To Life #2 / 1996 / AOC / M • Ron Hightower's White Chicks #03 / 1993 / LBO / M • Ron Hightower's White Chicks #12 / 1994 / LBO / M • A Round Behind / 1995 / PEP / M • Rump Reamers / 1994 / TTV / M • Sabrina Starlet / 1994 / SC / M • Saki's Private Party / 1995 / TTV / M • Screamers (Gourmet) / 1995 / ONA / M • Sean Michaels On The Road #03: Beverly Hills / 1993 / VT / M • The Secret Life Of Nina Hartley / 1994 / VC / M • The Seduction Of Annah Marie / 1996 / VT / M • Selina / 1993 / XCI / M • Sex Circus / 1994 / VIM / M • Sex In Black & White / 1995 / OD / M • Sex In Dangerous Places / 1994 / OD / M • Sex On The Run #1 / 1994 / TTV / M • Sex Professionals / 1994 / LIP / F • The Sex Therapist / 1995 / GO / M • Sexual Instinct #2 / 1994 / DR / M • Shades Of Lust / 1993 / TP / M • Shameless Lady / 1993 / ME / M • Shayla's Home Repair / 1993 / EVN / M • Shayla's Swim Party / 1997 / VC / M • She Quest / 1994 / OD / M • The Shocking Truth #2 / 1996 / DWO / M • Sisters / 1993 / ZA / M • Skid Row / 1994 / SC / M • Sleepless / 1993 / VD / M • Sorority Sex Kittens #3 / 1996 / VC / M • Spread The Wealth / 1993 / DR / M • Stacked With Honors / 1993 / DR / M • Star Attraction / 1995 / VT / M • Stardust #5 / 1996 / VI / M • Sticky Lips / 1993 / EX / M • Stiff Competition #2 / 1994 / CA / M • Stories Of Seduction / 1996 / MID / M • Stranger At The Backdoor / 1994 / CC / M • Stripper Nurses / 1994 / PE / M • Stud Finders / 1995 / ONA / M • Style #3 / 1996 / VT / M • Submission / 1994 / WP / M • Superstar Sex Challenge #1 / 1994 / VC / M • Superstar Sex Challenge #2 / 1994 / VC / M • Superstar Sex Challenge #3 / 1994 / VC / M • Sweet Revenge / 1996 / WAV / M • Tail Taggers #105 / 1993 / WV / M • Tail Taggers #112 / 1993 / WV / M • Tail Taggers #114: Booty Brunch / 1994 / WV / M • Telephone Expose / 1995 / VC / M • Tonya's List / 1994 / FD / M • Totally Real / 1996 / CA / M • Ultimate Gang Bang #1 / 1994 / HW / M • Underground #2: Subway To Sodom / 1996 / SC / M • Underground #3: Sit On This / 1996 / SC / M • Used And Abused #1 / 1994 / SFP / M • The Usual Anal Suspects / 1996 / CC / M • Venom #7 / 1996 / VD / M • Welcome To Bondage: Sahara / 1994 / BON / B • Whackers / 1995 / PP / M • What's Up, Tiger Pussy? / 1995

/ VC / M • Wild & Wicked #7 / 1996 / VT / M • Witness For The Penetration / 1994 / PEP / M • A Woman Scorned / 1995 / CA / M

SAHARAH SANDS *see* **Sahara Sands**

SAIKO NAKANO

Club Fantasy / 1996 / AVE / M • Jacuzzi Lust / 1996 / AVE / M

SAKAKU ASUKA

Love Fluid / 1996 / AVV / M

SAKE *see* **Saki**

SAKI *(Sake, Saki St Jermaine, Kitty (Saki), Alexis (Saki), Satina (Saki), Satina LaRouche)*

Ugly Oriental girl supposedly born in Tokyo (more likely somewhere South of the border). First picture was **Backdoor To Paradise** (Elite).

69th Street / 1993 / VIM / M • The Adventures Of Mr. Tootsie Pole #2 / 1995 / LBO / M • AHV #24: Party Girls / 1992 / EVN / M • Amateurama #03 / 1992 / RTP / F • Ambushed / 1990 / SE / M • Anal Addiction #2 / 1990 / SO / M • Anal Adventures (Dragon) / 1992 / DRP / M • Anal Alice / 1992 / AFV • Anal Asian Fantasies / 1996 / HO / M • Anal Attraction #2 / 1993 / AFV / C • Anal Climax #1 / 1991 / ROB / M • Anal Extasy / 1992 / ROB / M • Anal Future / 1992 / VC / M • Anal Inferno / 1992 / ROB / M • Anal International / 1992 / HW / M • Anal Madness / 1992 / ROB / M • Anal Orgasms / 1992 / DRP / M • Anal Pandemonium / 1994 / TTV / M • The Anals Of History #1 / 1991 / MID / M • Anything Butt Love / 1990 / PL / M • Asian / 1995 / CDI / C • Asian Angel / 1993 / VEX / C • Asian Boom Boom Girls / 1997 / HO / M • Asian Exotica / 1995 / EVN / M • Asian Heat #04: House Of The Rising Sun / 1993 / SC / M • Asian Heat #05: The Joy Suck Club / 1994 / SC / M • Asian Invasion / 1993 / IP / M • Asian Persuasion / 1993 / WV / M • Back To Black #2 / 1992 / VEX / C • Back To The Orient / 1992 / HW / M • Backdoor To Hollywood #13 / 1990 / CDI / M • Backdoor To Paradise / 1990 / ELV / M • Backstage Entrance #1 / 1992 / FH / M • Backstage Entrance #2 / 1992 / FH / M • Beach Bunny / 1994 / V99 / M • Bed, Butts & Breakfast / 1990 / LV / M • Behind The Backdoor #4 / 1990 / EVN / M • The Best Of Both Worlds #2 / 1986 / MID / G • The Best Of Oriental Anal #1 / 1994 / ROB / C • Bi Claudius / 1994 / BIL / G • Bi George / 1994 / BIL / G • Bi This! / 1995 / BIL / G • The Bi Valley / 1994 / BIL / G • Big Murray's New-Cummers #09: Oriental Lovers / 1993 / FD / M • The Big Winner #1 / 1991 / CDP / B • Black Ass Masters #2 / 1995 / GLI / M • Black Is Back / 1993 / HW / M • Black Mail / 1990 / TAO / C • Blue Angel / 1992 / AFV / M • Bobby Hollander's Maneaters #06 / 1993 / SFP / M • Bobby Hollander's Sweet Cheeks #106 / 1993 / QUA / M • Body Slammers #03 / 1993 / SBP / B • Bootylicious: China Town / 1995 / JMP / M • Breast Worx #19 / 1992 / LBO / M • Breast Worx #24 / 1992 / LBO / M • Broad Of Directors / 1992 / PEP / M • Bubble Butts #04 / 1992 / LBO / M • Bubble Butts #07 / 1992 / LBO / M • Bubble Butts #20 / 1992 / LBO / M • Bum Rap / 1990 / PLV / B • The Burma Road #1 / 1994 / LBO / C • The Burma Road #2 / 1994 / LBO / C • Burning Desire / 1992 / CDI / M • Butt Bandits #4 / 1996 / VD / C • Butt Light:

Queen Of Rears / 1992 / STR / M • Butt Naked #1 / 1990 / OD / M • The Butt Sisters Do Denver / 1994 / MID / M • Buttsizer, King Of Rears #1 / 1992 / EVN / M • Carnal Carnival / 1992 / FC / M • Catfighting Students / 1995 / PRE / C • Cats In A Storm / 199? / NAP / B • Caught From Behind #13 / 1990 / HO / M • Caught From Behind #16: The Reunion / 1992 / HO / M • Colossal Orgy #1 / 1993 / HW / M • Confessions #1 / 1992 / OD / M • Corporate Bi Out / 1994 / BIL / G • Dark Dreams / 1992 / WV / M • Deep Cheeks #1 / 1991 / ROB / M • Deep Cheeks #2 / 1991 / ROB / M • Double Penetration #5 / 1992 / WV / C • Double Penetration #6 / 1993 / WV / C • Double Take / 1991 / BIZ / B • Double The Pleasure / 1990 / SE / M • Double Wong Dong / 1995 / LV / M • Dr Finger's House Of Lesbians / 1996 / SC / M • The Dragon Lady #3: Tales From The Bed #2 / 1992 / WV / M • The Dream Machine / 1992 / CDI / M • Drive Bi / 1994 / BIL / G • Driving Miss Daisy Crazy #2 / 1992 / WV / M • Escape To The Party / 1994 / ELP / M • Fag Hags / 1991 / FC / G • The Finishing Touch / 1994 / DR / M • Foreign Bodies / 1991 / IN / M • Fortune Cookie / 1992 / VI / M • Freaks Of Leather #1 / 1993 / IF / M • Fresh Tits Of Bel Air / 1992 / OD / M • Gang Bang Bitches #03 / 1994 / PP / M • Gazongas #04 / 1993 / LEI / C • A Geisha's Secret / 1993 / VI / M • Girlfriends / 1995 / SC / M • Girls In The Night / 1990 / LE / M • Girls Will Be Boys #2 / 1990 / PL / F • Girls Will Be Boys #3 / 1991 / PL / F • Girls Will Be Boys #4 / 1991 / PL / F • Girls, Girls And More Girls / 1990 / LV / F • Giving It To Barbii / 1990 / TOR / M • Glitz Tits #02 / 1992 / GLI / M • Gold Diggers / 1993 / IN / M • Good Bi Girl / 1994 / BIL / G • Hannibal Lickter / 1992 / MID / M • Hermaphrodites / 1996 / REB / C • Hershe Highway #3 / 1990 / HO / M • Hillary Vamp's Private Collection #07 / 1992 / HVD / M • Hillary Vamp's Private Collection #17 / 1992 / HOV / M • Ho' Style Takeover / 1993 / FH / M • Hollywood Assets / 1990 / FH / M • Hometown Honeys #5 / 1993 / VEX / M • Hot Bi Summer / 1994 / BIL / G • Hot Foot / 1991 / PLV / B • Hot Summer Knights / 1991 / LV / M • I Am Desire / 1992 / WV / M • I Dream Of Tiffany / 1993 / IF / M • I Remember When / 1992 / ATL / M • If These Walls Could Talk (Director's Cut) / 1993 / MET / M • If These Walls Could Talk #2: Burning Secrets / 1993 / CV / M • If You Can't Lick 'em...Join 'em / 1996 / BAC / F • In Loving Color #4 / 1993 / VT / M • In Pursuit Of Passion / 1990 / V99 / M • Interviews At The Hard Wok Cafe / 1996 / LOF / M • It's Only Love / 1992 / VEX / M • Jugsy (Western) / 1992 / WV / M • Juicy Lips / 1991 / PL / F • Kink World: The Seduction Of Nena / 1993 / PL / M • Kinky Debutante Interviews #01 / 1994 / IP / M • Kinky Orientals / 1994 / FH / M • Kiss Is A Rebel With A Cause / 1993 / WV / M • The Last American Sex Goddess / 1993 / IF / M • Leather Unleashed / 1995 / GO / M • Leg...Ends #06 / 1992 / PRE / F • Lesbian Lingerie Fantasy #2 / 1989 / ESP / F • Lesbian Lingerie Fantasy #3 / 1989 / ESP / F • Lesbian Mystery Theatre: The Case Of The Deadly Dyke / 1994 / LIP / F • Lesbian Pros And Amateurs #09 / 1992 / GO / F • Lesbian Pros And Amateurs #10 / 1992 /

GO / F • Lips / 1994 / FC / M • Living For Love / 1993 / V99 / M • Lust For Leather / 1993 / IF / M • Main Street, U.S.A. / 1992 / PP / M • The Makeup Room #1 / 1992 / VC / M • The Makeup Room #2 / 1992 / VC / M • Making It Big / 1990 / TOR / M • Medieval Dungeon Master / 1993 / BON / B • Mike Hott: #132 Chessie And Satina #1 / 1991 / MHV / F • Mike Hott: #133 Chessie And Satina #2 / 1991 / MHV / F • Mike Hott: #134 Satina Solo / 1991 / MHV / F • Mike Hott: #150 Two Girl Spanking Session / 1991 / MHV / F • Mike Hott: #151 Four Girl Spanking Session / 1991 / MHV / F • Mike Hott: #175 Dusty And Satina / 1991 / MHV / F • Mike Hott: #179 Satina's Shoe Fetish / 1990 / MHV / F • Mike Hott: #242 Fuck The Boss #02 / 1993 / MHV / M • Mike Hott: #317 Girls Who Swallow Cum #01 / 1995 / MHV / C • Mike Hott: #331 Lesbian Sluts #21 / 1996 / MHV / F • Mike Hott: Cum Cocktails #2 / 1995 / MHV / C • Mixed Apples / 1996 / APP / G • Money Honey / 1990 / TOR / M • Moon Godesses #1 / 1992 / VIM / M • The Most Dangerous Game / 1996 / HO / M • Nasty Fuckin' Movies #09: Saki's Six Man Sexation #1 / 1992 / RUM / M • Nasty Girls #1 (1990-CDI) / 1990 / CIN / M • Nasty Jack's Homemade Vid. #01 / 1990 / CDI / M • Night Of Passion / 1993 / BIA / C • Night Vibes / 1990 / KNI / M • Night Wish / 1992 / CDI / M • Odyssey 30 Min: #264: / 1992 / OD / M • Odyssey Triple Play #70: Three By Threeway / 1994 / OD / M • Office Manners And Double Punishment / 1992 / TAO / B • Older And Anal #2 / 1995 / FC / M • One Night In The Valley / 1996 / CA / M • Oral Madness #1 / 1991 / OD / M • Oral Majority #09 / 1992 / WV / C • Orient Sexpress / 1996 / AVI / M • Oriental Anal Sluts / 1993 / WV / C • Oriental Oddballs #1 / 1994 / FH / M • Oriental Treatment #3: The Lost Empress / 1991 / AFV / M • Oriental Treatment #4: The Demon Lover / 1992 / AFV / M • Our Bang #05 / 1992 / GLI / M • Our Bang #08 / 1992 / GLI / M • P.S.: Back Alley Cats #06 / 1992 / PSP / F • Pai Gow Video #01: Asian Beauties / 1993 / EVN / M • Pai Gow Video #04: Tails Of The Town / 1994 / EVN / M • Pai Gow Video #05: California Asians / 1994 / EVN / M • Party Favors / 1993 / VEX / M • Passion For Fashion / 1992 / PEP / G • Passion Prescription / 1990 / V99 / M • Pearl Necklace: Amorous Amateurs #21 / 1993 / SEE / M • Penetrating Thoughts / 1992 / LV / M • Pleasure Chest / 1993 / IF / M • Pony Girl #1: In Harness / 1985 / CS / B • Positively Pagan #05 / 1993 / ATA / M • Positively Pagan #06 / 1993 / ATA / M • Principles Of Lust / 1992 / WV / M • Putting On The Ritz / 1990 / VEX / M • Raw Talent: Bang 'er 34 Times / 1992 / RTP / M • Ready, Willing & Anal / 1992 / OD / M • Reel Sex #05: Lesbian Toy Part / 1994 / SPP / F • Rock Groupies In Heat / 1995 / LV / M • Rubber Dungeon Of Pain / 1993 / SBP / B • Rump Humpers #06 / 1992 / GLI / M • Saints & Sinners / 1992 / PEP / M • Saki's Bedtime Stories / 1995 / TTV / M • Saki's House Party / 1990 / KNI / M • Saki's Private Party / 1995 / TTV / M • Semper Bi / 1994 / PEP / G • Sensual Solos #03 / 1994 / AVI / F • Sex Drive / 1993 / VEX / M • Sex In A Singles Bar / 1992 / VC / M • Sex Starved She-Males /

1995 / MET / G • Sexual Harassment / 1996 / TTV / M • Shipwrecked / 1992 / CDI / M • Single Girl Masturbation #3 / 1989 / ESP / F • Six Stud Swingathon #01 / 1992 / VAL / M • Six Stud Swingathon #02 / 1992 / RUM / M • Slammin' Granny In The Fanny / 1995 / GLI / M • Something New / 1991 / FH / M • Stasha's Adult School / 1993 / CDI / G • Student Fetish Videos: Best Of Foot Worship #02 / 1994 / PRE / C • Student Fetish Videos: Catfighting #01 / 1991 / PLV / B • Student Fetish Videos: Catfighting #03 / 1991 / PRE / B • Student Fetish Videos: Catfighting #04 / 1992 / PRE / B • Student Fetish Videos: Foot Worship #02 / 1990 / PRE / B • Summertime Boobs / 1994 / LEI / M • Super Bi Bowl / 1995 / BIL / G • Supermarket Babes In Heat / 1992 / OD / M • Sushi Butts / 1994 / SCL / M • The Sweet Sweet Back #3: Sho' Nuff Got Dat Woodski / 1994 / FH / M • These Buns For Hire / 1990 / LV / M • Things Mommy Taught Me / 1990 / KNI / M • Tight Fit #07 / 1994 / GO / M • Tight Fit #10 / 1994 / GO / M • Tight Tushies #1 / 1994 / SFP / M • Tit Tales #3 / 1991 / FC / M • Tit Tales #4 / 1993 / FC / M • Titillation #2 / 1990 / SE / M • Titillation #3 / 1991 / SE / M • Titty-Titty Bang-Bang / 1992 / FC / C • Toes 'n' Cons / 1996 / PRE / S • Toys Bi Us / 1993 / BIL / G • Transister Act / 1994 / HSV / G • Transsexual Try Outs / 1993 / HSV / G • TV Nation #2 / 1995 / HW / G • Ultimate Anal Gang Bang #3 / 1993 / HW / M • Ultimate Gang Bang #1 / 1994 / HW / M • Up The Ying Yang #1 / 1994 / CC / M • Weird And Bizarre Bondage / 1991 / FC / C • Welcum To My Place / 1990 / ZA / M • What's The Lesbian Doing In My Pirate Movie? / 1995 / LIP / F • Wild Cats / 1991 / PRE / B • Wild Orgies #11 / 1994 / AFI / M • Wild Orgies #14 / 1994 / AFI / M • Will And Ed's Bogus Gang Bang / 1992 / MID / M • Wolfen Tickle / 1995 / SBP / B

SAKI ST JAMES
Awol / 1994 / SBP / B

SAKI ST JERMAINE see Saki

SAL LANGFORD
Lusty Ladies #04 / 1983 / 4P / M

SAL PONTINI see Star Index I

SAL SABINO
Blonde At Both Ends / 1993 / TGA / M

SAL VITELLI see Star Index I

SALEM
Not too pretty older girl with reddish brown or dark blonde hair, 26 years old in 1994, enhanced medium tits, flat ass. Too tall.
Anal Virgins Of America #07 / 1994 / FOR / M • Anal Vision #25 / 1994 / LBO / M • Double D Dykes #14 / 1994 / GO / F • Four Screws And An Anal / 1994 / NEY / M • Hot Chicks Do L.A. / 1994 / EVN / F • Mr. Peepers Amateur Home Videos #89: Stiffy Stuffer / 1994 / LBO / M • Titties 'n Cream #1 / 1994 / FC / M • Video Virgins #14 / 1994 / NS / M

SALEM GRAVES
Swedish Erotica #76 / 1994 / CA / M • Tail Taggers #123 / 1994 / WV / M

SALEMA
Splato: Sexual Fantasies #05 / 1996 / SPL / M

SALEMIA
The Cumm Brothers #07: Honeymoon On Uranus / 1995 / OD / M • High Heeled & Horny #3 / 1995 / LBO / M • How To Make

A Model #06: Many Happy Returns / 1995 / LBO / M • Nature Girls #2: Get Wet / 1995 / WIV / F • Pussy Hunt #08 / 1995 / LEI / M

SALENA
Blue Vanities #584 / 1996 / FFL / M

SALINA
Blue Vanities #513 / 1992 / FFL / M • More Black Dirty Debutantes / 1994 / 4P / M

SALINA (KIKI) see Kiki (blonde)

SALINA (ST CLAIR) see Selina St Clair

SALLAI
The Betrayal Of Innocence #1: The Awakening Of Marika / 1993 / CC / M • The Betrayal Of Innocence #2: The Decadence / 1993 / CC / M • The Betrayal Of Innocence #3: The Choice / 1993 / CC / M

SALLEY
TV Birdcage Rage #2 / 1996 / GLI / G

SALLMATA
Chateau Duval / 1996 / HDE / M

SALLY
Blue Vanities #169 (New) / 1996 / FFL / M • Blue Vanities #169 (Old) / 1991 / FFL / M • Blue Vanities #512 / 1992 / FFL / M • Blue Vanities #524 / 1993 / FFL / M • Blue Vanities #569 / 1996 / FFL / M • Harry Horndog #23: The Final Flick / 1993 / ZA / M • Impulse #01: Memories Of An Italian Slut / 1995 / MBP / M • Odyssey Amateur #71: When Harry Wet Sally / 1991 / OD / M • Shaved #03 / 1992 / RB / F • Wrasslin She-Babes #07 / 1996 / SOW / M • Wrasslin She-Babes #08 / 1996 / SOW / M • Wrasslin She-Babes #09 / 1996 / SOW / M • Wrasslin She-Babes #10 / 1996 / SOW / M

SALLY (ZUMIRA) see Zumira

SALLY BOND see Star Index I

SALLY BREY
Bedtime Video #02 / 1984 / GO / M

SALLY BROOKS see Star Index I

SALLY DALLY
Dental Nurse / 1973 / VXP / M

SALLY DOUGLAS see Star Index I

SALLY DOYAWANNA
Filthy First Timers #1 / 1996 / EL / M

SALLY FEELS
Old Wave Hookers #2 / 1995 / PL / M • Sex Over 40 #2 / 1994 / PL / M

SALLY FISHER
White Hot / 1984 / VXP / M

SALLY FOREMEAT see Star Index I

SALLY JORDAN
Vixens (Avc) / 19?? / AVC / M

SALLY KIRK see Stephanie Page

SALLY LA CASTRO see Star Index I

SALLY LABOIS
Prey Of A Call Girl / 1975 / ALP / M

SALLY LAID see Sally Layd

SALLY LAYD (Sally Laid, Mustang Sally Layd, Sally Williamson)
None too pretty slutty-looking blonde with masses of curly hair (reddish-blonde), large breasts and the attitude of a greasy spoon waitress. Born 2/14/68 in Baltimore, MD and de-virginized at 15. 5'5" tall, 120lbs, 34DD-25-34. Another story has her birthdate as 10/22/61—who can tell which is right.
The Adventures Of Mr. Tootsie Pole #1 / 1995 / LBO / M • Adventures Of Mustang Sally Layd / 1995 / LBO / C • Anal Agony / 1994 / ZA / M • Anal All Stars / 1994 / CA / M • Anal Asian #2: The Won-Ton Woman / 1994 / IN / M • Anal Generation / 1995 / PE / M • Anal Nitrate / 1995 / PE / M • Anal Vi-

sion #24 / 1994 / LBO / M • Analtown USA #03 / 1995 / NIT / M • Ass Busters Incorporated / 1996 / BLC / M • Ass Dweller / 1994 / WIV / M • Assmania!! #1 / 1994 / ME / M • Babewatch #2 / 1994 / CC / M • The Backdoor Bandit / 1994 / LV / M • Badlands #1 / 1994 / PEP / M • Badlands #2: Back Into Hell / 1994 / PEP / M • Big & Busty Centerfolds / 1996 / DGD / F • Big Bust Babes #19 / 1994 / AFI / M • Big Bust Babes #20 / 1994 / AFI / M • Big Bust Babes #35 / 1996 / AFI / M • Big Knockers #13 / 1995 / TV / M • Big Knockers #14 / 1995 / TV / M • Big Knockers #21: Best Of Lesbian #2 / 1995 / TV / C • Black Attack / 1994 / ZA / M • The Black Avenger #1: The Titty Romp / 1996 / OUP / C • Boobies / 1995 / RTP / M • The Bottom Dweller Part Deux / 1994 / EL / M • Breast Collection #02 / 1995 / LBO / C • The Breast Files #2 / 1994 / AVI / M • Breastman's Wet T-Shirt Contest / 1994 / EVN / M • The Bridges Of Anal County / 1996 / PV0 / C • Bun Busters #14 / 1994 / LBO / M • Busty Babes In Heat #3 / 1995 / BTO / M • Butt Busters / 1995 / EX / M • The Butt Sisters Do Daytona / 1995 / MID / M • The Butt Sisters Do New York / 1994 / MID / M • The Butt Sisters Do Sturgis / 1994 / MID / M • Butthead Dreams: Big Boating Bonanza / 1994 / FH / M • Butthead Dreams: Mission Impenetrable / 1994 / FH / M • Candy's Custom Car Wash / 1995 / FC / M • Centerfold Celebrities '94 #2 / 1994 / SFP / M • The Crack / 1994 / LV / M • Cross Cuntry Vacation / 1995 / CC / M • Dead Aim / 1994 / PEP / M • Diamond In The Raw / 1996 / XCI / M • Dirty Bob's #23: Tampa Teasers / 1995 / FLP / S • Double D Amateurs #15 / 1994 / JMP / M • Double D Dykes #13 / 1994 / GO / F • Double D Dykes #24 / 1995 / GO / F • Double D Housewives / 1994 / PV / M • Double D Nurses / 1994 / PV / M • The Dragon Lady #7: Tales From The Bed #6 / 1994 / WV / M • The Ebony Connection #1 / 1994 / LBO / C • Erotica Optique / 1994 / SUF / M • Euro-Max #4: / 1995 / SC / M • First Time Lesbians #13 / 1994 / JMP / F • Fishin' For Lust / 1996 / WST / M • Forbidden Subjects #2 / 1994 / FC / M • Full Moon Fever / 1994 / LBO / M • Gang Bang Bitches #02 / 1994 / PP / M • The Girls From Butthole Ridge / 1994 / ZA / M • The Girls From Hootersville #06 / 1994 / SFP / M • Goldenbush / 1996 / AVI / M • Greek Week / 1994 / CV / M • Heatwaves / 1994 / LE / M • High Heel Harlots #05 / 1994 / SFP / M • The Hitch-Hiker #02: Dangerous Curves / 1994 / WMG / M • The Hitch-Hiker #06: Salty Dog / 1994 / WMG / M • Hot Diamond / 1995 / LE / M • Hot Tight Asses #05 / 1994 / TCK / M • Hot Tight Asses #10 / 1995 / TCK / M • Hotel Sodom #02 / 1995 / SNA / M • Hotel Sodom #06 / 1995 / SNA / M • Housewife Lust #1 / 1995 / TV / F • Howard Sperm's Private Parties / 1994 / LBO / M • In Search Of The Perfect Blow Job / 1995 / OD / M • Junkyard Dykes #01 / 1994 / ZA / F • Keyholes / 1995 / OD / M • Lick-A-Thon #2 / 1996 / HW / C • M Series #19 / 1994 / LBO / M • Make Me Watch / 1994 / PV / M • Mellon Man #01 / 1994 / AVI / M • Models Etc. / 1995 / LV / M • The Mountie / 1994 / PP / M • My Desire / 1996 / NIT / M • N.Y. Video Magazine #03 / 1995 / OUP / M • Nasty Dreams / 1994 /

PRK / M • Nasty Nymphos #07 / 1994 / ANA / M • The Nympho Files / 1995 / NIT / M • Nymphos: They Can't Help It...Really! / 1996 / P69 / M • Odyssey 30 Min: #398: Lay Down Sally / 1993 / OD / M • On The Run / 1995 / SC / M • Ona Zee's Black Label #1: Sex Hunger / 1996 / ONA / C • Pearl Necklace: Thee Bush League #29 / 1994 / SEE / M • Poison / 1994 / VI / M • Poop Shute Debutantes / 1995 / LBO / M • Positions Wanted: Experienced Only / 1993 / PV / M • Private Audition / 1995 / EVN / M • Private Film #12 / 1994 / OD / M • Private Film #14 / 1994 / OD / M • Private Video Magazine #09 / 1994 / OD / M • Pussyman Auditions #18 / 1996 / SNA / M • Rectal Rodeo / 1994 / ZA / M • Rumpman: Caught In An Anal Avalanche / 1995 / HW / M • Rxx For A Gangbang / 1994 / ZA / M • Sex Academy #3: The Art Of Real Sex / 1994 / ONA / M • Sex Trek #4: The Next Orgasm / 1994 / ME / M • Sex Trek #5: Deep Space Sex / 1994 / ME / M • Sex-A-Fari / 1994 / LV / M • Sexual Impulse / 1995 / VD / M • Slammed / 1995 / PV / M • Slave Quarters / 1995 / PRE / B • Sluthunt #1 / 1995 / BIP / F • Snatch Motors / 1995 / VC / M • Tail Taggers #116 / 1993 / WV / M • Take This Wad And Shove It! / 1994 / ZA / M • Tinsel Town Tales / 1995 / NOT / M • Tits / 1995 / AVI / M • Titties 'n Cream #1 / 1994 / FC / M • Titty City #2 / 1995 / TIW / C • Titty Town #1 / 1994 / HW / M • Topless Brain Surgeons / 1995 / LE / M • Trailer Trash / 1994 / VC / M • Treasure Chest / 1994 / LV / M • Twists Of The Heart / 1995 / NIT / M • The Watering Hole / 1994 / HO / M • A Week And A Half In The Life Of A Prostitute / 1997 / EL / M • Wet Deal / 1994 / FD / M • Wet Nurses #2 / 1995 / LE / M • Why Things Burn / 1994 / LBO / M • Witness For The Penetration / 1994 / PEP / M • Working Girls / 1995 / FH / M • Xxxanadu / 1994 / HW / M

SALLY MACK *see* **Paula Wain**

SALLY MANE *see* **Star Index I**

SALLY MARTIN
A Climax Of Blue Power / 1974 / EVI / M

SALLY MCNEIL
Not In My Neighborhood / 1993 / IPR / B

SALLY O'BRIEN *see* **Star Index I**

SALLY O'KEEFE *see* **Star Index I**

SALLY O'NEIL
Waterpower / 1975 / VHL / M

SALLY PARADISE *see* **Star Index I**

SALLY PARKS
Bedtime Video #05 / 1984 / GO / M

SALLY PETERSON *see* **Star Index I**

SALLY RAND *see* **Star Index I**

SALLY ROBERTS
Bondage Memories #03 / 1994 / BON / C • Erotic Fantasies #5 / 1983 / CV / C • Fit To Be Tied / 1984 / BON / B • Grand Prix / cr75 / COV / M • It's Only A Game / 1988 / BON / B • Sally Roberts In Bondage #1 / 1985 / 4P / B • Sally Roberts In Bondage #2 / 1985 / 4P / B • Sally Roberts In Bondage #3 / 1985 / 4P / B • Sally Roberts In Bondage #4 / 1985 / 4P / B • Sally Roberts In Bondage #5 / 1985 / 4P / B • Sally Roberts In Bondage #6 / 1985 / 4P / B • Testing Her Powers / 1987 / BON / B

SALLY ROSE *see* **Tamara Longley**

SALLY RUTH *see* **Star Index I**

SALLY SCHAEFFER *see* **Star Index I**

SALLY SHAW

Bedtime Video #07 / 1984 / GO / M

SALLY SVENSON
Impulse #06: / 1996 / MBP / M

SALLY SWIFT *see* **Jennifer West**

SALLY SYBER SEX
Virtual She-Male / 1995 / HSV / G

SALLY VEN YU BERG
Hardcore: The Films Of Richard Kern #1 / 1991 / FTV / M

SALLY VIXEN
18 And Anxious / cr78 / CDI / M

SALLY WILLIAMSON *see* **Sally Layd**

SALLY WITHERS
Teenage Cowgirls / 1973 / ALP / M

SALOME
Big Bust Black Legends / 1991 / BTO / C • Breast Of Britain #8 / 1990 / BTO / S • More Dirty Debutantes #44 / 1995 / 4P / M

SALVADOR DURAN
Club Privado / 1995 / KP / M

SALVATORE
Amateur Lusty Latins #2 / 1997 / SUF / M

SAM
Bikini Seasons / 1993 / PHV / F • Blow For Blow / 1992 / ZA / M • Frank Henenlotter's XXX Hardcore Horrors: Mad Love... / 1996 / SOW / M • Fresh Meat #2 / 1996 / PL / M • Lewd In Liverpool / 1995 / VC / M • The Mad Love Of The Red Hot Vampire / 1971 / SOW / M • Victoria's Amateurs #01 / 1992 / VGA / M

SAM (MAX HARDCORE) *see* **Max Hardcore**

SAM ABDUL
Bi-Conflict / 1994 / FST / G • Conflict Of Interest / 1994 / FST / G • The Fine Line / 1990 / SO / M

SAM ARTHUR *see* **Star Index I**

SAM BALDWIN
Dixie Ray Hollywood Star / 1983 / CA / M

SAM CONNERS *see* **Star Index I**

SAM COOPER
Anal Health Club Babes / 1995 / EVN / M • The Hollywood Starlet Search / 1995 / SC / M • Latex #1 / 1994 / VC / M • Midnight Dreams / 1994 / WV / M • Milli Vanilla / 1994 / TP / M • Vivid At Home #02 / 1994 / VI / M

SAM DEAN *see* **Star Index I**

SAM DIXSON
Lost In Vegas / 1996 / AWV / G

SAM FAILUS *see* **Star Index I**

SAM FRANKLIN *see* **Star Index I**

SAM GETSMORE
Made In The Hood / 1995 / HBE / M

SAM HAGGARD *see* **Star Index I**

SAM HODGES
Fade To Rio / 1984 / VHL / M

SAM JOHNSON *see* **Jim Sparks**

SAM KAMIEL *see* **Star Index I**

SAM KELLY *see* **Star Index I**

SAM KINNEY
Sex Boat / 1980 / VCX / M

SAM LITO
Sex Boat / 1980 / VCX / M

SAM MANN
Roller Blade / 1985 / NWW / S • Thunder And Mud / 1990 / RCA / B

SAM MARCH *see* **Star Index I**

SAM MENNING
Bachelorette Party / 1984 / JVV / M • Daughters Of Emmanuelle / 1982 / VCX / M • Wacked Waitresses / 1986 / CS / B

SAM NEUWAVE *see* **Star Index I**

SAM RITTER
Mechanics Bi Day, Lube Job Bi Night /

1995 / SP0 / G • Transsexual Prostitutes #2 / 1997 / DFI / G

SAM SAXON
East Coast Sluts #04: New York City / 1995 / PL / M • N.Y. Video Magazine #02 / 1995 / OUP / M • Purple Pain / 1995 / OUP / B

SAM SCHAD *see* **Gino Colbert**

SAM SHAD *see* **Gino Colbert**

SAM SHAFT
$ex 4 Fun & Profit / 1996 / SPR / M • Amateur Models For Hire / 1996 / MP0 / M • Amateurama #01 / 1992 / RTP / M • Amateurama #04 / 1992 / RTP / M • Amateurama #06 / 1993 / RTP / M • Anal Receivers / 3996 / MP0 / M • Anal Toy Story / 1996 / MP0 / M • Back Rent / 1996 / MP0 / M • Casting Couch Tips / 1996 / MP0 / M • Every Woman Wants A Penis #2 / 1996 / MID / M • Homegrown Video #043 / 1990 / HOV / M • HomeGrown Video #468: Lust American Style / 1996 / HOV / C • Hungry Humpers / 1996 / SP / M • In My Ass, Please! / 1996 / SP / M • Innocent Girls Of Legal Age #3 / 1996 / MP0 / M • Innocent Little Girls #1 / 1996 / MP0 / M • Innocent Little Girls #2 / 1996 / MP0 / M • Interview With A Tramp / 1996 / SP / M • Kink Inc. / 1996 / MP0 / M • Live Sex Net / 1996 / SPR / M • Raw Talent: Motel Room Fantasies / 1992 / RTP / M • Rimmers #1 / 1996 / MP0 / M • Rimmers #2 / 1996 / MP0 / M • Sam Gets Shafted / 1996 / MP0 / M • Sam Shaft's Anal Thrusts #2 / 1992 / RTP / M • Sam Shaft's Anal Thrusts #3 / 1993 / RTP / M • Sam Shaft's Best Anal Thrusts / 1994 / RTP / C • Sam Shaft's Public Flashing #1 / 1994 / RTP / M • Sam Shaft's Public Flashing #2 / 1994 / RTP / M • Sodom Bottoms / 1996 / SP / M • Special Attention / 1996 / MP0 / M • Tender Box / 1996 / MP0 / M

SAM SMYTHE *see* **Max Hardcore**

SAM SPEED *see* **Robert Bolla**

SAM STANFORD
[Oral Models / 197? / ... / M

SAM STOVE
Secluded Passion / 1983 / VHL / M

SAM STRONG
The Adventures Of Peeping Tom #3 / 1996 / OD / M • Bootylicious: It's A Butt Thang / 1994 / JMP / M • Eighteen & Easy / 1996 / SC / M • Lactamania #2: The Squirt Fest / 1995 / TTV / M • Lactamania #3 / 1995 / TTV / M • More Black Dirty Debutantes #3 / 1994 / 4P / M • More Black Dirty Debutantes #5 / 1995 / 4P / M • Pick Up Lines #08 / 1996 / OD / M • Ready To Drop #05 / 1995 / FC / M • Ready To Drop #06 / 1995 / FC / M • Ready To Drop #07 / 1995 / FC / M • Ready To Drop #08 / 1995 / FC / M • Up And Cummers #13 / 1994 / 4P / M

SAM TORN *see* **Star Index I**

SAM WATSON
Bottom Busters / 1973 / BLT / M

SAM WESTON
Private Film #01 / 1993 / OD / M

SAM WESTON (SPIN) *see* **Anthony Spinelli**

SAM WYNN *see* **Star Index I**

SAMANTHA
Amateur Nights #14 / 1996 / HO / M • Angle, Trish, Linda, Samantha / 1990 / PLV / B • AVP #7026: Samantha Scores Again—The Playoffs / 1991 / AVP / M • AVP #7027: Samantha Scores Again—The Championship / 1991 / AVP / M • The Best

Of Hot Body Video Magazine / 1994 / CG / C • Breast Worx #23 / 1992 / LBO / M • Bright Tails #1 / 1993 / STP / B • The Cumm Brothers #09: Chewin' The Bush / 1995 / OD / M • Cumm For Dinner / 1995 / BCP / M • Dirty Dave's #4 / 1996 / XPR / M • Eurotica #10 / 1996 / XC / M • Filthy First Timers #2: Innocence Lost / 1996 / EL / M • Fresh Faces #03 / 1995 / EVN / M • Green Piece Of Ass #1 / 1994 / RTP / M • Hard Core Beginners #05 / 1995 / LEI / M • Hollywood Amateurs #03 / 1994 / MID / M • HomeGrown Video #453: / 1995 / HOV / M • Hose Jobs / 1995 / VEX / M • Hot Body Video Magazine: Beverly Hills Wet T-Shirt Contest / 1994 / CG / F • Hot Legs #1 / 1990 / PLV / B • Intimate Interviews #4 / 1996 / NIT / M • Jan B: Girl Play / 1996 / JB0 / F • The Janitor / 1995 / CS / B • Joe Elliot's College Girls #29 / 1994 / JOE / M • Jus' Knockin' Boots #2: Black On Line / 1996 / NIT / M • Luscious Lips / 1994 / ORE / C • Micro X Video #1 / 1992 / VIP / M • Micro X Video #2 / 1992 / YDI / M • My Master, My Love / 1975 / BL / B • New Faces, Hot Bodies #11 / 1993 / STP / M • Pearl Necklace: Amorous Amateurs #02 / 1992 / SEE / M • Pearl Necklace: Amorous Amateurs #03 / 1992 / SEE / M • Pearl Necklace: Facial #01 / 1994 / SEE / C • Prima #11: Dr. Max In Hollywood / 1995 / MBP / M • Profiles #10: / 1997 / XPR / M • Pussy Fest Of The Northwest #1 / 1995 / NIT / M • Pussy Hunt #04 / 1994 / LEI / M • Pussy Hunt #13 / 1995 / LEI / M • Reel Life Video #48: Double D Girlfriends / 1996 / RLF / F • Return Of The Knickers Inspector / 1994 / CS / B • Rock 'n' Roll Rocco / 1997 / EA / M • RSK: Samantha #1 / 1993 / RSK / F • Samantha's Situation / 1995 / GAL / B • Samantha, You Cocksucker / 1992 / RUM / M • Sin City Cycle Sluts #2 / 1995 / SC / F • Skirts & Flirts #02 / 1997 / XPR / F • Snatch Masters #09 / 1995 / LEI / M • Triple Header / 1987 / AIR / C • Victoria's Amateurs #01 / 1992 / VGA / M • Video Virgins #07 / 1993 / NS / M • Video Virgins #12 / 1994 / NS / M

SAMANTHA (ARIEL) *see* **Ariel Anderson**
SAMANTHA (JORD. LEE) *see* **Jordan Lee**
SAMANTHA AMOUR *see* **Star Index I**
SAMANTHA ANDERSON
Pearl Necklace: Premier Sessions #07 / 1996 / SEE / M
SAMANTHA BUSH
Creme De La Face #10: Cum Dome / 1995 / OD / M • The Doctor Is In #1 / 1995 / NIT / M • Pussy Fest Of The Northwest #4 / 1995 / NIT / M • Sex Lessons / 1996 / NIT / M
SAMANTHA CARDIN *see* **Monique Cardin**
SAMANTHA CASH
Seka's Teenage Diary / 1984 / HO / C
SAMANTHA DIAMONDS
Caribbean Sunset / 1996 / PL / M
SAMANTHA FONG
Hong Kong Hookers / 1984 / AMB / M • Swindle / 1991 / CEL / S
SAMANTHA FOX *(Stacia Micula, Stasha Bergoff)*
Hard looking brunette who in later movies developed a very womanly body.
The 8th Annual Erotic Film Awards / 1984 /

SE / C • Afternoon Delights / 1981 / CA / M • Amanda By Night #1 / 1981 / CA / M • Angie, Undercover Cop / 1980 / MSI / M • Auto-Erotic Practices / 1980 / VCR / F • Babe / 1982 / AR / M • Babylon Gold / 1983 / COM / C • Babylon Pink #1 / 1979 / COM / M • Bad Penny / 1978 / QX / M • Behind The Scenes Of An Adult Movie / 1983 / CV / M • Beyond The Blue / cr78 / SVE / M • Blue Ecstasy / 1980 / CA / M • Blue Magic / 1981 / QX / M • Blue Shorts / cr83 / COM / C • Blue Vanities #066 / 1988 / FFL / M • Blue Voodoo / 1983 / VD / M • Bon Appetit / 1980 / QX / M • Burlexxx / 1984 / VC / M • C.O.D. / 1981 / VES / S • Caballero Preview Tape #1 / 1982 / CA / C • Caballero Preview Tape #2 / 1983 / CA / C • Caballero Preview Tape #3 / 1984 / CA / C • Candi Girl / 1979 / PVX / M • Captives / 1983 / BIZ / B • Centerfold Fever / 1981 / VXP / M • Chastity Kidd / 1983 / COM / M • Classic Erotica Special / 1985 / SVE / M • Coed Fever / 1980 / CA / M • Corruption / 1983 / VC / M • Critics' Choice #2 / 1984 / SE / C • Dallas School Girls / 1981 / VCX / M • Delivery Boys / 1984 / NWW / S • Devil In Miss Jones #2 / 1983 / VC / M • Dinner With Samantha / 1983 / PTV / M • Dirty Looks / 1982 / VC / C • Dixie Ray Hollywood Star / 1983 / CA / M • Double Your Pleasure / 1978 / CV / M • Dr Love And His House Of Perversions / 1978 / VC / M • Dracula Exotica / 1980 / TVX / M • Electric Blue: Cosmic Coeds / 1985 / CA / M • Electric Blue: World Nudes Tonight / 1985 / CA / C • Erotic Fantasies #2 / 1983 / CV / C • Erotic Fantasies #6 / 1984 / CV / C • Erotic Fantasies #7 / 1984 / CV / C • Erotic Gold #2 / 1985 / VEN / M • The Erotic World Of Vanessa #1 / 1983 / VCR / C • The Erotic World Of Vanessa #2 / 1984 / VCR / C • Fascination / 1980 / QX / M • The Filthy Rich / 1981 / CA / M • For The Love Of Pleasure / 1979 / SE / M • Foxtrot / 1982 / COM / M • Foxy Boxing / 1982 / AVC / M • French Kiss / 1979 / PVX / M • Games Women Play #1 / 1980 / CA / M • A Girl Like That / 1979 / CDC / M • A Girl's Best Friend / 1981 / QX / M • Girls U.S.A. / 1980 / AIR / M • Her Name Was Lisa / 1979 / VC / M • Here Comes The Bride / 1977 / CV / M • Honey Throat / 1980 / CV / M • Honeysuckle Rose / 1979 / CA / M • Hot Ones / 1982 / SUP / C • I, The Jury / 1982 / 2CF / S • In Love / 1983 / VC / M • Irresistible #1 / 1982 / SE / M • Jack 'n' Jill #1 / 1979 / VXP / M • Jack 'n' Jill #2 / 1984 / VC / M • Legends Of Porn #1 / 1987 / CV / C • Legends Of Porn #3 / 1991 / MET / C • Liquid A$$ets / 1982 / CA / M • Loop Hole / cr80 / ... / M • The Love Syndrome / 1978 / CV / M • Love-In Arrangement / 1981 / VXP / M • Luscious / 1980 / VXP / M • Midnight Blue #1 / 1980 / VXP / M • Mystique / 1979 / CA / M • A Night To Dismember / 1983 / MPI / S • The Nurses Are Coming / 1985 / VCR / C • October Silk / 1980 / COM / M • Odyssey / 1977 / VC / M • Once Upon A Secretary / 1983 / GO / M • Only The Best #2 / 1989 / CV / C • Outlaw Ladies #1 / 1981 / VC / M • Penetration #2 / 1984 / AVC / M • People / 1978 / QX / M • Physical #1 / 1981 / SUP / M • The Pink Ladies / 1980 / VC / M • Platinum Paradise / 1980 / COM / M • The Playgirl / 1982 / CA / M • Potpourri / 1981 / TGA / M • Princess Seka /

1980 / VC / M • Prized Possession / cr80 / ... / M • Pussycat Ranch / 1978 / CV / M • Queen Of Harts / 1986 / BLT / C • Robin's Nest / 1979 / BL / M • Roommates / 1982 / VXP / M • Satin Suite / 1979 / QX / M • The Seduction Of Cindy / 1980 / VC / M • Seka Is Tara / 1981 / VC / M • Sex Appeal / 1986 / VES / S • Showgirl #03: Vanessa Del Rio's Fantasies / 1981 / VC / M • Showgirl #16: Samantha Fox's Fantasies / 1983 / VCR / M • Six Faces Of Samantha / 1984 / AA / M • Sizzle / 1979 / QX / M • Slammer Girls / 1987 / LIV / S • Spitfire / 1984 / COM / M • Streetwalkin' / 1985 / VES / S • Swedish Erotica #43 / 1982 / CA / M • Swedish Sorority Girls / 1978 / CV / M • Sweet Surrender / 1980 / VCX / M • Sweethearts / 1986 / SE / C • The Tale Of Tiffany Lust / 1981 / CA / M • Talk Of The Town #1 / cr82 / VC0 / S • Talk Of The Town #2 / cr82 / VC0 / S • That Lucky Stiff / 1979 / QX / M • This Lady Is A Tramp / 1980 / CV / M • The Tiffany Minx / 1981 / SAT / M • Tigresses...And Other Man-Eaters / 1979 / VXP / M • Undercovers / 1982 / CA / M • VCA Previews #2 / 1988 / VC / C • Violated / 1984 / VES / S • Wanda Whips Wall Street / 1982 / VXP / M • Warrior Queen / 1987 / VES / S • Women In Love / 1980 / CA / M • Working Girls / 1984 / BMQ / M • [Porn Stars At Play / 1980 / ... / M
SAMANTHA FUN
All The Loving Couples / 1979 / KIT / M
SAMANTHA GIBSON
Enforcing The Code / 1994 / TVI / B
SAMANTHA HALL *(Crystal (Sam. Hall))*
Bubble Butts #15 / 1992 / LBO / M • Mike Hott: #104 Nanette And Ali And The Phantom Cock / 1990 / MHV / M • Nina Hartley's Professional Amateur Tournament #2 / 1990 / BKD / M • Oriental Treatment #2: The Pearl Divers / 1989 / AR / M • Positively Pagan #03 / 1991 / ATA / M • Rapture Girls #1: Tiffany & Crystal / 1991 / OD / M • Wild Fire / 1990 / WV / C
SAMANTHA HARLEY
Society Affairs / 1982 / CA / M
SAMANTHA J. TIMMS
The Hottest Show In Town / 1974 / ... / M
SAMANTHA KING *see* **Monique Cardin**
SAMANTHA LAKE
Bright Tails #1 / 1993 / STP / B
SAMANTHA MCCLAREN *see* **Star Index I**
SAMANTHA MOORE
Final Blow / 19?? / BL / M
SAMANTHA MORGAN *see* **Tamara Morgan**
SAMANTHA PETERS *see* **Star Index I**
SAMANTHA RUSH *see* **Star Index I**
SAMANTHA SABBATH
Creme De La Face #17: Semen For Seven / 1996 / OD / M
SAMANTHA SAXSON
Suck It Off / 1995 / DV / M
SAMANTHA SCOTT
Beyond The Valley Of The Dolls / 1970 / CBS / S • Brand Of Shame / 1986 / SOW / S • Girls Will Be Boys / 1990 / PL / F
SAMANTHA SEX
Top Model / 1995 / SC / M
SAMANTHA SHAMAL
Private Film #06 / 1994 / OD / M • Private Film #07 / 1994 / OD / M • Private Video Magazine #06 / 1993 / OD / M • Private Video Magazine #07 / 1994 / OD / M • Pri-

vate Video Magazine #08 / 1994 / OD / M
SAMANTHA SINN
N.Y. Video Magazine #05 / 1995 / OUP / M
SAMANTHA ST JAMES *see Star Index I*
SAMANTHA STRONG
Hefty blonde with originally small flabby and
then enhanced large tits. Little or no per-
sonality.
The $50,000,000 Cherry / 1987 / VD / M •
The Adventures Of Billy Blues / 1990 / HO
/ M • All For One / 1988 / CIN / M • All
Hands On Dick / 1988 / STA / G • All In The
Name Of Love / 1992 / IF / M • Anal Extasy
/ 1992 / ROB / M • Anal Inferno / 1992 /
ROB / M • Anal Madness / 1992 / ROB / M
• Around The World With Samantha Strong
/ 1989 / V99 / M • The Awakening / 1992 /
SC / M • Backside To The Future #2 / 1988
/ ZA / M • Backstage / 1988 / CDI / M • The
Battle Of The Breast Queens / 1989 / INS /
C • The Best Of Andrew Blake / 1993 / CA
/ C • Bi Day...Bi Night / 1988 / PV / G • Bil-
lionaire Girls Club / 1988 / LVI / C • Blonde
Bitch, Black Bitch / 1988 / NAP / B • Blow-
ing The Whistle / 1986 / VIP / M • Boobs,
Butts And Bloopers #1 / 1990 / HO / M •
Boobs, Butts And Bloopers #2 / 1990 / HO
/ M • Bootsie / 1984 / CC / M • Bored
Games / 1988 / ALF / M • Bustin' Out /
1988 / VEX / M • By Day Bi Night / 1989 /
LV / G • Can't Beat The Feeling / 1988 /
VEX / M • Chance Meetings / 1988 / VEX /
M • Chestmates / 1988 / VEX / M • Cock-
tails / 1990 / HO / M • Coming On Strong /
1989 / CA / C • Crystal Blue / 1987 / VD /
M • Dark Dreams / 1992 / WV / M • Debbie
Does 'em All #1 / 1985 / CV / M • Debbie
Does 'em All #2 / 1988 / CV / M • Deep In-
side Samantha Strong / 1992 / CDI / C •
Deep Throat #2 / 1986 / AR / M • Doctor
Feelgood / 1988 / CDI / M • Dreams / 1987
/ AR / M • The Easy Way / 1990 / VC / M •
Ebony And The Blonde / 1988 / NAP / B •
Erotic Tales / 1989 / V99 / M • Erotic Tele-
vision Video / 1988 / VD / M • Erotika /
1994 / WV / M • Excitable / 1992 / IF / M •
Fantasy Nights / 1990 / VC / M • Fast Girls
#2 / 1988 / DIS / M • Flesh In Ecstasy #02:
Samantha Strong / 1987 / GO / C • Flesh
In Ecstasy #04: Jeanna Fine / 1987 / GO /
C • Fringe Benefits / 1992 / IF / M • Gidget
Goes Bi / 1990 / STA / G • A Girl Named
Sam / 1988 / CC / M • Girls Of The Double
D #02 / 1987 / CDI / M • Golden Globes /
1989 / VEX / M • Good Vibrations / 1991 /
PM / M • The Greatest American Blonde /
1987 / WV / C • Hawaii Vice #2 / 1989 / CDI
/ M • Hawaii Vice #3 / 1988 / CIN / M •
Hawaii Vice #4 / 1989 / CIN / M • The
Heiress / 1988 / VI / M • HHHHot! TV #1 /
1988 / CDI / M • HHHHot! TV #2 / 1988 /
CDI / M • Holly Does Hollywood #2 / 1987
/ VEX / M • Hot Licks At The Pussycat Club
/ 1990 / WV / C • Hungry #1 / 1992 / SC /
M • Hungry #2 / 1993 / SC / M • If These
Walls Could Talk (Director's Cut) / 1993 /
MET / M • Images Of Desire / 1990 / PM /
M • In-N-Out With John Leslie / 1988 / WV
/ C • Interactive / 1994 / SC / M • Jewel Of
The Nite / 1986 / WV / M • Kascha &
Friends / 1988 / CIN / M • Keyhole #168:
Robo-Cocks / 1989 / KEH / M • Les Be
Friends / 1988 / WV / C • Maid To Fight /
1988 / NAP / B • Mammary Lane / 1988 /
VT / C • The Master Of Pleasure / 1988 /
VD / M • Merry X Miss / 1986 / VIP / M •

Misadventures Of The Bang Gang / 1987 /
AR / M • Never Say Good Bi / 1989 / STA /
G • Night Of Passion / 1993 / BIA / C •
Nightmare On Dyke Street / 1992 / PL / M
• No Man's Land #01 / 1988 / VT / C • Noth-
ing But Girls, Girls, Girls / 1988 / CDI / M •
Only The Best Of Debbie / 1992 / MET / C
• Only The Strong Survive / 1988 / ZA / M •
Oral Majority #04 / 1987 / WV / C • Oral
Majority #10 / 1993 / WV / C • Oral Major-
ity #13 / 1995 / WV / C • The Out Of Towner
/ 1987 / CDI / M • Paris Blues / 1990 / WV
/ C • Parliament: Hot Foxes #1 / 1988 / PM
/ F • Parliament: Lesbian Lovers #2 / 1988
/ PM / F • Parliament: Samantha Strong #1
/ 1986 / PM / M • Parliament: Teasers #2 /
1988 / PM / F • Parliament: Three Way Lust
/ 1988 / PM / M • Parliament: Woman's
Touch / 1988 / PM / F • Peepers / 1988 /
CV / M • Peggy Sue / 1987 / VT / M •
Phone Sex Girls #1 / 1987 / VT / M • Phone
Sex Girls #2 / 1987 / VT / M • Play It Again,
Samantha / 1986 / EVN / M • Precious As-
sets / cr87 / VEX / M • Precious Gems /
1988 / CV / M • Princess Of Darkness /
1987 / VEX / M • Proposals / 1988 / CC / M
• Rapture / 1990 / SC / M • Rearbusters /
1988 / LVI / C • Renegade / 1990 / CIN / M
• Sam's Fantasy / 1990 / CIN / M • Saman-
tha & Company / 1996 / PL / M • Saman-
tha's Private Fantasies / 1994 / WV / M •
Samantha, I Love You / 1988 / WV / C •
Satin Angels / 1986 / WV / M • The Scent
Of Samantha / 1988 / VEX / C • Secrets /
1990 / CA / M • Silence Of The Buns / 1992
/ WV / M • Sin City: The Movie / 1992 / SC
/ M • Spooked / 1989 / VEX / M • Star-
bangers #05 / 1993 / FPI / M • Starship In-
tercourse / 1987 / DR / M • Strong Lan-
guage / 1989 / IN / M • Strong Rays / 1988
/ IN / M • Strong Sensations / 1996 / PL / M
• Super Blondes / 1989 / VEX / M • Switch
Hitters #3: Squeeze Play / 1988 / IN / G •
Take My Wife, Please / 1993 / WP / M •
Teasers: Champagne Reunion / 1988 /
MET / M • Teasers: Poor Little Rich Girl /
1988 / MET / M • Teasers: Porno Princess
/ 1988 / MET / M • Teasers: Watch Me
Sparkle / 1988 / MET / M • This Could Be
The Night / 1993 / IF / M • Toys 4 Us #1 /
1987 / WV / C • Toys 4 Us #3: Follow The
Leader / 1990 / WV / C • Tres Riche / 1986
/ CLV / M • Wet Weekend / 1987 / MAC / M
• Wise Girls / 1989 / IN / C
SAMANTHA SWEET *see Jordan Lee*
SAMANTHA SWONG
The Desirous Wife / 1988 / PL / M
SAMANTHA WILKES
Stardust #1 / 1996 / VI / M
SAMANTHA WINTERS *see Star Index I*
SAMANTHA YORK
Not too pretty brunette with so so body. 5'4",
long brown hair, brown eyes, 36-24-36.
American Indian tattoo on her left breast
and an island sunset and bird on belly near
her right leg to cover an appendectomy
scar. First professional video was **Anal
Starlets**.
$exce$$ / 1993 / CA / M • A&B AB#408:
Private Dick / 1993 / A&B / M • A'mature:
Karrie Takes It All / 1992 / AVP / F • Adven-
tures Of The DP Boys: Triple Penetration
Girls / 1993 / HW / M • Amateur Lesbians
#18: Jamie / 1992 / GO / F • Amateur Les-
bians #19: Sophia / 1992 / GO / F • American Swinger Video Magazine #04 / 1993 /

ZA / M • American Swinger Video Maga-
zine #05 / 1993 / ZA / M • Anal Gang
Bangers #02 / 1993 / GLI / M • Anal House
Party / 1993 / IP / M • Anal International /
1992 / HW / M • Anal Starlets / 1991 / ROB
/ M • Animal Attraction / 1994 / IF / M • Any-
thing You Ever Wanted To Know About Sex
/ 1993 / VEX / M • Ass-Capades / 1992 /
HW / M • Awakening In Blue / 1991 / PL /
M • The Babes Of Bonerville / 1995 / VEX
/ C • Back To Black #2 / 1992 / VEX / C •
The Backway Inn #3 / 1993 / FD / M • Bat-
tling Bruisers / 1993 / SBP / B • Big Mur-
ray's New-Cummers #07: Swinging in the
"A" / 1993 / FD / M • Bigger / 1991 / PL / M
• Bitches In Heat / 1994 / PL / C • Bobby
Hollander's Maneaters #01 / 1993 / SFP /
M • Bobby Hollander's Sweet Cheeks #104
/ 1993 / QUA / M • Bondage Constrictor /
1994 / VTF / B • The Boneheads / 1992 /
PL / M • Bring On The Night / 1994 / VEX /
M • Bun Busters #05 / 1993 / LBO / M • Butt
Woman #3 / 1992 / FH / M • Butt's Up, Doc
#4 / 1994 / GO / M • Carnival Of Knowl-
edge / 1992 / XCI / M • Cat Fight / 1992 /
ONH / M • Caught From Behind #17 / 1992
/ HO / M • Classified Spanking / 1991 /
BON / B • Deep Cheeks #1 / 1991 / ROB /
M • Deep Cheeks #2 / 1991 / ROB / M •
Deliciously Teri / 1993 / IF / M • Desert Of
Fear / 1993 / BON / B • The Dirtiest Girl In
The World / 1992 / ZA / M • Dirty Bob's #05:
Vegas MasterpieCES / 1992 / FLP / S •
Dirty Danyel / 1994 / V99 / M • Dirty Doc's
Housecalls #08 / 1994 / LV / M • Easy
Pussy / 1991 / ROB / M • Edward Penis-
hands #3 / 1991 / VT / M • Enema Bondage
/ 1992 / BIZ / B • The Fluffer #1 / 1993 / FD
/ M • Foot Hookers / 1994 / SBP / B •
Freaks Of Leather #2 / 1994 / IF / C • A Gift
Of Sam / 1992 / YOE / M • A Girl's Affair
#05 / 1994 / FD / F • The Girls From Hoot-
ersville #03 / 1993 / SFP / M • Hitched And
Bound! / 1994 / VTF / B • The Hypnotist /
1994 / SBP / B • If These Walls Could Talk
#1: Wicked Whispers / 1993 / MET / M • If
These Walls Could Talk #2: Burning Se-
crets / 1993 / CV / M • Immaculate Erection
/ 1992 / VD / M • Infamous Crimes Against
Nature / 1993 / SUM / M • It Just Doesn't
Get Any Bigger / 1992 / BRE / M • Juicy
Treats / 1991 / ROB / M • Knockout / 1994
/ VEX / M • The Legend And The Legacy /
1992 / BRE / F • Les Wrestle / 1994 / SBP
/ B • Licking Legends #1 / 1992 / LE / F •
Licking Legends #2 / 1992 / LE / F • Love
Potion / 1993 / WV / M • The Magnificent 7
/ 1994 / VTF / B • The Merry Widows / 1993
/ VC / M • Mistress Jacqueline's Slave
School / 1992 / BIZ / B • Mr. Peepers Am-
ateur Home Videos #41: Getting Off For
Bad Beh / 1992 / LBO / M • Mr. Peepers
Amateur Home Videos #52: Tail Wackers /
1992 / LBO / M • Mr. Peepers Amateur
Home Videos #62: Private Pussy Party /
1992 / LBO / M • Much More Than A
Mouthful #3 / 1993 / VEX / M • Naughty
Butt Nice / 1993 / IF / M • Neighborhood
Watch #20 / 1992 / LBO / M • Never Never
Land / 1992 / PL / M • P.S.: Back Alley Cats
#02 / 1992 / PSP / F • Pearl Necklace:
Amorous Amateurs #19 / 1992 / SEE / M •
Pearl Necklace: Thee Bush League: The
Best Of Oral #01 / 1993 / SEE / C • Pearl
Necklace: Thee Bush League #14 / 1993 /
SEE / M • Petite & Sweet / 1994 / V99 / M

• Positively Pagan #01 / 1991 / ATA / M •
Positively Pagan #02 / 1991 / ATA / M •
Positively Pagan #04 / 1991 / ATA / M •
Positively Pagan #05 / 1993 / ATA / M • Private Label / 1993 / GLI / M • Professor
Butts / 1994 / SBP / F • Raunchy Porno
Picture Show / 1992 / FC / M • Reel Sex
#05: Lesbian Toy Part / 1994 / SPP / F •
Revealed / 1992 / VT / M • Rites Of Passage: Transformation Of A Student To A
Slave / 1992 / BIZ / B • Robin Head / 1991
/ CC / M • Ron Hightower's White Chicks
#02 / 1993 / LBO / M • S&M Pleasure Series: The Gift / 1994 / VTF / B • Samantha's
Two-Way Dream / 1992 / BRE / M • Sensual Solos #02 / 1993 / AVI / F • Sex Drive
/ 1993 / VEX / M • Spanked And Whipped /
1994 / VTF / B • Spanking At The Manor /
1994 / VTF / B • Spanking Good Salary /
1993 / VTF / B • Stiff Competition #2 / 1994
/ CA / M • Suburban Swingers / 1993 / IF /
M • Summer's End / 1991 / ROB / M • Sunrise Mystery / 1992 / FD / M • Taboo #10 /
1992 / IN / M • Taboo #11: Crazy On You /
1993 / IN / M • Taboo #12 / 1994 / MET / M
• Taboo #13 / 1994 / IN / M • Tail Taggers
#114: Booty Brunch / 1994 / WV / M • Take
It Like A Man / 1994 / IF / M • This Could
Be The Night / 1993 / IF / M • Tiffany Lords
Straps One On #1 / 1994 / WIV / F • Tiffany
Lords Straps One On #2 / 1994 / WIV / F •
Tight Rope / 1993 / VTF / B • Toe Teasers
#1 / 1993 / SBP / B • Toe Teasers #2 / 1993
/ SBP / B • Too Sexy / 1992 / MID / M • Top
Heavy / 1993 / IF / M • Tori Welles Goes
Behind The Scenes / 1992 / FD / M • Twin
Cheeks #4 / 1991 / CIN / M • Wet And
Wanton / 1992 / BRE / F • Whipped And
Waxed / 1993 / SBP / B • Willie Wanker
And The Fun Factory / 1994 / FD / M • You
Bet Your Buns / 1992 / ZA / M

SAMARA
Everything Is Not Relative / 1994 / EL / M

SAMAS
The Sex Machine / 1971 / SOW / M

SAMERA *see* **Zumira**

SAMI
Dirty Water / 1994 / VSL / B • Topless Lightweight Spectacular: Alex Jordan Vs. Tina...
/ 1994 / VSL / B • Welcome To Bondage:
Sami / 1993 / BON / B • Welcome To
Bondage: Starlets #2 / 1994 / BON / C

SAMIR *see* **Star Index I**

SAMIRA
Pussy Fest Of The Northwest #4 / 1995 /
NIT / M • Rodney's Rookies #1 / 1996 / NIT
/ M • The Sodomizer #2 / 1995 / SC / M

SAMMIE JAMES
Private Film #08 / 1994 / OD / M

SAMMY
Dangerous Behinds #2 / 1996 / HW / M •
Kinky College Cunts #04 / 1993 / NS / F

SAMMY COLE *see* **Star Index I**

SAMMY SHUNT
Erotic Fantasies #4 / 1983 / CV / C

SAMMY SPANX *see* **Star Index I**

SAMMY TEED
Honeypie / 1975 / VC / M

SAMMY TEEN
True Legends Of Adult Cinema: The Cult
Superstars / 1993 / VC / C

SAMSON
50 And Still Pumping! / 1994 / EMC / M •
Kitty Foxx's Kinky Kapers #01 / 1995 / TTV
/ M

SANA FEY

Filthy First Timers #7 / 1997 / EL / M

SANDAY DEMPSEY *see* **Sandy Dempsey**

SANDEE CAREY *see* **Sandi Carey**

SANDI
Blue Vanities #511 / 1992 / FFL / M •
HomeGrown Video #452: Make Me Cum! /
1995 / HOV / M • New Faces, Hot Bodies
#13 / 1994 / STP / M • Uncle Roy's Amateur Home Video #20 / 1993 / VIM / M

SANDI (BRIG. AIME) *see* **Brigitte Aime**

SANDI BEACH *(Sandi Beech)*
Petite blonde with medium tits and passable
face. 21 years old in 1994 and 5'3" tall,
34C-22-32. Despite the alleged "22" she
doesn't look like she has a tight waist. As of
September 1995 she has had her tits expanded to grotesque size and has put on
some weight.
113 Cherry Lane / 1994 / FOR / M • The 4th
Vixxen / 1995 / EMC / M • The Adventures
Of Studman #3 / 1994 / AFV / M • Amateur
Gay Girls / 1995 / LEI / C • The Anal Adventures Of Suzy Super Slut #3 / 1994 / IPI
/ M • Aroused #2 / 1995 / VI / M • Babes Illustrated #4 / 1995 / IN / F • Badgirls #4:
Jayebird / 1995 / VI / M • Beach Mistress /
1994 / XCI / M • Big & Busty Superstars /
1996 / DGD / F • Blue Balls / 1995 / VEX /
C • Breastman's Bikini Pool Party / 1995 /
EVN / M • The Butt Sisters Do Boston /
1995 / MID / M • Butthead Dreams: Down
In The Bush / 1995 / FH / M • Concrete
Heat / 1996 / XCI / M • Cross Cuntry Vacation / 1995 / CC / M • The Dinner Party /
1995 / ERA / M • Erotic Appetites / 1995 /
IN / M • Evil Temptations #1 / 1995 / ULP /
M • The Girl Next Door #2 / 1994 / VT / M
• Heidi's Girls / 1995 / GO / M • Hotel
Sodom #05: Tammi Ann Bends Over /
1995 / SNA / M • Lay Of The Land / 1995 /
LE / M • Life's A Beach, Then You're
Fucked / 1995 / FRM / M • Naked Desert /
1995 / VI / M • Naughty By Night / 1995 /
DR / M • New Wave Hookers #4 / 1994 /
VC / M • The Other Side / 1995 / ERA / M
• Passenger 69 #2 / 1994 / IP / M • Private
Eyes / 1995 / LE / M • Public Access / 1995
/ VC / M • Public Places #1 / 1994 / SC / M
• Pussyclips #05 / 1994 / SNA / M • Pussyman #10: Butts, Butts & More Butts / 1995
/ SNA / M • Raw Sex #01 / 1994 / ERW / M
• Reality & Fantasy / 1994 / DR / M • Rod
Wood / 1995 / LE / M • Ruthless Affairs /
1995 / LE / M • Sabotage / 1994 / CA / M •
Screamers (Gourmet) / 1995 / ONA / M •
Secret Of Her Suckcess / 1994 / VC / M •
Sex #3: After Seven (Vivid) / 1994 / VI / M
• Sex Alert / 1995 / PV / M • Snatch Masters #04 / 1995 / LEI / M • Snatch Masters
#06 / 1995 / LEI / M • Snatch Masters #12
/ 1995 / LEI / M • Some Like It Wet / 1995
/ LE / M • Sorority Stewardesses #1 / 1995
/ PE / M • Sorority Stewardesses #2 / 1995
/ PE / M • Studio Girls / 1995 / SUF / F •
Surf Babes / 1995 / LE / M • Swedish Erotica #76 / 1994 / CA / M • Tails From The
Crack / 1995 / HW / M • A Taste Of Fanny
/ 1994 / FH / M • Tight Shots #2 / 1994 / VI
/ M • Topless Stewardesses / 1995 / PV / M
• Up And Cummers #14 / 1994 / 4P / M •
Up And Cummers #15 / 1994 / 4P / M • Up
And Cummers #26 / 1996 / 4P / M • Visions
#2 / 1995 / ERA / M • Wet Nurses #2 / 1995
/ LE / M • The X-Rated OJ Truth... / 1995 /
MID / M

SANDI BEECH *see* **Sandi Beach**

SANDI CAREY *(Sandra Carey, Sandy
Carey, Sandy Cary, Sandee Carey)*
Blonde with small tits, pretty face, short hair,
slim body, nasty L-shaped Caesarian scar
(some movies only).
The Beauties And The Beast / 1973 / AP0
/ S • Bucky Beaver's Double Softies #06 /
1996 / SOW / S • The Chateau / 1973 / ALP
/ B • City Women / 1972 / SVE / M • Class
Reunion / 1972 / PS / S • The Devil's Garden / 1970 / SOW / S • Door To Door
Salesman / cr70 / ... / M • The Elevator /
1972 / ALP / M • The Hawaiian Split / 1971
/ SOW / S • I'm No Virgin / 1971 / WWV /
M • Kinky Potpourri #32 / 199? / SVE / C •
Love Boccaccio Style / 1970 / SOW / S •
Love On Top / 1971 / CV / M • The Loves
Of Mary Jane / 1989 / BWV / C • Midnight
Hustler / 1972 / ALP / M • Mysterious Jane
/ 1981 / LUN / S • Naked Encounters / 1974
/ SOW / M • Oriental Ecstasy Girls / 1974 /
... / M • Pastries / 1975 / ALP / M • Sex As
You Like It / 1972 / SVE / M • She-Devils Of
the S.S. / 1969 / AME / S • Snow Bunnies
/ 1970 / NFV / S • A Touch Of Sex / 1972 /
AR / M • Tropic Of Passion / 1971 / NGV /
M • Wham Bam Thank You Spaceman /
1973 / BPI / S • [The Whip And The Chain
/ 1970 / ... / M

SANDI DEMPSEY *see* **Sandy Dempsey**
SANDI FELDMAN *see* **Sandi Pinney**
SANDI FOXX *see* **Sandy Foxx**
SANDI KING *see* **Sandy King**

SANDI KING (AMAT)
AVP #9100: The Casting Call / 1992 / AVP
/ M

SANDI NELSON *see* **Star Index I**
SANDI PENNY *see* **Sandi Pinney**

SANDI PINNEY *(Sandi Penny, Sandy
Penny, Sandi Feldman, Sandy Feldman, Sandi Pinney, Sandra Rogan)*
Tall blonde with horsey but passable face, long
curly hair, small/medium tits, lithe body.
Baby Face #1 / 1977 / VC / M • Boiling
Point / 1978 / SE / M • Dream Girl / 1974 /
AVC / M • Erotic Fantasies #1 / 1983 / CV
/ C • Foxy Lady / 1978 / CV / M • Her Last
Fling / 1977 / HIF / M • Mary! Mary! / 1977
/ SE / M • Pink Lips / 1977 / VCX / M • Reflections / 1977 / VCX / M • The Spirit Of
Seventy Six / 1976 / NGV / M • Superstar
John Holmes / 1979 / AVC / M • That's
Porno / 1979 / CV / C • The Untamed /
1978 / VCX / M • V—The Hot One / 1978 /
CV / M

SANDI STONE
Limo Connection / 1983 / VC / M

SANDI SUAREZ *see* **Star Index I**
SANDI WEINSTEIN *see* **Star Index I**
SANDINE *see* **Star Index I**

SANDRA
A&B AB#478: Sandra / 1994 / A&B / M •
Adventures Of The DP Boys: Back In Town
/ 1994 / HW / M • Best Of Buttman #2 /
1993 / EA / C • Black Mystique #01 / 1993
/ VT / F • Blue Vanities #004 / 1987 / FFL /
M • Blue Vanities #548 / 1994 / FFL / M •
Blue Vanities #565 / 1995 / FFL / M • Blue
Vanities #572 / 1995 / FFL / M • Body
Tease / 1992 / VER / F • Buttman Goes To
Rio #2 / 1991 / EA / M • Dirty Blue Movies
#03 / 1992 / JTV / M • Drop Sex: Wipe The
Floor / 1997 / JLP / M • Erotic Westernscapes / 1994 / PHV / S • Fat Ends / 1989
/ 4P / M • Girls From Girdleville / 1992 /

ERK / M • Harry Horndog #02: Amateur Oriental Orgasms #1 / 1992 / ZA / M • Helen Does Holland / 1996 / VC / M • The Nurses Are Cumming #1 / 1996 / LBO / C • Onanie #2 / 1995 / MET / F • Pick Up Lines #12 / 1997 / OD / M • Ron Hightower's White Chicks #02 / 1993 / LBO / M • Ron Hightower's White Chicks #03 / 1993 / LBO / M • Sandra's Fantasies / 1995 / DIP / F • Sandra's Submission / 1994 / GAL / B • The Thief, The Girl & The Detective / 1996 / HDE / M • Toredo / 1996 / ROX / M

SANDRA (SENORA) *see* Senora

SANDRA BEACH
Lady Luck / 1975 / VCX / M

SANDRA BLAST
Odyssey / 1977 / VC / M

SANDRA CAREY *see* Sandi Carey

SANDRA CARSON
Bucky Beaver's XXX Dragon Art Theatre Double Feature #11 / 1996 / SOW / M • San Francisco Ball / 1971 / SOW / S

SANDRA CASSAND
Blue Vanities #582 / 1996 / FFL / M

SANDRA CHASE *see* Star Index I

SANDRA CLINTON *see* Brazil

SANDRA CUMMINGS *see* Star Index I

SANDRA DARK
Private Gold #11: The Pyramid #1 / 1996 / OD / M

SANDRA DEAN
Nicole: The Story Of O / 1972 / CLX / M

SANDRA DEE
Grateful Grandma's Gang Bang / 1994 / FC / M • Lesbian Mystery Theatre: The Case Of The Deadly Dyke / 1994 / LIP / F • Ron Hightower's White Chicks #14 / 1994 / LBO / M

SANDRA DEE RAMONA *see* Star Index I

SANDRA DEMPSEY *see* Sandy Dempsey

SANDRA ELITE *see* Star Index I

SANDRA FAY *see* Star Index I

SANDRA GABINCERA
Reel People #03 / 1989 / PP / M

SANDRA GEE *see* Star Index I

SANDRA GREY
Ejacula #1 / 1992 / VC / M • Ejacula #2 / 1992 / VC / M

SANDRA HENRY
M Series #10 / 1993 / LBO / M

SANDRA HILLMAN *see* Star Index I

SANDRA JANIERO
More Dirty Debutantes #32 / 1994 / 4P / M • Up And Cummers #07 / 1994 / 4P / M

SANDRA KING *see* Sandy King

SANDRA KYOTO
Bucky Beaver's XXX Dragon Art Theatre Double Feature #10 / 1996 / SOW / M • Sins Of Sandra / cr72 / SOW / M

SANDRA LEE
Blue Vanities #030 / 1988 / FFL / M

SANDRA LOVE
Primal / 1994 / PHV / S • Viola Video #108: Sondra Love On Tour / 1995 / PEV / M • Wet / 1994 / PHV / F

SANDRA MARGOT *see* Tiffany Million

SANDRA MARSH *see* Star Index I

SANDRA MARTIN
Peaches And Cream / 1982 / SE / M • Sweet Taste Of Honey / 1977 / ALP / M

SANDRA MILLER *see* Star Index I

SANDRA MORGAN *see* Traci Starr

SANDRA MYORGIA *see* Traci Starr

SANDRA NOVA

Backdoor Club / 1986 / CA / M • Backdoor Lust / 1987 / CV / C • Insatiable Janine / 1988 / CA / M • The Way She Was / 1987 / CA / M

SANDRA PETERSON
Born Erect / cr80 / CA / M

SANDRA RICE
Blue Vanities #197 / 1993 / FFL / M

SANDRA ROCKET
Breaker Beauties / 1977 / VHL / M

SANDRA ROGAN *see* Sandi Pinney

SANDRA SCREAM *(Sondra Scream)*
Anal Attack / 1991 / ZA / M • Black Balled / 1990 / ZA / M • Blonde Bombshell / 1991 / CC / M • Boobs, Butts And Bloopers #2 / 1990 / HO / M • Breasts And Beyond #2 / 1991 / ME / M • Bruce Seven's Favorite Endings #1 / 1991 / EL / C • Busting Out / 199? / NAP / F • Catalina Five-O: White Coral, Blue Death / 1990 / CIN / M • Catalina: Sabotage / 1991 / CDI / M • Catalina: Tiger Shark / 1991 / CDI / M • Catalina: Treasure Island / 1991 / CDI / M • Cooler Girls / 1994 / MID / C • The Danger Zone / 1990 / SO / M • Desire / 1990 / VC / M • Double The Pleasure / 1990 / SE / M • Dreams Cum True / 1990 / HO / M • Evil Woman / 1990 / LE / M • Eyewitness Nudes / 1990 / VC / M • Gettin' Wet / 1990 / VC / M • Girls In Heat / 1991 / ZA / F • Hard Core Cafe / 1991 / PL / M • Hard Core Cafe Revisited / 1991 / PL / M • Hard To Thrill / 1991 / CIN / M • Hot On Her Tail / 1990 / CA / M • I Said A Butt Light #2 / 1990 / LV / M • In Too Deep / 1992 / AFD / M • The Journey: Oral Majority / 1991 / WV / M • Juicy Sex Scandals / 1991 / VD / M • Legend #3 / 1991 / LE / M • Lucky Break / 1991 / SE / M • Maiden Heaven #1 / 1992 / MID / F • Mamm's The Word / 1991 / ZA / M • Maneaters (1992-Vidco) / 1992 / VD / C • Model Wife / 1991 / CA / M • Naughty Nurses / 1992 / VD / C • New Wave Hookers #2 / 1991 / VC / M • Nurse Nancy / 1991 / CA / M • A Rising Star / 1991 / HO / M • Scream In The Middle Of The Night / 1990 / CC / M • Snatched To The Future / 1991 / EL / F • The Spectacle / 1991 / IN / M • The Stranger Beside Me / 1991 / WV / M • Twin Cheeks #2 / 1991 / CIN / M • Two Of A Kind / 1990 / LV / M

SANDRA SLEEZE *see* Star Index I

SANDRA SOMMERS *(Sandra Summers)*
Not too pretty, inflated large tits that look like they're only attached by skin, older, short reddish-brown hair, tattoo on left belly, clit ring, scar (probably old C-section) from pussy to belly button. Supposedly 25 years old in 1996 (looks a lot older), comes from South Carolina, and was de-virginized at 16. Rumor has it that as of 1996 she was married to Tony Montana but then quickly divorced.
Bedtime Stories / 1996 / VC / M • Big Boob Bangeroo #6 / 1996 / TTV / M • Big Boob Bangeroo #8 / 1996 / TTV / M • Big Bust Babes #38 / 1996 / AFI / M • Double D Dykes #27 / 1995 / GO / F • Fresh Faces #12 / 1996 / EVN / M • Hardcore Confidential #1 / 1996 / TEP / M • Lingerie / 1996 / RAS / M • My First Time #7 / 1996 / NS / M • The Violation Of Paisley Hunter / 1996 / JMP / F

SANDRA STEEL
The Story of Bobby / cr80 / BIZ / B

SANDRA STONE *see* Sheila Stone

SANDRA SUMMERS *see* Sandra Sommers

SANDRA SUMMERS (86) *see* Sandy Summers

SANDRA SWEAT
MASH'ed / cr75 / ALP / M

SANDRA THOMPSON
Blue Confessions / 1983 / VCR / M

SANDRA WINTERS *(Summer Brown)*
China Girl / 1974 / SE / M

SANDRINE
Anabolic Import #01: Anal X / 1994 / ANA / M • Hell To Pay / 1996 / OUP / B • Impulse #01: Memories Of An Italian Slut / 1995 / MBP / M • Journey Into Hellfire / 1995 / GAL / B • Lusting, London Style / 1992 / VC / M • Magma: Deep Inside Janine / 1994 / MET / M • Magma: Dirty Diana / 1994 / MET / M • Magma: Double Anal / 1994 / MET / M • Magma: Horny Bulls / 1994 / MET / M • Magma: Insatiable Lust / 1995 / MET / M • Magma: Nymphettes / 1993 / MET / M • Magma: Tanja's Horny Nights / 1994 / MET / M • N.Y. Video Magazine #04 / 1995 / OUP / M • New York City Lesbian Gang Bang / 1995 / OUP / F • Private Video Magazine #04 / 1993 / OD / M • Streets Of New York #06 / 1996 / PL / M

SANDRINE MARTIN
Cunt Of Monte Cristo / 1996 / SPL / M

SANDRINE VAN HERPE
Sacred Doll / 1995 / FRF / M

SANDY
30 Men For Sandy / 1995 / SC / M • A&B AB#282: Interracial Couple / 1991 / A&B / F • A&B AB#305: Sandy's Treats / 1991 / A&B / M • A&B AB#307: Interracial Anal Sex / 1991 / A&B / M • A&B AB#317: Super Girl And Super Grandma / 1991 / A&B / F • A&B AB#323: Male Slaves / 1991 / A&B / G • Anal Virgins Of America #05 / 1993 / FOR / M • Beach Bum Amateur's #20 / 1992 / MID / M • Big Murray's New-Cummers #15: Rump Humpers / 1993 / FD / M • Blow Job Blvd #1 / 1993 / SC / M • Blue Vanities #051 / 1988 / FFL / M • Blue Vanities #516 / 1992 / FFL / M • Blue Vanities #539 / 1993 / FFL / M • Blue Vanities #541 / 1994 / FFL / M • Breast Wishes #06 / 1991 / LBO / M • The Burma Road #1 / 1994 / LBO / C • The Burma Road #2 / 1994 / LBO / C • California Girl: Amateur Nude Auditions / 1995 / PME / S • Catching Snapper / 1995 / XCI / M • Cowgirls / 1996 / GLI / M • Creme De La Face #07 / 1995 / OD / M • Creme De La Face #15: Showroom Sex / 1996 / OD / M • Dirty Doc's Housecalls #03 / 1993 / LV / M • Down And Out #2 / 1992 / CDP / B • Eurotica #13 / 1996 / XC / M • Fag Hags / 1991 / FC / G • FTV #19: Topless Lingerie Cat-Fight / 1996 / FT / B • Girls Of The Night / 1985 / CA / M • Hot Body Competition: Beverly Hill's Miniskirt Madness Cont. / 1996 / CG / F • Hot Legs #2 / 1990 / PLV / B • House Of Sex #03: Banging Sandy / 1994 / RTP / M • Just The Way You Like It #1: Sandy's Milk / 1994 / JEG / M • Kim's Convention Couples / 1995 / VAL / M • Lisa And Sandy: East Meets West / 1992 / LOD / F • Odyssey 30 Min: The Cocksucking Redhead / 1992 / OD / M • Penetration #1 / 1984 / AVC / M • Sandy In The Woods / 1993 / BON / B • Sandy Insatiable / 1995 / EA / M • Sandy's Lakeside Ordeal #1 / 1993 / BON / B • Sandy's Lakeside Ordeal

#2 / 1993 / BON / B • Sandy's: 10 Days In China / 1994 / SM / F • Spank Fu / 1993 / TAO / B • Super Sampler #5 / 1994 / LOD / C • Whipped Cream / 1996 / EA / M • Wrasslin She-Babes #10 / 1996 / SOW / M

SANDY (K. SAUNDERS) see Kim Saunders

SANDY (SONJA) see Sonja

SANDY ALLEN see Star Index I

SANDY BEACH
Coming In America / 1988 / VEX / M • Pretty In Black / 1986 / WET / M

SANDY BECKER see Star Index I

SANDY BERNHARDT
Contact / 1975 / VC / M

SANDY BLUE
Bi-Ceps / 1986 / LA / C • The Rod Garetto Story / 1995 / FC / C

SANDY BOLES
Young And Foolish / 197? / IHV / M

SANDY BOTTOM see Star Index I

SANDY BROWN
Naughty Network / 1981 / CA / M

SANDY CAREY see Sandi Carey

SANDY CARY see Sandi Carey

SANDY DAY see Star Index I

SANDY DEMPSEY *(Sandra Dempsey, Sandi Dempsey, Sanday Dempsey)*
Long-haired brunette with a young and curvaceous body, large tits, nice smile, white skin.
Afternoon Tease / cr72 / VCX / S • The Baby Sister / 1972 / ... / M • The Black Alley Cats / 1971 / SOW / S • City Women / 1972 / SVE / M • College Girls / cr73 / VXP / M • Connie & Floyd / 1973 / SVE / M • Country Hooker / 1970 / BPI / S • If You Don't Stop It You'll Go Blind / 1977 / MED / S • Johnny Wadd / 1973 / ALP / M • Legends Of Porn #1 / 1987 / CV / C • Liberty / 197? / CID / M • Little Miss Innocence / 1978 / ACV / S • The Loves Of Mary Jane / 1989 / BWV / C • Nipples / 1973 / ALP / M • Oriental Ecstasy Girls / 1974 / ... / M • Panorama Blue / 1974 / ALP / S • Poor Cecily / 1973 / ALF / S • Sex And The Single Vampire / 1970 / ALP / S • Sex As You Like It / 1972 / SVE / M • Sex Psycho / 1971 / SOW / M • Shot On Location / 1972 / ALP / S • Skin Flick Madness / 1971 / ALP / S • Swinging Cheerleaders / 1974 / MV1 / S • Swinging Genie / 1970 / ALP / M • A Touch Of Sex / 1972 / AR / M • Tough Guns / 1972 / ALP / S • Tropic Of Passion / 1971 / NGV / M • Video Vixens / 1972 / VES / S • [The Suckers / 1969 / ... / S

SANDY DONALDSON
Shiela's Deep Desires / 1986 ⁄ HO / M

SANDY DUNES see Star Index I

SANDY EATON
Blue Vanities #558 / 1994 / FFL / M

SANDY EILEEN see Star Index I

SANDY FELDMAN see Sandi Pinney

SANDY FIELDS see Star Index I

SANDY FLIER
Blue Vanities #552 / 1994 / FFL / M

SANDY FOXX *(Sandi Foxx)*
Angela, The Fireworks Woman / 1975 / VC / M • Blue Vanities #192 / 1993 / FFL / M • Certified Mail / 1975 / CDC / M • Cry Rape / 1975 / ASR / M • Defiance / 1974 / ALP / B • Lickity Split / 1974 / COM / M • Satan Was A Lady / 1977 / ALP / M • Slip Up / 1974 / ALP / M • Sunset Strip Girls / 1975 / TGA / M • Take Off / 1978 / VXP / M

SANDY FRANKEL

Bucky Beaver's XXX Dragon Art Theatre Double Feature #11 / 1996 / SOW / M • Teenage Fantasies #1 / 1972 / SOW / M

SANDY GAZELLE see Star Index I

SANDY HANSEN
Birthday Surprise / 1988 / BON / B

SANDY HILL
The Gypsy Ball / 1979 / ENC / M

SANDY JOHNSON
Gas Pump Girls / 1978 / WWV / S • H.O.T.S. / 1979 / VES / S • Love Mexican Style / cr75 / BLT / M • Modern Love #2 / 1992 / CPV / S

SANDY JONES see Sandy Summers

SANDY KANE see Star Index I

SANDY KERR
Ole / 1971 / KIT / M

SANDY KING *(Sandra King, Sandi King)*
Afrodisiac #1 / 1987 / CC / M • Bizarre Sorceress / 1979 / STM / B • Bucky Beaver's XXX Dragon Art Theatre Double Feature #25 / 1996 / SOW / M • Double Header / cr73 / BL / M • Erotic Mystique / 19?? / BL / M • Good Girl, Bad Girl / 1984 / SE / M • Head / 1985 / LA / M • Hot Lips / 1984 / VC / M • Lady On Top / cr73 / BL / M • Pleasure Cruise / 1972 / WV / M • Secluded Passion / 1983 / VHL / M • Thirst For Passion / 1988 / TRB / M • Urges In Young Girls / 1984 / VC / M • [The Gang's All Here / cr85 / STM / M

SANDY KLINE see Star Index I

SANDY LANE see Star Index I

SANDY LARADO
Starlet Nights / 1982 / XTR / M

SANDY LEE
Creme De La Face #08: Wanna Blow Job / 1995 / OD / M

SANDY LESTER
Spanked Young Tails / 1996 / BIZ / B

SANDY LONG see Crystal Sync

SANDY LORENZO
More Dirty Debutantes #47 / 1995 / 4P / M

SANDY LUE
The Doctor Is In #3: Achy Breaky Tarts / 1995 / NIT / M • Nothing Like Nurse Nookie #3 / 1996 / NIT / M • Pussy Fest Of The Northwest #1 / 1995 / NIT / M • Pussy Fest Of The Northwest #4 / 1995 / NIT / M

SANDY MARLOW
Blue Vanities #115 / 1988 / FFL / M

SANDY MORELLI see Star Index I

SANDY MOUNDS
50 And Still Gangbangin'! / 1995 / EMC / M

SANDY PENNY see Sandi Pinney

SANDY PINNEY see Sandi Pinney

SANDY RAVEN see Star Index I

SANDY REED
Layover / 1985 / HO / M • Maximum #6 / 1983 / CA / M • Snack Time / 1983 / HO / M

SANDY RUSSELL
Bunbusters / 1984 / VCR / M

SANDY SEALS see Star Index I

SANDY SONNERS
The Wrong Woman / 1990 / LE / M

SANDY STEEL
Man To Maiden / 1984 / BIZ / B

SANDY STRAM see Star Index I

SANDY SUMMERS *(Sandra Summers (86), Sandy Jones)*
Lithe petite brunette with small tits and a punk rock hairstyle.
1001 Erotic Nights #2 / 1987 / VC / M • Cavalcade Of Stars / 1985 / VCR / C • Dial A Dick / 1986 / AVC / M • Dollface / 1987 /

CV / M • Dr Truth's Great Sex / 1986 / VD / M • Girls Of The Chorus Line / 1986 / CLV / M • Harem Girls / 1986 / SE / M • Heavy Breathing / 1986 / CV / M • Indecent Itch / 1985 / VCR / M • Indecent Wives / 1985 / HO / M • Intimate Entry / 1988 / V99 / C • Lucky Charm / 1986 / AVC / C • Parliament: Shaved #1 / 1986 / PM / F • Showgirls / 1985 / SE / M

SANDY SUNSHINE see Star Index I

SANDY TAYLOR see Lynn Ray

SANDY TAYLOR (75) see Star Index I

SANDY WARNER
Deep Stroke / 1980 / CV / M

SANDY WEST
Blue Vanities #222 / 1994 / FFL / M

SANJA SORRELLO see Star Index I

SANTINO LEE *(Michael Santino, Michael Dushane)*
Black male who seems to be bald and wears a cap most of the time. Michael Dushane is from **Wild Widow**.
The Adventures Of Peeping Tom #2 / 1996 / OD / M • The Adventures Of Peeping Tom #3 / 1996 / OD / M • Afro American Dream Girls #1 / 1996 / DR / M • Afro American Dream Girls #2 / 1996 / DR / M • Anal Cannibals / 1996 / ZA / M • Anal Virgins Of America #07 / 1994 / FOR / M • Anna Amore's Fantasy Gang Bang / 1996 / FC / M • Ariana's Dirty Dancers: The Professionals / 1996 / 4P / M • Backstage Pass / 1994 / SC / M • Bang City #7: Carolina's Anal Gang Bang / 1995 / SC / M • Beyond Reality #2: Anal Expedition / 1996 / EXQ / M • Beyond Reality #3: Stand Erect! / 1996 / EXQ / M • Big Babies In Budapest / 1996 / EL / M • Big Bust Babes #20 / 1994 / AFI / M • Big Bust Babes #21 / 1994 / AFI / M • Black Centerfolds #1 / 1996 / DR / M • Black Centerfolds #2 / 1996 / DR / M • Black Centerfolds #3 / 1996 / MID / M • Black Centerfolds #4 / 1996 / MID / M • Black Cheerleader Search #02 / 1996 / ROB / M • Black Cheerleader Search #03 / 1996 / ROB / M • Black Cheerleader Search #04 / 1996 / ROB / M • Black Cheerleader Search #07 / 1996 / IVC / M • Black Fantasies #14 / 1996 / HW / M • Black Gangbangers #12 / 1996 / HW / M • Black White Festival / 1996 / P69 / M • The Blues #2 / 1994 / VT / M • Bottom Dweller: The Final Voyage / 1996 / EL / M • California Blacks / 1994 / V99 / M • Carolina's D.P. Anal Gangbang / 1996 / FC / M • Caught From Behind #21 / 1995 / HO / M • Cheatin' / 1994 / FD / M • China's House Party / 1996 / HW / M • Decadence / 1996 / VC / M • Dirty & Kinky Mature Women #08 / 1996 / C69 / M • Dirty & Kinky Mature Women #10 / 1996 / C69 / M • Dirty Tails / 1996 / SC / M • Doin' The Nasty / 1996 / AVI / M • Double Anal Alternatives / 1996 / EL / M • Double Dicked #1 / 1996 / RAS / M • Erotica Optique / 1994 / SUF / M • European Sex TV / 1996 / EL / M • A Fairy's Tail / 1996 / TTV / M • Hardcore Confidential #2 / 1996 / TEP / M • Hidden Camera #19 / 1994 / JMP / M • Hidden Camera #20 / 1994 / JMP / M • House Of Sex #14: All Black Gang Bang / 1994 / RTP / M • Lockdown / 1996 / NIT / M • M Series #20 / 1994 / LBO / M • M Series #23 / 1994 / LBO / M • Macin' #1 / 1996 / SMP / M • Macin' #2: Macadocious / 1996 / SMP / M • Microslut / 1996 / TTV / M • Milli Vanilla /

1994 / TP / M • My Baby Got Back #08 / 1996 / VT / M • My First Time #4 / 1996 / NS / M • Nba: Nuttin' Butt Ass / 1996 / SMP / M • New Girls In Town #6 / 1994 / CC / M • Odyssey Triple Play #90: Black & White In Loving Color / 1995 / OD / M • Perverted Stories #06 / 1996 / JMP / M • The Return Of Dr Blacklove / 1996 / CC / M • Sarah's Inheritance / 1995 / WIV / M • Savage Fury #3 / 1994 / VEX / M • Sista! #5 / 1996 / VT / F • Sodomania #17: Simply Makes U Tingle / 1996 / EL / M • Sodomania #18: Shame Based / 1996 / EL / M • Sodomania: Slop Shots / 1996 / EL / C • Span's Garden Party / 1996 / HW / M • Summer Dreams / 1996 / TEP / M • Swedish Erotica #76 / 1994 / CA / M • Swedish Erotica #84 / 1995 / CA / M • Swinging Couples #04 / 1994 / GO / M • Tailz From Da Hood #3 / 1996 / AVI / M • Takin' It To The Limit #7: Debauched / 1996 / BS / M • Thermonuclear Sex / 1996 / EL / M • Underground #2: Subway To Sodom / 1996 / SC / M • Underground #3: Sit On This / 1996 / SC / M • Up And Cummers #39 / 1996 / RWP / M • Up Your Ass #1 / 1996 / ANA / M • White Trash Whore / 1996 / JMP / M • Wild Orgies #03 / 1994 / AFI / M • Wild Widow / 1996 / NIT / M • Women Of Color #1 / 1994 / ANA / M

SANYEN SUNNY
Ultraflesh / 1980 / GO / M

SAPHIRE
How To Make A College Co-Ed / 1995 / VG0 / M

SAPHIRE (SUKOYA) *see* **Sukoya**

SAPHYR
Club Privado / 1995 / KP / M

SAPPHO *see Star Index I*

SARA
AVP #9121: The Date / 1991 / AVP / M • Bend Over Brazilian Babes #1 / 1993 / EA / M • Bend Over Brazilian Babes #2 / 1993 / EA / M • College Video Virgins #07 / 1996 / AOC / M • GRG: Sara's Seductive Interview / 1995 / GRG / F • Joe Elliot's College Girls #35 / 1994 / JOE / M • Micro X Video #3 / 1992 / YDI / M • Pearl Necklace: Amorous Amateurs #01 / 1992 / SEE / M • Pearl Necklace: Facial #01 / 1994 / SEE / C • Sex On The Saddle: Wicked Women Of The Wild West / 1994 / CPG / S

SARA (RICKY LEE) *see* **Ricky Lee**

SARA BERNARD
Black Sister, White Brother / 1987 / AT / M • Dick Of Death / 1985 / VCR / M • Flesh And Fantasy / 1985 / VC / M • Girl Busters / 1985 / VC / M • Give It To Me / 1984 / SE / M • Hot Licks / 1984 / SE / M • Hot Rockers / 1985 / IVP / M • Indiana Joan In The Black Hole Of Mammoo / 1984 / VC / M • Long Hard Nights / 1984 / ELH / M • A Passage Thru Pamela / 1985 / VC / G • Taboo American Style #3: Nina Becomes An Actress / 1985 / VC / M • Taboo American Style #4: The Exciting Conclusion / 1985 / VC / M • Tickled Pink / 1985 / VC / M • VCA Previews #4 / 1988 / VC / C • The Voyeur / 1985 / VC / M

SARA BLOOM
Mafia Girls / 1972 / SOW / M

SARA CANE
Ball & Chain / 1994 / GOT / B • Damaged Goods / 1995 / GOT / B • Dangerous Desires (Gotham) / 1994 / GOT / B • Judgement / 1994 / GOT / B • Lesbian Submission / 1994 / PL / B • Losing Control / 1995

/ GOT / B • Marquesa's Dungeon / 1994 / GOT / B • Masters Of Dominance / 1996 / GOT / C • Playthings / 1995 / GOT / B • The Princess Slave / 1994 / BIZ / B • Pussy Tamer #2 / 1993 / BIZ / B • Ravaged / 1994 / GOT / B • Savage Torture / 1994 / PL / B • The Spirit Of My Master / 1994 / BIZ / B • Toe Tales #11 / 1993 / GOT / B • Toe Tales #13 / 1994 / GOT / B • Toe Tales #14 / 1994 / GOT / B • Toe Tales #15 / 1994 / GOT / B • Toe Tales #16 / 1994 / GOT / B • Toe Tales #18 / 1994 / GOT / B • Toe Tales #20 / 1995 / GOT / B • Toe Tales #24 / 1995 / GOT / C • Toe Tales #26 / 1995 / GOT / B

SARA CONNELLY
Triple Play (Vh) / cr75 / VC / M

SARA CRUZ *see Star Index I*

SARA HEART *see* **Tera Heart**

SARA JANE HAMILTON *(Sarah Jane Hamilton, Victoria Secret, Victoria Secrett, Victoria Seerett)*
Started as a reasonable looker (see **2 Hung, 2 Tung**) but then developed into just another huge titted English import. Born April 15, 1971 in London, England. Supposedly she can "squirt" when she comes (yeah, sure!). De-virginized at age thirteen.
2 Hung 2 Tung / 1992 / MID / M • America's Raunchiest Home Videos #25: Victoria's Secretions / 1992 / ZA / M • American Buttman In London / 1991 / EA / M • American Swinger Video Magazine #07 / 1993 / ZA / M • Bad Girls Get Punished / 1994 / NTP / B • Badlands #1 / 1994 / PEP / M • Badlands #2: Back Into Hell / 1994 / PEP / M • Beach Ball / 1994 / SC / M • Big Knockers #16 / 1995 / TV / M • Big Knockers #17 / 1995 / TV / M • The British Are Coming / 1993 / ZA / M • Bubble Butts #07 / 1992 / LBO / M • Buck Naked In The 21st Century / 1993 / EVN / M • Bums Away / 1995 / PRE / C • The Busty Kittens / 1995 / NAP / F • Butt's Motel #6 / 1994 / EX / M • Butthead Dreams / 1994 / FH / M • Carnal College #2 / 1993 / AFV / M • Cheatin' / 1994 / FD / M • Chemical Reaction / 1995 / CC / M • The Cumming Of Sarah Jane #1 / 1993 / AFV / M • The Cumming Of Sarah Jane #2 / 1993 / AFV / M • Dead Ends / 1992 / PRE / B • Deep Inside Misty Rain / 1995 / VC / C • Double D Dykes #08 / 1993 / GO / F • Double D Dykes #10 / 1993 / GO / F • Double D Dykes #11 / 1993 / GO / F • Double Decadence / 1995 / NOT / M • Erotica Optique / 1994 / SUF / M • The Exchange / 1995 / BON / B • Exstasy / 1995 / WV / M • Extreme Sex #2: The Dungeon / 1994 / VI / M • The Face / 1994 / PP / M • Feathermates / 1992 / PRE / B • The First Live Bettie Page Interview / 1996 / SBI / S • Flood Control / 1992 / PRE / B • Foreign Tongues #2: Mesmerized / 1995 / VI / M • Forever Payne / 1994 / BS / B • Generally Horny Hospital / 1995 / IMV / M • A Girl's Affair #01 / 1992 / FD / F • Girls On Duty / 1994 / LE / M • The Great American Boobs To Kill For Dance Contest / 1995 / PEP / C • Greek Week / 1994 / CV / M • Harry Horndog #23: The Final Flick / 1993 / ZA / M • Hits & Misses / 1992 / PRE / B • Hollywood Confidential / 1995 / TWP / B • The Hollywood Starlet Search / 1995 / SC / M • How To Give Pleasure To A Woman By A Woman / 1995 / SEM / F • I Touch Myself / 1994 / IP / F • Immortal Desire / 1993 / VI / M • In The Bush / 1994 / PP / M • Indecent

Offer / 1993 / AFV / M • Jetstream / 1993 / AMP / M • Kym Wilde's On The Edge #21 / 1995 / RB / B • Laugh Factory / 1995 / PRE / C • Legal Briefs / 1996 / EX / M • Lesbian Mystery Theatre: The Case Of The Deadly Dyke / 1994 / LIP / F • Lesbian Pros And Amateurs #15 / 1992 / GO / F • Lesbian Pros And Amateurs #16 / 1992 / GO / F • Love Bunnies #06 / 1994 / FPI / F • Lydia's Web / 1994 / TWP / B • Mind Games / 1995 / IMV / M • Never Trust A Slave / 1996 / BON / B • No Quarter Given / 199? / NAP / B • Once A Slave / 1995 / HOM / B • P.K. & Company / 1995 / CV / M • Pajama Party X #1 / 1994 / VC / M • Pajama Party X #2 / 1994 / VC / M • Plaything #2 / 1995 / VI / M • Pretending / 1993 / CV / M • Prison World / 1994 / NTP / B • The Queens Of Mean / 1994 / NTP / B • Rainbird / 1994 / EMC / M • Rainwoman #05 / 1992 / CC / M • Rainwoman #06 / 1993 / CC / M • Rainwoman #07: In The Rainforest / 1993 / CC / M • Rare Ends / 1996 / PRE / C • Rear Ended / 1992 / CS / B • Reel Life / 1993 / ZA / M • Riot Grrrls / 1994 / SC / M • Safari Jane / 1995 / ERA / M • Sarah Jane's Love Bunnies #01 / 1993 / FPI / F • Sarah Jane's Love Bunnies #02 / 1993 / FPI / F • Sarah Jane's Love Bunnies #03 / 1993 / FPI / F • Sarah Jane's Love Bunnies #04 / 1993 / FPI / F • Sarah Jane's Love Bunnies #05 / 1993 / FPI / F • Secret Rendez-Vous / 1994 / XCI / M • Sex Lives Of Clowns / 1994 / VC / M • Slippery When Wet / 1994 / LEI / C • Songbird / 1993 / AMP / M • Spread The Wealth / 1993 / DR / M • Starbangers #03 / 1993 / ZA / M • Steam / 1993 / AMP / M • Strippers Inc. #1 / 1994 / ONA / M • Takin' It To The Limit #2 / 1994 / BS / M • Titty City #1 / 1995 / TIW / M • Top Debs #3: Riding Academy / 1993 / GO / M • Top Debs #4: Sex Boat / 1993 / GO / M • Uncle Roy's Amateur Home Video #05 / 1992 / VIM / M • Uncle Roy's Amateur Home Video #06 / 1992 / VIM / M • Uncle Roy's Best Of The Best: Red Hots / 1993 / VIM / C • Unplugged / 1995 / CC / M • Viva Viviana / 1994 / PME / F • Whackers / 1995 / PP / M • When The Mistress Is Away... / 1995 / HAC / B • Where The Boys Aren't #6 / 1995 / VI / F • Wild Roomies / 1994 / VC / M • Will & Ed's Keister Easter / 1992 / MID / M • The XXX Files: Lust In Space / 1995 / IMV / M • [Into The Forrest / 19?? / ... / M • [Liquid Lady / 19?? / ... / M

SARA LANE *see Star Index I*

SARA MAPLES
Dirty And Kinky Mature Women #1 / 1995 / C69 / M

SARA MELO *see Star Index I*

SARA NICHOLSON *see* **Jennifer Jordan**

SARA ST. JAMES
Captured On Camera / 1997 / BON / B • Erotic Eye / 1995 / DGD / S • Hot Body Competition: Bikinis & Bikes Contest / 1996 / CG / F • Nicole's Revenge / 1995 / MID / F • Nude Bowling Party / 1995 / BRI / S • Playboy: The Girls Of The Internet / 1995 / UNI / F • Spy Trap / 1995 / BON / B • Unruly Slaves #1 / 1995 / BON / B • Unruly Slaves #2 / 1995 / BON / B

SARA WALKER *see Star Index I*

SARA WALTERS
Sex In Black & White / 1995 / OD / M

SARA WINE *see* **Christy Canyon**

SARAH

Blue Vanities #510 / 1992 / FFL / M • Blue Vanities #538 / 1993 / FFL / M • British Cunts Are Cumming! / 1996 / SPL / M • Max Gold #1 / 1996 / XPR / C • Penthouse: Great Pet Hunt #1 / 1992 / PET / F • Spanked Senseless / 1995 / BIZ / B • Triple X Video Magazine #03 / 1995 / OD / M • World Sex Tour #7 / 1996 / ANA / M

SARAH BARNES see Jenny Baxter
SARAH BELLOMO see Roxanne Blaze
SARAH CLAUDIA see Star Index I
SARAH DAWCETT see Rhonda Jo Petty
SARAH DIGSIT
They Shall Overcome / 1974 / VST / M
SARAH DUVALL see Star Index I
SARAH HARRIS see Loni Sanders
SARAH HEART
Anal Destroyer / 1994 / ZA / M • Cherry Poppers #09: Misbehavin' / 1995 / ZA / M • Gang Bang Virgin #1 / 1994 / HO / M • Hollywood Amateurs #12 / 1994 / MID / M • Nasty Newcummers #07 / 1995 / MET / M
SARAH JANE HAMILTON see Sara Jane Hamilton
SARAH L.
Bucky Beaver's XXX Dragon Art Theatre Double Feature #04 / 1996 / SOW / M • Revelations / 1974 / SOW / M
SARAH LAKE see Star Index I
SARAH LE-ANNE HAYLEY
Buttman's British Moderately Big Tit Adventure / 1994 / EA / M
SARAH LEE
Busty Nymphos / 1996 / H&S / M
SARAH LESINI
Magma: Hot Service / 1995 / MET / M
SARAH LORHMAN
Star Of The Orient / 1978 / VIP / M
SARAH LYNN
Buffy Malibu's Nasty Girls #07 / 1994 / ANA / F • Much More Than A Mouthful #2 / 1988 / VEX / M
SARAH MAPLES
Grateful Grandma's Gang Bang / 1994 / FC / M
SARAH MICHELOB see Star Index I
SARAH MILLS see Kathy Riley
SARAH NICHOLSON see Jennifer Jordan
SARAH O'HARA see Star Index I
SARAH SCOTT
Anal Injury / 1994 / ZA / M
SARAH SHELDON see Star Index I
SARAH SIMMS see Star Index I
SARAH SMITH
Spiteful Housewives Spanked / 1995 / BIZ / B
SARAH SUMMERS see Star Index I
SARAH VACHE
Sweet Punkin...I Love You / 1975 / VC / M
SARAH WALKER see Star Index I
SARAH WILLIAMS
American Nympho In London / 1987 / VD / M • The Baroness / 1987 / VD / M • The French Maid's Flogging / 1995 / BIZ / B • Hard Core Cafe / 1988 / VD / M • Hot Nights And Dirty Days / 1988 / VD / M • International Phone Sex Girls #1 / 1988 / VD / M
SARAH YOUNG
Hamlet: For The Love Of Ophelia #2 / 1996 / IP / M • Sarah & Friends #1 / 1995 / SYC / M • Sarah & Friends #5 / 1995 / SYC / M • Sarah & Friends #7 / 1995 / PL / M
SARDE RENAUD
Girls With Curves #1 / 1985 / CV / M

SARINA see Star Index I
SARON
Deep Inside Dirty Debutantes #11 / 1996 / 4P / M
SARONA
Geisha Slave / 1985 / BIZ / B • Menage De Sade / 1987 / BIZ / B • Mistress Sarona's School Of Discipline / 1987 / BIZ / B • Private Quarters / 1987 / BIZ / B • Terri's Lesson In Bondage / 1979 / BIZ / B
SASCHA *(Sasha (Dutch))*
Blonde with medium enhanced tits. Quite pretty with a tight body.
The Anal-Europe Series #01: The Fisherman's Wife / 1992 / LV / M • Illusions #1 / 1992 / IF / M • Sodomania #02: More Tails / 1992 / EL / M • Student Fetish Videos: Best of Catfighting #03 / 1995 / PRE / C • Student Fetish Videos: Catfighting #13 / 1994 / PRE / B • Student Fetish Videos: Spanking #17 / 1994 / PRE / B • Thinking Of You / 1992 / LV / F • Torrid Tonisha / 1992 / VEX / M • Wild Girls / 1993 / LV / F • Women Of Influence / 1993 / LV / F • [European Invasion / cr93 / A&E / M
SASCHA (STRANGE) see Sasha Strange
SASCHA ATZENBACH see Star Index I
SASCHA CHONG
Black Dirty Debutantes / 1993 / 4P / M
SASCHA HEHN
[Schulmadchen-Report 4: Was Eltern Oft Verzweifeln LaBt / 1972 / ... / M
SASCHA KING see Star Index I
SASHA
A-Z Of Lesbian Love / 1996 / PAL / F • Back East Babes #2 / 1996 / NIT / M • Catch Of The Day #2 / 1995 / VG0 / M • China Bitch / 1989 / PV / C • Diamonds / 1996 / HDE / M • Double D Dykes #10 / 1993 / GO / F • Floor Play / 1989 / PLV / B • Foot Lights / 1988 / BIZ / B • Foot Teasers / 1988 / BIZ / B • Footgames In Bondage / 1992 / BIZ / C • The Long & Short Of It / 1992 / RUM / F • Penthouse: 25th Anniversary Pet Of The Year Spectacular / 1994 / A*V / F • Shane's World #6: Slumber Party / 1996 / OD / F • Student Fetish Videos: Best Of Foot Worship #02 / 1994 / PRE / C • Student Fetish Videos: Best Of Spanking #02 / 1993 / PRE / C • Student Fetish Videos: Foot Worship #07 / 1992 / PRE / B • Student Fetish Videos: Foot Worship #08 / 1992 / PRE / B • Student Fetish Videos: Spanking #07 / 1992 / PRE / B • Take It Like A Man / 1994 / IF / M • Tisa Marie: Finger Lickin' Good / 1991 / SXI / F • Trampled / 1993 / STM / B • Wet Workout: Shape Up, Then Strip Down / 1995 / PME / S
SASHA (BLACK)
Pearl Necklace: Amorous Amateurs #01 / 1992 / SEE / M • Pearl Necklace: Amorous Amateurs #03 / 1992 / SEE / M • Pearl Necklace: Amorous Amateurs #05 / 1992 / SEE / M • Pearl Necklace: Amorous Amateurs #09 / 1992 / SEE / M • Pearl Necklace: Facial #01 / 1994 / SEE / C • Pearl Necklace: Thee Bush League #25 / 1993 / SEE / M
SASHA (BRITISH) *(Sasha Suxx)*
Blonde sometimes with dark curly hair, very pretty face, tight body and waist, narrow hips, petite body. British sometimes sounding too pushy and knowing.
Cherry Poppers #13: Anal Pajama Party / 1996 / ZA / M • Freshness Counts / 1996 /

EL / M • Triple X Video Magazine #13 / 1996 / OD / M • Up And Cummers #26 / 1996 / 4P / M
SASHA (CHANEL) see Chanel (1992)
SASHA (DESIREE FOX) see Desiree Fox
SASHA (DUTCH) see Sascha
SASHA (S/M)
Bitter She-Males / 1992 / BIZ / G • Bone Appetit: A She-Male Seduction / 1994 / BIZ / G • Chicks With Dicks #1: A Slick And Slippery Oil Orgy / 1992 / BIZ / B • Defiant TV's / 1994 / BIZ / G • Shopping With A Transvestite: In A Boy, Out A Girl / 1992 / BIZ / G • Transsexual Passions #2 / 1994 / BIZ / G • TV Blondes Do It Best / 1992 / BIZ / G • TV Dildo Fantasy #1 / 1992 / BIZ / G • TV Dungeon / 1992 / BIZ / G • TV Ladies Room / 1993 / BIZ / G • TV Panty Party / 1994 / BIZ / G • TV Phone Sex / 1992 / BIZ / G • TV Reform School / 1992 / BIZ / G • TV Room / 1993 / BIZ / G • TVs Teased And Tormented / 1995 / BIZ / G
SASHA (STRANGE) see Sasha Strange
SASHA GABOR *(Kirk Reynolds, J. Bandit, James Bandit, Alex Gabor, Alexander Gabor, Garet Adkins)*
Heavy set male with a resemblence to Burt Reynolds.
40 The Hard Way / 1991 / OD / M • A'mature: Snatching Sasha / 1991 / AVP / M • Amber Aroused / 1985 / CA / M • Anal Angels #1 / 1986 / VEX / M • Angel's Back / 1988 / IN / M • As Cute As They Cum / 1990 / VEX / M • Asspiring Actresses / 1989 / CA / M • Assuming The Position / 1989 / V99 / M • AVP #7024: Bodyguard Bang / 1991 / AVP / M • B.Y.O.B. / 1984 / VD / M • Backdoor To Hollywood #04 / 1988 / CDI / M • Battling Beauties / 1983 / ACV / B • Beauties And The Beast / 1990 / AFV / M • Behind The Backdoor #3 / 1989 / EVN / M • Best Chest In The West / 1984 / ACV / S • Best Of Caught From Behind #2 / 1988 / HO / C • Beverly Hills Exposed / 1985 / SE / M • The Big Gun / 1989 / FAN / M • Black Angel / 1987 / CC / M • Blame It On The Heat / 1989 / VC / M • Blue Heaven / 1990 / IF / M • Body Games / 1987 / DR / M • Born For Love / 1987 / ... / M • The Buttnicks #1 / 1990 / VEX / M • Cagney & Stacey / 1984 / AT / M • California Blondes #02 / 1987 / VEX / M • Camera Shy / 1990 / IN / M • Caught From Behind #08 / 1988 / HO / M • Centerfold Celebrities #4 / 1983 / VC / M • Centerfold Celebrities #5 / 1983 / VC / M • Cherry Busters / 1984 / VIV / M • Creamy Cheeks / 1986 / VEX / M • Dangerous / 1989 / PV / M • Debbie Does 'em All #3 / 1989 / CV / M • Deep In Deanna Jones / 1989 / EVN / M • Deep Inside Rachel Ashley / 1987 / VEX / M • Deep Inside Viviana / 1992 / VEX / C • Deep Throat #5 / 1990 / AR / M • Devil In Vanity / 1990 / CC / M • Dirty Diane / 1989 / V99 / M • Dirty Harriet / 1986 / SAT / M • Dirty Pictures / 1985 / SUP / M • Double Black Fantasy / 1987 / CC / C • Double Penetration #1 / 1985 / WV / M • Dreams In The Forbidden Zone / 1989 / PCP / M • Dress To Thrill / 1986 / FAS / S • Dressed To Thrill / 1986 / CDI / M • E.X. / 1986 / SUP / M • Ebony Humpers #1 / 1986 / VEX / M • Erotic Rendezvous / 1988 / VEX / M • Every Woman Has A Fantasy #1 / 1984 / VC / M • Flesh In Ecstasy #06: Elle Rio / 1987 / GO / C • For Your Lips Only / 1989

/ FAZ / M • Fun In A Bun / 1990 / LV / M • Gang Bangs #1 / 1985 / VCR / M • Gazongas #01 / 1987 / VEX / M • Get Me While I'm Hot / 1988 / PV / M • Ginger (1984-Vivid) / 1984 / VI / M • Heartless / 1989 / REB / M • Heartthrobs / 1985 / CA / M • High Rollers / 1987 / VEX / M • Holly Does Hollywood #3 / 1989 / VEX / M • Hollywood Hustle #1 / 1990 / V99 / M • The Hollywood Starlet Search / 1995 / SC / M • The Honeymoon: The Bride's Running Behind / 1990 / 4P / M • Hot And Nasty! / 1986 / V99 / C • I Want Your Sex / 1990 / FAZ / M • Images Of Desire / 1990 / PM / M • Immoral Majority / 1986 / HTV / M • In Charm's Way / 1987 / IN / M • In Search Of The Golden Bone / 1986 / CA / M • Indecent Proposals / 1988 / SEX / M • Indecent Proposals / 1991 / V99 / M • Jane Bond Meets Thunderballs / 1986 / VD / M • Kascha & Friends / 1988 / CIN / M • Ladies Man / 1990 / REB / M • Love On The Borderline / 1987 / IN / M • Lusty Adventurer / 1985 / GO / M • Magic Pool / 1988 / VD / M • Making It Big / 1990 / TOR / M • Making The Grade / 1989 / IN / M • Miss American Dream / 1985 / CIV / M • Money Honey / 1990 / TOR / M • My Wildest Dreams / 1988 / IN / C • Naked Lust / 1985 / SE / M • Nasty Habits Are Hard To Break / 1986 / 4P / M • Naturally Sweet / 1989 / VEX / M • Naughty Neighbors / 1986 / VEX / M • Night On The Town / 1990 / V99 / M • Night Prowlers / 1985 / MAP / M • Night Watch / 1990 / VEX / M • Nikki And The Pom-Pom Girls / 1987 / VEX / M • No Strings Attached / 1990 / ERO / M • One Flew Over The Cuckoo's Breast / 1989 / FAZ / M • One For The Road / 1989 / V99 / M • One Hot Night Of Passion / 1985 / COL / C • One More Time / 1990 / VEX / M • Open House (CDI) / 1989 / CDI / M • Oriental Jade / 1985 / VC / M • Party Animals / 1987 / VEX / M • Party Animals / 1994 / VEX / C • Party In The Rear / 1989 / LV / M • Peek-A-Boo / 1987 / VEX / M • Platinum Princess / 1988 / VEX / M • Playing Dirty / 1989 / VEX / M • Playing The Field / 1990 / VEX / M • The Pleasure Hunt / 1985 / NSV / M • Pleasure Principle / 1988 / VEX / M • Power Play (Venus 99) / 1990 / V99 / M • Prescription For Passion / 1984 / VD / M • Raising Hell / 1987 / VD / M • Rebecca's / 1983 / AVC / M • Saki's House Party / 1990 / KNI / M • The Secret Diaries / 1990 / V99 / M • Sex And The Single Girl / 1990 / FAN / M • Sex Charades / 1990 / VEX / M • Sex Crazed / 1989 / VEX / M • Sex Sluts In The Slammer / 1988 / FAN / M • Shades Of Passion / 1985 / CA / M • She's America's Most Wanted / 1990 / VEX / M • Sky Pies / 1985 / GO / M • Slumber Party / 1990 / LV / M • Soul Games / 1988 / PV / C • Sounds Of Sex / 1985 / CA / M • Space Virgins / 1990 / VEX / M • Stag Party / 1986 / ACV / S • Street Heat / 1984 / VC / M • Sulka's Daughter / 1984 / MET / G • Super Sex / 1986 / MAP / M • Sweet Nothings / 1987 / HO / M • Take It To The Limit / 1990 / V99 / M • Tamara's Dreams / 1989 / VEX / M • Tasty / 1985 / CA / M • Ticket To Ride / 1990 / LV / M • Titillation #2 / 1990 / SE / M • Tough Girls Don't Dance / 1987 / SEV / M • Tracey And The Bandit / 1987 / LA / M • Tracey's Love Chamber / 1987 / AR / M • Undressed For Success / 1990 / V99 / M •

Up Up And Away / 1984 / CA / M • Vas-O-Line Alley / 1985 / VC / M • Wet, Wild And Wicked / 1984 / SE / M • Who Reamed Rosie Rabbit? #2 / 1989 / FAN / M • Wild Nurses In Lust / 1986 / PLY / M • Wildfire / 1989 / EVN / M • The Year Of The Sex Dragon / 1986 / PV / M

SASHA KING *see* **Sasha Strange**

SASHA LYNN
Hose Jobs / 1995 / VEX / M

SASHA PENDAVIS *see* **Champagne Pendarvis**

SASHA RAMONE
Boiling Point / 1978 / SE / M

SASHA ROUSA *see* **Star Index I**

SASHA SAVAGE
Not too pretty hefty blonde with tree trunk thighs. Looks like a hooker and seems to permanently chew gum.
Adventures Of The DP Boys: The Hollywood Bubble Butts / 1993 / HW / M • All "A" / 1994 / SFP / C • Anal Intruder #07 / 1993 / CC / M • Bobby Hollander's Maneaters #05 / 1993 / SFP / M • Bobby Hollander's Rookie Nookie #02 / 1993 / SFP / M • Dirty Bob's #06: NiCESt NoviCES / 1992 / FLP / S • First Time Lesbians #03 / 1993 / JMP / F • Girls Will Be Boys #6 / 1993 / PL / F • Immortal Desire / 1993 / VI / M • Needful Sins / 1993 / WV / M • Odyssey Triple Play #70: Three By Threeway / 1994 / OD / M • Straight A Students / 1993 / MET / M • Toppers #13 / 1993 / TV / M • Toppers #16 / 1993 / TV / M • Toppers #17 / 1993 / TV / M • Toppers #22 / 1993 / TV / C • Toppers & Whoppers / 1994 / PRE / C

SASHA STERLING
Mystic Tales Of The Orient / 1994 / PRK / M

SASHA STRANGE *(Sasha (Strange), Sasha Taylor, Sascha (Strange), Sasha King, Sasha Tayler)*
20th Century Fox / 1989 / FAZ / M • The Adventures Of Buttman / 1989 / EA / M • Army Brat #2 / 1989 / LV / M • The Aroused / 1989 / IN / M • Bad Habits / 1993 / VC / M • Best Of Buttman #1 / 1991 / EA / C • The Big Tease #2 / 1990 / VC / M • Bored Housewife / 1989 / CIN / M • Brat Force / 1989 / VI / M • Breaststroke #1 / 1988 / EX / M • Butt's Motel #1 / 1989 / EX / M • Dirty Books / 1990 / V99 / M • For Her Pleasure Only / 1989 / FAZ / M • Girls Like Us / cr88 / IN / C • Girls Of The Double D #06 / 1989 / CIN / M • Girls Will Be Girls / 1988 / LV / F • The Great Sex Contest #2 / 1989 / LV / M • Hot In The City / 1989 / VEX / M • Hot Palms / 1989 / GO / M • Mystery Of The Golden Lotus / 1989 / HU / M • No Man's Land / 803 / 1989 / VT / F • Nurse Tails / 1994 / VC / M • Play Christy For Me / 1990 / CAY / M • Playin' Dirty / 1990 / VC / M • Plenty Of Pleasure / 1990 / WET / M • Risque Business / 1989 / V99 / M • Rock 'n' Roll Heaven / 1989 / EA / M • Sex Crazed / 1989 / VEX / M • She's A Boy / 1989 / LV / G • Single She-Male Singles Bar / 1990 / STA / G • Slick Honey / 1989 / VC / M • Snatched / 1989 / VI / M • Spellbound / 1989 / LV / M • Stolen Kisses / 1989 / VD / M • Strange Curves / 1989 / VC / M • Super Ball / 1989 / VWA / M • Torrid Without A Cause #1 / 1989 / VI / M • Tour De Trans / 1989 / STA / G • True Confessions Of Hyapatia Lee / 1989 / VI / M • Vixens / 1989 / LV / F • Who Shaved Trinity Loren? / 1988

/ EX / M

SASHA SUXX *see* **Sasha (British)**
SASHA SWEET *(Honey Bee (Sasha))*
Black Masters: Den Of Punishment / 1996 / GOT / B • Black Masters: Hidden Fear / 1996 / GOT / B • Black Masters: Red Flesh / 1996 / GOT / B • Black Masters: Seduction In Bondage / 1996 / GOT / B • Blow Below The Belt / 1995 / GOT / B • Corrected Deception / 1994 / STM / B • Crack Up / 1994 / GOT / B • Cruel Lessons / 1996 / GOT / B • Dirty / 1993 / FD / C • Dirty Bob's #24: The Big O! / 1996 / FLP / M • Dirty Dancers #1 / 1994 / 4P / M • Hell To Pay / 1996 / OUP / B • Hoetown / 1994 / STM / F • Intimate Interviews #4 / 1996 / NIT / M • Judgement / 1994 / GOT / B • Jug Humpers / 1995 / V99 / C • Kittens #7 / 1995 / CC / F • Lesbian Submission / 1994 / PL / B • Losing Control / 1995 / GOT / B • Master's Frenzy / 1994 / GOT / B • Masters Of Dominance / 1996 / GOT / C • Mind Mirror / 1994 / LAP / M • Mistress From Hell / 1996 / GOT / B • Mr. Pink And The Hotel Harlots / 1996 / ORG / F • N.Y. Video Magazine #01 / 1994 / OUP / M • N.Y. Video Magazine #02 / 1995 / OUP / M • N.Y. Video Magazine #03 / 1995 / OUP / M • N.Y. Video Magazine #04 / 1995 / OUP / M • N.Y. Video Magazine #05 / 1995 / OUP / M • N.Y. Video Magazine #06 / 1995 / OUP / M • N.Y. Video Magazine #07 / 1996 / OUP / M • N.Y. Video Magazine #08 / 1996 / OUP / M • N.Y. Video Magazine #09 / 1996 / OUP / M • N.Y. Video Magazine #10 / 1996 / OUP / M • New York City Lesbian Gang Bang / 1995 / OUP / F • The Payoff / 1994 / GOT / B • Pitfalls Of Sasha / 1995 / GOT / B • Private Pleasures / 1994 / STM / F • Revenge & Punishment / 1995 / GOT / B • Road Trippin' #02: New York City / 1994 / OUP / F • Savage Torture / 1994 / PL / B • Seductive TV / 1995 / GOT / G • Sex Between The Scenes / 1994 / LAP / M • Snatch Masters #05 / 1995 / LEI / M • Toe Tales #11 / 1993 / GOT / B • Toe Tales #16 / 1994 / GOT / B • Toe Tales #17 / 1994 / GOT / B • Toe Tales #18 / 1994 / GOT / B • Toe Tales #19 / 1994 / GOT / B • Toe Tales #20 / 1995 / GOT / B • Toe Tales #22 / 1995 / GOT / B • Toe Tales #23 / 1995 / GOT / B • Toe Tales #24 / 1995 / GOT / C • Toe Tales #25 / 1995 / GOT / B • Toe Tales #27 / 1995 / GOT / B • Toe Tales #28 / 1995 / GOT / B • Toe Tales #29 / 1995 / GOT / B • Toe Tales #30 / 1995 / GOT / C • Toe Tales #31 / 1995 / GOT / B • Toe Tales #33 / 1996 / GOT / B • Toe Tales #34 / 1996 / GOT / B • Toe Tales #35 / 1996 / GOT / B • Toe Tales #36 / 1996 / GOT / B • Toe Tales #37 / 1996 / GOT / B • Toe Tales #38 / 1996 / GOT / B • Toe Tales #39 / 1996 / GOT / B • Trained Transvestites / 1995 / STM / B • Transvestite Ordeal / 1994 / GOT / G • TV Roommate / 1996 / GOT / G • TV Trained To Perform / 1994 / STM / G • Twisted Rage / 1995 / GOT / B • Very Bad Girls / 1995 / GOT / B • Worthless Wives / 1996 / GOT / B

SASHA TAYLER *see* **Sasha Strange**
SASHA TAYLOR *see* **Sasha Strange**
SASHA THE DESTROYER
Amazon Trample / 1995 / IBN / B
SASHA VINNI
Making Of The "Carousel Girls" Calendar / 1994 / DGD / S • Penthouse: 1993 Pet Of

The Year Playoff / 1993 / PET / F • Penthouse: 1994 Pet Of The Year Winners / 1994 / PET / F • Sex Off The Runway / 1991 / GMI / M • Zazel / 1996 / CV / M

SASHA WELLS
Filthy First Timers #3: Tearing Down The Walls Of Shame / 1996 / EL / M • Filthy First Timers #4 / 1996 / EL / M

SASHIA DEMUIS *see Star Index I*

SASHIA LENE *see Jessica James*

SASHYA
Bondage "Sybian" Rides / 1994 / PSE / B

SASKIA
Latent Image: Saskia / 1994 / LAT / F • Russian Model Magazine #1 / 1996 / IP / M

SASSY
AVP #9126: Photo Finish / 1991 / AVP / M • AVP #9155: Group Therapy #2 / 1991 / AVP / M • Deep Inside Annie Sprinkle / 1981 / VXP / M • Under The Skirt #1 / 1995 / KAE / F

SASSY DOUGLAS
[Snow Balling / 197? / ... / M

SASUKI YAWADO
Honey Sex / 1996 / AVE / M

SATANIA
Hollywood Amateurs #16 / 1995 / MID / M • Mickey Ray's Sex Search #05: Deep Inside / 1995 / WIV / M • Mike Hott: #291 Cunt Of The Month: Satania / 1995 / MHV / M • Mike Hott: #292 Three-Sum Sluts #03 / 1995 / MHV / M • Pussy Lotto / 1995 / WIV / M • Titan's Gonzo Video Magazine #02 / 1996 / TEG / M

SATCHA *see Star Index I*

SATIN
Anal Witness #1 / 1996 / LBO / M • Prima #11: Dr. Max In Hollywood / 1995 / MBP / M

SATIN (BLACK)
Black Street Hookers #2 / 1996 / DFI / M

SATIN CHEEKS *see Satin Sheets*

SATIN DECK *see Star Index I*

SATIN DOLL
Fresh Faces #09 / 1996 / EVN / M

SATIN SHEETS *(Satin Cheeks)*
Not too pretty, dark blonde or brown hair, needs major dental work, medium droopy tits, lithe body, tattoos on left tit (words) and left shoulder back.
19 & Naughty #1 / 1994 / SKV / M • Adventures Of The DP Boys: At The French Riviera / 1994 / HW / M • Amateur Dreams #3 / 1994 / DR / M • Amateur Dreams #4 / 1994 / DR / M • Beaver Hunt #03 / 1994 / LEI / M • Butt Hunt #05 / 1995 / LEI / M • Creme De La Face #03 / 1994 / OD / M • Creme De La Face #04 / 1994 / OD / M • First Time Lesbians #20 / 1994 / JMP / F • Florence Hump / 1994 / AFI / M • Hollywood Amateurs #04 / 1994 / MID / M • Hollywood Starlets Adventure #02 / 1995 / AVS / M • Teacher's Pet #2 / 1994 / WMG / M • Titanic Orgy / 1995 / PEP / M

SATIN SUMMER
69th Street Vice / 1984 / VC / M • Afrodisiac #1 / 1987 / CC / M • Afrodisiac #2 / 1989 / CC / M • Black Girls In Heat / 1985 / PL / M • Black Licorice / 1985 / CDI / M • Black Sister, White Brother / 1987 / AT / M • Cocktales / 1985 / AT / M • Ebony & Ivory Sisters / 1985 / PL / C • Flesh And Fantasy / 1985 / VC / M • Hot Fudge / 1984 / VC / M • Indiana Joan In The Black Hole Of Mammoo / 1984 / VC / M • Midnight Pink / 1987 / WV / M • Pretty In Black / 1986 /

WET / M • Rearbusters / 1988 / LVI / C • Romancing The Bone / 1984 / VC / M • Shameful Desires In Black & White Girls / 1984 / PL / M • The South Bronx Story / 1986 / CC / M • Young Girls Do #1: Troublemakers / 1995 / CDI / M

SATINA (SAKI) *see Saki*

SATINA LAROUCHE *see Saki*

SATIVA
More Dirty Debutantes #43 / 1995 / 4P / M • Nostalgia Blue / 1976 / VC / M

SATOMI LIN *see Satomi Suzuki*

SATOMI SUZUKI *(Satumi, Satomi Lin, Fusako, Fusoko)*
Young-looking petite Japanese girl with very nicely shaped small breasts. She's a bit flat on the ass and needs lots of dental work. 22 years old in 1994 and was de-virginized at 16.
Adventures Of The DP Boys: Tokyo Tramps / 1994 / HW / M • Anal Angel / 1994 / EX / M • Anal Legend / 1994 / ROB / M • Anal Lover #3 / 1994 / ROB / M • Anal Oriental Sorority / 1994 / LBO / M • Anal Rookies #2 / 1994 / ROB / M • Anal Savage #2 / 1994 / ROB / M • Anal Spitfire / 1994 / ROB / M • Anal Summer / 1994 / ROB / M • Anal Vision #27 / 1994 / LBO / M • Backdoor To Taiwan / 1994 / LV / M • The Best Of Black Anal #1 / 1995 / ROB / C • The Best Of Oriental Anal #1 / 1994 / ROB / C • Black Hollywood Amateurs #07 / 1995 / MID / M • Booty Mistress / 1994 / ROB / M • Bun Busters #20 / 1994 / LBO / M • Casting Call #06 / 1994 / SO / M • Dirty Doc's Housecalls #17 / 1994 / LV / M • East Vs West: Battle Of The Gang Bangs / 1994 / TTV / M • Fortune Nookie / 1994 / PPP / M • Horny Henry's Oriental Adventure / 1994 / TTV / M • I Can't Believe I Did The Whole Team! / 1994 / FPI / M • Kinky Debutante Interviews #02 / 1994 / IP / M • Kinky Orientals / 1994 / FH / M • Little Miss Anal / 1994 / ROB / M • Lovin' Spoonfuls #4 / 1995 / 4P / C • Miss D.P. Butterfly / 1995 / TIW / M • More Dirty Debutantes #33 / 1994 / 4P / M • Nasty Nymphos #03 / 1994 / ANA / M • New Ends #08 / 1994 / 4P / M • New Girls In Town #5 / 1994 / CC / M • Oriental Oddballs #1 / 1994 / FH / M • Perverted #1: The Babysitters / 1994 / ZA / M • Private Video Magazine #13 / 1994 / OD / M • Pussyclips #01 / 1994 / SNA / M • Slut Safari #3 / 1994 / FC / M • Smooth As Silk / 1994 / EMC / M • Stiff Competition #2 / 1994 / CA / M • Sushi Butts / 1994 / SCL / M • Sweat 'n' Bullets / 1995 / MID / M • Tight Fit #02 / 1994 / GO / M • Up And Cummers #12 / 1994 / 4P / M • Up And Cummers #15 / 1994 / 4P / M • Video Virgins #11 / 1994 / NS / M • Wild Orgies #05 / 1994 / AFI / M

SATUMI *see Satomi Suzuki*

SATUNI IKO
Tight Shots #1 / 1994 / VI / M

SATYN *see Star Index I*

SAUD IBLIS
Afrodisiac #2 / 1989 / CC / M • Tickled Pink / 1985 / VC / M • VCA Previews #4 / 1988 / VC / C

SAVAGE SKI
All "A" / 1994 / SFP / C • Bobby Hollander's Rookie Nookie #07 / 1993 / SFP / M

SAVANNA
Bondage Magic / 1996 / JAM / B • Christine's Bondage Fantasies / 1996 / JAM / B

SAVANNA CIARA

Sam Gets Shafted / 1996 / MP0 / M

SAVANNAH *(Silver, Silver Kane, Silver Cain, Silver Cane, Shannon Wilsey, Shannon Ward)*
Passable face, large rock solid tits, lithe body. The epitome of lazy sex. 5'6", 105lbs, 34D-22-30. The Silver Kane name was used prior to breast enhancement. Shannon Wilsey is her real name. Born October 9, 1970 and started in porn in 1990. Romantically linked to Greg Allman and Pauly Shore. On Sunday July 11, 1994 when returning home she crashed into a picket fence in her car and damaged her face. This upset her so much she took a gun and blew her brains out.
Adult Video News 1992 Awards / 1992 / VC / M • Amateur American Style #30 / 1992 / AR / F • America's Dirtiest Home Videos #03 / 1991 / VEX / M • America's Dirtiest Home Videos #07 / 1991 / VEX / M • Angels / 1992 / VC / A • Autoerotica #1 / 1991 / EX / M • Autoerotica #2 / 1991 / EX / M • Battle Of The Superstars / 1993 / VI / M • Best Of Foot Worship #3 / 1992 / BIZ / C • Blonde Forces #1 / 1991 / CC / M • Blonde Savage / 1991 / CDI / M • Bums Away / 1995 / PRE / C • Cheatin' Hearts / 1991 / VEX / M • Circus Of Lesbians / 1995 / VI / C • Crazy On You / 1991 / IF / M • Deep Inside Racquel Darrian / 1994 / VC / C • Deep Inside Savannah / 1993 / VC / C • Desire / 1990 / VC / M • Dirty Dave's American Amateurs #03 / 1992 / AR / M • Ecstasy / 1991 / LE / M • The Eliminators / 1991 / BIZ / B • End Results / 1991 / PRE / C • The Erotic Adventures Of The Three Musketeers / 1992 / CEL / S • Every Man's Fancy / 1991 / V99 / M • Flash Floods / 1991 / PRE / C • Forever / 1991 / LE / M • Foxy Hellcats Of Wrestling #1 / 1991 / CDP / B • Foxy Hellcats Of Wrestling #2 / 1991 / CDP / B • Gazongas #03 / 1991 / VEX / M • Ghoul School / 1990 / CVH / S • Girls Of Sin / 1994 / PL / C • Happy Endings / 1990 / BIZ / B • Hole In One / 1993 / IF / M • Hollywood X-Posed #1 / 1992 / VIM / C • Hometown Honeys #2 / 1991 / VEX / M • Hot Blondes / 1991 / VEX / C • Hot Body Video Magazine #08 / 1994 / CG / S • Hot Savannah Nights / 1991 / VEX / M • Hot Spot / 1991 / CDI / M • House Of Sleeping Beauties #1 / 1992 / VI / M • House Of Sleeping Beauties #2 / 1992 / VI / M • Hurts So Good / 1991 / VEX / M • The Hustlers / 1993 / MID / M • Indian Summer #1 / 1991 / VI / M • Indian Summer #2: Sandstorm / 1991 / VI / M • The Invisible Maniac / 1990 / REP / S • Kinky Nurses / 1995 / VEX / C • Laying The Ghost / 1991 / VC / M • Leg...Ends #03 / 1991 / BIZ / F • Legal Tender (1990-R) / 1990 / PRS / S • Lick-A-Thon #2 / 1996 / HW / C • Love Seats / 1994 / PRE / C • Made In Heaven / 1991 / PP / M • Nasty Jack's Homemade Vid. #08 / 1990 / CDI / M • Nasty Reputation / 1991 / VEX / M • Naughty Butt Nice / 1993 / IF / M • Naughty Nymphs / 1991 / VEX / C • New Wave Hookers #2 / 1991 / VC / M • No Boys Allowed / 1991 / VC / F • On Trial #1: In Defense Of Savannah / 1991 / VI / M • On Trial #2: Oral Arguments / 1991 / VI / M • On Trial #3: Takin' It To The Jury / 1992 / VI / M • On Trial #4: The Verdict / 1992 / VI / M • Pajama Party / 1993 / CV / C • Perfect Endings / 1994 / PLV / B • Pink To Pink

/ 1993 / VI / C • Racquel's Addiction / 1991 / VC / M • Reflections Of Innocence / 1991 / VEX / C • Roxy / 1991 / VC / M • Runaway / 1992 / VI / M • The Savannah Affair / 1993 / CDI / M • Savannah R.N. / 1992 / HW / M • Savannah Superstar / 1992 / VI / M • Savannah's Last Stand / 1993 / VI / M • Shipwrecked / 1991 / VEX / C • Sinderella #1 / 1992 / VI / M • Sinderella #2 / 1992 / VI / M • Skippy, Jiff & Jam / 1990 / CIA / M • Smarty Pants / 1992 / VEX / M • Sometime Sweet Savannah / 1994 / IF / M • Sorority House Massacre #2: Nighty Nightmare / 1990 / WAR / S • Southern Accents / 1992 / VEX / M • The Spectacle / 1991 / IN / M • Speedster / 1992 / VI / M • Starbangers #01 / 1993 / BIG / M • Student Fetish Videos: Best Of Foot Worship #03 / 1995 / PRE / C • Suburban Swingers / 1993 / IF / M • Summertime Boobs / 1994 / LEI / M • Surf City Sex / 1991 / CIA / M • Sweet Cheeks (1991-Vid Excl) / 1991 / VEX / C • Sweet Stuff / 1991 / V99 / M • The Taming Of Savannah / 1993 / VI / M • Telemates / 1991 / V99 / M • Three Girl Tickle #2 / 1996 / SY / B • Tight Fit / 1991 / VEX / C • Troublemaker / 1991 / VEX / M • True Legends Of Adult Cinema: The Modern Era / 1992 / VC / C • Turn Up The Heat / 1991 / VEX / C • The Vision / 1991 / LE / M • Vow Of Passion / 1991 / VI / M • Wet Event / 1992 / IF / M • What Kind of Girls Do You Think We Are? / 1991 / VEX / C • Where The Boys Aren't #4 / 1992 / VI / F • Wild Thing / 1994 / IF / M • [Camp Fear / 1991 / ... / S

SAVERA RAY see Star Index I
SAVIDA see Star Index I
SAYOKO AMANO see Star Index I
SCARLET
Analtown USA #08 / 1995 / NIT / M • Bad Side Of Town / 1993 / AFD / M • Bun Busters #21 / 1994 / LBO / M • Creme De La Face #12: Pretty Faces To Cum On / 1995 / OD / M • Cum Buttered Corn Holes #3 / 1996 / NIT / C • The Cumm Brothers #11: Oh Cum On Ye Faces / 1995 / OD / M • Cutie Pies / 1995 / TTV / M • Dance Beaver / 1995 / CZV / M • Decadent / 1991 / WV / M • Dirty Bob's #24: The Big O! / 1996 / FLP / M • Drop Outs / 1995 / PRE / B • Essence / 1996 / SO / M • First Time Lesbians #22 / 1994 / JMP / F • Forbidden Subjects #4 / 1995 / FC / M • Foreign Fucks / 1995 / FOR / M • Hollywood Starlets Adventure #02 / 1995 / AVS / M • Kinky Peep Shows: Anals & Orals / 1995 / SUF / M • M Series #29 / 1994 / LBO / M • M Series #30 / 1994 / LBO / M • Mike Hott: #392 / 1996 / MHV / M • The Older Women's Sperm Bank #2 / 1996 / SUF / M • The Older Women's Sperm Bank #3: Red Hot Grandmas / 1996 / SUF / M • The Older Women's Sperm Bank #4 / 1996 / SUF / M • Orgies Orgies Orgies / 1994 / WV / M • Pussy Hunt #06 / 1994 / LEI / M • Pussyclips #10 / 1995 / SNA / M • Ron Hightower's White Chicks #16 / 1994 / LBO / M • Scarlet And Pump-Her-Nickel / 1992 / RUM / M • Student Fetish Videos: Catfighting #13 / 1994 / PRE / B • Student Fetish Videos: The Enema #17 / 1995 / PRE / B • Student Fetish Videos: Foot Worship #13 / 1994 / PRE / B • Swedish Erotica #79 / 1994 / CA / M • Tail Taggers #129: / 1994 / WV / M • Triple Play / 1994 / PRE / B • Welcome To Paradise / 1994 / IF / M

SCARLET (BIG TITS) see Star Index I
SCARLET (SCHARLEAU) see Scarlett Scharleau
SCARLET BEGONIA
The Phantom Of The Montague Stage / 1997 / HO / M
SCARLET FEVER (96) (Jennifer Jo Smith)
Long dark brown hair, plucked eyebrows, passable face, medium/large droopy tits, flabby womanly body, Southern accent. According to her she comes from Mobile AL, is either 21 or 18 years old (depending on the movie all of which are in 1996), and was de-virginized at 15. She also says she tells the truth but obviously doesn't. Jennifer Jo Smith is the name she uses in **My First Time #7**.
Butt Sluts #6 / 1996 / ROB / F • Enemates #12 / 1996 / BIZ / B • Freaky Tailz / 1996 / AVI / M • Hit Parade / 1996 / PRE / B • Lesbian Pooper Sluts / 1996 / ROB / F • My First Time #7 / 1996 / NS / M • Sole Search / 1996 / PRE / B • Student Fetish Videos: Spanking #22 / 1996 / PRE / B • Student Fetish Videos: Tickling #13 / 1996 / SFV / B • Venom #5 / 1996 / VD / M • Video Virgins #33 / 1996 / NS / M • Young & Natural #15 / 1996 / TV / F • Young & Natural #16 / 1996 / TV / F • Young & Natural #18 / 1996 / TV / C
SCARLET FEVER (SCS) see Scarlett Scharleau
SCARLET HARLOT
House Of Chicks: Masturbation Memoirs #1 / 1995 / HOC / F
SCARLET JONES
Anal Annie And The Backdoor Housewives / 1984 / LIP / F • Butter Me Up / 1984 / CHX / M
SCARLET LA RUE see Donna Anne
SCARLET MALIBU
Anal Receivers / 3996 / MPO / M • The Crackster / 1996 / OUP / M • Creme De La Face #15: Showroom Sex / 1996 / OD / M • Interview With A Tramp / 1996 / SP / M • Nothing Like Nurse Nookie #2 / 1996 / NIT / M • Orgy Camera #1 / 1995 / EVN / M • Vortex / 1995 / MET / M • Young And Anal #3 / 1995 / JMP / M
SCARLET ROSE see Lacy Rose
SCARLET SCARBEAU see Scarlett Scharleau
SCARLET SHARBEAU see Scarlett Scharleau
SCARLET SMITH
Sex Crimes 2084 / 1985 / SE / M • Slammer Girls / 1987 / LIV / S
SCARLET WIND
Radical Affairs Video Magazine #09 / 1995 / ME / M • Up And Cummers #20 / 1995 / 4P / M
SCARLET WINDSOR (Megan Bradley)
English. Very pretty blonde with medium tits, tight waist, narrow hips and a nice little butt.
Backdoor To Hollywood #10 / 1989 / CIN / M • Devil In The Blue Dress / 1989 / ME / M • Girls Of The Double D #01 / 1986 / CDI / M • The Hustler / 1989 / CDI / M • Jealous Lovers / 1989 / CDI / M • Low Blows: The Private Collection / 1989 / ME / M • Make Me Sweat / 1989 / CIN / M • Sky Foxes / 1987 / VC / M • Super Tramp / 1989 / VD / M
SCARLETT (Scrarlotte, Michelle (Scar-

lett), Scarlett O'Hara)
Reddish-brown hair, very white skin consistent with being a natural redhead, medium firm tits, 28 in 1993, no freckles, squarish face, quite pretty. Masses of tattoos as follows: large one on left tit that looks like a leaping cat; leaf on her left back shoulder; and a dagger on her right outside bicep. Has a husband/boyfriend called Harley who has a Svengali-like beard.
Anal Vision #22 / 1993 / LBO / M • Beach Bum Amateur's #31 / 1993 / MID / M • Biff Malibu's Totally Nasty Home Videos #40 / 1993 / ANA / M • Buffy Malibu's Nasty Girls #11 / 1996 / ANA / F • Bun Busters #04 / 1993 / LBO / M • Casting Call #05 / 1994 / SO / M • Cherry Poppers #09: Misbehavin' / 1995 / ZA / M • Dirty Doc's Housecalls #03 / 1993 / LV / M • Eighteen #3 / 1996 / SC / M • Frankenfoot / 1993 / SBP / B • The Knocker Room / 1993 / GO / M • Master Of Masters #1 / 1995 / BBB / B • Mike Hott: #269 Cunt Of The Month: Scarlett / 1994 / MHV / M • Mike Hott: #272 Jack Off On My Cunt #01 / 1994 / MHV / M • Mike Hott: #315 Cum In My Mouth #02 / 1995 / MHV / C • Nasty Nymphos #14 / 1996 / ANA / M • Playtex / 1996 / GLI / M • Sodomania #16: Sexxy Pistols / 1996 / EL / M • Student Fetish Videos: Best of Catfighting #03 / 1995 / PRE / C • Student Fetish Videos: Best Of Foot Worship #03 / 1995 / PRE / C • Triple Flay / 1995 / PRE / B • Vagina Beach / 1995 / FH / M • Video Virgins #05 / 1993 / NS / M
SCARLETT (BIG)
Anal Maidens Three / 1996 / BOT / M • Designated Hitters / 1995 / PRE / B • Leg...Ends #15 / 1995 / PRE / F
SCARLETT FEVER (SCS) see Scarlett Scharleau
SCARLETT KENNEDY see Sue Nero
SCARLETT KNIGHT see Star Index I
SCARLETT O
Big redhead—not too pretty.
Anal Intruder #03 / 1989 / CC / M • Charlie's Girls #2 / 1989 / CC / M • Dirty Diane / 1989 / V99 / M • The Great Sex Contest #2 / 1989 / LV / M • Hershe Highway #1 / 1989 / HO / M • Hershe Highway #2 / 1989 / HO / M • No Man's Land #03 / 1989 / VT / F • Risque Business / 1989 / V99 / M • Sex Crazed / 1989 / VEX / M • Wetness For The Prosecution / 1989 / LV / M
SCARLETT O'HARA see Scarlett
SCARLETT SCHARLEAU (Scarlet Fever (SCS), Scarlett Fever (SCS), Scarlet (Scharleau), Scarlet Sharbeau, Scarlet Scarbeau)
Pudgy looking blonde with small tits.
69th Street Vice / 1984 / VC / M • Angela In Wonderland / 1986 / VD / M • Bi Bi American Style / cr85 / MET / G • Black Licorice / 1985 / CDI / M • Black Sister, White Brother / 1987 / AT / M • Black Voodoo / 1987 / FOV / M • Blowing Your Mind / 1984 / RSV / M • Chocolate Candy #3 / 1986 / VD / M • Close Friends / 1987 / CC / G • Confessions Of A Middle Aged Nympho / 1986 / WET / M • Cravings / 1987 / VC / M • Deep Throat #2 / 1986 / AR / M • Double Trouble / 1986 / DRV / M • Fannie's Fantail / 1985 / VC / M • Flesh And Fantasy / 1985 / VC / M • Hot Licks / 1984 / SE / M • Lorelei / 1984 / CV / M • Love Hammer / 1988 / VXP / M • No Man's Land #01 / 1988 / VT

/ C • Officer's Discipline / 1985 / BIZ / B • Secret Mistress / 1986 / VD / M • Sex Sounds / 1989 / PL / M • Shameful Desires In Black & White Girls / 1984 / PL / M • A Taste Of Pink / 1985 / VXP / M • Thunderstorm / 1987 / VC / M • Times Square Comes Alive / 1984 / VC / M • Tongues Of Fire / 1987 / BIZ / F • Toothless People / 1988 / SUV / M • Ultrasex / 1987 / VC / M • Vas-O-Line Alley / 1985 / VC / M • Video Tramp #2 / 1988 / TME / M

SCENESSIATURA
Essence Of A Woman / 1995 / ONA / M

SCHANEL
Black Casting Couch #1 / 1993 / WP / M • Chocolate Bunnies #03 / 1995 / LBO / C • Odyssey Triple Play #55: Black & White & Up The Ass / 1994 / OD / M • SVE: Spanks For The Memories / 1994 / SVE / B

SCHERELL *see* **Cherelle**

SCOCA O.
Private Gold #09: Private Dancer / 1996 / OD / M

SCORPIO DEE
Every Nerd Has A Fantasy / 1996 / FC / M

SCOTLAND
Homegrown Video #419: Reigning Pussycats And Horndogs / 1994 / HOV / M

SCOTT
Beach Bum Amateur's #20 / 1992 / MID / M • Biff Malibu's Totally Nasty Home Videos #31 / 1993 / ANA / M • British Butt Search / 1995 / VC / M • Catch Of The Day #5 / 1996 / VG0 / M • Dixie Debutantes #1 / 1996 / MYS / M • GVC: Sweet Dominance #127 / 1983 / GO / B • HomeGrown Video #465: Bong The Schlong / 1996 / HOV / M • HomeGrown Video #470: Heroes, Torpedoes & Grinders / 1996 / HOV / M • J.E.G.: Christy, Tim And Scott / 1995 / JEG / M • Mr. Peepers Amateur Home Videos #63: Sexual Soiree / 1992 / LBO / M • Nasty Fuckin' Movies #19: Fuck Me...Fresh Meat / 1993 / RUM / M • Neighborhood Watch #37: Pelvic Thrusters / 1993 / LBO / M • The Other Side Of Debbie / 1991 / CC / M • Stevi's: He Dreams Of Jeanie / 1994 / SSV / M

SCOTT ADAMS
Tobianna: A Gang Bang Fantasy / 1993 / FC / M

SCOTT ALLEN
Bound Brats / 1994 / BON / B • Delusions / 1983 / PRC / M • Personal Trainer (Ibn) / 1995 / IBN / B

SCOTT APOLLO
Behind The Backdoor #1 / 1986 / EVN / M • California Blondes #01 / 1986 / VEX / M • Cream Dreams / 1986 / VEX / M • Fun In The Sun / 1988 / EVN / C • The Ladies Room / 1987 / CA / M • Traci's Big Trick / 1987 / VAS / M

SCOTT BAKER *(Scott Thompson Baker)*
The Thompson as a middle name comes from **Cleo/Leo.**
Afrodisiac #2 / 1989 / CC / M • Angela In Wonderland / 1986 / VD / M • Bad Blood / 1989 / AE / S • Banana Split / 1991 / LBO / B • Bizarre World Of Scott Baker / 1992 / CAS / B • Bizarre's Dracula #1 / 1995 / BIZ / B • Bizarre's Dracula #2 / 1995 / BIZ / B • Blindfold / 1996 / GOT / B • Bordello...House Of The Rising Sun / 1985 / SE / M • Captive Sessions / 1994 / GOT / B • Cleo/Leo / 1989 / NWW / S • The Crack Of Dawn / 1989 / GLE / M • Cruel Turn-

about / 1990 / PL / B • Date With A Mistress / 1995 / BIZ / B • Daughters Of Discipline / 1993 / GOT / B • The Dean's Spanking / 1995 / STM / B • Debi Diamond: Mega Mistress / 1995 / BIZ / B • Deep Inside Trading / 1986 / AR / M • Delivery Boys / 1984 / NWW / S • Doctors Of Pain / 1995 / BIZ / B • Dr Of Pain / 1995 / BIZ / B • The Enema Bandit Strikes Again / 1995 / BIZ / B • Enslaved / 1995 / GOT / B • The Erotic Adventures Of Bedman And Throbbin / 1989 / VWA / M • Firm Hands / 1996 / GOT / B • Flames Of Submission / 1995 / GOT / B • Footgames In Bondage / 1992 / BIZ / C • Gillie's Isle / 1990 / GOT / M • The Golden Rule / 1993 / GOT / B • Hot Talk Radio / 1989 / VWA / M • Hung Jury / 1989 / VWA / M • Hyperkink / 1989 / VWA / M • In The Pink / 1983 / CA / M • Jack 'n' Jill #2 / 1984 / VC / M • Kiss My Ass / 1994 / GOT / B • Last Resort / 1994 / GOT / B • Mind Mirror / 1994 / LAP / M • The Mistress And The Prince / 1995 / STM / B • Mistress Cherri's Basic (Slave) Training / 1992 / CAS / B • Mistress From Hell / 1996 / GOT / B • Mother Load #2 / 1994 / GOT / B • Murder By Sex / 1993 / LAP / M • Naked Prey / 1996 / GOT / B • New York Nights / 1994 / ... / S • New York's Finest / 1988 / AE / S • No Respect / 1995 / GOT / B • Nurses Bound By Duty / 1996 / BIZ / B • Oriental Treatment / 1995 / GOT / B • Prisoners Of Pain / 1994 / BIZ / B • Raw Talent #3 / 1988 / VC / M • Revenge & Punishment / 1995 / GOT / B • Rites Of Passion / 1988 / FEM / M • Rough Games / 1994 / GOT / B • Ruling Methods / 1994 / GOT / B • Screw The Right Thing / 1990 / VWA / M • Secrets In The Attic #1 / 1994 / STM / B • Secrets In The Attic #2: Extreme Measures / 1994 / STM / B • Sex Between The Scenes / 1994 / LAP / M • Sex Crimes 2084 / 1985 / SE / M • Sex Drive / 1984 / VXP / M • Shame On You / 1995 / GOT / B • Slammer Girls / 1987 / LIV / S • Slaves Night Out / 1995 / COC / B • Slaves' Night Out / 1990 / COC / B • Striptease #1 / 1995 / PL / M • Stroke Of Nine / 1994 / GOT / B • Submission Of Ariana / 1995 / BIZ / B • Third Degree / 1992 / GOT / B • Thrilled To Death / 1988 / REP / S • Throbbin' Hood / 1987 / VD / M • Toe Tales #03 / 1992 / GOT / B • Toe Tales #04 / 1992 / GOT / B • Toe Tales #06 / 1993 / GOT / B • Toe Tales #07 / 1993 / GOT / B • Toe Tales #08 / 1993 / GOT / B • Toe Tales #09 / 1993 / GOT / B • Toe Tales #10 / 1993 / GOT / B • Toe Tales #12 / 1994 / GOT / C • Toe Tales #16 / 1994 / GOT / B • Toe Tales #17 / 1994 / GOT / B • Toe Tales #18 / 1994 / GOT / B • Toe Tales #21 / 1995 / GOT / B • Toe Tales #23 / 1995 / GOT / B • Toe Tales #24 / 1995 / GOT / C • Toe Tales #26 / 1995 / GOT / B • Toe Tales #27 / 1995 / GOT / B • Toe Tales #28 / 1995 / GOT / B • Toe Tales #29 / 1995 / GOT / B • Toe Tales #32 / 1996 / GOT / B • Toe Tales #35 / 1996 / GOT / B • Toe Tales #36 / 1996 / GOT / B • Toe Tales #37 / 1996 / GOT / B • Toe Tales #38 / 1996 / GOT / B • Toe Tales #39 / 1996 / GOT / B • The Training #2 / 1994 / BIZ / B • Transvestite Ordeal / 1994 / GOT / G • Trial And Error / 1994 / GOT / B • TV Roommate / 1996 / GOT / G • TV's Dilemma / 1993 / GOT / G • Twilight Pink #2 / 1982 / VC / M • Urban Heat / 1985 / FEM / M • VGA: Don't Defy

Domino / 1991 / VGA / B • VGA: Spanks-A-Lot / 1993 / VGA / B • The Voyeur / 1985 / VC / M • Web Of The Mistress / 1994 / GOT / B • Wildest Dreams / 1987 / VES / S

SCOTT BALDWIN
Our Trespasses / 1996 / AWV / G

SCOTT BOISVERT *see* **Alex Sanders**

SCOTT C. *see* **Alex Sanders**

SCOTT COOK *see* **Star Index I**

SCOTT D'BONE
Filthy First Timers #1 / 1996 / EL / M

SCOTT DANIELS *see* **Star Index I**

SCOTT DAVIS
Journal Of O #1: Servant Slave / 1994 / ONA / B • Journal Of O #2 / 1994 / ONA / B • Ona Zee's Learning The Ropes #10: Chains Of Love / 1994 / ONA / B • Ona Zee's Learning The Ropes #11: Chains Required / 1994 / ONA / B

SCOTT GALLEGOS *see* **Jonathan Morgan**

SCOTT HAMPTON
Ginger's Private Party / 1985 / VI / M

SCOTT HARDMAN
Bi-Conflict / 1994 / FST / G • Bi-Sex Pleasures / 1993 / PL / G • Conflict Of Interest / 1994 / FST / G • Inside Of Me / 1993 / PL / G

SCOTT HARRIS
Palm Springs Or Bust / 1994 / BTO / M

SCOTT IRISH *(Scott Shamrock)*
Scott Shamrock is from **Up All Night.** Was shot (not fatally) in the LA riots in 1992. Sandy haired tall male with small dick.
1-800-934-BOOB / 1992 / VD / C • 18 Candles / 1989 / LA / M • 69 Pump Street / 1988 / ZA / M • Adultery / 1989 / PP / M • The Adultress / 1987 / CA / M • All For One / 1988 / CIN / M • Amazing Tails #1 / 1987 / CA / M • Amber Lynn's Peter Meter / 1988 / 3HV / C • American Dream Girls #1 / 1986 / VEX / M • Anal Addiction #3 / 1991 / SO / M • Anal Angels #1 / 1986 / VEX / M • Anal Encounters #7: Enter Through The Rear / 1992 / VC / M • Anal Fury / 1992 / ROB / M • Angel Kelly Raw / 1987 / FAN / M • Anything Goes / 1993 / VD / C • Army Brat #1 / 1987 / VI / M • The Art Of Passion / 1987 / CA / M • Asian Silk / 1992 / VI / M • Assford Wives / 1992 / ATL / M • Autoerotica #2 / 1991 / EX / M • Backdoor Black #1 / 1992 / WV / C • Backdoor To Hollywood #02 / 1986 / CDI / M • Backdoor To Hollywood #04 / 1988 / CDI / M • Backing In #3 / 1991 / WV / C • The Backway Inn #1 / 1992 / FD / M • Banana Splits / 1987 / 3HV / M • Barbara The Barbarian / 1987 / SE / M • Batteries Included / 1988 / 3HV / M • The Battle Of the Breast Queens / 1989 / INS / C • Bazooka County #2 / 1989 / CC / M • Beach Bum Amateur's #02 / 1992 / MID / M • The Best Little Whorehouse In Beverly Hills / 1986 / CDI / M • The Best Of Oriental Anal #1 / 1994 / ROB / C • Betrayal / 1992 / XCI / M • Between My Breasts #02 / 1986 / L&W / S • Between My Breasts #11 / 1990 / BTO / M • The Big Thrill / 1989 / VD / M • Black Angel / 1987 / CC / M • Black Sensations / 1987 / VEX / M • Black Valley Girls #2 / 1989 / DR / M • Black, White And Blue / 1989 / E&I / M • Blondie / 1985 / TAR / M • Blowing The Whistle / 1986 / VIP / M • Body Shop / 1984 / VCX / M • Boobs, Butts And Bloopers #1 / 1990 / HO / M • Bored Housewife / 1989 / CIN / M • Brainteasers / 1991 / ZA / M • The Brat Pack /

1989 / VWA / M • Breaststroke #2 / 1989 / EX / M • Bring On The Virgins / 1989 / CA / M • Bringing Up Brat / 1987 / VI / M • Bringing Up The Rear / 1993 / VD / C • Busen Extra #1 / 1991 / BTO / M • California Gigolo / 1987 / VD / M • Call Girl Academy / 1990 / V99 / M • Can't Beat The Feeling / 1988 / VEX / M • Cat & Mouse #1 / 1992 / XCI / M • Caught From Behind #12 / 1989 / HO / M • The Chameleon / 1989 / VC / M • Changing Partners / 1989 / FAZ / M • Charm School / 1986 / VI / M • Charmed Forces / 1987 / VI / M • Cheek To Cheek / 1986 / VEX / M • Cheerleader Academy / 1986 / PL / M • Cheri Taylor Is Tasty And Tight / 1991 / ZA / M • Circus Acts / 1987 / SE / C • Club Bed / 1987 / CIX / M • Club Head (EVN) #2 / 1989 / EVN / C • Coming On Strong / 1989 / CA / C • Confessions #2 / 1992 / OD / M • Convenience Store Girls / 1986 / VD / M • Cream Dreams / 1986 / VEX / M • Debbie Does 'em All #3 / 1989 / CV / M • Deep Blue / 1989 / PV / M • Deep Inside Keisha / 1994 / VC / C • Deep Inside Nikki Sinn / 1996 / VC / C • Deep Inside Victoria Paris / 1993 / VC / C • Deep Throat #3 / 1989 / AR / M • Devil In Vanity / 1990 / CC / M • The Dinner Party / 1986 / WV / M • Don't Worry Be Sexy / 1989 / EVN / C • Double Black Fantasy / 1987 / CC / C • Double Penetration #4 / 1991 / WV / C • Double Standards / 1986 / VC / M • Double Trouble / 1988 / V99 / M • Double Whammy / 1986 / LA / M • Dreams Of Misty / 1984 / VCX / M • Easy Lovers / 1987 / SE / M • Erotic Aerobics / 1984 / VC / M • Erotic Radio WSEX / 1983 / VC / M • Erotic Therapy / 1987 / CDI / M • Escort To Ecstasy / 1987 / 3HV / M • Family Secrets / 1985 / AMB / M • Fast Girls #1 / 1987 / GBX / M • Fatal Seduction / 1988 / CDI / M • Feel The Heat / 1989 / VEX / M • Free And Foxy / 1986 / VCX / C • From Kascha With Love / 1988 / CDI / M • Gerein' Up / 1992 / VC / M • Gillie's Isle / 1990 / GOT / M • Ginger Snaps / 1987 / VI / M • The Girls Of Ball Street / 1988 / VEX / M • The Girls Of Rodeo Drive / 1987 / BAD / M • Girls Of The Double D #01 / 1986 / CDI / M • Girls Of The Double D #02 / 1987 / CDI / M • Girls Of The Double D #09 / 1989 / CDI / M • Going Down With Amber / 1987 / 4P / M • Gold LeMay / 1991 / VIM / M • The Great Sex Contest #2 / 1989 / LV / M • Head Clinic / 1987 / AVC / M • Heart Of Stone / 1990 / FAN / M • Heather's Home Movies / 1989 / VWA / M • Heraldo: Streetwalkers Of NY / 1990 / GOT / M • Here's Looking At You / 1988 / V99 / M • Hershe Highway #2 / 1989 / HO / M • Hidden Desire / 1989 / HO / M • Holly Does Hollywood #3 / 1989 / VEX / M • Hometown Honeys #1 / 1986 / VEX / M • Hot Blondes / 1988 / VEX / M • Hot Dreams / 1989 / VEX / M • Hot Dreams / 1991 / VEX / M • The Hot Lick Cafe / 1990 / AMB / M • Hot To Swap / 1988 / VEX / M • House Of The Rising Moon / 1986 / VD / M • Hung Jury / 1989 / VWA / M • Hungry / 1990 / GLE / M • Hyapatia Lee's Arcade Series #01 / 1988 / ZA / C • Hyapatia Lee's Arcade Series #02 / 1988 / ZA / C • Hyapatia Lee's Sexy / 1986 / SE / M • I Do #3 / 1992 / VI / M • I Wanna Be Teased / 1984 / SE / M • Icy Hot / 1990 / MID / M • Infidelity / 1988 / 4P / M • Innocent Obsession / 1989 / FC /

M • Innocent Seduction / 1988 / VC / M • Innocent Taboo / 1986 / VD / M • Introducing Barbii / 1987 / CDI / M • The Invisible Girl / 1989 / VI / M • Jane Bond Meets Thunderballs / 1986 / VD / M • Just For Tonight / 1992 / VC / M • Kascha's Blues / 1988 / CDI / M • The Kink / 1988 / WV / M • Kinky / 1987 / SE / M • Kissin' Cousins / 1984 / PL / M • Krystal Balling / 1988 / PL / M • L.A.D.P. / 1991 / PL / M • The Ladies Room / 1987 / CA / M • The Last Girl Scout / 1992 / PL / M • Laying Down The Law #1 / 1992 / AFV / M • Laying Down The Law #2 / 1992 / AFV / M • Lays Of Our Lives / 1988 / ZA / M • The Legend Of Sleepy Hollow / 1989 / LE / M • Lessons With My Aunt / 1986 / SHO / M • The Life Of The Party / 1991 / ZA / M • Like A Virgin #2 / 1986 / AT / M • Little American Maid / 1987 / VCX / M • Little Girls Of The Streets / 1984 / CV / M • A Live Nude Girl / 1989 / VWA / M • Loose Caboose / 1987 / 4P / M • Loose Ends #3 / 1987 / BS / M • Lottery Fever / 1985 / BEA / M • Love On The Borderline / 1987 / IN / M • Love Probe / 1986 / VT / M • Made In Japan / 1992 / VI / M • Making It In New York / 1989 / PLD / M • Mammary Lane / 1988 / VT / C • Married With Hormones #2 / 1992 / PL / M • Mistaken Identity / 1990 / CC / M • Moist To The Touch / 1991 / DR / M • More Chocolate Candy / 1986 / VD / M • My Pretty Go Between / 1985 / VC / M • Naked Edge / 1992 / LE / M • Naturally Sweet / 1989 / VEX / M • Naughty Ninja Girls / 1987 / LA / M • Naughty Nymphs / 1986 / VEX / M • Naughty Nymphs / 1991 / VEX / C • New Sensations / 1990 / CC / M • The Nicole Stanton Story #1 / 1989 / CA • The Nicole Stanton Story #2 / 1989 / CA / M • Night Games / 1986 / WV / M • Night Of The Living Debbies / 1989 / EX / M • Nightmare On Dyke Street / 1992 / PL / M • Nooner / 1986 / AVC / M • Oh! You Beautiful Doll / 1990 / ZA / M • On My Lips / 1989 / PV / M • On The Make / 1988 / V99 / M • On Trial #1: In Defense Of Savannah / 1991 / VI / M • On Trial #2: Oral Arguments / 1991 / VI / M • On Trial #3: Takin' It To The Jury / 1992 / VI / M • On Trial #4: The Verdict / 1992 / VI / M • Open House (CDI) / 1989 / CDI / M • The Outlaw / 1989 / VD / M • Parliament: Samantha Strong #1 / 1986 / PM / M • Party Dolls / 1992 / VEX / M • Party In The Rear / 1989 / LV / M • Peggy Sue / 1987 / VT / M • Penetrating Thoughts / 1992 / LV / M • Phone Sex Girls #1 / 1987 / VT / M • Power Play (Venus 99) / 1990 / V99 / M • Prince Of Beverly Hills #1 / 1987 / VEX / M • Princess Charming / 1987 / AVC / C • Private Encounters / 1987 / SE / M • A Pussy Called Wanda #1 / 1992 / DR / M • Pussy Whipped / 1991 / PL / B • Rambone Meets The Double Penetrators / 1987 / WET / M • Raw Sewage / 1989 / FC / M • Rent-A-Butt / 1992 / VC / M • Risque Business / 1989 / V99 / M • Rituals / 1989 / V99 / M • Rock Her / 1992 / LV / M • Romancing The Butt / 1992 / ATL / M • Saddletramp / 1988 / VD / M • Santa Comes Again / 1990 / GLE / M • Scorcher / 1992 / GO / M • The Screamer / 1991 / CA / M • Search For An Angel / 1988 / WV / M • Secret Cravings / 1989 / V99 / M • Sex On The Town / 1989 / V99 / M • Sex Slaves / 1986 / VEX / M • Sex With A Stranger / 1986 / AVC / M • Sexscape / 1986 / CA / M

• Sextrology / 1987 / CA / M • Sexy And 18 / 1987 / SE / M • Shaved Pink / 1986 / WET / M • She Comes Undone / 1987 / AIR / C • She-Male Nurse / 1989 / LV / G • Sheena In Wonderland / 1987 / 3HV / M • Simply Irresistible / 1988 / CC / M • The Sins Of Angel Kelly / 1987 / FAN / C • Sins Of The Wealthy #2 / 1986 / CLV / M • Sleeping With Everybody / 1992 / MID / C • Slumber Party / 1990 / LV / M • The Slutty Professor / 1989 / VWA / M • Smooth As Silk / 1987 / VIP / M • Sounds Of Sex / 1985 / CA / M • Spanish Fly / 1987 / CA / M • Spend The Holidays With Barbii / 1987 / CDI / M • Spread Sheets / 1991 / DR / M • Starship Intercourse / 1987 / DR / M • A Sticky Situation / 1987 / CA / M • Strange Curves / 1989 / VC / M • Street Heat / 1984 / VC / M • Strictly Business / 1987 / VD / M • Strong Language / 1989 / IN / M • Sugarpussy Jeans / 1986 / TEM / M • Super Ball / 1989 / VWA / M • Surf, Sand And Sex / 1987 / SE / M • Sweet Dreams / 1991 / VC / M • Switch Hitters #4: The Grand Slam / 1989 / IN / G • Taboo #06 / 1988 / IN / M • Taija's Tasty Treats / 1988 / EXP / C • Taking It To The Streets / 1987 / CDI / M • A Taste Of Pleasure / 1988 / AVC / M • A Taste Of Tori Welles / 1990 / PIN / C • Tasty / 1985 / CA / M • Telemates / 1988 / STA / M • Telemates / 1991 / V99 / M • Temple Of Lust / 1992 / VC / M • To Snatch A Thief / 1989 / PLD / M • A Tongue Is Born / 1990 / ERU / M • Tori Welles Exposed / 1990 / VD / C • Torrid House / 1989 / VI / M • Tracy Takes Paris / 1987 / VIP / M • Transparent Desires / 1991 / LV / M • Tricks Of The Trade / 1988 / CA / M • Triple Xposure / 1986 / VD / M • Twin Cheeks #3 / 1991 / CIN / M • Two Women & A Man / 1988 / VEX / M • Two Women & A Man / 1991 / VEX / C • Undercover Angel / 1988 / IN / M • Unthinkable / 1984 / SE / M • Up All Night / 1986 / CC / M • Very Sexy Ballet / 1988 / CA / M • Video Tramp #2 / 1988 / TME / M • Virgin Spring / 1991 / FAZ / M • Wet And Wild #1 / 1986 / VEX / M • Wet Tails / 1989 / PL / M • What Kind Of Girls Do You Think We Are? / 1986 / VEX / M • What Kind Of Girls Do You Think We Are? / 1991 / VEX / C • What's Love Got To Do With It / 1989 / WV / M • What's Up Doc / 1988 / SEV / M • White Chocolate / 1987 / PEN / M • Who Shaved Lynn Lemay? / 1989 / EX / M • Whore Of The Roses / 1990 / AFV / M • Wicked Sensations #2 / 1989 / DR / M • Wicked Wenches / 1988 / LA / M • Wild In The Woods / 1988 / VEX / M • Wild Nurses In Lust / 1986 / PLY / M • Wishful Thinking / 1992 / VC / M • The World According To Ginger / 1985 / VI / M • The X-Team / 1984 / CV / M • XXX Workout / 1987 / VEX / M • You Bet Your Butt / 1992 / VC / M

SCOTT JAMES
Starlet Nights / 1982 / XTR / M • Taboo American Style #4: The Exciting Conclusion / 1985 / VC / M

SCOTT JAMES (DAVIS) *see* **Mark Davis**

SCOTT JOHNSON *(Simple Johnson, Cecil Johnson)*
Afrodisiac #1 / 1987 / CC / M • Secluded Passion / 1983 / VHL / M • Treasure Box / 1981 / VC / M • True Legends Of Adult Cinema: The Cult Superstars / 1993 / VC / C

SCOTT LONG
Margarita On The Rocks / 1994 / SFP / M

SCOTT LONG (GREGOR) *see* Gregor Samsa
SCOTT MALLORY *(Scott Malory, Mal O'Ree, Mal O'Rae, Slave K.)*
Up until 1995, this guy was the editor of *Hustler Erotic Video Guide* and still occasionally writes articles for them. He seems to be particularly interested in being dominated but doesn't seem too picky about the quality of his women.
Afternoon With Goddess Sondra / 1992 / SSP / B • Ass Openers! #1 / 1995 / TCK / C • Aurora's Secret Diary / 1985 / LA / M • Beneath My Heels / 1990 / BEB / B • Bizarre Encounters / 1986 / 4P / B • Blue Views / 1990 / CDI / M • Boss Bitch! / 1992 / RB / B • Crisp Bottoms / 1988 / PLV / B • Cumming Clean / 1991 / FL / M • Cunning Coeds / 1985 / IVP / M • Deep Inside Annie Sprinkle / 1981 / VXP / M • Foot Mistress / 1986 / BIZ / B • Foot Worship #1 / 1992 / VER / B • Gangbang Girl #04 / 1992 / ANA / M • Gangbang Girl #05 / 1992 / ANA / M • Gangbang Girl #06 / 1992 / ANA / M • Gangbang Girl #07 / 1992 / ANA / M • Gangbang Girl #08 / 1992 / ANA / M • Hot Tight Asses #04 / 1993 / TCK / M • Latex Slave / 1992 / RB / B • Nails / 1993 / SSP / B • Notorious / 1992 / SC / M • Painful Mistake (Dungeon) / 1993 / PL / B • Pussyman #04: The Celebration / 1993 / SNA / M • Realities #1 / 1991 / ZA / M • The Satisfiers Of Alpha Blue / 1980 / AVC / M • Star Struck / 1991 / AFV / M • Starlets / 1985 / 4P / M • Stud Puppy / 1992 / STM / B • Submission Position #608 / 1988 / CTS / B • The Tasting / 1991 / EX / M • Tortured Passions / 1994 / PL / B • The Torturous Infidel / 1994 / PL / B • Wild Goose Chase / 1990 / EA / M • Women On Top / 1995 / BON / B
SCOTT MALORY *see* Scott Mallory
SCOTT MANSFIELD *see Star Index I*
SCOTT MITCHELL
Fatal Instinct / 1992 / NLH / S • Playboy: Inside Out #1 / 1992 / PLA / S • Rocky Mountains / 1991 / IF / M
SCOTT MURPHY
Erotic Fantasies #5 / 1983 / CV / C
SCOTT O'HARA
Double Standards / 1988 / BIL / G • Switch Hitters #2: Swinging Both Ways / 1987 / IN / G
SCOTT PARIS
Bedtime Video #05 / 1984 / GO / M
SCOTT PETERSON
Love Scenes #2 / 1992 / B/F / S • Retail Slut / 1989 / LV / M
SCOTT PRESTON *see* Mich Igan
SCOTT RAY
Bedtime Video #06 / 1984 / GO / M
SCOTT RAYMER *see Star Index I*
SCOTT RUSSELL
Secret Sex #3: The Takeover / 1994 / CAT / G
SCOTT SCHWARTZ *see* Scottie Schwartz
SCOTT SEDGEWICK *see Star Index I*
SCOTT SHAMROCK *see* Scott Irish
SCOTT SHY *see Star Index I*
SCOTT SINCLAIR
L.A. Tool & Die / 1979 / TMX / G
SCOTT SOUTHERLAND
Anal Virgins Of America #06 / 1994 / FOR / M
SCOTT ST JAMES *see* Mich Igan

SCOTT STERLING *see Star Index I*
SCOTT STRONG *see Star Index I*
SCOTT STYLES
Cloud 900 / 1996 / EYE / M • The Dinner Party #2: The Buffet / 1996 / ULI / M • Dominique's Inheritance / 1996 / CVC / M • Eighteen & Easy / 1996 / SC / M • Eternal Lust / 1996 / VC / M • Hypnotic Hookers #2 / 1996 / NIT / M • Pick Up Lines #06 / 1996 / OD / M • Shayla's Swim Party / 1997 / VC / M • Takin' It To The Limit #9: Rear Action View / 1996 / BS / M • Thermonuclear Sex / 1996 / EL / M
SCOTT SUMMERS *see Star Index I*
SCOTT SUTHERLAND
Hose Jobs / 1995 / VEX / M • Knockout / 1994 / VEX / M
SCOTT TAYLOR *see Star Index I*
SCOTT TAZER *see* Nick East
SCOTT THOMAS *see Star Index I*
SCOTT THOMPSON BAKER *see* Scott Baker
SCOTT THUMPER *see Star Index I*
SCOTT TRACY
Private Film #10 / 1994 / OD / M
SCOTT TURNER *see* Nick East
SCOTT WAINWRIGHT *see* Gregor Samsa
SCOTT WALKER
Dog Walker / 1994 / EA / M
SCOTT WARBUCK *see Star Index I*
SCOTT WATSON *see Star Index I*
SCOTT WEBER *see Star Index I*
SCOTT WIDOWMAKER *see Star Index I*
SCOTTIE SCHWARTZ *(Sol Schwartz, Robert Jay, Scott Schwartz)*
Small guy who was apparently a child star in the real movies appearing in **The Toy** with Richard Pryor and others.
A Christmas Story / 1983 / MGM / S • Comeback / 1995 / VI / M • Corrected Deception / 1994 / STM / B • Fear / 1988 / ... / S • Hellfire Mistress / 1996 / OUP / B • House Of Pain / 1996 / OUP / B • Humiliating Bind / 1996 / STM / B • Kidco / 1984 / FOX / S • Macin' #2: Macadocious / 1996 / SMP / M • Masked Mistress / 1994 / STM / B • Mistress Of Depravity / 1993 / GOT / B • Savate / 1994 / APE / S • Scotty's X-Rated Adventure / 1996 / WP / M • Shock 'em Dead / 1990 / AE / S • The Show / 1995 / VI / M • Silver Screen Confidential / 1996 / WP / M • A Time To Live / 1985 / ... / S • Toe Tales #05 / 1993 / GOT / B • The Toy / 1982 / C3S / S
SCOTTY
Mixed Titty Tumbles / 1990 / NPA / B
SCRAPPY *see Star Index I*
SCRAPY
Butt-Nanza / 1995 / WV / M
SCRARLOTTE *see* Scarlett
SCRATCH
Scratch: Return To Witch Fountain / 1993 / SCR / M • Scratch: Synergy #1: The Catch / 1992 / SCR / M • Scratch: Synergy #2: The Match / 1992 / SCR / M • Scratch: Synergy #3: The Make / 1992 / SCR / M
SCREAMIN' RACHEL
The Mistress And The Prince / 1995 / STM / B • A Peek Over The Wall / 1995 / STM / G
SEAN
Big Bust Babes #14 / 1993 / AFI / M • Harry Horndog #20: Love Puppies #6 / 1993 / ZA / M • Pearl Necklace: Amorous Amateurs #01 / 1992 / SEE / M • Pearl Necklace:

Amorous Amateurs #08 / 1992 / SEE / M • Slaves' Night Out / 1990 / COC / B
SEAN (SHONE TAYLOR) *see* Shone Taylor
SEAN ALEXANDER *see Star Index I*
SEAN AMERSON *see* Sean King
SEAN BONNERY
Beach Bum Amateur's #10 / 1992 / MID / M • C-Hunt #01: Pandemonium / 1995 / PEV / M • C-Hunt #02: Hot Pockets / 1995 / PEV / M • Canadian Beaver Hunt #1 / 1996 / PL / M • East Coast Sluts #07: Tampa Bay / 1995 / PL / M • Jus' Knockin' Boots #2: Black On Line / 1996 / NIT / M • Pearl Necklace: Amorous Amateurs #16 / 1992 / SEE / M • Pearl Necklace: Amorous Amateurs #17 / 1992 / SEE / M • Pearl Necklace: Amorous Amateurs #18 / 1992 / SEE / M • Pearl Necklace: Amorous Amateurs #20 / 1992 / SEE / M • Pearl Necklace: Amorous Amateurs #23 / 1993 / SEE / M • Pearl Necklace: Amorous Amateurs #25 / 1993 / SEE / M • Pearl Necklace: Amorous Amateurs #26 / 1993 / SEE / M • Pearl Necklace: Amorous Amateurs #30 / 1993 / SEE / M • Pearl Necklace: Amorous Amateurs #31 / 1993 / SEE / M • Pearl Necklace: Amorous Amateurs #33 / 1992 / SEE / M • Pearl Necklace: Amorous Amateurs #35 / 1993 / SEE / M • Pearl Necklace: Amorous Amateurs #38 / 1993 / SEE / M • Pearl Necklace: Amorous Amateurs #39 / 1993 / SEE / M • Pearl Necklace: Amorous Amateurs #40 / 1994 / SEE / M • Pearl Necklace: Amorous Amateurs #41 / 1994 / SEE / M • Pearl Necklace: Premier Sessions #02 / 1993 / SEE / M • Pearl Necklace: Thee Bush League #01 / 1992 / SEE / M • Pearl Necklace: Thee Bush League #13 / 1993 / SEE / M • Pearl Necklace: Thee Bush League #14 / 1993 / SEE / M • Pearl Necklace: Thee Bush League #16 / 1993 / SEE / M • Pearl Necklace: Thee Bush League #18 / 1993 / SEE / M • Pearl Necklace: Thee Bush League #26 / 1993 / SEE / M • Pearl Necklace: Thee Bush League #27 / 1993 / SEE / M • Pearl Necklace: Thee Bush League #28 / 1994 / SEE / M • Sunset In Paradise / 1996 / PL / M
SEAN BRANCATO *see Star Index I*
SEAN BRUCE
The Seductress / 1982 / VC / M
SEAN DESMOND
All About Annette / 1982 / SE / C
SEAN DUKE *see Star Index I*
SEAN ELLIOT
Firestorm #1 / 1984 / COM / M • Mascara / 1982 / CA / M • Peepholes / 1982 / AVC / M • Scoundrels / 1982 / COM / M • The Widespread Scandals Of Lydia Lace / 1983 / CA / M
SEAN FOX
Bi Dream Of Genie / 1990 / BIN / G • Switch Hitters #5: The Night Games / 1990 / IN / G
SEAN FRANCOIS
Open Lips / 1983 / AVO / M
SEAN HUNTER *see Star Index I*
SEAN KING *(Sean Amerson)*
Girls On Fire / 1985 / VCX / M • Marina Vice / 1985 / PEN / M
SEAN KNIGHT *see Star Index I*
SEAN KOCKERY
6969 Mel'hose Place / 1995 / VG0 / M
SEAN LAWRENCE

Bi-Surprise / 1988 / MET / G
SEAN MCCOURTNEY *see Star Index I*
SEAN MICHAELS *(Shawn Michael, Andre Allen, Jan Michaels, Shaun Michaels, Sean Peters)*
2 Hung 2 Tung / 1992 / MID / M • 4 Bi 4 / 1994 / BIN / G • 40 The Hard Way / 1991 / OD / M • 900 Desert Strip / 1991 / XPI / M • Adam & Eve's House Party #2: Bachelor Party / 1996 / VC / M • The Adventures Of Buck Naked / 1994 / OD / M • The Adventures Of Mr. Tootsie Pole #1 / 1995 / LBO / M • The Adventures Of Mr. Tootsie Pole #2 / 1995 / LBO / M • The Adventures Of Peeping Tom #1 / 1996 / OD / M • The Adventures Of Peeping Tom #2 / 1996 / OD / M • The Adventures Of Seymore Butts / 1992 / FH / M • After Midnight / 1994 / IN / M • AHV #15: That's The Way / 1991 / EVN / M • The All American Girl / 1991 / PP / M • All Inside Eva / 1991 / PL / M • All That Jism / 1994 / VD / M • Alley Cats / 1995 / VC / M • Always Anal / 1995 / AVI / C • Amadeus Mozart / 1996 / XC / M • Ambitious Blondes / 1992 / VIM / M • Ambushed / 1990 / SE / M • America's Raunchiest Home Videos #63: / 1993 / ZA / M • America's Raunchiest Home Videos #78: Stairway To Anal / 1993 / ZA / M • The Anal Adventures Of Bruce Seven / 1996 / BS / C • Anal Agony / 1994 / ZA / M • Anal All Stars / 1994 / CA / M • Anal Analysis (Heatwave) / 1992 / HW / M • Anal Angels #2 / 1990 / VEX / C • Anal Anonymous / 1994 / ZA / M • Anal Asian #2: The Won-Ton Woman / 1994 / IN / M • Anal Attack / 1991 / ZA / M • Anal Blues / 1994 / PEP / M • Anal Breakdown / 1994 / ROB / M • Anal Climax #1 / 1991 / ROB / M • Anal Climax #3 / 1993 / ROB / M • Anal Co-Ed / 1993 / ROB / M • The Anal Diary Of Misty Rain / 1993 / EL / M • Anal Encounters #3: Back In The Dark One / 1991 / VC / M • Anal Fury / 1992 / ROB / M • Anal Generation / 1995 / PE / M • Anal International / 1992 / HW / M • Anal Kitten / 1992 / ROB / M • Anal Palace / 1995 / VC / M • Anal Pussycat / 1995 / ROB / M • Anal Rampage #1 / 1992 / ROB / M • Anal Revolution / 1991 / ROB / M • Anal Rookies #1 / 1992 / ROB / M • Anal Savage #1 / 1992 / ROB / M • Anal Sensation / 1993 / ROB / M • Anal Siege / 1993 / ROB / M • Anal Sluts & Sweethearts #1 / 1992 / ROB / M • Anal Sluts & Sweethearts #2 / 1993 / ROB / M • Anal Sluts & Sweethearts #3 / 1995 / ROB / M • Anal Spitfire / 1994 / ROB / M • The Anal Starlets / 1991 / ROB / M • The Anal Team / 1993 / LV / M • Anal Thrills / 1992 / ROB / M • Anal Thunder #1 / 1993 / ROB / M • Anal Vision #09 / 1993 / LBO / M • Anal Vision #24 / 1994 / LBO / M • Anal With An Oriental Slant / 1993 / ROB / M • Anus & Andy / 1993 / ZA / M • The Anus Family / 1991 / CC / M • Anything Butt Love / 1990 / PL / M • Arabian Nights / 1993 / WP / M • The Artist / 1994 / HO / M • As Nasty As She Wants To Be / 1990 / IN / M • Ashlyn Rising / 1995 / VI / M • Asian Appetite / 1993 / HO / M • Asses Galore #4: Extreme Noise Terror / 1996 / DFI / M • Attack Of The 50 Foot Hooker / 1994 / OD / M • Babes / 1991 / CIN / M • The Back Doors (Western) / 1991 / WV / M • Backdoor Black #1 / 1992 / WV / C • Backdoor Black #2 / 1993 / WV / C • Backdoor To Holly-

wood #13 / 1990 / CDI / M • The Backpackers #3 / 1991 / IN / M • The Backway Inn #2 / 1992 / FD / M • Bad Habits / 1990 / WV / M • Behind The Scenes: The Making Of The Wil & Ed Movies / 1992 / MID / M • Best Gang Bangs / 1996 / DFI / C • The Best Of Black Anal #1 / 1995 / ROB / C • Best Of Caught From Behind #5 / 1991 / HO / C • The Best Of Oriental Anal #1 / 1994 / ROB / C • The Best Of Sean Michaels / 1994 / VT / C • Between A Rock And A Hot Place / 1989 / VEX / M • Beyond Reality #2: Anal Expedition / 1996 / EXQ / M • Bianca Trump's Towers / 1992 / LV / M • Big Black Dicks / 1993 / GO / C • The Bigger They Come / 1993 / VD / C • Black & Blue / 1990 / SO / M • Black & Gold / 1990 / CIN / M • Black Analyst #2 / 1995 / VEX / M • Black Attack / 1994 / ZA / M • The Black Avenger #1: The Titty Romp / 1996 / OUP / C • Black Balled / 1990 / ZA / M • Black Beauty (Coast To Coast) / 1994 / CC / M • Black Booty / 1993 / ZA / M • Black Buttman #01 / 1993 / CC / M • Black Buttman #02 / 1994 / CC / M • Black By Popular Demand / 1992 / ZA / M • Black Cheerleader Search #09 / 1996 / IVC / M • Black Detail #1 / 1994 / VT / M • Black Detail #2 / 1994 / VT / M • Black For More / 1993 / ZA / M • Black In The Saddle / 1990 / ZA / M • Black In The Saddle Again / 1991 / ZA / M • Black Jack City #1 / 1991 / VT / M • Black Jack City #2: Black's Revenge / 1992 / HW / M • Black Mariah / 1991 / FC / M • Black Nurse Fantasies / 1994 / CA / M • Black Obsession / 1991 / ZA / M • Black Satin / 1994 / IN / M • Black Studies / 1992 / GO / M • Black Studs & Little White Trash / 1995 / ROB / M • Black Velvet #1 / 1992 / CC / M • Black Velvet #2 / 1993 / CC / M • Black Velvet #3 / 1994 / CC / M • Black, White And Blue / 1989 / E&I / M • Blackballed / 1994 / VI / C • Blackbroad Jungle / 1994 / IN / M • Blackman / 1989 / PL / M • Blacks & Blondes #36 / 1986 / WV / M • Blacks & Blondes: The Movie / 1989 / WV / M • Blazing Butts / 1991 / LV / M • Blow Job Bonnie / 1992 / CC / M • The Blues #1 / 1992 / VT / M • The Blues #2 / 1994 / VT / M • Body Of Innocence / 1993 / WP / M • Body Triple / 1991 / VC / M • Booty By Nature / 1994 / WP / M • Booty Ho #2 / 1995 / ROB / M • The Breast Things In Life Are Free / 1991 / LV / M • Breathless / 1991 / WV / M • Brooklyn Nights / 1994 / OD / M • Brother Act / 1992 / PL / M • Brothers Bangin' / 1995 / ANA / M • Bubbles / 1991 / IF / M • Buns And Roses (LV) / 1990 / LV / M • Bunz-Eye / 1992 / ROB / M • Butt Banged Bicycle Babes / 1994 / ANA / M • Butt Naked #1 / 1990 / OD / M • Butt Row Unplugged / 1996 / ABS / M • The Butt Sisters Do Baltimore / 1995 / MID / M • The Butt Sisters Do Chicago / 1995 / MID / M • The Butt Sisters Do Cleveland / 1994 / MID / M • Butt's Up, Doc #1 / 1992 / GO / M • Butt's Up, Doc #2 / 1992 / GO / M • Butt's Up, Doc #3 / 1992 / GO / M • Buttman Vs Buttwoman / 1992 / EL / M • Buttman's Revenge / 1992 / EA / M • Butts Afire / 1992 / PMV / M • Butts Of Steel / 1994 / BLC / M • California Blacks / 1994 / V99 / M • Can't Touch This / 1991 / PL / M • Casanova #4 / 1993 / SC / M • Casting Call #08 / 1994 / SO / M • Caught From Behind #14 / 1990 / HO / M • Caught From Behind #15 / 1991 /

HO / M • Changing Partners / 1989 / FAZ / M • Checkmate / 1996 / SNA / M • Cheeks #3 / 1990 / CC / M • China Black / 1992 / IN / M • College Girl / 1990 / VEX / M • Con Jobs / 1990 / V99 / M • The Crack / 1994 / LV / M • The Crack Of Dawn / 1989 / GLE / M • The Crimson Kiss / 1993 / WV / M • Cumback Pussy #1 / 1996 / EL / M • Cumback Pussy #2: Crawling Back For More / 1996 / EL / M • Cumback Pussy #3: Coast To Coast Rump Romp / 1996 / EL / M • Cumback Pussy #5: Groopin' / 1996 / EL / M • Cumback Pussy #6: All-Star Poop Chute Salute / 1997 / EL / M • Cumback Pussy #7: NUGIRLZ / 1997 / EL / M • Cycle Sluts / 1992 / CC / M • The Danger Zone / 1990 / SO / M • Dark Justice / 1992 / ZA / M • Dark Obsessions / 1993 / WV / M • Dark Room / 1994 / VT / M • Dead Aim / 1994 / PEP / M • Dear John / 1993 / VI / M • Deep Cheeks #1 / 1991 / ROB / M • Deep Inside Jeanna Fine / 1992 / VC / C • Deep Inside Nicole London / 1995 / VC / C • Defying The Odds / 1995 / OD / M • Depraved / 1990 / IN / M • Desert Moon / 1994 / SPI / M • The Devil In Grandma Jones / 1994 / FC / M • The Devil Made Her Do It / 1992 / HO / M • Dick & Jane Sneak On The Set / 1993 / AVI / M • The Dinner Party #1 / 1994 / ULI / M • The Dinner Party #2: The Buffet / 1996 / ULI / M • Director's Wet Dreams / 1996 / BBE / M • Dirty Little Mind / 1994 / IP / M • Dirty Stories #5 / 1996 / PE / M • The Dong Show #01 / 1990 / AMB / M • Double Anal Alternatives / 1996 / EL / M • Double Penetration #4 / 1991 / WV / C • Down 4 Busine$$ / 1989 / GMI / M • Dr Freckle & Mr Jive / 1995 / IN / M • Dr Rear / 1995 / CC / M • The Dragon Lady #2: Tales From the Bed / 1992 / WV / M • Dream Lover / 1991 / WV / M • Dreams Of A Gigolo / 1996 / SNA / M • Drink Of Love / 1990 / V99 / M • Driving Miss Daisy Crazy #2 / 1992 / WV / M • Drop Sex: Wipe The Floor / 1997 / JLP / M • Earthquake Girls / 1990 / CC / M • East L.A. Law / 1991 / WV / M • Easy Way Out / 1989 / OD / M • Ebony Love / 1992 / VT / C • Electropussy / 1995 / CC / M • The Erotic Adventures Of Fanny Annie / 1991 / WV / M • Erotica / 1992 / CC / M • Euro-Sex Collection #01 / 1996 / IN0 / M • Executions On Butt Row / 1996 / EA / M • Extreme Sex #1: The Club / 1994 / VI / M • Extreme Sex #2: The Dungeon / 1994 / VI / M • Extreme Sex #3: Wired / 1994 / VI / M • Face Jam / 1996 / VC / M • Faithless Companions / 1992 / WV / M • Fame Is A Whore On Butt Row / 1996 / ABS / M • Family Affairs / 1990 / VD / M • Fantasies Of Alicia / 1995 / VT / M • Fashion Sluts #8 / 1996 / ABS / M • For Your Lips Only / 1989 / FAZ / M • Foreign Bodies / 1991 / IN / M • Fresh Meat (John Leslie) #3 / 1996 / EA / M • Fresh Tits Of Bel Air / 1992 / OD / M • From A Whisper To A Scream / 1993 / GO / M • Full Blown / 1992 / GO / M • Gang Bang Fury #1 / 1992 / ROB / M • Gang Bang Pussycat / 1992 / ROB / M • Gang Bang Thrills / 1992 / ROB / M • Gangbang Girl #07 / 1992 / ANA / M • Gangbang Girl #08 / 1992 / ANA / M • Gangbang Girl #12 / 1993 / ANA / M • Gangbang Girl #13 / 1994 / ANA / M • Gangbang Girl #14 / 1994 / ANA / M • Gangbang Girl #15 / 1995 / ANA / M • Gangbang Girl #16 / 1995 / ANA / M •

• Tail Of The Scorpion / 1990 / ELP / M • Tail Taggers #101 / 1993 / WV / M • Tail Taggers #102 / 1993 / WV / M • Tail Taggers #104 / 1993 / WV / M • Tail Taggers #105 / 1993 / WV / M • Tail Taggers #108: Vibro Love / 1993 / WV / M • Take My Wife, Please / 1993 / WP / M • Takin' It To The Limit #1 / 1994 / BS / M • Takin' It To The Limit #2 / 1994 / BS / M • Takin' It To The Limit #3 / 1994 / BS / M • Takin' It To The Limit #7: Debauched / 1996 / BS / M • Takin' It To The Limit #8: Hooked On Crack / 1996 / BS / M • Takin' It To The Limit #9: Rear Action View / 1996 / BS / M • Tequilla Sunset / 1989 / V99 / M • The Thief, The Girl & The Detective / 1996 / HDE / M • Things Mommy Taught Me / 1990 / KNI / M • Tight Pucker / 1992 / WV / M • Tight Tushies #1 / 1994 / SFP / M • Titillation #3 / 1991 / SE / M • A Touch Of Gold / 1990 / IN / M • Toyz / 1993 / MID / M • Treasure Chest / 1994 / LV / M • Twilight / 1991 / ZA / M • Two Of A Kind / 1993 / PL / M • Two Sides Of A Lady / 1994 / HDE / M • Two Sisters / 1992 / WV / M • Two-Pac / 1996 / VT / M • Uninhibited / 1993 / ANT / S • Unplugged / 1995 / CC / M • Up And Cummers #01 / 1993 / 4P / M • Up And Cummers #05 / 1993 / 4P / M • Up And Cummers #06 / 1993 / 4P / M • Up And Cummers #13 / 1994 / 4P / M • Up Your Ass #1 / 1996 / ANA / M • Up Your Ass #3 / 1996 / ANA / M • Valley Of The Sluts / 1991 / OD / M • Virgin Dreams / 1996 / EA / M • The Voyeur #2 / 1994 / EA / M • The Voyeur #6 / 1996 / EA / M • Wanda Does Transylvania / 1990 / V99 / M • Wanda Whips The Dragon Lady / 1990 / V99 / M • Waterbabies #2 / 1992 / CC / M • White Men Can't Hump / 1992 / CC / M • Who Reamed Rosie Rabbit? #2 / 1989 / FAN / M • Who Shaved Cassi Nova? / 1989 / EX / M • Whoomp! There She Is / 1993 / AVI / M • Whore'n / 1996 / AB / M • Whoreo / 1995 / BIP / M • Wicked Thoughts / 1992 / PL / M • Wil And Ed's Excellent Boner Christmas / 1991 / MID / M • Wild Goose Chase / 1990 / EA / M • Wild Side / 1991 / GO / M • Witness For The Penetration / 1994 / PEP / M • Wives Of The Rich And Famous / 1989 / V99 / M • Women Of Color #1 / 1994 / ANA / M • Women Of Color #2 / 1994 / ANA / M • Women's Penitentiary / 1992 / VIM / M • The Wonder Rears / 1990 / SO / M • World Cup / 1990 / PL / M • World Sex Tour #1 / 1995 / ANA / M • World Sex Tour #2 / 1995 / ANA / M • You Can Touch This / 1991 / EVN / M • You Go Girl! (Video Team) / 1995 / VT / M

SEAN PETERS *see* **Sean Michaels**

SEAN POST *see* **Star Index I**

SEAN POWERS

Lady Zazu's Daughter / 1971 / ALP / M

SEAN RAMHURST

Private Dancers / 1996 / RAS / M

SEAN RICHARDS

She-Male Slut House / 1994 / HEA / G

SEAN RICKS *see* **Shawn Ricks**

SEAN RIDER *(Stan Wilder, Sean Ryder)*

Young, reasonably presentable white male. Has appeared in gay movies.

1-900-FUCK #3 / 1995 / SO / M • 2 Wongs Make A White / 1996 / FC / M • A List / 1996 / SO / M • Abducted / 1996 / ZA / M • Addictive Desires / 1994 / OD / M • The Adventures Of Peeping Tom #2 / 1996 / OD /

M • All About Teri Weigel / 1996 / XCI / M • America's Raunchiest Home Videos #72: / 1993 / ZA / M • Anal Bandits / 1996 / SO / M • Anal Disciples #1 / 1996 / ZA / M • Anal Disciples #2: The Anal Conflict / 1996 / ZA / M • Anal Institution #1 / 1996 / ZA / M • Anal Interrogation / 1995 / ZA / M • Anal Jeopardy / 1996 / ZA / M • Anal League / 1996 / IN / M • Anal Portrait / 1996 / ZA / M • Anal Rippers #1: The Beginning / 1995 / ZA / M • Anal Sex / 1996 / ZA / M • Anything You Ever Wanted To Know About Sex / 1993 / VEX / M • Ariana's Dirty Dancers: The Professionals / 1996 / 4P / M • The Artist / 1994 / HO / M • Asian Pussyman Auditions / 1996 / SNA / M • Ass Kisser: A Love Story / 1995 / PEP / M • Ass Openers! #2 / 1995 / TCK / C • The Backdoor Bradys / 1995 / PL / M • Batbabe / 1995 / PL / M • Bi The Rear Window / 1994 / BIL / G • Bi-Laddin / 1994 / BIN / G • The Big One / 1995 / HO / M • Bigger Than Life / 1995 / IF / M • Born 2 B Wild / 1995 / PL / M • Breeders / 1996 / MET / M • Bring On The Night / 1994 / VEX / M • Careless / 1993 / PP / M • Carnal Garden / 1996 / KLP / M • Caught From Behind #21 / 1995 / HO / M • Cherry Poppers #12: Playing Nookie / 1995 / ZA / M • The Complete & Total Anal Workout #1 / 1995 / ZA / M • Compulsion (Amazing) / 1996 / MET / M • Conquest / 1996 / WP / M • Courting Libido / 1995 / HIV / G • Cumback Pussy #7: NUGIRLZ / 1997 / EL / M • Daydreams, Nightdreams / 1996 / VC / M • Debauchery / 1995 / MET / M • Decadent Obsession / 1995 / OD / M • Deceit / 1996 / ZA / M • Deep Focus / 1995 / VC / M • Deja Vu / 1993 / XCI / M • Dementia / 1995 / IP / M • Desperado / 1994 / SC / M • Dick & Jane Go To A Bachelor Party (#17) / 1996 / AVI / M • Dim Sum (Eating Chinese) / 1996 / SUF / M • Dirty Dancers #8 / 1996 / 4P / M • Dirty Laundry #1 / 1994 / CV / M • Dirty Mind / 1995 / VEX / M • Dirty Tricks #1: Just A Bunch Of Whores / 1995 / EA / M • Double Anal Alternatives / 1996 / EL / M • Dreams Of A Gigolo / 1996 / SNA / M • Drop Sex: Wipe The Floor / 1997 / JLP / M • Eighteen #1 / 1996 / SC / M • Enigma / 1995 / MET / M • Erotic World Of Anne Spice / 1995 / WV / M • Executions On Butt Row / 1996 / EA / M • Fame Is A Whore On Butt Row / 1996 / ABS / M • Fantasy Fuchs / 1996 / PLP / C • Fast Forward / 1995 / CA / M • Fixing A Hole / 1995 / XCI / M • Frendz? #1 / 1996 / RAS / M • Frendz? #2 / 1996 / RAS / M • Fresh Meat (John Leslie) #2 / 1995 / EA / M • From China With Love / 1993 / ZA / M • Gang Bang Bitches #01 / 1994 / PP / M • Gang Bang Bitches #02 / 1994 / PP / M • Gang Bang Bitches #03 / 1994 / PP / M • Gang Bang Bitches #05 / 1995 / PP / M • Gang Bang Bitches #06 / 1995 / PP / M • Gang Bang Bitches #09 / 1995 / PP / M • Gang Bang Bitches #10 / 1995 / PP / M • Gang Bang Bitches #11 / 1995 / PP / M • Gangbang Girl #16 / 1995 / ANA / M • Girls Of The Panty Raid / 1995 / VT / M • Harry Horndog #20: Love Puppies #6 / 1993 / ZA / M • Harry Horndog #21: Birthday Orgy / 1993 / ZA / M • Head First / 1995 / OD / M • Head Trip / 1995 / VC / M • Heatwaves / 1994 / LE / M • Helen & Louise / 1996 / HDE / M • Hidden Camera #10 / 1993 / JMP / M • Hollywood Temps / 1993 / ZA / M

• Hot Tight Asses #03 / 1993 / TCK / M • Hot Tight Asses #15 / 1996 / TCK / M • Hotwired / 1996 / VC / M • Intense / 1996 / MET / M • Intense Perversions #3 / 1996 / PL / M • Intersextion / 1994 / HO / M • Jailhouse Nurses / 1995 / SC / M • Jenna Ink / 1996 / WP / M • Kiss Is A Rebel With A Cause / 1993 / WV / M • Latex #2 / 1995 / VC / M • Legal Briefs / 1996 / EX / M • Legs / 1996 / ZA / M • Love Exchange / 1995 / DR / M • Made For A Gangbang / 1995 / ZA / M • Masque / 1995 / VC / M • Memories / 1996 / ZA / M • Miss Anal #1 / 1995 / C69 / M • Naked Juice / 1995 / OD / G • Naked Reunion / 1993 / VI / M • Needful Sins / 1993 / WV / M • The Night Of The Coyote / 1993 / MED / M • Nightshift Nurses #2 / 1996 / VC / M • Odyssey 30 Min: #294: / 1992 / OD / M • Orgies Orgies Orgies / 1994 / WV / M • Out Of My Mind / 1995 / PL / M • P.K. & Company / 1995 / CV / M • Paging Betty / 1994 / VC / M • Perverted Women / 1995 / SC / M • Pick Up Lines #02 / 1995 / 4P / M • Pick Up Lines #03 / 1995 / 4P / M • Pick Up Lines #04 / 1995 / 4P / M • Pick Up Lines #05 / 1996 / OD / M • Pick Up Lines #13 / 1997 / OD / M • The Portrait Of Dorie Grey / 1996 / KLP / M • Possessed / 1996 / MET / M • Princess Of Thieves / 1994 / SC / M • Private Stories #09 / 1996 / OD / M • Psychoanal Therapy / 1994 / CA / M • Pussyman #14: Dreams Of A Gigolo / 1996 / SNA / M • Pussyman Auditions #18 / 1996 / SNA / M • Red Door Diaries #1 / 1995 / ZA / M • Red Door Diaries #2 / 1996 / ZA / M • Scorched / 1995 / ONA / M • Seekers / 1994 / CA / M • Sensual Spirits / 1995 / LE / M • Sex Bandits / 1995 / VC / M • Sex Drive / 1993 / VEX / M • Sideshow Freaks / 1996 / ZA / M • Sinnocence / 1995 / CDI / M • Sleaze Please!—December Edition / 1994 / FH / M • Sodomania: Slop Shots / 1996 / EL / C • Spinners #1 (Wicked) / 1995 / WP / M • Spinners #2 (Wicked) / 1996 / WP / M • Split Decision / 1993 / FD / M • Star Girl / 1996 / ERA / M • Starbangers #01 / 1993 / BIG / M • Starbangers #05 / 1993 / FPI / M • Starbangers #06 / 1994 / FPI / M • Starbangers #08 / 1996 / FPI / M • Stuff Your Face #1 / 1994 / JMP / M • Stuff Your Face #2 / 1995 / JMP / M • Stuff Your Face #3 / 1995 / JMP / M • Sunset's Anal & D.P. Gangbang / 1996 / PL / M • Tail Taggers #130 / 1994 / WV / M • Tales From The Clit / 1993 / OD / M • A Tall Tail / 1996 / FC / M • Taxi Girls #3: Killer On The Loose / 1993 / MED / M • Timepiece / 1994 / CV / M • Top Heavy / 1993 / IF / M • Topless Brain Surgeons / 1995 / LE / M • Turnabout / 1996 / CTP / M • Two Too Much / 1996 / MET / M • Vagabonds / 1996 / ERA / M • Virgin Killers: Second Rampage / 1995 / PEP / M • Virgin Killers: The Killing Spree / 1995 / PEP / M • Wet Nurses #2 / 1995 / LE / M • While You Were Dreaming / 1995 / WV / M • A Woman Scorned / 1995 / CA / M • Women Behaving Badly / 1996 / RAS / M • Working Girls / 1995 / FH / M • Young And Anal #2 / 1995 / JMP / M • Young Girls Do #1: Troublemakers / 1995 / CDI / M

SEAN RYDER *see* **Sean Rider**

SEAN SULLIVAN

Ladies Nights / 1980 / VC / M • Las Vegas Lady / 1981 / VCX / M • Peaches And Cream / 1982 / SE / M

SEAN TAYLOR *see* **Shone Taylor**
SEAN THOMAS *see* **Shone Taylor**
SEAN WEBB
Erotica Optique / 1994 / SUF / M
SEANA RYAN
Captured Beauty / 1995 / SAE / B • Penthouse: 1995 Pet Of The Year Playoff / 1994 / PET / F • Penthouse: 25th Anniversary Swimsuit Video / 1994 / A*V / F • Penthouse: The Girls Of Penthouse #3 / 1995 / PET / S • Penthouse: Miami Hot Talk / 1996 / PET / S • Penthouse: Pet Rocks / 1995 / PET / S • Penthouse: Satin & Lace #2 / 1992 / PET / F • Penthouse: The Ultimate Pet Games / 1996 / PET / S
SEATTLE
Forbidden Subjects #1 / 1994 / FC / M • Forbidden Subjects #2 / 1994 / FC / M • High Heeled & Horny #1 / 1994 / LBO / M • M Series #29 / 1994 / LBO / M • M Series #30 / 1994 / LBO / M
SEBASTIAN
America's Raunchiest Home Videos #70: / 1993 / ZA / M • N.Y. Video Magazine #07 / 1996 / OUP / M • Nothing Butt Amateurs #01 / 1993 / AFI / M • Up And Cummers #11 / 1994 / 4P / M
SEBASTIAN (BEAU MIC) *see* **Beau Michaels**
SEBASTIAN LORD *see* **Star Index I**
SEBASTIAN MITCHELL
Streets Of New York #07 / 1996 / PL / M
SEBASTIAN SAVAGE
A Reason To Die / 1994 / PEP / M
SECRET
Butt Hunt #06 / 1995 / LEI / M • Green Piece Of Ass #1 / 1994 / RTP / M • Hard Core Beginners #11 / 1995 / LEI / M
SEDUCTION *(Suduction)*
Long brown hair, too tall, horrible enhanced rock-solid large tits, marginal face, clit ring, tattoos on inside right thigh, outside of both calves, and above belly button, thick body. 21 years old in 1996 and was de-virginized at 16. Says her measurements are 36-21-36 which seem very strange numbers.
The Adventures Of Peeping Tom #4 / 1997 / OD / M • African Angels #1 / 1996 / NIT / M • Anal Jammin' & Slammin' / 1996 / ROB / M • Assy #2 / 1996 / JMP / M • Borsky's Back Door Bitches / 1996 / ROB / M • Butthole Sweetheart / 1996 / ROB / M • Fashion Passion / 1997 / TEP / M • Interracial Video Virgins #01 / 1996 / NS / M • More Dirty Debutantes #58 / 1996 / 4P / M • Sodomania #21: Degenerate Lifestyles! / 1997 / EL / M
SEILVIA
Russian Model Magazine #1 / 1996 / IP / M
SEKA *(Dorothy H. Patton, Lynda Grasser)*
Platinum blonde with droopy large tits and later firm large enhanced tits, womanly body. Expressionless. First movie was **Lust at First Bite**. Real name is Dorothy Hundley Patton. She was married to Ken Yontz at one stage.
The 8th Annual Erotic Film Awards / 1984 / SE / C • Amazing Sex Stories #2 / 1987 / SUV / C • American Garter / 1993 / VC / M • The Angel In Mr. Holmes / 1988 / WV / C • Any Time, Any Place / 1981 / CA0 / M • Aunt Peg / 1980 / CV / M • Backdoor Girls / 1983 / VCR / C • Beauty And The Beast / 1982 / KEN / S • The Best Of Gail Palmer / 1981 / WWV / C • Best Of Hot Shorts #01 / 1987 / VCR / C • The Best Of Seka / 1993

/ ... / C • Between The Sheets / 1982 / CA / M • Beyond Desire / 1986 / VC / M • Beyond Shame / 1980 / VEP / M • Blacks & Blondes #54 / 1989 / WV / M • Blonde Fire / 1979 / EVI / M • Blonde Heat (VCA) / 1985 / VC / M • Blondes Have More Fun / 1980 / SE / M • Blue Ribbon Blue / 1984 / CA / C • Blue Vanities #045 (New) / 1988 / FFL / M • Blue Vanities #045 (Old) / 1988 / FFL / M • Blue Vanities #046 (Old) / 1988 / FFL / M • Blue Vanities #047 (Old) / 1988 / FFL / M • Blue Vanities #048 / 1988 / FFL / M • Blue Vanities #049 / 1988 / FFL / M • Blue Vanities #053 / 1988 / FFL / M • Blue Vanities #058 / 1988 / FFL / M • Blue Vanities #062 / 1988 / FFL / M • Blue Vanities #064 / 1988 / FFL / M • Blue Vanities #067 / 1988 / FFL / M • Blue Vanities #069 / 1988 / FFL / M • Blue Vanities #070 / 1988 / FFL / M • Blue Vanities #071 / 1988 / FFL / M • Blue Vanities #072 / 1988 / FFL / M • Blue Vanities #077 / 1988 / FFL / M • Blue Vanities #084 / 1988 / FFL / M • Blue Vanities #085 / 1988 / FFL / M • Blue Vanities #243 / 1996 / FFL / M • Blue Vanities #533 / 1993 / FFL / M • Caballero Preview Tape #2 / 1983 / CA / C • Careful, He May Be Watching / 1986 / CA / M • Carnal Encounters Of The Barest Kind / 1978 / VOY / C • Carnal Highways / 1980 / HIF / M • The Case Of The Missing Seka Master / 1993 / VCX / C • Classic Erotica #2 / 1980 / SVE / M • Classic Seka #1 / 1988 / AR / C • Classic Seka #2 / 1988 / SUV / C • Classic Swedish Erotica #03 / 1986 / CA / C • Classic Swedish Erotica #16 / 1986 / CA / C • Classic Swedish Erotica #27 / 1987 / CA / C • Confessions Of Seka / 1981 / SAT / M • Couples In Love / 19?? / ... / M • Cum Shot Revue #2 / 1985 / HO / C • Danish Erotica #1 / 1980 / CA / M • Danish Erotica #2 / 1980 / CA / M • Dark Desires / 1989 / BMV / C • Diamond Collection #03 / 1979 / CDI / M • Double Pleasure / 1985 / VCR / M • Downstairs, Upstairs / 1980 / SE / M • Electric Blue #004 / 1981 / CA / S • Electric Blue #007 / 1982 / CA / S • Erotic Gold #1 / 1985 / VEN / M • Erotic Gold #2 / 1985 / VEN / M • Erotic Interlude / 1981 / CA / M • The Erotic World Of Seka / 1983 / VCR / C • Exhausted / 1981 / CA / C • F / 1980 / GO / M • Flight Sensations / 1983 / VC / C • Football Widow / 1979 / SCO / M • Forbidden Worlds / 1988 / GO / C • Free And Foxy / 1986 / VCX / C • French Erotica: Inside Hollywood / 1980 / AR / M • French Erotica: Love Story / 1980 / AR / M • French Erotica: Report Card / 1980 / AR / M • Girls! Girls! Girls! #1 / 1986 / VCS / C • Heavenly Desire / 1979 / WV / M • High School Report Card / 1979 / CA / M • Hot Shorts: Seka / 1986 / VCR / C • Inside Seka / 1980 / VXP / M • Jawbreakers / 1985 / VEN / C • A Lacy Affair #2 / 1985 / HO / C • Legends Of Porn #1 / 1987 / CV / C • Legends Of Porn #2 / 1989 / CV / C • Limited Edition #17 / 1980 / AVC / M • Limited Edition #18 / 1980 / AVC / M • Long Hard Summer / 1989 / BMV / C • Love Goddesses / 1981 / VC / M • Love Notes / 1986 / HO / C • Love Story / 1979 / SCO / M • The Loves Of Mary Jane / 1989 / BWV / C • Loving Lips / 1987 / AMB / C • Lust At First Bite / 1978 / VC / M • Lust Vegas Joyride / 1986 / LIM / M • Men Don't Leave / 1989 / WAR / S •

My Sister Seka / 1981 / CA / M • Olympic Fever / 1979 / AR / M • On White Satin / 1980 / VCX / M • Oriental Temptations / 1984 / CV / C • Party #1 / 1979 / NAT / M • Party #2 / 1979 / NAT / M • Plato's, The Movie / 1980 / SE / M • Playboy: The Girls Of Radio / 1995 / UNI / F • Porn In The USA #2 / 1987 / VEN / C • Princess Seka / 1980 / VC / M • Prisoner Of Paradise / 1980 / VCX / M • Puss-O-Rama / 1975 / BLT / C • Queen Of Harts / 1986 / BLT / C • Ready, Willing & Anal (Vidco) / 1993 / VD / C • Regency #41: Jambo / cr81 / RHV / M • Rockin' With Seka / 1980 / WV / M • The Seduction Of Cindy / 1980 / VC / M • The Seduction Of Seka / 1981 / AVC / M • Seka In Heat / 1988 / BMV / C • Seka Is Tara / 1981 / VC / M • Seka The Platinum Goddess / 1987 / WV / C • Seka's Fantasies / 1981 / CA / M • Seka's Teenage Diary / 1984 / HO / C • Sensuous Caterer / 197? / HAV / S • Sex Club / 1986 / ... / M • The Sex Game / 1987 / SE / C • Sex On The Orient Express / 1991 / VC / C • Showgirl #02: Seka's Fantasies / 1981 / VCR / M • Snow Honeys / 1983 / VC / M • Splashing / 1986 / VCS / C • Sunny Days / cr80 / BOC / M • Super-Ware Party / 1979 / AR / M • Swedish Erotica #07 / 1980 / CA / M • Swedish Erotica #11 / 1980 / CA / M • Swedish Erotica #15 / 1980 / CA / M • Swedish Erotica #16 / 1980 / CA / M • Swedish Erotica #17 / 1980 / CA / M • Swedish Erotica #18 / 1980 / CA / M • Swedish Erotica #19 / 1980 / CA / M • Swedish Erotica #21 / 1980 / CA / M • Swedish Erotica #22 / 1980 / CA / M • Swedish Erotica #23 / 1980 / CA / M • Swedish Erotica #25 / 1980 / CA / M • Swedish Erotica #26 / 1980 / CA / M • Swedish Erotica #27 / 1980 / CA / M • Swedish Erotica #28 / 1980 / CA / M • Swedish Erotica #31 / 1980 / CA / M • Swedish Erotica #34 / 1980 / CA / M • Swedish Erotica #43 / 1982 / CA / M • Swedish Erotica #44 / 1982 / CA / M • Swedish Erotica #45 / 1983 / CA / M • Swedish Erotica Hard #00: Seka Special! / 1992 / OD / C • Swedish Erotica Hard #06: Seka—Takes Her Men / 1992 / OD / C • Swedish Erotica Hard #13: Cum Shots With Seka / 1992 / OD / C • Swedish Erotica Hard #22: Seka & Desiree: Sex 101 / 1992 / OD / C • Swedish Erotica Superstar #1: Seka / 1983 / CA / C • Swedish Erotica Superstar #2: Brigette Monet / 1983 / CA / C • Sweet Alice / 1983 / VCX / M • Teenage Desires / 1975 / IVP / M • That's Erotic / 1979 / CV / C • Triple Header / 1987 / AIR / C • True Legends Of Adult Cinema: The Golden Age / 1992 / VC / C • Ultraflesh / 1980 / GO / M • VCA Previews #2 / 1988 / VC / C • VCA Previews #4 / 1988 / VC / C • Wine Me, Dine Me, 69 Me / 1989 / COL / C • [Fuck Me, Suck Me, Eat Me / 1990 / ... / M • [Moonchild And Flames / 19?? / ... / M
SELEN
A Private Love Affair / 1996 / IP / M
SELENA *(Jan (Selena), Selene)*
Pretty brunette with shoulder length hair, small/medium tits, large-framed too tall body, nice skin, prominent tan lines, little girl voice, tight waist, washboard flat belly, and a nice personality. Used to work at Denny's as a waitress.

1-900-FUCK #1 / 1995 / SO / M • Anal Freaks / 1994 / KWP / M • Ass Kisser: A Love Story / 1995 / PEP / M • Beach Mistress / 1994 / XCI / M • Big Tit Racket / 1995 / PEP / M • Blindfold / 1994 / SC / M • Brenda: Back To Beverly Hills 9021A / 1994 / CA / M • Brunette Roulette / 1996 / LE / M • Buffy's Anal Adventure / 1996 / CDI / M • Buffy's First Encounter / 1995 / CIN / M • Call Me / 1995 / CV / M • The Cheater / 1994 / XCI / M • Dangerous Games / 1995 / VI / M • Devil In A Wet T-Shirt / 1995 / SPI / M • Dirty Tricks #1: Just A Bunch Of Whores / 1995 / EA / M • Erotic Aquatics #2 / 1996 / MLV / F • The Erotic Artist / 1995 / VC / M • French Twist / 1995 / IN / M • Girls Of The Ivy Leagues / 1994 / VT / M • Gun Runner / 1996 / CIN / M • Heartbeat / 1995 / PP / M • Hollywood Boulevard / 1995 / CV / M • The Horny Hiker / 1995 / LE / M • Joanie Pneumatic / 1996 / PL / M • Love Spice / 1995 / ERA / M • Mile High Thrills / 1995 / VIM / M • Motel Matches / 1996 / LE / M • Oriental Girls In Heat / 1995 / IF / M • Passage To Pleasure / 1995 / LE / M • The Passion / 1995 / IP / M • Patriot X / 1995 / LE / M • The Pawn Shop / 1996 / MID / M • Penetrator #2: Grudge Day / 1995 / PL / M • Phantasm / 1995 / WP / M • Pick Up Lines #06 / 1996 / OD / M • Private Desires / 1995 / LE / M • Private Matters / 1995 / EMC / M • Pumphouse Sluts / 1996 / CC / M • Rainwoman #09: Wetlands / 1995 / CC / M • Rebel Without A Condom / 1996 / ERA / M • Selena Under Siege / 1995 / XCI / M • Sexual Overdrive / 1996 / LE / M • Six Degrees Of Penetration / 1996 / PP / M • Snake Pit / 1996 / DWO / M • Some Like It Hard / 1995 / VC / M • Star Girl / 1996 / ERA / M • Strip Search / 1995 / CV / M • Stripping For Your Lover / 1995 / NIV / F • A Tall Tail / 1996 / FC / M • Temptation / 1994 / VC / M • Totally Real / 1996 / CA / M • Under Siege / 1995 / XCI / M • Under The Covers / 1996 / GO / M • Unleashed / 1996 / SAE / M • Up And Cummers #16 / 1994 / 4P / M • The Usual Anal Suspects / 1996 / CC / M • Vagabonds / 1996 / ERA / M • The Voyeur #3 / 1995 / EA / M • Whackers / 1995 / PP / M • Whore House / 1995 / IPI / M

SELENA KYLE
She-Mails / 1993 / PL / G

SELENA STEELE
Adult Video News 1992 Awards / 1992 / VC / M • Amateur American Style #06 / 1990 / AR / M • American Garter / 1993 / VC / M • Anything That Moves / 1992 / VC / M • The Barlow Affairs / 1991 / XCI / M • The Best Of The Gangbang Girl Series / 1995 / ANA / C • The Chameleon / 1989 / VC / M • Cumming Clean / 1991 / FL / M • Curse Of The Catwoman / 1990 / VC / M • Deep Inside Centerfold Girls / 1991 / VC / M • Deep Inside Racquel Darrian / 1994 / VC / C • Deep Inside Selena Steele / 1993 / VC / C • Gangbang Girl #07 / 1992 / ANA / M • Gangbang Girl #08 / 1992 / ANA / M • Hate To See You Go / 1990 / VC / M • The Last Resort / 1990 / VC / M • Lez Go Crazy / 1992 / HW / C • Magma: Bizarre Dreams / 1994 / MET / M • Mr. Fun's Mondo Adventure / 1993 / VC / M • Oh, What A Night! / 1990 / VC / M • Playin' Dirty / 1990 / VC / M • Positively Pagan #06 / 1993 / ATA / M

• Raunch #02 / 1990 / CC / M • Selena's Secrets / 1991 / MIN / M • Sirens / 1991 / VC / M • Slick Honey / 1989 / VC / M • Sorority Sex Kittens #1 / 1992 / VC / M • Sorority Sex Kittens #2 / 1993 / VC / M • Steele Butt / 1993 / AFV / M • The Tease / 1990 / VC / M • Toy Box Lingerie Show / 1991 / ESP / S • True Legends Of Adult Cinema: The Modern Era / 1992 / VC / C • The Visualizer / 1992 / VC / M • The Wild And The Innocent / 1990 / CC / M

SELENE see Selena

SELINA
Ladies In Leather / 1995 / GO / M • Mr. Peepers Amateur Home Videos #41: Getting Off For Bad Beh / 1992 / LBO / M • OUTS: Selina / 1992 / OUT / F

SELINA FABRE *(Felina Fabre, Ida)*
Older looking blonde who seems to like sex and looks similar to Taylor Wayne but they are defintely not the same person. Speaks with an accent but I can't tell what. Felina Fabre is from **Blue Angel**. Ida is from **Dick-tation**.
Anal Attraction #2 / 1993 / AFV / C • Blue Angel / 1991 / SE / M • Bunz-Eye / 1992 / ROB / M • The Butler Did It / 1991 / FH / M • Dick-Tation / 1991 / AFV / M • Dirty Business / 1992 / CV / M • French Open / 1990 / OD / M • Jewel Of The Orient / 1991 / VEX / M • Opening Night / 1991 / AR / M • Orgy On The Ranch / 1991 / NLE / M • Ready, Willing & Anal / 1992 / OD / M • Someone Sent Me A Girl / 1991 / FH / M • Summer Lovers / 1991 / VEX / M • The Ultimate Pleasure / 1991 / MET / G • Up The Gulf / 1991 / AR / M

SELINA ST CLAIR *(Jessica (Selina St), Celina (Selina St), Salina (St Clair))*
Brunette with rock hard medium to large enhanced tits, lithe body, nice skin, quite pretty. 24 years old in 1994 and was de-virginized at 17. Has done some regular Hollywood bit parts and then went to college prior to getting into the porno industry.
Adventures Of The DP Boys: Janet And Da Boyz / 1994 / HW / M • All The President's Women / 1994 / LV / M • Bodywaves / 1994 / ELP / M • The Bottom Dweller Part Deux / 1994 / EL / M • Breastman Goes To Breastland #2 / 1993 / EVN / M • Bun Busters #12 / 1993 / LBO / M • The Butt Sisters Do Sturgis / 1994 / MID / M • Colossal Orgy #3 / 1994 / HW / M • Dirty Doc's Housecalls #06 / 1993 / LV / M • Double Crossed / 1994 / MID / M • The Face / 1994 / PP / M • First Time Lesbians #13 / 1994 / JMP / F • First Time Lesbians #16 / 1994 / JMP / F • Gang Bang Diaries #3 / 1994 / SFP / M • The Great Pretenders / 1994 / FD / M • Hidden Camera #14 / 1994 / JMP / M • In X-Cess / 1994 / LV / M • Intercourse With The Vampyre #1 / 1994 / SC / M • Luscious Lickin' Lesbians / 1995 / TIE / F • Mike Hott: #257 Cunt of the Month: Selina / 1993 / MHV / M • Mr. Peepers Amateur Home Videos #81: It Beats A Rosy Palm / 1993 / LBO / M • Mr. Peepers Amateur Home Videos #84: She Put the Bra in Braz / 1994 / LBO / M • My Boyfriend's Black / 1994 / FD / M • Paging Betty / 1994 / VC / M • R.E.A.L. #1 / 1994 / LV / F • Rosie: The Neighborhood Slut / 1994 / VIM / M • Satin & Lace / 1994 / WP / M • Selina / 1993 / XCI / M • Tight Tushies #1 / 1994 / SFP / M • Up And Cummers #09 / 1994 / 4P / M •

Video Virgins #11 / 1994 / NS / M • Wendy Whoppers: Psychic Healer / 1994 / PEP / M

SELINA STARR see Star Index I

SELINA STORM see Star Index I

SELINE DE VOUX see Celine De Voux

SENNA
Anal Romp / 1995 / LIP / F

SENORA *(Sandra (Senora))*
Small hispanic girl with small tits and a nice body despite having had two daughters. 21 years old. Has a tattoo on her right back shoulder with a name "Vamiss" or similar.
Deep Inside Dirty Debutantes #09 / 1993 / 4P / M • M Series #12 / 1993 / LBO / M • Odyssey Triple Play #43: Anal Creaming & Reaming / 1993 / OD / M

SENSA RAGGI
Buttman's European Vacation #3 / 1995 / EA / M

SENTA
Blue Vanities #541 / 1994 / FFL / M

SEPHIA
Young Sluts In Heat #2 / 1996 / PL / M

SEPIA RAY
The Best Of Black White & Pink Inside / 1996 / CV / C • The Black Mystique / 1986 / CV / M • Chocolate Delights #2 / 1985 / TAG / C • Ebony Superstars / 1988 / VC / C • Taste Of The Best #3 / 1988 / PIN / C

SEPP ATZINGER see Star Index I

SEPTEMBER RAINES
Bareback Riders / 1992 / VEX / M • Hot Box / 1995 / V99 / C • Illusions #1 / 1992 / IF / M • Star Struck / 1992 / VEX / M

SEQUOIA see Sukoya

SERA
Harry Horndog #19: Anal Lovers #3 / 1993 / ZA / M

SERENA *(Marilyn Berg, Serena Blacquelord)*
Passable face, medium tits, short usually reddish-blonde hair although in early loops she had black or dark brown curly hair. Supposedly had a major drug problem.
800 Fantasy Lane / 1979 / GO / M • Abduction Of Lorelei / 1978 / BL / M • Afternoon Delights / 1981 / CA / M • All The King's Ladies / 1981 / SUP / M • Anal Annie And The Backdoor Housewives / 1984 / LIP / F • Anticipation / 1982 / HIF / M • Aunt Peg / 1980 / CV / M • Auto-Erotic Practices / 1980 / VCR / F • Backdoor Girls / 1983 / VCR / C • Behind The Brown Door / 1986 / VCR / C • The Best Of Raffaelli #2 / 1980 / DIM / M • Blonde In Black Silk / 1979 / QX / M • Blue Confessions / 1983 / VCR / M • Blue Ribbon Blue / 1984 / CA / C • Blue Vanities #016 (New) / 1988 / FFL / M • Blue Vanities #056 / 1988 / FFL / M • Blue Vanities #069 / 1988 / FFL / M • Blue Vanities #071 / 1988 / FFL / M • Blue Vanities #080 / 1988 / FFL / M • Blue Vanities #203 / 1993 / FFL / M • Blue Vanities #246 / 1995 / FFL / M • Blue Vanities #522 / 1993 / FFL / M • Blue Vanities #547 / 1994 / FFL / M • Blue Voodoo / 1983 / VD / M • Blue's Velvet / 1979 / ECV / M • Bound / 1979 / BIZ / B • Bucky Beaver's XXX Dragon Art Theatre Double Feature #01 / 1996 / SOW / M • Caballero Preview Tape #3 / 1984 / CA / C • Candi Girl / 1979 / PVX / M • Captives / 1983 / BIZ / B • Carnal Encounters Of The Barest Kind / 1978 / VOY / C • Chained / cr76 / BIZ / B • Cherry-Ettes For Hire / 1984 / 4P / M • Chopstix / 1979 / TVX / M • Clas-

sic Erotica #2 / 1980 / SVE / M • Classic Swedish Erotica #09 / 1986 / CA / C • Coed Fever / 1980 / CA / M • Collectors Series #07 / 1990 / TAO / B • Deep Rub / 1979 / VC / M • Desire For Men / 1981 / MIT / M • Double Pleasure / 1985 / VCR / M • The Ecstasy Girls #1 / 1979 / CA / M • Educating Serena / 1985 / 4P / M • Erotic Fantasies #7 / 1984 / CV / C • Erotic Gold #1 / 1985 / VEN / M • Erotic Gold #2 / 1985 / VEN / M • Every Which Way She Can / 1981 / CA / M • Extremes / 1981 / CA / M • Fantasex Island / 1983 / NSV / M • Fantasm / 1976 / VS / S • Fantasm Cums Again / 1977 / VS / S • Fantasy Follies #1 / 1983 / VC / M • Fantasy Follies #2 / 1983 / VC / M • Female Athletes / 1977 / VXP / M • Fetish Fever / 1993 / CA / C • For The Love Of Pleasure / 1979 / SE / M • Forbidden Worlds / 1988 / GO / C • Fulfilling Young Cups / 1978 / ... / M • Getting Off / 1979 / VIP / M • GVC: Reincarnation Of Serena #121 / 1983 / GO / M • Hardcore / 1979 / C3S / S • Heavenly Desire / 1979 / WV / M • High School Honeys / 1974 / SOW / M • Honey Throat / 1980 / CV / M • Honeypie / 1975 / VC / M • Honeysuckle Rose / 1979 / CA / M • Honkytonk Nights / 1978 / TWV / S • Hot Bodies (Ventura) / 1984 / VEN / C • Hot Cookies / 1977 / WWV / M • Hot Honey / 1977 / VXP / M • Hot Love / 1981 / SAT / M • Hot Ones / 1982 / SUP / C • Hot Skin In 3D / 1977 / ... / M • Insatiable #1 / 1980 / CA / M • Inside Desiree Cousteau / 1979 / VCX / M • Inspiration / 1981 / CHX / M • Intimate Realities #1 / 1983 / VC / M • Jive Turkey / 1976 / MUN / S • Joe #2 / cr80 / BL / M • John Holmes And The All-Star Sex Queens / 1984 / AMB / M • John Holmes Exposed / 1978 / AVC / C • The Journey Of O / 1975 / TVX / M • K-Sex / 1976 / VCR / M • Legends Of Porn #1 / 1987 / CV / C • Long Jeanne Silver / 1977 / VC / M • Love Notes / 1986 / HO / C • Lust At First Bite / 1978 / VC / M • Mafia Girls / 1972 / SOW / M • Mai Lin Vs Serena / 1982 / HIF / M • The Maids / 1973 / ... / M • Marilyn And The Senator / 1974 / HIF / M • Massage Parlor Wife / 1971 / SOW / S • Never So Deep / 1981 / VCX / M • New York Babes / 1979 / AR / M • Night Flight / cr80 / CRE / M • Olympic Fever / 1979 / AR / M • Only The Best From Europe / 1989 / CV / C • Passion Toys / 1985 / VCR / C • People / 1978 / QX / M • Physical #1 / 1981 / SUP / M • The Pleasure Palace / 1978 / CV / M • PP #2 / cr80 / BL / M • Princess Seka / 1980 / VC / M • Queen Of Harts / 1986 / BLT / C • Rolls Royce #02 / 1980 / ... / C • Screwples / 1979 / CA / M • The Seduction Of Cindy / 1980 / VC / M • Sensual Encounters Of Every Kind / 1978 / SE / M • Sensual Fire / 1979 / HIF / M • Sensuous Caterer / 197? / HAV / S • The Sensuous Detective / 1979 / VC / M • Serena, An Adult Fairy Tale / 1979 / VEN / M • Sexual Heights / 1981 / ... / M • Showgirl #08: Serena's Fantasies / 1983 / VCR / M • Showgirl #11: Merle Michaels' Fantasies / 1983 / VCR / M • Small Town Girls / 1979 / CXV / M • Spanking Scenes #04 / cr80 / TAO / C • Submission Of Serena / cr78 / SVE / B • Summertime Blue / 1979 / VCX / M • Swedish Erotica #02 / 1980 / CA / M • Swedish Erotica #08 / 1980 / CA / M • Swedish Erotica #10 / 1980 / CA

/ M • Swedish Erotica #12 / 1980 / CA / M • Swedish Erotica #45 / 1983 / CA / M • Sweet Cakes / 1976 / VC / M • Take Me Down / 1986 / CV / M • Tales From The Chateau / 1987 / BON / B • A Taste Of Sugar / 1978 / AR / M • Taxi Girls #1 / 1980 / WV / M • Teenage Cruisers / 1977 / VCX / M • Teenage Playmates / 1979 / LOV / M • Tenderloins / 19?? / ... / M • That's Erotic / 1979 / CV / C • That's Porno / 1979 / CV / C • Trashi / 1980 / CA / M • A Tribute To The King / 1985 / VCX / C • Triple Header / 1987 / AIR / C • True Legends Of Adult Cinema: Unsung Superstars / 1993 / VC / C • Ultraflesh / 1980 / GO / M • VCA Previews #2 / 1988 / VC / C • Weekend Tail / 1987 / VD / M • Wine Me, Dine Me, 69 Me / 1989 / COL / C • Wrestling Classics #2 / 1984 / CDP / B • [Chained, Whipped, Flogged, Beaten And Peed On / 1976 / ... / M

SERENA (OTHER)
AVP #7032: Just Drop On Bi / 1990 / AVP / F • Club Deb #3 / 1996 / MET / M • Creme De La Face #10: Cum Dome / 1995 / OD / M • Creme De La Face #11: Cum Plasterers / 1995 / OD / M • The Cumm Brothers #15: Hot Primal Sex / 1996 / OD / M • Finger Pleasures #4 / 1995 / PL / F • Fresh Faces #12 / 1996 / EVN / M • Nothing Like Nurse Nookie #2 / 1996 / NIT / M • Odyssey Triple Play #75: Interracial Anal Threesome / 1994 / OD / M • Q Balls #1 / 1996 / TTV / M • Q Balls #2 / 1996 / TTV / M • Rimmers #2 / 1996 / MP0 / M

SERENA BLACQUELORD *see* Serena
SERENA HEIGHTS *see Star Index I*
SERENA LEBEC *see Star Index I*
SERENA ROBINSON *see* Rachel Ryan
SERENA SANDERS *see Star Index I*
SERENA SAPPHIRE
Pussy Hunt #06 / 1994 / LEI / M
SERENA SAUNDERS
She-Male Encounters #09: She-Male Confidential / 1984 / MET / G
SERENA STEELE
Anal Vision #27 / 1994 / LBO / M
SERENA SUTAY *see Star Index I*
SERENA TITANON
San Francisco Lesbians #5 / 1994 / PL / F
SERENITY (WILDE) *see* Serenity Wilde
SERENITY WILDE *(Serenity (Wilde))*
Blonde with inflated tits who seems to be dick shy. Was 23 in 1993 and for 16 years used to be a ballet dancer (she looks too big for this but maybe that's why she's no longer one). Born in Missouri. Father was in the army.
1-900-FUCK #2 / 1995 / SO / M • Anal Ecstacy Girls #2 / 1993 / ROB / F • Andy / 1993 / ZA / M • Assent Of A Woman / 1993 / DR / M • The Best Of Strippers Inc / 1996 / ONA / C • Bombshell / 1996 / ME / M • Cat Lickers #4 / 1995 / ME / F • Cheerleader Strippers / 1996 / PE / M • Cry Baby / 1995 / CV / M • The Darker Side Of Shayla #2 / 1993 / PL / M • The Devil In Miss Jones #5: The Inferno / 1994 / VC / M • Eleventh Annual AVN Awards / 1994 / VC / M • En Garde / 1993 / DR / M • Erotic Visions / 1995 / ULI / M • First Time Ever #2 / 1996 / PE / F • For The Money #1 / 1993 / FH / M • For The Money #2 / 1993 / FH / M • Girls Will Be Boys #5 / 1993 / PL / F • Girls Will Be Boys #6 / 1993 / PL / F • Hillbilly Honeys / 1996 / WP / M • Hollywood

Spa / 1996 / WP / M • Immortal Desire / 1993 / VI / M • Inferno #1 / 1993 / SC / M • Inferno #2 / 1993 / SC / M • Jenna's Built For Speed / 1997 / WP / F • Jennifer Ate / 1993 / XCI / F • Lip Service / 1995 / WP / M • The Look / 1993 / WP / M • Lost Angels / 1997 / WP / M • The Mechanic / 1995 / VOY / M • Monkey Wrench / 1995 / BEP / M • Positively Pagan #06 / 1993 / ATA / M • Scotty's X-Rated Adventure / 1996 / WP / M • Sex On The Strip: The Lusty Ladies Of Las Vagas / 1993 / CPG / F • Sorority Sex Kittens #3 / 1996 / VC / M • Stacked With Honors / 1993 / DR / M • Strippers Inc. #3 / 1994 / ONA / M • Strippers Inc. #4 / 1995 / ONA / M • Taboo #14: Kissing Cousins / 1995 / IN / M • Taboo #15 / 1995 / IN / M • Temptation Of Serenity / 1994 / WP / M • The Time Machine / 1996 / WP / M • Toppers #05 / 1993 / TV / M • Toppers #20 / 1993 / TV / M • Toppers #23 / 1994 / TV / M • Toppers #26 / 1994 / TV / M • Toppers #32 / 1994 / TV / C • Up And Cummers: The Movie / 1994 / 4P / M • Within & Without You / 1993 / WP / M

SERENNA LEE
Girls Around The World #27 / 1995 / BTO / M • H&S: Sarenna Lee / 199? / H&S / M • Tit To Tit #4 / 1996 / BTO / S
SERGE
Aerienne's Surprise / 1995 / WIV / M
SERGE BONGHART
Cheap Sluts And The Guys Who Fuck Them / 1994 / MET / M • Connie & Floyd / 1973 / SVE / M
SERGEI NOVOTNY
Ultraflesh / 1980 / GO / M
SERGIO (CLAUDIO C) *see* Claudio Cazzo
SERGIO CALLUCI *see Star Index I*
SERGIO DEMON
Foreign Tongues #1: Going Down / 1995 / VI / M • Foreign Tongues #2: Mesmerized / 1995 / VI / M
SERGIO INGESIAS
Girls Of The Third Reich / 1985 / FC / M
SERGIO LEONARDO
Body Lust / 1980 / VC / M
SERINA *see* Rachel Ryan
SERINA ROBINSON *see* Rachel Ryan
SERPENTINA
Dyke's Discipline / 1994 / PL / F
SERRANI
Mr. Peepers Amateur Home Videos #23: Wetting the Wick / 1991 / LBO / M
SERRENA
Mike Hott: #333 Bonus Cunt: Serrena / 1995 / MHV / M
SERRI
Blue Vanities #195 / 1993 / FFL / S
SETH
HomeGrown Video #455 / 1995 / HOV / M
SETH CARSON
Tranny Hill: Sweet Surrender / 1994 / HSV / G
SETH DAMIAN *see* Jill Kelly
SETH GECKO
Babe Wire / 1996 / HW / M • Booty And The Ho' Fish / 1996 / RAS / M • Golden Rod / 1996 / SPI / M • Thunder And Lightning / 1996 / MID / M
SETH PERKINS
Tight Spot / 1996 / WV / M
SETH WAGNER *see Star Index I*
SETINA RAY *see Star Index I*
SEVERA LEE

Dear Fanny / 1984 / CV / M

SEVERITY
Wet Screams / 1996 / BON / B

SEX KITTEN
Bitch School / 1996 / BON / B • Final Orgy / 1996 / BON / B

SEXUAL CHOCOLATE
Black Street Hookers #3 / 1996 / DFI / M

SEXY BLACK
Black Snatch #2 / 1996 / DFI / F

SEXY SADE
Heartbreaker / 1991 / IF / M • Texas Towers / 1993 / IF / M

SEYMORE BUTTS
Backdoor To Buttsville / 1995 / ULI / M • Buttman's Ultimate Workout / 1990 / EA / M • Deep Behind The Scenes With Seymore Butts #1 / 1995 / ULI / M • Dirty Bob's #18: Under The Boardwalk! / 1995 / FLP / S • Dirty Bob's #27: Laid Back In L.A.! / 1996 / FLP / S • Eleventh Annual AVN Awards / 1994 / VC / M • Gangbang Girl #07 / 1992 / ANA / M • Monkey Business / 1996 / ULI / M • Private Video Magazine #09 / 1994 / OD / M • Sex Academy #5: The Art Of Pulp Fiction / 1994 / ONA / M • Seymore & Shane Do Ireland / 1994 / ULI / M • Seymore & Shane Live On Tour / 1995 / ULI / M • Seymore & Shane Meet Kathy Willets, The Naughty Nymph / 1994 / ULI / M • Seymore & Shane Mount Tiffany / 1994 / FH / M • Seymore & Shane On The Loose / 1994 / ULI / M • Seymore & Shane Playing With Fire / 1994 / ULI / M • Seymore Butts & The Honeymooners / 1992 / FH / M • Seymore Butts Goes Deep Inside Shane / 1994 / FH / M • Seymore Butts Goes Nuts / 1994 / FH / M • Seymore Butts In Paradise / 1993 / FH / M • Seymore Butts Swings / 1992 / FH / M • Seymore Butts: Big Boobs In Buttsville / 1996 / FH / M • Seymore Butts: Blow Me #1 / 1996 / ULI / M • Seymore Butts: My Travels With The Tramp / 1994 / FH / M • Seymore Butts: Slippin' In Through The Out Door / 1996 / FH / M • Squirters / 1996 / ULI / M • Yvonne's Odyssey / 1995 / BS / B

SEYMORE CANYON
The Loves Of Mary Jane / 1989 / BWV / C • A Touch Of Sex / 1972 / AR / M

SEYMOUR
Badgirls #1: Lockdown / 1994 / VI / M • Badgirls #2: Strip Search / 1994 / VI / M

SEYMOUR ASHLEY *see* Ashley Moore
SEYMOUR LOVE *see* Dave Copeland
SHA-SHA
Black Hollywood Amateurs #01 / 1995 / MID / M • Black Hollywood Amateurs #14 / 1995 / MID / M • Black Hollywood Amateurs #15 / 1995 / MID / M • Black Hollywood Amateurs #16 / 1995 / MID / M • Ebony Erotica #12: Pussy Posse / 1993 / GO / M • Girl's Towne #2 / 1994 / FC / F • Girlz Towne #11 / 1995 / FC / F

SHABLEE
50 And Still Pumping! / 1994 / EMC / M • Adventures Of The DP Boys: The Golden Girls / 1995 / HW / M • Butt Bangers Ball #1 / 1996 / TTV / M • D.P. Grannies / 1995 / JMP / M • Dirty And Kinky Mature Women #3 / 1995 / C69 / M • The Fabulous 50's Girls Ride Again / 1994 / EMC / M • Geriatric Valley Girls / 1995 / FC / M • Golden Oldies #1 / 1995 / TTV / M • Golden Oldies #2 / 1995 / TTV / M • Granny Bangers / 1995 / MET / M • Kinky Debutante Inter-

views #03 / 1994 / IP / M • Kitty Foxx's Kinky Kapers #03 / 1995 / TTV / M • Kitty's Kinky Capers / 1996 / TTV / M • Middle Aged Maidens / 1995 / GLI / M • Mike Hott: #280 Horny Couples #18 / 1995 / MHV / M • Old Wives' Tails / 1995 / EMC / M • Older And Anal #1 / 1995 / FC / M • Slammin' Granny In The Fanny / 1995 / GLI / M • Swedish Erotica #82 / 1995 / CA / M

SHABONA HUNTER *see* Siobhan Hunter
SHADE
Strap-On Sally #01: Strap-On Psycho / 1993 / PL / F • Strap-On Sally #02: Ariana Bottoms Out / 1993 / PL / F

SHADOW
Cumback Pussy #7: NUGIRLZ / 1997 / EL / M • Filthy First Timers #6 / 1997 / EL / M • Lucky Ladies #104 / 1992 / STI / M • Northwest Pecker Trek #2: Evergreen, Ever Horny / 1994 / LBO / M • Northwest Pecker Trek #6: Two Girls For Every Boy / 1995 / LBO / M

SHADOW NEVA
Candy Goes To Hollywood / 1979 / VCX / M

SHADOW THOMAS
She Male Dicktation / 1994 / HEA / G

SHADOWLYN NEVA
Sweet Savage / 1978 / ALP / M

SHADY O'TOOLE
School For Wayward Wives / 1993 / BIZ / B • Truth Or Dare / 1993 / VI / M

SHADY O'TOOLE (JAY) *see* Jay Ashley
SHAELYNN *see* Star Index I
SHAHE
Black Fantasies #13 / 1996 / HW / M • Black Gangbangers #11 / 1996 / HW / M

SHAIME *see* Stephanie Page
SHAKA *see* Champagne Pendarvis
SHAKER LEWIS *see* Star Index I
SHALEEN *see* Shelene
SHALEENA SPRINGIER *see* Star Index I
SHALENE *see* Shelene
SHALIMA *see* Shalimar
SHALIMAR *(Shalima, Letizia Bisset, Letizia Shalimar, Chantal (Shalimar))*
Slim Italian girl with small tits and a large tattoo of a dagger and snake on right thigh.
Amadeus Mozart / 1996 / XC / M • Hamlet: For The Love Of Ophelia #1 / 1996 / IP / M • Hamlet: For The Love Of Ophelia #2 / 1996 / IP / M • The Joy Club / 1996 / XC / M • Juliet & Romeo / 1996 / XC / M • Midnight Obsession / 1995 / XC / M • Never Say Never To Rocco Siffredi / 1995 / EA / M • Paprika / 1995 / XC / M • Private Film #19 / 1994 / OD / M • Private Video Magazine #13 / 1994 / OD / M • Robin Thief Of Wives / 1996 / XC / M • Sex Penitentiary / 1996 / XC / M

SHALIMAR (S/M)
Bus Stop Tales #04 / 1989 / PRI / M • Dreams Of Misty / 1984 / VCX / M • She Studs #02 / 1991 / BIZ / G • Trisexual Encounters #02 / 1985 / PL / G

SHAME *see* Stephanie Page
SHAMISHA
Slut Safari #3 / 1994 / FC / M

SHANA
Double Crossed / 1994 / MID / M • Florida Girls On Film / 1994 / DGD / F

SHANA (GRANT) *see* Shauna Grant
SHANA CAROL *see* Star Index I
SHANA DOHERTY
Up And Cummers #22 / 1995 / RWP / M

SHANA EVANS *see* Shauna Evans
SHANA KANE
Cats Have Claws / 1988 / NAP / B • Kicking Ass / 1988 / NAP / B • To Tame A Burglar / 1990 / NAP / B

SHANA LEE
Real Sex Magazine #02 / 1997 / HO / M

SHANA LEE (1973)
Four Women In Trouble / 1973 / AXV / M

SHANA O'BRIEN *see* Shauna O'Brien
SHANA VOTAR *see* Star Index I
SHANAE FOXX
Ass Masters (Leisure) #06 / 1995 / LEI / M • New Pussy Hunt #19 / 1996 / LEI / C • The New Snatch Masters #22 / 1996 / LEI / C

SHANDRA
Making Of The "Carousel Girls" Calendar / 1994 / DGD / S • More Dirty Debutantes #45 / 1995 / 4P / M • More Dirty Debutantes #46 / 1995 / 4P / M

SHANE *(Lisa (Shane))*
Long blonde hair, large enhanced tits (reasonable job, you would never know they're not natural if you didn't see an earlier version), passable face, bubbly personality verging on the "too pushy", tall, body is a little on the womanly side. However in **MDD #47** you see her at age 19 (probably about 1989): adorable little brunette with a very tight body, small tits (she calls them "avocadoes"), pretty face, sweet personality. Mall jailbait!
Backdoor To Buttsville / 1995 / ULI / M • Bruce Seven: A Compendium Of His Most Graphic Scenes Vol 6 / 1994 / BS / C • Butt Watch #03 / 1994 / FH / M • Butt Watch #04 / 1994 / FH / M • D.P. Grannies / 1995 / JMP / M • Dick & Jane Do The Strip / 1994 / AVI / M • Dirty And Kinky Mature Women #1 / 1995 / C69 / M • Dirty Bob's #18: Under The Boardwalk! / 1995 / FLP / S • Dirty Bob's #19: Over The Boardwalk! / 1995 / FLP / S • Dirty Bob's #25: Porn Never Sleeps! / 1996 / FLP / S • Dungeon Builder's Punishment / 1996 / STM / B • Eleventh Annual AVN Awards / 1994 / VC / M • House Of Slaves / 1995 / HOM / B • Julie's Diary / 1995 / LBO / M • More Dirty Debutantes #47 / 1995 / 4P / M • Overkill / 1994 / BS / B • Philmore Butts Meets The Freak / 1995 / SUF / M • A Pool Party At Seymores #1 / 1995 / ULI / M • A Pool Party At Seymores #2 / 1995 / ULI / M • Private Video Magazine #09 / 1994 / OD / M • Profiles #03: House Dick / 1995 / XPR / M • Seymore & Shane Do Ireland / 1994 / ULI / M • Seymore & Shane Live On Tour / 1995 / ULI / M • Seymore & Shane Meet Kathy Willets, The Naughty Nymph / 1994 / ULI / M • Seymore & Shane Mount Tiffany / 1994 / FH / M • Seymore & Shane On The Loose / 1994 / ULI / M • Seymore & Shane Playing With Fire / 1994 / ULI / M • Seymore Butts & His Mystery Girl / 1993 / FH / M • Seymore Butts Goes Deep Inside Shane / 1994 / FH / M • Seymore Butts Goes Nuts / 1994 / FH / M • Seymore Butts In Paradise / 1993 / FH / M • Seymore Butts: Bustin' Out My Best Anal / 1995 / FH / C • Seymore Butts: My Travels With The Tramp / 1994 / FH / M • Shane Superstar / 1995 / FH / C • Shane's Ultimate Fantasy / 1994 / BS / B • Shane's World #1 / 1996 / OD / M • Shane's World #2 / 1996 / OD / M • Shane's World #3 / 1996 / OD / M •

Shane's World #4 / 1996 / OD / M •
Shane's World #5 / 1996 / OD / M •
Shane's World #6: Slumber Party / 1996 /
OD / F • Shane's World #7 / 1996 / OD / M
• Sleaze Please!—August Edition / 1994 /
FH / M • Sleaze Please!—October Edition
/ 1994 / FH / M • Sodomania...And Then
Some!!! A Compendium / 1995 / EL / C •
Yvonne's Odyssey / 1995 / BS / B

SHANE (MALE)
Dirty Dancers #8 / 1996 / 4P / M • The Girls
Of Fantasex #2 / 1996 / NIT / M • New Girls
In Town #6 / 1994 / CC / M

SHANE (NIKKI) *see* **Nikki Shane**

SHANE (OLD)
Geriatric Valley Girls / 1995 / FC / M • Older
And Anal #2 / 1995 / FC / M

SHANE FISHMANN *see* **Shane Hunter**

SHANE HUNTER *(Barry (Shane Hunter),*
Shane Fishmann)
Barry (**Breast Worx #1**). Is this the same as
Barry Wood (**King Tongue Meets Anal**
Woman)? Married to Trinity Loren at one
stage.
Aja / 1988 / PL / M • Anal Analysis (Heat-
wave) / 1992 / HW / M • Anal Attraction #1
/ 1988 / 3HV / M • Anal Dawn / 1991 / AMB
/ M • Ass-Capades / 1992 / HW / M • Back
To Back #2 / 1992 / FC / C • Backdoor
Lambada / 1990 / GO / M • Backdoor To
Hollywood #06 / 1989 / CIN / M • Behind
The Backdoor #2 / 1989 / EVN / M • Big
Boob Boat Ride #1 / 1992 / FC / M • Big
Bust Babes #04 / 1988 / AFI / M • Biloxi
Babes / 1988 / WV / M • Blame It On The
Heat / 1989 / VC / M • Bored Housewife /
1989 / CIN / M • Breast Friends / 1991 / PL
/ M • Breast Worx #01 / 1991 / LBO / M •
Breast Worx #06 / 1991 / LBO / M • Bright
Lights, Big Titties / 1989 / CA / M • Broad-
way Babes / 1993 / FH / F • Butt's Motel #2
/ 1989 / EX / M • The Buttnicks #1 / 1990 /
VEX / M • Couples Club #2 / 1989 / BON /
B • Dreams In The Forbidden Zone / 1989
/ PCP / M • Fat Ends / 1989 / 4P / M • Fat-
liners #1 / 1990 / EX / M • Gangbang Girl
#04 / 1992 / ANA / M • Girls Of The Double
D #03 / 1988 / CDI / M • Girls Of The Dou-
ble D #04 / 1989 / CDI / M • The Golden
Gals / 1989 / BTO / M • Hardcore Plumpers
/ 1991 / BTO / M • Hawaii Vice #2 / 1989 /
CDI / M • Hot Licks / 1990 / CDI / M • Hot
Palms / 1989 / GO / M • In Your Face #2 /
1992 / PL / M • King Tongue Meets Anal
Woman / 1990 / PL / M • Lawyers In Heat /
1989 / CDI / M • Leave It To Cleavage #2 /
1989 / EVN / M • Life In The Fat Lane #3 /
1990 / FC / M • Madame X / 1989 / EVN /
M • Making It In New York / 1989 / PLD / M
• Naughty Neighbors / 1989 / CA / M • Per-
sonal Touch #4 / 1989 / AR / M • Playing
With A Full Dick / 1988 / PL / M • Ready To
Drop #01 / 1990 / FC / M • Ready To Drop
#02 / 1992 / FC / M • The Return Of The A
Team / 1988 / WV / M • Roll-X Girls / 1989
/ DYV / M • Soaked To The Bone / 1989 /
IN / M • Starbangers #05 / 1993 / FPI / M •
A Taste Of Sahara / 1990 / PIN / C • Temp-
tations Of An Angel / 1989 / PEN / M • This
One's For You / 1989 / AR / M • Tit In A
Wringer / 1993 / FC / M • Tit Tales #1 / 1989
/ 4P / M • Tit Tales #2 / 1990 / FC / M • To
Snatch A Thief / 1989 / PLD / M • A Trip
Down Mammary Lane / 1991 / FC / M •
Triple Header / 1990 / KNI / M • Who
Shaved Trinity Loren? / 1988 / EX / M

SHANE MICHAELS *see* **Star Index I**

SHANE PIERCE
Painless Steel #4 / 1996 / FLV / M

SHANE STEVENS *see* **Star Index I**

SHANE TAYLOR *see* **Shone Taylor**

SHANE TYLER
Short-haired blonde with a pretty face, lithe
body, medium droopy tits (one is slightly
smaller than the other), good tan lines with
the imprint of the *Playboy* bunny made by
the sun just above her pussy. Married to
Michael Mark.
Buttslammers #08: The Ultimate Invasion /
1994 / BS / F • Dirty Bob's #23: Tampa
Teasers / 1995 / FLP / S • Dirty Dancers #1
/ 1994 / 4P / M • Dirty Dancers #2 / 1994 /
4P / M • East Coast Sluts #03: South
Florida / 1995 / PL / M • Everything Is Not
Relative / 1994 / EL / M • Lydia's Web /
1994 / TWP / B • Obsession / 1994 / BS /
B • Sodomania #18: Shame Based / 1996
/ EL / M • Strap-On Sally #03: Thigh Har-
ness Terror / 1994 / PL / F • Strap-On Sally
#04: Double Penetration Dykes / 1994 / PL
/ F • Sunset Rides Again / 1995 / VC / M •
Tight Shots #1 / 1994 / VI / M • Up And
Cummers #17 / 1994 / 4P / M • Up And
Cummers #27 / 1996 / ERW / M • Up And
Cummers #31 / 1996 / 4P / M • Up And
Cummers #39 / 1996 / RWP / M • The
Voyeur #2 / 1994 / EA / M • Whiplash /
1996 / DFI / M

SHANEL *see* **Chanel (1992)**

SHANEL DUBOIS
Breast Worx #36 / 1992 / LBO / M • Chocolate Bunnies #02 / 1995 / LBO / C

SHANELLE STAXX
Score Busty Centerfolds #2 / 1995 / BTO /
M

SHANEN STEELE
Chicks, Licks And Dirty Tricks / 1993 / ME
/ F • I'll Do Anything But... / 1992 / CA / M •
Jiggly Queens #1 / 1993 / LE / M • Kym
Wilde's On The Edge #05 / 1993 / RB / B •
Penthouse: 25th Anniversary Swimsuit
Video / 1994 / A*V / F • Style #1 / 1992 / VT
/ M • Waterbabies #2 / 1992 / CC / M

SHANG
The Best Of East Coast Sluts / 1995 / PL /
C

SHANITA
Interracial 247 / 1995 / CC / M

SHANNA
Blue Vanities #577 / 1995 / FFL / M • More
Dirty Debutantes #19 / 1993 / 4P / M •
Steal This Heart (Director's) / 1993 / CV /
M

SHANNA (DEST. LANE) *see* **Destini**
Lane

SHANNA CURTIS *see* **Star Index I**

SHANNA DOVE *see* **Star Index I**

SHANNA EVANS
Deep Blue / 1989 / PV / M • A Very Debauched Girl / 1988 / PL / M

SHANNA KAY *see* **Shauna Rose**

SHANNA KRAMER
K-Sex / 1976 / VCR / M

SHANNA LEIGH
Sista! #2 / 1994 / VT / F

SHANNA MCCOULLACH *see* **Shanna**
McCullough

SHANNA MCCULLOUGH *(Shanna Mc-*
Coullach, Marcia Gray, Shauna McUl-
loh)
Reddish-brunette with a womanly body,
medium tits with barely visible areola,

passable face, a bit too big on the hips and
butt. In her return in 1996 she has had her
tits enhanced to large size and is just porno
fodder.
Acts Of Love / 1989 / ... / M • Addicted To
Love / 1988 / WAV / M • Adultery / 1986 /
DR / M • All For His Ladies / 1987 / PP / C
• All The Way In / 1984 / VC / M • Angel
Kelly Raw / 1987 / FAN / M • Angel Puss /
1988 / VC / M • Angel Rising / 1988 / IN /
M • At The Pornies / 1989 / VC / M • Babes
Illustrated #5 / 1996 / IN / F • Babylon Pink
#2 / 1988 / COM / M • Babylon Pink #3 /
1988 / COM / M • Ball In The Family / 1988
/ VWA / M • Ball Street / 1988 / CA / M • The
Beat Goes On / 1987 / VCR / C • Bedside
Brat / 1988 / VI / M • Behind Blue Eyes #2
/ 1988 / ZA / M • Best Of Talk Dirty To Me
#01 / 1991 / DR / C • Bi 'n' Large / 1992 /
VD / C • The Big Bang / 1988 / WET / M •
The Bitch / 1988 / FAN / M • Blonde On The
Run / 1985 / PV / M • Blue Ice / 1985 / CA
/ M • Blue Movie / 1989 / VD / M • Bobby
Sox / 1996 / VI / S • Body Games / 1987 /
DR / M • Body Girls / 1983 / SE / M • The
Boss / 1987 / FAN / M • Bound And
Gagged #04 / 1991 / RB / B • Bound To
Tease #3 / 1989 / BON / C • Brat On The
Run / 1987 / VI / M • Breakin' In / 1986 / WV
/ M • Broadway Brat / 1988 / VI / M • Cali-
fornia Taboo / 1986 / VC / M • Captain
Hooker & Peter Porn / 1987 / VD / M •
Careful, He May Be Watching / 1986 / CA /
M • Chastity Johnson / 1985 / AVC / M •
Cheri's On Fire / 1986 / V99 / M • Club Ex-
otica #1 / 1985 / WV / M • Club Exotica #2
/ 1985 / WV / M • Club Sex / 1989 / GO / M
• Color Me Amber / 1985 / VC / M • Com-
petition / 1989 / BON / B • Conflict / 1988 /
VD / M • Corporate Affairs / 1986 / SE / M
• Couples Club #1 / 1988 / BON / B • Cou-
ples Club #2 / 1989 / BON / B • Crazy With
The Heat #1 / 1986 / CV / M • Dangerous
Desire / 1986 / NSV / M • The De Renzy
Tapes / 1990 / CA / C • Dead Pit / 1989 /
IMP / S • Debbie Class Of '88 / 1987 / CC
/ M • Debbie Does 'em All #1 / 1985 / CV /
M • Deep Inside Ona Zee / 1992 / VC / C •
Deep Inside Shanna Mccullough / 1992 /
VC / C • Deviations / 1983 / SE / M • Dia-
mond Collection #51 / 1984 / CIN / M •
Dirty 30's Cinema: Patti Petite / 1986 / PV
/ C • Dr Juice's Lust Potion / 1986 / TEM /
M • Dy-Nasty / 1988 / SE / M • Ecstasy /
1986 / PP / M • The Erotic Adventures Of
Bonnie & Clyde / 1988 / GO / M • Erotic En-
counters (Interludes) / 1993 / NIV / S •
Erotica S.F. / 1994 / ORP / M • Expert
Tease / 1988 / CC / M • Expose Me Again
/ 1996 / CV / M • Exposure / 1988 / VD / M
• Falcon Breast / 1987 / CDI / M • Fatal
Passion / 1988 / CC / M • The Final Taboo
/ 1988 / CA / M • The Fire Inside / 1988 /
VC / C • The First Taboo / 1989 / LA / M •
For His Eyes Only / 1989 / PL / M • For
Your Love / 1988 / IN / M • The French
Connexxxion / 1991 / VC / M • French Let-
ters / 1984 / CA / M • The Gift / 1996 / FEM
/ M • Girls Like Us / cr88 / IN / C • Girls On
Fire / 1985 / VCX / M • Girlworld #2 / 1988
/ LIP / F • Glamour Girls / 1987 / SE / M •
Goin' Down Slow / 1988 / VC / M • The
Good Time Girls / 1985 / VEX / M • Good
To The Last Drop / 1986 / VCS / C • Grind
/ 1988 / CV / M • Guess Who Came At Din-
ner? / 1987 / FAN / M • Hands Off / 1988 /

PP / M • A Hard Act To Swallow / 1988 / VT / M • Hard Choices / 1987 / CA / M • Hard To Swallow / 1985 / PV / M • Harlem Candy / 1987 / WET / M • Haulin' 'n' Ballin' / 1988 / MET / G • Hawaii Vice #7 / 1989 / CDI / M • HHHHot! TV #1 / 1988 / CDI / M • Hornet's Nest / 1996 / ONA / M • Horneymooners #1 / 1988 / VXP / M • Horneymooners #2 / 1988 / VXP / M • The Hot Box Invasion / 1987 / AMB / M • Hot Nights And Hard Bodies / 1986 / VD / M • Hottest Ticket / 1987 / WV / C • House Of Sexual Fantasies / 1987 / GO / M • Housewife From Hell / 1994 / TRI / S • The Hungry Heart / 1996 / AOP / M • The Huntress / 1987 / IN / M • Insatiable #2 / 1984 / CA / M • It's Incredible / 1985 / SE / M • KTSX-69 / 1988 / CA / M • Kym Wilde's On The Edge #13 / 1994 / RB / B • L'Amour / 1984 / CA / M • L.A. Raw / 1986 / SE / M • The Last Condom / 1988 / PP / M • Leather For Lovers #1 / 1992 / LFL / M • Lesbian Lovers / 1988 / GO / F • Lesbian Nymphos / 1988 / GO / C • Let's Get It On With Amber Lynn / 1986 / VC / M • Let's Get Physical (Hyapatia Lee's) / 1984 / CA / M • Let's Talk Anal / 1996 / ESF / M • Licensed To Thrill / 1990 / VC / M • Liquid Love / 1988 / CA / M • Little Orphan Dusty #2 / 1981 / VIS / M • Living Doll / 1987 / WV / M • Lost Innocence / 1988 / PV / M • Love At First Sight / 1987 / SE / C • Love Lies / 1988 / IN / M • A Lover For Susan / 1987 / CLV / M • Lust Connection / 1988 / VT / M • The Magic Touch / 1985 / CV / M • Makeout / 1988 / VT / M • Making Ends Meet / 1988 / VT / M • Malibu Express / 1984 / MCA / S • Mardi Gras Passions / 1987 / MET / M • Material Girl / 1986 / VD / M • Meat Market / 1992 / SEX / C • Memoirs Of A Chambermaid / 1987 / FIR / M • Monaco Falcon / 1990 / VC / M • Moonlusting #1 / 1986 / WV / M • Moonlusting #2 / 1987 / WV / M • Motel Sweets / 1987 / VD / M • My Bare Lady / 1989 / ME / M • N.Y. Video Magazine #09 / 1996 / OUP / M • Naked Stranger / 1987 / CDI / M • Nasty Lady / 1984 / CV / M • Nasty Nymphos #16 / 1996 / ANA / M • Night Moves / 1983 / SUP / M • Nightmare On Porn Street / 1988 / ME / M • No Man's Land #14 / 1996 / VT / F • No One To Love / 1987 / PP / M • Nymphette #2 / 1986 / WV / M • On The Loose & Hot To Trot / 1987 / CA / M • Ona Zee's Doll House #3 / 1995 / ONA / F • Once Upon A Temptress / 1988 / CA / M • Only The Best Of The Erotic Eighties / 1992 / VC / C • Only The Best Of Women With Women / 1988 / CV / C • Only The Very Best On Video / 1992 / VC / C • Oral Majority #04 / 1987 / WV / C • Oral Majority #05 / 1987 / WV / C • Oral Majority #06 / 1988 / WV / C • Oral Majority Black #1 / 1987 / WV / C • Orgies / 1987 / WV / C • Our Dinner With Andrea / 1988 / CA / M • Outlaw Ladies #2 / 1988 / VC / M • Pajama Party Bondage / 1993 / BON / B • The Passion Within / 1986 / MAP / M • Passionate Heiress / 1987 / CA / M • Passionate Partners: The Guide For Daring Lovers / 1993 / PHV / S • Passions Of Sin / 1996 / NIT / M • The Pearl Divers / 1988 / VWA / M • Pearl Necklace: Amorous Amateurs #05 / 1992 / SEE / M • Peeping Tom / 1986 / CV / M • Perversion / 1984 / AVC / M • Phantom X / 1989 / VC / M • Phone Mates / 1988 / CA / M • Physical #2

/ 1985 / SUP / M • Physical Attraction / 1984 / MAP / M • The Pink Panties / 1985 / NSV / M • Playboy: House Of The Rising Sun / 1996 / UNI / S • The Pleasure Game / 1988 / CA / M • Porn Star Confidential / 1996 / ESF / M • Prom Girls / 1988 / CA / M • Provocative Pleasures / 1988 / VC / C • The PTX Club / 1988 / GO / M • Punished Princess / 1992 / HOM / B • Rachel Ryan Exposed / 1990 / WV / C • Raging Hormones / 1988 / VXP / M • Raising Hell / 1987 / VD / M • Rated Sex / 1986 / SE / M • Saddletramp / 1988 / VD / M • Satisfaction Jackson / 1988 / CA / M • Screwdriver / 1988 / CC / C • Sex Asylum #3 / 1988 / VI / M • The Sex Dancer / 1986 / NSV / M • Sex Life Of A Porn Star / 1986 / ELH / M • The Sex Life Of Mata Hari / 1989 / GO / M • Sex Lives Of The Rich And Famous #1 / 1988 / VC / M • Sex Lives Of The Rich And Famous #2 / 1989 / VC / M • The Sexaholic / 1988 / VC / M • Sexline You're On The Air / 1986 / CAT / M • Sexy Delights #2 / 1987 / CLV / M • Shame On Shanna / 1989 / DR / C • Shanna McCullough's College Bound / 1992 / BON / B • Shanna's Bondage Fantasy #1 / 1993 / BON / B • Shanna's Bondage Fantasy #2 / 1993 / BON / B • Shanna's Final Fling / 1991 / ME / M • Shanna Shaved #04 / 1992 / RB / F • She's So Fine #2 / 1988 / VC / M • Showdown / 1986 / CA / M • Sin Tax / 1996 / ZA / M • The Sins Of Angel Kelly / 1987 / FAN / C • Sinset Boulevard / 1987 / WV / M • The Slut / 1988 / FAN / M • Smooth Operator / 1986 / AR / M • Spoiled / 1987 / VD / M • St. Tropez Lust / 1990 / VC / M • St. X-Where #2 / 1988 / VD / M • Starbangers #10 / 1997 / ZA / M • Strictly Business / 1987 / VD / M • Sweat #2 / 1988 / PP / M • Sweet Cream / 1991 / VC / C • Talk Dirty To Me #04 / 1986 / DR / M • Talk Dirty To Me #05 / 1987 / DR / M • Talk Dirty To Me #06 / 1989 / DR / M • Talk Dirty to Me One More Time #2 / 1988 / PP / C • Taxi Girls #2: In Search Of Toni / 1986 / ELD / M • Tell Me Something Dirty / 1991 / NWV / M • Temptations Of An Angel / 1989 / PEN / M • Tender And Wild / 1989 / MTP / M • This Is Your Sex Life / 1987 / VD / M • Tight Fit / 1987 / V99 / M • Tight Fit / 1991 / VEX / C • Tight Spot / 1996 / WV / M • Too Hot To Handle / 1989 / WET / F • The Toy Box / 1996 / ONA / M • Triple Header / 1986 / SE / C • True Legends Of Adult Cinema: The Erotic Eighties / 1992 / VC / C • Type Cast / 1986 / AR / M • Unnatural Phenomenon #2 / 1986 / WV / M • Untamed Passions / 1987 / CV / C • Up Your Ass #2 / 1996 / ANA / M • Valentine's Wonderland / 1992 / LIP / F • Video Voyeur #1 / 1988 / VT / C • What's Up Doc / 1988 / SEV / M • Where There's Smoke There's Fire / 1987 / FAN / M • White Bun Busters / 1985 / VC / M • Who Came In The Backdoor? / 1987 / PV / M • Wild Fire / 1990 / WV / C • Wild Things #2 / 1986 / CV / M • Wise Girls / 1989 / IN / C • Women In Uniform / 1986 / TEM / M • WPINK-TV #3 / 1988 / PV / M • The X-Terminator / 1986 / PV / M • Xstasy / 1986 / NSV / M • Yank My Doodle, It's A Dandy / 1985 / GOM / M • The Young And The Wrestling #1 / 1988 / PL / M • Young Girls Do / 1984 / ELH / M • [Luck & Stupid / 1996 / ... / S • [Sisters Of Sin / 1996 / ... / S • [Virgin Desire / 1996 / ... / S

SHANNA ROSE *see Shauna Rose*

SHANNA SIMMS
She Male Service / 1994 / HEA / G

SHANNE
Her Name Is Asia / 1996 / SUF / M

SHANNON
AVP #8010: Bi-Bi Shannon / 1990 / AVP / F • AVP #8011: Initiating Shannon / 1990 / AVP / M • The Best Of Fabulous Flashers / 1996 / DGD / F • Body Tease / 1992 / VER / F • Bun Busters #11 / 1993 / LBO / M • Odyssey Triple Play #10: Shannon Goes Solo / 1992 / OD / M • The Sodomizer #5: Destination Moon / 1996 / SC / M • Southern: Previews #1 / 1992 / SSH / C • Swedish Erotica #27 / 1980 / CA / M

SHANNON (S/M) *(Catherine Crystal)*
Shannon is the name used by this transsexual prior to the operation and Catherine is the name used after.
Bi-Ceps / 1986 / LA / C • Bizarre People / 1982 / BIZ / G • Forbidden Desires / 1984 / BIZ / G • Forbidden Dreams / 1984 / BIZ / G • Go For It / 1984 / VC / M • Le Sex De Femme #3 / 1989 / AFI / C • Legs / 1986 / AMB / M • Looking For Mr Goodsex / 1984 / CC / M • Mama's Boy / 1984 / VD / M • Many Faces Of Shannon / 1988 / VC / C • The Postman Always Comes Twice / 1986 / AMB / M • Roommate In Bondage / 1983 / BIZ / B • Screw / 1985 / CV / M • Shannon / 1982 / BIZ / G • Shannon Shows Off / 1993 / HAC / G • She-Male Desires / 1989 / VC / C • She-Male Encounters #11: She-Male Roommates / 1986 / MET / G • Skintight / 1991 / VER / F • Transformation #2 / 199? / BIZ / G • Trisexual Encounters #01 / 1985 / PL / G • Trisexual Encounters #02 / 1985 / PL / G • Trisexual Encounters #05 / 1986 / PL / G • Trisexual Encounters #06 / 1987 / PL / G • Twice A Virgin / 1984 / PL / G

SHANNON BELL *see Star Index I*

SHANNON CARSE *see William Rotsler*

SHANNON DAVIS
Suze's Centerfolds #7 / 1983 / CA / M

SHANNON GOLD
Dirty Hairy's Amateurs #04: Black Dicks White Lips / 1995 / GOT / M

SHANNON HURTS *see Natalie Harris*

SHANNON HURTZ *see Natalie Harris*

SHANNON KNOWLES
Sex, Truth & Videotape #1 / 1995 / DOC / M • Sex, Truth & Videotape #2 / 1996 / DOC / M

SHANNON MOORE
Black Cheerleader Search #09 / 1996 / IVC / M • Black Snatch #1 / 1996 / DFI / F

SHANNON O'ROURKE *see Star Index I*

SHANNON RUSH
Pretty brunette with small tits (first few movies, later enhanced to watermelon size), lithe body and a nice butt. De-virginized at 15. Supposedly comes from Florida and is a dancer.
Abused / 1996 / ZA / M • Anal Fever / 1996 / ROB / M • Anal Party Girls / 1996 / GV / M • Anal Princess #2 / 1996 / VC / M • At The Mistress' Mercy / 1996 / OUP / B • Backdoor Diaries / 1995 / BBE / M • Beauty's Punishment / 1996 / BIZ / B • The Best Of East Coast Sluts / 1995 / PL / C • Call Of The Wild / 1995 / AFI / M • Celebrity Sluts And Tabloid Tramps / 1996 / LV / M • Cheerleaders In Bondage #1 / 1994 / GOT / B • Cheerleaders In Bondage #2 / 1995 /

GOT / B • Chronicles Of Pain #1 / 1996 / BIZ / B • Dirty Dancers #1 / 1994 / 4P / M • Dresden Diary #14: Ecstasy In Hell / 1996 / BIZ / B • East Coast Sluts #03: South Florida / 1995 / PL / M • Exotic Car Models #1 / 1996 / INO / F • Frendz? #1 / 1996 / RAS / M • Get Lucky / 1996 / NIT / M • Hard Core Beginners #10 / 1995 / LEI / M • Interview's Big Boob Bonanza / 1996 / LV / M • The Kiss / 1995 / WP / M • Kiss My Ass / 1994 / GOT / B • Leather Bound Dykes From Hell #7 / 1996 / BIZ / B • Male Order Brides / 1996 / RAS / M • Masters Of Dominance / 1996 / GOT / C • Microslut / 1996 / TTV / M • N.Y. Video Magazine #01 / 1994 / OUP / M • N.Y. Video Magazine #03 / 1995 / OUP / M • N.Y. Video Magazine #07 / 1996 / OUP / M • Nina Hartley's Guide To Swinging / 1996 / A&E / M • Philmore Butts Meets The Palm Beach Nymphomaniac Kathy Wille / 1995 / SUF / M • Pitfalls Of Sasha / 1995 / GOT / B • Playmates Of The Rich And Famous / 1995 / BBE / M • Red Door Diaries #2 / 1996 / ZA / M • Sapphire Unleashed / 1996 / OUP / B • Strap-On Sally #03: Thigh Harness Terror / 1994 / PL / F • Strap-On Sally #04: Double Penetration Dykes / 1994 / PL / F • Streets Of New York #03 / 1994 / PL / M • Toe Tales #18 / 1994 / GOT / B • Toe Tales #19 / 1994 / GOT / B • Video Virgins #22 / 1995 / NS / M • Waterworld: The Enema Movie / 1996 / BIZ / B

SHANNON TWILL *see Star Index I*
SHANNON WARD *see Savannah*
SHANNON WEST
Flesh Gordon #1 / 1974 / FAC / S • The Loves Of Mary Jane / 1989 / BWV / C • A Touch Of Sex / 1972 / AR / M
SHANNON WHITE
Buttman's British Moderately Big Tit Adventure / 1994 / EA / M
SHANNON WHITE (HART) *see Heather Hart*
SHANNON WILSEY *see Savannah*
SHANTE
Mike Hott: #121 Shante / 1989 / MHV / F
SHANTEL
A&B AB#272: The Sexiest Home-Made Videos #2 / 1991 / A&B / C
SHANTEL DAY *see Shantell Day*
SHANTELL DAY (Shantel Day, Rhonda Shantel)
Best Of Caught From Behind #2 / 1988 / HO / C • Caught From Behind #02: The Sequel / 1983 / HO / M • Dirty 30's Cinema: Janey Robbins & Shantell / 1986 / PV / C • Every Woman Has A Fantasy #1 / 1984 / VC / M • The Good Time Girls / 1985 / VEX / M • Hottest Parties / 1988 / VC / C
SHANTELLE *see Star Index I*
SHANTI
Limited Edition #16 / 1980 / AVC / M
SHANTREL
More Dirty Debutantes #36 / 1994 / 4P / M
SHARAR DESIRE
The Training #1 / 1984 / BIZ / B
SHAREE
Blue Vanities #129 / 1990 / FFL / M
SHARI ALEXANDER
Getting Lucky / 1983 / CA / M
SHARI ANDERSON *see Star Index I*
SHARI KAY *see Star Index I*
SHARI SLOAN *see Dana Dylan*
SHARI SLOANE *see Dana Dylan*
SHARI STEWART

Blonde On Black / 1986 / CC / F • Brown Sugar / 1984 / VC / M • Chocolate Candy #1 / 1984 / VD / M • Ebony Dreams / 1988 / PIN / C • The Midnight Zone / 1986 / IN / M
SHARICE *see Sharise*
SHARISE (Charise, Sharice, Alisha Jordean, Sherise, Sherice, Amber Woods)
Tall lithe blonde with firm tight body and small breasts. Alisha is from **Erectnophobia**. Used to be girlfriend of Nick E but they split up in 1993. As of late 1993, she has retired from the business. Seems to have returned in 1994 in **Video Virgins #14** where she says she's 21 years old. Amber Woods is the credit in **Anal Persuasion** and most subsequent movies and in her return she now has two eyes tattooed on her back.
976-76DD / 1993 / VI / M • Amateur Lesbians #15: Courtney / 1991 / GO / F • Amateur Lesbians #17: Sharise / 1992 / GO / F • America's Dirtiest Home Videos #08 / 1992 / VEX / M • America's Raunchiest Home Videos #22: City Lites / 1992 / ZA / M • American Pie / 1995 / WAV / M • Anal Adventures #1: Anal Executive / 1991 / VC / M • Anal Analysis / 1992 / ZA / M • Anal Angel / 1991 / ZA / M • Anal Disciples #1 / 1996 / ZA / M • Anal Disciples #2: The Anal Conflict / 1996 / ZA / M • Anal Ecstacy Girls #1 / 1993 / ROB / F • Anal Persuasion / 1994 / EX / M • Anal Woman #2 / 1993 / PL / M • Ass Kisser: A Love Story / 1995 / PEP / M • Backdoor Smugglers / 1994 / JAV / M • Battlestar Orgasmica / 1992 / EVN / M • Bedlam / 1995 / WAV / M • Bend Over Babes #3 / 1992 / EA / M • Best Butt(e) In The West #1 / 1992 / CC / M • Bossy Babes / 1993 / TCK / M • Boudoir Babe / 1996 / VMX / M • The Butt Sisters Do Daytona / 1995 / MID / M • Butt Woman #2 / 1992 / FH / M • California Pizza Girls / 1992 / EVN / M • Chasey Saves The World / 1996 / VI / M • Club Anal #1 / 1993 / ROB / F • Dallas Does Debbie / 1992 / PL / M • The Darker Side Of Shayla #2 / 1993 / PL / M • Deep Inside Ariana / 1995 / VC / C • Deep Inside Shanna Mccullough / 1992 / VC / C • Denim / 1991 / LE / M • Diamond In The Rough / 1993 / BIA / C • Dick & Jane Go To Northridge / 1994 / AVI / M • Do The White Thing / 1992 / ZA / M • The Doll House / 1995 / CV / M • Employee's Entrance In The Rear / 1996 / CC / M • Erectnophobia #1 / 1991 / MID / M • Eve Of Seduction / 1991 / CDI / M • Fame Has A Fantasy #3 / 1995 / VC / M • Fame Is A Whore On Butt Row / 1996 / ABS / M • Fast Track / 1992 / LIP / F • Fishin' For Lust / 1996 / WST / M • Fixing A Hole / 1995 / XCI / M • Flexxx #3 / 1995 / VT / M • Forever Young / 1994 / VI / M • Fox Fever / 1991 / LV / M • Gazongo / 1995 / PEP / M • Generally Horny Hospital / 1995 / IMV / M • Gold Diggers / 1993 / IN / M • Hard Core Beginners #04 / 1995 / LEI / M • The Hills Have Thighs / 1992 / MID / C • Hocus Poke-Us / 1991 / HO / M • Hooray For Hineywood / 1991 / MID / M • Hose Jobs / 1995 / VEX / M • Hot Tight Asses #10 / 1995 / TCK / M • Hourman Is Here / 1994 / CC / M • How To Have Anal Sex / 1993 / A&E / M • How To Love Your Lover / 1992 / XII / S • I Remember When / 1992 / ATL / M • In Your Face #2 / 1992 / PL / M • In

Your Face #4 / 1996 / PL / M • Interview: Barely Legal / 1995 / LV / M • Lady M's Anything Nasty #01: Pink Pussy Party / 1996 / AVI / F • Maiden Heaven #1 / 1992 / MID / F • Maliboobies / 1993 / CDI / F • Mind Trips / 1992 / FH / M • Mr. Fun's Mondo Adventure / 1993 / VC / M • Mr. Peepers Amateur Home Videos #20: Motel Dick / 1991 / LBO / M • Mr. Peepers Amateur Home Videos #26: Hole For Lease / 1991 / LBO / M • Mr. Peepers Amateur Home Videos #29: Going Down Payment / 1991 / LBO / M • Naked Bun 2 1/2 / 1991 / WV / M • Natural Born Thriller / 1994 / CC / M • A New Girlfriend / 1991 / XPI / M • Nighttime Stories / 1991 / LE / M • Nookie Cookies / 1993 / CDI / F • Nothing But Trouble / 1991 / CIN / M • Ona Zee's Learning The Ropes #11: Chains Required / 1994 / ONA / B • Out Of The Blue #1 / 1991 / VI / M • Out Of The Blue #2 / 1992 / VI / M • Passage To Pleasure / 1995 / LE / M • Pearl Of The Orient / 1995 / IN / M • Persuasion / 1995 / LE / M • The Phoenix #2 / 1992 / VI / M • The Pink Persuader / 1992 / LBO / M • Power Butt / 1994 / VI / C • Private Audition / 1995 / EVN / M • The Psychic / 1993 / CC / M • Public Enemy / 1995 / GO / M • Public Places #1 / 1994 / SC / M • Radio-Active / 1992 / SC / M • Rock Me / 1994 / CC / M • Rugburn / 1993 / LE / M • Scorcher / 1992 / GO / M • The Seduction Of Mary / 1992 / VC / M • Sex In A Singles Bar / 1992 / VC / M • Sex Symphony / 1992 / VC / M • Sex Trek #2: The Search For Sperm / 1991 / ME / M • Sexual Olympics #1: The Trials / 1992 / VT / M • Sexual Olympics #2: The Finals / 1992 / VT / M • A Shot In The Pants / 1995 / HO / M • Sittin' Pretty #2 / 1992 / DR / M • Soft And Wild / 1991 / LV / M • Star Girl / 1996 / ERA / M • Strippers Inc. #2 / 1994 / ONA / M • Sweet Dreams / 1991 / VC / M • Telesex #2 / 1992 / VI / M • Three Hearts / 1995 / CC / M • Tori Welles Goes Behind The Scenes / 1992 / FD / M • Transitions: An Anal Adventure / 1993 / PL / M • True Sex / 1994 / EMC / M • Turnabout / 1996 / CTP / M • Unlike A Virgin / 1991 / HO / M • Up The Ying Yang / 1995 / CC / M • The Usual Anal Suspects / 1996 / CC / M • Vagabonds / 1996 / ERA / M • Venus Of The Nile / 1991 / WV / M • Video Virgins #14 / 1994 / NS / M • Wild Flower #2 / 1992 / VI / M • With The Devil In Her Rear / 1992 / WV / M
SHARLA
Blue Vanities #116 / 1988 / FFL / M
SHARLA MAYNES
Hookers Holiday / cr70 / AXV / M
SHARLA O'SHEA *see Star Index I*
SHARLYN ALEXANDER *see Laurien Dominique*
SHARON
A&B AB#030: Grandma's House / 1990 / A&B / M • A&B AB#115: Cry Uncle / 1990 / A&B / M • Aerienne's Surprise / 1995 / WIV / M • Amateur Lesbians #28: Sharon / 1992 / GO / F • Bi-Bi Love Amateurs #1 / 1993 / SFP / G • Blue Vanities #527 / 1993 / FFL / M • Blue Vanities #530 / 1993 / FFL / M • Blue Vanities #533 / 1993 / FFL / M • Blue Vanities #534 / 1993 / FFL / M • Blue Vanities #555 / 1994 / FFL / M • Brabusters #1 / 1981 / CA / S • Cherry Poppers #07: Li'l Darlin's / 1994 / ZA / M • High Heels In Heat #3 / 1989 / RSV / F • Mistress Son-

dra's TV Discipline / 1990 / B&D / B • Penthouse: 1995 Pet Of The Year Playoff / 1994 / PET / F • Penthouse: The Girls Of Penthouse #3 / 1995 / PET / S • Raw Talent: Fetish Of The Month #01 / 1994 / RTP / G • Wedding Rituals / 1995 / DVP / M • Wrasslin She-Babes #05 / 1996 / SOW / M

SHARON ADAMS
F / 1980 / GO / M

SHARON ALEXANDER *see* **Laurien Dominique**

SHARON ASNES
Lesbian Orgy / 1980 / WID / F

SHARON AXIS
Housemother's Discipline #5 / 1994 / RB / B

SHARON BELL
Black Gangbangers #06 / 1995 / HW / M • Black Women, White Men #6 / 1995 / FC / M • Coco's House Party / 1995 / HW / M • Dirty And Kinky Mature Women #4 / 1995 / C69 / M • The Erotic Adventures Of Johnny Soiree / 1995 / LBO / M • Interracial Escorts / 1995 / GO / M • Sexual Impulse / 1995 / VD / M • Shades Of Color #1 / 1995 / LBO / M • Sharon's House Party / 1995 / HW / M • Snatch Masters #10 / 1995 / LEI / M • Tailz From Da Hood #2 / 1995 / AVI / M

SHARON BLACK
More Than A Voyeur / cr73 / SEP / M

SHARON BOXWORTH *see* **Ginger Snap**

SHARON CAIN *see* **Sharon Kane**

SHARON CANE *see* **Sharon Kane**

SHARON CHRISTY *see* **Star Index I**

SHARON CULP
Daddy / 1978 / BL / M • Do You Wanna Be Loved? / 1977 / AR / M

SHARON DAY *see* **Star Index I**

SHARON DRIVER *see* **Star Index I**

SHARON GOODHEART
Private Film #12 / 1994 / OD / M

SHARON HEAD
Bankok Connection / 1979 / CA / M

SHARON JONES
Ass Thrashing / 1995 / RB / B • More Punished Cheeks / 1994 / RB / B

SHARON KANE (Shirley Wood, Shirley Woods, Jennifer Walker, Jennifer Holmes, Sheri Vaughan, Sharon Cain, De Je Vou, Barbie Mathews, Sharon Malberg, Sharon Cane)
Blonde who can act quite well but who has long outlasted her one handed welcome. Her boyfriend was Michael Bruce who died of testicular cancer in 1985. Born February 24, 1956 per **Bloopers #2**.
4 Bi 4 / 1994 / BIN / G • 69th Street Vice / 1984 / VC / M • Action In Black / 1993 / FD / M • Adultery / 1989 / PP / M • Alexandra / 1984 / VC / M • All-Star Softball Game / 1995 / SAB / G • America's Most Wanted Girl / 1989 / IN / M • Anal Arsenal / 1994 / OD / M • Angels Bi Day, Devils Bi Night / 1990 / FC / G • The Art Of Passion / 1987 / CA / M • Assumed Innocence / 1990 / AR / M • Aunt Peg / 1980 / CV / M • Aunt Peg's Fulfillment / 1980 / CV / M • Awol / 1994 / SBP / B • B-Witched / 1994 / PEP / G • Baby Love & Beau / 1979 / TVX / M • Baby-lon Blue / 1983 / VXP / M • Babylon Pink #2 / 1988 / COM / M • Babylon Pink #3 / 1988 / COM / A • Bad Boy's Punishment / 1993 / BIZ / B • Banana Slits / 1993 / STM / F • Bare Bottom Treatment / 1993 / RB / B • Be Careful What You Wish For / 1993 / VC / G

• Bedrooms And Boardrooms / 1992 / DR / M • The Best Of Both Worlds #2 / 1986 / MID / G • The Best Of Gail Palmer / 1981 / WWV / C • The Best Of Hot Heels / 1992 / BIZ / B • Bi & Large / 1994 / STA / G • Bi 'n' Large / 1994 / PL / G • Bi 'n' Sell / 1990 / VC / G • Bi And Busty / 1991 / STA / G • Bi Anonymous / 1993 / BIL / G • Bi Bi Birdie / 1993 / BIL / G • Bi Chill / 1994 / BIL / G • Bi Intruder / 1991 / STA / G • The Bi-Linguist / 1993 / BIL / G • Bi Medicine / 1991 / STA / G • Bi Night / 1989 / PL / G • The Bi Valley / 1994 / BIL / G • Bi-Conflict / 1994 / FST / G • Bi-Inferno / 1992 / VEX / G • Bi-Laddin / 1994 / BIN / G • The Bi-Ologist / 1993 / ... / G • Bi-Ology: The Making Of Mr Right / 1992 / CAT / G • Bi-Sexual Anal #1 / 1994 / RTP / G • Bi-Swingers / 1991 / PL / G • Bi-Ways / 1991 / PL / C • Bi-Wicked / 1994 / BIN / G • Big Switch #3: Bachelor Party / 1991 / CAT / G • The Big Tease #1 / 1990 / VC / M • The Big Tease #2 / 1990 / VC / M • The Big Thrill / 1989 / VD / M • Bimbo Boys / 1995 / PL / C • Biography: Kaitlyn Ashley / 1996 / SC / C • The Bitches Of Westwood / 1987 / CA / M • Black Balled / 1990 / ZA / M • Black Sister, White Brother / 1987 / AT / M • Blackman & Anal Woman #2 / 1990 / PL / M • Blondes On Fire / 1987 / VCR / C • Bloopers #2 / 1991 / GO / C • Blowing In Style / 1989 / EA / M • Blue Confessions / 1983 / VCR / M • Blue Jeans / 1982 / VXP / M • Blue Vanities #005 / 1987 / FFL / M • Blue Vanities #016 (Old) / 1988 / FFL / M • Blue Vanities #048 / 1988 / FFL / M • Blue Vanities #079 / 1988 / FFL / M • Blue Vanities #086 / 1988 / FFL / M • Bodies In Heat #2 / 1989 / DR / M • Bondage Memories #03 / 1994 / BON / C • The Book / 1990 / IF / M • Book Of Love / 1992 / VC / M • Born For Love / 1987 / ... / M • Both My Lovers / 1994 / ... / G • Bound To Be Punk / 1990 / BON / B • Boxed Lunches / 1989 / ... / M • Breast Worx #25 / 1992 / LBO / M • Breast Worx #29 / 1992 / LBO / M • Bring On The Virgins / 1989 / CA / M • Brooke Does College / 1984 / VC / M • Buffy Malibu's Totally Nasty All-Girl Home Videos #04 / 1993 / ANA / F • Bunny's Office Fantasies / 1984 / VC / M • Burlexxx / 1984 / VC / M • Bush Pilots #2 / 1991 / VC / M • Caballero Preview Tape #3 / 1984 / CA / C • Caballero Preview Tape #4 / 1985 / CA / C • California Blondes #06 / 1992 / VD / C • California Hot Wax / 1992 / ... / S • Call Girls In Action / 1989 / CV / M • Camp Beaverlake #2 / 1991 / AFV / M • Candy Goes To Hollywood / 1979 / VCX / M • Cape Lere / 1992 / CC / M • The Casting Couch / 1983 / GO / M • Catalina Sixty-Nine / 1991 / AR / M • Catwalk #1 / 1995 / SC / M • Catwalk #2 / 1995 / SC / M • Chain Gang / 1994 / OD / F • Champagne For Breakfast / 1980 / SE / M • Changing Partners / 1989 / FAZ / M • Channel 69 / 1996 / CC / M • Cheerleader Nurses #1 / 1993 / VC / M • Cheerleader Nurses #2 / 1993 / VC / M • Chopstix / 1979 / TVX / M • Chronicles Of Pain #3: Slave Traders / 1996 / BIZ / B • Chug-A-Lug Girls #3 / 1993 / VT / M • Classic Swedish Erotica #22 / 1986 / CA / C • Climax / 1985 / CA / M • Club Lez / 1990 / PL / F • Coming In Style / 1986 / CA / M • Coming Out Bi / 1995 / IN / G • Compulsive Behavior / 1995 / PI / M • Conflict / 1988 / VD / M • Conflict Of Interest / 1994

/ FST / G • Contract / 1995 / LON / B • Contract For Service / 1994 / NTP / B • Courting Libido / 1995 / HIV / G • Cravings / 1987 / VC / M • Crossing Over / 1990 / IN / M • Cult Of The Whip / 1995 / LON / B • Daddy's Little Girls / 1983 / CA / M • Dallas Does Debbie / 1992 / PL / M • Dance To The Whip / 1996 / LBO / B • Days Gone Bi / 1994 / BIN / G • De Blond / 1989 / EA / M • The De Renzy Tapes / 1990 / CA / C • Debbie Class Of '89 / 1989 / CC / M • Debutante Training / 1995 / PL / B • A Decent Proposal / 1993 / BIL / G • Deep Inside Nikki Sinn / 1996 / VC / C • Deep Inside Ona Zee / 1992 / VC / C • Deep Inside Raquel / 1992 / CDI / C • Deep Passage / 1984 / VCR / C • Deep Rub / 1979 / VC / M • Defiance: The Art Of Spanking / 1996 / BIZ / B • Delusions Of Grandeur / cr85 / DRV / B • Designing She-Males / 1994 / HEA / G • Devil In Miss Jones #2 / 1983 / VC / M • Dial 666 For Lust / 1991 / AFV / M • Diaries Of Fire And Ice #1 / 1989 / VC / M • Diaries Of Fire And Ice #2 / 1989 / VC / M • Diary Of A Tormented TV / 1995 / BIZ / G • Dick Of Death / 1985 / VCR / M • Dirty Doc's Housecalls #13 / 1994 / LV / M • Dirty Lingerie / 1990 / VD / M • Dirty Movies / 1989 / VD / M • Domina #2: Every Inch A Lady / 1996 / LBO / G • Domina #4 / 1996 / LBO / G • Domina #6 / 1996 / LBO / B • Domina #8 / 1996 / LBO / B • Dominique Goes Bi / 1994 / STA / G • Dragon Lady / 1995 / SP0 / G • Dream Bound / 1995 / BON / B • Dreams Bi-Night / 1989 / PL / G • Dreams Of Desires / 1995 / ONA / M • Driven Home / 1995 / CSP / G • Dump Site / 1989 / BIZ / C • Dungeon Queens / 1995 / BIZ / G • Earth Girls Are Sleazy / 1990 / SO / M • Earthquake Girls / 1990 / CC / M • Easy Lovers / 1987 / SE / M • Ebony & Ivory Sisters / 1985 / PL / C • Education Of The Dominatrix / 1993 / HOM / B • Elegant Bargain / 1994 / FD / C • The Eliminators / 1991 / BIZ / B • Enemarathon / 1987 / BIZ / B • Enemates #01 / 1988 / BIZ / B • Enemates #03 / 1991 / BIZ / B • Entertainment Bi-Night / 1989 / PL / G • Erica Boyer: Non-Stop / 1988 / VD / C • Erotic Dimensions #2: Black Desire / 1982 / NSV / M • Erotic Fantasies #6 / 1984 / CV / C • Exposed / 1980 / SE / M • Exposed / 1993 / HOM / B • Extremes / 1981 / CA / M • Falling Stars / 1996 / PRE / C • Fantasy / 1978 / VCX / M • Fantasy Valley Ranch #1 / 1987 / BON / B • Fantasy World / 1979 / WWV / M • Fashion Dolls / 1985 / LA / M • Fashion Fantasies / 1986 / VC / M • Femme / 1984 / VC / M • Femmes On Fire / 1988 / VC / F • Final Exam #1 / 1987 / BON / B • Final Exam #2 / 1988 / BON / B • The Fine Line / 1990 / SO / M • Finely Back / 1990 / PL / F • The Finer Things In Life / 1990 / PL / F • Finger Pleasures #5 / 1996 / PL / F • Firestorm #1 / 1984 / COM / M • Firestorm #2: The Angel Blade / 1986 / COM / M • Firestorm #3 / 1986 / COM / M • Firm / 1993 / MID / M • First Annual XRCO Awards / 1984 / AVC / C • Fit To Be Tied / 1991 / BS / S • Flame's Bondage Bash / 1994 / BIZ / B • Flash Floods / 1991 / PRE / C • Flasher / 1986 / VD / M • Flesh And Fantasy / 1985 / VC / M • The Flintbones / 1992 / FR / M • The Foot Client / 1993 / SBP / B • For Sale Bi Owner / 1994 / ... / G • For The Love Of Pleasure / 1979 / SE / M

• Forbidden Forrest / 1994 / BON / B • Forbidden Fruit #4 / 1990 / MET / G • Forced Love / 1990 / LV / M • Four Alarm / 1991 / SE / M • Frankenhunter, Queen Of The Porno Zombies / 1989 / GMI / M • Freedom Of Choice / 1984 / VHL / M • The French Invasion / 1993 / LBO / M • G-Strings / 1984 / COM / M • Gangbang Girl #10 / 1993 / ANA / M • Generation Sex #1 / 1996 / VT / M • Geranalmo / 1994 / PL / M • Gere Up / 1991 / LV / C • Get Bi Tonight / 1991 / PL / G • A Girl's Best Friend (Madison Is) / 1990 / PL / F • Girls Gone Bad #1 / 1990 / GO / F • Girls Gone Bad #2: The Breakout / 1990 / GO / F • Girls Gone Bad #3: Back To The Slammer / 1991 / GO / F • Girls Gone Bad #4: Cell Block Riot / 1991 / GO / F • Girls Just Wanna Have Girls #3 / 1994 / HIO / F • Girls Like Us / cr88 / IN / C • The Girls Of Porn / 1989 / FRV / F • Girls Will Be Girls / 1988 / LV / F • The Girls' Club / 1990 / VC / F • Godmother / 1991 / AWV / F • The Good Stuff / 1989 / BON / C • Good Things Come In Small Packages / 1989 / CA / M • Good Vibrations #1: Self Satisfaction With A Vibrator / 1991 / VT / M • Great Balls Of Fire / 1989 / FAZ / M • Happy Endings / 1990 / BIZ / B • Hard Rockin' Babes / 1987 / VD / F • Head / 1985 / LA / M • Head Co-Ed Society / 1989 / VT / M • Heatwave #1 / 1992 / FH / F • Heaven's Touch / 1983 / CA / M • Hollywood Confidential / 1995 / TWP / B • Hollywood Swingers #04 / 1992 / LBO / M • Hot Dreams / 1983 / CA / M • Hot Legs / 1979 / VCX / M • Hot Licks / 1984 / SE / M • Hot Lunch / 1978 / SE / M • Hot Rockers / 1985 / IVP / M • Hot Shoes / 1992 / BIZ / B • Hot Wire / 1985 / VXP / M • House Of Sex #16: Dirty Oral Three Ways / 1994 / RTP / M • House Of Torture / 1994 / PL / B • House On Paradise Beach / 1996 / VC / M • Hyperkink / 1989 / VWA / M • Hypersexuals / 1984 / VC / M • I Do #1 / 1989 / VI / M • I Ream A Jeannie / 1990 / GLE / M • I Wanna Be A Lesbian / 1993 / HSV / F • If You Can't Lick 'em...Join 'em / 1996 / BAC / F • If You're Nasty / 1991 / PL / F • Illicit Affairs / 1989 / VD / M • In Miss Appleby's Face / 1994 / CAW / B • In The Heat Of The Night / 1990 / CDI / M • In The Scope / 1996 / VI / M • In Your Face #1 / 1992 / PL / M • Incredible Dreams #1 / 1992 / BIZ / B • Incredible Dreams #2 / 1992 / BIZ / B • The Initiation Of Cynthia / 1985 / VXP / M • Inner Blues / 1987 / VD / M • Inside Desiree Cousteau / 1979 / VCX / M • Interview With A She-Male / 1995 / PL / G • Intimate Action #1 / 1983 / INP / M • Intimate Action #2 / 1983 / INP / M • Intimate Explosions / 1982 / ... / C • Introducing Tracey Wynn / 1991 / PL / M • Itty Bitty Titty Committee #1 / 1990 / PL / F • Jaded / 1989 / 4P / M • Jailhouse Cock / 1993 / IP / M • Joined: The Siamese Twins / 1989 / PL / M • Juice Box / 1990 / AFV / M • Juicy Lips / 1991 / PL / F • Karen's Bi-Line / 1989 / MET / G • Kidnapped By Pirates / 1995 / LON / B • Kinky Business #1 / 1984 / DR / M • Kinky Business #2 / 1989 / DR / M • Kinky Kittens / 1995 / STM / C • Kinky Lesbians #02 / 1993 / BIZ / B • Kinky Sluts / 1988 / MIR / C • Kiss Of The Whip / 1996 / BON / B • The Kitty Kat Club / 1990 / PL / F • Kym Wilde's On The Edge #29 / 1995 / RB / B • Lace / 1989 / VT / F • Ladies In Combat / 1991 / PRE / B • The Last X-Rated Movie #1 / 1990 / COM / M • The Last X-Rated Movie #2 / 1990 / COM / M • The Last X-Rated Movie #3 / 1990 / COM / M • The Last X-Rated Movie #4 / 1990 / COM / M • Latex #2 / 1995 / VC / M • Latex Submission #1 / 1992 / BIZ / B • Leather / 1989 / VT / F • Leather And Lace / 1989 / VT / F • Leather Bound Dykes From Hell #1 / 1994 / BIZ / F • Leather Bound Dykes From Hell #2 / 1994 / BIZ / F • Leather Bound Dykes From Hell #3 / 1994 / BIZ / F • Leather Bound Dykes From Hell #4 / 1995 / BIZ / F • Leather Bound Dykes From Hell #8 / 1996 / BIZ / B • Leg...Ends #04 / 1991 / PRE / F • Legends Of Porn #3 / 1991 / MET / C • Lesbo A Go-Go / 1991 / PL / F • Letters From The Heart / 1991 / AWV / M • Letters Of Love / 1985 / CA / M • Liquid A$$ets / 1982 / CA / M • Little Miss Dangerous / 1989 / SO / M • Long Play / 1995 / 3XP / G • Love Goddesses / 1981 / VC / M • The Love Nest / 1989 / CA / M • Love Shack / 1990 / CC / M • Loving Friends / 1975 / AXV / M • Lusty Ladies / 1994 / MET / F • Made To Order / 1975 / AXV / M • Maiden Heaven #1 / 1992 / MID / F • Maiden Heaven #2 / 1992 / MID / F • Maidens Of Servitude #1 / 1993 / STM / B • Maidens Of Servitude #2: Obeisance / 1994 / STM / B • Maidens Of Servitude #3: A Jealous Bind / 1994 / STM / B • Make Me Feel It / 1984 / SE / M • Man In Chains / 1995 / HOM / B • Man Made Pussy / 1994 / HEA / G • The Many Loves Of Jennifer / 1991 / VC0 / S • Married Men With Men On The Side / 1996 / BHE / G • Married With She-Males / 1993 / PL / G • Master Of Ecstasy / 1997 / BON / B • The Mating Game / 1992 / PL / G • Maximum Head / 1987 / SE / M • Messy Mouth / 1994 / CA / C • Midnight Fire / 1990 / HU / M • Miss Bondwell's Reformatory / 1994 / LON / B • Miss Matches / 1996 / PRE / C • The Mistake / 1989 / CDP / B • Mistress Kane: Lessons In Terror / 1996 / BIZ / B • Mistress Kane: Town In Torment / 1996 / BIZ / B • Mistress Of Cruelty / cr94 / HOM / B • Mistresses At War #02 / 1993 / BIZ / B • Misty's First Whipping / 1994 / LON / B • Mixed Apples / 1996 / APP / G • Mixing It Up / 1991 / LV / C • More Than Friends / 1995 / KDP / G • Ms. Magnificent / 1979 / SE / M • My Sister's Husband / 1996 / AWV / G • Mystery Of The Golden Lotus / 1989 / HU / M • Naked Scents / 1984 / VC / M • Nasty Girls (1983-VCX) / 1983 / VCX / M • Nasty Nurse / 1990 / TAO / B • National Pornographic #1: Lesbians / 1987 / 4P / C • Never Say Never / 1994 / SC / M • Never Sleep Alone / 1984 / CA / M • The New Barbarians #1 / 1990 / VC / M • The New Barbarians #2 / 1990 / VC / M • Night Hunger / 1983 / AVC / M • The Night Temptress / 1989 / HU / M • Nightdreams #3 / 1991 / VC / M • No Man's Land #07 / 1993 / VT / F • No Man's Land #09 / 1994 / VT / F • Nydp Trannie / 1996 / WP / G • Obey Me Bitch #1 / 1992 / BIZ / B • Obey Me Bitch #2 / 1992 / BIZ / B • Obey Me Bitch #3 / 1992 / BIZ / B • Obey Me Bitch #4 / 1993 / BIZ / B • Office Heels / 1992 / BIZ / B • On Trial #3: Takin' It To The Jury / 1992 / VI / M • On Trial #4: The Verdict / 1992 / VI / M • Once A Slave / 1995 / HOM / B • One Way At A Time / 1979 / CA / M • Only The Best #2 / 1989 / CV / C • Only The Best #3 / 1990 / CV / C • Only The Best Of The Erotic Eighties / 1992 / VC / C • Only The Best Of Women With Women / 1988 / CV / C • Only The Very Best On Film / 1992 / VC / C • Oral Support / 1989 / V99 / M • The Other Side Of Debbie / 1991 / CC / M • The Oui Girls / 1981 / VHL / M • Our Dinner With Andrea / 1988 / CA / M • Outlaw Ladies #2 / 1988 / VC / M • Overnight Sensation / 1991 / XCI / M • Painful Secrets Of A TV / 1996 / BIZ / G • Painted / 1990 / INH / G • Party Partners / 1994 / STA / G • A Passage Thru Pamela / 1985 / VC / G • Perils Of Paula / 1989 / CA / M • Phantom Of The Cabaret #1 / 1989 / VC / M • Phantom Of The Cabaret #2 / 1989 / VC / M • Phone Sex Fantasies / 1984 / QX / M • Picture Me Bound / 1995 / LON / B • Playboy's Night Dreams / 1993 / PLA / S • Playboy: Inside Out #4 / 1993 / UNI / S • The Playgirl / 1982 / CA / M • Playthings / 1980 / VC / M • Please Don't Tell / 1995 / CEN / G • The Pleasures Of Innocence / 1985 / VC / M • Pointers / 1990 / LV / M • Positive Positions / 1989 / VEX / M • Possessions / 1992 / HW / M • Potpourri / 1981 / TGA / M • Power Blonde / 1988 / AVC / M • The Power Dykes / 1993 / BIZ / B • Preppies / 1982 / VES / S • Pretty Peaches #1 / 1978 / MIT / M • Private School Girls / 1983 / CA / M • Pump It Up / 1990 / LV / M • Punished Cheater / 1994 / STM / B • Punished She Fighters / 1992 / BIZ / B • Punishment Of Ashley Renee / 1993 / BON / B • Purple Rubber / 1993 / STM / B • Puss 'n' Boots / 1982 / VXP / M • Pyromaniac / 1990 / SO / M • Ravaged / 1990 / CIN / M • Ready, Willing & Anal (Cv) / 1993 / CV / C • Real Magnolias / 1990 / AWV / M • Red Hot Fire Girls / 1989 / VD / M • Release Me / 1996 / VT / M • Remembering Times Gone Bi / 1995 / AWV / G • Renegade / 1990 / CIN / M • Restrained By Desire / 1994 / NTP / B • Return To Alpha Blue / 1984 / AVC / M • Revenge Of The Bi Dolls / 1994 / CAT / G • Rippin' 'n' Strippin' #1 / 1987 / BON / B • Rippin' 'n' Strippin' #2 / 1988 / BON / B • Rising Star / 1985 / CA / M • Robin Head / 1991 / CC / M • Rock 'n' Roll Heaven / 1989 / EA / M • Rockhard (Coast) / 1996 / CC / M • Rolls Royce #02 / 1980 / ... / C • Rolls Royce #04 / 1980 / ... / C • Romancing The Bone / 1984 / VC / M • Ron Hightower's White Chicks #06 / 1993 / LBO / M • Runaway Slaves / 1995 / HOM / B • Saki's Bedtime Stories / 1995 / TTV / M • Saki's Private Party / 1995 / TTV / M • Saturday Night Special / 1989 / DR / M • Scared Stiff / 1992 / PL / B • Scenes They Wouldn't Let Me Shoot / 1984 / VC / M • Score Of Sex / 1995 / BAC / G • Sea Of Desire / 1990 / AR / M • Secluded Passion / 1983 / VHL / M • The Secret (USA) / 1990 / SO / M • Secret Diary #1 / 1994 / TAW / M • The Secret Dungeon / 1993 / HOM / B • Secret Games / 1995 / BON / B • Secret Lives / 1994 / SC / F • Secret Recipe / 1990 / PL / F • Secret Sex #2: The Sex Radicals / 1994 / CAT / G • Secret Sex #3: The Takeover / 1994 / CAT / G • Semper Bi / 1994 / PEP / G • Separated / 1989 / INH / M • Sex About Town / 1990 / LV / M • Sex Crimes 2084 / 1985 / SE / M • Sex Drive / 1984 / VXP / M • Sex Ed With Lil' Red / 1983 / TGA / M • Sex Freaks / 1995 / EA / M • Sex Wars / 1984 / EXF / M • Sexcapades / 1983 / VC / M • Sextrology / 1987 / CA / M • Sexual Healing / 1996 / SC / M • Sexually Altered States / 1986 / VC / M • Shameful Desires In Black & White Girls / 1984 / PL / M • Sharon And Karen / 1989 / LV / G • Sharon Kane Star Bound / 1990 / BON / B • Sharon Kane's TV Tamer / 1993 / BIZ / G • Sharon's Painful Persuasions / 1996 / SIL / B • Shauna: Every Man's Fantasy / 1985 / CA / C • She Male Service / 1994 / HEA / G • She Studs #05 / 1990 / BIZ / G • She Studs #06 / 1990 / BIZ / G • She's So Fine #1 / 1985 / VC / M • She's So Fine #2 / 1988 / VC / M • She-Male Call Girls / 1996 / BIZ / G • She-Male Encounters #21: Psychic She Males / 1994 / MET / G • She-Male Instinct / 1995 / BCP / G • She-Male Nymphos / 1995 / MET / G • She-Male Seduction / 1995 / MET / G • She-Male She Devils / 1996 / BIZ / G • She-Male Shenanigans / 1994 / HSV / G • She Male Spirits Of The Night / 1991 / VC / G • She-Male Trouble / 1994 / HEA / G • She-Male Undercover / 1990 / STA / G • She-Male Voyager / 1994 / HEA / G • She-Males In Torment #3 / 1995 / BIZ / G • Showgirl #08: Serena's Fantasies / 1983 / VCR / M • Showgirl #17: Phaedra Grant's Fantasies / 1983 / VCR / M • Silver Tongue / 1989 / CA / M • Sinderella's Revenge / 1992 / HOM / B • Single White She-Male / 1993 / PL / G • Sinners #1 / 1988 / COM / M • Sinners #2 / 1988 / COM / M • Sinners #3 / 1989 / COM / M • Sissy's Hot Summer / 1979 / CA / M • Sizzling She Males / 1995 / MET / G • Slammer Girls / 1987 / LIV / S • Slightly Used / 1987 / VD / M • Slit Skirts / 1983 / VXP / M • Slow Burn / 1991 / VC / M • Sluts In Slavery / 1995 / LBO / B • SM TV #2 / 1995 / FC / G • Small Town Girls / 1979 / CXV / M • Smooth And Easy / 1990 / XCV / M • Smooth As Silk / 1987 / VIP / M • Sniff Doggy Style / 1994 / PL / M • So Fine / 1992 / VT / C • Sorority Pink #1 / 1989 / CV / M • Sorority Pink #2 / 1989 / CV / M • Sorority Sex Kittens #1 / 1992 / VC / M • Sorority Sex Kittens #2 / 1993 / VC / M • Spanked In Lingerie / 1985 / LA / B • Spiked Heel Diaries #1 / 1994 / BIZ / B • Spiked Heel Diaries #2 / 1994 / BIZ / B • Splendor In The Ass #1 / 1989 / CA / M • Stairway To Paradise / 1990 / VC / M • Stasha's Diary / 1991 / CIN / G • Steel Garters / 1992 / CAT / G • The Story Of Pain / 1992 / PL / B • Strange Night On Earth / 1993 / PEP / G • Stranger At The Backdoor / 1994 / CC / M • Strap On Anal Attitude / 1994 / SCL / M • Strictly Business / 1987 / VD / M • Strip For The Whip / 1997 / BON / B • A Stroke At Midnight / 1993 / LBO / M • Submissive Exposure Profile #5: Keli Thomas / 1996 / STM / C • Succulent Toes / 1995 / STM / B • Suck Channel / 1991 / VIM / M • Summer School / 1979 / VCX / M • Super Enemates #1 / 1994 / PRE / C • Suzie Superstar...The Search Continues / 1988 / CV / M • The Swap #1 / 1990 / VI / M • Swedish Erotica #01 / 1980 / CA / M • Swedish Erotica #04 / 1980 / CA / M • Swedish Erotica #11 / 1980 / CA / M • Sweet Dreams Suzan / 1980 / CA / M • Sweet Seduction / 1990 / LV / M • Sweet Tarts / 1993 / STM / B • Swing Shift / 1989 / PL / G • Swingers Ink / 1990 / VC / M • Switch Hitters #5: The Night Games / 1990 / IN / G • Switch Hitters #8 / 1995 / IN / G •

Switch Hitters #9 / 1995 / IN / G • Taboo American Style #4: The Exciting Conclusion / 1985 / VC / M • Taija's Tasty Treats / 1988 / EXP / C • Tailiens #2 / 1992 / FD / M • Tailiens #3 / 1992 / FD / M • Tales Of The Backside / 1985 / VCR / C • Talk Dirty To Me #01 / 1980 / CA / M • Talk Dirty To Me #05 / 1987 / DR / M • The Tantric Guide To Sexual Potency And Extended Orgasm / 1994 / A&E / M • Tanya Foxx Star Bound / 1989 / BON / B • A Taste Of Stephanie / 1990 / PIN / C • Tattle Tales / 1989 / SE / M • Taxi Girls #4: Daughter Of Lust / 1994 / CA / M • That's Outrageous / 1983 / CA / M • Theatre Of Seduction #1 / 1990 / BON / B • Theatre Of Seduction #2 / 1990 / BON / B • The Therapist / 1992 / VC / M • Thirst For Passion / 1988 / TRB / M • Throat...12 Years After / 1984 / VC / M • Tickled Pink / 1985 / VC / M • Toys Bi Us / 1993 / BIL / G • Tracy Star Bound / 1991 / BON / B • Trans Europe Express / 1989 / VC / G • Transitions (TV) / 1993 / HSV / G • Transsexual 6900 / 1990 / LV / G • Transsexual Domination / 1990 / BIZ / B • Triangle / 1989 / VI / M • Trisexual Encounters #10 / 1990 / PL / G • Trisexual Encounters #12 / 1990 / PL / G • Trouble For Two / 1994 / BON / B • True Legends Of Adult Cinema: The Erotic Eighties / 1992 / VC / C • True Legends Of Adult Cinema: The Golden Age / 1992 / VC / C • True Legends Of Adult Cinema: Unsung Superstars / 1993 / VC / C • Turn On With Kelly Nichols / 1984 / CA / M • TV Dildo Fantasy #2 / 1996 / BIZ / G • TV Nation #1 / 1995 / HW / G • TV Nation #2 / 1995 / HW / G • TVs In Leather And Pain / 1996 / BIZ / G • TVs Teased And Tormented / 1995 / BIZ / G • Twilight Pink #2 / 1982 / VC / M • Udderly Fantastic / 1983 / TGA / C • The Ultimate Fantasy / 1995 / CV / M • Ultrasex / 1987 / VC / M • Untamed Passion / 1991 / VEX / M • Urban Cowgirls / 1980 / CA / M • Urban Heat / 1985 / FEM / M • Urges In Young Girls / 1984 / VC / M • Val Girls / 1990 / PL / F • Victoria's Secret / 1989 / SO / M • Viet Tran / 1996 / LBO / G • Violated / 1984 / VES / S • Vista Valley PTA / 1980 / CV / M • The Voyeur / 1985 / VC / M • A Weekend In Bondage / 1994 / BIZ / B • Wendy's Bi Adventure / 1994 / STA / M • Wet Dreams / 1984 / CA / M • Wet Kisses / 1988 / V99 / M • What's Love Got To Do With It / 1989 / WV / M • When She Was Bad / 1983 / CA / M • Where The Bi's Are / 1994 / BIN / G • Who Shaved Cassi Nova? / 1989 / EX / M • Who Shaved Lynn Lemay? / 1989 / EX / M • Whose Fantasy Is It, Anyway? / 1983 / AVC / M • Wicked Sensations #2 / 1989 / DR / M • Wicked Wenches / 1988 / LA / M • The Widespread Scandals Of Lydia Lace / 1983 / CA / M • Wildheart / 1989 / IN / M • Winner Takes All / 1995 / LON / B • The Women / 1993 / CAT / F • Women At Play / 1984 / SE / M • Women On Top / 1995 / BON / B • Worthy Women / 1990 / AWV / M • The Wrath Of Kane / 1995 / BON / B • The Wright Stuff / 1991 / AFV / M • X-Rated Bloopers #2/ 1986 / AR / M • Yes, My Lady / 1984 / VHL / B • Young Doctors In Lust / 1979 / NSV / M • Young Girls In Tight Jeans / 1989 / VD / M • [Erotic Dimensions Vols 1 To 8 / 1983 / NSV / C • [Office Fantasies / 1984 / ... / M • [The River Made To Drown In / 1996 / ... / M • [Sharon Kane's Guide

To Great Lovemaking / 199? / ... / M • [Sun Drenched She Males / 1994 / ... / G • [Toe Job / 1990 / ... / B • [TV Parties Tonight / 1993 / ... / G

SHARON KAUFMAN
The Love Couch / 1977 / VC / M

SHARON KELLY see Colleen Brennan

SHARON KLISER see Star Index I

SHARON LATE see Star Index I

SHARON LEE
Anal Cuties #2 / 1992 / ROB / M • Buck's Excellent Transsexual Adventure / 1989 / STA / G • Inch Bi Inch / 1989 / STA / G • Motor Psycho / 1965 / RMV / S • She-Male Nurse / 1989 / LV / G • Single She-Male Singles Bar / 1990 / STA / G • Tour De Trans / 1989 / STA / G • Wrasslin She-Babes #07 / 1996 / SOW / M • Wrasslin She-Babes #08 / 1996 / SOW / M

SHARON LIPS
A&B AB#516: Slutty Wife #1 / 1995 / A&B / M • A&B AB#517: Slutty Wife #2 / 1995 / A&B / M • A&B AB#520: Slutty Wife #3 / 1995 / A&B / M • A&B AB#539: Slutty Wife Returns / 1995 / A&B / M • A&B AB#546: Slutty Wife #4 / 1995 / A&B / M • A&B AB#557: Slutty Wife #5 / 1995 / A&B / M • A&B AB#568: Slutty Wife #6 / 1995 / A&B / M

SHARON LOVE
The Beat Goes On / 1987 / VCR / C

SHARON LUCAS see Star Index I

SHARON MAGNUSSON
Swedish Sex / 1996 / PL / M

SHARON MALBERG see Sharon Kane

SHARON MCINTYRE see Kathleen Kristel

SHARON MILLS see Star Index I

SHARON MITCHELL
Angular mannish brunette with small tits. Was married at one time to Jason Dean. Started in the business in 1975.
The $50,000,000 Cherry / 1987 / VD / M • 1-800-TIME / 1990 / IF / M • 2002: A Sex Odyssey / 1985 / DR / M • 52 Pick-Up / 1986 / MED / S • 69 Pump Street / 1988 / ZA / M • Adam & Eve's House Party #2: Bachelor Party / 1996 / VC / M • Aerobics Girls Club / 1986 / 4P / F • All The King's Ladies / 1981 / SUP / M • Amazing Sex Stories #2 / 1987 / SUV / C • Amber & Sharon Do Paris #1 / 1985 / PAA / M • Amber & Sharon Do Paris #2 / 1985 / PAA / M • Amber Lynn's Hotline 976 / 1987 / VCR / M • Amber Pays The Rent / 1986 / VT / M • The Amorous Adventures Of Janette Littledove / 1988 / AR / M • Anal Future / 1992 / VC / M • Another Kind Of Love / 1985 / CV / M • At The Mercy Of Mistress Jacqueline / 1993 / STM / B • The Autobiography Of Herman Flogger / 1986 / AVC / M • B&D Sorority / 1991 / BON / B • Backside To The Future #1 / 1986 / ZA / M • Bad Barbara / cr77 / BL / M • Barbara Broadcast / 1977 / VC / M • Barbara Dare's Bad / 1988 / SE / C • Barbara Dare's Roman Holiday / 1987 / SE / M • Barbii Bound / 1988 / BON / B • Bare Essentials / 1987 / VEX / M • Bedtime Stories / 1989 / WV / M • The Best Little Whorehouse In Hong Kong / 1987 / SE / M • Best Of Bruce Seven #3 / 1990 / BIZ / C • Best Of Bruce Seven #4 / 1990 / BIZ / C • The Best Of Flame / 1994 / BIZ / C • Beverly Hills Cox / 1986 / CA / M • Bi & Large / 1994 / STA / G • Bi Dream Of Genie / 1990 / BIN / G • The

Bi Spy / 1991 / STA / G • The Bi-Analyst / 1991 / STA / G • Bi-Heat #05 / 1987 / ZA / G • Bi-Heat #06 / 1987 / ZA / G • Bi-Heat #07 / 1987 / ZA / G • Bi-Heat #08 / 1988 / ZA / G • Bi-Heat #08 To #10 / 1988 / ZA / G • The Big Gun / 1989 / FAN / M • Bionca On Fire / 1988 / 4P / M • Bizarre Mistress Series: Mistress Jacqueline / 1992 / BIZ / C • Bizarre Mistress Series: Sharon Mitchell / 1992 / BIZ / C • Black Balled / 1990 / ZA / M • Black Bimbos In Heat / 1989 / MIR / C • Black Trisexual Encounters #2 / 1985 / LA / G • Black Trisexual Encounters #4 / 1986 / LA / G • Blacks & Blondes #37 / 1986 / WV / M • Blazing Bedrooms / 1987 / LA / M • Blonde Velvet / 1976 / COL / M • Bloopers #1 / cr90 / GO / C • Blue Jeans / 1982 / VXP / M • Blue Ribbon Blue / 1984 / CA / C • Blue Vanities #057 / 1988 / FFL / M • Blue Vanities #086 / 1988 / FFL / M • Blue Vanities #128 / 1990 / FFL / M • Blue Vanities #246 / 1995 / FFL / M • Blue Voodoo / 1983 / VD / M • Blush: Suburban Dykes / 1991 / BLV / F • Bobby Hollander's Maneaters #01 / 1993 / SFP / M • Body Shop / 1984 / VCX / M • Bold Obsession / 1983 / NSV / M • Bondage Academy #1 / 1991 / BON / B • Bondage Academy #2 / 1991 / BON / B • Bondage Across The Border / 1993 / B&D / B • Bondage Watch #2 / 1996 / STM / B • Boobs, Butts And Bloopers #2 / 1990 / HO / M • Born To Be Bad / 1987 / CV / M • Boss Bitch In Bondage / 199? / LON / B • The Boss's Boy Toy / 1992 / STM / B • Bossy Mistresses / 1993 / STM / B • Both Ends Burning / 1987 / VC / M • Bound To Be Loved / 1993 / ... / B • Bound To Tease #2 / 1989 / BON / C • Bound To Tease #3 / 1989 / BON / C • Breaker Beauties / 1977 / VHL / M • Breakin' In / 1986 / WV / M • A Brief Affair / 1982 / CA / M • Bubble Butts #16 / 1992 / LBO / M • Buns And Roses (V9) / 1990 / V99 / M • C-Hunt / 1985 / PL / M • Caballero Preview Tape #2 / 1983 / CA / C • Caballero Preview Tape #3 / 1984 / CA / C • Caballero Preview Tape #4 / 1985 / CA / C • Cafe Flesh / 1982 / VC / M • Cagney & Stacey / 1984 / AT / M • Captain Lust And The Amorous Contessa / 1977 / IHV / M • Careena #1 / 1987 / WV / C • Careena #2: A Star On The Rise / 1988 / WV / C • Carnal College / 1987 / VT / M • Carnal Games / 1978 / BL / M • Cat On A Hot Sin Roof / 1989 / LV / M • Chains Of Passion / 1993 / PL / B • China White / 1986 / WV / M • Chuck & Di In Heat / 1986 / DR / M • Chug-A-Lug Girls #2 / 1993 / VT / M • Class Of Nuke 'em High #2: Subhumanoid Meltdown / 1991 / MED / S • Club Exotica #1 / 1985 / WV / M • Club Exotica #2 / 1985 / WV / M • Club Ginger / 1986 / VI / M • Cock Robin / 1989 / SUE / M • Colossal Orgy #1 / 1993 / HW / M • Colossal Orgy #3 / 1994 / HW / M • Come To Me / cr80 / AIR / C • Coming On Strong / 1989 / CA / C • Confessions Of A Middle Aged Nympho / 1986 / WET / M • Consenting Adults / 1981 / VXP / M • Cracked Ice / 1977 / PVX / M • Crocodile Blondee #2 / 1988 / VCX / M • Dames / 1985 / SE / M • Dangerous Assignment / 1993 / BS / B • Dangerous Curves / 1985 / CV / M • Dangerous Women / 1987 / WET / M • Dark Desires / 1989 / BMV / C • Days Gone Bi / 1988 / ZA / G • Deep Throat Girls / 1986 / ELH / M • Defiance, The Spanking

Saga / 1992 / BIZ / B • Desperate Women / 1986 / VD / M • Devil In Miss Dare / 1986 / AVC / C • Devil In Miss Jones #2 / 1983 / VC / M • Dial P For Pleasure / 19?? / BL / M • Dirty Blonde / 1984 / VXP / M • Dirty Bob's #27: Laid Back In L.A.! / 1996 / FLP / S • Dirty Books / 1990 / V99 / M • Dirty Lilly / 1975 / VXP / M • Disciples Of Discipline / 1994 / STM / B • Doctor Blacklove / 1987 / CC / M • Domination Blue / 1976 / SVE / B • The Domination Of Summer #1 / 1994 / BIZ / B • The Domination Of Summer #2 / 1994 / BIZ / B • Don't Worry Be Sexy / 1989 / EVN / C • Doogan's Woman / 1978 / S&L / M • Dr Blacklove #1 / 1987 / CC / M • Dragon Lady / 1995 / SP0 / C • Dream Caller Bondage / 1993 / BON / B • Dream Lovers / 1987 / CA / M • Dreams Bi-Night / 1989 / PL / G • Dresden Diary #03 / 1989 / BIZ / B • Dresden Diary #04 / 1989 / BIZ / B • Dresden Diary #05: Invasion of Privacy / 1992 / BIZ / B • Dungeon De Sade / 1993 / FC / B • Electric Blue: Cosmic Coeds / 1985 / CA / M • Electric Blue: World Nudes Tonight / 1985 / CA / C • End Of Innocence / 1986 / AR / M • Endless Nights / 1988 / CDI / M • The Enema Bandit / 1994 / BIZ / B • The Enema Bandit Returns / 1995 / BIZ / B • Enema Bondage / 1992 / BIZ / B • Enema Obedience #1 / 1992 / BIZ / B • Enema Obedience #2 / 1994 / BIZ / B • Enema Obedience #3: The Ultimate Punishment / 1994 / BIZ / B • Erica Boyer: Non-Stop / 1988 / VD / C • Erotic Aerobics / 1984 / VC / M • Every Which Way She Can / 1981 / CA / M • The Experiment / 1983 / BIZ / B • Exploring Young Girls / 1978 / ALP / M • Eye Of The Tigress / 1988 / VD / M • Fantasy Doctor / 1993 / PL / B • Fantasy Follies #2 / 1983 / VC / M • Fascination / 1980 / QX / M • Feels Like Silk / 1983 / SE / M • Female Persuasion / 1990 / SO / F • Firestorm #1 / 1984 / COM / M • Firestorm #2: The Angel Blade / 1986 / COM / M • Firestorm #3 / 1986 / COM / M • Flesh For Fantasies / 1986 / TAM / M • Flesh In Ecstasy #09: Nikki Charm / 1987 / GO / C • Fondle With Care / 1989 / VEX / M • Foxtrot / 1982 / COM / M • French Classmates / 1977 / PVI / M • French Kittens / 1985 / VC / C • French Teen / 1977 / CV / M • Friday The 13th #2 / 1989 / VD / M • From Paris With Lust / 1985 / PEN / M • From The Heart / 1996 / XCI / M • Furburgers / 1987 / VD / M • Gang-Way / 1984 / ECO / C • Gangbang Girl #02 / 1992 / ANA / M • Generation Sex #1 / 1996 / VT / M • Get Bi Tonight / 1991 / PL / G • Getting Personal / 1986 / CA / M • Ginger's Greatest Boy/Girl Hits / 1987 / VI / C • Ginger's Greatest Girl/Girl Hits / 1986 / VI / C • Girl Country / 1990 / CC / F • Girl Crazy / 1989 / CDI / F • Girl Toys / 1986 / DR / M • A Girl's Affair #01 / 1992 / FD / F • Girls Gone Bad #4: Cell Block Riot / 1991 / GO / F • Girls Gone Bad #5: Mexican Justice / 1991 / GO / F • The Girls Of Porn / 1989 / FRV / F • The Girls On F Street / 1986 / AVC / M • Girls That Talk Dirty / 1986 / VCS / C • Girls, Girls And More Girls / 1990 / LV / F • Girls, Girls, Girls, Girls / 1993 / FD / C • Girlworld #1 / 1987 / LIP / F • Girlworld #2 / 1988 / LIP / F • Girlworld #3 / 1989 / LIP / F • The Golden Gals / 1989 / BTO / M • Good Girl, Bad Girl / 1984 / SE / M • Grand Prixxx / 1987 / CA / M • Hanna

Does Her Sisters / 1986 / HUR / M • Hard Rockin' Babes / 1987 / VD / F • Harlem Honies #2: Nasty In New York / 1994 / CC / M • Harlequin Affair / 1985 / CIX / M • Have I Got A Girl For You / 1989 / VEX / M • Head Clinic / 1987 / AVC / M • Heat Wave / 1977 / COM / M • Heidi A / 1985 / PL / M • Hell Cats / 1996 / HO / F • Her Every Wish / 1988 / GO / M • HHHHot! TV #1 / 1988 / CDI / M • HHHHot! TV #2 / 1988 / CDI / M • Holly's Hollywood / 1992 / STM / F • Hollywood Undercover / 1989 / BWV / C • Hometown Honeys #3 / 1989 / VEX / M • Honeymoon Harlots / 1986 / AVC / M • Hot Dreams / 1983 / CA / M • Hot Services / 1989 / WET / M • Hotel California / 1986 / WV / M • How Do You Like It? / 1985 / CA / M • I Love LA #2 / 1989 / PEN / C • I Remember When / 1992 / ATL / M • In Charm's Way / 1987 / IN / M • Inch Bi Inch / 1989 / STA / G • Infamous Crimes Against Nature / 1993 / SUM / M • Innocent Seduction / 1988 / VC / M • Inside Sharon Mitchell / 1989 / ZA / C • Intimate Desires / 1978 / VEP / M • Invitation Only / 1989 / AMB / M • Jail Bait / 1976 / VC / M • Jawbreakers / 1985 / VEN / C • Jewels Of The Night / 1986 / SE / M • Joanna Storm On Fire / 1985 / VIV / M • Joint Venture / 1977 / ELV / M • Journal Of O #1: Servant Slave / 1994 / ONA / B • Joy / 1977 / QX / M • The Joys Of Masturbation / 1988 / M&M / M • K-Sex / 1976 / VCR / M • Kamikaze Hearts / 1986 / FAC / S • Kinky / 1987 / SE / M • The Kiss / 1986 / SC / M • Kiss Thy Mistress' Feet #1 / 1990 / BIZ / B • Kiss Thy Mistress' Feet #2 / 1990 / BIZ / B • Knights In Black Satin / 1990 / VEX / M • Krystal Balling / 1988 / PL / M • Kym Wilde's On The Edge #38 / 1996 / RB / B • The Ladies Room / 1987 / CA / M • Lady Lust / 1984 / CA / M • Lair Of The Bondage Bandits / 1991 / HOM / B • The Last X-Rated Movie #1 / 1990 / COM / M • The Last X-Rated Movie #2 / 1990 / COM / M • The Last X-Rated Movie #3 / 1990 / COM / M • The Last X-Rated Movie #4 / 1990 / COM / M • Latex Foot Torture / 1993 / SBP / B • Latex Submission #1 / 1992 / BIZ / B • Lays Of Our Lives / 1988 / ZA / M • Le Sex De Femme #5 / 1990 / AFI / C • Le Striptease / 1983 / GLD / S • Learn Your Lessons / 1992 / BIZ / B • Leather & Lace / 1987 / SE / C • Leather Bound Dykes From Hell #1 / 1994 / BIZ / F • Leather Bound Dykes From Hell #2 / 1994 / BIZ / F • Leather Bound Dykes From Hell #3 / 1994 / BIZ / F • Leather Bound Dykes From Hell #4 / 1995 / BIZ / F • Legends Of Porn #1 / 1987 / CV / C • Legends Of Porn #3 / 1991 / MET / C • Les Lesbos Of Paris #1 / 1985 / LIP / F • Les Lesbos Of Paris #2 / 1985 / LIP / F • Les Nympho Teens / 1977 / ... / M • Lesbian Nymphos / 1988 / GO / C • Lesbian Sex, Power & Money / 1994 / STM / F • Lesbians, Bondage & Blackjack / 1991 / BIZ / B • Lessons In Humiliation / 1991 / BIZ / B • Lick My Lips / 1990 / LV / M • Like A Virgin #2 / 1986 / AT / M • Lipstick Lesbians / 1993 / STM / F • Liquid Love / 1988 / CA / M • Lisa Meets Mr Big / cr75 / VHL / M • The Little Blue Box / 1978 / BL / M • Living Doll / 1987 / WV / M • The Load Warriors #1 / 1987 / VD / M • The Load Warriors #2 / 1987 / VD / M • Loose Morals / 1987 / HO / M • The Loves Of Mary Jane / 1989 / BWV / C • Luscious /

1980 / VXP / M • Lust At First Bite / 1978 / VC / M • Lust Bug / 1985 / HO / M • Lust Italian Style / 1987 / CA / M • Lust Weekend / 1987 / CA / M • The Madame's Boudoir / 1993 / STM / B • Magic Girls / 1983 / SVE / M • Making It Big / 1984 / CV / M • Mammary Lane / 1988 / VT / C • Maneaters / 1983 / VC / M • Maniac / 1980 / MED / S • Marathon / 1982 / CA / M • Matronly Stern Spankings / 1994 / STM / B • Maxine / 1987 / EXF / M • Midnight Fantasies / 1989 / VEX / M • Midnight Heat / 1982 / VC / M • Miss Sharon Mitchell's Diaries #1 / 1995 / STM / B • Mistress Jacqueline's Slave School / 1992 / BIZ / B • Mistress Rules / 1995 / STM / B • Mistress Sharon's Girl Toy / 1995 / STM / B • Mistresses And Slaves: The Best Of Bruce Seven / 1991 / BEB / C • Mitzi's Honor / 1987 / TAM / M • Moonglow / 1989 / IN / M • My Sex-Rated Wife / 1977 / … / M • Mystery Of The Golden Lotus / 1989 / HU / M • The Naked Truth / 1990 / SE / M • Nasty Dancers #2 / 1996 / STM / B • Nasty Girls (1983-VCX) / 1983 / VCX / M • Nasty Lovers / 1987 / SE / C • The National Transsexual / 1990 / GO / G • Never Sleep Alone / 1984 / CA / M • Night Hunger / 1983 / AVC / M • Night Moves / 1983 / SUP / M • Night Of The Juggler / 1980 / MED / S • Night Vibes / 1990 / KNI / M • No Man's Land #02 / 1988 / VT / F • No Man's Land #08: Eight Women Who Ate Women / 1993 / VT / F • Nymphette #1 / 1986 / WV / M • Odyssey / 1977 / VC / M • Only The Best #3 / 1990 / CV / C • Only The Best Of Girls With Curves / 1992 / CV / C • Only The Best Of Oral / 1989 / CV / C • Open For Business / 1983 / AMB / M • Open House (Vid Exc) / 1989 / VEX / M • Oral Majority #02 / 1987 / WV / C • Oral Majority #03 / 1986 / WV / C • Oral Majority #05 / 1987 / WV / C • Orgies / 1987 / WV / C • Oriental Oddballs #1 / 1994 / FH / M • Paddled Payoff / 1993 / STM / B • Parliament: Lonesome Ladies #1 / 1987 / PM / F • Parliament: Teasers #1 / 1986 / PM / F • Party Partners / 1994 / STA / G • Passion Princess / 1991 / VEX / M • The Passion Seekers / cr78 / SIL / S • Passionate Lee / 1984 / CRE / M • The Penetration Of Elle Rio / 1987 / GO / M • Perfect Girl / 1991 / VEX / M • Personal Touch #1 / 1983 / AR / M • Phone Sex Girls #1 / 1987 / VT / M • Physical #2 / 1985 / SUP / M • Play It Again, Samantha / 1986 / EVN / M • The Poonies / 1985 / VI / M • Porsche / 1990 / NSV / M • Porsche Lynn, Vault Mistress #1 / 1994 / BIZ / B • Porsche Lynn, Vault Mistress #2 / 1994 / BIZ / B • Portraits Of Pleasure / 1974 / BL / M • Princess Charming / 1987 / AVC / C • Profiles In Discipline #01: The Mistress Is A Lady / 1994 / STM / C • Promises In The Dark / 1991 / CIN / G • Pure Energy / 1990 / VEX / M • The Queens Of Mean / 1994 / NTP / B • Ready, Willing & Anal (Cv) / 1993 / CV / C • Real Men Eat Keisha / 1986 / VC / M • Rearbusters / 1988 / LVI / C • The Red Room And Other Places / 1992 / COM / C • The Return Of Dr Blacklove / 1996 / CC / M • Rites Of Passage: Transformation Of A Student To A Slave / 1992 / BIZ / B • Rocky #1 / 1976 / MGM / S • Rough Draft / 1986 / VEN / M • Rubber Reamed Fuckholes / 1994 / MET / C • S&M Pleasure Series:

The Assistant / 1994 / VTF / B • Sacrificed To Love / 1986 / CDI / M • San Fernando Valley Girls / 1983 / CA / M • The Satisfiers Of Alpha Blue / 1980 / AVC / M • Scoundrels / 1982 / COM / M • Sean Michaels On The Road #07: New York / 1993 / VT / M • Secret Dreams Of Mona Q / 1977 / AR / M • The Secret Life Of Herbert Dingle / 1994 / TTV / M • The Seduction Of Cindy / 1980 / VC / M • The Seduction Of Lana Shore / 1984 / PL / M • Sex Asylum #1 / 1985 / VI / M • Sex Charades / 1990 / VEX / M • Sex For Hire / 1989 / HOE / C • Sex Maniacs / 1987 / JOY / C • Sexcapades / 1983 / VC / M • Sexually Altered States / 1986 / VC / M • Seymore Butts In The Love Shack / 1992 / FH / M • Sharon Mitchell's Sex Clinic #01 / 1993 / FC / M • Sharon Mitchell's Sex Clinic #02 / 1993 / FC / M • She Comes In Colors / 1987 / AMB / M • She Studs #01 / 1990 / BIZ / G • She's No Angel / cr75 / AXV / M • She's So Fine #1 / 1985 / VC / M • She-Male Encounters #03: Juicy Jennifer / 1981 / MET / G • She-Male Encounters #04: Jaded Jennifer / 1981 / MET / G • She-Male Sanitarium / 1988 / VD / G • She-Males In Bondage / 1995 / FC / G • Sheer Delight / 1984 / VC / M • Show Your Love / 1984 / VC / M • Showdown / 1986 / CA / M • Simply Irresistible / 1900 / CC / M • Sin Of Lust / 1976 / SVE / M • Sinners #1 / 1988 / COM / M • Sinners #2 / 1988 / COM / M • Sinners #3 / 1989 / COM / M • Sins Of Nina Hartley / 1989 / MIR / C • Skin Dive / 1988 / AVC / M • Skin Flicks / 1978 / AVC / M • Slaves In Heat / 1991 / BIZ / B • SM TV #1 / 1995 / FC / G • SM TV #2 / 1995 / FC / G • Smoker / 1983 / VC / M • Smothered, Bound & Tickled / 1993 / STM / B • Snake Eyes #1 / 1984 / COM / M • Snake Eyes #2 / 1987 / COM / M • Sodomania #06: Gangs And Bangs And Other Thangs / 1993 / EL / M • Soul Kiss This / 1988 / VCR / C • Space Virgins / 1984 / CRE / M • Spank! / 1992 / STM / B • Spiked Heel Diaries #2 / 1994 / BIZ / B • Spitfire / 1984 / COM / M • Split Decision / 1989 / MET / G • The Starmaker / 1982 / VC / M • Starship Intercourse / 1987 / DR / M • Stasha's Last Kiss / 1993 / VEX / G • Stiletto / 1994 / WAV / M • Student Enemas / 1996 / PRE / C • Student Fetish Videos: Catfighting #02 / 1991 / PLV / B • Student Fetish Videos: The Enema #05 / 1991 / PRE / B • Student Fetish Videos: Foot Worship #04 / 1992 / PRE / B • Submissive Exposure Profile #5: Keli Thomas / 1996 / STM / C • Succulent Toes / 1994 / PL / B • Succulent Toes / 1995 / STM / B • Suck Channel / 1991 / VIM / M • Sulka's Wedding / 1983 / MET / G • Summer Lovers / 1987 / WET / M • Surfside Sex / 1985 / PV / M • Suze's Centerfolds #7 / 1983 / CA / M • Suzie Superstar #1 / 1983 / CV / M • Swedish Erotica #40 / 1981 / CA / M • Swedish Erotica #46 / 1983 / CA / M • Sweet Things / 1987 / VC / M • Taija Is Sizzling Hot / 1986 / VT / M • Taija's Tasty Treats / 1988 / EXP / C • Tail For Sale / 1988 / VD / M • Tales From The Whip / 1993 / HOM / B • Talk Dirty To Me #04 / 1986 / DR / M • The Taming Of Rebecca / 1982 / SVE / B • A Taste Of Angel / 1989 / PIN / C • A Taste Of Bette / 1978 / VHL / M • A Taste Of Money / 1983 / AT / M • A Taste Of Sharon / 1990 / PIN / C • The Teacher's

Pet / 1985 / WV / M • Teenage Housewife / 1976 / BL / M • Teenage Pajama Party / 1977 / VC / M • That Lady From Rio / 1976 / VXP / M • That's My Daughter / 1982 / NGV / M • Their Absolute Property / 1994 / STM / B • This Bun's For You / 1989 / FAN / M • Thought You'd Never Ask / 1986 / CA / M • Threshold Of Fear / 1993 / BON / B • Throat...12 Years After / 1984 / VC / M • Toe-Tally Foot-Age / 1992 / STM / C • Touch Me In The Morning / 1982 / CA / M • A Touch Of Desire / 1983 / VCR / C • Traci's Big Trick / 1987 / VAS / M • Trans Europe Express / 1989 / VC / G • Trapped By The Mistress / 1991 / BIZ / B • Trashi / 1980 / CA / M • The Travails Of June / 1976 / VHL / M • Tres Riche / 1986 / CLV / M • Triple Xposure / 1986 / VD / M • Trisexual Encounters #04 / 1986 / PL / G • Trisexual Encounters #05 / 1986 / PL / G • Two On The Tongue / 1988 / TAM / C • Two Timer / 19?? / BL / M • The Ultimate / 1991 / BON / B • The Ultimate Climax / 1989 / V99 / M • The Ultimate Fantasy / 1995 / CV / M • Undercovers / 1982 / CA / M • Uninhibited / 1989 / VC / G • The Violation Of Claudia / 1977 / QX / M • Visions / 1977 / QX / M • The Wacky World Of X-Rated Bloopers / 1989 / GO / M • Wanda Whips Wall Street / 1982 / VXP / M • Waterpower / 1975 / VHL / M • Weekend Blues / 1990 / IN / M • A Weekend In Bondage / 1994 / BIZ / B • Wet Dreams 2001 / 1987 / VD / M • Wet Kisses / 1986 / SE / M • Wet Pink / 1989 / PL / F • Wet Shots (Vcr) / 1983 / VCR / C • Wet Tails / 1989 / PL / M • When She Was Bad / 1983 / CA / M • The Widespread Scandals Of Lydia Lace / 1983 / CA / M • Wild Dallas Honey / 1985 / VCX / M • Wild In The Sheets / 1984 / WET / M • Witchcraft 2000 / 1994 / GLI / M • With Love, Lisa / 1985 / CA / C • With Love, Littledove / 1988 / AR / M • With Love, Loni / 1985 / CA / C • A Woman's Touch / 1988 / ZA / F • Women At Play / 1984 / SE / M • Women Who Control The Family Jewels #2 / 1993 / STM / C • The World According To Ginger / 1985 / VI / M • The World Of Henry Paris / 1981 / VC / C • X-Rated Bloopers #1 / 1984 / AR / M • X-TV #2 / 1989 / PL / C • [More Than A Handful / 1991 / … / M • [Older Women Are Sexy #2 / 19?? / … / M • [Suburban Dykes / 1990 / … / F

SHARON MONTGOMERY
Caught! / 1985 / BIZ / B • Curiosity Excited The Kat / 1984 / BIZ / B • Master Control / 1985 / CS / B

SHARON NESTLE *see Star Index I*
SHARON NICKLE
Corsetry 101 / 1996 / ESF / B

SHARON PETERS
The Reel Sex World #02 / 1994 / WP / M • The Reel Sex World #03 / 1994 / WP / M

SHARON REGIS *see Star Index I*
SHARON ROSE
Powerbone / 1976 / VC / M • The Voyeur / 1985 / VC / M

SHARON SAINT *see Star Index I*
SHARON SANDERS *see Star Index I*
SHARON SANDS
The Dominator / 1992 / GOT / B • Masters Of Dominance / 1996 / GOT / C • No Pain, No Gain / 1992 / GOT / B • Spanking It Red / 1993 / GOT / B • Toe Tales #02 / 1992 / GOT / B • Toe Tales #05 / 1993 / GOT / B • TV Encounter / 1992 / GOT / G

SHARON SHARALOT
San Francisco Lesbians #3 / 1993 / PL / F
SHARON STEWART see Star Index I
SHARON SWALLOW
One For The Road / 1989 / V99 / M • Oral Support / 1989 / V99 / M • Positively Pagan #04 / 1991 / ATA / M
SHARON SWEETWATER see Star Index I
SHARON TAYLOR see Star Index I
SHARON TEMPLE
Sexhibition #3 / 1996 / SUF / M
SHARON THORPE *(Joanna Savage)*
Blonde or light brown hair, shoulder length, small to medium tits, marginal face, not petite, lithe body, a little flat on the butt. In some movies (e.g. **3 A.M.**) she seems to have a Caesarian scar.
3 A.M. / 1975 / ALP / M • All About Annette / 1982 / SE / C • All Night Long / 1975 / SE / M • Artful Lover / cr75 / BOC / M • Baby Rosemary / 1975 / SE / M • Black Widow's Nest / 1976 / ... / M • Blue Vanities #003 / 1987 / FFL / M • Blue Vanities #048 / 1988 / FFL / M • Bucky Beaver's XXX Dragon Art Theatre Double Feature #03 / 1996 / SOW / M • Bucky Beaver's XXX Dragon Art Theatre Double Feature #04 / 1996 / SOW / M • Cadillac Named Desire / cr79 / IHV / M • Candy Stripers #1 / 1978 / ALP / M • Carnal Haven / 1976 / SVE / M • Ceremony, The Ritual Of Love / 1976 / AVC / M • China Girl / 1974 / SE / M • Classic Swedish Erotica #18 / 1986 / CA / C • Classic Swedish Erotica #28 / 1987 / CA / C • Coming Attractions / 1976 / VEP / M • Fantastic Orgy / 197? / ... / M • Fantasy Girls / 1974 / VC / M • Fantasy In Blue / 1975 / IHV / M • Femmes De Sade / 1976 / ALP / M • First Annual XRCO Awards / 1984 / AVC / C • Honeypie / 1975 / VC / M • Jackpot / 1979 / VCX / M • Jane Bond And The Girl From AUNTIE / 1979 / VCI / M • Legends Of Porn #1 / 1987 / CV / C • Little Angel Puss / cr76 / SVE / M • Love Scenes For Loving Couples / 1987 / CV / C • Love Slaves / 1976 / VCR / M • Marilyn And The Senator / 1974 / HIF / M • Mary! Mary! / 1977 / SE / M • Me, Myself & I / 1987 / SE / C • Milk Chocolate / cr75 / VIS / M • Odalisque / 19?? / ASR / M • One Of A Kind / 1976 / SVE / M • Only The Best #2 / 1989 / CV / C • Overnight Sensation / 1976 / AR / M • Please, Please Me / 1976 / AR / M • Rings Of Passion / 1976 / VXP / G • School For Hookers / 1974 / SOW / M • The Seduction Of Lyn Carter / 1974 / ALP / M • Sex World / 1978 / SE / M • Sharon's Rosebud / 1974 / SOW / M • Sodom & Gomorrah / 1974 / MIT / M • Tapestry Of Passion / 1976 / SE / M • True Legends Of Adult Cinema: Unsung Superstars / 1993 / VC / C • The Untamed / 1978 / VCX / M • Valerie / 1975 / VCX / M • Visions Of Clair / 1977 / WWV / M • Young, Hot And Nasty / cr88 / BWV / C • [Confessions Of Miss Bonnie / cr75 / ... / M • [Hard Times At The Employoyment Office / cr75 / ... / M
SHARON VEGAS see Susan Vegas
SHARON WEST
Tight Tushies #1 / 1994 / SFP / M
SHARON WESTOVER see Star Index I
SHARON WISE
Blue Vanities #130 / 1990 / FFL / M
SHARON WOLFEN
Love Theatre / cr80 / VC / M

SHARON WRIGHT see Star Index I
SHARON YORKE see Star Index I
SHARONA BONNER see Becky LeBeau
SHARRON MARKS
Babes Of The Bay #1 / 1994 / LIP / F
SHARY GRAHAM see Greta Carlson
SHASTA ROSE see Star Index I
SHAUN COSTELLO see Russ Carlson
SHAUN EASTON
The National Transsexual / 1990 / GO / G • She Studs #02 / 1991 / BIZ / G • Trisexual Encounters #01 / 1985 / PL / G
SHAUN MASON
You Turn Me On / 1986 / LIM / M
SHAUN MICHAEL (GIRL) see Shaun Michelle
SHAUN MICHAELS see Sean Michaels
SHAUN MICHELLE *(Shawn Michelle, Shaun Michael (girl))*
Dark blonde with long straight hair, small tits, lithe body.
Amber Aroused / 1985 / CA / M • Bedtime Tales / 1985 / SE / M • Bizarre Encounters / 1986 / 4P / B • Body Shop / 1984 / VCX / M • California Valley Girls / 1983 / HO / M • College Lesbians / 1983 / JAN / F • Dreams Of Misty / 1984 / VCX / M • Erotic Aerobics / 1984 / VC / M • Fantasy Follies #1 / 1983 / VC / M • Flesh & Laces #2 / 1983 / CA / M • Flesh Pond / 1983 / VC / M • Forbidden Dreams / 1984 / BIZ / G • Fox Fever's Catfight Action / 1984 / VCR / B • Foxholes / 1983 / SE / M • Girls On Fire / 1985 / VCX / M • The Heartbreak Girl / 1985 / GO / M • I Love LA #1 / 1986 / PEN / C • Little Girls Lost / 1982 / VC / M • Making It Big / 1984 / CV / M • My Pretty Go Between / 1985 / VC / M • The Newcomers / 1983 / VCX / M • On The Wet Side / 1987 / V99 / M • Sensuous Moments / 1983 / VIV / M • Sheer Delight / 1984 / VC / M • Sounds Of Sex / 1985 / CA / M • Stacey's Hot Rod / 1983 / CV / M • Stolen Lust / 1985 / AAH / M • Swedish Erotica #63 / 1985 / CA / M • Swedish Erotica #64 / 1985 / CA / M • Too Much Too Soon / 1983 / VCX / M • Twice A Virgin / 1984 / PL / G • Up To No Good / 1986 / CDI / M • Watch My Lips / 1985 / AAH / M
SHAUN TAYLOR see Shone Taylor
SHAUNA
Bubble Butts #06 / 1992 / LBO / M • Homegrown Video #294 / 1990 / HOV / M • HomeGrown Video #458: Cream Pie For Dessert / 1995 / HOV / C • HomeGrown Video #468: Lust American Style / 1996 / HOV / C
SHAUNA ADAMS
Bucky Beaver's XXX Dragon Art Theatre Double Feature #03 / 1996 / SOW / M • School For Hookers / 1974 / SOW / M
SHAUNA EVANS *(Shawna Evans, Shana Evans, Beth Fix)*
Off color (probably a mixture of black and Polynesian) girl, not too pretty, black curly hair, medium tits, marginal body, mole, skin tag or lump on outside left shoulder and another on her chest between her tits.
Corrupt Desires / 1984 / MET / M • Diamond Collection #54 / 1984 / CIN / M • Fallen Angels / 1983 / VES / M • Fleshdance / 1983 / SE / M • Getting Lucky / 1983 / CA / M • GVC: Women Who Seduce Men #123 / 1982 / GO / M • Intimate Realities #1 / 1983 / VC / M • On My Lips / 1989 / PV / M • Rockin' Erotica / 1987 / SE / C •

Salt & Pepper / 1986 / VCS / C • Sweethearts / 1986 / SE / C
SHAUNA GRANT *(Shana (Grant), Caille Aimes, Colleen Applegate, Callie Aims)*
Very pretty golden slightly curly haired natural blonde with a tight waist, a Midwestern girl next door look, almost perfect medium breasts, slightly too long in the trunk, and not as narrow on the hips as she could be (the last two are being really picky). Her performance in the cot however was only marginal giving the impression (confirmed by posthumous interviews with others) that she really didn't like performing sex on screen. She unfortunately committed suicide on March 23, 1984 (aged 20) using a 22 cal rifle (an imitation M16). She shot herself through the right temple and the bullet exited the body and lodged in the wall. She was on life support for 24 hours before they pulled the plug. Colleen Applegate was her real (birth name) and she came from Farmington, MN. The subject of a **Frontline** documentary called **Death Of A Porn Star** and from that documentary: tried to commit suicide while in high school (pills); left MN with boyfriend, Mike Marcel; agent was Jim South of World Modelling; de-virginized at 16; **Maximum #4** was first video, followed by **Paper Dolls**; moved in with drug dealer, Jake Erlich, who was in jail when she killed herself; had an abortion and contracted herpes while in the business. In early movies (**Flesh And Laces** for example) her breasts look natural, slightly smaller and less firm than in (say) **Glitter**. One wonders if she wasn't using saline injections to pump them up for these movies. Certainley there aren't any enhancement scars.
The 8th Annual Erotic Film Awards / 1984 / SE / C • All American Girls #2: In Heat / 1983 / CA / M • Bad Girls #4 / 1984 / GO / M • Believe It or Not: Hollywood Sex Scandals / 1987 / ... / M • The Bigger The Better / 1986 / SE / C • Bloopers #2 / 1991 / GO / C • Blue Vanities #030 / 1988 / FFL / M • Blue Vanities #064 / 1988 / FFL / M • Blue Vanities #069 / 1988 / FFL / M • Caballero Preview Tape #4 / 1985 / CA / C • Candy's Bedtime Story / 1983 / CA / M • Celebrity Presents Celebrity / 1986 / VEP / C • Centerfold Celebrities #2 / 1983 / VC / M • Centerfold Celebrities #3 / 1983 / VC / M • Collection #08 / 1984 / CA / M • Fallen Angels / 1983 / VES / M • Feels Like Silk / 1983 / SE / M • Flesh & Laces #1 / 1983 / CA / M • Flesh & Laces #2 / 1983 / CA / M • Glitter / 1983 / CA / M • Golden Girls #05 / 1982 / SVE / M • Golden Girls, The Movie / 1984 / SE / M • Gourmet Quickies: Shauna Grant #1 #701 / 1983 / GO / C • Gourmet Quickies: Shauna Grant #2 #718 / 1985 / GO / C • Gourmet Quickies: Shauna Grant / Trinity Loren #725 / 1984 / GO / C • GVC: Dreams Of Pleasure #120 / 1983 / GO / M • GVC: Paper Dolls #117 / 1983 / GO / F • GVC: Party Stripper #130 / 1983 / GO / M • GVC: Shauna, Blonde Superstar #132 / 1984 / GO / C • GVC: Suburban Lust #128 / 1983 / GO / M • GVC: Valley Vixens #124 / 1983 / GO / M • Legends Of Porn #2 / 1989 / CV / C • Lusty Ladies #04 / 1983 / 4P / M • Maneaters / 1983 / VC / M • Maximum #4 / 1983 / CA / M • Nudes In Limbo / 1983 / MCA / S • Only

The Best #1 / 1986 / CV / C • Only The Best Of The Erotic Eighties / 1992 / VC / C • Parliament: Shauna Grant #1 / 1988 / PM / C • Parliament: Super Head #1 / 1989 / PM / C • Peeping Tom / 1983 / DIM / M • Penthouse: Love Stories / 1986 / A*V / S • Penthouse: On The Wild Side / 1988 / A*V / S • Personal Touch #1 / 1983 / AR / M • Personal Touch #2 / 1983 / AR / M • Private School Girls / 1983 / CA / M • Sex Games / 1983 / CA / M • Shauna Grant: The Early Years / 1988 / PV / C • Shauna: Every Man's Fantasy / 1985 / CA / C • Summer Camp Girls / 1983 / CA / M • Suze's Centerfolds #7 / 1983 / CA / M • Suzie Superstar #1 / 1983 / CV / M • Swedish Erotica #45 / 1983 / CA / M • Swedish Erotica Superstar #2: Brigette Monet / 1983 / CA / C • Swedish Erotica Superstar #4: Shauna Grant / 1984 / CA / C • Sweethearts / 1986 / SE / C • True Legends Of Adult Cinema: The Erotic Eighties / 1992 / VC / C • Virginia / 1983 / CA / M • The Wacky World Of X-Rated Bloopers / 1989 / GO / M • X-Rated Bloopers #1 / 1984 / AR / M • X-Rated Bloopers #2 / 1986 / AR / M • The Young Like It Hot / 1983 / CA / M

SHAUNA MCCULLOH *see* **Shanna McCullough**

SHAUNA O'BRIEN *(Shana O'Brien, Stevie Jean, Stevie Joan, Shawna O'Brien)*

Beverly Hills Workout / 1993 / PHV / S • Hot Body Video Magazine #08 / 1994 / CG / S • The Pamela Principle #2: Seduce Me / 1994 / IMP / S • Penthouse: 1993 Pet Of The Year Playoff / 1993 / PET / F • Penthouse: 1993 Pet Of The Year Winners / 1993 / PET / F • Penthouse: Behind The Scenes / 1995 / PET / F • Penthouse: The Girls Of Penthouse #3 / 1995 / PET / S • Penthouse: Party With The Pets / 1994 / PET / S • Penthouse: Satin & Lace #1 / 1992 / PET / F • Penthouse: Satin & Lace #2 / 1992 / PET / F • Playboy's Rising Stars And Sexy Starlets / 1996 / UNI / S • Primal / 1994 / PHV / S

SHAUNA ROSE *(Shaunna, Shawna (Rose), Shanna Kay, Shanna Rose, Shawna Rose)*

This is a not-too-pretty older woman with a relatively small body and an "I'll do anything" type of attitude.

The Absolute Worst Of Amateur #1 / 1993 / VEX / M • Amateur Lesbians #21: Daphne / 1992 / GO / F • Amateurs Exposed #01 / 1993 / CV / M • America's Dirtiest Home Videos #09 / 1992 / VEX / M • America's Raunchiest Home Videos #13: Beauty And The Beach / 1992 / ZA / M • American Dream Girls #2 / 1994 / LEI / M • Anal Delights #1 / 1992 / ROB / M • Anything That Moves / 1992 / VC / M • Auction #1 / 1992 / BIZ / B • Auction #2 / 1992 / BIZ / B • Backstage Pass / 1992 / VEX / M • Bareback Riders / 1992 / VEX / M • Biff Malibu's Totally Nasty Home Videos #02 / 1992 / ANA / M • Biff Malibu's Totally Nasty Home Videos #15 / 1992 / ANA / M • Biff Malibu's Totally Nasty Home Videos #36 / 1993 / ANA / M • The Bigger They Come / 1993 / VD / C • Blow Out / 1991 / IF / M • Breast Worx #16 / 1991 / LBO / M • Bubble Butts #21 / 1993 / LBO / M • Dark Dreams / 1992 / WV / M • Decadent Delights / 1992 / IF / M • Dirty Danyel / 1994 / V99 / M • Dirty

Deeds / 1992 / IF / M • Dr F #2: Bad Medicine / 1990 / WV / M • Erotic Oddities / 1993 / LEI / C • Gazonga Goddess #2 / 1994 / IF / M • Guess Who? / 1991 / EX / M • Hillary Vamp's Private Collection #15 / 1992 / HVD / M • Hillary Vamp's Private Collection #31 / 1992 / HOV / M • Humongous Hooters / 1993 / IF / M • I'll Do Anything But... / 1992 / CA / M • In Deep With The Devil / 1991 / ME / M • Mad Maxine / 1992 / AFV / M • Make Me Sweat / 1994 / V99 / M • Midnight Angels #01 / 1993 / MID / F • Mix Up / 1992 / IF / M • Mr. Peepers Amateur Home Videos #53: Dirty Laundry / 1992 / LBO / M • Naughty Butt Nice / 1993 / IF / M • New Pussy Hunt #26 / 1996 / LEI / C • One Night Love Affair / 1991 / IF / M • One Of A Kind / 1992 / VEX / M • Opportunity Knocks / 1990 / HO / M • Organic Facials / cr91 / GLI / M • The Pink Persuader / 1992 / LBO / M • Raw Talent: Deep Inside Shana's Ass / 1993 / FH / M • Rock Her / 1992 / LV / M • Rump Humpers #01 / 1992 / GLI / M • Rump Humpers #02 / 1992 / GLI / M • Rump Humpers #03 / 1992 / GLI / M • The Servants Of Midnight / 1992 / CDI / M • Shooting Star / 1993 / XCI / M • Six Plus One #2 / 1993 / VEX / C • Southern Accents / 1992 / VEX / M • Student Nurses / 1991 / CA / M • Uncle Roy's Amateur Home Video #17 / 1993 / VIM / M • Uncle Roy's Amateur Home Video #19 / 1993 / VIM / M • The Way They Wuz / 1996 / SHS / C • Wet & Wicked / 1992 / VEX / M • Wilde At Heart / 1992 / VEX / M • X-TV / 1992 / CA / C • You Said A Mouthful / 1992 / IF / M

SHAUNA STEVENS *see* **Star Index I**

SHAUNDRA SWEET *see* **Chandra Sweet**

SHAUNNA *see* **Shauna Rose**

SHAUNNA BEARD

Immortal Desire / 1993 / VI / M

SHAUNNA HORN *see* **Sheena Horne**

SHAWN

Big Bust Babes #12 / 1993 / AFI / M • Breast Worx #01 / 1991 / LBO / M

SHAWN DEVEREAUX *(Abundavita)*

Europe In The Raw! / 1963 / RMV / S • Fandango / 1969 / SOW / S • Mondo Topless #1 / 1966 / RMV / S • The Seven Minutes / 1971 / STO / S

SHAWN E. *(Shawnee (Shawn E.))*

Oriental, Long straight black hair, large seemingly natural tits, lithe white body, marginal face, too pushy. 20 years old in 1996 and comes from Thailand.

2 Wongs Make A White / 1996 / FC / M • Anal Asian Fantasies / 1996 / HO / M • Anal Crash Test Dummies / 1997 / ROB / M • Asian Boom Boom Girls / 1997 / HO / M • Asses Galore #2: No Remorse...No Repent / 1996 / DFI / M • Butthole Bunnies / 1996 / ROB / F • Deep Dippin' Anal Babes / 1996 / ROB / F • Delinquents On Butt Row / 1996 / EA / M • Dick & Jane Go To A Bachelor Party (#17) / 1996 / AVI / M • Eternal Lust / 1996 / VC / M • Ethnic Cheerleader Search #1 / 1996 / WIC / M • Intense Perversions #4 / 1996 / PL / M • Lollipop Shoppe #1 / 1996 / SC / M • Mike Hott: #375 Girls Who Swallow Cum #05 / 1996 / MHV / C • Mike Hott: #382 Cunt Of The Month: Shawn E. / 1996 / MHV / M • Mike Hott: #384 Three-Sum Sluts #16 / 1996 / MHV / M • Mike Hott: #385 Lesbian Sluts #29 / 1996 / MHV / F • Mike Hott: #390 /

1996 / MHV / M • More Dirty Debutantes #52 / 1996 / 4P / M • More Dirty Debutantes #54 / 1996 / 4P / M • Mutiny On The Booty / 1996 / FC / M • Nineteen #2 / 1996 / FOR / M • Point Of Entry / 1996 / WP / M • Up And Cummers #34 / 1996 / 4P / M • Up And Cummers #35 / 1996 / 4P / M • Valentina: Princess Of The Forest / 1996 / SC / M • Video Virgins #29 / 1996 / NS / M

SHAWN HARRIS *see* **Star Index I**

SHAWN JUSTIN

Like Father Like Son / 1996 / AWV / G • Marine Code Of Silence: Don't Ask Don't Tell / 1996 / BHE / G • Married Men With Men On The Side / 1996 / BHE / G • Score Of Sex / 1995 / BAC / G

SHAWN LEE *see* **Malia**

SHAWN MICHAEL *see* **Sean Michaels**

SHAWN MICHELLE *see* **Shaun Michelle**

SHAWN NELSON *see* **Star Index I**

SHAWN RICKS *(Andy (Shawn Ricks), Sean Ricks)*

Immature male who was the lover of or married to Sydney St. James. According to the gossip broke up in early 1995.

Alex Jordan's First Timers #01 / 1993 / OD / M • America's Raunchiest Home Videos #61: / 1993 / ZA / M • America's Raunchiest Home Videos #64: / 1993 / ZA / M • Anal Brat / 1993 / FL / M • Anal Explosions #2 / 1996 / NIT / M • Anal Intruder #08: Rich Girls Gone Bad / 1993 / CC / M • Anal Virgins #02 / 1996 / NS / M • Anal Virgins #03 / 1996 / NS / M • The Anal-Europe Series #08: / 1995 / LV / M • Anus The Menace / 1993 / CC / M • Babe Watch #4 / 1995 / SC / M • Back In Style / 1993 / VI / M • Bad Attitude #1 / 1995 / LV / M • Bad Attitude #2 / 1995 / LV / M • Bad To The Bone / 1996 / ULP / M • Badgirls #1: Lockdown / 1994 / VI / M • Badgirls #2: Strip Search / 1994 / VI / M • Badgirls #6: Ridin' Into Town / 1995 / VI / M • Behind The Blackout / 1993 / HW / M • Best Of Buttman #2 / 1993 / EA / C • Beverly Hills Blondes #1 / 1995 / LV / M • Beverly Hills Blondes #2 / 1995 / LV / M • Big Bust Babes #17 / 1993 / AFI / M • Big Murray's New-Cummers #23: Naughty Nymphettes / 1993 / FD / M • Biography: Kaitlyn Ashley / 1996 / SC / C • Bobby Hollander's Maneaters #07 / 1993 / SFP / M • Bondage Memories #04 / 1994 / BON / C • The Booty Guard / 1993 / IP / M • Bootylicious: Baby Got Booty / 1996 / JMP / M • The Bottom Dweller 33 1/3 / 1995 / EL / M • Bust A Move / 1993 / SC / M • Butt Camp / 1993 / HW / C • Butt Watch #02 / 1993 / FH / M • Buttman's Bubble Butt Babes / 1996 / EA / M • Buzzzz! / 1993 / OD / M • Casting Call #16 / 1995 / SO / M • Caught & Bound / 1993 / BON / B • Cheap Shots / 1994 / PRE / B • Chug-A-Lug Girls #3 / 1993 / VT / M • Controlled / 1994 / FD / M • Crime Doesn't Pay / 1993 / BS / B • Crotch Tied / 1996 / STM / B • Defending Your Soul / 1995 / EX / M • Designer Bodies / 1993 / VI / M • Dick At Nite / 1993 / MET / M • Diva / 1993 / XCI / M • Double Decadence / 1995 / NOT / M • Double Penetration Virgins #01 / 1993 / LE / M • Dynamite Brat / 1995 / LV / M • Eclipse / 1993 / SC / M • Eighteen #2 / 1996 / SC / M • Erotic Dripping Orientals / 1993 / WV / M • Fantasy Exchange / 1993 / VI / M • The Farmer's Daughters / 1994 / LV / M • Forbidden Cravings / 1996 / VC / M • Gang-

(well, maybe not grotesque but certainly too big and hard). Definitely not Traci Starr. Was aged 22 when she did her first movie, **Curious**, for Legend.

Adam & Eve's House Party #5 / 1996 / VC / M • Anal Crack Master / 1994 / ROB / M • Anal Ecstacy Girls #2 / 1993 / ROB / F • Anal Idol / 1994 / ROB / M • Anal Thunder #2 / 1993 / ROB / M • Anal Woman #2 / 1993 / PL / M • Ass Freaks #1 / 1993 / ROB / F • Assy Sassy #1 / 1994 / ROB / F • The Bitches / 1993 / LIP / F • Booty Sister #1 / 1993 / ROB / M • Butt Sluts #2 / 1993 / ROB / F • Candy Factory / 1994 / PE / M • Car Wash Angels / 1995 / VC / M • Carnival Of Knowledge / 1992 / XCI / M • Chasey Revealed / 1994 / WP / M • The Cockateer #2 / 1992 / LE / M • Conquest / 1996 / WP / M • County Line / 1993 / PEP / M • Curious / 1992 / LE / M • The Darker Side Of Shayla #1 / 1993 / PL / M • The Darker Side Of Shayla #2 / 1993 / PL / M • Daydreams, Nightdreams / 1996 / VC / M • Dig It / 1994 / FD / C • Dirty Looks / 1994 / VI / M • Diva #2: Deep In Glamour / 1996 / VC / F • Elements Of Desire / 1994 / ULI / M • Eleventh Annual AVN Awards / 1994 / VC / M • Eternal Lust / 1996 / VC / M • First Time Ever #2 / 1996 / PE / F • For The Money #1 / 1993 / FH / M • For The Money #2 / 1993 / FH / M • The Fury / 1993 / WIV / M • Head Trip / 1995 / VC / M • Hungry #1 / 1992 / SC / M • Hungry #2 / 1993 / SC / M • Inferno #1 / 1993 / SC / M • Inferno #2 / 1993 / SC / M • Jenna's Built For Speed / 1997 / WP / F • Jezebel #2 / 1993 / SC / M • Latex #2 / 1995 / VC / M • Lesbian Dating Game / 1993 / LIP / F • Lesbian Love Connection / 1992 / LIP / F • The Look / 1993 / WP / M • Lost Angels / 1997 / WP / M • Marked #1 / 1993 / FD / M • Marked #2 / 1993 / FD / M • Mind Shadows #1 / 1993 / FD / M • Mind Shadows #2 / 1993 / FD / M • N.Y. Video Magazine #07 / 1996 / OUP / M • Naked Truth #1 / 1993 / FH / M • Naked Truth #2 / 1993 / FH / M • Nightshift Nurses #2 / 1996 / VC / M • Outlaws / 1993 / SC / M • Professor Sticky's Anatomy 3X #01 / 1992 / FC / M • Restrained By Desire / 1994 / NTP / B • Sex #2: Fate (Vca) / 1995 / VC / M • Sex Trek #3: The Wrath Of Bob / 1992 / ME / M • Sexmares / 1993 / FH / M • Shayla's Gang / 1994 / WP / M • Shayla's Home Repair / 1993 / EVN / M • Shayla's Swim Party / 1997 / VC / M • Slapped Around Sluts / 1995 / PL / B • Smells Like...Sex / 1995 / VC / M • Sorority Sex Kittens #1 / 1992 / VC / M • Sorority Sex Kittens #2 / 1993 / VC / M • Sorority Sex Kittens #3 / 1996 / VC / M • Split Tail Lovers / 1994 / ROB / F • Stick It In The Rear #2 / 1993 / PL / M • Strap-On Sally #09: / 1996 / PL / F • Streets Of New York #08 / 1996 / PL / M • Strictly For Pleasure / 1994 / ONA / B • Stripper Nurses / 1994 / PE / M • Striptease #1 / 1995 / PL / M • Striptease #2 / 1995 / PL / M • Take The A Train / 1993 / MID / M • Transitions: An Anal Adventure / 1993 / PL / M • Trashy Ladies / 1993 / LIP / F • Virtual Reality / 1993 / EX / M • Waves Of Passion / 1993 / PL / M • Wild In Motion / 1992 / PL / M • Wild Innocence / 1992 / PL / M • Within & Without You / 1993 / WP / M

SHAYLA LAWRENCE *see* **Shayla LaVeaux**

SHAYNA JO

Mike Hott: Older Girls #13 / 1996 / MHV / C • Oldies But Goodies / 1995 / WIV / M

SHAYNE LEE *see* **Lorraine Day**

SHEBA SILAS *see* **Star Index I**

SHEELA DERLY

The Ultimate Pleasure / 1977 / HIF / M

SHEENA

Any Way They're Tied / 1993 / HAC / B • Buttman's Inferno / 1993 / EA / M • Chronicles Of Lust #1 / 1994 / HOV / M • Chronicles Of Lust #2 / 1996 / XPR / M • Eric Kroll's Fetish #1 / 1994 / ERK / M • FTV #21: New Boss In Town / 1996 / FT / B • FTV #22: Muscle Thrill / 1996 / FT / B • FTV #32: Fist Filet / 1996 / FT / B • FTV #33: Tara's Revenge / 1996 / FT / B • HomeGrown Video #468: Lust American Style / 1996 / HOV / C • Homegrown Video: Here Comes Sheena / 1994 / HOV / M • Homegrown Video: How To Achieve G-Spot Orgasms / 1994 / HOV / M • The Imprisonment Of Sheena / 1994 / BON / B • Kissing Kaylan / 1995 / CC / M • New Ends #04 / 1993 / 4P / M • New Girls In Town #5 / 1994 / CC / M • No Man's Land #10 / 1994 / VT / F • Pajama Party X #1 / 1994 / VC / M • Pajama Party X #2 / 1994 / VC / M • Princess Of Persia / 1993 / IP / M • Romance & Fantasy / 1995 / VEX / M • Sex And Money / 1994 / DGD / S • Seymore Butts & His Mystery Girl / 1993 / FH / M • Sheena's Bondage Dreams / 1994 / BON / B • Snatch Masters #02 / 1994 / LEI / M • Tail Taggers #115 / 1993 / WV / M • Valentine's Challenge / 1992 / LIP / F • Valentine's Wonderland / 1992 / LIP / F • The Voyeur #1 / 1994 / EA / M • Yellow Waters #1 / 1985 / BAK / F • Yellow Waters #2 / 1985 / BAK / F

SHEENA FIELDS *see* **Star Index I**

SHEENA HEIDENBORG *see* **Star Index I**

SHEENA HORNE (Debbie Houston, Lauren Lanceford, Shaunna Horn, Debbie Berle)

Oriental overtones, small breasts, very sweet. First movie was **Hannah Does Her Sisters**. Supposedly quit the business because of a weak heart.

Adult Video Therapist / 1987 / CLV / C • The Anal-ist #2 / 1986 / VEX / M • Angel Of The Night / 1985 / IN / M • The Autobiography Of Herman Flogger / 1986 / AVC / M • Behind Blue Eyes #1 / 1986 / ME / M • Beyond The Denver Dynasty / 1988 / CA / M • The Bottom Line / 1986 / WV / M • The Brazilian Connection / 1988 / CA / M • California Fever / 1987 / CV / M • Charm School / 1986 / VI / M • Convenience Store Girls / 1986 / VD / M • Cum Shot Revue #2 / 1985 / HO / C • Deep Throat #2 / 1986 / AR / M • The Desk Top Dolls / 1990 / BAD / C • Devil In Miss Dare / 1986 / AVC / C • Dirty Blondes / 1986 / CDI / M • Dr Truth's Great Sex / 1986 / VD / M • Escort To Ecstasy / 1987 / 3HV / M • Extreme Heat / 1987 / ME / M • Girls Like Us / cr88 / IN / C • The Girls Of Rodeo Drive / 1987 / BAD / M • Girls Of The Chorus Line / 1986 / CLV / M • Hanna Does Her Sisters / 1986 / HUR / M • Having It All / 1985 / IN / M • Hot Gun / 1986 / CA / M • The Huntress / 1987 / IN / M • Imaginary Lovers / 1986 / ME / M • Jane Bond Meets Thunderballs / 1986 / VD / M • L.A. Raw / 1986 / SE / M • The Life & Loves Of Nikki Charm / 1986 / MAL / M • The

Moon Girls / 1990 / ME / C • Nicki / 1987 / VI / M • Nightshift Nurses #1 / 1988 / VC / M • Nightshift Nurses #2 / 1996 / VC / M • Nina Does 'em All / 1988 / 3HV / C • Nooner / 1986 / AVC / M • Only The Best Of Peepers / 1992 / CV / C • Pajama Party / 1993 / CV / C • Pornocchio / 1987 / ME / M • Princess Charming / 1987 / AVC / C • Rambone Meets The Double Penetrators / 1987 / WET / M • Raw Talent #2 / 1987 / VC / M • Rich & Sassy / 1986 / VSE / M • The Rising / 1987 / SUV / M • Sex Aliens / 1987 / CA / M • Sex With A Stranger / 1986 / AVC / M • Sheena In Wonderland / 1987 / 3HV / M • Sheer Haven / 1989 / DR / C • Sky Foxes / 1987 / VC / M • Starlet Screen Test / 1990 / NST / S • Sweet Nothings / 1987 / HO / M • Tailgunners / 1985 / WET / M • Tales Of Taija Rae / 1989 / DR / M • Temperatures Rising / 1986 / VT / M • Thy Neighbour's Wife / 1986 / DR / M • Two To Tango / 1987 / TEM / M • Wise Girls / 1989 / IN / C • Young And Innocent / 1987 / HO / M

SHEENA MARIE

Big Bust Scream Queens / 1994 / BTO / M • Big Busty #36 / 198? / H&S / S

SHEENA SATAY *see* **Star Index I**

SHEENA WESTON

The Prize Package / 1993 / HSV / G • Surprise Package / 1993 / HSV / G • Transfigured / 1993 / HSV / G

SHEER DELIGHT *see* **Cher Delight**

SHEHERAZADE

Buttman In Barcelona / 1996 / EA / M

SHEIKY

Sweet Black Cherries #4 / 1996 / TTV / M

SHEILA

Buttman Goes To Rio #3 / 1992 / EA / M • The Girls Of Summer / 1995 / VT / M • Hardcore Schoolgirls #3: Legal And Eager / 1995 / XPR / M • Rosa / Francesca / 1995 / XC / M • Swedish Erotica #04 / 1980 / CA / M • Virgin Killers: The Killing Spree / 1995 / PEP / M • Wrasslin She-Babes #13 / 1996 / SOW / M

SHEILA (M. MASGLOW) *see* **Melinda Masglow**

SHEILA BLUE *see* **Star Index I**

SHEILA DEVLIN

Take Off / 1978 / VXP / M

SHEILA GALORE

Bucky Beaver's XXX Dragon Art Theatre Double Feature #13 / 1996 / SOW / M • Tomatoes / cr70 / SOW / M

SHEILA JONES *see* **Star Index I**

SHEILA KELLY (Jenny Blue)

Not too pretty flabby Australian girl.

Aussie Vice / 1989 / PM / M • Australian Connection / 1989 / PM / M • Bushwackers / 1990 / PM / M • Dick Tracer / 1990 / PM / M • Diedre In Danger / 1990 / VI / M • Images Of Desire / 1990 / PM / M • The New Barbarians #1 / 1990 / VC / M • The New Barbarians #2 / 1990 / VC / M • Outback Assignment / 1991 / VD / M • Phone Sex Girls: Australia / 1989 / PM / M • Sexual Healer / 1991 / CA / M

SHEILA LORRAINE

The Honeymoon: The Bride's Running Behind / 1990 / 4P / M

SHEILA PARIS *see* **Star Index I**

SHEILA PARKS *see* **Star Index I**

SHEILA ROSS *see* **Star Index I**

SHEILA SANDERS *see* **Harley (Sheila)**

SHEILA STONE (Sandra Stone, Shelia

Stone, Sheri Stone)
Not too pretty blonde with some surplus poundage and medium to large tits.
Anal Co-Ed / 1993 / ROB / M • Anal Sensation / 1993 / ROB / M • Animal Attraction / 1994 / IF / M • Bedtime Tales / 1995 / IF / M • Biff Malibu's Totally Nasty Home Videos #16 / 1992 / ANA / M • Boomeranal / 1992 / CC / M • Breast Worx #34 / 1992 / LBO / M • Bringing Up The Rear / 1993 / VD / C • Casting Call #14 / 1995 / SO / M • Centerfold / 1992 / VC / M • Cinderella Society / 1993 / GO / M • Dick & Jane Big Breast Adventure / 1993 / AVI / M • Essence Of A Woman / 1995 / ONA / M • Face Dance #1 / 1992 / EA / M • Face Dance #2 / 1992 / EA / M • Feds In Bed / 1993 / HO / M • Girls Around The World #29 / 1995 / BTO / M • Girls Gone Bad #7: Misfits Of Society / 1992 / GO / F • Girls, Girls, Girls, Girls / 1993 / FD / C • Head Lines / 1992 / SC / M • Hidden Obsessions / 1992 / BFP / M • KBBS: Weekend With Alicia Rio & Sheila Stone / 1992 / KBB / M • Lesbian Pros And Amateurs #20 / 1993 / GO / F • Looks Like A Million / 1992 / LV / M • The Lovers / 1993 / HO / M • Malcolm XXX / 1992 / OD / M • More Dirty Debutantes #05 / 1990 / 4P / M • More Than A Woman / 1994 / H&S / M • Mr. Fun's Mondo Adventure / 1993 / VC / M • Radical Affairs Video Magazine #02 / 1992 / ME / M • Radical Affairs Video Magazine #03 / 1992 / ME / M • Raising Kane / 1992 / FD / M • Raunch #05 / 1992 / CC / M • The Seductress / 1992 / ZA / M • Sex Ranch / 1993 / VC / M • Seymore Butts In The Love Shack / 1992 / FH / M • Seymore Butts: Bustin' Out My Best Anal / 1995 / FH / C • Splendor In The Ass #2 / 1992 / CA / M • Toppers #25 / 1994 / TV / M • Toppers #27 / 1994 / TV / M • Toppers #28 / 1994 / TV / M • Toppers #32 / 1994 / TV / C • Unfaithful Entry / 1992 / DR / M • Wild Girls / 1993 / LV / F • Will & Ed Are Geeks In Heat / 1994 / MID / M • Will & Ed's Back To Class / 1992 / MID / M • You Bet Your Buns / 1992 / ZA / M

SHEILA STUART
The Case Of The Full Moon Murders / 1971 / SOW / M • Love Games / 1975 / SAT / M

SHEILA TAYLOR
[The Gang's All Here / cr85 / STM / M

SHELBY
Arch Worship / 1995 / PRE / B • Big Murray's New-Cummers #30: Couples At Play / 1995 / FD / M • Detention Cell #101 / 1995 / VTF / B • Dungeon Of Despair / 199? / CS / B • The Erotic Adventures Of Fanny Annie / 1991 / WV / M • Giggles / 1992 / PRE / B • The Keys Please / 1993 / TAO / B • Lube Job / 1994 / PRE / B • Personal Trainer (Cs) / 1995 / CS / B • Reel Life Video #32: / 1995 / RLF / M • Reel Life Video #38: Toy Stories / 1995 / RLF / F • Reel Life Video: Britt & Iron John / 1995 / RLF / F • Reel Life Video: Brunettes In Heat / 1995 / RLF / F • Ropeburn / 1994 / VTF / B • Slap Happy / 1994 / PRE / B • Stroke Play / 1994 / PLV / B • Student Fetish Videos: Catfighting #12 / 1994 / PRE / B • Student Fetish Videos: The Enema #10 / 1993 / PRE / B • Student Fetish Videos: The Enema #16 / 1994 / PRE / B • Student Fetish Videos: Spanking

#10 / 1993 / PRE / B • Student Fetish Videos: Spanking #16 / 1994 / PRE / B • Student Fetish Videos: Tickling #07 / 1992 / SFV / B • Tied & Tickled #23: Tickling Dick / 1994 / CS / B

SHELBY (LEAH LYONS) *see* Leah Lyons
SHELBY (STEVENS) *see* Shelby Stevens
SHELBY LANE *see* Tamara Landry
SHELBY STEVENS *(Shelby (Stevens), Bobby Sue)*
Blonde with nice smile and hard cantaloupes but a nice figure otherwise who almost always appears with her boyfriend/husband, Ian Daniels (as of late 1994, they had broken up). Was 24 years old in 1993 and had her first sexual experience at 18.
1-900-FUCK #2 / 1995 / SO / M • 10,000 Anal Maniacs #2 / 1994 / FOR / M • The Adventures Of Major Morehead / 1994 / SC / M • Alex Jordan's First Timers #04 / 1994 / OD / M • All That Jism / 1994 / VD / M • Amateur Lesbians #43: Poppy / 1993 / GO / F • America's Raunchiest Home Videos #71: / 1993 / ZA / M • Anal Secrets (After Dark) / 1994 / AFD / M • Angel Eyes / 1995 / IN / M • Arch Villains / 1995 / PRE / B • The Art Of Deception / 1996 / BON / B • Assy Sassy #3 / 1995 / ROB / F • Babes Illustrated #3 / 1995 / IN / F • Badd Girls / 1994 / SC / F • Battling Bitches #1 / 1995 / BIZ / B • Because I Can / 1995 / BEP / M • The Best Of Buttslammers / 1995 / BS / C • Bi Bitches In Heat / 1996 / BIZ / F • Big Bust Babes #20 / 1994 / AFI / M • Big Bust Babes #21 / 1994 / AFI / M • Big Knockers #08 / 1994 / TV / M • Big Knockers #09 / 1995 / TV / M • Big Knockers #10 / 1995 / TV / M • Big Knockers #20 / 1995 / TV / C • Big Knockers #21: Best Of Lesbian #2 / 1995 / TV / C • Black Bamboo / 1995 / IN / M • Black Buttman #02 / 1994 / CC / M • Blonde Temptation / 1995 / IF / M • Bloopers & Boners / 1996 / VI / M • Bobby Hollander's Rookie Nookie #11 / 1993 / SFP / M • Boobs A Poppin' / 1994 / TTV / M • Bra Busters #04 / 1993 / LBO / M • Brassiere To Eternity / 1994 / PEP / F • Breast Collection #04 / 1995 / LBO / C • Breastman Does The Twin Towers / 1993 / EVN / M • Buffy Malibu's Nasty Girls #06 / 1994 / ANA / F • Buffy Malibu's Nasty Girls #08 / 1995 / ANA / F • The Butt Sisters Do Denver / 1994 / MID / M • Buttslammers #09: Fade To Anal / 1995 / BS / F • Buttslammers #10: Lust On The Internet / 1995 / BS / F • Buttslammers #13: The Madness Continues / 1996 / BS / F • California Covet / 1995 / CA / M • Car Wash Angels / 1995 / VC / M • Casanova #4 / 1993 / SC / M • Channel Blonde / 1994 / VI / M • Chronicles Of Pain #2 / 1996 / BIZ / B • Chronicles Of Pain #3: Slave Traders / 1996 / BIZ / B • Chronicles Of Pain #4: Tools Of The Trade / 1996 / BIZ / B • A Clockwork Orgy / 1995 / PL / M • Comeback / 1995 / VI / M • Confessions Of A Slutty Nurse / 1994 / VIM / M • The Couch Trap / 1993 / ELP / M • Cousin Bubba Country Corn Porn #01 / 1994 / VIM / M • Cousin Bubba Country Corn Porn #02 / 1994 / VIM / M • Cover To Cover / 1995 / WP / M • Cream / 1993 / SC / M • Crew Sluts / 1994 / KWP / M • Cum & Get Me / 1995 / PL / F • Debi Diamond: Mega Mistress / 1995 / BIZ / B • Deep Inside Juli Ashton / 1996 / VC / C • Deep Inside Kait-

lyn Ashley / 1995 / VC / C • Designs On Women / 1994 / IN / F • Desperate / 1995 / WP / M • Devil In A Wet T-Shirt / 1995 / SPI / M • Dirty Bob's #08: LAid Over In L.A. / 1993 / FLP / S • Dirty Bob's #09: Orlando Orgasms / 1993 / FLP / S • Dirty Bob's #18: Under The Boardwalk! / 1995 / FLP / S • Dirty Bob's #19: Over The Boardwalk! / 1995 / FLP / S • Dirty Doc's Housecalls #02 / 1993 / LV / M • Dream House / 1995 / XPR / M • Dresden Diary #11: Endangered Secrets / 1994 / BIZ / B • Dun-Hur #1 / 1994 / SC / M • Electropussy / 1995 / CC / M • Encore / 1995 / VI / M • Escape To The Party / 1994 / ELP / M • Everybody Wants Some / 1996 / EXQ / F • Evil Temptations #2 / 1995 / ULP / M • Fetish Finishing School / 1995 / HOM / B • Fire & Ice / 1995 / LV / M • First Time Ever #1 / 1995 / PE / F • First Time Lesbians #08 / 1993 / JMP / F • Flesh / 1996 / EA / M • The French Way / 1994 / HOV / M • Future Doms #1 / 1996 / BIZ / B • Gangbang Girl #12 / 1993 / ANA / M • A Girl's Affair #03 / 1993 / FD / F • A Girl's Affair #05 / 1994 / FD / F • The Girls From Hootersville #04 / 1993 / SFP / M • The Girls From Hootersville #05 / 1994 / SFP / M • Go Ahead...Eat Me! / 1995 / KWP / M • Hard Squeeze / 1994 / EMC / M • Heart Breaker / 1994 / CA / M • Heidi's High Heeled Hookers / 1995 / BBE / M • Hollywood '94: Butts Abound / 1993 / ELP / M • Hollywood Hillbillies / 1996 / LE / M • Hostile Takeover: Bitch Bosses / 1995 / BIZ / B • Indecent Interview / 1995 / PL / F • Invitation To The Blues / 1994 / LE / M • The Joy Dick Club / 1994 / MID / M • Junkyard Dykes #02 / 1994 / ZA / F • Kelly Jaye Close-Up / 1994 / VI / M • Kinky Fantasies / 1994 / KWP / M • Kittens #7 / 1995 / CC / F • Kitty Kat Club / 1994 / SC / F • Ladies Room / 1994 / SC / F • Leather Bound Dykes From Hell #5 / 1995 / BIZ / B • Leather Bound Dykes From Hell #8 / 1996 / BIZ / B • Lesbian Climax / 1995 / ROB / F • Lessons In Bondage / 1995 / HOM / B • Lick-A-Thon #2 / 1996 / HW / C • Love Potion 69 / 1994 / VC / M • Mask Of Innocence / 1996 / WP / B • The Mechanic / 1995 / VOY / M • Melissa's Wish / 1993 / LON / B • Mike Hott: #247 Cunt of the Month: Shelby / 1993 / MHV / M • Mistress (1993-HOM) / 1994 / HOM / B • Mistress Kane: Lessons In Terror / 1996 / BIZ / B • Mistress Kane: Town In Torment / 1996 / BIZ / B • Mistress Of The Mansion / 1994 / CV / M • Misty Rain: Wrestling Terror / 1995 / BIZ / B • Monkey Wrench / 1995 / BEP / M • More Than A Handful #6: Life Under The Big Top / 1994 / MET / M • More Than A Whore / 1995 / OD / M • Mr. Peepers Amateur Home Videos #74: C Foam Surfer / 1993 / LBO / M • Mr. Peepers Amateur Home Videos #86: Tit A Ton / 1994 / LBO / M • Neighbors / 1994 / LE / M • No Man's Land #11 / 1995 / VT / F • Nude Awakenings / 1996 / PP / M • Nurses Bound By Duty / 1996 / BIZ / B • Odyssey 30 Min: #384: Shelby The Slut / 1993 / OD / M • Odyssey Triple Play #91: Bone Appetite / 1995 / OD / M • Odyssey Triple Play #97: The Anal Game / 1995 / OD / M • On The Rise / 1994 / EX / M • Party Pack #2 / 1994 / LE / F • Perplexed / 1994 / FD / M • Picture Perfect (Cal Vista) / 1995 / CV / M • Prisoners Of Pain / 1994 / BIZ / B • Profiles

#07: Sexworld / 1996 / XPR / M • Psychoanal Therapy / 1994 / CA / M • Public Access / 1995 / VC / M • Pulp Friction / 1994 / PP / M • Raincoat Fantasies / 1993 / ELP / M • Raunch #09 / 1993 / CC / M • Raunch #10: Uncut Jewel / 1994 / CC / M • Raunchy Remedy / 1993 / ELP / M • Revenge Of The Pussy Suckers From Mars / 1994 / PP / M • Ring Of Passion / 1994 / ERA / M • Runaway Slaves / 1995 / HOM / B • Scrue / 1995 / VI / M • Secret Diary #2 / 1995 / MID / M • The Seduction Of Marylin Star / 1994 / VT / M • Seekers / 1994 / CA / M • Sex Fugitives / 1993 / LE / M • Sex On The Saddle: Wicked Women Of The Wild West / 1994 / CPG / S • Sex On The Strip: The Lusty Ladies Of Las Vagas / 1993 / CPG / F • Sex Party / 1995 / KWP / M • The Sexual Solution #1 / 1995 / LE / M • Sexual Trilogy #03 / 1994 / SFP / M • Shelby's Forbidden Fears / 1995 / BIZ / B • Silent Women / 1995 / ERA / M • Six Degrees Of Penetration / 1996 / PP / M • Slave Of Fashion / 1993 / LON / B • Sleaze Please!—August Edition / 1994 / FH / M • Snatch Masters #05 / 1995 / LEI / M • Sodomania #14: C**t Lickin', C*m Drinkin' Bitches / 1995 / EL / M • Something Blue / 1995 / CC / M • Sorority Stewardesses #1 / 1995 / PE / M • Sorority Stewardesses #2 / 1995 / PE / M • Southern: Jennifer / 1993 / SSH / F • Spiked Heel Diaries #3 / 1995 / BIZ / B • Spin For Sex / 1994 / IN / M • Stand By Your Man / 1994 / CV / M • Star Crossed / 1995 / VC / M • Strip Poker / 1995 / PEP / M • Submission / 1994 / WP / M • Submission To Ecstasy / 1995 / NTP / B • Summer Of '69 / 1994 / MID / M • Super Enemates #2 / 1996 / PRE / C • Supermodel #1 / 1994 / VI / M • Sweat 'n' Bullets / 1995 / MID / M • Sweet Cheerleaders Spanked / 1996 / BIZ / B • Swinging Couples #02 / 1993 / GO / M • Takin' It To The Limit #4 / 1995 / BS / M • Titty Slickers #2 / 1994 / LE / M • Titty Troop / 1995 / CC / M • The Training #2 / 1994 / BIZ / B • Tramps / 1996 / MID / M • A Trip Through Pain / 1995 / BS / B • Unleashed / 1996 / SAE / M • Video Virgins #09 / 1993 / NS / M • Wanted / 1995 / DR / M • Wet 'n' Wicked / 1995 / BEP / F • What's The Lesbian Doing In My Pirate Movie? / 1995 / LIP / F • Whips And Chains / 1995 / BS / B • Whispered Secrets Of The Call Girls / 1995 / TVE / F • Wild Roomies / 1994 / VC / M • Xxxanadu / 1994 / HW / M

SHELBY STONE
Buttman's Big Tit Adventure #3 / 1995 / EA / M

SHELBY TAYLOR
Eat At Dave's #1 / 1995 / SP / M

SHELDON
Reel Life Video #03: Julie, Sheldon and Jeff / 1994 / RLF / M

SHELDON AUSTIN
Dog Walker / 1994 / EA / M

SHELENE *(Darla O'Brien, Darla O'Brian, Shalene, Shaleen, Charlene (Shelene))*
Blonde with enhanced tits and so so face. She was 24 in 1993.
America's Raunchiest Home Videos #47: / 1993 / ZA / M • Anal Climax #3 / 1993 / ROB / M • Anal Sensation / 1993 / ROB / M • Biff Malibu's Totally Nasty Home Videos #36 / 1993 / ANA / M • Breast Worx #41 /

1993 / LBO / M • Butt Woman #5 / 1993 / FH / M • The Fluffer #1 / 1993 / FD / M • Heatwave #2 / 1993 / FH / F • Infamous Crimes Against Nature / 1993 / SUM / M • Kelly Eighteen #1 / 1993 / LE / M • Kelly Eighteen #2 / 1993 / LE / M • Lesbian Pros And Amateurs #21 / 1993 / GO / F • Lesbian Pros And Amateurs #22 / 1993 / GO / F • Mr. Peepers Amateur Home Videos #77: Facial Coverage / 1993 / LBO / M • The Nymphette / 1993 / CA / M • The Rehearsal / 1993 / VC / M • Seymore Butts Meets The Cumback Brat / 1993 / FH / M • Tender Loving Care / 1994 / BRI / S • Wendy Whoppers: Razorwoman / 1993 / PEP / M • Whispers Away / 1993 / CIN / M

SHELIA
Birds And Beads / 1974 / VC / M • Blue Vanities #512 / 1992 / FFL / M • Great Of Britain #6 / 1990 / BTO / S • Home Maid Memories #1 / 1994 / BON / C • Jak's Back / 1992 / BON / B • Playboy's Girls Of Hooters / 1995 / PLA / S • The Seductive Secretary / 1995 / GO / M • Shang-Hai Slits / 1994 / ORE / C • Super Bi Bowl / 1995 / BIL / G • Uncle Roy's Amateur Home Video #20 / 1993 / VIM / M • Video Virgins #06 / 1993 / NS / M

SHELIA BELL
Punished Cheeks / 1992 / RB / B • Shaved #04 / 1992 / RB / F

SHELIA I. ROSSI
Sexual Communication / 19?? / HIF / M

SHELIA SHORE
Ripe & Ready (Infinity) / 1995 / IF / M • Snatch Masters #06 / 1995 / LEI / M

SHELIA STONE *see* **Sheila Stone**

SHELL
A Party In My Tight Pussy / 1994 / MET / M • Sally's Palace Of Delight / cr76 / CV / M

SHELL KUGLER
Sodom & Gomorrah / 1974 / MIT / M

SHELL SEWARD
Eruption / 1977 / VCX / M

SHELL SILAS *see* **Star Index I**

SHELLEY
Mixed Titty Tumbles / 1990 / NPA / B

SHELLEY ABELS *see* **Georgina Spelvin**

SHELLEY RENEE
Bare-Chested, Bare-Breasted, Big-Busted, Wet T-Shirt Video / 1990 / NAP / B • The Battle Of The Busty Blondes / 1994 / NAP / B • Wrestling Challenge / 1990 / NAP / B

SHELLI
Goldilocks And The 3 Bares / 1996 / LBO / B • Neighborhood Watch #10 / 1991 / LBO / M • No Mercy For The Bitches / 1996 / LBO / B

SHELLY
Aerienne's Surprise / 1995 / WIV / M • Amateur Nights #05 / 1990 / HO / M • America's Raunchiest Home Videos #42: Swimsuit Sherrie / 1992 / ZA / M • Blue Vanities #521 / 1993 / FFL / M • Blue Vanities #577 / 1995 / FFL / M • Full Moon Video #22: Elite Fantasy Girls / 1992 / FAP / F • Harry Horndog #14: Love Puppies #3 / 1992 / ZA / M • Hollywood Amateurs #13 / 1994 / MID / M • Honey, I Blew Everybody #2 / 1992 / MID / M • J.E.G.: Amateurs Only #10 / 1996 / JEG / M • J.E.G.: Shelly's Pregnant Slam #1 / 1995 / JEG / M • Joe Elliot's College Girls #45 / 1996 / JOE / M • KBBS: Weekend With Laurel Canyon / 1992 / KBB / M • Kinky College Cunts #03 / 1993 / NS / F • Match #3: Battling Babes / 1995 / NPA

/ B • Neighborhood Watch #27 / 1992 / LBO / M • Shane's World #3 / 1996 / OD / M • Trample Goddess #2 / 1994 / VVO / B • Under The Skirt #1 / 1995 / KAE / F • Wedding Rituals / 1995 / DVP / M

SHELLY (DEE DEE) *see* **Dee Dee Reeves**

SHELLY DAVIS *see* **Star Index I**

SHELLY DYNAH MYTE
American Sex Fantasy / 1975 / IHV / M

SHELLY HUMMER
Cooler Girls / 1994 / MID / C

SHELLY JENSEN
Creme De La Face #16: Ladies Licking / 1996 / OD / M • Red Rumpers #01 / 1996 / LBO / B

SHELLY LEE *see* **Star Index I**

SHELLY LINX
Penthouse Pleasures / 19?? / VST / M

SHELLY LYONS
Addicted To Lust / 1996 / NIT / M • Birthday Bash / 1995 / BOT / M • Cabin Fever / 1995 / ERA / M • Fresh Faces #03 / 1995 / EVN / M • Henry's Big Boob Adventure / 1996 / HO / M • Interview With A Tramp / 1996 / SP / M • Nature Girls #2: Get Wet / 1995 / WIV / F • Pussy Hunt #09 / 1995 / LEI / M • Rimmers #1 / 1996 / MP0 / M • Up The Middle / 1995 / V99 / M • Video Virgins #27 / 1996 / NS / M

SHELLY MARS *see* **Star Index I**

SHELLY MATHEWS *see* **Star Index I**

SHELLY MICHAELS
Maximum Desade / 1995 / ZFX / B • Story Of Sweet Nicole / 1992 / ZFX / B

SHELLY O'HARA
Hot Sweet Honey / 1985 / VEP / M • Naughty Girls In Heat / 1986 / SE / M

SHELLY RAE *see* **Debi Diamond**

SHELLY REY *see* **Debi Diamond**

SHELLY SAND
Fast Girls #1 / 1987 / GBX / M • Imaginary Lovers / 1986 / ME / M • Jane Bond Meets Thunderballs / 1986 / VD / M • Virgin Heat / 1986 / TEM / M

SHELLY SUMMERS
Juice / 19?? / COM / M

SHELLY SUPREME *see* **Chelly Supreme**

SHELLY WILDE
Euro-Snatch / 1996 / SNA / M

SHELLY YORK
L.A. Tool & Die / 1979 / TMX / G

SHEMP BEAVER
Pussy Hunt #12 / 1995 / LEI / M

SHENA
AVP #9161: Boy Toy...The Video / 1991 / AVP / M • AVP #9162: Rise And Shine / 1990 / AVP / F • AVP #9163: Stood Up...Again / 1990 / AVP / F • Fantasy Photography: Hot Date / 1995 / FAP / F

SHENA TURNER
Naughty Network / 1981 / CA / M

SHENEQUA
Black Knockers #05 / 1995 / TV / M • Bootylicious: It's A Bootyful Thing / 1996 / JMP / M

SHER DELIGHT *see* **Cher Delight**

SHERA BENTLI
Private Film #05 / 1993 / OD / M

SHERAZADE
Games Women Play / 1995 / XC / M • Private Film #09 / 1994 / OD / M

SHEREE NORTH
Blue Vanities #580 / 1996 / FFL / M • [Jake Spanner, Private Eye / 1989 / ... / S

SHEREE SHERCUM
Ski Sluts / 1995 / LV / M • Snatch Masters

#08 / 1995 / LEI / M
SHEREE SMITH *see Star Index I*
SHERI
Full Moon Video #10: Squat City / 1994 / FAP / F • Homegrown Video #357 / 1991 / HOV / M • School For Hookers / 1974 / SOW / M • Teasedance Masturbation #3 / 1994 / MAV / F
SHERI GAVNER *see Cheri Janvier*
SHERI LAKE
Ass Thrashing / 1995 / RB / B • Bound And Gagged #01 / 1991 / RB / B • Bruised Buns / 1992 / RB / B • Finger Pleasures #5 / 1996 / PL / F • Firm Bottom Discipline / 1992 / RB / B • Housemother's Discipline #4 / 1992 / RB / B • Shaved #09 / 1995 / RB / F • Sorority Initiation / 1992 / RB / B • Spanking Dreams / 1992 / RB / B • Strict Stepmother / 1992 / RB / B
SHERI SLOAN *see Dana Dylan*
SHERI SPALDING *see Star Index I*
SHERI ST CLAIR *(Sheri St Cloud, Kim Kafkaloff, Cheri St Clair, Debbie Moore, Sheri St James)*
Kim Kafkaloff in **Sex Appeal** (a non-porno movie). Debbie Moore is from **Wet Sex**.
The Adultress / 1987 / CA / M • Aroused / 1985 / VIV / M • Bachelorette Party / 1984 / JVV / M • Back Road To Paradise / 1984 / CDI / M • Backdoor Bandits / 1989 / MIR / C • Backdoor Lust / 1987 / CV / C • Backdoor Romance / 1984 / VIV / M • Backing In #2 / 1990 / WV / C • Beaverly Hills Cop / 1985 / SE / M • Bent Over The Rent / 1984 / SKJ / B • Between The Cheeks #1 / 1985 / VC / M • Beverly Hills Cox / 1986 / CA / M • Beverly Hills Heat / 1985 / VEP / M • Bi-Coastal / 1985 / LAV / G • Bizarre Encounters / 1986 / 4P / B • Black 'n' White In Color / 1987 / VCR / C • Black Silk Secrets / 1989 / VC / C • Blonde Desire / 1984 / AIR / M • Blondie / 1985 / TAR / M • Blowing The Whistle / 1986 / VIP / M • Blue Dream Lover / 1985 / TAR / M • Bodies By Jackie / 1985 / IVP / M • Bottoms Up #07 / 1986 / AVC / C • Candy Stripers #2 / 1985 / AR / M • Charm School / 1986 / VI / M • Cherry Tricks / 1985 / VPE / M • Circus Acts / 1987 / SE / C • Coffee & Cream / 1984 / AVC / M • Color Me Amber / 1985 / VC / M • Corporate Assets / 1985 / SE / M • Cunning Coeds / 1985 / IVP / M • Dames / 1985 / SE / M • Deep Inside Trading / 1986 / AR / M • Desperate Women / 1986 / VD / M • Diamond Collection #79 / 1986 / CDI / M • Diamond Collection #80 / 1986 / CDI / M • Double Desires / 1988 / PIN / C • Double Penetration Fever / 1989 / MIR / C • Dr Penetration / 1986 / WET / M • Dream Lover / 1985 / CDI / M • Erotic Penetration / 1987 / HO / C • Family Secrets / 1985 / AMB / M • Fantasy Land / 1984 / LA / M • Fashion Passion / 1985 / VD / M • Firefoxes / 1985 / PLY / M • Flash Trance / 1985 / IVP / M • Flesh For Fantasies / 1986 / TAM / M • Foxy Brown / 1984 / VC / M • Ginger: The Movie / 1988 / PV / C • Girl Games / 1987 / PL / C • Girls On Girls / 1987 / SE / C • Girls That Talk Dirty / 1986 / VCS / C • Good Girls Do / 1984 / HO / M • Greek Lady / 1985 / TGA / M • Hot Chocolate #2 / 1986 / PLY / M • Hot Gypsy Love / 1985 / CDI / M • Hot Sweet Honey / 1985 / VEP / M • I Love A Girl In A Uniform / 1989 / VC / C • I Love LA #1 / 1986 / PEN / C • I Love LA #2 / 1989 / PEN / C • Illusions Of

Ecstasy / 1985 / NSV / M • Jacqueline / 1986 / MAP / M • John Holmes, The Man, The Legend / 1995 / EVN / C • Kiss Of The Gypsy / 1986 / WV / M • The Ladies In Lace Party / 1985 / MAP / M • Ladies Of The 80's / 1985 / PV / M • Le Sex De Femme #4 / 1989 / AFI / C • The Life & Loves Of Nikki Charm / 1986 / MAL / M • Lingerie Party / 1987 / SE / C • Little American Maid / 1987 / VCX / M • Little Girls Talking Dirty / 1984 / VCX / M • Little Girls, Dirty Desires / 1984 / JVV / M • Little Miss Innocence / 1987 / CA / M • Lonely Lady / 1984 / VC / M • The Long Ranger / 1987 / VCX / M • Loose Ends #3 / 1987 / BS / M • Love At First Sight / 1987 / SE / C • Love Button / 1985 / AVC / M • Lucky In Love #2 / 1988 / SEV / M • Lust In America / 1985 / VCX / M • Lust In The Fast Lane / 1984 / PV / M • Lusty Adventurer / 1985 / GO / M • Make Me Want It / 1986 / CA / M • Mama's Boy / 1984 / VD / M • Marilyn Chambers' Private Fantasies #4 / 1983 / CA / M • The Melting Spot / 1985 / VSE / M • Miami Spice #1 / 1987 / CA / M • Miami Spice #2 / 1988 / CA / M • Naughty Girls In Heat / 1986 / SE / M • Nicki / 1987 / VI / M • Nymphette #2 / 1986 / WV / M • Obsession / 1985 / HO / M • Pacific Intrigue / 1987 / AMB / M • Pajama Party / 1993 / CV / C • Party Girls / 1988 / MAP / M • Peeping Tom / 1986 / CV / M • Perfect Partners / 1986 / CV / M • Playpen / 1987 / VC / M • Please Don't Stop / 1986 / CV / M • Rear Entry / 1985 / VCR / C • The Return Of Johnny Wadd / 1986 / PEN / M • Sailing Into Ecstasy / 1986 / VCX / M • Secrets / 1984 / HO / M • The Seduction Of Lana Shore / 1984 / PL / M • Sex Appeal / 1986 / VES / S • Sex Busters / 1984 / PLY / M • Sex Crimes 2084 / 1985 / SE / M • Sex Drive / 1984 / VXP / M • Sex-A-Vision / 1985 / DR / M • Sex-O-Gram / 1986 / LA / M • She-Male Encounters #10: She-Male Vacation / 1986 / MET / G • Sheri's Gotta Have It / 1985 / LIM / C • Sheri's Wild Dream / 19?? / LIM / C • Sinful Pleasures / 1987 / HO / C • Sizzling Suburbia / 1985 / CDI / M • Slammer Girls / 1987 / LIV / S • Soaking Wet / 1985 / CV / M • Soft Warm Rain / 1987 / VD / M • Spanish Fly / 1987 / CA / M • Strip Search / 1987 / SEV / M • Super Sex / 1986 / MAP / M • Suzy's Birthday Bang / 1985 / CDI / M • Swedish Erotica #58 / 1984 / CA / M • Swedish Erotica #64 / 1985 / CA / M • Swedish Erotica #65 / 1985 / CA / M • Sweet Revenge / 1986 / ZA / M • Sweet Surrender / 1985 / AVC / M • Swinging Shift / 1985 / CDI / M • Talk Dirty To Me #04 / 1986 / DR / M • Terms Of Employment / 1984 / LA / M • This Babe's For You / 1984 / TAR / M • This Stud's For You / 1986 / MAP / C • Tight And Tender / 1985 / CA / M • Tight Squeeze / 1986 / AVC / M • Traci Who? / 1987 / AVC / C • A Tribute To The King / 1985 / VCX / C • Two On The Tongue / 1988 / TAM / C • User Friendly #1 / 1990 / LV / M • User Friendly #2 / 1990 / LV / M • Vas-O-Line Alley / 1985 / VC / M • Venus Of The Nile / 1991 / WV / M • The Voyeur / 1985 / VC / M • Voyeur's Delight / 1986 / VCS / C • Wet Sex / 1984 / CA / M • What Are Friends For? / 1985 / MAP / M • White Trash / 1986 / PV / M • Wild Orgies / 1986 / SE / C • Wild Toga Party / 1985 / VD / M • A Woman's Touch / 1988 / ZA / F

• Working Girls / 1985 / CA / M • Young And Naughty / 1984 / HO / M
SHERI ST CLOUD *see Sheri St Clair*
SHERI ST JAMES *see Sheri St Clair*
SHERI STONE *see Sheila Stone*
SHERI SUZETTE
Saturday Matinee Series #4 / 1996 / VCX / C
SHERI VAUGHAN *see Sharon Kane*
SHERICE *see Sharise*
SHERIE AVELINE *see Star Index I*
SHERISE *see Sharise*
SHERISSE *see Star Index I*
SHERMAINE
Black Hollywood Amateurs #15 / 1995 / MID / M
SHERMAN RICHMOND
Marriage And Other Four Letter Words / 1974 / VC / M
SHERMAN TORGEN
Hard Candy / 1977 / ... / M
SHERRI
Bucky Beaver's XXX Dragon Art Theatre Double Feature #03 / 1996 / SOW / M • Limited Edition #24 / 1984 / AVC / M • Once In A Blue Moon / 1991 / CC / M • Pearl Necklace: Amorous Amateurs #22 / 1993 / SEE / M • Sherri's Sessions #1 / 1994 / STP / B • Sherri's Sessions #2 / 1994 / STP / B
SHERRI (G.CARLSON) *see Greta Carlson*
SHERRI GRAHAM *see Greta Carlson*
SHERRI TART *see Rikki O'Neal*
SHERRIE *see Uschi Digart*
SHERRIE D'LYTE
Big Bust Babes #03 / 1988 / AFI / M
SHERRIE DEGRAFF
Resurrection Of Eve / 1973 / MIT / M
SHERRIE O'NEAL
Art Of Femininity #2 / 1988 / LEO / G • She-Male Encounters #17: Sorority / 1987 / MET / G
SHERRIE SMITH
Sex Boat / 1980 / VCX / M
SHERRY
A&B AB#446: Slutty Wife Returns / 1996 / A&B / M • Amateurs In Action #4 / 1995 / MET / M • Black Street Hookers #4: The Streets Of San Francisco / 1996 / DFI / M • Blue Vanities #518 / 1993 / FFL / M • Blue Vanities #520 / 1993 / FFL / M • Deep Waterworld / 1995 / HW / M • Full Moon Video #31: The Old Lady & The Who? / 1994 / FAP / M • Home Movie Production #06 / 1990 / DR / M • Neighborhood Watch #02 / 1991 / LBO / M • Sex Over 40 #2 / 1994 / PL / M • Sherry's Punishment / 1993 / BON / B • Waterworld Deep / 1995 / HW / M
SHERRY ANDERSON *see Elaine Southern*
SHERRY BLUE *see Star Index I*
SHERRY CARTER *see Star Index I*
SHERRY CASS
The Bite / 1975 / SVE / M
SHERRY EVANS
Bachelor's Paradise / 1986 / VEX / M • Backdoor Brides #2: The Honeymoon / 1986 / PV / M • Behind The Backdoor #1 / 1986 / EVN / M • Dr Truth's Great Sex / 1986 / VD / M • French Cleaners / 1986 / VCR / M • Going Down With Amber / 1987 / 4P / M • Loose Caboose / 1987 / 4P / M • Queen Of Spades / 1986 / VD / M • To Live & Shave In LA / 1986 / WET / M
SHERRY GARCIA

Donna Young: Sherry Garcia #1 / 1995 / DY / F
SHERRY KAY
The Loves Of Mary Jane / 1989 / BWV / C • A Touch Of Sex / 1972 / AR / M
SHERRY LIPPS
The Girls Of Fantasex #2 / 1996 / NIT / M • Julie's Diary / 1995 / LBO / M
SHERRY LYNN
Blue Vanities #558 / 1994 / FFL / M
SHERRY MOORE *see Star Index I*
SHERRY SWELLS
Raw Talent: Bang 'er 40 Times / 1992 / RTP / M
SHERRY TUFTS *see Star Index I*
SHERYL
Girls Games Of Summer #4 / 1994 / NIV / S • Reel Life Video #38: Toy Stories / 1995 / RLF / F • Siren / 1996 / WV1 / F
SHEURLEY
Rump Man: Goes To Cannes / 1995 / HW / M
SHEYENNE *see Star Index I*
SHIDA KARAI
A Widow's Affair / 1996 / AVV / M
SHILO
GRG: Pussy Licking Ladies / 1994 / GRG / F
SHILOE
Anal Camera #11 / 1995 / EVN / M • Fresh Faces #08 / 1995 / EVN / M • Lady Luck / 1995 / PMV / M
SHIMA
Anything Goes / 1995 / NAP / B • Oriental Conquest / 1995 / NAP / B
SHIMON PERESS
The Fantasy Booth / 1993 / ONA / M
SHINELLA
Anita / 1996 / BLC / M
SHIRA GOODLOW
Two Way Mirror / 1985 / CV / M
SHIREE *see Star Index I*
SHIREEN STARK *see Star Index I*
SHIRLEY
A&B AB#316: I Like It Deep / 1991 / A&B / M • Blue Vanities #516 / 1992 / FFL / M • Blue Vanities #517 / 1992 / FFL / M • Club Doma Global #4 / 1994 / VER / B • Girls With Curves #1 / 1985 / CV / M • Kinky College Cunts #16 / 1993 / NS / F
SHIRLEY CAT
Big Abner / 19?? / VXP / M
SHIRLEY COX *see Star Index I*
SHIRLEY DICKSON
Nylon / 1995 / VI / M
SHIRLEY DUKE *see Laurie Blue*
SHIRLEY MCCRACKEN
Sex Boat / 1980 / VCX / M
SHIRLEY PETERS *see Star Index I*
SHIRLEY THOMPSON *see Honey Wilder*
SHIRLEY WOOD *see Sharon Kane*
SHIRLEY WOODS *see Sharon Kane*
SHIVA
Bright Tails #5 / 1995 / STP / B
SHOBHAN HUNTER *see Siobhan Hunter*
SHOE SUCKING SALESMN *see Star Index I*
SHOLANDA
Black Mystique #03 / 1994 / VT / F
SHONA *see Star Index I*
SHONE TAYLOR *(Shone Tee, Shore Tee, Sean Taylor, Shane Taylor, Sean Thomas, Shawn Taylor, Tyler Hudson, Sean (Shone Taylor), Shaun Taylor)*
Addicted To Love / 1988 / WAV / M • Amber

Aroused / 1985 / CA / M • Barbara Dare's Prime Choice / 1987 / SE / C • Barbara The Barbarian / 1987 / SE / M • Before She Says I Do / 1984 / MAP / M • Beverly Hills Cox / 1986 / CA / M • Beverly Hills Heat / 1985 / VEP / M • Black Bimbos In Heat / 1989 / MIR / C • Born To Be Wild / 1987 / SE / M • Brat On The Run / 1987 / VI / M • Breaking It #1 / 1984 / COL / M • Broadway Fannie Rose / 1986 / CA / M • Campus Cuties / 1986 / CA / M • Captain Hooker & Peter Porn / 1987 / VD / M • Casino Of Lust / 1984 / AT / M • Charming Cheapies #1: Joy's Many Loves / 1985 / 4P / M • Charming Cheapies #2: No Holes Barred / 1985 / 4P / M • Chastity Johnson / 1985 / AVC / M • The Chocolate Fudge Factory / 1987 / PIN / M • Chocolate Kisses / 1986 / CA / M • Circus Acts / 1987 / SE / C • Corporate Affairs / 1986 / SE / M • Crazy With The Heat #1 / 1986 / CV / M • Daddy Doesn't Know / 1984 / HO / M • Dames / 1985 / SE / M • Dance Fever / 1985 / VCR / M • Debbie Does The Devil In Dallas / 1987 / SE / M • Deep Inside Ginger Lynn / 1986 / SE / C • Deep Obsession / 1987 / WV / M • Dial F For Fantasy / 1984 / PL / M • Double Dare / 1986 / SE / M • Double Your Pleasure / 1989 / VEX / M • Dr Lust / 1987 / VC / M • Dream Lovers / 1987 / CA / M • Dynamic Vices / 1987 / VC / M • Fondle With Care / 1989 / VEX / M • Freeway Honey / 1985 / VC / M • Gettin' Ready / 1985 / CDI / M • Gimme An X / 1993 / VD / C • Girl Toys / 1986 / DR / M • Girls Of The Third Reich / 1985 / FC / M • Golddiggers #1 / 1985 / VC / M • Good Girls Do / 1984 / HO / M • The Good, The Bad, And The Horny / 1985 / VCX / M • Hollywood Undercover / 1989 / BWV / C • Hot Flashes / 1984 / VC / M • Hot Gun / 1986 / CA / M • Hyapatia Lee's Arcade Series #01 / 1988 / ZA / C • Ice Cream #3: Naked Eyes / 1984 / VC / M • Inn Of Sin / 1988 / VT / M • Jacqueline / 1986 / MAP / M • Jewel Of The Nite / 1986 / WV / M • Joanna's Dreams / 1988 / SEV / M • Late After Dark / 1985 / BAN / M • Liquid Love / 1988 / CA / M • Little Girls Of The Streets / 1984 / CV / M • Little Girls, Dirty Desires / 1984 / JVV / M • Little Shop Of Whores / 1987 / VI / M • Lonely Lady / 1984 / VC / M • Loose Ends #1 / 1984 / 4P / M • Lucky In Love #1 / 1985 / BAN / M • Lust Connection / 1988 / VT / M • Lust In America / 1985 / VCX / M • Mad Sex / 1986 / VD / M • The Melting Spot / 1985 / VSE / M • Miss Adventures / 1989 / VEX / M • Mouthwatering / 1986 / BRA / M • Mrs. Rodgers Neighborhood / 1988 / EVN / C • My Pretty Go Between / 1985 / VC / M • Naughty Angels / 1984 / VC / M • Nightfire / 1987 / LA / M • Older Women With Young Boys / 1984 / CC / M • One Night At A Time / 1984 / PV / M • Only The Best Of Barbara Dare / 1990 / CV / C • The Passion Within / 1986 / MAP / M • Passionate Lee / 1984 / CRE / M • The Perfect Weekend / 1984 / AVC / M • The Pleasure Game / 1988 / CA / M • Pleasure Productions #07 / 1984 / VCR / M • Princess Charming / 1987 / AVC / C • Raising Hell / 1987 / VD / M • Reel People #02 / 1984 / AR / M • Revenge Of The Babes #1 / 1985 / LA / M • Sailing Into Ecstasy / 1986 / VCX / M • Samantha, I Love You / 1988 / WV / C • Satin Angels / 1986 / WV / M • Screwdriver / 1988 / CC / C • Sex

F/X / 1986 / VPE / M • Sex Waves / 1984 / EXF / M • Sex-A-Vision / 1985 / DR / M • Shameless Desire / 1989 / VEX / M • She Comes In Colors / 1987 / AMB / M • Sinful Pleasures / 1987 / HO / C • The Sleazy Detective / 1988 / VD / M • Sophisticated Lady / 1988 / SEX / M • St. X-Where #1 / 1986 / VD / M • Star Gazers / 1986 / CA / M • Stiff Competition #1 / 1984 / CA / M • Swedish Erotica #67 / 1985 / CA / M • Swedish Erotica #71 / 1986 / CA / M • Swedish Erotica #72 / 1986 / CA / M • Sweet Things / 1987 / VC / M • Swinging Shift / 1985 / CDI / M • Taboo #05 / 1986 / IN / M • Tailspin / 1987 / AVC / M • A Taste Of Nikki Charm / 1989 / PIN / C • Teasers: Poor Little Rich Girl / 1988 / MET / M • Teasers: Porno Princess / 1988 / MET / M • Terms Of Employment / 1984 / LA / M • Tight Fit / 1987 / V99 / M • Tight Fit / 1991 / VEX / C • Tight Squeeze / 1986 / AVC / M • Tongue 'n Cheek (Vca) / 1984 / VC / M • Torrid Zone / 1987 / MIR / M • Treasure Box / 1986 / PEN / M • The Ultimate Thrill / 1988 / PIN / C • Wet Kisses / 1986 / SE / M • Wild Weekend / 1984 / HO / M • The Woman Who Loved Men / 1984 / SE / M • Xstasy / 1986 / NSV / M • Yiddish Erotica #1 / 1986 / SE / C • You Bring Out The Animal In Me / 1987 / MIR / M • Young Nurses In Love / 1987 / VC / M
SHONE TEE *see Shone Taylor*
SHONNA LYNN
Petite girl with some mixture of black but a light skin, not too pretty face, small to medium tits, short frizzy blonde hair, nice little butt. After a while she gradually improved and then in early 1996 had her tits enhanced to cantaloupe level.
19 & Naughty #2 / 1995 / SKV / M • Adam & Eve's House Party #3: Swing Party / 1996 / VC / M • Adventures Of The DP Boys: Sicilian Sluts / 1995 / HW / M • Adventures Of The DP Boys: The Golden Girls / 1995 / HW / M • Amateurs Exposed #07 / 1995 / CV / M • Anal Cannibals / 1996 / ZA / M • Anal Connection / 1996 / ZA / M • Anal Delinquent #3 / 1995 / ROB / M • Anal Dynomite / 1995 / ROB / M • Anal Institution #2 / 1996 / ZA / M • Anal Plaything #2 / 1995 / ROB / M • Anal Romp / 1995 / LIP / F • Anal Tight Ass / 1995 / ROB / M • Anal Tramps / 1996 / LIP / F • Analtown USA #04 / 1995 / NIT / M • Ass Angels / 1996 / PAL / F • Assy Sassy #3 / 1995 / ROB / F • Babes Illustrated #4 / 1995 / IN / F • Behind The Mask / 1995 / XC / M • Bend Over Babes #4 / 1996 / EA / M • The Best Of Strippers Inc / 1996 / ONA / C • Black Buttwatch / 1995 / FH / M • Blue Saloon / 1996 / ME / M • Bootylicious: Big Badd Booty / 1995 / JMP / M • Butt Jammers #05 / 1996 / SC / F • Butt Motors / 1995 / VC / M • Butt Sluts #5 / 1995 / ROB / F • Butt X Files #2: Anal Abduction / 1995 / WIV / M • Buttslammers #11: / 1996 / BS / F • By Myself / 1996 / PL / F • Casting Call #16 / 1995 / SO / M • Chasey Revealed / 1994 / WP / M • Cherry Poppers #09: Misbehavin' / 1995 / ZA / M • Club Anal #3 / 1995 / ROB / F • The Complete & Total Anal Workout #2 / 1996 / ZA / M • Contrast / 1995 / CA / M • Deep Cheeks #5 / 1995 / ROB / M • Depraved Fantasies #4 / 1995 / FPI / M • Dirty Old Men #2 / 1995 / IP / M • Double Anal Alternatives / 1996 / EL / M • Double D Dykes #21 / 1995 / GO / F •

Erotic Newcummers Vol 1 #3: Anal Adventures / 1996 / DR / M • Exstasy / 1995 / WV / M • Fresh Faces #05 / 1995 / EVN / M • Hardcore Fantasies #1 / 1996 / LV / M • Hollywood Halloween Sex Ball / 1996 / EUR / M • Hot Tight Asses #13 / 1995 / TCK / M • House Of Hoochies / 1996 / DDP / M • Interracial Anal #03: Black And White All Over / 1995 / AFI / M • Interview: Naturals / 1995 / LV / M • Kittens & Vamps #2 / 1995 / ROB / F • Lesbian Climax / 1995 / ROB / F • Masturbation Ages 20 To 45 / 1996 / C69 / F • Mike Hott: #289 Three-Sum Sluts #02 / 1995 / MHV / M • Mike Hott: #321 Lesbian Sluts #20 / 1995 / MHV / F • Mike Hott: #324 Cum In My Cunt #06 / 1995 / MHV / C • Mike Hott: #325 Bonus Cunt: Shonna Lynn / 1995 / MHV / M • Mike Hott: #326 Cum In My Mouth #03 / 1995 / MHV / C • Miss Anal #2 / 1995 / C69 / M • More Dirty Debutantes #38 / 1995 / 4P / M • Muff Divers #2 / 1996 / TV / F • My Baby Got Back #08 / 1996 / VT / M • Nasty Newcummers: Black Edition / 1995 / MET / M • New Money / 1995 / ULP / M • The New Snatch Masters #15 / 1995 / LEI / C • Ona Zee's Doll House #2 / 1995 / ONA / F • Poop Dreams / 1995 / ULP / M • Private Gold #12: The Pyramid #2 / 1996 / OD / M • Pussyman Auditions #08 / 1995 / SNA / M • Reverse Gang Bang / 1995 / JMP / M • Rump Man: Sex On The Beach / 1995 / HW / M • Rump-Shaker #4 / 1995 / HW / M • Samantha & Company / 1996 / PL / M • Sleazy Streets / 1995 / PEP / M • Sodomania #12: Raw Filth / 1995 / EL / M • Sodomania: Slop Shots / 1996 / EL / C • Sodomize Me!!! / 1996 / SPR / M • Sperm Bitches / 1995 / ZA / M • Steam / 1996 / ULP / M • Strippers Inc. #5 / 1995 / ONA / M • Tail Taggers #130 / 1994 / WV / M • Tails Of Desire / 1995 / GO / M • Takin' It To The Limit #7: Debauched / 1996 / BS / M • Tight Fit #11 / 1995 / GO / M • Tight Fit #13 / 1995 / GO / M • Up And Cummers #25 / 1995 / 4P / M • Up Your Ass #1 / 1996 / ANA / M • Video Virgins #16 / 1994 / NS / M • Vivid Raw #1 / 1996 / VI / M • Waiting To XXX-Hale / 1996 / MET / M • Wet Daydreams / 1996 / XCI / M • Wild Orgies #17 / 1995 / AFI / M • Young & Natural #09 / 1995 / PRE / C • Young & Natural #10 / 1995 / PRE / F • Young & Natural #12 / 1996 / TV / F • Young & Natural #13 / 1996 / TV / F • Young & Natural #18 / 1996 / TV / C • Young Girls Do #1: Troublemakers / 1995 / CDI / M

SHORDIE
New Faces, Hot Bodies #09 / 1993 / STP / M • New Faces, Hot Bodies #21 / 1996 / STP / C

SHORE TEE *see* **Shone Taylor**

SHORT STUD *(Little Louie, Pu Pu, Louis Shortstud)*
Dwarf, gnome, or whaterver the politically correct term is for a mature male about three feet high.
Bloopers #2 / 1991 / GO / C • Call Me Angel, Sir / 1976 / ALP / M • Downstairs, Upstairs / 1980 / SE / M • Fantasex Island / 1983 / NSV / M • GVC: Bizarre Women #129 / 1982 / GO / M • Kate And The Indians / 1980 / SE / M • Let My Puppets Come / 1975 / CA / M • Long Hard Summer / 1989 / BMV / C • Merry X Miss / 1986 / VIP / M • Perversion / 1984 / AVC / M • Samurai Dick

/ 1984 / VC / M • Spreading Joy / 1984 / IN / M • Ultraflesh / 1980 / GO / M • Visions / 1977 / QX / M • The Wacky World Of X-Rated Bloopers / 1989 / GO / M

SHORTIE
Dragon Lady's Domination Technique / 1995 / STM / B • Oriental Dominatrix / 1995 / STM / B

SHORTY ROBERTS *see* **Star Index I**

SHWALLICA
Black Bitches In Heat #2 / 1995 / GDV / M

SHYANN STARR
Cyber-Sex Love Junkies / 1996 / BBE / M

SHYANNE
Fresh Faces #01 / 1994 / EVN / M • Wicked Fantasies / 1996 / CO2 / M

SHYLA FOXXX *(Shayla Foxxx)*
Marginal face, enhanced tits, shoulder length straggly black hair, 5'4" tall, 40DD-24-36, 188lbs, supposedly Puerto Rican, 22 years old in 1995.
Amazing #1 / 1996 / MET / M • Babes Illustrated #5 / 1996 / IN / F • Enigma / 1995 / MET / M • Gothic / 1995 / MET / M • Intense / 1996 / MET / M • Risque Burlesque #2 / 1996 / IN / M • Taboo #16 / 1996 / CV / M • Two Too Much / 1996 / MET / M

SIA *see* **Star Index I**

SIAMESE
Asses Galore #1: From L.A. To Brazil / 1996 / DFI / M

SIAN
Ben Dover's 9th / 1996 / VC / M

SIARA
Neighborhood Nookie #1 / 1996 / RAS / M

SIBBAN HUNTER *see* **Siobhan Hunter**

SIBIL FINE *see* **Star Index I**

SIBYLLE RAUCH
Born For Love / 1987 / … / M • Dirty Business / 1995 / WIV / M • Sex Dreams / 1995 / C69 / M

SID *see* **Star Index I**

SID DEUCE
Long-haired blonde with rock solid enchanced large tits, passable face (looks a lot like Seth Damian facially), lithe body, large tattoo on left shoulder back, good tan lines.
Adult Affairs / 1994 / VC / M • The All Girl Anal Orgy / 1996 / BAC / F • Anal Bandits / 1996 / SO / M • Anal League / 1996 / IN / M • Anal Maniacs #4 / 1995 / WP / M • Anal Maniacs #5 / 1996 / WP / M • Anal Princess #1 / 1996 / VC / M • Ass Ventura: Crack Detective / 1996 / PL / M • Assmania!! #2 / 1995 / ME / M • Bare Ass In The Park / 1995 / PEP / M • Best Butt(e) In The West #2 / 1995 / CC / M • Beverly Hills Blondes #2 / 1995 / LV / M • Big & Busty Centerfolds / 1996 / DGD / F • Big Bust Babes #27 / 1995 / AFI / M • Brian Sparks: Virtually Unreal #2 / 1996 / ALD / M • Buffy Malibu's Nasty Girls #10 / 1996 / ANA / F • Car Wash Angels / 1995 / VC / M • Cat Lickers #3 / 1995 / ME / F • Cheerleader Strippers / 1996 / PE / M • Club Decca / 1996 / BAC / F • Cockpit / 1996 / SC / M • The Come On / 1995 / EX / M • Deep Behind The Scenes With Seymore Butts #1 / 1995 / ULI / M • Deep Seven / 1996 / VC / M • Delaid Delivery / 1995 / EX / M • The Deviant Doctor / 1996 / NS / M • Dirty Stories #1 / 1995 / PE / M • Dreams Of A Gigolo / 1996 / SNA / M • Drilling For Gold / 1995 / ME / M • Eternal Lust / 1996 / VC / M • Every Nerd Has A Fantasy / 1996 / FC / M • Finger Pleasures #6 / 1996 / PL / F • Forever

/ 1995 / SC / M • Frendz? #1 / 1996 / RAS / M • Frendz? #2 / 1996 / RAS / M • Generation Sex #1 / 1996 / VT / M • Generation Sex #2: Nature's Revenge / 1996 / VT / M • Girls Of The Athletic Department / 1995 / VT / M • Girls Of The Panty Raid / 1995 / VT / M • Golddiggers #2 / 1995 / VC / M • Hellriders / 1995 / SC / M • Hotel California / 1995 / MID / M • The Hungry Heart / 1996 / AOP / M • Juliette's Desires / 1996 / LE / M • Kia Unmasked / 1995 / LE / M • Killer Tits / 1995 / LE / M • Kink #1 / 1995 / ROB / M • Kym Wilde's On The Edge #28 / 1995 / RB / B • Lollipops #2 / 1996 / SC / M • Love Dancers / 1995 / ME / M • Man Killer / 1996 / SC / M • Midget Goes Hawaiian / 1995 / FC / M • Midget On Milligan's Island / 1995 / FC / M • Moondance / 1996 / VT / M • The Night Shift / 1995 / LE / M • No Man's Land #12 / 1995 / VT / F • Odyssey 30 Min: #548: / 1995 / OD / M • Oral Addiction / 1995 / VI / M • The Palace Of Pleasure / 1995 / ULI / M • The Pawn Shop / 1996 / MID / M • Penetrator #2: Grudge Day / 1995 / PL / M • Philmore Butts Adventures In Paradise / 1996 / SUF / M • Philmore Butts Lake Poontang / 1996 / SUF / M • Philmore Butts Meets The Freak / 1995 / SUF / M • Pick Up Lines #10 / 1997 / OD / M • Plumb And Dumber / 1995 / PP / M • Point Of Entry / 1996 / WP / M • A Pool Party At Seymores #1 / 1995 / ULI / M • A Pool Party At Seymores #2 / 1995 / ULI / M • Pristine #1 / 1996 / CA / M • Pristine #2 / 1996 / CA / M • Private Stories #08 / 1996 / OD / M • Pussyclips #10 / 1995 / SNA / M • Pussyman #14: Dreams Of A Gigolo / 1996 / SNA / M • Pussyman Auditions #08 / 1995 / SNA / M • Pussyman's Nite Club Party #1 / 1996 / SNA / M • Pussyman's Nite Club Party #2 / 1997 / SNA / M • Radical Affairs Video Magazine #09 / 1995 / ME / M • Rockhard (Coast) / 1996 / CC / M • Shane's World #1 / 1996 / OD / M • Shave Tails #4 / 1995 / SO / M • Sinnocence / 1995 / CDI / M • Sluthunt #3 / 1996 / BIP / F • Snatch Masters #11 / 1995 / LEI / M • Sodomania #13: Your Lucky Number / 1995 / EL / M • Sodomania: Slop Shots / 1996 / EL / C • Solo Adventures / 1996 / AB / F • Something Blue / 1995 / CC / M • Sorority Cheerleaders / 1996 / PL / M • Spinners #2 (Wicked) / 1996 / WP / M • Street Workers / 1995 / ME / M • Stupid And Stupider / 1995 / SO / M • Take It Inside / 1995 / PEP / M • Thin Ice / 1996 / ONA / M • Tit Tease #1 / 1995 / VT / M • Topless Brain Surgeons / 1995 / LE / M • Trick Shots / 1995 / PV / M • The Ultimate Fantasy / 1995 / CV / M • Undercover / 1996 / VC / M • Up And Cummers #22 / 1995 / RWP / M • The Voyeur #5 / 1995 / EA / M • The Wanderer #1: Road Tails / 1995 / CDI / M • Wet Nurses #2 / 1995 / LE / M • XXX / 1996 / TEP / M • Young Girls Do #2: Sweet Meat / 1995 / CDI / M

SID RENO
Induced Pleasure / 1995 / ERA / M

SIDNEY
Adventures Of The DP Boys: At The French Riviera / 1994 / HW / M • Anal Addict / 1995 / ROB / M • Booty Bitch / 1995 / ROB / M • Bubbles / 1993 / KBR / S • Buttslammers #11: / 1996 / BS / F • Hollywood Amateurs #20 / 1995 / MID / M • Max #07: French Kiss / 1995 / XPR / M • The

New Ass Masters #08 / 1996 / LEI / C • Notorious / 1995 / MET / M • Pole Cats / 1993 / KBR / S • Pussy Hunt #12 / 1995 / LEI / M • Sweet Things / 1996 / FF / C • TVs In Trouble #2 / 1991 / BIZ / G • The Violation Of Rachel Love / 1995 / JMP / F • Virgin Killers: The Killing Spree / 1995 / PEP / M

SIDNEY BROWNSTREET
Bizarre Styles / 1981 / ALP / B

SIDNEY DERKO *see Star Index I*

SIDNEY FELLOWS
Purely Physical / 1982 / SE / M

SIDNEY NEIKERK
The 8th Annual Erotic Film Awards / 1984 / SE / C

SIDNEY SPADE
Dracula Exotica / 1980 / TVX / M

SIDNEY ST JMAES *see* **Sydney St James**

SIDNEY STREET
Helen Does Holland / 1996 / VC / M

SIDNEY STRONGMAN
Talking Trash #1 / 1995 / HW / M

SIDONIE
Euro-Max #1: Frisky In France / 1995 / SC / M • Eurotica #02 / 1995 / XC / M • Private Film #11 / 1994 / OD / M • Private Film #13 / 1994 / OD / M • Sandy Insatiable / 1995 / EA / M

SIDONIE LAVOUR
Private Video Magazine #10 / 1994 / OD / M

SIEGFRIED
Porno X-Treme #2: Club Bizarre / 1995 / SC / M • Porno X-Treme #4: Wet Dream / 1995 / SC / M • Skin #3 / 1995 / ERQ / M

SIEGFRIED CELLIER
Erotic Pleasures / 1976 / CA / M • [Les Plaisirs Fous / 1976 / … / M

SIEGLUND
Euromania #2 / 1996 / AOC / M

SIEGMAR DEUBNER *see Star Index I*

SIENNA
Filthy First Timers #7 / 1997 / EL / M

SIERRA
Adorable little brunette with originally small tits but as of fall 1993 she has had them enhanced to a large size. Fortunately the job was reasonably well done and they still seem quite flexible. Nice butt, slim but not ultra-tight waist, pretty face. Strangely no interviews or **MDD** type scenes up to November 1993 and then in **Nasty Nymphos #01** you finally get some information but you see why there haven't been any interviews. She sounds about 50 cents on the dollar. Either that or she's on some illicit substance. She says she's 19 years old (1993) and was born in Ventura CA. The latter is probably untrue because she hesitates a moment before replying. Even so that would make her very close to under age when she started. As of mid-1994 she was supposedly pregnant.
America's Raunchiest Home Videos #30: Hot Afternoon / 1992 / ZA / M • American Garter / 1993 / VC / M • Anal Climax #3 / 1993 / ROB / M • Anal Co-Ed / 1993 / ROB / M • Anal Distraction / 1993 / PEP / M • Anal Hunger / 1994 / ROB / M • Anal Orgy / 1993 / DRP / M • Anal Playground / 1995 / CA / M • Anal Rookies #2 / 1994 / ROB / M • Anal Savage #2 / 1994 / ROB / M • Anal Sensation / 1993 / ROB / M • Anal Woman #2 / 1993 / PL / M • Anniversary / 1992 / FOR / M • Arabian Nights / 1993 / WP / M

• Asian Persuasion / 1993 / WV / M • Ass Masters (Leisure) #04 / 1995 / LEI / M • The Basket Trick / 1993 / PL / M • Behind The Backdoor #6 / 1993 / EVN / M • The Best Of The Gangbang Girl Series #2 / 1995 / ANA / C • The Big Shave / 1993 / PEP / M • Big Tits And Fat Fannies #10 / 1994 / BTO / M • Bikini Beach #1 / 1993 / CC / M • Bikini Beach #2 / 1993 / CC / M • Bikini Beach #3 / 1993 / CC / F • Black To Basics / 1992 / ZA / M • A Blaze Of Glory / 1993 / ME / M • Blazing Boners / 1992 / MID / M • Blind Spot / 1993 / VI / M • Bobby Hollander's Maneaters #08 / 1993 / SFP / M • Broad Of Directors / 1992 / PEP / M • The Brothel / 1993 / OD / M • Buffy Malibu's Totally Nasty All-Girl Home Videos #05 / 1993 / ANA / F • Butt Sluts #1 / 1993 / ROB / F • Butthead & Beaver / 1993 / HW / M • Carnal Carnival / 1992 / FC / M • Casanova #2 / 1993 / SC / M • Casual Lies / 1992 / CA / M • The Catburglar / 1994 / PL / M • Chicks, Licks And Dirty Tricks / 1993 / ME / F • Chinatown / 1994 / SC / M • Club Anal #1 / 1993 / ROB / F • Constant Craving / 1992 / VD / M • The Creasemaster's Wife / 1993 / VC / M • Deep Inside Ariana / 1995 / VC / C • Defending Your Sex Life / 1992 / LE / M • The Devil Made Her Do It / 1992 / HO / M • Dick At Nite / 1993 / MET / M • The Dirtiest Girl In The World / 1992 / ZA / M • Double Decadence / 1995 / NOT / M • Double Penetration Virgins #02: The Second Cumming / 1994 / LE / M • Dream Strokes / 1994 / WIV / M • Dripping With Desire / 1992 / DR / M • Eleventh Annual AVN Awards / 1994 / VC / M • Face Dance #1 / 1992 / EA / M • Face Dance #2 / 1992 / EA / M • Facesitter #1 / 1992 / CC / M • Feds In Bed / 1993 / HO / M • Foolproof / 1994 / VC / M • French Open / 1993 / PV / M • French Open Part Deux / 1993 / MET / M • Frenzy / 1992 / SC / M • Gangbang Girl #12 / 1993 / ANA / M • Gimme An X / 1993 / VD / C • The Girls' Club / 1993 / VD / C • Good Vibrations / 1993 / ZA / M • Head First / 1993 / LE / M • Herman's Bed / 1992 / HO / M • Homegrown Video: Sexy Solos Of Beautiful Women / 1995 / HOV / F • Hot Box / 1995 / V99 / C • Hot For Teacher / 1993 / VD / M • How To Have Oral Sex / 1993 / A&E / M • Jan B: Jan & Sierra / 1995 / JBO / F • Kadillac & Devell / 1993 / ZA / M • Kinky Nurses / 1995 / VEX / C • A Kiss Before Dying / 1993 / CDI / M • Kittens #4: Bodybuilding Bitches / 1993 / CC / F • The Lady In Red / 1993 / VC / M • Lap Of Luxury / 1994 / WIV / M • The Last Of The Muff Divers / 1992 / MID / M • Laugh Factory / 1995 / PRE / C • A League Of Their Moan / 1992 / EVN / M • Lesbian Dating Game / 1993 / LIP / F • Let's Party / 1993 / VC / M • Lethal Lolita / 1993 / LE / M • Love Potion / 1993 / WV / M • The Lovers / 1993 / HO / M • The Magic Box / 1993 / TP / M • Maliboobies / 1993 / CDI / F • Malibu Blue / 1992 / LE / M • Mask / 1993 / VI / M • Mo' White Trash / 1993 / MET / M • The Money Hole / 1993 / VD / M • Mr. Peepers Amateur Home Videos #66: Ready In Red / z993 / LBO / M • Mr. Peepers Amateur Home Videos #73: Carnal Capture / 1993 / LBO / C • Naked Truth #1 / 1993 / FH / M • Nasty Fuckin' Movies #23 / 1994 / RUM / M • Nasty Nymphos #01 / 1993 / ANA / M •

Neutron Man / 1993 / HO / M • Night Wish / 1992 / CDI / M • Nobody's Looking / 1993 / VC / M • The Nymphette / 1993 / CA / M • Odyssey 30 Min: #199: / 1992 / OD / M • Odyssey Triple Play #32: Cum-Loving Nasty Girls / 1993 / OD / M • One In A Million / 1992 / HW / M • Oral Majority #11 / 1994 / WV / C • P.J. Sparxx On Fire / 1992 / MID / C • Prelude / 1992 / VT / M • Principles Of Lust / 1992 / WV / M • The Psychic / 1993 / CC / M • Pussy Galore / 1993 / VD / C • A Pussy To Die For / 1992 / CA / M • Pussywoman #1: Sisters In Sin / 1994 / CC / M • The Reel Sex World #04: Laid In Hawaii / 1994 / WP / M • Reel Sex World #05 / 1994 / WP / M • Riot Grrrls / 1994 / SC / M • The Room Mate / 1995 / EX / M • Savannah Superstar / 1992 / VI / M • Seven Good Women / 1993 / HO / F • Sex Stories / 1992 / VC / M • Sexed / 1993 / HO / M • Seymore Butts & His Mystery Girl / 1993 / FH / M • Seymore Butts & The Honeymooners / 1992 / FH / M • Seymore Butts: Bustin' Out My Best Anal / 1995 / FH / C • Single White Nympho / 1992 / MID / M • Slave To Love / 1993 / ROB / M • Snatch Masters #06 / 1995 / LEI / M • Sodom & Gomorrah / 1992 / OD / M • Sodomania #02: More Tails / 1992 / EL / M • Sodomania #07: Deep Down Inside / 1993 / EL / M • Sodomania: The Baddest Of The Best...And Then Some / 1994 / EL / C • Splendor In The Ass #2 / 1992 / CA / M • Steal This Heart #1 / 1993 / CV / M • Steal This Heart #2 / 1993 / CV / M • Steal This Heart (Director's) / 1993 / CV / M • Straight A's / 1993 / VC / M • Super Groupie / 1993 / PL / M • Surfer Girl / 1992 / PP / M • Tickled Pink / 1993 / LE / F • Totally Tasteless Video #02 / 1994 / TTV / M • The Truth Laid Bare / 1993 / ZA / M • Two Sisters / 1992 / WV / M • Ultra Head / 1992 / CA / M • Unchained Melanie / 1992 / VC / M • Unrefined / 1993 / CC / M • Virtual Sex / 1993 / VC / M • W.A.S.P. / 1992 / CC / M • Warm Pink / 1992 / LE / M • Waves Of Passion / 1993 / PL / M • Wicked Wish / 1992 / LE / M • Wild Things #3 / 1992 / MET / M • Willing Women / 1993 / VD / C • WPINK-TV #4 / 1993 / PV / M

SIERRA BLAZE *see* Christine Woods

SIERRA SHARON *see Star Index I*

SIERRA STUART *see* Ciera

SIGI
Der Mosen-Pflucker / 1995 / KRM / M

SIGI BUCHNER *see Star Index I*

SIGRID RASMUSSEN *see Star Index I*

SIGRUN THEIL
Caballero Preview Tape #1 / 1982 / CA / C • Laura's Desires / 1978 / LA / M

SIKKI NIXX *(Edward Penishands, Sin (Sikki Nixx), Michael Shaw)*
Tattooed young male with an emaciated body. SO of Jeanna Fine at one point but now believed to be on the run from the mob.
Anal Starlets / 1991 / ROB / M • The Backpackers #2 / 1990 / IN / M • The Bad News Brat / 1991 / VI / M • Best Of Edward Penishands / 1993 / VT / C • Black Jack City #1 / 1991 / VT / M • Blue Jeans Brat / 1991 / VI / M • Brandy & Alexander / 1991 / VC / M • Cat & Mouse #1 / 1992 / XCI / M • Caught From Behind #15 / 1991 / HO / M • Cycle Sluts / 1992 / CC / M • Dark Star / 1991 / VI / M • Deep Cheeks #3 / 1992 / ROB / M • Deep Inside Jeanna Fine / 1992

/ VC / C • Deep Inside Victoria Paris / 1993 / VC / C • Edward Penishands #1 / 1991 / VT / M • Edward Penishands #2 / 1991 / VT / M • Edward Penishands #3 / 1991 / VT / M • The Fine Line / 1990 / SO / M • The God Daughter #4 / 1992 / AFV / M • Headbangers Balls / 1991 / PL / M • Hothouse Rose #1 / 1991 / VC / M • How To Deep Throat Your Lover / 1994 / A&E / M • In Your Face #2 / 1992 / PL / M • Let's Party / 1993 / VC / M • The Mark Of Zara / 1990 / XCI / M • The Midas Touch / 1991 / VT / M • More Dirty Debutantes #07 / 1991 / 4P / M • More Dirty Debutantes #08 / 1991 / 4P / M • The New Kid On The Block / 1991 / VD / M • Play School / 1990 / SO / M • Safecracker / 1991 / CC / M • Summer's End / 1991 / ROB / M • Valleys Of The Moon / 1991 / SC / M • Zane's World / 1992 / ZA / M • Zara's Revenge / 1991 / XCI / M

SILHOUETTE
The Keys Please / 1993 / TAO / B

SILJ CONJUS
Matrimony Intrigue / 1995 / WIV / M

SILK see **Brooke Lee**

SILKA
Up And Cummers #11 / 1994 / 4P / M

SILKY
Odyssey 30 Min: #346: Kitty, Silky, and Studz / 1993 / OD / M • Odyssey Triple Play #73: Oriental Sexpress / 1994 / OD / M

SILVA MISER see **Sylvia Benedict**

SILVER see **Savannah**

SILVER CAIN see **Savannah**

SILVER CANE see **Savannah**

SILVER DAWN see **Star Index I**

SILVER FORREST
Adult Video News 1992 Awards / 1992 / VC / M • Butt Freak #1 / 1992 / EA / M • Buttman's European Vacation #1 / 1991 / EA / M • Ebony Love / 1992 / VT / C • Lethal Passion / 1991 / PL / M • Penthouse: Satin & Lace #1 / 1992 / PET / F • Raunch #04: Silver Melts / 1991 / CC / M • Sean Michaels On The Road #05: Amsterdam And Rotterdam / 1993 / VT / M • Sean Michaels On The Road #06: France & Belgium / 1993 / VT / M • Silver Elegance / 1992 / VT / M • Silver Seduction / 1992 / VT / M • Silver Sensations / 1992 / VT / M • Sterling Silver / 1992 / CC / M

SILVER KANE see **Savannah**

SILVER MOON
Hot Sex In Bangkok / 1974 / MED / M

SILVER SATINE
Black Jailbait / 1984 / PL / M • Hot Chocolate #1 / 1984 / TAG / M

SILVER STAR
First Time At Cherry High / 1984 / VC / M • Good Girl, Bad Girl / 1984 / SE / M • Great Sexpectations / 1984 / VC / M • The Stimulators / 1983 / VC / M • The T & A Team / 1984 / VC / M

SILVER STUDD
Big Boob Celebration / 1994 / BTO / M

SILVIA
Bend Over Brazilian Babes #1 / 1993 / EA / M • Buttman's Orgies / 1996 / EA / M • European Sex TV / 1996 / EL / M • Lewd In Liverpool / 1995 / VC / M • Prague By Night #2 / 1996 / EA / M

SILVIA (MOHLMANN) see **Silvia Mohlmann**

SILVIA MAY
High Heeled & Horny #2 / 1995 / LBO / M

SILVIA MOHLMANN *(Sylvia Mohlmann, Sylvia (Mohlmann), Silvia (Mohlmann))*
Short dark brown hair, German, medium to large rock solid enhanced tits, passable face, lithe body, so so skin.
100% Amateur #02: Back Door And More / 1995 / OD / M • Blindfold / 1994 / SC / M • Girls Of Sorority Row / 1994 / VT / M • Girls Of The Athletic Department / 1995 / VT / M • Harry Horndog #30: Love Puppies #7 / 1995 / FPI / M • The New Butt Hunt #13 / 1995 / LEI / C • Private Eyes / 1995 / LE / M • Pussy Hunt #08 / 1995 / LEI / M • Rod Wood / 1995 / LE / M • Sgt. Peckers Lonely Hearts Club Gang Bang / 1995 / AMP / M • Snatch Masters #02 / 1994 / LEI / M • Streetwalkers / 1995 / HO / M

SILVIA RYDER *(Sylvia Ryder, Sylvia (Ryder))*
Brunette with medium/large sized slightly droopy natural tits. Pretty. Good skin. Very tight body and very tight waist. A butt that is the standard to which most porno actresses can only hope to equal now (1994) that Heather Hunter has retired. Nice personality. 19 years old in 1993 and supposedly not de-virginized until 18 (somehow I doubt it).
Anal Crack Master / 1994 / ROB / M • Anal Idol / 1994 / ROB / M • Babes Illustrated #2 / 1994 / IN / F • Cuntrol / 1994 / MID / F • New Ends #06 / 1994 / 4P / M • Satin & Lace / 1994 / WP / M • Secret Lives / 1994 / SC / F

SILVIE RAUCH
Dirty Business / 1995 / WIV / M

SILVIO
Private Film #15 / 1994 / OD / M

SILVIO BELLO see **Star Index I**

SILVIO EVANGELISTA
All Grown Up / 1996 / XC / M • Don Salvatore: The Last Sicilian / 1995 / XC / M • Virility / 1996 / XC / M

SILVIO LADO
Juliet & Romeo / 1996 / XC / M • Midnight Obsession / 1995 / XC / M • Robin Thief Of Wives / 1996 / XC / M

SILVIO LUDI
Essence Of A Woman / 1995 / ONA / M

SILYA
Video Virgins #16 / 1994 / NS / M

SIMEONE LA CRUZ see **Star Index I**

SIMON
Dick & Jane In San Francisco / 1996 / AVI / M • Sodomania #17: Simply Makes U Tingle / 1996 / EL / M • Thermonuclear Sex / 1996 / EL / M

SIMON (JENNIFER ST) see **Jennifer Stewart**

SIMON MCNULTY see **Star Index I**

SIMON SANTANA see **Star Index I**

SIMON SULLIVAN
Infidel / 1996 / WV / M

SIMONA
Limited Edition #15 / 1980 / AVC / M

SIMONA VALLI
1001 Nights / 1996 / IP / M • Anabolic Import #02: Anal X / 1991 / ANA / M • Della Borsa / 1995 / WIV / M • Doctor, Doctor: Show Me Everything / 1995 / VMX / M • The Erotic Adventures Of Alladin X / 1995 / IP / M • The Husband / 1995 / WIV / M • The Last Train #1 / 1995 / BHE / M • The Last Train #2 / 1995 / BHE / M • The Last Vamp / 1996 / IP / M • Le Parfum De Mathilde / 1994 / VI / M • Marco Polo / 1995

/ SC / M • Matrimony Intrigue / 1995 / WIV / M • A Merry Widow / 1996 / SPI / M • Miss Liberty / 1996 / IP / M • Paradise Villa / 1995 / WIV / M • Secrets Of Madame X #2 / 1995 / WIV / M • Seduction Italiano / 1995 / WIV / M • Sex Penitentiary / 1996 / XC / M

SIMONA WING
Beyond Your Wildest Dreams / 1980 / CAT / M • Playthings / 1980 / VC / M • VCA Previews #2 / 1988 / VC / C

SIMONE
Amazon Heat #1 / 1996 / CC / M • Asses Galore #1: From L.A. To Brazil / 1996 / DFI / M • Bi-Bi Love Amateurs #2 / 1993 / SFP / G • Blue Vanities #572 / 1995 / FFL / M • Bottoms Up #02 / 1983 / AVC / C • A Dirty Western #1 / 1992 / FD / F • A Girl's Affair #01 / 1992 / FD / F • A Midsummer Night's Bondage / 1993 / ARL / B • Nurse's Schoolgirl Enema / 1990 / BIZ / B • Painless Steel #4 / 1996 / FLV / M • Private Gold #06: Cape Town #2 / 1996 / OD / M • Private Stories #05 / 1995 / OD / M • Private Video Magazine #22 / 1995 / OD / M • Reel Life Video #38: Toy Stories / 1995 / RLF / F • Reel Life Video: Brunettes In Heat / 1995 / RLF / F • Saturday Matinee Series #3 / 1996 / VCX / C • Southern Belles #2 / 1995 / HOV / M • That's Erotic / 1979 / CV / C • Tongue In Cheek / 1994 / LE / M • Triple X Video Magazine #08 / 1995 / OD / M • Triple X Video Magazine #09 / 1995 / OD / M

SIMONE (DOMINIQUE) see **Dominique Simone**

SIMONE DEVON
Dresden Diary #01 / 1986 / BIZ / B • Dresden Diary #02 / 1986 / BIZ / B

SIMONE FALLIQUE see **Star Index I**

SIMONE JOHNSON see **Star Index I**

SIMONE LASH see **Rayne**

SIMONE SINCLAIR see **Star Index I**

SIMONE ST JOHN see **Star Index I**

SIMONE STEAVENS
FTV #02: Wrestling Friends / 1996 / FT / B

SIMONE TAYLOR see **Chelsea Ann**

SIMONE VALDEZ
Gina, The Foxy Lady / cr79 / COV / M

SIMPLE JOHNSON see **Scott Johnson**

SIN
The Butt Sisters Do Washington D.C. / 1995 / MID / M • Rebel Without A Condom / 1996 / ERA / M

SIN (SIKKI NIXX) see **Sikki Nixx**

SIN FASHION
Beaver & Buttcheeks / 1993 / DR / M

SINA SOLARA
Sperm Injection / 1995 / PL / M

SINAMEN
Filthy First Timers #6 / 1997 / EL / M

SINAMMON see **Lea**

SINAMON (CINNAMON) see **Cinnamon**

SINBAD O'CONNOR see **Star Index I**

SINDEE
Hard Core Beginners #05 / 1995 / LEI / M

SINDEE COXX *(Cindee Cox)*
Blonde with shoulder length hair, not a particularly tight waist, small to medium tits, 22 years old and de-virginized at 14, 5'5" tall, 36-24-36 (all in 1994). Supposedly **Video Virgins #12** was really her first video. According to interviews she has never done anal on screen (that is: with a dick—the plastic type only counts if you count a guy screwing a love doll as intercourse) and the

apparent anal in **Anal Anonymous** wasn't her. On re-review of the movie this statement seems accurate—the butt looks like Kaitlyn Ashley. Grew up in Long Island, NY and got married before moving to CA. About the end of 1995 her tits were enhanced to large cantaloupe size and she acquired a large tattoo on her left shoulder back.

100% Amateur #13: / 1995 / OD / M • 4 Of A Kind / 1995 / BON / B • Adam & Eve's House Party #1 / 1995 / VC / M • Adam & Eve's House Party #2: Bachelor Party / 1996 / VC / M • Alice In Analand / 1994 / SC / M • Allure / 1996 / WP / M • The Anal Adventures Of Bruce Seven / 1996 / BS / C • Anal Anonymous / 1994 / ZA / M • Anal Bad Girls / 1994 / ROB / F • Anal Secrets (After Dark) / 1994 / AFD / M • Asses Galore #2: No Remorse...No Repent / 1996 / DFI / M • Assy Sassy #2 / 1994 / ROB / F • Babe Watch Beach / 1996 / SC / M • Babes Illustrated #3 / 1995 / IN / F • Babes Illustrated #4 / 1995 / IN / F • Babewatch #2 / 1994 / CC / M • Bad Girls #5 / 1994 / GO / M • Badgirls #5: Maximum Babes / 1995 / VI / M • Badgirls #6: Ridin' Into Town / 1995 / VI / M • Badgirls #7: Lust Confined / 1995 / VI / M • Beach Ball / 1994 / SC / M • The Best Of Strippers Inc / 1996 / ONA / C • Betrayed / 1996 / WP / M • Bizarre Desires / 1995 / ROB / F • Bondage Fantasy #1 / 1995 / BON / B • Bondage Fantasy #2 / 1995 / BON / B • Brassiere To Eternity / 1994 / PEP / F • Breeders / 1996 / MET / M • Buffy Malibu's Nasty Girls #08 / 1995 / ANA / F • Bun Busters #15 / 1994 / LBO / M • Burbank Sperm Bank / 1996 / CIN / M • Busty Backdoor Nurses / 1996 / PL / M • Butt Jammers #01 / 1995 / SC / F • Butt Jammers #03 / 1995 / SC / F • Butt Jammers #04 / 1995 / SC / F • Butt Jammers #05 / 1996 / SC / F • Butt Sluts #3 / 1994 / ROB / F • Butt Sluts #4 / 1995 / ROB / F • Buttslammers #07: Indecent Decadence / 1994 / BS / F • Buttslammers #08: The Ultimate Invasion / 1994 / BS / F • Buttslammers #11: / 1996 / BS / F • Buttslammers #13: The Madness Continues / 1996 / BS / F • Call Me / 1995 / CV / M • Car Wash Angels / 1995 / VC / M • Carnival / 1995 / PV / M • Channel 69 / 1996 / CC / M • Cheerleader Strippers / 1996 / PE / M • Cloud 900 / 1996 / EYE / M • Cockpit / 1996 / SC / M • Creme De Femme / 1994 / 4P / F • Crew Sluts / 1994 / KWP / M • Deep Inside Juli Ashton / 1996 / VC / C • Deep Inside Kaitlyn Ashley / 1995 / VC / C • Deep Inside Misty Rain / 1995 / VC / C • Deep Inside Sindee Coxx / 1996 / VC / C • The Devil In Miss Jones #5: The Inferno / 1994 / VC / M • Dildo Debutantes / 1995 / CA / F • Dirty Doc's Housecalls #15 / 1994 / LV / M • Dirty Minds / 1996 / NIT / M • Dirty Work / 1995 / VC / M • Diva #1: Caught In The Act / 1996 / VC / F • The Divine Marquis / 1995 / ONA / B • Dominant Jean / 1996 / CC / M • Domination Nation / 1996 / VI / M • Dreams Of A Gigolo / 1996 / SNA / M • Dreams Of Desires / 1995 / ONA / M • Employee's Entrance In The Rear / 1996 / CC / M • Fantasy Chamber / 1994 / ULI / M • Finger Pleasures #4 / 1995 / PL / F • Firecrackers / 1994 / HW / M • Fleshmates / 1994 / ERA / M • From The Heart / 1996 / XCI / M • Full House / 1995 / BON / B •

Generation X / 1995 / WAV / M • Getting Personal / 1995 / PE / M • A Girl's Affair #06 / 1995 / FD / F • A Girl's Affair #07 / 1995 / FD / F • Girly Video Magazine #3 / 1995 / BEP / M • Golddiggers #3 / 1995 / VC / M • Happy Ass Lesbians / 1994 / ROB / F • Hardcore Fantasies #4 / 1996 / LV / M • Heavenly Yours / 1995 / CV / M • The Hollywood Starlet Search / 1995 / SC / M • Hornet's Nest / 1996 / ONA / M • Illicit Entry / 1995 / WAV / M • In The Scope / 1996 / VI / M • Indecent Interview / 1995 / PL / F • The Initiation / 1995 / FD / M • Intense Perversions #2 / 1996 / PL / M • Interview With A Milkman / 1996 / VI / M • Interview With A Vibrator / 1996 / WAV / M • Kym Wilde's On The Edge #19 / 1995 / RB / B • Kym Wilde's On The Edge #21 / 1995 / RB / B • Kym Wilde's On The Edge #22 / 1995 / RB / B • Legend #5: The Legend Continues / 1994 / LE / M • Lesbian Bitches #1 / 1994 / ROB / F • Lesbian Bitches #2 / 1994 / ROB / F • Lesbian Mystery Theatre: The Case Of The Deadly Dyke / 1994 / LIP / F • Lesbian Social Club / 1995 / ROB / F • Lost Angels / 1997 / WP / M • Love Me, Love My Butt #2 / 1994 / ROB / F • Lydia's Web / 1994 / TWP / B • Microslut / 1996 / TTV / M • Midnight Snacks / 1995 / KLP / M • The Mile High Club / 1995 / PL / M • Models Etc. / 1995 / LV / M • N.Y. Video Magazine #05 / 1995 / OUP / M • The Naked Truth / 1995 / VI / M • Natural Born Thriller / 1994 / CC / M • Naughty By Night / 1995 / DR / M • Night Nurses / 1995 / WAV / M • Nightmare On Lesbian Street / 1995 / LIP / F • Nightshift Nurses #2 / 1996 / VC / M • No Man's Land #11 / 1995 / VT / F • No Man's Land #13 / 1996 / VT / F • No Man's Land #16 / 1996 / VT / F • Nudist Colony Vacation / 1996 / NIT / M • Once A Slave / 1995 / HOM / B • Out Of Love / 1995 / VI / M • Party Pack #2 / 1994 / LE / F • The Portrait Of Dorie Grey / 1996 / KLP / M • Primal Instinct / 1996 / SNA / M • Primarily Yours / 1996 / CA / M • Prisoners Of Payne / 1995 / NIT / B • Pristine #1 / 1996 / CA / M • Pristine #2 / 1996 / CA / M • Punished Innocence / 1994 / BS / B • Pure Filth / 1995 / RV / M • Pussyman #12: Sticky Fingers / 1995 / SNA / M • Pussyman #14: Dreams Of A Gigolo / 1996 / SNA / M • Pussyman Auditions #10 / 1995 / SNA / M • R.E.A.L. #2 / 1994 / LV / F • Raunch #10: Uncut Jewel / 1994 / CC / M • Rebel Cheerleaders / 1995 / VI / M • Rock Me / 1994 / CC / M • The Savage / 1994 / SC / M • Secret Games / 1995 / BON / B • Secret Lives / 1994 / SC / F • The Seductive Secretary / 1995 / GO / M • Sex Alert / 1995 / PV / M • Sex Kitten / 1995 / SC / M • Sex Machine / 1995 / VI / M • Sex-A-Fari / 1994 / LV / M • Sexual Overdrive / 1996 / LE / M • Shaving Grace / 1996 / GO / M • Show & Tell / 1996 / VI / M • Sideshow Freaks / 1996 / ZA / M • Silver Screen Confidential / 1996 / WP / M • Sin City Cycle Sluts #1 / 1995 / SC / F • Sin City Cycle Sluts #2 / 1995 / SC / F • Sin Tax / 1996 / ZA / M • Sluthunt #3 / 1996 / BIP / F • Sorority Cheerleaders / 1996 / PL / M • Sorority Sex Kittens #3 / 1996 / VC / M • Star Flash / 1996 / VT / M • The Stiff / 1995 / WAV / M • Stowaway / 1995 / LE / M • Strap-On Sally #05: Chantilly's French Kiss / 1995 / PL / F • Strippers Inc. #1 / 1994 / ONA / M • Strippers Inc. #2 / 1994 /

ONA / M • Sweet Smell Of Excess / 1996 / CIN / M • The Temple Of Poon / 1996 / PE / M • The Time Machine / 1996 / WP / M • Trained By Payne / 1994 / ONA / B • Unchained Marylin / 1996 / VT / M • Under The Pink / 1994 / ROB / F • Upbeat Love #2 / 1995 / CV / M • Vice / 1994 / WAV / M • Video Dominatrix / 1996 / LON / B • Video Virgins #12 / 1994 / NS / M • Violation / 1996 / LE / M • The Violation Of Felecia / 1995 / JMP / F • Virgin Hotline / 1996 / LVP / F • Visual Fantasies / 1995 / LE / M • Wet Faces #1 / 1997 / SC / C • Wheel Of Obsession / 1996 / TWP / B • Where The Boys Aren't #6 / 1995 / VI / F • Whore'n / 1996 / AB / M • Wicked At Heart / 1995 / WP / M • Wicked Ways #2: Education Of A D.P. Virgin / 1995 / WP / M • Wicked Ways #3: An All-Anal Slutfest / 1995 / WP / M • Wide Open Spaces / 1995 / VC / F • XXX / 1996 / TEP / M • XXX Channel / 1996 / VT / M

SINDEE MOORE
Blue Vanities #016 (New) / 1988 / FFL / M • Blue Vanities #222 / 1994 / FFL / M

SINDEE WILLIAMS
Gangbang In The Fat Lane / 1996 / FC / M • When The Fat Lady Sings / 1996 / EX / M

SINDI RIDBER *see Star Index I*

SINDY
Sexy Country Girl / 1991 / PL / M

SINDY CLAIR
Sodomania #10: Euro/American Again / 1994 / EL / M

SINDY DIX
Huge Grant On The Sunset Strip / 1995 / EVN / M

SINDY WILLIAMS
Heavyweight Contenders / 1996 / HW / M

SINGH LOW *see Andrea True*

SINJA DESIREE
New Clits On The Block / 1995 / DBM / M

SINN DO ME *see Star Index I*

SINNAMON *(Cinnamon (Sinnamon))*
Black girl with straight shoulder length hair, gap in front teeth, protruding belly button, medium-sized empty skin tags for tits, not fat but not tight body. 20 years old in 1994 and de-virginized at 12.

Adventures Of The DP Boys: Backyard Boogie / 1994 / HW / M • Adventures Of The DP Boys: Chocolate City / 1994 / HW / M • Alex Jordan's First Timers #06 / 1994 / OD / M • Amateur Black: Starlets / 1995 / SUF / M • America's Raunchiest Home Videos #48: / 1993 / ZA / M • Anal Nymphettes / 1995 / LIP / F • Analtown USA #02 / 1995 / NIT / M • Ass Masters (Leisure) #05 / 1995 / LEI / M • Babes Of The Bay #2 / 1995 / LIP / F • Behind The Black Door #3 / 1994 / MID / M • The Best Little Whorehouse In Tijuana / 1995 / HBE / M • The Black Butt Sisters Do Baltimore / 1995 / MID / M • The Black Butt Sisters Do Boston / 1995 / MID / M • The Black Butt Sisters Do Detroit / 1995 / MID / M • The Black Butt Sisters Do Los Angeles / 1995 / MID / M • The Black Butt Sisters Do New York / 1995 / MID / M • Black Casting Couch #2 / 1994 / WP / M • Black Fantasies #09 / 1995 / HW / M • Black Fantasies #10 / 1995 / HW / M • Black Fantasies #11 / 1996 / HW / M • Black Hollywood Amateurs #03 / 1995 / MID / M • Black Hollywood Amateurs #11 / 1995 / MID / M • Black Hollywood Amateurs #14 / 1995 / MID / M • Black Hollywood Amateurs #21 / 1996 / MID / M • Black Juice Bombs / 1996 / NIT / C • Black Nurse Fantasies / 1994 / CA / M • Black Orgies #21 / 1994 / GO / M • Black Orgies #26 / 1994 / GO / M • Black Orgies #29 / 1994 / GO / M • Black Talez N Da Hood / 1996 / APP / M • Black Women, White Men #7 / 1995 / FC / M • Brooklyn Nights / 1994 / OD / M • Chocolate Bunnies #01 / 1995 / LBO / C • Chocolate Bunnies #02 / 1995 / LBO / C • Chocolate Bunnies #04 / 1995 / LBO / C • Cracklyn / 1994 / HW / M • Crazy Times / 1995 / BS / B • The Cumm Brothers #03: Go To Traffic School / 1994 / OD / M • Da Booty Call / 1994 / HW / M • Dream's House Party / 1995 / HW / M • The Ebony Connection #2 / 1994 / LBO / C • Ebony Erotica #22: Fade To Black / 1994 / GO / M • Ebony Erotica #23: Black Betty / 1994 / GO / M • First Time Lesbians #19 / 1994 / JMP / F • Fishbone / 1994 / WIV / F • Long From Dong / 1995 / FH / M • M Series #22 / 1994 / LBO / M • M Series #27 / 1994 / LBO / M • Mr. Peepers Amateur Home Videos #88: A For Effort / 1994 / LBO / M • Nasty Newcummers: Black Edition / 1995 / MET / M • Odyssey Triple Play #90: Black & White In Loving Color / 1995 / OD / M • The Players Club / 1994 / HW / M • Pumps In Da Rump #1 / 1994 / HW / M • Slaves Of Artemis / 1996 / BON / B • Sleazy Streets / 1995 / PEP / M • Sugar Daddies / 1995 / FPI / M • Summer Of '69 / 1994 / MID / M • Sweet Black Cherries #3 / 1996 / TTV / M • The Sweet Sweet Back #2: Double Thaanng Dat Black Hole / 1994 / FH / M • Tails From The Hood / 1995 / FH / M • Video Virgins #13 / 1994 / NS / M • White Boys & Black Bitches / 1995 / ROB / M • Winter Heat / 1994 / MID / M • Women Of Color #2 / 1994 / ANA / M • The World's Biggest Gang Bang #1 / 1995 / FPI / M

SINTHIA BLACK
American Dream Girls #2 / 1994 / LEI / M

SIO BHAM HUNTER *see* **Siobhan Hunter**

SIOBHAN HUNTER *(Shabona Hunter, Kim Wong, Sio Bham Hunter, Shobhan Hunter, Sibban Hunter)*
Tall brunette with small tits and not a tight body (but not fat). A bit flat on the rear end. Facially, she wouldn't win any beauty contest but she's not ugly. Kim Wong is from **Best Little Whorehouse in Hong Kong**. Sio Bham Hunter is from **Sex Derby**.
10 1/2 Weeks / 1986 / SE / M • Adultery / 1986 / DR / M • Angel's Back / 1988 / IN / M • Back To Rears / 1988 / VI / M • Barbara Dare's Bad / 1988 / SE / C • Barbara Dare's Prime Choice / 1987 / SE / C • Bedroom Thighs / 1986 / VXP / M • The Best Little Whorehouse In Hong Kong / 1987 / SE / M • Bi American Style / cr85 / MET / G • Bi-Heat #08 To #10 / 1988 / ZA / G • The Bitch Is Back / 1988 / FAN / M • Bizarre Dildo Obsession / 1989 / BIZ / B • Bodies In Heat #2 / 1989 / DR / M • The Brat / 1986 / VI / M • Breakin' In / 1986 / WV / M • Candy Stripers #3 / 1986 / AR / M • Crocodile Blondee #1 / 1987 / CA0 / M • Debbie Does Dishes #3 / 1987 / AVC / M • Deep Inside Trading / 1986 / AR / M • Despicable Dames / 1986 / CC / M • Divorce Court Expose #1 / 1986 / VD / M • Divorce Court Expose #2 / 1987 / VD / M • Dreams Of Desire / 1988 / BIZ / F • The Erotic Ad-

ventures Of Chi Chi Chan / 1988 / VWA / M • The Flirt / 1987 / VWA / M • Frankenhunter, Queen Of The Porno Zombies / 1989 / GMI / M • Fresh! / 1987 / VXP / M • Girls Together / 1985 / GO / C • The Golden Gals / 1989 / BTO / M • Good Evening Vietnam / 1987 / WV / M • Hard Times / 1990 / GLE / M • The Heiress / 1988 / VI / M • Hidden Fantasies / 1986 / VD / M • Honeybuns #2: Grecian Formula / 1987 / WV / C • Hot Property / 1989 / EXH / C • Hotel California / 1986 / WV / M • Hottest Ticket / 1987 / WV / C • Inside Sharon Mitchell / 1989 / ZA / C • Krazy 4 You / 1987 / 4P / M • Krystal Balling / 1988 / PL / M • Lesbian Fantasies / 1990 / BIZ / F • Lilith Unleashed / 1986 / VC / M • A Little Bit Of Honey / 1987 / WET / M • Little Red Riding Hood / 1988 / WV / M • Little Shop Of Whores / 1987 / VI / M • Living Doll / 1987 / WV / M • Loose Ends #3 / 1987 / BS / M • A Lover For Susan / 1987 / CLV / M • Male Domination #14 / 1990 / BIZ / C • Moans & Groans / 1987 / 4P / M • Moonlusting #1 / 1986 / WV / M • Moonlusting #2 / 1987 / WV / M • Nasty Lovers / 1987 / SE / C • Nightshift Nurses #1 / 1988 / VC / M • Nudes At Eleven #2 / 1987 / AVC / M • Nurse's Schoolgirl Enema / 1990 / BIZ / B • The Oddest Couple / 1986 / VC / M • Only The Best Of Barbara Dare / 1990 / CV / C • Open House (Vid Exc) / 1989 / VEX / M • Oral Majority #03 / 1986 / WV / C • Oral Majority #04 / 1987 / WV / C • Oral Majority #05 / 1987 / WV / C • Oral Majority #06 / 1988 / WV / C • Oversexed / 1986 / VXP / M • Parted Lips / 1986 / QX / M • Pink Baroness / 1988 / VWA / M • Pink Clam / 1986 / RLV / M • Playpen / 1987 / VC / M • The Pleasure Chest / 1988 / VWA / M • Pretty Peaches #2 / 1987 / VC / M • Princess Of Penetration / 1988 / VXP / M • Punished By Two / 1990 / BIZ / B • Raging Hormones / 1988 / VXP / M • Raising Hell / 1987 / VD / M • Rambone: The First Time / 1985 / JOH / M • Raw Talent #3 / 1988 / VC / M • The Red Head / 1989 / VWA / M • The Right Tool For The Job / 1988 / VXP / M • Rio Heat / 1986 / VD / M • Robofox #2 / 1988 / FAN / M • The Screwables / 1992 / RUM / M • Secret Mistress / 1986 / VD / M • Secret Of My Sex-Cess / 1988 / CV / M • Sensual Escape / 1988 / FEM / M • Seven Minutes In Heaven / 1986 / VXP / M • Sex Crimes 2084 / 1985 / SE / M • Sex Derby / 1986 / GO / M • Sex Styles Of The Rich & Famous / 1986 / VXP / M • Sex Tips For Modern Women / 1987 / VXP / M • Sexually Altered States / 1986 / VC / M • Shoot To Thrill / 1988 / VWA / M • Simply Outrageous / 1989 / VC / C • Soft Warm Rain / 1987 / VD / M • Still The Brat / 1988 / VI / M • Summer Lovers / 1987 / WET / M • Suzie Creamcheese / 1988 / VWA / M • Sweet Revenge / 1986 / ZA / M • Sweet Spread / 1986 / VXP / M • The Sweet Spurt Of Youth / 1988 / WV / M • Temptations Of The Flesh / 1986 / VD / M • Three Daughters / 1986 / FEM / M • Tracey And The Bandit / 1987 / LA / M • Twentysomething #1 / 1988 / VI / M • Twentysomething #2 / 1988 / VI / M • VCA Previews #4 / 1988 / VC / C • Viper's Place / 1988 / VD / M • Wet Dreams 2001 / 1987 / VD / M • Where The Sun Never Shines / 1990 / IN / C • Wild Oral Erotica / 1988 / VD / C • Wimps / 1987

/ LIV / S • A Woman's Touch / 1988 / ZA / F • Wrong Arm Of The Law / 1987 / ZA / M • Young Nympho's / 1986 / VD / M

SIOUXSIE SAX
Cheeks #2: The Bitter End / 1989 / CC / M

SIR BIFFORD BOSCO
Mistress In Training / 1996 / STM / B

SIR EDMOND *see* **Star Index I**

SIR GEORGE PAYNE *see* **George Payne**

SIR JOHN
Black Masters: Seduction In Bondage / 1996 / GOT / B

SIR KENNETH *see* **Star Index I**

SIR MICHAEL
Abducted For Pleasure / 1990 / BIZ / B • Auction #1 / 1992 / BIZ / B • Auction #2 / 1992 / BIZ / B • The Best Of Flame / 1994 / BIZ / C • The Best Of Hot Heels / 1992 / BIZ / B • Bizarre Master Series: Sir Michael / 1992 / BIZ / C • Bond-Aid / 1992 / STM / B • Bondage Proposal / 1993 / STM / B • Bondage Seduction / 1992 / STM / B • Bound Biker Babes #1 / 1991 / STM / B • Bound Biker Babes #2 / 1993 / STM / B • Bunnie's Bondage Land / 1994 / STM / C • Defiance: Spanking And Beyond / 1993 / PRE / B • Defiance: The Ultimate Spanking / 1993 / BIZ / B • Disciples Of Bondage / 1992 / STM / B • The Education Of Karen / 1993 / BIZ / B • First Training / 1987 / BIZ / B • Hot Shoes / 1992 / BIZ / B • Incredible Dreams #1 / 1992 / BIZ / B • Incredible Dreams #2 / 1992 / BIZ / B • Latex Submission #1 / 1992 / BIZ / B • Latex Submission #2 / 1992 / BIZ / B • Leather And Tether / 1993 / STM / C • Leather Lair #3 / 1993 / STM / B • Lessons In Humiliation / 1991 / BIZ / B • Male Domination #10 / 1990 / BIZ / C • Master, Mistress And Slaves / cr85 / BIZ / B • Obey Me Bitch #1 / 1992 / BIZ / B • Obey Me Bitch #2 / 1992 / BIZ / B • Obey Me Bitch #3 / 1992 / BIZ / B • Obey Me Bitch #4 / 1993 / BIZ / B • Office Heels / 1992 / BIZ / B • Profiles In Discipline #02: Naughty Angel / 1994 / STM / C • Rendezvous With Destiny / 1984 / LA / B • Return To Leather Lair / 1993 / STM / B • School For Wayward Wives / 1993 / BIZ / B • Show Them No Mercy #1 / 1991 / STM / B • Show Them No Mercy #2 / 1991 / STM / B • Spanked Ecstasy / 1991 / BIZ / B • Spanking Tutor / 1985 / BIZ / B • Storehouse Of Agony #1 / 1993 / BIZ / B • Storehouse Of Agony #2 / 1992 / BIZ / B • Submission Of Susie / 1993 / BIZ / B • TV Husband, Submissive Wife / cr83 / BIZ / B • TVs In Trouble #2 / 1991 / BIZ / G • Working Girls In Bondage / 1991 / BIZ / B

SIR MIDIAN
Jacklyn's Attitude Adjustment / 1995 / JAM / B

SIR STEPHEN
Painful Mistake (Blowfish) / 1994 / BLP / B

SIR TOMMY
Made In The Hood / 1995 / HBE / M

SIR WILLIAM
Damaged Goods / 1995 / GOT / B • Masters Of Dominance / 1996 / GOT / C • Playthings / 1995 / GOT / B • Very Bad Girls / 1995 / GOT / B

SIRENA
Horny Brits Take It In The Bum / 1997 / ROB / M

SIRIA
Lovin' Spoonfuls #3 / 1995 / 4P / C • More Dirty Debutantes #15 / 1992 / 4P / M

SISKA *see* **Chelsea Lynx**

SISSY
Amateur Hours #19 / 1990 / AFI / M • The Best Of The Big Boob Battles / 1993 / CDP / C • Blue Vanities #529 / 1993 / FFL / M • Mike Hott: #142 Sissy And Chamice #1 / 1991 / MHV / F • Mike Hott: #143 Sissy And Chamice #2 / 1991 / MHV / F

SISSY CANE *see* **Star Index I**

SISSY PIRJO-LEENA
All American Super Bitches / 1984 / BIZ / B • Porno Screentests / 1982 / VC / M

SISTER X *see* **Star Index I**

SITINA
Vivid At Home #01 / 1994 / VI / M

SKARLETTE
Hollywood Amateurs #05 / 1994 / MID / M

SKEETER *see* **Star Index I**

SKEETS STODDARD
Blue Magic / 1981 / QX / M

SKIP
Shaved Submission / 1996 / GAL / B

SKIP BENNET
Erotic Interlude / 1981 / CA / M

SKIP BROOKS
Bedtime Video #07 / 1984 / GO / M

SKIP BURTON
Linda Lovelace For President / 1975 / ... / C

SKIP CANASI
Star 84: Tina Marie / 1984 / VEX / M

SKIP CHESTER
The Loves Of Mary Jane / 1989 / BWV / C • A Touch Of Sex / 1972 / AR / M

SKIP JONES *see* **Mark Saunders**

SKIP LAYTON *see* **Blake Palmer**

SKIP ROBBINS *see* **Blake Palmer**

SKIP SHIT
Erotic Ecstasy / 1994 / MAX / M • In Search Of The Brown Eye: An Anal Adventure / 1995 / MAX / M • Odyssey Triple Play #79: Dildos Dykes & Dicks / 1994 / OD / M • Private Request / 1994 / GLI / M

SKIP SMITH
My Wildest Date / 1995 / HO / M

SKIP STOKEY *see* **Blake Palmer**

SKIP STROKE *see* **Blake Palmer**

SKIPPER WICE
Limo Connection / 1983 / VC / M • Tight Assets / cr80 / VC / M

SKY
Fantasy In Oil #2 / 1996 / CAW / B • Hot Body Competition: Bikinis & Bikes Contest / 1996 / CG / F

SKY SAND *see* **Star Index I**

SKY WALKERR
Up And Cummers #25 / 1995 / 4P / M

SKYE *see* **Star Index I**

SKYE BLUE
A very hard nut crusher. 5'4" and 109lbs in 1996.
Assent Of A Woman / 1993 / DR / M • Awakening Of The Cats / 1994 / NAP / B • Backdoor Brides #4 / 1993 / PV / M • Battling Bitches #2 / 1995 / BIZ / B • Beyond Reality #1 / 1995 / EXQ / M • Beyond The Borderline / 1996 / STM / B • Bi Bitches In Heat / 1996 / BIZ / F • Big Knockers #06 / 1994 / TV / M • Big Knockers #09 / 1995 / TV / M • Big Knockers #15 / 1995 / TV / M • Big Knockers #17 / 1995 / TV / M • Big Knockers #20 / 1995 / TV / C • Big Knockers #21: Best Of Lesbian #2 / 1995 / TV / C • Borderline (Starmaker) / 1995 / STM / B • Bright Tails #5 / 1995 / STP / B • Broadway Babes / 1993 / FH / F • Burning Desires /

1994 / BS / B • Buttslammers #07: Indecent Decadence / 1994 / BS / F • Casanova #1 / 1993 / SC / M • Casanova #2 / 1993 / SC / M • Chronicles Of Pain #2 / 1996 / BIZ / B • College Cruelty / 1995 / FFE / B • Compete And Seduce / 1994 / NAP / B • Dark Secrets / 1995 / MID / S • Date With A Mistress / 1995 / BIZ / B • Designated Hitters / 1995 / PRE / B • Dirty Bob's #18: Under The Boardwalk! / 1995 / FLP / S • Dirty Bob's #19: Over The Boardwalk! / 1995 / FLP / S • The Domination Of Summer #1 / 1994 / BIZ / B • The Domination Of Summer #2 / 1994 / BIZ / B • Don't Try This At Home / 1994 / FPI / M • Double D Dykes #27 / 1995 / GO / F • Down And Out / 1995 / PRE / B • Dresden Diary #11: Endangered Secrets / 1994 / BIZ / B • Dresden Diary #12: / 1995 / BIZ / B • Dresden Diary #13: / 1995 / BIZ / B • Drop Outs / 1995 / PRE / B • The Enema Bandit / 1994 / BIZ / B • The Enema Bandit Returns / 1995 / BIZ / B • The Enema Bandit Strikes Again / 1995 / BIZ / B • Enema Obedience #2 / 1994 / BIZ / B • Fantasy Flings #03 / 1995 / WP / M • Flush Dance / 1996 / PRE / C • Foot Masters / 1995 / PRE / B • Funny Ladies / 1996 / PRE / B • Future Doms #1 / 1996 / BIZ / B • Future Doms #2 / 1996 / BIZ / B • Girls With Curves #2 / 1994 / CV / M • Hell Cats / 1996 / HO / F • Hello Norma Jeane / 1994 / VT / M • Hidden Obsessions / 1992 / BFP / M • High Heeled & Horny #1 / 1994 / LBO / M • Hostile Takeover: Bitch Bosses / 1995 / BIZ / B • Kittens #6 / 1994 / CC / F • Leather Bound Dykes From Hell #6 / 1995 / BIZ / B • Leg...Ends #14 / 1995 / PRE / F • Lesbian Kink Trilogy #2 / 1995 / STM / F • Licking Legends #1 / 1992 / LE / F • Licking Legends #2 / 1992 / LE / F • Lipstick Lesbians #1: Massage Parlor Dykes / 1994 / ZA / F • Major Exposure / 1995 / PL / F • Mellon Man #02 / 1994 / AVI / M • The Most Dangerous Game / 1996 / HO / M • Nasty Dancers #2 / 1996 / STM / B • New Faces, Hot Bodies #18 / 1995 / STP / M • Northwest Pecker Trek #4: Laid In Latte Land / 1994 / LBO / M • Notorious / 1992 / SC / M • Odyssey 30 Min: #244: / 1992 / OD / F • Over The Borderline / 1995 / STM / B • Panties / 1993 / VD / M • Porsche Lynn, Vault Mistress #1 / 1994 / BIZ / B • Porsche Lynn, Vault Mistress #2 / 1994 / BIZ / B • Positively Pagan #06 / 1993 / ATA / M • Primal / 1995 / MET / M • Prisoners Of Pain / 1994 / BIZ / B • Pussy Pursuits: The Best Of Skye And Summer / 1995 / AMX / C • Radical Affairs Video Magazine #04 / 1992 / ME / M • Raw Footage / 1996 / VC / M • Revenge Of The Brat / 1995 / NAP / B • Rollover / 1996 / NIT / M • Shelby's Forbidden Fears / 1995 / BIZ / B • Skye's The Limit / 1995 / BON / B • Soap Opera Sluts / 1996 / AFI / M • Sordid Stories / 1994 / AMP / M • Spiked Heel Diaries #4 / 1995 / BIZ / B • The Submission Of Alicia Rio / 1996 / BIZ / B • Summer's Surrender / 1996 / STM / B • Takin' It To The Limit #9: Rear Action View / 1996 / BS / M • Tame The Wild Brat / 1995 / NAP / B • To Snatch A Thief / 1996 / BON / B • Toe Tales #31 / 1995 / GOT / B • Toe Tales #36 / 1996 / GOT / B • Toe-Tail Torture / 1996 / STM / B • A Touch Of Leather / 1994 / BS / B • The Training #2 / 1994 / BIZ / B • The Training

#3 / 1995 / BIZ / B • Tropical Bondage Vacation / 1996 / STM / B • Wasted / 1995 / PRE / B • Waterworld: The Enema Club / 1996 / BIZ / B • What's A Nice Girl Like You Doing In An Anal Movie? / 1995 / AMP / M • WPINK-TV #4 / 1993 / PV / M

SKYE JOHNSON
Our Trespasses / 1996 / AWV / G

SKYE RYDER
After The Party / 1993 / AMF / B • Final Test / 1993 / GOT / B • Forbidden Ways / 1994 / GOT / B • Masters Of Dominance / 1996 / GOT / C • Severe Penalties / 1993 / GOT / B • Show No Mercy / 1993 / GOT / B • Spanking It Red / 1993 / GOT / B • Taming Of Laura / 1994 / GOT / B • Toe Tales #05 / 1993 / GOT / B • Toe Tales #08 / 1993 / GOT / B • Toe Tales #10 / 1993 / GOT / B • Tormented / 1993 / GOT / B • VGA: Down In Dorothy's Dungeon / 1993 / VGA / B • VGA: Mistress Cherri's Pool Party / 1993 / VGA / B

SKYLA WOODS
Pretty brunette with long straight hair, tiny/small tits, lithe body and a tattoo. What sort of tattoo, you might ask? One that has to be seen to be believed. Imagine shaving the girl's pubic hair (actually you can't tell if her pubic hair is completely shaven) and tattooing in place both back and front a pair of blue/black lace (with some design work) panties. The back is slightly higher than panties would be, forming an image of a triangular necklace with the bottom of the triangle pointing to her ass crack, and the sides don't go all the way around. Freak appeal and a pity on an otherwise attractive girl.
Cumback Pussy #5: Groopin' / 1996 / EL / M • Dick & Jane's Video Mail: From Virginville (#4) / 1996 / AVI / M • Drop Sex: Wipe The Floor / 1997 / JLP / M • Macin' #2: Macadocious / 1996 / SMP / M • More Dirty Debutantes #62 / 1997 / SBV / M • Sexhibition #2 / 1996 / SUF / M • Sinboy #3: The Island Of Dr. Moron / 1996 / SC / M • Undercover / 1996 / VC / M

SKYY BLEAU
AVP #7030: Working It Up, Working It Out / 1991 / AVP / M

SLAMMA JAMMA
Git Yo' Ass On Da Bus! / 1996 / HW / M

SLAVE 59
Taped, Tied & Tormented / 1996 / ATO / B

SLAVE ANGEL *see* **Star Index I**

SLAVE BEA
Bondage Memories #02 / 1993 / BON / C • Slave Bea, Basement Bound / 1993 / BON / B

SLAVE BERNIE
Dungeon Play / 1995 / IBN / B • Manhater / 1995 / IBN / B • To Serve Keisha / 1995 / IBN / B

SLAVE BILL
I Command! You Obey! / 1994 / TVI / B

SLAVE BILLY
Task Mistress / 1995 / IBN / B

SLAVE BOB *see* **Star Index I**

SLAVE BOY
The New Submit To Me #1 / 1996 / SY / B

SLAVE CARL
Battling Mistresses / 1995 / IBN / B • Sexual HerASSment / 1995 / IBN / B • Stalker's Punishment / 1995 / IBN / B

SLAVE CHRIS
The Computer Date / 1994 / ATO / B • Mag-

ical Mistresses: Jennifer And Artemis / 1993 / RSV / B • Mother & Daughter From Hell / 1996 / ATO / B

SLAVE D.
Spanknight #01 / 1992 / RB / B • Spanknight #02 / 1992 / RB / B

SLAVE DANNY BOY
Corporal Affair #1 / 1995 / IBN / B • Corporal Affair #2 / 1995 / IBN / B • Power Games / 1992 / STM / B • Profiles In Discipline #02: Naughty Angel / 1994 / STM / C

SLAVE DAVE
Velvet / 1995 / SPI / M

SLAVE DAVID see Star Index I

SLAVE DAWN
Learn Your Lessons / 1992 / BIZ / B

SLAVE DENNIS
Play Mistress For Me / 1995 / IBN / B

SLAVE DONNIE
Blonde Bombshells / 1992 / VER / B • Cruel Heels / 1991 / SSP / B • Dazzling Dominants / 1991 / RSV / B • Mistress Elle's Golden Cuffs / 1993 / RSV / B • Mistress Elle's Transgression Of Reality / 1993 / RSV / B • A Session With Mistress Sondra / 1990 / RSV / B

SLAVE ED
Bizarre Styles / 1981 / ALP / B

SLAVE ELLIS see Star Index I

SLAVE FRANK
Learn Your Lessons / 1992 / BIZ / B

SLAVE GARY
Jennifer's Revenge / 1995 / IBN / B

SLAVE GEORGE see Star Index I

SLAVE ILANA see Star Index I

SLAVE IRA
Ira's Ordeal / 198? / BON / B

SLAVE JACK
Ariana's Domain / 1996 / GOT / B • The Collector / cr83 / BIZ / B • Deranged / 1994 / GOT / B • Private Quarters / 1987 / BIZ / B • Toe Tales #19 / 1994 / GOT / B • Toe Tales #24 / 1995 / GOT / C

SLAVE JACKIE
Bondage Memories #03 / 1994 / BON / C • Taught To Obey / 1988 / BIZ / B

SLAVE JAMES
Dinner With Andres / 1991 / Z/N / B • Dungeon Builder's Punishment / 1994 / STM / B • Playing At Leah's / 1994 / LLF / B • Rendezvous With A BBS Mistress / 1995 / IBN / B • Secrets In The Attic #2: Extreme Measures / 1994 / STM / B • Secrets in the Attic #4: Purchased And Punished / 1994 / STM / B • Sexual HerASSment / 1995 / IBN / B • TS Trains TV Hubby / 1994 / STM / G

SLAVE JERRY
Cry Babies (Gotham) / 1995 / GOT / B • Flames Of Submission / 1995 / GOT / B • Slave Traders / 1995 / GOT / B • Toe Tales #22 / 1995 / GOT / B

SLAVE JIM
Annie Sprinkle's Fantasy Salon / 1990 / VER / B • Dazzling Dominants / 1991 / RSV / B • French-Pumped Femmes #1 / 1989 / RSV / G

SLAVE JOHN see Star Index I

SLAVE JOSEPH
Bizarre Mistress Series: Mistress Jacqueline / 1992 / BIZ / C • The Many Faces of Mistress Jacqueline / 1990 / BIZ / B • Natural Born Dominants / 1995 / IBN / B

SLAVE JULIAN see Star Index I

SLAVE JULIETTE see Star Index I

SLAVE K. see Scott Mallory

SLAVE KEN

Smothered / 1995 / LLF / B

SLAVE MARTA
Red Boot Diaries / 1992 / STM / B

SLAVE MATT
In Your Face / 1995 / IBN / B • MatboXer / 1995 / IBN / B • Payback Time / 1995 / IBN / B • Tied, Trampled, Terminated / 1995 / IBN / B

SLAVE MAX
Dungeon Madness / 1995 / IBN / B

SLAVE MICHAEL
Learn Your Lessons / 1992 / BIZ / B • Toe Tales #29 / 1995 / GOT / B

SLAVE NIKKI
The Analyst / 1990 / SOR / B

SLAVE P.O.D. see Star Index I

SLAVE PETER see Star Index I

SLAVE ROXANNE
I Command! You Obey! / 1994 / TVI / B

SLAVE S
Sessions With A Slave / cr90 / BON / B

SLAVE SCOTT
Lazy Boy / 1995 / ATO / B

SLAVE SEAN
Forgive Them Not #01 / 1993 / STM / B • Forgive Them Not #02 / 1993 / STM / B • Profiles In Discipline #04: Mistress Domino / 1994 / STM / C

SLAVE SLUT
Real Breasts Real Torment / 1995 / BON / C • Real People Real Bondage #2 / 1996 / BON / C

SLAVE SOPHIA
Visit To Mistress Debbie's / 1991 / COC / B

SLAVE SPANKY
Blow Below The Belt / 1995 / GOT / B • Degraded / 1995 / GOT / B • Deranged / 1994 / GOT / B • The Dominator / 1992 / GOT / B • Enslaved / 1995 / GOT / B • Mistress For Bad Boys / 1993 / GOT / B • Sailor Beware / 1993 / GOT / B • Toe Tales #02 / 1992 / GOT / B • Toe Tales #09 / 1993 / GOT / B • Toe Tales #12 / 1994 / GOT / C • Toe Tales #17 / 1994 / GOT / B • Toe Tales #18 / 1994 / GOT / B • Toe Tales #31 / 1995 / GOT / B • Toe Tales #32 / 1996 / GOT / B • Toe Tales #34 / 1996 / GOT / B • Toe Tales #36 / 1996 / GOT / B • Toe Tales #37 / 1996 / GOT / B • Toe Tales #39 / 1996 / GOT / B • Transvestite Ordeal / 1994 / GOT / G • Web Of The Mistress / 1994 / GOT / B

SLAVE STEPHANIE see Star Index I

SLAVE TONY see Star Index I

SLAVE VINNIE
Clear And Present Anger / 1995 / IBN / B

SLAVE WALTER
12 Steps To Domination / 1995 / IBN / B • Always Bet On Blond / 1995 / IBN / B • Amazon Trample / 1995 / IBN / B • Behavior Modification / 1995 / IBN / B • Bound To Like It / 1995 / IBN / B • The Controller / 1995 / IBN / B • Demolition Dom / 1995 / IBN / B • Dominant Neighbors From Hell / 1995 / IBN / B • Dominant Smoker / 1995 / IBN / B • Feminine Brutality / 1995 / IBN / B • German Marks #1 / 1995 / IBN / B • German Marks #2 / 1995 / IBN / B • The Goddesses Must Be Crazy / 1995 / IBN / B • Interrogation Dom #2 / 1995 / IBN / B • Kickin' Ass / 1995 / IBN / B • No Justice...No Piece / 1995 / IBN / B • Obedience Training / 1995 / IBN / B • Operation: Mistress / 1995 / IBN / B • Sensuous Asian Dominance / 1995 / IBN / B • To Serve Keisha / 1995 / IBN / B • Trample Bimbo /

1995 / IBN / B • True Ties / 1995 / IBN / B • A Whole Lotta Crushin' Going On / 1995 / IBN / B

SLAVE WILLIE
Knotty Nurse Domination / 1995 / IBN / B

SLAVE X see Star Index I

SLAVE YOHAN
The Fetish Files / 1995 / IBN / B

SLAVE ZERO see Star Index I

SLAVEBOY MARK
Housebreaking / 1995 / GOT / B

SLAVICA
Lust At First Bite / 1978 / VC / M

SLEDGE HAMMER
Intense Perversions #1 / 1995 / PL / M • Intense Perversions #2 / 1996 / PL / M

SLEEPIE LA BEEF
Sunny / 1979 / VC / M

SLICK
Bi-Bi Love Amateurs #2 / 1993 / SFP / G

SLIM GRADY see Bud Wise

SLIM GREEN see Star Index I

SLIM JIM
Black Fantasies #11 / 1996 / HW / M • Black Knockers #06 / 1995 / TV / M • Perverted Stories #06 / 1996 / JMP / M

SLISH
Kitty Foxx's Kinky Kapers #02 / 1995 / TTV / M

SLOAN
Spanked In Spades / 1995 / STM / B

SLOANE see Star Index I

SLOANE WINTERS
Bondage Memories #04 / 1994 / BON / C • Bound To Tease #5 / 1990 / BON / C • Lesbian Sex, Power & Money / 1994 / STM / F • Nancy Crew Meets Dr. Freidastein / cr90 / BON / B • Spanking, Spanking And More / 1990 / BON / B • Wild Thing / 1989 / BON / B

SLONE
Bobby Hollander's Rookie Nookie #10 / 1993 / MET / M

SLUG MARTIN see Star Index I

SLY
Attention: Ropes & Gags / 1994 / BON / B • Patio Bondage / 1994 / BON / B

SMART ALEC TIM
House Of Pain / 1996 / OUP / B

SMITH WESSON see Star Index I

SMOKEY
Horny Henry's Swinging Adventures / 1994 / TTV / M

SMOKEY UNIT see Star Index I

SMOOTHIE F.
Made In The Hood / 1995 / HBE / M

SMOTHERED MALE see Star Index I

SNAGGLE PUSSY
Gum Me Bare #1 / 1994 / GLI / M

SNAKE see Star Index I

SNOW see Angel Snow

SOCORRO CHATUYE
Ona Zee's Learning The Ropes #06: Lesbian Bondage / 1992 / ONA / B • Ona Zee's Learning The Ropes #07: At Lady Laura's / 1992 / ONA / B

SOFIA see Sophia

SOFIA FERRARI (Sophia Ferrari, Nikki (Sofia F.))
Italian. Not too pretty with large enhanced tits and a womanly body. Born Mar 4, 1966, San Remo, Italy; de-virginized at 19.
Adam & Eve's House Party #4 / 1996 / VC / M • The Adventures Of Peeping Tom #1 / 1996 / OD / M • Alexis Goes To Hell / 1996 / EXQ / B • Anal & 3-Way Play / 1995 / GLI

/ M • Anal 3-Way Play / 1995 / GLI / M • The Anal Adventures Of Max Hardcore: Love Hurts / 1994 / ZA / M • Anal Bandits / 1996 / SO / M • Anal Camera #16 / 1996 / EVN / M • Anal Cannibals / 1996 / ZA / M • Anal Destroyer / 1994 / ZA / M • Anal Fugitive / 1995 / PEP / M • Anal Glamour Girls / 1995 / ME / M • Anal Princess #1 / 1996 / VC / M • Anal Rippers #2: The Unveiling / 1996 / ZA / M • Anal Sex Freaks / 1996 / ZA / M • Ass Lover's Special / 1996 / PE / M • Ass Masters (Leisure) #04 / 1995 / LEI / M • Backdoor To Buttsville / 1995 / ULI / M • Bad To The Bone / 1996 / ULP / M • The Big One / 1995 / HO / M • Bizarre Desires / 1995 / ROB / F • Black & Booty-Full / 1996 / ROB / M • Bootylicious: Hoochie Ho's / 1995 / JMP / M • The Bottom Dweller 33 1/3 / 1995 / EL / M • Brunette Roulette / 1996 / LE / M • Buffy's Nude Camera-Party / 1996 / CIN / M • Burlesxxx / 1996 / VT / M • Bushwoman: She Takes Two / 1996 / RAS / M • Butt Hunt #10 / 1995 / LEI / M • Casting Call #12 / 1995 / MET / M • Channel 69 / 1996 / CC / M • Circus Sluts / 1995 / LV / M • Club Deb #3 / 1996 / MET / M • The Complete & Total Anal Workout #1 / 1995 / ZA / M • Corporate Justice / 1996 / TEP / M • Crack Attack! / 1996 / PE / M • Cum Duttered Corn Holes #1 / 1996 / NIT / C • Cum Buttered Corn Holes #3 / 1996 / NIT / C • D.P. Party Tonite / 1995 / JMP / M • Dark Eyes / 1995 / FC / M • Deceit / 1996 / ZA / M • The Dinner Party #2: The Buffet / 1996 / ULI / M • Dream House / 1995 / XPR / M • The Erotic Artist / 1995 / VC / M • European Sex TV / 1996 / EL / M • Fellatio Fanatics / 1996 / NIT / M • Femme Fatale / 1996 / CIN / M • Flexxx #2 / 1995 / VT / M • Friendly Fire / 1996 / EDP / M • Gangland Bangers / 1995 / VC / M • Generation Sex #1 / 1996 / VT / M • Generation Sex #2: Nature's Revenge / 1996 / VT / M • Golddiggers #3 / 1995 / VC / M • Gun Runner / 1996 / CIN / M • The Happy Office / 1996 / NIT / M • Hienie's Heroes / 1995 / VC / M • The Hitch-Hiker #10: Rolling & Reaming / 1995 / WMG / M • Hollywood Sex Tour / 1995 / VC / M • Hot Parts / 1996 / NIT / M • Hot Tight Asses #15 / 1996 / TCK / M • Hot Tight Asses #17 / 1996 / TCK / M • Hotel California / 1995 / MID / M • Hypnotic Hookers #1 / 1996 / NIT / M • In The Can With Oj / 1994 / HCV / M • Incantation / 1996 / FC / M • Indiscreet! Video Magazine #1 / 1995 / FH / M • The Initiation / 1995 / FD / M • Intense Perversions #3 / 1996 / LV / M • Interview's Anal Queens / 1996 / LV / M • Jizz Glazed Goo Guzzlers #2 / 1996 / NIT / C • Lady M's Anything Nasty #01: Pink Pussy Party / 1996 / AVI / F • Lady's Choice / 1995 / VD / M • Lana Exposed / 1995 / VT / M • Legend #6: / 1996 / LE / M • Lesbian Bitches #2 / 1994 / ROB / F • Lesbian Debutante #03 / 1996 / IP / F • Lesbian Social Club / 1995 / ROB / F • Lust Runner / 1995 / VC / M • Male Order Brides / 1996 / RAS / M • Max #03 / 1995 / FWE / M • Max Gold #1 / 1996 / XPR / C • Mickey Ray's Sex Search #06 / 1996 / WIV / M • Mike Hott: #351 Three-Sum Sluts #11 / 1996 / MHV / M • The Mile High Club / 1995 / PL / M • More Than A Handful #6: Life Under The Big Top / 1994 / MET / M •

Mutual Consent / 1995 / VC / M • Nasty Nymphos #07 / 1994 / ANA / M • Neighborhood Slut / 1996 / LV / M • The New Ass Masters #08 / 1996 / LEI / C • New Pussy Hunt #18 / 1995 / LEI / C • Nineteen #3 / 1996 / FOR / M • Nudist Colony Vacation / 1996 / NIT / M • Persia's Back / 1994 / VT / M • Perverted Stories #08 / 1996 / JMP / M • Pick Up Lines #05 / 1996 / OD / M • Priceless / 1995 / WP / M • Pure / 1996 / WP / M • Puritan Video Magazine #03 / 1996 / LE / M • The Real Deal #3 / 1996 / FC / M • Renegades #2 / 1995 / SC / M • Reverse Gang Bang / 1995 / JMP / M • Rumpman's Backdoor Sailing / 1996 / HW / M • Secret Of Her Suckcess / 1994 / VC / M • Sensual Spirits / 1995 / LE / M • Sex In Black & White / 1995 / OD / M • The Shocking Truth #1 / 1996 / DWO / M • Snatch Masters #01 / 1994 / LEI / M • Snatch Masters #02 / 1994 / LEI / M • Snatch Masters #11 / 1995 / LEI / M • Snatch Motors / 1995 / VC / M • Sodomania #12: Raw Filth / 1995 / EL / M • Sodomania #16: Sexxy Pistols / 1996 / EL / M • Sodomania: Slop Shots / 1996 / EL / C • Sofia: A Gang Bang Fantasy / 1994 / FC / M • Some Like It Hard / 1995 / VC / M • The Spa / 1996 / RAS / M • Steamy Sins / 1996 / IN / M • Stories Of Seduction / 1996 / MID / M • Strange Lesbian Taloo / 1996 / BAC / F • Student Fetish Videos: The Enema #19 / 1995 / PRE / B • Suzi Bungholeo / 1995 / ROB / M • Tainted Love / 1996 / VC / M • Takin' It To The Limit #4 / 1995 / BS / M • Thunder And Lightning / 1996 / MID / M • Thunder Road / 1995 / SC / M • Tight Fit #11 / 1995 / GO / M • Timepiece / 1994 / CV / M • Tits / 1995 / AVI / M • Titties 'n Cream #3 / 1995 / FC / M • Undercover / 1996 / VC / M • Underground #3: Sit On This / 1996 / SC / M • Venom #3 / 1996 / VD / M • Venom #6 / 1996 / CA / M • The Voyeur #4 / 1995 / EA / M • Wacky Weekend / 1995 / SUF / M • Waterbabies #3 / 1996 / CC / M • Wet Faces #1 / 1997 / SC / C • What's The Lesbian Doing In My Pirate Movie? / 1995 / LIP / F • Wicked Ways #2: Education Of A D.P. Virgin / 1995 / WP / M • World Class Ass / 1995 / FC / M • XXX Channel / 1996 / VT / M

SOFIA LUREN *see* Sophia

SOFIE BRATTLUND
Detained / 1996 / PL / M

SOL
A Touch Of Danger / 1994 / STM / B

SOL SCHWARTZ *see* Scottie Schwartz

SOL WEINER
The Taking Of Christina / 1975 / NGV / M

SOLANGE *see* Gyn Seng

SOLANGE DUMONT *see* Star Index I

SOLEIL
Joe Elliot's College Girls #43 / 1996 / JOE / M • Suck Channel / 1991 / VIM / M

SOLEIL AVALON
Journal Of O #2 / 1994 / ONA / B • More Dirty Debutantes #35 / 1994 / 4P / M • Snatch Masters #07 / 1995 / LEI / M • Sugar Daddies / 1995 / FPI / M

SOLVEIG
The Adventures Of Peeping Tom #3 / 1996 / OD / M • Afro American Dream Girls #1 / 1996 / DR / M • Afro American Dream Girls #2 / 1996 / DR / M • Anal Honeypie / 1996 / ROB / M • Black Centerfolds #4 / 1996 / MID / M • Black Cheerleader Search #11 / 1997 / IVC / M • Black Lube Job Girls /

1995 / SUF / M • Black Snatch #1 / 1996 / DFI / F • Booty Bang #1 / 1996 / HW / M • Bootylicious: Baby Got Booty / 1996 / JMP / M • Bow Down Backstreet / 1996 / HW / M • Breastman's Triple X Cellent Adventure / 1995 / EVN / M • Contrast / 1995 / CA / M • Coochie's Under Fire / 1996 / HW / F • Da Booty Bang #2 / 1996 / HW / M • Dreamgirls: Fort Lauderdale / 1996 / DR / M • Finger Pleasures #6 / 1996 / PL / F • Gang Bang Butthole Surfin' / 1996 / ROB / M • Girlz N The Hood #5 / 1995 / HW / M • Hardcore Debutantes #02 / 1996 / TEP / M • If You Can't Lick 'em...Join 'em / 1996 / BAC / F • In Da Booty / 1996 / LV / M • Kym Wilde's On The Edge #25 / 1995 / RB / B • Kym Wilde's On The Edge #32 / 1996 / RB / B • Licorice Lollipops: Back To School / 1996 / HW / M • Licorice Lollipops: Summer Break / 1996 / HW / M • Look What I Found On The Street #01 / 1996 / CC / M • Miss Judge / 1997 / VI / M • Painful Desire / 1996 / BON / B • Punishing The Sluts / 1996 / RB / B • Ron Hightower's Casting Couch #1 / 1995 / FC / M • Showtime / 1996 / VT / M • Skeezers / 1996 / LV / M • Sweet Black Cherries #1 / 1996 / TTV / M • Video Virgins #25 / 1995 / NS / M • Vivid Raw #4 / 1996 / VI / M

SOLVIEG
Booty Bang #2 / 1996 / HW / M • Hardcore Fantasies #5 / 1996 / LV / M • Takin' It To The Limit #9: Rear Action View / 1996 / BS / M

SOMMER KNIGHT *see* Star Index I

SOMOA
P.L.O.W.: Punk Ladies Of Wrestling / 1996 / GOT / B

SONA DA SILVIA
Private Film #22 / 1995 / OD / M

SONA ROME *see* Gina Rome

SONDA WITKINS *see* Star Index I

SONDRA DARK
Odyssey Triple Play #03: Anal Olympics / 1992 / OD / M

SONDRA LAW
Sound Of Love / 1981 / CA / M

SONDRA ORTEGA
More Dirty Debutantes #37 / 1995 / 4P / M

SONDRA REY *(Mistress Sondra, Goddess Sondra)*
Older blonde who just does B&D.
Afternoon With Goddess Sondra / 1992 / SSP / B • Babes In Bondage / 1991 / BIZ / B • Big Tit Torment / 1994 / SSP / B • Blonde Bitches / 1993 / SSP / B • Blonde Bombshells / 1992 / VER / B • Boss Bitch! / 1992 / RB / B • Chessie's Home Videos #17: C.E.S. Show / 1995 / CHM / M • Chessie's Home Videos #47A: Chessie In Charge / 1995 / CHM / B • Chessie's Home Videos #47B: The Taming Of Chessie / 1995 / CHM / B • Chessie's Home Videos #48: Big Boob Bondage / 1995 / CHM / B • Chessie's Home Videos #50: Goddess In Training / 1995 / CHM / B • Cruel Heels / 1991 / SSP / B • Daddy Gets Punished / 1990 / PL / B • Female Domination #1: Babes In Bondage / 1991 / BEB / B • Female Domination #2 / 1991 / BIZ / B • Foot Licking Fantasy / 1993 / SSP / B • Heel Fashions / 1993 / SSP / B • Latex Slave / 1992 / RB / B • Learn Your Lessons / 1992 / BIZ / B • Male Domination #17 / 1990 / BIZ / C • Man Training / 1993 / RB / B • Mistress Sondra's Playthings / 1990 / BON / B

• Mistress Sondra's TV Discipline / 1990 / B&D / B • Nails / 1993 / SSP / B • Nothing But Contempt / 1990 / PL / B • Painful Lesson (Red Board) / 1992 / RB / B • Punished By The Latex Mistress / 1992 / BIZ / B • A Session With Mistress Sondra / 1990 / RSV / B • Spanknight #01 / 1992 / RB / B • Spanknight #02 / 1992 / RB / B • Strict Mistress / 1992 / RB / B • Strict Stepmother / 1992 / RB / B • The Taming Of Kay / 1993 / SSP / B • Warehouse Slaves Discipline / 1990 / BIZ / B • Working Girls In Bondage / 1991 / BIZ / B • Worshipping Goddess Sondra / 1993 / VER / B

SONDRA SCREAM *see* **Sandra Scream**

SONDRA STILLMAN *see* **Lois Ayers**

SONIA
Eurotica #05 / 1996 / XC / M • Eurotica #06 / 1996 / XC / M • Homegrown Video #372 / 1991 / HOV / M • Private Stories #09 / 1996 / OD / M

SONIA CARR
The Black Chill / 1986 / WET / M

SONIA DEGLI ESPOSTI
Sex Penitentiary / 1996 / XC / M

SONIA FLICKER *see* **Alexandria (1976)**

SONIA FYRE *see* **Star Index I**

SONIA VEGA
Club Privado / 1995 / KP / M

SONIYA
Creme De La Face #12: Pretty Faces To Cum On / 1995 / OD / M

SONJA *(Cindy Lee, Sandy (Sonja), Sonya (Sonja))*
Thin bodied blonde, brunette or reddish blonde (i.e. she changes color all the time) with almost translucent skin and soft down on her arms. Quite pretty but her personality (which sounds affected) leaves something to be desired and doesn't gell with her looks. Seems to have very good taste in underwear so she looks sexy without looking slutty.
Amateur Lesbians #24: Sondra / 1992 / GO / F • America's Dirtiest Home Videos #05 / 1991 / VEX / M • Anal Encounters #8 / 1992 / VC / M • Assford Wives / 1992 / ATL / M • Autoerotica #1 / 1991 / EX / M • Autoerotica #2 / 1991 / EX / M • The Babe / 1992 / EX / M • Backdoor To Russia #1 / 1992 / VC / M • Backdoor To Russia #2 / 1993 / VC / M • Bad Attitude / 1992 / CDI / M • Behind The Backdoor #5 / 1992 / EVN / M • The Best Rears Of Our Lives / 1992 / OD / M • The Bigger They Come / 1993 / VD / C • Biker Chicks In Love / 1991 / LE / M • Blow Out / 1991 / IF / M • Busted / 1992 / HO / M • Butt Seriously Folks / 1994 / AFV / M • Club Josephine / 1991 / AR / F • Collectible / 1991 / LE / M • Coming Clean / 1992 / ME / M • The Dirty Little Mind of Martin Fink / 1991 / ME / M • Dream Date / 1992 / HO / M • Executive Positions / 1991 / V99 / M • Fever / 1992 / CA / M • Full Moon Fever / 1992 / PEP / M • Hard Ride / 1992 / WV / M • I Remember When / 1992 / ATL / M • I'll Do Anything But... / 1992 / CA / M • In Deep With The Devil / 1991 / ME / M • Little Secrets / 1991 / LE / M • Maiden Heaven #1 / 1992 / MID / F • Mind Games / 1992 / CDI / M • Muff 'n' Jeff / 1992 / ZA / M • Other People's Honey / 1991 / HW / M • Perks / 1992 / ZA / M • Rent-A-Butt / 1992 / VC / M • Rocky Mountains / 1991 / IF / M • Romancing The Butt / 1992 / ATL / M • The Seducers / 1992 / ZA / M • The Ser-

vants Of Midnight / 1992 / CDI / M • She Likes To Watch / 1992 / EVN / M • This Butt Lite Is For You / 1992 / ATL / M • To The Rear / 1992 / VC / M • Too Sexy / 1992 / MID / M • X-TV / 1992 / CA / C • You Said A Mouthful / 1992 / IF / M

SONJA (1994)
3 Mistresses Of The Mansion / 1994 / STM / B • Buttman's Big Butt Backdoor Babes / 1995 / EA / M • Dr Discipline #1 / 1994 / STM / B • Dr Discipline #2: Appointment With Pain / 1994 / STM / B • M Series #24 / 1994 / LBO / M • Spanking Tea Party / 1994 / STM / B • Teacher's Pet #1 / 1994 / WMG / M

SONJA (HUNG)
Nba: Nuttin' Butt Ass / 1996 / SMP / M • Porno X-Treme #2: Club Bizarre / 1995 / SC / M • Porno X-Treme #4: Wet Dream / 1995 / SC / M

SONJA KLAES *see* **Star Index I**

SONNY
Homegrown Video #179 / 1990 / HOV / M • Homegrown Video #425: The Best Of Brandy / 1994 / HOV / M • Ultraflesh / 1980 / GO / M

SONNY BONDERO
Dirty Dave's #2 / 1996 / XPR / M • Dirty Dave's #4 / 1996 / XPR / M • Filthy First Timers #1 / 1996 / EL / M • Filthy First Timers #2: Innocence Lost / 1996 / EL / M • Filthy First Timers #3: Tearing Down The Walls Of Shame / 1996 / EL / M • Filthy First Timers #4 / 1996 / EL / M • Filthy First Timers #5 / 1997 / EL / M • Filthy First Timers #6 / 1997 / EL / M

SONNY DAZE
Beneath The Cane / 1992 / BON / B • Bondage Memories #04 / 1994 / BON / C • Classified Spanking / 1991 / BON / B • Collected Spankings #1 / 1992 / BON / C • Collected Spankings #2 / 1992 / BON / C • Forbidden Fantasies / 1991 / BON / B • A Grand Obsession / 1992 / B&D / B • Old Fashioned Spankings / 1991 / BON / B • On Your Bare Bottom / 1992 / BON / B • Red Bottom Blues / 199? / BON / B • Ropemasters / cr90 / BON / B • She'll Take A Spanking / 199? / BON / B • Spank Me, Spank Me, Spank Me / 199? / BON / B • Spanked Shopper & Other Tales / 1991 / BON / C • Spanking Tails / 1993 / BON / B • To Taste The Strap / 199? / BON / B

SONNY DINER *see* **Star Index I**

SONNY FRANZESE
A Dirty Western #1 / 1973 / AR / M • Saturday Matinee Series #3 / 1996 / VCX / C

SONNY LANDHAM *(Doug Jackson)*
Reasonably famous (e.g. **48 Hours**) movie actor subsequent to a considerable number of roles in porno movies. Supposedly was married to Marlene Willoughby at one time.
48 Hours / 1982 / PAR / S • The Best Of The Best #2 / 1983 / FOX / S • Big Abner / 19?? / VXP / M • The Bite / 1975 / SVE / M • Come Fly With Us / 1974 / QX / M • Defiance / 1974 / ALP / B • The Dirty Dozen: The Next Mission / 1985 / MGM / S • Fleshburn / 1984 / MED / S • Happy Days / 1974 / IHV / M • The Honey Cup / cr76 / VXP / M • Hot Shots / 1974 / COM / M • Illusion Of Love / 1975 / COM / M • Lock Up / 1989 / LIV / S • The Love Bus / 1974 / OSC / M • Misbehavin' / 1979 / VXP / M • The Passions Of Carol / 1975 / VXP / M • Predator

#1 / 1987 / FOX / S • The Private Afternoons Of Pamela Mann / 1974 / TVX / M • Slippery When Wet / 1976 / VXP / M • Special Order / cr75 / BL / M • Steam Heat / 1980 / COM / M • Sylvia / 1976 / VCX / M • Taxi Dancers / 1993 / AIP / S • Three Days To A Kill / 1991 / HBO / S • The Trouble With Young Stuff / 1976 / VC / M • Virgin Snow / 1976 / VXP / M • [The Switch / 1974 / ... / S

SONNY LUSTIG
Confessions Of A Woman / 1976 / SE / M • The Untamed / 1978 / VCX / M

SONNY MCKAY *see* **Sunny McKay**

SONNY RUMBERG
Tight Tushies #1 / 1994 / SFP / M

SONOMA
Creme De La Face #02 / 1994 / OD / M • Mr. Peepers Amateur Home Videos #83: Roni And The Private's / 1994 / LBO / M • Mr. Peepers Amateur Home Videos #84: She Put the Bra in Braz / 1994 / LBO / M • Mr. Peepers Amateur Home Videos #85: Hand Puppet Job / 1994 / LBO / M • Mr. Peepers Nastiest #3 / 1995 / LBO / C • Southern Belles #1 / 1994 / HOV / M

SONORA
Hollywood Starlets Adventure #03 / 1995 / AVS / M • The Notorious Cleopatra / 1970 / SOW / S

SONYA
Bend Over Brazilian Babes #2 / 1993 / EA / M • Blue Vanities #528 / 1993 / FFL / M • Firestorm #2: The Angel Blade / 1986 / COM / M • Firestorm #3 / 1986 / COM / M • GRG: Suburban Slut / 1995 / GRG / M • GRG: The Long And The Short Of It / 1995 / GRG / M • The Mountainous Mams Of Alyssa Alps / 1993 / NAP / S • New Faces, Hot Bodies #14 / 1994 / STP / M • Penthouse: Ready To Ride / 1992 / PET / F • Slapped Senseless / 1993 / NAP / B • Trial Of The Tits / 1994 / NAP / B • U Witness: Pregnant And Horny As Hell I & II / 1995 / MSP / M • Viva Viviana / 1994 / PME / F

SONYA (SONJA) *see* **Sonja**

SONYA RAIN *see* **Star Index I**

SONYA SPIZER *see* **Star Index I**

SONYA SUMMERS
Beyond Shame / 1980 / VEP / M • Beyond Your Wildest Dreams / 1980 / CAT / M • Forbidden Entry / 1984 / VCR / M • High School Memories / 1980 / VCX / M • Ladies Nights / 1980 / VC / M • Naughty Fantasy / 1986 / CA / M • Never So Deep / 1981 / VCX / M • Please, Mr Postman / 1981 / VC / M • Tales Of The Backside / 1985 / VCR / C • Urban Cowgirls / 1980 / CA / M • Wicked Schoolgirls / 1981 / SVE / M • Wicked Sensations #1 / 1981 / CA / M

SOO LIN *see* **Star Index I**

SOPHIA *(Sofia Luren, Sofia)*
Ugly white girl who has a thin body and a penchant for anals.
Adventures In Paradise / 1992 / VEX / M • The Adventures Of Seymore Butts / 1992 / FH / M • Amateur Lesbians #19: Sophia / 1992 / GO / F • America's Raunchiest Home Videos #16: Sophia's Yankee Doodle / 1992 / ZA / M • America's Raunchiest Home Videos #18: Anal Crunch / 1992 / ZA / M • America's Raunchiest Home Videos #20: Penthouse Pussy Power / 1992 / ZA / M • The Anal Adventures Of Max Hardcore: Sunset Boulevard / 1992 / ZA / M • Bi On The Fourth Of July / 1994 / BIL / G • Blue

Moon / 1992 / AFV / M • Foot Hookers / 1994 / SBP / B • Lesbian Pros And Amateurs #11 / 1992 / GO / F • Lesbian Pros And Amateurs #12 / 1992 / GO / F • Mr. Peepers Amateur Home Videos #48: Dialing For Services / 1992 / LBO / M • Our Bang #02 / 1992 / GLI / M • Our Bang #04 / 1992 / GLI / M • Seymore Butts & The Honeymooners / 1992 / FH / M • Uncle Roy's Amateur Home Video #03 / 1992 / VIM / M • Uncle Roy's Amateur Home Video #06 / 1992 / VIM / M • Uncle Roy's Best Of The Best: Brazen Brunettes / 1993 / VIM / C • Uncle Roy's Best Of The Best: Cornhole Classics / 1992 / VIM / C

SOPHIA (BLACK)
Butt-Nanza / 1995 / WV / M • Girlz Towne #07 / 1995 / FC / F • You Go Girl! (Video Team) / 1995 / VT / M

SOPHIA (OTHER)
Bikini Watch / 1996 / PHV / F • Creme De La Face #12: Pretty Faces To Cum On / 1995 / OD / M • Dr Freckle & Mr Jive / 1995 / IN / M • Girls Next Door / 1996 / ANE / M • Nothing Like Nurse Nookie #1 / 1995 / NIT / M • Swimming Pool Orgy / 1995 / FRF / M

SOPHIA CAPRI
The Breast Files #3 / 1994 / AVI / M • Detective Covergirls / 1996 / CUC / B • Dirty Bob's #25: Porn Never Sleeps! / 1996 / FLP / S • Dirty Dirty Debutantes #3 / 1996 / 4P / M • Fashion Sluts #8 / 1996 / ABS / M • Filthy Little Bitches / 1996 / APP / F • Goldenbush / 1996 / AVI / M • Hollywood Amateurs #29 / 1996 / MID / M • Star Girl / 1996 / ERA / M • Vagabonds / 1996 / ERA / M • Video Virgins #27 / 1996 / NS / M • Wedding Night Blues / 1995 / EMC / M

SOPHIA CHARM
Black Bunbusters / 1985 / VC / M • House Of The Rising Moon / 1986 / VD / M • Tailgunners / 1985 / WET / M

SOPHIA DAWN
Blue Vanities #581 / 1996 / FFL / M

SOPHIA FERRARI see Sofia Ferrari

SOPHIA LA MAN
A Peek Over The Wall / 1995 / STM / G

SOPHIA LAWRENCE
Donna Young: Sophia Lawrence #1 / 1995 / DY / F

SOPHIA LOVE
Spanked And Whipped / 1994 / VTF / B

SOPHIA SOLANO
Blue Vanities #533 / 1993 / FFL / M • The Erotic World Of Seka / 1983 / VCR / C • Seka's Fantasies / 1981 / CA / M

SOPHIA STAKS
Attack Of The Killer Dildos / 1996 / RAS / M • Boobwatch #1 / 1996 / SC / M

SOPHIE
Anal Delights #3 / 1993 / ROB / M • Blue Vanities #521 / 1993 / FFL / M • Creme De La Face #03 / 1994 / OD / M • Eurotica #10 / 1996 / XC / M • Magma: Nymphettes / 1993 / MET / M • Magma: Party Extreme / 1995 / MET / M • Magma: Shopping Anal / 1994 / MET / M • New Faces, Hot Bodies #04 / 1992 / STP / M • New Faces, Hot Bodies #05 / 1992 / STP / M • New Faces, Hot Bodies #06 / 1993 / STP / M • New Faces, Hot Bodies #07 / 1993 / STP / M • New Faces, Hot Bodies #15 / 1994 / STP / M • New Faces, Hot Bodies #21 / 1996 / STP / C • Seymore Butts Goes Nuts / 1994 / FH / M • Student Fetish Videos: Tickling

#11 / 1995 / SFV / B

SOPHIE CALL
Drop Sex: Wipe The Floor / 1997 / JLP / M

SOPHIE DAVISON see Star Index I

SOPHIE DUFLOT
Hot Babes / cr78 / CIG / M • Shared With Strangers / 1985 / CV / M

SOPHIE DUPONT see Star Index I

SOPHIE FENNINGTON see Star Index I

SOPHIE FRENCH
Behind Closed Doors / 1996 / GOT / B • Enter Into Slavery / 1996 / GOT / B • Toe Tales #34 / 1996 / GOT / B • Toe Tales #36 / 1996 / GOT / B • Toe Tales #37 / 1996 / GOT / B

SOPHIE GARNIER see Star Index I

SOPHIE PARENT see Star Index I

SOPHIE RIO
100% Amateur #09: Asians & Latinas / 1995 / OD / M • Analtown USA #07 / 1995 / NIT / M • Analtown USA #08 / 1995 / NIT / M • Crew Sluts / 1996 / NOT / M • Cum Buttered Corn Holes #2 / 1996 / NIT / C • Dirty & Kinky Mature Women #08 / 1996 / C69 / M • Fuck Jasmin / 1997 / MET / M • Intense / 1996 / MET / M • Interview: Bun Busters / 1995 / LV / M • Leg Show #1 / 1995 / NIT / M • Mike Hott: #359 Bonus Cunt: Sophia Rio / 1996 / MHV / M • Mike Hott: #360 Cum In My Cunt #08 / 1995 / MHV / C • Mike Hott: #369 Cum In My Mouth #05 / 1996 / MHV / C • Mike Hott: #378 Fuck The Boss #8 / 1996 / MHV / M • Nasty Nymphos #15 / 1996 / ANA / M • Nothing Like Nurse Nookie #3 / 1996 / NIT / M • Philmore Butts Strikes Gold / 1996 / SUF / M • Santa Is Coming All Over Town / 1996 / EVN / M • Sexhibition #1 / 1996 / SUF / M • Sexhibition #2 / 1996 / SUF / M • Too Hot / 1996 / LV / M • Vortex / 1995 / MET / M • Wild Cherries / 1996 / SC / F

SOPHIE ZILLERS see Star Index I

SOPHIEN
World Sex Tour #4 / 1996 / ANA / M

SOREN HANSEN
Bordello / 1973 / AR / M

SOYOYA see Sukoya

SPANISH FLY
Showtime / 1996 / VT / M

SPANKY SNATCH
Butthead Dreams: Mission Impenetrable / 1994 / FH / M

SPARCY WILLIS see Sparky Vasc

SPARKLE DENSMORE see Frankie Leigh

SPARKLE PLENTY see Star Index I

SPARKY
Ona Zee's Learning The Ropes #07: At Lady Laura's / 1992 / ONA / B

SPARKY (VASC) see Sparky Vasc

SPARKY GOLDBERG see Sparky Vasc

SPARKY VASC *(Sparky Goldberg, Sparcy Willis, Sparky (Vasc))*
Pudgy black girl with large belly and large droopy tits. Sparky Goldberg is from **Casting Couch** and Willis is from **Peaches And Cream**. Born in NY but frequent performer in the early eighties in the O'Farrell Theatre.

The Casting Couch / 1983 / GO / M • Dark Angel / 1983 / VC / M • Flesh & Laces #1 / 1983 / CA / M • Kamikaze Hearts / 1986 / FAC / S • Peaches And Cream / 1982 / SE / M • TV Husband, Submissive Wife / cr83 / BIZ / B • Ultraflesh / 1980 / GO / M

SPAULDING GRAY

Farmers Daughters / 1975 / VC / M • The Opening Of Misty Beethoven / 1976 / VC / M

SPENDER TRAVIS
On White Satin / 1980 / VCX / M

SPICE
Small/medium tits, passable face, nose ring, clit ring, belly button ring, tongue pin, short dark brown hair, tall (6'0"), lithe body; tattoos on left shoulder back (bearded male head), left shoulder outside, left hip (name), and around belly button (three fishes). Supposedly German but speaks flawless English.

African Angels #1 / 1996 / NIT / M • Anal Witness #1 / 1996 / LBO / M • Borsky's Back Door Bitches / 1996 / ROB / M • Breastman's Hot Legs Contest / 1996 / ... / M • Brooklyn Nights / 1994 / OD / M • Brunette Roulette / 1996 / LE / M • Burbank Sperm Bank / 1996 / CIN / M • Eighteen #3 / 1996 / SC / M • Eternal Lust / 1996 / VC / M • The Happy Office / 1996 / NIT / M • Here Comes Elska / 1997 / XPR / M • Hypnotic Hookers #2 / 1996 / NIT / M • Incantation / 1996 / FC / M • The Shocking Truth #1 / 1996 / DWO / M • Sin-A-Matic / 1996 / VI / M • TV Nation #1 / 1995 / HW / G

SPIDER
Magma: Huge Cum Shots / 1995 / MET / M

SPIDER WEBB
Erotic Tattooing And Piercing #1 / 1986 / FLV / M • S.O.S. / 1975 / QX / M

SPIDERMAN
Spanking Scenes #04 / cr80 / TAO / C

SPIKE ADRIAN see Alan Adrian

SPIKETTE
The Angel In Mr. Holmes / 1988 / WV / C • Chain Of Command / 1991 / GOT / B • The Dominator / 1992 / GOT / B • A Lesson Well Taut / 1994 / GOT / B • Mistress Of The Whip / 1996 / GOT / C • Night Calls / 1993 / GOT / B • No Pain, No Gain / 1992 / GOT / B • The Shah Of Pain / 1993 / JOB / B • Toe Tales #01 / 1992 / GOT / B • Toe Tales #02 / 1992 / GOT / B • Toe Tales #12 / 1994 / GOT / C

SPOKE-N-FREEWHEEL see Star Index I

SPONTANEOUS XTASY
Ass Masters (Leisure) #06 / 1995 / LEI / M • Big & Busty Centerfolds / 1996 / DGD / F • Black Beauty (Las Vegas) / 1995 / LV / M • The Black Butt Sisters Do Miami / 1995 / MID / M • The Black Butt Sisters Do New York / 1995 / MID / M • Black Fantasies #07 / 1995 / HW / M • Black Gangbangers #05 / 1995 / HW / M • Black Hollywood Amateurs #07 / 1995 / MID / M • Black Hollywood Amateurs #10 / 1995 / MID / M • Black Hollywood Amateurs #17 / 1995 / MID / M • Black Knockers #13 / 1995 / TV / M • Black Leather / Black Skin / 1995 / VT / B • Black Orgies #33 / 1995 / GO / M • Black Orgies #34 / 1995 / GO / M • Black Sensations: Models In Heat / 1995 / SUF / M • Black Women, White Men #8 / 1995 / FC / M • Blacks N' Blue / 1995 / VT / B • Boob Tube Lube / 1996 / RAS / M • Booty Bang #2 / 1996 / HW / M • Bow Down Backstreet / 1996 / HW / M • Butt-Nanza / 1995 / WV / M • Coochie's Under Fire / 1996 / HW / F • Crimson Thighs / 1995 / HW / M • Da Booty Bang #2 / 1996 / HW / M • Gazongas Galore #1 / 1996 / NIT / C • Girlz Towne #07 / 1995 / FC / F • Girlz Towne #11 / 1995 / FC / F • Girlz Towne

#12 / 1995 / FC / F • Git Yo' Ass On Da Bus! / 1996 / HW / M • Interview's Dark And Delicious / 1996 / LV / M • Interview: Dark And Delicious / 1996 / LV / M • Juicy's Houseparty / 1995 / HW / M • Kym Wilde's On The Edge #37 / 1996 / RB / B • Leather / 1995 / LE / M • Liar's Poke Her / 1995 / NIW / M • Lockdown / 1996 / NIT / M • Long From Dong / 1995 / FH / M • Miss Nude International / 1996 / LE / M • Mistress 'n Da Hood / 1995 / VT / B • Paint It Black / 1995 / EVN / M • The Players Club / 1994 / HW / M • Pussy Hunt #15 / 1995 / LEI / M • Rump-Shaker #4 / 1995 / HW / M • Sista! #3 / 1995 / VT / F • Sistaz In Chains / 1995 / VT / B • Sittin' On Da Krome / 1995 / HW / M • Skeezers / 1996 / LV / M • Span's Garden Party / 1996 / HW / M • Student Fetish Videos: Catfighting #14 / 1994 / PRE / B • Student Fetish Videos: The Enema #19 / 1995 / PRE / B • Student Fetish Videos: Foot Worship #15 / 1995 / PRE / B • Tails From The Hood / 1995 / FH / M • Titties 'n Cream #3 / 1995 / FC / M • Titty Town #2 / 1995 / HW / M

SPRING FINLAY *(Pat Finley, Bonnie Lain)*
Redhead with red pubic hair, white skin, long straight hair, medium firm tits, lithe body. Pat Finley is from **Coming Attractions**. Bonnie is from **Baby Doll**.
Baby Doll / 1975 / AR / M • Cherry Truckers / 1979 / ALP / M • Coming Attractions / 1976 / VEP / M • Dixie / 1976 / VHL / M • The Girls In The Band / 1976 / SVE / M • Maid In Sweden / 197? / SIL / M • Revelations / 1974 / SOW / M • The Starlets / 1976 / RAV / M • Three Shades Of Flesh / 1976 / IVP / M

SPRING T. DEE *see* **Spring Taylor**
SPRING TAYLOR *(Spring Taylor Dee, Spring T. Dee)*
The Bimbo #1 / 1985 / VXP / M • The Bimbo #2: The Homecoming / 1986 / RLV / M • C.T. Coed Teasers / 1978 / VXP / M • Hot Licks / 1984 / SE / M • Inside Everybody / 1984 / AVC / M • Lady Madonna / 1985 / RLV / M • Long Hard Nights / 1984 / ELH / M • Miami Vice Girls / 1984 / RLV / M • Pretty In Black / 1986 / WET / M • Return To Alpha Blue / 1984 / AVC / M • Sleazy Susan / 1986 / VXP / M • The South Bronx Story / 1986 / CC / M • Temptations Of The Flesh / 1986 / VD / M

SPRING TAYLOR DEE *see* **Spring Taylor**
SQUIRT *see* **Fallon**
ST ELMO *see* **Elmer Fox**
ST NICK
Comeback / 1995 / VI / M
ST PETER *see* **Herb Nitke**
STACEE
Odyssey Triple Play #04: Leena & Stacee / 1992 / OD / F
STACEY
A&B GB#060: Mary, Janet & Stacey / 1992 / A&B / M • Amateur Nights #10 / 1990 / HO / M • Bi 'n' Sell / 1990 / VC / G • Blue Vanities #194 / 1993 / FFL / M • Jamie Gillis: The Private Collection Vol #2 / 1991 / SC / F • Lucky Ladies #101 / 1992 / STI / M • Mike Hott: #386 / 1996 / MHV / M • Mike Hott: #390 / 1996 / MHV / M • Mike Hott: #391 / 1996 / MHV / M
STACEY (VICTORIA L) *see* **Victoria Lee**
STACEY DELAVAN *see* **Paula Winters**
STACEY DEVOLIN *see* **Paula Winters**
STACEY DONOVAN *(Camilla (Stacey D),*

Tracy Donovan, Ashley Britton, Kelly Howe, Kelly Howell, Ashly Britton)
First movie was **Bouncing Buns**. Rather tall, pretty face, blonde hair, small tits, tight waist, good tan lines. Was a covergirl for *Seventeen* prior to appearing in her first porno. Generally hated by the porn industry because of her co-operation with the Meese Commission.
Adult Video Therapist / 1987 / CLV / C • Angels Of Passion / 1986 / CDI / M • Baby Face #2 / 1987 / VC / M • Backside To The Future #1 / 1986 / ZA / M • Bad Girls #3 / 1984 / COL / M • The Best Of Black White & Pink Inside / 1996 / CV / C • Best Of Bruce Seven #3 / 1990 / BIZ / C • Best Of Hot Shorts #01 / 1987 / VCR / C • The Better Sex Video Series #5: Sharing Fantasies / 1992 / LEA / M • Bondage Interludes #2 / 1983 / BIZ / B • Bouncing Buns / 1983 / VC / M • Breezy / 1985 / VCR / M • Cagney & Stacey / 1984 / AT / M • Caught By Surprise / 1987 / CDI / M • Cinderella / 1985 / VEL / M • Convenience Store Girls / 1986 / VD / M • Cum Shot Revue #3 / 1988 / HO / C • Deep Inside Traci / 1986 / CDI / C • Dial A Dick / 1986 / AVC / M • Dirty Dreams / 1987 / CA / M • Dirty Girls / 1984 / MIT / M • Dr Penetration / 1986 / WET / M • Dreamwalk / 1989 / COM / M • The Ecstasy Girls #2 / 1986 / CA / M • Erica Boyer: Non-Stop / 1988 / VD / C • Flaming Tongues #1 / 1984 / MET / F • Gentlemen Prefer Ginger / 1985 / VI / M • Ginger's Hawaiian Scrapbook / 1988 / GO / C • Girls Of Sin / 1994 / PL / C • Girls Of The Chorus Line / 1986 / CLV / M • Girls That Love Girls / 1984 / CA / F • Girls Together / 1985 / GO / C • Gourmet Quickies: Stacey Donovan #706 / 1985 / GO / C • Gourmet Quickies: Stacey Donovan / Heather Wayne #728 / 1985 / GO / C • GVC: Lost In Lust #134 / 1984 / GO / M • GVC: Olympix Affair #137 / 1985 / GO / M • Having It All / 1985 / IN / M • Hindsight / 1985 / IN / M • Holiday For Angels / 1987 / IN / M • Hot Pink / 1985 / VCR / F • Hustler #17 / 1984 / CA0 / M • I Know What Girls Like / 1986 / WET / G • Innocence Lost / 1987 / CAT / G • It's My Body / 1985 / CDI / M • Jane Bond Meets Thunderballs / 1986 / VD / M • Juggs / 1984 / VCR / M • Just Another Pretty Face / 1985 / AVC / M • Lady Madonna / 1985 / RLV / M • The Last X-Rated Movie #1 / 1990 / COM / M • The Last X-Rated Movie #2 / 1990 / COM / M • The Layout / 1986 / CDI / M • Legends Of Porn #2 / 1989 / CV / C • Letters Of Love / 1985 / CA / M • A Little Bit Of Hanky Panky / 1984 / GO / M • Lover's Lane / 1986 / SE / M • The Lust Detector / 1986 / PIN / M • Lusty Adventurer / 1985 / GO / M • Make Me Want It / 1986 / CA / M • Miami Spice #2 / 1988 / CA / M • Moving In / 1986 / CV / M • Naked Lust / 1985 / SE / M • Nasty Nights / 1988 / PL / C • Naughty Nurses / 1986 / VEX / M • New York Vice / 1984 / CC / M • The Night Of The Headhunter / 1985 / WV / M • Only The Best Of Anal / 1992 / MET / C • Oral Majority #01 / 1986 / WV / C • Outlaw Women / 1983 / LIP / F • Palomino Heat / 1985 / COM / F • Panty Raid / 1984 / GO / M • Parliament: Blondes Have More Fun / 1989 / PM / C • Parliament: Fanny / 1987 / PM / F • Parliament: Finger Friggin' #1 / 1986 / PM / F • Parliament: Lesbian Lovers

#1 / 1986 / PM / F • Parliament: Woman's Touch / 1988 / PM / F • A Passage To Ecstasy / 1985 / CDI / M • Passion Pit / 1985 / SE / M • Passions / 1985 / MIT / M • Penthouse: The Girls Of Penthouse #1 / 1984 / VES / S • The Pink Lagoon: A Sex Romp In Paradise / 1984 / GO / M • Playing For Passion / 1987 / IN / M • The Pleasure Maze / 1986 / PL / M • Pleasure Productions #06 / 1984 / VCR / M • Pleasure Productions #09 / 1985 / VCR / M • Pleasure Productions #11 / 1985 / VCR / M • Pleasure Productions #12 / 1985 / VCR / M • Secret Mistress / 1986 / VD / M • Seduction Of Jennifer / 1986 / HO / M • Sex Dreams On Maple Street / 1985 / WV / M • Sex For Hire / 1989 / HOE / C • Sexy Delights #1 / 1986 / CLV / M • Showgirls / 1985 / SE / M • Slip Into Ginger & Amber / 1986 / MAP / C • Splashing / 1986 / VCS / C • Summer Break / 1985 / VEX / M • Surrender In Paradise / 1984 / GO / M • Switch Hitters #1 / 1987 / IN / G • Taija's Satin Seduction / 1987 / CDI / M • Tailhouse Rock / 1985 / WV / M • A Taste Of Candy / 1985 / LA / M • Tasty / 1985 / CA / M • This Stud's For You / 1986 / MAP / C • Thrill Street Blues / 1985 / WV / M • Too Good To Be True / 1984 / MAP / M • Traci Who? / 1987 / AVC / C • Tracy Dick / 1985 / WV / M • Triple Header / 1986 / SE / C • The Ultimate O / 1985 / NSV / M • The Ultimate Thrill / 1988 / PIN / C • Up All Night / 1986 / CC / M • Up Up And Away / 1984 / CA / M • The Wacky World Of X-Rated Bloopers / 1989 / GO / M • Where The Girls Are / 1984 / VEX / M • White Women / 1986 / CC / M • Wise Girls / 1989 / IN / C • The Woman In Pink / 1984 / SE / M • Women's Secret Desires / 1983 / LIP / F • Young Nympho's / 1986 / VD / M
STACEY G. *see* **Star Index I**
STACEY K. *see* **Stacy King**
STACEY LORDS *see* **Staci Lords**
STACEY LORRENNA
Immortal Desire / 1993 / VI / M
STACEY NICHOLS *(Lori (Stacey Nich.), Laura King)*
Dirty blonde girl similar in looks to Stacey Donovan but with a bit more flesh. Lori is from **Breakfast With Tiffany**. Laura King is from **Moist to the Touch**. Allegedly got pregnant in 1992 and had a spontaneous abortion. As of very late 1994 or early 1995 she has had her tits expanded to humongous size.
8-Ball: Westside Gang Bang / 1995 / PL / M • The Adventures Of Buttgirl & Wonder Wench / 1991 / AFV / M • After Hours Bondage / 1993 / BON / B • AHV #09: Get Down On It / 1991 / EVN / M • AHV #11: Head First / 1991 / EVN / M • America's Dirtiest Home Videos #09 / 1992 / VEX / M • Anal Carnival / 1992 / ROB / M • Anal Encounters #1 / 1991 / VC / M • Anal Encounters #2 / 1991 / VC / M • Anal Encounters #5: Deliveries In The Rear / 1992 / VC / M • Anal Encounters #6 / 1992 / VC / M • Anal Encounters #7: Enter Through The Rear / 1992 / VC / M • Anal Fugitive / 1995 / PEP / M • Anal Invader / 1995 / PEP / M • Anal Maniacs #3 / 1995 / WP / M • Anal Takeover / 1993 / PEP / M • Anal Therapy #2 / 1993 / FD / M • The Anus Family / 1991 / CC / M • As Sweet As They Come / 1992 / V99 / M • Ass Kisser: A Love Story / 1995 / PEP / M • Baccarat #1 / 1991

/ FH / M • Baccarat #2 / 1991 / FH / M • Back Seat Bush / 1992 / LV / M • The Backdoor Bradys / 1995 / PL / M • The Backdoor Club / 1992 / LV / M • Backdoor Suite / 1992 / EX / M • Backing In #4 / 1993 / WV / C • Backing In #5 / 1994 / WV / C • Backing In #7 / 1995 / WV / C • Backstage Entrance #1 / 1992 / FH / M • Backstage Entrance #2 / 1992 / FH / M • Backstage Pass / 1992 / VEX / M • The Backway Inn #1 / 1992 / FD / M • The Backway Inn #2 / 1992 / FD / M • Behind The Backdoor #6 / 1993 / EVN / M • Bianca Trump's Towers / 1992 / LV / M • Big Knockers #13 / 1995 / TV / M • Big Knockers #17 / 1995 / TV / M • Big Knockers #21: Best Of Lesbian #2 / 1995 / TV / C • The Big Shave / 1993 / PEP / M • The Box / 1992 / EX / M • Breakfast At Tiffany's / 1994 / IF / M • Breakfast With Tiffany / 1990 / HO / M • Breastman's Bikini Pool Party / 1995 / EVN / M • Bubble Butts #14 / 1992 / LBO / M • Bubbles / 1991 / IF / M • Burn / 1991 / LE / M • Burning Desire / 1992 / CDI / M • The Bust Blondes In The USA / 1995 / NAP / F • Butt's Up, Doc #1 / 1992 / GO / M • Butt's Up, Doc #4 / 1994 / GO / M • Butterfly / 1993 / OD / M • Butties / 1992 / VC / M • Caged Fury / 1993 / DR / M • Canned Heat / 1995 / IN / M • Cape Rear / 1992 / WV / M • Caught From Behind #18 / 1993 / HO / M • Charm School / 1993 / PEP / M • Cheeks #8 / 1995 / CC / M • Cheerleader Nurses #1 / 1993 / VC / M • Cheerleader Nurses #2 / 1993 / VC / M • Cold As Ice / 1994 / IN / M • College Cuties / 1995 / LE / M • Confessions #1 / 1992 / OD / M • Cum To Dinner / 1991 / HO / M • Cycle Sluts / 1992 / CC / M • Dark Dreams / 1992 / WV / M • Decadent Delights / 1992 / IF / M • Deep Inside Centerfold Girls / 1991 / VC / M • Designs On Women / 1994 / IN / F • Double D Dykes #19 / 1995 / GO / F • Double Penetration #5 / 1992 / WV / C • Double Penetration #6 / 1993 / WV / C • Double Penetration #7 / 1994 / WV / C • The Dragon Lady #2: Tales From the Bed / 1992 / WV / M • The Dragon Lady #5: Tales From The Bed #4 / 1993 / WV / M • Ebony Princess / 1994 / IN / M • Erotic Oddities / 1993 / LEI / C • Fast Cars And Fast Women / 1992 / LV / M • Flashpoint / 1991 / AFV / M • Flesh And Boner / 1993 / WV / M • Foreign Affairs / 1991 / LE / M • Forever Yours / 1992 / CDI / M • Four Weddings And A Honeymoon / 1995 / PL / M • Frankie And Joanie / 1991 / HW / M • French Twist / 1995 / IN / M • Gazongo / 1995 / PEP / M • Ghost To Ghost / 1991 / CC / M • A Girl's Affair #02 / 1993 / FD / F • A Girl's Affair #03 / 1993 / FD / F • A Girl's Affair #06 / 1995 / FD / F • Girls Will Be Boys #5 / 1993 / PL / F • The God Daughter #1 / 1991 / AFV / M • The God Daughter #2 / 1991 / AFV / M • Goldenbush / 1996 / AVI / M • Guess Who? / 1991 / EX / M • Hard To Thrill / 1991 / CIN / M • The Harder Way / 1991 / AR / M • Heartbeat / 1995 / PP / M • Heidi's Girls / 1995 / GO / M • Her Obsession / 1991 / MID / M • Hocus Poke-Us / 1991 / HO / M • Hollywood Boulevard / 1995 / CV / M • Hollywood's Hills / 1992 / LV / M • Home Maid Memories #2 / 1994 / BON / C • Hot Leather #2 / 1995 / GO / M • Hot To Trot / 1994 / IF / M • House Of Spartacus #2 / 1993 / IF / M • House Pet / 1992 / V99 / M • Housewife Lust #2 / 1995

/ TV / F • I'm No Dummy / 1991 / HO / M • If Dreams Come True / 1991 / AFV / M • Inside Of Me / 1993 / PL / G • Intimate Spys / 1992 / FOR / M • The Joi Fuk Club / 1993 / WV / M • Just For The Hell Of It / 1991 / CA / M • Kia Unmasked / 1995 / LE / M • Killer Tits / 1995 / LE / M • Kinky Cameraman #4 / 1996 / LEI / C • Kiss It Goodbye / 1991 / SE / M • Lesbian Pros And Amateurs #26 / 1993 / GO / F • Long Hot Summer / 1992 / CDI / M • Love Spice / 1995 / ERA / M • Midnight Orgy / 1994 / MID / C • Mind Games / 1995 / IMV / M • Miracle On 69th Street / 1992 / HW / M • Modern Love / 1991 / FAZ / M • Moist To The Touch / 1991 / DR / M • Moon Godesses #1 / 1992 / VIM / M • Mr. Peepers Amateur Home Videos #18: Puss in Boots / 1991 / LBO / M • Mr. Peepers Amateur Home Videos #22: Emergency Lip Service / 1991 / LBO / M • Mr. Peepers Amateur Home Videos #42: Great American Tails / 1992 / LBO / M • Mr. Peepers Casting Couch / 1991 / LBO / M • Mr. Peepers Nastiest #4 / 1995 / LBO / C • Mummy Dearest #3: The Parting / 1991 / LV / M • My Anal Valentine / 1993 / FD / M • My Secret Lover / 1992 / XCI / M • Naked Bun 2 1/2 / 1991 / WV / M • Naked Goddess #1 / 1991 / VC / M • Naked Goddess #2 / 1991 / VC / M • Nasty Jack's Homemade Vid. #39 / 1991 / CDI / M • Nasty Reputation / 1991 / VEX / M • Naughty By Nature / 1992 / IF / M • New Pussy Hunt #25 / 1996 / LEI / C • No Man's Land #11 / 1995 / VT / F • The One And Only / 1993 / FD / M • Opie Goes To South Central / 1995 / PP / M • Oral Majority #09 / 1992 / WV / C • Oral Majority #13 / 1995 / WV / C • Overnight Sensation / 1991 / XCI / M • Pearl Of The Orient / 1995 / IN / M • Peep Land / 1992 / FH / M • The Poetry Of The Flesh / 1993 / PEP / M • Private Matters / 1995 / EMC / M • Professor Butts / 1994 / SBP / F • Raw Talent: Bang 'er 05 Times / 1991 / RTP / M • Raw Talent: Bang 'er Megamix 1 / 1994 / RTP / C • A Rear And Pleasant Danger / 1995 / PP / M • A Reason To Die / 1994 / PEP / M • Red Hot Lover / 1995 / CV / M • Rent-A-Butt / 1992 / VC / M • Ride 'em Hard / 1992 / LV / M • Ride The Pink Lady / 1993 / WV / M • Rock Her / 1992 / LV / M • Runnin' Hot / 1992 / LV / M • Sensual Spirits / 1995 / LE / M • Sex Symphony / 1992 / VC / M • Sexual Healing / 1992 / LV / M • Shave Tails #3 / 1994 / SO / M • Shock / 1995 / LE / M • Snatch Motors / 1995 / VC / M • Sorority Sex Kittens #1 / 1992 / VC / M • Sorority Sex Kittens #2 / 1993 / VC / M • Spread Sheets / 1991 / DR / M • Student Fetish Videos: Catfighting #01 / 1991 / PLV / B • Student Fetish Videos: Catfighting #05 / 1992 / PRE / B • Student Fetish Videos: The Enema #01 / 1990 / PRE / B • Student Fetish Videos: The Enema #02 / 1990 / SFV / B • Student Fetish Videos: Foot Worship #01 / 1990 / PRE / B • Student Fetish Videos: Foot Worship #02 / 1990 / PRE / B • Student Fetish Videos: Foot Worship #08 / 1992 / PRE / B • Student Fetish Videos: Spanking #01 / 1990 / PLV / B • Student Fetish Videos: Spanking #02 / 1990 / SFV / B • Stupid And Stupider / 1995 / SO / M • Sugar Daddies / 1995 / FPI / M • Sweet A$ Money / 1994 / MID / M • Sweet As Honey / 1992 / LV / M • Tail Taggers #104 / 1993 /

WV / M • Tail Taggers #110 / 1993 / WV / M • Tail Taggers #113: Behind The Scenes / 1994 / WV / M • Tail Taggers #125 / 1994 / WV / M • Tailgate Party / 1990 / HO / M • Tails Of Tribeca / 1993 / HW / M • Take It Inside / 1995 / PEP / M • Talk Dirty To Me #09 / 1992 / DR / M • Teri Diver's Bedtime Tales / 1993 / FD / M • Thighs & Dolls / 1993 / PEP / M • Tit Tease #1 / 1995 / VT / M • Tits / 1995 / AVI / M • Transformation / 1996 / XCI / M • Transformed / 1991 / MET / M • Twice As Hard / 1992 / IF / M • Twilight / 1991 / ZA / M • Twin Peeks / 1990 / DR / M • Two Of A Kind / 1993 / PL / M • Two Times A Virgin / 1991 / AR / M • Unfaithful Entry / 1992 / DR / M • Unzipped / 1991 / WV / M • The Wanderer #1: Road Tails / 1995 / CDI / M • Wee Wee's Big Misadventure / 1991 / FH / M • Wild & Wicked #5 / 1995 / VT / M • Will And Ed's Bogus Gang Bang / 1992 / MID / M • Willie Wanker At The Fudge Packing Factory / 1995 / FD / M • With Love / 1995 / FD / M • Working Stiffs / 1993 / FD / M

STACEY NICHOLS (OTH)
Blacks & Blondes #36 / 1986 / WV / M

STACEY NIX *see* **Barbara Dare**

STACEY OWEN
10 Years Of Big Busts #1 / 1989 / BTO / C • The World Of Double-D #2 / 199? / H&S / S

STACEY PEACH
The Inseminator #1 / 1994 / LBO / M • The Inseminator #2: Domination Day / 1994 / LBO / M

STACEY POOLE *see* **Paula Winters**

STACEY WILLIAMS
Anal Anarchy / 1995 / VC / M • Sports Illustrated 1994 Swimsuit Issue Video / 1994 / WAR / S

STACI
Ebony Erotica #12: Pussy Posse / 1993 / GO / M • Hot Body Competition: Hot Pants Contest / 1996 / CG / F

STACI LEE *see* **Star Index I**

STACI LORDS *(Stacey Lords)*
Bimbo Bowlers From Boston / 1990 / ZA / M • Blame It On The Heat / 1989 / VC / M • Breaststroke #3 / 1989 / EX / M • Breathless / 1989 / CIN / M • Charmed Again / 1989 / VI / M • Denim Dolls #1 / 1989 / CDI / M • Easy Lover / 1989 / EX / M • Exiles / 1991 / VT / M • For Her Pleasure Only / 1989 / FAZ / M • From Japan With Love / 1990 / SLV / M • Future Lust / 1989 / ME / M • The Girl With The Blue Jeans Off / 1989 / FAZ / M • Graduation Ball / 1989 / CAE / M • Hard Bodies / 1989 / CDI / M • Hard Sell / 1990 / VC / M • Heart Breaker / 1989 / LE / M • Hot In The City / 1989 / VEX / M • In The Flesh / 1990 / IN / M • Introducing Charli / 1989 / CIN / M • Juggernaut / 1990 / EX / M • Kisses Don't Lie / 1989 / PL / M • L.A. Fantasies / 1990 / WV / C • The Last Temptation / 1988 / VD / M • Leather And Lace Revisited / 1991 / VT / F • Lonely Is The Night / 1990 / V99 / M • Mistaken Identity / 1990 / CC / M • Moondance / 1991 / WV / M • New Sensations / 1990 / CC / M • Oral Majority #07 / 1989 / WV / C • Paris Blues / 1990 / WV / C • Play Christy For Me / 1990 / CAY / M • The Red Baron / 1989 / FAN / M • Rock 'n' Roll Heaven / 1989 / EA / M • Route 69 / 1989 / OD / M • Sex Flex / 1989 / CDI / M • A Sexual Obsession / 1989 / PP / M • Single Girl Mas-

turbation #2 / 1989 / ESP / F • Splendor In The Ass #1 / 1989 / CA / M • Stairway To Heaven / 1989 / ME / M • Touched / 1990 / VI / M • Undercover Angel / 1988 / IN / M • Unforgivable / 1989 / IN / M • Veil / 1990 / VI / M • Welcome To The House Of Fur Pi / 1989 / GO / M • Wet Fingers / 1990 / HIO / M • What's Love Got To Do With It / 1989 / WV / M • Who Reamed Rosie Rabbit? #1 / 1989 / FAN / M • X Dreams / 1989 / CA / M • Young Girls In Tight Jeans / 1989 / VD / M

STACI MILKAVITCH
More Dirty Debutantes #48 / 1995 / 4P / M • More Dirty Debutantes #49 / 1995 / 4P / M

STACI PAO see Star Index I

STACI STAXX
Busty Porno Queens / 1996 / H&S / M • On Location In Palm Springs / 1996 / H&S / S

STACI VALENTINE
Short blonde hair, passable face, lithe body, rock-solid cantaloupes, too wide on the hips, marginal skin, and a reasonably tight waist. 5'4" tall, 110lbs, 36C-25-35, 25 years old in 1996. De-virginized at 15. Late 1996 has increased to a DD.
Abused / 1996 / ZA / M • Allure / 1996 / WP / M • Anal Connection / 1996 / ZA / M • Anal Professor / 1996 / ZA / M • Anal Virgins #02 / 1996 / NS / M • Asses Galore #3: Pure Evil / 1996 / DFI / M • Bikini Beach #4 / 1996 / CC / M • Crack Attack! / 1996 / PE / M • Cumming Clean (1996—Caballero) / 1996 / CA / M • Deadly Sin / 1996 / ONA / M • Director's Wet Dreams / 1996 / BBE / M • Dominant Jean / 1996 / CC / M • Eternal Lust / 1996 / VC / M • Executions On Butt Row / 1996 / EA / M • Expose Me Again / 1996 / CV / M • From The Heart / 1996 / XCI / M • Hell Hole / 1996 / ZA / M • Hillbilly Honeys / 1996 / WP / M • Hollywood Confidential / 1996 / SC / M • In Cold Sweat / 1996 / VI / M • Indecent Exposures / 1996 / MID / M • Memories / 1996 / ZA / M • Micky Ray's Hot Shots #01 / 1996 / DIG / M • Mystique / 1996 / SC / M • Nasty Nymphos #13 / 1996 / ANA / M • Philmore Butts All American Butt Search / 1996 / SUF / M • Pick Up Lines #06 / 1996 / OD / M • Playtime / 1996 / VI / M • Primarily Yours / 1996 / CA / M • Pussyman Auditions #20 / 1996 / SNA / M • Satyr / 1996 / WP / M • Sorority Sex Kittens #3 / 1996 / VC / M • Stardust #5 / 1996 / VI / M • Up And Cummers #31 / 1996 / 4P / M • Up Close & Personal #3 / 1996 / IPI / M • Video Virgins #29 / 1996 / NS / M

STACI VAUGHN
As Sweet As Can Be / 1993 / V99 / M • Booberella / 1992 / BTO / M • Casting Call (Venus 99) / 1993 / V99 / M • Living For Love / 1993 / V99 / M • Taste The Pleasure / 1996 / LEI / C

STACIA MICULA see Samantha Fox

STACIE
The Kiss / 1995 / WP / M

STACIE SOMERS
More Punished Cheeks / 1994 / RB / B • Tight Asses / 1994 / RB / B

STACY
Black Street Hookers #4: The Streets Of San Francisco / 1996 / DFI / M • Bosoms Triple X / 1990 / BTO / M • Catfighting Students / 1995 / PRE / C • Full Moon Video #19: Toys For Twats / 1994 / FAP / F • Girls

Games Of Summer #4 / 1994 / NIV / S • HomeGrown Video #473: Furpie Feast #3 / 1997 / HOV / C • Intimate Interviews #3 / 1996 / NIT / M • Mike Hott: #204 Lesbian Sluts #05 / 1992 / MHV / F • More Dirty Debutantes #07 / 1991 / 4P / M • Nasty Newcummers #10 / 1995 / MET / M • New Faces, Hot Bodies #18 / 1995 / STP / M • Rope Dance / 1994 / VIG / B • Shane's World #5 / 1996 / OD / M • Shaved #01 / 1991 / RB / F

STACY (MIA POWERS) see Mia Powers

STACY AUSTIN see Star Index I

STACY BELLE
Fat and not-too-pretty with a tattoo of a mouth on her breasts and a 'Property of...' tattoo on her rear end.
Amateur Hours #06 / 1990 / AFI / M • America's Dirtiest Home Videos #04 / 1991 / VEX / M • America's Dirtiest Home Videos #05 / 1991 / VEX / M • America's Dirtiest Home Videos #06 / 1991 / AMA / M • America's Dirtiest Home Videos #14 / 1992 / VEX / M • Assinine / 1990 / CC / M • Best Of Foot Worship #3 / 1992 / BIZ / C • Bum Rap / 1990 / PLV / B • The Dane Harlow Story / 1990 / IF / M • Dane's Brothel / 1990 / IF / G • Deep Dreams / 1990 / IN / M • The Girls Of Cooze / 1992 / V99 / C • In Pursuit Of Passion / 1990 / V99 / M • It Happened At Midnight / 1990 / IN / M • Lady Badass / 1990 / V99 / M • Lady Of The House / 1990 / VEX / M • Love Ghost / 1990 / WV / M • Mike Hott: #150 Two Girl Spanking Session / 1991 / MHV / F • Mike Hott: #151 Four Girl Spanking Session / 1991 / MHV / F • Nasty Jack's Homemade Vid. #06 / 1990 / CDI / M • Nasty Jack's Homemade Vid. #22 / 1991 / CDI / M • Next Door Neighbors #17 / 1990 / BON / M • The Pawnbroker / 1990 / IF / M • The Perfect Pet / 1991 / VEX / C • Putting On The Ritz / 1990 / VEX / M • Randy And Dane / 1991 / IF / G • Rear Admiral / 1990 / ZA / M • Send Me An Angel / 1990 / V99 / M • Sunny After Dark / 1990 / WV / M • Women In Charge / 1990 / VEX / M • The Wonder Rears / 1990 / SO / M • Young Buns #2 / 1990 / WV / M

STACY BLAIR
Blushing Bottoms / 1992 / RB / B • Butt Busting / 1996 / RB / B • Domestic Training / 1992 / RB / B • Finger Pleasures #5 / 1996 / PL / F • Finger Pleasures #6 / 1996 / PL / F • Naughty Boys #1 / 1992 / RB / B • Naughty Boys #2 / 1992 / RB / B • Naughty Sisters #1 / 1992 / RB / B • Painful Lesson (Red Board) / 1992 / RB / B • Uncle Jamie's Double Trouble / 1992 / RB / B • Young Sluts In Heat #1 / 1996 / PL / M

STACY BLUE
Insane Desires / cr78 / ... / M • The Last Sex Act / cr78 / S&L / M • Lenny's Comeback / cr78 / CIN / M • Sexercise Clinic / cr78 / INT / M • Way Down Deep / cr78 / PYR / M

STACY DEE
C-Hunt #05: Wett Worx / 1996 / PEV / M

STACY EVANS (Stacy Goldman)
Blonde, lithe body, small tits, reasonably pretty, tattoo on right belly.
Desires Within Young Girls / 1977 / CA / M • The Ecstasy Girls #1 / 1979 / CA / M • The Erotic Adventures Of Candy / 1978 / VCX / M • Stalag 69 / 1982 / VHL / S • Taxi Girls #1 / 1980 / WV / M • The Untamed / 1978 /

VCX / M

STACY FREEMAN
Fair Warning / 1995 / ZFX / B

STACY GOLDMAN see Stacy Evans

STACY HOLMES
One Of A Kind / 1976 / SVE / M

STACY JONES
Creme De La Face #17: Semen For Seven / 1996 / OD / M

STACY KING (Stacey K.)
Long dark blonde or reddish hair (depending on the movie), passable almost pretty face, tongue pin, large natural tits, 38D-25-38, womanly body, tattoo around left bicep, another around left ankle, another large one on her left tit, and yet another on her right shoulder back. De-virginized at 14. Seems to have a quite pleasant tomboyish personality.
Ass Masters (Leisure) #04 / 1995 / LEI / M • Behind The Backdoor #7 / 1995 / EVN / M • Big Boob Bangeroo #6 / 1996 / TTV / M • Butt Bangers Ball #2 / 1996 / TTV / M • Butt Hunt #07 / 1995 / LEI / M • Casting Call #13 / 1995 / SO / M • Crunch Bunch / 1995 / PRE / C • The Cumm Brothers #08: Escape From Uranus / 1995 / OD / M • Cute Cuddly Bubbly Butts / 1996 / TTV / M • Delaid Delivery / 1995 / EX / M • Dirty Dirty Debutantes #1 / 1995 / 4P / M • Dirty Old Men #2 / 1995 / IP / M • Enemates #11 / 1995 / BIZ / B • Fresh Faces #06 / 1995 / EVN / M • High Heeled & Horny #4 / 1995 / LBO / M • Hollywood Starlets Adventure #05 / 1995 / AVS / M • J.E.G.: Pregnant Expose #1 (#31) / 1996 / JEG / F • Kinky Peep Shows: Anals & Orals / 1995 / SUF / M • Knocked-Up Nymphos #2 / 1996 / GLI / M • Lactamania #4 / 1996 / TTV / M • Leg...Ends #16 / 1996 / PRE / F • Mike Hott: #320 Three-Sum Sluts #06 / 1995 / MHV / M • Mike Hott: #324 Cum In My Cunt #06 / 1995 / MHV / C • Mike Hott: #331 Lesbian Sluts #21 / 1996 / MHV / F • Mike Hott: #366 Lactating Lesbians / 1996 / MHV / F • Mike Hott: #372 Stacey Pregnant / 1996 / MHV / M • Mike Hott: #378 Fuck The Boss #8 / 1996 / MHV / M • Mike Hott: #387 Girls Who Lap Cum From Cunts #04 / 1996 / MHV / M • Muff Divers #2 / 1996 / TV / F • Muff Divers #3 / 1996 / TV / F • The New Babysitter / 1995 / GO / M • The New Snatch Masters #16 / 1995 / LEI / C • Nothing Like Nurse Nookie #2 / 1996 / NIT / M • Odyssey 30 Min: #558: / 1995 / OD / M • Pounding Ass / 1995 / VMX / M • Ready To Drop #11 / 1996 / FC / M • Ready To Drop #12 / 1996 / FC / M • Throbbing Threesomes / 1996 / NIT / M • Toes 'n' Cons / 1996 / PRE / S • Young & Natural #06 / 1995 / PRE / F • Young & Natural #09 / 1995 / PRE / C • Young & Natural #12 / 1996 / TV / F • Young & Natural #14 / 1996 / TV / F

STACY LANE
Student Fetish Videos: Bondage #02 / 1996 / PRE / B • Student Fetish Videos: Tickling #12 / 1995 / SFV / B

STACY MORGAN
Private Film #07 / 1994 / OD / M

STACY POOL see Paula Winters

STACY SPELLING
Fashion Sluts #2 / 1995 / ABS / M • The Voyeur #4 / 1995 / EA / M

STACY ST JAMES see Sydney St James
STACY WALLER see Star Index I

STACY/TAMMY *(Tammy (Stacy/Tammy))*
This girl uses a common name in one movie and another in another. Grrr! However she's pretty enough to put up with the ID problems. According to **Anal Virgins #01** she's 21 years old in 1996 and was de-virginized at 16. She also says she's an anal virgin and from the performance maybe she's telling the truth. Very tight little body, perhaps a tad thin on the legs, small to medium tits, long straight blonde hair, nice personality, tight waist, narrow hips, nice little butt, slightly too much acne.
Anal Virgins #01 / 1996 / NS / M • Analtown USA #05 / 1995 / NIT / M • Video Virgins #26 / 1996 / NS / M

STALLION
Titties 'n Cream #1 / 1994 / FC / M

STAN
ABA: Double Feature #2 / 1996 / ALP / M • At Home With Stan And Bobbie / 1996 / SHL / B • HomeGrown Video #444: / 1995 / HOV / M • HomeGrown Video #458: Cream Pie For Dessert / 1995 / HOV / C • Magma: Dirty Diana / 1994 / MET / M • Magma: Horny & Greedy / 1993 / MET / M • Magma: Live And Learn / 1995 / MET / M • Magma: Tanja's Horny Nights / 1994 / MET / M • Rip-Off Of Millie / cr78 / VHL / M

STAN FIKE
Bottom Busters / 1973 / BLT / M

STAN JACOBS
My Sister Seka / 1981 / CA / M

STAN LEE see Star Index I
STAN OLIVER see Star Index I
STAN TANNER see Star Index I
STAN WILDER see Sean Rider

STANDA
Buttman's Orgies / 1996 / EA / M • Prague By Night #1 / 1996 / EA / M • Prague By Night #2 / 1996 / EA / M

STANFORD GROSSMAN see Star Index I

STANILAS PIOTR
Cherry Busters / 1995 / WIV / M • Jura Sexe / 1995 / JP / G

STANISLAS
Triple X Video Magazine #03 / 1995 / OD / M • Triple X Video Magazine #10 / 1995 / OD / M • Triple X Video Magazine #11 / 1995 / OD / M • Triple X Video Magazine #12 / 1996 / OD / M

STANLEY
New Faces, Hot Bodies #12 / 1993 / STP / M

STANLEY CAMEL see Star Index I
STANLEY LATZ see Star Index I
STANLEY MIRANDA see Star Index I

STAR
Alex Jordan's First Timers #02 / 1993 / OD / M • Amateur Hours #05 / 1990 / AFI / M • Casting Call #10 / 1994 / MET / M • Creme De Femme #4 / 1981 / AVC / C • Harlem Honies #2: Nasty In New York / 1994 / CC / M • HomeGrown Video #434: Forrest Hump / 1994 / HOV / M • HomeGrown Video #473: Furpie Feast #3 / 1997 / HOV / C • Honey Drippers / 1992 / ROB / F • Kittens & Vamps #1 / 1993 / ROB / F • Lesbian Lockup / 1993 / ROB / F • Limited Edition #21 / 1981 / AVC / M • Limited Edition #22 / 1981 / AVC / M • New Faces, Hot Bodies #04 / 1992 / STP / M • New Faces, Hot Bodies #05 / 1992 / STP / M • New Faces, Hot Bodies #09 / 1993 / STP / M • New Faces, Hot Bodies #21 / 1996 / STP /

C • Ona Zee's Doll House #1 / 1995 / ONA / F
STAR (WOOD) see Star Wood
STAR CHAMBERS see Star Index I
STAR CHANDLER *(Tabita Star Chandler, Ruby Richards)*
Thin, quite pretty redhead who originally only did bondage movies but in 1995 migrated to explicit under the name Ruby Richards. From **Bondage Outcall** (early 1994) she says she is 26 years old and has been doing bondage for about two years. In late 1996 or early 1997 she married Greg Dark.
Batbabe / 1995 / PL / M • Beauty's Punishment / 1996 / BIZ / B • Beauty's Revenge / 1996 / BIZ / B • Bondage Outcall / 1994 / BON / B • Born 2 B Wild / 1995 / PL / M • Boss Bitch From Bondage Hell / 1996 / LBO / B • Bright Tails #2 / 1994 / STP / B • Buffy Malibu's Nasty Girls #10 / 1996 / ANA / F • Butt Jammers #03 / 1995 / SC / F • The Butt Sisters Do Seattle / 1995 / MID / M • Buttslammers #11: / 1996 / BS / F • Buttslammers #12: Anal Madness / 1996 / BS / F • Captured On Camera / 1997 / BON / B • Caught & Punished / 1996 / EXQ / B • Chronicles Of Pain #1 / 1996 / BIZ / B • Cinderella In Chains #1 / 1996 / LBO / B • Cinderella In Chains #3 / 1996 / LBO / B • The Come On / 1995 / EX / M • The Contessa De Sade / 1996 / LBO / B • Cries From The Dungeon / cr94 / HOM / B • The Dean Of Discipline / 1996 / HAC / B • Desire & Submission #1 / 1994 / HAC / B • Desire & Submission #2 / 1994 / HAC / B • The Disciplinarians / 1996 / LON / B • The Divine Marquis / 1995 / ONA / B • Dresden Diary #14: Ecstasy In Hell / 1996 / BIZ / B • Dresden Diary #15: / 1996 / BIZ / B • Dungeon Of The Borgias / 1993 / HOM / B • Education Of The Dominatrix / 1993 / HOM / B • Electropussy / 1995 / CC / M • The Exchange / 1995 / BON / B • Exposed / 1993 / HOM / B • Finger Pleasures #3 / 1995 / PL / F • Gallery Of Pain / 1995 / BON / B • Goldilocks And The 3 Bares / 1996 / LBO / B • Hellfire Society / 19?? / HOM / B • Home Maid Memories #1 / 1994 / BON / C • Hootersville (Legend) / 1995 / LE / M • Innocent's Initiation / 1996 / BON / B • Interrogation South American Style / 1995 / LBO / B • Kym Wilde's On The Edge #29 / 1995 / RB / B • Lair Of The Bondage Bandits / 1991 / HOM / B • Leather Bound Dykes From Hell #7 / 1996 / BIZ / B • Little Shop Of Tortures / 1996 / LBO / B • Mistress (1993-HOM) / 1994 / HOM / B • Mistress Of Misery / 1996 / LBO / B • Never Trust A Slave / 1996 / BON / B • Phantom And The Whip / 1993 / VTF / B • Prisoners Of Payne / 1995 / NIT / B • The Punishment Of Red Riding Hood / 1996 / LBO / B • Pussyman's House Party #1 / 1996 / SNA / M • Pussyman's House Party #2 / 1996 / SNA / M • Queen Of The Lash / 1993 / LON / B • Sadistic Sisters / 1996 / BON / B • Sensuous Torture / 1996 / BS / B • The Shocking Truth #1 / 1996 / DWO / M • The Shocking Truth #2 / 1996 / DWO / M • The Slaves Of Alexis Payne / 1995 / LON / B • Sold Into Slavery / 1996 / BON / B • Spiked Heel Diaries #5 / 1995 / BIZ / B • The Story Of Ouch! / 1996 / LBO / B • Student Fetish Videos: Bondage #02 / 1996 / PRE / B • Student Fetish Videos: Catfighting #16 / 1996 / PRE / B • Student Fetish Videos:

The Enema #20 / 1996 / PRE / B • Till She Screams / 1992 / HOM / B • Totally Ona: The Best Of Ona Zee / 1996 / ONA / C • Two For The Price Of One / 1993 / BON / B • Voo Doo / 1995 / VTF / B • White Slavers / 1996 / LBO / B • Will Of Iron / 1991 / HOM / B
STAR HILLS
On White Satin / 1980 / VCX / M • Skintight / 1981 / CA / M
STAR LEMORE
Tailz From Da Hood #3 / 1996 / AVI / M
STAR MURPHY
Reel Classics #1 / 1996 / H&S / M
STAR TREK
Impulse #05: When I Was 20... / 1995 / MBP / M
STAR WEATHERLY see Kimberly Carson
STAR WOOD *(Starr Wood, Starr Would, Starr Hills, Star (Wood))*
Tall brunette, small tits, passable face, skin is only so-so.
All American Girls #1 / 1982 / CA / M • Calendar Girl '83 / 1983 / CXV / M • Daisy May / 1979 / VC / M • Fantasy World / 1979 / WWV / M • Femmes De Sade / 1976 / ALP / M • Irresistible #1 / 1982 / SE / M • Ladies Nights / 1980 / VC / M • Ms. Magnificent / 1979 / SE / M • Playthings / 1980 / VC / M • Same Time Every Year / 1981 / VHL / M • Sweet Dreams Suzan / 1980 / CA / M • Taboo #01 / 1980 / VCX / M • VCA Previews #2 / 1988 / VC / C
STAR-LING
Piglitz: Pudgy Porkers / 1996 / GLI / M
STARBUCK
Video Virgins #16 / 1994 / NS / M
STARBUCK (KEN) see Ken Starbuck
STARLENE
Creme De La Face #14: Kiss My Cum / 1996 / OD / M • Love Chunks / 1996 / TTV / M
STARLING
New Faces, Hot Bodies #14 / 1994 / STP / M • Salsa & Spice #4 / 1996 / TTV / M • Salsa & Spice #5 / 1997 / TTV / M
STARLYN SIMONE
Angel Above, Devil Below / 1974 / CV / M • Love On Top / 1971 / CV / M • Sleazy Rider (Phoenix) / 19?? / PHO / M
STARR
Blue Vanities #508 / 1992 / FFL / M • Hardcore Confidential #2 / 1996 / TEP / M • Licorice Lollipops: Summer Break / 1996 / HW / M
STARR DAMONE
Black Bottom Girlz / 1994 / CA / M • Black Nurse Fantasies / 1994 / CA / M • Hollywood Amateurs #04 / 1994 / MID / M • Sexual Misconduct / 1994 / VD / C • Swedish Erotica #75 / 1994 / CA / M • Video Virgins #13 / 1994 / NS / M
STARR HILLS see Star Wood
STARR JOHNSON see Star Index I
STARR LANE
Triple Play / 1983 / HO / M
STARR MURPHY
Big Bust Vixens / 1984 / BTO / S • Blue Vanities #558 / 1994 / FFL / M
STARR WOOD see Star Wood
STARR WOULD see Star Wood
STARRY KNIGHTS
Opie Goes To South Central / 1995 / PP / M • Palm Springs Or Bust / 1994 / BTO / M
STASHA *(Angelo (Stasha))*

Pretty blonde transexual, 36-26-36, born Mar 24, 1969, 5'7" tall. Slightly too pudgy but does act like a female. Allegedly died of leukemia in April 1993. Did some gay movies under the name of Angelo.
Crossing The Line / 1993 / STA / G • Double Impact / 1992 / CDI / G • The Eyes Of A Stranger / 1992 / CDI / G • Fire & Ice / 1992 / CDI / G • More Than A Woman / 1992 / CDI / G • Mystery Date / 1992 / CDI / G • Night Breed / 1992 / CDI / G • Passion For Fashion / 1992 / PEP / G • The Perfect Girl / 1992 / CDI / G • Prime Offender / 1993 / PEP / M • Promises In The Dark / 1991 / CIN / G • Split Personality / 1991 / CIN / G • Stasha's Adult School / 1993 / CDI / G • Stasha's Diary / 1991 / CIN / G • Stasha's Last Kiss / 1993 / VEX / G • Stasha: Portrait Of A Swinger / 1992 / CDI / G • Strange Night On Earth / 1993 / PEP / G

STASHA (BLACK)
Black Street Hookers #4: The Streets Of San Francisco / 1996 / DFI / M

STASHA (FRENCH)
Private Film #09 / 1994 / OD / M

STASHA BERGOFF *see* Samantha Fox

STAY C *see* Star Index I

STEAVIE STARR
Anal Vision #26 / 1994 / LBO / M • Boobwatch #1 / 1996 / SC / M • Both Ends Burning / 1993 / HW / M • Erotic Desires / 1994 / MAX / M • First Time Lesbians #18 / 1994 / JMP / F • Gonzo Groups & Gang Bangs / 1994 / GLI / M • More Dirty Debutantes #33 / 1994 / 4P / M • Reel People #06 / 1995 / PP / M • Rosie: The Neighborhood Slut / 1994 / VIM / M • Video Virgins #10 / 1993 / NS / M • Voices In My Bed / 1993 / VI / M • Xcitement: The Movie / 1993 / XCI / M

STEAVIE STONE *(Jessica Stone)*
Hefty blonde with large flabby tits and lots of flab elsewhere. In **I Want A Divorce** she has a mole on her chin but it could be just a zit and therefore not good ID.
Bubble Butts #25 / 1993 / LBO / M • I Want A Divorce / 1993 / ZA / M • Nothing Butt Amateurs #01 / 1993 / AFI / M • Positively Pagan #08 / 1993 / ATA / M • Tail Taggers #104 / 1993 / WV / M

STEDLA *see* Zumira

STEDNA *see* Zumira

STEF EISEN
Bucky Beaver's XXX Dragon Art Theatre Double Feature #01 / 1996 / SOW / M • Hitler's Harlots / cr73 / SOW / M

STEFAN PEACH *see* Star Index I

STEFANI *see* Stephanie (1990)

STEFANIA SARTORI
Buttman's Big Butt Backdoor Babes / 1995 / EA / M • Essence Of A Woman / 1995 / ONA / M • Hotel Fear / 1996 / ONA / M • Juliet & Romeo / 1996 / XC / M • Robin Thief Of Wives / 1996 / XC / M • Sleeping Booty / 1995 / EL / M • Sodomania #14: C**t Lickin', C*m Drinkin' Bitches / 1995 / EL / M • Sodomania: Slop Shots / 1996 / EL / C • World Sex Tour #1 / 1995 / ANA / M

STEFANIE DE PARIS
Magma: Showtime Cunts / 1994 / MET / M

STEFFEN THOMAS
New Clits On The Block / 1995 / DBM / M

STEFFI *(Meesha (Steffi))*
Quite pretty brunette with small tits, 22 years old, tight body and waist. De-virginized at

16 during lunchtime. Comes from upstate NY. 34B-23-34 (the B she admits is a "small B"). Up to the time of **MDD #26** she says she has only had 5 men. After about three movies she had her tits done and they became rock hard, medium sized.
Anal Knights In Hollywood #1 / 1993 / MET / M • Backdoor To Harley-Wood #3 / 1993 / AFV / M • The Cumming Of Sarah Jane #2 / 1993 / AFV / M • Debbie Does Dallas Again / 1994 / AFV / M • Dirty Doc's Housecalls #02 / 1993 / LV / M • Double D Dykes #12 / 1993 / GO / F • Eleventh Annual AVN Awards / 1994 / VC / M • First Time Lesbians #07 / 1993 / JMP / F • Haunting Dreams #1 / 1993 / LV / M • Heidi Does Hollywood / 1993 / AFV / M • Mistress Of The Mansion / 1994 / CV / M • More Dirty Debutantes #26 / 1993 / 4P / M • New Girls In Town #4 / 1993 / CC / M • Pleasure Dome: The Genesis Chamber / 1994 / AFV / M • Saturday Night Porn #3 / 1993 / AFV / M • Sexy Nurses #2 / 1994 / CV / M • Sindy Does Anal / 1993 / AFV / M • Sindy Does Anal Again / 1994 / AFV / M • Sindy's Sexercise Workout / 1994 / AFV / M • Video Virgins #07 / 1993 / NS / M

STEFFI (1984)
Foxy Brown / 1984 / VC / M

STEFFINE STONE *see* Melissa Melendez

STELA *see* Star Index I

STELLA
Blue Vanities #501 / 1992 / FFL / M • Blush: Burlez Live! #2 / 1993 / FAT / F • Eurotica #04 / 1996 / XC / M • Eurotica #13 / 1996 / XC / M • Mike Hott: #391 / 1996 / MHV / M • Mike Hott: #393 / 1996 / MHV / M • Sheer Panties / 1979 / SE / C • Stella's Contest / cr88 / BON / B • Wrasslin She-Babes #05 / 1996 / SOW / M

STELLA BLUE *see* Angela Summers

STELLA DESIRE
Papa's Got A Brand New Jag / 1995 / GOT / M

STELLA MANSFIELD
Disciples Of Discipline / 1996 / BON / B

STELLA ROCCI
Private Film #27 / 1995 / OD / M • Private Film #28 / 1995 / OD / M

STELLA SCOTT *see* Star Index I

STELLA STAR
After The Lights Go Out / 1989 / VEX / M • All Hands On Dick / 1988 / STA / G • Back On Top / 1988 / FAZ / M • Best Body In Town / 1989 / FAZ / F • Busting Loose / 1989 / AMB / F • Call Girl Academy / 1990 / V99 / M • Family Thighs / 1989 / AR / M • The Girls Are Bustin' Loose / 1988 / AMB / F • Imagination X-Posed / 1989 / 4P / M • Missy Impossible / 1989 / CAR / M • Mix-N-Match / 1989 / LV / G • My Pleasure / 1992 / CS / B • Strykin' It Deep / 1989 / V10 / M • Super Blondes / 1989 / VEX / M • Telemates / 1988 / STA / M • Telemates / 1991 / V99 / M • Twentysomething #3 / 1989 / VI / M

STELLA STEVEN
The Taming Of Rebecca / 1982 / SVE / B

STELLA WORTH
Dark Dreams / 1971 / ALP / M

STELLA ZINE
Intimate Interviews #2 / 1996 / NIT / M

STENA VIBEN
Swedish Vip Magazine #1 / 1995 / PL / M

STEPH *see* Lady Stephanie

STEPHAN KRAEMER
The Anal-Europe Series #03: The Museum Of The Living Art / 1993 / LV / M • The Anal-Europe Series #04: Anal Recall / 1993 / LV / M • Club DV8 #2 / 1993 / SC / M • Nasty Nymphos #02 / 1994 / ANA / M • Picture Me Naked / 1993 / LE / M • Prima #08: Sex Camping / 1995 / MBP / M • Prime Offender / 1993 / PEP / M • Virtual Reality / 1993 / EX / M

STEPHAN ROY
Angel Buns / 1981 / QX / M

STEPHAN WOLFE
Denni O' #3: Fanta-Sea Of Cum / 1996 / SP / M • Denni O' #4: Beach Ballin' / 1996 / SP / M • Denni O' #5: / 1996 / SP / M • Flexxx #4 / 1995 / VT / M • Telephone Expose / 1995 / VC / M

STEPHANE MAURY
Felicia / 1975 / QX / M

STEPHANI *see* Star Index I

STEPHANIA
Private Film #25 / 1995 / OD / M

STEPHANIE
Adventures Of The DP Boys: Back In Town / 1994 / HW / M • Afternoon Delights / 1995 / FC / M • Ash Prod: We Aim To Tease / 1995 / ASH / M • Beach Bum Amateur's #21 / 1993 / MID / F • Big Busty #37 / 198? / H&S / S • Blue Vanities #549 / 1994 / FFL / M • Bras And Panties #1 / 199? / H&S / S • Butt Hunt #04 / 1995 / LEI / M • Caged Heat #1 / 1974 / ST0 / S • Cries From The Dungeon / cr94 / HOM / B • Debauchery / 1995 / MET / M • Dementia / 1995 / IP / M • Destiny & April In Bondage / 1993 / BON / B • Dragxina, Queen Of The Underworld / 1995 / MET / G • Erotic Westernscapes / 1994 / PHV / S • Eurotica #03 / 1995 / XC / M • Eurotica #04 / 1996 / XC / M • The Girls From Hootersville #07 / 1994 / SFP / M • The Girls Of Fantasex #1 / 1996 / NIT / M • Hot Body Competition: Hot Pants Contest / 1996 / CG / F • I Want To Be A Mistress / cr86 / BIZ / B • Lewd In Liverpool / 1995 / VC / M • Little Big Girls / 1996 / VC / M • Magma: Bizarre Games / 1996 / MET / M • Naughty Nanny / 1995 / DIP / F • Nu-West Screen Test #1 / 1988 / NUV / F • Our Sorority / 1993 / SHL / B • Out Of My Mind / 1995 / PL / M • Primal / 1994 / PHV / S • Pussy Hunt #14 / 1995 / LEI / M • Ripe & Ready (Infinity) / 1995 / IF / M • Sex Dreams / 1995 / C69 / M • Shannon Shows Off / 1993 / HAC / G • Sodomania #15: Warning! / 1996 / EL / M • Stephanie: After Hours / 1995 / DIP / F

STEPHANIE (1990) *(Stefani)*
Amateur Lesbians #10: Stephanie / 1991 / GO / F • Between My Breasts #13 / 1990 / BTO / S • Between My Breasts #14 / 1991 / BTO / S • The Buttnicks #2 / 1991 / HIO / M • Derrier / 1991 / CC / M • More Dirty Debutantes #09 / 1991 / 4P / M • Nasty Jack's Homemade Vid. #31 / 1991 / CDI / M • Pearl Necklace: Amorous Amateurs #05 / 1992 / SEE / M • Shaved #02 / 1992 / RB / F

STEPHANIE ADAMS
First obvious appearence in **The Book**. Penthouse Pet for January 1990 and centerfold in *Penthouse* in January 1988 at age of 19. Adorable tight little body from the waist down. Boobs are natural but a trifle too large. In her return in mid-1994 she has put on some flab and lost the accolade of "tight

little body".

As Sweet As They Come / 1992 / V99 / M • The Book / 1990 / IF / M • Cat's Meow / 1991 / VEX / M • Centerfold Strippers / 1994 / ME / M • Deep Dreams / 1990 / IN / M • Heartbreaker / 1991 / IF / M • Hot Meat / 1990 / V99 / M • Indecent Proposals / 1991 / V99 / M • Lady Badass / 1990 / V99 / M • Lonely And Blue / 1990 / VEX / M • Looking For Love / 1991 / VEX / M • Masked Ball / 1992 / IF / M • New Pussy Hunt #26 / 1996 / LEI / C • Party Favors / 1993 / VEX / M • Putting On The Ritz / 1990 / VEX / M • Send Me An Angel / 1990 / V99 / M • Sexual Persuasion / 1991 / V99 / M • A Touch Of Mink / 1990 / V99 / M

STEPHANIE AUSTIN *see Star Index I*
STEPHANIE BISHOP *see Viper*
STEPHANIE BOND *see Star Index I*
STEPHANIE BOYD
The Awakening Of Emily / 1976 / CDI / M
STEPHANIE BRADLEY *see Star Index I*
STEPHANIE COLE *see Star Index I*
STEPHANIE DUKALLE *see* **Stephanie DuValle**
STEPHANIE DUVALLE *(Thumper, E. Thumper, Stephanie DuKalle, Menette, Stephanie Right, Monique (S. DuValle))*
Tight bodied blonde with enhanced (not too big) tits, tattoo of a horse on her back just above her ass crack. Works in mud wrestling at the Hollywood Tropicana. 23 years old in 1993 and was de-virginized at 14. 34-26-34. Sweet smile and very pretty face. Born in Trenton NJ. As of mid-1994 she has had her tits further enhanced to large size in a very bad job (see **Rump-Shaker #3**). Originally hung around with Dick Nasty but about 1994 they apparently broke up. In 1995 seems to have gone through further enhancement to almost watermelon size plus she's looking worn out. Dick Nasty seeems to be back in the picture too.
Adventures Of The DP Boys: At The French Riviera / 1994 / HW / M • Amateur Orgies #15 / 1992 / AFI / M • Amateur Orgies #19 / 1992 / AFI / M • Anal Alice / 1992 / AFV / M • Anal Angels #6 / 1996 / VEX / C • Anal Ski Vacation / 1993 / ANA / M • The Anal Team / 1993 / LV / M • Anal Variations #01 / 1993 / FH / M • Anal Virgins Of America #02 / 1993 / FOR / M • The Anal-Europe Series #06: Anal Luck / 1993 / LV / M • Ass, Gas & The Mystical GLOP / 1997 / EL / M • Attack Of The Killer Dildos / 1996 / RAS / M • Backdoor Magic / 1994 / LV / M • Beach Bum Amateur's #37 / 1993 / MID / M • Beverly Hills Bikini Company / 1996 / NIT / M • Biff Malibu's Totally Nasty Home Videos #24 / 1992 / ANA / M • Big Murray's New-Cummers #02: Las Vegas Swingers / 1992 / FD / M • Big Murray's New-Cummers #03: Orgy 'Til Dawn / 1992 / FD / M • Big Murray's New-Cummers #05: Luscious Lesbos / 1993 / FD / F • Big Murray's New-Cummers #06: Men & Women / 1993 / FD / M • Bimbette: Adventures In Anal Land / 1996 / TEP / M • Bimbonese 101 / 1993 / PL / M • The Blonde & The Beautiful #2 / 1993 / LV / M • The Blowjob Adventures Of Doctor Fellatio / 1997 / EL / M • Blue Moon / 1992 / AFV / M • Bobby Hollander's Rookie Nookie #04 / 1993 / SFP / M • Bobby Hollander's Rookie Nookie #05 / 1993 / SFP / M • The Bold, The Bald & The

Beautiful / 1993 / VIM / M • Boob Acres / 1996 / HW / M • Boob Tube Lube / 1996 / RAS / M • The Breast Of Breastmen / 1995 / EVN / C • Brian Sparks: Virtually Unreal #2 / 1996 / ALD / M • Broken Vows / 1996 / ULP / M • Buffy Malibu's Totally Nasty All-Girl Home Videos #02 / 1992 / ANA / F • Bun Busters #01 / 1993 / LBO / M • Bunny Bleu: A Gang Bang Fantasy / 1994 / FC / M • Butt Hole In-One / 1994 / AFV / M • Butt Woman #4 / 1993 / FH / M • Butt Woman #5 / 1993 / FH / M • The Cable Girl / 1996 / NIT / M • Cannes 93: Broads Abroad / 1993 / ELP / M • Casanova #4 / 1993 / SC / M • Casting Call #02 / 1993 / SO / M • The Catburglar / 1994 / PL / M • Caught From Behind #23 / 1995 / HO / M • Cheating Hearts / 1994 / AFI / M • Cloud 900 / 1996 / EYE / M • Club DV8 #1 / 1993 / SC / M • Colossal Orgy #1 / 1993 / HW / M • Colossal Orgy #2 / 1994 / HW / M • Colossal Orgy #3 / 1994 / HW / M • Corporate Justice / 1996 / TEP / M • Deep Throat #6 / 1992 / AFV / M • Designer Bodies / 1993 / VI / M • Dirty Diner #02 / 1993 / GLI / M • Diva #2: Deep In Glamour / 1996 / VC / F • Double Crossed / 1994 / MID / M • The Dragon Lady #5: Tales From The Bed #4 / 1993 / WV / M • The Ebony Connection #4 / 1994 / LBO / C • F-Channel / 1994 / AFV / F • Flashback / 1993 / SC / M • Forbidden / 1996 / SC / M • French Open Part Deux / 1993 / MET / M • Gang Bang Diaries #3 / 1994 / SFP / M • Gangbang Girl #11 / 1993 / ANA / M • Girly Video Magazine #3 / 1995 / BEP / M • Goldilocks And The 3 Bi Bears / 1997 / TTV / G • Guttman's Hollywood Adventure / 1993 / PL / M • Hardcore Fantasies #1 / 1996 / LV / M • Hardcore Fantasies #5 / 1996 / LV / M • The Heart Breaker / 1996 / MID / M • Henry's Big Boob Adventure / 1996 / HO / M • Hollywood Swingers #08 / 1993 / LBO / M • Hooters And The Blowjobs / 1996 / HW / M • Horny Henry's Peeping Adventures / 1994 / TTV / M • Horny Henry's Swinging Adventures / 1994 / TTV / M • Hot & Horny Amateurs #1 / 1994 / ... / M • Hot Tight Asses #17 / 1996 / TCK / M • House Of Sex #04: Banging Menette / 1994 / RTP / M • How To Make A Model #02: Got Her In Bed / 1993 / QUA / M • The Hunt / 1996 / ULP / M • Indecent Proposition / 1993 / LV / M • Interview's Anal Queens / 1996 / LV / M • Interview's Big Boob Bonanza / 1996 / LV / M • The Joy Dick Club / 1994 / MID / M • Kool Ass / 1996 / BOT / M • Ladies Lovin' Ladies #3 / 1993 / AFV / F • Lady Luck / 1995 / PMV / M • Lesbian Castle: No Kings Allowed / 1994 / LIP / F • Lesbian Pros And Amateurs #23 / 1993 / GO / F • Lollipops #2 / 1996 / SC / M • Love Potion 69 / 1994 / VC / M • M Series #11 / 1993 / LBO / M • M Series #17 / 1993 / LBO / M • Main Course / 1992 / FL / M • Mike Hott: #221 Horny Couples #09 / 1992 / MHV / M • Mike Hott: #222 Lesbian Sluts #10 / 1992 / MHV / F • Mike Hott: #268 Cum In My Mouth #01 / 1994 / MHV / C • Mike Hott: #349 Girls Who Swallow Cum #03 / 1996 / MHV / C • Mike Hott: #354 Three-Sum Sluts #12 / 1996 / MHV / M • Mike Hott: #371 Horny Couples #19 / 1996 / MHV / M • Mister Stickypants / 1996 / LV / M • Mr. Peepers Amateur Home Videos #66: Ready In Red / z993 / LBO / M • Mr. Peep-

ers Amateur Home Videos #68: A Tough Load To Swallow / 1993 / LBO / M • Naked Scandal #1 / 1995 / SPI / M • Naked Scandal #2 / 1996 / SPI / M • Naughty / 1996 / LV / M • Neighborhood Slut / 1996 / LV / M • The New Ass Masters #11 / 1996 / LEI / C • The New Ass Masters #15 / 1996 / LEI / C • New Girls In Town #7 / 1994 / CC / M • Nookie Ranch / 1996 / NIT / M • Nydp Pink / 1994 / HW / M • Nympho Zombie Coeds / 1993 / VIM / M • Once Upon An Anus / 1993 / LV / M • Pick Up Lines #10 / 1997 / OD / M • Pleasure Dome: The Genesis Chamber / 1994 / AFV / M • Point Of Entry / 1996 / WP / M • Positively Pagan #11 / 1993 / ATA / M • Positively Pagan #12 / 1993 / ATA / M • Private Video Magazine #03 / 1993 / OD / M • Profiles #08: Triple Ecstacy / 1996 / XPR / M • Pudsucker / 1994 / MID / M • Raincoat Fantasies / 1993 / ELP / M • Rears In Windows / 1993 / FH / M • Rituals / 1993 / SC / M • Rump-Shaker #3 / 1994 / HW / M • Rumpman's Backdoor Sailing / 1996 / HW / M • Sex Police 2000 / 1992 / AFV / M • Sexorcist / 1994 / HW / M • Sexperiment / 1996 / ULP / M • Seymore Butts & His Mystery Girl / 1993 / FH / M • Seymore Butts Swings / 1992 / FH / M • Seymore Butts: Bustin' Out My Best Anal / 1995 / FH / C • Sleeping With Seattle / 1993 / LV / M • Sneek Peeks #2 / 1993 / OCV / M • Soap Opera Sluts / 1996 / AFI / M • The Spa / 1996 / RAS / M • Steele Butt / 1993 / AFV / M • Superstar Sex Challenge #2 / 1994 / VC / M • Surfin' The Net / 1996 / RAS / M • Surrogate Lover / 1992 / TP / M • Tales From The Casting Couch / 1992 / ... / M • Tight Fit #15 / 1996 / GO / M • Trouble In Paradise / 1996 / ULP / M • Ultimate Orgy #1 / 1992 / GLI / M • Unbalanced Chemicals / 1996 / SUF / M • Valentine's Challenge / 1992 / LIP / F • Video Virgins #06 / 1993 / NS / M • White Bitches In Heat / 1995 / GDV / M • White Stockings / 1994 / BHS / M • Wicked Thoughts / 1992 / PL / M • Witchcraft 2000 / 1994 / GLI / M • Woman 2 Woman #1 / 1993 / SOF / F • WPINK-TV #5 / 1993 / PV / M

STEPHANIE EBST
10 Years Of Big Busts #3 / 199? / BTO / C
STEPHANIE ELDER
Campus Girl / 1972 / VXP / M
STEPHANIE G. *see Star Index I*
STEPHANIE HART-ROGER *(Carol Anne)*
British with a nice but well fleshed body and an attitude of a high class call girl.
Buttman's British Moderately Big Tit Adventure / 1994 / EA / M • The Inseminator #1 / 1994 / LBO / M • The Inseminator #2: Domination Day / 1994 / LBO / M • Mike Hott: #190 Jilly / 1992 / MHV / M • Mike Hott: Apple Asses #14 / 1992 / MHV / F • Private Film #03 / 1993 / OD / M • Private Film #06 / 1994 / OD / M • Private Film #10 / 1994 / OD / M • Private Video Magazine #06 / 1993 / OD / M • Private Video Magazine #09 / 1994 / OD / M • Sodomania #08: The London Sessions / 1994 / EL / M
STEPHANIE PAGE *(Shame, Jinny Lynne, Camille (Step. Page), Shaime, Laura (Step. Page), Sally Kirk)*
Not to be confused with Stephanie Rage. Brunette with big natural tits. Known as Shame in **Pink Recall** and **Forever** and Laura in **More Dirty Debutanes #03**. Jinny

Lynne is from **Head Nurse**. Sally Kirk is from **White Satin Nights**.

40 The Hard Way / 1991 / OD / M • Against All Bods / 1991 / VEX / M • Amateur Nights #04 / 1990 / HO / M • The Come On: Skip's Video Guide To Scoring Chicks / 1991 / LE / M • Forever / 1991 / LE / M • Head Nurse / 1990 / V99 / M • The Heat Of The Moment / 1990 / IN / M • More Dirty Debutantes #03 / 1990 / 4P / M • Mystified / 1991 / V99 / M • Nightdreams #2 / 1990 / VC / M • Nightdreams #3 / 1991 / VC / M • Pink Recall / 1991 / CA / C • Put It In Gere / 1991 / CA / M • Queen Of Midnight / 1991 / V99 / M • Speedtrap / 1992 / VC / M • Talk Dirty To Me #08 / 1990 / DR / M • Unzipped / 1991 / WV / M • White Satin Nights / 1991 / V99 / M

STEPHANIE RAGE *(Rebecca Rage)*
Passable trailer park blonde with originally small tits, later enhanced to cantaloupes. First Movie was **Magic Fingers**. Aged 23 in 1989, comes from Baltimore, 100 lbs, 34C-22-34. Well how things change. In 1994 she was 24 (slow ageing?) 5'4" tall 105lbs and 34C-24-34.

Aerobisex Girls #2 / 1989 / LIP / F • Another Day, Another Million / 1993 / BON / B • Assumed Innocence / 1990 / AR / M • B*A*S*H / 1989 / BIZ / C • Back To Rears / 1988 / VI / M • Batteries Included / 1988 / 3HV / M • Best Of Foot Worship #2 / 1989 / BIZ / C • Beverly Hills Seduction / 1988 / WV / M • Big Boob Conflict / 1994 / NAP / B • Big Boob Tease / 1993 / NAP / F • Big Bust Fantasies / 1995 / PME / F • The Big E #08 / 1988 / BIZ / B • The Big Pink / 1989 / VWA / M • Bionca, Just For You / 1989 / BON / F • The Bitch Is Back / 1988 / FAN / M • Black Rage / 1988 / ZA / M • Blonde Conquest / 1995 / NAP / B • Bondage Memories #01 / 1993 / BON / C • Broadcast Nudes / 1988 / EVN / M • Busty Babes Milking Duel / 1996 / NAP / B • The Busty Kittens / 1995 / NAP / F • California Blondes #01 / 1986 / VEX / M • California Blondes #02 / 1987 / VEX / M • Cats Will Duel / 1993 / NAP / B • Cheating American Style / 1988 / WV / M • Circus Of Lesbians / 1995 / VI / C • City Of Rage / 1989 / EVN / M • The Contessa / 1989 / VC / M • Crackdown / 1988 / BIZ / B • Cramped Spaces / 1989 / PLV / B • Creamy Cheeks / 1986 / VEX / M • Crocodile Blondee #2 / 1988 / VCX / M • Crossed Nipples / 1994 / NAP / B • Dance Fire / 1989 / EA / M • The Days Of Our Wives / 1988 / GO / M • Dirty Prancing / 1987 / EVN / M • Dump Site / 1989 / BIZ / C • The End Zone / 1993 / PRE / B • Face To Face #1 / 1994 / NAP / B • Face To Face #2: The Domination / 1994 / NAP / B • Fantasy Girls / 1988 / CA / M • Filet-O-Breast / 1988 / AVC / M • The First of April / 1988 / VI / M • The Flirt / 1987 / VWA / M • Foot Teasers / 1988 / BIZ / B • Frisky Fables / 1988 / LV / M • The Fun House / 1988 / SEV / C • Ghostly Estate / 1989 / BON / B • Giggles / 1992 / PRE / B • The Girls Of Mardi Gras / 1994 / P10 / S • The Girls Of The B.L.O. / 1988 / VWA / M • Girls Of Treasure Island / 1988 / CV / M • Gland Slam / 1995 / PRE / B • Hard Rockin' Babes / 1987 / VD / F • Haunted Passions / 1990 / FC / M • Hawaii Vice #1 / 1988 / CIN / M • Hawaii Vice #2 / 1989 / CDI / M • Hawaii Vice #3 / 1988 / CIN / M • Hawaii

Vice #6 / 1989 / CDI / M • Hawaii Vice: Reflections / 1990 / CIN / C • The Heiress / 1988 / VI / M • Here's Looking At You / 1988 / V99 / M • Horneymooners #1 / 1988 / VXP / M • Horneymooners #2 / 1988 / VXP / M • Hot Buns / 1988 / BIZ / B • Illicit Affairs / 1989 / VD / M • Immorals #1: Broken Hearts / 1989 / AR / M • Inner Pink #1 / 1988 / LIP / F • Inner Pink #2 / 1989 / LIP / F • Island Girls #1 / 1990 / CDI / C • Island Girls #2: Fun In The Sun / 1990 / CDI / C • Island Girls #3: Rip Tide / 1991 / CDI / C • It Takes Hair To Be A Woman / 1995 / NAP / B • Jeff Stryker's How to Enlarge Your Penis / 1990 / VC / M • Juice Box / 1990 / AFV / M • K.U.N.T.-TV / 1988 / WV / M • Last Rumba In Paris / 1989 / VC / M • Latent Image: Stephanie Rage—Outrageous / 1994 / LAT / F • Laugh Factory / 1995 / PRE / C • Leg...Ends #01 / 1988 / BIZ / F • Leg...Ends #09 / 1994 / PRE / F • Loose Ends #1 / 1984 / 4P / M • Loose Lifestyles / 1988 / CA / M • Lucy Makes It Big / 1987 / ME / M • Lust Weekend / 1987 / CA / M • Magic Fingers / 1987 / ME / M • Making It In New York / 1989 / PLD / M • Megasex / 1988 / EVN / M • The Moon Girls / 1990 / ME / C • More Unbelievable Orgies / 1989 / EVN / C • Mrs. Rodger's Neighborhood / 1988 / EVN / C • National Poontang's Summer Vacation / 1990 / FC / M • Naughty Neighbors / 1986 / VEX / M • A Night At The Waxworks / 1990 / IF / M • No Mercy For The Witches / 1992 / HOM / B • No More Mr Nice Guy / 1989 / GO / M • Oral Majority #07 / 1989 / WV / C • The Oversexual Tourist / 1989 / VEX / M • Parliament: Ass Parade #1 / 1988 / PM / F • Parliament: Finger Friggin' #2 / 1988 / PM / F • Partners In Sex / 1988 / FAN / M • Party Animals / 1987 / VEX / M • Party Animals / 1994 / VEX / C • The Pearl Divers / 1988 / VWA / M • Pink Baroness / 1988 / VWA / M • Platinum Princess / 1988 / VEX / M • Queen Of The Lash / 1993 / LON / B • The Queens Of Mean / 1994 / NTP / B • The Rage Meets The Foxxx / 1994 / NAP / B • The Rage Of Stephanie / 199? / NAP / B • Raging Hormones / 1988 / VXP / M • Raging Weekend / 1988 / GO / M • Raw Talent #3 / 1988 / VC / M • Rip Off #1 / 1988 / BIZ / B • Rip Off #2 / 1988 / PLV / B • Robofox #2 / 1988 / FAN / M • Rollover & Cell Blocks / 1988 / PLV / B • Screaming Rage / 1988 / LV / C • Sea Of Desire / 1990 / AR / M • Seduction Of Stephanie / 19?? / GO / C • Sex In Dangerous Places / 1988 / VI / M • Sharon's Painful Persuasions / 1996 / SIL / B • Shoot To Thrill / 1988 / VWA / M • Skin Dive / 1988 / AVC / M • Slumber Party Reunion / 1987 / AR / M • Stephanie's Outrageous / 1988 / LV / C • Stephanie, Just For You / 1989 / BON / F • Sucker / 1988 / VWA / M • Super Leg-Ends / 1992 / PRE / C • The Sweet Spurt of Youth / 1988 / WV / M • A Taste Of Stephanie / 1990 / PIN / C • Tattle Tales / 1989 / SE / M • Terrors Of The Inquisition / 1992 / HOM / B • Three By Three / 1989 / LV / C • Three Men And A Lady / 1988 / EVN / M • Tickled! / 1989 / BIZ / C • To Snatch A Thief / 1989 / PLD / M • Toys, Not Boys #3 / 1991 / FC / C • Tricks Of The Trade / 1988 / CA / M • Twisted Sisters / 1988 / ZA / M • Ubangis On Uranus / 1987 / WV / M • Unbelievable Orgies #1 / 1987 / EVN / C • Underwater

Vixens / 1993 / NAP / B • The Vanessa Obsession / 1987 / VCX / C • Very Sexy Ballet / 1988 / CA / M • The Wacky World Of X-Rated Bloopers / 1989 / GO / M • The Way They Were / 1990 / CDI / M • When Love Came To Town / 1989 / EVN / M • Wrong Arm Of The Law / 1987 / ZA / M

STEPHANIE RENO
Bedroom Dispute / 1988 / NAP / B • Cowgals And Injuns / 1988 / NAP / B • Just Reno / 1988 / NAP / F • Kim Meets Reno / 1988 / NAP / B • Office Dispute / 1988 / NAP / B • Salt And Pepper Blues / 1988 / NAP / B • The Taking Of Reno / 1988 / NAP / B

STEPHANIE RIGHT *see* **Stephanie Du-Valle**

STEPHANIE ROSS
Laura's Desires / 1978 / CA / M

STEPHANIE SCHICK *see* **Pandora Peaks**

STEPHANIE SILVER
Buttman In Barcelona / 1996 / EA / M • Rock 'n' Roll Rocco / 1997 / EA / M

STEPHANIE SUNSHINE *see Star Index I*

STEPHANIE SWIFT *(China Cat)*
Wonderful body with black shoulder length hair, marginal face, small/medium firm nicely shaped tits, tight waist, long thighs, pencil eraser nipples, and narrow hips. Looks very similar to Georgette Sanders. I don't believe she is Oriental despite the alternate name. She says she weighs 110lbs and won't tell her age but it's around 19 in 1995.

2 Wongs Make A White / 1996 / FC / M • Adam & Eve's House Party #5 / 1996 / VC / M • The Anal Adventures Of Max Hardcore: Hombre / 1995 / ZA / M • Anal Anarchy / 1995 / VC / M • Asses Galore #1: From L.A. To Brazil / 1996 / DFI / M • Asses Galore #5: T.T. Vs The World / 1996 / DFI / M • Babe Watch #5 / 1996 / VC / M • Bad Boyz / 1996 / VT / M • Bangkok Dreams / 1996 / SUF / M • Blaze / 1996 / WAV / M • Born Bad / 1996 / WAV / M • Butthole Bunnies / 1996 / ROB / F • Casting Call #11 / 1995 / MET / M • Casting Call #16 / 1995 / SO / M • Cat Lickers #4 / 1995 / ME / F • Cheerleader Strippers / 1996 / PE / M • Cherry Poppers #10: Sweet And Sassy / 1995 / ZA / M • Cloud 900 / 1996 / EYE / M • Cumback Pussy #6: All-Star Poop Chute Salute / 1997 / EL / M • Deep Behind The Scenes With Seymore Butts #1 / 1995 / ULI / M • Deep Dippin' Anal Babes / 1996 / ROB / F • Delinquents On Butt Row / 1996 / EA / M • Dick & Jane Go To A Bachelor Party (#17) / 1996 / AVI / M • The Dinner Party #2: The Buffet / 1996 / ULI / M • Dream House / 1995 / XPR / M • The End / 1995 / VI / M • Euro-Max #4: / 1995 / SC / M • Face Jam / 1996 / VC / M • Filthy Little Bitches / 1996 / APP / F • Final Obsession / 1996 / LE / M • Finger Sluts #1 / 1996 / LV / F • Freaknic / 1996 / IN / M • Fresh Meat (John Leslie) #2 / 1995 / EA / M • HomeGrown Video #463: Cum And Get It / 1995 / HOV / M • The Horny Hiker / 1995 / LE / M • In Cold Sweat / 1996 / VI / M • Lollipop Shoppe #1 / 1996 / SC / M • Lotus / 1996 / VI / M • The Many Faces Of P.J. Sparxx / 1996 / WP / M • Masque / 1995 / VC / M • Max #04: The Harder They Come / 1995 / FWE / M • Micky Ray's Hot Shots #01 / 1996 / DIG / M • Mike Hott: #288 Cunt

of the Month: Stephanie / 1995 / MHV / M • Mike Hott: #356 Girls Who Lap Cum From Cunts #01 / 1996 / MHV / M • Mind Set / 1996 / VI / M • Misty Rain's Anal Orgy / 1994 / FRM / M • More Dirty Debutantes #44 / 1995 / 4P / M • The Night Of The Living Bed / 1996 / LE / M • No Man's Land #15 / 1996 / VT / F • Nothing Sacred / 1995 / LE / M • Ona Zee's Doll House #4 / 1996 / ONA / F • Over Exposed / 1996 / ULP / M • The Palace Of Pleasure / 1995 / ULI / M • Passage To Pleasure / 1995 / LE / M • Passions Of Sin / 1996 / NIT / M • Pick Up Lines #01 / 1995 / 4P / M • Private Desires / 1995 / LE / M • Profiles #01 / 1995 / XPR / M • Profiles #02 / 1995 / XPR / M • Profiles #08: Triple Ecstacy / 1996 / XPR / M • Pussyman Auditions #21 / 1996 / SNA / M • Rainwoman #10: The Tenth Anniversary Edition / 1996 / CC / M • Rebel Without A Condom / 1996 / ERA / M • Roller Babes / 1996 / ERA / M • The Seduction Of Annah Marie / 1996 / VT / M • Sex 4 Life / 1995 / XPR / M • Sex Freaks / 1995 / EA / M • Shadows Of Lust / 1996 / NIT / M • Shayla's Swim Party / 1997 / VC / M • Show & Tell / 1996 / VI / M • Smoke & Mirrors / 1996 / PL / M • Squirters / 1996 / ULI / M • Star Girl / 1996 / ERA / M • The Swing / 1996 / VI / M • Turnabout / 1996 / CTP / M • Undercover / 1996 / VC / M • Up And Cummers #29 / 1996 / ERW / M • Vagabonds / 1996 / ERA / M • Venom #6 / 1996 / CA / M • Video Virgins #23 / 1995 / NS / M • Video Virgins #24 / 1996 / NS / M • Video Virgins #32 / 1996 / NS / M • Virgin Dreams / 1996 / EA / M • Virgins / 1995 / ERA / M • War Whores / 1996 / EL / M • Wedding Night Blues / 1995 / EMC / M • What's In It 4 Me / 1995 / TEG / M • Whiplash / 1996 / DFI / M • XXX / 1996 / TEP / M • Yin Yang Oriental Love Bang #3: Bangkok Dreams / 1996 / SUF / M

STEPHANIE TAYLOR see Laurie Smith
STEPHANIE WOLF
Eat At Dave's #6 / 1996 / SP / M
STEPHANIE YOUNG see Justina Lynn
STEPHEN
AVP #7025: Cum Specialist / 1991 / AVP / M • Skin #2 / 1995 / ERQ / M
STEPHEN ANNOUT
Pai Gow Video #04: Tails Of The Town / 1994 / EVN / M
STEPHEN BENTLY
Love Lips / 1976 / VC / M
STEPHEN DANIELS see Star Index I
STEPHEN DOUGLAS see Steve Douglas
STEPHEN EVANS
The Blonde Goddess / 1982 / VXP / M • Snack Time / 1983 / HO / M
STEPHEN RAYE see Star Index I
STEPHEN REYNOLDS (Steve Reynolds)
Tickled Pink / 1985 / VC / M • The Voyeur / 1985 / VC / M
STEPHEN ROBERTS see Star Index I
STEPHEN SCOTT
Erotic Obsession / 1994 / IN / M
STEPHEN ST. CROIX see Steven St. Croix
STEPHEN STEINBERG
Two Lives Of Jennifer / 1979 / VHL / M
STEPHEN WILCOX see Star Index I
STEPHENNIE
By Myself / 1996 / PL / F
STEPPY

The Betrayal Of Innocence #1: The Awakening Of Marika / 1993 / CC / M • The Betrayal Of Innocence #2: The Decadence / 1993 / CC / M • The Betrayal Of Innocence #3: The Choice / 1993 / CC / M
STERLING ROD
Twilight Pink #1 / 1980 / AR / M
STEVE
Amateur Nights #08 / 1990 / HO / M • Between My Breasts #15 / 1991 / BTO / M • Big Bust Babes #14 / 1993 / AFI / M • The Bondage Club #2 / 1987 / LON / B • Desolation / 1992 / BON / B • The Dong Show #03 / 1990 / AMB / M • Duke Of Knockers #2 / 1995 / BTO / M • English Muffins / 1995 / VC / M • Gangbang Girl #09 / 1993 / ANA / M • Harry Horndog #16: Love Puppies #4 / 1992 / ZA / M • Home Maid Memories #2 / 1994 / BON / C • Homegrown Video #358 / 1991 / HOV / M • Kitty's Kinky Capers / 1996 / TTV / M • Lovers, An Intimate Portrait #2: Jennifer & Steve / 1994 / FEM / M • Mike Hott: #120 Dildo Debbie, Dusty, Mike And Steve / 1990 / MHV / M • Mr. Peeppers Amateur Home Videos #64: Proposition 69 / 1992 / LBO / M • Neighborhood Watch #28 / 1992 / LBO / M • Next Door Neighbors #05 / 1989 / BON / M • Odyssey Triple Play #60: Interracial Facial / 1994 / OD / M • Pearl Necklace: Amorous Amateurs #38 / 1993 / SEE / M • Pearl Necklace: Premier Sessions #02 / 1993 / SEE / M • Pearl Necklace: Thee Bush League #27 / 1993 / SEE / M • Red Riding She Male / 1995 / PL / G • Shane's World #3 / 1996 / OD / M • SVE: Swing Time / 1993 / SVE / M • Uncle Roy's Amateur Home Video #18 / 1993 / VIM / M • Uncle Roy's Amateur Home Video #19 / 1993 / VIM / M
STEVE (TENNESSEE) see Star Index I
STEVE ANTHONY see Star Index I
STEVE AUSTIN (Wise Mark, Mark Wise, Wisemark, Steve Sucksi)
Lummox like white male who can't make up his mind about his name.
18 Candles / 1989 / LA / M • The Adventures Of Peeping Tom #3 / 1996 / OD / M • America's Dirtiest Home Videos #05 / 1991 / VEX / M • America's Dirtiest Home Videos #14 / 1992 / VEX / M • America's Raunchiest Home Videos #73: / 1993 / ZA / M • Barbii Unleashed / 1988 / 4P / M • Be Careful What You Wish For / 1993 / VC / G • Bi Dream Of Genie / 1990 / BIN / G • Big Murray's New-Cummers #01: Blondes Have More... / 1992 / FD / M • Black Babes / 1995 / LV / M • Black Street Hookers #5: The Mean Streets Of Washington D.C. / 1997 / DFI / M • Blonde Temptation / 1995 / IF / M • The Book / 1990 / IF / M • Breast Wishes #10 / 1992 / LBO / M • Breast Wishes #12 / 1993 / LBO / M • Breast Worx #35 / 1992 / LBO / M • Breast Worx #39 / 1992 / LBO / M • Career Girls / 1996 / OUP / M • Chance Meetings / 1988 / VEX / M • Cheek Busters / 1990 / FH / M • Cheeks #6 / 1992 / CC / M • Cherry Poppers #12: Playing Nookie / 1995 / ZA / M • A Clockwork Orgy / 1995 / PL / M • Coming Attractions / 1995 / WHP / M • Decadence / 1994 / WHP / M • Deep Throat #5 / 1990 / AR / M • Dirty Doc's Housecalls #03 / 1993 / LV / M • Dirty Doc's Housecalls #04 / 1993 / LV / M • Eight Is Never Enough / 1993 / ZA / M • Erotic Angel / 1994 / ERA / M • Fondle

With Care / 1989 / VEX / M • The Freak Club / 1994 / VMX / M • Fresh Meat (John Leslie) #1 / 1994 / EA / M • Fuck U: Girls Of The Packed-10 / 1995 / ZA / M • The Girls From Hootersville #02 / 1993 / SFP / M • Glitz Tits #02 / 1992 / GLI / M • The Great American Boobs To Kill For Dance Contest / 1995 / PEP / C • Heidi Does Hollywood / 1993 / AFV / M • Hindfeld / 1993 / PI / M • Hollywood Swingers #06 / 1992 / LBO / M • Honey, I Blew Everybody #2 / 1992 / MID / M • In Your Face #4 / 1996 / PL / M • Indecent / 1993 / XCI / M • Into The Fire / 1994 / ZA / M • Lawnmower Woman / 1992 / MID / M • Lethal Passion / 1991 / PL / M • Lips / 1994 / FC / M • Littledove's Cup / 1988 / FOV / M • Long Dark Shadow / 1994 / LE / M • The Mistress (1993-Caballero) / 1993 / CA / M • MR. Peeppers Amateur Home Videos #30: Bearded Clam On the Hal / 1991 / LBO / M • Mr. Peeppers Amateur Home Videos #44: A Royal Reaming / 1992 / LBO / M • Mr. Peeppers Amateur Home Videos #62: Private Pussy Party / 1992 / LBO / M • Mr. Peeppers Amateur Home Videos #63: Sexual Soiree / 1992 / LBO / M • Mr. Peeppers Amateur Home Videos #72: Dirty Diary / 1993 / LBO / M • My Evil Twin / 1994 / LE / M • My Wife Is A Call Girl / 1989 / FAZ / M • Nasty Jack's Homemade Vid. #02 / 1990 / CDI / M • Neighborhood Watch #33 / 1992 / LBO / M • Neighborhood Watch #34 / 1992 / LBO / M • Neighborhood Watch #38: Pearlie's Curlie's / 1993 / LBO / M • New Girls In Town #1 / 1990 / CC / M • Nutts About Butts / 1994 / LE / M • Older & Bolder In San Francisco / 1996 / TEP / M • Paging Betty / 1994 / VC / M • Party Animals / 1994 / VEX / C • Passionate Lips / 1990 / OD / M • Perfect Endings / 1994 / PLV / B • Push It To The Limit / 1988 / EVN / M • Radioactive / 1990 / VIP / M • Riding Miss Daisy / 1990 / VEX / M • Risque Burlesque #1 / 1994 / IN / M • Rocky-X #2 / 1988 / PEN / M • Saki's Private Party / 1995 / TTV / M • She Quest / 1994 / OD / M • Sindy Does Anal / 1993 / AFV / M • The Starlet / 1991 / PP / M • Straight A's / 1993 / VC / M • Summer Dreams / 1996 / TEP / M • Summer Of '69 / 1994 / MID / M • Sumo Sue And The Fat Ladies Of Wrestling / 1988 / FAN / M • Swinging Couples #02 / 1993 / GO / M • Tip Tap Toe / 1995 / PRE / C • Toe Nuts / 1994 / PRE / B • Uninhibited Love / 1994 / VPN / M • The Voyeur #3 / 1995 / EA / M • Wedding Vows / 1994 / ZA / M • Where The Boys Aren't #3 / 1990 / VI / F • Whiplash / 1996 / DFI / M • Women On Fire / 1995 / LBO / M
STEVE BALINT
The Jade Pussycat / 1977 / CA / M
STEVE BAXTER
Sweet Humility / 1995 / STM / B
STEVE BLANDER see Star Index I
STEVE BOYD
[Kansas City Trucking Company / 1976 / TMX / G
STEVE BRAMBLE see Star Index I
STEVE BRIDGES
Sunny / 1979 / VC / M
STEVE CAGLIONE see Star Index I
STEVE CANNON see Star Index I
STEVE CARSON see Star Index I
STEVE CATANIA
Private School Girls / 1983 / CA / M

STEVE CHASE *see Star Index I*
STEVE CLARK *see Steve Drake*
STEVE COOLS
Journal Of Love / 1970 / ALP / M
STEVE CROW
Buck's Excellent Transsexual Adventure / 1989 / STA / G
STEVE D.
Cluster Fuck #01 / 1993 / MAX / M
STEVE DANTE *see Craig Roberts*
STEVE DARBY *see Star Index I*
STEVE DARE
Canadian Beaver Hunt #3 / 1996 / PL / M •
Canadian Beaver Hunt #4 / 1996 / PL / M
STEVE DAVIS *see Star Index I*
STEVE DOUGLAS *(Stephen Douglas, Steven Douglas, Doug Ross, Doug Rossi)*
Alexandra / 1984 / VC / M • All American Girls #1 / 1982 / CA / M • Blue Interview / 1983 / VCR / M • Caught From Behind #01 / 1982 / HO / M • Centerfold Celebrities #1 / 1982 / VC / M • Centerfold Celebrities #2 / 1983 / VC / M • Daughters Of Emmanuelle / 1982 / VCX / M • Fantasies Of Jennifer Faye / 1983 / GO / M • Little Kimmi Johnson / 1983 / VEP / M • Mama's Boy / 1984 / VD / M • Personal Touch #2 / 1983 / AR / M • Stud Hunters / 1984 / CA / M • Tomboy / 1983 / VCX / M • Triple Play / 1983 / HO / M • Up 'n' Coming / 1983 / CA / M • Video Virgins #04 / 1993 / NS / M • Why Gentlemen Prefer Blondes / 1983 / HO / C • X-Rated Bloopers #1 / 1984 / AR / M
STEVE DRAKE *(Steve Goldberg, Steve Clark, Steve Nadel, Steve Nadelman, Dwight Lightning)*
Steve Nadelman is from **Crazy With The Heat**. Retired from porn in the late eighties while married to Dina DeVille (see entry) and then returned in the early nineties. 5'11" tall. Steve Clark in **Too Young To Know**. Steve Nadel in **Hindsight**. Dwight Lightning in **The Wizard Of Aahs**.
The $50,000,000 Cherry / 1987 / VD / M • 1001 Erotic Nights #2 / 1987 / VC / M • The Adventures Of Buttgirl & Wonder Wench / 1991 / AFV / M • The Adventures Of Studman #1 / 1994 / AFV / M • The Adventures Of Studman #2 / 1994 / AFV / M • The Adventures Of Studman #3 / 1994 / AFV / M • Age Of Consent / 1985 / AVC / M • Alexandria, I Love You / 1993 / AFV / M • All That Glitters / 1992 / LV / M • Amber Lynn's Peter Meter / 1988 / 3HV / C • America's Raunchiest Home Videos #12: Bimbo Ballers From Brt / 1992 / ZA / M • America's Raunchiest Home Videos #20: Penthouse Pussy Power / 1992 / ZA / M • American Garter / 1993 / VC / M • The Anal Adventures Of Suzy Super Slut #2 / 1994 / AFV / M • The Anal Adventures Of Suzy Super Slut #3 / 1994 / IPI / M • Anal Angels #6 / 1996 / VEX / C • Anal Asspirations / 1993 / LV / M • Anal Attraction #2 / 1993 / AFV / C • Anal Nature / 1993 / AFD / M • Anal Orgy / 1993 / DRP / M • The Anal-Europe Series #01: The Fisherman's Wife / 1992 / LV / M • The Anal-Europe Series #03: The Museum Of The Living Art / 1993 / LV / M • The Anal-Europe Series #04: Anal Recall / 1993 / LV / M • Angels Of Passion / 1986 / CDI / M • Anonymous / 1993 / VI / M • Another Dirty Western / 1992 / AFV / M • Anything That Moves / 1992 / VC / M • Aroused

#2 / 1995 / VI / M • Ass Openers! #2 / 1995 / TCK / C • Attack Of The 50 Foot Hooker / 1994 / OD / M • B.L.O.W. / 1992 / LV / M • Baccarat #1 / 1991 / FH / M • Baccarat #2 / 1991 / FH / M • Back Seat Bush / 1992 / LV / M • Backdoor Club #1 / 1996 / VEX / C • The Backdoor Club / 1992 / LV / M • Backdoor Magic / 1994 / LV / M • Backdoor To Harley-Wood #3 / 1993 / AFV / M • Backdoor To The City Of Sin / 1993 / ANA / M • Backstage Entrance #1 / 1992 / FH / M • Backstage Entrance #2 / 1992 / FH / M • Bad Attitude / 1992 / CDI / M • Bad To The Bone / 1992 / LE / M • Badgirls #1: Lockdown / 1994 / VI / M • Bangin' With The Home Girls / 1991 / AFV / M • Battle Of The Stars #1 / 1985 / NSV / M • Battle Of The Titans / 1986 / AVC / M • Beach Mistress / 1994 / XCI / M • Before She Says I Do / 1984 / MAP / M • Behind The Brown Door / 1994 / PE / M • Best Butt(e) In The West #1 / 1992 / CC / M • Betrayed / 1996 / WP / M • Between Her Thighs / 1992 / CDI / M • Between The Cheeks #3 / 1993 / VC / M • Beverly Hills Copulator / 1986 / ... / M • Beverly Hills Wives / 1985 / CV / M • Beyond The Casting Couch / 1986 / VD / M • Biff Malibu's Totally Nasty Home Videos #02 / 1992 / ANA / M • Biff Malibu's Totally Nasty Home Videos #19 / 1992 / ANA / M • The Big Bang #1 / 1993 / LV / M • Biker Chicks In Love / 1991 / LE / M • Black & White Affair / 1984 / VD / M • Black Holes In Space / 1987 / 4P / M • Black Orchid / 1993 / WV / M • Black Streets / 1994 / LE / M • Blinded By Love / 1993 / OD / M • The Blonde & The Beautiful #1 / 1993 / LV / M • The Blonde & The Beautiful #2 / 1993 / LV / M • Blow Job Bonnie / 1992 / CC / M • Blue Angel / 1992 / AFV / M • Blue Angel / 1992 / AFV / M • Blue Balls / 1995 / VEX / C • Blue Bayou / 1993 / VC / M • Bone Therapy / 1992 / LV / M • Bottoms Up #06 / 1986 / AVC / C • Breaking And Entering / 1991 / AFV / M • Breast Wishes #11 / 1993 / LBO / M • Breast Worx #21 / 1992 / LBO / M • Breastman Does The Himalayas / 1993 / EVN / M • Breastman's Anal Adventure / 1993 / EVN / M • Breeders / 1996 / MET / M • Breezy / 1985 / VCR / M • Bunny Bleu: A Gang Bang Fantasy / 1994 / FC / M • Business And Pleasure / 1992 / AFV / M • Bust A Move / 1993 / SC / M • Busty Wrestling Babes / 1986 / VD / M • Butt Camp / 1993 / HW / C • Butt Of Steel / 1994 / LV / M • The Butt Sisters Do Baltimore / 1995 / MID / M • The Butt Sisters Do Boston / 1995 / MID / M • The Butt Sisters Do Chicago / 1995 / MID / M • The Butt Sisters Do Daytona / 1995 / MID / M • The Butt Sisters Do Hawaii / 1995 / MID / M • The Butt Sisters Do New York / 1994 / MID / M • The Butt Sisters Do Philadelphia / 1995 / MID / M • The Butt Sisters Do Seattle / 1995 / MID / M • The Butt Sisters Do Sturgis / 1994 / MID / M • Butt Woman #2 / 1992 / FH / M • Butt Woman #3 / 1992 / FH / M • C-Hunt / 1985 / PL / M • Caddy Shack-Up / 1986 / VD / M • California Gigolo / 1987 / VD / M • Candy Factory / 1994 / PE / M • Captain Hooker & Peter Porn / 1987 / VD / M • Cat Alley / 1986 / AVC / M • The Catburglar / 1994 / PL / M • Caught Looking / 1995 / CC / M • Centerfold / 1992 / VC / M • Charm School / 1986 / VI / M • Chastity And The Starlets / 1986 / RAV / M

• The Cheater / 1994 / XCI / M • Checkmate / 1992 / CDI / M • Cheeks #5: The Ultimate Butt / 1991 / CC / M • Christmas Carol / 1993 / LV / M • Christy Canyon: She's Back / 1995 / TTV / C • Club DV8 #1 / 1993 / SC / M • Club DV8 #2 / 1993 / SC / M • Club Midnight / 1992 / LV / M • The Coach's Daughter / 1991 / AR / M • Come As You Are / 1985 / SUV / M • Coming Out / 1993 / VD / M • Committed / 1992 / LE / M • Concrete Heat / 1996 / XCI / M • Confessions #1 / 1992 / OD / M • Convenience Store Girls / 1986 / VD / M • Corporate Affairs / 1996 / CC / M • Crazy With The Heat #1 / 1986 / CV / M • The Creasemaster's Wife / 1993 / VC / M • The Crimson Kiss / 1993 / WV / M • Cross Cuntry Vacation / 1995 / CC / M • Crystal Blue / 1987 / VD / M • Cyrano / 1991 / PL / M • Dance Fever / 1985 / VCR / M • Dark Tunnels / 1994 / LV / M • The Darker Side Of Shayla #1 / 1993 / PL / M • Daydreams, Nightdreams / 1996 / VC / M • Deadly Sin / 1996 / ONA / M • Dear John / 1993 / VI / M • Debbie Does Dallas Again / 1994 / AFV / M • Decadent Obsession / 1995 / OD / M • Deception (1995-Executive) / 1995 / EX / M • Deep C Diver / 1992 / LV / M • Deep Focus / 1995 / VC / M • Deep Inside Ariana / 1995 / VC / C • Deep Inside Brittany O'connell / 1996 / VC / C • Deep Inside Kelly O'Dell / 1994 / VC / C • Deep Inside Nikki Dial / 1994 / VC / C • Deep Inside Tracey / 1987 / CDI / C • Deep Inside Victoria Paris / 1993 / VC / C • Deep Throat Girls / 1986 / ELH / M • Defending Your Sex Life / 1992 / LE / M • Defenseless / 1992 / CDI / M • Deliveries In The Rear #1 / 1985 / AVC / M • Denim / 1991 / LE / M • Desperately Seeking Suzie / 1985 / VD / M • Dial A Dick / 1986 / AVC / M • Dial F For Fantasy / 1984 / PL / M • Dial N For Nikki / 1993 / PEP / M • Diamond Collection #62 / 1984 / CDI / M • Diary Of A Geisha / 1995 / WV / C • Dickman & Throbbin / 1985 / WV / M • The Dinner Party #1 / 1994 / ULI / M • The Dinner Party / 1995 / ERA / M • Dirty Laundry #2 / 1994 / CV / M • Dirty Shary / 1985 / VD / M • Dirty Thoughts / 1992 / LE / M • Doctor Desire / 1984 / VD / M • Don't Tell Daddy #1 / 1985 / PL / C • Double Dare / 1986 / SE / M • Double Down / 1993 / LBO / M • Double Insertion / 1986 / 4P / M • Dr Lust / 1987 / VC / M • The Dragon Lady #5: Tales From The Bed #4 / 1993 / WV / M • The Dragon Lady #6: Tales From The Bed #5 / 1993 / WV / M • Dream Lovers / 1987 / CA / M • Dressed To Thrill / 1986 / CDI / M • E Three / 1985 / GO / M • Easy Cum...Easy Go / 1985 / BAN / M • Ebony & Ivory Fantasies / 1988 / VD / C • Eighteen #2 / 1996 / SC / M • Electropussy / 1995 / CC / M • Eleventh Annual AVN Awards / 1994 / VC / M • The Elixir / 1992 / CDI / M • The End / 1995 / VI / M • The Erotic Adventures Of The Three Musketeers / 1992 / CEL / S • Erotic Appetites / 1995 / IN / M • The Erotic Artist / 1995 / VC / M • Erotic Fiction / 1995 / LE / M • Erotic Heights / 1991 / AR / M • Erotic Newcummers Vol 1 #3: Anal Adventures / 1996 / DR / M • Erotic Newcummers Vol 1 #4 / 1996 / DR / M • Erotic Newcummers Vol 1 #5 / 1996 / DR / M • Erotic World Of Anne Spice / 1995 / WV / M • Erotique / 1992 / VC / M • Eternal Lust / 1996 / VC / M • Euroslut #1: French Tart / 1993 / CC /

M • Every Woman Has A Fantasy #3 / 1995 / VC / M • Exstasy / 1995 / WV / M • Face Dance #1 / 1992 / EA / M • Face Dance #2 / 1992 / EA / M • Facesitter #2 / 1993 / CC / M • Faithless Companions / 1992 / WV / M • Th Fanny / 1997 / WP / M • Fantasy Chamber / 1987 / VT / M • Fantasy Chamber / 1994 / ULI / M • Fantasy Fuchs / 1996 / PLP / C • Fashion Plate / 1995 / WAV / M • Fast Cars And Fast Women / 1992 / LV / M • Feds In Bed / 1993 / HO / M • The Fire Down Below / 1992 / CDI / M • Flamenco Ecstasy / 1996 / UEF / M • Flesh And Boner / 1993 / WV / M • Flesh Fire / 1985 / AVC / M • Flesh For Fantasies / 1986 / TAM / M • Flesh In Ecstasy #02: Samantha Strong / 1987 / GO / C • Fluff Dreams / 1995 / SUF / M • Foolproof / 1994 / VC / M • For The Fun Of It / 1986 / SEV / M • Frankenstein / 1994 / SC / M • French Open Part Deux / 1993 / MET / M • The Fun House / 1988 / SEV / C • The Fury / 1993 / WIV / M • Gangbang Girl #01 / 1992 / ANA / M • Gangbang Girl #02 / 1992 / ANA / M • Gangbang Girl #03 / 1992 / ANA / M • Gangbang Girl #12 / 1993 / ANA / M • Gangbang Girl #15 / 1995 / ANA / M • Ganggstas Paradise / 1995 / AVI / M • Gemini / 1994 / SC / M • Genie's Dirty Girls / 1987 / VCX / M • Gentlemen Prefer Ginger / 1985 / VI / M • Gettin' Ready / 1985 / CDI / M • Ginger On The Rocks / 1985 / VI / M • Ginger's Greatest Boy/Girl Hits / 1987 / VI / C • Girls And Guns / 1992 / KBR / M • Girls Of Sin / 1994 / PL / C • The Girls Of Summer / 1992 / FOR / M • Glamour Girl #5 / 1985 / CDI / M • Glamour Girl #6 / 1985 / CDI / M • Glamour Girl #8 / 1985 / CDI / M • The God Daughter #2 / 1991 / AFV / M • Gold Diggers / 1993 / IN / M • Golddiggers #1 / 1985 / VC / M • Gone Wild / 1993 / LV / M • The Greatest American Blonde / 1987 / WV / C • Guess Who Came To Dinner / 1992 / AFV / M • Guilty By Seduction / 1993 / PI / M • GVC: Broadcast Babes #138 / 1985 / GO / M • Hard To Stop #1 / 1992 / VC / M • Haunting Dreams #1 / 1993 / LV / M • Haunting Dreams #2 / 1993 / LV / M • Hawaiian Heat #1 / 1995 / CC / M • Hawaiian Heat #2 / 1995 / CC / M • Head Again / 1992 / AFV / M • Head First / 1993 / LE / M • Head First / 1995 / OD / M • Heartbreaker / 1992 / CDI / M • Heat / 1995 / WAV / M • Heatwaves / 1994 / LE / M • Heaven Scent (Las Vegas) / 1993 / LV / M • Heidi A / 1985 / PL / M • Heidi Does Hollywood / 1993 / AFV / M • Heidigate / 1993 / HO / M • Hidden Camera #14 / 1994 / JMP / M • Hidden Desires / 1992 / CDI / M • Hidden Obsessions / 1992 / BFP / M • Hindsight / 1985 / IN / M • Holly Does Hollywood #1 / 1985 / VEX / M • Hollywood Confidential / 1996 / SC / M • Hollywood Vice / 1985 / VD / M • Hookers Of Hollywood / 1994 / LE / M • Hootersville (Legend) / 1995 / LE / M • Hornet's Nest / 1996 / ONA / M • The Horny Hiker / 1995 / LE / M • Hot Cars, Nasty Women / 1985 / WV / M • Hot Gun / 1986 / CA / M • Hot Seat / 1986 / AVC / M • Hot Sweet Honey / 1985 / VEP / M • Hot Tails / 1984 / VEN / M • Hot Tight Asses #03 / 1993 / TCK / M • Hot Tight Asses #04 / 1993 / TCK / M • Hot Tight Asses #05 / 1994 / TCK / M • Hotel Sodom #04: Free Parking In Rear / 1995 / SNA / M • Hotel Sodom #05: Tammi Ann

Bends Over / 1995 / SNA / M • Hotel Sodom #10 / 1996 / SNA / M • Hottest Parties / 1988 / VC / C • House Of Blue Dreams / 1985 / WV / M • House Of Sleeping Beauties #1 / 1992 / VI / M • House Of Sleeping Beauties #2 / 1992 / VI / M • The House Of Strange Desires / 1985 / NSV / M • I Love A Girl In A Uniform / 1989 / VC / C • I Want It All / 1995 / WAV / M • Ice Woman #1 / 1993 / VI / M • Ice Woman #2 / 1993 / VI / M • If Dreams Come True / 1991 / AFV / M • Imaginary Lovers / 1986 / ME / M • Immoral Support / 1992 / AFV / M • In Search Of The Perfect Blow Job / 1995 / OD / M • In The Line Of Desire / 1996 / MID / M • In The Scope / 1996 / VI / M • In-N-Out With John Leslie / 1988 / WV / C • Indecent Exposures / 1996 / MID / M • Indecent Itch / 1985 / VCR / M • Indecent Proposition / 1993 / LV / M • Inferno #1 / 1993 / SC / M • Inside Candy Samples / 1984 / CV / M • Interview With A Milkman / 1996 / VI / M • Into The Gap / 1991 / LE / M • It's Blondage, The Video / 1994 / VI / M • Jean Genie / 1985 / CA / M • Jezebel #1 / 1993 / SC / M • Jezebel #2 / 1993 / SC / M • Joanie Pneumatic / 1996 / PL / M • The Joi Fuk Club / 1993 / WV / M • The Joy-Stick Girls / 1986 / CLV / M • Jugsy (X-Citement) / 1992 / XCI / M • Juranal Park / 1993 / OD / M • Just Another Pretty Face / 1985 / AVC / M • Just Friends / 1991 / AFV / M • Kinkyvision #1 / 1986 / 3HV / M • Kiss Of The Dragon Lady / 1986 / SEV / M • L.A. Topless / 1994 / LE / M • Lacy's Hot Anal Summer / 1992 / LV / M • Ladies Of The 80's / 1985 / PV / M • Lap Of Luxury / 1994 / WIV / M • The Last Action Whore / 1993 / LV / M • Lather / 1991 / LE / M • Lay Of The Land / 1995 / LE / M • Laying Down The Law #1 / 1992 / AFV / M • Laying Down The Law #2 / 1992 / AFV / M • Layover / 1994 / VI / M • Leena Goes Pro / 1992 / VT / M • Leena's Early Experiences / 1995 / OD / C • Legend #3 / 1991 / LE / M • Legend #5: The Legend Continues / 1994 / LE / M • License To Thrill / 1985 / VD / M • Lies Of Passion / 1992 / LV / M • The Life & Loves Of Nikki Charm / 1986 / MAL / M • Life's A Beach, Then You're Fucked / 1995 / FRM / M • Liquid Love / 1988 / CA / M • Little Girl Blue / 1995 / RHS / M • Little Girls, Dirty Desires / 1984 / JVV / M • Little Secrets / 1991 / LE / M • Live Sex / 1994 / LE / M • Living Doll / 1987 / WV / M • Living Doll / 1992 / CDI / M • Long Dark Shadow / 1994 / LE / M • Long Hot Summer / 1992 / CDI / M • Looking For Mr Goodsex / 1984 / CC / M • Looks Like A Million / 1992 / LV / M • Loose Ends #1 / 1984 / 4P / M • Losing Control / 1985 / CDI / M • Love Exchange / 1995 / DR / M • The Love Scene / 1985 / CDI / M • Lucky Charm / 1986 / AVC / C • Lucky Lady / 1995 / CV / M • Luscious Lucy In Love / 1986 / AVC / M • The Lust Potion Of Doctor F / 1985 / WV / M • Lust Weekend / 1987 / CA / M • Madame A / 1992 / LV / M • The Magic Touch / 1985 / CV / M • Make Me Want It / 1986 / CA / M • The Makeup Room #2 / 1992 / VC / M • Malibu Blue / 1992 / LE / M • Marilyn Chambers' Private Fantasies #5 / 1985 / CA / M • The Masseuse #2 / 1994 / VI / M • A Mid-Slumber's Night Dream / 1985 / 4P / M • The Midnight Zone / 1986 / IN / M • Mile High Thrills / 1995 / VIM / M • Mind Games /

1992 / CDI / M • Mind Shadows #1 / 1993 / FD / M • Mind Shadows #2 / 1993 / FD / M • Miracle On 69th Street / 1992 / HW / M • Miss Passion / 1984 / VD / M • Mistress To Sin / 1994 / LV / M • Model's Memoirs / 1993 / IP / M • The Modelling Studio / 1984 / GO / M • More Than A Handful / 1993 / CA / C • Mother's Pride / 1985 / DIM / M • Muffy The Vampire Layer / 1992 / LV / M • Murphie's Brown / 1992 / LV / M • Musical Bedrooms / 1993 / AFV / M • My Evil Twin / 1994 / LE / M • Naked Edge / 1992 / LE / M • Naked Night / 1985 / VCR / M • Nasty Nymphos #06 / 1994 / ANA / M • Nasty Nymphos #16 / 1996 / ANA / M • Native Tongue / 1993 / VI / M • Naughty By Night / 1995 / DR / M • New Wave Hookers #1 / 1984 / VC / M • The Newcomers / 1983 / VCX / M • Nice 'n' Tight / 1985 / AIR / M • Nicki / 1987 / VI / M • Night Moods / 1985 / AVC / M • Night Of Loving Dangerously / 1984 / PV / M • Night Prowlers / 1985 / MAP / M • Nighttime Stories / 1991 / LE / M • Nikki And The Pom-Pom Girls / 1987 / VEX / M • Nikki Never Says No / 1992 / LE / M • Nikki's Bon Voyage / 1993 / VC / M • Nikki's Nightlife / 1992 / IN / M • No Motive / 1994 / MID / M • Nothing But Trouble / 1991 / CIN / M • Nothing Butt The Truth / 1993 / AFV / M • Nothing Sacred / 1995 / LE / M • Nudes At Eleven #1 / 1986 / AVC / M • Nutts About Butts / 1994 / LE / M • Old Wives' Tails / 1995 / EMC / M • Older Men With Younger Women #2 / 1994 / CC / M • On The Come Line / 1993 / MID / M • Once Upon An Anus / 1993 / LV / M • One In A Million / 1992 / HW / M • Open Lips / 1994 / WV / M • Open Up Tracy / 1984 / VD / M • Oral Majority #04 / 1987 / WV / C • The Orgy #1 / 1993 / EMC / M • The Orgy #2 / 1993 / EMC / M • The Orgy #3 / 1993 / EMC / M • Orgy Attack / 1993 / DRP / M • Oriental Treatment #4: The Demon Lover / 1992 / AFV / M • The Other Side Of Lianna / 1984 / LA / M • Our Major Is Sex / 1984 / VD / M • Passage To Pleasure / 1995 / LE / M • Passenger 69 #2 / 1994 / IP / M • The Passion / 1995 / IP / M • Passion's Prisoners / 1994 / LV / M • Peep Land / 1992 / FH / M • Perfect Fit / 1985 / DR / M • Phantasm / 1995 / WP / M • The Phantom Of The Montague Stage / 1997 / HO / M • Pick Up Lines #03 / 1995 / 4P / M • Pick Up Lines #09 / 1996 / OD / M • Pick Up Lines #11 / 1997 / OD / M • Pick Up Lines #12 / 1997 / OD / M • Picture Me Naked / 1993 / LE / M • The Player / 1995 / VI / M • Playing For Passion / 1987 / IN / M • Pleasure Dome: The Genesis Chamber / 1994 / AFV / M • The Pleasure Girl / 1994 / GO / M • The Pleasure Hunt #2 / 1985 / NSV / M • Political Party / 1985 / AVC / M • Poor Little Rich Girl #1 / 1992 / XCI / M • Poor Little Rich Girl #2 / 1992 / XCI / M • Porn In The USA #1 / 1986 / WV / C • A Portrait Of Dorian / 1992 / OD / M • Portrait Of Lust / 1984 / CC / M • Prescription For Lust / 1995 / NIT / M • Prescription For Pleasure / 1993 / HW / M • Primarily Yours / 1996 / CA / M • Private Audition / 1995 / EVN / M • Private Desires / 1995 / LE / M • Private Eyes / 1995 / LE / M • Private Love Affairs / 1985 / VCR / C • The Proposal / 1993 / HO / M • Public Places #1 / 1994 / SC / M • Public Places #2 / 1995 / SC / M • Puppy Love / 1992 / AFV / M • Pussyclips #04 / 1994 / SNA / M

• Pussyclips #05 / 1994 / SNA / M • Pussyman #01: The Search / 1993 / CC / M • Pussyman #02: The Prize / 1993 / CC / M • Pussyman #03: The Search Continues / 1993 / SNA / M • Pussyman #04: The Celebration / 1993 / SNA / M • Pussyman #05: Captive Audience / 1994 / SNA / M • Pussyman #06: House Of Games / 1994 / SNA / M • Pussyman #07: On The Dark Side / 1994 / SNA / M • Pussyman #11: Prime Cuts / 1995 / SNA / C • Pussyman Auditions #13 / 1995 / SNA / M • Puttin' Her Ass On The Line / 1991 / DR / M • Quantum Deep / 1993 / HW / M • R & R / 1994 / VC / M • Radical Affairs Video Magazine #04 / 1992 / ME / M • Raging Hormones / 1992 / LE / M • Rainwoman #07: In The Rainforest / 1993 / CC / M • Rainwoman #08 / 1994 / CC / M • Raunch #09 / 1993 / CC / M • Raven / 1985 / VCR / M • Raw Sex #01 / 1994 / ERW / M • Rear Ended / 1985 / WV / M • Red Hot Pepper / 1986 / V99 / M • Red Light / 1994 / SC / S • Red On The Noodle Like A Swance On A Poodle / 1990 / FC / C • The Reel World #4 / 1995 / FOR / M • Reflections / 1995 / FD / M • Ride The Pink Lady / 1993 / WV / M • Rocket Girls / 1993 / VC / M • Rod Wood / 1995 / LE / M • Roman Goddess / 1992 / HW / M • Rumors / 1992 / FL / M • Satin Dolls / 1985 / CV / M • Satin Shadows / 1991 / CIN / M • Savannah's Last Stand / 1993 / VI / M • Schoolgirl By Day / 1985 / LA / M • Science Friction / 1986 / AXT / M • Scorched / 1995 / ONA / M • Screwballs / 1991 / AFV / M • Secret Rendez-Vous / 1994 / XCI / M • Secret Seductions #1 / 1995 / LV / M • Secret Seductions #2 / 1995 / ULP / M • Seduced / 1992 / VD / M • See-Thru / 1992 / LE / M • Selena Under Siege / 1995 / XCI / M • The Servants Of Midnight / 1992 / CDI / M • Servin' It Up / 1993 / VC / M • Sex #2: Fate (Vca) / 1995 / VC / M • Sex Asylum #1 / 1985 / VI / M • Sex Bandits / 1995 / VC / M • Sex Busters / 1984 / PLY / M • The Sex Game / 1987 / SE / C • Sex In Black & White / 1995 / OD / M • Sex Kitten / 1995 / SC / M • Sex Machine / 1986 / LA / M • Sex Ranch / 1993 / VC / M • Sex Secrets Of High Priced Call Girls / 1995 / MID / M • Sexmares / 1993 / FH / M • The Sexual Solution #1 / 1995 / LE / M • Shame / 1994 / VI / M • Shipwrecked / 1992 / CDI / M • Showgirls / 1985 / SE / M • Silent Stranger / 1992 / VI / M • Silk Stockings: The Black Widow / 1994 / SPI / M • Silver Sensations / 1992 / VT / M • Sindy Does Anal / 1993 / AFV / M • Sindy Does Anal Again / 1994 / AFV / M • Sindy's Sexercise Workout / 1994 / AFV / M • Single Tight Female / 1992 / LV / M • Single White Woman / 1992 / FD / M • Ski Bunnies #2 / 1994 / HW / M • Skin Games / 1986 / VEX / M • Skin Games / 1991 / VEX / C • Slip Into Ginger & Amber / 1986 / MAP / C • Slow Burn / 1991 / VC / M • Snatch Masters #12 / 1995 / LEI / M • Sodom & Gomorrah / 1992 / OD / M • Soft Tail / 1991 / IN / M • Sore Throat / 1985 / GO / M • Sorority Pink #3 / 1992 / SP / M • Sorority Sex Kittens #2 / 1993 / VC / M • Southern Side Up / 1992 / LV / M • Spanish Fly / 1992 / LE / M • Special Treatment / 1991 / AFV / M • Spermacus / 1993 / PI / M • Star 85: Kari Fox / 1985 / VEX / M • Starlets / 1985 / 4P / M • Steady As She Blows /

1993 / LV / M • Steamy Windows / 1993 / VI / M • A Sticky Situation / 1987 / CA / M • Stiff Competition #1 / 1984 / CA / M • Stolen Hearts / 1991 / AFV / M • Stretchin' The Rear / 1995 / PE / M • Summer Games / 1992 / HW / M • Sunset's Anal & D.P. Gangbang / 1996 / PL / M • Swedish Erotica #56 / 1984 / CA / M • Swedish Erotica #58 / 1984 / CA / M • Swedish Erotica #59 / 1984 / CA / M • Swedish Erotica #69 / 1985 / CA / M • Sweet Little Things / 1985 / COL / M • Sweet Revenge / 1997 / KBE / M • Sweet Things / 1987 / VC / M • Switch Hitters #1 / 1987 / IN / G • Taboo #13 / 1994 / IN / M • Taija / 1986 / WV / C • Taija's Satin Seduction / 1987 / CDI / M • Tail Taggers #102 / 1993 / WV / M • Tail Taggers #103 / 1993 / WV / M • Tail Taggers #104 / 1993 / WV / M • Tail Taggers #107 / 1993 / WV / M • Tail Taggers #111 / 1993 / WV / M • Tail Taggers #114: Booty Brunch / 1994 / WV / M • Take The A Train / 1993 / MID / M • Tales From The Chateau / 1987 / BON / B • Talk Dirty To Me #08 / 1990 / DR / M • Talk Dirty To Me #10 / 1996 / DR / M • The Tantric Guide To Sexual Potency And Extended Orgasm / 1994 / A&E / M • A Taste Of Angel / 1989 / PIN / C • A Taste Of Fanny / 1994 / FH / M • Taste Of The Best #1 / 1988 / PIN / C • Taste Of The Best #2 / 1988 / PIN / C • A Taste Of Viper / 1990 / PIN / C • Tasty / 1985 / CA / M • Taxi Girls #3: Killer On The Loose / 1993 / MED / M • Taylor Wayne's World / 1992 / AFV / M • The Teacher's Pet / 1993 / LV / M • Things Change / 1992 / MET / M • Things Change #2: Letting Go / 1992 / CV / M • This Stud's For You / 1986 / MAP / C • This Year's Model / 1996 / WAV / M • The Three Musketeers #1 / 1992 / FD / M • The Three Musketeers #2 / 1992 / FD / M • Tight And Tender / 1985 / CA / M • The Tigress / 1995 / VIM / M • Tit City #1 / 1993 / SC / M • Titty Bar #2 / 1994 / LE / M • Titty Slickers #2 / 1994 / LE / M • Too Good To Be True / 1984 / MAP / M • Too Young To Know / 1984 / CC / M • Traci Who? / 1987 / AVC / C • Trailer Trash / 1994 / VC / M • Transaction #1 / 1986 / WET / M • Trash In The Can / 1993 / LV / M • Trashy Lady / 1985 / MAP / M • Tres Riche / 1986 / CLV / M • Triple X Video Magazine #17 / 1996 / OD / M • Tunnel Of Love / 1986 / CLV / M • Tunnel Of Lust / 1993 / LV / M • Tush / 1992 / ZA / M • Two Times A Virgin / 1991 / AR / M • Two To Tango / 1987 / TEM / M • The Ultimate Thrill / 1988 / PIN / C • The Unashamed / 1993 / FD / M • Up And Cummers #16 / 1994 / 4P / M • Up Close & Personal #1 / 1996 / IPI / M • Up Close & Personal #2 / 1996 / IPI / M • Up Close & Personal #3 / 1996 / IPI / M • V.I.C.E. #2 / 1991 / AFV / M • Vampire's Kiss / 1993 / AVI / M • Video Store Vixens / 1986 / PL / M • Virgin Heat / 1986 / TEM / M • Virgins / 1995 / ERA / M • Virtual Reality / 1993 / EX / M • Visions Of Desire / 1994 / DR / M • W.A.S.P. / 1992 / CC / M • Wall To Wall / 1985 / VD / M • Watch My Lips / 1985 / AAH / M • Web Of Desire / 1993 / OD / M • Wedding Night Blues / 1995 / EMC / M • Wee Wee's Big Misadventure / 1991 / FH / M • Weird Fantasy / 1986 / LA / M • Wet 'n' Bare With Barbara Dare / 1988 / NEO / C • Wet Deal / 1994 / FD / M • Wet Faces #1 / 1997 / SC / C • Wet In The Saddle / 1994 / ME / M •

Wet Nurses #1 / 1994 / LE / M • What's Up, Tiger Pussy? / 1995 / VC / M • While You Were Dreaming / 1995 / WV / M • Whispered Lies / 1993 / LBO / M • White Wedding / 1995 / VI / M • Wicked At Heart / 1995 / WP / M • Wicked Wish / 1992 / LE / M • Wild & Wicked #1 / 1991 / VT / M • Wild Hearts / 1992 / SC / M • Wild Innocence / 1992 / PL / M • Wild Things #3 / 1992 / MET / M • Wild Weekend / 1984 / HO / M • The Wild Wild West / 1986 / SE / M • Wilder At Heart / 1993 / ANA / M • The Wizard Of AHH's / 1985 / SE / M • The Woman In Pink / 1984 / SE / M • The Wong Side Of Town / 1992 / LV / M • The World According To Ginger / 1985 / VI / M • X-Tales / 1995 / VIM / M • The X-Terminator / 1986 / PV / M

STEVE EVENT *see Star Index I*

STEVE FLOWERS

Young Sluts In Heat #1 / 1996 / PL / M • Young Sluts In Heat #2 / 1996 / PL / M

STEVE GOLDBERG *see Steve Drake*

STEVE GREEN *see Star Index I*

STEVE HANNA *see Star Index I*

STEVE HARPER *see Star Index I*

STEVE HARROD *see Star Index I*

STEVE HATCHER *(Jake Williams, Ben Handy, Hatcher, Jake East)*

Dark blonde haired (most of the time long) male with a tattoo on his right shoulder. Married to Chanel (1992) but divorced in 1993. 28 years old in 1995.

'Ho! 'Ho! 'Ho! / 1993 / WP / M • 9-Ball: Geisha Gang Bang / 1994 / PL / M • Abducted / 1996 / ZA / M • Abused / 1996 / ZA / M • Altered Paradise / 1995 / LE / M • Amateur Orgies #33 / 1993 / AFI / M • American Beauty #2 / 1994 / FOR / M • Anal Academy / 1996 / ZA / M • Anal Anarchy / 1995 / VC / M • Anal Aristocrat / 1995 / KWP / M • Anal Blues / 1994 / PEP / M • Anal Camera #05 / 1995 / EVN / M • Anal Cannibals / 1996 / ZA / M • Anal Chiropractor / 1995 / PEP / M • Anal Connection / 1996 / ZA / M • Anal Delivery / 1996 / ZA / M • Anal Disciples #1 / 1996 / ZA / M • Anal Disciples #2: The Anal Conflict / 1996 / ZA / M • Anal Explosions #1 / 1996 / NIT / M • Anal Institution #1 / 1996 / ZA / M • Anal Institution #2 / 1996 / ZA / M • Anal Institution #3 / 1996 / ZA / M • Anal Interrogation / 1995 / ZA / M • Anal Jeopardy / 1996 / ZA / M • Anal Lover #1 / 1992 / ROB / M • Anal Portrait / 1996 / ZA / M • Anal Princess #1 / 1996 / VC / M • Anal Princess #2 / 1996 / VC / M • Anal Professor / 1996 / ZA / M • Anal Rippers #1: The Beginning / 1995 / ZA / M • Anal Rippers #2: The Unveiling / 1996 / ZA / M • Anal Runaway / 1996 / ZA / M • Anal Sex / 1996 / ZA / M • Anal Sex Freaks / 1996 / ZA / M • Anal Shame / 1995 / VD / M • Anal Takeover / 1993 / PEP / M • Anal Talisman / 1996 / ZA / M • Anal Virgins Of America #03 / 1993 / FOR / M • Anal Webb / 1995 / ZA / M • Anal, Facial & Interracial / 1996 / FC / M • Anals, Inc / 1995 / ZA / M • Analtown USA #04 / 1995 / NIT / M • Anything Goes / 1996 / OUP / M • Anything That Moves / 1992 / VC / M • Ariana's Dirty Dancers: The Professionals / 1996 / 4P / M • Asses Galore #1: From L.A. To Brazil / 1996 / DFI / M • Babewatch #2 / 1994 / CC / M • Bachelor Party #1 / 1993 / FPI / M • Bachelor Party #2 / 1993 / FPI / M • Back In Style / 1993 / VI / M • Bad

Company / 1994 / VI / M • Badlands #1 / 1994 / PEP / M • Badlands #2: Back Into Hell / 1994 / PEP / M • Batwoman & Catgirl / 1992 / HW / M • The Bet / 1993 / VT / M • Biff Malibu's Totally Nasty Home Videos #30 / 1993 / ANA / M • Big Boob Boat Ride #2 / 1995 / FC / M • Big Bust Babes #15 / 1993 / AFI / M • Big Bust Babes #30 / 1995 / AFI / M • Big Bust Bangers #1 / 1994 / AMP / M • Big Town / 1993 / PP / M • Black Satin / 1994 / IN / M • Black Tie Affair / 1993 / VEX / M • Blackbroad Jungle / 1994 / IN / M • Blondes / 1995 / MET / M • Bodywaves / 1994 / ELP / M • Booby Prize / 1995 / PEP / M • Boogie In The Butt / 1993 / WIV / M • The Breast Of Breastmen / 1995 / EVN / C • Breastman Does The Twin Towers / 1993 / EVN / M • Breastman's Wet T-Shirt Contest / 1994 / EVN / M • Broad Of Directors / 1992 / PEP / M • Broken Vows / 1996 / ULP / M • Buck Naked In The 21st Century / 1993 / EVN / M • Buffy's First Encounter / 1995 / CIN / M • Buffy's Malibu Adventure / 1995 / CDI / M • Bunny Bleu: A Gang Bang Fantasy / 1994 / FC / M • Burning Desire / 1992 / CDI / M • Butt Bangers Ball / 1994 / FPI / M • Butt Camp / 1993 / HW / C • The Butt Connection / 1993 / TIW / M • Butt Jammers / 1994 / WIV / M • Butt Row Unplugged / 1996 / ABS / M • The Butt Sisters Do Hawaii / 1995 / MID / M • The Butt Sisters Do New York / 1994 / MID / M • Butt Woman #3 / 1992 / FH / M • Butt's Motel #6 / 1994 / EX / M • Butterfly / 1993 / OD / M • Butthole Sweetheart / 1996 / ROB / M • Buttman In The Crack / 1996 / EA / M • Buttman's Bubble Butt Babes / 1996 / EA / M • Buttmasters / 1994 / AMP / M • Butts Up / 1994 / CA / M • Buttsizer, King Of Rears #1 / 1992 / EVN / M • Candy / 1995 / MET / M • Carnal College #2 / 1993 / AFV / M • Caught From Behind #16: The Reunion / 1992 / HO / M • Caught From Behind #18 / 1993 / HO / M • Caught From Behind #21 / 1995 / HO / M • Caught From Behind #22 / 1995 / HO / M • Caught From Behind #24 / 1996 / HO / M • The Cellar Dweller / 1996 / EL / M • Centerfold Celebrities '94 #2 / 1994 / SFP / M • Checkmate / 1992 / CDI / M • Cheek To Cheek / 1997 / EL / M • Cliff Banger / 1993 / HW / M • Colossal Orgy #1 / 1993 / HW / M • The Complete & Total Anal Workout #1 / 1995 / ZA / M • The Complete & Total Anal Workout #2 / 1996 / ZA / M • Compulsion (Amazing) / 1996 / MET / M • Confessions Of A Slutty Nurse / 1994 / VIM / M • County Line / 1993 / PEP / M • Crack Attack! / 1996 / PE / M • Cum Buttered Corn Holes #1 / 1996 / NIT / C • Cumming Clean (1996—Caballero) / 1996 / CA / M • The Cumming Of Sarah Jane #1 / 1993 / AFV / M • The Cumming Of Sarah Jane #2 / 1993 / AFV / M • The D.J. / 1992 / VC / M • The D.P. Man #1 / 1992 / FD / M • Dead Aim / 1994 / PEP / M • Debauchery / 1995 / MET / M • Deceit / 1996 / ZA / M • Deep Inside Nikki Sinn / 1996 / VC / C • Depraved Fantasies #1 / 1993 / FPI / M • Desert Moon / 1994 / SPI / M • Dirt Bags / 1994 / FPI / M • Dirty Dancers #6 / 1995 / 4P / M • Dirty Minds / 1996 / NIT / M • Diva / 1993 / XCI / M • Dog Walker / 1994 / EA / M • Dominant Jean / 1996 / CC / M • Dorm Girls / 1992 / VC / M • Double D Nurses / 1994 / PV / M • Double Penetration #6 / 1993 / WV / C • Dou-

ble Penetration Virgins #06: DP Diner / 1995 / JMP / M • Dp #2: The Mighty Fhucks / 1994 / FC / M • The Dream Machine / 1992 / CDI / M • Dukes Of Anal / 1996 / VC / M • East Vs West: Battle Of The Gang Bangs / 1994 / TTV / M • Ebony Princess / 1994 / IN / M • Eight Is Never Enough / 1993 / ZA / M • Eighteen #1 / 1996 / SC / M • En Garde / 1993 / DR / M • Enigma / 1995 / MET / M • The Erotic Adventures Of The Three Musketeers / 1992 / CEL / S • Eternal Lust / 1996 / VC / M • Every Nerd Has A Fantasy / 1996 / FC / M • Executions On Butt Row / 1996 / EA / M • A Fairy's Tail / 1996 / TTV / M • Fashion Passion / 1997 / TEP / M • Flesh / 1996 / EA / M • Fleshmates / 1994 / ERA / M • Flexxx #2 / 1995 / VT / M • For The Money #2 / 1993 / FH / M • Frat Girls / 1993 / VC / M • French Vanilla / 1994 / HW / M • Fuck Jasmin / 1997 / MET / M • Fuck U: Girls Of The Packed-10 / 1995 / ZA / M • Gang Bang Bitches #01 / 1994 / PP / M • Gang Bang Bitches #02 / 1994 / PP / M • Gang Bang Bitches #03 / 1994 / PP / M • Gang Bang Bitches #04 / 1995 / PP / M • Gang Bang Bitches #05 / 1995 / PP / M • Gang Bang Bitches #06 / 1995 / PP / M • Gang Bang Bitches #07 / 1995 / PP / M • Gang Bang Bitches #09 / 1995 / PP / M • Gang Bang Bitches #10 / 1995 / PP / M • Gangbang Girl #10 / 1993 / ANA / M • Gangbang Girl #13 / 1994 / ANA / M • Gangbang Sluts / 1994 / VMX / M • Gazongas Galore #1 / 1996 / NIT / C • Ghost Town / 1995 / WAV / M • The Girl In Room 69 / 1994 / VC / M • The Girl Next Door #2 / 1994 / VT / M • The Good, The Bad & The Nasty / 1992 / VC / M • Granny Bangers / 1995 / MET / M • The Great American Boobs To Kill For Dance Contest / 1995 / PEP / C • The Great Pretenders / 1994 / FD / M • Greek Week / 1994 / CV / M • Hannibal Lickter / 1992 / MID / M • Hard As A Rock / 1992 / ZA / M • Hardware / 1996 / ZA / M • The Hardwood Chronicles / 1995 / XCI / M • Haunted Nights / 1993 / WP / M • Heartbeat / 1995 / PP / M • Heavyweight Contenders / 1996 / HW / M • Hell Hole / 1996 / ZA / M • Hellfire / 1995 / MET / M • Hillbilly Honeys / 1996 / WP / M • Hispanic Orgies #04 / 1993 / GO / M • The Hitch-Hiker #06: Salty Dog / 1994 / WMG / M • Hollywood Boulevard / 1995 / CV / M • Hollywood Legs / 1996 / NIT / M • Hopeless Romantic / 1992 / LE / M • Horny Henry's Strange Adventure / 1995 / TTV / M • Hot Blooded / 1994 / ERA / M • Hot Parts / 1996 / NIT / M • Hot Property / 1993 / PEP / M • Hot Tight Asses #14 / 1995 / TCK / M • Hot Tight Asses #16 / 1996 / TCK / M • Hot Tight Asses #18 / 1996 / TCK / M • Hot Wishes / 1995 / LE / M • Hotel Sodom #02 / 1995 / SNA / M • Hotel Sodom #04: Free Parking In Rear / 1995 / SNA / M • Hotel Sodom #05: Tammi Ann Bends Over / 1995 / SNA / M • Hotel Sodom #10 / 1996 / SNA / M • House Of Anal / 1995 / NOT / M • House Of Hoochies / 1996 / DDP / M • In The Bush / 1994 / PP / M • Indecent Offer / 1993 / AFV / M • Insatiable Nurses / 1992 / VIM / M • Inside Job / 1992 / ZA / M • Intense / 1996 / MET / M • Invitation To The Blues / 1994 / LE / M • Juranal Park / 1993 / OD / M • Just Jasmin / 1996 / AMP / M • Just My Imagination / 1993 / WP / M • Keyholes /

1995 / OD / M • Kink #2 / 1995 / ROB / M • Kink: Police Chronicles / 1995 / ROB / M • Lactamania #4 / 1996 / TTV / M • Lap Of Luxury / 1994 / WIV / M • Latex And Lace / 1996 / BBE / M • A League Of Their Moan / 1992 / EVN / M • Leena Is Nasty / 1994 / OD / M • Leg Show #2 / 1996 / NIT / M • Legal Briefs / 1996 / EX / M • Legend #4: Critic's Choice / 1992 / LE / M • Legs / 1996 / ZA / M • Living Doll / 1992 / CDI / M • Loose Jeans / 1996 / GO / M • Love Spice / 1995 / ERA / M • Lust & Desire / 1996 / WV / M • Many Happy Returns / 1995 / NIT / M • Million Dollar Buns / 1996 / MYS / M • Mistress Of The Mansion / 1994 / CV / M • More Than A Handful #5: California Or Bust / 1994 / MET / M • More Than A Handful #6: Life Under The Big Top / 1994 / MET / M • Mystique / 1996 / SC / M • N.Y.D.P. / 1994 / PEP / M • Nasty Dreams / 1994 / PRK / M • Nasty Nymphos #02 / 1994 / ANA / M • Native Tongue / 1993 / VI / M • Nineteen #8 / 1997 / FOR / M • No Bust Babes / 1992 / AFI / M • Nookie Of The Year / 1993 / HW / M • Objective: D.P. / 1993 / PEP / M • The Orgy #3 / 1993 / EMC / M • The Original Wicked Woman / 1993 / WP / M • The Other Side Of Chelsea / 1993 / XCI / M • Out Of My Mind / 1995 / PL / M • The Panty Parlor / 1996 / VIM / M • Passion / 1996 / SC / M • Peepshow / 1994 / OD / M • Performer Of The Year / 1994 / WP / M • Persia's Back / 1994 / VT / M • Perverted #1: The Babysitters / 1994 / ZA / M • Pizza Sluts: They Deliver / 1995 / XCI / M • Pornographic Priestess / 1992 / CA / M • The Portrait Of Dorie Grey / 1996 / KLP / M • Possessed / 1996 / MET / M • The Power & The Passion / 1993 / CDI / M • Prescription For Pleasure / 1993 / HW / M • Pretty Anal Ladies / 1996 / ANE / M • Private Dancer (CDI) / 1992 / CDI / M • Private Matters / 1995 / EMC / M • Private Video Magazine #05 / 1993 / OD / M • Professor Sticky's Anatomy 3X #01 / 1992 / FC / M • Professor Sticky's Anatomy 3X #02 / 1992 / FC / M • Provocative / 1994 / LE / M • Psychoanal Therapy / 1994 / CA / M • Pure Smut / 1996 / GO / M • Puritan Video Magazine #09 / 1997 / LE / M • Pussyclips #03 / 1994 / SNA / M • Pussyman #05: Captive Audience / 1994 / SNA / M • Pussyman #13: Lips / 1996 / SNA / M • Pussyman Auditions #02 / 1995 / SNA / M • Pussyman's House Party #1 / 1996 / SNA / M • Pussyman's House Party #2 / 1996 / SNA / M • Radical Affairs Video Magazine #01 / 1992 / ME / M • Raunch #08 / 1993 / CC / M • The Real Deal #1 / 1994 / FC / M • Realities #2 / 1992 / ZA / M • Rectal Rodeo / 1994 / ZA / M • Red Door Diaries #1 / 1995 / ZA / M • Red Hot Coeds / 1993 / VIM / M • Reflections / 1996 / ZA / M • Release Me / 1996 / VT / M • Return Engagement / 1995 / VI / M • Revealed / 1992 / VT / M • Revenge Of The Pussy Suckers From Mars / 1994 / PP / M • Ring Of Passion / 1994 / ERA / M • Rituals / 1993 / SC / M • Road Kill / 1995 / CA / M • Roly Poly Gang Bang / 1995 / HW / M • A Round Behind / 1995 / PEP / M • Roxy Rider Is In Control / 1996 / NIT / M • Rump Reamers / 1994 / TTV / M • Rumpman: Caught In An Anal Avalanche / 1995 / HW / M • Saints & Sinners / 1992 / PEP / M • Saturday Night Porn #3 / 1993 / AFV / M • Savannah's Last

Stand / 1993 / VI / M • The Secret Life Of Herbert Dingle / 1994 / TTV / M • Secret Urges (Vidco) / 1994 / VD / C • Seekers / 1994 / CA / M • The Servants Of Midnight / 1992 / CDI / M • Sex Circus / 1994 / VIM / M • Sex In Strange Places: The Sphincter Zone / 1994 / FPI / M • Sex Stories / 1992 / VC / M • Sexorcist / 1994 / HW / M • Sexual Olympics #1: The Trials / 1992 / VT / M • Sexual Olympics #2: The Finals / 1992 / VT / M • Seymore Butts & The Honeymooners / 1992 / FH / M • Shame / 1994 / VI / M • A Shaver Among Us / 1992 / ZA / M • Shayla's Home Repair / 1993 / EVN / M • She Quest / 1994 / OD / M • Shooting Gallery / 1996 / EL / M • Sideshow Freaks / 1996 / ZA / M • Sin City: The Movie / 1992 / SC / M • Sinister Sister / 1997 / WP / M • Slammed / 1995 / PV / M • Sleazy Streets / 1995 / PEP / M • Sluts, Butts And Pussy / 1996 / DFI / M • Smeers / 1992 / PL / M • Sodom Chronicles / 1995 / FH / M • Sorority Sex Kittens #3 / 1996 / VC / M • Stacked Deck / 1994 / IN / M • Star Crossed / 1995 / VC / M • Starbangers #01 / 1993 / BIG / M • Starbangers #04 / 1993 / FPI / M • Starbangers #05 / 1993 / FPI / M • Starbangers #08 / 1996 / FPI / M • Starbangers #09 / 1996 / ZA / M • Starbangers #10 / 1997 / ZA / M • Strip Show / 1996 / CA / M • Stripping / 1995 / NIT / M • Striptease / 1995 / SPI / M • Style #2 / 1994 / VT / M • Suburban Buttnicks Forever / 1995 / CC / M • Supermarket Babes In Heat / 1992 / OD / M • Surfer Girl / 1992 / PP / M • Sweet Target / 1992 / CDI / M • Swinging Couples #02 / 1993 / GO / M • Taboo #10 / 1992 / IN / M • Taboo #11: Crazy On You / 1993 / IN / M • Takin' It To The Limit #2 / 1994 / BS / M • A Tall Tail / 1996 / FC / M • Temptation / 1994 / VC / M • This Girl Is Freaky / 1996 / NIT / M • The Time Machine / 1996 / WP / M • Tinsel Town Tales / 1995 / NOT / M • Titanic Orgy / 1995 / PEP / M • Titty City #1 / 1995 / TIW / M • Titty Town #1 / 1994 / HW / M • To Shave And Shave Not / 1994 / PEP / M • Too Sexy / 1992 / MID / M • Top Debs #3: Riding Academy / 1993 / GO / M • Totally Depraved / 1996 / SC / M • Trailer Trash / 1994 / VC / M • Treacherous / 1995 / VD / M • Twist Of Fate / 1996 / WP / M • Two Too Much / 1996 / MET / M • Ultimate Anal Gang Bang #3 / 1995 / HW / M • Ultimate Orgy #1 / 1992 / GLI / M • Valentino's Euro-Invasion / 1997 / SC / M • Virgin Dreams / 1996 / EA / M • The Wanderer #2: Slippery When Wet / 1995 / CDI / M • War Whores / 1996 / EL / M • Wendy Whoppers: Environmental Attorney / 1993 / PEP / M • Wendy Whoppers: Ninja CPA / 1993 / PEP / M • Wendy Whoppers: Prison Love Doll / 1994 / PEP / M • Wendy Whoppers: Psychic Healer / 1994 / PEP / M • Wendy Whoppers: Ufo Tracker / 1994 / PEP / M • White Men Can't Iron On Butt Row / 1997 / ABS / M • Wicked Ways #3: An All-Anal Slutfest / 1995 / WP / M • Wild & Wicked #7 / 1996 / VT / M • Wild Widow / 1996 / NIT / M • Willie Wanker At The Fudge Packing Factory / 1995 / FD / M • Willie Wanker At The Sushi Bar / 1995 / FD / M • Willing Women / 1993 / VD / C • With The Devil In Her Rear / 1992 / WV / M • Witness For The Penetration / 1994 / PEP / M • X-Rated Blondes / 1992 / VD / C • XXX / 1996 / TEP / M

STEVE HENNESSEY
Black Chicks In Heat / 1988 / VC / M • Nightshift Nurses #1 / 1988 / VC / M • Nightshift Nurses #2 / 1996 / VC / M
STEVE HOLLYWOOD
Amateur Nights #16 / 1997 / HO / M
STEVE HORNER see Star Index I
STEVE HOUSTON *(Rex Houston, John (Steve Houston))*
Seems to be Alicia Rio's boyfriend or husband. Almost Home Alone / 1993 / SFP / M • Anal Romance / 1993 / LV / M • Anal Vision #11 / 1993 / LBO / M • Attack Of The 50 Foot Hooker / 1994 / OD / M • Beach Bunny / 1994 / V99 / M • Bobby Hollander's Maneaters #05 / 1993 / SFP / M • Bun Busters #12 / 1993 / LBO / M • The Butt Connection / 1993 / TIW / M • The Butt Sisters Do Las Vegas / 1994 / MID / M • Cum Buttered Corn Holes #3 / 1996 / NIT / C • Dirty Dancers #9 / 1996 / HO / M • Dirty Looks / 1994 / VI / M • The Erotic Artist / 1995 / VC / M • Fantasies Of Alicia / 1995 / VT / M • Frathouse Sexcapades / 1993 / SFP / M • The Girls From Hootersville #02 / 1993 / SFP / M • Hypnotic Hookers #1 / 1996 / NIT / M • Kym Wilde's On The Edge #12 / 1994 / RB / B • La Princesa Anal / 1993 / ROB / M • Lovebone Invasion / 1993 / PL / M • M Series #08 / 1993 / LBO / M • M Series #13 / 1993 / LBO / M • Mindsex / 1993 / MPA / M • Mutiny On The Booty / 1996 / FC / M • Neighborhood Watch #21 / 1992 / LBO / M • New Pussy Hunt #28 / 1997 / LEI / C • The Night Of The Coyote / 1993 / MED / M • Nookie Of The Year / 1993 / HW / M • Puritan Video Magazine #03 / 1996 / LE / M • Reflections Of Rio / 1993 / WP / M • Risque Burlesque #1 / 1994 / IN / M • Sean Michaels On The Road #01: The Barrio / 1993 / VT / M • Show Business / 1995 / LV / M • Ski Bunnies #1 / 1994 / HW / M • Steam / 1993 / AMP / M • Taxi Girls #4: Daughter Of Lust / 1994 / CA / M • Wild & Wicked #6 / 1995 / VT / M • Within & Without You / 1993 / WP / M
STEVE JOHNS
Erotic Dripping Orientals / 1993 / WV / M
STEVE JUSTICE
Temptation Of Serenity / 1994 / WP / M • The Time Machine / 1996 / WP / M
STEVE KENNEDY
Black & Beyond: The Darker Sid / 1990 / INH / G • Kitty Foxx's Kinky Kapers #01 / 1995 / TTV / M • Kitty Foxx's Kinky Kapers #02 / 1995 / TTV / M
STEVE KING
Eyes Of A Dreamer / 1983 / S&L / M
STEVE KNIGHT
How To Make A Model #03: Sunshine & Melons / 1994 / QUA / M • Mr. Peepers Amateur Home Videos #94: Calendar Cleavage / 1994 / LBO / M
STEVE LACEY
Sweet Cheeks / 1980 / VCX / M
STEVE LAPARITI
The Whipped Voyeur's Lesbian Sex Show / 1994 / PL / F
STEVE LARSON
Eat At Dave's #7 / 1996 / SP / M
STEVE LERNER
California Heat / cr75 / BL / M
STEVE M. see Star Index I
STEVE MALINO see Star Index I
STEVE MALONEY

Princess Seka / 1980 / VC / M
STEVE MARACHUK
Hot Sex In Bangkok / 1974 / MED / M • Hot Target / 1985 / LIV / S
STEVE MARKS
Secret Sex #3: The Takeover / 1994 / CAT / G
STEVE MARKSON
Love Mexican Style / cr75 / BLT / M
STEVE MARLOW
Dixie Ray Hollywood Star / 1983 / CA / M
STEVE MARSHALL
Debbie Does Dallas #1 / 1978 / VC / M
STEVE MARTY
Inside Desiree Cousteau / 1979 / VCX / M
STEVE MASON
The Amateurs / 1984 / VCX / M • A Bride For Brenda / 1968 / SOW / S
STEVE MASTERS
Krystal Balling / 1988 / PL / M • Ron Hightower's Casting Couch #1 / 1995 / FC / M
STEVE MICHAELS
Dirty Hairy's Shove It Up My Ass / 1996 / GOT / M
STEVE MILESTONE see Star Index I
STEVE MITCHELL see Carter Stevens
STEVE MORGAN
The Bride's Initiation / 1976 / VIP / M
STEVE NACY
Tickle Thy Slaves / 1995 / SBP / B
STEVE NADEL see Steve Drake
STEVE NADELMAN see Steve Drake
STEVE NOLTE
Alice In Whiteland / 1988 / VC / M • Debbie For President / 1988 / CC / M • Debbie Goes To Hawaii / 1988 / VC / M • Dirty Laundry / 1988 / PP / M • Hot Rods / 1988 / VEX / M • Jane Bond Meets Thunderthighs / 1988 / VD / M • Satisfaction Jackson / 1988 / CA / M • The Slut / 1988 / FAN / M • Three For All / 1988 / PL / M
STEVE OLSEN see Star Index I
STEVE PARKER
Married Men With Men On The Side / 1996 / BHE / G
STEVE PARKS
The Erotic Aventures Of Lolita / 1982 / VXP / M
STEVE PERRY *(Ben Dover (S. Perry), Steven Perry)*
English sleazy director and performer.
Alley Cats / 1995 / VC / M • Banned In Britain / 1995 / VC / M • Ben Dover's 9th / 1996 / VC / M • British Babe Hunt / 1996 / VC / M • British Butt Search / 1995 / VC / M • The British Connection / 1996 / VC / M • Buttman's Bubble Butt Babes / 1996 / EA / M • Different Strokes / 1996 / VC / M • Duke Of Knockers #1 / 1992 / BTO / M • Duke Of Knockers #2 / 1995 / BTO / M • English Class / 1995 / VC / M • English Muffins / 1995 / VC / M • Fresh Cheeks / 1995 / VC / M • Kinky Ladies Of London / 1995 / VC / M • Lewd In Liverpool / 1995 / VC / M • Little Big Girls / 1996 / VC / M • Lusting, London Style / 1992 / VC / M • Royal Ass Force / 1996 / VC / M
STEVE POWERS *(Eric Swenson, Kevin Olsen)*
Sleazy looking biker type with a tattoo on his right arm. Eric Swenson is from **Lusty Ladies #04**. Kevin Olsen is from **Hindsight**.
Amber Lynn's Peter Meter / 1988 / 3HV / C • Amber Pays The Rent / 1986 / VT / M • Aroused / 1985 / VIV / M • Bachelor's Par-

adise / 1986 / VEX / M • Backdoor Babes / 1985 / WET / M • The Beat Goes On / 1987 / VCR / C • Before She Says I Do / 1984 / MAP / M • Best Of Caught From Behind #1 / 1987 / HO / C • Between The Cheeks #1 / 1985 / VC / M • Black Holes In Space / 1987 / 4P / M • Black Throat / 1985 / VC / M • Blacks & Blondes #32 / 1986 / WV / M • Blondie / 1985 / TAR / M • Blue Dream Lover / 1985 / TAR / M • Blue Views / 1990 / CDI / M • Born To Run / 1985 / WV / M • C-Hunt / 1985 / PL / M • Cagney & Stacey / 1984 / AT / M • Caught From Behind #04: Nasty Young Girls / 1985 / HO / M • Coming Holmes / 1985 / VD / M • Confessions Of Candy / 1984 / VC / M • Deep Inside Vanessa Del Rio / 1986 / VC / M • The Desk Top Dolls / 1990 / BAD / C • Devil In Miss Jones #3: A New Beginning / 1986 / VC / M • Devil In Miss Jones #4: The Final Outrage / 1987 / VC / M • Double Insertion / 1986 / 4P / M • Double Penetration #1 / 1985 / WV / M • Double Penetration #2 / 1986 / WV / C • Double Penetration #3 / 1986 / WV / C • Ebony & Ivory Fantasies / 1988 / VD / C • Erica Boyer: Non-Stop / 1988 / VD / C • The Erotic World Of Cody Nicole / 1984 / VCR / C • Farmers Daughters / 1985 / WV / M • For Your Thighs Only / 1985 / WV / M • Funky Brewster / 1986 / DR / M • Gang Bangs #1 / 1985 / VCR / M • Ginger And Spice / 1986 / VI / M • Girls Just Want To...Have Fun / 1984 / SE / M • Headhunters / 1984 / VC / M • Heidi A / 1985 / PL / M • Hindsight / 1985 / IN / M • Hollywood Pink / 1985 / HO / M • Honeybuns #1 / 1987 / WV / C • Hot And Nasty! / 1986 / V99 / C • Hot Flashes / 1984 / VC / M • Hot Sweet Honey / 1985 / VEP / M • Hot Tails / 1984 / VEN / M • House Of Blue Dreams / 1985 / WV / M • House Of The Rising Moon / 1986 / VD / M • Imaginary Lovers / 1986 / ME / M • Indecent Wives / 1985 / HO / M • Intimate Couples / 1984 / VCX / M • Joy Toys / 1985 / WET / M • Kinkyvision #1 / 1986 / 3HV / M • Kiss Of The Married Woman / 1986 / WV / M • Lady Cassanova / 1985 / AVC / M • The Layout / 1986 / CDI / M • Let Me Tell Ya 'Bout Black Chicks / 1985 / VC / M • Like A Virgin #2 / 1986 / AT / M • Lingerie Party / 1987 / SE / C • Loose Morals / 1987 / HO / M • The Lust Detector / 1986 / PIN / M • Lusty Ladies #04 / 1983 / 4P / M • Mad Jack Beyond Thunderdome / 1986 / WET / M • Mammary Lane / 1988 / VT / C • Marilyn Chambers' Private Fantasies #2 / 1983 / CA / M • A Mid-Slumber's Night Dream / 1985 / 4P / M • Miss Passion / 1984 / VD / M • The Modelling Studio / 1984 / GO / M • Naughty Angels / 1984 / VC / M • Naughty Nanette / 1984 / VC / M • New Wave Hookers #1 / 1984 / VC / M • The Night Of The Headhunter / 1985 / WV / M • Nymphette #1 / 1986 / WV / M • Old Guys & Dolls #2 / 1995 / PL / M • Only The Very Best On Video / 1992 / VC / C • Oral Majority #01 / 1986 / WV / C • Oral Majority #03 / 1986 / WV / C • Orgies / 1987 / WV / C • Parliament: Dirty Blondes #1 / 1991 / PM / F • Penetration #1 / 1984 / AVC / M • Personal Touch #3 / 1983 / AR / M • Pleasure Productions #04 / 1984 / VCR / M • Rambone The Destroyer / 1985 / WET / M • Return To Sex 5th Avenue / 1985 / WV / M • Rich Quick, Private Dick / 1984 / CA / M • Rump

Humpers / 1985 / WET / M • The Seduction Of Lana Shore / 1984 / PL / M • Sensuous Tales / 1984 / VCR / C • Sex 5th Avenue / 1985 / WV / M • Sex Asylum #1 / 1985 / VI / M • Sex Beat / 1985 / WV / M • Sex For Hire / 1989 / HOE / C • Shave Tail / 1984 / AMB / M • Shaved / 1984 / VCR / M • Sin City / 1986 / WET / M • Sleeping With Everybody / 1992 / MID / C • Soul Kiss This / 1988 / VCR / C • Spermbusters / 1984 / AT / M • A Star Is Porn / 1985 / PL / M • Stripteaser / 1986 / LA / M • Sunny Side Up / 1984 / VC / M • Super Models Do LA / 1986 / AT / M • Surfside Sex / 1985 / PV / M • Taija Is Sizzling Hot / 1986 / VT / M • Tailenders / 1985 / WET / M • Tailgunners / 1985 / WET / M • Tailhouse Rock / 1985 / WV / M • A Taste Of Genie / 1986 / 4P / M • Tasty / 1985 / CA / M • This Butt's For You / 1986 / PME / M • Tongue 'n Cheek (Vca) / 1984 / VC / M • Tunnel Of Love / 1986 / CLV / M • Ubangis On Uranus / 1987 / WV / M • Up Desiree Lane / 1984 / VC / M • VCA Previews #4 / 1988 / VC / C • What Gets Me Hot / 1984 / ISV / M • White Bun Busters / 1985 / CLV / M • Wide World Of Sex / 1987 / CLV / C • Young Nurses In Love / 1987 / VC / M

STEVE PUMPKIN
Sharon In The Rough-House / 1976 / LA / M

STEVE RADO see Star Index I
STEVE REGIS
B-Witched / 1994 / PEP / G • Bi Bi Birdie / 1993 / BIL / G • Bi Chill / 1994 / BIL / G • The Bi-Linguist / 1993 / BIL / G • Days Gone Bi / 1994 / BIN / G

STEVE REYNOLDS see Stephen Reynolds
STEVE RICHARDS
Between The Cheeks #1 / 1985 / VC / M • Virgin Dreams / 1976 / BMV / M

STEVE RIDEOUT
L.A. Tool & Die / 1979 / TMX / G

STEVE RIGHT
Switch Hitters #2: Swinging Both Ways / 1987 / IN / G

STEVE ROBERTS
Head Waitress / 1984 / VC / M • Mouthful Of Love / 1984 / VC / M • Princess Seka / 1980 / VC / M • Taboo American Style #4: The Exciting Conclusion / 1985 / VC / M

STEVE ROGERS
Kitty Foxx's Kinky Kapers #01 / 1995 / TTV / M

STEVE ROSS
Switch Hitters #3: Squeeze Play / 1988 / IN / G • The Switch Is On / 1985 / CAT / G

STEVE RYDER
Big Switch #3: Bachelor Party / 1991 / CAT / G

STEVE SANDERS see David Sanders
STEVE SAUNDERS see David Sanders
STEVE SAVAGE see Star Index I
STEVE SAYADIAN see Rinse Dream
STEVE SCHLONG see Star Index I
STEVE SHAME
Oriental Techniques Of Pain And Pleasure / 1983 / ALP / B

STEVE SIQQUA
The Unholy Child / 1972 / AVC / M

STEVE SIX
Anal Camera #14 / 1996 / EVN / M • Anal Reunion / 1996 / EVN / M • Dangerous Behinds #2 / 1996 / HW / M • Fresh Faces #10 / 1996 / EVN / M • Orgy Camera #2 /

1996 / EVN / M
STEVE SLAMMER
Ready To Drop #01 / 1990 / FC / M
STEVE SPAIN
Interview With A She-Male / 1995 / PL / G • Sex Starved She-Males / 1995 / MET / G • She-Male Call Girls / 1996 / BIZ / G • She-Male Nymphos / 1995 / MET / G • She-Male Seduction / 1995 / MET / G
STEVE ST. CROIX see Steven St. Croix
STEVE STARR see Star Index I
STEVE STIX
Naked Mockey-Rayna / 1996 / EVN / M • Orgy Camera #1 / 1995 / EVN / M • Pure Anal / 1996 / MET / M
STEVE STORM
N.Y. Video Magazine #03 / 1995 / OUP / M • Primal Submission / A Glutton For Punishment / 1995 / OUP / B
STEVE SUCKSI see Steve Austin
STEVE TAYLOR
Country & Western Cuties #2: Naked Pie Eating Contest / 1996 / EVN / M • Dirty Minds / 1996 / NIT / M
STEVE THE DUDE see Star Index I
STEVE THORP
Buttman's Bouncin' British Babes / 1994 / EA / M • Sodomania #08: The London Sessions / 1994 / EL / M
STEVE TUCKER see Ashley Moore
STEVE VEGAS (The Flash)
All The Right Motions / 1990 / DR / M • Behind Closed Doors / 1990 / VI / M • Behind You All The Way #1 / 1990 / SO / M • Behind You All The Way #2 / 1990 / SO / M • Black Mail / 1990 / TAO / C • Blackman & Anal Woman #2 / 1990 / PL / M • Butt's Motel #4 / 1989 / EX / M • Changing Partners / 1989 / FAZ / M • Cheaters / 1990 / LE / M • Diedre In Danger / 1990 / VI / M • Dream Dates / 1990 / V99 / M • Dutch Masters / 1990 / IN / M • Great Balls Of Fire / 1989 / FAZ / M • The Hardriders / 1990 / 4P / M • Haunted Passions / 1990 / FC / M • Heart Of Stone / 1990 / FAN / M • Heraldo: Streetwalkers Of NY / 1990 / GOT / M • Hollywood Knights #3 / 1991 / PCP / M • Home Maid Memories #1 / 1994 / BON / C • In The Jeans / 1990 / ME / M • Internal Affair / 1990 / V99 / M • Kinky Couples / 1990 / VD / M • Lickety Pink / 1990 / ME / M • Little Miss Dangerous / 1989 / SO / M • National Poontang's Summer Vacation / 1990 / FC / M • Next Door Neighbors #21 / 1990 / BON / M • No Strings Attached / 1990 / ERO / M • Oral Addiction / 1989 / LV / M • Paradise Road / 1990 / WV / M • Santa Comes Again / 1990 / GLE / M • Sea Of Lust / 1990 / FAN / M • Sex Lives On Porno Tape / 1992 / VC / C • Shadow Dancers #1 / 1989 / EA / M • Sharon And Karen / 1989 / LV / G • The Shaving / 1989 / SO / M • The Smart Ass #1 / 1990 / VT / M • The Smart Ass #2: Rusty's Revenge / 1990 / VT / M • Sorceress / 1990 / GO / M • Susan & Steve Vegas Bound For You / 199? / BON / B • Talk Dirty To Me #07 / 1990 / DR / M • Three Wishes #1 / 1991 / CDP / B • Three Wishes #2 / 1991 / CDP / B • Untamed Passion / 1991 / VEX / M • Virgin Busters / 1989 / LV / M • When Larry Ate Sally / 1989 / EX / M • The Whore / 1989 / CA / M • Wise Ass! / 1990 / FH / M
STEVE VETTE
Island Of Love / 1983 / CV / M
STEVE WADE

Erotic Dimensions #1: Ripe / 1982 / NSV / M

STEVE WARD
The Butt Sisters Do The Twin Cities / 1996 / MID / M

STEVE WAYNE *see Star Index I*

STEVE YORK
Buttman's British Moderately Big Tit Adventure / 1994 / EA / M

STEVE ZIPLOW *see Star Index I*
STEVEN BLACKWELL *see Star Index I*
STEVEN CHASE *see Anthony Lawton*
STEVEN CRAIG *see Star Index I*
STEVEN DOUGLAS *see Steve Douglas*
STEVEN GRANT
The Seduction Of Seka / 1981 / AVC / M

STEVEN GRIMES
Pink Champagne / 1979 / CV / M

STEVEN HILL *see Star Index I*

STEVEN JAWORSKI
Campus Girl / 1972 / VXP / M

STEVEN KNITE *see Star Index I*
STEVEN LARK *see Star Index I*
STEVEN LOCKWOOD
Bordello...House Of The Rising Sun / 1985 / SE / M • Naked Scents / 1984 / VC / M • Sensual Escape / 1988 / FEM / M • Taboo American Style #4: The Exciting Conclusion / 1985 / VC / M

STEVEN LONG
Baby Doll / 1975 / AR / M

STEVEN MARKS
Bi-Conflict / 1994 / FST / G • Conflict Of Interest / 1994 / FST / G • Courting Libido / 1995 / HIV / G

STEVEN MICHAELS
Stuff Your Ass #3 / 1996 / JMP / M

STEVEN MITCHELL *see Carter Stevens*
STEVEN NIXON
Party Girl / 1995 / LV / M

STEVEN PERRY *see Steve Perry*
STEVEN REILLY
The Little French Maid / 1981 / VCX / M

STEVEN RICCI
Looking Good / 1984 / ABV / M

STEVEN SCOTT *see Star Index I*
STEVEN SHELDON *see Star Index I*
STEVEN SPECK
Audition For Pain / 1996 / VTF / B • The Intruders: Office Call / 1995 / VTF / B • Lesson In Spanking / 1996 / VTF / B

STEVEN ST JOX
Depraved Fantasies #2 / 1994 / FPI / M

STEVEN ST. CROIX *(Stephen St. Croix, Steve St. Croix, Jake Rider, Joey Renada)*
$exce$$ / 1993 / CA / M • 13th Annual Adult Video News Awards / 1996 / VC / S • The 4th Vixxen / 1995 / EMC / M • 69th Street / 1993 / VIM / M • The Absolute Worst Of Amateur #1 / 1993 / VEX / M • Affairs Of The Heart / 1993 / VI / M • All-Star Anal Interviews #1 / 1995 / LEI / M • Almost Home Alone / 1993 / SFP / M • Amateur Orgies #19 / 1992 / AFI / M • Amateur Orgies #20 / 1992 / AFI / M • American Beauty #1 / 1993 / FOR / M • American Beauty #2 / 1994 / FOR / M • Anal Arsenal / 1994 / OD / M • Anal Generation / 1995 / PE / M • Anal Takeover / 1993 / PEP / M • Anal Virgins Of America #10 / 1994 / FOR / M • Animal Instinct / 1993 / VI / M • Arabian Nights / 1993 / WP / M • Assent Of A Woman / 1993 / DR / M • Assmania!! #1 / 1994 / ME / M • Attic Toys / 1994 / ERA / M • Attitude / 1995 / VC / M • Back Door Mistress / 1994 / GO / M •

Backing In #6 / 1994 / WV / C • Bangkok Nights / 1994 / VI / M • The Bashful Blonde From Beautiful Bendover / 1993 / PEP / M • Beaver & Buttcheeks / 1993 / DR / M • Beaver Hunt #01 / 1994 / LEI / M • The Beaverly Hillbillies / 1993 / IP / M • Behind The Backdoor #6 / 1993 / EVN / M • Best Butt(e) In The West #2 / 1995 / CC / M • The Best Of Strippers Inc / 1996 / ONA / C • Big Bust Bangers #2 / 1994 / AMP / M • Big Murray's New-Cummers #06: Men & Women / 1993 / FD / M • Big Town / 1993 / PP / M • Bimbonese 101 / 1993 / PL / M • Bitch / 1993 / VIM / M • Black Velvet #3 / 1994 / CC / M • A Blaze Of Glory / 1993 / ME / M • Blind Spot / 1993 / VI / M • Blinded By Love / 1993 / OD / M • Blindfold / 1994 / SC / M • Blonde In Blue Flannel / 1995 / CA / M • Bloopers & Boners / 1996 / VI / M • Blue Movie / 1995 / WP / M • Bobby Sox / 1996 / VI / S • Body Language / 1995 / VI / M • Body Work / 1993 / MET / M • Bonnie & Clyde #3 / 1994 / VI / M • Bonnie & Clyde #4 / 1994 / VI / M • The Boob Tube / 1993 / MET / M • Boobtown / 1995 / VC / M • Booty By Nature / 1994 / WP / M • Bordello / 1995 / VI / M • Borderline (Vivid) / 1995 / VI / M • Both Ends Burning / 1993 / HW / M • Bottoms Up (1993-Hollywood) / 1993 / HO / M • Breast Wishes #12 / 1993 / LBO / M • Breast Worx #42 / 1993 / LBO / M • Breastman Goes To Breastland #2 / 1993 / EVN / M • Bring On The Night / 1994 / VEX / M • Bunmasters / 1995 / VC / M • Bustline / 1993 / LE / M • Butt Bandits #4 / 1996 / VD / C • Butt Banged Cycle Sluts / 1995 / ANA / M • Butt Freak #2 / 1996 / EA / M • The Butt Sisters / 1993 / MID / M • Buttman's Wet Dream / 1994 / EA / M • Butts Up / 1994 / CA / M • Cajun Heat / 1993 / SC / M • The Cathouse / 1994 / VI / M • Caught From Behind #18 / 1993 / HO / M • Caught From Behind #19 / 1994 / HO / M • Caught In The Act (1995-Wave) / 1995 / WAV / M • Centerfold Strippers / 1994 / ME / M • Chasey Saves The World / 1996 / VI / M • Chasin' The Fifties / 1994 / WP / M • Chateau Du Cheeks / 1994 / VC / M • Cheating / 1994 / VI / M • Chinatown / 1994 / SC / M • Cinesex #1 / 1995 / CV / M • Cinesex #2 / 1994 / CV / M • Cloud 9 / 1995 / VI / M • College Cuties / 1995 / LE / M • Comeback / 1995 / VI / M • The Comix / 1995 / VI / M • The Corruption Of Christina / 1993 / WP / M • The Coven #1 / 1993 / VI / M • Cry Baby / 1995 / CV / M • Cumback Pussy #1 / 1996 / EL / M • Cumming Of Ass / 1995 / TP / M • Cynthia And The Pocket Rocket / 1995 / CV / M • Dangerous Games / 1995 / VI / M • The Darker Side / 1994 / HO / M • Dear Diary / 1995 / WP / M • Deep Behind The Scenes With Seymore Butts #1 / 1995 / ULI / M • Deep Behind The Scenes With Seymore Butts #2 / 1995 / ULI / M • Deep Cover / 1993 / WP / M • Deep Inside Kaitlyn Ashley / 1995 / VC / C • Deep Inside Tyffany Million / 1995 / VC / C • Deep Throat #6 / 1992 / AFV / M • Demolition Woman #1 / 1994 / IP / M • Desperate / 1995 / WP / M • Diary Of A Geisha / 1995 / WV / C • Dirty Little Lies / 1993 / VT / M • Dirty Little Mind / 1994 / IP / M • Dirty Little Secrets / 1995 / WAV / M • Dirty Looks / 1994 / VI / M • Dirty Stories #2 / 1995 / PE / M • Dirty Tricks #1: Just A Bunch Of Whores / 1995 / EA / M • Dog

Walker / 1994 / EA / M • Doggie Style / 1994 / CA / M • Double Cross (Wicked) / 1995 / WP / M • Double Down / 1993 / LBO / M • Dr Butts #3 / 1993 / 4P / M • The Dragon Lady #5: Tales From The Bed #4 / 1993 / WV / M • Drilling For Gold / 1995 / ME / M • Eight Is Never Enough / 1993 / ZA / M • Eleventh Annual AVN Awards / 1994 / VC / M • Euphoria / 1993 / CA / M • Euroslut #1: French Tart / 1993 / CC / M • Euroslut #2 / 1994 / CC / M • Every Woman Has A Fantasy #3 / 1995 / VC / M • Extreme Close-Up / 1996 / VI / M • The F Zone / 1995 / WP / M • Fantasy Chamber / 1994 / ULI / M • Fire Down Below / 1994 / GO / M • Flashback / 1993 / SC / M • Flesh Shopping Network #1 / 1995 / MID / M • Fluff Dreams / 1995 / SUF / M • Foreign Tongues #2: Mesmerized / 1995 / VI / M • Forever Young / 1994 / VI / M • Fresh Meat (John Leslie) #2 / 1995 / EA / M • Gangbang Girl #12 / 1993 / ANA / M • Gangbusters / 1995 / VC / M • Gangland Bangers / 1995 / VC / M • Generally Horny Hospital / 1995 / IMV / M • Geranalmo / 1994 / PL / M • Ghosts / 1994 / EMC / M • The Girl With The Heart-Shaped Tattoo / 1995 / WAV / M • Glen And Glenda / 1994 / CA / M • The Golden Touch / 1995 / WP / M • Gonzo Groups & Gang Bangs / 1994 / GLI / M • Good Pussy / 1994 / VIM / M • Good Vibrations / 1993 / ZA / M • The Governess / 1993 / WP / M • The Grind / 1995 / XC / M • Hard Feelings / 1995 / VI / M • Hard-On Copy / 1994 / WV / M • Haunted Nights / 1993 / WP / M • Head Trip / 1995 / VC / M • Heat / 1995 / WAV / M • Heatseekers / 1996 / PE / M • Ho' Style Takeover / 1993 / FH / M • Hollywood Scandal: The Heidi Flesh Story / 1993 / IP / M • Hollywood Swingers #08 / 1993 / LBO / M • Hot Tight Asses #05 / 1994 / TCK / M • Hot To Trot / 1994 / IF / M • Hotel Sodom #01 / 1995 / SNA / M • Hotel Sodom #02 / 1995 / SNA / M • Hotel Sodom #06 / 1995 / SNA / M • Hotel Sodom #10 / 1996 / SNA / M • House Arrest / 1995 / CV / M • If These Walls Could Talk (Director's Cut) / 1993 / MET / M • If These Walls Could Talk #1: Wicked Whispers / 1993 / MET / M • If These Walls Could Talk #2: Burning Secrets / 1993 / CV / M • Illicit Entry / 1995 / WAV / M • In Cold Sweat / 1996 / VI / M • Inferno #2 / 1993 / SC / M • Internal Affairs / 1995 / VI / M • Island Of Lust / 1995 / XCI / M • Jailhouse Cock / 1993 / IP / M • Jordan Lee: Anal Queen / 1997 / SC / C • Julia Ann: Superstar / 1995 / WAV / M • Kinky Cameraman #2 / 1996 / LEI / C • The Kiss / 1995 / WP / M • A Kiss Before Dying / 1993 / CDI / M • Lap Of Luxury / 1994 / WIV / M • The Legend Of Barbi-Q And Little Fawn / 1994 / CA / M • Lethal Affairs / 1996 / VI / M • Lip Service / 1995 / WP / M • Lollipop Lickers / 1996 / V99 / C • Loose Morals / 1995 / EX / M • Love Tryst / 1995 / VPN / M • The Lovers / 1993 / HO / M • Lunachick / 1995 / VI / M • Lust Runner / 1995 / VC / M • Many Happy Returns / 1995 / NIT / M • Mask / 1993 / VI / M • The Masseuse #2 / 1994 / VI / M • The Mating Pot / 1994 / LBO / M • Midnight Snacks / 1995 / KLP / M • Mind Set / 1996 / VI / M • Mo' Honey / 1993 / FH / M • The Money Hole / 1993 / VD / M • Moon Godesses #2 / 1993 / VIM / M • More Than A Handful #4

/ 1994 / MET / M • Mr. Peepers Amateur Home Videos #68: A Tough Load To Swallow / 1993 / LBO / M • My Cousin Ginny / 1993 / MET / M • My Generation / 1994 / HO / M • N.Y.D.P. / 1994 / PEP / M • Naked Ambition / 1995 / VC / M • Naked Desert / 1995 / VI / M • The Naked Truth / 1995 / VI / M • The New Butt Hunt #19 / 1996 / LEI / C • New Lovers / 1993 / VI / M • New Pussy Hunt #24 / 1996 / LEI / C • Night Nurses / 1995 / WAV / M • Night Play / 1995 / WAV / M • Night Train / 1993 / VI / M • Nightbreed / 1995 / VI / M • Nikki Loves Rocco / 1996 / VI / M • No Motive / 1994 / MID / M • Nylon / 1995 / VI / M • Objective: D.P. / 1993 / PEP / M • Obsessions In Lace / 1994 / PL / M • On The Run / 1995 / SC / M • Oral Majority #13 / 1995 / WV / C • Oral Obsession #2 / 1995 / VI / M • The Orgy #1 / 1993 / EMC / M • The Orgy #2 / 1993 / EMC / M • The Orgy #3 / 1993 / EMC / M • The Original Wicked Woman / 1993 / WP / M • Paging Betty / 1994 / VC / M • The Palace Of Pleasure / 1995 / ULI / M • Parlor Games / 1993 / VI / M • Petite & Sweet / 1994 / V99 / M • Pleasureland / 1996 / VI / M • A Pool Party At Seymores #2 / 1995 / ULI / M • Pretending / 1993 / CV / M • Priceless / 1995 / WP / M • Prisoner Of Love / 1995 / CV / M • Private Request / 1994 / GLI / M • Private Video Magazine #21 / 1995 / OD / M • Public Access / 1995 / VC / M • Pulse / 1994 / EX / M • Pussy Whipped / 1994 / FOR / M • Pussyclips #01 / 1994 / SNA / M • Pussyclips #06 / 1995 / SNA / M • Pussyman #03: The Search Continues / 1993 / SNA / M • Pussyman #04: The Celebration / 1993 / SNA / M • Pussyman #07: On The Dark Side / 1994 / SNA / M • Pussyman #08: The Squirt Queens / 1994 / SNA / M • Pussyman #09: Feeding Frenzy / 1995 / SNA / M • Pussyman #11: Prime Cuts / 1995 / SNA / C • Pussywoman #2 / 1994 / CC / M • Quantum Deep / 1993 / HW / M • Radical Affairs Video Magazine #06 / 1993 / ME / M • The Reel Sex World #01 / 1993 / WP / M • The Reel Sex World #02 / 1994 / WP / M • The Reel Sex World #03 / 1994 / WP / M • The Reel Sex World #04: Laid In Hawaii / 1994 / WP / M • Reel Sex World #05 / 1994 / WP / M • Return Engagement / 1995 / VI / M • Ring Of Passion / 1993 / WV / M • Riot Grrrls / 1994 / SC / M • The Romeo Syndrome / 1995 / SC / M • Rosie: The Neighborhood Slut / 1994 / VIM / M • Sabotage / 1994 / CA / M • Satin & Lace / 1994 / WP / M • The Savannah Affair / 1993 / CDI / M • The Scarlet Woman / 1994 / WP / M • The Sex Connection / 1993 / VC / M • Sex Gallery / 1995 / WAV / M • Sex In Abissi / 1993 / WIV / M • Sex Machine / 1995 / VI / M • Sex Punk 2000 / 1993 / FOR / M • Sex Trek #4: The Next Orgasm / 1994 / ME / M • Sex Trek #5: Deep Space Sex / 1994 / ME / M • Sexed / 1993 / HO / M • Sexual Healing / 1994 / VI / M • Shameless Lady / 1993 / ME / M • Shayla's Home Repair / 1993 / EVN / M • Shiver / 1993 / FOR / M • The Show / 1995 / VI / M • Silent Women / 1995 / ERA / M • Silk Stockings: The Black Widow / 1994 / SPI / M • Sista Act / 1994 / AVI / M • Sister Snatch #1 / 1994 / SNA / M • Sister Snatch #2 / 1995 / SNA / M • Skin Hunger / 1995 / MET / M • Sleeping Single / 1994 / CC / M • Slippery Slopes / 1995 /

ME / M • Sluts In Suburbia / 1994 / GLI / M • Smart Ass Delinquent / 1993 / VT / M • Smoke Screen / 1995 / WAV / M • Sniff Doggy Style / 1994 / PL / M • Some Like It Hard / 1995 / VC / M • The Spa / 1993 / VC / M • Spirit Guide / 1995 / IN / M • The Stand-Up / 1994 / VC / M • The Star / 1994 / HO / M • Starbangers #04 / 1993 / FPI / M • Stardust #1 / 1996 / VI / M • Stardust #2 / 1996 / VI / M • Stardust #3 / 1996 / VI / M • Stardust #4 / 1996 / VI / M • Stardust #5 / 1996 / VI / M • The Stiff / 1995 / WAV / M • Strippers Inc. #2 / 1994 / ONA / M • Striptease / 1995 / SPI / M • Suburban Buttnicks Forever / 1995 / CC / M • Suggestive Behavior / 1996 / VI / M • Supermodel #1 / 1994 / VI / M • Supermodel #2 / 1994 / VI / M • Sweet Revenge / 1996 / WAV / M • The Swing / 1996 / VI / M • Tail Taggers #101 / 1993 / WV / M • Tail Taggers #106 / 1993 / WV / M • Tail Taggers #120 / 1994 / WV / M • Talking Trash #2 / 1995 / HW / M • Tempted / 1994 / VI / M • Tender Loving Care / 1995 / WP / M • Tight Ends In Motion / 1993 / TP / M • Titty Bar #1 / 1993 / LE / M • Twelth Annual Avn Awards / 1995 / VC / M • Two Sides Of A Lady / 1994 / HDE / M • Undercover Lover / 1992 / CV / M • Uninhibited Love / 1994 / VPN / M • Vagina Town / 1993 / CA / M • Victoria With An "A" / 1994 / PL / M • Virgin / 1993 / HW / M • Virtual Reality Sixty Nine / 1995 / WP / M • Visions Of Desire / 1994 / DR / M • Visions Of Seduction / 1994 / SC / M • Voices In My Bed / 1993 / VI / M • The Voyeur #1 / 1994 / EA / M • The Voyeur #5 / 1995 / EA / M • Western Nights / 1994 / WP / M • Wet Silk #1 / 1995 / SC / C • Whispered Lies / 1993 / LBO / M • Whoppers #6 / 1993 / VEX / F • Wild Breed / 1995 / SC / M • Wild Desires / 1994 / MAX / M • Yankee Rose / 1994 / LE / M

STEVEN STEINBERG
Slave Of Pleasure / 1978 / BL / M
STEVEN STRONG
Anal Nation #2 / 1990 / CC / M • Bardot / 1991 / VI / M • Blue Fox / 1991 / VI / M • New Girls In Town #2 / 1992 / CC / M • New Girls In Town #7 / 1994 / CC / M • Twister / 1992 / CC / M • Two Hearts / 1991 / VI / M
STEVEN TAYLOR (BEAU) *see* **Beau Michaels**
STEVEN TRUNK
Elodie Does The U.S.A. / 1995 / PPR / M
STEVEN TYLER *see* **Star Index I**
STEVEN VENTURA *see* **Star Index I**
STEVEN WEST *see* **Star Index I**
STEVI *(Lisa (Stevi), Stevi Secret, Linda (Stevi))*
Producer along with husband Stevie and sometimes star in a series of amateur productions. Sub-contractor for some of the pro-am series. Was 24 in 1993.
America's Raunchiest Home Videos #28: Anal Aerobics / 1992 / ZA / M • Beach Bum Amateur's #09 / 1992 / MID / M • Desolation / 1992 / BON / B • Dirty Bob's #03: Xplicit Interviews / 1992 / FLP / S • Dirty Bob's #05: Vegas MasterpieCES / 1992 / FLP / S • Gemini: Sex Packs #01 / 1993 / FAP / M • GM #137: Stevi's First Amateur Video / 1992 / GMV / M • GM #138: The Peeping Tom / 1993 / GMV / F • Home Maid Memories #2 / 1994 / BON / C • House Play (Bon Vue) / 1994 / BON / B • Odyssey 30 Min: #323: Don't Show Your

Friends / 1993 / OD / M • Seymore Butts & His Mystery Girl / 1993 / FH / M • Stevi's: Foot Sex / 1994 / SSV / F • Stevi's: Hot Night / 1993 / SSV / F • Stevi's: How Short Do You Want It? / 1994 / SSV / F • Stevi's: I'm Sorry, Daddy / 1993 / SSV / B • Stevi's: Oral Lover's Delight / 1992 / SSV / M • Stevi's: Pantyhose Superheroes / 1995 / SSV / F • Stevi's: Slip Sliding Away / 1993 / SSV / F • Stevi's: Smoke Screen / 1996 / SSV / F • Stevi's: Stevi Shaves Her Head / 1993 / SSV / S • Stevi's: Stevi's Second Shaved Shoot / 1995 / SSV / S • Stevi's: Stevi's XXX Sex Previews / 1995 / SSV / C • Stevi's: Stevie Tries Bondage / 1993 / SSV / B • Stevi's: The Casting Couch / 1993 / SSV / F • Stevi's: The Heart Shaped Bed / 1992 / SSV / F • SVE: Cheap Thrills #3: Self-Satisfaction / 1992 / SVE / F • SVE: Red Hot / 1992 / SVE / M • VGA: Bureau Of Discipline #1 / 1993 / VGA / B
STEVI HICKS *(Shawna (Stevi Hicks))*
Reasonably pretty blonde with a petite frame and a squarish face. Nice personality.
Bobby Hollander's Maneaters #11 / 1994 / SFP / M • Sexual Trilogy #03 / 1994 / SFP / M
STEVI SECRET *see* **Stevi**
STEVIE
The Best Of Fabulous Flashers / 1996 / DGD / F • Big Sister Substitute / 1990 / LEO / G • Casting Call #09 / 1995 / SO / M • D-Cup Delights / 1987 / VCR / M • Female Mimics International: Behind The Scenes / 1988 / LEO / G • Ona Zee's Date With Dallas / 1992 / ONA / M • Our Bang #04 / 1992 / GLI / M • Parliament: Dildo Babes #2 / 1988 / PM / F • Penthouse: The Girls Of Penthouse #3 / 1995 / PET / S • Regarding Hiney / 1991 / CC / M • Stevie Loves It / 1995 / GAL / B • Stevie's Bondage Seduction #1 / 1995 / IBN / B • Stevie's Bondage Seduction #2 / 1995 / GAL / B
STEVIE B.
Bondage Boot Camp / 1988 / TAN / B • The Bondage Club #4 / 1990 / LON / B • The Bondage Club #5 / 1990 / LON / B
STEVIE CONRAD
Up And Cummers #28 / 1996 / ERW / M
STEVIE G.
In Your Face #4 / 1996 / PL / M
STEVIE HART
Senior Sexcapades #1 / 1995 / PL / M
STEVIE JEAN *see* **Shauna O'Brien**
STEVIE JOAN *see* **Shauna O'Brien**
STEVIE LIX *see* **Star Index I**
STEVIE O
Western Nights / 1994 / WP / M
STEVIE RECT
Dick & Jane In The Mountains / 1994 / AVI / M
STEVIE STARR
A Tall Tail / 1996 / FC / M
STEVIE TAYLOR
Bare Elegance / 1984 / MAP / M • Before She Says I Do / 1984 / MAP / M • Caught From Behind #03 / 1985 / HO / M • Dangerous / 1989 / PV / M • Dream Lover / 1985 / CDI / M • Erotic Zones #1 / 1985 / CA / M • Fantasies Unltd. / 1985 / CDI / M • Flesh Fire / 1985 / AVC / M • Lust At The Top / 1985 / CDI / M • Orifice Party / 1985 / GOM / M • Portrait Of Desire / 1985 / IVP / M • The Ribald Tales Of Canterbury / 1986 / CA / M • Secrets / 1984 / HO / M •

Sinfully Yours / 1984 / HO / M • Swedish Erotica #57 / 1984 / CA / M • Swedish Erotica Featurettes #5 / 1990 / CA / M • A Taste Of Paradise / 1984 / HO / M • Teenage Games / 1985 / HO / M • Too Naughty To Say No / 1984 / CA / M • Working Girls / 1985 / CA / M

STEVIE WOOD
Going Down Under / 1993 / OD / M

STEWARD GALLANT *see Star Index I*

STEWART HARRIS *see Star Index I*

STIKKY NIRK
Kitty's Kinky Capers / 1996 / TTV / M

STINA
Triple X Video Magazine #10 / 1995 / OD / M

STONE BLACK
Marine Code Of Silence: Don't Ask Don't Tell / 1996 / BHE / G

STORM
AVP #7017: Sex By Storm / 1990 / AVP / M • Natural Response / 1996 / GPI / G • Painted / 1990 / INH / G

STORM CLOUD
Dark Dreams / 1971 / ALP / M

STORM STARR
Weekend Roulette / 1975 / VCX / M

STORMI *see Liz Alexander*

STORMY
Black Cheerleader Search #07 / 1996 / IVC / M • Catfighting Lesbians / 1991 / BIZ / F • Dildo Fantasy Party / 1990 / BIZ / F • Girl Lovers / 1990 / BIZ / F • Golden Moments / 1985 / BAK / F • Lesbian Catfights / 1990 / BIZ / B • Lesbian Obsession / 1990 / BIZ / B • Naughty New Orleans / 1962 / SOW / S

STORMY GALE
50 And Still Gangbangin'! / 1995 / EMC / M • Adventures Of The DP Boys: The Golden Girls / 1995 / HW / M • Butt Bangers Ball #2 / 1996 / TTV / M • Dirty And Kinky Mature Women #3 / 1995 / C69 / M • Golden Oldies #4 / 1996 / TTV / M • Granny Bangers / 1995 / MET / A / M • Masturbation Ages 20 To 45 / 1996 / C69 / F • Mike Hott: #282 Three-Sum Sluts #01 / 1995 / MHV / M • Older And Anal #1 / 1995 / FC / M • Sugar Mommies / 1995 / FPI / M • The Ultimate Climax / 1996 / EMC / M

STORMY SHORES
Behind The Blackout / 1993 / HW / M • Black Babes In Heat / 1993 / VIM / M • Black Bitches In Heat #2 / 1995 / GDV / M • Black Fire / 1993 / VIM / M • Black Is Back / 1993 / HW / M • Black Nurse Fantasies / 1994 / CA / M • Black Women, White Men #7 / 1995 / FC / M • Dark Passions #01 / 1993 / AFV / M • M Series #05 / 1993 / LBO / M • Rump-Shaker #1 / 1993 / HW / M

STORMY WEATHER (DA) *see Davia Ardell*

STORMY WEATHERS (AA) *see Anna Amore*

STORY GAIL
Aged To Perfection #3 / 1995 / TTV / M

STRAWBERRY
Black Casting Couch #2 / 1994 / WP / M

STRAWBERRY DELIGHT
The Girls Of Fantasex #2 / 1996 / NIT / M

STRETCH
AVP #9146: Ready, Set, -uck / 1990 / AVP / M • Southern Belles #5 / 1995 / XPR / M

STRETCH LAREDO
N.Y. Video Magazine #09 / 1996 / OUP / M

STU GREENWALD *see Star Index I*

STUART
Dirty Dancers #6 / 1995 / 4P / M

STUART HEMPLE *see Ken Scudder*

STUART HEMPOLE *see Ken Scudder*

STUART LANCASTER *(Stud Lancaster)*
Beneath The Valley Of The Ultra-Vixens / 1979 / RMV / S • Faster Pussycat, Kill...Kill / 1966 / RMV / S • Good Morning...And Goodbye / 1967 / RMV / S • Mantis In Lace / 1968 / BPI / S • Mudhoney / 1965 / RMV / S • The Secret Sex Lives Of Romeo And Juliet / 1968 / PS / S • The Seven Minutes / 1971 / ST0 / S • Starlet / 1969 / SOW / S • Supervixens / 1975 / RMV / S • Thar She Blows! / 1969 / SOW / S • Wilbur And The Baby Factory / 1970 / SOW / S

STUART SERKMAN
Bedtime Video #07 / 1984 / GO / M

STUD LANCASTER *see Stuart Lancaster*

STUDLEY DORIGHT *see Star Index I*

STUDLEY LAMONT
Wedding Vows / 1994 / ZA / M

STUDLEY POWERS *see Star Index I*

STUDS CHAVALLO *see Star Index I*

STUDS LONGER
They Shall Overcome / 1974 / VST / M

STUDZ
Odyssey 30 Min: #346: Kitty, Silky, and Studz / 1993 / OD / M • Odyssey Triple Play #73: Oriental Sexpress / 1994 / OD / M

STUMPY PENGUINO
Kink: Police Chronicles / 1995 / ROB / M

STYLES *see Niva Styles*

SU ANN
Bastille Erotica / 1996 / P69 / M • Private Film #15 / 1994 / OD / M • Private Film #16 / 1994 / OD / M • Private Film #17 / 1994 / OD / M • Private Video Magazine #14 / 1994 / OD / M

SUANN
Eurotica #08 / 1996 / XC / M

SUB-OH
San Francisco Lesbians #3 / 1993 / PL / F • San Francisco Lesbians #4 / 1993 / PL / F

SUDUCTION *see Seduction*

SUE
Blue Vanities #195 / 1993 / FFL / M • Blue Vanities #517 / 1992 / FFL / M • Blue Vanities #531 / 1993 / FFL / M • Blue Vanities #533 / 1993 / FFL / M • Blue Vanities #554 / 1994 / FFL / M • California Girl: Amateur Nude Auditions / 1995 / PME / S • Dirty Stories #3 / 1995 / PE / M • Full Moon Video #10: Squat City / 1994 / FAP / F • Hometown Girls / 1984 / CDP / F • Joe Elliot's Asian College Girls #02 / 1995 / JOE / M • Joe Elliot's College Girls #39 / 1994 / JOE / F • Kinky College Cunts #23 / 1993 / NS / F • Midnight Angels #03 / 1993 / MID / F • Pearl Necklace: Thee Bush League #20 / 1993 / SEE / M • Royal Ass Force / 1996 / VC / M

SUE BRIGHT *see Star Index I*

SUE CAROL
The Goodbye Girls / 1979 / CDI / M • Once...And For All / 1979 / HLV / M • Prisoner Of Paradise / 1980 / VCX / M

SUE CASH *(Cash (Sue), Casha (Sue))*
Tall brunette with long hair and not very good white skin. Medium sized natural tits.

All "A" / 1994 / SFP / C • America's Raunchiest Home Videos #54: / 1993 / ZA / M • America's Raunchiest Home Videos

#57 / 1993 / ZA / M • America's Raunchiest Home Videos #58: / 1993 / ZA / M • Anal Sluts & Sweethearts #2 / 1993 / ROB / M • Anal Urge / 1993 / ROB / M • Anal Vision #14 / 1993 / LBO / M • Anal-Holics / 1993 / AFV / M • Bobby Hollander's Rookie Nookie #03 / 1993 / SFP / M • Bobby Hollander's Rookie Nookie #06 / 1993 / SFP / M • Candy Snacker / 1993 / WIV / M • Double D Domination / 1993 / BIZ / B • Flashback / 1993 / SC / M • Freaks Of Leather #2 / 1994 / IF / C • Gang Bang Cummers / 1993 / ROB / M • Humongous Hooters / 1993 / IF / M • Kink World: The Seduction Of Nena / 1993 / PL / M • Ladies Lovin' Ladies #3 / 1993 / AFV / F • Much More Than A Mouthful #4 / 1994 / VEX / M • Nasty Nymphos #01 / 1993 / ANA / M • New Girls In Town #3 / 1993 / CC / M • No Man's Land #07 / 1993 / VT / F • Nurse Tails / 1994 / VC / M • Pearl Necklace: Premier Sessions #07 / 1996 / SEE / M • Ring Of Passion / 1993 / WV / M • Sensual Solos #02 / 1993 / AVI / F • Sharon Starlet / 1993 / WIV / M • Slave To Love / 1993 / ROB / M • Slaves Bound For Passion / 1994 / BIZ / B • Straight A Students / 1993 / MET / M • Voluptuous / 1993 / CA / M • Warehouse Wenches #1 / 1994 / BIZ / B • Warehouse Wenches #2 / 1994 / BIZ / B • Woman 2 Woman #1 / 1993 / SOF / F

SUE COLLINS
Gift Of Love / 1979 / ... / M

SUE DENIM
Command Performance / cr75 / LA / M • Prey Of A Call Girl / 1975 / ALP / M

SUE DUNN
Eager Beaver / 1975 / AVC / M • Fantasy Fever / 1975 / AVC / M • Mortgage Of Sin / 1975 / CA / M • Y-All Come / 1975 / CDC / M

SUE FLOSSEN
Sunny / 1979 / VC / M

SUE FRANKEL
Bucky Beaver's XXX Dragon Art Theatre Double Feature #11 / 1996 / SOW / M • Teenage Fantasies #1 / 1972 / SOW / M

SUE HERD *see Star Index I*

SUE HICKS
The Devil's Playground / 1974 / VC / M

SUE HOLLAND
Sex Boat / 1980 / VCX / M

SUE KELLY *see Star Index I*

SUE LEE
Fantasy Club: Luau Orgy / 1980 / WV / M

SUE LEE (SUZY) *see Suzy Lee*

SUE LION *see Star Index I*

SUE LONG
Girls U.S.A. / 1980 / AIR / M

SUE LYNN
Alm Bums / 1995 / DBM / M • Roman Orgy / 1991 / PL / M • Two Senoritas / 197? / VHL / M

SUE MITCHELL
Ski Ball / 19?? / BOC / M

SUE NERO *(Scarlett Kennedy, Susan Shields)*
Really ugly dark blonde/brunette with shoulder length curly hair, very large tits and a hefty body. Roseanne would be better. De-virginized at 16.

11 / 1980 / VCX / M • Ball Game / 1980 / CA / M • Bedtime Video #07 / 1984 / GO / M • Behind The Brown Door / 1986 / VCR / C • Beyond Your Wildest Dreams / 1980 / CAT / M • Big Busty #05 / 198? / BTO / M

• Black Heat / 1986 / VCR / C • Blue Vanities #003 / 1987 / FFL / M • Blue Vanities #044 (Old) / 1988 / FFL / M • Blue Vanities #077 / 1988 / FFL / M • Blue Vanities #086 / 1988 / FFL / M • Blue Vanities #092 / 1988 / FFL / M • Blue Vanities #108 / 1988 / FFL / M • Blue Vanities #204 / 1993 / FFL / M • Blue Vanities #222 / 1994 / FFL / M • Blue Vanities #240 / 1995 / FFL / M • Blue Vanities #241 / 1995 / FFL / M • Blue Vanities #251 / 1996 / FFL / M • Blue Vanities #534 / 1993 / FFL / M • Blue Vanities #535 / 1993 / FFL / M • Blue Vanities #536 / 1993 / FFL / M • Blue Vanities #537 / 1993 / FFL / M • Blue Vanities #589 / 1996 / FFL / M • Bust Lust / cr83 / BIZ / B • Busty Bitches / 1990 / BIZ / S • Cab-O-Lay / 1988 / PL / M • The Casting Couch / 1983 / GO / M • Catfighting Lesbians / 1991 / BIZ / F • Centerfold Fever / 1981 / VXP / M • Classic Swedish Erotica #09 / 1986 / CA / C • Coming In Style / 1986 / CA / M • Creme De Femme #1 / 1981 / AVC / C • Creme De Femme #2 / 1981 / AVC / C • Creme De Femme #4 / 1981 / AVC / C • Daisy May / 1979 / VC / M • Diamond Collection #01 / 1979 / SVE / M • Dildo Fantasy Party / 1990 / BIZ / F • Dildoe Action / cr85 / STM / B • Double D Domination / 1993 / BIZ / B • Ebony Erotica / 1985 / VCR / C • Erotic Fantasies #5 / 1983 / CV / C • Every Body / 1992 / LAP / M • Exposed / 1980 / SE / M • Extremes / 1981 / CA / M • Fannie's Fantail / 1985 / VC / M • Fantasy / 1978 / VCX / M • Fantasy Peeps: Solo Girls / 1985 / 4P / M • Fashion Dolls / 1985 / LA / M • Fetish Fever / 1993 / CA / C • For The Love Of Pleasure / 1979 / SE / M • Freedom Of Choice / 1984 / VHL / M • G-Strings / 1984 / COM / M • G...They're Big / 1981 / TGA / C • Garage Girls / 1981 / CV / M • Girl Lovers / 1990 / BIZ / F • Girls Just Wanna Have Girls #2 / 1990 / HIO / F • Head / 1985 / LA / M • Hot Service / 19?? / CDI / M • Hot Shorts: Sue Nero / 1986 / VCR / C • The Hot Tip / 1986 / VXP / M • In Love / 1983 / VC / M • Inside Desiree Cousteau / 1979 / VCX / M • Le Sex De Femme #3 / 1989 / AFI / C • Lesbian Catfights / 1990 / BIZ / B • Limited Edition #04 / 1979 / AVC / M • Limited Edition #21 / 1981 / AVC / M • Love Dreams / 1981 / CA / M • Luscious / 1980 / VXP / M • Lust Vegas Joyride / 1986 / LIM / M • Mammary Lane / 1988 / VT / C • Mandy's Executive Sweet / 1982 / AVC / M • Midnight Heat / 1982 / VC / M • Murder By Sex / 1993 / LAP / M • One Way At A Time / 1979 / CA / M • Only The Best Of Breasts / 1987 / CV / C • Pretty In Black / 1986 / WET / M • Private Showings / 1992 / STM / B • Pro Ball Cheerleaders / 1979 / AVC / M • Secluded Passion / 1983 / VHL / M • The Sensuous Detective / 1979 / VHL / M • Sex World Girls / 1987 / AR / M • Showgirl #06: Sue Nero's Fantasies / 1983 / VCR / M • Showgirl #17: Phaedra Grant's Fantasies / 1983 / VCR / M • Sinners #2 / 1988 / COM / M • Sissy's Hot Summer / 1979 / CA / M • Smothering Boobs / cr83 / BIZ / B • Spitfire / 1984 / COM / M • Street Star / cr82 / DRV / M • Sunset Strip Girls / 1975 / TGA / M • Supergirls Do The Navy / 1984 / VC / M • Superstar Masturbation / 1990 / BIZ / F • Toothless People / 1988 / SUV / M • Tracey Adams' Girls School / 1993 / BIZ / B • Tracey's Love Chamber / 1987 / AR / M •

Tropic Of Desire / 1979 / WWV / M • Warehouse Wenches #1 / 1994 / BIZ / B • Watermelon Babes / 1984 / VCR / M • Wet Shots (Vcr) / 1983 / VCR / C • The Widespread Scandals Of Lydia Lace / 1983 / CA / M

SUE PEARLMAN *see* **Tawny Pearl**
SUE PERLMAN *see* **Tawny Pearl**
SUE RAVAN
Cafe Flesh / 1982 / VC / M
SUE REMILFIELD *see Star Index I*
SUE RICHARDS *see* **Bree Anthony**
SUE ROWAN *see* **Bree Anthony**
SUE SNOW
Blue Vanities #514 / 1992 / FFL / M
SUE SUE
Woman In The Window / 1986 / TEM / M
SUE SWAN
People / 1978 / QX / M
SUE SWANSON
Hong Kong Hookers / 1984 / AMB / M • A Touch Of Desire / 1983 / VCR / C
SUE THOMAS *see Star Index I*
SUE VAUGHAN
Blue Vanities #580 / 1996 / FFL / M
SUE WADSWORTH *see Star Index I*
SUE WILLIAMS
Bizarre Styles / 1981 / ALP / B
SUE YU *see Star Index I*
SUE-ANN HAYES *see Star Index I*
SUEDE
Spotlight: Sybian Overload / 1995 / SPV / F
SUELE
Yellow Fever / 1994 / ORE / C
SUGAR
Babewatch Video Magazine #1 / 1994 / ERI / F • Green Piece Of Ass #4 / 1994 / RTP / M • She-Male Encounters #03: Juicy Jennifer / 1981 / MET / G • The Sweet Sweet Back #2: Double Thaanng Dat Black Hole / 1994 / FH / M
SUGAR BROWN *see* **Angel Kelly**
SUGAR NICOLE
She-Male Encounters #07: Divine Atrocities #1 / 1981 / MET / G • She-Male Encounters #08: Divine Atrocities #2 / 1981 / MET / G
SUGAR RAY
As Sweet As They Come / 1992 / V99 / M • Biff Malibu's Totally Nasty Home Videos #15 / 1992 / ANA / M • California Blacks / 1994 / V99 / M • Ebony Erotica #01: Black Narcissys / 1993 / GO / M • Gangbang Girl #08 / 1992 / ANA / M • Gangbang Girl #09 / 1993 / ANA / M • Gazonga Goddess #1 / 1993 / IF / M • Mr. Peepers Amateur Home Videos #53: Dirty Laundry / 1992 / LBO / M • Much More Than A Mouthful #3 / 1993 / VEX / M • Nothing Else Matters / 1992 / V99 / C • One Of A Kind / 1992 / VEX / M • Wet & Wicked / 1992 / VEX / M • Wilde At Heart / 1992 / VEX / M
SUGAR RAY SIMPSON *see Star Index I*
SUGURO TOSHIAKI
Academy Of Sex / 1995 / AVV / M
SUI CHUNG
Game Instructor / 1996 / AVV / M
SUJI HAYASHI
Triple Sex Play / 1985 / ORC / M
SUKI *see Star Index I*
SUKI SWEET
Creme De La Face #08: Wanna Blow Job / 1995 / OD / M
SUKI YU *see Star Index I*
SUKOWA *see* **Sukoya**

SUKOYA *(Sequoia, Holly Davidson, Amber Midnight, Soyoya, Amber Savage, Sukowa, Saphire (Sukoya), Lisa (Sukoya))*
Dark skinned but doesn't look Oriental or black. Tattoo on left hip and serpent on left breast. Big tits (natural) and flat ass. Looks a little like Mia Powers. Amber Midnight is from **Knights in Black Satin**. 5'10", 120 lbs, 36C-24-34, grew up in Albequerque NM. Amber Savage is from **Bush League**.
The Absolute Worst Of Amateur #1 / 1993 / VEX / M • AHV #02: Orgy Express / 1991 / EVN / M • All For You, Baby / 1990 / VEX / M • Amateur Lesbians #02: Dominique / 1991 / GO / F • Amateur Lesbians #03: April / 1991 / GO / F • Amateur Nights #08 / 1990 / HO / M • Amateurama #02 / 1992 / RTP / F • America's Dirtiest Home Videos #04 / 1991 / VEX / M • America's Dirtiest Home Videos #06 / 1991 / AMA / M • America's Dirtiest Home Videos #14 / 1992 / VEX / M • Anal Amateurs / 1992 / VD / M • Babes / 1991 / CIN / M • Bi Dream Of Genie / 1990 / BIN / G • Bi-Bi Love Amateurs #1 / 1993 / SFP / G • The Bondage Adventures Of Randy Ranger / 1994 / SBP / B • Bondage Memories #04 / 1994 / BON / C • The Bondage Producer / 1991 / BON / B • Breast Worx #17 / 1991 / LBO / M • Bush League #1 / 1990 / CC / M • Candy Ass / 1990 / V99 / M • Cat Fight / 1992 / ONH / C • Catfighting Students / 1995 / PRE / C • College Girl / 1990 / VEX / M • Dirty Blue Movies #04 / 1993 / JTV / F • Dr F #2: Bad Medicine / 1990 / WV / M • Eternal Bliss / 1990 / AFV / M • Every Man Should Have One / 1991 / VEX / M • Giving It To Barbii / 1990 / TOR / M • Great Expectations / 1990 / V99 / M • Great Expectations / 1992 / VEX / C • Harness Hannah At The Strap-On Ho Down / 1994 / WIV / F • Harness Hannah At The Strap-On Palace / 1994 / WIV / F • Hidden Pleasures / 1990 / VEX / M • Hollywood Hustle #1 / 1990 / V99 / M • Hollywood Hustle #2 / 1990 / V99 / M • Hot Licks / 1990 / CDI / M • Hot Shoes / 1992 / BIZ / B • In Pursuit Of Passion / 1990 / V99 / M • In The Jeans Again / 1990 / ME / M • Joy-Fm #07 / 1994 / BHS / M • Joy-Fm #11 / 1994 / BHS / M • Joy-Fm #12 / 1994 / BHS / M • Knights In Black Satin / 1990 / VEX / M • Latex Submission #1 / 1992 / BIZ / B • Leg Lovers / 03 / 1991 / BIZ / F • Lesbian Mystery Theatre: The Case Of The Deadly Dyke / 1994 / LIP / F • A Little Bit Pregnant / 1995 / SO / M • Living In Sin / 1990 / VEX / M • Making It Big / 1990 / TOR / M • Mike Hott: #146 Janice And Sukoya #1 / 1991 / MHV / F • Mike Hott: #147 Janice And Sukoya #2 / 1991 / MHV / F • Mike Hott: #149 Sukoya Solo / 1991 / MHV / F • Mistress Of Shadows / 1995 / HOM / B • Money Honey / 1990 / TOR / M • Money, Money, Money / 1993 / FD / M • Mr. Peepers Amateur Home Videos #12: Like It! Lick It! / 1991 / LBO / M • Mr. Peepers Amateur Home Videos #54: Cooking With Cum!! / 1992 / LBO / M • Mr. Peepers Amateur Home Videos #56: Hindsight Is Brownish / 1992 / LBO / M • Mr. Peepers Amateur Home Videos #64: Proposition 69 / 1992 / LBO / M • Nasty Fuckin' Movies #09: Saki's Six Man Sexation #1 / 1992 / RUM / M • Nasty Jack's Homemade Vid. #28 / 1991 / CDI / M • The New Barbarians

#2 / 1990 / VC / M • Obey Me Bitch #2 / 1992 / BIZ / B • Obey Me Bitch #3 / 1992 / BIZ / B • Obey Me Bitch #4 / 1993 / BIZ / B • Office Heels / 1992 / BIZ / B • One Of These Nights / 1991 / V99 / M • Oral Majority #08 / 1990 / WV / C • Passion Princess / 1991 / VEX / M • Perfect Girl / 1991 / VEX / M • Private Bound / 1994 / VTF / B • Punished Lesbians / 1992 / PL / B • Randy And Dane / 1991 / IF / G • Raunchy Porno Picture Show / 1992 / FC / M • Raw Talent: Bang 'er 07 Times / 1992 / RTP / M • Raw Talent: Bang 'er Megamix 1 / 1994 / RTP / C • Raw Talent: Fetish Of The Month #06 / 1994 / RTP / G • Robin Head / 1991 / CC / M • Rump Humpers #08 / 1992 / GLI / M • Scented Secrets / 1990 / CIN / M • Secret Dreams / 1991 / VEX / M • Sex Acts & Video Tape / 1990 / AFV / M • Sex Pistol / 1990 / CDI / M • Shades Of Bondage / 1991 / BON / B • The Shaving / 1989 / SO / M • She-Male Sex Clinic / 1991 / VC / G • She Male Spirits Of The Night / 1991 / VC / G • Six Stud Swingathon #01 / 1992 / VAL / M • Six Stud Swingathon #02 / 1992 / RUM / M • Student Fetish Videos: The Enema #05 / 1991 / PRE / B • Supertung / 1990 / LA / M • Suzanne's Grand Affair / 1990 / CV / M • Sweet Chastity / 1990 / EVN / M • Ultimate Orgy #3 / 1992 / GLI / M • We're No Angels / 1990 / CIN / M • Weekend Blues / 1990 / IN / M • Wild At Heart / 1990 / CDI / M

SULKA
Angel's Vengeance / 1995 / VMX / M • Beauty And The Beast / 1982 / KEN / S • Caballero Preview Tape #3 / 1984 / CA / C • Dream Lovers / 1980 / MET / G • Electric Blue #006 / 1982 / CA / S • Madness / cr80 / VTE / S • Marathon / 1982 / CA / M • She-Male Encounters #01: Tanatalizing Toni / 1981 / MET / G • She-Male Encounters #07: Divine Atrocities #1 / 1981 / MET / G • She-Male Encounters #19: Toga Party / 1989 / MET / G • She-Male Encounters #20: Switched / 1989 / MET / G • She-Male Tales / 1990 / MET / G • Sulka And Candy / 1992 / BIZ / C • Sulka's Daughter / 1984 / MET / G • Sulka's Nightclub / 1989 / VT / G • Sulka's Wedding / 1983 / MET / G • A Taste Of Sulka / 1989 / MET / C • Transformation Of Sulka / 1981 / BIZ / G

SULLY
Hell Cats / 1996 / HO / F

SULTAN T.
Private Gold #09: Private Dancer / 1996 / OD / M

SULTRY SERENA *see Star Index I*

SULTRY SUSAN
Blue Vanities #500 / 1992 / FFL / M

SULTRY SYLVIA
She-Male Encounters #02: Carnal Candy / 1981 / MET / G

SUM YUNG GAI *see Star Index I*

SUMMER
Black Knockers #06 / 1995 / TV / M • Shaved #01 / 1991 / RB / F • Skirts & Flirts #01 / 1997 / XPR / F

SUMMER BROWN *see Sandra Winters*

SUMMER COLLINS
Amazing Hardcore #1: Blow Jobs / 1997 / MET / M • The Cumm Brothers #15: Hot Primal Sex / 1996 / OD / M • Filthy First Timers #1 / 1996 / EL / M

SUMMER CUMMINGS
Brain dead partner of Skye Blue with huge tits.

Arsenal Of Fear / 1993 / BS / B • Bar Bizarre / 1996 / WP / B • Battling Bitches #2 / 1995 / BIZ / B • Beyond Reality #1 / 1995 / EXQ / M • Beyond The Borderline / 1996 / STM / B • Bi Bitches In Heat / 1996 / BIZ / F • Big Busty Whoppers / 1994 / PME / F • Big Knockers #06 / 1994 / TV / M • Big Knockers #07 / 1994 / TV / M • Big Knockers #15 / 1995 / TV / M • Bizarre's Dracula #1 / 1995 / BIZ / B • Blame It On Bambi / 1992 / BS / B • Blushing Bottoms / 1992 / RB / B • Borderline (Starmaker) / 1995 / STM / B • Bound And Gagged #01 / 1991 / RB / B • Bright Tails #5 / 1995 / STP / B • Burning Desires / 1994 / BS / B • Buttslammers #07: Indecent Decadence / 1994 / BS / F • Chronicles Of Pain #2 / 1996 / BIZ / B • College Cruelty / 1995 / FFE / B • Cruel Passions / 1992 / BS / B • Daddy Gets Punished / 1990 / PL / B • Dark Secrets / 1995 / MID / S • Date With A Mistress / 1995 / BIZ / B • Designated Hitters / 1995 / PRE / B • Dirty Bob's #18: Under The Boardwalk! / 1995 / FLP / S • Dirty Bob's #19: Over The Boardwalk! / 1995 / FLP / S • Dominated Dudes / 1992 / PL / B • The Domination Of Summer #1 / 1994 / BIZ / B • The Domination Of Summer #2 / 1994 / BIZ / B • Don't Try This At Home / 1994 / FPI / M • Double D Dykes #27 / 1995 / GO / F • Down And Out / 1995 / PRE / B • Dresden Diary #11: Endangered Secrets / 1994 / BIZ / B • Dresden Diary #12: / 1995 / BIZ / B • Dresden Diary #13: / 1995 / BIZ / B • Drop Outs / 1995 / PRE / B • The Enema Bandit Returns / 1995 / BIZ / B • Enema Obedience #2 / 1994 / BIZ / B • Enemates #11 / 1995 / BIZ / B • Fantasy Flings #03 / 1995 / WP / M • Flush Dance / 1996 / PRE / C • Foot Masters / 1995 / PRE / B • Funny Ladies / 1996 / PRE / B • Future Doms #1 / 1996 / BIZ / B • Future Doms #2 / 1996 / BIZ / B • Girls With Curves #2 / 1994 / CV / M • Hell Cats / 1996 / HO / F • Hello Norma Jeane / 1994 / VT / M • Her Personal Touch / 1996 / STM / F • High Heeled & Horny #1 / 1994 / LBO / M • Hostile Takeover: Bitch Bosses / 1995 / BIZ / B • Humongous Hooters / 1995 / PME / F • Kittens #6 / 1994 / CC / F • Leather Bound Dykes From Hell #6 / 1995 / BIZ / B • Leg...Ends #15 / 1995 / PRE / F • Lesbian Kink Trilogy #2 / 1995 / STM / F • Lipstick Lesbians #1: Massage Parlor Dykes / 1994 / ZA / F • Major Exposure / 1995 / PL / F • Mellon Man #02 / 1994 / AVI / M • The Most Dangerous Game / 1996 / HO / M • Nasty Dancers #2 / 1996 / STM / B • Naughty Boys #1 / 1992 / RB / B • Naughty Boys #2 / 1992 / RB / B • New Faces, Hot Bodies #01 / 1992 / STP / M • New Faces, Hot Bodies #08 / 1993 / STP / M • New Faces, Hot Bodies #18 / 1995 / STP / M • Northwest Pecker Trek #4: Laid In Latte Land / 1994 / LBO / M • Over The Borderline / 1995 / STM / B • Painful Pleasures / 1993 / BS / B • Porsche Lynn, Vault Mistress #1 / 1994 / BIZ / B • Porsche Lynn, Vault Mistress #2 / 1994 / BIZ / B • The Power Of Summer #1: Revenge / 1992 / BS / B • The Power Of Summer #2: Reward / 1992 / BS / B • Primal / 1995 / MET / M • Prisoners Of Pain / 1994 / BIZ / B • Pussy Pursuits: The Best Of Skye And Summer / 1995 / AMX / C • Raw Footage / 1996 / VC / M • Rollover / 1996 / NIT / M •

Roommate's Revenge / 1992 / RB / B • Shelby's Forbidden Fears / 1995 / BIZ / B • Skin #6: The 6th Sense / 1996 / ERQ / M • Skye's The Limit / 1995 / BON / B • Soap Opera Sluts / 1996 / AFI / M • Sordid Stories / 1994 / AMP / M • Spanking Debutantes / 1992 / RB / B • Spiked Heel Diaries #4 / 1995 / BIZ / B • The Submission Of Alicia Rio / 1996 / BIZ / B • Summer's Surrender / 1996 / STM / B • Sweet Cheerleaders Spanked / 1996 / BIZ / B • Take Out Torture / 1990 / PL / B • Takin' It To The Limit #9: Rear Action View / 1996 / BS / M • To Snatch A Thief / 1996 / BON / B • Toe-Tail Torture / 1996 / STM / B • A Touch Of Leather / 1994 / BS / B • The Training #2 / 1994 / BIZ / B • The Training #3 / 1995 / BIZ / B • Tropical Bondage Vacation / 1996 / STM / B • Whacked! / 1993 / BS / B • What's A Nice Girl Like You Doing In An Anal Movie? / 1995 / AMP / M

SUMMER KNIGHT *(Summer Knights)*
She prefers to be called Summer Knight (without the S). Born Feb 26, 1961, 36D-24-34 in Berkely CA. She got enhanced from a small C to a D in 1986 and has regretted it ever since. However in **Bangin' With The Home Girls** she looks like she has un-enhanced tits; they're still large but aren't the hard watermelons of 1992/3.

6000 Lash Lane / 1994 / LON / B • Adventures Of Buttwoman #1 / 1991 / EL / F • America's Raunchiest Home Videos #05: Sasha Gets Stuffed / 1992 / ZA / M • America's Raunchiest Home Videos #15: Outrageous Reaming / 1992 / ZA / M • B.L.O.W. / 1992 / LV / M • Back Seat Bush / 1992 / LV / M • Backdoor To Russia #3 / 1993 / VC / M • Backstage Entrance #1 / 1992 / FH / M • Bad Girls Get Punished / 1994 / NTP / B • Bangin' With The Home Girls / 1991 / AFV / M • Bar Bizarre / 1996 / WP / B • Bend Over Babes #3 / 1992 / EA / M • Biff Malibu's Totally Nasty Home Videos #04 / 1992 / ANA / M • Big Busted Dream Girls / 1995 / PME / S • Big Busty Whoppers / 1994 / PME / F • Bikini Beach #1 / 1993 / CC / M • Bikini Beach #2 / 1993 / CC / M • Bikini Beach #3 / 1993 / CC / M • Blonde Justice #1 / 1993 / VI / M • Blonde Justice #2 / 1993 / VI / M • Boobs On Fire / 1993 / NAP / F • The Bottom Dweller / 1993 / EL / M • Breast Worx #29 / 1992 / LBO / M • Breast Worx #38 / 1992 / LBO / M • Breast Worx #39 / 1992 / LBO / M • Breast Worx #42 / 1993 / LBO / M • Bubble Butts #17 / 1992 / LBO / M • Buffy Malibu's Totally Nasty All-Girl Home Videos #01 / 1992 / ANA / F • Cats Will Duel / 1993 / NAP / B • Cinderella In Chains #3 / 1996 / LBO / M • Circus Of Lesbians / 1995 / VI / C • Clan Of The Cave Woman / 1992 / NAP / B • Contract For Service / 1994 / NTP / B • Crazed #1 / 1992 / VI / M • Crazed #2 / 1992 / VI / M • Defeat And Humiliate / 1995 / NAP / B • Defenseless / 1992 / CDI / M • Desire & Submission #1 / 1994 / HAC / B • Desire & Submission #2 / 1994 / HAC / B • Diary Of A Mistress / 1995 / HOM / B • The Disciplinarians / 1996 / LON / B • Dominant's Dilemma / 1993 / LON / B • Double D Dykes #06 / 1992 / GO / F • Dr Feelgood Sex Psychiatrist / 1994 / LV / M • Eleventh Annual AVN Awards / 1994 / VC / M • The Enema Bandit / 1994 / BIZ / B • Extreme Passion / 1993 / WP / M • Fantasy Girls /

1994 / PME / F • Firm / 1993 / MID / M • First Time Ever #1 / 1995 / PE / F • Frat Girls / 1993 / VC / M • The Fun Bunch / 1992 / ... / M • The God Daughter #1 / 1991 / AFV / M • Groupies / 1993 / AFV / F • Her Darkest Desire / 1993 / HOM / B • Hidden Desires / 1992 / CDI / M • Hot Summer Knights / 1991 / LV / M • Hotel Sex / 1992 / AFV / M • Innocent's Initiation / 1996 / BON / B • Insatiable Nurses / 1992 / VIM / M • Kinky Cameraman #1 / 1996 / LEI / C • Kiss Of The Whip / 1996 / BON / B • Kittens #4: Bodybuilding Bitches / 1993 / CC / F • Knight Of Conquest / 1994 / NAP / B • Knight Shadows / 1992 / BS / B • Kym Wilde's On The Edge #11 / 1994 / RB / B • Leave It To Bondage / 1994 / BON / B • Long Hot Summer / 1992 / CDI / M • Mortal Passions / 1995 / FD / M • Mr. Peepers Amateur Home Videos #48: Dialing For Services / 1992 / LBO / M • Naughty Nights / 1996 / PLP / C • Neighbors / 1994 / LE / M • Night Blooms / 1997 / BON / B • Nightmare Of Discipline / 1993 / NTP / B • Nude Secretaries / 1994 / EDE / S • Odyssey 30 Min: #190: The Other Fucking Roommate / 1991 / OD / M • Odyssey Triple Play #29: Spontaneous & Raw 3-Ways / 1993 / OD / M • Painful Lessons (Bruce Seven) / 1992 / BS / B • Pajama Party X #1 / 1994 / VC / M • Pajama Party X #2 / 1994 / VC / M • The Phoenix #1 / 1992 / VI / M • The Phoenix #2 / 1992 / VI / M • Possessions / 1992 / HW / M • Pretty Cheeks / 1994 / RB / B • Pretty In Peach / 1992 / VI / M • Pussyman #01: The Search / 1993 / CC / M • Pussyman #02: The Prize / 1993 / CC / M • Pussyman #03: The Search Continues / 1993 / SNA / M • Pussyman #04: The Celebration / 1993 / SNA / M • Pussyman #05: Captive Audience / 1994 / SNA / M • Pussyman #06: House Of Games / 1994 / SNA / M • Pussyman #08: The Squirt Queens / 1994 / SNA / M • Pussyman #09: Feeding Frenzy / 1995 / SNA / M • Pussyman #11: Prime Cuts / 1995 / SNA / C • Reality & Fantasy / 1994 / DR / M • Red Hot Coeds / 1993 / VIM / M • Revolt Of The Slaves / 1996 / LBO / B • Rocket Girls / 1993 / VC / M • The Secret Dungeon / 1993 / HOM / B • Secret Rendez-Vous / 1994 / XCI / M • Seymore Butts In The Love Shack / 1992 / FH / M • Shades Of Blue / 1992 / VC / M • Smeers / 1992 / PL / M • Sorority Pink #3 / 1992 / SP / M • Sorority Sex Kittens #1 / 1992 / VC / M • Sorority Sex Kittens #2 / 1993 / VC / M • Special Request #3 / 1993 / HOM / B • Speedster / 1992 / VI / M • Stolen Fantasies / 1995 / LON / B • Street Angels / 1992 / LV / M • Street Girl Named Desire / 1992 / FD / M • Stripper Nurses / 1994 / PE / M • Summer Knight's Foot Tease / 1994 / JBV / F • SVE: Cheap Thrills #2: The More The Merrier / 1992 / SVE / M • Sweet As Honey / 1992 / LV / M • Tailiens #2 / 1992 / FD / M • Tied Temptations / 1996 / BON / B • Toppers #25 / 1994 / TV / M • Toppers #26 / 1994 / TV / M • Toppers #27 / 1994 / TV / M • Toppers #31 / 1994 / TV / C • Toppers #32 / 1994 / TV / C • Uncle Roy's Amateur Home Video #04 / 1992 / VIM / M • Uncle Roy's Amateur Home Video #14 / 1992 / VIM / M • Uncle Roy's Best Of The Best: Close Shaves / 1992 / VIM / C • Underwater Vixens / 1993 / NAP / B • Unfaithful Entry /

1992 / DR / M • When Mams Collide / 1992 / NAP / B • Where The Girls Play / 1992 / CC / F • White Chicks Can't Hump / 1992 / FD / M

SUMMER KNIGHTS *see* **Summer Knight**

SUMMER ROSE *(Vikki Drake, Goldie (S.Rose), Treonnia, Susie Sipes, Carressa, Carressa Nature (SR), Caressa Nature (SR), Heather Martin (SR))*
2002: A Sex Odyssey / 1985 / DR / M • Amber Lynn's Personal Best / 1986 / VD / M • America's Dirtiest Home Videos #09 / 1992 / VEX / M • Anal Reamers / 1986 / 4P / M • Aurora's Secret Diary / 1985 / LA / M • B*A*S*H / 1989 / BIZ / C • Back Road To Paradise / 1984 / CDI / M • Back To Back #1 / 1987 / 4P / C • Backdoor Babes / 1985 / WET / M • Backdoor Lust / 1987 / CV / C • Bare Waves / 1986 / VD / M • Behind The Backdoor #2 / 1989 / EVN / M • Best Of Foot Worship #3 / 1992 / BIZ / C • Between The Cheeks #1 / 1985 / VC / M • Black Bunbusters / 1985 / VC / M • Black Reamers / 1986 / 4P / M • Black With Sugar / 1989 / CIN / M • Blacks & Blondes #10 / 1986 / WV / M • Blacks & Blondes #16 / 1986 / WV / M • Blows Job / 1989 / BIZ / B • Blue Dream Lover / 1985 / TAR / M • Breaking It #2 / 1989 / GO / M • Bunbusters / 1984 / VCR / M • The Call Girl / 1986 / VD / M • Campus Cuties / 1986 / CA / M • Can Heat / 1988 / PLV / B • Chastity Johnson / 1985 / AVC / M • Cheri Taylor Is Tasty And Tight / 1991 / ZA / M • Club Head (EVN) #2 / 1989 / EVN / C • Coffee & Cream / 1984 / AVC / M • The Color Black / 1986 / WET / M • Deep Undercover / 1989 / PV / M • Dial F For Fantasy / 1984 / PL / M • Don't Tell Daddy #1 / 1985 / PL / C • Double Desires / 1988 / PIN / C • Double Penetration Fever / 1989 / MIR / C • Down And Dirty In Beverly Hills / 1986 / CV / M • Dump Site / 1989 / BIZ / C • Enemates #01 / 1988 / BIZ / B • The Erotic Adventures Of Bedman And Throbbin / 1989 / VWA / M • Family Secrets / 1985 / AMB / M • Fantasies Unltd. / 1985 / CDI / M • Female Aggressors / 1986 / LAV / M • Foot Mistress / 1986 / BIZ / B • Goin' Down / 1985 / VC / M • The Good, The Bad, And The Horny / 1985 / VCX / M • Grand Opening / 1985 / AT / M • Greek Lady / 1985 / TGA / M • Headgames / 1985 / WV / M • Hollywood Undercover / 1989 / BWV / C • Hometown Honeys #3 / 1989 / VEX / M • Horny Toed / 1989 / BIZ / S • Hot Cars, Nasty Women / 1985 / WV / M • Hot Seats / 1989 / PLV / B • Hot Tails / 1984 / VEN / M • The Hottest Show In Town / 1987 / VIP / M • Hungry / 1990 / GLE / M • The Idol / 1985 / WV / M • Jean Genie / 1985 / CA / M • John Holmes, The Man, The Legend / 1995 / EVN / C • Kissin' Cousins / 1984 / PL / M • Lady Cassanova / 1985 / AVC / M • Life Is Butt A Dream / 1989 / V99 / M • The Life Of The Party / 1991 / ZA / M • Lip Service / 1987 / BIK / C • Little Miss Innocence / 1987 / CA / M • Living In A Wet Dream / 1986 / PEN / C • Loose Ends #1 / 1984 / 4P / M • Loving Lips / 1987 / AMB / C • Loving Spoonfulls / 1987 / 4P / C • Lust In America / 1985 / VCX / M • Lustfully Seeking Susan / 1985 / PLY / M • Mad Sex / 1986 / VD / M • Marina Heat / 1985 / CV / M • Marina Vice / 1985 / PEN / M • The Melting Spot / 1985 / VSE / M • The Naked Bun / 1989 / VWA /

M • The Newcomers / 1983 / VCX / M • Nightfire / 1987 / LA / M • No Man's Land #03 / 1989 / VT / F • Nooner / 1985 / AMB / M • Older Men With Young Girls / 1985 / CC / M • Only The Best Of Anal / 1992 / MET / C • Only The Best Of Women With Women / 1988 / CV / C • Oral Majority #03 / 1986 / WV / C • Orgies / 1987 / WV / C • Penetration #4 / 1984 / AVC / M • Perversion / 1984 / AVC / M • Pipe Dreams / 1985 / 4P / M • The Plumber Cometh / 1985 / 4P / M • Porsche Lynn, Every Man's Dream / 1988 / CC / C • The Pregnant Babysitter / 1984 / WV / M • Prescription For Passion / 1984 / VD / M • Princess Charming / 1987 / AVC / C • Rocky-X #1 / 1986 / PEN / M • Royally Flushed / 1987 / BIZ / B • Rump Humpers / 1985 / WET / M • Schoolgirl By Day / 1985 / LA / M • Sex 5th Avenue / 1985 / WV / M • Sex F/X / 1986 / VPE / M • Sexual Pursuit / 1985 / AT / M • She's A Good Lust Charm / 1987 / LA / C • Slap Happy / 1994 / PRE / B • The Sleazy Detective / 1988 / VD / M • Sore Throat / 1985 / GO / M • Stolen Lust / 1985 / AAH / M • Student Fetish Videos: Foot Worship #03 / 1991 / PRE / B • Swedish Erotica #64 / 1985 / CA / M • Tails Of The Town / 1988 / WV / M • A Taste Of Candy / 1985 / LA / M • Taste Of The Best #2 / 1988 / PIN / C • Torrid / 1989 / VI / M • A Tribute To The King / 1985 / VCX / C • Triple Xposure / 1986 / VD / M • Two Tons Of Fun #1 / 1985 / 4P / C • Ubangis On Uranus / 1987 / WV / M • Up To No Good / 1986 / CDI / M • Visions Of Jeannie / 1986 / VD / M • Water Nymph / 1987 / LIM / M • Wetness For The Prosecution / 1989 / LV / M • What's Love Got To Do With It / 1989 / WV / M • Where The Boys Aren't #1 / 1989 / VI / F • Wild Toga Party / 1985 / VD / M • Yankee Seduction / 1984 / WV / M

SUMMER SARAH
Young Sluts In Heat #2 / 1996 / PL / M

SUMMER ST CERLY
Art Of Femininity #2 / 1988 / LEO / G • I Was A She-Male For The FBI / 1987 / SEA / G • The Mysteries Of Transsexualism Explored #1 / 1987 / OZE / G • Parliament: Hard TV #1 / 1988 / PM / G • She Studs #02 / 1991 / BIZ / G • She-Male Encounters #05: Orgy At The Poysinberry Bar #1 / 1987 / MET / G • She-Male Encounters #09: She-Male Confidential / 1984 / MET / G • She-Male Encounters #10: She-Male Vacation / 1986 / MET / G • She-Male Encounters #11: She-Male Roommates / 1986 / MET / G • She-Male Encounters #12: Orgy At The Poysinberry #2 / 1987 / MET / G • She-Male Encounters #13: She-Male Reformatory / 1987 / MET / G • She-Male Encounters #14: She-Male Wrestlers / 1987 / MET / G • She-Male Sanitarium / 1988 / VD / G • Squalor Motel / 1985 / SE / M • Trisexual Encounters #01 / 1985 / PL / G • Trisexual Encounters #02 / 1985 / PL / G

SUNDAE
Lickin' Good / 1995 / TVI / F • A Sundae Kinda Love / 1995 / TVI / M • Whipped Cream / 1995 / TVI / M

SUNDAE BRUNCH
Bun Busters #21 / 1994 / LBO / M • The Cumm Brothers #05: These Nuts For Hire / 1994 / OD / M • High Heeled & Horny #1 / 1994 / LBO / M • Northwest Pecker Trek

#4: Laid In Latte Land / 1994 / LBO / M • Northwest Pecker Trek #5: Cumming In King County / 1995 / LBO / M

SUNDANCE
Ona Zee's Date With Dallas / 1992 / ONA / M • Pussy Hunt #10 / 1995 / LEI / M • Wet And Wild #2 / 1995 / VEX / M

SUNE PILGAARD see Star Index I

SUNEE see Star Index I

SUNN LEE see Star Index I

SUNNY
Blue Vanities #573 / 1996 / FFL / M • Bootylicious: Big Badd Booty / 1995 / JMP / M • Interview: Chocolate Treats / 1995 / LV / M • Pussy Hunt #09 / 1995 / LEI / M • Real People Real Bondage #1 / 1995 / BON / C • Sunny In Bondage / 1993 / BON / B

SUNNY (BLONDE)
Anal Lickers And Cummers / 1996 / ROB / M • Hardcore Debutantes #03 / 1997 / TEP / M • More Dirty Debutantes #57 / 1996 / 4P / M • Wild Assed Pooper Slut / 1996 / ROB / M

SUNNY (NIKKI WYLDE) see Nikki Wylde

SUNNY DAY
Creme De La Face #18: Cum Mops / 1997 / OD / M • I Am For Sale / 1968 / SOW / S

SUNNY DAYE *(Alexandra Day)*
Best Of Buttman #2 / 1993 / EA / C • Blondes On Fire / 1987 / VCR / C • Body Double / 1984 / C3S / S • Bunbusters / 1984 / VCR / M • Creamy Cheeks / 1986 / VEX / M • Double Heat / 1986 / LA / M • Erotic Images / 1983 / VES / S • The Erotic World Of Sunny Day / 1984 / VCR / C • Future Sodom / 1988 / VD / M • Hot Yachts / 1987 / VEX / M • Inner Blues / 1987 / VD / M • Jack Hammer / 1987 / ZA / M • Joys Of Erotica #111 / 1984 / VCR / C • Joys Of Erotica #113 / 1984 / VCR / C • Leg...Ends #01 / 1988 / BIZ / F • Loose Lifestyles / 1988 / CA / M • Max Bedroom / 1987 / ZA / M • Naughty Neighbors / 1986 / VEX / M • Naughty Nurses / 1982 / VCR / M • Parliament: California Blondes #1 / 1987 / PM / F • Pleasure Productions #03 / 1984 / VCR / M • Pleasure Productions #04 / 1984 / VCR / M • Pleasure Productions #05 / 1984 / VCR / M • Sex Search / 1988 / IN / S • Shipwrecked / 1991 / VEX / C • Super Leg-Ends / 1992 / PRE / C

SUNNY DELIGHT
Bobby Hollander's Rookie Nookie #01 / 1993 / SFP / M • Bobby Hollander's Rookie Nookie #05 / 1993 / SFP / M • How To Make A Model #02: Got Her In Bed / 1993 / QUA / M • How To Make A Model #03: Sunshine & Melons / 1994 / QUA / M • Mr. Peepers Amateur Home Videos #94: Calendar Cleavage / 1994 / LBO / M • Uncle Roy's Amateur Home Video #18 / 1993 / VIM / M

SUNNY GLICK
Confessions Of Candy / 1984 / VC / M • Hot Flashes / 1984 / VC / M • Sizzling Summer / 1984 / VC / M • Spreading Joy / 1988 / VC / M • Taking Off / 1984 / VC / M • Young Nurses In Love / 1987 / VC / M

SUNNY MCKAY *(Kim McKay, Kim Barry, Sonny McKay)*
Australian blonde with small tits, lithe body and a passable face.
Alone / 1993 / OD / M • Amazing Tails #4 / 1990 / CA / M • Back To Nature / 1990 / CA / M • Backdoor Black #1 / 1992 / WV / C •

Behind Blue Eyes #3 / 1989 / ME / M • The Best Of Andrew Blake / 1993 / CA / C • Big Game / 1990 / LV / M • Black And Horny / 1994 / MET / M • Blackballed / 1994 / VI / C • Blue Bayou / 1993 / VC / M • Boobs, Butts And Bloopers #2 / 1990 / HO / M • Bruce Seven's Favorite Endings #1 / 1991 / EL / C • Buttman's European Vacation #1 / 1991 / EA / M • Buttman's Ultimate Workout / 1990 / EA / M • Camp Beaverlake #2 / 1991 / AFV / M • Carnal College #1 / 1991 / AFV / F • Catalina Five-O: White Coral, Blue Death / 1990 / CIN / M • Catalina Sixty-Nine / 1991 / AR / M • Catalina: Treasure Island / 1991 / CDI / M • Cocktails / 1990 / HO / M • Confessions Of A Chauffeur / 1990 / DR / M • Deep Inside P.J. Sparxx / 1995 / VC / C • Doop Throat #5 / 1990 / AR / M • Dial A Sailor / 1990 / PM / M • Dick-Tation / 1991 / AFV / M • Diedre In Danger / 1990 / VI / M • Dream Cream'n / 1991 / AR / M • The Dream Merchants / 1990 / CDI / M • Driving Miss Daisy Crazy #2 / 1992 / WV / M • Eternity / 1990 / SC / M • Everything Goes / 1990 / SE / M • Eyewitness Nudes / 1990 / VC / M • Fantasy Escorts / 1993 / FOR / M • Female Persuasion / 1990 / SO / F • Girls, Girls And More Girls / 1990 / LV / F • Hard Talk / 1992 / VC / M • Heart To Heart / 1990 / LE / M • The Heat Of The Moment / 1990 / IN / M • Heather Hunted / 1990 / VI / M • Heatwave #1 / 1992 / FH / F • Hot Diggity Dog / 1990 / ME / M • Hump Up The Volume / 1991 / AR / M • Immorals #3: Stroked / 1991 / SC / M • The Landlady / 1990 / VI / M • Lesbian Love Connection / 1992 / LIP / F • Loose Lips / 1990 / VC / M • Lost In Paradise / 1990 / CA / M • Lover's Trance / 1990 / LE / M • Lucky Break / 1991 / SE / M • Magma: After Eight / 1995 / MET / M • Magma: Double Anal / 1994 / MET / M • Mischief / 1991 / WV / M • Mummy Dearest #2: The Unwrapping / 1990 / LV / M • Opening Night / 1991 / AR / M • Outback Assignment / 1991 / VD / M • A Paler Shade Of Blue / 1991 / CC / M • Playin' With Fire / 1993 / LV / M • Prima #08: Sex Camping / 1995 / MBP / M • Prisoner Of Lust / 1991 / VC / F • Raunch #01 / 1990 / CC / M • Ready Freddy? / 1992 / FH / M • Scandanavian Double Features #4 / 1996 / PL / M • Scarlet Fantasy / 1990 / VI / M • Secrets / 1990 / CA / M • Sex Dreams / 1995 / C69 / M • Sexual Healer / 1991 / CA / M • Singles Holiday / 1990 / PM / M • Sittin' Pretty #1 / 1990 / DR / M • Sittin' Pretty #2 / 1992 / DR / M • Slip Of The Tongue / 1990 / SE / M • Steamy Windows / 1990 / VC / M • Sunny After Dark / 1990 / WV / M • Taboo #08 / 1990 / IN / M • The Therapist / 1992 / VC / M • Torch #1 / 1990 / VI / M • A Touch Of Gold / 1990 / IN / M • The Truth Laid Bare / 1993 / ZA / M • Up The Gulf / 1991 / AR / M • V.I.C.E. #1 / 1991 / AFV / M • Vegas #4: Joker's Wild / 1990 / CDI / M • Vegas #5: Blackjack / 1991 / CIN / M • Wet 'n' Working / 1990 / EA / F • Wire Desire / 1991 / XCI / M • You Can Touch This / 1991 / EVN / M

SUNNY NELSON see Star Index I

SUNNY NICK see Star Index I

SUNNY RAY *(Lita Dodge)*
Older brunette with a falling apart body and enhanced medium tits. Big frame.
America's Raunchiest Home Videos #74: /

1993 / ZA / M • The Bet / 1993 / VT / M • The Beverly Thrillbillies / 1993 / ZA / M • Bra Busters #05 / 1993 / LBO / M • Erotic Newcummers Vol 1 #2: Texas Twisters / 1993 / DR / M • M Series #13 / 1993 / LBO / M • New Girls In Town #4 / 1993 / CC / M • Sean Michaels On The Road #09: St. Louis / 1994 / VT / M

SUNNY STUD see Star Index I

SUNNY SUMMERS see Star Index I

SUNSET
Lesbian Pros And Amateurs #06 / 1992 / GO / F

SUNSET OLIVES
Private Video Magazine #19 / 1994 / OD / M

SUNSET THOMAS *(Diane (Sunset T))*
Little body and pretty cheeky face with a tight waist even while pregnant. Nice skin, blue eyes. From the interview in **Deep Inside Dirty Debutantes #01** she had had a baby boy about 5 months previous to the filming. She comes from Tenessee and was 20 in 1992. She grew up in Daytona Beach Florida. Before her pregnancy she was 34AA-24-34. During it she got huge and now she's 36C-24-36.
13th Annual Adult Video News Awards / 1996 / VC / S • Adventures In Paradise / 1992 / VEX / M • The Adventures Of Buttwoman #2: Behind Bars / 1992 / EL / F • Amateur Hours #61 / 1993 / AFI / M • Amateur Hours #68 / 1994 / AFI / M • Amateur Lesbians #40: Sunset / 1993 / GO / F • Amateur Orgies #07 / 1992 / AFI / M • Amateur Orgies #08 / 1992 / AFI / M • Amateur Orgies #12 / 1992 / AFI / M • Amateur Orgies #13 / 1992 / AFI / M • Amateur Orgies #16 / 1992 / AFI / M • America's Dirtiest Home Videos #04 / 1991 / VEX / M • America's Dirtiest Home Videos #07 / 1991 / VEX / M • America's Dirtiest Home Videos #14 / 1992 / VEX / M • Anal Avenue / 1992 / LV / M • Anal Ski Vacation / 1993 / ANA / M • Animal Instinct / 1996 / DTV / M • Asian Invasion / 1993 / IP / M • Babenet / 1995 / VC / M • Backing In #4 / 1993 / WV / C • Bare Market / 1993 / VC / M • Beach Bum Amateur's #14 / 1992 / MID / M • Beach Bum Amateur's #16 / 1992 / MID / M • Biography: Sunset Thomas / 1995 / SC / C • Black Orchid / 1993 / WV / M • Blow Job Baby / 1993 / CC / M • Bone Therapy / 1992 / LV / M • Bubble Butts #16 / 1992 / LBO / M • Cajun Heat / 1993 / SC / M • Caribbean Sunset / 1996 / PL / M • Chameleons: Not The Sequel / 1991 / VC / M • Cinderella Society / 1993 / GO / M • Club DV8 #1 / 1993 / SC / M • Club DV8 #2 / 1993 / SC / M • Club Midnight / 1992 / LV / M • Confessions / 1992 / PL / M • Cyberanal / 1995 / VC / M • Death Dancers / 1993 / 3SR / S • Debbie Does Dallas Again / 1994 / AFV / M • Deep Inside Dirty Debutantes #01 / 1992 / 4P / M • Deep Throat #6 / 1992 / AFV / M • Delicious (VCX-1993) / 1993 / VCX / M • Dick & Jane Go To Hollywood #1 / 1993 / AVI / M • Dirty Bob's #18: Under The Boardwalk! / 1995 / FLP / S • Dirty Bob's #19: Over The Boardwalk! / 1995 / FLP / S • Double D Dykes #06 / 1992 / GO / F • Double Decadence / 1995 / NOT / M • Double Penetration Virgins #01 / 1993 / LE / M • Flashback / 1993 / SC / M • Frenzy / 1992 / SC / M • Gang Bang Fury #1 / 1992 / ROB / M • Gang Bang Pussy-

cat / 1992 / ROB / M • Gang Bang Thrills / 1992 / ROB / M • Gypsy Queen / 1995 / CC / M • Hidden Obsessions / 1992 / BFP / M • Hillary Vamp's Private Collection #09 / 1992 / HVD / M • Hollywood Studs / 1993 / FD / M • Hollywood Teasers #01 / 1992 / LBO / F • If Looks Could Kill / 1992 / V99 / M • Inferno #1 / 1993 / SC / M • Inferno #2 / 1993 / SC / M • Inner Pink #3 / 1994 / LIP / F • Intervidnet #1: Special Delivery / 1994 / IVN / M • Jezebel #1 / 1993 / SC / M • Jezebel #2 / 1993 / SC / M • The Last Good Sex / 1992 / FD / M • Latex #1 / 1994 / VC / M • Latex #2 / 1995 / VC / M • Leena / 1992 / VT / M • Les Femmes Erotiques / 1993 / BFP / M • Lesbians In Tight Shorts / 1992 / LV / F • Looks Like A Million / 1992 / LV / M • The Love Doctor / 1992 / HIP / M • Love Letters #1 / 1993 / SC / M • Love Letters #2 / 1993 / SC / M • Maiden Heaven #1 / 1992 / MID / F • Mike Hott: #185 Cunt Of The Month: Sunset / 1990 / MHV / M • Mike Hott: #194 Sunset Thomas, Very Pregnant / 1994 / MHV / M • Mike Hott: #215 Lesbian Sluts #08 / 1992 / MHV / F • Mike Hott: Apple Asses #09 / 1992 / MHV / F • Mike Hott: Cum Cocktails #2 / 1995 / MHV / C • Mistress (1993-HOM) / 1993 / HOM / B • Misty's First Whipping / 1994 / LON / B • Mix Up / 1992 / IF / M • Mona Lisa / 1992 / LV / M • Mr. Peepers Amateur Home Videos #25: The 25th Anniversary Ed / 1991 / LBO / M • Mr. Peepers Amateur Home Videos #29: Going Down Payment / 1991 / LBO / M • Mr. Peepers Nastiest #6 / 1995 / LBO / C • Muffy The Vampire Layer / 1992 / LV / M • N.Y. Video Magazine #09 / 1996 / OUP / M • Native Tongue / 1993 / VI / M • Neighborhood Watch #07: Made Up To Go Down / 1991 / LBO / M • Nobody's Looking / 1993 / VC / M • Nookie Court / 1992 / AFV / M • Odyssey Triple Play #39: Triple Play Three Way #2 / 1993 / OD / M • The Oh! Zone / 1995 / VC / M • Once In A Lifetime / 1996 / VC / C • Opposite Attraction / 1992 / VEX / M • Our Bang #10 / 1993 / GLI / M • Pajama Party X #3 / 1994 / VC / M • Pearl Necklace: Thee Bush League: The Best Of Oral #01 / 1993 / SEE / C • Pearl Necklace: Thee Bush League #10 / 1993 / SEE / M • The Pink Lady Detective Agency: Case Of The Twisted Sister / 1994 / IN / M • Pleasure Dome: The Genesis Chamber / 1994 / AFV / M • Positively Pagan #06 / 1993 / ATA / M • Raunch #06: French Kiss / 1992 / CC / M • Ready To Drop #02 / 1992 / FC / M • Red Beaver Bonanza / 1992 / TCP / M • Savannah's Last Stand / 1993 / VI / M • Sensual Solos #01 / 1993 / AVI / F • Sex #1 (Vca) / 1994 / VC / M • Sex #2: Fate (Vca) / 1995 / VC / M • Silky Thighs / 1994 / ERA / M • Star Crossed / 1995 / VC / M • Sunset In Paradise / 1996 / PL / M • Sunset Rides Again / 1995 / VC / M • Sunset Strippers / 199? / CRI / S • Sunset Strips / 1996 / SUE / S • Sunset Thomas Live / 1994 / KBR / F • Sunset's Anal & D.P. Gangbang / 1996 / PL / M • Taboo #11: Crazy On You / 1993 / IN / M • The Tempest / 1993 / SC / M • Temptation / 1994 / VC / M • Teri's Fantasies / 1993 / VEX / M • Toredo / 1996 / ROX / M • Ultimate Orgy #2 / 1992 / GLI / M • Ultimate Orgy #3 / 1992 / GLI / M • Unbridled / 1995 / PPI / M • Undercover Lover / 1992 / CV / M • The Way They Wuz / 1996 / SHS

/ C • Welcome To Bondage: Starlets #2 / 1994 / BON / C • Welcome To Bondage: Sunset Thomas / 1993 / BON / B • Wet Memories / 1993 / WV / M • Witchcraft #4: Virgin Heart / 1993 / AE / S • Working Girl / 1993 / VI / M

SUNSHINE
Big Murray's New-Cummers #11: Willing & Able / 1993 / FD / M • Black Street Hookers #2 / 1996 / DFI / M • Blue Vanities #539 / 1993 / FFL / M • Burning Desire / 1983 / HO / M • Guttman's Hollywood Adventure / 1993 / PL / M • Harry Horndog #11: Love Puppies #2 / 1992 / ZA / M • Harry Horndog #12: Harry's Xmas Party / 1992 / ZA / M • Pearl Necklace: Amorous Amateurs #24 / 1993 / SEE / M • Pearl Necklace: Thee Bush League #13 / 1993 / SEE / M • Sweet Secrets / 1977 / VCS / M

SUNSHINE (BLONDE)
Filthy First Timers #6 / 1997 / EL / M

SUNSHINE DAWN
Natural Response / 1996 / GPI / G

SUNSHINE WOODS
College Girls / cr73 / VXP / M

SUPER MARIO *see* **Mario (English)**

SURAYA *see Star Index I*

SURAYA JAMAL
The Way Of Sex / 1995 / DBV / M

SURICA JOHNSON
Bad Girls #1 / 1981 / GO / M

SUSAN
A&B AB#123: Sexy Blondes / 1990 / A&B / F • A&B AB#224: Wild Women / 1990 / A&B / F • Amateurs In Action #4 / 1995 / MET / M • American Connection Video Magazine #03 / 1993 / ZA / M • Bend Over Babes #4 / 1996 / EA / M • Big Titted Tarts / 1994 / PL / C • Blue Vanities #170 (New) / 1996 / FFL / M • Blue Vanities #170 (Old) / 1991 / FFL / M • Blue Vanities #502 / 1992 / FFL / M • Blue Vanities #534 / 1993 / FFL / M • Blue Vanities #538 / 1993 / FFL / M • Blue Vanities #543 / 1994 / FFL / M • Blue Vanities #544 / 1994 / FFL / M • Blue Vanities #547 / 1994 / FFL / M • Blue Vanities #574 / 1996 / FFL / M • Blue Vanities #579 / 1995 / FFL / M • Creme De Femme #4 / 1981 / AVC / C • Eric Kroll's Bondage #1 / 1994 / ERK / M • Full Moon Video #22: Elite Fantasy Girls / 1992 / FAP / F • Home-Grown Video #463: Cum And Get It / 1995 / HOV / M • Joe Elliot's College Girls #30 / 1994 / JOE / M • Latent Image: Christine & Susan / 1993 / LAT / F • Limited Edition #19 / 1980 / AVC / M • Mr. Peepers Nastiest #2 / 1995 / LBO / C • Penetration (Anabolic) #3 / 1995 / ANA / M • Penthouse: All-Pet Workout / 1993 / NIV / F • Private Video Magazine #24 / 1995 / OD / M • Southern Belles #8 / 1997 / XPR / M • Starlet Screen Test / 1990 / NST / S • Titanic Tits #10 / 198? / L&W / S • Triple X Video Magazine #01 / 1995 / OD / M

SUSAN ADLE *(Audrey Lang)*
Pretty, small-titted blonde.
Heavenly Desire / 1979 / WV / M • Screwples / 1979 / CA / M • Steamy Sirens / 1984 / AIR / C • Triple Header / 1987 / AIR / C

SUSAN BARRETT *see Star Index I*

SUSAN BATES
Erotic Fantasies: Women With Women / 1984 / CV / C • Visions Of Clair / 1977 / WWV / M

SUSAN BESSON *see Star Index I*

SUSAN BLAIR

Bondage Memories #03 / 1994 / BON / C • Fit To Be Tied / 1984 / BON / B • It's Only A Game / 1988 / BON / B • Punished Cheeks / 1992 / RB / B • Sally Roberts In Bondage #5 / 1985 / 4P / B • Sally Roberts In Bondage #6 / 1985 / 4P / B • Shaved #04 / 1992 / RB / F • Testing Her Powers / 1987 / BON / B

SUSAN BLAUSTIEN
Sore Throat / 1985 / GO / M

SUSAN BLUE *see* **Connie Peterson**

SUSAN BOONE *see Star Index I*

SUSAN BRADLEY
Crocodile Blondee #1 / 1987 / CA0 / M

SUSAN BRADY *see Star Index I*

SUSAN CATHERINE
Little Angel Puss / cr76 / SVE / M • Lollipop Palace / 1973 / VCX / M • Night Pleasures / 1975 / WWV / M

SUSAN CHANG
Body Candy / 1980 / VIS / M

SUSAN CHERRY *see Star Index I*

SUSAN CLARE
Nylon / 1995 / VI / M

SUSAN CONO *see Star Index I*

SUSAN COWLING
Love Secrets / 1976 / VIP / M

SUSAN CRITZ *see Star Index I*

SUSAN DAVID *see Star Index I*

SUSAN DAVIS *see Star Index I*

SUSAN DE ANGELIS
The Good Girls Of Godiva High / 1979 / VCX / M

SUSAN DEASY *see Star Index I*

SUSAN DELOIR *see Star Index I*

SUSAN DEMPSEY
Little Me & Marla Strangelove / 1979 / ALP / M • Marriage And Other Four Letter Words / 1974 / VC / M

SUSAN DEVLIN *see Star Index I*

SUSAN DRAFTRON *see Star Index I*

SUSAN DREGER
[Ripoff / 1984 / ... / M

SUSAN DUBOIS
Mother Load #1 / 1993 / GOT / B • Mother Load #2 / 1994 / GOT / B

SUSAN ELLIS
Naughty Schoolgirls Revenge / 1994 / BIZ / B

SUSAN FIELDS *see Star Index I*

SUSAN FINNIGAN
Erecter Sex #5: Oral Fantasies / cr72 / AR / M • Water People / cr72 / AXV / M

SUSAN FLETCHER
Blue Vanities #510 / 1992 / FFL / M

SUSAN FOXWORTH *see Star Index I*

SUSAN FUENTES *see Star Index I*

SUSAN GART *see* **Susan Hart**

SUSAN GRIFFIN *see Star Index I*

SUSAN HARRIS *see Star Index I*

SUSAN HART *(Susan Gart, Suzi Hart)*
Slightly chubby in her later movies. Brunette with curly hair and a nice personality.
Adult 45 #01 / 1985 / DR / C • Back To Class #1 / 1984 / DR / M • Bad Girls #4 / 1984 / GO / M • Best Of Hot Shorts #01 / 1987 / VCR / C • The Big Thrill / 1984 / ECS / M • Breaking It #1 / 1984 / COL / M • Candy Girls #4 / 19?? / AVC / M • Celebration / 1984 / GO / C • Cheap Thrills / 1984 / RLV / M • China & Silk / 1984 / MAP / M • Coming Holmes / 1985 / VD / M • Deep Chill / cr85 / AT / M • Doctor Desire / 1984 / VD / M • Dream Lover / 1985 / CDI / M • The End Zone / 1987 / LA / C • Erotic Fantasies #5 / 1983 / CV / C • Fantasy

Land / 1984 / LA / M • Forbidden Fruit / 1985 / PV / M • Gang Bangs #1 / 1985 / VCR / M • Good Girls Do / 1984 / HO / M • Gourmet Premier: Beyond Arousal / Diva Does The Director 905 / cr85 / GO / M • Heartthrobs / 1985 / CA / M • Hot Girls In Love / 1984 / VIV / C • Hot Shorts: Susan Hart / 1986 / VCR / C • I Want It All / 1984 / VD / M • Ice Cream #3: Naked Eyes / 1984 / VC / M • Illusions Of Ecstasy / 1985 / NSV / M • Ladies Of The Knight / 1984 / GO / M • Lay Down And Deliver / 1989 / VWA / M • Layover / 1985 / HO / M • Lesbian Nymphos / 1988 / GO / C • Limited Edition #29 / 1984 / AVC / M • Lust American Style / 1985 / WV / M • Lusty Adventurer / 1985 / GO / M • Make Me Want It / 1986 / CA / M • Night Prowlers / 1985 / MAP / M • Oriental Jade / 1985 / VC / M • Our Major Is Sex / 1984 / VD / M • Perfect Fit / 1985 / DR / M • Photoflesh / 1984 / HO / M • The Pleasure Hunt #2 / 1985 / NSV / M • The Pussywillows / 1985 / SUV / M • Radio K-KUM / 1984 / HO / M • Rich Bitch / 1985 / HO / M • Sexaholic / 1985 / AVC / M • Sexsations / 1984 / NSV / M • Sinful Pleasures / 1987 / HO / C • Sister Dearest / 1984 / DR / M • Slumber Party / 1984 / HO / M • Spreading Joy / 1984 / IN / M • Stiff Competition #1 / 1984 / CA / M • Sweet Cheeks / 1987 / VCR / C • Tales Of Taija Rae / 1989 / DR / M • Talk Dirty To Me #03 / 1986 / DR / M • Treasure Chest / 1985 / GO / M • Victoria's Secret Desires / 1983 / S&L / C • Wet Sex / 1984 / CA / M • What Gets Me Hot / 1984 / ISV / M • Wild Weekend / 1984 / HO / M • Wings Of Passion / 1984 / HO / M • With Love From Ginger / 1986 / HO / C • With Love From Susan / 1988 / HO / C

SUSAN HART (SPECIAL) *see Star Index I*

SUSAN HERBST *see Star Index I*

SUSAN HERZOG *see Star Index I*

SUSAN HILL *see Star Index I*

SUSAN HOLMES *see Star Index I*

SUSAN HOWARD *see Star Index I*

SUSAN HUNT *see Star Index I*

SUSAN HURLEY
The Journey Of O / 1975 / TVX / M

SUSAN JAMES *see Star Index I*

SUSAN JENSEN *see Constance Money*

SUSAN KAY
Erotic Dimensions: Bold Fantasies / 1982 / NSV / M • The Mistress #1 / 1983 / CV / M • Suzie Superstar #2 / 1985 / CV / M

SUSAN KAYE *see Lynx Cannon*

SUSAN KEY *see Star Index I*

SUSAN KIGER
Angels Brigade / 1979 / LIV / S • Deadly Love / 1976 / EXF / M • Galaxina / 1980 / MCA / S • H.O.T.S. / 1979 / VES / S • The Happy Hooker Goes To Hollywood / 1980 / VES / S • House Of Death / 1982 / VIG / S • The Return / 1980 / AE / S • Seven / 1979 / LIV / S

SUSAN KOOL *see Nikki Wylde*

SUSAN KUCHINSKI *see Lynx Cannon*

SUSAN LACOSS *see Star Index I*

SUSAN LADD
Bedtime Video #02 / 1984 / GO / M

SUSAN LANDAU
All About Sex / 1970 / AR / M

SUSAN LAWRENCE
Old Wave Hookers #1 / 1995 / PL / M

SUSAN LEBEAU *see Star Index I*

SUSAN LIBERACE
Sex Styles Of The Rich & Famous / 1986 / VXP / M

SUSAN LION
Blacks & Blondes #12 / 1986 / WV / M

SUSAN LION (N. WEST) *see Nichole West*

SUSAN MANSON *(Susan Mason)*
Angela Takes A Dare / 1988 / FAZ / M • Backdoor To Hollywood #07 / 1989 / CIN / M • Best Body In Town / 1989 / FAZ / F • Cheek-A-Boo / 1988 / LV / M • Debbie's Love Spell / 1988 / STM / M • Girls Will Be Girls / 1988 / LV / F • Leather Clad Mistress / 19?? / STM / B • Lesbian Fantasies / 1990 / BIZ / F • Miss Adventures / 1989 / VEX / M • Sugar Tongues / 1992 / STM / C • Whoregasm / cr87 / FTV / M

SUSAN MARLOW
Doogan's Woman / 1978 / S&L / M

SUSAN MASON *see Susan Manson*

SUSAN MCBAIN *(Suzie Humphfree, Suzy Humphree)*
Brunette with shoulder length hair, small tits, lithe body, nice butt. Gives the impression she's on something in most of her performances.
Anna Obsessed / 1978 / ALP / M • Auto-Erotic Practices / 1980 / VCR / F • Bad Barbara / cr77 / BL / M • Barbara Broadcast / 1977 / VC / M • Blonde Velvet / 1976 / COL / M • Blue Vanities #059 / 1988 / FFL / M • Blue Vanities #204 / 1993 / FFL / M • Blue Vanities #536 / 1993 / FFL / M • Candy Lips / 1975 / CXV / M • A Coming Of Angels / 1977 / CA / M • Doogan's Woman / 1978 / S&L / M • Farmers Daughters / 1975 / VC / M • Heat Wave / 1977 / COM / M • Jawbreakers / 1985 / VEN / C • Legends Of Porn #2 / 1989 / CV / C • Maraschino Cherry / 1978 / QX / M • Miss Kinsey's Report / 19?? / BL / M • Odyssey / 1977 / VC / M • One Last Score / 1978 / CDI / M • Portraits Of Pleasure / 1974 / BL / M • Powerbone / 1976 / VC / M • Revenge Of The Rope Masters / 1979 / ... / B • Rollerbabies / 1976 / VC / M • Sharon / 1977 / AR / M • Showgirl #04: Tina Russell Classics / 1981 / VCR / M • Snow Honeys / 1983 / VC / M • Sweetheart / 1976 / SVE / M • Teenage Housewife / 1976 / BL / M • That's Erotic / 1979 / CV / C • That's Porno / 1979 / CV / C • Two Timer / 19?? / BL / M • Virgin Dreams / 1976 / BMV / M • Visions / 1977 / QX / M • Voluptuous Predators / cr76 / VHL / M • [Fuck Me, Suck Me, Eat Me / 1990 / ... / M • [Ganja And Hess / 1973 / VIG / S

SUSAN MCKINNEY *see Star Index I*

SUSAN MCQUIRY *see Star Index I*

SUSAN MICHELLE
Bankok Connection / 1979 / CA / M

SUSAN MILES *see Star Index I*

SUSAN MILLS
Summer Girls / 1986 / HO / C

SUSAN MOORE *see Patti Sebring*

SUSAN MORNING
Resurrection Of Eve / 1973 / MIT / M

SUSAN MYERS
Young, Hot And Nasty / cr88 / BWV / C

SUSAN NADIR
A Scent Of Heather / 1981 / VXP / M

SUSAN NICOLE
Big Boob Bangeroo #1 / 1995 / TTV / M • Big Boob Bangeroo #4 / 1995 / TTV / M

SUSAN NILE

Erotic Dimensions: Explode / 1982 / NSV / M • Erotic Dimensions: Macho Women / 1982 / NSV / M

SUSAN NORRIS *see Star Index I*

SUSAN O'DAY *see Star Index I*

SUSAN PALMER
Spanking Video #1: Sports College / 1995 / MET / B • Spanking Video #4: Sports Comeback / 1995 / MET / B

SUSAN PETERS
Princess Seka / 1980 / VC / M

SUSAN PRESLEY *see Star Index I*

SUSAN RODGERS
Beach Bum Amateur's #02 / 1992 / MID / M

SUSAN ROSEBUSH *see Star Index I*

SUSAN SANDS
Love Roots / 1987 / LIM / M • Love Under 16 / cr75 / VST / M • Pleasure Productions #11 / 1985 / VCR / M • Rear Entry / 1985 / VCR / C

SUSAN SEAFORTH
Dear Throat / 1979 / HLV / M

SUSAN SHAW *see Star Index I*

SUSAN SHEA
New Faces, Hot Bodies #04 / 1992 / STP / M • New Faces, Hot Bodies #06 / 1993 / STP / M • New Faces, Hot Bodies #07 / 1993 / STP / M • New Faces, Hot Bodies #21 / 1996 / STP / C

SUSAN SHIELDS *see Sue Nero*

SUSAN SINCLAIR *see Star Index I*

SUSAN SLOAN *(Rose Cranston, Carol Russo, Iris Flouret, Judy Watt, Nova Kane, Carol Russa)*
Typical seventies flower child with a lithe teenage body, marginal skin, small tits, pretty face, short dark hair.
Angela, The Fireworks Woman / 1975 / VC / M • Anyone But My Husband / 1975 / VC / M • Heavy Load / 1975 / COM / M • Illusion Of Love / 1975 / COM / M • The Naughty Victorians / 1975 / VC / M • The Passions Of Carol / 1975 / VXP / M • Winter Heat / 1975 / AVC / M

SUSAN SMREKER *see Mimi Morgan*

SUSAN SONG-LI *see Star Index I*

SUSAN SPARKLE *see Star Index I*

SUSAN STEWART
Mantis In Lace / 1968 / BPI / S • Mona The Virgin Nymph / 1970 / ALP / M

SUSAN STRONG *see Star Index I*

SUSAN SUMMERS
R/H Productions #5001: A Friendly Encounter Of A Sexual Kind / 1995 / R/H / M

SUSAN SVELTE
Twilight Pink #1 / 1980 / AR / M

SUSAN TAYLOR *see Star Index I*

SUSAN TERETITOFF
They Shall Overcome / 1974 / VST / M

SUSAN THOMAS
Karla / 19?? / ... / M • Love Mexican Style / cr75 / BLT / M

SUSAN VEGAS *(Sharon Vegas, Susanne Vargas)*
Born May 7, 1955.
All The Right Motions / 1990 / DR / M • Bed, Butts & Breakfast / 1990 / LV / M • Behind Closed Doors / 1990 / VI / M • Behind You All The Way #1 / 1990 / SO / M • Behind You All The Way #2 / 1990 / SO / M • The Big E #09 / 1990 / BIZ / B • Black Mail / 1990 / TAO / C • Blackman & Anal Woman #2 / 1990 / PL / M • Bloopers #2 / 1991 / GO / C • Bums Away / 1995 / PRE / C • Butt's Motel #4 / 1989 / EX / M • Changing

Partners / 1989 / FAZ / M • Cheaters / 1990 / LE / M • Dead Ends / 1992 / PRE / B • Diedre In Danger / 1990 / VI / M • Dream Dates / 1990 / V99 / M • Dutch Masters / 1990 / IN / M • Feathermates / 1992 / PRE / B • Flood Control / 1992 / PRE / B • Girls Will Be Boys #2 / 1990 / PL / F • Great Balls Of Fire / 1989 / FAZ / M • The Hardriders / 1990 / 4P / M • Haunted Passions / 1990 / FC / M • Heart Of Stone / 1990 / FAN / M • Heraldo: Streetwalkers Of NY / 1990 / GOT / M • Hits & Misses / 1992 / PRE / B • Hollywood Knights #3 / 1991 / PCP / M • Home Maid Memories #1 / 1994 / BON / C • Hot Salsa / 1988 / AR / M • Hot Spot / 1990 / PL / F • In The Jeans / 1990 / ME / M • Internal Affair / 1990 / V99 / M • Itty Bitty Titty Committee #1 / 1990 / PL / F • Kinky Couples / 1990 / VD / M • Legs And Lingerie #2 / 1990 / BEB / F • Lesbian Lingerie Fantasy #2 / 1989 / ESP / F • Lesbian Lingerie Fantasy #3 / 1989 / ESP / F • Lickety Pink / 1990 / ME / M • National Poontang's Summer Vacation / 1990 / FC / M • Next Door Neighbors #21 / 1990 / BON / M • No Strings Attached / 1990 / ERO / M • Oral Addiction / 1989 / LV / M • Paradise Road / 1990 / WV / M • Passion From Behind / 1990 / LV / M • Rare Ends / 1996 / PRE / C • Santa Comes Again / 1990 / GLE / M • Sea Of Lust / 1990 / FAN / M • Sex Lives On Porno Tape / 1992 / VC / C • Sex On Location / 1989 / KIS / M • Shadow Dancers #1 / 1989 / EA / M • Shadow Dancers #2 / 1989 / EA / M • Sharon And Karen / 1989 / LV / G • The Shaving / 1989 / SO / M • Single Girl Masturbation #3 / 1989 / ESP / F • The Smart Ass #1 / 1990 / VT / M • The Smart Ass #2: Rusty's Revenge / 1990 / VT / M • Sorceress / 1990 / GO / M • Susan & Steve Vegas Bound For You / 199? / BON / B • Talk Dirty To Me #07 / 1990 / DR / M • Untamed Passion / 1991 / VEX / M • Virgin Busters / 1989 / LV / M • When Larry Ate Sally / 1989 / EX / M • The Whore / 1989 / CA / M • Wildfire / 1989 / EVN / M • Wise Ass! / 1990 / FH / M • Young Cheeks / 1990 / BEB / B

SUSAN VEGAS (OTHER)
Hot Channels / 1973 / AR / M

SUSAN WALLACE
Stacey's Hot Rod / 1983 / CV / M

SUSAN WEST *see Star Index I*

SUSAN WHITE
Finger Pleasures #1 / 1995 / PL / F • Housemother's Discipline #6 / 1994 / RB / B • Scream Queen's Naked Christmas / 1996 / AHE / C • Shaved #07 / 1995 / RB / F

SUSAN WILDE
Come Get Me / 1983 / VEL / M • Confessions Of A Nymph / 1985 / VCR / M • The Erotic World Of Rene Summers / 1984 / VCR / C • Virginia / 1983 / CA / M

SUSAN WONG *see Star Index I*

SUSAN YAMA *see Star Index I*

SUSANA DEL ALBA
Club Privado / 1995 / KP / M

SUSANNA
New Faces, Hot Bodies #18 / 1995 / STP / M • Wrasslin She-Babes #08 / 1996 / SOW / M

SUSANNA BRITTON *(Barbara Peckinpaugh)*
Blonde, looks a little like Robin Everette.
Bad Girls #2 / 1983 / GO / M • Basic Train-

ing / 1984 / VES / S • Best Chest In The West / 1984 / ACV / S • The Blonde Goddess / 1982 / VXP / M • Body Double / 1984 / C3S / S • Erotic Images / 1983 / VES / S • Homework / 1982 / MCA / S • Love Skills: A Guide To The Pleasures Of Sex / 1984 / MCA / S • Lust And The Law / 1991 / GO / C • Penthouse: Love Stories / 1986 / A*V / S • Roller Blade / 1985 / NWW / S • Shadows Run Black / 1984 / VES / S • The Witching / 1972 / PAV / S • [Nudes In Limbo / 1983 / ... / S

SUSANNA CANTONA
The Joy Club / 1996 / XC / M

SUSANNA CARLI
Sex Penitentiary / 1996 / XC / M

SUSANNA CATONE
A Merry Widow / 1996 / SPI / M

SUSANNA FRENCH *see Suzannah French*

SUSANNA KATONA
Midnight Obsession / 1995 / XC / M • Prima #09: ASSassins / 1995 / MBP / M

SUSANNA KRISTINA
Hamlet: For The Love Of Ophelia #1 / 1996 / IP / M

SUSANNA LETTIERI
Paprika / 1995 / XC / M

SUSANNAH DYER *see Star Index I*

SUSANNAH FRENCH *see Suzannah French*

SUSANNAH WEST *see Star Index I*

SUSANNE
Erika Bella: Euroslut / 1995 / EL / M • Hot New Imports / 1996 / XC / M • Magma: Body Cocktails / 1995 / MET / M • Magma: Claudine In Action / 1996 / MET / M • Magma: Test Fuck / 1995 / MET / M

SUSANNE BRECHT
10 Years Of Big Busts #2 / 1990 / BTO / C • Big Boobs Around The World #1 / 1990 / BTO / M • Bosom Buddies / 1990 / BTO / F • H&S: Susanne Brecht / 199? / H&S / S • The World Of Double-D #1 / 199? / H&S / S

SUSANNE LOUISE
Erotic Dimensions: A Woman's Lust / 1982 / NSV / M

SUSANNE SILK
Erotic Dimensions: A Woman's Lust / 1982 / NSV / M

SUSANNE VARGAS *see Susan Vegas*

SUSAYE LONDON
Centerfold Fever / 1981 / VXP / M • Chorus Call / 1978 / TVX / M • Exploring Young Girls / 1978 / ALP / M • Fiona On Fire / 1978 / VC / M • Take Off / 1978 / VXP / M • Teenage Runaways / 1977 / WWV / M • Visions / 1977 / QX / M

SUSHI
Q Balls #1 / 1996 / TTV / M • Q Balls #2 / 1996 / TTV / M

SUSHI YUNG
Tokohama Mamma / 1994 / ORE / C

SUSI
Sleeping Booty / 1995 / EL / M • Sodomania: Slop Shots / 1996 / EL / C

SUSI DEWALL *see Star Index I*

SUSI SUSHI *see Star Index I*

SUSIE
Blue Vanities #515 / 1992 / FFL / M • Blue Vanities #568 / 1995 / FFL / M • Crazy On You / 1991 / IF / M • Hollywood Amateurs #04 / 1994 / MID / M • Hot Legs #2 / 1990 / PLV / B • Mr. Peepers Amateur Home Videos #25: The 25th Anniversary Ed /

1991 / LBO / M • Nasty Jack's Kloset Klassics #03 / 1991 / CDI / M • Sweet Sunshine / 1995 / IF / M

SUSIE CARLSON *see Star Index I*

SUSIE GOLD
Dr Love And His House Of Perversions / 1978 / VC / M

SUSIE MID-AMERICA *see Suzie Cassidy*

SUSIE NG
Pai Gow Video #08: Asian Fantasies / 1995 / EVN / M

SUSIE Q.
Mr. Peepers Nastiest #6 / 1995 / LBO / C

SUSIE SIPES *see Summer Rose*

SUSIE SUCKER
The Coming Of Angie / cr73 / TGA / M

SUSIE SUNG LEE *see Suzy Lee*

SUSIE WALKE
Swap Meet / 1984 / VD / M

SUSSIE TELL
Swedish Vip Magazine #1 / 1995 / PL / M • Swedish Vip Magazine #2 / 1995 / PL / M

SUSY BARON
The Love Couch / 1977 / VC / M

SUSY DEWS
Vanessa's Hot Nights / 1984 / SVE / M

SUSY REYNOLDS
Erotic Fantasies #6 / 1984 / CV / C

SUTA
Joe Elliot's College Girls #28 / 1994 / JOE / M

SUZAN KANE
Spanking In Shining Armor / 1995 / IBN / B

SUZANNAH
New Faces, Hot Bodies #20 / 1996 / STP / M • Private Film #02 / 1993 / OD / M

SUZANNAH ASH
Little Darlings / 1981 / VEP / M

SUZANNAH FRENCH *(Susanna French, Susannah French)*
Horse faced blonde with large droopy tits and a womanly body. Was married to Billy Dee at one stage.
All Day Suckers / cr77 / BOC / M • Any Time, Any Place / 1981 / CA0 / M • Aunt Peg's Fulfillment / 1980 / CV / M • Behind The Scenes Of An Adult Movie / 1983 / CV / M • Blazing Zippers / 1974 / SE / M • Blondes Have More Fun / 1980 / SE / M • Casanova #2 / 1976 / CA / M • Classic Erotica #3 / 1980 / SVE / M • Erotic Fantasies #2 / 1983 / CV / C • Erotic Fantasies #3 / 1983 / CV / C • Jawbreakers / 1985 / VEN / C • My First Time / 1976 / GO / M • Only The Best #1 / 1986 / CV / C • Only The Best #2 / 1989 / CV / C • The Other Side Of Julie / 1978 / CV / M • Skin On Skin / 1981 / CV / M • Stormy / 1980 / CV / M • Swedish Erotica #12 / 1980 / CA / M • Swedish Erotica #22 / 1980 / CA / M • Swedish Erotica #30 / 1980 / CA / M • Swedish Erotica #51 / 1983 / CA / M • Taboo #07 / 1980 / IN / M • Undulations / 1980 / VC / M • Wicked Sensations #1 / 1981 / CA / M

SUZANNE
Blue Vanities #511 / 1992 / FFL / M • HomeGrown Video #461: Splendor In The Grasp / 1995 / HOV / M • Magma: Sperm Dreams / 1990 / MET / M

SUZANNE (BRAZIL)
Max World #4: Let's Party / 1996 / XPR / M

SUZANNE ALEXANDER *see Marie Mason*

SUZANNE BLAKE *see Star Index I*

SUZANNE CHARMAINE

Fastlane Fuck-Holes! / 1994 / MET / M •
Supercharger / cr75 / CV / M

SUZANNE CHASE
Shake Well Before Using / 9990 / LV / M •
Titty-Titty Bang-Bang / 1992 / FC / C •
Toys, Not Boys #3 / 1991 / FC / C • A Trip
Down Mammary Lane / 1991 / FC / M

SUZANNE CHEESE
Command Performance / cr75 / LA / M •
Prey Of A Call Girl / 1975 / ALP / M

SUZANNE FIELDS see Cindy Stokes

SUZANNE HAMILTON see Star Index I

SUZANNE HOPPER
Overnight Sensation / 1976 / AR / M

SUZANNE MYERS see Cris Cassidy

SUZANNE PERRY
GVC: Private Nurses #126 / cr84 / GO / M

SUZANNE RAVEN see Star Index I

SUZANNE RAY
Sharon In The Rough-House / 1976 / LA /
M

SUZANNE RIVER
Resurrection Of Eve / 1973 / MIT / M

SUZANNE SILK see Star Index I

SUZANNE ST LORRAINE
Bad Medicine / 1990 / VEX / M • Blue Fire
/ 1991 / V99 / M • College Girl / 1990 / VEX
/ M • Delicate Matters / 1989 / VEX / M •
Hidden Pleasures / 1990 / VEX / M • Inti-
mate Affairs / 1990 / VEX / M • Kinky
Nurses / 1995 / VEX / C • Knights In Black
Satin / 1990 / VEX / M • Living In Sin / 1990
/ VEX / M • Night Watch / 1990 / VEX / M •
Passion Princess / 1991 / VEX / M • Per-
fect Girl / 1991 / VEX / M • Playing The
Field / 1990 / VEX / M • Secret Dreams /
1991 / VEX / M • Secret Obsession / 1990
/ V99 / M • Summer Dreams / 1990 / VEX
/ M • Suzanne's Grand Affair / 1990 / CV /
M • Sweet Tease / 1990 / VEX / M

SUZANNE TANNORIE see Star Index I

SUZANNE TYSON see Star Index I

SUZANNE VEGAS
Reel Classics #3 / 1996 / H&S / M

SUZANNE WRIGHT see Cris Cassidy

SUZE
Barby's On Butt Row / 1996 / ABS / M •
The Voyeur #7: Live In Europe #1 / 1996 /
JLP / M

SUZE RANDALL
Electric Blue #006 / 1982 / CA / S • Electric
Blue: Wickedly Wild West / 1985 / CA / C •
Erotic Eye / 1995 / DGD / S • Kiss And Tell
/ 1980 / CA / M • Miss Passion / 1984 / VD
/ M • Not A Love Story / 1980 / ... / M •
Suze's Centerfolds #9 / 1985 / CA / M

SUZETTE
Blue Vanities #116 / 1988 / FFL / M •
Bondage Classix #05: Painful Lesson /
198? / BON / B • Bucky Beaver's XXX
Dragon Art Theatre Double Feature #03 /
1996 / SOW / M • First Training / 1987 / BIZ
/ B • Girls Of The Ivy League / 1994 / NIV /
F • Glittering Gartered Girls / 1993 / RSV /
B • Long Legged Ladies / 1993 / VER / M •
Mr. Peepors Amateur Home Movies #24:
The Sleazy Riders / 1991 / LBO / M •
Nookie Professor #1 / 1996 / AVS / M • Old
Bitches / 1996 / GLI / M • Peek-A-Boo /
1953 / SOW / S • School Dayze / 1987 /
BON / B • School For Hookers / 1974 /
SOW / M • Sorority Lingerie Party / 1995 /
NIV / F • The Ultimate Master / cr87 / BIZ /
B

**SUZETTE ALEXANDER see Marie
Mason**

SUZETTE HOLLAND see Cris Cassidy

SUZETTE JONES see Star Index I

SUZETTE LEFEVRE see Fi Fi Bardot

SUZETTE WEST
Blue Vanities #585 / 1996 / FFL / M

SUZI
The Adventures Of Buttgirl & Wonder
Wench / 1991 / AFV / M • Into The Gap /
1991 / LE / M • New Faces, Hot Bodies #22
/ 1996 / STP / M • Prescription For Pain #3:
Bad Medicine / 1993 / BON / B

SUZI BARTLETT
Behind The Backdoor #3 / 1989 / EVN / M
• Beyond Innocence / 1990 / VCR / F •
Forced Love / 1990 / LV / M • Girls Gone
Bad #2: The Breakout / 1990 / GO / F •
Heather's Home Movies / 1989 / VWA / M
• Hot Talk Radio / 1989 / VWA / M • King
Tung: Bustin' The Royal Hienies / 1990 /
LA / M • Midnight Fire / 1990 / HU / M • My
Friend, My Lover / 1990 / FIR / M •
Odyssey 30 Min: #102: / 1991 / OD / F •
Secretaries / 1990 / PL / F • Sno Bunnies /
1990 / PL / F • Sorceress / 1990 / GO / M •
Star 90 / 1990 / CAY / M • Tit Tales #1 /
1989 / 4P / M • Tit Tales #2 / 1990 / FC / M
• A Touch Of Gold / 1990 / IN / M • Toys,
Not Boys #1 / 1991 / FC / C • Toys, Not
Boys #3 / 1991 / FC / C • The Two Janes /
1990 / WV / M

SUZI CHONG
The Burma Road #4 / 1996 / LBO / C

SUZI FLYNT
Sugar In The Raw / 1975 / AVC / M

SUZI HART see Susan Hart

SUZI J. see Penny Lane

SUZI LEE
Joe Elliot's College Girls #43 / 1996 / JOE
/ M

SUZI MAY see Star Index I

SUZI SPARKS
10 Years Of Big Busts #3 / 199? / BTO / C
• Breast Worx #01 / 1991 / LBO / M •
Golden Nuggets #13: The Celebration /
1990 / H&S / S • Introducing Suzie Sparks
/ 199? / H&S / S • My Dinner With Suzie
Sparks / 199? / H&S / S • The Very Best Of
Breasts #2 / 1996 / H&S / S

SUZI SWALLOW
Dance Beaver / 1995 / CZV / M

SUZI WAHL
Kim's Convention Couples / 1995 / VAL / M

SUZI WEST see Star Index I

SUZIE
America's Raunchiest Home Videos #05:
Sasha Gets Stuffed / 1992 / ZA / M • AVP
#9136: Solo Suzie / 1990 / AVP / F • Blow
Out / 1991 / IF / M • Horny For Anal / 1995
/ TIE / M • Kinky College Cunts #03 / 1993
/ NS / F • Kinky College Cunts #08 / 1993 /
NS / F • Kinky College Cunts #11 / 1993 /
NS / M • Kinky College Cunts #18 / 1993 /
NS / F • Neighborhood Watch #14: The
Beaver Cleaver / 1991 / LBO / M

SUZIE BOOBIES
Big Boob Lottery / 1993 / BTO / M • Big
Boob Tease / 1993 / NAP / F • Big Bust
Scream Queens / 1994 / BTO / M • Girls
Around The World #04 / 1991 / BTO / M •
Heavenly Bodies / 1993 / NAP / B • South-
ern: Previews #1 / 1992 / SSH / C • Viva Vi-
viana / 1994 / PME / F

SUZIE CASSIDY *(Suzie Mid-America,*
Susie Mid-America)
Formerly a reviewer for the industry advertis-
ing magazine. Long crinkly reddish-blonde

hair, white skin, passable face, small tits,
lithe body, and a very dark tattoo on her left
tit.
Dirty Dancers #6 / 1995 / 4P / M • Young &
Natural #07 / 1995 / PRE / F • Young &
Natural #09 / 1995 / PRE / C • Young &
Natural #10 / 1995 / PRE / F • Young &
Natural #11 / 1995 / PRE / F • Young & Nat-
ural #18 / 1996 / TV / C

SUZIE FANTASY
Positively Pagan #05 / 1993 / ATA / M

SUZIE FARRELL
Loose Times At Ridley High / 1984 / VCX /
M • Personal Touch #2 / 1983 / AR / M

SUZIE HOMEMAKER
The Trainers / cr83 / BIZ / B

SUZIE HUMPHREE see Susan McBain

SUZIE HUNTER see Star Index I

SUZIE MATHEWS *(Cindy (Suzie Mathew),*
Gretchen (Suzie Mat))
Blonde with a rectangular body and small tits.
The Adventures Of Buttwoman #2: Behind
Bars / 1992 / EL / F • Arsenal Of Fear /
1993 / BS / B • Blame It On Bambi / 1992 /
BS / B • Bobby Hollander's Rookie Nookie
#07 / 1993 / SFP / M • Bruce Seven: A
Compendium Of His Most Graphic Scenes
Vol 6 / 1994 / BS / C • Butt Freak #1 / 1992
/ EA / M • Buttman Vs Buttwoman / 1992 /
EL / M • Buttman's Revenge / 1992 / EA /
M • Buttslammers #03: The Ultimate
Dream / 1993 / BS / F • Buttslammers #06:
Over The Edge / 1994 / BS / F • The Ec-
stasy Of Payne / 1994 / BS / B • Mike Hott:
Apple Asses #05 / 1992 / MHV / F • Mis-
tress Gretchen And Christy / 1993 / BON /
B • Party Of Payne / 1993 / BS / B • Shine
My Chrome / 1993 / BON / B • Stevi's:
Cindy's Pantyhose Tease / 1994 / SSV / F
• Stevi's: Foot Sex / 1994 / SSV / F •
Stevi's: Pantyhose Seduction / 1995 / SSV
/ F • Stevi's: Stevi's XXX Sex Previews /
1995 / SSV / C • Stevi's: Suzie Mathews'
Dirty Home Movie / 1993 / SSV / M • Takin'
It To The Limit #1 / 1994 / BS / M • VGA:
Bureau Of Discipline #2 / 1993 / VGA / B •
Whacked! / 1993 / BS / B

SUZIE MERCEDES
The Anal Adventures Of Max Hardcore:
Hombre / 1995 / ZA / M • The Hitch-Hiker
#12: Southern Exposure / 1995 / VIM / M

SUZIE MID-AMERICA see Suzie Cassidy

SUZIE MITCHELL see Star Index I

SUZIE MUFFET see Star Index I

SUZIE Q
Lingerie Dreams #2 / 1994 / PHV / F •
Nasty Calendar / 1991 / XPI / M • The
Wright Stuff / 1991 / AFV / M

SUZIE SPARKLE see Nancy Dare

SUZIE SUZUKI *(Cherry Blossom)*
Older-looking Oriental with medium tits and a
lithe body.
Adam & Eve's House Party #2: Bachelor
Party / 1996 / VC / M • Anal Hanky-Panky /
1997 / ROB / M • Anal Load Lickers / 1996
/ ROB / M • Anal Tight Ass / 1995 / ROB /
M • Anal Toy Story / 1996 / MP0 / M • Anal
Tramps / 1996 / LIP / F • Anal Trashy Ass /
1995 / ROB / M • Asian Exotica / 1995 /
EVN / M • Assy Sassy #3 / 1995 / ROB / F
• Bangkok Boobarella / 1996 / BTO / M •
Bangkok Dreams / 1996 / SUF / M • Be-
yond Reality #3: Stand Erect! / 1996 / EXQ
/ M • Black & Booty-Full / 1996 / ROB / M •
Cheek To Cheek / 1997 / EL / M • Debu-
tante Dreams / 1995 / 4P / M • Deep Dish

Booty Pie / 1996 / ROB / M • Dick & Jane Go To Hong Kong / 1995 / AVI / M • Dim Sum (Eating Chinese) / 1996 / SUF / M • Far East Fantasy / 1995 / SUF / M • Her Name Is Asia / 1996 / SUF / M • The Hungry Heart / 1996 / AOP / M • In The Line Of Desire / 1996 / MID / M • Lotus / 1996 / VI / M • Malibu Ass Blasters / 1996 / ROB / M • More Dirty Debutantes #41 / 1995 / 4P / M • Nasty Nymphos #12 / 1996 / ANA / M • Over Eighteen #02 / 1997 / HW / M • Pai Gow Video #10: Asian Vacation / 1995 / EVN / M • Rectal Raiders / 1997 / ROB / M • Streets Of New York #08 / 1996 / PL / M • Suzi Bungholeo / 1995 / ROB / M • Suzi's Wild Anal Ride / 1997 / ROB / M • Takin' It To The Limit #9: Rear Action View / 1996 / BS / M • The Twin Peaks Of Mount Fuji / 1996 / SUF / M • Virgin Dreams / 1996 / EA / M • World Famous Dirty Debutantes / 1995 / 4P / S • Yin Yang Oriental Love Bang #1 / 1996 / SUF / M • Yin Yang Oriental Love Bang #3: Bangkok Dreams / 1996 / SUF / M

SUZIE WONG
Burning Desire / 1983 / HO / M • Toys, Not Boys #3 / 1991 / FC / C

SUZY
The All-Conference Nude Workout / 1995 / NIV / S • Blue Vanities #501 / 1992 / FFL / M • Full Moon Video #01: Suzy's Backseat Blow-Jobs / 1994 / FAP / M • Mr. Peepers Amateur Home Videos #03: Satin 'n' Face / 1991 / LBO / M • Mr. Peepers Nastiest #5 / 1995 / LBO / C

SUZY ANDERSSON see Star Index I
SUZY BARRETT
Blue Vanities #514 / 1992 / FFL / M
SUZY CAT see Suzy Gato
SUZY CHANG
Mr. Peepers Amateur Home Videos #14: Gushing Pussy / 1991 / LBO / M
SUZY CHUNG
The Kowloon Connection / 1973 / VCX / M • Oriental Kitten / 1973 / VCX / M
SUZY GATO (Suzy Cat)
Long straight reddish brown/black hair, large eyes, medium/large tits, passable face, lithe body, tall. Seems enthusiastic. Probably Hispanic although her first movies seemed to be Hungarian.
Amateur Lusty Latins #2 / 1997 / SUF / M • Asses Galore #6: Fallen Angels / 1996 / DFI / M • Diamonds / 1996 / HDE / M • Essence Of A Woman / 1995 / ONA / M • Gangbang Girl #19 / 1996 / ANA / M • Sodomania #17: Simply Makes U Tingle / 1996 / EL / M • Somewhere Under The Rainbow #1 / 1995 / HW / M • White Men Can't Iron On Butt Row / 1997 / ABS / M • World Sex Tour #1 / 1995 / ANA / M • World Sex Tour #2 / 1995 / ANA / M
SUZY HUMPFREE see Susan McBain
SUZY KAYE
A Girl Like That / 1979 / CDC / M • The Sexpert / 1975 / VEP / M
SUZY LEE (Susie Sung Lee, Sue Lee (Suzy))
The Erotic Adventures Of Chi Chi Chan / 1988 / VWA / M • Heather / 1989 / VWA / M • The Pleasure Chest / 1988 / VWA / M • Prescription For Passion / 1984 / VD / M
SUZY MANDEL
Blonde Ambition / 1981 / QX / M • Confessions Of A Driving Instructor / 1976 / ... / S • Intimate Games / 1976 / ... / S • The Play-

birds / 1978 / ... / S
SUZY Q
Anita / 1996 / BLC / M
SUZY Q see Laurel Canyon
SUZY REYNOLDS see Star Index I
SUZY ROSS
[Oral Models / 197? / ... / M
SUZY SPAIN see Tanya Fox
SUZY SPATZ see Star Index I
SUZY ST JAMES see Krystina King
SUZY STARR see Star Index I
SUZY SUITE
Foreplay / 1982 / VC / M
SUZY WHITEBOND
Marilyn Chambers' Private Fantasies #4 / 1983 / CA / M
SUZZETTE
Girls On Girls / 1983 / VC / F
SVEN
100% Amateur #19: / 1996 / OD / M
SVEN CHRISTIAN see Ray Dennis Steckler
SVEN JENSEN
Tight Delight / 1985 / VXP / M • [So Many Men, So Little Time / 19?? / BL / G
SVEN STROBYE
Sexual Customs In Scandinavia / cr73 / QX / M
SVENA
Girlfriends / 1983 / MIT / M • Hustler Video Magazine #1 / 1983 / SE / M
SVETA
Private Gold #11: The Pyramid #1 / 1996 / OD / M • Russian Model Magazine #1 / 1996 / IP / M
SVETLANA
F / 1980 / GO / M • Russian Model Magazine #2 / 1996 / IP / M
SWALLO see Star Index I
SWAN
Fantasy Photography: Afternoon Delights / 1995 / FAP / F
SWEEDEN KAJ see Star Index I
SWEET 'N LO
Throbbing Threesomes / 1996 / NIT / M
SWEET CHARITY see Star Index I
SWEET CHASTITY see Star Index I
SWEET HART see Star Index I
SWEET JANINE
Ona Zee's Learning The Ropes #07: At Lady Laura's / 1992 / ONA / B
SWEET LORRAINE
Black 'n' White In Color / 1987 / VCR / C • Foxy Brown / 1984 / VC / M • The Seduction Of Lana Shore / 1984 / PL / M
SWEET SUE
Blue Vanities #584 / 1996 / FFL / M
SWEETIE PIE see Sweety Py
SWEETNESS see Star Index I
SWEETY PY (Sweetie Pie, Tetra Dearr, Tedra Dear, Tedra DeArr, Dixie Downes, Tedra, Juliette (Sweety Py))
Tall blonde with a womanly body, small droopy tits, big butt, marginal face, lots of cellulite in butt and upper thighs. Has two kids of school age.
Adventures Of The DP Boys: D.P. Nurses / 1995 / HW / M • The All Girl Anal Orgy / 1996 / BAC / F • Anal Anonymous / 1995 / SO / M • Anal Camera #06 / 1995 / EVN / M • Anal Crybabies / 1996 / BAC / M • Anal Maidens Three / 1996 / BOT / M • Anal Misconduct / 1995 / VD / M • Analtown USA #02 / 1995 / NIT / M • Another Fuckin' Anal Movie / 1996 / ROB / M • Ass Masters (Leisure) #02 / 1995 / LEI / M • Ateball:

More Than A Mouthful / 1995 / ATE / F • Babenet / 1995 / VC / M • Bad Attitude #2 / 1995 / LV / M • Bad To The Bone / 1996 / ULP / M • Bang City #1: Kelly's Anal Gang Bang / 1995 / SC / M • Bang City #6: Bugger's Banquet / 1995 / SC / M • Bareback / 1996 / LE / M • Beyond Reality #2: Anal Expedition / 1996 / EXQ / M • Bitches In Heat #1: Locked In the Basement / 1995 / ZA / M • Black Hose Bag / 1996 / ROB / M • Blonde In Blue Flannel / 1995 / CA / M • The Blowjob Adventures Of Doctor Fellatio / 1997 / EL / M • Boudoir Babe / 1996 / VMX / M • Broken Vows / 1996 / ULP / M • Butt Alley / 1995 / VMX / M • Buttman's Big Butt Backdoor Babes / 1995 / EA / M • Carnal Country / 1996 / NIT / M • Caught From Behind #20 / 1995 / HO / M • Cum Buttered Corn Holes #1 / 1996 / NIT / C • Cum On Inn / 1995 / TEG / M • Deep Inside Anal Camera / 1996 / EVN / C • Deep Waterworld / 1995 / HW / M • Dementia / 1995 / IP / M • Dildo Debutantes / 1995 / CA / F • Dixie Downes Gang Bang / 1996 / FC / M • DPTV: Double Penetration Television / 1996 / SUF / M • Dream Butt / 1995 / VMX / M • Dream Reamin' / 1995 / LV / M • Fashion Sluts #1 / 1995 / ABS / M • Flappers / 1995 / EMC / M • Frendz? #2 / 1996 / RAS / M • The Happy Office / 1996 / NIT / M • Hardcore Fantasies #3 / 1996 / LV / M • Hollywood Amateurs #15 / 1995 / MID / M • Hollywood Amateurs #23 / 1995 / MID / M • Hollywood Amateurs #26 / 1995 / MID / M • Horny Henry's Snowballing Adventure / 1995 / TTV / M • In The Crack / 1995 / VMX / M • Inspector Croissant: The Case Of The Missing Pinky / 1995 / FC / M • Interview's Anal Queens / 1996 / LV / M • Interview's Hard Bodied Harlots / 1996 / LV / M • Interview: Bun Busters / 1995 / LV / M • Ir4: Inrearendence Day / 1996 / HW / M • It Could Happen To You / 1996 / HW / M • A Lady / 1995 / FD / M • Lady Luck / 1995 / PMV / M • Lesbian Debutante #01 / 1996 / IP / F • Mike Hott: #320 Three-Sum Sluts #06 / 1995 / MHV / M • More Than A Mouthful #1 / 1995 / VEX / F • Nasty Newcummers #09 / 1995 / MET / M • New Pussy Hunt #25 / 1996 / LEI / C • Nikki Arizona's Tomboys / 1995 / GAL / M • Oh My Gush / 1995 / OD / M • The Oh! Zone / 1995 / VC / M • Party Girl / 1995 / LV / M • Patty Plenty's Gang Bang / 1995 / NIT / M • Perverted Stories #01 / 1995 / JMP / M • Peyton's Place / 1996 / ULP / M • Pierced Punctured And Perverted / 1995 / FC / M • Pounding Ass / 1995 / VMX / M • Pussyman Auditions #04 / 1995 / SNA / M • The Real Deal #2 / 1995 / FC / M • Release Me / 1996 / VT / M • Ron Hightower's Casting Couch #1 / 1995 / FC / M • Rump Man: Sex On The Beach / 1995 / HW / M • Samantha & Company / 1996 / PL / M • Tails From The Crack / 1995 / HW / M • Takin' It To The Limit #9: Rear Action View / 1996 / BS / M • Talking Trash #1 / 1995 / HW / M • Tight Fit #14 / 1995 / GO / M • The Tigress / 1995 / VIM / M • Tripper Stripper / 1995 / VMX / M • Venom #7 / 1996 / VD / M • Waterworld Deep / 1995 / HW / M
SWETTA SILVESTRU
Jungle Heat / 1995 / LUM / M
SWIE OBERMAN
Inside Marilyn / 1984 / CA / M
SY KATZ

The Unholy Child / 1972 / AVC / M
SYBELLE DENNIGER *see* Sybil Danning
SYBIL DANNING *(Sybil Danninger, Sybelle Denniger)*
Sybil Danninger is from **The Long Swift Sword Of Siegfried**.
Amazon Women On The Moon / 1987 / MCA / S • Bluebeard / 1972 / LIV / S • Chained Heat #1 / 1983 / VES / S • The Erotic Adventures Of Pinocchio / 1971 / JLT / S • Famous T & A / 1982 / WIZ / C • The Long Swift Sword Of Siegfried / 1971 / SOW / S • Malibu Express / 1984 / MCA / S • Panther Squad / 1984 / VES / S • Phantom Empire / 1987 / PRS / S • Reform School Girls / 1986 / NWW / S • The Tomb / 1986 / TRW / S • Warrior Queen / 1987 / VES / S • Young Lady Chatterly #2 / 1985 / LIV / S
SYBIL DANNINGER *see* Sybil Danning
SYBIL HARTLEY
San Francisco Lesbians #5 / 1994 / PL / F • San Francisco Lesbians #6 / 1994 / PL / F
SYBIL KIDD *see* Anthony Spinelli
SYBIL LANSON
Private Video Magazine #10 / 1994 / OD / M
SYBIL WRAP *see* Star Index I
SYBILLE LANSON
Private Film #10 / 1994 / OD / M
SYDNEY
Butt Freak #2 / 1996 / EA / M • Casting Call #14 / 1995 / SO / M • HomeGrown Video #434: Forrest Hump / 1994 / HOV / M • Lovers, An Intimate Portrait #1: Sydney & Ray / 1993 / FEM / M • Tailz From Da Hood #4 / 1996 / AVI / M
SYDNEY BROOKS
Buffy Malibu's Nasty Girls #10 / 1996 / ANA / F • Buttslammers #12: Anal Madness / 1996 / BS / F
SYDNEY DANCE *(Dominique Bouche, Sydney Sanchez, Sydney Grace, Tiffany Torres, Danger, Marie Monelle, Dominique Torres, Harmony (Sydney D))*
Pudgy fat faced, not too pretty brunette with a flat ass. 23 years old in 1993 and was de-virginized at 17.
Alice In Analand / 1994 / SC / M • Amateurs Exposed #05 / 1995 / CV / M • Anal Delinquent #2 / 1994 / ROB / M • Anal Hunger / 1994 / ROB / M • Anal Innocence #2 / 1993 / ROB / M • Anal Knights In Hollywood #1 / 1993 / MET / M • Anal Overtures / 1993 / AFD / M • Anal Rampage #2 / 1993 / ROB / M • Anal Rookies #2 / 1994 / ROB / M • Anal Virgins Of America #05 / 1993 / FOR / M • Anal Vision #13 / 1993 / LBO / M • Anal Vision #14 / 1993 / LBO / M • Aroused #1 / 1994 / VI / M • Bachelor Party #2 / 1993 / FPI / M • Beach Ball / 1994 / SC / M • Big Bust Babes #17 / 1993 / AFI / M • Big Bust Babes #19 / 1994 / AFI / M • Big Knockers #05 / 1994 / TV / M • Big Knockers #07 / 1994 / TV / M • Big Knockers #09 / 1995 / TV / M • Big Knockers #20 / 1995 / TV / C • Bobby Hollander's Sweet Cheeks #111 / 1994 / WV / M • The Bottom Dweller Part Deux / 1994 / EL / M • The Breast Of Breastmen / 1995 / EVN / C • The Bridges Of Anal County / 1996 / PVO / C • Busty Babes In Heat #1 / 1993 / BTO / M • The Busty Foxxxes Of Napali Video / 1994 /

NAP / F • Buttman's Inferno / 1993 / EA / M • Buttslammers #06: Over The Edge / 1994 / BS / F • Cherry Poppers #03: School's Out / 1994 / ZA / M • Chinatown / 1994 / SC / M • Creme De La Face #02 / 1994 / OD / M • The Devil In Grandma Jones / 1994 / FC / M • Dick & Jane Go To Mexico / 1994 / AVI / M • Different Strokes / 1994 / PRE / B • Dirty Dating Service #03 / 1994 / WP / M • Double D Amateurs #04 / 1993 / JMP / M • Double D Amateurs #11 / 1993 / JMP / M • Double D Dykes #13 / 1994 / GO / F • Double D Housewives / 1994 / PV / M • Double Penetration Virgins #05: Go To Hell / 1994 / BB0 / M • Erotic Newcummers Vol 1 #1: Capitol Desires / 1993 / DR / M • Erotic Newcummers Vol 1 #2: Texas Twisters / 1993 / DR / M • F-Channel / 1994 / AFV / F • Gang Bang Bitches #03 / 1994 / PP / M • Gang Bang Bitches #10 / 1995 / PP / M • Gang Bang Diaries #2 / 1993 / SFP / M • Gang Bang Jizz Jammers / 1994 / ROB / M • Gas Works / 1994 / PRE / B • The Girls From Hootersville #03 / 1993 / SFP / M • Glitz Tits #07 / 1993 / GLI / M • Glitz Tits #08 / 1994 / GLI / M • Gonzo Groups & Gang Bangs / 1994 / GLI / M • Greek Week / 1994 / CV / M • Harry Horndog #22: Huge Hooters / 1993 / ZA / M • Hispanic Orgies #06 / 1993 / GO / M • Hispanic Orgies #07 / 1994 / GO / M • Hot Wishes / 1995 / LE / M • Interview With A Vamp / 1994 / ANA / M • Ladies Room / 1994 / SC / F • M Series #17 / 1993 / LBO / M • Nasty Newcummers #03 / 1994 / MET / M • Nasty Nymphos #02 / 1994 / ANA / M • Odyssey Triple Play #80: Couple Play / 1994 / OD / M • Open Lips / 1994 / WV / M • Private Video Magazine #09 / 1994 / OD / M • Pussyclips #03 / 1994 / SNA / M • Pussyman #07: On The Dark Side / 1994 / SNA / M • Red Light / 1994 / SC / S • The Room Mate / 1995 / EX / M • Rosie: The Neighborhood Slut / 1994 / VIM / M • Rump Humpers #18 / 1994 / GLI / M • Sarah Jane's Love Bunnies #04 / 1993 / FPI / F • Secret Rendez-Vous / 1994 / XCI / M • Sex In Dangerous Places / 1994 / OD / M • Sex Secrets Of High Priced Call Girls / 1995 / MID / M • Sexual Trilogy #01 / 1993 / SFP / M • Sexual Trilogy #05 / 1994 / SFP / M • Sista Act / 1994 / AVI / M • So I Married A Lesbian / 9993 / WV / M • Student Fetish Videos: Spanking #16 / 1994 / PRE / B • Student Fetish Videos: Tickling #10 / 1994 / SFV / B • Taboo #13 / 1994 / IN / M • Tail Taggers #103 / 1993 / WV / M • Tail Taggers #107 / 1993 / WV / M • Tail Taggers #109 / 1993 / WV / M • Tail Taggers #120 / 1994 / WV / M • Takin' It To The Limit #1 / 1994 / BS / M • Taxi Girls #3: Killer On The Loose / 1993 / MED / M • Triple Flay / 1995 / PRE / B • Triple Play / 1994 / PRE / B • Video Virgins #09 / 1993 / NS / M • Video Virgins #10 / 1993 / NS / M • Vivid At Home #01 / 1994 / VI / M • Wild Orgies #02 / 1994 / AFI / M • Willie Wanker And The Fun Factory / 1994 / FD / M
SYDNEY GRACE *see* Sydney Dance
SYDNEY SANCHEZ *see* Sydney Dance
SYDNEY ST JAMES *(Stacy St James, Sidney St Jmaes)*
Slutty blonde with un-enhanced small tits and a look of Casey Williams, made coarse. Married to Shawn Ricks. As from third quarter 1993 she has had her tits expanded—rock

hard but not too big.
Alexandria, I Love You / 1993 / AFV / M • Always / 1993 / XCI / M • Anal Brat / 1993 / FL / M • Anal Intruder #08: Rich Girls Gone Bad / 1993 / CC / M • Anus The Menace / 1993 / CC / M • Assy Sassy #3 / 1995 / ROB / F • The Beaverly Hillbillies / 1993 / IP / M • Best Of Buttman #2 / 1993 / EA / C • The Best Of Buttslammers / 1995 / BS / C • Beverly Hills Blondes #2 / 1995 / LV / M • Biography: Kaitlyn Ashley / 1996 / SC / C • Bobby Hollander's Maneaters #07 / 1993 / SFP / M • The Booty Guard / 1993 / IP / M • Butt Freak #2 / 1996 / EA / M • Butt Sluts #5 / 1995 / ROB / F • Butt Watch #01 / 1993 / FH / M • Butt Watch #02 / 1993 / FH / M • Buttslammers #02: The Awakening Of Felicia / 1993 / BS / F • Buttslammers #03: The Ultimate Dream / 1993 / BS / F • Buttslammers #10: Lust On The Internet / 1995 / BS / F • Car Wash Angels / 1995 / VC / M • Caught & Bound / 1993 / BON / B • Cheap Shots / 1994 / PRE / B • Chug-A-Lug Girls #3 / 1993 / VT / M • Crime Doesn't Pay / 1993 / BS / B • Defending Your Soul / 1995 / EX / M • Delicious Passions / 1993 / ROB / F • Dirty Stories #3 / 1995 / PE / M • Diva / 1993 / XCI / M • Eclipse / 1993 / SC / M • Girls Off Duty / 1994 / LE / M • Hollywood In Your Face / 1993 / VC / M • Hot Tight Asses #06 / 1994 / TCK / M • Hot Tight Asses #12 / 1995 / TCK / M • Junkyard Dykes #02 / 1994 / ZA / F • Lesbian Climax / 1995 / ROB / F • Love On The Run—401 / 1994 / APH / M • The Magic Box / 1993 / TP / M • Mainstream / 1993 / PRE / B • Mindsex / 1993 / MPA / M • More Than A Whore / 1995 / OD / M • New Money / 1995 / ULP / M • No Fly Zone / 1993 / LE / F • Nothing Butt The Truth / 1993 / AFV / M • Odyssey 30 Min: #309: Sewing And Blowing / 1993 / OD / M • Ona Zee's Doll House #1 / 1995 / ONA / F • Ona Zee's Learning The Ropes #12: Couples / 1995 / ONA / B • Ona Zee's Learning The Ropes #13: Best Of Male Submission / 1996 / ONA / C • The Orgy #1 / 1993 / EMC / M • Painful Cheeks / 1994 / BS / B • Painful Pleasures / 1993 / BS / B • Patent Leather / 1995 / CA / M • Philmore Butts Meets The Freak / 1995 / SUF / M • A Pool Party At Seymores #1 / 1995 / ULI / M • A Pool Party At Seymores #2 / 1995 / ULI / M • Prescription For Pain #2: The Ultimate Pain / 1993 / BON / B • Prime Time Slime #03 / 1994 / GLI / M • Real Tickets #1 / 1994 / VC / M • Real Tickets #2 / 1994 / VC / M • Rituals / 1993 / SC / M • Screamers (Ona Zee) / 1995 / ONA / M • Sean Michaels On The Road #08: Chicago / 1993 / VT / M • The Search For Canadian Beaver / 1995 / LIP / F • Sex On The Run #1 / 1994 / TTV / M • Sex On The Run #2 / 1994 / TTV / M • Sex Professionals / 1994 / LIP / F • Shameless Lady / 1993 / ME / M • Skin To Skin / 1993 / LE / M • Smokin' Buns / 1993 / PRE / B • Spinners #1 (Wicked) / 1995 / WP / M • Spread The Wealth / 1993 / DR / M • Student Fetish Videos: Best of Enema #03 / 1994 / PRE / C • The Submission Of Felecia / 1993 / BS / B • Taste Of Shame / 1994 / ROB / F • Tip Tap Toe / 1995 / PRE / C • Toe Biz / 1993 / PRE / S • Up Against It / 1993 / ZA / M • Up And Cummers #01 / 1993 / 4P / M • Whispered Secrets Of The Call Girls / 1995 / TVE / F • Xcitement: The

Movie / 1993 / XCI / M

SYLVAIN MANDAR see Star Index I

SYLVANA VALENTINE see Star Index I

SYLVIA

Anita / 1996 / BLC / M • Blue Vanities #509 / 1992 / FFL / M • Bosoms Triple X / 1990 / BTO / M • Bright Tails #4 / 1994 / STP / B • Bright Tails #8 / 1996 / STP / B • Cheryl Hanson: Cover Girl / 1981 / SE / M • Chocolate Cherries #2 / 1990 / CC / M • Everybody's Girl / 19?? / SOW / S • Lee Nover: The Search For The Perfect Butt / 1996 / IP / M • Letters From A Slave / 1995 / AOC / M • Lovin' Spoonfuls #4 / 1995 / 4P / C • The Ultimate Pleasure / 1995 / LEI / M • Wedding Rituals / 1995 / DVP / M

SYLVIA (BRAZ) see Star Index I

SYLVIA (MOHLMANN) see Silvia Mohlmann

SYLVIA (RYDER) see Silvia Ryder

SYLVIA BATZOCCI

Big Babies In Budapest / 1996 / EL / M

SYLVIA BENEDICT (Lisa Lang, Sylvia Moser, Buffy St John, Buffy St Johns, Silva Miser)

Reasonably pretty blonde with small slightly droopy tits, tattoo on right shoulder back and another on the back of her right hand, not a tight waist but within acceptable limits.

Bad Girls #1 / 1981 / GO / M • Bare Elegance / 1984 / MAP / M • The Best Of Blondes / 1986 / VCR / C • The Bitch Goddess / cr82 / BIZ / B • Black Sensations / 1987 / VEX / M • Breezy / 1985 / VCR / M • Classic Erotica #9 / 1996 / SVE / M • Collection #06 / 1984 / CA / M • The Erotic World Of Sylvia Benedict (#5) / 1983 / VCR / C • Gourmet Quickies: Buffy #708 / 1985 / GO / C • Hot Shorts: Sylvia Benedict / 1986 / VCR / C • Hot Sweet Honey / 1985 / VEP / M • Joys Of Erotica #109 / 1984 / VCR / C • Joys Of Erotica #114 / 1984 / VCR / C • Ladies In Heat / 1986 / PV / F • Loving Spoonfulls / 1987 / 4P / C • Lusty Ladies #01 / 1983 / 4P / M • Lusty Ladies #09 / 1984 / 4P / M • Naked Lust / 1985 / SE / M • Nasty Habits Are Hard To Break / 1986 / 4P / M • Passion Toys / 1985 / VCR / C • Pleasure Productions #01 / 1984 / VCR / M • Pleasure Productions #12 / 1985 / VCR / M • Sex Boat / 1980 / VCX / M

SYLVIA BOURDON

Candy's Candy / 1976 / BL / M • French Blue / 1974 / ... / M • Penetration / 1975 / SAT / M

SYLVIA COOPMAN

Visions Of Lust / 1983 / GO / M

SYLVIA CRYSTAL

Hard Core Beginners #06 / 1995 / LEI / M

SYLVIA DANIELS see Star Index I

SYLVIA DUVAL

Aerienne's Surprise / 1995 / WIV / M

SYLVIA HENRI see Star Index I

SYLVIA HOLLAND

Black Trisexual Encounters #4 / 1986 / LA / G • Forbidden Fruit #1 / 1987 / MET / G • The National Transsexual / 1990 / GO / G • She Studs #01 / 1990 / BIZ / G • She-Male Desires / 1989 / VC / C • Trisexual Encounters #04 / 1986 / PL / G • TV Encounter / 1992 / GOT / G

SYLVIA MAY

Lusty Lap Dancers #2 / 1994 / HO / M

SYLVIA MOHLMANN see Silvia Mohlmann

SYLVIA MOSER see Sylvia Benedict

SYLVIA PESCA see Star Index I

SYLVIA REASONER see Star Index I

SYLVIA REYNARD see Star Index I

SYLVIA RODGERS

Boiling Point / 1978 / SE / M • Girls! Girls! Girls! #1 / 1986 / VCS / C

SYLVIA RYDER see Silvia Ryder

SYLVIA SOPIA

Private Film #27 / 1995 / OD / M • Private Film #28 / 1995 / OD / M

SYLVIA SVENSON

Suck It Off / 1995 / DV / M

SYLVIA T. see Star Index I

SYLVIE

Hustler Honeys #1 / 1988 / VC / S • Magma: Deep Inside Janine / 1994 / MET / M • Magma: Horny & Greedy / 1993 / MET / M • Private Film #05 / 1993 / OD / M • Private Film #09 / 1994 / OD / M • Pumps In Da Rump #1 / 1994 / HW / M

SYLVIE DESSARTE

[Cathy, Fille Soumise / 1977 / ... / M

SYLVIE SCOTT see Star Index I

SYLVIE SHATZ

[Indecences 1930 / 1977 / ... / M

SYLVIO MATA

Butt Hole In-One / 1994 / AFV / M • Climax At The Melting Pot #1 / 1996 / AVS / M • Kinky Debutante Interviews #03 / 1994 / IP / M • Made In The Hood / 1995 / HBE / M • Tail Taggers #124 / 1994 / WV / M

SYNTHIA

New Faces, Hot Bodies #08 / 1993 / STP / M • New Faces, Hot Bodies #21 / 1996 / STP / C

SYREETA TAYLOR

Afrodisiac #1 / 1987 / CC / M • Black Angels / 1985 / VC / M • Black Girls In Heat / 1985 / PL / M • Black To Africa / 1987 / PL / C • Chocolate Bon-Bons / 1985 / PL / M • Hot Fudge / 1984 / VC / M • Jumpin' Black Flesh / 1987 / BTV / C

SZA SZA BRATOWSKI see Star Index I

SZILUIA KALMAN

True Stories #1 / 1993 / SC / M • True Stories #2 / 1993 / SC / M

SZILVIA

Fazano's Student Bodies / 1995 / EL / M • Nasty Travel Tails #01 / 1993 / CC / M

SZILVIA DEMETES

True Stories #1 / 1993 / SC / M • True Stories #2 / 1993 / SC / M

SZILVIA SZIBGGIO

True Stories #1 / 1993 / SC / M • True Stories #2 / 1993 / SC / M

SZOLI

Sluts 'n' Angels In Budapest / 1994 / EL / M

T-BONE see Star Index I

T. CHARLES see Star Index I

T. REX

Bang City #6: Bugger's Banquet / 1995 / SC / M

T.C.

Ass Tales / 1991 / PL / M • Beettlejizum / 1991 / PL / M • Bikini Seasons / 1993 / PHV / F • Class Ass / 1992 / PL / M • Mr. Big / 1991 / PL / M • Stick It In The Rear #1 / 1991 / PL / M • Unlaced / 1992 / PL / M

T.C. (BLACK)

Lactamania #2: The Squirt Fest / 1995 / TTV / M

T.C. (RICK BOWE) see Rick Bowe

T.J.

Anal Assault / 1995 / PEV / C • Pearl Necklace: Thee Bush League: The Best Of Oral

#01 / 1993 / SEE / C • Pearl Necklace: Thee Bush League #02 / 1992 / SEE / M • Pleasure Beach / 19?? / VC / M • Switch Hitters #5: The Night Games / 1990 / IN / G

T.J. CARSON (Betsy Ward)

Extreme Close-Up / 1981 / VC / M • Please Me! / cr86 / LIM / M • Taboo #01 / 1980 / VCX / M • Young Doctors In Lust / 1979 / NSV / M

T.J. SCOTT see Star Index I

T.J. SLOAN

No Reservations / 1995 / MN0 / G

T.J. STRYKER see Star Index I

T.J. SWAN see Star Index I

T.T. BOY (TT Boyd, Max Reynolds, Max Cash, Harry Dutchman (TTB), Bark Star, Butch (T.T. Boy))

Has a brother (Lex Baldwin) in the gay movies.

$exce$$ / 1993 / CA / M • 1-800-934-BOOB / 1992 / VD / C • 1-800-TIME / 1990 / IF / M • 10,000 Anal Maniacs #2 / 1994 / FOR / M • 13th Annual Adult Video News Awards / 1996 / VC / S • The 4th Vixxen / 1995 / EMC / M • A Is For Asia / 1996 / 4P / M • Ace Mulholland / 1995 / ERA / M • Acts Of Confession / 1991 / PP / M • The Adventures Of Billy Blues / 1990 / HO / M • The Adventures Of Major Morehead / 1994 / SC / M • The Adventures Of Seymore Butts / 1992 / FH / M • Alice In Hollywierd / 1992 / ZA / M • All Amateur Perfect 10's / 1995 / LEI / M • All In The Name Of Love / 1992 / IF / M • All That Jism / 1994 / VD / M • Alley Cat / 1991 / CIN / M • Alone And Dripping / 1991 / LV / M • Always / 1993 / XCI / M • Always Anal / 1995 / AVI / C • Amateur Nights #04 / 1990 / HO / M • Ambushed / 1990 / SE / M • Americans Most Wanted / 1991 / HO / M • Anal Addiction #3 / 1991 / SO / M • Anal Addicts / 1994 / KWP / M • Anal Adventures #2: Bodacious Buns / 1991 / VC / M • Anal Adventures #3: Can Her! / 1991 / VC / M • Anal Adventures #4: Doin' Her Up! / 1992 / VC / M • Anal Alley / 1996 / FD / M • Anal Analysis / 1992 / ZA / M • Anal Anarchy / 1995 / VC / M • Anal Angel / 1991 / ZA / M • Anal Arsenal / 1994 / OD / M • Anal Asian #1 / 1992 / IN / M • Anal Breakdown / 1994 / ROB / M • Anal Candy Ass / 1994 / ROB / M • Anal Climax #1 / 1991 / ROB / M • Anal Climax #4 / 1996 / ROB / M • Anal Cornhole Cutie / 1996 / ROB / M • Anal Crack Master / 1994 / ROB / M • Anal Crash Test Dummies / 1997 / ROB / M • Anal Cuties #1 / 1992 / ROB / M • Anal Cuties #3 / 1992 / ROB / M • Anal Deep Rider / 1994 / ROB / M • Anal Delights #1 / 1992 / ROB / M • Anal Delinquent #1 / 1993 / ROB / M • Anal Delinquent #2 / 1994 / ROB / M • Anal Delinquent #3 / 1995 / ROB / M • The Anal Diary Of Misty Rain / 1993 / EL / M • Anal Distraction / 1993 / PEP / M • Anal Dynomite / 1995 / ROB / M • Anal Encounters #5: Deliveries In The Rear / 1992 / VC / M • Anal Encounters #7: Enter Through The Rear / 1992 / VC / M • Anal Encounters #8 / 1992 / VC / M • Anal Extasy / 1992 / ROB / M • Anal Fever / 1996 / ROB / M • Anal Fireball / 1996 / ROB / M • Anal Generation / 1995 / PE / M • Anal Hanky-Panky / 1997 / ROB / M • Anal Heartbreaker / 1995 / ROB / M • Anal Hellraiser #1 / 1995 / ROB / M • Anal Hellraiser #2 / 1995 / ROB / M • Anal Honeypie / 1996 / ROB / M • Anal Hounds & Bitches / 1994

Debi Diamond / 1995 / VC / C • Deep Inside Juli Ashton / 1996 / VC / C • Deep Inside Kaitlyn Ashley / 1995 / VC / C • Deep Inside Nicole London / 1995 / VC / C • Deep Inside P.J. Sparxx / 1995 / VC / C • Deep Inside Savannah / 1993 / VC / C • Deep Inside Selena Steele / 1993 / VC / C • Defenseless / 1992 / CDI / M • Deja Vu / 1993 / XCI / M • Denim Dolls #2 / 1990 / CDI / M • Der Champion / 1995 / BTO / M • Designer Genes / 1990 / VI / M • The Devil In Miss Jones #5: The Inferno / 1994 / VC / M • Dial A For Anal / 1994 / CA / M • Dial A Nurse / 1992 / VD / M • Dial N For Nikki / 1993 / PEP / M • Diamond In The Rough / 1993 / BIA / C • Dick At Nite / 1993 / MET / M • Digital Lust / 1990 / SE / M • The Dirtiest Girl In The World / 1992 / ZA / M • Dirty Business / 1992 / CV / M • Dirty Little Mind / 1994 / IP / M • Dirty Work / 1995 / VC / M • Do Me Nurses / 1995 / LE / M • Doggie Style / 1994 / CA / M • Domination Nation / 1996 / VI / M • Don't Bother To Knock / 1991 / FAZ / M • Double Detail / 1992 / SO / M • Double Penetration #4 / 1991 / WV / C • Double Penetration #5 / 1992 / WV / C • Double Penetration #6 / 1993 / WV / C • Double The Pleasure / 1990 / SE / M • Dr Hooters / 1991 / PL / M • The Dragon Lady #2: Tales From the Bed / 1992 / WV / M • The Dragon Lady #5: Tales From The Bed #4 / 1993 / WV / M • The Dragon Lady #7: Tales From The Bed #6 / 1994 / WV / M • Dream Date / 1992 / HO / M • Dream Lover / 1991 / WV / M • Dream Lust / 1995 / NIT / M • The Dream Team / 1995 / VT / M • Dreams / 1995 / VC / M • Drilling For Gold / 1995 / ME / M • Drink Of Love / 1990 / V99 / M • Dripping With Desire / 1992 / DR / M • East L.A. Law / 1991 / WV / M • Easy Pickin's / 1990 / LV / M • The Edge / 1995 / SC / M • Edward Penishands #2 / 1991 / VT / M • Eight Is Never Enough / 1993 / ZA / M • Eleventh Annual AVN Awards / 1994 / VC / M • The Elixir / 1992 / CDI / M • En Garde / 1993 / DR / M • The End / 1992 / SC / M • Entangled / 1996 / KLP / M • The Erotic Adventures Of Fanny Annie / 1991 / WV / M • Erotic Dripping Orientals / 1993 / WV / M • Erotic Newcummers Vol 1 #1: Capitol Desires / 1993 / DR / M • Erotika / 1994 / WV / M • Euphoria / 1993 / CA / M • Even More Dangerous / 1990 / SO / M • Every Man Should Have One / 1991 / VEX / M • Every Woman Has A Fantasy #3 / 1995 / VC / M • Every Woman Has A Secret / 1991 / ROB / M • Everybody's Playmates / 1992 / CA / C • Executive Suites / 1993 / PL / M • The Exhibitionist / 1991 / VD / M • Exit In Rear / 1993 / XCI / M • Exotic Tastes / 1995 / VEX / C • The Eye Of The Needle / 1991 / CIN / M • Facesitter #1 / 1992 / CC / M • Facesitter #3 / 1994 / CC / M • Fantasies Of Marylin / 1995 / VT / M • Fantasy Chamber / 1994 / ULI / M • Fantasy Inc. / 1995 / CV / M • Fashion Sluts #3 / 1995 / ABS / M • Fashion Sluts #7 / 1996 / ABS / M • Father Of The Babe / 1993 / ZA / M • Fetish Fever / 1993 / CA / C • Fever / 1992 / CA / M • Film Buff / 1994 / WP / M • The Fire Down Below / 1990 / IN / M • Firm Offer / 1995 / SC / M • Flesh For Fantasy / 1994 / CV / M • Flying High #1 / 1992 / HO / M • Flying High #2 / 1992 / HO / M • Foolish Pleasure / 1992 / VD / M • Forbidden Cravings / 1996 / VC / M • Forever / 1995 / SC / M • Forever Yours / 1992 / CDI / M • Fortysomething #2 / 1991 / LE / M • Four Alarm / 1991 / SE / M • Frankie And Joanie / 1991 / HW / M • The French Invasion / 1993 / LBO / M • Fresh Tits Of Bel Air / 1992 / OD / M • From Brazil With Love / 1992 / ZA / M • From China With Love / 1993 / ZA / M • From The Heart / 1996 / XCI / M • Full Moon Fever / 1992 / PEP / M • Full Moon Fever / 1994 / LBO / M • Gang Bang Butthole Surfin' / 1996 / ROB / M • Gang Bang Cummers / 1993 / ROB / M • Gang Bang Dollies / 1996 / ROB / M • Gang Bang Face Bath #1 / 1993 / ROB / M • Gang Bang Face Bath #2 / 1994 / ROB / M • Gang Bang Face Bath #3 / 1994 / ROB / M • Gang Bang Fury #1 / 1992 / ROB / M • Gang Bang Jizz Jammers / 1994 / ROB / M • Gang Bang Jizz Queen / 1995 / ROB / M • Gang Bang Nymphette / 1994 / ROB / M • Gang Bang Pussycat / 1992 / ROB / M • Gang Bang Wild Style #1 / 1993 / ROB / M • Gang Bang Wild Style #2 / 1994 / ROB / M • Gangbang Girl #12 / 1993 / ANA / M • Gangbang Sluts / 1994 / VMX / M • Gangbusters / 1995 / VC / M • Geranalmo / 1994 / PL / M • Ghost To Ghost / 1991 / CC / M • Gimme An X / 1993 / VD / C • The Girl Next Door #1 / 1994 / VT / M • The Girl With The Heart-Shaped Tattoo / 1995 / WAV / M • Girls Of Sin / 1994 / PL / C • The Girls Of Summer / 1992 / FOR / M • Girls Off Duty / 1994 / LE / M • Girls With Big Jugs / 1995 / V99 / M • Girlz N The Hood #1 / 1991 / HW / M • Glamour Girl / 1991 / VEX / M • Glen And Glenda / 1994 / CA / M • Glitter Girls / 1992 / V99 / M • The Goddess / 1993 / ZA / M • Golddiggers #3 / 1995 / VC / M • Good Vibrations / 1993 / ZA / M • The Good, The Bed, And The Snuggly / 1993 / ZA / M • Grandma Does Dallas / 1990 / FC / M • The Great American Boobs To Kill For Dance Contest / 1995 / PEP / C • Hard Feelings / 1991 / V99 / M • Hard Headed / 1994 / LE / M • The Hard Line / 1993 / PEP / M • Hard To Stop #2 / 1992 / VC / M • Hard To Thrill / 1991 / CIN / M • Hard-On Copy / 1994 / WV / M • Harder, She Craved / 1995 / VC / M • Harlots From Hootersville / 1994 / BLC / M • Haunted Nights / 1993 / WP / M • Having It All / 1991 / VEX / M • Head First / 1995 / OD / M • Head Trip / 1995 / VC / M • Heart Breaker / 1994 / CA / M • Heartbreaker / 1992 / CDI / M • Heatseekers / 1991 / IN / M • Heavenscent / 1993 / ZA / M • Hellriders / 1995 / SC / M • Hexxxed / 1994 / VT / M • Hidden Agenda / 1992 / XCI / M • Hidden Desires / 1992 / CDI / M • Hienie's Heroes / 1995 / VC / M • Hindfeld / 1993 / PI / M • The Hindlick Maneuver / 1991 / CC / M • Hole In One / 1994 / HO / M • Home But Not Alone / 1991 / WV / M • Horny Brits Take It In The Bum / 1997 / ROB / M • Hot For Teacher / 1993 / VD / M • Hot Line / 1991 / VC / M • Hot Property / 1993 / PEP / M • Hot Sweet 'n' Sticky / 1992 / CA / C • Hot Tight Asses #01 / 1992 / TCK / M • Hot Tight Asses #03 / 1993 / TCK / M • Hot Tight Asses #04 / 1993 / TCK / M • Hot Tight Asses #07 / 1994 / TCK / M • Hot Tight Asses #08 / 1994 / TCK / M • Hot Tight Asses #10 / 1995 / TCK / M • Hot Tight Asses #11 / 1995 / TCK / M • Hot Tight Asses #12 / 1995 / TCK / M • Hot Tight Asses #13 / 1995 / TCK / M • Hot Tight Asses #15 / 1996 / TCK / M • Hot Tight Asses #16 / 1996 / TCK / M • Hot Tight Asses #17 / 1996 / TCK / M • Hot Tight Asses #18 / 1996 / TCK / M • Hotel California / 1995 / MID / M • Hotel Fantasy / 1995 / IN / M • Hotel Sodom #05: Tammi Ann Bends Over / 1995 / SNA / M • Hotel Sodom #09 / 1996 / SNA / M • Hothouse Rose #1 / 1991 / VC / M • House Arrest / 1995 / CV / M • How To Love Your Lover / 1992 / XII / S • Hump Up The Volume / 1991 / AR / M • I Am Desire / 1992 / WV / M • I Said A Butt Light #2 / 1990 / LV / M • I Want A Divorce / 1993 / ZA / M • I Want To Be Nasty / 1991 / XCV / M • I'll Do Anything But... / 1992 / CA / M • I'm No Dummy / 1991 / HO / M • I'm So Horny, Baby / 1997 / ROB / M • I'm Too Sexy / 1992 / CA / M • If Looks Could Kill / 1992 / V99 / M • Images Of Desire / 1990 / PM / M • Imagine / 1991 / LV / M • Immaculate Erection / 1992 / VD / M • Impact / 1995 / SC / M • In Too Deep / 1992 / AFD / M • Initiation Of Kylie / 1995 / VT / M • An Innocent Woman / 1991 / FAZ / M • Intense Perversions #2 / 1996 / PL / M • Interactive / 1993 / VD / M • Internal Affairs / 1992 / CDI / M • Introducing Danielle / 1990 / CDI / M • Introducing Tracey Wynn / 1991 / PL / M • Island Of Lust / 1995 / XCI / M • Jaded Love / 1994 / CA / M • Jizz Glazed Goo Guzzlers #1 / 1996 / NIT / C • Jordan Lee: Anal Queen / 1997 / SC / C • The Journey: Oral Majority / 1991 / WV / M • Jug Humpers / 1995 / V99 / C • Jugsy (Western) / 1992 / WV / M • Juice Box / 1990 / AFV / M • Juicy Cheerleaders / 1995 / LE / M • Juicy Sex Scandals / 1991 / VD / M • Juicy Treats / 1991 / ROB / M • Jungle Jive / 1992 / VD / M • Junk Yard Dogs / 1991 / FC / M • Junkyard Anal / 1994 / JAV / M • Just For The Hell Of It / 1991 / CA / M • Kadillac & Devell / 1993 / ZA / M • The Key to Love / 1992 / ZA / M • Kink: Police Chronicles / 1995 / ROB / M • The Kiss / 1995 / WP / M • Kiss Is A Rebel With A Cause / 1993 / WV / M • Kiss It Goodbye / 1991 / SE / M • Kittens #5 / 1994 / CC / F • Knockin' Da Booty / 1993 / WP / M • L.A. Stories / 1990 / VI / M • La Princesa Anal / 1993 / ROB / M • Lady Badass / 1990 / V99 / M • Lady Sterling Takes It Up The Arse / 1997 / ROB / M • Lady's Choice / 1995 / VD / M • Laid In Heaven / 1991 / VC / M • Laid Off / 1990 / CA / M • The Last Good Sex / 1992 / FD / M • Last Tango In Rio / 1991 / DR / M • Latex #2 / 1995 / VC / M • Lay Lady Lay / 1991 / VEX / M • Laying The Ghost / 1991 / VC / M • Leading Lady / 1991 / V99 / M • Legend #4: Critic's Choice / 1992 / LE / M • Let's Play Doctor / 1994 / PV / M • Lethal Passion / 1991 / PL / M • Lick My Lips / 1990 / LV / M • Life In The Fat Lane #2 / 1990 / FC / M • Lingerie / 1995 / SC / M • A Little Christmas Tail / 1991 / ZA / M • Little Miss Anal / 1994 / ROB / M • A Little Nookie / 1991 / VD / M • Little Secrets / 1991 / LE / M • Lollipop Lickers / 1996 / V99 / C • Lonely And Blue / 1990 / VEX / M • Lonely Hearts / 1995 / VC / M • Loose Lips / 1990 / VC / M • Loose Morals / 1995 / EX / M • Lotus / 1996 / VI / M • Love Ghost / 1990 / WV / M • Love Hurts / 1992 / VD / M • Love Potion / 1993 / WV / M • The Lovers / 1993 / HO / M • Lovin' Every

1996 / MET / M • Sporting Illustrated / 1990 / HO / M • Stacked With Honors / 1993 / DR / M • The Stand-Up / 1994 / VC / M • Star Attraction / 1995 / VT / M • Star Spangled Blacks / 1994 / VEX / M • Starbangers #03 / 1993 / ZA / M • Starbangers #04 / 1993 / FPI / M • Starbangers #06 / 1994 / FPI / M • Stardust #5 / 1996 / VI / M • The Starlet / 1991 / PP / M • The Starlet / 1995 / SC / M • Sterling Silver / 1992 / CC / M • Strange Behavior / 1991 / VD / M • The Stranger Beside Me / 1991 / WV / M • Street Heat / 1992 / CDI / M • Stripper Nurses / 1994 / PE / M • Style #2 / 1994 / VT / M • Summer Lovers / 1991 / VEX / M • Sun Bunnies #1 / 1991 / SC / M • Sunny After Dark / 1990 / WV / M • Super Groupie / 1993 / PL / M • Super Hornio Brothers #1 / 1993 / MID / M • Super Hornio Brothers #2 / 1993 / MID / M • Surfside Sex #2 / 1992 / LV / M • Swedish Erotica #82 / 1995 / CA / M • Swedish Erotica #85 / 1995 / CA / M • Sweet Cheeks (1991-Vid Excl) / 1991 / VEX / C • Sweet Licks / 1991 / MID / M • Sweet Poison / 1991 / CDI / M • Sweet Stuff / 1991 / V99 / M • Sweet Target / 1992 / CDI / M • Swing Into...Spring / 1995 / KWP / M • T.T.'s Oriental Adventure / 1992 / OD / M • Tail Taggers #101 / 1993 / WV / M • Tail Taggers #102 / 1993 / WV / M • Tail Taggers #104 / 1993 / WV / M • Tail Taggers #105 / 1993 / WV / M • Tail Taggers #107 / 1993 / WV / M • Tail Taggers #108: Vibro Love / 1993 / WV / M • Tail Taggers #109 / 1993 / WV / M • Tail Taggers #110 / 1993 / WV / M • Tail Taggers #117 / 1993 / WV / M • Tail Taggers #119 / 1994 / WV / M • Tail Taggers #120 / 1994 / WV / M • Tail Taggers #121: Behind The Lens / 1994 / WV / M • Tail Taggers #122: Anal Delight / 1994 / WV / M • Tail Taggers #123 / 1994 / WV / M • Tail Taggers #124 / 1994 / WV / M • Tail Taggers #125 / 1994 / WV / M • Tail Taggers #126 / 1994 / WV / M • Tail Taggers #127: / 1994 / WV / M • Tail Taggers #128: / 1994 / WV / M • Tailiens #1 / 1992 / FD / M • Tails Of Tribeca / 1993 / HW / M • Tainted Love / 1996 / VC / M • Take My Wife, Please / 1993 / WP / M • Takin' It To The Limit #1 / 1994 / BS / M • Tales From Sodom / 1994 / BLC / M • Tales From The Backside / 1993 / VC / M • Talk Dirty To Me #09 / 1992 / DR / M • Talking Trash #2 / 1995 / HW / M • A Taste Of Ecstasy / 1991 / CIN / M • A Taste Of Patricia Kennedy / 1992 / VD / C • The Tease / 1990 / VC / M • Telesex #1 / 1992 / VI / M • Telesex #2 / 1992 / VI / M • Tender Loving Care / 1995 / WP / M • Tenth Annual Adult Video News Awards / 1993 / VC / M • The Therapist / 1992 / VC / M • Things Mommy Taught Me / 1990 / KNI / M • Things That Go Hump In the Night / 1991 / LV / M • Three Men And A Hooker / 1991 / WV / M • The Three Muskatits / 1994 / PL / M • Thunder Road / 1995 / SC / M • Tight Lips / 1994 / CA / M • Tight Squeeze / 1992 / SC / M • Tit For Tat / 1994 / PEP / M • Tits / 1995 / AVI / M • Titty Bar #1 / 1993 / LE / M • Titty Slickers #1 / 1991 / LE / M • Titty Town #1 / 1994 / HW / M • The Tongue / 1995 / OD / M • Tongue In Cheek / 1994 / LE / M • The Tonya Hard-On Story / 1994 / GO / M • Top It Off / 1990 / VC / M • Total Exposure / 1992 / CDI / M • Treacherous / 1995 / VD / M • Troublemaker / 1991 / VEX / M • True Legends Of

Adult Cinema: The Modern Era / 1992 / VC / C • Tush / 1992 / ZA / M • Twin Cheeks #3 / 1991 / CIN / M • Twin Cheeks #4 / 1991 / CIN / M • Twisted / 1990 / VI / M • Two In The Bush / 1991 / EX / M • The Two Janes / 1990 / WV / M • Two Sisters / 1992 / WV / M • Two Women / 1992 / ROB / M • Undercover Lover / 1993 / VC / M • Unlike A Virgin / 1991 / HO / M • Untamed Cowgirls Of The Wild West #01: The Pillow Biters / 1992 / ZA / M • Untamed Cowgirls Of The Wild West #02: Jammy Glands... / 1993 / ZA / M • Unveil My Love / 1991 / HO / M • Unzipped / 1991 / WV / M • The Valley Girl Connection / 1994 / IN / M • Valleys Of The Moon / 1991 / SC / M • Vampire's Kiss / 1993 / AVI / M • Vanity / 1992 / HO / M • Vegas #4: Joker's Wild / 1990 / CDI / M • Venom #3 / 1996 / VD / M • Venom #5 / 1996 / VD / M • Venom #6 / 1996 / CA / M • Venus Of The Nile / 1991 / WV / M • Victim Of Love #2 / 1992 / VI / M • Victoria's Secret Life / 1992 / WV / M • Virgin Dreams / 1996 / EA / M • Virgin Spring / 1991 / FAZ / M • Visions #1 / 1995 / ERA / M • The Visualizer / 1992 / VC / M • Voluptuous / 1993 / CA / M • The Voyeur #5 / 1995 / EA / M • Voyeur Video / 1992 / ZA / M • Walking Small / 1992 / ZA / M • Wanda Whips The Dragon Lady / 1990 / V99 / M • Washington D.P. / 1993 / PEP / M • Waterbabies #1 / 1992 / CC / M • Weekend At Joey's / 1995 / ERA / M • Wendy Whoppers: Ninja CPA / 1993 / PEP / M • Western Nights / 1994 / WP / M • Wet Faces #1 / 1997 / SC / C • What You Are In The Dark / 1995 / KLP / M • What's Up, Tiger Pussy? / 1995 / VC / M • Whiplash / 1996 / DFI / M • Whispers / 1992 / HO / M • White Boys & Black Bitches / 1995 / ROB / M • White Lies / 1990 / VEX / M • White Men Can't Iron On Butt Row / 1997 / ABS / M • White Satin Nights / 1991 / V99 / M • White Wedding / 1994 / V99 / M • Whitey's On The Moon / 1996 / ROB / M • Why Things Burn / 1994 / LBO / M • Wicked / 1991 / XCI / M • Wicked As She Seems / 1993 / WP / M • Wild & Wicked #1 / 1991 / VT / M • Wild & Wicked #2 / 1992 / VT / M • Wild & Wicked #3 / 1993 / VT / M • Wild & Wicked #5 / 1995 / VT / M • Wild & Wicked #6 / 1995 / VT / M • Wild Assed Pooper Slut / 1996 / ROB / M • Wild Breed / 1995 / SC / M • Wild Goose Chase / 1990 / EA / M • The Wild Thing / 1992 / HO / M • Wild Things #3 / 1992 / MET / M • The Wild Wild Chest #3 / 1996 / HO / C • Wilder At Heart / 1993 / ANA / M • Wishful Thinking / 1992 / VC / M • Women In Charge / 1990 / VEX / M • The X-Producers / 1991 / XPI / M • X-Rated Blondes / 1992 / VD / C • X-TV / 1992 / CA / C • Young Buns #2 / 1990 / WV / M

TAB VIGA
The Unholy Child / 1972 / AVC / M

TABATHA CASH *(Tabetha Cash, Tabitha Cash)*
According to **MDD #20**, she's 18, was devirginized at 14 and has been with the same male ever since. She says she's Italian with 50% Japanese but lives in Paris and doesn't speak Japanese. She has a mole on her left face and a tattoo on her right breast. Enhanced medium to large tits.

1001 Nights / 1996 / IP / M • Anal Delights #3 / 1993 / ROB / M • The Anal-Europe Series #03: The Museum Of The Living Art /

1993 / LV / M • The Anal-Europe Series #04: Anal Recall / 1993 / LV / M • The Anal-Europe Series #05: Anal European Vacation / 1993 / LV / M • Animal Instinct / 1993 / VI / M • Booty Sister #1 / 1993 / ROB / M • Buffy Malibu's Nasty Girls #06 / 1994 / ANA / F • Casanova #1 / 1993 / SC / M • Casanova #2 / 1993 / SC / M • Club Anal #2 / 1993 / ROB / F • Deep Inside Dirty Debutantes #05 / 1993 / 4P / M • Delicious Passions / 1993 / ROB / F • Dr Butts #3 / 1993 / 4P / M • The Erotic Adventures Of Alladin X / 1995 / IP / M • Euroslut #1: French Tart / 1993 / CC / M • Facesitter #2 / 1993 / CC / M • Femme Fatale / 1993 / SC / M • Gangbang Girl #09 / 1993 / ANA / M • Guttman's Paris Vacation / 1993 / PL / M • Hardcore Copy / 1993 / PL / M • Lovin' Spoonfuls #3 / 1995 / 4P / C • Lovin' Spoonfuls #6 / 1996 / 4P / C • Magma: Spezial: Anal Ii / 1994 / MET / M • Marco Polo / 1995 / SC / M • More Dirty Debutantes #20 / 1993 / 4P / M • More Dirty Debutantes #23 / 1993 / 4P / M • More Dirty Debutantes #26 / 1993 / 4P / M • More Dirty Debutantes #29 / 1994 / 4P / M • Nasty Nymphos #01 / 1993 / ANA / M • New Ends #01 / 1993 / 4P / M • Night Train / 1993 / VI / M • Private Film #02 / 1993 / OD / M • Raunch #06: French Kiss / 1992 / CC / M • Seymore Butts Goes Nuts / 1994 / FH / M • Sodomania #03: Foreign Objects / 1993 / EL / M • Sodomania: The Baddest Of The Best...And Then Some / 1994 / EL / C • Tales From The Zipper #1 / 1993 / ME / M • Taste Of Shame / 1994 / ROB / F • Up And Cummers: The Movie / 1994 / 4P / M • The Wacky World Of Ed Powers / 1996 / 4P / C • The Worst Porno Ever Made With The Best Sex / 1993 / PL / M • [European Invasion / cr93 / A&E / M • [Rai / 199? / ... / M

TABATHA PARIS *see* **Nikki Cherry**
TABATHA ROGERS *see* **Star Index I**
TABATHA TOWERS
Horny Henry's Peeping Adventures / 1994 / TTV / M • Tabatha's Super Video / 1993 / H&S / S • Tit To Tit #4 / 1996 / BTO / S
TABBATHA FOX *see* **Tabitha Fox**
TABBETHA FOX *see* **Tabitha Fox**
TABETHA CASH *see* **Tabatha Cash**
TABITA STAR CHANDLER *see* **Star Chandler**
TABITHA
Back East Babes #1 / 1996 / NIT / M • Buttman's Double Adventure / 1993 / EA / M • Hellfire Society / 19?? / HOM / B • Intimate Interviews #1 / 1996 / NIT / M

TABITHA (1995) *(Nadine (Tabitha))*
Long curly dark brown hair, passable face, getting plump body, fading tattoo on her left tit, medium tits, nice smile. As of mid 1996 has had her tits enhanced to large.

Adam & Eve's House Party #5 / 1996 / VC / M • All That: Black Women's Fantasies / 1996 / VT / M • Anal Addict / 1995 / ROB / M • Anal Hellraiser #2 / 1995 / ROB / M • Anal Maniacs #3 / 1995 / WP / M • As Easy As A Bunch Of Cunts / 1996 / ROB / F • Assy Sassy #3 / 1995 / ROB / F • Black And White Revisited / 1995 / VT / F • Black Cream Queens / 1996 / APP / F • Booty Bitch / 1995 / ROB / M • Booty Ho #3 / 1995 / ROB / M • Borderline (Vivid) / 1995 / VI / M • Butt Banged Cycle Sluts / 1995 / ANA / M • Butt Motors / 1995 / VC / M • The

Butt Sisters Do Seattle / 1995 / MID / M • Butt Sluts #5 / 1995 / ROB / F • Casting Call #14 / 1995 / SO / M • Casting Call #16 / 1995 / SO / M • Casting Call #18 / 1996 / SO / M • Centerfold / 1995 / SC / M • Corn Hole Kittens / 1996 / ROB / F • Dark Desires #1 (Infin—1995) / 1995 / IF / M • Debi Diamond's Dirty Dykes #1 / 1995 / FD / F • Decadence / 1995 / AMP / M • Dirty Stories #3 / 1995 / PE / M • Enemates #12 / 1996 / BIZ / B • Everybody Wants Some / 1996 / EXQ / F • Fashion Sluts #2 / 1995 / ABS / M • Fresh Meat (John Leslie) #2 / 1995 / EA / M • Hawaiian Buttwatch / 1995 / SUF / M • Helen & Louise / 1996 / HDE / M • The Hitch-Hiker #13: Highway To Hell / 1995 / VIM / M • Hollywood On Ice / 1995 / VT / M • Hot Tight Asses #12 / 1995 / TCK / M • Hot Tight Asses #15 / 1996 / TCK / M • Intense Perversions #1 / 1995 / PL / M • Interracial Anal #03: Black And White All Over / 1995 / AFI / M • Lesbian C*Nt Whores / 1996 / ROB / F • Lesbian Climax / 1995 / ROB / F • Life's A Beach, Then You're Fucked / 1995 / FRM / M • Man Killer / 1996 / SC / M • Mistress 'n Da Hood / 1995 / VT / B • More Than A Whore / 1995 / OD / M • My Baby Got Back #07 / 1995 / VT / M • My Baby Got Back #08 / 1996 / VT / M • My Wildest Date / 1995 / HO / M • The New Snatch Masters #13 / 1995 / LEI / C • NYDP Blue / 1996 / WP / M • Once In A Lifetime / 1996 / VC / C • Perverted #3: The Parents / 1995 / ZA / M • Perverted Stories #04 / 1995 / JMP / M • Philmore Butts Hawaiian Anal Adventure / 1995 / SUF / M • Philmore Butts Meets The Freak / 1995 / SUF / M • Pick Up Lines #01 / 1995 / 4P / M • Plaything #2 / 1995 / VI / M • A Pool Party At Seymores #1 / 1995 / ULI / M • A Pool Party At Seymores #2 / 1995 / ULI / M • Poop Dreams / 1995 / ULP / M • Profiles #01 / 1995 / XPR / M • Rim Job Rita / 1994 / SC / M • Shayla's Swim Party / 1997 / VC / M • Sista! #3 / 1995 / VT / F • Sista! #4 / 1996 / VT / F • Sluts, Butts And Pussy / 1996 / DFI / M • So Bad / 1995 / VT / M • Top Debs #6: Rear Entry Girls / 1995 / GO / M • Tropical Taboo / 1995 / HO / M • Two Pac / 1996 / VT / M • Video Virgins #27 / 1996 / NS / M • Video Virgins #30 / 1996 / NS / M • The Voyeur #5 / 1995 / EA / M • Waiting For The Man / 1996 / VT / M • The Watering Hole / 1994 / HO / M

TABITHA (STEVENS) see Tabitha Stevens

TABITHA CASH see Tabatha Cash

TABITHA FOX *(Tabbatha Fox, Tabbetha Fox)*

Anal Angels / 1996 / PRE / B • As Sweet As They Come / 1992 / V99 / M • Assinine / 1990 / CC / M • Bondage Master / 1994 / CS / B • Bum Rap / 1990 / PLV / B • Dangerous / 1989 / PV / M • Debbie Does 'em All #3 / 1989 / CV / M • Drink Of Love / 1990 / V99 / M • Fantasy Lover / 1995 / V99 / C • Flash Floods / 1991 / PRE / C • Head Nurse / 1990 / V99 / M • Making The Grade / 1989 / IN / M • One For The Road / 1989 / V99 / M • One More Time / 1990 / VEX / M • Only The Best Of Debbie / 1992 / MET / C • Playing The Field / 1990 / VEX / M • Sex Kittens / 1990 / VEX / F • Sex She Wrote / 1991 / VEX / M • Sexual Persuasion / 1991 / V99 / M • Suite Sensations / 1988 / SEX / M • Summer Dreams / 1990 /

VEX / M • White Satin Nights / 1991 / V99 / M

TABITHA GAYLE

GRG: Ladies Only Affair / 1995 / GRG / F

TABITHA JORDAN see Debi Jointed

TABITHA LOMBARDO see Isabella Rovetti

TABITHA STEVENS *(Tabitha (Stevens), Lisa Lamborghini)*

Not the same as the girl of the same name in late 1995.

Backdoor To Hollywood #12 / 1990 / CIN / M • Bazooka County #2 / 1989 / CC / M • The Big Rock / 1988 / FOV / M • Buns And Roses (V9) / 1990 / V99 / M • Camera Shy / 1990 / IN / M • Future Lust / 1989 / ME / M • Girls Of The Double D #10 / 1989 / CDI / M • Hollywood Hustle #1 / 1000 / V99 / M • Introducing Tabitha / 1990 / CIN / M • Kym Wilde's On The Edge #33 / 1996 / RB / B • Love Thirsty / 1990 / IN / M • Lust Horizons / 1992 / PL / G • Making It In New York / 1989 / PLD / M • No Body Like...Tabitha / 1991 / MAG / F • On Stage And In Color / 1991 / VIP / M • Once Upon A Time / 1989 / VEX / M • Radioactive / 1990 / VIP / M • She's No Angel #1 / 1990 / V99 / M • She's Ready / 1990 / CDI / M • Speedtrap / 1992 / VC / M • Stairway To Heaven / 1989 / ME / M • Take It To The Limit / 1990 / V99 / M • To Snatch A Thief / 1989 / PLD / M • Under The Law / 1989 / AFV / M • Weekend Blues / 1990 / IN / M

TABITHA STEVENS (95)

Blonde with a passable face and large rock-solid enhanced tits. Tight body otherwise. 25 years old in 1995. Not the same as the 1990 girl. Originally from NY but spent her teenage years in Las Vegas NV and now lives in CA. De-virginized at 14.

Anything Goes / 1996 / OUP / M • Aqua Brats / 1996 / NAP / B • Blade / 1996 / MID / M • By Myself / 1996 / PL / F • Corporate Justice / 1996 / TEP / M • Exotic Car Models #1 / 1996 / IN0 / F • Fellatio Fanatics / 1996 / NIT / M • Finger Pleasures #5 / 1996 / PL / F • Finger Pleasures #6 / 1996 / PL / F • Frankenpenis / 1995 / LEI / M • Frendz? #1 / 1996 / RAS / M • Girly Video Magazine #4 / 1996 / BEP / M • Glory Days / 1996 / IN / M • Head Trip / 1995 / VC / M • In Your Face #4 / 1996 / PL / M • Interview's Blonde Bombshells / 1995 / LV / M • Interview: Silicone Sisters / 1996 / LV / M • Kym Wilde's On The Edge #29 / 1995 / RB / B • Kym Wilde's On The Edge #37 / 1996 / RB / B • Labyrinth Of The Lash / 1996 / BON / B • Lesbian Connection / 1996 / SUF / F • Lesbian Debutante #01 / 1996 / IP / F • Loose Jeans / 1996 / GO / M • Mask Of Innocence / 1996 / WP / B • Maui Waui / 1996 / PE / M • Microslut / 1996 / TTV / M • Million Dollar Buns / 1996 / MYS / M • Naughty Nights / 1996 / PLP / C • New Pussy Hunt #25 / 1996 / LEI / C • Nikki Loves Rocco / 1996 / VI / M • Philmore Butts Adventures In Paradise / 1996 / SUF / M • Philmore Butts Meets The Freak / 1995 / SUF / M • Pick Up Lines #12 / 1997 / OD / M • Pussyman Auditions #12 / 1995 / SNA / M • Rear Window / 1996 / NIT / M • Rolling Thunder / 1995 / VI / M • Rollover / 1996 / NIT / M • Samantha & Company / 1996 / PL / M • Sex Drives Of The Rich And Famous / 1996 / ERA / M • Sinboy #2: Yo' Ass Is Mine / 1996 / SC / M • Sinboy #3:

The Island Of Dr. Moron / 1996 / SC / M • Soap Opera Sluts / 1996 / AFI / M • Solo Adventures / 1996 / AB / F • Sorority Cheerleaders / 1996 / PL / M • Steam / 1996 / ULP / M • Strong Sensations / 1996 / PL / M • Sweet As Honey / 1996 / NIT / M • Sweet Things / 1996 / FF / C • Too Hot / 1996 / LV / M • Totally Depraved / 1996 / SC / M • Unbalanced Chemicals / 1996 / SUF / M • Velvet / 1995 / SPI / M • Video Virgins #26 / 1996 / NS / M • Voyeur Strippers / 1996 / PL / F • The Wicked Web / 1996 / WP / M • XXX Channel / 1996 / VT / M

TABOLINA see Tobianna

TABOO

Anal, Facial & Interracial / 1996 / FC / M • Black And White Hevisited / 1995 / VT / F • Black Babes / 1995 / LV / M • The Body System / 1996 / FD / M • The Case Of The Black Booty / 1996 / LV / M • Cum To Drink Of It / 1996 / BCP / M • The Cumm Brothers #10: Night Of The Giving Head / 1995 / OD / M • Dirty Dirty Debutantes #1 / 1995 / 4P / M • Dirty Stories #3 / 1995 / PE / M • Dr Whacks Treatment / 1996 / VTF / B • Fashion Sluts #3 / 1995 / ABS / M • Fit To Be Tied / 1996 / PL / B • Full Moon Madness / 1995 / CA / M • Hard Core Beginners #12 / 1995 / LEI / M • The Hardwood Chronicles / 1995 / XCI / M • Here Comes Magoof #2 / 1995 / VC / M • Hollywood Amateurs #26 / 1995 / MID / M • Illicit Affairs / 1996 / XC / M • The Kiss / 1995 / WP / M • Mike Hott: #332 Girls Who Swallow Cum #02 / 1995 / MHV / C • Mike Hott: #338 Lesbian Sluts #22 / 1996 / MHV / F • Mike Hott: #339 Cum In My Mouth #04 / 1996 / MHV / C • Mike Hott: #345 Cum In My Cunt #07 / 1995 / MHV / C • Mike Hott: #350 Bonus Cunt: Taboo / 1996 / MHV / M • The New Snatch Masters #21 / 1996 / LEI / C • Nikki Loves Rocco / 1996 / VI / M • Pick Up Lines #02 / 1995 / 4P / M • Pizza Sluts: They Deliver / 1995 / XCI / M • Pure Smut / 1996 / GO / M • Pussyman Auditions #09 / 1995 / SNA / M • Pussyman's House Party #1 / 1996 / SNA / M • Pussyman's House Party #2 / 1996 / SNA / M • So Bad / 1995 / VT / M • Special Attention / 1996 / MP0 / M • Tails From The Hood / 1995 / FH / M • Tailz From Da Hood #5 / 1996 / AVI / M • Tender Box / 1996 / MP0 / M • Throbbing Threesomes / 1996 / NIT / M • Video Virgins #25 / 1995 / NS / M

TAD see Star Index I

TAD BRONSON

Bi-Golly / 1993 / BIL / G • Wings Of Change / 1993 / HSV / G

TAD MARTIN see Star Index I

TAD TYLER

Openhanded Marriage / 1990 / RB / B

TADESHI ITOH see Star Index I

TAE see Brooke Ashley

TAE TOMOKO

The Sex Exchange / 1996 / AVV / M

TAFALDA

Amsterdam Nights #2 / 1996 / VC / M

TAFFY

Black Valley Girls #1 / 1986 / 4R / M • Detroit Dames / 1988 / DR / C • Get Me While I'm Hot / 1988 / PV / M • Soul Games / 1988 / PV / C

TAHOE JONATHON see Star Index I

TAI PEH

Magma: Huge Cum Shots / 1995 / MET / M

TAIJA DAWN
Asses Galore #4: Extreme Noise Terror / 1996 / DFI / M • Black Fantasies #16 / 1996 / HW / M • Black Hollywood Amateurs #25 / 1996 / MID / M • Black Knockers #11 / 1995 / TV / M • Booty Bang #1 / 1996 / HW / M • Bootylicious: Bitches & Ho's / 1996 / JMP / M • Bootylicious: Yo Bitch / 1996 / JMP / M • Interview: Dark And Delicious / 1996 / LV / M • Licorice Lollipops: Back To School / 1996 / HW / M • Tailz From Da Hood #4 / 1996 / AVI / M • Tailz From Da Hood #5 / 1996 / AVI / M • Vivid Raw #4 / 1996 / VI / M • Young And Anal #5 / 1996 / JMP / M

TAIJA RAE
69th Street Vice / 1984 / VC / M • Amber Pays The Rent / 1986 / VT / M • American Babylon / 1985 / PV / M • Baby Face #2 / 1987 / VC / M • Backdoor Club / 1986 / CA / M • Backdoor Lust / 1987 / CV / C • The Best Little Whorehouse In San Francisco / 1984 / LA / M • Best Of Talk Dirty To Me #01 / 1991 / DR / C • Big Gulp #2 / 1987 / VIP / C • Bootsie / 1984 / CC / M • Bordello...House Of The Rising Sun / 1985 / SE / M • Breakin' In / 1986 / WV / M • Campus Cuties / 1986 / CA / M • Candy Stripers #2 / 1985 / AR / M • Celebration / 1984 / GO / C • Chastity And The Starlets / 1986 / RAV / M • Cherry Tricks / 1985 / VPE / M • Christine's Secret / 1986 / FEM / M • Climax / 1985 / CA / M • Club Exotica #1 / 1985 / WV / M • Club Exotica #2 / 1985 / WV / M • Cum Blasted Cuties / 1993 / GO / C • Dangerous Stuff / 1985 / COM / M • Debbie Does 'em All #1 / 1985 / CV / M • Decadence / 1986 / VD / M • Delivery Boys / 1984 / NWW / S • Desperate Women / 1986 / VD / M • Doin' The Harlem Shuffle / 1986 / CA / M • Double Trouble / 1986 / DRV / M • Dr Penetration / 1986 / WET / M • Dream Girls / 1986 / VC / M • Driller / 1984 / VC / M • Eaten Alive / 1985 / VXP / M • Erotic Zones #3 / 1986 / CA / M • Ex-Connection / 1986 / SEV / M • Exposure / 1988 / VD / M • Fashion Dolls / 1985 / LA / M • Fashion Fantasies / 1986 / VC / M • Fashion Passion / 1985 / VD / M • The Fire Inside / 1988 / VC / C • Flesh And Fantasy / 1985 / VC / M • Furburgers / 1987 / VD / M • Girls That Talk Dirty / 1986 / VCS / C • Give It To Me / 1984 / SE / M • Good Girl, Bad Girl / 1984 / SE / M • Good Morning Taija Rae / 1988 / VCX / M • The Greatest American Blonde / 1987 / WV / C • Hard To Be Good / 1988 / VD / M • Hometown Honeys #1 / 1986 / VEX / M • Hostage Girls / 1984 / VC / M • The Hot Box Invasion / 1987 / AMB / M • Hot Licks At The Pussycat Club / 1990 / WV / C • Hot Rockers / 1985 / IVP / M • Hottest Parties / 1988 / VC / C • Immorals #4: Choice Cuts / 1991 / SC / M • In-N-Out With John Leslie / 1988 / WV / C • Inner Blues / 1987 / VD / M • Inside Little Oral Annie / 1984 / VXP / M • Jack 'n' Jill #2 / 1984 / VC / M • Jailhouse Girls / 1984 / VC / M • Jewel Of The Nite / 1986 / WV / M • Ladies Of The Knight / 1984 / GO / M • Legends Of Porn #2 / 1989 / CV / C • Les Be Friends / 1988 / WV / C • Little Oral Annie Takes Manhattan / 1985 / VXP / M • Littledove's Cup / 1988 / FOV / M • Living Doll / 1987 / WV / M • Long Hard Nights / 1984 / ELH / M • Looking For Mr Goodsex / 1984 / CC / M • Make Me Feel It / 1984 /

SE / M • Mardi Gras Passions / 1987 / MET / M • Mitzi's Honor / 1987 / TAM / M • Monkey Business / 1987 / SEV / M • Moonlusting #1 / 1986 / WV / M • Motel Sweets / 1987 / VD / M • Mouthwatering / 1986 / BRA / M • Naked Scents / 1984 / VC / M • Only The Best Of Oral / 1989 / CV / C • Only The Best Of The Erotic Eighties / 1992 / VC / C • Oral Majority #02 / 1987 / WV / C • Oral Majority #03 / 1986 / WV / C • Orgies / 1987 / WV / C • Paris Blues / 1990 / WV / C • Parliament: Dildo Babes #2 / 1988 / PM / F • Parliament: Dirty Blondes #1 / 1991 / PM / F • Parliament: Eating Pussy #1 / 1989 / PM / C • Parliament: Finger Friggin' #1 / 1986 / PM / F • Parliament: Lonesome Ladies #2 / 1985 / PM / F • Parliament: Sweet Starlets #1 / 1986 / PM / F • Play Me Again, Vanessa / 1986 / VC / M • Raw Talent #1 / 1984 / VC / M • Return To Alpha Blue / 1984 / AVC / M • Rock Hard / 1985 / CV / M • Samantha, I Love You / 1988 / WV / C • Satin Angels / 1986 / WV / M • Scenes They Wouldn't Let Me Shoot / 1984 / VC / M • Secret Mistress / 1986 / VD / M • Sex Appeal / 1986 / VES / S • Sex Crimes 2084 / 1985 / SE / M • Sex Drive / 1984 / VXP / M • Sex Life Of A Porn Star / 1986 / ELH / M • Sex On The Set / 1984 / RLV / M • Sex Spa USA / 1984 / VC / M • Sexually Altered States / 1986 / VC / M • Shades Of Passion / 1985 / CA / M • She's So Fine #1 / 1985 / VC / M • Sleazy Rider / 1990 / FOV / M • Smooth As Silk / 1987 / VIP / M • Splash / 1990 / WV / C • Splashing / 1986 / VCS / C • Spoiled / 1987 / VD / M • Star 85: Kari Fox / 1985 / VEX / M • Star Angel / 1986 / COM / M • Supergirls Do General Hospital / 1984 / VC / M • Supergirls Do The Navy / 1984 / VC / M • Swedish Erotica #69 / 1985 / CA / M • Swedish Erotica #70 / 1985 / CA / M • Taboo American Style #1: The Ruthless Beginning / 1985 / VC / M • Taboo American Style #2: The Story Continues / 1985 / VC / M • Taija / 1986 / WV / C • Taija Is Sizzling Hot / 1986 / VT / M • Taija's Satin Seduction / 1987 / CDI / M • Taija's Tasty Treats / 1988 / EXP / C • Tales Of Taija Rae / 1989 / DR / M • Talk Dirty To Me #04 / 1986 / DR / M • A Taste Of Taija Rae / 1989 / PIN / C • Taste Of The Best #2 / 1988 / PIN / C • Teasers: The Inheritance / 1988 / MET / M • This Is Your Sex Life / 1987 / VD / M • Tickled Pink / 1985 / VC / M • Toy Box Lingerie Show / 1991 / ESP / S • Toys 4 Us #3: Follow The Leader / 1990 / WV / C • Traci Lords' Fantasies / 1986 / CA / C • Tracy In Heaven (Rewrite) / 1986 / WV / M • Triple Header / 1986 / SE / C • Turn On With Kelly Nichols / 1984 / CA / M • Twins / 1986 / WV / M • The Ultimate Thrill / 1988 / PIN / C • Unveiled / 1987 / VC / M • Urban Heat / 1985 / FEM / M • VCA Previews #3 / 1988 / VC / C • VCA Previews #4 / 1988 / VC / C • The Voyeur / 1985 / VC / M • Wet Dreams / 1984 / CA / M • Wild Orgies / 1986 / SE / C • Winner Take All / 1986 / SEV / M • Wish You Were Here / 1984 / VXP / M • With Love, Lisa / 1985 / CA / C • World Of Good, Safe & Unusual Sex / 1987 / ... / M • WPINK-TV #3 / 1988 / PV / M • Young Nympho's / 1986 / VD / M

TAIMAK
[No More Dirty Deals / 1994 / V-I / S

TAIRO IKEDA

Honey Sex / 1996 / AVE / M

TAJ MAHAL
Amateur Lesbians #41: Kelli / 1993 / GO / F • Amateur Lesbians #42: Rosie Lee / 1993 / GO / F • Big Murray's New-Cummers #18: Crazy Cuties / 1993 / FD / M • Big Murray's New-Cummers #22: Exotic Erotica / 1993 / FD / M • Captain Bob's Lust Boat #2 / 1993 / FCP / M • Deep Inside Dirty Debutantes #07 / 1993 / 4P / M • First Time Lesbians #04 / 1993 / JMP / F • Girls Will Be Boys #5 / 1993 / PL / F • Girls Will Be Boys #6 / 1993 / PL / F • Harlem Honies #2: Nasty In New York / 1994 / CC / M • Hollywood Swingers #08 / 1993 / LBO / M • How To Make A Model #03: Sunshine & Melons / 1994 / QUA / M • Kym Wilde's On The Edge #06 / 1993 / RB / B • More Bad Girl Handling / 1994 / RB / B • More Dirty Debutantes #21 / 1993 / 4P / M • More Dirty Debutantes #30 / 1994 / 4P / M • Odyssey Triple Play #65: Black & White & Spread All Over / 1994 / OD / M • Odyssey Triple Play #74: Conjugal Couples / 1994 / OD / M • Pearl Necklace: Thee Bush League #14 / 1993 / SEE / M • Shaved #06 / 1993 / RB / F • Student Fetish Videos: Best of Enema #03 / 1994 / PRE / C • Student Fetish Videos: Catfighting #07 / 1993 / PRE / B • Student Fetish Videos: The Enema #11 / 1994 / PRE / B • Student Fetish Videos: Foot Worship #09 / 1993 / PRE / B

TAJ MONROE *see Star Index I*

TAJA
The All American Girl / 1989 / FAN / M • Black Mystique #07 / 1994 / VT / F • Black Mystique #08 / 1994 / VT / F • Cat Scratch Fever / 1989 / FAZ / M • Handle With Care / 1989 / FAZ / M • Midnight Baller / 1989 / PL / M • More Than Friends / 1989 / FAZ / M • Wet Pink / 1989 / PL / F

TAKAKO AOMORI *see Star Index I*

TAKAO IKEDA
Club Fantasy / 1996 / AVE / M

TAKAO OTA
Private Escort / 1996 / AVE / M

TAKEISHI TANAKA
Erotic Nurses / 1996 / AVE / M

TAKESHI NAIGAIKE
Bondage Of The Rising Sun / 1996 / BON / B • Captured On Camera / 1997 / BON / B

TAKO *see Star Index I*

TAKORA MODA
A Widow's Affair / 1996 / AVV / M

TALANNA
Big Bad Biker Bitches / 1994 / TTV / M • Freaky Flix / 1995 / TTV / C • Rollie Pollie Chicks / 1996 / TTV / M

TALIA
Amateur Hours #19 / 1990 / AFI / M • Amateur Night #01 / 1990 / HME / M • Open Window #17: Hardcore Interview / 1990 / ZA / M

TALIA (MALIA) *see Malia*

TALIA GENEVA *see Talia James*

TALIA JAMES *(Talia Geneva)*
Talia Geneva is from **Head Nurse**. Unconfirmed reports that she committed suicide.
Bad Habits / 1990 / WV / M • Best Of Buttman #2 / 1993 / EA / C • Black Stockings / 1990 / VD / M • Blue Heaven / 1990 / IF / M • Buttman's Ultimate Workout / 1990 / EA / M • Double Penetration #4 / 1991 / WV / C • Head Nurse / 1990 / V99 /

M • Laze / 1990 / ZA / M • Naked Lunch / 1995 / LEI / M • Odyssey Amateur #49: Gangbanging Nymphette / 1991 / OD / M • P.S.: Back Alley Cats #01 / 1992 / PSP / F • P.S.: Back Alley Cats #05 / 1992 / PSP / F • Paris By Night / 1990 / IN / M • The Price Was Right / 1994 / PAE / M • Steal Breeze / 1990 / SO / M • Sunny After Dark / 1990 / WV / M • The X-Producers / 1991 / XPI / M • Young Buns #2 / 1990 / WV / M

TALIA STAWN
Gold LeMay / 1991 / VIM / M

TALIESIN *see* **Will Jarvis**

TALL JOHN *see* **Star Index I**

TALLULAH
Odyssey Triple Play #96: Anal Option #2 / 1995 / OD / M

TALLY
Bad She-Males / 1994 / HSV / G • Bi On The Fourth Of July / 1994 / BIL / G • Knock Outs / 1992 / HHV / S • Tranny Hill: Sweet Surrender / 1994 / HSV / G

TALLY BRITTANY *(Tally Chanel)*
Free Ride / 1986 / LIV / S • Sex Appeal / 1986 / VES / S • Slammer Girls / 1987 / LIV / S • Warrior Queen / 1987 / VES / S

TALLY CHANEL *see* **Tally Brittany**

TALON *see* **Mona Lisa**

TALORE
Black Mystique #09 / 1994 / VT / F • Fun Zone / 1994 / PRE / B • Student Fetish Videos: Best of Enema #03 / 1994 / PRE / C • Student Fetish Videos: The Enema #15 / 1994 / PRE / B • Student Fetish Videos: Spanking #16 / 1994 / PRE / B • Student Fetish Videos: Tickling #10 / 1994 / SFV / B

TAMARA
Black Video Virgins #1 / 1996 / NS / M • Breast Worx #13 / 1992 / LBO / M • Dirty Blue Movies #04 / 1993 / JTV / F • Odyssey 30 Min: #195: Tamara's First Anal Adventure / 1991 / OD / M • Rendezvous With Destiny / 1984 / LA / B • Skirts & Flirts #02 / 1997 / XPR / F

TAMARA (LONGLEY) *see* **Tamara Longley**

TAMARA CHANG *see* **Tamara Longley**

TAMARA DWANEY *see* **Star Index I**

TAMARA LANDRY *(Shelby Lane)*
American Sweethearts / 1993 / LBO / S • Beach Babes From Beyond #1 / 1993 / BRI / S • Bel Air Babes / 1995 / PL / F • The Pamela Principle #1 / 1992 / IMP / S • R.S.V.P. / 1983 / VES / S • Strike A Pose / 1993 / PME / S

TAMARA LEE *(Pamela Self)*
Amazing Tails #5 / 1990 / CA / M • Anal Intruder #03 / 1989 / CC / M • Bazooka County #2 / 1989 / CC / M • Biff Malibu's Totally Nasty Home Videos #03 / 1992 / ANA / M • The Big Gun / 1989 / FAN / M • The Book / 1990 / IF / M • Born For Porn / 1989 / FAZ / M • Breaststroke #2 / 1989 / EX / M • Cat On A Hot Sin Roof / 1989 / LV / M • Cum To Dinner / 1991 / HO / M • Dangerous / 1989 / PV / M • Deep Throat #5 / 1990 / AR / M • Denim Dolls #2 / 1990 / CDI / M • Dynamite Darlene Lupone / 1996 / H&S / S • Entertainment L.A. Style / 1990 / HO / M • Foolish Pleasures / 1989 / ME / M • Girls Of The Double D #06 / 1989 / CIN / M • Girls Of The Double D #13 / 1990 / CDI / M • Girls Of The Double D #14 / 1990 / CIN / M • Hard At Work / 1989 / VEX / M • Haunted Passions / 1990 / FC / M • Holly

Does Hollywood #3 / 1989 / VEX / M • Hotel Paradise / 1989 / CA / M • The Invisible Girl / 1989 / VI / M • Laid Off / 1990 / CA / M • Late Night For Lovers / 1989 / ME / M • Leading Lady / 1991 / V99 / M • Live In, Love In / 1989 / ME / M • Lost Lovers / 1990 / VEX / M • Lunar Lust / 2990 / HO / M • The Mistress #2 / 1990 / CV / M • National Poontang's Summer Vacation / 1990 / FC / M • Naturally Sweet / 1989 / VEX / M • Neighborhood Watch #03 / 1991 / LBO / M • New Girls In Town #1 / 1990 / CC / M • Night On The Town / 1990 / V99 / M • One Flew Over The Cuckoo's Breast / 1989 / FAZ / M • Open House (CDI) / 1989 / CDI / M • Oral Hijinx / 1990 / ERU / M • Pleasure Principle / 1990 / FAZ / M • The Pleasure Seekers / 1990 / VD / M • Pure Energy / 1990 / VEX / M • Ready, Willing & Anal (Cv) / 1993 / CV / C • Rituals / 1989 / V99 / M • Secret Cravings / 1989 / V99 / M • Sex Appraisals / 1990 / HO / M • Sex Kittens / 1990 / VEX / F • Soft Bodies: Curves Ahead / 1991 / SB / F • Sweet Temptations / 1989 / V99 / M • Tamara's Dreams / 1989 / VEX / M • Torrid House / 1989 / VI / M • The Ultimate Climax / 1989 / V99 / M • Vegas #1: Royal Flush / 1990 / CIN / M • Wild Goose Chase / 1990 / EA / M

TAMARA LINGLEY *see* **Tamara Longley**

TAMARA LONGLEY *(Tamara Lingley, Tamara Chang, Tamera Longly, Blaire Richmond, Tamara (Longley), Sally Rose)*
Husky voiced brunette/dark blonde with small tits, small areola, good tan lines, and a lean body. Tamara Chang is from **Yellow Fever**. Blaire Richmond is from **Suze's Centerfolds #6**. Sally Rose is from **Inside Everybody**.
2002: A Sex Odyssey / 1985 / DR / M • Alien Lust / 1985 / AVC / M • Amber Lynn's Personal Best / 1986 / VD / M • Bachelor's Paradise / 1986 / VEX / M • Backdoor To Hollywood #01 / 1986 / CDI / M • Bare Waves / 1986 / VD / M • Best Of Caught From Behind #1 / 1987 / HO / C • Beverly Hills Exposed / 1985 / SE / M • Bi-Sexual Fantasies / 1984 / LAV / G • Black On White / 1987 / PL / C • Black To Africa / 1987 / PL / C • Bondage Classix #09: Andrea's Fault / 1987 / BON / B • Bondage Memories #02 / 1993 / BON / C • C-Hunt / 1985 / PL / M • Caught From Behind #03 / 1985 / HO / M • Chastity Johnson / 1985 / AVC / M • Circus Acts / 1987 / SE / C • Collection #09 / 1985 / CA / M • Corporate Assets / 1985 / SE / M • Crazy With The Heat #1 / 1986 / CV / M • Cunning Coeds / 1985 / IVP / M • Deep Chill / cr85 / AT / M • Desire / 1983 / VCX / M • Devil In Miss Jones #4: The Final Outrage / 1987 / VC / M • Double Heat / 1986 / LA / M • Easy Cum...Easy Go / 1985 / BAN / M • Erotic Aerobics / 1984 / VC / M • The Eyes Of Eddie Mars / 1984 / CV / M • Family Secrets / 1985 / AMB / M • Fantasies Unltd. / 1985 / CDI / M • Fantasy Follies #1 / 1983 / VC / M • Fashion Passion / 1985 / VD / M • Flash Trance / 1985 / IVP / M • Flesh & Laces #1 / 1983 / CA / M • Flesh & Laces #2 / 1983 / CA / M • For The Fun Of It / 1986 / SEV / M • The Fun House / 1988 / SEV / C • Ginger On The Rocks / 1985 / VI / M • Girl Games / 1987 / PL / C • The Girls Of The A Team #1 / 1985 / WV / M • Harle-

quin Affair / 1985 / CIX / M • Head & Tails / 1988 / VD / M • Honeybuns #2: Grecian Formula / 1987 / WV / C • The House Of Strange Desires / 1985 / NSV / M • I Love A Girl In A Uniform / 1989 / VC / C • Inside Everybody / 1984 / AVC / M • Joanna Storm On Fire / 1985 / VIV / M • Kiss Of The Married Woman / 1986 / WV / M • Ladies Of The 80's / 1985 / PV / M • Legacy Of Lust / 1985 / CA / M • Lip Service / 1988 / LV / C • Lucky Charm / 1986 / AVC / C • Lust With The Stranger / 1986 / MAP / M • Me, Myself & I / 1987 / SE / C • The More the Merrier / 1989 / VC / C • Naughty Girls In Heat / 1986 / SE / M • Nightfire / 1987 / LA / M • Older Men With Young Girls / 1985 / CC / M • Only The Best Of Men's And Women's Fantasies / 1988 / CV / C • Only The Best Of Oral / 1989 / CV / C • Oral Majority #04 / 1987 / WV / C • Oriental Lesbian Fantasies / 1984 / PL / F • The Other Side Of Lianna / 1984 / LA / M • Parliament: Dildo Babes #1 / 1986 / PM / F • Parliament: Tip Top #1 / 1986 / PM / F • Perfect Partners / 1986 / CV / M • Playpen / 1987 / VC / M • Please Don't Stop / 1986 / CV / M • The Pleasure Seekers / 1985 / AT / M • Princess Charming / 1987 / AVC / C • Pulsating Flesh / 1986 / VC / M • Real Men Eat Keisha / 1986 / VC / M • Rubber Reamed Fuckholes / 1994 / MET / C • Scent Of A Woman / 1985 / GO / M • Sex 5th Avenue / 1985 / WV / M • Sex Academy / 1985 / PLY / M • Sex Maniacs / 1987 / JOY / C • Sex-A-Vision / 1985 / DR / M • Sexpertease / 1985 / VD / M • She's A Boy Toy / 1985 / DR / M • Showdown / 1985 / BON / B • The Sleazy Detective / 1988 / VD / M • Slippery When Wet / 1986 / PL / M • A Star Is Porn / 1985 / PL / M • Suze's Centerfolds #6 / 1981 / CA / M • Tales From The Chateau / 1987 / BON / B • Taste Of The Best #2 / 1988 / PIN / C • Tawnee...Be Good! / 1988 / LV / M • This Stud's For You / 1986 / MAP / C • Threesomes / 1994 / CA / C • Tight Fit / 1987 / V99 / M • To Lust In LA / 1986 / LA / M • Treasure Box / 1986 / PEN / M • Trinity Brown / 1984 / CV / M • Unthinkable / 1984 / SE / M • VCA Previews #4 / 1988 / VC / C • Visions Of Jeannie / 1986 / VD / M • Voyeur's Delight / 1986 / VCS / C • The Wacky World Of X-Rated Bloopers / 1989 / GO / M • What Are Friends For? / 1985 / MAP / M • Wicked Wenches / 1988 / LA / M • Women Who Love Girls / 1989 / CLV / C • WPINK-TV #1 / 1985 / PV / M • Yellow Fever / 1984 / PL / M • Yiddish Erotica #1 / 1986 / SE / C • [Bare Mountain / 1985 / GO / M

TAMARA LYNN *see* **Star Index I**

TAMARA LYNNE *see* **Star Index I**

TAMARA MACANDREWS
An Unnatural Act #1 / 1984 / DR / M

TAMARA MORGAN *(Samantha Morgan)*
Samantha Morgan is from **Chopstix**.
Chopstix / 1979 / TVX / M • Girls In Blue / 1987 / VCX / C • Little Girls Blue #1 / 1977 / VCX / M

TAMARA SKYE *see* **Star Index I**

TAMARA WEST
The Blonde Goddess / 1982 / VXP / M • Twilight Pink #2 / 1982 / VC / M • Wild Innocents / 1982 / VCX / M

TAMARA WHITE *see* **Ariel Knight**

TAMARA WILD *see* **Kiss**

TAMERA LONGLY *see* **Tamara Longley**

TAMEYA JEWELS *(Jameya Jewels, Jamena Jewels)*

Big Bust Babes #36 / 1996 / AFI / M • Double D Dykes #25 / 1995 / GO / F • Hardcore Confidential #1 / 1996 / TEP / M • Lingerie / 1996 / RAS / M • Mike Hott: #365 Lesbian Sluts #26 / 1996 / MHV / F • Mike Hott: #369 Cum In My Mouth #05 / 1996 / MHV / C • Mike Hott: #383 Bonus Cunt: Tameya Jewels / 1996 / MHV / M • Perverted Stories #06 / 1996 / JMP / M • Young And Anal #4 / 1996 / JMP / M

TAMI

The All-Conference Nude Workout / 1995 / NIV / S • Black Hollywood Amateurs #05 / 1995 / MID / M • Black Hollywood Amateurs #06 / 1995 / MID / M • Ebony Assets / 1994 / VBE / M • Green Piece Of Ass #5 / 1994 / RTP / M • HomeGrown Video #464: Liza, We Love You / 1995 / HOV / M • Horny Old Broads / 1995 / FPI / M • Sean Michaels On The Road #10: Seattle / 1994 / VT / M

TAMI LEE CURTIS *(Tamy Dody, Tammy Dodi, Crystal Waters)*

Aerobics Girls Club / 1986 / 4P / F • Backdoor Babes / 1985 / WET / M • Bedtime Stories / 1989 / WV / M • Chastity And The Starlets / 1986 / RAV / M • Double Messages / 1987 / MOV / M • Inner Blues / 1987 / VD / M • Innocent Seduction / 1988 / VC / M • Keisha / 1987 / VD / M • Little American Maid / 1987 / VCX / M • The Long Ranger / 1987 / VCX / M • On The Wet Side / 1987 / V99 / M • Rear Ended / 1985 / WV / M • Rough Draft / 1986 / VEN / M • Sex-O-Gram / 1986 / LA / M • Starved For Affection / 1985 / AVC / M

TAMI REED

The Likes Of Louise / 197? / BL / M

TAMI ROCHE

Between My Breasts #06 / 1989 / BTO / M • Between My Breasts #09 / 1990 / BTO / M • Between My Breasts #15 / 1991 / BTO / M • Big Bust Strippers #01 / 1990 / BTO / F • Big Busty #22 / 198? / H&S / S • Here It Is: Burlesque / 1979 / VES / S

TAMI THOMAS

On White Satin / 1980 / VCX / M

TAMI WHITE *see* **Ariel Knight**

TAMIE TREVOR *see* **Star Index I**

TAMIKA

Ready To Drop #10 / 1996 / FC / M

TAMIKA (MENAGE) *see* **Menage Trois**

TAMIR

Sexhibition #3 / 1996 / SUF / M

TAMISHA *see* **Loving More**

TAMISHA ALLURE *see* **Loving More**

TAMMI

The Anal Adventures Of Max Hardcore: Love Hurts / 1994 / ZA / M • Full Moon Video #35: Wild Side Couples: The School HeadMaste / 1995 / FAP / M • Southern Belles #5 / 1995 / XPR / M

TAMMI ANN *(Tammy Ann, Tammi Fallon, Tammi Ann Fallon)*

Thin, somewhat emaciated very young looking blonde with tiny tits, pencil eraser nipples and a tight girl-like body. Nice laugh and pleasant personality. 22 years old in 1993. Used to park aircraft at LAX (?).

Ace In The Hole / 1995 / PL / M • The Adventures Of Mr. Tootsie Pole #2 / 1995 / LBO / M • The Anal Adventures Of Max Hardcore: Video Games / 1994 / ZA / M •

Anal Al's Adventures / 1995 / PL / M • Anal Angels #4 / 1995 / VEX / C • Anal Angels #6 / 1996 / VEX / C • Anal Bad Girls / 1994 / ROB / F • Anal Candy Ass / 1994 / ROB / M • Anal Deep Rider / 1994 / ROB / M • The Anal Diary Of Misty Rain / 1993 / EL / M • Anal Legend / 1994 / ROB / M • Anal Summer / 1994 / ROB / M • Anal Vision #19 / 1993 / LBO / M • The Ass Master #05 / 1994 / GLI / M • Badgirls #3: Cell Block 69 / 1994 / VI / M • Because I Can / 1995 / BEP / M • Booty Mistress / 1994 / ROB / M • Buffy Malibu's Nasty Girls #07 / 1994 / ANA / F • Bun Busters #07 / 1993 / LBO / M • The Butt Detective / 1994 / VC / M • Butt Jammers #03 / 1995 / SC / F • Butt Jammers #04 / 1995 / SC / F • Butt Love / 1995 / AB / M • Butt Motors / 1995 / VC / M • Butt Sluts #4 / 1995 / ROB / F • Butthunt / 1994 / AFV / M • Buttmasters / 1994 / AMP / M • Buttslammers #04: Down And Dirty / 1993 / BS / F • Buttslammers #05: Quake, Rattle & Roll! / 1994 / BS / F • Buttslammers #06: Over The Edge / 1994 / BS / F • Candy Factory / 1994 / PE / M • Car Wash Angels / 1995 / VC / M • Casting Call #04 / 1993 / SO / M • Cherry Poppers #01 / 1993 / ZA / M • Coming Of Age / 1995 / VEX / C • Creme De Femme / 1994 / 4P / F • Cum & Get Me / 1995 / PL / F • Cunthunt / 1995 / AB / F • Debbie Does Dallas Again / 1994 / AFV / M • Demolition Woman #2 / 1994 / IP / M • Depraved Fantasies #1 / 1993 / FPI / M • The Devil In Miss Jones #5: The Inferno / 1994 / VC / M • The Ebony Connection #2 / 1994 / LBO / C • Euro-Max #3: / 1995 / SC / M • Extreme Sex #1: The Club / 1994 / VI / M • Extreme Sex #3: Wired / 1994 / VI / M • Extreme Sex #4: The Experiment / 1995 / VI / M • The Fantasy Booth / 1993 / ONA / M • Finger Pleasures #3 / 1995 / PL / F • Flipside / 1996 / VI / M • Girls With Curves #2 / 1994 / CV / M • Girly Video Magazine #5 / 1996 / BEP / M • Hard-On Copy / 1994 / WV / M • Hello Norma Jeane / 1994 / VT / M • The Hitch-Hiker #01: Wide Open Spaces / 1993 / WMG / M • Hollywood Lesbians / 1995 / ROB / F • Hose Jobs / 1995 / VEX / M • Hotel Sodom #05: Tammi Ann Bends Over / 1995 / SNA / M • Indecent Interview / 1995 / PL / F • Intercourse With The Vampyre #1 / 1994 / SC / M • Intercourse With The Vampyre #2 / 1994 / SC / M • Just A Girl / 1996 / AB / M • Just Lesbians / 1995 / NOT / F • Kinky Cameraman #2 / 1996 / LEI / C • Kym Wilde's On The Edge #20 / 1995 / RB / B • Layover / 1994 / VI / M • Lesbian Mystery Theatre: The Case Of The Deadly Dyke / 1994 / LIP / F • Little Girl Blue / 1995 / RHS / M • Live Sex / 1994 / LE / M • Love Bunnies #06 / 1994 / FPI / F • Love Bunnies #07 / 1994 / FPI / F • Lust Runner / 1995 / VC / M • M Series #15 / 1993 / LBO / M • Major Fucking Slut / 1995 / BIP / M • Misty @ Midnight / 1995 / LE / M • N.Y. Video Magazine #06 / 1995 / OUP / M • The Naked Fugitive / 1995 / CA / M • Nasty Nymphos #04 / 1994 / ANA / M • Naughty In Nature / 1994 / PL / M • The New Butt Hunt #15 / 1995 / LEI / C • New Wave Hookers #4 / 1994 / VC / M • Nylon / 1995 / VI / M • Older Men With Younger Women #2 / 1994 / CC / M • Oral Majority #13 / 1995 / WV / C • Outrageous Sex / 1995 / BIP / F • The Pain Connection /

1994 / BS / B • Passion's Prisoners / 1994 / LV / M • Petite & Sweet / 1994 / V99 / M • Pleasure Dome: The Genesis Chamber / 1994 / AFV / M • Private Film #24 / 1995 / OD / M • Private Film #25 / 1995 / OD / M • Private Film #26 / 1995 / OD / M • Private Performance / 1994 / EX / M • Private Video Magazine #09 / 1994 / OD / M • Private Video Magazine #25 / 1995 / OD / M • Profiles #07: Sexworld / 1996 / XPR / M • Pure Filth / 1995 / RV / M • Pussy Tales / 1993 / SC / F • Pussyclips #05 / 1994 / SNA / M • Pussyman #09: Feeding Frenzy / 1995 / SNA / M • Pussyman #12: Sticky Fingers / 1995 / SNA / M • R.E.A.L. #2 / 1994 / LV / F • Raunch #10: Uncut Jewel / 1994 / CC / M • Reservoir Bitches / 1994 / BIP / M • Rump Man: Goes To Cannes / 1995 / HW / M • Savage Liasons / 1995 / BEP / F • Sex Machine / 1994 / VT / M • Sinboy #2: Yo' Ass Is Mine / 1996 / SC / M • Sindy Does Anal Again / 1994 / AFV / M • Sindy's Sexercise Workout / 1994 / AFV / M • Sloppy Seconds / 1994 / PE / M • Sluthunt #2 / 1995 / BIP / F • Sodomania #07: Deep Down Inside / 1993 / EL / M • Sodomania...And Then Some!!! A Compendium / 1995 / EL / C • Sodomania: Slop Shots / 1996 / EL / C • Solo Adventures / 1996 / AB / F • Sorority Stewardesses #1 / 1995 / PE / M • Sorority Stewardesses #2 / 1995 / PE / M • Stripper Nurses / 1994 / PE / M • Superstar Sex Challenge #1 / 1994 / VC / M • Taboo #15 / 1995 / IN / M • Tactical Sex Force / 1994 / IN / M • Tail Taggers #117 / 1993 / WV / M • Tail Taggers #120 / 1994 / WV / M • Takin' It To The Limit #1 / 1994 / BS / M • Takin' It Up The Butt / 1995 / IF / C • Triple X Video Magazine #01 / 1995 / OD / M • Triple X Video Magazine #02 / 1995 / OD / M • Trouble Maker / 1995 / VI / M • Vice / 1994 / WAV / M • Video Virgins #08 / 1993 / NS / M • The Violation Of Felecia / 1995 / JMP / F • The Violation Of Rachel Love / 1995 / JMP / F • Vivid At Home #01 / 1994 / VI / M • Water Worked / 1995 / AB / F • Where The Girls Sweat...Not The Sequel / 1996 / EL / F • Wild Dreams / 1995 / V99 / M • Wild Things #4 / 1994 / CV / M • A World Of Hurt / 1994 / BS / B • Young & Natural #07 / 1995 / PRE / F • Young & Natural #09 / 1995 / PRE / C • Young & Natural #10 / 1995 / PRE / F • Young & Natural #13 / 1996 / TV / F

TAMMI ANN FALLON *see* **Tammi Ann**

TAMMI FALLON *see* **Tammi Ann**

TAMMIE CLARK *see* **Star Index I**

TAMMIE LUST

Cherry Poppers #06: Pretty And Pink / 1994 / ZA / M

TAMMY

A&B AB#391: Sexy Blondes / 1991 / A&B / M • A&B AB#448: Girlfriends / 1996 / A&B / F • Blue Vanities #522 / 1993 / FFL / M • C.T. Coed Teasers / 1978 / VXP / M • The Erotic Aventures Of Lolita / 1982 / VXP / M • Full Moon Video #24: Wild Side Couples / 1992 / FAP / M • Full Moon Video #1F: Tammy's First Punishment / 1994 / FAP / B • HomeGrown Video #473: Furpie Feast #3 / 1997 / HOV / C • Ready To Drop #09 / 1995 / FC / M • Tales Of A Cathouse / 1994 / BRI / S

TAMMY (STACY/TAMMY) *see* **Stacy/Tammy**

TAMMY ALLEN
Nasty Girls #2 (1990-CDI) / 1990 / CDI / M
TAMMY ANN see Tammi Ann
TAMMY DODI see Tami Lee Curtis
TAMMY DOWNS see Tammy Reynolds
TAMMY HART see Rayann Drew
TAMMY KNIGHT see Star Index I
TAMMY LAMB
Golden Girls #31 / 1985 / CA / M • Lusty Ladies #03 / 1983 / SVE / M • Scoundrels / 1982 / COM / M • Star Angel / 1986 / COM / M
TAMMY LANE see Vanessa D'Oro
TAMMY LYNN
Poop Shute Debutantes / 1995 / LBO / M • Student Fetish Videos: Foot Worship #17 / 1995 / PRE / B • Student Fetish Videos: Spanking #20 / 1995 / PRE / R
TAMMY MONROE *(Darcy Derringer, Courtney Hill)*
Started as a redhead with medium sized tits and a tattoo on the left one. Became blonde, had the tits enhanced to a grotesque size and removed the tattoo. Tiny girl with a very hard attitude. In 1990 reportedly married one of the members of Slaughter, a heavy metal group, and quit the business. Returned in 1993. Is this the same as Michelle Carelli in *Love Scenes #1*? Now (1996) reportedly married to Chuck Zane (of Zane Entertainment).
Amazing Tails #4 / 1990 / CA / M • Anal Intruder #07 / 1993 / CC / M • Anal Vision #06 / 1992 / LBO / M • Beach Blanket Bondage / 1993 / BON / B • Biff Malibu's Totally Nasty Home Videos #16 / 1992 / ANA / M • Big Bust Casting Call / 1993 / PME / S • Blonde Beaver Bonanza / 1992 / TCP / M • Bob Lyons: Big Tits, Nude Slits, and a Six Foot Snake / 1992 / BLY / M • Bondage Fantasies #1 / 1989 / BIZ / B • Bondage Fantasies #2 / 1989 / BIZ / B • Bossy Babes / 1993 / TCK / M • Breast Worx #31 / 1992 / LBO / M • The British Are Coming / 1993 / ZA / M • California Pizza Girls / 1992 / EVN / M • Cat & Mouse #2 / 1993 / XCI / M • Cheri Taylor Is Tasty And Tight / 1991 / ZA / M • Coming Of Age / 1989 / CA / M • Dark Destiny / 1992 / BS / B • The Darker Side / 1994 / HO / M • Deep Inside Keisha / 1994 / VC / C • Dirty Bob's #04: SliCES Of ViCES / 1992 / FLP / S • Double D Dykes #07 / 1992 / GO / F • Dresden Mistress #3 / 1989 / BIZ / B • Eleventh Annual AVN Awards / 1994 / VC / M • The Erotic Adventures Of Bedman And Throbbin / 1989 / VWA / M • Family Affairs / 1990 / VD / M • Fantasy Girls / 1994 / PME / F • Father Of The Babe / 1993 / ZA / M • Frankenhunter, Queen Of The Porno Zombies / 1989 / GMI / M • Frat Girls Of Double D / 1993 / PP / M • Glitz Tits #01 / 1992 / GLI / M • The Goddess / 1993 / ZA / M • Good Things Come In Small Packages / 1989 / CA / M • The Good, The Bed, And The Snuggly / 1993 / ZA / M • Hard Times / 1990 / GLE / M • Head Lock / 1989 / VD / M • Hot Sweet 'n' Sticky / 1992 / CA / C • How To Give Pleasure To A Woman By A Woman / 1995 / SEM / F • How To Make A Model #04: Facial Cream Girls / 1994 / LBO / M • Hung Jury / 1989 / VWA / M • Hyperkink / 1989 / VWA / M • Intimate Secrets / 1993 / PME / F • Jennifer 69 / 1992 / PL / M • Jiggly Queens #1 / 1993 / LE / M • Kinky Couples / 1990 / VD / M • Kiss My

Grits / 1989 / CA / M • Kym Wilde Sessions #3 / 1993 / RB / B • Kym Wilde's On The Edge #01 / 1993 / RB / B • L.A. Woman / 1990 / PHV / F • Leg...Ends #08 / 1993 / PRE / F • Leg...Ends #11 / 1994 / PRE / F • Lesbian Pros And Amateurs #17 / 1992 / GO / F • The Long & Short Of It / 1992 / RUM / F • Mellon Man #02 / 1994 / AVI / M • More Than A Handful / 1993 / CA / C • My Secret Lover / 1992 / XCI / M • The Naked Bun / 1989 / VWA / M • New Hardcore Beginners #20 / 1996 / LEI / C • Night Trips #2 / 1990 / CA / M • Nookie Cookies / 1993 / CDI / F • The Outlaw / 1989 / VD / M • Party Pack #2 / 1994 / LE / F • Pretty Peaches #3 / 1989 / VC / M • The Red Head / 1989 / VWA / M • The Screwables / 1992 / RUM / M • Servin' It Up / 1993 / VC / M • Sex Bandits / 1992 / ZA / M • Sex Toy / 1993 / CA / C • The Sexual Zone / 1989 / EX / M • Sheer Ecstasy / 1993 / IF / M • Sins Of Tami Monroe / 1991 / CA / C • Sisters / 1993 / ZA / M • Sorority Sex Kittens #2 / 1993 / VC / M • Student Fetish Videos: Best of Catfighting #02 / 1994 / PRE / C • Student Fetish Videos: Best Of Foot Worship #03 / 1995 / PRE / C • Student Fetish Videos: Catfighting #10 / 1994 / PRE / B • Student Fetish Videos: Foot Worship #09 / 1994 / PRE / B • Student Fetish Videos: Spanking #13 / 1994 / PRE / B • SVE: Screentest Sex #1 / 1992 / SVE / M • Swedish Erotica Featurettes #1 / 1989 / CA / M • Swedish Erotica Featurettes #3 / 1989 / CA / M • Swedish Erotica Featurettes #4 / 1990 / CA / M • Swedish Erotica Featurettes #5 / 1990 / CA / M • Tami Monroe Tied At Home / 1993 / BON / B • The Taming Of Tami / 1990 / CA / M • A Taste Of Cheri / 1990 / PIN / C • A Taste Of Tori Welles / 1990 / PIN / C • Toppers #04 / 1993 / TV / M • Toppers #05 / 1993 / TV / M • Toppers #08 / 1993 / TV / M • Toppers #10 / 1993 / TV / M • Toppers #12 / 1993 / TV / C • Toppers #30 / 1994 / TV / C • Twice As Nice / 1989 / VWA / M • Twin Freaks / 1992 / ZA / M • Untamed Cowgirls Of The Wild West #01: The Pillow Biters / 1992 / ZA / M • Untamed Cowgirls Of The Wild West #02: Jammy Glands... / 1993 / ZA / M • Up Against It / 1993 / ZA / M • The Violation Of Tori Welles / 1990 / VD / C • Vogue / 1994 / VD / C • Welcome To Bondage: Starlets #2 / 1994 / BON / C • Wet & Wild Tami Monroe / 1991 / CA / C • Who Killed Holly Hollywood? / 1993 / VC / M • X-Rated Blondes / 1992 / VD / C
TAMMY PARKS
Attack Of The 60 Foot Centerfold / 1995 / NEH / S • The Dinner Party #1 / 1994 / ULI / M • Droid Gunner / 1995 / NEH / S • Erotic Visions / 1995 / ULI / M • Nude Bowling Party / 1995 / BRI / S • Penthouse: Women In & Out Of Uniform / 1994 / A*V / S • Strap-On Sally #08: Strap-On Cock Fight / 1995 / PL / F
TAMMY PEAR
Nanci Blue / 1979 / SE / M
TAMMY RAE see Tawny Rae
TAMMY REYNOLDS *(Tammy Downs)*
Alexandra The Greatest / 1990 / NAP / F • Banana Splits / 1987 / 3HV / M • The Battle Of the Breast Queens / 1989 / INS / C • Beyond The Denver Dynasty / 1988 / CA / M • Big Busted Goddesses Of L.A. / 1991 /

NAP / S • The Blonde And The Brunette / 1989 / NAP / B • Bright Lights, Big Titties / 1989 / CA / M • California Cherries / 1987 / EVN / M • Dana Lynn's Hot All Over / 1987 / V99 / M • Debbie Does Dallas #5 / 1988 / VEX / M • Deep Inside Ona Zee / 1992 / VC / C • Dream Match / 1989 / NAP / B • Filet-O-Breast / 1988 / AVC / M • Gazongas #02 / 1988 / VEX / M • Girls Of The Double D #04 / 1989 / CDI / M • Heart Of Stone / 1990 / FAN / M • Hot Blondes / 1988 / VEX / M • Hot Meat / 1990 / V99 / M • Introducing Micki Marsaille / 1990 / NAP / F • Just For The Thrill Of It / 1989 / V99 / M • La Bimbo / 1987 / PEN / M • Megasex / 1988 / EVN / M • The Pillowman / 1988 / VC / M • Sex On Location / 1989 / KIS / M • Travelling Companion / 1989 / NAP / B • When Big Busted Cats Tangle / 1990 / NAP / B • Wildfire / 1989 / EVN / M • [Berlin Caper / 1989 / ... / M
TAMMY TILDEN
GVC: Hotel Hooker #113 / 1975 / GO / M
TAMMY TWAT see Star Index I
TAMMY TWILIGHT
Blue Vanities #094 / 1988 / FFL / M
TAMMY WHITE see Ariel Knight
TAMRA
Roni Raye: Playful Playmates / 1996 / RR / F
TAMY DODY see Tami Lee Curtis
TAN LEE DUC
Midnight Fantasies / 1992 / VIM / M
TANA see Laurie Cameron
TANA TAMLIN see Laurie Cameron
TANAZ
More Dirty Debutantes #50 / 1996 / 4P / M
TANDEE
Mike Hott: #258 Horny Couples #16 / 1994 / MHV / M
TANGERINE DANTE see Star Index I
TANI ENGLAND
Pony Girl #2: At The Ranch / 1986 / CS / B
TANIA
Buttman's Double Adventure / 1993 / EA / M • Julie's Diary / 1995 / LBO / M • The Mysteries Of Transsexualism Explored #1 / 1987 / OZE / G
TANIA BUSSELIER
Douce Penetrations / 1975 / LUM / M • Sensations / 1975 / ALP / M
TANIA LA RUSSA
Prima #14: Hotel Europa / 1996 / MBP / M
TANIA LARIVIERE
Betty Bleu / 1996 / IP / M • Tania's Lustexzesse / 1994 / MET / M
TANIA RUSSOF
Private Film #27 / 1995 / OD / M • Private Film #28 / 1995 / OD / M • Private Gold #11: The Pyramid #1 / 1996 / OD / M • Private Gold #12: The Pyramid #2 / 1996 / OD / M • Private Video Magazine #17 / 1994 / OD / M • Triple X Video Magazine #01 / 1995 / OD / M • Triple X Video Magazine #02 / 1995 / OD / M • Triple X Video Magazine #04 / 1995 / OD / M • Triple X Video Magazine #12 / 1996 / OD / M
TANIA TASARA
New Pussy Hunt #17 / 1995 / LEI / M • Video Virgins #18 / 1994 / NS / M
TANIKA
HomeGrown Video #446: Slam Bam Thank You Ma'am! / 1995 / HOV / M
TANJA see Star Index I
TANJA DEVRIES see Tanya DeVries
TANJA GOLD

Ass Masters (Leisure) #02 / 1995 / LEI / M • Swedish Erotica #84 / 1995 / CA / M • Video Virgins #19 / 1994 / NS / M
TANJA LORD
Von Sex Gier Besessen / 1995 / PF / M
TANJA MAN *see Star Index I*
TANJA RATTER *see Star Index I*
TANJE ROE
The Voyeur #3 / 1995 / EA / M
TANK TOP SMITH *see Star Index I*
TANNER COLE *see Ted Wilson*
TANNER REEVES
Bi-Conflict / 1994 / FST / G • Bi-Wicked / 1994 / BIN / G • Conflict Of Interest / 1994 / FST / G • Long Play / 1995 / 3XP / G • More Than Friends / 1995 / KDP / G • Re-membering Times Gone Bi / 1995 / AWV / G • Where The Bi's Are / 1994 / BIN / G
TANO ROCCO *see Rocco Siffredi*
TANO SAKAMOTO
Private Escort / 1996 / AVE / M
TANTALA *see Star Index I*
TANTALA MORGAN *see Star Index I*
TANTALA NAVE *see Tantala Ray*
TANTALA RAY *(Darcy Nychols, Mistress Tantala, Tantala Nave, Darcy Nichols)*
Assault Of The Party Nerds #1 / 1989 / PRS / S • Back To Back #1 / 1987 / 4P / C • Best Of Bruce Seven #3 / 1990 / BIZ / C • Beverly Hills Cox / 1986 / CA / M • Bizarre Encounters / 1986 / 4P / B • Body Slam / 1987 / 4P / B • Bratgirl / 1989 / VI / M • Cafe Flesh / 1982 / VC / M • Celebrity Presents Celebrity / 1986 / VEP / C • Centerfold Celebrities #4 / 1983 / VC / M • Chicks In Black Leather / 1989 / VC / C • Computer Girls / 1983 / LIP / F • Crazy With The Heat #1 / 1986 / CV / M • Daisy Chain / 1984 / IN / M • Dear Fanny / 1984 / CV / M • Des-perate Women / 1986 / VD / M • Don't Tell Daddy #1 / 1985 / PL / C • Dreams Of Misty / 1984 / VCX / M • Fantasy Mansion / 1983 / BIZ / B • Fox Fever's Catfight Action / 1984 / VCR / B • Heart Breaker / 1985 / TAR / C • The Hottest Show In Town / 1987 / VIP / M • Kinky Sluts / 1988 / MIR / C • Let Me Tell Ya 'Bout Fat Chicks #1 / 1986 / 4P / C • Love Scenes For Loving Couples / 1987 / CV / C • Love To Mother / 1984 / VIV / M • Loving Spoonfulls / 1987 / 4P / C • Lusty Couples (Come To) / cr85 / CHX / M • Mad About You / 1987 / VC / M • Mama's Boy / 1984 / VD / M • Marilyn Chambers' Private Fantasies #2 / 1983 / CA / M • Mar-ilyn Chambers' Private Fantasies #3 / 1983 / CA / M • Marilyn Chambers' Private Fan-tasies #5 / 1985 / CA / M • Mistresses And Slaves: The Best Of Bruce Seven / 1991 / BEB / C • Motel Sweets / 1987 / VD / M • Nasty Habits Are Hard To Break / 1986 / 4P / M • Only The Best Of Anal / 1992 / MET / C • Out For Blood / 1990 / VI / M • Pacific Intrigue / 1987 / AMB / M • Passion For Bondage / 1983 / BIZ / B • Personal Touch #3 / 1983 / AR / M • The Rocky Porno Video Show / 1986 / 4P / M • Schoolgirl By Day / 1985 / LA / M • Slammer Girls / 1987 / LIV / S • Sounds Of Sex / 1985 / CA / M • Squalor Motel / 1985 / SE / M • Star Virgin / 1979 / CXV / M • Submission Position #608 / 1988 / CTS / B • Tantala's Fat Rack / 1990 / FC / B • A Taste Of Cherry / 1985 / CV / M • Wet, Wild And Wicked / 1984 / SE / M • What's My Punishment / 1983 / BIZ / B
TANTALIZING TONY

She-Male Encounters #01: Tanatalizing Toni / 1981 / MET / G • She-Male Encoun-ters #02: Carnal Candy / 1981 / MET / G • She-Male Encounters #08: Divine Atroci-ties #2 / 1981 / MET / G
TANYA
A&B GB#044: Tanya Eats It All / 1992 / A&B / M • Amateur Lesbians #18: Jamie / 1992 / GO / F • Amateur Lesbians #35: Meo / 1993 / GO / F • Amateur Lesbians #36: Candi / 1993 / GO / F • The Analyst / 1990 / SOR / B • Blacks & Blondes #13 / 1986 / WV / M • Blue Vanities #533 / 1993 / FFL / M • Blue Vanities #550 / 1994 / FFL / M • Blue Vanities #568 / 1995 / FFL / M • Bobby Hollander's Rookie Nookie #12 / 1993 / SFP / M • Bucky Beaver's XXX Dragon Art Theatre Double Feature #06 / 1996 / SOW / M • Cruel Turnabout / 1990 / PL / B • Double D Amateurs #05 / 1993 / JMP / M • Fangs Of Steel / Sexual Cutting / 1996 / FLV / M • Finishing School / 1975 / SOW / M • Frankenfoot / 1993 / SBP / B • Frat House / 1979 / NGV / M • Hard Core Beginners #07 / 1995 / LEI / M • Just The Way You Like It #3: Tanya And Company / 1994 / JEG / M • Lovin' Spoonfuls #8 / 1996 / 4P / C • Magma: Anal Wedding / 1995 / MET / M • Mr. Peepers Amateur Home Videos #86: Tit A Ton / 1994 / LBO / M • Perversity In Paris / 1994 / AVI / M • Snatch Masters #04 / 1995 / LEI / M • Top Debs #1: Prom Night / 1992 / GO / M • Toredo / 1996 / ROX / M • VGA: Spanks-A-Lot / 1993 / VGA / B
TANYA (ZUMIRA) *see Zumira*
TANYA ARTHUR *see Star Index I*
TANYA BLAKE *see Star Index I*
TANYA BROWN *see Star Index I*
TANYA CORTEZ *see Star Index I*
TANYA DEVRIES *(Tanja DeVries, Lola (Tanya DeVries), Tonya DeVries, Anja Schreiner)*
The Adventures Of Buttman / 1989 / EA / M • The Best Of Andrew Blake / 1993 / CA / C • Best Of Buttman #1 / 1991 / EA / C • Dou-ble Jeopardy / 1990 / HO / M • Dutch Mas-ters / 1990 / IN / M • Dutch Treat / 1989 / BON / B • Foreign Affairs / 1992 / VT / C • Hidden Desire / 1989 / HO / M • Insatiable Immigrants / 1989 / VT / M • Kiss My Grits / 1989 / CA / M • Lust In The Woods / 1990 / VI / M • Night Trips #1 / 1989 / CA / M • Postcards From Abroad / 1991 / CA / C • Rainwoman #02 / 1990 / CC / M • Swedish Erotica Featurettes #3 / 1989 / CA / M
TANYA DORSEY *see Star Index I*
TANYA EVENS
Deep Blue / 1989 / PV / M • On My Lips / 1989 / PV / M
TANYA FOX *(Kim Pare, Suzy Spain, Kim Parker, Katja (Tanya Fox), Laurn Hall)*
Short blonde with quite a pretty face and small tits but a big butt. Is this also Kim Park-land?
Amazing Tails #2 / 1987 / CA / M • Anal An-gels #1 / 1986 / VEX / M • Ashley Renee In Jeopardy / 1991 / HOM / B • Backdoor Brides #2: The Honeymoon / 1986 / PV / M • Backdoor Summer #1 / 1988 / PV / C • Backdoor To Hollywood #02 / 1986 / CDI / M • Backdoor To Hollywood #03 / 1987 / CDI / M • Behind The Backdoor #1 / 1986 / EVN / M • The Best Of Backdoor To Holly-wood / 1990 / CIN / C • Best Of Caught From Behind #1 / 1987 / HO / C • Best Of

Caught From Behind #2 / 1988 / HO / C • Best Of Caught From Behind #5 / 1991 / HO / C • The Best Of Hot Heels / 1992 / BIZ / B • The Big Thrill / 1989 / VD / M • Bionca, Just For You / 1989 / BON / F • Bizarre Mistress Series: Mistress Destiny / 1992 / BIZ / C • Black Heat / 1986 / VC / M • Black Lava / 1986 / WET / M • Blacks & Blondes #32 / 1986 / WV / M • Blows Job / 1989 / BIZ / B • Bondage Memories #03 / 1994 / BON / C • Bondage Memories #04 / 1994 / BON / C • Born To Run / 1985 / WV / M • Bound To Tease #1 / 1988 / BON / C • Bound To Tease #2 / 1989 / BON / C • Bring On The Virgins / 1989 / CA / M • Busting Loose / 1989 / AMB / F • Caddy Shack-Up / 1986 / VD / M • Captured Cop #1: Deadly Explosion / 1991 / BON / B • Captured Cop #2: The Stakeout / 1991 / BON / B • Captured Cop #3: Double Cross / 1991 / BON / B • Careena #2: A Star On The Rise / 1988 / WV / C • The Cat Club / 1987 / SE / M • Caught From Behind #05: Blondes & Blacks / 1986 / HO / M • Caught From Behind #06 / 1986 / HO / M • Caught From Behind #08 / 1988 / HO / M • Caught From Behind #09 / 1988 / HO / M • Caught From Behind #10 / 1989 / HO / M • Caught In The Act / 1992 / BON / B • Caught, Pun-ished And Caged / 1991 / BIZ / B • Chan-nel 69 / 1986 / LA / M • Cheap Shots / 1994 / PRE / B • Collected Spankings #1 / 1992 / BON / C • Criss-Cross / 1993 / BON / B • A Date With Destiny / 1992 / BIZ / B • The De Renzy Tapes / 1990 / CA / C • Decep-tion (1995-B&D) / 1995 / BON / B • Desert Heat / 1992 / BON / B • Deutsch Marks / 1992 / BON / B • Dialing For Desires / 1988 / 4P / M • Dirty Harriet / 1986 / SAT / M • Disciples Of Discipline / 1994 / STM / B • Doctor Feelgood / 1988 / CDI / M • Double Agents / 1988 / VXP / M • Double Black Fantasy / 1987 / CC / C • Double Penetra-tion #1 / 1985 / WV / M • Double Penetra-tion #2 / 1986 / WV / C • Double Penetra-tion #3 / 1986 / WV / C • Double Play / 1993 / CA / C • The Duchess / 1994 / CS / B • Dungeon De Sade / 1993 / FC / B • Ed-ucating Laurel / 1988 / BON / B • Erotic Penetration / 1987 / HO / C • Fettered Femmes / 1994 / BON / B • Fighting Mad / 1990 / NAP / B • Fresh Tender Asses / 1994 / RB / B • Funky Brewster / 1986 / DR .' M • Ghostest With The Mostest / 1988 / CA / M • Girl Crazy / 1989 / CDI / F • The Girls Are Bustin' Loose / 1988 / AMB / F • Girls Don't Lie / 1990 / IN / F • Girls Of Cell Block F / 1985 / WV / M • Going Down With Amber / 1987 / 4P / M • Grafenberg Girls Go Fishing / 1987 / MIT / M • Grand Slam / 1990 / PRE / B • Having It All / 1985 / IN / M • Head Clinic / 1987 / AVC / M • Holiday For Angels / 1987 / IN / M • Honeybuns #1 / 1987 / WV / C • Honeybuns #2: Grecian Formula / 1987 / WV / C • Hot Blood / 1990 / NAP / B • Hot Shoes / 1992 / BIZ / B • House Of Blue Dreams / 1985 / WV / M • House Of Sexual Fantasies / 1987 / GO / M • I Am Curious Black / 1986 / WET / M • Incessant / 1988 / CAD / G • Incredible Dreams #1 / 1992 / BIZ / B • Incredible Dreams #2 / 1992 / BIZ / B • Innocence Lost / 1988 / CA / M • Interracial Sex / 1987 / M&M / M • Introducing Kascha / 1988 / CDI / M • Invasion Of The Lust Snatchers / 1988 / 4P / M • The Joys Of Masturbation /

1988 / M&M / M • K.U.N.T.-TV / 1988 / WV / M • Kinky / 1987 / SE / M • KTSX-69 / 1988 / CA / M • Kym Wilde's On The Edge #09 / 1994 / RB / B • Latex Foot Torture / 1993 / SBP / B • Latex Slaves / cr87 / GOT / B • Latex Submission #1 / 1992 / BIZ / B • Latex Submission #2 / 1992 / BIZ / B • Laurel's Continuing Education / 1988 / BON / B • Let's Talk Dirty / 1987 / SE / M • Lilli Xene And Tanya Fox's Espionage Interrogation / 1993 / RSV / B • A Little Romance / 1986 / HO / M • Loose Caboose / 1987 / 4P / M • Love Hammer / 1988 / VXP / M • Lust, Ties & Videotape / 1993 / BON / B • Michelle Monroe Star Bound / 1990 / BON / B • My Wife Is A Call Girl / 1989 / FAZ / M • Naughty Nymphs / 1986 / VEX / M • Naughty Nymphs / 1991 / VEX / C • Night Shift Latex Slaves / 1991 / GOT / B • Obey Me Bitch #1 / 1992 / BIZ / B • Obey Me Bitch #2 / 1992 / BIZ / B • Obey Me Bitch #3 / 1992 / BIZ / B • Obey Me Bitch #4 / 1993 / BIZ / B • Office Heels / 1992 / BIZ / B • Oral Majority #01 / 1986 / WV / C • Oral Majority #03 / 1986 / WV / C • Oral Majority Black #1 / 1987 / WV / C • Orgies / 1987 / WV / C • Our Sorority / 1993 / SHL / B • Paddled Payoff / 1993 / STM / B • Panting At The Opera / 1988 / VXP / M • Parliament: Lesbian Lovers #2 / 1988 / PM / F • Parliament: Teasers #2 / 1988 / PM / F • Parliament: Woman's Touch / 1988 / PM / F • The Penetration Of Elle Rio / 1987 / GO / M • The Penitent / 1992 / BON / B • Playing For Passion / 1987 / IN / M • Please, Mistress! / 1993 / SV / B • Porn Star's Day Off / 1990 / FAZ / M • Primary Pleasure / 1987 / VXP / M • Professor Probe And The Spirit Of Sex / 1986 / ADU / M • Profiles In Discipline #01: The Mistress Is A Lady / 1994 / STM / C • The Punisher / 1994 / BON / B • Rainy Days #1 / 1991 / BON / B • Rainy Days #2 / 1991 / BON / B • Rambone Meets The Double Penetrators / 1987 / WET / M • Return To Sex 5th Avenue / 1985 / WV / M • Sex Beat / 1985 / WV / M • Sexy And 18 / 1987 / SE / M • Sharon Kane Star Bound / 1990 / BON / B • Shaved Pink / 1986 / WET / M • Shiela's Deep Desires / 1986 / HO / M • A Slave For The Bride / 1991 / BIZ / B • Slaves Bound For Passion / 1994 / BIZ / B • Slumber Party Reunion / 1987 / AR / M • Spanked Shopper & Other Tales / 1991 / BON / C • Spanking Tails / 1993 / BON / B • Spanking, Spanking And More / 1990 / BON / B • Split Decision / 1989 / MET / G • Stephanie, Just For You / 1989 / BON / F • Storehouse Of Agony #2 / 1992 / BIZ / B • Student Fetish Videos: The Enema #09 / 1992 / PRE / B • Student Fetish Videos: Spanking #08 / 1992 / PRE / B • Student Fetish Videos: Tickling #06 / 1992 / SFV / B • Surfside Sex / 1988 / CA / M • Sweet Surrender / 1991 / BIZ / B • Sweet Surrender / 1991 / BIZ / B • Taija's Satin Seduction / 1987 / CDI / M • Tales By Taylor / 1989 / AMB / M • Tanya Fox's Bondage Fantasies / 1993 / BON / B • Tanya Foxx After Hours / 1993 / BON / B • Tanya Foxx Star Bound / 1989 / BON / B • Tanya Foxx: A Diary Of Torment / 1995 / BON / B • Tanya Foxx: Suspended In Time / 1996 / BON / C • Taste For Submission / 1991 / LON / C • They Call My Sugar Candie / 1989 / SUE / M • Three Men And A Barbi /

1989 / FAN / M • Tie Me, Tease Me / 1994 / CS / B • Title Shots / 1995 / PRE / B • To Taste The Strap / 199? / BON / B • Toys 4 Us #2 / 1987 / WV / C • Tracey Adams' Girls School / 1993 / BIZ / B • Tracy Star Bound / 1991 / BON / B • TV Terrorists: Hostage Sluts / 1993 / BIZ / G • Two To Tango / 1987 / TEM / M • Ubangis On Uranus / 1987 / WV / M • Ultimate Submissives #3: Best of Tanya Fox / 1995 / BIZ / C • Underground #2: Subway To Sodom / 1996 / SC / M • Underground #3: Sit On This / 1996 / SC / M • The Wacky World Of X-Rated Bloopers / 1989 / GO / M • Warehouse Wenches #1 / 1994 / BIZ / B • Warehouse Wenches #2 / 1994 / BIZ / B • Wet 'n' Bare With Barbara Dare / 1988 / NEO / M • Whitey's On The Moon / 1996 / ROB / M • Wild Thing / 1989 / BON / B • Xcitement: The Movie / 1993 / XCI / M • XXX Workout / 1987 / VEX / M • Young Cheeks / 1990 / BEB / B • The Zebra Club / 1986 / VSE / M • [T&A #01 / 1989 / ... / C

TANYA FOX (TINA) *see* Tina Lindstrom

TANYA GERRADO *see* Zumira

TANYA HANEY *see Star Index I*

TANYA HARRISON *see Star Index I*

TANYA HARTLAY
My First Time #4 / 1996 / NS / M • Pussyman Auditions #18 / 1996 / SNA / M

TANYA HUNTER *see Star Index I*

TANYA HYDE
Score Busty Centerfolds #2 / 1995 / BTO / M

TANYA LARIVIERE
Hamlet: For The Love Of Ophelia #2 / 1996 / IP / M • Magma: Hot Business / 1995 / MET / M • Magma: Tanja's Horny Nights / 1994 / MET / M • Marquis De Sade / 1995 / IP / M • Nymphos: They Can't Help It...Really! / 1996 / P69 / M • Paris Chic / 1996 / SAE / M • Rump Man: Goes To Cannes / 1995 / HW / M • Up And Cummers #15 / 1994 / 4P / M

TANYA LAWSON
Passable face, shoulder length very curly dark blonde/light brown hair, lithe body, small/medium tits.
All The Way In / 1984 / VC / M • The Best Of Ron Jeremy / 1990 / WET / C • Blowing Your Mind / 1984 / RSV / M • Corruption / 1983 / VC / M • Erotic Radio WSEX / 1983 / VC / M • First Time At Cherry High / 1984 / VC / M • Flash Pants / 1983 / VC / M • Fleshdance / 1983 / SE / M • Fleshdance Fever / 1984 / SAT / M • Great Sexpectations / 1984 / VC / M • Hypersexuals / 1984 / VC / M • Kinky Business #1 / 1984 / DR / M • Only The Best #2 / 1989 / CV / C • The Pleasures Of Innocence / 1985 / VC / M • Porn Star Of The Year Contest / 1984 / VWA / M • Sex On The Set / 1984 / RLV / M • Shame On Shanna / 1989 / DR / C • Silk, Satin & Sex / 1983 / SE / M • Striptease / 1983 / VC / M • Succulent / 1983 / VXP / M • The T & A Team / 1984 / VC / M • Twilight Pink #2 / 1982 / VC / M • An Unnatural Act #1 / 1984 / DR / M • VCA Previews #3 / 1988 / VC / C • Whose Fantasy Is It, Anyway? / 1983 / AVC / M

TANYA LEE *see* Tanya Rivers

TANYA LOWSAN
A Very Debauched Girl / 1988 / PL / M

TANYA MARIE *see Star Index I*

TANYA MOORE
Breastman's Triple X Cellent Adventure /

1995 / EVN / M • Hollywood Amateurs #27 / 1996 / MID / M • Live Sex Net / 1996 / SPR / M

TANYA NAUGHTISKYA
More Dirty Debutantes #49 / 1995 / 4P / M

TANYA NORDIC *see Star Index I*

TANYA RIO
The Enforcer / 199? / NAP / B • Magnificent Seven / 1991 / NAP / F

TANYA RIVERS *(Hillary Winters, Cody (T. Rivers), Michelle (T. Rivers), Nicole (T. Rivers), Nicole Sweet, Tanya Lee)*
Brunette/dark blonde with a slightly oriental look. Has the hair and eyes of Brigitte Monroe and the coloration and skin of Kascha. A bit pudgy around the middle. Hillary Winters from **Cheeks #5**. Cody from **Temple Of Lust #1**. Michelle from **Two For The Price Of One**. First appeared in **MDD #09** where she was credited as either Nicole or Nicole Sweet. She's half Japanese and half Caucasian.
2 Hung 2 Tung / 1992 / MID / M • Behind The Blinds / 1992 / VIM / M • Brats In Bondage / 1993 / LON / B • Cheeks #5: The Ultimate Butt / 1991 / CC / M • Close Quarters / 1992 / ME / M • Ghost Writer / 1992 / LE / M • Girls And Guns / 1992 / KBR / M • Home Maid Memories #1 / 1994 / BON / C • Hooked / 1992 / SC / M • Lesbian Pros And Amateurs #11 / 1992 / GO / F • Love Scenes #2 / 1992 / B/F / S • Memories / 1992 / LE / M • More Dirty Debutantes #09 / 1991 / 4P / M • More Dirty Debutantes #25 / 1993 / 4P / M • Naked Edge / 1992 / LE / M • Neighborhood Watch #09: Dial-A-Slut / 1991 / LBO / M • Neighborhood Watch #13: Teasers and Crumpets / 1991 / LBO / M • Temple Of Lust / 1992 / VC / M • Two For The Price Of One / 1993 / BON / B • Wet Faces #1 / 1997 / SC / C • Wild Hearts / 1992 / SC / M

TANYA ROBERTSON *see Star Index I*

TANYA RUSSOF
Triple X Video Magazine #09 / 1995 / OD / M

TANYA SALAMA *see* Tanya Summers

TANYA SCICLLY *see Star Index I*

TANYA SCOTT
Eyes Of A Dreamer / 1983 / S&L / M

TANYA SENATA *see Star Index I*

TANYA SHEA *see Star Index I*

TANYA SICILY *see Star Index I*

TANYA SPICER *see Star Index I*

TANYA STORM *(Niki (one K), Cindi Snow, Cindy Snow)*
Brunette with a tattoo on her right breast, large floppy tits and a slobby but not horrible body.
AC/DC #2 / 1994 / HP / G • Adventures Of The DP Boys: Hooter County / 1995 / HW / M • AHV #22: Hello, I Love You / 1992 / EVN / M • Amateur Lesbians #27: Megan / 1992 / GO / F • Amateur Lesbians #28: Sharon / 1992 / GO / F • Amateur Lesbians #39: Tiffany / 1993 / GO / F • Amateur Lesbians #40: Sunset / 1993 / GO / F • Amateur Orgies #12 / 1992 / AFI / M • Amateur Orgies #13 / 1992 / AFI / M • Amateur Orgies #16 / 1992 / AFI / M • America's Raunchiest Home Videos #17: This Butt's For You / 1992 / ZA / M • America's Raunchiest Home Videos #51: / 1993 / ZA / M • American Connection Video Magazine #02 / 1992 / ZA / M • Anal Camera #02 / 1994 / EVN / M • Anal Gang Bangers #02

/ 1993 / GLI / M • Anal Orgasms / 1992 / DRP / M • Anal Oriental Sorority / 1994 / LBO / M • Anal Therapy #2 / 1993 / FD / M • Asian Persuasion / 1993 / WV / M • Beach Bum Amateur's #04 / 1992 / MID / M • Beach Bunny / 1994 / V99 / M • Big Bust Babes #21 / 1994 / AFI / M • Big Murray's New-Cummers #21: Double Penetration One / 1993 / FD / M • Big Murray's New-Cummers #23: Naughty Nymphettes / 1993 / FD / M • Black Buttman #02 / 1994 / CC / M • Black Men Can Hump / 1992 / FH / M • The Bodacious Boat Orgy #1 / 1993 / GLI / M • Bubble Butts #05 / 1992 / LBO / M • The Butt Boss / 1993 / VD / M • Coming Out / 1993 / VD / M • Dark Passions #02 / 1993 / AFV / M • Dead Ends / 1992 / PRE / B • The Dickheads #2 / 1993 / MID / M • Double D Amateurs #22 / 1994 / JMP / M • The Dragon Lady #3: Tales From The Bed #2 / 1992 / WV / M • Ene-mates #06 / 1992 / BIZ / B • Erotika / 1994 / WV / M • Feathermates / 1992 / PRE / B • The Freak Club / 1994 / VMX / M • A Girl's Affair #05 / 1994 / FD / F • Glitz Tits #05 / 1993 / GLI / M • Hedonism #01 / 1993 / FH / M • Hidden Camera #03 / 1993 / JMP / M • Hillary Vamp's Private Collection #19 / 1992 / HOV / M • Hillary Vamp's Private Collection #20 / 1992 / HOV / M • Hits & Misses / 1992 / PRE / B • Hometown Honeys #4 / 1993 / VEX / M • House Of Sex #05: Banging Corby And Tanya / 1994 / RTP / M • In Your Face #1 / 1992 / PL / M • Inside Of Me / 1993 / PL / G • J.E.G.: Tanya And Company #3 / 1995 / JEG / M • The Joy Dick Club / 1994 / MID / M • Jugsy (X-Citement) / 1992 / XCI / M • Kiss Is A Rebel With A Cause / 1993 / WV / M • Knockout / 1994 / VEX / M • Leg...Ends #07 / 1993 / PRE / F • Leg...Ends #08 / 1993 / PRE / F • Lesbian Lingerie Fantasy #6 / 1991 / ESP / F • Lust / 1993 / FH / M • The Magnificent 7 / 1994 / VTF / B • Mid-night Angels #02 / 1993 / MID / F • Midnight Dreams / 1994 / WV / M • Mike Hott: #205 Lesbian Sluts #06 / 1992 / MHV / F • Mike Hott: #213 Horny Couples #07 / 1992 / MHV / M • Nasty Cracks / 1992 / PRE / B • Nasty Fuckin' Movies #12: Rub My Twat / 1992 / RUM / F • Neighborhood Watch #26: / 1992 / LBO / M • Neighborhood Watch #28 / 1992 / LBO / M • Odyssey 30 Min: #176: Tanya And The Two Hard Cocks / 1991 / OD / M • Odyssey 30 Min: #186: / 1991 / OD / M • Odyssey Triple Play #22: Interracial Double Penetration / 1993 / OD / M • Only The Best Of Barbara Dare / 1990 / CV / C • Our Bang #01 / 1992 / GLI / M • Our Bang #02 / 1992 / GLI / M • Our Bang #03 / 1992 / GLI / M • Our Bang #05 / 1992 / GLI / M • Our Bang #06 / 1992 / GLI / M • Our Bang #07 / 1992 / GLI / M • Our Bang #08 / 1992 / GLI / M • Our Bang #10 / 1993 / GLI / M • Overnight Sensation / 1991 / XCI / M • Phone Fantasy #1 / 1992 / ATL / M • Phone Fantasy #2 / 1992 / ATL / M • Positively Pagan #02 / 1991 / ATA / M • Positively Pagan #12 / 1993 / ATA / M • The Prince Of Lies / 1992 / LE / M • Raging Waters / 1992 / PRE / B • Raw Talent: Bang 'er 33 Times / 1992 / RTP / M • Raw Talent: Hedonism #1 / 1993 / FH / M • Raw Talent: Swing Rave / 1993 / FH / M • Raw Talent: Top Bang / 1994 / RTP / M • Ron High-tower's White Chicks #05 / 1993 / LBO / M

• Rump Humpers #12 / 1993 / GLI / M • Sharon Mitchell's Sex Clinic #02 / 1993 / FC / M • Sheer Ecstasy / 1993 / IF / M • Sniff Doggy Style / 1994 / PL / M • Sole Survivors / 1996 / PRE / C • Student Fetish Videos: Best Of Foot Worship #02 / 1994 / PRE / C • Student Fetish Videos: Best Of Spanking #02 / 1993 / PRE / C • Student Fetish Videos: Foot Worship #08 / 1992 / PRE / B • Student Fetish Videos: Spanking #07 / 1992 / PRE / B • Supermarket Babes In Heat / 1992 / OD / M • Swing Rave / 1993 / EVN / M • Titties 'n Cream #2 / 1995 / FC / M • Titty City #1 / 1995 / TIW / M • Toe Hold / 1992 / PRE / B • Toe Teasers #2 / 1993 / SBP / B • Ultimate Orgy #2 / 1992 / GLI / M • Victoria's Amateurs #02 / 1992 / VGA / M • Victoria's Amateurs #03 / 1992 / VGA / M • Voyeurism #1 / 1993 / FH / M • White Men Can't Hump / 1992 / CC / M • Willie Wanker And The Fun Factory / 1994 / FD / M

TANYA SUMMERS *(Tanya Salama, Tonya Summer)*
Not too pretty Iranian girl with medium tits and a hard attitude. 25 years old in 1993. 5'6", 34B-24-35, 110lbs.
America's Raunchiest Home Videos #65: / 1993 / ZA / M • Biff Malibu's Totally Nasty Home Videos #35 / 1993 / ANA / M • Breastman Does The Himalayas / 1993 / EVN / M • Coming Out / 1993 / VD / M • The Cumming Of Sarah Jane #1 / 1993 / AFV / M • Lovin' Spoonfuls #5 / 1996 / 4P / C • Midnight Madness / 1993 / DR / M • Mr. Peepers Amateur Home Videos #76: Sixty Nine Plus Seven / 1993 / LBO / M • Princess Of Persia / 1993 / IP / M • Raunch #07 / 1993 / CC / M • Seymore Butts Meets The Cumback Brat / 1993 / FH / M • Top-pers #15 / 1993 / TV / M • Toppers #16 / 1993 / TV / M • Toppers #17 / 1993 / TV / M • Video Virgins #03 / 1993 / NS / M • Vir-gin Tales #01 / 1993 / 4P / M • Virtual Sex / 1993 / VC / M

TANYA T. TICKLER
The Collegiates / 1971 / BL / M • It Hap-pened In Hollywood / 1973 / WWV / M

TANYA TAILOR
The All Girl Anal Orgy / 1996 / BAC / F

TANYA TASHARA see Autumn Daye

TANYA TAYLOR see Star Index I

TANYA TEASE
Time For Action / 1993 / CS / B

TANYA TUCKER see Brazil

TANYA TURNER
Class Reunion / cr77 / BL / F

TANYA VICKERS see Star Index I

TANZI
Dynasty's Anal Brat Pack / 1996 / OUP / F • Southern Belles #6 / 1996 / XPR / M

TAO
Geisha Io Go / 1994 / PPP / M • Jungle Heat / 1995 / LUM / M • The Last Vamp / 1996 / IP / M • Miss Liberty / 1996 / IP / M • Virility / 1996 / XC / M

TARA
Breast Worx #21 / 1992 / LBO / M • Class Reunion / cr77 / BL / F • Crystal Images / 1995 / INB / M • Lonely And Blue / 1990 / VEX / M • Sodomania #09: Doin' Time / 1994 / EL / M • Wet / 1994 / PHV / F • Wide Open / 1994 / GLI / M • [Hotel Flesh / 1983 / CV / M

TARA (SPANISH)

The Anal Adventures Of Max Hardcore: Cafe Life / 1994 / ZA / M • The Hitch-Hiker #06: Salty Dog / 1994 / WMG / M

TARA AIRE *(Bobbi Jackson, Bobby Jackson, Bobbie Jackson)*
Reddish blonde with droopy medium tits and a marginal body.
Babe / 1982 / AR / M • Bedroom Fantasies / 1983 / ... / M • Big Bust Babes #03 / 1988 / AFI / M • Campus Capers / 1982 / VC / M • Centerspread Girls / 1982 / CA / M • Cof-fee, Tea Or Me / 1984 / CV / M • Dallas School Girls / 1981 / VCX / M • Desire / 1983 / VCX / M • Fleshdance Fever / 1984 / SAT / M • The Girl From S.E.X. / 1982 / CA / M • Girlfriends / 1983 / MIT / M • Golden Girls #33 / 1988 / CA / M • GVC: The Babysitter #107 / 1983 / GO / M • GVC: Danielle's Girlfriends #116 / cr83 / GO / F • GVC: Lust Weekend #103 / 1980 / GO / M • GVC: Women Who Love Women #115 / cr83 / GO / F • I Want To Be Bad / 1984 / CV / M • Intimate Realities #2 / 1983 / VC / M • Joanna Storm On Fire / 1985 / VIV / M • Lingerie / 1983 / CDI / M • Lusty Ladies #11 / 1984 / 4P / M • Lusty Ladies #12 / 1984 / 4P / M • Nasty Lady / 1984 / CV / M • Never So Deep / 1981 / VCX / M • Pleasure Zone / 1984 / SE / M • Private School Girls / 1983 / CA / M • Puss 'n' Boots / 1982 / VXP / M • Sex Appeal / 1984 / ABV / M • Society Affairs / 1982 / CA / M • Striptease / 1983 / VC / M • Summer Camp Girls / 1983 / CA / M • Summer Of '72 / 1982 / CA / M • Suzie Superstar #1 / 1983 / CV / M • Swedish Erotica #09 / 1980 / CA / M • Swedish Erotica #33 / 1980 / CA / M • Swedish Erotica #41 / 1982 / CA / M • Swedish Erotica Superstar #4: Shauna Grant / 1984 / CA / C • Thigh High / 1983 / ... / M • Tight Assets / cr80 / VC / M

TARA ALEXANDER *(Tara Smith)*
October Silk / 1980 / COM / M

TARA BELLES see Star Index I

TARA BLAIR see Star Index I

TARA BLAKE
Breaststroke #2 / 1989 / EX / M • Butt's Motel #2 / 1989 / EX / M • Deep Inside Trading / 1986 / AR / M • Holly Does Holly-wood #3 / 1989 / VEX / M • The Invisible Girl / 1989 / VI / M • Secret Cravings / 1989 / V99 / M • The Sex Detective / 1987 / GO / M • The Wacky World Of X-Rated Bloop-ers / 1989 / GO / M

TARA CHANG
Beach House / 1981 / CA / C • Burning De-sire / 1983 / HO / M • Revenge & Punish-ment / 1996 / ALP / M • A Woman's Tor-ment / 1977 / VC / M

TARA COLLINS see Tianna

TARA DOUGLAS see Star Index I

TARA FLYNN
Any Time, Any Place / 1981 / CA0 / M • Centerfold Celebrities #2 / 1983 / VC / M • Centerfold Celebrities #3 / 1983 / VC / M • Hot Dallas Nights / 1981 / VCX / M • Lim-ited Edition #23 / 1983 / AVC / M

TARA GOLD
Ugly blonde with a pudgy porcine body.
Amateur Lesbians #31: Lacy / 1992 / GO / F • Amateur Lesbians #32: Tara / 1992 / GO / F • Amateur Orgies #18 / 1992 / AFI / M • Amateur Orgies #26 / 1993 / AFI / M • Anal Avenue / 1992 / LV / M • Balling In-stinct / 1992 / FH / M • The Bare-Assed Naked Gun / 1992 / MID / M • Beach Bum

Amateur's #04 / 1992 / MID / M • Beach Bum Amateur's #25 / 1993 / MID / M • Beaverjuice / 1992 / LV / M • Behind The Blinds / 1992 / VIM / M • Bend Over Babes #3 / 1992 / EA / M • Biff Malibu's Totally Nasty Home Videos #20 / 1992 / ANA / M • Biff Malibu's Totally Nasty Home Videos #36 / 1993 / ANA / M • Big Bust Babes #09 / 1992 / AFI / M • Big Busty Whoppers / 1994 / PME / F • Biggies #04 / 1992 / XPI / M • Boobs On Fire / 1993 / NAP / F • Breast Collection #03 / 1995 / LBO / C • Breast Wishes #05 / 1991 / LBO / M • Breast Wishes #06 / 1991 / LBO / M • Breast Worx #17 / 1991 / LBO / M • Breast Worx #20 / 1992 / LBO / M • Breast Worx #26 / 1992 / LBO / M • Breast Worx #33 / 1992 / LBO / M • Breastman Goes To Breastland #1 / 1993 / PRE / B • The Bust Things In Life Are Free / 1994 / NAP / S • Butt Freak #2 / 1996 / EA / M • Double D Amateurs #01 / 1993 / JMP / M • Double D Amateurs #02 / 1993 / JMP / M • Double D Dykes #05 / 1992 / GO / F • Enemates #07 / 1992 / PRE / B • Excitable / 1992 / IF / M • Fast Cars And Fast Women / 1992 / LV / M • Flood Control / 1992 / PRE / B • Home Maid Memories #1 / 1994 / BON / C • Honeymooned / 1992 / PRE / B • It's Only Love / 1992 / VEX / M • Jak's Back / 1992 / BON / B • Just My Imagination / 1993 / WP / M • Leg...Ends #08 / 1993 / PRE / F • Make Me Sweat / 1994 / V99 / M • Masquerade (1992-Usa) / 1992 / SC / M • More Dirty Debutantes #43 / 1995 / 4P / M • One In A Million / 1992 / HW / M • Party Favors / 1993 / VEX / M • The Savannah Affair / 1993 / CDI / M • A Scent Of Leather / 1992 / IF / M • Sexual Healing / 1992 / LV / M • Summer Games / 1992 / HW / M • Super Enemates #1 / 1994 / PRE / C • Tit For Tat / 1994 / PEP / M • Wanderlust / 1992 / LE / M • Welcome To Bondage: Starlets #1 / 1993 / BON / C • Welcome To Bondage: Tara Gold / 1992 / BON / B • Wendy Whoppers: Brain Surgeon / 1993 / PEP / M

TARA HART *see* **Tera Heart**
TARA HUPP
Aunt Peg Goes To Hollywood / 1982 / CA / M
TARA JANE
The Coming Of Angie / cr73 / TGA / M
TARA KING
Private Film #17 / 1994 / OD / M
TARA LANE *see* **Star Index I**
TARA MANN *see* **Star Index I**
TARA MARIKO *see* **Mariko**
TARA MONROE
Supposedly the sister of Tammy Monroe. Small girl with humongous tits and a reasonably pretty face. Long brown hair. Apart from the tits she has a nice tight body. 4'11" tall.
Aroused #1 / 1994 / VI / M • Barrio Bitches / 1994 / SC / F • Beaver & Buttcheeks / 1993 / DR / M • Big & Busty Country Line Dancing / 1995 / SEM / S • Bonnie & Clyde #3 / 1994 / VI / M • Bonnie & Clyde #4 / 1994 / VI / M • Boob-O-Rama #3 / 1995 / WNW / M • Breastman Goes To Breastland #2 / 1993 / EVN / M • Buffy Malibu's Nasty Girls #07 / 1994 / ANA / F • Eight Is Never Enough / 1993 / ZA / M • Eleventh Annual AVN Awards / 1994 / VC / M • Gangbang Girl #12 / 1993 / ANA / M • Intercourse With The Vampyre #1 / 1994 / SC / M • Inter-

course With The Vampyre #2 / 1994 / SC / M • L.A. Topless / 1994 / LE / M • Little Magicians / 1993 / ANA / M • The Man Who Loves Women / 1994 / VC / M • Nasty Nymphos #03 / 1994 / ANA / M • Night And Day #2 / 1993 / VT / M • No Man's Land #08: Eight Women Who Ate Women / 1993 / VT / F • Off Duty Porn Stars / 1994 / VC / M • Porn In The Pen / 1993 / LE / F • Reds / 1993 / LE / F • The Reel Sex World #01 / 1993 / WP / M • Secret Rendez-Vous / 1994 / XCI / M • Sex Machine / 1994 / VT / M • Shameless Lady / 1993 / ME / M • Show & Tell / 1994 / ELP / M • Sisters / 1993 / ZA / M • Sodomania #06: Gangs And Bangs And Other Thangs / 1993 / EL / M • Student Fetish Videos: Best of Catfighting #02 / 1994 / PRE / C • Student Fetish Videos: Best Of Foot Worship #02 / 1994 / PRE / C • Student Fetish Videos: Best Of Spanking #03 / 1995 / PRE / C • Student Fetish Videos: Catfighting #08 / 1993 / PRE / B • Student Fetish Videos: Spanking #11 / 1993 / PRE / B • Subway / 1994 / SC / M • Toppers #11 / 1993 / TV / C • Toppers #14 / 1993 / TV / M • Toppers #15 / 1993 / TV / M • Toppers #18 / 1993 / TV / M • Toppers #21 / 1993 / TV / C • Toppers #22 / 1993 / TV / C • Toppers #30 / 1994 / TV / C • Toppers & Whoppers #1 / 1994 / PRE / C • Wet Nurses #1 / 1994 / LE / M • Women Of Color #1 / 1994 / ANA / M

TARA NOVA *see* **Kassi Nova**
TARA O'HARA
Hillary Vamp's Private Collection #23 / 1992 / HOV / M • Our Bang #03 / 1992 / GLI / M • Positively Pagan #02 / 1991 / ATA / M • Positively Pagan #04 / 1991 / ATA / M • Vegas Reunion / 1992 / TOP / M
TARA PERET *see* **Star Index I**
TARA SMITH *see* **Tara Alexander**
TARA TITANIUM
FTV #09: Cast Iron Bitch #1 / 1996 / FT / B • FTV #10: Cast Iron Bitch #2 / 1996 / FT / B • FTV #14: Big Bust Boxing / 1996 / FT / B • FTV #15: Mixed Boxing Punch Out / 1996 / FT / B • FTV #16: He's Mine / 1996 / FT / B • FTV #17: Double Trouble / 1996 / FT / B • FTV #21: New Boss In Town / 1996 / FT / B • FTV #28: Femme Fatale / Black & Blue / 1996 / FT / B • FTV #33: Tara's Revenge / 1996 / FT / B • FTV #44: Tight Tamali And Bam Jam / 1996 / FT / B • FTV #46: One Lump Or Two? / 1996 / FT / B • FTV #48: Bare Breasted Boxing / 1996 / FT / B • FTV #74: Big Bust Challenge #1 / 1996 / FT / B • FTV #75: Big Bust Challenge #2 / 1996 / FT / B
TARA WINE *see* **Christy Canyon**
TARDAC
Alien Probe #2 / 1994 / ZFX / B
TAREN STEELE
Long light brown hair, very pretty face, small/medium tits, tight waist, nice butt.
American Tushy! / 1996 / ULI / M • Cat Lickers #4 / 1995 / ME / F • Cumback Pussy #6: All-Star Poop Chute Salute / 1997 / EL / M • Diva #1: Caught In The Act / 1996 / VC / F • Monkey Business / 1996 / ULI / M • Strap-On Sally #09: / 1996 / PL / F
TASHA
Anal Auditions #1 / 1996 / XPR / M • Booty Babes / 1993 / ROB / F • Buffy Malibu's Nasty Girls #07 / 1994 / ANA / F • Butt Jammers #02 / 1995 / SC / F • Creme De La

Face #14: Kiss My Cum / 1996 / OD / M • Midnight Dancers / 1993 / MID / S • Nothing Like Nurse Nookie #4 / 1996 / NIT / M • Penthouse: Great Pet Hunt #1 / 1992 / PET / F • Red Rumpers #01 / 1996 / LBO / B • Sweet Lips & Buns / 1993 / ROB / F • Trapped / 1996 / VI / M
TASHA (1972)
Lunch / 1972 / VC / M
TASHA (N. SKYLER) *see* **Natasha Skyler**
TASHA BLADES
Latex #1 / 1994 / VC / M • Pussy Hunt #14 / 1995 / LEI / M
TASHA DEAN *see* **Star Index I**
TASHA MOY
Finger Pleasures #1 / 1995 / PL / F • Shaved #08 / 1995 / RB / F
TASHA RAY *see* **Star Index I**
TASHA VAUX *see* **Tasha Voux**
TASHA VOUX *(Tasha Vaux)*
Not too pretty NY-based blonde with a very flexible body which she can bend into lots of unusual shapes. Medium tits.
69th Street Vice / 1984 / VC / M • Abducted For Pleasure / 1990 / BIZ / B • Anal Intruder #01 / 1986 / CC / M • Angela In Wonderland / 1986 / VD / M • Angels With Sticky Faces / 1991 / VD / M • The Ass Has It / 1992 / KEE / B • Babes In Bondage / 1991 / BIZ / B • Bad Attitude / 1987 / CC / M • Barely Legal / 1985 / CDI / M • Basic Desire / cr85 / STM / B • The Best Of Trained Transvestites / 1990 / BIZ / G • Bi-Heat #02 / 1987 / ZA / G • Bi-Heat #03 / 1987 / ZA / G • Bi-Heat #04 / 1987 / ZA / G • Bi-Heat #07 / 1987 / ZA / G • Big Busted Lesbians At Play / 1991 / BIZ / F • Bizarre Master Series: Sir Michael / 1992 / BIZ / C • Black Angels / 1985 / VC / M • Black Flesh / 1986 / LA / M • Black Goddesses / cr85 / STM / B • Black Madam Sadista / 1992 / BIZ / B • Black On White / 1987 / PL / C • Black Sister, White Brother / 1987 / AT / M • Blowing Your Mind / 1984 / RSV / M • Bondage Fantasies #1 / 1989 / BIZ / B • Bondage Fantasies #2 / 1989 / BIZ / B • Bondage Games #2 / 1991 / BIZ / B • Bondage Seduction / 1992 / STM / B • Bound Biker Babes #2 / 1993 / STM / B • Bunny's Lesson In Pain / 1992 / PL / B • Catfighting Lesbians / 1991 / BIZ / F • Chatsworth Hall / 1989 / BIZ / B • Chocolate Bon-Bons / 1985 / PL / M • Cravings / 1987 / VC / M • Critical Positions / 1987 / VXP / M • Days Gone Bi / 1988 / ZA / G • Deep & Wet / 1986 / VD / M • Deep Throat #2 / 1986 / AR / M • Delusions Of Grandeur / cr85 / DRV / B • Dildo Fantasy Party / 1990 / BIZ / F • Dirty / 1993 / FD / C • Dominant Nurses / 1990 / ... / B • Dreamwalk / 1989 / COM / M • Dresden Mistress #1 / 1988 / BIZ / B • Dresden Mistress #3 / 1989 / BIZ / B • Ebony & Ivory Sisters / 1985 / PL / C • Endless Nights / 1988 / CDI / M • Erotic Moments / 1985 / CDI / C • Fannie's Fantail / 1985 / VC / M • Fashion Dolls / 1985 / LA / M • Female Domination #1: Babes In Bondage / 1991 / BEB / B • Flesh And Fantasy / 1985 / VC / M • Flipside: A Backdoor Adventure / 1985 / CV / M • Full Service Butler / 1993 / KEE / B • A Gift For The Master / 1990 / BIZ / B • Girl Lovers / 1990 / BIZ / F • Girls Just Wanna Have Girls #2 / 1990 / HIO / C • Girls U.S.A. / 1980 / AIR / M • Hard Times / 1990 / GLE / M • Harem Girls / 1986 / SE / M • Hidden Fantasies /

1986 / VD / M • Hog Tied And Spanked / 1991 / BIZ / B • Homegrown Video #323 / 1990 / HOV / M • Homegrown Video #325 / 1990 / HOV / M • Hot Service / 19?? / CDI / M • I Creme With Genie / 1991 / PL / M • Journey Into Pain #2 / 1989 / BIZ / B • Kellie Everts #080 / 1990 / KEE / B • Kellie Everts #083 / 1990 / KEE / B • Kellie Everts #089 / 1993 / KEE / B • Kellie Everts #101 / 1993 / KEE / B • Kellie Everts #102 / 1993 / KEE / B • Kellie Everts #107 / 1992 / KEE / B • Kellie Everts #108 / 1992 / KEE / B • Kittens #2 / 1991 / CC / F • Krazy 4 You / 1987 / 4P / M • The Last X-Rated Movie / 1990 / COM / M • The Last X-Rated Movie #2 / 1990 / COM / M • The Last X-Rated Movie #3 / 1990 / COM / M • The Last X-Rated Movie #4 / 1990 / COM / M • Leather Lair #3 / 1990 / STM / B • Leather Lust Mistress / 1989 / BIZ / B • Lesbian Catfights / 1990 / BIZ / B • Lesbian Dildo Bondage #2 / 1990 / BIZ / B • Lesbian Dildo Fever #1 / 1989 / BIZ / F • Lesbian Dildo Fever #2 / 1989 / BIZ / F • Lesbian Fantasies / 1990 / BIZ / F • Lesbian Love Slave / 1989 / KEE / B • Lesbian Pussy Power / 1992 / BIZ / B • Lesbian She Fights #1 / 1992 / BIZ / B • Lesbian She Fights #2 / 1992 / BIZ / B • Lilith Unleashed / 1986 / VC / M • Long Hard Nights / 1984 / ELH / M • Lovers, An Intimate Portrait #1: Sydney & Ray / 1993 / FEM / M • Lustfire / 1991 / LA / C • Lusty Licking Lesbians / 198? / JAN / F • Male Domination #16 / 1990 / BIZ / C • Male Domination #17 / 1990 / BIZ / C • Mind Mirror / 1994 / LAP / M • Moans & Groans / 1987 / 4P / M • Mouth To Mouth / 1986 / CC / M • Naked Scents / 1984 / VC / M • The Oddest Couple / 1986 / VC / M • Officer's Discipline / 1985 / BIZ / B • Our Naked Eyes / 1988 / TME / M • Passion Chain / 1987 / ZA / M • Pinned And Smothered / 1992 / BIZ / B • The Power of DeSade / 1992 / BIZ / B • Private Showings / 1992 / STM / B • Punished She Fighters / 1992 / BIZ / B • Raw Talent #2 / 1987 / VC / M • Red Tails #2 / 1993 / STM / B • Rich Bitches / 1993 / KEE / B • Romancing The Bone / 1984 / VC / M • The Screwables / 1992 / RUM / M • Secret Fantasies Of Submissive Women / 1992 / BIZ / B • Secret Urges (Starmaker) / 1994 / STM / F • Sex Between The Scenes / 1994 / LAP / M • Sexpot / 1987 / VXP / M • Silence Of The G.A.M.S. / 1992 / CA / M • Sinners #1 / 1988 / COM / M • Sinners #2 / 1988 / COM / M • Sinners #3 / 1989 / COM / M • Slavegirls In Suspension / 19?? / STM / B • Slumber Party Reunion / 1987 / AR / M • Snake Eyes #2 / 1987 / COM / M • Snatching A Peep / 1989 / NOP / M • Spanked Ecstasy / 1991 / BIZ / B • Spanked In Lingerie / 1985 / LA / B • Submission Of Susie / 1993 / BIZ / B • Sweet Revenge / 1986 / ZA / M • Temptations Of The Flesh / 1986 / VD / M • There's Magic In The Air / 1987 / AR / M • Thrilled To Death / 1988 / REP / S • Tickled Pink / 1985 / VC / M • Tied For The Master / 1991 / BIZ / B • Times Square Comes Alive / 1984 / VC / M • Training Academy / 1984 / LA / B • Transsexual Trouble / 1991 / CIN / G • True Legends Of Adult Cinema: The Cult Superstars / 1993 / VC / C • True Legends Of Adult Cinema: The Erotic Eighties / 1992 / VC / C • Ultrasex / 1987 / VC / M • Vas-O-Line Alley /

1985 / VC / M • VCA Previews #4 / 1988 / VC / C • Virginia's TV Initiation / 1992 / STM / G • Warehouse Slaves Discipline / 1990 / BIZ / B • Working Girls In Bondage / 1991 / BIZ / B • Wrecked 'em / 1985 / CC / M • Wrestling Beauties #1 / 1985 / BIZ / B
TASHA WELCH
Bip Tease / 1996 / BON / B • Bondage Fantasy #1 / 1995 / BON / B • Disciples Of Discipline / 1996 / BON / B • Eight Babes A Week / 1996 / DGD / F • Gallery Of Pain / 1995 / BON / B • Labyrinth Of The Lash / 1996 / BON / B • Little Shop Of Tortures / 1996 / LBO / B • Party Of The Dammed / 1996 / BON / B • Red Rumpers #01 / 1996 / LBO / B • Rough-House Room-Mates / 1996 / NAP / B • Thoroughly Thrashed / 1996 / NAP / B • Tricked & Tied / 1996 / VTF / B • Vagabondage / 1996 / B&D / B
TASHAWNA see Star Index I
TASHI MAY
Kym Wilde's On The Edge #30 / 1995 / RB / B
TASHI MOY
Housemother's Discipline #6 / 1994 / RB / B • Old Guys & Dolls #1 / 1995 / PL / M
TASMIN
British Cunts Are Cumming! / 1996 / SPL / M
TASTY FREEZE see Star Index I
TATIA LOGAN see Star Index I
TATIANA
Eurotica #06 / 1996 / XC / M • Eurotica #12 / 1996 / XC / M
TATIANA (TIANNA) see Tianna
TATIANA BERNARD see Star Index I
TATIANA BOBROVA
Horny Henry's Euro Adventure / 1995 / TTV / M
TATIANA VANKOVA
Lil' Women: Vacation / 1996 / EUR / M • Skin #5: The 5th Column / 1996 / ERQ / M
TATIANNA
Biff Malibu's Totally Nasty Home Videos #09 / 1992 / ANA / M • Dirty Dixie / 1992 / IF / M • Fringe Benefits / 1992 / IF / M • More Dirty Debutantes #13 / 1992 / 4P / M
TATIANNA (CORTEZ) see Tatianna Cortez
TATIANNA (E. JAMA) see Elizabeth Jama
TATIANNA CORTEZ *(Tatianna (Cortez), Trina (Tatianna))*
Passable face with a mole on her left chin, shoulder length brown hair, curvaceous body, and medium tits. In *MDD #53* (1996) she says she's 22 years old, was de-virginized at 16, was originally Mexican, and did bondage videos for the last three years (none known by me). In the same movie you also see a performance at age 18 where she just masturbates.
The Adventures Of Peeping Tom #2 / 1996 / OD / M • The Adventures Of Peeping Tom #3 / 1996 / OD / M • Anal Lovebud / 1996 / ROB / M • Asses Galore #2: No Remorse...No Repent / 1996 / DFI / M • Assy #2 / 1996 / JMP / M • Backdoor Play / 1996 / AVI / M • Betrayed / 1996 / WP / M • Butt Sluts #6 / 1996 / ROB / F • The Clock Strikes Bizarre On Butt Row / 1996 / ABS / M • Deep Dish Booty Pie / 1996 / ROB / M • Dick & Jane's Video Mail: From Virginville (#4) / 1996 / AVI / M • Erotic Bondage / 1996 / ONA / B • Extreme Close-Up / 1996 / VI / M • Face Jam / 1996 / VC / M • First

Whores Club / 1996 / ERA / M • Generation Sex #2: Nature's Revenge / 1996 / VT / M • Hillbilly Honeys / 1996 / WP / M • Hot Wired / 1996 / VC / M • Hotwired / 1996 / VC / M • In The Line Of Desire / 1996 / MID / M • Intense Perversions #4 / 1996 / PL / M • Joanie Pneumatic / 1996 / PL / M • Lesbian Pooper Sluts / 1996 / ROB / F • Lisa / 1997 / SC / M • Lollipop Shoppe #1 / 1996 / SC / M • Malibu Ass Blasters / 1996 / ROB / M • More Dirty Debutantes #53 / 1996 / 4P / M • Muff Divers #2 / 1996 / TV / F • N.Y. Video Magazine #08 / 1996 / OUP / M • Night Vision / 1996 / WP / M • Numba 1 Ass Fucka / 1996 / ROB / M • Ona Zee's Doll House #4 / 1996 / ONA / F • Passions Of Sin / 1996 / NIT / M • Pick Up Lines #06 / 1996 / OD / M • Pick Up Lines #07 / 1996 / OD / M • Puritan Video Magazine #03 / 1996 / LE / M • Rainwoman #10: The Tenth Anniversary Edition / 1996 / CC / M • Risque Burlesque #2 / 1996 / IN / M • Sex Hungry Butthole Sluts / 1996 / ROB / M • Sexhibition #2 / 1996 / SUF / M • Seymore Butts: Big Boobs In Buttsville / 1996 / FH / M • She's No Angel / 1996 / ERA / S • Sweet Revenge / 1997 / KBE / M • Takin' It To The Limit #8: Hooked On Crack / 1996 / BS / M • The Time Machine / 1996 / WP / M • Totally Depraved / 1996 / SC / M • Undercover / 1996 / VC / M • Up And Cummers #33 / 1996 / 4P / M • Video Virgins #29 / 1996 / NS / M • Waterbabies #3 / 1996 / CC / M • Wet 'n' Wicked / 1995 / BEP / F • Young & Natural #20 / 1996 / TV / F • Young & Natural #21 / 1996 / TV / F
TATSUO MORI
Triple Sex Play / 1985 / ORC / M
TATTIANA
Tattiana's Terror / 1996 / GAL / B
TATTOO
Backdoor Diaries / 1995 / BBE / M • Indecent Obsessions / 1995 / BBE / M
TATTOO DANNY see Star Index I
TATYANA
Dirty Dancers #4 / 1995 / 4P / M • Dirty Stories #1 / 1995 / PE / M • Penitentiary / 1995 / HW / M • Pick Up Lines #01 / 1995 / 4P / M • Up And Cummers #18 / 1995 / 4P / M
TATYANA MARADINO see Star Index I
TATYANA TIGHERA
The Thief, The Girl & The Detective / 1996 / HDE / M
TAWN MASTREY see Star Index I
TAWNEE (DOWNS) see Tawny Downs
TAWNEE (LEE) see Tawni Lee
TAWNEE LUCCI see Vanessa D'Oro
TAWNI see Tawni Lee
TAWNI LEE *(Liz Turner, Tawnee (Lee), Tawni)*
Blonde with small tits. See also Tawny Downs which may have some of Tawni Lee's movies and vice-versa.
Assinine / 1990 / CC / M • Boobs, Butts And Bloopers #1 / 1990 / HO / M • Caught From Behind #09 / 1988 / HO / M • From Rags To Riches / 1988 / CDI / M • I Can't Get No...Satisfaction / 1988 / CDI / M • Salsa Break / 1989 / EA / M • Tawnee...Be Good! / 1988 / LV / M • Very Sexy Ballet / 1988 / CA / M • The Way They Were / 1990 / CDI / M
TAWNY
The Adventures Of Buttwoman #2: Behind Bars / 1992 / EL / F • The Bottom Dweller / 1993 / EL / M • Bound To Be Tickled / 1994

/ VTF / B • Breast Worx #36 / 1992 / LBO / M • Catch Of The Day #5 / 1996 / VG0 / M • Doctor DeAngelo / 1994 / CS / B • Girly Video Magazine #4 / 1996 / BEP / M • Love Letters / 1992 / ELP / F • The Magnificent 7 / 1994 / VTF / B • Muffy The Vampire Layer / 1992 / LV / M • Odyssey 30 Min: Tawny Loves Come In Her Face / 1992 / OD / M • Strange Passions / 1993 / BS / B • Striptease #2 / 1995 / PL / M • Student Fetish Videos: Best Of Foot Worship #02 / 1994 / PRE / C • Student Fetish Videos: Foot Worship #07 / 1992 / PRE / B • Student Fetish Videos: Foot Worship #08 / 1992 / PRE / B • Student Fetish Videos: Spanking #07 / 1992 / PRE / B • Uncle Roy's Amateur Home Video #15 / 1992 / VIM / M • Wrasslin She-Babes #10 / 1996 / SOW / M

TAWNY (T. MINX) see Tiffany Minx

TAWNY DOWNS *(Lee (Tawny Downs), Amy Berens, Tawnee (Downs))*
Dark haired with a nice slim body and very prominent eyebrows. See also Tawni Lee who may have some of Tawny Downs movies and vice-versa.

Ali Boobie & The 40 D's / 1988 / 3DV / M • The Beverly Thrillbillies / 1987 / EVN / M • Carnal Possessions / 1988 / VEX / M • Carnal Possessions / 1991 / VEX / M • Caught From Behind #09 / 1988 / HO / M • Cheek-A-Boo / 1988 / LV / M • City Of Rage / 1989 / EVN / M • Club Head (EVN) #1 / 1987 / EVN / C • Feel The Heat / 1989 / VEX / M • Flesh For Frankenstein / 1987 / VEX / M • Fun In A Bun / 1990 / LV / M • Girl Crazy / 1989 / CDI / F • The Girls Of Cooze / 1992 / V99 / C • Girls Will Be Girls / 1988 / LV / F • Here's Looking At You / 1988 / V99 / M • Hot Rods / 1988 / VEX / M • How To Get A "Head" / 1988 / CV / M • Leave It To Cleavage #1 / 1988 / GO / M • The Legend Of Reggie D. / 1989 / EA / M • Megasex / 1988 / EVN / M • Nothing But Girls, Girls, Girls / 1988 / CDI / M • Parliament: Bottoms #2 / 1988 / PM / C • Parliament: Dildo Babes #2 / 1988 / PM / F • Parliament: Hot Legs #1 / 1988 / PM / F • Parliament: Licking Lesbians #1 / 1988 / PM / F • Reflections Of Innocence / 1988 / SEX / M • Reflections Of Innocence / 1991 / VEX / C • Surfside Sex / 1988 / CA / M • A Taste Of Tawnee / 1988 / LV / C • Three By Three / 1989 / LV / C • Unbelievable Orgies #1 / 1987 / EVN / C • Where The Sun Never Shines / 1990 / IN / C

TAWNY FOX
The Affairs Of Miss Roberts / 19?? / ... / M

TAWNY LITTLE
Blue Vanities #537 / 1993 / FFL / M

TAWNY MARONA see Star Index I

TAWNY PEAKS
Big Busty #51 / 1994 / BTO / S • Girls Around The World #21: Tawny Peaks & Friends / 1995 / BTO / M • Girls Around The World #27 / 1995 / BTO / M • Girls Around The World #28 / 1995 / BTO / S • On Location: Boob Cruise / 1996 / H&S / S

TAWNY PEAR see Tawny Pearl

TAWNY PEARL *(Sue Pearlman, Loni Henderson, Sue Perlman, Lauri Pearl, Tawny Pear)*
Passable face, long straight blonde hair, very good body with medium firm tits and very tight waist. Nice smile.

Ball Game / 1980 / CA / M • Blondes On

Fire / 1987 / VCR / C • Blue Vanities #030 / 1988 / FFL / M • Blue Vanities #044 (Old) / 1988 / FFL / M • Blue Vanities #053 / 1988 / FFL / M • Blue Vanities #061 / 1988 / FFL / M • Blue Vanities #066 / 1988 / FFL / M • Blue Vanities #095 / 1988 / FFL / M • Blue Vanities #253 / 1996 / FFL / M • Budding Blondes / 1979 / TGA / C • Coed Fever / 1980 / CA / M • Endless Lust / 1983 / VC / M • Extremes / 1981 / CA / M • Fantasy Peeps: Three For Love / 1985 / 4P / M • Fantasy Peeps: Untamed Desires / 1985 / 4P / M • Fantasy Peeps: Women In Love / 1985 / 4P / M • Frat House / 1979 / NGV / M • The Goodbye Girls / 1979 / CDI / M • Joys Of Erotica #102 / 1980 / VCR / C • Limited Edition #06 / 1979 / AVC / M • Limited Edition #12 / 1980 / AVC / M • Limited Edition #14 / 1980 / AVC / M • Loving Lesbos / 1983 / VCR / C • Lusty Ladies #14 / 1984 / 4P / F • The Master And Mrs. Johnson / 1980 / SAT / M • Mrs. Rodger's Neighborhood / 1988 / EVN / C • Nanci Blue / 1979 / SE / M • National Pornographic #1: Lesbians / 1987 / 4P / C • Only The Best Of Oral / 1989 / CV / C • Party #1 / 1979 / NAT / M • Party #2 / 1979 / NAT / M • Pink Champagne / 1979 / CV / M • Plato's, The Movie / 1980 / SE / M • Pleasure Productions #02 / 1984 / VCR / M • Potpourri / 1981 / TGA / M • Rolls Royce #04 / 1980 / ... / C • Service Entrance / 1979 / REG / C • Sex Ed With Lil' Red / 1983 / TGA / M • Sexual Heights / 1981 / ... / M • Showgirl #08: Serena's Fantasies / 1983 / VCR / M • Showgirl #14: Kitty Shane's Fantasies / 1983 / VCR / M • Showgirl #15: Taylor Evans' Fantasies / 1983 / VCR / M • Taboo #01 / 1980 / VCX / M • Tinsel Town / 1980 / VC / M • Toys, Not Boys #1 / 1991 / FC / C • Trouble Down Below / 1981 / CA / M • Ultraflesh / 1980 / GO / M • Weekend Fantasy / 1980 / VCX / M • [Burning Wild / 1979 / SIL / M • [Sex Pageant / 1978 / ... / M • [Three For Love / 1983 / ... / M • [Untamed Desires / 1985 / ... / M • [Women In Love / 1985 / ... / M

TAWNY RAE *(Toni Ray, Tammy Rae)*
Older (27 in 1996), not too pretty, light brown out-of-control hair, hefty body that looks like it's falling apart, loss of belly muscle tone, large tits.

Amateur Nights #13 / 1996 / HO / M • The Desert Cafe / 1996 / NIT / M • Domina #6 / 1996 / LBO / B • Domina #8 / 1996 / LBO / B • Look What I Found On The Street #01 / 1996 / CC / M • Mike Hott: #384 Three-Sum Sluts #16 / 1996 / MHV / M • Mike Hott: #385 Lesbian Sluts #29 / 1996 / MHV / F • Mike Hott: #386 / 1996 / MHV / M • Mike Hott: #387 Girls Who Lap Cum From Cunts #04 / 1996 / MHV / M • Mike Hott: #390 / 1996 / MHV / M • Mike Hott: #391 / 1996 / MHV / M • My First Time #6 / 1996 / NS / M • Nektar / 1996 / BAC / M • Nineteen #2 / 1996 / FOR / M • Take All Cummers / 1996 / HO / M • Video Virgins #31 / 1996 / NS / M

TAWNY WINTERS
More Punished Cheeks / 1994 / RB / B

TAYASHI MOTOYOSHI see Star Index I

TAYJA
Black Snatch #1 / 1996 / DFI / F

TAYLNN see Jalynn

TAYLOR
Bedtime Stories / 1996 / VC / M • Cheap

Tricks #1 / 1996 / PAV / M • First Time Lesbians #17 / 1994 / JMP / F • Fresh Cheeks / 1995 / VC / M • Gangbang Girl #12 / 1993 / ANA / M • Glittering Gartered Girls / 1993 / RSV / B • Hot Body Competition: Hot Pants Contest / 1996 / CG / F • Jus' Knockin' Boots #1: Fade To Black / 1996 / NIT / M • Long Legged Ladies / 1993 / VER / M • Pearl Necklace: Amorous Amateurs #36 / 1993 / SEE / M • Pearl Necklace: Amorous Amateurs #37 / 1993 / SEE / M • Pearl Necklace: Premier Sessions #01 / 1993 / SEE / M • Pearl Necklace: Premier Sessions #07 / 1996 / SEE / M • Pearl Necklace: Thee Bush League #24 / 1993 / SEE / M • Southern Belles #1 / 1994 / HOV / M • Toe Teasers #3 / 1994 / SRP / B • Under The Skirt #2 / 1995 / KAE / F

TAYLOR (SEVENTIES) see Star Index I

TAYLOR ADAMS
Intimate Couples / 1984 / VCX / M

TAYLOR BLACK
The Farmer's Daughter / 1995 / TEG / M

TAYLOR BRITTEN
Charade / 1993 / HSV / G

TAYLOR DANE see Paula Harlow

TAYLOR DANTE
Afro American Dream Girls #2 / 1996 / DR / M • Amateur Black: Sexpots / 1996 / SUF / M • Black Centerfolds #3 / 1996 / MID / M • Black Centerfolds #4 / 1996 / MID / M • Black Fantasies #15 / 1996 / HW / M • Black Knockers #06 / 1995 / TV / M • Black Video Virgins #1 / 1996 / NS / M • Bootylicious: Baby Got Booty / 1996 / JMP / M • Bootylicious: It's A Bootyful Thing / 1996 / JMP / M • The Butt Sisters Do Washington D.C. / 1995 / MID / M • Double Dicked #1 / 1996 / RAS / M • Girls II Women / 1996 / AVI / M • In Da Booty / 1996 / LV / M • Jiggly Queens #3 / 1996 / LE / M • Tailz From Da Hood #4 / 1996 / AVI / M • Yo' Where's Homey? / 1996 / SUF / M

TAYLOR EVANS *(Ashley Grant, Ashley West, Ashley Brown, Brooke West(T.Evans), Morgan Lee, Rolly Evans, Ashley Welles, Ellie May Jackson, Vanessa Taylor, Lee Brown)*
Blonde with medium tits, marginal face, and a womanly body.

Afrodisiac #2 / 1989 / CC / M • Anal Annie And The Magic Dildo / 1984 / LIP / F • The Angel In Mr. Holmes / 1988 / WV / C • Angela In Wonderland / 1986 / VD / M • Barely Legal / 1985 / CDI / M • The Best Of Anal Annie: The Girl-Girl Adventures / 1993 / LIP / C • Bi Bi American Style / cr85 / MET / G • Bi-Surprise / 1988 / MET / G • The Bimbo #2: The Homecoming / 1986 / RLV / M • Black Heat / 1986 / VCR / C • Carnal Competition / 1985 / WV / C • Centerfold Celebrities #5 / 1983 / VC / M • Cinderella / 1985 / VEL / M • Classic Erotica #8 / 1985 / SVE / M • Classic Swedish Erotica #26 / 1987 / CA / C • Cocktales / 1985 / AT / M • Coffee, Tea Or Me / 1984 / CV / M • Debbie Does Dallas #2 / 1980 / VC / M • Decadence / 1986 / VD / M • Deep Throat #2 / 1986 / AR / M • Down And Dirty / 1985 / LBO / M • Eaten Alive / 1985 / VXP / M • Erotic Moments / 1985 / CDI / C • The Erotic World Of Linda Wong / 1985 / VIV / M • The Erotic World Of Vanessa #1 / 1983 / VCR / C • Fannie's Fantail / 1985 / VC / M • Feel The Heat / 1985 / AAH / M • Femalien / 1996 / SCI / S • For Love And Lust

/ 1985 / AVC / M • Gang-Way / 1984 / ECO / C • Grind / 1988 / CV / M • Harem Girls / 1986 / SE / M • Haulin' 'n' Ballin' / 1988 / MET / G • Hot Service / 19?? / CDI / M • In All The Right Places / 1986 / VD / M • John Holmes, The Lost Films / 1988 / PEN / C • Lady Madonna / 1985 / RLV / M • Let's Get It On With Amber Lynn / 1986 / VC / M • Limited Edition #11 / 1980 / AVC / M • Limited Edition #12 / 1980 / AVC / M • Lingerie Girls / 1987 / … / F • Lusty Ladies #09 / 1984 / 4P / M • Mrs. Rodger's Neighborhood / 1988 / EVN / C • Nasty Nights / 1988 / PL / C • Naughty Cheerleaders / 1985 / HO / M • Passion Pit / 1985 / SE / M • Pleasure Productions #03 / 1984 / VCR / M • Pleasure Zone / 1984 / SE / M • Pretty Peaches #2 / 1987 / VC / M • Private Encounters / 1987 / SE / M • Rear Action Girls #2 / 1985 / LIP / F • Rear Entry / 1985 / VCR / C • Scriptease / 1984 / WV / C • Secret Loves / 1986 / CDI / M • Sex Dreams On Maple Street / 1985 / WV / M • Sex Machine / 1986 / LA / M • Sex Styles Of The Rich & Famous / 1986 / VXP / M • Sex Wars / 1984 / EXF / M • Sexcapades / 1983 / VC / M • Showgirl #10: Candida Royale's Fantasies / 1983 / VCR / M • Showgirl #15: Taylor Evans' Fantasies / 1983 / VCR / M • Sleazy Susan / 1986 / VXP / M • Split Decision / 1989 / MET / G • Tasty / 1985 / CA / M • This Is Your Sex Life / 1987 / VD / M • Tough Cookie / cr78 / M$M / C • Ultrasex / 1987 / VC / M • Unnatural Phenomenon #2 / 1986 / WV / M • Virgin Vessel / 1985 / WV / C • Walk On The Wild Side / 1987 / CDI / M • The Way They Were / 1990 / CDI / M • Wild Things #1 / 1985 / CV / M • Working Girls / 1985 / CA / M • [Untamed Desires / 1985 / … / M

TAYLOR FINE
Creme De La Face #03 / 1994 / OD / M • Creme De La Face #04 / 1994 / OD / M

TAYLOR HAYES
13th Annual Adult Video News Awards / 1996 / VC / S • Bare Essentials / 1995 / NIV / F • Boobtown / 1995 / VC / M • The Complete Guide To Sexual Positions / 1996 / PME / S • Deep Behind The Scenes With Seymore Butts #1 / 1995 / ULI / M • Deep Behind The Scenes With Seymore Butts #2 / 1995 / ULI / M • Hienie's Heroes / 1995 / VC / M • Lust Runner / 1995 / VC / M • Monkey Business / 1996 / ULI / M • Naked Dolls / 1995 / NIV / F • A Pool Party At Seymores #2 / 1995 / ULI / M • Seymore Butts: Slippin' In Through The Out Door / 1996 / FH / M • Squirters / 1996 / ULI / M

TAYLOR HINES see **Star Index I**

TAYLOR HUDSON see **Chi Chi La Rue**

TAYLOR LAMBORNE
Ancient Secrets Of Sexual Ecstasy / 1996 / HIG / M

TAYLOR LEIGH see **Star Index I**

TAYLOR MAISON
The Immoral Miss Teeze / 1987 / CV / M

TAYLOR MORE
Up And Cummers #04 / 1993 / 4P / M • Up And Cummers #07 / 1994 / 4P / M • Up And Cummers #09 / 1994 / 4P / M • Up And Cummers #19 / 1995 / 4P / M

TAYLOR PORRELLI
Score Of Sex / 1995 / BAC / G

TAYLOR ROSE
Dirty Dancers #7 / 1996 / 4P / M • Where The Girls Sweat...Not The Sequel / 1996 / EL / F

TAYLOR SINCLAIR
Delinquents On Butt Row / 1996 / EA / M • Detective Covergirls / 1996 / CUC / B

TAYLOR THOMAS
Anal Crybabies / 1996 / BAC / M

TAYLOR TROUBLE
The Horny Housewife / 1996 / HO / M

TAYLOR WANE see **Taylor Wayne**

TAYLOR WAYNE *(Taylor Wane, Joanna (T. Wayne), Fayrin Heitz, Farron Hytes, Farran Hytes, Farryn Heights, Joanna G., Joanna Gee, Joanna T., Maggie Snatcher)*
Started out with large droopy ugly tits and had them made even uglier. Blonde 5'3" 38DD-22-32, 24 years old (in 1993), born in England and has been in the US for about 5 years (also as of 1993). First movie was **Female Persuasion**. Fayrin Heitz comes from **Love Letters (1991)**. Joanna G. is from **Gettin' Wet**. Supposedly engaged to photographer Laurien. Married him on Aug 7, 1993 in Las Vegas.
Above And Beyond / 1990 / PNP / G • The Adventures Of Breastman / 1992 / EVN / M • The Adventures Of Buttgirl & Wonder Wench / 1991 / AFV / M • Amateur Lesbians #01: Leanna / 1991 / GO / F • Amateur Lesbians #06: Taylor / 1991 / GO / F • Amateur Lesbians #14: Avalon / 1991 / GO / F • Amateur Lesbians #17: Sharise / 1992 / GO / F • Anal Orgasms / 1992 / DRP / M • Anniversary / 1992 / FOR / M • Another Dirty Western / 1992 / AFV / M • Assault With A Friendly Weapon / 1990 / DAY / M • Backdoor To Cannes / 1993 / VC / M • Bad Influence / 1991 / CDI / M • Batwoman & Catgirl / 1992 / HW / M • Bazooka County #3 / 1991 / CC / M • Best Of Bi And Beyond / 1992 / PNP / C • Big Boob Tease / 1993 / NAP / F • The Big Bust / 1992 / FPI / M • Big Titted Tarts / 1994 / PL / C • The Bimbo #2 / 1992 / AFV / M • The Blonde & The Beautiful #1 / 1993 / LV / M • The Blonde & The Beautiful #2 / 1993 / LV / M • Blonde Ambition / 1991 / CIN / M • Blonde Beaver Bonanza / 1992 / TCP / M • Body Music #2 / 1990 / DR / M • Bosom Buddies / 1990 / BTO / F • Breaking And Entering / 1991 / AFV / M • Breast Worx #08 / 1991 / LBO / M • Broad Of Directors / 1992 / PEP / M • Busty Porno Queens / 1996 / H&S / M • California Taxi Girls / 1991 / AFV / M • The Cannes Sex Fest / 1992 / SFP / M • Catalina Five-O: White Coral, Blue Death / 1990 / CIN / M • Cheesecake / 1991 / VC / M • Club Josephine / 1991 / AR / F • The Coach's Daughter / 1991 / AR / M • Confessions #1 / 1992 / OD / M • Cum On Line / 1991 / XPI / M • Dark Star / 1991 / VI / M • Deep Inside Savannah / 1993 / VC / C • Desert Fox / 1990 / VD / M • Devil's Agenda & Miss Jones / 1991 / AR / M • Dial 666 For Lust / 1991 / AFV / M • Dig It / 1994 / FD / C • Encino Woman / 1992 / VIM / M • Endangered / 1992 / PP / M • Enemates #03 / 1991 / BIZ / B • Every Woman Has A Secret / 1991 / ROB / M • Exiles / 1991 / VT / M • Exposure Images #22: Taylor Wane / 1992 / EXI / F • Eyewitness Nudes / 1990 / VC / M • Female Persuasion / 1990 / SO / F • The Fire Down Below / 1992 / CDI / M • Flashpoint / 1991 / AFV / M • Flying High #2 / 1992 / HO / M • Four Alarm / 1991 / SE / M • Gettin' Wet / 1990 / VC / M • Girl Friends / 1990 / PL / F • The God Daughter #2 / 1991 / AFV / M • The God Daughter #3 / 1992 / AFV / M • The God Daughter #4 / 1992 / AFV / M • Groupies / 1993 / AFV / F • Guess Who Came To Dinner / 1992 / AFV / M • The Harley Girls / 1991 / AR / F • Head Again / 1992 / AFV / M • Hollywood's Hills / 1992 / LV / M • Hooter Heaven / 1992 / CA / M • Hot Line / 1991 / VC / M • Hotel Sex / 1992 / AFV / M • I'm No Dummy / 1991 / HO / M • If Dreams Come True / 1991 / AFV / M • Introducing Tracey Wynn / 1991 / PL / M • Just Friends / 1991 / AFV / M • Kiss And Tell / 1992 / AFV / M • Ladies In Combat / 1991 / PRE / B • Ladies Lovin' Ladies #1 / 1990 / AR / F • Ladies Lovin' Ladies #2 / 1992 / AR / F • Ladies Lovin' Ladies #4 / 1992 / AFV / F • The Last Blonde / 1991 / IN / M • Laugh Factory / 1995 / PRE / C • Laying Down The Law #1 / 1992 / AFV / M • Laying Down The Law #2 / 1992 / AFV / M • Laying The Ghost / 1991 / VC / M • A League Of Their Moan / 1992 / EVN / M • Leather And Lace Revisited / 1991 / VT / F • Leg...Ends #04 / 1991 / PRE / F • Lesbian Lingerie Fantasy #4 / 1990 / ESP / F • Lesbian Pros And Amateurs #16 / 1992 / GO / F • Lesbo A Go-Go / 1990 / PL / F • Lethal Woman / 1991 / CIN / M • Lies Of Passion / 1992 / LV / M • Love Letters / 1991 / VI / M • Love Letters / 1992 / ELP / F • Maneater (1992-Las Vegas) / 1992 / LV / M • Maneaters (1992-Vidco) / 1992 / VD / C • Mind Trips / 1992 / FH / M • Mirage #1 / 1991 / VC / M • Mirage #2 / 1992 / VC / M • Miss Matches / 1996 / PRE / C • More Dirty Debutantes #06 / 1990 / 4P / M • Mr. Peepers Amateur Home Videos #02: Bachelorette Party / 1991 / LBO / M • Mr. Peepers Amateur Home Videos #04: Hot English Muff / 1991 / LBO / M • Mr. Peepers Amateur Home Videos #10: Red Rider & Little Shav / 1991 / LBO / M • Mr. Peepers Amateur Home Videos #12: Like It! Lick It! / 1991 / LBO / M • Mr. Peepers Nastiest #5 / 1995 / LBO / C • Nasty Jack's Homemade Vid. #29 / 1991 / CDI / M • Nookie Court / 1992 / AFV / M • Object Of Desire / 1991 / FAZ / M • Obsession / 1991 / CDI / M • On The Prowl #2 / 1991 / SC / M • Oriental Treatment #4: The Demon Lover / 1992 / AFV / M • The Party / 1992 / CDI / M • Peekers / 1993 / MID / M • The Poetry Of The Flesh / 1993 / PEP / M • The Power & The Passion / 1993 / CDI / M • Precious Peaks / 1990 / ZA / M • Principles Of Lust / 1992 / WV / M • Quickies / 1992 / AFV / M • The Rage Of Stephanie / 199? / NAP / B • Raunch #05 / 1992 / CC / M • Raw #2 / 1994 / AFV / M • Riviera Heat / 1993 / FD / M • Roxy / 1991 / VC / M • Rumors / 1992 / FL / M • Runnin' Hot / 1992 / LV / M • Screwballs / 1991 / AFV / M • Secret Diary #1 / 1994 / TAW / M • Secret Diary #2 / 1995 / MID / M • Selena's Secrets / 1991 / MIN / M • Sexcalibur / 1992 / FD / M • Seymore & Shane Mount Tiffany / 1994 / FH / M • Seymore Butts Rides Again / 1992 / FH / M • Single Girl Masturbation #4 / 1990 / ESP / F • Single Tight Female / 1992 / LV / M • Skin Deep / 1991 / CIN / M • Sole Food / 1992 / PRE / B • Special Treatment / 1991 / AFV / M • Stolen Hearts / 1991 / AFV / M • Street Walkers / 1990 / PL / M • Super Cakes / 1994 / CA / C • Super Enemates #1 / 1994 / PRE / C •

Surfer Girl / 1992 / PP / M • Sweet Cheeks (1991-Prestige) / 1991 / PRE / B • Sweet Poison / 1991 / CDI / M • A Tale Of Two Titties #2 / 1992 / AFV / M • Taylor Wayne's World / 1992 / AFV / M • Toppers #02 / 1992 / TV / M • Up The Gulf / 1991 / AR / M • V.I.C.E. #2 / 1991 / AFV / M • Voo Doo Soup / 1996 / ... / S • W.A.S.P. / 1992 / CC / M • The Wild Wild Chest #3 / 1996 / HO / C • X Factor: The Next Generation / 1991 / HO / M • X-Rated Blondes / 1992 / VD / C
TAYLOR YOUNG
Part of a pair of identical twins (the other is Brooke Young). Lithe body, pretty face, small tits. Not the same as her namesake in **Make Me Sweat**.
ABA: Double Feature #3 / 1996 / ALP / M • Cannonball Run / 1981 / 2CF / S • Cherry Hustlers / 1977 / VEN / M • Double Your Pleasure / 1978 / CV / M • Erotic Fantasies #1 / 1983 / CV / C • Hot Bodies (Ventura) / 1984 / VEN / C • Jawbreakers / 1985 / VEN / C • John Holmes, The Lost Films / 1988 / PEN / C • Reunion (Vanessa Del Rio's) / 1977 / LIM / M • Saturday Matinee Series #2 / 1996 / VCX / C • Sweet Cakes / 1976 / VC / M • Teenage Twins / 1976 / VCX / M • Thunderbuns / 1976 / VCX / C
TAYLOR YOUNG (NOT 2) see Star Index I
TAYLORE ST. CLAIR
Captured Beauty / 1995 / SAE / B • Erotic Visions / 1995 / ULI / M • Paris Chic / 1996 / SAE / M • Penthouse: Miami Hot Talk / 1996 / PET / S • Soft Bodies: Show 'n Tell / 1995 / SB / F • Up And Cummers #19 / 1995 / 4P / M • Virtual Encounters / 1996 / SCI / S
TAYME MASTERS see Star Index I
TAYNE
J.E.G.: Tayne's First Fuck / 1995 / JEG / M
TAZ
America's Raunchiest Home Videos #71: / 1993 / ZA / M • America's Raunchiest Home Videos #72: / 1993 / ZA / M • Bound For Therapy / 1991 / BIZ / B • Dirty Dave's #4 / 1996 / XPR / M • Filthy First Timers #3: Tearing Down The Walls Of Shame / 1996 / EL / M • Mike Hott: #385 Lesbian Sluts #29 / 1996 / MHV / F • Odyssey 30 Min: #355: Menage A Fuck / 1993 / OD / M • Odyssey Triple Play #94: Triple Decker Sex Sandwich / 1995 / OD / M
TAZ ACTION
Toys Bi Us / 1993 / BIL / G • Transsexual Try Outs / 1993 / HSV / G
TAZDIER see Star Index I
TAZZ
Dirty & Kinky Mature Women #10 / 1996 / C69 / M
TEAL see Star Index I
TEAL (JEN) see Jen Teal
TEAL DARE see Heather Wayne
TEAP
Global Girls / 1996 / GO / F
TED
ABA: Double Feature #2 / 1996 / ALP / M • Nothing Butt Amateurs #01 / 1993 / AFI / M • Pearl Necklace: Premier Sessions #01 / 1993 / SEE / M • Rip-Off Of Millie / cr78 / VHL / M
TED ARMSTRONG
Teenage Cowgirls / 1973 / ALP / M
TED C. BEEJUN
Girls On Fire / 1985 / VCX / M
TED COX

Above And Beyond / 1990 / PNP / G • Bi And Beyond #5 / 1990 / INH / G • Bimbo Boys / 1995 / PL / C • Black & Beyond: The Darker Sid / 1990 / INH / G • Courting Libido / 1995 / HIV / G • Good Boy, Bad Girl / 1990 / VT / G • She-Male Tales / 1990 / MET / G • The Stroke / 1990 / SO / M • Switch Hitters #5: The Night Games / 1990 / IN / G
TED CRAIG see Michael J. Cox
TED DEVIN
The Satisfiers Of Alpha Blue / 1980 / AVC / M
TED DUNCAN see Star Index I
TED GORLEY see Star Index I
TED HARLOW see Star Index I
TED HEAD
Winter Heat / 1994 / MID / M
TED KESEY
Eager Beaver / 1975 / AVC / M • Pleasure Island / 1975 / TGA / M • Sex Museum / 1976 / AXV / M • Y-All Come / 1975 / CDC / M
TED MARTIN see Star Index I
TED MCKNIGHT see Star Index I
TED PARAMORE see Harold Lime
TED REEMS
Nicole: The Story Of O / 1972 / CLX / M
TED ROTER *(Peter Balakoff, Tovia Israel, Tovia Borodyn)*
Soft spoken male with an accent. Ted Roter is his normal name as a director.
Little Girls Lost / 1982 / VC / M • One Page Of Love / 1980 / VCX / M • Paul, Lisa And Caroline / 1976 / SE / M • Prison Babies / 1976 / ... / M • The Psychiatrist / 1978 / VC / M • Scandalous Simone / 1985 / SE / M • Wild Nurses In Lust / 1986 / PLY / M
TED SANDERS
Bottom Busters / 1973 / BLT / M
TED SHAW see Star Index I
TED STREET see Star Index I
TED SUGAR see Star Index I
TED WANSLEY
The She-Male Who Stole Christmas / 1993 / HSV / G
TED WILLIAMS
Caught In The Middle / 1985 / CDI / M • The Poonies / 1985 / VI / M • The Teacher's Pet / 1985 / WV / M
TED WILSON *(Biff Wilson, Conner Henry, Tanner Cole)*
The Biff Wilson is from **Spring Break**. Conner Henry is from **American Built**. Tanner Cole is from **The Anals of History #2**. Rumored to be the husband of Debi Diamond at one stage. This guy became a Mormon and moved to Salt Lake City.
All That Glitters / 1992 / LV / M • Amateurs Exposed #02 / 1993 / CV / M • America's Dirtiest Home Videos #05 / 1991 / VEX / M • America's Raunchiest Home Videos #18: Anal Crunch / 1992 / ZA / M • American Built / 1992 / LE / M • Anal Future / 1992 / VC / M • The Anals Of History #1 / 1991 / MID / M • The Anals Of History #2 / 1992 / MID / M • Back In The Pen / 1992 / FH / M • Back Seat Bush / 1992 / LV / M • Balling Instinct / 1992 / FH / M • The Bare-Assed Naked Gun / 1992 / MID / M • Bazooka County #4 / 1992 / CC / M • Beaverjuice / 1992 / LV / M • Biggies #04 / 1992 / XPI / M • Breast Wishes #05 / 1991 / LBO / M • Breast Wishes #06 / 1991 / LBO / M • Breast Wishes #07 / 1992 / LBO / M • Breast Worx #10 / 1991 / LBO / M • Breast

Worx #11 / 1991 / LBO / M • Breast Worx #12 / 1991 / LBO / M • Breast Worx #14 / 1992 / LBO / M • Breast Worx #16 / 1991 / LBO / M • Breast Worx #20 / 1992 / LBO / M • Breast Worx #29 / 1992 / LBO / M • Breast Worx #33 / 1992 / LBO / M • Bubble Butts #04 / 1992 / LBO / M • Bubble Butts #06 / 1992 / LBO / M • Bubble Butts #07 / 1992 / LBO / M • Bubble Butts #09 / 1992 / LBO / M • Bubble Butts #10 / 1992 / LBO / M • Bubble Butts #14 / 1992 / LBO / M • Bubble Butts #18 / 1992 / LBO / M • The Burma Road #1 / 1994 / LBO / C • The Burma Road #2 / 1994 / LBO / C • Butt Light: Queen Of Rears / 1992 / STR / M • Butt Seriously Folks / 1994 / AFV / M • Cycle Sluts / 1992 / CC / M • Decadent Delights / 1992 / IF / M • The Dragon Lady #3: Tales From The Bed #2 / 1992 / WV / M • Driving Miss Daisy Crazy #2 / 1992 / WV / M • Elvis Slept Here / 1992 / LE / M • Fast Girls #3 / 1992 / XPI / M • Foxes / 1992 / FL / M • Gangbang Girl #07 / 1992 / ANA / M • Gangbang Girl #08 / 1992 / ANA / M • Head & Tails / 1988 / VD / M • Head Again / 1992 / AFV / M • Heartbreaker / 1991 / IF / M • Hillary Vamp's Private Collection #07 / 1992 / HVD / M • Hollywood Swingers #02 / 1992 / LBO / M • Hollywood Swingers #04 / 1992 / LBO / M • Hot Pie Delivery / 1993 / AFV / M • Immoral Support / 1992 / AFV / M • In Your Face #1 / 1992 / PL / M • Just One Look / 1993 / V99 / M • Kiss And Tell / 1992 / AFV / M • Laying Down The Law #1 / 1992 / AFV / M • Little Muffy Johnson / 1985 / VEP / M • Mr. Peepers Amateur Home Videos #19: How Deep My Love? / 1991 / LBO / M • Mr. Peepers Amateur Home Videos #42: Great American Tails / 1992 / LBO / M • Mr. Peepers Amateur Home Videos #43: Gym-Nastiness / 1992 / LBO / M • Mr. Peepers Amateur Home Videos #44: A Royal Reaming / 1992 / LBO / M • Mr. Peepers Amateur Home Videos #46: A Schnitzel In The Bush / 1992 / LBO / M • Mr. Peepers Amateur Home Videos #47: Sigma Cum Louder / 1992 / LBO / M • Mr. Peepers Amateur Home Videos #50: All That Glitters / 1992 / LBO / M • Mummy Dearest #3: The Parting / 1991 / LV / M • Nasty Jack's Kloset Klassics #02 / 1991 / CDI / M • Neighborhood Watch #07: Made Up To Go Down / 1991 / LBO / M • Neighborhood Watch #09: Dial-A-Slut / 1991 / LBO / M • Neighborhood Watch #17: Burning The Sausage / 1992 / LBO / M • Neighborhood Watch #20 / 1992 / LBO / M • Neighborhood Watch #21 / 1992 / LBO / M • Night Moods / 1985 / AVC / M • Nookie Court / 1992 / AFV / M • Odyssey Amateur #30: Angela & Ted's Anal Adventure / 1991 / OD / M • Odyssey Amateur #73: Lori's Oral Luau / 1991 / OD / M • Oral Majority #10 / 1993 / WV / C • Oriental Anal Sluts / 1993 / WV / C • Party Favors / 1993 / VEX / M • Pearl Necklace: Thee Bush League #09 / 1993 / SEE / M • Penetrating Thoughts / 1992 / LV / M • Principles Of Lust / 1992 / WV / M • Ready Freddy? / 1992 / FH / M • Rear Ended / 1985 / WV / M • Rock & Roll Fantasies / 1992 / FL / M • Romance & Fantasy / 1995 / VEX / M • Rumors / 1992 / FL / M • Rump Humpers #01 / 1992 / GLI / M • Rump Humpers #02 / 1992 / GLI / M • Score 4 Me / 1991 / XPI / M • Sexual Healing / 1992 / LV / M • Seymore Butts Rides Again / 1992 / FH / M • Southern Side Up / 1992 / LV / M • Spring Break / 1992 / PL / M • Texas Towers / 1993 / IF / M • Tickets To Paradise / 1992 / XPI / M • Two Sisters / 1992 / WV / M • Udderly Fantastic / 1993 / IF / M • Uncle Roy's Amateur Home Video #01 / 1992 / VIM / M • Vampirass / 1992 / VC / M • You Said A Mouthful / 1992 / IF / M

TEDDI
Drop Outs / 1995 / PRE / B • Leg...Ends #14 / 1995 / PRE / F • The Players Club / 1994 / HW / M

TEDDI AUSTIN
Alumni Girls / 1996 / GO / M • Amateur Lesbians #29: Ari / 1992 / GO / F • Amateur Lesbians #31: Lacy / 1992 / GO / F • Amateur Lesbians #32: Tara / 1992 / GO / F • America's Raunchiest Home Videos #22: City Lites / 1992 / ZA / M • Anal Kitten / 1992 / ROB / M • Anal Lover #2 / 1993 / ROB / M • Anal Orgy / 1993 / DRP / M • Anal Savage #1 / 1992 / ROB / M • Anal With An Oriental Slant / 1993 / ROB / M • The Anals Of History #1 / 1991 / MID / M • Ashlyn Gere: The Savage Mistress / 1992 / BIZ / B • Auction #1 / 1992 / BIZ / B • Auction #2 / 1992 / BIZ / B • Backdoor To Russia #1 / 1992 / VC / M • Backdoor To Russia #2 / 1993 / VC / M • Banana Slits / 1993 / STM / F • The Bare Truth / 1994 / FD / C • Beach Bum Amateur's #05 / 1992 / MID / M • The Best Of Flame / 1994 / BIZ / C • Biff Malibu's Totally Nasty Home Videos #06 / 1992 / ANA / M • Biff Malibu's Totally Nasty Home Videos #18 / 1992 / ANA / M • Biff Malibu's Totally Nasty Home Videos #39 / 1993 / ANA / M • Big Murray's New-Cummers #12: In The Pink / 1993 / FD / M • Big Murray's New-Cummers #13: Hot Tight Ladies / 1993 / FD / M • Blue Moon / 1992 / AFV / M • Bond-Aid / 1992 / STM / B • Bondage Seduction / 1992 / STM / B • Bound Biker Babes #2 / 1993 / STM / B • Breast Collection #02 / 1995 / LBO / C • Breast Worx #23 / 1992 / LBO / M • Breast Worx #25 / 1992 / LBO / M • Breast Worx #36 / 1992 / LBO / M • Bubble Butts #09 / 1992 / LBO / M • Bubble Butts #18 / 1992 / LBO / M • Buffy The Vamp / 1992 / FD / M • Buttman's Revenge / 1992 / EA / M • Creation Of Karen: Tormented & Transformed / 1993 / BIZ / B • Creme De La Face #02 / 1994 / OD / M • Deep Butt / 1994 / MID / C • Delicious (VCX-1993) / 1993 / VCX / M • Designated Hitters / 1995 / PRE / B • The Domination Of Summer #1 / 1994 / BIZ / B • The Domination Of Summer #2 / 1994 / BIZ / B • Double D Domination / 1993 / BIZ / B • Dresden Diary #06: The Hellfire Legend / 1992 / BIZ / B • Dresden Diary #07 / 1992 / BIZ / B • Dresden Diary #08 / 1992 / BIZ / B • Dresden Diary #09 / 1993 / BIZ / B • Dresden Diary #10: Punishment For Their Sins / 1993 / BIZ / B • The Education Of Karen / 1993 / BIZ / B • The End Zone / 1993 / PRE / B • Endangered / 1992 / PP / M • The Enema Bandit Returns / 1995 / BIZ / B • Enema Obedience #2 / 1994 / BIZ / B • Enema Obedience #3: The Ultimate Punishment / 1994 / BIZ / B • Enemates #07 / 1992 / PRE / B • Giggles / 1992 / PRE / B • Harry Horndog #01: Amateur Double Penetration #1 / 1992 / ZA / M • Hollywood Swingers #02 / 1992 / LBO / M • I Made Marian / 1993 / PEP / M • Incredible

Dreams #2 / 1992 / BIZ / B • Just One Look / 1993 / V99 / M • L.A. Rear / 1992 / FD / M • Leg...Ends #10 / 1994 / PRE / F • Licking Legends #1 / 1992 / LE / F • Licking Legends #2 / 1992 / LE / F • Made To Order / 1994 / FD / C • Matronly Stern Spankings / 1994 / STM / B • Mike Hott: #200 Lesbian Sluts #03 / 1992 / MHV / F • Mike Hott: #206 Horny Couples #04 / 1992 / MHV / M • Mike Hott: #257 Cunt of the Month: Selina / 1993 / MHV / M • Motel Hell / 1992 / PL / M • Mr. Peepers Amateur Home Videos #44: A Royal Reaming / 1992 / LBO / M • Mr. Peepers Amateur Home Videos #47: Sigma Cum Louder / 1992 / LBO / M • Ms: Two Cocks In A Pussy / 1992 / MSP / M • Ms: Your Nasty Neighbors #2 / 1993 / MSP / M • Night Wish / 1992 / CDI / M • Nookie Cookies / 1993 / CDI / F • Odyssey 30 Min: #185: Floppy Tit Gang Bang / 1991 / OD / M • On A Platter / 1994 / FD / M • Parlor Games / 1992 / VT / M • Porsche Lynn, Vault Mistress #1 / 1994 / BIZ / B • Porsche Lynn, Vault Mistress #2 / 1994 / BIZ / B • Positively Pagan #04 / 1991 / ATA / M • The Power & The Passion / 1993 / CDI / M • Profiles In Discipline #01: The Mistress Is A Lady / 1994 / STM / C • Pussy Tamer #2 / 1993 / BIZ / B • Running Mates / 1993 / PRE / B • Sex Heist / 1992 / WV / M • Sex Ranch / 1993 / VC / M • Sex Stories / 1992 / VC / M • Soda Jerk / 1992 / ZA / M • Spank! / 1992 / STM / B • The Spirit Of My Master / 1994 / BIZ / B • Spring Break / 1992 / PL / M • Storehouse Of Agony #1 / 1993 / BIZ / B • Storehouse Of Agony #2 / 1992 / BIZ / B • To Serve...Protect...And Submit / 1994 / BIZ / B • Tracey's Academy Of DD Dominance / 1993 / BIZ / B • Triple Flay / 1995 / PRE / B • TV Toilet Challenge / 1993 / BIZ / G • Twin Peaks / 1993 / PL / M • Ultimate Submissives #2: Best of Teddi Austin / 1995 / BIZ / C • Vampirass / 1992 / VC / M • Vice Versa / 1992 / FD / M • Virginia's TV Initiation / 1992 / STM / G • Way Inside Lee Caroll / 1992 / VIM / M • Wendy Is Watching / 1993 / ELP / M • Will & Ed's Keister Easter / 1992 / MID / M • Women's Penitentiary / 1992 / VIM / M • Yank Fest / 1994 / FD / C • Zane's World / 1992 / ZA / M

TEDDI BARRETT
Alumni Girls / 1996 / GO / M • Anal Witness #1 / 1996 / LBO / M • Another Fuckin' Anal Movie / 1996 / ROB / M • The Crackster / 1996 / OUP / M • The Generation Gap / 1996 / LV / M • Hot Tight Asses #17 / 1996 / TCK / M • The Ultimate Climax / 1996 / EMC / M • Venom #3 / 1996 / VD / M • Viet Tran / 1996 / LBO / G • Waves Of Passion / 1996 / ERA / M

TEDDY
Shave Me / 1994 / RTP / F

TEDDY (LANA WOODS) see Lana Woods

TEDDY (ZUMIRA) see Zumira

TEDDY BARE
The Love Couch / 1977 / VC / M

TEDDY GONZALES
P.L.O.W.: Punk Ladies Of Wrestling / 1996 / GOT / B

TEDDY KING
Midnight Hustle / 1978 / VC / M

TEDDY STEELE see Star Index I

TEDRA see Sweety Py

TEDRA DEAR see Sweety Py

TEDRA DEARR see Sweety Py

TEE
Paint It Black / 1995 / EVN / M • Secrets In The Attic #1 / 1994 / STM / B • Secrets In The Attic #2: Extreme Measures / 1994 / STM / B

TEENA
Limited Edition #15 / 1980 / AVC / M

TEENA PAGON
Black, White & Red All Over / 1984 / EXF / C • The Erotic World Of Seka / 1983 / VCR / C • Triangle Of Lust / 1983 / VCR / M

TEESHA NOIR
More Black Dirty Debutantes #4 / 1995 / 4P / M

TEIGHLOR
Dr Butts #1 / 1991 / 4P / M • Fatliners #1 / 1990 / EX / M • Fatliners #2 / 1991 / EX / M • Freak Show / 1991 / FC / M • Life In The Fat Lane #1 / 1990 / FC / M • Life In The Fat Lane #2 / 1990 / FC / M • More To Love #2 / 1995 / TTV / M

TEISHA see Star Index I

TELLY STALONE see Star Index I

TEMPEST STORM (Ann Banks)
Blue Vanities #115 / 1988 / FFL / M • Buxom Beautease / 19?? / SOW / S • Grindhouse Follies: First Row #01 / 1993 / SOW / M • Kiss Me, Baby / 1957 / SOW / S • A Night In Hollywood / 1953 / SOW / S • Paris After Midnight / 1951 / SOW / S • Reel Classics #4 / 1996 / H&S / M • Shock-O-Rama / 1955 / SOW / S • Teaserama / 1954 / SOW / S • Varietease / 1955 / SOW / S

TEMPTATION
Booty And The Ho' Bitch / 1995 / JMP / M • Bootylicious: Booty & The Ho Bitch / 1996 / JMP / M • Butt-Nanza / 1995 / WV / M

TEMPTRESS MINA
Video Virgins #32 / 1996 / NS / M

TEMPYST
Creme De La Face #16: Ladies Licking / 1996 / OD / M

TENA LOUISE
Girls Of The Panty Raid / 1995 / VT / M

TENAY ALDRICH
American Pie / 1980 / SE / M

TENE
Girl's Towne #1 / 1994 / FC / F

TENIAL
Ebony Erotica #11: Harlem Knights / 1993 / GO / M

TENMEI KANO see Star Index I

TEO
Prague By Night #1 / 1996 / EA / M • Prague By Night #2 / 1996 / EA / M

TEQUILA see Star Index I

TERA HEART (Tara Hart, Sara Heart, LeAnn (Tera Heart))
Cute brunette with the body proportions of Nikki Valentine but a prettier face. Has a tattoo on right shoulder. Goes under some other name in **More Dirty Debutantes #6** but not possible to tell what. As of the end of 1994, she has put on lots of weight and had her tits enhanced to large rock-solid proportions.
10,000 Anal Maniacs #2 / 1994 / FOR / M • 900 Desert Strip / 1991 / XPI / M • Above The Knee / 1994 / WAV / M • Ace Mulholland / 1995 / ERA / M • The Adventures Of Major Morehead / 1994 / SC / M • Amateur Lesbians #04: Tera / 1991 / GO / F • Amateur Lesbians #09: Meschel / 1991 / GO / F • Amateur Lesbians #12: Kimberly / 1991 /

GO / F • Amateur Lesbians #33: Mackala / 1992 / GO / F • America's Dirtiest Home Videos #03 / 1991 / VEX / M • Anal Alien / 1994 / CC / M • Anal Centerfold / 1995 / ROB / M • Anal Generation / 1995 / PE / M • Anal Hellraiser #1 / 1995 / ROB / M • Anal Insatiable / 1995 / ROB / M • Anal Maniacs #1 / 1994 / WP / M • Aroused #2 / 1995 / VI / M • Ashlyn Rising / 1995 / VI / M • Backdoor To Buttsville / 1995 / ULI / M • Backdoor To Harley-Wood #2 / 1990 / AFV / M • The Backpackers #2 / 1990 / IN / M • Big Knockers #14 / 1995 / TV / M • Big Knockers #15 / 1995 / TV / M • Big Knockers #20 / 1995 / TV / C • Blonde / 1995 / LE / M • Blue Movie / 1995 / WP / M • Boiling Point / 1994 / WAV / M • Boobs, Butts And Bloopers #2 / 1990 / HO / M • Breakfast With Tiffany / 1990 / HO / M • Bunmasters / 1995 / VC / M • Butt Hunt #04 / 1995 / LEI / M • Buttslammers #10: Lust On The Internet / 1995 / BS / F • Canned Heat / 1995 / IN / M • Cat Lickers #3 / 1995 / ME / F • Club Erotica / 1996 / IN / M • Creme De Femme / 1994 / 4P / F • Cry Baby / 1995 / CV / M • Cumming Clean / 1991 / FL / M • Desire / 1990 / VC / M • Desperate / 1995 / WP / M • Dirty Bob's #23: Tampa Teasers / 1995 / FLP / S • Do It American Amateur Style / 1992 / EAA / M • The Dream Team / 1995 / VT / M • Dreams Cum True / 1990 / HO / M • Dyke Bar / 1991 / PL / F • Erotic Fiction / 1995 / LE / M • Eyewitness Nudes / 1990 / VC / M • Fantasies Of Tera / 1995 / VT / M • Fast Forward / 1995 / CA / M • Film Buff / 1994 / WP / M • Fire Down Below / 1994 / GO / M • Firm Offer / 1995 / SC / M • French Open / 1990 / OD / M • Gettin' Wet / 1990 / VC / M • A Girl's Affair #07 / 1995 / FD / F • The Golden Touch / 1995 / WP / M • The Grunge Girl Chronicles / 1995 / MAX / M • Hard Core Beginners #12 / 1995 / LEI / M • The Harley Girls / 1991 / AR / F • Hawaiian Heat #1 / 1995 / CC / M • Hawaiian Heat #2 / 1995 / CC / M • Hienie's Heroes / 1995 / VC / M • Hole In One / 1994 / HO / M • The Hooker / 1995 / LOT / M • Hooters / 1996 / MID / C • Hot Tight Asses #08 / 1994 / TCK / M • Hot Tight Asses #10 / 1995 / TCK / M • Hotel Sodom #04: Free Parking In Rear / 1995 / SNA / M • Hotel Sodom #06 / 1995 / SNA / M • Hotel Sodom #09 / 1996 / SNA / M • Housewife Lust #2 / 1995 / TV / F • Keyholes / 1995 / OD / M • A Lacy Affair #4 / 1991 / HO / F • Lingerie / 1995 / SC / M • Long Dark Shadow / 1994 / LE / M • Lover Under Cover / 1995 / ERA / M • Midnight Snacks / 1995 / KLP / M • More Dirty Debutantes #06 / 1990 / 4P / M • My 500 Pound Vibrator / 1991 / LV / C • My Evil Twin / 1994 / LE / M • Naked Ambition / 1995 / VC / M • Nasty Nymphos #05 / 1994 / ANA / M • Nightmare Visions / 1994 / ERA / M • Nightvision / 1995 / VI / M • No Man's Land #12 / 1995 / VT / F • Nothing Like A Dame #1 / 1995 / IN / M • Nurse Nancy / 1991 / CA / M • Nutts About Butts / 1994 / LE / M • The Passion / 1995 / IP / M • Perverted #1: The Babysitters / 1994 / ZA / M • Public Access / 1995 / VC / M • Public Places #2 / 1995 / SC / M • Rear Admiral / 1990 / ZA / M • Rockin' The Boat / 1990 / VI / M • Rod Wood / 1995 / LE / M • Sex Academy #2: The Art Of Talking Dirty / 1994 / ONA / M • Sex Academy #3: The Art Of Real Sex

/ 1994 / ONA / M • Sex Academy #4: The Art Of Anal / 1994 / ONA / M • Sex Suites / 1995 / TP / M • Sex Trek #4: The Next Orgasm / 1994 / ME / M • Sex Trek #5: Deep Space Sex / 1994 / ME / M • Silent Women / 1995 / ERA / M • Sin Asylum / 1995 / CV / M • Skippy, Jiff & Jam / 1990 / CIA / M • The Smart Ass Vacation / 1990 / VT / M • Spirit Guide / 1995 / IN / M • Stiletto / 1994 / WAV / M • Streetwalkers / 1995 / HO / M • Sudden Urge / 1990 / IN / M • Surf City Sex / 1991 / CIA / M • Swedish Erotica #75 / 1994 / CA / M • Tailgate Party / 1990 / HO / M • Temptation Of Serenity / 1994 / WP / M • Three's A Crowd / 1990 / HO / M • Torch #2 / 1990 / VI / M • Twelfth Annual Avn Awards / 1995 / VC / M • Twisted / 1990 / VI / M • Vice / 1994 / WAV / M • Wanted / 1995 / DR / M • The Watering Hole / 1994 / HO / M • Western Nights / 1994 / WP / M • Whispered Secrets Of The Call Girls / 1995 / TVE / F • Wicked At Heart / 1995 / WP / M • Wicked Fascination / 1991 / CIN / M • Wicked Thoughts / 1991 / AFV / M • Wild & Wicked #5 / 1995 / VT / M • The Wild Wild Chest #1 / 1990 / HO / M • Wildcats / 1995 / WP / M • Wilde Palms / 1994 / XCI / M • Women On Fire / 1995 / LBO / M

TERA MCGAVIN *see Star Index I*
TERA NOVA *see Kassi Nova*
TERENCE MCNIGHT
Opie Goes To South Central / 1995 / PP / M
TERENCE SCANLON
Confessions Of A Woman / 1976 / SE / M
TERENCE SCANLON (KEN *see* **Ken Scudder**
TERESA
Blue Vanities #539 / 1993 / FFL / M • Bobby Hollander's Sweet Cheeks #102 / 1992 / WV / M • Mike Hott: #367 Girls Who Lap Cum From Cunts #02 / 1996 / MHV / M • Mr. Peepers Nastiest #5 / 1995 / LBO / C • Score Busty Centerfolds #1 / 1995 / BTO / S
TERESA (CZECH)
Dirty Dirty Debutantes #7 / 1996 / 4P / M • More Dirty Debutantes #40 / 1995 / 4P / M • More Dirty Debutantes #41 / 1995 / 4P / M • More Dirty Debutantes #42 / 1995 / 4P / M
TERESA BISMARK
The Big Thing / 1973 / VHL / M
TERESA GOLLUM
The Joy Of Fooling Around / 1978 / CV / M
TERESA JONES
Eat At The Blue Fox / 1983 / VC / M • Groupies Galore / 1983 / VC / M • Stacey's Hot Rod / 1983 / CV / M
TERESA ORLOWSKI
Backdoor Lust / 1987 / CV / C • Double Desires / 1988 / PIN / C • Foxy Lady #1 / 1985 / PL / M • Foxy Lady #2 / 1986 / PL / M • Foxy Lady #3 / 1986 / PL / M • Foxy Lady's Candid Camera #1 / 1986 / LA / M • Go For It / 1984 / VC / M • Only The Best From Europe / 1989 / CV / C • Only The Best Of Breasts / 1987 / CV / C • Only The Best Of Oral / 1989 / CV / C • Simply Outrageous / 1989 / VC / C • Teresa, The Woman Who Loves Men / 1985 / CV / M • The Woman Who Loves Men / 1985 / CA / M
TERESA SVENSSON
The Second Coming Of Eva / 1974 / ALP / M

TERESA TEASE
America's Raunchiest Home Videos #50: / 1993 / ZA / M • Big Boob Bangeroo #1 / 1995 / TTV / M • Black Centerfold Celebrities / 1993 / MID / M • Black Fantasies #09 / 1995 / HW / M • Black Fantasies #10 / 1995 / HW / M • Black Velvet #2 / 1993 / CC / M • Brown Sugar From The Hood / 1996 / MID / M • Dangerous Behinds #2 / 1996 / HW / M • Dark Alleys #01 / 1992 / FC / M • Dark Alleys #02 / 1992 / FC / M • Ebony Erotica #07: Sepia Salute / 1993 / GO / M • Freaky Flix / 1995 / TTV / C • Henry's Big Boob Adventure / 1996 / HO / M • Hooters In The 'hood / 1995 / TTV / M • Lactamania #1 / 1994 / TTV / M • Mo' Honey / 1993 / FH / M • Ready To Drop #03 / 1994 / FC / M • Sweet Black Cherries #1 / 1996 / TTV / M • Sweet Black Cherries #2 / 1996 / TTV / M • Tit Tales #4 / 1993 / FC / M
TERI
Blue Vanities #572 / 1995 / FFL / M • Blush: Private Pleasures / 1993 / FAT / F • Blush: Shadow / 1993 / FAT / F • Hollywood Confidential #2 / 1983 / PRC / M • Homegrown Video #374 / 1992 / HOV / M • Monkey Business / 1996 / ULI / M
TERI BROWN
Sheila's Payoff / 1977 / VCX / M
TERI DIVER *(Terry Diver, Teri Driver)*
Reddish-blonde with enhanced medium to large tits and an attitude.
3 Wives / 1993 / VT / M • The 4th Vixxen / 1995 / EMC / M • Alice In Hollywierd / 1992 / ZA / M • All That Glitters / 1992 / LV / M • Ambitious Blondes / 1992 / VIM / M • America's Raunchiest Home Videos #02: Cooking with Hot Sauce / 1991 / ZA / M • Anal Adventures #4: Doin' Her Up! / 1992 / VC / M • Anal Intruder #09: The Butt From Another Planet / 1995 / CC / M • The Analizer / 1994 / VD / M • Anything That Moves / 1992 / VC / M • The Babe / 1992 / EX / M • Bad To The Bone / 1992 / LE / M • Bazooka County #4 / 1992 / CC / M • Bedroom Bondage / 1994 / LON / B • Bedtime Stories / 1992 / CDI / M • The Big E #10 / 1992 / PRE / B • Big Titted Tarts / 1994 / PL / C • Bigger / 1991 / PL / M • Bikini City / 1991 / CC / M • Black By Popular Demand / 1992 / ZA / M • Black In The Saddle Again / 1991 / ZA / M • Blonde Ice #2 / 1993 / EX / M • Bloopers & Boners / 1996 / VI / M • Body Work / 1993 / MET / M • Bondage Slut / 1994 / HOM / B • The Boneheads / 1992 / PL / M • Brainteasers / 1991 / ZA / M • Brats In Bondage / 1993 / LON / B • The Brothel / 1993 / OD / M • Bubbles / 1991 / IF / M • Burn / 1991 / LE / M • Bush Wacked / 1991 / ZA / M • Busted / 1992 / HO / M • Cajun Heat / 1993 / SC / M • California Pony Girls / 1992 / STM / B • Cat & Mouse #2 / 1993 / XCI / M • Catfighting Students / 1995 / PRE / C • Cinnamon Twist / 1993 / OD / M • Colossal Orgy #1 / 1993 / HW / M • Colossal Orgy #2 / 1994 / HW / M • Compulsive Behavior / 1995 / PI / M • Cookie 'n' Cream / 1992 / ME / M • Cumming Of Ass / 1995 / TP / M • The D.P. Man #1 / 1992 / FD / M • Dark Justice / 1992 / ZA / M • Dear John / 1993 / VI / M • Deception / 1991 / XCI / M • Deep C Diver / 1992 / LV / M • Deep Inside Victoria Paris / 1993 / VC / C • Deja Vu / 1993 / XCI / M • Denim / 1991 / LE / M • Diver Down /

1992 / CC / M • Dr Feelgood Sex Psychiatrist / 1994 / LV / M • Dungeon Delight / 1995 / LON / B • Edward Penishands #3 / 1991 / VT / M • Erotique / 1992 / VC / M • The Eye Of The Needle / 1991 / CIN / M • Fast Track / 1992 / LIP / F • Genie In A Bikini / 1991 / ZA / M • A Girl's Affair #01 / 1992 / FD / F • A Girl's Affair #03 / 1993 / FD / F • Girls Just Wanna Have Girls #3 / 1994 / HIO / F • Girls Will Be Boys #5 / 1993 / PL / F • Girls Will Be Boys #6 / 1993 / PL / F • Gold LeMay / 1991 / VIM / M • Golden Arches / 1992 / PRE / B • Good Vibrations #1: Self Satisfaction With A Vibrator / 1991 / VT / M • The Governess / 1993 / WP / M • Guilty By Seduction / 1993 / PI / M • Hard Rider / 1992 / IN / M • Hard Talk / 1992 / VC / M • Hard To Stop #2 / 1992 / VC / M • Hard Whips For Soft Bodies / 1993 / NTP / B • Her Darkest Desire / 1993 / HOM / B • Hollywood Swingers #02 / 1992 / LBO / M • Hollywood Teasers #03 / 1992 / LBO / M • Hot Flushes / 1992 / PRE / B • Hot Summer Knights / 1991 / LV / M • Hourman Is Here / 1994 / CC / M • House Pet / 1992 / V99 / M • How To Love Your Lover / 1992 / XII / S • I Was An Undercover Slave / 1994 / HOM / B • If These Walls Could Talk (Director's Cut) / 1993 / MET / M • If These Walls Could Talk #1: Wicked Whispers / 1993 / MET / M • If These Walls Could Talk #2: Burning Secrets / 1993 / CV / M • Insatiable Nurses / 1992 / VIM / M • Intersextion / 1994 / HO / M • Into The Gap / 1991 / LE / M • It's A Wonderful Sexlife / 1991 / LE / M • Jungle Jive / 1992 / VD / M • Junkyard Anal / 1994 / JAV / M • Juranal Park / 1993 / OD / M • Just For The Hell Of It / 1991 / CA / M • Just For Tonight / 1992 / VC / M • Kinky Roommates / 1992 / TP / M • Leg...Ends #07 / 1993 / PRE / F • Lesbian Kink Trilogy #1 / 1992 / STM / F • Little Big Dong / 1992 / ZA / M • Live Sex / 1994 / LE / M • Made For A Gangbang / 1995 / ZA / M • Major Exposure / 1995 / PL / F • Masquerade / 1995 / HO / M • Mastering The Male / 1995 / RB / B • The Merry Widows / 1993 / VC / M • Mr. Peepers Amateur Home Videos #19: How Deep My Love? / 1991 / LBO / M • Muff 'n' Jeff / 1992 / ZA / M • My Cousin Ginny / 1993 / MET / M • My Secret Lover / 1992 / XCI / M • Nasty Jack's Kloset Klassics #02 / 1991 / CDI / M • Nasty Jack's Kloset Klassics #04 / 1991 / CDI / M • Natural Born Thrillers / 1994 / LV / M • Neighborhood Watch #05 / 1991 / LBO / M • Nipples / 1994 / FOR / F • No Man's Land #05 / 1992 / VT / F • No Men 4 Miles / 1992 / LV / F • Odds 'n' Ends / 1992 / PRE / B • Oral Madness #2 / 1992 / OD / M • Oral Majority #09 / 1992 / WV / C • Oral Majority #12 / 1994 / WV / C • Pajama Party / 1993 / CV / C • Paper Tiger / 1992 / VI / M • Passion's Prisoners / 1994 / LV / M • Popped Tarts / 1992 / RB / B • Pops / 1994 / PL / M • A Portrait Of Dorian / 1992 / OD / M • Primal Desires / 1993 / EX / M • Private Pleasures / 1994 / STM / F • Pulse / 1994 / EX / M • Puttin' Out / 1992 / VD / M • Putting It All Behind #2: Star Treatment / 1994 / IN / M • Rainbows / 1992 / VT / F • Rainwoman #05 / 1992 / CC / M • Realities #2 / 1992 / ZA / M • Red Hot Coeds / 1993 / VIM / M • Reds / 1993 / LE / F • Roman Goddess / 1992 / HW / M • Runnin' Hot / 1992 / LV / M • The

Screamer / 1991 / CA / M • The Seduction Of Mary / 1992 / VC / M • Sex Nurses / 1991 / VIR / M • Sexual Instinct #2 / 1994 / DR / M • Sexual Olympics #1: The Trials / 1992 / VT / M • Sexual Olympics #2: The Finals / 1992 / VT / M • Seymore Butts In The Love Shack / 1992 / FH / M • Seymore Butts Rides Again / 1992 / FH / M • The Sin-A-Bun Girls / 1995 / OD / M • Sittin' Pretty #2 / 1992 / DR / M • Slaves Of The Warrior Queen / 1993 / HOM / B • Slow Dancing / 1990 / VI / M • So You Wanna Be A Porn Star #1: The Russians Are Cumming / 1994 / WHP / M • Sole Food / 1992 / PRE / B • Sorority Sex Kittens #1 / 1992 / VC / M • Sorority Sex Kittens #2 / 1993 / VC / M • Street Angels / 1992 / LV / M • Street Heat / 1992 / CDI / M • Student Fetish Videos: Catfighting #03 / 1991 / PRE / B • Student Fetish Videos: Catfighting #04 / 1992 / PRE / B • Student Fetish Videos: The Enema #07 / 1992 / PRE / B • Student Fetish Videos: Tickling #04 / 1992 / SFV / B • Stylin' / 1994 / FD / M • Surfside Sex #1 / 1991 / LV / F • Sweet Alicia Rio / 1992 / FH / M • Taboo #10 / 1992 / IN / M • Taboo #11: Crazy On You / 1993 / IN / M • Tailiens #3 / 1992 / FD / M • Tangled / 1994 / PL / M • Tarts In Torment / 1993 / LBO / B • A Taste Of K.C. Williams / 1992 / VD / C • Telesex #2 / 1992 / VI / M • Teri Diver's Bedtime Tales / 1993 / FD / M • The Tiffany Minx Affair / 1992 / FOR / M • Tight Asses / 1994 / RB / B • Tight Pucker / 1992 / WV / M • Titty Slickers #1 / 1991 / LE / M • Toni Welles Goes Behind The Scenes / 1992 / FD / M • Transparent Desires / 1991 / LV / M • Truth And Bare / 1991 / LV / M • Up For Grabs / 1991 / FH / M • Use It Or Lose It / 1994 / CA / M • Wee Wee's Big Misadventure / 1991 / FH / M • Where There's Sparxx, There's Fire / 1991 / LV / M • Wicked Thoughts / 1991 / AFV / M • Wicked Wenches / 1991 / LV / M • Wild & Wicked #2 / 1992 / VT / M • Wishful Thinking / 1992 / VC / M • With The Devil In Her Rear / 1992 / WV / M • The Women / 1993 / CAT / F • Women Of Color / 1991 / PL / F

TERI DONOVAN *see Star Index I*
TERI DRIVER *see Teri Diver*
TERI GALKO *see Loni Sanders*
TERI HANNON
French Erotica: Report Card / 1980 / AR / M • High School Report Card / 1979 / CA / M • L.A. Tool & Die / 1979 / TMX / G • [The Raw Report / 1978 / ... / M
TERI LYNN (A. RAIN) *see Angelica Rain*
TERI MARTINE
Blue Vanities #567 / 1995 / FFL / M • Maids In Bondage /The Bondage Girls / 1985 / 4P / B
TERI MCNEILE
Big Busted Goddesses Of L.A. / 1991 / NAP / S • Cat-Fight Dream / 1988 / NAP / B • Dominated / 1988 / NAP / B • The Taming Of Teri #1 / 1988 / NAP / B • The Taming Of Teri #2 / 1988 / NAP / B • Topless Trio / 1988 / NAP / B
TERI MORGAN
Body Lust / 1980 / VC / M • Lorelei / 1984 / CV / M
TERI REYNOLDS *see Star Index I*
TERI ST JAMES *see Star Index I*
TERI WEIGEL *(Teri Weigle)*
Brunette with big inflated tits but an tight body otherwise. She is married to Murrill Maglio

(what taste!). Born in Florida. Modelled for Saks and *Seventeen* and was then a *Playboy* Playmate (April 1986). Appeared as an extra in **Predator #2**. Breast size in May 92 is 36DD. First sex scene was in **Inferno**. 33 years old in 1995 and still married to the same guy whom she calls "Merle".
All About Teri Weigel / 1996 / XCI / M • Auntie Lee's Meat Pies / 1992 / C3S / S • The Banker / 1989 / AE / S • The Barlow Affairs / 1991 / XCI / M • Battle Of The Superstars / 1993 / VI / M • Bloopers & Boners / 1996 / VI / M • Burning Desire / 1992 / CDI / M • Cheerleader Camp / 1987 / PAR / S • Circus Of Lesbians / 1995 / VI / C • Deliciously Teri / 1993 / IF / M • Dick & Jane Do The Strip / 1994 / AVI / M • Encore / 1995 / VI / M • Everybody's Playmates / 1992 / CA / C • Far From Home / 1989 / VES / S • Friends & Lovers #1 / 1991 / VT / M • Friends & Lovers #2 / 1991 / VT / M • Glitch! / 1988 / AE / S • The Housewife In Heat / 1991 / PL / M • I Dream Of Teri / 1993 / IF / M • Illusions #1 / 1992 / IF / M • Illusions #2 / 1992 / IF / M • Inferno / 1991 / XCI / M • Innocent Blood / 1992 / WAR / S • The Last Act / 1995 / VI / M • The Last American Sex Goddess / 1993 / IF / M • The Last Temptation Of Teri / 1991 / IF / M • Lingerie Busters / 1991 / FH / M • Marked For Death / 1990 / FOX / S • Midwest: At The Ponderosa / 1992 / MV0 / S • Miss Nude North America #1 / 1995 / VOY / S • Miss Nude North America #2 / 1995 / VOY / S • More Dirty Debutantes #09 / 1991 / 4P / M • Night Visitor / 1989 / MGM / S • Penthouse: Fast Cars, Fantasy Women / 1992 / PET / F • Playboy Video Calendar 1988 / 1987 / PLA / S • Playboy Video Centerfold: Teri Weigel / 1985 / PLA / F • Playboy's Erotic Fantasies #1 / 1987 / UNI / S • Playboy's Erotic Fantasies #2 / 1990 / UNI / S • Playboy's Girls Of Rock & Roll / 1985 / PLA / S • Playboy's Sexy Lingerie #2 / 1989 / HBO / S • Playboy's Sexy Lingerie #3 / 1991 / HBO / S • Playboy: Inside Out #3 / 1993 / UNI / S • Playboy: Secrets Of Euro Massage / 1991 / PLA / S • Playboy: Secrets Of Making Love To The Same Person Forever / 1991 / HBO / S • Playboy: Wet & Wild #1 / 1989 / HBO / S • Playboy: Wet & Wild #2 / 1990 / HBO / S • Predator #2 / 1990 / FOX / S • Private Dancer (CDI) / 1992 / CDI / M • Raunch #03 / 1991 / CC / M • Return Of The Killer Tomatoes / 1988 / NWW / S • Savage Beach / 1989 / C3S / S • Sex Scenes / 1992 / VD / C • Sheer Ecstasy / 1993 / IF / M • Spellbound / 1991 / CDI / M • Starr / 1991 / CA / M • A Taste Of Teri / 1994 / FF / C • Teri Weigel's Little Pepper / 1992 / CDI / M • Teri's Fantasies / 1993 / VEX / M • Totally Teri / 1992 / IF / M • Wet Event / 1992 / IF / M • Wicked / 1991 / XCI / M • Wicked Fascination / 1991 / CIN / M • [La Camionista / 19?? / ... / M • [Masquerade (1992-Italy) / 1992 / ... / S
TERI WEIGLE *see Teri Weigel*
TERI WHITMORE
More On The Job Training / 1994 / RB / B
TERMITE *see Star Index I*
TERRA
Blue Vanities #534 / 1993 / FFL / M
TERRENCE MCKNIGHT
8-Ball: Westside Gang Bang / 1995 / PL / M
TERRI

Biff Malibu's Totally Nasty Home Videos #19 / 1992 / ANA / M • Blonde Temptress / 1989 / LOD / F • Blue Vanities #529 / 1993 / FFL / M • Body Tease / 1992 / VER / F • High Heels In Heat #1 / 1988 / RSV / F • High Heels In Heat #3 / 1989 / RSV / F • Real Women...Real Fantasies! / 1996 / WSD / F • Skintight / 1991 / VER / F

TERRI BENOUM *see* Adrienne Bellaire

TERRI CARTER *see Star Index I*

TERRI COPELAND *see Star Index I*

TERRI DOLAN *(Terry Dolan, Gloria Harrison)*

Gloria Harrison is from **Coed Fever**.
Coed Fever / 1980 / CA / M • Sex Boat / 1980 / VCX / M • Star Virgin / 1979 / CXV / M • Ultraflesh / 1980 / GO / M

TERRI EASTERN
Birds And Beads / 1974 / VC / M

TERRI ELLIS
Black Cheerleader Search #02 / 1996 / ROB / M • More Black Dirty Debutantes #6 / 1996 / 4P / M

TERRI GORDON
Forbidden Dreams / 1984 / BIZ / G • Twice A Virgin / 1984 / PL / G

TERRI HALL *(National Velvet)*

Not too pretty brunette with medium tits and a mole on her belly just to the left of midline. Supposedly she was a ballet dancer at one stage (well, it's a change from nudie bar dancer). As of 1995 she is reportedly dead from cancer.

Alice In Wonderland / 1976 / CA / M • Babylon Gold / 1983 / COM / C • Blue Vanities #239 / 1995 / FFL / M • Blue Vanities #244 / 1995 / FFL / M • Bucky Beaver's XXX Dragon Art Theatre Double Feature #02 / 1996 / SOW / M • Classic Erotica #3 / 1980 / SVE / M • The Devil Inside Her / 1977 / ALP / M • Divine Obsession / 1976 / TVX / M • Dominatrix Without Mercy / 1976 / ALP / B • The Double Exposure Of Holly / 1977 / TVX / M • Ecstasy In Blue / 1976 / ALP / M • Electric Blue #006 / 1982 / CA / S • Electric Blue: Caribbean Cruise / 1984 / CA / S • Fantasex / 1976 / COM / M • Farewell Scarlett / 1976 / COM / M • Feelings / 1977 / VC / M • Frank Henenlotter's XXX Hardcore Horrors #05 / 1996 / SOW / M • Gums / 1976 / AVC / M • The Honeymooners / 1978 / CV / M • Honeypie / 1975 / VC / M • Legacy Of Satan / 19?? / APB / S • Legends Of Porn #1 / 1987 / CV / C • My Sex-Rated Wife / 1977 / ... / M • Odyssey / 1977 / VC / M • Once Over Nightly / 197? / VXP / M • Only The Very Best On Film / 1992 / VC / C • The Opening Of Misty Beethoven / 1976 / VC / M • Oriental Blue / 1975 / ALP / M • Pornocopia Sensual / 1976 / VHL / M • Rollerbabies / 1976 / VC / M • Seduction / 1974 / VXP / M • Sex Wish / 1976 / CV / M • The Story Of Joanna / 1975 / VHL / M • Sugar Britches / 1980 / VCX / C • Suzie's Take Out Service / 1975 / CDC / M • Sweetheart / 1976 / SVE / M • The Taking Of Christina / 1975 / NGV / M • Teenage Pajama Party / 1977 / VC / M • Terri's Revenge / 1974 / ALP / M • That's Porno / 1979 / CV / C • Through The Looking Glass / 1976 / ALP / M • Unwilling Lovers / 197? / SVE / M • VCA Previews #2 / 1988 / VC / C • Virgin Dreams / 1976 / BMV / M • The World Of Henry Paris / 1981 / VC / C • [Ganja And Hess / 1973 / VIG / S

TERRI HAMPTON *see Star Index I*

TERRI JOHNSON *(Lynn Harris, Judy Medford)*

Petite gap-toothed blonde.
Below The Belt / 1971 / SOW / S • Blue Vanities #508 / 1992 / FFL / M • Blue Vanities #513 / 1992 / FFL / M • Class Reunion / 1972 / PS / S • The Cocktail Hostesses / 1972 / ... / S • The Erotic Adventures Of Zorro / 1969 / SOW / S • Flesh Gordon #1 / 1974 / FAC / S • The Hand Of Pleasure / 1971 / SOW / S • In Sarah's Eyes / 1975 / VHL / M • Little Miss Innocence / 1978 / ACV / S • The Love Couch / 1977 / VC / M • Midnight Plowboy / 1973 / SOW / S • Pleasure Unlimited / 1972 / PS / S • Snow Bunnies / 1970 / NFV / S • The Stewardesses / 1969 / SOW / S • Video Vixens / 1972 / VES / S • Wanda, The Sadistic Hypnotist / 1967 / SOW / S

TERRI LEE *see* Keanna

TERRI NELSON *see Star Index I*

TERRI RITTER
The Bitch Goddess / cr82 / BIZ / B

TERRI RUGGIERO
The Pay-Off / cr70 / VHL / M

TERRI STEELE
Pink Champagne / 1979 / CV / M

TERRI STEVENS
The Erotic Adventures Of Lolita / 1982 / VXP / M

TERRI TRIP
Limo Connection / 1983 / VC / M

TERRI TYLER *see Star Index I*

TERRY
The Betrayal Of Innocence #1: The Awakening Of Marika / 1993 / CC / M • The Betrayal Of Innocence #2: The Decadence / 1993 / CC / M • The Betrayal Of Innocence #3: The Choice / 1993 / CC / M • Black Cheerleader Search #05 / 1996 / IVC / M • Black Cheerleader Search #10 / 1997 / IVC / M • Blue Vanities #112 / 1988 / FFL / M • Blue Vanities #510 / 1992 / FFL / M • Blue Vanities #554 / 1994 / FFL / M • Bus Stop Tales #03 / 1989 / PRI / M • Fetish High Heels And Corsets / 1987 / RSV / G • Mike Hott: #176 Terry And Lisa / 1990 / MHV / M • Raw Talent: Fetish Of The Month #01 / 1994 / RTP / G • She-Male Encounters #22: She-Male Mystique / 1995 / MET / G

TERRY AUSTIN
Candy Lips / 1975 / CXV / M • Heat Wave / 1977 / COM / M

TERRY DIVER *see* Teri Diver

TERRY DOLAN *see* Terri Dolan

TERRY FLAME
Heat Wave / 1977 / COM / M

TERRY GALE
Blue Vanities #551 / 1994 / FFL / M

TERRY GALKO *see* Loni Sanders

TERRY GLENN
The Love Couch / 1977 / VC / M

TERRY GRUBBER *see Star Index I*

TERRY HIGGINS
Blue Vanities #514 / 1992 / FFL / M

TERRY ISAH
How To Make A College Co-Ed / 1995 / VG0 / M

TERRY JEAN
Blue Vanities #115 / 1988 / FFL / M

TERRY KEELER
Erotic Interlude / 1981 / CA / M

TERRY LARSEN
Keyhole / 1977 / SE / M

TERRY LEE
Bedtime Video #04 / 1984 / GO / M

TERRY LESTER
Just Deserts / 1991 / BIZ / B

TERRY LLOYD *see Star Index I*

TERRY LYNN
The Ginger Effect / 1985 / VI / M • Ginger's Greatest Girl/Girl Hits / 1986 / VI / C • Ready, Willing & Anal (Cv) / 1993 / CV / C

TERRY MAXWELL *see* Marlene Willoughby

TERRY MILLER
ABA: Double Feature #1 / 1996 / ALP / M • Fanny Hill / 1975 / TGA / M

TERRY MORGAN
Fantasy Mansion / 1983 / BIZ / B

TERRY MORRIS
Close Up / 19?? / BOC / M

TERRY MOUND
Most Valuable Slut / 1973 / HLV / M

TERRY PEPPER
Beyond The Valley Of The Ultra Milkmaids / 1984 / 4P / F • Blue Vanities #029 / 1988 / FFL / M • Blue Vanities #534 / 1993 / FFL / M

TERRY PERRY
Backdoor Brides #1 / 1985 / PV / M

TERRY PETTERS
Blue Vanities #581 / 1996 / FFL / M

TERRY RICH
The Violation Of Missy / 1996 / JMP / F

TERRY ROCKS *see* Terry Thomas

TERRY RUGGEIRO
[Payoff / 197? / ... / M

TERRY RYDER
Girls U.S.A. / 1980 / AIR / M

TERRY SMITH
Kitty's Kinky Capers / 1996 / TTV / M

TERRY SWEENEY *see Star Index I*

TERRY TEDESCHI *see* Tony Tedeschi

TERRY THOMAS *(Terry Rocks, Terry Tyler, Larry White)*

Boyfriend or husband of Crystal Wilder.
10,000 Anal Maniacs #1 / 1993 / FOR / M • Adult Video Nudes / 1993 / VC / M • Anal Intruder #07 / 1993 / CC / M • Anal Squeeze / 1993 / FOR / M • Anal Taboo / 1993 / ROB / M • Ass Openers! #1 / 1995 / TCK / C • The Bashful Blonde From Beautiful Bendover / 1993 / PEP / M • Bazooka County #5: The Jugs / 1993 / CC / M • The Bet / 1993 / VT / M • The Beverly Thrillbillies / 1993 / ZA / M • Bikini Beach #1 / 1993 / CC / M • Blinded By Love / 1993 / OD / M • Blonde Justice #2 / 1993 / VI / M • Blow For Blow / 1992 / ZA / M • Bobby Hollander's Sweet Cheeks #101 / 1992 / WV / M • Body Of Innocence / 1993 / WP / M • Body Work / 1993 / MET / M • Boogie In The Butt / 1993 / WIV / M • The Boss / 1993 / VT / M • Breast Worx #37 / 1992 / LBO / M • Breastman's Anal Adventure / 1993 / EVN / M • Bronco Millie / 1992 / ZA / M • The Brothel / 1993 / OD / M • Bubble Butts #14 / 1992 / LBO / M • Burgundy Blues / 1993 / MET / M • Bush League #2 / 1992 / CC / M • The Butt Boss / 1993 / VD / M • Butt Darling / 1994 / WIV / M • Butt Hole Boulevard / 1993 / CA / M • The Butt Sisters / 1993 / MID / M • Butts Afire / 1992 / PMV / M • Caged Fury / 1993 / DR / M • Cheeks #6 / 1992 / CC / M • Cheerleader Nurses #1 / 1993 / VC / M • Chug-A-Lug Girls #2 / 1993 / VT / M • Cinnamon Twist / 1993 / OD / M • The Corruption Of Christina / 1993 / WP / M • Deep Butt / 1994 / MID / C • Deep Cover / 1993 / WP / M • Deep Inside Crystal Wilder / 1995 / VC

/ C • Dial N Again / 1993 / PEP / M • Dirty Little Lies / 1993 / VT / M • The Dragon Lady #4: Tales From The Bed #3 / 1992 / WV / M • Dream House / 1995 / XPR / M • Eight Is Never Enough / 1993 / ZA / M • En Garde / 1993 / DR / M • Endlessly / 1993 / VI / M • Erotic Newcummers Vol 1 #2: Texas Twisters / 1993 / DR / M • The Fluffer #1 / 1993 / FD / M • Frenzy / 1992 / SC / M • Full Moon Bay / 1993 / VI / M • Gang Bang Wild Style #1 / 1993 / ROB / M • Gangbang Girl #12 / 1993 / ANA / M • Gimme An X / 1993 / VD / C • The Governess / 1993 / WP / M • Harry Horndog #10: Love Puppies #1 / 1992 / ZA / M • Hootermania / 1994 / VC / M • Hot For Teacher / 1993 / VD / M • Hot Property / 1993 / PEP / M • Hot Tight Asses #02 / 1993 / TCK / M • Hot Tight Asses #04 / 1993 / TCK / M • House Of The Rising Sun / 1993 / TCK / M • Hyapatia Obsessed / 1993 / EX / M • Interactive / 1993 / VD / M • Juranal Park / 1993 / OD / M • Kelly Eighteen #2 / 1993 / LE / M • Knockin' Da Booty / 1993 / WP / M • The Lady In Red / 1993 / VC / M • The Last Anal Hero / 1993 / OD / M • Lawnmower Woman / 1992 / MID / M • Loopholes / 1993 / TP / M • Masquerade (1992-Usa) / 1992 / SC / M • Mind Shadows #1 / 1993 / FD / M • Mind Shadows #2 / 1993 / FD / M • The Mistress (1993-Caballero) / 1993 / CA / M • Model's Memoirs / 1993 / IP / M • More Than A Handful #2 / 1993 / MET / M • More Than A Handful #3 / 1993 / MET / M • My Cousin Ginny / 1993 / MET / M • Naked Truth #2 / 1993 / FH / M • Neighborhood Watch #36 / 1992 / LBO / M • New Wave Hookers #3 / 1993 / VC / M • Night Creatures / 1992 / PL / M • No Man's Land #06 / 1992 / VT / F • Nothing Personal / 1993 / CA / M • Objective: D.P. / 1993 / PEP / M • Odyssey 30 Min: #205: / 1992 / OD / M • Odyssey Triple Play #33: 3 Back-Door Boinkers / 1993 / OD / M • One Of Our Porn Stars Is Missing / 1993 / OD / M • The Orgy #2 / 1993 / EMC / M • P.J. Sparxx On Fire / 1992 / MID / C • Panties / 1993 / VD / M • Professor Sticky's Anatomy 3X #02 / 1992 / FC / M • Rear Entry / 1993 / LEI / M • Secret Services / 1993 / PEP / M • Seduced / 1992 / VD / M • Sex #1 (Vivid) / 1993 / VI / M • Sex #2 (Vivid) / 1993 / VI / M • Sharon Starlet / 1993 / WIV / M • Shear Ecstasy / 1993 / PEP / M • Single White Nympho / 1992 / MID / M • A Slow Hand / 1992 / FD / M • Southern Cumfort / 1993 / HO / M • Starbangers #02 / 1993 / BIG / M • A Stripper Named Desire / 1993 / CC / M • Sun Bunnies #2: The Pink Cheek Tales / 1992 / SC / M • Teri's Fantasies / 1993 / VEX / M • Truth Or Dare / 1993 / VI / M • Unsolved Double Penetration / 1993 / PEP / M • Up And Coming Executive / 1993 / TP / M • The Uptown Girl / 1992 / ZA / M • Virtual Reality / 1993 / EX / M • Web Of Desire / 1993 / OD / M • Who Killed Holly Hollywood? / 1993 / VC / M • Wilder At Heart / 1993 / ANA / M • Working Girl / 1993 / VI / M • You Bet Your Buns / 1992 / ZA / M

TERRY TYLER *see* **Terry Thomas**
TERRY VOGUE *see* **Star Index I**
TERRY WALSH *see* **Star Index I**
TERRY WAYNE
The Necklace #3 / 1994 / ZFX / B • Night Prowler #3: Master Of Reality / 1995 / ZFX

/ B
TERRY X.
Nightclub / 1996 / SC / M
TERRY YOUNG *see* **Star Index I**
TERRY YULE
Dracula Exotica / 1980 / TVX / M
TERUYO AKAI *see* **Star Index I**
TESHA
Look What I Found On The Street #01 / 1996 / CC / M
TESLA BROWN
Black Fire / 1993 / VIM / M • Captain Bob's Lust Boat #2 / 1993 / FCP / M • Dark Passions #01 / 1993 / AFV / M • More Dirty Debutantes #26 / 1993 / 4P / M • Totally Tasteless Video #02 / 1994 / TTV / M
TESS
Blue Vanities #539 / 1993 / FFL / M • Homegrown Video #418: Looks As Good As It Feels / 1994 / HOV / M • HomeGrown Video #456 / 1995 / HOV / M • Painless Steel #3 / 1996 / FLV / M • Rawhide / 1994 / BIZ / B • Sweet Brown Sugar / 1994 / AVI / M
TESS (FERRE) *see* **Tess Ferre**
TESS ARMSTRONG *see* **Tess Newhart**
TESS FERRARI *see* **Tess Ferre**
TESS FERRE *(Tess Ferrari, Tess Petre, Tess (Ferre), Tess Terre)*
Not the same as Ali Moore although there is some resemblance.
Alien Lust / 1985 / AVC / M • B.Y.O.B. / 1984 / VD / M • Beverly Hills Cox / 1986 / CA / M • Beverly Hills Heat / 1985 / VEP / M • Don't Tell Daddy #1 / 1985 / PL / C • Evil Angel / 1986 / VCR / M • Heartthrobs / 1985 / CA / M • Hindsight / 1985 / IN / M • If My Mother Only Knew / 1985 / CA / M • John Holmes, The Man, The Legend / 1995 / EVN / C • Kiss Of The Gypsy / 1986 / WV / M • Looking For Mr Goodsex / 1984 / CC / M • Love Button / 1985 / AVC / M • Lust With The Stranger / 1986 / MAP / M • Marina Vice / 1985 / PEN / M • One Night In Bangkok / 1985 / CA / M • Oriental Jade / 1985 / VC / M • Playing For Passion / 1987 / IN / M • Portrait Of Desire / 1985 / IVP / M • Pulsating Flesh / 1986 / VC / M • Real Men Eat Keisha / 1986 / VC / M • Screw / 1985 / CV / M • Showdown / 1985 / BON / B • Showdown / 1986 / CA / M • Starved For Affection / 1985 / AVC / M • Swedish Erotica #61 / 1984 / CA / M • Swedish Erotica #63 / 1985 / CA / M • Swedish Erotica #67 / 1985 / CA / M • Sweet Surrender / 1985 / AVC / M • A Taste Of Cherry / 1985 / CV / M • Teacher's Pets / 1985 / AVC / M • Traci Who? / 1987 / AVC / C • Wild Things #1 / 1985 / CV / M • The Woman In Pink / 1984 / SE / M • You're The Boss / 1985 / VD / M
TESS FINLANDIA
Never So Deep / 1981 / VCX / M
TESS MAYO *see* **Star Index I**
TESS NEWHART *(Tess Armstrong, Linda Lou (Tess N.))*
Dark blonde or light brown hair, brown eyes, pretty, tiny tits, faint tattoo on right shoulder back, 26 years old and de-virginized at 16. Seems to have the down-to-earth practicality of Natalie Harris (Corby Wells) but is prettier.
100% Amateur #02: Back Door And More / 1995 / OD / M • The Adventures Of Studman #1 / 1994 / AFV / M • Altered Paradise / 1995 / LE / M • The Anal Adventures

Of Suzy Super Slut #1 / 1994 / AFV / M • The Anal Adventures Of Suzy Super Slut #3 / 1994 / IPI / M • Anal Al's Adventures / 1995 / PL / M • Anal Camera #03 / 1994 / EVN / M • Anal Hunger / 1994 / ROB / M • Anal Invader / 1995 / PEP / M • Anal Plaything #1 / 1994 / ROB / M • Anal Rookies #2 / 1994 / ROB / M • Anal Savage #2 / 1994 / ROB / M • Anal Secrets (After Dark) / 1994 / AFD / M • Anal Therapy #3 / 1994 / FD / M • Analtown USA #01 / 1995 / NIT / M • Bare Ass In The Park / 1995 / PEP / M • Behind The Brown Door / 1994 / PE / M • Big Murray's New-Cummers #28: Rump Humpers #2 / 1995 / FD / M • Big Tit Racket / 1995 / PEP / M • Black Ass Masters #2 / 1995 / GLI / M • Black Studs & Little White Trash / 1995 / ROB / M • Butt Hunt #02 / 1994 / LEI / M • Butt Hunt #08 / 1995 / LEI / M • The Butt Sisters Do Cleveland / 1994 / MID / M • The Butt Sisters Do Sturgis / 1994 / MID / M • The Cumm Brothers #05: These Nuts For Hire / 1994 / OD / M • Deep Space 69 / 1994 / HW / M • Dildo Debutantes / 1995 / CA / F • End Around / 1994 / PRE / B • Enemates #09 / 1994 / BIZ / B • The Farmer's Daughters / 1994 / LV / M • First Time Lesbians #15 / 1994 / JMP / F • Fun Zone / 1994 / PRE / B • Gang Bang Bitches #05 / 1995 / PP / M • Gang Bang Bitches #09 / 1995 / PP / M • Gas Works / 1994 / PRE / B • Go Ahead...Eat Me! / 1995 / KWP / M • The Gypsy Queen / 1996 / CC / M • Happy Ass Lesbians / 1994 / ROB / F • Junkyard Anal / 1994 / JAV / M • Kinky Fantasies / 1994 / KWP / M • Lady's Choice / 1995 / VD / M • Lap Of Luxury / 1994 / WIV / M • Laugh Factory / 1995 / PRE / C • Leg...Ends #13 / 1995 / PRE / F • Lesbian Bitches #1 / 1994 / ROB / F • Lesbian Mystery Theatre: The Case Of The Deadly Dyke / 1994 / LIP / F • Lusty Lap Dancers #2 / 1994 / HO / M • Max #02 / 1994 / FWE / M • Max Gold #1 / 1996 / XPR / C • Mighty Man #1: Virgins In The Forest / 1994 / LE / M • Mike Hott: #278 Cunt of the Month: Tess 12-94 / 1994 / MHV / M • Mike Hott: #289 Three-Sum Sluts #02 / 1995 / MHV / M • Mike Hott: #295 Older Gals #07 / 1995 / MHV / F • Mike Hott: #299 Jordan Hart & Friends #2 / 1995 / MHV / M • Mike Hott: #307 Lesbian Sluts #18 / 1995 / MHV / F • Mike Hott: #312 Lesbian Sluts #19 / 1995 / MHV / F • Mike Hott: #315 Cum In My Mouth #02 / 1995 / MHV / C • Mike Hott: #317 Girls Who Swallow Cum #01 / 1995 / MHV / C • Mike Hott: #321 Lesbian Sluts #20 / 1995 / MHV / F • Mike Hott: #367 Girls Who Lap Cum From Cunts #02 / 1996 / MHV / M • Mike Hott: #378 Fuck The Boss #8 / 1996 / MHV / M • Mr. Peepers Amateur Home Videos #89: Stiffy Stuffer / 1994 / LBO / M • Mr. Peepers Amateur Home Videos #90: Back Door Bonanza / 1994 / LBO / M • Mr. Peepers Amateur Home Videos #93: Creative Fornication / 1994 / LBO / M • Nasty Newcummers #09 / 1995 / MET / M • Nasty Nymphos #05 / 1994 / ANA / M • Natural Born Thriller / 1994 / CC / M • Older Men With Younger Women #2 / 1994 / CC / M • Prime Cuts #1 / 1994 / FOR / M • Prime Cuts #2 / 1994 / FOR / M • Private Diaries #1: Christina / 1995 / AVI / M • Provocative / 1994 / LE / M • R.E.A.L. #2 / 1994 / LV / F • A Rear And Pleasant Danger / 1995 /

PP / M • Sex Party / 1995 / KWP / M • Sex-A-Fari / 1994 / LV / M • Shave Tails #3 / 1994 / SO / M • Sluts In Suburbia / 1994 / GLI / M • Snatch Patch / 1995 / LE / M • So You Wanna Be A Porn Star #1: The Russians Are Cumming / 1994 / WHP / M • Star Crossed / 1995 / VC / M • Strange Sex In Strange Places / 1994 / ZA / M • Strap-On Sally #05: Chantilly's French Kiss / 1995 / PL / F • Strap-On Sally #06: Triple Penetration Trollop / 1995 / PL / F • Strip Poker / 1995 / PEP / M • Student Fetish Videos: The Enema #17 / 1995 / PRE / B • Student Fetish Videos: Foot Worship #14 / 1995 / PRE / B • Student Fetish Videos: Spanking #18 / 1995 / PRE / B • Sweet A$ Money / 1994 / MID / M • Tail Taggers #124 / 1994 / WV / M • Tongue In Cheek / 1994 / LE / M • The Tonya Hard-On Story / 1994 / GO / M • Top Debs #5: Deb Of The Month / 1994 / GO / M • Under The Pink / 1994 / ROB / F • Up The Middle / 1995 / V99 / M • Video Virgins #11 / 1994 / NS / M • Walk On The Wild Side / 1994 / VIM / M • Willie Wanker At The Fudge Packing Factory / 1995 / FD / M

TESS PETRE *see* **Tess Ferre**

TESS TERRE *see* **Tess Ferre**

TESS WATERS
The Hitch-Hiker #09: Back Road Detour / 1994 / WMG / M

TESSA KAHN *(Dynasti)*
Indonesian who says she was born in Bali (sure!—Bali, CA more likely) 24 years old in 1993, tall Oriental, medium tits, tight waist, very self-confident.
Lovin' Spoonfuls #6 / 1996 / 4P / C • More Dirty Debutantes #27 / 1993 / 4P / M • More Dirty Debutantes #29 / 1994 / 4P / M • New Ends #08 / 1994 / 4P / M

TESSIE LYNN *see* **Laura Fujiyama**

TETCHIE
Anal Oriental Sorority / 1994 / LBO / M

TETRA DEARR *see* **Sweety Py**

TEX ANTHONY
Bi Bi Love / 1986 / LAV / G • Bi-Sexual Fantasies / 1984 / LAV / G • The Big Switch / 1985 / LAV / G • Cabaret Sin / 1987 / IN / M • The National Transsexual / 1990 / GO / G • Trisexual Encounters #04 / 1986 / PL / G • Tropical Lust / 1987 / MET / M

TEX FORD
All The Senator's Girls / 1977 / CA / M

TEX THE WONDER DICK
[The Raw Report / 1978 / ... / M

TEXAS
Black Knockers #12 / 1995 / TV / M

TEXAS MILLIE *see* **Texas Milly**

TEXAS MILLY *(Natasha (Texas M), Millie, Texas Millie, Jara (Texas M), Andrea (Texas M))*
Pretty blonde with curly hair, petite, very dark pussy and ass crack, small tits with prominent areola, nice smile, passable to pretty face, not tight on waist, mole on belly just to right of her belly button. Supposedly from Brazil (bullshit—no accent) and de-virginized at 15.
Anal Camera #07 / 1995 / EVN / M • Deep Inside Anal Camera / 1996 / EVN / C • Fresh Faces #03 / 1995 / EVN / M • Hard Core Beginners #04 / 1995 / LEI / M • Pussy Hunt #13 / 1995 / LEI / M • Pussyman Auditions #02 / 1995 / SNA / M • Video Virgins #20 / 1995 / NS / M

TEXAS SWEETS

Fresh Faces #05 / 1995 / EVN / M

THAK
New Faces, Hot Bodies #14 / 1994 / STP / M

THE BONE RANGER
Up And Cummers #08 / 1994 / 4P / M

THE CONTESSA *see* **Star Index I**

THE COUNT *see* **Star Index I**

THE DELIVERY BOY
Clear And Present Anger / 1995 / IBN / B

THE DUDE *see* **Star Index I**

THE DUNGEON MASTER
Discipline / 1994 / TVI / B

THE EGG *see* **Star Index I**

THE FLASH *see* **Steve Vegas**

THE FROGMAN
Anal League / 1996 / IN / M

THE GOLDEN GHOST *see* **Jim Holliday**

THE GREAT WALDO *see* **David Christopher**

THE HORSLEYS
Spank Me, Spank Me, Spank Me / 199? / BON / B

THE INCREDIBLE BULK
Suburban Swingers / 1993 / IF / M • Take It Like A Man / 1994 / IF / M

THE ITALIAN STALLION *see* **Star Index I**

THE LEATHER MASTER
Discipline / 1994 / TVI / B • Return To Leather Lair / 1993 / STM / B

THE MASKED LADY
More Dirty Debutantes #32 / 1994 / 4P / M

THE MASKED ONE
By Myself / 1996 / PL / F

THE NERDS *see* **Star Index I**

THE PET
S&M Pet Control / 1995 / SBP / B

THE PIPER
Aged To Perfection #3 / 1995 / TTV / M

THE RIPPER *see* **Star Index I**

THE SHERIFF
Philmore Butts Goes Wild! / 1996 / SUF / M

THE VOYEUR
Julie: A First Time Submissive In A Dungeon / 1996 / DHP / B

THE X-MAN
Blonde / 1995 / LE / M • The Dirty Little Mind of Martin Fink / 1991 / ME / M • Jack The Stripper / 1992 / ME / M • Radical Affairs Video Magazine #01 / 1992 / ME / M • Sodom & Gomorrah / 1992 / OD / M

THEE ELMA PETTI *see* **Star Index I**

THELMA
Blue Vanities #538 / 1993 / FFL / M

THELMA RULE *see* **Star Index I**

THEODORA DUNCAN *see* **Roseanne Farrow**

THEODORE
Odyssey Triple Play #63: Orient Express / 1994 / OD / M

THERESA
Lesbian Pros And Amateurs #02 / 1992 / GO / F • Penthouse: The Girls Of Penthouse #2 / 1993 / PET / S • Thunder Boobs / 1995 / BTO / M

THERESA CASALE
AVP #9110: Eight Balls & Peeping Toms / 1991 / AVP / M

THERESA FLASH
Butt Watch #06 / 1994 / FH / M

THERESA GUNN
Anal Toy Story / 1996 / MP0 / M • Back Rent / 1996 / MP0 / M • Emerald: Princess Of The Night / 1996 / FC / M • Latin Fever #3 / 1996 / C69 / M • Sodomize Me!!! /

1996 / SPR / M

THERESA LEECH
Twilight / 1996 / ESN / M

THERESA OSOVKY
Double Pleasure / 1995 / XYS / M

THERESA ROXX
East Coast Sluts #08: Atlantic City / 1995 / PL / M • Fresh Meat #2 / 1996 / PL / M • Strap-On Sally #07: Face Dildo Frenzy / 1995 / PL / F • Strap-On Sally #08: Strap-On Cock Fight / 1995 / PL / F

THERESA WHITE
Menage De Sade / 1987 / BIZ / B

THIERRY
Cindy Puts Out / 1996 / OLL / M

THIERRY DE BREM
[Rentre C'est Bon / 1977 / ... / M

THIERRY WINNER *see* **Star Index I**

THILO
Hot New Imports / 1996 / XC / M

THOM GLARDON
Sodom & Gomorrah / 1974 / MIT / M

THOMAS
Feelings / 1977 / VC / M • Wrestling Classics #2 / 1984 / CDP / B

THOMAS APPLETREE
Silver Screen Confidential / 1996 / WP / M

THOMAS CHIN *see* **Star Index I**

THOMAS FRANCINI *see* **Blair Harris**

THOMAS GANGE
Big Titted Tarts / 1994 / PL / C

THOMAS HARDING
Return Of The Knickers Inspector / 1994 / CS / B

THOMAS HOOKS *see* **Star Index I**

THOMAS JR.
The Voyeur #8: Live In Europe #2 / 1996 / JLP / M

THOMAS LILIUS
The Wild Women / 1996 / PL / M

THOMAS LILLIUS
Scandanavian Double Features #1 / 1996 / PL / M

THOMAS LONG *see* **Star Index I**

THOMAS MITCHELL
The Girls In The Band / 1976 / SVE / M

THOMAS PAINE
Chickie / 1975 / CA / M

THOMAS PARKER *see* **Christian Parker**

THOMAS RYDER
Bottom Dweller: The Final Voyage / 1996 / EL / M

THOMAS SMITH
Le Parfum De Mathilde / 1994 / VI / M

THOMAS SWEETWOOD *see* **Thomas Wood**

THOMAS TRINGLER *see* **Star Index I**

THOMAS WOOD *(Thomas Sweetwood, William Kerwin)*
The Adventures Of Lucky Pierre / 1961 / SOW / S • Bell, Bare And Beautiful / 1963 / SOW / S • Boinng / 1962 / SOW / S • Goldilocks And The Three Bares / 1962 / ... / S • My Third Wife George / 1969 / SOW / S • Scum Of The Earth / 1963 / SOW / S • Suburban Roulette / 1967 / SOW / S • [Living Venus / 1960 / ... / S

THOMASINA *see* **Star Index I**

THOR
AVP #9161: Boy Toy...The Video / 1991 / AVP / M

THOR CRUISE *see* **Star Index I**

THOR SOUTHERN *see* **Star Index I**

THORSTEN JEWSKI
Dirty Business / 1995 / WIV / M

THRASHER *see* **Star Index I**

THUMPER *see* **Stephanie DuValle**

THUMPER (MALE)
Forbidden Fantasies #1 / 1995 / ZA / M

THUNDER
Bottom Dweller: The Final Voyage / 1996 / EL / M

THUVIA
Temptations / 1976 / VXP / M

TI'BOURG TAIME *see* **Star Index I**

TIA *(Tia Yarbough)*
Plasticized large older blonde with enhanced (some say natural) large tits, older, flabby belly, not too pretty face, and tattoos on her left tit (faded) and left belly. Tia Yarbough is from **Big Boob Bangaroo #6**. 36 years old in 1996.
Ass, Gas & The Mystical GLOP / 1997 / EL / M • Backdoor Diaries / 1995 / BBE / M • Bad To The Bone / 1996 / ULP / M • Bel Air Babes / 1996 / SUF / M • Beverly Hills Bikini Company / 1996 / NIT / M • Big Boob Bangeroo #5 / 1996 / TTV / M • Big Boob Bangeroo #6 / 1996 / TTV / M • Big Bust Babes #30 / 1995 / AFI / M • Big Bust Babes #35 / 1996 / AFI / M • Big Bust Babes #39 / 1996 / AFI / M • Big Busty Major Babes / 1996 / NAP / F • Breastman's Hot Legs Contest / 1996 / ... / M • Breastman's Triple X Cellent Adventure / 1995 / EVN / M • Buffy Malibu's Nasty Girls #09 / 1995 / ANA / F • Buffy's Nude Camera-Party / 1996 / CIN / M • Buttsizer #3: Return Of The King Of Rears / 1995 / EVN / M • Casting Call #14 / 1995 / SO / M • Climax At The Melting Pot #2 / 1996 / AVS / M • Crew Sluts / 1996 / NOT / M • The Cumm Brothers #11: Oh Cum On Ye Faces / 1995 / OD / M • Cyber-Sex Love Junkies / 1996 / BBE / M • Dirty & Kinky Mature Women #08 / 1996 / C69 / M • Double D Dykes #20 / 1995 / GO / F • Double D Dykes #22 / 1995 / GO / F • Double D Dykes #24 / 1995 / GO / F • Double D Dykes #25 / 1995 / GO / F • Feature Speciale: The Ultimate Squirt / 1996 / ANE / M • Geriatric Valley Girls / 1995 / FC / M • The Girls Of Summer / 1995 / VT / M • Hardcore Fantasies #1 / 1996 / LV / M • Hardcore Schoolgirls #3: Legal And Eager / 1995 / XPR / M • Head Nurse / 1996 / RAS / M • Heavy Breathing / 1996 / NIT / M • Incantation / 1996 / FC / M • Interracial Escorts / 1995 / GO / M • Jingle Balls / 1996 / EVN / M • Lesbian Nights / 1996 / AVI / F • Middle Aged Sex Maniacs / 1995 / SUF / M • Mike Hott: #286 Fuck The Boss #06 / 1996 / MHV / M • Mike Hott: #329 Cunt Of The Month: Tia / 1995 / MHV / M • Mike Hott: #331 Lesbian Sluts #21 / 1996 / MHV / F • Mike Hott: #332 Girls Who Swallow Cum #02 / 1995 / MHV / C • Mike Hott: #339 Cum In My Mouth #04 / 1996 / MHV / C • Mike Hott: #342 Three-Sum Sluts #10 / 1995 / MHV / M • Mike Hott: #345 Cum In My Cunt #07 / 1995 / MHV / C • Mike Hott: #348 Lesbian Sluts #23 / 1996 / MHV / F • Mike Hott: #387 Girls Who Lap Cum From Cunts #04 / 1996 / MHV / M • Mile High Thrills / 1995 / VIM / M • Mondo Extreme / 1996 / SHS / M • Nookie Professor #2 / 1996 / AVS / M • Nothing Like Nurse Nookie #1 / 1995 / NIT / M • The Older Women's Sperm Bank #2 / 1996 / SUF / M • Oldies But Goodies / 1995 / WIV / M • Orgy Camera #1 / 1995 / EVN / M • Orgy Camera #2 / 1996 / EVN / M • Pussyman Auditions #15 / 1995 / SNA / M

• Pussyman's House Party #1 / 1996 / SNA / M • Pussyman's House Party #2 / 1996 / SNA / M • Red Hots / 1996 / PL / M • Senior Stimulation / 1996 / CC / M • Sexual Overdrive / 1996 / LE / M • A Shot In The Pink / 1995 / BBE / M • The Strippers / 1995 / GO / M • Surfin' The Net / 1996 / RAS / M • Tia's Holiday Gang Bang / 1995 / HO / M • The Tigress / 1995 / VIM / M • Trading Partners / 1995 / GO / M • Unbalanced Chemicals / 1996 / SUF / M • Using Your Assets To Get A Head / 1996 / OUP / F • The Violation Of Rachel Love / 1995 / JMP / F • The Wanderer #2: Slippery When Wet / 1995 / CDI / M • Whammin' & Jammin' At The Hard Cock Ole / 1996 / GLI / M • You Bet Your Ass / 1991 / EA / B

TIA (MEXICAN)
Dick & Jane Go To Mexico / 1994 / AVI / M

TIA (ORIENTAL)
More Dirty Debutantes #23 / 1993 / 4P / M

TIA DE ANGELO *see* **Kandi Valentine**

TIA FORD *see* **Star Index I**

TIA MARIE
Lady M's Anything Nasty #01: Pink Pussy Party / 1996 / AVI / F

TIA VON DAVIS
ABA: Double Feature #3 / 1996 / ALP / M • Blow Some My Way / 1977 / VHL / M • Mount Of Venus / 1975 / ... / M • Saturday Matinee Series #2 / 1996 / VCX / C • Teenage Twins / 1976 / VCX / M

TIA YARBOUGH *see* **Tia**

TIANA
Passionate Lovers / 1991 / PL / M

TIANA (1994)
Anal Vision #22 / 1993 / LBO / M • The Superhawk Girls...And Their Fabulous Toys / 1996 / GLI / C

TIANA CAMBRIDGE
Bondage Boot Camp / 1988 / TAN / B • The Bondage Club #4 / 1990 / LON / B

TIANA MENDEZ
The Psychiatrist / 1978 / VC / M

TIANA REGAL *see* **Tianna Scott**

TIANNA *(Tara Collins, Tatiana (Tianna))*
Older slim blonde with small tits. Quite pretty but very aggresive. Tatiana is from **Forgiveable**. Born November 30, 1963 according to **Bloopers #2**. Was married to Patrick Collins, the head of Elegant Angel but as of 1995 had split up.
Above And Beyond / 1990 / PNP / G • Adult Video News 1992 Awards / 1992 / VC / M • The Adventures Of Buttman / 1989 / EA / M • Adventures Of Buttwoman #1 / 1991 / EL / F • The Adventures Of Buttwoman #2: Behind Bars / 1992 / EL / F • The All American Girl / 1991 / PP / M • Amazons From Burbank / 1990 / PL / F • Anal Revolution / 1991 / ROB / M • Backdoor To Russia #1 / 1992 / VC / M • Backdoor To Russia #2 / 1993 / VC / M • The Bad News Brat / 1991 / VI / M • Beach Blanket Brat / 1989 / VI / M • Best Of Bi And Beyond / 1992 / PNP / C • Best Of Bruce Seven #1 / 1990 / BIZ / C • Best Of Bruce Seven #3 / 1990 / BIZ / C • Best Of Buttman #1 / 1991 / EA / C • The Best Of Buttslammers / 1995 / BS / C • The Better Sex Video Series #1: The Better Sex Basics / 1991 / LEA / M • The Better Sex Video Series #2: Advanced Sex Techniques / 1991 / LEA / M • The Better Sex Video Series #3: Sex Games and Toys / 1991 / LEA / M • Between The Cheeks #2 / 1990 / VC / M • Bi And Beyond #5 / 1990

/ INH / G • Bi Cycling / 1989 / FC / G • The Bi-Ologist / 1993 / ... / G • Big Titted Tarts / 1994 / PL / C • Bitches In Heat / 1994 / PL / C • Bizarre Mistress Series: Sharon Mitchell / 1992 / BIZ / C • Black & Beyond: The Darker Sid / 1990 / INH / G • Black Studies / 1992 / GO / M • Bloopers #2 / 1991 / GO / C • Blowing In Style / 1989 / EA / M • Bruce Seven's Favorite Endings #1 / 1991 / EL / C • Bruce Seven: A Compendium Of His Most Graphic Scenes Vol 1 / 1991 / BS / C • Butt Freak #1 / 1992 / EA / M • Buttman Goes To Rio #4 / 1993 / EA / M • Buttman Vs Buttwoman / 1992 / EL / M • Buttman's Big Tit Adventure #1 / 1992 / EA / M • Buttman's Double Adventure / 1993 / EA / M • Buttman's Revenge / 1992 / EA / M • Buttslammers #01 / 1993 / BS / F • Buttslammers #02: The Awakening Of Felicia / 1993 / BS / F • Buttslammers #05: Quake, Rattle & Roll! / 1994 / BS / F • Buttwoman Back In Budapest / 1993 / EL / M • Buttwoman In Budapest / 1992 / EA / M • Canadian Beaver Hunt #3 / 1996 / PL / M • The Challenge / 1990 / EA / B • Cherry Red / 1993 / RB / B • Cool Sheets / 1989 / PP / M • Corruption / 1990 / CC / M • Dallas Does Debbie / 1992 / PL / M • Deep Inside Centerfold Girls / 1991 / VC / M • Deep Inside Debi Diamond / 1995 / VC / C • Deep Inside Jeanna Fine / 1992 / VC / C • Deep Inside Keisha / 1994 / VC / C • Deep Throat #4 / 1990 / AR / M • Denim Dolls #1 / 1989 / CDI / M • Dominating Girlfriends #1 / 1992 / PL / B • Dominating Girlfriends #2 / 1992 / PL / B • Dresden Diary #03 / 1989 / BIZ / B • Dresden Diary #04 / 1989 / BIZ / B • Easy Pussy / 1991 / ROB / M • The Easy Way / 1990 / VC / M • Easy Way Out / 1989 / OD / M • Eleventh Annual AVN Awards / 1994 / VC / M • Fit To Be Tied / 1991 / BS / B • G Squad / 1990 / SO / G • Gang Bangs #2 / 1989 / EA / M • Ghost Lusters / 1990 / EL / F • Girls Gone Bad #1 / 1990 / GO / F • Girls Gone Bad #2: The Breakout / 1990 / GO / F • Girls Gone Bad #3: Back To The Slammer / 1991 / GO / F • Girls Gone Bad #4: Cell Block Riot / 1991 / GO / F • Girls Gone Bad #5: Mexican Justice / 1991 / GO / F • Girls Of Sin / 1994 / PL / C • Hard On The Press / 1991 / AWV / M • The Hardriders / 1990 / 4P / M • Hollywood Bikini Party Girls / 1989 / VC / M • Honey Drippers / 1992 / ROB / F • House Of Dark Dreams #1 / 1990 / BS / B • House Of Dark Dreams #2 / 1990 / BS / B • The Hungarian Connection / 1992 / EA / M • I Dream Of Christy / 1989 / CAY / M • Indian Summer #1 / 1991 / VI / M • Indian Summer #2: Sandstorm / 1991 / VI / M • Intimate Journey / 1993 / VI / M • Introducing Tabitha / 1990 / CIN / M • Itty Bitty Titty Committee #1 / 1990 / PL / F • Jail Babes #1 / 1990 / PL / F • Joined: The Siamese Twins / 1989 / PL / M • Kittens #1 / 1990 / CC / F • Lace / 1989 / VT / F • The Last Temptation / 1988 / VD / M • Leather / 1989 / VT / F • Leather And Lace / 1989 / VT / F • Leather And Lace Revisited / 1991 / VT / F • Lesbian Pros And Amateurs #15 / 1992 / GO / F • Letters From The Heart / 1991 / AWV / M • Lick-A-Thon #2 / 1996 / HW / C • Lips On Lips / 1989 / LIP / F • Little Miss Dangerous / 1989 / SO / M • Loose Ends #6 / 1989 / 4P / M • Making The Grade / 1989 / IN / M • Masturbation Madness /

1991 / 5KS / F • Meat Market / 1992 / SEX / C • Mistaken Identity / 1990 / CC / M • Nasty Girls #3 (1990-Plum) / 1990 / PP / M • Never Enough / 1990 / PP / M • The New Barbarians #1 / 1990 / VC / M • The New Barbarians #2 / 1990 / VC / M • New Sensations / 1990 / CC / M • Nightdreams #2 / 1990 / VC / M • Nightdreams #3 / 1991 / VC / M • Nothing To Hide #2 / 1993 / CV / M • The Only Game In Town / 1991 / VC / M • Only The Best Of Barbara Dare / 1990 / CV / C • Only The Very Best On Video / 1992 / VC / C • Pajama Party / 1993 / CV / C • Parliament: Lesbian Seduction #1 / 1990 / PM / F • Parliament: Lesbian Seduction #2 / 1990 / PM / C • Party Doll A Go-Go #1 / 1991 / VC / M • Party Doll A Go-Go #2 / 1991 / VC / M • Party Dolls / 1992 / VEX / M • The Penthouse / 1989 / PP / M • Play Me / 1989 / VI / M • Pony Girls / 1993 / ROB / F • The Power Of Summer #2: Reward / 1992 / BS / B • Pretty Peaches #3 / 1989 / VC / M • Queen Of Hearts #2: Hearts On Fire / 1990 / PL / M • Rapture / 1990 / SC / M • Rayne Storm / 1991 / VI / M • Route 69 / 1989 / OD / M • Runaway / 1992 / VI / M • Savage Fury #2 / 1989 / CAY / M • Secretaries / 1990 / PL / F • Separated / 1989 / INH / M • Sex Lives On Porno Tape / 1992 / VC / C • The Sex Symbol / 1991 / GO / M • A Sexual Obsession / 1989 / PP / M • Shadow Dancers #1 / 1989 / EA / M • Shadow Dancers #2 / 1989 / EA / M • Shadows In The Dark / 1990 / 4P / M • Shaved Sinners #3 / 1990 / VT / M • Sno Bunnies / 1990 / PL / F • Sodomania #07: Deep Down Inside / 1993 / EL / M • Sodomania: Smokin' Sextions / 1996 / EL / C • Sorority Pink #1 / 1989 / CV / M • Sorority Pink #2 / 1989 / CV / M • Stairway To Paradise / 1990 / VC / M • Steamy Windows / 1990 / VC / M • Studio Sex / 1990 / FH / M • Super Tramp / 1989 / VD / M • Sweet Chastity / 1990 / EVN / M • Tailspin #1 / 1991 / VT / M • Talk Dirty To Me #07 / 1990 / DR / M • Thrill Seekers / 1990 / BS / B • A Tongue Is Born / 1990 / ERU / M • True Legends Of Adult Cinema: The Modern Era / 1992 / VC / C • TV Nation #1 / 1995 / HW / G • Two In The Bush / 1991 / EX / M • The Unauthorized Biography Of Rob Blow / 1990 / LV / M • Uncut Diamond / 1989 / IN / M • Unforgivable / 1989 / IN / M • Waterbabies #1 / 1992 / CC / M • Welcome To The House Of Fur Pi / 1989 / GO / M • Wet 'n' Working / 1990 / EA / F • Where The Girls Play / 1992 / CC / F • Where The Girls Sweat #1 / 1990 / EA / F • Where The Girls Sweat #2 / 1991 / EL / F • Whore Of The Roses / 1990 / AFV / M • Why Do You Want To be In An Adult Video / 1990 / PM / F • X-Rated Bloopers #2 / 1986 / AR / M

TIANNA SCOTT *(Tiana Regal)*
Blonde with a nice tight waist but not particularly pretty.
Anal Co-Ed / 1993 / ROB / M • Bay City Hot Licks / 1993 / ROB / F • Biff Malibu's Totally Nasty Home Videos #33 / 1993 / ANA / M • Buffy Malibu's Totally Nasty All-Girl Home Videos #02 / 1992 / ANA / F • Kittens & Vamps #1 / 1993 / ROB / F • Sweet Lips & Buns / 1993 / ROB / F

TIANNA TAYLOR *(Raven (T.Taylor), Chanel (T.Taylor))*
A large reddish brunette with a big nose and big

enhanced hard tits. Piggish eyes. Avoid.
The Adventures Of Breastman / 1992 / EVN / M • Alice In Hollywierd / 1992 / ZA / M • Anal Analysis (Heatwave) / 1992 / HW / M • Anal Asian / 1994 / VEX / M • Anal Virgins Of America #01 / 1993 / FOR / M • Anything That Moves / 1992 / VC / M • Babe Magnet / 1994 / IN / M • Bat Bitch #2 / 1990 / FAZ / M • Battle Of The Superstars / 1993 / VI / M • Beach Bunny / 1994 / V99 / M • The Best Rears Of Our Lives / 1992 / OD / M • Betrayal / 1992 / XCI / M • The Big Bust / 1992 / FPI / M • Big Bust Babes #10 / 1992 / AFI / M • Big Bust Babes #12 / 1993 / AFI / M • Big Bust Platinum: Superstar Strip Tease / 1993 / PME / F • Blue Heaven / 1990 / IF / M • Breast Wishes #12 / 1993 / LBO / M • Bush Pilots #1 / 1990 / VC / M • Checkmate / 1992 / CDI / M • Committed / 1992 / LE / M • Cookie 'n' Cream / 1992 / ME / M • The Coven #1 / 1993 / VI / M • Dark Dreams / 1992 / WV / M • Defying The Odds / 1995 / OD / M • Dick & Jane In San Francisco / 1996 / AVI / M • Dickin' Around / 1994 / VEX / M • Dirty Dixie / 1992 / IF / M • Double D Dykes #04 / 1992 / GO / F • Double D Dykes #08 / 1993 / GO / F • Double D Dykes #12 / 1993 / GO / F • Encino Woman / 1992 / VIM / M • Fireball #1 / 1994 / VI / C • Flesh And Boner / 1993 / WV / M • Fresh Tits Of Bel Air / 1992 / OD / M • Gerein' Up / 1992 / VC / M • The Girl Has Assets / 1990 / LV / M • The Girls Of Summer / 1992 / FOR / M • The Great American Boobs To Kill For Dance Contest / 1995 / PEP / C • Hooter Heaven / 1992 / CA / M • Hootermania / 1994 / VC / M • Hot Property / 1993 / PEP / M • I Love LA #2 / 1989 / PEN / C • Illusions #1 / 1992 / IF / M • Inside Of Me / 1993 / PL / G • Internal Affairs / 1992 / CDI / M • Jiggly Queens #1 / 1993 / LE / M • Lesbian Pros And Amateurs #19 / 1993 / GO / F • Lesbian Pros And Amateurs #25 / 1993 / GO / F • Lez Go Crazy / 1992 / HW / C • Love Hurts / 1992 / VD / M • Macin' #1 / 1996 / SMP / M • Maliboobies / 1993 / CDI / F • Man Of Steel / 1992 / IF / M • Miracle On 69th Street / 1992 / HW / M • More Than A Handful #2 / 1993 / MET / M • Nookie Cookies / 1993 / CDI / F • Nookie Of The Year / 1993 / HW / M • Oral Majority #09 / 1992 / WV / C • Oriental Temptations / 1992 / WV / M • Perks / 1992 / ZA / M • Pretty In Peach / 1992 / VI / M • Raunch #04: Silver Melts / 1991 / CC / M • Samantha's Private Fantasies / 1994 / WV / M • The Seducers / 1992 / ZA / M • The Servants Of Midnight / 1992 / CDI / M • Seymore Butts In The Love Shack / 1992 / FH / M • Seymore Butts Rides Again / 1992 / FH / M • Silence Of The Buns / 1992 / WV / M • Silk Elegance / 1991 / VIM / M • Silver Elegance / 1992 / VT / M • Spin For Sex / 1994 / IN / M • Sporting Illustrated / 1990 / HO / M • Starlet / 1994 / VI / M • Summer Games / 1992 / HW / M • Surprise!!! / 1994 / VI / M • Sweet Dreams / 1991 / VC / M • Sweet Seduction / 1990 / LV / M • Tails From The Tower / 1993 / AFI / M • Take It To The Limit / 1992 / VEX / M • Tempting Tianna / 1992 / V99 / M • Totally Teri / 1992 / IF / M • Undress To Thrill / 1994 / VI / M • Victoria's Secret Life / 1992 / WV / M • Wendy Whoppers: Ufo Tracker / 1994 / PEP / M • Wet & Wicked / 1992 / VEX / M

• The Wild Thing / 1992 / HO / M • X-TV / 1992 / CA / C

TIANNA TEMPTRESS
Buffy Malibu's Nasty Girls #06 / 1994 / ANA / F • The Finishing Touch / 1994 / DR / M • Nasty Nymphos #03 / 1994 / ANA / M

TIARA *see* Tiarra

TIARA O'MALLEY
Rhinestone Cowgirls / 1981 / SE / M

TIARA WEST *(Tiarra (West), Nikki Prince (West))*
Blonde, big tits and ugly.
Alley Cat / 1991 / CIN / M • Blonde Savage / 1991 / CDI / M • Captain Butt's Beach / 1992 / LV / M • Casual Sex / 1991 / GO / M • The Eternal Idol / 1992 / CDI / M • Eve Of Seduction / 1991 / CDI / M • Grandma Does Dallas / 1990 / FC / M • Heart To Heart / 1990 / LE / M • Hershe Highway #4 / 1991 / HO / M • In Deep With The Devil / 1991 / ME / M • Into The Gap / 1991 / LE / M • Juicy Sex Scandals / 1991 / VD / M • Nightfire / 1991 / CIN / M • Private Places / 1992 / VC / M • Pro Ball / 1991 / VD / M • Raunch #02 / 1990 / CC / M • Satin Shadows / 1991 / CIN / M • Shifting Gere / 1990 / VT / M • Southern Comfort / 1991 / CIN / M • Venus: Wings Of Seduction / 1991 / CDI / M

TIARA WHITE *see* Tiarra

TIARRA *(Tiara, Nikki Prince (Tiarra, Tiara White))*
Pretty with small tits, long straight blonde hair, lithe tight body, lots of moles on chest and sides. Nikki Prince is from **Scream In The Middle Of The Night**.
Beyond Innocence / 1990 / VCR / F • Body Music #2 / 1990 / DR / M • Double D Dykes #14 / 1994 / GO / F • Eat 'em And Smile / 1990 / ME / M • Fortysomething #1 / 1990 / LE / M • Hothouse Rose #1 / 1991 / VC / M • House Of Dark Dreams #2 / 1990 / BS / B • Laid Off / 1990 / CA / M • The Magic Box / 1990 / SO / M • Making Tracks / 1990 / DR / M • Modern Love / 1991 / FAZ / M • A Night At The Waxworks / 1990 / IF / M • No Tell Motel / 1990 / ZA / M • Racquel In Paradise / 1990 / VC / M • Scream In The Middle Of The Night / 1990 / CC / M • Strange Behavior / 1991 / VD / M • Wire Desire / 1991 / XCI / M

TIARRA (WEST) *see* Tiara West

TIAZ
Buttman's Big Tit Adventure #3 / 1995 / EA / M

TIBAR MARTINI
Prima #14: Hotel Europa / 1996 / MBP / M

TICE BUNE
Bushwoman: She Takes Two / 1996 / RAS / M • Interview With A Tramp / 1996 / SP / C

TICO PATTERSON *see* Star Index I
TIEGER *see* Chelsea Manchester

TIERRA
Canadian Beaver Hunt #3 / 1996 / PL / M

TIESHA
Black Street Hookers #3 / 1996 / DFI / M

TIFANI
Creme De Femme / 1994 / 4P / F

TIFFAN DUPONTE *see* Tiffany DuPont
TIFFANIE STORM *see* Tiffany Storm
TIFFANT DUPONTE *see* Tiffany DuPont

TIFFANY
A&B AB#128: Deep Holed Lady / 1990 / A&B / F • A&B AB#129: Biggest Pussy / 1990 / A&B / F • A&B AB#166: Big Girls /

1990 / A&B / F • Ball Busters / 1991 / FH / M • Bra Busters #06 / 1993 / LBO / M • Buttman's Double Adventure / 1993 / EA / M • Classic Swedish Erotica #13 / 1986 / CA / C • Czech Mate / 1996 / BAC / M • Dildo Bitches / 1995 / LAF / F • FTV #52: Busty Blood Bath / 1996 / FT / B • FTV #53: Topless Boxing Terror / 1996 / FT / B • FTV #54: Punch Me Harder / 1996 / FT / B • FTV #61: Boss Lady #1 / 1996 / FT / B • FTV #63: DD Domination #1 / 1996 / FT / B • FTV #64: Blonde Bust Battle / 1996 / FT / B • FTV #69: Boxing Boob Bash / 1996 / FT / B • FTV #78: Cat's Claws / 1996 / FT / B • Girls Games Of Summer #4 / 1994 / NIV / S • The Good Stuff / 1989 / BON / C • Hot Body Hall Of Fame: Tracy Dali / 1995 / CG / F • Hot Body Video Magazine: Red Hot / 1995 / CG / S • Hot Body Video Magazine: Southern Belle / 1994 / CG / F • Just The Way You Like It #4: Tiffany Oh So Tasty / 1994 / JEG / M • Leg...Ends #03 / 1991 / BIZ / F • Lovelace Meets Miss Jones / 1975 / AVC / M • Luscious Lips / 1994 / ORE / C • Mardi Gras Passions / 1987 / MET / M • Midnight Angels #01 / 1993 / MID / F • Mike Hott: #209 Tiffany / 1993 / MHV / M • New Faces, Hot Bodies #12 / 1993 / STP / M • Odyssey Amateur #02: Tiffany's Special Talents / 1991 / OD / M • Odyssey Amateur #29: Breakfast At Tiffany's / 1991 / OD / M • Pussy Tales / 1993 / SC / F • Raquel Untamed / 1990 / CIN / M • The Royal Court Collection / 1993 / VER / S • She'll Take A Spanking / 199? / BON / B • Skintight / 1991 / VER / F • Sorority Lingerie Party / 1995 / NIV / F • Southern Belles #7 / 1996 / XPR / M • Southern: Previews #2 / 1992 / SSH / C • Toppers #12 / 1993 / TV / C • Wild Things #2 / 1986 / CV / M • World Sex Tour #7 / 1996 / ANA / M

TIFFANY (BRITTANY) *see* **Brittany**
TIFFANY (CZECH) *see* **Tiffany (Polish)**
TIFFANY (EVA FL) *see* **Eva Tiffany**
TIFFANY (POLISH) *(Tiffany (Czech), Amy (Polish))*
Blonde with shoulder length straight hair, passable face, medium tits, getting-plump body. 23 years old in 1996 and was de-virginized at 16. Somewhat confused as to where she's from. In one movie she says she's Polish, in another Czech and in a third she came from Poland via Czechoslovakia. It really doesn't matter, I suppose.
Airotica / 1996 / SC / M • My First Time #7 / 1996 / NS / M • Promises And Lies / 1996 / NIT / M • Real Sex Magazine #01 / 1996 / HO / M • Video Virgins #32 / 1996 / NS / M

TIFFANY ANDREWS
Canadian Beaver Hunt #4 / 1996 / PL / M

TIFFANY ANNE (CLA) *see* **Chasey Laine**

TIFFANY BEANE
Strip Poker / 1995 / PEP / M

TIFFANY BENCH *see* **Star Index I**

TIFFANY BLAKE
The Beat Goes On / 1987 / VCR / C • Blacks & Blondes #13 / 1986 / WV / M • Caught In The Middle / 1985 / CDI / M • The Fine Art Of Cunnilingus / 1985 / VCR / M • Girls Of Cell Block F / 1985 / WV / M • Graduation Ball / 1989 / CAE / M • The Heat Is On / 1985 / WV / M • Heatwaves / 1987 / LAV / G • The Hottest Show In Town

/ 1987 / VIP / M • Indecent Itch / 1985 / VCR / M • Irresistible #2 / 1986 / SE / M • Joanna's Dreams / 1988 / SEV / M • Loose Morals / 1987 / HO / M • Lost Innocence / 1988 / PV / M • Lust Bug / 1985 / HO / M • Made In Germany / 1988 / FAZ / M • Make My Night / 1985 / CIN / M • Orgies / 1987 / WV / C • Pool Party / 1991 / CIN / M • The Pussywillows / 1985 / SUV / M • Revenge Of The Babes #2 / 1987 / PL / M • Satania / 1986 / DR / M • Saturday Night Beaver / 1986 / EVN / M • Sensuous Singles: Trinity Loren / 1987 / VCR / F • The Sex Detective / 1987 / GO / M • Sex F/X / 1986 / VPE / M • Sex Maniacs / 1987 / JOY / C • Sex Shoot / 1985 / AT / M • Sex The Hard Way / 1985 / CV / M • Sexual Pursuit / 1985 / AT / M • Spermbusters / 1984 / AT / M • St. X-Where #1 / 1986 / VD / M • Surfside Sex / 1985 / PV / M • Sweet Tricks / 1987 / TEM / M • Tailhouse Rock / 1985 / WV / M • The Teacher's Pet / 1985 / WV / M • Toys 4 Us #2 / 1987 / WV / C • Tracy Dick / 1985 / WV / M • The Twilight Moan / 1985 / WV / M • Two Timing Tracie / 1985 / V20 / M • Wicked Whispers / 1985 / VD / M

TIFFANY CLARK
Pretty, slim brunette with small tits and a tight body.
Angel Buns / 1981 / QX / M • Babe / 1982 / AR / M • Babes In Toyland / 1988 / COM / C • Babylon Gold / 1983 / COM / C • Back To Back #1 / 1987 / 4P / C • Ball Game / 1980 / CA / M • The Bizarre World Of F.J. Lincoln / 19?? / VHL / C • Blue Vanities #042 (New) / 1988 / FFL / M • Blue Vanities #533 / 1993 / FFL / M • Blue Vanities #535 / 1993 / FFL / M • Bondage Photo Session / 1990 / BIZ / B • Caballero Preview Tape #2 / 1983 / CA / C • Caballero Preview Tape #4 / 1985 / CA / C • Carnal Competition / 1985 / WV / C • Centerfold Fever / 1981 / VXP / M • The Champ / 1984 / WV / M • Cherry-Ettes For Hire / 1984 / 4P / M • Cocktales / 1985 / AT / M • Corruption / 1983 / VC / M • Creme De Femme #3 / 1981 / AVC / C • Dallas School Girls / 1981 / VCX / M • Dangerous Stuff / 1985 / COM / M • Dick Of Death / 1985 / VCR / M • Every Man's Fancy / 1983 / BIZ / B • Fantasy Follies #1 / 1983 / VC / M • Fantasy Follies #2 / 1983 / VC / M • Firestorm #2: The Angel Blade / 1986 / COM / M • Firestorm #3 / 1986 / COM / M • Five Card Stud / 1990 / BIZ / B • Foxtrot / 1982 / COM / M • Freedom Of Choice / 1984 / VHL / M • Ginger (1984-Vivid) / 1984 / VI / M • Glitter / 1983 / CA / M • Go For It / 1984 / VC / M • The Goodbye Girls / 1979 / CDI / M • Hot Dreams / 1983 / CA / M • Hot Love / 1981 / SAT / M • Hot Pink / 1985 / VCR / F • Hot Stuff / 1984 / VXP / M • Kinky Tricks / 1978 / VEP / M • Liquid A$$ets / 1982 / CA / M • Loop Hole / cr80 / ... / M • Maneaters / 1983 / VC / M • Mascara / 1982 / CA / M • Mrs. Rodger's Neighborhood / 1988 / EVN / C • Nasty Girls (1983-VCX) / 1983 / VCX / M • Never Say No / 1983 / ... / M • Night Flight / cr80 / CRE / M • The Oui Girls / 1981 / VHL / M • Pandora's Mirror / 1981 / CA / M • Passion Toys / 1985 / VCR / C • Pink Champagne / 1979 / CV / M • The Playgirl / 1982 / CA / M • Pleasure Productions #12 / 1985 / VCR / M • Same Time Every Year / 1981 / VHL / M • The Satisfiers Of Alpha Blue / 1980 / AVC / M • Scenes

They Wouldn't Let Me Shoot / 1984 / VC / M • Scoundrels / 1982 / COM / M • Sex On The Set / 1984 / RLV / M • Sexcapades / 1983 / VC / M • Shacking Up / 1985 / VXP / M • Silk, Satin & Sex / 1983 / SE / M • Simply Outrageous / 1989 / VC / C • Society Affairs / 1982 / CA / M • Swedish Erotica Superstar #4: Shauna Grant / 1984 / CA / C • Tales From The Chateau / 1987 / BON / B • Tarot Temptress / 1985 / AA / M • That's Outrageous / 1983 / CA / M • Tight Delight / 1985 / VXP / M • Trouble For Two / 1994 / BON / B • Twilight Pink #1 / 1980 / AR / M • Viva Vanessa The Undresser / 1984 / VC / M • What Would Your Mother Say? / 1981 / HAV / M • Wild Innocents / 1982 / VCX / M • Yes, My Lady / 1984 / VHL / B

TIFFANY DUPONT *(Tiffany Duponte, Tiffan Duponte, Tiffany Duponte, Tiffant Duponte, Christina DuPonte)*
69 Park Avenue / 1995 / ELH / M • Backing In #1 / 1990 / WV / C • Blondes! Blondes! Blondes! / 1986 / VCS / C • Dangerous Women / 1987 / WET / M • Lifestyles Of The Blonde And Dirty / 1987 / WET / M • Lustfully Seeking Susan / 1985 / PLY / M • Play Me Again, Vanessa / 1986 / VC / M • Rated Sex / 1986 / SE / M • Sex Academy / 1985 / PLY / M • Shaved Bunnies / 1985 / LIP / F • Showgirls / 1985 / SE / M • Tuff Stuff / 1987 / WET / M

TIFFANY DUPONTE *see* **Tiffany DuPont**
TIFFANY GLEASON *see* **Star Index I**

TIFFANY HALL
East Coast Sluts #05: North Carolina / 1995 / PL / M

TIFFANY JORDAN
Bondage Memories #03 / 1994 / BON / C • D-Cup Delights / 1987 / VCR / M • My Wildest Date / 1989 / FOV / M • School Dayze / 1987 / BON / B • Sex For Secrets / 1987 / VCR / M

TIFFANY LANE *(Tiffany Wild, Rose Wilde, Tiffany Rose, Tiffany Love)*
Died 1988 (car crash). This girl is white (or close to) with a large tattoo on her left shoulder and upper arm.
The Adventures Of Dick Black, Black Dick / 1987 / DR / M • Behind The Black Door / 1987 / VEX / M • Black Sensations / 1987 / VEX / M • Cat 'nipped / 1995 / PLV / B • Chocolate Chips / 1987 / VD / M • Chocolate Dreams (Venus 99) / 1987 / V99 / M • Club Taboo / 1987 / MET / G • Enemarathon / 1987 / BIZ / B • Girlworld #1 / 1987 / LIP / F • Mr. Peepers Nastiest #4 / 1995 / LBO / C • Naughty Ninja Girls / 1987 / LA / M • Night Games / 1986 / WV / M • Reamin' Reunion / 1988 / CC / M • Splash Dance / 1987 / AR / M • Wet And Wild #1 / 1986 / VEX / M

TIFFANY LONG *see* **Tiffany Wong**

TIFFANY LORDS
American Dream Girls #2 / 1994 / LEI / M • Bloopers & Behind The Scenes / 1995 / LEI / M • Butt Whore / 1994 / WIV / M • Dirty Laundry / 1994 / HOH / M • Harness Hannah At The Strap-On Ho Down / 1994 / WIV / F • John Wayne Bobbitt Uncut / 1994 / LEI / M • Lust What The Doctor Ordered / 1994 / WIV / M • Pussy Hunt #07 / 1994 / LEI / M • Tiffany Lords Straps One On #1 / 1994 / WIV / F • Tiffany Lords Straps One On #2 / 1994 / WIV / F

TIFFANY LOVE *see* **Tiffany Lane**

TIFFANY LYNN *see Star Index I*

TIFFANY MELLON *see Tiffany Million*

TIFFANY MIDNIGHT *see Star Index I*

TIFFANY MILLION *(Tiffany Mellon, Tyffany Million, Sandra Margot)*
Blonde who used to be in GLOW (some female wrestling team) and has does a lot of B movies. Was married and has a daughter. Aged body. First movie was **Twister**. She was 27 (born 1966) in 1993. There is a **Hard Copy** interview with her called **The Making of a Porn Star**. In 1994 was 127lbs, 5'6" tall and 38-26-34. As of 1994 was married to Ritchie Razor. Divorced from him in 1995.
13th Annual Adult Video News Awards / 1996 / VC / S • The Adventures Of Mr. Tuolsie Pole #1 / 1995 / LBO / M • American Angels / 199? / ... / S • American Garter / 1993 / VC / M • The Anal Adventures Of Bruce Seven / 1996 / BS / C • The Awakening / 1992 / SC / M • B.L.O.W. / 1992 / LV / M • Back Door Mistress / 1994 / GO / M • The Beverly Hillbillies / 1993 / IP / M • Big & Busty Superstars / 1996 / DGD / F • Big Bust Platinum: Superstar Strip Tease / 1993 / PME / F • Bloopers (Video Team) / 1994 / VT / M • Body And Soul / 1992 / OD / M • Body Of Influence / 1993 / AE / S • Borderline (Vivid) / 1995 / VI / M • The Boss / 1993 / VT / M • Breast Worx #38 / 1992 / LBO / M • Buttslammers #04: Down And Dirty / 1993 / BS / F • Caged Fury / 1990 / C3S / S • Calendar Girl / 1993 / C3S / S • A Cameo Appearence / 1992 / VI / M • Carnival Of Flesh / 1996 / NIT / M • Climax 2000 #1 / 1994 / CC / M • Climax 2000 #2 / 1994 / CC / M • Compulsive Behavior / 1995 / PI / M • The Creasemaster / 1993 / VC / M • The Creasemaster's Wife / 1993 / VC / M • Deep Inside Tyffany Million / 1995 / VC / C • Demon Wind / 1990 / PAR / S • Dirty Books / 1992 / VC / M • Dirty Little Mind / 1994 / IP / M • Eleventh Annual AVN Awards / 1994 / VC / M • Exstasy / 1995 / WV / M • Face Dance #1 / 1992 / EA / M • Face Dance #2 / 1992 / EA / M • The Fantasy Booth / 1993 / ONA / M • The Fluffer #2 / 1993 / FD / M • Generally Horny Hospital / 1995 / IMV / M • Girls Off Duty / 1994 / LE / M • The Great American Boobs To Kill For Dance Contest / 1995 / PEP / C • Haunting Dreams #2 / 1993 / LV / M • Heatseekers / 1996 / PE / M • Hidden Agenda / 1992 / XCI / M • Hollywood Swingers #01 / 1992 / LBO / M • Hourman Is Here / 1994 / CC / M • I Touch Myself / 1994 / IP / F • Jailhouse Cock / 1993 / IP / M • A Kiss Before Dying / 1993 / CDI / M • Kittens #4: Bodybuilding Bitches / 1993 / CC / F • Kym Wilde's On The Edge #03 / 1993 / RB / B • Latex #1 / 1994 / VC / M • Latex #2 / 1995 / VC / M • Leena's Early Experiences / 1995 / OD / C • Legacy Of Love / 1992 / LE / M • Lies Of Passion / 1992 / LV / M • The Living End / 1992 / OD / M • Looks Like A Million / 1992 / LV / M • Lunachick / 1995 / VI / M • The Makeup Room #1 / 1992 / VC / M • The Makeup Room #2 / 1992 / VC / M • Mind Games / 1995 / IMV / M • Motel Sex #3 / 1995 / RAP / M • The Naked Pen / 1992 / VC / M • New Wave Hookers #3 / 1993 / VC / M • One In A Million / 1992 / HW / M • Out Of The Blue #2 / 1992 / VI / M • The Passion / 1995 / IP / M • Phone

Fantasy #1 / 1992 / ATL / M • Phone Fantasy #2 / 1992 / ATL / M • Pleasure Dome: The Genesis Chamber / 1994 / AFV / M • Pops / 1994 / PL / M • Positively Pagan #06 / 1993 / ATA / M • Prime Target / 1991 / HHV / S • Ring Of Desire / 1995 / LBO / M • Russian Roulette / 1995 / NIT / M • Sex #1 (Vca) / 1994 / VC / M • Sex #2: Fate (Vca) / 1995 / VC / M • Shades Of Blue / 1992 / VC / M • Silk Stockings: The Black Widow / 1994 / SPI / M • The Sleeping Car / 1990 / VMA / S • Smeers / 1992 / PL / M • Splatman / 1992 / FR / M • Starbangers #06 / 1994 / FPI / M • Strippers Inc. #2 / 1994 / ONA / M • Strippers Inc. #3 / 1994 / ONA / M • Strippers Inc. #4 / 1995 / ONA / M • A Stroke At Midnight / 1993 / LBO / M • Swoot Targot / 1002 / CDI / M • Takin' It To The Limit #3 / 1994 / BS / M • Tales From Sodom / 1994 / BLC / M • Tangled / 1994 / PL / M • Taxi Girls #3: Killer On The Loose / 1993 / MED / M • The Temple Of Poon / 1996 / PE / M • Titty Bar #2 / 1994 / LE / M • Twister / 1992 / CC / M • Twists Of The Heart / 1995 / NIT / M • The Tyffany Million Diaries / 1995 / IMV / C • Untamed Cowgirls Of The Wild West #01: The Pillow Biters / 1992 / ZA / M • Untamed Cowgirls Of The Wild West #02: Jammy Glands... / 1993 / ZA / M • Vice Versa / 1992 / FD / M • Whispered Lies / 1993 / LBO / M • Why Things Burn / 1994 / LBO / M • The Wicked One / 1995 / WP / M • Wild Things #3 / 1992 / MET / M • The World's Biggest Gang Bang #2 / 1996 / FPI / M • The XXX Files: Lust In Space / 1995 / IMV / M • [Kill, Kill, Overkill / 199? / ... / S

TIFFANY MINX *(Tiffany Mynx, Tawny (T. Minx), Angelica (T. Minx))*
Pretty dark (depending on movie) blonde with droopy medium tits and a lithe body. Tattoo on the back of the right shoulder. Born Oct 10, 1971 in Upland, CA (22 in 1992). As of 1992 has a child, Nathan. As of 1997 has two children.
1-800-934-BOOB / 1992 / VD / C • Always / 1993 / XCI / M • America's Raunchiest Home Videos #35: Nothing Butt / 1992 / ZA / M • American Built / 1992 / LE / M • Anal Adventures (Dragon) / 1992 / DRP / M • The Anal Adventures Of Max Hardcore: Between The Lines / 1993 / ZA / M • Anal Rampage #1 / 1992 / ROB / M • Anal Romance / 1993 / LV / M • Anal Rookies #1 / 1992 / ROB / M • Anal Sluts & Sweethearts #1 / 1992 / ROB / M • Anonymous / 1993 / VI / M • Babes Illustrated #1 / 1994 / IN / F • Babes Illustrated #5 / 1996 / IN / F • Backdoor Black #2 / 1993 / WV / C • Backdoor To Cannes / 1993 / VC / M • Backdoor To The City Of Sin / 1993 / ANA / M • Bad Habits / 1993 / VC / M • Batwoman & Catgirl / 1992 / HW / M • Best Butt(e) In The West #1 / 1992 / CC / M • The Best Of Oriental Anal #1 / 1994 / ROB / C • Bikini Beach #1 / 1993 / CC / M • Bikini Beach #2 / 1993 / CC / M • Bikini Beach #3 / 1993 / CC / F • Black To Basics / 1992 / ZA / M • Blonde Justice #1 / 1993 / VI / M • Blonde Justice #2 / 1993 / VI / M • Blue Bayou / 1993 / VC / M • The Boss / 1993 / VT / M • The Bottom Dweller / 1993 / EL / M • Broadway Babes / 1993 / FH / F • Bubble Butts #12 / 1992 / LBO / M • Butt Bandits #4 / 1996 / VD / C • Butt Camp / 1993 / HW / C • Butt Jammers / 1994 / WIV / M • Butt

Light: Queen Of Rears / 1992 / STR / M • Butt Of Steel / 1994 / LV / M • The Butt Sisters Do Sturgis / 1994 / MID / M • Butt Sluts #3 / 1994 / ROB / F • Butt Woman #4 / 1993 / FH / M • Butt Woman #5 / 1993 / FH / M • Butt's Up, Doc #3 / 1992 / GO / M • The Buttnicks #3 / 1992 / CC / M • Buttslammers #01 / 1993 / BS / F • Buttslammers #05: Quake, Rattle & Roll! / 1994 / BS / F • Caged Fury / 1993 / DR / M • California Pizza Girls / 1992 / EVN / M • Captain Butt's Beach / 1992 / LV / M • Carnal Interludes / 1995 / NOT / M • Casual Lies / 1992 / CA / M • Chasin' The Fifties / 1994 / WP / M • Cheek To Cheek / 1997 / EL / M • Cheerleader Nurses #1 / 1993 / VC / M • Cheerleader Nurses #2 / 1993 / VC / M • Choorloador Strippora / 1006 / PE / M • Chicks, Licks And Dirty Tricks / 1993 / ME / F • College Cuties / 1995 / LE / M • Coming Of Fortune / 1994 / EX / M • Compulsive Behavior / 1995 / PI / M • Courting Libido / 1995 / HIV / G • The Creasemaster / 1993 / VC / M • Cumback Pussy #4: Get Some!!! / 1996 / EL / M • Cumback Pussy #6: All-Star Poop Chute Salute / 1997 / EL / M • Cuntrol / 1994 / MID / F • The D.J. / 1992 / VC / M • The D.P. Man #2 / 1992 / FD / M • Dark Obsessions / 1993 / WV / M • Deep Inside Crystal Wilder / 1995 / VC / C • Deep Inside Juli Ashton / 1996 / VC / C • Deep Inside Kaitlyn Ashley / 1995 / VC / C • Deep Inside Kelly O'Dell / 1994 / VC / C • Deep Inside Nikki Sinn / 1996 / VC / C • Deep Inside Racquel Darrian / 1994 / VC / C • Deep Inside Tiffany Mynx / 1994 / VC / C • Deep Throat #6 / 1992 / AFV / M • Delicious (Midnight-1993) / 1993 / MID / M • Delicious (VCX-1993) / 1993 / VCX / M • Dirty Bob's #10: Sleeping Late In Seattle / 1993 / FLP / S • Dirty Work / 1995 / VC / M • Double Detail / 1992 / SO / M • Elements Of Desire / 1994 / ULI / M • Eleventh Annual AVN Awards / 1994 / VC / M • En Garde / 1993 / DR / M • Endlessly / 1993 / VI / M • Erectnophobia #2 / 1992 / MID / M • Face Dance #1 / 1992 / EA / M • Face Dance #2 / 1992 / EA / M • Facesitter #2 / 1993 / CC / M • The Fantasy Booth / 1993 / ONA / M • Film Buff / 1994 / WP / M • First Time Ever #1 / 1995 / PE / F • First Time Ever #2 / 1996 / PE / F • Flying High #1 / 1992 / HO / M • Foolish Pleasure / 1992 / VD / M • Forbidden / 1992 / FOR / M • Ghosts / 1994 / EMC / M • Girls Just Wanna Have Girls #3 / 1994 / HIO / F • Girls Will Be Boys #5 / 1993 / PL / F • The Good, The Bad & The Nasty / 1992 / VC / M • Hard As A Rock / 1992 / ZA / M • Head Lines / 1992 / SC / M • Heatwave #2 / 1993 / FH / F • Hexxxed / 1994 / VT / M • Honey, I Blew Everybody #1 / 1992 / MID / M • Honey, I Blew Everybody #2 / 1992 / MID / M • Hookers Of Hollywood / 1994 / LE / M • Hot Sweet 'n' Sticky / 1992 / CA / C • House Arrest / 1995 / CV / M • I Am Desire / 1992 / WV / M • In Search Of The Perfect Blow Job / 1995 / OD / M • Independence Night / 1996 / SC / M • Inner Pink #3 / 1994 / LIP / F • Inside Job / 1992 / ZA / M • Interview With A Vamp / 1994 / ANA / M • Legend #4: Critic's Choice / 1992 / LE / M • Lesbian Dating Game / 1993 / LIP / F • Lesbian Pros And Amateurs #21 / 1993 / GO / F • The Living End / 1992 / OD / M • Loopholes / 1993 / TP / M • Love Me, Love

My Butt #2 / 1994 / ROB / F • Lusty Ladies / 1994 / MET / F • The Magic Box / 1993 / TP / M • Midnight Angels #01 / 1993 / MID / F • Midnight Angels #02 / 1993 / MID / F • Midnight Confessions / 1992 / XCI / M • Midnight Madness / 1993 / DR / M • Mr. Peepers Amateur Home Videos #50: All That Glitters / 1992 / LBO / M • Musical Bedrooms / 1993 / AFV / M • Mutual Consent / 1995 / VC / M • My Cousin Ginny / 1993 / MET / M • Nikki At Night / 1993 / LE / M • Nikki Never Says No / 1992 / LE / M • No Fear / 1996 / IN / F • No Man's Land #09 / 1994 / VT / F • Nurse Tails / 1994 / VC / M • Oral Majority #12 / 1994 / WV / C • Pajama Party X #2 / 1994 / VC / M • The Party / 1992 / CDI / M • Passion / 1996 / SC / M • Penthouse: Ready To Ride / 1992 / PET / F • Pink To Pink / 1993 / VI / C • Portrait Of Lust / 1992 / WV / M • Private Dancer (CDI) / 1992 / CDI / M • Pubic Eye / 1992 / HW / M • Puritan Video Magazine #09 / 1997 / LE / M • Pussyman #02: The Prize / 1993 / CC / M • Quantum Deep / 1993 / HW / M • The Quest / 1994 / SC / M • R & R / 1994 / VC / M • R.E.A.L. #1 / 1994 / LV / F • Raunch #05 / 1992 / CC / M • Real Tickets #1 / 1994 / VC / M • Real Tickets #2 / 1994 / VC / M • Return To Melrose Place / 1993 / HW / M • Rocket Girls / 1993 / VC / M • Roto-Rammer / 1993 / I.V / M • Sabotage / 1994 / CA / M • Saints & Sinners / 1992 / PEP / M • Sassy Pleasures / 1993 / RB / B • Satisfaction / 1992 / LE / M • Scent Of A Wild Woman / 1993 / EVN / C • Search For The Perfect Blow-Job / 1995 / OD / M • Secret Urges (Vidco) / 1994 / VD / C • Servin' It Up / 1993 / VC / M • Sexvision / 1992 / HO / M • Shooting Gallery / 1996 / EL / M • Silk Stockings: The Black Widow / 1994 / SPI / M • Single White She-Male / 1993 / PL / G • Single White Woman / 1992 / FD / M • Sister Snatch #1 / 1994 / SNA / M • Sister Snatch #2 / 1995 / SNA / M • Sloppy Seconds / 1994 / PE / M • Sodomania #01: Tales Of Perversity / 1992 / EL / M • Sodomania #02: More Tails / 1992 / EL / M • Sodomania #03: Foreign Objects / 1993 / EL / M • Sodomania #04: Further On Down The Road / 1993 / EL / M • Sodomania #05: Euro-American Style / 1993 / EL / M • Sodomania #09: Doin' Time / 1994 / EL / M • Sodomania #18: Shame Based / 1996 / EL / M • Sodomania: The Baddest Of The Best...And Then Some / 1994 / EL / C • Sorority Sex Kittens #1 / 1992 / VC / M • Sorority Sex Kittens #2 / 1993 / VC / M • Sorority Sex Kittens #3 / 1996 / VC / M • Spread The Wealth / 1993 / DR / M • Stacked With Honors / 1993 / DR / M • Stocking Stuffers / 1992 / LV / M • Stripper Nurses / 1994 / PE / M • Submission / 1994 / WP / M • Supermarket Babes In Heat / 1992 / OD / M • Superstar Sex Challenge #1 / 1994 / VC / M • Superstar Sex Challenge #2 / 1994 / VC / M • Superstar Sex Challenge #3 / 1994 / VC / M • Sure Bet / 1995 / CV / M • Sweet Target / 1992 / CDI / M • Taboo #10 / 1992 / IN / M • Tailiens #1 / 1992 / FD / M • Tailiens #2 / 1992 / FD / M • Thermonuclear Sex / 1996 / EL / M • The Tiffany Minx Affair / 1992 / FOR / M • Tiffany Minx Wildcat / 1993 / MID / C • Tight Spot / 1992 / VD / M • Totally Naked / 1994 / VC / M • Trailer Trash / 1994 / VC / M • Unbridled Lust / 1995 / NOT / F • Undercover Lover / 1992 / CV / M • User Friendly / 1992 / VT / M • Virtual Sex / 1993 / VC / M • Visions Of Desire / 1994 / DR / M • Wicked As She Seems / 1993 / WP / M • Wicked Ways #1: Interview With The Anal Queen / 1994 / WP / M • Wild & Wicked #7 / 1996 / VT / M • Wild Flower #2 / 1992 / VI / M • Wilder At Heart / 1993 / ANA / M • Will & Ed's Back To Class / 1992 / MID / M

TIFFANY MYNX *see* **Tiffany Minx**
TIFFANY RAY *see* **Tiffany Taylor**
TIFFANY RENE *see* **Rene Tiffany**
TIFFANY ROSE *see* **Tiffany Lane**
TIFFANY STARK
Student Fetish Videos: Best of Catfighting #03 / 1995 / PRE / C • Student Fetish Videos: Foot Worship #16 / 1995 / PRE / B • Student Fetish Videos: Spanking #20 / 1995 / PRE / B

TIFFANY STEWART
Touch Me / 1971 / SE / M • Tropic Of Passion / 1971 / NGV / M

TIFFANY STORM (*Tiffanie Storm, Mary Moons, Lisa D'Amona, Lisa De Angelo, Lisa D., Lisa D'Amone*)
Lisa D. is from **Black Moon Rising**. In 1988 was 25 years old and 34D-24-33.
The Adventures Of Dick Black, Black Dick / 1987 / DR / M • Amber Pays The Rent / 1986 / VT / M • The Anal-ist #2 / 1986 / VEX / M • Anything Butt Love / 1990 / PL / M • Backdoor Brides #2: The Honeymoon / 1986 / PV / M • Backdoor Brides #3 / 1988 / PV / M • Backdoor Summer #1 / 1988 / PV / C • Backdoor Summer #2 / 1989 / PV / C • Backdoor To Hollywood #03 / 1987 / CDI / M • Backdoor To Hollywood #04 / 1988 / CDI / M • Banana Splits / 1987 / 3HV / M • Behind Blue Eyes #1 / 1986 / ME / M • Best Of Foot Worship #2 / 1989 / BIZ / C • Best Of Foot Worship #3 / 1992 / BIZ / C • The Big E #09 / 1990 / BIZ / B • Black Lava / 1986 / WET / M • Black Rage / 1988 / ZA / M • Breast Friends / 1991 / PL / M • The Bride / 1986 / WV / M • Broadway Fannie Rose / 1986 / CA / M • Busting Out / 199? / NAP / F • California Native / 1988 / CDI / M • Campfire Girls / 1988 / SE / M • Candy's Little Sister Sugar / 1988 / VD / M • Cat 'nipped / 1995 / PLV / B • Caught From Behind #08 / 1988 / HO / M • Cheeks #1 / 1988 / CC / M • Chocolate Chips / 1987 / VD / M • Crystal Blue / 1987 / VD / M • Debbie Does The Devil In Dallas / 1987 / SE / M • Deep Obsession / 1987 / WV / M • Deep Throat Girls / 1986 / ELH / M • Dialing For Desires / 1988 / 4P / M • Dirty 30's Cinema: Tiffanie Storm / 1986 / PV / C • Double D Dykes #03 / 1992 / GO / F • Double Play / 1993 / CA / C • Dreams / 1987 / AR / M • Dump Site / 1989 / BIZ / C • The Eliminators / 1991 / BIZ / B • Enemaced / 1988 / PLV / B • Enemates #03 / 1991 / BIZ / B • Fade To Black / 1988 / CDI / M • Fantasy Chamber / 1987 / VT / M • Fantasy Confidential / 1988 / GO / M • Feet First / 1988 / BIZ / S • Foot Lights / 1988 / BIZ / B • Foot Teasers / 1988 / BIZ / B • From Kascha With Love / 1988 / CDI / M • Full Metal Bikini / 1988 / PEN / M • Furburgers / 1987 / VD / M • Get It Straight / 1989 / CDI / M • The Girls Of The B.L.O. / 1988 / VWA / M • Girls Of The Double D #02 / 1987 / CDI / M • A Hard Act To Swallow / 1988 / VT / M • Harem Girls / 1986 / SE / M • Harem Candy / 1987 / WET / M • Hot Black Moon Rising Forever / 1988 / ZA / M • Hot Buns / 1988 / BIZ / B • Hot Pink And Chocolate Brown / 1988 / PV / M • House Of Sexual Fantasies / 1987 / GO / M • House Of The Rising Moon / 1986 / VD / M • I Am Curious Black / 1986 / WET / M • I Found My Thrill On Cheri Hill / 1988 / PL / M • Immoral Majority / 1986 / HTV / M • In A Crystal Fantasy / 1988 / VD / M • Inner Pink #1 / 1988 / LIP / F • Interracial Anal Bonanza / 1993 / CA / C • Jane Bond Meets The Man With The Golden Rod / 1987 / VD / M • John Holmes, The Lost Films / 1988 / PEN / C • Juicy Lips / 1991 / PL / F • Kascha's Blues / 1988 / CDI / M • L.A. Raw / 1986 / SE / M • La Boomba / 1987 / VCX / M • Ladies In Combat / 1991 / PRE / B • Leg...Ends #01 / 1988 / BIZ / F • Lesbian Appliance Guide: Tools, Toys & Tits #2 / 1994 / GO / F • Lethal Woman #1 / 1988 / SEV / M • Lethal Woman #2 / 1988 / SEV / M • Lingerie Vixens / 199? / NAP / B • Living In A Wet Dream / 1986 / PEN / C • Love At First Sight / 1987 / SE / C • Lucky In Love #2 / 1988 / SEV / M • Lusty Layout / 1986 / PV / M • Makeout / 1988 / VT / M • Meltdown / 1990 / LV / M • Misadventures Of The Bang Gang / 1987 / AR / M • The Moon Girls / 1990 / ME / C • Moonlusting #2 / 1987 / WV / M • The Naked Truth / 1990 / SE / M • Nasty Lovers / 1987 / SE / C • Night Games / 1986 / WV / M • No Man's Land #01 / 1988 / VT / C • The One And Only / 1987 / VCR / C • Oral Hijinx / 1990 / ERU / M • Oriental Spice / 1990 / SE / M • Parliament: Anal Babes #1 / 1989 / PM / F • Parliament: Finger Friggin' #2 / 1988 / PM / F • Parliament: Queens Of Double Penetration #1 / 1991 / PM / F • Parliament: Samantha Strong #1 / 1986 / PM / M • Piece Of Heaven / 1988 / CDI / M • Pink Baroness / 1988 / VWA / M • Playboy Video Centerfold: Tiffany Storm / 1992 / UNI / S • Punished Princess / 1992 / HOM / B • Push It To The Limit / 1988 / EVN / M • Ramb-Ohh #2 / 1988 / PV / M • Rapture Girls #1: Tiffany & Crystal / 1991 / OD / M • Real Magnolias / 1990 / AWV / M • The Red Hot Roadrunner / 1987 / VD / M • Ride A Pink Lady / 1986 / SE / M • Screaming Rage / 1988 / LV / C • Secret Recipe / 1990 / PL / F • Seduction By Fire / 1987 / VD / M • Sex Search / 1988 / IN / S • Shame On Shanna / 1989 / DR / C • Sins Of Nina Hartley / 1989 / MIR / C • Sleeping With Everybody / 1992 / MID / C • Slightly Used / 1987 / VD / M • Splash Dance / 1987 / AR / M • Starship Intercourse / 1987 / DR / M • Strip Search / 1987 / SEV / M • Super Enemates #1 / 1994 / PRE / C • Super Leg-Ends / 1992 / PRE / C • Supersluts Of Wrestling / 1986 / VD / M • Sweet Addiction / 1988 / CIN / M • Sweet Chocolate / 1987 / VD / M • Sweet Sensations / 1989 / SEX / M • Taboo #06 / 1988 / IN / M • Tailgunners / 1985 / WET / M • A Taste Of Tiffanie / 1990 / PIN / C • That Ole Black Magic / 1988 / CDI / M • This Is Your Sex Life / 1987 / VD / M • Top Heavy / 1988 / VD / M • Toppers #03 / 1993 / TV / M • Toppers #04 / 1993 / TV / M • Toppers #08 / 1993 / TV / M • Tough Girls Don't Dance / 1987 / SEV / M • The Way They Were / 1990 / CDI / M • Weekend Delights / 1992 / V99 / M • White Trash, Black Splash / 1988 / WET / M • Who Came In The Backdoor? / 1987 /

PV / M • Woman To Woman / 1989 / ZA / C • The Year Of The Sex Dragon / 1986 / PV / M • Young And Innocent / 1987 / HO / M • Young Cheeks / 1990 / BEB / B

TIFFANY TAYLOR *(Tiffany Ray)*
This is not Janet Jacmee. This girl looks like a young Annette Haven in her prime with dark hair and small hanging tits.
Biff Malibu's Totally Nasty Home Videos #14 / 1992 / ANA / M • Biff Malibu's Totally Nasty Home Videos #29 / 1993 / ANA / M • Oral Majority #11 / 1994 / WV / C • Positively Pagan #02 / 1991 / ATA / M • Principles Of Lust / 1992 / WV / M • Savannah Superstar / 1992 / VI / M • Sex Off The Runway / 1991 / GMI / M • Two Sisters / 1992 / WV / M • Welcome To Bondage: Tiffany Taylor / 1992 / BON / B

TIFFANY TORRES *see* **Sydney Dance**

TIFFANY TOWERS
The Best Of Tiffany Towers / 1996 / H&S / C • Big Bust Scream Queens / 1994 / BTO / M • Big Busty #49 / 1995 / BTO / S • Booberella / 1992 / BTO / M • Breakfast At Tiffany's / 1994 / IF / M • Exposure Images #02: Tiffany Towers / 1992 / EXI / F • Gazongas #04 / 1993 / LEI / C • Girls Around The World #14 / 199? / BTO / M • The Girls Of Daytona / 1993 / BTO / S • Girls With Big Jugs / 1995 / V99 / M • Heavenly Hooters / 1994 / IF / M • Hometown Honeys #4 / 1993 / VEX / M • Hump Tiffany Towers / 199? / H&S / M • I Dream Of Tiffany / 1993 / IF / M • Jugs Of Joy / 1994 / LEI / C • On Location In Palm Springs / 1996 / H&S / S • On Location In The Bahamas / 1996 / H&S / S • Score Busty Covergirls #3 / 1995 / BTO / S • Seymore & Shane Mount Tiffany / 1994 / FH / M • Seymore & Shane On The Loose / 1994 / ULI / M • Texas Towers / 1993 / IF / M • Tiffany And Tonisha, Lover Girls / 1993 / LEI / F • Tiffany I Love You / 1994 / IF / M • Tiffany Tonight / 1993 / LEI / M • Tiffany's Last Stand / 1993 / LEI / M • Tommyknockers / 1994 / CC / M • Udderly Fantastic / 1993 / IF / M • The Ultimate Pleasure / 1995 / LEI / M • Whoppers #3 / 1993 / VEX / F • Whoppers #6 / 1993 / VEX / F • Zena Hardcore Special / 1994 / BTO / M

TIFFANY WILD *see* **Tiffany Lane**

TIFFANY WILLIS *see* **Cynthia Brooks**

TIFFANY WONG *(Tiffany Long)*
Oriental with too big (enhanced) tits for her ethnic background.
Amateur Lesbians #39: Tiffany / 1993 / GO / F • Asian Heat #02: Satin Angels / 1993 / SC / M • Back In Action / 1992 / FD / M • Biff Malibu's Totally Nasty Home Videos #17 / 1992 / ANA / M • Buffy Malibu's Totally Nasty All-Girl Home Videos #01 / 1992 / ANA / F • The Burma Road #3 / 1996 / LBO / C • The Burma Road #4 / 1996 / LBO / C • Dirty Dating Service #01 / 1993 / WP / M • First Time Lesbians #18 / 1994 / JMP / F • Major Slut / 1993 / LV / M • Mike Hott: #214 Lesbian Sluts #07 / 1992 / MHV / F • Mr. Peepers Amateur Home Videos #66: Ready In Red / z993 / LBO / M • Mr. Peepers Amateur Home Videos #69: Love Tunnel / 1993 / LBO / M • Neighborhood Watch #40: / 1993 / LBO / M • The Wong Side Of Town / 1992 / LV / M

TIGER
Blush: Burlez Live! #1 / 1993 / FAT / F • Wrestling Classics #2 / 1984 / CDP / B

TIGER LILLY *see* **Star Index I**

TIGGER JAMES *see* **Star Index I**

TIGR *see* **Chelsea Manchester**

TIGR MENNETT *see* **Chelsea Manchester**

TIGR MINETTE *see* **Chelsea Manchester**

TIGRE (S/M)
She-Male Encounters #06: Trilogy Of The Bizarre / 1981 / MET / G

TIKA
Adultress / 1995 / WIV / M

TIKI
More Bad Girl Handling / 1994 / RB / B • Shaved #05 / 1993 / RB / F

TIKKY
Private Gold #13: The Pyramid #3 / 1996 / OD / M

TILLIE TREMBLE *see* **Star Index I**

TIM
Bi-Bi Love Amateurs #4 / 1994 / QUA / G • Breast Worx #04 / 1991 / LBO / M • Breast Worx #05 / 1991 / LBO / M • Breast Worx #17 / 1991 / LBO / M • Bubble Butts #04 / 1992 / LBO / M • Fresh Cheeks / 1995 / VC / M • HomeGrown Video #455 / 1995 / HOV / M • HomeGrown Video #463: Cum And Get It / 1995 / HOV / M • J.E.G.: Christy, Tim And Scott / 1995 / JEG / M • Nothing Butt Amateurs #01 / 1993 / AFI / M

TIM BAKER
She-Mails / 1993 / PL / G

TIM BALE
Fantastic Voyeur / 1975 / AVC / M

TIM BANGER *see* **Star Index I**

TIM BARNETT
Driven Home / 1995 / CSP / G

TIM BEAU *see* **Star Index I**

TIM BOYD
Bi Dream Of Genie / 1994 / BIL / G • Bi The Book / 1996 / MID / G • The Bi Valley / 1994 / BIL / G • Corporate Bi Out / 1994 / BIL / G • Days Gone Bi / 1994 / BIN / G • Good Bi Girl / 1994 / BIL / G • Mixed Apples / 1996 / APP / G • Pom Pom She-Males / 1994 / HEA / G

TIM BURR *see* **Star Index I**

TIM CANYON *see* **Tim Lake**

TIM COLE
The Naked Truth / 1995 / VI / M • Nightshift Nurses #2 / 1996 / VC / M • Sorority Sex Kittens #3 / 1996 / VC / M

TIM CONNELLY *see* **Dick Howard**

TIM CRUISE *see* **Star Index I**

TIM DENNIS
Kiss And Tell / 1980 / CA / M

TIM FAIRBANKS
Dream Girls / 1986 / VC / M

TIM FIELDS *see* **Star Index I**

TIM GISH
Resurrection Of Eve / 1973 / MIT / M

TIM HARRIS
Ben Dover's 9th / 1996 / VC / M

TIM JACOBS *see* **Star Index I**

TIM JOHNSON *see* **Cal Jammer**

TIM KAUFMAN
Seduce Me Tonight / 1984 / AT / M

TIM KNIGHT
Anal Reamers / 1986 / 4P / M • Charming Cheapies #3: Day And Night / 1985 / 4P / M • Pipe Dreams / 1985 / 4P / M

TIM LAKE *(Tom Becker, R. Tomy, Tim Canyon, Ferrell Timlake, Farrell Timlake)*
Tom Becker is from the credits of **Bubble Butts #1** but could be incorrect in which case a pseudonym would be Tom Dobbs.

Together with his wife, Alyssa Jarreau, he now (1993) owns HomeGrown Video.
30 Days In The Hole / 1993 / ZA / M • A&B GB#072: Chessie Does It / 1990 / A&B / M • Adventures Of The DP Boys: Back In The Bush / 1993 / HW / M • Alice In Hollywierd / 1992 / ZA / M • Amateur Nights #02 / 1989 / HO / M • America's Raunchiest Home Videos #20: Penthouse Pussy Power / 1992 / ZA / M • America's Raunchiest Home Videos #25: Victoria's Secretions / 1992 / ZA / M • America's Raunchiest Home Videos #73: / 1993 / ZA / M • America's Raunchiest Home Videos #74: / 1993 / ZA / M • American Garter / 1993 / VC / M • The Anal Adventures Of Max Hardcore: Video Games / 1994 / ZA / M • Anal Anarchy / 1995 / VC / M • Anal Asian #1 / 1992 / IN / M • Anal Vision #08 / 1993 / LBO / M • Anal Vision #11 / 1993 / LBO / M • Anal Vision #14 / 1993 / LBO / M • Anal Vision #17 / 1993 / LBO / M • Anal Vision #19 / 1993 / LBO / M • Anything That Moves / 1992 / VC / M • The Awakening / 1992 / SC / M • Backing In #4 / 1993 / WV / C • Backing In #7 / 1995 / WV / C • Bardot / 1991 / VI / M • Blonde Justice #1 / 1993 / VI / M • Blonde Justice #2 / 1993 / VI / M • Book Of Love / 1992 / VC / M • Bra Busters #04 / 1993 / LBO / M • Bra Busters #05 / 1993 / LBO / M • Bubble Butts #01 / 1992 / LBO / M • Bubble Butts #02 / 1992 / LBO / M • Bubble Butts #19 / 1992 / LBO / M • Bubble Butts #20 / 1992 / LBO / M • Bubble Butts #25 / 1993 / LBO / M • Bubble Butts #26 / 1993 / LBO / M • Bubble Butts #28 / 1993 / LBO / M • Bun Busters #05 / 1993 / LBO / M • Bun Busters #06 / 1993 / LBO / M • Bun Busters #07 / 1993 / LBO / M • Bun Busters #08 / 1993 / LBO / M • Bun Busters #09 / 1993 / LBO / M • Bun Busters #16 / 1994 / LBO / M • Butt Freak #2 / 1996 / EA / M • Butt Love / 1995 / AB / M • Butt Woman #3 / 1992 / FH / M • Butt Woman #5 / 1993 / FH / M • Buttman's Inferno / 1993 / EA / M • The Buttnicks #3 / 1992 / CC / M • Casting Call #04 / 1993 / SO / M • Casting Call #05 / 1994 / SO / M • Chameleons: Not The Sequel / 1991 / VC / M • Cherry Poppers #01 / 1993 / ZA / M • Chocolate Bunnies #02 / 1995 / LBO / C • Cinnamon Twist / 1993 / OD / M • Crazed #1 / 1992 / VI / M • Crazed #2 / 1992 / VI / M • The Creasemaster / 1993 / VC / M • Dark Obsessions / 1993 / WV / M • Deep Inside Selena Steele / 1993 / VC / C • Diamond In The Rough / 1993 / BIA / C • Dorm Girls / 1992 / VC / M • Dream House / 1995 / XPR / M • Erotic Dripping Orientals / 1993 / WV / M • The Fluffer #1 / 1993 / FD / M • The French Way / 1994 / HOV / M • Gangbang Girl #13 / 1994 / ANA / M • Guttman's Paris Vacation / 1993 / PL / M • Hard Ride / 1992 / WV / M • Hidden Camera #08 / 1993 / JMP / M • Hidden Camera #10 / 1993 / JMP / M • Hidden Camera #12 / 1993 / JMP / M • The Hitch-Hiker #01: Wide Open Spaces / 1993 / WMG / M • The Hitch-Hiker #02: Dangerous Curves / 1994 / WMG / M • The Hitch-Hiker #03: No Exit / 1994 / WMG / M • The Hitch-Hiker #04: Max Overdrive / 1994 / WMG / M • The Hitch-Hiker #05: Traffic Jam / 1994 / WMG / M • The Hitch-Hiker #06: Salty Dog / 1994 / WMG / M • The Hitch-Hiker #07: Life In The Fast Lane / 1994 / WMG / M • The

Hitch-Hiker #08: On The Trail / 1994 / WMG / M • The Hitch-Hiker #09: Back Road Detour / 1994 / WMG / M • The Hitch-Hiker #10: Rolling & Reaming / 1995 / WMG / M • Hollywood Swingers #07 / 1993 / LBO / M • Homegrown Video #419: Reigning Pussycats And Horndogs / 1994 / HOV / M • HomeGrown Video #442: / 1995 / HOV / M • HomeGrown Video #445: Sex Kittens / 1995 / HOV / M • Homegrown Video: Here Comes Anna Malle / 1994 / HOV / M • Homegrown Video: Here Comes Sheena / 1994 / HOV / M • Hooray For Hineywood / 1991 / MID / M • Hot Summer Knights / 1991 / LV / M • Howard Sperm's Private Parties / 1994 / LBO / M • In The Can With Oj / 1994 / HCV / M • In Your Face #2 / 1992 / PL / M • Kinky Roommates / 1992 / TP / M • Love Letters #2 / 1993 / SC / M • Lust Crimes / 1992 / WV / M • M Series #11 / 1993 / LBO / M • Mad Maxine / 1992 / AFV / M • Midsummer Love Story / 1993 / WV / M • Misty Rain's Anal Orgy / 1994 / FRM / M • More Dirty Debutantes #13 / 1992 / 4P / M • Mr. Fun's Mondo Adventure / 1993 / VC / M • Mr. Peepers Amateur Home Videos #26: Hole For Lease / 1991 / LBO / M • Mr. Peepers Amateur Home Videos #32: Fingers in the Honey Po / 1991 / LBO / M • Mr. Peepers Amateur Home Videos #49: Up And Cumming #2 / 1992 / LBO / M • Mr. Peepers Amateur Home Videos #68: A Tough Load To Swallow / 1993 / LBO / M • Mr. Peepers Amateur Home Videos #70: New Tits On The Block / 1993 / LBO / M • Mr. Peepers Amateur Home Videos #73: Carnal Capture / 1993 / LBO / M • Mr. Peepers Amateur Home Videos #77: Facial Coverage / 1993 / LBO / M • My Cousin Ginny / 1993 / MET / M • My Way / 1993 / CA / M • Naked Goddess #1 / 1991 / VC / M • Nasty Fuckin' Movies #09: Saki's Six Man Sexation #1 / 1992 / RUM / M • Neighborhood Watch #37: Pelvic Thrusters / 1993 / LBO / M • New Pussy Hunt #21 / 1996 / LEI / C • Nina Hartley's Lifestyles Party / 1995 / FRM / M • Odyssey Triple Play #43: Anal Creaming & Reaming / 1993 / OD / M • Odyssey Triple Play #73: Oriental Sexpress / 1994 / OD / M • Pearl Necklace: Thee Bush League #25 / 1993 / SEE / M • Pearl Necklace: Thee Bush League #28 / 1994 / SEE / M • The Pink Persuader / 1992 / LBO / M • Portrait Of Lust / 1992 / WV / M • Private Film #18 / 1994 / OD / M • Private Video Magazine #02 / 1993 / OD / M • Private Video Magazine #09 / 1994 / OD / M • Professor Sticky's Anatomy 3X #01 / 1992 / FC / M • Profiles #01 / 1995 / XPR / M • Profiles #03: House Dick / 1995 / XPR / M • Profiles #05: Planet Lust / 1995 / XPR / M • Profiles #07: Sexworld / 1996 / XPR / M • Profiles #08: Triple Ecstacy / 1996 / XPR / M • Profiles #10: / 1997 / XPR / M • Radical Affairs Video Magazine #05 / 1993 / ME / M • Raquel Released / 1991 / VI / M • Realities #2 / 1992 / ZA / M • Rump Humpers #05 / 1992 / GLI / M • Rump Humpers #06 / 1992 / GLI / M • Sex 4 Life / 1995 / XPR / M • Sex Fugitives / 1993 / LE / M • Sorority Sex Kittens #1 / 1992 / VC / M • Sorority Sex Kittens #3 / 1996 / VC / M • The Stranger / 1996 / BEP / M • Strippers Inc. #1 / 1994 / ONA / M • Undercover Lover / 1993 / VC / M • Untamed Cowgirls Of The

Wild West #02: Jammy Glands... / 1993 / ZA / M • Victim Of Love #1 / 1992 / VI / M • Victim Of Love #2 / 1992 / VI / M • Welcome To Dallas / 1991 / VI / M • Wet Memories / 1993 / WV / M • Whispered Lies / 1993 / LBO / M • With The Devil In Her Rear / 1992 / WV / M • The Worst Porno Ever Made With The Best Sex / 1993 / PL / M • WPINK-TV #4 / 1993 / PV / M • WPINK-TV #5 / 1993 / PV / M

TIM LEBARON *see Star Index I*

TIM LLOYD *see Star Index I*

TIM LONG *see Harry Reems*

TIM LOWE

Angels Bi Day, Devils Bi Night / 1990 / FC / G • Bi Madness / 1991 / STA / G • Blazing Nova / 1989 / LV / M • Every Which Way / 1990 / V10 / G • Get Bi Tonight / 1991 / PL / G • The Offering / 1988 / INH / G • Real Magnolias / 1990 / AWV / M • Uninhibited / 1989 / VC / G

TIM MILLER

Nineteen #1 / 1996 / FOR / M

TIM NEWSOME *see Star Index I*

TIM NUGENT

Family Affair / 1979 / MIT / M

TIM RICHARDS

Ready To Drop #02 / 1992 / FC / M

TIM RUSSELL

Talk Dirty To Me #02 / 1982 / CA / M

TIM RYAN

Double Trouble / 1988 / V99 / M • Miss Adventures / 1989 / VEX / M • The Squirt / 1988 / AR / M • Under The Law / 1989 / AFV / M

TIM S.

Man Training / 1993 / RB / B

TIM SKI

Naughty Network / 1981 / CA / M

TIM WADD *see Star Index I*

TIM WAKEFIELD *see Jake Steed*

TIM WHITFIELD *see Jake Steed*

TIM WINFIELD *see Jake Steed*

TIM WOODFIELD *see Jake Steed*

TIMBER

Amazing Hardcore #1: Blow Jobs / 1997 / MET / M • Delirium / 1996 / MET / M • Enigma / 1995 / MET / M • Hot Tight Asses #16 / 1996 / TCK / M • Interview's Southern Comfort / 1996 / LV / M • Pure Anal / 1996 / MET / M

TIMEA

European Sex TV / 1996 / EL / M • Feuchte Muschies / 1995 / KRM / M • Itsy Bitsy Gang Bang / 1996 / HW / M • Private Stories #04 / 1995 / OD / M • Somewhere Under The Rainbow #1 / 1995 / HW / M

TIMEO KISS

Dirty Stories #5 / 1996 / PE / M

TIMI *see Star Index I*

TIMI LEE

The Jade Pussycat / 1977 / CA / M

TIMMI LANE *see Star Index I*

TIMMY *see Star Index I*

TIMOTHY BLACKSTONE *see Star Index I*

TIMOTHY MALTRAVERS

Naughty Schoolgirls Revenge / 1994 / BIZ / B

TIMOTHY PARIS *see Star Index I*

TIMOTHY RYAN *see Star Index I*

TIMY JOY

Dirty Stories #4 / 1995 / PE / M

TINA

A&B AB#138: Shaved Teen / 1990 / A&B / M • A&B AB#219: Tina My Love / 1990 /

A&B / M • A&B AB#477: Tina / 1994 / A&B / M • A&B FL#01 /]995 / A&B / S • ABA: Double Feature #2 / 1996 / ALP / M • African Angels #2 / 1996 / NIT / M • Amateur Nights #15 / 1997 / HO / M • Angel's Vengeance / 1995 / VMX / M • Ass Tales / 1991 / PL / M • Black Mystique #01 / 1993 / VT / F • Black Street Hookers #4: The Streets Of San Francisco / 1996 / DFI / M • Blue Vanities #506 / 1992 / FFL / M • Blue Vanities #526 / 1993 / FFL / M • Blue Vanities #529 / 1993 / FFL / M • Blue Vanities #541 / 1994 / FFL / M • Breast Worx #10 / 1991 / LBO / M • Bright Tails #4 / 1994 / STP / B • Bubble Butts #06 / 1992 / LBO / M • Class Ass / 1992 / PL / M • Creme De La Face #13: Nine Nasty Nymphs / 1995 / OD / M • Debi Diamond's Dirty Dykes #1 / 1995 / FD / F • Dirty Water / 1994 / VSL / B • Double D Dykes #07 / 1992 / GO / F • Ebony Erotica #03: Black Adonis / 1993 / GO / M • Foxx Tales / 1996 / TTV / M • Full Moon Video #35: Wild Side Couples: The School HeadMaste / 1995 / FAP / M • Hidden Camera #21 / 1994 / JMP / M • Home-Grown Video #435: Seasoned To Perfection / 1994 / HOV / M • Julie's Diary / 1995 / LBO / M • Lesbian Pros And Amateurs #05 / 1992 / GO / F • Mo' Honey / 1993 / FH / M • Mr. Big / 1991 / PL / M • Mr. Peepers Amateur Home Videos #82: Born To Swing! / 1993 / LBO / M • Mr. Peepers Nastiest #5 / 1995 / LBO / C • New Faces, Hot Bodies #15 / 1994 / STP / M • The New Snatch Masters #14 / 1995 / LEI / C • Odyssey Triple Play #55: Black & White & Up The Ass / 1994 / OD / M • Old Fashioned Spankings / 1991 / BON / B • OUTS: Tina / 1994 / OUT / F • Pearl Necklace: Premier Sessions #05 / 1994 / SEE / M • Pearl Necklace: Thee Bush League #12 / 1993 / SEE / M • Penthouse: Great Pet Hunt #1 / 1992 / PET / F • Rip-Off Of Millie / cr78 / VHL / M • Sex In Dangerous Places / 1988 / VI / M • Silk 'n' Spanking / 1994 / VER / M • Sistal #1 / 1993 / VT / F • Steam Heat / 1980 / COM / M • Swedish Sex / 1996 / PL / M • To Taste The Strap / 199? / BON / B • Topless Lightweight Spectacular: Alex Jordan Vs. Tina... / 1994 / VSL / B • Virgins Of Video #09 / 1993 / YDI / M • Wrasslin She-Babes #05 / 1996 / SOW / M • Wrasslin She-Babes #08 / 1996 / SOW / M

TINA (B. MONET) *see Brigitte Monet*

TINA ALAMEDA *see Star Index I*

TINA AMES *see Star Index I*

TINA ANTON

Melissa's Wish / 1993 / LON / B

TINA ARIA *see Star Index I*

TINA ASHLEY *see Tina Ross*

TINA AUSTIN *see China Leigh*

TINA BLAIR

Aerobisex Girls #1 / 1983 / LIP / F • Blue Confessions / 1983 / VCR / M • Blue Vanities #087 / 1988 / FFL / M • Blue Vanities #533 / 1993 / FFL / M • Cover Girl Fantasies #1 / 1983 / VCR / C • Going Both Ways / 1984 / LIP / G • Odds And Ends / 1981 / TGA / M • Showgirl #07: Arcadia Lake's Fantasies / 1983 / VCR / M • The Twilight Moan / 1985 / WV / M • Udderly Fantastic / 1983 / TGA / C • Women's Secret Desires / 1983 / LIP / F • Yummy Nymphs / 1983 / TGA / C

TINA BURNER

Butt Naked #1 / 1990 / OD / M
TINA CHERI
Busty Debutantes / 1996 / H&S / M • Girls Around The World #24 / 1995 / BTO / S • Hard Core Beginners #12 / 1995 / LEI / M • Naughty Nights / 1996 / PLP / C • New Pussy Hunt #20 / 1996 / LEI / C
TINA CRUISE see Star Index I
TINA DAVIS
Black Taboo #1 / 1984 / JVV / M • Ebony Orgies / 1987 / SE / C • Hot Chocolate #1 / 1984 / TAG / M
TINA DODGE see Star Index I
TINA EVANS see Star Index I
TINA FOXX see Tina Lindstrom
TINA FRASCATTI
White Hot / 1984 / VXP / M
TINA GORDON *(Tina ,Jordan (Gordon))*
50 Ways To Lick Your Lover / 1989 / ZA / M • Assuming The Position / 1989 / V99 / M • Caught From Behind #12 / 1989 / HO / M • Easy Way Out / 1989 / OD / M • Girls Gone Bad #1 / 1990 / GO / F • The Hustler / 1989 / CDI / M • Jealous Lovers / 1989 / CDI / M • Parliament: Lesbian Seduction #1 / 1990 / PM / F • Tattle Tales / 1989 / SE / M
TINA GRAHAM see Star Index I
TINA HARLOW see Kristi Myst
TINA HART see Star Index I
TINA HOLLAWAY
Fantasy Peeps: Black On White / 1985 / 4P / M • Fantasy Peeps: Solo Girls / 1985 / 4P / M
TINA HUTTON see Star Index I
TINA JACKSON see Star Index I
TINA JORDAN
Naughty Network / 1981 / CA / M
TINA JORDAN (GORDON) see Tina Gordon
TINA LATOUR
Don Salvatore: The Last Sicilian / 1995 / XC / M • Gillie's Isle / 1990 / GOT / M • The Golden Gals / 1989 / BTO / M • Virility / 1996 / XC / M
TINA LINDSTROM *(Tina Foxx, Tanya Fox (Tina), Prudence Myers)*
Petite British girl with red or brown or dark blonde hair depending on the movie. Distinctive accent. Small tits, nice butt, not so tight on the waist, quite pretty.
Alone / 1993 / OD / F • Bondage Asylum / 1995 / LON / B • Heidi & Elke / 1995 / SHL / B • Kidnapped By Pirates / 1995 / LON / B • Lessons From The Mistress / 1994 / BON / B • Lipstick Lesbians / 1993 / STM / F • Sorority Sex Kittens #2 / 1993 / VC / M • Spanking Tails / 1993 / BON / B • Student Fetish Videos: Catfighting #07 / 1993 / PRE / B • Student Fetish Videos: Foot Worship #09 / 1993 / PRE / B • Student Fetish Videos: Spanking #10 / 1993 / PRE / B • Tales From The Zipper #1 / 1993 / ME / M • Threshold Of Fear / 1993 / BON / B • Video Virgins #03 / 1993 / NS / M • The Wager / 1993 / TAO / B
TINA LOREN see Star Index I
TINA LOUISE
Blue Vanities #204 / 1993 / FFL / M • Blue Vanities #222 / 1994 / FFL / M • The Seduction Of Seka / 1981 / AVC / M • That's Erotic / 1979 / CV / C • That's Porno / 1979 / CV / C
TINA LOVE
C-Hunt #01: Pandemonium / 1995 / PEV / M
TINA LYNN

Cruel Passions / 1992 / BS / B • Dances With Pain / 1992 / BS / B • Dark Destiny / 1992 / BS / B • Hot Rod To Hell #2 / 1992 / BS / B
TINA LYNN (1976)
Jail Bait / 1976 / VC / M
TINA LYNN (B.LONDON) see Brook London
TINA MADISON
Blue Vanities #580 / 1996 / FFL / M
TINA MARIE
Hershe Highway #5: Backdoor Blues / 1996 / HO / M • Lovin' Spoonfuls #8 / 1996 / 4P / C
TINA MARIE (VICT. J) see Victoria Jackson
TINA MENNETT see Chelsea Manchester
TINA MONET see Star Index I
TINA MONTANA see Star Index I
TINA MORGAN see Star Index I
TINA ORCHID (C.LEIGH see China Leigh
TINA OWEN
Anal Auditions / 1995 / VMX / M • Anal Playground / 1995 / CA / M • Ass Masters (Leisure) #03 / 1995 / LEI / M • Ateball: More Than A Mouthful / 1995 / ATE / F • Back Door Babewatch / 1995 / IF / C • Blonde Temptation / 1995 / IF / M • Butts Up / 1994 / CA / M • D.P. Grannies / 1995 / JMP / M • Double D Dykes #18 / 1995 / GO / F • Double D Dykes #19 / 1995 / GO / F • East Vs West: Battle Of The Gang Bangs / 1994 / TTV / M • Hard Core Beginners #03 / 1995 / LEI / M • Horny Old Broads / 1995 / FPI / M • Hot Leather #1 / 1995 / GO / M • Lactamania #2: The Squirt Fest / 1995 / TTV / M • Lactamania #3 / 1995 / TTV / M • More Than A Mouthful #1 / 1995 / VEX / F • The New Ass Masters #08 / 1996 / LEI / C • New Pussy Hunt #20 / 1996 / LEI / C • Older And Anal #2 / 1995 / FC / M • Rumpman: Caught In An Anal Avalanche / 1995 / HW / M • Senior Stimulation / 1996 / CC / M • Snatch Masters #08 / 1995 / LEI / M • Tight Fit #13 / 1995 / GO / M
TINA PASCAL see Star Index I
TINA PEREZ
Desire Kills / 1996 / SUM / M
TINA ROBERTS see Star Index I
TINA RONIE see Tina Ross
TINA RONNIE see Tina Ross
TINA ROSS *(Lauren Wilde, Tina Ronnie, Tina Ashley, Kristy Bond, Kristy Boyd, Lauren Summers, Kresten Boyd, Tina Ronie)*
Died 1984. First Movie is **Let's Talk Sex**. Pretty face, gorgeous little body with tight waist, narrow hips, good skin, small to medium tits.
Alexandra / 1984 / VC / M • Bad Girls #4 / 1984 / GO / M • Bubblegum / 1982 / VC / M • Centerfold Celebrities #1 / 1982 / VC / M • Golden Girls #06 / 1983 / SVE / M • Golden Girls #24 / 1984 / CA / M • Golden Girls, The Movie / 1984 / SE / M • Let's Talk Sex / 1982 / CA / M • Tomboy / 1983 / VCX / M • VCA Previews #3 / 1988 / VC / C
TINA ROSS (J. WEST) see Jennifer West
TINA RUSSELL *(Dianna Baker, Linda Sanderson, Christina Russell)*
Reasonably pretty with long black hair, medium tits and a slightly chunky body. Died in May 1981 of bone cancer (alternatively reported as a burst blood vessel in the

stomach due to annorexia, but this might be consequent to cancer) at the age of 31 (born 1949). Born in Williamsport PA. Married to Jason Russell.
Bedroom Bedlam / 1973 / VHL / M • The Big Thing / 1973 / VHL / M • Birds And Beads / 1974 / VC / M • Blow Hard / 1973 / CV / M • Blue Vanities #011 (Old) / 1988 / FFL / M • Blue Vanities #013 / 1988 / FFL / M • Blue Vanities #104 / 1988 / FFL / M • Blue Vanities #244 / 1995 / FFL / M • Blue Vanities #248 / 1995 / FFL / M • Blue Vanities #532 / 1993 / FFL / M • Blue Vanities #533 / 1993 / FFL / M • Blue Vanities #560 / 1994 / FFL / M • Bottoms Up / 1974 / SOW / M • Bucky Beaver's XXX Dragon Art Theatre Double Feature #03 / 1996 / SOW / M • Bucky Beaver's XXX Dragon Art Theatre Double Feature #05 / 1996 / SOW / M • Campus Girl / 1972 / VXP / M • Cheap Sluts And The Guys Who Fuck Them / 1994 / MET / M • Classic Erotica #5 / 1985 / SVE / M • Dark Dreams / 1971 / ALP / M • The Debauchers / 1972 / QX / M • Devil's Due / 1974 / ALP / M • Dr Teen Dilemma / 1973 / VHL / M • Ebony Erotica / 1985 / SVE / C • The Erotic Memoirs Of A Male Chauvinist Pig / 1973 / QX / M • Fantasy Peeps: Sensuous Delights / 1984 / 4P / M • Fantasy Peeps: Solo Girls / 1985 / 4P / M • Fantasy Peeps: Untamed Desires / 1985 / 4P / M • The Filthiest Show In Town / 1975 / … / M • First Annual XRCO Awards / 1984 / AVC / C • French Kittens / 1985 / VC / C • French Postcard Girls / 1977 / VC / M • French Schoolgirls / 1973 / AVC / M • French Wives / 1970 / VC / M • Girls In Passion / 1979 / VHL / M • The Hardy Girls / cr71 / ALP / M • Honeymoon Suite / 1974 / VHL / M • Hypnorotica / 1972 / EVI / M • Is There Sex After Death? / 1970 / … / S • Joe Rock Superstar / cr76 / ALP / M • Kinky Potpourri #31 / 199? / SVE / C • Lady Zazu's Daughter / 1971 / ALP / M • Legends Of Porn #1 / 1987 / CV / C • Linda Can't Stop / cr73 / VHL / M • Madame Zenobia / 1973 / HOE / S • Meatball / 1972 / VCX / M • The Newcomers / 1973 / VSH / M • Not Just Another Woman / 1974 / … / M • Penetration / 1976 / MV1 / S • Personals / 1972 / COM / M • Pleasure Motel / 197? / CV / M • Possessed / 1976 / VCX / M • Presidential Peepers / 1975 / … / M • Private Secretary / 1973 / … / M • Revolving Teens / 1974 / SEP / M • Road Service / cr73 / VHL / M • School For Hookers / 1974 / SOW / M • Sex U.S.A / 1970 / SEP / M • Sexual Customs In Scandinavia / cr73 / QX / M • Showgirl #04: Tina Russell Classics / 1981 / VCR / M • Sleepyhead / 1973 / VXP / M • Steam Heat / 1980 / COM / M • Sunset Strip Girls / 1975 / TGA / M • That's Erotic / 1979 / CV / C • A Time To Love / 1971 / ALP / M • Too Many Cocks In Me! / 1992 / MET / M • True Legends Of Adult Cinema: The Golden Age / 1992 / VC / C • The Undergraduate / 19?? / KOV / M • Violated / 1973 / PVX / M • Wait Till He Comes In Me! / 1994 / MET / M • Whatever Happened To Miss September? / 1973 / ALP / M • The Whistle Blowers / cr72 / … / M
TINA SCHWARTZ
Sluts 'n' Angels In Budapest / 1994 / EL / M • Sodomania #10: Euro/American Again / 1994 / EL / M • Sodomania #11: In Your

Face / 1994 / EL / M

TINA SIOUX
Beaver Hunt #03 / 1994 / LEI / M • Desire Kills / 1996 / SUM / M • Pussyclips #04 / 1994 / SNA / M • Take It Like A Man / 1994 / IF / M

TINA SOVELL *see Star Index I*

TINA SUMMERS
More Dirty Debutantes #49 / 1995 / 4P / M

TINA TAI
Dirty Dirty Debutantes #8 / 1996 / 4P / M • More Dirty Debutantes #51 / 1996 / 4P / M • More Dirty Debutantes #57 / 1996 / 4P / M

TINA TALON
Hollywood Amateurs #28 / 1996 / MID / M • Sam Gets Shafted / 1996 / MP0 / M • Sodomize Me!!! / 1996 / SPR / M

TINA TARGET *see Star Index I*

TINA TAYLOR *see Star Index I*

TINA TAYLOR (TYLER) *see Tina Tyler*

TINA TEDESCHI *see Tina Tyler*

TINA TEENA
Black Casting Couch #1 / 1993 / WP / M • Black Velvet #2 / 1993 / CC / M • Uncle Roy's Amateur Home Video #19 / 1993 / VIM / M

TINA TEMPEST *see Star Index I*

TINA TERESA
Fleshdance Fever / 1984 / SAT / M

TINA TERIFIQUE
Slam Dunk / 1993 / NAP / B • Tina On Top / 1993 / NAP / B • Warrior Queen Of The Zulus / 1993 / NAP / B

TINA TRYON
Eager Beaver / 1975 / AVC / M • Fantasy Fever / 1975 / AVC / M • Mortgage Of Sin / 1975 / CA / M • Y-All Come / 1975 / CDC / M

TINA TURNON
The Bimbo #2: The Homecoming / 1986 / RLV / M • Black Knockers #09 / 1995 / TV / M

TINA TYLER *(Tina Tedeschi, Delilah Savage, Tina Taylor (Tyler), Christina Tyler)*
Not too pretty brunette with a reasonable body and nice skin who married Tony Tedeschi in 1993. Divorced in 1994.
1-900-FUCK #1 / 1995 / SO / M • Adult Video Nudes / 1993 / VC / M • Affairs Of The Heart / 1993 / VI / M • Bad Company / 1994 / VI / M • Biff Malibu's Totally Nasty Home Videos #37 / 1993 / ANA / M • The Big Shave / 1993 / PEP / M • Big Town / 1993 / PP / M • Black Is Back / 1993 / HW / M • The Blues #1 / 1992 / VT / M • Body Work / 1993 / MET / M • Brassiere To Eternity / 1994 / PEP / F • Buffy Malibu's Totally Nasty All-Girl Home Videos #05 / 1993 / ANA / F • Butt Woman #4 / 1993 / FH / M • Careless / 1993 / PP / M • Casanova #1 / 1993 / SC / M • Casanova #2 / 1993 / SC / M • The Cathouse / 1994 / VI / M • Cliff Banger / 1993 / HW / M • Deep Throat #6 / 1992 / AFV / M • Desert Moon / 1994 / SPI / M • Dirty Laundry #1 / 1994 / CV / M • Dirty Laundry #2 / 1994 / CV / M • Dominoes / 1993 / VI / M • Double D Dykes #12 / 1993 / GO / F • Double Load #1 / 1993 / HW / M • Dungeon De Sade / 1993 / FC / B • Erotic Escape / 1995 / FH / M • Euro-Max #1: Frisky In France / 1995 / SC / M • Euro-Max #3: / 1995 / SC / M • Face Dance #1 / 1992 / EA / M • Face Dance #2 / 1992 / EA / M • Foolproof / 1994 / VC / M • Forever Young / 1994 / VI / M • Forget Me Not

/ 1994 / FH / M • Gangbang Girl #10 / 1993 / ANA / M • The Go-Go Girls / 1994 / EVN / M • The Good, The Bed, And The Snuggly / 1993 / ZA / M • Hard Squeeze / 1994 / EMC / M • Hindfeld / 1993 / PI / M • Hollywood Swingers #07 / 1993 / LBO / M • Hollywood Temps / 1993 / ZA / M • Horny Henry's French Adventure / 1994 / TTV / M • Hot Property / 1993 / PEP / M • In The Bush / 1994 / PP / M • Juranal Park / 1993 / OD / M • Just My Imagination / 1993 / WP / M • A Kiss Before Dying / 1993 / CDI / M • Leena Meets Frankenstein / 1993 / OD / M • Let's Party / 1993 / VC / M • Lick-A-Thon #2 / 1996 / HW / C • Lovebone Invasion / 1993 / PL / M • Midnight Madness / 1993 / DR / M • Mike Hott: #223 Cunt Of The Month: Tina Tyler / 1993 / MHV / M • Mike Hott: Fuck The Boss #01 / 1993 / MHV / M • More Than A Handful #5: California Or Bust / 1994 / MET / M • My Cousin Ginny / 1993 / MET / M • Naked Reunion / 1993 / VI / M • Nasty Nymphos #13 / 1996 / ANA / M • Naughty Nights / 1996 / PLP / C • Night Of Seduction / 1994 / VC / M • Night Seduction / 1995 / VC / M • Ona Zee's Learning The Ropes #09: The Training Continues / 1992 / ONA / B • One Of Our Porn Stars Is Missing / 1993 / OD / M • Passenger 69 #2 / 1994 / IP / M • Peepshow / 1994 / OD / M • Private Video Magazine #18 / 1994 / OD / M • Pulp Friction / 1994 / PP / M • Raunch #06: French Kiss / 1992 / CC / M • Read My Lips: No More Bush / 1992 / HW / M • Reflections Of Rio / 1993 / WP / M • Revenge Of The Bi Dolls / 1994 / CAT / G • Revenge Of The Pussy Suckers From Mars / 1994 / PP / M • Ron Hightower's White Chicks #15 / 1994 / LBO / M • The Savannah Affair / 1993 / CDI / M • Sharon Mitchell's Sex Clinic #01 / 1993 / FC / M • Shear Ecstasy / 1993 / PEP / M • So You Want To Be In The Movies? / 1994 / VC / M • The Star / 1995 / CC / M • Strippers Inc. #2 / 1994 / ONA / M • Tangled / 1994 / PL / M • Tempted / 1994 / VI / M • Titanic Orgy / 1995 / PEP / M • To Shave And Shave Not / 1994 / PEP / M • Video Virgins #01 / 1992 / NS / M • Video Virgins #05 / 1993 / NS / M • Virtual Sex / 1993 / VC / M • Web Of Desire / 1993 / OD / M • Wendy Whoppers: Brain Surgeon / 1993 / PEP / M • Wendy Whoppers: Environmental Attorney / 1993 / PEP / M • Wendy Whoppers: Ninja CPA / 1993 / PEP / M • Wendy Whoppers: Park Ranger / 1993 / PEP / M • What's Butt Got To Do With It? / 1993 / HW / M • Wide Open Spaces / 1995 / VC / F

TINA VEVILLE *see Star Index I*

TINA WADE *see Star Index I*

TINA WALLACE *see Star Index I*

TINA WILDE
Viola Video #109: Backdoor Bavarian Babes / 1995 / PEV / M

TINA WONG *see China Leigh*

TINISHA SCOTT *see Star Index I*

TINKERBELL
Blue Vanities #042 (New) / 1988 / FFL / M

TINO
Bondage Memories #04 / 1994 / BON / C • The Bondage Producer / 1991 / BON / B

TINY
Bootylicious: Booty & The Ho Bitch / 1996 / JMP / M

TINY AYRES *see Star Index I*

TINY DORRITT *see Star Index I*

TINY JOHNSON *see Star Index I*

TINY MARY *see Victoria Jackson*

TINY RITTLE *see Star Index I*

TINY SHOWBIZ *see Star Index I*

TIPPI LONDON *see Star Index I*

TIPPI PETERLAAN
Bi Bi European Style / 1990 / PL / G • Get Bi Tonight / 1991 / PL / G

TIPPI ROCKS *see Star Index I*

TIPSY *see Star Index I*

TISA *see Vanity*

TISA MARIE
Studio Xiii: Spanx Honey / 1992 / SXI / B • Tisa Marie: Finger Lickin' Good / 1991 / SXI / F

TISH AMBROSE *(J.T. Ambrose)*
Not too pretty ball buster with womanly body, reddish brown curly long hair, medium to large tits with a large mole on the top of the left one.
Amber Lynn's Peter Meter / 1988 / 3HV / C • American Babylon / 1985 / PV / M • Anal Angels #1 / 1986 / VEX / M • Babylon Blue / 1983 / VXP / M • The Best Of Ron Jeremy / 1990 / WET / C • Black Lava / 1986 / WET / M • Black To The Future / 1986 / VD / M • Bordello...House Of The Rising Sun / 1985 / SE / M • Cabaret Sin / 1987 / IN / M • Cherry Cheesecake / 1984 / AR / M • Circus Acts / 1987 / SE / C • Climax / 1985 / CA / M • Corporate Assets / 1985 / SE / M • Corruption / 1983 / VC / M • The Cosmopolitan Girls / 1982 / VC / M • Dames / 1985 / SE / M • Decadence / 1986 / VD / M • Don't Tell Daddy #1 / 1985 / PL / C • The Ecstasy Girls #2 / 1986 / CA / M • Empire Of The Sins / 1988 / IN / M • Erica Boyer: Non-Stop / 1988 / VD / C • The Erotic World Of Angel Cash / 1983 / VXP / M • Erotic Zones #2 / 1985 / CA / M • Escort To Ecstasy / 1987 / 3HV / M • Femme / 1984 / VC / M • Firestorm #2: The Angel Blade / 1986 / COM / M • Firestorm #3 / 1986 / COM / M • Freedom Of Choice / 1984 / VHL / M • The Girls Of Rodeo Drive / 1987 / BAD / M • Girls! Girls! Girls! #1 / 1986 / VCS / C • Glitter / 1983 / CA / M • Head / 1985 / LA / M • Hot Buns / 1988 / BIZ / B • Hot Lips / 1984 / VC / M • Hot Seat / 1986 / AVC / M • Hyapatia Lee's Arcade Series #02 / 1988 / ZA / C • In Love / 1983 / VC / M • Interracial Anal Bonanza / 1993 / CA / C • Le Sex De Femme #3 / 1989 / AFI / C • Lilith Unleashed / 1986 / VC / M • Luscious Lucy In Love / 1986 / AVC / M • Maneaters / 1983 / VC / M • Midnight Heat / 1982 / VC / M • Moon Rivers / 1994 / PRE / B • Naked Scents / 1984 / VC / M • Nudes At Eleven #1 / 1986 / AVC / M • One Night In Bangkok / 1985 / CA / M • Only The Best Of Anal / 1992 / MET / C • Perfection / 1985 / VD / M • Pleasure Island / 1984 / AR / M • The Pleasures Of Innocence / 1985 / VC / M • Private School Girls / 1983 / CA / M • Puss 'n' Boots / 1982 / VXP / M • Raw Talent #1 / 1984 / VC / M • The Red Garter / 1986 / SE / M • Rich & Sassy / 1986 / VSE / M • Scenes They Wouldn't Let Me Shoot / 1984 / VC / M • Sex Aliens / 1987 / CA / M • Smear My Ass With Cum / 1993 / EX / C • The Starmaker / 1982 / VC / M • Street Star / cr82 / DRV / M • Swedish Erotica #67 / 1985 / CA / M • A Taste Of Cherry / 1985 / CV / M • Tickled! / 1989 / BIZ / C • Tunnel Of Love / 1986 / CLV / M • Urban Heat /

1985 / FEM / M • Urges In Young Girls / 1984 / VC / M • VCA Previews #4 / 1988 / VC / C • The Voyeur / 1985 / VC / M • Wanda Whips Wall Street / 1982 / VXP / M • Wide World Of Sex / 1987 / CLV / C

TISH ASHLEY see Star Index I

TISH MARTIN see Star Index I

TITANIC TONI
10 Years Of Big Busts #1 / 1989 / BTO / C • Big Busty #29 / 198? / H&S / S • Breast Of Britain #4 / 1990 / BTO / S • Busen Extra #1 / 1991 / BTO / M • Busty Babes In Heat #2 / 1993 / BTO / M • European Cleavage Queens / 199? / H&S / S • The Very Best Of Breasts #1 / 1996 / H&S / S

TITIAN see Carol Titian

TITO MARINO
Bi Bi Banjee Boyz / 1994 / PL / G

TITTI
Impulse #02: The Film / 1995 / MBP / M

TITUS MOODY
A Dirty Western #2: Smoking Guns / 1994 / CV / M • Escape To Passion / 1970 / SOW / S • Hollywood She Wolves / 197? / SE / M • [S.M.U.T. / 197? / ... / S

TITUS STING see Star Index I

TITZIANNA REDFORD see Joanna Redford

TIV DAVENPORT
Every Inch A Lady / 1975 / QX / M

TIZANIA REDFORD see Joanna Redford

TOBIANNA *(Tabolina, Tobianna Monroe, Monroe Tobiana, Tobyana, Monroe (Tobianna))*
Tall, not-too-pretty blonde with medium to large tits and a falling apart body who admits she's 30 years old.
Bobby Hollander's Maneaters #10 / 1993 / SFP / M • Bobby Hollander's Rookie Nookie #13 / 1993 / SFP / M • Breast Collection #02 / 1995 / LBO / C • Bun Busters #14 / 1994 / LBO / M • Cheeks #7: Mirror Image / 1994 / CC / M • Desperado / 1994 / SC / M • Double D Amateurs #14 / 1994 / JMP / M • M Series #18 / 1994 / LBO / M • Mr. Peepers Amateur Home Videos #82: Born To Swing! / 1993 / LBO / M • Mr. Peepers Nastiest #3 / 1995 / LBO / C • Nasty Nymphos #03 / 1994 / ANA / M • Princess Of Thieves / 1994 / SC / M • Special Reserve / 1994 / VC / M • Tobianna: A Gang Bang Fantasy / 1993 / FC / M

TOBIANNA MONROE see Tobianna

TOBY DAMMIT
Black Fire / 1993 / VIM / M • Black Magic #1 / 1993 / VIM / M • The Bold, The Bald & The Beautiful / 1993 / VIM / M • Cousin Bubba Country Corn Porn #01 / 1994 / VIM / M • Cousin Bubba Country Corn Porn #02 / 1994 / VIM / M • Crew Sluts / 1996 / NOT / M • Double Crossed / 1994 / MID / M • Dun-Hur #1 / 1994 / SC / M • Golden Rod / 1996 / SPI / M • My Wildest Date / 1995 / HO / M • Nympho Zombie Coeds / 1993 / VIM / M • Porno Bizarro / 1995 / GLI / M • Pudsucker / 1994 / MID / M • Sneek Peeks #2 / 1993 / OCV / M • Sodomania #21: Degenerate Lifestyles! / 1997 / EL / M • Steele Butt / 1993 / AFV / M • Suck Channel / 1991 / VIM / M • Uncle Roy's Amateur Home Video #21 / 1993 / VIM / M • Uncle Roy's Amateur Home Video #22 / 1993 / VIM / M

TOBY PHILLIPS see Paul Thomas

TOBYANA see Tobianna

TOCCATA MUSK see Star Index I

TOD COUCH
A Coming Of Angels, The Sequel / 1985 / CA / M

TODD
Hollywood Swingers #03 / 1992 / LBO / M • Hustler Video Magazine #1 / 1983 / SE / M • Victoria's Amateurs #03 / 1992 / VGA / M

TODD (JOR. SMITH) see Jordan Smith

TODD BARON see Star Index I

TODD BRUNTTI
Pick Up Lines #13 / 1997 / OD / M

TODD CANYON see Star Index I

TODD E. see Jordan Smith

TODD GRINDER
Most Valuable Slut / 1973 / HLV / M

TODD JONES see Star Index I

TODD KELLER
Getting Lucky / 1983 / CA / M

TODD KNIGHT
The Best Of Both Worlds #2 / 1986 / MID / G • Primal She-Male / 1996 / HSV / G

TODD MASON see Star Index I

TODD MOSS
Bi-Conflict / 1994 / FST / G • Conflict Of Interest / 1994 / FST / G

TODD PEMBROOKE see Star Index I

TODD SCHWARTZ
Dirty Danyel / 1994 / V99 / M

TODD STEVENS
Mr. Blue / 1996 / JSP / G

TODD STINGER
Once...And For All / 1979 / HLV / M

TODD STUDD see Star Index I

TODD TANNER see Star Index I

TODD WHITE
Oriental Girls In Heat / 1995 / IF / M

TOKO B.
Private Gold #09: Private Dancer / 1996 / OD / M

TOKYO
The Psychiatrist / 1978 / VC / M • Ring Of Desire / 1981 / SE / M

TOLDI GYORGY
Sirens / 1995 / GOU / M

TOM
Aged To Perfection #3 / 1995 / TTV / M • Amateur Hours #04 / 1989 / AFI / M • Amateur Hours #09 / 1990 / AFI / M • Amateur Nights #05 / 1990 / HO / M • Amateurs In Action #4 / 1995 / MET / M • AVP #9164: The Voyeur / 1990 / AVP / F • Breast Worx #05 / 1991 / LBO / M • Bubble Butts Gold #2 / 1994 / LBO / M • Bun Busters #18 / 1994 / LBO / M • Canadian Beaver Hunt #2 / 1996 / PL / M • Casting Couch Cuties #1 / 1994 / WP / M • FTV #31: Trio Of Terror / 1996 / FT / B • FTV #38: Wrestling Tough / 1996 / FT / B • FTV #39: Balls In A Bunch / 1996 / FT / B • FTV #40: Triple Terror / 1996 / FT / B • FTV #66: Squeeze Me Tighter / 1996 / FT / B • Hardcore Male/Female Oil Wrestling / 1996 / JSP / M • High Heeled & Horny #3 / 1995 / LBO / M • Homegrown Video #350 / 1991 / HOV / M • Homegrown Video #355 / 1991 / HOV / M • Homegrown Video #357 / 1991 / HOV / M • HomeGrown Video #472: Everyday People / 1996 / HOV / M • HomeGrown Video #473: Furpie Feast #3 / 1997 / HOV / C • Horny For Anal / 1995 / TIE / M • Hungry Humpers / 1996 / SP / M • Neighborhood Watch #17: Burning The Sausage / 1992 / LBO / M • Northwest Pecker Trek #1 / 1994 / LBO / M • Pussy Fest Of The Northwest #3 / 1995 / NIT / M • Stevi's: Love And The

Blade / 1994 / SSV / M • Teacher's Pet #1 / 1994 / WMG / M • Wrasslin She-Babes #07 / 1996 / SOW / M

TOM ALLEN
Triangle Of Love / cr78 / ASR / M

TOM ANDERSON see Star Index I

TOM BAKER
Secret Dreams Of Mona Q / 1977 / AR / M

TOM BANNISTER see Star Index I

TOM BECKER see Tim Lake

TOM BELMAN see Star Index I

TOM BERG
Resurrection Of Eve / 1973 / MIT / M

TOM BETTMAN
Viola Video #105: / 1995 / PEV / M

TOM BLACK see Ian Daniels

TOM BLAKE see Star Index I

TOM BOWDEN JR
The Scavengers / 1969 / ALP / S • Sodom & Gomorrah / 1974 / MIT / M

TOM BYRON
This is also Sal Langford or Jim Hopson but it's not possible to tell which (see **Lusty Ladies #04**). First movie was **GVC: Anything Goes.**
'Ho! 'Ho! 'Ho! / 1993 / WP / M • 1-800-934-BOOB / 1992 / VD / C • 10 1/2 Weeks / 1986 / SE / M • 2002: A Sex Odyssey / 1985 / DR / M • 3 Wives / 1993 / VT / M • 4F Dating Service / 1989 / AR / M • 52 Pick-Up / 1986 / MED / S • 69 Park Avenue / 1985 / ELH / M • A Is For Asia / 1996 / 4P / M • A.S.S.(Anal Security Squad) / 1988 / VD / M • Above The Knee / 1994 / WAV / M • Adult 45 #01 / 1985 / DR / C • Adult Affairs / 1994 / VC / M • Adult Video News 1991 Awards / 1991 / VC / M • Adult Video News 1992 Awards / 1992 / VC / M • Adults Only / 1995 / BOT / M • The Adventures Of Billy Blues / 1990 / HO / M • The Adventures Of Buttman / 1989 / EA / M • The Adventures Of Studman #3 / 1994 / AFV / M • After Midnight / 1994 / IN / M • Aja / 1988 / PL / M • All Amateur Perfect 10's / 1995 / LEI / M • All American Girls #2: In Heat / 1983 / CA / M • All For One / 1988 / CIN / M • All For You, Baby / 1990 / VEX / M • All In The Family / 1985 / VCR / M • Alone And Dripping / 1991 / LV / M • Amazing Tails #1 / 1987 / CA / M • Amazing Tails #2 / 1987 / CA / M • Amazing Tails #3 / 1987 / CA / M • Amazing Tails #4 / 1990 / CA / M • Amazing Tails #5 / 1990 / CA / M • Amber Lynn's Peter Meter / 1988 / 3HV / C • Amber Lynn: She's Back / 1995 / TTV / C • Amber's Desires / 1985 / CA / M • America's Raunchiest Home Videos #73: / 1993 / ZA / M • American Fan Club Prowl / 1996 / VT / M • American Nympho In London / 1987 / VD / M • American Pie / 1995 / WAV / M • American Sweethearts / 1996 / PL / M • Anal Addict / 1995 / ROB / M • Anal Addiction #1 / 1990 / SO / M • Anal Adventures #1: Anal Executive / 1991 / VC / M • Anal Adventures #2: Bodacious Buns / 1991 / VC / M • Anal Adventures #4: Doin' Her Up! / 1992 / VC / M • The Anal Adventures Of Bruce Seven / 1996 / BS / C • The Anal Adventures Of Suzy Super Slut #1 / 1994 / AFV / M • Anal Alley / 1990 / ME / M • Anal Anarchy / 1995 / VC / M • Anal Assassins / 1991 / IN / M • Anal Booty Burner / 1996 / ROB / M • Anal Breakdown / 1994 / ROB / M • Anal Candy Ass / 1994 / ROB / M • Anal Carnival / 1992 / ROB / M • Anal Centerfold / 1995 / ROB / M • Anal Climax #1 / 1991 /

Run / 1987 / VI / M • Bratgirl / 1989 / VI / M • The Brazilian Connection / 1988 / CA / M • Breakfast With Tiffany / 1990 / HO / M • Breaking It #1 / 1984 / COL / M • Breast Collection #03 / 1995 / LBO / C • Breast Collection #04 / 1995 / LBO / C • The Breast Files #1 / 1994 / AVI / M • Breastman's Anal Adventure / 1993 / EVN / M • Breasts And Beyond #1 / 1991 / ME / M • Breezy / 1985 / VCR / M • The Bride / 1986 / WV / M • The Bridges Of Anal County / 1996 / PVO / C • Bringing Up Brat / 1987 / VI / M • Broadway Brat / 1988 / VI / M • Buffy The Vamp / 1992 / FD / M • Built For Sex (Angela Baron's) / 1988 / FAZ / C • Bun Busters #07 / 1993 / LBO / M • Bun For The Money / 1990 / FH / M • Bunbusters / 1984 / VCR / M • Bung-Ho Baboo / 1991 / FC / M • Burgundy Blues / 1993 / MET / M • Burning Desire / 1992 / CDI / M • Bush Pilots #1 / 1990 / VC / M • Bust A Move / 1993 / SC / M • Busted / 1989 / CA / M • Busty Backdoor Nurses / 1996 / PL / M • Butt Banged Cycle Sluts / 1995 / ANA / M • The Butt Detective / 1994 / VC / M • Butt Freak #2 / 1996 / EA / M • Butt Jammers / 1994 / WIV / M • Butt Naked #2 / 1994 / OD / M • The Butt Sisters Do Baltimore / 1995 / MID / M • The Butt Sisters Do Daytona / 1995 / MID / M • The Butt Sisters Do New Orleans / 1995 / MID / M • The Butt Stops Here / 1991 / LV / M • Butt Watch #03 / 1994 / FH / M • Butt Watch #06 / 1994 / FH / M • Butt's Up, Doc #3 / 1992 / GO / M • Butthead & Beaver / 1993 / HW / M • Butthead Dreams / 1994 / FH / M • Butthole Sweetheart / 1996 / ROB / M • Butties / 1992 / VC / M • Buttman In The Crack / 1996 / EA / M • Buttman's Big Tit Adventure #1 / 1992 / EA / M • Buttman's Bubble Butt Babes / 1996 / EA / M • Buttman's Ultimate Workout / 1990 / EA / M • Buttman's Wet Dream / 1994 / EA / M • Buttwiser / 1992 / HW / M • Cabaret Sin / 1987 / IN / M • California Blondes #06 / 1992 / VD / C • California Covet / 1995 / CA / M • California Native / 1988 / CDI / M • A Cameo Appearance / 1992 / VI / M • Campus Cuties / 1986 / CA / M • Candy Snacker / 1993 / WIV / M • Car Wash Angels / 1995 / VC / M • Careena #1 / 1987 / WV / C • Careena #2: A Star On The Rise / 1988 / WV / C • Carnal College #2 / 1993 / AFV / M • Carnal Invasions / 1996 / NIT / M • Carnival Of Knowledge / 1992 / XCI / M • The Case Of The Cockney Cupcake / 1989 / ME / M • Casino Of Lust / 1984 / AT / M • Casual Lies / 1992 / CA / M • Cat Alley / 1986 / AVC / M • Cat Fight / 1992 / ONH / M • Catalina: Undercover / 1991 / CIN / M • Caught From Behind #02: The Sequel / 1983 / HO / M • Caught From Behind #04: Nasty Young Girls / 1985 / HO / M • Caught From Behind #06 / 1986 / HO / M • Caught From Behind #09 / 1988 / HO / M • Caught From Behind #10 / 1989 / HO / M • Caught In The Act / 1987 / WV / M • Centerfold Celebrities #1 / 1982 / VC / M • Certifiably Anal / 1993 / ROB / M • The Chameleon / 1989 / VC / M • Charm School / 1986 / VI / M • Charmed And Dangerous / 1987 / VI / M • Chasey Saves The World / 1996 / VI / M • Chastity And The Starlets / 1986 / RAV / M • Cheaters / 1990 / LE / M • Cheating / 1986 / SEV / M • Cheek To Cheek / 1997 / EL / M • Cheek-A-Boo / 1988 / LV / M •

Cheeks #2: The Bitter End / 1989 / CC / M • Cheerleader Academy / 1986 / PL / M • Chicks On Sex / 1991 / FH / M • Chocolate Kisses / 1986 / CA / M • Chronicles Of Pain #1 / 1996 / BIZ / B • Chronicles Of Pain #2 / 1996 / BIZ / B • Chronicles Of Pain #4: Tools Of The Trade / 1996 / BIZ / B • Clean And Dirty / 1990 / ME / M • The Clock Strikes Bizarre On Butt Row / 1996 / ABS / M • Club DV8 #2 / 1993 / SC / M • Club Erotica / 1996 / IN / M • Club Ginger / 1986 / VI / M • Club Head / 1990 / CA / M • Cold As Ice / 1994 / IN / M • College Cuties / 1995 / LE / M • The Come On: Skip's Video Guide To Scoring Chicks / 1991 / LE / M • Coming Attractions / 1995 / WHP / M • Coming Of Age / 1989 / CA / M • Coming On Strong / 1989 / CA / C • Competent People / 1994 / FD / C • Compulsion (Amazing) / 1996 / MET / M • Compulsive Behavior / 1995 / PI / M • Confessions Of A Nymph / 1985 / VCR / M • Conflict / 1988 / VD / M • Conquest / 1996 / WP / M • Controlled / 1994 / FD / M • Country Girl / 1985 / AVC / M • Covergirl / 1994 / WP / M • Covergirl / 1996 / LE / M • Crack Attack! / 1996 / PE / M • Crash In The Rear / 1992 / HW / C • The Creasemaster's Wife / 1993 / VC / M • Crystal Balls / 1986 / DR / M • Cum Shot Revue #2 / 1985 / HO / C • Cum To Dinner / 1991 / HO / M • Cumback Pussy #1 / 1996 / EL / M • Cumback Pussy #2: Crawling Back For More / 1996 / EL / M • Cumback Pussy #3: Coast To Coast Rump Romp / 1996 / EL / M • Cumback Pussy #4: Get Some!!! / 1996 / EL / M • Cumback Pussy #5: Groopin' / 1996 / EL / M • Cumback Pussy #6: All-Star Poop Chute Salute / 1997 / EL / M • Cumback Pussy #7: NU-GIRLZ / 1997 / EL / M • The Cumming Of Sarah Jane #1 / 1993 / AFV / M • The Cumming Of Sarah Jane #2 / 1993 / AFV / M • Curse Of The Catwoman / 1990 / VC / M • D-Cup Dating Service / 1991 / ME / M • Dane's Surprise / 1991 / IF / G • Dark Dreams / 1992 / WV / M • The Darker Side Of Shayla #1 / 1993 / PL / M • The Darker Side Of Shayla #2 / 1993 / PL / M • Day Dreams / 1993 / CV / M • De Blond / 1989 / EA / M • The De Renzy Tapes / 1990 / CA / C • Dear Bridgette / 1992 / ZA / M • Dear John / 1993 / VI / M • Debbie 4 Hire / 1988 / AVC / M • Debbie Does Dallas Again / 1994 / AFV / M • Debbie Goes To Hawaii / 1988 / VD / C • The Debutante / 1986 / BEA / M • Decadence / 1996 / VC / M • Deep Cheeks #1 / 1991 / ROB / M • Deep Cheeks #3 / 1992 / ROB / M • Deep Cheeks #4 / 1993 / ROB / M • Deep Cheeks #5 / 1995 / ROB / M • Deep Cover / 1993 / WP / M • Deep Dish Booty Pie / 1996 / ROB / M • Deep Inside Ariana / 1995 / VC / C • Deep Inside Brittany O'connell / 1996 / VC / C • Deep Inside Charli / 1990 / CDI / C • Deep Inside Debi Diamond / 1995 / VC / C • Deep Inside Deidre Holland / 1993 / VC / C • Deep Inside Ginger Lynn / 1986 / SE / C • Deep Inside Jeanna Fine / 1992 / VC / C • Deep Inside Juli Ashton / 1996 / VC / C • Deep Inside Kelly O'Dell / 1994 / VC / C • Deep Inside Misty Rain / 1995 / VC / C • Deep Inside Nikki Sinn / 1996 / VC / C • Deep Inside Ona Zee / 1992 / VC / C • Deep Inside Racquel Darrian / 1994 / VC / C • Deep Inside Samantha Strong / 1992 / CDI / C • Deep Inside

Shanna Mccullough / 1992 / VC / C • Deep Inside Tracey / 1987 / CDI / C • Deep Inside Traci / 1986 / CDI / C • Deep Inside Vanessa Del Rio / 1986 / VC / M • Deep Inside Victoria / 1992 / CDI / C • Deep Obsession / 1987 / WV / M • Deep Seven / 1996 / VC / M • Deep Throat Girls / 1986 / ELH / M • Deeper! Harder! Faster! / 1986 / VCS / C • Deja Vu / 1993 / XCI / M • Delinquents On Butt Row / 1996 / EA / M • The Desert Cafe / 1996 / NIT / M • Desire Kills / 1996 / SUM / M • The Desk Top Dolls / 1990 / BAD / C • Despicable Dames / 1986 / CC / M • Devil In Miss Jones #3: A New Beginning / 1986 / VC / M • Devil In Miss Jones #4: The Final Outrage / 1987 / VC / M • The Devil In Miss Jones #5: The Inferno / 1994 / VC / M • Devil In The Blue Dress / 1989 / ME / M • The Devil Made Her Do It / 1992 / HO / M • Dial A Nurse / 1992 / VD / M • Dial A Sailor / 1990 / PM / M • Dial F For Fantasy / 1984 / PL / M • Diamond Collection #57 / 1984 / CIN / M • Diamond Collection #58 / 1984 / CDI / M • Diamond Collection #68 / 1985 / CDI / M • Diamond Collection #80 / 1986 / CDI / M • Diamond Head / 1987 / AVC / M • Diary Of A Bad Girl / 1986 / SUP / M • Diary Of A Geisha / 1995 / WV / C • Dick & Jane Go The Strip / 1994 / AVI / M • Dickman & Throbbin / 1985 / WV / M • The Dinner Party #2: The Buffet / 1996 / ULI / M • Dirty 30's Cinema: Ginger Lynn / 1986 / PV / C • Dirty 30's Cinema: Patti Petite / 1986 / PV / C • Dirty Dancers #7 / 1996 / 4P / M • Dirty Dreams / 1987 / CA / M • Dirty Girls / 1984 / MIT / M • Dirty Looks / 1990 / IN / M • Dirty Movies / 1989 / VD / M • Dirty Pictures / 1985 / SUP / M • Dirty Pictures / 1988 / CA / M • Dirty Prancing / 1987 / EVN / M • Dirty Stories #1 / 1995 / PE / M • Dirty Stories #3 / 1995 / PE / M • Dirty Work / 1995 / VC / M • Divine Decadence / 1988 / CA / M • Doctor Feelgood / 1988 / CDI / M • Dog Walker / 1994 / EA / M • The Doll House / 1995 / CV / M • Dominated Dudes / 1992 / PL / B • Domination / 1994 / WP / M • Domination Of Tammy / 1983 / JAN / B • Dominoes / 1993 / VI / M • Don't Bother To Knock / 1991 / FAZ / M • Don't Tell Daddy #1 / 1985 / PL / C • Double Anal Alternatives / 1996 / EL / M • Double Desires / 1988 / PIN / C • Double Penetration #1 / 1985 / WV / M • Double Penetration #2 / 1986 / WV / C • Double Penetration #3 / 1986 / WV / C • Double Penetration #5 / 1992 / WV / C • Double Penetration Fever / 1989 / MIR / C • Double Whammy / 1986 / LA / M • Double Your Pleasure / 1989 / VEX / M • Dr Butts #3 / 1993 / 4P / M • Dr Penetration / 1986 / WET / M • Draghixa With An X / 1994 / EX / M • The Dragon Lady #2: Tales From the Bed / 1992 / WV / M • The Dragon Lady #7: Tales From The Bed #6 / 1994 / WV / M • Dream Girls / 1986 / VC / M • Dream Lover / 1985 / CDI / M • Dream Lover / 1995 / SC / M • Dream Strokes / 1994 / WIV / M • Dreams / 1987 / AR / M • Dreams In The Forbidden Zone / 1989 / PCP / M • Dreams Of Candace Hart / 1991 / VI / M • Dreams Of Desires / 1995 / ONA / M • Dreamwalk / 1989 / COM / M • Dresden Diary #14: Ecstasy In Hell / 1996 / BIZ / B • Dresden Diary #15: / 1996 / BIZ / B • Dresden Diary #16: / 1996 / BIZ / B • Dressed To Tease / 1992 / RB / B • Earth

Girls Are Sleazy / 1990 / SO / M • Easy Pussy / 1991 / ROB / M • The Easy Way / 1990 / VC / M • Eat 'em And Smile / 1990 / ME / M • Ecstasy / 1986 / PP / M • Ecstasy / 1991 / LE / M • Eight Is Never Enough / 1993 / ZA / M • Electric Blue #011 / 1983 / CA / S • Electric Blue: Desiree Cousteau / 1983 / CA / C • Electric Blue: World Nudes Tonight / 1985 / CA / C • The Eleventh Commandment / 1987 / WAV / M • Empire Of The Sins / 1988 / IN / M • The Enchantress / 1985 / 4P / M • Encore / 1995 / VI / M • Entangled / 1996 / KLP / M • Entertainment L.A. Style / 1990 / HO / M • Erotic Express / 1983 / CV / M • Erotic Newcummers Vol 1 #4 / 1996 / DR / M • Erotic Television Video / 1988 / VD / M • Erotic World Of Anne Spice / 1995 / WV / M • The Erotic World Of Candy Shields / 1984 / VCR / C • The Erotic World Of Rene Summers / 1984 / VCR / C • The Erotic World Of Sunny Day / 1984 / VCR / C • Erotic Zones #3 / 1986 / CA / M • Escort Girls #1 / 198? / LVI / C • Escort To Ecstasy / 1987 / 3HV / M • Eternal Lust / 1996 / VC / M • Eternity / 1990 / SC / M • Every Man's Dream, Every Woman's Nightmare / 1988 / CC / C • Every Woman Has A Fantasy #3 / 1995 / VC / M • Everything Goes / 1990 / SE / M • Executive Suites / 1993 / PL / M • The Exhibitionist / 1991 / VD / M • Exstasy / 1995 / WV / M • Extreme Passion / 1993 / WP / M • Extreme Sex #1: The Club / 1994 / VI / M • Extreme Sex #3: Wired / 1994 / VI / M • Extreme Sex #4: The Experiment / 1995 / VI / M • Eye Of The Tigress / 1988 / VD / M • Eyewitness Nudes / 1990 / VC / M • Face Dance #1 / 1992 / EA / M • Face Dance #2 / 1992 / EA / M • Fade To Black / 1988 / CDI / M • Fame Is A Whore On Butt Row / 1996 / ABS / M • Famous Ta-Ta's #1 / 1986 / VCS / C • Fantasy Du Jour / 1995 / FH / M • Fantasy Girls / 1988 / CA / M • Fantasy Inc. / 1995 / CV / M • Fantasy Nights / 1990 / VC / M • Fashion Plate / 1995 / WAV / M • Fashion Sluts #2 / 1995 / ABS / M • Fashion sluts #5: Ethnic Ecstasy / 1995 / ABS / M • Fashion Sluts #6 / 1995 / ABS / M • Fashion Sluts #7 / 1996 / ABS / M • Film Buff / 1994 / WP / M • Filthy First Timers #6 / 1997 / EL / M • Filthy First Timers #7 / 1997 / EL / M • Fire & Ice: Caught In The Act / 1995 / WP / M • Fire Down Below / 1994 / GO / M • The Fire Inside / 1988 / VC / C • Firm Offer / 1995 / SC / M • First Annual XRCO Awards / 1984 / AVC / C • Flashback / 1993 / SC / M • Flesh And Ecstasy / 1985 / VD / M • Flesh For Fantasy / 1994 / CV / M • Flesh Shopping Network #1 / 1995 / MID / M • Flipside / 1996 / VI / M • The Fluffer #1 / 1993 / FD / M • Foolish Pleasure / 1992 / VD / M • For Love Or Money / 1994 / AFI / M • For The Money #1 / 1993 / FH / M • For Your Thighs Only / 1985 / WV / M • Forbidden / 1992 / FOR / M • Forbidden Bodies / 1986 / HU / M • Forbidden Cravings / 1996 / VC / M • Forbidden Entry / 1984 / VCR / M • Forbidden Fruit / 1985 / PV / M • Forbidden Subjects #1 / 1994 / FC / M • Forbidden Subjects #2 / 1994 / FC / M • Foreign Affairs / 1991 / LE / M • Forever / 1991 / LE / M • Fortysomething / 1990 / LE / M • Four Screws And An Anal / 1994 / NEY / M • Four Weddings And A Honeymoon / 1995 / PL / M • Foxy Boxing / 1982 / AVC / M • The

Freak Club / 1994 / VMX / M • Frenzy / 1992 / SC / M • Fresh Meat (John Leslie) #1 / 1994 / EA / M • Fresh Meat (John Leslie) #2 / 1995 / EA / M • Fresh Meat (John Leslie) #3 / 1996 / EA / M • Friday The 13th #2 / 1989 / VD / M • From Japan With Love / 1990 / SLV / M • From Sweden With Love / 1989 / ZA / M • Frontin' Da Booty / 1994 / WP / M • Full Moon Fever / 1994 / LBO / M • Full Throttle Girls: Boredom Pulled The Trigger / 1993 / VIM / M • Future Doms #1 / 1996 / BIZ / B • Future Doms #2 / 1996 / BIZ / B • Future Lust / 1989 / ME / M • Games Couples Play / 1987 / HO / M • Gang Bang Butthole Surfin' / 1996 / ROB / M • Gang Bang Cummers / 1993 / ROB / M • Gang Bang Face Bath #1 / 1993 / ROB / M • Gang Bang Face Bath #2 / 1994 / ROB / M • Gang Bang Face Bath #3 / 1994 / ROB / M • Gang Bang Face Bath #4 / 1995 / ROB / M • Gang Bang Fury #1 / 1992 / ROB / M • Gang Bang Fury #2 / 1996 / ROB / M • Gang Bang Jizz Jammers / 1994 / ROB / M • Gang Bang Jizz Queen / 1995 / ROB / M • Gang Bang Nymphette / 1994 / ROB / M • Gang Bang Thrills / 1992 / ROB / M • Gang Bang Wild Style #2 / 1994 / ROB / M • Gang Bangs #1 / 1985 / VCR / M • Gang Bangs #2 / 1989 / EA / M • Gangbang Girl #12 / 1993 / ANA / M • Gangbang Girl #13 / 1994 / ANA / M • Gangbang Girl #14 / 1994 / ANA / M • Gangbang Girl #15 / 1995 / ANA / M • Gangbang Girl #17 / 1995 / ANA / M • Gangbang Girl #19 / 1996 / ANA / M • Gazongas #03 / 1991 / VEX / M • Gazongo / 1995 / PEP / M • Generation X / 1995 / WAV / M • Genie In A Bikini / 1991 / ZA / M • Gettin' Wet / 1990 / VC / M • Getting Personal / 1986 / CA / M • Ghost Town / 1995 / WAV / M • Ghostest With The Mostest / 1988 / CA / M • Gimme An X / 1993 / VD / C • Ginger (1984-Vivid) / 1984 / VI / M • Ginger Does Them All / 1988 / CV / M • The Ginger Effect / 1985 / VI / M • Ginger In Ecstasy / 1987 / GO / C • Ginger On The Rocks / 1985 / VI / M • Ginger Snaps / 1987 / VI / M • Ginger Then And Now / 1990 / VI / C • Ginger's Greatest Boy/Girl Hits / 1987 / VI / C • Ginger's Private Party / 1985 / VI / M • Ginger: The Movie / 1988 / PV / C • The Girl Has Assets / 1990 / LV / M • The Girl With The Heart-Shaped Tattoo / 1995 / WAV / M • Girls Of Cell Block F / 1985 / WV / M • Girls Of Paradise #1 / 1986 / PV / C • The Girls Of Rodeo Drive / 1987 / BAD / M • Girls Of Sin / 1994 / PL / C • The Girls Of The A Team #1 / 1985 / WV / M • Girls Of The Double D #03 / 1988 / CDI / M • Girls Of The Double D #05 / 1988 / CIN / M • Girls Of The Double D #06 / 1989 / CIN / M • Girls Of The Double D #11 / 1990 / CIN / M • Girls Of The Double D #13 / 1990 / CDI / M • Girly Video Magazine #3 / 1995 / BEP / M • Girlz N The Hood #2 / 1992 / HW / M • Glamour Girl #1 / 1984 / CDI / M • Glamour Girl #2 / 1984 / CDI / M • Glamour Girl #3 / 1984 / CDI / M • Glamour Girl #4 / 1984 / CDI / M • Glory Days / 1996 / IN / M • Go Ahead...Eat Me! / 1995 / KWP / M • Goin' Down Slow / 1988 / VC / M • Golden Girls #15 / 1984 / CA / M • Golden Girls #16 / 1984 / CA / M • Golden Girls #17 / 1984 / CA / M • Golden Girls #18 / 1984 / CA / M • Golden Girls #20 / 1984 / CA / M • Golden Girls #23 / 1984 / CA / M

• Golden Girls #28 / 1985 / CA / M • Golden Girls #29 / 1985 / CA / M • Good Girls Do / 1984 / HO / M • The Good, The Bad, And The D-Cup / 1991 / GO / C • Goodtime Charli / 1989 / CIN / M • Gorgeous / 1990 / CA / M • Gorgeous / 1995 / MET / M • Gourmet Premier: Lust X 4 / Raven's Rendezvous #901 / cr85 / GO / M • Gourmet Quickies: Shauna Grant #1 #701 / 1983 / GO / C • Graduation Ball / 1989 / CAE / M • Grafenberg Girls Go Fishing / 1987 / MIT / M • Grand Opening / 1985 / AT / M • Greek Week / 1994 / CV / M • Growing Up / 1990 / GO / M • GVC: Anything Goes #119 / 1983 / GO / M • GVC: Shauna, Blonde Superstar #132 / 1984 / GO / C • GVC: Suburban Lust #128 / 1983 / GO / M • GVC: Valley Vixens #124 / 1983 / GO / M • A Handful Of Summers / 1991 / ME / M • Handle With Care / 1989 / FAZ / M • Hard Choices / 1987 / CA / M • Hard Core Cafe / 1988 / VD / M • Hard To Stop #2 / 1992 / VC / M • Hard To Swallow / 1985 / PV / M • Hard-On Copy / 1994 / WV / M • Hardcore Copy / 1993 / PL / M • Harlequin Affair / 1985 / CIX / M • Having It All / 1985 / IN / M • Hawaii Vice #7 / 1989 / CDI / M • Hawaii Vice #8 / 1990 / CIN / M • Head Clinic / 1987 / AVC / M • Head First / 1995 / OD / M • Head Shots / 1995 / VI / M • Headgames / 1985 / WV / M • Heart Breaker / 1989 / LE / M • Heart To Heart / 1990 / LE / M • Heather Hunted / 1990 / VI / M • Heidi Does Hollywood / 1993 / AFV / M • Heidi's Girls / 1995 / GO / M • Hershe Highway #4 / 1991 / HO / M • Hienie's Heroes / 1995 / VC / M • The Hind-Lick Maneuver / 1991 / GO / C • The Hitch-Hiker #08: On The Trail / 1994 / WMG / M • Ho' Style Takeover / 1993 / FH / M • Hocus Poke-Us / 1991 / HO / M • Hole In One / 1993 / IF / M • Holiday For Angels / 1987 / IN / M • Hollywood Undercover / 1989 / BWV / C • Home Bodies / 1988 / VEX / M • Home But Not Alone / 1991 / WV / M • Home Movies Ltd #1 / 1983 / SE / M • Honeybuns #1 / 1987 / WV / C • Honeybuns #2: Grecian Formula / 1987 / WV / C • Honkytonk Angels / 1988 / IN / C • Horny Brits Take It In The Bum / 1997 / ROB / M • Hospitality Sweet / 1988 / WV / M • Hot And Nasty! / 1986 / V99 / C • The Hot Box Invasion / 1987 / AMB / M • Hot Diggity Dog / 1990 / ME / M • Hot In The City / 1989 / VEX / M • Hot Nights And Dirty Days / 1988 / VD / M • Hot Nights At The Blue Note Cafe / 1985 / WV / M • Hot Property / 1989 / EXH / C • Hot Rocks / 1986 / WET / M • Hot Shots / 1992 / VD / C • Hot Wired / 1996 / VC / M • Hot Wishes / 1995 / LE / M • Hotel Fantasy / 1995 / IN / M • Hotel Sodom #01 / 1995 / SNA / M • Hotel Sodom #02 / 1995 / SNA / M • Hotel Sodom #03 / 1995 / SNA / M • Hotel Sodom #04: Free Parking In Rear / 1995 / SNA / M • Hotel Sodom #08 / 1995 / SNA / M • Hotel Sodom #10 / 1996 / SNA / M • Hothouse Rose #1 / 1991 / VC / M • Hothouse Rose #2 / 1992 / VC / M • Hottest Parties / 1988 / VC / C • Hottest Ticket / 1987 / WV / C • Hotwired / 1996 / VC / M • House Of Blue Dreams / 1985 / WV / M • House Of Sleeping Beauties #1 / 1992 / VI / M • House Of Sleeping Beauties #2 / 1992 / VI / M • The House On Chasey Lane / 1995 / VI / M • How Do You Like It? / 1985

Nikki's Last Stand / 1993 / VC / M • Nineteen #1 / 1996 / FOR / M • No Tell Motel / 1995 / CV / M • Nobody's Looking / 1993 / VC / M • Nooner / 1986 / AVC / M • Nothing Personal / 1990 / IN / M • Nothing Sacred / 1995 / LE / M • Nudes At Eleven #1 / 1986 / AVC / M • Numba 1 Ass Fucka / 1996 / ROB / M • Nurse Tails / 1994 / VC / M • NYDP Blue / 1996 / WP / M • Nymphette #2 / 1986 / WV / M • Nymphobrat / 1989 / VI / M • Object Of Desire / 1991 / FAZ / M • Object(s) Of My Desire / 1988 / V99 / M • Obsession / 1991 / CDI / M • Office Girls / 1989 / CA / M • Oh! You Beautiful Doll / 1990 / ZA / M • Older Women With Young Boys / 1984 / CC / M • On Golden Blonde / 1984 / PV / M • On The Job Training / 1991 / RB / B • On The Loose & Hot To Trot / 1987 / CA / M • On Your Honor / 1989 / LE / M • Once Upon A Madonna / 1985 / PV / M • One Night Stand / 1990 / LE / M • One Wife To Give / 1989 / ZA / M • Only The Best #3 / 1990 / CV / C • Only The Best Of Breasts / 1987 / CV / C • Only The Best Of Men's And Women's Fantasies / 1988 / CV / C • Only The Best Of Oral / 1989 / CV / C • Only The Best Of The Erotic Eighties / 1992 / VC / C • Only The Very Best On Video / 1992 / VC / C • Only With A Married Woman / 1990 / LE / M • Open Up Tracy / 1984 / VD / M • Oral Clinic / 1990 / DAY / M • Oral Hijinx / 1990 / ERU / M • Oral Majority #01 / 1986 / WV / C • Oral Majority #02 / 1987 / WV / C • Oral Majority #03 / 1986 / WV / C • Oral Majority #04 / 1987 / WV / C • Oral Majority #05 / 1987 / WV / C • Oral Majority #09 / 1992 / WV / C • Oral Majority #10 / 1993 / WV / C • Orgies / 1987 / WV / C • The Orgy #2 / 1993 / EMC / M • The Orgy #3 / 1993 / EMC / M • Oriental Anal Sluts / 1993 / WV / C • Oriental Lust / 1983 / GO / M • The Original Wicked Woman / 1993 / WP / M • The Other Side Of Pleasure / 1987 / SEV / M • Out Of Love / 1995 / VI / M • Outback Assignment / 1991 / VD / M • Outlaw Ladies #2 / 1988 / VC / M • Outrageous Foreplay / 1987 / WV / M • The Oval Office / 1991 / LV / M • Paddle Tales / 1992 / BON / B • A Paler Shade Of Blue / 1991 / CC / M • Panties / 1993 / VD / M • Parliament: Ass Masters #1 / 1987 / PM / M • Parliament: Shauna Grant #1 / 1988 / PM / C • Parliament: Three Way Lust / 1988 / PM / M • Parlor Games / 1993 / VI / M • Party Doll / 1990 / VC / M • Party Doll A Go-Go #1 / 1991 / VC / M • Party Doll A Go-Go #2 / 1991 / VC / M • Passage To Pleasure / 1995 / LE / M • Passenger 69 #1 / 1994 / IP / M • The Passion Potion / 1995 / WP / M • Passionate Angels / 1990 / HO / M • Passionate Heiress / 1987 / CA / M • Passionate Lips / 1990 / OD / M • Penetration #1 / 1984 / AVC / M • Penetration #3 / 1984 / AVC / M • Penetrator #2: Grudge Day / 1995 / PL / M • The Perfect Brat / 1989 / VI / M • Perfect Fit / 1985 / DR / M • Perfection / 1985 / VD / M • Personal Touch #2 / 1983 / AR / M • Personalities / 1991 / PL / M • Perverted #1: The Babysitters / 1994 / ZA / M • Phantasm / 1995 / WP / M • Phantom X / 1989 / VC / M • Phone Fantasy #2 / 1992 / ATL / M • Photo Play / 1995 / VI / M • Photoflesh / 1984 / HO / M • Physical #2 / 1985 / SUP / M • Piece Of Heaven / 1988 / CDI / M • The Pink Pussycat / 1992

/ CA / M • Play Christy For Me / 1990 / CAY / M • Play It Again, Samantha / 1986 / EVN / M • Playin' Dirty / 1990 / VC / M • Playing With A Full Dick / 1988 / PL / M • Playing With Fire / 1983 / IN / M • Plaything #1 / 1995 / VI / M • Plaything #2 / 1995 / VI / M • The Pleasure Hunt #2 / 1985 / NSV / M • Pleasure Is My Business / 1989 / EX / M • Pleasure Productions #04 / 1984 / VCR / M • Pleasure Productions #07 / 1984 / VCR / M • Pleasure Productions #08 / 1984 / VCR / M • Pleasure Productions #11 / 1985 / VCR / M • Pleasure Productions #12 / 1985 / VCR / M • The Pleasure Seekers / 1990 / VD / M • Pool Party / 1991 / CIN / M • A Pool Party At Seymores #1 / 1995 / ULI / M • A Pool Party At Seymores #2 / 1995 / ULI / M • Poor Little Rich Girl #1 / 1992 / XCI / M • Poor Little Rich Girl #2 / 1992 / XCI / M • Porn Star's Day Off / 1990 / FAZ / M • Porsche Lynn, Every Man's Dream / 1988 / CC / C • Possessions / 1992 / HW / M • Postcards From Abroad / 1991 / CA / C • Pouring It On / 1993 / CV / M • Power Play (Bruce Seven) / 1990 / BS / B • Precious Peaks / 1990 / ZA / M • Prescription For Pleasure / 1993 / HW / M • Pretty As You Feel / 1984 / PV / M • Prince Of Beverly Hills #1 / 1987 / VEX / M • Princess Of The Night / 1990 / VD / M • Prisoner Of Love / 1991 / ME / M • Private Moments / 1983 / CV / M • Private Performance / 1994 / EX / M • Private Teacher / 1983 / CA / M • Private Video Magazine #08 / 1994 / OD / M • Project Ginger / 1985 / VI / M • Prom Girls / 1988 / CA / M • The Psychic / 1993 / CC / M • Pumping Ethel / 1988 / PV / M • Punishing The Sluts / 1996 / RB / B • Pure Sex / 1988 / FAN / C • Purely Sexual / 1991 / HO / M • A Pussy Called Wanda #2 / 1992 / DR / M • Pussy Whipped / 1991 / PL / B • Pussyman #01: The Search / 1993 / CC / M • Pussyman #02: The Prize / 1993 / CC / M • Pussyman Auditions #18 / 1996 / SNA / M • The Pussywillows / 1985 / SUV / M • Pussywoman #1: Sisters In Sin / 1994 / CC / M • Pussywoman #2 / 1994 / CC / M • Pussywoman #3 / 1995 / CC / M • Putting It All Behind #1 / 1991 / IN / M • Rachel Ryan / 1988 / WV / C • Radical Affairs Video Magazine #02 / 1992 / ME / M • Radio K-KUM / 1984 / HO / M • Radio-Active / 1992 / SC / M • Rainbird / 1994 / EMC / M • Ramb-Ohh #1 / 1986 / PV / M • Rambone The Destroyer / 1985 / WET / M • Rapture / 1990 / SC / M • Rated Sex / 1986 / SE / M • Raunch #05 / 1992 / CC / M • Raunch #06: French Kiss / 1992 / CC / M • Raunch #10: Uncut Jewel / 1994 / CC / M • Raunchy Ranch / 1991 / AFV / M • Raw Naked In Your Face / 1997 / ROB / M • Rayne Storm / 1991 / VI / M • Ready, Willing & Anal (Cv) / 1993 / CV / C • Realities #1 / 1991 / ZA / M • A Rear And Pleasant Danger / 1995 / PP / M • Rearbusters / 1988 / LVI / C • Rebel Cheerleaders / 1995 / VI / M • Rectal Raiders / 1997 / ROB / M • Red Hot Fire Girls / 1989 / VD / M • Red Hots / 1996 / PL / M • Reflections Of Innocence / 1988 / SEX / M • Reflections Of Innocence / 1991 / VEX / C • The Rehearsal / 1993 / VC / M • Restless Nights / 1987 / SEV / M • Return Engagement / 1995 / VI / M • Return To Sex 5th Avenue / 1985 / WV / M • Rhapsody / 1993 / VT / M • Ride 'em Hard

/ 1992 / LV / M • The Rise Of The Roman Empress #2 / 1990 / PV / M • A Rising Star / 1991 / HO / M • Risque Burlesque #2 / 1996 / IN / M • Road Kill / 1995 / CA / M • Robofox #1 / 1987 / FAN / M • Rock 'n' Roll Heaven / 1989 / EA / M • Rock Me / 1994 / CC / M • Rockin' The Boat / 1990 / VI / M • The Rocky Porno Video Show / 1986 / 4P / M • Romeo And Juliet #1 / 1987 / WV / M • Romeo And Juliet #2 / 1988 / WV / M • Ruthless Affairs / 1995 / LE / M • Sabotage / 1994 / CA / M • Safecracker / 1991 / CC / M • Samantha & Company / 1996 / PL / M • Samantha And The Deep Throat Girls / 1988 / CV / M • Samantha's Private Fantasies / 1994 / WV / M • Satin & Lace / 1994 / WP / M • Saturday Matinee Series #4 / 1996 / VCX / C • Saturday Night Porn #1 / 1993 / AFV / M • Satyr / 1996 / WP / M • Scandalous / 1989 / CC / M • The Scarlet Bride / 1989 / VI / M • Scarlet Fantasy / 1990 / VI / M • The Scarlet Woman / 1994 / WP / M • The Screamer / 1991 / CA / M • Screaming Rage / 1988 / LV / C • Screwdriver / 1988 / CC / C • Sea Of Love / 1990 / CIN / M • The Search For Pink October / 1990 / EX / M • The Secret Life Of Nina Hartley / 1994 / VC / M • Secret Of Her Suckcess / 1994 / VC / M • Secret Urges (Vidco) / 1994 / VD / C • The Seduction Of Julia Ann / 1993 / VT / M • Seeing Red / 1993 / VI / M • Sensuous / 1991 / LV / M • Sex #1 (Vivid) / 1993 / VI / M • Sex #2 (Vivid) / 1993 / VI / M • Sex #3: After Seven (Vivid) / 1994 / VI / M • Sex 5th Avenue / 1985 / WV / M • Sex Academy #2: The Art Of Talking Dirty / 1994 / ONA / M • Sex And The Happy Landlord / 1988 / CDI / M • Sex Asylum #2 / 1986 / VI / M • Sex For Hire / 1989 / HOE / C • Sex Freaks / 1995 / EA / M • The Sex Game / 1987 / SE / C • The Sex Goddess / 1984 / GO / M • Sex Hungry Butthole Sluts / 1996 / ROB / M • Sex In Strange Places: The Sphincter Zone / 1994 / FPI / M • Sex Liners / 1991 / CIN / M • Sex Lives Of The Rich And Beautiful / 1988 / CA / M • Sex Machine / 1995 / VI / M • Sex Maniacs / 1987 / JOY / C • Sex Party / 1995 / KWP / M • Sex Shoot / 1985 / AT / M • Sex Suites / 1995 / TP / M • Sex Toys / 1985 / CA / M • Sexophrenia / 1993 / VC / M • Sexpertease / 1985 / VD / M • Sexscape / 1986 / CA / M • Sextectives / 1989 / CIN / M • Sexual Fantasies / 1993 / ... / C • Sexual Healer / 1991 / CA / M • Sexual Power / 1988 / CV / M • Sexy And 18 / 1987 / SE / M • Sexy Nurses #2 / 1994 / CV / M • Seymore Butts: Big Boobs In Buttsville / 1996 / FH / M • Seymore Butts: Slippin' In Through The Out Door / 1996 / FH / M • Sgt. Peckers Lonely Hearts Club Gang Bang / 1995 / AMP / M • Shades Of Blue / 1992 / VC / M • Shades Of Ecstasy / 1983 / HO / M • Shadows In The Dark / 1990 / 4P / M • Shameless / 1995 / VC / M • Shane's World #1 / 1996 / OD / M • Shanna's Final Fling / 1991 / ME / M • Shauna Grant: The Early Years / 1988 / PV / C • Shaved / 1984 / VCR / M • Shayla's Gang / 1994 / WP / M • She'll Take A Spanking / 199? / BON / B • She's Got The Juice / 1990 / CDI / M • She's Ready / 1990 / CDI / M • She's So Fine #2 / 1988 / VC / M • Sheer Bedlam / 1986 / VI / M • Shiela's Deep Desires / 1986 / HO / M • Shifting Gere / 1990 / VT / M • Shot From Behind /

• Video Tramp #1 / 1985 / AA / M • Video Virgins #19 / 1994 / NS / M • Video Virgins #27 / 1996 / NS / M • Viper's Place / 1988 / VD / M • Virgin Dreams / 1996 / EA / M • The Vision / 1991 / LE / M • Visual Fantasies / 1995 / LE / M • Vivid Raw #3: Double Header / 1996 / VI / M • Voices In My Bed / 1993 / VI / M • Vow Of Passion / 1991 / VI / M • The Voyeur #1 / 1994 / EA / M • The Voyeur #3 / 1995 / EA / M • Voyeur Video / 1992 / ZA / M • Voyeur's Delight / 1986 / VCS / C • The Wacky World Of X-Rated Bloopers / 1989 / GO / M • Waiting To XXX-Hale / 1996 / MET / M • Wanted / 1995 / DR / M • Warm Pink / 1992 / LE / M • Waterbabies #1 / 1992 / CC / M • Waterworld: The Enema Club / 1996 / BIZ / B • Waves Of Passion / 1993 / PL / M • The Way They Were / 1990 / CDI / M • A Way With Wood / 1995 / HOM / B • Web Of Desire / 1993 / OD / M • Weird Sex / 1995 / GO / M • Westside Tori / 1989 / ERO / M • Wet Science / 1986 / PLY / M • What About Boob? / 1993 / CV / M • What Gets Me Hot / 1984 / ISV / M • Where The Sun Never Shines / 1990 / IN / C • While You Were Dreaming / 1995 / WV / M • White Boys & Black Bitches / 1995 / ROB / M • White Bun Busters / 1985 / VC / M • White Men Can't Iron On Butt Row / 1997 / ABS / M • White Trash / 1986 / PV / M • White Women / 1986 / CC / M • Who Came In The Backdoor? / 1987 / PV / M • The Whore / 1989 / CA / M • Whore House / 1995 / IPI / M • The Whore Of The Worlds / 1985 / PV / M • Wicked As She Seems / 1993 / WP / M • Wicked At Heart / 1995 / WP / M • Wicked Fascination / 1991 / CIN / M • The Wicked One / 1995 / WP / M • Wicked Ways #2: Education Of A D.P. Virgin / 1995 / WP / M • The Wicked Web / 1996 / WP / M • Wicked Woman / 1994 / HO / M • Wild & Wicked #1 / 1991 / VT / M • Wild & Wicked #3 / 1993 / VT / M • Wild & Wicked #6 / 1995 / VT / M • Wild Assed Pooper Slut / 1996 / ROB / M • The Wild Brat / 1988 / VI / M • Wild Breed / 1995 / SC / M • Wild Buck / 1993 / STY / M • Wild Flower #2 / 1992 / VI / M • Wild In Motion / 1992 / PL / M • Wild In The Wilderness / 1988 / SE / M • Wild Things #1 / 1985 / CV / M • Wild Weekend / 1984 / HO / M • The Wild Wild West / 1986 / SE / M • Willie Wanker And The Fun Factory / 1994 / FD / M • Willie Wanker At The Fudge Packing Factory / 1995 / FD / M • Willing Women / 1993 / VD / C • Wings Of Passion / 1984 / HO / M • Wire Desire / 1991 / XCI / M • Wise Ass! / 1990 / FH / M • The Witching Hour / 1992 / FOR / M • With Love From Ginger / 1986 / HO / C • With Love From Susan / 1988 / HO / C • Within & Without You / 1993 / WP / M • The Woman In Pink / 1984 / SE / M • The Woman Who Loved Men / 1984 / SE / M • Women On Top / 1995 / BON / B • Women Who Spank Men / 1995 / SHL / B • Working Stiffs / 1993 / FD / M • World Sex Tour #6 / 1996 / ANA / M • World Sex Tour #7 / 1996 / ANA / M • WPINK-TV #3 / 1988 / PV / M • Wrapped Up / 1992 / VD / C • The Wrong Woman / 1990 / LE / M • X-TV #1 / 1986 / PL / C • X-TV / 1992 / CA / C • XXX Channel / 1996 / VT / M • The XXX Files: Lust In Space / 1995 / IMV / M • Yank Fest / 1994 / FD / C • The Year Of The Sex Dragon / 1986 / PV / M • You Make Me Wet

/ 1985 / SVE / M • Young And Naughty / 1984 / HO / M • Young Girls In Tight Jeans / 1989 / VD / M • Zane's World / 1992 / ZA / M

TOM CANTRELL *see Star Index I*
TOM CARLTON
Sodom & Gomorrah / 1974 / MIT / M
TOM CARTWRIGHT *see Star Index I*
TOM CHAPMAN *(Tom Thomas, Mike Jones (T.Chap.))*
Credited as Mike Jones in **Perfect Girl (1992)** and **Fire & Ice.**
1-900-FUCK #1 / 1995 / SO / M • The A Chronicles / 1992 / CC / M • Against All Bods / 1991 / VEX / M • Alley Cat / 1991 / CIN / M • America's Raunchiest Home Videos #25: Victoria's Secretions / 1992 / ZA / M • America's Raunchiest Home Videos #29: Love Box / 1992 / ZA / M • America's Raunchiest Home Videos #32: Model of Lust / 1992 / ZA / M • America's Raunchiest Home Videos #34: The Big Splash / 1992 / ZA / M • Anal All Stars / 1994 / CA / M • Anal Anonymous / 1995 / SO / M • Anal Asian / 1994 / VEX / M • Anal Delights #1 / 1992 / ROB / M • Anal Encounters #1 / 1991 / VC / M • Anal Encounters #7: Enter Through The Rear / 1992 / VC / M • Anal Intruder #09: The Butt From Another Planet / 1995 / CC / M • Anal Maniacs #3 / 1995 / WP / M • Anal Nation #2 / 1990 / CC / M • Anal Woman #3 / 1995 / PL / M • Animal Attraction / 1994 / IF / M • Any Port In The Storm / 1991 / LV / M • Anything Goes / 1993 / VD / C • The Babe / 1992 / EX / M • Back In Action / 1992 / FD / M • Backdoor To Russia #1 / 1992 / VC / M • Backdoor To Russia #2 / 1993 / VC / M • Backdoor To Russia #3 / 1993 / VC / M • Backstage Entrance #2 / 1992 / FH / M • Bad Side Of Town / 1993 / AFD / M • Bad To The Bone / 1992 / LE / M • Ball Busters / 1991 / FH / M • Beach Bum Amateur's #12 / 1992 / MID / M • Beach Bum Amateur's #14 / 1992 / MID / M • Beaver Ridge / 1991 / VC / M • Behind The Backdoor #4 / 1990 / EVN / M • Behind The Backdoor #5 / 1992 / EVN / M • Behind The Brown Door / 1994 / PE / M • Biff Malibu's Totally Nasty Home Videos #12 / 1992 / ANA / M • Biff Malibu's Totally Nasty Home Videos #21 / 1992 / ANA / M • Biggies #04 / 1992 / XPI / M • Biker Chicks In Love / 1991 / LE / M • The Bimbo #1 / 1992 / AFV / M • The Bimbo #2 / 1992 / AFV / M • Black Jack City #1 / 1991 / VT / M • Black Nurse Fantasies / 1994 / CA / M • Blindfold / 1994 / SC / M • Blonde Bombshell / 1991 / CC / M • Blow Out / 1991 / IF / M • Blue Angel / 1992 / AFV / M • Bonfire Of The Panties / 1990 / CC / M • Bonnie & Clyde #1 / 1992 / VI / M • Bonnie & Clyde #2 / 1992 / VI / M • Boomeranal / 1992 / CC / M • Boudoir Babe / 1996 / VMX / M • The Box / 1992 / EX / M • Bunmasters / 1995 / VC / M • Butt Naked #1 / 1990 / OD / M • Butt Row Unplugged / 1996 / ABS / M • The Butt, The Boobs, The Lips / 1996 / C69 / M • The Butt-nicks #2 / 1991 / HIO / M • Butts Up / 1994 / CA / M • Carnival / 1995 / PV / M • Caught From Behind #20 / 1995 / HO / M • Cheeks #4: A Backstreet Affair / 1991 / CC / M • Cheeks #8 / 1995 / CC / M • Cheesecake / 1991 / VC / M • City Of Sin / 1991 / LV / M • Cold As Ice / 1994 / IN / M • Coming Out / 1993 / VD / M • Crazy On You / 1991 / IF

/ M • Dance Naked / 1995 / PEP / M • Date Night / 1992 / V99 / M • Debbie Class Of '95 / 1995 / CC / M • Debbie Does Wall Street / 1991 / VC / M • Decadence / 1994 / WHP / M • Decadent / 1991 / WV / M • Deep Inside Centerfold Girls / 1991 / VC / • Deep Inside Nikki Sinn / 1996 / VC / C • Deep Inside Selena Steele / 1993 / VC / C • Deep Inside Viviana / 1992 / VEX / C • Defending Your Sex Life / 1992 / LE / M • Deja Vu / 1993 / XCI / M • Desert Fox / 1990 / VD / M • The Determinator #2 / 1991 / VIM / M • Dial 666 For Lust / 1991 / AFV / M • Dig It / 1994 / FD / C • Dirty Dixie / 1992 / IF / M • Dirty Thoughts / 1992 / LE / M • Dirty Tricks / 1993 / CC / M • Diver Down / 1992 / CC / M • Double Crossing / 1991 / IN / M • Double D Amateurs #22 / 1994 / JMP / M • Double The Pleasure / 1990 / SE / M • Dream Lover / 1991 / WV / M • The Drifter / 1995 / CV / M • East L.A. Law / 1991 / WV / M • The End / 1992 / SC / M • Erectnophobia #2 / 1992 / MID / M • The Erotic Adventures Of Fanny Annie / 1991 / WV / M • Eternity / 1991 / CDI / M • Executive Positions / 1991 / V99 / M • Executive Suites / 1993 / PL / M • The Exhibitionist / 1991 / VD / M • Exiles / 1991 / VT / M • Fashion Sluts #1 / 1995 / ABS / M • Fashion Sluts #4 / 1995 / ABS / M • Fire & Ice / 1992 / CDI / G • Four Weddings And A Honeymoon / 1995 / PL / M • Frat Girls / 1993 / VC / M • Fresh Meat (John Leslie) #1 / 1994 / EA / M • Friends & Lovers #1 / 1991 / VT / M • Frontin' Da Booty / 1994 / WP / M • Gangbang Girl #01 / 1992 / ANA / M • Gangbang Girl #02 / 1992 / ANA / M • Gangbang Girl #03 / 1992 / ANA / M • Gangbang Girl #06 / 1992 / ANA / M • Gangbang Girl #08 / 1992 / ANA / M • Getting Personal / 1995 / PE / M • Ghost Writer / 1992 / LE / M • Girl's School / 1994 / ERA / M • Glamour Girl / 1991 / VEX / M • The God Daughter #3 / 1992 / AFV / M • The God Daughter #4 / 1992 / AFV / M • The Good, The Bed, And The Snuggly / 1993 / ZA / M • Great Expectations / 1992 / VEX / C • Guess Who? / 1991 / EX / M • Heartbeats / 1992 / LE / M • Hershe Highway #4 / 1991 / HO / M • Hometown Honeys #5 / 1993 / VEX / M • Hooked / 1992 / SC / M • Hose Jobs / 1995 / VEX / M • Hot On Her Tail / 1990 / CA / M • Hotel Sodom #03 / 1995 / SNA / M • Hotel Sodom #06 / 1995 / SNA / M • Hotel Sodom #07 / 1995 / SNA / M • Hotel Sodom #09 / 1996 / SNA / M • Hothouse Rose #1 / 1991 / VC / M • House Of Sleeping Beauties #2 / 1992 / VI / M • House Pet / 1992 / V99 / M • The Housewife In Heat / 1991 / PL / M • If Dreams Come True / 1991 / AFV / M • Illusions #2 / 1992 / IF / M • In Excess / 1991 / CA / M • Interactive / 1994 / SC / M • Into The Gap / 1991 / LE / M • It's A Wonderful Sexlife / 1991 / LE / M • Kink #1 / 1995 / ROB / M • Kiss And Tell / 1992 / AFV / M • L.A. Rear / 1992 / FD / M • Laying Down The Law #2 / 1992 / AFV / M • A Little Nookie / 1991 / VD / M • Living For Love / 1993 / V99 / M • Lonely Hearts / 1995 / VC / M • Looking For Love / 1991 / VEX / M • Lust For Love / 1991 / VC / M • Maid For Service / 1990 / LV / M • Manbait #2 / 1992 / VC / M • Maneater / 1995 / ERA / M • Masked Ball / 1992 / IF / M • Masquerade / 1995 / HO / M • The Mile High Club / 1995 / PL / M • Mi-

TOMMY GALLO
Look What I Found On The Street #01 / 1996 / CC / M

TOMMY GRANT *see Star Index I*

TOMMY GUNN
50 And Still Gangbangin'! / 1995 / EMC / M • Ass, Gas & The Mystical GLOP / 1997 / EL / M • Ben Dover & Barbie / 1995 / SUF / M • Beverly Hills Bikini Company / 1996 / NIT / M • Black Women, White Men #7 / 1995 / FC / M • Black Women, White Men #8 / 1995 / FC / M • Bound & Shaved / 1994 / BON / B • Catching Snapper / 1995 / XCI / M • Cloud 900 / 1996 / EYE / M • Crew Sluts / 1996 / NOT / M • Dirty Diner #3 / 1996 / SC / M • Domination Nation / 1996 / VI / M • Dominique's Inheritance / 1996 / CVC / M • Double Dicked #2 / 1996 / RAS / M • Eighteen & Easy / 1996 / SC / M • Emerald: Princess Of The Night / 1996 / FC / M • Forbidden Fantasies #3 / 1995 / ZA / M • Frendz? #2 / 1996 / RAS / M • Hollywood Amateurs #25 / 1995 / MID / M • Hot Amateur Nights / 1996 / WV / M • In Cold Sweat / 1996 / VI / M • Incantation / 1996 / FC / M • Kinky Debutante Interviews #09 / 1995 / IP / M • Knocked-Up Nymphos #1 / 1996 / GLI / M • Latin Fever #3 / 1996 / C69 / M • The Line Up / 1996 / CDI / M • Living On The Edge / 1997 / DWO / M • Mike Hott: #367 Girls Who Lap Cum From Cunts #02 / 1996 / MHV / M • Mike Hott: #368 Three-Sum Sluts #13 / 1996 / MHV / M • Mike Hott: #372 Stacey Pregnant / 1996 / MHV / M • Mike Hott: #380 Girls Who Lap Cum From Cunts #03 / 1996 / MHV / C • Mike Hott: #384 Three-Sum Sluts #16 / 1996 / MHV / M • Mike Hott: #386 / 1996 / MHV / M • Mike Hott: #387 Girls Who Lap Cum From Cunts #04 / 1996 / MHV / M • Mike Hott: #390 / 1996 / MHV / M • Mike Hott: #391 / 1996 / MHV / M • Mike Hott: #393 / 1996 / MHV / M • Monkey Gang Bang / 1996 / NOT / M • My First Time #6 / 1996 / NS / M • Nasty Newcummers #11 / 1995 / MET / M • Next...! / 1996 / CDI / M • Nineteen #2 / 1996 / FOR / M • Nineteen #3 / 1996 / FOR / M • Over Eighteen #02 / 1997 / HW / M • Perverted Stories #11 / 1996 / JMP / M • Peyton's Place / 1996 / ULP / M • Pussyman's Nite Club Party #1 / 1996 / SNA / M • Pussyman's Nite Club Party #2 / 1997 / SNA / M • The Shocking Truth #1 / 1996 / DWO / M • The Shocking Truth #2 / 1996 / DWO / M • Show & Tell / 1996 / VI / M • Slutsville U.S.A. / 1995 / VMX / M • Sticky Fingers / 1996 / WV / M • Stripping / 1995 / NIT / M • Stuff Your Ass #3 / 1996 / JMP / M • Stuff Your Face #4 / 1996 / JMP / M • Summer Dreams / 1996 / TEP / M • Trapped / 1996 / VI / M • Triple Penetration Debutante Sluts #2 / 1996 / BAC / M • Valley Cooze / 1996 / SC / M • Wet Daydreams / 1996 / XCI / M • What Women Want / 1996 / SUF / M • White Trash Whore / 1996 / JMP / M

TOMMY HAWK *see Star Index I*

TOMMY JUNIOR *see Star Index I*

TOMMY K.
Bound Buns / 1994 / GAL / B

TOMMY KAYE
Back East Babes #2 / 1996 / NIT / M • Back East Babes #3 / 1996 / NIT / M • Intimate Interviews #1 / 1996 / NIT / M • Intimate Interviews #3 / 1996 / NIT / M • Intimate Interviews #4 / 1996 / NIT / M

TOMMY LA ROC
Caught From Behind #02: The Sequel / 1983 / HO / M • Country Comfort / 1981 / SE / M • Flash / 1980 / CA / M • Hard Worker / cr80 / AVC / M • Limited Edition #16 / 1980 / AVC / M • Mrs. Smith's Erotic Holiday / 1982 / VCX / M • Star Babe / 1977 / CA / M • Undercovers / 1982 / CA / M

TOMMY LEIGH *see Star Index I*

TOMMY LONG
Sugar In The Raw / 1975 / AVC / M

TOMMY T. *see Star Index I*

TOMMY TATAS
Big Busty #45 / 1994 / BTO / S • Girls Around The World #13: Lynn LeMay And Friends / 1994 / BTO / M

TOMMY TOOLE
Bucky Beaver's XXX Dragon Art Theatre Double Feature #13 / 1996 / SOW / M • Tomatoes / cr70 / SOW / M

TOMMY WINCHESTER *see Star Index I*

TOMMY X.
Mellon Man #07 / 1996 / AVI / M

TOMY TAYLOR *see Star Index I*

TON SINTILLA *see Star Index I*

TONDELAYO
Dark Passions #01 / 1993 / AFV / M

TONEY
Courting Libido / 1995 / HIV / G

TONG *see Star Index I*

TONI
A&B GB#023: The Team Is Here / 1992 / A&B / M • African Angels #2 / 1996 / NIT / M • Afro American Dream Girls #1 / 1996 / DR / M • Angie, Trish, Linda, Samantha / 1990 / PLV / B • Art Of Sex / 1992 / FD / M • Back East Babes #3 / 1996 / NIT / M • Banned In Britain / 1995 / VC / M • Blue Vanities #509 / 1992 / FFL / M • Blue Vanities #538 / 1993 / FFL / M • Blue Vanities #577 / 1995 / FFL / M • Blush: Burlez Live! #1 / 1993 / FAT / F • Bobby Hollander's Rookie Nookie #09 / 1993 / SFP / M • Borderline (Vivid) / 1995 / VI / M • Club Deb #4 / 1996 / MET / M • Dangerous Behinds #1 / 1995 / HW / M • Dirty Dancers #8 / 1996 / 4P / M • Double D Dykes #22 / 1995 / GO / F • The Fantasy Realm #1 / 1990 / RUM / M • Hot Body Competition: Beverly Hill's Miniskirt Madness Cont. / 1996 / CG / F • Hot Body Hall Of Fame: Christy Carrera / 1996 / CG / F • Hot Legs #1 / 1990 / PLV / B • Jiggly Queens #3 / 1996 / LE / M • New Ends #03 / 1993 / 4P / M • New Ends #09 / 1994 / 4P / M • Nothing Sacred / 1995 / LE / M • Philmore Butts Lake Poontang / 1996 / SUF / M • Reel Life Video #48: Double D Girlfriends / 1996 / RLF / F • Sex Freaks / 1995 / EA / M • The Show / 1995 / VI / M • SVE: Screentest Sex #3 / 1993 / SVE / M • Swap Meat / 1995 / GLI / M • TV Shoestore Fantasy #1 / 1991 / BIZ / G • TVs In Trouble #2 / 1991 / BIZ / G • Uncle Roy's Amateur Home Video #16 / 1992 / VIM / M • Wrasslin She-Babes #08 / 1996 / SOW / M • Wrasslin She-Babes #09 / 1996 / SOW / M

TONI ADRIAN
Agony Of Love, Lace And Lash / cr73 / SOW / M • Bucky Beaver's XXX Dragon Art Theatre Double Feature #14 / 1996 / SOW / M

TONI ALESSANDRINI
40 The Hard Way / 1991 / OD / M • The Lascivious Ladies Of Dr Lipo / 1991 / OD /

M • Mickey Ray's Sex Search #06 / 1996 / WIV / M • Mind, Body & Soul / 1992 / AIP / S • Thunder And Lightning / 1996 / MID / M • Vice Academy #2 / 1990 / PRS / S • Vice Academy #3 / 1991 / PRS / S

TONI ALLINI *see Star Index I*

TONI BROOKS
Careful, He May Be Watching / 1986 / CA / M • Passions / 1985 / MIT / M

TONI BUSH *see Star Index I*

TONI CHASE
America's Raunchiest Home Videos #34: The Big Splash / 1992 / ZA / M • Anal Therapy #1 / 1992 / FD / M • Beach Bum Amateur's #12 / 1992 / MID / M • Beach Bum Amateur's #15 / 1992 / MID / M • Beach Bum Amateur's #16 / 1992 / MID / M • Biff Malibu's Totally Nasty Home Videos #12 / 1992 / ANA / M • Bondage Beginner / 1993 / BON / B • Double D Dykes #04 / 1992 / GO / F • Manwiched / 1992 / FPI / M • Native Tongue / 1993 / VI / M • New Girls In Town #2 / 1992 / CC / M • Odyssey 30 Min: #196: The Adorable Toni Chase / 1991 / OD / M • Our Bang #08 / 1992 / GLI / M • Our Bang #10 / 1993 / GLI / M • Positively Pagan #01 / 1991 / ATA / M • Positively Pagan #04 / 1991 / ATA / M • Raging Hormones / 1992 / LE / M • Soda Jerk / 1992 / ZA / M • Wild Flower #2 / 1992 / VI / M

TONI CHAVEZ *see Star Index I*

TONI CHRISTIAN *see Kim Alexis*

TONI COUCHEZ
Girls, Girls, Girls, Girls / 1993 / FD / C • Midnight Fantasies / 1992 / VIM / M • Zane's World / 1992 / ZA / M

TONI HINZ
Filthy First Timers #7 / 1997 / EL / M

TONI JAMES (Loni James)
Pretty blonde with shoulder length hair, lithe tight body, tight waist, small tits, nice little butt. 20 years old in 1996 and at that time girlfriend of Steve Drake. Comes from Englewood CA.
Euroflesh: Dentro Il Vulcano / 1996 / SC / M • Th Fanny / 1997 / WP / M • Fashion Passion / 1997 / TEP / M • Nasty Nymphos #16 / 1996 / ANA / M • The Phantom Of The Montague Stage / 1997 / HO / M • Pick Up Lines #12 / 1997 / OD / M • Real Sex Magazine #02 / 1997 / HO / M • Sweet Revenge / 1997 / KBE / M

TONI KERNES *see Star Index I*

TONI LEE
Loose Times At Ridley High / 1984 / VCX / M • Saturday Matinee Series #4 / 1996 / VCX / C

TONI LEE OLIVER
The Girls On F Street / 1966 / AVC / B

TONI LYNN *see Star Index I*

TONI MOE *see Star Index I*

TONI MORENO
Sex Roulette / 1979 / CA / M

TONI O'BRIEN
Dixie Debutantes #1 / 1996 / MYS / M

TONI PANTHER
The Sexaholic / 1988 / VC / M

TONI RAM
Live Bi-Me / 1990 / PL / G

TONI RAY *see Tawny Rae*

TONI RENEE *see Star Index I*

TONI RIBAS
Club Privado / 1995 / KP / M

TONI ROAM *see Star Index I*

TONI ROME
Sex Wish / 1976 / CV / M

TONI SCOTT *(Angela Dermer)*
This girl looks very like Marlene Willoughby (see **Passions Of Carol**).
Meter Maids / 1974 / SIL / M • The Passions Of Carol / 1975 / VXP / M • The Pleasure Masters / 1975 / AST / M • Satisfaction Guaranteed / 1972 / AXV / M

TONI STARK see Star Index I

TONI STARR see Star Index I

TONI STEINER
The Girls In The Band / 1976 / SVE / M

TONI THOMAS see Star Index I

TONI WOLFE
The Whipped Voyeur's Lesbian Sex Show / 1994 / PL / F

TONIE STORIE
Snatch Masters #03 / 1994 / LEI / M

TONISHA
Butthole Bunnies / 1996 / ROB / F • U Witness: Video Three-Pak #3 / 1995 / MSP / M

TONISHA MILLS
Not too pretty blonde. After one performance (see **MDD #25**) she had a nose and breast job. She is (after breast enhancement) 34DD-25-34, 110 lbs 5'3" and is aged 21 in 1992. In May 7, 1994 she gave birth to a baby girl. Returned in 1997 with badly stretched watermelons and the usual attitude of a too-old performer. Small tattoo on left ankle.
Alone And Dripping / 1991 / LV / M • Amateur Hours #46 / 1992 / AFI / M • Ambitious Blondes / 1992 / VIM / M • America's Dirtiest Home Videos #05 / 1991 / VEX / M • America's Dirtiest Home Videos #08 / 1992 / VEX / M • America's Dirtiest Home Videos #11 / 1992 / VEX / M • Anal Adventures #3: Can Her! / 1991 / VC / M • Bazooka County #4 / 1992 / CC / M • Bi Dream Of Genie / 1990 / BIN / G • Big Busty Major Babes / 1996 / NAP / F • Bikini City / 1991 / CC / M • Butt's Motel #5 / 1990 / EX / M • Candy Stripers #4 / 1990 / AR / M • Carnal Possessions / 1991 / VEX / M • Cheek Busters / 1990 / FH / M • Dane's Surprise / 1991 / IF / G • Deep Dreams / 1990 / IN / M • Dirty Dave's American Amateurs #13 / 1992 / AR / M • The Dong Show #03 / 1990 / AMB / M • Drink Of Love / 1990 / V99 / M • Ejacula #1 / 1992 / VC / M • Ejacula #2 / 1992 / VC / M • Encino Woman / 1992 / VIM / M • Every Man Should Have One / 1991 / VEX / M • Excitable / 1992 / IF / M • The Fire Down Below / 1992 / CDI / M • Fresh Tits Of Bel Air / 1992 / OD / M • Good Girls, Naughty Nights / 1996 / LEI / C • Halloweenie / 1991 / PL / M • Hannibal Lickter / 1992 / MID / M • Hard Feelings / 1991 / V99 / M • Have I Got A Girl For You / 1989 / VEX / M • Heartbreaker / 1991 / IF / M • Heavenly Hooters / 1994 / IF / M • Hot Cherries / 1990 / CC / F • House Of Spartacus #1 / 1993 / IF / M • House Of Spartacus #2 / 1993 / IF / M • How To Love Your Lover / 1992 / XII / S • Impulse #03: Evening In Venice / 1995 / MBP / M • Impulse #09: / 1996 / MBP / M • Insatiable Nurses / 1992 / VIM / M • Laid Off / 1990 / CA / M • The Lethal Squirt / 1990 / AR / M • Man Of Steel / 1992 / IF / M • Married With Hormones #2 / 1992 / PL / M • The Merry Widows / 1993 / VC / M • Mind Games / 1992 / CDI / M • More Dirty Debutantes #25 / 1993 / 4P / M • Naked Buns 8 1/2 / 1992 / CC / M • Nice Fuckin' Movie! / 1997 / EL / M • No Men 4 Miles / 1992 / LV

/ F • Odyssey Amateur #75: Sindy! / 1991 / OD / M • The Party / 1992 / CDI / M • Queen Of Midnight / 1991 / V99 / M • Rear Estates / 1991 / … / M • Ride 'em Cowgirl / 1991 / V99 / M • Scenes From A Crystal Ball / 1992 / ZA / M • Sex Acts & Video Tape / 1990 / AFV / M • Sex She Wrote / 1991 / VEX / M • The Sexual Limits / 1992 / VC / M • Sexvision / 1992 / HO / M • She's The Boss / 1992 / VIM / M • Skin Games / 1991 / VEX / C • Sodomania #21: Degenerate Lifestyles! / 1997 / EL / M • Surfside Sex #1 / 1991 / LV / F • Surfside Sex #2 / 1992 / LV / M • Tiffany And Tonisha, Lover Girls / 1993 / LEI / F • Titty Slickers #1 / 1991 / LE / M • Toppers #21 / 1993 / TV / C • Toppers #24 / 1994 / TV / M • Toppers #31 / 1994 / TV / C • Torrid Tonisha / 1992 / VEX / M • Two Women & A Man / 1991 / VEX / C • Untamed Passion / 1991 / VEX / M • Wacs / 1992 / PP / M • Wet Paint / 1990 / DR / M • Whoppers #3 / 1993 / VEX / F • The Wild Wild Chest #3 / 1996 / HO / C

TONNY
Hollywood Amateurs #21 / 1995 / MID / M

TONTALAYA
Black Clits And White Dicks / cr86 / JAN / M • Ebony & Ivory Sisters / 1985 / PL / C • Lusty Licking Lesbians / 198? / JAN / F

TONY
Amateur Nights #15 / 1997 / HO / M • AVP #9139: At Home / 1991 / AVP / M • Bizarre Fantasies / 1983 / BIZ / B • Bus Stop Tales #02 / 1989 / PRI / M • California Girl: Amateur Nude Auditions / 1995 / PME / S • Cindy Puts Out / 1996 / OLL / M • FTV #13: Crotch Crunch / 1996 / FT / B • FTV #28: Femme Fatale / Black & Blue / 1996 / FT / B • FTV #29: Boss Lady And Black & Blue / 1996 / FT / B • FTV #47: Hold Me Hurt Me / 1996 / FT / B • FTV #56: Leg Lock Of Love / 1996 / FT / B • Gigi Gives It Away / 1995 / FRF / M • Hardcore Male/Female Oil Wrestling / 1996 / JSP / M • Hollywood Amateurs #03 / 1994 / MID / M • Hollywood Amateurs #04 / 1994 / MID / M • Hollywood Amateurs #06 / 1994 / MID / M • Home-Grown Video #434: Forrest Hump / 1994 / HOV / M • HomeGrown Video #461: Splendor In The Grasp / 1995 / HOV / M • It Could Happen To You / 1996 / HW / M • Mistress Brigit's Footsteps / 1993 / NEP / B • Next Door Neighbors #05 / 1989 / BON / M • She Studs #05 / 1990 / BIZ / G • Titties 'n Cream #1 / 1994 / FC / M • Titty Town #2 / 1995 / HW / M • Veronica The Screenwriting Hooker / 1996 / LE / M

TONY ALTERA
Alana: A Gang Bang Fantasy / 1993 / FC / M • Breastman's Triple X Cellent Adventure / 1995 / EVN / M • Country & Western Cuties #2: Naked Pie Eating Contest / 1996 / EVN / M • Jingle Balls / 1996 / EVN / M

TONY BELIZE
Julia Ann: Superstar / 1995 / WAV / M • The Stiff / 1995 / WAV / M

TONY BELMONTE
The Best Little He/She House In Texas / 1993 / HSV / G • Bi Watch / 1994 / BIN / G • Bi-Sex Pleasures / 1993 / PL / G • Bone Appetit: A She-Male Seduction / 1994 / BIZ / G • A Decent Proposal / 1993 / BIL / G • Defiant TV's / 1994 / BIZ / G • Gilligan's Bi-Land / 1994 / PL / G • Man In Chains / 1995 / HOM / B • Married With She-Males / 1993

/ PL / G • Mistresses At War #01 / 1993 / BIZ / B • Mistresses At War #02 / 1993 / BIZ / B • Queens From Outer Space / 1993 / HSV / G • She's The Boss / 1993 / BIL / G • She-Mails / 1993 / PL / G • She-Male Trouble / 1994 / HEA / G • Sizzling She Males / 1995 / MET / G • Transexual Blvd / 1994 / PL / G • Transsexual Passions #2 / 1994 / BIZ / G • Transvestite Tour Guide / 1993 / HSV / G • TV Panty Party / 1994 / BIZ / G

TONY BINDER see Star Index I

TONY BLUE
Invasion Of The Love Drones / 1977 / ALP / M • The Vixens Of Kung Fu: A Tale Of Yin Yang / 1975 / VC / M

TONY BOND see Star Index I

TONY BROOKS see Star Index I

TONY BULLET
The Crackster / 1996 / OUP / M

TONY BURKE see Star Index I

TONY CASSANO
Carnal Olympics / 1983 / CA / M

TONY CHRISTIAN see Kim Alexis

TONY COHN
Teenage Cruisers / 1977 / VCX / M

TONY COLLINS
The Fantasy Booth / 1993 / ONA / M

TONY COLUMBO
The Butt Sisters Do Daytona / 1995 / MID / M • N.Y. Video Magazine #02 / 1995 / OUP / M

TONY CORTEZ
A Dirty Western #2: Smoking Guns / 1994 / CV / M

TONY CUMMINGS see Star Index I

TONY DAVID see Star Index I

TONY DAVIS
All Hands On Dick / 1988 / STA / G • Bi 'n' Sell / 1990 / VC / G • Bi Mistake / 1989 / VI / G • Blow Bi Blow / 1988 / MET / G • Hotel Transylvania #2 / 1990 / LIP / G • Hung Guns / 1988 / STA / G • Innocent Bi Standers / 1989 / LV / G • Matters In Hand / 1989 / STA / G • Sex Crazed / 1989 / VEX / M • Sharon And Karen / 1989 / LV / G • She-Male Cocksuckers / 1993 / LEO / G • She-Male Nurse / 1989 / LV / G • TV Training Center / 1993 / LEO / G

TONY DEE
Black Heat / 1986 / VCR / C • Long From Dong / 1995 / FH / M • Toe Tales #01 / 1992 / GOT / B • Wet Kisses / 1988 / V99 / M

TONY DEPRIMA see Star Index I

TONY DEXTER see Star Index I

TONY DOBBS see Star Index I

TONY DOUGLASS see Star Index I

TONY EL-LAY
The Best Little Whorehouse In Beverly Hills / 1986 / CDI / M • Black 'n' Blew / 1988 / VC / M • Black 'n' White In Color / 1987 / VCR / C • Black Bad Girls / 1985 / PLY / M • Black Beauties / 1987 / SE / C • Black Heat / 1986 / VCR / C • Black Jailbait / 1984 / PL / M • Black Lava / 1986 / WET / M • Black Taboo #1 / 1984 / JVV / M • Blacks Have More Fun / 1985 / AVC / M • Chocolate Candy #1 / 1984 / VD / M • Chocolate Delights #1 / 1985 / TAG / C • Chocolate Delights #2 / 1985 / TAG / C • Dark Brothers, Dark Sisters / 1986 / VCS / C • Ebony Orgies / 1987 / SE / C • Ebony Superstars / 1988 / VC / C • Foxy Brown / 1984 / VC / M • French Cleaners / 1986 / VCR / M • The Godmother #1 / 1987 / VC / M • The Godmother #2 / 1988 / VC / M •

Philmore Butts Meets The Freak / 1995 / SUF / M • Philmore Butts Meets The Palm Beach Nymphomaniac Kathy Wille / 1995 / SUF / M • Philmore Butts On The Prowl / 1995 / SUF / M • Philmore Butts Spring Break / 1996 / SUF / M • Philmore Butts Strikes Gold / 1996 / SUF / M • Pick Up Lines #03 / 1995 / 4P / M • Picture Me Naked / 1993 / LE / M • Playin' Hard To Get / 1994 / VEX / M • Pleasure Party (Gourmet) / 1985 / GO / M • A Pool Party At Seymores #1 / 1995 / ULI / M • Poop Dreams / 1995 / ULP / M • Porsche Lynn, Every Man's Dream / 1988 / CC / C • Precious Cargo / 1993 / VIM / M • Prime Choice #1 / 1995 / RAS / M • Private Request / 1994 / GLI / M • Pussy Hunt #12 / 1995 / LEI / M • Pussy Hunt #14 / 1995 / LEI / M • Pussyman #05: Captive Audience / 1994 / SNA / M • Pussyman Auditions #03 / 1995 / SNA / M • Pussyman Auditions #04 / 1995 / SNA / M • Pussyman Auditions #06 / 1995 / SNA / M • Pussyman Auditions #23 / 1996 / SNA / M • Queen Of Hearts #3: Heartless / 1992 / PL / M • Quickies / 1992 / AFV / M • Racially Motivated / 1994 / LV / M • Read My Lips: No More Bush / 1992 / HW / M • Rear Ended / 1995 / WV / M • Rear Entry / 1995 / LEI / M • Rear Window / 1996 / NIT / M • Red On The Noodle Like A Swance On A Poodle / 1990 / FC / C • Renegades #2 / 1995 / SC / M • The Ribald Tales Of Canterbury / 1986 / CA / M • Ripe & Ready (Infinity) / 1995 / IF / M • Rock Groupies In Heat / 1995 / LV / M • Roller Babes / 1996 / ERA / M • Rump Reamers / 1994 / TTV / M • Rump-Shaker #2 / 1993 / HW / M • Sabrina Starlet / 1994 / SC / M • Satin Finish / 1985 / SUV / M • Savage Fury #1 / 1985 / VEX / M • Savage Fury #3 / 1994 / VEX / M • Secret Seductions #1 / 1995 / LV / M • Secret Seductions #2 / 1995 / ULP / M • Secrets / 1984 / HO / M • The Seductress / 1992 / ZA / M • Sex Beat / 1985 / WV / M • The Sex Dancer / 1986 / NSV / M • Sex Detective / 1994 / LV / M • Sex On The Beach Hawaiian Style #1 / 1995 / ULP / M • Sex On The Beach Hawaiian Style #2 / 1995 / ULP / M • Sex Scientist / 1992 / FD / M • Sex Star Competition / 1985 / PL / M • Sex The Hard Way / 1985 / CV / M • Sex, Truth & Videotape #1 / 1995 / DOC / M • Sex, Truth & Videotape #2 / 1996 / DOC / M • Sexline You're On The Air / 1986 / CAT / M • Sexorcist / 1994 / HW / M • Seymore Butts & The Honeymooners / 1992 / FH / M • Seymore Butts Goes Deep Inside Shane / 1994 / FH / M • Seymore Butts Rides Again / 1992 / FH / M • Seymore Butts Swings / 1992 / FH / M • Seymore Butts: Bustin' Out My Best Anal / 1995 / FH / C • Seymore Butts: My Travels With The Tramp / 1994 / FH / M • Sheer Ecstasy / 1993 / IF / M • Show Business / 1995 / LV / M • Sinfully Yours / 1984 / HO / M • Sins Of Wealthy Wives / 1989 / CDI / C • Six Plus One #2 / 1993 / VEX / C • Ski Sluts / 1995 / LV / M • Skin Dive / 1996 / SC / M • Skin Games / 1991 / VEX / C • Sleeping With Seattle / 1993 / LV / M • Slippery When Wet / 1986 / PL / M • Sluts In Suburbia / 1994 / GLI / M • Smeers / 1992 / PL / M • Smoke & Mirrors / 1996 / PL / M • Snow Bunnies #1 / 1995 / SC / M • Snow Bunnies #2 / 1995 / SC / M • Soap Me Up! / 1993 / FD / M • Sorority Sex Kittens #1 / 1992 /

VC / M • Spanish Fly / 1993 / VEX / M • Spies / 1986 / PL / M • Squirt Squad / 1995 / AMP / M • Starbangers #06 / 1994 / FPI / M • Steele Butt / 1993 / AFV / M • Straight A's / 1994 / AMP / M • Street Girl Named Desire / 1992 / FD / M • Striptease / 1995 / SPI / M • Suburban Nymphos / 1994 / ATL / M • Suburban Swingers / 1993 / IF / M • Summertime Boobs / 1994 / LEI / M • Sweet Cheeks / 1987 / VCR / C • Swinging Couples #04 / 1994 / GO / M • A Tale Of Two Titties #2 / 1992 / AFV / M • Tampa Spice / 1996 / SUF / M • The Teacher's Pet / 1993 / LV / M • Temperatures Rising / 1986 / VT / M • The Temple Of Poon / 1996 / PE / M • The Thief / 1994 / SC / M • This Could Be The Night / 1993 / IF / M • Thunder And Lightning / 1996 / MID / M • Thunder Road / 1995 / SC / M • Tight Spot / 1996 / WV / M • Tinseltown Wives / 1992 / AFV / M • Tonight's The Night / 1992 / V99 / M • The Tonya Hard-On Story / 1994 / GO / M • Too Cute For Words / 1992 / V99 / M • Top Debs #5: Deb Of The Month / 1994 / GO / M • Top Heavy / 1993 / IF / M • Topless Brain Surgeons / 1995 / LE / M • Tracy In Heaven (Orig 1985) / 1985 / WV / M • Tracy In Heaven (Rewrite) / 1986 / WV / M • Trash In The Can / 1993 / LV / M • Treasure Chest / 1994 / LV / M • Trick Shots / 1995 / PV / M • Tropical Taboo / 1995 / HO / M • The Trouble With Traci / 1984 / CHA / C • Tunnel Of Lust / 1993 / LV / M • Twice As Hard / 1992 / IF / M • Ultimate Gang Bang #1 / 1994 / HW / M • The Ultimate Squirting Machine / 1994 / FPI / M • Unbalanced Chemicals / 1996 / SUF / M • Uncle Roy's Amateur Home Video #11 / 1992 / VIM / M • Uncle Roy's Amateur Home Video #12 / 1992 / VIM / M • Up & In / 1985 / AA / M • Up The Middle / 1995 / V99 / M • Up To No Good / 1986 / CDI / M • Video Paradise / 1988 / ZA / M • Video Virgins #21 / 1995 / NS / M • Video Virgins #23 / 1995 / NS / M • Virgin / 1993 / HW / M • Visions #1 / 1995 / ERA / M • Visions #2 / 1995 / ERA / M • The Visualizer / 1992 / VC / M • Vote Pink / 1984 / VD / M • Wacky Weekend / 1995 / SUF / M • Walk On The Wild Side / 1994 / VIM / M • Waves Of Passion / 1996 / ERA / M • The Way They Wuz / 1996 / SHS / C • Welcome To Paradise / 1994 / IF / M • Wet & Wicked / 1992 / VEX / M • Wet Faces #1 / 1997 / SC / C • Wet, Wild And Willing / 1993 / V99 / M • Whispered Lies / 1993 / LBO / M • Whorelock / 1993 / LV / M • Wide Open / 1994 / GLI / M • Wild Desires / 1994 / MAX / M • Wilde At Heart / 1992 / VEX / M • Wilde Palms / 1994 / XCI / M • The Woman In Pink / 1984 / SE / M • Women Who Love Men, Men Who Love Women / 1993 / FD / C • The X-Terminator / 1986 / PV / M • Yin Yang Oriental Love Bang #1 / 1996 / SUF / M • Yin Yang Oriental Love Bang #2 / 1996 / SUF / M • You're The Boss / 1985 / VD / M

TONY MAZZIOTTI *see Star Index I*

TONY MONTANA *(Tony Romano, JoJo (Tony Montana), Julio (Tony Montana), Julio Gonzales)*

Tony Romana is from **Jane Bond Meets Octopussy**. Married to Sandra Sommers in late 1996 and then divorced.

The Adultress / 1987 / CA / M • The Adventures Of Buttgirl & Wonder Wench / 1991 / AFV / M • AHV #02: Orgy Express /

1991 / EVN / M • AHV #03: Porking In The Rear / 1991 / EVN / M • AHV #33: To The Baja And Back / 1993 / EVN / M • AHV #34: Ring My Bell / 1993 / EVN / M • Aja / 1988 / PL / M • Amazing Tails #1 / 1987 / CA / M • Amazing Tails #3 / 1987 / CA / M • Amber Lynn's Hotline 976 / 1987 / VCR / M • Anal 247 / 1995 / CC / M • Anal Angels #2 / 1990 / VEX / C • Anal Brat / 1993 / FL / M • Anal House Party / 1993 / IP / M • Anal Nation #2 / 1990 / CC / M • Anal Playground / 1995 / CA / M • Anal Pleasures / 1988 / AVC / M • Anal Virgins Of America #07 / 1994 / FOR / M • Angelica / 1989 / ARG / M • As Cute As They Cum / 1990 / VEX / M • As Nasty As She Wants To Be / 1990 / IN / M • Assmania!! #2 / 1995 / ME / M • Assuming The Position / 1989 / V99 / M • Backdoor Club #1 / 1996 / VEX / C • Backdoor Smugglers / 1994 / JAV / M • Backdoor To Harley-Wood #2 / 1990 / AFV / M • The Backpackers #3 / 1991 / IN / M • Backstage Pass / 1994 / SC / M • Bad Medicine / 1990 / VEX / M • Bar-B-Que Gang Bang / 1994 / JMP / M • Bazooka County #2 / 1989 / CC / M • Bed, Butts & Breakfast / 1990 / LV / M • Bedtime Stories / 1996 / VC / M • Before She Says I Do / 1984 / MAP / M • Behind The Backdoor #3 / 1989 / EVN / M • Between A Rock And A Hot Place / 1989 / VEX / M • Beverly Hills Geisha / 1992 / V99 / M • Beyond The Senses / 1986 / AVC / M • The Bi Spy / 1991 / STA / G • Biff Malibu's Totally Nasty Home Videos #33 / 1993 / ANA / M • Big Bad Biker Bitches / 1994 / TTV / M • Black Sensations / 1987 / VEX / M • Blue Fire / 1991 / V99 / M • Blue Heaven / 1990 / IF / M • Blue Lace / 1986 / SE / M • Bo-Dacious / 1989 / V99 / M • Bobby Hollander's Maneaters #10 / 1993 / SFP / M • Bobby Hollander's Rookie Nookie #04 / 1993 / SFP / M • Body Triple / 1991 / VC / M • The Book / 1990 / IF / M • Borderline (Vivid) / 1995 / VI / M • The Bottom Line / 1986 / WV / M • The Brazilian Connection / 1988 / CA / M • Breakfast With Tiffany / 1990 / HO / M • Breast Worx #03 / 1991 / LBO / M • Brooklyn Nights / 1994 / OD / M • Bun Busters #14 / 1994 / LBO / M • Bunny Bleu: A Gang Bang Fantasy / 1994 / FC / M • Burgundy Blues / 1993 / MET / M • The Butt, The Boobs, The Lips / 1996 / C69 / M • The Buttnicks #1 / 1990 / VEX / M • California Blondes #01 / 1986 / VEX / M • California Blondes #03 / 1991 / VD / C • California Blondes #06 / 1992 / VD / C • Camera Shy / 1990 / IN / M • Carnal Possessions / 1991 / VEX / M • Catfights #3 / 1987 / OHV / B • Caught From Behind #10 / 1989 / HO / M • Cheerleader Academy / 1986 / PL / M • Chills / 1989 / LV / M • Club Head (EVN) #2 / 1989 / EVN / C • College Girl / 1990 / VEX / M • Colossal Orgy #1 / 1993 / HW / M • Coming Alive / 1988 / LV / M • Coming Attractions / 1995 / WHP / M • Coming In America / 1988 / VEX / M • Con Jobs / 1990 / V99 / M • Confessions Of A Chauffeur / 1990 / DR / M • Cream Dreams / 1986 / VEX / M • Creamy Cheeks / 1986 / VEX / M • Cumming Clean / 1991 / FL / M • Daddy's Girls / 1985 / LA / M • The Dane Harlow Story / 1990 / IF / M • Dane's Brothel / 1990 / IF / G • Dane's Party / 1991 / IF / G • Dane's Surprise / 1991 / IF / G • Dangerous / 1989 / PV / M

• Dark Side Of The Moon / 1986 / VD / M • Deep In Deanna Jones / 1989 / EVN / M • Deep In The Bush / 1990 / KIS / M • Deep Throat #4 / 1990 / AR / M • Depraved / 1990 / IN / M • The Desk Top Dolls / 1990 / BAD / C • Desperado / 1994 / SC / M • Dirty Blondes / 1986 / CDI / M • Dirty Harriet / 1986 / SAT / M • Dirty Tricks / 1990 / VEX / M • Double Dicked #1 / 1996 / RAS / M • Double Trouble / 1988 / V99 / M • Double Whammy / 1986 / LA / M • Double Your Pleasure / 1989 / VEX / M • Dreams Cum True / 1990 / HO / M • Erotic Dreams / 1987 / HO / M • Every Man's Fancy / 1991 / V99 / M • Every Woman Has A Secret / 1991 / ROB / M • The Fabulous 50's Girls #1 / 1994 / EMC / M • Fantasy Drive / 1990 / VEX / M • Fantasy Fuchs / 1996 / PLP / C • Feel The Heat / 1989 / VEX / M • Flesh In Ecstasy #01: Blondie / 1987 / GO / C • Flesh In Ecstasy #04: Jeanna Fine / 1987 / GO / C • Flesh In Ecstasy #12: Blondie / 1987 / GO / C • Forbidden Subjects #2 / 1994 / FC / M • Foreign Bodies / 1991 / IN / M • Four Screws And An Anal / 1994 / NEY / M • Games Women Play / 1995 / XC / M • The Gang Bang Story / 1993 / IP / M • Gang Bang Virgin #2 / 1995 / HO / M • Gangbang Girl #01 / 1992 / ANA / M • Gangbang Girl #02 / 1992 / ANA / M • Gangbang Girl #09 / 1993 / ANA / M • Gangbang Girl #10 / 1993 / ANA / M • Gangbang Girl #11 / 1993 / ANA / M • Gangbang Girl #12 / 1993 / ANA / M • Gangbang Girl #13 / 1994 / ANA / M • Gangland Bangers / 1995 / VC / M • The Gentlemen's Club / 1986 / WV / M • Girls Of The Bamboo Palace / 1989 / VEX / M • Girlz In The Hood #3: Erotic Justice / 1993 / HW / M • Going Down With Amber / 1987 / 4P / M • Hard At Work / 1989 / VEX / M • Hard Choices / 1987 / CA / M • Hard Core Beginners #03 / 1995 / LEI / M • Having It All / 1991 / VEX / M • Head Nurse / 1996 / RAS / M • Heather's Secrets / 1990 / VEX / M • Helen & Louise / 1996 / HDE / M • The Hitch-Hiker #15: Cat & Mouse / 1995 / VIM / M • Holly Does Hollywood #4 / 1990 / CAY / M • Hollywood Hustle #2 / 1990 / V99 / M • Honkytonk Angels / 1988 / IN / C • Hot Dreams / 1989 / VEX / M • Hot Savannah Nights / 1991 / VEX / M • Hot Services / 1989 / WET / M • Hot Summer Nites / 1988 / VEX / M • Hot Tight Asses #11 / 1995 / TCK / M • Humongous Squirting Knockers / 1992 / CA / C • Hurts So Good / 1991 / VEX / M • Hyapatia Lee's Sexy / 1986 / SE / M • I Dream Of Christy / 1989 / CAY / M • I Love Juicy / 1993 / ZA / M • In Pursuit Of Passion / 1990 / V99 / M • Indecent / 1993 / XCI / M • It Happened At Midnight / 1990 / IN / M • Jane Bond Meets Octopussy / 1986 / VD / M • Jewel Of The Orient / 1991 / VEX / M • Juicy Cheerleaders / 1995 / LE / M • Junkyard Anal / 1994 / JAV / M • Just Between Friends / 1988 / VEX / M • Keep It Cumming / 1990 / V99 / M • Keyhole #167: Ass Eaters / 1989 / KEH / M • Knights In Black Satin / 1990 / VEX / M • Lactamania #1 / 1994 / TTV / M • Ladies Man / 1990 / REB / M • The Ladies Room / 1987 / CA / M • Lady Badass / 1990 / V99 / M • Lady Of The House / 1990 / VEX / M • The Last Blonde / 1991 / IN / M • Lay Lady Lay / 1991 / VEX / M • Leading Lady / 1991 / V99 / M • Life Is Butt A Dream /

1989 / V99 / M • Lingerie / 1996 / RAS / M • A Little Dove-Tale / 1987 / IN / M • Little Shop Of Whores / 1987 / VI / M • Living In Sin / 1990 / VEX / M • Lonely Is The Night / 1990 / V99 / M • Looking For Love / 1991 / VEX / M • Loose Caboose / 1987 / 4P / M • Loose Lifestyles / 1988 / CA / M • Love On The Borderline / 1987 / IN / M • Love On The Line / 1990 / SO / M • Love Thirsty / 1990 / IN / M • Lucy Has A Ball / 1987 / ME / M • Lucy Makes It Big / 1987 / ME / M • Lust Letters / 1988 / CA / M • Lustful Obsessions / 1996 / NOT / M • Mad Love / 1988 / VC / M • Madame X / 1989 / EVN / M • The Mark Of Zara / 1990 / XCI / M • Masked Ball / 1992 / IF / M • Miami Spice #1 / 1987 / CA / M • Milli Vanilla / 1994 / TP / M • Mindsex / 1993 / MPA / M • Mistress Memoirs #2 / 1993 / PL / C • The Model / 1991 / HO / M • Model Wife / 1991 / CA / M • The Most Dangerous Game / 1996 / HO / M • Mr. Peepers Amateur Home Videos #12: Like It! Lick It! / 1991 / LBO / M • Mr. Peepers Amateur Home Videos #76: Sixty Nine Plus Seven / 1993 / LBO / M • Mr. Peepers Amateur Home Videos #82: Born To Swing! / 1993 / LBO / M • Mr. Peepers Amateur Home Videos #89: Stiffy Stuffer / 1994 / LBO / M • Mr. Peepers Amateur Home Videos #90: Back Door Bonanza / 1994 / LBO / M • My 500 Pound Vibrator / 1991 / LV / C • The Naked Truth / 1990 / SE / M • Nasty Nymphos #03 / 1994 / ANA / M • Nasty Nymphos #04 / 1994 / ANA / M • Nasty Nymphos #06 / 1994 / ANA / M • Nasty Nymphos #09 / 1995 / ANA / M • Nasty Reputation / 1991 / VEX / M • Naughty Neighbors / 1986 / VEX / M • Nena Cherry's Dp Gang Bang / 1996 / NIT / M • The New Ass Masters #11 / 1996 / LEI / C • The New Butt Hunt #13 / 1995 / LEI / C • New Girls In Town #3 / 1993 / CC / M • The New Snatch Masters #20 / 1996 / LEI / C • New Wave Hookers #2 / 1991 / VC / M • The Night Of The Coyote / 1993 / MED / M • Night Vibes / 1990 / KNI / M • Nina Does 'em All / 1988 / 3HV / C • No Strings Attached / 1990 / ERO / M • Object(s) Of My Desire / 1988 / V99 / M • Old Throat And D.P. / 1993 / FC / M • One Of These Nights / 1991 / V99 / M • Opportunity Knocks / 1990 / HO / M • Parliament: Blondes Have More Fun / 1989 / PM / C • Parliament: California Blondes #1 / 1987 / PM / F • Passion Prescription / 1990 / V99 / M • Patty Plenty's Gang Bang / 1995 / NIT / M • The Perfect Pet / 1991 / VEX / C • Philmore Butts Meets The Freak / 1995 / SUF / M • The Pillowman / 1988 / VC / M • Positions Wanted / 1990 / VI / M • Positive Positions / 1989 / VEX / M • Power Of The Pussy / 1995 / LEI / M • Princess Of The Night / 1990 / VD / M • Princess Of Thieves / 1994 / SC / M • Promises In The Dark / 1991 / CIN / G • Proposals / 1988 / CC / M • Pumping Irene #1 / 1986 / FAN / M • Pumping Irene #2 / 1986 / FAN / M • Purple Haze / 1991 / WV / M • Pussyman Auditions #01 / 1995 / SNA / M • Pussyman Auditions #09 / 1995 / SNA / M • Pussyman Auditions #10 / 1995 / SNA / M • Pussyman Auditions #14 / 1995 / SNA / M • Putting On The Ritz / 1990 / VEX / M • Radioactive / 1990 / VIP / M • Raw Silk / 1996 / RAS / M • Rear Admiral / 1990 / ZA / M • Rear Entry / 1995 / LEI / M • Rearbusters / 1988 / LVI

/ C • Reckless Passion / 1986 / ME / M • Riding Miss Daisy / 1990 / VEX / M • A Rising Star / 1991 / HO / M • Risque Business / 1989 / V99 / M • The Rock Hard Files / 1991 / VEX / M • Ron Hightower's White Chicks #11 / 1994 / LBO / M • Rump Humpers / 1985 / WET / M • Savage Fury #2 / 1989 / CAY / M • The Scent Of Samantha / 1988 / VEX / C • Scorched / 1995 / ONA / M • The Seduction Of Marylin Star / 1995 / VT / M • Send Me An Angel / 1990 / V99 / M • Seriously Anal / 1996 / ONA / M • Sex Aliens / 1987 / CA / M • Sex Crazed / 1989 / VEX / M • Sex Express / 1991 / SE / M • Sex On The Town / 1989 / V99 / M • Sex She Wrote / 1991 / VEX / M • Sexual Persuasion / 1991 / V99 / M • Shaved Sinners #2 / 1987 / VT / M • Sheets Of San Francisco / 1986 / AVC / M • Snow White And The Seven Weenies / 1989 / FAN / M • Sodomania #12: Raw Filth / 1995 / EL / M • Sodomania: Slop Shots / 1996 / EL / C • Soft And Wild / 1991 / LV / M • Soft Caresses / 1988 / VEX / M • Some Like It Hard / 1995 / VC / M • Space Virgins / 1990 / VEX / M • Space Vixens / 1987 / V99 / M • Spanish Rose / 1991 / VEX / M • Special Reserve / 1994 / VC / M • The Squirt Bunny / 1989 / ERU / M • Stand-In Studs / 1989 / V99 / M • Star 90 / 1990 / CAY / M • Stasha's Diary / 1991 / CIN / G • Steam Heat / 1989 / VEX / M • Suburban Seduction / 1991 / HO / M • Supersluts Of Wrestling / 1986 / VD / M • Sure Bet / 1995 / CV / M • Suzie Superstar #3 / 1989 / CV / M • Sweat #1 / 1986 / PP / M • Sweat Shop / 1991 / EVN / M • Swedish Erotica #73 / 1986 / CA / M • Swedish Erotica #85 / 1995 / CA / M • Sweet Sensations / 1989 / SEX / M • Sweet Temptations / 1989 / V99 / M • Swing & Swap #02 / 1990 / CDI / M • Taija's Satin Seduction / 1987 / CDI / M • Tail Of The Scorpion / 1990 / ELP / M • Tail Taggers #123 / 1994 / WV / M • A Taste Of Ariel / 1989 / PIN / C • A Taste Of Madison / 1992 / VD / C • A Taste Of Purple Passion / 1990 / CA / C • A Taste Of Stephanie / 1990 / PIN / C • Taxi Girls #3: Killer On The Loose / 1993 / MED / M • Taxi Girls #4: Daughter Of Lust / 1994 / CA / M • Teach Me Tonight / 1990 / VEX / M • Teasers: Heavenly Bodies / 1988 / MET / M • Teasers: Hot Pursuit / 1988 / MET / M • Telemates / 1988 / STA / M • Telemates / 1991 / V99 / M • Tequilla Sunset / 1989 / V99 / M • Thy Neighbour's Wife / 1986 / DR / M • Tia's Holiday Gang Bang / 1995 / HO / M • Tight Fit #03 / 1994 / GO / M • Tight Fit #04 / 1994 / GO / M • Tight Fit #05 / 1994 / GO / M • To Live & Shave In LA / 1986 / WET / M • Tobianna: A Gang Bang Fantasy / 1993 / FC / M • Tonight's The Night / 1992 / V99 / M • Too Hot To Stop / 1989 / V99 / M • Too Naughty To Say No / 1984 / CA / M • Tropical Temptations / 1989 / VEX / M • Troublemaker / 1991 / VEX / M • Turn Up The Heat / 1988 / SEX / M • Turn Up The Heat / 1991 / VEX / C • Twin Cheeks #1 / 1990 / CIN / M • Twin Cheeks #2 / 1991 / CIN / M • Two To Tango / 1987 / TEM / M • Two Women & A Man / 1988 / VEX / M • Two Women & A Man / 1991 / VEX / C • The Ultimate Pleasure / 1995 / LEI / M • Uninhibited / 1993 / ANT / S • The Vanessa Obsession / 1987 / VCX / C • Video Virgins #12 / 1994 / NS / M • Video

Virgins #14 / 1994 / NS / M • Video Virgins #18 / 1994 / NS / M • Viviana's Dude Ranch / 1992 / IF / M • Vote Pink / 1984 / VD / M • The Voyeur #1 / 1994 / EA / M • Voyeur's Fantasies / 1996 / C69 / M • Wanda Does Transylvania / 1990 / V99 / M • Wanda Whips The Dragon Lady / 1990 / V99 / M • Waterworld Deep / 1995 / HW / M • Weekend Blues / 1990 / IN / M • Westside Tori / 1989 / ERO / M • Wet And Wild #1 / 1986 / VEX / M • Wet Science / 1986 / PLY / M • Wetness For The Prosecution / 1989 / LV / M • Whatever Turns You On / 1987 / CA / M • Where The Sun Never Shines / 1990 / IN / C • White Satin Nights / 1991 / V99 / M • Wild Orgies #06 / 1994 / AFI / M • Wild Orgies #08 / 1994 / AFI / M • X-TV #1 / 1986 / PL / C • XXX Workout / 1987 / VEX / M

TONY MORENA *see Star Index I*
TONY NACIVERS *see Joey Silvera*
TONY PAGE *see Star Index I*
TONY PALERMO
Conflict Of Interest / 1994 / FST / G
TONY PANTERA
Dun-Hur #1 / 1994 / SC / M
TONY PEPPER
Charming Cheapies #4: Duelling Dildos / 1985 / 4P / F
TONY PEREZ
Anyone But My Husband / 1975 / VC / M • Beach House / 1981 / CA / C • Dear Pam / 1976 / CA / M • From Holly With Love / 1977 / CA / M • The New York City Woman / 1979 / VC / C • Only The Very Best On Film / 1992 / VC / C • Sweet Punkin...I Love You / 1975 / VC / M • VCA Previews #2 / 1988 / VC / C
TONY PETERS *see Star Index I*
TONY PIEKARZ
Palm Springs Or Bust / 1994 / BTO / M
TONY RAMOS *see Star Index I*
TONY RIBAS
Anal Pow Wow / 1995 / XC / M
TONY RICH *see Star Index I*
TONY RICHARDS
Alice In Wonderland / 1976 / CA / M • Doogan's Woman / 1978 / S&L / M • Exploring Young Girls / 1978 / ALP / M • Highway Hookers / 1976 / SVE / M • In Sarah's Eyes / 1975 / VHL / M • One Last Fling / cr76 / CPL / M • Peaches And Cream / 1982 / SE / M • Reunion (Vanessa Del Rio's) / 1977 / LIM / M
TONY ROMAN
Beach Bum Amateur's #38 / 1993 / MID / M • Laguna Nights / 1995 / FH / M
TONY ROMANO *see Tony Montana*
TONY ROME
VGA: Bureau Of Discipline #1 / 1993 / VGA / B • VGA: Bureau Of Discipline #3 / 1993 / VGA / B
TONY RUSSO *see Star Index I*
TONY SALUMERI *see Star Index I*
TONY SALVANO
Breastman's Anal Adventure / 1993 / EVN / M • Country & Western Cuties #2: Naked Pie Eating Contest / 1996 / EVN / M • Hollywood Assets / 1990 / FH / M • To Shave And Shave Not / 1994 / PEP / M
TONY SANTINO
Nasty Girls (1983-VCX) / 1983 / VCX / M • Peaches And Cream / 1982 / SE / M • Sexcapades / 1983 / VC / M
TONY SAVAGE
Too Good To Be True / 1984 / MAP / M

TONY SCINTILA *see Star Index I*
TONY SCOTT
Hardgore / 1973 / ALP / M
TONY SPEED
Kitty Foxx's Kinky Kapers #01 / 1995 / TTV / M
TONY SPJUTH
Swedish Sex / 1996 / PL / M
TONY STALLONE
Executions On Butt Row / 1996 / EA / M
TONY STANS
Bedtime Video #06 / 1984 / GO / M
TONY STARR
Dungeons of Europe: An S & M Trilogy / 1988 / MAR / B
TONY STERN *see Star Index I*
TONY STONE
Playpen / 1987 / VC / M
TONY SUAVE *see Star Index I*
TONY T. *see Tony Tedeschi*
TONY TANDOORI *see Tony Tedeschi*
TONY TEDERICHI *see Tony Tedeschi*
TONY TEDESCHI *(Tony Tandoori, Tony T., Tony Tederichi, Tony Tedeschy, Bryan Cobb, Terry Tedeschi)*
Tony Tandoori is from **Cheeks #4** and Bryan Cobb is from **Bubble Butts #05**.
1-800-934-BOOB / 1992 / VD / C • A Is For Asia / 1996 / 4P / M • Ace Mulholland / 1995 / ERA / M • Adult Video Nudes / 1993 / VC / M • The Adventures Of Breastman / 1992 / EVN / M • Affairs Of The Heart / 1993 / VI / M • America's Raunchiest Home Videos #23: Video Virgin / 1992 / ZA / M • American Blonde / 1993 / VI / M • American Garter / 1993 / VC / M • Anal Adventures (Dragon) / 1992 / DRP / M • The Anal Adventures Of Suzy Super Slut #2 / 1994 / AFV / M • Anal Alley / 1996 / FD / M • Anal Angels #3 / 1995 / VEX / C • Anal Babes / 1995 / PPR / M • Anal Intruder #09: The Butt From Another Planet / 1995 / CC / M • Anal Orgasms / 1992 / DRP / M • Anal Duty / 1993 / DRP / M • Anal Virgins Of America #05 / 1993 / FOR / M • Anal Vision #10 / 1993 / LBO / M • Angel Baby / 1995 / SC / M • Anything That Moves / 1992 / VC / M • Arizona Gold / 1996 / KLP / M • Aroused #1 / 1994 / VI / M • Asian Persuasion / 1993 / WV / M • Babe Magnet / 1994 / IN / M • Babe Watch #1 / 1994 / SC / M • Babe Watch #2 / 1994 / SC / M • Babenet / 1995 / VC / M • Backhand / 1995 / SC / M • Backing In #4 / 1993 / WV / C • Backstage Pass / 1994 / SC / M • Badgirls #1: Lockdown / 1994 / VI / M • Badgirls #5: Maximum Babes / 1995 / VI / M • Badgirls #7: Lust Confined / 1995 / VI / M • Battlestar Orgasmica / 1992 / EVN / M • Batwoman & Catgirl / 1992 / HW / M • Beach Ball / 1994 / SC / M • Beaver & Buttface / 1995 / SC / M • Bed & Breakfast / 1995 / WAV / M • Bedazzled / 1993 / OD / M • The Best Of Strippers Inc / 1996 / ONA / C • Between The Cheeks #3 / 1993 / VC / M • Beyond Reality #3: Stand Erect! / 1996 / EXQ / M • Biff Malibu's Totally Nasty Home Videos #38 / 1993 / ANA / M • Big Boob Boat Butt Ride / 1996 / FC / M • Big Bust Babes #08 / 1991 / AFI / M • The Big One / 1995 / HO / M • The Big Pink / 1995 / MID / M • Black Streets / 1994 / LE / M • Blade / 1996 / MID / M • Blaze / 1996 / WAV / M • Blonde Beaver Bonanza / 1992 / TCP / M • Blonde In Blue Flannel / 1995 / CA / M • Blonde Justice #1 / 1993 / VI / M • Blonde Justice

#2 / 1993 / VI / M • Blonde Justice #3 / 1994 / VI / M • Bloopers & Boners / 1996 / VI / M • Blue Bayou / 1993 / VC / M • Blue Movie / 1995 / WP / M • Body Work / 1993 / MET / M • Bonnie & Clyde #4 / 1994 / VI / M • The Boob Tube / 1993 / MET / M • Boomeranal / 1992 / CC / M • Bra Busters #01 / 1993 / LBO / M • Breastman Does The Himalayas / 1993 / EVN / M • Breastman Goes To Breastland #1 / 1993 / EVN / M • Breastman's Anal Adventure / 1993 / EVN / M • Broad Of Directors / 1992 / PEP / M • Bubble Butts #05 / 1992 / LBO / M • Busty Backdoor Nurses / 1996 / PL / M • Butt Bandits #4 / 1996 / VD / C • Butt Banged Cycle Sluts / 1995 / ANA / M • Butt Camp / 1993 / HW / C • The Butt Sisters Do New York / 1994 / MID / M • Butt Woman #2 / 1992 / FH / M • Butt Woman #4 / 1993 / FH / M • Butt Woman #5 / 1993 / FH / M • Buttsizer, King Of Rears #1 / 1992 / EVN / M • Buttsizer, King Of Rears #2 / 1992 / EVN / M • Buttsizer #3: Return Of The King Of Rears / 1995 / EVN / M • California Pizza Girls / 1992 / EVN / M • Candy Snacker / 1993 / WIV / M • Carnal Garden / 1996 / KLP / M • Catwalk #1 / 1995 / SC / M • Catwalk #2 / 1995 / SC / M • Chasey Saves The World / 1996 / VI / M • Checkmate / 1992 / CDI / M • Cheeks #4: A Backstreet Affair / 1991 / CC / M • Chow Down / 1994 / VI / M • Chug-A-Lug Girls #6 / 1995 / VT / M • Cinesex #2 / 1994 / CV / M • Climax 2000 #1 / 1994 / CC / M • Climax 2000 #2 / 1994 / CC / M • Close To The Edge / 1994 / VI / M • Colossal Orgy #1 / 1993 / HW / M • Colossal Orgy #2 / 1994 / HW / M • Colossal Orgy #3 / 1994 / HW / M • Comeback / 1995 / VI / M • Coming Of Age / 1995 / VEX / C • Confessions / 1992 / PL / M • Corporate Affairs / 1996 / CC / M • Cynthia And The Pocket Rocket / 1995 / CV / M • The D.J. / 1992 / VC / M • De Sade / 1994 / SC / M • Decadent Dreams / 1996 / ME / M • Deep Dish Booty Pie / 1996 / ROB / M • Deep Inside Brittany O'connell / 1996 / VC / C • Deep Inside Keisha / 1994 / VC / C • Deep Inside Nicole London / 1995 / VC / C • Deep Inside Nikki Sinn / 1996 / VC / C • Deep Inside Tiffany Mynx / 1994 / VC / C • Deep Inside Tyffany Million / 1995 / VC / C • Delicious (VCX-1993) / 1993 / VCX / M • Demolition Woman #2 / 1994 / IP / M • Dominoes / 1993 / VI / M • Double Load #1 / 1993 / HW / M • Dun-Hur #1 / 1994 / SC / M • The Edge / 1995 / SC / M • Eleventh Annual AVN Awards / 1994 / VC / M • Endangered / 1992 / PP / M • Entangled / 1996 / KLP / M • Erotic Obsession / 1994 / IN / M • Eternal Lust / 1996 / VC / M • Euro Studs / 1996 / SC / C • Every Nerd's Big Boob Boat Butt Ride / 1996 / FC / M • Expose Me Again / 1996 / CV / M • EXXXtra Parts: Interview With A Hermaphrodite / 1995 / PL / M • Face Dance #1 / 1992 / EA / M • Face Dance #2 / 1992 / EA / M • Face Jam / 1996 / VC / M • Facesitter #2 / 1993 / CC / M • Facesitter #3 / 1994 / CC / M • Falling In Love Again / 1993 / PMV / M • Th Fanny / 1997 / WP / M • Fantasy Chamber / 1994 / ULI / M • Fingers / 1993 / LE / M • Flesh Mountain / 1994 / VI / C • The Flintbones / 1992 / FR / M • Flipside / 1996 / VI / M • Foolproof / 1994 / VC / M • Forbidden Cravings / 1996 / VC / M • Forbidden Pleasures / 1995 / ERA / M •

Foreign Tongues #1: Going Down / 1995 / VI / M • Foreign Tongues #2: Mesmerized / 1995 / VI / M • Forever / 1995 / SC / M • Forever Yours / 1992 / CDI / M • Forget Me Not / 1994 / FH / M • Frankenstein / 1994 / SC / M • Fresh Meat (John Leslie) #1 / 1994 / EA / M • From The Heart / 1996 / XCI / M • Full Blown / 1992 / GO / M • Full Moon Madness / 1995 / CA / M • Gangbang Girl #09 / 1993 / ANA / M • Gangbang Girl #10 / 1993 / ANA / M • Gangbang Girl #11 / 1993 / ANA / M • Gangbang Girl #14 / 1994 / ANA / M • Gangbang Girl #16 / 1995 / ANA / M • Gangbang Girl #18 / 1996 / ANA / M • Gangbusters / 1995 / VC / M • Gemini / 1994 / SC / M • Ghost Town / 1995 / WAV / M • Ghosts / 1995 / WV / M • The Girl With The Heart-Shaped Tattoo / 1995 / WAV / M • Girls Off Duty / 1994 / LE / M • The Good, The Bad & The Nasty / 1992 / VC / M • The Governess / 1993 / WP / M • Hardcore / 1994 / VI / M • Harry Horndog #01: Amateur Double Penetration #1 / 1992 / ZA / M • The Heist / 1996 / WAV / M • Hellriders / 1995 / SC / M • Hienie's Heroes / 1995 / VC / M • Hollywood Confidential / 1996 / SC / M • Hollywood Swingers #07 / 1993 / LBO / M • Hollywood Temps / 1993 / ZA / M • Homegrown Video: At Home With Britt Morgan / 1990 / HOV / M • Honey, I Blew Everybody #1 / 1992 / MID / M • Hookers Of Hollywood / 1994 / LE / M • Hooters / 1996 / MID / C • Hootersville (Legend) / 1995 / LE / M • Hornet's Nest / 1996 / ONA / M • The Horny Housewife / 1996 / HO / M • Hourman Is Here / 1994 / CC / M • House Of Sleeping Beauties #1 / 1992 / VI / M • House Of Sleeping Beauties #2 / 1992 / VI / M • Ice Woman #1 / 1993 / VI / M • Ice Woman #2 / 1993 / VI / M • Immortal Desire / 1993 / VI / M • Impact / 1995 / SC / M • In Your Face #1 / 1992 / PL / M • In Your Face #2 / 1992 / PL / M • In Your Face #3 / 1995 / PL / M • In Your Face #4 / 1996 / PL / M • Independence Night / 1996 / SC / M • Induced Pleasure / 1995 / ERA / M • Intersextion / 1994 / HO / M • Island Of Lust / 1995 / XCI / M • Jaded Love / 1994 / CA / M • Jailhouse Cock / 1993 / IP / M • Jenna Loves Rocco / 1996 / WAV / M • Jordan Lee: Anal Queen / 1997 / SC / C • Juranal Park / 1993 / OD / M • Keyholes / 1995 / OD / M • Killer Tits / 1995 / LE / M • Kink World: The Seduction Of Nena / 1993 / PL / M • Kittens #5 / 1994 / CC / F • L.A. Topless / 1994 / LE / M • La Femme Vanessa / 1995 / SC / M • Ladies Room / 1994 / SC / F • Layover / 1994 / VI / M • A League Of Their Moan / 1992 / EVN / M • Leena Meets Frankenstein / 1993 / OD / M • Let's Party / 1993 / VC / M • Lethal Affairs / 1996 / VI / M • Lingerie / 1995 / SC / M • Little Big Dong / 1992 / PL / M • Live Sex / 1994 / LE / M • The Love Doctor / 1992 / HIP / M • Lover Under Cover / 1995 / ERA / M • Malibu Ass Blasters / 1996 / ROB / M • Malibu Madam / 1995 / CC / M • Manwiched / 1992 / FPI / M • The Masseuse #2 / 1994 / VI / M • Midget Goes Hawaiian / 1995 / FC / M • Midget On Milligan's Island / 1995 / FC / M • Midnight Madness / 1993 / DR / M • Midnight Snacks / 1995 / KLP / M • Mighty Man #1: Virgins In The Forest / 1994 / LE / M • Mike Hott: #223 Cunt Of The Month: Tina Tyler / 1993 / MHV / M • Miss Nude International / 1993 / LE / M • Mr. Peepers Amateur Home Videos #58: Penthouse Pussy Power / 1992 / LBO / M • My Cousin Ginny / 1993 / MET / M • Mystique / 1996 / SC / M • Naked & Nasty / 1995 / WP / M • The Naked Fugitive / 1995 / CA / M • Naked Reunion / 1993 / VI / M • Nasty Nymphos #02 / 1994 / ANA / M • Natural Wonders / 1993 / VI / M • Naughty By Night / 1995 / DR / M • The New Ass Masters #08 / 1996 / LEI / C • The New Babysitter / 1995 / GO / M • New Lovers / 1993 / VI / M • The New Snatch Masters #18 / 1996 / LEI / C • New Wave Hookers #3 / 1993 / VC / M • New Wave Hookers #4 / 1994 / VC / M • Night Tales / 1996 / VC / M • Night Vision / 1996 / WP / M • Night Wish / 1992 / CDI / M • Nightclub / 1996 / SC / M • Nightmare Visions / 1994 / ERA / M • Nikki Loves Rocco / 1996 / VI / M • No Motive / 1994 / MID / M • Nobody's Looking / 1993 / VC / M • Nothing Like A Dame #1 / 1995 / IN / M • Nothing Like A Dame #2 / 1995 / IN / M • Nothing Sacred / 1995 / LE / M • Odyssey 30 Min: #161: Hush, Hush, Sweet Charlotte / 1991 / OD / M • Odyssey 30 Min: #185: Floppy Tit Gang Bang / 1991 / OD / M • Odyssey 30 Min: #306: / 1993 / OD / M • Odyssey Triple Play #23: Redheads' Fuckfest / 1993 / OD / M • Odyssey Triple Play #43: Anal Creaming & Reaming / 1993 / OD / M • Odyssey Triple Play #62: Gang Bangs All Around / 1994 / OD / M • Off Duty Porn Stars / 1994 / VC / M • On The Run / 1995 / SC / M • One Of Our Porn Stars Is Missing / 1993 / OD / M • Orgy Attack / 1993 / DRP / M • Other People's Honey / 1991 / HW / M • Our Bang #05 / 1992 / GLI / M • Our Bang #08 / 1992 / GLI / M • Paper Tiger / 1992 / VI / M • The Party / 1992 / CDI / M • Party House / 1995 / WAV / M • Passage To Pleasure / 1995 / LE / M • Passenger 69 #1 / 1994 / IP / M • Passion For Fashion / 1992 / PEP / G • The Passion Potion / 1995 / WP / M • Phone Fantasy #1 / 1992 / ATL / M • Phone Fantasy #2 / 1992 / ATL / M • Plaything #1 / 1995 / VI / M • Playtime / 1996 / VI / M • Pops / 1994 / PL / M • Pornographic Priestess / 1992 / CA / M • The Portrait Of Dorie Grey / 1996 / KLP / M • Portrait Of Lust / 1992 / WV / M • The Power & The Passion / 1993 / CDI / M • Pretending / 1993 / CV / M • Priceless / 1995 / WP / M • Pristine #2 / 1996 / CA / M • Private Dancer (CDI) / 1992 / CDI / M • Public Access / 1995 / VC / M • Pussy Hunt #06 / 1994 / LEI / M • Quantum Deep / 1993 / HW / M • Queen Of Hearts #3: Heartless / 1992 / PL / M • R & R / 1994 / VC / M • Rainwoman #10: The Tenth Anniversary Edition / 1996 / CC / M • Raw Footage / 1996 / VC / M • Razor's Edge / 1995 / ONA / M • Read My Lips: No More Bush / 1992 / HW / M • Red Beaver Bonanza / 1992 / TCP / M • Red Light / 1994 / SC / S • The Reel World #3: Trouble In Paradise / 1995 / FOR / M • Renegades #1 / 1994 / SC / M • Renegades #2 / 1995 / SC / M • Return Engagement / 1995 / VI / M • Return To Melrose Place / 1993 / HW / M • Risque Burlesque #1 / 1994 / IN / M • Risque Burlesque #2 / 1996 / IN / M • Rugburn / 1993 / LE / M • Saints & Sinners / 1992 / PEP / M • The Savage / 1994 / SC / M • Savannah R.N. / 1992 / HW / M • Scandal / 1995 / VI / M • Scenes From A Crystal Ball / 1992 / ZA / M • The Seduction Of Annah Marie / 1996 / VT / M • Sensations #1 / 1996 / SC / M • Sensations #2 / 1996 / SC / M • Sensual Recluse / 1994 / EX / M • The Servants Of Midnight / 1992 / CDI / M • Sex Kitten / 1995 / SC / M • Sex Raiders / 1996 / WAV / M • Sex Wish / 1992 / WV / M • Sexual Instinct #2 / 1994 / DR / M • Sexual Misconduct / 1994 / VD / C • Sexvision / 1992 / HO / M • Shame / 1994 / VI / M • Sharon Mitchell's Sex Clinic #01 / 1993 / FC / M • Sharon Starlet / 1993 / WIV / M • The Show / 1995 / VI / M • Silver Screen Confidential / 1996 / WP / M • Sin Asylum / 1995 / CV / M • Ski Bunnies #1 / 1994 / HW / M • Skid Row / 1994 / SC / M • Skin Dive / 1996 / SC / M • Skin Hunger / 1995 / MET / M • Slammed / 1995 / PV / M • Smeers / 1992 / PL / M • Smells Like...Sex / 1995 / VC / M • Smooth Ride / 1996 / WP / M • Snow Bunnies #1 / 1995 / SC / M • Snow Bunnies #2 / 1995 / SC / M • So You Want To Be In The Movies? / 1994 / VC / M • Sodomania #01: Tales Of Perversity / 1992 / EL / M • Sodomania #04: Further On Down The Road / 1993 / EL / M • Sodomania: The Baddest Of The Best...And Then Some / 1994 / EL / C • Sorority Cheerleaders / 1996 / PL / M • Spin For Sex / 1994 / IN / M • Splatman / 1992 / FR / M • Star Flash / 1996 / VT / M • Stardust #3 / 1996 / VI / M • Starlet / 1994 / VI / M • The Starlet / 1995 / SC / M • Steal This Heart #1 / 1993 / CV / M • Steal This Heart #2 / 1993 / CV / M • Steal This Heart (Director's) / 1993 / CV / M • Strippers Inc. #4 / 1995 / ONA / M • Strippers Inc. #5 / 1995 / ONA / M • Style #3 / 1996 / VT / M • Subway / 1994 / SC / M • Sue / 1995 / VC / M • Suggestive Behavior / 1996 / VI / M • Suite 18 / 1994 / VI / M • Superboobs / 1994 / LE / M • Supermarket Babes In Heat / 1992 / OD / M • Surfer Girl / 1992 / PP / M • Surprise!!! / 1994 / VI / M • The Swap #2 / 1994 / VI / M • Tail Taggers #127: / 1994 / WV / M • Tailz From Da Hood #4 / 1996 / AVI / M • Tangled / 1994 / PL / M • Temptation Of Serenity / 1994 / WP / M • The Thief / 1994 / SC / M • Thunder Road / 1995 / SC / M • Tight Lips / 1994 / CA / M • Tight Spot / 1992 / VD / M • Tit Tales #4 / 1993 / FC / M • Titty Bar #2 / 1994 / LE / M • Tongue In Cheek / 1994 / LE / M • Trailer Trash / 1994 / VC / M • Trouble Maker / 1995 / VI / M • True Sex / 1994 / EMC / M • Twist Of Fate / 1996 / WP / M • Ultimate Orgy #3 / 1992 / GLI / M • Unchained Marylin / 1996 / VT / M • Uncle Roy's Amateur Home Video #10 / 1992 / VIM / M • Undercover / 1996 / VC / M • Vagablonde / 1994 / VI / M • Venom #2 / 1996 / VD / M • Venom #3 / 1996 / VD / M • Venom #4 / 1996 / VD / M • Venom #5 / 1996 / VD / M • Video Virgins #01 / 1992 / NS / M • Video Virgins #06 / 1993 / NS / M • Virgin Dreams / 1996 / EA / M • Virtual Sex / 1993 / VC / M • Visions #1 / 1995 / ERA / M • Visions #2 / 1995 / ERA / M • Wacs / 1992 / PP / M • Walking Small / 1992 / ZA / M • Web Of Desire / 1993 / OD / M • Weekend At Joey's / 1995 / ERA / M • Wendy Whoppers: Brain Surgeon / 1993 / PEP / M • Western Nights / 1994 / WP / M • Wet Faces #1 / 1997 / SC / C • Wet Memories / 1993 / WV / M • Wet Nurses #1 / 1994 / LE / M • White Men Can Hump / 1992 / EVN /

M • The Wicked One / 1995 / WP / M • Wicked Thoughts / 1992 / PL / M • Wilde Palms / 1994 / XCI / M • Work Of Art / 1995 / LE / M • Working Stiffs / 1993 / FD / M

TONY TEDESCHY *see* **Tony Tedeschi**

TONY THE SCAMMER
Interrogation Dom #1 / 1995 / IBN / B

TONY TIMSON
Willie Wanker And The Fun Factory / 1994 / FD / M

TONY TORO
Bi Bi Banjee Boyz / 1994 / PL / G

TONY TURCO *see* **Star Index I**

TONY TUSCANY
Private Gold #05: Cape Town #1 / 1996 / OD / M

TONY VALENTINO *see* **Star Index I**

TONY VARGAS
Cocks In Frocks #1 / 1996 / TTV / G

TONY VENICAR *see* **Star Index I**

TONY VITO
Every Inch A Lady / 1975 / QX / M

TONY WELLS *see* **Star Index I**

TONYA
AVP #9154: Group Therapy #1 / 1991 / AVP / M • Blue Vanities #559 / 1994 / FFL / M • Deep Behind The Scenes With Seymore Butts #2 / 1995 / ULI / M • Retail Slut / 1989 / LV / M

TONYA DEVRIES *see* **Tanya DeVries**

TONYA HARDING
Tonya & Jeff's Wedding Night / 1994 / PET / M

TONYA SUMMER *see* **Tanya Summers**

TONYAKO MAGUSA
Sex For Money / 1985 / ORC / M

TOO TALL TERESA *see* **Star Index I**

TOOTSIE
Fresh Faces #09 / 1996 / EVN / M • Thunderthighs / 1984 / TGA / M

TOOTSIE ROBUSTA *see* **Tootsie Robysto**

TOOTSIE ROBYSTO *(Tootsie Robusta)*
Unknown girl. Probably large titted brunette, not too pretty.
Heavy Load / 1975 / COM / M • Sweet Punkin...I Love You / 1975 / VC / M

TOP JIMMY
Hexxxed / 1994 / VT / M

TOPAZ
Rich Quick, Private Dick / 1984 / CA / M • Sharon Mitchell's Sex Clinic #02 / 1993 / FC / M • Spanking In Shining Armor / 1995 / IBN / B • Strange Night On Earth / 1993 / PEP / G • Tit In A Wringer / 1993 / FC / M • Yankee Seduction / 1984 / WV / M

TORI
Generation Sex #2: Nature's Revenge / 1996 / VT / M • GRG: Private Moments #312: Analize Me / 1996 / GRG / M • Pearl Necklace: Amorous Amateurs #19 / 1992 / SEE / M

TORI (SHORT HAIR)
Anal Auditions #2 / 1996 / LE / M • Eighteen #3 / 1996 / SC / M • More Dirty Debutantes #57 / 1996 / 4P / M

TORI D.
Fame Is A Whore On Butt Row / 1996 / ABS / M

TORI DOUGLAS
Snack Time / 1983 / HO / M

TORI HOUSTON *see* **Star Index I**

TORI SINCLAIR
Visions Of Seduction / 1994 / SC / M

TORI STORIE
Short black hair, large natural tits, very pushy,

marginal facially, fleshy body. Says she comes from NY.
Anal Camera #06 / 1995 / EVN / M • Bigger Than Life / 1995 / IF / M • Butthead Dreams: Exposed / 1995 / FH / M • Hollywood Amateurs #14 / 1995 / MID / M • In Search Of The Brown Eye: An Anal Adventure / 1995 / MAX / M • Nightmare On Lesbian Street / 1995 / LIP / F • Oriental Girls In Heat / 1995 / IF / M • Snatch Masters #01 / 1994 / LEI / M

TORI SUE *see* **Star Index I**

TORI WELLES *(Brittani Paris)*
First movie was **The Offering**. Has had previously floppy breasts enhanced to enormous proportions. Married Paul Norman in June/July 1990. Had her breast implants removed in late 91 because of problems with them. Divorced from Paul Norman in 1994/5.
1-800-934-BOOB / 1992 / VD / C • Adam & Eve's Guide To A G-Spot Orgasm / 1994 / VI / M • Adult Video News 1991 Awards / 1991 / VC / M • Andrew Blake's Girls / 1992 / CA / C • Bend Over Babes #1 / 1990 / EA / M • The Best Of Andrew Blake / 1993 / CA / C • The Better Sex Video Series #7: Advanced Sexual Fantasies / 1992 / LEA / M • Bratgirl / 1989 / VI / M • Busted / 1989 / CA / M • Butt's Motel #2 / 1989 / EX / M • The Chameleon / 1989 / VC / M • Coming Of Age / 1989 / CA / M • Controlled / 1994 / FD / M • Doubletake / 1989 / CC / M • Edward Penishands #1 / 1991 / VT / M • Edward Penishands #3 / 1991 / VT / M • Flesh Mountain / 1994 / VI / C • Foolish Pleasures / 1989 / ME / M • Girl Crazy / 1989 / CDI / F • Head Lock / 1989 / VD / M • How To Achieve Multiple Orgasms / 1994 / A&E / M • Ice Cream Man / 1995 / APE / S • The Invisible Girl / 1989 / VI / M • Late Night For Lovers / 1989 / ME / M • Live In, Love In / 1989 / ME / M • Maneaters (1992-Vidco) / 1992 / VD / C • Miss Directed / 1990 / VI / M • Mystic Pieces / 1989 / EA / M • Night Trips #1 / 1989 / CA / M • The Offering / 1988 / INH / G • One Wife To Give / 1989 / ZA / M • Out For Blood / 1990 / VI / M • The Outlaw / 1989 / VD / M • Pajama Party / 1993 / CV / C • Postcards From Abroad / 1991 / CA / C • The Scarlet Bride / 1989 / VI / M • The Scarlet Mistress / 1990 / VI / M • Sextectives / 1989 / CIN / M • Sins Of Tami Monroe / 1991 / CA / C • Sleeping Beauty Aroused / 1989 / VI / M • Splash Shots / 1989 / CC / M • Swedish Erotica Featurettes #1 / 1989 / CA / M • Swedish Erotica Featurettes #2 / 1989 / CA / M • Swedish Erotica Featurettes #3 / 1989 / CA / M • A Taste Of Tami Monroe / 1990 / PIN / C • A Taste Of Tori Welles / 1990 / PIN / C • A Taste Of Victoria Paris / 1990 / PIN / C • Too Hot To Stop / 1989 / V99 / M • Tori Welles Exposed / 1990 / VD / C • Torrid / 1989 / VI / M • Torrid House / 1989 / VI / M • Torrid Without A Cause #1 / 1989 / VI / M • Torrid Without A Cause #2 / 1990 / VI / M • Trouble / 1989 / VD / M • True Confessions Of Tori Welles / 1989 / VI / M • True Legends Of Adult Cinema: The Modern Era / 1992 / VC / C • Twentysomething #3 / 1989 / VI / M • The Violation Of Tori Welles / 1990 / VD / C • Vogue / 1994 / VD / C • Westside Tori / 1989 / ERO / M • Where The Boys Aren't #1 / 1989 / VI / F • Where The Boys Aren't #3 / 1990 / VI / F •

Women Of Color / 1991 / PL / F

TORREY
The End Zone / 1993 / PRE / B • Giggles / 1992 / PRE / B • Gland Slam / 1995 / PRE / B • Leg...Ends #09 / 1994 / PRE / F

TORY TAMAS
Sirens / 1995 / GOU / M

TOSH
Backdoor Pleasures #1 / 1993 / MAV / M • Odyssey Amateur #25: Tosh & Her Backdoor Lovers / 1991 / OD / M

TOSHA *see* **Star Index I**

TOSHI *see* **Star Index I**

TOSHIA *see* **Star Index I**

TOT
The Betrayal Of Innocence #1: The Awakening Of Marika / 1993 / CC / M • The Betrayal Of Innocence #2: The Decadence / 1993 / CC / M • The Betrayal Of Innocence #3: The Choice / 1993 / CC / M

TOVIA BORODYN *see* **Ted Roter**

TOVIA ISRAEL *see* **Ted Roter**

TOY *(LaWanda Peabody, Toy Clayton)*
Huge natural breasted not too pretty black girl.
All That Jism / 1994 / VD / M • Amateur Lesbians #32: Tara / 1992 / GO / F • Anal Alien / 1994 / CC / M • Anal Virgins Of America #08 / 1994 / FOR / M • Animal Attraction / 1994 / IF / M • Back To Black #2 / 1992 / VEX / C • Biff Malibu's Totally Nasty Home Videos #19 / 1992 / ANA / M • Big Boob Boat Ride #2 / 1995 / FC / M • Big Bust Babes #10 / 1992 / AFI / M • Big Bust Babes #16 / 1993 / AFI / M • Bizarre Mistress Series: Mistress Jacqueline / 1992 / BIZ / C • Black Babes / 1995 / LV / M • Black Beauties #2 / 1992 / VIM / M • Black Bottom Girlz / 1994 / CA / M • The Black Butt Sisters Do Baltimore / 1995 / MID / M • The Black Butt Sisters Do Chicago / 1995 / MID / M • The Black Butt Sisters Do Detroit / 1995 / MID / M • Black Fantasies #07 / 1995 / HW / M • Black Fantasies #09 / 1995 / HW / M • Black Fantasies #10 / 1995 / HW / M • Black Fantasies #11 / 1996 / HW / M • Black Hollywood Amateurs #15 / 1995 / MID / M • Black Hollywood Amateurs #16 / 1995 / MID / M • Black Knockers #02 / 1995 / TV / M • Black Nurse Fantasies / 1994 / CA / M • Black On Black (1994-Midnight) / 1994 / MID / C • Black Talez N Da Hood / 1996 / APP / M • Black Women, White Men #1 / 1995 / FC / M • Black Women, White Men #2 / 1995 / FC / M • Black Women, White Men #5 / 1995 / FC / M • Black Women, White Men #6 / 1995 / FC / M • Black Women, White Men #8 / 1995 / FC / M • The Blues #1 / 1992 / VT / M • Boobytrap...The Next Generation / 1992 / HW / M • Boomerwang / 1992 / MID / M • Breast Worx #33 / 1992 / LBO / M • Breast Worx #39 / 1992 / LBO / M • Busty Babes In Heat #1 / 1993 / BTO / M • Butt Light: Queen Of Rears / 1992 / STR / M • The Case Of The Black Booty / 1996 / LV / M • Chocolate Bunnies #03 / 1995 / LBO / C • Danger-Ass / 1992 / MID / M • Dark Alleys #02 / 1992 / FC / M • Dark Alleys #07 / 1992 / FC / M • Dark Alleys #08 / 1992 / FC / M • Dirty Dominique / 1994 / V99 / M • Double D Dykes #04 / 1992 / GO / F • Double D Dykes #14 / 1994 / GO / F • Ebony Erotica #02: Midnight Madness / 1993 / GO / M • Ebony Erotica #35: Midnight Toy / 1995 / GO / M • Female Domination #1: Babes In Bondage / 1991 / BEB

/ B • Gimme Some Head / 1994 / VT / M • Girlz N The Hood #4 / 1994 / HW / M • In Loving Color #4 / 1993 / VT / M • Learn Your Lessons / 1992 / BIZ / B • Malcolm XXX / 1992 / OD / M • Missed You / 1995 / RTP / M • Mo' Honey / 1993 / FH / M • More Than A Handful #5: California Or Bust / 1994 / MET / M • Ms. Fix-It / 1994 / PRK / M • One Lay At A Time / 1992 / V99 / M • Rocks / 1993 / VT / M • Seymore Butts Swings / 1992 / FH / M • Smarty Pants / 1992 / VEX / M • Superstar Masturbation / 1990 / BIZ / F • SVE: Screentest Sex #1 / 1992 / SVE / M • Tit In A Wringer / 1993 / FC / M • Titanic Orgy / 1995 / PEP / M • Toppers #21 / 1993 / TV / C • Toppers #23 / 1994 / TV / M • Toppers #25 / 1994 / TV / M • Toppers #27 / 1994 / TV / M • Toppers #30 / 1994 / TV / C • Toppers #31 / 1994 / TV / C • Toppers #32 / 1994 / TV / C • Twice As Hard / 1992 / IF / M • The Very Best Of Breasts #1 / 1996 / H&S / S

TOY (OTHER)
Bizarre Mistress Series: Mistress Destiny / 1992 / BIZ / C • A Date With Destiny / 1992 / BIZ / B • Tied And Taunted / 1992 / JAN / B

TOY SIN *see* **Regina Bardot**
TOYMASTER
Rumor (1995) has it that he's dead but how and why is not known.
The Anniversary / 1994 / PSE / B • Arcade Slut / 1994 / PSE / B • Bondage "Sybian" Rides / 1994 / PSE / B • HomeGrown Video #468: Lust American Style / 1996 / HOV / C • Homegrown Video: How To Achieve G-Spot Orgasms / 1994 / HOV / M
TOYOTA
Lee Nover: The Search For The Perfect Butt / 1996 / IP / M
TRACEY
Amateur Nights #08 / 1990 / HO / M • Between My Breasts #12 / 1990 / BTO / M • Swingers Confidential #1 / 1995 / FC / M
TRACEY ADAMS *(Debbie Blaisdell, Tracy Roams)*
Pretty but tall brunette with large tits, lithe body and narrow hips. Debbie Blaisdell is from **The Lost Empire** (not a porno movie). **Bella** and **A Scent Of Heather** are not this Tracey Adams. Tracy Roams is from **Candy Stripers #4**. Rumor has it that she's a confirmed lesbian and as of 1997 has been living with the same girl for seven years. Screwing Ron Jeremy is enough to turn anyone off hetero sex!
2002: A Sex Odyssey / 1985 / DR / M • Adam & Eve's Guide To A G-Spot Orgasm / 1994 / VI / M • Addicted To Love / 1988 / WAV / M • The Adventures Of Buttman / 1989 / EA / M • Alexandra The Greatest / 1990 / NAP / F • All Night Long / 1990 / NWV / C • All The Right Motions / 1990 / DR / M • Amanda By Night #2 / 1987 / CA / M • Amazing Sex Stories #1 / 1986 / SUV / M • Amazing Sex Stories #2 / 1987 / SUV / C • Amber Lynn's Hotline 976 / 1987 / VCR / M • American Nympho In London / 1987 / VD / M • Angel Gets Even / 1987 / FAN / M • Angela Baron Series #1 / 1988 / VD / C • Angela Baron Series #2 / 1988 / VD / C • Angela Baron Series #3 / 1988 / VD / C • Angela Baron Series #4 / 1988 / VD / C • Angela Baron Series #5 / 1988 / VD / C • Angela Baron Series #6 / 1988 / VD / C • Angels Of Passion / 1986 / CDI /

M • Army Brat #2 / 1989 / VI / M • As The Spirit Moves You / 1990 / LV / M • Attack Of The Monster Mammaries / 1987 / LA / C • Aussie Exchange Girls / 1990 / PM / M • Aussie Maid In America / 1990 / PM / M • Back To Rears / 1988 / VI / M • Backdoor Club / 1986 / CA / M • Backdoor Summer #2 / 1989 / PV / C • The Baroness / 1987 / VD / M • The Beat Goes On / 1987 / VCR / C • Beauty And The Beast #1 / 1988 / VC / M • Beauty And The Beast #2 / 1990 / VC / M • Best Of Buttman #1 / 1991 / EA / C • The Better Sex Video Series #6: Acting Out Your Fantasies / 1992 / LEA / M • Bi-Bi-Baby / 1990 / CDI / G • Big Bust Babes #08 / 1991 / AFI / M • Big Bust Babes #13 / 1993 / AFI / M • Big Bust Babes #20 / 1994 / AFI / M • The Big Thrill / 1989 / VD / M • Big Titted Tarts / 1994 / PL / C • Bimbo Cheerleaders From Outer Space / 1988 / FAN / M • Blame It On The Heat / 1989 / VC / M • Blonde Ice #1 / 1990 / EX / M • Boobs, Butts And Bloopers #2 / 1990 / HO / M • Breakfast With Tiffany / 1990 / HO / M • Breastography, Lesson #1 / 1987 / VCR / M • Built For Sex (Angela Baron's) / 1988 / FAZ / C • Busted / 1989 / CA / M • Buttman's Big Tit Adventure #1 / 1992 / EA / M • California Native / 1988 / CDI / M • Campus Cuties / 1986 / CA / M • Candy Stripers #4 / 1990 / AR / M • Caught In The Middle / 1985 / CDI / M • Chastity Johnson / 1985 / AVC / M • Cherry Tricks / 1985 / VPE / M • Classic Pics / 1988 / PP / C • Clinique / 1989 / VC / M • Cocktails / 1990 / HO / M • Confessions #2 / 1992 / OD / M • The Cumming Of Sarah Jane #1 / 1993 / AFV / M • D-Cup Dating Service / 1991 / ME / M • Dangerous Desire / 1986 / NSV / M • Dark Corners / 1991 / LV / M • De Blond / 1989 / EA / M • Deep Blue / 1989 / PV / M • Deep Inside Barbie / 1989 / CDI / C • Deep Inside Keisha / 1994 / VC / C • Deep Inside Shanna Mccullough / 1992 / VC / C • Deep Inside Tracey / 1987 / CDI / C • Deep Throat #3 / 1989 / AR / M • Demin Dolls #2 / 1990 / CDI / M • Depraved Innocent / 1986 / VD / M • The Devil In Mr Holmes / 1988 / PV / M • Dirty Argus Spritzt Zuruck / 1993 / MET / M • Dirty Dreams / 1987 / CA / M • Dirty Pictures / 1988 / CA / M • The Domination Of Summer #2 / 1994 / BIZ / B • Double D Domination / 1993 / BIZ / B • Double D Dykes #09 / 1993 / GO / F • Double D Dykes #02 / 1992 / GO • Double Your Pleasure / 1989 / VEX / M • Dr Hooters / 1991 / PL / M • Dream Lovers / 1987 / CA / M • Eat 'em And Smile / 1990 / ME / M • Eaten Alive / 1985 / VXP / M • Educating Kascha / 1989 / CIN / M • The End Of The Innocence / 1989 / IN / M • The Enema Bandit / 1994 / BIZ / B • The Enema Bandit Returns / 1995 / BIZ / B • Enema Obedience #2 / 1994 / BIZ / B • Enema Obedience #3: The Ultimate Punishment / 1994 / BIZ / B • Enrapture / 1990 / ATL / S • Eternity / 1990 / SC / M • Fatal Seduction / 1988 / CDI / M • First Impressions / 1989 / ... / C • Flame / 1989 / ARG / M • Flame's Bondage Bash / 1994 / BIZ / B • Flesh In Ecstasy #07: Brittany Stryker / 1987 / GO / C • Flesh In Ecstasy #08: Traci Adams / 1987 / GO / C • Flying High With Rikki Lee / 1992 / VEX / C • Flying High With Tracey Adams / 1987 / VEX / M • Fondle With Care / 1989 / VEX / M • The French Con-

nexxxion / 1991 / VC / M • Gang Bangs #2 / 1989 / EA / M • Gazongas #03 / 1991 / VEX / M • Gettin' Ready / 1985 / CDI / M • Gimme An X / 1993 / VD / C • Girl Crazy / 1989 / CDI / F • Girls Of The Double D #07 / 1989 / CIN / M • Girls Of The Double D #09 / 1989 / CDI / M • Girls Of The Double D #10 / 1989 / CDI / M • Girls Of The Double D #12 / 1990 / CDI / M • Girls Of The Double D #13 / 1990 / CDI / M • Girlworld #3 / 1989 / LIP / F • Goddess Of Love / 1986 / CDI / M • Grafenberg Girls Go Fishing / 1987 / MIT / M • The Great Sex Contest #1 / 1988 / LV / M • Hands Off / 1988 / PP / M • Hard Core Cafe / 1988 / VD / M • Hard Sell / 1990 / VC / M • Hard Talk / 1992 / VC / M • Hawaii Vice #5 / 1989 / CDI / M • Hawaii Vice #6 / 1989 / CDI / M • Heraldo: Streetwalkers Of NY / 1990 / GOT / M • Hot Licks At The Pussycat Club / 1990 / WV / C • Hot Nights And Dirty Days / 1988 / VD / M • Hot Number / 1987 / WET / M • Hot Seat / 1986 / AVC / M • Hot Shorts: Tracey Adams / 1986 / VCR / C • Hotel Paradise / 1989 / CA / M • How To Achieve Multiple Orgasms / 1994 / A&E / M • I Cream Of Genie / 1988 / SE / M • I Ream A Jeannie / 1990 / GLE / M • I Want To Be Nasty / 1991 / XCV / M • In The Jeans / 1990 / ME / M • International Phone Sex Girls #1 / 1988 / VD / M • Introducing Barbii / 1987 / CDI / M • Introducing Charli / 1989 / CIN / M • Invasion Of The Samurai Sluts From Hell / 1988 / FAZ / M • Jacqueline / 1986 / MAP / M • Jetstream / 1993 / AMP / M • The Joy Of Sec's / 1989 / VEX / M • Killer / 1991 / SC / M • Late After Dark / 1985 / BAN / M • Le Hot Club / 1987 / WV / M • Leather Bound Dykes From Hell #1 / 1994 / BIZ / F • Leather Bound Dykes From Hell #2 / 1994 / BIZ / F • Leather Bound Dykes From Hell #3 / 1994 / BIZ / F • Leather Bound Dykes From Hell #4 / 1995 / BIZ / F • Leave It To Cleavage #1 / 1988 / GO / M • Legal Tender (1990-X) / 1990 / VC / M • Legends Of Porn #2 / 1989 / CV / C • Les Be Friends / 1988 / WV / C • Lesbian Pros And Amateurs #09 / 1992 / GO / F • Let's Get Wet / 1987 / WV / M • Lethal Passion / 1991 / PL / M • Licensed To Thrill / 1990 / VC / M • Lips On Lips / 1989 / LIP / F • The Lost Empire / 1983 / LIV / S • Lottery Fever / 1985 / BEA / M • Love Probe / 1986 / VT / M • Lover's Lane / 1986 / SE / M • Lucky In Love #1 / 1985 / BAN / M • Lust College / 1989 / ... / M • Lust On The Orient X-Press / 1986 / CA / M • Made In Germany / 1988 / FAZ / M • Magma: Pussy Jobs / 1994 / MET / M • Make My Night / 1985 / CIN / M • Mammary Lane / 1988 / VT / C • Marina Heat / 1985 / CV / M • Mind Trips / 1992 / FH / M • The Mischief Maker / 1987 / SE / M • Monaco Falcon / 1990 / VC / M • Monkey Business / 1987 / SEV / M • Moonlusting #1 / 1986 / WV / M • Moonlusting #2 / 1987 / WV / M • Mouthwatering / 1986 / BRA / M • Nasty Nights / 1988 / PL / C • Naughty 90's / 1990 / HO / M • Nicki / 1987 / VI / M • Night Games / 1986 / WV / M • Nikki's Nightlife / 1992 / IN / M • No Man's Land #01 / 1988 / VT / C • Nudes At Eleven #1 / 1986 / AVC / M • Object(s) Of My Desire / 1988 / V99 / M • On My Lips / 1989 / PV / M • Only The Best Of Peepers / 1992 / CV / C • Oral Majority #06 / 1988 / WV / C • Peeping Tom / 1986 / CV / M • Piece Of

Heaven / 1988 / CDI / M • The Pleasure Game / 1988 / CA / M • The Pleasure Maze / 1986 / PL / M • Pleasure Principle / 1988 / VEX / M • Porn On The 4th Of July / 1990 / IN / M • Porsche Lynn, Vault Mistress #1 / 1994 / BIZ / B • Porsche Lynn, Vault Mistress #2 / 1994 / BIZ / B • Pretty Peaches #2 / 1987 / VC / M • Pretty Peaches #3 / 1989 / VC / M • Private & Confidential / 1990 / AR / M • Rachel Ryan / 1988 / WV / C • Racquel's Treasure Hunt / 1990 / VC / M • Ramb-Ohh #2 / 1988 / PV / M • Rears / 1987 / VI / M • The Red Garter / 1986 / SE / M • Red Hot Fire Girls / 1989 / VD / M • Revenge By Lust / 1986 / VCR / M • Revenge Of The Babes #1 / 1985 / LA / M • Revenge Of The Babes #2 / 1987 / PL / M • The Rise Of The Roman Empress #1 / 1986 / PV / M • Sailing Into Ecstasy / 1986 / VCX / M • Samantha And The Deep Throat Girls / 1988 / CV / M • Santa Comes Again / 1990 / GLE / M • Screen Test / 1985 / C3S / S • Seduction Of Tracy / 19?? / GO / C • The Sensual Massage Video / 1993 / … / M • Sex Asylum #3 / 1988 / VI / M • Sex Contest / 1988 / LV / M • Sex Derby / 1986 / GO / M • The Sex Detective / 1987 / GO / M • Sex F/X / 1986 / VPE / M • Sex Machine / 1986 / LA / M • Sex Sluts In The Slammer / 1988 / FAN / M • Sex Soviet Style #1 / 1992 / EVN / M • Sex Soviet Style #2 / 1992 / EVN / M • Sex World Girls / 1987 / AR / M • Sexline You're On The Air / 1986 / CAT / M • Sextectives / 1989 / CIN / M • Shades Of Passion / 1985 / CA / M • Sins Of The Wealthy #2 / 1986 / CLV / M • Sleepwalker / 1990 / XCI / M • Soft Warm Rain / 1987 / VD / M • Spielzeug Des Teufels / 1993 / MET / M • Spiked Heel Diaries #1 / 1994 / BIZ / B • Spiked Heel Diaries #2 / 1994 / BIZ / B • Splash Shots / 1989 / CC / M • St. Tropez Lust / 1990 / VC / M • Starbangers #04 / 1993 / FPI / M • Strange Love / 1987 / WV / M • Strangers When We Meet / 1990 / VCR / M • Student Affairs / 1988 / VES / S • Swedish Erotica #67 / 1985 / CA / M • Swedish Erotica #70 / 1985 / CA / M • Swingers Ink / 1990 / VC / M • Tailspin / 1987 / AVC / M • Talk Dirty To Me #05 / 1987 / DR / M • Talk Dirty To Me #06 / 1989 / DR / M • Talk Dirty To Me #07 / 1990 / DR / M • A Taste Of Nikki Charm / 1989 / PIN / C • A Taste Of Rachel / 1990 / PIN / C • This Is Your Sex Life / 1987 / VD / M • Too Hot To Handle / 1989 / WET / F • Too Hot To Touch #2 / 1993 / CV / M • Toppers #11 / 1993 / TV / C • Toppers #13 / 1993 / TV / M • Toppers #14 / 1993 / TV / M • Toppers #16 / 1993 / TV / M • Toppers #21 / 1993 / TV / C • Toppers #22 / 1993 / TV / C • Toppers & Whoppers #2 / 1994 / PRE / C • Torrid Zone / 1987 / MIR / M • Tracey Adams' Girls School / 1993 / BIZ / B • Tracey And The Bandit / 1987 / LA / M • Tracey's Academy Of DD Dominance / 1993 / BIZ / B • Tracey's Love Chamber / 1987 / AR / M • Tracy Takes Paris / 1987 / VIP / M • The Ultimate Lover / 1986 / VD / M • Ultimate Submissives #2: Best of Teddi Austin / 1995 / BIZ / C • The Ultimate Thrill / 1988 / PIN / C • Unleashed Lust / 1989 / VC / C • Valleys Of The Moon / 1991 / SC / M • VCA Previews #4 / 1988 / VC / C • Visions Of Jeannie / 1986 / VD / M • The Wacky World Of X-Rated Bloopers / 1989 / GO / M • A Weekend In Bondage / 1994 /

BIZ / B • Weird Fantasy / 1986 / LA / M • Wet Dreams 2001 / 1987 / VD / M • The Whore / 1989 / CA / M • The Wild Wild Chest #3 / 1996 / HO / C • Wildest Dreams / 1987 / VES / S • Wimps / 1987 / LIV / S • WPINK-TV #3 / 1988 / PV / M • Wrestling Tongues / 1990 / NAP / B • X Dreams / 1989 / CA / M • X Factor: The Next Generation / 1991 / HO / M • [Nude Aerobics #1 / 199? / … / S

TRACEY ALLEN
America's Raunchiest Home Videos #70: / 1993 / ZA / M • Anal Virgins Of America #04 / 1993 / FOR / M • Beach Bum Amateur's #32 / 1993 / MID / M • Bobby Hollander's Maneaters #08 / 1993 / SFP / M • Mr. Peepers Amateur Home Videos #71: I Dream Of Creamy / 1993 / LBO / M • The Orgy #2 / 1993 / EMC / M • Payne-Full Revenge / 1995 / BS / B • Suburban Nymphos / 1994 / ATL / M • Takin' It To The Limit #6 / 1995 / BS / M • Video Virgins #06 / 1993 / NS / M

TRACEY AUSTIN
Black On White / 1987 / PL / C • Coffee & Cream / 1984 / AVC / M • I Like To Be Watched / 1984 / VD / M • Sinful Sisters / 1986 / VEX / M • Spies / 1986 / PL / M • Stripteaser / 1986 / LA / M • Swedish Erotica #58 / 1984 / CA / M • You Make Me Wet / 1985 / SVE / M

TRACEY BUTLER
Bad Company / 1978 / CV / M

TRACEY CHRISTIANSEN
Hell To Pay / 1996 / OUP / B

TRACEY LORI *see* Tracy Love

TRACEY PRINCE *(Traci Prince, Medea, Julie (Tracey P))*
Not too pretty blonde/redhead who could do with a nose job.
Adventures Of The DP Boys: Back In The Bush / 1993 / HW / M • Amateur Orgies #23 / 1993 / AFI / M • Amateur Orgies #26 / 1993 / AFI / M • Amateur Orgies #32 / 1993 / AFI / M • American Swinger Video Magazine #05 / 1993 / ZA / M • Anal Asspirations / 1993 / LV / M • Babe Patrol / 1993 / FOR / M • Backdoor Magic / 1994 / LV / M • Badd Girls / 1994 / SC / F • Battle Of The Glands / 1994 / LV / F • Bi Watch / 1994 / BIN / G • Biff Malibu's Totally Nasty Home Videos #34 / 1993 / ANA / M • Big Murray's New-Cummers #05: Luscious Lesbos / 1993 / FD / F • Bobby Hollander's Maneaters #10 / 1993 / SFP / M • The Breast Of Breastmen / 1995 / EVN / C • Buffy Malibu's Totally Nasty All-Girl Home Videos #04 / 1993 / ANA / F • The Butt Boss / 1993 / VD / M • Butt Of Steel / 1994 / LV / M • Butt Watch #02 / 1993 / FH / M • Cajun Heat / 1993 / SC / M • Club DOM / 1994 / SBP / B • Competent People / 1994 / FD / C • Days Gone Bi / 1994 / BIN / G • Deep Inside Brittany O'connell / 1996 / VC / C • Dirty Dating Service #02 / 1993 / WP / M • Erotic Newcummers Vol 1 #1: Capitol Desires / 1993 / DR / M • First Time Lesbians #03 / 1993 / JMP / F • First Time Lesbians #04 / 1993 / JMP / F • Foxxxy Lady / 1992 / HW / M • The Fury / 1993 / WIV / M • Guttman's Hollywood Adventure / 1993 / PL / M • Hindfeld / 1993 / PI / M • The Howard Sperm Show / 1993 / LV / M • The Intruders: Office Call / 1995 / VTF / B • Ladies Lovin' Ladies #3 / 1993 / AFV / F • Laugh Factory / 1995 / PRE / C • Little

Shop Of Tickle / 1995 / SBP / B • Love Letters #2 / 1993 / SC / M • Love Potion 69 / 1994 / VC / M • M Series #06 / 1993 / LBO / M • M Series #15 / 1993 / LBO / M • The Man Who Loved Women / 1993 / SC / M • Margarita On The Rocks / 1994 / SFP / M • Mike Hott: #220 Cunt Of The Month: Traci / 1993 / MHV / M • Mike Hott: #225 Lesbian Sluts #11 / 1993 / MHV / F • Mike Hott: #242 Fuck The Boss #02 / 1993 / MHV / M • Miss Anal America / 1993 / LV / M • Mr. Peepers Amateur Home Videos #72: Dirty Diary / 1993 / LBO / M • Mr. Peepers Amateur Home Videos #78: She Dreams Of Weenie / 1993 / LBO / M • Neighborhood Watch #40: / 1993 / LBO / M • New Girls In Town #3 / 1993 / CC / M • Nothing Personal / 1993 / CA / M • Nympho Zombie Coeds / 1993 / VIM / M • Obey Thy Feet / 1994 / SBP / B • Odyssey 30 Min: #332: / 1993 / OD / M • On The Come Line / 1993 / MID / M • Once Upon An Anus / 1993 / LV / M • The Orgy #2 / 1993 / EMC / M • Oriental Sorority Secrets / 1992 / VIM / M • Outlaws / 1993 / SC / M • Photo Bound / 1994 / VTF / B • Prince Of Ties / 1994 / BON / B • Real People Real Bondage #2 / 1996 / BON / C • The Rehearsal / 1993 / VC / M • S&M Playtime / 1995 / SBP / B • A Scent Of A Girl / 1993 / LV / M • Sean Michaels On The Road #01: The Barrio / 1993 / VT / M • Sex Academy #2: The Art Of Talking Dirty / 1994 / ONA / M • Seymore Butts & His Mystery Girl / 1993 / FH / M • Seymore Butts: Bustin' Out My Best Anal / 1995 / FH / C • She-Male Trouble / 1994 / HEA / G • Sleeping With Seattle / 1993 / LV / M • Sneek Peeks #2 / 1993 / OCV / M • Soap Me Up! / 1993 / FD / M • Star Struck / 1991 / AFV / M • Ultimate Orgy #1 / 1992 / GLI / M • Video Virgins #02 / 1992 / NS / M • Wild Girls / 1993 / LV / F

TRACEY WINN *see* Tracey Wynn

TRACEY WOLFE *see* Casey Williams

TRACEY WYNN *(Angelique (T. Wynn), Tracey Winn)*
Very pretty but too big brunette from Riverside CA. Lives with David Angel (what taste!). Her first was a g/g with Zara in a **Zara's Revenge**. In **Starr** and **Zara's Revenge** she is credited as Angelique. As of 1992, she was 5'9", 150lbs, 36B-27-38.
2 Hung 2 Tung / 1992 / MID / M • Amateur Lesbians #23: Sherri / 1992 / GO / F • Amateur Lesbians #24: Sondra / 1992 / GO / F • America's Raunchiest Home Videos #07: A Fucking Beauty / 1991 / ZA / M • Anal Adventures (Dragon) / 1992 / DRP / M • The Anals Of History #1 / 1991 / MID / M • Anything That Moves / 1992 / VC / M • The Back Doors (Executive) / 1991 / EX / M • Backstage Entrance #1 / 1992 / FH / M • Backstage Entrance #2 / 1992 / FH / M • Bad To The Bone / 1992 / LE / M • Between The Bars / 1992 / FH / M • Biff Malibu's Totally Nasty Home Videos #06 / 1992 / ANA / M • Big Switch #3: Bachelor Party / 1991 / CAT / G • Biker Chicks In Love / 1991 / LE / M • The Boneheads / 1992 / PL / M • Buttsizer, King Of Rears #1 / 1992 / EVN / M • Chameleons: Not The Sequel / 1991 / VC / M • Collectible / 1991 / LE / M • Cumming Clean / 1991 / FL / M • Deep Inside Selena Steele / 1993 / VC / C • Denim / 1991 / LE / M • Dirty Business / 1992 / CV / M • The Dirty Little Mind of Martin Fink / 1991 / ME

/ M • Dirty Thoughts / 1992 / LE / M • The Erotic Adventures Of The Three Musketeers / 1992 / CEL / S • Foreign Affairs / 1991 / LE / M • Forever Yours / 1992 / CDI / M • French Open / 1990 / OD / M • Friends & Lovers #1 / 1991 / VT / M • Ghost Writer / 1992 / LE / M • Girl Gone Bad #6: On Parole / 1992 / GO / F • Heartbeats / 1992 / LE / M • In Your Face #1 / 1992 / PL / M • In Your Face #2 / 1992 / PL / M • Introducing Tracey Wynn / 1991 / PL / M • L.A.D.P. / 1991 / PL / M • Lesbian Pros And Amateurs #08 / 1992 / GO / F • Lingerie Busters / 1991 / FH / M • Naked Edge / 1992 / LE / M • The Naked Pen / 1992 / VC / M • The Penetrator #1 / 1991 / PL / M • Perks / 1992 / ZA / M • Private Dancer (CDI) / 1992 / ME / M • Radical Affairs Video Magazine #02 / 1992 / ME / M • Raunch #03 / 1991 / CC / M • Rocket Girls / 1993 / VC / M • Saints & Sinners / 1992 / PEP / M • Scorcher / 1992 / GO / M • Sex Bi-Lex / 1993 / CAT / G • Soft And Wild / 1991 / LV / M • Southern Exposure / 1991 / LE / M • Starr / 1991 / CA / M • Steel Garters / 1992 / CAT / G • Supermarket Babes In Heat / 1992 / OD / M • Sweet Licks / 1991 / MID / M • The Three Musketeers #1 / 1992 / FD / M • The Three Musketeers #2 / 1992 / FD / M • Tori Welles Goes Behind The Scenes / 1992 / FD / M • Two Women / 1992 / ROB / M • Wet Faces #1 / 1997 / SC / C • Wild Hearts / 1992 / SC / M • Zara's Revenge / 1991 / XCI / M

TRACI
AVP #7033: The Repair Man / 1991 / AVP / M • Candyman #02 / 1992 / GLI / M • First Time Lesbians #07 / 1993 / JMP / F • TV Birdcage Rage #2 / 1996 / GLI / G

TRACI DIAMOND see Trisha Diamond

TRACI DUZIT (Nicole Blanc)
Amateur Coed Frolics / 1985 / SUN / M • Amber Aroused / 1985 / CA / M • Beverly Hills Exposed / 1985 / SE / M • Camp Beaverlake #1 / 1984 / AR / M • Centerfold Celebrities #4 / 1983 / VC / M • Centerfold Celebrities #5 / 1983 / VC / M • Cherry Busters / 1984 / VIV / M • Come As You Are / 1985 / SUV / M • Famous Ta-Ta's #1 / 1986 / VCS / C • Future Voyeur / 1985 / SUV / M • GVC: Family Affair / 1983 / GO / M • Hot Flashes / 1984 / VC / M • Personal Touch #3 / 1983 / AR / M • Raffles / 1988 / VC / M • Scared Stiff / 1984 / PV / M • Screen Play / 1984 / XTR / M • Squalor Motel / 1985 / SE / M • Wet, Wild And Wicked / 1984 / SE / M • Young Nurses In Love / 1987 / VC / M

TRACI LIGHT
Fame Is A Whore On Butt Row / 1996 / ABS / M

TRACI LORDS (Nora Kuzma, Nora Louise Kuzma, Kristie Nussman)
First movie was **What Gets Me Hot**. Born May 7, 1968 in Steubenville, Ohio, and therefore underage for most of her movies. Blonde with big tits, an unpleasant personality, flabby body, and marginal face. Married in 1990 to Brook Yeaton.
Adult 45 #01 / 1985 / DR / C • Another Roll In The Hay / 1985 / COL / M • Aroused / 1985 / VIV / M • Bad Girls #3 / 1984 / COL / M • Battle Of The Stars #1 / 1985 / NSV / M • Beverly Hills Copulator / 1986 / ... / M • Black Throat / 1985 / VC / M • Breaking It #1 / 1984 / COL / M • Caballero Preview

Tape #5 / 1986 / CA / C • Country Girl / 1985 / AVC / M • Cry-Baby / 1990 / MCA / S • Deep Inside Traci / 1986 / CDI / C • Desperate Crimes / 1993 / AIP / S • Diamond Collection #69 / 1985 / CDI / M • Diamond Collection #73 / 1985 / CDI / M • Diamond Collection #75 / 1985 / CDI / M • Diamond Collection #76 / 1985 / CDI / M • Diamond Collection #89 / 1986 / CDI / M • Diamond Preview Tape / 1985 / CDI / C • Dirty Pictures / 1985 / SUP / M • Dream Lover / 1985 / CDI / M • Educating Mandy / 1985 / CDI / M • Electric Blue: Beverly Hills Wives / cr85 / CA / S • Electric Blue: Hard Times / 1985 / CA / M • Erotic Gold #1 / 1985 / VEN / M • Erotic Zones #1 / 1985 / CA / M • Fantasy Club #69 / 1985 / WV / M • Fast Food / 1989 / FHV / S • First Annual XRCO Awards / 1984 / AVC / C • Future Voyeur / 1985 / SUV / M • Gourmet Quickies: Traci Lords #723 / 1984 / GO / C • The Grafenberg Spot / 1985 / MIT / M • Harlequin Affair / 1985 / CIX / M • Holly Does Hollywood #1 / 1985 / VEX / M • Hollywood Heartbreakers / 1985 / VEX / M • Hot Pink / 1985 / VCR / F • Hot Shorts: Raven / 1986 / VCR / C • Ice / 1993 / PME / S • Inside Danielle / 1985 / VC / C • Intent To Kill / 1992 / PME / S • It's My Body / 1985 / CDI / M • Jean Genie / 1985 / CA / M • Joys Of Erotica #110 / 1984 / VCR / C • Joys Of Erotica #114 / 1984 / VCR / C • Just Another Pretty Face / 1985 / AVC / M • Kinky Business #1 / 1984 / DR / M • The Ladies In Lace Party / 1985 / MAP / M • Laser Moon / 1992 / HHV / S • Love Bites / 1985 / CA / M • Lust In The Fast Lane / 1984 / PV / M • Marilyn Chambers' Private Fantasies #5 / 1985 / CA / M • Marilyn Chambers' Private Fantasies #6 / 1985 / CA / M • Miss Passion / 1984 / VD / M • More Than A Handful #1 / 1985 / CV / C • New Wave Hookers #1 / 1984 / VC / M • Night Of Loving Dangerously / 1984 / PV / M • Not Of This Earth / 1994 / MGM / S • The Nutt House / 1995 / TRI / S • Nympherotica / 1984 / COL / M • One Hot Night Of Passion / 1985 / COL / C • Open Up Tracy / 1984 / VD / M • Passion Pit / 1985 / SE / M • The Peek A Boo Gang / 1985 / COL / M • Perfect Fit / 1985 / DR / M • Physical #2 / 1985 / SUP / M • Pleasure Party (Gourmet) / 1985 / GO / M • Pleasure Productions #09 / 1985 / VCR / M • Pleasure Productions #10 / 1985 / VCR / M • Plughead Rewired: Circuitry Man #2 / 1993 / C3S / S • Pony Girl #1: In Harness / 1985 / CS / S • Porn In The USA #1 / 1986 / WV / C • Portrait Of Lust / 1984 / CC / M • Raw Nerve / 1991 / AIP / S • Serial Mom / 1994 / HBS / S • Sex 5th Avenue / 1985 / WV / M • The Sex Goddess / 1984 / GO / M • Sex Shoot / 1985 / AT / M • Sex Waves / 1984 / EXF / M • Shock 'em Dead / 1990 / AE / S • Sister Dearest / 1984 / DR / M • Sizzling Suburbia / 1985 / CDI / M • Skinner / 1995 / APE / S • Splashing / 1986 / VCS / C • Suzie Superstar #2 / 1985 / CV / M • Swedish Erotica #56 / 1984 / CA / M • Swedish Erotica #57 / 1984 / CA / M • Swedish Erotica #60 / 1984 / CA / M • Swedish Erotica #61 / 1984 / CA / M • Swedish Erotica #62 / 1984 / CA / M • Swedish Erotica Hard #17: Amber & Christy's Sex Party / 1992 / OD / C • Sweet Little Things / 1985 / COL / M • Tailhouse Rock / 1985 / WV / M • Talk Dirty

To Me #03 / 1986 / DR / M • A Taste Of Traci / 1990 / PIN / C • Those Young Girls / 1984 / PV / M • A Time To Die / 1991 / PME / S • The Tommyknockers / 1993 / VMA / S • Traci Lords' Fantasies / 1986 / CA / C • Traci Takes Tokyo / 1986 / TLC / M • Traci, I Love You / 1987 / CA / M • Tracie Lords / 1984 / CIT / M • Tracy Dick / 1985 / WV / M • Tracy In Heaven (Orig 1985) / 1985 / WV / M • Two Timing Tracie / 1985 / V20 / M • Virtuosity / 1995 / ... / S • Warm Up With Traci Lords / 199? / FRV / S • We Love To Tease / 1985 / VD / M • What Gets Me Hot / 1984 / ISV / M • Wild Things #1 / 1985 / CV / M • Young Girls Do / 1984 / ELH / M • [As Good As Dead / 1994 / ... / S • [Boxing Babes / 1990 / AIP / M • [Dragstrip Girl / 1994 / ... / M • [Embassy Girls / 1985 / ... / M • [Naked Movie Stars / 19?? / ... / S • [Red Hot Rock #1 / cr85 / ... / S • [Reincarnation Of Don Juan / 1985 / ... / M • [Screamers / cr84 / ... / M

TRACI MILKAVITCH
More Dirty Debutantes #56 / 1996 / 4P / M

TRACI NELSON
Pretty, innocent sounding, small breasted brunette.
Dougie Hoser: The World's Youngest Gynaecologist / 1990 / VT / M

TRACI O'CONNOR
The Van / 1995 / ZFX / B

TRACI O'NEILL see Tracy O'Neill

TRACI PRINCE see Tracey Prince

TRACI STARR (Tracy Star, Sandra Myorgia, Sandra Morgan)
Seen in **More Dirty Debutantes #04** where she does an anal with Ed, this girl has small breasts, a cheeky face, great smile and short page boy hair. Supposedly 23 in 1992.
Girl Gone Bad #6: On Parole / 1992 / GO / F • More Dirty Debutantes #04 / 1990 / 4P / M • Rocky Mountains / 1991 / IF / M • Tracy Star Bound / 1991 / BON / B • Wil And Ed's Excellent Boner Christmas / 1991 / MID / M • Will And Ed: The Curse Of Poona / 1994 / MID / C

TRACI TAME see Star Index I

TRACI TEMPLETON
Maids In Bondage /The Bondage Girls / 1985 / 4P / B

TRACI TOPPS
10 Years Of Big Busts #3 / 199? / BTO / C • Big Bust Blondes / 1992 / BTO / F • Exposure Images #03: Traci Topps / 1992 / EXI / F • Girls Around The World #27 / 1995 / BTO / M • H&S: Traci Topps / 199? / H&S / S • Score Busty Covergirls #5 / 1995 / BTO / S

TRACI TOYOTA
Yin Yang Oriental Love Bang #1 / 1996 / SUF / M

TRACI WOLFE
Bum Rap / 1990 / PLV / B • End Results / 1991 / PRE / C • Hot Foot / 1991 / PLV / B

TRACIE
Student Fetish Videos: Best of Catfighting #03 / 1995 / PRE / C • Student Fetish Videos: Best of Enema #03 / 1994 / PRE / C • Student Fetish Videos: Catfighting #12 / 1994 / PRE / B • Student Fetish Videos: The Enema #15 / 1994 / PRE / B • Student Fetish Videos: Spanking #15 / 1994 / PRE / B

TRACY
Blue Vanities #528 / 1993 / FFL / M • Blue Vanities #547 / 1994 / FFL / M • Blue Van-

ities #572 / 1995 / FFL / M • Bra Busters #04 / 1993 / LBO / M • Bubble Butts #28 / 1993 / LBO / M • Co-Ed In Bondage / 1996 / GAL / B • Creme De Femme #4 / 1981 / AVC / C • Dirty Debutantes / 1990 / 4P / M • Harry Horndog #22: Huge Hooters / 1993 / ZA / M • Hollywood Amateurs #06 / 1994 / MID / M • HomeGrown Video #446: Slam Bam Thank You Ma'am! / 1995 / HOV / M • Joe Elliot's College Girls #47 / 1996 / JOE / F • Kinky College Cunts #21 / 1993 / NS / M • Lesbian Pros And Amateurs #10 / 1992 / GO / F • Limited Edition #19 / 1980 / AVC / M • Limited Edition #20 / 1980 / AVC / M • Mr. Peepers Amateur Home Videos #76: Sixty Nine Plus Seven / 1993 / LBO / M • New Busom Brits / 199? / H&S / S • Pantyhose Teasers #1 / 1991 / JBV / S

TRACY (CASEY WILL.) see Casey Williams

TRACY ADAMS (1980)
Not the same as THE Tracey Adams. This one is pretty and slim with small breasts. There's something strange about her pubic hair, however, with the line at the top being covered by what look like petals in **Bella**. Maybe she has a Caesarian scar?
Bella / 1980 / AR / M • Fascination / 1980 / QX / M • A Scent Of Heather / 1981 / VXP / M

TRACY BOOKER
Ebony Erotica / 1985 / SVE / C

TRACY BURR
Busty Babes In Heat #2 / 1993 / BTO / M

TRACY CARRERA
Bionic Babes / 1986 / 4P / M

TRACY CHRISTIANSEN
N.Y. Video Magazine #08 / 1996 / OUP / M • Over The Knee / 1996 / OUP / B • Strap-On Sally #09: / 1996 / PL / F

TRACY DIONE see Patti Petite

TRACY DONOVAN see Stacey Donovan

TRACY EDWARDS
The Desirous Wife / 1988 / PL / M

TRACY ESCOBAR see Star Index I

TRACY EVANS see Star Index I

TRACY FONTE
Ball Game / 1980 / CA / M

TRACY G.
Cluster Fuck #01 / 1993 / MAX / M

TRACY GIBB
Buttman's European Vacation #2 / 1992 / EA / M • Girls Around The World #05 / 1992 / BTO / S • Mammary Manor / 1992 / BTO / M • Tit To Tit #1 / 1994 / BTO / M

TRACY HANNA see Star Index I

TRACY JONES see Star Index I

TRACY KITTRIDGE see Kelli Dylan

TRACY LOVE *(Love, Tracey Lori, Love Hanson)*
Blonde with shoulder length hair, medium tits, passable face, tight waist, lithe body, nice little butt, 21 years old in 1995. Very bubbly personality but sounds a little retarded.
A List / 1996 / SO / M • Abducted / 1996 / ZA / M • The Adventures Of Peeping Tom #1 / 1996 / OD / M • Anal Cornhole Cutie / 1996 / ROB / M • Anal Fever / 1996 / ROB / M • Anal Fireball / 1996 / ROB / M • Anal Lovebud / 1996 / ROB / M • Anal Nurses / 1996 / LBO / M • Anal Sex / 1996 / ZA / M • Anal Talisman / 1996 / ZA / M • Analtown USA #10 / 1996 / NIT / M • Babes Illustrated #5 / 1996 / IN / F • Backfield In Motion / 1995 / VT / M • Carnal Garden / 1996 / KLP / M • Corporate Justice / 1996 / TEP

/ M • Cum Buttered Corn Holes #1 / 1996 / NIT / C • Entangled / 1996 / KLP / M • Erotic Newcummers Vol 1 #4 / 1996 / DR / M • Everybody Wants Some / 1996 / EXQ / F • Exotic Car Models #1 / 1996 / IN0 / F • Fashion Sluts #6 / 1995 / ABS / M • Gang Bang Butthole Surfin' / 1996 / ROB / M • Gang Bang Dollies / 1996 / ROB / M • Hardcore Fantasies #4 / 1996 / LV / M • Hardcore Fantasies #5 / 1996 / LV / M • The Hitch-Hiker #15: Cat & Mouse / 1995 / VIM / M • Hollywood Halloween Sex Ball / 1996 / EUR / M • Hollywood Hookers / 1996 / DWV / M • Hot Tight Asses #15 / 1996 / TCK / M • Lesbian Debutante #03 / 1996 / IP / F • Max #12: Spread Eagle / 1996 / LE / M • Memories / 1996 / ZA / M • Naked & Nasty / 1995 / WP / M • Pick Up Lines #03 / 1995 / 4P / M • Pick Up Lines #04 / 1995 / 4P / M • The Portrait Of Dorie Grey / 1996 / KLP / M • Sex Hungry Butthole Sluts / 1996 / ROB / M • The Shocking Truth #1 / 1996 / DWO / M • The Show / 1995 / VI / M • Sinboy #1 / 1996 / SC / M • Sinnocence / 1995 / CDI / M • Smooth Ride / 1996 / WP / M • Spinners #2 (Wicked) / 1996 / WP / M • Talk Dirty To Me #10 / 1996 / DR / M • The Time Machine / 1996 / WP / M • Up Close & Personal #1 / 1996 / IPI / M • Up Your Ass #1 / 1996 / ANA / M • What You Are In The Dark / 1995 / KLP / M

TRACY MAJORS see Star Index I

TRACY MCSHEA
The Love Couch / 1977 / VC / M

TRACY NPELT see Star Index I

TRACY O'NEALL see Tracy O'Neill

TRACY O'NEIL see Tracy O'Neill

TRACY O'NEILL *(Traci O'Neill, Tracy O'Neil, Tracy O'Neall)*
China De Sade / 1977 / ALP / M • Inside Babysitter / 1977 / MID / M • The Liberation Of Honeydoll Jones / 1978 / VCX / M • Lipps & Mccain / 1978 / VC / M • Love Secrets / 1976 / VIP / M • The Other Side Of Julie / 1978 / CV / M • She Comes Undone / 1987 / AIR / C • Sweet Folds Of Flesh / 19?? / AST / M • Thoroughly Amorous Amy / 1978 / VCX / M • V—The Hot One / 1978 / CV / M

TRACY QUARTERMAIN see Star Index I

TRACY ROAMS see Tracey Adams

TRACY SCOTT
All American Hustler / cr73 / SOW / M • Bucky Beaver's XXX Dragon Art Theatre Double Feature #28 / 1996 / SOW / M

TRACY SLASH
The Girls Of Klit House / 1984 / LIP / F

TRACY STAR see Traci Starr

TRACY TAYLOR see Star Index I

TRACY TWINS see Star Index I

TRACY TYME
Dirty Dave's #3 / 1996 / XPR / M • Dirty Dave's #4 / 1996 / XPR / M • Nineteen #6 / 1996 / FOR / M

TRACY VALDIS see Star Index I

TRACY WALTON see Star Index I

TRACY WEST
Assent Of A Woman / 1993 / DR / M • Awakening Of The Cats / 1994 / NAP / B • Backdoor Brides #4 / 1993 / PV / M • Broadway Babes / 1993 / FH / F • Bruce Seven: A Compendium Of His Most Graphic Scenes Vol 6 / 1994 / BS / C • Casanova #1 / 1993 / SC / M • Casanova #2 / 1993 / SC / M • Compete And Seduce

/ 1994 / NAP / B • Elements Of Desire / 1994 / ULI / M • Girls Around The World #11 / 199? / BTO / S • Girls Around The World #26 / 1995 / BTO / S • Hidden Obsessions / 1992 / BFP / M • Licking Legends #1 / 1992 / LE / F • Licking Legends #2 / 1992 / LE / F • Notorious / 1992 / SC / M • Odyssey 30 Min: #244: / 1992 / OD / F • Panties / 1993 / VD / M • Positively Pagan #06 / 1993 / ATA / M • Punished Innocence / 1994 / BS / B • Radical Affairs Video Magazine #04 / 1992 / ME / M • Wicked Pleasures / 1995 / BS / B • WPINK-TV #4 / 1993 / PV / M

TRACY WOLFE see Casey Williams

TRANCE
1-900-SPANKME Ext.1 / 1994 / BON / B • 1-900-SPANKME Ext.2 / 1994 / BON / B

TRANSELVANIA
Hermaphrodites / 1996 / REB / C • Opposite Attraction / 1992 / VEX / M

TRAUMA MOMA
Master's Touch #2: Punished Slave Girls / 1994 / FAP / B • Master's Touch #6: Dom's In Distress / 1995 / FAP / B • The Price Is Wrong / 1995 / SV / B

TRAVIS KIDD
Red Riding She Male / 1995 / PL / G

TRAVIS LEE *(Travis Taylor)*
Boyfriend or husband of Josalynn Taylor.
Belly Of The Beast / 1993 / ZFX / B • Captain Bob's Pussy Patrol / 1993 / FCP / M • Dance Macabre / 1993 / ZFX / B • Dirty Dating Service #02 / 1993 / WP / M • Dirty Deeds Done Cheap / 1993 / ZFX / B • Fair Warning / 1995 / ZFX / B • Fantasy Flings #01 / 1993 / WP / M • Futureshock / 1993 / ZFX / B • Guinea Pigs #3 / 1993 / ZFX / B • Harry Horndog #17: Love Puppies #5 / 1993 / ZA / M • Highway To Hell / 1993 / ZFX / B • Mind Shadows #2 / 1993 / FD / M • Mr. Peepers Amateur Home Videos #72: Dirty Diary / 1993 / LBO / M • Mr. Peepers Amateur Home Videos #75: Trio In Rio / 1993 / LBO / M • Nasty Newcummers #02 / 1993 / MET / M • The Necklace #1 / 1994 / ZFX / B • The Necklace #3 / 1994 / ZFX / B • New Faces, Hot Bodies #07 / 1993 / STP / M • New Faces, Hot Bodies #21 / 1996 / STP / C • Night Prowler #1 / 1993 / ZFX / B • Night Prowler #3: Master Of Reality / 1995 / ZFX / B • Night Prowler #5 / 1995 / ZFX / B • Odyssey Triple Play #66: Cum-Crazed Couples / 1994 / OD / M • Odyssey Triple Play #70: Three By Threeway / 1994 / OD / M • Odyssey Triple Play #79: Dildos Dykes & Dicks / 1994 / OD / M • Pearl Necklace: Thee Bush League #16 / 1993 / SEE / M • Pearl Necklace: Thee Bush League #18 / 1993 / SEE / M • Phantacide Peepshow / 1996 / ZFX / B • Tiffany Twisted / 1993 / ZFX / B • Video Pirates #5: A Bullet To Bite / 1995 / ZFX / B

TRAVIS O'NEIL see Star Index I

TRAVIS TAYLOR see Travis Lee

TRE DWEEB
We Be Bangin' 24/7 / 1996 / FD / M

TREALLA
Mother Nature's Bulging Bellies / 1995 / LIP / F

TREANNA see Aurora

TREASURE see Star Index I

TREASURE CHEST see Greta Carlson

TREBLE HART see Heidi Nelson

TREE
In Search Of The Perfect Blow Job / 1995

/ OD / M

TRENT
Kinky Debutante Interviews #10 / 1995 / IP / M

TRENT MATTHEWS
Lady Dick / 1993 / HSV / G

TRENT ROELAN
Anal Interrogation / 1995 / ZA / M • Anal Playground / 1995 / CA / M • Arches Of Triumph / 1995 / PRE / S • Big Black & Beautiful Gang Bang / 1995 / HO / M • Club Kiss / 1995 / ONA / M • Deep Cheeks #5 / 1995 / ROB / M • Deep Inside Kaitlyn Ashley / 1995 / VC / C • Hit Ladies / 1995 / PRE / B • Hollywood Amateurs #23 / 1995 / MID / M • Hollywood Sex Tour / 1995 / VC / M • Keyholes / 1995 / OD / M • Lolita / 1995 / SC / M • The Night Shift / 1995 / LE / M • Swat Team / 1995 / PRE / B • The Voyeur #5 / 1995 / EA / M

TRENT WESTWOOD
Fantasy Flings #03 / 1995 / WP / M • Tootsies & Footsies / 1994 / LBO / M

TREONNA see Aurora

TREONNIA see Summer Rose

TRES DOVER see Fay Burd

TREVELYN
FTV #02: Wrestling Friends / 1996 / FT / B

TREVOR KNIGHT
Filthy First Timers #4 / 1996 / EL / M

TREVOR MAMMIK
Virgin Snow / 1976 / VXP / M

TREVOR WILLIAMS see Star Index I

TREXSURE see Star Index I

TREY TEMPEST
Bi Madness / 1991 / STA / G

TREZ see Star Index I

TREZINA
Black Women, White Men #1 / 1995 / FC / M

TRICIA
Kinky College Cunts #05 / 1993 / NS / F

TRICIA ASCOTT
Sweet Surrender / 1980 / VCX / M

TRICIA DEVERAUX (Jennifer Huss)
Tall dark blonde or light brown long hair in the sixties style, passable face, lithe body, medium tits, good skin with a golden down visible on tapes with good reproduction, 20 years old, good bottom tan lines, comes from Ohio. The outstanding thing about this girl are not her looks but her personality—she actually seems to like sex and draws a favorable response from the males. Jennifer Huss is from **Vamps: Deadly Dreamgirls**. As of 1997, supposedly married to Robert Black.
Anal Cornhole Cutie / 1996 / ROB / M • Anal Fireball / 1996 / ROB / M • Anal Honeypie / 1996 / ROB / M • Ass, Gas & The Mystical GLOP / 1997 / EL / M • Asses Galore #3: Pure Evil / 1996 / DFI / M • Asses Galore #5: T.T. Vs The World / 1996 / DFI / M • Barby's On Butt Row / 1996 / ABS / M • The Blowjob Adventures Of Doctor Fellatio / 1997 / EL / M • Blue Saloon / 1996 / ME / M • The Cellar Dweller / 1996 / EL / M • Cumback Pussy #1 / 1996 / EL / M • Dirty Debutantes #2 / 1996 / 4P / M • Dirty Tricks #2: This Ain't Love / 1996 / EA / M • Eternal Lust / 1996 / VC / M • Fashion Sluts #7 / 1996 / ABS / M • Gang Bang Dollies / 1996 / ROB / M • Gangbang Girl #17 / 1995 / ANA / M • Hypnotic Hookers #2 / 1996 / NIT / M • Kink: Police Chronicles / 1995 / ROB / M • Nasty Nymphos #11 / 1995 /

ANA / M • Nasty Nymphos #16 / 1996 / ANA / M • Nektar / 1996 / BAC / M • No Man's Land #15 / 1996 / VT / F • Perverted Stories #10 / 1996 / JMP / M • Private Dancers / 1996 / RAS / M • Private Gold #16: Summer Wind / 1997 / OD / M • Profiles #08: Triple Ecstacy / 1996 / XPR / M • Puritan Video Magazine #05 / 1996 / LE / M • Scotty's X-Rated Adventure / 1996 / WP / M • Sexual Atrocities / 1996 / EL / M • The Shocking Truth #1 / 1996 / DWO / M • Sin-A-Matic / 1996 / VI / M • Smoke & Mirrors / 1996 / PL / M • Sorority Sex Kittens #3 / 1996 / VC / M • Triple X Video Magazine #17 / 1996 / OD / M • Vamps: Deadly Dreamgirls / 1996 / EJF / S • Violation / 1996 / LE / M • The Voyeur #6 / 1996 / EA / M • War Whores / 1996 / EL / M • A Week And A Half In The Life Of A Prostitute / 1997 / EL / M • Young & Natural #13 / 1996 / TV / F • Young & Natural #14 / 1996 / TV / F • Young & Natural #15 / 1996 / TV / F • Young & Natural #18 / 1996 / TV / C

TRICIA GRAHAM see Star Index I

TRICIA JEN see Trisha Yin

TRICIA LAKE see Star Index I

TRICIA LANGSTON
Pink Champagne / 1979 / CV / M

TRICIA MARTIN
Love Mexican Style / cr75 / BLT / M

TRICIA RUSSELL see Star Index I

TRICIA YIN see Trisha Yin

TRICK TONY see J.P. Anthony

TRICKSY JAMESON
Double Trouble: Spanking English Style / 1996 / BIZ / B

TRICKY DICK
The Coming Of Angie / cr73 / TGA / M

TRIER
New Faces, Hot Bodies #20 / 1996 / STP / M

TRINA
Foxx Tales / 1996 / TTV / M • HomeGrown Video #435: Seasoned To Perfection / 1994 / HOV / M • HomeGrown Video #472: Everyday People / 1996 / HOV / M

TRINA (MARIE SHARP) see Marie Sharp

TRINA (TATIANNA) see Tatianna Cortez

TRINA TRIBAD
French-Pumped Femmes #1 / 1989 / RSV / G • Wet Dream On Maple Street / 1988 / FAN / M

TRINIDAD
100% Amateur #16: Bkack On White / 1995 / OD / M • Anal 247 / 1995 / CC / M • Ass Masters (Leisure) #06 / 1995 / LEI / M • Color Me Anal / 1995 / ME / M • Girls II Women / 1996 / AVI / M • Interracial 247 / 1995 / CC / M • More Black Dirty Debutantes #4 / 1995 / 4P / M • Sarah's Inheritance / 1995 / WIV / M • Snatch Masters #12 / 1995 / LEI / M • Tailz From Da Hood #3 / 1996 / AVI / M • Up And Cummers #24 / 1995 / 4P / M • Video Virgins #17 / 1994 / NS / M • What's The Lesbian Doing In My Pirate Movie? / 1995 / LIP / F

TRINITY
100% Amateur #19: / 1996 / OD / M

TRINITY BARNES see Trinity Loren

TRINITY LANE (Kim Reed, Christina Clark, Christine Clark)
Amazonian blonde with short hair and small tits who looks like a bigger version of Stacey Nichols. Very bad skin. Supposedly 29 years old in 1994 and was devirginized at 12.

Anal Camera #04 / 1995 / EVN / M • Bobby Hollander's Sweet Cheeks #112 / 1994 / QUA / M • Boiling Point / 1994 / WAV / M • Butthunt / 1994 / AFV / F • Deep Inside Dirty Debutantes #10 / 1993 / 4P / M • Double Decadence / 1995 / NOT / M • Fantasy Du Jour / 1995 / FH / M • Love Thrust / 1995 / ERA / M • Love Tryst / 1995 / VPN / M • Mike Hott: #260 Cunt of the Month: Trinity / 1994 / MHV / M • Mike Hott: #277 Cum In My Cunt #2 / 1994 / MHV / M • Mike Hott: #307 Lesbian Sluts #18 / 1995 / MHV / F • New Girls In Town #4 / 1993 / CC / M • Night Crawlers / 1994 / SC / M • The Pink Lady Detective Agency: Case Of The Twisted Sister / 1994 / IN / M • Prime Cuts #1 / 1994 / FOR / M • Prime Cuts #2 / 1994 / FOR / M • Hidin' The Big One / 1994 / TEG / M • Rocco Unleashed / 1994 / SC / M • The Room Mate / 1995 / EX / M • Sexy Nurses #2 / 1994 / CV / M • Star Struck / 1994 / ERA / M • Tight Fit #01 / 1994 / GO / M • Used And Abused #2 / 1995 / SFP / M • Video Virgins #11 / 1994 / NS / M • Visual Fantasies / 1995 / LE / M • Working Girls / 1995 / FH / M

TRINITY LOREN (Trinity Barnes)
Not too pretty fat blonde. Married to Shane Hunter at one stage.
Above And Beyond / 1990 / PNP / G • The Adventures Of Breastman / 1992 / EVN / M • AHV #02: Orgy Express / 1991 / EVN / M • AHV #03: Porking In The Rear / 1991 / EVN / M • Aja / 1988 / PL / M • Amateur Lesbians #01: Leanna / 1991 / GO / F • Amateur Lesbians #02: Dominique / 1991 / GO / F • Amateur Lesbians #07: Holly / 1991 / GO / F • Amateur Lesbians #08: Trixie / 1991 / GO / F • The Amateurs / 1984 / VCX / M • Amazing Tails #1 / 1987 / CA / M • Amazing Tails #2 / 1987 / CA / M • Amazing Tails #3 / 1987 / CA / M • American Dream Girls #1 / 1986 / VEX / M • Anal Analysis (Heatwave) / 1992 / HW / M • Anal Attraction #1 / 1988 / 3HV / M • Anal Dawn / 1991 / AMB / M • Anal Pleasures / 1988 / AVC / M • Angels Of Passion / 1986 / CDI / M • Arches Of Triumph / 1995 / PRE / S • The Aroused / 1989 / IN / M • Ass-Capades / 1992 / HW / M • Attack Of The Monster Mammaries / 1987 / LA / C • Awesome #01 / 1986 / 4P / C • Back To Back #2 / 1992 / FC / C • Backdoor Lambada / 1990 / GO / M • Backdoor To Hollywood #01 / 1986 / CDI / M • Backdoor To Hollywood #02 / 1986 / CDI / M • Backdoor To Hollywood #06 / 1989 / CIN / M • Backing In #3 / 1991 / WV / C • Bare Essence / 1989 / EA / M • The Battle Of The Breast Queens / 1989 / INS / C • Battle Of The Ultra Milkmaids / 1992 / LET / M • The Beat Goes On / 1987 / VCR / C • Bedrooms And Boardrooms / 1992 / DR / M • Beefeaters / 1989 / PV / M • Behind The Backdoor #2 / 1989 / EVN / M • Best Of Bi And Beyond / 1992 / PNP / C • Best Of Caught From Behind #1 / 1987 / HO / C • Best Of Caught From Behind #3 / 1989 / HO / C • Best Of Foot Worship #3 / 1992 / BIZ / C • Big Boob Boat Ride #1 / 1992 / FC / M • Big Bust Babes #04 / 1988 / AFI / M • Big Bust Babes #06 / 1991 / AFI / F • Big Bust Casting Call / 1993 / PME / S • Big Busty #47 / 1994 / BTO / S • Big Tit Orgy #01 / 1987 / H&S / M • Big Titted Tarts / 1994 / PL / C • Big Top Cabaret #1 / 1986 / BTO / M • Biloxi Babes / 1988 / WV / M •

Blonde On The Run / 1985 / PV / M • Body Slam / 1987 / 4P / B • Bored Housewife / 1989 / CIN / M • Bouncin' In The U.S.A. / 1986 / H&S / S • Bound To Tease #3 / 1989 / BON / C • Breakfast With Tiffany / 1990 / HO / M • Breast Collection #01 / 1995 / LBO / C • Breast Collection #03 / 1995 / LBO / C • Breast Friends / 1991 / PL / M • Breast Wishes #05 / 1991 / LBO / M • Breast Worx #01 / 1991 / LBO / M • Breast Worx #06 / 1991 / LBO / M • Breast Worx #22 / 1992 / LBO / M • Breastography, Lesson #1 / 1987 / VCR / M • Breaststroke #1 / 1988 / EX / M • Breaststroke #2 / 1989 / EX / M • Bright Lights, Big Titties / 1989 / CA / M • Bubble Butts #10 / 1992 / LBO / M • Bum Rap / 1990 / PLV / B • Bums Away / 1995 / PRE / C • But...Can She Type? / 1989 / CDI / M • Butt's Motel #2 / 1989 / EX / M • The Buttnicks #1 / 1990 / VEX / M • Caught From Behind #06 / 1986 / HO / M • Caught From Behind #16: The Reunion / 1992 / HO / M • Cheesecake / 1991 / VC / M • City Of Rage / 1989 / EVN / M • Class Of Nuke 'em High #2: Subhumanoid Meltdown / 1991 / MED / S • Club Head (EVN) #2 / 1989 / EVN / C • Club Josephine / 1991 / AR / F • The Coach's Daughter / 1991 / AR / M • Controlled / 1990 / BS / B • Couples Club #1 / 1988 / BON / B • Couples Club #2 / 1989 / BON / B • Cyrano / 1991 / PL / M • Dance Fire / 1989 / EA / M • Deep C Diver / 1992 / LV / M • Depraved Innocent / 1986 / VD / M • Dirty 30's Cinema: Patti Petite / 1986 / PV / C • Dirty 30's Cinema: Trinity Loren / 1986 / PV / C • The Doctor's In / 1986 / CDI / M • Doin' The Harlem Shuffle / 1986 / CA / M • Double D-Cup Dates / 1994 / BTO / M • Double The Pleasure / 1990 / SE / M • Dr Hooters / 1991 / PL / M • Dreams In The Forbidden Zone / 1989 / PCP / M • Dump Site / 1989 / BIZ / C • Educating Kascha / 1989 / CIN / M • Ex-Connection / 1986 / SEV / M • Exiles / 1991 / VT / M • Exposure Images #19: Trinity Loren / 1992 / EXI / F • Fat Ends / 1989 / 4P / M • Fatliners #1 / 1990 / EX / M • Feet First / 1988 / BIZ / S • Filet-O-Breast / 1988 / AVC / M • Flying High #2 / 1992 / HO / M • Fortysomething #1 / 1990 / LE / M • Full Bodied: Trinity Loren / 1990 / H&S / S • Full Moon Fever / 1992 / PEP / M • Funny Ladies / 1996 / PRE / B • Ginger's Hawaiian Scrapbook / 1988 / GO / C • Girls Like Us / cr88 / IN / C • Girls Of The Double D #03 / 1988 / CDI / M • Girls Of The Double D #04 / 1989 / CDI / M • Girls Of The Double D #05 / 1988 / CIN / M • Girls Of The Double D #08 / 1989 / CDI / M • Girls Of Treasure Island / 1988 / CV / M • The Golden Gals / 1989 / BTO / M • Gourmet Quickies: Shauna Grant / Trinity Loren #725 / 1984 / GO / C • Gourmet Quickies: Trinity Loren / Jacquelyn Brooks #726 / 1985 / GO / C • Hardcore Plumpers / 1991 / BTO / M • The Harley Girls / 1991 / AR / F • Having It All / 1985 / IN / M • Hawaii Vice #8 / 1990 / CIN / M • Honkytonk Angels / 1988 / IN / C • Hooter Heaven / 1992 / CA / M • Horny Toed / 1989 / BIZ / S • Hot Foot / 1991 / PLV / B • Hot Licks / 1990 / CDI / M • Hot Line / 1991 / VC / M • I Am Desire / 1992 / WV / M • I Love X / 1992 / FC / C • I'm No Dummy / 1991 / HO / M • Innocence Lost / 1988 / CA / M • Internal Affairs / 1992 / CDI / M • King Tongue

Meets Anal Woman / 1990 / PL / M • Kiss Of The Married Woman / 1986 / WV / M • A Lacy Affair #4 / 1991 / HO / F • Lawyers In Heat / 1989 / CDI / M • The Layout / 1986 / CDI / M • Le Sex De Femme #3 / 1989 / AFI / C • A League Of Their Moan / 1992 / EVN / M • Leather And Lace Revisited / 1991 / VT / F • Leave It To Cleavage #2 / 1989 / EVN / M • Lez Go Crazy / 1992 / HW / C • Lifestyles Of The Black And Famous / 1986 / WET / M • A Little Romance / 1986 / HO / M • Loving Spoonfulls / 1987 / 4P / C • Mad Sex / 1986 / VD / M • Making It In New York / 1989 / PLD / M • Midnight Pink / 1987 / WV / M • Mirage #1 / 1991 / VC / M • Mirage #2 / 1992 / VC / M • More Unbelievable Orgies / 1989 / EVN / C • Mystic Pieces / 1989 / EA / M • Naughty Neighbors / 1989 / CA / M • Nina, Just For You / 1989 / BON / F • Only The Best Of Barbara Dare / 1990 / CV / C • Orgies / 1987 / WV / C • Other People's Honey / 1991 / HW / M • Parliament: Licking Lesbians #2 / 1989 / PM / F • Personal Touch #4 / 1989 / AR / M • Playing With A Full Dick / 1988 / PL / M • Porn Star's Day Off / 1990 / FAZ / M • The Price Is Right / 1992 / VT / C • Rachel Ryan / 1988 / WV / C • Ready To Drop #01 / 1990 / FC / M • The Return Of The A Team / 1988 / WV / M • Sensuous Singles: Trinity Loren / 1987 / VCR / F • Sex Slaves / 1986 / VEX / M • Sex Star Competition / 1985 / PL / M • Sexaholics / 1987 / VCX / M • Sinderella's Revenge / 1992 / HOM / B • Sins Of Wealthy Wives / 1989 / CDI / C • Sirens / 1991 / VC / M • Soaked To The Bone / 1989 / IN / M • Sorority Pink #1 / 1989 / CV / M • Sorority Pink #2 / 1989 / CV / M • Southern Side Up / 1992 / LV / M • Special Interest / 1990 / GO / C • Special Treatment / 1991 / AFV / M • Student Fetish Videos: Catfighting #02 / 1991 / PLV / B • Student Fetish Videos: The Enema #02 / 1990 / SFV / B • Super Cakes / 1994 / CA / C • Super Leg-Ends / 1992 / PRE / C • Super Sex / 1986 / MAP / M • Supersluts Of Wrestling / 1986 / VD / M • Surfer Girl / 1992 / PP / M • Surfside Sex / 1988 / CA / M • Sweet Cheeks / 1987 / VCR / C • Tailgunners / 1985 / WET / M • Tantala's Fat Rack / 1990 / FC / B • A Taste Of Genie / 1986 / 4P / M • A Taste Of Trinity Loren / 1990 / PIN / C • Teasers: Saturday Lovers / 1988 / MET / M • Temptations / 1989 / DR / M • Temptations Of An Angel / 1989 / PEN / M • This One's For You / 1989 / AR / M • Tit Tales #1 / 1989 / 4P / M • Tit Tales #2 / 1990 / FC / M • Tit Tales #3 / 1991 / FC / M • Tit To Tit #1 / 1994 / BTO / M • Titty-Titty Bang-Bang / 1992 / FC / C • To Live & Shave In LA / 1986 / WET / M • To Snatch A Thief / 1989 / PLD / M • Tooth And Nail / 1988 / NAP / B • Toys, Not Boys #1 / 1991 / FC / C • Toys, Not Boys #3 / 1991 / FC / C • Transaction #1 / 1986 / WET / M • Trinity Bound At Home / 1990 / BON / B • Trinity, Just For You / 1989 / BON / F • A Trip Down Mammary Lane / 1991 / FC / M • Triple Header / 1990 / KNI / M • The Twilight Moan / 1985 / WV / M • Twin Peaks / 1993 / PL / M • Video Paradise / 1988 / ZA / M • Vixens / 1989 / LV / F • Wenches / 1991 / VT / F • Wet Dream On Maple Street / 1988 / FAN / M • Who Shaved Trinity Loren? / 1988 / EX / M • Wild Things #3 / 1992 / MET / M • Winner

Take All / 1986 / SEV / M • A Woman's Touch / 1988 / ZA / F • The X-Terminator / 1986 / PV / M • [Berlin Caper / 1989 / ... / M • [Palm Springs Weekend / 19?? / ... / M

TRISH
Angie, Trish, Linda, Samantha / 1990 / PLV / B • Big Murray's New-Cummers #01: Blondes Have More... / 1992 / FD / M • Big Murray's New-Cummers #02: Las Vegas Swingers / 1992 / FD / M • Blackmail Bondage / 1993 / BON / B • Blue Vanities #502 / 1992 / FFL / M • Hot Legs #1 / 1990 / PLV / B • Stevi's: Trish & Robert / 1993 / SSV / M

TRISH (1996)
Anal Virgins #03 / 1996 / NS / M • Hardcore Debutantes #03 / 1997 / TEP / M • Video Virgins #32 / 1996 / NS / M

TRISH ADAMS
Brats In Bondage / 1993 / LON / B • Hellfire Society / 19?? / HOM / B • Her Darkest Desire / 1993 / HOM / B

TRISH COLE
Triangle Of Love / cr78 / ASR / M

TRISH HORNE
Carnal Carnival / cr78 / VCX / M

TRISH MARS
Daddy's Girls / 1985 / LA / M

TRISHA
AVP #7016: Can I See Your Dickie? / 1990 / AVP / M • Big Boobs Around The World #1 / 1990 / BTO / M • Big British Plumpers / 1989 / BTO / M • Crack Attack! / 1996 / PE / M • H&S: Trisha / 199? / H&S / S • Lesbian Love Dolls / 1995 / LIP / F • Real People Real Bondage #1 / 1995 / BON / C

TRISHA COLE
Cheeks #6 / 1992 / CC / M • Creme De La Face #17: Semen For Seven / 1996 / OD / M • The Cumm Brothers #17: Goo Guy Gone Bad / 1996 / OD / M • Hardcore Debutantes #03 / 1997 / TEP / M • Santa Is Coming All Over Town / 1996 / EVN / M • Sodom Bottoms / 1996 / SP / M

TRISHA DIAMOND *(Traci Diamond)*
French, 20 years old, firm lithe body, tight waist, good skin, nice butt, medium sized breasts, blonde with long straight hair, minimal English but nice personality and seems to like sex.
The Anal-Europe Series #05: Anal European Vacation / 1993 / LV / M • Buffy Malibu's Nasty Girls #06 / 1994 / ANA / F • Club Anal #2 / 1993 / ROB / F • Dr Butts #3 / 1993 / 4P / M • Lovin' Spoonfuls #6 / 1996 / 4P / C • More Dirty Debutantes #27 / 1993 / 4P / M • Taste Of Shame / 1994 / ROB / F • Up And Cummers: The Movie / 1994 / 4P / M • [European Invasion / cr93 / A&E / M

TRISHA INGLE
Little Girls Blue #2 / 1983 / VCX / M

TRISHA LAE *see Star Index I*

TRISHA VENUS
Bedtime Video #04 / 1984 / GO / M

TRISHA VERON
Sex Off The Runway / 1991 / GMI / M

TRISHA YEN *see Trisha Yin*

TRISHA YIN *(Tricia Yin, Trisha Yen, Mimi Wong, Tricia Jen, Mimi Yen)*
Oriental with a very petite doll-like body, nice medium (for her size) tits, pretty with a nice smile. Personality wise she seems a little too forward and in control. In 1993 was 19 years old, 5' tall, 87lbs and of Vietnamese/Japanese ancestry. In 1995 she has added nipple rings and a belly button ring.

As of mid 1996 she was allegedly dying of metasticized cancer. America's Raunchiest Home Videos #75: / 1993 / ZA / M • Asian Heat #04: House Of The Rising Sun / 1993 / SC / M • Asian Heat #05: The Joy Suck Club / 1994 / SC / M • Bodywaves / 1994 / ELP / M • Bordello / 1995 / VI / M • Butterfly / 1993 / OD / M • Butthead Dreams: Mission Impenetrable / 1994 / FH / M • Chow Down / 1994 / VI / M • Colossal Orgy #1 / 1993 / HW / M • Colossal Orgy #3 / 1994 / HW / M • Cream / 1993 / SC / M • The Dean's Spanking / 1995 / STM / B • Demolition Woman #1 / 1994 / IP / M • Demolition Woman #2 / 1994 / IP / M • Diary Of A Geisha / 1995 / WV / C • Dirty Bob's #14: Can Hams! / 1994 / FLP / S • Dollars And Yen / 1994 / FH / M • The Dragon Lady #7: Tales From The Bed #6 / 1994 / WV / M • Dragon Lady's Domination Technique / 1995 / STM / B • Eclipse / 1993 / SC / M • Erotica Optique / 1994 / SUF / M • Escape To The Party / 1994 / ELP / M • Extreme Sex #4: The Experiment / 1995 / VI / M • First Time Lesbians #14 / 1994 / JMP / F • Games Women Play / 1995 / XC / M • Geisha To Go / 1994 / PPP / M • A Girl's Affair #04 / 1994 / FD / F • The Grind / 1995 / XC / M • Hard-On Copy / 1994 / WV / M • Hidden Camera #12 / 1993 / JMP / M • Kinky Orientals / 1994 / FH / M • Kittens #6 / 1994 / CC / F • Kym Wilde's On The Edge #28 / 1995 / RB / B • Latex #2 / 1995 / VC / M • Lesbian Kink Trilogy #2 / 1995 / STM / F • Makin' It / 1994 / A&E / M • Mike Hott: #252 Horny Couples #15 / 1994 / MHV / M • Mike Hott: #282 Three-Sum Sluts #01 / 1995 / MHV / M • The Mistress And The Prince / 1995 / STM / B • Moist Thighs / 1995 / STM / F • More Dirty Debutantes #28 / 1994 / 4P / M • Mystic Tales Of The Orient / 1994 / PRK / M • Oriental Dominatrix / 1995 / STM / B • Oriental Oddballs #2 / 1994 / FH / M • Pai Gow Video #05: California Asians / 1994 / EVN / M • Pai Gow Video #07: East Meets West / 1995 / EVN / M • Pai Gow Video #08: Asian Fantasies / 1995 / EVN / M • R & R / 1994 / VC / M • Red Light / 1994 / SC / S • Ridin' The Big One / 1994 / TEG / M • Secret Desires / 1994 / ORE / C • Seekers / 1994 / CA / M • Sex Secrets Of High Priced Call Girls / 1995 / MID / M • Spanked Geisha Girl / 1995 / STM / B • Stiff Competition #2 / 1994 / CA / M • Strap-On Sally #05: Chantilly's French Kiss / 1995 / PL / F • Strap-On Sally #06: Triple Penetration Trollop / 1995 / PL / F • Temple Of Love / 1995 / STM / B • Tricia's Painful Pleasure / 1995 / STM / B • Truck Stop Angel / 1994 / CC / M • Two Can Chew / 1995 / FD / M • Ultimate Gang Bang #1 / 1994 / HW / M • Up And Cummers: The Movie / 1994 / 4P / M • Up The Ying Yang #1 / 1994 / CC / M • Video Virgins #07 / 1993 / NS / M • Virtual Encounters / 1996 / SCI / S • Wet Faces #1 / 1997 / SC / C • Xcitement: The Movie / 1993 / XCI / M • Yin Yang Oriental Love Bang #2 / 1996 / SUF / M

TRISTAN
Sidone Bi / 1995 / FRF / G

TRISTE
The French Canal / 1995 / DVP / G

TRIX
Blue Vanities #553 / 1994 / FFL / M

TRIXI HEINEN *see Star Index I*

TRIXIE
Babes Of The Bay #1 / 1994 / LIP / F • Homegrown Video #418: Looks As Good As It Feels / 1994 / HOV / M • Wrestling Classics #2 / 1984 / CDP / B

TRIXIE SOMMERS
Limited Edition #04 / 1979 / AVC / M

TRIXIE TYALOR *see Trixie Tyler*

TRIXIE TYLER *(Trixie Tyalor, Barbara Wood (Trix))*
Not too good looking slutty blonde. Trixie Tyalor (sic) is from **Pink Card**. Born March 2, 1968 in San Bernadino, CA.
Adventures Of Buttwoman #1 / 1991 / EL / F • AHV #01: Three Way Wonders / 1991 / EVN / M • Amateur Lesbians #07: Holly / 1991 / GO / F • Amateur Lesbians #08: Trixie / 1991 / GO / F • America's Raunchiest Home Videos #05: Sasha Gets Stuffed / 1992 / ZA / M • Anal Carnival / 1992 / ROB / M • Anal Delights #1 / 1992 / ROB / M • Anal Innocence #1 / 1991 / ROB / M • Anal Starlets / 1991 / ROB / M • Anal Therapy #1 / 1992 / FD / M • The Anals Of History #1 / 1991 / MID / M • Animal Instincts / 1991 / VEX / M • Art Of Sex / 1992 / FD / M • Autobiography Of A Whip / 1991 / BS / B • Back In Action / 1992 / FD / M • Backdoor To Russia #1 / 1992 / VC / M • Backdoor To Russia #2 / 1993 / VC / M • Backdoor To Russia #3 / 1993 / VC / M • The Bad News Brat / 1991 / VI / M • Bangin' With The Home Girls / 1991 / AFV / M • The Best Of Black Anal #1 / 1995 / ROB / C • Best Of Buttman #1 / 1991 / EA / C • Best Of Buttman #2 / 1993 / EA / C • The Best Of The Gangbang Girl Series #2 / 1995 / ANA / C • The Best Of The Gangbang Girl Series / 1995 / ANA / C • Beyond It All / 1991 / PAL / G • Biff Malibu's Totally Nasty Home Videos #28 / 1992 / ANA / M • Blue Fox / 1991 / VI / M • Body Fire / 1991 / LV / M • Book Of Love / 1992 / VC / M • Bound For Pleasure / 1991 / BS / B • Breast Worx #27 / 1992 / LBO / M • Bruce Seven: A Compendium Of His Most Graphic Scenes Vol 3 / 1992 / BS / C • Bruce Seven: A Compendium Of His Most Graphic Scenes Vol 4 / 1993 / BS / C • The Butler Did It / 1991 / FH / M • Butt Freak #2 / 1996 / EA / M • Butties / 1992 / VC / M • Cannes Heat / 1992 / FD / M • City Of Sin / 1991 / LV / M • Cries From The Dungeon / cr94 / HOM / B • Dallas Does Debbie / 1992 / PL / M • Dances With Foxes / 1991 / CC / M • The Danger Zone / 1990 / SO / M • Dark Star / 1991 / VI / M • Dominating Girlfriends #2 / 1992 / PL / B • European Debutantes #01 / 1995 / IP / M • European Debutantes #03 / 1995 / IP / M • Exotic Tastes / 1995 / VEX / C • The Fear Zone / 1991 / BS / B • Fit To Be Tied / 1991 / BS / B • The Flintbones / 1992 / FR / M • The Flirt / 1992 / EVN / M • Forever / 1991 / LE / M • Full Moon Video #34: Wild Side Couples—From Head To Toe / 1995 / FAP / M • Gangbang Girl #01 / 1992 / ANA / M • Gangbang Girl #02 / 1992 / ANA / M • Girl Friends / 1990 / PL / F • Girls Gone Bad #4: Cell Block Riot / 1991 / GO / F • Girls Gone Bad #5: Mexican Justice / 1991 / GO / F • Girls, Girls, Girls / 1993 / FD / C • Head Talk / 1991 / ZA / M • The Hills Have Thighs / 1992 / MID / C • Hothouse Rose #1 / 1991 / VC / M • Hothouse Rose #2 / 1992 / VC / M • House Of Torture / 1993 / PL / B •

Hush...My Mother Might Hear Us / 1993 / FL / M • If You're Nasty / 1991 / PL / F • In Your Face #2 / 1992 / PL / M • Indiscretions / 1991 / PP / M • Infamous Crimes Against Nature / 1993 / SUM / M • Junk Yard Dogs / 1991 / FC / M • L.A. Rear / 1992 / FD / M • Lesbian Pros And Amateurs #14 / 1992 / GO / F • Lust Horizons / 1992 / PL / G • The Master & The Slave / 1993 / BON / B • Master's Touch #4: Pain's World / 1995 / FAP / B • The Mating Game / 1992 / PL / G • Midnight Caller / 1992 / MID / M • Mirage #2 / 1992 / VC / M • Miss 21st Century / 1991 / ZA / M • Modern Torture / 1992 / PL / B • Mona Lisa / 1992 / LV / M • Motel Hell / 1992 / PL / M • Mr. Peepers Amateur Home Videos #13: Backdoor Doctor / 1991 / LBO / M • Mr. Peepers Amateur Home Videos #15: When Company Comes / 1991 / LBO / M • Mr. Peepers Amateur Home Videos #17: No Holes Barred / 1991 / LBO / M • My 500 Pound Vibrator / 1991 / LV / C • My Anal Valentine / 1993 / FD / M • Nasty Reputation / 1991 / VEX / M • Neighborhood Watch #03 / 1991 / LBO / M • No Mercy For The Witches / 1992 / HOM / B • Nothing Serious / 1990 / EX / M • The Nurses Are Cumming #2 / 1996 / LBO / C • The One And Only / 1993 / FD / M • Openhanded Girlfriends / 1992 / RB / B • Openhanded Marriage / 1990 / RB / B • Orgy On The Ranch / 1991 / NLE / M • Pajama Party / 1993 / CV / C • Parlor Games / 1992 / VT / M • The Penetrator #1 / 1991 / PL / M • Pink Card / 1991 / FH / M • The Pink Pussycat / 1992 / CA / M • Private Places / 1992 / VC / M • Pubic Eye / 1992 / HW / M • Puttin' Her Ass On The Line / 1991 / DR / M • Racquel In Paradise / 1990 / VC / M • Raquel Released / 1991 / VI / M • Realities #1 / 1991 / ZA / M • Red Beaver Bonanza / 1992 / TCP / M • Ripe & Ready (Infinity) / 1995 / IF / M • Riviera Heat / 1993 / FD / M • Rockin' The Boat / 1990 / VI / M • Scared Stiff / 1992 / PL / B • The Seductress / 1992 / ZA / M • The Sex Symbol / 1991 / GO / M • Sittin' Pretty #1 / 1990 / DR / M • Sluts In Slavery / 1995 / LBO / B • Soda Jerk / 1992 / ZA / M • Sporting Illustrated / 1990 / HO / M • Spring Break / 1992 / PL / M • The Story Of Pain / 1992 / PL / B • Street Girl Named Desire / 1992 / FD / M • Summer's End / 1991 / ROB / M • Takin' It Off / 1994 / DGD / S • Tales From The Backside / 1993 / VC / M • Talk Dirty To Me #08 / 1990 / DR / M • Titty-Titty Bang-Bang / 1992 / FC / C • To The Rear / 1992 / VC / M • Torch #2 / 1990 / VI / M • Tortured Passions / 1994 / PL / B • The Torturous Infidel / 1994 / PL / B • Twin Peeks / 1990 / DR / M • VGA: Cutting Room Floor #1 / 1993 / VGA / M • VGA: Sorry Salesman / 1993 / VGA / B • VGA: Spanking Sampler #2 / 1992 / VGA / B • A Vision In Heather / 1991 / VI / M • The War Of The Hoses / 1991 / NLE / M • Where There's Sparxx, There's Fire / 1991 / LV / M • Zane's World / 1992 / ZA / M

TRIXY JOHNSON
Spiteful Housewives Spanked / 1995 / BIZ / B

TROUBLE
Fashion Sluts #8 / 1996 / ABS / M

TROY
Bi-Bi Love Amateurs #3 / 1993 / QUA / G

TROY (MICHAEL J COX) *see Michael J.*

Cox

TROY BALLOU
Sodomania #04: Further On Down The Road / 1993 / EL / M

TROY BENJAMIN
More Dirty Debutantes #56 / 1996 / 4P / M

TROY BENNY *see* Carlos Tobalina

TROY BERG *see* Troy Tanner

TROY COLLINS *see Star Index I*

TROY HART *see Star Index I*

TROY LANIER *see* Troy Tanner

TROY LEE
The Big One / 1995 / HO / M • The Night Shift / 1995 / LE / M • Renegades #1 / 1994 / SC / M

TROY NEXUS
Cocks In Frocks #2 / 1996 / TTV / G

TROY RAMSEY *see Star Index I*

TROY RICHARDS *see Star Index I*

TROY SCALPINI
Dr Bizarro / 1978 / ALP / B

TROY STEELE
Marine Code Of Silence: Don't Ask Don't Tell / 1996 / BHE / G

TROY TANIER *see* Troy Tanner

TROY TANNER *(Troy Trainer, Troy Tannier, Troy Tanier, Troy Lanier, Troy Berg)*
Emaciated looking male with black hair and very white skin. SO of Kari Fox at one point.
Amazing Sex Stories #2 / 1987 / SUV / C • Amber Pays The Rent / 1986 / VT / M • The Anal-ist #2 / 1986 / VEX / M • Backdoor To Hollywood #03 / 1987 / CDI / M • Backdoor To Hollywood #04 / 1988 / CDI / M • Beyond The Denver Dynasty / 1988 / CA / M • Blonde Fantasy / 1988 / CC / M • Blonde On The Run / 1985 / PV / M • Bondage Playmates / Taut Adventure / 1987 / BIZ / B • California Reaming / 1985 / WV / M • Caught From Behind #06 / 1986 / HO / M • Crystal Balls / 1986 / DR / M • Deep Inside Vanessa Del Rio / 1986 / VC / M • Devil In Miss Jones #3: A New Beginning / 1986 / VC / M • Devil In Miss Jones #4: The Final Outrage / 1987 / VC / M • The Ecstasy Girls #2 / 1986 / CA / M • Every Woman Has A Fantasy #2 / 1986 / VC / M • Gentlemen Prefer Ginger / 1985 / VI / M • Getting LA'd / 1986 / PV / M • Girls Of The Double D #02 / 1987 / CDI / M • Goddess Of Love / 1986 / CDI / M • Going Down With Amber / 1987 / 4P / M • Hollywood Vice / 1985 / VD / M • Hometown Honeys #1 / 1986 / VEX / M • Hot Nights At The Blue Note Cafe / 1985 / WV / M • Hottest Parties / 1988 / VC / C • Indecent Itch / 1985 / VCR / M • Introducing Barbii / 1987 / CDI / M • Kiss Of The Dragon Lady / 1986 / SEV / M • The Layout / 1986 / CDI / M • Loose Caboose / 1987 / 4P / M • Loose Ends #2 / 1986 / 4P / M • Lust Letters / 1988 / CA / M • Naughty Ninja Girls / 1987 / LA / M • Night Games / 1986 / WV / M • Oral Majority #06 / 1988 / WV / C • Project Ginger / 1985 / VI / M • Rambone The Destroyer / 1985 / WET / M • Rated Sex / 1986 / SE / M • Ready, Willing & Anal (Cv) / 1993 / CV / C • Rears / 1987 / VI / M • Return To Sex 5th Avenue / 1985 / WV / M • Scent Of A Woman / 1985 / GO / M • Secret Lessons #1 / 1986 / BIZ / B • Sinful Sisters / 1986 / VEX / M • Skin Games / 1986 / VEX / M • Smooth As Silk / 1987 / VIP / M • Star 85: Kari Fox / 1985 / VEX / M • A Taste Of Tawnee / 1988 / LV

/ C • Tawnee...Be Good! / 1988 / LV / M • Teasers: Frustrated Housewife / 1988 / MET / M • Tickle Time / 1987 / BIZ / B • Traci's Big Trick / 1987 / VAS / M • WPINK-TV #2 / 1986 / PV / M • The X-Terminator / 1986 / PV / M

TROY TANNIER *see* Troy Tanner

TROY TRAINER *see* Troy Tanner

TROYE LANE *see Star Index I*

TRUDY
Blue Vanities #527 / 1993 / FFL / M • Buffy Malibu's Totally Nasty All-Girl Home Videos #03 / 1992 / ANA / F • The Older Women's Sperm Bank #6 / 1996 / SUF / M

TRUDY MARSEN
Sex Boat / 1980 / VCX / M

TRUDY TRUE
Ancient Amateurs #1 / 1996 / LOF / M

TRUDY WAYNE
Blue Vanities #556 / 1994 / FFL / M • Teaserama / 1954 / SOW / S • Varietease / 1955 / SOW / S

TRULEY *see Star Index I*

TRULY SCRUMPTIOUS *see* Courtney

TSANG KONG
Wild Cherry / 1983 / ORC / M

TSUNAMI
Pai Gow Video #09: Naked Asians / 1995 / EVN / M

TSUNEO SHIRAYAMA
Sexually Yours / 1996 / AVE / M

TSUYAKO HIME *see Star Index I*

TT BOYD *see* T.T. Boy

TUESDAY
C-Hunt #01: Pandemonium / 1995 / PEV / M

TUESDAY BLUE *see Star Index I*

TULIP BUFFS
Bottom Busters / 1973 / BLT / M

TUNDE
Buttwoman Back In Budapest / 1993 / EL / M • Buttwoman In Budapest / 1992 / EA / M • Frank Thring's Double Penetration #1 / 1995 / XPR / M • The Hungarian Connection / 1992 / EA / M • Penetration (Anabolic) #3 / 1995 / ANA / M • Prague By Night #1 / 1996 / EA / M • Private Gold #12: The Pyramid #2 / 1996 / OD / M • Private Gold #14: Sweet Lady #1 / 1997 / OD / M • Sleeping Booty / 1995 / EL / M • Thermonuclear Sex / 1996 / EL / M

TUNISIA *see Star Index I*

TUPPY OWENS
Sensations / 1975 / ALP / M • Sex Maniac's Ball / 1995 / AOC / S

TURK LYNN *see* Turk Lyon

TURK LYON *(Robert Lyon, Robert Magatoney, Turk Lynn)*
Robert Magatoney is from *Cry For Cindy*.
Baby Face #1 / 1977 / VC / M • Bad Company / 1978 / CV / M • The Best Of Alex De Renzy #1 / 1983 / VC / C • Candy Goes To Hollywood / 1979 / VCX / M • Ceremony, The Ritual Of Love / 1976 / AVC / M • Cry For Cindy / 1976 / AR / M • Desires Within Young Girls / 1977 / CA / M • Dixie / 1976 / VHL / M • The Ecstasy Girls #1 / 1979 / CA / M • The Erotic Adventures Of Candy / 1978 / VCX / M • Erotic Fantasies #1 / 1983 / CV / C • Erotic Fantasies #4 / 1983 / CV / C • Femmes De Sade / 1976 / ALP / M • Flight Sensations / 1983 / VC / C • Frat House / 1979 / NGV / M • Hot Dallas Nights / 1981 / VCX / M • Hot Rackets / 1979 / CV / M • Judgement Day / 1976 / CV / M • Limited Edition #03 / 1979 / AVC / M • Limited

Edition #04 / 1979 / AVC / M • Little Girls Blue #1 / 1977 / VCX / M • Little Orphan Dusty #1 / 1978 / ALP / M • Love Slaves / 1976 / VCR / M • Midnight Hustle / 1978 / VC / M • Naked Afternoon / 1976 / CV / M • Night Pleasures / 1975 / WWV / M • One Of A Kind / 1976 / SVE / M • Pretty Peaches #1 / 1978 / MIT / M • Pro Ball Cheerleaders / 1979 / AVC / M • Sensual Encounters Of Every Kind / 1978 / SE / M • Seven Into Snowy / 1977 / VC / M • Sex Boat / 1980 / VCX / M • Taboo #01 / 1980 / VCX / M • The Velvet Edge / cr76 / SE / M

TURK TURPIN *see Star Index I*

TUSHIMA BREAST
Asian Tigress / 1994 / NAP / B • The Challenge Of Tushima / 1994 / NAP / B • Mean Streak / 1994 / NAP / B • The Taming Of Tushima / 1994 / NAP / B

TUTU
Filthy First Timers #5 / 1997 / EL / M

TWINKLE STAR
Black Casting Couch #2 / 1994 / WP / M

TWINKY *see Star Index I*

TWYLA LOVE
Nina's Knockouts / 1987 / AVC / C

TY FOX
Revenge Of The Bi Dolls / 1994 / CAT / G

TY JONES *see Star Index I*

TY KOLBY
Soft Warm Rain / 1987 / VD / M • Tracey And The Bandit / 1987 / LA / M

TY RUSSELL
4 Bi 4 / 1994 / BIN / G • Las Vegas She-Males / 1995 / BCP / G

TY SPEARS *see Star Index I*

TY WALKER
Transister Act / 1994 / HSV / G

TY WINTERS *see Star Index I*

TYFFANY MILLION *see* Tiffany Million

TYGR
The Hollywood Starlet Search / 1995 / SC / M

TYLEENA
Sweet Black Cherries #2 / 1996 / TTV / M

TYLENE DEVINE
Paddle Tales / 1992 / BON / B • She'll Take A Spanking / 199? / BON / B

TYLER
Long straight blonde hair, pretty/passable face with bushy black eyebrows, small/medium tits with very small areola, lithe body and a tight waist. Comes from Ohio and was in the navy before becoming a dancer and then porno performer. 21 years old in 1996 and de-virginized at 18.
Anal Virgins #03 / 1996 / NS / M • Asses Galore #4: Extreme Noise Terror / 1996 / DFI / M • Bootylicious: Baby Got Booty / 1996 / JMP / M • Cirque Du Sex #2 / 1996 / VT / M • Cloud 900 / 1996 / EYE / M • Country Girl / 1996 / VC / M • Dirty Diner #3 / 1996 / SC / M • Eighteen #2 / 1996 / SC / M • Eternal Lust / 1996 / VC / M • Fame Is A Whore On Butt Row / 1996 / ABS / M • First Time Lesbians #21 / 1994 / JMP / F • From The Heart / 1996 / XCI / M • I Wanna Be A Porn Star #2 / 1996 / 4P / M • Lollipop Shoppe #2 / 1996 / SC / M • Up And Cummers #38 / 1996 / RWP / M • Video Virgins #31 / 1996 / NS / M • Waves Of Passion / 1996 / ERA / M

TYLER (BRUNETTE)
Kinky Peep Shows: Anals & Orals / 1995 / SUF / M

TYLER (OTHER)

6000 Lash Lane / 1994 / LON / B • Dominant's Dilemma / 1993 / LON / B
TYLER BLAZE
Anal Witness #2: No Prisoners / 1996 / LBO / M
TYLER COLE *see Star Index I*
TYLER GIBSON *see Star Index I*
TYLER HORNE *(Tyler Reynolds, Jason Welles, Jason Wells, Y. Tyler Horn, Pencil Sharp)*
The Analyst / 1975 / ALP / M • Behind The Green Door #1 / 1972 / MIT / M • Bottom Busters / 1973 / BLT / M • Cavalcade Of Stars / 1985 / VCR / C • Count The Ways / 1976 / CA / M • Daddy / 1978 / BL / M • Dental Nurse / 1973 / VXP / M • Do You Wanna Be Loved? / 1977 / AR / M • Fantasy Girls / 1974 / VC / M • Femmoe Do Sade / 1976 / ALP / M • Inside Marilyn Chambers / 1975 / MIT / M • Limited Edition #08 / 1979 / AVC / M • Little Angel Puss / cr76 / SVE / M • Long Hard Summer / 1989 / BMV / C • Mary! Mary! / 1977 / SE / M • Midnight Hustle / 1978 / VC / M • Most Valuable Slut / 1973 / HLV / M • The Pleasure Masters / 1975 / AST / M • Randy, The Electric Lady / 1978 / VC / M • Reflections / 1977 / VCX / M • Resurrection Of Eve / 1973 / MIT / M • San Francisco Original 200s Special / 1980 / SVE / C • Seka In Heat / 1988 / BMV / C • Sexual Awareness / cr72 / CDC / M • She's A Boy Toy / 1985 / DR / M • Sodom & Gomorrah / 1974 / MIT / M • The Spirit Of Seventy Six / 1976 / NGV / M • Star Babe / 1977 / CA / M • Starlet Nights / 1982 / XTR / M • Sweet Savage / 1978 / ALP / M • Teeny Buns / 1977 / VC / M • That's Porno / 1979 / CV / C • Ultraflesh / 1980 / GO / M • Young Love / 1973 / VCX / M
TYLER HUDSON *see Shone Taylor*
TYLER MOORE *see Star Index I*
TYLER REGAN
Secret Sex #2: The Sex Radicals / 1994 / CAT / G
TYLER REYNOLDS *see Tyler Horne*
TYLER SCOTT
Foxy Boxing / 1982 / AVC / M
TYLER SWEET
The Dinner Party #2: The Buffet / 1996 / ULI / M
TYLISSA
Latin Plump Humpers #1 / 1995 / TTV / M • Latin Plump Humpers #2 / 1995 / TTV / M • Makin' Bacon / 1994 / WIV / M
TYRA BACKS
Black Knockers #12 / 1995 / TV / M
TYRA BELMONT
Rusty Boner's Late Night Videos #1 / 1995 / RHV / M
TYRA LAYS
Beverly She-Males / 1994 / PL / G • Bone Appetit: A She-Male Seduction / 1994 / BIZ / G • Defiant TV's / 1994 / BIZ / G • Kink #2 / 1995 / ROB / M • Mr. Madonna / 1994 / FPI / G • Shaved She-Males / 1994 / PL / G • Tranny Claus / 1994 / HEA / G • Tranny Jerk-Fest / 1995 / VC / G • Transsexual Passions #2 / 1994 / BIZ / G • TV Panty Party / 1994 / BIZ / G • TVs Teased And Tormented / 1995 / BIZ / G
TYRON FLOWER
Blue Vanities #182 / 1993 / FFL / M
TYRONE
AVP #9127: The Doctor Is In / 1991 / AVP / M • HomeGrown Video #461: Splendor In

The Grasp / 1995 / HOV / M • Reel Life Video #25: The Drip / 1995 / RLF / M • Reel Life Video #37: Heavy Honies / 1995 / RLF / M
TYRONE BROWNE
The Bite / 1975 / SVE / M
U. HEIDI SOHLER *see Uschi Digart*
U.U.
Magma: Anal Wedding / 1995 / MET / M
UGO ROSS
Ejacula #1 / 1992 / VC / M • Ejacula #2 / 1992 / VC / M • Impulse #02: The Film / 1995 / MBP / M
ULLA
Ancient Secrets Of Sexual Ecstasy / 1996 / HIG / M • Blue Vanities #513 / 1992 / FFL / M • Blue Vanities #528 / 1993 / FFL / M • Magma: Shopping Anal / 1994 / MET / M • Titanic Tits #03 / 198? / L&W / S
ULLA BJERGSKOV
Bordello / 1973 / AR / M
ULRIKE BUTZ
Practice Makes Perfect / 1983 / MED / S • Veil Of Lust / 1973 / BL / M • [Junge Madchen Mogen's HeiB, Hausfrauen Noch HeiBer / 1973 / ... / M • [Krankenschwestern-Report / 1972 / ... / M • [Schulmadchen-Report 4: Was Eltern Oft Verzweifeln LaBt / 1972 / ... / M
ULTRA MAX *see Linda Vale*
ULTRA MAXINE *see Linda Vale*
UMA *see Umma*
UMAYA
Alm Bums / 1995 / DBM / M • Roman Orgy / 1991 / PL / M
UMMA *(Uma)*
Quite sweet Oriental/black girl who comes from Brooklyn. 19 years old in 1993, 5'3" tall, 34C-23-34, medium to large tits, tight body and nice boy-like butt. Very pleasant personality.
Anal Knights In Hollywood #2 / 1993 / MET / M • Anal Queen / 1994 / FPI / M • Asian Heat #04: House Of The Rising Sun / 1993 / SC / M • Asian Heat #05: The Joy Suck Club / 1994 / SC / M • Beach Bum Amateur's #35 / 1993 / MID / M • Bi-Sexual Anal #2 / 1994 / RTP / G • Black Orgies #17 / 1993 / AFI / M • Black Orgies #18 / 1993 / AFI / M • Bobby Hollander's Maneaters #10 / 1993 / SFP / M • Cherry Poppers #02: Barely Legal / 1994 / ZA / M • Creme De La Face #01 / 1994 / OD / M • The Cumm Brothers #02: Goin' To A Ho' Down / 1994 / OD / M • Cuntz #1 / 1994 / RTP / M • Cuntz #2 / 1994 / RTP / M • Cuntz #3 / 1994 / RTP / M • Cuntz #4 / 1994 / RTP / M • Dark Secrets / 1995 / MID / S • Depraved Fantasies #3 / 1994 / FPI / M • Depraved Fantasies #4 / 1995 / FPI / M • The Devil In Grandma Jones / 1994 / FC / M • Diary Of A Geisha / 1995 / WV / C • Dirt Bags / 1994 / FPI / M • Dirty Doc's Housecalls #14 / 1994 / LV / M • Dungeon Dykes #2 / 1994 / FPI / F • Electro Sex / 1994 / FPI / M • End Of Innocence / 1994 / WIV / M • Eskimo Gang Bang / 1994 / HW / M • First Time Lesbians #11 / 1993 / JMP / F • First Time Lesbians #15 / 1994 / JMP / F • Gang Bang Diaries #1 / 1993 / SFP / M • Girlz Towne #09 / 1995 / FC / F • Girlz Towne #10 / 1995 / FC / F • Guess What? / 1994 / FPI / G • Harry Horndog #29: Anal Lovers #5 / 1995 / FPI / M • Hidden Camera #12 / 1993 / JMP / M • Hidden Camera: Interracial Special / 1994 / JMP / M • High Heel Harlots #03 /

1994 / SFP / M • The Hitch-Hiker #02: Dangerous Curves / 1994 / WMG / M • Horny Old Broads / 1995 / FPI / M • House Of Sex #15: Dirty Anal Three Ways / 1994 / RTP / M • Kim's House Party / 1995 / HW / M • Kinky Orientals / 1994 / FH / M • Lessons In Love / 1995 / SPI / M • Love Bunnies #09 / 1994 / FPI / F • Love Bunnies #10 / 1994 / FPI / F • Lovin' Spoonfuls #3 / 1995 / 4P / C • Mike Hott: #254 Cunt of the Month: Uma 9-93 / 1993 / MHV / M • More Dirty Debutantes #22 / 1993 / 4P / M • More Dirty Debutantes #25 / 1993 / 4P / M • My Boyfriend's Black / 1994 / FD / M • My Cum Is Oozing From Umma's Ass / 1994 / RTP / M • Odyssey 30 Min: #381: I Want Some Dark Meat / 1993 / OD / M • One For The Gusher / 1995 / AMP / M • Oriental Oddballs #2 / 1994 / FH / M • Private Video Magazine #09 / 1994 / OD / M • Pussy Tales / 1993 / SC / F • Queen Of The Bizarre / 1994 / AMP / G • Raw Sex #01 / 1994 / ERW / M • Sex In Dangerous Places / 1994 / OD / M • Sexual Trilogy #02 / 1993 / SFP / M • Sexual Trilogy #05 / 1994 / SFP / M • A Step Beyond / 1994 / AMP / G • Strap On Anal Attitude / 1994 / SCL / M • Stylin' / 1994 / FD / M • Tail Taggers #119 / 1994 / WV / M • Up And Cummers #16 / 1994 / 4P / M • Up And Cummers #21 / 1995 / RWP / M • Up And Cummers: The Movie / 1994 / 4P / M • Used And Abused #1 / 1994 / CC / M • What's A Nice Girl Like You Doing In An Anal Movie? / 1995 / AMP / M • Where The Bi's Are / 1994 / BIN / G
UNCLE CHACH *see Star Index I*
UNCLE MILTIE *see Michael Morrison*
UNCLE ROY *see Star Index I*
UNCLE WILLY *see Star Index I*
UNIQUE LOVE
Fatliners #1 / 1990 / EX / M • Life In The Fat Lane #1 / 1990 / FC / M • Life In The Fat Lane #2 / 1990 / FC / M • Night Lessons / 1990 / V99 / M • Not So Innocent / 1989 / VEX / M
URANUS *see Star Index I*
URSOLYA
Bedtime Story Italiano / 1995 / UGO / M
URSULA
The Adventures Of Peeping Tom #2 / 1996 / OD / M • Big Busty #05 / 198? / BTO / M • Big Busty #10 / 198? / H&S / M • Blue Vanities #167 (New) / 1996 / FFL / M • Blue Vanities #167 (Old) / 1991 / FFL / M • Blue Vanities #580 / 1996 / FFL / M • Career Girls / 1996 / OUP / M • Misty Rain's Anal Orgy / 1994 / FRM / M • Nba: Nuttin' Butt Ass / 1996 / SMP / M • Wrasslin She-Babes #05 / 1996 / SOW / M
URSULA (HUNG)
Deep Behind The Scenes With Seymore Butts #2 / 1995 / ULI / M • Fazano's Student Bodies / 1995 / EL / M
URSULA AUSTIN
Babylon Gold / 1983 / COM / C • Come With Me, My Love / 1976 / PVX / M • Fiona On Fire / 1978 / VC / M • Heat Wave / 1977 / COM / M • Slippery When Wet / 1976 / VXP / M • Take Off / 1978 / VXP / M • The Travails Of June / 1976 / VHL / M
URSULA BRANDWYN *see Star Index I*
URSULA FONTAINE
Pleasure So Deep / 1983 / AT / M
URSULA KARNAT *see Star Index I*
URSULA KRUSCH

Girlworld #4 / 1989 / LIP / F • She-Male Encounters #18: Murder She-Male Wrote / 1987 / MET / G

URSULA PASSARELL *see* **Vanessa del Rio**

URSULA TOUCHE *see* **Star Index I**

URSULA TRUCK
Dangerous / 1996 / SNA / M

URSULA WHITE
French Erotic Fantasies / 1978 / ... / M • Harlot / 1983 / VEP / M

USCHI *see* **Star Index I**

USCHI DEVON *see* **Uschi Digart**

USCHI DIGARD *see* **Uschi Digart**

USCHI DIGART *(Astrid Lillimor, Heidi Sohler, U. Heidi Sohler, Uschi Digard, Uschi Devon, Marni, Sherrie, Elke Von, Inge Pinson, Ronnie Roundheels, Edie Swenson)*
Huge breasted long haired blonde. 44-26-35 Born Aug 15, 1948 in Stockholm, Sweden. Very popular as a print model and allegedly worked for a while as an interpreter at the UN. All sources seem to indicate she never performed sex on screen.
40 Plus / 1987 / MFM / M • All The Lovin' Kinfolk / 197? / AA / S • The Beauties And Thc Beast / 1973 / AP0 / S • Below The Belt / 1971 / SOW / S • Beneath The Valley Of The Ultra-Vixens / 1979 / RMV / S • Best Of Richard Rank #1 / 1987 / GO / F • The Best Of Sex And Violence / 1981 / WIZ / C • Big Bust Babes #02 / 1984 / AFI / M • Big Bust Loops #01 / 1993 / SOW / M • Big Bust Loops #15 / 1994 / SOW / M • The Big Snatch / 1968 / SOW / S • The Black Alley Cats / 1971 / SOW / S • Blood Sabbath / 1972 / JLT / S • Blue Vanities / 028 / 1988 / FFL / M • Blue Vanities #042 (Old) / 1988 / FFL / M • Blue Vanities #046 (Old) / 1988 / FFL / M • Blue Vanities #051 / 1988 / FFL / M • Blue Vanities #052 / 1988 / FFL / M • Blue Vanities #125 / 1990 / FFL / M • Blue Vanities #132 / 1991 / FFL / M • Blue Vanities #513 / 1992 / FFL / M • Blue Vanities #547 / 1994 / FFL / M • Blue Vanities #557 / 1994 / FFL / M • Bondage Pleasures #1 / 1981 / 4P / B • Bondage Pleasures #2 / 1981 / 4P / B • Brabusters #2 / 1982 / CA / S • Can I Do It...Till I Need Glasses? / 1977 / MED / S • Cherry, Harry And Raquel / 1969 / RMV / S • Chesty Anderson USN / 1975 / WV0 / S • A Climax Of Blue Power / 1974 / EVI / M • Dr Sex / 1964 / SOW / S • Drop Out / 1972 / ... / S • The Erotic Adventures Of Pinocchio / 1971 / JLT / S • Even Devils Pray / 1970 / ALP / S • The Erotic Dreams Of Casanova / 1970 / SOW / S • Famous T & A / 1982 / WIZ / C • Fantasm / 1976 / VS / S • Fantasm Cums Again / 1977 / VS / S • Female Chauvinists / 1975 / ... / M • Fringe Benefits / 1975 / IHV / M • Girls On Girls / 1983 / VC / F • Girls On The Road / 1973 / UNV / S • The Godson / 1971 / BPI / S • Gunblast / 1974 / ... / S • The Hawaiian Split / 1971 / SOW / S • Hollywood Babylon / 1972 / AIR / S • Honey Buns / cr75 / BL / M • I Want You / 1970 / ALP / M • If You Don't Stop It You'll Go Blind / 1977 / MED / S • Ilsa, Keeper Of The Oil Sheik's Harem / 1975 / AME / S • Ilsa, She Wolf Of The SS / 1974 / VID / S • John Holmes And The All-Star Sex Queens / 1984 / AMB / M • Kentucky Fried Movie / 1977 / MED / S • The Killer Elite / 1975 / MGM / S • Last Days Of Pompeii / 1975 /

... / S • Le Sex De Femme #1 / 1989 / AFI / C • Le Sex De Femme #5 / 1990 / AFI / C • The Magic Mirror / 1970 / ALP / S • The Maids / 1973 / ... / M • Norma Isn't Quite Normal / 1969 / SOW / S • Oddly Coupled / 1970 / SOW / S • The Only House In Town / 1971 / SOW / S • Panorama Blue / 1974 / ALP / S • Pastries / 1975 / ALP / M • Poor Cecily / 1973 / ALF / S • Prison Girls / 1973 / ... / S • Private Arrangement / 1970 / SOW / S • Sandra: The Making Of A Woman / 1970 / SOW / S • The Scavengers / 1969 / ALP / S • The Secret Sex Lives Of Romeo And Juliet / 1968 / PS / S • The Seven Minutes / 1971 / ST0 / S • The Sex Machine / 1971 / SOW / M • Sex, Love And Happiness / 1973 / ... / S • She-Devils Of the S.S. / 1969 / AME / S • Skin Flick Madness / 1971 / ALP / S • Street Of 1000 Pleasures / 1970 / SOW / S • Superchick / 1971 / PRS / S • Supervixens / 1975 / RMV / S • Swingers Massacre / 1975 / SVE / S • The Toy Box / 1971 / BPI / S • Truck Stop Women / 1974 / VES / S • Uschi's Hollywood Adventure / 1972 / SOW / S • Where Does It Hurt? / 1972 / ... / S • Wild Honey / 1969 / SOW / S • Wrasslin She-Babes #07 / 1996 / SOW / M • Wrasslin She-Babes #10 / 1996 / SOW / M • Wrasslin She-Babes #11 / 1996 / SOW / M • [Big Boobs #1 / 19?? / ... / M • [Big Boobs #2 / 19?? / ... / M • [The Big Bounce / 1978 / ... / S • [The Black Gestapo / 1975 / UNV / S • [Blood Hunger / 197? / ... / S • [Catholic High School Girls In Trouble / cr70 / ... / S • [Cum Together / 19?? / ... / M • [The Dirt Gang / 197? / ... / S • [Dr Feelgood / 1972 / ... / S • [Fantasy / 1977 / ... / S • [Farok Universota / 1972 / ... / S • [Getting Into Heaven / 1971 / ... / S • [Heads Of Tails / 197? / ... / S • [Inside Amy / 1975 / ... / S • [Kitty Can't Help It / 1975 / ... / S • [Love Secrets Of The Kama Sutra / 1976 / ... / S • [The Marauders / 1969 / ... / S • [The Midnight Graduate / 1970 / ... / S • [Naked...Are The Cheaters / 1971 / ... / S • [Old King Cock / 19?? / ... / M • [The Politicians / 197? / ... / S • [Raquel Motel / 1970 / ... / S • [Runaway Hormones / 1973 / ... / S • [Satisfaction Guaranteed (2) / 1972 / ... / S • [Thaw The Frigid Bird / 197? / ... / M • [Uschi In Bondage / 1971 / ... / B • [Woman On Woman / 197? / ... / M • [The World Is Just A B Movie / 1971 / ... / S

USCHI HORN
Inside Marilyn / 1984 / CA / M • Inside Olinka / 1993 / CA / C

USCHI KAMAT *see* **Star Index I**

USHI DANSK
Deep Throat Girls / cr75 / ... / M

UTA ERICKSON *(Uta Erikson)*
German girl who appeared in the early seventies.
Bacchanale / 1972 / ALP / M • Dynamite / 1971 / VXP / M • The Kiss Of Her Flesh / 1968 / SOW / S • Mnasidika / 1969 / ALP / S • The Ultimate Degenerate / 1969 / SOW / S

UTA ERIKSON *see* **Uta Erickson**

UWE BRINKMAN *see* **Star Index I**

V. GREY
Toe Tales #26 / 1995 / GOT / B

V. HART *see* **Veronica Hart**

V. HOWARD
Breaker Beauties / 1977 / VHL / M

V.A.

Magma: Anal Teenies / 1994 / MET / M • Magma: Live And Learn / 1995 / MET / M • Magma: Sperm-Crazy / 1994 / MET / M

VAL
Blue Vanities #505 / 1992 / FFL / M • Blue Vanities #573 / 1996 / FFL / M • Love Letters / 1992 / ELP / F

VAL HALLA
Blue Vanities #543 / 1994 / FFL / M

VAL SILVER
Pussy Hunt #11 / 1995 / LEI / M

VAL SMITH
Blue Vanities #517 / 1992 / FFL / M

VALDESTA *see* **Star Index I**

VALENTINA
Canadian Beaver Hunt #1 / 1996 / PL / M • Erika Bella: Euroslut / 1995 / EL / M • Frank Thring's Double Penetration #2 / 1996 / XPR / M • Hamlet: For The Love Of Ophelia #1 / 1996 / IP / M • Marquis De Sade / 1995 / IP / M • Passion In Venice / 1995 / ULI / M • Sluts 'n' Angels In Budapest / 1994 / EL / M • Virility / 1996 / XC / M

VALENTINA (A. TYLER) *see* **Amanda Tyler**

VALENTINA (N. PINK) *see* **Nikki Pink**

VALENTINA DEFEO
Prima #14: Hotel Europa / 1996 / MBP / M

VALENTINA MARTINEZ
Hamlet: For The Love Of Ophelia #2 / 1996 / IP / M

VALENTINA VECRU
Private Gold #04: Amazonas / 1996 / OD / M • Private Stories #06 / 1995 / OD / M • Private Stories #07 / 1996 / OD / M • Private Stories #09 / 1996 / OD / M • Triple X Video Magazine #05 / 1995 / OD / M • Triple X Video Magazine #10 / 1995 / OD / M

VALENTINA VELASQUEZ
Prima #09: ASSassins / 1995 / MBP / M • Private Gold #08: The Longest Night / 1996 / OD / M • The Sex Clinic / 1995 / WIV / M • World Sex Tour #4 / 1996 / ANA / M

VALENTINE
Black Balled / 1984 / AMB / M • Dirty Dancers #7 / 1996 / 4P / M • In Your Face #4 / 1996 / PL / M • Kym Wilde's On The Edge #29 / 1995 / RB / B • Nightclub / 1996 / SC / M • Sadistic Sisters / 1996 / BON / B • The Story Of Ouch! / 1996 / LBO / B • Student Fetish Videos: Bondage #02 / 1996 / PRE / B • Student Fetish Videos: Catfighting #16 / 1996 / PRE / B • Student Fetish Videos: The Enema #20 / 1996 / PRE / B • Tied Temptations / 1996 / BON / B • Valentine's Challenge / 1992 / LIP / F • Valentine's Wonderland / 1992 / LIP / F • Virgin Killers: Second Rampage / 1995 / PEP / M • The Voyeur #6 / 1996 / EA / M • Young & Natural #06 / 1995 / PRE / F • Young & Natural #08 / 1995 / PRE / F • Young & Natural #09 / 1995 / PRE / C • Young & Natural #10 / 1995 / PRE / F • Young & Natural #11 / 1995 / PRE / F • Young & Natural #18 / 1996 / TV / C

VALENTINO
Anal Crack Master / 1994 / ROB / M • Bad Medicine / 1990 / VEX / M • New Ends #06 / 1994 / 4P / M

VALENTINO REY
Distinctive looking male with blonde hair slicked back, hatchet face and protruding eyes. Think *arts nouveaux* or thirties gigolo.
8-Ball: Westside Gang Bang / 1995 / PL /

M • 9-Ball: Geisha Gang Bang / 1994 / PL / M • All Grown Up / 1996 / XC / M • Amadeus Mozart / 1996 / XC / M • Anal All Stars / 1994 / CA / M • Anal Maidens Three / 1996 / BOT / M • The Anal-Europe Series #07: / 1994 / LV / M • Backing In #7 / 1995 / WV / C • Bad Attitude #2 / 1995 / LV / M • Bang City #1: Kelly's Anal Gang Bang / 1995 / SC / M • Bang City #4: Gina's Anal Gang Bang / 1995 / SC / M • Bar-B-Que Gang Bang / 1994 / JMP / M • The Big Stick-Up / 1994 / WV / M • Black Beach / 1995 / LV / M • Black Beauty (Las Vegas) / 1995 / LV / M • Black Orgies #35 / 1995 / GO / M • Blonde Temptation / 1995 / IF / M • The Butt Sisters Do Denver / 1994 / MID / M • Buttman In Barcelona / 1996 / EA / M • Buttman In The Crack / 1996 / FA / M • Buttman's Bubble Butt Babes / 1996 / EA / M • Buttman's Wet Dream / 1994 / EA / M • Cinesex #1 / 1995 / CV / M • Cinesex #2 / 1994 / CV / M • Cry Babies #1: Anal Scream / 1995 / ZA / M • D.P. Grannies / 1995 / JMP / M • Dangerous / 1996 / SNA / M • Dirty And Kinky Mature Women #1 / 1995 / C69 / M • Don Salvatore: The Last Sicilian / 1995 / XC / M • Dream's House Party / 1995 / HW / M • Drop Sex: Wipe The Floor / 1997 / JLP / M • East Vs West: Battle Of The Gang Bangs / 1994 / TTV / M • Ebony Erotica #26: Night Shift / 1994 / GO / M • Ebony Princess / 1994 / IN / M • Frank Thring's Double Penetration #3 / 1996 / XPR / M • Gang Bang Bitches #03 / 1994 / PP / M • Gang Bang Virgin #1 / 1994 / HO / M • Gang Bang Virgin #2 / 1995 / HO / M • Granny Bangers / 1995 / MET / M • Hellfire / 1995 / MET / M • Holly's Holiday Gang Bang / 1994 / LBO / M • Horny Brits Take It In The Bum / 1997 / ROB / M • Hot Tight Asses #08 / 1994 / TCK / M • In Search Of The Brown Eye: An Anal Adventure / 1995 / MAX / M • In The Can With Oj / 1994 / HCV / M • Indiscreet! Video Magazine #1 / 1995 / FH / M • Kimberly Kupps Gets Black Balled / 1996 / NIT / M • Layover / 1994 / VI / M • Maverdick / 1995 / WV / M • Mo' Booty #4 / 1995 / TIW / M • Models Etc. / 1995 / LV / M • The New Butt Hunt #19 / 1996 / LEI / C • Odyssey 30 Min: #538: / 1995 / OD / M • Oral Majority #13 / 1995 / WV / C • Oriental Gang Bang / 1995 / HO / M • Passion In Venice / 1995 / ULI / M • Penetration (Anabolic) #3 / 1995 / ANA / M • Penetration (Anabolic) #4 / 1996 / ANA / M • The Pleasure Girl / 1994 / GO / M • Primal Instinct / 1996 / SNA / M • Prime Choice #1 / 1995 / RAS / M • Prime Choice #2 / 1995 / RAS / M • Profiles #01 / 1995 / XPR / M • Profiles #03: House Dick / 1995 / XPR / M • Pussyman Auditions #13 / 1995 / SNA / M • Pussyman's Nite Club Party #1 / 1996 / SNA / M • Pussyman's Nite Club Party #2 / 1997 / SNA / M • Racially Motivated / 1994 / LV / M • Sherlock Homie / 1995 / IN / M • Snatch Masters #03 / 1994 / LEI / M • Starbangers #08 / 1996 / FPI / M • Sweat 'n' Bullets / 1995 / MID / M • Swedish Erotica #79 / 1994 / CA / M • Takin' It To The Limit #4 / 1995 / BS / M • Toredo / 1996 / ROX / M • Triple X Video Magazine #16 / 1996 / OD / M • Ultimate Anal Gang Bang #3 / 1995 / HW / M • The Ultimate Squirting Machine / 1994 / FPI / M • Valentino's Asian Invasion / 1997 / SC / M • Valentino's Euro-Invasion / 1997

/ SC / M • Virility / 1996 / XC / M • The Voyeur #2 / 1994 / EA / M • Wild Orgies #14 / 1994 / AFI / M • Zena's Gang Bang / 1995 / HO / M

VALERIA *(Corrina Lindero, Corinna, Valeria Box, Corinna Taylor)*
Not too pretty gray blonde with small to medium sized natural tits and good tan lines. Mole or birthmark on her belly just above the bikini line and to the left of midline. Blue eyes and not-tight waist. Born Frankfurt, Germany, was 19 years old in 1993 and was de-virginized at 14. 5'11" tall. Works with boyfriend or husband, J.P. Anthony. First movie was **Breastman's Anal Adventure**. As of early 1996 they have broken up and she has returned to Germany.

Act Of Submission / 1995 / OUP / B • The Adventures Of Buck Naked / 1994 / OD / M • Alice In Annaland / 1994 / SC / M • Amateur Orgies #27 / 1993 / AFI / M • Anal Chiropractor / 1995 / PEP / M • Anal Vision #16 / 1993 / LBO / M • The Anal-Europe Series #06: Anal Luck / 1993 / LV / M • Ass Angels / 1996 / PAL / F • The Backdoor Bandit / 1994 / LV / M • Backdoor Boogie / 1994 / TEG / M • Badd Girls / 1994 / SC / F • The Beaverly Hillbillies / 1993 / IP / M • Big Murray's New-Cummers #18: Crazy Cuties / 1993 / FD / M • Black Attack / 1994 / ZA / M • Boogie In The Butt / 1993 / WIV / M • Brassiere To Eternity / 1994 / PEP / F • Breastman Goes To Breastland #2 / 1993 / EVN / M • Breastman's Anal Adventure / 1993 / EVN / M • The Bridges Of Anal County / 1996 / PV0 / C • The Butt Connection / 1993 / TIW / M • Butt Darling / 1994 / WIV / M • Butt Jammers #05 / 1996 / SC / F • Butt Watch #02 / 1993 / FH / M • Caged Fury / 1993 / DR / M • Captain Bob's Lust Boat #2 / 1993 / FCP / M • Carnal Interludes / 1995 / NOT / M • Chateau Of Torment / 1995 / STM / B • Club Anal #2 / 1993 / ROB / F • Cousin Bubba Country Corn Porn #01 / 1994 / VIM / M • The Crack / 1994 / LV / M • Deep Cover / 1993 / WP / M • Deep Inside Tiffany Mynx / 1994 / VC / C • Delicious Passions / 1993 / ROB / F • Designs On Women / 1994 / IN / F • Desperado / 1994 / SC / M • Diamond Meets Valeria / 1995 / DIP / F • Dick & Jane Do The Strip / 1994 / AVI / M • Different Strokes / 1994 / PRE / B • Dirty Bob's #08: LAid Over In L.A. / 1993 / FLP / S • Dirty Bob's #18: Under The Boardwalk! / 1995 / FLP / S • Dirty Bob's #19: Over The Boardwalk! / 1995 / FLP / S • A Dirty Western #2: Smoking Guns / 1994 / CV / M • Dirty Work / 1995 / VC / M • Diva / 1993 / XCI / M • Dungeon Discipline / 1996 / STM / B • The Ebony Connection #4 / 1994 / LBO / C • Eclipse / 1993 / SC / M • Enemates #09 / 1994 / BIZ / B • Euroslut #1: French Tart / 1993 / CC / M • Explicit Entry / 1995 / LE / M • Extreme Passion / 1993 / WP / M • Fire Down Below / 1994 / GO / M • First Time Lesbians #06 / 1993 / JMP / F • Florence Hump / 1994 / AFI / M • Fluff Dreams / 1995 / SUF / M • For Love Or Money / 1994 / AFI / M • Forever Young / 1994 / VI / M • The Freak Club / 1994 / VMX / M • Fun "4" All / 1994 / PRE / B • Fun Zone / 1994 / PRE / B • A Girl's Affair #03 / 1993 / FD / F • A Girl's Affair #04 / 1994 / FD / F • A Girl's Affair #05 / 1994 / FD / F • The Great Pre-

tenders / 1994 / FD / M • Hot Chicks Do L.A. / 1994 / EVN / F • Hot Tight Asses #04 / 1993 / TCK / M • Hotel Sodom #07 / 1995 / SNA / M • In X-Cess / 1994 / LV / M • Induced Pleasure / 1995 / ERA / M • Jiggly Queens #2 / 1994 / LE / M • Junkyard Dykes #01 / 1994 / ZA / F • Junkyard Dykes #03 / 1994 / ZA / F • Kinky Cameraman #4 / 1996 / LEI / C • Kitty Kat Club / 1994 / SC / F • Kym Wilde's On The Edge #09 / 1994 / RB / B • Lap Of Luxury / 1994 / WIV / M • Laugh Factory / 1995 / PRE / C • Leg...Ends #12 / 1994 / PRE / F • Lube Job / 1994 / PRE / B • M Series #07 / 1993 / LBO / M • M Series #10 / 1993 / LBO / M • Midnight Dreams / 1994 / WV / M • Mind Games / 1995 / IMV / M • Mistress Rules / 1995 / STM / B • Mysteria / 1995 / NIT / M • N.Y. Video Magazine #06 / 1995 / OUP / M • A Night Of Hell / 1993 / LBO / B • No Man's Land #10 / 1994 / VT / F • Nookie Of The Year / 1993 / HW / M • Old Throat And D.P. / 1993 / FC / M • Ona Zee's Learning The Ropes #11: Chains Required / 1994 / ONA / B • One For The Gusher / 1995 / AMP / M • Open Lips / 1994 / WV / M • Oral Majority #12 / 1994 / WV / C • The Orgy #1 / 1993 / EMC / M • The Orgy #2 / 1993 / EMC / M • The Orgy #3 / 1993 / EMC / M • Pearl Of The Orient / 1995 / IN / M • Perverted #1: The Babysitters / 1994 / ZA / M • Pure Filth / 1995 / RV / M • Pussy Posse / 1993 / CC / M • Reckless / 1995 / NOT / M • Release Me Please / 1995 / VTF / B • Ring Of Passion / 1994 / ERA / M • Rocco Unleashed / 1994 / SC / M • Ron Hightower's White Chicks #01 / 1993 / LBO / M • Russian Roulette / 1995 / NIT / M • Sabotage / 1994 / CA / M • The Search For Canadian Beaver / 1995 / LIP / F • Secret Urges (Vidco) / 1994 / VD / C • Sex Academy #1 / 1993 / ONA / M • Shades Of Passion / 1995 / NOT / M • Star Struck / 1994 / ERA / M • Stiff Competition #2 / 1994 / CA / M • Stud Finders / 1995 / ONA / M • Student Fetish Videos: Best of Catfighting #03 / 1995 / PRE / C • Student Fetish Videos: Catfighting #14 / 1994 / PRE / B • Student Fetish Videos: The Enema #18 / 1995 / PRE / B • Student Fetish Videos: Foot Worship #15 / 1995 / PRE / B • Sue / 1995 / VC / M • Tail Taggers #111 / 1993 / WV / M • Tail Taggers #118 / 1993 / WV / M • Taste Of Shame / 1994 / ROB / F • Texas Crude / 1995 / NIT / M • Title Shots / 1995 / PRE / B • Triple Flay / 1995 / PRE / B • Triple Play / 1994 / PRE / B • Twists Of The Heart / 1995 / NIT / M • Two Of A Kind / 1993 / PL / M • Ultimate Gang Bang #1 / 1994 / HW / M • Ultimate Orgy #1 / 1992 / GLI / M • Unbridled Lust / 1995 / NOT / F • Up And Cummers: The Movie / 1994 / 4P / M • Valeria Gets Fucked / 1995 / DIP / M • The Violation Of Rachel Love / 1995 / JMP / F • Voices In My Bed / 1993 / VI / M • Weak-Ends / 1995 / PRE / B • Wendy Whoppers: Prison Love Doll / 1994 / PEP / M • Wilder At Heart / 1993 / ANA / M • X-Tales / 1995 / VIM / M

VALERIA BLACK
I Know What Girls Like / 1986 / WET / G
VALERIA BLUE
French Schoolgirls / 1973 / AVC / M
VALERIA BONDARENKO
True Stories #1 / 1993 / SC / M • True Stories #2 / 1993 / SC / M

VALERIA BOX *see* Valeria
VALERIA DEL MONTE
Sex Penitentiary / 1996 / XC / M
VALERIE
A&B AB#163: The Plumber / 1990 / A&B /
F • A&B AB#182: Watch Me Spank Me /
1990 / A&B / M • A&B AB#200: Bachelor
Party / 1990 / A&B / M • A&B AB#201:
Pussy Galore / 1990 / A&B / F • A&B
AB#205: Strippers Choice / 1990 / A&B / M
• Anabolic Import #01: Anal X / 1994 / ANA
/ M • Best Exotic Dancers In The Usa /
1995 / PME / S • Blue Vanities #194 / 1993
/ FFL / M • Blue Vanities #573 / 1996 / FFL
/ M • The Cross Of Lust / 1995 / CL0 / M •
Dick & Jane Penetrate Paris / 1994 / AVI /
M • European Cleavage Queens / 199? /
H&S / S • Eurotica #03 / 1995 / XC / M •
Eurotica #06 / 1996 / XC / M • Girls Of
France / 1991 / BTO / M • Hardcore
Male/Female Oil Wrestling / 1996 / JSP / M
• Ladies In Leather / 1995 / GO / M • Love
Mexican Style / cr75 / BLT / M • Magma:
Hot Business / 1995 / MET / M • Magma:
Shopping Anal / 1994 / MET / M • Quebec
Perversity #5 / 1996 / IN0 / M • Skin #2 /
1995 / ERQ / M • Swedish Erotica #37 /
1981 / CA / M • Up And Cummers #27 /
1996 / ERW / M • Veronica The Screen-
writing Hooker / 1996 / LE / M
VALERIE (ZUMIRA) *see* Zumira
VALERIE ADAMI
Odyssey / 1977 / VC / M
VALERIE ADAMS
Seduction Of Joyce / 1977 / BL / M
VALERIE ASHLEY *see Star Index I*
VALERIE BOISSEL
Helena / 19?? / WWV / M
VALERIE BRAND *see Star Index I*
VALERIE CLARK
John Holmes And The All-Star Sex Queens
/ 1984 / AMB / M
VALERIE DARLYN *(Lotta Leggs, Valerie
Paulson)*
Too tall reasonably pretty girl with medium
droopy tits.
Fantasex Island / 1983 / NSV / M • Fantasy
World / 1979 / WWV / M • Flight Sensa-
tions / 1983 / VC / C • Forbidden Entry /
1984 / VCR / M • Screwples / 1979 / CA /
M • Serena, An Adult Fairy Tale / 1979 /
VEN / M • Sexsations / 1984 / NSV / M •
Showgirl #08: Serena's Fantasies / 1983 /
VCR / M • Small Town Girls / 1979 / CXV /
M • Taboo #01 / 1980 / VCX / M • Tales Of
The Backside / 1985 / VCR / C • Young
Doctors In Lust / 1979 / NSV / M
VALERIE DEVINE
The Unsuspecting Repairman #1 / 1995 /
TVI / B
VALERIE DRISKELL
Erotic Fantasies #1 / 1983 / CV / C • Erotic
Fantasies #4 / 1983 / CV / C • Erotic Fan-
tasies: John Leslie / 1985 / CV / C • Foxy
Lady / 1978 / CV / M
VALERIE DUBOIS
Command Performance / cr75 / LA / M •
Prey Of A Call Girl / 1975 / ALP / M
VALERIE FRANKLIN *see Star Index I*
VALERIE HART *see* Veronica Hart
VALERIE HARTE *see* April Rayne
VALERIE JOHNSON
Agony Of Love, Lace And Lash / cr73 /
SOW / M • Bucky Beaver's XXX Dragon Art
Theatre Double Feature #14 / 1996 / SOW
/ M

VALERIE LA VEAU *see Star Index I*
VALERIE LOVE
Classical Romance / 1984 / MAP / M
VALERIE MARRON
Blow Hard / 1973 / CV / M • Cheap Sluts
And The Guys Who Fuck Them / 1994 /
MET / M • Wet Rainbow / 1973 / AR / M
VALERIE MORGENSTERN
Waterpower / 1975 / VHL / M
VALERIE PARKER *see Star Index I*
VALERIE PAULSON *see* Valerie Darlyn
VALERIE PETCHER *see Star Index I*
VALERIE RAY CLARK
Blue Vanities #122 / 1990 / FFL / M
VALERIE ROBERTS *see Star Index I*
VALERIE ST CLOUD
Barbara Dare's Roman Holiday / 1987 / SE
/ M • Lust Italian Style / 1987 / CA / M •
Porsche / 1990 / NSV / M
VALERIE STONE *see* Diedre Holland
VALERIE SUE
Bedtime Video #05 / 1984 / GO / M
VALERIE VAN OWEN *see* Chanel (1992)
VALERIE VINAI *see Star Index I*
VALHALLA *(Audrey Lane, Gema Talons,
Gema (Valhalla), Judy Lynn)*
Audrey Lane is from **Lesbian Lingerie Fan-
tasy #4.**
4 Of A Kind / 1995 / BON / B • 40 The Hard
Way / 1991 / OD / M • Amateur Lesbians
#05: Missy / 1991 / GO / F • Anal Illusions
/ 1991 / LV / M • Blonde Forces #1 / 1991 /
CC / M • Box Of Slavegirls / 1995 / LON /
B • Fantasy Abduction / 1997 / BON / B •
The Fetish Files / 1995 / IBN / B • Final
Orgy / 1996 / BON / B • Full House / 1995
/ BON / B • Gangbang Bitches / 1996 / LON
/ B • Girls In Heat / 1991 / ZA / F • Heavy
Petting / 1991 / SE / M • Lady & The
Champ / 1991 / AFV / M • The Lascivious
Ladies Of Dr Lipo / 1991 / OD / M • Lesbian
Lingerie Fantasy #4 / 1990 / ESP / F •
Maiden Heaven #2 / 1992 / MID / F • Main
Course / 1992 / FL / M • Mistress Calling /
1995 / IBN / B • Mistress Of Misery / 1996
/ LBO / B • Mondo Bitches / 1991 / LBO / B
• Mr. Peepers Amateur Home Videos #05:
Hot To Trot / 1991 / LBO / M • Mr. Peepers
Amateur Home Videos #11: Fur Pie Smor-
gasbord / 1991 / LBO / M • Pain In The
Rent / 1996 / BON / B • Pink Card / 1991 /
FH / M • Play Mistress For Me / 1995 / IBN
/ B • Portraits Of Pain / 1995 / B&D / B • Pro
Ball / 1991 / VD / M • Quadruple Trample /
1995 / IBN / B • Right On Track / 1995 / IBN
/ B • Single Girl Masturbation #4 / 1990 /
ESP / F • Slave Sisters / 1995 / LON / B •
Sneek Peeks #1 / 1993 / FL / M • Stalker's
Punishment / 1995 / IBN / B • Step To The
Rear / 1991 / VD / M • Taped, Tied & Tor-
mented / 1996 / ATO / B • Task Mistress /
1995 / IBN / B • Tell Me What To Do / 1991
/ CA / M • To The Rear / 1992 / VC / M •
Toying Around / 1992 / FL / M • Trans-
formed / 1995 / BON / B • The Ultimate Sex
/ 1992 / MET / G
VALKYRA
Blue Vanities #115 / 1988 / FFL / M • Taste
For Submission / 1991 / LON / C
VALY VERDY
Della Borsa / 1995 / WIV / M • The Hus-
band / 1995 / WIV / M • Private Film #05 /
1993 / OD / M • Private Film #09 / 1994 /
OD / M
VAMPIRELLA
[In Due Di Dietro / 19?? / ... / M

VAN DAMAGE
6969 Mel'hose Place / 1995 / VG0 / M •
Catch Of The Day #1 / 1995 / VG0 / M •
Catch Of The Day #2 / 1995 / VG0 / M •
Catch Of The Day #3 / 1996 / VG0 / M •
Catch Of The Day #4 / 1996 / VG0 / M •
Catch Of The Day #5 / 1996 / VG0 / M •
Catch Of The Day #6 / 1996 / VG0 / M •
Cumback Pussy #7: NUGIRLZ / 1997 / EL
/ M • Dirty Dave's #3 / 1996 / XPR / M •
Dirty Dave's #4 / 1996 / XPR / M • Filthy
First Timers #1 / 1996 / EL / M • Filthy First
Timers #2: Innocence Lost / 1996 / EL / M
• Filthy First Timers #3: Tearing Down The
Walls Of Shame / 1996 / EL / M • Filthy
First Timers #4 / 1996 / EL / M • Filthy First
Timers #5 / 1997 / EL / M • Filthy First
Timers #6 / 1997 / EL / M • Filthy First
Timers #7 / 1997 / EL / M • Girly Video
Magazine #4 / 1996 / BEP / M • How To
Make A College Co-Ed / 1995 / VG0 / M •
War Whores / 1996 / EL / M • Western
Whores Hotel / 1996 / VG0 / M
VAN HERPE
Just One Day / 1995 / DBM / M
VAN HOUSTON
Snatch Motors / 1995 / VC / M
VAN KAMP
Just One Day / 1995 / DBM / M
VAN LEIBERMANN
Anal In The Alps / 1996 / P69 / M
VAN STAR *see Star Index I*
VANCE ERIKSON #3 *see Star Index I*
VANDA
Beverly She-Males / 1994 / PL / G • Middle
Aged Maidens / 1995 / GLI / M • Penetra-
tion (Anabolic) #1 / 1995 / ANA / M •
Shaved She-Males / 1994 / PL / G • She-
Mails / 1993 / PL / G • Tranny Jerk-Fest /
1995 / VC / G • Wet Mask / 1995 / SC / M
VANDA FULL
She Male Sex Kittens / 1995 / MET / G •
She Male Sluts / 1995 / KDP / G
VANELLA
Passion Procession / 19?? / ASR / M
VANELLA SIMMS *see* Vanilla Sims
VANELLA WILLIAMS *see* Vanilla Sims
VANESA
Sweet Black Cherries #3 / 1996 / TTV / M
VANESA ROMAN *see Star Index I*
VANESSA
African Angels #1 / 1996 / NIT / M • All
American Super Bitches / 1984 / BIZ / B •
The Best Of Fabulous Flashers / 1996 /
DGD / F • Black Cheerleader Search #02 /
1996 / ROB / M • Black Knockers #02 /
1995 / TV / M • Casting Couch Cuties #1 /
1994 / WP / M • Diaries Of Fire And Ice #1
/ 1989 / VC / M • Diaries Of Fire And Ice #2
/ 1989 / VC / M • Eurotica #09 / 1996 / XC
/ M • Girls Games Of Summer #4 / 1994 /
NIV / S • GM #110: Inside Vanessa / 1992
/ GMV / F • Hard Core Beginners #07 /
1995 / LEI / M • HomeGrown Video #456 /
1995 / HOV / M • Hot Body Video Maga-
zine #08 / 1994 / CG / S • Magma: Trans-
Games / 1995 / MET / G • Miss Judge /
1997 / VI / M • New Busom Brits / 199? /
H&S / S • Northwest Pecker Trek #3:
Ducks & Dicks / 1994 / LBO / M • North-
west Pecker Trek #5: Cumming In King
County / 1995 / LBO / M • Odyssey Ama-
teur #44: Vanessa's Fantasy / 1991 / OD /
M • Penthouse: Great Pet Hunt #1 / 1992 /
PET / F • Pick Up Lines #12 / 1997 / OD /
M • Rendezvous With Destiny / 1984 / LA /

B • Spanking Tutor / 1985 / BIZ / B • Stevi's: The Heart Shaped Bed / 1992 / SSV / F • Tiger Eye: Vanessa / 1995 / TEV / F • Tongue 'n Cheek (Red Light) / 1984 / RLV / M • Training Academy / 1984 / LA / B • Up And Cummers #15 / 1994 / 4P / M

VANESSA (CHANTE) see Chante

VANESSA (D'ORO) see Vanessa D'Oro

VANESSA (FRENCH) *(Nancy (Vanessa))*
Petite not too pretty girl with small tits, lithe body, long wavy black hair. Looks Indian (from Asia). Says she's French. 20 years old in 1996 and de-virginized at 18. At one stage she says she's from Mauritius which would explain her insistence on being French and her mixed Chinese/black/French/British ancestry.
Asses Galore #7: Lunatic Fringe / 1996 / DFI / M • Barby's On Butt Row / 1996 / ABS / M • Black Street Hookers #4: The Streets Of San Francisco / 1996 / DFI / M • Cumback Pussy #5: Groopin' / 1996 / EL / M • Drop Sex: Wipe The Floor / 1997 / JLP / M • Ethnic Cheerleader Search #1 / 1996 / WIC / M • The Hitch-Hiker #17: Dead End / 1996 / VIM / M • Interracial Video Virgins #01 / 1996 / NS / M • Living On The Edge / 1997 / DWO / M • Nasty Nymphos #15 / 1996 / ANA / M • Nba: Nuttin' Butt Ass / 1996 / SMP / M • Pick Up Lines #07 / 1996 / OD / M

VANESSA (HUNGARY)
Bottom Dweller: The Final Voyage / 1996 / EL / M

VANESSA BURLIE see Star Index I

VANESSA CHASE *(Chase (female), Vanessa Drake, Chasey (Vanessa))*
Not too pretty brunette who was 18 in 1993 and was de-virginized at 14. Bad hair, medium tits, very white skin, a sad look, pudgy face, falling apart body and revolting crotch acne. Has improved somewhat over time especially in regards to the hair and acne.
The Anal Adventures Of Max Hardcore: Full Throttle / 1994 / ZA / M • Anal Agony / 1994 / ZA / M • Anal All Stars / 1994 / CA / M • Anal Anonymous / 1994 / ZA / M • Anal Dynomite / 1995 / ROB / M • Anal Innocence #3 / 1994 / ROB / M • Anal Plaything #2 / 1995 / ROB / M • Anal Sweetheart / 1994 / ROB / M • Anal Vision #23 / 1994 / LBO / M • Anal Vision #24 / 1994 / LBO / M • Attitude / 1995 / VC / M • Backdoor To Buttsville / 1995 / ULI / M • Badd Girls / 1994 / SC / F • Black Studs & Little White Trash / 1995 / ROB / M • Bootylicious: White Trash / 1995 / JMP / M • Brooklyn Nights / 1994 / OD / M • Brothers Bangin' / 1995 / ANA / M • Buffy Malibu's Nasty Girls #08 / 1995 / ANA / F • Bun Busters #15 / 1994 / LBO / M • Butt Banged Cycle Sluts / 1995 / ANA / M • The Butt Detective / 1994 / VC / M • Buttman's Big Butt Backdoor Babes / 1995 / EA / M • Casting Call #05 / 1994 / SO / M • Catwalk #1 / 1995 / SC / M • Catwalk #2 / 1995 / SC / M • Cherry Poppers #05: Playtime / 1994 / ZA / M • Cross Cuntry Vacation / 1995 / CC / M • Cyberanal / 1995 / VC / M • The Devil In Miss Jones #5: The Inferno / 1994 / VC / M • The Dinner Party #1 / 1994 / ULI / M • Dirty Doc's Housecalls #16 / 1994 / LV / M • Domination / 1994 / WP / M • Double Decadence / 1995 / NOT / M • Double Penetration Virgins #05: Go To Hell / 1994 / BBO / M • Dr Freckle & Mr Jive / 1995 / IN

/ M • Dun-Hur #1 / 1994 / SC / M • Erotic Appetites / 1995 / IN / M • Erotic Obsession / 1994 / IN / M • Erotica Optique / 1994 / SUF / M • Every Woman Has A Fantasy #3 / 1995 / VC / M • Fantasy Chamber / 1994 / ULI / M • Gangbang Girl #14 / 1994 / ANA / M • Girls II Women / 1996 / AVI / M • Heavenly Yours / 1995 / CV / M • Homegrown Video: Here Comes Anna Malle / 1994 / HOV / M • Hot In The Saddle / 1994 / ERA / M • Hotel Sodom #02 / 1995 / SNA / M • Hotel Sodom #04: Free Parking In Rear / 1995 / SNA / M • Hotel Sodom #06 / 1995 / SNA / M • Hotel Sodom #10 / 1996 / SNA / M • La Femme Vanessa / 1995 / SC / M • Laguna Nights / 1995 / FH / M • Lessons In Love / 1995 / SPI / M • Lovin' Spoonfuls #4 / 1995 / 4P / C • Lucky Lady / 1995 / CV / M • Midnight Snacks / 1995 / KLP / M • Misfits / 1994 / CV / M • Misty @ Midnight / 1995 / LE / M • My Baby Got Back #04 / 1994 / VT / M • Naked Ambition / 1995 / VC / M • Nasty Backdoor Nurses / 1994 / LBO / M • Nasty Newcummers #04 / 1994 / MET / M • Nasty Nymphos #06 / 1994 / ANA / M • New Girls In Town #5 / 1994 / CC / M • No Tell Motel / 1995 / CV / M • The Nurses Are Cumming #2 / 1996 / LBO / C • Photo Opportunity / 1994 / VC / M • Private Film #12 / 1994 / OD / M • Private Film #14 / 1994 / OD / M • Private Stories #01 / 1995 / OD / M • Private Video Magazine #09 / 1994 / OD / M • Private Video Magazine #10 / 1994 / OD / M • Private Video Magazine #19 / 1994 / OD / M • Profiles #03: House Dick / 1995 / XPR / M • Pussyclips #06 / 1995 / SNA / M • Pussywoman #3 / 1995 / CC / M • Put 'em On Da Glass / 1994 / VT / M • Rxx For A Gangbang / 1994 / ZA / M • Sex 4 Life / 1995 / XPR / M • Sex In Black & White / 1995 / OD / M • Sexual Misconduct / 1994 / VD / C • Seymore & Shane Do Ireland / 1994 / ULI / M • Seymore & Shane Mount Tiffany / 1994 / FH / M • Seymore & Shane Playing With Fire / 1994 / ULI / M • Sista! #2 / 1994 / VT / F • Sister Snatch #2 / 1995 / SNA / M • Snatch Masters #06 / 1995 / LEI / M • Sodomania #09: Doin' Time / 1994 / EL / M • Sodomania #10: Euro/American Again / 1994 / EL / M • Sodomania #12: Raw Filth / 1995 / EL / M • Sodomania: Slop Shots / 1996 / EL / C • Sodomania: Smokin' Sextions / 1996 / EL / C • Strange Sex In Strange Places / 1994 / ZA / M • Submission / 1994 / WP / M • Supermodel #1 / 1994 / VI / M • Supermodel #2 / 1994 / VI / M • The Sweet Sweet Back #2: Double Thaanng Dat Black Hole / 1994 / FH / M • Tail Taggers #115 / 1993 / WV / M • Tail Taggers #120 / 1994 / WV / M • Tail Taggers #122: Anal Delight / 1994 / WV / M • Takin' It To The Limit #4 / 1995 / BS / M • Unmistakably You / 1995 / CV / M • Up And Cummers #17 / 1994 / 4P / M • Upbeat Love #1 / 1994 / CV / M • Video Virgins #09 / 1993 / NS / M • Wanted / 1995 / DR / M • Whore House / 1995 / IPI / M • Wild Orgies #04 / 1994 / AFI / M • Women Of Color #2 / 1994 / ANA / M • Young Nurses In Lust / 1994 / LBO / M

VANESSA COLE
Dirty Prancing / 1987 / EVN / M • Fun In The Sun / 1988 / EVN / C • In-N-Out With John Leslie / 1988 / WV / C • La Bimbo / 1987 / PEN / M • Le Hot Club / 1987 / WV

/ M • Megasex / 1988 / EVN / M • The Night Before / 1987 / WV / M

VANESSA D'AMOURE see Star Index I

VANESSA D'ORO *(Vanessa (D'Oro), Tammy Lane, Tawnee Lucci)*
Brunette with a womanly body and large enhanced tits.
Best Of Talk Dirty To Me #02 / 1991 / DR / C • Black Silk Secrets / 1989 / VC / C • Down And Dirty In Beverly Hills / 1986 / CV / M • Female Aggressors / 1986 / LAV / M • The Filthy Rich / 1989 / LA / M • Girls Gone Bad #3: Back To The Slammer / 1991 / GO / F • Girls Gone Bad #4: Cell Block Riot / 1991 / GO / F • Hawaiian Heat #1 / 1995 / CC / M • Hawaiian Heat #2 / 1995 / CC / M • Hottest Ticket / 1987 / WV / C • I Love A Girl In A Uniform / 1989 / VC / C • Just The Two Of Us / 1985 / WV / M • Lesbian Pros And Amateurs #02 / 1992 / GO / F • Living In A Wet Dream / 1986 / PEN / C • Neighborhood Watch #08: Extended Foreplay / 1991 / LBO / M • Only The Best Of Breasts / 1987 / CV / C • Pink And Pretty / 1986 / CA / M • Rocky-X #1 / 1986 / PEN / M • Saturday Night Beaver / 1986 / EVN / M • Super Sex / 1986 / MAP / M • Tales Of Taija Rae / 1989 / DR / M • Talk Dirty To Me #04 / 1986 / DR / M • Taste Of The Best #1 / 1988 / PIN / C • The Thrill Of It / 1986 / CAT / M • To Lust In LA / 1986 / LA / M

VANESSA DANTE
Bite The Black Bullets / 1995 / ME / M • Black Cheerleader Search #09 / 1996 / IVC / M • Black Knockers #05 / 1995 / TV / M • Black Snatch #1 / 1996 / DFI / F • Black Video Virgins #1 / 1996 / NS / M • The Girls Of Summer / 1995 / VT / M • Girls II Women / 1996 / AVI / M • Kool Ass / 1996 / BOT / M • More Dirty Debutantes #61 / 1997 / SBV / M • Yo' Where's Homey? / 1996 / SUF / M

VANESSA DAWNE see Star Index I

VANESSA DEL RIO *(Ursula Passarell, Anna Maria Sanchez)*
Ugly looking Hispanic; a real ball buster.
ABA: Double Feature #4 / 1996 / ALP / M • ABA: Double Feature #5 / 1996 / ALP / M • Afternoon Delights / 1981 / CA / M • Amazing Sex Stories #2 / 1987 / SUV / C • Anal Ultra Vixens / 197? / ALP / M • Angie, Undercover Cop / 1980 / MSI / M • Aphrodesia's Diary / 1984 / CA / M • Appointment With Agony / cr80 / AVO / B • Auto-Erotic Practices / 1980 / VCR / F • Babylon Gold / 1983 / COM / C • Babylon Pink #1 / 1979 / COM / M • Backdoor Girls / 1983 / VCR / C • Beauty / 1981 / VC / M • Behind The Brown Door / 1986 / VCR / C • Best Of Hot Shorts #01 / 1987 / VCR / C • Between The Sheets / 1982 / CA / M • Beyond Desire / 1986 / VC / M • Big Gulp #1 / 1986 / VIP / C • Bizarre Styles / 1981 / ALP / F • Blue Vanities #044 (New) / 1988 / FFL / M • Blue Vanities #062 / 1988 / FFL / M • Blue Vanities #066 / 1988 / FFL / M • Blue Vanities #090 / 1988 / FFL / M • Blue Vanities #240 / 1995 / FFL / M • Blue Vanities #241 / 1995 / FFL / M • Blue Vanities #250 / 1996 / FFL / M • Blue Vanities #534 / 1993 / FFL / M • Blue Voodoo / 1983 / VD / M • Breaker Beauties / 1977 / VHL / M • Caballero Preview Tape #1 / 1982 / CA / C • Caballero Preview Tape #2 / 1983 / CA / C • Caballero Preview Tape #3 / 1984 / CA / C • Caballero Preview Tape #4 / 1985 / CA / C

• Cherry Hustlers / 1977 / VEN / M • China Doll / 1976 / VC / M • Classic Erotica #2 / 1980 / SVE / M • Classic Erotica #8 / 1985 / SVE / M • Classic Erotica Special / 1985 / SVE / M • Coed Fever / 1980 / CA / M • Come Softly / 1977 / TVX / M • Come To Me / cr80 / AIR / C • Come With Me, My Love / 1976 / PVX / M • Corruption / 1983 / VC / M • The Dancers / 1981 / VCX / M • Daughters Of Discipline #1 / 197? / AVO / B • Deep Inside Vanessa Del Rio / 1986 / VC / M • Devil In Miss Jones #3: A New Beginning / 1986 / VC / M • Dirty Bob's #25: Porn Never Sleeps! / 1996 / FLP / S • Dirty Looks / 1982 / VC / C • Domination Blue / 1976 / SVE / B • Dominatrix Without Mercy / 1976 / ALP / B • Double Pleasure / 1985 / VCR / M • Dr Lust / 1987 / VC / M • Dracula Exotica / 1980 / TVX / M • Dynamic Vices / 1987 / VC / M • Electric Blue #006 / 1982 / CA / S • Emergency Nurse / 1978 / … / M • Erotic Gold #2 / 1985 / VEN / M • The Erotic World Of Crystal Dawn (#3) / 1983 / VCR / C • The Erotic World Of Vanessa #1 / 1983 / VCR / C • The Erotic World Of Vanessa #2 / 1984 / VCR / C • Exploring Young Girls / 1978 / ALP / M • Fantasy Peeps: Solo Girls / 1985 / 4P / M • Fantasy Peeps: Women In Love / 1985 / 4P / M • Fetish Fever / 1993 / CA / C • The Filthy Rich / 1981 / CA / M • The Final Test / 197? / RLV / B • Fire In Francesca / cr77 / ASR / M • Foxholes / 1983 / SE / M • Foxtrot / 1982 / COM / M • Fulfilling Young Cups / 1978 / … / M • Fury In Alice / 1976 / SVE / M • Girls In Passion / 1979 / VHL / M • Girls U.S.A. / 1980 / AIR / M • Gourmet Quickies: Vanessa Del Rio #710 / 1984 / GO / C • GVC: Bizarre Moods #111 / cr83 / GO / M • GVC: Forbidden Ways #114 / 1978 / GO / M • GVC: Private Nurses #126 / cr84 / GO / M • GVC: Real Estate #109 / 198? / GO / M • Her Name Was Lisa / 1979 / VC / M • Historic Erotica: Celebrity Sinners / 1992 / GMI / M • Hollywood Goes Hard / 19?? / AVO / B • Hot Shorts: Vanessa Del Rio / 1986 / VCR / C • Hot Spots / 1984 / BTO / C • House Of DeSade / 1975 / ALP / B • Jabberwalk #2 / 1982 / … / S • Jack 'n' Jill #1 / 1979 / VXP / M • Jacquette / cr77 / CDI / M • Jawbreakers / 1985 / VEN / C • Joint Venture / 1977 / ELV / M • Justine: A Matter Of Innocence / 1980 / SAT / M • Kinky Potpourri #24 / 199? / SVE / C • Kinky Potpourri #29 / 1997 / SVE / C • Kinky Potpourri #33 / 1997 / SVE / C • Ladies In Love / 19?? / PLY / C • The Lady Vanessa / 1985 / HOR / C • Legends Of Porn #1 / 1987 / CV / C • Lips: The Passage To Pleasure / 1981 / CA / M • Love-In Arrangement / 1981 / VXP / M • Luscious / 1980 / VXP / M • Magic Girls / 1983 / SVE / M • Midnight Blue #1 / 1980 / VXP / M • Midnight Desires / 1976 / VXP / M • Naughty Nurses / 1982 / VCR / M • New York Babes / 1979 / AR / M • Night Of Submission / 1976 / BIZ / M • The Nurses Are Coming / 1985 / VCR / C • Odyssey / 1977 / VC / M • The One And Only / 1987 / VCR / C • Only The Very Best On Film / 1992 / VC / C • Parliament: Ass Masters #1 / 1987 / PM / M • The Pink Ladies / 1980 / VC / M • Platinum Paradise / 1980 / COM / M • Play Me Again, Vanessa / 1986 / VC / M • Pleasure #1 / 1985 / LA / M • Pleasure #4 / 1990 / BTO / M • Porn In The USA #2 /

1987 / VEN / C • Rearbusters / 1988 / LVI / C • The Red Room And Other Places / 1992 / COM / C • Reunion (Vanessa Del Rio's) / 1977 / LIM / M • A Scent Of Heather / 1981 / VXP / M • The Seduction Of Cindy / 1980 / VC / M • Sex Maniac's Guide To The Usa / 1982 / KEN / S • Showgirl #02: Seka's Fantasies / 1981 / VCR / M • Showgirl #03: Vanessa Del Rio's Fantasies / 1981 / VCR / M • Showgirl #06: Sue Nero's Fantasies / 1983 / VCR / M • Showgirl #16: Samantha Fox's Fantasies / 1983 / VCR / M • Silk, Satin & Sex / 1983 / SE / M • Sin Of Lust / 1976 / SVE / M • Sister Midnight / 19?? / … / M • Snow Honeys / 1983 / VC / M • Swedish Erotica #20 / 1980 / CA / M • Swedish Erotica #29 / 1980 / CA / M • Swedish Erotica #43 / 1982 / CA / M • Swedish Erotica #44 / 1982 / CA / M • Take Off / 1978 / VXP / M • The Tale Of Tiffany Lust / 1981 / CA / M • A Taste Of Vanessa De Rio / 1990 / PIN / C • Teenage Bikers / 197? / SIL / B • Temptations / 1976 / VXP / M • That Lady From Rio / 1976 / VXP / M • That's Erotic / 1979 / CV / C • That's Porno / 1979 / CV / C • Tigresses...And Other Man-Eaters / 1979 / VXP / M • Too Young To Care / cr73 / BOC / M • Top Secret / 1982 / BIZ / B • True Legends Of Adult Cinema: The Golden Age / 1992 / VC / C • The Vanessa Obsession / 1987 / VCX / C • Vanessa's Bed Of Pleasure / 1983 / SVE / M • Vanessa's Hot Nights / 1984 / SVE / M • Vanessa...Maid In Manhattan / 1984 / VC / M • VCA Previews #2 / 1988 / VC / C • VCA Previews #3 / 1988 / VC / C • VCA Previews #4 / 1988 / VC / C • Venessa In Heat / 1995 / … / C • Victims Of Love / 1975 / ALP / M • Video Kixs Magazine #4 / 1983 / GLD / S • Video Kixs Magazine #6 / 1983 / GLD / M • Virgin Snow / 1976 / VXP / M • Viva Vanessa The Undresser / 1984 / VC / M • Wet Shots (Vcr) / 1983 / VCR / C • When She Was Bad / 1983 / CA / M • Women In Love / 1980 / CA / M • [Carole / 1983 / … / M • [Gulp / cr75 / … / M • [The Lady Vanessa / 1993 / … / M • [Vanessa's Dirty Deeds / 19?? / SVE / M

VANESSA DRAKE *see* **Vanessa Chase**
VANESSA FORTUNATO *see* **Star Index I**
VANESSA JACKSON
Florence Rump / 1995 / SUF / M
VANESSA JORSON *see* **Clair Dia**
VANESSA LA CRUZ
Anal Intruder #01 / 1986 / CC / M • The South Bronx Story / 1986 / CC / M
VANESSA MELVILLE *see* **Star Index I**
VANESSA MOORE
African Angels #3 / 1996 / NIT / M • The Cumm Brothers #17: Goo Guy Gone Bad / 1996 / OD / M • Nothing Like Nurse Nookie #2 / 1996 / NIT / M
VANESSA PANTHER
Sean Michaels On The Road #06: France & Belgium / 1993 / VT / M
VANESSA PARKER *see* **Star Index I**
VANESSA PRIDE *see* **Star Index I**
VANESSA ROSE
Ass Masters (Leisure) #01 / 1995 / LEI / M • Back Door Babewatch / 1995 / IF / C • Fresh Faces #05 / 1995 / EVN / M
VANESSA STEELE (EC) *see* **Evon Crawford**
VANESSA TAYLOR *see* **Taylor Evans**
VANESSA TIBBS
California Gigolo / 1979 / WWV / M

VANESSA VALENTY
World Cup / 1990 / PL / M
VANESSA WILLIS
Shiela's Deep Desires / 1986 / HO / M
VANESSA YONI
Dream House / 1995 / XPR / M
VANILLA
100% Amateur #01: Double Penetration Sensation / 1995 / OD / M • African Angels #2 / 1996 / NIT / M
VANILLA JOY *see* **Star Index I**
VANILLA SIMS *(Vanella Simms, Vanilla Williams, Vanella Williams)*
Blonde emaciated dancer with a tight body and depending on the movie either small droopy or enhanced medium tits. Not ugly but not too pretty either.
The Anal Adventures Of Max Hardcore: Wildlife / 1994 / ZA / M • Anal Anonymous / 1994 / ZA / M • Anal Maniacs #1 / 1994 / WP / M • Bun Busters #17 / 1994 / LBO / M • Butt Hunt #02 / 1994 / LEI / M • Cherry Poppers #03: School's Out / 1994 / ZA / M • Dirty Doc's Housecalls #15 / 1994 / LV / M • Hidden Camera #18 / 1994 / JMP / M • The Hitch-Hiker #03: No Exit / 1994 / WMG / M • House Of Sex #11: Dirty Anal Gang Bangs / 1994 / RTP / M • Petite & Sweet / 1994 / V99 / M • Secret Diary #1 / 1994 / TAW / M
VANILLA WILLIAMS *see* **Vanilla Sims**
VANITY *(Tisa)*
The Italian Stallion is her boyfriend. In 1995 is working as a hooker in Hollywood and looks like she may be under the influence of some illicit substance. Had two kids which she lost presumably as a result of her hooker/drug activities.
Angel Of The Island / 1988 / IN / M • The Bottom Line / 1990 / AMB / M • Devil In Vanity / 1990 / CC / M • Erotic Tales / 1989 / V99 / M • Heidi Fleiss: Hollywood Madam / 1995 / BMG / S • Hometown Honeys #3 / 1989 / VEX / M • The Oversexual Tourist / 1989 / VEX / M • Risque Business / 1989 / V99 / M • Sex Kittens / 1990 / VEX / F • South Beach / 1992 / PRS / S • Tropical Temptations / 1989 / VEX / M
VANITY (D.D. WINT) *see* **D.D. Winters**
VANITY (OTHER)
Fantasy Photography: Cheri's Passion / 1995 / FAP / F • Private Gold #05: Cape Town #1 / 1996 / OD / M
VANITY FAIR
The Love Couch / 1977 / VC / M
VANITY H.
New Ends #05 / 1993 / 4P / M • Private Film #04 / 1993 / OD / M • Up And Cummers #11 / 1994 / 4P / M
VANNA
Penthouse: Great Pet Hunt #1 / 1992 / PET / F • Pussyman's Nite Club Party #1 / 1996 / SNA / M • Up And Cummers #19 / 1995 / 4P / M
VANNA BLANC *see* **Star Index I**
VANNA LACE
Big Busted Goddesses Of Beverly Hills / 1996 / NAP / S • Dressed To Dominate / 1996 / NAP / B • Venus' Playhouse / 1994 / VDL / S
VANNA PAYMORE *see* **Jeanna Fine**
VANNAH
Pussyman's Nite Club Party #2 / 1997 / SNA / M
VANYA *see* **Sabrina Bliss**
VARMINT *see* **Star Index I**

VASAS
The Betrayal Of Innocence #1: The Awakening Of Marika / 1993 / CC / M • The Betrayal Of Innocence #2: The Decadence / 1993 / CC / M • The Betrayal Of Innocence #3: The Choice / 1993 / CC / M

VAUGHAN MEADER
Linda Lovelace For President / 1975 / ... / C

VAUGHN MITCHELL
Mystique / 1979 / CA / M

VEE SUMMERS see Star Index I

VEGAS
Southern Belles #4 / 1995 / HOV / M

VEGAS VIC
The Bottom Dweller 33 1/3 / 1995 / EL / M

VELDA CARRERA
Plastic Workshop / 1995 / LAF / M

VELVET
A&B AB#181: Horny Housewife / 1990 / A&B / M • A&B AB#202: Seductive Night / 1990 / A&B / M • A&B AB#208: Velvet My Lover / 1990 / A&B / F • A&B AB#215: Anal Sex Session / 1990 / A&B / M • A&B AB#329: Velvet's Striptease & Lingerie Show / 1991 / A&B / F • A&B AB#330: Velvet Takes It All / 1991 / A&B / M • A&B AB#376: Velvet Is Back / 1991 / A&B / M • A&B AB#530: Masters / 1995 / A&B / B • A&B GB#001: Cum Bath / 1992 / A&B / M • A&B GB#003: Cum Together—Velvet And Ginger / 1992 / A&B / M • AVP #7024: Bodyguard Bang / 1991 / AVP / M • AVP #9012: Slow & Easy, Long & Hard / 1990 / AVP / M • Black Mystique #10 / 1994 / VT / F • Dark Passions #03 / 1995 / AFV / M • Dirty Dancers #7 / 1996 / 4P / M • Times Square Comes Alive / 1984 / VC / M

VELVET BLUE
Adventures Of The DP Boys: At The French Riviera / 1994 / HW / M • Amateur Dreams #3 / 1994 / DR / M • Amateur Dreams #4 / 1994 / DR / M • Beaver Hunt #03 / 1994 / LEI / M • First Time Lesbians #20 / 1994 / JMP / F • Florence Hump / 1994 / AFI / M • Fresh Faces #01 / 1994 / EVN / M • Titanic Orgy / 1995 / PEP / M

VELVET BUSCH see Star Index I

VELVET SOMMER see Velvet Summers

VELVET SUMMERS *(Little Velvet Sommer, Velvet Sommer)*
Cute very petite (4'11") brunette with shoulder length hair, passable face, small tits, small tattoo on her left chest above her tit, tight waist. 30-24-30 and 21 years old in 1982.
Dr Bizarro / 1978 / ALP / B • Education Of Velvet / 1983 / BIZ / B • Hitchhiker / 1983 / AVC / M • Housebroken / 1983 / BIZ / B • Never Sleep Alone / 1984 / CA / M • Night Hunger / 1983 / AVC / M • Peepholes / 1982 / AVC / M • Sex Stalker / 1983 / MPP / M • Sweet Little Sister/The Dreamer / 1983 / SHO / M • Tales Of The Bizarre / 1983 / ALP / B • The Taming Of Rebecca / 1982 / SVE / B • Twilight Pink #2 / 1982 / VC / M • Wicked Schoolgirls / 1981 / SVE / M

VELVET TOUCH *(Lady Samantha)*
This is a fat white female aged about 50.
All For You, Baby / 1990 / VEX / M • Belle Of The Ball / 1989 / V99 / M • Butt Hunt #05 / 1995 / LEI / M • Depraved / 1990 / IN / M • Dream Dates / 1990 / V99 / M • Oral Support / 1989 / V99 / M • Red Hot And Ready / 1990 / V99 / M • A Touch Of Mink / 1990 / V99 / M

VENDETTE
The Stimulators / 1983 / VC / M

VENESSA
Mickey Ray's Sex Search #01: Sliding In / 1994 / WIV / M

VENESSA ROSO
Horny Henry's London Adventure / 1995 / TTV / M

VENESSA STEELE see Evon Crawford

VENNA MACGREGOR
The Psychiatrist / 1978 / VC / M

VENOM
A Lowdown Dirty Game / 1996 / LBO / M

VENUS
Girls In Heat / 1995 / WIV / M • The Husband / 1995 / WIV / M • The Last Train #1 / 1995 / BHE / M • The Last Train #2 / 1995 / BHE / M • M Series #07 / 1993 / LBO / M • Peek-A-Boo / 1953 / SOW / S

VENUS CHANTELL
Anal Intruder #01 / 1986 / CC / M • Bitch Queendom / 1987 / BIZ / B

VENUS DELIGHT
Angel Of Passion / 1991 / CPV / S • Best Chest 14 / 1994 / CAW / B • Checkmate / 1995 / WAV / M • Desert Starm (030 Min) / 1993 / NAP / B • Desert Starm (120 Min) / 1993 / NAP / C • Dressed To Dominate / 1996 / NAP / B • Get You Wet / 1992 / NAP / S • Heavenly Bodies / 1993 / NAP / B • Marathon Woman / 1996 / CAW / B • Miss Nude World International Pageant / 1996 / WAT / F • The Model And The Showgirl / 1995 / NAP / B • Queen Of The Harem / 1993 / NAP / B • Sex Magic / 1996 / CAW / B • Sex On The Strip: The Lusty Ladies Of Las Vagas / 1993 / CPG / F • Venus' Playhouse / 1994 / VDL / S • World Duos Championship Finals / 1994 / PME / S • World Duos Championship Semi-Finals / 1994 / PME / S

VENUS GUILLEN see Venus/Persia

VENUS MIEL
Twilight Pink #2 / 1982 / VC / M

VENUS/PERSIA *(Venus Guillen)*
Black girl with quite a pretty face but an ugly fat body and huge tits.
The Adventures Of Breastman / 1992 / EVN / M • Adventures Of The DP Boys: Chocolate City / 1994 / HW / M • Adventures Of The DP Boys: The Blacks Are Cumming / 1994 / HW / M • Alice In Pornoland / 1996 / IP / M • Amateur Lesbians #32: Tara / 1992 / GO / F • America's Raunchiest Home Videos #67: / 1993 / ZA / M • Anal Adventures (Dragon) / 1992 / DRP / M • Anal Delights #2 / 1992 / ROB / M • Anal Encounters #8 / 1992 / VC / M • Anal International / 1992 / HW / M • Anal Orgasms / 1992 / DRP / M • Anal Sexual Silence / 1993 / IP / M • Ass Openers! #1 / 1995 / TCK / C • Ass Openers! #2 / 1995 / TCK / C • Backdoor To The City Of Sin / 1993 / ANA / M • Backing In #4 / 1993 / WV / C • Bareback Riders / 1992 / VEX / M • The Bashful Blonde From Beautiful Bendover / 1993 / PEP / M • Beach Bum Amateur's #08 / 1992 / MID / M • Beach Bum Amateur's #11 / 1992 / MID / M • The Best Of Black Anal #1 / 1995 / ROB / C • The Best Of Sean Michaels / 1994 / VT / C • The Best Rears Of Our Lives / 1992 / OD / M • Big Bust Babes #08 / 1991 / AFI / M • Big Bust Babes #16 / 1993 / AFI / M • Big Man's Ebony Dreams / 1996 / LOK / M • Black Beauties #1 / 1992 / VIM / M • Black

Buttman #01 / 1993 / CC / M • Black Fantasies #09 / 1995 / HW / M • Black Fantasies #10 / 1995 / HW / M • Black Hollywood Amateurs #20 / 1995 / MID / M • Black Jack City #4 / 1994 / HW / M • Black Leather / Black Skin / 1995 / VT / B • Black Mystique #07 / 1994 / VT / F • Black Mystique #08 / 1994 / VT / F • Black On Black (1994-Midnight) / 1994 / MID / C • Black Velvet #1 / 1992 / CC / M • Blacks N' Blue / 1995 / VT / B • Boomerwang / 1992 / MID / M • Breast Collection #02 / 1995 / LBO / C • Breast Collection #03 / 1995 / LBO / C • Breast Worx #25 / 1992 / LBO / M • Breast Worx #32 / 1992 / LBO / M • Breast Worx #35 / 1992 / LBO / M • Brown Sugar From The Hood / 1996 / MID / M • Bunz-Eye / 1992 / ROB / M • Butties / 1992 / VC / M • Chessie's Home Videos #19: Girl On Girl / 1995 / CHM / F • Chocolate Bunnies #01 / 1995 / LBO / C • Chocolate Bunnies #02 / 1995 / LBO / C • Chocolate Bunnies #03 / 1995 / LBO / C • Chocolate Bunnies #04 / 1995 / LBO / C • Chocolate Bunnies #06 / 1996 / LBO / C • Danger-Ass / 1992 / MID / M • Dark Passions #03 / 1995 / AFV / M • The Dirtiest Girl In The World / 1992 / ZA / M • Dirty Dixie / 1992 / IF / M • Double D Dykes #02 / 1992 / GO / F • Double D Dykes #06 / 1992 / GO / F • Double Penetration #6 / 1993 / WV / C • The Dream Team / 1995 / VT / M • Driving Miss Daisy Crazy #2 / 1992 / WV / M • The Ebony Connection #1 / 1994 / LBO / C • Ebony Erotica / 1995 / VT / M • Encino Woman / 1992 / VIM / M • Exposure Images #26: Persia / 1995 / EXI / F • Extraterrestrial Virgins / 1995 / VIT / M • Fantasies Of Persia / 1995 / VT / M • Firm / 1993 / MID / M • Foreign Affairs / 1992 / VT / C • Full Service / 1993 / GO / M • The Girls From Hootersville #02 / 1993 / SFP / M • Girlz N The Hood #2 / 1992 / HW / M • Girlz N The Hood #4 / 1994 / HW / M • Hard Ride / 1992 / WV / M • Hometown Honeys #5 / 1993 / VEX / M • Hot Tight Asses #01 / 1992 / TCK / M • Impulse #05: When I Was 20... / 1995 / MBP / M • In Loving Color #1 / 1992 / VT / M • In Loving Color #2 / 1992 / VT / M • In Loving Color #3 / 1992 / VT / M • In Loving Color #4 / 1993 / VT / M • Interracial Affairs / 1996 / FC / M • Knockin' Da Booty / 1993 / WP / M • Lettre Da Rimini / 1995 / MID / M • Lust Crimes / 1992 / WV / M • M Series #26 / 1994 / LBO / M • Main Street, U.S.A. / 1992 / PP / M • Midsummer Love Story / 1993 / WV / M • Mission Hard / 1995 / XC / M • Mo' Booty #4 / 1995 / TIW / M • More Than A Handful #3 / 1993 / MET / M • My Baby Got Back #01 / 1992 / VT / M • My Baby Got Back #02 / 1993 / VT / M • My Baby Got Back #03 / 1995 / VT / M • My Baby Got Back #05 / 1995 / VT / M • Odyssey 30 Min: #198B: Venus Cures More Than Throbbing Dick / 1991 / OD / M • Odyssey Triple Play #27: Black & White Adventures / 1993 / OD / M • One Lay At A Time / 1992 / V99 / M • One Night Love Affair / 1991 / IF / M • Party Dolls / 1992 / VEX / M • Persia's Back / 1994 / VT / M • Persia's Fantasies / 1995 / VT / M • The Pick Up / 1993 / MID / M • Portrait Of Lust / 1992 / WV / M • Positively Pagan #04 / 1991 / ATA / M • The Power & The Passion / 1993 / CDI / M • Prima #04: The Editing Room / 1995 / MBP / M • The Prince Of Lies / 1992 / LE / M •

Private Dancer (CDI) / 1992 / CDI / M • Pubic Eye / 1992 / HW / M • Rocks / 1993 / VT / M • Rocky Mountains / 1991 / IF / M • Sex Bandits / 1992 / ZA / M • Sex In Uniform / 1992 / BIJ / M • Sex Wish / 1992 / WV / M • Shoot To Thrill / 1992 / WV / M • Star Spangled Blacks / 1994 / VEX / M • Supermarket Babes In Heat / 1992 / OD / M • Tailiens #3 / 1992 / FD / M • Tails Of Tribeca / 1993 / HW / M • Tales From The Backside / 1993 / VC / M • Tits And Tongues / 1993 / NAP / B • Twin Peaks / 1993 / PL / M • Undercover Lover / 1993 / VC / M • What's Butt Got To Do With It? / 1993 / HW / M • White Men Can Hump / 1992 / EVN / M • With The Devil In Her Rear / 1992 / WV / M • You Bet Your Butt / 1992 / VC / M

VERA
Blue Vanities #578 / 1995 / FFL / M • Magma: Puszta Teenies / 1995 / MET / M • Rocco Goes To Prague / 1995 / EA / M • Sex On The Beach!: Spring Break Texas Style / 1994 / CPG / F • Vera Vera / 1973 / CLX / M

VERA BUTLER see Nina DePonca

VERA NOVAK
Blue Vanities #517 / 1992 / FFL / M

VERA SAXBE
The Unholy Child / 1972 / AVC / M

VERA SWEN
Von Sex Gier Besessen / 1995 / PF / M

VERCINIA *(Babygirl, Baby (Vercinia))*
Pretty black girl with corn rolls and a sort of topknot, medium natural tits, nice butt, petite, slim but not emaciated, full pubic bush and hairy (!) belly. Birthmark on right waist.
Anal Spitfire / 1994 / ROB / M • The Best Of Black Anal #1 / 1995 / ROB / C • Black Bottom Girls / 1994 / ME / M • Black Centerfolds #4 / 1996 / MID / M • Black Cheerleader Search #10 / 1997 / IVC / M • Black Snatch #1 / 1996 / DFI / F • Little Miss Anal / 1994 / ROB / M • Sista! #2 / 1994 / VT / F

VERE DEDKO
The Swing Thing / 1973 / TGA / M

VERI KNOTTI see Veri Knotty

VERI KNOTTY *(Veri Knotti, Fanny Wolfe)*
Ugly girl with droopy medium-to-large tits who can tie her labia minora in a knot, hence the name. In **Auto-Erotic Practices** she says the last name is spelt with a "y". Unconfirmed rumor that she is dead.
Auto-Erotic Practices / 1980 / VCR / F • Bedtime Video #06 / 1984 / GO / M • Beyond Shame / 1980 / VEP / M • Blue Ecstasy / 1980 / CA / M • Blue Vanities #536 / 1993 / FFL / M • California Gigolo / 1979 / WWV / M • Captain Lust And The Amorous Contessa / 1977 / IHV / M • Centerfold Fever / 1981 / VXP / M • Dirty Looks / 1982 / VC / C • For The Love Of Pleasure / 1979 / SE / M • A Girl's Best Friend / 1981 / QX / M • GVC: Strange Family / 1977 / GO / M • Heat Wave / 1977 / COM / M • Jail Bait / 1976 / VC / M • Loose Threads / 1979 / S&L / M • The Nurses Are Coming / 1985 / VCR / C • Sizzle / 1979 / QX / M • Sweet Surrender / 1980 / VCX / M • This Lady Is A Tramp / 1980 / CV / M • Vanessa's Bed Of Pleasure / 1983 / SVE / M • Women In Love / 1980 / CA / M

VERMILLION see Star Index I

VERN ROSSI

A Dirty Western #1 / 1973 / AR / M • Saturday Matinee Series #3 / 1996 / VCX / C

VERNA QUICK
18 And Anxious / cr78 / CDI / M • Insane Lovers / 1978 / VIS / M • Small Change / 1978 / CDC / M

VERNON VON BERGDORF see Star Index I

VERONA
Limited Edition #16 / 1980 / AVC / M

VERONA LAKE see Kitty Monroe

VERONICA
Ashley Rene & Veronica: Bondage Buddies / 1994 / BON / B • The Bitch Squirms & Squiggles #1 / 1993 / BON / B • The Bitch Squirms & Squiggles #2 / 1993 / BON / B • Blackmail Bondage / 1993 / BON / B • Blue Vanities #531 / 1993 / FFL / M • Buffy Malibu's Totally Nasty All-Girl Home Videos #03 / 1992 / ANA / F • Delinquent Renter / 1994 / BON / B • The Escapades Of Marie Maiden / 1993 / RSV / G • Fantasy In Oil #1 / 1996 / CAW / B • Girls Around The World #29 / 1995 / BTO / M • Homegrown Video #344 / 1991 / HOV / M • Hot Body Competition: The Beverly Hill's Naughty Nightie C. / 1995 / CG / F • Intimate Interviews #4 / 1996 / NIT / M • Match #4: Hellcats / 1995 / NPA / B • New Faces, Hot Bodies #19 / 1995 / STP / M • Real People Real Bondage #1 / 1995 / BON / C • Stevi's: Phone Sex / 1993 / SSV / M • Student Fetish Videos: Catfighting #12 / 1994 / PRE / B • Student Fetish Videos: The Enema #15 / 1994 / PRE / B • Student Fetish Videos: Spanking #15 / 1994 / PRE / B • Submissive Stripper / 1995 / GAL / B • VGA: Bureau Of Discipline #3 / 1993 / VGA / B

VERONICA (LAKE) see Veronica Lake

VERONICA (LOUISI) *(Louisi (Veronica))*
Brazilian, marginal face, small/medium tits, long black hair, lithe body, white skin, tattoo on left shoulder back and another tiny one on her right bicep.
Fashion Passion / 1997 / TEP / M • Real Sex Magazine #02 / 1997 / HO / M

VERONICA (ZUMIRA) see Zumira

VERONICA ADAMS
One Last Fling / cr76 / CPL / M

VERONICA ANDERS see Star Index I

VERONICA BRASIL see Veronica Castillo

VERONICA BRAZIL see Veronica Castillo

VERONICA CALIENTE see Veronica Castillo

VERONICA CASTILLO *(Veronica Rio, Veronica Brazil, Veronica Florez, Veronica Caliente, Veronica Brasil)*
Not too pretty krinkly haired dark blonde with one of the worst tit jobs on record—humongous and ugly. The rest of her body is OK. Born Oct 12, 1958 in Rio De Janeiro, Brazil. Was a stripper and dancer before she turned to pornos.
All About Teri Weigel / 1996 / XCI / M • Anal Angels #6 / 1996 / VEX / C • Anal Nymphettes / 1995 / LIP / F • Ass Busters Incorporated / 1996 / BLC / M • Ass Openers! #2 / 1995 / TCK / C • Big Bust Babes #16 / 1993 / AFI / M • Big Bust Babes #17 / 1993 / AFI / M • Big Busty Whoppers / 1994 / PME / F • Bigggum's / 1995 / GLI / C • Black Butt Jungle / 1993 / ME / M • Black Orgies #14 / 1993 / AFI / M • Bloop-

ers & Behind The Scenes / 1995 / LEI / M • Booty In The House / 1993 / WP / M • Bra Busters #05 / 1993 / LBO / M • Bra Busters #06 / 1993 / LBO / M • Breast Collection #04 / 1995 / LBO / C • The Breast Of Breastmen / 1995 / EVN / C • Breastman Does The Twin Towers / 1993 / EVN / M • Busty Babes In Heat #1 / 1993 / BTO / M • Busty Porno Queens / 1996 / H&S / M • Centerfold Celebrities '94 #1 / 1994 / SFP / M • Cheeks #7: Mirror Image / 1994 / CC / M • Chocolate Bunnies #03 / 1995 / LBO / C • Crossed Nipples / 1994 / NAP / B • Crotch To Crotch: Latex Madness / 1996 / NAP / B • Der Champion / 1995 / BTO / M • Dick & Jane Big Breast Adventure / 1993 / AVI / M • Dick & Jane Sneak On The Set / 1993 / AVI / M • Dirty Bob's #08: LAid Over In L.A. / 1993 / FLP / S • Dirty Bob's #10: Sleeping Late In Seattle / 1993 / FLP / S • Dirty Bob's #19: Over The Boardwalk! / 1995 / FLP / S • Dirty Mind / 1995 / VEX / M • Double D Amateurs #08 / 1993 / JMP / M • Eruption Of Jealousy / 1996 / NAP / B • Exotic Tastes / 1995 / VEX / C • Fantasy Flings #01 / 1993 / WP / M • Fantasy Fuchs / 1996 / PLP / C • Gazonga Goddess #2 / 1994 / IF / M • The Girls From Hootersville #04 / 1993 / SFP / M • Glitz Tits #06 / 1993 / GLI / M • Glitz Tits #07 / 1993 / GLI / M • Gringa / 1996 / NAP / B • High Heel Harlots #02 / 1993 / SFP / M • Hispanic Orgies #01 / 1993 / GO / M • Hispanic Orgies #03 / 1993 / GO / M • Hooters In The 'hood / 1995 / TTV / M • Hot Tight Asses #04 / 1993 / TCK / M • How To Make A Model #04: Facial Cream Girls / 1994 / LBO / M • Interview's Foreign Affair / 1996 / LV / M • John Wayne Bobbitt Uncut / 1994 / LEI / M • Kinky Cameraman #4 / 1996 / LEI / C • Knockout / 1994 / VEX / M • Latex Lioness / 1996 / NAP / B • Latina Rumble / 1996 / NAP / B • M Series #16 / 1993 / LBO / M • Mike Hott: #251 Cunt of the Month: Veronica / 1993 / MHV / M • More Than A Handful #4 / 1994 / MET / M • Mr. Peepers Amateur Home Videos #84: She Put the Bra in Braz / 1994 / LBO / M • The Night Of The Coyote / 1993 / MED / M • Odyssey Triple Play #78: South American Senoritas / 1994 / OD / M • Sarah Jane's Love Bunnies #05 / 1993 / FPI / F • Sexual Trilogy #02 / 1993 / SFP / M • Shades Of Erotica #02 / 1994 / GLI / M • Special Reserve / 1994 / VC / M • Stewardesses Behind Bars / 1994 / HW / M • Student Fetish Videos: Best of Enema #03 / 1994 / PRE / C • Switch Hitters #8 / 1995 / IN / G • Switch Hitters #9 / 1995 / IN / G • Titty City #2 / 1995 / TIW / C • Toppers #21 / 1993 / TV / C • Toppers #23 / 1994 / TV / M • Toppers #24 / 1994 / TV / M • Toppers #27 / 1994 / TV / M • Toppers #31 / 1994 / TV / C • Toppers #32 / 1994 / TV / C • Truck Stop Angel / 1994 / CC / M • Video Virgins #07 / 1993 / NS / M • Whoomp! There She Is / 1993 / AVI / M

VERONICA COUSTEAU
Veronica's Kiss / 1979 / VCI / M

VERONICA DOLL
50 Ways To Lick Your Lover / 1989 / ZA / M • Buttman's European Vacation #1 / 1991 / EA / M • From Sweden With Love / 1989 / ZA / M • Girls Don't Lie / 1990 / IN / F • House Of Dreams / 1990 / CA / M • The Moon Girls / 1990 / ME / C • Oh! You Beautiful Doll / 1990 / ZA / M • Payne In The Be-

hind / 1993 / AMF / C • A Rare Starlet / 1987 / ME / M • Woman To Woman / 1989 / ZA / C

VERONICA ERICKSON *(Erica Erickson)*
Beyond The Valley Of The Dolls / 1970 / CBS / S • Fanny Hill: Memoirs Of A Woman Of Pleasure / 1964 / PAV / S

VERONICA FLOREZ *see* **Veronica Castillo**

VERONICA HALL
Bored Housewife / 1989 / CIN / M • Buttslammers #06: Over The Edge / 1994 / BS / F • The Catwoman / 1988 / VC / M • The Erotic Adventures Of Bedman And Throbbin / 1989 / VWA / M • Flesh For Frankenstein / 1987 / VEX / M • Girl Crazy / 1989 / CDI / F • The Naked Bun / 1989 / VWA / M • The Offering / 1988 / INH / G • Peeping Passions / 1989 / CAE / M • Pleasure Is My Business / 1989 / EX / M • Sex Sluts From Beyond The Galaxy / 1991 / LBO / C

VERONICA HART *(Randy Styles, Jane Hamilton, V. Hart, Victoria Holt, Valerie Hart)*
Blonde with a very distinctive face (not ugly but not pretty either), a good screen presence, medium tits, and an OK but not particularly lithe body. Randy Styles is the box credits of **Games Women Play #1**. Victoria Holt is from **Afternoon Delights**.
8 To 4 / 1981 / CA / M • Afternoon Delights / 1981 / CA / M • Alexandra / 1984 / VC / M • Alien Intruder / 1993 / PME / S • Amanda By Night #1 / 1981 / CA / M • Amanda By Night #2 / 1987 / CA / M • Amazing Sex Stories #2 / 1987 / SUV / C • American Desire / 1981 / CA / M • American Garter / 1993 / VC / M • Angel Buns / 1981 / QX / M • Babe / 1982 / AR / M • Babylon Gold / 1983 / COM / C • Be Careful What You Wish For / 1993 / VC / G • Beauty / 1981 / VC / M • Beauty School / 1993 / IMP / S • Bedroom Eyes #2 / 1989 / VMA / S • Behind The Scenes Of An Adult Movie / 1983 / CV / M • Between The Sheets / 1982 / CA / M • Black Orchid / 1993 / WV / M • Bloodsucking Pharoahs Of Pittsburgh / 1995 / PAR / S • Blowing Your Mind / 1984 / RSV / M • Blue Magic / 1981 / QX / M • Blue Ribbon Blue / 1984 / CA / C • Caballero Preview Tape #1 / 1982 / CA / C • Caballero Preview Tape #2 / 1983 / CA / C • Caballero Preview Tape #3 / 1984 / CA / C • Caballero Preview Tape #4 / 1985 / CA / C • Centerspread Girls / 1982 / CA / M • Cleo/Leo / 1989 / NWW / S • Confessions Of Seka / 1981 / SAT / M • Deathmask / 1983 / PRS / S • Delicious / 1981 / VXP / M • Delivery Boys / 1984 / NWW / S • Deranged / 1987 / REP / S • Dixie Ray Hollywood Star / 1983 / CA / M • The Ecstasy Girls #2 / 1986 / CA / M • Electric Blue #002 / 1986 / CA / S • Electric Blue #005 / 1982 / CA / S • Electric Blue: Cosmic Coeds / 1985 / CA / M • Electric Blue: Search For A Star / 1985 / CA / M • Electric Blue: Wickedly Wild West / 1985 / CA / C • Electric Blue: World Nudes Tonight / 1985 / CA / C • Enrapture / 1990 / ATL / S • Fascination / 1980 / QX / M • The Final Taboo / 1988 / CA / M • Firestorm #1 / 1984 / COM / M • Foxtrot / 1982 / COM / M • Games Women Play #1 / 1980 / CA / M • A Girl's Best Friend / 1981 / QX / M • Good Vibrations #1: Self Satisfaction With A Vibrator /

1991 / VT / M • Good Vibrations #2: A Couples Guide To Vibrator Use / 1991 / VT / M • Heaven's Touch / 1983 / CA / M • Hollywood Erotic Film Festival / 1987 / PAR / S • If Looks Could Kill / 1987 / REP / S • In Love / 1983 / VC / M • Indecent Exposure / 1981 / CA / M • Latex #1 / 1994 / VC / M • Legends Of Porn #1 / 1987 / CV / C • Liquid A$$ets / 1982 / CA / M • Little Girls Lost / 1982 / VC / M • Midnight Blue #2 / 1980 / VXP / M • Model Behavior / 1983 / LIV / S • My Surrender / 1996 / A&E / M • Neon Nights / 1981 / COM / M • New York's Finest / 1988 / AE / S • Night On The Town / 1982 / KEN / S • No Man's Land #10 / 1994 / VT / F • Nylon / 1995 / VI / M • Once Upon A Secretary / 1983 / GO / M • Only The Very Best On Film / 1992 / VC / C • Outlaw Ladies #1 / 1981 / VC / M • Pandora's Mirror / 1981 / CA / M • Party Girls / 1989 / NWW / S • The Playgirl / 1982 / CA / M • Porn Star Of The Year Contest / 1984 / VWA / M • Princess Seka / 1980 / VC / M • Private School Girls / 1983 / CA / M • Puss 'n' Boots / 1982 / VXP / M • Queen Of Harts / 1986 / BLT / C • R.S.V.P. / 1983 / VES / S • Real Tickets #1 / 1994 / VC / M • Real Tickets #2 / 1994 / VC / M • Risque Burlesque #2 / 1996 / IN / M • Roommates / 1982 / VXP / M • Ruby / 1992 / C3S / S • Satisfaction Jackson / 1988 / CA / M • A Scent Of Heather / 1981 / VXP / M • The Seduction Of Cindy / 1980 / VC / M • Seka Is Tara / 1981 / VC / M • Sensations / 1987 / AE / S • Sex Academy #1 / 1993 / ONA / M • Sex Appeal / 1986 / VES / S • Sex Maniac's Guide To The Usa / 1982 / KEN / S • Sexpot / 1988 / AE / S • Silk, Satin & Sex / 1983 / SE / M • Slammer Girls / 1987 / LIV / S • Society Affairs / 1982 / CA / M • The Starmaker / 1982 / VC / M • Stephanie's Lust Story / 1983 / VC / M • Student Affairs / 1988 / VES / S • The Tale Of Tiffany Lust / 1981 / CA / M • Touch Me In The Morning / 1982 / CA / M • Twilight Pink #1 / 1980 / AR / M • Two Hearts / 1991 / VI / M • The Ultimate Fantasy / 1995 / CV / M • Urban Cowgirls / 1980 / CA / M • VCA Previews #2 / 1988 / VC / C • Wanda Whips Wall Street / 1982 / VXP / M • Wildest Dreams / 1987 / VES / S • Wimps / 1987 / LIV / S • Women In Love / 1980 / CA / M • Young Nurses In Love / 1986 / VES / S

VERONICA KEYS
Latent Image: Blow Baby Blow / 1994 / LAT / F

VERONICA KRANTZ *see* **Star Index I**

VERONICA LAKE *(Veronica (Lake), Veronica Sage, Veronica Sanders, Cici (Veronica Lake), Veronica Page, Jewel Night, Jewel (Night))*
Not the regular movie star (who is dead), this is a very pretty small brunette/redhead with a very tight body, very tight waist, reddish pussy hair, pale not-suntanned body, small conical tits with large areola and a nice smile. In **Visions Of Desire** she sounds like she might have an Irish accent which would be consistent with her looks. Born August 7, 1973 in Van Nuys, CA and supposedly devirginized at 14. Used to work at Bank Of America. As of late 1994 she has had her tits enhanced to rock solid medium size and done something to her nose—a write-off now, unfortunately.
The Adventures Of Buck Naked / 1994 /

OD / M • Alex Jordan's First Timers #04 / 1994 / OD / M • American Beauty #2 / 1994 / FOR / M • American Blonde / 1993 / VI / M • Anal Innocence #2 / 1993 / ROB / M • Anal Rampage #2 / 1993 / ROB / M • Anal Vision #20 / 1993 / LBO / M • Animal Instinct / 1993 / VI / M • Beverly Hills Sex Party / 1993 / EX / M • Boogie In The Butt / 1993 / WIV / M • Bun Busters #09 / 1993 / LBO / M • The Butt Sisters Do Detroit / 1993 / MID / M • The Butt Sisters Do Los Angeles / 1993 / MID / M • Carlita's Backway / 1993 / OD / M • Casting Call #04 / 1993 / SO / M • Certifiably Anal / 1993 / ROB / M • Cherry Poppers #01 / 1993 / ZA / M • Club Anal #2 / 1993 / ROB / F • Dick & Jane In The Mountains / 1994 / AVI / M • The Dinner Party #1 / 1994 / ULI / M • Exit In Rear / 1993 / XCI / M • Explicit Entry / 1995 / LE / M • First Time Lesbians #15 / 1994 / JMP / F • Gorgeous / 1995 / MET / M • Kept Women / 1995 / LE / M • Kittens #5 / 1994 / CC / F • Love Bunnies #06 / 1994 / FPI / F • Lovin' Spoonfuls #3 / 1995 / 4P / C • The Mating Pot / 1994 / LBO / M • New Ends #07 / 1994 / 4P / M • New Wave Hookers #4 / 1994 / VC / M • Patriot X / 1995 / LE / M • Raunch #10: Uncut Jewel / 1994 / CC / M • Riot Grrrls / 1994 / SC / M • Ski Bunnies #1 / 1994 / HW / M • Ski Bunnies #2 / 1994 / HW / M • Surprise!!! / 1994 / VI / M • The Swap #2 / 1994 / VI / M • Tail Taggers #112 / 1993 / WV / M • Taste Of Shame / 1994 / ROB / F • Up And Cummers #06 / 1993 / 4P / M • Up And Cummers #25 / 1995 / 4P / M • Vagina Town / 1993 / CA / M • Visions #1 / 1995 / ERA / M • Visions Of Desire / 1993 / HO / M

VERONICA LANE *(Jenni (Veronica Lane)*
Blonde with long straight fine hair, droopy medium tits, clit ring, belly button ring, lithe body, pleasant personality. Was 19 years old in 1995 and says she was de-virginized at 14.
Dirty Bob's #21: Squeaky-Clean / 1995 / FLP / S • Dirty Stories #3 / 1995 / PE / M • Fashion Sluts #4 / 1995 / ABS / M • Hand Jobs #1 / 1994 / MAV / M • HomeGrown Video #445: Sex Kittens / 1995 / HOV / M • Max #04: The Harder They Come / 1995 / FWE / M • Nasty Newcummers #14 / 1995 / MET / M • Sleeping Booty / 1995 / EL / M • Sodomania #15: Warning! / 1996 / EL / M • Sodomania: Slop Shots / 1996 / EL / C • Southern Belles #3 / 1995 / HOV / M • Video Virgins #22 / 1995 / NS / M

VERONICA MELLON *see* **Star Index I**

VERONICA MONET
Porn Star Confidential / 1996 / ESF / M • Real Women...Real Fantasies! / 1996 / WSD / F

VERONICA MOON
Man To Maiden / 1984 / BIZ / B • The Story of Bobby / cr80 / BIZ / B

VERONICA NELSON
The Birthday Ball / 1975 / VHL / M

VERONICA NOSHER
Euro Extremities #25 / 199? / SVE / C

VERONICA PAGE *see* **Veronica Lake**

VERONICA PINK *see* **Star Index I**

VERONICA POND *see* **Star Index I**

VERONICA RIO *see* **Veronica Castillo**

VERONICA SAGE *see* **Veronica Lake**

VERONICA SANDERS *see* **Veronica Lake**

VERONICA TANNER
Sexplorations / 1991 / VC / C
VERONICA TAYLOR *see Star Index I*
VERONICA VALDEZ
Back Door Babewatch / 1995 / IF / C • Glamour Girl / 1991 / VEX / M • Leading Lady / 1991 / V99 / M
VERONICA VERA
Bare Witness / 1991 / VER / B • Consenting Adults / 1981 / VXP / M • Deep Inside Trading / 1986 / AR / M • Getting Ahead / 1983 / PL / M • A History Of Corsets / 1987 / VER / S • I Know What Girls Like / 1986 / WET / G • Latex Lovers / cr83 / VD / B • Night Hunger / 1983 / AVC / M • Portrait Of A Sexual Evolutionary / cr90 / ... / C • Rebecca's Dream / cr83 / VD / B • Sex Maniac's Ball / 1995 / AOC / S • She Comes In Colors / 1987 / AMB / M • Times Square Comes Alive / 1984 / VC / M
VERONICA VICIOUS
Destiny & April In Bondage / 1993 / BON / B
VERONIKA
Buttman's European Vacation #3 / 1995 / EA / M • Buttwoman Back In Budapest / 1993 / FI / M • Eurotica #02 / 1995 / XC / M • Prague By Night #2 / 1996 / EA / M
VERONIKA ROCKET
Only The Very Best On Film / 1992 / VC / C • Smoker / 1983 / VC / M
VERONIKA RYD
Swedish Vip Magazine #1 / 1995 / PL / M
VERONIQUE
Dr Max And The Oral Girls / 1995 / VIT / M • Homegrown Video #419: Reigning Pussycats And Horndogs / 1994 / HOV / M • Magma: Spezial: Anal Ii / 1994 / MET / M • Penetration (Anabolic) #1 / 1995 / ANA / M • Veronica The Screenwriting Hooker / 1996 / LE / M
VERONIQUE LACAN *see Star Index I*
VERONIQUE LEFAY
Private Film #04 / 1993 / OD / M
VERONIQUE MAUGARSKY
[Jouissances / 1976 / ... / M • [Rentre C'est Bon / 1977 / ... / M
VERONIQUE MONET *see Star Index I*
VERONIQUE RICH *see Star Index I*
VERUSCHKA
Bizarre Styles / 1981 / ALP / B
VIC BUTLER *see Star Index I*
VIC DARE
Lickity Split / 1974 / COM / M
VIC DE MILLE
Ass Attack / 1995 / PL / M
VIC DEVOID *see Star Index I*
VIC FALCOLN *see Herschel Savage*
VIC FALCON *see Herschel Savage*
VIC FALCONE *see Herschel Savage*
VIC HALL
Las Vegas She-Males / 1995 / BCP / G • Mechanics Bi Day, Lube Job Bi Night / 1995 / SP0 / G • To Bi For / 1996 / PL / G
VIC MORE
The Bottom Dweller Part Deux / 1994 / EL / M
VIC NIXON *see Rick Bowe*
VIC ROCK
Bizarre Styles / 1981 / ALP / B
VIC STUART
One Page Of Love / 1980 / VCX / M
VICCI
Penetration (Flash) #2 / 1995 / FLV / M
VICK SAMANA *see Star Index I*
VICKA *see Victoria Queen*

VICKI
A&B FL#03: More Flashing Fun / 1995 / A&B / S • Best Butt(e) In The West #1 / 1992 / CC / M • Blue Vanities #571 / 1995 / FFL / M • I Want To Be A Mistress / cr86 / BIZ / B • Sandy's: Bicycle Trail Humpers / 1994 / SM / F
VICKI (D. ROGERS) *see Danielle Rogers*
VICKI BENNET
Great Grandma Gets Her Cookies / 1995 / FC / M
VICKI BLAIR
Pudgy. 5'3", 36-26-36, 21 in 1991.
Anal Annie's All-Girl Escort Service / 1990 / LIP / F • Bi Night / 1989 / PL / G • Bi-Dacious / 1989 / PL / G • Deep Inside Keisha / 1994 / VC / C • Entertainment Bi-Night / 1989 / PL / G • Get Bi Tonight / 1991 / PL / G • Girlworld #3 / 1989 / LIP / F • Live Bi-Me / 1990 / PL / G • Pretty Peaches #3 / 1989 / VC / M • Reel People #03 / 1989 / PP / M • Stunt Woman / 1990 / LIP / F
VICKI GLUCK
Lust Flight 2000 / 1978 / VHL / M • Olympic Fever / 1979 / AR / M
VICKI KAUFMAN
Teenage Madam / 1979 / CXV / M • The Ultimate Pleasure / 1977 / HIF / M
VICKI KENNEDY
Blue Vanities #517 / 1992 / FFL / M • Blue Vanities #582 / 1996 / FFL / M
VICKI LARSEN *see Debra Lynn*
VICKI LOVE
Blue Vanities #028 / 1988 / FFL / M
VICKI LYNN
Bottom Busters / 1973 / BLT / M
VICKI LYON *see Star Index I*
VICKI MEILLEUR *see Le Le Adams*
VICKI MILES *(Allison Louise Downe, Bunny Downe)*
Boinng / 1962 / SOW / S • Goldilocks And The Three Bares / 1962 / ... / S • Nature Girl / 1962 / SOW / S • Nature's Playmates / 1962 / SOW / S • Scum Of The Earth / 1963 / SOW / S • Suburban Roulette / 1967 / SOW / S
VICKI POWERS *see Star Index I*
VICKI RAY *see Star Index I*
VICKI REDFIELD *see Star Index I*
VICKI STANTON *see Star Index I*
VICKI TRIMBLE
Sex Boat / 1980 / VCX / M
VICKI VICKERS *see Raven*
VICKIE
Blue Vanities #516 / 1992 / FFL / M
VICKIE BLACK
Pleasure Productions #01 / 1984 / VCR / M
VICKIE PETERS
The Awakening Of Sally / 1984 / VCR / M
VICKY
A&B AB#309: Horny Housewife / 1991 / A&B / M • A&B AB#391: Sexy Blondes / 1991 / A&B / M • A&B AB#395: Cum Dripping Ladies / 1990 / A&B / M • Hamlet: For The Love Of Ophelia #1 / 1996 / IP / M • Hamlet: For The Love Of Ophelia #2 / 1996 / IP / M • Latin Plump Humpers #2 / 1995 / TTV / M • Latin Plump Humpers #3 / 1995 / TTV / M • Marquis De Sade / 1995 / IP / M • Salsa & Spice #1 / 1995 / TTV / M • TV Shoestore Fantasy #1 / 1991 / BIZ / G • TVs In Trouble #2 / 1991 / BIZ / G
VICKY (DEBRA LYNN) *see Debra Lynn*
VICKY ASHLEY
Blue Vanities #581 / 1996 / FFL / M
VICKY CARNAL

Limited Edition #07 / 1979 / AVC / M
VICKY EDWARDS *see Star Index I*
VICKY LARSEN *see Debra Lynn*
VICKY LINDSAY *(Anita Crest)*
Ceremony, The Ritual Of Love / 1976 / AVC / M • Lipps & Mccain / 1978 / VC / M • Pizza Girls (We Deliver) / 1978 / VCX / M • Student Bodies / 1975 / VC / M
VICKY PRINCIPAL *see Star Index I*
VICKY STEELE
My Sister Seka / 1981 / CA / M
VICKY VAIN
Student Fetish Videos: Bondage #01 / 1995 / PRE / B • Student Fetish Videos: Catfighting #16 / 1996 / PRE / B • Student Fetish Videos: Foot Worship #17 / 1995 / PRE / B
VICKY VICKERS *see Raven*
VICKY WEST
Born Erect / cr80 / CA / M
VICTOR
She Studs #05 / 1990 / BIZ / G • Toe Tales #13 / 1994 / GOT / B
VICTOR AIRWAE
The Phantom Of The Montague Stage / 1997 / HO / M
VICTOR ALTER *see Marshall Efron*
VICTOR BUTLER *see Star Index I*
VICTOR DIAMOND
Tobianna: A Gang Bang Fantasy / 1993 / FC / M
VICTOR LAMOUR *see Star Index I*
VICTOR PONTI *see Star Index I*
VICTOR SUAVE
Night Crawlers / 1994 / SC / M
VICTOR SUVIUS
Breaker Beauties / 1977 / VHL / M
VICTOR VALENTINO
Fresh Faces #05 / 1995 / EVN / M
VICTORIA
4 Of A Kind / 1995 / BON / B • Amazon Heat #1 / 1996 / CC / M • The Best Of Fabulous Flashers / 1996 / DGD / F • Bondage Workout / 1995 / GAL / B • Dirty Blue Movies #04 / 1993 / JTV / F • Dr Pussy's Tasty Tails #1 / 1993 / SHV / F • Fabulous Flashers #2 / 1996 / DGD / F • Florida Girls On Film / 1994 / DGD / F • Full House / 1995 / BON / B • Homegrown Video #414: Pussy Hairstylist / 1994 / HOV / M • Lesbian Orgy / 1980 / WID / F • No Man's Land #09 / 1994 / VT / F • Our Bang #04 / 1992 / GLI / M • Private Video Magazine #19 / 1994 / OD / M • Swedish Vip Magazine #2 / 1995 / PL / M • Toe Tales #14 / 1994 / GOT / B
VICTORIA (D.O'DAINE) *see Diane O'-Daine*
VICTORIA ADAMS
Bad Girl Handling / 1993 / RB / B • Shaved #05 / 1993 / RB / F
VICTORIA ANDREWS
Fairly tall brunette with small tits and some loss of belly muscle tone. However, she's quite pretty (perhaps a bit too long nose) with good skin, a slightly tomboyish attitude and seems to enjoy sex. Born October 11, 1968 in Watertown, NY. In 1995 has had tits expanded to 38D and is 5'9" tall, 124lbs.
Anal Justice / 1994 / ROB / M • Assy Sassy #2 / 1994 / ROB / F • Butt Sluts #3 / 1994 / ROB / F • Butt Watch #06 / 1994 / FH / M • C-Hunt #01: Pandemonium / 1995 / PEV / M • Chemical Reaction / 1995 / CC / M • Chug-A-Lug Girls #4 / 1994 / VT / M • Cir-

cus Of Lesbians / 1995 / VI / C • Close To The Edge / 1994 / VI / M • Defending Your Soul / 1995 / EX / M • Demolition Woman #2 / 1994 / IP / M • Dick & Jane Go To Northridge / 1994 / AVI / M • Dick & Jane Up, Down And All Around / 1994 / AVI / M • Elements Of Desire / 1994 / ULI / M • Gang Bang Face Bath #3 / 1994 / ROB / M • Hard Headed / 1994 / LE / M • Hookers Of Hollywood / 1994 / LE / M • Kelly Jaye Close-Up / 1994 / VI / M • Live Sex / 1994 / LE / M • Love Me, Love My Butt #2 / 1994 / ROB / F • New Positions / 1994 / PV / M • Night Of Seduction / 1994 / VC / M • Night Seduction / 1995 / VC / M • No Man's Land #10 / 1994 / VT / F • Passenger 69 #1 / 1994 / IP / M • Passenger 69 #2 / 1994 / IP / M • Pearl Necklace: Amorous Amateurs #37 / 1993 / SEE / M • Pearl Necklace: Amorous Amateurs #38 / 1993 / SEE / M • Pearl Necklace: Amorous Amateurs #40 / 1994 / SEE / M • Peepshow / 1994 / OD / M • Prime Cuts #1 / 1994 / FOR / M • Prime Cuts #2 / 1994 / FOR / M • Private Video Magazine #09 / 1994 / OD / M • R & R / 1994 / VC / M • The Real Story Of Tonya & Nancy / 1994 / EX / M • Sex Professionals / 1994 / LIP / F • Sexual Instinct #2 / 1994 / DR / M • Tech: Victoria Andrews #1 / 1993 / TWA / M • Victoria With An "A" / 1994 / PL / M • Visions Of Seduction / 1994 / SC / M • Wedding Vows / 1994 / ZA / M

VICTORIA CORSAUNT *see* **Victoria Corsaut**

VICTORIA CORSAUT *(Victoria Corsaw, Victoria Corsaunt)*
Not too pretty, long blonde hair, big nose, pushy disposition, very white skin, reddish blonde pubic hair, small tits, womanly body.
Breaker Beauties / 1977 / VHL / M • Dirty Mary / cr77 / BL / M • Doctor Yes / 1978 / VIS / M • Mrs. Rodger's Neighborhood / 1988 / EVN / C • Pop-Porn: Safari Club / 1992 / 4P / M • Safari Club / 1977 / 4P / M • Skin Flicks / 1978 / AVC / M • Visions / 1977 / QX / M

VICTORIA CORSAW *see* **Victoria Corsaut**

VICTORIA DANE *see Star Index I*

VICTORIA GOLD *(Angelica (V. Gold), Corrina (V. Gold))*
Blonde with long straight hair and large droopy tits, not too good skin and a reasonably tight body. Her chest size is 34D (in **Beach Bum Amateurs #40** she couldn't remember). From **New Ends #09**: 18 years old and was 13 when de-virginized. As of mid-1996 there seems to be another Victoria Gold who was described (in **Video Virgins #31**) as 20 years old from Miami FL, de-virginized at 15, young looking face, large cantaloupes, long blonde hair, passable face and not a tight waist.
A List / 1996 / SO / M • Ace In The Hole / 1995 / PL / M • Anal Al's Adventures / 1995 / PL / M • Beach Bum Amateur's #39 / 1993 / MID / M • Beach Bum Amateur's #40 / 1993 / MID / M • Bun Busters #10 / 1993 / LBO / M • Butthunt / 1994 / AFV / F • The Clock Strikes Bizarre On Butt Row / 1996 / ABS / M • Hit Parade / 1996 / PRE / B • The Hustlers / 1993 / MID / M • Kinky Cameraman #4 / 1996 / LEI / C • Leg...Ends #17 / 1996 / PRE / F • Look What I Found On The Street #01 / 1996 / CC / M • Naughty

In Nature / 1994 / PL / M • New Ends #09 / 1994 / 4P / M • Ona Zee's Doll House #4 / 1996 / ONA / F • Pleasure Dome: The Genesis Chamber / 1994 / AFV / M • Sabrina Starlet / 1994 / SC / M • Sexhibition #2 / 1996 / SUF / M • Sole Search / 1996 / PRE / B • Squirters / 1996 / ULI / M • Thin Ice / 1996 / ONA / M • Video Virgins #30 / 1996 / NS / M • Video Virgins #31 / 1996 / NS / M • Virgin Hotline / 1996 / LVP / F • Wild Dreams / 1995 / V99 / M

VICTORIA GUNN *see Star Index I*

VICTORIA HARTE *see Star Index I*

VICTORIA HILL
Profiles #10: / 1997 / XPR / M • Puritan Video Magazine #09 / 1997 / LE / M • White Men Can't Iron On Butt Row / 1997 / ABS / M

VICTORIA HOLT *see* **Veronica Hart**

VICTORIA JACKSON *(Tina Marie (Vict. J), Anne Marie Jackson, Tiny Mary, Lyn Richards)*
Brunette with a pretty face and large (39D) droopy tits. In 1982 she was 18 years old and 5'11" tall. De-virginized at 15. She retired in 1986 and was married to Mark Carriere of Leisure Time Entertainment but then divorced.
Bad Girls #4 / 1984 / GO / M • Body Shop / 1984 / VCX / M • Detroit Dames / 1988 / DR / C • Firestorm #1 / 1984 / COM / M • First Time Lesbians (Gourmet) / 1987 / GO / F • Go For It / 1984 / VC / M • Golden Girls #05 / 1982 / SVE / M • Golden Girls #23 / 1984 / CA / M • The Good Time Girls / 1985 / VEX / M • GVC: Companions #122 / 1983 / GO / F • GVC: Paper Dolls #117 / 1983 / GO / F • Lingerie / 1983 / CDI / M • Naughty Girls Need Love Too / 1983 / SE / M • Never Sleep Alone / 1984 / CA / M • The Red Room And Other Places / 1992 / COM / C • Star 84: Tina Marie / 1984 / VEX / M • Teasin' & Pleasin' / 1988 / LBO / F • Up 'n' Coming / 1983 / CA / M • Where The Girls Are / 1984 / VEX / M • Woman Times Four / 1983 / LIP / F

VICTORIA JACOBS
Sex Over 40 #1 / 1994 / PL / M • Sex Over 40 #2 / 1994 / PL / M

VICTORIA KNOLL
Bad Girls #1 / 1981 / GO / M • Indecent Exposure / 1981 / CA / M

VICTORIA LAID
Hose Jobs / 1995 / VEX / M

VICTORIA LEE *(Cassandra Lee (Vict), Stacey (Victoria L))*
Shoulder length black hair in a page boy cut, small tits, marginal face, lithe body, tight waist, shaven pussy, tattoo around her belly button and another small one on her right butt. De-virginized at 15.
Anal Health Club Babes / 1995 / EVN / M • Boss Bitch From Bondage Hell / 1996 / LBO / B • Butt Hunt #07 / 1995 / LEI / M • Cherry Poppers #15: Mischievous Maidens / 1996 / ZA / M • Creme De La Face #14: Kiss My Cum / 1996 / OD / M • Creme De La Face #16: Ladies Licking / 1996 / OD / M • The Cumm Brothers #14: Buttdraft / 1995 / OD / M • Deceit / 1996 / ZA / M • Double Penetration Virgins: DP Therapy / 1996 / JMP / M • Fresh Faces #12 / 1996 / EVN / M • Girl's School / 1994 / ERA / M • Girls Of The Ivy Leagues / 1994 / VT / M • Hard Core Beginners #04 / 1995 / LEI / M • Hardcore Fantasies #2 / 1996 /

LV / M • Interview's Hard Bodied Harlots / 1996 / LV / M • Jizz Glazed Goo Guzzlers #1 / 1996 / NIT / C • Jug Humpers / 1995 / V99 / C • Latin Fever #3 / 1996 / C69 / M • Lay Of The Land / 1995 / LE / M • Lotus Blossoms / 1996 / SUF / M • Mike Hott: #367 Girls Who Lap Cum From Cunts #02 / 1996 / MHV / M • Motel Matches / 1996 / LE / M • Mystic Tales Of The Orient / 1994 / PRK / M • The New Ass Masters #09 / 1996 / LEI / C • New Ends #10 / 1995 / 4P / M • The New Snatch Masters #16 / 1995 / LEI / C • The Night Of The Living Bed / 1996 / LE / M • Nineteen #4 / 1996 / FOR / M • Nineteen #5 / 1996 / FOR / M • Ona Zee's Learning The Ropes #11: Chains Required / 1994 / ONA / B • Outlaw Sluts / 1996 / RAS / M • Paradise Found / 1995 / LE / M • Prime Choice #6 / 1996 / RAS / M • Private Eyes / 1995 / LE / M • Pussy Hunt #06 / 1994 / LEI / M • Pussy Whipped / 1994 / FOR / M • The Scam / 1996 / LV / M • The Sodomizer #3 / 1996 / SC / M • The Sodomizer #4 / 1996 / SC / M • The Spank Master / 1996 / PRE / B • Student Fetish Videos: Best Of Foot Worship #03 / 1995 / PRE / C • Student Fetish Videos: The Enema #17 / 1995 / PRE / B • Student Fetish Videos: Foot Worship #14 / 1995 / PRE / B • Student Fetish Videos: Spanking #18 / 1995 / PRE / B • Summer Dreams / 1996 / TEP / M • Tailz From Da Hood #5 / 1996 / AVI / M • Video Virgins #19 / 1994 / NS / M • Wild Orgies #16 / 1995 / AFI / M • Witches Are Bitches / 1996 / NIT / M • Yin Yang Oriental Love Bang #5: Lotus Blossoms / 1996 / SUF / M

VICTORIA LEE (78)
Lure Of The Triangle / 1978 / VC / M

VICTORIA LONG
Private Film #22 / 1995 / OD / M

VICTORIA M.
Private Gold #09: Private Dancer / 1996 / OD / M

VICTORIA MATHESON *(Victoria Robinson)*
A&B GB#022 / 1992 / A&B / M • A&B GB#025: She Cut Our Dicks Off / 1992 / A&B / M • America's Raunchiest Home Videos #33: Anal Engagement / 1992 / ZA / M • Biff Malibu's Totally Nasty Home Videos #12 / 1992 / ANA / M • Butt Woman #3 / 1992 / FH / M

VICTORIA MAXWELL
Spanking Video #1: Sports College / 1995 / MET / B • Spanking Video #4: Sports Comeback / 1995 / MET / B

VICTORIA NITE
Anal Vision #28 / 1994 / LBO / M • Bun Busters #19 / 1994 / LBO / M

VICTORIA PAGAN *see* **Alana Blue**

VICTORIA PARIS
The epitome of the dumb blonde (but she plays unsuitable drama roles) with, in later movies, huge enhanced tits.
20th Century Fox / 1989 / FAZ / M • Adult Video News 1991 Awards / 1991 / VC / M • The Adventures Of Buttman / 1989 / EA / M • The All American Girl / 1989 / FAN / M • The Babe / 1992 / EX / M • The Backdoor Club / 1992 / LV / M • Bare-Chested, Bare-Breasted, Big-Busted, Wet T-Shirt Video / 1990 / NAP / B • Barflies / 1990 / ZA / M • Beauty And The Beast #2 / 1990 / VC / M • Beaverjuice / 1992 / LV / M • Behind Closed Doors / 1990 / VI / M • Behind The

Scenes: The Making Of The Wil & Ed Movies / 1992 / MID / M • The Best Of Andrew Blake / 1993 / CA / C • Best Of Buttman #1 / 1991 / EA / C • The Best Of Buttslammers / 1995 / BS / C • Between My Breasts #11 / 1990 / BTO / M • Big Bust Platinum: Superstar Strip Tease / 1993 / PME / F • Big-Busted Cat-Fight Fantasy / 1990 / NAP / B • Big-Busted Cell-Mates / 1990 / NAP / B • The Bigger They Come, The Harder They fall / 1990 / NAP / B • Bimbo Bowlers From Buffalo / 1989 / ZA / M • Black Beauty (Ebony & Ivory) / 1989 / E&I / M • Black Obsession / 1991 / ZA / M • Body Music #1 / 1989 / DR / M • The Breast Things In Life Are Free / 1991 / LV / M • Breathless / 1991 / WV / M • Bruce Seven's Favorite Endings #1 / 1991 / EL / C • Bruce Seven: A Compendium Of His Most Graphic Scenes Vol 1 / 1991 / BS / C • Busted / 1989 / CA / M • Buttslammers #01 / 1993 / BS / F • Cat-Fight Angels / 1990 / NAP / B • The Chameleon / 1989 / VC / M • Clinique / 1989 / VC / M • The Contessa / 1989 / VC / M • Cool Sheets / 1989 / PP / M • Decadence / 1996 / VC / M • Deep Inside Victoria / 1992 / CDI / C • Deep Inside Victoria Paris / 1993 / VC / C • Deep Throat #4 / 1990 / AR / M • Deep Throat #5 / 1990 / AR / M • Designing Babes / 1990 / GOT / M • Dirty Lingerie / 1990 / VD / M • Duel Of The Cats / 1990 / NAP / B • Easy Way Out / 1989 / OD / M • Erotique / 1992 / VC / M • Fantasy Nights / 1990 / VC / M • Farmer's Daughter / 1989 / FAZ / M • Fast Cars And Fast Women / 1992 / LV / M • Flesh Mountain / 1994 / VI / C • Forbidden / 1992 / FOR / M • Gang Bangs #2 / 1989 / EA / M • Ghost Lusters / 1990 / EL / F • The Girl With The Blue Jeans Off / 1989 / FAZ / M • Girls Of The Double D #07 / 1989 / CIN / M • Girls Of The Double D #09 / 1989 / CDI / M • Girls Of The Double D #14 / 1990 / CIN / M • Good Things Come In Small Packages / 1989 / CA / M • Handle With Care / 1989 / FAZ / M • Head Co-Ed Society / 1989 / VT / M • The Hot Lick Cafe / 1990 / AMB / M • Hotel Paradise / 1989 / CA / M • Hothouse Rose #1 / 1991 / VC / M • Hothouse Rose #2 / 1992 / VC / M • House Of Dark Dreams #1 / 1990 / BS / B • House Of Dark Dreams #2 / 1990 / BS / B • Illicit Affairs / 1989 / VD / M • Images Of Desire / 1990 / PM / M • Introducing Tracey Wynn / 1991 / PL / M • Introducing Victoria Paris / 1990 / NAP / F • Lady In Blue / 1990 / CIN / M • Last Rumba In Paris / 1989 / VC / M • Late Night For Lovers / 1989 / ME / M • Laze / 1990 / ZA / M • Legal Tender (1990-X) / 1990 / VC / M • Lesbian Pros And Amateurs #10 / 1992 / GO / F • Lesbians In Tight Shorts / 1992 / LV / F • Lesbo Power Tools / 1994 / CA / C • Licking Legends #2 / 1992 / LE / F • Lies Of Passion / 1992 / LV / M • Life, Love And Divorce / 1990 / LV / M • Live In, Love In / 1989 / ME / M • Lost In Vegas / 1996 / AWV / G • Made To Order / 1994 / FD / C • Mamm's The Word / 1991 / ZA / M • Mind Trips / 1992 / FH / M • Miracle On 69th Street / 1992 / HW / M • Mischief In The Mansion / 1989 / LE / M • My Wildest Date / 1989 / FOV / M • Mystery Of The Golden Lotus / 1989 / HU / M • Mystic Pieces / 1989 / EA / M • Naughty Neighbors / 1989 / CA / M • The New Barbarians

#1 / 1990 / VC / M • The New Barbarians #2 / 1990 / VC / M • Night Trips #1 / 1989 / CA / M • On Your Honor / 1989 / LE / M • Only The Best Of The Erotic Eighties / 1992 / VC / C • Oral Madness #1 / 1991 / OD / M • Oral Madness #2 / 1992 / OD / M • Pajama Party / 1993 / CV / C • Paris Burning / 1989 / CC / M • Paris By Night / 1990 / IN / M • Parliament: Licking Lesbians #2 / 1989 / PM / F • Parliament: Sweet Starlets #2 / 1986 / PM / F • Party Doll / 1990 / VC / M • Passionate Angels / 1990 / HO / M • Pretty Peaches #3 / 1989 / VC / M • Pyromaniac / 1990 / SO / M • Ready Freddy? / 1992 / FH / M • Ready, Willing & Anal / 1992 / OD / M • Roadgirls / 1990 / DR / M • Rocket Girls / 1993 / VC / M • Roman Goddess / 1992 / HW / M • Russian Roulette / 1995 / NIT / M • Sam's Fantasy / 1990 / CIN / M • The Secret (USA) / 1990 / SO / M • The Seduction Of Mary / 1992 / VC / M • Sex Toy / 1993 / CA / C • Sex Under Glass / 1992 / VC / M • Sextectives / 1989 / CIN / M • Shadows In The Dark / 1990 / 4P / M • Silver Tongue / 1989 / CA / M • Slipping It In / 1992 / FD / M • Snatched To The Future / 1991 / EL / F • Sorority Sex Kittens #1 / 1992 / VC / M • Sorority Sex Kittens #2 / 1993 / VC / M • Sorority Sex Kittens #3 / 1996 / VC / M • Stairway To Paradise / 1990 / VC / M • Stolen Kisses / 1989 / VD / M • Strange Curves / 1989 / VC / M • Super Cakes / 1994 / CA / C • Swedish Erotica Featurettes #2 / 1989 / CA / M • A Taste Of Victoria Paris / 1990 / PIN / C • Temptations / 1989 / DR / M • Tori Welles Exposed / 1990 / VD / C • Trouble / 1989 / VD / M • True Legends Of Adult Cinema: The Cult Superstars / 1993 / VC / C • True Legends Of Adult Cinema: The Erotic Eighties / 1992 / VC / C • True Legends Of Adult Cinema: The Modern Era / 1992 / VC / C • Two Sisters / 1992 / WV / M • Two Women / 1992 / ROB / M • Vegas #1: Royal Flush / 1990 / CIN / M • Vegas #2: Snake Eyes / 1990 / CIN / M • Vegas #3: Let It Ride / 1990 / CIN / M • Vegas #4: Joker's Wild / 1990 / CDI / M • Vegas #5: Blackjack / 1991 / CIN / M • Veil / 1990 / VI / M • Victoria Victorious / 1990 / NAP / B • Victoria's Secret / 1989 / SO / M • Victoria's Secret Life / 1992 / WV / M • Vogue / 1994 / VD / C • Voodoo Lust: The Possession / 1989 / PCP / M • Wet Fingers / 1990 / HIO / M • Who Reamed Rosie Rabbit? #1 / 1989 / FAN / M • Wil And Ed's Excellent Boner Christmas / 1991 / MID / M • Will And Ed's Bogus Gang Bang / 1992 / MID / M • Will And Ed: The Curse Of Poona / 1994 / MID / C • Women's Penitentiary / 1992 / VIM / M • X Dreams / 1989 / CA / M

VICTORIA QUEEN *(Queen Victoria, Viktoria (Queen), Vicka)*
Russian, very pretty face, lithe tight body, tight waist, narrow hips, washboard flat belly, nice smile, short dark red hair, nice butt. Downer: enhanced rock solid cantaloupes. Another downer which is not apparent in her Hungarian tapes: she's 5'11" tall.

Big Babies In Budapest / 1996 / EL / M • Bottom Dweller: The Final Voyage / 1996 / EL / M • The Coming Of Nikita / 1995 / EL / M • Cumback Pussy #2: Crawling Back For More / 1996 / EL / M • Decadence / 1996 / VC / M • Dirty Dirty Debutantes #6 /

1996 / 4P / M • Dirty Stories #5 / 1996 / PE / M • Diva #1: Caught In The Act / 1996 / VC / F • Diva #2: Deep In Glamour / 1996 / VC / F • Max #08: The Fugitive / 1995 / XPR / M • Penetration (Anabolic) #2 / 1995 / ANA / M • Pick Up Lines #07 / 1996 / OD / M • Sodomania: Slop Shots / 1996 / EL / C • Thermonuclear Sex / 1996 / EL / M

VICTORIA QUEST
The Sinful Pleasures Of Reverend Star / 1976 / … / M

VICTORIA QUINN *see* **Alexandria Quinn**

VICTORIA REEVES
Beneath My Heels / 1990 / BEB / B

VICTORIA RINK
Garters And Lace / 1975 / SE / M

VICTORIA ROBINSON *see* **Victoria Matheson**

VICTORIA ROSET
Private Gold #04: Amazonas / 1996 / OD / M

VICTORIA SANDS
ABA: Double Feature #4 / 1996 / ALP / M • Daughters Of Discipline #2 / 1983 / AVO / B • Painmania / 1983 / AVO / B

VICTORIA SCARLETT
Bums Away / 1995 / PRE / C

VICTORIA SECRET *see* **Sara Jane Hamilton**

VICTORIA SECRETT *see* **Sara Jane Hamilton**

VICTORIA SEERETT *see* **Sara Jane Hamilton**

VICTORIA SELLERS
Celebrity Sluts And Tabloid Tramps / 1996 / LV / M • Warlords / 1988 / VMA / S

VICTORIA SLICK
Baby Cakes / 1982 / SE / M • The Blonde Next Door / 1982 / GO / M • Body Magic / 1982 / SE / M • Captives / 1983 / BIZ / B • Centerspread Girls / 1982 / CA / M • Erotic Dimensions #1: Ripe / 1982 / NSV / M • Erotic Dimensions #2: Black Desire / 1982 / NSV / M • Erotic Dimensions #3: My Way! / 1982 / NSV / M • Erotic Dimensions #4: The Exhibitionist / 1982 / NSV / M • Erotic Dimensions #9: The Fantasy Trade / 1982 / NSV / M • Erotic Dimensions: Aggressive Women / 1982 / NSV / M • Erotic Dimensions: Explicit / 1982 / NSV / M • Erotic Dimensions: I Want To Watch / 1982 / NSV / M • Erotic Dimensions: Macho Women / 1982 / NSV / M • Erotic Dimensions: The Wild Life / 1982 / NSV / M • Never So Deep / 1981 / VCX / M • Victoria's Secret Desires / 1983 / S&L / C • [Erotic Dimensions Vols 1 To 8 / 1983 / NSV / C

VICTORIA STANTON *see* **Star Index I**

VICTORIA STARR
Overnight Sensation / 1976 / AR / M

VICTORIA STARR (KYM) *see* **Kym Wilde**

VICTORIA TAYLOR *see* **Star Index I**

VICTORIA VETRI *(Angela Dorian)*
Playmate of the year in 1968. Allegedly she is dead.
Invasion Of The Bee Girls / 1973 / EHE / S

VICTORIA VIXXEN
Belly Of The Beast / 1993 / ZFX / B • Erotic Bondage Confessions / 1992 / ZFX / B • Fresh Faces #02 / 1994 / EVN / M • Guinea Pigs #2 / 1993 / ZFX / B • Highway To Hell / 1993 / ZFX / B • Meanstreak / 1993 / ZFX / B • The Misadventures Of Lois Payne / 1995 / ZFX / B • Night Prowler #1 / 1993 / ZFX / B • Spread Eagle / 1992 / ZFX / B

VICTORIA WATT

Teenage Cousins / cr76 / SOW / M
VICTORIA WILDE *see* **Gina Carrera**
VICTORIA WINTER
The Liberation Of Honeydoll Jones / 1978 / VCX / M • Swedish Erotica #03 / 1980 / CA / M • Swedish Erotica #08 / 1980 / CA / M • Teenage Fantasies #2 / 1980 / AR / M
VIDA
Breast Worx #01 / 1991 / LBO / M • Bubble Butts #05 / 1992 / LBO / M • Mr. Peepers Amateur Home Videos #10: Red Rider & Little Shav / 1991 / LBO / M • Mr. Peepers Amateur Home Videos #25: The 25th Anniversary Ed / 1991 / LBO / M
VIDA GARMAN
The Wild Women / 1996 / PL / M
VIDEO PAUL *see* **Max Hardcore**
VIDYA *see* **Star Index I**
VIENNA HALL
Black Detail #1 / 1994 / VT / M • Black Detail #2 / 1994 / VT / M • Doin' The Nasty / 1996 / AVI / M • New Girls In Town #5 / 1994 / CC / M • Vienna's Place / 1996 / VCX / M
VIETTA
Hirsute Lovers #1 / 1995 / BTO / M • Tit To Tit #1 / 1994 / BTO / M
VIJU KREM
Bloodsucking Freaks / 1975 / VES / B • MASH'ed / cr75 / ALP / M
VIKI
Penetration (Anabolic) #2 / 1995 / ANA / M
VIKKI
A&B AB#541: Sexy Rusty Waters / 1995 / A&B / F • A&B AB#545: Vikki Gets Wild / 1995 / A&B / B
VIKKI DRAKE *see* **Summer Rose**
VIKKI VAIN
Reality & Fantasy / 1994 / DR / M
VIKTORIA (QUEEN) *see* **Victoria Queen**
VIKTORIA KARUALY
True Stories #1 / 1993 / SC / M • True Stories #2 / 1993 / SC / M
VIKTORIA LAZA
True Stories #1 / 1993 / SC / M • True Stories #2 / 1993 / SC / M
VILMA BROWN
Loose Times At Ridley High / 1984 / VCX / M • Saturday Matinee Series #4 / 1996 / VCX / C
VINCE
Alexandra's Pampered Pet / 1993 / LEO / G • New Faces, Hot Bodies #18 / 1995 / STP / M
VINCE ALANTER
Bedtime Video #05 / 1984 / GO / M
VINCE BALBOA *see* **Star Index I**
VINCE DEL RIO *see* **Star Index I**
VINCE DUCA
American Pie / 1980 / SE / M
VINCE HARRINGTON
Bi Claudius / 1994 / BIL / G • Bi-Wicked / 1994 / BIN / G • Transvestite Tour Guide / 1993 / HSV / G
VINCE JAFFE
Bucky Beaver's XXX Dragon Art Theatre Double Feature #11 / 1996 / SOW / M • San Francisco Ball / 1971 / SOW / S
VINCE LAROCK
HomeGrown Video #435: Seasoned To Perfection / 1994 / HOV / M
VINCE LONG
Butt Hunt #09 / 1995 / LEI / M • Hard Core Beginners #09 / 1995 / LEI / M • Hard Core Beginners #11 / 1995 / LEI / M • Pussy Hunt #13 / 1995 / LEI / M

VINCE NEIL
The Hollywood Starlet Search / 1995 / SC / M
VINCE ROCKLAND
Coming Out Bi / 1995 / IN / G
VINCE ROMAN *see* **Star Index I**
VINCE VOYEUR
29 years old in 1995.
13th Annual Adult Video News Awards / 1996 / VC / S • 9-Ball: Geisha Gang Bang / 1994 / PL / M • Adam & Eve's House Party #1 / 1995 / VC / M • The Adventures Of Peeping Tom #4 / 1997 / OD / M • Airotica / 1996 / SC / M • Alice In Analand / 1994 / SC / M • Altered Paradise / 1995 / LE / M • The Anal Adventures Of Bruce Seven / 1996 / BS / C • Anal Cornhole Cutie / 1996 / ROB / M • Anal Crash Test Dummies / 1997 / ROB / M • Anal Fireball / 1996 / ROB / M • Anal Fugitive / 1995 / PEP / M • Anal Intruder #09: The Butt From Another Planet / 1995 / CC / M • Anal Intruder #10 / 1995 / CC / M • Anal Invader / 1995 / PEP / M • Anal Jammin' & Slammin' / 1996 / ROB / M • Anal Lickers And Cummers / 1996 / ROB / M • Anal Load Lickers / 1996 / ROB / M • Anal Portrait / 1996 / ZA / M • Anal Shame / 1995 / VD / M • Anal Talisman / 1996 / ZA / M • Angel Eyes / 1995 / IN / M • Angels In Flight / 1995 / NIT / M • Another Fuckin' Anal Movie / 1996 / ROB / M • Asses Galore #3: Pure Evil / 1996 / DFI / M • Badgirls #3: Cell Block 69 / 1994 / VI / M • Badgirls #4: Jayebird / 1995 / VI / M • Barby's On Butt Row / 1996 / ABS / M • Bare Ass In The Park / 1995 / PEP / M • The Best Of Strippers Inc / 1996 / ONA / C • Betrayed / 1996 / WP / M • Big Thingiees / 1996 / BEP / M • Big Tit Racket / 1995 / PEP / M • Bikini Beach #4 / 1996 / CC / M • Black & Booty-Full / 1996 / ROB / M • Blaze / 1996 / WAV / M • Bloopers & Boners / 1996 / VI / M • Body Language / 1995 / VI / M • Boobwatch #1 / 1996 / SC / M • Booby Prize / 1995 / PEP / M • Borsky's Back Door Bitches / 1996 / ROB / M • Busty Backdoor Nurses / 1996 / PL / M • Butt Bandits #4 / 1996 / VD / C • The Butt Sisters Do Boston / 1995 / MID / M • Butthead Dreams / 1994 / FH / M • Butthead Dreams: Down In The Bush / 1995 / FH / M • Call Me / 1995 / CV / M • Caribbean Sunset / 1996 / PL / M • The Clock Strikes Bizarre On Butt Row / 1996 / ABS / M • A Clockwork Orgy / 1995 / PL / M • Club Erotica / 1996 / IN / M • Cold As Ice / 1994 / IN / M • The Comix / 1995 / VI / M • Concrete Heat / 1996 / XCI / M • Conquest / 1996 / WP / M • Crack Attack! / 1996 / PE / M • Crazy With The Heat #3 / 1994 / CV / M • Cybersex / 1996 / WAV / M • Decadence / 1996 / VC / M • Deep Focus / 1995 / VC / M • Deep Inside Ariana / 1995 / VC / C • Deep Inside Brittany O'connell / 1996 / VC / C • Deep Inside Juli Ashton / 1996 / VC / C • Deep Seven / 1996 / VC / M • Delirium / 1996 / MET / M • Desert Moon / 1994 / SPI / M • The Devil In Miss Jones #5: The Inferno / 1994 / VC / M • The Dinner Party #1 / 1994 / ULI / M • Director's Wet Dreams / 1996 / BBE / M • Dirty Little Ass Slut / 1995 / KWP / M • Dirty Tricks #1: Just A Bunch Of Whores / 1995 / EA / M • Dirty Tricks #2: This Ain't Love / 1996 / EA / M • Dreams / 1995 / VC / M • Drop Sex: Wipe The Floor / 1997 / JLP / M • Encore /

1995 / VI / M • The End / 1995 / VI / M • Erotic Newcummers Vol 1 #3: Anal Adventures / 1996 / DR / M • Erotic Newcummers Vol 1 #4 / 1996 / DR / M • Erotic Newcummers Vol 1 #5 / 1996 / DR / M • Erotika / 1994 / WV / M • Every Woman Has A Fantasy #3 / 1995 / VC / M • Extreme Sex #3: Wired / 1994 / VI / M • Extreme Sex #4: The Experiment / 1995 / VI / M • EXXXtra Parts: Interview With a Hermaphrodite / 1995 / PL / M • Fantasy Chamber / 1994 / ULI / M • Fashion Plate / 1995 / WAV / M • Fire & Ice: Caught In The Act / 1995 / WP / M • Fixing A Hole / 1995 / XCI / M • Flesh / 1996 / EA / M • Flexxx #1 / 1994 / VT / M • Flexxx #2 / 1995 / VT / M • French Roommate / 1995 / C69 / M • French Vanilla / 1994 / HW / M • Full Moon Madness / 1995 / CA / M • Gang Bang Bitches #05 / 1995 / PP / M • Gang Bang Bitches #06 / 1995 / PP / M • Gang Bang Bitches #07 / 1995 / PP / M • Gang Bang Bitches #08 / 1995 / PP / M • Gang Bang Bitches #09 / 1995 / PP / M • Gang Bang Dollies / 1996 / ROB / M • Gang Bang Fury #2 / 1996 / ROB / M • Gangbang Girl #14 / 1994 / ANA / M • Gangbang Girl #15 / 1995 / ANA / M • Gangbang Girl #17 / 1995 / ANA / M • Gangbang Girl #18 / 1996 / ANA / M • Gangland Bangers / 1995 / VC / M • Gazongo / 1995 / PEP / M • Get Lucky / 1996 / NIT / M • Girl's School / 1994 / ERA / M • Girls With Curves #2 / 1994 / CV / M • Girly Video Magazine #1 / 1995 / BEP / M • Golddiggers #2 / 1995 / VC / M • Golddiggers #3 / 1995 / VC / M • Gorgeous / 1995 / MET / M • The Gypsy Queen / 1996 / CC / M • Hard Core Beginners #12 / 1995 / LEI / M • Hard Evidence / 1996 / WP / M • Hard Feelings / 1995 / VI / M • Hard Squeeze / 1994 / EMC / M • Hard-On Copy / 1994 / WV / M • Harder, She Craved / 1995 / VC / M • Head First / 1995 / OD / M • Head Shots / 1995 / VI / M • Head To Head / 1996 / VI / M • Head Trip / 1995 / VC / M • Heat / 1995 / WAV / M • Heatseekers / 1996 / PE / M • The Heist / 1996 / WAV / M • Hello Norma Jeane / 1994 / VT / M • Hollywood Confidential / 1996 / SC / M • Homegrown Video #420: Straight Into The Corner Pocket / 1994 / HOV / M • Hot Tight Asses #16 / 1996 / TCK / M • Hot Tight Asses #17 / 1996 / TCK / M • I'm So Horny, Baby / 1997 / ROB / M • Illicit Entry / 1995 / WAV / M • In The Line Of Desire / 1996 / MID / M • In Your Face #3 / 1995 / PL / M • In Your Face #4 / 1996 / PL / M • Indecent Exposures / 1996 / MID / M • Intense Perversions #3 / 1996 / PL / M • Intense Perversions #4 / 1996 / PL / M • Joanie Pneumatic / 1996 / PL / M • Kissing Kaylan / 1995 / CC / M • Kym Wilde's On The Edge #29 / 1995 / RB / B • Latex #1 / 1994 / VC / M • Latex #2 / 1995 / VC / M • Lip Service / 1995 / WP / M • Little Girl Lost / 1995 / SC / M • Lollipop Shoppe #1 / 1996 / SC / M • Lost Angels / 1997 / WP / M • Love Exchange / 1995 / DR / M • Love Spice / 1995 / ERA / M • Loving You Always / 1994 / IN / M • Lucky Lady / 1995 / CV / M • Made For A Gangbang / 1995 / ZA / M • The Many Faces Of P.J. Sparxx / 1996 / WP / M • Many Happy Returns / 1995 / NIT / M • Masque / 1995 / VC / M • The Mechanic / 1995 / VOY / M • Midnight Dreams / 1994 / WV / M • Mile High Thrills / 1995 /

VIM / M • Misty @ Midnight / 1995 / LE / M • Monkey Wrench / 1995 / BEP / M • Mutual Consent / 1995 / VC / M • Mysteria / 1995 / NIT / M • The Naked Fugitive / 1995 / CA / M • Naked Scandal #1 / 1995 / SPI / M • Naked Scandal #2 / 1996 / SPI / M • Nasty Nymphos #13 / 1996 / ANA / M • Nasty Nymphos #14 / 1996 / ANA / M • Nasty Nymphos #15 / 1996 / ANA / M • Nasty Nymphos #16 / 1996 / ANA / M • Naughty Nights / 1996 / PLP / C • Nektar / 1996 / BAC / M • New Pussy Hunt #21 / 1996 / LEI / C • New Wave Hookers #4 / 1994 / VC / M • On The Rise / 1994 / EX / M • Once In A Lifetime / 1996 / VC / C • Open Lips / 1994 / WV / M • Oral Majority #13 / 1995 / WV / C • Oral Obsession #2 / 1995 / VI / M • P.K. & Company / 1995 / CV / M • Pajama Party X #1 / 1994 / VC / M • Pajama Party X #2 / 1994 / VC / M • Party House / 1995 / WAV / M • The Passion Potion / 1995 / WP / M • Pearl Of The Orient / 1995 / IN / M • Penthouse: Kama Sutra #2 / 1994 / A*V / S • Pick Up Lines #01 / 1995 / 4P / M • Pick Up Lines #02 / 1995 / 4P / M • Pick Up Lines #03 / 1995 / 4P / M • Pick Up Lines #05 / 1996 / OD / M • Pick Up Linee #08 / 1996 / OD / M • Pick Up Lines #11 / 1997 / OD / M • Pick Up Lines #12 / 1997 / OD / M • Pick Up Lines #13 / 1997 / OD / M • The Pleasure Girl / 1994 / GO / M • Point Of Entry / 1996 / WP / M • Primal Instinct / 1996 / SNA / M • Private Matters / 1995 / EMC / M • Private Stories #01 / 1995 / OD / M • Profiles #06: Super Model Orgy / 1996 / XPR / M • Pulp Friction / 1994 / PP / M • Pure / 1996 / WP / M • Puritan Video Magazine #03 / 1996 / LE / M • Puritan Video Magazine #05 / 1996 / LE / M • Pussyman #15: The Bone Voyage Bash / 1997 / SNA / M • Pussyman Auditions #02 / 1995 / SNA / M • Pussyman Auditions #12 / 1995 / SNA / M • Pussyman Auditions #22 / 1996 / SNA / M • Pussywoman #3 / 1995 / CC / M • Putting It All Behind #2: Star Treatment / 1994 / IN / M • Rainwoman #09: Wetlands / 1995 / CC / M • Raunch #10: Uncut Jewel / 1994 / CC / M • Raw Footage / 1996 / VC / M • A Rear And Pleasant Danger / 1995 / PP / M • Red Hot Honeys / 1994 / IF / M • Red Hot Lover / 1995 / CV / M • Reflections / 1995 / FD / M • Reservoir Bitches / 1994 / BIP / M • Revenge Of The Bi Dolls / 1994 / CAT / G • Revenge Of The Pussy Suckers From Mars / 1994 / PP / M • The Right Connection / 1995 / VC / M • Sabrina The Booty Queen / 1997 / ROB / M • Safari Jane / 1995 / ERA / M • Samantha & Company / 1996 / PL / M • Samantha's Private Fantasies / 1994 / WV / M • Scotty's X-Rated Adventure / 1996 / WP / M • Secret Services / 1995 / CV / M • Selena Under Siege / 1995 / XCI / M • Sensual Spirits / 1995 / LE / M • Sex Academy #5: The Art Of Pulp Fiction / 1994 / ONA / M • Sex Bandits / 1995 / VC / M • Sex Raiders / 1996 / WAV / M • Sex Secrets Of A Mistress / 1995 / VI / M • Sex Suites / 1995 / TP / M • Sexhibition #1 / 1996 / SUF / M • Sexhibition #2 / 1996 / SUF / M • The Sexual Solution #1 / 1995 / LE / M • Seymore & Shane Meet Kathy Willets, The Naughty Nymph / 1994 / ULI / M • Seymore & Shane Playing With Fire / 1994 / ULI / M • Shame / 1994 / VI / M • Shameless / 1995 / VC / M • Shane's

World #2 / 1996 / OD / M • Shock / 1995 / LE / M • A Shot In The Pants / 1995 / HO / M • The Show / 1995 / VI / M • Silk Stockings: The Black Widow / 1994 / SPI / M • Sin-A-Matic / 1996 / VI / M • Smells Like...Sex / 1995 / VC / M • Snake Pit / 1996 / DWO / M • Some Like It Wet / 1995 / LE / M • Something Blue / 1995 / CC / M • Sorority Cheerleaders / 1996 / PL / M • Stand By Your Man / 1994 / CV / M • Star Attraction / 1995 / VT / M • Star Crossed / 1995 / VC / M • Starbangers #08 / 1996 / FPI / M • Stories Of Seduction / 1996 / MID / M • Street Legal / 1995 / WAV / M • Strippers Inc. #4 / 1995 / ONA / M • Striptease / 1995 / SPI / M • Strong Sensations / 1996 / PL / M • Style #3 / 1996 / VT / M • Suburban Buttnicks Forever / 1995 / CC / M • Sunset In Paradise / 1996 / PL / M • Sure Bet / 1995 / CV / M • Surf Babes / 1995 / LE / M • Suzi Bungholeo / 1995 / ROB / M • Sweet A$ Money / 1994 / MID / M • The Swing / 1996 / VI / M • Taboo #14: Kissing Cousins / 1995 / IN / M • Taboo #15 / 1995 / IN / M • Tail Taggers #121: Behind The Lens / 1994 / WV / M • Tainted Love / 1996 / VC / M • Take It Inside / 1995 / PEP / M • Takin' It To The Limit #3 / 1994 / BS / M • Takin' It To The Limit #4 / 1995 / BS / M • Talk Dirty To Me #10 / 1996 / DR / M • A Taste Of Fanny / 1994 / FH / M • Temptation / 1994 / VC / M • Texas Crude / 1995 / NIT / M • Thunder Boobs / 1995 / BTO / M • The Tigress / 1995 / VIM / M • Timepiece / 1994 / CV / M • Titanic Orgy / 1995 / PEP / M • Tits A Wonderful Life / 1994 / CV / M • Twists Of The Heart / 1995 / NIT / M • Unleashed / 1996 / SAE / M • Unplugged / 1995 / CC / M • Up And Cummers #19 / 1995 / 4P / M • Up And Cummers #25 / 1995 / 4P / M • Up And Cummers #26 / 1996 / 4P / M • Up And Cummers #27 / 1996 / ERW / M • Up And Cummers #29 / 1996 / ERW / M • Up And Cummers #30 / 1996 / 4P / M • Up And Cummers #31 / 1996 / 4P / M • Up And Cummers #32 / 1996 / 4P / M • Up And Cummers #33 / 1996 / 4P / M • Up And Cummers #34 / 1996 / 4P / M • Up And Cummers #35 / 1996 / 4P / M • Up And Cummers #39 / 1996 / RWP / M • Upbeat Love #2 / 1995 / CV / M • View Point / 1995 / VI / M • Virgins / 1995 / ERA / M • Virtual Encounters / 1996 / SCI / S • Wedding Night Blues / 1995 / EMC / M • What's Up, Tiger Pussy? / 1995 / VC / M • White Men Can't Iron On Butt Row / 1997 / ABS / M • Whitey's On The Moon / 1996 / ROB / M • The Wicked Web / 1996 / WP / M • Wild Assed Pooper Slut / 1996 / ROB / M • Willie Wanker At The Fudge Packing Factory / 1995 / FD / M • Willie Wanker At The Sushi Bar / 1995 / FD / M • World Sex Tour #6 / 1996 / ANA / M • World Sex Tour #7 / 1996 / ANA / M • X-Tales / 1995 / VIM / M • XXX Channel / 1996 / VT / M

VINCENT BOYDELL
Seduce Me Tonight / 1984 / AT / M
VINCENT CALABRESE
Spanking Double Feature / 1994 / SHL / B
VINCENT DEMARCO
Natural Response / 1996 / GPI / G
VINCENT GUAGE
Sex #1 (Vca) / 1994 / VC / M
VINCENT STEPHENS
Sex Rituals Of The Occult / 1970 / ALP / M

• Thar She Blows! / 1969 / SOW / S • [The Suckers / 1969 / ... / S
VINCENTA
Joe Elliot's College Girls #47 / 1996 / JOE / F
VINEKO MOMOYAMA see Star Index I
VINNIE DEMARCO see Felipe
VINNIE SPIT
4 Of A Kind / 1995 / BON / B • Full House / 1995 / BON / B
VINNY LA MARCA see Felipe
VINNY ROSSI
Flash Backs / 1990 / BON / B
VIOLA
Penetration (Anabolic) #1 / 1995 / ANA / M
VIOLET
The Big E #08 / 1988 / BIZ / B • Blood Bath / 1995 / FLV / B • Super Sampler #5 / 1994 / LOD / C
VIOLET BLISS
[Mountain Orgy / 197? / ... / M
VIOLET REASON see Star Index I
VIOLET SWEETSEAT see Star Index I
VIOLETTE WILDE see Star Index I
VIPER *(Stephanie Bishop)*
Was 28 in 1988. Spent some time in the Marines. In 1989 got breasts enlarged to grotesque proportions. Tattoos all over her body.
4F Dating Service / 1989 / AR / M • Amazing Tails #4 / 1990 / CA / M • Ambushed / 1990 / SE / M • Anal Attraction #2 / 1993 / AFV / C • Anything Goes / 1993 / VD / C • Aunty V's Panty Boy / 1991 / LEO / B • Awesome Assets / 1985 / 4P / M • Back To Back #2 / 1992 / FC / C • Backdoor Lust / 1987 / CV / C • Backdoor To Harley-Wood #1 / 1990 / AFV / M • Backdoor To Hollywood #03 / 1987 / CDI / M • Backing In #1 / 1990 / WV / C • Backing In #2 / 1990 / WV / C • The Best Little Whorehouse In Hong Kong / 1987 / SE / M • Best Of Caught From Behind #5 / 1991 / HO / C • Black & Gold / 1990 / CIN / M • Black Angel / 1987 / CC / M • Black On White / 1987 / PL / C • Black Taboo #2 / 1986 / SE / M • Blacks & Blondes #46 / 1987 / WV / M • Blowing The Whistle / 1986 / VIP / M • Blue Views / 1990 / CDI / M • Body Slam / 1987 / 4P / B • Bondage Classix #13: Class Of 86 #2 / 1991 / BON / B • Born To Be Bad / 1987 / CV / M • Born To Be Wild / 1987 / SE / M • Born To Suck Cock / 1994 / MET / C • Breathless / 1991 / WV / M • Broadcast Nudes / 1988 / EVN / M • Butt Naked #1 / 1990 / OD / M • Captain Hooker & Peter Porn / 1987 / VD / M • The Cat Club / 1987 / SE / M • Caught From Behind #09 / 1988 / HO / M • Cheek To Cheek / 1986 / VEX / M • Debbie Does The Devil In Dallas / 1987 / SE / M • Detroit Dames / 1988 / DR / C • Deviled X / 1987 / 4P / M • Don't Get Them Wet / 1987 / VD / M • Dreams In The Forbidden Zone / 1989 / PCP / M • Ebony Ecstacy / 1988 / HIO / C • The Erotic Adventures Of Bonnie & Clyde / 1988 / GO / M • Erotic Heights / 1991 / AR / M • Fantasy Nights / 1990 / VC / M • Fast Girls #1 / 1987 / GBX / M • Fire In The Hole / 1989 / ... / C • Foot Lights / 1988 / BIZ / B • Forbidden Fruit #2 / 1987 / MET / G • Frat Brats / 1990 / VC / M • Freak Show / 1991 / FC / M • Fun In The Sun / 1988 / EVN / C • Future Sodom / 1988 / VD / M • Girls Of Silicone Valley / 1991 / FC / M • The Godmother #1 / 1987 / VC / M • Graduation Ball

/ 1989 / CAE / M • Hard Road To Victory / 1989 / WV / C • Heavy Petting / 1991 / SE / M • The Hindlick Maneuver / 1991 / CC / M • Hospitality Sweet / 1988 / WV / M • Hotel California / 1986 / WV / M • Hyapatia Lee's Arcade Series #01 / 1988 / ZA / C • Hyapatia Lee's Arcade Series #02 / 1988 / ZA / C • I Love X / 1992 / FC / C • Images Of Desire / 1990 / PM / M • Immorals #1: Broken Hearts / 1989 / AR / M • Immorals #2: The Good, The Bad, And The Banged / 1990 / AR / M • Immorals #3: Stroked / 1991 / SC / M • Immorals #4: Choice Cuts / 1991 / SC / M • Inner Blues / 1987 / VD / M • International Phone Sex Girls #5 / 1991 / PM / M • Jane Bond Meets The Man With The Golden Rod / 1987 / VD / M • Jane Bond Meets Thunderballs / 1986 / VD / M • Kiss My Asp / 1989 / EXH / M • Leather Jackets / 1990 / C3S / S • Leave It To Cleavage #1 / 1988 / GO / M • Lesbian Lovers / 1988 / GO / F • Lessons In Lust / 1987 / LA / M • Let's Talk Dirty / 1987 / SE / M • Lingerie Party / 1987 / SE / C • A Little Bit Of Honey / 1987 / WET / M • Loose Ends #4 / 1988 / 4P / M • Lust College / 1989 / ... / M • The Masseuse #1 / 1990 / VI / M • Midnight Fire / 1990 / HU / M • The Mile High Girls / 1987 / CA / M • Mondo Bitches / 1991 / LBO / B • Moondance / 1991 / WV / M • More Dirty Debutantes #03 / 1990 / 4P / M • The More the Merrier / 1989 / VC / C • Mystery Of The Golden Lotus / 1989 / HU / M • Nasty Girls #1 (1990-CDI) / 1990 / CIN / M • Night Vibes / 1990 / KNI / M • Oral Majority #06 / 1988 / WV / C • The Other Side Of Pleasure / 1987 / SEV / M • Pacific Intrigue / 1987 / AMB / M • Parliament: Anal Babes #1 / 1989 / PM / F • Parliament: Ass Masters #1 / 1987 / PM / M • Parliament: Ass Parade #1 / 1988 / PM / F • Parliament: Bare Assets / 1988 / PM / F • Parliament: Finger Friggin' #2 / 1988 / PM / F • Parliament: Hard TV #1 / 1988 / PM / G • Parliament: Licking Lesbians #1 / 1988 / PM / F • Parliament: Shaved #2 / 1988 / PM / F • The Penetration Of Elle Rio / 1987 / GO / M • Phone Sex Girls #5 / 1990 / TOR / M • Pool Party / 1991 / CIN / M • Possession / 1990 / CIN / M • Princess Of The Night / 1990 / VD / M • Raunchy Porno Picture Show / 1992 / FC / M • Saki's House Party / 1990 / KNI / M • Satania / 1986 / DR / M • School Dayze / 1987 / BON / B • Selena's Secrets / 1991 / MIN / M • The Sex Life Of Mata Hari / 1989 / GO / M • She-Male Encounters #13: She-Male Reformatory / 1987 / MET / G • She-Male Encounters #14: She-Male Wrestlers / 1987 / MET / G • She-Male Sex Toys / 1993 / SC / G • She-Male Tales / 1990 / MET / G • Smooth As Silk / 1987 / VIP / M • Spanish Fly / 1987 / CA / M • Suburban Seduction / 1991 / HO / M • Sugarpussy Jeans / 1986 / TEM / M • Taste Of The Best #1 / 1988 / PIN / C • A Taste Of Viper / 1990 / PIN / C • Tickled! / 1989 / BIZ / C • Tit Tales #3 / 1991 / FC / M • Titillation #2 / 1990 / SE / M • Titty-Titty Bang-Bang / 1992 / FC / C • Toy Box Lingerie Show / 1991 / ESP / S • Toying Around / 1992 / FL / M • Tracy Takes Paris / 1987 / VIP / M • Trisexual Encounters #06 / 1987 / PL / G • Ubangis On Uranus / 1987 / WV / M • Up The Ying Yang / 1991 / EVN / C • Vice Academy #4 / 1994 / PRS / S • Viper's

Place / 1988 / VD / M • Voodoo Lust: The Possession / 1989 / PCP / M • The Wacky World Of X-Rated Bloopers / 1989 / GO / M • Weird And Bizarre Bondage / 1991 / FC / C • White Trash / 1986 / PV / M • [More Than A Handful / 1991 / ... / M

VIRGINIA
Blue Vanities #518 / 1993 / FFL / M • Breast Of Britain #2 / 1987 / BTO / M • Breast Of Britain #4 / 1990 / BTO / S • Busty Superstars #1 / 199? / H&S / S • A Peek Over The Wall / 1995 / STM / G • Trained Transvestites / 1995 / STM / B

VIRGINIA BELL
Bell, Bare And Beautiful / 1963 / SOW / S • Blue Vanities #110 / 1988 / FFL / M • Blue Vanities #514 / 1992 / FFL / M • Blue Vanities #515 / 1992 / FFL / M • Blue Vanities #526 / 1993 / FFL / M • Blue Vanities #555 / 1994 / FFL / M • Blue Vanities #568 / 1995 / FFL / M • Busty Beauties / 199? / SVE / M • Reel Classics #1 / 1996 / H&S / M • Reel Classics #3 / 1996 / H&S / M • Titanic Tits #03 / 198? / L&W / S

VIRGINIA FENWAY see Star Index I

VIRGINIA GIRITLIAN
Thundercrack! / 1974 / LUM / M

VIRGINIA ICE
Itsy Bitsy Gang Bang / 1996 / HW / M • Somewhere Under The Rainbow #2 / 1995 / HW / M

VIRGINIA LANE *(Virginia Layne)*
Bi Bi Love / 1986 / LAV / G • Bi-Sexual Fantasies / 1984 / LAV / G • Passion By Fire / 1986 / LAV / G

VIRGINIA LAYNE see Virginia Lane

VIRGINIA LEWIS
Poor Little Rich Girls / 1994 / SHL / B

VIRGINIA MULLER see Star Index I

VIRGINIA PAYMORE see Jeanna Fine

VIRGINIA SANDRADO see Star Index I

VIRGINIA SLIM see Star Index I

VIRGINIA THOMPSON
Ole / 1971 / KIT / M

VIRGINIA VIGNON see Star Index I

VIRGINIE
Adultress / 1995 / WIV / M • Anabolic Import #07: Anal X / 1995 / ANA / M • Eurotica #10 / 1996 / XC / M • Sappho Connection / 19?? / LIP / F

VISION
Reddish brown or reddish blonde hair, so so face, medium droopy tits, cellulite in the buttocks and upper thighs, freckles, tattoo on right hip and another on her right shoulder back, a little pudgy.
1-900-SPANKME Ext.1 / 1994 / BON / B • 100% Amateur #10: / 1995 / OD / M • Anal Angels #4 / 1995 / VEX / C • Anal Vision #25 / 1994 / LBO / M • Beach Bum Amateur's #40 / 1993 / MID / M • Bobby Hollander's Sweet Cheeks #111 / 1994 / WV / M • Butt Hunt #01 / 1994 / LEI / M • Heels & Toes #1 / 1994 / BON / F • Nasty Newcummers #04 / 1994 / MET / M • Oh My Gush / 1995 / OD / M • Photo Opportunity / 1994 / VC / M • Rear Entry / 1995 / LEI / M • Sex In Dangerous Places / 1994 / OD / M • Slut Safari #1 / 1994 / FC / M • Spank-O-Rama / 1994 / BON / B • Video Virgins #10 / 1993 / NS / M • Wet And Wild #2 / 1995 / VEX / M

VITO
Bang City #4: Gina's Anal Gang Bang / 1995 / SC / M

VITORIO

Feuchte Muschies / 1995 / KRM / M

VITTORIO PARRINI
Sex Penitentiary / 1996 / XC / M

VIVA
Black Beauty (Las Vegas) / 1995 / LV / M • Black Hollywood Amateurs #03 / 1995 / MID / M • Blue Vanities #207 / 1993 / FFL / M • Forbidden Subjects #4 / 1995 / FC / M • GVC: Party Girl #102 / 1981 / GO / M • Hot Child In The City / 1979 / PVX / M • More Black Dirty Debutantes #5 / 1995 / 4P / M

VIVA KENVIEL
Striptease #1 / 1995 / PL / M • Striptease #2 / 1995 / PL / M

VIVA KNIEVAL
P.L.O.W.: Punk Ladies Of Wrestling / 1996 / GOT / B

VIVECA ASH
Invasion Of The Love Drones / 1977 / ALP / M

VIVEN NADOS
Lil' Women: Vacation / 1996 / EUR / M

VIVIAN
Body English / 1993 / PL / M • Butt Hole In-One / 1994 / AFV / M • The Erotic Adventures Of Johnny Soiree / 1995 / LBO / M • The Sweet Sweet Back #3: Sho' Nuff Got Dat Woodski / 1994 / FH / M • World Sex Tour #4 / 1996 / ANA / M

VIVIAN (1994)
Bi Love Lucy / 1994 / PL / G • Creme De La Face #05 / 1994 / OD / M • Dirty Doc's Housecalls #19 / 1994 / LV / M • Northwest Pecker Trek #3: Ducks & Dicks / 1994 / LBO / M • Northwest Pecker Trek #4: Laid In Latte Land / 1994 / LBO / M • Reel People #07 / 1995 / PP / M

VIVIAN (BRAZ)
Buttman Goes To Rio #3 / 1992 / EA / M

VIVIAN (LATE 80S)
The Mistake / 1989 / CDP / B

VIVIAN (LEY) see Vivian Ley

VIVIAN GREEN
Toe Tales #27 / 1995 / GOT / B

VIVIAN LEE see Vivian Ley

VIVIAN LEY *(Vivian (Ley), Vivian Lee, Viviana (V. Ley), June Lee (V. Ley), Vivian Tran)*
Not too pretty Oriental (supposedly Thai) girl with small droopy tits, 18 years old in 1994, OK butt, loss of belly muscle tone. Wears braces in her first movies. De-virginized at 15.
Anal Vision #26 / 1994 / LBO / M • Anal Vision #27 / 1994 / LBO / M • Anal Vision #28 / 1994 / LBO / M • Back Door Asians / 1995 / EVN / M • Black Orgies #22 / 1994 / GO / M • Bobby Hollander's Sweet Cheeks #109 / 1994 / WV / M • The Burma Road #1 / 1994 / LBO / C • The Burma Road #2 / 1994 / LBO / C • Cherry Poppers #04: Ripe 'n' Ready / 1994 / ZA / M • Fantasy Flings #02 / 1994 / WP / M • Geisha To Go / 1994 / PPP / M • Green Piece Of Ass #2 / 1994 / RTP / M • Harness Hannah At The Strap-On Palace / 1994 / WIV / F • The Hitch-Hiker #03: No Exit / 1994 / WMG / M • The Hitch-Hiker #04: Max Overdrive / 1994 / WMG / M • Hollywood Starlets Adventure #02 / 1995 / AVS / M • Home Nurses Anal Adventure / 1994 / LBO / M • Horny Henry's Peeping Adventures / 1994 / TTV / M • I Can't Believe I Did The Whole Team! / 1994 / FPI / M • Kinky Debutante Interviews #02 / 1994 / IP / M • Kinky Orientals

/ 1994 / FH / M • My Baby Got Back #04 / 1994 / VT / M • Nasty Nymphos #03 / 1994 / ANA / M • New Ends #07 / 1994 / 4P / M • Oriental Gang Bang Fantasy / 1994 / FC / M • Pai Gow Video #06: New Wave Orientals / 1994 / EVN / M • Pussy Hunt #05 / 1994 / LEI / M • R & R / 1994 / VC / M • Slut Safari #3 / 1994 / FC / M • Tail Taggers #121: Behind The Lens / 1994 / WV / M • The Ultimate Squirting Machine / 1994 / FPI / M • Video Virgins #11 / 1994 / NS / M • Wild Orgies #04 / 1994 / AFI / M

VIVIAN MAYER
Blue Vanities #519 / 1993 / FFL / M

VIVIAN PARKS
Bucky Beaver's XXX Dragon Art Theatre Double Feature #02 / 1996 / SOW / M • The Rites Of Uranus / 1975 / SOW / M

VIVIAN THOMAS
Flaming Tongues #1 / 1984 / MET / F • Palomino Heat / 1985 / COM / F

VIVIAN TRAN see Vivian Ley

VIVIAN VEE
Teacher's Pet #3 / 1995 / APP / M

VIVIANA
Against All Bods / 1991 / VEX / M • Amateur American Style #27 / 1992 / AR / M • Animal Instincts / 1991 / VEX / M • Big Bust Fantasies / 1995 / PME / F • Breasts And Beyond #1 / 1991 / ME / M • Breasts And Beyond #2 / 1991 / ME / M • Catalina: Tiger Shark / 1991 / CDI / M • D-Cup Dating Service / 1991 / ME / M • Deep Inside Viviana / 1992 / VEX / C • Desire / 1990 / VC / M • Dr Hooters / 1991 / PL / M • Executive Positions / 1991 / V99 / M • Ghost To Ghost / 1991 / CC / M • Glamour Girl / 1991 / VEX / M • Glitter Girls / 1992 / V99 / M • Hard To Thrill / 1991 / CIN / M • Hot On Her Tail / 1990 / CA / M • More Than A Mouthful #1 / 1991 / VEX / M • More Than A Mouthful #2 / 1991 / VEX / M • Nasty Jack's Homemade Vid. #15 / 1991 / CDI / M • Physically Fit / 1991 / V99 / C • Spanish Rose / 1991 / VEX / M • Titty-Titty Bang-Bang / 1992 / FC / C • Tonight's The Night / 1992 / V99 / M • A Trip Down Mammary Lane / 1991 / FC / M • Viva Vivian / 1994 / PME / F • Viviana's Dude Ranch / 1992 / IF / M • Wet, Wild And Willing / 1993 / V99 / M

VIVIANA (V. LEY) see Vivian Ley

VIVIEN
Ejacula #1 / 1992 / VC / M • Ejacula #2 / 1992 / VC / M

VIVIENNE (HUNGARY)
Pretty or not so pretty depending on the lighting of the movie and the color of the hair plus has a tendency to screw up her face during sex which does nothing for her prettiness. The closer she gets to black hair instead of the dark red preferred by the Eastern Europeans the better she looks. Otherwise she has a petite body, medium very nicely shaped tits, nice butt and good skin.
Asses Galore #7: Lunatic Fringe / 1996 / DFI / M • Lee Nover: The Search For The Perfect Butt / 1996 / IP / M • More Dirty Debutantes #62 / 1997 / SBV / M • Pick Up Lines #13 / 1997 / OD / M • Streets Of New York #07 / 1996 / PL / M • Valentino's Euro-Invasion / 1997 / SC / M • White Men Can't Iron On Butt Row / 1997 / ABS / M

VIVIENNE CLASH
Private Film #27 / 1995 / OD / M • Private Film #28 / 1995 / OD / M • Private Stories #04 / 1995 / OD / M • Triple X Video Mag-

azine #06 / 1995 / OD / M • Triple X Video Magazine #07 / 1995 / OD / M

VIVIENNE WARREN
Blue Vanities #516 / 1992 / FFL / M • Blue Vanities #581 / 1996 / FFL / M

VIXEN see Star Index I

VIXEN (VIXXEN) see Vixxen

VIXEN LADOUR
I'm A Curious She-Male / 1993 / HSV / G

VIXEN RED see Star Index I

VIXEN WILD see Star Index I

VIXENE see Brigitte Aime

VIXXEN *(Vixen (Vixxen), Angel (Vixxen))*
Thin girl with strawberry blonde hair, small tits (natural), nice skin, tight butt and waist (32B-23-34). Reasonably pretty but sounds a little slutty. Tattoo on her left ankle. Not to be confused with a fat blonde who appears in the bondage and big tit movies. Comes from Illinois. In 1995 had her tits enhanced to large rock-solid cantaloupes (34D). Angel is the name used in some of her early AVP amateurs.
30 Days In The Hole / 1993 / ZA / M • Ace In The Hole / 1995 / PL / M • America's Raunchiest Home Videos #73: / 1993 / ZA / M • American Blonde / 1993 / VI / M • The Anal Adventures Of Max Hardcore: Wildlife / 1994 / ZA / M • Anal Al's Adventures / 1995 / PL / M • Anal Aspirations / 1993 / LV / M • The Anal Diary Of Misty Rain / 1993 / EL / M • Anal Vision #17 / 1993 / LBO / M • Anal Vision #19 / 1993 / LBO / M • The Ass Master #06 / 1994 / GLI / M • Assmania!! #2 / 1995 / ME / M • AVP #9146: Ready, Set, -uck / 1990 / AVP / M • AVP #9150: Babes In Joyland / 1990 / AVP / F • Babe Magnet / 1994 / IN / M • Babes Illustrated #1 / 1994 / IN / F • Baby Doll / 1994 / SC / M • Back In Style / 1993 / VI / M • The Big Bang #1 / 1993 / LV / M • Blonde Angel / 1994 / VI / M • Blonde Forces #2 / 1994 / CC / M • The Bottom Dweller Part Deux / 1994 / EL / M • Bruce Seven: A Compendium Of His Most Graphic Scenes Vol 6 / 1994 / BS / C • Buffy Malibu's Totally Nasty All-Girl Home Videos #05 / 1993 / ANA / F • Bun Busters #05 / 1993 / LBO / M • Butthead & Beaver / 1993 / HW / M • Butthunt / 1994 / AFV / F • Buttslammers #05: Quake, Rattle & Roll! / 1994 / BS / F • Buttslammers #08: The Ultimate Invasion / 1994 / BS / F • Casting Call #04 / 1993 / SO / M • Climax 2000 #1 / 1994 / CC / M • Close To The Edge / 1994 / VI / M • Colossal Orgy #1 / 1993 / HW / M • Colossal Orgy #2 / 1994 / HW / M • The Couch Trap / 1993 / ELP / M • Cum & Get Me / 1995 / PL / F • Debutante Training / 1995 / PL / B • Dirty Bob's #09: Orlando Orgasms / 1993 / FLP / S • Dirty Bob's #11: Vegas Blues #1 / 1994 / FLP / S • Dirty Bob's #23: Tampa Teasers / 1995 / FLP / S • Diva / 1993 / XCI / M • Double Crossed / 1994 / MID / M • Dungeon Dykes #1 / 1994 / FPI / F • Eclipse / 1993 / SC / M • Euro Studs / 1996 / SC / C • Fantastic Facials / 1994 / PEV / C • Feet And Head / 1994 / SV / M • First Time Lesbians #08 / 1993 / JMP / F • The Flirt / 1995 / GO / M • Fresh Tender Asses / 1994 / RB / B • GRG: Dripping Wet Dykes / 1994 / GRG / B • GRG: Garage Gang Bang / 1993 / GRG / M • GRG: Vixxen's Nympho Gang Bang / 1993 / GRG / M • Haunting Dreams #1 / 1993 / LV / M • Haunting Dreams #2 / 1993 / LV /

M • Heatwaves / 1994 / LE / M • Heidi Does Hollywood / 1993 / AFV / M • Hexxxed / 1994 / VT / M • Hidden Camera #06 / 1993 / JMP / M • Hidden Camera #08 / 1993 / JMP / M • Hole In One / 1994 / HO / M • Hollywood '94: Butts Abound / 1993 / ELP / M • I Touch Myself / 1994 / IP / F • Indecent Interview / 1995 / PL / F • Intercourse With The Vampyre #1 / 1994 / SC / M • Intercourse With The Vampyre #2 / 1994 / SC / M • Junkyard Dykes #01 / 1994 / ZA / F • Lusty Ladies / 1994 / MET / F • Madame Hollywood / 1993 / LE / M • Nasty Fuckin' Movies #18: Lesbian Audition / 1993 / RUM / M • Nasty Nymphos #01 / 1993 / ANA / M • Neighbors / 1994 / LE / M • New Wave Hookers #4 / 1994 / VC / M • No Man's Land #10 / 1994 / VT / F • Odyssey 30 Min: #354: Three Cocks For Vixxen / 1993 / OD / M • Odyssey Triple Play #71: Bodacious Blondes / 1994 / OD / M • Odyssey Triple Play #89: Group Sex Grab Bag / 1995 / OD / M • Oral Obsession #1 / 1994 / VI / M • Outrageous Sex / 1995 / BIP / F • Overkill / 1994 / BS / B • Pearl Necklace: Thee Bush League #24 / 1993 / SEE / M • Pretending / 1993 / CV / M • Private Video Magazine #05 / 1993 / OD / M • Psychoanal Therapy / 1994 / CA / M • Pulse / 1994 / EX / M • Pussyman #04: The Celebration / 1993 / SNA / M • The Quest / 1994 / SC / M • R.E.A.L. #1 / 1994 / LV / F • Raunch #09 / 1993 / CC / M • Revenge Of The Bi Dolls / 1994 / CAT / G • Riot Grrrls / 1994 / SC / M • The Seduction Of Julia Ann / 1993 / VT / M • Sex Therapy Ward / 1995 / LBO / M • Sexual Trilogy #02 / 1993 / SFP / M • Songbird / 1993 / AMP / M • Spectator Sport / 1993 / VVO / B • Steady As She Blows / 1993 / LV / M • Supermodel #2 / 1994 / VI / M • Surprise!!! / 1994 / VI / M • Takin' It To The Limit #1 / 1994 / BS / M • Takin' It To The Limit #4 / 1995 / BS / M • Tales From The Clit / 1993 / OD / M • The Teacher's Pet / 1993 / LV / M • Top Debs #5: Deb Of The Month / 1994 / GO / M • Up And Cummers #03 / 1993 / 4P / M • Up And Cummers: The Movie / 1994 / 4P / M • Use It Or Lose It / 1994 / CA / M • Vicci's Revenge / 1994 / L&L / B • The Way They Wuz / 1996 / SHS / C • The Whipping Post / 1995 / BS / B • Whorelock / 1993 / LV / M • Wicked Pleasures / 1995 / BS / B • Wild Things #4 / 1994 / CV / M

VIXXEN VAUGHN
Reasonably pretty blonde with long straight hair, medium enhanced tits, large tattoo on chest just above left breast, one on right belly and another on her right shoulder back. A bit big in the butt. Her SO (as of 1994) is Greg Wilcocks (known as (just) Greg in the B&D movies).
Beyond Domination / 1996 / GOT / B • Black Masters: Den Of Punishment / 1996 / GOT / B • Black Masters: Restrained / 1995 / GOT / B • Black Masters: Trapped / 1995 / GOT / B • Blindfold / 1996 / GOT / B • Dirty Dancers #2 / 1994 / 4P / M • Drastic Measures / 1996 / GOT / B • Extreme Guilt / 1996 / GOT / B • Masters Of Dominance / 1996 / GOT / C • Mistress From Hell / 1996 / GOT / B • On Your Knees / 1995 / GOT / B • Road Trippin' #01: New York City / 1994 / OUP / F • Road Trippin' #02: New York City / 1994 / OUP / F • Road Trippin' #03: New York City / 1994 / OUP / M •

Strap-On Sally #03: Thigh Harness Terror / 1994 / PL / F • Strap-On Sally #04: Double Penetration Dykes / 1994 / PL / F • Toe Tales #21 / 1995 / GOT / B • Toe Tales #23 / 1995 / GOT / B • Toe Tales #24 / 1995 / GOT / C

VLAD
Spank-O-Rama / 1994 / BON / B

VLADIMIR
100% Amateur #15: / 1995 / OD / M • Back East Babes #1 / 1996 / NIT / M • Bright Tails #7 / 1995 / STP / B • Cumm For Dinner / 1995 / BCP / M • Eternal Bonds / 1995 / RHV / B • New Faces, Hot Bodies #17 / 1995 / STP / M • Northwest Pecker Trek #2: Evergreen, Ever Horny / 1994 / LBO / M • Northwest Pecker Trek #3: Ducks & Dicks / 1994 / LBO / M • Northwest Pecker Trek #4: Laid In Latte Land / 1994 / LBO / M • Northwest Pecker Trek #6: Two Girls For Every Boy / 1995 / LBO / M • Profiles #03: House Dick / 1995 / XPR / M • Pussy Fest Of The Northwest #1 / 1995 / NIT / M • Pussy Fest Of The Northwest #2 / 1995 / NIT / M • Rusty Boner's Late Night Videos #1 / 1995 / RHV / M • Spanked In Spades / 1995 / STM / B • Teacher's Pet #1 / 1994 / WMG / M • Under The Cum Cum Tree / 1996 / BCP / M

VLADIMIR CORREA *(Marcelo Matter, Marcello (V.Correa))*
Anal Woman #2 / 1993 / PL / M • Anal Woman #3 / 1995 / PL / M • Bi 'n' Large / 1992 / VD / C • Bi And Busty / 1991 / STA / G • Bi Dream Of Genie / 1990 / BIN / G • Bi-Inferno / 1992 / VEX / G • The Big Shave / 1993 / PEP / M • Buttman Goes To Rio #1 / 1990 / EA / M • Club Taboo / 1987 / MET / G • Double Standards / 1988 / BIL / G • Haulin' 'n' Ballin' / 1988 / MET / G • Herman's Other Head / 1992 / LV / M • I Ream A Jeannie / 1990 / GLE / M • Incessant / 1988 / CAD / G • Just My Imagination / 1993 / WP / M • Night Breed / 1992 / CDI / G • Obsessions In Lace / 1994 / PL / M • Pay The Lady / 1987 / VXP / M • The Rod Garetto Story / 1995 / FC / C • Stasha's Last Kiss / 1993 / VEX / G • Stick It In The Rear #2 / 1993 / PL / M • Transitions: An Anal Adventure / 1993 / PL / M • Wishbone / 1988 / VXP / M

VLOTKA KUMSKOVA
More Dirty Debutantes #51 / 1996 / 4P / M

VOLKER HART
Viola Video #107: Private Party / 1995 / PEV / M

VON
FTV #03: Queen Boxer & Mixed Fist / 1996 / FT / B

VON VON LINDENBERG
[No More Dirty Deals / 1994 / V-I / S

VONDA PATTERSON
Butt Bangers Ball #1 / 1996 / TTV / M • Golden Oldies #3 / 1995 / TTV / M • Golden Oldies #5 / 1996 / TTV / M • Lesbian Lust Bust / 1995 / GLI / F

VTA KAZAMA
Academy Of Sex / 1995 / AVV / M

W. SMITH
Blue Vanities #555 / 1994 / FFL / M

W.O. WILLIAMS
Like A Virgin #1 / 1985 / AT / M

W.P. DREMAK
Dirty Lilly / 1975 / VXP / M • Draws / 1976 / VIG / S • If Looks Could Kill / 1987 / REP / S • Take Off / 1978 / VXP / M • Visions / 1977 / QX / M • Wimps / 1987 / LIV / S

WAD ZILLA
Forbidden Fantasies #2 / 1995 / ZA / M

WADE NICHOLS *(Wade Parker, Dennis Parker)*
Died in 1985. Supposedly blew his brains out when he found out he had AIDS. Worked on the TV soap **Edge of Night**.
Bang Bang You Got It / 1975 / VXP / M • Barbara Broadcast / 1977 / VC / M • Beach House / 1981 / CA / C • Blonde Ambition / 1981 / QX / M • Blue Voodoo / 1983 / VD / M • Breaker Beauties / 1977 / VHL / M • Call Me Angel, Sir / 1976 / ALP / M • Captain Lust And The Amorous Contessa / 1977 / IHV / M • Dirty Looks / 1982 / VC / C • Exploring Young Girls / 1978 / ALP / M • Honeymoon Haven / 1977 / QX / M • Jail Bait / 1976 / VC / M • Jawbreakers / 1985 / VEN / C • Long Hard Summer / 1989 / BMV / C • Love You / 1980 / CA / M • Lucky Charm / 1986 / AVC / C • Magic Girls / 1983 / SVE / M • Maraschino Cherry / 1978 / QX / M • My Sex-Rated Wife / 1977 / ... / M • Odyssey / 1977 / VC / M • Pussycat Ranch / 1978 / CV / M • Raw Footage / 1977 / CA / M • Secret Dreams Of Mona Q / 1977 / AR / M • Steamy Sirens / 1984 / AIR / C • Summer Of Laura / 1975 / CXV / M • Sweetheart / 1976 / SVE / M • Take Off / 1978 / VXP / M • Teenage Pajama Party / 1978 / VXP / M • Teenage Runaways / 1977 / WWV / M • Triple Header / 1987 / AIR / C • Underage / 1974 / IHV / M • Virgin Dreams / 1976 / BMV / M • Visions / 1977 / QX / M

WADE PARKER see **Wade Nichols**

WAGNER
Gang Bang Bitches #01 / 1994 / PP / M • Gang Bang Bitches #02 / 1994 / PP / M • Wild Orgies #15 / 1995 / AFI / M

WALDO
Bi-Bi Love Amateurs #4 / 1994 / QUA / G

WALDO GRADE
Matinee Idol / 1984 / VC / M

WALDO PIPER see Star Index I

WALDO SHORT see Star Index I

WALLY HUGHES see Star Index I

WALLY SEGAP
Platinum Paradise / 1980 / COM / M

WALLY SHERWOOD
Welcome To SM / 1996 / ESF / B

WALLY WHARTON
Cheerleaders' Wild Weekend / cr77 / VES / S • Dirty Bob's #17: Tampa Teasers! / 1994 / FLP / S • Double Crossed / 1994 / MID / M • Eclipse / 1993 / SC / M • Golden Rod / 1996 / SPI / M • Lessons In Love / 1995 / SPI / M • Naked Scandal #1 / 1995 / SPI / M • Naked Scandal #2 / 1996 / SPI / M • Supermodel #1 / 1994 / VI / M • Sweat 'n' Bullets / 1995 / MID / M • Thunder And Mud / 1990 / RCA / B • Velvet / 1995 / SPI / M

WALT DAVIS
Evil Come Evil Go / 1972 / ST0 / S • Sex Psycho / 1971 / SOW / M

WALT TURNER
The Joy Of Fooling Around / 1978 / CV / M

WALTER BUSTELLI
[Die Madchenhandler / 1972 / ... / M

WALTER ELECTRIC
Mad Love / 1988 / VC / M • Old Guys & Dolls #1 / 1995 / PL / M

WALTER FEUCHTENBERG
[Schulmadchen-Report 4: Was Eltern Oft Verzweifeln LaBt / 1972 / ... / M

WALTER GABARRON see Star Index I

WALTER HILL
G.I. Executioner / 1971 / VES / S • Private Film #12 / 1994 / OD / M

WALTER KRAUSE
The Long Swift Sword Of Siegfried / 1971 / SOW / S • Rx For Sex / 1983 / AT / M

WALTER KUPPERS see Star Index I

WALTER MCDILLON
Dangerous / 1996 / SNA / M • Primal Instinct / 1996 / SNA / M

WALTER MORENO
Euroflesh: Dentro Il Vulcano / 1996 / SC / M

WALTER SMITTY see Star Index I

WALTER WOLF see Star Index I

WANDA
100% Amateur #18: / 1995 / OD / M • Blue Vanities #534 / 1993 / FFL / M • Bun Busters #15 / 1994 / LBO / M • The Hitch-Hiker #07: Life In The Fast Lane / 1994 / WMG / M • Limited Edition #25 / 1984 / AVC / M

WANDA (S/M)
Secret Dreams Of Mona Q / 1977 / AR / M

WANDA ALVEREZ
Blue Vanities #204 / 1993 / FFL / M

WANDA B. UGLEE see Star Index I

WANDA BRUCE see Star Index I

WANDA DENOIR see Star Index I

WANDA GETZ see Star Index I

WANDA LAPAR
Waterfront Honey / 19?? / XTR / M

WANDA LONG
Party #1 / 1979 / NAT / M

WANDA QUICK
The Nurses Are Coming / 1985 / VCR / C • Yummy Nymphs / 1983 / TGA / C

WANDA SCOTT
Prisoners Of Love / 19?? / BL / M

WANDA SIMMONS
The Rose And The Bee / 19?? / VST / M

WANDA WERNER
Young Sluts In Heat #1 / 1996 / PL / M • Young Sluts In Heat #2 / 1996 / PL / M

WANDA WILSON see Star Index I

WANNITA
Black Bitches In Heat #2 / 1995 / GDV / M

WARD SUMMERS see **Cecil Howard**

WARREN
HomeGrown Video #473: Furpie Feast #3 / 1997 / HOV / C • Swingers Confidential #1 / 1995 / FC / M

WARREN EVANS see **Russ Carlson**

WARREN REECE
Blow Dry / 1977 / SVE / M

WARREN SCOTT *(Warren Stone)*
Anal Chiropractor / 1995 / PEP / M • Anal Interrogation / 1995 / ZA / M • Anal Party Girls / 1996 / GV / M • Anal Webb / 1995 / ZA / M • Bad Attitude #1 / 1995 / LV / M • Bad Attitude #2 / 1995 / LV / M • Behind The Mask / 1995 / XC / M • Beyond Reality #1 / 1995 / EXQ / M • Big Black & Beautiful Gang Bang / 1995 / HO / M • Black Bamboo / 1995 / IN / M • Black Gangbangers #08 / 1995 / HW / M • Crimson Thighs / 1995 / HW / M • Cum On Inn / 1995 / TEG / M • D.P. Grannies / 1995 / JMP / M • Decadence / 1995 / AMP / M • Dirty Dancers #5 / 1995 / 4P / M • Dirty Tricks #1: Just A Bunch Of Whores / 1995 / EA / M • Dream Reamin' / 1995 / LV / M • Filthy First Timers #1 / 1996 / EL / M • Filthy First Timers #3: Tearing Down The Walls

Of Shame / 1996 / EL / M • Full Metal Babes / 1995 / LE / M • Ganggstas Paradise / 1995 / AVI / M • Girly Video Magazine #4 / 1996 / BEP / M • Granny Bangers / 1995 / MET / M • The Hardwood Chronicles / 1995 / XCI / M • Here Comes Magoof #1 / 1995 / VC / M • Hollywood Amateurs #17 / 1995 / MID / M • Hollywood Amateurs #21 / 1995 / MID / M • Hollywood Amateurs #31 / 1996 / MID / M • Hot Box / 1995 / V09 / C • Interview With A Vibrator / 1996 / WAV / M • Major Fucking Whore / 1995 / BEP / M • The Meatman / 1995 / OUP / M • Mellon Man #05 / 1995 / AVI / M • Mike Hott: #317 Girls Who Swallow Cum #01 / 1995 / MHV / C • Mike Hott: #324 Bonus Cunt: Brandie Rio / 1996 / MHV / M • Mike Hott: #329 Cunt Of The Month: Tia / 1995 / MHV / M • Mike Hott: #336 Three-Sum Sluts #09 / 1995 / MHV / M • Mike Hott: #349 Girls Who Swallow Cum #03 / 1996 / MHV / C • The Naked Fugitive / 1995 / CA / M • Naked Scandal #1 / 1995 / SPI / M • Naked Scandal #2 / 1996 / SPI / M • Nasty Newcummers #09 / 1995 / MET / M • Nasty Newcummers #10 / 1995 / MET / M • Nasty Newcummers #11 / 1995 / MET / M • Nasty Newcummers #12 / 1995 / MET / M • NYDP Blue / 1996 / WP / M • Odyssey 30 Min: #538: / 1995 / OD / M • Odyssey 30 Min: #547: / 1995 / OD / M • Odyssey 30 Min: #553: / 1995 / OD / M • Penitentiary / 1995 / HW / M • Perverted Stories #01 / 1995 / JMP / M • Perverted Stories #06 / 1996 / JMP / M • Perverted Stories #09 / 1996 / JMP / M • Pizzas, Hot Tubs & Bimbos / 1995 / SUF / M • Profiles #01 / 1995 / XPR / M • Puritan Video Magazine #01 / 1996 / LE / M • Raunch Ranch / 1995 / LE / M • Red Door Diaries #1 / 1995 / ZA / M • Reminiscing / 1995 / LE / M • Ron Hightower's Casting Couch #2 / 1995 / FC / M • A Round Behind / 1995 / PEP / M • Sittin' On Da Krome / 1995 / HW / M • Small Top Bitches / 1996 / AVI / M • The Social Club / 1995 / LE / M • Stardust #4 / 1996 / VI / M • Stripping / 1995 / NIT / M • Stuff Your Ass #2 / 1995 / JMP / M • Tails Of Desire / 1995 / GO / M • Talking Trash #1 / 1995 / HW / M • Tight Fit #14 / 1995 / GO / M • The Voyeur #5 / 1995 / EA / M • Western Whores Hotel / 1996 / VG0 / M • Whackers / 1995 / PP / M • What Women Want / 1996 / SUF / M • Young And Anal #3 / 1995 / JMP / M

WARREN STONE *see* **Warren Scott**
WARRREN SCOTT
Hollywood Amateurs #26 / 1995 / MID / M
WAYNE
Black Fantasies #07 / 1995 / HW / M • Pornocchio / 1987 / ME / M
WAYNE CONDON
The Loves Of Mary Jane / 1989 / BWV / C • A Touch Of Sex / 1972 / AR / M
WAYNE CREWS
Betrayed / 1996 / WP / M • Conquest / 1996 / WP / M
WAYNE DANIELS *see* **Star Index I**
WAYNE DAVIS *see* **Star Index I**
WAYNE JOHNSON
Teenage Cowgirls / 1973 / ALP / M
WAYNE NICHOLS
Hot Pursuit / 1983 / VC / M
WAYNE REYNOLDS
Ring Of Desire / 1981 / SE / M • Stephanie's Lust Story / 1983 / VC / M

WAYNE SOMMERS *see* **Wayne Sommers**
WAYNE STEVENS *see* **Star Index I**
WAYNE STEVENS (SUMM) *see* **Wayne Summers**
WAYNE SUMMERS *(Dino Alba, Dean Alba, Dino, Wayne Stevens (Summ), Wayne Sommers, Randy Summers)*
Wayne Stevens is from **KTSX 69**. Dino Alba is from **Charmed Again**. Note this is not Beau Michaels.
1-800-TIME / 1990 / IF / M • The Absolute Worst Of Amateur #1 / 1993 / VEX / M • Adult Video News 1991 Awards / 1991 / VC / M • Amateur Nights #05 / 1990 / HO / M • Amazing Tails #4 / 1990 / CA / M • America's Dirtiest Home Videos #04 / 1991 / VEX / M • America's Dirtiest Home Videos #14 / 1992 / VEX / M • America's Raunchiest Home Videos #05: Sasha Gets Stuffed / 1992 / ZA / M • America's Raunchiest Home Videos #08: Who Was That Masked Mn / 1991 / ZA / M • America's Raunchiest Home Videos #13: Beauty And The Beach / 1992 / ZA / M • America's Raunchiest Home Videos #14: Janet's Big Lunch / 1992 / ZA / M • Anal Analysis (Heatwave) / 1992 / HW / M • Anal Encounters #2 / 1991 / VC / M • Anal Encounters #3: Back In The Dark One / 1991 / VC / M • Anal Heat / 1990 / ZA / M • Anal Nation #1 / 1990 / CC / M • Anal Nation #2 / 1990 / CC / M • The Anus Family / 1991 / CC / M • The Back Doors (Western) / 1991 / WV / M • Backdoor To Russia #1 / 1992 / VC / M • Backstage Entrance #1 / 1992 / FH / M • Backstage Entrance #2 / 1992 / FH / M • Bad Attitude / 1992 / CDI / M • Ball Busters / 1991 / FH / M • Bangin' With The Home Girls / 1991 / AFV / M • Beach Bum Amateur's #06 / 1992 / MID / M • Between The Cheeks #2 / 1990 / VC / M • Bi Dream Of Genie / 1990 / BIN / G • Bi-Bi-Baby / 1990 / CDI / G • Big Bust Babes #10 / 1992 / AFI / M • Big Titted Tarts / 1994 / PL / C • The Bimbo #1 / 1992 / AFV / M • The Bimbo #2 / 1992 / AFV / M • Black Mariah / 1991 / FC / M • Black On White / 1991 / VT / F • Blazing Boners / 1992 / MID / M • Blue Angel / 1992 / AFV / M • Blue Angel / 1992 / AFV / M • Blue Heaven / 1990 / IF / M • Boobs, Butts And Bloopers #2 / 1990 / HO / M • The Book / 1990 / IF / M • Booty And The Ho' Fish / 1996 / RAS / M • Bra Busters #03 / 1993 / LBO / M • Breakfast With Tiffany / 1990 / HO / M • Breaking And Entering / 1991 / AFV / M • Bubbles / 1991 / IF / M • Butt Seriously Folks / 1994 / AFV / M • Butt Woman #1 / 1990 / FH / M • California Taxi Girls / 1991 / AFV / M • Candy Ass / 1990 / V99 / M • Catalina: Treasure Island / 1991 / CDI / M • Caught From Behind #13 / 1990 / HO / M • Caught From Behind #15 / 1991 / HO / M • Charmed Again / 1989 / VI / M • Cheeks #3 / 1990 / CC / M • Cheeks #6 / 1992 / CC / M • The Coach's Daughter / 1991 / AR / M • Cocktails / 1990 / HO / M • The Coming Of Christy / 1990 / CAY / M • Crazed #1 / 1992 / VI / M • Crazed #2 / 1992 / VI / M • Cumming Clean / 1991 / FL / M • D-Cup Dating Service / 1991 / ME / M • Dane's Surprise / 1991 / IF / G • Deep Throat #4 / 1990 / AR / M • Deep Throat #5 / 1990 / AR / M • Dream Cream'n / 1991 / AR / M • The Dream Merchants / 1990 / CDI / M • East L.A. Law / 1991 / WV / M •

Entertainment L.A. Style / 1990 / HO / M • The Erotic Adventures Of Fanny Annie / 1991 / WV / M • The Erotic Adventures Of The Three Musketeers / 1992 / CEL / S • Exiles / 1991 / VT / M • Eyewitness Nudes / 1990 / VC / M • The Flintbones / 1992 / FR / M • Gangbang Girl #05 / 1992 / ANA / M • Genital Hospital / 1987 / SE / M • Girls Of Silicone Valley / 1991 / FC / M • Girls Of The Double D #14 / 1990 / CIN / M • Great Expectations / 1990 / V99 / M • Great Expectations / 1992 / VEX / C • Halloweenie / 1991 / PL / M • Hate To See You Go / 1990 / VC / M • Head Nurse / 1996 / RAS / M • Hidden Desire / 1989 / HO / M • Holly Does Hollywood #4 / 1990 / CAY / M • Hollywood Bikini Party Girls / 1989 / VC / M • Home But Not Alone / 1991 / WV / M • Honey, I Blew Everybody #1 / 1992 / MID / M • Hooked / 1992 / SC / M • Hot Pie Delivery / 1993 / AFV / M • Hothouse Rose #1 / 1991 / VC / M • Hump Up The Volume / 1991 / AR / M • I Remember When / 1992 / ATL / M • Images Of Desire / 1990 / PM / M • Immoral Support / 1992 / AFV / M • Immorals #3: Stroked / 1991 / SC / M • Immorals #4: Choice Cuts / 1991 / SC / M • In Your Face #2 / 1992 / PL / M • Indian Summer #1 / 1991 / VI / M • Indian Summer #2: Sandstorm / 1991 / VI / M • Insatiable Immigrants / 1989 / VT / M • The Journey: Oral Majority / 1991 / WV / M • Kimberly Kupps Gets 5 A's / 1996 / NIT / M • Kiss And Tell / 1992 / AFV / M • Lady Badass / 1990 / V99 / M • Laid In Heaven / 1991 / VC / M • Laying Down The Law #1 / 1992 / AFV / M • Laying Down The Law #2 / 1992 / AFV / M • Lethal Love / 1990 / DAY / M • Lethal Passion / 1991 / PL / M • Lickety Pink / 1990 / ME / M • Love Letters / 1991 / VI / M • Lust Fever / 1991 / FH / M • Mad Maxine / 1992 / AFV / M • Make Me Over, Baby / 1996 / LOF / M • Marked #1 / 1993 / FD / M • The Midas Touch / 1991 / VT / M • Nasty Girls #1 (1990-CDI) / 1990 / CIN / M • Nasty Girls #2 (1990-CDI) / 1990 / CDI / M • Nasty Girls #3 (1990-CDI) / 1990 / CDI / M • Nasty Jack's Homemade Vid. #01 / 1990 / CDI / M • Nasty Jack's Homemade Vid. #22 / 1991 / CDI / M • New Girls In Town #1 / 1990 / CC / M • A Night At The Waxworks / 1990 / IF / M • Night Lessons / 1990 / V99 / M • The Night Temptress / 1989 / HU / M • No Time For Love / 1991 / VI / M • Nookie Court / 1992 / AFV / M • Not So Innocent / 1989 / VEX / M • Oh, What A Night! / 1990 / VC / M • Opportunity Knocks / 1990 / HO / M • Oral Hijinx / 1990 / ERU / M • Oriental Treatment #3: The Lost Empress / 1991 / AFV / M • Oriental Treatment #4: The Demon Lover / 1992 / AFV / M • Other People's Honey / 1991 / HW / M • Out Of The Blue #1 / 1991 / VI / M • P.J. Sparxx On Fire / 1992 / MID / C • A Paler Shade Of Blue / 1991 / CC / M • Passion Princess / 1991 / VEX / M • The Pawnbroker / 1990 / IF / M • Pay 4 Play / 1996 / RAS / M • The Penetration Of Elle Rio / 1987 / GO / M • Prime Choice #8 / 1996 / RAS / M • Quickies / 1992 / AFV / M • Radioactive / 1990 / VIP / M • Rainwoman #02 / 1990 / CC / M • Ravaged Rivalry / 1990 / HO / M • Rearing Rachel / 1990 / ZA / M • The Rebel / 1990 / CIN / M • Red Hot And Ready / 1990 / V99 / M • Ride 'em Cowgirl / 1991 / V99 / M • Rock & Roll Fantasies /

1992 / FL / M • The Rookies / 1991 / VC / M • Saki's House Party / 1990 / KNI / M • Savage Fury #2 / 1989 / CAY / M • Scream In The Middle Of The Night / 1990 / CC / M • Send Me An Angel / 1990 / V99 / M • Sex Lives On Porno Tape / 1992 / VC / C • The Sexual Limits / 1992 / VC / M • Sexual Olympics #1: The Trials / 1992 / VT / M • Sexual Olympics #2: The Finals / 1992 / VT / M • Sexy Nurses #1 On And Off Duty / 1990 / CV / M • She's Got The Juice / 1990 / CDI / M • Sin City: The Movie / 1992 / SC / M • Single White Nympho / 1992 / MID / M • The Specialist / 1990 / HO / M • The Spectacle / 1991 / IN / M • Speedtrap / 1992 / VC / M • Sporting Illustrated / 1990 / HO / M • The Strip / 1992 / SC / M • Surf City Sex / 1991 / CIA / M • Suzanne's Grand Affair / 1990 / HO / M • A Tale Of Two Titties #1 / 1990 / AR / M • A Tale Of Two Titties #2 / 1992 / AFV / M • Taylor Wayne's World / 1992 / AFV / M • Teach Me Tonight / 1990 / VEX / M • Tequila Sunset / 1989 / V99 / M • Things That Go Hump in the Night / 1991 / LV / M • Three Men And A Geisha / 1990 / HO / M • Three Men And A Hooker / 1991 / WV / M • The Three Musketeers #1 / 1992 / FD / M • The Three Musketeers #2 / 1992 / FD / M • Three's A Crowd / 1990 / HO / M • Titty-Titty Bang-Bang / 1992 / FC / C • Too Sexy / 1992 / MID / M • Torch #2 / 1990 / VI / M • Torrid Tonisha / 1992 / VEX / M • Total Reball / 1990 / CC / M • Totally Tasteless Video #02 / 1994 / TTV / M • Touched / 1990 / VI / M • A Trip Down Mammary Lane / 1991 / FC / M • Twin Peaks / 1993 / PL / M • Unzipped / 1991 / WV / M • Up The Gulf / 1991 / AR / M • Valleys Of The Moon / 1991 / SC / M • Welcum To My Place / 1990 / ZA / M • Wet Faces #1 / 1997 / SC / C • Whiplash / 1996 / DFI / M • Wild Hearts / 1992 / SC / M • The Wild Wild Chest #1 / 1990 / HO / M • Will And Ed's Bogus Gang Bang / 1992 / MID / M

WAYNE THOMAS see Star Index I
WAYNE WILLIAMS
Sexorcist Devil / 1974 / CXV / M
WAYNE WINYARD
Bucky Beaver's XXX Dragon Art Theatre Double Feature #02 / 1996 / SOW / M • The Rites Of Uranus / 1975 / SOW / M
WAYNE WRIGHT
Gazonga Goddess #1 / 1993 / IF / M • Makin' It / 1994 / A&E / M • Suburban Swingers / 1993 / IF / M • Summertime Boobs / 1994 / LEI / M
WEDNESDAY
Frizzy haired dark blonde with a thin tight body and hard enhanced medium tits. Very bad skin faculty.
American Beauty #1 / 1993 / FOR / M • Beaver & Buttcheeks / 1993 / DR / M • Big & Busty Country Line Dancing / 1995 / SEM / S • Buffy Malibu's Totally Nasty All-Girl Home Videos #05 / 1993 / ANA / F • Buffy Malibu's Nasty Girls #08 / 1995 / ANA / F • The Couch Trap / 1993 / ELP / M • Escape To The Party / 1994 / ELP / M • Fabulous Flashers #1 / 1995 / DGD / F • Gangbang Girl #12 / 1993 / ANA / M • Hollywood '94: Butts Abound / 1993 / ELP / M • Love Potion 69 / 1994 / VC / M • The Man Who Loves Women / 1994 / VC / M • Nasty Nymphos #01 / 1993 / ANA / M • Nasty Nymphos #02 / 1994 / ANA / M • Nasty

Nymphos #04 / 1994 / ANA / M • The Orgy #2 / 1993 / EMC / M • Porn In The Pen / 1993 / LE / F • Raunchy Remedy / 1993 / ELP / M • Reds / 1993 / LE / F • The Reel Sex World #01 / 1993 / WP / M • Sex Machine / 1994 / VT / M • Show & Tell / 1994 / ELP / M • Sisters / 1993 / ZA / M • Sodomania #06: Gangs And Bangs And Other Thangs / 1993 / EL / M • Sodomania #07: Deep Down Inside / 1993 / EL / M • Sodomania: Slop Shots / 1996 / EL / C • Sodomania: Smokin' Sextions / 1996 / EL / C • Student Fetish Videos: Best of Catfighting #02 / 1994 / PRE / C • Student Fetish Videos: Best Of Foot Worship #02 / 1994 / PRE / C • Student Fetish Videos: Catfighting #08 / 1993 / PRE / B • Student Fetish Videos: Spanking #11 / 1993 / PRE / B • Toppers #17 / 1993 / TV / M • Toppers #18 / 1993 / TV / M • Toppers #22 / 1993 / TV / C • Toppers #24 / 1994 / TV / M • Toppers #31 / 1994 / TV / C

WEDNESDAY (1994)
Bubble Butts Gold #2 / 1994 / LBO / M • Bun Busters #18 / 1994 / LBO / M • High Heeled & Horny #3 / 1995 / LBO / M • Northwest Pecker Trek #1 / 1994 / LBO / M • Northwest Pecker Trek #2: Evergreen, Ever Horny / 1994 / LBO / M • Pussy Fest Of The Northwest #3 / 1995 / NIT / M • Teacher's Pet #1 / 1994 / WMG / M
WELFE
Forbidden Subjects #1 / 1994 / FC / M
WELLS PHARGOE
Bra Busters #05 / 1993 / LBO / M • Bubble Butts #14 / 1992 / LBO / M • High Heel Harlots #01 / 1993 / SFP / M • Hollywood Swingers #01 / 1992 / LBO / M
WENDELL
Neighborhood Watch #17: Burning The Sausage / 1992 / LBO / M
WENDI (H.LERE) see Heather Lere
WENDI WESTBROOK
Under Lock And Key / 1994 / IMP / S
WENDY
Afternoon Delights / 1995 / FC / M • Blue Vanities #500 / 1992 / FFL / M • Blue Vanities #515 / 1992 / FFL / M • Bondage Audition / 1995 / GAL / B • British Butt Search / 1995 / VC / M • The Girls Of Fantasex #1 / 1996 / NIT / M • House Of Sex #06: Banging Wendy, Kitty, Corby and Connie / 1994 / RTP / M • House Of Sex #08: Banging Wendy / 1994 / RTP / M • J.E.G.: Wendy Worth Watching / 1995 / JEG / M • Jack Strap / 1995 / RTP / M • Kinky Ladies Of London / 1995 / VC / M • Mr. Peepers Nastiest #4 / 1995 / LBO / C • Private Video Magazine #07 / 1994 / OD / M • Private Video Magazine #08 / 1994 / OD / M • Reel Life Video #30: Welcome To The Bi World! / 1996 / RLF / F • Secret Desires / 1994 / ORE / C • Stevi's: Wendy's Garterbelt Tease / 1994 / SSV / F
WENDY (H.LERE) see Heather Lere
WENDY (LEANNA FOXXX) see Leanna Foxxx
WENDY BROWN
Motel Sex #1 / 1995 / FAP / M
WENDY C. IWANOW see Bianca Trump
WENDY DU NEAR
Shades Of Blue #1 / 1982 / ASV / M
WENDY FOSTER see Star Index I
WENDY HART see Star Index I
WENDY LIONS see Anthony Spinelli
WENDY LUTON

Blue Vanities #517 / 1992 / FFL / M
WENDY O. WILLIAMS
800 Fantasy Lane / 1979 / GO / M • Candy Goes To Hollywood / 1979 / VCX / M • Forbidden Worlds / 1988 / GO / C • Pucker Up And Bark Like A Dog / 1987 / FHV / S • Reform School Girls / 1986 / NWW / S
WENDY PETERS see Star Index I
WENDY PIMKNEE
Sex Boat / 1980 / VCX / M
WENDY PIPPIN
Horny Henry's Peeping Adventures / 1994 / TTV / M
WENDY SANDERS see Star Index I
WENDY STUART
Model Behavior / 1983 / LIV / S • Never Sleep Alone / 1984 / CA / M
WENDY SUE
Snatch Masters #12 / 1995 / LEI / M
WENDY SWEENEY
Blue Vanities #577 / 1995 / FFL / M
WENDY SWEENY
Blue Vanities #165 (New) / 1996 / FFL / M
WENDY TALBERT
Blue Vanities #125 / 1990 / FFL / M • Blue Vanities #559 / 1994 / FFL / M
WENDY WALKER see Star Index I
WENDY WATERS
More Dirty Debutantes #03 / 1990 / 4P / M • Taboo #08 / 1990 / IN / M
WENDY WHOPPERS
Small girl with enormous ugly inflated tits. Allegedly, pre-breast-enhacement she weighed 93lbs and after, 107lbs.
Best Of Wendy Whoppers / 1995 / LEI / C • Big Boob Ball / 1995 / IF / C • Big Boob Bikini Bash / 1995 / BTO / M • Big Bust Babes #11 / 1992 / AFI / M • Big Busty Whoppers / 1994 / PME / F • Bigger Than Life / 1995 / IF / M • The Bottom Dweller / 1993 / EL / M • The Breast Of Breastmen / 1995 / EVN / C • Breastman Goes To Breastland #1 / 1993 / EVN / M • Busty Angels / 1996 / IF / C • Busty Babes / 1995 / NAP / F • Dick & Jane Do The Strip / 1994 / AVI / M • Double Load #1 / 1993 / HW / M • Double Load #2 / 1994 / HW / M • Eleventh Annual AVN Awards / 1994 / VC / M • Frat Girls Of Double D / 1993 / PP / M • Freaks Of Leather #1 / 1993 / IF / M • Hometown Honeys #5 / 1993 / VEX / M • Humongous Hooters / 1995 / PME / F • Hump Wendy Whoppers / 199? / H&S / M • Jiggly Queens #1 / 1993 / LE / M • Jugs Of Joy / 1994 / LEI / C • Kelly Eighteen #2 / 1993 / LE / M • Lollipop Lickers / 1996 / V99 / C • More Than A Handful #2 / 1993 / MET / M • Much More Than A Mouthful #3 / 1993 / VEX / M • Palm Springs Or Bust / 1994 / BTO / M • Score Busty Covergirls #6 / 1995 / BTO / S • Sodomania: The Baddest Of The Best...And Then Some / 1994 / EL / C • Tit To Tit #3 / 1995 / BTO / M • Titillator / 1994 / HW / C • Top Heavy / 1993 / IF / M • Toppers #03 / 1993 / TV / M • Toppers #04 / 1993 / TV / M • Toppers #08 / 1993 / TV / M • Toppers #11 / 1993 / TV / C • Toppers #12 / 1993 / TV / C • Toppers #30 / 1994 / TV / C • Toppers & Whoppers #1 / 1994 / PRE / C • Wendy Whoppers: Bomb Squad / 1993 / PEP / M • Wendy Whoppers: Brain Surgeon / 1993 / PEP / M • Wendy Whoppers: Environmental Attorney / 1993 / PEP / M • Wendy Whoppers: Ninja CPA / 1993 / PEP / M • Wendy Whoppers: Park Ranger / 1993 / PEP / M • Wendy

Whoppers: Prison Love Doll / 1994 / PEP / M • Wendy Whoppers: Psychic Healer / 1994 / PEP / M • Wendy Whoppers: Razorwoman / 1993 / PEP / M • Wendy Whoppers: Ufo Tracker / 1994 / PEP / M • Wendy's Bi Adventure / 1994 / STA / M • Whoppers #3 / 1993 / VEX / F • Whoppers #6 / 1993 / VEX / F

WENDY WILLIS
Something For Everybody / 1975 / ... / M

WENDY WILSON
Down Mammary Lane #4 / 1989 / BTO / F • Pregnant Mamas / 1984 / CPL / M

WENDY WONG see Star Index I

WENDY WOOD see Star Index I

WENDY WOOLY
The Cumm Brothers #16: Deja Goo / 1996 / OD / M

WES
Black Casting Couch #2 / 1994 / WP / M • Slut Safari #2 / 1994 / FC / M

WES ARMOUR see Star Index I

WES BROWN see Anthony Spinelli

WES CRAVEN see Star Index I

WES DANIELS
Beyond It All / 1991 / PAL / G • The Bi-Linguist / 1993 / BIL / G • Bimbo Boys / 1995 / PL / C • Steel Garters / 1992 / CAT / G

WES HAILEY see Star Index I

WES HEALY
Black Gangbangers #01 / 1994 / HW / M • Dirty Dating Service #05 / 1994 / WP / M

WES OWENS
Bump 'n' Grind / 1994 / HW / M • Rump-Shaker #3 / 1994 / HW / M

WESLEY ARTUR
The Vixens Of Kung Fu: A Tale Of Yin Yang / 1975 / VC / M

WESLEY EMERSON
Around The World In 80 Ways / 1968 / ... / S • Sex #1 (Vca) / 1994 / VC / M • Striptease / 1983 / VC / M

WESLEY T. BROWN
All That: Black Women's Fantasies / 1996 / VT / M

WESS
Ron Hightower's White Chicks #05 / 1993 / LBO / M • Ron Hightower's White Chicks #07 / 1993 / LBO / M

WESSEL PETERMAN see Star Index I

WEST REGENT
Bucky Beaver's XXX Dragon Art Theatre Double Feature #02 / 1996 / SOW / M • The Rites Of Uranus / 1975 / SOW / M

WESTIN CHASE
Anal Party Girls / 1996 / GV / M • Catch Of The Day #4 / 1996 / VG0 / M • Dirty Dancers #6 / 1995 / 4P / M • Girly Video Magazine #4 / 1996 / BEP / M • Lust & Desire / 1996 / WV / M • Mike Hott: #340 Cunt Of The Month: Westin Chase / 1996 / MHV / M • Mike Hott: #348 Lesbian Sluts #23 / 1996 / MHV / F • Mike Hott: #349 Girls Who Swallow Cum #03 / 1996 / MHV / C

WHISTLER'S GRANDMA see Star Index I

WHITLEY BANKS see Destini Lane

WHITNEY
Big Murray's New-Cummers #29: Tools Of The Trade / 1995 / FD / M

WHITNEY (DEST. LANE) see Destini Lane

WHITNEY ADAMS
Black Clits And White Dicks / cr86 / JAN / M • Journey Into Bondage / 1989 / BIZ / B • Sugar Tongues / 1992 / STM / C • Vanilla

& Fudge / 1988 / JAN / M • [The Gang's All Here / cr85 / STM / M

WHITNEY BANKS see Destini Lane

WHITNEY COLE
Doctor Feelgood / 1988 / CDI / M

WHITNEY PRESCOTT see Joi Reno

WHITNEY PRICE see Beverly Glen

WHITNEY PRINCE see Beverly Glen

WHITNEY ROGUE
N.Y. Video Magazine #07 / 1996 / OUP / M

WHITNEY VALENTINE
Bad Mama Jama And The Fat Ladies Of The Evening / 1989 / VT / M • Bad Mama Jama Busts Out / 1989 / VT / M • Fatliners #2 / 1991 / EX / M • Innocent Obsession / 1989 / FC / M • Life In The Fat Lane #1 / 1990 / FC / M • Life In The Fat Lane #2 / 1990 / FC / M • Ready To Drop #01 / 1990 / FC / M • Titty-Titty Bang-Bang / 1992 / FC / C

WHITNEY WONDERS
Yet another large inflated titted brunette. Born May 22, 1973 in Los Angeles CA and de-virginized at 13. Performs as a dancer.
Anal Aristocrat / 1995 / KWP / M • Babes Illustrated #4 / 1995 / IN / F • Big Knockers #09 / 1995 / TV / M • Big Knockers #13 / 1995 / TV / M • Big Knockers #20 / 1995 / TV / C • Big Knockers #21: Best Of Lesbian #2 / 1995 / TV / C • Black Bamboo / 1995 / IN / M • Boobtown / 1995 / VC / M • Breastman's Wild West Adventure / 1995 / EVN / M • The Busty Kittens / 1995 / NAP / F • Butthead Dreams: Down In The Bush / 1995 / FH / M • Concrete Heat / 1996 / XCI / M • Depraved Fantasies #4 / 1995 / FPI / M • Double D Dykes #16 / 1995 / GO / F • Double D Dykes #20 / 1995 / GO / F • Down & Dirty / 1995 / NAP / B • Flexxx #3 / 1995 / VT / M • Gang Bang Bitches #08 / 1995 / PP / M • Gazongo / 1995 / PEP / M • A Girl's Affair #08 / 1995 / FD / F • Girls Of Sorority Row / 1994 / VT / M • High Heeled & Horny #2 / 1995 / LBO / M • House Of Hoochies / 1996 / DDP / M • Housewife Lust #1 / 1995 / TV / F • How To Make A Model #05: Back To Innocence / 1994 / LBO / M • Lusty Lap Dancers #1 / 1994 / HO / M • Lusty Lap Dancers #2 / 1994 / HO / M • Mellon Man #03 / 1994 / AVI / M • Mellon Man #06 / 1995 / AVI / M • More Than A Handful #6: Life Under The Big Top / 1994 / MET / M • New Pussy Hunt #25 / 1996 / LEI / C • The New Snatch Masters #16 / 1995 / LEI / C • Nightmare On Lesbian Street / 1995 / LIP / F • The Panty Parlor / 1996 / VIM / M • Plumb And Dumber / 1995 / PP / M • Pussy Hunt #13 / 1995 / LEI / M • Pussyman Auditions #05 / 1995 / SNA / M • Reel People #08 / 1995 / PP / M • Shave Tails #2 / 1994 / SO / M • A Shot In The Pants / 1995 / HO / M • Sluthunt #2 / 1995 / BIP / F • Southern: Whitney / 1995 / SSH / F • Spinners #1 (Wicked) / 1995 / WP / M • Stupid And Stupider / 1995 / SO / M • Thunder Boobs / 1995 / BTO / M • Tit Tease #1 / 1995 / VT / M • Titty Town #2 / 1995 / HW / M • Trump Your Ass / 1996 / NAP / B • The Wanderer #1: Road Tails / 1995 / CDI / M • Water Worked / 1995 / AB / F • Wet 'n' Wicked / 1995 / BEP / F • A Woman Scorned / 1995 / CA / M

WILBUR
FTV #10: Cast Iron Bitch #2 / 1996 / FT / B • FTV #12: Two Against A Wimp / 1996 / FT / B • FTV #15: Mixed Boxing Punch Out /

1996 / FT / B • FTV #17: Double Trouble / 1996 / FT / B

WILD BILL
The Best Of East Coast Sluts / 1995 / PL / C • Big Butts Of The Wild West / 1993 / BTO / M • Big Tits And Fat Fannies #01 / 1989 / BTO / M • Body Shop / 1984 / VCX / M • Double D Harem / 1988 / L&W / M • East Coast Sluts #01: New Jersey / 1995 / PL / M • Fat & Hungry 200 Plus / 1991 / BTO / M • Interstate 95 Amateurs #1 / 1995 / RHV / M • Nasty Newcummers #12 / 1995 / MET / M • Private Diaries #1: Christina / 1995 / AVI / M • Real Sex Magazine #01 / 1996 / HO / M • Rusty Boner's Late Night Videos #1 / 1995 / RHV / M

WILD HORSE
She Male Goddesses / 1994 / MET / G

WILD ORCHID
Black Magic #1 / 1993 / VIM / M

WILD OSCAR (Wilde Oscar, Chris Oscar, Eron, Chris Sterling, Oscar Wilde)
Small older balding guy who seems to be the husband/lover of Nici Sterling.
The Adventures Of Peeping Tom #1 / 1996 / OD / M • American Fan Club Prowl / 1996 / VT / M • Anal Therapy #4 / 1996 / FD / M • Backdoor Club #1 / 1996 / VEX / C • Best Butt(e) In The West #2 / 1995 / CC / M • Beyond Reality #1 / 1995 / EXQ / M • Blue Dreams / 1996 / SC / M • Bushwoman: She Takes Two / 1996 / RAS / M • Butt Bandits #4 / 1996 / VD / C • The Butt Sisters Do The Twin Cities / 1996 / MID / M • Buttman's Bouncin' British Babes / 1994 / EA / M • Caught From Behind #22 / 1995 / HO / M • Gangbang Girl #15 / 1995 / ANA / M • Gangbang Girl #17 / 1995 / ANA / M • Golden Rod / 1996 / SPI / M • Hornet's Nest / 1996 / ONA / M • The Hungry Heart / 1996 / AOP / M • Love Exchange / 1995 / DR / M • Malibu Madam / 1995 / CC / M • My Surrender / 1996 / A&E / M • Nici Sterling's DP Gang Bang / 1996 / FC / M • One Night In The Valley / 1996 / CA / M • Philmore Butts Las Vegas Vacation / 1995 / SUF / M • Pick Up Lines #02 / 1995 / 4P / M • Pick Up Lines #04 / 1995 / 4P / M • Pick Up Lines #05 / 1996 / OD / M • Pick Up Lines #06 / 1996 / OD / M • Pick Up Lines #07 / 1996 / OD / M • Prime Choice #2 / 1995 / RAS / M • Private Video Magazine #16 / 1994 / OD / M • Puritan Video Magazine #02 / 1996 / LE / M • Pussyman Auditions #03 / 1995 / SNA / M • Rainwoman #09: Wetlands / 1995 / CC / M • Rainwoman #10: The Tenth Anniversary Edition / 1996 / CC / M • Raw Silk / 1996 / RAS / M • Royal Ass Force / 1996 / VC / M • Sinboy #3: The Island Of Dr. Moron / 1996 / SC / M • Sleeping Booty / 1995 / EL / M • Smells Like...Sex / 1995 / VC / M • Snake Pit / 1996 / DWO / M • Sodomania #15: Warning! / 1996 / EL / M • Sodomania: Slop Shots / 1996 / EL / C • Up Close & Personal #2 / 1996 / IPI / M • Valentina: Princess Of The Forest / 1996 / SC / M • Venom #4 / 1996 / VD / M • Venom #5 / 1996 / VD / M • Video Virgins #21 / 1995 / NS / M • Vivid Raw #3: Double Header / 1996 / VI / M • Wet Faces #1 / 1997 / SC / C

WILD PANTERA (Inga Pantera)
Goddess Of Love / 1986 / CDI / M • The Lust Detector / 1986 / PIN / M

WILD ROSE

Sex On The Run #2 / 1994 / TTV / M
WILDE OSCAR *see* **Wild Oscar**
WILDFLOWER *see* **Star Index I**
WILDSYDE MIKE
Dirty Dancers #3 / 1995 / 4P / M
WILEY PIZZA BOY
DOM And DOMer / 1995 / IBN / B
WILFRED HYDE GOON *see* **Star Index I**
WILL
Ona Zee's Date With Dallas / 1992 / ONA /
M • Reel Life Video #49: / 1996 / RLF / F
WILL BOGAS *see* **Will Ravage**
WILL CLARK
Night Walk / 1995 / HIV / G
WILL DIVIDE
Bikini Beach #1 / 1993 / CC / M • Bikini
Beach #4 / 1996 / CC / M • Bikini City /
1991 / CC / M • Pussyman #01: The
Search / 1993 / CC / M • Pussyman #02:
The Prize / 1993 / CC / M • Pussyman #03:
The Search Continues / 1993 / SNA / M •
Pussyman #04: The Celebration / 1993 /
SNA / M • Pussyman #05: Captive Audi-
ence / 1994 / SNA / M • Pussyman #06:
House Of Games / 1994 / SNA / M • Pussy-
man #07: On The Dark Side / 1994 / SNA /
M • Pussyman #08: The Squirt Queens /
1994 / SNA / M • Pussyman #09: Feeding
Frenzy / 1995 / SNA / M • Pussyman #10:
Butts, Butts & More Butts / 1995 / SNA / M
• Pussyman #12: Sticky Fingers / 1995 /
SNA / M • Rainwoman #10: The Tenth An-
niversary Edition / 1996 / CC / M
WILL GETZ
Party Club / 1996 / C69 / M • The Sex Ther-
apist / 1995 / GO / M
WILL JARVIS *(Taliesin, Adam Oren Ladd)*
AHV #01: Three Way Wonders / 1991 /
EVN / M • Amateur Dreams #3 / 1994 / DR
/ M • Angela In Wonderland / 1986 / VD / M
• Bi Bi American Style / cr85 / MET / G •
Candy Stripers #2 / 1985 / AR / M • Colos-
sal Orgy #1 / 1993 / HW / M • Colossal
Orgy #3 / 1994 / HW / M • Every Nerd Has
A Fantasy / 1996 / FC / M • Exstasy / 1995
/ WV / M • The Fabulous 50's Girls Ride
Again / 1994 / EMC / M • Huge Grant On
The Sunset Strip / 1995 / EVN / M • Midget
On Milligan's Island / 1995 / FC / M • Mr.
Peepers Amateur Home Videos #03: Satin
'n' Face / 1991 / LBO / M • Naked Scandal
#1 / 1995 / SPI / M • Naked Scandal #2 /
1996 / SPI / M • Nasty Fuckin' Movies #09:
Saki's Six Man Sexation #1 / 1992 / RUM /
M • Nina Hartley's Professional Amateur
Tournament #2 / 1990 / BKD / M • Odyssey
30 Min: #102: / 1991 / OD / F • Odyssey 30
Min: #230: / 1992 / OD / M • Odyssey 30
Min: #242: / 1992 / OD / M • Odyssey Triple
Play #62: Gang Bangs All Around / 1994 /
OD / M • Orgy Camera #1 / 1995 / EVN / M
• Our Bang #01 / 1992 / GLI / M • Our Bang
#02 / 1992 / GLI / M • Our Bang #03 / 1992
/ GLI / M • Our Bang #04 / 1992 / GLI / M •
Our Bang #07 / 1992 / GLI / M • Our Naked
Eyes / 1988 / TME / M • Over 50 / 1994 /
GLI / M • Positively Pagan #01 / 1991 / ATA
/ M • Positively Pagan #02 / 1991 / ATA / M
• Positively Pagan #03 / 1991 / ATA / M •
Positively Pagan #04 / 1991 / ATA / M •
Positively Pagan #05 / 1993 / ATA / M •
Positively Pagan #07 / 1993 / ATA / M •
Positively Pagan #08 / 1993 / ATA / M •
Positively Pagan #11 / 1993 / ATA / M •
Positively Pagan #12 / 1993 / ATA / M •
Raw Talent #2 / 1987 / VC / M • Raw Tal-

ent: Bang 'er 07 Times / 1992 / RTP / M •
Raw Talent: Bang 'er 14 Times / 1992 /
RTP / M • Raw Talent: Bang 'er 26 Times /
1992 / RTP / M • Raw Talent: Bang 'er 34
Times / 1992 / RTP / M • Return To Alpha
Blue / 1984 / AVC / M • Roly Poly Gang
Bang / 1995 / HW / M • Stuff Your Ass #2 /
1995 / JMP / M • Supergirls Do General
Hospital / 1984 / VC / M • A Tasty Kind Of
Love / 1987 / LV / M • Taylor Made / 1989 /
DR / M • There's Magic In The Air / 1987 /
AR / M • Undercover Carol / 1990 / FAN /
M • Valentino's Euro-Invasion / 1997 / SC /
M • Video Tramp #2 / 1988 / TME / M • Viva
Vanessa The Undresser / 1984 / VC / M •
Wild Orgies #19 / 1995 / AFI / M
WILL LONG
Frank Henenlotter's XXX Hardcore Hor-
rors: Mad Love... / 1996 / SOW / M • The
Mad Love Of The Red Hot Vampire / 1971
/ SOW / M
WILL RAVAGE *(Will Bogas)*
Brother of Guy DeSilva and part of the Bogas
Brothers. The other one is Alex San Paolo.
Aged To Perfection #3 / 1995 / TTV / M •
Amateur Nights #11 / 1996 / HO / M • Am-
ateur Nights #12 / 1996 / HO / M • Amateur
Nights #13 / 1996 / HO / M • Anal Asian
Fantasies / 1996 / HO / M • Asian Boom
Boom Girls / 1997 / HO / M • Big Boob
Bangeroo #1 / 1995 / TTV / M • Big Boob
Bangeroo #2 / 1995 / TTV / M • Big Boob
Bangeroo #3 / 1996 / TTV / M • Big Boob
Bangeroo #4 / 1995 / TTV / M • Big Boob
Bangeroo #5 / 1996 / TTV / M • Big Boob
Bangeroo #6 / 1996 / TTV / M • Big Boob
Bangeroo #7 / 1996 / TTV / M • Big Boob
Bangeroo #8 / 1996 / TTV / M • Butt
Bangers Ball #1 / 1996 / TTV / M • Butt
Bangers Ball #2 / 1996 / TTV / M • Cute
Cuddly Bubbly Butts / 1996 / TTV / M •
Cutie Pies / 1995 / TTV / M • Dirty & Kinky
Mature Women #07 / 1996 / C69 / M • Dirty
& Kinky Mature Women #09 / 1996 / C69 /
M • Golden Oldies #1 / 1995 / TTV / M •
Golden Oldies #2 / 1995 / TTV / M • Golden
Oldies #3 / 1995 / TTV / M • Golden Oldies
#4 / 1996 / TTV / M • Golden Oldies #5 /
1996 / TTV / M • Golden Oldies #6 / 1996 /
TTV / M • Hershe Highway #5: Backdoor
Blues / 1996 / HO / M • Hooters In The
'hood / 1995 / TTV / M • Lactamania #2:
The Squirt Fest / 1995 / TTV / M • Las
Vegas Big Boob Hospitality Sweet / 1997 /
HO / M • Latin Fever #1 / 1996 / C69 / M •
Latin Fever #2 / 1996 / C69 / M • Latin
Plump Humpers #1 / 1995 / TTV / M • Latin
Plump Humpers #2 / 1995 / TTV / M • Latin
Plump Humpers #3 / 1995 / TTV / M • Lil'
Latin Cutie Pies / 1996 / CDI / M • Love
Chunks / 1996 / TTV / M • More To Love #2
/ 1995 / TTV / M • Muffmania / 1995 / TTV
/ M • Q Balls #1 / 1996 / TTV / M • Q Balls
#2 / 1996 / TTV / M • Ready To Drop #09 /
1995 / FC / M • Ready To Drop #10 / 1996
/ FC / M • Ready To Drop #12 / 1996 / FC
/ M • Rollie Pollie Chicks / 1996 / TTV / M •
Salsa & Spice #1 / 1995 / TTV / M • Salsa
& Spice #2: Latin Lust / 1996 / TTV / M •
Salsa & Spice #3 / 1996 / TTV / M • Salsa
& Spice #4 / 1996 / TTV / M • Salsa &
Spice #5 / 1997 / TTV / M • Sexual Ha-
rassment / 1996 / TTV / M • Sweet Black
Cherries #2 / 1996 / TTV / M • Sweet Black
Cherries #3 / 1996 / TTV / M • Sweet Black
Cherries #4 / 1996 / TTV / M • Sweet Black

Cherries #5 / 1996 / TTV / M • Sweet Black
Cherries #6 / 1996 / TTV / M • Take All
Cummers / 1996 / HO / M
WILL SEAGERS
Bi-Surprise / 1988 / MET / G • L.A. Tool &
Die / 1979 / TMX / G
WILL STOKES *see* **Star Index I**
WILL THOMAS
Dixie Ray Hollywood Star / 1983 / CA / M
WILLI WONDERFUL
Canadian Beaver Hunt #3 / 1996 / PL / M
WILLIAM BARNES *see* **Star Index I**
WILLIAM BASIL
The Stewardesses / 1969 / SOW / S • The
Stewardesses / 1981 / CA / M
WILLIAM BOOTH
Chickie / 1975 / CA / M
WILLIAM CONSTANTINO
Campus Girl / 1972 / VXP / M
WILLIAM DREW *see* **Star Index I**
WILLIAM HATFIELD *see* **Star Index I**
WILLIAM HILL
Tale Of Bearded Clam / cr71 / PYR / M
WILLIAM HOWELL *see* **Star Index I**
WILLIAM HUNT *see* **Star Index I**
WILLIAM KERWIN *see* **Thomas Wood**
WILLIAM LEE *see* **Star Index I**
WILLIAM LOVE *see* **Star Index I**
WILLIAM LOWEN *see* **Star Index I**
WILLIAM LUX
Bedtime Video #03 / 1984 / GO / M
WILLIAM MARGOLD *(Bill Margold,
Regina Jax, Moms Margold)*
Sleazy but articulate raincoater who as well as
being an actor was the SO of Drea and then
Viper. Used to run Reb's Pretty Girl agency.
The Angel In Mr. Holmes / 1988 / WV / C •
The Anus Family / 1991 / CC / M • Any
Time, Any Place / 1981 / CA0 / M • Audi-
tions / 1978 / MEA / S • Back In The Pen /
1992 / FH / M • Backdoor To Paradise /
1990 / ELV / M • Balling Instinct / 1992 / FH
/ M • Black Men Can Hump / 1992 / FH / M
• Bloopers #2 / 1991 / GO / C • Blue Ice /
1985 / CA / M • Blue Moon / 1992 / AFV /
M • Blue Views / 1990 / CDI / M • Bodies In
Heat #1 / 1983 / CA / M • Bondage Classix
#13: Class Of 86 #2 / 1991 / BON / B •
Born To Be Wild / 1987 / SE / M • Born To
Burn / 1987 / HOT / M • Broadcast Nudes /
1988 / EVN / M • Bucky Beaver's XXX
Dragon Art Theatre Double Feature #01 /
1996 / SOW / M • Butt Watch #01 / 1993 /
FH / M • Butt Watch #03 / 1994 / FH / M •
Butt Watch #06 / 1994 / FH / M • Butt's
Motel #3 / 1989 / EX / M • Carnal Encoun-
ters Of The Barest Kind / 1978 / VOY / C •
Casanova #2 / 1976 / CA / M • The Cat
Club / 1987 / SE / M • Chastity And The
Starlets / 1986 / RAV / M • Chicks In Black
Leather / 1989 / VC / C • The Chocolate
Fudge Factory / 1987 / PIN / M • Classic
Seka #1 / 1988 / AR / C • Classic Seka #2
/ 1988 / SUV / C • Corporate Assets / 1985
/ SE / M • The Crackster / 1996 / OUP / M
• Cunning Coeds / 1985 / IVP / M • Debbie
Does The Devil In Dallas / 1987 / SE / M •
Desire / 1983 / VCX / M • Desire Kills /
1996 / SUM / M • Detroit Dames / 1988 /
DR / C • Deviled X / 1987 / 4P / M • Dial F
For Fantasy / 1984 / PL / M • Dirty Bob's
#17: Tampa Teasers! / 1994 / FLP / S • Di-
vorce Court Expose #1 / 1986 / VD / M • Di-
vorce Court Expose #2 / 1987 / VD / M •
Don't Get Them Wet / 1987 / VD / M • Don't
Tell Daddy #1 / 1985 / PL / C • Double

Standards / 1986 / VC / M • Dr Strange Sex / 1985 / CA / M • Endless Lust / 1983 / VC / M • The Erotic Adventures Of Peter Galore / 1973 / ALP / M • Erotic Aerobics / 1984 / VC / M • Erotic Radio WSEX / 1983 / VC / M • Eternal Bliss / 1990 / AFV / M • The Eyes Of Eddie Mars / 1984 / CV / M • Fantasm / 1976 / VS / S • Fantasy Follies #1 / 1983 / VC / M • Fantasy Follies #2 / 1983 / VC / M • Feels Like Silk / 1983 / SE / M • First Annual XRCO Awards / 1984 / AVC / C • Flesh & Laces #1 / 1983 / CA / M • Foot Lights / 1988 / BIZ / B • Football Widow / 1979 / SCO / M • Fox Fever's Catfight Action / 1984 / VCR / B • Foxxxy Lady / 1992 / HW / M • Free And Foxy / 1986 / VCX / C • French Erotica: Inside Hollywood / 1980 / AR / M • French Erotica: Love Story / 1980 / AR / M • French Erotica: Report Card / 1980 / AR / M • From Japan With Love / 1990 / SLV / M • Future Sodom / 1988 / VD / M • The Girl From S.E.X. / 1982 / CA / M • The Good Time Girls / 1985 / VEX / M • Good To The Last Drop / 1986 / VCS / C • GVC: Reincarnation Of Serena #121 / 1983 / GO / M • High School Honeys / 1974 / SOW / M • High School Report Card / 1979 / CA / M • Hot Skin In 3D / 1977 / ... / M • Hush...My Mother Might Hear Us / 1993 / FL / M • Hyapatia Lee's Arcade Series #02 / 1988 / ZA / C • Immorals #1: Broken Hearts / 1989 / AR / M • Immorals #2: The Good, The Bad, And The Banged / 1990 / AR / M • Immorals #3: Stroked / 1991 / SC / M • Immorals #4: Choice Cuts / 1991 / SC / M • Inner Blues / 1987 / VD / M • Intimate Lessons / 1982 / VC / M • Jack Hammer / 1987 / ZA / M • A Lacy Affair #1 / 1983 / HO / F • Las Vegas Girls / 1983 / HIF / M • Leather & Lace / 1987 / SE / C • Leave It To Cleavage #1 / 1988 / GO / M • Let's Talk Dirty / 1987 / SE / M • Little American Maid / 1987 / VCX / M • Little Girls Lost / 1982 / VC / M • Love Goddesses / 1981 / VC / M • Love Story / 1979 / SCO / M • Lust At First Bite / 1978 / VC / M • Lust Flight 2000 / 1978 / VHL / M • Lust Inferno / 1982 / CA / M • Main Course / 1992 / FL / M • Marathon / 1982 / CA / M • Marilyn And The Senator / 1974 / HIF / M • The Master And Mrs. Johnson / 1980 / SAT / M • Max Bedroom / 1987 / ZA / M • Maxine / 1987 / EXF / M • Megasex / 1988 / EVN / M • The Midnight Zone / 1986 / IN / M • Mocha Magic / 1992 / FH / M • Mystery Of The Golden Lotus / 1989 / HU / M • Night Flight / cr80 / CRE / M • Nympho Zombie Coeds / 1993 / VIM / M • Olympic Fever / 1979 / AR / M • One Page Of Love / 1980 / VCX / M • Only The Best Of Men's And Women's Fantasies / 1988 / CV / C • Only The Best Of Oral / 1989 / CV / C • Oriental Sorority Secrets / 1992 / VIM / M • Oriental Treatment #2: The Pearl Divers / 1989 / AR / M • The Other Side Of Lianna / 1984 / LA / M • Panorama Blue / 1974 / ALP / S • Passionate Lee / 1984 / CRE / M • Paul, Lisa And Caroline / 1976 / SE / M • Pink Champagne / 1979 / CV / M • Plato's, The Movie / 1980 / SE / M • Pleasure Dome / 1982 / SE / M • A Pool Party At Seymores #1 / 1995 / ULI / M • A Pool Party At Seymores #2 / 1995 / ULI / M • Positively Pagan #04 / 1991 / ATA / M • The Psychiatrist / 1978 / VC / M • Pubic Eye / 1992 / HW / M • Pudsucker / 1994 / MID /

M • Ring Of Desire / 1981 / SE / M • Satania / 1986 / DR / M • School Dayze / 1987 / BON / B • Sexcalibur / 1982 / SE / M • Seymore Butts Rides Again / 1992 / FH / M • Shane's World #2 / 1996 / OD / M • Sheer Delight / 1984 / VC / M • Showdown / 1985 / BON / B • Sleaze Please!—August Edition / 1994 / FH / M • Sleaze Please!—September Edition / 1994 / FH / M • Sleaze Please!—October Edition / 1994 / FH / M • Sleaze Please!—November Edition / 1994 / FH / M • Sleaze Please!—December Edition / 1994 / FH / M • Sneek Peeks #1 / 1993 / FL / M • Sneek Peeks #2 / 1993 / OCV / M • Soap Me Up! / 1993 / FD / M • Spoiled Rich / 1989 / CC / M • Star Struck / 1991 / AFV / M • Stephanie's Lust Story / 1983 / VC / M • Stiff Competition #2 / 1994 / CA / M • Super-Ware Party / 1979 / AR / M • Sweet Alice / 1983 / VCX / M • Sweet Surrender / 1985 / AVC / M • A Taste Of Viper / 1990 / PIN / C • The Tasting / 1991 / EX / M • Teenage Cruisers / 1977 / VCX / M • Three Men And A Lady / 1988 / EVN / M • Tickled! / 1989 / BIZ / C • Tight Fit / 1991 / VEX / C • Tinsel Town / 1980 / VC / M • Too Much Too Soon / 1983 / VCX / M • Too Young To Know / 1984 / CC / M • Toying Around / 1992 / FL / M • The Ultimate Fantasy / 1995 / CV / M • Voodoo Lust: The Possession / 1989 / PCP / M • Wacked Waitresses / 1986 / CS / B • Weekend Fantasy / 1980 / VCX / M • Wendy Is Watching / 1993 / ELP / M • What Would Your Mother Say? / 1981 / HAV / M • When Love Came To Town / 1989 / EVN / M • Winter Heat / 1994 / MID / M • The Wright Stuff / 1991 / AFV / M • The Young Like It Hot / 1983 / CA / M • [The Raw Report / 1978 / ... / M

WILLIAM MORGAN
One Last Score / 1978 / CDI / M
WILLIAM MORINI see Russ Carlson
WILLIAM OSBORNE
ABA: Double Feature #2 / 1996 / ALP / M • Fannie / 1975 / ALP / M
WILLIAM ROTSLER *(Shannon Carse)*
The Agony Of Love / 1965 / SOW / S • The Girl With The Hungry Eyes / 1967 / SOW / S • Mantis In Lace / 1968 / BPI / S • The Notorious Daughter Of Fanny Hill / 1966 / SOW / S • The Secret Sex Lives Of Romeo And Juliet / 1968 / PS / S
WILLIAM SCHRAFFT
Boiling Point / 1978 / SE / M
WILLIAM SHELL
All Inside Eva / 1991 / PL / M • Passionate Lovers / 1991 / PL / M
WILLIAM SPAN see Star Index I
WILLIAM SWEET see Star Index I
WILLIAM WHITROCK
Buttmasters / 1994 / AMP / M
WILLIAM WINEHARDT see Star Index I
WILLIE
Blue Vanities #510 / 1992 / FFL / M • Blue Vanities #569 / 1996 / FFL / M • China Lee's Bachelorette Party / 1995 / RHV / M
WILLIE BEAM
All The Loving Couples / 1979 / KIT / M
WILLIE BRACK see Star Index I
WILLIE CUMOUT see Star Index I
WILLIE FILMORE
The Loves Of Mary Jane / 1989 / BWV / C • A Touch Of Sex / 1972 / AR / M
WILLIE MILLER see Star Index I
WILLMA
Blue Vanities #574 / 1996 / FFL / M

WILLOW
Bobby Hollander's Sweet Cheeks #111 / 1994 / WV / M • Bun Busters #17 / 1994 / LBO / M • Casting Couch Cuties #1 / 1994 / WP / M • Cousin Bubba Country Corn Porn #02 / 1994 / VIM / M • The Cumm Brothers #03: Go To Traffic School / 1994 / OD / M • Double Penetration Virgins #05: Go To Hell / 1994 / BB0 / M • Nasty Backdoor Nurses / 1994 / LBO / M
WILLY MONTANA see Star Index I
WILLY SCHULTES
[Krankenschwestern-Report / 1972 / ... / M
WILLY WANTAUGH
Transformation Of Alicia / 19?? / BIZ / G
WILLY WEBER
My Sister Seka / 1981 / CA / M
WILSON MCGAVER
ABA: Double Feature #1 / 1996 / ALP / M • Fanny Hill / 1975 / TGA / M
WILT TORRANCE see Star Index I
WIMP see Star Index I
WINDY
Blue Vanities #167 (New) / 1996 / FFL / M • Blue Vanities #167 (Old) / 1991 / FFL / M • Homegrown Video #390 / 1993 / HOV / M • HomeGrown Video #458: Cream Pie For Dessert / 1995 / HOV / C • Limited Edition #24 / 1984 / AVC / M • Reed: Windy #1 / 1991 / RED / M • Reed: Windy #2 / 1991 / RED / M
WINDY DIABLO
Summer Girls / 1986 / HO / C
WINDY LANE
Blue Vanities #068 / 1988 / FFL / M
WINDY WILLS see Star Index I
WINNIE COOPER
Nasty Nymphos #16 / 1996 / ANA / M
WINSTON
Goldilocks And The 3 Bi Bears / 1997 / TTV / G
WINSTON CLEAT
Up 'n' Coming / 1983 / CA / M
WINSTON FONTE *(Rick Fonte)*
Black male.
The Loves Of Mary Jane / 1989 / BWV / C • Pink Champagne / 1979 / CV / M • A Touch Of Sex / 1972 / AR / M
WINTER
Northwest Pecker Trek #1 / 1994 / LBO / M • Pussy Fest Of The Northwest #3 / 1995 / NIT / M
WINTER LAYNE
Redhead with a very white body, enhanced medium to large tits, marginal face, bely button ring, large tattoo where her pussy hair should be and another (flower) on her left butt. Supposedly 21 in 1994 but looks older.
The Best Of Strippers Inc / 1996 / ONA / C • Breastman's Wild West Adventure / 1995 / EVN / M • Butthead Dreams: Down In The Bush / 1995 / FH / M • Cumming Unscrewed / 1995 / TEG / F • Dancing Dominant Damsels / 1994 / RSV / B • Dirty Bob's #22: Lube! / 1995 / FLP / S • Exstasy / 1995 / WV / M • First Time Lesbians #18 / 1994 / JMP / F • Hard Core Beginners #09 / 1995 / LEI / M • High Heeled & Horny #4 / 1995 / LBO / M • Ona Zee's Doll House #2 / 1995 / ONA / F • Reel People #10 / 1995 / PP / M • Ridin' The Big One / 1994 / TEG / M • Sex Academy #5: The Art Of Pulp Fiction / 1994 / ONA / M • Shave Tails #4 / 1995 / SO / M • Snatch Masters #09 / 1995 / LEI / M • Titan's Amateur Video

Magazine #01 / 1995 / TEG / M • Who's In Charge (Titan) / 1995 / TEG / M

WIRLYN DERVICH
American Sex Fantasy / 1975 / IHV / M

WISE MARK *see* **Steve Austin**

WISEMARK *see* **Steve Austin**

WOLF
The Case Of The Missing Seka Master / 1993 / VCX / C

WOLF HARNISCH
[Schulmadchen-Report 4: Was Eltern Oft Verzweifeln LaBt / 1972 / ... / M

WOLF SAVAGE
100% Amateur #11: / 1995 / OD / M • 100% Amateur #15: / 1995 / OD / M • African Angels #2 / 1996 / NIT / M • Amateur A Cuppers / 1993 / VEX / C • America's Raunchiest Home Videos #66: / 1993 / ZA / M • Analtown USA #07 / 1995 / NIT / M • Analtown USA #08 / 1995 / NIT / M • Black Beauties #2 / 1992 / VIM / M • Black Booty / 1995 / UBP / M • Black Juice Bombs / 1996 / NIT / C • Bootylicious: White Trash / 1995 / JMP / M • Bun Busters #02 / 1993 / LBO / M • Bun Busters #03 / 1993 / LBO / M • Bun Busters #11 / 1993 / LBO / M • The Burma Road #1 / 1994 / LBO / C • The Burma Road #2 / 1994 / LBO / C • Creme De La Face #05 / 1994 / OD / M • Creme De La Face #07 / 1995 / OD / M • Creme De La Face #08: Wanna Blow Job / 1995 / OD / M • Creme De La Face #10: Cum Dome / 1995 / OD / M • Creme De La Face #11: Cum Plasterers / 1995 / OD / M • Creme De La Face #13: Nine Nasty Nymphs / 1995 / OD / M • Creme De La Face #15: Showroom Sex / 1996 / OD / M • Creme De La Face #16: Ladies Licking / 1996 / OD / M • Creme De La Face #17: Semen For Seven / 1996 / OD / M • Creme De La Face #18: Cum Mops / 1997 / OD / M • Cum Buttered Corn Holes #3 / 1996 / NIT / C • The Cumm Brothers #01 / 1993 / OD / M • The Cumm Brothers #02: Goin' To A Ho' Down / 1994 / OD / M • The Cumm Brothers #03: Go To Traffic School / 1994 / OD / M • The Cumm Brothers #04: Laid Off & Laid / 1994 / OD / M • The Cumm Brothers #05: These Nuts For Hire / 1994 / OD / M • The Cumm Brothers #06: Hook, Line And Sphincter / 1995 / OD / M • The Cumm Brothers #07: Honeymoon On Uranus / 1995 / OD / M • The Cumm Brothers #08: Escape From Uranus / 1995 / OD / M • The Cumm Brothers #09: Chewin' The Bush / 1995 / OD / M • The Cumm Brothers #10: Night Of The Giving Head / 1995 / OD / M • The Cumm Brothers #11: Oh Cum On Ye Faces / 1995 / OD / M • The Cumm Brothers #12: Two GOOS For Every Girl / 1995 / OD / M • The Cumm Brothers #13: Rump Rangers / 1996 / OD / M • The Cumm Brothers #14: Buttdraft / 1995 / OD / M • The Cumm Brothers #15: Hot Primal Sex / 1996 / OD / M • The Cumm Brothers #16: Deja Goo / 1996 / OD / M • The Cumm Brothers #17: Goo Guy Gone Bad / 1996 / OD / M • Cummin' 'round The Mountain / 1996 / BCP / M • Dirty Dating Service #01 / 1993 / WP / M • Dirty Dating Service #02 / 1993 / WP / M • Dirty Dating Service #03 / 1994 / WP / M • Dirty Dating Service #04 / 1994 / WP / M • Dirty Dating Service #05 / 1994 / WP / M • Dirty Dating Service #06 / 1994 / WP / M • The Doctor Is In #1 / 1995 / NIT / M • The Doctor Is In #2: Pussy Pox

/ 1995 / NIT / M • Fantasy Flings #01 / 1993 / WP / M • Gang Bang Diaries #2 / 1993 / SFP / M • Gang Bang Diaries #5 / 1994 / SFP / M • The Girls From Hootersville #01 / 1993 / SFP / M • Girls Just Wanna Have Cum / 1995 / HO / M • High Heeled & Horny #1 / 1994 / LBO / M • Hillary Vamp's Private Collection #17 / 1992 / HOV / M • Hollywood Swingers #08 / 1993 / LBO / M • Hollywood Swingers #10 / 1993 / LBO / M • The Journey: Oral Majority / 1991 / WV / M • The Joy Dick Club / 1994 / MID / M • Lusty Lap Dancers #2 / 1994 / HO / M • M Series #01 / 1993 / LBO / M • M Series #21 / 1994 / LBO / M • M Series #24 / 1994 / LBO / M • M Series #26 / 1994 / LBO / M • M Series #28 / 1994 / LBO / M • M Series #29 / 1994 / LBO / M • M Series #30 / 1994 / LBO / M • Mr. Peepers Amateur Home Videos #78: She Dreams Of Weenie / 1993 / LBO / M • Neighborhood Watch #18: Smokin' In Bed / 1992 / LBO / M • Neighborhood Watch #40: / 1993 / LBO / M • Nothing Like Nurse Nookie #1 / 1995 / NIT / M • Nothing Like Nurse Nookie #2 / 1996 / NIT / M • Nothing Like Nurse Nookie #3 / 1996 / NIT / M • Nothing Like Nurse Nookie #4 / 1996 / NIT / M • Nothing Like Nurse Nookie #5 / 1996 / NIT / M • Odyssey 30 Min: #282: / 1992 / OD / M • Odyssey Triple Play #59: Two On Two Fuckfest / 1994 / OD / M • Odyssey Triple Play #74: Conjugal Couples / 1994 / OD / M • Odyssey Triple Play #75: Interracial Anal Threesome / 1994 / OD / M • Private Label / 1993 / GLI / M • Rodney's Rookies #1 / 1996 / NIT / M • The Savage / 1994 / SC / M • The Sodomizer #2 / 1995 / SC / M • The Sodomizer #4 / 1996 / SC / M • The Sodomizer #6 / 1996 / SC / M • Teacher's Pet #2 / 1994 / WMG / M • Teacher's Pet #4 / 1995 / APP / M • Throbbing Threesomes / 1996 / NIT / M • Uncle Roy's Amateur Home Video #01 / 1992 / VIM / M • Uncle Roy's Amateur Home Video #06 / 1992 / VIM / M • Witches Are Bitches / 1996 / NIT / M

WOLF WOMYN *see* **Star Index I**

WOLFF BANE
Queen Of The Bizarre / 1994 / AMP / G

WOLFGANG
House Of Anal / 1995 / NOT / M • Porno X-Treme #2: Club Bizarre / 1995 / SC / M • Porno X-Treme #4: Wet Dream / 1995 / SC / M • Pure Anal / 1996 / MET / M • Tia's Holiday Gang Bang / 1995 / HO / M

WOLFGANG JANSEN
[Schulmadchen-Report 4: Was Eltern Oft Verzweifeln LaBt / 1972 / ... / M

WOODY
Bi-Bi Love Amateurs #2 / 1993 / SFP / G • The Lustful Turk / 1968 / SOW / S

WOODY BLAIN *see* **Star Index I**

WOODY HARRELSON
[The People vs. Larry Flynt / 1996 / C3S / S

WOODY LONG *(Dick Nasty (W. Long), Nasty Dan, Brewster Cocburn, Buster Cockburn, Boy Toy, Brian Curtis, Bryan Kurtis, Brian Curtin)*
Bewster Cocburn is from **Anal Attack**..
10,000 Anal Maniacs #1 / 1993 / FOR / M • Alexandria, I Love You / 1993 / AFV / M • America's Raunchiest Home Videos #01: Some Serious Sex / 1991 / ZA / M • America's Raunchiest Home Videos #02: Cook-

ing with Hot Sauce / 1991 / ZA / M • America's Raunchiest Home Videos #07: A Fucking Beauty / 1991 / ZA / M • Anal Attack / 1991 / ZA / M • Anal Inquisition / 1996 / ZA / M • Anal Ski Vacation / 1993 / ANA / M • The Anal-Europe Series #01: The Fisherman's Wife / 1992 / LV / M • Another Dirty Western / 1992 / AFV / M • Backdoor To Harley-Wood #3 / 1993 / AFV / M • Bare Market / 1993 / VC / M • Bend Over Babes #3 / 1992 / EA / M • Best Butt(e) In The West #1 / 1992 / CC / M • Best Of Bruce Seven #3 / 1990 / BIZ / C • The Bet / 1993 / VT / M • Biff Malibu's Totally Nasty Home Videos #01 / 1992 / ANA / M • Biff Malibu's Totally Nasty Home Videos #18 / 1992 / ANA / M • Big Town / 1993 / PP / M • Black Tie Affair / 1993 / VEX / M • Blonde Bombshell / 1991 / CC / M • Bouncing Buns / 1983 / VC / M • Breast Worx #18 / 1992 / LBO / M • Breasts And Beyond #2 / 1991 / ME / M • Bustin' Thru / 1993 / LV / M • Butt Freak #1 / 1992 / EA / M • Butt Freak #2 / 1996 / EA / M • Buttman In The Crack / 1996 / EA / M • Buttman's Big Tit Adventure #1 / 1992 / EA / M • Buttman's Revenge / 1992 / EA / M • Casanova #3 / 1993 / SC / M • Caught In The Act (1995-Wave) / 1995 / WAV / M • Chameleons: Not The Sequel / 1991 / VC / M • Chateau Du Cheeks / 1994 / VC / M • Daddy Doesn't Know / 1984 / HO / M • The Danger Zone / 1990 / SO / M • Dangerous Curves / 1995 / VC / M • Deep Cheeks #2 / 1991 / ROB / M • Deep Cover / 1993 / WP / M • Deep Inside Nicole London / 1995 / VC / C • Defending Your Sex Life / 1992 / LE / M • Dial N Again / 1993 / PEP / M • Dial N For Nikki / 1993 / PEP / M • Double The Pleasure / 1990 / SE / M • Elements Of Desire / 1994 / ULI / M • Eleventh Annual AVN Awards / 1994 / VC / M • Erotic Radio WSEX / 1983 / VC / M • Evil Woman / 1990 / LE / M • Face Dance #1 / 1992 / EA / M • The Fine Line / 1990 / SO / M • Gangbang Girl #02 / 1992 / ANA / M • Gangbang Girl #03 / 1992 / ANA / M • Gangbang Girl #04 / 1992 / ANA / M • Gangbang Girl #05 / 1992 / ANA / M • Gangbang Girl #06 / 1992 / ANA / M • Gangbang Girl #08 / 1992 / ANA / M • Gangbang Girl #16 / 1995 / ANA / M • Gangbang Girl #17 / 1995 / ANA / M • Gangbang Girl #18 / 1996 / ANA / M • Guilty By Seduction / 1993 / PI / M • Halloweenie / 1991 / PL / M • Hard Core Cafe / 1991 / PL / M • Hard Core Cafe Revisited / 1991 / PL / M • Hard To Stop #1 / 1992 / VC / M • Hard To Stop #2 / 1992 / VC / M • Haunted Nights / 1993 / WP / M • Heavenscent / 1993 / ZA / M • Heidi Does Hollywood / 1993 / AFV / M • Hidden Obsessions / 1992 / BFP / M • Hollywood Ho' House / 1994 / VC / M • Hollywood Scandal: The Heidi Flesh Story / 1993 / IP / M • Hot On Her Tail / 1990 / CA / M • How To Love Your Lover / 1992 / XII / S • Hungry #1 / 1992 / SC / M • Hungry #2 / 1993 / SC / M • In Too Deep / 1992 / AFD / M • The Journey: Oral Majority / 1991 / WV / M • Juicy Sex Scandals / 1991 / VD / M • Juicy Treats / 1991 / ROB / M • Junk Yard Dogs / 1991 / FC / M • Just For The Hell Of It / 1991 / CA / M • Leena / 1992 / VT / M • Legend #3 / 1991 / LE / M • The Look / 1993 / WP / M • The Makeup Room #2 / 1992 / VC / M • Maneaters (1992-Vidco) / 1992 / VD /

C • Model Wife / 1991 / CA / M • My Secret Lover / 1992 / XCI / M • Naked Buns 8 1/2 / 1992 / CC / M • The Natural / 1993 / VT / M • Naughty Nurses / 1992 / VD / C • Nobody's Looking / 1993 / VC / M • Notorious / 1992 / SC / M • Nurse Nancy / 1991 / CA / M • On Trial #3: Takin' It To The Jury / 1992 / VI / M • On Trial #4: The Verdict / 1992 / VI / M • Oral Madness #1 / 1991 / OD / M • The Orgy #2 / 1993 / EMC / M • The Orgy #3 / 1993 / EMC / M • The Original Wicked Woman / 1993 / WP / M • Passion For Bondage / 1983 / BIZ / B • The Penetrator #1 / 1991 / PL / M • Plan 69 From Outer Space / 1993 / CA / M • Poison / 1994 / VI / M • Prime Choice #5 / 1996 / RAS / M • Raunch #08 / 1993 / CC / M • Regarding Hiney / 1991 / CC / M • Rocket Girls / 1993 / VC / M • Saturday Night Porn #3 / 1993 / AFV / M • Scream In The Middle Of The Night / 1990 / CC / M • The Seduction Of Julia Ann / 1993 / VT / M • Sex Under Glass / 1992 / VC / M • Sexdrive #1: Topdown Girl / 1993 / OD / M • Sexy Nurses #2 / 1994 / CV / M • Shameless / 1991 / SC / M • Shiver / 1993 / FOR / M • Silk Elegance / 1991 / VIM / M • Sindy Does Anal / 1993 / AFV / M • Sindy Does Anal Again / 1994 / AFV / M • Sindy's Sexercise Workout / 1994 / AFV / M • Single Tight Female / 1992 / LV / M • Smooth Ride / 1996 / WP / M • Southern Cumfort / 1993 / HO / M • The Spectacle / 1991 / IN / M • Starbangers #08 / 1996 / FPI / M • Stasha's Adult School / 1993 / CDI / G • Stocking Stuffers / 1992 / LV / M • The Stranger Beside Me / 1991 / WV / M • Sun Bunnies #1 / 1991 / SC / M • Surfside Sex / 1988 / CA / M • Things Change / 1992 / MET / M • Things Change #1: My First Time / 1992 / CV / M • Things Change #2: Letting Go / 1992 / CV / M • Truth And Bare / 1991 / LV / M • Twin Cheeks #2 / 1991 / CIN / M • Twin Cheeks #4 / 1991 / CIN / M • Two Of A Kind / 1991 / ZA / M • Unrefined / 1993 / CC / M • Up And Cummers #04 / 1993 / 4P / M • Vow Of Passion / 1991 / VI / M • Warm Pink / 1992 / LE / M • Wet Faces #1 / 1997 / SC / C • Where There's Sparxx, There's Fire / 1991 / LV / M • Wicked Women / 1993 / ME / M • Wild Innocence / 1992 / PL / M

WOOP see Star Index I
WYNNE COLBURN see Star Index I
XANDRA
S&M On The Ranch: Training The New Pony Girl / 1994 / VER / B
XAVIER
Sidone Bi / 1995 / FRF / G
XAVIER BONGO see Star Index I
XENA
Pick Up Lines #12 / 1997 / OD / M
XENIA (AXINIA) see Axinia
XOSHII
Booty Babes / 1993 / ROB / F • Ebony Erotica #12: Pussy Posse / 1993 / GO / M • Honey Drippers / 1992 / ROB / F • Kittens & Vamps #1 / 1993 / ROB / F • Lesbian Lockup / 1993 / ROB / F • Pony Girls / 1993 / ROB / F • Ron Hightower's White Chicks #02 / 1993 / LBO / M • Sweet Lips & Buns / 1993 / ROB / F • Thrill Seekers / 1993 / ROB / F
XOUIZIT see Lil Lee
XRISTIAN ROSS
Bi Chill / 1994 / BIL / G • My She-Male

Valentine / 1994 / HSV / G • The She-Male Who Stole Christmas / 1993 / HSV / G
XSTASY LANE see Star Index I
Y. TYLER HORN see Tyler Horne
YAIICHI MATSURA
Erotic Nurses / 1996 / AVE / M
YAMABAYASHI YOSHIHIR
Virgin Cover Girl / 1996 / AVE / M
YANA
Rocco Goes To Prague / 1995 / EA / M
YANI BEN-ITZHAR
Young Sluts In Heat #2 / 1996 / PL / M
YANK LEVINE
Behind The Green Door #1 / 1972 / MIT / M • Sodom & Gomorrah / 1974 / MIT / M
YANNA
Private Gold #12: The Pyramid #2 / 1996 / OD / M
YASHI see Star Index I
YASMINE
Black Mystique #11 / 1995 / VT / F • Bootylicious: EZ Street / 1995 / JMP / M • Brothers Bangin' / 1995 / ANA / M • Girl's Towne #2 / 1994 / FC / F • Girlz Towne #12 / 1995 / FC / F • More Black Dirty Debutantes #4 / 1995 / 4P / M
YASMINE (KASSI NOVA) see Kassi Nova
YASMINE PENDARVIS *(Monique Seabrook, Yasmine Pendavis)*
Black girl with tight body, passable face, and tiny tits with a mole on the bottom of the right one.
Black Cheerleader Jungle Jerk-Off / 1996 / WIC / F • Black Cheerleader Search #01 / 1996 / ROB / M • Booty Sister #2 / 1996 / ROB / M • The Brat Pack / 1989 / VWA / M • The Case Of The Black Booty / 1996 / LV / M • The Crack Of Dawn / 1989 / GLE / M • Essence / 1996 / SO / M • Flesh / 1996 / EA / M • Ganggstas Paradise / 1995 / AVI / M • Heather Hunter's Bedtime Stories / 1991 / GLE / C • Heather's Home Movies / 1989 / VWA / M • Hollywood Amateurs #09 / 1994 / MID / M • I Want It All / 1995 / WAV / M • Interview's Dark And Delicious / 1996 / LV / M • Interview: Dark And Delicious / 1996 / LV / M • My Baby Got Back #07 / 1995 / VT / M • My Baby Got Back #08 / 1996 / VT / M • NYDP Blue / 1996 / WP / M • Pick Up Lines #04 / 1995 / 4P / M • Pussyman's House Party #1 / 1996 / SNA / M • Pussyman's House Party #2 / 1996 / SNA / M • Screw The Right Thing / 1990 / VWA / M • Sista! #3 / 1995 / VT / F • Sista! #4 / 1996 / VT / F • Small Top Bitches / 1996 / AVI / M • Tailz From Da Hood #3 / 1996 / AVI / M • Toot Z Roll / 1995 / WP / M • Two-Pac / 1996 / VT / M • [Adult Stars Close Up: Nasty / 199? / ... / M
YASMINE PENDAVIS see Yasmine Pendarvis
YASU YAMATO see Star Index I
YASUHARA ARUGA
Erotic Nurses / 1996 / AVE / M
YDI see Star Index I
YELENA SAMARINA
[Le Journal Intime D'Une Nymphomane / 1972 / ... / M
YENINAS
Foreskin Gump / 1994 / LE / M
YO YO
Adventures Of The DP Boys: South Of The Border / 1995 / HW / M • Chocolate Cherries #2 / 1990 / CC / M
YOHAN

When The Fat Lady Sings / 1996 / EX / M
YOHO MIHARA
G-String Geisha / 1978 / ORC / M
YOKO
Classic Swedish Erotica #17 / 1986 / CA / C • Diamond Snatch / 1977 / COM / M • Inn Of Sin / 1988 / VT / M • Oriental Taboo / 1985 / CDI / M • The Seduction Of Tessa / cr86 / CA / M
YOKO SAKAMOTO
Jacuzzi Lust / 1996 / AVE / M
YOKO SEKI see Dallas Miko
YOKO SUZUKI see Star Index I
YOKO WONG
Anal Annie And The Willing Husbands / 1984 / LIP / M • Anal Annie Just Can't Say No / 1984 / LIP / M • Backdoor Romance / 1984 / VIV / M • Backing In #1 / 1990 / WV / C • Beyond Taboo / 1984 / VIV / M • The Dragon Lady #1 / 1988 / WV / C • Girl On The Run / 1985 / VC / M • You Turn Me On / 1986 / LIM / M
YOLAND GREEN see Star Index I
YOLANDA
Big Tits And Fat Fannies #10 / 1994 / BTO / M • Candyman #06 / 1993 / GLI / M • Cherry Poppin #01 / 1994 / CDY / M • Dick & Jane Go To Mexico / 1994 / AVI / M • Eric Kroll's Fetish #2 / 1994 / ERK / M • Gourmet Premier: Between Rooms / Rear Entry #911 / cr85 / GO / M • Rump Humpers #02 / 1992 / GLI / M • Three Sexateers / 1970 / SOW / S
YOLANDA BONNEA
Mystique / 1979 / CA / M
YOLANDA BORKHURST see Star Index I
YOLANDA CLARK
GVC: Companions #122 / 1983 / GO / F • GVC: Family Affair / 1983 / GO / M
YOLANDA KNIGHT see Star Index I
YOLANDA SAVALAS
Expose Me, Lovely / 1976 / QX / M • Her Name Was Lisa / 1979 / VC / M • Revenge Of The Rope Masters / 1979 / ... / B • Rollerbabies / 1976 / VC / M
YOLANDA SMITH
Love Airlines / 1978 / SE / M
YOLIE see Star Index I
YOLINDA
Raw Talent: Bang 'er 31 Times / 1992 / RTP / M
YORK POWERS
Long Play / 1995 / 3XP / G
YORYEK YEZNO
Dark Dreams / 1971 / ALP / M
YOSHIKO MANDA see Star Index I
YOSHIKO TANAKA
Club Fantasy / 1996 / AVE / M
YOSHIKO YAKAMORA
More Dirty Debutantes #31 / 1994 / 4P / M • New Ends #07 / 1994 / 4P / M
YOSHIZO KENEKAZA see Star Index I
YOUKO HONDA
A Widow's Affair / 1996 / AVV / M
YOUNG DOC
Intense Perversions #4 / 1996 / PL / M
YOUNG PARTNA DUDE
Best Gang Bangs / 1996 / DFI / C • Sluts, Butts And Pussy / 1996 / DFI / M
YOYO see Joey Murphy
YSIDRO WALTERS
Jezebel / 1979 / CV / M
YUAN SLAVE
Sexual Initiation Of A Married Woman / 1984 / VD / M

YUBA *see Star Index I*

YUCARI TACUCHI
The Kimono / 1983 / ORC / M

YUKIKO FUJIMAKI
Erotic Nurses / 1996 / AVE / M

YUKIKO SASAKI
Snow Country / 1984 / ORC / M

YUKIKO SHIOYAMA
Unchained Instinct / 1996 / AVE / M

YUKO *see Star Index I*

YUKO MIZUNOKI
The Sex Exchange / 1996 / AVV / M

YUMI KAMAMOTO
Club Fantasy / 1996 / AVE / M

YUMIKA HAYASHI
Sexually Yours / 1996 / AVE / M

YURI KLIMA
Russian Girls / 1996 / WV / M

YURIKO HISHIMI
Lust In Old Edo / 1978 / ORC / M

YUTAKA TAKEDA
Sexually Yours / 1996 / AVE / M

YVAN SLAVE *see Star Index I*

YVE SOLEIL
Flash Pants / 1983 / VC / M

YVES
Anabolic Import #01: Anal X / 1994 / ANA / M • Anal In The Alps / 1996 / P69 / M • Dick & Jane Penetrate Paris / 1994 / AVI / M • Magma: Anal Teenies / 1994 / MET / M • Magma: Double Anal / 1994 / MET / M • The Voyeur #7: Live In Europe #1 / 1996 / JLP / M • World Sex Tour #4 / 1996 / ANA / M

YVES BAILLARD *see Yves Baillat*

YVES BAILLAT *(Yves Baillard)*
Anal Magic / 1995 / XC / M • Anal Pow Wow / 1995 / XC / M • Chateau Duval / 1996 / HDE / M • Cherry Busters / 1995 / WIV / M • Diamonds / 1996 / HDE / M • Ejacula #1 / 1992 / VC / M • Ejacula #2 / 1992 / VC / M • Extraterrestrial Virgins / 1995 / VIT / M • Games Women Play / 1995 / XC / M • The Grind / 1995 / XC / M • Impulse #01: Memories Of An Italian Slut / 1995 / MBP / M • Impulse #08: The A Channel / 1996 / MBP / M • Jura Sexe / 1995 / JP / G • Lettre Da Rimini / 1995 / MID / M • Magma: Old And Young / 1995 / MET / M • Mission Hard / 1995 / XC / M • Prima #08: Sex Camping / 1995 / MBP / M • Private Film #22 / 1995 / OD / M • Private Film #24 / 1995 / OD / M • Private Film #25 / 1995 / OD / M • Private Film #26 / 1995 / OD / M • Private Film #27 / 1995 / OD / M • Private Film #28 / 1995 / OD / M • Private Video Magazine #22 / 1995 / OD / M • Private Video Magazine #23 / 1995 / OD / M • Private Video Magazine #24 / 1995 / OD / M • Private Video Magazine #25 / 1995 / OD / M • Private Video Magazine #26 / 1995 / OD / M • Rosa / Francesca / 1995 / XC / M • Sex Scandals / 1995 / XC / M • Skin #3 / 1995 / ERQ / M • The Thief, The Girl & The Detective / 1996 / HDE / M • Triple X Video Magazine #01 / 1995 / OD / M • Triple X Video Magazine #02 / 1995 / OD / M • Triple X Video Magazine #03 / 1995 / OD / M • Triple X Video Magazine #04 / 1995 / OD / M • Triple X Video Magazine #05 / 1995 / OD / M • Triple X Video Magazine #06 / 1995 / OD / M • Triple X Video Magazine #07 / 1995 / OD / M • Triple X Video Magazine #08 / 1995 / OD / M • Triple X Video Magazine #09 / 1995 / OD / M • Triple X Video Magazine #10 /

1995 / OD / M

YVES CALLAS *see Star Index I*

YVES CHAMPINION
Perversity In Paris / 1994 / AVI / M

YVES TONIGUE *see Star Index I*

YVETTE
America's Raunchiest Home Videos #52: / 1993 / ZA / M • Breast Of Britain #6 / 1990 / BTO / S • Breast Of Britain #9 / 1990 / BTO / M • Dangerous Behinds #1 / 1995 / HW / M • Hot Body Video Magazine: Southern Belle / 1994 / CG / F • Limited Edition #12 / 1980 / AVC / M • Limited Edition #14 / 1980 / AVC / M • M.O. #2 / 1995 / STP / F • New Faces, Hot Bodies #08 / 1993 / STP / M • New Faces, Hot Bodies #19 / 1995 / STP / M • New Faces, Hot Bodies #21 / 1996 / STP / C • New Faces, Hot Bodies #22 / 1996 / STP / M • Pole Cats / 1993 / KBR / S • Raw Talent: Bang 'er 25 Times / 1992 / RTP / M • Suze's Centerfolds #9 / 1985 / CA / M • Sweet Black Cherries #1 / 1996 / TTV / M • Toy Time #5: / 1996 / STP / F • Triple X Video Magazine #07 / 1995 / OD / M • Uncle Roy's Amateur Home Video #14 / 1992 / VIM / M • Uncle Roy's Amateur Home Video #18 / 1993 / VIM / M

YVETTE (S/M)
Bizarre People / 1982 / BIZ / G • She-Males Behind Closed Doors / 1991 / RSV / G

YVETTE BRANDON
Oriental Treatment #1 / 1978 / AR / M • Star Of The Orient / 1978 / VIP / M • Wild River Girls / 1977 / IVP / M

YVETTE COLE *see Star Index I*

YVETTE HIVER *see Star Index I*

YVETTE LARUE *see Star Index I*

YVON
Adultress / 1995 / WIV / M

YVONNE
The Black Bunch / 1970 / SOW / S • Blue Vanities #114 / 1988 / FFL / M • Blue Vanities #567 / 1995 / FFL / M • Erotic Visions / 1995 / ULI / M • Girl's Towne #1 / 1994 / FC / F • Girl's Towne #2 / 1994 / FC / F • I Do #2 / 1990 / VI / M • Mike Hott: #251 Cunt of the Month: Veronica / 1993 / MHV / M • Secrets in the Attic #3: Trials Of Acceptance / 1994 / STM / B • Secrets in the Attic #4: Purchased And Punished / 1994 / STM / B • Strap-On Sally #05: Chantilly's French Kiss / 1995 / PL / F

YVONNE (KELLY TRUMP) *see Kelly Trump*

YVONNE (ROSIE LEE) *(Rosie Lee, Yvonne Scott)*
Quite pretty older blonde with a tight waist and small hips. Originally had medium sized tits which she had expanded to grotesque proportions. English and was the SO of Mark Davis at one stage. Yvonne Scott is from **The Player**.
Amateur Lesbians #41: Kelli / 1993 / GO / F • Amateur Lesbians #42: Rosie Lee / 1993 / GO / F • Angel Eyes / 1995 / IN / M • Backdoor To Buttsville / 1995 / ULI / M • Bad Luck For Bad Girls / 1996 / EXQ / B • Badgirls #6: Ridin' Into Town / 1995 / VI / M • Beauty's Punishment / 1996 / BIZ / B • Beauty's Revenge / 1996 / BIZ / B • Big Murray's New-Cummers #22: Exotic Erotica / 1993 / FD / M • Body English / 1993 / PL / M • Bruce Seven: A Compendium Of His Most Graphic Scenes Vol 6 / 1994 / BS

/ C • Buffy Malibu's Nasty Girls #07 / 1994 / ANA / F • Buffy Malibu's Nasty Girls #10 / 1996 / ANA / F • Buffy Malibu's Nasty Girls #11 / 1996 / ANA / F • Busty Backdoor Nurses / 1996 / PL / M • Butt Banged Bicycle Babes / 1994 / ANA / M • The Butt Sisters Do Denver / 1994 / MID / M • Butt Watch #01 / 1993 / FH / M • Butt Watch #02 / 1993 / FH / M • Butt Watch #03 / 1994 / FH / M • Buttslammers #10: Lust On The Internet / 1995 / BS / F • Buttslammers #11: / 1996 / BS / F • Buttslammers #12: Anal Madness / 1996 / BS / F • Buttslammers #13: The Madness Continues / 1996 / BS / F • Checkmate / 1995 / WAV / M • Chronicles Of Pain #1 / 1996 / BIZ / B • Chronicles Of Pain #2 / 1996 / BIZ / B • The Dinner Party #1 / 1994 / ULI / M • Double D Dykes #16 / 1995 / GO / F • Dresden Diary #14: Ecstasy In Hell / 1996 / BIZ / B • Dresden Diary #15: / 1996 / BIZ / B • Everybody Wants Some / 1996 / EXQ / F • Future Doms #1 / 1996 / BIZ / B • A Girl's Affair #02 / 1993 / FD / F • Golddiggers #2 / 1995 / VC / M • Golddiggers #3 / 1995 / VC / M • Heat / 1995 / WAV / M • Hush...My Mother Might Hear Us / 1993 / FL / M • I Love Lesbians / 1995 / ERW / F • Intense Perversions #2 / 1996 / PL / M • Jiggly Queens #2 / 1994 / LE / M • Legend #5: The Legend Continues / 1994 / LE / M • Lesbian Connection / 1996 / SUF / F • Little Girl Lost / 1995 / SC / M • Mr. Peepers Amateur Home Videos #76: Sixty Nine Plus Seven / 1993 / LBO / M • Naked Scandal #1 / 1995 / SPI / M • Naked Scandal #2 / 1996 / SPI / M • Nasty Nymphos #04 / 1994 / ANA / M • New Wave Hookers #4 / 1994 / VC / M • Passenger 69 #1 / 1994 / IP / M • Philmore Butts Goes Wild! / 1996 / SUF / M • Philmore Butts Meets The Palm Beach Nymphomaniac Kathy Willie / 1995 / SUF / M • The Player / 1995 / VI / M • A Pool Party At Seymores #1 / 1995 / ULI / M • Puritan Video Magazine #01 / 1996 / LE / M • Pussy Hunt #05 / 1994 / LEI / M • Renegades #1 / 1994 / SC / M • Sex Raiders / 1996 / WAV / M • Sex Therapy Ward / 1995 / LBO / M • Seymore & Shane Do Ireland / 1994 / ULI / M • Seymore & Shane Meet Kathy Willets, The Naughty Nymph / 1994 / ULI / M • Seymore & Shane On The Loose / 1994 / ULI / M • Seymore & Shane Playing With Fire / 1994 / ULI / M • Seymore Butts Goes Nuts / 1994 / FH / M • Seymore Butts: Bustin' Out My Best Anal / 1995 / FH / C • Seymore Butts: My Travels With The Tramp / 1994 / FH / M • Shane's World #1 / 1996 / OD / M • Shane's World #2 / 1996 / OD / M • Shane's World #3 / 1996 / OD / M • Shane's World #5 / 1996 / OD / M • Shane's World #6: Slumber Party / 1996 / OD / F • Shane's World #7 / 1996 / OD / M • Sleaze Please!—August Edition / 1994 / FH / M • Sleaze Please!—September Edition / 1994 / FH / M • Sleaze Please!—November Edition / 1994 / FH / M • Sodomania...And Then Some!!! A Compendium / 1995 / EL / C • Spiked Heel Diaries #5 / 1995 / BIZ / B • Stiletto / 1994 / WAV / M • Strap-On Sally #06: Triple Penetration Trollop / 1995 / PL / F • Sunset And Divine: The British Experience / 1996 / LEI / M • Sweet Cheerleaders Spanked / 1996 / BIZ / B • Tainted Love / 1996 / VC / M • Takin' It To The Limit #5 / 1995 / BS / M •

The Theory Of Relativity / 1994 / EL / M • Up And Cummers #06 / 1993 / 4P / M • Up And Cummers #07 / 1994 / 4P / M • Waterworld: The Enema Club / 1996 / BIZ / B • Waterworld: The Enema Movie / 1996 / BIZ / B • Weird Sex / 1995 / GO / M • Wildcats / 1995 / WP / M • Yvonne's Odyssey / 1995 / BS / B

YVONNE ANDREA *see Star Index I*

YVONNE DAVIS
Bedtime Video #09 / 1984 / GO / M • Desert Passion / 1992 / CPV / S

YVONNE ELDERS *see Star Index I*

YVONNE EVIER *see Star Index I*

YVONNE FRANCE
Viola Video #104: Miss France To Visit / 1995 / PEV / M

YVONNE GREEN *see Star Index I*

YVONNE MASTERS *see Star Index I*

YVONNE MCKINNON
Impulse #06: / 1996 / MBP / M

YVONNE PRICE
Black Lust / 1983 / VCR / C • Ebony Erotica / 1985 / VCR / C • Pleasure Productions #12 / 1985 / VCR / M

YVONNE RIVERS
Bucky Beaver's XXX Dragon Art Theatre Double Feature #15 / 1996 / SOW / M • Left At The Altar / 1974 / SOW / M

YVONNE WELDON *see Star Index I*

YVONNE ZOLLIKER
The Young Seducers / 1971 / BL / M

Z.Z. ZSAR
Kinky Villa / 1995 / PL / M • Sperm Injection / 1995 / PL / M

ZABOU
The Perils Of Gwendoline In The Land Of The Yik Yak / 1984 / LIV / S • Rebecca Lord's World Tour #1: French Edition / 1995 / WP / M • The Streets Of Paris / 1996 / SC / M • [Suivez Mon Regard / 1986 / ... / S

ZACH YOUNGBLOOD
Bang City #2: China's Anal Gang Bang / 1995 / SC / M • Bang City #3: Fallon's Anal Gang Bang / 1995 / SC / M

ZACHERY ADAMS *see Zake Thomas*

ZACHERY STRONG
Resurrection Of Eve / 1973 / MIT / M

ZACHERY THOMAS *see Zake Thomas*

ZACK (R.J. REYNOLDS) *see R.J. Reynolds*

ZACK MATHIAS *see Star Index I*

ZACK THOMAS *see Zake Thomas*

ZACK TYLOR *see Star Index I*

ZAK SPEARS
Secret Sex #2: The Sex Radicals / 1994 / CAT / G

ZAK THOMAS *see Zake Thomas*

ZAKE THOMAS *(Zack Thomas, Zak Thomas, Zachery Thomas, Jack Thomas, Zachery Adams)*
Husband to Sunset Thomas. Was 30 in 1993. Used to be a gigolo in Daytona Beach, FL.
The Absolute Worst Of Amateur #1 / 1993 / VEX / M • Adventures In Paradise / 1992 / VEX / M • All Amateur Perfect 10's / 1995 / LEI / M • Amateur Orgies #07 / 1992 / AFI / M • Amateur Orgies #10 / 1992 / AFI / M • Amateur Orgies #12 / 1992 / AFI / M • Amateur Orgies #13 / 1992 / AFI / M • Amateur Orgies #15 / 1992 / AFI / M • Amateur Orgies #16 / 1992 / AFI / M • America's Dirtiest Home Videos #04 / 1991 / VEX / M • America's Dirtiest Home Videos #07 / 1991 / VEX / M • America's Dirtiest Home Videos

#09 / 1992 / VEX / M • America's Raunchiest Home Videos #22: City Lites / 1992 / ZA / M • America's Raunchiest Home Videos #26: Tiptoe Thru The 2 Lips / 1992 / ZA / M • America's Raunchiest Home Videos #27: Here Cums Ginger! / 1992 / ZA / M • America's Raunchiest Home Videos #47: / 1993 / ZA / M • American Dream Girls #2 / 1994 / LEI / M • Anal Avenue / 1992 / LV / M • Anal Ski Vacation / 1993 / ANA / M • Asian Heat #02: Satin Angels / 1993 / SC / M • Asian Heat #03: Tales Of The Golden Lotus / 1993 / SC / M • Asian Invasion / 1993 / IP / M • Babenet / 1995 / VC / M • Backing In #4 / 1993 / WV / C • Beach Bum Amateur's #03 / 1992 / MID / M • Beach Bum Amateur's #14 / 1992 / MID / M • Beach Bum Amateur's #16 / 1992 / MID / M • Beach Bum Amateur's #30 / 1993 / MID / M • Bend Over Backwards / 1993 / VIM / M • Best Gang Bangs / 1996 / DFI / C • Black Orchid / 1993 / WV / M • The Booty Guard / 1993 / IP / M • Breakfast At Tiffany's / 1994 / IF / M • Bubble Butts #05 / 1992 / LBO / M • Bubble Butts #16 / 1992 / LBO / M • Butt Whore / 1994 / WIV / M • Cajun Heat / 1993 / SC / M • Careless / 1993 / PP / M • Chameleons: Not The Sequel / 1991 / VC / M • Cinderella Society / 1993 / GO / M • Club DV8 #2 / 1993 / SC / M • The Creasemaster's Wife / 1993 / VC / M • Cyberanal / 1995 / VC / M • Deep Inside Dirty Debutantes #01 / 1992 / 4P / M • Deep Throat #6 / 1992 / AFV / M • Delicious (VCX-1993) / 1993 / VCX / M • Dick & Jane Go To Hollywood #1 / 1993 / AVI / M • Dirty Dancers #8 / 1996 / 4P / M • Dirty Laundry / 1994 / HOH / M • Double Decadence / 1995 / NOT / M • Double Penetration Virgins #01 / 1993 / LE / M • End Of Innocence / 1994 / WIV / M • Femme Fatale / 1993 / SC / M • Flashback / 1993 / SC / M • The Fucking Elvises / 1994 / GLI / M • Gang Bang Fury #1 / 1992 / ROB / M • Gangbang Girl #09 / 1993 / ANA / M • Geisha To Go / 1994 / PPP / M • The Girls From Hootersville #07 / 1994 / SFP / M • Glitz Tits #01 / 1992 / GLI / M • Glitz Tits #06 / 1993 / GLI / M • Gypsy Queen / 1995 / CC / M • Hard Core Beginners #02 / 1995 / LEI / M • Hard Core Beginners #03 / 1995 / LEI / M • Hard Core Beginners #05 / 1995 / LEI / M • Hard Core Beginners #06 / 1995 / LEI / M • Hard Core Beginners #09 / 1995 / LEI / M • Hard To Hold / 1993 / IF / M • High Heel Harlots #04 / 1994 / SFP / M • Hillary Vamp's Private Collection 09 / 1992 / HVD / M • Hillary Vamp's Private Collection #24 / 1992 / HOV / M • Hillary Vamp's Private Collection #31 / 1992 / HOV / M • Hometown Girl / 1994 / VEX / M • Hose Jobs / 1995 / VEX / M • Humongous Hooters / 1993 / IF / M • I Dream Of Teri / 1993 / IF / M • Inferno #1 / 1993 / SC / M • Inferno #2 / 1993 / SC / M • Jezebel #1 / 1993 / SC / M • Jezebel #2 / 1993 / SC / M • Kinky Debutante Interviews #03 / 1994 / IP / M • The Last Action Whore / 1993 / LV / M • The Last Good Sex / 1992 / FD / M • Latex #1 / 1994 / VC / M • Leena / 1992 / VT / M • The Love Doctor / 1992 / HIP / M • Love Letters #1 / 1993 / SC / M • Love Letters #2 / 1993 / SC / M • Mike Hott: #194 Sunset Thomas, Very Pregnant / 1994 / MHV / M • Mike Hott: #243 Cunt of the Month: Krista / 1993 / MHV / M • Mr.

Peepers Amateur Home Videos #25: The 25th Anniversary Ed / 1991 / LBO / M • Mr. Peepers Amateur Home Videos #82: Born To Swing! / 1993 / LBO / M • Ms. Fix-It / 1994 / PRK / M • Muffy The Vampire Layer / 1992 / LV / M • Naked Lunch / 1995 / LEI / M • Neighborhood Watch #16: Dirty Laundry / 1992 / LBO / M • Neighborhood Watch #18: Smokin' In Bed / 1992 / LBO / M • The New Butt Hunt #13 / 1995 / LEI / C • New Pussy Hunt #18 / 1995 / LEI / C • On The Come Line / 1993 / MID / M • Once In A Lifetime / 1996 / VC / C • Opposite Attraction / 1992 / VEX / M • Our Bang #10 / 1993 / GLI / M • Paper Tiger / 1992 / VI / M • Pearl Necklace: Amorous Amateurs #33 / 1992 / SEE / M • Pearl Necklace: Thee Bush League #10 / 1993 / SEE / M • Penetrating Thoughts / 1992 / LV / M • The Pink Lady Detective Agency: Case Of The Twisted Sister / 1994 / IN / M • The Pink Pussycat / 1992 / CA / M • Princess Of Persia / 1993 / IP / M • Profiles #04: Lust Lessons / 1995 / XPR / M • Pussy Hunt #04 / 1994 / LEI / M • Pussy Hunt #05 / 1994 / LEI / M • Ready To Drop #02 / 1992 / FC / M • Sex #2: Fate (Vca) / 1995 / VC / M • Sex Secrets Of High Priced Call Girls / 1995 / MID / M • Stiff Competition #2 / 1994 / CA / M • Straight A's / 1994 / AMP / M • Sunset Rides Again / 1995 / VC / M • Sunset's Anal & D.P. Gangbang / 1996 / PL / M • Sweet Sunshine / 1995 / IF / M • Temptation / 1994 / VC / M • Too Fast For Love / 1992 / IF / M • Toredo / 1996 / ROX / M • Uncle Roy's Amateur Home Video #01 / 1992 / VIM / M • Undercover Lover / 1992 / CV / M • Victoria's Secret Life / 1992 / WV / M • Wet Memories / 1993 / WV / M • Wicked Thoughts / 1992 / PL / M • Working Girl / 1993 / VI / M

ZANA QUE *see Kitty Yung*

ZANDY ROSE
Aged To Perfection #3 / 1995 / TTV / M • Every Granny Has A Fantasy / 1996 / GLI / M • Golden Oldies #5 / 1996 / TTV / M • Golden Oldies #6 / 1996 / TTV / M • Kitty Foxx's Kinky Kapers #03 / 1995 / TTV / M • Mike Hott: Older Girls #13 / 1996 / MHV / C • Old Bitches / 1996 / GLI / M

ZAP LOCKER
Ejacula #1 / 1992 / VC / M • Ejacula #2 / 1992 / VC / M

ZARA
Blue Vanities #565 / 1995 / FFL / M

ZARA WHITES *(Paulina Peters, Amy Kooiman)*
Paulina Peters is from **Anal Nation**. Amy Kooiman is from **Latent Image's Amy Kooiman**.
Adult Video News 1991 Awards / 1991 / VC / M • Adult Video News 1992 Awards / 1992 / VC / M • Anal Nation #1 / 1990 / CC / M • Andrew Blake's Girls / 1992 / CA / C • As Dirty As She Wants To Be / 1990 / ME / M • The Best Of Andrew Blake / 1993 / CA / C • Blue Angel / 1991 / SE / M • Bruce Seven: A Compendium Of His Most Graphic Scenes Vol 1 / 1991 / BS / C • Butt Freak #1 / 1992 / EA / M • Buttman's European Vacation #1 / 1991 / EA / M • Buttman's Ultimate Workout / 1990 / EA / M • Casual Sex / 1991 / GO / M • Catalina: Sabotage / 1991 / CDI / M • Catalina: Tiger Shark / 1991 / CDI / M • Catalina: Undercover / 1991 / CIN / M • The Challenge / 1990 / EA

/ B • Crossing Over / 1990 / IN / M • Curse Of The Catwoman / 1990 / VC / M • Desire / 1990 / VC / M • French Open / 1990 / OD / M • Gorgeous / 1990 / CA / M • Heavy Petting / 1991 / SE / M • House Of Dreams / 1990 / CA / M • Indiscretions / 1991 / PP / M • A Journey Into Darkness / 1991 / BS / B • Kiss It Goodbye / 1991 / SE / M • Latent Image: Amy Kooiman / 1991 / LAT / F • Lethal Woman / 1991 / CIN / M • The Mark Of Zara / 1990 / XCI / M • Model Wife / 1991 / CA / M • More Dirty Debutantes #07 / 1991 / 4P / M • The Mystery Of Payne / 1991 / BS / B • Naughty Nurses / 1992 / VD / C • Nurse Nancy / 1991 / CA / M • Object Of Desire / 1991 / FAZ / M • Obsession / 1991 / CDI / M • Postcards From Abroad / 1991 / CA / C • Ready, Willing & Anal / 1992 / OD / M • Sophisticated Lady / 1991 / CIN / M • Spellbound / 1991 / CDI / M • Titillation #3 / 1991 / SE / M • Wicked Fascination / 1991 / CIN / M • Zara's Revenge / 1991 / XCI / M

ZARAH
Gigi Gives It Away / 1995 / FRF / M

ZARRAH
Honey Drippers / 1992 / ROB / F • Kittens & Vamps #1 / 1993 / ROB / F • Lesbian Lockup / 1993 / ROB / F

ZASU KNIGHT
More Dirty Debutantes #63 / 1997 / SBV / M • White Men Can't Iron On Butt Row / 1997 / ABS / M

ZAZA
Transaction #1 / 1986 / WET / M

ZDENA
Toredo / 1996 / ROX / M

ZEBEDY COLT
The Affairs Of Janice / 1975 / ALP / M • The Devil Inside Her / 1977 / ALP / M • Dutch Treat / 1977 / VHL / M • Every Man's Fantasy / 1985 / IN / M • Farmers Daughters / 1975 / VC / M • Frank Henenlotter's XXX Hardcore Horrors #05 / 1996 / SOW / M • French Kittens / 1985 / VC / C • Georgia Peach / 1977 / COM / M • Hot Flashes / 1984 / VC / M • Hot Nurses / 1977 / CA / M • In The Pink / 1983 / CA / M • Love In Strange Places / 1977 / CA / M • Playgirls Of Munich / 1977 / VC / M • Raffles / 1988 / VC / M • Seka Is Tara / 1981 / VC / M • Sex Wish / 1976 / CV / M • Sharon / 1977 / AR / M • Sherlick Holmes / cr75 / SVE / M • Sizzling Summer / 1984 / VC / M • Spreading Joy / 1988 / VC / M • The Story Of Joanna / 1975 / VHL / M • Unwilling Lovers / 197? / SVE / M • Virgin Dreams / 1976 / BMV / M • Young Nurses In Love / 1987 / VC / M

ZED *see Star Index I*

ZEE
Joe Elliot's College Girls #33 / 1994 / JOE / M

ZEENA LEE
Finger Pleasures #2 / 1995 / PL / F • Shaved #08 / 1995 / RB / F

ZEKE
Cherry Poppers #15: Mischievous Maidens / 1996 / ZA / M

ZELDA STARR *see Star Index I*

ZELMA
Tropic Of Passion / 1971 / NGV / M

ZEN
Bun Busters #14 / 1994 / LBO / M • Odyssey Triple Play #98: Three Ways To Sunday / 1995 / OD / M • Sexual Trilogy

#02 / 1993 / SFP / M • Sexual Trilogy #04 / 1994 / SFP / M

ZEN BUCKAROO *see Star Index I*

ZENA
Bi The Time You Get Back / 1995 / BIN / G • The Bitch Biker #1: The Long Road Home / 1994 / RBP / F • Night Moods / 1985 / AVC / M

ZENA FULSOM
Exposure Images #06: Zena Fulsom / 1992 / EXI / F • Further Escapades Of Zena / 199? / H&S / S • H&S: Zena #1 / 1991 / H&S / M • H&S: Zena #2 / 1991 / H&S / M • Introducing Zena Fulsom / 199? / H&S / S • The Zena Fulsom Story / 1993 / BTO / S • Zena Hardcore Special / 1994 / BTO / M

ZENA GRANGER
[Sex Hungry Twins / 197? / ... / M

ZENA ZATORI
N.Y. Video Magazine #08 / 1996 / OUP / M

ZENIA DAMAGE *see Lynx Cannon*

ZENZA RAGGI
Amsterdam Nights #1 / 1996 / BLC / M • The Way Of Sex / 1995 / DBV / M • Chateau Duval / 1996 / HDE / M • Diamonds / 1996 / HDE / M • Dirty Tricks #2: This Ain't Love / 1996 / EA / M • Fresh Meat (John Leslie) #3 / 1996 / EA / M • Hose Jobs / 1995 / VEX / M • Private Gold #02: Friends In Sex / 1995 / OD / M • Private Gold #03: The Chase / 1996 / OD / M • Private Gold #04: Amazonas / 1996 / OD / M • Private Gold #08: The Longest Night / 1996 / OD / M • Private Gold #09: Private Dancer / 1996 / OD / M • Private Gold #10: Sins / 1996 / OD / M • Private Stories #05 / 1995 / OD / M • Private Stories #06 / 1995 / OD / M • Sodomania #20: For Members Only / 1997 / EL / M • Triple X Video Magazine #10 / 1995 / OD / M • Triple X Video Magazine #12 / 1996 / OD / M • The Voyeur #6 / 1996 / EA / M • The Voyeur #7: Live In Europe #1 / 1996 / JLP / M

ZERINA DREAMS
FTV #25: Big Bust Domination / 1996 / FT / B • FTV #26: Smother Queen / 1996 / FT / B • FTV #43: The Enforcer / 1996 / FT / B

ZEUS *see Damian Zeus*

ZEXX-EE
Video Virgins #31 / 1996 / NS / M

ZHOL WALTON
Dirty Stories #5 / 1996 / PE / M

ZIARA TAX
Dyke's Discipline / 1994 / PL / F

ZIARIE
Gillie's Isle / 1990 / GOT / M

ZIE UVA (ZOE) *see Star Index I*

ZINA (LISA ANN) *see Lisa Ann*

ZINA DEAN
50 And Still Gangbangin'! / 1995 / EMC / M • Anal Camera #09 / 1995 / EVN / M • Anal Virgins Of America #10 / 1994 / FOR / M • Ass Busters / 1995 / VMX / C • Ass Masters (Leisure) #03 / 1995 / LEI / M • Butt Bangers Ball #1 / 1996 / TTV / M • Creme De La Face #06 / 1995 / OD / M • The Cumm Brothers #15: Hot Primal Sex / 1996 / OD / M • Fortysomething And Still Hot / 1995 / SUF / M • Gangbang At The O.K. Corral / 1994 / FPI / M • Golden Oldies #1 / 1995 / TTV / M • Golden Oldies #2 / 1995 / TTV / M • Golden Oldies #3 / 1995 / TTV / M • High Heeled & Horny #1 / 1994 / LBO / M • Hollywood Amateurs #09 / 1994 / MID / M • Middle Aged Sex Mani-

acs / 1995 / SUF / M • Old Wives' Tails / 1995 / EMC / M • Older And Anal #1 / 1995 / FC / M • The Older Women's Sperm Bank #3: Red Hot Grandmas / 1996 / SUF / M • Oldies But Goodies / 1995 / WIV / M • Orgies Orgies Orgies / 1994 / WV / M • Rainwoman #09: Wetlands / 1995 / CC / M • Reel People #11 / 1995 / PP / M • Snatch Patch / 1995 / LE / M • Straight A's / 1994 / AMP / M • Sugar Mommies / 1995 / FPI / M • Tail Taggers #129: / 1994 / WV / M • Tight Fit #08 / 1994 / GO / M • Under The Cum Cum Tree / 1996 / BCP / M • Voyeur's Fantasies / 1996 / C69 / M • Wicked Waxxx Worxxx / 1995 / HW / M • Wild Orgies #12 / 1994 / AFI / M • The World's Biggest Gang Bang #1 / 1995 / FPI / M • Zena's Gang Bang / 1995 / HO / M

ZINA REEL *see Star Index I*

ZINA SUNSHINE *see Lisa Ann*

ZITA
The Betrayal Of Innocence #1: The Awakening Of Marika / 1993 / CC / M • The Betrayal Of Innocence #2: The Decadence / 1993 / CC / M • The Betrayal Of Innocence #3: The Choice / 1993 / CC / M

ZITA BENESIC
True Stories #2 / 1993 / SC / M

ZOE
Joe Elliot's College Girls #31 / 1994 / JOE / M • The Latex Dungeon / 1992 / GOT / B • Lesbian Sleaze / 1994 / PL / F • Toe Tales #03 / 1992 / GOT / B

ZOE FRIEDRICH
The Collegiates / 1971 / BL / M

ZOE HILTON
Bon Appetite / 1985 / TGA / C • Showgirl #14: Kitty Shane's Fantasies / 1983 / VCR / M • Torch Of Desire / 1983 / REG / M

ZOE JARDINE *see Star Index I*

ZOE LOVE *see Star Index I*

ZOE LUCIEN
French Heat / 1975 / VC / M

ZOE MANISO
Finger Pleasures #1 / 1995 / PL / F • Shaved #07 / 1995 / RB / F

ZOE MARLOWE
Naughty Girls Need Love Too / 1983 / SE / M

ZOEY
Voluptuous #2 / 199? / H&S / M • Voluptuous #3 / 199? / H&S / M

ZOEY MILES *see Star Index I*

ZOLI
The Betrayal Of Innocence #1: The Awakening Of Marika / 1993 / CC / M • The Betrayal Of Innocence #2: The Decadence / 1993 / CC / M • The Betrayal Of Innocence #3: The Choice / 1993 / CC / M • Dick & Jane In Budapest / 1993 / AVI / M • Dick & Jane Return To Hungary / 1993 / OAP / M • The Witch's Tail / 1994 / GOU / M

ZOLKIN *see Star Index I*

ZOLLY
Angel's Vengeance / 1995 / VMX / M • Mission Hard / 1995 / XC / M

ZOLT WALTON
Hotel Fear / 1996 / ONA / M

ZOLTAN
Frank Thring's Double Penetration #1 / 1995 / XPR / M • Itsy Bitsy Gang Bang / 1996 / HW / M • Porno X-Treme #2: Club Bizarre / 1995 / SC / M • Porno X-Treme #4: Wet Dream / 1995 / SC / M • Sodomania #11: In Your Face / 1994 / EL / M • Somewhere Under The Rainbow #1 / 1995

/ HW / M • Somewhere Under The Rainbow #2 / 1995 / HW / M

ZOLTAN HESS
The Voyeur #7: Live In Europe #1 / 1996 / JLP / M • The Voyeur #8: Live In Europe #2 / 1996 / JLP / M

ZOLTAN KABAI
Jungle Heat / 1995 / LUM / M • Lil' Women: Vacation / 1996 / EUR / M • True Stories #1 / 1993 / SC / M • True Stories #2 / 1993 / SC / M

ZOLTAN KRUCSAY
The Coming Of Nikita / 1995 / EL / M

ZOLTAN ROSCY
Private Gold #02: Friends In Sex / 1995 / OD / M

ZOLTAN TOTH
True Stories #1 / 1993 / SC / M • True Stories #2 / 1993 / SC / M

ZOR'A
Christine's Bondage Fantasies / 1996 / JAM / B

ZORAN
The Voyeur #8: Live In Europe #2 / 1996 / JLP / M

ZORENA
Desire / 1990 / VC / M

ZORRO
Kellie Everts #035 / 1989 / KEE / B • Kellie Everts #036 / 1989 / KEE / B • Transsexual Prostitutes #2 / 1997 / DFI / G

ZORYNA DREAMS
Big Bust Scream Queens / 1994 / BTO / M • Girls Around The World #13: Lynn LeMay And Friends / 1994 / BTO / M • Juicy Treats / 1991 / ROB / M • Palm Springs Or Bust / 1994 / BTO / M • Studio Bust Out / 1994 / BTO / M

ZSA ZSA
Somewhere Under The Rainbow #1 / 1995 / HW / M

ZSA ZSA CORTEZ *see Star Index I*

ZSASZA
The Betrayal Of Innocence #1: The Awakening Of Marika / 1993 / CC / M • The Betrayal Of Innocence #2: The Decadence / 1993 / CC / M • The Betrayal Of Innocence #3: The Choice / 1993 / CC / M

ZSUSANNA SKOUPY
Diamonds / 1996 / HDE / M

ZSUZSANNA
Thermonuclear Sex / 1996 / EL / M

ZUKI *see Star Index I*

ZULA *see Star Index I*

ZUMARIA *see Zumira*

ZUMIRA *(Zumaria, Margarita Espana, Shayla (Zumira), Teddy (Zumira), Donzella Danzig, Donella Danzig, Donald Danzig (sic), Donella Danzing, Tanya Gerrado, Tanya (Zumira), Maria (Zumira), Kedina, Dedina, Adriani, Samera, Grocier, Bobina, Kadina, Brea, Gail (Zumira), Brigitte (Zumira), Veronica (Zumira), Stedla, Dajilla, Sally (Zumira), Valerie (Zumira), Stedna, Gabrielle (Zumira))*
Tight bodied dark complexioned Hispanic (she says French) girl with a limited command of English. Small tits, reddish brown hair, pretty face, 22 years old in 1993, pencil eraser nipples. According to her in **MDD #28**, she's 23 (1993) and comes from Argentina via Brooklyn. Since she has changed her name in almost every movie, I think she's a pathological liar.
30 Days In The Hole / 1993 / ZA / M • Alice

In Analand / 1994 / SC / M • Amateur Dreams #3 / 1994 / DR / M • Anal Oriental Sorority / 1994 / LBO / M • Anal Pow Wow #08 / 1994 / XC / M • Anal Virgins Of America / 1994 / FOR / M • Anal Vision #19 / 1993 / LBO / M • Beach Bum Amateur's #34 / 1993 / MID / M • The Blues #2 / 1994 / VT / M • Brassiere To Eternity / 1994 / PEP / F • Bubble Butts Gold #2 / 1994 / LBO / M • Bun Busters #07 / 1993 / LBO / M • Bun Busters #10 / 1993 / LBO / M • Bun Busters #13 / 1994 / LBO / M • Cherry Poppers #01 / 1993 / ZA / M • Creme De La Face #01 / 1994 / OD / M • Creme De La Face #02 / 1994 / OD / M • The Cumm Brothers #03: Go To Traffic School / 1994 / OD / M • The Cumm Brothers #07: Honeymoon On Uranus / 1995 / OD / M • Dick & Jane Go To Mexico / 1994 / AVI / M • Dirty Doc's Housecalls #04 / 1993 / LV / M • Dr Fraud's Female Fantasies / 1993 / AM / M • Ebony Erotica #17: Black Power / 1994 / GO / M • Gang Bang Bitches #02 / 1994 / PP / M • Gang Bang Diaries #4 / 1994 / SFP / M • Hidden Camera #11 / 1993 / JMP / M • The Hitch-Hiker #01: Wide Open Spaces / 1993 / WMG / M • Hose Jobs / 1995 / VEX / M • Koko Is Cumin' At Cha / 1994 / AVI / M • M Series #17 / 1993 / LBO / M • M Series #25 / 1994 / LBO / M • Max #01 / 1994 / FWE / M • Max Gold #1 / 1996 / XPR / C • Milli Vanilla / 1994 / TP / M • More Dirty Debutantes #28 / 1994 / 4P / M • More Dirty Debutantes #29 / 1994 / 4P / M • Nasty Newcummers #03 / 1994 / MET / M • Naughty Nicole / 1994 / SC / M • Naughty Senorita / 1994 / WIV / M • Odyssey Triple Play #72: Backdoor Score / 1994 / OD / M • Raw Sex #02 / 1995 / ERW / M • Ron Hightower's White Chicks #13 / 1994 / LBO / M • Tail Taggers #123 / 1994 / WV / M • Tight Fit #03 / 1994 / GO / M • Tight Fit #06 / 1994 / GO / M • Triple Play / 1994 / PRE / B • Up And Cummers #12 / 1994 / 4P / M • Video Virgins #07 / 1993 / NS / M • Women Of Color #1 / 1994 / ANA / M

ZUZANA
Prague By Night #1 / 1996 / EA / M

ZYLECKO PRINCESS *see Carol Titian*

Movie Names'
Cross-References

$exce$$ • Sexcess

(Hot & Saucy) Pizza Girls (We Deliver) • Pizza Girls (We Deliver)

(This Film Is) All About... • All About Sex

10 Years Of Big Busts #1 • Ten Years Of Big Busts

1001 Erotic Nights #1 • Hard Arabian Nights

10th Annual Adult Video News Awards • Tenth Annual Adult Video News Awards

11th Annual Adult Video News Awards • Eleventh Annual AVN Awards

12th Annual Adult Video News Awards • Twelth Annual Avn Awards

13th Annual Adult Video News Awards • Adult Video News 1996 Awards

18 And Anxious (1996) • Eighteen #1

18 And Anxious (Cr78) • Eighteen And Anxious (Cr78)

2 Baggers • Two Baggers

2 Hot 2 Touch • Too Hot To Touch #2

2 Hung 2 Tung • Too Hung To Tongue

2 Janes • The Two Janes

2 Of A Kind • Two Of A Kind (1993)

2 Times A Virgin • Two Times A Virgin

2 Women And A Man • Two Women & A Man (1988)

2002: A Sex Odyssey • A Sex Odyssey

20th Century Fox • 20th Century Lady

20th Century Lady • 20th Century Fox

24 Heures D'Un Americain A Paris • Paris Ooh-La-La!

3 A.M. • Three A.M.

3 Beauties And A Maid • Three Beauties And A Maid

3 Men And A Hooker • Three Men And A Hooker

3 Shades Of Flesh • Three Shades Of Flesh

3-Way Lust • Parliament: Three Way Lust

37.2o Le Matin • Betty Blue (French)

4 Bi 4 • Four Bi Four

4 Of A Kind • Four Of A Kind

50 & Sizzlin' • 50 Enni In Calore

50 Enni In Calore • 50 & Sizzlin'

50 Ways To Lick Your Lover • 50 Ways To Please Your Lover

50 Ways To Please Your Lover • 50 Ways To Lick Your Lover

6 Faces Of Samantha • Six Faces Of Samantha

69 Park Avenue • Uptown Fantasies

7 Good Women • Seven Good Women

7 Into Snowy • Seven Into Snowy

9 Lives Of A Wet Pussycat • Nine Lives Of A Wet Pussycat

9 To Sex • Scandanavian Double Features

#3

The A Chronicles • The Anal Chronicle

A Estranha Hosperaria Dos Prazeres • The Strange Hostel Of Naked Pleasures

A Team #1 • The Girls Of The A Team #1

A Team #2 • The Return Of The A Team

A Team #3: Hardbreak Ridge • Hardbreak Ridge

A Team #3: Heartbreak Ridge • Hardbreak Ridge

A&B AB#027: Gang Bang Girl • A&B GB#027: The Invitation Party #1

A&B AB#028: Britt Takes On 35 • A&B GB#028: The Invitation Party #28

A&B AB#059: Ginger's Gang Bang • A&B GB#059: Ginger

A&B AB#073: Cum Eating Anal Fucking Gang Bang • A&B GB#073: Chessi Does It Again

A&B AB#116: Blowjobs For All • A&B GB#116: Blow Jobs For All

A&B AB#324: Bridget • A&B AB#472: Bridget

A&B AB#472: Bridget • A&B AB#324: Bridget

A&B GB#027: The Invitation Party #1 • A&B AB#027: Gang Bang Girl

A&B GB#028: The Invitation Party #28 • A&B AB#028: Britt Takes On 35

A&B GB#034: Hot Wild And Sexy • A&B GB#070: Hot Wild And Sexy

A&B GB#059: Ginger • A&B AB#059: Ginger's Gang Bang

A&B GB#070: Hot Wild And Sexy • A&B GB#034: Hot Wild And Sexy

A&B GB#073: Chessi Does It Again • A&B AB#073: Cum Eating Anal Fucking Gang Bang

A&B GB#116: Blow Jobs For All • A&B AB#116: Blowjobs For All

The A-Train • Take The A Train

A.S.S.(Anal Security Squad) • Anal Security Squad

Acque Di Primavera • Torrents Of Spring

Adam & Eve's House Party #1 • House Party (VCA)

Adult Affairs • Nina Hartley's Adult Affairs

Adult Cartoons #1 • Dirty Little Adult Cartoons #1

Adult Cartoons #2 • King Dick

Adult Fairytales • Fairy Tales

Adult Video News 1993 Awards • Tenth Annual Adult Video News Awards

Adult Video News 1994 Awards • Eleventh Annual AVN Awards

Adult Video News 1995 Awards • Twelth Annual Avn Awards

Adult Video News 1996 Awards • 13th Annual Adult Video News Awards

Adultery For Fun And Profit • Bucky Beavers #111

Adultress Abduction • The Taking Of Christina

The Adventures Of Buttgirl & Wonder Wench • Buttgirl & Wonder Wench

Adventures Of Buttwoman #1 • Buttwoman #1

The Adventures Of Buttwoman #2: Behind Bars • Buttwoman #2: Behind Bars

The Adventures Of Dickman & Throbbin • Dickman & Throbbin

The Adventures Of Major Morehead • Major Morehead

Adventures Of Mighty Man #1 • Mighty Man #1: Virgins In The Forest

The Adventures Of Neutron Man • Neutron Man

The Adventures Of Peeping Tom #1 • The Video Adventures Of Peeping Tom • Peeping Tom #1

The Adventures Of Rich Quick, Private Dick • Rich Quick, Private Dick

The Adventures Of Sabrina Starlet • Sabrina Starlet

Adventures Of Sherlick Holmes • Sherlick Holmes

The Adventures Of Suzy Super Slut #3 • The Anal Adventures Of Suzy Super Slut #3

Adventures Of The Cockateer • The Cockateer #1

Adventures Of Tracy Dick • Tracy Dick

Aerobics Girls Club • Aerobisex Girls' Club

Aerobisex Girls' Club • Aerobics Girls Club

Agent 69 • Emmanuelle In Denmark • Agent 69 I Skyttens Tegn • I Skyttens Tegn

Agent 69 I Skyttens Tegn • Agent 69

Agent OOSex • The Erotic Adventures Of Peter Galore

Aggressive Women (1983) • Erotic Dimensions: Aggressive Women

Agony Of Lace, Lash And Love • Agony Of Love, Lace And Lash

Agony Of Love, Lace And Lash • Agony Of Lace, Lash And Love

Ai No Corrida • In The Realm Of The Senses

Al Terego's Anal Alternatives • Double Anal Alternatives

The Alcove • L'Alcova

Alex De Renzy's Girlfriends • Girlfriends (1983)

Alex De Renzy's Moving In • Moving In

Bottoms #2 • Parliament: Bottoms #2

Bottoms Up (1974) • *The Magical Ring*

The Box Lunch Club • The Hot Lunch Club

Breakdown • Sexual Breakdown

Breaker Beauties • *Mel's And Vanessa's Diner* • *The New Mel's And Vanessa's Diner* • *Mother Truckers*

Breastman Back In Breastland #2 • Breastman Goes To Breastland #2

Breastman Goes To Breastland #2 • *Breastman Back In Breastland #2*

Breastman's Ultimate Orgy • Ultimate Orgy #1

Breeders (1984) • Corporal Collectors #5: Breeders

Briar Patch Dolls • Brier Patch Dolls

Bridal Sweet • The Wedding

Brier Patch Dolls • *Briar Patch Dolls*

Bring Your Own Body • B.Y.O.B.

British Babe Hunt • *Ben Dover's British Babe Hunt*

British Butt Search • *Ben Dover's British Butt Search*

The British Connection • *Ben Dover's British Connection*

Britt Morgan Takes It On The Chin • Superstars Of Porn (PI) #03

Broadcast Babes • GVC: Broadcast Babes #138

Brooke Does College • *Brooke Goes To College*

Brooke Goes To College • Brooke Does College

Brothers Grime X-Rated Cartoons #1 • *Gonad The Barbarian*

Brothers Grime X-Rated Cartoons #2 • *Offenders Of The Universe*

Brothers Grime X-Rated Cartoons #3 • *Pandora...An Erotic Trilogy*

Brown Sugar (1984) • *Satin Sugar*

Bruce Seven's Diverse Endings • Bruce Seven's Favorite Endings #1

Bruce Seven's Favorite Endings #1 • *Bruce Seven's Diverse Endings*

Bruce Seven: A Compendium Of His Most Graphic Scenes Vol 5 • *Best Of Felecia*

Brutal Nights Of Emmanuelle • Emmanuelle In America

Buck Adams' Frankenstein • Frankenstein (1994)

Bucky Beaver's XXX Dragon Art Theatre Double Feature #01 • *Dragon Art Theatre #01*

Bucky Beavers #050 • Mona The Virgin Nymph

Bucky Beavers #065 • Man And Wife

Bucky Beavers #066 • He And She

Bucky Beavers #067 • The Art Of Marriage

Bucky Beavers #068 • The Coming Thing

Bucky Beavers #069 • American Sexual Revolution

Bucky Beavers #070 • The History Of Pornography

Bucky Beavers #071 • The Sexual Secrets Of Marijuana

Bucky Beavers #072 • Censorship In Denmark

Bucky Beavers #073 • The Nurses

Bucky Beavers #075 • Sexo-Weirdo

Bucky Beavers #076 • School Girl

Bucky Beavers #077 • What About Jane?

Bucky Beavers #078 • Kitty's Pleasure Palace

Bucky Beavers #079 • Tijuana Blue

Bucky Beavers #080 • Girl In The Basket

Bucky Beavers #081 • School For Sex

Bucky Beavers #082 • Smash Or How To Get Hung

Bucky Beavers #083 • Mafia Girls (1969)

Bucky Beavers #084 • Lady Zazu's Daughter

Bucky Beavers #085 • Night Of The Animals

Bucky Beavers #111 • Adultery For Fun And Profit

Bucky Beavers #112 • The Sex Machine (1971)

Bucky Beavers #113 • Electro Sex '75 (1970)

Bucky Beavers #114 • Journal Of Love

Bucky Beavers #115 • Mondo Porno

Bucky Beavers #116 • Teenage Cousins

Bucky Beavers #117 • The Ideal Marriage

Bucky Beavers #118 • Erotography

Bucky Beavers #119 • Uschi's Hollywood Adventure

Bucky Beavers #120 • Missus Little's Dude Ranch

Bucky Beavers #129 • Devil's Due

Buffy And The Boys • Fantasy Photography: Buffy And The Boys

Bummer! • The Sadist

Bunny's Office Fantasies • *What Happened In Bunny's Office*

Buns In The USA • Teeny Buns

Burglars In The Bedroom • Any Time, Any Place

Burning Desires (1974) • Inside Georgina Spelvin

Burning Secrets • If These Walls Could Talk #2: Burning Secrets

Burning Snow • Swedish Playbirds

Business As Usual • Loose Threads

Bust Out (1973) • Convict's Women

Bust Out (1994) • Studio Bust Out

Bustin' Loose (1985) • Treasure Chest (1985)

Bustin' Loose (1993) • Bustin' Thru

Bustin' Out My Best Anal • Seymore Butts: Bustin' Out My Best Anal

Bustin' Thru • *Bustin' Loose (1993)*

Busty Beauties Of The Seventies • Down Mammary Lane #4

Busty Centerfolds #1 • Score Busty Centerfolds #1

Busty Covergirls #1 • Score Busty Covergirls #1

Butt Freak #2 • *Buttman's Butt Freak Ii*

Butt Hole Boulevard • *California Cruizin: Butt Hole Boulevard*

Butt Light #1 • I Said A Butt Light #1

Butt Light #2 • I Said A Butt Light #2

Butt Light: Queen Of Rears • *The Rump Ranger*

The Butt Sisters • *The Anal Adventures Of The Butt Sisters*

The Butt Stops Here • *This Butt Stops Here*

Butt's #3 • Butt's Motel #3

Butt's Motel #3 • *Butt's #3*

Butterflies • *Young Butterflies* • Lifterskan

Butterfly (1993) • *X Butterfly*

Buttgirl & Wonder Wench • The Adventures Of Buttgirl & Wonder Wench

Butthead & Beaver • *The Backdoor Adventures Of Butthead & The Beaver*

Buttman Back In Rio • Buttman Goes To Rio #2

Buttman Goes To Rio #2 • *Buttman Back In Rio*

Buttman Meets Buttwoman • Buttman Vs Buttwoman

Buttman Vs Buttwoman • *Buttman Meets Buttwoman*

Buttman's Big Tit Adventure #1 • *Big Tit Adventure*

Buttman's Butt Freak Ii • Butt Freak #2

The Buttnicks #2 • *The Buttnicks Vacation*

The Buttnicks #3 • *Suburban Buttnicks*

The Buttnicks #4: The Black Buttnicks • *The Black Buttnicks*

The Buttnicks Vacation • The Buttnicks #2

Buttslammers #01 • *All The Girls Are Buttslammers*

Buttwoman #1 • Adventures Of Buttwoman #1

Buttwoman #2: Behind Bars • The Adventures Of Buttwoman #2: Behind Bars

Buttwoman Does Budapest • Buttwoman In Budapest

Buttwoman In Budapest • *Buttwoman Does Budapest*

Bye Bye Monkey • *Ciao Maschio* • Reve De Singe

C.O.D. • *Snap*

Cadillak & Devell • Kadillac & Devell

Caged Heat #1 • *Renegade Girls*

Caged Virgins • *Requiem For A Vampire* • *Vierges Et Vampires* • *Crazed Virgins* • *The Crazed Vampire* • *Dungeon Of Terror* • *Sex Vampires* • *Virgins And Vampires*

Caged Women (1984) • Emmanuelle In Hell

California Asians • Pai Gow Video #05: California Asians

California Blondes (Parliam.) • Parliament: California Blondes #1

The California Connection • The Erotic Adventures Of Peter Galore

California Creamin' • Golden Girls, The Movie

California Cruizin: Butt Hole Boulevard • Butt Hole Boulevard

California Cruizin: Slummin' Hood Girls • Slummin' Hood Girlz

California Dreaming • California Reaming

California Gigolo (1987) • *The Touchables*

California Reaming • *California Dreaming*

California Surfer Girls • Teenage Surfer Girls

Cambridge Blues • Spanking Video #3: Cambridge Blues

Cameo Is Revealed • Revealed

Camp Beaverlake #2 • *Return To Camp Beaverlake*

Campus Capers • *Crammin' Cuties*

Can Her! • Anal Adventures #3: Can Her!

Canadian Beaver • The Search For Canadian Beaver

Candi Girl • *Jet Sex*

Candida Royale's Fantasies • Showgirl #10: Candida Royale's Fantasies

Candy's Hot Interview • Candy's Sweet Interview

Candy's Sweet Interview • *Candy's Hot Interview*

Cannes Fantasies • Private Film #16

Cannibal • Jungle Holocaust

Cannibal Ferrox • Make Them Die Slowly

Cannibal Island • *David Friedman's Road Show Rarities #07: Cannibal Island*

Cannonball • F

Captain Lust And The Amorous Contessa • *Captain Lust and the Pirate Women* • *The Pirate Women*

Captain Lust and the Pirate Women • Cap-

Creme Rinse • *Cream Rinse*

Crew Sluts (1996) • *Tales From The Road: Crew Sluts*

Crocodile Blondee #1 • *A Taste Of Amber (Cabaret)*

Crocodile Blondee #2 • *First Bite*

Cruel Passion • Justine (1977)

Cruising For Sex • Teenage Cruisers

Cry Uncle • *American Oddballs* • *Super Dick*

Crystal Blue Persuasion • Persuasion

Crystal Dawn's Fantasies • Showgirl #05: Crystal Dawn's Fantasies

Cum Rain, Cum Shine • *Come Rain, Come Shine*

Cumback Pussy #1 • *Tom Byron's Cumback Pussy #1*

Cumm For Dinner • *Rodney Moore's Cum For Dinner*

Cummin' At Cha • Koko Is Cumin' At Cha

The Cumming Of Sarah Jane #2 • *Second Cumming Of Sarah Jane*

Curse Of The Demon Womb • Urotsukidoji #2: Curse Of The Demon Womb

Curse Of The Living Dead • Demoniacs

Cutthroat Commandos • She-Devils Of the S.S.

Cutthroats • She-Devils Of The S.S.

Cyberzone • Droid Gunner

Cycle Sluts (1995) • Sin City Cycle Sluts #1

D'ardenelle • Harem

Daddy • *My Heart Belongs To Daddy* • Her Heart Belongs To Daddy

Daddy's Darling Daughters • *Darling Nikki*

Daddy's Girls (1992) • Wild Hearts (1992)

Daisy Mae • Dalsy May

Daisy May • *Daisy Mae*

Dale's House Of Anal • House Of Anal

Damaged Goods (1937) • *David Friedman's Road Show Rarities #11: Damaged Goods* • Forbidden Desires (1937) • Marriage Forbidden

Damaged Goods (1975) • Little Girl...Big Tease

Dames • *Sassy Ladies*

Damiano's People • People

Danger (Curves Ahead) • Diedre In Danger

Dangerous Curves Ahead • Diedre In Danger

Dangerous Desires (1994) • Passion's Prisoners

Dangerous Obsession • *The Devil's Honey* • La Miel Del Diablo • Il Miele Del Diavolo

Dangerous When Wet (Amber Lynn Is) • Amber Lynn Is Dangerous When Wet

Danielle On Fire • Limo Connection

Danielle's Dirty Deeds • *Dirty Deeds Done, Danielle*

Danielle's Girlfriends • GVC: Danielle's Girlfriends #116

Danielle, Blonde Superstar • GVC: Danielle, Blonde Superstar #131

Dark & Sweet #1 • Parliament: Dark & Sweet #1

Dark Angel • *The Devil Wore High Heels*

Dark Mission • *Flowers Of Evil* • The Heroin Deal

Darling Daughter • Loving Daughter

Darling Nikki • Daddy's Darling Daughters

Das Verbotene Paradies • Forbidden Paradise

Date With Dallas • Ona Zee's Date With Dallas

Date With Death (1975) • The Taking Of Christina

The Daughter • I, A Woman #3

Daughters Of Darkness (1971) • *The Promise Of Red Lips* • The Red Lips • Erzebeth • La Rouge Aux Levres • Blut An Den Lippen

Daughters Of Emmanuelle • *Never 2 Deep*

Daughters Of Lesbos • *Dominique In Daughters Of Lesbos*

David Friedman's Road Show Rarities #01: Teaserama • Teaserama

David Friedman's Road Show Rarities #02: Varietease • Varietease

David Freidman's Road Show Rarities #03: Guilty Parents • Guilty Parents

David Freidman's Road Show Rarities #04: Marihuana • Marihuana

David Friedman's Road Show Rarities #05: Child Brides • Child Brides

David Friedman's Road Show Rarities #06: Mau Mau • Mau Mau

David Friedman's Road Show Rarities #07: Cannibal Island • Cannibal Island

David Friedman's Road Show Rarities #08: Samurai • Samurai

David Friedman's Road Show Rarities #09: Kiss Me, Baby • Kiss Me, Baby

David Friedman's Road Show Rarities #10: Peek-A-Boo • Peek-A-Boo (1953)

David Friedman's Road Show Rarities #11: Damaged Goods • Damaged Goods (1937)

Dawn Of Woman • Dreams Of Misty

Day Of The Woman • I Spit On Your Grave

A Day That's Hot & Heavy • Hot & Heavy (1989)

Day-Dream • Asian Erotic Cinema: Day-Dream

De Sade 70 • *Eugenie...The Story Of Her Journey Into Perversion*

De Sade's Justine • Justine (1977)

Deadly Love • *Hot Nasties*

Death Game • The Seducers (1977)

Death In A French Garden • Peril

Death's Ecstacy • The Beast

Debbie Does Dallas #1 • *The Games People Play*

Debbie Does Dishes #2 • Blazing Mattresses

Debbie Does The Devil In Dallas • *Sex Bowl*

Debbie's Love Spell • *Magical Seduction*

Debi Diamond's Dirty Panties • *Dirty Panties*

Debi, You're A Fucking Slut • *You're A Fucking Slut #1*

The Debutante • *Texas Twats*

The Decadent Adventures Of Generation XXX • *Generation Xxx*

Decadent Dames • Despicable Dames

Decendance Of Grace • *Descendants Of Grace*

Deception (1995-Executive) • *A Moment Of Lust*

The Decline And Fall Of Lacey Bodine • Lacey Bodine (The Decline And Fall Of)

Deena Duos & Friends • *Girls Around The World #20: Deena Duos & Friends*

Deep Desires (1986) • *Shiela's Deep Desires*

Deep Dreams • *Sweet Dreams Are Made Of This*

Deep Ghost (1984) • Scared Stiff (1984)

Deep Inside Shane • Seymore Butts Goes Deep Inside Shane

Deep Spikes • Discipline Collectors #1: Deep Spikes

Deep Throat Girls (1986) • *Hummers*

Defiance • *The Defiance Of Good*

The Defiance Of Good • Defiance

Delinquent School Girls • *Bad Girls (1974)*

Delires Porn • Sexy

Delirios De Um Anormal • Hallucinations Of A Deranged Mind

Delirious • Sexy

Deliveries In The Rear #2 • Tailspin (1987)

Delivery Girls • Fast Girls #1

Delusions (1973) • Violated (1973)

Delusions (1983) • *Hollywood Confidential #1* • Memories Of Amanda • Erotic Auditions • Screaming Orgasm

Demon Keeper (1994) • Tales From The Crypt Presents Demon Knight

Demon Knight • Tales From The Crypt Presents Demon Knight

Demoniacs • *Les Demoniaques* • Two Virgins For Satan • Tina The Perverse Pirate • Curse Of The Living Dead

Den Pornografiske Jungfrun • Veil Of Lust

Denni O' #1 • *The Spectacular Denni O'Brien*

Denni O' #2 • Insatiable Denni O' #2

Dentro Il Vulcano • Euroflesh: Dentro Il Vulcano

Descendants Of Grace • Decendance Of Grace

Desire (1979) • Object Of Desire (1979)

Desire (1990) • *Andrew Blake's Desire* • The Art Of Desire

Desire In The Night • *A Little Sex In The Night*

The Desirous Wife • *Karin Moglie Vigliosa*

Desperado (1992) • Bonnie & Clyde #2

Desperately Pleasing Debbie • *White Women*

Desperately Sleazy Susan • *Sleazy Susan*

Despicable Dames • *Decadent Dames*

Destiny • *Porsche Lynn's Destiny*

The Devil In Miss Jones #5: The Inferno • Dmj5

Devil In The Flesh • *Le Diable Au Corps* • Il Diavolo In Corpo

The Devil Wore High Heels • Dark Angel

Devil's Camera • Scum Of The Earth

Devil's Due • *Bucky Beavers #129*

The Devil's Honey • Dangerous Obsession

Devious Girls • The Venus Trap

Diary Of A Nudist • *Nature Camp Confidential*

Diary Of A Sex Goddess • *Hot Night* • Sexstar Search

The Diary Of Casanova • Casanova #3 (1993)

A Dairy Of Torment • Tanya Foxx: A Diary Of Torment

Dick & Jane In Budapest • *Dick & Jane In Hungary*

Dick & Jane In Hungary • Dick & Jane In Budapest

Dick At Nite • *Nite Time TV*

The Dickheads #2 • *Return Of The Dickheads* • Dickheads (Part Deux)

Dickheads (Part Deux) • The Dickheads #2

Dickman & Throbbin • *The Adventures Of Dickman & Throbbin* • The Erotic Adventures Of Dickman & Throbbin

Die Flucht Der Schwarzen Schwestern • Veil Of Lust

Die Jungfrau Und Die Peitsche • Eugenie...The Story Of Her Journey Into Perversion

Die Nichten Der Frau Oberst • Come Play With Me #1

Woman
Marsha, The Erotic Housewife • *Marsha, The Exotic Housewife*
Marsha, The Exotic Housewife • Marsha, The Erotic Housewife
Mary Flegus, Mary Flegus • Doctor Yes
Mary! Mary! • *Money Honey (1977)*
Maryanne's Honeymoon Suite • Honeymoon Suite
MASH'd • MASH'ed
MASH'ed • *SMASH'd* • *MASH'd*
Master Of Reality • Night Prowler #3: Master Of Reality
Mata Hari • The Sex Life Of Mata Hari
The Mating Pot • *The Melting Pot*
A Matter Of Taste • Oralism
Mau Mau • *David Friedman's Road Show Rarities #06: Mau Mau*
Max Hardcore #01 • *The Anal Adventures Of Max Hardcore: Adventures In Shopping*
Max World #1 • *The World According To Max: Southern Cross*
Meduses • L'Annee Des Meduses
Megavixens • Cherry, Harry And Raquel
Mel's And Vanessa's Diner • Breaker Beauties
The Melting Pot • The Mating Pot
Memoirs Of A Male Chauvinist Pig • The Erotic Memoirs Of A Male Chauvinist Pig
The Memoirs Of Fanny Hill • Fanny Hill
Memories Of Amanda • Delusions (1983)
Men...I Eat Them • Felicia
Menage • *Evening Dress* • *Tenue De Soiree*
Meridian • *Phantoms*
Merle Michaels' Fantasies • Showgirl #11: Merle Michaels' Fantasies
Mesmerized • Foreign Tongues #2: Mesmerized
Michael Bruno's Private Label • Private Label
Micro X Video #1 • *Micro X Video: New Frontier* • New Frontier
Micro X Video: New Frontier • Micro X Video #1
Midnight Plowboy • *Sunset Girls*
Mighty Man #1: Virgins In The Forest • *Adventures Of Mighty Man #1*
Mike Horner's Around Frisco • Around Frisco
Mike South's Southern Belles • Southern Belles #1
The Milkmaid • Maid In Sweden
Millenium Countdown • [Camp Fear
Millie's Homecoming • Lady Zazu's Daughter
Million Dollar Mona • Nipples (1973)
The Millionaire • Bondage Classix #17: The Millionaire
Misfits Of Society • Girls Gone Bad #7: Misfits Of Society
Miss Demeanor • Where The Girls Play
Miss September • Whatever Happened To Miss September?
Missus Little's Dude Ranch • *Bucky Beavers #120*
The Mistress And The Slave • The Punishment Of Anne
Mistress Angelina's World Of Male Torture • World Of Male Torture
Mistress Domino's • An Evening At Mistress Dominos
Mistress Electra • *My Mistress Electra*
Mistress Elsa's Latex Sex Camp • *Latex

Sex Camp
Mistress Marianne's Slave Of Love • Bondage Classix #04: Mistress Marianne's Slave Of Love
Mistress Sarona's School Of Discipline • *Sarona's School Of Discipline*
Mistress Sensei's House Of Pain • House Of Pain
Mobile Home Girls • *Jouissances A Domicile* • *Jouissances Roulantes*
The Mole • El Topo
A Moment Of Lust • Deception (1995-Executive)
Moment To Moment • *In Ogni Posto, In Ogni Momento*
Momma's Boy • Mama's Boy
Mona Lisa • *A Portrait Of Mona Lisa*
Mona The Virgin Nymph • *Bucky Beavers #050*
Mona's Place • Fandango
Mondo Girls • *Mondo Topless #1*
Mondo Porno • *Bucky Beavers #115*
Mondo Topless #1 • *Mondo Girls*
Money Buys Happiness • Tight Assets
Money For Nothing: Sex For Free • Private Film #10
Money Honey (1977) • Mary! Mary!
The Monsters Are Loose • The Thrill Killers
The Moon In The Gutter • *La Lune Dans Le Caniveau*
More Games Women Play • *Games Women Play #2*
More Reel People Pt 2 • Reel People #02
More Reel People Pt 3 • Reel People #03
More Sorority Stewardesses • Sorority Stewardesses #2
More Than Just Summer Lovers • Summer Lovers (1987)
More To Love #2 • *Much More To Love*
More Women Without Men • Women Without Men #2
Most Valuable Pussy • Most Valuable Slut
Most Valuable Slut • *Most Valuable Pussy*
Mote Med Djavulen • Veil Of Lust
Motel Lust • Nice 'n' Tight
Mother • *Up Your Teddy Bear*
Mother Truckers • Breaker Beauties
Motor Mods And Rockers • Motor Psycho
Motor Psycho • *Motor Mods And Rockers*
Moving In • *Alex De Renzy's Moving In*
Mr. E. Woman • Transaction #2
Mr. Peepers Casting Couch • *Casting Couch (1991)*
Mr. Peter's Pets • *Petey's Sweeties*
Mrs. Winter's Lover • *Confidences Pornographiques De Lady Winter*
Ms. Behaved • *Lil' Ms. Behaved*
Much More To Love • More To Love #2
Muddy Mama • Riverboat Mama
She-Male #18 Murder She-Male Wrote • She-Male Encounters #18: Murder She-Male Wrote
Murder, Baby • Dixie Ray Hollywood Star
The Museum Of The Living Art • The Anal-Europe Series #03: The Museum Of The Living Art
The Muskatits • The Three Muskatits
Mustaa Valkoisella • [Black On White (1967)
My Ass #2 • My Black Ass
My Black Ass • *My Ass #2*
My First Time (1976) • The First Time
My Gun Is Hard • Street Heat (1984)
My Heart Belongs To Daddy • Daddy
My Mistress Electra • Mistress Electra
My Sister Seka • *I Remember Seka*

My Sister Seymour? #2 • Almost Sisters
My Tail Is Hot • Panties Inferno
My Tale Is Told • Panties Inferno
My Teenage Daughter • Keyhole (1977)
My Way! (1983) • Erotic Dimensions #3: My Way!
My Wife The Hooker • French Erotica: My Wife The Hooker
N.Y. Babes • New York Babes
Naked Afternoon • *Thomasina Kelly*
Naked As Nature Intended • As Nature Intended
Naked Desire • The Face
Naked Dreams Of The Naughty Nerd • The Bachelor's Dreams
Naked Eyes • Ice Cream #3: Naked Eyes
The Naked Kiss • *The Iron Kiss*
Naked Paradise • Emmanuelle In Egypt
Naked Pursuit • *Kofun*
Naked Street Girls • Confessions Of The Sex Slaves
Nalale In Casa D'appuntamento • Love By Appointment
Nasty (1994) • Leena Is Nasty
Nasty As She Wants To Be • As Nasty As She Wants To Be
Nasty Girls #3 (1990-CDI) • *Innocence Lost (1990)*
Nasty Nurses • *Tender Loving Care (1983)*
National Lampoon Goes To The Movies • *National Lampoon's Movie Madness*
National Lampoon's Movie Madness • National Lampoon Goes To The Movies
National Poontang's Sex Vacation • *National Poontang's Summer Vacation*
National Poontang's Summer Vacation • National Poontang's Sex Vacation
Native American Love Techniques • Snakedance
Nature Camp Confidential • Diary Of A Nudist
Nature Girl • *Blaze Starr Goes Nudist* • *Nature Girl (1962)*
Nature Girl (1962) • Nature Girl
Naughty Fantasy • *Naughty French Fantasies* • *Naughty Little French Fantasys* • *House Of Ill Repute*
Naughty French Fantasies • Naughty Fantasy
Naughty Girls • Naughty Girls Need Love Too
Naughty Girls Need Love Too • Naughty Girls
Naughty Little French Fantasys • Naughty Fantasy
Naughty Notions • Coming Attractions
The Naughty Victorians • *A Man With A Maid*
Naval Discipline • Spanking Video #2: Naval Discipline
Nba: Nuttin' Butt Ass • *Nuttin' Butt Ass*
Nea • *A Young Emmanuelle*
Necromancy • *The Witching*
Necronomicon • Succubus
Neptune's Daughter • Wet Tails
Network Sex • GVC: Network Sex #104
Neutron Man • *The Adventures Of Neutron Man*
Never 2 Deep • Daughters Of Emmanuelle
Never Cry Devil • Night Visitor
The New Black Emmanuelle • Black Emmanuelle #2
The New Erotic Adventures Of Cassanova • Casanova #2 (1976)
New Frontier • Micro X Video #1
The New Mel's And Vanessa's Diner •

Reel People #03 • *More Reel People Pt 3*

Reel Sex #02: Splash Party • *Splash Party*

Reflections (1977) • *Teenage Reflections*

Reincarnation Of Serena • GVC: Reincarnation Of Serena #121

Renee, Summer Of '69 • Summer Of '69

Renegade (1990) • *Heartthrob (1990)*

Renegade Girls • Caged Heat #1

Renegade Raiders • The Scavengers

Requiem For A Vampire • Caged Virgins

Reservoir Bitches • *Reservoir Bitches*

Resevoir Bitches • Reservoir Bitches

The Return • *The Alien's Return*

Return Engagement • *Drive-In Dreams*

The Return Of Dr Blacklove • *Dr Blacklove #2*

The Return Of Dr F • Dr F #2: Bad Medicine

The Return Of The A Team • *The Girls Of The A Team #2* • *A Team #2*

The Return Of The Bimbo • The Bimbo #2 (1992)

Return Of The Cheerleader Nurses • Cheerleader Nurses #2

Return Of The Dickheads • The Dickheads #2

Return Of The Fabulous 50 Girls • The Fabulous 50's Girls #2

Return To A Tale Of Two Tittie • A Tale Of Two Titties #2

Return To Bazooka County • Bazooka County #2

Return To Camp Beaverlake • Camp Beaverlake #2

Return To Melrose Place • *Back To Melrose Place*

Return To Sex 5th Avenue • *Sex 5th Avenue #2*

Reunion (Vanessa Del Rio's) • *Vanessa's Wild Reunion* • *Vanessa Gets It!*

Reve De Singe • Bye Bye Monkey

Revealed • *Cameo Is Revealed*

Revelations (1974) • *A Portrait Of Two Women*

The Revenge Of Bonnie & Clyde • Bonnie & Clyde #4

Revenge Of The Alien Dimension • Lethal Woman #2 (1988)

Revenge Of The Pussy Suckers From Mars • *Pussy Suckers From Mars*

Revenge Of The Smart Ass • The Smart Ass #2: Rusty's Revenge

Rich Girls Gone Bad • Anal Intruder #08: Rich Girls Gone Bad

Rich Quick, Private Dick • *The Adventures Of Rich Quick, Private Dick*

The Right Stiff • *Embassy Girls #5*

Ring Of Passion (1994) • *Hot Properties (1994)*

Ripe • Erotic Dimensions #1: Ripe

The Rise Of The Roman Empress #2 • *The Lust Resort*

Rites Of Passion • *Star Director Series #2*

Ritual Of The Maniacs • Awakenings Of The Beast

Riverboat Mama • *Muddy Mama*

Robovixens • Batteries Included

Rock 'em Dead • Shock 'em Dead

Rockin' With Seka • *Seka Fallen Angel* • *Seka's Cruise*

Rodney Moore's Cum For Dinner • Cumm For Dinner

Roman Orgy • *Oriental Night*

Ron Hightower's Casting Couch #1 • *Casting Couch (Ron Hightower)*

Ron Hightower's Ebony Erotica #01: Black

Narcisssys • Ebony Erotica #01: Black Narcissys

Rooster: Spurs Of Death! • *Spurs Of Death!*

Rosa / Francesca • *Francesca & Rosa*

Rosebud • Growing Up (1980)

The Rosebud Beach Hotel • *The Big Lobby* • *The No-Tell Hotel*

Rosey Red And Cheeky • Rosie Red And Cheeky

Rosie Red And Cheeky • *Rosey Red And Cheeky*

Rote Lippen • Sadisterotica

Roto Reamer • Double Insertion

Roxy (1991) • *Virgins On The Run*

Royal Ass Force • *Ben Dover's British Royal Ass Force*

The Rump Ranger • Butt Light: Queen Of Rears

Rumpman In And Out Of Africa • *In And Out Of Africa (1996)*

Run Swinger Run • *Nude On The Run*

Runaway (1991) • Killer

Running Wild • Wild In The Wilderness (1984)

Russian Girls • *Girls From Russia*

Rusty Boner's Back East Babes #1 • Back East Babes #1

Rusty Boner's Bondage Videos: Eternal Bonds • Eternal Bonds

Rx For Passion • Inside Candy Samples

S&M Pleasure Series: The Assistant • *The Assistant*

S&M Pleasure Series: The Contract • *The Contract (1994)*

S&M Pleasure Series: The Gift • *The Gift*

S&M Pleasure Series: The Tomb • *The Tomb*

S.O.S. • *Screw On Screen*

Sabrina Starlet • *The Adventures Of Sabrina Starlet*

Saddle Tramp Women • Tough Guns

The Sadist • Bummer!

Sadisterotica • *Rote Lippen* • *El Caso De Las Dos Bellezas* • *Red Lips (1967)*

Salo' O Le 120 Giornate Di Sodoma • Salo, Or The 120 Days Of Sodom

Salo, Or The 120 Days Of Sodom • *Salo' O Le 120 Giornate Di Sodoma*

Salopis De Chaintes • Gang Bang Gang Bang

Salsa & Spice #5 • *Salsa And Spice Cinco*

Salsa And Spice Cinco • Salsa & Spice #5

Samantha Fox's Fantasies • Showgirl #16: Samantha Fox's Fantasies

Samantha Strong #1 • Parliament: Samantha Strong #1

Samba • *Private Film #22*

Samurai • *David Friedman's Road Show Rarities #08: Samurai*

San Francisco Cosmopolitan Club Amateur Night • San Francisco Cosmopolitan Club Amateur Night

Sandra • Sandra: The Making Of A Woman

Sandra: The Making Of A Woman • *Sandra* • *I Am Sandra*

Sandstorm • Indian Summer #2: Sandstorm

Santa Claus Comes Twice • Spreading Joy (1984)

Santa Comes But Once A Year • Spreading Joy (1984)

Santa Comes Twice • Spreading Joy (1984)

Sarona's School Of Discipline • Mistress Sarona's School Of Discipline

Sassy Ladies • Dames

Satin Angels (1993) • Asian Heat #02: Satin Angels

Satin Seduction • Taija's Satin Seduction

Satin Sugar • Brown Sugar (1984)

Satisfaction (1988) • I Can't Get No...Satisfaction

Saturday Lovers • Teasers: Saturday Lovers

Saturday Night At Canoga Park • Saturday Night Porn #1

Saturday Night Porn #1 • *Saturday Night At Canoga Park*

Savage Passion (1969) • The Ramrodder

Savannah On Trial • On Trial #1: In Defense Of Savannah

Savate • *The Fighter*

Scandanavian Double Features #1 • *The Horny Female*

Scandanavian Double Features #2 • *Possessed By Lust*

Scandanavian Double Features #3 • *9 To Sex* • *Sex Service*

Scandanavian Double Features #4 • *Cat & Ermine* • *A Man's Dream*

Scared Stiff (1984) • *Deep Ghost (1984)*

Scarlet Fantasy • *Secret Fantasy*

The Scavengers • *Rebel Vixens* • *Ambush!* • *Renegade Raiders* • The Grabbers

Scenes They Wouldn't Let Me Shoot • *Great Director Series #1*

The Scent Of Mathilde • Le Parfum De Mathilde

School For Hookers • *Three Cheers For Bju*

School For Sex • *Bucky Beavers #081*

School Girl • *Bucky Beavers #076*

Schoolgirl's Reunion • *College Girl Reunion*

Schwanzgeil • Magma: Horny For Cock

Scooter Trash • Down & Dirty Scooter Trash

Score Busty Centerfolds #1 • *Busty Centerfolds #1*

Score Busty Covergirls #1 • *Busty Covergirls #1*

Scorpion's Tail • La Coda Dello Scorpione

Scoundrels • Rainbow Jam

Scream In The Middle Of The Night • *Scream In The Night*

Scream In The Night • Scream In The Middle Of The Night

A Scream In The Streets • *Girls In The Streets* • *Scream Street*

Scream Queen Hot Tub Party • Hollywood Scream Queen Hot Tub Party

Scream Street • A Scream In The Streets

Screamers (1994) • *Halsning Fran Budapest*

Screaming Orgasm • Delusions (1983)

Screw • *Screw Magazine Video #1*

Screw Magazine Video #1 • Screw

Screw On Screen • S.O.S.

Screwdriver (1988) • *Screwdriver Saloon*

Screwdriver Saloon • Screwdriver (1988)

Screwface • Marked For Death

Screwing Around (1990) • Hustler #17

Scum Of The Earth • *Devil's Camera*

Sean Michael's Jam • Jam

Sean Michaels Sex Machine • Sex Machine (1994)

Sean Michaels Up Your Ass • Up Your Ass #1

Sean Michaels' Bad Girls • Bad Girls (1994)

The Search For Canadian Beaver • *Cana-*

Spanking Video #3: Cambridge Blues • *Cambridge Blues*

Spanking Video #4: Sports Comeback • *Sports Complex*

The Spectacular Denni O'Brien • *Denni O' #1*

Sperma-Traume • Magma: Sperm Dreams

Sphincter Lickin' Good • Historic Erotica #1: Sphincter Lickin' Good

Spies • *Spys 'r' Us* • *Spies & Butts*

Spies & Butts • Spies

The Spirit Of Seventy Six • *Seventeen Seventy Sex*

Splash Party • Reel Sex #02: Splash Party

Sports College • Spanking Video #1: Sports College

Sports Complex • Spanking Video #4: Sports Comeback

Spread For Action • Spread The Action

Spread The Action • *Spread For Action*

Spread The Wealth • *Share The Wealth*

Spreading Joy (1984) • *Santa Comes Twice* • *Santa Comes But Once A Year* • *Santa Claus Comes Twice*

Spreading Joy (1988) • *Babylon Nights*

Spring Break • *Totally Outrageous Spring Break*

Spring Break USA • Spring Fever USA

Spring Fever USA • *Lauderdale* • *Spring Break USA*

Spring Symphony • *Fruhlingssinfonie*

Spurs Of Death! • Rooster: Spurs Of Death!

Spys 'r' Us • Spies

Squirters • *Seymore's Squirters*

Stage Girls • Hostage Girls

Star Director Series #1 • A Taste Of Ambrosia

Star Director Series #2 • Rites Of Passion

Star Director Series #3 • Sensual Escape

Star Flix: Girls Who Love To Suck • Loving Lips

Star Of The Orient • Asian Love Bunnies

The Starlets (1976) • *The X-Rated Starlets*

Starlets (1985) • *Hollywood Starlets*

Stasha: Portrait Of A Swinger • *Portrait Of A Swinger*

Stay As You Are • *Stay The Way You Are* • *Cosi Como Sei*

Stay The Way You Are • Stay As You Are

Steamin' Hot • Princess Seka

Steamy Dreams • *Dreams (Cr70)* • *Feelings (cr70)*

Steamy Sirens (1983) • I'm Yours

Steamy Windows (1993) • *Windows*

Stephanie's Outrageous • *Outrageous (1988)*

Stephen King's Tommyknockers • The Tommyknockers (1993)

The Stepsister • Sinderella #2

Sticky Fingers (Cr70) • Sticky Wagons

Sticky Wagons • *Sticky Fingers (Cr70)* • *Dr Carstairs 1869 Love Root Elixir*

Still Hard To Stop • Hard To Stop #2

Stocks And Blondes • Wanda Whips Wall Street

The Story Of O #1 • *L'Histoire D'O*

The Story Of O • Nicole: The Story Of O

The Story Of O Continues: Fruits Of Passion • *Les Fruits De La Passion* • *The Fruits Of Passion*

Straight To The Top • In And Out (In Beverly Hills)

The Strange Case Of Dr Jeckell & Ms Hide • Dr Jeckell & Ms Hide

Strange Family • GVC: Strange Family

The Strange Hostel Of Naked Pleasures • *A Estranha Hosperaria Dos Prazeres*

The Strange Loves Of Dr Sex • Dr Sex

Strange Portfolio Of Jekyll And Hyde • The Jekyll And Hyde Portfolio

Strange Sex • Beyond Shame

Strangers When We Mate • Love With A Proper Stranger

Strap-On Ho Down • Harness Hannah At The Strap-On Ho Down

Strap-On Palace • Harness Hannah At The Strap-On Palace

Street Heat (1984) • *My Gun Is Hard*

Street Of 1000 Pleasures • *Penthouse Playgirls*

Strickly Sex • Nipples (1973)

Strip Tease #1 (1986) • Parliament: Strip Tease #1

Striptease College • The Art Of Burlesque

Stud Wars • Battle Of The Stars #3: Stud Wars

Student Bodies • Carnal College (1975) • Young Students • Hot Students

Student Enema • Enema Affair / Student Enema

Student Union • Harrad Summer

Studio Bust Out • *Bust Out (1994)*

A Study In Sex • Private Gold #01: Study In Sex

Stuff Your Face #2 • *Stuff Your Face Again*

Stuff Your Face Again • Stuff Your Face #2

Suburban Buttnicks • The Buttnicks #3

Suburban Lust • GVC: Suburban Lust #128

Success • The American Success Company

Succubus • Necronomicon

Suck Channel • Climb To Sex-Dome #3

Sucker For A Job • Blue Interview

The Sucking • Lust At First Bite

Sue Nero's Fantasies • Showgirl #06: Sue Nero's Fantasies

Sugar Daddy Dirty Dave's #2 • Dirty Dave's #2

Sultry Black Dolls • Parliament: Sultry Black Dolls

Summer Beach House • GVC: Summer Beach House #106

Summer In Heat • Hot Revenge

Summer Lovers (1987) • More Than Just Summer Lovers

Summer Of '69 • Renee, Summer Of '69

Sun Bunnies #2: The Pink Cheek Tales • *Backside Out*

Sunset Girls • Midnight Plowboy

Super Dick • Cry Uncle

Super Head #1 • Parliament: Super Head #1

Super Plumpers Of The Seventies • Down Mammary Lane #3

Super Seka • Princess Seka

Super Wrestling Sluts Of Hollywood • Supersluts Of Wrestling

Supersluts Of Wrestling • *Super Wrestling Sluts Of Hollywood*

Superstar Brigitte Monet • Swedish Erotica Superstar #2: Brigitte Monet

Superstar Janey Robbins • Swedish Erotica Superstar #3: Janey Robbins

Superstar John Holmes • John Holmes Superstar

Superstar Seka • Swedish Erotica Superstar #1: Seka

Swedish Erotica Superstar 4: Shauna Grant • Swedish Erotica Superstar #4: Shauna Grant

Superstars Of Porn (PI) #01 • *Shayla Sluts It Up*

Superstars Of Porn (PI) #02 • *Chantilly Lace's Anal Lust*

Superstars Of Porn (PI) #03 • *Britt Morgan Takes It On The Chin*

Superstars Of Porn (PI) #04 • *Nina Hartley: A Twat-Soaked Tribute*

Superstars Of Porn (PI) #05 • *Kaitlyn Ashley: Cum Guzzling Tramp*

Superstars Of Porn (PI) #06 • *Racquel Darrian Rides Again*

Superstars Of Porn (PI) #07 • *Madison: Gutter Mouth Cock Hound*

Superstars Of Porn (PI) #08 • *Jeanna Fine: Bottomless Throat*

Supervixens • Supervixens Eruption • Vixens (1975)

Supervixens Eruption • Supervixens

Surfer Girls (1976) • Teenage Surfer Girls

Surfside Sex (1985) • *Malibu Swingers* • *Pleasure Party (Coast)*

The Surrogate • *Blind Rage*

Suze Randall's Erotic Eye • Erotic Eye

Suzie's Birthday Bang • Suzy's Birthday Bang

Suzy's Birthday Bang • *Suzie's Birthday Bang*

Swedish Erotica Superstar #1: Seka • *Superstar Seka*

Swedish Erotica Superstar #2: Brigitte Monet • *Superstar Brigitte Monet*

Swedish Erotica Superstar #3: Janey Robbins • *Superstar Janey Robbins*

Swedish Erotica Superstar #4: Shauna Grant • *Shauna Grant, Superstar* • *Swedish Erotica Superstar 4: Shauna Grant*

Swedish Gas Pump Girls • Friendly Favors

Swedish Minx • [Justine Och Juliette

Swedish Playbirds • Burning Snow

Sweet Dominance • GVC: Sweet Dominance #127

Sweet Dreams (1975) • Finishing School

Sweet Dreams (1978) • *Les Mauvais Rencontres* • *French Flesh*

Sweet Dreams (1986) • Hyapatia Lee's Secret Dreams

Sweet Dreams Are Made Of This • Deep Dreams

Sweet Erotica • Blue Heat

Sweet Hitchhiker • Girl On The Run

Sweet Penetrations • Douce Penetrations

Sweet Smell Of Love • From Woman To Woman To Woman

Sweet Spot • Jail Bait

Sweet Starlets #1 • Parliament: Sweet Starlets #1

Sweet Starlets #2 • Parliament: Sweet Starlets #2

Sweet Suzy, Dutchess Of Doom • Blacksnake!

Sweet Taste Of Honey (1972) • Hot Sister

Sweethearts #1 • Parliament: Sweethearts #1

Swing Into Spring (1983) • I Never Say No

The Swingin' Stewardesses • *Die Stewardessen*

Swinging Wives • *The Hottest Report Yet*

The Switch (1978) • The Con Artists

Switched • She-Male Encounters #20: Switched

T&A Academy • H.O.T.S.

Ta Mej I Dalen • Practice Makes Perfect (1975)

Tabatha Towers & Julie Juggs • Tabatha's

Sam
[Mane • The Dwelling

The Marquise Of O • [Die Marquise Von
O...

[Masquerade (1992-Italy) • [Bissi Istinti

[Mauvais Sang • The Night Is Young

[Midnight Gigolo • [Voglia Di Guardare •
[Christina

[Miss Stone's Thing • [Sensuous Wife

The Mother And The Whore • [La Maman
Et La Putain

The Murri Affair • [La Grande Bourgeoise

The Nesting • [Phobia

[Never Steal Anything Wet • [Catalina
Caper

The Night Digger • The Road Builder

[Night In A Cemetery • [La Rose De Fer

The Night Is Young • [Mauvais Sang

[Nippon Konchuki • The Insect Woman

[Office Love-In • [Swinging Secretary

[Palm Springs Weekend • [Super Vogliose
Di Maschi

[Parties Fines • [Indecences 1930

[Pesticide • [Les Raisins De La Mort

[Phobia • The Nesting

[Playing With Fire (French) • [Le Jeu Avec
Le Feu

The Pleasure • [Il Piacere

The Pocket Lover • [Lover Boy

[Poliziotto Sprint • [Highway Racer

[Porno Poker • [Una Partita Senza Carte

[Pour Le Peau D'un Flic • [Whirlpool

[Queen Of The Vampires • [Viol Du Vampire

[Quien Puede Matar A Un Nino? • [Island
Of The Damned

The Raisins Of Death • [Les Raisins De La
Mort

[Rapt De Nymphettes • [Je Brule De
Partout

[Raw Meat • [Deathline

The Road Builder • The Night Digger

[Road To Salina • [Sur La Route De Salina
• [La Route De Salina

[S.S. Bordello • [Bordell Ss • [Freudenhaus
42

[S.S. Girls • Deported Women Of The SS
Special Section

Sechs Schwedinnen Von Der Tankstelle •
[Swedish Erotic Sensations

[Sensuous Wife • [Miss Stone's Thing

[Sex And The Vampire • [Le Frisson Des
Vampires

[Sex And Voodoo • [Il Pavone Nero

[Sicarius: The Midnight Party • The Loves
Of Irina

[Sinner • Le Journal Intime D'Une
Nymphomane

[Stau • [Traffic Jam

The Story Of Sin • [Dzieje Grezechu

[Super Cool • [Body Fever

[Super Vogliose Di Maschi • [Palm Springs
Weekend

[Supremes Jouissances • [Jouissances

[Sur La Route De Salina • [Road To Salina

[Swedish Erotic Sensations • Sechs
Schwedinnen Von Der Tankstelle

[Swinging Secretary • [Office Love-In

[Target: Murder • L'Uomo Piu Velenoso Del
Cobra

Tell Me That You Love Me, Junie Moon •
Just Tell Me That You Love Me, Junie
Moon

[Tenderness Of The Wolves • [Zartlichkeit
Der Wolfe

[Terror Of The Vampires • [Le Frisson Des

Vampires
[Torture Castle • [Bacchanales Sexuelles

[Traffic Jam • [Le Grand Embouteillage •
[Stau • L'Ingorgo: Una Storia Impossible

[Un Mauvais Fils • A Bad Son

[Una Partita Senza Carte • [Porno Poker

[Une Flamme Dans Mon Coeur • A Flame
In My Heart

[United Trash: Die Spalte • [Die Spalte

[Vampire Nest • [Levres De Sang

[Vampire Women • [Viol Du Vampire

[Viol Du Vampire • [Queen Of The Vampires • [Female Vampires • [Vampire
Women

[Voglia Di Guardare • [Midnight Gigolo

[Whirlpool • [Pour Le Peau D'un Flic

[Would You Kill A Child • [Island Of The
Dammed

[Yacula • The Loves Of Irina

[Zartlichkeit Der Wolfe • [Tenderness Of
The Wolves

Distributor/Manufacturer Codes

Code	Name	Code	Name	Code	Name
210	210 Productions	AMP	Amazing Pictures	BAN	Banana Video
21F	21st Century Films	AMR	Ambient Rose	BAS	Badlands Studios
2CF	20th Century Fox	AMS	American Sunbathing	BB0	Big Bang Video
3DV	Trident Video	AMX	American Exotica	BBB	Boston Baked Bondage
3HV	Three Hearts Video	ANA	Anabolic Video	BBE	BBE Video/Films
3O6	Triple-O-Six Prod.	ANE	Annaka Entertain.	BBI	Black Bird Video
3SR	III Star Releasing	ANF	Anita F.	BBV	Bare Bottom Video
3VH	Tri-Vid Home Video	ANI	Anime 18	BCP	Blue Coral Product.
3WO	Tri World	ANN	Annie Video	BCS	BCS Productions
3XP	Triple X Productions	ANT	Antigua Pictures	BCV	Bobcat Video
4P	4-Play Video	AOC	Astral Ocean Cinema	BEA	Beaver Busters
4R	Four Rivers Video	AOP	Alpha Omega Product.	BEB	Bean Blossom
4S	Four Seas Film	AP0	Applause Video	BEC	Becky Sunshine Amat.
5KS	Five K Sales	AP1	Albedo Productions	BEE	Bee Video Production
7SP	Seven Star Productn	APB	Abacus Productions	BEL	Bellagio
A&B	A&B Video	APE	A-Pix Entertainment	BEP	Bella Pictures
A&E	Adam & Eve	APH	Aphrodite Video	BET	Bedtime Theatre
A*V	A*Vision Entertainmt	APP	Apple Video	BEV	Bel-Air Video
AA	American Adult	AQA	Aqua Video	BFP	Blue Frame Product.
AAH	AAHS Video	AR	Arrow Film & Video	BFV	Best Film & Video
AB	Al Borda Video	AR0	Arista	BHE	Brickhouse Enterpris
ABA	Abandon Video	ARG	Argen Home Video	BHS	BHS Video
ABS	All Blew Shirts Vid.	ARI	Aries	BIA	Big Apple Video
ABV	ABV West	ARL	Arlo Productions	BIG	Big Time Pictures
AC0	Asian Connection Vid	ASH	Ash Productions	BIJ	Bijou Video
ACE	Ace Video	ASR	Astro	BIK	Bikini Video
ACO	Acorn Films	ASS	Associated Video Grp	BIL	Bi Line Productions
ACP	Alley Cat Production	AST	Astronics	BIN	Bi-Now Productions
ACV	Active Home Video	ASV	Astra Video	BIP	B.I.G. Productions
ADF	Adventure Films	AT	Atom Home Video	BIS	Bisex Video
ADU	Adult Video	ATA	ATAXI	BIZ	Bizarre Video
ADV	AD Video	ATE	Ateball Productions	BKD	B.K. Distributing
AE	Academy Entertain.	ATL	Atlas	BL	Blue Video
AEG	Atlantis Enter. Grp.	ATO	Antone Antics	BLA	Blast Video
AFD	After Dark Video	AUD	Audubon Video	BLB	Black & Blue
AFI	AFVC (Gourmet Video)	AVC	AVC	BLC	Blue Coyote Pictures
AFR	Afrocentrix Product.	AVD	AVID Video	BLE	Brianna Lee Video
AFV	A.F.V. Releasing	AVE	AVE Entertainment	BLP	Blowfish Productions
AGF	Atlantic Group Films	AVI	AVICA Entertainment	BLT	Black Triangle Video
AHE	American Home Enter.	AVO	Avon Production	BLU	Blu-Pix
AHP	AHPA Enteprises	AVP	Amature Video Prod.	BLV	Blush Video
AIA	Amateurs In Action	AVS	AVS Ltd	BLY	Bob Lyons Video
AIP	A.I.P. Home Video	AVV	AsiaView Video	BMA	Blu Market Video
AIR	AIR Video	AWF	Award Films Internat	BMG	BMG Video
AJA	AJA Video	AWP	August West Product.	BMQ	Blue Marquee Video
ALB	Albumin Video	AWV	All Worlds Video	BMV	Black Market Video
ALD	Aldo Entertainment	AXF	Axel Film Corp.	BN	Boudoir Noir
ALF	Alpha France Video	AXI	Axis Films Internat.	BOB	Bob Bouchard
ALL	Allied Video	AXT	AXTC	BOC	Boccaccio 100
ALP	Alpha Blue Archives	AXV	Action X Video	BOK	Bookstore Video
ALS	All Sex Video	B&D	B & D Pleasures	BON	Bon Vue Video
AM	Action Management	B/F	B/Fore Productions	BOP	Bondo Productions
AMA	Amateur Home Video	BAC	Bacchus Releasing	BOS	Bossa Productions
AMB	Ambassador	BAD	Bad Girl Video	BOT	Bottom Line Prod
AME	American Video Corp	BAJ	Baja Video	BOV	Bob's Video
AMF	Amsterdam Films	BAK	Baker Video	BPI	Blank Productions In
AMO	Amour Prod.	BAL	Ball Buster Video	BPM	Black Pussy Mania

LON	London Enterprises	NEO	Neon Video	PIP	Private Eye Product.
LOR	Lorimar	NEP	New Esoteric Press	PKP	Paul Kiener Product.
LOT	Lotus	NEY	Nighteyes Theater P.	PL	Pleasure Productions
LOV	Love Television	NFV	Nite Flight Video	PLA	Playboy Video
LRH	L'il Red Hen Product	NGV	Night Games Video	PLD	Pleasure Dome
LUC	Lucy Video	NIL	Niles	PLP	Platinum Pictures
LUM	Luminous Film & Vid.	NIT	Nitro Productions	PLS	Pleasure Series
LUN	Luna Video	NIV	NightVision	PLV	Platinum Video
LV	Las Vegas Video	NIW	Nitewatch Video	PLY	Playtime Video
LVI	Limousine Video	NLE	Night Light Express	PM	Parliament Video
LVP	Liquid Video Prod.	NLH	New Line Home Video	PME	Pacific Media Enter.
LVV	Live Video	NMP	NMPC Video	PMV	Private Moments Vid.
M$M	Million $ Movie	NOP	Night Owl Production	PN	Pearl Necklace Video
M&M	M and M	NOT	Notorious Pictures	PNP	Paul Norman Product.
MAC	Mark Curtis	NOU	Nouveaux Video	POL	Polygram Home Video
MAE	Magnum Entertainment	NPA	New Path Video	PP	Plum Productions
MAG	Magic Video	NS	New Sensations	PP0	Purfect Productions
MAI	Main Attraction Vid.	NST	New Star Video	PPI	Passionate Pictures
MAJ	Majestic Home Video	NSV	Now Showing Video	PPP	Pink Pearl Product.
MAL	Malibu Movies	NT0	Nasty Treats Video	PPR	Passion Productions
MAP	Masterpiece	NTP	New Twist Production	PPV	Patty Plenty Video
MAR	Marathon Films	NTV	Night Time Video	PRC	Producers Concepts
MAS	Mastervision	NUV	Nu-West Video Prod.	PRE	Prestige Video
MAV	Milton's Amateur Vid	NVI	New Vision	PRF	Private Film
MAX	Maximum Video	NWV	Nightwatch Video	PRI	Privert Video
MBP	Max Bellocchio Prod.	NWW	New World Video	PRK	Pretty Kitty Prod.
MCA	MCA Home Video	NYF	New Yorker Video	PRO	Pro-Am Video
ME	Moonlight Entertain.	NYM	Nympherotica	PRP	Priapism Home Video
MEA	Meda Video	OAP	Oasis Productions	PRS	Prism Entertainment
MED	Media International	OCV	Oceanfront Video	PRV	Private Video
MEL	Melody Films	OD	Odyssey Group Video	PS	Private Screenings
MET	Metro Home Video	ODI	Odyssey Internation.	PSE	Private Sessions
MEV	Metro Video	OHV	Olympia Home Video	PSP	P.S. Productions
MFM	MFM	OLL	Ooh La La Production	PTV	Pillow Talk Video
MGM	MGM/UA	ONA	Ona Zee Productions	PUB	Publishing Magazine
MHV	Mike Hott Video	ONH	On Hand Productions	PUP	Pin Up Productions
MID	Midnight Film & Vid.	ORC	Orchid Video	PV	Paradise Visuals
MIN	Minky Productions	ORE	Orient Express	PV0	Pricebusters Video
MIR	Mirage Video	ORG	Organic Video	PV1	Phantom Video
MIT	Mitchell Brothers	ORI	Orion Home Video	PVI	Premier Video
MIV	Mark IV	ORP	Oranj Productions	PVX	PVX
MKS	MKS Productions	OSC	Oscar Tripe	PYE	Pyramid Entertain.
MLB	Mike Lebell's Video	OSH	Ocean Shores	PYR	Pop Your Rocks Video
MLV	Magic Lamp Video	OUP	Outlaw Productions	QUA	Quackenbush Video
MM1	Magic Moments Video	OUT	O.U.T.'s Glamour Vid	QX	Quality X
MMA	Magma	OVP	Omanko Video Product	R/H	R/H Productions
MMV	Mr. Mustard Video	OZE	OZ Entertainment	RAI	Raincoat Productions
MN0	Minotaur	P10	Perfect 10 Video	RAM	Ramar
MNT	MNTEX Entertainment	P69	Passport 69 Video	RAP	RAM Video
MOG	Morning Glory	PAA	Paris-American Video	RAS	Raw Silk Video
MON	Monarch Home Video	PAC	Pacific Ocean	RAV	Rainbow Video
MOV	Mondo Video	PAE	Passion Entertain.	RAW	Rawhide Video
MP	Media Products	PAL	Paladin Video	RB	Red Board Video
MP0	Masked Pictures	PAN	Pandora Productions	RBP	Rick Bolton Product.
MP1	Maximum Perversion	PAP	Parallel Pictures	RCA	RCA
MPA	Marina Pacific	PAR	Paramount Home Video	RCV	R.C. Video
MPI	MPI Video	PAS	Passion Video	RDC	RD Communications
MPP	Mr. Puppy Production	PAV	Paragon Video	REB	Rebel Video
MSC	M. Schmidt	PCP	Pure Class Product.	RED	Reed Brothers, The
MSI	MSI Video	PCV	Pink Champagne Video	REE	Reel Pleasure
MSP	MS Productions	PE	Plush Entertainment	REG	Regal Home Video
MTP	Mandy Turner Prod.	PEA	Peach Entertainment	REN	Rendo Films
MUN	Movies Unlimited	PEI	PEI Corporation	REP	Republic Pictures
MV	Millenium Video	PEK	Peekaboo Home Video	REV	REV Productions
MV0	Midwest Video	PEN	Penguin Productions	RFC	Rene Fashion Co
MV1	Monterey Video	PEP	Pepper Productions	RHI	Rhino Home Video
MVI	Magnum Video	PER	Personal Touch	RHS	Red Hot Video
MYS	Mystic Productions	PET	Penthouse Video	RHV	Regency Home Video
NA0	New Age Pictures	PEV	Pearl Visuals	RIV	Riviera
NAN	Naughty Neighbors	PEY	Peeling Eyeball Vid.	RLF	Reel Life Video
NAP	Napali Video	PF	Power Film	RLV	Red Light Video
NAS	Nasty Man Production	PGV	Pai Gow Video	RMV	RM Video Russ Meyer
NAT	National Video	PHO	Phoenix	ROB	Rosebud Video
NAV	New Age Video	PHV	Player Home Video	ROM	Romance Home Video
NEH	New Horizons Home V.	PI	Pinnacle	ROP	Rocket Pictures
NEI	Neighbor Girls	PIN	Pink Video	ROR	Raunch-O-Rama

ROX	Roxci Films	SPL	Splato Video	TIS	Tistok Malic Video
ROY	Royal Video	SPP	Spectacular Pictures	TIW	Tidal Wave Pictures
RP	Riyo Productions	SPR	S.S. Productions	TLC	Traci Lords Company
RPG	RPG Video	SPV	Spotlight Video	TLE	Torchlight Entertain
RR	Roni Raye (Amateur)	SS	Spectra Series	TLV	TLC Video
RSK	RSK Productions	SSH	Southern Shore Video	TME	TM Entertainment
RSP	Roxy Starr Product.	SSP	Strictly Sondra Prod	TMM	Third Millenium Magi
RSV	R.S.V.P.	SST	SexStar Video	TMV	Tempe Video
RTP	Raw Talent Product.	SSV	Stevi's Secrets Vide	TMX	TMX
RUM	Rumpus Distributors	ST0	Strange Video	TNT	TNT Video
RV	Realistic Video	ST2	Studio 2000	TO1	Top Video
RVE	Revolution Entertain	STA	Stallion Video	TOA	TOA Media
RWP	Randy West Product.	STD	Standard Video	TOD	Today's Art Video
S&L	S & L Video	STE	Stan's Video Exchan.	TOP	Tara O'Hara Product
S&S	Supersound & Sight	STI	Stardata Internation	TOR	Torrid Video
SAB	Sabin Publishing	STK	Steel Kittens	TOT	Turn on TV
SAE	Studio A Entertain.	STM	Starmaker Video	TOU	Touchstone Home Vid
SAM	Samuels Company, The	STP	Starbright Product.	TP	Total Video Product.
SAT	Select-A-Tape	STR	Stroker Video	TPA	T. Page
SAV	Satellite Video	STT	Stryker Tool Company	TRB	Tribeca
SB	Soft Bodies	STU	Studio Entertainment	TRI	Triboro Video
SBI	Susan Block Institut	STV	Star Video	TRP	Ted Roter Production
SBP	Sinclair Blue Prod.	STY	Stryker Productions	TRW	Trans World Entert.
SBV	Sky Blue Video	SUB	Sunburst	TSS	Trans Studios
SC	Sin City Video	SUE	Sunset Entertainment	TTV	Totally Tasteless Vd
SCI	Surrender Cinema	SUF	Sunshine Films	TUX	Tuxedo Network
SCL	Sigma Cum Laude	SUL	Sultan Entertainment	TV	Topper Video
SCO	Scorpio	SUM	Summit Pictures	TVD	TVD
SCR	Scratch Video	SUN	Sundance Productions	TVE	TalkView Entertain.
SCS	Stone City Sales	SUP	Superior Video	TVI	Talon Videos Inc
SDP	Sundown Productions	SUS	Sunshine Erotica	TVV	TV Video
SE	Select/Essex	SUV	Superstar Video	TVX	TVX
SE0	Shanachie Entertain.	SUZ	Suzy's Secrets	TWA	Tech's Warehouse
SEA	Seabag Productions	SV	Scarry Video	TWE	Tori Welles Prod
SEE	Southseas Entertain.	SV0	Susan's Video	TWI	Twilight Video
SEM	SEMG Films	SV1	Strand/VCI Entertain	TWP	Twist Productions
SEN	Senorita Video	SV2	Sex-O-Vision	TWV	Tapeworm Video
SEP	Scorched Earth Prod.	SVE	S.V.E.	TYV	Tycoon Video
SEV	S.E.V.P.	SVI	Super Video	TZV	TZ Video
SEX	Sextasy Video	SVL	Swan Video Ltd	UA	United Artists
SFI	Sea Films Inc	SWE	S.W. Enterprises	UBP	Ultra Black Product.
SFO	Superfox Video	SXI	Studio XIII	UCV	Urban Classics Video
SFP	Silver Foxx Product.	SY	Solefully Yours	UEF	Ultimate Euro Films
SFV	Student Fetish Video	SYC	Sarah Young Commun.	UGO	UGO Video
SGE	Savage	T&A	T & A Video	ULI	Ultimate Video
SGI	Sushi Roll Internat.	T-B	T-Bone Studios	ULP	Unlimited Production
SGO	Samuel Goldwyn	T-Z	T-Z Video	ULS	Ultrasexxx Video
SGV	Shapiro/Glickenhaus	TAB	Tabu Video	UNI	UNI Distribution
SHA	Shackle Video	TAG	Target Video	UNP	Unique Pictures
SHF	Shoeshine Films	TAM	Tamarack Productions	UNQ	Unique Video
SHL	Shadow Lane Video	TAN	Tantric Productions	UNT	United Video
SHM	She-Man Studios	TAO	TAO Productions	UNV	Unicorn Video
SHO	Showcase Video	TAR	Tara Video	USA	USA Home Video
SHS	Shooting Star Video	TAV	Tanagra Video	UWV	U Witness Video
SHV	Savage Heart Video	TAW	Taylor Wane Product.	V-I	VCI
SIL	Silhouette Video	TBP	Tom Boka Productions	V10	Video 10 Productions
SIS	Silver State	TBV	Toy Box Video	V20	Video 2000
SIV	Sinclair Video Lib.	TCK	TCKS Entertainment	V99	Venus 99 Video
SKJ	SKJ Productions	TCP	Two Cool Productions	VAE	Video-Audio Electron
SKV	Sex Kitten Video	TDG	Tee Dee Gee Ltd	VAL	Video Alternatives
SLV	Sir Lloyd Video	TDH	Twisted Dreams H.V.	VAM	Vidamerica
SM	Sandy's Modelling	TEG	Titan Entertainment	VAS	Valley Star
SMP	Sean Michaels Prod.	TEM	Tempo-High Class Pro	VBE	Van Brunt Entertain.
SNA	Snatch Productions	TEP	Tight Ends Product.	VBM	VBM
SNO	Snowflake Films	TEV	Tiger Eye Video	VBV	VB Video
SO	Soho Video	TGA	TGA	VC	VCA
SOF	Softouch Video	TGE	Trans Global Enter.	VC0	VC-II
SOG	Solid Gold Video	THA	Top Hat Video	VC1	Video Communications
SOH	Sohard Productions	THN	The Naturists	VCI	Video City Product.
SOR	Sorel Productions	THO	Thorn E.M.I	VCL	Video Clinic (AMA)
SOV	Southwest Video	THP	Twat House Pictures	VCR	VCR
SOW	Something Weird Vid.	THT	Threat Theatre Int.	VCS	Video Classics
SP	Sticky Pictures	THV	Thanksgiving Video	VCX	VCX
SP0	S.B. Pictures	TIE	Tiffany Entertainm.	VD	Vidco Home Video
SPE	SpreadEagle Video	TIF	Tiffany Collection	VDL	VDL Productions
SPI	Sterling Pictures	TIG	Tigress Entertain.	VDM	Video Dimensions